SCOTT

2000
Standard Postage Stamp Catalogue

ONE HUNDRED AND FIFTY-SIXTH EDITION IN SIX VOLUMES

VOLUME 1

UNITED STATES
and Affiliated Territories

UNITED NATIONS

COUNTRIES OF THE WORLD

A-B

VICE PRESIDENT/PUBLISHER	Stuart J. Morrissey
EDITOR	James E. Kloetzel
ASSOCIATE EDITOR	William W. Cummings
VALUING EDITOR	Martin J. Frankevicz
NEW ISSUES EDITOR	David C. Akin
COMPUTER CONTROL COORDINATOR	Denise Oder
EDITORIAL ASSISTANTS	Judith E. Bertrand, Beth Brown
ART/PRODUCTION DIRECTOR	Janine C. S. Apple
PRODUCTION COORDINATOR	Nancy S. Martin
MARKETING/SALES DIRECTOR	William Fay
ADVERTISING	Sabrina D. Morton
CIRCULATION/PRODUCT PROMOTION MANAGER	Tim Wagner

Released April 1999
Includes New Stamp Listings through the March, 1999 *Scott Stamp Monthly* Catalogue Update

Copyright© 1999 by

Scott Publishing Co.

911 Vandemark Road, Sidney, OH 45365-0828
A division of AMOS PRESS, INC., publishers of *Linn's Stamp News, Coin World, Cars & Parts* magazine and *The Sidney Daily News*.

CONSIGNMENTS WANTED
When you're ready to sell, we're ready to take action!

When you consign your collection to SUPERIOR, you will receive...

- ✔ Professional Operations
- ✔ International Expertise
- ✔ A Worldwide Marketplace
- ✔ Personalized Service
- ✔ No Shortage of Money

ONE CALL IS ALL IT TAKES
Be assured that each and every detail will be professionally handled by one of the most experienced names in the stamp industry

Ask about our Senior Discount!

Alan Lipkin
I. Michael Orenstein

Superior Stamp & Coin

9478 WEST OLYMPIC BOULEVARD, BEVERLY HILLS, CALIFORNIA 90212-4246
TOLL FREE (800) 421-0754 TEL (310) 203-9855 FAX (310) 203-8037 INTERNET www.superiorSC.com

BONDED CALIFORNIA AUCTIONEERS

© Copywright 1999. A-Mark Auction Galleries, Inc. Lic. No. 146637300697 • Mark E. Goldberg Lic. No. 146637300699

Value Priced Stockbooks

Stockbooks are a classic and convenient storage alternative for many collectors. These German-made stockbooks feature heavyweight archival quality paper with 9 pockets on each page. The 8½" x 11⅜" pages are bound inside a handsome leatherette grain cover and include glassine interleaving between the pages for added protection. The Value Priced Stockbooks are available in two page styles, the white page stockbooks feature glassine pockets while the black page variety includes clear acetate pockets

Value Priced Stockbooks are available from your favorite dealer or direct from Scott Publishing Co. P.O. Box 828
Sidney OH 45365-0828
www.scottonline.com

SCOTT

White Page Stockbooks Glassine Pockets

Item	Color	Pages	Retail
SW16BL	Blue	16 pages	$5.95
SW16GR	Green	16 pages	$5.95
SW16RD	Red	16 pages	$5.95

Black Page Stockbooks Acetate Pockets

Item	Color	Pages	Retail
ST16GR	Red	16 pages	$9.95
ST16GR	Green	16 pages	$9.95
ST16BL	Blue	16 pages	$9.95
ST16BK	Black	16 pages	$9.95
ST32RD	Red	32 pages	$14.95
ST32GR	Green	32 pages	$14.95
ST32BL	Blue	32 pages	$14.95
ST32BK	Black	32 pages	$14.95
ST64RD	Red	64 pages	$27.95
ST64GR	Green	64 pages	$27.95
ST64BL	Blue	64 pages	$27.95
ST64BK	Black	64 pages	$27.95

To order call 1-800-572-6885

Table of Contents

Letter from the Publisher	5A
Acknowledgments	7A
Information on Philatelic Societies	8A
Information on Catalogue Values, Grade and Condition	12A
Grading Illustrations	13A, 14A
Gum Chart	15A
Catalogue Listing Policy	17A
Understanding the Listings	18A
Special Notices	20A
Abbreviations	21A
Basic Stamp Information	22A
Terminology	30A
Currency Conversion	33A
Colonies, Former Colonies, Offices, Territories Controlled by Parent States	35A
The British Commonwealth of Nations	36A
Common Design Types	38A
United States	1
Subject Index of Regular and Air Post Issues	84
United Nations	146
Countries of the World A-B	167
2000 Volume 1 Catalogue Number Additions, Deletions & Changes	885
British Colonial and Crown Agents Watermarks	887
Dies of British Colonial Stamps Referred to in the Catalogue	887
Illustrated Identifier	888
Index and Identifier	**902**
Index to Advertisers	910
Dealer Directory Yellow Pages	911
Pronunciation Symbols	926

See Volumes 2 through 6 for Countries of the World, C-Z

Volume 2: C-F
Volume 3: G-I
Volume 4: J-O
Volume 5: P-Sl
Volume 6: So-Z

Scott Publishing Mission Statement

The Scott Publishing Team exists to serve the recreational,
educational and commercial hobby needs of stamp collectors and dealers.
We strive to set the industry standard for philatelic information and products by developing and
providing goods that help collectors identify, value, organize and present their collections.
Quality customer service is, and will continue to be, our highest priority.
We aspire toward achieving total customer satisfaction.

Copyright Notice

The contents of this book are owned exclusively by Scott Publishing Co. and all rights thereto are reserved under the Pan American and Universal Copyright Conventions.

Copyright @1999 by Scott Publishing Co., Sidney, OH. Printed in U.S.A.

COPYRIGHT NOTE
Permission is hereby given for the use of material in this book and covered by copyright if:
  (a) The material is used in advertising matter, circulars or price lists for the purpose of offering stamps for sale or purchase at the prices listed therein; and
  (b) Such use is incidental to the business of buying and selling stamps and is limited in scope and length, i.e., it does not cover a substantial portion of the total number of stamps issued by any country or of any special category of stamps of any country; and
  (c) Such material is not used as part of any catalogue, stamp album or computerized or other system based upon the Scott catalogue numbers, or in any updated valuations of stamps not offered for sale or purchase; and
  (d) Such use is not competitive with the business of the copyright owner; and
  (e) Such use is for editorial purposes in publications in the form of articles or commentary, except for computer software or the serialization of books in such publications, for which separate written permission is required.
  Any use of the material in this book which does not satisfy all the foregoing conditions is forbidden in any form unless permission in each instance is given in writing by the copyright owner.

Trademark Notice

The terms SCOTT, SCOTT'S, SCOTT CATALOGUE NUMBERING SYSTEM, SCOTT CATALOGUE NUMBER, SCOTT NUMBER and abbreviations thereof, are trademarks of Scott Publishing Co., used to identify its publications and its copyrighted system for identifying and classifying postage stamps for dealers and collectors. These trademarks are to be used only with the prior consent of Scott Publishing Co.
  No part of this work may be reproduced in any form or by any means, electronic or mechanical, including photocopying, without permission in writing from Scott Publishing Co., P.O. Box 828, Sidney, OH 45365-0828.

ISBN 0-89487-250-8

Library of Congress Card No. 2-3301

ScottMounts

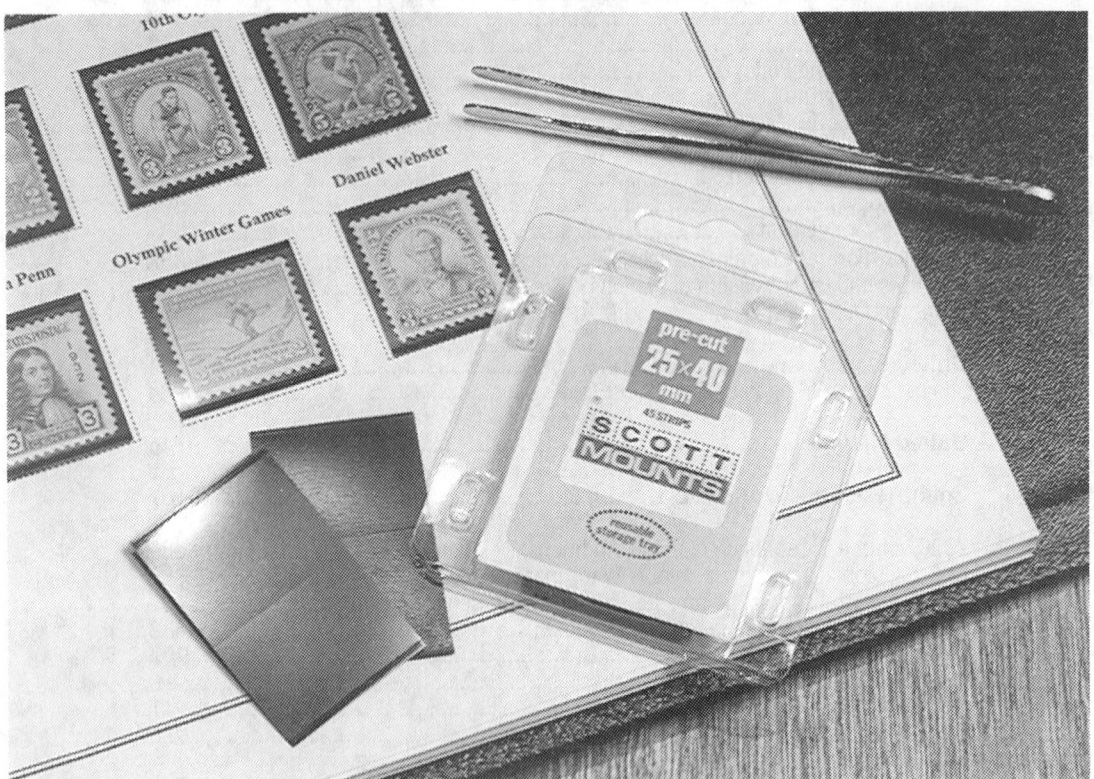

For stamp presentation unequaled in beauty and clarity, insist on ScottMounts. Made of 100% inert polystyrol foil, ScottMounts protect your stamps from the harmful effects of dust and moisture. Available in your choice of clear or black backs, ScottMounts are center-split across the back for easy insertion of stamps and feature crystal clear mount faces. Double layers of gum assure stay-put bonding on the album page. Discover the quality and value ScottMounts have to offer.

ScottMounts are available from your favorite stamp dealer or direct from:

Scott Publishing Co.
P.O. Box 828 Sidney OH 45365-0828
www.scottonline.com

Discover the quality and value ScottMounts have to offer. For a complete list of ScottMount sizes or a free sample pack call or write Scott Publishing Co.

SCOTT
1-800-572-6885

Scott Publishing Co.

911 VANDEMARK ROAD, SIDNEY, OHIO 45365   937-498-0802

Dear Scott Catalogue User:

Since the cover of this catalogue bears the year 2000 it probably feels like the start of the millennium to some. But you don't have to wait for 2000 to observe vast changes sweeping the philatelic landscape.

The internet has dramatically altered the way stamp business is conducted. Some dealers have quit stamp shows for websites. New collectors, who have their own ideas on how much stamps are worth, are outbidding traditionalists online for cheaper stamps. Although high-end auctions are still held offline you can view just about any fancy auction catalog online at Stampauctioncentral.com. Stamp collecting supplies of every description are available at Scottonline.com (sorry, couldn't resist the plug).

There are approximately 11,000 value changes since the last edition of Volume 1. A portion of these changes already has appeared in the *U.S. Specialized,* but the vast majority are new to this volume. There also are more editorial changes than ever.

And now for the self-imposed interview:

What's hot in U.S. Postage?

Grills, 1869 Pictorials, Banknotes and Special Printings.

For example, Scott 80, the 5 cent "A" grill (all-over grill), jumps to $80,000 used from $50,000. Scott 82, the 3 cent "B" grill, shoots to $160,000 used from $100,000. The famous 1 cent "Z" grill, Scott 85A, is now valued at $935,000.

The 1869 Pictorials continue their advance of recent years. The 1 cent buff, Scott 112, bumps to $550 unused and $140 used, from $525 unused and $125 used last year, and the 2 cent brown, Scott 113, climbs to $500 unused and $50 used, from $450 unused and $45 used. The higher denominations also move upward.

Among the Banknote issues, a particularly noteworthy increase is seen in the 1870 30 cent black grilled stamp, Scott 143, which skyrockets to $9,500 unused and $2,000 used, from $9,000 unused and $1,500 used. Scott 192-204, the 1880 Special Printings of the 1879 issue, see significant increases for all values that did not increase last year and further increases for some values that did.

The gap between unused and mint never hinged has widened in some areas, such as the 1893 Columbians, where mint never-hinged values move upward while unused hinged values remain static. The same trend is noted in the First Bureau issue of 1894-1898.

The extremely scarce perf. 12x10 or perf. 10x12 varieties of the normally perf. 10 Washington-Franklin stamps of 1914-15, have been dramatically raised due to their appearance and sale at auction in 1998. For example, Scott 424a, the perf. 12x10 1 cent green, leaps to $1,750 unused and $1,500 used, from $850 unused and $750 used last year.

All of the imperforate vertically or imperforate horizontally varieties of the 1934 National Parks set, Scott 740-749, see rather large value increases either mint never hinged only, or more usually both unused and mint never hinged. Scott 2466b, the "Bronx blue" color variety of the 1995 32 cent Ferryboat coil, is valued unused for the first time at $6. The 1994 Recalled Legends of the West pane of 20, Scott 2870, moves to $175 from $160.

Early postage dues and officials rise in value in unused condition. There are also many changes in postal stationery. Scott U157, the 1881 2 cent vermilion on amber cut square, skyrockets to $35,000 unused, from $15,000.

What has changed with A-B Countries?

Nearly 1,600 values have been revised in Austria and well over 1,000 changes were made in Antigua. Other countries with many significant value changes include Aden, Aitutaki, Anguilla, Bosnia & Herzegovina, Botswana and Burundi.

In Austria, many of the stamps of the classic period show increases. The Dollfuss stamp, Scott 380, remains at $900 in mint never-hinged condition. The single stamp from the WIPA sheet, Scott B111a, increases in hinged condition to $375 from $350. The Occupation stamps of 1918 show sharp increases.

The biggest change in Belgium is the listing of stamps in never-hinged condition starting with the 1919 set depicting King Albert wearing a trench helmet, Scott 124-137. Belgium features about 400 changes, mostly all in the early postage issues including the helmet set which increased slightly.

Aden's beautiful 1937 Dhows set, Scott 1-12, bumps up a bit as do other sets of the country. Burundi, which is usually not regarded as a hotbed of stamp value activity, shows many substantial increases. Most are wildlife or flower topicals.

What about editorial changes?

For U.S.: Additional informative and warning footnotes have been added. For example, collectors are warned to watch for plentiful fakes in the marketplace of the 1 cent-10 cent coils, Scott 348-356.

A footnote appears below the imperforate error of the "F" rate Flower stamp, Scott 2517a, warning collectors not to confuse this imperforate with the imperforate coil variety, Scott 2518a. The different design measurements are given.

In a significant expansion of the postal stationery listings, surcharged envelopes from the 1920-25 period have been further specialized by the addition of minor variety listings for the die types of the envelopes that were surcharged.

For editorial consistency, several minor-lettered se-tenant pairs have been renumbered to make the multiple a minor variety of the last Scott major number making up the multiple. This brings these items in line with the listing style elsewhere in the catalogue for se-tenant multiples.

For A-B countries: Values for never-hinged sets and singles have been added in Austria, Antigua, Ascension and Belgium.

In Belgium's classic issues, a note has been added to alert collectors to the two sizes of Scott 10-12. In the Scott 13-16 and 18-22 sets, the values are stated as being for particular perforations – perf. 14 for the Scott 13-16 set, and perf. 15 for the other set. Other perforations of these stamps will be valued in the Scott *Classic Specialized Catalogue.* Sizes have been added to the listings for Scott 127 and 128, the 1919 King Albert in Trench Helmet 10c and 15c values.

Belgium Scott 141b has been deleted as all examples known are said to be fakes.

What can you do to improve your collection and add more enjoyment to your favorite hobby?

Go online. Surf the web. Participate in online auctions. Check out your favorite dealers website. Visit Linn's www.zillionsofstamps.com. Take advantage of the search feature available on many sites to find more material. Communicate with your fellow collectors via email. It's easy.

If you don't have a computer go get one. You will not regret it. Prices on hardware have come down dramatically. The internet and email are the greatest thing to hit the hobby since the folded hinge.

Happy Collecting,

Stuart Morrissey/Publisher

P.S. Start planning now for Stamp Show 2000, which promises to be a truly great stamp show and millennium celebration. Stamp Show 2000 will take place in London from May 22 to May 29, 2000.

National Albums

SCOTT NATIONAL SERIES

The National series offers a panoramic view of our country's heritage through postage stamps. It is the most complete and comprehensive U.S. album series you can buy. There are spaces for every major U.S. stamp listed in the Scott Catalogue, including Special Printings, Newspaper stamps and much more.

* Pages printed on one side.
* All spaces identified by Scott numbers.
* All major variety of stamps or either illustrated or described.
* Chemically neutral paper protects stamps.

Item			Retail
100NTL1	1845-1934	97 pgs	$29.95
100NTL2	1935-1976	108 pgs	$29.95
100NTL3	1977-1993	110 pgs	$29.95
100NTL4	1994-1998	101 pgs	$29.95

Supplemented in March. Back supplements available.

Computer Vended Postage
103CVP0 1989-1994 11 pgs $3.95

National Blank Pages (Border B)
ACC120 20 per pack $6.95

National Quad Blank Pages (Border B)
ACC121 20 per pack $6.95

National Album Package

Get everything you need to house and value your collection in one convenient and affordable package. There's never been a better or more economical way to get the album pages, accessories and catalogues you need to build a better collection for one low price.

The National Album Package Include

1	National Pages Part 1 1845 - 1934 97 pgs.
1	National Pages Part 2 1935 - 1976 108 pgs.
1	National Pages Part 3 1977 - 1993 110 pgs.
1	National Pages Part 4 1994 - 1997 81 pgs.
4	Large three-ring binders
4	Large Slipcases
4	Black Protector Fly Sheets
4	National Album Labels
1	ScottMount Assortment (Item 966B)
1	Current U.S. Specialized Catalogue

SET PRICE $259.00

1-800-572-6885
www.scottonline.com

Scott albums are available from your favorite stamp dealer or direct from:

Scott Publishing Co.
P.O. Box 828
Sidney OH 45365-0828

Acknowledgments

Our appreciation and gratitude go to the following individuals who have assisted us in preparing information included in the 2000 Scott Catalogues. Some helpers prefer anonymity. These individuals have generously shared their stamp knowledge with others through the medium of the Scott Catalogue.

Those who follow provided information that is in addition to the hundreds of dealer price lists and advertisements and scores of auction catalogues and realizations which were used in producing the catalogue values. It is from those noted here that we have been able to obtain information on items not normally seen in published lists and advertisements. Support from these people goes beyond data leading to catalogue values, for they also are key to editorial changes.

Mario R. Alcala
A.R. Allison (Orange Free State Study Circle)
Robert Ausubel
Don Bakos
Jules K. Beck
Vladimir Berrio-Lemm (Centro de Filatelistas Independientes de Panama)
John Birkinbine II
George W. Brett
Roger S. Brody
A. Bryan Camarda
Alan C. Campbell
Nathan Carlin
Richard A. Champagne
Charles Chesloe (Tribuna Stamp Co.)
Henry Chlanda
Dr. Leonard Cohen (Marlen Stamps & Coins, Ltd.)
Laurie Conrad
Frank D. Correl
Andrew Cronin (Canadian Society of Russian Philately)
William T. Crowe
Bob Dumaine (Sam Houston Duck Company)
William S. Dunn
Stephen G. Esrati
Leon Finik (Loral Stamps)
Henry Fisher
Joseph E. Foley (Eire Philatelic Association)
Marvin Frey
Huguette Gagnon (Ethiopian Philatelic Society)
Bob Genisol (Sultan Stamp Center)
Robert Greenwald
Fred F. Gregory
Rudolf Hamar (Estonian Philatelic Society)
Erich E. Hamm (Philactica)
John B. Head
Robert R. Hegland
Clifford O. Herrick (Fidelity Trading Company)
Lee H. Hill, Jr.
Dr. Eugene H. Holmok (Tatra Stamps, Reg'd.)
Jack R. Hughes (Fellowship of Samoa Specialists)
Wilson Hulme
Jack Ince (West Africa Study Circle)
Eric Jackson
John I. Jamieson (Saskatoon Stamp Centre)
Peter C. Jeannopoulos
Stanford M. Katz
Dr. James W. Kerr
Charles F. Kezbers
William A. Litle
Pedro Llach (Filatelia Llach S.L.)
George W. MacLellan
F. Brian Marshall (Sarawak Specialists' Society)
Marilyn R. Mattke
Dr. Hector R. Mena (Society of Costa Rica Collectors)

Jack E. Molesworth (Jack E. Molesworth, Inc.)
William E. Mooz
Gary M. Morris (Pacific Midwest Co.)
Peter Mosiondz, Jr.
Bruce M. Moyer (Valley Stamp & Coin, Inc.)
Richard H. Muller (Richard's Stamps)
Erik B. Nagel
John E. Pearson (Pittwater Philatelic Service)
Robert H. Penn (Spanish Philatelic Society)
Donald J. Peterson
Vernon W. Pickering
Stanley M. Piller (Stanley M. Piller & Associates)
Stephen Radin
Siddique Mahmudur Rahman (Bangladesh Institute of Philatelic Studies)
Michael Rogers (Michael Rogers, Inc.)
Jon W. Rose
Larry Rosenblum (Great Britain Collectors Club)
Frans H. A. Rummens (American Society for Netherlands Philately)
Richard H. Salz
Theodosios Sampson (Superior Stamp & Coin)
Jacques C. Schiff, Jr. (Jacques C. Schiff, Jr., Inc.)
Bernard Seckler (Fine Arts Philatelists)
F. Burton Sellers
Michael Shamilzadeh
J. Randall Shoemaker (Professional Stamp Experts, Inc.)
Jeff Siddiqui (Pakistan Study Circle)
Sergio & Liane Sismondo (The Classic Collector)
Dr. Russell V. Skavaril (St. Helena, Ascension & Tristan da Cunha Philatelic Society)
Dr. Hubert C. Skinner
Mark Stucker
Glenn Tjia (Quality Philatelics)
Scott R. Trepel (Siegel Auction Galleries, Inc.)
Ming W. Tsang (Hong Kong Stamp Society)
James O. Vadeboncoeur (Mexico-Elmhurst Philatelic Society International)
Xavier Verbeck
Jerome S. Wagshal
Richard A. Washburn
Giana Wayman
Raymond H. Weill
William R. Weiss, Jr. (Weiss Philatelics)
John M. Wilson
Robert F. Yacano (K-Line Philippines)
Val Zabijaka
Dr. Michal Zika (Album)

A special acknowledgment to Liane and Sergio Sismondo of The Classic Collector for their extraordinary assistance and knowledge sharing that has aided in the preparation of this year's Standard and Classic Specialized Catalogues.

Addresses, Telephone Numbers, Web Sites, E-Mail Addresses of General & Specialized Philatelic Societies

Collectors can contact the following groups for information about the philately of the areas within the scope of these societies, or inquire about membership in these groups. Aside from the general societies, we limit this list to groups that specialize in particular fields of philately, particular areas covered by the Scott Standard Postage Stamp Catalogue, and topical groups. Many more specialized philatelic societies exist than those listed below. These addresses were compiled in January 1999, and are, to the best of our knowledge, correct and current. Groups should inform the editors of address changes whenever they occur. The editors also want to hear from other such specialized groups not listed.

Unless otherwise noted all website addresses begin with http://

General "Umbrella" Societies

American Philatelic Society
PO Box 8000
State College PA 16803
Ph: (814) 237-3803
www.west.net/~stamps1/aps.html
E-mail: relamb@stamps.org

American Stamp Dealers' Association
Joseph Savarese
3 School St.
Glen Cove NY 11542
Ph: (516) 759-7000
www.amerstampdlrs.com
E-mail: asda@erols.com

International Society of Worldwide Stamp Collectors
Anthony Zollo
PO Box 150407
Lufkin TX 75915-0407
www.frontiernet/~stamptmf/iswsc.html
E-mail: stamptmf@frontiernet.net

Junior Philatelists of America
Ellie Chapman
PO Box 850
Boalsburg PA 16827-0850
www.jpastamps.org
E-mail: jpaellie@aol.com

Royal Philatelic Society
41 Devonshire Place
London, United Kingdom W1N 1PE

Royal Philatelic Society of Canada
PO Box 929, Station Q
Toronto, ON, Canada M4T 2P1
www.interlog.com/~rspc
E-mail: rpsc@interlog.com

Groups focusing on fields or aspects found in world-wide philately (some may cover U.S. area only)

American Air Mail Society
Stephen Reinhard
PO Box 110
Mineola NY 11501
ourworld.compuserve.com/homepages/aams/
E-mail: sr1501@aol.com

American First Day Cover Society
Douglas Kelsey
PO Box 65960
Tucson AZ 85728-5960
Ph: (520) 321-0880
E-mail: afdcs@aol.com

American Revenue Association
Bruce Miller
511 South First Ave., #332
Arcadia CA 91006

American Topical Association
Paul E. Tyler
PO Box 50820
Albuquerque NM 87181-0820
E-mail: ATAStamps@aol.com

Errors, Freaks and Oddities Collectors Club
Jim McDevitt
138 East Lakemont Dr.
Kingsland GA 31548
Ph: (912) 729-1573
E-mail: cwouscg@aol.com

First Issues Collectors Club
Peter F. Kaminski
1347 Prosser Drive
Sycamore IL 60178
Ph: (815) 895-2819
E-mail: pkaminsk@niu.edu

National Duck Stamp Collectors Society
Anthony J. Monico
PO Box 43, Harleysville PA 19438-0043

No Value Identified Club
Albert Sauvanet
Le Clos Royal B, Boulevard des Pas Enchantes
St. Sebastien-sur Loire, France 44230
E-mail: alain.vailly@irin.univ_nantes.fr

The Perfins Club
Kurt Ottenheimer
462 West Walnut St.
Long Beach NY 11561
E-mail: oak462@juno.com

Post Mark Collectors Club
David Proulx
7629 Homestead Drive
Baldwinsville NY 13027
E-mail: stampdance@baldcom.net

Postal History Society
Kalman V. Illyefalvi
8207 Daren Court
Pikesville MD 21208-2211
Ph: (410) 653-0665

Precancel Stamp Society
176 Bent Pine Hill
North Wales PA 19454
Ph: (215) 368-6082

United Postal Stationery Society
Joann Thomas
PO Box 48, Redlands CA 92373
www.uh.edu/~lib19/upss.htm

Groups focusing on U.S. area philately as covered in the Standard Catalogue

Bureau Issues Association
David G. Lee
PO Box 2641
Reston VA 20195-0641
www.delphi.com/stamps/clubs/bia.html

Canal Zone Study Group
Richard H. Salz
60 27th Ave.
San Francisco CA 94121

Carriers and Locals Society
Steven M. Roth
PO Box 57160
Washington DC 20036
Ph: (202) 293-6813
E-mail: smroth@wizard.net

Confederate Stamp Alliance
Richard L. Calhoun
PO Box 581
Mt. Prospect IL 60056-0581

Hawaiian Philatelic Society
Kay H. Hoke
PO Box 10115
Honolulu HI 96816-0115
Ph: (808) 521-5721
www.stampshows.com/hps.html
E-mail: bannan@pixi.com

Plate Number Coil Collectors Club
Gene C. Trinks
3603 Bellows Court
Troy MI 48083
www.geocities.com/Heartland/Hills/6283
E-mail: gctrinks@tir.com

United Nations Philatelists
Blanton Clement, Jr.
292 Springdale Terrace
Yardley PA 19067-3421

U.S. Cancellation Club
Roger Rhoads
3 Ruthana Way
Hockessin DE 19707
www.geocities.com/athens/2088/usschome.htm
E-mail: rrrhoads@aol.com

U.S. Philatelic Classics Society
Mark D. Rogers
PO Box 80708
Austin TX 78708-0708
www.scruz.net/~eho/uspcs
E-mail: mdr3@swbell.net

U.S. Possessions Philatelic Society
David S. Durbin
1608 S. 22nd St.
Blue Springs MO 64015
Ph: (816) 224-3666

Groups focusing on philately of foreign countries or regions

American Society of Polar Philatelists (Antarctic areas)
Richard Julian
1153 Fairview Dr.
York PA 17403
E-mail: rajulian@netrax.net

Australian States Study Circle
Ben Palmer
GPO 1751
Sydney, N.S.W., Australia 1043

American Belgian Philatelic Society
Kenneth L. Costilow
621 Virginius Dr.
Virginia Beach VA 23452-4417
Ph: (757) 463-6081
E-mail: klc32@erols.com

Bermuda Collectors Society
Thomas J. McMahon
PO Box 1949
Stuart FL 34995

Brazil Philatelic Association
Kurt Ottenheimer
462 West Walnut St.
Long Beach NY 11561
E-mail: oak462@juno.com

British Caribbean Philatelic Study Group
Gale J. Raymond
Bali-Hai, PO Box 228
Sugar Land TX 77478-0228

British North America Philatelic Society (Canada & Provinces)
Alexander Unwin
PO Box 1686
Bellevue WA 98009-1686
www.wep.ab.ca/bnaps
E-mail: alecunwin@msn.com

British West Indies Study Circle
W. Clary Holt
PO Drawer 59
Burlington NC 27216
Ph: (336) 227-7461

Burma Philatelic Study Circle
A. Meech
7208 91st Ave.
Edmonton, AB, Canada T6B 0R8
E-mail: ameech@telusplanet.net

Ceylon Study Group
R. W. P. Frost
42 Lonsdale Road, Cannington
Bridgewater, Somerset, United Kingdom TA5 2JS

China Stamp Society
Paul H. Gault
PO Box 20711
Columbus OH 43220
www.azstarnet.com/~gersten/China.Stamp.Society.html
E-mail: gault.1@osu.edu

Colombia / Panama Philatelic Study Group
PO Box 2245
El Cajon CA 92021
E-mail: jimacross@juno.com

Society of Costa Rica Collectors
Dr. Hector R. Mena
PO Box 14831
Baton Rouge LA 70808
www.intersurf.com/~hrmena
E-mail: hrmena@intersurf.com

Croatian Philatelic Society (Croatia & other Balkan areas)
Ekrem Spahich
502 Romero, PO Box 696
Fritch TX 79036-0696
Ph: (806) 857-0129
www.hrnet.org/cps
E-mail: ou812@arn.net

Society for Czechoslovak Philately
Robert T. Cossaboom
PO Box 25332
Scott AFB IL 62225-0332
www.erols.com/sibpost
E-mail: klfck1@aol.com

East Africa Study Circle
John G. Harvey
22 High Street
Mepal, Cambridgeshire, United Kingdom CB6 2AW

Estonian Philatelic Society
Rudolf Hamar
1912 Nugget Drive
Felton CA 95018

Ethiopian Philatelic Society
Huguette Gagnon
110-10662 151A Street
Surrey, BC, Canada V3R 8T3
Ph: (604) 584-1701

Falkland Islands Philatelic Study Group
Carl J. Faulkner
Williams Inn, On-the-Green
Williamstown MA 01267-2620
Ph: (413) 458-9371

Faroe Islands Study Circle
Norman Hudson
28 Enfield Road
Ellesmere Port, South Wirral, United Kingdom L65 8BY

France & Colonies Philatelic Society
Walter Parshall
103 Spruce St.
Bloomfield NJ 07003-3514

Germany Philatelic Society
PO Box 779
Arnold MD 21012-4779
www.gps.nu
E-mail: germanyphilatelic@juno.com

German Democratic Republic Study Group of the German Philatelic Society
Ken Lawrence
PO Box 8040
State College PA 16803-8040

Great Britain Collectors Club
Janet Gordon
PO Box 42324
Cincinnati OH 45242-0324
www.gbstamps.com/gbcc
E-mail: jangnp@aol.com

Hellenic Philatelic Society of America (Greece and related areas)
Dr. Nicholas Asimakopulos
541 Cedar Hill Ave.
Wyckoff NJ 07481
Ph: (201) 447-6262

International Society of Guatemala Collectors
Mrs. Mae Vignola
105 22nd Ave.
San Francisco CA 94121

Haiti Philatelic Society
Ubaldo Del Toro
5709 Marble Archway
Alexandria VA 22310
E-mail: u007ubi@aol.com

Honduras Collectors Club
Jeff Brasor
PO Box 173
Coconut Creek FL 33097

Hong Kong Stamp Society
Dr. An-Min Chung
120 Deerfield Rd.
Broomall PA 19008
Ph: (215) 576-6850

Hungary Philatelic Society
Thomas Phillips
PO Box 1162
Fairfield CT 06432-1162

India Study Circle
John Warren
PO Box 7326
Washington DC 20044
Ph: (202) 564-6876
E-mail: warren.john@epamail.epa.gov

Indian Ocean Study Circle
K. B. Fitton
50 Firlands
Weybridge, Surrey, United Kingdom KT13 0HR
E-mail: keithfitton@intonet.co.uk

Society of Indochina Philatelists
Paul Blake
1466 Hamilton Way
San Jose CA 95125

Iran Philatelic Study Circle
David J. Armacost
PO Box 33381
Phoenix AZ 85067

Eire Philatelic Association (Ireland)
Myron G. Hill III
PO Box 1210
College Park, MD 20741-1210
http://ourworld.compuserve.com/homepages/aranman/epa.htm
E-mail: mhill@radix.net

Society of Israel Philatelists
Paul S. Aufrichtig
300 East 42nd St.
New York NY 10017

International Society for Japanese Philately
Kenneth Kamholz
PO Box 1283
Haddonfield NJ 08033
www.west.net/~lmevans/isjp.html
E-mail: kamholz@uscom.com

Korea Stamp Society
William M. Collyer
PO Box 4158
Saticoy CA 93007-0158

Latin American Philatelic Society
Piet Steen
197 Pembina Ave.
Hinton, AB, Canada T7V 2B2

Latvian Philatelic Society
J. Ronis
7 Lowes Ave.
Brampton, ON, Canada L6X 1R8

Liberian Philatelic Society
William Thomas Lockard
PO Box 106
Wellston OH 45692
Ph: (740) 384-2020
E-mail: tlockard@zoomnet.net

Liechtenstudy USA (Liechtenstein)
Ralph Schneider
PO Box 23049
Belleville IL 62223
Ph: (618) 277-8543
www.rschneiderstamps.com/info.html
E-mail: rsstamps@aol.com

Lithuanian Philatelic Society
John Variakojis
3715 W. 68th St.
Chicago IL 60629
Ph: (773) 585-8649
E-mail: variakojis@earthlink.net

Malta Study Circle
J.G.C. Lander
Waterdale House, Chequers Lane, Waterdale, Watford, Hertfordshire, United Kingdom, WD2 7LP
E-mail: Lander.JGC@btinternet.com

Mexico-Elmhurst Philatelic Society International
David Pietsch
PO Box 50997
Irvine CA 92619-0997
E-mail: mepsi@msn.com

Society for Moroccan and Tunisian Philately
206, bld. Pereire, 75017 Paris, France
http://members.aol.com/Jhaik5811/p1E.html
E-mail: jhaik5814@aol.com

Nepal & Tibet Philatelic Study Group
Roger D. Skinner
1020 Covington Road
Los Altos CA 94022-5003
Ph: (415) 968-4163

American Society of Netherlands Philately
Jan Enthoven
W6428 Riverview Drive
Onalaska WI 54650
Ph: (608) 781-8612
www.cs.cornell.edu/Info/People/aswin/NL/neth
E-mail: jenthoven@centuryinter.net

Nicaragua Study Group
Erick Rodriguez
11817 S.W. 11th St.
Miami FL 33184-2501
clubs.yahoo.com/clubs/nicaraguastudygroup
E-mail: nsgsec@yahoo.com

Society of Australasian Specialists / Oceania
Henry Bateman
PO Box 4862, Monroe LA 71211
Ph: (800) 571-0293
E-mail: ck100@iamerica.net

Orange Free State Study Circle
J. R. Stroud
28 Oxford St.
Burnham-on-sea, Somerset, United Kingdom TA8 1LQ
www.ofssc.org

Pacific Islands Study Group
John Ray
24 Woodvale Avenue
London, United Kingdom SE25 4AE
dspace.dial.pipex.com/jray/pisc.html
E-mail: jray@dial.pipex.com

Pakistan Study Circle
Jeff Siddiqui
PO Box 7002
Lynnwood WA 98046
E-mail: jeffsiddiqui@msn.com

Papuan Philatelic Society
Steven Zirinsky
PO Box 49, Ansonia Station
New York NY 10023
Ph: (212) 665-0765
E-mail: szirinsky@compuserve.com

International Philippine Philatelic Society
Robert F. Yacano
PO Box 100
Toast NC 27049
Ph: (336) 783-0768

Pitcairn Islands Study Group
Nelson A. L. Weller
2940 Wesleyan Lane
Winston-Salem NC 27106
Ph: (910) 724-6398
E-mail: nalweller@juno.com

Plebiscite-Memel-Saar Study Group of the German Philatelic Society
Clay Wallace
100 Lark Court
Alamo CA 94507
E-mail: clay.wallace@brightware.com

Polonus Philatelic Society (Poland)
Roman H. Strzelecki
PO Box 458
Berwyn IL 60402
Ph: (708) 749-9345

International Society for Portuguese Philately
Clyde Homen
1491 Bonnie View Rd.
Hollister CA 95023-5117
E-mail: cjh@hollinet.com

Rhodesian Study Circle
William R. Wallace
PO Box 16381
San Francisco CA 94116
E-mail: bwall8rscr@earthlink.net

Romanian Chapter of Croatian Philatelic Society
Dan Demetriade
PO Box 09700
Detroit MI 48209

Canadian Society of Russian Philately
Andrew Cronin
PO Box 5722, Station A
Toronto, ON, Canada M5W 1P2
Ph: (905) 764-8968

Rossica Society of Russian Philately
George G. Werbizky
409 Jones Rd.
Vestal NY 13850-3246

Ryukyu Philatelic Specialist Society
Carmine J. DiVincenzo
PO Box 381
Clayton CA 94517-0381

St. Helena, Ascension & Tristan Da Cunha Philatelic Society
Dr. Russell V. Skavaril
222 East Torrance Road
Columbus OH 43214-3834
Ph: (614) 262-3046
http://ourworld.compuserve.com/homepages/st_helena_ascen_tdc

St. Pierre & Miquelon Philatelic Society
David Salovey
PO Box 464
New York NY 10014-0464

Associated Collectors of El Salvador
Jeff Brasor
PO Box 173
Coconut Creek FL 33097

Fellowship of Samoa Specialists
Jack R. Hughes
1541 Wellington St.
Oakland CA 94602-1751

Sarawak Specialists' Society
Stu Leven
4031 Samson Way
San Jose CA 95124-3733
E-mail: stulev@ix.netcom.com

Scandinavian Collectors Club
Donald B. Brent
PO Box 13196
El Cajon CA 92020
www.nb.net/~downs/scc/scc.htm
E-mail: dbrent47@sprynet.com

Philatelic Society for Greater Southern Africa
William C. Brooks VI
200 East 30th, Apt. 144
San Bernardino CA 92404-2302
Ph: (602)839-8796
E-mail: lawrence@enuxsa.eas.asu.edu

Spanish Philatelic Society
Robert H. Penn
1108 Walnut Drive
Danielsville PA 18038
Ph: (610) 767-6793

Sudan Study Group
N. D. Collier
34 Padleys Lane
Burton Joyce, Nottingham,
United Kingdom NG14 5BZ

American Helvetia Philatelic Society (Switzerland, Liechtenstein)
Richard T. Hall
PO Box 666
Manhattan Beach CA 90267-0666
E-mail: rtavish@pacbell.net

Tannu Tuva Collectors Society
Ken Simon
513 Sixth Ave. So.
Lake Worth FL 33460-4507
Ph: (561) 588-5954
www.seflin.org/tuva
E-mail: p003115b@pb.seflin.org

Society for Thai Philately
H. R. Blakeney
PO Box 25644
Oklahoma City OK 73125
E-mail: HRBlakeney@aol.com

Tonga/Tin Can Mail Study Circle
Laurence L. Benson
1832 Jean Ave.
Tallahassee FL 32308-5227
Ph: (850) 877-7001
members.aol.com/tongajan/ttcmsc.html
E-mail: LLBenson@aol.com

Turkish and Ottoman Philatelic Society
Robert Stuchell
173 Valley Stream Lane
Wayne PA 19087

Ukrainian Philatelic & Numismatic Society
Bohdan O. Pauk
PO Box 11184
Chicago IL 60611-0184
Ph: (773) 276-0355
E-mail: yurko@warwick.net

Vatican Philatelic Society
Sal Quinonez
2 Aldersgate, Apt. 119
Riverhead NY 11901
Ph: (516) 727-6426

West Africa Study Circle
Jack Ince
PO Box 858
Stirling, ON, Canada K0K 3E0
Ph: (613) 395-1926
ourworld.compuserve.com/homepages/FrankWalton
E-mail: pamjack@bel.auracom.com

Western Australia Study Group
Brian Pope
PO Box 423
Claremont, Western Australia,
Australia 6910

Yugoslavia Study Group of the Croatian Philatelic Society
Michael Lenard
1514 North 3rd Ave.
Wausau WI 54401

Topical Groups

American Indian Philatelic Society
Charles Eson
128 Western Ave.
Altamont NY 12009

Americana Unit
Dennis Dengel
17 Peckham Rd.
Poughkeepsie NY 12603-2018
www.philately.com/society_news/americana_unit.htm
E-mail: 70363.3621@compuserve.com

Astronomy Study Unit
George Young
PO Box 632
Tewksbury MA 01876-0632
Ph: (978) 851-8283
www.fandm.edu/departments/astronomy/miscell/astunit.html
E-mail: george-young@msn.com

Bicycle Stamp Club
Norman Batho
358 Iverson Place
East Windsor NJ 08520
Ph: (609) 448-9547
E-mail: normbatho@worldnet.att.net

Canadiana Study Unit
John Peebles
PO Box 3262, Station "A"
London, ON, Canada N6A 4K3
E-mail: john.peebles@odyssey.on.ca

Captain Cook Study Unit
Brian P. Sandford
173 Minuteman Dr.
Concord MA 01742-1923
freespace.virgin.net/chris.jones/ccsu.htm
E-mail: borehami@williscorroon.com

Casey Jones Railroad Unit
Oliver Atchison
PO Box 31631
San Francisco CA 94131-0631
Ph: (415) 648-8057
E-mail: casey_jones@gowebway.com

Cats on Stamps Study Unit
Mary Ann Brown
3006 Wade Rd.
Durham NC 27705

Chemistry & Physics Study Unit
Dr. Roland Hirsch
20458 Water Point Lane
Germantown MD 20874
E-mail: rfhirsch@erols.com

Chess on Stamps Study Unit
Anne Kasonic
7625 County Road #153
Interlaken NY 14847
www.iglobal.net/home/reott/stamps1.htm#cossu
E-mail: akasonic@epix.net

Christmas Philatelic Club
Linda Lawrence
312 Northwood Drive
Lexington KY 40505
Ph: (606) 293-0151
www.hwcn.org/link/cpc
E-mail: stamplinda@aol.com

Christopher Columbus Philatelic Society
Donald R. Ager
PO Box 71
Hillsboro NH 03244
Ph: (603) 464-5379
E-mail: don_ager@conknet.com

Collectors of Religion on Stamps
Verna Shackleton
425 North Linwood Avenue #110
Appleton WI 54914
Ph: (920) 734-2417
www.powemetonline.com/corosec/coros1.htm
E-mail: corosec@powernetonline.com

Dogs on Stamps Study Unit
Morris Raskin
202A Newport Rd.
Cranbury NJ 08512
Ph: (609) 655-7411
E-mail: mraskin@worldnet.att.net

Earth's Physical Features Study Group
Fred Klein
515 Magdalena Ave.
Los Altos CA 94024
www.philately.com/society_news/earths_physical.htm

Embroidery, Stitchery, Textile Unit
Helen N. Cushman
1001 Genter St., Apt. 9H
La Jolla CA 92037
Ph: (619) 459-1194

Europa Study Unit
Hank Klos
PO Box 611
Bensenville IL 60106
E-mail: eunity@aol.com

Fine & Performing Arts
Ruth Richards
10393 Derby Dr.
Laurel MD 20723
www.philately.com/society_news/fap.htm
E-mail: bersec@aol.com

Gay & Lesbian History on Stamps Club
Joe Petronie
PO Box 515981
Dallas TX 75251-5981
E-mail: glhsc@aol.com

Gems, Minerals & Jewelry Study Group
George Young
PO Box 632
Tewksbury MA 01876-0632
Ph: (978) 851-8283
www.rockhounds.com/rockshop/gmjsuapp.txt
E-mail: george-young@msn.com

Graphics Philately Association
Mark Winnegrad
1450 Parkchester Road
Bronx NY 10462

Journalists, Authors & Poets on Stamps
Louis Forster
7561 East 24th Court
Wichita KS 67226

Lighthouse Stamp Society
Dalene Thomas
8612 West Warren Lane
Lakewood CO 80227-2352
Ph: (303) 986-6620
www.users.uswest.net/~dalene1
E-mail: dalene1@uswest.net

Lions International Stamp Club
John Bargus
RR #1
Mill Bay, BC, Canada V0R 2P0
Ph: (250) 743-5782

Mask Study Unit
Carolyn Weber
PO Box 2542
Oxnard CA 93034
www.philately.com/society_news/masks.htm

Mathematical Study Unit
Estelle Buccino
5615 Glenwood Rd.
Bethesda MD 20817
Ph: (301) 718-8898

Medical Subjects Unit
Dr. Frederick C. Skvara
PO Box 6228
Bridgewater NJ 08807

Mesoamerican Archeology Study Unit
Chris Moser
PO Box 1442
Riverside CA 92502
E-mail:cmoser@ci.riverside.ca.us

Napoleonic Age Philatelists
Ken Berry
7513 Clayton Dr.
Oklahoma City OK 73132-5636
Ph: (405) 721-0044

Parachute Study Group
Bill Wickert
3348 Clubhouse Road
Virginia Beach VA 23452-5339
Ph: (757) 486-3614

Petroleum Philatelic Society International
Linda W. Corwin
5427 Pine Springs Court
Conroe TX 77304

Philatelic Computing Study Group
Robert de Violini
PO Box 5025
Oxnard CA 93031
www.west.net/~stamps1/pcsg/pcsg.html
E-mail: dviolini@west.net

Philatelic Music Circle
Cathleen Osborne
PO Box 1781
Sequim WA 98382
Ph: (360) 683-6373
www.stampshows.com/pmc.html

Rainbow Study Unit
Shirley Sutton
PO Box 37
Lone Pine, AB, Canada T0G 1M0
Ph: (304) 584-2268
E-mail: george-young@msn.com

Rotary on Stamps Unit
Donald Fiery
PO Box 333
Hanover PA 17331
Ph: (717) 632-8921

Scouts on Stamps Society International
Carl Schauer
PO Box 526
Belen NM 87002
Ph: (505) 864-0098
www.sossi.org
E-mail: rfrank@sossi.org

Ships on Stamps Unit
Robert Stuckert
2750 Highway 21 East
Paint Lick KY 40461
Ph: (606) 925-4901

Space Unit
Carmine Torrisi
PO Box 780241
Maspeth NY 11378
Ph: (718) 386-7882
stargate.1usa.com/stamps/

Sports Philatelists International
Margaret Jones
5310 Lindenwood Ave.
St. Louis MO 63109-1758
www.concentric.net/~laimins/spi.html

Stamps on Stamps / Centenary Unit
William Critzer
13385 Country Way
Los Altos Hills CA 94022
Ph: (650) 941-1567
http://ourworld.compuserve.com/homepages/soscu
E-mail: willcrit@aol.com

Windmill Study Unit
Walter J. Hollien
PO Box 346
Long Valley NJ 07853-0346

Wine on Stamps Study Unit
James D. Crum
5132 Sepulveda
San Bernardino CA 92404-1134
Ph: (909) 886-3186
E-mail: jdakcrum@aol.com

Women on Stamps Study Unit
Phebe Quattrucci
259 Middle Road
Falmouth ME 04105

Zeppelin Collectors Club
Cheryl Ganz
PO Box A3843
Chicago IL 60690-3843

Expertizing Services

The following organizations will, for a fee, provide expert opinions about stamps submitted to them. Collectors should contact these organizations to find out about their fees and requirements before submitting philatelic material to them. The listing of these groups here is not intended as an endorsement by Scott Publishing Co.

General Expertizing Services

American Philatelic Expertizing Service (a service of the American Philatelic Society)
PO Box 8000
State College PA 16803
Ph: (814) 237-3808
Fax: (814) 237-6128
www.west.net/~stamps1/aps.html
E-mail: ambristo@stamps.org
Areas of Expertise: Worldwide

B. P. A. Expertising, Ltd.
PO Box 137
Leatherhead, Surrey, United Kingdom KT22 0RG
E-mail: sec.bpa@tcom.co.uk
Areas of Expertise: British Commonwealth, Great Britain, Classics of Europe, South America and the Far East

Philatelic Foundation
501 Fifth Ave., Rm. 1901
New York NY 10017
Areas of Expertise: U.S. & Worldwide

Professional Stamp Experts
PO Box 43-0055
Miami FL 33243-0055
Ph: (305) 971-9010
Fax: (305) 259-4701
www.stampexperts.com
E-mail: randyshoemaker@netscape.net
Areas of Expertise: Stamps and covers of U.S., U.S. Possessions, British Commonwealth

Royal Philatelic Society Expert Committee
41 Devonshire Place
London, United Kingdom W1N 1PE
Areas of Expertise: All

Expertizing Services Covering Specific Fields Or Countries

Canadian Society of Russian Philately Expertizing Service
PO Box 5722, Station A
Toronto, ON, Canada M5W 1P2
Fax: (416)932-0853
Areas of Expertise: Russian areas

Confederate Stamp Alliance Authentication Service
522 Old State Road
Lincoln DE 19960-9797
Ph: (302) 422-2656
Fax: (302) 424-1990
www.webuystamps.com/csaauth.htm
E-mail: trish@ce.net
Areas of Expertise: Confederate stamps and postal history

Croatian Philatelic Society Expertizing Service
PO Box 696
Fritch TX 79036-0696
Ph: (806) 857-0129
E-mail: ou812@arn.net
Areas of Expertise: Croatia and other Balkan areas

Errors, Freaks and Oddities Collectors Club Expertizing Service
138 East Lakemont Dr.
Kingsland GA 31548
Ph: (912) 729-1573
Areas of Expertise: U.S. errors, freaks and oddities

Estonian Philatelic Society Expertizing Service
39 Clafford Lane
Melville NY 11747
Ph: (516) 421-2078
E-mail: esto4@aol.com
Areas of Expertise: Estonia

Hawaiian Philatelic Society Expertizing Service
PO Box 10115
Honolulu HI 96816-0115
Areas of Expertise: Hawaii

Hong Kong Stamp Society Expertizing Service
PO Box 206
Glenside PA 19038
Fax: (215) 576-6850
Areas of Expertise: Hong Kong

International Society for Japanese Philately Expertizing Committee
32 King James Court
Staten Island NY 10308-2910
Ph: (718) 227-5229
Areas of Expertise: Japan and related areas, except WWII Japanese Occupation issues

International Society for Portuguese Philately Expertizing Service
PO Box 43146
Philadelphia PA 19129-3146
Ph: (215) 843-2106
Fax: (215) 843-2106
E-mail: s.s.washburne@worldnet.att.net
Areas of Expertise: Portugal and colonies

Mexico-Elmhurst Philatelic Society International Expertization
PO Box 26644
Austin TX 78755
Areas of Expertise: Mexico

Philatelic Society for Greater Southern Africa Expert Panel
13955 W. 30th Ave.
Golden CO 80401
Areas of Expertise: Entire South and South West Africa area, Bechuanalands, Basutoland, Swaziland

Ryukyu Philatelic Specialist Society Expertizing Service
1710 Buena Vista Ave.
Spring Valley CA 91977-4458
Ph: (619) 697-3205
Areas of Expertise: Ryukyu Islands

Ukrainian Philatelic & Numismatic Society Expertizing Service
30552 Dell Lane
Warren MI 48092-1862
Ph: (810) 751-5754
Areas of Expertise: Ukraine, Western Ukraine

V. G. Greene Philatelic Research Foundation
Box 100, First Canadian Place
Toronto, ON, Canada M5X 1B2
Ph: (416) 863-4593
Fax: (416) 863-4592
Areas of Expertise: British North America

Information on Catalogue Values, Grade and Condition

Catalogue Value

The Scott Catalogue value is a retail value; that is, an amount you could expect to pay for a stamp in the grade of Very Fine with no faults. Any exceptions to the grade valued will be noted in the text. The general introduction on the following pages and the individual section introductions further explain the type of material that is valued. The value listed for any given stamp is a reference that reflects recent actual dealer selling prices for that item.

Dealer retail price lists, public auction results, published prices in advertising and individual solicitation of retail prices from dealers, collectors and specialty organizations have been used in establishing the values found in this catalogue. Scott Publishing Co. values stamps, but Scott is not a company engaged in the business of buying and selling stamps as a dealer.

Use this catalogue as a guide for buying and selling. The actual price you pay for a stamp may be higher or lower than the catalogue value because of many different factors, including the amount of personal service a dealer offers, or increased or decreased interest in the country or topic represented by a stamp or set. An item may occasionally be offered at a lower price as a "loss leader," or as part of a special sale. You also may obtain an item inexpensively at public auction because of little interest at that time or as part of a large lot.

Stamps that are of a lesser grade than Very Fine, or those with condition problems, generally trade at lower prices than those given in this catalogue. Stamps of exceptional quality in both grade and condition often command higher prices than those listed.

Values for pre-1900 unused issues are for stamps with approximately half or more of their original gum. Stamps with most or all of their original gum may be expected to sell for more, and stamps with less than half of their original gum may be expected to sell for somewhat less than the values listed. On rarer stamps, it may be expected that the original gum will be somewhat more disturbed than it will be on more common issues. Post-1900 unused issues are assumed to have full original gum. From breakpoints in most countries' listings, stamps are valued as never hinged, due to the wide availability of stamps in that condition. These notations are prominently placed in the listings and in the country information preceding the listings. Some countries also feature listings with dual values for hinged and never-hinged stamps.

Grade

A stamp's grade and condition are crucial to its value. The accompanying illustrations show examples of Very Fine stamps from different time periods, along with examples of stamps in Fine to Very Fine and Extremely Fine grades as points of reference.

FINE stamps (illustrations not shown) have designs that are noticeably off center on two sides. Imperforate stamps may have small margins, and earlier issues may show the design touching one edge of the stamp design. For perforated stamps, perfs may barely clear the design on one side, and very early issues normally will have the perforations slightly cutting into the design. Used stamps may have heavier than usual cancellations.

FINE-VERY FINE stamps may be somewhat off center on one side, or slightly off center on two sides. Imperforate stamps will have two margins of at least normal size, and the design will not touch any edge. For perforated stamps, the perfs are well clear of the design, but are still noticeably off center. *However, early issues of a country may be printed in such a way that the design naturally is very close to the edges. In these cases, the perforations may cut into the design very slightly.* Used stamps will not have a cancellation that detracts from the design.

VERY FINE stamps may be slightly off center on one side, but the design will be well clear of the edge. The stamp will present a nice, balanced appearance. Imperforate stamps will have three normal-sized margins. *However, early issues of many countries may be printed in such a way that the perforations may touch the design on one or more sides. Where this is the case, a boxed note will be found defining the centering and margins of the stamps being valued.* Used stamps will have light or otherwise neat cancellations. This is the grade used to establish Scott Catalogue values.

EXTREMELY FINE stamps are close to being perfectly centered. Imperforate stamps will have even margins that are larger than normal. Even the earliest perforated issues will have perforations clear of the design on all sides.

Condition

Grade addresses only centering and (for used stamps) cancellation. *Condition* refers to factors other than grade that affect a stamp's desirability.

Factors that can increase the value of a stamp include exceptionally wide margins, particularly fresh color, the presence of selvage, and plate or die varieties. Unusual cancels on used stamps (particularly those of the 19th century) can greatly enhance their value as well.

Factors other than faults that decrease the value of a stamp include loss of original gum, regumming, a hinge remnant or foreign object adhering to the gum, natural inclusions, straight edges, and markings or notations applied by collectors or dealers.

Faults include missing pieces, tears, pin or other holes, surface scuffs, thin spots, creases, toning, short or pulled perforations, clipped perforations, oxidation or other forms of color changelings, soiling, stains, and such man-made changes as reperforations or the chemical removal or lightening of a cancellation.

Scott Publishing Co. recognizes that there is no formally enforced grading scheme for postage stamps, and that the final price you pay or obtain for a stamp will be determined by individual agreement at the time of transaction.

On the following two pages are illustrations of various stamps from countries appearing in this volume. These stamps are arranged by country, and they represent early or important issues that are often found in widely different grades in the marketplace. The editors believe the illustrations will prove useful in showing the margin size and centering that will be seen on the various issues.

In addition to the matters of margin size and centering, collectors are reminded that the very fine stamps valued in the Scott catalogues also will possess fresh color and intact perforations, and they will be free from defects.

Most examples shown are computer – manipulated images made from single digitized master illustrations.

INTRODUCTION

13A

Fine-Very Fine →

SCOTT CATALOGUES VALUE STAMPS IN THIS GRADE
Very Fine →

Extremely Fine →

Fine-Very Fine →

SCOTT CATALOGUES VALUE STAMPS IN THIS GRADE
Very Fine →

Extremely Fine →

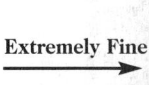

14A INTRODUCTION

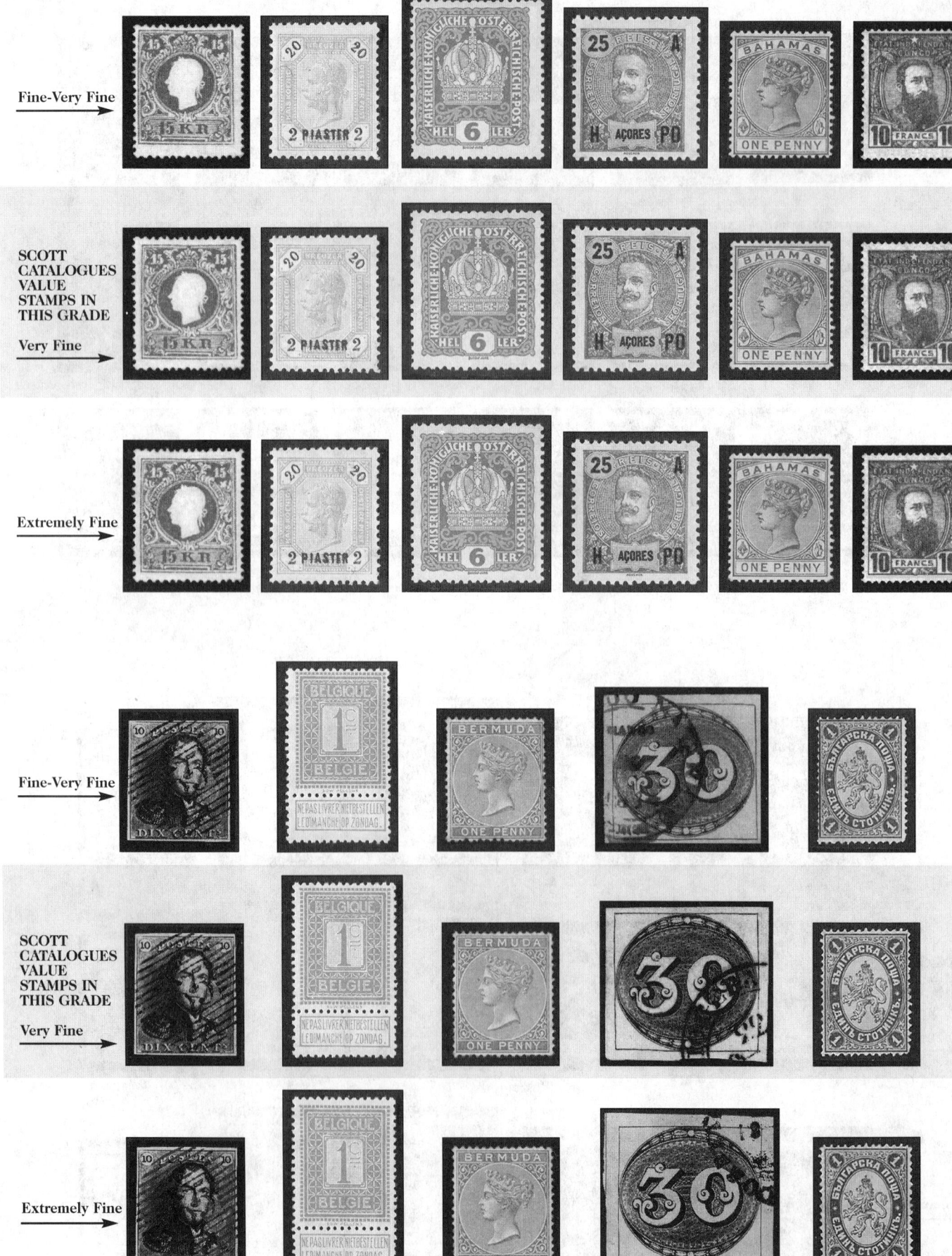

INTRODUCTION

15A

For purposes of helping to determine the gum condition and value of an unused stamp, Scott Publishing Co. presents the following chart which details different gum conditions and indicates how the conditions correlate with the Scott values for unused stamps. Used together, the Illustrated Grading Chart on the previous pages and this Illustrated Gum Chart should allow catalogue users to better understand the grade and gum condition of stamps valued in the Scott catalogues.

Gum Categories:	MINT N.H.	ORIGINAL GUM (O.G.)					NO GUM
	Mint Never Hinged *Free from any disturbance*	**Lightly Hinged** *Faint impression of a removed hinge over a small area*	**Hinge Mark or Remnant** *Prominent hinged spot with part or all of the hinge remaining*	**Large part o.g.** *Approximately half or more of the gum intact*	**Small part o.g.** *Approximately less than half of the gum intact*	**No gum** *Only if issued with gum*
Commonly Used Symbol:	★★	★	★	★	★	(★)
Pre-1900 Issues (Pre-1890 for U.S.)	*Very fine pre-1900 stamps in these categories trade at a premium over Scott value*			Scott Value for "Unused"		Scott "No Gum" listings for selected unused classic stamps
From 1900 to breakpoints for listings of never-hinged stamps	Scott "Never Hinged" listings for selected unused stamps	Scott Value for "Unused" (Actual value will be affected by the degree of hinging of the full o.g.)				
From breakpoints noted for many countries	Scott Value for "Unused"					

Never Hinged (NH; ★★): A never-hinged stamp will have full original gum that will have no hinge mark or disturbance. The presence of an expertizer's mark does not disqualify a stamp from this designation.

Original Gum (OG; ★): Pre-1900 stamps should have approximately half or more of their original gum. On rarer stamps, it may be expected that the original gum will be somewhat more disturbed that it will be on more common issues. Post-1900 stamps should have full original gum. Original gum will show some disturbance caused by a previous hinge(s) which may be present or entirely removed. The actual value of a post-1900 stamp will be affected by the degree of hinging of the full original gum.

Disturbed Original Gum: Gum showing noticeable effects of humidity, climate or hinging over more than half of the gum. The significance of gum disturbance in valuing a stamp in any of the Original Gum categories depends on the degree of disturbance, the rarity and normal gum condition of the issue and other variables affecting quality.

Regummed (RG; (★)): A regummed stamp is a stamp without gum that has had some type of gum privately applied at a time after it was issued. This normally is done to deceive collectors and/or dealers into thinking that the stamp has original gum and therefore has a higher value. A regummed stamp is considered the same as a stamp with none of its original gum for purposes of grading.

Catalogue Tabs

Looking up listings in the Scott Catalogue has never been easier!

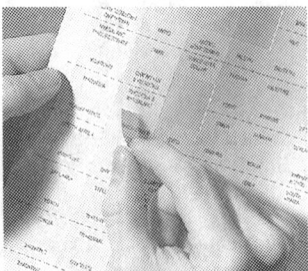

1. Scott Catalogue Tabs make referencing listings quick and easy. Simply select the country name or specialty area from the sheet.

2. Affix a portion of the tab to the appropriate page. Fold tab in half at the dotted line.

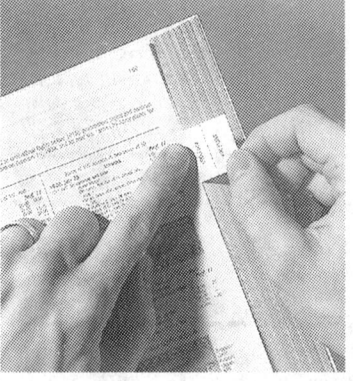

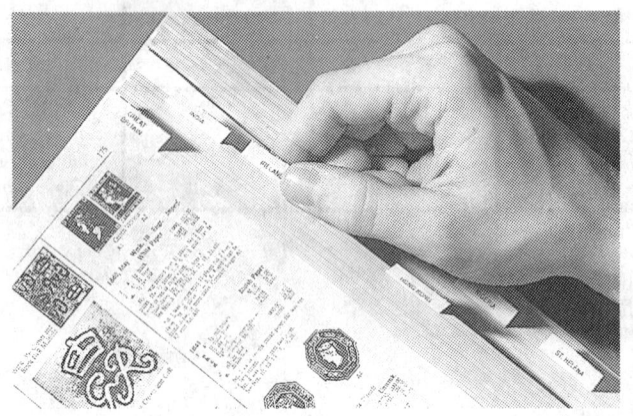

3. Use the tabs to reference catalogue listings. Blank tabs also included.

Tabs available for each Volume of the Scott Catalogue

CT1	Catalogue Tabs Volume 1 *U.S. and Countries A - B*	$2.95	**CT5**	Catalogue Tabs Volume 5 *Countries P - Slovenia*	$2.95
CT2	Catalogue Tabs Volume 2 *Countries C - F*	$2.95	**CT6**	Catalogue Tabs Volume 6 *Countries Solomon Islands - Z*	$2.95
CT3	Catalogue Tabs Volume 3 *Countries G - I*	$2.95	**CLGT6**	Catalogue Tabs *U.S. Specialized*	$2.95
CT4	Catalogue Tabs Volume 4 *Countries J - O*	$2.95	**CLGTC**	Catalogue Tabs *Classic Specialized*	$2.95

Scott Catalogue Tabs are available from your favorite stamp dealer or direct from:

1-800-572-6885
P.O. Box 828 Sidney OH 45365-0828
www.scottonline.com

Catalogue Listing Policy

It is the intent of Scott Publishing Co. to list all postage stamps of the world in the *Scott Standard Postage Stamp Catalogue*. The only strict criteria for listing is that stamps be decreed legal for postage by the issuing country. Whether the primary intent of issuing a given stamp or set was for sale to postal patrons or to stamp collectors is not part of our listing criteria. Scott's role is to provide basic comprehensive postage stamp information. It is up to each stamp collector to choose which items to include in a collection.

It is Scott's objective to seek reasons why a stamp should be listed, rather than why it should not. Nevertheless, there are certain types of items that will not be listed. These include the following:

1. Unissued items that are not officially distributed or released by the issuing postal authority. Even if such a stamp is "accidentally" distributed to the philatelic or even postal market, it remains unissued. If such items are officially issued at a later date by the country, they will be listed. Unissued items consist of those that have been printed and then held from sale for reasons such as change in government, errors found on stamps or something deemed objectionable about a stamp subject or design.

2. Stamps "issued" by non-existent postal entities or fantasy countries, such as Nagaland, Occusi-Ambeno, Staffa, Sedang, Torres Straits and others.

3. Semi-official or unofficial items not required for postage. Examples include items issued by private agencies for their own express services. When such items are required for delivery, or are valid as prepayment of postage, they are listed.

4. Local stamps issued for local use only. Postage stamps issued by governments specifically for "domestic" use, such as Haiti Scott 219-228, or the United States non-denominated stamps, are not considered to be locals, since they are valid for postage throughout the country of origin.

5. Items not valid for postal use. For example, a few countries have issued souvenir sheets that are not valid for postage. This area also includes a number of worldwide charity labels (some denominated) that do not pay postage.

6. Intentional varieties, such as imperforate stamps that look like their perforated counterparts and are issued in very small quantities. These are often controlled issues intended for speculation.

7. Items distributed by the issuing government only to a limited group, such as a stamp club, philatelic exhibition or a single stamp dealer, and later brought to market at inflated prices. These items normally will be included in a footnote.

The fact that a stamp has been used successfully as postage, even on international mail, is not in itself sufficient proof that it was legitimately issued. Numerous examples of so-called stamps from non-existent countries are known to have been used to post letters that have successfully passed through the international mail system.

There are certain items that are subject to interpretation. When a stamp falls outside our specifications, it may be listed along with a cautionary footnote.

A number of factors are considered in our approach to analyzing how a stamp is listed. The following list of factors is presented to share with you, the catalogue user, the complexity of the listing process.

Additional printings — "Additional printings" of a previously issued stamp may range from an item that is totally different to cases where it is impossible to differentiate from the original. At least a minor number (a small-letter suffix) is assigned if there is a distinct change in stamp shade, noticeably redrawn design, or a significantly different perforation measurement. A major number (numeral or numeral and capital-letter combination) is assigned if the editors feel the "additional printing" is sufficiently different from the original that it constitutes a different issue.

Commemoratives — Where practical, commemoratives with the same theme are placed in a set. For example, the U.S. Civil War Centenniel set of 1961-65 and the Constitution Bicentennial series of 1989-90 appear as sets. Countries such as Japan and Korea issue such material on a regular basis, with an announced, or at least predictable, number of stamps known in advance. Occasionally, however, stamp sets that were released over a period of years have been separated. Appropriately placed footnotes will guide you to each set's continuation.

Definitive sets — Blocks of numbers generally have been reserved for definitive sets, based on previous experience with any given country. If a few more stamps were issued in a set than originally expected, they often have been inserted into the original set with a capital-letter suffix, such as U.S. Scott 1059A. If it appears that many more stamps than the originally allotted block will be released before the set is completed, a new block of numbers will be reserved, with the original one being closed off. In some cases, such as the British Machin Head series or the U.S. Transportation and Great Americans series, several blocks of numbers exist. Appropriately placed footnotes will guide you to each set's continuation.

New country — Membership in the Universal Postal Union is not a consideration for listing status or order of placement within the catalogue. The index will tell you in what volume or page number the listings begin.

"No release date" items — The amount of information available for any given stamp issue varies greatly from country to country and even from time to time. Extremely comprehensive information about new stamps is available from some countries well before the stamps are released. By contrast some countries do not provide information about stamps or release dates. Most countries, however, fall between these extremes. A country may provide denominations or subjects of stamps from upcoming issues that are not issued as planned. Sometimes, philatelic agencies, those private firms hired to represent countries, add these later-issued items to sets well after the formal release date. This time period can range from weeks to years. If these items were officially released by the country, they will be added to the appropriate spot in the set. In many cases, the specific release date of a stamp or set of stamps may never be known.

Overprints — The color of an overprint is always noted if it is other than black. Where more than one color of ink has been used on overprints of a single set, the color used is noted. Early overprint and surcharge illustrations were altered to prevent their use by forgers.

Se-tenants — Connected stamps of differing features (se-tenants) will be listed in the format most commonly collected. This includes pairs, blocks or larger multiples. Se-tenant units are not always symmetrical. An example is Australia Scott 508, which is a block of seven stamps. If the stamps are primarily collected as a unit, the major number may be assigned to the multiple, with minors going to each component stamp. In cases where continuous-design or other unit se-tenants will receive significant postal use, each stamp is given a major Scott number listing. This includes issues from the United States, Canada, Germany and Great Britain, for example.

Understanding the Listings

On the opposite page is an enlarged "typical" listing from this catalogue. Below are detailed explanations of each of the highlighted parts of the listing.

① Scott number — Scott catalogue numbers are used to identify specific items when buying, selling or trading stamps. Each listed postage stamp from every country has a unique Scott catalogue number. Therefore, Germany Scott 99, for example, can only refer to a single stamp. Although the Scott catalogue usually lists stamps in chronological order by date of issue, there are exceptions. When a country has issued a set of stamps over a period of time, those stamps within the set are kept together without regard to date of issue. This follows the normal collecting approach of keeping stamps in their natural sets.

When a country issues a set of stamps over a period of time, a group of consecutive catalogue numbers is reserved for the stamps in that set, as issued. If that group of numbers proves to be too few, capital-letter suffixes, such as "A" or "B," may be added to existing numbers to create enough catalogue numbers to cover all items in the set. A capital-letter suffix indicates a major Scott catalogue number listing. Scott uses a suffix letter only once. Therefore, a catalogue number listing with a capital-letter prefix will not also be found with the same letter (lower case) used as a minor-letter listing. If there is a Scott 16A in a set, for example, there will not also be a Scott 16a.

Suffix letters are not cumulative. A minor variety of Scott 16A would be Scott 16b, not Scott 16Ab. Any exceptions, such as Great Britain Scott 358cp, are clearly indicated.

There are times when a reserved block of Scott catalogue numbers is too large for a set, leaving some numbers unused. Such gaps in the numbering sequence also occur when the catalogue editors move an item's listing elsewhere or have removed it entirely from the catalogue. Scott does not attempt to account for every possible number, but rather attempts to assure that each stamp is assigned its own number.

Scott numbers designating regular postage normally are only numerals. Scott numbers for other types of stamps, such as air post, semipostal, postal tax, postage due, occupation and others have a prefix consisting of one or more capital letters or a combination of numerals and capital letters.

② Illustration number — Illustration or design-type numbers are used to identify each catalogue illustration. For most sets, the lowest face-value stamp is shown. It then serves as an example of the basic design approach for other stamps not illustrated. Where more than one stamp use the same illustration number, but have differences in design, the design paragraph or the description line clearly indicates the design on each stamp not illustrated. Where there are both vertical and horizontal designs in a set, a single illustration may be used, with the exceptions noted in the design paragraph or description line.

When an illustration is followed by a lower-case letter in parentheses, such as "A2(b)," the trailing letter indicates which overprint or surcharge illustration applies.

Illustrations normally are 75 percent of the original size of the stamp. An effort has been made to note all illustrations not illustrated at that percentage. Virtually all souvenir sheet illustrations are reduced even more. Overprints and surcharges are shown at 100 percent of their original size, unless otherwise noted. In some cases, the illustration will be placed above the set, between listings or omitted completely. Overprint and surcharge illustrations are not placed in this catalogue for purposes of expertizing stamps.

③ Paper color — The color of a stamp's paper is noted in italic type when the paper used is not white.

④ Listing styles — There are two principal types of catalogue listings: major and minor.

Major listings are in a larger type style than minor listings. The catalogue number is a numeral that can be found with or without a capital-letter suffix, and with or without a prefix.

Minor listings are in a smaller type style and have a small-letter suffix or (if the listing immediately follows that of the major number) may show only the letter. These listings identify a variety of the major item. Examples include perforation, color, watermark or printing method differences, multiples (some souvenir sheets, booklet panes and se-tenant combinations), and singles of multiples.

Examples of major number listings include 16, 28A, B97, C13A, 10N5, and 10N6A. Examples of minor numbers are 16a and C13b.

⑤ Basic information about a stamp or set — Introducing each stamp issue is a small section (usually a line listing) of basic information about a stamp or set. This section normally includes the date of issue, method of printing, perforation, watermark and, sometimes, some additional information of note. *Printing method, perforation and watermark apply to the following sets until a change is noted.* Stamps created by overprinting or surcharging previous issues are assumed to have the same perforation, watermark and printing method as the original. Dates of issue are as precise as Scott is able to confirm and often reflect the dates on first-day covers, rather than the actual date of release.

⑥ Denomination — This normally refers to the face value of the stamp; that is, the cost of the unused stamp at the post office at the time of issue. When a denomination is shown in parentheses, it does not appear on the stamp. This includes the non-denominated stamps of the United States, Brazil and Great Britain, for example.

⑦ Color or other description — This area provides information to solidify identification of a stamp. In many recent cases, a description of the stamp design appears in this space, rather than a listing of colors.

⑧ Year of issue — In stamp sets that have been released in a period that spans more than a year, the number shown in parentheses is the year that stamp first appeared. Stamps without a date appeared during the first year of the issue. Dates are not always given for minor varieties.

⑨ Value unused and Value used — The Scott catalogue values are based on stamps that are in a grade of Very Fine unless stated otherwise. Unused values refer to items that have not seen postal, revenue or any other duty for which they were intended. Pre-1900 unused stamps that were issued with gum must have at least most of their original gum. Later issues are assumed to have full original gum. From breakpoints specified in most countries' listings, stamps are valued as never hinged. Stamps issued without gum are noted. Modern issues with PVA or other synthetic adhesives may appear ungummed. Self-adhesive stamps are valued as appearing undisturbed on their original backing paper. For a more detailed explanation of these values, please see the "Catalogue Value," "Condition" and "Understanding Valuing Notations" elsewhere in this introduction.

In some cases, where used stamps are more valuable than unused stamps, the value is for an example with a contemporaneous cancel, rather than a modern cancel or a smudge or other unclear marking. For those stamps that were released for postal and fiscal purposes, the used value represents a postally used stamp. Stamps with revenue cancels generally sell for less.

⑩ Changes in basic set information — Bold type is used to show any changes in the basic data given for a set of stamps. This includes perforation differences from one stamp to the next or a different paper, printing method or watermark.

⑪ Total value of a set — The total value of sets of three or more stamps issued after 1900 are shown. The set line also notes the range of Scott numbers and total number of stamps included in the grouping.

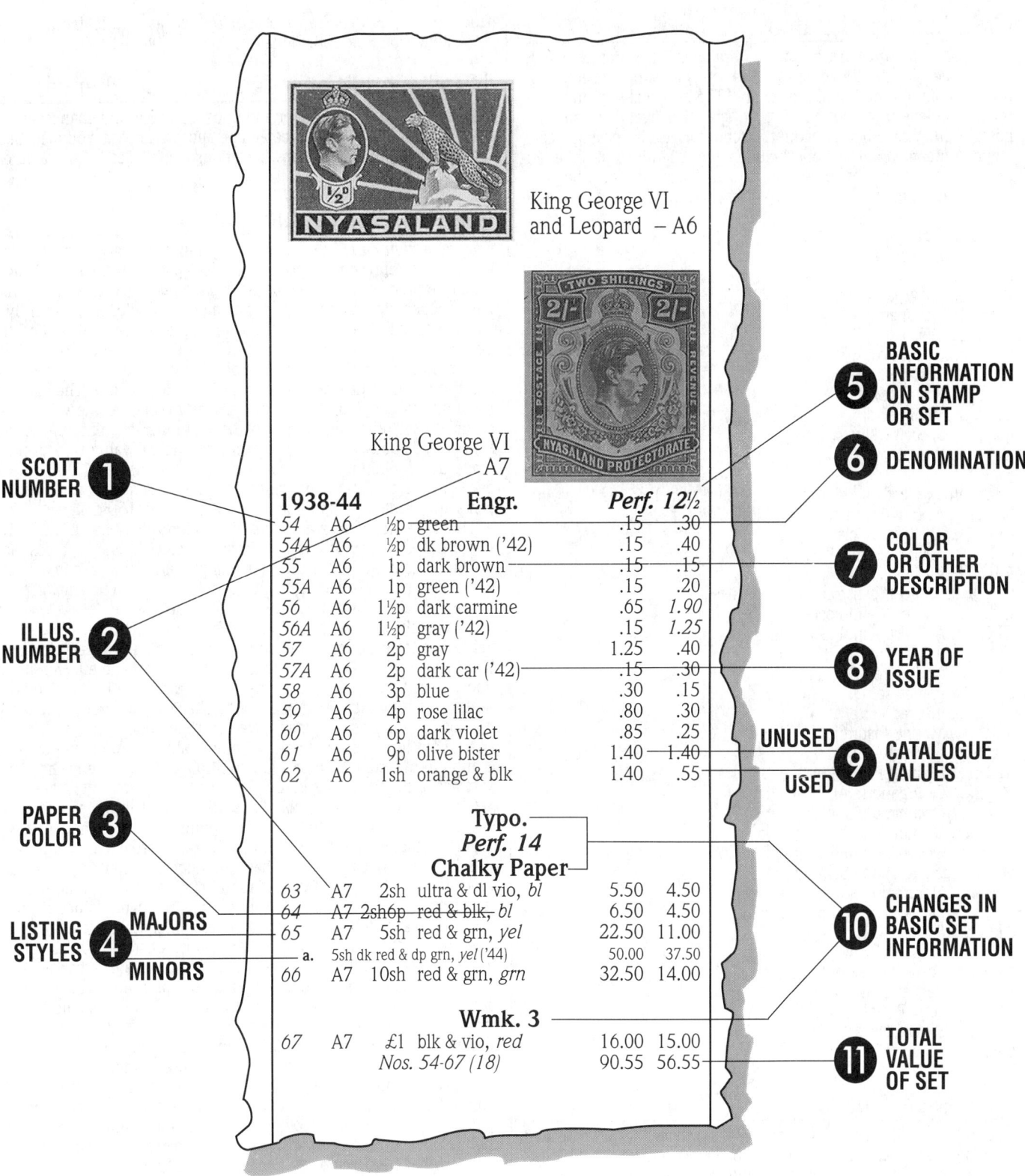

Special Notices

Classification of stamps

The *Scott Standard Postage Stamp Catalogue* lists stamps by country of issue. The next level of organization is a listing by section on the basis of the function of the stamps. The principal sections cover regular postage, semi-postal, air post, special delivery, registration, postage due and other categories. Except for regular postage, catalogue numbers for all sections include a prefix letter (or number-letter combination) denoting the class to which a given stamp belongs.

The following is a listing of the most commonly used catalogue prefixes.

Prefix....Category
C ....Air Post
M............Military
P ....Newspaper
N ....Occupation - Regular Issues
O ....Official
Q ....Parcel Post
J..............Postage Due
RA ....Postal Tax
B.............Semi-Postal
E.............Special Delivery
MR ....War Tax

Other prefixes used by more than one country include the following:
H ....Acknowledgment of Receipt
CO.........Air Post Official
CQ.........Air Post Parcel Post
RAC.......Air Post Postal Tax
CF..........Air Post Registration
CB ....Air Post Semi-Postal
CBO.......Air Post Semi-Postal Official
CE ....Air Post Special Delivery
EY..........Authorized Delivery
S ....Franchise
G ....Insured Letter
GY ....Marine Insurance
MC ....Military Air Post
MQ........Military Parcel Post
NC.........Occupation - Air Post
NO.........Occupation - Official
NJ ....Occupation - Postage Due
NRA.......Occupation - Postal Tax
NB ....Occupation - Semi-Postal
NE ....Occupation - Special Delivery
QY ....Parcel Post Authorized Delivery
AR ....Postal-fiscal
RAJ ....Postal Tax Due
RAB ....Postal Tax Semi-Postal
F.............Registration
EB..........Semi-Postal Special Delivery
EO ....Special Delivery Official
QE ....Special Handling

New issue listings

Updates to this catalogue appear each month in the *Scott Stamp Monthly* magazine. Included in this update are additions to the listings of countries found in the *Scott Standard Postage Stamp Catalogue* and the *Specialized Catalogue of United States Stamps*, as well as corrections and updates to current editions of this catalogue.

From time to time there will be changes in the final listings of stamps from the *Scott Stamp Monthly* to the next edition of the catalogue. This occurs as more information about certain stamps or sets becomes available.

The catalogue update section of the *Scott Stamp Monthly* is the most timely presentation of this material available. Annual subscriptions to the *Scott Stamp Monthly* are available from Scott Publishing Co., Box 828, Sidney, OH 45365-0828.

Number additions, deletions and changes

A listing of catalogue number additions, deletions and changes from the previous edition of the catalogue appears in each volume. See Catalogue Number Additions, Deletions & Changes in the table of contents for the location of this list.

Understanding valuing notations

The *minimum catalogue value* of an individual stamp or set is 15 cents. This represents a portion of the cost incurred by a dealer when he prepares an individual stamp for resale. As a point of philatelic-economic fact, the lower the value shown for an item in this catalogue, the greater the percentage of that value is attributed to dealer mark up and profit margin. In many cases, such as the 15-cent minimum value, that price does not cover the labor or other costs involved with stocking it as an individual stamp. The sum of minimum values in a set does not properly represent the value of a complete set primarily composed of a number of minimum-value stamps, nor does the sum represent the actual value of a packet made up of minimum-value stamps. Thus a packet of 1,000 different common stamps — each of which has a catalogue value of 15 cents — normally sells for considerably less than 150 dollars!

The *absence of a retail value* for a stamp does not necessarily suggest that a stamp is scarce or rare. In the U.S. listings, a dash in the value column means that the stamp is known in a stated form or variety, but information is either lacking or insufficient for purposes of establishing a usable catalogue value.

Stamp values in *italics* generally refer to items that are difficult to value accurately. For expensive items, such as those priced at $1,000 or higher, a value in italics indicates that the affected item trades very seldom. For inexpensive items, a value in italics represents a warning. One example is a "blocked" issue where the issuing postal administration may have controlled one stamp in a set in an attempt to make the whole set more valuable. Another example is an item that sold at an extreme multiple of face value in the marketplace at the time of its issue.

One type of warning to collectors that appears in the catalogue is illustrated by a stamp that is valued considerably higher in used condition than it is as unused. In this case, collectors are cautioned to be certain the used version has a genuine and contemporaneous cancellation. The type of cancellation on a stamp can be an important factor in determining its sale price. Catalogue values do not apply to fiscal or telegraph cancels, unless otherwise noted.

Some countries have released back issues of stamps in canceled-to-order form, sometimes covering as much as a 10-year period. The Scott Catalogue values for used stamps reflect canceled-to-order material when such stamps are found to predominate in the marketplace for the issue involved. Notes frequently appear in the stamp listings to specify which items are valued as canceled-to-order, or if there is a premium for postally used examples.

Many countries sell canceled-to-order stamps at a marked reduction of face value. Countries that sell or have sold canceled-to-order stamps at *full* face value include Australia, Netherlands, France and Switzerland. It may be almost impossible to identify such stamps if the gum has been removed, because official government canceling devices are used. Postally used copies of these items on cover, however, are usually worth more than the canceled-to-order stamps with original gum.

Abbreviations

Scott Publishing Co. uses a consistent set of abbreviations throughout this catalogue to conserve space, while still providing necessary information.

COLOR ABBREVIATIONS

amb.....amber	crim.....crimson	ol.........olive
anil......aniline	cr.........cream	olvn.....olivine
ap........apple	dk........dark	org.......orange
aqua.....aquamarine	dl.........dull	pck......peacock
az........azure	dp........deep	pnksh...pinkish
bis.......bister	db........drab	Prus.....Prussian
bl........blue	emer....emerald	pur.......purple
bld.......blood	gldn.....golden	redsh...reddish
blk.......black	grysh....grayish	res.......reseda
bril......brilliant	grn.......green	ros.......rosine
brn.......brown	grnsh...greenish	ryl........royal
brnsh...brownish	hel.......heliotrope	sal........salmon
brnz.....bronze	hn........henna	saph.....sapphire
brt.......bright	ind.......indigo	scar......scarlet
brnt.....burnt	int........intense	sep.......sepia
car.......carmine	lav.......lavender	sien......sienna
cer.......cerise	lem......lemon	sil........silver
chlky....chalky	lil.........lilac	sl.........slate
cham...chamois	lt..........light	stl........steel
chnt.....chestnut	mag.....magenta	turq.....turquoise
choc....chocolate	man.....manila	ultra.....ultramarine
chr......chrome	mar......maroon	Ven......Venetian
cit........citron	mv........mauve	ver.......vermilion
cl.........claret	multi....multicolored	vio.......violet
cob......cobalt	mlky....milky	yel.......yellow
cop......copper	myr......myrtle	yelsh...yellowish

When no color is given for an overprint or surcharge, black is the color used. Abbreviations for colors used for overprints and surcharges include: "(B)" or "(Blk)," black; "(Bl)," blue; "(R)," red; and "(G)," green.

Additional abbreviations in this catalogue are shown below:

Adm. ....Administration
AFL ....American Federation of Labor
Anniv. ....Anniversary
APS ....American Philatelic Society
Assoc. ....Association
ASSR. ....Autonomous Soviet Socialist Republic
b.....................Born
BEP ....Bureau of Engraving and Printing
Bicent. ....Bicentennial
Bklt.................Booklet
Brit. ....British
btwn...............Between
Bur. ....Bureau
c. or ca............Circa
Cat. ....Catalogue
Cent. ....Centennial, century, centenary
CIO ....Congress of Industrial Organizations
Conf. ....Conference
Cong...............Congress
Cpl. ....Corporal
CTO ....Canceled to order
d.....................Died
Dbl. ....Double
EKU................Earliest known use
Engr................Engraved
Exhib..............Exhibition
Expo................Exposition
Fed. ....Federation
GB..................Great Britain
Gen. ....General
GPO ....General post office
Horiz. ....Horizontal
Imperf.............Imperforate
Impt. ....Imprint
Intl. ....International
Invtd...............Inverted
L.....................Left
Lieut., lt...........Lieutenant
Litho...............Lithographed
LL...................Lower left
LR ....Lower right
mm.................Millimeter
Ms...................Manuscript
Natl. ....National
No...................Number
NY..................New York
NYC ....New York City
Ovpt. ....Overprint
Ovptd. ....Overprinted
P.....................Plate number
Perf.................Perforated, perforation
Phil. ....Philatelic
Photo..............Photogravure
PO ....Post office
Pr. ....Pair
P.R. ....Puerto Rico
Prec. ....Precancel, precanceled
Pres. ....President
PTT ....Post, Telephone and Telegraph
Rio..................Rio de Janeiro
Sgt. ....Sergeant
Soc. ....Society
Souv. ....Souvenir
SSR ....Soviet Socialist Republic, see ASSR
St.....................Saint, street
Surch...............Surcharge
Typo. ....Typographed
UL ....Upper left
Unwmkd. ....Unwatermarked
UPU ....Universal Postal Union
UR ....Upper Right
US ....United States
USPOD ....United States Post Office Department
USSR ....Union of Soviet Socialist Republics
Vert. ....Vertical
VP ....Vice president
Wmk. ....Watermark
Wmkd. ....Watermarked
WWI ....World War I
WWII ....World War II

Examination

Scott Publishing Co. will not comment upon the genuineness, grade or condition of stamps, because of the time and responsibility involved. Rather, there are several expertizing groups that undertake this work for both collectors and dealers. Neither will Scott Publishing Co. appraise or identify philatelic material. The company cannot take responsibility for unsolicited stamps or covers sent by individuals.

How to order from your dealer

When ordering stamps from a dealer, it is not necessary to write the full description of a stamp as listed in this catalogue. All you need is the name of the country, the Scott catalogue number and whether the desired item is unused or used. For example, "Japan Scott 422 unused" is sufficient to identify the unused stamp of Japan listed as "422 A206 5y brown."

Basic Stamp Information

A stamp collector's knowledge of the combined elements that make a given stamp issue unique determines his or her ability to identify stamps. These elements include paper, watermark, method of separation, printing, design and gum. On the following pages each of these important areas is briefly described.

Paper

Paper is an organic material composed of a compacted weave of cellulose fibers and generally formed into sheets. Paper used to print stamps may be manufactured in sheets, or it may have been part of a large roll (called a web) before being cut to size. The fibers most often used to create paper on which stamps are printed include bark, wood, straw and certain grasses. In many cases, linen or cotton rags have been added for greater strength and durability. Grinding, bleaching, cooking and rinsing these raw fibers reduces them to a slushy pulp, referred to by paper makers as "stuff." Sizing and, sometimes, coloring matter is added to the pulp to make different types of finished paper.

After the stuff is prepared, it is poured onto sieve-like frames that allow the water to run off, while retaining the matted pulp. As fibers fall onto the screen and are held by gravity, they form a natural weave that will later hold the paper together. If the screen has metal bits that are formed into letters or images attached, it leaves slightly thinned areas on the paper. These are called watermarks.

When the stuff is almost dry, it is passed under pressure through smooth or engraved rollers - dandy rolls - or placed between cloth in a press to be flattened and dried.

Stamp paper falls broadly into two types: wove and laid. The nature of the surface of the frame onto which the pulp is first deposited causes the differences in appearance between the two. If the surface is smooth and even, the paper will be of fairly uniform texture throughout. This is known as *wove paper*. Early papermaking machines poured the pulp onto a continuously circulating web of felt, but modern machines feed the pulp onto a cloth-like screen made of closely interwoven fine wires. This paper, when held to a light, will show little dots or points very close together. The proper name for this is "wire wove," but the type is still considered wove. Any U.S. or British stamp printed after 1880 will serve as an example of wire wove paper.

Closely spaced parallel wires, with cross wires at wider intervals, make up the frames used for what is known as *laid paper*. A greater thickness of the pulp will settle between the wires. The paper, when held to a light, will show alternate light and dark lines. The spacing and the thickness of the lines may vary, but on any one sheet of paper they are all alike. See Russia Scott 31-38 for examples of laid paper.

Batonne, from the French word meaning "a staff," is a term used if the lines in the paper are spaced quite far apart, like the printed ruling on a writing tablet. Batonne paper may be either wove or laid. If laid, fine laid lines can be seen between the batons. The laid lines, which are a form of watermark, may be geometrical figures such as squares, diamonds, rectangles or wavy lines.

Quadrille is the term used when the lines in the paper form little squares. *Oblong quadrille* is the term used when rectangles, rather than squares, are formed. See Mexico-Guadalajara Scott 35-37 for examples of oblong quadrille paper.

Paper also is classified as thick or thin, hard or soft, and by color if dye is added during manufacture. Such colors may include yellowish, greenish, bluish and reddish.

Brief explanations of other types of paper used for printing stamps, as well as examples, follow.

Pelure — Pelure paper is a very thin, hard and often brittle paper that is sometimes bluish or grayish in appearance. See Serbia Scott 169-170.

Native — This is a term applied to handmade papers used to produce some of the early stamps of the Indian states. Stamps printed on native paper may be expected to display various natural inclusions that are normal and do not negatively affect value. Japanese paper, originally made of mulberry fibers and rice flour, is part of this group. See Japan Scott 1-18.

Manila — This type of paper is often used to make stamped envelopes and wrappers. It is a coarse-textured stock, usually smooth on one side and rough on the other. A variety of colors of manila paper exist, but the most common range is yellowish-brown.

Silk — Introduced by the British in 1847 as a safeguard against counterfeiting, silk paper contains bits of colored silk thread scattered throughout. The density of these fibers varies greatly and can include as few as one fiber per stamp or hundreds. U.S. revenue Scott R152 is a good example of an easy-to-identify silk paper stamp.

Silk-thread paper has uninterrupted threads of colored silk arranged so that one or more threads run through the stamp or postal stationery. See Great Britain Scott 5-6 and Switzerland Scott 14-19.

Granite — Filled with minute cloth or colored paper fibers of various colors and lengths, granite paper should not be confused with either type of silk paper. Austria Scott 172-175 and a number of Swiss stamps are examples of granite paper.

Chalky — A chalk-like substance coats the surface of chalky paper to discourage the cleaning and reuse of canceled stamps, as well as to provide a smoother, more acceptable printing surface. Because the designs of stamps printed on chalky paper are imprinted on what is often a water-soluble coating, any attempt to remove a cancellation will destroy the stamp. *Do not soak these stamps in any fluid.* To remove a stamp printed on chalky paper from an envelope, wet the paper from underneath the stamp until the gum dissolves enough to release the stamp from the paper. See St. Kitts-Nevis Scott 89-90 for examples of stamps printed on this type of chalky paper.

India — Another name for this paper, originally introduced from China about 1750, is "China Paper." It is a thin, opaque paper often used for plate and die proofs by many countries.

Double — In philately, the term double paper has two distinct meanings. The first is a two-ply paper, usually a combination of a thick and a thin sheet, joined during manufacture. This type was used experimentally as a means to discourage the reuse of stamps.

The design is printed on the thin paper. Any attempt to remove a cancellation would destroy the design. U.S. Scott 158 and other Banknote-era stamps exist on this form of double paper.

The second type of double paper occurs on a rotary press, when the end of one paper roll, or web, is affixed to the next roll to save time feeding the paper through the press. Stamp designs are printed over the joined paper and, if overlooked by inspectors, may get into post office stocks.

Goldbeater's Skin — This type of paper was used for the 1866 issue of Prussia, and was a tough, translucent paper. The design was printed in reverse on the back of the stamp, and the gum applied over the printing. It is impossible to remove stamps printed on this type of paper from the paper to which they are affixed without destroying the design.

Ribbed — Ribbed paper has an uneven, corrugated surface made by passing the paper through ridged rollers. This type exists on some copies of U.S. Scott 156-165.

Various other substances, or substrates, have been used for stamp manufacture, including wood, aluminum, copper, silver and gold foil, plastic, and silk and cotton fabrics.

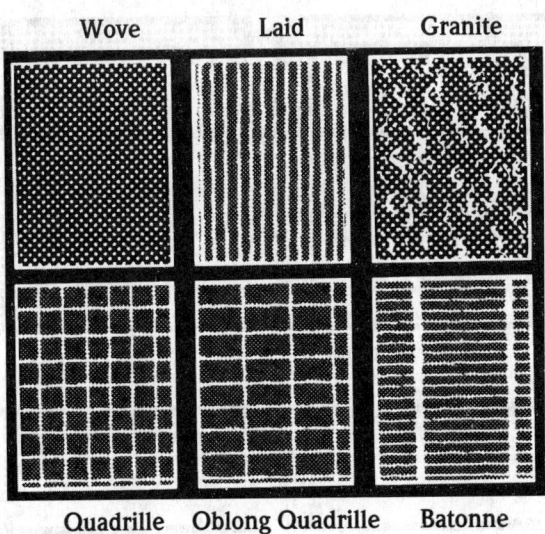

Watermarks

Watermarks are an integral part of some papers. They are formed in the process of paper manufacture. Watermarks consist of small designs, formed of wire or cut from metal and soldered to the surface of the mold or, sometimes, on the dandy roll. The designs may be in the form of crowns, stars, anchors, letters or other characters or symbols. These pieces of metal - known in the paper-making industry as "bits" - impress a design into the paper. The design sometimes may be seen by holding the stamp to the light. Some are more easily seen with a watermark detector. This important tool is a small black tray into which a stamp is placed face down and dampened with a fast-evaporating watermark detection fluid that brings up the watermark image in the form of dark lines against a lighter background. These dark lines are the thinner areas of the paper known as the watermark. Some watermarks are extremely difficult to locate, due to either a faint impression, watermark location or the color of the stamp. There also are electric watermark detectors that come with plastic filter disks of various colors. The disks neutralize the color of the stamp, permitting the watermark to be seen more easily.

Multiple watermarks of Crown Agents and Burma

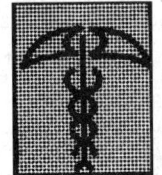

Watermarks of Uruguay, Vatican City and Jamaica

WARNING: Some inks used in the photogravure process dissolve in watermark fluids (Please see the section on Soluble Printing Inks). Also, see "chalky paper."

Watermarks may be found normal, reversed, inverted, reversed and inverted, sideways or diagonal, as seen from the back of the stamp.

The relationship of watermark to stamp design depends on the position of the printing plates or how paper is fed through the press. On machine-made paper, watermarks normally are read from right to left. The design is repeated closely throughout the sheet in a "multiple-watermark design." In a "sheet watermark," the design appears only once on the sheet, but extends over many stamps. Individual stamps may carry only a small fraction or none of the watermark.

"Marginal watermarks" occur in the margins of sheets or panes of stamps. They occur on the outside border of paper (ostensibly outside the area where stamps are to be printed). A large row of letters may spell the name of the country or the manufacturer of the paper, or a border of lines may appear. Careless press feeding may cause parts of these letters and/or lines to show on stamps of the outer row of a pane.

Soluble Printing Inks

WARNING: Most stamp colors are permanent; that is, they are not seriously affected by short-term exposure to light or water. Many colors, especially of modern inks, fade from excessive exposure to light. There are stamps printed with inks that dissolve easily in water or in fluids used to detect watermarks. Use of these inks was intentional to prevent the removal of cancellations. Water affects all aniline inks, those on so-called safety paper and some photogravure printings - all such inks are known as *fugitive colors. Removal from paper of such stamps requires care and alternatives to traditional soaking.*

Separation

"Separation" is the general term used to describe methods used to separate stamps. The three standard forms currently in use are perforating, rouletting and die-cutting. These methods are done during the stamp production process, after printing. Sometimes these methods are done on-press or sometimes as a separate step. The earliest issues, such as the 1840 Penny Black of Great Britain (Scott 1), did not have any means provided for separation. It was expected the stamps would be cut apart with scissors or folded and torn. These are examples of imperforate stamps. Many stamps were first issued in imperforate formats and were later issued with perforations. Therefore, care must be observed in buying single imperforate stamps to be certain they were issued imperforate and are not perforated copies that have been altered by having the perforations trimmed away. Stamps issued imperforate usually are valued as singles. However, imperforate varieties of normally perforated stamps should be collected in pairs or larger pieces as indisputable evidence of their imperforate character.

PERFORATION

The chief style of separation of stamps, and the one that is in almost universal use today, is perforating. By this process, paper between the stamps is cut away in a line of holes, usually round, leaving little bridges of paper between the stamps to hold them together. Some types of perforation, such as hyphen-hole perfs, can be confused with roulettes, but a close visual inspection reveals that paper has been removed. The little perforation bridges, which project from the stamp when it is torn from the pane, are called the teeth of the perforation.

As the size of the perforation is sometimes the only way to differentiate between two otherwise identical stamps, it is necessary to be able to accurately measure and describe them. This is done with a perforation gauge, usually a ruler-like device that has dots or graduated lines to show how many perforations may be counted in the space of two centimeters. Two centimeters is the space universally adopted in which to measure perforations.

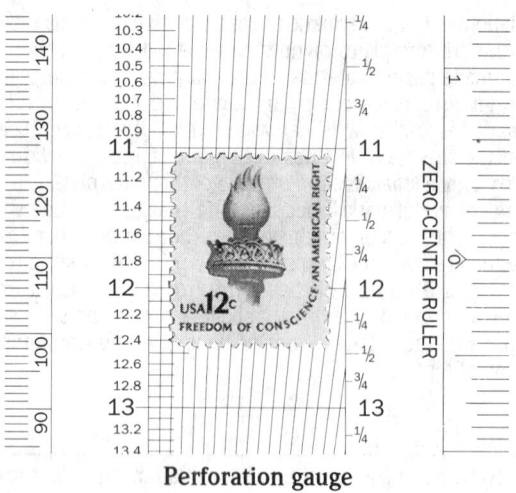

Perforation gauge

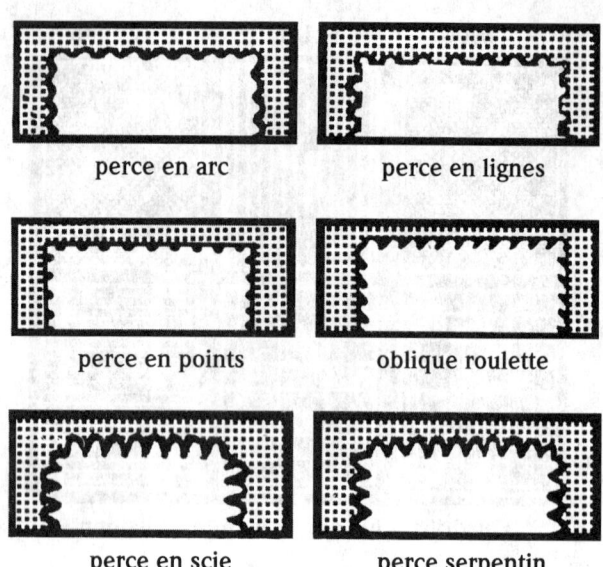

To measure a stamp, run it along the gauge until the dots on it fit exactly into the perforations of the stamp. If you are using a graduated-line perforation gauge, simply slide the stamp along the surface until the lines on the gauge perfectly project from the center of the bridges or holes. The number to the side of the line of dots or lines that fit the stamp's perforation is the measurement. For example, an "11" means that 11 perforations fit between two centimeters. The description of the stamp therefore is "perf. 11." If the gauge of the perforations on the top and bottom of a stamp differs from that on the sides, the result is what is known as *compound perforations*. In measuring compound perforations, the gauge at top and bottom is always given first, then the sides. Thus, a stamp that measures 11 at top and bottom and 10 1/2 at the sides is "perf. 11 x 10 1/2." See U.S. Scott 632-642 for examples of compound perforations.

Stamps also are known with perforations different on three or all four sides. Descriptions of such items are clockwise, beginning with the top of the stamp.

A perforation with small holes and teeth close together is a "fine perforation." One with large holes and teeth far apart is a "coarse perforation." Holes that are jagged, rather than clean-cut, are "rough perforations." *Blind perforations* are the slight impressions left by the perforating pins if they fail to puncture the paper. Multiples of stamps showing blind perforations may command a slight premium over normally perforated stamps.

The term *syncopated perfs* describes intentional irregularities in the perforations. The earliest form was used by the Netherlands from 1925-33, where holes were omitted to create distinctive patterns. Beginning in 1992, Great Britain has used an oval perforation to help prevent counterfeiting. Several other countries have started using the oval perfs.

A new type of perforation, still primarily used for postal stationery, is known as microperfs. Microperfs are tiny perforations (in some cases hundreds of holes per two centimeters) that allows items to be intentionally separated very easily, while not accidentally breaking apart as easily as standard perforations. These are not currently measured or differentiated by size, as are standard perforations.

ROULETTING

In rouletting, the stamp paper is cut partly or wholly through, with no paper removed. In perforating, some paper is removed. Rouletting derives its name from the French roulette, a spur-like wheel. As the wheel is rolled over the paper, each point makes a small cut. The number of cuts made in a two-centimeter space determines the gauge of the roulette, just as the number of perforations in two centimeters determines the gauge of the perforation.

The shape and arrangement of the teeth on the wheels varies. Various roulette types generally carry French names:

Perce en lignes - rouletted in lines. The paper receives short, straight cuts in lines. This is the most common type of rouletting. See Mexico Scott 500.

Perce en points - pin-rouletted. This differs from a small perforation because no paper is removed, although round, equidistant holes are pricked through the paper. See Mexico Scott 242-256.

Perce en arc and *perce en scie* - pierced in an arc or saw-toothed designs, forming half circles or small triangles. See Hanover (German States) Scott 25-29.

Perce en serpentin - serpentine roulettes. The cuts form a serpentine or wavy line. See Brunswick (German States) Scott 13-18.

Once again, no paper is removed by these processes, leaving the stamps easily separated, but closely attached.

DIE-CUTTING

The third major form of stamp separation is die-cutting. This is a method where a die in the pattern of separation is created that later cuts the stamp paper in a stroke motion. Although some standard stamps bear die-cut perforations, this process is primarily used for self-adhesive postage stamps. Die-cutting can appear in straight lines, such as U.S. Scott 2522, shapes, such as U.S. Scott 1551, or imitating the appearance of perforations, such as New Zealand Scott 935A and 935B.

Printing Processes

ENGRAVING (Intaglio, Line-engraving, Etching)

Master die — The initial operation in the process of line engraving is making the master die. The die is a small, flat block of softened steel upon which the stamp design is recess engraved in reverse.

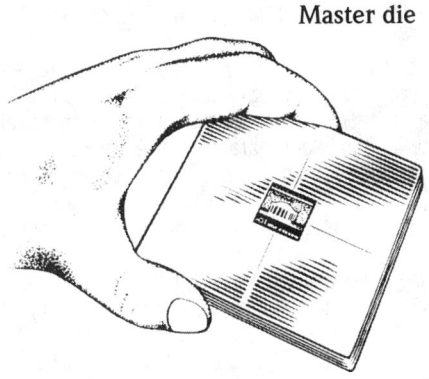

Master die

Photographic reduction of the original art is made to the appropriate size. It then serves as a tracing guide for the initial outline of the design. The engraver lightly traces the design on the steel with his graver, then slowly works the design until it is completed. At various points during the engraving process, the engraver hand-inks the die and makes an impression to check his progress. These are known as progressive die proofs. After completion of the engraving, the die is hardened to withstand the stress and pressures of later transfer operations.

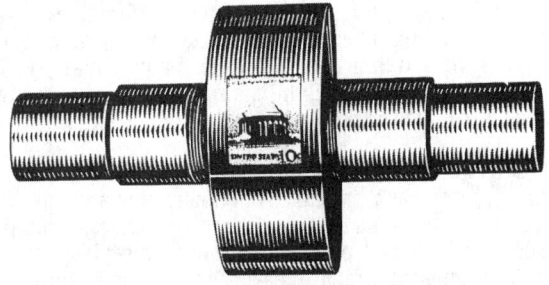

Transfer roll

Transfer roll — Next is production of the transfer roll that, as the name implies, is the medium used to transfer the subject from the master die to the printing plate. A blank roll of soft steel, mounted on a mandrel, is placed under the bearers of the transfer press to allow it to roll freely on its axis. The hardened die is placed on the bed of the press and the face of the transfer roll is applied to the die, under pressure. The bed or the roll is then rocked back and forth under increasing pressure, until the soft steel of the roll is forced into every engraved line of the die. The resulting impression on the roll is known as a "relief" or a "relief transfer." The engraved image is now positive in appearance and stands out from the steel. After the required number of reliefs are "rocked in," the soft steel transfer roll is hardened.

Different flaws may occur during the relief process. A defective relief may occur during the rocking in process because of a minute piece of foreign material lodging on the die, or some other cause. Imperfections in the steel of the transfer roll may result in a breaking away of parts of the design. This is known as a relief break, which will show up on finished stamps as small, unprinted areas. If a damaged relief remains in use, it will transfer a repeating defect to the plate. Deliberate alterations of reliefs sometimes occur. "Altered reliefs" designate these changed conditions.

Plate — The final step in pre-printing production is the making of the printing plate. A flat piece of soft steel replaces the die on the bed of the transfer press. One of the reliefs on the transfer roll is positioned over this soft steel. Position, or layout, dots determine the correct position on the plate. The dots have been lightly marked on the plate in advance. After the correct position of the relief is determined, the design is rocked in by following the same method used in making the transfer roll. The difference is that this time the image is being transferred from the transfer roll, rather than to it. Once the design is entered on the plate, it appears in reverse and is recessed. There are as many transfers entered on the plate as there are subjects printed on the sheet of stamps. It is during this process that double and shifted transfers occur, as well as re-entries. These are the result of improperly entered images that have not been properly burnished out prior to rocking in a new image.

Modern siderography processes, such as those used by the U.S. Bureau of Engraving and Printing, involve an automated form of rocking designs in on preformed cylindrical printing sleeves. The same process also allows for easier removal and re-entry of worn images right on the sleeve.

Transferring the design to the plate

Following the entering of the required transfers on the plate, the position dots, layout dots and lines, scratches and other markings generally are burnished out. Added at this time by the siderographer are any required *guide lines, plate numbers* or other *marginal markings*. The plate is then hand-inked and a proof impression is taken. This is known as a plate proof. If the impression is approved, the plate is machined for fitting onto the press, is hardened and sent to the plate vault ready for use.

On press, the plate is inked and the surface is automatically wiped clean, leaving ink only in the recessed lines. Paper is then forced under pressure into the engraved recessed lines, thereby receiving the ink. Thus, the ink lines on engraved stamps are slightly raised, and slight depressions (debossing) occur on the back of the stamp. Prior to the advent of modern high-speed presses and more advanced ink formulations, paper had to be dampened before receiving the ink. This sometimes led to uneven shrinkage by the time the stamps were perforated, resulting in improperly perforated stamps, or misperfs. Newer presses use drier paper, thus both *wet* and *dry printings* exist on some stamps.

Rotary Press — Until 1914, only flat plates were used to print engraved stamps. Rotary press printing was introduced in 1914, and slowly spread. Some countries still use flat-plate printing.

After approval of the plate proof, older *rotary press plates* require additional machining. They are curved to fit the press cylinder. "Gripper slots" are cut into the back of each plate to receive the "grippers," which hold the plate securely on the press. The plate is then hardened. Stamps printed from these bent rotary press plates are longer or wider than the same stamps printed from flat-plate presses. The stretching of the plate during the curving process is what causes this distortion.

Re-entry — To execute a re-entry on a flat plate, the transfer roll is re-applied to the plate, often at some time after its first use on the press. Worn-out designs can be resharpened by carefully burnishing out the original image and re-entering it from the transfer roll. If the original impression has not been sufficiently removed and the transfer roll is not precisely in line with the remaining impression, the resulting double transfer will make the re-entry obvious. If the registration is true, a re-entry may be difficult or impossible to distinguish. Sometimes a stamp printed from a successful re-entry is identified by having a much sharper and clearer impression than its neighbors. With the advent of rotary presses, post-press re-entries were not possible. After a plate was curved for the rotary press, it was impossible to make a re-entry. This is because the plate had already been bent once (with the design distorted).

However, with the introduction of the previously mentioned modern-style siderography machines, entries are made to the preformed cylindrical printing sleeve. Such sleeves are dechromed and softened. This allows individual images to be burnished out and re-entered on the curved sleeve. The sleeve is then rechromed, resulting in longer press life.

Double Transfer — This is a description of the condition of a transfer on a plate that shows evidence of a duplication of all, or a portion of the design. It usually is the result of the changing of the registration between the transfer roll and the plate during the rocking in of the original entry. Double transfers also occur when only a portion of the design has been rocked in and improper positioning is noted. If the worker elected not to burnish out the partial or completed design, a strong double transfer will occur for part or all of the design.

It sometimes is necessary to remove the original transfer from a plate and repeat the process a second time. If the finished reworked image shows traces of the original impression, attributable to incomplete burnishing, the result is a partial double transfer.

With the modern automatic machines mentioned previously, double transfers are all but impossible to create. Those partially doubled images on stamps printed from such sleeves are more than likely re-entries, rather than true double transfers.

Re-engraved — Alterations to a stamp design are sometimes necessary after some stamps have been printed. In some cases, either the original die or the actual printing plate may have its "temper" drawn (softened), and the design will be re-cut. The resulting impressions from such a re-engraved die or plate may differ slightly from the original issue, and are known as "re-engraved." If the alteration was made to the master die, all future printings will be consistently different from the original. If alterations were made to the printing plate, each altered stamp on the plate will be slightly different from each other, allowing specialists to reconstruct a complete printing plate.

Dropped Transfers — If an impression from the transfer roll has not been properly placed, a dropped transfer may occur. The final stamp image will appear obviously out of line with its neighbors.

Short Transfer — Sometimes a transfer roll is not rocked its entire length when entering a transfer onto a plate. As a result, the finished transfer on the plate fails to show the complete design, and the finished stamp will have an incomplete design printed. This is known as a "short transfer." U.S. Scott No. 8 is a good example of a short transfer.

TYPOGRAPHY (Letterpress, Surface Printing, Flexography, Dry Offset, High Etch)

Although the word "Typography" is obsolete as a term describing a printing method, it was the accepted term throughout the first century of postage stamps. Therefore, appropriate Scott listings in this catalogue refer to typographed stamps. The current term for this form of printing, however, is "letterpress."

As it relates to the production of postage stamps, letterpress printing is the reverse of engraving. Rather than having recessed areas trap the ink and deposit it on paper, only the raised areas of the design are inked. This is comparable to the type of printing seen by inking and using an ordinary rubber stamp. Letterpress includes all printing where the design is above the surface area, whether it is wood, metal or, in some instances, hardened rubber or polymer plastic.

For most letterpress-printed stamps, the engraved master is made in much the same manner as for engraved stamps. In this instance, however, an additional step is needed. The design is transferred to another surface before being transferred to the transfer roll. In this way, the transfer roll has a recessed stamp design, rather than one done in relief. This makes the printing areas on the final plate raised, or relief areas.

For less-detailed stamps of the 19th century, the area on the die not used as a printing surface was cut away, leaving the surface area raised. The original die was then reproduced by stereotyping or electrotyping. The resulting electrotypes were assembled in the required number and format of the desired sheet of stamps. The plate used in printing the stamps was an electroplate of these assembled electrotypes.

Once the final letterpress plates are created, ink is applied to the raised surface and the pressure of the press transfers the ink impression to the paper. In contrast to engraving, the fine lines of letterpress are impressed on the surface of the stamp, leaving a debossed surface. When viewed from the back (as on a typewritten page), the corresponding line work on the stamp will be raised slightly (embossed) above the surface.

PHOTOGRAVURE (Gravure, Rotogravure, Heliogravure)

In this process, the basic principles of photography are applied to a chemically sensitized metal plate, rather than photographic paper. The design is transferred photographically to the plate through a halftone, or dot-matrix screen, breaking the reproduction into tiny dots. The plate is treated chemically and the dots form depressions, called cells, of varying depths and diameters, depending on the degrees of shade in the design. Then, like engraving, ink is applied to the plate and the surface is wiped clean. This leaves ink in the tiny cells that is lifted out and deposited on the paper when it is pressed against the plate.

Gravure is most often used for multicolored stamps, generally using the three primary colors (red, yellow and blue) and black. By varying the dot matrix pattern and density of these colors, virtually any color can be reproduced. A typical full-color gravure stamp will be created from four printing cylinders (one for each color). The original multicolored image will have been photographically separated into its component colors.

For examples of the first photogravure stamps printed (1914), see Bavaria Scott 94-114.

LITHOGRAPHY (Offset Lithography, Stone Lithography, Dilitho, Planography, Collotype)

The principle that oil and water do not mix is the basis for lithography. The stamp design is drawn by hand or transferred from engraving to the surface of a lithographic stone or metal plate in a greasy (oily) substance. This oily substance holds the ink, which will later be transferred to the paper. The stone (or plate) is wet with an acid fluid, causing it to repel the printing ink in all areas not covered by the greasy substance.

Transfer paper is used to transfer the design from the original stone or plate. A series of duplicate transfers are grouped and, in turn, transferred to the final printing plate.

Photolithography — The application of photographic processes to lithography. This process allows greater flexibility of design, related to use of halftone screens combined with line work. Unlike photogravure or engraving, this process can allow large, solid areas to be printed.

Offset — A refinement of the lithographic process. A rubber-covered blanket cylinder takes the impression from the inked lithographic plate. From the "blanket" the impression is *offset* or transferred to the paper. Greater flexibility and speed are the principal reasons offset printing has largely displaced lithography. The term "lithography" covers both processes, and results are almost identical.

EMBOSSED (Relief) Printing

Embossing, not considered one of the four main printing types, is a method in which the design first is sunk into the metal of the die. Printing is done against a yielding platen, such as leather or linoleum. The platen is forced into the depression of the die, thus forming the design on the paper in relief. This process is often used for metallic inks.

Embossing may be done without color (see Sardinia Scott 4-6); with color printed around the embossed area (see Great Britain Scott 5 and most U.S. envelopes); and with color in exact registration with the embossed subject (see Canada Scott 656-657).

COMBINATION PRINTINGS

Sometimes two or even three printing methods are combined in producing stamps. In these cases, such as Austria Scott 933, the stamp's dual printing technique can be determined by studying the individual characteristics of each printing type (intaglio and offset). A few stamps, such as Singapore Scott 684-684A, combine as many as three of the four major printing types (offset, intaglio and letterpress). When this is done it often indicates the incorporation of security devices against counterfeiting.

INK COLORS

Inks or colored papers used in stamp printing often are of mineral origin, although there are numerous examples of organic-based pigments. As a general rule, organic-based pigments are far more subject to varieties and change than those of mineral-based origin.

The appearance of any given color on a stamp may be affected by many aspects, including printing variations, light, color of paper, aging and chemical alterations.

Numerous printing variations may be observed. Heavier pressure or inking will cause a more intense color, while slight interruptions in the ink feed or lighter impressions will cause a lighter appearance. Stamps printed in the same color by water-based and solvent-based inks can differ significantly in appearance. This affects several stamps in the U.S. Prominent Americans series. Hand-mixed ink formulas (primarily from the 19th century) produced under different conditions (humidity and temperature) account for notable color variations in early printings of the same stamp (see U.S. Scott 248-250, 279B, for example). Different sources of pigment can also result in significant differences in color.

Light exposure and aging are closely related in the way they affect stamp color. Both eventually break down the ink and fade colors, so that a carefully kept stamp may differ significantly in color from an identical copy that has been exposed to light. If stamps are exposed to light either intentionally or accidentally, their colors can be faded or completely changed in some cases.

Papers of different quality and consistency used for the same stamp printing may affect color appearance. Most pelure papers, for example, show a richer color when compared with wove or laid papers. See Russia Scott 181a, for an example of this effect.

The very nature of the printing processes can cause a variety of differences in shades or hues of the same stamp. Some of these shades are scarcer than others, and are of particular interest to the advanced collector.

Luminescence

All forms of tagged stamps fall under the general category of luminescence. Within this broad category is fluorescence, dealing with forms of tagging visible under longwave ultraviolet light, and phosphorescence, which deals with tagging visible only under shortwave light. Phosphorescence leaves an afterglow and fluorescence does not. These treated stamps show up in a range of different colors when exposed to UV light. The differing wavelengths of the light activates the tagging material, making it glow in various colors that usually serve different mail processing purposes.

Intentional tagging is a post-World War II phenomenon, brought about by the increased literacy rate and rapidly growing mail volume. It was one of several answers to the problem of the need for more automated mail processes. Early tagged stamps served the purpose of triggering machines to separate different types of mail. A natural outgrowth was to also use the signal to trigger machines that faced all envelopes the same way and canceled them.

Tagged stamps come in many different forms. Some tagged stamps have luminescent shapes or images imprinted on them as a form of security device. Others have blocks (United States), stripes, frames (South Africa and Canada), overall coatings (United States), bars (Great Britain and Canada) and many other types. Some types of tagging are even mixed in with the pigmented printing ink (Australia Scott 366, Netherlands Scott 478 and U.S. Scott 1359 and 2443).

The means of applying taggant to stamps differs as much as the intended purposes for the stamps. The most common form of tagging is a coating applied to the surface of the printed stamp. Since the taggant ink is frequently invisible except under UV light, it does not interfere with the appearance of the stamp. Another common application is the use of phosphored papers. In this case the paper itself either has a coating of taggant applied before the stamp is printed or has taggant applied during the papermaking process, incorporating it into the fibers. This is currently in use in the United States. A similar form is the application of a fluorescent coating either to the finished paper or during the papermaking process. This type of tagging has been extensively used by Australia and Germany.

Many countries now use tagging in various forms to either expedite mail handling or to serve as a printing security device against counterfeiting. Following the introduction of tagged stamps for public use in 1959 by Great Britain, other countries have steadily joined the parade. Among those are Germany (1961); Canada and Denmark (1962); United States, Australia, France and Switzerland (1963); Belgium and Japan (1966); Sweden and Norway (1967); Italy (1968); and Russia (1969). Since then, many other countries have begun using forms of tagging, including Brazil, China, Czechoslovakia, Hong Kong, Guatemala, Indonesia, Israel, Lithuania, Luxembourg, Netherlands, Penrhyn Islands, Portugal, St. Vincent, Singapore, South Africa, Spain and Sweden to name a few.

In some cases, including United States, Canada, Great Britain and Switzerland, stamps were released both with and without tagging. Many of these were released during each country's experimental period. Tagged and untagged versions are listed for the aforementioned countries and are noted in some other countries' listings. For at least a few stamps, the experimentally tagged version is worth far more than its untagged counterpart, such as the 1963 experimental tagged version of France Scott 1024.

In some cases, luminescent varieties of stamps were inadvertently created. Several Russian stamps, for example, sport highly fluorescent ink that was not intended as a form of tagging. Older stamps, such as early U.S. postage dues, can be positively identified by the use of UV light, since the organic ink used has become slightly fluorescent over time. Other stamps, such as Austria Scott 70a-82a (varnish bars) and Obock Scott 46-64 (printed quadrille lines), have become fluorescent over time.

Various fluorescent substances have been added to paper to make it appear brighter. These optical brightners, as they are known, greatly affect the appearance of the stamp under UV light. The brightest of these is known as Hi-Brite paper. These paper varieties are beyond the scope of the Scott Catalogue.

Shortwave UV light also is used extensively in expertizing, since each form of paper has its own fluorescent characteristics that are impossible to perfectly match. It is therefore a simple matter to detect filled thins, added perforation teeth and other alterations that involve the addition of paper. UV light also is used to examine stamps that have had cancels chemically removed and for other purposes as well.

Gum

The Illustrated Gum Chart in the first part of this introduction shows and defines various types of gum condition. Because gum condition has an important impact on the value of unused stamps, we recommend studying this chart and the accompanying text carefully.

The gum on the back of a stamp may be shiny, dull, smooth, rough, dark, white, colored or tinted. Most stamp gumming adhesives use gum arabic or dextrine as a base. Certain polymers such as polyvinyl alcohol (PVA) have been used extensively since World War II.

The *Scott Standard Postage Stamp Catalogue* does not list items by types of gum. The *Scott Specialized Catalogue of United States Stamps* does differentiate among some types of gum for certain issues.

Reprints of stamps may have gum differing from the original issues. In addition, some countries have used different gum formulas for different seasons. These adhesives have different properties that may become more apparent over time.

Many stamps have been issued without gum, and the catalogue will note this fact. See United States Scott PR33-PR56. Sometimes, gum may have been removed to preserve the stamp. Germany Scott B68, for example, has a highly acidic gum that eventually destroys the stamps. This item is valued in the catalogue with gum removed.

Reprints and Reissues

These are impressions of stamps (usually obsolete) made from the original plates or stones. If they are valid for postage and reproduce obsolete issues (such as U.S. Scott 102-111), the stamps are *reissues*. If they are from current issues, they are designated as *second, third*, etc., *printing*. If designated for a particular purpose, they are called *special printings*.

When special printings are not valid for postage, but are made from original dies and plates by authorized persons, they are *official reprints*. *Private reprints* are made from the original plates and dies by private hands. An example of a private reprint is that of the 1871-1932 reprints made from the original die of the 1845 New Haven, Conn., postmaster's provisional. *Official reproductions* or imitations are made from new dies and plates by government authorization. Scott will list those reissues that are valid for postage if they differ significantly from the original printing.

The U.S. government made special printings of its first postage stamps in 1875. Produced were official imitations of the first two stamps (listed as Scott 3-4), reprints of the demonetized pre-1861 issues (Scott 40-47) and reissues of the 1861 stamps, the 1869 stamps and the then-current 1875 denominations. Even though the official imitations and the reprints were not valid for postage, Scott lists all of these U.S. special printings.

Most reprints or reissues differ slightly from the original stamp in some characteristic, such as gum, paper, perforation, color or watermark. Sometimes the details are followed so meticulously that only a student of that specific stamp is able to distinguish the reprint or reissue from the original.

Remainders and Canceled to Order

Some countries sell their stock of old stamps when a new issue replaces them. To avoid postal use, the *remainders* usually are canceled with a punch hole, a heavy line or bar, or a more-or-less regular-looking cancellation. The most famous merchant of remainders was Nicholas F. Seebeck. In the 1880s and 1890s, he arranged printing contracts between the Hamilton Bank Note Co., of which he was a director, and several Central and South American countries. The contracts provided that the plates and all remainders of the yearly issues became the property of Hamilton. Seebeck saw to it that ample stock remained. The "Seebecks," both remainders and reprints, were standard packet fillers for decades.

Some countries also issue stamps *canceled-to-order (CTO)*, either in sheets with original gum or stuck onto pieces of paper or envelopes and canceled. Such CTO items generally are worth less than postally used stamps. In cases where the CTO material is far more prevalent in the marketplace than postally used examples, the catalogue value relates to the CTO examples, with postally used examples noted as premium items. Most CTOs can be detected by the presence of gum. However, as the CTO practice goes back at least to 1885, the gum inevitably has been soaked off some stamps so they could pass as postally used. The normally applied postmarks usually differ slightly from standard postmarks, and specialists are able to tell the difference. When applied individually to envelopes by philatelically minded persons, CTO material is known as *favor canceled* and generally sells at large discounts.

Cinderellas and Facsimiles

Cinderella is a catch-all term used by stamp collectors to describe phantoms, fantasies, bogus items, municipal issues, exhibition seals, local revenues, transportation stamps, labels, poster stamps and many other types of items. Some cinderella collectors include in their collections local postage issues, telegraph stamps, essays and proofs, forgeries and counterfeits.

A *fantasy* is an adhesive created for a nonexistent stamp-issuing authority. Fantasy items range from imaginary countries (Occusi-Ambeno, Kingdom of Sedang, Principality of Trinidad or Torres Straits), to non-existent locals (Winans City Post), or nonexistent transportation lines (McRobish & Co.'s Acapulco-San Francisco Line).

On the other hand, if the entity exists and could have issued stamps (but did not) or was known to have issued other stamps, the items are considered *bogus* stamps. These would include the Mormon postage stamps of Utah, S. Allan Taylor's Guatemala and Paraguay inventions, the propaganda issues for the South Moluccas and the adhesives of the Page & Keyes local post of Boston.

Phantoms is another term for both fantasy and bogus issues.

Facsimiles are copies or imitations made to represent original stamps, but which do not pretend to be originals. A catalogue illustration is such a facsimile. Illustrations from the Moens catalogue of the last century were occasionally colored and passed off as stamps. Since the beginning of stamp collecting, facsimiles have been made for collectors as space fillers or for reference. They often carry the word "facsimile," "falsch" (German), "sanko" or "mozo" (Japanese), or "faux" (French) overprinted on the face or stamped on the back. Unfortunately, over the years a number of these items have had fake cancels applied over the facsimile notation and have been passed off as genuine.

Forgeries and Counterfeits

Forgeries and counterfeits have been with philately virtually from the beginning of stamp production. Over time, the terminology for the two has been used interchangeably. Although both forgeries and counterfeits are reproductions of stamps, the purposes behind their creation differ considerably.

Among specialists there is an increasing movement to more specifically define such items. Although there is no universally accepted terminology, we feel the following definitions most closely mirror the items and their purposes as they are currently defined.

Forgeries (also often referred to as *Counterfeits*) are reproductions of genuine stamps that have been created to defraud collectors. Such spurious items first appeared on the market around 1860, and most old-time collections contain one or more. Many are crude and easily spotted, but some can deceive experts.

An important supplier of these early philatelic forgeries was the Hamburg printer Gebruder Spiro. Many others with reputations in this craft included S. Allan Taylor, George Hussey, James Chute, George Forune, Benjamin & Sarpy, Julius Goldner, E. Oneglia and L.H. Mercier. Among the noted 20th-century forgers were Francois Fournier, Jean Sperati and the prolific Raoul DeThuin.

Forgeries may be complete replications, or they may be genuine stamps altered to resemble a scarcer (and more valuable) type. Most forgeries, particularly those of rare stamps, are worth only a small fraction of the value of a genuine example, but a few types, created by some of the most notable forgers, such as Sperati, can be worth as much or more than the genuine. Fraudulently produced copies are known of most classic rarities and many medium-priced stamps.

In addition to rare stamps, large numbers of common 19th- and early 20th-century stamps were forged to supply stamps to the early packet trade. Many can still be easily found. Few new philatelic forgeries have appeared in recent decades. Successful imitation of well-engraved work is virtually impossible. It has proven far easier to produce a fake by altering a genuine stamp than to duplicate a stamp completely.

Counterfeit (also often referred to as *Postal Counterfeit* or *Postal Forgery*) is the term generally applied to reproductions of stamps that have been created to defraud the government of revenue. Such items usually are created at the time a stamp is current and, in some cases, are hard to detect. Because most counterfeits are seized when the perpetrator is captured, postal counterfeits, particularly used on cover, are usually worth much more than a genuine example to specialists. The first postal counterfeit was of Spain's 4-cuarto carmine of 1854 (the real one is Scott 25). Apparently, the counterfeiters were not satisfied with their first version, which is now very scarce, and they soon created an engraved counterfeit, which is common. Postal counterfeits quickly followed in Austria, Naples, Sardinia and the Roman States. They have since been created in many other countries as well, including the United States.

An infamous counterfeit to defraud the government is the 1-shilling Great Britain "Stock Exchange" forgery of 1872, used on telegraph forms at the exchange that year. The stamp escaped detection until a stamp dealer noticed it in 1898.

Fakes

Fakes are genuine stamps altered in some way to make them more desirable. One student of this part of stamp collecting has estimated that by the 1950s more than 30,000 varieties of fakes were known. That number has grown greatly since then. The widespread existence of fakes makes it important for stamp collectors to study their philatelic holdings and use relevant literature. Likewise, collectors should buy from reputable dealers who guarantee their stamps and make full and prompt refunds should a purchased item be declared faked or altered by some mutually agreed-upon authority. Because fakes always have some genuine characteristics, it is not always possible to obtain unanimous agreement among experts regarding specific items. These students may change their opinions as philatelic knowledge increases. More than 80 percent of all fakes on the philatelic market today are regummed, reperforated (or perforated for the first time), or bear forged overprints, surcharges or cancellations.

Stamps can be chemically treated to alter or eliminate colors. For example, a pale rose stamp can be re-colored to resemble a blue shade of high market value. In other cases, treated stamps can be made to resemble missing color varieties. Designs may be changed by painting, or a stroke or a dot added or bleached out to turn an ordinary variety into a seemingly scarcer stamp. Part of a stamp can be bleached and reprinted in a different version, achieving an inverted center or frame. Margins can be added or repairs done so deceptively that the stamps move from the "repaired" into the "fake" category.

Fakers have not left the backs of the stamps untouched either. They may create false watermarks, add fake grills or press out genuine grills. A thin India paper proof may be glued onto a thicker backing to create the appearance an issued stamp, or a proof printed on cardboard may be shaved down and perforated to resemble a stamp. Silk threads are impressed into paper and stamps have been split so that a rare paper variety is added to an otherwise inexpensive stamp. The most common treatment to the back of a stamp, however, is regumming.

Some in the business of faking stamps have openly advertised fool-proof application of "original gum" to stamps that lack it, although most publications now ban such ads from their pages. It is believed that very few early stamps have survived without being hinged. The large number of never-hinged examples of such earlier material offered for sale thus suggests the widespread extent of regumming activity. Regumming also may be used to hide repairs or thin spots. Dipping the stamp into watermark fluid, or examining it under longwave ultraviolet light often will reveal these flaws.

Fakers also tamper with separations. Ingenious ways to add margins are known. Perforated wide-margin stamps may be falsely represented as imperforate when trimmed. Reperforating is commonly done to create scarce coil or perforation varieties, and to eliminate the naturally occurring straight-edge stamps found in sheet margin positions of many earlier issues. Custom has made straight-edged stamps less desirable. Fakers have obliged by perforating straight-edged stamps so that many are now uncommon, if not rare.

Another fertile field for the faker is that of overprints, surcharges and cancellations. The forging of rare surcharges or overprints began in the 1880s or 1890s. These forgeries are sometimes difficult to detect, but experts have identified almost all. Occasionally, overprints or cancellations are removed to create non-overprinted stamps or seemingly unused items. This is most commonly done by removing a manuscript cancel to make a stamp resemble an unused example. "SPECIMEN" overprints may be removed by scraping and repainting to create non-overprinted varieties. Fakers use inexpensive revenues or pen-canceled stamps to generate unused stamps for further faking by adding other markings. The quartz lamp or UV lamp and a high-powered magnifying glass help to easily detect removed cancellations.

The bigger problem, however, is the addition of overprints, surcharges or cancellations - many with such precision that they are very difficult to ascertain. Plating of the stamps or the overprint can be an important method of detection.

Fake postmarks may range from many spurious fancy cancellations to a host of markings applied to transatlantic covers, to adding normally appearing postmarks to definitives of some countries with stamps that are valued far higher used than unused. With the increased popularity of cover collecting, and the widespread interest in postal history, a fertile new field for fakers has come about. Some have tried to create entire covers. Others specialize in adding stamps, tied by fake cancellations, to genuine stampless covers, or replacing less expensive or damaged stamps with more valuable ones. Detailed study of postal rates in effect at the time a cover in question was mailed, including the analysis of each handstamp used during the period, ink analysis and similar techniques, usually will unmask the fraud.

Restoration and Repairs

Scott Publishing Co. bases its catalogue values on stamps that are free of defects and otherwise meet the standards set forth earlier in this introduction. Most stamp collectors desire to have the finest copy of an item possible. Even within given grading categories there are variances. This leads to a controversial practice that is not defined in any universal manner: stamp *restoration*.

There are broad differences of opinion about what is permissible when it comes to restoration. Carefully applying a soft eraser to a stamp or cover to remove light soiling is one form of restoration, as is washing a stamp in mild soap and water to clean it. These are fairly accepted forms of restoration. More severe forms of restoration include pressing out creases or removing stains caused by tape.

To what degree each of these is acceptable is dependent upon the individual situation. Further along the spectrum is the freshening of a stamp's color by removing oxide build-up or the effects of wax paper left next to stamps shipped to the tropics.

At some point in this spectrum the concept of *repair* replaces that of restoration. Repairs include filling thin spots, mending tears by reweaving or adding a missing perforation tooth. Regumming stamps may have been acceptable as a restoration or repair technique many decades ago, but today it is considered a form of fakery.

Restored stamps may or may not sell at a discount, and it is possible that the value of individual restored items may be enhanced over that of their pre-restoration state. Specific situations dictate the resultant value of such an item. Repaired stamps sell at substantial discounts from the value of sound stamps.

Terminology

Booklets — Many countries have issued stamps in small booklets for the convenience of users. This idea continues to become increasingly popular in many countries. Booklets have been issued in many sizes and forms, often with advertising on the covers, the panes of stamps or on the interleaving.

The panes used in booklets may be printed from special plates or made from regular sheets. All panes from booklets issued by the United States and many from those of other countries contain stamps that are straight edged on the sides, but perforated between. Others are distinguished by orientation of watermark or other identifying features. Any stamp-like unit in the pane, either printed or blank, that is not a postage stamp, is considered to be a *label* in the catalogue listings.

Scott lists and values booklet panes only. Complete booklets are listed and valued in only a few cases, such as Grenada Scott 1055 and some forms of British prestige booklets. Individual booklet panes are listed only when they are not fashioned from existing sheet stamps and, therefore, are identifiable from their sheet stamp counterparts.

Panes usually do not have a used value assigned to them because there is little market activity for used booklet panes, even though many exist used and there is some demand for them.

Cancellations — The marks or obliterations put on stamps by postal authorities to show that they have performed service and to prevent their reuse are known as cancellations. If the marking is made with a pen, it is considered a "pen cancel." When the location of the post office appears in the marking, it is a "town cancellation." A "postmark" is technically any postal marking, but in practice the term generally is applied to a town cancellation with a date. When calling attention to a cause or celebration, the marking is known as a "slogan cancellation." Many other types and styles of cancellations exist, such as duplex, numerals, targets, fancy and others. See also "precancels," below.

Coil Stamps — These are stamps that are issued in rolls for use in dispensers, affixing and vending machines. Those coils of the United States, Canada, Sweden and some other countries are perforated horizontally or vertically only, with the outer edges imperforate. Coil stamps of some countries, such as Great Britain and Germany, are perforated on all four sides and may in some cases be distinguished from their sheet stamp counterparts by watermarks, counting numbers on the reverse or other means.

Covers — Entire envelopes, with or without adhesive postage stamps, that have passed through the mail and bear postal or other markings of philatelic interest are known as covers. Before the introduction of envelopes in about 1840, people folded letters and wrote the address on the outside. Some people covered their letters with an extra sheet of paper on the outside for the address, producing the term "cover." Used airletter sheets, stamped envelopes and other items of postal stationery also are considered covers.

Errors — Stamps that have some major, consistent, unintentional deviation from the normal are considered errors. Errors include, but are not limited to, missing or wrong colors, wrong paper, wrong watermarks, inverted centers or frames on multicolor printing, inverted or missing surcharges or overprints, double impressions, missing perforations and others. Factually wrong or misspelled information, if it appears on all examples of a stamp, are not considered errors in the true sense of the word. They are errors of design. Inconsistent or randomly appearing items, such as misperfs or color shifts, are classified as freaks.

Overprints and Surcharges — Overprinting involves applying wording or design elements over an already existing stamp. Overprints can be used to alter the place of use (such as "Canal Zone" on U.S. stamps), to adapt them for a special purpose ("Porto" on Denmark's 1913-20 regular issues for use as postage due stamps, Scott J1-J7) or to commemorate a special occasion (United States Scott 647-648).

A *surcharge* is a form of overprint that changes or restates the face value of a stamp or piece of postal stationery.

Surcharges and overprints may be handstamped, typeset or, occasionally, lithographed or engraved. A few hand-written overprints and surcharges are known.

Precancels — Stamps that are canceled before they are placed in the mail are known as precancels. Precanceling usually is done to expedite the handling of large mailings and generally allow the affected mail pieces to skip certain phases of mail handling.

In the United States, precancellations generally identified the point of origin; that is, the city and state. This information appeared across the face of the stamp, usually centered between parallel lines. More recently, bureau precancels retained the parallel lines, but the city and state designations were dropped. Recent coils have a service inscription that is present on the original printing plate. These show the mail service paid for by the stamp. Since these stamps are not intended to receive further cancellations when used as intended, they are considered precancels. Such items often do not have parallel lines as part of the precancellation.

In France, the abbreviation *Affranchts* in a semicircle together with the word *Postes* is the general form of precancel in use. Belgian precancellations usually appear in a box in which the name of the city appears. Netherlands precancels have the name of the city enclosed between concentric circles, sometimes called a "lifesaver." Precancellations of other countries usually follow these patterns, but may be any arrangement of bars, boxes and city names.

Precancels are listed in the Scott catalogues only if the precancel changes the denomination (Belgium Scott 477-478); if the precanceled stamp is different from the non-precanceled version (such as untagged U.S. precancels); or if the stamp exists only precanceled (France Scott 1096-1099, U.S. Scott 2265).

Proofs and Essays — Proofs are impressions taken from an approved die, plate or stone in which the design and color are the same as the stamp issued to the public. Trial color proofs are impressions taken from approved dies, plates or stones in colors that vary from the final version. An essay is the impression of a design that differs in some way from the issued stamp. "Progressive die proofs" generally are considered to be essays.

Provisionals — These are stamps that are issued on short notice and intended for temporary use pending the arrival of regular issues. They usually are issued to meet such contingencies as changes in government or currency, shortage of necessary postage values or military occupation.

During the 1840s, postmasters in certain American cities issued stamps that were valid only at specific post offices. In 1861, postmasters of the Confederate States also issued stamps with limited validity. Both of these examples are known as "postmaster's provisionals."

Se-tenant — This term refers to an unsevered pair, strip or block of stamps that differ in design, denomination or overprint.

Unless the se-tenant item has a continuous design (see U.S. Scott 1451a, 1694a) the stamps do not have to be in the same order as shown in the catalogue (see U.S. Scott 2158a).

Specimens — The Universal Postal Union required member nations to send samples of all stamps they released into service to the International Bureau in Switzerland. Member nations of the UPU received these specimens as samples of what stamps were valid for postage. Many are overprinted, handstamped or initial-perforated "Specimen," "Canceled" or "Muestra." Some are marked with bars across the denominations (China-Taiwan), punched holes (Czechoslovakia) or back inscriptions (Mongolia).

Stamps distributed to government officials or for publicity purposes, and stamps submitted by private security printers for official approval, also may receive such defacements.

The previously described defacement markings prevent postal use, and all such items generally are known as "specimens."

Tete Beche — This term describes a pair of stamps in which one is upside down in relation to the other. Some of these are the result of intentional sheet arrangements, such as Morocco Scott B10-B11. Others occurred when one or more electrotypes accidentally were placed upside down on the plate, such as Colombia Scott 57a. Separation of the tete-beche stamps, of course, destroys the tete beche variety.

Looking for some of stamp collecting's most fascinating and entertaining issues?

Subscribe to Scott Stamp Monthly

Every month you'll find a wide variety of articles, columns and departments for all collecting interests. Whether it's a tale about an amazing stamp find, a feature about some of your favorite stamps or the latest listing of stamp releases from around the world, you'll find it on the pages of *Scott Stamp Monthly*.

Scott Stamp Monthly offers a level of entertainment not found in a news publication. With features such as "Fun in Philately," "Lesser Known Rarities," "Snapshots," "Amazing Stamp Stories," and "Free For All".

For instance, our monthly "Free For All" column allows you to add stamps, covers and products to your collection simply by sending us a stamped, self-addressed envelope. This feature alone usually covers the cost of your subscription.

In addition, as a subscriber, you'll enjoy huge savings on the entire line of Scott products through the *Scott Stamp Monthly* Advantage Program.

Original and intriguing articles, listings of all the new issues, free stamps and huge savings all add up to a great magazine. You won't find a better deal in stamp collecting. Save more than $18 off the cover price. To subscribe, call:

12 Issues Only $17.95

1-800-572-6885

Subscribe today!

SCOTT

P.O. Box 828 Sidney OH 45365-0828
www.scottonline.com

Currency Conversion

Country	Dollar	Pound	S Franc	Guilder	Yen	Lira	HK Dollar	D-Mark	Fr Franc	Cdn Dollar	Aust Dollar
Australia	1.6313	2.7288	1.1870	0.8608	0.0140	0.0010	0.2106	0.9700	0.2894	1.0520	....
Canada	1.5507	2.5940	1.1284	0.8183	0.0133	0.0009	0.2002	0.9221	0.2751	....	.09506
France	5.6360	9.4279	4.1010	2.9741	0.0485	0.0034	0.7276	3.3514	....	3.6345	3.4549
Germany	1.6817	2.8131	1.2237	0.8874	0.0145	0.0010	0.2171	....	0.2984	1.0845	1.0309
Hong Kong	7.7455	12.957	5.6360	4.0873	0.0666	0.0047	....	4.6058	1.3743	4.9948	4.7481
Italy	1665.30	2785.71	1211.74	878.79	14.325	....	215.00	990.25	295.48	1073.90	1020.84
Japan	116.25	194.47	84.592	61.348	....	0.0698	15.009	69.129	20.627	74.969	71.265
Netherlands	1.8950	3.17	1.3789	....	0.0163	0.0011	0.2447	1.1268	0.3362	1.2220	1.1617
Switzerland	1.3743	2.2989	....	0.7252	0.0118	0.0008	0.1774	0.8172	0.2438	0.8862	0.8425
U.K.	0.5978	....	0.4350	0.3155	0.0051	0.0004	0.0772	0.3555	0.1061	0.3855	0.3665
U.S.	....	1.6728	0.7276	0.5277	0.0086	0.0006	0.1291	0.5946	0.1774	0.6449	0.6130

Country	Currency	U.S. $ Equiv.
Afghanistan	afghani	.0002
Aitutaki	New Zealand dollar	.5235
Albania	lek	.0072
Algeria	dinar	.0166
Andorra (French)	franc	.1774
Andorra (Spanish)	peseta	.0069
Angola	kwanza	.00001
Anguilla	East Caribbean dollar	.3703
Antigua	East Caribbean dollar	.3703
Argentina	peso	1.00
Aruba	guilder	.5586
Ascension	British pound	1.6728
Australia	dollar	.6130
Australian Antarctic Territory	dollar	.6130
Austria	schilling	.0847
Azerbaijan	manat	.00025
Bahamas	dollar	1.00
Bahrain	dinar	2.63
Bangladesh	taka	.0206
Barbados	dollar	.4972
Barbuda	East Caribbean dollar	.3703
Belgium	franc	.0288
Belize	dollar	.5000
Benin	Community of French Africa (CFA) franc	.00177
Bermuda	dollar	1.00
Bhutan	ngultrum	.0235
Bolivia	boliviano	.1177
Botswana	pula	.2239
Brazil	real	.8282
British Antarctic Territory	British pound	1.6728
British Indian Ocean Territory	British pound	1.6728
Brunei	dollar	.6035
Bulgaria	lev	.0006
Burkina Faso	CFA franc	.00177
Burma	kyat	.1625
Burundi	franc	.0021
United Nations-New York	U.S. dollar	1.00
United Nations-Geneva	Swiss franc	.7276
United Nations-Vienna	Austria shilling	.0847
United States	dollar	1.00

*Source: **Wall Street Journal** Dec. 28 1998. Figures reflect values as of Dec. 25, 1998.*

Stock Pages

Hagner-style stock pages offer convenience and flexibility. Pages are produced on thick, archival-quality paper with acetate pockets glued from the bottom of each pocket. They're ideal for the topical collector who may require various page styles to store a complete collection. Multi-hole punch fits most binder types. Available in 9 different page formats. 8 1/2" x 11" size accomodates every size stamp.

Sold in packages of 10.
Available with pockets on one side or both sides.
"D" in item number denotes two-sided page.

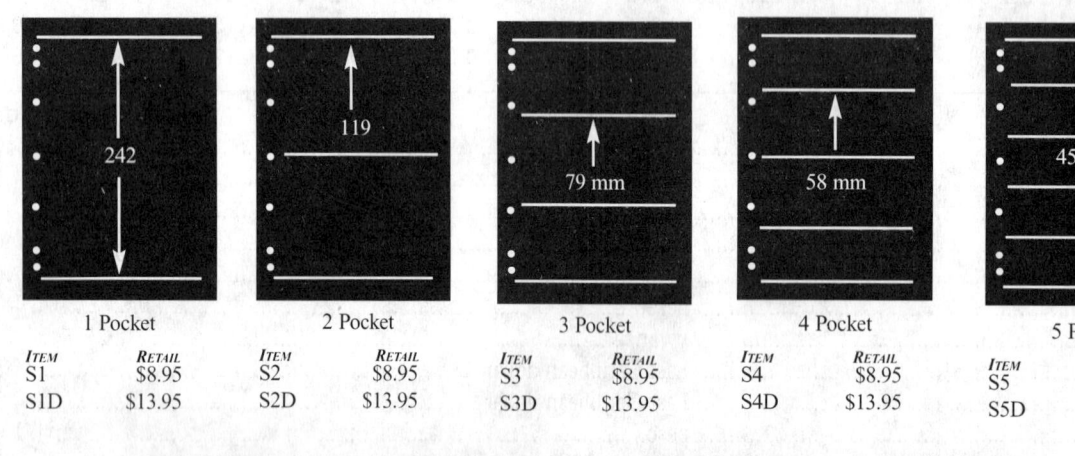

1 Pocket	2 Pocket	3 Pocket	4 Pocket	5 Pocket
Item S1 *Retail* $8.95	*Item* S2 *Retail* $8.95	*Item* S3 *Retail* $8.95	*Item* S4 *Retail* $8.95	*Item* S5 *Retail* $8.95
S1D $13.95	S2D $13.95	S3D $13.95	S4D $13.95	S5D $13.95

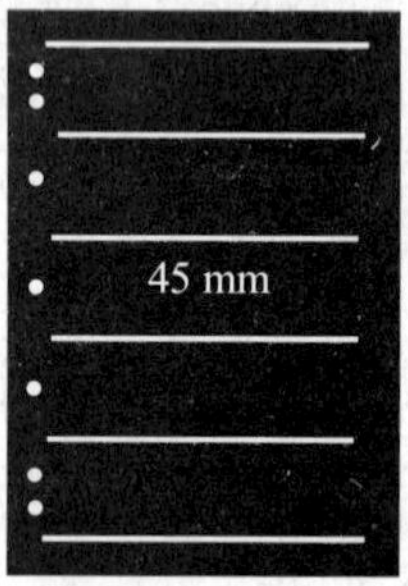

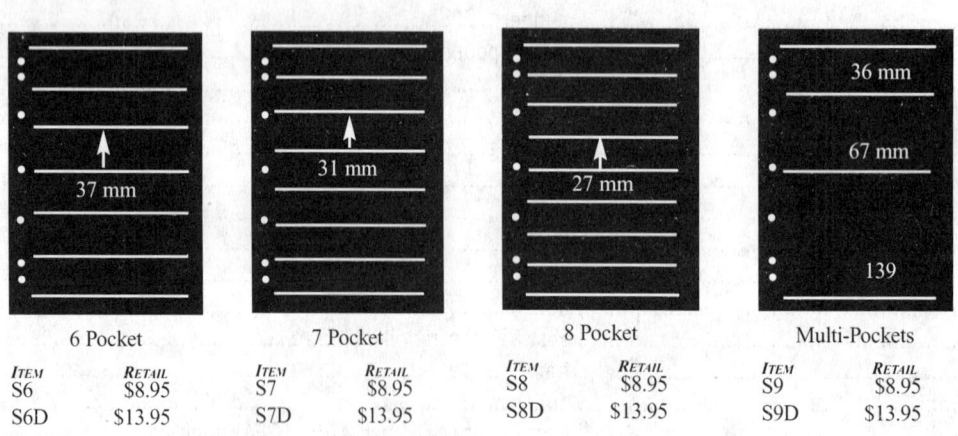

6 Pocket	7 Pocket	8 Pocket	Multi-Pockets
Item S6 *Retail* $8.95	*Item* S7 *Retail* $8.95	*Item* S8 *Retail* $8.95	*Item* S9 *Retail* $8.95
S6D $13.95	S7D $13.95	S8D $13.95	S9D $13.95

STOCK PAGE BINDER AND SLIPCASE
Keep all your stock pages neat and tidy with binder and accompanying slipcase. Available in two colors.

Item	Color	Retail
SSBSRD	Red	$19.95
SSBSBL	Blue	$19.95

Available from your favorite dealer or direct from:

Box 828 Sidney OH 45365-0828
1-800-572-6885
www.scottonline.com

Colonies, Former Colonies, Offices, Territories Controlled by Parent States

Belgium
Belgian Congo
Ruanda-Urundi

Denmark
Danish West Indies
Faroe Islands
Greenland
Iceland

Finland
Aland Islands

France

COLONIES PAST AND PRESENT, CONTROLLED TERRITORIES
Afars & Issas, Territory of
Alaouites
Alexandretta
Algeria
Alsace & Lorraine
Anjouan
Annam & Tonkin
Benin
Cambodia (Khmer)
Cameroun
Castellorizo
Chad
Cilicia
Cochin China
Comoro Islands
Dahomey
Diego Suarez
Djibouti (Somali Coast)
Fezzan
French Congo
French Equatorial Africa
French Guiana
French Guinea
French India
French Morocco
French Polynesia (Oceania)
French Southern & Antarctic Territories
French Sudan
French West Africa
Gabon
Germany
Ghadames
Grand Comoro
Guadeloupe
Indo-China
Inini
Ivory Coast
Laos
Latakia
Lebanon
Madagascar
Martinique
Mauritania
Mayotte
Memel
Middle Congo
Moheli
New Caledonia
New Hebrides
Niger Territory
Nossi-Be
Obock
Reunion
Rouad, Ile
Ste.-Marie de Madagascar
St. Pierre & Miquelon
Senegal
Senegambia & Niger
Somali Coast
Syria
Tahiti
Togo
Tunisia
Ubangi-Shari
Upper Senegal & Niger
Upper Volta
Viet Nam
Wallis & Futuna Islands

POST OFFICES IN FOREIGN COUNTRIES
China
Crete
Egypt
Turkish Empire
Zanzibar

Germany

EARLY STATES
Baden
Bavaria
Bergedorf
Bremen
Brunswick
Hamburg
Hanover
Lubeck
Mecklenburg-Schwerin
Mecklenburg-Strelitz
Oldenburg
Prussia
Saxony
Schleswig-Holstein
Wurttemberg

FORMER COLONIES
Cameroun (Kamerun)
Caroline Islands
German East Africa
German New Guinea
German South-West Africa
Kiauchau
Mariana Islands
Marshall Islands
Samoa
Togo

Italy

EARLY STATES
Modena
Parma
Romagna
Roman States
Sardinia
Tuscany
Two Sicilies
   Naples
   Neapolitan Provinces
   Sicily

FORMER COLONIES, CONTROLLED TERRITORIES, OCCUPATION AREAS
Aegean Islands
   Calimno (Calino)
   Caso
   Cos (Coo)
   Karki (Carchi)
   Leros (Lero)
   Lipso
   Nisiros (Nisiro)
   Patmos (Patmo)
   Piscopi
   Rodi (Rhodes)
   Scarpanto
   Simi
   Stampalia
Castellorizo
Corfu
Cyrenaica
Eritrea
Ethiopia (Abyssinia)
Fiume
Ionian Islands
   Cephalonia
   Ithaca
   Paxos
Italian East Africa
Libya
Oltre Giuba
Saseno
Somalia (Italian Somaliland)
Tripolitania

POST OFFICES IN FOREIGN COUNTRIES
"ESTERO"*
Austria
China
   Peking
   Tientsin
Crete
Tripoli
Turkish Empire
   Constantinople
   Durazzo
   Janina
Jerusalem
Salonika
Scutari
Smyrna
Valona

*Stamps overprinted "ESTERO" were used in various parts of the world.

Netherlands
Aruba
Netherlands Antilles (Curacao)
Netherlands Indies
Netherlands New Guinea
Surinam (Dutch Guiana)

Portugal

COLONIES PAST AND PRESENT, CONTROLLED TERRITORIES
Angola
Angra
Azores
Cape Verde
Funchal
Horta
Inhambane
Kionga
Lourenco Marques
Macao
Madeira
Mozambique
Mozambique Co.
Nyassa
Ponta Delgada
Portuguese Africa
Portuguese Congo
Portuguese Guinea
Portuguese India
Quelimane
St. Thomas & Prince Islands
Tete
Timor
Zambezia

Russia

ALLIED TERRITORIES AND REPUBLICS, OCCUPATION AREAS
Armenia
Aunus (Olonets)
Azerbaijan
Batum
Estonia
Far Eastern Republic
Georgia
Karelia
Latvia
Lithuania
North Ingermanland
Ostland
Russian Turkestan
Siberia
South Russia
Tannu Tuva
Transcaucasian Fed. Republics
Ukraine
Wenden (Livonia)
Western Ukraine

Spain

COLONIES PAST AND PRESENT, CONTROLLED TERRITORIES
Aguera, La
Cape Juby
Cuba
Elobey, Annobon & Corisco
Fernando Po
Ifni
Mariana Islands
Philippines
Puerto Rico
Rio de Oro
Rio Muni
Spanish Guinea
Spanish Morocco
Spanish Sahara
Spanish West Africa

POST OFFICES IN FOREIGN COUNTRIES
Morocco
Tangier
Tetuan

British Commonwealth of Nations
Dominions, Colonies, Territories, Offices and Independent Members

Comprising stamps of the British Commonwealth and associated nations.

A strict observance of technicalities would bar some or all of the stamps listed under Burma, Ireland, Kuwait, Nepal, New Republic, Orange Free State, Samoa, South Africa, South-West Africa, Stellaland, Sudan, Swaziland, the two Transvaal Republics and others but these are included for the convenience of collectors.

1. Great Britain

Great Britain: Including England, Scotland, Wales and Northern Ireland.

2. The Dominions, Present and Past

AUSTRALIA
The Commonwealth of Australia was proclaimed on January 1, 1901. It consists of six former colonies as follows:

New South Wales	Victoria
Queensland	Tasmania
South Australia	Western Australia

Territories belonging to, or administered by Australia: Australian Antarctic Territory, Christmas Island, Cocos (Keeling) Islands, Nauru, New Guinea, Norfolk Island, Papua New Guinea.

CANADA
The Dominion of Canada was created by the British North America Act in 1867. The following provinces were former separate colonies and issued postage stamps:

British Columbia and Vancouver Island	Newfoundland
New Brunswick	Nova Scotia
	Prince Edward Island

FIJI
The colony of Fiji became an independent nation with dominion status on Oct. 10, 1970.

GHANA
This state came into existence Mar. 6, 1957, with dominion status. It consists of the former colony of the Gold Coast and the Trusteeship Territory of Togoland. Ghana became a republic July 1, 1960.

INDIA
The Republic of India was inaugurated on January 26, 1950. It succeeded the Dominion of India which was proclaimed August 15, 1947, when the former Empire of India was divided into Pakistan and the Union of India. The Republic is composed of about 40 predominantly Hindu states of three classes: governor's provinces, chief commissioner's provinces and princely states. India also has various territories, such as the Andaman and Nicobar Islands.

The old Empire of India was a federation of British India and the native states. The more important princely states were autonomous. Of the more than 700 Indian states, these 43 are familiar names to philatelists because of their postage stamps.

CONVENTION STATES
Chamba	Jhind
Faridkot	Nabha
Gwalior	Patiala

NATIVE FEUDATORY STATES
Alwar	Jammu
Bahawalpur	Jammu and Kashmir
Bamra	Jasdan
Barwani	Jhalawar
Bhopal	Jhind (1875-76)
Bhor	Kashmir
Bijawar	Kishangarh
Bundi	Las Bela
Bussahir	Morvi
Charkhari	Nandgaon
Cochin	Nowanuggur
Dhar	Orchha
Duttia	Poonch
Faridkot (1879-85)	Rajpeepla
Hyderabad	Sirmur
Idar	Soruth
Indore	Travancore
Jaipur	Wadhwan

NEW ZEALAND
Became a dominion on September 26, 1907. The following islands and territories are, or have been, administered by New Zealand:

Aitutaki	Ross Dependency
Cook Islands (Rarotonga)	Samoa (Western Samoa)
Niue	Tokelau Islands
Penrhyn	

PAKISTAN
The Republic of Pakistan was proclaimed March 23, 1956. It succeeded the Dominion which was proclaimed August 15, 1947. It is made up of all or part of several Moslem provinces and various districts of the former Empire of India, including Bahawalpur and Las Bela. Pakistan withdrew from the Commonwealth in 1972.

SOUTH AFRICA
Under the terms of the South African Act (1909) the self-governing colonies of Cape of Good Hope, Natal, Orange River Colony and Transvaal united on May 31, 1910, to form the Union of South Africa. It became an independent republic May 3, 1961.

Under the terms of the Treaty of Versailles, South-West Africa, formerly German South-West Africa, was mandated to the Union of South Africa.

SRI LANKA (CEYLON)
The Dominion of Ceylon was proclaimed February 4, 1948. The island had been a Crown Colony from 1802 until then. On May 22, 1972, Ceylon became the Republic of Sri Lanka.

3. Colonies, Past and Present; Controlled Territory and Independent Members of the Commonwealth

Aden	Bechuanaland
Aitutaki	Bechuanaland Prot.
Antigua	Belize
Ascension	Bermuda
Bahamas	Botswana
Bahrain	British Antarctic Territory
Bangladesh	British Central Africa
Barbados	British Columbia and Vancouver Island
Barbuda	
Basutoland	British East Africa
Batum	British Guiana

British Honduras
British Indian Ocean Territory
British New Guinea
British Solomon Islands
British Somaliland
Brunei
Burma
Bushire
Cameroons
Cape of Good Hope
Cayman Islands
Christmas Island
Cocos (Keeling) Islands
Cook Islands
Crete,
  British Administration
Cyprus
Dominica
East Africa & Uganda
  Protectorates
Egypt
Falkland Islands
Fiji
Gambia
German East Africa
Gibraltar
Gilbert Islands
Gilbert & Ellice Islands
Gold Coast
Grenada
Griqualand West
Guernsey
Guyana
Heligoland
Hong Kong
Indian Native States
  (see India)
Ionian Islands
Jamaica
Jersey

Kenya
Kenya, Uganda & Tanzania
Kuwait
Labuan
Lagos
Leeward Islands
Lesotho
Madagascar
Malawi
Malaya
  Federated Malay States
  Johore
  Kedah
  Kelantan
  Malacca
  Negri Sembilan
  Pahang
  Penang
  Perak
  Perlis
  Selangor
  Singapore
  Sungei Ujong
  Trengganu
Malaysia
Maldive Islands
Malta
Man, Isle of
Mauritius
Mesopotamia
Montserrat
Muscat
Namibia
Natal
Nauru
Nevis
New Britain
New Brunswick
Newfoundland
New Guinea

New Hebrides
New Republic
New South Wales
Niger Coast Protectorate
Nigeria
Niue
Norfolk Island
North Borneo
Northern Nigeria
Northern Rhodesia
North West Pacific Islands
Nova Scotia
Nyasaland Protectorate
Oman
Orange River Colony
Palestine
Papua New Guinea
Penrhyn Island
Pitcairn Islands
Prince Edward Island
Queensland
Rhodesia
Rhodesia & Nyasaland
Ross Dependency
Sabah
St. Christopher
St. Helena
St. Kitts
St. Kitts-Nevis-Anguilla
St. Lucia
St. Vincent
Samoa
Sarawak
Seychelles
Sierra Leone
Solomon Islands
Somaliland Protectorate
South Arabia
South Australia
South Georgia

Southern Nigeria
Southern Rhodesia
South-West Africa
Stellaland
Straits Settlements
Sudan
Swaziland
Tanganyika
Tanzania
Tasmania
Tobago
Togo
Tokelau Islands
Tonga
Transvaal
Trinidad
Trinidad and Tobago
Tristan da Cunha
Trucial States
Turks and Caicos
Turks Islands
Tuvalu
Uganda
United Arab Emirates
Victoria
Virgin Islands
Western Australia
Zambia
Zanzibar
Zululand

POST OFFICES IN FOREIGN COUNTRIES
Africa
  East Africa Forces
  Middle East Forces
Bangkok
China
Morocco
Turkish Empire

COLLECT THE SCOTT WAY WITH

British Commonwealth Albums

SCOTT ALBUMS FEATURE:

- High quality chemically neutral paper printed on one side. •
- All spaces identified by Scott numbers with either illustrations or descriptions. •
- All pages have matching borders. •
- Pages contain general postage issues, as well as complete back-of-the book materials. •
- Albums supplemented annually. •

For a complete list of Scott British Commonwealth albums available contact your local dealer,
or call Scott Publishing at 1-800-5SCOTT5 or write to P.O. Box 828, Sidney, OH 45365.

Common Design Types

Pictured in this section are issues where one illustration has been used for a number of countries in the Catalogue. Not included in this section are overprinted stamps or those issues which are illustrated in each country.

EUROPA

Europa, 1956

The design symbolizing the cooperation among the six countries comprising the Coal and Steel Community is illustrated in each country.

Belgium	496-497
France	805-806
Germany	748-749
Italy	715-716
Luxembourg	318-320
Netherlands	368-369

Europa, 1958

"E" and Dove — CD1

European Postal Union at the service of European integration.

1958, Sept. 13

Belgium	527-528
France	889-890
Germany	790-791
Italy	750-751
Luxembourg	341-343
Netherlands	375-376
Saar	317-318

Europa, 1959

6-Link Endless Chain – CD2

1959, Sept. 19

Belgium	536-537
France	929-930
Germany	805-806
Italy	791-792
Luxembourg	354-355
Netherlands	379-380

Europa, 1960

19-Spoke Wheel – CD3

First anniversary of the establishment of C.E.P.T. (Conference Europeenne des Administrations des Postes et des Telecommunications.)
The spokes symbolize the 19 founding members of the Conference.

1960, Sept.

Belgium	553-554
Denmark	379
Finland	376-377
France	970-971
Germany	818-820
Great Britain	377-378
Greece	688
Iceland	327-328
Ireland	175-176
Italy	809-810
Luxembourg	374-375
Netherlands	385-386
Norway	387
Portugal	866-867
Spain	941-942
Sweden	562-563
Switzerland	400-401
Turkey	1493-1494

Europa, 1961

19 Doves Flying as One – CD4

The 19 doves represent the 19 members of the Conference of European Postal and Telecommunications Administrations C.E.P.T.

1961-62

Belgium	572-573
Cyprus	201-203
France	1005-1006
Germany	844-845
Great Britain	383-384
Greece	718-719
Iceland	340-341
Italy	845-846
Luxembourg	382-383
Netherlands	387-388
Spain	1010-1011
Switzerland	410-411
Turkey	1518-1520

Europa, 1962

Young Tree with 19 Leaves CD5

The 19 leaves represent the 19 original members of C.E.P.T.

1962-63

Belgium	582-583
Cyprus	219-221
France	1045-1046
Germany	852-853
Greece	739-740
Iceland	348-349
Ireland	184-185
Italy	860-861
Luxembourg	386-387
Netherlands	394-395
Norway	414-415
Switzerland	416-417
Turkey	1553-1555

Europa, 1963

Stylized Links, Symbolizing Unity – CD6

1963, Sept.

Belgium	598-599
Cyprus	229-231
Finland	419
France	1074-1075
Germany	867-868
Greece	768-769
Iceland	357-358
Ireland	188-189
Italy	880-881
Luxembourg	403-404
Netherlands	416-417
Norway	441-442
Switzerland	429
Turkey	1602-1603

Europa, 1964

Symbolic Daisy – CD7

5th anniversary of the establishment of C.E.P.T. The 22 petals of the flower symbolize the 22 members of the Conference.

1964, Sept.

Austria	738
Belgium	614-615
Cyprus	244-246
France	1109-1110
Germany	897-898
Greece	801-802
Iceland	367-368
Ireland	196-197
Italy	894-895
Luxembourg	411-412
Monaco	590-591
Netherlands	428-429
Norway	458
Portugal	931-933
Spain	1262-1263
Switzerland	438-439
Turkey	1628-1629

Europa, 1965

Leaves and "Fruit" CD8

1965

Belgium	636-637
Cyprus	262-264
Finland	437
France	1131-1132
Germany	934-935
Greece	833-834
Iceland	375-376
Ireland	204-205
Italy	915-916
Luxembourg	432-433
Monaco	616-617
Netherlands	438-439
Norway	475-476
Portugal	958-960
Switzerland	469
Turkey	1665-1666

Europa, 1966

Symbolic Sailboat – CD9

1966, Sept.

Andorra, French	172
Belgium	675-676
Cyprus	275-277
France	1163-1164
Germany	963-964
Greece	862-863
Iceland	384-385
Ireland	216-217
Italy	942-943
Liechtenstein	415
Luxembourg	440-441
Monaco	639-640
Netherlands	441-442
Norway	496-497
Portugal	980-982
Switzerland	477-478
Turkey	1718-1719

Europa, 1967

Cogwheels CD10

1967

Andorra, French	174-175
Belgium	688-689
Cyprus	297-299
France	1178-1179
Germany	969-970
Greece	891-892
Iceland	389-390
Ireland	232-233
Italy	951-952
Liechtenstein	420
Luxembourg	449-450
Monaco	669-670
Netherlands	444-447
Norway	504-505
Portugal	994-996
Spain	1465-1466
Switzerland	482
Turkey	B120-B121

Europa, 1968

Golden Key with C.E.P.T. Emblem CD11

1968

Andorra, French	182-183
Belgium	705-706
Cyprus	314-316
France	1209-1210
Germany	983-984
Greece	916-917
Iceland	395-396
Ireland	242-243
Italy	979-980
Liechtenstein	442
Luxembourg	466-467
Monaco	689-691
Netherlands	452-453
Portugal	1019-1021
San Marino	687
Spain	1526
Turkey	1775-1776

Europa, 1969

"EUROPA" and "CEPT" – CD12

Tenth anniversary of C.E.P.T.

1969

Andorra, French	188-189
Austria	837
Belgium	718-719
Cyprus	326-328
Denmark	458
Finland	483
France	1245-1246
Germany	996-997
Great Britain	585
Greece	947-948
Iceland	406-407
Ireland	270-271
Italy	1000-1001
Liechtenstein	453
Luxembourg	474-475
Monaco	722-724
Netherlands	475-476
Norway	533-534
Portugal	1038-1040
San Marino	701-702
Spain	1567

COMMON DESIGN TYPES

Sweden 814-816
Switzerland 500-501
Turkey 1799-1800
Vatican 470-472
Yugoslavia 1003-1004

Europa, 1970

Interwoven Threads
CD13

1970
Andorra, French 196-197
Belgium 741-742
Cyprus 340-342
France 1271-1272
Germany 1018-1019
Greece 985, 987
Iceland 420-421
Ireland 279-281
Italy 1013-1014
Liechtenstein 470
Luxembourg 489-490
Monaco 768-770
Netherlands 483-484
Portugal 1060-1062
San Marino 729-730
Spain 1607
Switzerland 515-516
Turkey 1848-1849
Yugoslavia 1024-1025

Europa, 1971

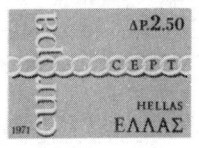

"Fraternity, Cooperation, Common Effort" – CD14

1971
Andorra, French 205-206
Belgium 803-804
Cyprus 365-367
Finland 504
France 1304
Germany 1064-1065
Greece 1029-1030
Iceland 429-430
Ireland 305-306
Italy 1038-1039
Liechtenstein 485
Luxembourg 500-501
Malta 425-427
Monaco 797-799
Netherlands 488-489
Portugal 1094-1096
San Marino 749-750
Spain 1675-1676
Switzerland 531-532
Turkey 1876-1877
Yugoslavia 1052-1053

Europa, 1972

Sparkles, Symbolic of Communications
CD15

1972
Andorra, French 210-211
Andorra, Spanish 62
Belgium 825-826
Cyprus 380-382
Finland 512-513
France 1341
Germany 1089-1090
Greece 1049-1050
Iceland 439-440
Ireland 316-317
Italy 1065-1066
Liechtenstein 504

Luxembourg 512-513
Malta 450-453
Monaco 831-832
Netherlands 494-495
Portugal 1141-1143
San Marino 771-772
Spain 1718
Switzerland 544-545
Turkey 1907-1908
Yugoslavia 1100-1101

Europa, 1973

Post Horn and Arrows
CD16

1973
Andorra, French 319-320
Andorra, Spanish 76
Belgium 839-840
Cyprus 396-398
Finland 526
France 1367
Germany 1114-1115
Greece 1090-1092
Iceland 447-448
Ireland 329-330
Italy 1108-1109
Liechtenstein 528-529
Luxembourg 523-524
Malta 469-471
Monaco 866-867
Netherlands 504-505
Norway 604-605
Portugal 1170-1172
San Marino 802-803
Spain 1753
Switzerland 580-581
Turkey 1935-1936
Yugoslavia 1138-1139

PORTUGAL & COLONIES
Vasco da Gama

Fleet Departing
CD20

Fleet Arriving at Calicut
CD21

Embarking at Rastello
CD22

Muse of History – CD23

San Gabriel, da Gama and Camoens – CD24

Archangel Gabriel, the Patron Saint
CD25

Flagship San Gabriel
CD26

Vasco da Gama
CD27

Fourth centenary of Vasco da Gama's discovery of the route to India.

1898
Azores 93-100
Macao 67-74
Madeira 37-44
Portugal 147-154
Port. Africa 1-8
Port. Congo 75-98
Port. India 189-196
St. Thomas & Prince Islands 170-193
Timor 45-52

Pombal

POSTAL TAX

POSTAL TAX DUES

Marquis de Pombal
CD28

Planning Reconstruction of Lisbon, 1755
CD29

Pombal Monument, Lisbon
CD30

Sebastiao Jose de Carvalho e Mello, Marquis de Pombal (1699-1782), statesman, rebuilt Lisbon after earthquake of 1755. Tax was for the erection of Pombal monument. Obligatory on all mail on certain days throughout the year.

Postal Tax Dues are inscribed "Multa."

1925
Angola RA1-RA3, RAJ1-RAJ3
Azores RA9-RA11, RAJ2-RAJ4
Cape Verde RA1-RA3, RAJ1-RAJ3
Macao RA1-RA3, RAJ1-RAJ3
Madeira RA1-RA3, RAJ1-RAJ3
Mozambique RA1-RA3, RAJ1-RAJ3
Nyassa RA1-RA3, RAJ1-RAJ3
Portugal RA11-RA13, RAJ2-RAJ4
Port. Guinea RA1-RA3, RAJ1-RAJ3
Port. India RA1-RA3, RAJ1-RAJ3
St. Thomas & Prince
  Islands RA1-RA3, RAJ1-RAJ3
Timor RA1-RA3, RAJ1-RAJ3

Vasco da Gama
CD34

Mousinho de Albuquerque
CD35

Dam
CD36

Prince Henry the Navigator – CD37

Affonso de Albuquerque
CD38

Plane over Globe
CD39

1938-39
Angola 274-291, C1-C9
Cape Verde 234-251, C1-C9
Macao 289-305, C7-C15
Mozambique 270-287, C1-C9
Port. Guinea 233-250, C1-C9
Port. India 439-453, C1-C8
St. Thomas & Prince
  Islands 302-319, 323-340, C1-C18
Timor 223-239, C1-C9

Lady of Fatima

Our Lady of the Rosary, Fatima, Portugal
CD40

1948-49
Angola 315-318
Cape Verde 266
Macao 336
Mozambique 325-328
Port. Guinea 271
Port. India 480
St. Thomas & Prince Islands 351
Timor 254

A souvenir sheet of 9 stamps was issued in 1951 to mark the extension of the 1950 Holy Year. The sheet contains: Angola No. 316, Cape Verde No. 266, Macao No. 336, Mozambique No. 325, Portuguese Guinea No. 271, Portuguese India Nos. 480, 485, St. Thomas & Prince Islands No. 351, Timor No. 254.

The sheet also contains a portrait of Pope Pius XII and is inscribed "Encerramento do Ano Santo, Fatima 1951." It was sold for 11 escudos.

Holy Year

Church Bells and Dove
CD41

Angel Holding Candelabra
CD42

Holy Year, 1950.
1950-51
Angola 331-332
Cape Verde 268-269
Macao 339-340
Mozambique 330-331
Port. Guinea 273-274
Port. India 490-491, 496-503
St. Thomas & Prince Islands 353-354
Timor 258-259

A souvenir sheet of 8 stamps was issued in 1951 to mark the extension of the Holy Year. The sheet contains: Angola No. 331, Cape Verde No. 269, Macao No. 340, Mozambique No. 331, Portuguese Guinea No. 275, Portuguese India No. 490, St. Thomas & Prince Islands No. 354, Timor No. 258, some with colors changed. The sheet contains doves and is inscribed "Encerramento do Ano Santo, Fatima 1951." It was sold for 17 escudos.

Holy Year Conclusion

Our Lady of Fatima
CD43

Conclusion of Holy Year. Sheets contain alternate vertical rows of stamps and labels bearing quotation from Pope Pius XII, different for each colony.
1951
Angola 357
Cape Verde 270
Macao 352
Mozambique 356
Port. Guinea 275
Port. India 506
St. Thomas & Prince Islands 355
Timor 270

Medical Congress

CD44

First National Congress of Tropical Medicine, Lisbon, 1952.
Each stamp has a different design.
1952
Angola 358
Cape Verde 287
Macao 364
Mozambique 359
Port. Guinea 276
Port. India 516
St. Thomas & Prince Islands 356
Timor 271

POSTAGE DUE STAMPS

CD45

1952
Angola J37-J42
Cape Verde J31-J36
Macao J53-J58
Mozambique J51-J56
Port. Guinea J40-J45
Port. India J47-J52
St. Thomas & Prince Islands J52-J57
Timor J31-J36

Sao Paulo

Father Manuel de Nobrega and View of Sao Paulo
CD46

Founding of Sao Paulo, Brazil, 400th anniv.
1954
Angola 385
Cape Verde 297
Macao 382
Mozambique 395
Port. Guinea 291
Port. India 530
St. Thomas & Prince Islands 369
Timor 279

Tropical Medicine Congress

CD47

Sixth International Congress for Tropical Medicine and Malaria, Lisbon, Sept. 1958.
Each stamp shows a different plant.
1958
Angola 409
Cape Verde 303
Macao 392
Mozambique 404
Port. Guinea 295
Port. India 569
St. Thomas & Prince Islands 371
Timor 289

Sports

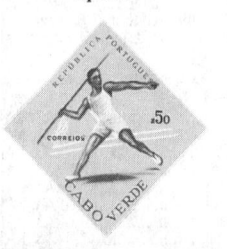

CD48

Each stamp shows a different sport.
1962
Angola 433-438
Cape Verde 320-325
Macao 394-399
Mozambique 424-429
Port. Guinea 299-304
St. Thomas & Prince Islands 374-379
Timor 313-318

Anti-Malaria

Anopheles Funestus and Malaria Eradication Symbol
CD49

World Health Organization drive to eradicate malaria.
1962
Angola 439
Cape Verde 326
Macao 400
Mozambique 430
Port. Guinea 305
St. Thomas & Prince Islands 380
Timor 319

Airline Anniversary

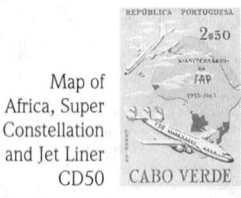

Map of Africa, Super Constellation and Jet Liner
CD50

Tenth anniversary of Transportes Aereos Portugueses (TAP).
1963
Angola 490
Cape Verde 327
Mozambique 434
Port. Guinea 318
St. Thomas & Prince Islands 381

National Overseas Bank

Antonio Teixeira de Sousa
CD51

Centenary of the National Overseas Bank of Portugal.
1964, May 16
Angola 509
Cape Verde 328
Port. Guinea 319
St. Thomas & Prince Islands 382
Timor 320

ITU

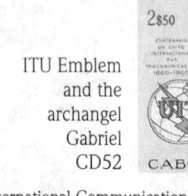

ITU Emblem and the archangel Gabriel
CD52

International Communications Union, Cent.
1965, May 17
Angola 511
Cape Verde 329
Macao 402
Mozambique 464
Port. Guinea 320
St. Thomas & Prince Islands 383
Timor 321

National Revolution

CD53

40th anniv. of the National Revolution.
Different buildings on each stamp.
1966, May 28
Angola 525
Cape Verde 338
Macao 403
Mozambique 465
Port. Guinea 329
St. Thomas & Prince Islands 392
Timor 322

Navy Club

CD54

Centenary of Portugal's Navy Club.
Each stamp has a different design.
1967, Jan. 31
Angola 527-528
Cape Verde 339-340
Macao 412-413
Mozambique 478-479
Port. Guinea 330-331
St. Thomas & Prince Islands 393-394
Timor 323-324

Admiral Coutinho

CD55

Centenary of the birth of Admiral Carlos Viegas Gago Coutinho (1869-1959), explorer and aviation pioneer.
Each stamp has a different design.
1969, Feb. 17
Angola 547
Cape Verde 355
Macao 417
Mozambique 484
Port. Guinea 335
St. Thomas & Prince Islands 397
Timor 335

Administration Reform

Luiz Augusto Rebello da Silva – CD56

Centenary of the administration reforms of the overseas territories.
1969, Sept. 25
Angola 549
Cape Verde 357
Macao 419
Mozambique 491
Port. Guinea 337
St. Thomas & Prince Islands 399
Timor 338

COMMON DESIGN TYPES

Marshal Carmona

CD57

Birth centenary of Marshal Antonio Oscar Carmona de Fragoso (1869-1951), President of Portugal.

Each stamp has a different design.

1970, Nov. 15
Angola	563
Cape Verde	359
Macao	422
Mozambique	493
Port. Guinea	340
St. Thomas & Prince Islands	403
Timor	341

Olympic Games

CD59

20th Olympic Games, Munich, Aug. 26-Sept. 11.

Each stamp shows a different sport.

1972, June 20
Angola	569
Cape Verde	361
Macao	426
Mozambique	504
Port. Guinea	342
St. Thomas & Prince Islands	408
Timor	343

Lisbon-Rio de Janeiro Flight

CD60

50th anniversary of the Lisbon to Rio de Janeiro flight by Arturo de Sacadura and Coutinho, March 30-June 5, 1922.

Each stamp shows a different stage of the flight.

1972, Sept. 20
Angola	570
Cape Verde	362
Macao	427
Mozambique	505
Port. Guinea	343
St. Thomas & Prince Islands	409
Timor	344

WMO Centenary

WMO Emblem – CD61

Centenary of international meterological cooperation.

1973, Dec. 15
Angola	571
Cape Verde	363
Macao	429
Mozambique	509
Port. Guinea	344
St. Thomas & Prince Islands	410
Timor	345

FRENCH COMMUNITY

Upper Volta can be found under Burkina Faso in Vol. 1

Madagascar can be found under Malagasy in Vol. 3

Colonial Exposition

People of French Empire CD70

Women's Heads CD71

France Showing Way to Civilization CD72

"Colonial Commerce" CD73

International Colonial Exposition, Paris.

1931
Cameroun	213-216
Chad	60-63
Dahomey	97-100
Fr. Guiana	152-155
Fr. Guinea	116-119
Fr. India	100-103
Fr. Polynesia	76-79
Fr. Sudan	102-105
Gabon	120-123
Guadeloupe	138-141
Indo-China	140-142
Ivory Coast	92-95
Madagascar	169-172
Martinique	129-132
Mauritania	65-68
Middle Congo	61-64
New Caledonia	176-179
Niger	73-76
Reunion	122-125
St. Pierre & Miquelon	132-135
Senegal	138-141
Somali Coast	135-138
Togo	254-257
Ubangi-Shari	82-85
Upper Volta	66-69
Wallis & Futuna Isls.	85-88

Paris International Exposition Colonial Arts Exposition

"Colonial Resources"
CD74   CD77

Overseas Commerce – CD75

Exposition Building and Women CD76

"France and the Empire" CD78

Cultural Treasures of the Colonies CD79

Souvenir sheets contain one imperf. stamp.

1937
Cameroun	217-222A
Dahomey	101-107
Fr. Equatorial Africa	27-32, 73
Fr. Guiana	162-168
Fr. Guinea	120-126
Fr. India	104-110
Fr. Polynesia	117-123
Fr. Sudan	106-112
Guadeloupe	148-154
Indo-China	193-199
Inini	41
Ivory Coast	152-158
Kwangchowan	132
Madagascar	191-197
Martinique	179-185
Mauritania	69-75
New Caledonia	208-214
Niger	72-83
Reunion	167-173
St. Pierre & Miquelon	165-171
Senegal	172-178
Somali Coast	139-145
Togo	258-264
Wallis & Futuna Isls.	89

Curie

Pierre and Marie Curie CD80

40th anniversary of the discovery of radium. The surtax was for the benefit of the Intl. Union for the Control of Cancer.

1938
Cameroun	B1
Cuba	B1-B2
Dahomey	B2
France	B76
Fr. Equatorial Africa	B1
Fr. Guiana	B3
Fr. Guinea	B2
Fr. India	B6
Fr. Polynesia	B5
Fr. Sudan	B1
Guadeloupe	B3
Indo-China	B14
Ivory Coast	B2
Madagascar	B2
Martinique	B2
Mauritania	B3
New Caledonia	B4
Niger	B1
Reunion	B4
St. Pierre & Miquelon	B3
Senegal	B2
Somali Coast	B2
Togo	B1

Caillie

Rene Caille and Map of Northwestern Africa - CD81

Death centenary of Rene Caillie (1799-1838), French explorer.

All three denominations exist with colony name omitted.

1939
Dahomey	108-110
Fr. Guinea	161-163
Fr. Sudan	113-115
Ivory Coast	160-162
Mauritania	109-111
Niger	84-86
Senegal	188-190
Togo	265-267

New York World's Fair

Natives and New York Skyline CD82

1939
Cameroun	223-224
Dahomey	111-112
Fr. Equatorial Africa	78-79
Fr. Guiana	169-170
Fr. Guinea	164-165
Fr. India	111-112
Fr. Polynesia	124-125
Fr. Sudan	116-117
Guadeloupe	155-156
Indo-China	203-204
Inini	42-43
Ivory Coast	163-164
Kwangchowan	121-122
Madagascar	209-210
Martinique	186-187
Mauritania	112-113
New Caledonia	215-216
Niger	87-88
Reunion	174-175
St. Pierre & Miquelon	205-206
Senegal	191-192
Somali Coast	179-180
Togo	268-269
Wallis & Futuna Isls.	90-91

French Revolution

Storming of the Bastille – CD83

French Revolution, 150th anniv. The surtax was for the defense of the colonies.

1939
Cameroun	B2-B6
Dahomey	B3-B7
Fr. Equatorial Africa	B4-B8, CB1
Fr. Guiana	B4-B8, CB1
Fr. Guinea	B3-B7
Fr. India	B7-B11
Fr. Polynesia	B6-B10, CB1
Fr. Sudan	B2-B6
Guadeloupe	B4-B8
Indo-China	B15-B19, CB1
Inini	B1-B5
Ivory Coast	B3-B7
Kwangchowan	B1-B5
Madagascar	B3-B7, CB1
Martinique	B3-B7
Mauritania	B4-B8
New Caledonia	B5-B9, CB1
Niger	B2-B6
Reunion	B5-B9, CB1
St. Pierre & Miquelon	B4-B8
Senegal	B4-B8, CB1
Somali Coast	B3-B7
Togo	B2-B6
Wallis & Futuna Isls.	B1-B5

COMMON DESIGN TYPES

Plane over Coastal Area
CD85

All five denominations exist with colony name omitted.

1940
Dahomey	C1-C5
Fr. Guinea	C1-C5
Fr. Sudan	C1-C5
Ivory Coast	C1-C5
Mauritania	C1-C5
Niger	C1-C5
Senegal	C12-C16
Togo	C1-C5

Colonial Infantryman
CD86

1941
Cameroun	B13B
Dahomey	B13
Fr. Equatorial Africa	B8B
Fr. Guiana	B10
Fr. Guinea	B13
Fr. India	B13
Fr. Polynesia	B12
Fr. Sudan	B12
Guadeloupe	B10
Indo-China	B19B
Inini	B7
Ivory Coast	B13
Kwangchowan	B7
Madagascar	B9
Martinique	B9
Mauritania	B14
New Caledonia	B11
Niger	B12
Reunion	B11
St. Pierre & Miquelon	B8B
Senegal	B14
Somali Coast	B9
Togo	B10B
Wallis & Futuna Isls.	B7

Cross of Lorraine & Four-motor Plane
CD87

1941-5
Cameroun	C1-C7
Fr. Equatorial Africa	C17-C23
Fr. Guiana	C9-C10
Fr. India	C1-C6
Fr. Polynesia	C3-C9
Fr. West Africa	C1-C3
Guadeloupe	C1-C2
Madagascar	C37-C43
Martinique	C1-C2
New Caledonia	C7-C13
Reunion	C18-C24
St. Pierre & Miquelon	C1-C7
Somali Coast	C1-C7

Transport Plane CD88

Caravan and Plane
CD89

1942
Dahomey	C6-C13
Fr. Guinea	C6-C13
Fr. Sudan	C6-C13
Ivory Coast	C6-C13
Mauritania	C6-C13
Niger	C6-C13
Senegal	C17-C25
Togo	C6-C13

Red Cross

Marianne
CD90

The surtax was for the French Red Cross and national relief.

1944
Cameroun	B28
Fr. Equatorial Africa	B38
Fr. Guiana	B12
Fr. India	B14
Fr. Polynesia	B13
Fr. West Africa	B1
Guadeloupe	B12
Madagascar	B15
Martinique	B11
New Caledonia	B13
Reunion	B15
St. Pierre & Miquelon	B13
Somali Coast	B13
Wallis & Futuna Isls.	B9

Eboue

CD91

Felix Eboue, first French colonial administrator to proclaim resistance to Germany after French surrender in World War II.

1945
Cameroun	296-297
Fr. Equatorial Africa	156-157
Fr. Guiana	171-172
Fr. India	210-211
Fr. Polynesia	150-151
Fr. West Africa	15-16
Guadeloupe	187-188
Madagascar	259-260
Martinique	196-197
New Caledonia	274-275
Reunion	238-239
St. Pierre & Miquelon	322-323
Somali Coast	238-239

Victory

Victory – CD92

European victory of the Allied Nations in World War II.

1946, May 8
Cameroun	C8
Fr. Equatorial Africa	C24
Fr. Guiana	C11
Fr. India	C7
Fr. Polynesia	C10
Fr. West Africa	C4
Guadeloupe	C3
Indo-China	C19
Madagascar	C44
Martinique	C3
New Caledonia	C14
Reunion	C25
St. Pierre & Miquelon	C8
Somali Coast	C8
Wallis & Futuna Isls.	C1

Chad to Rhine

Leclerc's Departure from Chad – CD93

Battle at Cufra Oasis – CD94

Tanks in Action, Mareth – CD95

Normandy Invasion – CD96

Entering Paris – CD97

Liberation of Strasbourg – CD98

"Chad to the Rhine" march, 1942-44, by Gen. Jacques Leclerc's column, later French 2nd Armored Division.

1946, June 6
Cameroun	C9-C14
Fr. Equatorial Africa	C25-C30
Fr. Guiana	C12-C17
Fr. India	C8-C13
Fr. Polynesia	C11-C16
Fr. West Africa	C5-C10
Guadeloupe	C4-C9
Indo-China	C20-C25
Madagascar	C45-C50
Martinique	C4-C9
New Caledonia	C15-C20
Reunion	C26-C31
St. Pierre & Miquelon	C9-C14
Somali Coast	C9-C14
Wallis & Futuna Isls.	C2-C7

UPU

French Colonials, Globe and Plane
CD99

Universal Postal Union, 75th anniv.

1949, July 4
Cameroun	C29
Fr. Equatorial Africa	C34
Fr. India	C17
Fr. Polynesia	C20
Fr. West Africa	C15
Indo-China	C26
Madagascar	C55
New Caledonia	C24
St. Pierre & Miquelon	C18
Somali Coast	C18
Togo	C18
Wallis & Futuna Isls.	C10

Tropical Medicine

Doctor Treating Infant
CD100

The surtax was for charitable work.

1950
Cameroun	B29
Fr. Equatorial Africa	B39
Fr. India	B15
Fr. Polynesia	B14
Fr. West Africa	B3
Madagascar	B17
New Caledonia	B14
St. Pierre & Miquelon	B14
Somali Coast	B14
Togo	B11

Military Medal

Medal, Early Marine and Colonial Soldier
CD101

Centenary of the creation of the French Military Medal.

1952
Cameroun	332
Comoro Isls.	39
Fr. Equatorial Africa	186
Fr. India	233
Fr. Polynesia	179
Fr. West Africa	57
Madagascar	286
New Caledonia	295
St. Pierre & Miquelon	345
Somali Coast	267
Togo	327
Wallis & Futuna Isls.	149

Liberation

Allied Landing, Victory Sign and Cross of Lorraine – CD102

COMMON DESIGN TYPES

Lberation of France, 10th anniv.

1954, June 6
Cameroun	C32
Comoro Isls.	C4
Fr. Equatorial Africa	C38
Fr. India	C18
Fr. Polynesia	C22
Fr. West Africa	C17
Madagascar	C57
New Caledonia	C25
St. Pierre & Miquelon	C19
Somali Coast	C19
Togo	C19
Wallis & Futuna Isls.	C11

FIDES

Plowmen
CD103

Efforts of FIDES, the Economic and Social Development Fund for Overseas Possessions (Fonds d' Investissement pour le Developpement Economique et Social).

Each stamp has a different design.

1956
Cameroun	326-329
Comoro Isls.	43
Fr. Polynesia	181
Fr. West Africa	65-72
Madagascar	292-295
New Caledonia	303
Somali Coast	268
Togo	331

Flower

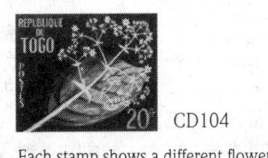

CD104

Each stamp shows a different flower.

1958-9
Cameroun	333
Comoro Isls.	45
Fr. Equatorial Africa	200-201
Fr. Polynesia	192
Fr. So. & Antarctic Terr.	11
Fr. West Africa	79-83
Madagascar	301-302
New Caledonia	304-305
St. Pierre & Miquelon	357
Somali Coast	270
Togo	348-349
Wallis & Futuna Isls.	152

Human Rights

Sun, Dove and U.N. Emblem – CD105

10th anniversary of the signing of the Universal Declaration of Human Rights.

1958
Comoro Isls.	44
Fr. Equatorial Africa	202
Fr. Polynesia	191
Fr. West Africa	85
Madagascar	300
New Caledonia	306
St. Pierre & Miquelon	356
Somali Coast	274
Wallis & Futuna Isls.	153

C.C.T.A.

CD106

Commission for Technical Cooperation in Africa south of the Sahara, 10th anniv.

1960
Cameroun	335
Cent. Africa	3
Chad	66
Congo, P.R.	90
Dahomey	138
Gabon	150
Ivory Coast	180
Madagascar	317
Mali	9
Mauritania	117
Niger	104
Upper Volta	89

Air Afrique, 1961

Modern and Ancient Africa, Map and Planes – CD107

Founding of Air Afrique (African Airlines).

1961-62
Cameroun	C37
Cent. Africa	C5
Chad	C7
Congo, P.R.	C5
Dahomey	C17
Gabon	C5
Ivory Coast	C18
Mauritania	C17
Niger	C22
Senegal	C31
Upper Volta	C4

Anti-Malaria

CD108

World Health Organization drive to eradicate malaria.

1962, Apr. 7
Cameroun	B36
Cent. Africa	B1
Chad	B1
Comoro Isls.	B1
Congo, P.R.	B3
Dahomey	B15
Gabon	B4
Ivory Coast	B15
Madagascar	B19
Mali	B1
Mauritania	B16
Niger	B14
Senegal	B16
Somali Coast	B15
Upper Volta	B1

Abidjan Games

CD109

Abidjan Games, Ivory Coast, Dec. 24-31, 1961. Each stamp shows a different sport.

1962
Chad	83-84
Cent. Africa	19-20
Congo, P.R.	103-104
Gabon	163-164, C6
Niger	109-111
Upper Volta	103-105

African and Malagasy Union

Flag of Union
CD110

First anniversary of the Union.

1962, Sept. 8
Cameroun	373
Cent. Africa	21
Chad	85
Congo, P.R.	105
Dahomey	155
Gabon	165
Ivory Coast	198
Madagascar	332
Mauritania	170
Niger	112
Senegal	211
Upper Volta	106

Telstar

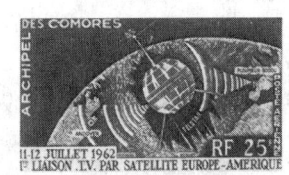

Telstar and Globe Showing Andover and Pleumeur-Bodou – CD111

First television connection of the United States and Europe through the Telstar satellite, July 11-12, 1962.

1962-63
Andorra, French	154
Comoro Isls.	C7
Fr. Polynesia	C29
Fr. So. & Antarctic Terr.	C5
New Caledonia	C33
Somali Coast	C31
St. Pierre & Miquelon	C26
Wallis & Futuna Isls.	C17

Freedom From Hunger

World Map and Wheat Emblem
CD112

U.N. Food and Agriculture Organization's "Freedom from Hunger" campaign.

1963, Mar. 21
Cameroun	B37-B38
Cent. Africa	B2
Chad	B2
Congo, P.R.	B4
Dahomey	B16
Gabon	B5
Ivory Coast	B16
Madagascar	B21
Mauritania	B17
Niger	B15
Senegal	B17
Upper Volta	B2

Red Cross Centenary

CD113

Centenary of the International Red Cross.

1963, Sept. 2
Comoro Isls.	55
Fr. Polynesia	205
New Caledonia	328
St. Pierre & Miquelon	367
Somali Coast	297
Wallis & Futuna Isls.	165

African Postal Union, 1963

UAMPT Emblem, Radio Masts, Plane and Mail
CD114

Establishment of the African and Malagasy Posts and Telecommunications Union.

1963, Sept. 8
Cameroun	C47
Cent. Africa	C10
Chad	C9
Congo, P.R.	C13
Dahomey	C19
Gabon	C13
Ivory Coast	C25
Madagascar	C75
Mauritania	C22
Niger	C27
Rwanda	36
Senegal	C32
Upper Volta	C9

Air Afrique, 1963

Symbols of Flight – CD115

First anniversary of Air Afrique and inauguration of DC-8 service.

1963, Nov. 19
Cameroun	C48
Chad	C10
Congo, P.R.	C14
Gabon	C18
Ivory Coast	C26
Mauritania	C26
Niger	C35
Senegal	C33

Europafrica

Europe and Africa Linked
CD116

Signing of an economic agreement between the European Economic Community and the African and Malagasy Union, Yaounde, Cameroun, July 20, 1963.
1963-64
Cameroun	402
Chad	C11
Cent. Africa	C12
Congo, P.R.	C16
Gabon	C19
Ivory Coast	217
Niger	C43
Upper Volta	C11

Human Rights

Scales of Justice and Globe — CD117

15th anniversary of the Universal Declaration of Human Rights.
1963, Dec. 10
Comoro Isls.	58
Fr. Polynesia	206
New Caledonia	329
St. Pierre & Miquelon	368
Somali Coast	300
Wallis & Futuna Isls.	166

PHILATEC

Stamp Album, Champs Elysees Palace and Horses of Marly — CD118

Intl. Philatelic and Postal Techniques Exhibition, Paris, June 5-21, 1964.
1963-64
Comoro Isls.	60
France	1078
Fr. Polynesia	207
New Caledonia	341
St. Pierre & Miquelon	369
Somali Coast	301
Wallis & Futuna Isls.	167

Cooperation

CD119

Cooperation between France and the French-speaking countries of Africa and Madagascar.
1964
Cameroun	409-410
Cent. Africa	39
Chad	103
Congo, P.R.	121
Dahomey	193
France	1111
Gabon	175
Ivory Coast	221
Madagascar	360
Mauritania	181
Niger	143
Senegal	236
Togo	495

ITU

Telegraph, Syncom Satellite and ITU Emblem — CD120

Intl. Telecommunication Union, Cent.
1965, May 17
Comoro Isls.	C14
Fr. Polynesia	C33
Fr. So. & Antarctic Terr.	C8
New Caledonia	C40
New Hebrides	124-125
St. Pierre & Miquelon	C29
Somali Coast	C36
Wallis & Futuna Isls.	C20

French Satellite A-1

Diamant Rocket and Launching Installation — CD121

Launching of France's first satellite, Nov. 26, 1965.
1965-66
Comoro Isls.	C15-C16
France	1137-1138
Fr. Polynesia	C40-C41
Fr. So. & Antarctic Terr.	C9-C10
New Caledonia	C44-C45
St. Pierre & Miquelon	C30-C31
Somali Coast	C39-C40
Wallis & Futuna Isls.	C22-C23

French Satellite D-1

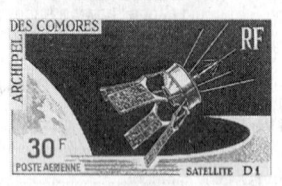

D-1 Satellite in Orbit — CD122

Launching of the D-1 satellite at Hammaguir, Algeria, Feb. 17, 1966.
1966
Comoro Isls.	C17
France	1148
Fr. Polynesia	C42
Fr. So. & Antarctic Terr.	C11
New Caledonia	C46
St. Pierre & Miquelon	C32
Somali Coast	C49
Wallis & Futuna Isls.	C24

Air Afrique, 1966

Planes and Air Afrique Emblem — CD123

Introduction of DC-8F planes by Air Afrique.
1966
Cameroun	C79
Cent. Africa	C35
Chad	C26
Congo, P.R.	C42
Dahomey	C42
Gabon	C47
Ivory Coast	C32
Mauritania	C57
Niger	C63
Senegal	C47
Togo	C54
Upper Volta	C31

African Postal Union, 1967

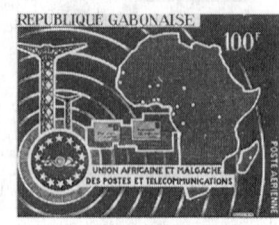

Telecommunications Symbols and Map of Africa — CD124

Fifth anniversary of the establishment of the African and Malagasy Union of Posts and Telecommunications, UAMPT.
1967
Cameroun	C90
Cent. Africa	C46
Chad	C37
Congo, P.R.	C57
Dahomey	C61
Gabon	C58
Ivory Coast	C34
Madagascar	C85
Mauritania	C65
Niger	C75
Rwanda	C1-C3
Senegal	C60
Togo	C81
Upper Volta	C50

Monetary Union

Gold Token of the Ashantis, 17-18th Centuries — CD125

West African Monetary Union, 5th anniv.
1967, Nov. 4
Dahomey	244
Ivory Coast	259
Mauritania	238
Niger	204
Senegal	294
Togo	623
Upper Volta	181

WHO Anniversary

Sun, Flowers and WHO Emblem — CD126

World Health Organization, 20th anniv.
1968, May 4
Afars & Issas	317
Comoro Isls.	73
Fr. Polynesia	241-242
Fr. So. & Antarctic Terr.	31
New Caledonia	367
St. Pierre & Miquelon	377
Wallis & Futuna Isls.	169

Human Rights Year

Human Rights Flame — CD127

1968, Aug. 10
Afars & Issas	322-323
Comoro Isls.	76
Fr. Polynesia	243-244
Fr. So. & Antarctic Terr.	32
New Caledonia	369
St. Pierre & Miquelon	382
Wallis & Futuna Isls.	170

2nd PHILEXAFRIQUE

CD128

Opening of PHILEXAFRIQUE, Abidjan, Feb. 14. Each stamp shows a local scene and stamp.
1969, Feb. 14
Cameroun	C118
Cent. Africa	C65
Chad	C48
Congo, P.R.	C77
Dahomey	C94
Gabon	C82
Ivory Coast	C38-C40
Madagascar	C92
Mali	C65
Mauritania	C80
Niger	C104
Senegal	C68
Togo	C104
Upper Volta	C62

Concorde

Concorde in Flight — CD129

First flight of the prototpye Concorde super-sonic plane at Toulouse, Mar. 1, 1969.
1969
Afars & Issas	C56
Comoro Isls.	C29
France	C42
Fr. Polynesia	C50
Fr. So. & Antarctic Terr.	C18
New Caledonia	C63
St. Pierre & Miquelon	C40
Wallis & Futuna Isls.	C30

Development Bank

Bank Emblem — CD130

African Development Bank, fifth anniv.
1969
Cameroun	499

COMMON DESIGN TYPES

Chad 217
Congo, P.R. 181-182
Ivory Coast 281
Mali 127-128
Mauritania 267
Niger 220
Senegal 317-318
Upper Volta 201

ILO

ILO Headquarters, Geneva, and Emblem – CD131

Intl. Labor Organization, 50th anniv.
1969-70
Afars & Issas 337
Comoro Isls. 83
Fr. Polynesia 251-252
Fr. So. & Antarctic Terr. 35
New Caledonia 379
St. Pierre & Miquelon 396
Wallis & Futuna Isls. 172

ASECNA

Map of Africa, Plane and Airport – CD132

10th anniversary of the Agency for the Security of Aerial Navigation in Africa and Madagascar (ASECNA, Agence pour la Securite de la Navigation Aerienne en Afrique et a Madagascar).
1969-70
Cameroun 500
Cent. Africa 119
Chad 222
Congo, P.R. 197
Dahomey 269
Gabon 260
Ivory Coast 287
Mali 130
Niger 221
Senegal 321
Upper Volta 204

U.P.U. Headquarters

CD133

New Universal Postal Union headquarters, Bern, Switzerland.
1970
Afars & Issas 342
Algeria 443
Cameroun 503-504
Cent. Africa 125
Chad 225
Comoro Isls. 84
Congo, P.R. 216
Fr. Polynesia 261-262
Fr. So. & Antarctic Terr. 36
Gabon 258
Ivory Coast 295
Madagascar 444
Mali 134-135
Mauritania 283
New Caledonia 382
Niger 231-232
St. Pierre & Miquelon 397-398
Senegal 328-329
Tunisia 535
Wallis & Futuna Isls. 173

De Gaulle

CD134

First anniversay of the death of Charles de Gaulle, (1890-1970), President of France.
1971-72
Afars & Issas 356-357
Comoro Isls. 104-105
France 1322-1325
Fr. Polynesia 270-271
Fr. So. & Antarctic Terr. 52-53
New Caledonia 393-394
Reunion 377, 380
St. Pierre & Miquelon 417-418
Wallis & Futuna Isls. 177-178

African Postal Union, 1971

UAMPT Building, Brazzaville, Congo – CD135

10th anniversary of the establishment of the African and Malagasy Posts and Telecommunications Union, UAMPT.
1971, Nov. 13
Cameroun C177
Cent. Africa C89
Chad C94
Congo, P.R. C136
Dahomey C146
Gabon C120
Ivory Coast C47
Mauritania C113
Niger C164
Rwanda C8
Senegal C105
Togo C166
Upper Volta C97

West African Monetary Union

African Couple, City, Village and Commemorative Coin – CD136

West African Monetary Union, 10th anniv.
1972, Nov. 2
Dahomey 300
Ivory Coast 331
Mauritania 299
Niger 258
Senegal 374
Togo 825
Upper Volta 280

African Postal Union, 1973

Telecommunications Symbols and Map of Africa – CD137

11th anniversary of the African and Malagasy Posts and Telecommunications Union (UAMPT).
1973, Sept. 12
Cameroun 574
Cent. Africa 194
Chad 294
Congo, P.R. 289
Dahomey 311
Gabon 320
Ivory Coast 361
Madagascar 500
Mauritania 304
Niger 287
Rwanda 540
Senegal 393
Togo 849
Upper Volta 297

Philexafrique II — Essen

CD138

CD139

Designs: Indigenous fauna, local and German stamps.

Types CD138-CD139 printed horizontally and vertically se-tenant in sheets of 10 (2x5). Label between horizontal pairs alternately commemoratives Philexafrique II, Libreville, Gabon, June 1978, and 2nd International Stamp Fair, Essen, Germany, Nov. 1-5.
1978-1979
Benin C285-C286
Central Africa C200-C201
Chad C238-C239
Congo Republic C245-C246
Djibouti C121-C122
Gabon C215-C216
Ivory Coast C64-C65
Mali C356-C357
Mauritania C185-C186
Niger C291-C292
Rwanda C12-C13
Senegal C146-C147
Togo C363-C364
Upper Volta C253-C254

BRITISH COMMONWEALTH OF NATIONS

The listings follow established trade practices when these issues are offered as units by dealers. The Peace issue, for example, includes only one stamp from the Indian state of Hyderabad. The U.P.U. issue includes the Egypt set. Pairs are included for those varieties issues with bilingual designs se-tenant.

Silver Jubilee

Windsor Castle and King George V
CD301

Reign of King George V, 25th anniv.
1935
Antigua 77-80
Ascension 33-36
Bahamas 92-95
Barbados 186-189
Basutoland 11-14
Bechuanaland Protectorate ... 117-120
Bermuda 100-103
British Guiana 223-226
British Honduras 108-111
Cayman Islands 81-84
Ceylon 260-263
Cyprus 136-139
Dominica 90-93
Falkland Islands 77-80
Fiji 110-113
Gambia 125-128
Gibraltar 100-103
Gilbert & Ellice Islands 33-36
Gold Coast 108-111
Grenada 124-127
Hong Kong 147-150
Jamaica 109-112
Kenya, Uganda, Tanganyika ... 42-45
Leeward Islands 96-99
Malta 184-187
Mauritius 204-207
Montserrat 85-88
Newfoundland 226-229
Nigeria 34-37
Northern Rhodesia 18-21
Nyasaland Protectorate 47-50
St. Helena 111-114
St. Kitts-Nevis 72-75
St. Lucia 91-94
St. Vincent 134-137
Seychelles 118-121
Sierra Leone 166-169
Solomon Islands 60-63
Somaliland Protectorate 77-80
Straits Settlements 213-216
Swaziland 20-23
Trinidad & Tobago 43-46
Turks & Caicos Islands 71-74
Virgin Islands 69-72

The following have different designs but are included in the omnibus set:
Great Britain 226-229
Offices in Morocco ... 67-70, 226-229, 422-425, 508-510
Australia 152-154
Canada 211-216
Cook Islands 98-100
India 142-148
Nauru 31-34
New Guinea 46-47
New Zealand 199-201
Niue 67-69
Papua 114-117
Samoa 163-165
South Africa 68-71
Southern Rhodesia 33-36
South-West Africa 121-124
249 stamps, Never Hinged $975.

Coronation

Queen Elizabeth and King George VI
CD302

1937

Aden	13-15
Antigua	81-83
Ascension	37-39
Bahamas	97-99
Barbados	190-192
Basutoland	15-17
Bechuanaland Protectorate	121-123
Bermuda	115-117
British Guiana	227-229
British Honduras	112-114
Cayman Islands	97-99
Ceylon	275-277
Cyprus	140-142
Dominica	94-96
Falkland Islands	81-83
Fiji	114-116
Gambia	129-131
Gibraltar	104-106
Gilbert & Ellice Islands	37-39
Gold Coast	112-114
Grenada	128-130
Hong Kong	151-153
Jamaica	113-115
Kenya, Uganda, Tanganyika	60-62
Leeward Islands	100-102
Malta	188-190
Mauritius	208-210
Montserrat	89-91
Newfoundland	230-232
Nigeria	50-52
Northern Rhodesia	22-24
Nyasaland Protectorate	51-53
St. Helena	115-117
St. Kitts-Nevis	76-78
St. Lucia	107-109
St. Vincent	138-140
Seychelles	122-124
Sierra Leone	170-172
Solomon Islands	64-66
Somaliland Protectorate	81-83
Straits Settlements	235-237
Swaziland	24-26
Trinidad & Tobago	47-49
Turks & Caicos Islands	75-77
Virgin Islands	73-75

The following have different designs but are included in the omnibus set:

Great Britain	234
Offices in Morocco	82, 439, 514
Canada	237
Cook Islands	109-111
Nauru	35-38
Newfoundland	233-243
New Guinea	48-51
New Zealand	223-225
Niue	70-72
Papua	118-121
South Africa	74-78
Southern Rhodesia	38-41
South-West Africa	125-132

202 stamps, Never Hinged $80.

Peace

King George VI and Parliament Buildings, London – CD303

Return to peace at the close of World War II.

1945-46

Aden	28-29
Antigua	96-97
Ascension	50-51
Bahamas	130-131
Barbados	207-208
Bermuda	131-132
British Guiana	242-243
British Honduras	127-128
Cayman Islands	112-113
Ceylon	293-294
Cyprus	156-157
Dominica	112-113
Falkland Islands	97-98
Falkland Islands Dep.	1L9-1L10
Fiji	137-138
Gambia	144-145
Gibraltar	119-120
Gilbert & Ellice Islands	52-53
Gold Coast	128-129
Grenada	143-144
Jamaica	136-137
Kenya, Uganda, Tanganyika	90-91
Leeward Islands	116-117
Malta	206-207
Mauritius	223-224
Montserrat	104-105
Nigeria	71-72
Northern Rhodesia	46-47
Nyasaland Protectorate	82-83
Pitcairn Island	9-10
St. Helena	128-129
St. Kitts-Nevis	91-92
St. Lucia	127-128
St. Vincent	152-153
Seychelles	149-150
Sierra Leone	186-187
Solomon Islands	80-81
Somaliland Protectorate	108-109
Trinidad & Tobago	62-63
Turks & Caicos Islands	90-91
Virgin Islands	88-89

The following have different designs but are included in the omnibus set:

Great Britain	264-265
Offices in Morocco	523-524
Aden	
Kathiri State of Seiyun	12-13
Qu'aiti State of Shihr and Mukalla	12-13
Australia	200-202
Basutoland	29-31
Bechuanaland Protectorate	137-139
Burma	66-69
Cook Islands	127-130
Hong Kong	174-175
India	195-198
Hyderabad	51
New Zealand	247-257
Niue	90-93
Pakistan-Bahawalpur	O16
Samoa	191-194
South Africa	100-102
Southern Rhodesia	67-70
South-West Africa	153-155
Swaziland	38-40
Zanzibar	222-223

164 stamps, Never Hinged $42.50.

Silver Wedding

King George VI and Queen Elizabeth
CD304   CD305

1948-49

Aden	30-31
Kathiri State of Seiyun	14-15
Qu'aiti State of Shihr and Mukalla	14-15
Antigua	98-99
Ascension	52-53
Bahamas	148-149
Barbados	210-211
Basutoland	39-40
Bechuanaland Protectorate	147-148
Bermuda	133-134
British Guiana	244-245
British Honduras	129-130
Cayman Islands	116-117
Cyprus	158-159
Dominica	114-115
Falkland Islands	99-100
Falkland Islands Dep.	1L11-1L12
Fiji	139-140
Gambia	146-147
Gibraltar	121-122
Gilbert & Ellice Islands	54-55
Gold Coast	142-143
Grenada	145-146
Hong Kong	178-179
Jamaica	138-139
Kenya, Uganda, Tanganyika	92-93
Leeward Islands	118-119
Malaya	
Johore	128-129
Kedah	55-56
Kelantan	44-45
Malacca	1-2
Negri Sembilan	36-37
Pahang	44-45
Penang	1-2
Perak	99-100
Perlis	1-2
Selangor	74-75
Trengganu	47-48
Malta	223-224
Mauritius	229-230
Montserrat	106-107
Nigeria	73-74
North Borneo	238-239
Northern Rhodesia	48-49
Nyasaland Protectorate	85-86
Pitcairn Island	11-12
St. Helena	130-131
St. Kitts-Nevis	93-94
St. Lucia	129-130
St. Vincent	154-155
Sarawak	174-175
Seychelles	151-152
Sierra Leone	188-189
Singapore	21-22
Solomon Islands	82-83
Somaliland Protectorate	110-111
Swaziland	48-49
Trinidad & Tobago	64-65
Turks & Caicos Islands	92-93
Virgin Islands	90-91
Zanzibar	224-225

The following have different designs but are included in the omnibus set:

Great Britain	267-268
Offices in Morocco	93-94, 525-526
Bahrain	62-63
Kuwait	82-83
Oman	25-26
South Africa	106
South-West Africa	159

138 stamps, Never Hinged $1,600.

U.P.U.

Mercury and Symbols of Communications – CD306

Plane, Ship and Hemispheres – CD307

Mercury Scattering Letters over Globe
CD308

U.P.U. Monument, Bern – CD309

Universal Postal Union, 75th anniversary.

1949

Aden	32-35
Kathiri State of Seiyun	16-19
Qu'aiti State of Shihr and Mukalla	16-19
Antigua	100-103
Ascension	57-60
Bahamas	150-153
Barbados	212-215
Basutoland	41-44
Bechuanaland Protectorate	149-152
Bermuda	138-141
British Guiana	246-249
British Honduras	137-140
Brunei	79-82
Cayman islands	118-121
Cyprus	160-163
Dominica	116-119
Falkland Islands	103-106
Falkland Islands Dep.	1L14-1L17
Fiji	141-144
Gambia	148-151
Gibraltar	123-126
Gilbert & Ellice Islands	56-59
Gold Coast	144-147
Grenada	147-150
Hong Kong	180-183
Jamaica	142-145
Kenya, Uganda, Tanganyika	94-97
Leeward Islands	126-129
Malaya	
Johore	151-154
Kedah	57-60
Kelantan	46-49
Malacca	18-21
Negri Sembilan	59-62
Pahang	46-49
Penang	23-26
Perak	101-104
Perlis	3-6
Selangor	76-79
Trengganu	49-52
Malta	225-228
Mauritius	231-234
Montserrat	108-111
New Hebrides	62-65
Nigeria	75-78
North Borneo	240-243
Northern Rhodesia	50-53
Nyasaland Protectorate	87-90
Pitcairn Islands	13-16
St. Helena	132-135
St. Kitts-Nevis	95-98
St. Lucia	131-134
St. Vincent	170-173
Sarawak	176-179
Seychelles	153-156
Sierra Leone	190-193
Singapore	23-26
Solomon Islands	84-87
Somaliland Protectorate	112-115
Southern Rhodesia	71-72
Swaziland	50-53
Tonga	87-90
Trinidad & Tobago	66-69
Turks & Caicos Islands	101-104
Virgin Islands	92-95
Zanzibar	226-229

The following have different designs but are included in the omnibus set:

Great Britain	276-279
Offices in Morocco	546-549
Australia	223
Bahrain	68-71
Burma	116-121
Ceylon	304-306
Egypt	281-283
India	223-226
Kuwait	89-92
Oman	31-34
Pakistan-Bahawalpur	26-29, O25-O28
South Africa	109-111
South-West Africa	160-162

315 stamps, Never Hinged $325.

COMMON DESIGN TYPES

University

Arms of University College
CD310

Alice, Princess of Athlone
CD311

1948 opening of University College of the West Indies at Jamaica.

1951
Antigua	104-105
Barbados	228-229
British Guiana	250-251
British Honduras	141-142
Dominica	120-121
Grenada	164-165
Jamaica	146-147
Leeward Islands	130-131
Montserrat	112-113
St. Kitts-Nevis	105-106
St. Lucia	149-150
St. Vincent	174-175
Trinidad & Tobago	70-71
Virgin Islands	96-97

28 stamps

Coronation

Queen Elizabeth II
CD312

1953
Aden	47
Kathiri State of Seiyun	28
Qu'aiti State of Shihr and Mukalla	28
Antigua	106
Ascension	61
Bahamas	157
Barbados	234
Basutoland	45
Bechuanaland Protectorate	153
Bermuda	142
British Guiana	252
British Honduras	143
Cayman Islands	150
Cyprus	167
Dominica	141
Falkland Islands	121
Falkland Islands Dependencies	1L18
Fiji	145
Gambia	152
Gibraltar	131
Gilbert & Ellice Islands	60
Gold Coast	160
Grenada	170
Hong Kong	184
Jamaica	153
Kenya, Uganda, Tanganyika	101
Leeward Islands	132
Malaya	
Johore	155
Kedah	82
Kelantan	71
Malacca	27
Negri Sembilan	63
Pahang	71
Penang	27
Perak	126
Perlis	28
Selangor	101
Trengganu	74
Malta	241
Mauritius	250
Montserrat	127
New Hebrides	77
Nigeria	79
North Borneo	260
Northern Rhodesia	60
Nyasaland Protectorate	96
Pitcairn	19
St. Helena	139
St. Kitts-Nevis	119
St. Lucia	156
St. Vincent	185
Sarawak	196
Seychelles	172
Sierra Leone	194
Singapore	27
Solomon Islands	88
Somaliland Protectorate	127
Swaziland	54
Trinidad & Tobago	84
Tristan da Cunha	13
Turks & Caicos Islands	118
Virgin Islands	114

The following have different designs but are included in the omnibus set:
Great Britain	313-316
Offices in Morocco	579-582
Australia	259-261
Bahrain	92-95
Canada	330
Ceylon	317
Cook Islands	145-146
Kuwait	113-116
New Zealand	280-284
Niue	104-105
Oman	52-55
Samoa	214-215
South Africa	192
Southern Rhodesia	80
South-West Africa	244-248
Tokelau Islands	4

106 stamps, Never Hinged $70.

Royal Visit 1953

Separate designs for each country for the visit of Queen Elizabeth II and the Duke of Edinburgh.

1953
Aden	62
Australia	267-269
Bermuda	163
Ceylon	318
Fiji	146
Gibraltar	146
Jamaica	154
Kenya, Uganda, Tanganyika	102
Malta	242
New Zealand	286-287

13 stamps

West Indies Federation

Map of the Caribbean – CD313

Federation of the West Indies, April 22, 1958.

1958
Antigua	122-124
Barbados	248-250
Dominica	161-163
Grenada	184-186
Jamaica	175-177
Montserrat	143-145
St. Kitts-Nevis	136-138
St. Lucia	170-172
St. Vincent	198-200
Trinidad & Tobago	86-88

30 stamps, Never Hinged $6.

Freedom from Hunger

Protein Food
CD314

U.N. Food and Agricultural Organization's "Freedom from Hunger" campaign.

1963
Aden	65
Antigua	133
Ascension	89
Bahamas	180
Basutoland	83
Bechuanaland Protectorate	194
Bermuda	192
British Guiana	271
British Honduras	179
Brunei	100
Cayman Islands	168
Dominica	181
Falkland Islands	146
Fiji	198
Gambia	172
Gibraltar	161
Gilbert & Ellice Islands	76
Grenada	190
Hong Kong	218
Malta	291
Mauritius	270
Montserrat	150
New Hebrides	93
North Borneo	296
Pitcairn	35
St. Helena	173
St. Lucia	179
St. Vincent	201
Sarawak	212
Seychelles	213
Solomon Islands	109
Swaziland	108
Tonga	127
Tristan da Cunha	68
Turks & Caicos Islands	138
Virgin Islands	140
Zanzibar	280

37 stamps

Red Cross Centenary

Red Cross and Elizabeth II – CD315

1963
Antigua	134-135
Ascension	90-91
Bahamas	183-184
Basutoland	84-85
Bechuanaland Protectorate	195-196
Bermuda	193-194
British Guiana	272-273
British Honduras	180-181
Cayman Islands	169-170
Dominica	182-183
Falkland Islands	147-148
Fiji	203-204
Gambia	173-174
Gibraltar	162-163
Gilbert & Ellice Islands	77-78
Grenada	191-192
Hong Kong	219-220
Jamaica	203-204
Malta	292-293
Mauritius	271-272
Montserrat	151-152
New Hebrides	94-95
Pitcairn Islands	36-37
St. Helena	174-175
St. Kitts-Nevis	143-144
St. Lucia	180-181
St. Vincent	202-203
Seychelles	214-215
Solomon Islands	110-111
South Arabia	1-2
Swaziland	109-110
Tonga	134-135
Tristan da Cunha	69-70
Turks & Caicos Islands	139-140
Virgin Islands	141-142

70 stamps

Shakespeare

Shakespeare Memorial Theatre, Stratford-on-Avon – CD316

400th anniversary of the birth of William Shakespeare.

1964
Antigua	151
Bahamas	201
Bechuanaland Protectorate	197
Cayman Islands	171
Dominica	184
Falkland Islands	149
Gambia	192
Gibraltar	164
Montserrat	153
St. Lucia	196
Turks & Caicos Islands	141
Virgin Islands	143

12 stamps

ITU

ITU Emblem
CD317

Intl. Telecommunication Union, cent.

1965
Antigua	153-154
Ascension	92-93
Bahamas	219-220
Barbados	265-266
Basutoland	101-102
Bechuanaland Protectorate	202-203
Bermuda	196-197
British Guiana	293-294
British Honduras	187-188
Brunei	116-117
Cayman Islands	172-173
Dominica	185-186
Falkland Islands	154-155
Fiji	211-212
Gibraltar	167-168
Gilbert & Ellice Islands	87-88
Grenada	205-206
Hong Kong	221-222
Mauritius	291-292
Montserrat	157-158
New Hebrides	108-109
Pitcairn Islands	52-53
St. Helena	180-181
St. Kitts-Nevis	163-164
St. Lucia	197-198
St. Vincent	224-225
Seychelles	218-219
Solomon Islands	126-127
Swaziland	115-116
Tristan da Cunha	85-86
Turks & Caicos Islands	142-143
Virgin Islands	159-160

64 stamps, Never Hinged $50.

Intl. Cooperation Year

ICY Emblem – CD318

1965
Antigua	155-156
Ascension	94-95
Bahamas	222-223
Basutoland	103-104
Bechuanaland Protectorate	204-205
Bermuda	199-200
British Guiana	295-296
British Honduras	189-190
Brunei	118-119
Cayman Islands	174-175
Dominica	187-188
Falkland Islands	156-157
Fiji	213-214
Gibraltar	169-170
Gilbert & Ellice Islands	104-105
Grenada	207-208
Hong Kong	223-224
Mauritius	293-294
Montserrat	176-177
New Hebrides	110-111
Pitcairn Islands	54-55
St. Helena	182-183
St. Kitts-Nevis	165-166
St. Lucia	199-200
Seychelles	220-221
Solomon Islands	143-144
South Arabia	17-18
Swaziland	117-118
Tristan da Cunha	87-88
Turks & Caicos Islands	144-145
Virgin Islands	161-162

62 stamps

Churchill Memorial

Winston Churchill and St. Paul's,
London, During Air Attack – CD319
1966
Antigua	157-160
Ascension	96-99
Bahamas	224-227
Barbados	281-284
Basutoland	105-108
Bechuanaland Protectorate	206-209
Bermuda	201-204
British Antarctic Territory	16-19
British Honduras	191-194
Brunei	120-123
Cayman Islands	176-179
Dominica	189-192
Falkland Islands	158-161
Fiji	215-218
Gibraltar	171-174
Gilbert & Ellice Islands	106-109
Grenada	209-212
Hong Kong	225-228
Mauritius	295-298
Montserrat	178-181
New Hebrides	112-115
Pitcairn Islands	56-59
St. Helena	184-187
St. Kitts-Nevis	167-170
St. Lucia	201-204
St. Vincent	241-244
Seychelles	222-225
Solomon Islands	145-148
South Arabia	19-22
Swaziland	119-122
Tristan da Cunha	89-92
Turks & Caicos Islands	146-149
Virgin Islands	163-166

132 stamps

Royal Visit, 1966

Queen Elizabeth II and Prince Philip
CD320

Caribbean visit, Feb. 4 - Mar. 6, 1966.
1966
Antigua	161-162
Bahamas	228-229
Barbados	285-286
British Guiana	299-300
Cayman Islands	180-181
Dominica	193-194
Grenada	213-214
Montserrat	182-183
St. Kitts-Nevis	171-172
St. Lucia	205-206
St. Vincent	245-246
Turks & Caicos Islands	150-151
Virgin Islands	167-168

26 stamps

World Cup Soccer

Soccer Player and Jules Rimet Cup
CD321

World Cup Soccer Championship, Wembley, England, July 11-30.
1966
Antigua	163-164
Ascension	100-101
Bahamas	245-246
Bermuda	205-206
Brunei	124-125
Cayman Islands	182-183
Dominica	195-196
Fiji	219-220
Gibraltar	175-176
Gilbert & Ellice Islands	125-126
Grenada	230-231
New Hebrides	116-117
Pitcairn Islands	60-61
St. Helena	188-189
St. Kitts-Nevis	173-174
St. Lucia	207-208
Seychelles	226-227
Solomon Islands	167-168
South Arabia	23-24
Tristan da Cunha	93-94

40 stamps

WHO Headquarters

World Health Organization Headquarters, Geneva – CD322
1966
Antigua	165-166
Ascension	102-103
Bahamas	247-248
Brunei	126-127
Cayman Islands	184-185
Dominica	197-198
Fiji	224-225
Gibraltar	180-181
Gilbert & Ellice Islands	127-128
Grenada	232-233
Hong Kong	229-230
Montserrat	184-185
New Hebrides	118-119
Pitcairn Islands	62-63
St. Helena	190-191
St. Kitts-Nevis	177-178
St. Lucia	209-210
St. Vincent	247-248
Seychelles	228-229
Solomon Islands	169-170
South Arabia	25-26
Tristan da Cunha	99-100

44 stamps

UNESCO Anniversary

"Education" – CD323
"Science" (Wheat ears & flask enclosing globe). "Culture" (lyre & columns).
20th anniversary of the UNESCO.
1966-67
Antigua	183-185
Ascension	108-110
Bahamas	249-251
Barbados	287-289
Bermuda	207-209
Brunei	128-130
Cayman Islands	186-188
Dominica	199-201
Gibraltar	183-185
Gilbert & Ellice Islands	129-131
Grenada	234-236
Hong Kong	231-233
Mauritius	299-301
Montserrat	186-188
New Hebrides	120-122
Pitcairn Islands	64-66
St. Helena	192-194
St. Kitts-Nevis	179-181
St. Lucia	211-213
St. Vincent	249-251
Seychelles	230-232
Solomon Islands	171-173
South Arabia	27-29
Swaziland	123-125
Tristan da Cunha	101-103
Turks & Caicos Islands	155-157
Virgin Islands	176-178

81 stamps

Silver Wedding, 1972

Queen Elizabeth II and Prince Philip
CD324

Designs: borders differ for each country.
1972
Anguilla	161-162
Antigua	295-296
Ascension	164-165
Bahamas	344-345
Bermuda	296-297
British Antarctic Territory	43-44
British Honduras	306-307
British Indian Ocean Territory	48-49
Brunei	186-187
Cayman Islands	304-305
Dominica	352-353
Falkland Islands	223-224
Fiji	328-329
Gibraltar	292-293
Gilbert & Ellice Islands	206-207
Grenada	466-467
Hong Kong	271-272
Montserrat	286-287
New Hebrides	169-170
Pitcairn Islands	127-128
St. Helena	271-272
St. Kitts-Nevis	257-258
St. Lucia	328-329
St. Vincent	344-345
Seychelles	309-310
Solomon Islands	248-249
South Georgia	35-36
Tristan da Cunha	178-179
Turks & Caicos Islands	257-258
Virgin Islands	241-242

60 stamps

Princess Anne's Wedding

Princess Anne and Mark Phillips
CD325

Wedding of Princess Anne and Mark Phillips, Nov. 14, 1973.
1973
Anguilla	179-180
Ascension	177-178
Belize	325-326
Bermuda	302-303
British Antarctic Territory	60-61
Cayman Islands	320-321
Falkland Islands	225-226
Gibraltar	305-306
Gilbert & Ellice Islands	216-217
Hong Kong	289-290
Montserrat	300-301
Pitcairn Island	135-136
St. Helena	277-278
St. Kitts-Nevis	274-275
St. Lucia	349-350
St. Vincent	358-359
St. Vincent Grenadines	1-2
Seychelles	311-312
Solomon Islands	259-260
South Georgia	37-38
Tristan da Cunha	189-190
Turks & Caicos Islands	286-287
Virgin Islands	260-261

44 stamps

Elizabeth II Coronation Anniv.

CD326   CD327

CD328

Designs: Royal and local beasts in heraldic form and simulated stonework. Portrait of Elizabeth II by Peter Grugeon.
25th anniversary of coronation of Queen Elizabeth II.
1978
Ascension	229
Barbados	474
Belize	397
British Antarctic Territory	71
Cayman Islands	404
Christmas Island	87
Falkland Islands	275
Fiji	384
Gambia	380
Gilbert Islands	312
Mauritius	464
New Hebrides	258
St. Helena	317
St. Kitts-Nevis	354
Samoa	472
Solomon Islands	368
South Georgia	51
Swaziland	302
Tristan da Cunha	238
Virgin Islands	337

20 sheets

Queen Mother Elizabeth's 80th Birthday

CD330

Designs: Photographs of Queen Mother Elizabeth. Falkland Islands issued in sheets of 50; others in sheets of 9.
1980
Ascension	261
Bermuda	401
Cayman Islands	443
Falkland Islands	305
Gambia	412
Gibraltar	393
Hong Kong	364
Pitcairn Islands	193
St. Helena	341
Samoa	532
Solomon Islands	426
Tristan da Cunha	277

12 stamps

COMMON DESIGN TYPES

Royal Wedding, 1981

Prince Charles and Lady Diana
CD331

Wedding of Charles, Prince of Wales, and Lady Diana Spencer, St. Paul's Cathedral, London, July 29, 1981.

1981
Antigua	623-625
Ascension	294-296
Barbados	547-549
Barbuda	497-499
Bermuda	412-414
Brunei	268-270
Cayman Islands	471-473
Dominica	701-703
Falkland Islands	324-326
Falkland Islands Dep.	1L59-1L61
Fiji	442-444
Gambia	426-428
Ghana	759-761
Grenada	1051-1053
Grenada Grenadines	440-443
Hong Kong	373-375
Jamaica	500-503
Lesotho	335-337
Maldive Islands	906-908
Mauritius	520-522
Norfolk Island	280-282
Pitcairn Islands	206-208
St. Helena	353-355
St. Lucia	543-545
Samoa	558-560
Sierra Leone	509-517
Solomon Islands	450-452
Swaziland	382-384
Tristan da Cunha	294-296
Turks & Caicos Islands	486-488
Caicos Island	8-10
Uganda	314-316
Vanuatu	308-310
Virgin Islands	406-408

Princess Diana

CD332   CD333

Designs: Photographs and portrait of Princess Diana, wedding or honeymoon photographs, royal residences, arms of issuing country. Portrait photograph by Clive Friend. Souvenir sheet margins show family tree, various people related to the princess. 21st birthday of Princess Diana of Wales, July 1.

1982
Antigua	663-666
Ascension	313-316
Bahamas	510-513
Barbados	585-588
Barbuda	544-546
British Antarctic Territory	92-95
Cayman Islands	486-489
Dominica	773-776
Falkland Islands	348-351
Falkland Islands Dep.	1L72-1L75
Fiji	470-473
Gambia	447-450
Grenada	1101A-1105
Grenada Grenadines	485-491
Lesotho	372-375
Maldive Islands	952-955
Mauritius	548-551
Pitcairn Islands	213-216
St. Helena	372-375
St. Lucia	591-594
Sierra Leone	531-534
Solomon Islands	471-474
Swaziland	406-409
Tristan da Cunha	310-313
Turks and Caicos Islands	530A-534
Virgin Islands	430-433

250th anniv. of first edition of Lloyd's List (shipping news publication) and of Lloyd's marine insurance.

CD335

Designs: First page of early edition of the list; historical ships, modern transportation or harbor scenes.

1984
Ascension	351-354
Bahamas	555-558
Barbados	627-630
Cayes of Belize	10-13
Cayman Islands	522-525
Falkland Islands	404-407
Fiji	509-512
Gambia	519-522
Mauritius	587-590
Nauru	280-283
St. Helena	412-415
Samoa	624-627
Seychelles	538-541
Solomon Islands	521-524
Vanuatu	368-371
Virgin Islands	466-469

Queen Mother 85th Birthday

CD336

Designs: Photographs tracing the life of the Queen Mother, Elizabeth. The high value in each set pictures the same photograph taken of the Queen Mother holding the infant Prince Henry.

1985
Ascension	372-376
Bahamas	580-584
Barbados	660-664
Bermuda	469-473
Falkland Islands	420-424
Falkland Islands Dep.	1L92-1L96
Fiji	531-535
Hong Kong	447-450
Jamaica	599-603
Mauritius	604-608
Norfolk Island	364-368
Pitcairn Islands	253-257
St. Helena	428-432
Samoa	649-653
Seychelles	567-571
Solomon Islands	543-547
Swaziland	476-480
Tristan da Cunha	372-376
Vanuatu	392-396
Zil Elwannyen Sesel	101-105

Queen Elizabeth II, 60th Birthday

CD337

1986, April 21
Ascension	389-393
Bahamas	592-596
Barbados	675-679
Bermuda	499-503
Cayman Islands	555-559
Falkland Islands	441-445
Fiji	544-548
Hong Kong	465-469
Jamaica	620-624
Kiribati	470-474
Mauritius	629-633
Papua New Guinea	640-644
Pitcairn Islands	270-274
St. Helena	451-455
Samoa	670-674
Seychelles	592-596
Solomon Islands	562-566
South Georgia	101-105
Swaziland	490-494
Tristan da Cunha	388-392
Vanuatu	414-418
Zambia	343-347
Zil Elwannyen Sesel	114-118

Royal Wedding

Marriage of Prince Andrew and Sarah Ferguson
CD338

1986, July 23
Ascension	399-400
Bahamas	602-603
Barbados	687-688
Cayman Islands	560-561
Jamaica	629-630
Pitcairn Islands	275-276
St. Helena	460-461
St. Kitts	181-182
Seychelles	602-603
Solomon Islands	567-568
Tristan da Cunha	397-398
Zambia	348-349
Zil Elwannyen Sesel	119-120

Queen Elizabeth II, 60th Birthday

Queen Elizabeth II Inspecting Guard, 1946
CD339

Designs: Photographs tracing the life of Queen Elizabeth II.

1986
Anguilla	674-677
Antigua	925-928
Barbuda	783-786
Dominica	950-953
Gambia	611-614
Grenada	1371-1374
Grenada Grenadines	749-752
Lesotho	531-534
Maldive Islands	1172-1175
Sierra Leone	760-763
Uganda	495-498

Royal Wedding, 1986

CD340

Designs: Photographs of Prince Andrew and Sarah Ferguson during courtship, engagement and marriage.

1986
Antigua	939-942
Barbuda	809-812
Dominica	970-973
Gambia	635-638
Grenada	1385-1388
Grenada Grenadines	758-761
Lesotho	545-548
Maldive Islands	1181-1184
Sierra Leone	769-772
Uganda	510-513

Lloyds of London, 300th Anniv.

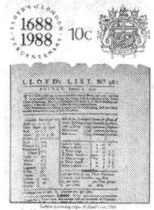

CD341

Designs: 17th century aspects of Lloyds, representations of each country's individual connections with Lloyds and publicized disasters insured by the organization.

1986
Ascension	454-457
Bahamas	655-658
Barbados	731-734
Bermuda	541-544
Falkland Islands	481-484
Liberia	1101-1104
Malawi	534-537
Nevis	571-574
St. Helena	501-504
St. Lucia	923-926
Seychelles	649-652
Solomon Islands	627-630
South Georgia	131-134
Trinidad & Tobago	484-487
Tristan da Cunha	439-442
Vanuatu	485-488
Zil Elwannyen Sesel	146-149

Moon Landing, 20th Anniv.

CD342

Designs: Equipment, crew photographs, spacecraft, official emblems and report profiles created for the Apollo Missions. Two stamps in each set are square in format rather than like the stamp shown; see individual country listings for more information.

1989
Ascension Is.	468-472
Bahamas	674-678
Belize	916-920
Kiribati	517-521
Liberia	1125-1129
Nevis	586-590
St. Kitts	248-252
Samoa	760-764
Seychelles	676-680
Solomon Islands	643-647
Vanuatu	507-511
Zil Elwannyen Sesel	154-158

COMMON DESIGN TYPES

Queen Mother, 90th Birthday

CD343 CD344

Designs: Portraits of Queen Elizabeth, the Queen Mother. See individual country listings for more information.

1990

Ascension Is.	491-492
Bahamas	698-699
Barbados	782-783
British Antarctic Territory	170-171
British Indian Ocean Territory	106-107
Cayman Islands	622-623
Falkland Islands	524-525
Kenya	527-528
Kiribati	555-556
Liberia	1145-1146
Pitcairn Islands	336-337
St. Helena	532-533
St. Lucia	969-970
Seychelles	710-711
Solomon Islands	671-672
South Georgia	143-144
Swaziland	565-566
Tristan da Cunha	480-481
Zil Elwannyen Sesel	171-172

Queen Elizabeth II, 65th Birthday, and Prince Philip, 70th Birthday

CD345 CD346

Designs: Portraits of Queen Elizabeth II and Prince Philip differ for each country. Printed in sheets of 10 + 5 labels (3 different) between. Stamps alternate, producing 5 different triptychs.

1991

Ascension Is.	505-506
Bahamas	730-731
Belize	969-970
Bermuda	617-618
Kiribati	571-572
Mauritius	733-734
Pitcairn Islands	348-349
St. Helena	554-555
St. Kitts	318-319
Samoa	790-791
Seychelles	723-724
Solomon Islands	688-689
South Georgia	149-150
Swaziland	586-587
Vanuatu	540-541
Zil Elwannyen Sesel	177-178

Royal Family Birthday, Anniversary

CD347

Queen Elizabeth II, 65th birthday, Charles and Diana, 10th wedding anniversary: Various photographs of Queen Elizabeth II, Prince Philip, Prince Charles, Princess Diana and their sons William and Henry.

1991

Antigua	1446-1455
Barbuda	1229-1238
Dominica	1328-1337
Gambia	1080-1089
Grenada	2006-2015
Grenada Grenadines	1331-1340
Guyana	2440-2451
Lesotho	871-875
Maldive Islands	1533-1542
Nevis	666-675
St. Vincent	1485-1494
St. Vincent Grenadines	769-778
Sierra Leone	1387-1396
Turks & Caicos Islands	913-922
Uganda	918-927

Queen Elizabeth II's Accession to the Throne, 40th Anniv.

CD348

CD349

Various photographs of Queen Elizabeth II with local Scenes.

1992 - CD348

Antigua	1513-1518
Barbuda	1306-1309
Dominica	1414-1419
Gambia	1172-1177
Grenada	2047-2052
Grenada Grenadines	1368-1373
Lesotho	881-885
Maldive Islands	1637-1642
Nevis	702-707
St. Vincent	1582-1587
St. Vincent Grenadines	829-834
Sierra Leone	1482-1487
Turks and Caicos Islands	978-987
Uganda	990-995
Virgin Islands	742-746

1992 - CD349

Ascension Islands	531-535
Bahamas	744-748
Bermuda	623-627
British Indian Ocean Territory	119-123
Cayman Islands	648-652
Falkland Islands	549-553
Gibraltar	605-609
Hong Kong	619-623
Kenya	563-567
Kiribati	582-586
Pitcairn Islands	362-366
St. Helena	570-574
St. Kitts	332-336
Samoa	805-809
Seychelles	734-738
Soloman Islands	708-712
South Georgia	157-161
Tristan da Cunha	508-512
Vanuatu	555-559
Zambia	561-565
Zil Elwannyen Sesel	183-187

Royal Air Force, 75th Anniversary

CD350

1993

Ascension	557-561
Bahamas	771-775
Barbados	842-846
Belize	1003-1008
Bermuda	648-651
British Indian Ocean Territory	136-140
Falkland Is.	573-577
Fiji	687-691
Montserrat	830-834
St. Kitts	351-355
Samoa	957-961

Royal Air Force, 80th Anniv.

Design CD 350 1993 Re-inscribed

1998

Ascension	697-701
Bahamas	907-911
British Indian Ocean Terr	198-202
Cayman Islands	754-758
Fiji	814-818
Gibraltar	755-759
Samoa	957-961
Trinidad & Tobago	
Tuvalu	763-767
Virgin Islands	879-883

Items without Scott numbers have not been received. Numbers will be assigned when the stamps are received.

End of World War II, 50th Anniv.

CD351

CD352

1995

Ascension	613-617
Bahamas	824-828
Barbados	891-895
Belize	1047-1050
British Indian Ocean Territory	163-167
Cayman Islands	704-708
Falkland Islands	634-638
Fiji	720-724
Kiribati	662-668
Liberia	1175-1179
Mauritius	803-805
St. Helena	646-654
St. Kitts	389-393
St. Lucia	1018-1022
Samoa	890-894
Solomon Islands	799-803
South Georgia & S. Sandwich Is.	198-200
Tristan da Cunha	562-566

UN, 50th Anniv.

CD353

1995

Bahamas	839-842
Barbados	901-904
Belize	1055-1058
Jamaica	847-851
Liberia	1187-1190
Mauritius	813-816
Pitcairn Islands	436-439
St. Kitts	398-401
St. Lucia	1023-1026
Samoa	900-903
Tristan da Cunha	568-571
Virgin Islands	807-810

Queen Elizabeth, 70th Birthday

CD354

1996

Ascension	632-635
British Antarctic Territory	240-243
British Indian Ocean Territory	176-180
Falkland Islands	653-657
Pitcairn Islands	446-449
St. Helena	672-676
Samoa	912-916
Tokelau	223-227
Tristan da Cunha	576-579
Virgin Islands	824-828

Diana, Princess of Wales (1961-97)

CD 355

1998

Ascension	696
Bahamas	901A-902
Barbados	950
Belize	1091
Bermuda	753
Botswana	659-663
British Antarctic Territory	258
British Indian Ocean Terr.	197
Cayman Islands	753
Falkland Islands	694
Fiji	819
Gibraltar	754
Kiribati	720
Namibia	909
Niue	706
Norfolk Island	644-645
Papua New Guinea	937
Pitcairn Islands	
St. Helena	711
St. Kitts	438
Samoa	956
Seycelles	802
Solomon Islands	866-867
South Georgia & South Sandwich Islands	
Tokelau	253
Tonga	980
Niuafo'ou	201
Tristan da Cunha	618
Tuvalu	762
Vanuatu	719

Items without Scott Numbers nave not been received. Numbers will be assigned when the stamps are received.

UNITED STATES

yü-ˌnī-təd 'stāts

GOVT. — Republic
AREA — 3,615,211 sq. mi.
POP. — 226,545,805 (1980)
CAPITAL — Washington, DC

In addition to the 50 States and the District of Columbia, the Republic includes Guam, the Commonwealth of Puerto Rico, the Virgin Islands, American Samoa, Wake, Midway, and a number of small islands in the Pacific Ocean, all of which use stamps of the United States.

100 Cents = 1 Dollar

Catalogue values for unused stamps in this country are for Never Hinged items, beginning with Scott 772 in the regular postage section, Scott C19 in the air post section, Scott E17 in the special delivery section, Scott FA1 in the certified mail section, Scott O127 in officials section, Scott J88 in the postage due section, Scott R733 in the revenues section, Scott RW1 in the hunting permit stamps section.

Watermarks

Wmk. 190- "USPS" in Single-lined Capitals

Wmk. 191- Double-lined "USPS" in Capitals

Wmk. 190PI - PIPS, used in the Philippines
Wmk. 191PI - PIPS, used in the Philippines
Wmk. 191C - US-C, used for Cuba
Wmk. 191R - USIR

PROVISIONAL ISSUES BY POSTMASTERS

Values for Envelopes are for entires.

Alexandria, Va.

A1

Type I - 40 asterisks in circle.
Type II - 39 asterisks in circle.

1846 Typeset *Imperf.*
1X1 A1 5c black, *buff*, Type I
  a. 5c black, *buff*, Type II   75,000.
1X2 A1 5c black, *blue*, Type I, on cover   —

All known copies of Nos. 1X1-1X2 are cut to shape.

Annapolis, Md.

ENVELOPE

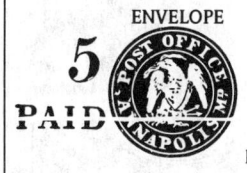

E1

1846
2XU1 E1 5c carmine red   210,000.

Handstamped impressions of the circular design with "2" in blue or red exist on envelopes and letter sheets. Values: blue $2,500, red $3,500.
A letter sheet exists with circular design and "5" handstamped in red. Values: blue $3,500, red $5,000.
A similar circular design in blue was used as a postmark.

Baltimore, Md.

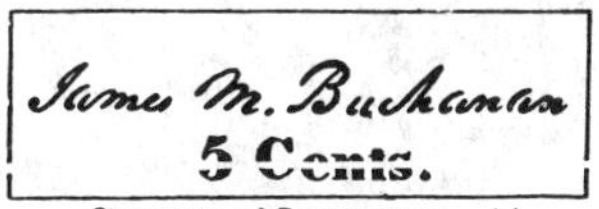

Signature of Postmaster — A1

1845 Engr. *Imperf.*
3X1 A1 5c black   5,000.
3X2 A1 10c black, on cover   50,000.
3X3 A1 5c black, *bluish* 65,000. 5,000.
3X4 A1 10c black, *bluish*   60,000.

Nos. 3X1-3X4 were printed from a plate of 12 (2x6) containing nine 5c and three 10c.

ENVELOPES

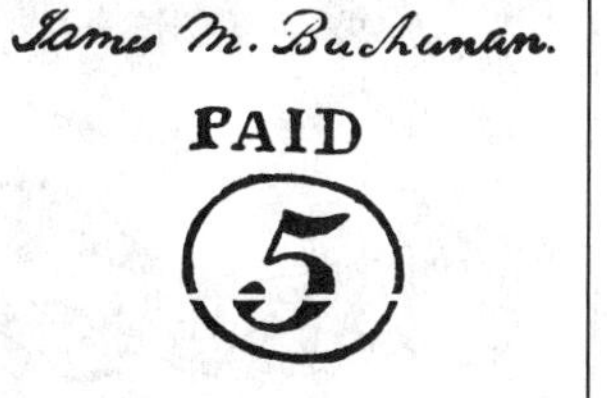

E1

1845 Handstamped
Various Papers
3XU1 E1 5c blue   6,000.
3XU2 E1 5c red   10,000.
3XU3 E1 10c blue   17,500.
3XU4 E1 10c red   20,000.

On the formerly listed "5+5" envelopes, the second "5" in oval is believed not to be part of the basic prepaid marking.

Boscawen, N. H.

A1

1846(?) Typeset *Imperf.*
4X1 A1 5c dull blue, *yellowish*, on cover   175,000.

Brattleboro, Vt.

Initials of Postmaster (FNP) — A1

Plate of 10 (5x2).

1846 Engr. *Imperf.*
5X1 A1 5c black, *buff*   9,000.

Lockport, N. Y.

A1

Handstamped, "5" in Black Ms
1846
6X1 A1 5c red, *buff*, on cover   150,000.

Millbury, Mass.

George Washington — A1

Printed from a Woodcut
1846 *Imperf.*
7X1 A1 5c blue, *bluish* 130,000. 20,000.

New Haven, Conn.

ENVELOPES

E1

1845 Handstamped
Signed in Blue, Black, Magenta or Red
8XU1 E1 5c red (Bl or M)   75,000.
8XU2 E1 5c red, *light bluish* (Bk)   100,000.
8XU3 E1 5c dull blue, *buff* (Bl)   100,000.
8XU4 E1 5c dull blue (Bl)   100,000.

Values of Nos. 8XU1-8XU4 are a guide to value. They are based on auction realizations and retail sales and take condition into consideration. All New Haven envelopes are of almost equal rarity. An entire of No. 8XU2 is the finest example known. The other envelopes are valued according to condition as much as rarity.

Reprints were made at various times between 1871 and 1932. They differ in shade and paper from the originals.

New York, N. Y.

George Washington — A1

Plate of 40 (5x8). Nos. 9X1-9X3 and varieties unused are valued without gum. Examples with original gum are extremely scarce and will command higher prices.

1845-46 Engr. *Imperf.*
Bluish Wove Paper
9X1 A1 5c blk, signed ACM,
  connected ('46)   1,300. 500.
  a. Signed ACM. AC connected   1,600. 550.
  b. Signed A.C.M.   3,750. 700.
  c. Signed MMJr   9,000.
  d. Signed RHM   13,000. 3,250.
  e. Without signature   3,250. 750.

These stamps were usually initialed "ACM" in magenta ink, as a control, before being sold or passed through the mails.
A plate of 9 (3x3) was made from which proofs were printed in black on white and deep blue papers; also in blue, green, brown and red on white bond paper.

1847 Engr. *Imperf.*
Blue Wove Paper
9X2 A1 5c blk, signed ACM,
  connected   6,500. 3,500.
  a. Signed RHM
  d. Without signature   11,000. 7,250.

On the listing example of No. 9X2a the "R" is illegible and does not match those of the other "RHM" signatures.

1847 Engr. *Imperf.*
Gray Wove Paper
9X3 A1 5c blk, signed ACM,
  connected   5,250. 2,100.
  a. Signed RHM   7,000.
  b. Without signature   7,000.

Providence, R.I.

A1    A2

1846 Engr. *Imperf.*
10X1 A1 5c gray black   400. 1,750.
10X2 A2 10c gray black   1,250. 15,000.
  a. Pair, #10X1-10X2   2,150.

Plate of 12 (3x4) contains 11-5c and 1-10c.
Reprints were made in 1898. Each stamp bears one of the following letters on the back: B. O. G. E. R. T. D. U. R. B. I. N. Value of 5c, $50; 10c, $125; sheet, $725.
Reprint singles or sheets without back print sell for more.

St. Louis, Mo.

Missouri Coat of Arms
A1   A2   A3

Unused are valued without gum.

1845-46 Engr. *Imperf.*
Greenish Wove Paper
11X1 A1 5c black   5,000. 2,750.
11X2 A2 10c black   4,500. 2,500.
11X3 A3 20c black   20,000.

Three varieties of 5c, 3 of 10c, 2 of 20c.

1846
Gray Lilac Paper
11X4 A1 5c black   — 4,250.
11X5 A2 10c black   4,500. 2,200.
11X6 A3 20c black   13,500.

One variety of 5c, 3 of 10c, 2 of 20c.

1847
Pelure Paper
11X7 A1 5c black *bluish*   — 6,250.
11X8 A2 10c black, *bluish*   6,250.
  a. Impression of 5c on back   —

Three varieties of 5c, 3 of 10c.
Used values are for pencanceled copies.

Tuscumbia, Ala.

ENVELOPE

E1

1861 Handstamped
12XU1 E1 3c dull red, *buff*   16,000.

See Confederate States Nos. 84XU1-84XU6.

UNITED STATES

GENERAL ISSUES
All Issues from 1847 to 1894 are Unwatermarked.

Benjamin Franklin — A1
George Washington — A2

1847, July 1   Engr.   Imperf.

1	A1	5c red brown, *bluish*	5,000.	600.
		No gum	2,600.	
a.		5c dark brown, *bluish*	5,000.	625.
		No gum	2,900.	
b.		5c orange brown, *bluish*	6,250.	700.
		No gum	3,500.	
c.		5c red orange, *bluish*	12,500.	5,000.
		No gum	8,000.	
d.		Double impression	—	
		Pen cancel		300.

The only known double impression shows part of the design doubled.

2	A2	10c black, *bluish*	26,000.	1,400.
		No gum	15,000.	
a.		Diagonal half used as 5c on cover		13,000.
b.		Vertical half used as 5c on cover		35,000.
c.		Horizontal half used as 5c on cover		—
		Pen cancel		750.

REPRODUCTIONS
Actually, official imitations made from new plates by order of the Post Office Department.

A3    A4

1875   Imperf.
Bluish Paper Without Gum

3	A3	5c red brown		850.
4	A4	10c black		1,100.

Reproductions. The letters R. W. H. & E. at the bottom of each stamp are less distinct on the reproductions than on the originals.

5c. On the originals the left side of the white shirt frill touches the oval on a level with the top of the "F" of "Five." On the reproductions it touches the oval about on a level with the top of the figure "5."

10c. On the reproductions, line of coat at left points to right tip of "X" and line of coat at right points to center of "S" of CENTS. On the originals, line of coat points to "T" of TEN and between "T" and "S" of CENTS. On the reproductions the eyes have a sleepy look, the line of the mouth is straighter, and in the curl of hair near the left cheek is a strong black dot, while the originals have only a faint one.

VALUES FOR VERY FINE STAMPS
Stamps are valued in the grade of very fine unless otherwise indicated.
Values for unused stamps with no gum are for examples with certificates of authenticity or examples sold with the buyer having the right of certification. Beware of unused, no gum stamps that are offered "as is." Expertization by competent authorities is recommended.

Franklin — A5

ONE CENT
Type I. Has complete curved lines outside the labels with "U.S. Postage" and "One Cent." The scrolls below the lower label are turned under, forming little balls. The ornaments at top are substantially complete.
Values for type I are for stamps showing the marked characteristics plainly. Copies of type I showing the balls indistinctly sell for much lower prices.
Type Ib. Same as I but balls below the bottom label are not so clear. The plumelike scrolls at bottom are not complete.

A6

Type Ia. Same as I at bottom but top ornaments and outer line at top are partly cut away.
Type Ic. Same as Ia, but bottom right plume and ball ornament incomplete. Bottom left plume complete or nearly complete.

A7

Type II. The little balls of the bottom scrolls and the bottoms of the lower plume ornaments are missing. The side ornaments are complete.

A8

Type III. The top and bottom curved lines outside the labels are broken in the middle. The side ornaments are complete.
Type IIIa. Similar to type III with the outer line broken at top or bottom but not both.

A9

Type IV. Similar to type II, but with the curved lines outside the labels recut at top or bottom or both.

Washington — A10

THREE CENTS
Type I. There is an outer frame line on all four sides.

Thomas Jefferson — A11

FIVE CENTS
Type I. There are projections on all four sides.

Washington — A12

A13

TEN CENTS
Type I. The "shells" at the lower corners are practically complete. The outer line below the label is very nearly complete. The outer lines are broken above the middle of the top label and the "X" in each upper corner.

Type II. The design is complete at the top. The outer line at the bottom is broken in the middle. The shells are partly cut away.

A14

Type III. The outer lines are broken above the top label and the "X" numerals. The outer line at the bottom and the shells are partly cut away, similar to Type II.

A15

Washington — A16

Type IV. The outer lines have been recut at top or bottom or both.
Types I, II, III and IV have complete ornaments at the sides of the stamps and three pearls at each outer edge of the bottom panel.

In Nos. 5-17, the 1c, 3c, and 12c have very small margins between the stamps. The 5c and 10c have moderate size margins. The values of these stamps take the margin size into consideration.
Values for No. 5A, 6b and 19b are for the less distinct positions. Best examples sell for more.
Values for No. 16 are for outer line recut at top. Other recuts sell for more.

1851-57   Imperf.

5	A5	1c blue, I	175,000.	31,000.

Values for No. 5 are for copies with margins touching or slightly cutting into the design. Value unused is for an example with no gum.

5A	A5	1c blue, Ib	11,500.	4,750.
		No gum	6,250.	
6	A6	1c blue, Ia ('57)	30,000.	8,500.
		No gum	19,000.	
b.		Type Ic	6,000.	1,400.
		No gum	3,750.	
7	A7	1c blue, II	975.	150.
		No gum	525.	
8	A8	1c blue, III	9,000.	2,400.
		No gum	5,500.	

Values for type III are for at least a 2mm break in each outer line. Examples of type III with wide breaks in outer lines command higher prices; those with small breaks sell for less.

8A	A8	1c blue, IIIa	4,000.	950.
		No gum	2,250.	

Stamps of type IIIa with bottom line broken command higher prices than those with top line broken. See note after No. 8 on width of break of outer lines.

9	A9	1c blue, IV ('52)	650.	125.
		No gum	375.	
a.		Printed on both sides, reverse inverted	—	
10	A10	3c org brown, I	2,600.	90.
		No gum	1,500.	
a.		Printed on both sides	—	
11	A10	3c dull red, I	225.	10.
		No gum	100.	
c.		Vertical half used as 1c on cover		5,000.
d.		Diagonal half used as 1c on cover		5,000.
e.		Double impression		5,000.
12	A11	5c red brown, I ('56)	16,000.	1,250.
		No gum	10,000.	
13	A12	10c green, I ('55)	13,000.	750.
		No gum	8,000.	
14	A13	10c green, II ('55)	3,100.	225.
		No gum	1,750.	
15	A14	10c green, III ('55)	3,100.	225.
		No gum	1,750.	
16	A15	10c green, IV ('55)	21,000.	1,500.
		No gum	13,500.	
17	A16	12c black	4,000.	325.
		No gum	2,400.	
a.		Diagonal half used as 6c on cover		2,500.
b.		Vertical half used as 6c on cover		8,500.
c.		Printed on both sides		10,000.

Same Designs as 1851-56 Issues

Franklin — A20

ONE CENT

UNITED STATES

Type V. Similar to type III of 1851-57 but with side ornaments partly cut away.

Washington — A21

THREE CENTS

Type II. The outer frame line has been removed at top and bottom. The side frame lines were recut so as to be continuous from the top to the bottom of the plate. Stamps from the top or bottom rows show the ends of the side frame lines and may be mistaken for type IIa.

Type IIa. The side frame lines extend only to the top and bottom of the stamp design.

Jefferson — A22

FIVE CENTS

Type II. The projections at top and bottom are partly cut away.

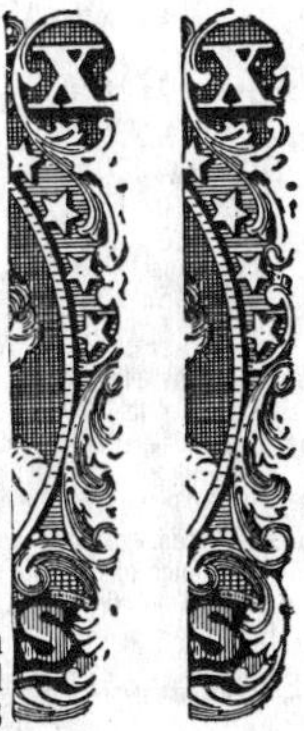

Washington (Two typical examples) — A23

TEN CENTS

Type V. The side ornaments are slightly cut away. Usually only one pearl remains at each end of the lower label but some copies show two or three pearls at the right side. At the bottom the outer line is complete and the shells nearly so. The outer lines at top are complete except over the right "X."

Washington A17    Franklin A18

Washington — A19

TWELVE CENTS
Plate I. Outer frame lines complete.
Plate III. Outer frame lines noticeably uneven or broken, sometimes partly missing.

Nos. 18-39 have small or very small margins. The values take into account the margin size.

1857-61			Perf. 15½	
18	A5	1c blue, type I ('61)	1,400.	500.
		No gum	850.	
19	A6	1c blue, type Ia	16,000.	4,500.
		No gum	10,000.	
b.		Type Ic	2,600.	1,100.
		No gum	1,750.	
20	A7	1c blue, type II	850.	240.
		No gum	500.	
21	A8	1c blue, type III	10,000.	1,700.
		No gum	5,500.	
22	A8	1c blue, type IIIa	1,600.	400.
		No gum	1,000.	
b.		Horiz. pair, imperf. btwn.		5,000.

One pair of No. 22b has been reported. Beware of pairs with blind perforations.

23	A9	1c blue, type IV	6,000.	550.
		No gum	3,750.	
24	A20	1c blue, type V	175.	40.
		No gum	90.	
b.		Laid paper		—
25	A10	3c rose, type I	1,900.	75.
		No gum	1,150.	
b.		Vert. pair, imperf. horiz.		10,000.
26	A21	3c dull red, type II	75.	5.
		No gum	30.	
a.		3c dull red, type IIa	200.	45.
		No gum	110.	
b.		Horiz. pair, imperf. vert., type II	4,000.	—
c.		Vert. pair, imperf. horiz., type II		—
d.		Horizontal pair, imperf. between, type II		—
e.		Dbl. impression, type II		2,500.
f.		Horiz. strip of 3, imperf. vert., type IIa, on cover		8,250.
27	A11	5c brick red, type I ('58)	15,000.	1,000.
		No gum	9,000.	
28	A11	5c red brown, type I	2,800.	450.
		No gum	1,600.	
b.		5c bright red brown	3,000.	600.
		No gum	1,800.	
28A	A11	5c Indian red, type I ('58)	20,000.	2,750.
		No gum	13,500.	
29	A11	5c brown, type I ('59)	1,800.	325.
		No gum	1,000.	
30	A22	5c org brown, type II ('61)	1,100.	1,000.
		No gum	650.	
30A	A22	5c brown, type II ('60)	1,500.	260.
		No gum	850.	
b.		Printed on both sides	4,000.	4,250.
31	A12	10c green, type I	13,000.	750.
		No gum	7,500.	
32	A13	10c green, type II	4,000.	275.
		No gum	2,600.	
33	A14	10c green, type III	4,000.	275.
		No gum	2,600.	
34	A15	10c green, type IV	25,000.	2,100.
		No gum	16,000.	
35	A23	10c green, type V ('59)	275.	65.
		No gum	150.	
36	A16	12c black, plate I	1,100.	190.
		No gum	700.	
a.		Diagonal half used as 6c on cover (I)		17,500.
b.		12c black, plate III ('59)	700.	170.
		No gum	425.	
c.		Horizontal pair, imperf. between (I)		12,500.
37	A17	24c gray lilac ('60)	1,200.	325.
a.		24c gray	1,200.	325.
		No gum	650.	
38	A18	30c orange ('60)	1,500.	425.
		No gum	850.	
39	A19	90c blue ('60)	2,500.	5,500.
		No gum	1,500.	
		Pen cancel		1,250.

See Die and Plate proofs in the Scott United States Specialized Catalogue for imperfs. of the 12c, 24c, 30c, 90c.

Genuine cancellations on the 90c are rare.

REPRINTS OF 1857-60 ISSUE
White Paper
Without Gum

1875			Perf. 12
40	A5	1c bright blue	550.
41	A10	3c scarlet	2,400.
42	A22	5c orange brown	1,000.
43	A12	10c blue green	2,000.
44	A16	12c greenish blk	2,500.
45	A17	24c black violet	2,500.
46	A18	30c yellow orange	2,500.
47	A19	90c deep blue	3,750.
		Nos. 40-47 (8)	17,200.

Nos. 41-46 are valued in the grade of fine. Nos. 40-47 exist imperf., value, set $25,000.

Essays - Trial Color Proofs

The paper of former Nos. 55-62 (Nos. 63E11e, 65-E15h, 67-E9e, 69-E6e, 72-E7h, Essay section, Nos. 70eTC, 71bTC, Trial Color Proof section, Scott U.S. Specialized) is thin and semitransparent. That of the postage issues is thicker and more opaque, except Nos. 62B, 70c and 70d.

Franklin — A24

1c - There is a dash under the tip of the ornament at right of the numeral in upper left corner. There is no dash on the essay.

Washington — A25

3c - Ornaments at corners are large and end in a small ball. The ornaments are smaller and there is no ball on the essay.

Jefferson — A26

5c - Leaflets appear at each corner. These do not appear on the essay.

Washington — A27

A27a

A27

10c - On A27 a heavy curved line appears below the stars and an outer line above them which does not appear on A27a.

Washington — A28

City Stamp Montreal
R. Cooperman, Philatelist

SELLING CANADA & BNA

- Largest Selection of Classic Canada (#1-65) Available in North America all grades: VG-Superb, (LH, NH)
- All Our Stamps Are Priced At "Fair Market Value" Not Inflated Retail!
- Famous Wholesale Dept. Catering to Dealers from Coast to Coast
- 72 page Canada/BNA- Worldwide (Including U.S.A.) Catalog Fully Illustrated- Free

Call Toll Free to discuss buying or selling

BUYING CANADA & BNA

Paying
Canada Postage...51% Face
Classics (#1-65) (F-VF)....................................up to 75% Scott
(#1-65) (with small faults)............................up to 1/4 Catalogue
Collections - Canada & World ....desperately needed
Errors & Varieties (anything)............................Top Dollar Paid
Dealers Stocks (complete or part) .....Immediate Cash Available

★ **OUR 18th YEAR** ★
1134 St. Catherine St. #709
Montreal, Quebec, Canada H3B 1H4
TEL (514)875-2596 FAX (514)875-2802
To buy & sell 1-800-615-2596

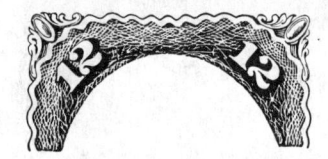

UNITED STATES

12c - Ovals and scrolls appear at each corners. These do not appear on the essay.

Washington A29

Franklin A30

Washington — A31

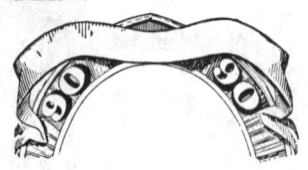

90c. Two pairs of parallel lines form an angle above the ribbon with "U. S. Postage"; between these lines is a row of dashes, and there is a point of color to the apex of the lower pair. These do not appear on the essay.

1861				**Perf. 12**
62B	A27a	10c dark green	6,000.	750.
		No gum	3,500.	

1861-62				**Perf. 12**
63	A24	1c blue	280.00	27.50
		No gum	130.00	
a.		1c ultramarine	650.00	225.00
		No gum	375.00	
b.		1c dark blue	475.00	55.00
		No gum	275.00	
c.		Laid paper	—	
d.		Vert. pair, imperf. horiz.	—	
e.		Printed on both sides	—	2,500.
64	A25	3c pink	6,000.	675.00
		No gum	3,600.	
a.		3c pigeon blood pink	14,000.	3,250.
		No gum	8,500.	
b.		3c rose pink	450.00	110.00
		No gum	225.00	
65	A25	3c rose	125.00	2.50
		No gum	55.00	
b.		Laid paper	—	
d.		Vert. pair, imperf. horiz.	3,500.	750.00
e.		Printed on both sides	2,000.	1,600.
f.		Double impression	—	6,000.

The 3c lake can be found under No. 66 in the Trial Color Proofs section of the Scott U.S. Specialized Catalogue. The imperf 3c lake under No. 66P in the same section. The imperf 3c rose can be found in the Die and Plate Proofs section of the Specialized.

67	A26	5c buff	15,000.	700.00
a.		5c brown yellow	15,000.	700.00
		No gum	9,000.	
b.		5c olive yellow	—	800.00

Values for Nos. 67, 67a, 67b reflect the normal small margins.

68	A27	10c yellow green	500.00	47.50
		No gum	250.00	
a.		10c dark green	525.00	50.00
		No gum	260.00	
b.		Vert. pair, imperf. horiz.	—	3,500.
69	A28	12c black	900.00	85.00
		No gum	550.00	
70	A29	24c red lilac ('62)	1,300.	125.00
		No gum	750.00	
a.		24c brown lilac	1,250.	115.00
		No gum	725.00	
b.		24c steel blue	6,500.	475.00
		No gum	4,250.	
c.		24c violet, thin paper	9,000.	900.00
		No gum	5,500.	
d.		24c pale gray violet, thin paper	2,250.	600.00
		No gum	1,400.	
71	A30	30c orange	1,100.	130.00
		No gum	675.00	
a.		Printed on both sides	—	—

Values for No. 71 are for copies with small margins, especially at sides. Large margined examples sell for much more.

72	A31	90c blue	2,200.	375.00
		No gum	1,350.	
a.		90c pale blue	2,200.	375.00
		No gum	1,350.	
b.		90c dark blue	2,400.	425.00
		No gum	1,500.	

Nos. 70c, 70d are on a thinner, harder and more transparent paper than Nos. 70, 70a, 70b, or the later Nos. 78, 78a, 78b and 78c.

VALUES FOR VERY FINE STAMPS
Stamps are valued in the grade of very fine unless otherwise indicated.
Values for unused stamps with no gum are for examples with certificates of authenticity or examples sold with the buyer having the right of certification. Beware of unused, no gum stamps that are offered "as is." Expertization by competent authorities is recommended.

Designs as 1861 Issue

Andrew Jackson A32

Abraham Lincoln A33

1861-66				**Perf. 12**
73	A32	2c black ('63)	300.00	45.00
		No gum	140.00	
a.		Vert. or diag. half used as 1c as part of 3c rate on cover		1,250.
b.		Diagonal half used alone as 1c on cover		3,000.
c.		Horiz. half used as 1c as part of 3c rate on cover		3,500.
d.		Laid paper	—	
e.		Printed on both sides	—	5,000.

The 3c scarlet can be found under No. 74 in the Scott U.S. Specialized Catalogue Trial Color Proofs section.

75	A26	5c red brown ('62)	3,750.	425.00
		No gum	2,100.	
76	A26	5c brown ('63)	800.00	100.00
		No gum	450.00	
a.		5c black brown	900.00	115.00
		No gum	500.00	
b.		Laid paper	—	
77	A33	15c black ('66)	1,100.	130.00
		No gum	600.00	
78	A29	24c lilac ('63)	750.00	85.00
		No gum	450.00	
a.		24c grayish lilac	750.00	85.00
		No gum	450.00	
b.		24c gray	750.00	85.00
		No gum	450.00	
c.		24c blackish violet	25,000.	1,750.
		No gum	17,500.	
d.		Printed on both sides	—	3,500.

Values for Nos. 75, 76, 76a reflect the normal small margins.

Grill

Same as 1861-66 Issues
Embossed with grills of various sizes

Grill with Points Up
Grills A and C were made by a roller covered with ridges shaped like an inverted V. Pressing the ridges into the stamp paper forced the paper into the pyramidal pits between the ridges, causing irregular breaks in the paper.
Grill B was made by a roller with raised bosses.

A. Grill covering the entire stamp

1867				**Perf. 12**
79	A25	3c rose	3,750.	850.
		No gum	2,250.	
b.		Printed on both sides		
80	A26	5c brown	—	80,000.
a.		5c dark brown		80,000.
81	A30	30c orange	—	50,000.

Nos. 79, 79b, are valued for fine - very fine centering but with minor perforation faults.
An essay which is often mistaken for No. 79 (#79-E15) shows the points of the grill as small squares faintly impressed in the paper, but not cutting through it. On No. 79 the grill breaks through the paper. Copies free from defects are rare.
Eight copies of Nos. 80 and 80a (four unused, four used), and eight copies of No. 81 (one institutionalized and not available to collectors) are

known. All are more or less faulty and/or off-center. Values are for off-center examples with small perforation faults.
The imperf. of the 3c rose can be found in the Scott U.S. Specialized Catalogue Die and Plate Proofs section.

B. Grill about 18x15mm (22 by 18 points)

82	A25	3c rose		160,000.

The four known copies of No. 82 are fine.

C. Grill about 13x16mm (16 to 17 by 18 to 21 points)

83	A25	3c rose	4,250.	800.
		No gum	2,500.	

The grilled area on each of four C grills in the sheet may total about 18x15mm when a normal C grill adjoins a fainter grill extending to the right or left edge of the stamp. This is caused by a partial erasure on the grill roller when it was changed to produce C grills instead of the all-over A grill.
The imperf. can be found in the Scott U.S. Specialized Catalogue Die and Plate Proofs section.

Grill with Points Down
The grills were produced by rollers with the surface covered by pyramidal bosses. On the Z grill the tips of the pyramids are very short horizontal ridges. On the D, E and F grills the ridges are vertical.

D. Grill about 12x14mm (15 by 17 to 18 points)

84	A32	2c black	12,500.	2,250.
		No gum	7,750.	

No. 84 is valued in the grade of fine.

85	A25	3c rose	4,500.	800.
		No gum	2,600.	

Z. Grill about 11x14mm (13 to 14 by 17 to 18 points)

85A	A24	1c blue		935,000.
85B	A32	2c black	5,000.	800.
		No gum	3,000.	
85C	A25	3c rose	8,500.	2,250.
		No gum	4,750.	
85D	A27	10c green		90,000.
85E	A28	12c black	7,000.	1,000.
		No gum	4,250.	
85F	A33	15c black		220,000.

Two copies of No. 85A are known. One is contained in the New York Public Library collection. Value represents 1998 auction sale price of the single example available to collectors.
Six copies of No. 85D are known. One is in the New York Public Library collection. Value is for a well-centered example with small faults.
Two copies of No. 85F are known. Value represents 1998 auction sale price of the much finer example.

E. Grill about 11x13mm (14 by 15 to 17 points)

86	A24	1c blue	2,250.	400.
		No gum	1,250.	
a.		1c dull blue	2,250.	375.
		No gum	1,250.	
87	A32	2c black	850.	100.
		No gum	475.	
a.		Half used as 1c on cover, diagonal or vert.		2,000.
88	A25	3c rose	600.	15.
		No gum	350.	
a.		3c lake red	650.	19.
		No gum	375.	
89	A27	10c green	3,500.	275.
		No gum	2,000.	
90	A28	12c black	3,500.	300.
		No gum	2,000.	
91	A33	15c black	6,500.	600.
		No gum	3,600.	

F. Grill about 9x13mm (11 to 12 by 15 to 17 points)

92	A24	1c blue	850.	160.
a.		1c pale blue	850.	160.
		No gum	475.	
93	A32	2c black	350.	37.50
		No gum	175.	
a.		Vert. or diag. half used as 1c as part of 3c rate on cover		1,250.
c.		Horiz. or diagonal half used alone as 1c on cover		2,500.
94	A25	3c red	300.	4.25
a.		3c rose	300.	4.25
		No gum	150.	
c.		Vert. pair, imperf. horiz.	1,050.	
d.		Printed on both sides	1,150.	

The imperf. 3c can be found in the Scott U.S. Specialized Catalogue Die and Plate Proofs section.

95	A26	5c brown	2,400.	600.
		No gum	1,350.	
a.		5c black brown	2,600.	650.
		No gum	1,500.	

Values for Nos. 95, 95a reflect the normal small margins.

96	A27	10c yellow green	1,900.	175.
a.		10c dark green	1,900.	175.
		No gum	1,200.	
97	A28	12c black	2,250.	200.
		No gum	1,350.	
98	A33	15c black	2,500.	275.
		No gum	1,500.	

Quality United States

We stock MINT, USED, PLATE BLOCKS, and BACK OF THE BOOK items from SUPERB GEMS to spacefillers. Call or write for your FREE U.S. pricelist!

We want to help you build the collection of your dreams whether it be a personalized collection or a prize exhibit. Give us a call today!

OVER 20 YEARS PHILATELIC EXPERIENCE!
QUALITY – PRICE – SERVICE – INTEGRITY

CHECK OUT OUR WEBPAGE:
See our ever changing site with lots of stamps and over 500 color photos.
http://members.aol.com/MALACKWEB

STEVE MALACK STAMPS
P.O. Box 5628, Endicott, NY 13763
607-862-9441 (phone /FAX)
E-mail us at Malackweb@aol.com

Buying & Selling

UNITED STATES

99	A29	24c gray lilac	4,000.	650.
		No gum	2,250.	
100	A30	30c orange	4,250.	625.
		No gum	2,500.	

Values for No. 100 are for copies with small margins, especially at sides. Large-margined examples sell for much more.

101	A31	90c blue	7,000.	1,150.
		No gum	4,000.	

Some authorities believe that more than one size of grill probably existed on one of the grill rolls.

Re-issue of 1861-66 Issues
Without Grill
Hard White Paper
White Crackly Gum

1875   *Perf. 12*

102	A24	1c blue	650.	950.
		No gum	400.	
103	A32	2c black	2,500.	4,500.
		No gum	1,600.	
104	A25	3c brown red	2,750.	5,000.
		No gum	1,800.	
105	A26	5c brown	2,100.	2,500.
		No gum	1,400.	
106	A27	10c green	2,250.	4,250.
		No gum	1,450.	
107	A28	12c black	3,000.	5,000.
		No gum	2,000.	
108	A33	15c black	3,000.	5,500.
		No gum	2,000.	
109	A29	24c deep violet	3,750.	7,000.
		No gum	2,500.	
110	A30	30c brownish org	4,000.	8,000.
		No gum	2,650.	
111	A31	90c blue	5,250.	40,000.
		No gum	3,500.	

These stamps can be distinguished from the 1861-66 issues by the shades and the paper which is hard and very white instead of yellowish. The gum is white and crackly.

Franklin — A34 
Post Horse and Rider — A35 
Locomotive — A36 
Washington — A37
Shield and Eagle — A38
S. S. Adriatic — A39
Landing of Columbus — A40

FIFTEEN CENTS
Type I. Picture unframed.

A40a

Type II. Picture framed.
Type III. Same as type I but without fringe of brown shading lines around central vignette.

"The Declaration of Independence" A41
Shield, Eagle and Flags A42 
Lincoln — A43 

G. Grill measuring 9½x9mm
(12 by 11 to 11½ points)

1869   *Perf. 12*

112	A34	1c buff	550.00	140.00
		No gum	300.00	
b.		Without grill	4,000.	
113	A35	2c brown	500.00	50.00
		No gum	260.00	
b.		Without grill	1,250.	
c.		Half used as 1c on cover, diagonal, vert. or horiz.		3,000.
d.		Printed on both sides		9,000.
114	A36	3c ultramarine	275.00	17.50
		No gum	140.00	
a.		Without grill	900.00	
b.		Vertical one third used as 1c on cover		—
c.		Vertical two thirds used as 2c on cover		4,000.
d.		Double impression		3,500.
e.		Printed on both sides		
115	A37	6c ultramarine	2,000.	180.00
		No gum	1,100.	
b.		Vertical half used as 3c on cover		
116	A38	10c yellow	1,600.	130.
		No gum	900.	
117	A39	12c green	1,600.	140.
		No gum	900.	
118	A40	15c brn & blue, Type I	6,000.	600.
		No gum	4,000.	
		Without grill	7,000.	
119	A40a	15c brn & blue, Type II	2,500.	250.
		No gum	1,400.	
b.		Center inverted	275,000.	17,500.
c.		Center dbl., one invtd.		35,000.
120	A41	24c green & vio	5,000.	700.
		No gum	3,250.	
a.		Without grill	7,250.	
b.		Center inverted	275,000.	20,000.
121	A42	30c ultra & car	5,500.	500.
		No gum	3,500.	
a.		Without grill	7,250.	
b.		Flags inverted	210,000.	75,000.
122	A43	90c car & black	7,500.	2,100.
		No gum	4,500.	
a.		Without grill	12,500.	

Values of varieties of Nos. 112-122 without grill are for copies with original gum.
Most copies of Nos. 119b, 120b are faulty. Values are for fine centered copies with only minimal faults.

Re-issues of the 1869 Issue
Without Grill
Hard White Paper
White Crackly Gum

1875   *Perf. 12*

123	A34	1c buff	475.	300.
		No gum	275.	
124	A35	2c brown	575.	425.
		No gum	350.	
125	A36	3c blue	4,250.	14,000.
		No gum	3,000.	

Used value for No. 125 is for an attractive copy with minimal faults.

126	A37	6c blue	1,200.	1,250.
		No gum	750.	
127	A38	10c yellow	1,850.	1,400.
		No gum	1,250.	
128	A39	12c green	2,000.	2,250.
		No gum	1,350.	
129	A40	15c brown & blue, type III	1,750.	900.
		No gum	1,100.	
a.		Imperf. horiz., single	2,500.	

Type III is same as type I but without fringe of brown shading lines around central vignette.

130	A41	24c green & violet	1,750.	1,050.
		No gum	1,100.	
131	A42	30c ultra & carmine	2,400.	2,000.
		No gum	1,700.	
132	A43	90c carmine & black	4,500.	4,500.
		No gum	3,000.	

1880-81   **Soft Porous Paper**

133	A34	1c buff	275.	175.
		No gum	135.	
a.		1c brown orange ('81)	210.	150.

No. 133 was issued with gum, No. 133a without gum.

Printed by the National Bank Note Company

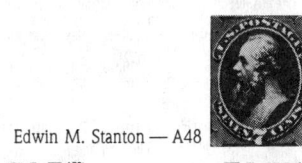

Franklin — A44
Jackson — A45
Washington — A46
Lincoln — A47
Edwin M. Stanton — A48
Jefferson — A49
Henry Clay — A50
Daniel Webster — A51
Gen. Winfield Scott A52 
Alexander Hamilton A53 
Commodore O. H. Perry — A54

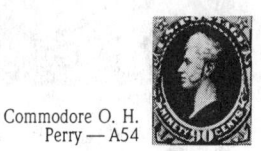

Two varieties of grill are known on this issue.

H. Grill about 10x12mm
(11 to 13 by 14 to 16 points)
On all values, 1c to 90c
I. Grill about 8½x10mm
(10 to 11 by 10 to 13 points)
On 1, 2, 3, 6, 7 and 15c

On the 1870-71 stamps the grill impressions are usually faint or incomplete. This is especially true of the H grill, which often shows only a few points.
Values for 1c - 7c are for stamps showing well-defined grills.

White Wove Paper

1870-71   *Perf. 12*

134	A44	1c ultramarine	1,400.	100.00
		No gum	700.00	
135	A45	2c red brown	850.00	60.00
		No gum	425.00	
a.		Diagonal half used as 1c on cover		
136	A46	3c green	600.00	15.00
		No gum	300.00	

The imperf. 3c can be found in the Scott U.S. Specialized Catalogue Die and Plate Proofs section.

137	A47	6c carmine	3,250.	450.
		No gum	1,750.	
138	A48	7c vermilion ('71)	2,250.	400.
		No gum	1,250.	
139	A49	10c brown	3,500.	650.
		No gum	1,900.	
140	A50	12c dull violet	17,500.	2,500.
		No gum	9,500.	
141	A51	15c orange	4,250.	1,000.
		No gum	2,400.	
142	A52	24c purple		6,500.

No. 142 is valued in the grade of fine.

143	A53	30c black	9,500.	2,000.
		No gum	6,000.	
144	A54	90c carmine	10,000.	1,300.
		No gum	6,250.	

Without Grill
White Wove Paper

1870-71   *Perf. 12*

145	A44	1c ultramarine	350.00	12.00
		No gum	175.00	
146	A45	2c red brown	250.00	7.50
		No gum	125.00	
a.		Half used as 1c on cover, diagonal or vert.		
c.		Double impression		

UNITED STATES

147	A46	3c green	250.00	1.10
		No gum	125.00	
a.		Printed on both sides		1,750.
b.		Double impression		1,250.

The imperf. 3c can be found in the Scott U.S. Specialized Catalogue Die and Plate Proofs section.

148	A47	6c carmine	525.00	20.00
		No gum	260.00	
a.		Vert. half used as 3c on cover		—
b.		Double impression		1,500.
149	A48	7c vermilion ('71)	600.00	85.00
		No gum	350.00	
150	A49	10c brown	525.00	17.50
		No gum	310.00	
151	A50	12c dull violet	1,300.	120.00
		No gum	725.00	
152	A51	15c bright orange	1,400.	120.00
		No gum	775.00	
a.		Double impression		1,500.
153	A52	24c purple	1,300.	120.00
		No gum	725.00	
154	A53	30c black	3,000.	150.00
		No gum	1,750.	
155	A54	90c carmine	3,000.	250.00
		No gum	1,750.	

Printed by the Continental Bank Note Co.

Designs of the 1870-71 Issue with secret marks on the values from 1c to 15c as described and illustrated below.

Franklin — A44a

1c. In pearl at left of numeral "1" is a small crescent.

Jackson — A45a

2c. Under the scroll at the left of "U. S." there is a small diagonal line. This mark seldom shows clearly. The stamp, No. 157, can be distinguished by its color.

Washington — A46a

3c. The under part of the upper tail of the left ribbon is heavily shaded.

Lincoln — A47a

6c. The first four vertical lines of the shading in the lower part of the left ribbon have been strengthened.

Stanton — A48a

7c. Two small semi-circles are drawn around the ends of the lines that outline the ball in the lower right hand corner.

Jefferson — A49a

10c. There is a small semi-circle in the scroll at the right end of the upper label.

Clay — A50a

12c. The balls of the figure "2" are crescent shaped.

Webster — A51a

15c. In the lower part of the triangle in the upper left corner two lines have been made heavier forming a "V." This mark can be found on some of the Continental and American (1879) printings, but not all stamps show it.

Secret marks were added to the dies of the 24c, 30c and 90c but new plates were not made from them. The various printings of these stamps can be distinguished only by the shades and paper.

White Wove Paper, thin to thick
Without Grill*

1873 *Perf. 12*

156	A44a	1c ultramarine	180.00	2.50
		No gum	95.00	
e.		With grill	2,000.	
f.		Imperf., pair		550.00
157	A45a	2c brown	325.00	15.00
		No gum	175.00	
c.		With grill	1,750.	700.00
d.		Double impression		—
e.		Vertical half used as 1c on cover		—
158	A46a	3c green	110.00	.30
		No gum	45.00	
e.		With grill	275.00	
h.		Horiz. pair, imperf. vert.		—
i.		Horiz. pair, imperf. btwn.		1,300.
j.		Double impression		1,250.
k.		Printed on both sides		—

The imperf. 3c, with and without grill, can be found in the Scott U.S. Specialized Catalogue Die and Plate Proofs section.

159	A47a	6c dull pink	375.00	15.00
		No gum	200.00	
b.		With grill	1,800.	
160	A48a	7c orange ver	800.00	75.00
		No gum	450.00	
a.		With grill	2,500.	
161	A49a	10c brown	550.00	16.00
		No gum	300.00	
c.		With grill	2,750.	
d.		Horiz. pair, imperf. btwn.		2,500.
162	A50a	12c black violet	1,350.	85.00
		No gum	725.00	
a.		With grill	4,250.	
163	A51a	15c yellow orange	1,500.	95.00
		No gum	800.00	
a.		With grill	4,250.	
164	A52	24c purple		—
165	A53	30c gray black	1,600.	90.00
		No gum	850.00	
c.		With grill	4,250.	
166	A54	90c rose carmine	2,400.	240.00
		No gum	1,475.	

The Philetelic Foundation has certified as genuine a 24c on vertically ribbed paper, and that is the stamp listed as No. 164. Specialists believe that only Continental used ribbed paper.

* All values except 24c, 90c exist with experimental (J) grill, about 7x9 1/2mm.

Special Printing of the 1873 Issue
Hard, White Wove Paper
Without Gum

1875 *Perf. 12*

167	A44a	1c ultramarine	9,000.	
168	A45a	2c dark brown	4,000.	
169	A46a	3c blue green	10,500.	—
170	A47a	6c dull rose	9,500.	
171	A48a	7c redsh vermilion	2,300.	
172	A49a	10c pale brown	9,500.	
173	A50a	12c dark violet	3,750.	
174	A51a	15c bright orange	9,500.	
175	A52	24c dull purple	2,250.	5,000.
176	A53	30c greenish black	7,000.	
177	A54	90c violet carmine	8,500.	

Although perforated, these stamps were usually cut apart with scissors. As a result, the perforations are often much mutilated and the design is frequently damaged.

These can be distinguished from the 1873 issue by the shades, also by the paper, which is very white instead of yellowish.

These and the subsequent issues listed under this heading are special printings of stamps then in current use which, together with the reprints and reissues, were made for sale to collectors. They were available for postage except for the Officials and demonetized issues.

Zachary Taylor — A55

Yellowish Wove Paper

1875, June 21 *Perf. 12*

178	A45a	2c vermilion	300.00	7.50
		No gum	160.00	
b.		Half used as 1c on cover		—
c.		With grill	500.00	

The imperf. 2c can be found in the Scott U.S. Specialized Catalogue Die and Plate Proofs section.

179	A55	5c blue	425.00	15.00
		No gum	210.00	
c.		With grill	1,500.	

Almost all of the stamps of the Continental Bank Note Co. printing including the Department stamps and some of the Newspaper stamps may be found upon a paper that shows more or less of the characteristics of a ribbed paper.

Special Printing of the 1875 Issue
Hard, White Wove Paper
Without Gum

1875

180	A45a	2c carmine ver	26,000.	
181	A55	5c bright blue	42,500.	

VALUES FOR VERY FINE STAMPS
Stamps are valued in the grade of very fine unless otherwise indicated.
Values for unused stamps with no gum are for examples with certificates of authenticity or examples sold with the buyer having the right of certification. Beware of unused, no gum stamps that are offered "as is." Expertization by competent authorities is recommended.

Printed by the American Bank Note Company
Same as 1870-75 Issues
Soft Porous Paper
Varying from Thin to Thick

1879 *Perf. 12*

182	A44a	1c dark ultra	240.00	2.25
		No gum	130.00	
183	A45a	2c vermilion	120.00	2.25
		No gum	60.00	
a.		Double impression		500.00
184	A46a	3c green	85.00	.30
		No gum	35.00	
b.		Double impression		—

The imperf. 3c can be found in the Scott U.S. Specialized Catalogue Die and Plate Proofs section.

185	A55	5c blue	425.00	12.00
		No gum	190.00	
186	A47a	6c pink	750.00	17.50
		No gum	400.00	
187	A49	10c brown (without secret mark)	1,500.	22.50
		No gum	825.00	
188	A49a	10c brown (with secret mark)	1,100.	22.50
		No gum	575.00	
189	A51a	15c red orange	300.00	21.00
		No gum	150.00	
190	A53	30c full black	900.00	55.00
		No gum	500.00	
191	A54	90c carmine	1,900.	240.00
		No gum	1,100.	

The ABN Co. used many Continental plates to print the postage, Departmental and Newspaper stamps. Therefore, stamps bearing the Continental imprint were not always its product.

The ABN Co. also used the National 90c plate and possibly the 30c plate.

Early printings of No. 188 were from Continental plates 302 and 303 which contained the normal secret mark of 1873. After those plates were re-entered by the ABN Co. in 1880, pairs or multiple pieces contained combinations of normal, hairline or missing marks. The pairs or other multiples usually found contain at least one hairline mark which tended to disappear as the plate wore.

ABN Co. plates 377 and 378 were made in 1881 from the National transfer roll of 1870. No. 187 from those plates has no secret mark.

Perf 12 Trial Color Proofs on gummed stamp paper exist, as does a 15c without the blue "SAMPLE" overprint.

The ABN Co. used many Continental plates to print the postage, Departmental and Newspaper stamps. Therefore, stamps bearing the Continental imprint were not always its product. The imperf. 90c can be found in the Scott U.S. Specialized Catalogue Die and Plate Proofs section.

Special Printing of the 1879 Issue
Soft Porous Paper
Without Gum

1880 *Perf. 12*

192	A44a	1c dark ultra	14,000.
193	A45a	2c black brown	7,000.
194	A46a	3c blue green	20,000.
195	A47a	6c dull rose	14,000.
196	A48a	7c scar vermilion	2,750.
197	A49a	10c deep brown	14,000.
198	A50a	12c black purple	4,250.
199	A51a	15c orange	14,000.
200	A52	24c dark violet	4,250.
201	A53	30c grnsh black	10,000.
202	A54	90c dull carmine	11,000.
203	A45a	2c scar vermilion	22,500.
204	A55	5c deep blue	38,500.

No. 197 was printed from Continental plate 302 (or 303) after plate was re-entered, therefore stamp may show normal, hairline or missing secret mark.

James A. Garfield — A56

1882, Apr. 10 *Perf. 12*

205	A56	5c yellow brown	190.00	7.00
		No gum	85.00	

Special Printing
Soft Porous Paper
Without Gum

1882

205C	A56	5c gray brown	25,000.

Designs of 1873 Re-engraved

Franklin — A44b

1c. The vertical lines in the upper part of the stamp have been so deepened that the background often appears to be solid. Lines of shading have been added to the upper arabesques.

Washington — A46b

3c. The shading at the sides of the central oval appears only about one-half the previous width. A short horizontal dash has been cut about 1mm below the "TS" of "CENTS."

Lincoln — A47b

6c. On the original stamps four vertical lines can be counted from the edge of the panel to the outside of the stamp. On the re-engraved stamps there are but three lines in the same place.

Jefferson — A49b

10c. On the original stamps there are five vertical lines between the left side of the oval and the edge of the shield. There are only four lines on the re-engraved stamps. In the lower part of the latter, also, the horizontal lines of the background have been strengthened.

1881-82 *Perf. 12*

206	A44b	1c gray blue	60.00	.75
		No gum	27.50	
207	A46b	3c blue green	60.00	.40
		No gum	27.50	
c.		Double impression		—

UNITED STATES

208	A47b	6c rose ('82)	425.00	65.00
		No gum	225.00	
a.		6c deep brown red	375.00	85.00
		No gum	190.00	
209	A49b	10c brown ('82)	120.00	3.50
		No gum	55.00	
b.		10c black brown	350.00	22.50
		No gum	200.00	
c.		Double impression		—
		Nos. 206-209 (4)	665.00	69.65

Specimen stamps without overprint exist in a brown shade that differs from No. 209 and in green. The unoverprinted brown specimen is cheaper than No. 209.

Washington A57  **Jackson A58**

1883, Oct. 1 — Perf. 12

210	A57	2c red brown	45.00	.30
		No gum	20.00	
211	A58	4c blue green	210.00	11.00
		No gum	95.00	

Imperfs. can be found in the Scott U.S. Specialized Catalogue Die and Plate Proofs section.

Special Printings of 1883 follow.

Special Printing
Soft Porous Paper

1883-85

211B	A57	2c pale red brown	550.	—
		No gum	300.	
c.		Horiz. pair, imperf. btwn.	2,000.	
211D	A58	4c deep blue green	21,000.	

No. 211D is without gum.

Franklin — A59

1887 — Perf. 12

212	A59	1c ultramarine	95.00	1.10
		No gum	37.50	
213	A57	2c green	35.00	.35
		No gum	12.50	
b.		Printed on both sides		—
214	A46b	3c vermilion	70.00	50.00
		No gum	32.50	
		Nos. 212-214 (3)	200.00	51.45

Imperf. 1c, 2c can be found in the Scott U.S. Specialized Catalogue Die and Plate Proofs section.

1888 — Perf. 12

215	A58	4c carmine	200.00	16.00
		No gum	90.00	
216	A56	5c indigo	200.00	9.00
		No gum	85.00	
217	A53	30c orange brown	425.00	90.00
		No gum	220.00	
218	A54	90c purple	1,100.	200.00
		No gum	650.00	
		Nos. 215-218 (4)	1,925.	315.00

Imperfs. can be found in the Scott U.S. Specialized Catalogue Die and Plate Proofs section.

Have you found a typo or other error in this catalogue?

Inform the editors via our web site or e-mail

sctcat@
scottonline.com

IMPORTANT INFORMATION REGARDING VALUES FOR NEVER-HINGED STAMPS

Collectors should be aware that the values given for never-hinged stamps from No. 219 on are for stamps in the grade of very fine. The never-hinged premium as a percentage of value will be larger for stamps in extremely fine or superb grades, and the premium will be smaller for fine-very fine, fine or poor examples. This is particularly true of the issues of the late-19th and early-20th centuries. For example, in the grade of very fine, an unused stamp from this time period may be valued at $100 hinged and $160 never hinged. The never-hinged premium is thus 60%. But in a grade of extremely fine, this same stamp will not only sell for more hinged, but the never-hinged premium will increase, perhaps to 100%-300% or more over the higher extremely fine value. In a grade of superb, a hinged copy will sell for much more than a very fine copy, and additionally the never-hinged premium will be much larger, perhaps as large as 300%-400% or more. On the other hand, the same stamp in a grade of fine or fine-very fine not only will sell for less than a very fine stamp in hinged condition, but additionally the never-hinged premium will be smaller than the never-hinged premium on a very fine stamp, perhaps as small as 15%-30%.

Please note that the above statements and percentages are NOT a formula for arriving at the values of stamps in hinged or never-hinged condition in the grades of fine, fine to very fine, extremely fine or superb. The percentages given apply only to the size of the premium for never-hinged condition that might be added to the stamp value for hinged condition. The marketplace will determine what this value will be for grades other than very fine. Further, the percentages given are only generalized estimates. Some stamps or grades may have percentages for never-hinged condition that are higher or lower than the ranges given.

Franklin — A60  **Washington — A61**

Jackson — A62 **Lincoln — A63**

Ulysses S. Grant — A64 **Garfield — A65**

William T. Sherman — A66  **Daniel Webster — A67**

Henry Clay — A68  **Jefferson — A69**

Perry — A70

1890-93 — Perf. 12

219	A60	1c dull blue	25.00	.25
		Never hinged	40.00	
219D	A61	2c lake	190.00	.60
		Never hinged	260.00	
220	A61	2c carmine	20.00	.25
		Never hinged	32.50	
a.		Cap on left "2"	65.00	2.00
		Never hinged	105.00	
c.		Cap on both "2's"	190.00	15.00
		Never hinged	300.00	
221	A62	3c purple	65.00	6.00
		Never hinged	105.00	
222	A63	4c dark brown	67.50	2.25
		Never hinged	110.00	
223	A64	5c chocolate	65.00	2.25
		Never hinged	105.00	
224	A65	6c brown red	67.50	18.00
		Never hinged	110.00	
225	A66	8c lilac ('93)	52.50	11.00
		Never hinged	85.00	
226	A67	10c green	140.00	2.75
		Never hinged	215.00	
227	A68	15c indigo	180.00	18.00
		Never hinged	275.00	
228	A69	30c black	300.00	25.00
		Never hinged	475.00	
229	A70	90c orange	450.00	115.00
		Never hinged	700.00	
		Nos. 219-229 (12)	1,622.	201.35

The "cap on right 2" variety is due to imperfect inking, not a plate defect.

Imperfs. can be found in the Scott U.S. Specialized Catalogue Die and Plate Proofs section.

Columbian Exposition Issue

Columbus in Sight of Land — A71

Landing of Columbus — A72

Flagship of Columbus — A73

Fleet of Columbus — A74

Columbus Soliciting Aid from Isabella — A75

Columbus Welcomed at Barcelona — A76

Columbus Restored to Favor — A77

Columbus Presenting Natives — A78

Columbus Announcing his Discovery — A79

Columbus at La Rábida — A80

Recall of Columbus — A81

Isabella Pledging her Jewels — A82

Columbus in Chains — A83

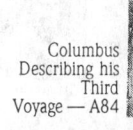

Columbus Describing his Third Voyage — A84

Isabella and Columbus — A85

Columbus — A86

1893 — Perf. 12

230	A71	1c deep blue	25.00	.40
		Never hinged	40.00	
231	A72	2c brown violet	22.50	.20
		Never hinged	35.00	
232	A73	3c green	62.50	15.00
		Never hinged	100.00	
233	A74	4c ultra	87.50	7.50
		Never hinged	140.00	
a.		4c blue (error)	17,000.	5,500.
		Never hinged	25,000.	
234	A75	5c chocolate	95.00	8.00
		Never hinged	150.00	
235	A76	6c purple	90.00	22.50
		Never hinged	145.00	
a.		6c red violet	90.00	22.50
		Never hinged	145.00	
236	A77	8c magenta	80.00	11.00
		Never hinged	125.00	
237	A78	10c black brown	135.00	8.00
		Never hinged	225.00	
238	A79	15c dark green	240.00	65.00
		Never hinged	400.00	
239	A80	30c orange brown	300.00	85.00
		Never hinged	500.00	
240	A81	50c slate blue	600.00	160.00
		Never hinged	1,000.	
241	A82	$1 salmon	1,500.	650.00
		Never hinged	2,500.	
		No gum	725.00	
242	A83	$2 brown red	1,550.	600.00
		Never hinged	2,500.	
		No gum	750.00	
243	A84	$3 yellow green	2,400.	1,000.
		Never hinged	4,000.	
		No gum	1,150.	
a.		$3 olive green	2,400.	975.00
		Never hinged	4,000.	
		No gum	1,150.	
244	A85	$4 crimson lake	3,250.	1,350.
		Never hinged	5,500.	
		No gum	1,500.	
a.		$4 rose carmine	3,250.	1,350.
		Never hinged	5,500.	
		No gum	1,500.	
245	A86	$5 black	3,750.	1,600.
		Never hinged	6,750.	
		No gum	1,750.	

World's Columbian Expo., Chicago, May 1-Oct. 30, 1893.

Nos. 230-245 are known imperf., but were not regularly issued. (See Scott U. S. Specialized Catalogue Die and Plate Proofs for the 2c.)

UNITED STATES

Never-Hinged Stamps
See note after No. 218 regarding premiums for never-hinged stamps.

Bureau Issues

Starting in 1894, the Bureau of Engraving and Printing at Washington has produced most U.S. postage stamps. Until 1965 Bureau-printed stamps were engraved except Nos. 525-536, which are offset. The combination of lithography and engraving (see No. 1253) was first used in 1964, and photogravure (see No. 1426) in 1971.

Franklin A87
Washington A88 
Jackson A89 
Lincoln A90 
Grant A91 
Garfield A92 
Sherman A93 
Webster A94 
Clay A95 
Jefferson A96 
Perry A97 
James Madison A98 
John Marshall — A99 

TWO CENTS

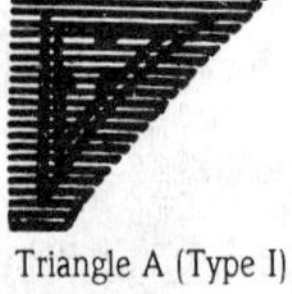

Triangle A (Type I)
Triangle B (Type II) 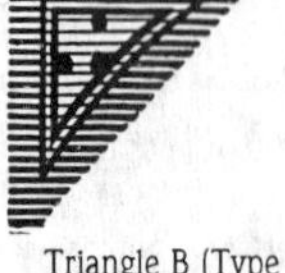

Type I. The horizontal lines of the ground work run across the triangle and are of the same thickness within it as without.

Type II. The horizontal lines cross the triangle but are thinner within it than without.

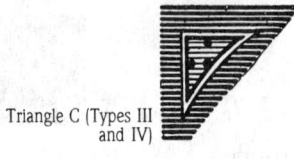

Triangle C (Types III and IV)

Type III. The horizontal lines do not cross the double frame lines of the triangle. The lines within the triangle are thin, as in type II. Otherwise, design as type II.

Type IV. Same triangle C as type III, but other design differences including, (1) re-cutting and lengthening of hairline, (2) shaded toga button, (3) strengthening of lines on sleeve, (4) additional dots on ear, (5) "T" of "TWO" straight at right, (6) background lines extend into white oval opposite "U" of "UNITED." Many other differences exist.

ONE DOLLAR

Type I

Type I. The circles enclosing "$1" are broken where they meet the curved line below "One Dollar." The 15 left vert. rows of impressions from plate 76 are Type I, the balance Type II.

Type II

Type II. The circles are complete.

1894		Unwmk.		Perf. 12
246	A87	1c ultramarine	29.00	4.00
		Never hinged	47.50	
247	A87	1c blue	60.00	2.00
		Never hinged	100.00	
248	A88	2c pink, Type I	25.00	3.00
		Never hinged	42.50	
249	A88	2c carmine lake, Type I	130.00	2.25
		Never hinged	220.00	
250	A88	2c car, Type I	27.50	.50
		Never hinged	45.00	
a.		2c rose, type I	27.50	.50
		Never hinged	45.00	
b.		2c scarlet, type I ('95)	27.50	.50
		Never hinged	45.00	
c.		Vert. pair, imperf. horiz.	1,500.	
d.		Horiz. pair, imperf. btwn.	1,500.	
251	A88	2c car, Type II	225.00	3.50
		Never hinged	375.00	
a.		2c scarlet, type II	225.00	3.50
		Never hinged	375.00	
252	A88	2c car, Type III	110.00	3.75
		Never hinged	180.00	
a.		2c scarlet, type III	110.00	3.75
		Never hinged	180.00	
b.		Horiz. pair, imperf. vert.	1,350.	
c.		Horiz. pair, imperf. btwn.	1,500.	
253	A89	3c purple	95.00	8.00
		Never hinged	160.00	
254	A90	4c dark brown	120.00	3.75
		Never hinged	200.00	
255	A91	5c chocolate	90.00	4.75
		Never hinged	150.00	
c.		Vert. pair, imperf. horiz.	1,750.	
256	A92	6c dull brown	140.00	21.00
		Never hinged	230.00	
a.		Vert. pair, imperf. horiz.	850.00	
257	A93	8c vio brn ('95)	130.00	14.00
		Never hinged	220.00	
258	A94	10c dark green	225.00	10.00
		Never hinged	375.00	
259	A95	15c dark blue	275.00	45.00
		Never hinged	450.00	
260	A96	50c orange	400.00	95.00
		Never hinged	675.00	
261	A97	$1 black, Type I	825.00	250.00
		Never hinged	1,375.	
		No gum	325.	
261A	A97	$1 black, Type II	2,000.	550.00
		Never hinged	3,400.	
		No gum	750.	
262	A98	$2 bright blue	2,750.	825.00
		Never hinged	4,600.	
		No gum	1,050.	
263	A99	$5 dark green	4,000.	1,750.
		Never hinged	6,750.	
		No gum	1,900.	

For imperfs. and the 2c pink, vert. pair, imperf. horiz., see Scott U. S. Specialized Catalogue Die and Plate Proofs.

Same as 1894 Issue

1895		Wmk. 191		Perf. 12
264	A87	1c blue	5.50	.25
		Never hinged	9.00	
265	A88	2c car, Type I	27.50	.80
		Never hinged	45.00	
266	A88	2c car, Type II	27.50	3.00
		Never hinged	45.00	
267	A88	2c car, Type III	5.00	.25
		Never hinged	8.25	
a.		2c pink, type III ('97)	5.50	.30
		Never hinged	9.00	
b.		2c vermilion, type III ('99)	25.00	—
c.		2c rose carmine, type III ('99)		

The three left vertical rows from plate 170 are Type II, the balance being Type III.

268	A89	3c purple	35.00	1.10
		Never hinged	57.50	
269	A90	4c dark brown	37.50	1.60
		Never hinged	62.50	
270	A91	5c chocolate	35.00	1.90
		Never hinged	57.50	
271	A92	6c dull brown	85.00	4.25
		Never hinged	140.00	
a.		Wmkd. USIR	2,250.	400.00
272	A93	8c violet brown	55.00	1.25
		Never hinged	90.00	
a.		Wmkd. USIR	1,750.	110.00
273	A94	10c dark green	75.00	1.50
		Never hinged	125.00	
274	A95	15c dark blue	200.00	9.00
		Never hinged	330.00	
275	A96	50c orange	260.00	20.00
		Never hinged	425.00	
a.		50c red orange	290.00	24.00
		Never hinged	475.00	
276	A97	$1 blk, Type I	600.00	65.00
		Never hinged	1,000.	
		No gum	175.00	
276A	A97	$1 blk, Type II	1,200.	140.00
		Never hinged	2,000.	
		No gum	400.00	
277	A98	$2 bright blue	975.00	300.00
		Never hinged	1,650.	
		No gum	350.00	
a.		$2 dark blue	975.00	300.00
		Never hinged	1,650.	
		No gum	350.00	
278	A99	$5 dark green	2,250.	425.00
		Never hinged	3,800.	
		No gum	850.	

For imperfs. and the 1c horiz. pair, imperf. vert., see Scott U. S. Specialized Catalogue Die and Plate Proofs.

For "I.R." overprints see Nos. R155-R158.

TEN CENTS

Type I

Type I. Tips of foliate ornaments do not impinge on white curved line below "TEN CENTS."

Type II

Type II. Tips of ornaments break curved line below "E" of "TEN" and "T" of "CENTS."

1898		Wmk. 191		Perf. 12
279	A87	1c deep green	9.00	.25
		Never hinged	15.00	
279B	A88	2c red, type IV ('99)	9.00	.25
		Never hinged	15.00	
c.		2c rose carmine, type IV ('99)	240.00	65.00
		Never hinged	400.00	
d.		2c orange red, type IV ('00)	10.00	.30
		Never hinged	17.00	
e.		Booklet pane of 6 ('00)	425.00	350.00
		Never hinged	700.00	
f.		2c carmine, type IV ('97)	10.00	.25
		Never hinged	17.00	
g.		2c pink, type IV ('97)	11.00	.35
		Never hinged	18.00	
h.		2c vermilion, type IV ('99)	10.00	.25
		Never hinged	17.00	
i.		2c brown orange, type IV ('99)	100.00	5.00
		Never hinged	170.00	
280	A90	4c rose brown	30.00	.90
		Never hinged	50.00	
a.		4c lilac brown	30.00	.90
		Never hinged	50.00	
b.		4c orange brown	30.00	.90
		Never hinged	50.00	
281	A91	5c dark blue	35.00	.75
		Never hinged	57.50	
282	A92	6c lake	45.00	2.50
		Never hinged	75.00	
a.		6c purple lake	55.00	3.50
		Never hinged	90.00	
282C	A94	10c brown, Type I	180.00	2.50
		Never hinged	300.00	
283	A94	10c org brown, Type II	110.00	2.00
		Never hinged	180.00	
284	A95	15c olive green	150.00	7.50
		Never hinged	250.00	
		Nos. 279-284 (8)	568.00	16.65

For "I.R." overprints see Nos. R153-R154.

VALUES FOR VERY FINE STAMPS
Please note: Stamps are valued in the grade of Very Fine unless otherwise indicated.

Trans-Mississippi Exposition Issue

Marquette on the Mississippi A100
Farming in the West — A101 
Indian Hunting Buffalo — A102 
Frémont on the Rocky Mountains A103 
Troops Guarding Wagon Train — A104 
Hardships of Emigration A105 
Western Mining Prospector A106 
Western Cattle in Storm — A107 
Mississippi River Bridge — A108 

1898, June 17		Wmk. 191		Perf. 12
285	A100	1c dk yel green	27.50	6.00
		Never hinged	47.50	
286	A101	2c copper red	25.00	1.50
		Never hinged	42.50	
287	A102	4c orange	140.00	21.00
		Never hinged	225.00	
288	A103	5c dull blue	130.00	19.00
		Never hinged	225.00	
289	A104	8c violet brown	175.00	37.50
		Never hinged	290.00	
a.		Vert. pair, imperf. horiz.	19,000.	
290	A105	10c gray violet	170.00	22.50
		Never hinged	275.00	
291	A106	50c sage green	600.00	170.00
		Never hinged	1,000.	
292	A107	$1 black	1,250.	500.00
		Never hinged	2,100.	
		No gum	600.	

UNITED STATES

293 A108 $2 orange brown 2,100. 850.00
    Never hinged 3,500.
    No gum 1,000.
Nos. 285-293 (9) 4,617. 1,627.

Trans-Mississippi Exposition, Omaha, Neb., June 1 to Nov. 1, 1898.

For "I.R." overprints see #R158A-R158B.

Never-Hinged Stamps
See note after No. 218 regarding premiums for never-hinged stamps.

Pan-American Exposition Issue

Fast Lake Navigation — A109
"Empire State" Express — A110 
Electric Automobile A111 
Bridge at Niagara Falls A112 
Canal Locks at Sault Ste. Marie — A113 
Fast Ocean Navigation — A114 

1901, May 1   Wmk. 191   *Perf. 12*

294 A109 1c green & black 18.00 3.00
    Never hinged 30.00
  a. Center inverted 10,000. 7,000.
    Never hinged 15,000.
295 A110 2c car & black 17.50 1.00
    Never hinged 29.00
  a. Center inverted 37,500. 16,000.
296 A111 4c dp red brn & black 80.00 15.00
    Never hinged 135.00
  a. Center inverted 20,000.
297 A112 5c ultra & black 95.00 14.00
    Never hinged 160.00
298 A113 8c brn vio & black 120.00 50.00
    Never hinged 200.00
299 A114 10c yel brn & black 170.00 25.00
    Never hinged 280.00
Nos. 294-299 (6) 500.50 108.00
Nos. 294-299, never hinged 834.00

Buffalo, NY, May 1-Nov. 1, 1901.

No. 296a was a special printing.

Almost all unused copies of Nos. 295a and 296a have partial or disturbed gum. Values are for examples with full original gum that is slightly disturbed.

Franklin A115
Washington A116 
Jackson A117 
Grant A118 
Lincoln A119 
Garfield A120 

Martha Washington A121
Webster A122 
Benjamin Harrison A123 
Clay A124 
Jefferson A125 
David G. Farragut A126 
Madison A127 
Marshall A128 

1902-03   Wmk. 191   *Perf. 12*

300 A115 1c blue grn ('03) 10.00 .20
    Never hinged 17.00
  b. Booklet pane of 6 525.00 —
    Never hinged 875.00
301 A116 2c carmine ('03) 14.00 .20
    Never hinged 22.50
  c. Booklet pane of 6 450.00 —
    Never hinged 750.00
302 A117 3c brt violet ('03) 50.00 2.75
    Never hinged 82.50
303 A118 4c brown ('03) 55.00 1.25
    Never hinged 90.00
304 A119 5c blue ('03) 55.00 1.50
    Never hinged 90.00
305 A120 6c claret ('03) 65.00 2.50
    Never hinged 110.00
306 A121 8c violet black 40.00 2.00
    Never hinged 67.50
307 A122 10c pale red brn ('03) 60.00 1.40
    Never hinged 100.00
308 A123 13c purple black 45.00 7.50
    Never hinged 75.00
309 A124 15c olive green ('03) 150.00 4.75
    Never hinged 250.00
310 A125 50c orange ('03) 425.00 22.50
    Never hinged 700.00
311 A126 $1 black ('03) 700.00 55.00
    Never hinged 1,200.
    No gum 160.00
312 A127 $2 dark blue ('03) 1,100. 170.00
    Never hinged 1,850.
    No gum 275.
313 A128 $5 dark green ('03) 2,750. 675.00
    Never hinged 4,600.
    No gum 825.
Nos. 300-313 (14) 5,519. 946.55

For listings of designs A127 and A128 with Perf. 10, see Nos. 479 and 480.

1906-08   *Imperf.*

314 A115 1c blue green 20.00 15.00
    Never hinged 32.50
314A A118 4c brown ('08) 27,500. 21,000.
315 A119 5c blue ('08) 290.00 425.00
    Never hinged 450.00

No. 314A was issued imperforate but all copies were privately perforated with large oblong perforations at the sides (Schermack type III).

Beware of copies of No. 303 with trimmed perforations and fake private perfs added.

Used copies of Nos. 314 & 315 must have contemporaneous cancels.

Coil Stamps

Imperforate stamps are known fraudulently perforated to resemble coil stamps and part perforate varieties.

1908   *Perf. 12 Horizontally*

316 A115 1c blue green, pair 90,000. —
317 A119 5c blue, pair 12,500. —
    Never hinged

Perf. 12 Vertically

318 A115 1c blue green, pair 8,500. —

Coil stamps for use in vending and affixing machines are perforated on two sides only, either horizontally or vertically. They were first issued in 1908, using perf. 12. This was changed to 8½ in 1910, and to 10 in 1914.

Imperforate sheets of certain denominations were sold to the vending machine companies which applied a variety of private perforations and separations.

Several values of the 1902 and later issues are found on an apparently coarse ribbed paper. This is caused by worn blankets on the printing press and is not a true paper variety.

Washington — A129

Type I   Type II

Type I. Leaf next to left "2" penetrates the border.

Type II. Strong line forming border left of leaf.

1903, Nov. 12   Wmk. 191   *Perf. 12*

319 A129 2c carmine (I) 5.25 .15
    Never hinged 8.75
  a. 2c lake (I) — —
  b. 2c carmine rose (I) 7.00 .35
    Never hinged 11.50
  c. 2c scarlet (I) 5.25 .25
    Never hinged 8.75
  d. Vert. pair, imperf. horiz. 3,500.
  e. Vert. pair, imperf. btwn. 1,100.
  f. 2c carmine (III) 6.75 .25
    Never hinged 11.00
  g. Booklet pane of 6, car (I) 110.00 150.00
    Never hinged 180.00
  h. As "g" (II) 240.00
    Never hinged 400.00
  i. 2c carmine (III) 25.00 50.00
    Never hinged 40.00
  j. 2c carmine rose (II) 19.00 .75
    Never hinged 30.00
  k. 2c scarlet (II) 16.00 .45
    Never hinged 25.00
  m. As "g," lake (I) 2,500.
  n. As "g," car rose (I) 160.00 160.00
    Never hinged 260.00
  p. As "g," scarlet (I) 150.00 150.00
    Never hinged 250.00
  q. As "g," lake (II) 190.00 250.00
    Never hinged 310.00

1906, Oct. 2   *Imperf.*

320 A129 2c carmine (I) 19.00 12.00
    Never hinged 30.00
  a. 2c lake (II) 50.00 40.00
    Never hinged 77.50
  b. 2c scarlet (I) 19.00 12.50
    Never hinged 30.00
  c. 2c carmine rose (I) 60.00 40.00
    Never hinged 95.00
  d. 2c carmine (II) —

Coil Stamps

1908   *Perf. 12 Horizontally*

321 A129 2c car, pair (I) 125,000. 170,000.

Four or five authenticated unused pairs are known. The used value is for a single on cover, of which 2 authenticated examples are known, both used from Indianapolis in 1908. Numerous counterfeits exist.

Perf. 12 Vertically

322 A129 2c carmine, pair 8,000. 5,500.

Louisiana Purchase Exposition
St. Louis, Mo., Apr. 30 - Dec. 1, 1904

Robert R. Livingston A130
Thomas Jefferson A131 
James Monroe — A132 
William McKinley A133 
Map of Louisiana Purchase — A134 

1904, Apr. 30   Wmk. 191   *Perf. 12*

323 A130 1c green 30.00 4.00
    Never hinged 47.50
324 A131 2c carmine 27.50 1.75
    Never hinged 45.00
  a. Vert. pair, imperf. horiz. 10,000.
325 A132 3c violet 90.00 30.00
    Never hinged 145.00
326 A133 5c dark blue 95.00 20.00
    Never hinged 150.00
327 A134 10c red brown 180.00 27.50
    Never hinged 290.00
Nos. 323-327 (5) 422.50 83.25
Nos. 323-327, never hinged 677.50

Jamestown Exposition Issue

Captain John Smith A135
Founding of Jamestown A136 
Pocahontas — A137 

1907   Wmk. 191   *Perf. 12*

328 A135 1c green 27.50 4.00
    Never hinged 45.00
329 A136 2c carmine 32.50 3.50
    Never hinged 52.50
330 A137 5c blue 130.00 27.50
    Never hinged 210.00
Nos. 328-330 (3) 190.00 35.00
Nos. 328-330, never hinged 307.50

Jamestown Expo., Hampton Roads, Va., Apr. 26 to Dec. 1.

Franklin A138
Washington A139 
Washington — A140 

There are several types of some of the 2c and 3c stamps of this and succeeding issues. These types are described under the dates when they first appeared.

Illustrations of Types I-VII of the 2c (A140) and Types I-IV of the 3c (A140) are reproduced by permission of H. L. Lindquist.

TYPE I

THREE CENTS

Type I. The top line of the toga rope is weak and the rope shading lines are thin. The fifth line from the left is missing.

The line between the lips is thin.

Used on both flat plate and rotary press printings.

1908-09 Wmk. 191 *Perf. 12*

331	A138 1c green	7.00	.15
	Never hinged	11.50	
a.	Booklet pane of 6	160.00	*140.00*
	Never hinged	240.00	
332	A139 2c carmine	6.50	.15
	Never hinged	10.50	
a.	Booklet pane of 6	135.00	*125.00*
	Never hinged	200.00	
333	A140 3c deep violet, Type I	32.50	2.50
	Never hinged	52.50	
334	A140 4c orange brown	40.00	1.00
	Never hinged	65.00	
335	A140 5c blue	50.00	2.00
	Never hinged	80.00	
336	A140 6c red orange	62.50	5.00
	Never hinged	100.00	
337	A140 8c olive green	47.50	2.50
	Never hinged	75.00	
338	A140 10c yellow ('09)	67.50	1.40
	Never hinged	110.00	
339	A140 13c blue green ('09)	40.00	19.00
	Never hinged	65.00	
340	A140 15c pale ultra ('09)	65.00	5.50
	Never hinged	105.00	
341	A140 50c violet ('09)	325.00	20.00
	Never hinged	525.00	
342	A140 $1 vio brown ('09)	500.00	75.00
	Never hinged	800.00	
	Nos. 331-342 (12)	1,243.	134.20

For listings of China Clay papers see the Scott U.S. Specialized Catalogue.

For listing of other perforated stamps of designs A138, A139 and A140 see

#357-366	Bluish Paper	
#374-382, 405-407	Single line wmk.	Perf. 12
#424-430	Single line wmk.	Perf. 10
#461	Single line wmk.	Perf. 11
#462-469	Unwmkd.	Perf. 10
#498-507	Unwmkd.	Perf. 11
#519	Double line wmk.	Perf. 11
#525-530, 536	Offset printing	
#538-546	Rotary press printing	

Imperf

343	A138 1c green	5.75	4.50
	Never hinged	9.00	
344	A139 2c carmine	7.00	3.00
	Never hinged	11.00	
345	A140 3c dp violet, Type I	13.00	20.00
	Never hinged	20.00	
346	A140 4c org brown ('09)	22.50	22.50
	Never hinged	35.00	
347	A140 5c blue ('09)	40.00	32.50
	Never hinged	62.50	
	Nos. 343-347 (5)	88.25	82.50

For listings of other imperforate stamps of designs A138, A139 and A140 see

#383 & 384, 408 & 409, 459	Single line wmk.
#481-485	Unwmkd.
#531-535	Offset printing

Coil Stamps

1908-10 *Perf. 12 Horizontally*

348	A138 1c green	30.00	17.00
	Never hinged	47.50	
349	A139 2c carmine ('09)	60.00	10.00
	Never hinged	95.00	
350	A140 4c orange brown ('10)	135.00	90.00
	Never hinged	220.00	
351	A140 5c blue ('09)	150.00	125.00
	Never hinged	240.00	
	Nos. 348-351 (4)	375.00	242.00

1909 *Perf. 12 Vertically*

352	A138 1c green	67.50	35.00
	Never hinged	110.00	
353	A139 2c carmine	75.00	10.00
	Never hinged	120.00	
354	A140 4c orange brown	165.00	70.00
	Never hinged	260.00	
355	A140 5c blue	175.00	90.00
	Never hinged	280.00	
356	A140 10c yellow	2,250.	1,050.
	Never hinged	3,100.	

Beware of stamps offered as No. 356 which may be examples of No. 338 with perforations trimmed at top and/or bottom. Beware also of plentiful fakes in the marketplace of Nos. 348-355. Authentication of all these coil stamps is advised.

For listings of other coil stamps of designs A138, A139 and A140 see

#385-396, 410-413, 441-458	Single line wmk.
#486-496	Unwmkd.

Bluish Paper

This was made with 35 per cent rag stock instead of all wood pulp. The grayish blue color goes through the paper showing clearly on the back as well as on the face.

1909 *Perf. 12*

357	A138 1c green	95.00	100.00
	Never hinged	150.00	
358	A139 2c carmine	90.00	100.00
	Never hinged	145.00	
359	A140 3c dp violet, Type I	1,800.	*2,100.*
	Never hinged	2,600.	
360	A140 4c orange brown	*19,000.*	
	Never hinged	25,000.	
361	A140 5c blue	4,500.	*5,250.*
	Never hinged	*6,250.*	
362	A140 6c red orange	1,350.	*1,600.*
	Never hinged	1,950.	
363	A140 8c olive green	*20,000.*	
	Never hinged	*26,000.*	
364	A140 10c yellow	1,600.	*1,850.*
	Never hinged	2,250.	
365	A140 13c blue green	2,800.	*2,100.*
	Never hinged	4,000.	
366	A140 15c pale ultra	1,350.	*1,600.*
	Never hinged	1,950.	

Nos. 360, 363 not regularly issued.

Lincoln Centenary of Birth Issue

Lincoln — A141

1909, Feb. 12 Wmk. 191 *Perf. 12*

367	A141 2c carmine	5.50	1.75
	Never hinged	8.00	

Imperf

368	A141 2c carmine	22.50	20.00
	Never hinged	35.00	

Bluish Paper

1909 *Perf. 12*

369	A141 2c carmine	225.00	240.00
	Never hinged	325.00	

Alaska-Yukon-Pacific Exposition Issue

William H. Seward — A142

1909, June 1 Wmk. 191 *Perf. 12*

370	A142 2c carmine	9.00	2.00
	Never hinged	13.00	

1909 *Imperf.*

371	A142 2c carmine	30.00	22.50
	Never hinged	42.50	

Seattle, Wash., June 1 to Oct. 16.

Hudson-Fulton Celebration Issue

"Half Moon" and Steamship A143

1909, Sept. 25 Wmk. 191 *Perf. 12*

372	A143 2c carmine	13.00	4.50
	Never hinged	18.00	

Imperf

373	A143 2c carmine	35.00	25.00
	Never hinged	47.50	

Tercentenary of the discovery of the Hudson River and Centenary of Robert Fulton's steamship.

Designs of 1908-09 Issue

1910-11 Wmk. 190 *Perf. 12*

374	A138 1c green	6.50	.20
	Never hinged	10.00	
a.	Booklet pane of 6	140.00	*100.00*
	Never hinged	210.00	
375	A139 2c carmine	6.50	.20
	Never hinged	10.00	
a.	Booklet pane of 6	95.00	*85.00*
	Never hinged	145.00	
376	A140 3c dp vio, Type I ('11)	19.00	1.40
	Never hinged	30.00	
377	A140 4c brown ('11)	30.00	.50
	Never hinged	47.50	
378	A140 5c blue ('11)	30.00	.50
	Never hinged	47.50	
379	A140 6c red orange ('11)	35.00	.70
	Never hinged	55.00	
380	A140 8c olive green ('11)	110.00	12.50
	Never hinged	175.00	
381	A140 10c yellow ('11)	100.00	3.75
	Never hinged	160.00	
382	A140 15c pale ultra ('11)	260.00	15.00
	Never hinged	425.00	
	Nos. 374-382 (9)	597.00	34.75

1910 *Imperf.*

383	A138 1c green	2.60	2.00
	Never hinged	4.00	
384	A139 2c carmine	4.25	2.50
	Never hinged	6.50	

Coil Stamps

1910 *Perf. 12 Horizontally*

385	A138 1c green	30.00	15.00
	Never hinged	47.50	
386	A139 2c carmine	55.00	20.00
	Never hinged	87.50	

1910-11 *Perf. 12 Vertically*

387	A138 1c green	125.00	50.00
	Never hinged	200.00	
388	A139 2c carmine	750.00	350.00
	Never hinged	1,150.	
389	A140 3c dp vio, Type I ('11)	*52,500.*	*10,000.*
	Never hinged	*80,000.*	

Stamps sold as No. 388 frequently are privately perforated examples of No. 384, or examples of No. 375 with top and/or bottom perfs trimmed.

Stamps offered as No. 389 sometimes are examples of No. 376 with top and/or bottom perfs trimmed.

Expertization by competent authorities is recommended.

1910 *Perf. 8 1/2 Horizontally*

390	A138 1c green	4.50	*6.00*
	Never hinged	7.25	
391	A139 2c carmine	35.00	12.50
	Never hinged	55.00	

1910-13 *Perf. 8 1/2 Vertically*

392	A138 1c green	20.00	19.00
	Never hinged	32.50	
393	A139 2c carmine	40.00	7.75
	Never hinged	65.00	
394	A140 3c dp vio, Type I ('11)	50.00	47.50
	Never hinged	80.00	
395	A140 4c brown ('12)	50.00	42.50
	Never hinged	80.00	
396	A140 5c blue ('13)	50.00	42.50
	Never hinged	80.00	
	Nos. 392-396 (5)	210.00	159.25

Panama-Pacific Exposition Issue

Vasco Nunez de Balboa — A144

Pedro Miguel Locks, Panama Canal — A145

Golden Gate — A146

Discovery of San Francisco Bay — A147

1913 Wmk. 190 *Perf. 12*

397	A144 1c green	17.50	1.50
	Never hinged	27.50	
398	A145 2c carmine	20.00	.50
	Never hinged	32.50	
399	A146 5c blue	75.00	9.50
	Never hinged	120.00	
400	A147 10c orange yellow	125.00	20.00
	Never hinged	200.00	
400A	A147 10c orange	210.00	16.00
	Never hinged	340.00	
	Nos. 397-400A (5)	447.50	47.50
	Nos. 397-400A, never hinged	720.00	

1914-15 *Perf. 10*

401	A144 1c green	25.00	5.50
	Never hinged	40.00	
402	A145 2c carmine ('15)	75.00	1.50
	Never hinged	120.00	
403	A146 5c blue ('15)	175.00	15.00
	Never hinged	280.00	
404	A147 10c orange ('15)	925.00	62.50
	Never hinged	1,425.	
	Nos. 401-404 (4)	1,200.	84.50
	Nos. 401-404, never hinged	1,865.	

San Francisco, Cal., Feb. 20 to Dec. 4.

TYPE I

TWO CENTS

Type I. There is one shading line in the first curve of the ribbon above the left "2" and one in the second curve of the ribbon above the right "2."

The button of the toga has a faint outline.

The top line of the toga rope, from the button to the front of the throat, is also very faint.

The shading lines at the face terminate in front of the ear with little or no joining, to form a lock of hair.

Used on both flat and rotary press printings.

1912-14 Wmk. 190 *Perf. 12*

405	A140 1c green	5.25	.15
	Never hinged	8.50	
a.	Vert. pair, imperf. horiz.	*650.00*	—
b.	Booklet pane of 6	60.00	*40.00*
	Never hinged	95.00	
406	A140 2c carmine, Type I	5.00	.15
	Never hinged	8.00	
a.	Booklet pane of 6	60.00	*60.00*
	Never hinged	95.00	
b.	Double impression	—	
c.	2c lake, type II	*350.00*	—
407	A140 7c black ('14)	80.00	11.00
	Never hinged	130.00	
	Nos. 405-407 (3)	90.25	11.30

1912 *Imperf.*

408	A140 1c green	1.15	.55
	Never hinged	1.75	
409	A140 2c carmine, Type I	1.40	.60
	Never hinged	2.10	

Coil Stamps

1912 *Perf. 8 1/2 Horizontally*

410	A140 1c green	6.00	4.00
	Never hinged	9.50	
411	A140 2c carmine, Type I	9.00	3.75
	Never hinged	14.50	

Perf. 8 1/2 Vertically

412	A140 1c green	22.50	5.50
	Never hinged	35.00	
413	A140 2c carmine, Type I	42.50	1.10
	Never hinged	67.50	
	Nos. 410-413 (4)	80.00	14.35

Franklin — A148

1912-14 Wmk. 190 *Perf. 12*

414	A148 8c pale olive green	45.00	1.25
	Never hinged	72.50	
415	A148 9c salmon red ('14)	55.00	12.50
	Never hinged	87.50	
416	A148 10c orange yellow	45.00	.40
	Never hinged	72.50	
a.	10c brown yellow	*400.00*	—
	Never hinged	*575.00*	
417	A148 12c claret brown ('14)	50.00	4.25
	Never hinged	80.00	
418	A148 15c gray	85.00	3.50
	Never hinged	135.00	
419	A148 20c ultra ('14)	200.00	15.00
	Never hinged	325.00	
420	A148 30c orange red ('14)	125.00	15.00
	Never hinged	200.00	
421	A148 50c violet ('14)	425.00	17.50
	Never hinged	700.00	
	Nos. 414-421 (8)	1,030.	69.40

No. 421 almost always has an offset of the frame lines on the back under the gum. No. 422 does not have this offset.

VALUES FOR VERY FINE STAMPS
Please note: Stamps are valued in the grade of Very Fine unless otherwise indicated.

UNITED STATES 11

1912, Feb. 12 Wmk. 191 *Perf. 12*

422 A148 50c violet 250.00 15.00
Never hinged 400.00
423 A148 $1 violet brown 525.00 60.00
Never hinged 825.00

Other stamps of type A148:

#431-440	Single line wmk.	Perf. 10
#460	Double line wmk.	Perf. 10
#470-478	Unwmkd.	Perf. 10
#508-518	Unwmkd.	Perf. 11

1914-15 Wmk. 190 *Perf. 10*

424 A140 1c green 2.30 .20
Never hinged 3.75
a. Perf. 12x10 *1,750. 1,500.*
b. Perf. 10x12 *750.00*
c. Vert. pair, imperf. horiz. *425.00 250.00*
d. Booklet pane of 6 4.75 *2.00*
Never hinged 7.25
e. As "d," imperf. *1,600.*

Most copies of No. 424b are precanceled Dayton, Ohio, to which the value applies.
All known examples of No. 424e are without gum.

425 A140 2c rose red, Type I 2.20 .20
Never hinged 3.50
c. Perf. 10x12 —
d. Perf. 12x10 *5,000. 2,000.*
e. Booklet pane of 6 16.00 *12.50*
Never hinged 25.00
426 A140 3c deep vio, Type I 14.00 1.25
Never hinged 22.50
427 A140 4c brown 35.00 .50
Never hinged 55.00
428 A140 5c blue 32.50 .50
Never hinged 52.50
a. Perf. 12x10 *4,000.*
429 A140 6c red orange 47.50 1.40
Never hinged 75.00
430 A140 7c black 85.00 4.00
Never hinged 135.00
431 A148 8c pale olive green 35.00 1.50
Never hinged 55.00
432 A148 9c salmon red 50.00 7.50
Never hinged 80.00
433 A148 10c orange yellow 47.50 .40
Never hinged 75.00
434 A148 11c dark green ('15) 22.50 7.50
Never hinged 35.00
435 A148 12c claret brown 26.00 4.00
Never hinged 41.00
a. 12c copper red 29.00 4.00
Never hinged 46.00
437 A148 15c gray 125.00 7.25
Never hinged 200.00
438 A148 20c ultra 210.00 4.00
Never hinged 340.00
439 A148 30c orange red 250.00 16.00
Never hinged 400.00
440 A148 50c violet ('15) 550.00 16.00
Never hinged 875.00
Nos. 424-440 (16) 1,534. 72.20

Coil Stamps

1914 *Perf. 10 Horizontally*

441 A140 1c green 1.00 1.00
Never hinged 1.55
442 A140 2c carmine, Type I 8.00 6.00
Never hinged 12.50

1914 *Perf. 10 Vertically*

443 A140 1c green 22.50 5.00
Never hinged 35.00
444 A140 2c carmine, Type I 35.00 1.50
Never hinged 52.50
445 A140 3c violet, Type I 220.00 125.00
Never hinged 340.00
446 A140 4c brown 120.00 42.50
Never hinged 190.00
447 A140 5c blue 42.50 27.50
Never hinged 65.00
Nos. 443-447 (5) 440.00 201.50

TYPE II

TWO CENTS
Type II. Shading lines in ribbons as on type I.
The toga button, rope, and shading lines are heavy.
The shading lines of the face at the lock of hair end in a strong vertical curved line.
Used on rotary press printings only.

TYPE III

TWO CENTS
Type III. Two lines of shading in the curves of the ribbons.
Other characteristics similar to type II.
Used on rotary press printings only.

Fraudulently altered copies of Type III (Nos. 455, 488, 492 and 540) have had one line of shading scraped off to make them resemble Type II (Nos. 454, 487, 491 and 539).

ROTARY PRESS STAMPS
The Rotary Press stamps are printed from plates that are curved to fit around a cylinder. This curvature produces stamps that are slightly larger, either horizontally or vertically, than those printed from flat plates. Stamps from flat plates measure about 18½-19mm wide by 22mm high. When the impressions are placed sideways on the curved plates the stamps are 19½-20mm wide; when they are placed vertically the stamps are 23mm high.

Coil Stamps
Rotary Press Printing

1915-16 *Perf. 10 Horizontally*

448 A140 1c green 6.00 3.25
Never hinged 9.50
449 A140 2c red, Type I 2,400. 450.00
Never hinged 3,500.
450 A140 2c car, Type III ('16) 9.50 3.00
Never hinged 15.00

1914-16 *Perf. 10 Vertically*

452 A140 1c green 9.50 2.00
Never hinged 15.00
453 A140 2c carmine rose, Type I 110.00 4.25
Never hinged 175.00
454 A140 2c red, Type II 82.50 10.00
Never hinged 130.00
455 A140 2c carmine, Type III 8.50 1.00
Never hinged 13.50
456 A140 3c violet, Type I ('16) 240.00 90.00
Never hinged 375.00
457 A140 4c brown ('16) 25.00 17.50
Never hinged 40.00
458 A140 5c blue ('16) 30.00 17.50
Never hinged 47.50
Nos. 452-458 (7) 505.50 142.25

1914, June 30 *Imperf.*

459 A140 2c car, Type I 250.00 *900.00*
Never hinged 350.00

No. 459 is a horizontal coil.
The used value is for a copy with a contemporaneous cancel.

Flat Plate Printings

1915, Feb. 8 Wmk. 191 *Perf. 10*

460 A148 $1 violet black 775.00 85.00
Never hinged 1,150.

1915, June 17 Wmk. 190 *Perf. 11*

461 A140 2c pale carmine red, Type I 125.00 *250.00*
Never hinged 180.00

Fraudulently perforated copies of No. 409 are offered as No. 461.
The used value is for a copy with a contemporaneous cancel.

Unwatermarked
From 1916 onward all postage stamps except Nos. 519 and 832b are on unwatermarked paper.

1916-17 Unwmk. *Perf. 10*

462 A140 1c green 6.50 .35
Never hinged 10.00
a. Booklet pane of 6 9.00 *1.60*
Never hinged 13.50
463 A140 2c carmine, Type I 4.25 .25
Never hinged 6.75
a. Booklet pane of 6 90.00 *45.00*
Never hinged 135.00
464 A140 3c violet, Type I 75.00 12.50
Never hinged 120.00
465 A140 4c orange brown 45.00 1.70
Never hinged 72.50
466 A140 5c blue 75.00 1.70
Never hinged 120.00
467 A140 5c car (error in plate of 2c, '17) 550.00 675.00
Never hinged 825.00
468 A140 6c red orange 95.00 7.00
Never hinged 150.00
469 A140 7c black 120.00 11.00
Never hinged 190.00
470 A148 8c olive green 57.50 5.50
Never hinged 92.50
471 A148 9c salmon red 57.50 14.00
Never hinged 97.50
472 A148 10c orange yel 105.00 1.25
Never hinged 165.00
473 A148 11c dark green 37.50 16.00
Never hinged 60.00
474 A148 12c claret brown 50.00 5.00
Never hinged 80.00
475 A148 15c gray 190.00 10.50
Never hinged 300.00
476 A148 20c lt ultra 240.00 12.00
Never hinged 375.00
476A A148 30c orange red *4,000.* —
Never hinged *5,250.*
477 A148 50c lt violet ('17) 950.00 60.00
Never hinged 1,500.
478 A148 $1 violet black 725.00 16.00
Never hinged 1,100.
Nos. 462-466,468-476,477-478 (16) 2,833. 174.75

No. 476A is valued in the grade of fine.

Types of 1903 Issue

1917, Mar. 22 *Perf. 10*

479 A127 $2 dark blue 300.00 40.00
Never hinged 500.00
480 A128 $5 light green 240.00 42.50
Never hinged 375.00

TYPE Ia

TWO CENTS
Type Ia. Design characteristics similar to type I except that all lines of design are stronger.
The toga button, toga rope and rope shading lines are heavy. The latter characteristics are those of type II, which, however, occur only on impressions from rotary plates.
Used only on flat plates 10208 and 10209.

TYPE II

THREE CENTS
Type II. The top line of the toga rope is strong and the rope shading lines are heavy and complete.
The line between the lips is heavy.
Used on both flat plate and rotary press printings.

1916-17 *Imperf.*

481 A140 1c green 1.00 .55
Never hinged 1.50
482 A140 2c carmine, Type I 1.50 1.25
Never hinged 2.25
482A A140 2c dp rose, Type Ia *11,000.*

No. 482A was issued imperforate but all copies were privately perforated with large oblong perforations at the sides (Schermack type III).

No. 500 exists with imperforate top sheet margin. Copies have been altered by trimming perforations. Some also have faked Schermack perfs.

483 A140 3c violet, Type I ('17) 14.00 7.50
Never hinged 21.00
484 A140 3c violet, Type II 11.00 5.00
Never hinged 16.50
485 A140 5c car (error in plate of 2c) ('17) *12,000.*

Although #485 is valued as a single stamp, such examples are not seen in the marketplace. The stamp is collected as the center stamps in a block of 9 with 8 #482 (value with #485 never hinged, $15,000) or as two center stamps in a block of 12 (value with both #485 never hinged, $26,000).

Coil Stamps
Rotary Press Printing

1916-19 *Perf. 10 Horizontally*

486 A140 1c green ('18) .90 .25
Never hinged 1.40
487 A140 2c car, Type II 14.00 3.00
Never hinged 22.50
488 A140 2c car, Type III ('19) 2.50 1.75
Never hinged 3.75
489 A140 3c violet, Type I ('17) 5.00 1.50
Never hinged 7.50
Nos. 486-489 (4) 22.40 6.50

1916-22 *Perf. 10 Vertically*

490 A140 1c green .55 .25
Never hinged .80
491 A140 2c car, Type II 2,100. 550.00
Never hinged 2,750.
492 A140 2c car, Type III 9.00 .25
Never hinged 14.00
493 A140 3c vio, Type I ('17) 16.00 3.00
Never hinged 25.00
494 A140 3c vio, Type II ('18) 10.00 1.00
Never hinged 15.00
495 A140 4c org brown ('17) 10.00 4.00
Never hinged 15.00
496 A140 5c blue ('19) 3.50 1.00
Never hinged 5.25
497 A148 10c orange yel ('22) 20.00 10.50
Never hinged 30.00
Nos. 490,492-497 (7) 69.05 20.00

See note above #448 regarding #487, 491.

Blind Perfs.
Listings of imperforate-between varieties are for examples which show no trace of "blind perfs.," traces of impressions from the perforating pins which do not cut into the paper.

Types of 1912-14 Issue

1917-19 Flat Plate Printings *Perf. 11*

498 A140 1c green .35 .25
Never hinged .60
a. Vert. pair, imperf. horiz. 175.00
b. Horiz. pair, imperf. btwn. 100.00
c. Vert. pair, imperf. btwn. *450.00* —
d. Double impression 175.00
e. Booklet pane of 6 2.50 *.50*
Never hinged 4.00
f. Booklet pane of 30 *1,000.*
Never hinged *1,300.*
499 A140 2c rose, Type I .35 .25
Never hinged .60
a. Vert. pair, imperf. horiz. 150.00
b. Horiz. pair, imperf. vert. 275.00 *150.00*
c. Vert. pair, imperf. btwn. *650.00 225.00*
e. Booklet pane of 6 4.00 *.65*
Never hinged 6.25
f. Booklet pane of 30 *27,500.*
Never hinged *33,000.*
g. Double impression 160.00 —
500 A140 2c deep rose, Type Ia 250.00 180.00
Never hinged 400.00
501 A140 3c lt violet, Type I 11.00 .25
Never hinged 17.50
b. Booklet pane of 6 70.00 *20.00*
Never hinged 110.00
c. Vert. pair, imperf. horiz. 350.00
d. Double impression 275.00
502 A140 3c dk violet, Type II 14.00 .40
Never hinged 22.50
b. Booklet pane of 6 60.00 *30.00*
Never hinged 92.50
c. Vert. pair, imperf. horiz. 250.00 125.00
d. Double impression 200.00
503 A140 4c brown 10.00 .25
Never hinged 16.00
b. Double impression —
504 A140 5c blue 9.00 .25
Never hinged 14.50
a. Horiz. pair, imperf. btwn. *2,500.* —
505 A140 5c rose (error in plate of 2c) 375.00 500.00
Never hinged 575.00
506 A140 6c red orange 12.50 .25
Never hinged 20.00
507 A140 7c black 27.50 1.10
Never hinged 45.00
508 A148 8c olive bister 12.00 .50
Never hinged 19.00
b. Vert. pair, imperf. btwn. — —
509 A148 9c salmon red 14.00 1.75
Never hinged 22.50
510 A148 10c orange yellow 17.00 .15
Never hinged 27.50
a. 10c brown yellow *350.00* —
Never hinged *525.00*
511 A148 11c lt green 9.00 2.50
Never hinged 14.50

512	A148	12c claret brown	9.00	.35
		Never hinged	14.50	
		12c brown carmine	9.50	.40
		Never hinged	15.00	
513	A148	13c apple green ('19)	11.00	6.00
		Never hinged	17.50	
514	A148	15c gray	37.50	1.00
		Never hinged	60.00	
515	A148	20c light ultra	47.50	.25
		Never hinged	75.00	
	b.	Vert. pair, imperf. btwn.	325.00	
	c.	Double impression	1,250.	

Beware of pairs with blind perforations inside the design of the top stamp that are offered as No. 515b.

516	A148	30c orange red	37.50	1.00
		Never hinged	60.00	
	b.	Double impression	—	
517	A148	50c red violet	67.50	.50
		Never hinged	110.00	
	b.	Vert. pair, imperf. btwn. & at bottom	1,750.	1,000.
518	A148	$1 violet brown	52.50	1.50
		Never hinged	85.00	
	b.	$1 deep brown	1,500.	825.00
		Never hinged	2,400.	
		Nos. 498-504,506-518 (20)	649.20	198.50

No. 518b is valued in the grade of fine to very fine.

Type of 1908-09 Issue
1917, Oct. 10   Wmk. 191   Perf. 11

519	A139	2c carmine	375.00	700.00
		Never hinged	600.00	

Fraudulently perforated copies of No. 344 are offered as No. 519.
The used value is for a stamp with a contemporaneous cancel.

Franklin — A149

1918, Aug. 19   Unwmk.   Perf. 11

523	A149	$2 orange red & blk	625.00	230.00
		Never hinged	950.00	
524	A149	$5 dp grn & black	220.00	35.00
		Never hinged	340.00	

See No. 547 for $2 carmine & black.

Types of 1912-14 Issue

TYPE IV

TWO CENTS
Type IV. Top line of toga rope is broken. Shading lines in toga button are so arranged that the curving of the first and last form a "D (reversed) ID."
Line of color in left "2" is very thin and usually broken.
Used on offset printings only.

TYPE V

TWO CENTS
Type V. Top line of toga is complete.
Five vertical shading lines in toga button.
Line of color in left "2" is very thin and usually broken.

Shading dots on the nose and lip are as indicated on the diagram.
Used on offset printings only.

TYPE Va

TWO CENTS
Type Va. Characteristics same as type V, except in shading dots of nose. Third row from bottom has 4 dots instead of 6. Overall height of type Va is 1/3mm less than type V.
Used on offset printings only.

TYPE VI

TWO CENTS
Type VI. General characteristics same as type V, except that line of color in left "2" is very heavy.
Used on offset printings only.

TYPE VII

TWO CENTS
Type VII. Line of color in left "2" is invariably continuous, clearly defined, and heavier than in type V or Va, but not as heavy as in type VI.
Additional vertical row of dots has been added to the upper lip.
Numerous additional dots have been added to hair on top of head.
Used on offset printings only.

The values of stamps in extremely fine to superb condition are greater than catalogue value.

TYPE III

THREE CENTS
Type III. The top line of the toga rope is strong but the fifth shading line is missing as in type I.
Center shading line of the toga button consists of two dashes with a central dot.
The "P" and "O" of "POSTAGE" are separated by a line of color.
The frame line at the bottom of the vignette is complete.
Used on offset printings only.

TYPE IV

THREE CENTS
Type IV. Shading lines of toga rope are complete. Second and fourth shading lines in toga button are broken in the middle and the third line is continuous with a dot in the center.
"P" and "O" of "POSTAGE" are joined.
Frame line at bottom of vignette is broken.
Used on offset printings only.

1918-20   Offset Printing   Perf. 11

525	A140	1c gray green	2.50	.50
		Never hinged	3.90	
	a.	1c dark green	2.75	.95
		Never hinged	4.25	
	c.	Horiz. pair, imperf. btwn.	100.00	
	d.	Double impression	27.50	25.00
526	A140	2c car, Type IV ('20)	27.50	3.50
		Never hinged	44.00	
527	A140	2c car, Type V ('20)	20.00	1.00
		Never hinged	32.50	
	a.	Double impression	60.00	10.00
	b.	Vert. pair, imperf. horiz.	600.00	
	c.	Horiz. pair, imperf. vert.	1,000.	—
528	A140	2c car, Type Va ('20)	9.00	.25
		Never hinged	14.50	
	c.	Double impression	27.50	
	g.	Vert. pair, imperf. btwn.	1,000.	
528A	A140	2c car, Type VI ('20)	52.50	1.50
		Never hinged	82.50	
	d.	Double impression	160.00	—
	f.	Vert. pair, imperf. horiz.	—	
	h.	Vert. pair, imperf. btwn.	1,000.	
528B	A140	2c car, Type VII ('20)	22.50	.35
		Never hinged	35.00	
	e.	Double impression	70.00	
529	A140	3c vio, Type III	3.25	.25
		Never hinged	5.25	
	a.	Double impression	32.50	—
	b.	Printed on both sides	450.00	
530	A140	3c pur, Type IV	1.60	.20
		Never hinged	2.50	
	a.	Double impression	20.00	6.00
	b.	Printed on both sides	250.00	
		Nos. 525-530 (8)	138.85	7.55

1918-20   Imperf.

531	A140	1c green ('19)	9.00	8.00
		Never hinged	14.50	
532	A140	2c car rose, Type IV ('20)	40.00	27.50
		Never hinged	62.50	
533	A140	2c car, Type V	150.00	80.00
		Never hinged	240.00	
534	A140	2c car, Type Va ('20)	11.00	6.50
		Never hinged	17.50	
534A	A140	2c car, Type VI ('20)	40.00	22.50
		Never hinged	62.50	
534B	A140	2c car, Type VII ('20)	1,700.	850.00
		Never hinged	2,500.	
535	A140	3c vio, Type IV	9.00	5.00
		Never hinged	14.50	
	a.	Double impression	100.00	—
		Nos. 531-534A,535 (6)	259.00	149.50

1919, Aug. 15   Perf. 12½

536	A140	1c gray green	17.50	20.00
		Never hinged	27.50	
	a.	Horiz. pair, imperf. vert.	700.00	

Victory Issue

"Victory" and Flags of the Allies — A150

Flat Plate Printing
1919, Mar. 3   Engr.   Perf. 11

537	A150	3c violet	9.50	3.25
		Never hinged	15.00	
	a.	3c deep red violet	550.00	150.00
		Never hinged	800.00	
	b.	3c light reddish violet	9.50	3.00
		Never hinged	15.00	
	c.	3c red violet	40.00	12.00
		Never hinged	62.50	

Victory of Allies in World War I.
No. 537a is valued in the grade of fine.

Rotary Press Printings

1919   Perf. 11x10
Size: 19½ to 20mm wide by 22 to 22¼mm high

538	A140	1c green	11.00	8.50
		Never hinged	16.50	
	a.	Vert. pair, imperf. horiz.	50.00	100.00
		Never hinged	75.00	
539	A140	2c carmine rose, Type II	2,800.	3,750.
		Never hinged	4,000.	
540	A140	2c carmine rose, Type III	12.00	8.50
		Never hinged	18.00	
	a.	Vert. pair, imperf. horiz.	50.00	100.00
		Never hinged	75.00	
	b.	Horiz. pair, imperf. vert.	750.00	
541	A140	3c vio, Type II	37.50	30.00
		Never hinged	57.50	

The part perforate varieties of Nos. 538a and 540a were issued in sheets and may be had in blocks; similar part perforate varieties, Nos. 490 and 492, are from coils and are found only in strips.
See note over No. 448 regarding No. 539.
No. 539 is valued in the grade of fine.

Size: 19x22½-22¾mm
1920, May 26   Perf. 10x11

542	A140	1c green	13.50	1.10
		Never hinged	20.00	

Size: 19x22½mm
1921   Perf. 10

543	A140	1c green	.50	.25
		Never hinged	.75	
	a.	Horiz. pair, imperf. btwn.	1,100.	

Size: 19x22½mm
1922   Perf. 11

544	A140	1c green	13,500.	3,250.
		Never hinged	20,000.	

No. 544 is valued in the grade of fine.

Size: 19½-20x22mm
1921   Perf. 11

545	A140	1c green	150.00	160.00
		Never hinged	240.00	
546	A140	2c car rose, Type III	100.00	150.00
		Never hinged	160.00	

Flat Plate Printing
1920, Nov. 1   Perf. 11

547	A149	$2 carmine & black	190.00	40.00
		Never hinged	300.00	

Pilgrim Tercentenary Issue

"Mayflower" A151

Landing of the Pilgrims A152

Signing of the Compact — A153

1920, Dec. 21 *Perf. 11*

548 A151 1c green	4.50	2.25
Never hinged	6.75	
549 A152 2c carmine rose	6.50	1.60
Never hinged	10.00	
550 A153 5c deep blue	42.50	12.50
Never hinged	65.00	
Nos. 548-550 (3)	53.50	16.35
Nos. 548-550, never hinged	81.75	

Tercentenary of the landing of the Pilgrims at Plymouth, Mass.

Nathan Hale
A154

Franklin
A155

Harding
A156

Washington
A157

Lincoln
A158

Martha Washington
A159

Theodore Roosevelt
A160

Garfield
A161

McKinley
A162

Grant
A163

Jefferson
A164

Monroe
A165

Rutherford B. Hayes
A166

Grover Cleveland
A167

American Indian
A168

Statue of Liberty
A169

Golden Gate — A170

Niagara Falls — A171

Buffalo
A172

Arlington Amphitheater
A173

Lincoln Memorial
A174

US Capitol
A175

Head of Freedom Statue, Capitol Dome — A176

1922-25 *Perf. 11*

551 A154 ½c olive brn ('25)	.15	.15
Never hinged	.25	
552 A155 1c dp green ('23)	1.40	.15
Never hinged	2.50	
a. Booket pane of 6	6.00	*.80*
Never hinged	9.50	
553 A156 1½c yel brn ('25)	2.60	.15
Never hinged	3.90	
554 A157 2c carmine ('23)	1.40	.15
Never hinged	2.20	
a. Horiz. pair, imperf. vert.	200.00	
b. Vert. pair, imperf. horiz.	*500.00*	
c. Booklet pane of 6	6.50	*1.50*
Never hinged	10.50	
555 A158 3c violet ('23)	18.00	1.00
Never hinged	28.50	
556 A159 4c yel brn ('23)	19.00	.25
Never hinged	30.00	
a. Vert. pair, imperf. horiz.	—	
557 A160 5c dark blue	19.00	.20
Never hinged	30.00	
a. Imperf., pair	*1,500.*	
b. Horiz. pair, imperf. vert.	—	
558 A161 6c red orange	35.00	.85
Never hinged	55.00	
559 A162 7c black ('23)	9.00	.55
Never hinged	13.50	
560 A163 8c olive grn ('23)	47.50	.60
Never hinged	75.00	
561 A164 9c rose ('23)	13.50	1.10
Never hinged	22.50	
562 A165 10c orange ('23)	18.00	.15
Never hinged	29.00	
a. Vert. pair, imperf. horiz.	*1,250.*	
b. Imperf., pair	*1,250.*	
563 A166 11c light blue	1.30	.40
Never hinged	2.20	
d. Imperf., pair		—
564 A167 12c brn vio ('23)	6.00	.15
Never hinged	9.50	
a. Horiz. pair, imperf. vert.	*1,000.*	
565 A168 14c blue ('23)	4.00	.75
Never hinged	6.50	
566 A169 15c gray	22.50	.15
Never hinged	37.50	
567 A170 20c car rose ('23)	21.00	.15
Never hinged	35.00	
a. Horiz. pair, imperf. vert.	*1,500.*	
568 A171 25c yellow green	18.00	.45
Never hinged	29.00	
b. Vert. pair, imperf. horiz.	*850.00*	
569 A172 30c olive brn ('23)	32.50	.35
Never hinged	52.50	
570 A173 50c lilac	55.00	.15
Never hinged	87.50	
571 A174 $1 vio black ('23)	45.00	.45
Never hinged	72.50	
572 A175 $2 dp blue ('23)	90.00	9.00
Never hinged	150.00	
573 A176 $5 car & bl ('23)	150.00	15.00
Never hinged	250.00	
a. $5 carmine lake & dark blue	175.00	16.00
Never hinged	280.00	
Nos. 551-573 (23)	629.85	32.30
Nos. 551-573, never hinged	1,023.	

For listings of other perforated stamps of designs A154 to A176 see

#578-579	Perf. 11x10
#581-591	Perf. 10
#594-595	Perf. 11
#632-642, 653, 692-696	Perf. 11x10½
#697-701	Perf. 10½x11

This series includes Nos. 622-623 (perf. 11).

1923-25 *Imperf.*

575 A155 1c green	7.50	5.00
Never hinged	11.50	
576 A156 1½c yel brn ('25)	1.60	1.50
Never hinged	2.40	
577 A157 2c carmine	1.75	1.25
Never hinged	2.60	
Nos. 575-577 (3)	10.85	7.75
Nos. 555-577, never hinged	16.50	

The 1½c A156 rotary press imperforate is listed as No. 631.

Rotary Press Printings

Perf. 11x10

578 A155 1c green	95.00	*140.00*
Never hinged	150.00	
579 A157 2c carmine	85.00	*125.00*
Never hinged	135.00	

Nos. 578-579 were made from coil waste of Nos. 597, 599 and measure approximately 19¾x22¼mm.

1923-26 *Perf. 10*

581 A155 1c green	9.50	.65
Never hinged	15.00	
582 A156 1½c brown ('25)	4.50	.60
Never hinged	7.25	
583 A157 2c carmine ('24)	2.50	.25
Never hinged	4.00	
a. Booklet pane of 6	85.00	*27.50*
Never hinged	130.00	
584 A158 3c violet ('25)	26.50	2.25
Never hinged	42.50	
585 A159 4c yel brn ('25)	16.00	.45
Never hinged	26.00	
586 A160 5c blue ('25)	16.00	.25
Never hinged	26.00	
a. Horiz. pair, imperf. btwn.		—
587 A161 6c red org ('25)	7.50	.35
Never hinged	12.00	
588 A162 7c black ('26)	10.50	5.50
Never hinged	17.00	
589 A163 8c ol grn ('26)	25.00	3.50
Never hinged	40.00	
590 A164 9c rose ('26)	5.00	2.25
Never hinged	8.00	
591 A165 10c orange ('25)	60.00	.25
Never hinged	95.00	
Nos. 581-591 (11)	183.00	16.30
Nos. 581-591, never hinged	292.75	

Perf. 11

594 A155 1c green	*18,000.*	5,500.
595 A157 2c carmine	275.	300.
Never hinged	425.	

Nos. 594-595 were made from coil waste of Nos. 597 and 599, and measure approximately 19¾x22¼mm.

No. 594 unused is valued without gum; both unused and used are valued with perforations just touching frameline on one side.

Perf. 11

596 A155 1c green		*60,000.*
Precanceled		*40,000.*

No. 596 was made from rotary press sheet waste and measures approximately 19¼x22½mm. A majority of the copies carry the Bureau precancel "Kansas City, Mo." No. 596 is valued in the grade of fine.

ROTARY PRESS DOUBLE PAPER

The web of paper used on rotary presses must be continuous, therefore any break in the paper must be lapped and pasted, causing the "double paper" varieties. These are no longer listed since they may occur on any rotary press stamp.

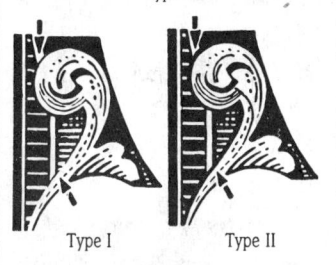

Type I

Type II

Type I

Type II

Type I. No heavy hair lines at top center of head. Outline of left acanthus scroll generally faint at top and toward base at left side.

Type II. The heavy hair lines at top center of head; two being outstanding in the white area. Outline of left acanthus scroll very strong and clearly defined at top (under left edge of lettered panel) and at lower curve (above and to left of numeral oval). Type II is found only on Nos. 599A and 634A.

Coil Stamps

Rotary Press Printing

1923-29 *Perf. 10 Vertically*

597 A155 1c green	.30	.15
Never hinged	.45	
598 A156 1½c brown ('25)	1.00	.15
Never hinged	1.50	
599 A157 2c car, Type I ('23)	.40	.15
Never hinged	.60	
599A A157 2c car, Type II ('29)	125.00	11.00
Never hinged	200.00	
600 A158 3c violet ('24)	7.25	.15
Never hinged	11.00	
601 A159 4c yellow brown	4.25	.35
Never hinged	6.50	
602 A160 5c dk bl ('24)	1.75	.15
Never hinged	2.60	
603 A165 10c orange ('24)	4.00	.15
Never hinged	6.00	

Perf. 10 Horizontally

604 A155 1c green ('24)	.35	.15
Never hinged	.50	
605 A156 1½c yel brn ('25)	.35	.15
Never hinged	.50	
606 A157 2c carmine	.35	.20
Never hinged	.50	
Nos. 597-599,600-606 (10)	20.00	1.75
Nos. 597-599, never hinged	30.15	

Harding Memorial Issue

Warren G. Harding — A177

Flat Plate Printing
(19¼x22¼mm)

1923, Sept. 1 *Perf. 11*

610 A177 2c black	.65	.15
Never hinged	1.00	
a. Horiz. pair, imperf. vert.	*1,750.*	

1923, Nov. 15 *Imperf.*

611 A177 2c black	6.50	4.00
Never hinged	10.00	

Rotary Press Printing
(19¼x22½mm)

1923, Sept. 12 *Perf. 10*

612 A177 2c black	16.00	1.75
Never hinged	24.00	

1923 *Perf. 11*

613 A177 2c black		*20,000.*

Tribute to President Warren G. Harding, who died August 2, 1923.

Nos. 610a, 613 valued in the grade of fine.

Huguenot-Walloon Tercentenary Issue

"New Netherland"
A178

Landing at Fort Orange — A179

Monument to Jan Ribault at Duvall County, Fla. — A180

Flat Plate Printings

1924, May 1 *Perf. 11*

614 A178 1c dark green	3.00	3.25
Never hinged	4.25	
615 A179 2c carmine rose	6.00	2.10
Never hinged	8.50	
616 A180 5c dark blue	25.00	12.50
Never hinged	35.00	
Nos. 614-616 (3)	34.00	17.85
Nos. 614-616, never hinged	47.75	

Tercentenary of the settling of the Walloons and in honor of the Huguenots.

UNITED STATES

Lexington-Concord Issue

Washington at Cambridge A181

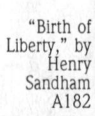

"Birth of Liberty," by Henry Sandham A182

The Minute Man, by Daniel Chester French A183

1925, Apr. 4		Perf. 11	
617 A181	1c deep green	2.80	2.40
	Never hinged	4.00	
618 A182	2c carmine rose	5.50	3.90
	Never hinged	7.75	
619 A183	5c dark blue	22.50	12.50
	Never hinged	32.50	
	Nos. 617-619 (3)	30.80	18.80
	Nos. 617-619, never hinged	44.25	

150th anniv. of the Battle of Lexington-Concord.

Norse-American Issue

Sloop "Restaurationen" A184

Viking Ship A185

1925, May 18		Perf. 11	
620 A184	2c carmine & black	4.00	3.00
	Never hinged	6.00	
621 A185	5c dk blue & black	15.00	10.50
	Never hinged	22.50	

100th anniv. of the arrival in NY on Oct. 9, 1825, of the sloop "Restaurationen" with the first group of immigrants from Norway to the US.

Benjamin Harrison A186

Woodrow Wilson A187

1925-26		Perf. 11	
622 A186	13c green ('26)	13.50	.45
	Never hinged	21.00	
623 A187	17c black	15.00	.25
	Never hinged	24.00	

Sesquicentennial Exposition Issue

Liberty Bell — A188

1926, May 10		Perf. 11	
627 A188	2c carmine rose	3.25	.50
	Never hinged	4.50	

150th anniv. of the Declaration of Independence, Philadelphia, June 1-Dec. 1.

Statue of John Ericsson A189

Alexander Hamilton's Battery A190

Ericsson Memorial Issue

1926, May 29		Perf. 11	
628 A189	5c gray lilac	6.50	3.25
	Never hinged	9.50	

John Ericsson, builder of the "Monitor."

Battle of White Plains Issue

1926, Oct. 18		Perf. 11	
629 A190	2c carmine rose	2.25	1.70
	Never hinged	3.25	
a.	Vertical pair, imperf. btwn.		

Battle of White Plains, NY, 150th anniv.

International Philatelic Exhibition
Souvenir Sheet

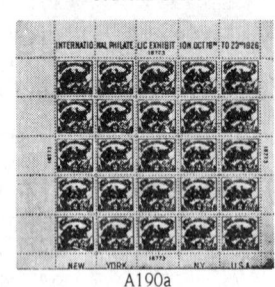

A190a

1926, Oct. 18		Perf. 11	
630 A190a	2c carmine rose, sheet of 25	400.00	450.00
	Never hinged	550.00	

Intl. Phil. Exhib. in NYC, Oct. 16-23. Size: 158-160¼x136-146½mm.
Condition Valued:
Centering: Overall centering will average very fine, but individual stamps may be better or worse.
Perforations: No folds along rows of perforations.
Gum: There may be some light gum bends but no gum creases.
Hinging: There may be hinge marks in the selvage and on up to two or three stamps, but no heavy hingling or hinge remnants in the ungummed portion of the wide selvage.
Margins: Top panes should have about ½ inch bottom margin and 1 inch top margin. Bottom panes should have about ½ inch top margin and just under ¾ inch bottom margin. Both will have one wide side (usually 1½ inches plus) and one narrow (½ inch) side margin. The wide margin corner will have a small diagonal notch on top panes.

Types of 1922-26
Rotary Press Printings

1926, Aug. 27		Imperf.	
631 A156	1½c yellow brown	2.00	1.70
	Never hinged	2.75	

1926-34		Perf. 11x10½	
632 A155	1c green ('27)	.15	.15
	Never hinged	.15	
a.	Booklet pane of 6	5.50	1.25
	Never hinged	7.00	
b.	Vert. pair, imperf. btwn.	1,600.	125.00
	Never hinged	2,500.	
633 A156	1½c yel brown ('27)	2.00	.15
	Never hinged	2.60	
634 A157	2c car, Type I	.15	.15
	Never hinged	.15	
b.	2c carmine lake		—
c.	Horiz. pair, imperf. btwn.	2,000.	
d.	Booklet pane of 6	1.75	.75
	Never hinged	2.50	
634A A157	2c car, Type II ('28)	350.00	13.50
	Never hinged	475.00	
635 A158	3c violet ('27)	.45	.15
	Never hinged	.55	
a.	3c bright violet ('34)	.25	.15
	Never hinged	.30	
636 A159	4c yel brown ('27)	2.25	.15
	Never hinged	3.00	
637 A160	5c dk blue ('27)	2.25	.15
	Never hinged	3.00	
638 A161	6c red orange ('27)	2.25	.15
	Never hinged	3.00	
639 A162	7c black ('27)	2.25	.15
	Never hinged	3.00	
a.	Vert. pair, imperf. btwn.	275.00	85.00
640 A163	8c ol grn ('27)	2.25	.15
	Never hinged	3.00	
641 A164	9c rose ('27)	2.25	.15
	Never hinged	3.00	
642 A165	10c orange ('27)	3.75	.15
	Never hinged	5.00	
	Nos. 632-634,635-642 (11)	20.00	1.65
	Nos. 632-634, 635-642 never hinged	26.45	

The 1½c, 2c, 4c, 5c, 6c, 8c imperf. (dry print) are printer's waste.
For ½c, 11c-50c see Nos. 653, 692-701.

Vermont Sesquicentennial Issue

Green Mountain Boy — A191

Flat Plate Printing

1927, Aug. 3		Perf. 11	
643 A191	2c carmine rose	1.40	.80
	Never hinged	2.00	

Battle of Bennington, Vt., and independence of the State of Vermont, 150th anniv.

The Surrender of General Burgoyne, by John Trumbull A192

Washington at Prayer A193

Burgoyne Campaign Issue

1927, Aug. 3		Perf. 11	
644 A192	2c carmine rose	3.50	2.10
	Never hinged	5.00	

Battles of Bennington, Oriskany, Fort Stanwix and Saratoga.

Valley Forge Issue

1928, May 26		Perf. 11	
645 A193	2c carmine rose	1.05	.40
	Never hinged	1.40	

150th anniv. of Washington's encampment at Valley Forge, Pa.

Battle of Monmouth Issue

No. 634 Overprinted **MOLLY PITCHER**

Rotary Press Printing

1928, Oct. 20		Perf. 11x10½	
646 A157	2c carmine	1.10	1.10
	Never hinged	1.45	
a.	"Pitcher" only		

The normal space between a vertical pair of the overprints is 18mm, but pairs are known with the space measuring 28mm.
150th anniv. of the Battle of Monmouth, NJ, and as a memorial to "Molly Pitcher" (Mary Ludwig Hays), the heroine of the battle.

Hawaii Sesquicentennial Issue

Nos. 634 and 637 Overprinted **HAWAII 1778 - 1928**

Rotary Press Printing

1928, Aug. 13		Perf. 11x10½	
647 A157	2c carmine	5.00	4.50
	Never hinged	6.75	
648 A160	5c dark blue	14.50	13.50
	Never hinged	20.00	

150th anniv. of the discovery of the Hawaiian Islands by Captain Cook.
These stamps were on sale at post offices in the Hawaiian Islands and at the Postal Agency in Washington, DC They were not on sale at post offices in the Continental US, though they were valid for postage there.
Normally the overprints were placed 18mm apart vertically, but pairs exist with a space of 28mm between the overprints.

Aeronautics Conference Issue

Wright Airplane A194

Globe and Airplane A195

Flat Plate Printing

1928, Dec. 12		Perf. 11	
649 A194	2c carmine rose	1.25	.80
	Never hinged	1.75	
650 A195	5c blue	5.25	3.25
	Never hinged	7.00	

Intl. Civil Aeronautics Conf. at Washington, DC, Dec. 12-14, 1928, and of the 25th anniv. of the 1st airplane flight by the Wright brothers, Dec. 17, 1903.

George Rogers Clark Issue

Surrender of Fort Sackville A196

1929, Feb. 25		Perf. 11	
651 A196	2c carmine & black	.65	.50
	Never hinged	.90	

150th anniv. of the surrender of Fort Sackville, the present site of Vincennes, Ind., to George Rogers Clark.

Type of 1925
Rotary Press Printing

1929, May 25		Perf. 11x10½	
653 A154	½c olive brown	.15	.15
	Never hinged	.20	

Edison's First Lamp A197

Maj. Gen. John Sullivan A198

Electric Light Jubilee Issue

1929	Flat Plate Printing	Perf. 11	
654 A197	2c carmine rose	.70	.70
	Never hinged	1.00	

Rotary Press Printing
Perf. 11x10½

655 A197	2c carmine rose	.65	.15
	Never hinged	.90	

Coil Stamp (Rotary Press)
Perf. 10 Vertically

656 A197	2c carmine rose	14.00	1.75
	Never hinged	20.00	
	Nos. 654-656 (3)	15.35	2.60

50th anniv. of invention of the incandescent lamp by Thomas Alva Edison, Oct. 21, 1879. Issued: No. 654, June 5; Nos. 655-656, June 11.

Sullivan Expedition Issue
Flat Plate Printing

1929, June 17		Perf. 11	
657 A198	2c carmine rose	.70	.60
	Never hinged	1.00	
a.	2c lake	175.00	—
	Never hinged	250.00	

150th anniv. of the Sullivan Expedition in NY State during the Revolutionary War.

Nos. 632-634, 635-642 Overprinted **Kans.**

Rotary Press Printing

1929		Perf. 11x10½	
658 A155	1c green	2.50	2.00
	Never hinged	3.50	
a.	Vert. pair, one without ovpt.	325.00	
659 A156	1½c brown	4.00	2.90
	Never hinged	5.50	
a.	Vert. pair, one without ovpt.	350.00	
660 A157	2c carmine	4.50	1.10
	Never hinged	6.25	
661 A158	3c violet	22.50	15.00
	Never hinged	31.00	
a.	Vert. pair, one without ovpt.	425.00	
662 A159	4c yellow brown	22.50	9.00
	Never hinged	31.00	
a.	Vert. pair, one without ovpt.	425.00	
663 A160	5c deep blue	14.00	9.75
	Never hinged	20.00	
664 A161	6c red orange	32.50	18.00
	Never hinged	45.00	
665 A162	7c black	30.00	27.50
	Never hinged	42.50	
a.	Vert. pair, one without ovpt.	425.00	
666 A163	8c olive green	110.00	75.00
	Never hinged	150.00	
667 A164	9c light rose	16.00	11.25
	Never hinged	22.50	

UNITED STATES

668	A165	10c orange yel		25.00	12.00
		Never hinged		34.00	
		Nos. 658-668 (11)		283.50	183.50
		Nos. 658-668, never hinged		391.25	

See note following No. 679.

Overprinted Nebr.

669	A155	1c green		4.00	2.25
		Never hinged		5.75	
a.		Vert. pair, one without ovpt.		300.00	
b.		No period after "Nebr."			
		(19338, 19339 UR 26, 36)		50.00	
670	A156	1½c brown		3.75	2.50
		Never hinged		5.25	
671	A157	2c carmine		3.75	1.30
		Never hinged		5.25	
672	A158	3c violet		15.00	12.00
		Never hinged		21.00	
a.		Vert. pair, one without ovpt.		425.00	
673	A159	4c yellow brown		22.50	15.00
		Never hinged		32.50	
674	A160	5c deep blue		20.00	15.00
		Never hinged		27.50	
675	A161	6c red orange		47.50	24.00
		Never hinged		65.00	
676	A162	7c black		27.50	18.00
		Never hinged		37.50	
677	A163	8c olive green		37.50	25.00
		Never hinged		52.50	
678	A164	9c light rose		42.50	27.50
		Never hinged		60.00	
a.		Vert. pair, one without ovpt.		650.00	
679	A165	10c orange yel		135.00	22.50
		Never hinged		190.00	
		Nos. 669-679 (11)		359.00	165.05
		Nos. 669-679, never hinged		502.25	

Nos. 658-660, 669-673, 677 and 678 are known with the overprints on vertical pairs spaced 32mm apart instead of the normal 22mm.

Important: Nos. 658-679 with original gum have either one horizontal gum breaker ridge per stamp or portions of two at the extreme top and bottom of the stamps, 21mm apart. Multiple complete gum breaker ridges indicate a fake overprint. Absence of the gum breaker ridges indicates either regumming or regumming and a fake overprint.

Gen. Anthony Wayne Memorial — A199

Lock No. 5, Monongahela River — A200

Battle of Fallen Timbers Issue
Flat Plate Printing
1929, Sept. 14 Perf. 11

680	A199	2c carmine rose		.80	.80
		Never hinged		1.10	

General Anthony Wayne memorial and the 135th anniv. of the Battle of Fallen Timbers, Ohio.

Ohio River Canalization Issue
1929, Oct. 19 Perf. 11

681	A200	2c carmine rose		.70	.65
		Never hinged		.90	

Completion of the Ohio River Canalization Project between Cairo, Ill. and Pittsburgh.

Massachusetts Bay Colony Issue

Mass. Bay Colony Seal — A201

1930, Apr. 8 Perf. 11

682	A201	2c carmine rose		.60	.50
		Never hinged		.80	

300th anniv. of the founding of the Massachusetts Bay Colony.

Carolina-Charleston Issue

Gov. Joseph West and Chief Shadoo, a Kiowa — A202

1930, Apr. 10 Perf. 11

683	A202	2c carmine rose		1.20	1.20
		Never hinged		1.60	

260th anniv. of the founding of the Province of Carolina, and the 250th anniv. of the City of Charleston, SC.

Warren G. Harding — A203

William H. Taft — A204

Type of 1922-26 Issue
Rotary Press Printing
1930 Perf. 11x10½

684	A203	1½c brown		.35	.15
		Never hinged		.45	
685	A204	4c brown		.90	.15
		Never hinged		1.25	

Coil Stamps
Perf. 10 Vertically

686	A203	1½c brown		1.80	.15
		Never hinged		2.50	
687	A204	4c brown		3.25	.45
		Never hinged		4.50	

Braddock's Field Issue

Statue of Col. George Washington — A205

Flat Plate Printing
1930, July 9 Perf. 11

688	A205	2c carmine rose		1.00	.85
		Never hinged		1.30	

175th anniv. of the Battle of Braddock's Field, otherwise the Battle of Monongahela.

General von Steuben — A206

General Casimir Pulaski — A207

Von Steuben Issue
1930, Sept. 17 Perf. 11

689	A206	2c carmine rose		.55	.55
		Never hinged		.70	
a.		Imperf., pair		2,500.	
		Never hinged		3,250.	

Gen. Baron Friedrich Wilhelm von Steuben (1730-1794), German soldier who served with distinction in American Revolution.

Pulaski Issue
1931, Jan. 16 Perf. 11

690	A207	2c carmine rose		.30	.15
		Never hinged		.40	

150th anniv. (in 1929) of the death of Gen. Count Casimir Pulaski (1748-1779), Polish patriot and hero of American Revolution.

Types of 1922-26
Rotary Press Printing
1931 Perf. 11x10½

692	A166	11c light blue		2.60	.15
		Never hinged		3.70	
693	A167	12c brown violet		5.50	.15
		Never hinged		7.75	
694	A186	13c yellow green		2.00	.15
		Never hinged		2.80	
695	A168	14c dark blue		3.75	.25
		Never hinged		5.25	
696	A169	15c gray		8.00	.15
		Never hinged		11.25	

Perf. 10½x11

697	A187	17c black		4.50	.15
		Never hinged		6.25	
698	A170	20c carmine rose		8.75	.15
		Never hinged		12.50	
699	A171	25c blue green		9.00	.15
		Never hinged		12.50	
700	A172	30c brown		17.50	.15
		Never hinged		25.00	
701	A173	50c lilac		40.00	.15
		Never hinged		55.00	
		Nos. 692-701 (10)		101.60	1.60
		Nos. 692-701, never hinged		142.00	

"The Greatest Mother" A208

Count de Rochambeau, Washington, Count de Grasse A209

Red Cross Issue
Flat Plate Printing
1931, May 21 Perf. 11

702	A208	2c black & red		.25	.15
		Never hinged		.30	
a.		Red cross omitted		40,000.	

50th anniv. of the founding of the American Red Cross Society.

Yorktown Issue
1931, Oct. 19 Perf. 11

703	A209	2c carmine rose & black		.40	.25
		Never hinged		.50	
a.		2c lake & black		4.50	.65
		Never hinged		6.25	
b.		2c dark lake & black		375.00	
		Never hinged		525.00	
c.		Horiz. pair, imperf. vert.		5,000.	
		Never hinged		6,250.	

Surrender of Yorktown, sesquicentennial.

Washington Bicentennial Issue
Various Portraits of George Washington

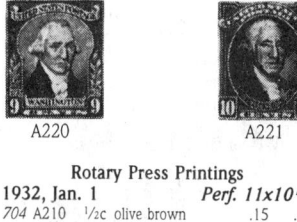

A210  A211

A212  A213

A214  A215

A216  A217

A218  A219

A220 A221

Rotary Press Printings
1932, Jan. 1 Perf. 11x10½

704	A210	½c olive brown		.15	.15
		Never hinged		.15	
705	A211	1c green		.15	.15
		Never hinged		.15	
706	A212	1½c brown		.40	.15
		Never hinged		.55	
707	A213	2c carmine rose		.15	.15
		Never hinged		.15	
708	A214	3c deep violet		.55	.15
		Never hinged		.80	
709	A215	4c light brown		.25	.15
		Never hinged		.35	
710	A216	5c blue		1.60	.15
		Never hinged		2.25	
711	A217	6c red orange		3.25	.15
		Never hinged		4.50	
712	A218	7c black		.25	.15
		Never hinged		.35	
713	A219	8c olive bister		2.75	.50
		Never hinged		3.75	
714	A220	9c pale red		2.40	.15
		Never hinged		3.25	
715	A221	10c orange yellow		10.00	.15
		Never hinged		14.00	
		Nos. 704-715 (12)		21.90	2.15
		Nos. 704-715, never hinged		30.25	

200th anniv. of the birth of Washington.

Skier — A222

Boy and Girl Planting Tree — A223

Olympic Winter Games Issue
Flat Plate Printing
1932, Jan. 25 Perf. 11

716	A222	2c carmine rose		.40	.20
		Never hinged		.50	

Olympic Winter Games, Lake Placid, NY, Feb. 4-13.

Arbor Day Issue
Rotary Press Printing
1932, Apr. 22 Perf. 11x10½

717	A223	2c carmine rose		.15	.15
		Never hinged		.20	

60th anniv. of the 1st observance of Arbor Day in Nebr., April, 1872, and the birth centenary of Julius Sterling Morton, who conceived the plan and the name "Arbor Day," while a member of the Nebr. State Board of Agriculture.

10th Olympic Games Issue

Runner at Starting Mark A224

Myron's Discobolus A225

1932, June 15 Perf. 11x10½

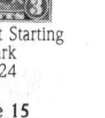

718	A224	3c violet		1.40	.15
		Never hinged		1.75	
719	A225	5c blue		2.20	.20
		Never hinged		2.75	

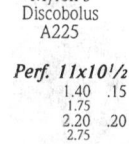

Los Angeles, Cal., July 30-Aug. 14.

Washington — A226

1932, June 16 Perf. 11x10½

720	A226	3c deep violet		.15	.15
		Never hinged		.20	
b.		Booklet pane of 6		37.50	5.00
		Never hinged		50.00	
c.		Vert. pair, imperf. btwn.		325.00	250.00
		Never hinged		425.00	

Coil Stamps
Rotary Press Printing
1932, June 24 Perf. 10 Vertically

721	A226	3c deep violet		2.75	.15
		Never hinged		3.50	

1932, Oct. 12 Perf. 10 Horizontally

722	A226	3c deep violet		1.50	.35
		Never hinged		2.00	

Garfield Type of 1922-26 Issue
1932, Aug. 18 Perf. 10 Vertically

723	A161	6c deep orange		11.00	.30
		Never hinged		14.50	

William Penn A227

Daniel Webster A228

UNITED STATES

William Penn Issue
Flat Plate Printing
1932, Oct. 24   *Perf. 11*
724 A227 3c violet   .25   .15
    Never hinged   .35
a. Vert. pair, imperf. horiz.

250th anniv. of the arrival in America of William Penn (1644-1718), English Quaker and founder of Pennsylvania.

Daniel Webster Issue
1932, Oct. 24   *Perf. 11*
725 A228 3c violet   .30   .25
    Never hinged   .40

Daniel Webster (1782-1852), statesman.

Georgia Bicentennial Issue

Gen. James Edward Oglethorpe — A229

1933, Feb. 12   *Perf. 11*
726 A229 3c violet   .25   .20
    Never hinged   .35

200th anniv. of the founding of the Colony of Georgia and James Edward Oglethorpe, who landed from England, Feb. 12th, 1733, and personally supervised the establishing of the colony.

Peace of 1783 Issue

Washington's Headquarters, Newburgh, NY — A230

Rotary Press Printing
1933, Apr. 19   *Perf. 10½x11*
727 A230 3c violet   .15   .15
    Never hinged   .20

150th anniv. of the Proclamation of Peace between the US and Great Britain at the end of the Revolutionary War.
See No. 752.

Century of Progress Issue

Restoration of Fort Dearborn A231    Federal Building at Chicago, 1933 A232

1933, May 25   *Perf. 10½x11*
728 A231 1c yellow green   .15   .15
    Never hinged   .20
729 A232 3c violet   .15   .15
    Never hinged   .20

"Century of Progress" Intl. Phil. Exhib., Chicago, 1933 and 100th anniv. of the incorporation of Chicago as a city.

American Philatelic Society Issue
Souvenir Sheets
Without Gum
Flat Plate Printing
1933, Aug. 25   *Imperf.*
730   Sheet of 25   27.50   27.50
a. A231 1c deep yellow green   .75   .45
731   Sheet of 25   25.00   25.00
a. A232 3c deep violet   .65   .45

Sheet measures 134x120mm.
See Nos. 766-767.

National Recovery Act Issue

Group of Workers — A233

Rotary Press Printing
1933, Aug. 15   *Perf. 10½x11*
732 A233 3c violet   .15   .15
    Never hinged   .20

Issued to direct attention to and arouse support of the Nation for the NRA.

Byrd Antarctic Issue

World Map on van der Grinten's Projection — A234

Flat Plate Printing
1933, Oct. 9   *Perf. 11*
733 A234 3c dark blue   .50   .50
    Never hinged   .60

Second Antarctic expedition of Rear Admiral Richard E. Byrd.
In addition to the 3 cents postage, letters sent by the ships of the expedition to be canceled in Little America were subject to a service charge of 50 cents each.
See Nos. 735, 753.

Kosciuszko Issue

Statue of Gen. Tadeusz Kosciuszko — A235

1933, Oct. 13   *Perf. 11*
734 A235 5c blue   .55   .25
    Never hinged   .65
a. Horiz. pair, imperf. vert.   2,250.
    Never hinged   2,800.

Gen. Tadeusz Kosciuszko (1746-1807), Polish soldier and statesman who served in American Revolution. 150th anniv. of grant of American citizenship.

National Stamp Exhibition Issue
Souvenir Sheet
Without Gum
1934, Feb. 10   *Imperf.*
735   Sheet of 6   12.50   10.00
a. A234 3c dark blue   2.00   1.65

Sheet measures 87x93mm. See #768.

Maryland Tercentenary Issue

"The Ark" and "The Dove" — A236

1934, Mar. 23   *Perf. 11*
736 A236 3c carmine rose   .15   .15
    Never hinged   .20

300th anniv. of the founding of Maryland.

Mothers of America Issue

Adaptation of Whistler's Portrait of his Mother A237

Rotary Press Printing
1934, May 2   *Perf. 11x10½*
737 A237 3c deep violet   .15   .15
    Never hinged   .20

Flat Plate Printing
Perf. 11
738 A237 3c deep violet   .15   .15
    Never hinged   .20

Mother's Day. See No. 754.

Wisconsin Tercentenary Issue

Nicolet's Landing A238

1934, July 7   *Perf. 11*
739 A238 3c deep violet   .15   .15
    Never hinged   .15
a. Vert. pair, imperf. horiz.   350.00

b. Horiz. pair, imperf. vert.   450.00
    Never hinged   575.00

Tercentenary of the arrival of French explorer Jean Nicolet at Green Bay, Wis.
See No. 755.

National Parks Issue

El Capitan, Yosemite (California) A239

Old Faithful, Yellowstone (Wyoming) A243

Grand Canyon (Arizona) A240

Mt. Rainier and Mirror Lake (Washington) A241

Mesa Verde (Colorado) A242

Crater Lake (Oregon) A244

Great Head, Acadia Park (Maine) A245

Great White Throne, Zion Park (Utah) A246

Great Smoky Mts. (North Carolina) A248

Mt. Rockwell (Mt. Sinopah) and Two Medicine Lake, Glacier Natl. Park (Montana) A247

1934   Flat Plate Printing   *Perf. 11*
740 A239 1c green   .15   .15
    Never hinged   .15
a. Vert. pair, imperf. horiz., with gum   450.00
    Never hinged   575.00
741 A240 2c red   .15   .15
    Never hinged   .15
a. Vert. pair, imperf. horiz., with gum   450.00
    Never hinged   575.00
b. Horiz. pair, imperf. vert., with gum   425.00
    Never hinged   550.00
742 A241 3c deep violet   .15   .15
    Never hinged   .15
a. Vert. pair, imperf. horiz., with gum   425.00
    Never hinged   550.00

743 A242 4c brown   .35   .40
    Never hinged   .45
a. Vert. pair, imperf. horiz., with gum   700.00
    Never hinged   1,000.
744 A243 5c blue   .70   .65
    Never hinged   .95
a. Horiz. pair, imperf. vert., with gum   500.00
    Never hinged   725.00
745 A244 6c dark blue   1.10   .85
    Never hinged   1.50
746 A245 7c black   .60   .75
    Never hinged   .85
a. Horiz. pair, imperf. vert., with gum   700.00
    Never hinged   1,000.
747 A246 8c sage green   1.60   1.50
    Never hinged   2.20
748 A247 9c red orange   1.50   .65
    Never hinged   2.10
749 A248 10c gray black   3.00   1.25
    Never hinged   4.25
    Nos. 740-749 (10)   9.30   6.50
    Nos. 740-749, never hinged   12.75

National Parks Year.
See Nos. 750-751, 756-765, 769-770, 797.

American Philatelic Society Issue
Souvenir Sheet
1934, Aug. 28   *Imperf.*
750   Sheet of 6   30.00   27.50
    Never hinged   37.50
a. A241 3c deep violet   3.50   3.25
    Never hinged   4.50

Sheet measures approximately 98x93mm. See #770.

Trans-Mississippi Philatelic Exposition Issue
Souvenir Sheet
1934, Oct. 10   *Imperf.*
751   Sheet of 6   12.50   12.50
    Never hinged   16.00
a. A239 1c green   1.40   1.60
    Never hinged   1.85

Sheet measures approximately 92x99mm. See #769.

Special Printing (Nos. 752-771)

"Issued for a limited time in full sheets as printed, and in blocks thereof, to meet the requirements of collectors and others who may be interested."—From Postal Bulletin, No. 16614.

Issuance of the following 20 stamps in complete sheets resulted from the protest of collectors and others at the practice of presenting, to certain government officials, complete sheets of unsevered panes, imperforate (except Nos. 752 and 753) and generally ungummed.

Without Gum.

Note. In 1940 the P.O. Department offered to and did gum full sheets of Nos. 754 to 771 sent in by owners.

Type of Peace Issue
Issued in sheets of 400
Rotary Press Printing
1935, Mar. 15   *Perf. 10½x11*
752 A230 3c violet   .15   .15

Type of Byrd Issue
Issued in sheets of 200
Flat Plate Printing
Perf. 11
753 A234 3c dark blue   .50   .45

No. 753 is similar to No. 733. Positive identification is by pairs or blocks showing a guide line between stamps. These lines are found only on No. 753.

Type of Mothers of America Issue
Issued in sheets of 200
Imperf
754 A237 3c deep violet   .55   .55

Type of Wisconsin Issue
Issued in sheets of 200
Imperf
755 A238 3c deep violet   .55   .55

Types of National Parks Issue
Issued in sheets of 200
Imperf
756 A239 1c green   .20   .20
757 A240 2c red   .25   .25
758 A241 3c deep violet   .50   .45
759 A242 4c brown   .95   .95
760 A243 5c blue   1.50   1.30
761 A244 6c dark blue   2.40   2.10
762 A245 7c black   1.50   1.40
763 A246 8c sage green   1.60   1.50
764 A247 9c red orange   1.90   1.65
765 A248 10c gray black   3.75   3.25
    Nos. 756-765 (10)   14.55   13.05

UNITED STATES

Souvenir Sheets
Type of Century of Progress Issue
Issued in sheets of 9 panes of 25 stamps each

Note: Single items from these sheets are identical with other varieties, 766 & 730, 766a & 730a, 767 & 731, 767a & 731a, 768 & 735, 768a & 735a, 769 & 756, 770 & 758. Positive identification is by blocks or pairs showing wide gutters between stamps. These wide gutters occur only on Nos. 766 to 770 and measure, horizontally, 13mm on Nos. 766-767; 16mm on No. 768, and 23mm on Nos. 769-770.

Imperf

766	Pane of 25	25.00	25.00
a.	A231 1c yellow green	.70	.40
767	Pane of 25	23.50	23.50
a.	A232 3c violet	.60	.40

National Exhibition Issue
Type of Byrd Issue
Issued in sheets of 25 panes of 6 stamps each

Imperf

768	Pane of 6	20.00	15.00
a.	A234 3c dark blue	2.80	2.40

Types of National Parks Issue
Issued in sheets of 20 panes of 6 stamps each

Imperf

769	Pane of 6	12.50	11.00
a.	A239 1c green	1.85	1.80
770	Pane of 6	30.00	24.00
a.	A241 3c deep violet	3.25	3.10

Type of Air Post Special Delivery
Issued in sheets of 200

Imperf

| 771 | APSD1 16c dark blue | 2.25 | 2.25 |

Catalogue values for unused stamps in this section, from this point to the end of the section, are for Never Hinged items.

Connecticut Tercentenary Issue

Charter Oak — A249

Rotary Press Printing
1935, Apr. 26   *Perf. 11x10½*
772 A249 3c violet   .15   .15

300th anniv. of the settlement of Conn.
See No. 778a.

California-Pacific Exposition Issue

View of San Diego Exposition A250

1935, May 29   *Perf. 11x10½*
773 A250 3c purple   .15   .15

California-Pacific Expo., San Diego.
See No. 778b.

Boulder Dam Issue

Boulder Dam — A251

Flat Plate Printing
1935, Sept. 30   *Perf. 11*
774 A251 3c purple   .15   .15

Dedication of Boulder Dam.

Michigan Centenary Issue

Michigan State Seal — A252

Rotary Press Printing
1935, Nov. 1   *Perf. 11x10½*
775 A252 3c purple   .15   .15

Advance celebration of Michigan statehood centenary. Michigan was admitted to Union Jan. 26, 1837.
See No. 778c.

Texas Centennial Issue

Sam Houston, Stephen F. Austin and the Alamo — A253

1936, Mar. 2   *Perf. 11x10½*
776 A253 3c purple   .15   .15

Centennial of Texas independence.
See No. 778d.

Rhode Island Tercentenary Issue

Statue of Roger Williams — A254

1936, May 4   *Perf. 10½x11*
777 A254 3c purple   .15   .15

Settlement of Rhode Island, 1636.

Third International Philatelic Exhibition Issue
Souvenir Sheet

A254a

Flat Plate Printing
1936, May 9   *Imperf.*
778 A254a Sheet of 4   1.75 1.75
 a. A249 3c violet   .40   .30
 b. A250 3c violet   .40   .30
 c. A252 3c violet   .40   .30
 d. A253 3c violet   .40   .30

Sheet measures 98x66mm.

Arkansas Centennial Issue

Arkansas Post, Old and New State Houses A255

Rotary Press Printing
1936, June 15   *Perf. 11x10½*
782 A255 3c purple   .15   .15

Centennial of Arkansas statehood.

Map of Oregon Territory A256

Susan B. Anthony A257

Oregon Territory Issue
1936, July 14   *Perf. 11x10½*
783 A256 3c purple   .15   .15

Centenary of Oregon Territory opening.

Susan B. Anthony Issue
1936, Aug. 26   *Perf. 11x10½*
784 A257 3c dark violet   .15   .15

Susan Brownell Anthony (1820-1906), woman suffrage advocate, honored on 16th anniv. of ratification of 19th Amendment granting American women the right to vote.

Army Issue

George Washington, Nathanael Greene and Mount Vernon — A258

Andrew Jackson, Winfield Scott and the Hermitage A259

Generals Sherman, Grant and Sheridan A260

Generals Robert E. Lee, "Stonewall" Jackson and Stratford Hall — A261

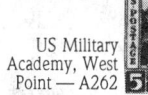

US Military Academy, West Point — A262

1936-37   *Perf. 11x10½*
785 A258 1c green   .15   .15
786 A259 2c carmine ('37)   .15   .15
787 A260 3c purple ('37)   .20   .15
788 A261 4c gray ('37)   .30   .15
789 A262 5c ultra ('37)   .60   .15
 Nos. 785-789 (5)   1.40   .75

Issued in honor of the United States Army.

Navy Issue

John Paul Jones and John Barry — A263

Stephen Decatur and Thomas MacDonough A264

Admirals David G. Farragut and David D. Porter — A265

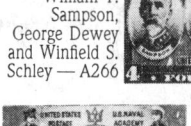

Admirals William T. Sampson, George Dewey and Winfield S. Schley — A266

Seal of US Naval Academy and Naval Cadets — A267

1936-37   *Perf. 11x10½*
790 A263 1c green   .15   .15
791 A264 2c carmine ('37)   .15   .15
792 A265 3c purple ('37)   .15   .15
793 A266 4c gray ('37)   .30   .15
794 A267 5c ultra ('37)   .60   .15
 Nos. 790-794 (5)   1.35   .75

Issued in honor of the United States Navy.

Northwest Ordinance Sesquicentennial Issue

Manasseh Cutler, Rufus Putnam and Map of Northwest Territory A268

1937, July 13   *Perf. 11x10½*
795 A268 3c red violet   .15   .15

150th anniv. of the adoption of the Ordinance of 1787 and the creation of the Northwest Territory.

Virginia Dare Issue

Virginia Dare and Parents — A269

Flat Plate Printing
1937, Aug. 18   *Perf. 11*
796 A269 5c gray blue   .20   .20

350th anniv. of the birth of Virginia Dare and the settlement at Roanoke Island. Virginia was the first child born in America of English parents (Aug. 18, 1587).

Society of Philatelic Americans
Souvenir Sheet

A269a

1937, Aug. 26   *Imperf.*
797 A269a 10c blue green   .60   .40

Sheet measures 67x78mm.

Constitution Sesquicentennial Issue

Signing of the Constitution A270

Rotary Press Printing
1937, Sept. 17   *Perf. 11x10½*
798 A270 3c bright red violet   .15   .15

Sesquicentennial of the Signing of the Constitution, Sept. 17, 1787.

Territorial Issues
Hawaii

Statue of Kamehameha I, Honolulu — A271

1937, Oct. 18   *Perf. 10½x11*
799 A271 3c violet   .15   .15

UNITED STATES

Alaska

Landscape with Mt. McKinley — A272

1937, Nov. 12   *Perf. 11x10½*
800 A272 3c violet   .15 .15

Puerto Rico

La Fortaleza, San Juan — A273

1937, Nov. 25   *Perf. 11x10½*
801 A273 3c bright violet   .15 .15

Virgin Islands

Charlotte Amalie — A274

1937, Dec. 15   *Perf. 11x10½*
802 A274 3c light violet   .15 .15

Presidential Issue

Benjamin Franklin A275
George Washington A276
Martha Washington A277
John Adams A278
Thomas Jefferson A279
James Madison A280
White House A281
James Monroe A282
John Q. Adams A283
Andrew Jackson A284
Martin Van Buren A285 
William H. Harrison A286
John Tyler A287
Zachary Taylor A289
Franklin Pierce A291
Abraham Lincoln A293
Ulysses S. Grant A295
Grover Cleveland A299
William McKinley A301
William Howard Taft A303
James K. Polk A288
Millard Fillmore A290
James Buchanan A292
Andrew Johnson A294
Rutherford B. Hayes A296
James A. Garfield A297
Chester A. Arthur A298
Benjamin Harrison A300
Theodore Roosevelt A302
Woodrow Wilson A304
Warren G. Harding A305 
Calvin Coolidge A306

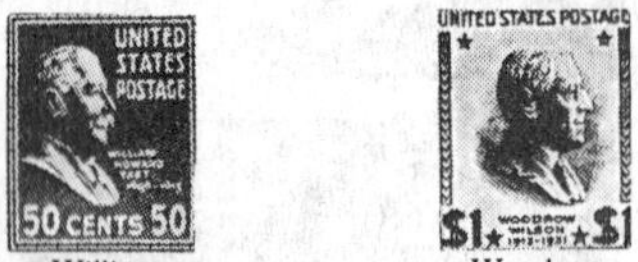

1938-54   *Perf. 11x10½*
803 A275 ½c deep orange   .15 .15
804 A276 1c green   .15 .15
   b. Booklet pane of 6   2.00 .75
805 A277 1½c bister brown   .15 .15
   b. Horiz. pair, imperf. btwn.   175.00 30.00
806 A278 2c rose carmine   .15 .15
   b. Booklet pane of 6   4.75 .75
807 A279 3c deep violet   .15 .15
   a. Booklet pane of 6   8.50 1.00
   b. Horiz. pair, imperf. btwn.   900.00 —
   c. Imperf., pair   2,500.
808 A280 4c red violet   .75 .15
809 A281 4½c dark gray   .15 .15
810 A282 5c bright blue   .20 .15
811 A283 6c red orange   .20 .15
812 A284 7c sepia   .25 .15
813 A285 8c olive green   .30 .15
814 A286 9c rose pink   .30 .15
815 A287 10c brown red   .25 .15
816 A288 11c ultra   .65 .15
817 A289 12c bright violet   .90 .15
818 A290 13c blue green   1.25 .15
819 A291 14c blue   .90 .15
820 A292 15c blue gray   .40 .15
821 A293 16c black   .90 .25
822 A294 17c rose red   .85 .15
823 A295 18c brown car   1.75 .15
824 A296 19c bright violet   1.25 .35
825 A297 20c brt blue green   .70 .15
826 A298 21c dull blue   1.25 .15
827 A299 22c vermilion   1.00 .40
828 A300 24c gray black   3.50 .20
829 A301 25c deep red lilac   .60 .15
830 A302 30c deep ultra   3.75 .15
831 A303 50c lt red violet   5.75 .15

Flat Plate Printing
Perf. 11

832 A304 $1 pur & black   7.00 .15
   a. Vert. pair, imperf. horiz.   1,500.
   b. Wmkd. USIR ('51)   250.00 65.00
   c. $1 red violet & black ('54)   6.00 .15
   d. As "c," vert. pair, imperf. horiz.   1,250.
   e. Vert. pair, imperf. btwn.   2,750.
   f. As "c," vert. pair, imperf. btwn.   7,000.
833 A305 $2 yel grn & blk   20.00 3.75
834 A306 $5 car & black   95.00 3.00
   a. $5 red brown & black   3,500. 1,500.
   Hinged   2,750.
Nos. 803-834 (32)   150.55 11.85

No. 832c is printed on thick white paper with smooth, colorless gum.
No. 834 can be chemically altered to resemble No. 834a. No. 834a should be purchased only with competent expert certification.
See Nos. 839-851.

Constitution Ratification Issue

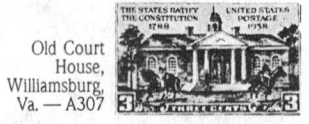

Old Court House, Williamsburg, Va. — A307

Rotary Press Printing

1938, June 21   *Perf. 11x10½*
835 A307 3c deep violet   .25 .15

150th anniv. of the ratification of the US Constitution.

Landing of the Swedes and Finns — A308
Statue Symbolizing Colonization of the West — A309

Swedish-Finnish Tercentenary Issue
Flat Plate Printing

1938, June 27   *Perf. 11*
836 A308 3c red violet   .15 .15

Tercentenary of the founding of the Swedish and Finnish settlement at Wilmington, Del.

Northwest Territory Issue
Rotary Press Printing

1938, July 15   *Perf. 11x10½*
837 A309 3c bright violet   .15 .15

Sesquicentennial of the settlement of the Northwest Territory.

Iowa Territory Centennial Issue

Old Capitol, Iowa City — A310

1938, Aug. 24   *Perf. 11x10½*
838 A310 3c violet   .15 .15

Centenary of Iowa Territory.

Presidential Types of 1938
Coil Stamps
Rotary Press Printing

1939   *Perf. 10 Vertically*
839 A276 1c green   .30 .15
840 A277 1½c bister brown   .30 .15
841 A278 2c rose carmine   .40 .15
842 A279 3c deep violet   .50 .15
843 A280 4c red violet   8.00 .40
844 A281 4½c dark gray   .70 .40
845 A282 5c bright blue   5.00 .35
846 A283 6c red orange   1.10 .20
847 A287 10c brown red   11.00 .50

Perf. 10 Horizontally
848 A276 1c green   .85 .15
849 A277 1½c bister brown   1.25 .30
850 A278 2c rose carmine   2.50 .40
851 A279 3c deep violet   2.25 .35
Nos. 839-851 (13)   34.15 3.65

"Tower of the Sun" A311
Trylon and Perisphere A312

Golden Gate International Exposition Issue
Rotary Press Printing

1939, Feb. 18   *Perf. 10½x11*
852 A311 3c bright purple   .15 .15

Golden Gate Intl. Expo., San Francisco.

New York World's Fair Issue

1939, Apr. 1   *Perf. 10½x11*
853 A312 3c deep purple   .15 .15

Washington Inauguration Issue

George Washington Taking Oath of Office — A313

Flat Plate Printing

1939, Apr. 30   *Perf. 11*
854 A313 3c bright red violet   .40 .15

Sesquicentennial of the inauguration of George Washington as 1st president.

Baseball Centennial Issue

Sand-lot Baseball Game — A314

UNITED STATES

Rotary Press Printing
1939, June 12   Perf. 11x10½
855 A314 3c violet   1.75   .15
  Centennial of baseball.

Panama Canal Issue
Theodore Roosevelt, Gen. George W. Goethals and Gaillard Cut — A315

Flat Plate Printing
1939, Aug. 15   Perf. 11
856 A315 3c deep red violet   .25   .15
  25th anniv. of the Panama Canal opening.

Printing Tercentenary Issue
Stephen Daye Press — A316

Rotary Press Printing
1939, Sept. 25   Perf. 10½x11
857 A316 3c violet   .15   .15
  300th anniv. of printing in Colonial America.

50th Anniversary of Statehood Issue.
Map of North and South Dakota, Montana and Washington A317

1939, Nov. 2   Perf. 11x10½
858 A317 3c rose violet   .15   .15
  50th anniv. of admission to Statehood of North Dakota, South Dakota, Montana and Washington.

Famous Americans Issues
Authors
Washington Irving A318 
James Fenimore Cooper A319 
Ralph Waldo Emerson A320 
Louisa May Alcott A321 
Samuel L. Clemens (Mark Twain) — A322

1940   Perf. 10½x11
859 A318 1c bright blue green   .15   .15
860 A319 2c rose carmine   .15   .15
861 A320 3c bright red violet   .15   .15
862 A321 5c ultra   .30   .20
863 A322 10c dark brown   1.65 1.20
  Nos. 859-863 (5)   2.40 1.85

Poets
Henry W. Longfellow A323 
John Greenleaf Whittier A324 
James Russell Lowell A325 
Walt Whitman A326 
James Whitcomb Riley — A327

1940   Perf. 10½x11
864 A323 1c bright blue green   .15   .15
865 A324 2c rose carmine   .15   .15
866 A325 3c bright red violet   .15   .15
867 A326 5c ultra   .35   .15
868 A327 10c dark brown   1.75 1.25
  Nos. 864-868 (5)   2.55 1.85

Educators
Horace Mann A328
Mark Hopkins A329 
Charles W. Eliot A330 
Frances E. Willard A331 
Booker T. Washington — A332

1940   Perf. 10½x11
869 A328 1c bright blue green   .15   .15
870 A329 2c rose carmine   .15   .15
871 A330 3c bright red violet   .15   .15
872 A331 5c ultra   .40   .20
873 A332 10c dark brown   1.25 1.10
  Nos. 869-873 (5)   2.10 1.75

Scientists
John James Audubon A333
Dr. Crawford W. Long A334
Luther Burbank A335
Dr. Walter Reed A336
Jane Addams — A337

1940   Perf. 10½x11
874 A333 1c bright blue green   .15   .15
875 A334 2c rose carmine   .15   .15
876 A335 3c bright red violet   .15   .15
877 A336 5c ultra   .25   .15
878 A337 10c dark brown   1.10   .85
  Nos. 874-878 (5)   1.80 1.45

Composers
Stephen Collins Foster — A338 
John Philip Sousa — A339 
Victor Herbert A340 
Edward MacDowell A341 
Ethelbert Nevin — A342

1940   Perf. 10½x11
879 A338 1c bright blue green   .15   .15
880 A339 2c rose carmine   .15   .15
881 A340 3c bright red violet   .15   .15
882 A341 5c ultra   .40   .20
883 A342 10c dark brown   3.75 1.20
  Nos. 879-883 (5)   4.60 1.85

Artists
Gilbert Charles Stuart A343 
James A. McNeill Whistler A344 
Augustus Saint-Gaudens A345 
Daniel Chester French A346 
Frederic Remington — A347

1940   Perf. 10½x11
884 A343 1c bright blue green   .15   .15
885 A344 2c rose carmine   .15   .15
886 A345 3c bright red violet   .15   .15
887 A346 5c ultra   .50   .20
888 A347 10c dark brown   1.75 1.25
  Nos. 884-888 (5)   2.70 1.90

Inventors
Eli Whitney A348 
Samuel F. B. Morse A349 
Cyrus Hall McCormick A350 
Elias Howe A351 
Alexander Graham Bell — A352

1940   Perf. 10½x11
889 A348 1c brt blue green   .15   .15
890 A349 2c rose carmine   .15   .15
891 A350 3c bright red violet   .25   .15
892 A351 5c ultra   1.10   .30
893 A352 10c dark brown   11.00 2.00
  Nos. 889-893 (5)   12.65 2.75
  Nos. 859-893 (35)   28.80 13.40

Pony Express Issue
Pony Express Rider — A353

1940, Apr. 3   Perf. 11x10½
894 A353 3c henna brown   .25   .15
  80th anniv. of the Pony Express.

Pan American Union Issue
The Three Graces from Botticelli's "Spring" — A354

1940, Apr. 14   Perf. 10½x11
895 A354 3c light violet   .20   .15
  Pan American Union founding, 50th anniv.

Idaho Statehood Issue
Idaho Capitol, Boise — A355

1940, July 3   Perf. 11x10½
896 A355 3c bright violet   .15   .15
  Idaho statehood, 50th anniv.

Wyoming Statehood Issue
Wyoming State Seal — A356

1940, July 10   Perf. 10½x11
897 A356 3c brown violet   .15   .15
  Wyoming statehood, 50th anniv.

UNITED STATES

Coronado Expedition Issue

"Coronado and His Captains" Painted by Gerald Cassidy A357

1940, Sept. 7		Perf. 11x10½
898 A357	3c violet	.15 .15

400th anniv. of the Coronado Expedition.

National Defense Issue

Statue of Liberty — A358

90-millimeter Anti-aircraft Gun — A359

Torch of Enlightenment — A360

1940, Oct. 16		Perf. 11x10½
899 A358	1c bright blue green	.15 .15
a.	Vert. pair, imperf. btwn.	650.00 —
b.	Horiz. pair, imperf. btwn.	40.00 —
900 A359	2c rose carmine	.15 .15
a.	Horiz. pair, imperf. btwn.	40.00 —
901 A360	3c bright violet	.15 .15
a.	Horiz. pair, imperf. btwn.	30.00 —
	Nos. 899-901 (3)	.45 .45

Thirteenth Amendment Issue

"Emancipation," Statue of Lincoln and Slave, by Thomas Ball — A361

1940, Oct. 20		Perf. 10½x11
902 A361	3c deep violet	.20 .15

75th anniv. of the 13th Amendment to the Constitution.

Vermont Statehood Issue

Vermont Capitol, Montpelier A362

1941, Mar. 4		Perf. 11x10½
903 A362	3c light violet	.15 .15

Vermont statehood, 150th anniv.

Kentucky Statehood Issue

Daniel Boone and Three Frontiersmen, from Mural by Gilbert White — A363

1942, June 1		Perf. 11x10½
904 A363	3c violet	.15 .15

Kentucky statehood, 150th anniv.

American Eagle A364

Lincoln, Sun Yat-sen and Map A365

Win the War Issue

1942, July 4		Perf. 11x10½
905 A364	3c violet	.15 .15
b.	3c purple	—

Chinese Resistance Issue

1942, July 7		Perf. 11x10½
906 A365	5c bright blue	.30 .20

Five years' resistance of the Chinese people to Japanese aggression.

Allegory of Victory A366

Liberty Holding Torch of Freedom and Enlightenment A367

Allied Nations Issue

1943, Jan. 14		Perf. 11x10½
907 A366	2c rose carmine	.15 .15

Four Freedoms Issue

1943, Feb. 12		Perf. 11x10½
908 A367	1c bright blue green	.15 .15

Overrun Countries Issue

Flag of Poland — A368

Frames Engraved, Centers Offset Letterpress
Rotary Press Printing

1943-44	Unwmk.	Perf. 12
909 A368	5c Poland	.20 .15
910 A368	5c Czechoslovakia	.20 .15
911 A368	5c Norway	.15 .15
912 A368	5c Luxembourg	.15 .15
913 A368	5c Netherlands	.15 .15
914 A368	5c Belgium	.15 .15
915 A368	5c France	.15 .15
916 A368	5c Greece	.35 .25
917 A368	5c Yugoslavia	.25 .15
918 A368	5c Albania	.20 .15
919 A368	5c Austria	.20 .15
920 A368	5c Denmark	.20 .15
921 A368	5c Korea ('44)	.15 .15
	Nos. 909-921 (13)	2.50 2.05

Transcontinental Railroad Issue

"Golden Spike Ceremony" Painting by John McQuarrie A369

Engraved; Rotary Press Printing

1944, May 10		Perf. 11x10½
922 A369	3c violet	.20 .15

75th anniv. of the completion of the first transcontinental railroad.

Steamship Issue

"Savannah" A370

1944, May 22		Perf. 11x10½
923 A370	3c violet	.15 .15

125th anniv. of the first steamship to cross the Atlantic Ocean.

Shop with Scott Publishing Co. 24 hours a day 7 days a week at www.scottonline.com

Telegraph Issue

Telegraph Wires and the First Transmitted Words "What Hath God Wrought" A371

1944, May 24		Perf. 11x10½
924 A371	3c bright red violet	.15 .15

100th anniv. of the 1st message transmitted by telegraph.

Philippines Issue

View of Corregidor A372

1944, Sept. 27		Perf. 11x10½
925 A372	3c deep violet	.15 .15

Final resistance of the US and Philippine defenders on Corregidor.

Motion Pictures, 50th Anniv.

Motion Picture Showing for the Armed Forces in South Pacific — A373

1944, Oct. 31		Perf. 11x10½
926 A373	3c deep violet	.15 .15

Florida Statehood Centenary

Old Florida Seal, St. Augustine Gates and State Capitol — A374

1945, Mar. 3		Perf. 11x10½
927 A374	3c bright red violet	.15 .15

United Nations Conference Issue

A375

1945, Apr. 25		Perf. 11x10½
928 A375	5c ultramarine	.15 .15

United Nations conference, San Francisco.

Iwo Jima (Marines) Issue

Marines Raising the Flag on Mt. Suribachi, Iwo Jima — A376

1945, July 11		Perf. 10½x11
929 A376	3c yellow green	.15 .15

Achievements of the US Marines in WWII.

Franklin D. Roosevelt Issue

Roosevelt and Hyde Park Home — A377

Roosevelt and "Little White House," Warm Springs, Georgia A378

Roosevelt and White House — A379

Roosevelt, Globe and Four Freedoms A380

1945-46		Perf. 11x10½
930 A377	1c blue green	.15 .15
931 A378	2c carmine rose	.15 .15
932 A379	3c purple	.15 .15
933 A380	5c bright blue ('46)	.15 .15
	Nos. 930-933 (4)	.60 .60

Franklin Delano Roosevelt (1882-1945).

Army Issue

US Troops Passing Arch of Triumph, Paris — A381

1945, Sept. 28		Perf. 11x10½
934 A381	3c olive	.15 .15

Achievements of the US Army in WWII.

Navy Issue

US Sailors — A382

1945, Oct. 27		Perf. 11x10½
935 A382	3c blue	.15 .15

Achievements of the US Navy in WWII.

Coast Guard Issue

Coast Guard Landing Craft and Supply Ship — A383

1945, Nov. 10		Perf. 11x10½
936 A383	3c bright blue green	.15 .15

Achievements of the US Coast Guard in WWII.

Alfred E. Smith A384

US and Texas State Flags A385

Alfred E. Smith Issue

1945, Nov. 26		Perf. 11x10½
937 A384	3c purple	.15 .15

Smith (1873-1944), governor of NY.

Texas Statehood Centenary

1945, Dec. 29		Perf. 11x10½
938 A385	3c dark blue	.15 .15

UNITED STATES

Merchant Marine Issue

Liberty Ship Unloading Cargo A386

Honorable Discharge Emblem A387

1946, Feb. 26   *Perf. 11x10½*
939 A386 3c blue green   .15 .15
Achievements of the US Merchant Marine in WWII.

Veterans of World War II Issue

1946, May 9   *Perf. 11x10½*
940 A387 3c dark violet   .15 .15
Issued to honor all veterans of WWII.

Tennessee Statehood, 150th Anniv.

Andrew Jackson, John Sevier and Tennessee Capitol — A388

1946, June 1   *Perf. 11x10½*
941 A388 3c dark violet   .15 .15

Iowa Statehood Centenary

Iowa State Flag and Map — A389

1946, Aug. 3   *Perf. 11x10½*
942 A389 3c deep blue   .15 .15

Smithsonian Institution Issue

Smithsonian Institution A390

1946, Aug. 10   *Perf. 11x10½*
943 A390 3c violet brown   .15 .15
Centenary of the establishment of the Smithsonian Institution, Washington, DC.

Kearny Expedition Issue

"Capture of Santa Fe" by Kenneth M. Chapman A391

1946, Oct. 16   *Perf. 11x10½*
944 A391 3c brown violet   .15 .15
Centenary of the entry of General Stephen Watts Kearny into Santa Fe.

Thomas Alva Edison Issue

Thomas A. Edison, Birth Centenary — A392

1947, Feb. 11   *Perf. 10½x11*
945 A392 3c bright red violet   .15 .15

Joseph Pulitzer Birth Centenary

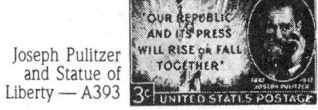

Joseph Pulitzer and Statue of Liberty — A393

1947, Apr. 10   *Perf. 11x10½*
946 A393 3c purple   .15 .15

US Postage Stamp Centenary

Washington and Franklin, Early and Modern Mail-carrying Vehicles A394

1947, May 17   *Perf. 11x10½*
947 A394 3c deep blue   .15 .15

Centenary International Philatelic Exhibition (CIPEX) Souvenir Sheet

A395

Flat Plate Printing
1947, May 19   *Imperf.*
948 A395 Sheet of 2   .55 .45
  a. A1 5c blue   .20 .20
  b. A2 10c brown orange   .25 .25
Sheet size varies: 96-98x66-68mm

Doctors Issue

"The Doctor," by Sir Luke Fildes — A396

Rotary Press Printing
1947, June 9   *Perf. 11x10½*
949 A396 3c brown violet   .15 .15
Issued to honor the physicians of America.

Utah Settlement Centenary

Pioneers Entering the Valley of Great Salt Lake — A397

1947, July 24   *Perf. 11x10½*
950 A397 3c dark violet   .15 .15

US Frigate Constitution Issue

Naval Architect's Drawing of Frigate Constitution A398

1947, Oct. 21   *Perf. 11x10½*
951 A398 3c blue green   .15 .15
150th anniv. of the launching of the US Frigate Constitution ("Old Ironsides").

Everglades National Park Issue

Great White Heron and Map of Florida — A399

1947, Dec. 5   *Perf. 10½x11*
952 A399 3c bright green   .15 .15
Dedication of Everglades Natl. Park, Florida, Dec. 6, 1947.

Dr. George Washington Carver Issue

Dr. George Washington Carver — A400

1948, Jan. 5   *Perf. 10½x11*
953 A400 3c bright red violet   .15 .15
5th anniv. of the death of Dr. George Washington Carver, scientist.

California Gold Centennial Issue

Sutter's Mill, Coloma, California A401

1948, Jan. 24   *Perf. 11x10½*
954 A401 3c dark violet   .15 .15
Discovery of gold in California, centenary.

Mississippi Territory, 150th Anniv.

Map, Seal and Gov. Winthrop Sargent — A402

1948, Apr. 7   *Perf. 11x10½*
955 A402 3c brown violet   .15 .15

Four Chaplains Issue

Four Chaplains and Sinking S. S. Dorchester A403

1948, May 28   *Perf. 11x10½*
956 A403 3c gray black   .15 .15
Honoring George L. Fox, Clark V. Poling, John P. Washington and Alexander D. Goode, the four chaplains who sacrificed their lives in the sinking of the SS Dorchester, Feb. 3, 1943.

Wisconsin Statehood Centenary

Map on Scroll and State Capitol A404

1948, May 29   *Perf. 11x10½*
957 A404 3c dark violet   .15 .15

Swedish Pioneer Issue

Swedish Pioneer with Covered Wagon Moving Westward A405

1948, June 4   *Perf. 11x10½*
958 A405 5c deep blue   .15 .15
Centenary of the coming of the Swedish pioneers to the Middle West.

Progress of Women Issue

Elizabeth Stanton, Carrie C. Catt and Lucretia Mott — A406

1948, July 19   *Perf. 11x10½*
959 A406 3c dark violet   .15 .15
Century of progress of American women.

William Allen White Issue

William Allen White, Editor and Author — A407

1948, July 31   *Perf. 10½x11*
960 A407 3c bright red violet   .15 .15

US-Canada Friendship Centenary

Niagara Railway Suspension Bridge — A408

1948, Aug. 2   *Perf. 11x10½*
961 A408 3c blue   .15 .15

Francis Scott Key Issue

Key and American Flags of 1814 and 1948 — A409

1948, Aug. 9   *Perf. 11x10½*
962 A409 3c rose pink   .15 .15
Francis Scott Key (1779-1843), Maryland lawyer and author of "The Star-Spangled Banner" (1813).

Salute to Youth Issue

Girl and Boy Carrying Books — A410

1948, Aug. 11   *Perf. 11x10½*
963 A410 3c deep blue   .15 .15
Youth of America and "Youth Month," Sept. 1948.

Oregon Territory Issue

John McLoughlin, Jason Lee and Wagon on Oregon Trail — A411

1948, Aug. 14   *Perf. 11x10½*
964 A411 3c brown red   .15 .15
Centenary of the establishment of Ore. Terr.

Chief Justice Harlan Fiske Stone — A412

Observatory, Palomar Mt., Cal. — A413

Harlan Fiske Stone Issue

1948, Aug. 25   *Perf. 10½x11*
965 A412 3c bright red violet   .15 .15

Palomar Mountain Observatory Issue

1948, Aug. 30   *Perf. 10½x11*
966 A413 3c blue   .15 .15
  a. Vert. pair, imperf btwn.   550.00

Clara Barton, 1821-1912

Founder of the American Red Cross (1882) — A414

1948, Sept. 7   *Perf. 11x10½*
967 A414 3c rose pink   .15 .15

UNITED STATES

Poultry Industry Issue

Light Brahma Rooster — A415

1948, Sept. 9   *Perf. 11x10½*
968 A415 3c sepia   .15 .15

Centenary of the establishment of the American poultry industry.

Gold Star Mothers Issue

Star and Palm Frond — A416

1948, Sept. 21   *Perf. 10½x11*
969 A416 3c orange yellow   .15 .15

Honoring mothers of deceased members of the US armed forces.

Fort Kearny Issue

Fort Kearny and Pioneer Group — A417

1948, Sept. 22   *Perf. 11x10½*
970 A417 3c violet   .15 .15

Cent. of the establishment of Fort Kearny, Nebr.

Volunteer Firemen Issue

Peter Stuyvesant; Early and Modern Fire Engines A418

1948, Oct. 4   *Perf. 11x10½*
971 A418 3c bright rose carmine   .15 .15

300th anniv. of the organization of the 1st volunteer firemen in America by Peter Stuyvesant (1592-1672), Dutch colonial gov. of New Netherland.

Indian Centennial Issue

Map of Indian Territory and Seals of Five Tribes A419

1948, Oct. 15   *Perf. 11x10½*
972 A419 3c dark brown   .15 .15

Cent. of the arrival in Indian Territory, later Okla., of the Five Civilized Indian Tribes.

Rough Riders Issue

Statue of Capt. William O. (Bucky) O'Neill A420

1948, Oct. 27   *Perf. 11x10½*
973 A420 3c violet brown   .15 .15

50th anniv. of the organization of the Rough Riders of the Spanish-American War.

Low and Girl Scout Emblem — A421

Will Rogers — A422

Juliette Low Issue

1948, Oct. 29   *Perf. 11x10½*
974 A421 3c blue green   .15 .15

Juliette Gordon Low (1860-1927), organizer of the Girl Scouts of America.

Will Rogers Issue

1948, Nov. 4   *Perf. 10½x11*
975 A422 3c bright red violet   .15 .15

Will Rogers, 1879-1935, humorist and political commentator.

Fort Bliss and Rocket A423

Moina Michael and Poppy Plant A424

Fort Bliss Centennial Issue

1948, Nov. 5   *Perf. 10½x11*
976 A423 3c henna brown   .15 .15

Centenary of Fort Bliss, Texas.

Moina Michael Issue

1948, Nov. 9   *Perf. 11x10½*
977 A424 3c rose pink   .15 .15

Michael (1870-1944), educator who originated (1918) Flanders Field Poppy Day idea as memorial to war dead.

Gettysburg Address Issue

Lincoln and Quotation from Gettysburg Address A425

1948, Nov. 19   *Perf. 11x10½*
978 A425 3c bright blue   .15 .15

85th anniv. of Abraham Lincoln's address at Gettysburg, Pa.

Torch and American Turners' Emblem A426

Joel Chandler Harris A427

American Turners Issue

1948, Nov. 20   *Perf. 10½x11*
979 A426 3c carmine   .15 .15

Centenary of the formation of the American Turners Society.

Joel Chandler Harris Issue

1948, Dec. 9   *Perf. 10½x11*
980 A427 3c bright red violet   .15 .15

Harris (1848-1908), editor and author.

Minnesota Territory Issue

Pioneer and Red River Oxcart — A428

1949, Mar. 3   *Perf. 10½x11*
981 A428 3c blue green   .15 .15

Cent. of the establishment of Minn. Terr.

Washington and Lee University Issue

George Washington, Robert E. Lee and University Building A429

1949, Apr. 12   *Perf. 11x10½*
982 A429 3c ultramarine   .15 .15

200th anniv. of the founding of Washington and Lee Univ.

Puerto Rico Election Issue

Puerto Rican Farmer Holding Cogwheel and Ballot Box — A430

1949, Apr. 27   *Perf. 11x10½*
983 A430 3c green   .15 .15

1st gubernatorial election in the Territory of P.R., Nov. 2, 1948.

Annapolis Tercentenary Issue

Stoddert's 1718 Map of Regions about Annapolis, Redrawn A431

1949, May 23   *Perf. 11x10½*
984 A431 3c aquamarine   .15 .15

300th anniv. of the founding of Annapolis, Md.

Union Soldier and GAR Veteran of 1949 — A432

Edgar Allan Poe — A433

GAR Issue

1949, Aug. 29   *Perf. 11x10½*
985 A432 3c bright rose carmine   .15 .15

Final encampment of the Grand Army of the Republic, Indianapolis, Aug. 28 to Sept. 1.

Edgar Allan Poe Issue

1949, Oct. 7   *Perf. 10½x11*
986 A433 3c bright red violet   .15 .15

Poe (1809-1849), writer and poet.

Coin, Symbolizing Fields of Banking Service A434

Samuel Gompers A435

Bankers Issue

1950, Jan. 3   *Perf. 11x10½*
987 A434 3c yellow green   .15 .15

75th anniv. of the formation of the American Bankers Assoc.

Samuel Gompers Issue

1950, Jan. 27   *Perf. 10½x11*
988 A435 3c bright red violet   .15 .15

Gompers (1850-1924), labor leader.

National Capital Sesquicentennial Issue

Statue of Freedom on Capitol Dome A436

Executive Mansion A437

Supreme Court Building — A438

United States Capitol — A439

1950   *Perf. 10½x11, 11x10½*
989 A436 3c bright blue   .15 .15
990 A437 3c deep green   .15 .15
991 A438 3c light violet   .15 .15
992 A439 3c bright red violet   .15 .15
Nos. 989-992 (4)   .60 .60

150th anniv. of the establishment of the National Capital, Washington, DC.
Issued: Apr. 20, June 12, Aug. 2 and Nov. 22.

Railroad Engineers Issue

"Casey" Jones and Locomotives of 1900 and 1950 A440

1950, Apr. 29   *Perf. 11x10½*
993 A440 3c violet brown   .15 .15

Kansas City, Missouri, Issue

Kansas City Skyline, 1950 and Westport Landing, 1850 — A441

1950, June 3   *Perf. 11x10½*
994 A441 3c violet   .15 .15

Cent. of the incorporation of Kansas City, Mo.

Boy Scouts Issue

Three Boys, Statue of Liberty and Scout Badge — A442

1950, June 30   *Perf. 11x10½*
995 A442 3c sepia   .15 .15

Honoring the BSA on the occasion of the 2nd Natl. Jamboree, held at Valley Forge, Pa.

Indiana Territory Issue

Gov. William Henry Harrison and First Indiana Capitol, Vincennes A443

1950, July 4   *Perf. 11x10½*
996 A443 3c bright blue   .15 .15

150th anniv. of the establishment of Ind. Terr.

UNITED STATES

California Statehood Centenary

Gold Miner, Pioneers and S.S. *Oregon* A444

1950, Sept. 9   *Perf. 11x10½*
997 A444 3c yellow orange   .15 .15

United Confederate Veterans Final Reunion Issue

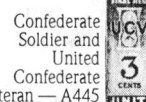

Confederate Soldier and United Confederate Veteran — A445

1951, May 30   *Perf. 11x10½*
998 A445 3c gray   .15 .15

Final reunion of the United Confederate Veterans, Norfolk, Va, May 30, 1951.

Nevada Settlement Centennial

Carson Valley, c. 1851 A446

1951, July 14   *Perf. 11x10½*
999 A446 3c light olive green   .15 .15

Landing of Cadillac Issue

Detroit Skyline and Cadillac Landing A447

1951, July 24   *Perf. 11x10½*
1000 A447 3c blue   .15 .15

250th anniv. of the landing of Antoine de la Mothe Cadillac at Detroit.

Colorado Statehood Issue

Colorado Capitol and Mount of the Holy Cross — A448

1951, Aug. 1   *Perf. 11x10½*
1001 A448 3c blue violet   .15 .15

Colorado statehood, 75th anniv. Design includes columbine and statue, "The Bronco Buster," by A. Phimister Proctor.

American Chemical Society Issue

A. C. S. Emblem and Symbols of Chemistry A449

1951, Sept. 4   *Perf. 11x10½*
1002 A449 3c violet brown   .15 .15

American Chemical Soc., 75th anniv.

Battle of Brooklyn Issue

Gen. George Washington Evacuating Army — A450

1951, Dec. 10   *Perf. 11x10½*
1003 A450 3c violet   .15 .15

175th anniv. of the Battle of Brooklyn. Design includes Fulton Ferry House.

Betsy Ross Issue

Betsy Ross Showing Flag to Gen. George Washington, Robert Morris and George Ross — A451

1952, Jan. 2   *Perf. 11x10½*
1004 A451 3c carmine rose   .15 .15

200th anniv. of the birth of Betsy Ross, maker of the 1st American flag.

4-H Club Issue

Farm, Club Emblem, Boy and Girl — A452

1952, Jan. 15   *Perf. 11x10½*
1005 A452 3c blue green   .15 .15

B. & O. Railroad Issue

Charter and Three Stages of Rail Transportation A453

1952, Feb. 28   *Perf. 11x10½*
1006 A453 3c bright blue   .15 .15

125th anniv. of the granting of a charter to the Baltimore and Ohio Railroad Company by the Maryland Legislature.

A. A. A., 50th Anniv.

School Girls and Safety Patrolman, Automobiles of 1902 and 1952 — A454

1952, Mar. 4   *Perf. 11x10½*
1007 A454 3c deep blue   .15 .15

Torch of Liberty and Globe A455

Spillway, Grand Coulee Dam A456

NATO Issue

1952, Apr. 4   *Perf. 11x10½*
1008 A455 3c deep violet   .15 .15

3rd anniv. of the signing of the North Atlantic Treaty.

Grand Coulee Dam Issue

1952, May 15   *Perf. 11x10½*
1009 A456 3c blue green   .15 .15

50 years of Federal cooperation in developing the resources of rivers and streams in the West.

Lafayette Issue

Marquis de Lafayette, Flags, Cannon and Landing Party — A457

1952, June 13   *Perf. 11x10½*
1010 A457 3c bright blue   .15 .15

175th anniv. of the arrival of Lafayette in America.

Mt. Rushmore Memorial Issue

Sculptured Heads on Mt. Rushmore — A458

1952, Aug. 11   *Perf. 10½x11*
1011 A458 3c blue green   .15 .15

25th anniv. of the dedication of the Mt. Rushmore Natl. Memorial.

Engineering Centennial Issue

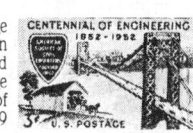

George Washington Bridge and Covered Bridge of 1850's — A459

1952, Sept. 6   *Perf. 11x10½*
1012 A459 3c violet blue   .15 .15

Centenary of the founding of the American Soc. of Civil Engineers.

Service Women Issue

Women of the Marine Corps, Army, Navy and Air Force — A460

1952, Sept. 11   *Perf. 11x10½*
1013 A460 3c deep blue   .15 .15

Honoring the women in the US Armed Services.

Gutenberg Bible Issue

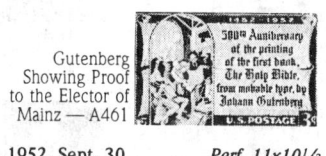

Gutenberg Showing Proof to the Elector of Mainz — A461

1952, Sept. 30   *Perf. 11x10½*
1014 A461 3c violet   .15 .15

500th anniv. of the printing of the 1st book, the Holy Bible, from movable type, by Johann Gutenberg.

Newspaper Boys Issue

Newspaper Boy, Torch and Group of Homes — A462

1952, Oct. 4   *Perf. 11x10½*
1015 A462 3c violet   .15 .15

Red Cross Issue

Globe, Sun and Cross — A463

Perf. 11x10½
1952, Nov. 21   Cross Typo.
1016 A463 3c deep blue & carmine   .15 .15

National Guard Issue

National Guardsman and Amphibious Landing A464

1953, Feb. 23   *Perf. 11x10½*
1017 A464 3c bright blue   .15 .15

Ohio Statehood Sesquicentennial

Map and Ohio State Seal — A465

1953, Mar. 2   *Perf. 11x10½*
1018 A465 3c chocolate   .15 .15

Washington Territory Issue

Medallion, Pioneers and Washington Scene — A466

1953, Mar. 2   *Perf. 11x10½*
1019 A466 3c green   .15 .15

Centenary of the organization of Washington Territory.

Louisiana Purchase, 150th Anniv.

Monroe, Livingston and Barbé-Marbois A467

1953, Apr. 30   *Perf. 11x10½*
1020 A467 3c violet brown   .15 .15

Opening of Japan Centennial Issue

Commodore Perry and 1st Anchorage off Tokyo Bay — A468

1953, July 14   *Perf. 11x10½*
1021 A468 5c green   .15 .15

Cent. of Commodore Matthew Calbraith Perry's negotiations with Japan, which opened her doors to foreign trade.

American Bar Association, 75th Anniv.

Section of Frieze, Supreme Court Room — A469

1953, Aug. 24   *Perf. 11x10½*
1022 A469 3c rose violet   .15 .15

Sagamore Hill Issue

Home of Theodore Roosevelt A470

1953, Sept. 14   *Perf. 11x10½*
1023 A470 3c yellow green   .15 .15

Opening of Sagamore Hill, Theodore Roosevelt's home, as a national shrine.

Future Farmers Issue

Agricultural Scene and Future Farmer — A471

1953, Oct. 13   *Perf. 11x10½*
1024 A471 3c deep blue   .15 .15

25th anniv. of the organization of Future Farmers of America.

UNITED STATES

Trucking Industry Issue

Truck, Farm and Distant City — A472

1953, Oct. 27   *Perf. 11x10½*
1025   A472   3c violet   .15   .15

Trucking Industry in the US, 50th anniv.

General Patton Issue

Gen. George S. Patton, Jr., and Tank in Action — A473

1953, Nov. 11   *Perf. 11x10½*
1026   A473   3c blue violet   .15   .15

Honoring Patton and the armored forces of the US army.

New York City, 300th Anniv.

Dutch Ship in New Amsterdam Harbor — A474

1953, Nov. 20   *Perf. 11x10½*
1027   A474   3c bright red violet   .15   .15

Gadsden Purchase Issue

Map and Pioneer Group — A475

1953, Dec. 30   *Perf. 11x10½*
1028   A475   3c copper brown   .15   .15

Centenary of James Gadsden's purchase of territory from Mexico, to adjust US-Mexico boundary.

Columbia University, 200th Anniv.

Low Memorial Library — A476

1954, Jan. 4   *Perf. 11x10½*
1029   A476   3c blue   .15   .15

Wet and Dry Printings

In 1953 the Bureau of Engraving and Printing began experiments in printing on "dry" paper (moisture content 5-10 per cent). In previous "wet" printings the paper had a moisture content of 13-35 per cent.

The new process required a thicker, stiffer paper, special types of inks and greater pressure to force the paper into the recessed plates. The "dry" printings show whiter paper, a higher sheen on the surface, feel thicker and stiffer, and the designs stand out more clearly than on the "wet" printings.

Nos. 832c and 1041 (flat plate) were the first "dry" printings to be issued of flat-plate, regular-issue stamps. No. 1063 was the first rotary-press stamp to be produced entirely by "dry" printing.

All postage stamps have been printed by the "dry" process since the late 1950's.

See the Scott Specialized Catalogue of United States Stamps for listings of the wet and dry printings and for No. 1033 on Silkote paper.

Liberty Issue

Franklin A477    Washington A478
Palace of the Governors, Santa Fe — A478a    Mount Vernon — A479 
Thomas Jefferson A480    Bunker Hill Monument, Mass. Flag, 1776 A481 
Statue of Liberty A482    Abraham Lincoln A483 
The Hermitage A484    James Monroe A485 
Theodore Roosevelt A486    Woodrow Wilson A487 
Statue of Liberty A488   A489  
John J. Pershing A489a    The Alamo A490 
Independence Hall — A491 
Statue of Liberty A491a    Benjamin Harrison A492 
John Jay A493    Monticello A494 
Paul Revere A495    Robert E. Lee A496 
John Marshall A497    Susan B. Anthony A498 
Patrick Henry A499    Alexander Hamilton A500 

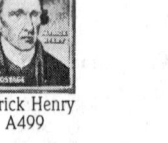

Perf. 11x10½, 10½x11

1954-68   **Rotary Press Printing**

1030	A477	½c red orange ('55)	.15	.15
1031	A478	1c dark green	.15	.15
1031A	A478a	1¼c turq ('60)	.15	.15
1032	A479	1½c brown carmine ('56)	.15	.15
1033	A480	2c car rose	.15	.15
1034	A481	2½c gray blue ('59)	.15	.15
1035	A482	3c deep violet	.15	.15
a.		Booklet pane of 6	4.00	.90
b.		Tagged ('66)	.25	.25
c.		Imperf., pair	2,000.	
d.		Horiz. pair, imperf. btwn.	—	
g.		As "a," vert. imperf. btwn.	5,000.	

No. 1057a measures about 19½x22mm; No. 1035c, about 18¾x22½mm.

1036	A483	4c red violet	.15	.15
a.		Booklet pane of 6 ('58)	2.75	.80
b.		Tagged ('63)	.50	.40
d.		As "a," imperf. horiz.		
1037	A484	4½c blue green ('59)	.15	.15
1038	A485	5c deep blue	.15	.15
1039	A486	6c car ('55)	.25	.15
1040	A487	7c rose carmine ('56)	.20	.15

Flat Plate Printing
Perf. 11
Size: 22.7mm high

1041	A488	8c dk vio blue & car	.25	.15
a.		Double impression of carmine	650.00	

Rotary Press Printing
Size: 22.9mm high

1041B	A488	8c dk vio blue & car	.25	.15

Giori Press Printing
Redrawn Design

1042	A489	8c dk vio bl & car rose ('58)	.20	.15

Rotary Press Printing
Perf. 11x10½, 10½x11

1042A	A489a	8c brown ('61)	.20	.15
1043	A490	9c rose lilac ('56)	.30	.15
1044	A491	10c rose lake ('56)	.15	.15
b.		Tagged ('66)	2.00	1.00

Giori Press Printing
Perf. 11

1044A	A491a	11c car & dk vio blue ('61)	.30	.15
c.		Tagged ('67)	2.00	1.60

Rotary Press Printing
Perf. 11x10½, 10½x11

1045	A492	12c red ('59)	.35	.15
a.		Tagged ('68)	.35	.15
1046	A493	15c rose lake ('58)	.60	.15
a.		Tagged ('66)	1.10	.35
1047	A494	20c ultra ('56)	.40	.15
1048	A495	25c green ('58)	1.10	.15
1049	A496	30c black ('55)	.70	.15
1050	A497	40c brown red ('55)	1.50	.15
1051	A498	50c brt purple ('55)	1.50	.15
1052	A499	$1 purple ('55)	5.00	.15

Flat Plate Printing
Perf. 11

1053	A500	$5 black ('56)	75.00	6.75
	Nos. 1030-1053 (28)		89.85	10.80

Luminescence

During 1963 quantities of certain issues (Nos. C64a, 1213b, 1213c and 1229a) were overprinted with phosphorescent coating, "tagged," for use in testing automated facing and canceling machines. Listings for tagged varieties of stamps previously issued without tagging start with Nos. 1035b and C59a.

The entire printings of Nos. 1238, 1278, 1280-1281, 1283B, 1286-1288, 1298-1305, 1323-1340, 1342-1362, 1364, and C69-C75 and all following listings, unless otherwise noted, were tagged.

Stamps tagged with zinc orthosilicate glow yellow green. Airmail stamps with calcium silicate overprint glow orange red. Both tagging overprints are activated only by shortwave ultraviolet light.

Coil Stamps
Perf. 10 Vert., Horiz. (1¼c, 4½c)

1954-73

1054	A478	1c dark green	.20	.15
b.		Imperf., pair	2,500.	.15
1054A	A478a	1¼c turq ('60)	.15	.15
1055	A480	2c rose car	.15	.15
a.		Tagged ('68)	.15	.15
b.		Imperf., pair (Bureau precanceled)		550.00
c.		As "a," imperf. pair	575.00	
1056	A481	2½c gray blue ('59)	.25	.25
1057	A482	3c dp violet	.15	.15
a.		Imperf., pair	1,750.	
b.		Tagged ('66)	1.00	.50

No. 1057a measures about 19½x22mm; No. 1035c, about 18¾x22½mm.

1058	A483	4c red vio ('58)	.15	.15
a.		Imperf., pair	110.00	70.00
1059	A484	4½c blue grn ('59)	1.50	1.20
1059A	A495	25c grn ('65)	.50	.30
b.		Tagged ('73)	.65	.50
c.		Imperf., pair	50.00	
	Nos. 1054-1059A (8)		3.05	2.50

Value for No. 1059c is for fine centering.

Nebraska Territory Issue

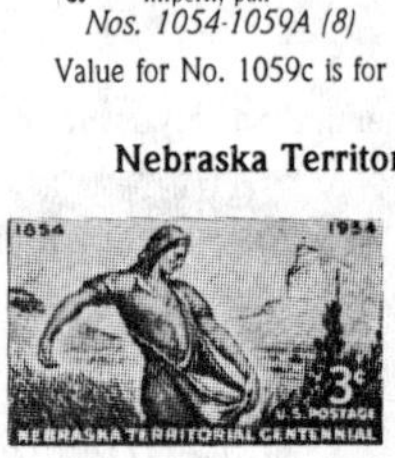

Mitchell Pass, Scotts Bluff and "The Sower," by Lee Lawrie — A507

1954, May 7   *Perf. 11x10½*
1060   A507   3c violet   .15   .15

Centenary of the establishment of the Nebraska Territory.

Kansas Territory Issue

Wheat Field and Pioneer Wagon Train — A508

1954, May 31   *Perf. 11x10½*
1061   A508   3c brown orange   .15   .15

Centenary of the establishment of the Kansas Territory.

UNITED STATES

George Eastman Issue

George Eastman (1854-1932), Inventor and Philanthropist — A509

1954, July 12   *Perf. 10½x11*
1062 A509 3c violet brown   .15 .15

Lewis and Clark Expedition Sesquicentennial

Landing of Lewis and Clark — A510

1954, July 28   *Perf. 11x10½*
1063 A510 3c violet brown   .15 .15

Pennsylvania Acad. of the Fine Arts

Charles Willson Peale in his Museum, Self-portrait — A511

1955, Jan. 15   *Perf. 10½x11*
1064 A511 3c violet brown   .15 .15

150th anniv. of the founding of the Pa. Acad. of the Fine Arts, Philadelphia.

Land Grant Colleges Issue

Open Book and Symbols of Subjects Taught — A512

1955, Feb. 12   *Perf. 11x10½*
1065 A512 3c green   .15 .15

Cent. of the founding of Mich. State College and Penn. State Univ., 1st of the land-grant institutions.

Rotary International, 50th Anniv.

Torch, Globe and Rotary Emblem — A513

1955, Feb. 23   *Perf. 11x10½*
1066 A513 8c deep blue   .20 .15

Armed Forces Reserve Issue

Marine, Coast Guard, Army, Navy, and Air Force Personnel A514

1955, May 21   *Perf. 11x10½*
1067 A514 3c purple   .15 .15

New Hampshire Issue

Great Stone Face — A515

1955, June 21   *Perf. 10½x11*
1068 A515 3c green   .15 .15

Honor NH on the occasion of the sesquicentennial of the discovery of the "Old Man of the Mountains."

Soo Locks Opening, Centenary

Map of Great Lakes and Two Steamers A516

1955, June 28   *Perf. 11x10½*
1069 A516 3c blue   .15 .15

Atoms for Peace Policy

Atomic Energy Encircling the Hemispheres A517

1955, July 28   *Perf. 11x10½*
1070 A517 3c deep blue   .15 .15

Fort Ticonderoga Bicentenary

Map of the Fort, Ethan Allen and Artillery A518

1955, Sept. 18   *Perf. 11x10½*
1071 A518 3c light brown   .15 .15

Andrew W. Mellon Issue

Andrew W. Mellon — A519

1955, Dec. 20   *Perf. 10½x11*
1072 A519 3c rose carmine   .15 .15

Mellon, US Sec. of the Treasury (1921-32), financier and art collector.

Benjamin Franklin Issue

"Franklin Taking Electricity from the Sky," by Benjamin West — A520

1956, Jan. 17   *Perf. 10½x11*
1073 A520 3c bright carmine   .15 .15

250th anniv. of the birth of Franklin.

Booker T. Washington Issue

Log Cabin — A521

1956, Apr. 5   *Perf. 11x10½*
1074 A521 3c deep blue   .15 .15

Washington (1856-1915), black educator.

Fifth Intl. Phil. Exhib. Issues Souvenir Sheet

A522

Flat Plate Printing

1956, Apr. 28   *Imperf.*
1075 A522 Sheet of 2   2.00 2.00
   a. A482 3c deep violet   .80 .80
   b. A488 8c dk vio bl & carmine   1.00 1.00

No. 1075 measures 108x73mm; Nos. 1075a and 1075b measure 24x28mm.

New York Coliseum and Columbus Monument A523

Rotary Press Printing

1956, Apr. 30   *Perf. 11x10½*
1076 A523 3c deep violet   .15 .15

FIPEX, New York City, Apr. 28-May 6.

Wildlife Conservation Issue

Wild Turkey A524

Pronghorn Antelope A525

King Salmon — A526

1956   *Perf. 11x10½*
1077 A524 3c rose lake   .15 .15
1078 A525 3c brown   .15 .15
1079 A526 3c blue green   .15 .15
   Nos. 1077-1079 (3)   .45 .45

Emphasizing the importance of Wildlife conservation in America.
Issued May 5, June 22 and Nov. 9.
See Nos. 1098, 1392.

Pure Food and Drug Laws, 50th Anniv.

Harvey W. Wiley — A527

1956, June 27   *Perf. 10½x11*
1080 A527 3c dark blue green   .15 .15

Wheatland Issue

President Buchanan's Home, "Wheatland," Lancaster, PA — A528

1956, Aug. 5   *Perf. 11x10½*
1081 A528 3c black brown   .15 .15

Labor Day Issue

Mosaic, AFL-CIO Headquarters — A529

1956, Sept. 3   *Perf. 10½x11*
1082 A529 3c deep blue   .15 .15

Nassau Hall Issue

Nassau Hall, Princeton, NJ — A530

1956, Sept. 22   *Perf. 11x10½*
1083 A530 3c black, orange   .15 .15

200th anniv. of Nassau Hall, Princeton University.

Devils Tower Issue

Devils Tower — A531

1956, Sept. 24   *Perf. 10½x11*
1084 A531 3c violet   .15 .15

50th anniv. of the Federal law providing for protection of American natural antiquities. Devils Tower Natl. Monument, Wyoming, is an outstanding example.

Children's Issue

Children of the World A532

1956, Dec. 15   *Perf. 11x10½*
1085 A532 3c dark blue   .15 .15

Promoting friendship among the world's children.

Alexander Hamilton Issue

Alexander Hamilton (1757-1804) and Federal Hall — A533

1957, Jan. 11   *Perf. 11x10½*
1086 A533 3c rose red   .15 .15

Polio Issue

Allegory — A534

1957, Jan. 15   *Perf. 10½x11*
1087 A534 3c red lilac   .15 .15

Honoring "those who helped fight polio," and 20th anniv. of the Natl. Foundation for Infantile Paralysis and the March of Dimes.

Coast and Geodetic Survey Issue

Flag of Coast and Geodetic Survey and Ships at Sea — A535

1957, Feb. 11   *Perf. 11x10½*
1088 A535 3c dark blue   .15 .15

150th anniv. of the establishment of the Coast and Geodetic Survey.

United States stamps can be mounted in the Scott National and Minuteman albums.

UNITED STATES

Architects Issue

Corinthian Capital and Mushroom Type Head and Shaft — A536

1957, Feb. 23   *Perf. 11x10½*
1089 A536 3c red lilac   .15   .15

Centenary of the American Institute of Architects.

Steel Industry Centenary

American Eagle and Pouring Ladle — A537

1957, May 22   *Perf. 10½x11*
1090 A537 3c bright ultra   .15   .15

International Naval Review Issue

Aircraft Carrier and Jamestown Festival Emblem A538

1957, June 10   *Perf. 11x10½*
1091 A538 3c blue green   .15   .15

Intl. Naval Review and Jamestown Festival.

Oklahoma Statehood, 50th Anniv.

Map of Oklahoma, Arrow and Atom Diagram A539

1957, June 14   *Perf. 11x10½*
1092 A539 3c dark blue   .15   .15

School Teachers Issue

Teacher and Pupils — A540

1957, July 1   *Perf. 11x10½*
1093 A540 3c rose lake   .15   .15

Honoring the school teachers of America.

Flag Issue

"Old Glory" (48 Stars) — A541

Giori Press Printing
1957, July 4   *Perf. 11*
1094 A541 4c dk blue & dp carmine   .15   .15

Shipbuilding Issue

"Virginia of Sagadahock" and Seal of Maine — A542

Rotary Press Printing
1957, Aug. 15   *Perf. 10½x11*
1095 A542 3c deep violet   .15   .15

350th anniv. of shipbuilding in America.

Champion of Liberty Issue

Ramon Magsaysay, (1907-1957), Philippines President — A543

Giori Press Printing
1957, Aug. 31   *Perf. 11*
1096 A543 8c carmine, ultra & ocher   .20   .15

For other Champion of Liberty issues, see Nos. 1110-1111, 1117-1118, 1125-1126, 1136-1137, 1147-1148, 1159-1160, 1165-1166, 1168-1169, 1174-1175.

Marquis de Lafayette A544

Whooping Cranes A545

Lafayette Bicentenary Issue
Rotary Press Printing
1957, Sept. 6   *Perf. 10½x11*
1097 A544 3c rose lake   .15   .15

Bicentenary of the birth of Lafayette.

Wildlife Conservation Issue
Giori Press Printing
1957, Nov. 22   *Perf. 11*
1098 A545 3c blue, ocher & green   .15   .15

Emphasizing the importance of Wildlife Conservation in America.

Bible, Hat and Quill Pen — A546

"Bountiful Earth" — A547

Religious Freedom Issue
Rotary Press Printing
1957, Dec. 27   *Perf. 10½x11*
1099 A546 3c black   .15   .15

Flushing Remonstrance, 300th anniv.

Gardening-Horticulture Issue
1958, Mar. 15
1100 A547 3c green   .15   .15

Garden clubs of America and cent. of the birth of Liberty Hyde Bailey, horticulturist.

Brussels Fair Issue

US Pavilion at Brussels A551

Rotary Press Printing
1958, Apr. 17   *Perf. 11x10½*
1104 A551 3c deep claret   .15   .15

Opening of the Universal and Intl. Exhib., Brussels, Apr. 17.

James Monroe Issue

James Monroe, by Gilbert Stuart — A552

1958, Apr. 28   *Perf. 11x10½*
1105 A552 3c purple   .15   .15

Monroe (1758-1831), 5th pres. of the US.

Minnesota Statehood Centenary

Minnesota Lakes and Pines — A553

Rotary Press Printing
1958, May 11
1106 A553 3c green   .15   .15

Geophysical Year (IGY, 1957-58)

Solar Disc and Hands from Michelangelo's "Creation of Adam" — A554

Giori Press Printing
1958, May 31   *Perf. 11*
1107 A554 3c black & red orange   .15   .15

Gunston Hall Issue

Gunston Hall, Virginia A555

Rotary Press Printing
1958, June 12   *Perf. 11x10½*
1108 A555 3c light green   .15   .15

Bicent. of Gunston Hall and honoring George Mason, author of the Constitution of Va. and the Va. Bill of Rights.

Mackinac Bridge A556

Simon Bolivar A557

Mackinac Bridge Issue
1958, June 25   *Perf. 10½x11*
1109 A556 3c bright greenish blue   .15   .15

Dedication of Mackinac Bridge, Mich.

Champion of Liberty Issue
Rotary Press Printing
1958, July 24   *Perf. 10½x11*
1110 A557 4c olive bister   .15   .15

Giori Press Printing
Perf. 11
1111 A557 8c carmine, ultra & ocher   .20   .15

Simon Bolivar, So. American freedom fighter.

Atlantic Cable Centennial Issue

Neptune, Globe and Mermaid A558

Rotary Press Printing
1958, Aug. 15   *Perf. 11x10½*
1112 A558 4c reddish purple   .15   .15

Centenary of the Atlantic Cable, linking the Eastern and Western hemispheres.

Lincoln Sesquicentennial Issue

Lincoln, by George Healy A559

Lincoln, by Gutzon Borglum A560

Abraham Lincoln and Stephen A. Douglas Debating A561

Lincoln, by Daniel Chester French — A562

1958-59   *Perf. 10½x11, 11x10½*
1113 A559 1c green ('59)   .15   .15
1114 A560 3c purple ('59)   .15   .15
1115 A561 4c sepia   .15   .15
1116 A562 4c dark blue ('59)   .15   .15
Nos. 1113-1116 (4)   .60   .60

No. 1114 also for the founding of Cooper Union cent., NYC. No. 1115 also for the Lincoln-Douglas debates, cent.
Issue dates: Nos. 1113, 1114, 1116, Feb. 12, Feb. 27 and May 30. No. 1115, Aug. 27.

Lajos Kossuth, (1802-1892) A563

Early Press and Hand Holding Quill A564

Champion of Liberty Issue
Rotary Press Printing
1958, Sept. 19   *Perf. 10½x11*
1117 A563 4c green   .15   .15

Giori Press Printing
Perf. 11
1118 A563 8c carmine, ultra & ocher   .20   .15

Kossuth, Hungarian freedom fighter.

Freedom of Press Issue
Rotary Press Printing
1958, Sept. 22   *Perf. 10½x11*
1119 A564 4c black   .15   .15

Honoring journalism and freedom of the press in connection with the 50th anniv. of the 1st School of Journalism at the Univ. of Mo.

Overland Mail Centenary

Mail Coach and Map of Southwest US — A565

1958, Oct. 10   *Perf. 11x10½*
1120 A565 4c crimson rose   .15   .15

Noah Webster A566

Forest Scene A567

UNITED STATES

Noah Webster Issue
1958, Oct. 16 — Perf. 10½x11
1121 A566 4c dark carmine rose .15 .15
Webster (1758-1843), lexicographer.

Forest Conservation Issue
Giori Press Printing
1958, Oct. 27 — Perf. 11
1122 A567 4c green, yel & brown .15 .15
Publicizing forest conservation and the protection of natural resources and honoring Theodore Roosevelt, a leading forest conservationist, on the cent. of his birth.

Fort Duquesne Issue

Occupation of Fort Duquesne — A568

Rotary Press Printing
1958, Nov. 25 — Perf. 11x10½
1123 A568 4c blue .15 .15
Bicentennial of Fort Duquesne (Fort Pitt).

Oregon Statehood Centenary

Covered Wagon and Mt. Hood — A569

1959, Feb. 14 — Perf. 11x10½
1124 A569 4c blue green .15 .15

José de San Martin — A570
NATO Emblem — A571 

Champion of Liberty Issue
Rotary Press Printing
1959, Feb. 25 — Perf. 10½x11
1125 A570 4c blue .15 .15
  a. Horiz. pair, imperf. btwn. 1,500.

Giori Press Printing
Perf. 11
1126 A570 8c car, ultra & ocher .20 .15
San Martin, South American soldier and statesman.

NATO Issue
Rotary Press Printing
1959, Apr. 1 — Perf. 10½x11
1127 A571 4c blue .15 .15
North Atlantic Treaty Organ., 10th anniv.

Arctic Explorations Issue

North Pole, Dog Sled and "Nautilus" A572

1959, Apr. 6 — Perf. 11x10½
1128 A572 4c brt greenish blue .15 .15
Conquest of the Arctic by land by Rear Admiral Robert Edwin Peary in 1909 and by sea by the submarine "Nautilus" in 1958.

World Peace Through World Trade Issue

Globe and Laurel — A573

1959, Apr. 20 — Perf. 11x10½
1129 A573 8c rose lake .20 .15
Issued in conjunction with the 17th Cong. of the Intl. Chamber of Commerce, Washington, DC, Apr. 19-25.

Silver Centennial Issue

Henry Comstock at Mount Davidson Site — A574

1959, June 8 — Perf. 11x10½
1130 A574 4c black .15 .15
Cent. of the discovery of silver at the Comstock Lode, Nev.

St. Lawrence Seaway Issue

Great Lakes, Maple Leaf and Eagle Emblems A575

Giori Press Printing
1959, June 26 — Perf. 11
1131 A575 4c red & dark blue .15 .15
Opening of the St. Lawrence Seaway, June 26, 1959. See Canada No. 387.

49-Star Flag Issue

US Flag, 1959 — A576

1959, July 4 — Perf. 11
1132 A576 4c ocher, dk blue & dp car .15 .15

Soil Conservation Issue

Modern Farm — A577

1959, Aug. 26
1133 A577 4c blue, green & ocher .15 .15
Tribute to farmers and ranchers who use soil and water conservation measures.

Petroleum Industry Issue

Oil Derrick — A578

Rotary Press Printing
1959, Aug. 27 — Perf. 10½x11
1134 A578 4c brown .15 .15
Cent. of the completion of the nation's 1st oil well at Titusville, Pa.

Dental Health Issue

Children A579

1959, Sept. 14 — Perf. 11x10½
1135 A579 4c green .15 .15
Publicizing dental health and cent. of the American Dental Assoc.

Ernst Reuter A580
Dr. Ephraim McDowell A581 

Champion of Liberty Issue
Rotary Press Printing
1959, Sept. 29 — Perf. 10½x11
1136 A580 4c gray .15 .15

Giori Press Printing
Perf. 11
1137 A580 8c carmine, ultra & ocher .20 .15
  a. Ocher omitted 3,750.
  b. Ultramarine omitted 3,750.
  c. Ocher & ultramarine omitted 4,000.
  d. All colors omitted —
Ernst Reuter, mayor of Berlin 1948-53.

Dr. Ephraim McDowell Issue
Rotary Press Printing
1959, Dec. 3 — Perf. 10½x11
1138 A581 4c rose lake .15 .15
  a. Vert. pair, imperf. btwn. 450.00
  b. Vert. pair, imperf. horiz. 350.00
Honoring McDowell on the 150th anniv. of the 1st successful ovarian operation performed in the US.

American Credo Issue

Quotation from Washington's Farewell Address, 1796 — A582
Benjamin Franklin Quotation A583 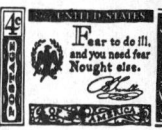
Thomas Jefferson Quotation A584 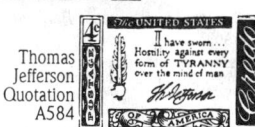
Francis Scott Key Quotation A585 
Abraham Lincoln Quotation A586 
Patrick Henry Quotation A587 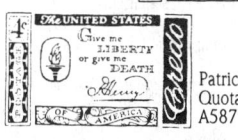

Giori Press Printing
1960-61 — Perf. 11
1139 A582 4c dk violet blue & car .15 .15
1140 A583 4c olive bister & green .15 .15
1141 A584 4c gray & vermilion .15 .15
1142 A585 4c carmine & dark blue .15 .15
1143 A586 4c magenta & green .15 .15
1144 A587 4c green & brown ('61) .15 .15
  Nos. 1139-1144 (6) .90 .90
Re-emphasizing the ideals upon which America was founded and honoring those great Americans who wrote or uttered the credos.
Issue dates: Jan. 20, Mar. 31, May 18, Sept. 14, Nov. 19, and Jan. 11.

Boy Scout Jubilee Issue

Boy Scout Giving Scout Sign — A588

Giori Press Printing
1960, Feb. 8 — Perf. 11
1145 A588 4c red, dk blue & dk bis .15 .15
Boy Scouts of America, 50th anniv.

Olympic Rings and Snowflake A589
Thomas G. Masaryk A590 

Olympic Winter Games Issue
Rotary Press Printing
1960, Feb. 18 — Perf. 10½x11
1146 A589 4c dull blue .15 .15
Opening of the 8th Olympic Winter Games, Squaw Valley, Feb. 18-29.

Champion of Liberty Issue
Rotary Press Printing
1960, Mar. 7 — Perf. 10½x11
1147 A590 4c blue .15 .15
  a. Vert. pair, imperf. btwn. 3,250.

Giori Press Printing
Perf. 11
1148 A590 8c carmine, ultra & ocher .20 .15
  a. Horiz. pair, imperf. btwn.
Masaryk, founder and pres. of Czechoslovakia (1918-35), on the 110th anniv. of his birth.

World Refugee Year Issue

Refugee Family Walking Toward New Life — A591

Rotary Press Printing
1960, Apr. 7 — Perf. 11x10½
1149 A591 4c gray black .15 .15
WRY, July 1, 1959-June 30, 1960.

Water Conservation Issue

Water, from Watershed to Consumer A592

Giori Press Printing
1960, Apr. 18 — Perf. 11
1150 A592 4c dk blue, brn org & green .15 .15
  a. Brown orange omitted
Stressing the importance of water conservation, and 7th Watershed Cong., Washington, DC.

UNITED STATES

SEATO Issue

SEATO Emblem — A593

Rotary Press Printing
1960, May 31 — Perf. 10½x11
1151 A593 4c blue .15 .15
a. Vert. pair, imperf. btwn. 175.00
South-East Asia Treaty Org. and the SEATO Conf., Washington, DC, May 31-June 3.

American Woman Issue

Mother and Daughter A594

1960, June 2 — Perf. 11x10½
1152 A594 4c deep violet .15 .15
A tribute to American women and their accomplishments in civic affairs, education, arts and industry.

50-Star Flag Issue

US Flag, 1960 — A595

Giori Press Printing
1960, July 4 — Perf. 11
1153 A595 4c dark blue & red .15 .15

Pony Express Centennial Issue

Pony Express Rider — A596

Rotary Press Printing
1960, July 19 — Perf. 11x10½
1154 A596 4c sepia .15 .15

Man in Wheelchair Operating Drill Press — A597

5th World Forestry Congress Seal — A598

Employ the Handicapped Issue

1960, Aug. 28 — Perf. 10½x11
1155 A597 4c dark blue .15 .15
Promoting employment of the physically handicapped and publicizing the 8th World Cong. of the Intl. Soc. for the Welfare of Cripples, NYC.

World Forestry Congress Issue

1960, Aug. 29
1156 A598 4c green .15 .15
5th World Forestry Cong., Seattle, Wash., Aug. 29-Sept. 10.

A599

A600

Mexican Independence Issue

Giori Press Printing
1960, Sept. 16 — Perf. 11
1157 A599 4c Independence Bell .15 .15
150th anniv. of Mexican independence. See Mexico No. 910.

US-Japan Treaty Issue

1960, Sept. 28 — Perf. 11
1158 A600 4c blue & pink .15 .15
Washington Monument and Cherry Blossoms
Cent. of the US-Japan Treaty of Amity and Commerce.

Ignacy Jan Paderewski A601

Robert A. Taft A602

Champion of Liberty Issue

Rotary Press Printing
1960, Oct. 8 — Perf. 10½x11
1159 A601 4c blue .15 .15

Giori Press Printing — Perf. 11
1160 A601 8c carmine, ultra & ocher .20 .15
Paderewski (1866-1941), Polish statesman and musician.

Senator Taft Memorial Issue

Rotary Press Printing
1960, Oct. 10 — Perf. 10½x11
1161 A602 4c dull violet .15 .15
Senator Taft (1889-1953), of Ohio.

Wheels of Freedom Issue

Globe and Steering Wheel with Tractor, Car and Truck — A603

1960, Oct. 15 — Perf. 11x10½
1162 A603 4c dark blue .15 .15
Honoring the automotive industry and in connection with the National Automobile Show, Detroit, Oct. 15-23.

Boys' Clubs of America Issue

Profile of a Boy — A604

Giori Press Printing
1960, Oct. 18 — Perf. 11
1163 A604 4c indigo, slate & rose red .15 .15
Cent. of the Boys' Clubs of America movement.

Automated Post Office Issue

Architect's Sketch of New Post Office, Providence, RI — A605

1960, Oct. 20 — Perf. 11
1164 A605 4c dk blue & carmine .15 .15
Opening of the 1st automated PO in the US.

Baron Gustaf Emil Mannerheim A606

Camp Fire Girls Emblem A607

Champion of Liberty Issue

Rotary Press Printing
1960, Oct. 26 — Perf. 10½x11
1165 A606 4c blue .15 .15

Giori Press Printing — Perf. 11
1166 A606 8c car, ultra & ocher .20 .15
Mannerheim (1867-1951), marshal and pres. of Finland.

Camp Fire Girls Issue

Giori Press Printing
1960, Nov. 1 — Perf. 11
1167 A607 4c dk blue & brt red .15 .15
50th anniv. of the Camp Fire Girls' movement and with their Golden Jubilee Convention celebration.

Giuseppe Garibaldi (1807-1882) A608

Walter F. George (1878-1957) A609

Champion of Liberty Issue

Rotary Press Printing
1960, Nov. 2 — Perf. 10½x11
1168 A608 4c green .15 .15

Giori Press Printing — Perf. 11
1169 A608 8c carmine, ultra & ocher .20 .15
Garibaldi, Italian patriot and freedom fighter.

Senator George Memorial Issue

Rotary Press Printing
1960, Nov. 5 — Perf. 10½x11
1170 A609 4c dull violet .15 .15
Senator Walter F. George of Georgia.

Andrew Carnegie A610

John Foster Dulles A611

Andrew Carnegie Issue

1960, Nov. 25
1171 A610 4c deep claret .15 .15
Carnegie (1835-1919), industrialist and philanthropist.

John Foster Dulles Memorial Issue

1960, Dec. 6 — Perf. 10½x11
1172 A611 4c dull violet .15 .15
John Foster Dulles (1888-1959), Sec. of State (1953-1959).

Echo I -- Communications for Peace Issue

Radio Waves Connecting Echo I and Earth — A612

1960, Dec. 15 — Perf. 11x10½
1173 A612 4c deep violet .15 .15
World's 1st communications satellite, Echo I, placed in orbit by NASA, Aug. 12, 1960.

Champion of Liberty Issue

Mahatma Gandhi — A613

Rotary Press Printing
1961, Jan. 26 — Perf. 10½x11
1174 A613 4c red orange .15 .15

Giori Press Printing — Perf. 11
1175 A613 8c carmine, ultra & ocher .20 .15
Mohandas K. Gandhi, leader in India's struggle for independence.

Range Conservation Issue

The Trail Boss and Modern Range — A614

Giori Press Printing
1961, Feb. 2 — Perf. 11
1176 A614 4c blue, slate & brown orange .15 .15
Importance of range conservation and meeting of the American Soc. of Range Management, Washington, DC. "The Trail Boss" from a drawing by Charles M. Russell is the Society's emblem.

Horace Greeley Issue

Horace Greeley (1811-1872), Publisher and Editor — A615

Rotary Press Printing
1961, Feb. 3 — Perf. 10½x11
1177 A615 4c dull violet .15 .15

Civil War Centennial Issue

Sea Coast Gun of 1861 — A616

Rifleman at Shiloh, 1862 — A617

Blue and Gray at Gettysburg, 1863 — A618

UNITED STATES

Battle of the Wilderness, 1864 — A619

Appomattox, 1865 — A620

1961-65   *Perf. 11x10½*
1178 A616 4c light green .15 .15
1179 A617 4c blk, *peach blossom* .15 .15

Giori Press Printing
Perf. 11
1180 A618 5c gray & blue .15 .15
1181 A619 5c dark red & black .15 .15
1182 A620 5c Prus blue & black .25 .15
   a. Horiz. pair, imperf. vert. 4,500.
   Nos. 1178-1182 (5) .85 .75

Cent. of the firing on Fort Sumter, No. 1178; cent. of the Battle of Shiloh, No. 1179; cent. of the Battle of Gettysburg, No. 1180; cent. of the Battle of the Wilderness, No. 1181; cent. of the surrender of Gen. Robert E. Lee to Lt. Gen. Ulysses S. Grant at Appomattox Court House, No. 1182.
Issue dates of Nos. 1178-1182: Apr. 12; Apr. 7, 1962; July 1, 1963; May 5, 1964; Apr. 9, 1965.

Kansas Statehood Centenary

Sunflower, Pioneer Couple and Stockade A621

Giori Press Printing
1961, May 10   *Perf. 11*
1183 A621 4c brn, dk red & grn, *yellow* .15 .15

Senator George W. Norris Issue

Norris and Norris Dam, Tenn. — A622

Rotary Press Printing
1961, July 11   *Perf. 11x10½*
1184 A622 4c blue green .15 .15

Norris (1861-1944) of Nebraska.

Naval Aviation, 50th Anniv.

Navy's First Plane (Curtiss A-1 of 1911) and Naval Air Wings — A623

1961, Aug. 20
1185 A623 4c blue .15 .15

Scales of Justice, Factory, Worker and Family A624

Remington's "Smoke Signal" A625

Workmen's Compensation Issue
1961, Sept. 4   *Perf. 10½x11*
1186 A624 4c ultra, *grayish* .15 .15

50th anniv. of the 1st successful Workmen's Compensation Law, enacted by the Wis. legislature.

Frederic Remington Issue
Giori Press Printing
1961, Oct. 4   *Perf. 11*
1187 A625 4c multicolored .15 .15

Frederic Remington (1861-1909), artist of the West. The design is from an oil painting, Amon Carter Museum of Western Art, Fort Worth, Texas.

Sun Yat-sen A626

Basketball A627

Republic of China, 50th Anniv.
Rotary Press Printing
1961, Oct. 10   *Perf. 10½x11*
1188 A626 4c blue .15 .15

Naismith-Basketball Issue
1961, Nov. 6   *Perf. 10½x11*
1189 A627 4c brown .15 .15

Honoring basketball and James A. Naismith (1861-1939), who invented the game in 1891.

Nursing Issue

Student Nurse Lighting Candle — A628

Giori Press Printing
1961, Dec. 28   *Perf. 11*
1190 A628 4c blue, green, org & blk .15 .15

New Mexico Statehood, 50th Anniv.

Shiprock A629

1962, Jan. 6   *Perf. 11*
1191 A629 4c lt blue, maroon & bis .15 .15

Arizona Statehood, 50th Anniv.

Giant Saguaro Cactus — A630

1962 Feb. 14   *Perf. 11*
1192 A630 4c car, vio blue & green .15 .15

Project Mercury Issue

"Friendship 7" Capsule and Globe — A631

1962, Feb. 20   *Perf. 11*
1193 A631 4c dark blue & yellow .15 .15

First orbital flight of a US astronaut, Lt. Col. John H. Glenn, Jr., Feb. 20, 1962. Imperfs. are printers waste.

Malaria Eradication Issue

Great Seal of US and WHO Symbol — A632

1962, Mar. 30   *Perf. 11*
1194 A632 4c blue & bister .15 .15

WHO drive to eradicate malaria.

Charles Evans Hughes A633

Space Needle and Monorail A634

Charles Evans Hughes Issue
Rotary Press Printing
1962, Apr. 11   *Perf. 10½x11*
1195 A633 4c black, *buff* .15 .15

Hughes (1862-1948), Gov. of NY, Chief Justice of the US.

Seattle World's Fair Issue
Giori Press Printing
1962, Apr. 25   *Perf. 11*
1196 A634 4c red & dark blue .15 .15

"Century 21" Intl. Expo., Seattle, Wash., Apr. 21-Oct. 21.

Louisiana Statehood Sesquicentennial

Riverboat on the Mississippi A635

1962, Apr. 30   *Perf. 11*
1197 A635 4c blue, dk sl grn & red .15 .15

Homestead Act Centenary

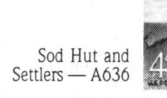

Sod Hut and Settlers — A636

Rotary Press Printing
1962, May 20   *Perf. 11x10½*
1198 A636 4c slate .15 .15

Girl Scout of America, 50th Anniv.

Senior Girl Scout and Flag — A637

1962, July 24   *Perf. 11x10½*
1199 A637 4c rose red .15 .15

Senator Brien McMahon Issue

Brien McMahon and Atomic Diagram A638

1962, July 28   *Perf. 11x10½*
1200 A638 4c violet .15 .15

Honoring Sen. McMahon, Conn., for his role in opening the way to peaceful uses of atomic energy.

Apprenticeship Issue

Machinist Handing Micrometer to Apprentice A639

1962, Aug. 31   *Perf. 11x10½*
1201 A639 4c black, *yellow bister* .15 .15

Natl. Apprenticeship Program and 25th anniv. of the Natl. Apprenticeship Act.

Sam Rayburn Issue

Sam Rayburn and Capitol — A640

Giori Press Printing
1962, Sept. 16   *Perf. 11*
1202 A640 4c dk blue & red brown .15 .15

Sam Rayburn (1882-1961), Speaker of the House of Representatives.

Dag Hammarskjold Issue

UN Headquarters and Dag Hammarskjold A641

Giori Press Printing
1962, Oct. 23   *Perf. 11*
1203 A641 4c black, brown & yellow .15 .15

Hammarskjold, Sec. Gen. of the UN, 1953-61.

Hammarskjold Special Printing
1962, Nov. 16
1204 A641 4c black, brn & yel (yel inverted) .15 .15

No. 1204 was issued following discovery of No. 1203 with yellow background inverted.

Wreath and Candles A642

Map of US and Lamp A643

Christmas Issue
Giori Press Printing
1962, Nov. 1   *Perf. 11*
1205 A642 4c green & red .15 .15

Higher Education Issue
1962, Nov. 14   *Perf. 11*
1206 A643 4c blue green & black .15 .15

Higher education's role in American cultural and industrial development in connection with the centenary celebrations of the signing of the law creating land-grant colleges and universities.

Winslow Homer Issue

"Breezing Up" — A644

1962, Dec. 15   *Perf. 11*
1207 A644 4c multicolored .15 .15
   a. Horiz. pair, imperf. btwn. & at right 6,750.

Winslow Homer (1836-1910), painter (showing his oil which hangs in the Natl. Gallery, Washington, DC).

Flag Issue

Flag over White House — A645

1963-66   *Perf. 11*
1208 A645 5c blue & red .15 .15
   a. Tagged ('66) .20 .15
   b. Horiz. pair, imperf. btwn.

Issue dates: #1208, Jan. 9. #1208a, Aug. 25.
Beware of pairs with faint blind perforations between offered as No. 1208b.

UNITED STATES

Regular Issue

Andrew Jackson A646

George Washington A650

Rotary Press Printing
1962-66   Perf. 11x10½
1209 A646 1c green ('63)   .15 .15
   a. Tagged ('66)   .15 .15
1213 A650 5c dark blue gray   .15 .15
   a. Booklet pane 5 + label   3.00 1.75
   b. Tagged ('63)   .50 .20
   c. As "a," tagged ('63)   2.00 1.50

See Luminescence note after No. 1053.
Three different messages are found on the label in No. 1213a, and two messages on that of No. 1213c.
Unused catalogue numbers (1210-1212, 1214-1224, 1226-1228) were left vacant for additional denominations in this regular series which were not produced.

Coil Stamps; Rotary Press
1962-66   Perf. 10 Vertically
1225 A646 1c green ('63)   .15 .15
   a. Tagged ('66)   .15 .15
1229 A650 5c dark blue gray   1.25 .15
   a. Tagged ('63)   1.25 .15
   b. Imperf., pair   400.00

Carolina Charter Issue

First Page of Carolina Charter — A662

Giori Press Printing
1963, Apr. 6   Perf. 11
1230 A662 5c dk carmine & brown   .15 .15

Carolina Charter, 1663, granting to 8 Englishmen lands, extending coast-to-coast roughly along the present border of Va. to the north and Fla. to the south. Original charter on display at Raleigh.

Food for Peace-Freedom from Hunger

Wheat — A663

1963, June 4   Perf. 11
1231 A663 5c green, buff & red   .15 .15

American "Food for Peace" program and FAO "Freedom from Hunger" campaign.

West Virginia Statehood Centenary

Map of West Virginia and State Capitol — A664

1963, June 20
1232 A664 5c green, red & blk   .15 .15

Emancipation Proclamation Issue

Severed Chain — A665

1963, Aug. 16   Perf. 11
1233 A665 5c dk blue, black & red   .15 .15

Cent. of Lincoln's Emancipation Proclamation, freeing about 3,000,000 slaves in 10 southern states.

Alliance for Progress Issue

Alliance Emblem A666

1963, Aug. 17
1234 A666 5c ultra & green   .15 .15

2nd anniv. of the Alliance for Progress, which aims to stimulate economic growth and raise living standards in Latin America.

Cordell Hull Issue

Cordell Hull (1871-1955), Sec. of State (1933-44) — A667

Rotary Press Printing
1963, Oct. 5   Perf. 10½x11
1235 A667 5c blue green   .15 .15

Eleanor Roosevelt Issue

Mrs. Franklin D. Roosevelt (1884-1962) A668

1963, Oct. 11   Perf. 11x10½
1236 A668 5c bright purple   .15 .15

Science Issue

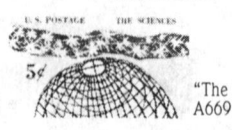

"The Universe" A669

Giori Press Printing
1963, Oct. 14   Perf. 11
1237 A669 5c Prus blue & black   .15 .15

Honoring the sciences and cent. of the Natl. Academy of Science.

Free City Mail Delivery Centenary

Letter Carrier, 1863 — A670

1963, Oct. 26   Tagged   Perf. 11
1238 A670 5c gray, dark blue & red   .15 .15

International Red Cross Centenary

Cuban Refugees on S.S. *Morning Light* and Red Cross Flag — A671

1963, Oct. 29   Perf. 11
1239 A671 5c bluish black & red   .15 .15

Christmas Issue

National Christmas Tree and White House — A672

1963, Nov. 1   Perf. 11
1240 A672 5c dk blue, bluish black & red   .15 .15
   a. Tagged   .65 .40

See Luminescence note after No. 1053.

"Columbia Jays" A673

Sam Houston A674

John James Audubon Issue
1963, Dec. 7   Perf. 11
1241 A673 5c dark blue & multi   .15 .15

John James Audubon (1785-1851), ornithologist and artist. The birds pictured are actually Collie's magpie jays.

Sam Houston Issue
Rotary Press Printing
1964, Jan. 10   Perf. 10½x11
1242 A674 5c black   .15 .15

Sam Houston (1793-1863), soldier, pres. of Texas, US senator.

Charles M. Russell Issue

"Jerked Down" — A675

Giori Press Printing
1964, Mar. 19   Perf. 11
1243 A675 5c indigo, red brn & olive   .15 .15

Russell (1864-1926), painter. The design is from a painting, Thomas Gilcrease Inst. of American History and Art, Tulsa, Okla.

New York World's Fair (1964-65)

Mall with Unisphere and "Rocket Thrower," by Donald De Lue — A676

Rotary Press Printing
1964, Apr. 22   Perf. 11x10½
1244 A676 5c blue green   .15 .15

John Muir Issue

John Muir (1838-1914), naturalist and conservationist and Redwood Forest — A677

Giori Press Printing
1964, Apr. 29   Perf. 11
1245 A677 5c brn, grn, yel grn & ol   .15 .15

Kennedy Memorial Issue

Pres. John F. Kennedy (1917-63) and Eternal Flame — A678

Rotary Press Printing
1964, May 29   Perf. 11x10½
1246 A678 5c blue gray   .15 .15

New Jersey Tercentenary Issue

Philip Carteret Landing at Elizabethtown, and Map of New Jersey — A679

1964, June 15   Perf. 10½x11
1247 A679 5c bright ultra   .15 .15

300th anniv. of English colonization of NJ. The design is from a mural by Howard Pyle in the Essex County Courthouse, Newark.

Nevada Statehood Centenary

Virginia City and Map of Nevada — A680

Giori Press Printing
1964, July 22   Perf. 11
1248 A680 5c red, yellow & blue   .15 .15

Flag A681

William Shakespeare A682

Register and Vote Issue
Giori Press Printing
1964, Aug. 1   Perf. 11
1249 A681 5c dark blue & red   .15 .15

Campaign to draw more voters to the polls.

Shakespeare Issue
Rotary Press Printing
1964, Aug. 14   Perf. 10½x11
1250 A682 5c black brown, *tan*   .15 .15

400th anniv. of the birth of Shakespeare (1564-1616).

Doctors Mayo Issue

Drs. William and Charles Mayo — A683

1964, Sept. 11   Perf. 10½x11
1251 A683 5c green   .15 .15

William (1861-1939) and his brother, Charles (1865-1939), surgeons who founded the Mayo Foundation for Medical Education and Research in affiliation with the Univ. of Minn. at Rochester. From a sculpture by James Earle Fraser.

American Music Issue

Lute, Horn, Laurel, Oak and Music Score — A684

Giori Press Printing
1964, Oct. 15   Perf. 11
Gray Paper with Blue Threads
1252 A684 5c red, black & blue   .15 .15
   a. Blue omitted   1,000.

50th anniv. of the founding of ASCAP (American Soc. of Composers, Authors and Publishers). Beware of copies offered as No. 1252a which have traces of blue.

UNITED STATES

Homemakers Issue

Farm Scene Sampler — A685

Lithographed, Engraved (Giori)
1964, Oct. 26   *Perf. 11*
1253 A685 5c multicolored   .15   .15

Honoring American women as homemakers and 50th anniv. of the passage of the Smith-Lever Act. By providing economic experts under an extension service of the US Dept. of Agriculture, this legislation helped to improve homelife.

Christmas Issue

Holly A686
Mistletoe A687    
Poinsettia A688
Sprig of Conifer A689

Giori Press Printing
1964, Nov. 9   *Perf. 11*
1254 A686 5c green, car & black   .25   .15
    a. Tagged   .60   .50
1255 A687 5c car, green & black   .25   .15
    a. Tagged   .60   .50
1256 A688 5c car, green & black   .25   .15
    a. Tagged   .60   .50
1257 A689 5c black, green & car   .25   .15
    a. Tagged   .60   .75
    b. Block of 4, #1254-1257   1.10   1.00
    c. Block of 4, #1254a-1257a   2.50   2.00

Tagged stamps issued Nov. 10.

Verrazano-Narrows Bridge Issue

Verrazano-Narrows Bridge and Map of NY Bay — A690

Rotary Press Printing
1964, Nov. 21   *Perf. 10½x11*
1258 A690 5c blue green   .15   .15

Opening of the Verrazano-Narrows Bridge connecting Staten Island and Brooklyn, NY.

Fine Arts Issue

Abstract Design by Stuart Davis — A691

Giori Press Printing
1964, Dec. 2   *Perf. 11*
1259 A691 5c ultra, blk & dull red   .15   .15

Amateur Radio Issue

Radio Waves and Dial — A692

Rotary Press Printing
1964, Dec. 15   *Perf. 10½x11*
1260 A692 5c red lilac   .15   .15

Honoring radio amateurs on the 50th anniv. of the American Radio Relay League.

Battle of New Orleans Issue

General Andrew Jackson and Sesquicentennial Medal — A693

Giori Press Printing
1965, Jan. 8   *Perf. 11*
1261 A693 5c dp car, violet blue & gray   .15   .15

Battle of New Orleans, Chalmette Plantation, Jan. 8-18, 1815, which established 150 years of peace and friendship between the US and Great Britain.

Discus Thrower A694
Microscope and Stethoscope A695 

Physical Fitness-Sokol Issue

1965, Feb. 15   *Perf. 11*
1262 A694 5c maroon & black   .15   .15

Importance of physical fitness and cent. of the founding of the Sokol (athletic) org. in America.

Crusade Against Cancer Issue

1965, Apr. 1   *Perf. 11*
1263 A695 5c blk, pur & red org   .15   .15

"Crusade Against Cancer" and stressing the importance of early diagnosis.

Churchill Memorial Issue

Winston Churchill — A696

Rotary Press Printing
1965, May 13   *Perf. 10½x11*
1264 A696 5c black   .15   .15

Sir Winston Spencer Churchill (1874-1965), British statesman and WWII leader.

Magna Carta Issue

Procession of Barons and King John's Crown A697

Giori Press Printing
1965, June 15   *Perf. 11*
1265 A697 5c blk, yel ocher & red lilac   .15   .15

750th anniv. of the Magna Carta, the basis of English and American common law.

International Cooperation Year Issue

ICY Emblem A698

1965, June 26   *Perf. 11*
1266 A698 5c dull blue & black   .15   .15

ICY, 1965, and 20th anniv. of the UN.

A699
Dante — A700 

Salvation Army Issue

1965, July 2   *Perf. 11*
1267 A699 5c red, black & dark blue   .15   .15

Cent. of the founding of the Salvation Army in London by William Booth.

Dante Alighieri Issue
Rotary Press Printing
1965, July 17   *Perf. 10½x11*
1268 A700 5c maroon, tan   .15   .15

Dante Alighieri (1265-1321), Italian poet. Design after a 16th cent. painting.

Herbert Hoover Issue

Pres. Herbert Clark Hoover (1874-1964) — A701

1965, Aug. 10   *Perf. 10½x11*
1269 A701 5c rose red   .15   .15

Robert Fulton Issue

Robert Fulton and Clermont A702

Giori Press Printing
1965, Aug. 19   *Perf. 11*
1270 A702 5c black & blue   .15   .15

Fulton (1765-1815), inventor of the 1st commercial steamship.

Settlement of Florida Issue

Spanish Explorer, Royal Flag of Spain and Ships — A703

1965, Aug. 28   **Giori Press Printing**
1271 A703 5c red, yel & blk   .15   .15
    a. Yellow omitted   425.00

400th anniv. of the settlement of Fla., and the 1st permanent European settlement in the continental US, St. Augustine, Fla. See Spain #1312.

Traffic Safety Issue

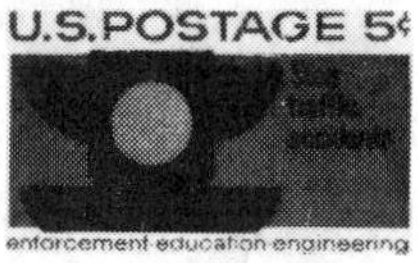

Traffic Signal A704

1965, Sept. 3   *Perf. 11*
1272 A704 5c emerald, black & red   .15   .15

Traffic safety and the prevention of traffic accidents.

John Singleton Copley Issue

Elizabeth Clarke Copley — A705

1965, Sept. 17
1273 A705 5c black, brown & olive   .15   .15

Copley (1738-1815), painter. The portrait of the artist's daughter is from the oil painting "The Copley Family," which hangs in the Natl. Gallery of Art, Washington, DC.

International Telecommunication Union Centenary

Gall Projection World Map and Radio Sine Wave — A706

1965, Oct. 6   *Perf. 11*
1274 A706 11c black, car & bister   .35   .20

Adlai E. Stevenson A707
Angel with Trumpet, 1840 Weather Vane A708 

Adlai E. Stevenson Issue

1965, Oct. 23   *Litho., Engr. (Giori)*
1275 A707 5c pale blue, blk, car & vio blue   .15   .15

Stevenson (1900-65), gov. of Ill., US ambassador to the UN.

Christmas Issue
Giori Press Printing
1965, Nov. 2   *Perf. 11*
1276 A708 5c car, dk ol grn & bis   .15   .15
    a. Tagged   .75   .25

Prominent Americans Issue

Thomas Jefferson A710 
Albert Gallatin A711

Frank Lloyd Wright and Guggenheim Museum, New York A712

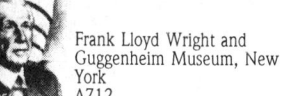

UNITED STATES

Francis Parkman A713

Lincoln A714

Washington A715

Washington (Redrawn) A715a

Franklin D. Roosevelt A716

Albert Einstein A717

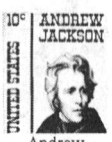

Andrew Jackson A718

Henry Ford, 1909 Model T A718a

John F. Kennedy A719

Oliver Wendell Holmes A720

George Catlett Marshall A721

Frederick Douglass A722

John Dewey A723

Thomas Paine — A724

Lucy Stone — A725

Eugene O'Neill A726

John Bassett Moore A727

Perf. 11x10½, 10½x11
1965-78 Rotary Press Printing
1278	A710	1c green, tagged		.15	.15
a.		Booklet pane of 8		1.00	.50
b.		Bklt. pane of 4 + 2 labels		.80	.30
c.		Untagged (Bureau precanceled)			
1279	A711	1¼c lt green		.15	.15
1280	A712	2c dk blue gray, tagged		.15	.15
a.		Booklet pane of 5 + label		1.25	.60
b.		Untagged (Bureau precanceled)			.15
c.		Booklet pane of 6		1.00	.50
1281	A713	3c vio, tagged		.15	.15
a.		Untagged (Bureau precanceled)			.15
1282	A714	4c black		.15	.15
a.		Tagged		.15	.15
1283	A715	5c blue		.15	.15
a.		Tagged		.15	.15
1283B	A715a	5c blue, tagged		.15	.15
d.		Untagged (Bureau precanceled)			.15
1284	A716	6c gray brown		.15	.15
a.		Tagged		.15	.15
b.		Booklet pane of 8		1.50	.75
c.		Booklet pane of 5 + label		1.50	.75
1285	A717	8c violet		.20	.15
a.		Tagged		.20	.15
1286	A718	10c lilac, tagged		.20	.15
b.		Untagged (Bureau precanceled)			.20
1286A	A718a	12c black, tagged		.25	.15
a.		Untagged (Bureau precanceled)			.25
1287	A719	13c brn, tagged		.30	.15
a.		Untagged (Bureau precanceled)			.35
1288	A720	15c magenta, tagged		.30	.15
a.		Untagged (Bureau precanceled)			.30
d.		Type II			.55

Type II: necktie does not touch coat at bottom.

Perf. 10
1288B	A720	15c magenta (from bklt. pane)		.30	.15
c.		Booklet pane of 8		2.50	1.75
e.		As "c," vert. imperf. btwn.			

Perf. 11x10½, 10½x11
1289	A721	20c deep olive		.40	.15
a.		Tagged		.40	.15
1290	A722	25c rose lake		.55	.15
a.		Tagged		.45	.15
b.		25c magenta		1.25	—
1291	A723	30c red lilac		.60	.15
a.		Tagged		.50	.15
1292	A724	40c blue black		.85	.15
a.		Tagged		.65	.15
1293	A725	50c rose magenta		1.00	.15
a.		Tagged		.80	.15
1294	A726	$1 dull purple		2.25	.15
a.		Tagged		1.65	.15
1295	A727	$5 gray black		9.50	2.25
a.		Tagged		8.00	2.00
		Nos. 1278-1295 (21)		17.90	5.25

On No. 1283B the highlights and shadows have been softened.

No. 1288B issued in booklets only. All stamps have one or two straight edges.

Issue dates (without tagging)—1965: 4c, Nov. 19.
1966: 5c, Feb. 22; 6c, Jan. 29; 8c, Mar. 14; $5, Dec. 3.
1967: 1¼c, Jan. 30; 20c, Oct. 24; 25c, Feb. 14; $1, Oct. 16.
1968: 30c, Oct. 21; 40c, Jan. 29; 50c, Aug. 13.
Dates for tagged: 1965: 4c, Dec. 1.
1966: 2c, June 8; 5c, Feb. 23; 6c, Dec. 29; 8c, July 6.
1967: 3c, Sept. 16; No. 1283B, Nov. 17; No. 1284b, Dec. 28; 10c, Mar. 15; 13c, May 29.
1968: 1c & No. 1284c, Jan. 12; No. 1280a, Jan. 8; 12c, July 30; 15c, Mar. 8.
1973: 20c, 25c, 30c, 40c, 50c, $1, $5, Apr. 3.
1978: No. 1288B, June 14.

Franklin D. Roosevelt — A727a

Coil Stamps
Rotary Press Printing
1966-81 Tagged Perf. 10 Horiz.
1297	A713	3c violet		.15	.15
a.		Imperf., pair		30.00	
b.		Untagged (Bureau precanceled)			.15
c.		As "b," imperf. pair			6.00
1298	A716	6c gray brn		.15	.15
a.		Imperf., pair		2,250.	

Perf. 10 Vertically
1299	A710	1c green		.15	.15
a.		Untagged (Bureau precanceled)			.15
b.		Imperf., pair		30.00	
1303	A714	4c black		.15	.15
a.		Untagged (Bureau precanceled)			.15
b.		Imperf., pair		900.00	
1304	A715	5c blue		.15	.15
a.		Untagged (Bureau precanceled)			.15
b.		Imperf., pair		175.00	
e.		As "a," imperf. pair			450.00

No. 1304b is valued in the grade of fine.

1304C	A715a	5c blue		.15	.15
d.		Imperf., pair		1,000.	
1305	A727a	6c gray brn		.15	.15
a.		Imperf., pair		75.00	
b.		Untagged (Bureau precanceled)			.20
1305E	A720	15c magenta		.25	.15
f.		Untagged (Bureau precanceled)			.30
g.		Imperf., pair		30.00	
h.		Pair, imperf. between		225.00	
i.		Type II		.35	.15
j.		Imperf., pair, type II		90.00	
1305C	A726	$1 dull pur		1.75	.20
d.		Imperf., pair		2,250.	
		Nos. 1297-1305C (9)		3.05	1.40

Issued: 1c, 1/12/68; 3c, 11/4/75; 4c, 5/28/66; #1304, 9/8/66; 6c, #1298, 12/28/67; #1305, 2/28/68; $1, 1/12/73; 15c, 6/14/78.

See Nos. 1393-1395, 1397-1402 for more Prominent Americans.

Migratory Bird Treaty Issue

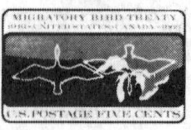

Migratory Birds over Canada-US Border — A728

Giori Press Printing
1966, Mar. 16 Perf. 11
1306	A728	5c blk, crim & dk blue		.15	.15

50th anniv. of the Migratory Bird Treaty between the US and Canada.

Humane Treatment of Animals Issue

Mongrel A729

Lithographed, Engraved (Giori)
1966, Apr. 9 Perf. 11
1307	A729	5c org brown & black		.15	.15

Humane treatment of all animals and cent. of the ASPCA.

Indiana Statehood Sesquicentennial

Sesquicentennial Seal; Map of Indiana with 19 Stars and Old Capitol at Corydon — A730

1966, Apr. 16 Giori Press Printing
1308	A730	5c yel, ocher & vio blue		.15	.15

American Circus Issue

Clown — A731

1966, May 2 Perf. 11
1309	A731	5c multicolored		.15	.15

Honoring the American circus on the cent. of the birth of John Ringling.

Sixth Intl. Phil. Exhib. Issues

Stamped Cover — A732

A733

Lithographed, Engraved (Giori)
1966, May Perf. 11
1310	A732	5c multicolored		.15	.15

Souvenir Sheet
Imperf
1311	A733	5c multicolored		.15	.15

SIPEX, Washington, DC, May 21-30.
No. 1311 measures 108x74mm.
Issue dates: #1310, 21st. #1311, 23rd.

"Freedom" Checking "Tyranny" A734

Polish Eagle and Cross A735

Bill of Rights, 175th Anniv.
Giori Press Printing
1966, July 1 Perf. 11
1312	A734	5c carmine, dk & lt blue		.15	.15

Polish Millennium Issue
Rotary Press Printing
1966, July 30 Perf. 10½x11
1313	A735	5c red		.15	.15

1000th anniv. of the adoption of Christianity in Poland.

Tagging Extended

During 1966 experimental use of tagged stamps was extended to the Cincinnati Postal Region covering offices in Indiana, Kentucky and Ohio. To supply these offices about 12 percent of the following nine issues (Nos. 1314-1322) were tagged.

National Park Service Issue

National Park Service Emblem — A736

Lithographed, Engraved (Giori)
1966, Aug. 25 Perf. 11
1314	A736	5c yel, black & green		.15	.15
a.		Tagged		.30	.25

50th anniv. of the Natl. Park Service of the Interior Dept. The design "Parkscape U.S.A." identifies Natl. Park Service facilities. No. 1314a was issued Aug. 26.

Marine Corps Reserve Issue

Combat Marine, 1966; Frogman; WW II Flier; WW I "Devil Dog" and Marine, 1775 — A737

Lithographed, Engraved (Giori)
1966, Aug. 29 Perf. 11
1315	A737	5c black, bister, red & ultra		.15	.15
a.		Tagged		.30	.30
b.		Black & bister (engr.) omitted		16,000.	

50th anniv. of the founding of the US Marine Corps Reserve.

General Federation of Women's Clubs

Women of 1890 and 1966 — A738

UNITED STATES

Giori Press Printing
1966, Sept. 12   *Perf. 11*
1316 A738 5c black, pink & blue   .15   .15
   a.   Tagged   .30   .20

75 years of service by the Gen. Fed. of Women's Clubs. No. 1316a was issued Sept. 13.

American Folklore Issue

Johnny Appleseed — A739

1966, Sept. 24   *Perf. 11*
1317 A739 5c green, red & black   .15   .15
   a.   Tagged   .30   .20

Johnny Appleseed, (John Chapman, 1774-1845), who wandered over 100,000 square miles planting apple trees, and who gave away and sold seedlings to Midwest pioneers. No. 1317a issued Sept. 26.

Beautification of America Issue

Jefferson Memorial, Tidal Basin and Cherry Blossoms A740

1966, Oct. 5   *Perf. 11*
1318 A740 5c emerald, pink & black   .15   .15
   a.   Tagged   .30   .20

Pres. Johnson's "Plant for a more beautiful America" campaign.

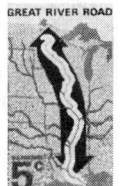

Central US Map With Great River Road — A741

Statue of Liberty and "Old Glory" — A742

Great River Road Issue
Lithographed, Engraved (Giori)
1966, Oct. 21   *Perf. 11*
1319 A741 5c ver, yellow, blue & green   .15   .15
   a.   Tagged   .30   .20

5,600-mile Great River Road connecting New Orleans with Kenora, Ontario, following the Mississippi most of the way. No. 1319a issued Oct. 22.

Savings Bond-Servicemen Issue
1966, Oct. 26
1320 A742 5c red, dk & lt blue, black   .15   .15
   a.   Tagged   .30   .20
   b.   Red, dark blue & black omitted   5,000.
   c.   Dark blue (engr.) omitted   9,000.

25th anniv. of US Savings Bonds, and to honor American servicemen. No. 1320a issued Oct. 27.

Christmas Issue

Madonna and Child, by Hans Memling — A743

Lithographed, Engraved (Giori)
1966, Nov. 1   *Perf. 11*
1321 A743 5c multicolored   .15   .15
   a.   Tagged   .30   .20

The design is from "Madonna and Child with Angels," by the Flemish artist Hans Memling (c. 1430-1494), National Gallery of Art, Washington, DC. No. 1321a was issued Nov. 2. See No. 1336.

Mary Cassatt Issue

"The Boating Party" — A744

Giori Press Printing
1966, Nov. 17   *Perf. 11*
1322 A744 5c multicolored   .15   .15
   a.   Tagged   .30   .25

Cassatt (1844-1926), painter. The original painting is in the Natl. Gallery of Art, Washington, DC.

National Grange Issue

Grange Poster, 1870 — A745

1967, Apr. 17   Tagged   *Perf. 11*
1323 A745 5c multicolored   .15   .15

Cent. of the founding of the National Grange, American farmers' organization.

Phosphor Tagging
From No. 1323 onward, all postage issues are tagged, unless otherwise noted.

Tagging Omitted
Inadvertent omissions of tagging occurred on Nos. 1238, 1278, 1281, 1298 and 1305. In addition most tagged issues from 1967 on exist with tagging unintentionally omitted.

Canada Centenary Issue

Canadian Landscape A746

Giori Press Printing
1967, May 25   *Perf. 11*
1324 A746 5c multicolored   .15   .15

Cent. of Canada's emergence as a nation.

Erie Canal Issue

Stern of Early Canal Boat — A747

Lithographed, Engraved (Giori)
1967, July 4   *Perf. 11*
1325 A747 5c multicolored   .15   .15

150th anniv. of the Erie Canal ground-breaking ceremony. The canal links Lake Erie and NYC.

"Peace"—Lions Issue

Peace Dove — A748

Giori Press Printing
1967, July 5   *Perf. 11*
Gray Paper with Blue Threads
1326 A748 5c blue, red & black   .15   .15

Publicizing the Search for Peace. This was the theme of an essay contest for young men and women sponsored by Lions Intl. on its 50th anniv.

Henry David Thoreau Issue

Henry David Thoreau (1817-1862), Writer — A749

1967, July 12
1327 A749 5c red, black & green   .15   .15

Nebraska Statehood Centenary

Hereford Steer and Corn — A750

Lithographed, Engraved (Giori)
1967, July 29   *Perf. 11*
1328 A750 5c dk red brn, lem & yel   .15   .15

Voice of America Issue

Radio Transmission Tower and Waves — A751

1967, Aug. 1   Giori Press Printing
1329 A751 5c red, blue, black & car   .15   .15

25th anniv. of the radio branch of the US Information Agency (USIA).

American Folklore Issue

Davy Crockett (1786-1836) and Scrub Pines — A752

Lithographed, Engraved (Giori)
1967, Aug. 17   *Perf. 11*
1330 A752 5c green, black & yellow   .15   .15
   a.   Vert. pair, imperf. btwn.   6,000.
   b.   Green (engr.) omitted   —
   c.   Black & green (engr.) omitted   —
   d.   Yellow & green (litho.) omitted   —

Crockett, frontiersman and congressman, died in defense of the Alamo.

A foldover on one pane created one each of Nos. 1330b-1330d. Part of the colors appear on the back of the selvage or stamps.

Space Accomplishments Issue

Space-Walking Astronaut — A753

Gemini 4 Capsule and Earth A754

Lithographed, Engraved (Giori)
1967, Sept. 29   *Perf. 11*
1331 A753 5c multicolored   .55   .15
1332 A754 5c multicolored   .55   .15
   b.   Pair, #1331-1332   1.25   1.25

US accomplishments in space.

View of Model City — A755

Finnish Coat of Arms — A756

Urban Planning Issue
Lithographed, Engraved (Giori)
1967, Oct. 2   *Perf. 11*
1333 A755 5c dk & lt blue, black   .15   .15

Importance of Urban Planning and the Intl. Conf. of the American Inst. of Planners, Washington, DC, Oct. 1-6.

Finnish Independence, 50th Anniv.
Engraved (Giori)
1967, Oct. 6   *Perf. 11*
1334 A756 5c blue   .15   .15

Thomas Eakins Issue

"The Biglin Brothers Racing" (Sculling on Schuylkill River, Philadelphia) A757

1967, Nov. 2   Photo.   *Perf. 12*
1335 A757 5c gold & multi   .15   .15

Eakins (1844-1916), painter and sculptor. The painting is in the Natl. Gallery of Art, Washington, DC.

Christmas Issue

Madonna and Child, by Hans Memling — A758

Lithographed, Engraved (Giori)
1967, Nov. 6   *Perf. 11*
1336 A758 5c multicolored   .15   .15

See note after No. 1321.

Magnolia — A759

Flag and White House — A760

Mississippi Statehood, 150th Anniv.
Giori Press Printing
1967, Dec. 11   *Perf. 11*
1337 A759 5c brt grnsh blue, green & red brown   .15   .15

Flag Issue
Giori Press Printing
1968-71   *Perf. 11*

Size: 19x22mm
1338 A760 6c dk blue, red & green   .15   .15
   k.   Vert. pair, imperf. btwn.   550.00
   s.   Red omitted

Vert. pairs have been offered as imperf. horiz. Some have had the gum washed off to remove blind perfs.

UNITED STATES

Coil Stamp
Multicolor Huck Press
Perf. 10 Vert.
Size: 18¼x21mm

1338A A760 6c dk blue, red & green ('69) .15 .15
  b. Imperf., pair 500.00

Multicolor Huck Press
Perf. 11x10½
Size: 18¼x21mm

1338D A760 6c dk blue, red & green ('70) .15 .15
  e. Horiz. pair, imperf. btwn. 175.00
1338F A760 8c multi ('71) .15 .15
  i. Vert. pair, imperf. 50.00
  j. Horiz. pair, imperf. btwn. 60.00
  p. Slate green omitted 450.00
  t. Horiz. pair, imperf. vert. —

Issued: #1338, Jan. 24, 1968; #1338A, May 30, 1969; #1338D, Aug. 7, 1970; 8c, May 10, 1971.

Coil Stamp
1971, May 10   *Perf. 10 Vert.*
Size: 18¼x21mm

1338G A760 8c multi ('71) .20 .15
  h. Imperf., pair 55.00

Farm House and Fields of Ripening Grain A761

Map of North and South America A762

Illinois Statehood, 150th Anniv.
Lithographed, Engraved (Giori)
1968, Feb. 12   *Perf. 11*
1339 A761 6c multicolored .15 .15

HemisFair '68 Issue
1968, Mar. 30   *Perf. 11*
1340 A762 6c blue, rose red & white .15 .15
  a. White omitted 1,500.

HemisFair '68 exhib. at San Antonio, Tex., Apr. 6-Oct. 6, for the 250th anniv. of San Antonio.

Airlift Issue

Eagle Holding Pennant A763

Lithographed, Engraved (Giori)
1968, Apr. 4   Untagged   *Perf. 11*
1341 A763 $1 sep, dk blue, ocher & brn red 2.25 1.25

Issued to pay for airlift of parcels from and to US ports to servicemen overseas and in Alaska, Hawaii and P.R. Valid for all regular postage.
On Apr. 26, 1969, the POD ruled that henceforth No. 1341 "may be used toward paying the postage or fees for special services on airmail articles."

"Youth"—Elks Issue

Girls and Boys — A764

Lithographed, Engraved (Giori)
1968, May 1   *Perf. 11*
1342 A764 6c ultra & orange red .15 .15

Support Our Youth program, and honoring the Benevolent and Protective Order of Elks, which extended its youth service program in observance of its centennial year.

Policeman and Small Boy — A765

Eagle Weather Vane — A766

Law and Order Issue
Giori Press Printing
1968, May 17   *Perf. 11*
1343 A765 6c chlky blue, blk & red .15 .15

The police as protector and friend and respect for law and order.

Register and Vote Issue
Lithographed, Engraved (Giori)
1968, June 27   *Perf. 11*
1344 A766 6c blk, yel & org .15 .15

Campaign to draw more voters to the polls. The weather vane is from an old house in the Russian Hill section of San Francisco.

Historic Flag Series

Ft. Moultrie, 1776 — A767

Ft. McHenry, 1795-1818 A768

Washington's Cruisers, 1775 — A769

Bennington, 1777 — A770

Rhode Island, 1775 — A771

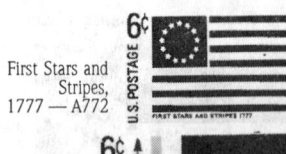

First Stars and Stripes, 1777 — A772

Bunker Hill, 1775 A773

Grand Union, 1776 — A774

Philadelphia Light Horse, 1775 A775

First Navy Jack, 1775 — A776

**Engraved (Giori) (#1345-1348, 1350):
Engr. & Litho. (#1349, 1351-1354)**
1968, July 4   *Perf. 11*
1345 A767 6c dark blue .40 .25
1346 A768 6c dk blue & red .30 .25
1347 A769 6c dk blue & ol green .25 .25
1348 A770 6c dk blue & red .25 .25
1349 A771 6c dk blue, yel & red .25 .25
1350 A772 6c dk blue & red .25 .25
1351 A773 6c dk bl, ol grn & red .25 .25
1352 A774 6c dk blue & red .25 .25
1353 A775 6c dk blue, yel & red .25 .25
1354 A776 6c dk blue, red & yel .25 .25
  Strip of 10, Nos. 1345-1354 2.75 2.75

Flags carried by American colonists and by citizens of the new United States. The flag sequence on the upper panes is as listed. On the lower panes the sequence is reversed with the Navy Jack in the 1st row and the Fort Moultrie flag in the 10th.

Walt Disney Issue

Disney and Children of the World — A777

1968, Sept. 11   Photo.   *Perf. 12*
1355 A777 6c multicolored .15 .15
  a. Ocher (Walt Disney, 6c, etc.) omitted 850. —
  b. Vert. pair, imperf. horiz. 750.
  c. Imperf., pair 675.
  d. Black omitted 2,000.
  e. Horiz. pair, imperf. btwn. 4,750.
  f. Blue omitted 2,250.

Disney (1901-1966), cartoonist, film producer, creator of Mickey Mouse.

Father Marquette Issue

Father Marquette and Louis Jolliet Exploring the Mississippi A778

Giori Press Printing
1968, Sept. 20   *Perf. 11*
1356 A778 6c black, apple green & org brn .15 .15

Father Jacques Marquette (1637-1675), French Jesuit missionary, who with Louis Jolliet explored the Mississippi and its tributaries.

American Folklore Issue
Daniel Boone (1734-1820)

Pennsylvania Rifle, Powder Horn, Tomahawk Pipe and Knife — A779

Lithographed, Engraved (Giori)
1968, Sept. 26   *Perf. 11*
1357 A779 6c yel, dp yel, mar & blk .15 .15

Daniel Boone, frontiersman and trapper.

Arkansas River Navigation Issue

Ship's Wheel, Power Transmission Tower and Barge — A780

1968, Oct. 1   *Perf. 11*
1358 A780 6c brt bl, dk bl & blk .15 .15

Opening of the Arkansas River to commercial navigation.

Leif Erikson Issue

Leif Erikson, by Stirling Calder — A781

1968, Oct. 9   Litho., Engr.   *Perf. 11*
1359 A781 6c lt gray brn & blk brn .15 .15

Erikson, 11th cent. Norse explorer, was the 1st European to set foot on the American continent, at a place he called Vinland. The statue by an American sculptor is in Reykjavik, Iceland.
The light gray brown ink carries the tagging element.

Cherokee Strip Issue

Homesteaders Racing to Cherokee Strip — A782

Rotary Press Printing
1968, Oct. 15   *Perf. 11x10½*
1360 A782 6c brown .15 .15

75th anniv. of the opening of the Cherokee Strip to settlers, Sept. 16, 1893.

John Trumbull Issue

Detail from "The Battle of Bunker's Hill" — A783

Lithographed, Engraved
1968, Oct. 18   *Perf. 11*
1361 A783 6c multicolored .15 .15

Trumbull (1756-1843), painter. The stamp shows Lt. Thomas Grosvenor and his attendant, Peter Salem. The painting is at Yale Univ., New Haven, CT.

Waterfowl Conservation Issue

Wood Ducks — A784

Lithographed, Engraved (Giori)
1968, Oct. 24   *Perf. 11*
1362 A784 6c black & multi .15 .15
  a. Vert. pair, imperf. btwn. 550.
  b. Red & dark blue omitted 1,100.
  c. Red omitted

Gabriel, from van Eyck's Annunciation A785

Chief Joseph, by Cyrenius Hall A786

Christmas Issue
Engraved (Multicolor Huck)
1968, Nov. 1   Tagged   *Perf. 11*
1363 A785 6c multicolored .15 .15
  a. Untagged .15 .15
  b. Imperf., pair, tagged 250.00
  c. Light yellow omitted 85.00
  d. Imperf., pair, untagged 325.00

"The Annunciation" by the 15th cent. Flemish artist Jan van Eyck is in the Natl. Gallery of Art, Washington, DC. No. 1363a was issued Nov. 2.

UNITED STATES

Luminescence
No. 1364 and all following postage stamps are tagged, unless otherwise noted.

American Indian Issue
Lithographed, Engraved (Giori)
1968, Nov. 4   *Perf. 11*
1364 A786 6c black & multi   .15   .15

Honoring American Indians and the opening of the Natl. Portrait Gallery, Oct. 5, 1968. Chief Joseph (Indian name Thunder Traveling over the Mountains) a leader of the Nez Percé tribe, was born c. 1840 in eastern Oregon and died at the Colesville Reservation in Washington in 1904.

Beautification of America Issue

Capitol, Azaleas and Tulips — A787

Washington Monument, Potomac River and Daffodils — A788

Poppies and Lupines along Highway — A789

Blooming Crabapples along Street — A790

Lithographed, Engraved (Giori)
1969, Jan. 16   *Perf. 11*
1365 A787 6c multicolored   .35   .15
1366 A788 6c multicolored   .35   .15
1367 A789 6c multicolored   .35   .15
1368 A790 6c multicolored   .35   .15
    a. Block of 4, #1365-1368   1.65   1.75

Natural Beauty Campaign for more beautiful cities, parks, highways and streets.

Eagle from Great Seal of US — A791

July Fourth, by Grandma Moses — A792

American Legion, 50th Anniv.
Lithographed, Engraved (Giori)
1969, Mar. 15   *Perf. 11*
1369 A791 6c red, blue & black   .15   .15

American Folklore Issue
Grandma Moses
Lithographed, Engraved (Giori)
1969, May 1   *Perf. 11*
1370 A792 6c multicolored   .15   .15
    a. Horiz. pair, imperf. btwn.   225.00
    b. Black and Prus blue omitted   900.00

Grandma Moses (Anna Mary Robertson Moses, 1860-1961), primitive painter of American life.
Beware of pairs with blind perfs. being offered as No. 1370a. No. 1370b often comes with mottled or disturbed gum. Such stamps sell for about two-thirds as much as copies with perfect gum.

Apollo 8 Issue

Moon Surface and Earth — A793

Giori Press Printing
1969, May 5   *Perf. 11*
1371 A793 6c black, blue & ocher   .15   .15

Apollo 8 mission, which put the 1st men into orbit around the moon, Dec. 21-27, 1968. Imperfs. exist from printer's waste.

William Christopher Handy Issue

W. C. Handy (1873-1958), Jazz Musician and Composer — A794

Lithographed, Engraved (Giori)
1969, May 17   *Perf. 11*
1372 A794 6c multicolored   .15   .15

California Settlement, 200th Anniv.

Carmel Mission Belfry — A795

1969, July 16   *Perf. 11*
1373 A795 6c multicolored   .15   .15

John Wesley Powell Issue

Powell Exploring Colorado River — A796

1969, Aug. 1   *Perf. 11*
1374 A796 6c multicolored   .15   .15

Powell (1834-1902), geologist and explorer of the Green and Colorado Rivers, 1869-1875.

Alabama Statehood, 150th Anniv.

Camellia and Yellow-shafted Flicker — A797

1969, Aug. 2   *Perf. 11*
1375 A797 6c multicolored   .15   .15

Botanical Congress Issue

Douglas Fir (Northwest) — A798

Lady's-slipper (Northeast) — A799

Ocotillo (Southwest) — A800

Franklinia (Southeast) — A801

Lithographed, Engraved (Giori)
1969, Aug. 23   *Perf. 11*
1376 A798 6c multicolored   .45   .15
1377 A799 6c multicolored   .45   .15
1378 A800 6c multicolored   .45   .15
1379 A801 6c multicolored   .45   .15
    a. Block of 4, #1376-1379   2.00   2.25

11th Intl. Botanical Cong., Seattle, Wash., Aug. 24-Sept. 2.

Dartmouth College Case Issue

Daniel Webster and Dartmouth Hall — A802

Rotary Press Printing
1969, Sept. 22   *Perf. 10½x11*
1380 A802 6c green   .15   .15

Sesquicentennial of the Dartmouth College case, argued by Daniel Webster before the Supreme Court, which reasserted the sanctity of contracts.

Professional Baseball Centenary

Batter — A803

Lithographed, Engraved (Giori)
1969, Sept. 24   *Perf. 11*
1381 A803 6c yel, red, black & green   .65   .15
    a. Black (1869-1969, United States. 6c, Professional Baseball) omitted   1,100.

Intercollegiate Football Centenary

Football Player and Coach — A804

1969, Sept. 26   *Perf. 11*
1382 A804 6c red & green   .15   .15

Dwight D. Eisenhower Issue

Dwight D. Eisenhower — A805

Giori Press Printing
1969, Oct. 14   *Perf. 11*
1383 A805 6c blue, black & red   .15   .15

Gen. Eisenhower, 34th Pres. (1890-1969).

Christmas Issue

Winter Sunday in Norway, Maine — A806

Engraved (Multicolor Huck)
1969, Nov. 3   *Perf. 11x10½*
1384 A806 6c dk green & multi   .15   .15
    Precanceled   .50
    b. Imperf., pair   1,100.
    c. Light green omitted   25.00
    d. Lt grn, red & yel omitted   1,000.
    e. Yellow omitted   2,250.
    g. Red & yellow omitted

The precancel value applies to the experimental precancel printed in four cities with the names between lines 4½mm apart: in black or green "ATLANTA, GA" and in green only "BALTIMORE, MD," "MEMPHIS, TN" and "NEW HAVEN, CT." They were sold freely to the public and could be used on any class of mail at all post offices during the experimental program and thereafter.
Most examples of No. 1384c show orange where the offset green was. Value is for this variety. Copies without orange sell for a premium.

Cured Child — A807

"Old Models" — A808

Hope for Crippled Issue
Lithographed, Engraved (Giori)
1969, Nov. 20   *Perf. 11*
1385 A807 6c multicolored   .15   .15

Issued to encourage the rehabilitation of crippled children and adults, and to honor the Natl. Soc. for Crippled Children and Adults (Easter Seal Soc.) on its 50th anniv.

William M. Harnett Issue
1969, Dec. 3   *Perf. 11*
1386 A808 6c multicolored   .15   .15

Harnett (1848-1892), painter. The painting is in the Museum of Fine Arts, Boston.

Natural History Issue

American Bald Eagle — A809

African Elephant Herd — A810

Tlingit Chief in Haida Ceremonial Canoe — A811

Brontosaurus, Stegosaurus and Allosaurus from Jurassic Period — A812

UNITED STATES

Lithographed, Engraved (Giori)
1970, May 6 — Perf. 11
- 1387 A809 6c multicolored .15 .15
- 1388 A810 6c multicolored .15 .15
- 1389 A811 6c multicolored .15 .15
- 1390 A812 6c multicolored .15 .15
  - a. Block of 4, #1387-1390 .50 .60

1969-1970 celebration of the cent. of the American Museum of Natural History in NYC. The design of No. 1390 is a detail from a mural by Rudolph Zallinger in Yale's Peabody Museum.

Maine Statehood Issue

Lighthouse at Two Lights, Maine — A813

Lithographed, Engraved (Giori)
1970, July 9 — Perf. 11
- 1391 A813 6c black & multi .15 .15

Sesquicentennial of Maine statehood. The painting by Edward Hopper (1882-1967) hangs in the Metropolitan Museum of Art, NYC.

Wildlife Conservation Issue

American Buffalo A814

Rotary Press Printing
1970, July 20 — Perf. 10½x11
- 1392 A814 6c black, light brown .15 .15

Regular Issue
Dwight David Eisenhower

A815 — Dot between "R" and "U" 
A815a — No dot between "R" and "U"

Benjamin Franklin A816 
USPS Emblem A817

Fiorello H. LaGuardia A817a 
Ernest Taylor Pyle A818

Dr. Elizabeth Blackwell A818a
Amadeo P. Giannini A818b 

Rotary (6c, 7c, 14c, 16c, 18c, 21c, #1395); Giori (#1394); Photo. (#1396)
Perf. 11x10½, 10½x11; 11 (#1394)
1970-74
- 1393 A815 6c dark blue gray .15 .15
  - a. Booklet pane of 8 1.50 .65
  - b. Booklet pane of 5 + label 1.50 .65
  - c. Untagged (Bureau precanceled)
- 1393D A816 7c brt blue ('72) .15 .15
  - e. Untagged (Bureau precanceled) .15
- 1394 A815a 8c blk, red & bl gray ('71) .15 .15
- 1395 A815 8c dp claret ('71) .20 .15
  - a. Booklet pane of 8 1.80 1.25
  - b. Booklet pane of 6 1.25 .90
  - c. Booklet pane of 4 + 2 labels ('72) 1.65 .80
  - d. Booklet pane of 7 + label ('72) 1.90 1.00
- 1396 A817 8c multi ('71) .15 .15
- 1397 A817a 14c gray brn ('72) .25 .15
- 1398 A818 16c brown ('71) .30 .15
  - a. Untagged (Bureau precanceled) .35
- 1399 A818a 18c violet ('74) .35 .15
- 1400 A818b 21c green ('73) .40 .15
  - Nos. 1393-1400 (9) 2.10 1.35

No. 1395 was issued in booklets only. All stamps have one or two straight edges.
Issued: 6c, 8/6/70; 7c, 10/20/72; #1394-1395, 5/10/71; #1396, 7/1/71; 14c, 4/24/72; 16c, 5/7/71; 18c, 1/23/74; 21c, 6/27/73.

Coil Stamps
1970-71 Rotary Press — Perf. 10 Vert.
- 1401 A815 6c dark blue gray .15 .15
  - a. Untagged (Bureau precanceled) .15
  - b. Imperf., pair 2,000.
- 1402 A815 8c deep claret .15 .15
  - a. Imperf., pair 45.00
  - b. Untagged (Bureau precanceled) .15
  - c. Pair, imperf. btwn. 6,250.

Issue dates: 6c, Aug. 6; 8c, May 10, 1971.

Edgar Lee Masters Issue

Edgar Lee Masters (1869-1950), Poet — A819

Lithographed, Engraved (Giori)
1970, Aug. 22 — Perf. 11
- 1405 A819 6c black & olive bister .15 .15

Woman Suffrage Issue

Suffragettes, 1920, and Woman Voter, 1970 — A820

Giori Press Printing
1970, Aug. 26 — Perf. 11
- 1406 A820 6c blue .15 .15

50th anniv. of the 19th Amendment, which gave women the vote.

South Carolina Issue

Symbols of South Carolina A821

Lithographed, Engraved (Giori)
1970, Sept. 12 — Perf. 11
- 1407 A821 6c bister, black & red .15 .15

300th anniv. of the founding of Charles Town (Charleston), the 1st permanent settlement of SC. Against a background of pine wood the line drawings of the design represent the economic and historic development of SC: the spire of St. Phillip's Church, Capitol, state flag, a ship, 17th cent. man and woman, a Fort Sumter cannon, barrels, cotton, tobacco and yellow jessamine.

Stone Mountain Memorial Issue

Robert E. Lee, Jefferson Davis and "Stonewall" Jackson — A822

Giori Press Printing
1970, Sept. 19 — Perf. 11
- 1408 A822 6c gray .15 .15

Dedication of the Stone Mountain Confederate Memorial, GA, May 9, 1970.

Fort Snelling Issue

Fort Snelling, Keelboat and Tepees — A823

Lithographed, Engraved (Giori)
1970, Oct. 17 — Perf. 11
- 1409 A823 6c yellow & multi .15 .15

150th anniv. of Fort Snelling, MN, which was an important outpost for the opening of the Northwest.

Anti-Pollution Issue

Globe and Wheat — A824
Globe and City — A825 
Globe and Bluegill — A826 
Globe and Seagull — A827 

1970, Oct. 28 Photo. — Perf. 11x10½
- 1410 A824 6c multicolored .20 .15
- 1411 A825 6c multicolored .20 .15
- 1412 A826 6c multicolored .20 .15
- 1413 A827 6c multicolored .20 .15
  - a. Block of 4, #1410-1413 1.00 1.25

Issued to focus attention on the mounting problems of pollution.

Christmas Issue

Nativity, by Lorenzo Lotto (1480-1556) A828
Tin and Cast-iron Locomotive A829 
Toy Horse on Wheels — A830 
Mechanical Tricycle A831 
Doll Carriage A832 

1970, Nov. 5 Photo. — Perf. 10½x11
- 1414 A828 6c multicolored .15 .15
  - a. Precanceled .15 .15
  - b. Black omitted 650.00
  - c. As "a," blue omitted 1,500.

Perf. 11x10½
- 1415 A829 6c multicolored .30 .15
  - a. Precanceled .75 .15
  - b. Black omitted 2,500.
- 1416 A830 6c multicolored .30 .15
  - a. Precanceled .75 .15
  - b. Black omitted 2,500.
  - c. Imperf., pair (#1416, 1418) 4,000.
- 1417 A831 6c multicolored .30 .15
  - a. Precanceled .75 .15
  - b. Black omitted 2,500.
- 1418 A832 6c multicolored .30 .15
  - a. Precanceled .75 .15
  - b. Block of 4, #1415-1418 1.25 1.50
  - c. As "b," precanceled 3.25 3.25
  - d. Black omitted 2,500.
  - Nos. 1414-1418 (5) 1.35 .75

Nos. 1415-1418 are antique Christmas toys. The precanceled stamps, Nos. 1414a-1418a, were furnished to 68 cities. The plates include two straight (No. 1414a) or two wavy (Nos. 1415a-1418a) black lines that make up the precancellation. Unused values are for copies with gum and used values are for copies with an additional cancellation or without gum.

United Nations, 25th Anniv.

"UN" and UN Emblem A833

Lithographed, Engraved (Giori)
1970, Nov. 20 — Perf. 11
- 1419 A833 6c black, ver & ultra .15 .15

Landing of the Pilgrims Issue

Mayflower and Pilgrims — A834

Lithographed, Engraved (Giori)
1970, Nov. 21 — Perf. 11
- 1420 A834 6c black, org, yel, brn, mag & blue .15 .15
  - a. Orange & yellow omitted 1,000.

Mayflower landing, 350th anniv.

Disabled Veterans and Servicemen Issue

A835
A836 

Lithographed, Engraved (Giori)
1970, Nov. 24 — Perf. 11
- 1421 A835 6c multicolored .15 .15

Engr.
- 1422 A836 6c dk blue, black & red .15 .15
  - a. Pair, #1421-1422 .25 .32

50th anniv. of the Disabled Veterans of America Organization (No. 1421); honoring the contribution of servicemen, particularly those who were prisoners of war or missing in action (No. 1422).

Ewe and Lamb A837
Douglas MacArthur A838 

American Wool Industry Issue
Lithographed, Engraved (Giori)
1971, Jan. 19 — Perf. 11
- 1423 A837 6c multicolored .15 .15
  - b. Teal blue ("United States") omitted

450th anniv. of the introduction of sheep to the No. American continent and the beginning of the American wool industry.

UNITED STATES

No. 1423b was caused by the misregistration of the intaglio printing.

Gen. Douglas MacArthur Issue
1971, Jan. 26   Giori Press Printing
1424 A838 6c black, red & dk blue   .15   .15

MacArthur (1880-1964), Chief of Staff, Supreme Commander for the Allied Powers in the Pacific Area during WW II and Supreme Commander in Japan after the war.

Blood Donor Issue
"Giving Blood Saves Lives" — A839

1971, Mar. 12   Perf. 11
1425 A839 6c lt blue, scar & indigo   .15   .15

Salute to blood donors and spur to participation in the blood donor program.

Missouri Sesquicentennial Issue
"Independence and the Opening of the West," Detail, by Thomas Hart Benton — A840

1971, May 8   Photo.   Perf. 11x10½
1426 A840 8c multicolored   .15   .15

The stamp design shows a Pawnee hunter-trapper and a group of settlers.

Wildlife Conservation Issue

Trout — A841

Alligator — A842

Polar Bear and Cubs — A843

California Condor — A844

Lithographed, Engraved (Giori)
1971, June 12   Perf. 11
1427 A841 8c multicolored   .15   .15
   a.   Red omitted   1,250.
1428 A842 8c multicolored   .15   .15
1429 A843 8c multicolored   .15   .15
1430 A844 8c multicolored   .15   .15
   Block of 4, #1427-1430   .80   .90
   b.   As "a," lt grn & dk grn omitted from #1427-1428   4,500.
   c.   As "a," red omitted from #1427, 1429-1430   9,000.

Antarctic Treaty Issue
Map of Antarctica — A845

1971, June 23   Giori Press Printing
1431 A845 8c red & dark blue   .15   .15

10th anniv. of the Antarctic Treaty pledging peaceful uses of and scientific cooperation in Antarctica.

American Revolution Bicentennial

Bicentennial Commission Emblem — A846

Lithographed, Engraved (Giori)
1971, July 4   Perf. 11
1432 A846 8c red, blue, gray & black   .20   .15
   a.   Gray & black omitted   750.00
   b.   Gray ("U.S. Postage 8c") omitted   1,250.

John Sloan Issue
The Wake of the Ferry — A847

1971, Aug. 2   Perf. 11
1433 A847 8c multicolored   .15   .15

Sloan (1871-1951), painter.

Space Achievement Decade Issue

Earth, Sun, Landing Craft on Moon — A848

Lunar Rover and Astronauts — A849

Lithographed, Engraved (Giori)
1971, Aug. 2   Perf. 11
1434 A848 8c blk, bl, yel & red   .15   .15
1435 A849 8c blk, bl, yel & red   .15   .15
   b.   Pair, #1434-1435   .40   .45
   d.   As "b," bl & red (litho.) omitted   1,500.

A decade of space achievements. Apollo 15 moon exploration mission July 26-Aug. 7.

Emily Elizabeth Dickinson — A850

Sentry Box, Morro Castle, San Juan — A851

Emily Dickinson Issue
Lithographed, Engraved (Giori)
1971, Aug. 28   Perf. 11
1436 A850 8c multi, *greenish*   .15   .15
   a.   Black & olive (engr.) omitted   950.
   b.   Pale rose omitted   7,500.
   c.   Red omitted

Dickinson (1830-1886), poet.

San Juan, PR, 450th Anniv.
1971, Sept. 12
1437 A851 8c multicolored   .15   .15

Young Woman Drug Addict — A852

Hands Reaching for CARE — A853

Prevent Drug Abuse Issue
1971, Oct. 5   Photo.   Perf. 10½x11
1438 A852 8c bl, dp bl & blk   .15   .15

Drug Abuse Prevention Week, Oct. 3-9.

CARE Issue
1971, Oct. 27
1439 A853 8c multicolored   .15   .15
   a.   Black omitted   4,750.

25th anniv. of CARE, a US-Canadian Cooperative for American Relief Everywhere.

Historic Preservation Issue

Decatur House, Washington, DC — A854

Whaling Ship Charles W. Morgan, Mystic, Conn. — A855

Cable Car, San Francisco — A856

San Xavier del Bac Mission, Tucson, Ariz. — A857

Lithographed, Engraved (Giori)
1971, Oct. 29   Buff Paper   Perf. 11
1440 A854 8c blk brn & ocher   .15   .15
1441 A855 8c blk brn & ocher   .15   .15
1442 A856 8c blk brn & ocher   .15   .15
1443 A857 8c blk brn & ocher   .15   .15
   a.   Block of 4, #1440-1443   .75   .85
   b.   As "a," black brown omitted   2,750.
   c.   As "a," ocher omitted

Christmas Issue

Adoration of the Shepherds, by Giorgione — A858

Partridge in a Pear Tree, by Jamie Wyeth — A859

1971, Nov. 10   Photo.   Perf. 10½x11
1444 A858 8c gold & multi   .15   .15
   a.   Gold omitted   600.00
1445 A859 8c multicolored   .15   .15

Sidney Lanier (1842-1881) — A860

Peace Corps Poster, by David Battle — A861

Sidney Lanier Issue
Giori Press Printing
1972, Feb. 3   Perf. 11
1446 A860 8c black, brown & lt blue   .15   .15

Lanier, poet, musician, lawyer, educator.

Peace Corps Issue
1972, Feb. 11   Photo.   Perf. 10½x11
1447 A861 8c dk blue, light blue & red   .15   .15

National Parks Centennial Issue

Hulk of Ship — A862

Cape Hatteras Lighthouse — A863

Laughing Gulls on Driftwood — A864

Laughing Gulls and Dune — A865

Wolf Trap Farm, Vienna, Va. — A866

Old Faithful, Yellowstone — A867

Mt. McKinley, Alaska — A868

UNITED STATES

Lithographed, Engraved (Giori)
1972   *Perf. 11*

1448	A862	2c black & multi	.15	.15
1449	A863	2c black & multi	.15	.15
1450	A864	2c black & multi	.15	.15
1451	A865	2c black & multi	.15	.15
a.		Block of 4, #1448-1451	.25	.25
b.		As "a," black (litho.) omitted	2,750.	
1452	A866	6c multicolored	.15	.15
1453	A867	8c blk, blue, brn & multi	.15	.15
1454	A868	15c black & multi	.30	.20

Cent. of Yellowstone Natl. Park, the 1st Natl. Park, and of the Natl. Park System. The four 2c stamps were issued for Cape Hatteras, NC, Natl. Seashore.

Issued: 2c, 4/5; 6c, 6/26; 8c, 3/1; 15c, 7/28. See No. C84.

Family Planning Issue

Family — A869

1972, Mar. 18

1455	A869	8c black & multi	.15	.15
a.		Yellow omitted	1,650.	
b.		Dark brown & olive omitted		
c.		Dark brown omitted	9,500	

American Bicentennial
Colonial American Craftsmen

Glassmaker A870

Silversmith A871

Wigmaker A872

Hatter — A873

1972, July 4   *Engr.*   *Perf. 11x10½*
Dull Yellow Paper

1456	A870	8c deep brown	.15	.15
1457	A871	8c deep brown	.15	.15
1458	A872	8c deep brown	.15	.15
1459	A873	8c deep brown	.15	.15
a.		Block of 4, #1456-1459	.65	.75

Olympic Games Issue

Bicycling and Olympic Rings — A874

Bobsledding A875

Running A876

1972, Aug. 17   *Photo.*   *Perf. 11x10½*

1460	A874	6c multicolored	.15	.15
1461	A875	8c multicolored	.15	.15
1462	A876	15c multicolored	.30	.20
		Nos. 1460-1462 (3)	.60	.50

11th Winter Olympic Games, Sapporo, Japan, Feb. 3-13, and 20th Summer Olympic Games, Munich, Germany, Aug. 26-Sept. 11. See No. C85.

Parent Teacher Association, 75th Anniv.

Blackboard A877

1972, Sept. 15   *Photo.*   *Perf. 11x10½*

1463	A877	8c yellow & black	.15	.15

Wildlife Conservation Issue

Fur Seals A878

Cardinal — A879

Brown Pelican A880

Bighorn Sheep A881

Lithographed, Engraved
1972, Sept. 20   *Perf. 11*

1464	A878	8c multicolored	.15	.15
1465	A879	8c multicolored	.15	.15
1466	A880	8c multicolored	.15	.15
1467	A881	8c multicolored	.15	.15
a.		Block of 4, #1464-1467	.65	.75
b.		As "a," brown omitted	4,000.	
c.		As "a," green & blue omitted	4,750.	
d.		As "a," red & brown omitted	4,500.	

Mail Order Issue

Rural Post Office Store — A882

1972, Sept. 27   *Photo.*   *Perf. 11x10½*

1468	A882	8c multicolored	.15	.15

Cent. of mail order business, originated by Aaron Montgomery Ward, Chicago.

Ordering on-line is QUICK! EASY! CONVENIENT!
www.scottonline.com

Osteopathic Medicine Issue

Man's Quest for Health — A883

1972, Oct. 9   *Photo.*   *Perf. 10½x11*

1469	A883	8c yel, org & dk brn	.15	.15

75th anniv. of the American Osteopathic Assoc., founded by Dr. Andrew T. Still.

American Folklore Issue

Tom Sawyer, by Norman Rockwell — A884

Lithographed, Engraved (Giori)
1972, Oct. 13   *Perf. 11*

1470	A884	8c black & multi	.15	.15
a.		Horiz. pair, imperf. btwn.	4,500.	
b.		Red & black (engr.) omitted	2,250.	
c.		Yellow & tan (litho.) omitted	2,400.	

Tom Sawyer, hero of "The Adventures of Tom Sawyer," by Mark Twain.

Angel from "Mary, Queen of Heaven" A885

Santa Claus A886

1972, Nov. 9   *Photo.*   *Perf. 10½x11*

1471	A885	8c multicolored	.15	.15
a.		Pink omitted	200.	
b.		Black omitted	4,000.	
1472	A886	8c multicolored	.15	.15

Design of No. 1471 shows detail from a painting by the Master of the St. Lucy Legend.

Pharmacy Issue

Mortar and Pestle, Bowl of Hygeia, 19th Century Medicine Bottles A887

Lithographed, Engraved (Giori)
1972, Nov. 10   *Perf. 11*

1473	A887	8c black & multi	.15	.15
a.		Blue & orange omitted	1,000.	
b.		Blue omitted	2,250.	
c.		Orange omitted	2,250.	

Honoring American druggists, and 120th anniv. of the American Pharmaceutical Assoc.

Stamp Collecting Issue

US No. 1 Under Magnifying Glass A888

1972, Nov. 17   *Perf. 11*

1474	A888	8c dark blue green, black & brown	.15	.15
a.		Black (litho.) omitted	1,000.	

Love Issue

"Love," by Robert Indiana A889

1973, Jan. 26   *Photo.*   *Perf. 11x10½*

1475	A889	8c red; emer & vio blue	.15	.15

American Bicentennial
Communications in Colonial Times

Printer and Patriots Examining Pamphlet A890

Posting a Broadside A891

Postrider A892

Drummer A893

1973   Giori Press Printing   *Perf. 11*

1476	A890	8c ultra, grnsh blk & red	.15	.15
1477	A891	8c black, ver & ultra	.15	.15

Lithographed, Engraved (Giori)

1478	A892	8c multicolored	.15	.15
1479	A893	8c multicolored	.15	.15
		Nos. 1476-1479 (4)	.60	.60

Issue dates: No. 1476, Feb. 16; No. 1477, Apr. 13; No. 1478, June 22; No. 1479, Sept. 28.

Boston Tea Party

British Merchantman A894

British Threemaster A895

Boats and Ship's Hull — A896

Boat and Dock — A897

Lithographed, Engraved (Giori)
1973, July 4   *Perf. 11*

1480	A894	8c black & multi	.15	.15
1481	A895	8c black & multi	.15	.15
1482	A896	8c black & multi	.15	.15
1483	A897	8c black & multi	.15	.15
a.		Block of 4, #1480-1483	.65	.75
b.		As "a," black (engr.) omitted	1,500.	
c.		As "a," black (litho.) omitted	1,500.	

UNITED STATES

American Arts Issue

Gershwin, Sportin' Life, Porgy and Bess — A898

Robinson Jeffers, Man and Children of Carmel with Burro A899

Henry Ossawa Tanner, Palette and Rainbow A900

Willa Cather, Pioneer Family and Covered Wagon A901

1973	Photo.		Perf. 11	
1484	A898	8c dp green & multi	.15	.15
a.		Vert. pair, imperf. horiz.	250.00	
1485	A899	8c Prus blue & multi	.15	.15
a.		Vert. pair, imperf. horiz.	250.00	
1486	A900	8c yel brown & multi	.15	.15
1487	A901	8c dp brown & multi	.15	.15
a.		Vert. pair, imperf. horiz.	275.00	
		Nos. 1484-1487 (4)	.60	.60

Honoring: No. 1484, George Gershwin (1898-1937), composer. No. 1485, Robinson Jeffers (1887-1962), poet. No. 1486, Henry Ossawa Tanner (1859-1937), black painter (portrait by Thomas Eakins). No. 1487, Willa Sibert Cather (1873-1947), novelist.
Issue dates: No. 1484, Feb. 28; No. 1485, Aug. 13; No. 1486, Sept. 10; No. 1487, Sept. 20.

Copernicus Issue

Nicolaus Copernicus (1473-1543), Polish Astronomer — A902

Lithographed, Engraved (Giori)
1973, Apr. 23			Perf. 11	
1488	A902	8c black & orange	.15	.15
a.		Orange omitted	1,000.	
b.		Black (engraved) omitted	1,300.	

The orange color can be chemically removed.

Postal Service Employees' Issue

Stamp Counter — A903

Mail Collection — A904

Letter Facing on Conveyor Belt — A905

Parcel Post Sorting — A906

Mail Canceling — A907

Manual Letter Routing — A908

Electronic Letter Routing — A909

Loading Mail on Truck — A910

Mailman — A911

Rural Mail Delivery — A912

1973, Apr. 30	Photo.	Perf. 10½x11	
1489	A903	8c multicolored	.15	.15
1490	A904	8c multicolored	.15	.15
1491	A905	8c multicolored	.15	.15
1492	A906	8c multicolored	.15	.15
1493	A907	8c multicolored	.15	.15
1494	A908	8c multicolored	.15	.15
1495	A909	8c multicolored	.15	.15
1496	A910	8c multicolored	.15	.15
1497	A911	8c multicolored	.15	.15
1498	A912	8c multicolored	.15	.15
a.		Strip of 10, Nos. 1489-1498	1.50	1.75

A tribute to USPS employees. Emerald inscription on back, printed beneath gum in water-soluble ink, includes the USPS emblem, "People Serving You" and a statement, differing for each of the 10 stamps, about some aspect of postal service.
Each stamp in top or bottom row has a tab with blue inscription enumerating various jobs in postal service.

Harry S Truman Issue

Harry S Truman, 33rd President (1884-1972) A913

Giori Press Printing
1973, May 8			Perf. 11	
1499	A913	8c car rose, black & blue	.15	.15

Electronics Progress Issue

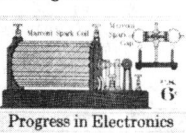

Marconi's Spark Coil and Gap — A914

Transistors and Printed Circuit Board A915

Microphone, Speaker, Vacuum Tube, TV Camera Tube — A916

Lithographed, Engraved (Giori)
1973, July 10			Perf. 11	
1500	A914	6c lilac & multi	.15	.15
1501	A915	8c tan & multi	.15	.15
a.		Black (inscriptions & "U.S. 8c") omitted	700.	
b.		Tan (background) & lilac omitted	1,500.	
1502	A916	15c gray green & multi	.30	.15
a.		Black (inscriptions & "U.S. 15c") omitted	1,500.	
		Nos. 1500-1502 (3)	.60	.45

No. 1501b hinged is ½ unhinged value.
See No. C86.

Lyndon B. Johnson Issue

Lyndon B. Johnson (1908-1973), 36th President — A917

1973, Aug. 27	Photo.		Perf. 11	
1503	A917	8c black & multi	.15	.15
a.		Horiz. pair, imperf. vert.	350.00	

Rural America Issue

Angus and Longhorn Cattle A918

Chautauqua Tent and Buggies A919

Wheat Fields and Train — A920

Lithographed, Engraved (Giori)
1973-74			Perf. 11	
1504	A918	8c multicolored	.15	.15
a.		Green & red brown omitted	1,000.	
b.		Vert. pair, imperf. between	—	
1505	A919	10c multicolored	.20	.15
a.		Black (litho.) omitted		
1506	A920	10c multicolored	.20	.15
a.		Black & blue (engr.) omitted	900.	
		Nos. 1504-1506 (3)	.55	.45

Cent. of introduction of Aberdeen Angus cattle to US (No. 1504); of Chautauqua Institution (No. 1505); of introduction of hard winter wheat into Kansas by Mennonite immigrants (No. 1506).
Issue dates: No. 1504, Oct. 5, 1973. No. 1505, Aug. 6, 1974. No. 1506, Aug. 16, 1974.

Christmas Issue

Small Cowper Madonna, by Raphael A921

Christmas Tree in Needlepoint A922

1973, Nov. 7	Photo.	Perf. 10½x11	
1507	A921	8c tan & multi	.15	.15
1508	A922	8c green & multi	.15	.15
a.		Vert. pair, imperf. btwn.	350.00	

50-Star and 13-Star Flags — A923

Jefferson Memorial and Signature — A924

Mail Transport — A925

Liberty Bell — A926

Multicolor Huck Press
1973-74	Tagged	Perf. 11x10½	
1509	A923	10c red & blue	.20	.15
a.		Horiz. pair, imperf. btwn.	60.	
b.		Blue omitted	175.	
c.		Vert. pair, imperf.	1,150.	
d.		Horiz. pair, imperf. vert.	1,000.	

Rotary Press Printing
1510	A924	10c blue	.20	.15
a.		Untagged (Bureau precanceled)		.20
b.		Booklet pane of 5 + label	1.65	.55
c.		Booklet pane of 8	1.65	.70
d.		Booklet pane of 6 ('74)	5.25	1.00
e.		Vert. pair, imperf. horiz.	525.00	
f.		Vert. pair, imperf. btwn.	—	
1511	A925	10c multi, photo	.20	.15
a.		Yellow omitted	65.00	

The yellow can be chemically removed.

Coil Stamps
Perf. 10 Vert.
Rotary Press Printing
1518	A926	6.3c brick red	.15	.15
a.		Untagged (Bureau precanceled)		.15
b.		Imperf., pair	225.00	
c.		As "a," imperf. pair	110.00	

Multicolor Huck Press
1519	A923	10c red & blue	.20	.15
a.		Imperf., pair	37.50	

Rotary Press Printing
1520	A924	10c blue	.25	.15
a.		Untagged (Bureau precanceled)		.25
b.		Imperf., pair	42.50	

Issued: #1509, 1519, 12/8/73; #1510, 1520, 12/14/73; #1511, 1/4/74; #1518, 10/1/74.

Veterans of Foreign Wars Issue

V.F.W. Emblem A928

Giori Press Printing
1974, Mar. 11			Perf. 11	
1525	A928	10c red & dark blue	.20	.15

75th anniv. of Veterans of Spanish American and other Foreign Wars.

UNITED STATES

Robert Frost Issue

Robert Frost (1874-1963), Poet — A929

Rotary Press Printing
1974, Mar. 26   *Perf. 10½x11*
1526   A929   10c black   .20   .15

EXPO '74 Issue

"Cosmic Jumper" A930

1974, Apr. 18   Photo.   *Perf. 11*
1527   A930   10c multicolored   .20   .15

EXPO '74, Spokane, Wash., May 4-Nov. 4. Theme, "Preserve the Environment."

Horse Racing Issue

Horses Rounding Turn — A931

1974, May 4   Photo.   *Perf. 11x10½*
1528   A931   10c yellow & multi   .20   .15
   a.   Blue ("Horse Racing") omitted   1,000.
   b.   Red ("U.S. postage 10 cents") omitted   —

Beware of stamps offered as No. 1528b that have traces of red.

Skylab Issue

Skylab — A932

Lithographed, Engraved (Giori)
1974, May 14   *Perf. 11*
1529   A932   10c multicolored   .20   .15
   a.   Vert. pair, imperf. btwn.   —

1st anniv. of the launching of Skylab and to honor all who participated in the Skylab projects.

Centenary of UPU Issue

Michelangelo, from "School of Athens," by Raphael — A933

"Five Feminine Virtues," by Hokusai — A934

Buying Sets
It is often less expensive to purchase complete sets than individual stamps that make up the set.

Old Time Letter Rack, by Peto — A935

Mlle. La Vergne, by Jean Liotard — A936

Lady Writing Letter, by Gerard Terborch — A937

Inkwell and Quill, by Jean Chardin — A938

Mrs. John Douglas, by Thomas Gainsborough A939

Don Antonio Noreiga, by Francisco de Goya A940

1974, June 6   Photo.   *Perf. 11*
1530   A933   10c multicolored   .20   .15
1531   A934   10c multicolored   .20   .15
1532   A935   10c multicolored   .20   .15
1533   A936   10c multicolored   .20   .15
1534   A937   10c multicolored   .20   .15
1535   A938   10c multicolored   .20   .15
1536   A939   10c multicolored   .20   .15
1537   A940   10c multicolored   .20   .15
   a.   Block or strip of 8, #1530-1537   1.60   1.60
   b.   As "a" (block), imperf. vert.   7,500.

Mineral Heritage Issue

Petrified Wood A941

Tourmaline — A942

Amethyst A943

Rhodochrosite — A944

Lithographed, Engraved (Giori)
1974, June 13   *Perf. 11*
1538   A941   10c lt blue & multi   .20   .15
   a.   Light blue & yellow omitted   —
1539   A942   10c lt blue & multi   .20   .15
   a.   Light blue omitted   —
   b.   Black & purple omitted   —
1540   A943   10c lt blue & multi   .20   .15
   a.   Light blue & yellow omitted   —
1541   A944   10c lt blue & multi   .20   .15
   a.   Block or strip of 4, #1538-1541   .80   .90
   b.   As "a," lt bl & yel omitted   2,000.
   c.   Light blue omitted   —
   d.   Black & red omitted   —

Kentucky Settlement Issue

Fort Harrod — A945

Lithographed, Engraved (Giori)
1974, June 15   *Perf. 11*
1542   A945   10c green & multi   .20   .15
   a.   Dull black (litho.) omitted   900.
   b.   Green (engr. & litho.), black (engr. & litho.), blue omitted   3,750.
   c.   Green (engr.) omitted   —
   d.   Grn (engr.), blk (litho.) omitted   —

American Bicentennial
First Continental Congress

Carpenters' Hall — A946

A947

A948

Independence Hall — A949

Giori Press Printing
1974, July 4   *Perf. 11*
1543   A946   10c dark blue & red   .20   .15
1544   A947   10c gray, dk blue & red   .20   .15
1545   A948   10c gray, dk blue & red   .20   .15
1546   A949   10c red & dark blue   .20   .15
   a.   Block of 4, #1543-1546   .80   .90

Energy Conservation Issue

Molecules and Drops of Gasoline and Oil — A950

Lithographed, Engraved (Giori)
1974, Sept. 23   *Perf. 11*
1547   A950   10c multicolored   .20   .15
   a.   Blue & orange omitted   900.
   b.   Orange & green omitted   750.
   c.   Green omitted   900.

To publicize the importance of conserving all forms of energy.

American Folklore Issue
Legend of Sleepy Hollow

Headless Horseman Pursuing Ichabod Crane A951

Lithographed, Engraved (Giori)
1974, Oct. 10   *Perf. 11*
1548   A951   10c dk blue, black, org & yel   .20   .15

Legend of Sleepy Hollow, by Washington Irving.

Retarded Children Issue

Retarded Child — A952

Giori Press Printing
1974, Oct. 12   *Perf. 11*
1549   A952   10c brn red & dk brn   .20   .15

Natl. Assoc. of Retarded Citizens.

Christmas Issue

Angel, from Perussis Altarpiece, 1480 — A953

"The Road-Winter," by Currier and Ives — A954

Dove Weather Vane, Mount Vernon A955

1974   Photo.   *Perf. 10½x11*
1550   A953   10c multicolored   .20   .15
   Perf. 11x10½
1551   A954   10c multicolored   .20   .15
   a.   Buff omitted   35.00

No. 1551a is difficult to identify. Competent expertization is necessary.

UNITED STATES

Die Cut, Paper Backing Rouletted
Self-adhesive
Inscribed "Precanceled"
Untagged

1552	A955	10c multicolored	.20 .15

Issued: #1550-1551, Oct. 23; #1552, Nov. 15.
Unused value of No. 1552 is for copy on rouletted paper backing as issued. Used value is for copy on piece, with or without postmark. Most copies are becoming discolored, probably from the adhesive. Unused and used values are for discolored copies.
Die cutting includes crossed slashes through dove, applied to prevent removal and re-use of stamp. The stamp will separate into layers if soaked.

American Arts Issue

Benjamin West, Self-portrait
A956

Paul Laurence Dunbar
A957

D. W. Griffith and Projector
A958

1975   **Photo.**   *Perf. 10½x11*
1553	A956	10c multicolored	.20 .15

Perf. 11
1554	A957	10c multicolored	.20 .15
a.		Imperf., pair	1,300.

Litho., Engr. (Giori)
1555	A958	10c multicolored	.20 .15
a.		Brown (engr.) omitted	750.
		Nos. 1553-1555 (3)	.60 .45

Honoring: West (1738-1820), painter (#1553). Dunbar (1872-1906), poet (#1554). David Lewelyn Wark Griffith (1875-1948), motion picture producer (#1555).
Issued: #1553, 2/10; #1554, 5/1; #1555, 5/27.

Space Issue

Pioneer 10 Passing Jupiter
A959

Mariner 10, Venus and Mercury
A960

Lithographed, Engraved (Giori)
1975   *Perf. 11*
1556	A959	10c lt yel, dk yel, red, blue, & 2 dk blues	.20 .15
a.		Red & dk yel omitted	1,500.
b.		Dk blues (engr.) omitted	950.
d.		Dark yellow omitted	

Imperfs. exist from printer's waste.

1557	A960	10c blk, red, ultra & bis	.20 .15
a.		Red omitted	600.
b.		Ultra & bister omitted	2,000.

US unmanned accomplishments in space. Pioneer 10 passed within 81,000 miles of Jupiter, Dec. 3, 1973. Mariner 10 explored Venus and Mercury in 1974, and Mercury again in Mar. 1975.
Issue dates: #1556, Feb. 28; #1557, Apr. 4.

Collective Bargaining Issue

"Labor and Management"
A961

1975, Mar. 13   **Photo.**   *Perf. 11*
1558	A961	10c multicolored	.20 .15

Collective Bargaining Law, enacted 1935 with Wagner Act. Imperfs. are printers waste.

American Bicentennial
Contributors to the Cause

Sybil Ludington
A962

Salem Poor
A963

Haym Salomon
A964

Peter Francisco
A965

1975, Mar. 25   **Photo.**   *Perf. 11x10½*
1559	A962	8c multicolored	.15 .15
a.		Back inscription omitted	275.00
1560	A963	10c multicolored	.20 .15
a.		Back inscription omitted	225.00
1561	A964	10c multicolored	.20 .15
a.		Back inscription omitted	250.00
b.		Red omitted	250.00
1562	A965	18c multicolored	.35 .20
		Nos. 1559-1562 (4)	.90 .65

Ludington, age 16, rallied militia Apr. 26, 1777. Poor, black freeman, fought in Battle of Bunker Hill. Salomon, Jewish immigrant, raised money to finance Revolutionary War. Francisco, Portuguese-French immigrant, joined Continental Army at 15.
Emerald inscription on back, printed beneath gum in water-soluble ink, gives thumbnail sketch of portrayed contributor.

Lexington-Concord Battle, 200th Anniv.

"Birth of Liberty," by Henry Sandham
A966

1975, Apr. 19   **Photo.**   *Perf. 11*
1563	A966	10c multicolored	.20 .15
a.		Vert. pair, imperf. horiz.	425.00

Battle of Bunker Hill, 200th Anniv.

Battle of Bunker Hill, by John Trumbull — A967

1975, June 17   *Perf. 11*
1564	A967	10c multicolored	.20 .15

Military Uniforms

Soldier with Flintlock Musket, Uniform Button — A968

Sailor with Grappling Hook, First Navy Jack, 1775 — A969

Marine with Musket, Full-rigged Ship — A970

Militiaman with Musket, Powder Horn — A971

1975, July 4   *Perf. 11*
1565	A968	10c multicolored	.20 .15
1566	A969	10c multicolored	.20 .15
1567	A970	10c multicolored	.20 .15
1568	A971	10c multicolored	.20 .15
a.		Block of 4, #1565-1568	.85 .90

Bicentenary of US Military Services.

Apollo Soyuz Space Issue

Apollo and Soyuz After Docking and Earth — A972

Spacecraft Before Docking, Earth and Project Emblem — A973

1975, July 15   **Photo.**   *Perf. 11*
1569	A972	10c multicolored	.20 .15
1570	A973	10c multicolored	.20 .15
a.		Pair, #1569-1570	.45 .40
c.		As "a", vert. pair, imperf. horiz.	2,000.

Apollo Soyuz space test project (Russo-American cooperation); launching, July 15; link-up, July 17. See Russia Nos. 4339-4340.

International Women's Year Issue

Worldwide Equality for Women
A974

1975, Aug. 26   **Photo.**   *Perf. 11x10½*
1571	A974	10c blue, org & dk blue	.20 .15

Postal Service Bicentennial Issue

Stagecoach and Trailer Truck
A975

Old and New Locomotives
A976

Early Mail Plane and Jet — A977

Satellite for Transmission of Mailgrams
A978

1975, Sept. 3   **Photo.**   *Perf. 11x10½*
1572	A975	10c multicolored	.20 .15
1573	A976	10c multicolored	.20 .15
1574	A977	10c multicolored	.20 .15
1575	A978	10c multicolored	.20 .15
a.		Block of 4, #1572-1575	.85 .90
b.		As "a", red ("10c") omitted	9,500.

World Peace Through Law Issue

Law Book, Olive Branch and Globe
A979

Giori Press Printing
1975, Sept. 29   *Perf. 11*
1576	A979	10c green, Prus blue & rose brown	.20 .15
a.		Horiz. pair, imperf. vert.	

A prelude to 7th World Conf. of the World Peace Through Law Center at Washington, DC, Oct. 12-17.

Banking and Commerce Issue

Engine Turning, Indian Head Penny and Morgan Silver Dollar
A980

Seated Liberty Quarter, $20 Gold (Double Eagle), Engine Turning
A981

Lithographed, Engraved (Giori)
1975, Oct. 6   *Perf. 11*
1577	A980	10c multicolored	.20 .15
1578	A981	10c multicolored	.20 .15
a.		Pair, #1577-1578	.40 .40
b.		As "a", brown & blue (litho.) omitted	2,250.
c.		As "a", brown, blue & yellow (litho.) omitted	2,750.

Banking and commerce in the US and for the Centennial Convention of the American Bankers Association.

Christmas Issue

Madonna, by Domenico Ghirlandaio
A982

Christmas Card, by Louis Prang, 1878
A983

1975, Oct. 14   **Photo.**   *Perf. 11*
1579	A982	(10c) multicolored	.20 .15
a.		Imperf., pair	110.00
1580	A983	(10c) multicolored	.20 .15
a.		Imperf., pair	120.00
b.		Perf. 10½x11	.60 .15

UNITED STATES

Americana Issue

Inkwell and Quill — A984 (1c)
Speaker's Stand — A985 (2c)
Early Ballot Box — A987 (3c)
Books, Bookmark, Eyeglasses — A988 (4c)
Dome of Capitol — A994 (9c)
Contemplation of Justice — A995 (10c)
Early American Printing Press — A996 (11c)
Torch — A997 (12c)
Liberty Bell — A998 (13c)
Eagle and Shield — A999 (13c)
Fort McHenry Flag — A1001 (15c)
Head, Statue of Liberty — A1002 (16c)
Old North Church, Boston — A1003 (24c)
Fort Nisqually — A1004 (28c)
Sandy Hook Lighthouse, NJ — A1005 (29c)
Morris Township School No. 2, Devils Lake, ND — A1006 (30c)
Iron "Betty" Lamp, 17th-18th Cent. — A1007 (50c)
Rush Lamp and Candle Holder — A1008 ($1.00)

Kerosene Table Lamp — A1009 ($2.00)
Railroad Conductor's Lantern, c. 1850 — A1010 ($5.00)

1975-81   Engr.   Perf. 11x10½

No.	Type	Description	Unused	Used
1581	A984	1c dk blue, *grnsh*	.15	.15
a.		Untagged (Bureau precanceled)	.15	.15
1582	A985	2c red brown, *grnsh*	.15	.15
a.		Untagged (Bureau precanceled)	.15	.15
b.		Cream paper ('81)	.15	
1584	A987	3c olive, *grnsh*	.15	.15
1585	A988	4c rose mag, *cr*	.15	.15
a.		Untagged (Bureau precanceled)		1.25

Size: 17½x20½mm

1590	A994	9c slate green	.45	.20
a.		Perf. 10	20.00	12.50

Size: 18½x22½mm

1591	A994	9c slate green, *gray*	.20	.15
a.		Untagged (Bureau precanceled)	.20	
1592	A995	10c violet, *gray*	.20	.15
1593	A996	11c orange, *gray*	.20	.15
1594	A997	12c brown red, *beige*	.25	.15
1595	A998	13c brown	.25	.15
a.		Booklet pane of 6	1.90	.75
b.		Booklet pane of 7 + label	1.75	.75
c.		Booklet pane of 8	2.00	1.00
d.		Booklet pane of 5 + label ('76)	1.50	.75
e.		Vert. pair, imperf btwn.	—	

Photo. Perf. 11

1596	A999	13c multicolored	.25	.15
a.		Imperf., pair	50.00	
b.		Yellow omitted	200.00	

Engr.

1597	A1001	15c gray, dk blue & red	.30	.15
a.		Vert. pair, imperf.	20.00	
b.		Gray omitted	700.00	
c.		Vert. strip of 3, imperf. btwn. & at top or bottom	—	

Perf. 11x10½

1598	A1001	15c gray, dk blue & red	.35	.15
a.		Booklet pane of 8	3.50	.80
1599	A1002	16c blue	.35	.15
1603	A1003	24c red, *blue*	.45	.15
1604	A1004	28c brown, *blue*	.55	.15
1605	A1005	29c blue, *blue*	.55	.15
1606	A1006	30c green, *blue*	.55	.15

Engr. & Litho. Perf. 11

1608	A1007	50c tan, black & org	.85	.15
a.		Black omitted	300.00	
b.		Vert. pair, imperf. horiz.	1,750.	

Beware of copies offered as No. 1608b that have blind perfs.

1610	A1008	$1 tan, brn, org & yel	1.75	.20
a.		Brown (engraved) omitted	275.	
b.		Tan, orange & yel omitted	350.	
c.		Brown inverted	15,000.	
1611	A1009	$2 tan, dk grn, org & yel	3.25	.75
1612	A1010	$5 tan, red brn, yel & org	7.50	1.75
		Nos. 1581-1612 (22)	18.85	5.60

Nos. 1590, 1590a, 1595, 1598 issued in booklets only. All stamps have one or two straight edges.
Years of issue: #1591, 1595-1596, 11c, 24c, 1975. #1590, 1c-4c, 10c, 1977. #1597-1598, 16c, 28c, 29c, $2, 1978. 30c-$1, $5, 1979. 12c, 1981.

Guitar A1011 (3.1c)
Saxhorns A1012 (7.7c)
Drum A1013 (7.9c)
Piano A1014 (8.4c)

Coil Stamps
Engr. Perf. 10 Vertically

1613	A1011	3.1c brown, *yel*	.15	.15
a.		Untagged (Bureau precanceled)		.50
b.		Imperf., pair	1,400.	
1614	A1012	7.7c brown, *brt yel*	.20	.15
a.		Untagged (Bureau precanceled)		.35
b.		As "a," imperf., pair	1,600.	
1615	A1013	7.9c carmine, *yel*	.20	.15
a.		Untagged (Bureau precanceled)		.20
b.		Imperf., pair	600.00	
1615C	A1014	8.4c dk blue, *yel*	.20	.15
d.		Untagged (Bureau precanceled)		.30
e.		As "d," pair, imperf. btwn.	75.00	
f.		As "d," imperf., pair	17.50	
1616	A994	9c sl green, *gray*	.20	.15
a.		Untagged (Bureau precanceled)		
b.		Imperf., pair	175.00	
c.		As "b," imperf., pair		.35
			700.00	
1617	A995	10c violet, *gray*	.20	.15
a.		Untagged (Bureau precanceled)		.25
b.		Imperf., pair	70.00	
1618	A998	13c brown	.25	.15
a.		Untagged (Bureau precanceled)		.45
b.		Imperf., pair	25.00	
g.		Pair, imperf. between		
h.		As "a," imperf., pair		
1618C	A1001	15c gray, dk blue & red	.40	.15
d.		Imperf., pair	25.00	
e.		Pair, imperf. between	150.00	
f.		Gray omitted	40.00	
1619	A1002	16c blue	.35	.15
a.		Huck press printing	.50	.15
		Nos. 1613-1619 (9)	2.15	1.35

The 15c was printed on two different presses. Huck press printings have white background without bluish tinge, are a fraction of a millimeter smaller and have block instead of overall tagging. Cottrell press printings show a joint line.
Years of issue: 9c, 13c, 1975. 7.7c, 7.9c, 1976. 10c, 1977. 8.4c, 15c, 16c, 1978. 3.1c, 1979.
See Nos. 1811, 1813, 1816.

13-Star Flag, Independence Hall A1015
Flag over Capitol A1016 

Multicolor Huck Press
1975-77   Perf. 11x10½

1622	A1015	13c dark blue & red	.25	.15
a.		Horiz. pair, imperf. btwn.	55.	
b.		Vert. pair, imperf.	1,100.	
c.		Perf. 11 ('81)	.65	.15
d.		As "c," vert. pair, imperf.	150.	
e.		Horiz. pair, imperf. vert.		

No. 1622 has large block tagging and nearly vertical multiple gum ridges. No. 1622c has small block tagging and flat gum.

1623	A1016	13c blue & red ('77)	.25	.15
a.		Booklet pane of 8 (1 #1590 and 7 #1623)	2.25	1.10
b.		Perf. 10	1.00	1.00
c.		Booklet pane of 8 (1 #1590a and 7 #1623b)	26.00	—
d.		Se-tenant pair, #1590 & 1623	.70	.70
e.		Se-tenant pair, #1590a & 1623b	22.50	20.00

Coil Stamp
Perf. 10 Vertically

1625	A1015	13c dark blue & red	.25	.15
a.		Imperf., pair	25.00	

Nos. 1623 and 1623b issued in booklets only. All stamps have one or two straight edges.

American Bicentennial — Spirit of '76

Drummer Boy A1019
Old Drummer A1020 
Fifer — A1021 

Designed after painting "The Spirit of '76," by Archibald M. Willard.

1976, Jan. 1   Photo.   Perf. 11

1629	A1019	13c multicolored	.20	.15
a.		Imperf., vert. pair		
1630	A1020	13c multicolored	.20	.15
1631	A1021	13c multicolored	.20	.15
a.		Strip of 3, #1629-1631	.60	.65
b.		As "a," imperf.	1,300.	
c.		Imperf., vert. pair #1631	800.	

Interphil Issue

"Interphil 76" A1022

Lithographed, Engraved (Giori)
1976, Jan. 17   Perf. 11

1632	A1022	13c dk blue, red & ultra	.20	.15

Interphil 76 Intl. Phil. Exhib., Philadelphia, Pa., May 29-June 6.

State Flags A1023-A1072

1976, Feb. 23   Photo.   Perf. 11

1633	A1023	13c Delaware	.25	.20
1634	A1024	13c Pennsylvania	.25	.20
1635	A1025	13c New Jersey	.25	.20
1636	A1026	13c Georgia	.25	.20
1637	A1027	13c Connecticut	.25	.20
1638	A1028	13c Massachusetts	.25	.20
1639	A1029	13c Maryland	.25	.20
1640	A1030	13c South Carolina	.25	.20
1641	A1031	13c New Hampshire	.25	.20
1642	A1032	13c Virginia	.25	.20
1643	A1033	13c New York	.25	.20
1644	A1034	13c North Carolina	.25	.20
1645	A1035	13c Rhode Island	.25	.20
1646	A1036	13c Vermont	.25	.20
1647	A1037	13c Kentucky	.25	.20
1648	A1038	13c Tennessee	.25	.20
1649	A1039	13c Ohio	.25	.20
1650	A1040	13c Louisiana	.25	.20
1651	A1041	13c Indiana	.25	.20
1652	A1042	13c Mississippi	.25	.20
1653	A1043	13c Illinois	.25	.20
1654	A1044	13c Alabama	.25	.20
1655	A1045	13c Maine	.25	.20
1656	A1046	13c Missouri	.25	.20
1657	A1047	13c Arkansas	.25	.20
1658	A1048	13c Michigan	.25	.20
1659	A1049	13c Florida	.25	.20
1660	A1050	13c Texas	.25	.20
1661	A1051	13c Iowa	.25	.20
1662	A1052	13c Wisconsin	.25	.20
1663	A1053	13c California	.25	.20
1664	A1054	13c Minnesota	.25	.20
1665	A1055	13c Oregon	.25	.20
1666	A1056	13c Kansas	.25	.20
1667	A1057	13c West Virginia	.25	.20
1668	A1058	13c Nevada	.25	.20
1669	A1059	13c Nebraska	.25	.20
1670	A1060	13c Colorado	.25	.20
1671	A1061	13c North Dakota	.25	.20
1672	A1062	13c South Dakota	.25	.20
1673	A1063	13c Montana	.25	.20
1674	A1064	13c Washington	.25	.20
1675	A1065	13c Idaho	.25	.20
1676	A1066	13c Wyoming	.25	.20
1677	A1067	13c Utah	.25	.20
1678	A1068	13c Oklahoma	.25	.20
1679	A1069	13c New Mexico	.25	.20
1680	A1070	13c Arizona	.25	.20
1681	A1071	13c Alaska	.25	.20
1682	A1072	13c Hawaii	.25	.20
a.		Pane of 50	13.00	—

Telephone Centenary Issue

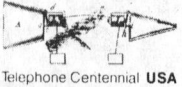

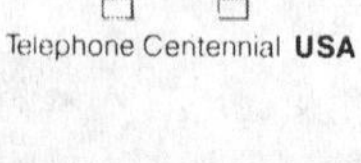

Alexander Graham Bell 13c
Bell's Telephone Patent Application
Telephone Centennial USA A1073

UNITED STATES

Engraved (Giori)
1976, Mar. 10   *Perf. 11*
1683 A1073 13c blk, pur & red, *tan*   .25   .15
1st telephone call by Alexander Graham Bell, Mar. 10, 1876.

Commercial Aviation Issue
Ford-Pullman Monoplane and Laird Swallow Biplane — A1074

1976, Mar. 19   Photo.   *Perf. 11*
1684 A1074 13c blue & multi   .25   .15
50th anniv. of 1st contract airmail flights: Dearborn, MI to Cleveland, OH, Feb. 15, 1926; and Pasco, WA to Elko, NV, Apr. 6, 1926.

Chemistry Issue
Various Flasks, Separatory Funnel, Computer Tape — A1075

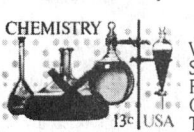

1976, Apr. 6   Photo.   *Perf. 11*
1685 A1075 13c multicolored   .25   .15
Honoring American chemists, cent. of the American Chemical Society.

Designs, from Left to Right, No. 1686: a, Two British officers. b, Gen. Benjamin Lincoln. c, George Washington. d, John Trumbull, Col. Cobb, von Steuben, Lafayette, Thomas Nelson. Alexander Hamilton, John Laurens, Walter Stewart, all vert.
No. 1687: a, John Adams, Roger Sherman, Robert R. Livingston. b, Jefferson, Franklin. c, Thomas Nelson, Jr., Francis Lewis, John Witherspoon, Samuel Huntington. d, John Hancock, Charles Thomson. e, George Read, John Dickinson, Edward Rutledge (a, d, vert., b, c, e, horiz.).
No. 1688: a, Boatsman. b, Washington. c, Flag bearer. d, Men in boat. e, Men on shore (a, d, horiz., b, c, e, vert.).
No. 1689: a, Two officers. b, Washington. c, Officer, black horse. d, Officer, white horse. e, Three soldiers (a, c, e, horiz., b, d, vert.).

1976, May 29   Litho.   *Perf. 11*
1686 A1076   Sheet of 5   3.25   —
   a.-e.   13c multi, any single   .45   .40
   f.   USA 13c omitted on "b," "c" & "d," imperf., untagged   —   2,250.
   g.   USA 13c omitted on "a" & "e"   450.   —
   h.   Imperf., untagged   —   2,250.
   i.   USA 13c omitted on "b", "c" & "d"   450.   —
   j.   USA 13c double on "b"   —   —
   k.   USA 13c omitted on "c" & "d"   800.   —
   l.   USA 13c omitted on "e"   500.   —
   m.   USA 13c omitted, imperf., untagged   —   —
   n.   As "g," imperf., untagged   —   —
1687 A1077   Sheet of 5   4.25   —
   a.-e.   18c multi, any single   .55   .55
   f.   Design & marginal inscriptions omitted   3,000.   —
   g.   USA 18c omitted on "a" & "c"   800.   —
   h.   USA 18c omitted on "b," "d" & "e"   500.   —
   i.   USA 18c omitted on "d"   550.   500.
   j.   Black omitted in design   2,000.   —
   k.   USA 18c omitted, imperf., untagged   3,000.   —
   m.   USA 18c omitted on "b" & "e"   500.   —
   n.   USA 18c omitted on "b" & "d"   —   —
   p.   Imperf., tagged   —   —
   q.   USA 18c omitted on "c"   —   —

1688 A1078   Sheet of 5   5.25   —
   a.-e.   24c multi, any single   .70   .70
   f.   USA 24c omitted, imperf., untagged   3,500.   —
   g.   USA 24c omitted on "d" & "e"   450.   450.
   h.   Design & marginal inscriptions omitted   3,250.   —
   i.   USA 24c omitted on "a," "b" & "c"   500.   —
   j.   Imperf., untagged   3,000.   —
   k.   USA 24c of "d" & "e" inverted   —   —
1689 A1079   Sheet of 5   6.25   —
   a.-e.   31c multi, any single   .85   .85
   f.   USA 31c omitted, imperf., untagged   2,750.   —
   g.   USA 31c omitted on "a" & "c"   450.   —
   h.   USA 31c omitted on "b," "d" & "e"   450.   —
   i.   USA 31c omitted on "e"   500.   —
   j.   Black omitted in design   2,000.   —
   k.   Imperf., untagged   —   —
   l.   USA 31c omitted on "d"   2,250.   —
   m.   USA 31c omitted on "a" "c" & "e"   —   —
   n.   As "m," imperf., untagged   —   —
   p.   As "h," imperf., untagged   2,500.   —
   q.   As "g," imperf., untagged   2,750.   —
   r.   USA 31c omitted on "d" & "e"   —   —

Nos. 1686-1689 (4)   19.00

Nos. 1688-1689 exist with inverted perforations.
Issued in connection with Interphil 76 Intl. Phil. Exhib., Philadelphia, Pa., May 29-June 6. Size of sheets: 203x152mm; stamps: 25x39$\frac{1}{2}$mm, 39$\frac{1}{2}$x25mm.

Benjamin Franklin Issue
Franklin and Map of North America, 1776 — A1080

Lithographed, Engraved (Giori)
1976, June 1   *Perf. 11*
1690 A1080 13c ultra & multi   .25   .15
   a.   Light blue omitted   300.00
American Bicentennial; Franklin (1706-1790), deputy postmaster general for the colonies (1753-1774) and statesman.
See Canada No. 691.

For all your stamp supply needs
www.scottonline.com

American Bicentennial Issue
Souvenir Sheets

Surrender of Cornwallis at Yorktown, by John Trumbull
A1076

Declaration of Independence, by John Trumbull
A1077

Washington Crossing the Delaware, by Emanuel Leutze/Eastman Johnson
A1078

Washington Reviewing Army at Valley Forge, by William T. Trego
A1079

UNITED STATES

American Bicentennial Issue

Declaration of Independence, by John Trumbull
JULY 4,1776 — A1081
JULY 4,1776 — A1082
JULY 4,1776 — A1083
JULY 4,1776 — A1084

1976, July 4	Photo.		Perf. 11	
1691	A1081	13c multicolored	.25	.15
1692	A1082	13c multicolored	.25	.15
1693	A1083	13c multicolored	.25	.15
1694	A1084	13c multicolored	.25	.15
a.		Strip of 4, #1691-1694	1.00	1.10

Olympic Games Issue

Diving A1085
Skiing A1086    
Running A1087
Skating A1088

1976, July 16	Photo.		Perf. 11	
1695	A1085	13c multicolored	.25	.15
1696	A1086	13c multicolored	.25	.15
1697	A1087	13c multicolored	.25	.15
1698	A1088	13c multicolored	.25	.15
a.		Block of 4, #1695-1698	1.10	1.10
b.		As "a," imperf.	750.00	

12th Winter Olympic Games, Innsbruck, Austria, Feb. 4-15, and 21st Summer Olympic Games, Montreal, Canada, July 17-Aug. 1.

Clara Maass Issue

Clara Maass, Newark German Hospital Pin — A1089

1976, Aug. 18	Photo.		Perf. 11	
1699	A1089	13c multicolored	.25	.15
a.		Horiz. pair, imperf. vert.	475.00	

Clara Maass (1876-1901), volunteer in fight against yellow fever, birth centenary.

Adolph S. Ochs Issue

Adolph S. Ochs (1858-1935), Publisher of the NY Times, 1896-1935 A1090

Giori Press Printing

1976, Sept. 18		Perf. 11	
1700 A1090 13c black & gray		.25	.15

Christmas Issue

Nativity, by John Singleton Copley A1091

"Winter Pastime," by Nathaniel Currier A1092

1976, Oct. 27	Photo.		Perf. 11	
1701	A1091	13c multicolored	.25	.15
a.		Imperf., pair	100.00	
1702	A1092	13c multicolored	.25	.15
a.		Imperf., pair	100.00	
1703	A1092	13c multicolored	.25	.15
a.		Imperf., pair	110.00	
b.		Vert. pair, imperf. btwn.		
d.		Red omitted	—	
e.		Yellow omitted	—	
		Nos. 1701-1703 (3)	.75	.45

No. 1702 has overall tagging. Lettering at base is black and usually ½mm below design. As a rule, no "snowflaking" in sky or pond. Pane of 50 has margins on 4 sides with slogans.

No. 1703 has block tagging the size of printed area. Lettering at base is gray black and usually ¾mm below design. "Snowflaking" generally in sky and pond. Pane has margin only at right or left, and no slogans. Copies are known with various amounts of red or yellow missing. Nos. 1703d and 1703e have the color totally omitted. Expertization is recommended.

American Bicentennial Issue
Washington at Princeton

Washington, Nassau Hall, Hessians, 13-Star Flag, by Charles Willson Peale — A1093

1977, Jan. 3	Photo.		Perf. 11	
1704	A1093	13c multicolored	.25	.15
a.		Horiz. pair, imperf. vert.	550.00	

Washington's victory at Princeton over Lord Cornwallis, bicentennial.

Sound Recording Issue

Tin Foil Phonograph A1094

Lithographed, Engraved (Giori)

1977, Mar. 23		Perf. 11	
1705 A1094 13c black & multi		.25	.15

Centenary of invention of the phonograph by Thomas Alva Edison, and development of sophisticated recording industry.

American Folk Art Issue
Pueblo Pottery

Pueblo Art USA 13c
Zia Pot — A1095

Pueblo Art USA 13c
San Ildefonso Pot — A1096

Pueblo Art USA 13c
Hopi Pot — A1097

Pueblo Art USA 13c
Acoma Pot — A1098

1977, Apr. 13	Photo.		Perf. 11	
1706	A1095	13c multicolored	.25	.15
1707	A1096	13c multicolored	.25	.15
1708	A1097	13c multicolored	.25	.15
1709	A1098	13c multicolored	.25	.15
a.		Block or strip of 4	1.00	1.00
b.		As "a," imperf.	2,500.	

Pueblo art, 1880-1920, from museums in NM, AZ and CO.

Lindbergh Flight Issue

Spirit of St. Louis A1099

1977, May 20	Photo.		Perf. 11	
1710	A1099	13c multicolored	.25	.15
a.		Imperf., pair	1,250.	

Charles A. Lindbergh's solo transatlantic flight from NY to Paris, 50th anniv.

Colorado Statehood Issue

Columbine and Rocky Mountains — A1100

1977, May 21	Photo.		Perf. 11	
1711	A1100	13c multicolored	.25	.15
a.		Horiz. pair, imperf. btwn.	600.00	
b.		Horiz. pair, imperf. vert.	900.00	

Colorado became a state in 1876.

Butterfly Issue

Swallowtail A1101
Checkerspot A1102 
Dogface A1103 

WEBSTER'S GEOGRAPHICAL DICTIONARY

Cities, countries, rivers and mountains - just about any proper name associated with geography can be found in this volume. All 48,000 entries appear in single alphabetical list for quick reference. An invaluable reference for the postal history buff.

Item Z600 Retail $24.95

The Webster's Geographical Dictionary is available from your favorite stamp dealer or direct from:

Scott Publishing Co. P.O. Box 828 Sidney OH 45365
www.scottonline.com
1-800-572-6885

UNITED STATES

Orange Tip — A1104

1977, June 6   Photo.   Perf. 11
1712 A1101 13c tan & multi   .25 .15
1713 A1102 13c tan & multi   .25 .15
1714 A1103 13c tan & multi   .25 .15
1715 A1104 13c tan & multi   .25 .15
   a. Block of 4, #1712-1715   1.00 1.00
   b. As "a," imperf. horiz.   15,000.

American Bicentennial Issues
Lafayette

Marquis de Lafayette — A1105

1977, June 13   Engr.   Perf. 11
1716 A1105 13c blue, black & red   .25 .15

200th anniv. of Lafayette's landing on the coast of SC, north of Charleston.

Skilled Hands for Independence

Seamstress A1106

Blacksmith A1107

Wheelwright A1108

Leatherworker A1109

1977, July 4   Photo.   Perf. 11
1717 A1106 13c multicolored   .25 .15
1718 A1107 13c multicolored   .25 .15
1719 A1108 13c multicolored   .25 .15
1720 A1109 13c multicolored   .25 .15
   a. Block of 4, #1717-1720   1.00 1.00

Peace Bridge Issue

Peace Bridge and Dove — A1110

1977, Aug. 4   Engr.   Perf. 11x10½
1721 A1110 13c blue   .25 .15

50th anniv. of the Peace Bridge, connecting Buffalo, NY with Fort Erie, Ontario.

American Bicentennial Issue
Battle of Oriskany

Herkimer at Oriskany, by Frederick Yohn A1111

1977, Aug. 6   Photo.   Perf. 11
1722 A1111 13c multicolored   .25 .15

200th anniv. of Battle of Oriskany, American Militia led by Brig. Gen. Nicholas Herkimer (1728-1777).

Energy Issue

Energy Conservation A1112

Energy Development A1113

1977, Oct. 20   Photo.   Perf. 11
1723 A1112 13c multicolored   .25 .15
1724 A1113 13c multicolored   .25 .15
   a. Pair, #1723-1724   .50 .50

Conservation and development of nation's energy resources.

Alta California Issue

Farm Houses A1114

Litho. & Engraved (Giori)
1977, Sept. 9   Perf. 11
1725 A1114 13c black & multi   .25 .15

El Pueblo de San José de Guadalupe, 1st civil settlement in Alta California, 200th anniv.

American Bicentennial Issue
Articles of Confederation

Members of Continental Congress in Conference A1115

Engraved (Giori)
1977, Sept. 30   Perf. 11
1726 A1115 13c red & brn, *cream*   .25 .15
   b. Red omitted
   c. Red & brown omitted

200th anniv. of drafting the Articles of Confederation, York Town, Pa.

No. 1726b also has most of the brown color omitted. No. 1726c must be collected as a transition multiple, certainly with No. 1726b and preferably also with No. 1726.

Talking Picture, 50th Anniv. Issue

Movie Projector and Phonograph A1116

Litho. & Engraved (Giori)
1977, Oct. 6   Perf. 11
1727 A1116 13c multicolored   .25 .15

American Bicentennial Issue
Surrender at Saratoga

Surrender of Burgoyne, by John Trumbull A1117

1977, Oct. 7   Photo.   Perf. 11
1728 A1117 13c multicolored   .25 .15

200th anniv. of Gen. John Burgoyne's surrender at Saratoga.

Christmas Issue

Washington at Valley Forge A1118

Rural Mailbox A1119

1977, Oct. 21   Photo.   Perf. 11
1729 A1118 13c multicolored   .25 .15
   a. Imperf., pair   75.00
1730 A1119 13c multicolored   .25 .15
   a. Imperf., pair   300.00

Carl Sandburg Issue

Carl Sandburg, by William A. Smith, 1952 — A1120

Engraved (Giori)
1978, Jan. 6   Perf. 11
1731 A1120 13c black & brown   .25 .15
   a. Brown omitted

Sandburg (1878-1967), poet, biographer and collector of American folk songs.

Captain Cook Issue

Capt. Cook, by Nathaniel Dance, 1776 A1121

"Resolution" and "Discovery," by John Webber A1122

Giori Press Printing
1978, Jan. 20   Perf. 11
1732 A1121 13c dark blue   .25 .15
1733 A1122 13c green   .25 .15
   a. Vert. pair, imperf. horiz.
   b. Pair, #1732-1733   .50 .50
   c. As "b," imperf. between   4,500.

Capt. James Cook, 200th anniv. of his arrival in Hawaii, at Waimea, Kauai, Jan. 20, 1778, and of his anchorage in Cook Inlet, near Anchorage, Alaska, June 1, 1778. Nos. 1732-1733 issued in panes of 50, containing 25 each of Nos. 1732-1733 including 5 No. 1732a. Design of No. 1733 is after etching "A View of Karakekooa in Owyhee."

Indian Head Penny, 1877 A1123

Eagle A1124

Roses — A1126

Engraved (Giori)
1978, Jan. 11   Perf. 11
1734 A1123 13c brown & blue green, *bister*   .25 .15
   a. Horiz. pair, imperf. vert.   300.00

1978, May 22   Photo.   Perf. 11
1735 A1124 (15c) orange   .25 .15
   a. Imperf., pair   110.00
   b. Vert. pair, imperf. horiz.   750.00

Engr.   Perf. 11x10½
1736 A1124 (15c) orange   .25 .15
   a. Booklet pane of 8   2.25 .90

See No. 1743

1978, July 11   Engr.   Perf. 10
1737 A1126 15c multicolored   .25 .15
   a. Booklet pane of 8   2.25 .90
   b. As "a," imperf.   —

Nos. 1736, 1737 issued in booklets only. All stamps have 1 or 2 straight edges.

Robertson Windmill, Williamsburg A1127

Old Windmill, Portsmouth A1128

Cape Cod Windmill, Eastham — A1129

Dutch Mill, Batavia — A1130

Southwestern Windmill — A1131

1980, Feb. 7   Engr.   Perf. 11
Booklet Stamps
1738 A1127 15c sepia, *yellow*   .30 .15
1739 A1128 15c sepia, *yellow*   .30 .15
1740 A1129 15c sepia, *yellow*   .30 .15
1741 A1130 15c sepia, *yellow*   .30 .15
1742 A1131 15c sepia, *yellow*   .30 .15
   a. Bklt. pane, 2 each #1738-1742   3.50 3.00
   b. Strip of 5, #1738-1742   1.50 1.40

Coil Stamp
1978, May 22   Engr.   Perf. 10 Vert.
1743 A1124 (15c) orange   .25 .15
   a. Imperf., pair   100.00

No. 1743a is valued in the grade of fine.

Black Heritage Issue

Harriet Tubman (1820-1913), Cart Carrying Slaves — A1133

1978, Feb. 1   Photo.   Perf. 10½x11
1744 A1133 13c multicolored   .25 .15

Tubman, born a slave, helped more than 300 slaves escape to freedom.

American Folk Art Issue
American Quilts, Basket Design
A1134 A1135 
A1136 A1137

1978, Mar. 8   Photo.   *Perf. 11*
1745 A1134 13c multicolored   .25   .15
1746 A1135 13c multicolored   .25   .15
1747 A1136 13c multicolored   .25   .15
1748 A1137 13c multicolored   .25   .15
    a.   Block of 4, #1745-1748   1.00   1.00

American Dance Issue
Ballet A1138 
Theater A1139
Folk Dance A1140 
Modern Dance A1141

1978, Apr. 26   Photo.   *Perf. 11*
1749 A1138 13c multicolored   .25   .15
1750 A1139 13c multicolored   .25   .15
1751 A1140 13c multicolored   .25   .15
1752 A1141 13c multicolored   .25   .15
    a.   Block of 4, #1749-1752   1.00   1.00

American Bicentennial Issue
French Alliance
Louis XVI and Franklin, Porcelain Sculpture by G. G. Sauvage — A1142

Giori Press Printing
1978, May 4   *Perf. 11*
1753 A1142 13c blue, black & red   .25   .15
Bicent. of French Alliance, signed in Paris, Feb. 6, 1778, and ratified by Continental Cong., May 4.

Early Cancer Detection Issue
Dr. George Papanicolaou (1883-1962), his Signature and Microscope — A1143

1978, May 18   Engr.   *Perf. 10½x11*
1754 A1143 13c brown   .25   .15
Papanicolaou, developer of Pap Test, early cancer detection in women.

Performing Arts Issues
Jimmie Rodgers and Locomotive A1144
George M. Cohan, "Yankee Doodle Dandy" and Stars A1145

1978   Photo.   *Perf. 11*
1755 A1144 13c multicolored   .25   .15
1756 A1145 15c multicolored   .25   .15
Rodgers (1897-1933), the "Singing Brakeman, Father of Country Music," and Cohan (1878-1942), actor and playwright.
Issue dates: #1755, May 24; #1756, July 3.

CAPEX Issue
Wildlife from Canadian-US Border — A1146

Litho. & Engr. (Giori)
1978, June 10   *Perf. 11*
1757 A1146   Block of 8   2.00   2.00
  a.   13c Cardinal   .25   .15
  b.   13c Mallard   .25   .15
  c.   13c Canada goose   .25   .15
  d.   13c Blue jay   .25   .15
  e.   13c Moose   .25   .15
  f.   13c Chipmunk   .25   .15
  g.   13c Red fox   .25   .15
  h.   13c Raccoon   .25   .15
  i.   Yellow, green, red, brown, blue, black (litho.) omitted   6,500.
  j.   Strip of 4 (a-d), imperf. vert.   —
  k.   Strip of 4 (e-h), imperf. vert.   —
CAPEX, Canadian Intl. Phil. Exhib., Toronto, Ont., June 9-18.

Photography Issue
Photographic Equipment A1147

1978, June 26   Photo.   *Perf. 11*
1758 A1147 15c multicolored   .30   .15

Viking Missions to Mars Issue
Viking 1 Lander Scooping Up Soil on Mars A1148

1978, July 20   Litho. & Engr.
1759 A1148 15c multicolored   .30   .15
2nd anniv. of landing of Viking 1 on Mars.

American Owls Issue
Great Gray Owl A1149
Saw-whet Owl A1150
Barred Owl A1151
Great Horned Owl A1152

1978, Aug. 26   Engr.   *Perf. 11*
1760 A1149 15c multicolored   .30   .15
1761 A1150 15c multicolored   .30   .15
1762 A1151 15c multicolored   .30   .15
1763 A1152 15c multicolored   .30   .15
    a.   Block of 4, #1760-1763   1.25   1.25

American Trees Issue
Giant Sequoia A1153 
White Pine A1154 
White Oak — A1155

Gray Birch A1156

1978, Oct. 9   Photo.   *Perf. 11*
1764 A1153 15c multicolored   .30   .15
1765 A1154 15c multicolored   .30   .15
1766 A1155 15c multicolored   .30   .15
1767 A1156 15c multicolored   .30   .15
    a.   Block of 4, #1764-1767   1.25   1.25
    b.   As "a," imperf. horiz.   12,500.

Christmas Issue
Madonna and Child with Cherubim, by Andrea della Robbia — A1157
Child on Hobby-horse and Christmas Trees — A1158

1978, Oct. 18   Photo.   *Perf. 11*
1768 A1157 15c blue & multi   .30   .15
    a.   Imperf., pair   90.00
1769 A1158 15c red & multi   .30   .15
    a.   Imperf., pair   100.00
    b.   Vert. pair, imperf. horiz.   2,250.
Value for #1768a is for an uncreased pair.

Robert F. Kennedy Issue
Robert F. Kennedy (1925-68), US Attorney General — A1159

1979, Jan. 12   Engr.   *Perf. 11*
1770 A1159 15c blue   .30   .15

Black Heritage Issue
Dr. Martin Luther King, Jr. (1929-68), and Civil Rights Marchers — A1160

1979, Jan. 13   Photo.   *Perf. 11*
1771 A1160 15c multicolored   .30   .15
    a.   Imperf., pair   —   .15
Civil rights leader.

Year of the Child Issue
Children A1161 International Year of the Child

1979, Feb. 15   Engr.   *Perf. 11*
1772 A1161 15c orange red   .30   .15
International Year of the Child.

John Steinbeck A1162
Albert Einstein A1163

UNITED STATES

John Steinbeck Issue
1979, Feb. 27   Engr.   *Perf. 10½x11*
1773 A1162 15c dark blue   .30   .15
John Ernst Steinbeck (1902-68), novelist.

Albert Einstein Issue
1979, Mar. 4   Engr.   *Perf. 10½x11*
1774 A1163 15c chocolate   .30   .15
Einstein (1879-1955), theoretical physicist.

American Folk Art Issue
Pennsylvania Toleware
Coffeepot A1164
Tea Caddy A1165    
Sugar Bowl A1166
Coffeepot A1167

1979, Apr. 19   Photo.   *Perf. 11*
1775 A1164 15c multicolored   .30   .15
1776 A1165 15c multicolored   .30   .15
1777 A1166 15c multicolored   .30   .15
1778 A1167 15c multicolored   .30   .15
    a. Block of 4, #1775-1778   1.25   1.25
    b. As "a," imperf. horiz.   4,250.

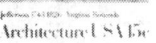

American Architecture Issue
Virginia Rotunda, by Thomas Jefferson — A1168
Baltimore Cathedral, by Benjamin Latrobe — A1169     
Boston State House, by Charles Bulfinch — A1170
Philadelphia Exchange, by William Strickland — A1171

1979, June 4   Engr.   *Perf. 11*
1779 A1168 15c black & brick red   .30   .15
1780 A1169 15c black & brick red   .30   .15
1781 A1170 15c black & brick red   .30   .15
1782 A1171 15c black & brick red   .30   .15
    a. Block of 4, #1779-1782   1.25   1.25

Endangered Flora Issue
Persistent Trillium A1172
Hawaiian Wild Broadbean A1173   
Contra Costa Wallflower A1174
Antioch Dunes Evening Primrose A1175

1979, June 7   Photo.   *Perf. 11*
1783 A1172 15c multicolored   .30   .15
1784 A1173 15c multicolored   .30   .15
1785 A1174 15c multicolored   .30   .15
1786 A1175 15c multicolored   .30   .15
    a. Block of 4, #1783-1786   1.25   1.25
    b. As "a," imperf.   600.00

Seeing Eye Dogs Issue
German Shepherd Leading Man — A1176

1979, June 15
1787 A1176 15c multicolored   .30   .15
    a. Imperf., pair   400.00

Special Olympics Issue
Child Holding Winner's Medal — A1177

1979, Aug. 9   *Perf. 11*
1788 A1177 15c multicolored   .30   .15
Special Olympics for special children, Brockport, NY, Aug. 8-13.

John Paul Jones Issue
John Paul Jones, by Charles Willson Peale — A1178

1979, Sept. 23   Photo.   *Perf. 11x12*
1789 A1178 15c multicolored   .30   .15
    a. Perf. 11   .30   .15
    b. Perf. 12   2,100.   1,000.
    c. Vert. pair, imperf. horiz.   200.
    d. As "a," vert. pair, imperf horiz.   160.

John Paul Jones (1747-1792), Naval Commander, American Revolution.
Imperfs., perf. or imperf. gutter pairs and blocks exist from printer's waste.

Olympic Games Issue
Javelin A1179
Running A1180 
Swimming A1181 
Rowing A1182 
Equestrian A1183

1979   Photo.   *Perf. 11*
1790 A1179 10c multicolored   .20   .20
1791 A1180 15c multicolored   .30   .15
1792 A1181 15c multicolored   .30   .15
1793 A1182 15c multicolored   .30   .15
1794 A1183 15c multicolored   .30   .15
    a. Block of 4, #1791-1794   1.25   1.25
    b. As "a," imperf.   1,600.

22nd Summer Olympic Games, Moscow, July 19-Aug. 3, 1980.
Issue dates: 10c, Sept. 5; 15c, Sept. 28.

Winter Olympic Games Issue
Speed Skating A1184 
Downhill Skiing A1185 
Ski Jump A1186 
Ice Hockey A1187

1980, Feb. 1   Photo.   *Perf. 11x10½*
1795 A1184 15c multicolored   .35   .15
    a. Perf. 11   1.05
1796 A1185 15c multicolored   .35   .15
    a. Perf. 11   1.05
1797 A1186 15c multicolored   .35   .15
    a. Perf. 11   1.05
1798 A1187 15c multicolored   .35   .15
    a. Perf. 11   1.05
    b. Block of 4, #1795-1798   1.50   1.40
    c. Block of 4, #1795a-1798a   4.25

13th Winter Olympic Games, Lake Placid, NY, Feb. 12-24.

Christmas Issue
Virgin and Child, by Gerard David — A1188
Santa Claus, Christmas Tree Ornament — A1189

1979, Oct. 18   Photo.   *Perf. 11*
1799 A1188 15c multicolored   .30   .15
    a. Imperf., pair   100.
    b. Vert. pair, imperf.   700.
    c. Vert. pair, imperf. btwn.   2,250.
1800 A1189 15c multicolored   .30   .15
    a. Green & yellow omitted   750.
    b. Green, yellow & tan omitted   800.

Nos. 1800a, 1800b always have the remaining colors misaligned.
No. 1800b is valued in the grade of fine.

Performing Arts Issue
Will Rogers (1879-1935), Actor and Humorist — A1190

1979, Nov. 4   Photo.   *Perf. 11*
1801 A1190 15c multicolored   .30   .15
    a. Imperf., pair   225.00

Viet Nam Veterans Issue
Ribbon for Viet Nam Service Medal A1191

1979, Nov. 11   Photo.   *Perf. 11*
1802 A1191 15c multicolored   .30   .15

A tribute to veterans of the Viet Nam War.

Performing Arts Issue
W.C. Fields (1880-1946), actor and comedian — A1192

1980, Jan. 29   Photo.   *Perf. 11*
1803 A1192 15c multicolored   .30   .15
    a. Imperf., pair

Black Heritage
Benjamin Banneker (1731-1806), Astronomer and Mathematician, Transverse — A1193

1980, Feb. 15   Photo.   *Perf. 11*
1804 A1193 15c multicolored   .30   .15
    a. Horiz. pair, imperf. vert.   800.00

Imperf. printer's waste has been fraudulently perforated to simulate No. 1804a. Legitimate examples of No. 1804a do not have colors misregistered.

UNITED STATES

Letter Writing

Letters Preserve Memories A1194
P.S. Write Soon A1195 
Letters Lift Spirits A1196 
Letters Shape Opinions A1197 

1980, Feb. 25
1805 A1194 15c multicolored .30 .15
1806 A1195 15c purple & multi .30 .15
1807 A1196 15c multicolored .30 .15
1808 A1195 15c green & multi .30 .15
1809 A1197 15c multicolored .30 .15
1810 A1195 15c red & multi .30 .15
  a. Vert. strip of 6 #1805-1810 1.85 2.00
    Nos. 1805-1810 (6) 1.80 .90

Natl. Letter Writing Week, Feb. 24-Mar. 1.

Americana Type

Weaver Violins — A1199

Coil Stamps

1980-81 Engr. Perf. 10 Vert.
1811 A984 1c dk blue, grnsh .15 .15
  a. Imperf., pair 175.00
1813 A1199 3.5c purple, yel .15 .15
  a. Untagged (Bureau precanceled, lines only) .15
  b. Imperf., pair 225.00
1816 A997 12c brown red, beige ('81) .25 .15
  a. Untagged (Bureau precanceled) .25
  b. Imperf., pair 200.00

A1207

1981, Mar. 15 Photo. Perf. 11x10½
1818 A1207 (18c) violet .35 .15

Engr. Perf. 10

Booklet Stamp

1819 A1207 (18c) violet .40 .15
  a. Booklet pane of 8 3.50 1.75

Coil Stamp
Perf. 10 Vert.
1820 A1207 (18c) violet .40 .15
  a. Imperf., pair 120.00
    Nos. 1818-1820 (3) 1.15 .45

Frances Perkins

Frances Perkins (1882-1965), Sec. of Labor, 1933-45 (1st Woman Cabinet Member) — A1208

1980, Apr. 10 Perf. 10½x11
1821 A1208 15c Prus blue .30 .15

Dolley Madison

Dolley Madison (1768-1849), First Lady, 1809-1817 — A1209

1980, May 20 Perf. 11
1822 A1209 15c red brown & sepia .30 .15

Emily Bissell

Emily Bissell (1861-1948), Social Worker; Introduced Christmas seals in US — A1210

1980, May 31
1823 A1210 15c black & red .30 .15
  a. Vert. pair, imperf. horiz. 400.00

Helen Keller

Helen Keller and Anne Sullivan — A1211

Litho. & Engr.
1980, June 27 Perf. 11
1824 A1211 15c multicolored .30 .15

Keller (1880-1968), blind and deaf writer and lecturer taught by Sullivan (1867-1936).

Veterans Administration

Veterans Administration Emblem A1212 
Gen. Bernardo de Galvez A1213

1980, July 21 Photo.
1825 A1212 15c car & vio bl .30 .15
  a. Horiz. pair, imperf. vert. 500.00

General Bernardo de Galvez

1980, July 23 Engr. Perf. 11
1826 A1213 15c multicolored .30 .15
  a. Red, brn & bl (engr.) omitted 800.
  b. Red, brn, bl (engr.), bl & yel (litho.) omitted 1,400.

Galvez (1746-1786), helped defeat British in Battle of Mobile, 1780.

Coral Reefs

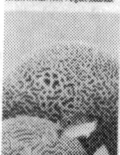

Brain Coral, Beaugregory Fish A1214
Elkhorn Coral, Porkfish A1215  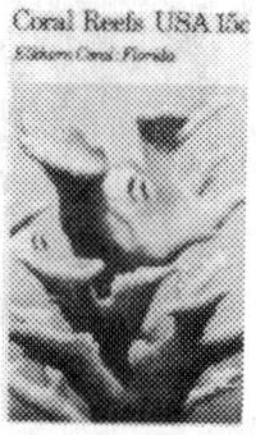
Chalice Coral, Moorish Idol Fish A1216 
Finger Coral, Sabertooth Blenny Fish A1217 

1980, Aug. 26 Photo. Perf. 11
1827 A1214 15c multicolored .30 .15
1828 A1215 15c multicolored .30 .15
1829 A1216 15c multicolored .30 .15
1830 A1217 15c multicolored .30 .15
  a. Block of 4, #1827-1830 1.25 1.10
  b. As "a," imperf. 1,250.
  c. As "a," vert. imperf. btwn. —
  d. As "a," imperf. vert. 3,000.

American Bald Eagle A1218
Edith Wharton A1219 

Organized Labor

1980, Sept. 1 Photo. Perf. 11
1831 A1218 15c multicolored .30 .15
  a. Imperf., pair 375.00

Edith Wharton

1980, Sept. 5 Engr. Perf. 10½x11
1832 A1219 15c purple .30 .15

Edith Wharton (1862-1937), writer.

American Education

"Homage to the Square: Glow," by Josef Albers — A1220

1980, Sept. 12 Photo. Perf. 11
1833 A1220 15c multicolored .30 .15
  a. Horiz. pair, imperf. btwn. 250.00

American Folk Art
Pacific Northwest Indian Masks

Heiltsuk, Bella Bella Tribe A1221
Chilkat Tlingit Tribe A1222 
Tlingit Tribe A1223 
Bella Coola Tribe A1224 

1980, Sept. 25
1834 A1221 15c multicolored .30 .15
1835 A1222 15c multicolored .30 .15
1836 A1223 15c multicolored .30 .15
1837 A1224 15c multicolored .30 .15
  a. Block of 4, #1834-1837 1.25 1.25

American Architecture

Smithsonian Institution, by James Renwick A1225
Trinity Church, Boston, by Henry Hobson Richardson A1226 
Pennsylvania Academy of Fine Arts, by Frank Furness A1227 
Lyndhurst, Tarrytown, NY, by Alexander Jackson Davis A1228 

1980, Oct. 9 Engr. Perf. 11
1838 A1225 15c black & brick red .30 .15
1839 A1226 15c black & brick red .30 .15
1840 A1227 15c black & brick red .30 .15
1841 A1228 15c black & brick red .30 .15
  a. Block of 4, #1838-1841 1.25 1.25

Christmas

Madonna and Child A1229
Wreath, Toys on Windowsill A1230 

1980, Oct. 31 Photo. Perf. 11
1842 A1229 15c multicolored .30 .15
  a. Imperf., pair 85.00

UNITED STATES

1843 A1230 15c multicolored .30 .15
   a. Imperf., pair 85.00
   b. Buff omitted 25.00
   c. Vert. pair, imperf. horiz.

No. 1843b is difficult to identify and should have a competent certificate.

Great Americans

A1231 Dorothea Dix USA 1c
A1232 Igor Stravinsky USA 2c
A1233 Henry Clay USA 3c
A1234 Carl Schurz 4c USA
A1235 Pearl Buck USA 5c
A1236 Walter Lippmann 6 USA
A1237 Abraham Baldwin USA 7
A1238 Henry Knox USA 8
A1239 Sylvanus Thayer USA 9c
A1240 Richard Russell USA 10c
A1241 Alden Partridge USA 11
A1242 Crazy Horse USA 13c
A1243 Sinclair Lewis USA 14
A1244 Rachel Carson USA 17c
A1245 George Mason USA 18c
A1246 Sequoyah 19c
A1247 Ralph Bunche USA 20c
A1248 Thomas H. Gallaudet USA 20c
A1249 Harry S Truman USA 20c
A1250 John J. Audubon USA 22

A1251 Frank C. Laubach USA 30c
A1252 Charles R Drew MD USA 35c
A1253 Robert Millikan 37c USA
A1254 Grenville Clark USA 39
A1255 Lillian M. Gilbreth USA 40c
A1256 Chester W. Nimitz USA 50

Perf. 11x10½, 11 (1, 6-11, 14, #1862, 22, 30, 39, 40, 50c)
1980-85 *Engr.*
1844 A1231 1c black .15 .15
   a. Imperf. pair 425.
   b. Vert. pair, imperf. btwn. and at bottom 3,000.
   d. Vert. pair, imperf. horiz.
1845 A1232 2c brown black .15 .15
1846 A1233 3c olive green .15 .15
1847 A1234 4c violet .15 .15
1848 A1235 5c henna brown .15 .15
1849 A1236 6c orange ver .15 .15
   a. Vert. pair, imperf. btwn. and at bottom 2,500.
1850 A1237 7c brt carmine .15 .15
1851 A1238 8c olive black .15 .15
1852 A1239 9c dark green .20 .15
1853 A1240 10c Prus blue .20 .15
   a. Vert. pair, imperf. btwn. & at bottom 1,100.
   b. Horiz. pair, imperf. btwn. 2,250.

Completely imperforate tagged or untagged stamps are from printer's waste.

1854 A1241 11c dark blue .25 .15
1855 A1242 13c lt maroon .25 .15
1856 A1243 14c slate green .25 .15
   a. Vert. pair, imperf. horiz. 150.
   b. Horiz. pair, imperf. btwn. 10.00
   d. All color omitted 1,900.

No. 1856d comes from a partially printed pane and should be collected as a vertical strip of 10, one stamp normal, one stamp transitional and 8 stamps with color omitted.

1857 A1244 17c green .35 .15
1858 A1245 18c dark blue .35 .15
1859 A1246 19c brown .40 .15
1860 A1247 20c claret .40 .15
1861 A1248 20c green .45 .15
1862 A1249 20c black .40 .15
1863 A1250 22c dk chalky blue .45 .15
   a. Vert. pair, imperf. horiz. 2,500.
   c. Horiz. pair, imperf. btwn. 2,500.
1864 A1251 30c olive gray .55 .15
1865 A1252 35c gray .70 .15
1866 A1253 37c blue .75 .15
1867 A1254 39c rose lilac .80 .15
   a. Vert. pair, imperf. horiz. 600.
   b. Horiz. pair, imperf. btwn. 2,000.
1868 A1255 40c dark green .80 .15
1869 A1256 50c brown .95 .15
   Nos. 1844-1869 (26) 9.70 3.90

Years of issue: 19c, 1980. 17c, 18c, 35c, 1981. No. 1860, 2c, 13c, 37c, 1982. No. 1861, 1c, 3c-5c, 1983. No. 1862, 10c, 30c, 40c, 1984. 6c-9c, 11c, 14c, 22c, 39c, 50c, 1985.

A1261 USA 15c Everett Dirksen
A1262 Whitney Moore Young Black Heritage USA 15c

Everett Dirksen
1981, Jan. 4 *Perf. 11*
1874 A1261 15c gray .30 .15
   a. All color omitted

Everett Dirksen (1896-1969), Senate Minority Leader, 1960-69.

No. 1874a comes from a paially printed pane and may be collected as either a vertical strip of 3 or 5 (1 or 3 stamps normal, one stamp transitional and one stamp with color omitted) or as a pair with one partially printed stamp.

Black Heritage
1981, Jan. 30 *Photo.* *Perf. 11*
1875 A1262 15c multicolored .30 .15

Whitney Moore Young (1921-71), civil rights leader.

Flowers

A1263 Rose USA 18c
A1264 Camellia USA 18c
A1265 Dahlia USA 18c
A1266 Lily USA 18c

1981, Apr. 23 *Perf. 11*
1876 A1263 18c multicolored .35 .15
1877 A1264 18c multicolored .35 .15
1878 A1265 18c multicolored .35 .15
1879 A1266 18c multicolored .35 .15
   a. Block of 4, #1876-1879 1.40 1.25

A1267-A1276

1981, May 14 *Engr.* *Perf. 11*
Booklet Stamps
1880 A1267 18c Bighorn .55 .15
1881 A1268 18c Puma .55 .15
1882 A1269 18c Harbor seal .55 .15
1883 A1270 18c Bison .55 .15
1884 A1271 18c Brown bear .55 .15
1885 A1272 18c Polar bear .55 .15
1886 A1273 18c Elk (wapiti) .55 .15
1887 A1274 18c Moose .55 .15
1888 A1275 18c White-tailed deer .55 .15
1889 A1276 18c Pronghorn .55 .15
   a. Bklt. pane of 10, #1880-1889 8.00 7.00
   Nos. 1880-1889 (10) 5.50 1.50

See No. 1949.

A1277
A1278 
A1279
A1280

Multicolor Huck Press
1981, Apr. 24 *Perf. 11*
1890 A1277 18c multicolored .35 .15
   a. Imperf., pair 110.00
   b. Vert. pair, imperf. horiz. 1,000.

Coil Stamp
Perf. 10 Vert.
1891 A1278 18c multicolored .35 .15
   a. Imperf., pair 20.00
   b. Pair, imperf. btwn.

Beware of pairs offered as imperf. between that have faint blind perfs.

Booklet Stamps
Perf. 11
1892 A1279 6c multicolored .50 .15
1893 A1280 18c multicolored .30 .15
   a. Booklet pane, 2 #1892, 6 #1893 3.00 2.25
   b. As "a," vert. imperf. btwn. 75.00
   c. Pair, #1892, 1893 .90 1.00

Bureau Precanceled Coils
Starting with No. 1895e, Bureau precanceled coil stamps are valued unused as well as used. The coils issued with dull finish gum may be difficult to distinguish. When used normally these stamps do not receive any postal markings so that used stamps with an additional post-cancellation of any kind are worth considerably less than the values shown here.

A1281 USA 20c (flag)

1981, Dec. 17 *Perf. 11*
1894 A1281 20c blk, dk blue & red .40 .15
   a. Vert. pair, imperf. 35.00
   b. Vert. pair, imperf. horiz. 600.00
   c. Dark blue omitted 90.00
   d. Black omitted 325.00

Coil Stamp
Perf. 10 Vertical
1895 A1281 20c blk, dk blue & red .35 .15
   a. Imperf., pair 8.50
   b. Black omitted 55.00
   c. Dark blue omitted 1,500.
   d. Pair, imperf. btwn. 1,250.
   e. Untagged (Bureau precanceled) .50 .50

Booklet Stamp
Perf. 11x10½
1896 A1281 20c blk, dk blue & red .35 .15
   a. Booklet pane of 6 2.50 2.00
   b. Booklet pane of 10 4.25 3.25

Transportation Coils

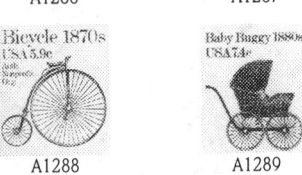

A1282 Omnibus 1880s USA 1c
A1283 Locomotive 1870s USA 2c
A1284 Handcar 1880s USA 3c
A1285 Stagecoach 1890s USA 4c
A1286 Motorcycle 1913 USA 5c
A1287 Sleigh 1880s USA 5.2c
A1288 Bicycle 1870s USA 5.9c
A1289 Baby Buggy 1880s USA 7.4c

49

UNITED STATES

A1290 — Mail Wagon 1880s USA 9.3c
A1291 — Hansom Cab 1890s USA 10.9c
A1292 — RR Caboose 1890s USA 11c
A1293 — Electric Auto 1917 USA 17c
A1294 — Surrey 1890s USA 18c
A1295 — Fire Pumper 1860s USA 20c

1981-84		Engr.	Perf. 10 Vert.	
1897	A1282	1c violet	.15	.15
b.		Imperf., pair	700.00	
1897A	A1283	2c black	.15	.15
a.		Imperf., pair	60.00	

For similar designs to the 1c and 2c, see Nos. 2225-2226.

1898	A1284	3c dk green	.15	.15
1898A	A1285	4c redsh brown	.15	.15
c.		Untagged (Bureau precanceled)	.15	.15
d.		As "b," imperf., pair	750.00	
		No. 1898A, imperf., pair	925.00	—
1899	A1286	5c gray green	.15	.15
a.		Imperf., pair	2,750.	
1900	A1287	5.2c carmine	.15	.15
a.		Untagged (Bureau precanceled)	.15	.15
1901	A1288	5.9c blue	.20	.15
a.		Untagged (Bureau precanceled, lines only)	.20	.20
b.		As "a," imperf., pair	200.00	
1902	A1289	7.4c brown	.20	.15
a.		Untagged (Bureau precanceled)	.20	.20
1903	A1290	9.3c car rose	.30	.20
a.		Untagged (Bureau precanceled, lines only)	.25	.25
b.		As "a," imperf., pair	125.00	
1904	A1291	10.9c purple	.25	.15
a.		Untagged (Bureau precanceled, lines only)	.25	.25
b.		As "a," imperf., pair	150.00	
1905	A1292	11c red	.25	.15
a.		Untagged	.25	.15
1906	A1293	17c ultra	.35	.15
a.		Untagged (Bureau precanceled, Presorted First Class)	.35	.35
b.		Imperf., pair	165.00	
c.		As "a," imperf., pair	650.00	
1907	A1294	18c dark brown	.35	.15
a.		Imperf., pair	160.00	
1908	A1295	20c vermilion	.35	.15
a.		Imperf., pair	110.00	
		Nos. 1897-1908 (14)	3.15	2.15

Years of issue: 9.3c, 17c-20c, 1981. 2c, 4c, 5.9c, 10.9c, 1982. 1c, 3c, 5c, 5.2c, 1983. 7.4c, 11c, 1984.

See Nos. 2123-2136, 2225-2231, 2252-2266, 2451-2468.

A1296 — $9.35 eagle

		Perf. 10 Vert. on 1 or 2 Sides		
1983, Aug. 12			Photo.	
1909	A1296	$9.35 multi	21.00	14.00
a.		Booklet pane of 3	65.00	

A1297 — The Gift of Self, American Red Cross 1881-1981
A1298 — Savings and Loans, Save USA 18c

American Red Cross Centennial
1981, May 1   Perf. 10½x11
1910   A1297   18c multicolored   .35   .15

Savings & Loan Sesquicentennial
1981, May 8   Perf. 11
1911   A1298   18c multicolored   .35   .15

Space Achievement

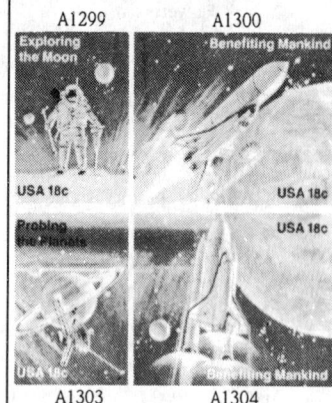

A1299 — Exploring the Moon
A1300 — Benefiting Mankind
A1301 — Probing the Planets
A1302 — Benefiting Mankind
A1303 — Benefiting Mankind
A1304 — Understanding the Sun
A1305 — Benefiting Mankind
A1306 — Comprehending the Universe

1981, May 21   Perf. 11

1912	A1299	18c multicolored	.35	.15
1913	A1300	18c multicolored	.35	.15
1914	A1301	18c multicolored	.35	.15
1915	A1302	18c multicolored	.35	.15
1916	A1303	18c multicolored	.35	.15
1917	A1304	18c multicolored	.35	.15
1918	A1305	18c multicolored	.35	.15
1919	A1306	18c multicolored	.35	.15
a.		Block of 8, #1912-1919	3.00	3.00
b.		As "a," imperf.	9,000.	

Professional Management

A1307 — Joseph Wharton

1981, June 18
1920   A1307   18c blue & black   .35   .15

Preservation of Wildlife Habitats

A1308 — Save Wetland Habitats
A1309 — Save Grassland Habitats
A1310 — Save Mountain Habitats 
A1311 — Save Woodland Habitats

1981, June 26

1921	A1308	18c multicolored	.35	.15
1922	A1309	18c multicolored	.35	.15
1923	A1310	18c multicolored	.35	.15
1924	A1311	18c multicolored	.35	.15
a.		Block of 4, #1921-1924	1.50	1.25

International Year of the Disabled

A1312 — Man Looking through Microscope, Disabled doesn't mean Unable

1981, June 29   Photo.   Perf. 11
1925   A1312   18c multicolored   .35   .15
   a.   Vert. pair, imperf. horiz.   2,750.

Edna St. Vincent Millay, 1892-1950

A1313

Litho. & Engr.
1981, July 10   Perf. 11
1926   A1313   18c multicolored   .35   .15
   a.   Black (engr., inscriptions) omitted   425.00   —

Alcoholism

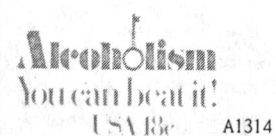

A1314 — Alcoholism You can beat it! USA 18c

1981, Aug. 19   Engr.   Perf. 11
1927   A1314   18c blue & black   .40   .15
   a.   Imperf., pair   450.
   b.   Vert. pair, imperf. horiz.   2,250.

American Architecture

A1315 — New York University Library by Sanford White
A1316 — Biltmore House by Richard Morris Hunt
A1317 — Palace of the Arts by Bernard Maybeck
A1318 — National Farmer's Bank by Louis Sullivan

1981, Aug. 28   Engr.   Perf. 11

1928	A1315	18c black & red	.40	.15
1929	A1316	18c black & red	.40	.15
1930	A1317	18c black & red	.40	.15
1931	A1318	18c black & red	.40	.15
a.		Block of 4, #1928-1931	1.65	1.50

Athletes

A1319 — Mildred Didrikson Zaharias
A1320 — Robert Tyre Jones

1981, Sept. 22   Engr.   Perf. 10½x11
1932   A1319   18c purple   .35   .15
1933   A1320   18c green   .35   .15

Frederic Remington, 1861-1909

A1321 — Coming Through the Rye

1981, Oct. 9   Perf. 11
1934   A1321   18c gray, green & brown   .35   .15
   a.   Vert. pair, imperf. btwn.   275.00
   b.   Brown omitted   550.00

James Hoban, 1762?-1831

A1322 — Irish-American Architect of White House

1981, Oct. 13   Photo.   Perf. 11
1935   A1322   18c multicolored   .35   .15
1936   A1322   20c multicolored   .35   .15
See Ireland No. 504.

American Bicentennial

A1323 — Battle of Yorktown
A1324 — Battle of Virginia Capes

Litho. & Engr.
1981, Oct. 16   Perf. 11
1937   A1323   18c multicolored   .35   .15
1938   A1324   18c multicolored   .35   .15
   a.   Pair, #1937-1938   .90   .75
   b.   As "a," black (engr., inscriptions) omitted   450.00

Footnotes near stamp listings often refer to other stamps of the same design.

UNITED STATES

Christmas

Madonna and Child, Botticelli — A1325
Felt Bear on Sled — A1326

1981, Oct. 28 Photo. Perf. 11
1939 A1325 (20c) multicolored .40 .15
  a. Imperf., pair 125.
  b. Vert. pair, imperf. horiz. 1,650.
1940 A1326 (20c) multicolored .40 .15
  a. Imperf., pair 350.
  b. Vert. pair, imperf. horiz. 2,500.

John Hanson, 1721-1783

First President of Continental Congress — A1327

1981, Nov. 5 Photo. Perf. 11
1941 A1327 20c multicolored .40 .15

Desert Plants

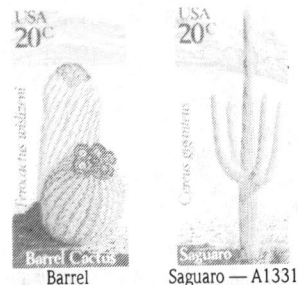

Barrel Cactus — A1328
Agave — A1329
Beavertail Cactus — A1330 
Saguaro — A1331

1981, Dec. 11 Litho. & Engr.
1942 A1328 20c multicolored .35 .15
1943 A1329 20c multicolored .35 .15
1944 A1330 20c multicolored .35 .15
1945 A1331 20c multicolored .35 .15
  a. Block of 4, #1942-1945 1.50 1.25
  b. As "a," deep brown omitted 7,500.
  c. No. 1945 imperf., vert. pair 5,250.

A1332   A1333   A1334

1981, Oct. 11 Photo. Perf. 11x10½
1946 A1332 (20c) multicolored .40 .15

Coil Stamp
Perf. 10 Vert.
1947 A1332 (20c) brown .60 .15
  a. Imperf., pair 1,750.

Booklet Stamp
Perf. 11x10½
1948 A1333 (20c) brown .40 .15
  a. Booklet pane of 10 4.50 3.00

1982, Jan. 8 Engr. Perf. 11
1949 A1334 20c dk blue (from bklt. pane) .50 .15
  a. Booklet pane of 10 5.00 2.50
  b. As "a," vert. imperf. btwn. 110.00
  c. Type II .50 .15
  d. As "c," booklet pane of 10 10.00

No. 1949 is 18¾mm wide and has overall tagging. No. 1949c is 18½mm wide and has block tagging.
See No. 1880.

Franklin Delano Roosevelt

A1335

1982, Jan. 30 Engr. Perf. 11
1950 A1335 20c blue .40 .15

A1336

1982, Feb. 1 Photo. Perf. 11x10½
1951 A1336 20c multicolored .65 .15
  a. Perf. 11 .40 .15
  b. Imperf., pair 350.00
  c. Blue omitted 225.00
  d. Yellow omitted

No. 1951c is valued in the grade of fine.

A1337   A1338-A1387

George Washington

1982, Feb. 22 Photo. Perf. 11
1952 A1337 20c multicolored .40 .15

State Birds & Flowers

1982, Apr. 14 Photo. Perf. 10½x11
1953 A1338 20c Alabama .50 .25
1954 A1339 20c Alaska .50 .25
1955 A1340 20c Arizona .50 .25
1956 A1341 20c Arkansas .50 .25
1957 A1342 20c California .50 .25
1958 A1343 20c Colorado .50 .25
1959 A1344 20c Connecticut .50 .25
1960 A1345 20c Delaware .50 .25
1961 A1346 20c Florida .50 .25
1962 A1347 20c Georgia .50 .25
1963 A1348 20c Hawaii .50 .25
1964 A1349 20c Idaho .50 .25
1965 A1350 20c Illinois .50 .25
1966 A1351 20c Indiana .50 .25
1967 A1352 20c Iowa .50 .25
1968 A1353 20c Kansas .50 .25
1969 A1354 20c Kentucky .50 .25
1970 A1355 20c Louisiana .50 .25
1971 A1356 20c Maine .50 .25
1972 A1357 20c Maryland .50 .25
1973 A1358 20c Massachusetts .50 .25
1974 A1359 20c Michigan .50 .25
1975 A1360 20c Minnesota .50 .25
1976 A1361 20c Mississippi .50 .25
1977 A1362 20c Missouri .50 .25
1978 A1363 20c Montana .50 .25
1979 A1364 20c Nebraska .50 .25
1980 A1365 20c Nevada .50 .25
1981 A1366 20c New Hampshire .50 .25
1982 A1367 20c New Jersey .50 .25
1983 A1368 20c New Mexico .50 .25
1984 A1369 20c New York .50 .25
1985 A1370 20c North Carolina .50 .25
1986 A1371 20c North Dakota .50 .25
1987 A1372 20c Ohio .50 .25
1988 A1373 20c Oklahoma .50 .25
1989 A1374 20c Oregon .50 .25
1990 A1375 20c Pennsylvania .50 .25
1991 A1376 20c Rhode Island .50 .25
1992 A1377 20c South Carolina .50 .25
1993 A1378 20c South Dakota .50 .25
1994 A1379 20c Tennessee .50 .25
1995 A1380 20c Texas .50 .25
1996 A1381 20c Utah .50 .25
1997 A1382 20c Vermont .50 .25
1998 A1383 20c Virginia .50 .25
1999 A1384 20c Washington .50 .25
2000 A1385 20c West Virginia .50 .25
2001 A1386 20c Wisconsin .50 .25
2002 A1387 20c Wyoming .50 .25
  a. #1953a-2002a, any single, perf. 11 .55 .30
  b. Pane of 50, perf. 10½x11 25.00
  c. Pane of 50, perf. 11 27.50
  d. Pane of 50, imperf. 27,500.

US-Netherlands

200th Anniv. of Diplomatic Recognition by the Netherlands — A1388

1982, Apr. 20 Photo. Perf. 11
2003 A1388 20c ver, brt blue & gray black .40 .15
  a. Imperf., pair 325.00

See Netherlands Nos. 640-641.

Library of Congress

A1389

1982, Apr. 21 Engr. Perf. 11
2004 A1389 20c red & black .40 .15

Consumer Education

A1390

Coil Stamp
1982, Apr. 27 Engr. Perf. 10 Vert.
2005 A1390 20c sky blue .55 .15
  a. Imperf., pair 100.00

Knoxville World's Fair

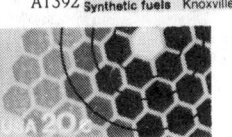

Solar energy — A1391
Synthetic fuels — A1392
Breeder reactor — A1393
Fossil fuels — A1394

1982, Apr. 29 Photo. Perf. 11
2006 A1391 20c multicolored .40 .15
2007 A1392 20c multicolored .40 .15
2008 A1393 20c multicolored .40 .15
2009 A1394 20c multicolored .40 .15
  a. Block of 4, #2006-2009 1.65 1.50

American Author, 1832-1899

Frontispiece from "Ragged Dick" — A1395

1982, Apr. 30 Engr. Perf. 11
2010 A1395 20c red & black, tan .40 .15
  a. Red & Black omitted

The Philatelic Foundation has issued a certificate for a pane of 50 with red and black colors omitted. Recognition of this error is by the paper and by a tiny residue of red ink from the tagging roller. The engraved plates did not strike the paper.

Aging Together

A1396

1982, May 21 Perf. 11
2011 A1396 20c brown .40 .15

A1397   A1398

Performing Arts

Design: Actors John, Ethel & Lionel Barrymore.

1982, June 8 Photo. Perf. 11
2012 A1397 20c multicolored .40 .15

Dr. Mary E. Walker, 1832-1919

1982, June 10 Photo. Perf. 11
2013 A1398 20c multicolored .40 .15

International Peace Garden

A1399

1982, June 30 Photo. Perf. 11
2014 A1399 20c multicolored .40 .15
  a. Black & green (engr.) omitted 275.00

A1400   A1401

America's Libraries

1982, July 13 Engr. Perf. 11
2015 A1400 20c red & black .40 .15
  a. Vert. pair, imperf. horiz. 325.00

Jackie Robinson, 1919-1972

1982, Aug. 2 Photo. Perf. 10½x11
2016 A1401 20c multicolored 1.10 .15

Touro Synagogue

A1402

Photogravure, Engraved
1982, Aug. 22 Perf. 11
2017 A1402 20c multicolored .40 .15
  a. Imperf., pair 2,500.

UNITED STATES

Wolf Trap Farm Park

A1403

1982, Sept. 1   **Photo.**   *Perf. 11*
2018   A1403   20c multicolored   .40   .15

American Architecture

Fallingwater, Mill Run, Pa., by Frank Lloyd Wright — A1404

Illinois Institute of Technology by Ludwig Mies van der Rohe — A1405

Gropius House, Lincoln, Mass., by Walter Gropius — A1406

Dulles Airport, by Eero Saarinen — A1407

1982, Sept. 30   **Engr.**   *Perf. 11*
2019   A1404   20c black & brown   .40   .15
2020   A1405   20c black & brown   .40   .15
2021   A1406   20c black & brown   .40   .15
2022   A1407   20c black & brown   .40   .15
    a.   Block of 4, #2019-2022   1.75   1.60

St. Francis of Assisi, 1182-1226

A1408

1982, Oct. 7   **Photo.**   *Perf. 11*
2023   A1408   20c multicolored   .40   .15

Ponce de Leon, 1527-1591

A1409

1982, Oct. 12   **Photo.**   *Perf. 11*
2024   A1409   20c multicolored   .40   .15
    a.   Imperf., pair   600.00
    b.   Vert. pair, Imperf. btwn. and at top   —

Christmas

A1410

A1411

A1412

A1413

A1414

A1415

1982, Nov. 3   **Photo.**   *Perf. 11*
2025   A1410   13c multicolored   .25   .15
    a.   Imperf., pair   650.00

1982, Oct. 28
2026   A1411   20c multicolored   .40   .15
    a.   Imperf., pair   150.00
    b.   Horiz. pair, imperf. vert.
    c.   Vert. pair, imperf. horiz.
2027   A1412   20c multicolored   .45   .15
2028   A1413   20c multicolored   .45   .15
2029   A1414   20c multicolored   .45   .15
2030   A1415   20c multicolored   .45   .15
    a.   Block of 4, #2027-2030   2.00   1.50
    b.   As "a," imperf.   3,000.
    c.   As "a," imperf. horiz.   3,250.
    Nos. 2025-2030 (6)   2.45   .90

Science & Industry

A1416

Litho. & Engr.
1983, Jan. 19   *Perf. 11*
2031   A1416   20c multicolored   .40   .15
    a.   Black (engr.) omitted   1,400.

Balloons

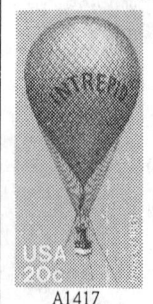

A1417

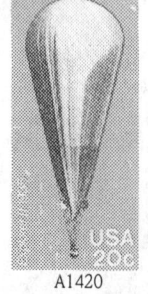

A1418

A1419

A1420

1983, Mar. 31   **Photo.**   *Perf. 11*
2032   A1417   20c multicolored   .40   .15
2033   A1418   20c multicolored   .40   .15
2034   A1419   20c multicolored   .40   .15
2035   A1420   20c multicolored   .40   .15
    a.   Block of 4, #2032-2035   1.65   1.50
    b.   As "a," imperf.   4,500.
    c.   As "a," right stamp perf., otherwise imperf.   4,500.

US-Sweden

A1421

1983, Mar. 24   **Engr.**   *Perf. 11*
2036   A1421   20c multicolored   .40   .15
See Sweden No. 1453.

Civilian Conservation Corps

A1422

1983, Apr. 5   **Photo.**   *Perf. 11*
2037   A1422   20c multicolored   .40   .15
    a.   Imperf., pair   2,500.
    b.   Vert. pair, imperf. horiz.   —

Joseph Priestley, 1733-1804

A1423

1983, Apr. 13   **Photo.**   *Perf. 11*
2038   A1423   20c multicolored   .40   .15

Voluntarism

A1424

1983, Apr. 20   **Engr.**   *Perf. 11*
2039   A1424   20c red & black   .40   .15
    a.   Imperf., pair   800.00

US-Germany

Concord, 1683 — A1425

1983, Apr. 29   *Perf. 11*
2040   A1425   20c brown   .40   .15
See Germany No. 1397.

Brooklyn Bridge

A1426

1983, May 17   **Engr.**   *Perf. 11*
2041   A1426   20c blue   .40   .15

T.V.A.

A1427

Photo. & Engr.
1983, May 18   *Perf. 11*
2042   A1427   20c multicolored   .40   .15

Physical Fitness

A1428

1983, May 14   **Photo.**   *Perf. 11*
2043   A1428   20c multicolored   .40   .15

Scott Joplin, 1868-1917

A1429

1983, June 9   **Photo.**
2044   A1429   20c multicolored   .40   .15
    a.   Imperf., pair   550.00

Medal of Honor

A1430

1983, June 7   **Litho. & Engr.**   *Perf. 11*
2045   A1430   20c multicolored   .40   .15
    a.   Red omitted   325.00

A1431

A1432

George Herman Ruth, 1895-1948

1983, July 6   **Engr.**   *Perf. 10½x11*
2046   A1431   20c blue   1.10   .15

Nathaniel Hawthorne, 1804-1864

1983, July 8   **Photo.**   *Perf. 11*
2047   A1432   20c multicolored   .40   .15

1984 Summer Olympics

Discus — A1433

UNITED STATES

High Jump
A1434

Archery
A1435

Boxing
A1436

1983, July 28   Photo.   *Perf. 11*
2048 A1433 13c multicolored   .35   .15
2049 A1434 13c multicolored   .35   .15
2050 A1435 13c multicolored   .35   .15
2051 A1436 13c multicolored   .35   .15
   a. Block of 4, #2048-2051   1.50   1.25

Signing of Treaty of Paris

John Adams, Franklin, John Jay, David Hartley A1437

1983, Sept. 2   Photo.   *Perf. 11*
2052 A1437 20c multicolored   .40   .15

Civil Service

A1438

1983, Sept. 9   Photo. & Engr.
2053 A1438 20c buff, blue & red   .40   .15

Metropolitan Opera

A1439

1983, Sept. 14   Litho. & Engr.
2054 A1439 20c yellow & maroon   .40   .15

American Inventors

A1440   Charles Steinmetz

Edwin Armstrong   A1441

A1442   Nikola Tesla

Philo T. Farnsworth   A1443

1983, Sept. 21   Litho. & Engr
2055 A1440 20c multicolored   .40   .15
2056 A1441 20c multicolored   .40   .15
2057 A1442 20c multicolored   .40   .15
2058 A1443 20c multicolored   .40   .15
   a. Block of 4, #2055-2058   1.60   1.25
   b. As "a," black omitted   450.00

Streetcars

A1444

A1445

A1446

A1447

1983, Oct. 8   Photo. & Engr.
2059 A1444 20c multicolored   .40   .15
2060 A1445 20c multicolored   .40   .15
2061 A1446 20c multicolored   .40   .15
2062 A1447 20c multicolored   .40   .15
   a. Block of 4, #2059-2062   1.70   1.40
   b. As "a," black omitted   475.00
   c. As "a," black omitted on #2059, 2061   —

Christmas

A1448

A1449

1983, Oct. 28   Photo.   *Perf. 11*
2063 A1448 20c multicolored   .40   .15
2064 A1449 20c multicolored   .40   .15
   a. Imperf., pair   175.00

A1450

Caribou and Alaska Pipeline — A1451

Martin Luther, 1483-1546

1983, Nov. 11   Photo.   *Perf. 11*
2065 A1450 20c multicolored   .40   .15

25th Anniv. of Alaska Statehood

1984, Jan. 3   Photo.   *Perf. 11*
2066 A1451 20c multicolored   .40   .15

Winter Olympic Games

Ice Dancing A1452   Downhill Skiing A1453

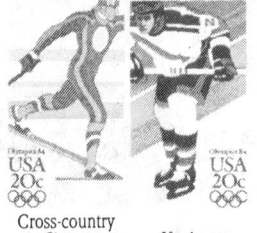

Cross-country Skiing A1454   Hockey A1455

1984, Jan. 6   *Perf. 10½x11*
2067 A1452 20c multicolored   .45   .15
2068 A1453 20c multicolored   .45   .15
2069 A1454 20c multicolored   .45   .15
2070 A1455 20c multicolored   .45   .15
   a. Block of 4, #2067-2070   1.85   1.50

14th Winter Olympic Games, Sarajevo, Yugoslavia, Feb. 8-19.

A1456

A1457

Federal Deposit Insurance Corp., 50th Anniv.

1984, Jan. 12   *Perf. 11*
2071 A1456 20c multicolored   .40   .15

Love

1984, Jan. 31   Photo. & Engr.
2072 A1457 20c multicolored   .40   .15
   a. Horiz. pair, imperf. vert.   175.00

Carter G. Woodson (1875-1950), Writer — A1458

A1459

Black Heritage Issue

1984, Feb. 1   Photo.
2073 A1458 20c multicolored   .40   .15
   a. Horiz. pair, imperf. vert.   1,750.

Soil and Water Conservation

1984, Feb. 6
2074 A1459 20c multicolored   .40   .15

50th Anniv. of Credit Union Act

Dollar Sign, Coin — A1460

1984, Feb. 10   Photo.   *Perf. 11*
2075 A1460 20c multicolored   .40   .15

Orchids

A1461

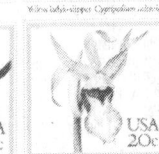

A1462

A1463

A1464

1984, Mar. 5
2076 A1461 20c Wild pink   .45   .15
2077 A1462 20c Yellow lady's-slipper   .45   .15
2078 A1463 20c Spreading pogonia   .45   .15
2079 A1464 20c Pacific calypso   .45   .15
   a. Block of 4, #2076-2079   1.85   1.50

25th Anniv. of Hawaii Statehood

Eastern Polynesian Canoe, Golden Plover, Mauna Loa Volcano A1465

1984, Mar. 12   Photo.   *Perf. 11*
2080 A1465 20c multicolored   .40   .15

National Archives

Abraham Lincoln, George Washington — A1466

1984, Apr. 16   Photo.   *Perf. 11*
2081 A1466 20c multicolored   .40   .15

Have you found a typo or other error in this catalogue?

Inform the editors via our web site or e-mail

sctcat@scottonline.com

UNITED STATES

1984 Los Angeles Olympics

Diving A1467
Long Jump A1468 
Wrestling A1469 
Kayak A1470 

1984, May 4   Perf. 11
2082 A1467 20c multicolored .50 .15
2083 A1468 20c multicolored .50 .15
2084 A1469 20c multicolored .50 .15
2085 A1470 20c multicolored .50 .15
   a. Block of 4, #2082-2085 2.25 1.90

New Orleans World Exposition

River Wildlife, Fresh water as a source of Life A1471

1984, May 11   Perf. 11
2086 A1471 20c multicolored .40 .15

Health Research

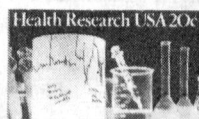

Lab Equipment A1472

1984, May 17   Perf. 11
2087 A1472 20c multicolored .40 .15

Actor Douglas Fairbanks (1883-1939) — A1473
A1474 

Performing Arts

1984, May 23   Photo. & Engr.
2088 A1473 20c multicolored .40 .15
   b. Horiz. pair, imperf btwn. —

Jim Thorpe, 1888-1953

1984, May 24   Engr.   Perf. 11
2089 A1474 20c dark brown .40 .15

Performing Arts

Tenor John McCormack (1884-1945) — A1475

1984, June 6   Photo.   Perf. 11
2090 A1475 20c multicolored .40 .15
   See Ireland No. 594.

25th Anniv. of St. Lawrence Seaway

Aerial View of Seaway, Freighters A1476

1984, June 26   Photo.   Perf. 11
2091 A1476 20c multicolored .40 .15

50th Anniv. of Waterfowl Preservation Act

"Mallards Dropping In," by Jay N. Darling A1477

1984, July 2   Engr.   Perf. 11
2092 A1477 20c blue .50 .15
   a. Horiz. pair, imperf. vert. 425.00
   See No. RW1.

A1478
Author — A1479 

Roanoke Voyages

1984, July 13   Photo.   Perf. 11
2093 A1478 20c multicolored .40 .15

Herman Melville (1819-1891)

1984, Aug. 1   Engr.   Perf. 11
2094 A1479 20c sage green .40 .15

Horace Moses (1862-1947)

Junior Achievement Founder — A1480

1984, Aug. 6   Engr.
2095 A1480 20c orange & dk brown .45 .15

Smokey Bear — A1481
Clemente, Puerto Rican Flag — A1482 

1984, Aug. 13   Litho. & Engr.
2096 A1481 20c multicolored .40 .15
   a. Horiz. pair, imperf. btwn. 300.
   b. Vert. pair, imperf. btwn. 275.
   c. Block of 4, imperf. btwn, vert. and horiz. 5,500.
   d. Horiz. pair, imperf. vert. 1,750.

Roberto Clemente (1934-1972)

1984, Aug. 17   Photo.   Perf. 11
2097 A1482 20c multicolored 1.40 .15
   a. Horiz. pair, imperf. vert. 1,900.

Dogs

Beagle, Boston Terrier A1483
Chesapeake Bay Retriever, Cocker Spaniel A1484 
Alaskan Malamute, Collie A1485 
Black & Tan Coonhound, American Foxhound A1486 

1984, Sept. 7   Photo.   Perf. 11
2098 A1483 20c multicolored .40 .15
2099 A1484 20c multicolored .40 .15
2100 A1485 20c multicolored .40 .15
2101 A1486 20c multicolored .40 .15
   a. Block of 4, #2098-2101 1.75 1.75

Crime Prevention

McGruff, The Crime Dog — A1487

1984, Sept. 26   Photo.   Perf. 11
2102 A1487 20c multicolored .40 .15

Hispanic Americans

A1488 A Proud Heritage USA 20

1984, Oct. 31   Photo.   Perf. 11
2103 A1488 20c multicolored .40 .15
   a. Vert. pair, imperf. horiz. 1,750.

Family Unity

A1489

1984, Oct. 1   Photo. & Engr.
2104 A1489 20c multicolored .40 .15
   a. Horiz. pair, imperf. vert. 550.00
   c. Vert. pair, imperf. btwn. and at bottom —

Eleanor Roosevelt

A1490

1984, Oct. 11   Engr.   Perf. 11
2105 A1490 20c deep blue .40 .15

Nation of Readers

Lincoln, Son Tad — A1491

1984, Oct. 16   Engr.   Perf. 11
2106 A1491 20c brown & maroon .40 .15

Christmas

Madonna and Child by Fra Filippo Lippi — A1492
Santa Claus — A1493 

1984, Oct. 30   Photo.   Perf. 11
2107 A1492 20c multicolored .40 .15
2108 A1493 20c multicolored .40 .15
   a. Horiz. pair, imperf. vert. 950.00
   No. 2108a is valued in the grade of fine.

UNITED STATES

Vietnam Veterans Memorial

Memorial Wall — A1494

1984, Nov. 10   Engr.   Perf. 10½
2109   A1494   20c multicolored   .40   .15

Performing Arts

Composer Jerome Kern (1885-1945) — A1495

1985, Jan. 23   Photo.   Perf. 11
2110   A1495   22c multicolored   .40   .15

A1496    A1497

1985, Feb. 1   Photo.   Perf. 11
2111   A1496   (22c) green   .55   .15
    a.   Vert. pair, imperf.   45.
    b.   Vert. pair, imperf. horiz.   1,350.

Coil Stamp
Perf. 10 Vert.
2112   A1496   (22c) green   .60   .15
    a.   Imperf., pair   50.00

Booklet Stamp
Perf. 11
2113   A1497   (22c) green   .80   .15
    b.   Booklet pane of 10   8.50   3.00
    c.   As "a," imperf. btwn. horiz.   —

A1498

Flag over Capitol Dome A1499

1985, Mar. 29   Engr.   Perf. 11
2114   A1498   22c blue, red & black   .40   .15

Coil Stamp
Perf. 10 Vert.
2115   A1498   22c blue, red & black   .40   .15
    a.   Imperf., pair   12.50
    b.   Inscribed "T" at bottom ('87)   .50   .15
    c.   Black field of stars   —   —

Booklet Stamp
Perf. 10 Horiz. on 1 or 2 Sides
2116   A1499   22c blue, red & black   .50   .15
    a.   Booklet pane of 5   2.50   1.25

Seashells

Frilled Dogwinkle A1500    Reticulated Helmet A1501

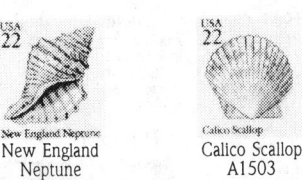

New England Neptune A1502   Calico Scallop A1503

Lightning Whelk — A1504

1985, Apr. 4   Engr.   Perf. 10
Booklet Stamps
2117   A1500   22c black & brown   .40   .15
2118   A1501   22c multicolored   .40   .15
2119   A1502   22c black & brown   .40   .15
2120   A1503   22c black & violet   .40   .15
2121   A1504   22c multicolored   .40   .15
    a.   Booklet pane of 10, 2 ea #2117-2121   4.00   2.50
    b.   As "a," violet omitted   850.00
    c.   As "a," vert. imperf. btwn.   600.00
    d.   As "a," imperf.   —
    e.   Strip of 5, #2117-2121   2.00   —

Eagle and Half Moon A1505

Type I. Washed out, dull appearance most evident in the black of the body of the eagle, and the red in the background between the eagle's shoulder and the moon. "$10.75" appears splotchy or grainy (P# 11111).
Type II. Brighter, more intense colors most evident in the black on the eagle's body, and red in the background. "$10.75" appears smoother, brighter, and less grainy (P# 22222).

Perf. 10 Vert. on 1 or 2 Sides
1985, Apr. 29   Photo.   Untagged
2122   A1505 $10.75 multi, type I   17.00   7.00
    a.   Booklet pane of 3   52.50
    b.   Type II   17.00
    c.   As "b," booklet pane of 3   52.50   —

Issued in booklets only.

Transportation Coils

A1506    A1507 
A1508   A1509 
A1510    A1511 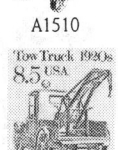 
A1512    A1513

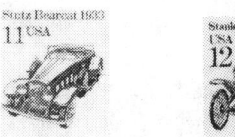

A1514    A1515
A1516    A1517 
A1518    A1519 

1985-87   Engr.   Perf. 10 Vert.
2123   A1506   3.4c dk bluish green   .15   .15
    a.   Untagged (Bureau precanceled)   .15   .15
2124   A1507   4.9c brn blk   .15   .15
    a.   Untagged (Bureau precanceled)   .20   .20
2125   A1508   5.5c deep mag   .15   .15
    a.   Untagged (Bureau precanceled)   .15   .15
2126   A1509   6c red brown   .15   .15
    a.   Untagged (Bureau precanceled)   .15   .15
    b.   As "a," imperf., pair   200.00
2127   A1510   7.1c lake   .15   .15
    a.   Untagged (Bureau precanceled)   .15   .15
2128   A1511   8.3c green   .20   .15
    a.   Untagged (Bureau precanceled)   .20   .20

For similar stamp see No. 2231.

2129   A1512   8.5c dk Prus green   .20   .15
    a.   Untagged (Bureau precanceled)   .20   .20
2130   A1513   10.1c slate blue   .25   .25
    a.   Untagged (Bureau precanceled)   .25   .25
    b.   As "a," imperf., pair   15.00
2131   A1514   11c dk green   .25   .15
2132   A1515   12c dk bl, type I   .25   .15
    a.   Untagged (Bureau precanceled)   .25   .25
    b.   Type II, untagged (Bureau precanceled)   .25   .25

Type II has "Stanley Steamer 1909" ½mm shorter (17½mm) than No. 2132 (18mm).

2133   A1516   12.5c olive green   .25   .15
    a.   Untagged (Bureau precanceled)   .25   .25
    b.   As "a," imperf., pair   55.00
2134   A1517   14c sky bl, type I   .30   .15
    a.   Imperf., pair   100.00
    b.   Type II   .30   .15

Type II design is ¼mm narrower (17¼mm) than No. 2134 (17½mm) and has block tagging. No. 2134 has overall tagging.

2135   A1518   17c sky blue   .30   .15
    a.   Imperf., pair   550.00
2136   A1519   25c org brown   .45   .15
    a.   Imperf., pair   10.00
    b.   Pair, imperf. between Nos. 2123-2136 (14)   3.20   2.10

Years of issue: 3.4c, 4.9c, 6c, 8.3c, 10.1c-14c, 1985. 5.5c, 17c, 25c, 1986. 7.1c, 8.5c, 1987.
See Nos. 1897-1908, 2225-2231, 2252-2266, 2451-2468.

Black Heritage Issue

Mary McLeod Bethune (1875-1955), Educator — A1520

1985, Mar. 5   Photo.   Perf. 11
2137   A1520   22c multicolored   .40   .15

Duck Decoys

Broadbill A1521
Mallard A1522 
Canvasback A1523 
Redhead A1524 

1985, Mar. 22   Photo.   Perf. 11
2138   A1521   22c multicolored   .60   .15
2139   A1522   22c multicolored   .60   .15
2140   A1523   22c multicolored   .60   .15
2141   A1524   22c multicolored   .60   .15
    a.   Block of 4, #2138-2141   3.75   2.25

Winter Special Olympics

Ice Skater, Emblem, Skier A1525

1985, Mar. 25   Photo.   Perf. 11
2142   A1525   22c multicolored   .40   .15
    a.   Vert. pair, imperf. horiz.   650.00

Love

A1526

1985, Apr. 17   Photo.
2143   A1526   22c multicolored   .40   .15
    a.   Imperf., pair   1,750.

Rural Electrification Administration

Electrified Farm A1527

1985, May 11   Photo. & Engr.
2144   A1527   22c multicolored   .45   .15
    a.   Vert. pair, imperf. btwn.   —

AMERIPEX '86

US No. 134 — A1528

1985, May 25   Litho. & Engr.
2145   A1528   22c multicolored   .40   .15
    a.   Red, black & blue omitted   200.
    b.   Red & black omitted   1,250.
    c.   Red omitted

UNITED STATES

US First Lady

Abigail Adams (1744-1818) — A1529

1985, June 14   Litho.   Perf. 11
2146 A1529 22c multicolored   .40   .15
  a.   Imperf., pair   275.00

Architect, Sculptor

Frederic Auguste Bartholdi (1834-1904), Statue of Liberty
A1530

1985, July 18   Litho. & Engr.
2147 A1530 22c multicolored   .40   .15
  a.   Black (engr.) omitted

Examples exist with most, but not all, of the engraved black omitted. Expertization of No. 2147a is recommended.

George Washington, Washington Monument
A1532

Envelopes
A1533

COIL STAMPS

1985   Photo.   Perf. 10 Vert.
2149 A1532 18c multicolored   .35   .15
  a.   Untagged (Bureau precanceled)   .35   .35
  b.   Imperf., pair   950.00
  c.   As "a," imperf., pair   800.00
2150 A1533 21.1c multicolored   .40   .15
  a.   Untagged (Bureau precanceled)   .40   .40

Issue dates: 18c, Nov. 6; 21.1c, Oct. 22. Precancellations on Nos. 2149a ("PRESORTED FIRST CLASS"), 2150a ("ZIP+4") do not have lines.

Korean War Veterans

American Troops Marching
A1535

1985, July 26   Engr.   Perf. 11
2152 A1535 22c gray grn & rose red   .40   .15

Social Security Act, 50th Anniv.

Men, Women, Children, Corinthian Columns
A1536

1985, Aug. 14   Photo.   Perf. 11
2153 A1536 22c deep blue & lt blue   .40   .15

World War I Veterans

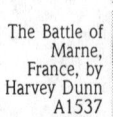

The Battle of Marne, France, by Harvey Dunn
A1537

1985, Aug. 26   Engr.   Perf. 11
2154 A1537 22c gray grn & rose red   .40   .15

Horses

Quarter Horse A1538
Morgan A1539 
Saddlebred A1540 
Appaloosa A1541 

1985, Sept. 25   Photo.   Perf. 11
2155 A1538 22c multicolored   .90   .15
2156 A1539 22c multicolored   .90   .15
2157 A1540 22c multicolored   .90   .15
2158 A1541 22c multicolored   .90   .15
  a.   Block of 4, #2155-2158   5.50   4.50

Public Education in America

Quill Pen, Apple, Spectacles, Penmanship Quiz — A1542

1985, Oct. 1   Photo.   Perf. 11
2159 A1542 22c multicolored   .45   .15

International Youth Year

YMCA Youth Camping, Cent. A1543
Boy Scouts, 75th Anniv. A1544 
Big Brothers/Big Sisters Fed., 40th Anniv. A1545 
Camp Fire, Inc., 75th Anniv. A1546 

1985, Oct. 7   Photo.   Perf. 11
2160 A1543 22c multicolored   .60   .15
2161 A1544 22c multicolored   .60   .15
2162 A1545 22c multicolored   .60   .15
2163 A1546 22c multicolored   .60   .15
  a.   Block of 4, #2160-2163   2.75   2.25

Help End Hunger

Youths and the Elderly Suffering from Malnutrition
A1547

1985, Oct. 15   Photo.
2164 A1547 22c multicolored   .45   .15

Christmas

Genoa Madonna, Enameled Terra-Cotta by Luca Della Robbia (1400-1482) — A1548

Poinsettia Plants
A1549

1985, Oct. 30   Photo.
2165 A1548 22c multicolored   .40   .15
  a.   Imperf., pair   100.00
2166 A1549 22c multicolored   .40   .15
  a.   Imperf., pair   130.00

Arkansas Statehood, 150th Anniv.

Old State House, Little Rock
A1550

1986, Jan. 3   Photo.   Perf. 11
2167 A1550 22c multicolored   .40   .15
  a.   Vert. pair, imperf. horiz.   —

Great Americans

Margaret Mitchell A1551
Mary Lyon A1552 
Paul Dudley White, MD A1553 
Father Flanagan A1554 
Hugo L. Black A1555 
Luis Muñoz Marin A1556 
Red Cloud A1557 
Julia Ward Howe A1558
Buffalo Bill Cody A1559 
(A1560)
Virginia Apgar A1561 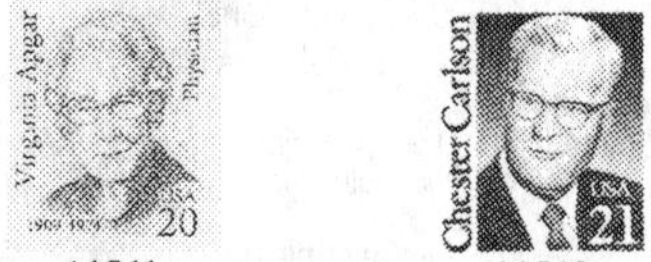
Chester Carlson A1562
Mary Cassatt A1563
Jack London A1564
Sitting Bull A1565 
Earl Warren A1566
Thomas Jefferson A1567 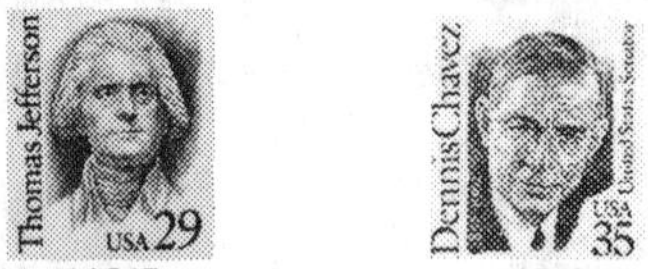
Dennis Chavez A1568
Claire Chennault A1569 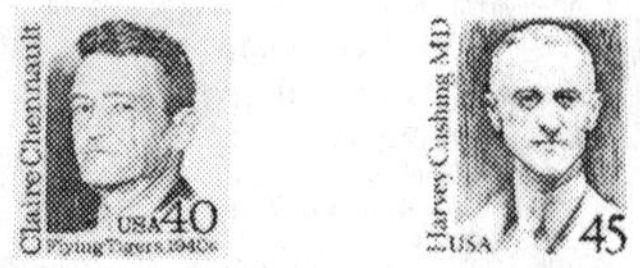
Harvey Cushing MD A1570
Hubert H Humphrey A1571 
John Harvard A1572
H.H. Hap Arnold A1573 
Wendell Willkie A1574
Bernard Revel A1575  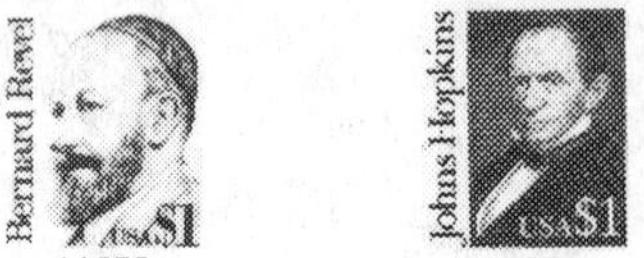
Johns Hopkins A1576
William Jennings Bryan A1577
Bret Harte A1578

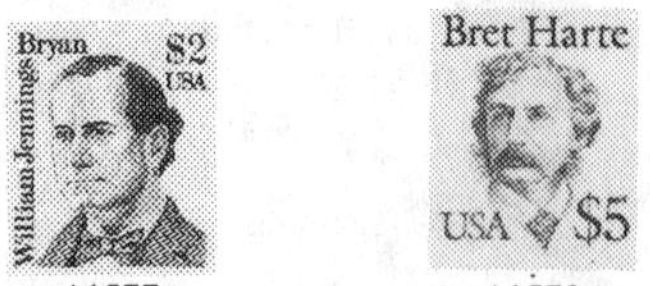

Perf. 11, 11½x11 (#2185), 11.1x11 (#2179)

1986-94   Engr.
2168 A1551 1c brnsh ver   .15   .15
2169 A1552 2c bright blue   .15   .15
  a.   Untagged   .15   .15
2170 A1553 3c bright blue   .15   .15
2171 A1554 4c blue violet   .15   .15
  a.   As #2171, untagged   .15   .15
  b.   4c grayish violet, untagged   .25   .15
2172 A1555 5c dk ol grn   .15   .15
2173 A1556 5c carmine   .15   .15
  a.   Untagged   .15   .15
2175 A1557 10c lake   .20   .15
  d.   carmine, phosphored paper (embedded taggant)   .25   .15

UNITED STATES

2176	A1558	14c crimson	.25	.15
2177	A1559	15c claret	.30	.15
2178	A1560	17c dull bl grn	.35	.15
2179	A1561	20c red brown	.40	.15
a.		20c orange brown	.40	.15
2180	A1562	21c blue vio	.40	.15
2181	A1563	23c purple	.45	.15
2182	A1564	25c blue	.45	.15
a.		Booklet pane of 10 ('88)	4.50	3.75
2183	A1565	28c myrtle grn	.50	.15
2184	A1566	29c blue	.55	.15
2185	A1567	29c indigo	.50	.15
2186	A1568	35c black	.65	.15
2187	A1569	40c dark blue	.70	.15
2188	A1570	45c bright blue	.85	.15
a.		45c blue, overall tagging ('90)	1.65	—
2189	A1571	52c purple	.90	.15
2190	A1572	56c scarlet	1.10	.15
2191	A1573	65c dark blue	1.20	.20
2192	A1574	75c dp magenta	1.30	.25
2193	A1575	$1 dk Prus grn	2.25	.50
2194	A1576	$1 deep blue	1.75	.50
2195	A1577	$2 brt violet	3.50	.50
2196	A1578	$5 copper red	8.00	1.00
	Nos. 2168-2196 (28)		27.45	6.20

Booklet Stamp
Perf. 10 on 2 or 3 sides

2197	A1564	25c blue ('88)	.45	.15
a.		Booklet pane of 6	3.00	2.25

Issued: #2182, 1/11/86; #2172, 2/27/86; $2, 3/19/86; 17c, 6/18/86; 1c, 6/30/86; 4c, 7/14/86; 56c, 9/3/86; 3c, 9/15/86; #2193, 9/23/86; 14c, 2/12/87; 2c, 2/28/87; 10c, 8/15/87; $5, 8/25/87; #2183a, 2197, 5/3/88; 15c, 6/6/88; 45c, 6/17/88; 21c, 10/21/88; 23c, 11/4/88; 65c, 11/5/88; #2194, 6/7/89; 28c, 9/14/89; #2173, 2/18/90; 40c, 9/6/90; 35c, 4/3/91; 52c, 6/3/91; 75c, 2/16/92; #2184, 3/9/92; #2185, 4/13/93; 20c, 10/24/94.

Stamp Collecting

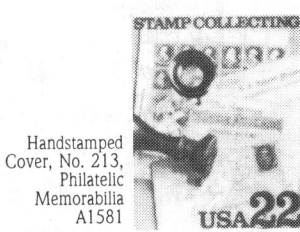

Handstamped Cover, No. 213, Philatelic Memorabilia A1581

Boy Examining Stamp Collection A1582

No. 836 Under Magnifying Glass, Sweden Nos. 268, 271 — A1583

1986 Presidents Miniature Sheet — A1584

Perf. 10 Vert. on 1 or 2 Sides

1986, Jan. 23   *Litho. & Engr.*
Booklet Stamps

2198	A1581	22c multicolored	.45	.15
2199	A1582	22c multicolored	.45	.15
2200	A1583	22c multicolored	.45	.15
2201	A1584	22c multicolored	.45	.15
a.		Bklt. pane of 4, #2198-2201	2.00	1.75
b.		As "a," black omitted on #2198, 2201	55.00	
c.		As "a," blue (litho.) omitted on #2198-2200	2,500.	
d.		As "a," buff (litho.) omitted	—	

See Sweden Nos. 1585-1588.

Love

A1585

Black Heritage Issue

A1586

1986, Jan. 30   *Photo.*   *Perf. 11*

2202	A1585	22c Puppy	.40	.15

1986, Feb. 4   *Photo.*   *Perf. 11*

2203	A1586	22c multicolored	.40	.15

Sojourner Truth (c. 1797-1883), abolitionist.

Republic of Texas, 150th Anniv.

Texas State Flag and Silver Spur — A1587

1986, Mar. 2   *Photo.*

2204	A1587	22c dk bl, dk red & grysh blk	.40	.15
a.		Horiz. pair, imperf. vert.	1,250.	
b.		Dark red omitted	2,750.	
c.		Dark blue omitted	8,500.	

Fish

Muskellunge — A1588

Atlantic Cod A1589

Largemouth Bass A1590

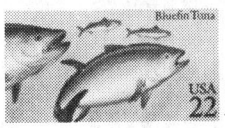

Bluefin Tuna A1591

Catfish A1592

Perf. 10 Horiz. on 1 or 2 Sides
1986, Mar. 21   *Photo.*
Booklet Stamps

2205	A1588	22c multicolored	.50	.15
2206	A1589	22c multicolored	.50	.15
2207	A1590	22c multicolored	.50	.15
2208	A1591	22c multicolored	.50	.15
2209	A1592	22c multicolored	.50	.15
a.		Bklt. pane of 5, #2205-2209	4.50	2.75

Public Hospitals

A1593

1986, Apr. 11   *Photo.*   *Perf. 11*

2210	A1593	22c multicolored	.40	.15
a.		Vert. pair, imperf. horiz.	300.	
b.		Horiz. pair, imperf. vert.	1,350.	

Performing Arts

Edward Kennedy "Duke" Ellington (1899-1974), Jazz Composer — A1594

1986, Apr. 29   *Photo.*   *Perf. 11*

2211	A1594	22c multicolored	.40	.15
a.		Vert. pair, imperf. horiz.	1,000.	—

Miniature Sheets

35 Presidents — A1599

No. 2216: a, Washington. b, John Adams. c, Jefferson. d, Madison. e, Monroe. f, John Quincy Adams. g, Jackson. h, Van Buren. i, Harrison.

No. 2217: a, Tyler. b, Polk. c, Taylor. d, Fillmore. e, Pierce. f, Buchanan. g, Lincoln. h, Andrew Johnson. i, Grant.

No. 2218: a, Hayes. b, Garfield. c, Arthur. d, Cleveland. e, Harrison. f, McKinley. g, Theodore Roosevelt. h, Taft. i, Wilson.

No. 2219: a, Harding. b, Coolidge. c, Hoover. d, Franklin Delano Roosevelt. e, White House. f, Truman. g, Eisenhower. h, Kennedy. i, Lyndon B. Johnson.

1986, May 22   *Litho. & Engr.*

2216		Sheet of 9	3.75	
a.-i.		A1599 22c any single	.40	.25
j.		Blue omitted	3,500.	
k.		Black inscription omitted	2,000.	
l.		Imperf.	10,500.	
2217		Sheet of 9	3.75	
a.-i.		A1599 22c any single	.40	.25
j.		Black inscription omitted	3,750.	
2218		Sheet of 9	3.75	
a.-i.		A1599 22c any single	.40	.25
j.		Brown omitted	3,000.	
k.		Black inscription omitted		
2219		Sheet of 9	3.75	
a.-i.		A1599 22c any single	.40	.25
j.		Blackish blue (engr.) inscription omitted on a.-b., d.-e., g.-h.	—	
	Nos. 2216-2219 (4)		15.00	

Issued at AMERIPEX '86 Intl. Phil. Exhib., Chicago, IL, May 22-June 1.

Arctic Explorers

Elisha Kent Kane A1600

Adolphus W. Greely A1601

Vilhjalmur Stefansson A1602

Robert E. Peary and Matthew Alexander Henson A1603

1986, May 28   *Photo.*   *Perf. 11*

2220	A1600	22c multicolored	.65	.15
2221	A1601	22c multicolored	.65	.15
2222	A1602	22c multicolored	.65	.15
2223	A1603	22c multicolored	.65	.15
a.		Block of 4, #2220-2223	2.75	2.25
b.		As "a," black (engr.) omitted	9,500.	
c.		As "a," #2220 & 2221 black (engr.) omitted	—	

Statue of Liberty, Cent. — A1604

1986, July 4   *Engr.*   *Perf. 11*

2224	A1604	22c scarlet & dark blue	.40	.15

See France No. 2014.

Transportation Coils
Types of 1982-85 and

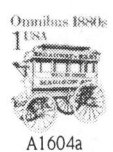

Omnibus 1880s A1604a

Locomotive 1870s A1604b

1986-87   *Engr.*   *Perf. 10 Vert.*

2225	A1604a	1c violet	.15	.15
a.		Untagged	.15	.15
b.		Imperf., pair	2,500.	
2226	A1604b	2c black ('87)	.15	.15
a.		Untagged	.15	.15
2228	A1285	4c reddish brown	.15	.15
b.		Imperf., pair	300.00	
2231	A1511	8.3c grn (Bureau precancel)	.20	.20
	Nos. 2225-2231 (4)		.65	.65

Issue dates: 1c, Nov. 26. 2c, Mar. 6. Earliest known usage of 4c, Aug. 15, 1986. 8.3c, Aug. 29. On No. 2228 "Stagecoach 1890s" is 17½mm long, on No. 1898A 19½mm long. On No. 2231 "Ambulance 1860s" is 18mm long, on No. 2128 18½mm long.

No. 2226 inscribed "2 USA;" No. 1897A inscribed "USA 2c."

Navajo Art

A1605   A1606

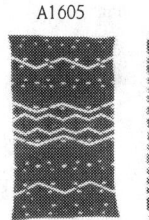

A1607    A1608

Blankets in the Museum of the American Indian and Lowe Art Museum.

1986, Sept. 4   *Litho. & Engr.*   *Perf. 11*

2235	A1605	22c multicolored	.45	.15
2236	A1606	22c multicolored	.45	.15
2237	A1607	22c multicolored	.45	.15
2238	A1608	22c multicolored	.45	.15
a.		Block of 4, #2235-2238	2.25	2.00
b.		As "a," blk (engr.) omitted	450.00	

UNITED STATES

Literary Arts

T. S. Eliot (1888-1965), Poet — A1609

1986, Sept. 26   Engr.   Perf. 11
2239 A1609 22c copper red   .40   .15

Woodcarved Figurines

Highlander Figure A1610
Ship Figurehead A1611
Nautical Figure A1612
Cigar Store Figure A1613

1986, Oct. 1   Photo.   Perf. 11
2240 A1610 22c multicolored   .40   .15
2241 A1611 22c multicolored   .40   .15
2242 A1612 22c multicolored   .40   .15
2243 A1613 22c multicolored   .40   .15
   a. Block of 4, #2240-2243   1.75   1.75
   b. As "a," imperf. vert.   1,500.

Christmas

Madonna, by Perugino (c. 1450-1523) A1614
Village Scene A1615 

1986, Oct. 24   Perf. 11
2244 A1614 22c multicolored   .40   .15
   a. Imperf., pair   —
2245 A1615 22c multicolored   .40   .15

Michigan Statehood Sesquicent.

White Pine — A1616

1987, Jan. 26   Photo.   Perf. 11
2246 A1616 22c multicolored   .40   .15

Pan American Games, Indianapolis, August 7-25

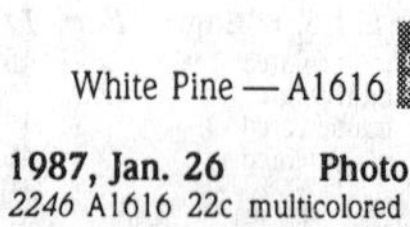

Runner in Full Stride A1617

1987, Jan. 29   Perf. 11
2247 A1617 22c multicolored   .15
   a. Silver omitted   1,500.

No. 2247a is valued in the grade of fine.

A1618
A1619 

Love
1987, Jan. 30   Photo.   Perf. 11½x11
2248 A1618 22c multicolored   .40   .15

Black Heritage
1987, Feb. 20   Photo.   Perf. 11
2249 A1619 22c multicolored   .40   .15

Jean Baptiste Pointe du Sable (c. 1750-1818), pioneer trader, founder of Chicago

A1620
A1621 

Performing Arts
Enrico Caruso (1873-1921), Opera Tenor
Photo. & Engr.
1987, Feb. 27   Perf. 11
2250 A1620 22c multicolored   .40   .15
   a. Black (engr.) omitted   5,000.

Girl Scouts, 75th Anniv.
Litho. & Engr.
1987, Mar. 12   Perf. 11
2251 A1621 22c 14 Achievement Badges   .40   .15
   a. All litho. colors omitted   2,500

All known examples of No. 2251a have been expertized, and certificate must accompany purchase.

Transportation Coils

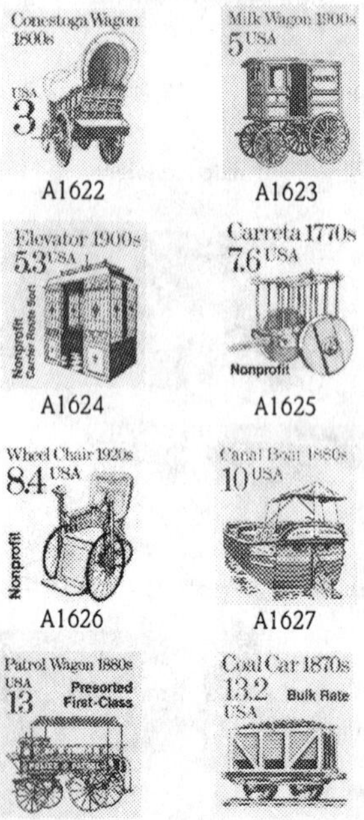

Conestoga Wagon 1800s A1622
Milk Wagon 1900s A1623
Elevator 1900s A1624
Carreta 1770s A1625
Wheel Chair 1920s A1626
Canal Boat 1880s A1627
Patrol Wagon 1880s A1628
Coal Car 1870s A1629

Tugboat 1900s A1630
Popcorn Wagon 1902 A1631 
Racing Car 1911 A1632 
Cable Car 1880s A1633
Fire Engine 1900s A1634 
Railroad Mail Car 1920s A1635 
Tandem Bicycle 1890s A1636 

1987-88   Engr.   Perf. 10 Vert.
2252 A1622 3c claret   .15   .15
   a. Untagged   .15   .15
2253 A1623 5c black   .15   .15
2254 A1624 5.3c blk (Bureau precanc. in scarlet)   .15   .15
2255 A1625 7.6c brn (Bureau precanc. in scarlet)   .15   .15
2256 A1626 8.4c dp clar (Bureau precanc. in red)   .15   .15
   a. Imperf., pair   750.00
2257 A1627 10c sky blue   .20   .15
2258 A1628 13c blk (Bureau precanc. in red)   .25   .25
2259 A1629 13.2c slate grn (Bureau precanc. in red)   .25   .25
   a. Imperf., pair   100.00
2260 A1630 15c violet   .25   .15
   c. Imperf., pair   800.00
2261 A1631 16.7c rose (Bureau precanc. in black)   .30   .30
   a. Imperf., pair   225.00

All known copies of No. 2261a are miscut top to bottom.

2262 A1632 17.5c dark violet   .30   .15
   a. Untagged (Bureau precancel)   .30   .30
   b. Imperf., pair   2,250.
2263 A1633 20c blue vio   .35   .15
   a. Imperf., pair   75.00
2264 A1634 20.5c rose (Bureau precanc. in black)   .40   .40
2265 A1635 21c olive grn (Bureau precanc. in red)   .40   .40
   a. Imperf., pair   65.00
2266 A1636 24.1c deep ultra (Bureau precancel)   .45   .45
Nos. 2252-2266 (15)   3.90   3.40

The 5.3c, 7.6c, 8.4c, 13c, 13.2c, 16.7c, 20.5c, 21c and 24.1c are only available precanceled and are untagged.

Years of issue: 5c, 10c, 17.5c, 1987; others, 1988.

See Nos. 1897-1908, 2123-2136, 2225-2231, 2451-2468.

Special Occasions

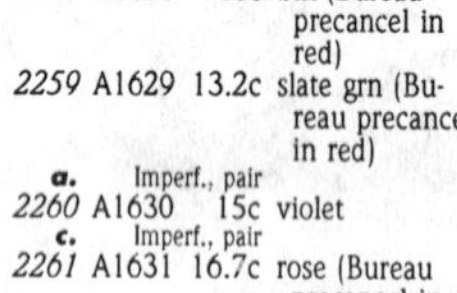

A1637
Get Well! A1638 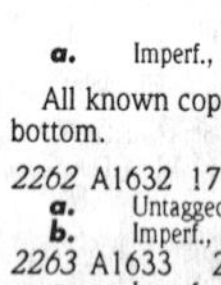
Thank You! A1639
Love You, Dad! A1640 
A1641
Happy Birthday! A1642 
Love You, Mother! A1643
Keep In Touch! A1644

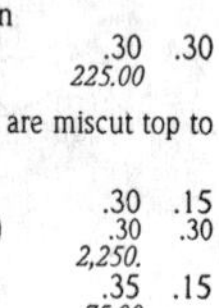

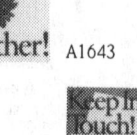

Perf. 10 on 1, 2, or 3 sides
1987, Apr. 20   Photo.
Booklet Stamps
2267 A1637 22c multicolored   .55   .15
2268 A1638 22c multicolored   .55   .15
2269 A1639 22c multicolored   .55   .15
2270 A1640 22c multicolored   .55   .15
2271 A1641 22c multicolored   .55   .15
2272 A1642 22c multicolored   .55   .15
2273 A1643 22c multicolored   .55   .15
2274 A1644 22c multicolored   .55   .15
   a. Bklt. pane of 10, #2268-2271, 2273-2274, 2 each #2267, 2272   8.00   5.00
Nos. 2267-2274 (8)   4.40   1.20

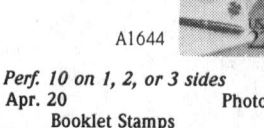

United Way Centenary

Six Profiles Uniting Communities A1645

Litho. & Engr.
1987, Apr. 28   Perf. 11
2275 A1645 22c multicolored   .40   .15

A1646
A1647 (Earth, Domestic USA) 
A1648
A1649 (Yosemite)
Pheasant A1649a
Grosbeak A1649b 
Owl A1649c 
Honeybee A1649d 

Photo., Engr. (No. 2280), Litho. & Engr. (No. 2281)
1987-88   Perf. 11
2276 A1646 22c multicolored   .40   .15
   a. Booklet pane of 20   8.50   —
   b. As "a." vert. pair, imperf. btwn.
2277 A1647 (25c) multi ('88)   .45   .15
2278 A1648 25c multi ('88)   .40   .15
Nos. 2276-2278 (3)   1.25   .45

UNITED STATES

Coil Stamps
Perf. 10 Vertical

2279	A1647	(25c) multi ('88)	.45	.15
a.		Imperf., pair	85.00	—
2280	A1649	25c Green trees ('88)	.45	.15
a.		Imperf., pair	30.00	
b.		Black trees	100.00	—
d.		Pair, imperf. btwn.	800.00	
2281	A1649d	25c multi ('88)	.45	.15
a.		Imperf., pair	45.00	
b.		Black (engr.) omitted	65.00	
c.		Black (litho.) omitted	550.00	
d.		Pair, imperf. between	1,000.	
e.		Yellow (litho.) omitted	1,250.	
		Nos. 2279-2281 (3)	1.35	.45

Beware of copies with traces of the litho. black that are offered as No. 2281c. Vertical pairs or blocks of No. 2281 and imperfs. with the engr. black missing are from printer's waste.

Booklet Stamps
Perf. 10 on 2 or 3 Sides, 11 on 2 or 3 sides (#2283)

2282	A1647	(25c) multi ('88)	.50	.15
a.		Booklet pane of 10	6.50	3.50

Vert. pairs, imperf between, are printer's waste. Other "varieties" probably exist.

2283	A1649a	25c multi ('88)	.50	.15
a.		Booklet pane of 10	6.00	3.50
b.		25c multi, red removed from sky	6.00	.15
c.		As "b," booklet pane of 10	65.00	
d.		As "a," horiz. imperf. between	2,250.	

Imperfs. are printer's waste.

2284	A1649b	25c multi ('88)	.45	.15
2285	A1649c	25c multi ('88)	.45	.15
b.		Bklt. pane of 10, 5 each Nos. 2284-2285	4.50	3.50
d.		Pair, Nos. 2284-2285	1.00	.25
2285A	A1648	25c multi ('88)	.45	.15
c.		Booklet pane of 6	2.75	2.00
		Nos. 2282-2285A (5)	2.35	.75

Issued: #2276, 5/9; #2277, 2279, 2282, 3/22; #2278, 5/6; #2280, 5/20; #2281, 9/2; #2283, 4/29; #2284-2285, 5/28; #2285A, 7/5.

North American Wildlife — A1650-A1699

1987, June 13   Photo.   Perf. 11

2286	A1650	22c Barn swallow	.85	.15
2287	A1651	22c Monarch butterfly	.85	.15
2288	A1652	22c Bighorn sheep	.85	.15
2289	A1653	22c Broad-tailed hummingbird	.85	.15
2290	A1654	22c Cottontail	.85	.15
2291	A1655	22c Osprey	.85	.15
2292	A1656	22c Mountain lion	.85	.15
2293	A1657	22c Luna moth	.85	.15
2294	A1658	22c Mule deer	.85	.15
2295	A1659	22c Gray squirrel	.85	.15
2296	A1660	22c Armadillo	.85	.15
2297	A1661	22c Eastern chipmunk	.85	.15
2298	A1662	22c Moose	.85	.15
2299	A1663	22c Black bear	.85	.15
2300	A1664	22c Tiger swallowtail	.85	.15
2301	A1665	22c Bobwhite	.85	.15
2302	A1666	22c Ringtail	.85	.15
2303	A1667	22c Red-winged blackbird	.85	.15
2304	A1668	22c American lobster	.85	.15
2305	A1669	22c Black-tailed jack rabbit	.85	.15
2306	A1670	22c Scarlet tanager	.85	.15
2307	A1671	22c Woodchuck	.85	.15
2308	A1672	22c Roseate spoonbill	.85	.15
2309	A1673	22c Bald eagle	.85	.15
2310	A1674	22c Alaskan brown bear	.85	.15
2311	A1675	22c Iiwi	.85	.15
2312	A1676	22c Badger	.85	.15
2313	A1677	22c Pronghorn	.85	.15
2314	A1678	22c River otter	.85	.15
2315	A1679	22c Ladybug	.85	.15
2316	A1680	22c Beaver	.85	.15
2317	A1681	22c White-tailed deer	.85	.15
2318	A1682	22c Blue jay	.85	.15
2319	A1683	22c Pika	.85	.15
2320	A1684	22c Bison	.85	.15
2321	A1685	22c Snowy egret	.85	.15
2322	A1686	22c Gray wolf	.85	.15
2323	A1687	22c Mountain goat	.85	.15
2324	A1688	22c Deer mouse	.85	.15
2325	A1689	22c Black-tailed prairie dog	.85	.15
2326	A1690	22c Box turtle	.85	.15
2327	A1691	22c Wolverine	.85	.15
2328	A1692	22c American elk	.85	.15
2329	A1693	22c California sea lion	.85	.15
2330	A1694	22c Mockingbird	.85	.15
2331	A1695	22c Raccoon	.85	.15
2332	A1696	22c Bobcat	.85	.15
2333	A1697	22c Black-footed ferret	.85	.15
2334	A1698	22c Canada goose	.85	.15
2335	A1699	22c Red fox	.85	.15
a.		Pane of 50, #2286-2335	47.50	
b.		2286b-2335b, any single, red omitted	—	

Ratification of the Constitution

Dec 7, 1787 USA — Delaware 22 — A1700
Dec 12, 1787 — Pennsylvania 22 — A1701
Dec 18, 1787 USA — New Jersey 22 — A1702 
January 2, 1788 — Georgia 22 — A1703
January 9, 1788 — Connecticut 22 — A1704
Feb 6, 1788 — Massachusetts 22 — A1705
April 28, 1788 USA — Maryland 22 — A1706 
May 23, 1788 USA — South Carolina 25 — A1707
June 21, 1788 — New Hampshire 22 — A1708
June 25, 1788 USA — Virginia 25 — A1709  
July 26, 1788 USA — New York 25 — A1710 
November 21, 1789 USA — North Carolina 25 — A1711
May 29, 1790 — Rhode Island — A1712

Litho. & Engr., Photo. (#2337, 2343-2344, 2347)

1987-90   Perf. 11

2336	A1700	22c multi	.40	.15
2337	A1701	22c multi	.40	.15
2338	A1702	22c multi	.40	.15
a.		Black (engr.) omitted	6,000.	
2339	A1703	22c multi ('88)	.40	.15
2340	A1704	22c multi ('88)	.40	.15
2341	A1705	22c dk blue & dk red ('88)	.40	.15
2342	A1706	22c multi ('88)	.40	.15
2343	A1707	25c multi ('88)	.45	.15
a.		Strip of 3, vert. imperf. btwn.		
2344	A1708	25c multi ('88)	.45	.15
2345	A1709	25c multi ('88)	.45	.15
2346	A1710	25c multi ('88)	.45	.15
2347	A1711	25c multi ('89)	.45	.15
2348	A1712	25c multi ('90)	.45	.15
		Nos. 2336-2348 (13)	5.50	1.95

Issued: #2336, 7/4; #2337, 8/26; #2338, 9/11; #2339, 1/6; #2340, 1/9; #2341, 2/6; 32342, 2/15; #2343, 5/23; #2344, 6/21; #2345, 6/25; #2346, 7/26; # 2347, 8/22; #2348, 5/29.

US-Morocco Diplomatic Relations Bicentennial

Friendship with Morocco 1787-1987
Arabesque, Dar Batha Palace, Fez — A1713

Litho. & Engr.

1987, July 18   Perf. 11

2349	A1713	22c scar & blk	.40	.15
		Black (engr.) omitted	350.00	

See Morocco No. 642.

Literary Arts

William Cuthbert Faulkner (1897-1962), Novelist — A1714

1987, Aug. 3   Engr.   Perf. 11

2350	A1714	22c bright green	.40	.15

Imperfs. are from printer's waste.

Folk Art Issue

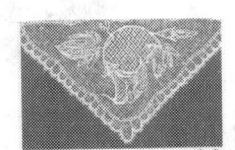

A1715 Lacemaking USA 22
A1716 Lacemaking USA 22
A1717 Lacemaking USA 22
Lacemaking USA 22 A1718

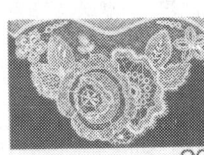

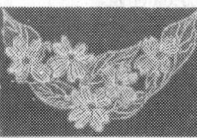

Litho. & Engr.

1987, Aug. 14   Perf. 11

2351	A1715	22c ultra & white	.45	.15
2352	A1716	22c ultra & white	.45	.15
2353	A1717	22c ultra & white	.45	.15
2354	A1718	22c ultra & white	.45	.15
a.		Block of 4, #2351-2354	1.90	1.90
b.		As "a," white omitted	1,000.	

Drafting of the Constitution Bicentennial

A1719 — The Bicentennial of the Constitution of the United States of America 1787-1987 USA 22
A1720 — We the people of the United States, in order to form a more perfect Union... Preamble, U.S. Constitution USA 22
A1721 — Establish justice, insure domestic tranquility, provide for the common defense, promote the general welfare... Preamble, U.S. Constitution USA 22
A1722 — And secure the blessings of liberty to ourselves and our posterity... Preamble, U.S. Constitution USA 22
A1723 — Do ordain and establish this Constitution for the United States of America. Preamble, U.S. Constitution USA 22

Perf. 10 Horiz. on 1 or 2 Sides

1987, Aug. 28   Booklet Stamps   Photo.

2355	A1719	22c multicolored	.50	.15
a.		Grayish grn (background) omitted		
2356	A1720	22c multicolored	.50	.15
a.		Grayish grn (background) omitted		
2357	A1721	22c multicolored	.50	.15
a.		Grayish grn (background) omitted		
2358	A1722	22c multicolored	.50	.15
a.		Grayish grn (background) omitted		
2359	A1723	22c multicolored	.50	.15
a.		Bklt. pane of 5, #2355-2359	2.50	2.25
b.		Grayish grn (background) omitted		

A1724 — U.S. Constitution 22
A1725 — CPA Certified Public Accountants 22

Signing of the Constitution
Litho. & Engr.

1987, Sept. 17   Perf. 11

2360	A1724	22c multicolored	.40	.15

Certified Public Accounting

1987, Sept. 21   Litho. & Engr.

2361	A1725	22c multicolored	1.90	.15
a.		Black (engr.) omitted	900.00	

59

UNITED STATES

Locomotives

Stourbridge Lion, 1829 A1726

Best Friend of Charleston, 1830 A1727

John Bull, 1831 A1728

Brother Jonathan, 1832 A1729

Gowan & Marx, 1839 A1730

Perf. 10 Horiz. on 1 or 2 Sides
1987, Oct. 1   **Booklet Stamps**
2362	A1726	22c multicolored	.55	.15
2363	A1727	22c multicolored	.55	.15
2364	A1728	22c multicolored	.55	.15
2365	A1729	22c multicolored	.55	.15
a.		Red omitted		
2366	A1730	22c multicolored	.55	.15
a.		Bklt. pane of 5, #2362-2366	2.75	2.50
b.		As "a," blk omitted on #2366		
c.		As No. 2366, blue omitted (single)	—	

Christmas

Moroni Madonna A1731

Christmas Ornaments A1732

1987, Oct. 23   Photo.   *Perf. 11*
2367	A1731	22c multicolored	.40	.15
2368	A1732	22c multicolored	.40	.15

1988 Winter Olympics, Calgary

Skiing — A1733

1988, Jan. 10   Photo.   *Perf. 11*
2369	A1733	22c multicolored	.40	.15

Find what you're looking for in the "Scott Stamp Monthly." New issue and topical listings, as well as fascinating features, are found in each issue. Please call 1-800-572-6885 for more information.

Australia Bicentennial

Caricature of Australian Koala and American Bald Eagle — A1734

1988, Jan. 10   Photo.   *Perf. 11*
2370	A1734	22c multicolored	.40	.15

See Australia No. 1052.

Black Heritage

James Weldon Johnson, 1871-1938, Author, Lyricist — A1735

1988, Feb. 2   Photo.   *Perf. 11*
2371	A1735	22c multicolored	.40	.15

Siamese, Exotic Shorthair A1736

Abyssinian, Himalayan A1737

Maine Coon, Burmese A1738

American Shorthair, Persian A1739

1988, Feb. 5   *Perf. 11*
2372	A1736	22c multicolored	.45	.15
2373	A1737	22c multicolored	.45	.15
2374	A1738	22c multicolored	.45	.15
2375	A1739	22c multicolored	.45	.15
a.		Block of 4, #2372-2375	1.90	1.90

American Sports Issues

Knute Rockne A1740

Francis Ouimet A1741

1988, Mar. 9   Litho. & Engr.
2376	A1740	22c multicolored	.40	.15

Knute Kenneth Rockne (1888-1931), Notre Dame football coach.

1988, June 13   Photo.   *Perf. 11*
2377	A1741	25c multicolored	.45	.15

Francis Ouimet (1893-1967), 1st amateur golfer to win the US Open Championship.

Love Issue

Rose — A1742

A1743

1988   Photo.   *Perf. 11*
2378	A1742	25c multicolored	.45	.15
a.		Imperf., pair	3,000.	
2379	A1743	45c multicolored	.65	.20

Issue dates: 25c, July 4; 45c, Aug. 8.

1988 Summer Olympics, Seoul

Gymnastic Rings A1744

1988, Aug. 19   Photo.   *Perf. 11*
2380	A1744	25c multicolored	.45	.15

Classic Automobiles

1928 Locomobile — A1745

1929 Pierce-Arrow A1746

1931 Cord A1747

1932 Packard A1748

1935 Duesenberg — A1749

Perf. 10 Horiz. on 1 or 2 Sides
1988, Aug. 25   Litho. & Engr.
Booklet Stamps
2381	A1745	25c multicolored	.50	.15
2382	A1746	25c multicolored	.50	.15
2383	A1747	25c multicolored	.50	.15
2384	A1748	25c multicolored	.50	.15
2385	A1749	25c multicolored	.50	.15
a.		Bklt. pane of 5, #2381-2385	5.25	2.25
		Nos. 2381-2385 (5)	2.50	.75

Antarctic Explorers

Nathaniel Palmer (1799-1877) A1750

Lt. Charles Wilkes (1798-1877) A1751

Richard E. Byrd (1888-1957) A1752

Lincoln Ellsworth (1880-1951) A1753

1988, Sept. 14   Photo.   *Perf. 11*
2386	A1750	25c multicolored	.65	.15
2387	A1751	25c multicolored	.65	.15
2388	A1752	25c multicolored	.65	.15
2389	A1753	25c multicolored	.65	.15
a.		Block of 4, #2386-2389	2.75	2.00
b.		Black (engr.) omitted	1,500.	
c.		As "a," imperf. horiz.	3,000.	

Folk Art Issue
Carousel Animals

Deer — A1754

Horse — A1755

Camel — A1756

Goat — A1757

1988, Oct. 1   Litho. & Engr.   *Perf. 11*
2390	A1754	25c multicolored	.65	.15
2391	A1755	25c multicolored	.65	.15
2392	A1756	25c multicolored	.65	.15
2393	A1757	25c multicolored	.65	.15
a.		Block of 4, #2390-2393	3.00	2.00

Express Mail Rate

Eagle in Flight — A1758

1988, Oct. 4   Litho. & Engr.   *Perf. 11*
2394	A1758	$8.75 multi	13.50	8.00

UNITED STATES

Special Occasions

Happy Birthday — A1759

Best Wishes — A1760

Thinking of You — A1761

Love You — A1762

Perf. 11 on 2 or 3 sides
1988, Oct. 22   Photo.
Booklet Stamps
2395	A1759	25c multicolored	.50	.15
2396	A1760	25c multicolored	.50	.15
a.		Bklt. pane of 6, 3 #2395 + 3 #2396 with gutter btwn.	3.50	3.25
2397	A1761	25c multicolored	.50	.15
2398	A1762	25c multicolored	.50	.15
a.		Bklt. pane of 6, 3 #2397 + 3 #2398 with gutter btwn.	3.50	3.25
b.		As "a," imperf. horiz.		
		Nos. 2395-2398 (4)	2.00	.60

Madonna and Child, by Botticelli A1763

One-horse Open Sleigh and Village Scene A1764

Litho. & Engr., Photo. (No. 2400)
1988, Oct. 20   Perf. 11½
2399	A1763	25c multicolored	.45	.15
a.		Gold omitted	30.00	
2400	A1764	25c multicolored	.45	.15

Montana Statehood Centennial

C.M. Russell and Friends, by Charles M. Russell (1865-1926) A1765

1989, Jan. 15   Litho. & Engr.   Perf. 11
2401	A1765	25c multicolored	.45	.15

Shop with Scott Publishing Co. 24 hours a day 7 days a week at www.scottonline.com

Black Heritage Issues

Asa Philip Randolph (1889-1979), Labor and Civil Rights Leader — A1766

1989, Feb. 3   Photo.   Perf. 11
2402	A1766	25c multicolored	.45	.15

North Dakota Statehood Centennial

A1767 North Dakota 1889

1989, Feb. 21   Perf. 11
2403	A1767	25c multicolored	.45	.15

Washington Statehood Centennial

A1768

1989, Feb. 22   Perf. 11
2404	A1768	25c multicolored	.45	.15

Steamboats

Experiment, 1788-1790 — A1769

Phoenix, 1809 — A1770

New Orleans, 1812 — A1771

Washington, 1816 — A1772

Walk in the Water, 1818 — A1773

Perf. 10 Horiz. on 1 or 2 sides
1989, Mar. 3   Litho. & Engr.
Booklet Stamps
2405	A1769	25c multicolored	.45	.15
2406	A1770	25c multicolored	.45	.15
2407	A1771	25c multicolored	.45	.15
2408	A1772	25c multicolored	.45	.15
2409	A1773	25c multicolored	.45	.15
a.		Bklt. pane of 5, #2405-2409	2.25	1.75

A1774

A1775

World Stamp Expo '89
Nov. 17-Dec. 3, Washington, DC
1989, Mar. 16   Litho. & Engr.   Perf. 11
2410	A1774	25c No. 122	.45	.15

Performing Arts

Arturo Toscanini (1867-1975), Italian Conductor

1989, Mar. 25   Photo.   Perf. 11
2411	A1775	25c multicolored	.45	.15

Constitution Bicentennial

House of Representatives A1776

Senate A1777

Executive Branch — A1778

Supreme Court — A1779

1989-90   Litho. & Engr.   Perf. 11
2412	A1776	25c multicolored	.45	.15
2413	A1777	25c multicolored	.45	.15
2414	A1778	25c multicolored	.45	.15
2415	A1779	25c multicolored	.45	.15
		Nos. 2412-2415 (4)	1.80	.60

Issue dates: #2412, Apr. 4; #2413, Apr. 6; #2414, Apr. 16. #2415, Feb. 2, 1990.

South Dakota State Centenary

State Flower, Pioneer Woman and Sod House on Grasslands A1780

1989, May 3   Photo.   Perf. 11
2416	A1780	25c multicolored	.45	.15

American Sports

Henry Louis "Lou" Gehrig (1903-1941), Baseball Player for the New York Yankees — A1781

1989, June 10   Photo.   Perf. 11
2417	A1781	25c multicolored	.50	.15

Literary Arts

Ernest Hemingway (1899-1961), Nobel Prize-winner for Literature, 1954 — A1782

1989, July 17   Photo.   Perf. 11
2418	A1782	25c multicolored	.45	.15

Moon Landing, 20th Anniv.

Raising the Flag on Lunar Surface, July 20, 1969 — A1783

Perf. 11x11½
1989, July 20   Litho. & Engr.
2419	A1783	$2.40 multicolored	4.00	2.00
a.		Black (engr.) omitted	2,750.	
b.		Imperf., pair	750.00	
c.		Black (litho.) omitted	4,750.	

Natl. Assoc. of Letter Carriers, Cent.

Letter Carriers A1784

1989, Aug. 30   Photo.   Perf. 11
2420	A1784	25c multicolored	.45	.15

Constitution Bicentennial

Bill of Rights — A1785

1989, Sept. 25   Litho. & Engr.   Perf. 11
2421	A1785	25c multicolored	.45	.15
a.		Black (engr.) omitted	375.00	

Prehistoric Animals

Tyrannosaurus Rex — A1786

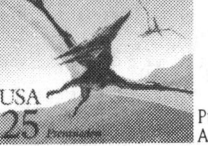

Pteranodon A1787

61

UNITED STATES

Stegosaurus
A1788

Brontosaurus
A1789

1989, Oct. 1   Litho. & Engr.   Perf. 11
2422	A1786	25c multicolored	.65	.15
2423	A1787	25c multicolored	.65	.15
2424	A1788	25c multicolored	.65	.15
2425	A1789	25c multicolored	.65	.15
a.		Block of 4, #2422-2425	3.00	2.00
b.		As "a," black (engr.) omitted	1,150.	

The correct name for "Brontosaurus" is "Apatosaurus."
No. 2425b is valued in the grade of fine.

Pre-Columbian America Issue

Southwest Carved Figure, A. D. 1150-1350 — A1790

Emblem of the Postal Union of the Americas and Spain (UPAE) and Southwestern Wood-carved Ritual Figure, Mogollon Culture, Mimbres Period, a Forerunner of the Hopi Indian Kachina Doll, A.D. 1150-1350.

1989, Oct. 12   Photo.   Perf. 11
2426	A1790	25c multicolored	.45	.15

Discovery of America, 500th anniv. (in 1992). See No. C121.

Christmas

Madonna and Child, by Caracci
A1791

Sleigh Full of Presents
A1792

**   Litho. & Engr.**
1989, Oct. 19   Perf. 11½
2427	A1791	25c multicolored	.45	.15
a.		Booklet pane of 10	4.75	3.50
b.		Red (litho.) omitted	900.00	
c.		As "a," imperf.		

**   Photo.**
**   Perf. 11**
2428	A1792	25c multicolored	.45	.15
a.		Vert. pair, imperf. horiz.	2,000.	

Booklet Stamp
Perf. 11½ on 2 or 3 sides
2429	A1792	25c multicolored	.45	.15
a.		Booklet pane of 10	4.75	3.50
b.		As "a," imperf. horiz.	—	
c.		Vert. pair, imperf. horiz.	—	
d.		As "a," red omitted	—	
e.		Imperf., pair	—	

Marked differences exist between Nos. 2428 and 2429: The runners on the sleigh in No. 2429 are twice as thick as those in No. 2428; in No. 2429 the package at upper left in the sleigh has a red bow, whereas the same package in No. 2428 has a red and black bow; and the ribbon on the upper right package in No. 2429 is green, whereas the same ribbon in No. 2428 is black.

Eagle and Shield — A1793

1989, Nov. 10   Photo.   Die Cut
Self-Adhesive
2431	A1793	25c multicolored	.50	.20
a.		Booklet pane of 18	11.00	
b.		Vert. pair, no die cutting between	850.00	
c.		Pair, no die cutting		

Issued unfolded in panes of 18; peelable paper backing is booklet cover. Sold for $5.
Also available in strips of 18 with stamps spaced for use in affixing machines to service first day covers. Sold for $5.
Sold in 15 test cities and through the philatelic agency only.

Souvenir Sheet

World Stamp Expo, Washington, DC, Nov. 17-Dec. 3 — A1794

1989, Nov. 17   Litho. & Engr.   Imperf.
2433	A1794	Sheet of 4	12.00	9.00
a.		90c like No. 122	2.00	1.75
b.		90c like No. 132TC (blue frame, brown center)	2.00	1.75
c.		90c like No. 132TC (green frame, blue center)	2.00	1.75
d.		90c like No. 132TC (scarlet frame, blue center)	2.00	1.75

Traditional Mail Delivery

Stagecoach, c. 1850 — A1795

Paddlewheel Steamer — A1796

Biplane
A1797

Depot-hack Type Automobile
A1798

**   Litho. & Engr.**
1989, Nov. 19   Perf. 11
2434	A1795	25c multicolored	.45	.15
2435	A1796	25c multicolored	.45	.15
2436	A1797	25c multicolored	.45	.15
2437	A1798	25c multicolored	.45	.15
a.		Block of 4, #2434-2437	2.00	2.00
b.		As "a," dk blue (engr.) omitted	1,000.	

No. 2437b is valued in the grade of fine. Very fine blocks exist and sell for somewhat more.

1989, Nov. 28   Imperf.
2438		Sheet of 4	4.00	1.75
a.	A1795	25c multicolored	.65	.25
b.	A1796	25c multicolored	.65	.25
c.	A1797	25c multicolored	.65	.25
d.	A1798	25c multicolored	.65	.25
e.		Dark blue & gray (engr.) omitted	1,100.	

20th Universal Postal Union Congress.

Idaho State Centenary

Mountain Bluebird, Sawtooth Mountains — A1799

1990, Jan. 6   Photo.   Perf. 11
2439	A1799	25c multicolored	.45	.15

Love Issue

A1800

1990, Jan. 18   Photo.   Perf. 12½x13
2440	A1800	25c brt bl, dk pink & emer grn	.45	.15
a.		Imperf., pair	850.00	

Booklet Stamp
Perf. 11½ on 2 or 3 sides
2441	A1800	25c ultra, brt pink & dk grn	.45	.15
a.		Booklet pane of 10	4.75	3.50
b.		As "a," bright pink omitted	2,250.	
c.		As "b," single stamp	225.	

No. 2441c may be obtained from booklet panes containing both normal and color-omitted stamps.

Black Heritage

Ida B. Wells (1862-1931), Journalist — A1801

1990, Feb. 1   Photo.   Perf. 11
2442	A1801	25c multicolored	.45	.15

Beach Umbrella — A1802

1990, Feb. 3   Photo.   Perf. 11
Booklet Stamp
2443	A1802	15c multicolored	.30	.15
a.		Booklet pane of 10	3.00	2.00
b.		As "a," blue omitted	2,000.	
c.		As No. 2443, blue omitted	180.	

Wyoming State Centenary

High Mountain Meadows, by Conrad Schwiering
A1803

1990, Feb. 23   Litho. & Engr.   Perf. 11
2444	A1803	25c multicolored	.45	.15
a.		Black (engr.) omitted	2,500.	

Classic Films

The Wizard of Oz — A1804

Gone With the Wind — A1805

Beau Geste
A1806

Stagecoach
A1807

1990, Mar. 23   Photo.   Perf. 11
2445	A1804	25c multicolored	1.00	.15
2446	A1805	25c multicolored	1.00	.15
2447	A1806	25c multicolored	1.00	.15
2448	A1807	25c multicolored	1.00	.15
a.		Block of 4, #2445-2448	4.50	3.50

Literary Arts Series

Marianne Craig Moore (1887-1972), Poet — A1808

1990, Apr. 18   Photo.   Perf. 11
2449	A1808	25c multicolored	.45	.15

TRANSPORTATION ISSUE

Steam Carriage 1866
A1810

Circus Wagon 1900s
A1811

Circus Wagon 1900s
A1811a

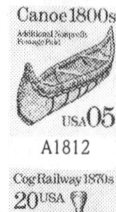

Canoe 1800s
A1812

Tractor Trailer
A1816

Cog Railway 1870s
A1822

Lunch Wagon 1890s
A1823

Ferryboat 1900s
A1825

Seaplane 1914
A1827

Engr., Photo. (#2452B, 2452D, 2454, 2458)
1990-95 Coil Stamps   Perf. 9.8 Vert.
Untagged: #2452B, 2452D, 2453, 2454, & 10c

2451	A1810	4c claret	.15	.15
a.		Imperf., pair	700.00	
b.		Untagged		
2452	A1811	5c carmine	.15	.15
a.		Untagged	.15	.15
c.		Imperf., pair	1,000.	
2452B	A1811	5c carmine	.15	.15
2452D	A1811a	5c carmine	.15	.15
a.		Imperf., pair		
2453	A1812	5c brn (Bureau precancel in gray)	.15	.15
a.		Imperf., pair	400.00	
b.		Gray omitted	—	
2454	A1812	5c red (Bureau precancel in gray)	.15	.15
2457	A1816	10c grn (Bureau precancel in gray)	.20	.20
a.		Imperf., pair	400.00	
2458	A1816	10c grn (Bureau precancel in black)	.20	.20
2463	A1822	20c green	.40	.15
a.		Imperf., pair	150.00	
2464	A1823	23c dark blue	.45	.15
a.		Imperf., pair	175.00	
2466	A1825	32c blue	.60	.15
a.				
		32c bright blue	6.00	—
2468	A1827	$1 blue & scar	1.75	.50
a.		Imperf., pair	2,500.	
		Nos. 2451-2468 (12)	4.50	2.25

Issued: $1, 4/20; #2452, 8/31; 4c, 1/25/91; #2453, 2457, 5/25/91; #2454, 10/22/91; 23c,

UNITED STATES

4/12/91; #2452B, 12/8/92; #2458, 5/25/94; #2452D, 3/20/95; 32c, 6/2/95; #2463, 6/9/95

This is an expanding set. Numbers will change if necessary.

Some pairs of No. 2468 appear to be imperf but have some blind perfs on the gum. Beware of copies with the gum removed.

Lighthouses

Admiralty Head, WA — A1829
Cape Hatteras, NC — A1830 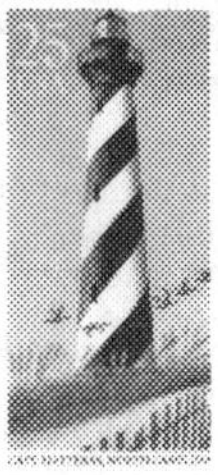
West Quoddy Head, ME — A1831
American Shoals, FL — A1832 
Sandy Hook, NJ — A1833 

Perf. 10 Vert. on 1 or 2 Sides
1990, Apr. 26   Litho. & Engr.
Booklet Stamps

2470	A1829 25c multicolored	.45	.15
2471	A1830 25c multicolored	.45	.15
2472	A1831 25c multicolored	.45	.15
2473	A1832 25c multicolored	.45	.15
2474	A1833 25c multicolored	.45	.15
a.	Bklt. pane of 5, #2470-2474	2.50	2.00
b.	As "a," white (USA 25) omitted	75.00	

Flag

A1834

1990, May 18   Photo.   *Die Cut*
Self-adhesive

2475	A1834 25c dk red & dk bl	.50	.25
a.	Pane of 12	6.00	

Sold only in panes of 12; peelable plastic backing inscribed in light ultramarine. Available for a test period of six months at 22 First National Bank automatic teller machines in Seattle.

Flora and Fauna Series

American Kestrel
A1840   A1841

Eastern Bluebird — A1842
Fawn — A1843 
Cardinal A1844 
Pumpkinseed Sunfish A1845 
Bobcat A1846 

Perf. 11, 11.2 (#2477)
1990-95   Litho.   Untagged

2476	A1840 1c multicolored	.15	.15
2477	A1841 1c multicolored	.15	.15
2478	A1842 3c multicolored	.15	.15

Photo.
Perf. 11½x11

2479	A1843 19c multicolored	.35	.15
b.	Red omitted	850.00	

On No. 2479b other colors are shifted.

2480	A1844 30c multicolored	.50	.15

Litho. & Engr.
Perf. 11

2481	A1845 45c multicolored	.80	.15
a.	Black (engr.) omitted	600.00	—
2482	A1846 $2 multicolored	3.00	1.25
a.	Black (engr.) omitted	350.00	
	Nos. 2476-2482 (7)	5.10	2.15

Issued: $2, 6/1/90; 19c, 3/11/91; 3c, 30c, #2476, 6/22/91; 45c, 12/2/92; #2477, 5/10/95. See No. 3044. Compare design A1842 with A2336.

Blue Jay — A1847
Wood Duck — A1848 
African Violets — A1849  
Peach — A1850 
Pear — A1851 
Red Squirrel — A1852 
Rose — A1853 
Pine Cone — A1854 

Booklet Stamps
1991-95   Perf. 10.9x9.8

2483	A1847 20c multicolored	.40	.15
a.	Booklet pane of 10	4.00	2.25

See No. 3053.

Perf. 10 on 2 or 3 Sides

2484	A1848 29c black & multi	.50	.15
a.	Booklet pane of 10	5.50	3.75
b.	As "a," horiz. imperf. between	—	

Perf. 11 on 2 or 3 Sides

2485	A1848 29c red & multi	.50	.15
a.	Booklet pane of 10	5.50	4.00
b.	Vert. pair, imperf. between	275.00	
c.	As "b," booklet pane of 10	1,500.	

Perf. 10x11 on 2 or 3 Sides

2486	A1849 29c multicolored	.50	.15
a.	Booklet pane of 10	5.50	4.00
2487	A1850 32c multicolored	.60	.15
2488	A1851 32c multicolored	.60	.15
a.	Booklet pane, 5 each #2487-2488	6.00	4.25
b.	Pair, #2487-2488	1.25	.30

Issued: #2484-2485, 4/12/91; #2486, 10/8/93; 20c, 6/15/95; 32c 7/8/95.

Booklet Stamps
1993   Photo.   *Die Cut*
Self-Adhesive

2489	A1852 29c multicolored	.50	.15
a.	Booklet pane of 18	10.00	
2490	A1853 29c red, green & black	.50	.15
a.	Booklet pane of 18	10.00	
2491	A1854 29c multicolored	.50	.15
a.	Booklet pane of 18	11.00	
b.	Horiz. pair, no die cutting between	—	

Issued: #2489, June 25; #2490, Aug. 19; #2491, Nov. 5.

Serpentine Die Cut

2492	A1853 32c pink, green & black	.60	.15
a.	Booklet pane of 20+label	12.00	
b.	Booklet pane of 15+label ('96)	8.75	
c.	Horiz. pair, no die cutting between	—	
d.	As "a," 2 stamps and parts of 7 others printed on backing liner	—	
e.	Booklet pane of 14	11.00	
f.	Booklet pane of 16	12.50	
2493	A1850 32c multicolored	.60	.15
2494	A1851 32c multicolored	.60	.15
a.	Booklet pane, 10 each #2493-2494+label	12.50	

Coil Stamps
Serpentine Die Cut Vert.

2495	A1850 32c multicolored	.60	.15
2495A	A1851 32c multicolored	.60	.15

See Nos. 3048-3049, 3053-3054.

Olympians

Jesse Owens, 1936 — A1855
Ray Ewry, 1900-08 — A1856 
Hazel Wightman, 1924 — A1857 
Eddie Eagan, 1920, 1932 — A1858 
Helene Madison, 1932 — A1859 

1990, July 6   Photo.   Perf. 11

2496	A1855 25c multicolored	.60	.15
2497	A1856 25c multicolored	.60	.15
2498	A1857 25c multicolored	.60	.15
2499	A1858 25c multicolored	.60	.15
2500	A1859 25c multicolored	.60	.15
a.	Strip of 5, 2496-2500	3.25	2.50

Indian Headdresses

Assiniboin A1860
Cheyenne A1861 
Comanche A1862 
Flathead A1863 
Shoshone A1864 

Perf. 11 on 2 or 3 sides
1990, Aug. 17   Litho. & Engr.
Booklet Stamps

2501	A1860 25c multicolored	.55	.15
2502	A1861 25c multicolored	.55	.15
2503	A1862 25c multicolored	.55	.15
2504	A1863 25c multicolored	.55	.15
2505	A1864 25c multicolored	.55	.15
a.	Bklt. pane, 2 each #2501-2505	5.50	3.50
b.	As "a," black (engr.) omitted	2,500.	
c.	Strip of 5, #2501-2505	2.75	1.00
d.	As "a," horiz. imperf. btwn.	—	

Micronesia, Marshall Islands

Canoe and Flag of the Federated States of Micronesia A1865

Stick Chart, Canoe and Flag of the Republic of the Marshall Islands A1866

1990, Sept. 28   Perf. 11

2506	A1865 25c multicolored	.45	.15
2507	A1866 25c multicolored	.45	.15
a.	Pair, #2506-2507	.90	.60
b.	As "a," black (engr.) omitted	4,000.	

See Micronesia Nos. 124-126 and Marshall Islands No. 381.

Sea Creatures

Killer Whales A1867

UNITED STATES

Northern Sea Lions A1868

Sea Otter A1869

Common Dolphin A1870

1990, Oct. 3   Litho. & Engr.   Perf. 11
2508 A1867 25c multicolored .45 .15
2509 A1868 25c multicolored .45 .15
2510 A1869 25c multicolored .45 .15
2511 A1870 25c multicolored .45 .15
   a. Block of 4, #2508-2511 1.90 1.75
   b. As "a," blk (engr.) omitted 1,200.
See Russia Nos. 5933-5936.

Pre-Columbian America Issue

Grand Canyon A1871

1990, Oct. 12   Photo.   Perf. 11
2512 A1871 25c multicolored .45 .15

Dwight David Eisenhower

A1872

1990, Oct. 13   Photo.   Perf. 11
2513 A1872 25c multicolored .45 .15
   a. Imperf., pair 2,250.

Christmas

Madonna and Child by Antonello da Messina — A1873

Christmas Tree — A1874

Litho. & Engr.   Perf. 11½
2514 A1873 25c multicolored .45 .15
   a. Booklet pane of 10 5.00 3.25

Photo.   Perf. 11
2515 A1874 25c multicolored .45 .15
   a. Vert. pair, imperf horiz. 1,100.

Perf. 11½x11 on 2 or 3 Sides
2516 A1874 25c multicolored .45 .15
   a. Booklet pane of 10 5.00 3.25
Nos. 2514-2516 (3) 1.35 .45

Marked differences exist between Nos. 2515 and 2516. The background red on No. 2515 is even while that on No. 2516 is splotchy. The bands across the tree and "GREETINGS" are blue green on No. 2515 and yellow green on No. 2516.

A1875

A1876

A1877

1991, Jan. 22   Photo.   Perf. 13
2517 A1875 (29c) yel, blk, red & yel grn .50 .15
   a. Imperf., pair 750.00
   b. Horiz. pair, imperf. vert. 1,250.

Do not confuse No. 2517a with No. 2518a. Design of No. 2517a measures 21½x17½mm; No. 2518a 21x18mm;

**Coil Stamp
Perf. 10 Vert.**
2518 A1875 (29c) yel, blk, dull red & dk yel grn .50 .15
   a. Imperf., pair 40.00
See note after No. 2517.

**Booklet Stamps
Perf. 11 on 2 or 3 Sides**
2519 A1875 (29c) yel, blk, dull red & dk grn .50 .15
   a. Booklet pane of 10 6.50 4.50
2520 A1875 (29c) pale yel, blk, red & brt grn .50 .15
   a. Booklet pane of 10 18.00 4.50

No. 2519 has bullseye perforations that measure approximately 11.2. No. 2520 has less pronounced black lines in the leaf, which is a much brighter green than on No. 2519.

**Litho.
Perf. 11**
2521 A1876 (4c) bister & car .15 .15
   a. Vert. pair, imperf. horiz. 125.00
   b. Imperf., pair —

**Photo.
Imperf., Die Cut
Self-Adhesive**
2522 A1877 (29c) blk, dk blue & red .50 .25
   a. Pane of 12 7.00

No. 2522 sold only in panes of 12; peelable plastic backing inscribed in light ultramarine. Available during a test period at 22 First National Bank automatic teller machines in Seattle.

Flag Over Mt. Rushmore A1878

Flower A1879

**1991, Mar. 29   Engr.   Perf. 10 Vert.
Coil Stamps**
2523 A1878 29c bl, red & claret .50 .15
   b. Imperf., pair 20.00
   c. Blue, red & brown 5.00 —

Photo.
2523A A1878 29c blue, red & brown .50 .15

On No. 2523A, USA and 29 are not outlined in white and appear farther from edge of design. Issue dates: #2523, Mar. 29. #2523A, July 4.

1991-92   Photo.   Perf. 11
2524 A1879 29c dull yel, blk, red & pale yel grn .50 .15
   a. Perf. 13x12½ .60 .15

**Coil Stamps
Roulette 10 Vert.**
2525 A1879 29c pale yel, blk, red & yel grn .50 .15

Perf. 10 Vert.
2526 A1879 29c pale yel, blk, red & yel grn .50 .15

**Perf. 11 on 2 or 3 Sides
Booklet Stamp**
2527 A1879 29c pale yel, blk, red & brt grn .50 .15
   a. Booklet pane of 10 5.50 3.50
   b. As "a," imperf. vert. 1,500.
   c. Horiz. pair, imperf. vert. 300.
   d. As "a," imperf horiz. 2,750.

Flower on No. 2524 has grainy appearance, inscriptions look rougher.
Issue dates: #2524, 2527, Apr. 5. #2525, Aug. 16. #2526, Mar. 3, 1992.

Flag, Olympic Rings — A1880

**Perf. 11 on 2 or 3 Sides
Booklet Stamp**
1991, Apr. 21   Photo.
2528 A1880 29c multicolored .50 .15
   a. Booklet pane of 10 5.25 3.50
   b. As "a," horiz. imperf. between

Fishing Boat — A1881

Balloon — A1882

**1991-94   Photo.   Perf. 9.8 Vert.
Coil Stamps**
2529 A1881 19c multicolored .35 .15
   a. Type II ('93) .35 .15
   b. As "a," untagged ('93) 1.00 .40
2529C A1881 19c multicolored .50 .15

Design of Type II stamps is created by a finer dot pattern. The vertical sides of "1" are smooth on Type II and jagged on Type I stamps.

No. 2529C has one loop of rope tying boat to piling, numerals and USA are taller and thinner.
Issued: No. 2529, 8/8/91; No. 2529C, 6/25/94.

Perf. 10 on 2 or 3 Sides
**1991, May 17   Photo.
Booklet Stamp**
2530 A1882 19c multicolored .35 .15
   a. Booklet pane of 10 3.50 2.75

Flags on Parade — A1883

Liberty Torch — A1884

1991, May 30   Photo.   Perf. 11
2531 A1883 29c multicolored .50 .15

**1991, June 25   Photo.   Die Cut
Booklet Pane
Self-Adhesive**
2531A A1884 29c blk, gold & grn .55 .25
   b. Booklet pane of 18 10.50
   c. Pair, imperf —

Switzerland, 700th Anniv.

A1887

1991, Feb. 22   Photo.   Perf. 11
2532 A1887 50c multicolored 1.00 .25
   a. Vert. pair, imperf horiz. 1,750.

Imperfs exist from printers' waste.
See Switzerland No. 888.

A1888

A1889

Vermont Statehood Bicentennial
1991, Mar. 1   Perf. 11
2533 A1888 29c multicolored .50 .15

Savings Bonds, 50th Anniv.
1991, Apr. 30   Photo.   Perf. 11
2534 A1889 29c multicolored .50 .15

Love

A1890

A1891

1991, May 9   Photo.   Perf. 12½x13
2535 A1890 29c multicolored .50 .15
   b. Imperf., pair .60 .15

**Perf. 11 on 2 or 3 Sides
Booklet Stamp**
2536 A1890 29c multicolored .50 .15
   a. Booklet pane of 10 5.25 3.50

"29" is closer to edge of design on No. 2536 than on No. 2535.

Perf. 11
2537 A1891 52c multicolored .90 .20

Literary Arts Series

William Saroyan A1892

1991, May 22   Photo.   Perf. 11
2538 A1892 29c multicolored .50 .15
See Russia No. 6002.

Eagle, Olympic Rings — A1893

1991, Sept. 29   Photo.   Perf. 11
2539 A1893 $1 gold & multi 1.75 .50

A1894

UNITED STATES

A1895

A1896

1991	Litho. & Engr.		Perf. 11
Untagged (#2541-2542)			
2540	A1894	$2.90 Priority	5.00	2.50
a.	Vert. pair, imperf horiz.		—
2541	A1895	$9.95 Domestic express	15.00	7.50
2542	A1896	$14 Intl. express	22.50	10.00
a.	Red (engr. inscriptions) omitted	1,500.	
	Nos. 2540-2542 (3)	42.50	20.00

Issued: $2.90, 7/7; $9.95, 6/16; $14, 8/31.

Priority Mail Rate

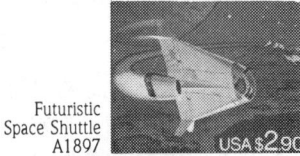

Futuristic Space Shuttle
A1897

Space Shuttle Challenger
A1898

Perf. 11x10½
1993, June 3   Litho. & Engr.
2543 A1897 $2.90 multicolored   5.00 2.25

Litho. & Engr.
1995, June 22   Perf. 11.2
2544 A1898 $3 multi, dated "1995"   5.25 2.25
  b.   Dated "1996"   5.25 2.25

Express Mail Rate

Space Shuttle Endeavour
A1898a

1995, Aug. 4   Litho. & Engr.   Perf. 11
2544A A1898a $10.75 multi   17.50 7.50

Fishing Flies

Royal Wulff
A1899

Jock Scott
A1900

Apte Tarpon Fly — A1901

Lefty's Deceiver
A1902

Muddler Minnow
A1903

Perf. 11 Horiz. on 1 or 2 Sides
1991, May 31   Photo.
Booklet Stamps
2545 A1899 29c multicolored   .55 .15
  a.   Black omitted   .55 —
2546 A1900 29c multicolored   .55 .15
  a.   Black omitted   .55 —
2547 A1901 29c multicolored   .55 .15
  a.   Black omitted   .55 —
2548 A1902 29c multicolored   .55 .15
2549 A1903 29c multicolored   .55 .15
  a.   Bklt. pane of 5, #2545-2549 3.00 2.50

Horiz. pairs, imperf. vert., exist from printers' waste.

Cole Porter
A1904

A1905

Performing Arts
Cole Porter (1891-1964), Composer
1991, June 8   Photo.   Perf. 11
2550 A1904 29c multicolored   .50 .15
  a.   Vert. pair, imperf. horiz.   650.00

Operations Desert Shield & Desert Storm
1991, July 2   Photo.   Perf. 11
2551 A1905 29c Southwest Asia
     service medal   .50 .15
  a.   Vert. pair, imperf horiz.   2,500.

Perf. 11 Vert. on 1 or 2 Sides
Booklet Stamp
2552 A1905 29c multicolored   .50 .15
  a.   Booklet pane of 5   2.75 2.25

No. 2552 is 20½mm wide stamp. Inscriptions are shorter than on No. 2551.

Summer Olympics

Pole Vault
A1907

Discus
A1908

Women's Sprints
A1909

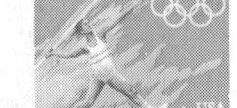

Javelin
A1910

Women's Hurdles
A1911

1991, July 12   Photo.   Perf. 11
2553 A1907 29c multicolored   .50 .15
2554 A1908 29c multicolored   .50 .15
2555 A1909 29c multicolored   .50 .15
2556 A1910 29c multicolored   .50 .15
2557 A1911 29c multicolored   .50 .15
  a.   Strip of #2553-2557   2.75 2.25

Numismatics

1858 Flying Eagle Cent, 1907 Standing Liberty Double Eagle, Series 1875 $1 Note, Series 1902 $10 National Currency Note — A1912

Litho. & Engr.
1991, Aug. 13   Perf. 11
2558 A1912 29c multicolored   .50 .15

World War II

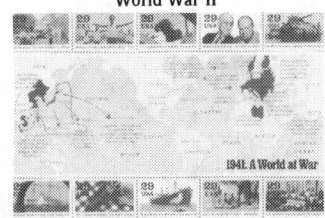

A1913

Designs and events of 1941: a, Military vehicles (Burma Road, 717-mile lifeline to China). b, Recruits (America's 1st peacetime draft). c, Shipments for allies (US supports allies with Lend-Lease Act). d, Roosevelt, Churchill (Atlantic Charter sets war aims of allies). e, Tank (America becomes the "arsenal of democracy"). f, Sinking of Destroyer Reuben James, Oct. 31. g, Gas mask, helmet (Civil defense mobilizes Americans at home). h, Liberty Ship, sea gull (1st Liberty ship delivered Dec. 30). i, Sinking ships (Japanese bomb Pearl Harbor, Dec. 7). j, Congress in session (US declares war on Japan, Dec. 8). Central label is the size of 15 stamps and shows world map, extent of Axis control.
Illustration reduced.

1991, Sept. 3   Litho. & Engr.   Perf. 11
2559 A1913 Block of 10   5.25 4.50
  a.-j. 29c any single   .50   .30
  k.   Black (engr.) omitted   10,000.

Basketball, 100th Anniversary

Basketball, Hoop, Players' Arms — A1914

1991, Aug. 28   Photo.   Perf. 11
2560 A1914 29c multicolored   .55 .15

District of Columbia Bicentennial

Capitol Building from Pennsylvania Avenue, Circa 1903
A1915

1991, Sept. 7   Litho. & Engr.   Perf. 11
2561 A1915 29c multicolored   .50 .15
  a.   Black (engr.) omitted   160.00

Comedians

Stan Laurel and Oliver Hardy
A1916

Edgar Bergen and Charlie McCarthy
A1917

Jack Benny
A1918

Fanny Brice
A1919

Bud Abbott and Lou Costello
A1920

Perf. 11 on 2 or 3 Sides
1991, Aug. 29   Litho. & Engr.
Booklet Stamps
2562 A1916 29c multicolored   .50 .15
2563 A1917 29c multicolored   .50 .15
2564 A1918 29c multicolored   .50 .15
2565 A1919 29c multicolored   .50 .15
2566 A1920 29c multicolored   .50 .15
  a.   Bklt. pane, 2 each #2562-2566   5.50 3.50
  b.   As "a," scarlet & bright violet
       (engr.) omitted   900.00
  c.   Strip of 5, #2562-2566   2.50 —

Black Heritage

Jan E. Matzeliger (1852-1889), Inventor — A1921

1991, Sept. 15   Photo.   Perf. 11
2567 A1921 29c multicolored   .50 .15
  a.   Horiz. pair, imperf. vert.   1,750.
  b.   Vert. pair, imperf. horiz.   1,500.
  c.   Imperf, pair   2,750.

Space Exploration

Mercury, Mariner 10
A1922

Venus, Mariner 2
A1923

65

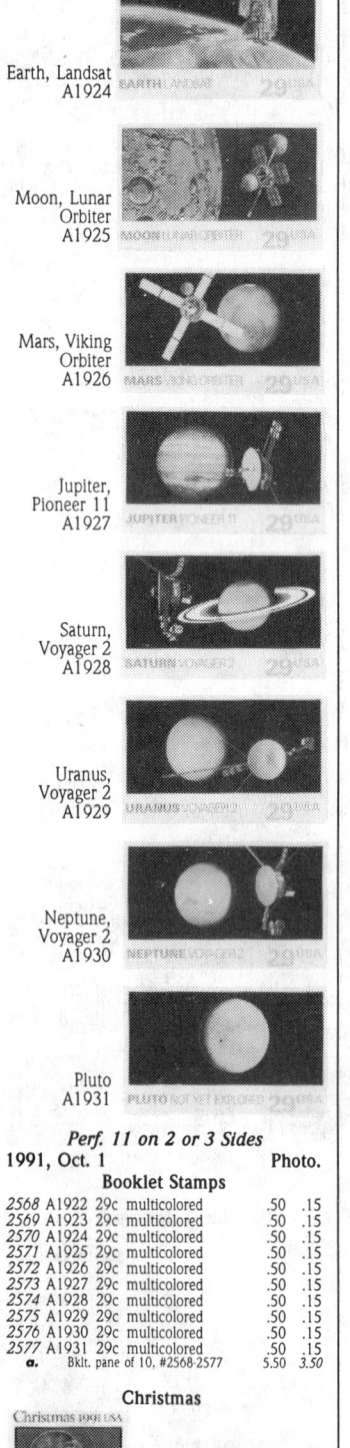

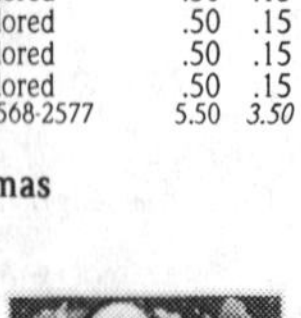

66 UNITED STATES

Earth, Landsat A1924
Moon, Lunar Orbiter A1925
Mars, Viking Orbiter A1926
Jupiter, Pioneer 11 A1927
Saturn, Voyager 2 A1928
Uranus, Voyager 2 A1929
Neptune, Voyager 2 A1930
Pluto A1931

Perf. 11 on 2 or 3 Sides
1991, Oct. 1   Photo.
Booklet Stamps

2568	A1922	29c multicolored	.50	.15
2569	A1923	29c multicolored	.50	.15
2570	A1924	29c multicolored	.50	.15
2571	A1925	29c multicolored	.50	.15
2572	A1926	29c multicolored	.50	.15
2573	A1927	29c multicolored	.50	.15
2574	A1928	29c multicolored	.50	.15
2575	A1929	29c multicolored	.50	.15
2576	A1930	29c multicolored	.50	.15
2577	A1931	29c multicolored	.50	.15
a.		Bklt. pane of 10, #2568-2577	5.50	3.50

Christmas

Madonna and Child by Antoniazzo Romano A1933
Santa Claus in Chimney A1934
Santa Checking List — A1935 
Santa with Present — A1936 
Santa at Fireplace — A1937 
Santa and Sleigh — A1938 

1991, Oct. 17   Litho. & Engr.   Perf. 11

2578	A1933	(29c) multicolored	.50	.15
a.		Booklet pane of 10	5.75	3.25
b.		As "a," single, red & black (engr.) omitted	3,500.	

Photo.

2579	A1934	(29c) multicolored	.50	.15
a.		Horiz. pair, imperf. vert.	400.00	
b.		Vert. pair, imperf. horiz.	625.00	

Booklet Stamps
Size: 25x18½mm

Perf. 11 on 2 or 3 Sides

2580	A1934	(29c) Type I	1.75	.15
2581	A1934	(29c) Type II	1.75	.15
a.		Pair, #2580, 2581	3.50	.25
b.		Bklt. pane, 2 each #2580, 2581	7.50	1.25
2582	A1935	(29c) multicolored	.50	.15
a.		Booklet pane of 4	2.00	1.25
2583	A1936	(29c) multicolored	.50	.15
a.		Booklet pane of 4	2.00	1.25
2584	A1937	(29c) multicolored	.50	.15
a.		Booklet pane of 4	2.00	1.25
2585	A1938	(29c) multicolored	.50	.15
a.		Booklet pane of 4	2.00	1.25
		Nos. 2578-2585 (8)	6.50	1.20

The extreme left brick in top row of chimney is missing from Type II, No. 2581.

A1939
A1942 
A1944 

James K. Polk (1795-1849)
1995, Nov. 2   Engr.   Perf. 11.2
2587 A1939 32c red brown   .60 .15

Surrender of Gen. John Burgoyne
1994, May 5   Engr.   Perf. 11.5
2590 A1942 $1 blue   1.90 .50

Washington and Jackson
1994, Aug. 19   Engr.   Perf. 11.5
2592 A1944 $5 slate green   8.00 2.50

Pledge of Allegiance — A1946
Eagle and Shield — A1947 
A1950 
Statue of Liberty — A1951 

Perf. 10 on 2 or 3 sides
1992-93   Photo.
Booklet Stamps

2593	A1946	29c black & multi	.50	.15
a.		Booklet pane of 10	5.25	4.25
b.		Perf. 11x10 on 2 or 3 sides	.50	.15
c.		As "b," booklet pane of 10	5.50	4.25

Perf. 11x10 on 2 or 3 Sides

2594	A1946	29c red & multi	.50	.15
a.		Booklet pane of 10	5.25	4.25
b.		Imperf., pair	900.00	

Denomination is red on #2594 and black on #2593.
Issue dates: #2593, Sept. 8. #2594, 1993.

1992-94   Litho. & Engr.   Die Cut
Self-Adhesive

2595	A1947	29c brown & multi	.50	.25
a.		Bklt. pane of 17 + label	13.00	
b.		Pair, no die cutting	250.00	
c.		Brown (engr.) omitted	500.00	
d.		As "a," no die cutting	2,000.	

Photo.

2596	A1947	29c green & multi	.50	.25
a.		Bklt. pane of 17 + label	12.00	
2597	A1947	29c red & multi	.50	.25
a.		Bklt. pane of 17 + label	10.00	
2598	A1950	29c red, cream & blue	.50	.15
a.		Booklet pane of 18	10.00	
2599	A1951	29c multicolored	.50	.15
a.		Booklet pane of 18	10.00	

Plate No. and inscription reads down on No. 2595a and up on Nos. 2596a-2597a. Design is sharper and more finely detailed on Nos. 2595, 2597.

Issued unfolded in panes of 17 + label; peelable paper backing is booklet cover. Sold for $5.
Issue dates: No. 2598, Feb. 4, 1994; No. 2599, June 24, 1994; others. Sept. 25, 1992.
See Nos. 3122, 3122E.

Bulk Rate A1956 
A1957 
A1959 
A1960

Flag Over White House — A1961

Perf. 10 Vert.
1991-93   Photo.   Untagged
Coil Stamps

2602	A1956	(10c) multicolored	.20	.15
a.		Imperf., pair	—	
2603	A1957	(10c) orange yel & multi	.20	.20
a.		Imperf., pair	30.00	
b.		Tagged	2.00	
2604	A1957	(10c) gold & multi	.20	.20
2605	A1959	23c multi (Bureau precancel in blue)	.40	.40
2606	A1960	23c multi (Bureau Precanceled)	.40	.40
2607	A1960	23c multi (Bureau precanceled)	.40	.40
c.		Imperf., pair	125.00	
2608	A1960	23c vio blue, red & blk (Bureau Precanceled)	.40	.40
		Imperf., pair		

"23" is 7mm long on No. 2607. "First Class" is 8½mm long on No. 2608.

Engr.

2609	A1961	29c blue & red	.50	.15
a.		Imperf., pair	20.00	
b.		Pair, imperf between	100.00	
		Nos. 2602-2609 (8)	2.70	2.30

Issue dates: #2602, Dec. 13. #2603-2604, May 29, 1993. #2605, Sept. 27. #2606, July 21, 1992. #2607, Oct. 9, 1992. #2608, May 14, 1993. 29c, Apr. 23, 1992.
See Nos. 2907, 3270-3271.

Winter Olympics

Hockey A1963
Figure Skating A1964 
Speed Skating A1965 
Skiing A1966 
Bobsledding A1967 

1992, Jan. 11   Photo.   Perf. 11

2611	A1963	29c multicolored	.50	.15
2612	A1964	29c multicolored	.50	.15
2613	A1965	29c multicolored	.50	.15
2614	A1966	29c multicolored	.50	.15
2615	A1967	29c multicolored	.50	.15
a.		Strip of 5, #2611-2615	2.75	2.25

A1968
A1969 

World Columbian Stamp Expo
1992, Jan. 24   Litho. & Engr.
2616 A1968 29c Detail from #129   .50 .15

Black Heritage
1992, Jan. 31   Litho. & Engr.   Perf. 11
2617 A1969 29c multicolored   .50 .15

W.E.B. Du Bois (1868-1963), writer and civil rights leader.

Love

A1970

1992, Feb. 6   Photo.   Perf. 11
2618 A1970 29c multicolored   .50 .15
    a.   Horiz. pair, imperf vert.   900.00

Olympic Baseball

A1971

1992, Apr. 3   Photo.   Perf. 11
2619 A1971 29c multicolored   .50 .15

UNITED STATES

Voyages of Columbus

Seeking Queen Isabella's Support — A1972

Crossing the Atlantic — A1973

Approaching Land — A1974

Coming Ashore — A1975

1992, Apr. 24 Litho. & Engr. Perf. 11
2620	A1972	29c multicolored	.50	.15
2621	A1973	29c multicolored	.50	.15
2622	A1974	29c multicolored	.50	.15
2623	A1975	29c multicolored	.50	.15
a.		Block of 4, #2620-2623	2.00	1.90

See Italy Nos. 1877-1880.

Voyages of Columbus
Souvenir Sheets

A1976

A1977

A1978

A1979

A1980

A1981

Illustrations reduced.
Margins on Nos. 2624-2628 are lithographed. Nos. 2624a-2628c, 2629 are similar in design to Nos. 230-245 but are dated 1492-1992.

Litho. & Engr.
1992, May 22 Perf. 10½

2624	A1976	Sheet of 3	1.75	—
a.		A71 1c deep blue	.15	.15
b.		A74 4c ultramarine	.15	.15
c.		A82 $1 salmon	1.65	1.00
d.		As No. 2624, imperf		
2625	A1977	Sheet of 3	6.75	—
a.		A72 2c brown violet	.15	.15
b.		A73 3c green	.15	.15
c.		A85 $4 crimson lake	6.50	4.00
d.		As No. 2625, imperf		
2626	A1978	Sheet of 3	1.40	—
a.		A75 5c chocolate	.15	.15
b.		A80 30c orange brown	.50	.30
c.		A81 50c slate blue	.80	.50
d.		As No. 2626, imperf		
2627	A1979	Sheet of 3	5.25	—
a.		A76 6c purple	.15	.15
b.		A77 8c magenta	.15	.15
c.		A84 $3 yellow green	4.75	3.00
d.		As No. 2627, imperf		
2628	A1980	Sheet of 3	3.75	—
a.		A78 10c black brown	.15	.15
b.		A79 15c dark green	.25	.15
c.		A83 $2 brown red	3.25	2.00
d.		As No. 2628, imperf		
2629	A1981	$5 Sheet of 1 Type A86	8.50	—
a.		Imperf		
		Nos. 2624-2629 (6)	27.40	

See Italy Nos. 1883-1888, Portugal Nos. 1918-1923 and Spain Nos. 2677-2682.

New York Stock Exchange Bicentennial

A1982

1992, May 17 Litho. & Engr. Perf. 11
2630	A1982	29c green, red & black	.50	.15

Space Accomplishments

Cosmonaut, US Space Shuttle — A1983

Astronaut, Russian Space Station — A1984

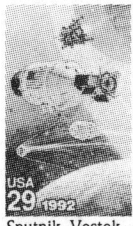

Sputnik, Vostok, Apollo Command & Lunar Modules — A1985

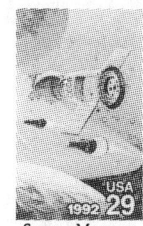

Soyuz, Mercury and Gemini Spacecraft — A1986

1992, May 29 Photo. Perf. 11
2631	A1983	29c multicolored	.50	.15
2632	A1984	29c multicolored	.50	.15
2633	A1985	29c multicolored	.50	.15
2634	A1986	29c multicolored	.50	.15
a.		Block of 4, #2631-2634	2.00	1.75

See Russia Nos. 6080-6083.

Alaska Highway, 50th Anniversary

A1987

1992, May 30 Litho. & Engr. Perf. 11
2635	A1987	29c multicolored	.50	.15
a.		Black (engr.) omitted	500.00	

Most known examples of No. 2635a have poor to fine centering. It is valued in the grade of fine. Very fine examples sell for much more.

Kentucky Statehood Bicentennial

A1988

1992, June 1 Photo. Perf. 11
2636	A1988	29c multicolored	.50	.15

Summer Olympics

Soccer — A1989

Gymnastics — A1990

Volleyball — A1991

Boxing — A1992

Swimming — A1993

1992, June 11 Photo. Perf. 11
2637	A1989	29c multicolored	.50	.15
2638	A1990	29c multicolored	.50	.15
2639	A1991	29c multicolored	.50	.15
2640	A1992	29c multicolored	.50	.15
2641	A1993	29c multicolored	.50	.15
a.		Strip of 5, #2637-2641	2.50	2.25

Hummingbirds

Ruby-throated — A1994

Broad-billed — A1995

Costa's — A1996

Rufous — A1997

Calliope — A1998

Perf. 11 Vert. on 1 or 2 sides
1992, June 15 Photo.
Booklet Stamps
2642	A1994	29c multicolored	.50	.15
2643	A1995	29c multicolored	.50	.15
2644	A1996	29c multicolored	.50	.15
2645	A1997	29c multicolored	.50	.15
2646	A1998	29c multicolored	.50	.15
a.		Bklt. pane of 5, #2642-2646	2.75	2.25

Wildflowers

A1999-A2048

UNITED STATES

1992, July 24 Litho. *Perf. 11*
2647	A1999	29c Indian paintbrush	.50	.15
2648	A2000	29c Fragrant water lily	.50	.15
2649	A2001	29c Meadow beauty	.50	.15
2650	A2002	29c Jack-in-the-pulpit	.50	.15
2651	A2003	29c California poppy	.50	.15
2652	A2004	29c Large-flowered trillium	.50	.15
2653	A2005	29c Tickseed	.50	.15
2654	A2006	29c Shooting star	.50	.15
2655	A2007	29c Stream violet	.50	.15
2656	A2008	29c Bluets	.50	.15
2657	A2009	29c Herb Robert	.50	.15
2658	A2010	29c Marsh marigold	.50	.15
2659	A2011	29c Sweet white violet	.50	.15
2660	A2012	29c Claret cup cactus	.50	.15
2661	A2013	29c White mountain avens	.50	.15
2662	A2014	29c Sessile bellwort	.50	.15
2663	A2015	29c Blue flag	.50	.15
2664	A2016	29c Harlequin lupine	.50	.15
2665	A2017	29c Twinflower	.50	.15
2666	A2018	29c Common sunflower	.50	.15
2667	A2019	29c Sego lily	.50	.15
2668	A2020	29c Virginia bluebells	.50	.15
2669	A2021	29c Ohi'a lehua	.50	.15
2670	A2022	29c Rosebud orchid	.50	.15
2671	A2023	29c Showy evening primrose	.50	.15
2672	A2024	29c Fringed gentian	.50	.15
2673	A2025	29c Yellow lady's slipper	.50	.15
2674	A2026	29c Passionflower	.50	.15
2675	A2027	29c Bunchberry	.50	.15
2676	A2028	29c Pasqueflower	.50	.15
2677	A2029	29c Round-lobed hepatica	.50	.15
2678	A2030	29c Wild columbine	.50	.15
2679	A2031	29c Fireweed	.50	.15
2680	A2032	29c Indian pond lily	.50	.15
2681	A2033	29c Turk's cap lily	.50	.15
2682	A2034	29c Dutchman's breeches	.50	.15
2683	A2035	29c Trumpet honeysuckle	.50	.15
2684	A2036	29c Jacob's ladder	.50	.15
2685	A2037	29c Plains prickly pear	.50	.15
2686	A2038	29c Moss campion	.50	.15
2687	A2039	29c Bearberry	.50	.15
2688	A2040	29c Mexican hat	.50	.15
2689	A2041	29c Harebell	.50	.15
2690	A2042	29c Desert five spot	.50	.15
2691	A2043	29c Smooth Solomon's seal	.50	.15
2692	A2044	29c Red maids	.50	.15
2693	A2045	29c Yellow skunk cabbage	.50	.15
2694	A2046	29c Rue anemone	.50	.15
2695	A2047	29c Standing cypress	.50	.15
2696	A2048	29c Wild flax	.50	.15
a.		Pane of 50, #2647-2696	25.00	—

World War II

A2049

Designs and events of 1942: a, B-25's take off to raid Tokyo, Apr. 18. b, Ration coupons (food and other commodities rationed). c, Divebomber and deck crewman (US wins Battle of the Coral Sea, May). d, Prisoners of war (Corregidor falls to Japanese, May 6). e, Dutch Harbor buildings on fire (Japan invades Aleutian Islands, June). f, Headphones, coded message (Allies decipher secret enemy codes). g, Yorktown lost, US wins at Midway. h, Woman with drill (millions of women join war effort). i, Marines land on Guadalcanal, Aug. 7. j, Tank in desert (Allies land in North Africa, Nov.). Central label is the size of 15 stamps and shows world map, extent of axis control.
Illustration reduced.

Litho. & Engr.
1992, Aug. 17 *Perf. 11*
2697		A2049 Block of 10	5.25	4.50
a.-j.		29c any single	.50	.30
k.		Red (litho.) omitted	10,000.	

Dorothy Parker — A2050

A2051

Literary Arts Series
1992, Aug. 22 Photo. *Perf. 11*
2698	A2050	29c multicolored	.50	.15

1992, Aug. 31 Photo. *Perf. 11*
2699	A2051	29c multicolored	.50	.15

Dr. Theodore von Karman (1881-1963), rocket scientist.

Minerals

Azurite — A2052
Copper — A2053 
Variscite — A2054 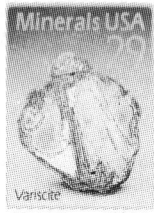
Wulfenite — A2055 

Litho. & Engr.
1992, Sept. 17 *Perf. 11*
2700	A2052	29c multicolored	.50	.15
2701	A2053	29c multicolored	.50	.15
2702	A2054	29c multicolored	.50	.15
2703	A2055	29c multicolored	.50	.15
a.		Block or strip of 4, #2700-2703	2.00	1.75
b.		As "a," silver (litho.) omitted	8,500.	
c.		As "a," red (litho.) omitted		

Juan Rodriguez Cabrillo

Cabrillo (d. 1543), Ship, Map of San Diego Bay Area — A2056

Litho. & Engr.
1992, Sept. 28 *Perf. 11*
2704	A2056	29c multicolored	.50	.15

Wild Animals

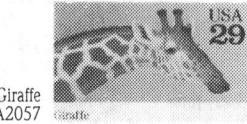

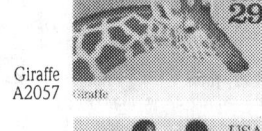

Giraffe A2057
Giant Panda A2058 
Flamingo A2059 
King Penguins A2060 
White Bengal Tiger A2061 

Perf. 11 Horiz. on 1 or 2 sides
1992, Oct. 1 Photo.
Booklet Stamps
2705	A2057	29c multicolored	.50	.15
2706	A2058	29c multicolored	.50	.15
2707	A2059	29c multicolored	.50	.15
2708	A2060	29c multicolored	.50	.15
2709	A2061	29c multicolored	.50	.15
a.		Booklet pane of 5, #2705-2709	2.50	2.00
b.		As "a," imperforate	3,000.	

Christmas

Madonna and Child, by Giovanni Bellini — A2062

A2063   A2064
A2065   A2066

1992 Litho. & Engr. *Perf. 11.2*
2710	A2062	29c multicolored	.50	.15
a.		Booklet pane of 10	5.25	3.50

Litho.
Perf. 11½x11
2711	A2063	29c multicolored	.50	.15
2712	A2064	29c multicolored	.50	.15
2713	A2065	29c multicolored	.50	.15
2714	A2066	29c multicolored	.50	.15
a.		Block of 4, #2711-2714	2.00	1.10

Booklet Stamps
Photo.
Perf. 11 on 2 or 3 Sides
2715	A2063	29c multicolored	.50	.15
2716	A2064	29c multicolored	.50	.15
2717	A2065	29c multicolored	.50	.15
2718	A2066	29c multicolored	.50	.15
a.		Bklt. pane of 4, #2715-2718	2.25	1.25
b.		As "a," imperf horiz.	—	
c.		As "a," imperf	—	

Self-Adhesive
Die Cut
2719	A2064	29c multicolored	.60	.15
a.		Booklet pane of 18	11.00	

Issued: #2710-2718, Oct. 22; #2719, Oct. 28. "Greetings" is 27mm long on Nos. 2711-2714, 25mm long on Nos. 2715-2718 and 21½mm long on No. 2719. Nos. 2715-2719 differ in color from Nos. 2711-2714.

Chinese New Year

Year of the Rooster A2067

1992, Dec. 30 Litho. & Engr. *Perf. 11*
2720	A2067	29c multicolored	.50	.15

American Music Series

Elvis Presley A2068
Oklahoma! A2069 
Hank Williams A2070 
Elvis Presley A2071 
Bill Haley A2072 
Clyde McPhatter A2073 
Ritchie Valens A2074 
Otis Redding A2075 
Buddy Holly A2076 
Dinah Washington A2077 

1993, Jan. 8 Photo. *Perf. 11*
2721	A2068	29c multicolored	.50	.15

1993, Mar. 30 Photo. *Perf. 10*
2722	A2069	29c multicolored	.50	.15

1993
2723	A2070	29c multicolored	.50	.15
a.		Perf. 11.2x11.4	20.00	3.00
2724	A2071	29c multicolored	.50	.15
2725	A2072	29c multicolored	.50	.15
2726	A2073	29c multicolored	.50	.15
2727	A2074	29c multicolored	.50	.15
2728	A2075	29c multicolored	.50	.15
2729	A2076	29c multicolored	.50	.15

UNITED STATES

2730	A2077	29c multicolored	.50	.15
a.		Vertical strip of 7, #2724-2730	3.50	—

Booklet Stamps
Perf. 11 Horiz.

2731	A2071	29c multicolored	.50	.15
2732	A2072	29c multicolored	.50	.15
2733	A2073	29c multicolored	.50	.15
2734	A2074	29c multicolored	.50	.15
2735	A2075	29c multicolored	.50	.15
2736	A2076	29c multicolored	.50	.15
2737	A2077	29c multicolored	.50	.15
a.		Booklet pane, 2 #2731, 1 each #2732-2737	4.25	2.25
b.		Booklet pane of 4, #2731, 2735-2737 + tab	2.25	1.50

Issued: No. 2723, June 9; others, June 16.
See Nos. 2769, 2771, 2775 and designs A2112-A2117.

Space Fantasy

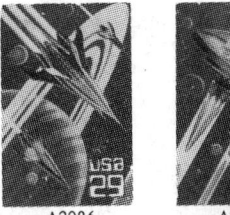

A2086
A2087 
A2088 
A2089 
A2090 

Perf. 11 Vert. on 1 or 2 Sides
1993, Jan. 25 — Photo.

Booklet Stamps

2741	A2086	29c multicolored	.50	.15
2742	A2087	29c multicolored	.50	.15
2743	A2088	29c multicolored	.50	.15
2744	A2089	29c multicolored	.50	.15
2745	A2090	29c multicolored	.50	.15
a.		Bklt. pane of 5, #2741-2745	2.50	2.00

Black Heritage

Percy Lavon Julian (1899-1975), Chemist — A2091

1993, Jan. 29 — Litho. & Engr. — Perf. 11

| 2746 | A2091 | 29c multicolored | .50 | .15 |

Oregon Trail

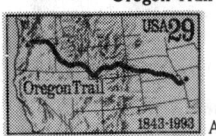

A2092

1993, Feb. 12 — Litho. & Engr. — Perf. 11

| 2747 | A2092 | 29c multicolored | .50 | .15 |

World University Games

A2093 World University Games Buffalo '93

1993, Feb. 25 — Photo. — Perf. 11

| 2748 | A2093 | 29c multicolored | .50 | .15 |

Grace Kelly (1929-1982)

Actress, Princess of Monaco — A2094

1993, Mar. 24 — Engr. — Perf. 11

| 2749 | A2094 | 29c blue | .50 | .15 |

See Monaco No. 1851.

Circus

Clown A2095
Ringmaster A2096 
Trapeze Artist A2097
Elephant A2098

Illustrations reduced.

1993, Apr. 6 — Litho. — Perf. 11

2750	A2095	29c multicolored	.50	.15
2751	A2096	29c multicolored	.50	.15
2752	A2097	29c multicolored	.50	.15
2753	A2098	29c multicolored	.50	.15
a.		Block of 4, #2750-2753	2.00	1.75

Cherokee Strip Land Run, Centennial

A2099

1993, Apr. 17 — Litho. & Engr. — Perf. 11

| 2754 | A2099 | 29c multicolored | .50 | .15 |

Dean Acheson (1893-1971)

Secretary of State — A2100

1993, Apr. 21 — Engr. — Perf. 11

| 2755 | A2100 | 29c greenish gray | .50 | .15 |

Sporting Horses

Steeplechase A2101
Thoroughbred Racing A2102 
Harness Racing A2103 
Polo A2104 

Perf. 11x11½
1993, May 1 — Litho. & Engr.

2756	A2101	29c multicolored	.50	.15
2757	A2102	29c multicolored	.50	.15
2758	A2103	29c multicolored	.50	.15
2759	A2104	29c multicolored	.50	.15
a.		Block of 4, #2756-2759	2.00	1.75
b.		As "a," black (engr.) omitted	1,750.	

Garden Flowers

Hyacinth A2105
Daffodil A2106
Tulip — A2107  
Iris — A2108 
Lilac — A2109 

1993, May 15 — Litho. & Engr. — Perf. 11 Vert.

2760	A2105	29c multicolored	.50	.15
2761	A2106	29c multicolored	.50	.15
2762	A2107	29c multicolored	.50	.15
2763	A2108	29c multicolored	.50	.15
2764	A2109	29c multicolored	.50	.15
a.		Booklet pane of 5, #2760-2764	2.50	2.00
b.		As "a," black (engr.) omitted	375.00	
c.		As "a," imperf.	3,000.	

World War II

A2110

Designs and events of 1943: a, Destroyers (Allied forces battle German U-boats). b, Military medics treat the wounded. c, Amphibious landing craft on beach (Sicily attacked by Allied forces, July). d, B-24s hit Ploesti refineries, August. e, V-mail delivers letters from home. f, PT boat (Italy invaded by Allies, Sept.). g, Nos. WS7, WS8, savings bonds (Bonds and stamps help war effort). h, "Willie and Joe" keep spirits high. i, Banner in window (Gold Stars mark World War II losses). j, Marines assault Tarawa, Nov.

Central label is the size of 15 stamps and shows world map with extent of Axis control and Allied operations.
Illustration reduced.

1993, May 31 — Litho. & Engr. — Perf. 11

| 2765 | A2110 | Block of 10 + label | 5.25 | 4.50 |
| a.-j. | | 29c any single | .50 | .30 |

Joe Louis (1914-1981)

A2111

1993, June 22 — Litho. & Engr. — Perf. 11

| 2766 | A2111 | 29c multicolored | .50 | .15 |

American Music Series
Oklahoma! Type and

Show Boat — A2112
Porgy & Bess — A2113 
My Fair Lady — A2114 

Perf. 11 Horiz. on 1 or 2 Sides
1993, July 14 — Photo.

Booklet Stamps

2767	A2112	29c multicolored	.50	.15
2768	A2113	29c multicolored	.50	.15
2769	A2069	29c multicolored	.50	.15
2770	A2114	29c multicolored	.50	.15
a.		Booklet pane of 4, #2767-2770	2.50	2.00

No. 2769 has smaller design size, brighter colors and shorter inscription than No. 2722, as well as a frameline around the design and other subtle design differences.

UNITED STATES

Hank Williams Type and
Patsy Cline 
A2115

The Carter Family
A2116

Bob Wills
A2117

1993, Sept. 25   Photo.   Perf. 10

2771	A2070	29c multicolored	.50	.15
2772	A2115	29c multicolored	.50	.15
2773	A2116	29c multicolored	.50	.15
2774	A2117	29c multicolored	.50	.15
a.		Block or horiz. strip of 4, #2771-2774	2.00	1.75

Booklet Stamps
Perf. 11 Horiz.
With Black Frameline

2775	A2070	29c multicolored	.50	.15
2776	A2116	29c multicolored	.50	.15
2777	A2115	29c multicolored	.50	.15
2778	A2117	29c multicolored	.50	.15
a.		Booklet pane of 4, #2775-2778	2.50	2.00
b.		As "a," imperf		

Inscription at left measures 27mm on No. 2771, 27½mm on No. 2723 and 22mm on No. 2775. No. 2723 shows only two tuning keys on guitar, while No. 2771 shows those two and parts of two others.

National Postal Museum

Independence Hall, Benjamin Franklin, Printing Press, Colonial Post Rider
A2118

Pony Express Rider, Civil War Soldier, Concord Stagecoach
A2119

JN-4H Biplane, Charles Lindbergh, Railway Mail Car, 1931 Model A Ford Mail Truck
A2120

California Gold Rush Miner's Letter, Nos. 39, 295, C3a, C13, Barcode and Circular Date Stamp
A2121

1993, July 30   Litho. & Engr.   Perf. 11

2779	A2118	29c multicolored	.50	.15
2780	A2119	29c multicolored	.50	.15
2781	A2120	29c multicolored	.50	.15
2782	A2121	29c multicolored	.50	.15
a.		Block or strip of 4, #2779-2782	2.00	1.75
b.		As "a," engr. maroon (USA/29) & black ("My Dear...") omitted	—	
c.		As "a," imperf	3,500.	

American Sign Language

A2122    A2123

Designs:

1993, Sept. 20   Photo.   Perf. 11½

2783	A2122	29c multicolored	.50	.15
2784	A2123	29c multicolored	.50	.15
a.		Pair, #2783-2784	1.00	.65

Classic Books

A2124    A2125

A2126    A2127

Designs: No. 2785, Rebecca of Sunnybrook Farm, by Kate Douglas Wiggin. No. 2786, Little House on the Prairie, by Laura Ingalls Wilder. No. 2787, The Adventures of Huckleberry Finn, by Mark Twain. No. 2788, Little Women, by Louisa May Alcott.

1993, Oct. 23   Litho. & Engr.   Perf. 11

2785	A2124	29c multicolored	.50	.15
2786	A2125	29c multicolored	.50	.15
2787	A2126	29c multicolored	.50	.15
2788	A2127	29c multicolored	.50	.15
a.		Block or horiz. strip of 4, #2785-2788	2.00	1.75
b.		As "a," imperf	3,000.	

Christmas

Madonna and Child in a Landscape, by Giovanni Battista Cima — A2128

Jack-in-the-Box
A2129

Red-Nosed Reindeer
A2130

Snowman
A2131

Toy Soldier Blowing Horn
A2132

1993, Oct. 21   Litho. & Engr.   Perf. 11

| 2789 | A2128 | 29c multicolored | .50 | .15 |

Booklet Stamp
Size: 18x25mm
Perf. 11½x11 on 2 or 3 Sides

2790	A2128	29c multicolored	.50	.15
a.		Booklet pane of 4	2.25	1.75
b.		Imperf pair	—	
c.		As "a," imperf		

No. 2790 has darker colors and smaller inscriptions than No. 2789.

1993   Photo.   Perf. 11½

2791	A2129	29c multicolored	.50	.15
2792	A2130	29c multicolored	.50	.15
2793	A2131	29c multicolored	.50	.15
2794	A2132	29c multicolored	.50	.15
a.		Block or strip of 4, #2791-2794	2.00	1.75

Booklet Stamps
Size: 18x21mm
Perf. 11x10 on 2 or 3 Sides

2795	A2132	29c multicolored	.50	.15
2796	A2131	29c multicolored	.50	.15
2797	A2130	29c multicolored	.50	.15
2798	A2129	29c multicolored	.50	.15
a.		Booklet pane, 3 each #2795-2796, 2 each #2797-2798	5.00	4.00
b.		Booklet pane, 3 each #2797-2798, 2 each #2795-2796	5.00	4.00

Self-Adhesive
Size: 19½x26½mm
Die Cut

2799	A2131	29c multicolored	.50	.15
2800	A2132	29c multicolored	.50	.15
2801	A2129	29c multicolored	.50	.15
2802	A2130	29c multicolored	.50	.15
a.		Bklt. pane, 3 each #2799-2802	7.00	

Size: 17x20mm

| 2803 | A2131 | 29c multicolored | .50 | .15 |
| a. | | Booklet pane of 18 | 10.00 | |

Issue dates: Nos. 2791-2798, Oct. 21; Nos. 2799-2803, Oct. 28.
Snowman on Nos. 2793, 2799 has three buttons and seven snowflakes beneath nose (placement differs on both stamps). No. 2796 has two buttons and five snowflakes beneath nose. No. 2803 has two orange buttons and four snowflakes beneath nose.

Mariana Islands

A2133

1993, Nov. 4   Litho. & Engr.   Perf. 11

| 2804 | A2133 | 29c multicolored | .50 | .15 |

Columbus' Landing in Puerto Rico, 500th Anniv.

A2134

1993, Nov. 19   Photo.   Perf. 11.2

| 2805 | A2134 | 29c multicolored | .50 | .15 |

AIDS Awareness

A2135

1993, Dec. 1   Photo.   Perf. 11.2

2806	A2135	29c black & red	.50	.15
a.		Perf. 11 vert. on 1 or 2 sides, from bklt. pane	.50	.15
b.		As "a," booklet pane of 5	2.50	2.00

Winter Olympics

Slalom — A2136   Luge — A2137

Ice Dancing
A2138

Cross-Country Skiing
A2139

Ice Hockey — A2140

1994, Jan. 6   Litho.   Perf. 11.2

2807	A2136	29c multicolored	.50	.15
2808	A2137	29c multicolored	.50	.15
2809	A2138	29c multicolored	.50	.15
2810	A2139	29c multicolored	.50	.15
2811	A2140	29c multicolored	.50	.15
a.		Strip of 5, #2807-2811	2.50	2.25

Edward R. Murrow, Journalist (1908-65)

A2141

1994, Jan. 21   Engr.   Perf. 11.2

| 2812 | A2141 | 29c brown | .50 | .15 |

Love

A2142    A2143

A2144

1994   Litho. & Engr.   Die Cut
Self-Adhesive (No. 2813)

| 2813 | A2142 | 29c multicolored | .50 | .15 |
| a. | | Booklet pane of 18 | 11.00 | |

Photo.
Perf. 10.9x11.1

| 2814 | A2143 | 29c multicolored | .50 | .15 |
| a. | | Booklet pane of 10 | 5.50 | 3.50 |

UNITED STATES

Litho. & Engr.
Perf. 11.1
2814C A2143 29c multicolored .50 .15
Photo. & Engr.
Perf. 11.2
2815 A2144 52c multicolored 1.00 .20

Size of No. 2814C is 20x28mm. No. 2814 is 18x24½mm.
Issued: No. 2813, Jan. 27. Nos. 2814-2815, Feb. 14. No. 2814C, June 24.
No. 2814 was issued in booklets only.

Black Heritage

Dr. Allison Davis (1902-83), Social Anthropologist, Educator — A2145

1994, Feb. 1   Engr.   Perf. 11.2
2816 A2145 29c red brown & brown .50 .15

Chinese New Year

Year of the Dog — A2146

1994, Feb. 5   Photo.   Perf. 11.2
2817 A2146 29c multicolored .50 .15

Buffalo Soldiers

A2147

Perf. 11.5x11.2
1994, Apr. 22   Litho. & Engr.
2818 A2147 29c multicolored .50 .15

Silent Screen Stars

Rudolph Valentino (1895-1926) A2148

Clara Bow (1905-65) A2149

Charlie Chaplin (1889-1977) A2150

Lon Chaney (1883-1930) A2151

John Gilbert (1895-1936) A2152

Zasu Pitts (1898-1963) A2153

Harold Lloyd (1894-1971) A2154

Keystone Cops A2155

Theda Bara (1885-1955) A2156

Buster Keaton (1895-1966) A2157

Litho. & Engr.
1994, Apr. 27   *Perf. 11.2*
2819 A2148 29c red, blk & brt vio .50 .15
2820 A2149 29c red, blk & brt vio .50 .15
2821 A2150 29c red, blk & brt vio .50 .15
2822 A2151 29c red, blk & brt vio .50 .15
2823 A2152 29c red, blk & brt vio .50 .15
2824 A2153 29c red, blk & brt vio .50 .15
2825 A2154 29c red, blk & brt vio .50 .15
2826 A2155 29c red, blk & brt vio .50 .15
2827 A2156 29c red, blk & brt vio .50 .15
2828 A2157 29c red, blk & brt vio .50 .15
  a. Block of 10, #2819-2828 5.00 4.00
  b. As "a," black (litho.) omitted
  c. As "a," black, red & brt vio (litho.) omitted —

Garden Flowers

Lily — A2158

Zinnia — A2159

Gladiola A2160

Marigold A2161

Rose — A2162

Perf. 10.9 Vert.
1994, Apr. 28   Litho. & Engr.
Booklet Stamps
2829 A2158 29c multicolored .50 .15
2830 A2159 29c multicolored .50 .15
2831 A2160 29c multicolored .50 .15
2832 A2161 29c multicolored .50 .15
2833 A2162 29c multicolored .50 .15
  a. Booklet pane of 5, #2829-2833 2.50
  b. As "a," imperf 2,500.
  c. As "a," black (engr.) omitted 425.00

1994 World Cup Soccer Championships

A2163

A2164

A2165

Design: 40c, Soccer player, diff.

1994, May 26   Photo.   Perf. 11.1
2834 A2163 29c multicolored .50 .15
2835 A2163 40c multicolored .80 .20
2836 A2164 50c multicolored 1.00 .20
  Nos. 2834-2836 (3) 2.30 .55

Souvenir Sheet
2837 A2165 Sheet of 3, #a.-c. 2.50 2.00

Nos. 2834-2836 are printed on phosphor-coated paper, while Nos. 2837a (29c), 2837b (40c), 2837c (50c) are block tagged. No. 2837c has a portion of the yellow map in the LR corner.

World War II

A2166

Designs and events of 1944: a, Allied forces retake New Guinea. b, P-51s escort B-17s on bombing raids. c, Troops running from landing craft (Allies in Normandy, D-Day, June 6). d, Airborne units spearhead attacks. e, Officer at periscope (Submarines shorten war in Pacific). f, Parade (Allies free Rome, June 4; Paris, Aug. 25). g, Soldier firing flamethrower (US troops clear Saipan bunkers). h, Red Ball Express speeds vital supplies. i, Battleship firing main battery (Battle for Leyte Gulf, Oct. 23-26). j, Soldiers in snow (Bastogne and Battle of the Bulge, Dec.).
Central label is size of 15 stamps and shows world map with extent of Axis control and Allied operations.
Illustration reduced.

Litho. & Engr.
1994, June 6   *Perf. 10.9*
2838 A2166 Block of 10 + label 5.25 4.50
  a.-j. 29c any single .50 .30

Norman Rockwell

A2167

A2168

Perf. 10.9x11.1
1994, July 1   Litho. & Engr.
2839 A2167 29c multicolored .50 .15

Souvenir Sheet
Litho.
2840 A2168 Sheet of 4 4.00 2.75
  a. 50c Freedom from Want 1.00 .65
  b. 50c Freedom from Fear 1.00 .65
  c. 50c Freedom of Speech 1.00 .65
  d. 50c Freedom of Worship 1.00 .65

Moon Landing, 25th Anniv.

A2169

A2170

1994, July 20   Litho.   Perf. 11.2x11.1
Miniature Sheet
2841 A2169 Sheet of 12 7.50 —
  a. 29c Single stamp .60 .60

Litho. & Engr.
Perf. 10.7x11.1
2842 A2170 $9.95 multicolored 17.50 7.50

Locomotives

Hudson's General A2171

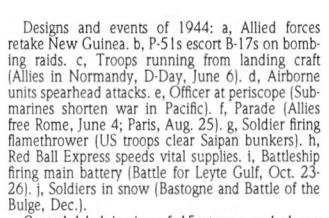

McQueen's Jupiter A2172

Eddy's No. 242 A2173

Ely's No. 10 A2174

UNITED STATES

Buchanan's
No. 999
A2175

1994, July 28   Photo.   Perf. 11 Horiz.
Booklet Stamps
2843	A2171	29c multicolored	.50	.15
2844	A2172	29c multicolored	.50	.15
2845	A2173	29c multicolored	.50	.15
2846	A2174	29c multicolored	.50	.15
2847	A2175	29c multicolored	.50	.15
a.		Booklet pane of 5, #2843-2847	2.50	2.00
b.		As "a," imperf		

George Meany, Labor Leader (1894-1980)

A2176 Labor Leader

1994, Aug. 16   Engr.   Perf. 11.1x11
| 2848 | A2176 | 29c blue | .50 | .15 |

American Music Series

Al Jolson
(1886-1950)
A2177

Bing Crosby
(1904-77)
A2178

Ethel Waters
(1896-1977)
A2179

Nat "King" Cole (1919-65)
A2180

Ethel Merman
(1908-84)
A2181

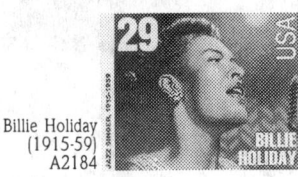

Bessie Smith
(1894-1937)
A2182

Muddy Waters
(1915-83)
A2183

Billie Holiday
(1915-59)
A2184

Robert Johnson
(1911-38)
A2185

Jimmy Rushing
(1902-72)
A2186

"Ma" Rainey
(1886-1939)
A2187

Mildred Bailey
(1907-51)
A2188

Howlin' Wolf
(1910-76)
A2189

1994   Photo.   Perf. 10.1x10.2
2849	A2177	29c multicolored	.50	.15
2850	A2178	29c multicolored	.50	.15
2851	A2179	29c multicolored	.50	.15
2852	A2180	29c multicolored	.50	.15
2853	A2181	29c multicolored	.50	.15
a.		Vert. strip of 5, #2849-2853	2.50	2.00

Perf. 11x10.8
Litho.
2854	A2182	29c multicolored	.50	.15
2855	A2183	29c multicolored	.50	.15
2856	A2184	29c multicolored	.50	.15
2857	A2185	29c multicolored	.50	.15
2858	A2186	29c multicolored	.50	.15
2859	A2187	29c multicolored	.50	.15
2860	A2188	29c multicolored	.50	.15
2861	A2189	29c multicolored	.50	.15
a.		Block of 9, #2854-2861 +1 additional stamp	4.50	3.50

Issued: Nos. 2849-2853, 9/1/94; Nos. 2854-2861, 9/17/94.

Literary Arts Series

James Thurber (1894-1961) — A2190

Litho. & Engr.
1994, Sept. 10   Perf. 11
| 2862 | A2190 | 29c multicolored | .50 | .15 |

Wonders Of The Sea

Diver, Motorboat
A2191

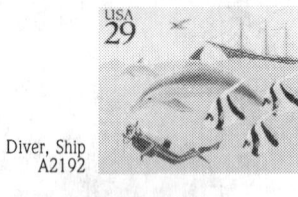

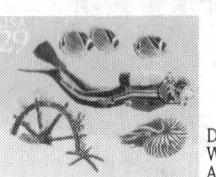

Diver, Ship
A2192

Diver, Ship's Wheel
A2193

Diver, Coral
A2194

1994, Oct. 3   Litho.   Perf. 11x10.9
2863	A2191	29c multicolored	.50	.15
2864	A2192	29c multicolored	.50	.15
2865	A2193	29c multicolored	.50	.15
2866	A2194	29c multicolored	.50	.15
a.		Block of 4, #2863-2866	2.00	1.50
b.		As "a," imperf	2,250.	

Cranes

Black-Necked
A2195

Whooping
A2196

Litho. & Engr.
1994, Oct. 9   Perf. 10.8x11
2867	A2195	29c multicolored	.50	.15
2868	A2196	29c multicolored	.50	.15
a.		Pair, #2867-2868	1.00	.65
b.		Black & magenta (engr.) omitted	—	

See People's Republic of China Nos. 2528-2529.

Legends Of The West
Miniature Pane

A2197

g. Bill Pickett (1870-1932) (Revised)

Designs: a, Home on the Range. b, Buffalo Bill Cody (1846-1917). c, Jim Bridger (1804-81). d, Annie Oakley (1860-1926). e, Native American Culture. f, Chief Joseph (c. 1840-1904). h, Bat Masterson (1853-1921). i, John C. Fremont (1813-90). j, Wyatt Earp (1848-1929). k, Nellie Cashman (c. 1849-1925). l, Charles Goodnight (1826-1929). m, Geronimo (1823-1909). n, Kit Carson (1809-68). o, Wild Bill Hickok (1837-76). p, Western Wildlife. q, Jim Beckwourth (c. 1798-1866). r, Bill Tilghman (1854-1924). s, Sacagawea (c. 1787-1812). t, Overland Mail.

1994, Oct. 18   Photo.   Perf. 10.1x10
2869	A2197	Pane of 20	12.00	—
a.-t.		29c any single	.60	.15
u.		As No. 2869, a.-e. imperf, f.-j. part perf.		

Legends Of The West (Recalled)
Miniature Pane

g. Bill Pickett (Recalled)

Nos. 2870b-2870d, 2870f-2870o, 2870q-2870s have a frameline around the vignette that is half the width of the frameline on similar stamps in No. 2869. Other design differences may exist.

1994   Photo.   Perf. 10.1x10
| 2870 | A2197 | 29c Pane of 20 | 175.00 | |

150,000 panes were made available through a drawing. Panes were delivered in an envelope. Value is for pane without envelope.

Christmas

Madonna and Child, by Elisabetta Sirani
A2200

Stocking
A2201

UNITED STATES

Santa Claus
A2202

Cardinal in Snow
A2203

Litho. & Engr.
1994, Oct. 20   *Perf. 11.1*
2871 A2200 29c multicolored   .50 .15
    a. Perf. 9.8x10.8, from bklt. pane   .50 .15
    b. As "a," booklet pane of 10   5.25 3.50
    c. As "a," imperf   —

Litho.
2872 A2201 29c multicolored   .50 .15
    a. Booklet pane of 20   10.50 3.00

Booklet Stamps
Photo.
Die Cut
Self-Adhesive
2873 A2202 29c multicolored   .50 .15
    a. Booklet pane of 12   6.25
2874 A2203 29c multicolored   .50 .15
    a. Booklet pane of 18   9.50

Bureau Of Engraving & Printing
Souvenir Sheet

A2204

1994, Nov. 3   Litho. & Engr.   *Perf. 11*
2875 A2204 Sheet of 4   15.00 —
    a. $2 Single stamp   3.00 1.25

Chinese New Year

Year of the Boar — A2205

1994, Dec. 30   Photo.   *Perf. 11.2x11.1*
2876 A2205 29c multicolored   .50 .15

A2206

Old Glory
A2207

Old Glory
USA G
For U.S. addresses only
A2208

Old Glory
USA G
For U.S. addresses only
A2208a

Old Glory
USA G
First-Class Presort
A2209

Old Glory
USA G
Nonprofit Presort
A2210

1994, Dec. 13   Litho.   *Perf. 11x10.8*
Untagged
2877 A2206 (3c) tan, bright blue & red   — .15
    a. Imperf., pair

Perf. 10.8x10.9
2878 A2206 (3c) tan, dark blue & red   .15 .15

Inscriptions on #2877 are in a thin typeface. Those on #2878 are in heavy, bold type.

Photo.
Perf. 11.2x11.1
Tagged
2879 A2207 (20c) black "G," yellow & multi   .40 .15

Perf. 11x10.9
2880 A2207 (20c) red "G," yellow & multi   .45 .15

Perf. 11.2x11.1
2881 A2208 (32c) black "G" & multi   .70 .15
    a. Booklet pane of 10   6.00 3.75

Perf. 11x10.9
2882 A2208 (32c) red "G" & multi   .60 .15

Distance on #2882 from bottom of red G to top of flag immediately above is 13 3/4mm. Illustration A2208a shows #2885 superimposed over #2882.

Booklet Stamps
Perf. 10x9.9 on 2 or 3 Sides
2883 A2208 (32c) black "G" & multi   .60 .15
    a. Booklet pane of 10   6.25 3.75

Perf. 10.9 on 2 or 3 Sides
2884 A2208 (32c) blue "G" & multi   .60 .15
    a. Booklet pane of 10   6.00 3.75
    b. As "a," imperf   —

Perf. 11x10.9 on 2 or 3 Sides
2885 A2208a (32c) red "G" & multi   .60 .15
    a. Booklet pane of 10   6.00 3.75
    b. Pair, imperf vert.

Distance on #2885 from bottom of red G to top of flag immediately above is 13 1/2mm. See note below #2882.

Old G
A2208b

Old G
A2208c

Self-Adhesive   *Die Cut*
2886 A2208b (32c) gray, blue, lt blue, red & blk   .60 .15
    a. Booklet pane of 18   11.00

No. 2886 is printed on pre-phosphored paper and has only a small number of blue shading dots in the white stripes immediately below the flag's blue field.

2887 A2208c (32c) black, blue & red   .60 .15
    a. Booklet pane of 18   11.00

No. 2887 has noticeable blue shading in the white stripes immediately below the blue field and has overall tagging.

COIL STAMPS
1994-95   *Perf. 9.8 Vert.*
2888 A2209 (25c) black "G"   .50 .15
2889 A2208 (32c) black "G"   .60 .15
    a. Imperf., pair
2890 A2208 (32c) blue "G"   .60 .15
2891 A2208 (32c) red "G"   .60 .15

Rouletted 9.8 Vert.
2892 A2208 (32c) red "G"   .60 .15

Perf. 9.8 Vert.
2893 A2210 (5c) green & multi   .15 .15

Nos. 2888-2892 issued 12/13/94. No. 2893 was only available through the Philatelic Fulfillment Center after its announcement 1/12/95.

Eagle and Shield Type of 1993 and:

Flag Over Porch
A2212

Butte
A2217

Mountain
A2218

Auto
A2220

Auto Tail Fin
A2223

Juke Box
A2225

Flag Over Field — A2230

1995-97   Photo.   *Perf. 10.4*
2897 A2212 32c multicolored   .60 .15
    a. Imperf., vert. pair   275.00

COIL STAMPS
Self-Adhesive (#2902B, 2904A-2904B, 2906-2907, 2910, 2912A-2912B, 2915-2915D, 2919-2921)
Photo.
Perf. 9.8 Vert.
2902 A2217 (5c) yel, red & bl   .15 .15
    a. Imperf., pair   750.00

Serpentine Die Cut 11.5 Vert.
2902B A2217 (5c) yellow, red & blue   .15 .15

Perf. 9.8 Vert.
2903 A2218 (5c) purple & multi   .20 .20

Letters of inscription "USA NONPROFIT ORG." outlined in purple on #2903.

2904 A2218 (5c) blue & multi   .20 .20
    c. Imperf., pair   750.00

Letters of inscription have no outline on #2904.

Serpentine Die Cut 11.2 Vert.
2904A A2218 (5c) pur & multi   .20 .20

Serpentine Die Cut 9.8 Vert.
2904B A2218 (5c) pur & multi   .20 .20

Letters of inscription outlined in purple on #2904B, not outlined on No. 2904A.

Perf. Perf. 9.8 Vert.
2905 A2220 (10c) blk, red brn & brn   .20 .20

Serpentine Die Cut 11.5 Vert.
2906 A2220 (10c) blk, brn & red brn   .20 .20
2907 A1957 (10c) gold & multi   .20 .20

Perf. 9.8 Vert.
2908 A2223 (15c) dk org yel & multi   .30 .30

No. 2908 has dark, bold colors, heavy shading lines and heavily shaded chrome.

2909 A2223 (15c) buff & multi   .30 .30

No. 2909 has shinier chrome, more subdued colors and finer details than No. 2908.

Serpentine Die Cut 11.5 Vert.
2910 A2223 (15c) buff & multi   .30 .30

Perf. 9.8 Vert.
2911 A2225 (25c) dk red, dk yel grn & multi   .50 .50

No. 2911 has dark, saturated colors and dark blue lines in the music selection board.

2912 A2225 (25c) brt org red, brt yel grn & multi   .50 .50

No. 2912 has bright colors, less shading and light blue lines in the music selection board.

Serpentine Die Cut 11.5 Vert.
2912A A2225 (25c) brt org red, brt yel grn & multi   .50 .50

Serpentine Die Cut 9.8 Vert.
2912B A2225 (25c) dark red, dark yellow green & multi   .50 .50

Perf. 9.8 Vert.
2913 A2212 32c bl, tan, brn, red & lt bl   .60 .15
    a. Imperf., pair   75.00

No. 2913 has pronounced light blue shading in the flag and red "1995" at left bottom. See No. 3132.

2914 A2212 32c bl, yel brn, red & gray   .60 .15

No. 2914 has pale gray shading in the flag and blue "1995" at left bottom.

Serpentine Die Cut 8.7 Vert.
2915 A2212 32c multicolored   .60 .30

Serpentine Die Cut 9.8 Vert.
2915A A2212 32c dk bl, tan, brn, red & lt bl   .60 .15
    h. Imperf., pair
    i. Tan omitted   —

On No. 2915Ai all other colors except brown are severly shifted.

Serpentine Die Cut 11.5 Vert.
2915B A2212 32c As #2915A   .60 .15

Serpentine Die Cut 10.9 Vert.
2915C A2212 32c As #2915A   .60 .15

Serpentine Die Cut 9.8 Vert.
2915D A2212 32c dk bl, tan, brn, red & lt bl   .60 .15

Die cutting on #2915D starts and ends with straight cuts and has 9 teeth between. Die cutting on #2915A has a straight cut at bottom and 11 teeth above. Stamps on multiples of No. 2915A touch, and are on a peelable backing the same size as the stamps, while those of No. 2915D are separated on the peelable backing, which is larger than the stamps.

No. 2915D has red "1997" at left bottom; No. 2915A has red "1996" at left bottom.

Sky on No. 3133 shows color gradation at lower right not on No. 2915D, and it has blue "1996" at left bottom.

Booklet Stamps
Perf. 10.8x9.8 on 2 or 3 Adjacent Sides
2916 A2212 32c bl, tan, brn, red & lt bl   .60 .15
    a. Booklet pane of 10   6.00
    b. As "a," imperf

Die Cut
2919 A2230 32c multicolored   .60 .15
    a. Booklet pane of 18   11.00
    b. Vert. pair, no die cutting btwn.

Serpentine Die Cut 8.7 on 2, 3 or 4 Adjacent Sides
2920 A2212 32c multi, large blue "1995" date   .60 .15
    a. Booklet pane of 20+label   12.00
    b. Small blue "1995" date   1.75 .25
    c. As "b," booklet pane of 20+label   37.50
    d. Serpentine die cut 11.3, blue "1996" date, from bklt. pane   .60 .15
    e. As "d," booklet pane of 10   6.00
    f. As #2920, pane of 15+label   9.00 —
    g. As "a," partial pane of 15, 3 stamps and parts of 7 stamps printed on backing liner   —
    h. As #2920, booklet pane of 15   9.00

No. 2920d is dated "1996." Date on No. 2920 is nearly twice as large as date on No. 2920b. No. 2920f comes in various configurations.

No. 2920h is a pane of 16 with one stamp removed. The missing stamp is the lower right stamp in the pane. No. 2920h cannot be made from No. 2920f, a pane of 15 + label. The label is located in the second or third row of the pane and is die cut. If the label is removed, an impression of the die cutting appears on the backing paper.

Serpentine Die Cut 9.8 on 2 or 3 Adjacent Sides
2921 A2212 32c dk bl, tan, brn, red & lt bl, red "1996" date   .60 .15
    a. Booklet pane of 10, red "1996" date   6.00
    b. As #2921, red "1997" date   .60 .15
    c. As "a," imperf
    d. Booklet pane of 5 + label, red "1997" date   3.25
    e. As "a," imperf

Issued: #2902, 2905, 3/10/95; #2908-2909, 2911-2912, 2919, 3/17/95; #2915, 2920, 4/18/95; #2897, 2913 2914, 2916, 5/19/95; #2920d, 1/20/96; #2904B, 2912B, 2915D 1/24/96; #2903-2904, 3/16/96; #2915A, 5/21/96; #2907, 2921, 5/21/96; #2902B, 2904A, 2906, 2910, 2912A, 2915B, 6/15/96; #2915C, 5/21/96; #2921d, 1/24/97.

See Nos. 3132-3133.

Great Americans Issue

A2248

A2249

UNITED STATES

A2250
A2251 
A2253 
A2255 
A2257 
A2258 

Perf. 11.1, 11.8x11.6 (#2942)

1995-98			Engr.	
2933	A2248	32c brown	.60	.15
2934	A2249	32c green	.60	.15
2935	A2250	32c lake	.60	.15
2936	A2251	32c blue	.60	.15
2938	A2253	46c carmine	.90	.15
2940	A2255	55c green	1.10	.20
2942	A2257	77c blue	1.50	.20
2943	A2258	78c bright violet	1.60	.20
a.		78c Dull violet	1.60	.20
b.		78c Pale violet	1.75	.30
		Nos. 2933-2943 (8)	7.50	1.35

Issued: #2933, 9/13; 46c, 10/20; 55c, 7/11; 78c, 8/18; #2934, 5/26/96; #2935, 4/3/98; #2936, 7/16/98; #2942, 11/9/98.
This is an expanding set. Nos. will change.

Love

Cherub from Sistine Madonna, by Raphael
A2263
A2264

Litho. & Engr.

1995, Feb. 1			Perf. 11.2	
2948	A2263	(32c) multicolored	.60	.15

Self-Adhesive
Die Cut

2949	A2264	(32c) multicolored	.60	.15
a.		Booklet pane of 20 + label	12.00	
b.		As No. 2949, red (engr.) omitted	1,000.	
c.		As "a," red (engr.) omitted	—	

Florida Statehood, 150th Anniv.
A2265

1995, Mar. 3   Litho.   Perf. 11.1
2950 A2265 32c multicolored   .60 .15

Earth Day

Earth Clean-Up
A2266

Solar Energy
A2267

Tree Planting
A2268

Beach Clean-Up
A2269

1995, Apr. 20   Litho.   Perf. 11.1x11

2951	A2266	32c multicolored	.60	.15
2952	A2267	32c multicolored	.60	.15
2953	A2268	32c multicolored	.60	.15
2954	A2269	32c multicolored	.60	.15
a.		Block of 4, #2951-2954	2.40	1.75

Richard M. Nixon

Richard M. Nixon, 37th President (1913-94) — A2270

Litho. & Engr.
1995, Apr. 26   Perf. 11.2
2955 A2270 32c multicolored   .60 .15
 a.   Red (engr.) omitted   1,350.

No. 2955 is known with red (engr. "Richard Nixon") inverted, and with red (engr.) omitted but only half of Nixon portrait present, both from printer's waste.
No. 2955a shows a complete Nixon portrait.

Black Heritage

Bessie Coleman (d. 1926), Aviator — A2271

1995, Apr. 27   Engr.   Perf. 11.2
2956 A2271 32c red & black   .60 .15

Love

A2272
A2273 

Cherubs from Sistine Madonna, by Raphael — A2274

Litho. & Engr.
1995, May 12   Perf. 11.2

2957	A2272	32c multicolored	.60	.15
2958	A2273	55c multicolored	1.10	.15

BOOKLET STAMPS
Perf. 9.8x10.8

2959	A2272	32c multicolored	.60	.15
a.		Booklet pane of 10	6.00	3.25
b.		As "a," imperf	—	

Self-Adhesive
Die Cut

2960	A2274	55c multicolored	1.10	.15
a.		Booklet pane of 20 + label	22.50	

Recreational Sports

Volleyball A2275
Softball A2276 
Bowling A2277 
Tennis A2278 
Golf A2279 

1995, May 20   Litho.   Perf. 11.2

2961	A2275	32c multicolored	.60	.15
2962	A2276	32c multicolored	.60	.15
2963	A2277	32c multicolored	.60	.15
2964	A2278	32c multicolored	.60	.15
2965	A2279	32c multicolored	.60	.15
a.		Vert. strip of 5, #2961-2965	3.00	2.00
b.		As "a," imperf	2,500.	
c.		As "a," yellow omitted	2,500.	
d.		As "a," yel, bl & mag omitted	2,500.	

Prisoners of War & Missing in Action

A2280

1995, May 29   Perf. 11.2
2966 A2280 32c multicolored   .60 .15

Legends of Hollywood

Marilyn Monroe (1926-62) — A2281

1995, June 1   Photo.   Perf. 11.1
2967 A2281 32c multicolored   .60 .15
 a.   Imperf., pair   600.00

Texas Statehood

A2282

1995, June 16   Litho.   Perf. 11.2
2968 A2282 32c multicolored   .60 .15

Great Lakes Lighthouses

Split Rock, Lake Superior
A2283

St. Joseph, Lake Michigan
A2284

Spectacle Reef, Lake Huron — A2285

Marblehead, Lake Erie — A2286

Thirty Mile Point, Lake Ontario — A2287

1995, June 17   Photo.   Perf. 11.2 Vert.
Booklet Stamps

2969	A2283	32c multicolored	.60	.15
2970	A2284	32c multicolored	.60	.15
2971	A2285	32c multicolored	.60	.15
2972	A2286	32c multicolored	.60	.15
2973	A2287	32c multicolored	.60	.15
a.		Booklet pane of 5, #2969-2973	3.00	2.25

U.N., 50th Anniv.

A2288

1995, June 26   Engr.   Perf. 11.2
2974 A2288 32c blue   .60 .15

Civil War

A2289

Designs: a, Monitor and Virginia. b, Robert E. Lee. c, Clara Barton. d, Ulysses S. Grant. e, Battle of Shiloh. f, Jefferson Davis. g, David Farragut. h, Frederick Douglass. i, Raphael Semmes. j, Abraham Lincoln. k, Harriet Tubman. l, Stand Watie. m, Joseph E. Johnston. n, Winfield Hancock. o, Mary Chestnut. p, Battle of Chancellorsville. q, William T. Sherman. r, Phoebe Pember. s, "Stonewall" Jackson. t, Battle of Gettysburg.

UNITED STATES

1995, June 29 Photo. Perf. 10.1
2975 A2289 Pane of 20   12.00   —
  a.-t.   32c any single   .60   .15
  u.   As "No. 2975," a.-e. imperf., f.-j.
        part perf   —
  v.   As "No. 2975," k.-t. imperf., f.-j.
        part perf   —
  w.   As "No. 2975," imperf   1,500.
  x.   Block of 9 (f.-h., k.-m., p.-r.), k.-
        l., p.-q. imperf vert.

Carousel Horses

A2290    A2291

A2292    A2293

1995, July 21 Litho. Perf. 11
2976 A2290 32c multicolored   .60   .15
2977 A2291 32c multicolored   .60   .15
2978 A2292 32c multicolored   .60   .15
2979 A2293 32c multicolored   .60   .15
  a.   Block of 4, #2976-2979   2.40   1.75

Woman Suffrage

A2294

Litho. & Engr.
1995, Aug. 26 Perf. 11.1x11
2980 A2294 32c multicolored   .60   .15
  a.   Black (engr.) omitted   500.00
  b.   Imperf, pair   1,600.

No. 2980a is valued in the grade of fine. Very fine examples sell for much more.

World War II

A2295

Designs and events of 1945: a, Marines raise flag on Iwo Jima. b, Fierce fighting frees Manila by March 3, 1945. c, Soldiers advancing (Okinawa, the last big battle). d, Destroyed bridge (US and Soviets link up at Elbe River). e, Allies liberate Holocaust survivors. f, Germany surrenders at Reims. g, Refugees (by 1945, World War II has uprooted millions). h, Truman announces Japan's surrender. i, Sailor kissing nurse (news of victory hits home). j, Hometowns honor their returning veterans.

Central label is size of 15 stamps and shows world map with extent of Axis control and Allied operations.
Illustration reduced.

Litho. & Engr.
1995, Sept. 2 Perf. 11.1
2981 A2295 Block of 10   6.00   4.50
  a.-j. 32c any single   .60   .30

American Music Series

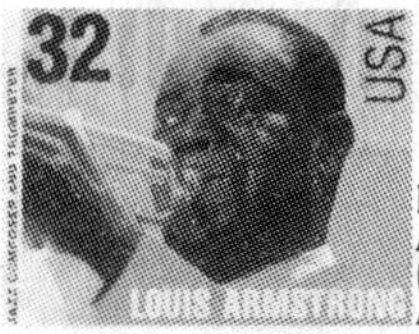

Louis Armstrong (1901-71) A2296

Coleman Hawkins (1904-69) A2297

James P. Johnson (1894-1955) A2298

Jelly Roll Morton (1890-1941) A2299

Charlie Parker (1920-55) A2300

Eubie Blake (1883-1983) A2301

Charles Mingus (1922-79) A2302

Thelonious Monk (1917-82) A2303

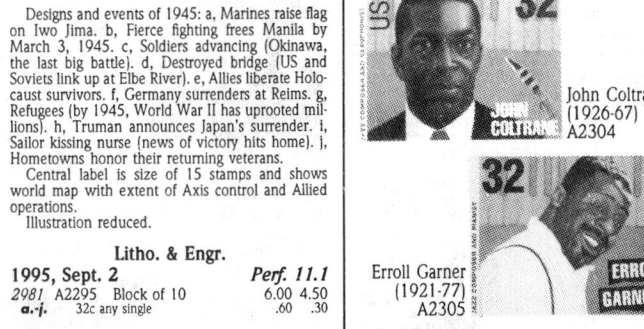

John Coltrane (1926-67) A2304

Erroll Garner (1921-77) A2305

1995   Litho.   Perf. 11.1x11
2982 A2296 32c white "32c"   .60   .15
2983 A2297 32c multicolored   .60   .15
2984 A2296 32c black "32c"   .60   .15
2985 A2298 32c multicolored   .60   .15
2986 A2299 32c multicolored   .60   .15
2987 A2300 32c multicolored   .60   .15
2988 A2301 32c multicolored   .60   .15
2989 A2302 32c multicolored   .60   .15
2990 A2303 32c multicolored   .60   .15
2991 A2304 32c multicolored   .60   .15
2992 A2305 32c multicolored   .60   .15
  a.   Vert. block of 10, #2983-2992,
       top selvage   6.00   —
  b.   As "a," dark blue (inscriptions)
       omitted

Issued: No. 2982, 9/1/95; others, 9/16/95.

Garden Flowers

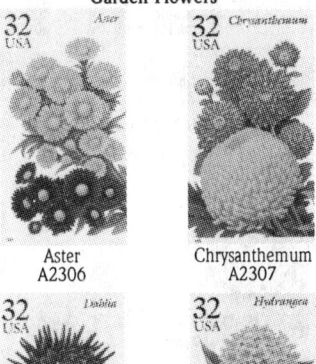

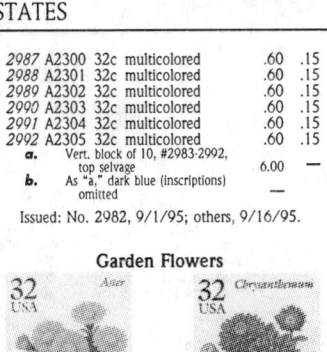

Aster A2306

Chrysanthemum A2307

Dahlia A2308

Hydrangea A2309

Rudbeckia — A2310

Perf. 10.9 Vert.
1995, Sept. 19 Litho. & Engr.
Booklet Stamps
2993 A2306 32c multicolored   .60   .15
2994 A2307 32c multicolored   .60   .15
2995 A2308 32c multicolored   .60   .15
2996 A2309 32c multicolored   .60   .15
2997 A2310 32c multicolored   .60   .15
  a.   Booklet pane of 5, #2993-2997 3.00 2.25

Eddie Rickenbacker (1890-1973), Aviator

A2311

1995, Sept. 25 Photo. Perf. 11.1
2998 A2311 60c multicolored   1.25   .25

Republic of Palau

A2312

1995, Sept. 29 Litho. Perf. 11.1
2999 A2312 32c multicolored   .60   .15

Comic Strips

A2313

Designs: a, The Yellow Kid. b, Katzenjammer Kids. c, Little Nemo in Slumberland. d, Bringing Up Father. e, Krazy Kat. f, Rube Goldberg's Inventions. g, Toonerville Folks. h, Gasoline Alley. i, Barney Google. j, Little Orphan Annie. k, Popeye. l, Blondie. m, Dick Tracy. n, Alley Oop. o, Nancy. p, Flash Gordon. q, Li'l Abner. r, Terry and the Pirates. s, Prince Valiant. t, Brenda Starr, Reporter.

1995, Oct. 1   Photo.   Perf. 10.1
3000 A2313 Pane of 20   12.00   —
  a.-t. 32c any single   .60   .15
  u.   As No. 3000, a.-h. imperf., i.-l.
       part perf   —
  v.   As No. 3000, m.-t. imperf., i.-l.
       part perf   —

Inscriptions on back of each stamp describe the comic strip.

U.S. Naval Academy, 150th Anniversary

A2314

1995, Oct. 10 Litho. Perf. 10.9
3001 A2314 32c multicolored   .60   .15

Literary Arts Series

Tennessee Williams (1911-83) A2315

1995, Oct. 13 Litho. Perf. 11.1
3002 A2315 32c multicolored   .60   .15

Christmas

Madonna and Child, by Giotto di Bondone — A2316

Santa Claus Entering Chimney A2317

Child Holding Jumping Jack A2318

Child Holding Tree — A2319

Santa Claus Working on Sled — A2320

UNITED STATES

Midnight Angel
A2321

Children Sledding
A2322

1995		Litho. & Engr.	Perf. 11.2
3003	A2316	32c multicolored	.60 .15
a.		Perf. 9.8x10.8, from bklt. pane	.60 .15
b.		As "a," booklet pane of 10	6.00 4.00
c.		As #3003, black (engr. denomination) omitted	—

Lithographed

3004	A2317	32c multicolored	.60 .15
3005	A2318	32c multicolored	.60 .15
3006	A2319	32c multicolored	.60 .15
3007	A2320	32c multicolored	.60 .15
a.		Block or strip of 4, #3004-3007	2.40 1.25
b.		Booklet pane of 10, 3 each #3004-3005, 2 each #3006-3007	6.00 4.00
c.		Booklet pane of 10, 2 each #3004-3005, 3 each #3006-3007	6.00 4.00
d.		As "a," imperf.	800.00

Self-Adhesive Stamps
Photogravure
Serpentine Die Cut

3008	A2320	32c multicolored	.60 .15
3009	A2318	32c multicolored	.60 .15
3010	A2317	32c multicolored	.60 .15
3011	A2319	32c multicolored	.60 .15
a.		Booklet pane of 20, 5 each #3008-3011 + label	12.00

Lithographed

3012	A2321	32c multicolored	.60 .15
a.		Booklet pane of 20 + label	12.00
c.		Booklet pane of 15 + label	9.00
d.		Booklet pane of 15	—

Colors of No. 3012c are deeper than those on #3012a. Label on #3012c has die-cutting, not found on label of #3012a.

No. 3012d is a pane of 16 with one stamp removed. The missing stamp is from the second row, either from the top or bottom, of the pane. No. 3012d cannot be made from No. 3012c, a pane of 15 + label. The label is die cut. If the label is removed, an impression of the die cutting appears on the backing paper.

Photogravure
Die Cut

3013	A2322	32c multicolored	.60 .15
a.		Booklet pane of 18	11.00

Self-Adhesive Coil Stamps
Serpentine Die Cut Vert.

3014	A2320	32c multicolored	.60 .30
3015	A2318	32c multicolored	.60 .30
3016	A2317	32c multicolored	.60 .30
3017	A2319	32c multicolored	.60 .30

Lithographed

| 3018 | A2321 | 32c multicolored | .60 .30 |

Nos. 3014-3018 were only available through the Philatelic Fulfillment Center in Kansas City.
Issued: #3003, 3012-3013, 3018, 10/19; #3004-3011, 3014-3017, 9/30.

Antique Automobiles

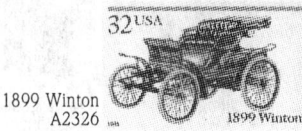

1893 Duryea
A2323

1894 Haynes
A2324

1898 Columbia
A2325

1899 Winton
A2326

1901 White
A2327

1995, Nov. 3		Photo.	Perf. 11.1
3019	A2323	32c multicolored	.60 .15
3020	A2324	32c multicolored	.60 .15
3021	A2325	32c multicolored	.60 .15
3022	A2326	32c multicolored	.60 .15
3023	A2327	32c multicolored	.60 .15
a.		Vert. or horiz. strip of 5, #3019-3023	3.00 2.00

Vert. and horiz. strips are all in different order.

Utah Statehood Centenary

Utah 1896 — Delicate Arch, Arches Natl. Park — A2328

1996, Jan. 4		Litho.	Perf. 11.1
3024	A2328	32c multicolored	.60 .15

Garden Flowers

Crocus A2329

Winter Aconite A2330

Pansy A2331

Snowdrop A2332

Anemone — A2333

Perf. 10.9 Vert.
1996, Jan. 19		Litho. & Engr.

Booklet Stamps

3025	A2329	32c multicolored	.60 .15
3026	A2330	32c multicolored	.60 .15
3027	A2331	32c multicolored	.60 .15
3028	A2332	32c multicolored	.60 .15
3029	A2333	32c multicolored	.60 .15
a.		Booklet pane of 5, #3025-3029	3.00 2.25
b.		As "a," imperf	—

Love

Cherub from Sistine Madonna, by Raphael — A2334

Serpentine Die Cut 11.3
1996, Jan. 20 Self-Adhesive
Booklet Stamp

3030	A2334	32c multicolored	.60 .15
a.		Booklet pane of 20 + label	12.00
b.		Booklet pane of 15 + label	9.00
c.		Red omitted	—

Flora and Fauna Series
Kestrel Type of 1995 and

Red-headed Woodpecker A2335

Eastern Bluebird A2336

Red Fox A2339

Ring-necked Pheasant A2350

1996-98		Litho.	Perf. 11.1
3032	A2335	2c multicolored	.15 .15
3033	A2336	3c multicolored	.15 .15

Serpentine Die Cut 11.5x11.3
Self-Adhesive

| 3036 | A2339 | $1 multicolored | 2.00 .50 |

COIL STAMP
Perf. 9.8 Vert.
| 3044 | A1841 | 1c multicolored | .15 .15 |

Issued: #3032, 2/2/96; #3033, 4/3/96; #3044, 1/20/96; #3036, 8/14/98.

Blue Jay & Rose Types of 1993-95
Serpentine Die Cut 10.4x10.8 on 3 Sides
1996-98			Photo.

Self-Adhesive
Booklet Stamps

3048	A1847	20c multicolored	.40 .15
a.		Booklet pane of 10	4.00

Serpentine Die Cut 11.3x11.7
3049	A1853	32c yellow, orange, green & black	.60 .15
a.		Booklet pane of 20 + label	12.00
b.		Booklet pane of 4	2.75
c.		Booklet pane of 5 + label	3.00
d.		Booklet pane of 6	3.60

Serpentine Die Cut 11.2 on 3 Sides
3050	A2350	20c multicolored	.40 .20
a.		Booklet pane of 10	4.00

Coil Stamps
Serpentine Die Cut 11.6 Vert.
| 3053 | A1847 | 20c multicolored | .40 .15 |

Serpentine Die Cut 9.8 Vert.
Litho.
Self-Adhesive

3054	A1853	32c yel, org, blk & grn	.60 .15
a.		Imperf, pair	—
b.		Blk, yel & grn omitted	—
c.		Blk, yel & grn omitted, imperf pair	—
d.		Black omitted	—
e.		Black omitted, imperf pair	—

Nos. 3054b and 3054d also are miscut and with shifted die cuttings.

| 3055 | A2350 | 20c multicolored | .40 .20 |

Issued: #3048, 3053, 8/2/96; #3049, 10/24/96; #3054, 8/1/97; #3050, 3055, 7/31/98.

Black Heritage

Ernest E. Just (1883-1941), Marine Biologist — A2358

1996, Feb. 1		Litho.	Perf. 11.1
3058	A2358	32c gray & black	.60 .15

Smithsonian Institution, 150th Anniversary

A2359

1996, Feb. 7			Perf. 11.1
3059	A2359	32c multicolored	.60 .15

Chinese New Year

Year of the Rat — A2360

1996, Feb. 8		Photo.	Perf. 11.1
3060	A2360	32c multicolored	.60 .15

Pioneers of Communication

Eadweard Muybridge (1830-1904), Photographer A2361

Ottmar Mergenthaler (1854-99), Inventor of Linotype A2362

Frederic E. Ives (1856-1937), Developer of Halftone Process A2363

William Dickson (1860-1935), Co-developer of Kinetoscope A2364

1996, Feb. 22		Litho.	Perf. 11.1x11
3061	A2361	32c multicolored	.60 .15
3062	A2362	32c multicolored	.60 .15
3063	A2363	32c multicolored	.60 .15
3064	A2364	32c multicolored	.60 .15
a.		Block or strip of 4, #3061-3064	2.40 1.75

Fulbright Scholarships, 50th Anniversary

A2365

1996, Feb. 28		Litho. & Engr.	Perf. 11.1
3065	A2365	32c multicolored	.60 .15

Jacqueline Cochran (1910-80), Pilot

A2366

UNITED STATES

Litho. & Engr.
1996, Mar. 9   Perf. 11.1
3066 A2366 50c multicolored   1.00   .20
   a.   Black (eng.) omitted   85.00

Marathon

A2367

1996, Apr. 11   Litho.   Perf. 11.1
3067 A2367 32c multicolored   .60   .15

1996 Summer Olympic Games

A2368

Designs: a, Decathlon (javelin). b, Canoeing. c, Women's running. d, Women's diving. e, Cycling. f, Freestyle wrestling. g, Women's gymnastics. h, Women's sailboarding. i, Shot put. j, Women's soccer. k, Beach volleyball. l, Rowing. m, Sprints. n, Women's swimming. o, Women's softball. p, Hurdles. q, Swimming. r, Gymnastics (pommel horse). s, Equestrian. t, Basketball.

1996, May 2   Photo.   Perf. 10.1
3068 A2368 Pane of 20   12.00   —
   a.-t.   32c any single   .60   .15
   u.   As No. 3068, imperf   —
   v.   As No. 3068, back inscriptions omitted on a, f, k, p, incorrect back inscriptions on others   —

Inscription on back of each stamp describes the sport shown.

Georgia O'Keeffe (1887-1986)

A2369

1996, May 23   Photo.   Perf. 11.6x11.4
3069 A2369 32c multicolored   .60   .15
   a.   Imperf, pair   250.00

Tennessee Statehood Bicentennial

A2370

1996, May 31   Photo.   Perf. 11.1
3070 A2370 32c multicolored   .60   .15

Booklet Stamp
Self-Adhesive
Serpentine Die Cut 9.9x10.8

3071 A2370 32c multicolored   .60   .30
   a.   Booklet pane of 20   12.00
   b.   Horiz. pair, no die cutting btwn.   —

American Indian Dances

Fancy A2371
Butterfly A2372 
Traditional A2373 
Raven A2374 
Hoop — A2375 

1996, June 7   Litho.   Perf. 11.1
3072 A2371 32c multicolored   .60   .15
3073 A2372 32c multicolored   .60   .15
3074 A2373 32c multicolored   .60   .15
3075 A2374 32c multicolored   .60   .15
3076 A2375 32c multicolored   .60   .15
   a.   Strip of 5, #3072-3076   3.00   1.75

Prehistoric Animals

Eohippus A2376
Woolly Mammoth A2377 
Mastodon A2378 
Saber-tooth Cat — A2379 

1996, June 8   Litho.   Perf. 11.1x11
3077 A2376 32c multicolored   .60   .15
3078 A2377 32c multicolored   .60   .15
3079 A2378 32c multicolored   .60   .15
3080 A2379 32c multicolored   .60   .15
   a.   Block or strip of 4, #3077-3080   2.40   1.50

A2380
A2381 

Breast Cancer Awareness
1996, June 15   Litho.   Perf. 11.1
3081 A2380 32c multicolored   .60   .15

Legends of Hollywood
James Dean (1931-55)
1996, June 24   Photo.   Perf. 11.1
3082 A2381 32c multicolored   .60   .15
   a.   Imperf. pair   450.00
   b.   As "a," red (USA 32c) omitted   —

Folk Heroes

A2382
A2383 
A2384 
A2385 

1996, July 11   Litho.   Perf. 11.1x11
3083 A2382 32c multicolored   .60   .15
3084 A2383 32c multicolored   .60   .15
3085 A2384 32c multicolored   .60   .15
3086 A2385 32c multicolored   .60   .15
   a.   Block or strip of 4, #3083-3086   2.40   1.50

Myron's Discobolus A2386
Young Corn, by Grant Wood A2387 

Centennial Olympic Games
1996, July 19   Engr.   Perf. 11.1
3087 A2386 32c brown   .60   .15
Sheet margin of the pane of 20 is lithographed.

Iowa Statehood, 150th Anniversary
1996, Aug. 1   Litho.   Perf. 11.1
3088 A2387 32c multicolored   .60   .15

Booklet Stamp
Self-Adhesive
Serpentine Die Cut 11.6x11.4
3089 A2387 32c multicolored   .60   .30
   a.   Booklet pane of 20   12.00

Rural Free Delivery, Cent.

A2388

Litho. & Engr.
1996, Aug. 7   Perf. 11.2x11
3090 A2388 32c multicolored   .60   .15

Riverboats

Robt. E. Lee — A2389
Sylvan Dell — A2390 
Far West A2391  
Rebecca Everingham A2392 
Bailey Gatzert A2393 

Self-Adhesive
Serpentine Die Cut 11x11.1
1996, Aug. 22   Photo.
3091 A2389 32c multicolored   .60   .15
3092 A2390 32c multicolored   .60   .15
3093 A2391 32c multicolored   .60   .15
3094 A2392 32c multicolored   .60   .15
3095 A2393 32c multicolored   .60   .15
   a.   Vert. strip of 5, #3091-3095   3.00   —
   b.   As "a," with special die cutting   75.00   —

The serpentine die cutting runs through the peelable backing to which Nos. 3091-3095 are affixed. No. 3095a exists with stamps in different sequences.

On the long side of each stamp in No. 3095b, the die cutting is missing 3 "perforations" between the stamps, one near each end and one in the middle. This allows a complete strip to be removed from the backing paper for use on a first day cover.

American Music Series
Big Band Leaders

Count Basie A2394
Tommy & Jimmy Dorsey A2395 
Glenn Miller A2396

UNITED STATES

Benny Goodman
A2397

Songwriters

Harold Arlen
A2398

Johnny Mercer
A2399

Dorothy Fields
A2400

Hoagy Carmichael
A2401

1996, Sept. 11	Litho.		Perf. 11.1x11
3096	A2394	32c multicolored	.60 .15
3097	A2395	32c multicolored	.60 .15
3098	A2396	32c multicolored	.60 .15
3099	A2397	32c multicolored	.60 .15
a.		Block or strip of 4, #3096-3099	2.40 1.50
3100	A2398	32c multicolored	.60 .15
3101	A2399	32c multicolored	.60 .15
3102	A2400	32c multicolored	.60 .15
3103	A2401	32c multicolored	.60 .15
a.		Block or strip of 4, #3100-3103	2.40 1.50

Literary Arts

F. Scott Fitzgerald (1896-1940)
A2402

1996, Sept. 27	Photo.		Perf. 11.1
3104	A2402	23c multicolored	.45 .15

Endangered Species

A2403

Designs: a, Black-footed ferret. b, Thick-billed parrot. c, Hawaiian monk seal. d, American crocodile. e, Ocelot. f, Schaus swallowtail butterfly. g, Wyoming toad. h, Brown pelican. i, California condor. j, Gila trout. k, San Francisco garter snake. l, Woodland caribou. m, Florida panther. n, Piping plover. o, Florida manatee.

1996, Oct. 2	Litho.		Perf. 11.1x11
3105	A2403	Pane of 15	9.00 —
a.-o.		32c any single	.60 .15

See Mexico No. 1995.

Computer Technology

A2404

		Perf. 10.9x11.1	
1996, Oct. 8		Litho. & Engr.	
3106	A2404	32c multicolored	.60 .15

Christmas

Madonna and Child from Adoration of the Shepherds, by Paolo de Matteis — A2405

Family at Fireplace
A2406

Decorating Tree
A2407

Dreaming of Santa Claus
A2408

Holiday Shopping
A2409

Skaters — A2410

1996		Litho. & Engr.	Perf. 11.1x11.2
3107	A2405	32c multicolored	.60 .15

Litho.
Perf. 11.3

3108	A2406	32c multicolored	.60 .15
3109	A2407	32c multicolored	.60 .15
3110	A2408	32c multicolored	.60 .15
3111	A2409	32c multicolored	.60 .15
a.		Block or strip of 4, #3108-3111	2.40 1.50
b.		Strip of 4, #3110-3111, 3108-3109, with #3109 imperf, #3108 imperf at right	—

Self-Adhesive Booklet Stamps
Litho. & Engr.
Serpentine Die Cut 10 on 2, 3 or 4 Sides

3112	A2405	32c multicolored	.60 .15
a.		Booklet pane of 20 + label	12.00
b.		No die cutting, pair	—
c.		As "a," no die cutting	—

Litho.
Serpentine Die Cut 11.8x11.5 on 2, 3 or 4 Sides

3113	A2406	32c multicolored	.60 .15
3114	A2407	32c multicolored	.60 .15
3115	A2408	32c multicolored	.60 .15
3116	A2409	32c multicolored	.60 .15
a.		Booklet pane, 5 ea #3113-3116	12.00

Photo.
Die Cut

3117	A2410	32c multicolored	.60 .15
a.		Booklet pane of 18	11.00

Issued: #3108-3111, 3113-3117, 10/8; #3107, 3112, 11/1.

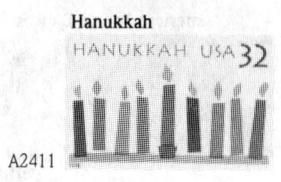

Hanukkah

A2411

Serpentine Die Cut 11.1
1996, Oct. 22			Photo.

Self-Adhesive

3118	A2411	32c multicolored	.60 .15

See Israel No. 1289.

Cycling
Souvenir Sheet

A2412

1996, Nov. 1	Photo.		Perf. 11x11.1
3119	A2412	Sheet of 2	2.00 2.00
a.		50c orange & multi	1.00 1.00
b.		50c blue green & multi	1.00 1.00

Chinese New Year

Year of the Ox — A2413

1997, Jan. 5			Photo.	Perf. 11.2
3120	A2413	32c multicolored		.60 .15

Black Heritage

Brig. Gen. Benjamin O. Davis, Sr. (1880-1970) — A2414

Self-Adhesive
Serpentine Die Cut 11.4

1997, Jan. 28			Litho.
3121	A2414	32c multicolored	.60 .15

Statue of Liberty Type of 1994
Serpentine Die Cut 11 on 2, 3 or 4 Sides

1997, Feb. 1			Photo.

Self-Adhesive

3122	A1951	32c red, lt bl, dk bl & yel	.60 .15
a.		Booklet pane of 20 + label	12.00
b.		Booklet pane of 4	3.20
c.		Booklet pane of 5 + label	3.00
d.		Booklet pane of 6	3.60
h.		As "a," no die cutting	—

Serpentine Die Cut 11.5x11.8 on 2, 3 or 4 Sides

1997			Photo.

Self-Adhesive

3122E	A1951	32c red, lt bl, dk bl & yel	.60 .15
f.		Booklet pane of 20 + label	12.00
g.		Booklet pane of 6	3.60

Love

Swans
A2415   A2416

Serpentine Die Cut 11.8x11.6 on 2, 3 or 4 Sides

1997, Feb. 7			Litho.

Self-Adhesive

3123	A2415	32c multicolored	.60 .15
a.		Booklet pane of 20 + label	12.00
b.		No die cutting, pair	—
c.		As "a," no die cutting	—
d.		As "a," black omitted	—

Serpentine Die Cut 11.6x11.8 on 2, 3 or 4 Sides

3124	A2416	55c multicolored	1.10 .15
a.		Booklet pane of 20 + label	22.00

Helping Children Learn

A2417

Serpentine Die Cut 11.6x11.7

1997, Feb. 18			Photo.

Self-Adhesive

3125	A2417	32c multicolored	.60 .15

Merian Botanical Prints

Citron, Moth, Larvae, Pupa, Beetle
A2418

Flowering Pineapple, Cockroaches
A2419

No. 3128 (r), No. 3129 (l), No. 3128a below

Serpentine Die Cut 10.9x10.2 on 2, 3 or 4 Sides

1997, Mar. 3			Photo.

Self-Adhesive

3126	A2418	32c multicolored	.60 .15
3127	A2419	32c multicolored	.60 .15
a.		Booklet pane of 20, 10 ea #3126-3127 + label	12.00

Size: 18.5x24mm
Serpentine Die Cut 11.2x10.8 on 2 or 3 Sides

3128	A2418	32c multicolored	.60 .15
a.		See footnote	.60
b.		Booklet pane of 5, 2 ea #3128-3129, 1 #3128a	3.00
3129	A2419	32c multicolored	.60 .15
a.		See footnote	
b.		Booklet pane of 5, 2 ea #3128-3129, 1 #3129a	3.00

Nos. 3128a-3129a are placed sideways on the pane and are serpentine die cut 11.2 on top and bottom, 10.8 on left side. The right side is 11.2 broken by a large perf where the stamp meets the vertical perforations of the two stamps above it. See illustration above.

UNITED STATES

Pacific '97

Sailing Ship — A2420

Stagecoach — A2421

1997, Mar. 13	Engr.		Perf. 11.2	
3130	A2420	32c blue	.60	.15
3131	A2421	32c red	.60	.15
a.		Pair, #3130-3131	1.25	.30

Juke Box and Flag Over Porch Types of 1995
COIL STAMPS

1997, Mar. 14	Photo.		Imperf.	
3132	A2225	(25c) brt org red, brt yel grn & multi	.50	.50

Tagged
Serpentine Die Cut 9.9 Vert.

| 3133 | A2212 | 32c dk bl, tan, brn, red & lt bl | .60 | .15 |

Nos. 3132-3133 were issued without backing paper. No. 3132 has simulated perforations ending in black bars at the top and bottom edges of the stamp.

Sky on No. 3133 shows color gradation at lower right that is not on Nos. 2915A or 2915D, and it has blue "1996" at left bottom.

Literary Arts

Thornton Wilder (1897-1975)
A2422

1997, Apr. 17	Litho.		Perf. 11.1	
3134	A2422	32c multicolored	.60	.15

Raoul Wallenberg (1912-47)

Wallenberg and Jewish Refugees
A2423

1997, Apr. 24	Litho.		Perf. 11.1	
3135	A2423	32c multicolored	.60	.15

Dinosaurs

A2424

Designs: a, Ceratosaurus. b, Camptosaurus. c, Camarasaurus. d, Brachiosaurus. e, Goniopholis. f, Stegosaurus. g, Allosaurus. h, Opisthias. i, Edmontonia. j, Einiosaurus. k, Daspletosaurus. l, Palaeosaniwa. m, Corythosaurus. n, Ornithomimus. o, Parasaurolophus.
Illustration reduced.

1997, May 1	Litho.		Perf. 11x11.1	
3136	A2424	Sheet of 15	9.00	
a.-o.		32c any single	.60	.15
p.		As #3136, bottom seven stamps imperf	—	

Bugs Bunny

A2425

Serpentine Die Cut 11

1997, May 22			Photo.	
3137		Pane of 10	6.00	
a.	A2425	32c single	.60	.15
b.		Booklet pane of 9	5.40	
c.		Booklet pane of 1	.60	

Die cutting on #3137b does not extend through the backing paper.

3138		Pane of 10	150.00	
a.	A2425	32c single	2.00	
b.		Booklet pane of 9	—	
c.		Booklet pane of 1, imperf	—	

Die cutting on #3138b extends through the backing paper. Used examples of #3138a are identical to those of #3137a.

An untagged promotional piece similar to No. 3137c exists on the same backing paper as the booklet pane, with the same design image, but without Bugs' signature and the single stamp. Replacing the stamp is an enlarged "32 / USA" in the same style as used on the stamp.

Pacific 97

Franklin A2426

Washington A2427

1997	Litho. & Engr.		Perf. 10.5x10.4	
3139		Sheet of 12	12.00	
a.	A2426	50c single	1.00	.50
3140		Sheet of 12	14.50	
a.	A2427	60c single	1.20	.60

Margins on Nos. 3139-3140 are lithographed.
Issued: No. 3139, 5/29, No. 3140, 5/30.

Marshall Plan, 50th Anniv.

Gen. George C. Marshall, Map of Europe
A2428

1997, June 4			Perf. 11.1	
3141	A2428	32c multicolored	.60	.15

Classic American Aircraft

A2429

Designs: a, Mustang. b, Model B. c, Cub. d, Vega. e, Alpha. f, B-10. g, Corsair. h, Stratojet. i, GeeBee. j, Staggerwing. k, Flying Fortress. l, Stearman. m, Constellation. n, Lightning. o, Peashooter. p, Tri-Motor. q, DC-3. r, 314 Clipper. s, Jenny. t, Wildcat.
Illustration reduced.

1997, July 19			Photo.	Perf. 10.1
3142	A2429	Pane of 20	12.00	
a.-t.		32c any single	.60	.15

Inscriptions on back of each stamp describe the airplane.

Football Coaches

Bear Bryant A2430

Pop Warner A2431

Vince Lombardi A2432

George Halas A2433

1997	Litho.		Perf. 11.2	
3143	A2430	32c multicolored	.60	.15
3144	A2431	32c multicolored	.60	.15
3145	A2432	32c multicolored	.60	.15
3146	A2433	32c multicolored	.60	.15
a.		Block or strip of 4, #3143-3146	2.40	—

With Red Bar Above Coach's Name
Perf. 11

3147	A2430	32c multicolored	.60	.30
3148	A2431	32c multicolored	.60	.30
3149	A2432	32c multicolored	.60	.30
3150	A2433	32c multicolored	.60	.30

Issued: #3143-3146, 7/25; #3147, 8/5; #3148, 8/7; #3149, 8/8; #3150, 8/16.

American Dolls

A2434

Designs: a, "Alabama Baby," and doll by Martha Chase. b, "Columbian Doll." c, Johnny Gruelle's "Raggedy Ann." d, Doll by Martha Chase. e, "American Child." f, "Baby Coos." g, Plains Indian. h, Doll by Izannah Walker. i, "Babyland Rag." j, "Scooties." k, Doll by Ludwig Greiner. l, "Betsy McCall." m, Percy Crosby's "Skippy." n, "Maggie Mix-up." o, Dolls by Albert Schoenhut.
Illustration reduced.

1997, July 28			Perf. 10.9x11.1	
3151	A2434	Pane of 15	9.00	
a.-o.		32c any single	.60	.15

A2435

A2436

Legends Of Hollywood
Humphrey Bogart (1899-1957)

1997, July 31			Photo.	Perf. 11.1
3152	A2435	32c multicolored	.60	.15

Perforations in corner of each stamp are star-shaped.

"The Start and Stripes Forever!"

1997, Aug. 21			Perf. 11.1	
3153	A2436	32c multicolored	.60	.15

American Music Series
Opera Singers

Lily Pons A2437

Richard Tucker A2438

Lawrence Tibbett A2439

Rosa Ponselle A2440

Classical Composers & Conductors

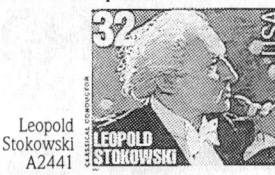

Leopold Stokowski A2441

Arthur Fiedler A2442

George Szell A2443

Eugene Ormandy A2444

Samuel Barber A2445

UNITED STATES

Ferde Grofé
A2446

Charles Ives
A2447

Louis Moreau Gottschalk
A2448

1997	Litho.		Perf. 11	
3154	A2437	32c multicolored	.60	.15
3155	A2438	32c multicolored	.60	.15
3156	A2439	32c multicolored	.60	.15
3157	A2440	32c multicolored	.60	.15
a.	Block or strip of 4, #3154-3157		2.40	—
3158	A2441	32c multicolored	.60	.15
3159	A2442	32c multicolored	.60	.15
3160	A2443	32c multicolored	.60	.15
3161	A2444	32c multicolored	.60	.15
3162	A2445	32c multicolored	.60	.15
3163	A2446	32c multicolored	.60	.15
3164	A2447	32c multicolored	.60	.15
3165	A2448	32c multicolored	.60	.15
a.	Block of 8, #3158-3165		4.80	—

Issued: #3154-3157, 9/10; #3158-3165, 9/12.

Padre Félix Varela (1788-1853)

A2449

1997, Sept. 15	Litho.	Perf. 11.2	
3166	A2449 32c purple	.60	.15

Department of the Air Force, 50th Anniv.

Thunderbirds Aerial Demonstration Squadron
A2450

1997, Sept. 18	Litho.	Perf. 11.2x11.1	
3167	A2450 32c multicolored	.60	.15

Beginning with #3167, a hidden 3-D design can be seen on some stamps when they are viewed with a special viewer sold by the post office.

Classic Movie Monsters

Lon Chaney as The Phantom of the Opera — A2451

Bela Lugosi as Dracula — A2452

Boris Karloff as Frankenstein's Monster — A2453

Boris Karloff as The Mummy — A2454

Lon Chaney, Jr. as The Wolf Man — A2455

1997, Sept. 30	Photo.	Perf. 10.2	
3168	A2451 32c multicolored	.60	.15
3169	A2452 32c multicolored	.60	.15
3170	A2453 32c multicolored	.60	.15
3171	A2454 32c multicolored	.60	.15
3172	A2455 32c multicolored	.60	.15
a.	Strip of 5, #3168-3172	3.00	—

First Supersonic Flight, 50th Anniv.

A2456

Serpentine Die Cut 11.4

1997, Oct. 14		Litho.
	Self-Adhesive	
3173	A2456 32c multicolored	.60 .15

Women In Military Service

A2457

1997, Oct. 18	Litho.	Perf. 11.1
3174	A2457 32c multicolored	.60 .15

Kwanzaa

A2458

Serpentine Die Cut 11

1996, Oct. 22		Photo.
	Self-Adhesive	
3175	A2458 32c multicolored	.60 .15

Christmas

Madonna and Child, by Sano di Pietro
A2459

Holly
A2460

Serpentine Die Cut 9.9 on 2, 3 or 4 Sides

1997		Litho.
	Booklet Stamps	
	Self-Adhesive	
3176	A2459 32c multicolored	.60 .15
a.	Booklet pane of 20 + label	12.00

Serpentine Die Cut 11.2x11.8 on 2, 3 or 4 Sides

3177	A2460 32c multicolored	.60 .15
a.	Booklet pane of 20 + label	12.00
b.	Booklet pane of 4	2.50
c.	Booklet pane of 5 + label	3.00
d.	Booklet pane of 6	3.75

Issued: No. 3176, 10/27; No. 3177, 10/30.

Mars Pathfinder Souvenir Sheet

Mars Rover Sojourner — A2461

Illustration reduced.

1997, Dec. 10	Photo.	Perf. 11x11.1
3178	A2461 $3 multicolored	6.00

The perforations at the bottom of the stamp include the letters "USA." Vertical rouletting extends from the vertical perforations of the stamp to the bottom of the souvenir sheet.

Chinese New Year

Year of the Tiger
A2462

1998, Jan. 5	Photo.	Perf. 11.2
3179	A2462 32c multicolored	.60 .15

A2463

A2464

Alpine Skiing

1998, Jan. 22	Litho.	Perf. 11.2
3180	A2463 32c multicolored	.60 .15

Black Heritage

Serpentine Die Cut 11.6x11.3

1998, Jan. 28		
	Self-Adhesive	
3181	A2464 32c sepia & black	.60 .15

Madam C.J. Walker (1867-1919), entrepreneur.

Celebrate the Century

1900s — A2465

1910s — A2466

1920s — A2467

1930s — A2468

No. 3182: a, Model T Ford. b, Theodore Roosevelt. c, Motion picture "The Great Train Robbery," 1903. d, Crayola Crayons introduced, 1903. e, St. Louis World's Fair, 1904. f, Design used on Hunt's Remedy stamp (#RS56), Pure Food & Drug Act, 1906. g, Wright Brothers first flight, Kitty Hawk, 1903. h, Boxing match shown in painting "Stag at Sharkey's," by George Bellows of the Ash Can School. i, Immigrants arrive. j, John Muir, preservationist. k, "Teddy" Bear created. l, W.E.B. Du Bois, social activist. m, Gibson Girl. n, First baseball World Series, 1903. o, Robie House, Chicago, designed by Frank Lloyd Wright.

No. 3183: a, Charlie Chaplin as the Little Tramp. b, Federal Reserve System created, 1913. c, George Washington Carver. d, Avant-garde art introduced at Armory Show, 1913. e, First transcontinental telephone line, 1914. f, Panama Canal opens, 1914. g, Jim Thorpe wins decathlon at Stockholm Olympics, 1912. h, Grand Canyon National Park, 1919. i, U.S. enters World War I. j, Boy Scouts started in 1910, Girl Scouts formed in 1912. k, Woodrow Wilson. l, First crossword puzzle published, 1913. m, Jack Dempsey wins heavyweight title, 1919. n, Construction toys. o, Child labor reform.

No. 3184: a, Babe Ruth. b, The Gatsby style. c, Prohibition enforced. d, Electric toy trains. e, 19th Amendment (woman voting). f, Emily Post's Etiquette. g, Margaret Mead, anthropologist. h, Flappers do the Charleston. i, Radio entertains America. j, Art Deco style (Chrysler Building). k, Jazz flourishes. l, Four Horsemen of Notre Dame. m, Lindbergh flies the Atlantic. n, American realism (The Automat, by Edward Hopper). o, Stock Market crash, 1929.

No. 3185: a, Franklin D. Roosevelt. b, The Empire State Building. c, 1st Issue of Life Magazine, 1936. d, Eleanor Roosevelt. e, FDR's New Deal. f,

UNITED STATES

Superman arrives, 1938. g, Household conveniences. h, "Snow White and the Seven Dwarfs," 1937. i, "Gone with the Wind," 1936. j, Jesse Owens. k, Streamline design. l, Golden Gate Bridge. m, America survives the Depression. n, Bobby Jones wins Grand Slam, 1938. o, The Monopoly Game.

Litho. & Engr. (#3182m, 3183f, 3184m, 3185b)

1998			Perf. 11.6	
3182	A2465	Pane of 15	9.00	—
a.-o.		32c any single	.60	.30
3183	A2466	Pane of 15	9.00	—
a.-o.		32c any single	.60	.30
3184	A2467	Pane of 15	9.00	—
a.-o.		32c any single	.60	.30
3185	A2468	Pane of 15	9.00	—
a.-o.		32c any single	.60	.30

Issued: #3182-3183, 2/3; #3184, 5/28; #3185, 9/10.
Numbers have been reserved for additional sheets in this set.

"Remember The Maine"

A2475

Litho. & Engr.

1998, Feb. 15			Perf. 11.2x11	
3192	A2475	32c red & black	.60	.15

Flowering Trees

Southern Magnolia — A2476
Blue Paloverde — A2477 
Yellow Poplar — A2478 
Prairie Crab Apple — A2479 
Pacific Dogwood — A2480 

Die Cut Perf 11.3

1998, Mar. 19   Litho.
Self-Adhesive

3193	A2476	32c multicolored	.60	.15
3194	A2477	32c multicolored	.60	.15
3195	A2478	32c multicolored	.60	.15
3196	A2479	32c multicolored	.60	.15
3197	A2480	32c multicolored	.60	.15
a.		Strip of 5, #3193-3197	3.00	

Alexander Calder (1898-1976), Sculptor

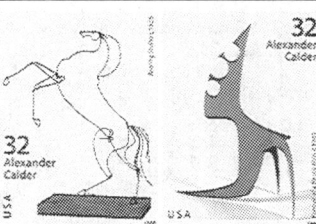

Black Cascade, 13 Verticals, 1959 — A2481
Untitled, 1965 — A2482
Rearing Stallion, 1928 — A2483
Portrait of a Young Man, c. 1945 — A2484
Un Effet du Japonais, 1945 — A2485 

1998, Mar. 25   Photo.   *Perf. 10.2*

3198	A2481	32c multicolored	.60	.15
3199	A2482	32c multicolored	.60	.15
3200	A2483	32c multicolored	.60	.15
3201	A2484	32c multicolored	.60	.15
3202	A2485	32c multicolored	.60	.15
a.		Strip of 5, #3198-3202	3.00	—

Cinco De Mayo

A2486

Serpentine Die Cut 11.7x10.9

1998, Apr. 16   Photo.
Self-Adhesive

3203	A2486	32c multicolored	.60	.15

See Mexico No. 2066.

A2487    A2488

Sylvester & Tweety

Serpentine Die Cut 11.1

1998, Apr. 27
Self-Adhesive

3204		Pane of 10	6.00	
a.		A2487 32c single	.60	.15
b.		Booklet pane of 9 #3204a	5.40	
c.		Booklet pane of 1 #3204a	.60	

Die cutting on #3204b does not extend through the backing paper.

3205		Pane of 10	10.00	
a.		A2487 32c single		.60
b.		Booklet pane of 9 #3205a	—	
c.		Booklet pane of 1, imperf.	—	

Die cutting on #3205a extends through the backing paper. Used examples of No. 3205a are identical to those of No. 3204a.

Wisconsin Statehood

Serpentine Die Cut 10.8x10.9

1998, May 29   Photo.
Self-Adhesive

3206	A2488	32c multicolored	.60	.30

See note after No. 3167.

Wetlands A2489
Diner A2490 

COIL STAMPS

1998   Photo.   *Perf. 10 Vert.*
Self-Adhesive (#3207A, 3208A)

3207	A2489	(5c) multicolored	.15	.15

Perf. 9.7 Vert.

3207A	A2489	(5c) multicolored	.15	.15

Perf. 10 Vert.

3208	A2490	(25c) multicolored	.50	.50

Serpentine Die Cut 9.7 Vert.

3208A	A2490	(25c) multicolored	.50	.50

Issued: #3207-3208, 6/5; #3208A, 9/30; #3207A, 12/14.

1898 Trans-Mississippi Stamps, Cent.

A2491

Litho. & Engr.

1998, June 18			Perf. 12x12.4	
3209	A2491	Sheet of 9	7.75	5.00
a.	A100	1c green & black	.15	.15
b.	A108	2c red brown & black	.15	.15
c.	A102	4c orange & black	.15	.15
d.	A103	5c blue & black	.15	.15
e.	A104	8c dark lilac & black	.15	.15
f.	A105	10c purple & black	.20	.15
g.	A106	50c green & black	1.00	.60
h.	A107	$1 red & black	2.00	1.25
i.	A101	$2 red brown & black	4.00	2.50

Vignettes on Nos. 3209b and 3209i are reversed in comparison to the original issue.

3210	A107	$1 Sheet of 9		
		#3209h	18.00	

Berlin Airlift, 50th Anniv.

A2492

1998, June 26   Photo.   *Perf. 11.2*

3211	A2492	32c multicolored	.60	.15

American Music Series

Huddie "Leadbelly" Ledbetter (1888-1949) A2493
Woody Guthrie (1912-67) A2494 
Sonny Terry (1911-86) A2495 
Josh White (1908-69) A2496 
Mahalia Jackson (1911-72) A2497
Roberta Martin (1917-69) A2498
Clara Ward (1924-73) A2499
Sister Rosetta Tharpe (1921-73) A2500

1998, June 26   *Perf. 10.1x10.2*

3212	A2493	32c multicolored	.60	.15
3213	A2494	32c multicolored	.60	.15
3214	A2495	32c multicolored	.60	.15
3215	A2496	32c multicolored	.60	.15
a.		Block or strip of 4, #3212-3215	2.40	—

1998, July 15   Photo.   *Perf. 10.1x10.3*

3216	A2497	32c multicolored	.60	.15
3217	A2498	32c multicolored	.60	.15
3218	A2499	32c multicolored	.60	.15
3219	A2500	32c multicolored	.60	.15
a.		Block or strip of 4, #3216-3219	2.40	—

Spanish Settlement of the Southwest

La Mision de San Miguel de San Gabriel, Española, NM — A2501

1998, July 11   Litho.   *Perf. 11.2*

3220	A2501	32c multicolored	.60	.15

Literary Arts

Stephen Vincent Benét (1898-43) A2502

1998, July 22   Litho.   *Perf. 11.2*

3221	A2502	32c multicolored	.60	.15

Tropical Birds

Antillean Euphonia A2503
Green-throated Carib — A2504 
Crested Honeycreeper A2505

UNITED STATES

Cardinal Honeyeater
A2506

1998, July 29   Litho.   Perf. 11.2
3222	A2503	32c multicolored	.60 .15
3223	A2504	32c multicolored	.60 .15
3224	A2505	32c multicolored	.60 .15
3225	A2506	32c multicolored	.60 .15
a.	Block of 4, #3222-3225		2.40

A2507 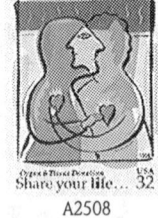   A2508

Legends of Hollywood
1998, Aug. 3   Photo.   Perf. 11.1
3226 A2507 32c multicolored   .60 .15

Alfred Hitchcock (1899-1980). Perforations in corner of each stamp are star-shaped. Hitchcock's profile in the UL corner of each stamp is laser cut.

Organ & Tissue Donation
Serpentine Die Cut 11.7
1998, Aug. 5   Photo.
Self-Adhesive
3227 A2508 32c multicolored   .60 .15

MODERN BICYCLE

A2509

Subscribe to stamp collecting's most entertaining read, Scott Stamp Monthly

Get 12 issues for only $17.95

To subscribe call 1-800-572-6885 or visit our web site at www.scottonline.com

---

COIL STAMPS
Serpentine Die Cut 9.8 Vert.
1998, Aug. 14   Photo.   Untagged
Self-Adhesive
3228 A2509 (10c) multicolored   .20 .15

Perf. 9.9 Vert.
3229 A2509 (10c) multicolored   .20 .15

Bright Eyes

Dog — A2510

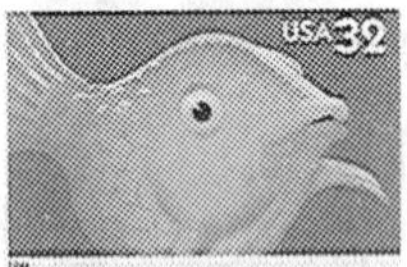

Fish — A2511

Cat — A2512

Parakeet A2513

Hamster A2514

Serpentine Die Cut 9.9
1998, Aug. 20   Photo.
Self-Adhesive
3230	A2510	32c multicolored	.60 .15
3231	A2511	32c multicolored	.60 .15
3232	A2512	32c multicolored	.60 .15
3233	A2513	32c multicolored	.60 .15
3234	A2514	32c multicolored	.60 .15
a.	Strip of 5, #3230-3234		3.00

See note after No. 3167.

Klondike Gold Rush, Centennial

A2515

1998, Aug. 21   Litho.   Perf. 11.1
3235 A2515 32c multicolored   .60 .15

American Art

A2516

1998, Aug. 27   Photo.   Perf. 10.2
3236	A2516	Pane of 20	12.00
a.-t.		32c any single	.60 .15

Paintings: a, "Portrait of Richard Mather," by John Foster. b, "Mrs. Elizabeth Freake and Baby Mary," by The Freake Limner. c, "Girl in Red Dress with Cat and Dog," by Ammi Phillips. d, "Rubens Peale with a Geranium," by Rembrandt Peale. e, "Long-billed Curlew, Numenius Longrostris," by John James Audubon. f, "Boatmen on the Missouri," by George Caleb Bingham. g, "Kindred Spirits," by Asher B. Durand. h, "The Westwood Children," by Joshua Johnson. i, "Music and Literature," by William Harnett. j, "The Fog Warning," by Winslow Homer. k, "The White Cloud, Head Chief of the Iowas," by George Catlin. l, "Cliffs of Green River," by Thomas Moran. m, "The Last of the Buffalo," by Alfred Bierstadt. n, "Niagara," by Frederic Edwin Church. o, "Breakfast in Bed," by Mary Cassatt. p, "Nighthawks," by Edward Hopper. q, "American Gothic," by Grant Wood. r, "Two Against the White," by Charles Sheeler. s, "Mahoning," by Franz Kline. t, "No. 12," by Mark Rothko.

Inscriptions on the back of each stamp describe the painting and the artist.

AMERICAN BALLET

A2517

1998, Sept. 16   Litho.   Perf. 10.9x11.1
3237 A2517 32c multicolored   .60 .15

SPACE DISCOVERY

A2518    A2519

A2520    A2521

A2522

1998, Oct. 1   Photo.   Perf. 11.1
3238	A2518	32c multicolored	.60 .15
3239	A2519	32c multicolored	.60 .15
3240	A2520	32c multicolored	.60 .15
3241	A2521	32c multicolored	.60 .15
3242	A2522	32c multicolored	.60 .15
a.	Strip of 5, #3238-3242		3.00 —

See note after No. 3167.

Giving and Sharing

A2523

Serpentine Die Cut 11.1
1998, Oct. 7   Photo.
Self-Adhesive
3243 A2523 32c multicolored   .60 .15

Christmas

Madonna and Child, Florence, 15th Cent. — A2524

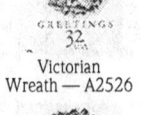

Evergreen Wreath — A2525   Victorian Wreath — A2526

Chili Pepper Wreath — A2527     Tropical Wreath — A2528

Serpentine Die Cut 10.1x9.9 on 2, 3 or 4 Sides
1998, Oct. 15   Litho.
Booklet Stamps
3244	A2524	32c multicolored	.60 .15
a.		Booklet pane of 20 + label	12.00

Serpentine Die Cut 11.3x11.6 on 2 or 3 Sides

3245	A2525	32c multicolored	.60	.15
3246	A2526	32c multicolored	.60	.15
3247	A2527	32c multicolored	.60	.15
3248	A2528	32c multicolored	.60	.15
a.		Booklet pane of 4, #3245-3248	2.50	
b.		Booklet pane of 5, #3245-3246, 3248, 2 #3247 + label	3.00	
c.		Booklet pane of 6, #3247-3248, 2 each #3245-3246	3.60	

Size: 23x30mm
Serpentine Die Cut 11.4x11.6 on 2, 3 or 4 Sides

3249	A2525	32c multicolored	.60	.15
3250	A2526	32c multicolored	.60	.15
3251	A2527	32c multicolored	.60	.15
3252	A2528	32c multicolored	.60	.15
a.		Block of 4, #3249-3252	2.40	
b.		Booklet pane, 5 each #3249-3252	12.00	

Weather Vane A2529
Uncle Sam A2530 
Uncle Sam's Hat — A2531 
Space Shuttle Landing — A2532 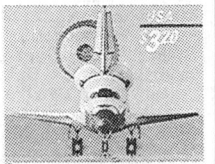
Piggyback Space Shuttle A2533 

1998   Litho.   Perf. 11.2
Self-Adhesive (#3259, 3261-3263, 3265-3269)

3257	A2529	(1c) multicolored	.15	.15
3258	A2529	(1c) multicolored	.15	.15

No. 3257 is 18mm high, has thin letters, white USA, and black 1998. No. 3258 is 17mm high, has thick letters, pale blue USA and blue 1998.

Photo.
Serpentine Die Cut 10.8

3259	A2530	22c multicolored	.45	.15

Perf. 11.2

3260	A2531	(33c) multicolored	.65	.15

Litho.
Serpentine Die Cut 11.5

3261	A2532	$3.20 multicolored	6.00	3.00
3262	A2533	$11.75 multicolored	22.50	11.50

COIL STAMPS
Photo.
Serpentine Die Cut 9.9 Vert.

3263	A2530	22c multicolored	.45	.15

Perf. 9.8 Vert.

3264	A2531	(33c) multicolored	.65	.15

Serpentine Die Cut 9.9 Vert.

3265	A2531	(33c) multicolored	.65	.15

Unused examples of No. 3265 are on backing paper the same size as the stamps.

Serpentine Die Cut 9.7 Vert.

3266	A2531	(33c) multicolored	.65	.15

Unused examples of No. 3266 are on backing paper larger than the stamps. Corners of stamps are rounded.

BOOKLET STAMPS
Serpentine Die Cut 9.9 on 2 or 3 Sides

3267	A2531	(33c) multicolored	.65	.15
a.		Booklet pane of 10	6.50	

Serpentine Die Cut 11.2x11.1 on 2, 3 or 4 Sides

3268	A2531	(33c) multicolored	.65	.15
a.		Booklet pane of 10	6.50	
b.		Booklet pane of 20 + label	13.00	

Die Cut 8 on 2, 3 or 4 Sides

3269	A2531	(33c) multicolored	.65	.15
a.		Booklet pane of 18	12.00	

Issued: No. 3262, 11/19; others, 11/9.

A2533

COIL STAMPS
1998, Dec. 14   Photo.   Perf. 9.9 Vert.

3270	A2533	(10c) multicolored	.20	.20

Serpentine Die Cut 9.9 Vert.
Self-Adhesive

3271	A2533	(10c) multicolored	.20	.20

Compare to Nos. 2602-2604, 2907.

Ordering on-line is
QUICK!
EASY!
CONVENIENT!
www.scottonline.com

Subject Index of Regular andAir Post Issues

Abbott, Bud 2566
Accounting, Certified Public 2361
Acheson, Dean 2755
Adams, Abigail 2146
Adams, John 806, 841, 850, 2216b
Adams, John Q. 811, 846, 2216f
Addams, Jane 878
Admiralty Head, WA, Lighthouse 2470
Adriatic, S.S. 117, 128
Adventures of Huckleberry Finn 2787
African Elephant Herd 1388
African Violet 2486
Agave 1943
Aging Together 2011
AIDS Awareness 2806
Aircraft 3142
Air Force, U.S. C49, 3167
Air Mail, 50th Anniversary C74
Air Service Emblem C5
Airborne Attack Units 2838d
Airlift 1341
Alabama Statehood 1375
Alamo, The 1043
Alaska Highway 2635
Alaska Purchase C70
Alaska Statehood 2066, C53
Alaska Territory 800
Alaska-Yukon Pacific Exposition 370, 371
Alaskan Brown Bear 2310
Albania, Flag 918
Alcoholism 1927
Alcott, Louisa May 862
Aleutian Islands, Japanese Invasion of .2697e
Alexandria, Virginia C40
Alger, Horatio 2010
Alley Oop 3000n
Alliance for Progress 1234
Allied Nations 907
Alligator 1428
Allosaurus 3136g
Alpha Airplane 3142e
Alpine Skiing 3180
Alta California 1725
Amateur Radio 1260
Ambulance 2128, 2231
American Arts 1484-1487,
1553-1554, 3236
American Automobile Association 1007
American Bald Eagle 1387
American Bar Association 1022
American Bicentennial 1456-1459,
1476-1479, 1480-1483, 1543-1546,
1559-1568, 1629-1631, 1686-1694,
1704, 1716-1720, 1722, 1726, 1728,
1753, 1937-1938, 2052
American Buffalo 1392
American Chemical Society 1002, 1685
American Crocodile 3105d
American Elk 2328
American Folklore 1317, 1330,
1357, 1370, 1470, 1548
American Indian 565, 695, 1364
American Indian Dances 3072-3076
American Institute of Architects 1089
American Kestrel 2476-2477, 3044
American Legion 1369
American Lobster 2304
American Music 1252, 2721-2737,
2767-2778, 2849-2861, 2982-2992,
3096-3103, 3154-3165, 3212-3219
American Philatelic Society 750
American Realism (art) 3184n
American Revolution Bicentennial 1432
American Shoals, FL, Lighthouse 2473
AMERIPEX '86 .... 2145, 2216-2219
Anemone 3029
Annapolis Tercentenary 984
Antarctic Treaty 1431, C130
Anthony, Susan B. 784, 1051
Antillean Euphonia 3222
Anti-aircraft Gun 900
Anti-Pollution 1410-1413
Apgar, Virginia.................................... 2179
Apollo 8 1371
Apollo-Soyuz Space Project 1569-1570
Appleseed, Johnny 1317
Appomattox Surrender 1182
Apprenticeship 1201
Apte Tarpon Fly 2547
Arbor Day 717
Architecture, American 1779-1782,
1838-1841, 1928-1931, 2019-2022
Arctic Explorations 1128
Arizona Statehood 1192
Arkansas River Navigation 1358
Arkansas Statehood 782, 2167
Arlen, Harold 3100
Arlington Amphitheater 570, 701
Armadillo 2296
Armed Forces Reserve 1067
Armory Show 3183d
Armstrong, Edwin 2056
Armstrong, Louis 2982, 2984
Army 785-789, 934
Army, Continental 1565
Arnold, H.H. "Hap" 2191
Arsenal of Democracy 2559e
Arthur, Chester A. 826, 2218c
Articles of Confederation 1726
Artists 884-888
Ash Can School 3182h
Art Deco Style 3184j
Assiniboin Headdress 2501
Aster 2993
Atomic Energy Act 1200
Atoms for Peace 1070
Audubon, John J. 874, 1241,
1863, 3236e, C71
Australia Bicentennial 2370
Austria, Flag 919
Authors 859-863
Automated Post Office 1164
Automobile, Electric 296
Automobiles 2381-2385,
2905-2906, 3019-3023
Automobile Tail Fin 2908-2910

B-10 Airplane 3142f
Baby Buggy 1902
Badger 2312
Bailey Gatzert Riverboat 3095
Bailey, Mildred 2860
Balboa, Vasco Nunez de 397, 401
Bald Eagle 2309
Baldwin, Abraham 1850
Ballet..3237
Balloons 2032-2035, 2530, C54
Ballot Box 1584
Baltimore & Ohio Railroad 1006
Bankers Association, American 987
Banking and Commerce 1577-1578
Banneker, Benjamin 1804
Bara, Theda 2827
Barber, Samuel 3162
Barney Google 3000i
Barn Swallow 2286
Barrel Cactus 1942
Barrymore, John, Ethel & Lionel 2012
Bartholdi, Frederic Auguste 2147
Barton, Clara 967, 2975c
Baseball 855, 1381, 2619
Basie, Count 3096
Basketball 1189, 2560
Bass, Largemouth 2207
Bastogne & Battle of the Bulge 2838j
Beacon on Rocky Mountains C11
Bearberry 2687
Beau Geste 2447
Beautification of America . 1318, 1365-1368
Beaver 2316
Beavertail Cactus 1944
Beckwourth, Jim 2869q, 2870
Belgium, Flag 914
Bell, Alexander Graham 893
Benedict, Ruth 2938
Benét, Stephen Vincent 3221
Benny, Jack 2564
Bergen, Edgar 2563
Bering Land Bridge C131
Berlin Airlift 3211
Bethune, Mary McLeod 2137
Bicycle 1901, 3228-3229
Bierstadt, Alfred................................3236m
Big Brothers/Big Sisters 2162
Bighorn Sheep 1467, 1880, 1949, 2288
Biglin Brothers 1335
Bill of Rights 1312, 2421
Bingham, George Caleb 3236f
Biplane 2436, 2438c
Birds and Flowers, State 1953-2002
Birds, Tropical 3222-3225
Birth of Liberty 618
Bison 1883, 2320
Bissell, Emily 1823
Black Bear 2299
Black Heritage 1744, 1771,
1804, 1875, 2016, 2044, 2073, 2137,
2203, 2249, 2371, 2402, 2442, 2567,
2617, 2746, 2816, 2956, 3058
Black, Hugo L. 2172
Black-footed Ferret 2333, 3105a
Black-necked Crane 2867
Black-tailed Jack Rabbit 2305
Black-tailed Prairie Dog 2325
Blackwell, Elizabeth 1399
Blair, Montgomery C66
Blake, Eubie 2988
Blondie 3000l
Blood Donor 1425
Blue Flag 2663
Blue Jay 1757d, 2318, 2483, 3048, 3053
Bluebird, Eastern 2478, 3033
Bluets 2656
Bobcat 2332, 2482
Bobwhite 2301
Bogart, Humphrey 3152
Bolivar, Simon 1110-1111
Books, Bookmark, and Eyeglasses 1585
Boone, Daniel 1357
Boston Tea Party 1480-1483
Botanical Prints by M. S. Merian .3126-3129
Botanical Congress 1376-1379
Boulder Dam 774
Bow, Clara 2820
Bowling.. 2963
Box Turtle 2326
Boy Scouts 995, 1145, 2161, 3183j
Boys' Clubs of America 1163
Brachiosaurus 3136d
Braddock's Field 688
Bread Wagon 2136
Breast Cancer Awareness 3081, B1
Breckinridge, Mary.............................2942
Brenda Starr 3000t
Brice, Fanny 2565
Bridge at Niagara Falls 297
Bridge, Mississippi River 293
Bridger, Jim 2869c, 2870
Bringing Up Father 3000d
Broad-billed Hummingbird 2643
Broad-tailed Hummingbird 2289
Brontosaurus 2425
Brooklyn Bridge 2041
Brooklyn, Battle of 1003
Brown Bear 1884
Brown Pelican 1466, 3105h
Brussels International Exhibition 1104
Bryan, William Jennings 2195
Bryant, Bear 3143, 3148
Buchanan, James 820, 2217f
Buchanan's No. 999 2847
Buck, Pearl 1848
Buckboard 2124
Buffalo 569, 700, 1392
Buffalo Soldiers 2818
Bugs Bunny 3137-3138
Bunchberry 2675
Bunche, Ralph 1860
Bunker Hill Monument 1034, 1056
Bunker Hill, Battle of 1564
Burbank, Luther 876
Bureau of Engraving and Printing 2875
Burgoyne 1728
Burgoyne Campaign 644
Burma Road 2559a
Butte.................................... 2902, 2902B
Butterflies 1712-1715, 3105f
Byrd Antarctic 733, 753, 768
Byrd, Richard E. 2388

Cable Car 2263
Caboose 1905
Cabrillo, Juan Rodriguez 2704
Cadillac, Landing of 1000
Calder, Alexander 3198-3202
California Condor 1430, 3105i
California Gold 954
California Poppy 2651
California Sea Lion 2329
California Settlement 1373
California Statehood 997
California-Pacific Exposition 773
Calliope Hummingbird 2646
Camarasaurus 3136c
Camellia 1877
Camp Fire Girls 1167
Camp Fire, Inc. 2163
Camptosaurus 3136b
Canada Centenary 1324
Canada Goose 1757c, 2334
Canada-U.S. Friendship 961
Canal Boat 2257
Canal Locks at Sault Ste. Marie 298
Cancer 1263, 1754
Canoe 2453, 2454
Cape Hatteras Lighthouse 2471
Cape Hatteras National Seashore 1448-1451
CAPEX '78 1757
Cardinal 1465, 1757a, 2480
Cardinal Honeyeater 3225
CARE 1439
Caribou, Woodland 3105l
Carlson, Chester 2180
Carmichael, Hoagy 3103
Carnegie, Andrew 1171
Carolina Charter 1230
Carolina-Charleston 683
Carousel Animals 2390-2393, 2976-2979
Carreta 2255
Carson, Kit 2869n, 2870
Carson, Rachael 1857
Carter Family 2773, 2777
Caruso, Enrico 2250
Carved Figures 2426, C121
Carver, George Washington 953, 3183c
Cashman, Nellie 2869k, 2870
Cassatt, Mary 1322, 2181, 3236o
Catfish 2209
Cather, Willa 1487
Catlin, George 3236k
Cats 2372-2375. 3232
Catt, Carrie Chapman 959
Cattle 1504
Celebrate the Century 3182-3191
Century of Progress 728-731, 766-767
Ceratosaurus 3136a
Certified Public Accounting 2361
Champions of Liberty 1096,
1110-1111, 1117-1118, 1125-1126,
1136-1137, 1147-1148, 1159-1160,
1165-1166, 1168-1169, 1174-1175
Chancellorsville, Battle of 2975p
Chaney, Lon 2822, 3168
Chaney, Lon, Jr. 3172
Chanute, Octave C93-C94
Chaplains, Four 956
Chaplin, Charlie 2821, 3183a
Chautauqua 1505
Chavez, Dennis 2186
Chemical Society, American 1002
Chemistry 1685
Chennault, Claire 2187
Cherokee Strip 1360, 2754
Chesnut, Mary 2975o
Cheyenne Headdress 2502
Chief Joseph 1364
Child Labor Reform 3183o
Children's Friendship 1085
China Clipper C20-C22
Chinese Resistance 906
Chipmunk 1757f, 2297
Christmas 1205, 1240,
1254-1257, 1276, 1321, 1336, 1363,
1384, 1414-1418, 1444-1445, 1471-
1472, 1507-1508, 1550-1552, 1579-
1580, 1701-1703, 1729-1730, 1768-
1769, 1799-1800, 1842-1843, 1939-
1940, 2025-2030, 2063-2064, 2107-
2108, 2165-2166, 2244-2245, 2367-
2368, 2399-2400, 2427-2429, 2514-
2516, 2578-2585, 2710-2719, 2789-
2803, 2871-2874, 3003-3018, 3107-
3117, 3176-3177, 3244-3252
Chrysanthemum 2994
Church, Frederick 3236n
Churchill, Winston S. 1264, 2559d

SUBJECT INDEX OF REGULAR AND AIR POST ISSUES 85

Cinco de Mayo ... 3203
CIPEX ... 948
Circus, American ... 1309, 2750-2753
Circus Wagon ... 2452, 2452B, 2452D
City Mail Delivery ... 1238
Civil Defense ... 2559g
Civil Service ... 2053
Civil War ... 1178-1182, 2975
Civilian Conservation Corps ... 2037
Claret Cup Cactus ... 2660
Clark, George Rogers ... 651
Clark, Grenville ... 1867
Clay, Henry ... 140, 151, 162, 173, 198, 227, 259, 274, 284, 309, 1846
Clemens, Samuel L. ... 863
Clemente, Roberto ... 2097
Cleveland, Grover ... 564, 693, 827, 2218d
Cline, Patsy ... 2772, 2777
Coal Car ... 2259
Coast and Geodetic Survey ... 1088
Coast Guard ... 936
Cochran, Jacqueline ... 3066
Cod, Atlantic ... 2206
Code Deciphering ... 2697f
Cody, Buffalo Bill ... 2177, 2869b, 2870
Cog Railroad ... 2463
Cohan, George M. ... 1756
Cole, Nat "King" ... 2852
Coleman, Bessie ... 2956
Collective Bargaining ... 1558
Colonial Communications ... 1476-1479
Colonial Craftsmen ... 1456-1459
Colorado Statehood ... 1001, 1711
Coltrane, John ... 2991
Columbia University ... 1029
Columbian Exposition . 230-245, 2624-2629
Columbus' Discovery ... 2426, 2512, 2620-2623, 2805, C121, C127, C131
Comanche Headdress ... 2503
Comedians ... 2562-2566
Comic Strips ... 3000
Commercial Aviation ... 1684
Common Sunflower ... 2666
Commonwealth of the Northern Mariana Islands ... 2804
Communications for Peace ... 1173
Compact, Signing of the ... 550
Composers ... 879-883, 3100-3103
Computer Technology ... 3106
Comstock, Henry ... 1130
Condor, California ... 1430, 3105i
Conestoga Wagon ... 2252
Confederate Veterans, United ... 998
Confederation, Articles of ... 1726
Connecticut Statehood ... 2340
Connecticut Tercentenary ... 772
Constellation Airplane ... 3142m
Constitution Bicentennial ... 2412-2414
Constitution Drafting ... 2355-2359
Constitution Ratification ... 835, 2336-2348
Constitution Signing ... 798, 2360
Constitution, U.S. Frigate ... 951
Construction Toys ... 3182n
Consumer Education ... 2005
Contemplation of Justice ... 1592, 1617
Continental Army ... 1565
Continental Congress ... 1543-1546
Continental Marines ... 1567
Continental Navy ... 1566
Contributors to the Cause ... 1559-1561
Cook, Capt. James ... 1732-1733
Coolidge, Calvin ... 834, 2219b
Cooper, Gary ... 2447
Cooper, James Fenimore ... 860
Copernicus, Nicolaus ... 1488
Copley, John Singleton ... 1273
Coral Reefs ... 1827-1830
Coral Sea, Battle of ... 2697c
Cord (automobile) ... 2383
Coronado Expedition ... 898
Corregidor ... 925, 2697d
Corsair Airplane ... 3142g
Corythosaurus ... 3136m
Costello, Lou ... 2566
Cottontail ... 2290
CPA ... 2361
Cranes ... 1097, 2867-2868
Crayola Crayons ... 3182d
Crazy Horse ... 1855
Credit Union Act ... 2075
Credo ... 1139-1144
Crested Honeycreeper ... 3224
Crime Prevention ... 2102
Crippled, Hope for ... 1385
Crockett, Davy ... 1330
Crocodile, American ... 3105d
Crocus ... 3025
Crosby, Bing ... 2850
Crossword Puzzle, First ... 3183l
Cub Airplane ... 3142c
Curtiss Jenny ... C1-C3, 3142s
Curtiss, Glenn ... C100
Cushing, Harvey ... 2188
Cycling ... 3119
Czechoslovakia, Flag ... 910

Daffodil ... 2761
Dahlia ... 1878, 2995
Dance, American ... 1749-1752
Dances, American Indian ... 3072-3076
Dante ... 1268
Dare, Virginia ... 796
Dartmouth College Case ... 1380
Daspletosaurus ... 3136k
Davis, Dr. Allison ... 2816
Davis, Benjamin O. ... 3121
Davis, Jefferson ... 2975f
DC-3 Airplane ... 3142q
DC-4 Skymaster .. C32-C33, C37, C39, C41
D-Day ... 2838c
De Haviland Biplane ... C6
Dean, James ... 3082
Declaration of Independence ... 120, 130, 627, 1691-1695
Declaration of War on Japan ... 2559j
Deer Mouse ... 2324
Defense, National ... 899-901
Delaware Statehood ... 2336
Delta Wing ... C77
Dempsey, Jack ... 3183m
Denmark, Flag ... 920
Dental Health ... 1135
Desert Fire Spot ... 2690
Desert Plants ... 1942-1945
Desert Shield/Desert Storm ... 2551-2552
Destroyer Reuben James ... 2559f
Devils Tower ... 1084
Dewey, John ... 1291
Dickinson, Emily ... 1436
Dickson, William ... 3064
Dick Tracy ... 3000m
Diner ... 3208, 3208A
Dinosaurs ... 2422-2425, 3136
Dirksen, Everett ... 1874
Disabled Veterans ... 1421
Disney, Walt ... 1355
District of Columbia ... 2561
Dix, Dorothea ... 1844
Doctors ... 949
Dog Sled ... 2135
Dogs ... 2098-2101, 3230
Dolls ... 3151
Dolphin ... 2511
Dome of Capitol ... 1590-1591, 1616
Dorsey, Tommy & Jimmy ... 3097
Douglass, Frederick ... 1290, 2975h
Dracula ... 3169
Drew, Charles R. ... 1865
Drug Abuse, Prevent ... 1438
Drum ... 1615
Du Bois, W.E.B. ... 2617, 3182l
Du Sable, Jean Baptiste Pointe ... 2249
Duck Decoys ... 2138-2141
Duck, Wood ... 2484-2485
Duesenberg ... 2385
Dulles, John Foster ... 1172
Dunbar, Paul Laurence ... 1554
Durand, Asher B. ... 3236g
Dutchman's Breeches ... 2682

Eagan, Eddie ... 2499
Eagle ... 1735-1736, 1743, 1818-1820, 1909, 1946-1948, 2111-2113, 2122, 2309, 2394, 2540, 2541, 2542, 2598, C48, C50, C67
Eagle and Shield ... 116, 127, 771, 1596, 2431, 2595-2597, 2602-2604, 2907, 3270-3271, CE1-CE2
Eagle Holding Shield, etc. ... 121, 131, C23
Eakins, Thomas ... 1335
Earhart, Amelia ... C68
Earp, Wyatt ... 2869j, 2870
Earth ... 2277, 2279, 2282, 2570
Earth Day ... 2951-2954
Eastern Bluebird ... 2478, 3033
Eastern Chipmunk ... 2297
Eastman, George ... 1062
Echo I ... 1173
Eddy's No. 242 ... 2845
Edison, Thomas A. ... 654-656, 945
Edmontonia ... 3136i
Education ... 1833
Educators ... 869-873
Einiosaurus ... 3136j
Einstein, Albert ... 1285, 1774
Eisenhower, Dwight D. ... 1383, 1393-1395, 1401-1402, 2219g, 2513
Electric Auto ... 296, 1906
Electric Light ... 654-656
Electric Toy Trains ... 3184d
Electronics ... 1500-1502, C86
Elevator ... 2254
Eliot, Charles W. ... 871
Eliot, T.S. ... 2239
Elk ... 1886
Elks, B.P.O. ... 1342
Ellington, "Duke" ... 2211
Ellsworth, Lincoln ... 2389
Ely's No. 10 ... 2846
Emancipation Proclamation ... 1233
Emerson, Ralph Waldo ... 861
Emigration, Hardships of ... 290
Empire State Express ... 295
Endangered Flora ... 1783-1786
Endangered Species ... 3105
Energy ... 1723-1724, 2006-2009
Energy Conservation ... 1547
Engineers, American Society of Civil ... 1012
Envelopes ... 2150
Eohippus ... 3077
Ericsson, John, Statue of ... 628
Erie Canal ... 1325
Erikson, Leif ... 1359
Etiquette ... 3184
Everglades ... 952
Ewry, Ray ... 2497
Executive Branch of Government ... 2414
Explorers ... 2024, 2093, 2220-2223, 2386-2389
EXPO '74 ... 1527

Fairbanks, Douglas ... 2088
Fallen Timbers, Battle of ... 680
Family Planning ... 1455
Family Unity ... 2104
Far West Riverboat ... 3093
Farley, Carl ... 2934
Farming in the West ... 286
Farnsworth, Philo T. ... 2058
Farragut, David G. ... 311, 2975g
Faulkner, William ... 2350
Fawn ... 2479
Federal Deposit Insurance Corp. ... 2071
Federal Reserve System ... 3183b
Federated States of Micronesia ... 2506
Ferret, Black-footed ... 2333, 3105a
Ferryboat ... 2466
Fiedler, Arthur ... 3159
Fields, Dorothy ... 3102
Fields, W.C. ... 1803
Fillmore, Millard ... 818, 2217d
Films ... 2445-2448
Finnish Independence ... 1334
FIPEX ... 1075
Fire Engine ... 2264
Fire Pumper ... 1908
Fireweed ... 2679
Fish ... 2205-2209, 3231
Fishing Boat ... 2529, 2529C
Fishing Flies ... 2545-2549
Fitzgerald, F. Scott ... 3104
Flag, Foreign ... 909-921
Flag, Fort McHenry ... 1597-1598, 1618, 1618C
Flag, U.S. ... 1094, 1132, 1153, 1208, 1338-1338G, 1345-1354, 1509, 1519, 1597, 1618C, 1622-1623, 1625, 1890-1891, 1893-1896, 2114-2116, 2276, 2278, 2280, 2285A, 2475, 2522, 2523, 2523A, 2528, 2531, 2593-2594, 2605-2609, 2879-2893, 2897, 2913-2916, 2919-2921, 3133
Flags, 50 States ... 1633-1682
Flamingo ... 2707
Flanagan, Father Edward Joseph ... 2171
Flappers ... 3184h
Flash Gordon ... 3000p
Flathead Headdress ... 2504
Florida Manatee ... 3105o
Florida Panther ... 3105m
Florida Settlement ... 1271
Florida Statehood ... 927, 2950
Flowers ... 1876-1879, 2076-2079, 2517-2520, 2524-2527, 2647-2696, 2760-2764, 2829-2833, 2993-2997, 3025-3029
Flowers and Birds, State ... 1953-2002
Flushing Remonstrance ... 1099
Flying Fortress Airplane ... 3142k
Folk Art, American ... 1706-1709, 1745-1748, 1775-1778, 1834-1837, 2240-2243, 2351-2354, 2390-2393
Food for Peace ... 1231
Football, Intercollegiate ... 1382
Ford, Henry ... 1286A
Forest Conservation ... 1122
Forestry Congress, 5th World ... 1156
Fort Bliss ... 976
Fort Duquesne ... 1123
Fort Kearny ... 970
Fort Nisqually ... 1604
Fort Orange, Landing at ... 615
Fort Snelling ... 1409
Fort Sumter ... 1178
Fort Ticonderoga ... 1071
Foster, John ... 3236a
Foster, Stephen Collins ... 879
Four Freedoms ... 908
Four-H Clubs ... 1005
Four Horseman of Notre Dame ... 3184l
Fox, Red ... 1757g, 3036
Fragrant Water Lily ... 2648
France, Flag ... 915
Francis of Assisi ... 2023
Francisco, Peter ... 1562
Frankenstein ... 3170
Franklin, Benjamin ... 1, 3, 5-5A, 6-8A, 9, 18-24, 38, 40, 46, 63, 71, 81, 85, 86, 92, 100, 102, 110, 112, 123, 133-134, 145, 156, 167, 182, 192, 206, 212, 219, 246-247, 264, 279, 300, 314, 316, 318, 331, 343, 348, 352, 357, 374, 383, 385, 387, 390, 392, 414-423, 431-440, 460, 470-478, 497, 508-518, 523-524, 547, 552, 575, 578, 581, 594, 596-597, 604, 632, 658, 669, 803, 1030, 1073, 1393D, 1690, 3139
Freedom from Hunger ... 1231
Freedom of the Press ... 1119
Fremont, John C. ... 2869i, 2870
Fremont on the Rocky Mountains ... 288
French Alliance ... 1753
French Revolution ... C120
French, Daniel Chester ... 887
Fringed Gentian ... 2672
Frost, Robert ... 1526
Fulbright Scholarships ... 3065
Fulton, Robert ... 1270
Fur Seal ... 1464
Future Farmers ... 1024
Futuristic Mail Delivery ... C122-C126

Gable, Clark & Leigh, Vivien ... 2446
Gadsden Purchase ... 1028
Gallatin, Albert ... 1279
Gallaudet, Thomas H. ... 1861
Galvez, Gen. Bernardo de ... 1826
Gandhi, Mahatma ... 1174-1175
Gardening-Horticulture ... 1100
Garfield, James A. ... 205, 205C, 216, 224, 256, 271, 282, 305, 558, 587, 638, 664, 675, 723, 825, 2218b
Garibaldi, Giuseppe ... 1168-1169
Garland, Judy ... 2445
Garner, Erroll ... 2992
Gasoline Alley ... 3000h

Gatsby Style ... 3184b
Geebee Airplane ... 3142i
Gehrig, Lou ... 2417
George, Walter F. ... 1170
Georgia Bicentennial ... 726
Georgia Statehood ... 2339
German Immigration ... 2040
Geronimo ... 2869m, 2870
Gershwin, George ... 1484
Gettysburg Address ... 978
Gettysburg, Battle of ... 1180, 2975t
Giannini, Amadeo P. ... 1400
Gibson Girl ... 3182m
Gila Trout ... 3105j
Gilbert, John ... 2823
Gilbreth, Lillian M. ... 1868
Giant Panda ... 2706
Giraffe ... 2705
Girl Scouts ... 974, 1199, 2251, 3182k
Giving & Sharing ... 3243
Gladiola ... 2831
Goddard, Robert H. ... C69
Gold Star Banner ... 2765i
Gold Star Mothers ... 969
Golden Gate ... 399, 403, 567, 698
Golden Gate Exposition ... 852
Golf ... 2965
Gompers, Samuel ... 988
Gone With the Wind ... 2446
Goniopholis ... 3136e
Goodman, Benny ... 3099
Goodnight, Charles ... 2869l, 2870
Gottschalk, Louis Moreau ... 3165
Graf Zeppelin ... C13-C15, C18
Grand Army of the Republic ... 985
Grand Canyon ... 2512, 3183h
Grand Coulee Dam ... 1009
Grange ... 1323
Grant, U.S. ... 223, 255, 270, 281, 303, 314, 560, 589, 640, 666, 677, 823, 2217i, 2975d
Gray Squirrel ... 2295
Gray Wolf ... 2322
Great River Road ... 1319
"Great Train Robbery, The" ... 3182c
Greece, Flag ... 916
Greeley, Horace ... 1177
Greely, Adolphus W. ... 2221
Green-throated Carib ... 3223
Griffith, D.W. ... 1555
Grofe', Ferde ... 3163
Grosbeak ... 2284
Guadalcanal, Battle of ... 2697i
Guitar ... 1613
Gunston Hall ... 1108
Gutenberg Bible ... 1014
Guthrie, Woody ... 3213

Haida Canoe ... 1389
Halas, George ... 3146, 3150
Hale, Nathan ... 551, 653
Haley, Bill ... 2725, 2732
Half Moon and Steamship ... 372-373
Hamilton, Alexander ... 143, 154, 165, 176, 190, 201, 217, 1053, 1086
Hamilton, Alice ... 2940
Hammarskjold, Dag ... 1203-1204
Hamster ... 3234
Hancock, Winfield ... 2975n
Handcar ... 1898
Handicapped ... 1155
Handy, W.C. ... 1372
Hansom Cab ... 1904
Hanson, John ... 1941
Hanukkah ... 3118
Happy New Year ... 2720, 2817, 2876, 3060, 3120, 3179
Harbor Seal ... 1882
Harding, Warren G. ... 553, 576, 582, 598, 605, 610-613, 631, 633, 659, 670, 684, 686, 833, 2219a
Hardy, Oliver ... 2562
Harebell ... 2689
Harlequin Lupine ... 2664
Harnett, William M. ... 1386, 3236i
Harris, Joel Chandler ... 980
Harrison, Benjamin ... 308, 622, 694, 828, 1045, 2218e
Harrison, William H. ... 814, 996, 2216i
Harte, Bret ... 2196
Harvard, John ... 2190
Hawaii ... C46
Hawaii Sesquicentennial ... 647-648
Hawaii Statehood ... 2080, C55
Hawaii Territory ... 799
Hawaiian Monk Seal ... 3105c
Hawkins, Coleman ... 2983
Hawthorne, Nathaniel ... 2047
Hayes, Rutherford B. . 563, 692, 824, 2218a
Head of Freedom Statue, Capitol Dome . 573
Health Research ... 2087
Helping Children Learn ... 3125
HemisFair '68 ... 1340
Hemingway, Ernest M. ... 2418
Henry, Patrick ... 1052
Henson, Matthew, & Peary, Robert E. . 2223
Herb Robert ... 2657
Herbert, Victor ... 881
Herkimer at Oriskany ... 1722
Hermitage, The ... 1037, 1059
Hershey, Milton ... 2933
Hickok, Wild Bill ... 2869o, 2870
Higher Education ... 1206
Hispanic Americans ... 2103
Historic Preservation ... 1440-1443
Hitchcock, Alfred ... 3226
Hoban, James ... 1935-1936
Holiday, Billie ... 2856
Holly, Buddy ... 2729, 2736
Holmes, Oliver Wendell ... 1288, 1288B, 1305E
Home on the Range ... 2869a, 2870
Homemakers ... 1253
Homer, Winslow ... 1207, 3236j
Homestead Act ... 1198
Honeybee ... 2281
Hoover, Herbert C. ... 1269, 2219c
Hopkins, Johns ... 2194
Hopkins, Mark ... 870
Hopper, Edward ... 3236p
Horse Racing ... 1528
Horses ... 2155-2158, 2756-2759
Horticulture ... 1100
Hospitals ... 2210
House of Representatives, U.S. ... 2412
Houston, Sam ... 1242
Hovercraft ... C123, C126b
Howe, Elias ... 892
Howe, Julia Ward ... 2176
Howlin' Wolf ... 2861
Hudson-Fulton Celebration ... 372-373
Hudson's General ... 2843
Hughes, Charles Evans ... 1195
Huguenot-Walloon Tercentenary ... 614-616
Hull, Cordell ... 1235
Humane Treatment of Animals ... 1307
Hummingbirds ... 2642-2646
Humphrey, Hubert ... 2189
Hunger, Help End ... 2164
Hyacinth ... 2760
Hydrangea ... 2996

Iceboat ... 2134
Idaho Statehood ... 896, 2439
Iiwi ... 2311
Illinois Statehood ... 1339
Immigrants Arrive ... 3182i
Independence Hall ... 1044
Independence Spirit, Rise of ... 1476-1479
Independence, Skilled Hands for 1717-1720
Indian Centenary ... 972
Indian Headdresses ... 2501-2505
Indian Head Penny ... 1734
Indian Hunting Buffalo ... 287
Indian Masks, Pacific Northwest 1834-1837
Indian Paintbrush ... 2647
Indian Pond Lily ... 2680
Indiana Statehood ... 1308
Indiana Territory ... 996
Inkwell and Quill ... 1581, 1811
Int'l Aeronautics Conference ... 649-650
International Cooperation Year ... 1266
International Geophysical Year ... 1107
International Peace Garden ... 2014
International Philatelic Exhibition ... 630, 778, 1075-1076, 1310-1311, 1632, 1757, 2145, 2216-2219
Int'l Telecommunications Union ... 1274
International Women's Year ... 1571
International Year of the Child ... 1772
International Year of the Disabled ... 1925
International Youth Year ... 2160-2163
Interphil 76 ... 1632
Inventors ... 889-893, 2055-2058
Iowa Statehood ... 942, 3088-3089
Iowa Territory ... 838
Iron "Betty" Lamp ... 1608
Iris ... 2763
Irving, Washington ... 859
Italy, Invasion of ... 2765f
Ives, Charles ... 3164
Ives, Frederic E. ... 3063
Iwo Jima ... 929

Jack-in-the-pulpit ... 2650
Jackson, Andrew ... 73, 84-85, 87, 93, 103, 135, 146, 157, 168, 178, 180, 183, 193, 203, 211, 211D, 215, 221, 253, 268, 302, 812, 941, 1209, 1225, 1286, 2216g, 2592
Jackson, Mahalia ... 3216
Jackson, "Stonewall" ... 2975s
Jacob's Ladder ... 2684
Jamestown Exposition ... 328-330
Jamestown Festival ... 1091
Jamestown, Founding of ... 329
Japan ... 1021, 1158
Jay, John ... 1046
Jazz Flourishes ... 3184k
Jeffers, Robinson ... 1485
Jefferson Memorial ... 1510, 1520
Jefferson, Thomas ... 12, 27-30A, 42, 67, 75-76, 80, 95, 105, 139, 150, 161, 172, 187-188, 197, 209, 228, 260, 275, 310, 324, 561, 590, 641, 667, 678, 807, 842, 851, 1033, 1055, 1278, 1299, 2185, 2216c
Jenny Airplane ... C1-C3, 3142s
Jet Airliner Silhouette ... C51-C52, C60-C61, C78, C82
Jock Scott ... 2546
John Henry ... 3085
Johnson, Andrew ... 822, 2217h
Johnson, James P. ... 2985
Johnson, James Weldon ... 2371
Johnson, Joshua ... 3236h
Johnson, Lyndon B. ... 1503, 2219i
Johnson, Robert ... 2857
Johnston, Joseph E. ... 2975m
Jolson, Al ... 2849
Jones, Casey ... 993
Jones, John Paul ... 1789
Jones, Robert Tyre ... 1933
Joplin, Scott ... 2044
Joseph, Chief ... 1364, 2869f, 2870
Juke Box ... 2911-2912B, 3132
Julian, Percy Lavon ... 2746
Jupiter ... 2573
Jupiter Balloon ... C54
Just, Ernest E. ... 3058

Kane, Elisha Kent ... 2220
Kansas City, Missouri ... 994
Kansas Statehood ... 1183
Kansas Territory ... 1061
Karloff, Boris ... 3170, 3171
Karman, Theodore von ... 2699
Katzenjammer Kids ... 3000b
Kearny Expedition ... 944
Keaton, Buster ... 2828
Keller, Helen, & Anne Sullivan ... 1824
Kelly, Grace ... 2749
Kennedy, John F. ... 1246, 1287, 2219h
Kennedy, Robert F. ... 1770
Kentucky Settlement ... 1542
Kentucky Statehood ... 904, 2636
Kern, Jerome ... 2110
Kerosene Table Lamp ... 1611
Kestrel, American ... 2476-2477, 3044
Key, Francis Scott ... 962
Keystone Cops ... 2826
Killer Whale ... 2508
King, Jr., Dr. Martin Luther ... 1771
King Penguins ... 2708
Kline, Franz ... 3236s
Klondike Gold Rush ... 3235
Knox, Henry ... 1851
Knoxville World's Fair ... 2006-2009
Korea, Flag ... 921
Kosciuszko, Gen. Tadeusz ... 734-735
Kossuth, Lajos ... 1117-1118
Krazy Kat ... 3000e
Kwanzaa ... 3175

Labor Day ... 1082
Lacemaking ... 2351-2354
Ladybug ... 2315
Lafayette, Marquis de ... 1010, 1097, 1716
LaGuardia, Fiorello H. ... 1397
Land-Grant Colleges ... 1065, 1206
Landing of Columbus ... 118-119, 129
Langley, Samuel P. ... C118
Lanier, Sidney ... 1446
Large-flowered Trillium ... 2652
Laubach, Frank C. ... 1864
Laurel, Stanley ... 2562
Law and Order ... 1343
Leadbelly (Huddie Ledbetter) ... 3212
Lee, Jason ... 964
Lee, Robert E. ... 1049, 2975b
Lefty's Deceiver ... 2548
Legend of Sleepy Hollow ... 1548
Legends of the West ... 2869-2870
Leigh, Vivien & Gable, Clark ... 2446
Lend Lease ... 2559c
Leon, Ponce de ... 2024
Letter Carriers ... 2420
Lewis and Clark Expedition ... 1063
Lewis, Sinclair ... 1856
Lexington-Concord ... 617-619, 1563
Leyte Gulf, Battle of ... 2838i
Liberation of Rome and Paris ... 2838f
Liberty Bell ... 627, 1518, 1595, 1618, C57, C62
Liberty Ships ... 2559h
Libraries, America's ... 2015
Library of Congress ... 2004
Lighthouses ... 1605, 2470-2474, 2969-2973
Lightning Airplane ... 3142n
Li'l Abner ... 3000q
Lilac ... 2764
Lily ... 1879, 2829
Limner, The Freake ... 3236b
Lincoln Memorial ... 571
Lincoln, Abraham ... 77, 85F, 91, 98, 108, 122, 132, 137, 148, 159, 170, 186, 195, 208, 222, 254, 269, 280, 304, 315, 317, 367-369, 555, 584, 600, 635, 661, 672, 821, 906, 978, 1036, 1058, 1113-1116, 1282, 1303, 2217g, 2433, 2975j, C59
Lincoln-Douglas Debates ... 1115
Lindbergh Flight ... 1710, 3184m
Lions International ... 1326
Lippmann, Walter ... 1849
Little House on the Prairie ... 2786
Little Nemo in Slumberland ... 3000c
Little Orphan Annie ... 3000j
Little Women ... 2788
Livingston, Robert R. ... 323
Lloyd, Harold ... 2825
Lockwood, Belva Ann ... 2178
Locomobile ... 2381
Locomotive ... 114, 125, 1897A, 2226, 2362-2366, 2843-2847
Lombardi, Vince ... 3145, 3147
London, Jack ... 2182, 2197
Long, Dr. Crawford W. ... 875
Longfellow, Henry W. ... 864
Louis, Joe ... 2766
Louisiana Purchase ... 1020
Louisiana Purchase Exposition ... 323-327
Louisiana Purchase, Map of ... 327
Louisiana Statehood ... 1197
Louisiana World Exposition ... 2086
Love ... 1475, 1951, 2072, 2143, 2202, 2248, 2378-2379, 2398, 2440-2441, 2535-2537, 2618, 2813-2815, 2948-2949, 2957-2960, 3030, 3123-3124
Low, Juliette Gordon ... 974
Lowell, James Russell ... 866
Luce, Henry R. ... 2935
Ludington, Sybil ... 1559
Lugosi, Bela ... 3169

Luna Moth	2293	Migratory Bird Treaty	1306
Lunch Wagon	2464	Mighty Casey	3083
Luther, Martin	2065	Military Medics	2765b
Luxembourg, Flag	912	Military Services Bicentenary	1565-1568
Lyon, Mary	2169	Military Uniforms	1565-1568
		Militia, American	1568
Maass, Clara	**1699**	Milk Wagon	2253
MacArthur, Gen. Douglas	1424	Millay, Edna St. Vincent	1926
MacDowell, Edward	882	Miller, Glenn	3098
Mackinac Bridge	1109	Millikan, Robert	1866
Madison, Dolley	1822	Mineral Heritage	1538-1541
Madison, Helene	2500	Mingus, Charles	2989
Madison, James	262, 277, 312, 479, 808, 843, 2216d, 2875a	Mining Prospector	291
Magna Carta	1265	Minnesota Statehood	1106
Magsaysay, Ramon	1096	Minnesota Territory	981
Mail Automobile	2437, 2438d	Minute Man, The	619
Mail Order Business	1468	Mississippi Statehood	1337
Mail Transport – ZIP Code	1511	Mississippi Territory	955
Mail Wagon	1903	Missouri Statehood	1426
Maine Statehood	1391	Mitchell, Margaret	2168
Malaria	1194	Mobile, Battle of	1826
Mallard	1757b	Mockingbird	2330
Mammoth, Woolly	3078	Model B Airplane	3142b
Manatee, Florida	3105o	Model T Ford	3182a
Mann, Horace	869	Monarch Butterfly	2287
Mannerheim, Baron Gustaf Emil.	1165-1166	Monitor and Virginia, Battle of	2975a
Map, U.S.	C7-C9	Monk, Thelonious	2990
Marathon	3067	Monmouth, Battle of	646
Marblehead Lighthouse	2972	Monroe, James	325, 562, 591, 603, 642, 668, 679, 810, 845, 1038, 1105, 2216e
Mariana Islands	2804	
Marigold	2832	Monroe, Marilyn	2967
Marine Corps Reserve	1315	Montana Statehood	858, 2401
Mariner 10	1557	Monticello	1047
Marines, Continental	1567	Moon	2571
Marines, World War II	929	Moon Landing	2419, 2841-2842, C76
Marquette on the Mississippi	285	Moon Rover	1435, C124, C126c
Marquette, Jacques	1356	Moore, John Bassett	1295
Mars	2572	Moore, Marianne	2449
Mars Pathfinder and Sojourner	3178	Moose	1757e, 1887, 2298
Marsh Marigold	2658	Moran, Thomas	3236l
Marshall, George C.	1289	Morocco-U.S. Diplomatic Relations	2349
Marshall Islands	2507	Morris Township School, N. Dakota	1606
Marshall, John	263, 278, 313, 480, 1050, 2415	Morse, Samuel F.B.	890
		Morton, Jelly Roll	2986
Marshall Plan	3141	Moses, (Grandma) Anna Mary Robertson	1370
Martin, Roberta	3217	Moses, Horace	2095
Maryland Statehood	2342	Moss Campion	2686
Maryland Tercentenary	736	Mothers of America	737-738, 754
Masaryk, Thomas G.	1148	Motion Pictures	926
Mason, George	1858	Motorcycle	1899
Massachusetts Bay Colony	682	Mott, Lucretia	959
Massachusetts Statehood	2341	Mount McKinley	1454
Masters, Edgar Lee	1405	Mount Rushmore	1011, 2523, 2523A, C88
Masterson, Bat	2869h, 2870	Mount Vernon	1032
Mastodon	3079	Mountain	2903-2904b
Mayflower	548	Mountain Goat	2323
Matzeliger, Jan	2567	Mountain Lion	2292
Mayo, Drs. William and Charles	1251	Muddler Minnow	2549
Mazzei, Philip	C98	Muir, John	1245, 3182j
McCormack, John	2090	Mule Deer	2294
McCormick, Cyrus Hall	891	Munmy, The	3171
McDowell, Dr. Ephraim	1138	Munoz Marin, Luis	2173
McKinley, William	326, 559, 588, 639, 665, 676, 829, 2218f	Murrow, Edward R.	2812
		Muskellunge	2205
McLoughlin, John	964	Mustang Airplane	3142a
McMahon, Brien	1200	Muybridge, Eadweard	3061
McPhatter, Clyde	2726, 2733	My Fair Lady	2770
McQueen's Jupiter	2844		
Mead, Margaret	3184c	**Naismith-Basketball**	**1189**
Meadow Beauty	2649	Nancy	3000o
Meany, George	2848	Nassau Hall	1083
Medal of Honor	2045	Nation of Readers	2106
Mellon, Andrew W.	1072	National Academy of Science	1237
Melville, Herman	2094	National Archives	2081
Mercer, Johnny	3101	National Capital Sesquicentennial	989-992
Merchant Marine	939	National Grange	1323
Mercury	2568	National Guard	1017
Mergenthaler, Ottmar	3062	National Letter Writing Week	1805-1810
Merman, Ethel	2853	National Park Service	1314
Metropolitan Opera	2054	National Parks	740-749, 756-765, 769-770, 1448-1454, C84
Mexican Hat	2688	
Mexican Independence	1157	National Postal Museum	2779-2782
Michael, Moina	977	National Recovery Administration	732
Michigan Centenary	775	National Stamp Exhibition	735
Michigan State College	1065	Native American Culture	2869e, 2870
Michigan Statehood	2246	NATO	1008, 1127
Micronesia, Federated States of	2506	Natural History Museum	1387-1390
Midway, Battle of	2697g		

Navajo Blankets	2235-2237	Overland Mail	1120, 2869t, 2870
Naval Aviation	1185	Overrun Countries	909-921
Naval Review	1091	Owens, Jesse	2496
Navigation, Lake	294	Owl	1760-1763, 2285
Navigation, Ocean	299		
Navy, Continental	1566	**P-51s Escorting B-17s**	**2838b**
Navy, U.S.	790-794, 935	Pacific 97	3130-3131, 3139-3140
Nebraska Statehood	1328	Packard	2384
Nebraska Territory	1060	Paderewski, Ignacy Jan	1159-1160
Neptune	2576	Paine, Thomas	1292
Netherlands	2003	Palace of the Governors Santa Fe	1031A, 1054A
Netherlands, Flag	913	Palaeosaniwa	3136l
Nevada Settlement	999	Palau	2999
Nevada Statehood	1248	Palmer, Nathaniel	2386
Nevin, Ethelbert	883	Palomar Observatory	966
New Guinea, Allied recapture of	2838a	Pan American Games	2247, C56
New Hampshire	1068	Pan American Union	895, C34
New Hampshire Statehood	2344	Pan-American Exposition	294-299
New Jersey Statehood	2338	Panama Canal	856, 3183f
New Jersey Tercentenary	1247	Panama Canal, Pedro Miguel Locks	398, 402
New Mexico Statehood	1191	
New Netherland	614	Panama-Pacific Exposition	397-404
New Orleans, Battle of	1261	Pansy	3027
New Sweden Settlement	C117	Panther, Florida	3105m
New York City	1027, C38	Papanicolaou, Dr. George	1754
New York Coliseum	1076	Parakeet	3233
New York Skyline & Statue of Liberty	C35	Parasaurolophus	3136o
New York Statehood	2346	Parent Teacher Association	1463
New York Stock Exchange	2630	Parker, Charlie	2987
New York World's Fair	853, 1244	Parker, Dorothy	2698
Newburgh, New York	727	Parkman, Francis	1281, 1297
Newspaper Boys	1015	Parrot, Thick-Billed	3105b
Niagara Falls	568, 699	Partridge, Alden	1854
Nimitz, Chester M.	1869	Pasqueflower	2676
Nineteenth Amendment	3184e	Passionflower	2674
Nixon, Richard	2955	Patrol Wagon	2258
Non-Denominated	1735-1736, 1743, 1818-1820, 1946-1948, 2111-2113, 2277, 2279, 2282, 2517-2522, 2602-2604, 2877-2893, 2902, 2905, 2908-2909, 2911-2912	Patton, Gen. George S., Jr.	1026
		Paul, Alice	2943
		Paul Bunyan	3084
		Peace Bridge	1721
		Peace Corps	1447
Norris, George W.	1184	Peace of 1783	727, 752
Norse-American	620, 621	Peacetime Draft	2559b
North African Invasion	2697j	Peach	2487, 2493, 2495
North Carolina Statehood	2347	Peale, Rembrandt	3236d
North Dakota Statehood	858, 2403	Pear	2488, 2494, 2495A
Northern Mariana Islands, Commonwealth of the	2804	Pearl Harbor	2559i
		Peary, Robert E., & Matthew Henson	2223
Northwest Ordinance	795	Peashooter Airplane	3142o
Northwest Territory	837	Pecos Bill	3086
Norway, Flag	911	Pember, Phoebe	2975r
Numismatics	2558	Penn, William	724
Nursing	1190	Pennsylvania Academy	1064
		Pennsylvania State University	1065
Oakley, Annie	**2869d, 2870**	Pennsylvania Statehood	2337
Ocelot	3105e	Pennsylvania Toleware	1775-1778
Ochs, Adolph S.	1700	Performing Arts	1755-1756, 1801, 1803, 2012, 2088, 2090, 2110, 2211, 2250, 2411
Oglethorpe, Gen. James Edward	726	
Ohi'a Lehua	2669	
Ohio River Canalization	681	Perkins, Frances	1821
Ohio Statehood	1018	Perry, Commodore Matthew C.	1021
Oil Wagon	2130	Perry, Commodore O.H.	144, 155, 166, 177, 191, 202, 218, 229, 261-261A, 276-276A
O'Keeffe, Georgia	3069	
Oklahoma! (musical)	2722, 2769	
Oklahoma Statehood	1092	Pershing, Gen. John J.	1042A
Old Faithful, Yellowstone	1453	Petroleum Industry	1134
Old North Church, Boston	1603	Phantom of the Opera, The	3168
Olympics	716, 718-719, 1146, 1460-1462, 1695-1698, 1790-1798, 2048-2051, 2067-2070, 2082-2085, 2369, 2380, 2528, 2496-2500, 2539-2542, 2553-2557, 2611-2615, 2619, 2637-2641, 2807-2811, 3068, 3087, C85, C97, C101-C112	Pharmacy	1473
		Pheasant	2283, 3050-3055
		Phillips, Ammi	3236c
		Photography	1758
		Physical Fitness	2043
		Physical Fitness-Sokol	1262
		Piano	1615C
Omnibus	1897, 2225	Pickett, Bill	2869g, 2870
O'Neill, Eugene	1294, 1305C	Pierce, Franklin	819, 2217e
Opisthias	3136h	Pierce-Arrow	2382
Orchids	2076-2079	Pika	2319
Oregon Statehood	1124	Pilgrim Tercentenary	548-550
Oregon Territory	783, 964	Pilgrims, Landing of the	549, 1420
Oregon Trail	2747	Pine Cone	2491
Organ & Tissue Donation	3227	Pioneer 10	1556
Organized Labor	1831	Piper, William	C129, C132
Oriskany, Battle of	1722	Piping Plover	3105n
Ormandy, Eugene	3161	Pitcher, Molly	646
Ornithomimus	3136n	Pitts, Zasu	2824
Osprey	2291	Plains Prickly Pear	2685
Osteopathic Medicine	1469	Plane and Globes	C89-C90
Ouimet, Francis	2377		

88 SUBJECT INDEX OF REGULAR AND AIR POST ISSUES

Pledge of Allegiance 2594, 2594B
Ploesti Refineries, Bombing of 2765d
Plover, Piping 3105n
Pluto 2577
Pocahontas 330
Poe, Edgar Allan 986
Poets 864-868
Poland, Flag 909
Polar Bear 1429, 1885
Polio 1087
Polish Millennium 1313
Polk, James K. 816, 2217b, 2587
Pons, Lily 3154
Ponselle, Rosa 3157
Pony Express 894, 1154
Poor, Salem 1560
Popcorn Wagon 2261
Popeye 3000k
Poppy, Memorial 977
Porgy & Bess 2768
Porter, Cole 2550
Post Horse & Rider 113, 124
Post, Emily 3182f
Post, Wiley C95-C96
Postal Service Bicentenary 1572-1575
Postal Service Employees 1489-1498
Poultry Industry 968
Powell, John Wesley 1374
Powered Flight C47
President of the United States 2216-2219
Presley, Elvis 2721, 2724, 2731
Priestley, Joseph 2038
Prince Valiant 3000s
Printing 857
Printing Press, Early American 1593
Prisoners of War/Missing in Action 2966
Professional Management 1920
Prohibition Enforced 3184c
Project Mercury 1193
Pronghorn 1889, 2313
Propeller and Radiator C4
PTA 1463
Pteranodon 2423
Public Education 2159
Pueblo Pottery 1706-1709
Puerto Rico Elections 983
Puerto Rico Territory 801
Pulaski, Gen. Casimir 690
Pulitzer, Joseph 946
Puma 1881
Pumpkinseed Sunfish 2481
Pure Food and Drug Act 3182f
Pushcart 2133
Pyle, Ernie T. 1398

Quilts 1745-1748
Quimby, Harriett C128

Raccoon 1757h, 2331
Racing Car 2262
Radio Entertains America................. 3184i
Railroad Conductor's Lantern 1612
Railroad Engineers 993
Railroad Mail Car 2265
Railroad, Transcontinental 922
Rainey, "Ma" 2859
Randolph, Asa Philip 2402
Range Conservation 1176
Ration Coupons 2697b
Rayburn, Sam 1202
Readers, Nation of 2106
Rebecca Everingham Riverboat 3094
Rebecca of Sunnybrook Farm 2785
Red Ball Express 2838h
Red Cloud 2175
Red Cross 702, 967, 1016, 1239, 1910
Red Fox 1757g, 2335
Red Maid 2692
Redding, Otis 2728, 2735
Red-headed Woodpecker 3032
Red-winged Blackbird 2303
Reed, Dr. Walter 877
Register and Vote 1249, 1344
Religious Freedom 1099
Remember The Maine 3192
Remington, Frederic 888, 1187, 1934
Reptiles, Age of 1390
Restaurationen, sloop 620
Retarded Children 1549
Reuter, Ernst 1136-1137
Revel, Bernard 2193
Revere, Paul 1048, 1059A
Rhode Island Statehood 2348
Rhode Island Tercentenary 777
Ribault, Jan, Monument to 616
Rickenbacker, Eddie 2998
Riley, James Whitcomb 868
Ringtail 2302
Rise of Spirit of Independence 1476-1479
River Otter 2314
Riverboats 3091-3095
Roanoke Voyages 2093
Robie House 3182o
Robinson, Jackie 2016
Robt. E. Lee Riverboat 3091
Rockne, Knute 2376
Rockwell, Norman 2839-2840
Rodgers, Jimmie 1755
Rogers, Will 975, 1801
Roosevelt, Eleanor 1236, 2105
Roosevelt, Franklin D. 930-933, 1284, 1298, 1305, 1950, 2219d, 2559d
Roosevelt, Theodore 557, 586, 602, 637, 663, 674, 830, 1039, 2218g, 3182b
Roseate Spoonbill 2308
Rosebud Orchid 2670
Roses 1737, 1876, 2378-2379, 2490, 2492, 2833, 3049, 3054
Ross, Betsy 1004
Rotary International 1066
Rothko, Mark....................................3236t
Rough Riders 973
Round-lobed Hepatica 2677
Royal Wulff 2545
Rube Goldberg 3000f
Ruby-throated Hummingbird 2642
Rudbeckia 2997
Rue Anemone 2694
Rufous Hummingbird 2645
Rural America 1504-1506
Rural Electrification Administration 2144
Rural Free Delivery 3090
Rush Lamp and Candle Holder 1610
Rushing, Jimmy 2858
Russell, Charles M. 1243
Russell, Richard 1853
Ruth, Babe 2046, 3184a

Saber-tooth Cat 3080
Sacagawea 2869s, 2870
Sagamore Hill 1023
Saguaro 1945
Saint-Gaudens, Augustus 886
St. Joseph Lighthouse 2970
St. Lawrence Seaway 1131, 2091
St. Louis World's Fair 3182e
Saipan, Battle of 2838g
Salomon, Haym 1561
Salvation Army 1267
San Francisco Bay, Discovery of 400-400A, 404
San Francisco Garter Snake 3105k
San Francisco-Oakland Bay Bridge C36
San Juan 1437
San Martin, Jose de 1125-1126
Sandburg, Carl 1731
Sandy Hook Lighthouse, New Jersey ... 1605
Saratoga, Surrender at 1728, 2590
Saroyan, William 2538
Saturn 2574
Save Our Air, Cities, Soil, Water 1410-1413
Savings & Loan 1911
Savings Bonds, 50th Anniv. 2534
Savings Bonds-Servicemen 1320
Sawyer, Tom 1470
Saxhorns 1614
Scarlet Tanager 2306
Schaus Swallowtail Butterfly 3105f
School Bus 2123
Schurz, Carl 1847
Science & Industry 2031
Science, National Academy of 1237
Scientists 874-878
Scott, Blanche Stuart C99
Scott, Gen. Winfield 142, 153, 175, 200
Sea Creatures 2508-2511
Sea Lions 2509
Sea Otter 2510
Seal, Hawaiin Monk 3105c
Seaplane 2468
Search for Peace 1326
Seashells 2117-2121
SEATO 1151
Seattle World's Fair 1196
Seeing Eye Dogs 1787
Sego Lily 2667
Semmes, Raphael 2975i
Senate, U.S. 2413
Sequoyah 1859
Serra, Father Junipero C116
Service Women 1013
Servicemen 1422
Servicemen-Savings Bonds 1320
Sesquicentennial Exposition 627
Sessile Bellwort 2662
Sevier, John 941
Seward, William H. 372-373
Shakespeare, William 1250
Sheeler, Charles 3236r
Sherman, William T. . 225, 257, 272, 2975a
Shiloh, Battle of 1179, 2975e
Shipbuilding 1095
Shooting Star 2654
Shoshone Headdress 2505
Show Boat 2767
Showy Evening Primrose 2671
Sicily, Invasion of............................ 2765c
Sign Language 2783-2784
Sikorsky, Igor C119
Silver Centennial 1130
SIPEX 1310-1311
Sitting Bull 2183
Skiing 3180
Skilled Hands for Independence . 1717-1720
Skylab 1529
Sleepy Hollow 1548
Sleigh 1900
Sloan, John 1433
Smith, Alfred E. 937
Smith, Bessie 2854
Smith, Capt. John 328
Smithsonian Institution 943, 3059
Smokey the Bear 2096
Smooth Soloman's Seal 2691
Snake, San Francisco Garter 3105k
Snowdrop 3028
Snowy Egret 2321
Social Security Act 2153
Society of Philatelic Americans 797
Soil Conservation 1133
Soil and Water Conservation 2074
Softball 2962
Sokol-Physical Fitness 1262
Soo Locks 1069
Sound Recording 1705
Sousa, John Philip 880
South Carolina Statehood 2343
South Carolina Tercentenary 1407
South Dakota Statehood 858, 2416
Space Accomplishments 1331-1332, 1529, 1556-1557, 1569-1570, 1759, 1912-1919, 2568-2577, 2631-2634
Space Achievement Decade 1434-1435
Space Discovery...........................3238-3242
Spacecraft C122, C126a
Space Fantasy 2543, 2741-2745
Space Shuttle 1913-1914, 1917-1918, 2544-2544A, 3261-3262, C125, C126d
Spanish-American War 3192
Spanish Settlement In Southwest 3220
Speaker's Stand 1582
Special Occasions 2267-2274, 2395-2398
Special Olympics 1788, 2142
Spectacle Reef Lighthouse 2971
Sperry, Lawrence and Elmer C114
Spirit of '76 1629-1631
Spirit of St. Louis C10
Split Rock Lighthouse 2969
Squirrel.. 2489
Stagecoach 1898A, 2228, 2434, 2438a
Stagecoach (film) 2448
Staggerwing Airplane 3142j
Stamp Centenary 947
Stamp Collecting 1474, 2198-2201
Standing Cypress 2695
Stanley Steamer 2132
Stanton, Edwin M. 138, 149, 160, 171, 196
Stanton, Elizabeth 959
Star Route Truck 2125
Stars C72-C73
Stars and "6" 1892
"Stars and Stripes Forever" 3153
State Birds and Flowers 1953-2002
State Flags 1633-1682
Statehood: North Dakota, South Dakota, Montana, Washington 858
Statue of Liberty 566, 696, 899, 1035, 1041-1042, 1044A, 1057, 1075, 1599, 1619, 2147, 2224, 2599, 3122, 3122E, C58, C63, C80, C87
Statue of Liberty & New York Skyline ... C35
Steam Carriage 2451
Steamboats 2405-2409, 2435, 2438b
Steamship Savannah 923
Stearman Airplane 3142l
Steel Industry 1090
Stefansson, Vilhjalmur 2222
Stegosaurus 2424, 3136f
Steinbeck, John 1773
Steinmetz, Charles 2055
Steuben, Baron Friedrich von 689
Stevenson, Adlai E. 1275
Stock Market Crash 3184o
Stokowski, Leopold 3158
Stone Mountain Memorial 1408
Stone, Harlan Fiske 965
Stone, Lucy 1293
Startojet Airplane 3142h
Stravinsky, Igor 1845
Stream Violet 2655
Streetcars 2059-2062
Stuart, Gilbert Charles 884
Stutz Bearcat 2131
Stuyvesant, Peter 971
Submarines in Pacific 2838e
Sullivan, Anne, and Helen Keller 1824
Sullivan, Maj. Gen. John 657
Sun Yat-sen 906, 1188
Supersonic Flight 3173
Supreme Court Bicentennial 2415
Supreme Court 991
Surrender of Burgoyne at Saratoga 2590
Surrender of Cornwallis at Yorktown .. 1686
Surrey 1907
Sweden-U.S. Treaty 2036
Swedish Pioneers 958
Swedish-Finnish Tercentenary 836
Sweet White Violet 2659
Switzerland, 700th Anniv. 2532
Sylvan Dell Riverboat 3092
Sylvester the Cat 3204-3205
Szell, George 3160

Taft, Robert A. 1161
Taft, William H. 685, 687, 831, 2218h
Talking Pictures 1727
Tandem Bicycle 2266
Tanner, Henry Ossawa 1486
Tarawa, Invasion of 2765j
Taylor, Zachary 179, 181, 185, 204, 817, 2217c
Teachers 1093
Teddy Bear Created 3182k
Telegraph Centenary 924
Telephone Centenary 1683
Tennessee Statehood 941, 3070-3071
Tennessee Valley Authority 2042
Tennis 2964
Terry and the Pirates 3000r
Terry, Sonny 3214
Tesla, Nikola 2057
Texas Independence 776
Texas Republic 2204
Texas Statehood 938, 2968
Tharpe, Rosetta 3219
Thayer, Sylvanus 1852
Thick-billed Parrot 3105b
Third International Philatelic Exhibition 778
Thirteenth Amendment 902
Thirty Mile Point Lighthouse 2973
Thoreau, Henry David 1327
Thorpe, Jim 2089, 3183g
314 Clipper Airplane 3142r
Thurber, James 2862

Entry	Number(s)
Tibbett, Lawrence	3156
Tickseed	2653
Tiger Swallowtail	2300
Tilghman, Bill	2869r, 2870
Toad, Wyoming	3105g
Tokyo Raid	2697a
Tom Sawyer	1470
Toonerville Folks	3000g
Torch	901, 1594, 1816, 2531A
Toscanini, Arturo	2411
Touro Synagogue	2017
Tow Truck	2129
Tractor	2127
Tractor Trailer	2457, 2458
Traditional Mail Delivery	2434-2438
Traffic Safety	1272
Transcontinental Telephone Line	3183e
Trans-Mississippi Exposition	285-293
Trans-Mississippi Philatelic Exposition	751
Trans-Mississippi Stamps, Cent.	3209-3210
Transpacific Airmail	C115
Transport Plane	C25-C31
Treaty of Paris	2052
Trees, American	1764-1767, 3193-3197
Tricycle	2126
Tri-Motor Airplane	3142p
Troops Guarding Train	289
Trout	1427, 3105j
Trucking Industry	1025
Truman, Harry S	1499, 1862, 2219f
Trumbull, John	1361
Trumpet Honeysuckle	2683
Truth, Sojourner	2203
Tubman, Harriet	1744, 2975k
Tucker, Richard	3155
Tugboat	2260
Tulip	2517-2520, 2524-2527, 2762
Tuna, Bluefin	2208
Turk's Cap Lily	2681
Turners, American Society of	979
Twain, Mark	863
Tweety Bird	3204-3205
Twinflower	2665
Tyler, John	815, 847, 2217a
Tyrannosaurus Rex	2422
U-boat Battles	2765a
Umbrella	2443
Uncle Sam	3259, 3263
Uncle Sam's Hat	3260, 3264-3269
United Confederate Veterans	998
United Nations	1419, 2974
United Nations Conference	928
U.S. Capitol	572, 992, C64-C65
U.S.-Canada Friendship	961
U.S.-Canada Peace Bridge	1721
U.S.-Japan Treaty	1158
U.S.-Morocco Diplomatic Relations	2349
U.S. Naval Academy	793, 3001
U.S.-Netherlands Diplomatic Relations	2003
U.S.-Sweden Treaty	2036
United Way	2275
Universal Postal Congress	2434-2438, C122-C126
Universal Postal Union	1530-1537, C42-C44
Uranus	2575
Urban Planning	1333
"USA"	C75-C81
USPS Emblem	1396
USPS Emblem & Olympic Rings	2539
Utah Settlement	950
Utah Statehood	3024
Valens, Ritchie	2727, 2734
Valentino, Rudolph	2819
Valley Forge	645, 1729
Van Buren, Martin	813, 2216h
Varela, Feliz	3166
Vega Airplane	3142d
Venus	2569
Vermont Sesquicentennial	643
Vermont Statehood	903, 2533
Verrazano-Narrows Bridge	1259
Verville, Alfred V.	C113
Veterans Administration	1825
Veterans of Foreign Wars	1525
Veterans, Korean War	2152
Veterans, Viet Nam War	1802
Veterans, World War I	2154
Veterans, World War II	940
Victory	537
Vietnam Veterans' Memorial	2109
Viking Missions to Mars	1759
Viking Ship	621
Violins	1813
Virgin Islands Territory	802
Virginia Bluebells	2668
Virginia Capes, Battle of	1938
Virginia Statehood	2345
V-mail	2765e
Voice of America	1329
Volleyball	2961
Voluntarism	2039
Volunteer Firemen	971
Von Karman, Theodore	2699
Voyages of Columbus	2620-2629
Walker, C. J.	**3181**
Walker, Dr. Mary E.	2013
Wallace, Lila and DeWitt	2936
Wallenberg, Raoul	3135
War Savings Bonds & Stamps	2765g
Ward, Clara	3218
Warner, Pop	3144, 3149
Warren, Earl	2184
Washington and Lee University	982
Washington at Cambridge	617
Washington Crossing the Delaware	1688
Washington Reviewing Army at Valley Forge	1689
Washington Statehood	858, 2404
Washington Territory	1019
Washington, Booker T.	873, 1074
Washington, D.C.	989-992, 2561
Washington, Dinah	2730, 2737
Washington, George	2, 4, 10-11, 13-17, 25-26, 31-37, 39, 41, 43-45, 47, 62B, 64-66, 68-70, 72, 74, 78-79, 82-83, 85, 85C-85E, 88-90, 94, 96-97, 99, 101, 104, 106-107, 109, 111, 115, 126, 136, 147, 158, 169, 184, 194, 207, 210-211, 213-214, 219D, 220, 248-252, 265-267, 279, 301, 319-322, 332-342, 344-347, 349-351, 353-356, 358-366, 375-382, 384, 386, 388-389, 391, 393-396, 405-413, 424-430, 441-450, 452-459, 461-469, 481-496, 498-507, 519, 525-528, 530-536, 538-546, 554, 577, 579, 583, 595, 599-599A, 606, 634-634A, 660, 671, 704-715, 720-722, 804, 829, 839, 848, 854, 947-948, 1003, 1031, 1054, 1213, 1229, 1283, 1283B, 1304, 1304C, 1686, 1688-1689, 1704, 1729, 1952, 2149, 2216a, 2592, 3140
Washington, Martha	306, 556, 585, 601, 636, 662, 673, 805, 840, 849
Water Conservation	1150
Waterfowl Conservation	1362
Waterfowl Preservation Act	2092
Waters, Ethel	2851
Waters, Muddy	2855
Watie, Stand	2975I
Wayne, Gen. Anthony	680
Wayne, John	2448
Weather Vane	3257-3258
Webster, Daniel	141, 152, 163, 174, 189, 199, 226, 258, 273, 282C, 283, 307, 725, 1380
Webster, Noah	1121
Wells, Ida B.	2442
West, Benjamin	1553
Western Cattle in Storm	292
Western Wildlife	2869p, 2870
West Point	789
West Quoddy Head, ME, Lighthouse	2472
West Virginia Statehood	1232
Wetlands	3207-3207A
Wharton, Edith	1832
Wharton, Joseph	1920
Wheat Fields	1506
Wheatland	1081
Wheel Chair	2256
Wheels of Freedom	1162
Whistler, James A. McNeill	885
White Bengal Tiger	2709
White House	809, 844, 2219e
White Mountain Avens	2661
White Plains, Battle of	629-630
White, Josh	3215
White, Paul Dudley	2170
White, William Allen	960
White-tailed Deer	1888, 2317
Whitman, Walt	867
Whitney, Eli	889
Whittier, John Greenleaf	865
Whooping Crane	1097, 2868
Wildcat Airplane	3142t
Wild Columbine	2678
Wild Flax	2696
Wild Animals	2705-2709
Wilder, Thornton	3134
Wilderness, Battle of the	1181
Wildlife Conservation	1921-1924, 2286-2335
Wildlife Conservation	1077-1079, 1098, 1392, 1427-1430, 1464-1467
Wiley, Harvey W.	1080
Wilkes, Lt. Charles	2387
Willard, Frances E.	872
Williams, Hank	2723, 2771, 2775
Williams, Tennessee	3002
Willie and Joe	2765h
Willkie, Wendell	2192
Wills, Bob	2774, 2778
Wilson, Woodrow	623, 697, 832, 1040, 2218i
Win the War	905
Windmills	1738-1742
Winged Airmail Envelope	C79-C83
Winged Globe	C12, C16-C17, C19, C24
Winter Aconite	3026
Wisconsin Statehood	957, 3206
Wisconsin Tercentenary	739, 755
Wizard of Oz, The	2445
Wolfman, The	3172
Wolf Trap Farm Park	1452, 2018
Wolverine	2327
Woman Suffrage	1406, 2980, 3184e
Women	1152
Women, Armed Services	1013, 3174
Women in War Effort	2697h
Women, Progress of	959
Womens' Clubs	1316
Wonders of the Sea	2863-2866
Wood Carvings	2240-2243
Woodchuck	2307
Wood Duck	2484-2485
Wood, Grant	3236q
Woodland Caribou	3105l
Woodpecker, Red-headed	3032
Woodson, Carter G.	2073
Wool Industry	1423
Woolly Mammoth	3078
Workman's Compensation	1186
World Columbian Stamp Expo	2616
World Cup Soccer Championships	2834-2837
World Peace Through Law	1576
World Peace Through World Trade	1129
World Refugee Year	1149
World Series	3182n
World Stamp Expo '89	2410, 2433
World's Fair	853, 1196, 1244, 2006-2009, 2086, 3182e
World University Games	2748
World War I, U.S. Involvement	3183i
World War II	2559, 2697, 2765, 2838, 2981
Wright Brothers	C45, C91-C92, 3182g
Wright, Frank Lloyd	1280
Wyoming Statehood	897, 2444
Wyoming Toad	3105g
Yellow Kid	**3000a**
Yellow Lady's Slipper	2673
Yellow Skunk Cabbage	2693
YMCA Youth Camping	2160
Yorktown, Battle of	1937
Yorktown, Surrender of	703
Yorktown, Sinking of the	2697g
Young, Whitney Moore	1875
Youth Month	963
Youth, Support Our	1342
Yugoslavia, Flag	917
Zaharias, Mildred Didrikson	**1932**
Zeppelin, Graf	C13-C15, C18
Zinnia	2830

UNITED STATES

SEMI-POSTAL STAMP

Breast Cancer Awareness

SP1

Serpentine Die Cut 11
1998, July 29   *Photo.*
Self-Adhesive
B1 SP1 (32c+8c) multicolored   .80   .60

AIR POST STAMPS

For prepayment of postage on all mailable matter sent by airmail.

Curtiss Jenny — AP1

Engraved (Flat Plate Printing)
1918   Unwmk.   *Perf. 11*
C1	AP1	6c orange	75.00 30.00
		Never hinged	110.00
C2	AP1	16c green	105.00 35.00
		Never hinged	155.00
C3	AP1	24c car rose & blue	105.00 35.00
		Never hinged	155.00
a.		Center inverted	150,000.
		Never hinged	175,000.
		Nos. C1-C3 (3)	285.00 100.00
		Nos. C1-C3, never hinged	420.00

UNITED STATES

Price Lists FREE

a. PRE-1940 USED
b. REVENUES
c. PRE-1940 MINT
d. BACK of BOOK
e. CUT SQUARES
f. MODERN MINT, USED, & PLATE BLOCKS

Stamp orders filled on the day received.
Send us your request soon!
Satisfaction Guaranteed!

LAURENCE L. WINUM
P.O. Box 247, Dept. M
Walden, NY 12586
APS 51900 • ARA 1970 • Est. 1964

1-800-914-8090

Wooden Propeller and Radiator — AP2

Emblem of Air Service — AP3

De Havilland Biplane — AP4

1923
C4	AP2	8c dark green	27.50 14.00
		Never hinged	40.00
C5	AP3	16c dark blue	105.00 30.00
		Never hinged	155.00
C6	AP4	24c carmine	120.00 30.00
		Never hinged	180.00
		Nos. C4-C6 (3)	252.50 74.00
		Nos. C4-C6, never hinged	375.00

Map of US and Two Mail Planes — AP5

1926-27
C7	AP5	10c dark blue	3.00 .35
		Never hinged	4.50
C8	AP5	15c olive brown	3.50 2.50
		Never hinged	5.25
C9	AP5	20c yellow green ('27)	9.00 2.00
		Never hinged	13.50
		Nos. C7-C9 (3)	15.50 4.85
		Nos. C7-C9, never hinged	23.25

Lindbergh's Airplane "Spirit of St. Louis" — AP6

1927, June 18
C10	AP6	10c dark blue	8.50 2.50
		Never hinged	12.50
a.		Booklet pane of 3	85.00 65.00
		Never hinged	120.00

Singles from No. C10a are imperf. at sides or imperf. at sides and bottom.

Nos. C1-C10 were available for ordinary postage.

Beacon on Rocky Mountains — AP7

1928, July 25   *Perf. 11*
C11	AP7	5c carmine & blue	5.25 .75
		Never hinged	8.00
a.		Vertical pair, imperf. btwn.	5,500.

Winged Globe — AP8

1930, Feb. 10   *Perf. 11*
Size: 46½x19mm
C12	AP8	5c violet	11.00 .50
		Never hinged	16.50
a.		Horiz. pair, imperf. btwn.	4,500.

See Nos. C16-C17, C19.

Graf Zeppelin Issue

Zeppelin over Atlantic Ocean — AP9

Zeppelin between Continents — AP10

Zeppelin Passing Globe — AP11

1930, Apr. 19   *Perf. 11*
C13	AP9	65c green	250.00 160.00
		Never hinged	360.00
C14	AP10	$1.30 brown	500.00 375.00
		Never hinged	725.00
C15	AP11	$2.60 blue	800.00 575.00
		Never hinged	1,150.
		Nos. C13-C15 (3)	1,550. 1,110.
		Nos. C13-C15, never hinged	2,235.

Issued for use on mail carried on first Europe-Pan-America round-trip flight of Graf Zeppelin, May, 1930.

Type of 1930 Issue
Rotary Press Printing
1931-32   *Perf. 10½x11*
Size: 47½x19mm
C16	AP8	5c violet	5.50 .60
		Never hinged	8.25
C17	AP8	8c olive bister ('32)	2.50 .40
		Never hinged	3.75

Century of Progress Issue

Airship "Graf Zeppelin" — AP12

Flat Plate Printing
1933, Oct. 2   *Perf. 11*
C18	AP12	50c green	75.00 70.00
		Never hinged	110.00

Flight of the "Graf Zeppelin" in Oct. 1933, to Miami, Akron and Chicago, and from the last city to Europe.

> Catalogue values for unused stamps in this section, from this point to the end of the section, are for Never Hinged items.

Type of 1930 Issue
Rotary Press Printing
1934, June 30   *Perf. 10½x11*
C19	AP8	6c dull orange	3.50 .25

Transpacific Issues

The "China Clipper" over the Pacific — AP13

Flat Plate Printing
1935, Nov. 22   *Perf. 11*
C20	AP13	25c blue	1.40 1.00

Issued to pay postage on mail carried on the Transpacific air post service inaugurated Nov. 22, 1935.

The "China Clipper" over the Pacific — AP14

1937, Feb. 15   *Perf. 11*
C21	AP14	20c green	11.00 1.75
C22	AP14	50c carmine	10.00 5.00

Eagle Holding Shield, Olive Branch and Arrows — AP15

1938, May 14   *Perf. 11*
C23	AP15	6c dk blue & carmine	.50 .15
a.		Vert. pair, imperf. horiz.	350.00
b.		Horiz. pair, imperf. vert.	12,500.

Transatlantic Issue

Winged Globe — AP16

1939, May 16   *Perf. 11*
C24	AP16	30c dull blue	10.50 1.50

Twin-Motored Transport Plane — AP17

Rotary Press Printing
1941-44   *Perf. 11x10½*
C25	AP17	6c carmine	.15 .15
a.		Booklet pane of 3 ('43)	5.00 1.50
b.		Horiz. pair, imperf. between	2,250.
C26	AP17	8c olive green ('44)	.20 .15
C27	AP17	10c violet	1.25 .20
C28	AP17	15c brown carmine	2.75 .35
C29	AP17	20c bright green	2.25 .30
C30	AP17	30c blue	2.50 .35
C31	AP17	50c orange	11.00 3.00
		Nos. C25-C31 (7)	20.10 4.50

Singles from No. C25a are imperf. at sides or imperf. at sides and bottom.

DC-4 Skymaster — AP18

1946, Sept. 25   *Perf. 11x10½*
C32	AP18	5c carmine	.15 .15

DC-4 Skymaster — AP19

1947, Mar. 26   *Perf. 10½x11*
C33	AP19	5c carmine	.15 .15

See Nos. C37, C39, C41.

Pan American Union Building, Washington, DC — AP20

Statue of Liberty and New York Skyline — AP21

Plane over San Francisco-Oakland Bay Bridge — AP22

1947   *Perf. 11x10½*
C34	AP20	10c black	.25 .15
C35	AP21	15c brt blue green	.35 .15
a.		Horiz. pair, imperf. between	2,000.
C36	AP22	25c blue	.85 .15
		Nos. C34-C36 (3)	1.45 .45

Coil Stamp
1948, Jan. 15   *Perf. 10 Horiz.*
C37	AP19	5c carmine	1.00 .80

UNITED STATES

New York City Issue

Map of Five Boroughs, Circular Band and Planes — AP23

1948, July 31   *Perf. 11x10½*
C38 AP23 5c bright carmine   .15   .15
50th anniv. of the consolidation of the 5 boroughs of NYC.

Type of 1947

1949, Jan. 18   *Perf. 10½x11*
C39 AP19 6c carmine   .15   .15
   a. Booklet pane of 6   10.00   5.00

Alexandria Bicentennial Issue

Home of John Carlyle, Alexandria Seal and Gadsby's Tavern — AP24

Rotary Press Printing

1949, May 11   *Perf. 11x10½*
C40 AP24 6c carmine   .15   .15
Founding of Alexandria, Va, 200th anniv.

Type of 1947
Coil Stamp

1949, Aug. 25   *Perf. 10 Horiz.*
C41 AP19 6c carmine   3.25   .15

Universal Postal Union Issue

Post Office Department Building AP25

Globe and Doves Carrying Messages AP26

Boeing Stratocruiser and Globe — AP27

1949   *Unwmk.*   *Perf. 11x10½*
C42 AP25 10c violet   .20   .20
C43 AP26 15c ultramarine   .30   .25
C44 AP27 25c rose carmine   .50   .40
   Nos. C42-C44 (3)   1.00   .85
75th anniv. of the UPU.

Wright Brothers Issue

Wilbur and Orville Wright and their Plane — AP28

1949, Dec. 17   *Perf. 11x10½*
C45 AP28 6c magenta   .15   .15
46th anniv. of the Wright Brothers' 1st flight, Dec. 17, 1903.

Diamond Head, Honolulu, Hawaii — AP29

1952, Mar. 26   *Perf. 11x10½*
C46 AP29 80c brt red violet   5.00   1.25

First Plane and Modern Plane AP30

Eagle in Flight AP31

Powered Flight Issue

1953, May 29   *Perf. 11x10½*
C47 AP30 6c carmine   .15   .15
50th anniversary of powered flight.

For Domestic Post Cards

1954, Sept. 3   *Perf. 11x10½*
C48 AP31 4c bright blue   .15   .15
See No. C50.

Air Force Issue

B-52 Stratofortress and F-104 Starfighters AP32

Rotary Press Printing

1957, Aug. 1   *Perf. 11x10½*
C49 AP32 6c blue   .15   .15
50th anniv. of US Air Force.

Flying Eagle Type of 1954
For Domestic Post Cards

1958, July 31   *Perf. 11x10½*
C50 AP31 5c rose red   .15   .15

Silhouette of Jet Airliner — AP33

1958, July 31   *Perf. 10½x11*
C51 AP33 7c blue   .15   .15
   a. Booklet pane of 6   14.00   7.00

Coil Stamp
Perf. 10 Horizontally
C52 AP33 7c blue   2.25   .15
See Nos. C60-C61.

Alaska Statehood Issue

Big Dipper, North Star and Map of Alaska — AP34

Rotary Press Printing

1959, Jan. 3   *Perf. 11x10½*
C53 AP34 7c dark blue   .15   .15
Alaska's admission to statehood.

Balloon Jupiter Issue

Balloon and Crowd — AP35

Giori Press Printing

1959, Aug. 17   *Perf. 11*
C54 AP35 7c dark blue & red   .15   .15
Cent. of the carrying of mail by the balloon Jupiter from Lafayette to Crawfordsville, Ind.

Hawaii Statehood Issue

Alii Warrior, Map of Hawaii and Star of Statehood AP36

Rotary Press Printing

1959, Aug. 21   *Perf. 11x10½*
C55 AP36 7c rose red   .15   .15
Hawaii's admission to statehood.

Pan American Games Issue

Runner Holding Torch — AP37

Giori Press Printing

1959, Aug. 27   *Perf. 11*
C56 AP37 10c violet blue & brt red   .25   .25
3rd Pan American Games, Chicago, Aug. 27-Sept. 7.

Liberty Bell — AP38

Statue of Liberty — AP39

Abraham Lincoln — AP40

Giori Press Printing

1959-66   *Perf. 11*
C57 AP38 10c blk & grn ('60)   1.25   .70
C58 AP39 15c black & orange   .35   .20
C59 AP40 25c blk & mar ('60)   .50   .15
   a. Tagged ('66)   .60   .30
   Nos. C57-C59 (3)   2.10   1.05

Luminescence
See note following No. 1053. "Tagged" varieties of untagged airmail stamps start with No. C59a and end with No. C67a.
Airmail stamps starting with No. C69 are tagged unless otherwise noted.

Type of 1958
Rotary Press Printing

1960, Aug. 12   *Perf. 10½x11*
C60 AP33 7c carmine   .15   .15
   a. Booklet pane of 6   17.50   8.00

Type of 1958
Coil Stamp

1960, Oct. 22   *Perf. 10 Horiz.*
C61 AP33 7c carmine   4.25   .25

Type of 1959-60 and

Statue of Liberty — AP41

Giori Press Printing

1961-67   *Perf. 11*
C62 AP38 13c black & red   .40   .15
   a. Tagged ('67)   .75   .50
C63 AP41 15c black & orange   .30   .15
   a. Tagged ('67)   .35   .20
   b. As "a," horiz. pair, imperf. vert.   15,000.
No. C63 has a gutter between the two parts of the design; No. C58 has none.

Jet Airliner Over Capitol — AP42

Rotary Press Printing

1962, Dec. 5   *Perf. 10½x11*
C64 AP42 8c carmine   .15   .15
   a. Tagged ('63)   .15   .15
   b. Booklet pane 5 + label   7.00   3.00
   c. As "b," tagged ('64)   2.00   .75
Three different messages are found on the label in No. C64b, and one on No. C64c.

Coil Stamp
Perf. 10 Horizontally
C65 AP42 8c carmine   .40   .15
   a. Tagged ('65)   .35   .15
The 1st luminescent tagged US issue was No. C64a issued Aug. 1, 1963, at Dayton, OH. Initial experiments there used tagged stamps and an automated facer-canceler to extract airmail as an aid to dispatch.

Montgomery Blair — AP43

Bald Eagle — AP44

Montgomery Blair Issue
Giori Press Printing

1963, May 3   *Unwmk.*   *Perf. 11*
C66 AP43 15c car, dp claret & blue   .60   .55
Blair (1813-1883), Postmaster Gen. (1861-64), who called the 1st Intl. Postal Conf., Paris, 1863, forerunner of the UPU.

For Domestic Post Cards
Rotary Press Printing

1963, July 12   *Perf. 11x10½*
C67 AP44 6c red   .15   .15
   a. Tagged ('67)   4.00   3.00

Amelia Earhart Issue

Amelia Earhart and Lockheed Electra — AP45

Giori Press Printing

1963, July 24   *Perf. 11*
C68 AP45 8c carmine & maroon   .20   .15
Earhart (1898-1937), 1st woman to fly across the Atlantic.

Dr. Robert H. Goddard Issue

Robert H. Goddard, Atlas Rocket and Launching Tower, Cape Kennedy AP46

1964, Oct. 5   *Unwmk.*   *Tagged*
C69 AP46 8c blue, red & bister   .40   .15
Goddard (1882-1945), physicist and pioneer rocket researcher.

Tlingit Totem, Southern Alaska AP47

"Columbia Jays," by Audubon AP48

UNITED STATES

Alaska Purchase Issue
Giori Press Printing
1967, Mar. 30   *Perf. 11*
C70 AP47 8c brown   .25   .15
  Cent. of the Alaska Purchase. The Tlingit totem is from the Alaska State Museum, Juneau.

1967, Apr. 26   *Perf. 11*
C71 AP48 20c multicolored   .80   .15
  See note after No. 1241.

50-Star Runway — AP49

Rotary Press Printing
1968, Jan. 5   Unwmk.   *Perf. 11x10½*
C72 AP49 10c carmine   .20   .15
  b. Booklet pane of 8   2.00   .75
  c. Booklet pane of 5 + label   3.75   .75

Coil Stamp
Perf. 10 Vertically
C73 AP49 10c carmine   .30   .15
  a. Imperf., pair   600.00

The $1 Air Lift stamp is listed as No. 1341.

Air Mail Service Issue

Curtiss Jenny — AP50

Lithographed, Engraved (Giori)
1968, May 15   *Perf. 11*
C74 AP50 10c blue, black & red   .25   .15
  a. Red (tail stripe) omitted
  50th anniv. of regularly scheduled US air mail service.

USA and Jet — AP51

1968, Nov. 22   *Perf. 11*
C75 AP51 20c red, blue & black   .35   .15
  See No. C81.

Moon Landing Issue

First Man on the Moon — AP52

Litho. & Engr. (Giori)
1969, Sept. 9   *Perf. 11*
C76 AP52 10c multicolored   .25   .15
  a. Rose red (litho.) omitted   500.00

Man's 1st landing on the moon, July 20, 1969. US astronauts Neil A. Armstrong and Col. Edwin E. Aldrin, Jr., with Lieut. Col. Michael Collins piloting Apollo 11.
On No. C76a, the litho. rose red is missing from the entire vignette—the dots on top of the yellow areas as well as the flag shoulder patch.

Type of 1968 and:

Silhouette of Delta Wing Plane — AP53

Silhouette of Jet Airliner — AP54

Winged Airmail Envelope — AP55

Statue of Liberty AP56

Design: 21c, "USA" and jet (as C75).

Rotary Press Printing
1971-73   *Perf. 10½x11*
C77 AP53 9c red   .20   .15

Perf. 11x10½
C78 AP54 11c carmine   .20   .15
  a. Booklet pane of 4 + 2 labels   1.25
  b. Untagged (Bureau precanceled)   .30
C79 AP55 13c carmine ('73)   .25   .15
  a. Booklet pane of 5 + label ('73)   1.50   .75
  b. Untagged (Bureau precanceled)   .30

Giori Press Printing
Perf. 11
C80 AP56 17c bluish black, red & dark green   .30   .15

Litho. & Engr. (Giori)
Perf. 11
C81 AP51 21c red, blue & black   .35   .15
  Nos. C77-C81 (5)   1.30   .75
  Issue dates: 9c, May 15; 11c, May 7; 17c, July 13; 21c, May 21, 1971; 13c, Nov. 16, 1973. The 9c was for use on domestic post cards. No. C78b is precanceled "WASHINGTON D.C." (or "DC") and No. C79b "WASHINGTON DC" for the use of Congressmen and the public.

Coil Stamps
Rotary Press Printing
1971-73   *Perf. 10 Vertically*
C82 AP54 11c carmine   .25   .15
  a. Imperf., pair   250.00
C83 AP55 13c carmine ('73)   .30   .15
  a. Imperf., pair   80.00
  Issue dates: 11c, May 7; 13c, Dec. 27.

National Parks Centennial Issue

Kii Statue and Temple, City of Refuge, Hawaii — AP57

Litho. & Engr. (Giori)
1972, May 3   *Perf. 11*
C84 AP57 11c orange & multi   .20   .15
  a. Blue & green (litho) omitted   1,000.
  Cent. of the Natl. Parks system. No. C84 shows view of the City of Refuge Natl. Historical Park at Honaunau.

Olympic Games Issue

Skiing and Olympic Rings — AP58

Photogravure (Andreotti)
1972, Aug. 17   *Perf. 11x10½*
C85 AP58 11c multicolored   .20   .15
  11th Winter Olympic Games, Sapporo, Japan, Feb. 3-13, and 20th Summer Olympic Games, Munich, Germany, Aug. 26-Sept. 11.

Electronics Progress Issue

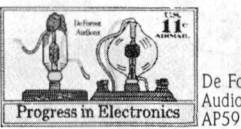

De Forest Audions AP59

Litho. & Engr. (Giori)
1973, July 10   *Perf. 11*
C86 AP59 11c multicolored   .20   .15
  a. Vermilion & olive (litho.) omitted   1,400.

Statue of Liberty AP60

Mt. Rushmore National Memorial AP61

1974   Giori Press Printing   *Perf. 11*
C87 AP60 18c car, black & ultra   .35   .25
C88 AP61 26c ultra, black & car   .50   .15
  Issue dates: 18c, Jan. 11; 26c, Jan. 2.

Plane and Globes — AP62

Plane, Globes and Flag — AP63

Giori Press Printing
1976, Jan. 2   *Perf. 11*
C89 AP62 25c ultra, red & black   .45   .15
C90 AP63 31c ultra, red & black   .50   .15

Wright Brothers Issue

Orville and Wilbur Wright, Flyer A — AP64

Wright Brothers, Flyer A and Shed — AP65

Litho. & Engr.
1978, Sept. 23   *Perf. 11*
C91 AP64 31c ultra & multi   .60   .30
C92 AP65 31c ultra & multi   .60   .30
  a. Vert. pair, #C91-C92   1.20   1.10
  b. As "a," ultramarine & black (engr.) omitted   800.00
  d. As "a," black, yellow, magenta, blue & brown (litho.) omitted   2,250.
  75th anniv. of 1st powered flight, Kill Devil Hill, NC, Dec. 17, 1903.

Octave Chanute Issue

Chanute and Biplane Hangglider AP66

Biplane Hanggliders and Chanute AP67

Litho. & Engr.
1979, Mar. 29   *Perf. 11*
C93 AP66 21c ultra & multi   .70   .30
C94 AP67 21c ultra & multi   .70   .30
  a. Vert. pair, #C93-C94   1.40   1.10
  b. As "a," ultramarine & black (engr.) omitted   4,500.
  Octave Chanute (1832-1910), civil engineer and aviation pioneer.

Wiley Post Issue

Wiley Post and "Winnie Mae" — AP68

NR-105 W, Post in Pressurized Suit, Portrait — AP69

Litho. & Engr.
1979, Nov. 20   *Perf. 11*
C95 AP68 25c ultra & multi   1.10   .35
C96 AP69 25c ultra & multi   1.10   .35
  a. Vert. pair, #C95-C96   2.25   1.25
  Post (1899-1935), 1st man to fly around the world alone and high-altitude flying pioneer.

Olympic Games Issue

High Jump — AP70

1979, Nov. 1   Photo.   *Perf. 11*
C97 AP70 31c multicolored   .65   .30
  22nd Olympic Games, Moscow, July 19-Aug. 3, 1980.

Philip Mazzei (1730-1816), Italian-born Political Writer — AP71

1980, Oct. 13   Photo.   *Perf. 11*
C98 AP71 40c multicolored   .75   .15
  a. Perf. 10½x11   4.50
  b. Imperf., pair   3,250.
  c. Horiz. pair, imperf. vert.

Blanche Stuart Scott (1886-1970) AP72

Glenn Curtiss (1878-1930) AP73

1980, Dec. 30
C99 AP72 28c multicolored   .55   .15
  a. Imperf., pair
C100 AP73 35c multicolored   .60   .15
  Scott, 1st woman pilot, and Curtiss, aviation pioneer and aircraft designer.

1984 Olympic Games

AP81

1983, June 17   *Perf. 11*
C101 AP81 28c Gymnast   1.00   .30
C102 AP81 28c Hurdler   1.00   .30
C103 AP81 28c Basketball   1.00   .30
C104 AP81 28c Soccer   1.00   .30
  a. Block of 4, #C101-C104   4.50   2.00
  b. As "a," imperf. vert.
  Nos. C101-C104 are vertical.

1983, Apr. 8
C105 AP81 40c Shot put   .90   .40
C106 AP81 40c Gymnast   .90   .40
C107 AP81 40c Swimmer   .90   .40
C108 AP81 40c Weightlifting   .90   .40
  b. Block of 4, #C105-C108   4.25   2.50
  d. As "b," imperf.   1,250.

UNITED STATES

1983, Nov. 4
C109	AP81	35c Women's fencing	.90	.50
C110	AP81	35c Cycling	.90	.50
C111	AP81	35c Women's volleyball	.90	.50
C112	AP81	35c Pole vaulting	.90	.50
a.		Block of 4, #C109-C112	4.00	3.00

33 Alfred V. Verville AP86

Lawrence and Elmer Sperry AP87

1985, Feb. 13   Photo.
C113	AP86	33c multicolored	.60	.20
a.		Imperf., pair	1,000.	
C114	AP87	39c multicolored	.70	.25
a.		Imperf., pair	1,400.	

Alfred V. Verville (1890-1970), aircraft designer, Lawrence Sperry (1892-1931), designer and pilot, and Elmer Sperry (1860-1930), inventor.

Transpacific Airmail AP88

1985, Feb. 15   Photo.
C115	AP88	44c multicolored	.80	.25
a.		Imperf., pair	1,000.	

Fr. Junipero Serra (1713-84)
California Missionary

Outline Map of Southern California, Portrait, San Gabriel Mission AP89

1985, Aug. 22   Photo.   Perf. 11
C116	AP89	44c multicolored	.90	.30
a.		Imperf., pair	1,500.	

Settling of New Sweden, 350th Anniv. AP90

Design: 17th Cent. European settler negotiating with two American Indians, map of New Sweden, the Swedish ships *Kalmar Nyckel* and *Fogel Grip*, based on an 18th cent. illustration from a Swedish book about the Colonies.

1988, Mar. 29   Litho. & Engr.
C117	AP90	44c multicolored	1.00	.25

See Finland No. 768 and Sweden No. 1672.

Samuel Pierpont Langley (1834-1906)
Astronomer, Aviation Pioneer and Inventor

Langley and Unmanned Aerodrome No. 5 — AP91

1988, May 14   Litho. & Engr.   Perf. 11
C118	AP91	45c multicolored	.85	.20

Igor Sikorsky (1889-1972)
Aeronautic Engineer

Sikorsky and VS300 Helicopter, 1939 — AP92

1988, June 23   Photo.   Perf. 11
C119	AP92	36c multicolored	.65	.20

French Revolution, Bicent.

Liberty, Equality and Fraternity — AP93

Perf. 11½x11
1989, July 14   Litho. & Engr.
C120	AP93	45c multicolored	.85	.20

See France Nos. 2143-2145a.

Pre-Columbian America Issue

UPAE Emblem and Southeastern Figure, *Key Marco Cat*, Calusa Culture, Pre-Columbian Mississippian Period, A.D. 700-1450 — AP94

1989, Oct. 12   Photo.   Perf. 11
C121	AP94	45c multicolored	.85	.20

Discovery of America, 500th anniv. (in 1992).

Futuristic Mail Delivery

Spacecraft AP95   Air-suspended Hover Car AP96

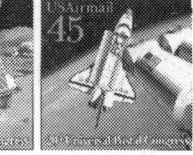

Moon Rover AP97   Space Shuttle AP98

1989, Nov. 27   Perf. 11
C122	AP95	45c multicolored	1.00	.40
C123	AP96	45c multicolored	1.00	.40
C124	AP97	45c multicolored	1.00	.40
C125	AP98	45c multicolored	1.00	.40
a.		Block of 4, Nos. C122-C125	4.00	3.00
b.		As "a," light blue (engr.) omitted	1,000.	

1989, Nov. 24   Litho. & Engr.   Imperf.
C126		Sheet of 4	4.25	3.25
a.		AP95 45c multicolored	.90	.50
b.		AP96 45c multicolored	.90	.50
c.		AP97 45c multicolored	.90	.50
d.		AP98 45c multicolored	.90	.50

World Stamp Expo '89, 20th UPU Congress. See Russia No. 5837.

Pre-Columbian America Issue

Tropical Coast AP99

1990, Oct. 12   Photo.   Perf. 11
C127	AP99	45c multicolored	.85	.20

Harriet Quimby, Bleriot Aircraft AP100

1991, Apr. 27   Photo.   Perf. 11
C128	AP100	50c multicolored	.90	.25
a.		Vert. pair, imperf. horiz.	2,000.	
b.		Perf. 11.2 ('93)	.90	.25

William T. Piper, Piper Cub AP101

1991, May 17
C129	AP101	40c multicolored	.80	.20

See No. C132.

Antarctic Treaty, 30th Anniv. AP102

1991, June 21   Photo.   Perf. 11
C130	AP102	50c multicolored	.90	.25

Pre-Columbian America Issue

First Americans Crossed Over From Asia — AP103

1991, Oct. 12   Photo.   Perf. 11
C131	AP103	50c multicolored	.90	.25

Piper Type of 1991
1993   Photo.   Perf. 11
C132	AP101	40c multicolored	.90	.20

Piper's hair touches top edge of design. Bullseye perf. 11.2.

AIR POST SPECIAL DELIVERY STAMPS

To provide for the payment of both the postage and the special delivery fee in one stamp.

Great Seal of United States — APSD1

Flat Plate Printing
1934   Unwmk.   Perf. 11
CE1	APSD1	16c dark blue	.60	.65
		Never hinged	.80	

For imperforate variety see No. 771.

1936
CE2	APSD1	16c red & blue	.40	.25
		Never hinged	.50	
a.		Horiz. pair, imperf. vert.	4,000.	

SPECIAL DELIVERY STAMPS

When affixed to any letter or article of mailable matter, secure immediate delivery, between 7 A.M. and midnight, at any post office.

Messenger Running SD1

Flat Plate Printing
1885   Unwmk.   Perf. 12
E1	SD1	10c blue	275.00	40.00
		Never hinged	465.00	

Messenger Running SD2

1888
E2	SD2	10c blue	250.00	15.00
		Never hinged	425.00	

1893
E3	SD2	10c orange	165.00	20.00
		Never hinged	275.00	

Messenger Running SD3

Line under "Ten Cents"
1894
E4	SD3	10c blue	600.00	25.00
		Never hinged	975.00	

1895   Wmk. 191
E5	SD3	10c blue	140.00	3.25
		Never hinged	215.00	
b.		Printed on both sides	—	

Messenger on Bicycle SD4

1902
E6	SD4	10c ultramarine	90.00	3.00
		Never hinged	135.00	
a.		10c blue	90.00	3.00
		Never hinged	135.00	

Helmet of Mercury and Olive Branch — SD5

1908
E7	SD5	10c green	55.00	35.00
		Never hinged	85.00	

1911   Wmk. 190   Perf. 12
E8	SD4	10c ultramarine	95.00	5.00
		Never hinged	140.00	
b.		10c violet blue	95.00	5.00
		Never hinged	140.00	

1914   Perf. 10
E9	SD4	10c ultramarine	160.00	6.00
		Never hinged	240.00	
a.		10c blue	190.00	6.00
		Never hinged	275.00	

1916   Unwmk.   Perf. 10
E10	SD4	10c pale ultra	265.00	25.00
		Never hinged	400.00	
a.		10c blue	290.00	25.00
		Never hinged	430.00	

1917   Perf. 11
E11	SD4	10c ultramarine	16.50	.50
		Never hinged	27.50	
b.		10c gray violet	16.50	.50
		Never hinged	27.50	
c.		10c blue	45.00	2.50
		Never hinged	70.00	

94 UNITED STATES

Postman and Motorcycle SD6

Post Office Truck — SD7

1922-25

E12	SD6 10c gray violet	27.50	.40
	Never hinged	40.00	
a.	10c deep ultramarine	32.50	.50
	Never hinged	47.50	
E13	SD6 15c deep orange ('25)	25.00	.90
	Never hinged	37.50	
E14	SD7 20c black ('25)	2.00	.85
	Never hinged	3.00	
	Nos. E12-E14 (3)	54.50	2.15

No. E12 measures 36x21½mm
No. E15 measures 36½x21¾mm
No. E13 measures 36½x21½mm
No. E16 measures 36¾x22¼mm
No. E14 measures 35½x21½mm
No. E19 measures 36¼x22mm

Rotary Press Printing

1927-31 *Perf. 11x10½*

E15	SD6 10c gray violet	.60	.15
	Never hinged	.80	
a.	10c red lilac	.60	.15
	Never hinged	.80	
b.	10c gray lilac	.60	.15
	Never hinged	.80	
c.	Horiz. pair, imperf. btwn.	300.00	
E16	SD6 15c orange ('31)	.70	.15
	Never hinged	.90	

Catalogue values for unused stamps in this section, from this point to the end of the section, are for Never Hinged items.

1944-51

E17	SD6 13c blue	.60	.15
E18	SD6 17c orange yellow	2.75	1.75
E19	SD7 20c black ('51)	1.25	.15
	Nos. E17-E19 (3)	4.60	2.05

Special Delivery Letter, Hand to Hand — SD8

1954-57 *Perf. 11x10½*

E20	SD8 20c deep blue	.40	.15
E21	SD8 30c lake ('57)	.50	.15

Arrows — SD9

Giori Press Printing

1969-71 *Perf. 11*

E22	SD9 45c car & vio blue	1.25	.25
E23	SD9 60c vio blue & car ('71)	1.25	.20

Issue dates: 45c, Nov. 21; 60c, May 10.

REGISTRATION STAMP

Issued for the prepayment of registry fees; not usable for postage.

Eagle — RS1

Wmk. 190

1911, Dec. 1 Engr. *Perf. 12*

F1	RS1 10c ultramarine	75.00	7.50
	Never hinged	115.00	

CERTIFIED MAIL STAMP

For use on first-class mail for which no indemnity value is claimed, but for which proof of mailing and proof of delivery are available at less cost than registered mail.

Catalogue values for unused stamps in this section are for Never Hinged items.

Letter Carrier — CM1

Rotary Press Printing

1955, June 6 Unwmk. *Perf. 10½x11*

FA1	CM1 15c red	.45	.30

POSTAGE DUE STAMPS

For affixing, by a postal clerk to any piece of mailable matter, to denote the amount to be collected from the addressee because of insufficient prepayment of postage.

Unused Values for Nos. J1-J14 are for stamps with full original gum.

D1

D2

Printed by the American Bank Note Company

1879 Unwmk. Engraved *Perf. 12*

J1	D1 1c brown	50.00	8.50
J2	D1 2c brown	325.00	7.50
J3	D1 3c brown	45.00	4.50
J4	D1 5c brown	525.00	45.00
J5	D1 10c brown	550.00	25.00
a.	Imperf., pair	*2,000.*	
J6	D1 30c brown	275.00	50.00
J7	D1 50c brown	425.00	60.00
	Nos. J1-J7 (7)	2,195.	200.50

Special Printing

1879

J8	D1 1c deep brown	*7,000.*	
J9	D1 2c deep brown	*5,000.*	
J10	D1 3c deep brown	*6,500.*	
J11	D1 5c deep brown	*5,000.*	
J12	D1 10c deep brown	*2,750.*	
J13	D1 30c deep brown	*2,750.*	
J14	D1 50c deep brown	*2,750.*	

1884

J15	D1 1c red brown	50.00	4.50
J16	D1 2c red brown	60.00	4.50
J17	D1 3c red brown	850.00	175.00
J18	D1 5c red brown	400.00	25.00
J19	D1 10c red brown	400.00	17.50
J20	D1 30c red brown	150.00	50.00
J21	D1 50c red brown	1,500.	175.00
	Nos. J15-J21 (7)	3,410.	451.50

1891

J22	D1 1c bright claret	22.50	1.00
J23	D1 2c bright claret	27.50	1.00
J24	D1 3c bright claret	55.00	8.00
J25	D1 5c bright claret	67.50	8.00
J26	D1 10c bright claret	110.00	17.50
J27	D1 30c bright claret	400.00	150.00
J28	D1 50c bright claret	425.00	150.00
	Nos. J22-J28 (7)	1,107.	335.50

See Die and Plate Proofs in the Scott U.S. Specialized for imperfs. on stamp paper.

Printed by the Bureau of Engraving and Printing

1894

J29	D2 1c vermilion	1,400.	325.
	Never hinged	2,250.	
J30	D2 2c vermilion	600.	125.
	Never hinged	950.	

1894

J31	D2 1c deep claret	40.00	6.00
	Never hinged	65.00	
b.	Vert. pair, imperf. horiz.	—	
J32	D2 2c deep claret	37.50	4.00
	Never hinged	60.00	
J33	D2 3c deep claret	150.00	30.00
	Never hinged	240.00	
J34	D2 5c deep claret	225.00	35.00
	Never hinged	360.00	
J35	D2 10c deep claret	225.00	25.00
	Never hinged	360.00	
J36	D2 30c deep claret	375.00	90.00
a.	30c carmine	375.00	100.00
	Never hinged	600.00	
b.	30c pale rose	310.00	85.00
	Never hinged	500.00	
J37	D2 50c deep claret	1,100.	250.00
	Never hinged	1,750.	
a.	50c pale rose	1,050.	250.00
	Never hinged	1,700.	
	Nos. J31-J37 (7)	2,152.	440.00

Shades are numerous in the 1894 and later issues.

See Die and Plate Proofs in the Scott U.S. Specialized for 1c imperf. on stamp paper.

1895 **Wmk. 191**

J38	D2 1c deep claret	8.00	.75
	Never hinged	13.00	
J39	D2 2c deep claret	8.00	.70
	Never hinged	13.00	
J40	D2 3c deep claret	50.00	1.75
	Never hinged	80.00	
J41	D2 5c deep claret	55.00	1.75
	Never hinged	87.50	
J42	D2 10c deep claret	57.50	3.50
	Never hinged	90.00	
J43	D2 30c deep claret	500.00	50.00
	Never hinged	800.00	
J44	D2 50c deep claret	300.00	37.50
	Never hinged	475.00	
	Nos. J38-J44 (7)	978.50	95.95

1910-12 **Wmk. 190**

J45	D2 1c deep claret	30.00	3.00
	Never hinged	47.50	
a.	1c rose carmine	27.50	3.00
	Never hinged	42.50	
J46	D2 2c deep claret	30.00	1.00
	Never hinged	45.00	
a.	2c rose carmine	27.50	1.00
	Never hinged	42.50	
J47	D2 3c deep claret	550.00	30.00
	Never hinged	875.00	
J48	D2 5c deep claret	85.00	6.50
	Never hinged	135.00	
a.	5c rose carmine	80.00	6.50
	Never hinged	130.00	
J49	D2 10c deep claret	110.00	12.50
	Never hinged	175.00	
a.	10c rose carmine	105.00	12.50
	Never hinged	170.00	
J50	D2 50c deep claret ('12)	850.00	120.00
	Never hinged	1,350.	
	Nos. J45-J50 (6)	1,655.	173.00

1914 *Perf. 10*

J52	D2 1c carmine lake	55.00	11.00
	Never hinged	87.50	
a.	1c dull rose	65.00	11.00
	Never hinged	105.00	
J53	D2 2c carmine lake	45.00	.40
	Never hinged	72.50	
a.	2c dull rose	50.00	.40
	Never hinged	80.00	
b.	2c vermilion	50.00	.40
	Never hinged	80.00	
J54	D2 3c carmine lake	825.00	37.50
	Never hinged	1,350.	
a.	3c dull rose	825.00	37.50
	Never hinged	1,350.	
J55	D2 5c carmine lake	36.00	2.50
	Never hinged	57.50	
a.	5c dull rose	36.00	2.50
	Never hinged	57.50	
J56	D2 10c carmine lake	55.00	2.00
	Never hinged	87.50	
a.	10c dull rose	65.00	2.00
	Never hinged	105.00	
J57	D2 30c carmine lake	225.00	17.50
	Never hinged	360.00	
J58	D2 50c carmine lake	*9,500.*	800.00
	Never hinged	*15,000.*	
	Nos. J52-J58 (7)	10,741.	870.90

1916 **Unwmk.** *Perf. 10*

J59	D2 1c rose	2,400.	300.00
	Never hinged	3,900.	
J60	D2 2c rose	150.00	20.00
	Never hinged	240.00	

1917 *Perf. 11*

J61	D2 1c carmine rose	2.75	.25
	Never hinged	4.50	
a.	1c rose red	2.75	.25
	Never hinged	4.50	
b.	1c deep claret	2.75	.25
	Never hinged	4.50	
J62	D2 2c carmine rose	2.50	.25
	Never hinged	4.00	
a.	2c rose red	2.50	.25
	Never hinged	4.00	
b.	2c deep claret	2.50	.25
	Never hinged	4.00	
J63	D2 3c carmine rose	11.00	.25
	Never hinged	17.50	
a.	3c rose red	11.00	.25
	Never hinged	17.50	
b.	3c deep claret	11.00	.35
	Never hinged	17.50	
J64	D2 5c carmine	11.00	.25
	Never hinged	17.50	
a.	5c rose red	11.00	.25
	Never hinged	17.50	
b.	5c deep claret	11.00	.25
	Never hinged	17.50	
J65	D2 10c carmine rose	17.00	.30
	Never hinged	27.50	
a.	10c rose red	17.00	.25
	Never hinged	27.50	
b.	10c deep claret	17.00	.25
	Never hinged	27.50	
J66	D2 30c carmine rose	87.50	.75
	Never hinged	140.00	
a.	30c deep claret	87.50	.75
	Never hinged	140.00	
J67	D2 50c carmine rose	110.00	.30
	Never hinged	175.00	
a.	50c rose red	110.00	.30
	Never hinged	175.00	
b.	50c deep claret	110.00	.30
	Never hinged	175.00	
	Nos. J61-J67 (7)	241.75	2.35

1925

J68	D2 ½c dull red	1.00	.25
	Never hinged	1.50	

D3

D4

1930 *Perf. 11*

J69	D3 ½c carmine	4.50	1.40
	Never hinged	6.00	
J70	D3 1c carmine	3.00	.25
	Never hinged	4.25	
J71	D3 2c carmine	4.00	.25
	Never hinged	5.75	
J72	D3 3c carmine	21.00	1.75
	Never hinged	32.50	
J73	D3 5c carmine	19.00	2.50
	Never hinged	30.00	
J74	D3 10c carmine	40.00	1.00
	Never hinged	65.00	
J75	D3 30c carmine	110.00	2.00
	Never hinged	160.00	
J76	D3 50c carmine	140.00	.75
	Never hinged	250.00	
J77	D4 $1 carmine	30.00	.25
	Never hinged	40.00	
a.	$1 scarlet	25.00	.25
	Never hinged	35.00	
J78	D4 $5 carmine	37.50	.25
	Never hinged	57.50	
a.	$5 scarlet	32.50	.25
	Never hinged	47.50	
	Nos. J69-J78 (10)	409.00	10.40

Rotary Press Printing

1931-56 *Perf. 11x10½*

J79	D3 ½c dull carmine	.90	.15
	Never hinged	1.30	
J80	D3 1c dull carmine	.20	.15
	Never hinged	.30	
J81	D3 2c dull carmine	.20	.15
	Never hinged	.30	
J82	D3 3c dull carmine	.25	.15
	Never hinged	.40	
J83	D3 5c dull carmine	.40	.15
	Never hinged	.60	
J84	D3 10c dull carmine	1.10	.15
	Never hinged	1.60	
J85	D3 30c dull carmine	7.50	.25
	Never hinged	10.00	
J86	D3 50c dull carmine	10.00	.25
	Never hinged	15.00	
J79a	D3 ½c scarlet	.90	.15
	Never hinged	1.30	
J80a	D3 1c scarlet	.20	.15
	Never hinged	.30	
J81a	D3 2c scarlet	.20	.15
	Never hinged	.30	
J82a	D3 3c scarlet	.25	.15
	Never hinged	.40	
J83a	D3 5c scarlet	.40	.15
	Never hinged	.60	
J84a	D3 10c scarlet	1.10	.15
	Never hinged	1.60	
J85a	D3 30c scarlet	7.50	.25
	Never hinged	10.00	
J86a	D3 50c scarlet	10.00	.25
	Never hinged	15.00	

Perf. 10½x11

J87	D4 $1 scarlet ('56)	35.00	.25
	Never hinged	52.50	
	Nos. J79-J87 (17)	76.10	3.05
	Nos. J79a-J86a (8)	20.55	1.40

Catalogue values for unused stamps in this section, from this point to the end of the section, are for Never Hinged items.

D5

Denominations added by rubber plates in an operation similar to precanceling.

Rotary Press Printing

Perf. 11x10½

1959, June 19 — Unwmk.

Denomination in Black

J88	D5	½c carmine rose	1.50	1.10
J89	D5	1c carmine rose	.15	.15
a.		"1 CENT" omitted	350.00	
b.		Pair, one without "1 CENT"	600.00	
J90	D5	2c carmine rose	.15	.15
J91	D5	3c carmine rose	.15	.15
a.		Pair, one without "3 CENTS"	700.00	
J92	D5	4c carmine rose	.15	.15
J93	D5	5c carmine rose	.15	.15
a.		Pair, one without "5 CENTS"	1,250.	
J94	D5	6c carmine rose	.15	.15
a.		Pair, one without "6 CENTS"	800.00	
J95	D5	7c carmine rose	.20	.15
J96	D5	8c carmine rose	.20	.15
a.		Pair, one without "8 CENTS"	850.00	
J97	D5	10c carmine rose	.20	.15
J98	D5	30c carmine rose	.75	.15
J99	D5	50c carmine rose	1.10	.15

Straight Numeral Outlined in Black

J100	D5	$1 carmine rose	2.00	.15
J101	D5	$5 carmine rose	9.00	.20
		Nos. J88-J101 (14)	15.85	3.10

All single copies with value omitted are catalogued as No. J89a.

1978-85

Denomination in Black

J102	D5	11c carmine rose	.25	.20
J103	D5	13c carmine rose	.25	.20
J104	D5	17c carmine rose ('85)	.40	.35
		Nos. J102-J104 (3)	.90	.75
		Nos. J88-J104 (17)	16.75	3.85

Issue dates: Jan. 2, 1978, June 10, 1985.

UNITED STATES OFFICES IN CHINA

Issued for sale by the postal agency at Shanghai, at their surcharged value in local currency. Valid to the amount of their original values for the prepayment of postage on mail dispatched from the US postal agency at Shanghai to addresses in the US.

Nos. 498-499, 502-504, 506-510, 512, 514-518 Surcharged

SHANGHAI
2¢
CHINA

1919 — Unwmk. — *Perf. 11*

K1	A140	2c on 1c green	25.00	*27.50*
		Never hinged	40.00	
K2	A140	4c on 2c rose, type I	25.00	*27.50*
		Never hinged	40.00	
K3	A140	6c on 3c vio, type II	50.00	*65.00*
		Never hinged	80.00	
K4	A140	8c on 4c brown	55.00	*65.00*
		Never hinged	87.50	
K5	A140	10c on 5c blue	60.00	*65.00*
		Never hinged	95.00	
K6	A140	12c on 6c red org	77.50	*95.00*
		Never hinged	125.00	
K7	A140	14c on 7c black	82.50	*110.00*
		Never hinged	130.00	
K8	A148	16c on 8c ol bis	60.00	*70.00*
		Never hinged	95.00	
a.		16c on 8c olive green	55.00	*60.00*
		Never hinged	87.50	
K9	A148	18c on 9c sal red	60.00	*75.00*
		Never hinged	95.00	
K10	A148	20c on 10c org yel	55.00	*60.00*
		Never hinged	87.50	
K11	A148	24c on 12c brn car	65.00	*70.00*
		Never hinged	105.00	
a.		24c on 12c claret brown	87.50	*110.00*
		Never hinged	140.00	
K12	A148	30c on 15c gray	82.50	*125.00*
		Never hinged	130.00	
K13	A148	40c on 20c dp ultra	125.00	*190.00*
		Never hinged	200.00	
K14	A148	60c on 30c org red	110.00	*160.00*
		Never hinged	175.00	
K15	A148	$1 on 50c lt vio	450.00	*550.00*
		Never hinged	725.00	
K16	A148	$2 on $1 vio brown	390.00	*450.00*
		Never hinged	625.00	
a.		Double surcharge	*4,250.*	*4,750.*
		Never hinged	*6,250.*	
		Nos. K1-K16 (16)	1,772.	2,205.

SHANGHAI
2 Cts.
CHINA

Nos. 498 and 528B Surcharged

1922, July 3

K17	A140	2c on 1c green	120.00	110.00
		Never hinged	190.00	
K18	A140	4c on 2c carmine, type VII	105.00	95.00
		Never hinged	170.00	

OFFICIAL STAMPS

The franking privilege having been abolished, as of July 1, 1873, these stamps were provided for each of the departments of Government for the prepayment of postage on official matter.

These stamps were supplanted on May 1, 1879, by penalty envelopes and on July 5, 1884, were declared obsolete.

Designs, except Post Office, resemble those illustrated but are not identical. Each bears the name of Department. Portraits are as follows: 1c, Franklin; 2c, Jackson; 3c, Washington; 6c, Lincoln; 7c, Stanton; 10c, Jefferson; 12c, Clay; 15c, Webster; 24c, Scott; 30c, Hamilton; 90c, Perry.

Grade, condition and original gum are very important in valuing #O1-O120 unused.

Printed by the Continental Bank Note Co.

Thin Hard Paper

O1

1873 — Unwmk. — Engr. — *Perf. 12*

Dept. of Agriculture

O1	O1	1c yellow	160.00	125.00
O2	O1	2c yellow	130.00	50.00
O3	O1	3c yellow	115.00	9.50
O4	O1	6c yellow	125.00	40.00
O5	O1	10c yellow	260.00	160.00
O6	O1	12c yellow	350.00	200.00
O7	O1	15c yellow	290.00	175.00
O8	O1	24c yellow	290.00	160.00
O9	O1	30c yellow	375.00	225.00
		Nos. O1-O9 (9)	2,095.	1,144.

Special printings overprinted "SPECIMEN" follow No. O120.

Executive Dept.

O10	O1	1c carmine	575.00	350.00
O11	O1	2c carmine	375.00	160.00
O12	O1	3c carmine	450.00	160.00
a.		3c violet rose	450.00	160.00
O13	O1	6c carmine	675.00	425.00
O14	O1	10c carmine	625.00	500.00
		Nos. O10-O14 (5)	2,700.	1,595.

Special printings overprinted "SPECIMEN" follow No. O120.

Dept. of the Interior

O15	O1	1c vermilion	35.00	8.00
O16	O1	2c vermilion	30.00	5.50
O17	O1	3c vermilion	47.50	5.00
O18	O1	6c vermilion	35.00	5.00
O19	O1	10c vermilion	35.00	10.00
O20	O1	12c vermilion	50.00	7.75
O21	O1	15c vermilion	85.00	17.00
O22	O1	24c vermilion	62.50	14.00
a.		Double impression		—
O23	O1	30c vermilion	85.00	14.00
O24	O1	90c vermilion	190.00	37.50
		Nos. O15-O24 (10)	655.00	123.75

Special printings overprinted "SPECIMEN" follow No. O120.

Dept. of Justice

O25	O1	1c purple	105.00	77.50
O26	O1	2c purple	175.00	82.50
O27	O1	3c purple	175.00	17.00
O28	O1	6c purple	160.00	25.00
O29	O1	10c purple	180.00	55.00
O30	O1	12c purple	140.00	37.50
O31	O1	15c purple	275.00	125.00
O32	O1	24c purple	700.00	275.00
O33	O1	30c purple	600.00	160.00
O34	O1	90c purple	900.00	425.00
		Nos. O25-O34 (10)	3,410.	1,279.

Special printings overprinted "SPECIMEN" follow No. O120.

Navy Dept.

O35	O1	1c ultramarine	75.00	37.50
a.		1c dull blue	85.00	40.00
O36	O1	2c ultramarine	60.00	17.00
a.		2c dull blue	70.00	15.00
O37	O1	3c ultramarine	60.00	8.00
a.		3c dull blue	70.00	11.00
O38	O1	6c ultramarine	60.00	14.00
a.		6c dull blue	70.00	14.50
O39	O1	7c ultramarine	375.00	140.00
a.		7c dull blue	425.00	150.00
O40	O1	10c ultramarine	80.00	27.50
a.		10c dull blue	85.00	27.50
O41	O1	12c ultramarine	95.00	25.00
O42	O1	15c ultramarine	175.00	50.00
O43	O1	24c ultramarine	175.00	55.00
a.		24c dull blue	200.00	—
O44	O1	30c ultramarine	140.00	27.50
O45	O1	90c ultramarine	700.00	175.00
a.		Double impression		*3,750.*
		Nos. O35-O45 (11)	1,995.	576.50

Special printings overprinted "SPECIMEN" follow No. O120.

O6

Post Office Dept.

O47	O6	1c black	12.50	5.00
O48	O6	2c black	16.00	4.00
a.		Double impression	325.00	300.00
O49	O6	3c black	5.25	1.25
a.		Printed on both sides		*3,000.*
O50	O6	6c black	16.00	3.25
a.		Diagonal half used as 3c on cover		*3,000.*
O51	O6	10c black	70.00	35.00
O52	O6	12c black	35.00	8.25
O53	O6	15c black	47.50	14.00
O54	O6	24c black	60.00	17.00
O55	O6	30c black	60.00	17.00
O56	O6	90c black	90.00	14.00
		Nos. O47-O56 (10)	412.25	118.75

Stamps of the POD are often on paper with a gray surface. This is due to insufficient wiping of the plates during printing.

Special printings overprinted "SPECIMEN" follow No. O120.

Seward — O8

Dept. of State

O57	O1	1c dark green	110.00	40.00
O58	O1	2c dark green	210.00	60.00
O59	O1	3c bright green	85.00	17.00
O60	O1	6c bright green	80.00	19.00
O61	O1	7c dark green	160.00	40.00
O62	O1	10c dark green	125.00	27.50
O63	O1	12c dark green	200.00	82.50
O64	O1	15c dark green	210.00	55.00
O65	O1	24c dark green	425.00	140.00
O66	O1	30c dark green	400.00	110.00
O67	O1	90c dark green	750.00	250.00
O68	O8	$2 green & black	850.00	650.00
O69	O8	$5 green & black	6,000.	3,250.
O70	O8	$10 green & black	4,000.	2,250.
O71	O8	$20 green & black	3,250.	1,700.

Special printings overprinted "SPECIMEN" follow No. O120.

Treasury Dept.

O72	O1	1c brown	37.50	4.50
O73	O1	2c brown	47.50	4.50
O74	O1	3c brown	32.50	1.70
a.		Double impression		—
O75	O1	6c brown	42.50	4.00
O76	O1	7c brown	90.00	22.50
O77	O1	10c brown	90.00	7.75
O78	O1	12c brown	90.00	6.00
O79	O1	15c brown	85.00	7.75
O80	O1	24c brown	425.00	65.00
O81	O1	30c brown	145.00	9.00
O82	O1	90c brown	150.00	10.00
		Nos. O72-O82 (11)	1,235.	142.70

Special printings overprinted "SPECIMEN" follow No. O120.

War Dept.

O83	O1	1c rose	140.00	7.25
O84	O1	2c rose	125.00	9.50
O85	O1	3c rose	130.00	2.75
O86	O1	6c rose	425.00	6.00
O87	O1	7c rose	125.00	72.50
O88	O1	10c rose	42.50	11.00
O89	O1	12c rose	145.00	9.00
O90	O1	15c rose	37.50	11.00
O91	O1	24c rose	37.50	6.75
O92	O1	30c rose	40.00	6.75
O93	O1	90c rose	90.00	40.00
		Nos. O83-O93 (11)	1,337.	182.50

Special printings overprinted "SPECIMEN" follow No. O120.

Printed by the American Bank Note Co.

1879 — Soft Porous Paper

Dept. of Agriculture

O94	O1	1c yel, no gum	3,000.	
O95	O1	3c yellow	290.00	55.00

Dept. of the Interior

O96	O1	1c vermilion	210.00	190.00
O97	O1	2c vermilion	4.00	1.60
O98	O1	3c vermilion	3.50	1.10
O99	O1	6c vermilion	5.25	5.50
O100	O1	10c vermilion	65.00	55.00
O101	O1	12c vermilion	125.00	90.00
O102	O1	15c vermilion	300.00	225.00
O103	O1	24c vermilion	*3,000.*	—

Dept. of Justice

O106	O1	3c bluish purple	85.00	55.00
O107	O1	6c bluish purple	190.00	160.00

Post Office Dept.

O108	O6	3c black	15.00	5.00

Treasury Dept.

O109	O1	3c brown	45.00	6.75
O110	O1	6c brown	85.00	35.00
O111	O1	10c brown	125.00	40.00
O112	O1	30c brown	1,250.	275.00
O113	O1	90c brown	2,000.	275.00
		Nos. O109-O113 (5)	3,505.	631.75

War Dept.

O114	O1	1c rose red	3.50	2.75
O115	O1	2c rose red	5.00	3.25
O116	O1	3c rose red	5.00	1.60
a.		Imperf., pair	*900.00*	
b.		Double impression	*750.00*	
O117	O1	6c rose red	4.50	1.40
O118	O1	10c rose red	37.50	37.50
O119	O1	12c rose red	30.00	10.00
O120	O1	30c rose red	80.00	67.50
		Nos. O114-O120 (7)	165.50	124.00

SPECIAL PRINTINGS

Special printings of Official stamps were made in 1875 at the time the other Reprints, Re-issues and Special Printings were printed. They are ungummed.

Although perforated, these stamps were sometimes (but not always) cut apart with scissors. As a result the perforations may be mutilated and the design damaged.

All values exist imperforate.

QUALITY U.S. Plate Blocks, Stamps, Specialists' Items, Especially Scott #1 to 715, C1-24, E1-14, O1-120, PR, B.O.B., Postal History, Specialized Collections, Officials & Newspapers also a specialty.

Builder of Specialized Collections...Inquire
Excellent stock. Complete Satisfaction Guaranteed.
Want Lists Serviced. We Will Quote Against Your Want List!
CALL OR WRITE! • WE ALSO BUY THE ABOVE MATERIAL!
QUALITY INVESTORS LTD.
ROBERT L. MARKOVITS Since 1958
Box 891, Middletown, NY 10940
Phone 914-343-2174 • Fax 914-342-2597

Printed by the Continental Bank Note Co.

Overprinted in Block Letters **SPECIMEN**

1875 *Perf. 12*
Thin, hard white paper
Type D

AGRICULTURE
Carmine Overprint

O1S	D	1c yellow	14.00
a.		"Specimen" error	700.00
b.		Small dotted "i" in "Specimen"	425.00
c.		Horiz. ribbed paper	20.00
O2S	D	2c yellow	27.50
a.		"Specimen" error	750.00
O3S	D	3c yellow	75.00
a.		"Specimen" error	3,000.
O4S	D	6c yellow	130.00
a.		"Specimen" error	5,500.
O5S	D	10c yellow	130.00
a.		"Specimen" error	3,250.
O6S	D	12c yellow	125.00
a.		"Specimen" error	3,750.
O7S	D	15c yellow	125.00
a.		"Specimen" error	3,250.
O8S	D	24c yellow	125.00
a.		"Specimen" error	3,250.
O9S	D	30c yellow	125.00
a.		"Specimen" error	3,250.
		Nos. O1S-O9S (9)	876.50

EXECUTIVE
Blue Overprint

O10S	D	1c carmine	14.00
a.		Small dotted "i" in "Specimen"	325.00
b.		Ribbed paper	20.00
O11S	D	2c carmine	27.50
O12S	D	3c carmine	27.50
O13S	D	6c carmine	27.50
O14S	D	10c carmine	27.50
		Nos. O10S-O14S (5)	124.00

INTERIOR
Blue Overprint

O15S	D	1c vermilion	27.50
O16S	D	2c vermilion	35.00
a.		"Specimen" error	3,750.
O17S	D	3c vermilion	475.00
O18S	D	6c vermilion	450.00
O19S	D	10c vermilion	450.00
O20S	D	12c vermilion	475.00
O21S	D	15c vermilion	475.00
O22S	D	24c vermilion	475.00
O23S	D	30c vermilion	475.00
O24S	D	90c vermilion	475.00
		Nos. O15S-O24S (10)	3,812.

JUSTICE
Blue Overprint

O25S	D	1c purple	15.00
a.		"Specimen" error	675.00
b.		Small dotted "i" in "Specimen"	275.00
c.		Horiz. ribbed paper	20.00
O26S	D	2c purple	30.00
a.		"Specimen" error	1,100.
O27S	D	3c purple	250.00
a.		"Specimen" error	3,750.
O28S	D	6c purple	250.00
O29S	D	10c purple	250.00
O30S	D	12c purple	250.00
a.		"Specimen" error	4,000.
O31S	D	15c purple	275.00
a.		"Specimen" error	4,000.
O32S	D	24c purple	300.00
a.		"Specimen" error	4,000.
O33S	D	30c purple	300.00
a.		"Specimen" error	4,000.
O34S	D	90c purple	325.00
		Nos. O25S-O34S (10)	2,245.

NAVY
Carmine Overprint

O35S	D	1c ultramarine	17.50
a.		"Specimen" error	550.00
O36S	D	2c ultramarine	35.00
a.		"Specimen" error	675.00
O37S	D	3c ultramarine	300.00
O38S	D	6c ultramarine	350.00
O39S	D	7c ultramarine	150.00
a.		"Specimen" error	3,000.
O40S	D	10c ultramarine	350.00
a.		"Specimen" error	4,250.
O41S	D	12c ultramarine	300.00
a.		"Specimen" error	4,000.
O42S	D	15c ultramarine	300.00
a.		"Specimen" error	7,500.
O43S	D	24c ultramarine	300.00
a.		"Specimen" error	4,000.
O44S	D	30c ultramarine	300.00
a.		"Specimen" error	4,500.
O45S	D	90c ultramarine	300.00
		Nos. O35S-O45S (11)	2,702.

POST OFFICE
Carmine Overprint

O47S	D	1c black	25.00
a.		"Specimen" error	650.00
b.		Inverted overprint	1,000.
O48S	D	2c black	65.00
a.		"Specimen" error	1,750.
O49S	D	3c black	450.00
O50S	D	6c black	425.00
O51S	D	10c black	275.00
a.		"Specimen" error	4,250.
O52S	D	12c black	400.00
O53S	D	15c black	475.00
a.		"Specimen" error	4,250.
O54S	D	24c black	425.00
a.		"Specimen" error	4,250.
O55S	D	30c black	425.00
O56S	D	90c black	425.00
a.		"Specimen" error	8,000.
		Nos. O47S-O56S (10)	3,390.

STATE
Carmine Overprint

O57S	D	1c bluish green	15.00
a.		"Specimen" error	400.00
b.		Small dotted "i" in "Specimen"	400.00
c.		Horiz. ribbed paper	20.00
O58S	D	2c bluish green	30.00
a.		"Specimen" error	550.00
O59S	D	3c bluish green	45.00
a.		"Specimen" error	2,000.
O60S	D	6c bluish green	95.00
a.		"Specimen" error	2,250.
O61S	D	7c bluish green	47.50
a.		"Specimen" error	1,750.
O62S	D	10c bluish green	180.00
a.		"Specimen" error	7,500.
O63S	D	12c bluish green	190.00
a.		"Specimen" error	3,500.
O64S	D	15c bluish green	180.00
O65S	D	24c bluish green	180.00
a.		"Specimen" error	3,500.
O66S	D	30c bluish green	180.00
a.		"Specimen" error	3,750.
O67S	D	90c bluish green	180.00
a.		"Specimen" error	3,750.
O68S	D	$2 green & black	7,250.
O69S	D	$5 green & black	12,000.
O70S	D	$10 green & black	16,000.
O71S	D	$20 green & black	19,000.
		Nos. O57S-O67S (11)	1,322.

TREASURY
Blue Overprint

O72S	D	1c dark brown	27.50
O73S	D	2c dark brown	130.00
O74S	D	3c dark brown	475.00
O75S	D	6c dark brown	425.00
O76S	D	7c dark brown	250.00
O77S	D	10c dark brown	450.00
O78S	D	12c dark brown	475.00
O79S	D	15c dark brown	475.00
O80S	D	24c dark brown	375.00
O81S	D	30c dark brown	500.00
O82S	D	90c dark brown	500.00
		Nos. O72S-O82S (11)	4,082.

WAR
Blue Overprint

O83S	D	1c deep rose	17.50
a.		"Specimen" error	550.00
O84S	D	2c deep rose	35.00
a.		"Specimen" error	1,000.
O85S	D	3c deep rose	350.00
a.		"Specimen" error	4,000.
O86S	D	6c deep rose	350.00
a.		"Specimen" error	4,250.
O87S	D	7c deep rose	72.50
a.		"Specimen" error	1,900.
O88S	D	10c deep rose	325.00
a.		"Specimen" error	4,250.
O89S	D	12c deep rose	375.00
a.		"Specimen" error	4,250.
O90S	D	15c deep rose	375.00
a.		"Specimen" error	4,250.
O91S	D	24c deep rose	375.00
a.		"Specimen" error	4,250.
O92S	D	30c deep rose	375.00
a.		"Specimen" error	4,250.
O93S	D	90c deep rose	375.00
a.		"Specimen" error	4,250.
		Nos. O83S-O93S (11)	3,025.

SOFT POROUS PAPER

1881 **EXECUTIVE**
Blue Overprint

O10xS	D	1c violet rose	45.00

NAVY
Carmine Overprint

O35xS	D	1c gray blue	50.00
a.		Double overprint	850.00

STATE
Carmine Overprint

O57xS	D	1c yellow green	200.00

Official Postal Savings Mail

These stamps were used to prepay postage on official correspondence of the Postal Savings Division of the POD. Discontinued Sept. 23, 1914.

O11

1911 **Wmk. 191**

O121	O11	2c black	14.00	1.50
		Never hinged	22.50	
O122	O11	50c dark green	140.00	40.00
		Never hinged	225.00	
O123	O11	$1 ultra	130.00	11.00
		Never hinged	210.00	

Wmk. 190

O124	O11	1c dark violet	7.50	1.50
		Never hinged	12.00	
O125	O11	2c black	45.00	5.50
		Never hinged	72.50	
O126	O11	10c carmine	17.00	1.60
		Never hinged	27.50	
		Nos. O121-O126 (6)	353.50	61.10

Catalogue values for unused stamps in this section, from this point to the end of the section, are for Never Hinged items.

Catalogue values for used stamps are for regularly used copies, not copies removed from first day covers.

Official Mail

O12    O13

Type O13 has frame line completely around blue design.

1983-85 Unwmk. Perf. 11

O127	O12	1c red, bl & blk	.15	.15
O128	O12	4c red, bl & blk	.15	.25
O129	O12	13c red, bl & blk	.45	.75
O129A	O12	14c red, bl & blk ('85)	.45	.50
O130	O12	17c red, bl & blk	.55	.40
O132	O12	$1 red, bl & blk	2.00	1.00
O133	O12	$5 red, bl & blk	9.00	5.00
		Nos. O127-O133 (7)	12.75	8.05

Coil Stamps
Perf. 10 Vert.

O135	O12	20c red, bl & blk	1.75	2.00
a.		Imperf., pair	2,000.	
O136	O12	22c red, bl & blk ('85)	.70	2.00

No. O129A does not have a "c" after the "14."

Inscribed: Postal Card Rate D

1985, Feb. 4 *Perf. 11*

O138	O12	(14c) red, bl & blk	5.25	5.00

Coil Stamps

Inscribed: No. O139, Domestic Letter Rate D. No. O140, Domestic Mail E.

1985-88 *Perf. 10 Vert.*

O138A	O13	15c red, bl & blk	.45	.50
O138B	O13	20c red, bl & blk	.45	.30
O139	O12	(22c) red, bl & blk	5.25	3.00
O140	O13	(25c) red, bl & blk	.75	2.00
O141	O13	25c red, bl & blk	.65	.50
a.		Imperf., pair	1,750.	
		Nos. O138A-O141 (5)	7.55	6.30

Issue dates: 1985; E, Mar. 22, 1988; 15c, June 11; 20c, May 19; 25c, June 11.
See Nos. O143, O145-O151, O153-O156.

1989, July 5 Litho. *Perf. 11*

O143	O13	1c red, blue & black	.15	.15

O14

1991, Jan. 22 Litho. *Perf. 10 Vert.*
Coil Stamp

O144	O14	(29c) red, blue & black	.75	.50

See No. O152.

Official Type of 1985
1991, May 24 Litho. *Perf. 10 Vert.*
Coil Stamp

O145	O13	29c red, blue & black	.65	.30

1991-93 *Perf. 11*

O146	O13	4c red, blue & black	.15	.30
O146A	O13	10c red, blue & black	.25	.30
O147	O13	19c red, blue & black	.40	.50
O148	O13	23c red, blue & black	.45	.30
a.		Imperf., pair	400.00	
O151	O13	$1 red, blue & black	2.00	.75

Nos. O146A, O151 have a line of microscopic printing below eagle. Nos. O147 and O148 have blue background made up of crosshatched lines, thicker lettering and thinner numerals.
Issued: #O146, 4/6; #O147, O148, 5/24; 10c, 10/19/93; #O151, 9/1993.

COIL STAMP
1994, Dec. 13 Litho. *Perf. 9.8 Vert.*
Inscribed: No. O152, For U.S. addresses only G.

O152	O14	(32c) red, blue & black	.65	—

Type of 1985
1995, May 9 Litho. *Perf. 9.8 Vert.*
COIL STAMP

O153	O13	32c red, blue & black	.65	.30

1995, May 9 *Perf. 11.2*

O154	O13	1c red, blue & black	.15	.15
O155	O13	20c red, blue & black	.45	.30
O156	O13	23c red, blue & black	.50	.30

Nos. O153-O156 have a line of microscopic text below the eagle.

NEWSPAPER STAMPS

For the prepayment of postage on bulk shipments of newspapers and periodicals. From 1875 on, the stamps were affixed to memorandums of mailing, canceled and retained by the post office. Discontinued on July 1, 1898.

Most used stamps of Nos. PR1-PR4, PR9-PR32, PR57-PR79 and PR81-PR89 are pen canceled (or uncanceled). Handstamp cancellations on any of these issues are rare and sell for much more than catalogue values which are for pen-canceled examples. Used values for Nos. PR102-PR125 are for stamps with handstamp cancellations.

Washington N1

Franklin N2

Lincoln — N3

UNITED STATES

Printed by the National Bank Note Co.
Thin Hard Paper, No Gum

1865 Unwmk. Typo. Perf. 12
Size: 51x95mm
Colored Border

PR1	N1	5c dark blue	350.00	—
a.		5c light blue	375.00	—
PR2	N2	10c blue green	140.00	—
a.		10c green	140.00	—
b.		Pelure paper	165.00	—
PR3	N3	25c orange red	190.00	—
a.		25c carmine red	220.00	—
b.		Pelure paper	190.00	—

White Border
Yellowish Paper

PR4	N1	5c light blue	87.50	—
a.		5c dark blue	87.50	—
b.		Pelure paper	87.50	—
	Nos. PR1-PR4 (4)		767.50	

Reprints of 1865 Issue
Printed by the National Bank Note Co.
Hard White Paper, Without Gum

1875

PR5	N1	5c dull blue	100.00
a.		Printed on both sides	
PR6	N2	10c dk bluish green	110.00
a.		Printed on both sides	2,000.
PR7	N3	25c dark carmine	135.00
	Nos. PR5-PR7 (3)		345.00

The 5c has white border, 10c and 25c have colored borders.

Printed by the American Bank Note Co.
Soft Porous Paper

1880
White Border

PR8	N1	5c dark blue	240.

Statue of Freedom — N4
"Justice" — N5 
Ceres — N6 
"Victory" — N7 
Clio — N8 
Minerva — N9 
Vesta — N10 
"Peace" — N11 

"Commerce" N12
Hebe N13 
Indian Maiden — N14 

Printed by the Continental Bank Note Co.
Engraved Thin Hard Paper

1875 Size: 24x35mm

PR9	N4	2c black	35.00	22.50
PR10	N4	3c black	40.00	25.00
PR11	N4	4c black	37.50	22.50
PR12	N4	6c black	45.00	25.00
PR13	N4	8c black	60.00	35.00
PR14	N4	9c black	120.00	80.00
PR15	N4	10c black	60.00	30.00
PR16	N5	12c rose	140.00	70.00
PR17	N5	24c rose	165.00	80.00
PR18	N5	36c rose	200.00	90.00
PR19	N5	48c rose	350.00	150.00
PR20	N5	60c rose	180.00	80.00
PR21	N5	72c rose	400.00	190.00
PR22	N5	84c rose	600.00	240.00
PR23	N5	96c rose	350.00	160.00
PR24	N6	$1.92 dark brn	450.00	200.00
PR25	N7	$3 vermilion	600.00	240.00
PR26	N8	$6 ultra	950.00	325.00
PR27	N9	$9 yellow	1,250.	400.00
PR28	N10	$12 blue grn	1,400.	525.00
PR29	N11	$24 dk gray vio	1,400.	525.00
PR30	N12	$36 brn rose	1,500.	625.00
PR31	N13	$48 red brn	2,100.	750.00
PR32	N14	$60 violet	2,100.	750.00

Special Printing of the 1875 Issue
Printed by the Continental Bank Note Co.
Hard White Paper
Without Gum

PR33	N4	2c gray black	225.
a.		Horizontally ribbed paper	225.
PR34	N4	3c gray black	240.
a.		Horizontally ribbed paper	250.
PR35	N4	4c gray black	275.
PR36	N4	6c gray black	325.
PR37	N4	8c gray black	400.
PR38	N4	9c gray black	450.
PR39	N4	10c gray black	550.
a.		Horizontally ribbed paper	600.
PR40	N5	12c pale rose	675.
PR41	N5	24c pale rose	950.
PR42	N5	36c pale rose	1,100.
PR43	N5	48c pale rose	1,250.
PR44	N5	60c pale rose	1,400.
PR45	N5	72c pale rose	1,900.
PR46	N5	84c pale rose	2,250.
PR47	N5	96c pale rose	3,250.
PR48	N6	$1.92 dk brown	9,000.
PR49	N7	$3 vermilion	17,500.
PR50	N8	$6 ultra	20,000.
PR51	N9	$9 yellow	35,000.
PR52	N10	$12 blue green	30,000.
PR53	N11	$24 dk gray vio	—
PR54	N12	$36 brown rose	—
PR55	N13	$48 red brown	—
PR56	N14	$60 violet	—

Nos. PR33 to PR56 exist imperf. but were not regularly issued. (See the Scott U.S. Specialized Catalogue.)

Printed by the American Bank Note Co.

1879
Soft Porous Paper

PR57	N4	2c black	15.00	5.50
PR58	N4	3c black	20.00	7.00
PR59	N4	4c black	17.50	7.00
PR60	N4	6c black	35.00	15.00
PR61	N4	8c black	35.00	15.00
PR62	N4	10c black	35.00	15.00
PR63	N5	12c red	150.00	45.00
PR64	N5	24c red	150.00	45.00
PR65	N5	36c red	400.00	190.00
PR66	N5	48c red	325.00	100.00
PR67	N5	60c red	275.00	90.00
a.		Imperf. pair	1,250.	
PR68	N5	72c red	525.00	180.00
PR69	N5	84c red	400.00	140.00
PR70	N5	96c red	250.00	90.00
PR71	N6	$1.92 pale brown	200.00	85.00
PR72	N7	$3 red ver	200.00	85.00
PR73	N8	$6 blue	325.00	140.00
PR74	N9	$9 orange	230.00	90.00
PR75	N10	$12 yellow grn	375.00	120.00
PR76	N11	$24 dk violet	425.00	160.00
PR77	N12	$36 Indian red	525.00	175.00
PR78	N13	$48 yellow brown	650.00	240.00
PR79	N14	$60 purple	650.00	240.00
	Nos. PR57-PR70 (14)		2,632.	894.50

See the Scott U.S. Specialized Catalogue Die and Plate Proof section for other imperforates.

Special Printing of the 1879 Issue
Printed by the American Bank Note Co.

1881

PR80	N4	2c intense black	500.00

1885

PR81	N4	1c black	17.50	7.50
PR82	N5	12c carmine	55.00	17.50
PR83	N5	24c carmine	57.50	20.00
PR84	N5	36c carmine	82.50	30.00
PR85	N5	48c carmine	120.00	45.00
PR86	N5	60c carmine	165.00	65.00
PR87	N5	72c carmine	175.00	70.00
PR88	N5	84c carmine	360.00	160.00
PR89	N5	96c carmine	275.00	120.00
	Nos. PR81-PR89 (9)		1,307.	535.00

See the Scott U.S. Specialized Catalogue Die and Plate Proof section for imperforates.

Printed by the Bureau of Engraving and Printing

1894 Soft Wove Paper

PR90	N4	1c intense black	150.00
PR91	N4	2c intense black	150.00
PR92	N4	4c intense black	160.00
PR93	N4	6c intense black	2,250.
PR94	N4	10c intense black	325.00
PR95	N5	12c carmine	875.00
PR96	N5	24c pink	875.00
PR97	N5	36c pink	10,000.
PR98	N5	60c pink	10,000.
PR99	N5	96c pink	12,500.
PR100	N7	$3 scarlet	15,000.
PR101	N8	$6 pale blue	19,000.

Statue of Freedom N15
"Justice" N16 
"Victory" N17
Clio — N18 
Vesta — N19 
"Peace" — N20 
"Commerce" N21 
Indian Maiden N22

1895 Unwmk.
Sizes: 1c-50c, 21x34mm,
$2-$100, 24x35mm

PR102	N15	1c black	60.00	12.50
	Never hinged		95.00	
PR103	N15	2c black	60.00	12.50
	Never hinged		95.00	
PR104	N15	5c black	80.00	20.00
	Never hinged		130.00	
PR105	N15	10c black	175.00	52.50
	Never hinged		275.00	
PR106	N16	25c carmine	250.00	55.00
	Never hinged		375.00	
PR107	N16	50c carmine	500.00	150.00
	Never hinged		775.00	
PR108	N17	$2 scarlet	600.00	110.00
	Never hinged		950.00	
PR109	N18	$5 ultra	850.00	225.00
	Never hinged		1,300.	
PR110	N19	$10 green	900.00	250.00
	Never hinged		1,400.	
PR111	N20	$20 slate	1,300.	450.00
	Never hinged		2,000.	
PR112	N21	$50 dull rose	1,400.	450.00
	Never hinged		2,150.	
PR113	N22	$100 purple	1,600.	525.00
	Never hinged		2,500.	
	Nos. PR102-PR113 (12)		7,775.	2,312.

1895-97 Wmk. 191

PR114	N15	1c black ('96)	6.00	4.00
	Never hinged		9.50	
PR115	N15	2c black	6.50	4.00
	Never hinged		10.00	
PR116	N15	5c black ('96)	10.00	6.50
	Never hinged		16.00	
PR117	N15	10c black	6.50	4.25
	Never hinged		10.00	
PR118	N16	25c carmine	12.50	10.00
	Never hinged		19.50	
PR119	N16	50c carmine	15.00	15.00
	Never hinged		24.00	
PR120	N17	$2 scar ('97)	20.00	22.50
	Never hinged		32.50	
PR121	N18	$5 dk blue ('96)	35.00	35.00
	Never hinged		55.00	
a.		$5 light blue	175.00	70.00
	Never hinged		280.00	
PR122	N19	$10 green ('96)	35.00	35.00
	Never hinged		55.00	
PR123	N20	$20 slate ('96)	37.50	37.50
	Never hinged		60.00	
PR124	N21	$50 dl rose ('97)	50.00	42.50
	Never hinged		80.00	
PR125	N22	$100 purple ('96)	55.00	47.50
	Never hinged		87.50	
	Nos. PR114-PR125 (12)		289.00	263.75

In 1899 the Government sold 26,989 sets of these stamps, but, as the stock of the high values was not sufficient to make up the required number, the $5, $10, $20, $50 and $100 were reprinted. These are virtually indistinguishable from earlier printings.

For overprints see Nos. R159-R160.

PARCEL POST STAMPS

Issued for the prepayment of postage on parcel post packages only.

Post Office Clerk — PP1
City Carrier — PP2 
Railway Postal Clerk — PP3 
Rural Carrier — PP4 
Mail Train — PP5

UNITED STATES

Steamship and Mail Tender — PP6

Automobile Service — PP7

Airplane Carrying Mail — PP8

Manufacturing PP9

Dairying PP10

Harvesting PP11

Fruit Growing PP12

1913		Engr.	Wmk. 190	Perf. 12	
Q1	PP1	1c carmine rose		4.75	1.30
		Never hinged		7.50	
Q2	PP2	2c carmine rose		6.00	1.00
		Never hinged		9.50	
Q3	PP3	3c carmine		10.00	5.25
		Never hinged		16.00	
Q4	PP4	4c carmine rose		30.00	2.50
		Never hinged		47.50	
Q5	PP5	5c carmine rose		25.00	2.00
		Never hinged		40.00	
Q6	PP6	10c carmine rose		45.00	2.50
		Never hinged		72.50	
Q7	PP7	15c carmine rose		60.00	10.00
		Never hinged		95.00	
Q8	PP8	20c carmine rose		120.00	20.00
		Never hinged		190.00	
Q9	PP9	25c carmine rose		60.00	6.00
		Never hinged		95.00	
Q10	PP10	50c carmine rose		250.00	37.50
		Never hinged		400.00	
Q11	PP11	75c carmine rose		80.00	30.00
		Never hinged		130.00	
Q12	PP12	$1 carmine rose		325.00	25.00
		Never hinged		525.00	
	Nos. Q1-Q12 (12)			1,015.	143.05

PARCEL POST POSTAGE DUE STAMPS

For affixing by a postal clerk, to any parcel post package, to denote the amount to be collected from the addressee because of insufficient prepayment of postage.

PPD1

1913		Engr.	Wmk. 190	Perf. 12	
JQ1	PPD1	1c dark green		9.00	4.00
		Never hinged		14.00	
JQ2	PPD1	2c dark green		70.00	16.00
		Never hinged		110.00	
JQ3	PPD1	5c dark green		12.50	5.25
		Never hinged		20.00	
JQ4	PPD1	10c dark green		150.00	40.00
		Never hinged		235.00	
JQ5	PPD1	25c dark green		85.00	4.75
		Never hinged		130.00	
	Nos. JQ1-JQ5 (5)			326.50	70.00

SPECIAL HANDLING STAMPS

For use on fourth-class mail to secure the same expeditious handling accorded to first-class mail matter.

PP13

1925-29		Unwmk.	Engr.	Perf. 11	
QE1	PP13	10c yellow grn ('28)		1.40	1.00
		Never hinged		2.10	
QE2	PP13	15c yellow grn ('28)		1.50	.90
		Never hinged		2.20	
QE3	PP13	20c yellow grn ('28)		2.25	1.50
		Never hinged		3.50	
QE4	PP13	25c yellow grn ('29)		19.00	7.50
		Never hinged		29.00	
a.		25c deep green ('25)		27.50	5.50
		Never hinged		42.50	
	Nos. QE1-QE4 (4)			24.15	10.90

COMPUTER VENDED POSTAGE

CVP1

CVP2

1989, Aug. 23 Tagged *Guillotined*
Self-Adhesive
Washington, DC, Machine 82
Any Date Other Than 1st Day

1	CVP1	25c 1st Class	6.00	—
a.		1st day dated, serial #12501-15500	4.50	
b.		1st day dated, serial #00001-12500	4.50	
c.		1st day dated, serial over #27500	—	
2	CVP1	$1 3rd Class	—	—
a.		1st day dated, serial #24501-27500	—	
b.		1st day dated, serial over #27500	—	
3	CVP2	$1.69 Parcel Post	—	—
a.		1st day dated, serial #21501-24500	—	
b.		1st day dated, serial over #27500	—	
4	CVP1	$2.40 Priority Mail	—	—
a.		1st day dated, serial #18501-21500	—	
b.		Priority Mail ($2.74), with bar code (CVP2)	100.00	
c.		1st day dated, serial over #27500	—	
5	CVP1	$8.75 Express Mail	—	—
a.		1st day dated, serial #15501-18500	—	
b.		1st day dated, serial over #27500	—	
	Nos. 1a-5a (5)		82.50	

Washington, DC, Machine 83
Any Date Other Than 1st Day

6	CVP1	25c 1st Class	6.00	—
a.		1st day dated, serial #12501-15500	4.50	
b.		1st day dated, serial #00001-12500	4.50	
c.		1st day dated, serial over #27500	—	
7	CVP1	$1 3rd Class	—	—
a.		1st day dated, serial #24501-27500	—	
b.		1st day dated, serial over #27500	—	
8	CVP2	$1.69 Parcel Post	—	—
a.		1st day dated, serial #21501-24500	—	
b.		1st day dated, serial over #27500	—	
9	CVP1	$2.40 Priority Mail	—	—
a.		1st day dated, serial #18501-21500	—	

b.		1st day dated, serial over #27500	—	
c.		Priority Mail ($2.74), with bar code (CVP2)	100.00	
10	CVP1	$8.75 Express Mail	—	—
a.		1st day dated, serial #15501-18500	—	
b.		1st day dated, serial over #27500	—	
	Nos. 6a-10a (5)		57.50	

1989, Sept. 1
Kensington, MD, Machine 82
Any Date Other Than 1st Day

11	CVP1	25c 1st Class	6.00	—
a.		1st day dated, serial #12501-15500	4.50	
b.		1st day dated, serial #00001-12500	4.50	
c.		1st day dated, serial over #27500	—	
12	CVP1	$1 3rd Class	—	—
a.		1st day dated, serial #24501-27500	—	
b.		1st day dated, serial over #27500	—	
13	CVP2	$1.69 Parcel Post	—	—
a.		1st day dated, serial #21501-24500	—	
b.		1st day dated, serial over #27500	—	
14	CVP1	$2.40 Priority Mail	—	—
a.		1st day dated, serial #18501-21500	—	
b.		1st day dated, serial over #27500	—	
c.		Priority Mail ($2.74), with bar code (CVP2)	100.00	
15	CVP1	$8.75 Express Mail	—	—
a.		1st day dated, serial #15501-18500	—	
b.		1st day dated, serial over #27500	—	
	Nos. 11a-15a (5)		57.50	
	Nos. 1b, 11b (2)		9.00	

Kensington, MD, Machine 83
Any Date Other Than 1st Day

16	CVP1	25c 1st Class	6.00	—
a.		1st day dated, serial #12501-15500	4.50	
b.		1st day dated, serial #00001-12500	4.50	
c.		1st day dated, serial over #27500	—	
17	CVP1	$1 3rd Class	—	—
a.		1st day dated, serial #24501-27500	—	
b.		1st day dated, serial over #27500	—	
18	CVP2	$1.69 Parcel Post	—	—
a.		1st day dated, serial #21501-24500	—	
b.		1st day dated, serial over #27500	—	
19	CVP1	$2.40 Priority Mail	—	—
a.		1st day dated, serial #18501-21500	—	
b.		1st day dated, serial over #27500	—	
c.		Priority Mail ($2.74), with bar code (CVP2)	100.00	
20	CVP1	$8.75 Express Mail	—	—
a.		1st day dated, serial #15501-18500	—	
b.		1st day dated, serial over #27500	—	
	Nos. 16a-20a (5)		57.50	
	Nos. 6b, 16b (2)		9.00	

1989, Nov.
Washington, DC, Machine 11

21	CVP1	25c 1st Class	150.00	—
a.		1st Class, with bar code (CVP2)	—	

Stamps in CVP1 design, probably certified 1st class, with $1.10 denomination exist.

22	CVP1	$1 3rd Class	500.00	—
23	CVP2	$1.69 Parcel Post	500.00	—
24	CVP1	$2.40 Priority Mail	500.00	—
a.		Priority Mail ($2.74), with bar code (CVP2)	—	
25	CVP1	$8.75 Express Mail	500.00	—

Washington, DC, Machine 12

| 26 | CVP1 | 25c 1st Class | 150.00 | — |

A $1.10 certified 1st Class stamp, dated Nov. 20, exists on cover.

| 27 | CVP1 | $1 3rd Class | — | — |

A $1.40 Third Class stamp of type CVP2, dated Dec. 1 is known on a Dec. 2 cover.

28	CVP2	$1.69 Parcel Post	—	—
29	CVP1	$2.40 Priority Mail	—	—
a.		Priority Mail ($2.74), with bar code (CVP2)	—	
30	CVP1	$8.75 Express Mail	—	—

An $8.50 Express Mail stamp, dated Dec. 2, exists on cover.

Type I — CVP3

Type II — CVP3

1992, Aug. 20 Engr. Perf. 10 Horiz. Coil Stamp

| 31 | CVP3 | 29c red & blue, type I | .60 | .25 |
| c. | | 32c, type II ('94) | .80 | .25 |

No. 31 was available in all denominations from 1c to $99.99. The listing is for the first class rate. Other denominations, se-tenant combinations, or "errors" will not be listed.

Type II denomination has large sans-serif numerals preceded by an asterisk measuring 2mm across. No. 31 has small numerals with serifs preceded by an asterisk 1 1/2mm across.

CVP4

1994, Feb. 19 Photo. Perf. 9.9 Vert. Coil Stamp

| 32 | CVP4 | 29c dark red & dark blue | .60 | .25 |

No. 32 was available in all denominations from 19c to $99.99. The listing is for the first class rate at time of issue. Other denominations, se-tenant combinations, or "errors" will not be listed.

1996, Jan. 26 Photo. Perf. 9.9 Vert.

| 33 | CVP4 | 32c bright red & blue | .60 | .25 |

Letters in "USA" on No. 33 are thicker than on No. 32. Numerous other design differences exist in the moire pattern and in the bunting. No. 33 has "1996" in the lower left corner; No. 32 has no date.

For No. 33, the 32c value has been listed because it was the first class rate at time of issue.

CARRIERS' STAMPS

OFFICIAL ISSUES

Issued by the US Government to facilitate payment of fees for delivering and collecting letters.

Franklin OC1

Eagle OC2

1851		Unwmk.	Engr.	Imperf.	
LO1	OC1	(1c) dull blue, *rose*		4,500.	5,000.
LO2	OC2	1c blue		25.00	50.00

1875

REPRINTS OF 1851 ISSUE
Without Gum

LO3	OC1	(1c) blue, *rose*, imperf.	50.00	
LO4	OC1	(1c) blue, perf. 12	2,500.	
LO5	OC2	1c blue, imperf.	25.00	
LO6	OC2	1c blue, perf. 12	190.00	

Reprints of the Franklin Carrier are printed in dark blue, instead of the dull blue or deep blue of the originals. The reprints of the Eagle carrier are on hard white paper, ungummed and sometimes perforated, and also on a coarse wove paper. Originals are on yellowish paper with brown gum.

SEMI-OFFICIAL ISSUES

Issued by officials or employees of the US Government for the purpose of securing or indicating payment of carriers' fees.

Baltimore, Md.

C1

1850-55		Typo.		Imperf.	
1LB1	C1	1c red, *bluish*		130.	130.
1LB2	C1	1c blue, *bluish*		160.	115.
a.		Bluish laid paper			
1LB3	C1	1c blue		120.	80.
		Laid paper		190.	130.
1LB4	C1	1c green		—	600.
1LB5	C1	1c red		500.	400.

Ten varieties.

UNITED STATES

C2, C3

1856   Typo.
1LB6 C2 1c blue   120.   80.
1LB7 C2 1c red   120.   80.
   Shades exist of Nos. 1LB6-1LB7.

1857
1LB8 C3 1c black   60.   45.
   a. "SENT"   90.   65.
   b. Short rays   90.   65.
1LB9 C3 1c red   90.   80.
   a. "SENT"   125.   100.
   b. Short rays   125.   100.
   Ten varieties of C3.

BOSTON, MASS.

C6, C7

1849-50   Typeset
3LB1 C6 1c blue   375.   180.
3LB2 C7 1c blue (shades), *slate*   190.   100.

CHARLESTON, S. C.

C8, C10

1849   Typo.
4LB1 C8 2c black, *brn rose*   4,000.   2,500.
4LB2 C8 2c black, *yellow*   2,500.

1854   Typeset
4LB3 C10 2c black   1,000.

C11

1849-50   Typeset
4LB5 C11 2c black, *bluish, pelure*   600.   450.
4LB7 C11 2c black, *yellow*   600.   750.
   Several varieties of C11.

C13, C14

C15

1851-58   Typeset
4LB8 C13 2c blk, *bluish*   225.   130.
   a. Period after "Paid"   450.   200.
   b. "Cens"   700.
   c. "Conours" and "Bents"
4LB9 C13 2c blk, *bluish, pelure*   475.   525.
4LB11 C14 (2c) blk, *bluish*   —   325.
4LB12 C14 (2c) blk, *bluish, pelure*   —   325.
4LB13 C15 (2c) blk, *bluish* ('58)   425.   200.
   a. Comma after "PAID"   1,000.
   b. No period after "Post"   1,300.
   Several varieties of C13.

C16, C17

1851-58   Typeset
4LB14 C16 2c black, *bluish*   550.   625.
4LB15 C17 2c black, *bluish*   700.   700.
   Several varieties of each.

C18

1858   Typeset
4LB16 C18 2c black, *bluish*   5,000.
   Several varieties.

Same as C19, but inscribed "Beckmann's City Post"

1860
4LB17 C19 2c black   —
   One copy exists, on cover.

C19, C20

1859   Typeset
4LB18 C19 2c black, *bluish*   3,000.
4LB19 C20 2c black, *bluish*   5,000.   —
4LB20 C20 2c black, *pink*   200.   —
4LB21 C20 2c black, *yellow*   175.

CINCINNATI, OHIO

C20a

1854   Litho.   Wove Paper
9LB1 C20a 2c brown   2,750.   2,750.

CLEVELAND, OHIO

C20b, C20c

1854   Wove Paper   Litho.
10LB1 C20b blue   2,000.   2,000.
   Vertically Laid Paper
10LB2 C20c 2c black, *bluish*   —   3,750.

LOUISVILLE, KY.

C21, C22

1857-58
5LB1 C21 (2c) bluish green   90.
5LB2 C22 (2c) blue ('58)   175.   175.
5LB3 C22 (2c) black ('58)   700.   1,750.

NEW YORK, N.Y.

C23

1842   Engr.
6LB1 C23 3c black, *grayish*   1,250.

Used copies are Carriers' stamps only when canceled with the regular government cancellation "U.S." in octagonal frame (see illustration), "U.S.CITY DESPATCH POST," or New York circular postmark. When canceled "FREE" in frame they were used as local stamps (see No. 40L1 in the Scott Specialized Catalogue of United States Stamps).

C24

1842-45   Engr.
Unsurfaced Paper, Colored Through
6LB2 C24 3c black, *rosy buff*   800.
6LB3 C24 3c blk, *light blue*   500.   500.
6LB4 C24 3c black, *green*   —
   Some authorities consider No. 6LB2 to be an essay, and No. 6LB4 to be a color changeling.

Glazed Paper, Surface Colored
6LB5 C24 3c black, *blue green* (shades)   175.   140.
   a. Double impression   500.
   b. 3c, black, *blue*   650.   200.
   c. As "b," double impression   750.
   d. 3c, black, *green*   1,000.   900.
   e. As "d," double impression

No. 6LB5 Surcharged in Red — C25

1846
6LB7 C25 2c on 3c, on cover   —
   The City Despatch 2c red is listed in the Scott United States Specialized Catalogue as a Local stamp.

C27

1849-50   Typo.
6LB9 C27 1c black, *rose*   90.   75.
6LB10 C27 1c black, *yellow*   90.   90.
6LB11 C27 1c black, *buff*   90.   75.
   a. Pair, one stamp sideways   1,000.

PHILADELPHIA, PA.

C28, C29

1849-50   Typeset
7LB1 C28 1c blk, *rose* (with letters L.P.)   275.
7LB2 C28 1c black, *rose* (with letter S)   750.
7LB3 C28 1c blk, *rose* (with letter H)   275.
7LB4 C28 1c blk, *rose* (with letters L.S.)   275.
7LB5 C28 1c black, *rose* (with letters J.J.)   3,250.
7LB6 C29 1c black, *rose*   225.   190.
7LB7 C29 1c black, *blue*, glazed   800.
7LB8 C29 1c blk, *ver*, glazed   700.
7LB9 C29 1c blk, *yel*, glazed   3,000.
   Several varieties of each.
   Nos. 7LB1-7LB9 normally received no cancellation.
   The 1c black on buff (unglazed), type C29, is believed to be a color changeling.

C30, C31

C32

1850-52   Litho.
7LB11 C30 1c gold, *black, glazed*   140.   105.
7LB12 C30 1c blue   300.   225.
7LB13 C30 1c black   —   550.
   25 varieties of C30.

Handstamped
7LB14 C31 1c blue, *buff*   2,250.
7LB16 C31 1c black   1,650.

1856(?)
7LB18 C32 1c black   900.   1,400.

Labels in these designs are not believed to be Carrier stamps.

ST. LOUIS, MO.

C36, C37

(Actual size) — C37

Several varieties.

1849   Litho.
8LB1 C36 2c black   4,000.   7,500.

1857   Litho.
8LB2 C37 2c blue   5,000.

Carrier stamps Nos. 9LB1, 10LB1-10LB2 are listed following No. 4LB21.

STAMPED ENVELOPES AND WRAPPERS

VALUES

Values are for cut squares in a grade of very fine. Very fine cut squares will have the design well centered within moderately large margins. Precanceled cut squares must include the entire pre-cancellation. Values for unused entires are for those without printed or manuscript address. Values for letter sheets are for folded entires. Unfolded copies sell for more. A "full corner" includes back and side flaps and commands a premium. (Entire envelopes and wrappers are listed in the Scott U.S. Specialized Catalogue.)

UNITED STATES

Wrappers are listed with envelopes of corresponding designs, and indicated by prefix letter "W" instead of "U."

Envelopes with the stamp printed by error in colorless embossing from an uninked die, are "albinos." They are worth more than normal, inked impressions. Albinos of earlier issues, canceled while current, are scarce.

The papers of these issues vary greatly in texture, and in color from yellowish to bluish white and from amber to dark buff.

"+" Some authorities claim that Nos. U37, U48, U49, U110, U124, U125, U130, U133A, U137A, U137B, U137C, W138, U145, U162, U178A, U185, U220, U285, U286, U298, U299, UO3, UO32, UO38, UO45 and UO45A (each with "+" before number) were not regularly issued and are not known to have been used.

Washington
U1   U2

U1 — "THREE" in short label with curved ends; 13mm wide at top.
U2 — "THREE" in short label with straight ends; 15½mm wide at top.

U3   U4

U3 — "THREE" in short label with octagon ends.
U4 — "THREE" in wide label with straight ends; 20mm wide at top.

U5   U6

U5 — "THREE" in medium wide label with curved ends; 14½mm wide at top.

U7   U8

U7 — "TEN" in short label; 15⅓mm wide at top.
U8 — "TEN" in wide label 20mm wide at top.

1853-55 On Diagonally Laid Paper

U1	U1	3c red	240.00	20.00
U2	U1	3c red, buff	80.00	11.00
U3	U2	3c red	900.00	35.00
U4	U2	3c red, buff	250.00	20.00
U5	U3	3c red ('54)	4,500.	375.00
U6	U3	3c red, buff ('54)	250.00	42.50
U7	U4	3c red	700.00	85.00
U8	U4	3c red, buff	1,500.	100.00
U9	U5	3c red ('54)	25.00	3.00
U10	U5	3c red, buff ('54)	15.00	3.00
U11	U6	6c red	170.00	65.00
U12	U6	6c red, buff	125.00	55.00
U13	U6	6c green	225.00	100.00
U14	U6	6c green, buff	200.00	80.00
U15	U7	10c green ('55)	200.00	70.00
U16	U7	10c green, buff ('55)	70.00	50.00
a.		10c pale green	70.00	45.00
U17	U8	10c green ('55)	250.00	100.00
a.		10c pale green	225.00	100.00
U18	U8	10c green, buff ('55)	125.00	60.00
a.		10c pale green	125.00	60.00

Nos. U9, U10, U11, U12, U13, U14, U17 and U18 have been reprinted on white and buff papers, wove or vertically laid, and are not known entire. The originals are on diagonally laid paper. Value of 8 reprints on laid, $225. Reprints on wove sell for more.

Franklin, Period after "POSTAGE."
U9   U10

U10 — Bust touches inner frame-line at front and back.

No period after "POSTAGE"
U11

Washington
U12

Envelopes are on diagonally laid paper. Wrappers on vertically or horizontally laid paper.

1860-61

U19	U9	1c blue, buff	30.00	15.00
W20	U9	1c blue, buff ('61)	65.00	50.00
W21	U9	1c blue, man ('61)	45.00	45.00
W22	U9	1c blue, org ('61)	2,750.	
U23	U10	1c blue, org	450.00	350.00
U24	U11	1c blue, buff	225.00	90.00
W25	U11	1c blue, man ('61)	3,250.	2,750.
U26	U12	3c red	27.50	13.00
U27	U12	3c red, buff	20.00	12.50
U28	U12+9	3c + 1c red & blue	325.00	240.00
U29	U12+9	3c + 1c red & blue, buff	275.00	225.00
U30	U12	6c red	2,400.	1,250.
U31	U12	6c red, buff	2,250.	900.00
U32	U12	10c green	1,200.	350.00
U33	U12	10c green, buff	1,100.	250.00

Nos. U26, U27, U30 to U33 have been reprinted on the same vertically laid paper as the reprints of the 1853-55 issue, and are not known entire. Value, Nos. U26-U27, $160; Nos. U30-U33, $100.

U13   U14

U15 **Washington** U16

Envelopes are on diagonally laid paper.

1861

U34	U13	3c pink	20.00	5.50
U35	U13	3c pink, buff	19.00	5.00
U36	U13	3c pink, bl (letter sheet)	75.00	50.00
+U37	U13	3c pink, org	3,500.	
U38	U14	6c pink	110.00	80.00
U39	U14	6c pink, buff	65.00	60.00
U40	U15	10c yellow green	32.50	30.00
a.		10c blue green	30.00	27.50
U41	U15	10c yel green, buff	27.50	27.50
a.		10c blue green, buff	27.50	27.50
U42	U16	12c red & brown, buff	180.00	160.00
a.		12c lake & brown, buff	800.00	
U43	U16	20c red & bl, buff	190.00	175.00
U44	U16	24c red & green, buff	200.00	175.00
a.		24c lake & green, sal	225.00	200.00
U45	U16	40c black & red, buff	300.00	300.00

Nos. U38 and U39 have been reprinted on the same papers as the reprints of the 1853-55 issue and are not known entire. Value of two reprints, $60.

Jackson — U17   Jackson — U18

"U.S. POSTAGE" above

U17 — The downstroke and tail of the "2" unite near the point.

U18 — The downstroke and tail of the "2" touch but do not merge.

Jackson — U19   Jackson — U20

"U.S. POST" above

U19 — Stamp measures 24 to 25mm in width.

U20 — Stamp measures 25½ to 26¼mm in width.

Envelopes are on diagonally laid paper. Wrappers on vertically or horizontally laid paper.

1863-64

U46	U17	2c black, buff	35.00	17.50
W47	U17	2c black, dk man	45.00	35.00
+U48	U18	2c black, buff	2,250.	
+U49	U18	2c black, orange	1,200.	
U50	U19	2c blk, buff ('64)	12.50	9.00
W51	U19	2c blk, buff ('64)	160.00	150.00
U52	U19	2c blk, org ('64)	11.00	9.00
W53	U19	2c black, dk man ('64)	37.50	25.00
U54	U20	2c blk, buff ('64)	12.50	9.00
W55	U20	2c blk, buff ('64)	75.00	55.00
W56	U20	2c blk, org ('64)	11.00	8.00
W57	U20	2c blk, lt man ('64)	12.50	11.50

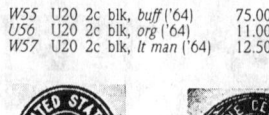

Washington
U21   U22

1864-65

U58	U21	3c pink	7.00	1.50
U59	U21	3c pink, buff	5.00	1.00
U60	U21	3c brown ('65)	42.50	27.50
U61	U21	3c brn, buff ('65)	42.50	25.00
U62	U21	6c pink	60.00	27.50
U63	U21	6c pink, buff	32.50	27.50
U64	U21	6c purple ('65)	45.00	27.50
U65	U21	6c pur, buff ('65)	40.00	19.00
U66	U22	9c lem, buff ('65)	400.00	250.00
U67	U22	9c org, buff ('65)	100.00	80.00
a.		9c orange yellow, buff	90.00	85.00
U68	U22	12c brn, buff ('65)	350.00	225.00
U69	U22	12c red brn, buff ('65)	85.00	55.00
U70	U22	18c red, buff ('65)	90.00	90.00
U71	U22	24c bl, buff ('65)	95.00	80.00
U72	U22	30c grn, buff ('65)	70.00	60.00
a.		30c yellow green, buff	60.00	72.50
U73	U22	40c rose, buff ('65)	90.00	225.00

Reay Issue

The engravings in this issue are finely executed.

Franklin — U23   Jackson — U24

U23 — Bust points to the end of the "N" of "ONE".

U24 — Bust narrow at back. Small, thick figures of value.

Washington — U25   Lincoln — U26

U25 — Queue projects below bust.

U26 — Neck very long at the back.

Stanton — U27   Jefferson — U28

U27 — Bust pointed at the back, figures "7" are normal.

U28 — Queue forms straight line with the bust.

Clay — U29   Webster — U30

U29 — Ear partly concealed by hair, mouth large, chin prominent.

U30 — Has side whiskers.

Scott — U31   Hamilton — U32

United Postal Stationery Society

• Bi-monthly Publications (news & research)
• Comprehensive Catalogs • Auctions

Learn more about this branch of philately.

UPSS Central Office
P.O. Box 48
Redlands, CA 92373

UNITED STATES

U31 — Straggling locks of hair at top of head; ornaments around the inner oval end in squares.

U32 — Back of bust very narrow, chin almost straight; labels containing figures of value are exactly parallel.

Perry — U33

U33 — Front of bust very narrow and pointed; inner lines of shields project very slightly beyond the oval.

1870-71

U74	U23	1c blue	32.50	27.50
a.		1c ultramarine	55.00	32.50
U75	U23	1c blue, amber	32.50	27.50
a.		1c ultramarine. amb	50.00	30.00
U76	U23	1c blue, org	17.50	15.00
W77	U23	1c blue, man	40.00	35.00
U78	U24	2c brown	37.50	15.00
U79	U24	2c brown, amb	15.00	8.50
U80	U24	2c brown, org	9.00	6.00
W81	U24	2c brown, man	25.00	20.00
U82	U25	3c green	6.50	.85
U83	U25	3c green, amb	5.75	1.90
U84	U25	3c green, cream	8.50	4.00
U85	U26	6c dark red	20.00	16.00
		6c vermilion	15.00	16.00
U86		6c dk red, amb	22.50	15.00
a.		6c vermilion. amber	21.00	15.00
U87	U26	6c dk red, cr	25.00	15.00
a.		6c vermilion. cream	22.50	15.00
U88	U27	7c ver, amb ('71)	45.00	180.00
U89	U28	10c olive black	550.00	425.00
U90	U28	10c ol blk, amb	550.00	425.00
U91	U28	10c brown	50.00	70.00
U92	U28	10c brn, amb	70.00	50.00
a.		10c dark brown. amb	60.00	60.00
U93	U29	12c plum	110.00	82.50
U94	U29	12c plum, amb	110.00	110.00
U95	U29	12c plum, cr	225.00	225.00
U96	U30	15c red orange	67.50	70.00
		15c orange	67.50	
U97	U30	15c red org, amb	140.00	180.00
		15c orange. amber	140.00	
U98	U30	15c red org, cr	240.00	225.00
		15c orange. cream	240.00	
U99	U31	24c purple	120.00	120.00
U100	U31	24c pur, amb	175.00	300.00
U101	U31	24c pur, cream	175.00	300.00
U102	U32	30c black	80.00	100.00
U103	U32	30c blk, amb	190.00	250.00
U104	U32	30c blk, cream	210.00	400.00
U105	U33	90c carmine	140.00	225.00
U106	U33	90c car, amb	325.00	400.00
U107	U33	90c car, cream	450.00	650.00

Plimpton Issue

The profiles in this issue are inferior to the fine engraving of the Reay issue.

U34   U35

U34 — Bust forms an angle at the back near the frame. Lettering poorly executed. Distinct circle in "O" of "POSTAGE."

U35 — Lower part of bust points to the end of the "E" in "ONE." Head inclined downward.

U36   U37

U36 — Bust narrow at back. Thin figures of value. The head of the "P" in "POSTAGE" is very narrow. The bust at front is broad and ends in sharp corners.

U37 — Bust broad. Figures of value in long ovals.

U38   U39

U38 — Similar to die 2 but the figure "2" at the left touches the oval.

U39 — Similar to die 2 but the "O" of "TWO" has the center netted instead of plain. The "G" of "POSTAGE" and the "C" of "CENTS" have diagonal crossline.

U40   U41

U40 — Bust broad; numerals in ovals short and thick.

U41 — Similar to die 5 but the ovals containing the numerals are much heavier. A diagonal line runs from the upper part of the "U" to the white frame-line.

U42   U43

U42 — Similar to die 5 but the middle stroke of "N" in "CENTS" is as thin as the vertical strokes.

U43 — Bottom of bust cut almost semi-circularly.

U44   U45

U44 — Thin lettering, long thin figures of value.

U45 — Thick lettering, well-formed figures of value, queue does not project below bust.

U46

U46 — Top of head egg-shaped; knot of queue well marked and projects triangularly.

Taylor — U47

Die 1   Die 2

Die 1 — Figures of value with thick curved tops.

Die 2 — Figures of value with long, thin tops.

U48   U49

U48 — Neck very short at the back.

U49 — Figures of value turned up at the ends.

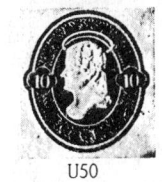

U50   U51

U50 — Very large head.

U51 — Knot of queue stands out prominently.

U52   U53

U52 — Ear prominent, chin receding.

U53 — No side whiskers, forelock projects above head.

U54   U55

U54 — Hair does not project; ornaments around the inner oval end in points.

U55 — Back of bust rather broad, chin slopes considerably; labels containing figures of value are not exactly parallel.

U56

U56 — Front of bust sloping; inner lines of shields project considerably into the inner oval.

1874-86

U34

U108	1c dark blue	95.00	70.00
a.	1c light blue	110.00	75.00
U109	1c dk blue, amb	120.00	75.00
+U110	1c dk blue, cr	1,000.	
U111	1c dk blue, org	20.00	16.00
a.	1c light blue. org	22.50	15.00
W112	1c dk blue, man	50.00	40.00

U35

U113	1c light blue	1.50	.75
a.	1c dark blue	7.50	7.50
U114	1c lt blue, amb	4.00	4.00
a.	1c dark blue. amb	15.00	10.00
U115	1c blue, cr	4.25	4.50
a.	1c dark blue. cr	17.50	8.00
U116	1c lt blue, org	.75	.40
a.	1c light blue. org	3.00	3.50
U117	1c lt bl, bl ('80)	5.75	5.25
U118	1c light blue, fawn ('79)	5.75	5.50
U119	1c lt blue, man ('86)	5.75	3.25
W120	1c lt blue, man	1.50	1.00
a.	1c lt blue. man	7.00	8.00
U121	1c lt blue, amb man ('86)	11.00	10.00

U36

U122	2c brown	90.00	37.50
U123	2c brown, amb	55.00	40.00
+U124	2c brown, cr	775.00	

+U125	2c brown, org	12,500.	
W126	2c brown, man	110.00	65.00
W127	2c ver, man	1,250.	250.00

U37

U128	2c brown	42.50	32.50
U129	2c brown, amb	65.00	37.50
+U130	2c brown, cr	40,000.	
W131	2c brown, man	15.00	15.00

U38

U132	2c brown	60.00	27.50
U133	2c brown, amb	190.00	55.00
+U133A	2c brown, cr	—	

U39

U134	2c brown	575.00	135.00
U135	2c brown, amb	400.00	110.00
U136	2c brown, org	45.00	27.50
W137	2c brown, man	60.00	35.00
+U137A	2c vermilion	18,500.	
+U137B	2c ver, amb	18,500.	
+U137C	2c ver, org	18,500.	
+W138	2c ver, man	17,500.	

U40

U139	2c brown ('75)	40.00	32.50
U140	2c brown, amb ('75)	75.00	62.50
U140A	2c brown, org ('75)	17,500.	
W141	2c brown, man ('75)	35.00	25.00
U142	2c ver ('75)	5.50	2.75
a.	2c pink	8.50	6.50
U143	2c ver, amber ('75)	5.50	2.75
U144	2c ver, cr ('75)	12.50	6.00
+U145	2c ver, org ('75)	12,500.	
U146	2c ver, bl ('80)	125.00	30.00
U147	2c ver, fawn ('75)	6.00	4.50
W148	2c ver, man ('75)	3.50	3.50

U41

U149	2c ver ('78)	45.00	30.00
a.	2c pink	45.00	30.00
U150	2c ver, amber ('78)	22.50	17.50
U151	2c ver, bl ('80)	12.50	9.00
a.	2c pink, blue	10.00	9.00
U152	2c ver, fawn ('78)	10.00	4.50

U42

U153	2c ver ('76)	55.00	25.00
U154	2c ver, amb ('76)	275.00	85.00
W155	2c ver, man ('76)	19.00	9.50

U43

U156	2c ver ('81)	600.00	130.00
U157	2c ver, amb ('81)	35,000.	15,000.
W158	2c ver, man ('81)	80.00	62.50

U44

U159	3c green	22.50	6.50
U160	3c green, amb	27.50	10.00
U161	3c green, cr	35.00	12.50
+U162	3c green, blue	—	

U45

U163	3c green	1.25	.25
U164	3c green, amb	1.40	.65
U165	3c green, cr	7.50	6.75
U166	3c green, blue	8.00	6.00
U167	3c green, fawn ('75)	4.50	3.50

U46

U168	3c green ('81)	500.00	55.00
U169	3c green, amb ('81)	225.00	100.00
U170	3c grn, bl ('81)	8,000.	2,250.
U171	3c green, fawn ('81)	40,000.	2,000.

U47

U172	5c blue, die 1 ('75)	10.00	8.00
U173	5c blue, die 1, amb ('75)	10.00	9.00
U174	5c blue, die 1, cr ('75)	90.00	40.00
U175	5c blue, die 1, bl ('75)	25.00	15.00
U176	5c blue, die 1, fawn ('75)	110.00	55.00
U177	5c blue, die 2 ('75)	7.50	6.50
U178	5c blue, die 2, amb ('75)	8.00	7.50
+U178A	5c blue, die 2, cr ('76)	4,250.	
U179	5c blue, die 2, blue ('75)	15.00	9.00
U180	5c blue, die 2, fawn ('75)	100.00	45.00

U48

U181	6c red	6.75	6.00
a.	6c vermilion	5.75	5.50
U182	6c red, amber	10.00	6.00
a.	6c vermilion. amber	10.00	6.00
U183	6c red, cream	20.00	12.50
a.	6c vermilion. cream	20.00	12.50
U184	6c red, fawn ('75)	17.50	12.50

U49

+U185	7c vermilion	1,500.	
U186	7c ver, amber	95.00	60.00

U50

U187	10c brown	32.50	20.00
U188	10c brown, amb	60.00	32.50

U51

U189	10c choc ('75)	7.50	4.25
a.	10c bister brown	8.50	5.00
b.	10c yellow ocher	1,250.	

101

UNITED STATES

U190		10c choc, amb ('75)	8.50	7.50
a.		10c bister brown, amb	8.50	7.50
b.		10c yellow ocher, amb	1,050.	
U191		10c brn, oriental buff ('86)	10.00	8.50
U192		10c brn, bl ('86)	12.50	8.50
a.		10c gray black, blue	11.00	7.50
b.		10c red brown, blue	11.00	7.50
U193		10c brown, man ('86)	14.00	10.00
a.		10c red brown, man	12.50	9.50
U194		10c brown, amb man ('86)	15.00	9.00
a.		10c red brown, amber manila	17.50	9.00

U52
U195		12c plum	180.00	85.00
U196		12c plum, amb	170.00	150.00
U197		12c plum, cream	225.00	175.00

U53
U198		15c orange	45.00	37.50
U199		15c orange, amb	135.00	100.00
U200		15c org, cream	350.00	350.00

U54
U201		24c purple	150.00	125.00
U202		24c purple, amb	160.00	125.00
U203		24c pur, cream	160.00	125.00

U55
U204		30c black	60.00	27.50
U205		30c black, amb	70.00	60.00
U206		30c black, cream	375.00	375.00
U207		30c blk, oriental buff ('86)	95.00	80.00
U208		30c blk, bl ('86)	100.00	80.00
U209		30c black, man ('86)	90.00	80.00
U210		30c black, amb man ('86)	125.00	80.00

U56
U211		90c carmine ('75)	125.00	80.00
U212		90c car, amb ('75)	160.00	225.00
U213		90c car, cr ('75)	1,300.	
U214		90c car, oriental buff ('86)	200.00	275.00
U215		90c car, bl ('86)	180.00	250.00
U216		90c car, man ('86)	160.00	250.00
U217		90c car, amb man ('86)	115.00	200.00

See Nos. U336-U347.

United States Centennial Issue

Single line under "POSTAGE" — U57
Double line under "POSTAGE" — U58 

1876
U218	U57	3c red	50.00	25.00
U219	U57	3c green	45.00	17.50
+U220	U58	3c red	25,000.	
U221	U58	3c green	52.50	22.50

Cent. of the US, and the World's Fair at Philadelphia. See No. U582.

Garfield — U59    Washington — U60

1882-86
U222	U59	5c brown	4.00	2.75
U223	U59	5c brown, amb	4.50	3.25
U224	U59	5c brn, oriental buff ('86)	110.00	70.00
U225	U59	5c brown, blue	60.00	35.00
U226	U59	5c brown, fawn	240.00	

1883, Oct.
U227	U60	2c red	3.50	2.25
a.		2c brown (error), entire	3,000.	
U228	U60	2c red, amber	4.50	2.75
U229	U60	2c red, blue	6.50	5.00
U230	U60	2c red, fawn	7.50	5.25

Wavy lines fine and clear — U61
Wavy lines thick and blurred — U62 

Four Wavy Lines in Oval

1883, Nov.
U231	U61	2c red	3.50	2.25
U232	U61	2c red, amber	4.50	3.75
U233	U61	2c red, blue	7.50	7.00
U234	U61	2c red, fawn	5.50	4.50
W235	U61	2c red, manila	15.00	6.00

1884, June
U236	U62	2c red	7.50	4.00
U237	U62	2c red, amber	11.00	10.00
U238	U62	2c red, blue	17.50	10.00
U239	U62	2c red, fawn	12.00	9.50

See Nos. U260-W269.

3½ links over left "2" — U63
2 links below right "2" — U64 

Round "O" in "TWO" — U65

U240	U63	2c red	65.00	40.00
U241	U63	2c red, amber	700.00	325.00
U242	U63	2c red, fawn	6,500.	
U243	U64	2c red	85.00	55.00
U244	U64	2c red, amber	160.00	75.00
U245	U64	2c red, blue	325.00	140.00
U246	U64	2c red, fawn	325.00	140.00
U247	U65	2c red	1,500.	350.00
U248	U65	2c red, amber	2,500.	850.00
U249	U65	2c red, fawn	600.00	375.00

See Nos. U270-U276.

Jackson — U66

Die 1 — Numeral at left is 2¾mm wide
Die 2 — Numeral at left is 3¼mm wide 

1883-86
U250	U66	4c grn, die 1	3.50	3.50
U251	U66	4c grn, die 1, amb	4.25	3.50
U252	U66	4c grn, die 1, oriental buff ('86)	7.50	9.00
U253	U66	4c grn, die 1, bl ('86)	7.50	6.50
U254	U66	4c grn, die 1, man ('86)	9.00	7.50
U255	U66	4c grn, die 1, amb man ('86)	17.50	10.00
U256	U66	4c grn, die 2	5.00	5.00
U257	U66	4c grn, die 2, amb	10.00	7.00
U258	U66	4c grn, die 2, man ('86)	9.50	7.50
U259	U66	4c grn, die 2, amb man ('86)	10.00	7.50

1884, May
U260	U61	2c brown	12.00	5.75
U261	U61	2c brown, amber	11.00	6.75
U262	U61	2c brn, blue	12.00	9.50
U263	U61	2c brn, fawn	11.00	9.00
W264	U61	2c brn, manila	12.50	10.00

1884, June — Retouched Die
U265	U62	2c brown	14.00	6.00
U266	U62	2c brn, amber	60.00	40.00
U267	U62	2c brn, blue	12.00	6.00
U268	U62	2c brn, fawn	14.00	11.00
W269	U62	2c brn, manila	20.00	15.00

2 Links Below Right "2"
U270	U64	2c brown	85.00	37.50
U271	U64	2c brn, amber	200.00	90.00
U272	U64	2c brn, fawn	3,500.	1,250.

Round "O" in "Two"
U273	U65	2c brown	160.00	80.00
U274	U65	2c brn, amber	200.00	80.00
U275	U65	2c brn, blue		15,000.
U276	U65	2c brn, fawn	825.00	650.00

Washington
U67   U68

U67 — Extremity of bust below the queue forms a point.

U68 — Extremity of bust is rounded.

Similar to U61
Two wavy lines in oval

1884-86
U277	U67	2c brown	.45	.15
a.		2c brown lake	20.00	22.50
U278	U67	2c brn, amber	.60	.45
a.		2c brown lake, amber	30.00	12.50
U279	U67	2c brn, oriental buff ('86)	2.60	2.00
U280	U67	2c brn, blue	2.25	2.00
U281	U67	2c brn, fawn	2.75	2.25
U282	U67	2c brn, man ('86)	9.00	4.00
W283	U67	2c brn, man	5.00	5.00
U284	U67	2c brn, amb man ('86)	5.50	5.75
+U285	U67	2c red	550.00	
+U286	U67	2c red, blue	250.00	
W287	U67	2c red, man	110.00	
U288	U68	2c brown	150.00	35.00
U289	U68	2c brn, amb	14.00	12.50
U290	U68	2c brn, blue	950.00	140.00
U291	U68	2c brn, fawn	20.00	19.00
W292	U68	2c brn, man	20.00	17.50

Grant — US1

1886 — Letter Sheet
U293	US1	2c green, entire	24.00	16.00

See the Scott U.S. Specialized Catalogue for perforation and inscription varieties.

Franklin U69   Washington U70

U70 — Bust points between 3rd and 4th notches of inner oval; "G" of "POSTAGE" has no bar.

U71    U72

U71 — Bust points between second and third notches of inner oval; "G" of "POSTAGE" has a bar; ear is indicated by one heavy line; one vertical line at corner of mouth.

U72 — Frame same as die 2; upper part of head more rounded; ear indicated by two curved lines with two locks of hair in front; two vertical lines at corner of mouth.

Jackson — U73

Grant — U74    U75

U74 — There is a space between the beard and the collar of the coat. A button is on the collar.

U75 — The collar touches the beard and there is no button.

1887-94
U294	U69	1c blue	.50	.20
U295	U69	1c dk bl ('94)	6.50	2.50
U296	U69	1c bl, amb ('94)	3.00	1.25
U297	U69	1c dk blue, amb ('94)	45.00	22.50
+U298	U69	1c bl, oriental buff ('94)	3,750.	
+U299	U69	1c bl, bl ('94)	8,000.	
U300	U69	1c bl, man ('94)	.65	.35
W301	U69	1c bl, man ('94)	.45	.30
U302	U69	1c dk blue, man ('94)	22.50	10.00
W303	U69	1c dk blue, man	12.00	9.50
U304	U69	1c bl, amb man	5.25	4.25
U305	U70	2c green	10.00	9.00
U306	U70	2c grn, amb	22.50	14.00
U307	U70	2c grn, oriental buff	75.00	30.00
U308	U70	2c grn, blue	8,000.	1,000.
U309	U70	2c grn, man	4,500.	500.00
U310	U70	2c grn, amb man	1,800.	1,250.
U311	U71	2c green	.30	.15
U312	U71	2c grn, amb	.40	.20
U313	U71	2c grn, oriental buff	.55	.25
U314	U71	2c grn, blue	.60	.30
U315	U71	2c grn, man	1.60	.50
W316	U71	2c grn, man	3.00	2.50
U317	U71	2c grn, amb man	2.50	1.90
U318	U72	2c green	110.00	12.50
U319	U72	2c grn, amb	160.00	25.00
U320	U72	2c grn, oriental buff	155.00	40.00
U321	U72	2c grn, blue	175.00	65.00
U322	U72	2c grn, man	150.00	65.00
U323	U72	2c grn, amb man	325.00	72.50
U324	U73	4c carmine	2.25	1.75
a.		4c lake	2.50	2.00
b.		4c scarlet ('94)	2.75	2.25
U325	U73	4c car, amb	2.50	2.25
a.		4c lake, amber	3.00	2.50
b.		4c scarlet, amber ('94)	3.00	3.25
U326	U73	4c car, oriental buff	5.25	3.00
a.		4c lake, oriental buff	6.00	3.50
U327	U73	4c car, blue	4.50	4.00
a.		4c lake, blue	4.50	4.00
U328	U73	4c car, man	6.25	5.50
a.		4c lake, manila	7.25	6.00
b.		4c pink, manila	7.50	4.50
U329	U73	4c car, amb man	4.25	2.75
a.		4c lake, amb manila	4.50	3.25
b.		4c pink, amb manila	5.25	3.25
U330	U74	5c blue	3.25	4.00
U331	U74	5c bl, amber	4.00	2.25
U332	U74	5c bl, oriental buff	4.25	3.75
U333	U74	5c bl, blue	8.00	5.50
U334	U75	5c blue ('94)	12.00	5.50
U335	U75	5c bl, amb ('94)	10.00	5.50
U336	U55	30c red brown	40.00	37.50
a.		30c yellow brown	45.00	45.00
b.		30c chocolate	45.00	47.50
U337	U55	30c red brn, amb	45.00	50.00
a.		30c yel brown, amber	42.50	42.50
b.		30c choc, amber	42.50	42.50
U338	U55	30c red brn, oriental buff	40.00	42.50
a.		30c yel brn, oriental buff	35.00	42.50
U339	U55	30c red brn, bl	40.00	42.50
a.		30c yellow brown, blue	35.00	42.50
U340	U55	30c red brn, manila	42.50	42.50
a.		30c brown, manila	40.00	37.50
U341	U55	30c red brown, amb man	47.50	27.50
a.		30c red brn, amber man	45.00	27.50
U342	U56	90c purple	60.00	70.00
U343	U56	90c pur, amb	75.00	75.00
U344	U56	90c pur, oriental buff	75.00	80.00
U345	U56	90c pur, blue	80.00	85.00
U346	U56	90c pur, man	80.00	85.00
U347	U56	90c pur, amb manila	85.00	85.00

UNITED STATES

Columbian Exposition Issue

Columbus and Liberty — U76

1893
U348	U76	1c deep blue	2.00	1.10
U349	U76	2c violet	1.75	.50
a.		2c dark slate (error)	1,750.	
U350	U76	5c chocolate	8.50	7.50
a.		5c slate brown (error)	750.00	750.00
U351	U76	10c slate brown	30.00	25.00
		Nos. U348-U351 (4)	42.25	34.10

Franklin U77 — Washington U78

U78 — Bust points to first notch of inner oval and is only slightly concave below.

U79 U80

U79 — Bust points to middle of second notch of inner oval and is quite hollow below. Queue has ribbon around it.

U80 — Same as die 2 but hair flowing and no ribbon around queue.

Lincoln — U81

Pointed but not draped.

U82 U83

U82 — Bust broad and draped.

U83 — Head larger, inner oval has no notches.

Grant — U84

Similar to designs of 1887-95 but smaller

1899
U352	U77	1c green	.55	.20
U353	U77	1c grn, amb	4.50	1.50
U354	U77	1c grn, oriental buff	10.00	2.75
U355	U77	1c grn, bl	11.00	7.50
U356	U77	1c grn, man	2.00	.95
W357	U77	1c grn, man	2.25	1.10
U358	U78	2c carmine	2.75	1.75
U359	U78	2c car, amb	17.50	14.00
U360	U78	2c car, oriental buff	17.50	8.00
U361	U78	2c car, blue	55.00	27.50
U362	U79	2c carmine	.30	.20
a.		2c dark lake	27.50	32.50
U363	U79	2c car, amb	1.00	.20
U364	U79	2c car, oriental buff	1.00	.20
U365	U79	2c car, blue	1.25	.55
W366	U79	2c car, man	6.00	3.25
U367	U80	2c carmine	4.00	2.75
U368	U80	2c car, amber	8.00	6.75
U369	U80	2c car, oriental buff	22.50	12.50
U370	U80	2c car, blue	11.00	10.00
U371	U81	4c brown	15.00	11.00
U372	U81	4c brn, amb	16.00	12.50
U373	U82	4c brown	6,250.	375.00
U374	U83	4c brown	10.00	8.00
U375	U83	4c brn, amb	37.50	17.50
W376	U83	4c brn, man	15.00	8.25
U377	U84	5c blue	9.50	9.50
U378	U84	5c blue, amb	12.50	12.50

Franklin U85 — Washington U86

U86 — One short and two long vertical lines at right of "CENTS."

Grant — U87 — Lincoln — U88

1903
U379	U85	1c green	.60	.20
U380	U85	1c green, amb	12.50	2.00
U381	U85	1c grn, oriental buff	12.50	2.50
U382	U85	1c green, blue	17.50	2.50
U383	U85	1c grn, manila	3.50	.90
W384	U85	1c grn, manila	1.25	.40
U385	U86	2c carmine	.35	.15
U386	U86	2c carmine, amb	1.75	.20
U387	U86	2c car, oriental buff	1.50	.30
U388	U86	2c carmine, blue	1.20	.50
U389	U86	2c car, manila	15.00	9.50
U390	U87	4c chocolate	20.00	11.00
U391	U87	4c choc, amber	19.00	12.50
W392	U87	4c choc, manila	18.00	12.50
U393	U88	5c blue	18.00	12.50
U394	U88	5c blue, amber	18.50	12.50

U89

The three lines at the right of "CENTS" and at the left of "TWO" are usually all short; the lettering is heavier and the ends of the ribbons slightly changed.

1904 Re-cut Die
U395	U89	2c carmine	.45	.20
U396	U89	2c car, amber	7.00	1.00
U397	U89	2c car, oriental buff	5.00	1.10
U398	U89	2c carmine, blue	3.25	.90
W399	U89	2c car, manila	11.00	9.50

Franklin — U90

Die 1 — Die 2 — Die 3 — Die 4

Die 1. Wide "D" in "UNITED."
Die 2. Narrow "D" in "UNITED."
Die 3. Wide "S-S" in "STATES" (1910).
Die 4. Sharp angle at back of bust, "N" and "E" of "ONE" are parallel (1912).

1907-16 Die 1
U400	U90	1c green	.25	.15
a.		Die 2	.75	.35
b.		Die 3	.75	.35
c.		Die 4	.65	.30
U401	U90	1c green, amber	.75	.40
a.		Die 2	.85	.70
b.		Die 3	.95	.75
c.		Die 4	.80	.65
U402	U90	1c grn, oriental buff	4.25	1.00
a.		Die 2	5.25	1.50
b.		Die 3	6.00	1.50
c.		Die 4	4.50	1.50
U403	U90	1c green, blue	4.75	1.50
a.		Die 2	4.75	1.50
b.		Die 3	4.75	3.00
c.		Die 4	4.00	1.50
U404	U90	1c grn, manila	2.75	1.90
a.		Die 2	3.50	3.00
W405	U90	1c grn, manila	.40	.25
a.		Die 2	40.00	25.00
b.		Die 3	6.00	4.00
c.		Die 4	40.00	

Die 1, Washington — U91

Die 2

Die 3

Die 4

Die 5

Die 6

Die 7

Die 8

Die 1. Oval "O" in "TWO" and "C" in "CENTS," front of bust broad.
Die 2. Similar to 1 but hair in two distinct locks at top of head.
Die 3. Round "O" in "TWO" and "C" in "CENTS," coarse lettering.
Die 4. Similar to 3 but lettering fine and clear, hair lines clearly embossed. Inner oval thin and clear.
Die 5. All "S's" wide (1910).
Die 6. Similar to 1 but front of bust narrow (1913).
Die 7. Similar to 6 but upper corner of front of bust cut away (1916).
Die 8. Similar to 7 but lower stroke of "S" in "CENTS" is a straight line. Hair as in Die 2 (1916).

Die I
U406	U91	2c brown red	.75	.15
a.		Die 2	27.50	6.25
b.		Die 3	.50	.20
U407	U91	2c brn red, amb	5.00	2.00
a.		Die 2	100.00	45.00
b.		Die 3	3.00	1.00
U408	U91	2c brown red, oriental buff	6.50	1.50
a.		Die 2	125.00	55.00
b.		Die 3	6.00	2.50
U409	U91	2c brn red, blue	4.25	1.75
a.		Die 2	125.00	100.00
b.		Die 3	4.25	1.50
W410	U91	2c brn red, man	40.00	32.50
U411	U91	2c carmine	.20	.15
a.		Die 2	.40	.20
b.		Die 3	.65	.35
c.		Die 4	.35	.20
d.		Die 5	.45	.30
e.		Die 6	.35	.20
f.		Die 7	12.50	10.00
g.		Die 8	13.00	10.00
h.		Die 1, with added impression of 1c grn (#U400), entire	325.00	
i.		Die 1, with added impression of 4c blk (#U416a), entire	300.00	
U412	U91	2c carmine, amb	.20	.15
a.		Die 2	.40	.25
b.		Die 3	1.25	.45
c.		Die 4	.35	.25
d.		Die 5	.55	.35
e.		Die 6	.50	.35
f.		Die 7	11.00	8.00
U413	U91	2c car, oriental buff	.40	.20
a.		Die 2	.50	.45
b.		Die 3	6.00	3.00
c.		Die 4	.35	.20
d.		Die 5	2.75	1.25
e.		Die 6	.50	.25
f.		Die 7	35.00	17.50
g.		Die 8	11.00	8.50
U414	U91	2c carmine, blue	.45	.20
a.		Die 2	.45	.35
b.		Die 3	.75	.60
c.		Die 4	.45	.25
d.		Die 5	.55	.30
e.		Die 6	.50	.35
f.		Die 7	12.50	7.50
g.		Die 8	12.50	7.50
W415	U91	2c car, manila	4.25	2.00
a.		Die 2	4.25	1.10
b.		Die 5	4.25	2.25
c.		Die 7	40.00	35.00

103

UNITED STATES

"F" 1mm from left "4" — Die 1
"F" 1¾mm from left "4" — Die 2 

U416	U90 4c black, die 2	3.75	2.25
a.	Die 1	4.25	3.00
U417	U90 4c black, amb, die 2	5.25	2.50
a.	Die 1	5.25	2.50

Die 1-Tall "F" in "FIVE"
Die 2-Short "F" in "FIVE" 

U418	U91 5c blue, die 2	6.00	2.25
a.	Die 1	6.00	2.25
b.	5c blue, buff, die 2 (error)	1,000.	
c.	5c blue, blue, die 2 (error)	1,000.	
d.	5c blue, blue, die 1 (error)	1,100.	
U419	U91 5c blue, amber, die 2	12.00	11.00
a.	Die 1	12.00	11.00

Franklin — U92

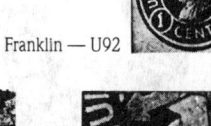

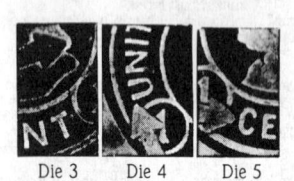

Die 1  / Die 2 / Die 3 / Die 4 / Die 5

(The 1c and 4c dies are the same except for figures of value.)
Die 1. UNITED nearer inner circle than outer circle.
Die 2. Large U; large NT closely spaced.
Die 3. Knob of hair at back of neck. Large NT widely spaced.
Die 4. UNITED nearer outer circle than inner circle.
Die 5. Narrow oval C, (also O and G).

1916-32

		Die 1	
U420	U92 1c green	.15	.15
a.	Die 2	90.00	55.00
b.	Die 3	.30	.15
c.	Die 4	.40	.40
d.	Die 5	.40	.35
U421	U92 1c grn, amber	.35	.30
a.	Die 2	300.00	175.00
b.	Die 3	1.00	.65
c.	Die 4	1.15	.85
d.	Die 5	.90	.55
U422	U92 1c grn, oriental buff	1.75	.90
a.	Die 4	3.75	1.25
U423	U92 1c green, blue	.40	.35
a.	Die 3	.75	.45
b.	Die 4	1.25	.65
c.	Die 5	.65	.35
U424	U92 1c grn, (unglazed) manila	6.00	4.00
W425	U92 1c grn, (unglazed) manila	.20	.15
a.	Die 3	140.00	125.00
U426	U92 1c grn, (glazed) brown ('20)	30.00	15.00
W427	U92 1c grn, (glazed) brown ('20)	60.00	
U428	U92 1c grn, (unglazed) brown ('20)	7.50	7.50

Die 1, Washington — U93

Die 2
Die 3 
Die 4 
Die 5 
Die 6 
Die 7 
Die 8 
Die 9 

(The 1½c, 2c, 3c, 5c, and 6c are the same except for figures of value.)
Die 1. Letters broad. Numerals vertical. Large head (9¼mm) from tip of nose to back of neck. E closer to inner circle than N of cents.
Die 2. Similar to 1; but U far from left circle.
Die 3. Similar to 2; but all inner circles very thin (Rejected Die).
Die 4. Similar to 1; but C very close to left circle.
Die 5. Small head (8¾mm) from tip of nose to back of neck. T and S of CENTS close at bottom.
Die 6. Similar to 5; but C close to left CENTS far apart at bottom. Left numeral slopes to right.
Die 7. Large head. Both numerals slope to right. Clean cut lettering. All letters T have short top strokes.
Die 8. Similar to 7; but all letters T have long top strokes.
Die 9. Narrow oval C (also O and G).

Die 1

U429	U93 2c carmine	.15	.15
a.	Die 2	9.00	6.00
b.	Die 3	30.00	25.00
c.	Die 4	9.00	7.50
d.	Die 5	.50	.35
e.	Die 6	.60	.30
f.	Die 7	.65	.25
g.	Die 8	.45	.20
h.	Die 9	.40	.20
i.	2c grn, error, die 1, entire	8,000.	
j.	2c car, die 1 with added impression of 1c grn (#U420), die 1	450.00	
k.	Die 1, with added impression of 4c blk (#U416a), entire	700.00	
l.	Die 1, with added impression of 1c grn (#U400), die 1, entire	500.00	
U430	U93 2c car, amber	.25	.15
a.	Die 2	9.25	7.50
b.	Die 4	20.00	10.00
c.	Die 5	1.10	.35
d.	Die 7	.95	.40
e.	Die 7	.70	.35
f.	Die 8	.60	.30
g.	Die 9	.50	.20
U431	U93 2c car, oriental buff	2.00	.65
a.	Die 2	100.00	40.00
b.	Die 4	30.00	30.00
c.	Die 5	2.75	1.75
d.	Die 6	3.00	2.00
e.	Die 7	2.75	1.75
U432	U93 2c carmine, blue	.20	.15
a.	Die 2	25.00	20.00
b.	Die 3	100.00	90.00
c.	Die 4	25.00	25.00
e.	Die 5	.80	.30
f.	Die 6	.85	.40
g.	Die 7	.75	.35
h.	Die 8	.60	.30
i.	Die 9	.90	.30
U432A	U93 2c car, manila, die 7, entire	25,000.	
W433	U93 2c car, manila	.25	.20
W434	U93 2c car, (glazed) brn ('20)	80.00	50.00
W435	U93 2c car, (unglazed) brn ('20)	85.00	50.00
U436	U93 3c dk violet	.50	.20
a.	3c purple ('32), die 1	.30	.15
b.	3c dark violet, die 5	1.65	.75
c.	3c dark violet, die 6	2.00	1.40
d.	3c dark violet, die 7	1.40	.95
e.	3c purple ('32), die 7	.60	.30
f.	3c purple ('32), die 9	.35	.20
g.	3c carmine (error), die 1	30.00	27.50
h.	3c carmine (error), die 5	32.50	30.00
i.	3c dk vio, die 1, with added impression of 1c grn (#U420), die 1, entire	600.00	
j.	3c dk vio, die 1, with added impression of 2c car (#U429), die 1, entire	700.00	—
U437	U93 3c dk violet, amb	3.00	1.25
a.	3c purple ('32), die 1	.30	.15
b.	3c dark vio, die 5	4.50	2.50
c.	3c dark vio, die 6	4.50	2.50
d.	3c dark vio, die 7	3.75	2.25
e.	3c purple ('32), die 7	.60	.15
f.	3c purple ('32), die 9	.50	.15
g.	3c carmine (error), die 5	450.00	275.00
h.	3c black (error), die 1	165.00	
U438	U93 3c dk vio, oriental buff	20.00	1.50
a.	Die 5	20.00	1.00
b.	Die 6	30.00	1.65
c.	Die 7	30.00	3.50
U439	U93 3c dk violet, bl	6.00	2.00
a.	3c purple ('32), die 1	.25	.20
b.	3c dark violet, die 5	6.50	4.00
c.	3c dark violet, die 6	6.00	4.25
d.	3c dark vio, die 7	9.00	5.50
e.	3c purple ('32), die 7	.55	.25
f.	3c purple ('32), die 9	.50	.20
g.	3c carmine (error), die 5	300.00	300.00
U440	U92 4c black	1.00	.60
a.	4c black with added impression of 2c car (#U429), die 1, entire	250.00	
U441	U92 4c black, amb	2.75	.85
U442	U92 4c black, bl ('21)	3.00	.85
U443	U93 5c blue	3.00	2.75
U444	U93 5c blue, amber	3.50	1.60
U445	U93 5c bl, blue ('21)	3.75	3.25

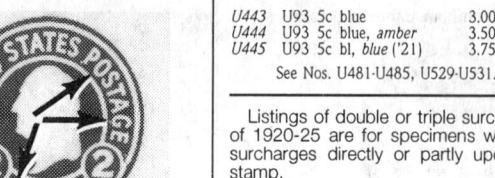

See Nos. U481-U485, U529-U531.

Listings of double or triple surcharges of 1920-25 are for specimens with the surcharges directly or partly upon the stamp.

Surcharged Type 1

2 CENTS

1920-21

U446	U93 2c on 3c dk vio (U436, die 1)	11.00	10.00
a.	Die 5 (U436b)	11.00	10.00

Surcharged Type 2

2

Rose Surcharge

U447	U93 2c on 3c dk vio (U436, die 1)	7.00	6.50
b.	Die 6 (U436c)	9.00	8.50

Black Surcharge

U447A	U93 2c on 2c car (U429, die 1)	—	
U447C	U93 2c on 2c car, amb (U430, die 1)	—	
U448	U93 2c on 3c dk vio (U436, die 1)	2.25	2.00
a.	Die 5 (U436b)	2.25	2.00
b.	Die 6 (U436c)	3.00	2.00
c.	Die 7 (U436d)	2.25	2.00
U449	U93 2c on 3c dk vio, amb (U437, die 1)	6.00	6.00
a.	Die 5 (U437b)	9.00	7.50
b.	Die 6 (U437c)	7.00	6.00
c.	Die 7 (U437d)	6.50	6.50
U450	U93 2c on 3c dk vio, oriental buff (U438, die 1)	15.00	14.00
a.	Die 5 (U438a)	15.00	14.00
b.	Die 6 (U438b)	15.00	14.00
c.	Die 7 (U438c)	100.00	90.00
U451	U93 2c on 3c dk vio, blue (U439, die 1)	11.00	10.00
b.	Die 5 (U439b)	11.00	10.00
c.	Die 6 (U439c)	11.00	10.00
d.	Die 7 (U439d)	22.50	20.00

Surcharged Type 3

2 |||| ||||

Bars 2mm apart

U451A	U90 2c on 1c grn (U400, die 1)	2,000.	
U452	U92 2c on 1c grn (U420, die 1)	1,750.	
a.	Die 3 (U420b)	1,750.	
b.	As No. U452, dbl. surch.	1,500.	
U453	U91 2c on 2c car (U411b, die 3)	1,500.	
a.	Die 1 (U411)	1,750.	
U453B	U91 2c on 2c car, bl (U414e, die 6)	1,250.	
U453C	U91 2c on 2c car, oriental buff (U413e, die 6)	1,100.	650.00
d.	Die 1 (U413)		
U454	U93 2c on 2c car (U429e, die 6)	77.50	
a.	Die 1 (U429)	150.00	
b.	Die 5 (U429d)	300.00	
c.	Die 7 (U429f)	77.50	
U455	U93 2c on 2c car, amb (U430, die 1)	1,250.	
a.	Die 6 (U430d)	1,250.	
b.	Die 7 (U430e)	1,250.	
U456	U93 2c on 2c car, oriental buff (U431a, die 2)	175.00	
a.	Die 5 (U431c)	175.00	
b.	Die 7 (U431e)	175.00	
c.	As #U456, double surcharge	225.00	
U457	U93 2c on 2c car, bl (U432f, die 6)	200.00	
a.	Die 5 (U432e)	250.00	
b.	Die 7 (U432g)	200.00	

UNITED STATES

U458	U93 2c on 3c dk vio (U436, die 1)	.45	.35
a.	Die 5 (U436b)	.45	.40
b.	Die 6 (U436c)	.45	.35
c.	Die 7 (U436d)	.45	.35
d.	As #U458, double surcharge	14.00	7.50
e.	As #U458, triple surcharge	35.00	
f.	As #U458, dbl. surch., one in magenta	65.00	
g.	As #U458, double surcharge, types 2 & 3	100.00	
h.	As "a," double surcharge	27.50	15.00
i.	As "a," triple surcharge	50.00	
j.	As "a," double surcharge, both magenta	65.00	
k.	As "b," double surcharge	16.00	8.00
l.	As "c," double surcharge	16.00	8.00
m.	As "c," triple surcharge	35.00	
U459	U93 2c on 3c dk vio, amb (U437c, die 6)	2.75	1.00
a.	Die 1 (U437)	3.50	1.00
b.	Die 5 (U437b)	3.50	1.00
c.	Die 7 (U437d)	2.75	1.00
d.	As No. U459, dbl. surch.	24.00	
e.	As "a," double surcharge	24.00	
f.	As "b," double surcharge	24.00	
g.	As "b," double surcharge, types 2 & 3	80.00	
h.	As "c," double surcharge	18.00	
U460	U93 2c on 3c dk vio, oriental buff (U438a, die 5)	2.50	1.00
a.	Die 1 (U438)	2.75	1.50
b.	Die 6 (U438b)	2.75	2.00
c.	As No. U460, double surcharge	12.50	
d.	As "a," double surcharge	12.50	
e.	As "b," double surcharge	12.50	
f.	As "b," triple surcharge	27.50	
U461	U93 2c on 3c dk vio, bl (U439, die 1)	4.00	1.00
a.	Die 5 (U439b)	4.00	1.00
b.	Die 6 (U439c)	4.00	2.00
c.	Die 7 (U439d)	10.00	6.00
d.	As No. U461, dbl. surch.	12.50	
e.	As "a," double surcharge	12.50	
f.	As "b," double surcharge	12.50	
g.	As "c," double surcharge	12.50	
U462	U87 2c on 4c choc (U390)	350.00	160.00
U463	U87 2c on 4c choc, amb (U391)	350.00	100.00
U463A	U90 2c on 4c blk (U416, die 2)	1,100.	375.00
U464	U93 2c on 5c bl (U443)	1,000.	

Surcharged Type 4

Similar to Type 3, but bars 1½mm apart.

U465	U92 2c on 1c grn (U420, die 1)	1,100.	
a.	Die 3 (U420b)	1,150.	
U466	U91 2c on 2c car (U411e, die 6)	7,500.	
U466A	U93 2c on 2c car (U429, die 1)	240.00	
c.	Die 5 (U429d)	375.00	
d.	Die 6 (U429e)	450.00	
e.	Die 7 (U429f)	325.00	
U466B	U93 2c on 2c car, amb (U430)	5,000.	
U467	U45 2c on 3c grn (U163)	225.00	
U468	U93 2c on 3c dk vio (U436, die 1)	.70	.45
a.	Die 5 (U436b)	.70	.50
b.	Die 6 (U436c)	.70	.50
c.	Die 7 (U436d)	.70	.50
d.	As No. U468, double surcharge	15.00	
e.	As No. U468, triple surcharge	20.00	
f.	As No. U468, dbl. surch., types 2 & 4	75.00	
g.	As "a," double surcharge	15.00	
h.	As "b," double surcharge	15.00	
i.	As "c," double surcharge	15.00	
j.	As "c," triple surcharge	20.00	
k.	As "c," inverted surcharge	75.00	
l.	2c on 3c car (error) (U436h)	450.00	
U469	U93 2c on 3c dk vio, ambcr (U437, die 1)	3.25	2.25
a.	Die 5 (U437b)	3.25	2.25
b.	Die 6 (U437c)	3.25	2.25
c.	Die 7 (U437d)	3.25	2.25
d.	As No. U469, dbl. surch.	20.00	
e.	As "a," double surcharge	20.00	
f.	As "a," double surcharge, types 2 & 4	60.00	
g.	As "b," double surcharge	20.00	
h.	As "c," double surcharge	20.00	
U470	U93 2c on 3c dk vio, oriental buff (U438, die 1)	4.25	2.50
a.	Die 5 (U438a)	4.25	2.50
b.	Die 6 (U438b)	4.25	2.50
c.	Die 7 (U438c)	35.00	32.50
d.	As No. U470, dbl. surch.	18.50	
e.	As No. U470, double surcharge, types 2 & 4	60.00	
f.	As "a," double surcharge	18.50	
g.	As "b," double surcharge	22.50	
U471	U93 2c on 3c dk vio, bl (U439, die 1)	3.75	1.75
a.	Die 5 (U439b)	3.75	1.75
b.	Die 6 (U439c)	3.75	1.75
c.	Die 7 (U439d)	10.00	6.00
d.	As No. U471, dbl. surch.	18.50	
e.	As No. U471, double surcharge, types 2 & 4	150.00	
f.	As "a," double surcharge	18.50	
g.	As "b," double surcharge	18.50	

U472	U87 2c on 4c choc (U390)	11.00	8.00
a.	Double surcharge	37.50	
U473	U87 2c on 4c choc, amb (U391)	15.00	10.00

1 CENT

Dbl. Surch., Type 4 and as above

U474	U93 2c on 1c on 3c dk vio (U436, die 1)	225.00	
a.	Die 5 (U436b)	300.00	
b.	Die 7 (U436d)	450.00	
U475	U93 2c on 1c on 3c dk vio, amb (U437, die 1)	225.00	

Surcharged Type 5

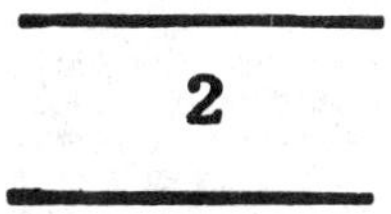

2

U476	U93 2c on 3c dk vio, amb (U437, die 1)	120.00	
a.	Die 6 (U437c)	600.00	
b.	As No. U476, double surcharge	—	

Surcharged Type 6

2

U477	U93 2c on 3c dk vio (U436, die 1)	100.00	
a.	Die 5 (U436b)	125.00	
b.	Die 6 (U436c)	150.00	
c.	Die 7 (U436d)	150.00	
U478	U93 2c on 3c dk vio, amb (U437, die 1)	200.00	

Handstamped Surcharge in Black or Violet—Type 7

U479	U93 2c on 3c dk vio (Bk) (U436b, die 5)	300.00	
a.	Die 1 (U436)	350.00	
b.	Die 7 (U436d)	300.00	
U480	U93 2c on 3c dk vio (V) (U436d, die 7)	2,500.	

Expertization by competent authorities is recommened for Nos. U479-U480.

Type of 1916-32 Issue

1925-34

Die 1

U481	U93 1½c brown	.15	.15
a.	Die 8	.60	.25
b.	1½c purple (error) ('34)	90.00	
U482	U93 1½c brown, amber	.90	.40
a.	Die 8	1.40	.75
U483	U93 1½c brn, bl	1.50	.95
a.	Die 8	1.75	1.25
U484	U93 1½c brown, manila	6.00	3.00
W485	U93 1½c brown, manila	.75	.15
a.	With added impression of No. W433	120.00	—

Surcharged Type 8
1½

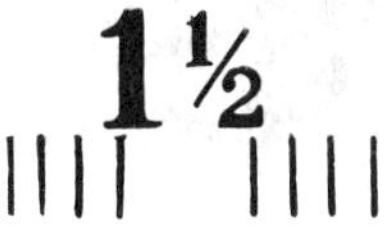

1925

U486	U71 1½c on 2c grn (U311)	675.00	
U487	U71 1½c on 2c grn, amb (U312)	850.00	
U488	U77 1½c on 1c grn (U352)	550.00	
U489	U77 1½c on 1c grn, amb (U353)	90.00	60.00
U490	U90 1½c on 1c grn (U400, die 1)	3.75	3.50
a.	Die 2 (U400a)	12.00	9.00
b.	Die 3 (U400b)	25.00	17.50
c.	Die 4 (U400c)	6.00	2.50
U491	U90 1½c on 1c grn (U401c, die 4)	4.25	2.25
a.	Die 1 (U401)	7.50	2.50
b.	Die 3 (U401a)	75.00	65.00
c.	Die 4 (U401b)	35.00	30.00
U492	U90 1½c on 1c grn, oriental buff (U402a, die 2)	200.00	80.00
a.	Die 4 (U402c)	500.00	80.00

U493	U90 1½c on 1c grn, bl (U403c, die 4)	75.00	52.50
a.	Die 2 (U403a)	75.00	52.50
U494	U90 1½c on 1c grn, man (U404, die 1)	210.00	72.50
a.	Die 3 (U404a)	250.00	
U495	U92 1½c on 1c grn (U420, die 1)	.45	.25
a.	Die 2 (U420a)	50.00	50.00
b.	Die 3 (U420b)	1.50	.60
c.	Die 4 (U420c)	1.65	.75
d.	As No. U495, dbl. surch.	4.00	1.90
e.	As "b," double surcharge	7.00	3.00
f.	As "c," double surcharge	6.00	3.00
U496	U92 1½c on 1c grn, amb (U421, die 1)	15.00	12.50
a.	Die 3 (U421b)	500.00	
b.	Die 4 (U421c)	15.00	12.50
U497	U92 1½c on 1c grn, oriental buff (U422, die 1)	3.00	1.90
a.	Die 4 (U422b)	50.00	
U498	U92 1½c on 1c grn, bl (U423c, die 4)	1.10	.75
a.	Die 1 (U423)	2.25	1.50
b.	Die 3 (U423b)	1.65	1.50
U499	U92 1½c on 1c grn, man (U424)	11.00	6.00
U500	U92 1½c on 1c grn, brn (unglazed) (U428)	55.00	30.00
U501	U93 1½c on 1c grn, brn (glazed) (U426)	55.00	25.00
U502	U93 1½c on 2c car (U429, die 1)	225.00	—
a.	Die 5 (U429d)	300.00	
b.	Die 7 (U429f)	300.00	
U503	U93 1½c on 2c car, oriental buff (U431c, die 5)	250.00	—
a.	Double surcharge		
b.	Dbl. surch., one inverted	525.00	
U504	U93 1½c on 2c car, bl (U432, die 1)	250.00	—
a.	Die 7 (U432g)		

On Envelopes of 1925

U505	U93 1½c on 1½c brn (U481, die 1)	400.00	
a.	Die 8 (U481a)	400.00	
U506	U93 1½c on 1½c brn, bl (U483a, die 8)	325.00	

The paper of No. U500 is not glazed and appears to be the same as that used for wrappers of 1920.

Surcharged Type 9
1½

Black Surcharge

U507	U69 1½c on 1c bl (U294)	1,400.	
U508	U77 1½c on 1c grn, amb (U353)	50.00	
U508A	U85 1½c on 1c grn (U379)	2,000.	
U509	U85 1½c on 1c grn, amb (U380)	12.00	10.00
a.	Double surcharge	25.00	
U509A	U85 1½c on 1c grn, oriental buff (U381)	50.00	40.00
U510	U90 1½c on 1c grn (U400, die 1)	2.00	1.25
b.	Die 2 (U400a)	6.00	4.00
c.	Die 3 (U400b)	16.00	8.00
d.	Die 4 (U400c)	3.00	1.25
e.	As No. U510, double surcharge	7.50	
U511	U90 1½c on 1c grn, amb (U401, die 1)	150.00	72.50
U512	U90 1½c on 1c grn, oriental buff (U402, die 1)	6.00	4.00
a.	Die 4 (U402c)	17.00	14.00
U513	U90 1½c on 1c grn, bl (U403, die 1)	5.00	2.50
a.	Die 3 (U403c)	5.00	4.00
U514	U90 1½c on 1c grn, man (U404, die 1)	22.50	9.00
a.	Die 3 (U404a)	50.00	37.50
U515	U92 1½c on 1c grn (U420, die 1)	.30	.20
a.	Die 2 (U420a)	20.00	15.00
b.	Die 3 (U420b)	.30	.20
c.	Die 4 (U420c)	.30	.20
d.	As No. U515, double surcharge	9.00	
e.	As No. U515, inverted surch.	9.00	
f.	As No. U515, triple surcharge	11.00	
g.	As No. U515, dbl. surch., one invtd., entire		
h.	As "b," double surcharge	6.00	
i.	As "b," inverted surcharge	9.00	
j.	As "b," triple surcharge	11.00	
k.	As "c," double surcharge	6.00	
l.	As "c," inverted surcharge	9.00	
U516	U92 1½c on 1c grn, amb (U421c, die 4)	40.00	25.00
a.	Die 1 (U421)	45.00	30.00
U517	U92 1½c on 1c grn, oriental buff (U422, die 1)	4.25	1.25
a.	Die 4 (U422a)	5.50	1.50

U518	U92 1½c on 1c grn, bl (U423b, die 4)	4.25	1.25
a.	Die 1 (U423)	6.50	2.50
b.	Die 3 (U423a)	20.00	7.50
c.	As "a," double surcharge	9.00	
U519	U92 1½c on 1c grn, man (U424)	20.00	10.00
a.	Double surcharge	27.50	
U520	U93 1½c on 2c car (U429, die 1)	250.00	—
a.	Die 5 (U429d)	250.00	
b.	Die 6 (U429e)	250.00	
c.	Die 7 (U429f)	250.00	

Magenta Surcharge

U521	U92 1½c on 1c grn (U420b, die 3)	4.25	3.50
a.	Double surcharge	25.00	

Sesquicentennial Exposition Issue

Liberty Bell — U94

Die 1. The center bar of "E" of "POSTAGE" is shorter than top bar.
Die 2. The center bar of "E" of "POSTAGE" is of same length as top bar.

1926

U522	U94 2c carmine, die 1	1.10	.50
a.	Die 2	6.50	3.75

See note below No. 627.

Washington Bicentennial Issue

Mount Vernon — U95

2 cent:
Die 1. "S" of "POSTAGE" normal.
Die 2. "S" of "POSTAGE" raised.

1932

U523	U95 1c olive green	.90	.80
U524	U95 1½c chocolate	1.75	1.50
U525	U95 2c car, die 1	.40	.20
a.	Die 2	70.00	16.00
b.	Die 1, blue, entire (error)	27,500.	
U526	U95 3c violet	1.75	.35
U527	U95 4c black	18.00	16.00
U528	U95 5c dark blue	3.75	3.50
	Nos. U523-U528 (6)	26.55	22.35

Bicen. of the birth of Washington.

1932   **Die 7**

U529	U93 6c orange	5.50	4.00
U530	U93 6c orange, amber	11.00	8.00
U531	U93 6c orange, blue	11.00	10.00

Franklin — U96   Washington — U97

Die 1   Die 2

Die 3

Die 1. Short (3½mm) and thick "1" in thick circle.
Die 2. Tall (4½mm) and thin "1" in thin circle; upper and lower bars of E in ONE long and 1mm from circle.
Die 3. As in Die 2, but E normal and 1½mm from circle.

1950

U532	U96 1c green, die 1	5.00	1.75
a.	Die 2	6.50	3.00
b.	Die 3	6.00	3.00
	Die 3, precanceled		.50

Die 1

Die 2

Die 3 Die 4

Die 1. Thick "2" in circle; toe of "2" is an acute angle.

Die 2. Thin "2" in thin circle; toe of "2" is almost right angle; line through stand of "E" in POSTAGE goes considerably below tip of chin; "N" of UNITED is tall; "O" of TWO is high.

Die 3. Thin "2" in thin circle; toe of "2" is almost right angle; short UN in UNITED: thin crossbar in A of STATES.

Die 4. Tall UN in UNITED; thick crossbar in A of STATES; otherwise like Die 3.

U533	U97 2c carmine, die 3	.75	.25
a.	Die 1	.75	.30
b.	Die 2	1.40	.85
c.	Die 4	1.30	.60

Die 1 Die 2

Die 3

Die 4 Die 5

Die 1. Thick and tall (4 1/2mm) "3" in thick circle; long top bars and short stems in T's of STATES.

Die 2. Thin and tall (4 1/2mm) "3" in medium circle; short top bars and long stems in T's of STATES.

Die 3. Thin and short (4mm) "3" in thin circle; lettering wider than Dies 1 and 2; line from left stand of N to stand of E is distinctly below tip of chin.

Die 4. Figure and letters as in Die 3. Line hits tip of chin; short N in UNITED and thin crossbar in A of STATES.

Die 5. Figure, letter and chin line as in Die 4; but tall N in UNITED and thick crossbar in A of STATES.

U534	U97 3c dk violet, die 4	.40	.20
a.	Die 1	2.00	.70
b.	Die 2	.75	.50
c.	Die 3	.50	.25
d.	Die 5	.80	.45

Washington — U98

1952

U535	U98 1 1/2c brown	5.00	3.50
	Precanceled		.50

Die 1 Die 2

Die 3

Die 1. Head high in oval (2mm below T of STATES). Circle near (1mm) bottom of colored oval.

Die 2. Head low in oval (3mm). Circle 1 1/2mm from edge of oval. Right leg of A of POSTAGE shorter than left. Short leg on P.

Die 3. Head centered in oval (2 1/2mm). Circle as in Die 2. Legs of A of POSTAGE about equal. Long leg on P.

1958

U536	U96 4c red violet, die 1	.75	.20
a.	Die 2	1.00	.20
b.	Die 3	1.00	.20

Nos. U429, U429f, U429h, U533, U533a-U533c Surcharged in Red at Left of Stamp - b

1958

U537	U93 2c + 2c car, die 1	3.00	1.50
a.	2c + 2c carmine, die 7	10.00	7.00
b.	2c + 2c carmine, die 9	5.00	5.00
U538	U97 2c + 2c car, die 1	.75	.20
a.	2c + 2c carmine, die 2	1.00	—
b.	2c + 2c carmine, die 3	.80	.25
c.	2c + 2c carmine, die 4	.80	—

Nos. U436a, U436e-U436f, U534a-U534d Surcharged in Green at Left of Stamp - a

U539	U93 3c + 1c pur, die 1	15.00	11.00
a.	3c + 1c purple, die 7	12.00	9.00
b.	3c + 1c purple, die 9	30.00	15.00
U540	U97 3c + 1c dk violet, die 3	.50	.15
a.	3c + 1c dk violet, die 2, entire	*1,000.*	—
b.	3c + 1c dark violet, die 4	.75	.15
c.	3c + 1c dark violet, die 5	.75	.15

See No. U545.

Franklin U99

Washington U100

Die 1 Die 2

Dies of 1 1/4c

Die 1. The "4" is 3mm high. Upper leaf in left cluster 2mm from "U."

Die 2. The "4" is 3 1/2mm high. Leaf clusters are larger. Upper leaf at left is 1mm from "U."

1960

U541	U99 1 1/4c turquoise, die 1	.70	.50
	Die 1, precanceled		.15
a.	Die 2, precanceled		1.50
U542	U100 2 1/2c dull blue	.80	.50
	Precanceled		.15

Precanceled Cut Squares

Precanceled envelopes do not normally receive another cancellation. Since the lack of a cancellation makes it impossible to distinguish between cut squares from used and unused envelopes, they are valued here as used only.

Pony Express Centennial Issue

Pony Express Rider U101

Envelope White Outside, Blue Inside

1960, July 19

U543	U101 4c brown	.60	.30

Abraham Lincoln — U102

Die 1 Die 2

Die 3

Die 1. Center bar of E of POSTAGE is above the middle. Center bar of E of STATES slants slightly upward. Nose sharper, more pointed. No offset ink specks inside envelope on back of die impression.

Die 2. Center bar of E in POSTAGE in middle. P of POSTAGE has short stem. Ink specks on back of die impression.

Die 3. FI of FIVE closer than Die 1 or 2. Second T of STATES seems taller than ES. Ink specks on back of die impression.

1962, Nov. 19

U544	U102 5c dark blue, die 2	.80	.20
a.	Die 1	.85	.25
b.	Die 3	.90	.35
c.	Die 2 with albino impression of 4c (#U536)	50.00	—
d.	Die 3 with albino impression of 4c (#U536)	70.00	—

No. U536 Surcharged Type "a" in Green at Left of Stamp

Two types of surcharge "a":

Type I. "U.S. POSTAGE" 18 1/2mm high. Serifs on cross of T both diagonal. Two lines of shading in C of CENT.

Type II. "U.S. POSTAGE" 17 1/2mm high. Right serif on cross of T is vertical. Three shading lines in C.

1962, Nov.

U545	U96 4c + 1c red vio, Type I	1.40	.50
a.	Type II	1.00	.50

New York World's Fair (1964-65)

Globe with Satellite Orbit U103

1964, Apr. 22

U546	U103 5c carmine rose	.60	.40

Liberty Bell — U104

Old Ironsides — U105

Eagle — U106

Head of Statue of Liberty — U107

1965-69 **Tagged (6c)**

U547	U104	1 1/4c brown		.15
U548	U104	1 4/10c brown ('68)		.15
U548A	U104	1 6/10c orange ('69)		.15
U549	U105	4c bright blue	.75	.15
U550	U106	5c bright purple	.75	.15
a.		Tagged ('67)	1.25	.15
U551	U107	6c lt green ('68)	.70	.15

Issue dates: 5c, Jan. 5; 1 1/4c, Jan. 6; 6c, Jan. 4; 1 4/10c, Mar. 26; 1 6/10c, June 16.

No. U550a has a luminescent panel 9x29mm at left of stamp. It glows yellow green under ultraviolet light.

Nos. U549-U550 Surcharged Types "b" and "a" in Red or Green at Left of Stamp

1968, Feb. 5

U552	U105 4c + 2c brt blue (R)	3.75	2.00
U553	U106 5c + 1c brt purple (G)	3.50	2.50
a.	Tagged	3.50	2.75

Tagging

Envelopes from No. U554 onward are tagged, with the tagging element in the ink unless otherwise noted.

Herman Melville Issue

Moby Dick — U108

1970, Mar. 7

U554	U108 6c light blue	.50	.15

Herman Melville (1819-91), writer, and the whaling industry.

Youth Conference Issue

Youth Conference Emblem U109

1971, Feb. 24

U555	U109 6c light blue	.75	.15

White House Conference on Youth, Estes Park, Colo., Apr. 18-22.

UNITED STATES
107

Bell Type of 1965-69 and

Eagle — U110

1971   **Untagged (1 7/10c)**
U556 U104 1 7/10c deep lilac   .15
U557 U110 8c bright ultra   .40   .15
Issue dates: 1 7/10c, May 10; 8c, May 6.

Nos. U551 and U555 Surcharged in Green at Left of Stamp

1971, May 16
U561 U107 6c + (2c) light green   1.00   .30
U562 U109 6c + (2c) light blue   2.00 1.60

Bowling Issue

Bowling Ball and Pin — U111

1971, Aug. 21
U563 U111 8c rose red   .50   .15
Salute to bowling and 7th World Tournament of the Intl. Bowling Fed., Milwaukee, WI.

Aging Conference Issue

Conference Symbol — U112

1971, Nov. 5
U564 U112 8c light blue   .50   .15
White House Conference on Aging, Washington, DC, Nov. 28-Dec. 2, 1971.

International Transportation Exhibition Issue

Transportation Exhibition Emblem U113

Illustration 2/3 actual size.

1972, May 2
U565 U113 8c ultra & rose red   .50   .15
US Intl. Transportation Exhib., Dulles Intl. Airport, Washington, May 27-June 4.

No. U557 Surcharged Type "b" in Ultramarine at Left of Stamp

1973, Dec. 1
U566 U110 8c + 2c bright ultra   .40   .15

Liberty Bell — U114

1973, Dec. 5
U567 U114 10c emerald   .40   .15

"Volunteer Yourself" — U115

1974, Aug. 23   **Untagged**
U568 U115 1 8/10c blue green   .15

US Tennis Centenary Issue

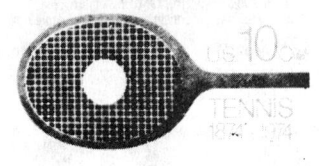

Tennis Racquet — U116

1974, Aug. 31
U569 U116 10c yel, brt blue & lt grn   .30   .20

Bicentennial Era Issue

The Seafaring Tradition--Compass Rose — U118

The American Homemaker--Quilt Pattern — U119

The American Farmer--Sheaf of Wheat U120

The American Doctor — U121

The American Craftsman--Tools, c. 1750 — U122

Designs (in brown on left side of envelope): 10c, Norwegian sloop Restaurationen. No. U572, Spinning wheel. No. U573, Plow. No. U574, Colonial era medical instruments and bottle. No. U575, Shaker rocking chair.

Light Brown Diagonally Laid Paper
1975-76
U571 U118 10c brown & blue   .30   .15
  a. Brown ("10c/USA," etc.) omitted, entire   125.00
U572 U119 13c brn & bl grn   .35   .15
  a. Brown ("13c/USA," etc.) omitted, entire   125.00
U573 U120 13c brn & brt grn   .35   .15
  a. Brown ("13c/USA," etc.) omitted, entire   125.00
U574 U121 13c brown & orange   .35   .15
  a. Brown ("13c/USA," etc.) omitted, entire   —
U575 U122 13c brown & car   .35   .15
  a. Brown ("13c/USA," etc.) omitted, entire   125.00

Issue dates: 10c, Oct. 13, 1975. No. U572, Feb. 2, 1976. No. U573, Mar. 15, 1976. No. U574, June 30, 1976. No. U575, Aug. 6, 1976.

Liberty Tree, Boston, 1646 — U123

1975, Nov. 8
U576 U123 13c orange brown   .30   .15

Precanceled Cut Squares
See note following No. U542.

Star and Pinweel — U124

U125

U126

Eagle — U127

"Uncle Sam" — U128

1976-78
U577 U124 2c red, untagged ('76)   .15
U578 U125 2.1c yel grn, untagged ('77)   .15
U579 U126 2.7c grn, untagged ('78)   .15
U580 U127 (15c) orange ('78)   .40   .15
U581 U128 15c red ('78)   .40   .15
Issue dates: 2c, Sept. 10; 2.1c June 3; 2.7c, July 5; A, May 22; 15c, June 3.

Bicentennial Issue

Centennial Envelope, 1876 — U129

1976, Oct. 15
U582 U129 13c emerald   .35   .15
See Nos. U218-U221.

Golf Issue

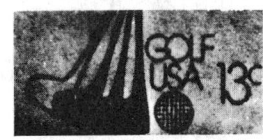

Golf Club in Motion and Golf Ball — U130

1977, Apr. 7
U583 U130 13c blk, bl & yel green   .45   .20
  a. Black omitted, entire
  b. Black & blue omitted, entire   550.00

Energy Issue

Energy Conservation U131

Energy Development U132

1977, Oct. 20
U584 U131 13c blk, red & yel   .40   .15
  a. Red & yel omitted, entire
  b. Yellow omitted, entire   —
  c. Black omitted, entire   —
  d. Black & red omitted, entire   475.00
U585 U132 13c blk, red & yel   .40   .15
Nos. U584-U585 have a luminescent panel at left of stamp.

Olive Branch and Star — U133

1978, July 28
U586 U133 15c on 16c blue   .35   .15
  a. Surcharge omitted, entire   400.00
  b. Surcharge on #U581, entire   —

Auto Racing Issue

Indianapolis 500 Racing Car — U134

1978, Sept. 2
U587 U134 15c red, blue & black   .35   .15
  a. Black omitted, entire   140.00
  b. Black & blue omitted, entire   —
  c. Red omitted, entire   —
  d. Red & blue omitted, entire   —
No. U576 Surcharged at left of Stamp Like No. U586

1978, Nov. 28   **Embossed**
U588 U123 15c on 13c org brown   .35   .15

Precanceled Cut Squares
See note following No. U542.

U135

Weaver Violins — U136

U137

Eagle — U138

Star — U139

Eagle U140

UNITED STATES

1979-82   Untagged (3.1c, 3.5c, 5.9c)
U589 U135 3.1c ultramarine .15
U590 U136 3.5c purple .15
U591 U137 5.9c brown .15
U592 U138 (18c) violet .45 .20
U593 U139 18c dark blue .45 .20
U594 U140 (20c) brown .45 .15

Issue dates: 3.1c, May 18; 3.5c, June 23; 5.9c, Feb. 17, 1982. #U592, Mar. 15, 1981; #U593, Apr. 2, 1981; #U594, Oct. 11, 1981.

Veterinary Medicine Issue

Seal of Veterinarians — U141

Design on left side of envelope shows 5 animals and a bird in brown and "Veterinary Medicine" in gray.

1979, July 24
U595 U141 15c brown & gray .35 .15
  a. Gray omitted, untagged, entire 700.00
  b. Brown omitted, entire —

Olympic Games Issue

U142

Design (multicolored on left side of envelope) shows two soccer players with ball.

1979, Dec. 10
U596 U142 15c red, green & black .60 .15
  a. Red & green omitted, untagged, entire 225.00
  b. Blk omitted, untagged, entire 225.00
  c. Black & green omitted, entire 225.00
  d. Red omitted, untagged, entire —

22nd Olympic Games, Moscow, July 19-Aug. 3, 1980.

Bicycling Issue

Highwheeler Bicycle — U143

Design (on left side of envelope) shows racing bicycle.

1980, May 16
U597 U143 15c bl & rose claret .40 .15
  a. Blue ("15c USA") omitted 100.00

America's Cup Yacht Races Issue

Racing Yacht — U144

1980, Sept. 15
U598 U144 15c light blue .40 .15

Italian Honeybee and Orange Blossoms — U145

Bee & Petals Colorless Embossed

1980, Oct. 10
U599 U145 15c multicolored .35 .15
  a. Brown ("USA 15c") omitted, entire 140.00

Design: Hand and braille colorless embossed

1981, Oct. 11
U600 U146 18c blue & red .45 .20
  a. Blue omitted, untagged, entire —

Capitol Dome — U147

1981, Nov. 13
U601 U147 20c deep magenta .45 .15

U148

Illustration reduced.

1982, June 15
U602 U148 20c dk blue, blk & mag .45 .15
  a. Dark blue omitted, entire —
  b. Dark blue & magenta omitted, entire —

The Purple Heart 1782 1982 USA 20c — U149

1982, Aug. 6
U603 U149 20c purple & black .45 .15

U150

1983, Mar. 21   Untagged
U604 U150 5.2c orange .15

Remember Our Paralyzed Veterans — U151

1983, Aug. 3
U605 U151 20c red, blue & black .45 .15
  a. Red omitted, entire —
  b. Blue omitted, entire —
  c. Red & black omitted, entire —
  d. Blue & black omitted, entire —
  e. Black omitted, entire 225.00

Small Business USA 20c — U152

Design shows storefronts at lower left. Stamp and design continue on back of envelope.

1984, May 7   Photo.
U606 U152 20c multicolored .50 .15

U153

1985, Feb. 1   Embossed
U607 U153 (22c) deep green .55 .15

Bison — U154

1985, Feb. 25   Embossed
U608 U154 22c violet brown .55 .15
  a. Untagged, precanceled with 3 blue lines .15

Frigate U.S.S. Constitution, "Old Ironsides" — U155

1985, May 3   Embossed Untagged
U609 U155 6c green blue .15

Mayflower — U156

1986, Dec. 4   Embossed Untagged Precanceled
U610 U156 8.5c black & gray .15

Stars — U157

1988, Mar. 26   Embossed & Typo.
U611 U157 25c dk bl & dk red .60 .15
  a. Dark red ("25") omitted, entire 85.00

Sea Gulls, Frigate USS Constellation — U158

Embossed & Typo.

1988, Apr. 12   Untagged
U612 U158 8.4c black & brt blue .15
  a. Black omitted, entire 600.00

Snowflake — U159

"Holiday Greetings!" inscribed at lower left.

1988, Sept. 8   Typo.
U613 U159 25c dark red & green .60 .25

Stars and "*Philatelic Mail*" Continuous in Dark Red Below Vignette — U160

1989, Mar. 10   Typo.
U614 U160 25c dk red & dp bl .50 .25

"USA" and Stars — U161

1989, July 10   Typo. Unwmk.
U615 U161 25c dk red & dp bl .50 .25
  a. Dark red omitted, entire —

Love — U162

1989, Sept. 25   Litho. & Typo. Unwmk.
U616 U162 25c dark red & blue .50 .25

Shuttle Docking at Space Station — U163

1989, Dec. 3   Typo. Unwmk.
U617 U163 25c ultramarine .60 .30
  a. Ultramarine omitted, entire 750.00

A hologram, visible through the die cut window to the right of "USA 25," is affixed to the inside of the envelope. Available only in No. 9 size. No. 9 envelopes are 225mm by 100mm.
See Nos. U625, U639.

UNITED STATES

Vince Lombardi Trophy, Football Players — U164

1990, Sept. 9   Litho.   Unwmk.
U618 U164 25c vermilion   .50   .25
A hologram, visible through the die cut window to the right of "USA 25," is affixed to the inside of the envelope.

Star — U165

Has embossed bars above and below the design.
1991, Jan. 24   Embossed & Typo.
U619 U165 29c ultra & rose   .60   .30
   a. Ultramarine omitted, entire
   b. Rose omitted, entire   —

Precanceled Cut Squares
See note following No. U542.

Birds — U166
Stamp and design continue on back of envelope.
1991, May 3   Typo.   Wmk.
Untagged
Precanceled
U620 U166 11.1c blue & red   .20

Love — U167
1991, May 9   Litho.
U621 U167 29c lt blue, maroon & brt rose   .60   .30
   a. Bright rose omitted, entire   500.00

Creating a Brighter World
Magazine Industry, 250th Anniv. — U168

Photo. & Typo.
1991, Oct. 7   Unwmk.
U622 U168 29c multicolored   .60   .30
The photogravure vignette, visible through the die cut window to the right of "USA 29," is affixed to the inside of the envelope. Available only in No. 10 size.

Star U169
Stamp and design continue on back of envelope.
1991, July 20   Typo.
U623 U169 29c ultra & rose   .60   .30
   a. Ultra omitted, entire
   Rose omitted, entire   —
Lined with a blue design to provide security for enclosures. Available only in No. 9 size.

Country Geese U170
1991, Nov. 8   Litho. & Typo.   Wmk.
U624 U170 29c blue gray & yellow   .60   .60

Space Shuttle Type of 1989
1992, Jan. 21   Typo.   Unwmk.
U625 U163 29c yellow green   .60   .25
A hologram, visible through the die cut window to the right of "USA 29," is affixed to the inside of the envelope. Available only in No. 10 size.
See No. U617a for envelopes with hologram only.

Western Americana U171

Typo. & Litho.
1992, Apr. 10   Unwmk.   *Die Cut*
U626 U171 29c multicolored   .60   .30
The lithographed vignette, visible through the die cut window to the right of "USA 29," is affixed to the inside of the envelope.

Hillebrandia — U172
Illustration reduced.
1992, Apr. 22
U627 U172 29c multicolored   .60   .30
The lithographed vignette, visible through the die cut window to the right of "29 USA," is affixed to the inside of the envelope.

U173

Typo. & Embossed
1992, May 19   Untagged
Precanceled
U628 U173 19.8c red & blue   .40

Disabled Americans 
U174
1992, July 22   Typo.   Unwmk.
U629 U174 29c red & blue   .60   .30

U175
Illustration reduced.
Typo. & Litho.
1993, Oct. 2   Unwmk.   *Die Cut*
U630 U175 29c multicolored   .60   .30
The lithographed vignette, visible through the die cut window to the right of "USA 29," is affixed to the inside of the envelope.

U176
Typo. & Embossed
1994, Sept. 17   Unwmk.
U631 U176 29c brown & black   .60   .30
   a. Black ("29/USA") omitted, entire
See No. U638.

Liberty Bell — U177
Typo. & Embossed
1995, Jan. 3   Unwmk.
U632 U177 32c greenish blue & blue   .65   .30
   a. Greenish blue omitted, entire
   b. Blue ("USA 32") omitted, entire   —

U178
Design size: 49x38mm (#U633), 53x44mm (#U634). Stamp and design continue on back of envelope.
1995   Typo.   Unwmk.
U633 U178 (32c) blue & red   .65   .30
U634 U178 (32c) blue & red   .65   .30
   a. Red color and tagging omitted, entire
   b. Blue omitted, entire   —
Originally, Nos. U633-U634 were only available through the Philatelic Fulfillment Center after their announcement 1/12/95.

U179
Design size: 58x25mm. Stamp and design continue on back of envelope.
1995, Mar. 10   Typo.   Unwmk.
Precanceled
U635 U179 (5c) green & red brown   .15

Graphic Eagle — U180
1995, Mar. 10   Typo.   Unwmk.
Precanceled
U636 U180 (10c) dark carmine & blue   .15

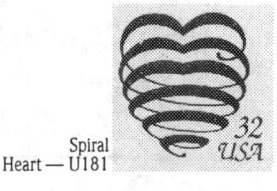

Spiral Heart — U181
1995, May 12   Typo.   Unwmk.
U637 U181 32c red, *light blue*   .65   .30

Liberty Bell Type of 1995
1995, May 16   Typo.   Unwmk.
U638 U177 32c greenish blue & blue   .65   .30

Space Shuttle Type of 1989
Unwmk.
1995, Sept. 22   Typo.   *Die Cut*
U639 U163 32c carmine rose   .65   .35
A hologram, visible through the die cut window to the right of "USA 32," is affixed to the inside of the envelope.

U182
Typo. & Litho.
1996, Apr. 20   Unwmk.   *Die Cut*
U640 U182 32c multicolored   .60   .30
The lithographed vignette, visible through the die cut window to the right of "USA 32c," is affixed to the inside of the envelope.

U183
1996, May 2
U641 U183 32c multicolored   .60   .30
   a. Black & red omitted, entire
   b. Blue & gold omitted, entire   —

AIR POST STAMPED ENVELOPES AND AIR LETTER SHEETS

UC1

UC2

UC1 — Vertical rudder is not semi-circular but slopes down to the left. The tail of the plane projects into the G of POSTAGE.

UC2 — Vertical rudder is semi-circular. The tail of the plane touches but does not project into the G of POSTAGE.

6c: Same as UC2 except 3 types of numeral.
Die 2a- Numeral "6" 6½mm wide.
Die 2b- Numeral "6" 6mm wide.
Die 2c- Numeral "6" 5½mm wide.
Die 3- Vertical rudder leans forward. S closer to O than to T of POSTAGE. E of POSTAGE has short center bar.

1929-44 **Embossed**

UC1 UC1 5c blue 3.50 2.00
UC2 UC2 5c blue 11.00 5.00
UC3 UC2 6c org, die 2a ('34) 1.45 .40
a. No. UC3 with added impression of 3c pur (#U436a), entire without border *3,000.*
UC4 UC2 6c org, die 2b ('42) 2.75 2.00
UC5 UC2 6c org, die 2c ('44) .75 .30
UC6 UC2 6c org, die 3 ('42) 1.00 .35
a. 6c org, *blue* (error), entire *3,500.* *2,400.*
UC7 UC2 8c olive green ('32) 13.00 3.50

Surcharged in black on envelopes indicated by numbers in brackets.

AIR 6¢ MAIL

1945

UC8 U93 6c on 2c (U429) 1.25 .65
a. 6c on 1c grn, error, (U420) *1,750.*
b. 6c on 3c purple, error, (U436a) *2,000.*
c. 6c on 3c purple, error, *amb* (U437a) *3,000.*
d. 6c on 3c vio, error, (U526) *3,000.*
UC9 U95 6c on 2c (U525) 75.00 40.00

Nos. UC8a-UC8d are known only entire.

Surcharged in Black on 6c Orange Air Post Envelopes without borders

REVALUED
5¢
P.O.DEPT.

1946

UC10 UC2 5c on 6c, die 2a 2.75 1.50
a. Double surcharge 60.00
UC11 UC2 5c on 6c, die 2b 9.00 5.50
UC12 UC2 5c on 6c, die 2c .75 .50
a. Double surcharge 60.00 60.00
UC13 UC2 5c on 6c, die 3 .80 .60
a. Double surcharge 60.00

The 6c borderless envelopes and the revalued envelopes were issued primarily for use to and from members of the armed forces.
The 5c rate came into effect Oct. 1, 1946.

AIR MAIL
5¢
5¢
UNITED STATES OF AMERICA
DC-4 Skymaster UC3

Die 1. The end of the wing at the right is a smooth curve. The juncture of the front end of the plane and the engine forms an acute angle. The first T of STATES and the E's of UNITED STATES lean to the left.
Die 2. The end of the wing at the right is a straight line. The juncture of the front end of the plane and the engine is wide open. The first T of STATES and the E's of UNITED STATES lean to the right.

1946 **Embossed**

UC14 UC3 5c carmine, die 1 .75 .20
UC15 UC3 5c carmine, die 2 .85 .25

See Nos. UC18, UC26.

DC-4 Skymaster — UC4

Letter Sheet for Foreign Postage
"Air Letter" on face, 2-line inscription on back.

1947, Apr. 29 **Typo.**

UC16 UC4 10c brt red, *pale bl*, entire 7.50 6.00
a. "Air Letter" on face, 4-line inscription on back ('51), entire 16.00 14.00
b. As "a," 10c chocolate, *pale bl*, entire 400.00
c. "Air Letter" and "Aerogramme" on face, 4-line inscription on back ('53), entire 45.00 12.50
d. As "c," 3-line inscription on back ('55), entire 8.00 8.00

AIR MAIL
5¢
5¢
U.S. POSTAGE STAMP CENTENARY
Washington and Franklin, Early and Modern Mail-carrying Vehicles — UC5

Embossed, Rotary Press Printing

1947, May 21

UC17 UC5 5c car, (22¼mm high) .40 .25
a. Flat plate (21¾mm high) .50 .30

Cent. of the 1st postage stamps issued by the US Government.

Type of 1946

Type I- 6's lean to right.
Type II- 6's upright.

1950, Sept. 22

UC18 UC3 6c carmine, Type I .35 .15
a. Type II .75 .25

Several other types differ slightly from the two listed.

Nos. UC14, UC15, UC18 Surcharged in Red at Left of Stamp

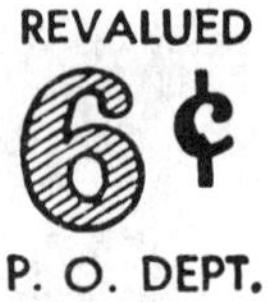
REVALUED
6¢
P. O. DEPT.

1951

UC19 UC3 6c on 5c car, die 1 .85 .50
UC20 UC3 6c on 5c car, die 2 .80 .50
a. 6c on 6c car, error, entire *1,500.*
b. 6c on 5c, double surcharge *250.00* —

Nos. UC14, UC15 and UC17 Surcharged in Red at Left of Stamp

REVALUED
6¢
P.O. DEPT.

1952

UC21 UC3 6c on 5c, die 1 27.50 17.50
UC22 UC3 6c on 5c, die 2 3.50 2.50
a. Double surcharge 75.00
UC23 UC5 6c on 5c, entire *1,850.*

The 6c on 4c black (No. U440) is believed to be a favor printing.

AIR MAIL 6¢
U.S. POSTAGE
Eagle in Flight — UC6

1956, May 2 **Embossed**

UC25 UC6 6c red .75 .50

FIPEX, NYC, Apr. 28-May 6. Two types exist, differing mainly in the clouds at top.

Skymaster Type of 1946

1958, July 31

UC26 UC3 7c blue .65 .50

Nos. UC3-UC5, UC18 and UC25 Surcharged in Green at Left of Stamp

U.S. POSTAGE
CENT

1958

UC27 UC2 6c + 1c, die 2a 250.00 225.00
UC28 UC2 6c + 1c, die 2b 65.00 75.00
UC29 UC2 6c + 1c, die 2c 37.50 50.00
UC30 UC3 6c + 1c, type I 1.00 .50
a. Type II 1.00 .50
UC31 UC6 6c + 1c 1.00 .50

U S POSTAGE
AIR MAIL 10¢
Jet Airliner — UC7

Letter Sheet for Foreign Postage.

Two types:
Type I - Back inscription in 3 lines.
Type II - Back inscription in 2 lines.

1958-59 **Typo.**

UC32 UC7 10c bl & red, *bl*, II ('59), entire 6.00 5.00
a. Type I ('58), entire 10.00 5.00
b. Red omitted, II, entire —
c. Blue omitted, II, entire —

US 7
Silhouette of Jet Airliner — UC8

1958, Nov. 21 **Embossed**

UC33 UC8 7c blue .60 .25

1960, Aug. 18

UC34 UC8 7c carmine .60 .25

Jet Plane and Globe — UC9

Letter Sheet for Foreign Postage

1961, Nov. 16 **Typo.**

UC35 UC9 11c red & bl, *bl*, entire 2.75 1.50
a. Red omitted, entire *875.00*
b. Blue omitted, entire *875.00*

AIR MAIL
US 8¢
UC10

8
UC11

1962, Nov. 17 **Embossed**

UC36 UC10 8c red .55 .15

1965, Jan. 7

UC37 UC11 8c red .35 .15
a. Tagged ('67) 1.25 .30

No. UC37a has a luminescent panel ⅜x1 inches at left of stamp. It glows orange red under ultraviolet light.

11¢ AIR MAIL
JOHN F. KENNEDY
U·S·A
Pres. John F. Kennedy and Jet Plane — UC12

Letter Sheets for Foreign Postage

1965-67 **Typo.**

UC38 UC12 11c red & dk bl, *blue*, entire 3.25 1.50
UC39 UC12 13c red & dk bl, *blue*, entire 3.00 1.50
a. Red omitted *500.00*
b. Dark blue omitted *500.00*

Issued: 11c, May 29, 1965; 13c, May 29, 1967.

TEN CENTS
U.S. AIR MAIL
UC13

1968, Jan. 8 **Tagged** **Embossed**

UC40 UC13 10c red .50 .15

No. UC37 Surcharged in Red at Left of Stamp

U. S. POSTAGE
2 CENTS

1968, Feb. 5

UC41 UC11 8c + 2c red .65 .15

Tagging
Envelopes and Letter Sheets from No. UC42 onward are tagged unless otherwise noted.

HUMAN RIGHTS YEAR
U.S. POSTAGE
13¢
Globes and Flock of Birds UC14

Letter Sheet for Foreign Postage

1968, Dec. 3 **Photo.**

UC42 UC14 13c gray, brn, org & blk, *blue*, entire 8.00 4.00
a. Orange omitted, entire —
b. Brown omitted, entire *400.00*
c. Black omitted, entire —

Intl. Human Rights Year, and 20th anniv. of the UN Declaration of Human Rights.

U.S.
11¢
AIR MAIL
UC15

1971, May 6 **Embossed**

UC43 UC15 11c red & blue .50 .15

usa
postage 15c
Birds in Flight and "usa" — UC16

Letter Sheet for Foreign Postage
"postage 15c" in Gray

1971, May 28 **Photo.**

UC44 UC16 15c gray, red, white & blue, *blue*, entire 1.50 1.10
a. "AEROGRAMME" added, entire 1.50 1.10

Folding instructions (2 steps) in capitals on No. UC44; (4 steps) in upper and lower case on No. UC44a. No. UC44a issued Dec. 13.
See No. UC46.

No. UC40 Surcharged in Green at Left of Stamp

POSTAGE
REVALUED

1971, June 28 **Embossed**

UC45 UC13 10c + (1c) red 1.50 .20

Letter Sheet for Foreign Postage
"usa" Type of 1971

Design: Three balloons and cloud at left in address section; no birds beside stamp.

"postage 15c" in Blue

1973, Feb. 10 **Photo.**

UC46 UC16 15c red, white & bl, *blue*, entire .75 .40

Hot Air Ballooning World Championships, Albuquerque, NM, Feb. 10-17. Folding instructions as on No. UC44a, with "INTERNATIONAL HOT AIR BALLOONING" added to inscription.

UNITED STATES

Bird in Flight — UC17

1973, Dec. 1 — Embossed
UC47 UC17 13c rose red .30 .15

Beginning with No. UC48 all letter sheets are for Foreign Postage unless noted otherwise.

UC18

1974, Jan. 4 — Photo.
UC48 UC18 18c red & blue, *blue*, entire .90 .30
 a. Red omitted, entire

UC19

Design: "NATO" and NATO emblem in multicolor at left in address section.

1974, Apr. 4 — Photo.
UC49 UC19 18c red & blue, *blue*, entire .90 .40

25th anniv. of NATO.

UC20

1976, Jan. 16 — Photo.
UC50 UC20 22c red & blue, *blue*, entire .90 .40

UC21

1978, Nov. 3 — Photo.
UC51 UC21 22c bl, *bl*, entire .70 .25

UC22

Design (multicolored in bottom left corner) shows discus thrower.

1979, Dec. 5 — Photo.
UC52 UC22 22c red, blk & grn, *bluish*, entire 1.50 .25

22nd Olympic Games, Moscow, July 19-Aug. 3, 1980.

UC23

Design shows Statue of Liberty at lower left. Inscribed "Tour the United States," folding area shows tourist attractions.

1980-81 — Photo.
UC53 UC23 30c bl, red & brn, *bl*, entire .65 .30
 a. Red ("30c") omitted, entire 75.00
UC54 UC23 30c yel, magenta, bl & blk, *bl*, entire ('81) .65 .30

Issued: Dec. 29, 1980; Sept. 21, 1981.

UC24

"Made in USA . . . world's best buys."

1982, Sept. 16 — Photo.
UC55 UC24 30c multi, *bl*, entire .65 .30

World Communications Year Issue

World Map Showing Locations of Satellite Tracking Stations — UC25

1983, Jan. 7 — Photo.
UC56 UC25 30c multi, *bl*, entire .65 .30

1984 Olympics

UC26

1983, Oct. 14 — Photo.
UC57 UC26 30c multi, *bl*, entire .65 .30

UC27

Design: Satellite over Earth at lower left, with Landsat photographs on folding area. Inscribed: Landsat views the Earth.

1985, Feb. 14 — Photo.
UC58 UC27 36c multi, *bl*, entire .70 .35

National Tourism Week

Urban Skyline UC28

1985, May 21 — Photo.
UC59 UC28 36c multi, *bl*, entire .70 .35
 a. Black omitted, entire

Mark Twain (1835-1910) and Halley's Comet

Comet Tail Viewed from Space — UC29

1985, Dec. 4 — Photo.
UC60 UC29 36c multi, entire .70 .35

UC30

1988, May 9 — Litho.
UC61 UC30 39c multi, entire .80 .40

Montgomery Blair and Pres. Lincoln — UC31

Design: Mail bags and text at lower left. Globe, locomotive, bust of Blair, UPU emblem and text contained on reverse folding area.

1989, Nov. 20 — Litho.
UC62 UC31 39c multi, entire .80 .40

UC32

1991, May 17 — Litho.
UC63 UC32 45c gray, red & blue, *blue*, entire .90 .45
 a. White paper, entire .90 .45

Thaddeus Lowe (1832-1913), Balloonist — UC33

Letter Sheet for Foreign Postage

1995, Sept. 23 — Litho.
UC64 UC33 50c multicolored, *blue* 1.00 .50

United States postal stationery can be mounted in the Scott U.S. Postal Stationery album.

POSTAL CARDS
"R.F." CONTROL OVERPRINT
STAMPED ENVELOPES
are listed in the Scott Specialized Catalogue of United States Stamps.
NEWSPAPER WRAPPERS
Included in listings of Stamped Envelopes with prefix "W" instead of "U"
LETTER SHEETS Included with Stamped Envelopes

OFFICIAL STAMPED ENVELOPES

Post Office Department

"2" 9mm high — UO1
"3" 9mm high — UO2 

"6" 9½mm high — UO3

1873
UO1 UO1 2c black, *lemon* 15.00 8.00
UO2 UO2 3c black, *lemon* 9.00 6.00
+UO3 UO2 3c black 20,000.
UO4 UO3 6c black, *lemon* 17.50 14.00

"2" 9¼mm high — UO4
"3" 9¼mm high — UO5 

"6" 10½mm high — UO6

1874-79
UO5 UO4 2c black, *lemon* 6.00 4.00
UO6 UO4 2c black 70.00 32.50
UO7 UO5 3c black, *lemon* 3.00 .75
UO8 UO5 3c black 1,500. 850.00
UO9 UO5 3c black, *amber* 45.00 35.00
UO10 UO5 3c black, *blue* 17,500.
UO11 UO5 3c blue, *blue* 15,000.
UO12 UO6 6c black, *lemon* 8.00 6.00
UO13 UO6 6c black 1,150.

Postal Service

UO7

1877
UO14 UO7 black 7.00 3.75
UO15 UO7 black, *amber* 55.00 27.50
UO16 UO7 blue, *amber* 50.00 30.00
UO17 UO7 blue, *blue* 8.00 6.00
Nos. UO14-UO17 (4) 120.00 67.25

War Department

Franklin — UO8
Jackson — UO9

UO8 — Bust points to the end of "N" of "ONE."
UO9 — Bust narrow at the back.

Washington UO10
Lincoln UO11 

UO10 — Queue projects below the bust.
UO11 — Neck very long at the back.

Jefferson — UO12
Clay — UO13 

UO12 — Queue forms straight line with bust.
UO13 — Ear partly concealed by hair, mouth large, chin prominent.

Webster — UO14
Scott — UO15 

UO14 — Has side whiskers.

Hamilton — UO16

Back of bust very narrow, chin almost straight; the labels containing the letters "U S" are exactly parallel.

1873

Reay Issue

UO18	UO8	1c dark red	525.00	300.00
UO19	UO9	2c dark red	850.00	425.00
UO20	UO10	3c dark red	60.00	40.00
UO21	UO10	3c dark red, amb		17,500.
UO22	UO10	3c dark red, cr	450.00	225.00
UO23	UO11	6c dark red	210.00	90.00
UO24	UO11	6c dark red, cr	2,250.	425.00
UO25	UO12	10c dark red	6,000.	350.00
UO26	UO13	12c dark red	110.00	50.00
UO27	UO14	15c dark red	110.00	55.00
UO28	UO15	24c dark red	110.00	50.00
UO29	UO16	30c dark red	450.00	150.00
UO30	UO8	1c vermilion	135.00	
WO31	UO8	1c ver, man	12.50	12.50
+UO32	UO9	2c vermilion	275.00	
WO33	UO9	2c ver, man	200.00	
UO34	UO10	3c vermilion	70.00	40.00
UO35	UO10	3c ver, amb	80.00	
UO36	UO10	3c ver, cr	15.00	12.50
UO37	UO11	6c vermilion	70.00	
+UO38	UO11	6c ver, cr	325.00	
UO39	UO12	10c vermilion	200.00	
UO40	UO13	12c vermilion	135.00	
UO41	UO14	15c vermilion	210.00	
UO42	UO15	24c vermilion	375.00	
UO43	UO16	30c vermilion	375.00	

UO17
UO18 

UO17--Bottom serif on "S" is thick and short, bust at bottom below hair forms sharp point.

UO18--Bottom serif on "S" is thick and short, front part of bust is rounded.

UO19
UO20 

UO19--Bottom serif on "S" is short, queue does not project below bust.
UO20--Neck very short at the back.

UO21
UO22 

UO21--Knot of queue stands out prominently.
UO22--Ear prominent, chin receding.

UO23
UO24 

UO23--Has no side whiskers, forelock projects above head.
UO24--Back of bust rather broad; chin slopes considerably; the labels containing letters "U S" are not exactly parallel.

1875

Plimpton Issue

UO44	UO17	1c red	120.00	80.00
+UO45	UO17	1c red, amb	750.00	
+UO45A	UO17	1c red, org	35,000.	
WO46	UO17	1c red, man	3.75	2.75
UO47	UO18	2c red	90.00	
UO48	UO18	2c red, amb	25.00	14.00
UO49	UO18	2c red, org	42.50	12.50
WO50	UO18	2c red, man	75.00	40.00
UO51	UO19	3c red	12.50	9.00
UO52	UO19	3c red, amb	14.00	9.00
UO53	UO19	3c red, cr	6.50	3.75
UO54	UO19	3c red, bl	3.50	2.75
UO55	UO19	3c red, fawn	4.50	2.75
UO56	UO20	6c red	40.00	30.00
UO57	UO20	6c red, amb	70.00	40.00
UO58	UO20	6c red, cr	175.00	87.50
UO59	UO21	10c red	150.00	82.50
UO60	UO21	10c red, amb	1,100.	
UO61	UO22	12c red	42.50	40.00
UO62	UO22	12c red, amb	625.00	
UO63	UO22	12c red, cr	600.00	
UO64	UO23	15c red	160.00	140.00
UO65	UO23	15c red, amb	700.00	
UO66	UO23	15c red, cr	675.00	
UO67	UO24	30c red	160.00	140.00
UO68	UO24	30c red, amb	900.00	
UO69	UO24	30c red, cr	900.00	

POSTAL SAVINGS STAMPED ENVELOPES

UO25

1911

UO70	UO25	1c green	60.00	20.00
UO71	UO25	1c grn, oriental buff	175.00	65.00
UO72	UO25	2c carmine	10.00	3.75
a.		2c carmine, manila (error)	1,900.	

Used Values
Catalogue values for regularly used entires. Those with first day cancels generally sell for much less.

OFFICIAL MAIL

UO26

1983, Jan. 12
UO73 UO26 20c blue, entire 1.25 30.00

UO27

1985, Feb. 26
UO74 UO27 22c blue, entire .90 5.00

UO28

1987, Mar. 2   Typo.
UO75 UO28 22c blue, entire .90 20.00
Used exclusively to mail US Savings Bonds.

UO29

1988, Mar. 22   Typo.
UO76 UO29 (25c) blk & bl, entire 1.00 20.00
Used exclusively to mail US Saving Bonds.

UO30

1988, Apr. 11   Embossed & Typo.
UO77 UO30 25c blk & blue, entire .75 5.00
  a. Denomination & lettering as No. UO78

UO31

1988, Apr. 11   Typo.
UO78 UO31 25c black & blue, entire .85 25.00
  a. Denomination & lettering as No. UO77
Used exclusively to mail US Saving Bonds.

Used Values
The appearance in the marketplace of postally used examples of the entires used to mail passports (Nos. UO79-UO82, UO86-UO87) is so infrequent that it currently is not possible to establish accurate values.

1990, Mar. 17   Typo.
UO79 UO31 45c blk & bl, entire 1.25 —
UO80 UO31 65c blk & bl, entire 1.60 —
Used exclusively to mail US passports.

UO32

Type UO32: sharp impression, stars and "E Pluribus Unum" are clear and distinct. Official is 14½mm long, USA is 17mm long.

1990, Aug. 10   Typo.
UO81 UO32 45c blk & bl, entire 1.25 —
UO82 UO32 65c blk & bl, entire 1.50 —
Used exclusively to mail US passports.

UO33

1991, Jan. 22   Typo.   Wmk.
UO83 UO33 (29c) blk & bl, entire 1.10 20.00
Used exclusively to mail US Saving Bonds.

UO34

1991, Apr. 6   Typo. & Embossed
UO84 UO34 29c black & blue, entire .70 2.00

UO35

1991, Apr. 17   Typo.   Wmk.
UO85 UO35 29c blk & bl, entire .70 20.00
Used exclusively to mail US Saving Bonds.

Consular Service, Bicent. — UO36

1992, July 10   Litho.   Unwmk.
UO86 UO36 52c blue & red, entire 1.25 —
UO87 UO36 75c blue & red, entire 1.75 —
Used exclusively to mail US passports.

UO37

Typo. & Embossed
1995, May 9   Unwmk.
UO88 UO37 32c blue & red, entire .75 10.00

UNITED STATES

OFFICIAL WRAPPERS
Included in listings of Official Stamped Envelopes with prefix letters "WO" instead of "UO"

REVENUE STAMPS

Nos. R1-R102 were used to pay taxes on documents and proprietary articles including playing cards. Until Dec. 25, 1862, the law stated that a revenue stamp could be used only for payment of the tax upon the particular instrument or article specified on its face. After that date stamps, except the Proprietary, could be used indiscriminately.

Values quoted are for pen-canceled copies. Stamps with handstamped cancellations sell at higher prices. Stamps canceled with cuts, punches or holes sell for less. See the Scott U.S. Specialized Catalogue.

General Issue
First Issue. Head of Washington in Oval. Various Frames as Illustrated.

Old Paper
Perf. 12

Nos. R1b to R42b, part perforate, occur perforated sometimes at sides only and sometimes at top and bottom only. The higher values, part perforate, are perforated at sides only. Imperforate and part perforate revenues often bring much more in pairs or blocks than as single copies.

The experimental silk paper is a variety of the old paper and has only a very few minute fragments of fiber.

Some of the stamps were in use eight years and were printed several times. Many color variations occurred, particularly when unstable pigments were used and the color was intended to be purple or violet, such as the 4c Proprietary, 30c and $2.50 stamps. Before 1868 dull colors predominate on these and the early red stamps. In later printings of the 4c Proprietary, 30c and $2.50 stamps, red predominates in the mixture, and on the dollar values the red is brighter. The early $1.90 stamp is dull purple, imperf. or perforated. In a later printing, perforated only, the purple is darker.

R1, R2, R3, R4, R5

1862-71
			Engr.
R1	R1	1c Express, red	1.25
a.		Imperf.	55.00
b.		Part perf.	35.00
d.		Silk paper	85.00
R2	R1	1c Playing Cards, red	130.00
a.		Imperf.	1,000.
b.		Part perf.	700.00
R3	R1	1c Proprietary, red	.50
a.		Imperf.	725.00
b.		Part perf.	120.00
d.		Silk paper	20.00
R4	R1	1c Telegraph, red	11.00
a.		Imperf.	375.00

R5	R2	2c Bank Check, blue	.25
a.		Imperf.	1.00
b.		Part perf.	1.75
c.		Vertical pair, imperf. between, old paper	400.00
R6	R2	2c Bank Check, orange	.25
b.		Part perf.	55.00
d.		Silk paper	240.00
e.		Old paper, green	375.00
R7	R2	2c Certificate, blue	25.00
a.		Imperf.	12.50
R8	R2	2c Certificate, orange	25.00
R9	R2	2c Express, blue	.40
a.		Imperf.	12.50
b.		Part perf.	20.00
R10	R2	2c Express, orange	7.50
b.		Part perf.	—
d.		Silk paper	60.00
R11	R2	2c Playing Cards, blue	4.00
b.		Part perf.	165.00
R12	R2	2c Playing Cards, orange	35.00
R13	R2	2c Proprietary, blue	.40
a.		Imperf.	350.00
b.		Part perf.	120.00
d.		Silk paper	50.00
e.		Ultramarine	170.00
R14	R2	2c Proprietary, orange	35.00
R15	R2	2c U.S. Int. Rev., orange ('64)	.15
d.		Silk paper	.25
e.		Old paper, green	500.00
R16	R3	3c For. Exch., green	3.50
b.		Part perf.	250.00
d.		Silk paper	45.00
R17	R3	3c Playing Cards, green ('63)	120.00
a.		Imperf.	8,500.
R18	R3	3c Proprietary, green	3.25
b.		Part perf.	275.00
d.		Silk paper	27.50
e.		Printed on both sides, old paper	1,600.
R19	R3	3c Telegraph, green	2.75
a.		Imperf.	55.00
b.		Part perf.	20.00
R20	R3	4c Inland Exch., brown ('63)	1.75
d.		Silk paper	45.00
R21	R3	4c Playing Cards, slate ('63)	500.00
R22	R3	4c Proprietary, purple	6.50
a.		Imperf.	—
b.		Part perf.	210.00
d.		Silk paper	60.00

Many shade and color variations of Nos. R21-R22. See foreword, "Revenue Stamps."

R23	R3	5c Agreement, red	.25
d.		Silk paper	1.50
R24	R3	5c Certificate, red	.25
a.		Imperf.	2.50
b.		Part perf.	11.00
d.		Silk paper	.35
R25	R3	5c Express, red	.30
a.		Imperf.	4.50
b.		Part perf.	5.00
R26	R3	5c Foreign Exchange, red	.30
b.		Part perf.	—
d.		Silk paper	175.00
R27	R3	5c Inland Exch., red	.25
a.		Imperf.	5.00
b.		Part perf.	3.75
d.		Silk paper	12.50
R28	R3	5c Playing Cards, red ('63)	17.50
R29	R3	5c Proprietary, red ('64)	22.50
d.		Silk paper	100.00
R30	R3	6c Inland Exch., org ('63)	1.75
d.		Silk paper	65.00
R31	R3	6c Proprietary, orange ('71)	1,600.

Nearly all copies of No. R31 are faulty or repaired and poorly centered.

The Catalogue value is for a fine centered copy with minor faults which do not detract from its appearance.

R32	R3	10c Bill of Lading, blue	1.00
a.		Imperf.	45.00
b.		Part perf.	200.00
R33	R3	10c Certificate, blue	.25
a.		Imperf.	120.00
b.		Part perf.	200.00
d.		Silk paper	5.00
R34	R3	10c Contract, blue	.35
b.		Part perf.	150.00
d.		Silk paper	2.25
e.		Ultramarine, part perf.	425.00
f.		Ultramarine, old paper	1.00
R35	R3	10c For. Exch., blue	7.00
d.		Silk paper	—
e.		ultra, old paper	9.75
R36	R3	10c Inland Exch., blue	.15
a.		Imperf.	175.00
b.		Part perf.	3.50
d.		Silk paper	27.50
R37	R3	10c Power of Attorney, blue	.50
a.		Imperf.	450.00
b.		Part perf.	15.00
R38	R3	10c Proprietary, blue ('64)	14.00
R39	R3	15c For. Exch., brown ('63)	14.00
R40	R3	15c Inland Exch., brown	1.25
a.		Imperf.	30.00
b.		Part perf.	12.50
R41	R3	20c For. Exch., red	32.50
a.		Imperf.	40.00
R42	R3	20c Inland Exch., red	.35
a.		Imperf.	15.00
b.		Part perf.	17.50
R43	R4	25c Bond, red	2.50
a.		Imperf.	145.00
b.		Part perf.	6.00
R44	R4	25c Certificate, red	.25
a.		Imperf.	10.00
b.		Part perf.	6.00
d.		Silk paper	2.75
f.		Printed on both sides, old paper	1,750.
		Impression of No. R48 on back, old paper	—
R45	R4	25c Entry of Goods, red	.75
a.		Imperf.	17.50
b.		Part perf.	65.00
d.		Silk paper	22.50
R46	R4	25c Insurance, red	.25
a.		Imperf.	10.00
b.		Part perf.	10.00
d.		Silk paper	4.50

R6, R7

R47	R4	25c Life Insurance, red	6.50
a.		Imperf.	35.00
b.		Part perf.	210.00
R48	R4	25c Power of Attorney, red	.30
a.		Imperf.	6.00
b.		Part perf.	27.50
R49	R4	25c Protest, red	6.75
a.		Imperf.	30.00
b.		Part perf.	260.00
R50	R4	25c Warehouse Receipt, red	22.50
a.		Imperf.	42.50
b.		Part perf.	235.00
R51	R4	30c For. Exch., lilac	52.50
a.		Imperf.	72.50
b.		Part perf.	950.00
R52	R4	30c Inland Exch., lilac	3.50
a.		Imperf.	47.50
b.		Part perf.	60.00

Many shade and color variations of Nos. R51-R52. See foreword, "Revenue Stamps."

R53	R4	40c Inland Exch., brown	3.50
a.		Imperf.	575.00
b.		Part perf.	7.00
R54	R5	50c Conveyance, blue	.15
a.		Imperf.	14.00
b.		Part perf.	1.60
d.		Silk paper	3.00
e.		Ultramarine, old paper	.25
f.		Ultramarine, silk paper	—
R55	R5	50c Entry of Goods, blue	.40
a.		Imperf.	12.00
b.		Part perf.	40.00
R56	R5	50c For. Exch., blue	5.00
a.		Imperf.	42.50
b.		Part perf.	40.00
R57	R5	50c Lease, blue	8.50
a.		Imperf.	24.00
b.		Part perf.	60.00
R58	R5	50c Life Insurance, blue	.90
a.		Imperf.	30.00
b.		Part perf.	45.00
R59	R5	50c Mortgage, blue	.90
a.		Imperf.	14.00
d.		Silk paper	2.50
R60	R5	50c Original Process, blue	.60
a.		Imperf.	3.00
b.		Part perf.	550.00
d.		Silk paper	1.60
R61	R5	50c Passage Ticket, blue	1.25
a.		Imperf.	72.50
b.		Part perf.	140.00
R62	R5	50c Probate of Will, blue	19.00
a.		Imperf.	35.00
b.		Part perf.	60.00
R63	R5	50c Surety Bond, blue	.30
a.		Imperf.	150.00
b.		Part perf.	2.50
e.		Ultramarine, old paper	.75
R64	R5	60c Inland Exch., org	6.00
a.		Imperf.	85.00
b.		Part perf.	47.50
d.		Silk paper	32.50
R65	R5	70c For. Exch., green	8.00
a.		Imperf.	325.00
b.		Part perf.	95.00
d.		Silk paper	47.50

R8, R9, R10, R11 (Illustration sideways)

Old Paper

R66	R6	$1 Conveyance, red	15.00
a.		Imperf.	12.00
b.		Part perf.	425.00
d.		Silk paper	85.00
R67	R6	$1 Entry of Goods, red	1.90
a.		Imperf.	32.50
b.		Part perf.	50.00
R68	R6	$1 For. Exch., red	.60
a.		Imperf.	60.00
b.		Part perf.	45.00
R69	R6	$1 Inland Exch., red	.45
a.		Imperf.	12.50
b.		Part perf.	300.00
d.		Silk paper	2.25

WANTED TO BUY
U.S. REVENUES & BACK-OF-BOOK
TOP PRICES PAID!   **CALL OR WRITE**

- Revenues
- Documentaries
- Tax Paids
- Match/Medicine
- Possessions
- State Revenues
- Classic U.S. Stamps
- Officials
- Proofs/Essays

BUYING!   WANT LISTS INVITED   SELLING!

GOLDEN PHILATELICS
Myrna Golden • Jack Golden
Post Office Box 484, Cederhurst, NY 11516
Phone (516) 791-1804 • Fax (516) 791-7846

R70 R6 $1 Lease, red 2.25
a. Imperf. 35.00
R71 R6 $1 Life Insurance, red 6.50
a. Imperf. 150.00
R72 R6 $1 Manifest, red 27.50
a. Imperf. 42.50
R73 R6 $1 Mortgage, red 175.00
a. Imperf. 20.00
R74 R6 $1 Passage Ticket, red 200.00
a. Imperf. 250.00
R75 R6 $1 Power of Attorney, red 2.10
a. Imperf. 72.50
R76 R6 $1 Probate of Will, red 35.00
a. Imperf. 70.00
R77 R7 $1.30 For. Exch., orange ('63) 55.00
a. Imperf. *3,000.*
R78 R7 $1.50 Inland Exch., blue 3.25
a. Imperf. 22.50
R79 R7 $1.60 For. Exch., green ('63) 105.00
a. Imperf. 900.00
R80 R7 $1.90 For. Exch., purple ('63) 90.00
a. Imperf. *3,750.*
d. Silk paper —

Many shade and color variations of No. R80. See foreword, "Revenue Stamps."

R81 R8 $2 Conveyance, red 2.75
a. Imperf. 100.00
b. Part perf. 1,300.
d. Silk paper 25.00
R82 R8 $2 Mortgage, red 3.00
a. Imperf. 100.00
d. Silk paper 55.00
R83 R8 $2 Probate of Will, red ('63) 50.00
a. Imperf. *3,250.*
R84 R8 $2.50 Inland Exch., pur ('63) 6.50
a. Imperf. 2,500.
d. Silk paper 20.00
R85 R8 $3 Charter Party, green 5.00
a. Imperf. 110.00
d. Silk paper 80.00
e. Printed on both sides *2,000.*
g. Impression of #RS208 on back *4,000.*
R86 R8 $3 Manifest, green 25.00
a. Imperf. 110.00
R87 R8 $3.50 Inland Exch., blue ('63) 45.00
a. Imperf. *2,750.*
e. Printed on both sides —

Many shade and color variations of the $2.50. See foreword, "Revenue Stamps." The $3.50 has stars in upper corners.

R88 R9 $5 Charter Party, red 6.00
a. Imperf. 240.00
d. Silk paper 65.00
R89 R9 $5 Conveyance, red 6.00
a. Imperf. 35.00
d. Silk paper 60.00
R90 R9 $5 Manifest, red 77.50
a. Imperf. 110.00
R91 R9 $5 Mortgage, red 17.00
a. Imperf. 110.00
R92 R9 $5 Probate of Will, red 17.50
a. Imperf. 475.00
R93 R9 $10 Charter Party, green 25.00
a. Imperf. 550.00
R94 R9 $10 Conveyance, green 60.00
a. Imperf. 90.00
R95 R9 $10 Mortgage, green 25.00
a. Imperf. 350.00
R96 R9 $10 Probate of Will, green 27.50
a. Imperf. 1,150.
R97 R10 $15 Mortgage, blue 120.00
a. Imperf. 1,100.
e. Ultramarine, old paper 190.00
R98 R10 $20 Conveyance, org 60.00
a. Imperf. 125.00
d. Silk paper 110.00
R99 R10 $20 Probate of Will, orange 1,050.
a. Imperf. 1,200.
R100 R10 $25 Mortgage, red ('63) 115.00
a. Imperf. 900.00
d. Silk paper 175.00
e. Horiz. pair, imperf. btwn., old paper *1,100.*
R101 R10 $50 U.S. Int. Rev., green ('63) 90.00
a. Imperf. 190.00
R102 R11 $200 U.S. Int. Rev., green & red ('64) 625.00
a. Imperf. 1,400.

DOCUMENTARY STAMPS

Second Issue

After release of the First Issue revenue stamps, the Bureau of Internal Revenue received many reports of fraudulent cleaning and re-use. The Bureau ordered a Second Issue with new designs and colors, using a patented "chameleon" paper which is usually slightly violet or pinkish, with silk fibers.

R12

R12a

R13a

R13

R13b

Head of Washington in Black within Octagon. Various Frames and Numeral Arrangements.

1871 *Perf. 12*

R103 R12 1c blue & black 35.00
Cut cancel 17.50
a. Inverted center *950.00*
R104 R12 2c blue & black 1.10
Cut cancel .20
a. Inverted center *3,750.*
R105 R12a 3c blue & black 15.00
Cut cancel 8.50
R106 R12a 4c blue & black 60.00
Cut cancel 30.00
R107 R12a 5c blue & black 1.50
Cut cancel .50
a. Inverted center *1,650.*
R108 R12a 6c blue & black 90.00
Cut cancel 50.00
R109 R12a 10c blue & black .90
Cut cancel .15
a. Inverted center *1,650.*
R110 R12a 15c blue & black 25.00
Cut cancel 14.00
R111 R12a 20c blue & black 5.50
Cut cancel 2.50
a. Inverted center *8,000.*

Head of Washington in Black within Circle
Various Frames

R112 R13 25c blue & black .60
Cut cancel .15
a. Inverted center *8,000.*
b. Sewing machine perf. 95.00
c. Perf. 8 275.00
R113 R13 30c blue & black 65.00
Cut cancel 35.00
R114 R13 40c blue & black 40.00
Cut cancel 20.00
R115 R13a 50c blue & black .60
Cut cancel .15
a. Sewing machine perf. 75.00
b. Inverted center 800.00
Inverted center, punch cancellation 220.00
R116 R13a 60c blue & black 90.00
Cut cancel 45.00
R117 R13a 70c blue & black 35.00
Cut cancel 17.50
a. Inverted center *2,750.*
R118 R13b $1 blue & black 3.00
Cut cancel 1.25
a. Inverted center *4,250.*
Invtd. center, punch cancel *750.*
R119 R13b $1.30 blue & black 275.00
Cut cancel 150.00
R120 R13b $1.50 blue & black 12.50
Cut cancel 7.00
a. Sewing machine perf. 450.00
R121 R13b $1.60 blue & black 325.00
Cut cancel 200.00
R122 R13b $1.90 blue & black 165.00
Cut cancel 90.00
R123 R13b $2 blue & black 15.00
Cut cancel 7.50
R124 R13b $2.50 blue & black 27.50
Cut cancel 15.00
R125 R13b $3 blue & black 30.00
Cut cancel 17.50
R126 R13b $3.50 blue & black 150.00
Cut cancel 75.00
R127 R13b $5 blue & black 17.50
Cut cancel 9.00
a. Inverted center *2,400.*
Invtd. center, punch cancel *650.*
R128 R13b $10 blue & black 100.00
Cut cancel 60.00
R129 R13b $20 blue & black 325.00
Cut cancel 200.00
R130 R13b $25 blue & black 325.00
Cut cancel 200.00
R131 R13b $50 blue & black 350.00
Cut cancel 225.00
R132 R13b $200 red, blue & blk *5,000.*
Cut cancel *2,750.*
R133 R13b $500 red org, grn & blk *12,500.*

Fraudulently produced inverted centers exist, some excellently made.

Value for No. R133 is for a very fine appearing example with a light cut cancel or with minor flaws.

Third Issue

Violet "Chameleon" Paper with Silk Fibers. Various Frames and Numeral Arrangements.

1871-72 *Perf. 12*

R134 R12 1c claret & blk ('72) 30.00
Cut cancel 17.50
R135 R12 2c orange & blk .20
Cut cancel .15
a. 2c vermilion & black (error) *550.00*
b. Inverted center 300.00
c. Imperf., pair —
R136 R12a 4c brown & blk ('72) 35.00
Cut cancel 17.50
R137 R12a 5c orange & black .25
Cut cancel .15
a. Inverted center *3,250.*
R138 R12a 6c orange & blk ('72) 35.00
Cut cancel 17.50
R139 R12a 15c brown & blk ('72) 8.50
Cut cancel 4.00
a. Inverted center *8,000.*
R140 R13 30c orange & blk ('72) 14.00
Cut cancel 7.00
a. Inverted center *2,250.*
R141 R13 40c brown & blk ('72) 30.00
Cut cancel 15.00
R142 R13 60c orange & blk ('72) 60.00
Cut cancel 30.00
R143 R13 70c green & blk ('72) 40.00
Cut cancel 20.00
R144 R13b $1 green & blk ('72) 1.35
Cut cancel .55
a. Inverted center *5,500.*
R145 R13b $2 ver & black ('72) 20.00
Cut cancel 12.50
R146 R13b $2.50 claret & blk ('72) 35.00
Cut cancel 20.00
a. Inverted center *13,500.*
R147 R13b $3 green & blk ('72) 35.00
Cut cancel 20.00
R148 R13b $5 ver & black ('72) 20.00
Cut cancel 10.00
R149 R13b $10 green & blk ('72) 75.00
Cut cancel 40.00
R150 R13b $20 orange & blk ('72) 475.00
Cut cancel 250.00
a. $20 vermilion & black (error) 600.00

1874 *Perf. 12*

R151 R12 2c orange & black, *green* .20
Cut cancel .15
a. Inverted center 350.00

Liberty — R14

1875-78

R152 R14 2c blue, *blue,* silk paper .15
b. Wmk. 191R ('78) .15
c. Wmk. 191R, rouletted 32.50
d. Vert. pair, imperf. horiz. 175.00
e. As "b," imperf., pair *250.00*

The rouletted stamps probably were introduced in 1881.

Nos. 279, 267, 279B, 272-274
Overprinted in Red or Blue

I. R.
a

I. R.
b

1898 **Wmk. 191** *Perf. 12*

R153 A87(a) 1c green (R) 3.00 2.50
R154 A87(b) 1c green (R) .15 .15
a. Overprint inverted 20.00 *17.50*
b. Overprint on back instead of face, inverted —
c. Pair, one without ovpt. —
R155 A88(b) 2c pink, type III (Bl) .20 .15
b. 2c carmine, type III .25 *.15*
c. As #R155, overprint inverted 4.50 *2.75*
d. Vert. pair, one without ovpt. *750.00*
e. Horiz. pair, one without ovpt. —
f. As #R155, overprinted on back instead of face, inverted —
R155A A88(b) 2c pink, type IV (Bl) .15 .15
g. 2c carmine, type IV .20 *.15*
h. As #R155A, overprint inverted 2.50 *1.75*

Handstamped Type "b"

R156 A93 8c vio brn *4,000.*
R157 A94 10c dark green *4,000.*
R158 A95 15c dark blue *4,750.*

Nos. R156-R158 were emergency provisionals, privately prepared, not officially issued.

Privately Prepared Provisionals

No. 285 Overprinted in Red

I. R.
L. H. C.

1898 **Wmk. 191** *Perf. 12*

R158A A100 1c dk yel grn *8,500.* *7,750.*

Same Overprinted "I.R./P.I.D. & Son" in Red

R158B A100 1c dk yel grn — *10,000.*

Nos. R158A-R158B were overprinted with federal government permission by the Purvis Printing Co. upon order of Capt. L.H. Chapman of the Chapman Steamboat Line. Both the Chapman line and P.I. Daprix & Son operated freight-carrying steamboats on the Erie Canal. The Chapman Line touched at Syracuse, Utica, Little Falls and Fort Plain; the Daprix boat ran between Utica and Rome. 250 of each stamp were overprinted.

Dr. Kilmer & Co. provisional overprints are listed in the Scott Specialized Catalogue of United States Stamps under Private Die Medicine Stamps, Nos. RS307-RS315.

Newspaper Stamp No. PR121 Surcharged Vertically in Red

INT. REV.
$5.
DOCUMENTARY.

1898 **Wmk. 191** *Perf. 12*

Reading Down

R159 N18 $5 on $5 dk blue 250.00 160.00

Reading Up

R160 N18 $5 on $5 dk blue 110.00 70.00

Battleship R15

Inscribed: "Series of 1898" and "Documentary."

1898 **Wmk. 191R** *Rouletted 5½*

R161 R15 ½c orange 2.00 *7.50*
R162 R15 ½c dark gray .25 .15
a. Vert. pair, imperf. horiz. 60.00
R163 R15 1c pale blue .15 .15
a. Vert. pair, imperf. horiz. 7.50
b. Imperf., pair *300.00*
R164 R15 2c carmine rose .25 .25
a. Vert. pair, imperf. horiz. 47.50
b. Imperf., pair 160.00
c. Horiz. pair, imperf. vert. —
R165 R15 3c dark blue 1.25 .15
R166 R15 4c pale rose .90 .15
a. Vert. pair, imperf. horiz. 90.00
R167 R15 5c lilac .20 .15
a. Pair, imperf. horiz. or vert. 175.00 125.00
b. Horiz. pair, imperf. btwn. *300.00*
R168 R15 10c dark brown 1.25 .15
a. Vert. pair, imperf. horiz. 27.50 27.50
b. Horiz. pair, imperf. vert. —
R169 R15 25c purple brown 1.25 .15
R170 R15 40c blue lilac 110.00 .60
Cut cancellation .30
R171 R15 50c slate violet 12.50 .15
a. Imperf., pair *300.00*
R172 R15 80c bister 65.00 .25
Cut cancellation .15

No. R167b may not be genuine.

Hyphen Hole Perf. 7

R163p 1c .25 .15
R164p 2c .30 .15
R165p 3c 11.00 .50
R166p 4c 4.00 1.10
R167p 5c 4.00 .15
R168p 10c 2.75 .15
R169p 25c 5.00 .25
R170p 40c 150.00 25.00
R171p 50c 20.00 .25
b. Horiz. pair, imperf. btwn. — *250.00*
R172p 80c 150.00 30.00

UNITED STATES

Commerce — R16

1898   Rouletted 5½
R173 R16	$1 dark green	8.00	.15
a.	Vert. pair, imperf. horiz.	—	
b.	Horiz. pair, imperf. vert.	—	300.00
p.	Hyphen hole perf. 7	15.00	.65
R174 R16	$3 dark brown	17.50	.85
	Cut cancellation		.15
a.	Horiz. pair, imperf. vert.		450.00
p.	Hyphen hole perf. 7	20.00	2.25
			.25
R175 R16	$5 orange red	22.50	1.40
	Cut cancellation		.20
R176 R16	$10 black	70.00	2.75
	Cut cancellation		.50
a.	Horiz. pair, imperf. vert.	—	
R177 R16	$30 red	210.00	110.00
	Cut cancellation		45.00
R178 R16	$50 gray brown	100.00	5.50
	Cut cancellation		2.00

There are 2 styles of rouletting for the 1898 proprietary and documentary stamps, an ordinary roulette 5½ and one where small rectangles of the paper are cut out, called hyphen hole perf. 7. Except for Nos. R161, R162 and R175-R178, all the stamps of the two series exist with both roulettes.

See Nos. R182-R183.

John Marshall — R17

Alexander Hamilton R18

James Madison R19

Inscribed "Series of 1898"
1899   Without Gum   Imperf.
R179 R17	$100 yel brn & black	120.00	30.00
	Cut cancellation		20.00
R180 R18	$500 car lake & black	725.00	500.00
	Cut cancellation		225.00
R181 R19	$1000 grn & blk	725.00	300.00
	Cut cancellation		110.00

See Nos. R224-R227, R246-R252, R282-R286.

Type of 1898
1900   Hyphen-Hole Perf. 7
R182 R16	$1 carmine	16.00	.50
	Cut cancellation		.15
R183 R16	$3 lake	120.00	45.00
	Cut cancellation		7.00

Surcharged in Black

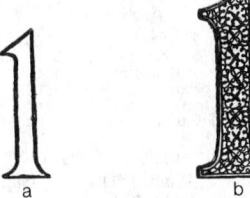

a   b

Surcharged type "a"
1900
R184 R16	$1 gray	11.00	.20
	Cut cancellation		.15
a.	Horiz. pair, imperf. vert.	125.00	
b.	Surcharge omitted		80.00
	As "b", cut cancellation		
R185 R16	$2 gray	9.00	.20
	Cut cancellation		.15
R186 R16	$3 gray	55.00	11.00
	Cut cancellation		3.00
R187 R16	$5 gray	37.50	6.50
	Cut cancellation		1.00
R188 R16	$10 gray	65.00	17.50
	Cut cancellation		3.00
R189 R16	$50 gray	650.00	400.00
	Cut cancellation		85.00

Surcharged type "b"
1902
R190 R16	$1 green	17.50	3.75
	Cut cancellation		.20
a.	Inverted surcharge		175.00
R191 R16	$2 carmine	15.00	1.30
	Cut cancellation		.25
a.	Surcharged as #R185	75.00	75.00
b.	Surch. as #R185, in vio	1,300.	
c.	Double surcharge	100.00	
d.	Triple surcharge		
R192 R16	$5 green	125.00	25.00
	Cut cancellation		4.00
a.	Surcharge omitted	140.00	
b.	Pair, one without surch.	325.00	
R193 R16	$10 green	325.00	125.00
	Cut cancellation		45.00
R194 R16	$50 green	950.00	800.00
	Cut cancellation		225.00

Warning: If Nos. R190-R194 are soaked, the center part of the surcharged numeral may wash off. Before surcharging, a square of soluble varnish was applied to the middle of some stamps.

R20   Liberty — R21

Inscribed "Series of 1914"
Offset Printing
1914   Wmk. 190   Perf. 10
R195 R20	½c rose	7.50	3.50
R196 R20	1c rose	1.40	.15
R197 R20	2c rose	2.00	.15
R198 R20	3c rose	47.50	30.00
R199 R20	4c rose	14.00	2.00
R200 R20	5c rose	4.00	.20
R201 R20	10c rose	3.25	.15
R202 R20	25c rose	27.50	.55
R203 R20	40c rose	17.50	1.00
R204 R20	50c rose	6.00	.15
R205 R20	80c rose	85.00	10.00
	Nos. R195-R205 (11)	215.65	47.85

Wmk. 191R
R206 R20	½c rose	1.50	.50
R207 R20	1c rose	.15	.15
R208 R20	2c rose	.15	.15
R209 R20	3c rose	1.40	.20
R210 R20	4c rose	3.50	.45
R211 R20	5c rose	1.75	.25
R212 R20	10c rose	.60	.15
R213 R20	25c rose	5.00	1.25
R214 R20	40c rose	65.00	12.50
	Cut cancellation		.45
R215 R20	50c rose	15.00	.25
R216 R20	80c rose	95.00	17.50
	Cut cancellation		1.00
	Nos. R206-R216 (11)	189.05	33.35

Engr.
R217 R21	$1 green	30.00	.30
	Cut cancellation		.15
a.	$1 yellow green	—	.15
R218 R21	$2 carmine	45.00	.50
	Cut cancellation		.15
R219 R21	$3 purple	55.00	2.00
	Cut cancellation		.20
R220 R21	$5 blue	47.50	2.75
	Cut cancellation		.15
R221 R21	$10 orange	110.00	5.00
	Cut cancellation		.75

R222 R21	$30 vermilion	225.00	11.00
	Cut cancellation		2.00
R223 R21	$50 violet	1,250.	800.00
	Cut cancellation		350.00

See #R240-R245, R257-R259, R276-R281.

Portrait Types of 1899 Inscribed "Series of 1915" (#R224), or "Series of 1914"
1914-15   Without Gum   Perf. 12
R224 R19	$60 brn (Lincoln)	—	100.00
	Cut cancellation		45.00
R225 R17	$100 grn (Washington)	60.00	40.00
	Cut cancellation		15.00
R226 R18	$500 blue	—	450.00
	Cut cancellation		200.00
R227 R19	$1000 orange	—	350.00
	Cut cancellation		150.00

The stamps of types R17, R18 and R19 in this and subsequent issues are issued in vert. strips of 4 which are imperf. at the top, bottom and right side; therefore, single copies are always imperf. on 1 or 2 sides.

R22

Offset Printing
1917   Wmk. 191R   Perf. 11
Size: 21x18mm
R228 R22	1c carmine rose	.15	.15
R229 R22	2c carmine rose	.15	.15
R230 R22	3c carmine rose	1.25	.35
R231 R22	4c carmine rose	.50	.15
R232 R22	5c carmine rose	.20	.15
R233 R22	8c carmine rose	1.75	.30
R234 R22	10c carmine rose	.35	.15
R235 R22	20c carmine rose	.60	.15
R236 R22	25c carmine rose	1.10	.15
R237 R22	40c carmine rose	1.50	.40
R238 R22	50c carmine rose	2.00	.15
R239 R22	80c carmine rose	5.00	.15
	Nos. R228-R239 (12)	14.55	2.40

Type of 1914 without "Series 1914"
1917-33   Engr.   Size: 18½x27½mm
R240 R21	$1 yellow green	6.50	.15
a.	$1 green	6.50	.15
R241 R21	$2 rose	11.00	.15
R242 R21	$3 violet	35.00	.75
	Cut cancellation		.15
R243 R21	$4 yellow brown ('33)	25.00	1.75
	Cut cancellation		.15
R244 R21	$5 dark blue	15.00	.25
	Cut cancellation		.15
R245 R21	$10 orange	30.00	.90
	Cut cancellation		.15

Portrait Types of 1899-1915 without "Series of" and Date
Portraits: $30, Grant. $100, Washington.
1917   Without Gum   Perf. 12
R246 R17	$30 dp org, grn numerals	45.00	10.00
	Cut cancellation		1.00
a.	Imperf., pair		750.00
b.	Numerals in blue	70.00	1.90
	As "b," cut cancellation		1.00
R247 R17	$60 brown	55.00	7.00
	Cut cancellation		.80
R248 R17	$100 green	32.50	1.00
	Cut cancellation		.35
R249 R18	$500 blue, red numerals	220.00	35.00
	Cut cancellation		10.00
a.	Numerals in orange		50.00
R250 R19	$1000 orange	125.00	12.50
	Cut cancellation		4.00
a.	Imperf., pair		900.00

See note after No. R227.

1928-29   Offset Printing   Perf. 10
R251 R22	2c carmine rose	2.00	1.50
R252 R22	4c carmine rose	.60	.20
R253 R22	4c carmine rose	5.50	3.75
R254 R22	5c carmine rose	1.25	.50
R255 R22	10c carmine rose	1.75	1.25
R256 R22	20c carmine rose	5.50	4.50
	Nos. R251-R256 (6)	16.60	11.70

Engr.
R257 R21	$1 green	85.00	30.00
	Cut cancellation		5.00
R258 R21	$2 rose	32.50	2.50
R259 R21	$10 orange	110.00	40.00
	Cut cancellation		25.00

1929   Offset Printing   Perf. 11x10
R260 R22	2c carmine rose	2.75	2.50
R261 R22	5c carmine rose	2.00	1.75
R262 R22	10c carmine rose	7.50	6.50
R263 R22	20c carmine rose	15.00	8.00

Used values for Nos. R264-R734 are for copies which are neither cut nor perforated with initials. Copies with cut cancellations or perforated initials are valued in the Scott U. S. Specialized Catalogue.

Types of 1917-33 Overprinted in Black   SERIES 1940
1940   Offset Printing   Perf. 11
R264 R22	1c rose pink	2.75	2.25
R265 R22	2c rose pink	2.75	1.75
R266 R22	3c rose pink	8.25	4.00
R267 R22	4c rose pink	3.50	.55
R268 R22	5c rose pink	3.75	.90
R269 R22	8c rose pink	14.00	12.50
R270 R22	10c rose pink	1.75	.45
R271 R22	20c rose pink	2.25	.60
R272 R22	25c rose pink	5.50	1.00
R273 R22	40c rose pink	5.50	.65
R274 R22	50c rose pink	6.00	.50
R275 R22	80c rose pink	10.00	.90
	Nos. R264-R275 (12)	66.00	26.05

Engr.
R276 R21	$1 green	32.50	.80
R277 R21	$2 rose	32.50	1.00
R278 R21	$3 violet	45.00	25.00
R279 R21	$4 yellow brown	80.00	30.00
R280 R21	$5 dark blue	45.00	11.00
R281 R21	$10 orange	100.00	27.50

Types of 1917 Handstamped in Green Like Nos. R264-R281
Without Gum   Perf. 12
R282 R17	$30 vermilion		500.
a.	With black 2-line handstamp in larger type		—
R283 R17	$60 brown		700.
	As #R282a, cut cancel		
R284 R17	$100 green		1,100.
R285 R18	$500 blue		1,400.
a.	As #R282a	2,250.	2,000.
b.	Blue handstamp, double transfer		
R286 R19	$1000 orange		650.

Alexander Hamilton — R23

Levi Woodbury — R24   Thomas Corwin — R25

Portraits: 2c, Oliver Wolcott, Jr. 3c, Samuel Dexter. 4c, Albert Gallatin. 5c, George Washington Campbell. 8c, Alexander Dallas. 10c, William H. Crawford. 20c, Richard Rush. 25c, Samuel D. Ingham. 40c, Louis McLane. 50c, William J. Duane. 80c, Roger B. Taney. $2, Thomas Ewing. $3, Walter Forward. $4, John Canfield Spencer. $5, George M. Bibb. $10, Robert J. Walker. $20, William M. Meredith. $50, James Guthrie. $60, Howell Cobb. $100, P. F. Thomas. $500, John Adams Dix. $1,000, Salmon P. Chase.

Overprinted in Black Like Nos. R264-R281
1940   Size: 19x22mm   Perf. 11
Various Portraits
R288 R23	1c carmine	4.00	3.00
R289 R23	2c carmine	4.50	2.75
R290 R23	3c carmine	17.50	9.00
R291 R23	4c carmine	40.00	20.00
R292 R23	5c carmine	3.00	.60
R293 R23	8c carmine	60.00	45.00
R294 R23	10c carmine	2.50	.45
R295 R23	20c carmine	3.75	2.50
R296 R23	25c carmine	2.75	.50
R297 R23	40c carmine	40.00	18.00
R298 R23	50c carmine	4.50	.40
R299 R23	80c carmine	85.00	60.00
	Nos. R288-R299 (12)	267.50	162.20

Size: 21½x36¼mm
R300 R24	$1 carmine	32.50	.50
R301 R24	$2 carmine	40.00	.75
R302 R24	$3 carmine	125.00	75.00
R303 R24	$4 carmine	65.00	30.00
R304 R24	$5 carmine	40.00	1.50
R305 R24	$10 carmine	70.00	5.00
R305A R24	$20 carmine	1,500.	550.00
b.	Imperf., pair		600.00

116 UNITED STATES

Size: 28½x42mm
Various Frame Designs
Perf. 12
Without Gum

R306	R25	$30 carmine	110.00	40.00
R306A	R25	$50 carmine	—	1,500.
R307	R25	$60 carmine	225.00	55.00
a.		Vert. pair, imperf. between		1,450.
R308	R25	$100 carmine	160.00	60.00
R309	R25	$500 carmine	—	1,250.
R310	R25	$1000 carmine	—	425.00

The $30 to $1,000 denominations in this and following similar issues, and the $2,500, $5,000 and $10,000 stamps of 1952-58 have straight edges on one or two sides. They were issued without gum through No. R723.

Overprinted in Black "SERIES 1941"

1941 Size: 19x22mm *Perf. 11*

R311	R23	1c carmine	3.00	2.25
R312	R23	2c carmine	3.00	.90
R313	R23	3c carmine	7.50	3.50
R314	R23	4c carmine	5.00	1.25
R315	R23	5c carmine	1.00	.25
R316	R23	8c carmine	14.00	7.50
R317	R23	10c carmine	1.25	.15
R318	R23	20c carmine	3.00	.45
R319	R23	25c carmine	1.75	.20
R320	R23	40c carmine	10.00	2.50
R321	R23	50c carmine	2.50	.15
R322	R23	80c carmine	45.00	10.00
		Nos. R311-R322 (12)	97.00	29.10

Size: 21½x36¼mm

R323	R24	$1 carmine	8.50	.25
R324	R24	$2 carmine	10.00	.35
R325	R24	$3 carmine	17.50	2.50
R326	R24	$4 carmine	27.50	15.00
R327	R24	$5 carmine	32.50	.60
R328	R24	$10 carmine	50.00	3.00
R329	R24	$20 carmine	500.00	175.00

Size: 28½x42mm
Perf. 12
Without Gum

R330	R25	$30 carmine	50.00	22.50
R331	R25	$50 carmine	175.00	150.00
R332	R25	$60 carmine	—	42.50
R333	R25	$100 carmine	45.00	17.50
R334	R25	$500 carmine	—	200.00
R335	R25	$1000 carmine	—	100.00

Overprinted in Black "SERIES 1942"

1942 Size: 19x22mm *Perf. 11*

R336	R23	1c carmine	.50	.45
R337	R23	2c carmine	.45	.45
R338	R23	3c carmine	.70	.60
R339	R23	4c carmine	1.20	.90
R340	R23	5c carmine	.45	.20
R341	R23	8c carmine	5.50	4.25
R342	R23	10c carmine	1.20	.25
R343	R23	20c carmine	1.20	.45
R344	R23	25c carmine	2.10	.45
R345	R23	40c carmine	4.75	1.20
R346	R23	50c carmine	3.00	.20
R347	R23	80c carmine	16.00	10.00
		Nos. R336-R347 (12)	37.05	19.40

Size: 21½x36¼mm

R348	R24	$1 carmine	7.50	.25
R349	R24	$2 carmine	9.00	.25
R350	R24	$3 carmine	15.00	2.00
R351	R24	$4 carmine	22.50	3.75
R352	R24	$5 carmine	25.00	.90
R353	R24	$10 carmine	55.00	2.50
R354	R24	$20 carmine	110.00	30.00

Size: 28½x42mm
Perf. 12
Without Gum

R355	R25	$30 carmine	40.00	20.00
R356	R25	$50 carmine	325.00	250.00
R357	R25	$60 carmine	675.00	625.00
R358	R25	$100 carmine	150.00	100.00
R359	R25	$500 carmine	—	200.00
R360	R25	$1000 carmine	—	100.00

Overprinted in Black "SERIES 1943"

1943 Size: 19x22mm *Perf. 11*

R361	R23	1c carmine	.60	.50
R362	R23	2c carmine	.45	.35
R363	R23	3c carmine	2.50	2.50
R364	R23	4c carmine	1.00	1.00
R365	R23	5c carmine	.50	.30
R366	R23	8c carmine	4.00	3.00
R367	R23	10c carmine	.60	.25
R368	R23	20c carmine	1.75	.60
R369	R23	25c carmine	1.50	.25
R370	R23	40c carmine	5.00	2.00
R371	R23	50c carmine	1.25	.15
R372	R23	80c carmine	12.50	5.50
		Nos. R361-R372 (12)	31.65	16.40

Size: 21½x36¼mm

R373	R24	$1 carmine	5.00	.35
R374	R24	$2 carmine	10.00	.25
R375	R24	$3 carmine	17.50	2.00
R376	R24	$4 carmine	22.50	3.00
R377	R24	$5 carmine	27.50	.50
R378	R24	$10 carmine	45.00	3.00
R379	R24	$20 carmine	95.00	20.00

Size: 28½x42mm
Perf. 12
Without Gum

R380	R25	$30 carmine	35.00	18.00
R381	R25	$50 carmine	67.50	25.00
R382	R25	$60 carmine	—	75.00
R383	R25	$100 carmine	—	10.00
R384	R25	$500 carmine	—	175.00
R385	R25	$1000 carmine	—	150.00

Overprinted in Black "Series 1944"

1944 Size: 19x22mm *Perf. 11*

R386	R23	1c carmine	.40	.35
R387	R23	2c carmine	.40	.35
R388	R23	3c carmine	.40	.35
R389	R23	4c carmine	.55	.50
R390	R23	5c carmine	.30	.15
R391	R23	8c carmine	1.75	1.25
R392	R23	10c carmine	.40	.15
R393	R23	20c carmine	.75	.20
R394	R23	25c carmine	1.40	.15
R395	R23	40c carmine	2.75	.60
R396	R23	50c carmine	3.00	.15
R397	R23	80c carmine	12.50	4.00
		Nos. R386-R397 (12)	24.60	8.20

Size: 21½x36¼mm

R398	R24	$1 carmine	5.50	.20
R399	R24	$2 carmine	8.00	.25
R400	R24	$3 carmine	12.50	1.50
R401	R24	$4 carmine	17.50	10.00
R402	R24	$5 carmine	20.00	.25
R403	R24	$10 carmine	37.50	1.25
R404	R24	$20 carmine	80.00	15.00

Size: 28½x42mm
Perf. 12
Without Gum

R405	R25	$30 carmine	50.00	20.00
R406	R25	$50 carmine	20.00	10.00
R407	R25	$60 carmine	100.00	45.00
R408	R25	$100 carmine	—	8.00
R409	R25	$500 carmine	—	1,200.
R410	R25	$1000 carmine	—	165.00

Overprinted in Black "Series 1945"

1945 Size: 19x22mm *Perf. 11*

R411	R23	1c carmine	.20	.20
R412	R23	2c carmine	.25	.20
R413	R23	3c carmine	.50	.45
R414	R23	4c carmine	.30	.30
R415	R23	5c carmine	.25	.15
R416	R23	8c carmine	4.25	2.00
R417	R23	10c carmine	.80	.15
R418	R23	20c carmine	4.50	1.00
R419	R23	25c carmine	1.10	.30
R420	R23	40c carmine	4.75	1.00
R421	R23	50c carmine	2.75	.20
R422	R23	80c carmine	17.50	8.00
		Nos. R411-R422 (12)	37.15	13.95

Size: 21½x36¼mm

R423	R24	$1 carmine	7.00	.15
R424	R24	$2 carmine	7.50	.25
R425	R24	$3 carmine	15.00	2.25
R426	R24	$4 carmine	20.00	3.00
R427	R24	$5 carmine	20.00	.40
R428	R24	$10 carmine	40.00	1.25
R429	R24	$20 carmine	90.00	11.00

Size: 28½x42mm
Without Gum
Perf. 12

R430	R25	$30 carmine	60.00	20.00
R431	R25	$50 carmine	65.00	25.00
R432	R25	$60 carmine	110.00	42.50
R433	R25	$100 carmine	—	12.00
R434	R25	$500 carmine	200.00	160.00
R435	R25	$1000 carmine	100.00	82.50

Overprinted in Black "Series 1946"

1946 Wmk. 191R *Perf. 11*
Size: 19x22mm

R436	R23	1c carmine	.20	.25
R437	R23	2c carmine	.35	.30
R438	R23	3c carmine	.35	.30
R439	R23	4c carmine	.60	.50
R440	R23	5c carmine	.30	.15
R441	R23	8c carmine	1.25	1.10
R442	R23	10c carmine	.70	.15
R443	R23	20c carmine	1.25	.40
R444	R23	25c carmine	4.00	.20
R445	R23	40c carmine	2.50	.75
R446	R23	50c carmine	3.00	.20
R447	R23	80c carmine	10.00	4.00
		Nos. R436-R447 (12)	24.50	8.30

Size: 21½x36¼mm

R448	R24	$1 carmine	7.00	.20
R449	R24	$2 carmine	10.00	.20
R450	R24	$3 carmine	15.00	5.00
R451	R24	$4 carmine	20.00	10.00
R452	R24	$5 carmine	20.00	.45
R453	R24	$10 carmine	40.00	1.50
R454	R24	$20 carmine	80.00	10.00

Size: 28½x42mm
Without Gum
Perf. 12

R455	R25	$30 carmine	40.00	12.00
R456	R25	$50 carmine	20.00	9.00
R457	R25	$60 carmine	40.00	16.00
R458	R25	$100 carmine	45.00	10.00
R459	R25	$500 carmine	—	100.00
R460	R25	$1000 carmine	—	100.00

Overprinted in Black "Series 1947"

1947 Wmk. 191R *Perf. 11*
Size: 19x22mm

R461	R23	1c carmine	.65	.50
R462	R23	2c carmine	.55	.50
R463	R23	3c carmine	.55	.50
R464	R23	4c carmine	.70	.60
R465	R23	5c carmine	.35	.30
R466	R23	8c carmine	1.20	.70
R467	R23	10c carmine	1.10	.25
R468	R23	20c carmine	1.80	.50
R469	R23	25c carmine	2.40	.60
R470	R23	40c carmine	3.75	.90
R471	R23	50c carmine	3.00	.25
R472	R23	80c carmine	8.25	6.00
		Nos. R461-R472 (12)	24.30	11.60

Size: 21½x36¼mm

R473	R24	$1 carmine	5.75	.25
R474	R24	$2 carmine	9.00	.50
R475	R24	$3 carmine	10.00	5.00
R476	R24	$4 carmine	11.00	4.50
R477	R24	$5 carmine	17.50	.50
R478	R24	$10 carmine	40.00	2.00
R479	R24	$20 carmine	60.00	10.00

Size: 28½x42mm
Perf. 12
Without Gum

R480	R25	$30 carmine	60.00	17.50
R481	R25	$50 carmine	30.00	12.00
R482	R25	$60 carmine	75.00	35.00
R483	R25	$100 carmine	30.00	10.00
R484	R25	$500 carmine	—	150.00
R485	R25	$1000 carmine	—	80.00

Overprinted in Black "Series 1948"

1948 Wmk. 191R *Perf. 11*
Size: 19x22mm

R486	R23	1c carmine	.25	.25
R487	R23	2c carmine	.35	.30
R488	R23	3c carmine	.45	.35
R489	R23	4c carmine	.40	.30
R490	R23	5c carmine	.35	.15
R491	R23	8c carmine	.75	.35
R492	R23	10c carmine	.60	.15
R493	R23	20c carmine	1.75	.30
R494	R23	25c carmine	1.50	.20
R495	R23	40c carmine	4.50	1.50
R496	R23	50c carmine	2.25	.15
R497	R23	80c carmine	7.00	4.50
		Nos. R486-R497 (12)	20.15	8.50

Size: 21½x36¼mm

R498	R24	$1 carmine	7.00	.20
R499	R24	$2 carmine	10.00	.20
R500	R24	$3 carmine	14.00	2.50
R501	R24	$4 carmine	20.00	2.75
R502	R24	$5 carmine	17.50	.50
R503	R24	$10 carmine	40.00	1.00
a.		Pair, one dated "1946"		—
R504	R24	$20 carmine	80.00	10.00

Size: 28½x42mm
Perf. 12
Without Gum

R505	R25	$30 carmine	40.00	20.00
R506	R25	$50 carmine	40.00	17.50
a.		Vert. pair, imperf. btwn.		—
R507	R25	$60 carmine	60.00	27.50
a.		Vert. pair, imperf. btwn.	1,100	
R508	R25	$100 carmine	50.00	10.00
a.		Vert. pair, imperf. btwn.	850.00	
R509	R25	$500 carmine	125.00	100.00
R510	R25	$1000 carmine	80.00	60.00

Overprinted in Black "Series 1949"

1949 Wmk. 191R *Perf. 11*
Size: 19x22mm

R511	R23	1c carmine	.25	.25
R512	R23	2c carmine	.55	.35
R513	R23	3c carmine	.40	.35
R514	R23	4c carmine	.60	.50
R515	R23	5c carmine	.35	.20
R516	R23	8c carmine	.70	.60
R517	R23	10c carmine	.40	.25
R518	R23	20c carmine	1.30	.60
R519	R23	25c carmine	1.80	.70
R520	R23	40c carmine	4.25	2.10
R521	R23	50c carmine	3.50	.30
R522	R23	80c carmine	8.50	4.75
		Nos. R511-R522 (12)	22.60	10.95

Size: 21½x36¼mm

R523	R24	$1 carmine	7.00	.40
R524	R24	$2 carmine	9.00	2.00
R525	R24	$3 carmine	14.00	6.00
R526	R24	$4 carmine	17.50	6.00
R527	R24	$5 carmine	17.50	2.25
R528	R24	$10 carmine	40.00	2.50
R529	R24	$20 carmine	80.00	9.00

Size: 28½x42mm
Perf. 12
Without Gum

R530	R25	$30 carmine	50.00	22.50
R531	R25	$50 carmine	60.00	35.00
R532	R25	$60 carmine	—	40.00
R533	R25	$100 carmine	45.00	15.00
R534	R25	$500 carmine	—	180.00
R535	R25	$1000 carmine	—	110.00

Overprinted in Black "Series 1950"

1950 Wmk. 191R *Perf. 11*
Size: 19x22mm

R536	R23	1c carmine	.20	.15
R537	R23	2c carmine	.30	.25
R538	R23	3c carmine	.35	.30
R539	R23	4c carmine	.50	.40
R540	R23	5c carmine	.30	.15
R541	R23	8c carmine	1.25	.65
R542	R23	10c carmine	.60	.20
R543	R23	20c carmine	1.00	.35
R544	R23	25c carmine	1.50	.35
R545	R23	40c carmine	3.25	1.75
R546	R23	50c carmine	4.00	.20
R547	R23	80c carmine	7.00	4.00
		Nos. R536-R547 (12)	20.25	8.75

Size: 21½x36¼mm

R548	R24	$1 carmine	7.00	.20
R549	R24	$2 carmine	9.00	2.00
R550	R24	$3 carmine	10.00	4.00
R551	R24	$4 carmine	14.00	5.00
R552	R24	$5 carmine	17.50	.75
R553	R24	$10 carmine	40.00	7.50
R554	R24	$20 carmine	80.00	8.50

Size: 28½x42mm
Perf. 12
Without Gum

R555	R25	$30 carmine	65.00	40.00
R556	R25	$50 carmine	40.00	14.00
a.		Vert. pair, imperf. horiz.		—
R557	R25	$60 carmine	—	50.00
R558	R25	$100 carmine	50.00	17.50
R559	R25	$500 carmine	—	100.00
R560	R25	$1000 carmine	—	75.00

Overprinted in Black "Series 1951"

1951 Wmk. 191R *Perf. 11*
Size: 19x22mm

R561	R23	1c carmine	.15	.15
R562	R23	2c carmine	.30	.25
R563	R23	3c carmine	.25	.25
R564	R23	4c carmine	.30	.25
R565	R23	5c carmine	.30	.20
R566	R23	8c carmine	1.00	.35
R567	R23	10c carmine	.55	.20
R568	R23	20c carmine	1.25	.45
R569	R23	25c carmine	1.25	.40
R570	R23	40c carmine	3.00	1.25
R571	R23	50c carmine	2.50	.35
R572	R23	80c carmine	6.00	2.50
		Nos. R561-R572 (12)	16.85	6.60

Size: 21½x36¼mm

R573	R24	$1 carmine	7.00	.20
R574	R24	$2 carmine	9.00	.50
R575	R24	$3 carmine	12.50	3.50
R576	R24	$4 carmine	17.50	5.00
R577	R24	$5 carmine	14.00	.60
R578	R24	$10 carmine	35.00	2.25
R579	R24	$20 carmine	75.00	8.50

Size: 28½x42mm
Perf. 12
Without Gum

R580	R25	$30 carmine	—	10.00
a.		Imperf., pair		750.00
R581	R25	$50 carmine	50.00	15.00
R582	R25	$60 carmine	—	40.00
R583	R25	$100 carmine	40.00	12.50
R584	R25	$500 carmine	125.00	82.50
R585	R25	$1000 carmine	—	95.00

Overprinted in Black "Series 1952"

Designs: 55c, $1.10, $1.65, $2.20, $2.75, $3.30, L. J. Gage; $2500, William Windom; $5000, C. J. Folger; $10,000, W. Q. Gresham.

1952 Wmk. 191R *Perf. 11*
Size: 19x22mm

R586	R23	1c carmine	.20	.15
R587	R23	2c carmine	.35	.25
R588	R23	3c carmine	.30	.25
R589	R23	4c carmine	.30	.25
R590	R23	5c carmine	.25	.15
R591	R23	8c carmine	.65	.45
R592	R23	10c carmine	.40	.20
R593	R23	20c carmine	1.00	.35
R594	R23	25c carmine	1.50	.40
R595	R23	40c carmine	3.00	1.00
R596	R23	50c carmine	2.75	.20
R597	R23	55c carmine	17.50	10.00
R598	R23	80c carmine	10.00	3.00
		Nos. R586-R598 (13)	38.20	16.65

Size: 21½x36¼mm

R599	R24	$1 carmine	5.00	1.50
R600	R24	$1.10 carmine	35.00	25.00
R601	R24	$1.65 carmine	125.00	45.00
R602	R24	$2 carmine	9.00	.65
R603	R24	$2.20 carmine	100.00	60.00

UNITED STATES 117

R604	R24	$2.75 carmine	110.00	60.00
R605	R24	$3 carmine	20.00	4.00
a.		Horiz. pair, imperf. btwn.	500.00	
R606	R24	$3.30 carmine	100.00	60.00
R607	R24	$4 carmine	17.50	4.00
R608	R24	$5 carmine	17.50	1.25
R609	R24	$10 carmine	35.00	1.25
R610	R24	$20 carmine	60.00	9.00

Size: 28 1/2x42mm

Perf. 12

Without Gum

R611	R25	$30 carmine	45.00	18.00
R612	R25	$50 carmine	40.00	12.00
R613	R25	$60 carmine	150.00	50.00
R614	R25	$100 carmine	35.00	8.00
R615	R25	$500 carmine	—	100.00
R616	R25	$1000 carmine	—	30.00
R617	R25	$2500 carmine	—	150.00
R618	R25	$5000 carmine	—	1,400.
R619	R25	$10,000 carmine	—	*1,250.*

Overprinted in Black "Series 1953"

1953 Wmk. 191R *Perf. 11*

Size: 19x22mm

R620	R23	1c carmine	.20	.15
R621	R23	2c carmine	.20	.15
R622	R23	3c carmine	.25	.20
R623	R23	4c carmine	.35	.25
R624	R23	5c carmine	.20	.15
a.		Vert. pair, imperf. horiz.	650.00	
R625	R23	8c carmine	.75	.35
R626	R23	10c carmine	.40	.20
R627	R23	20c carmine	.75	.40
R628	R23	25c carmine	1.00	.50
R629	R23	40c carmine	1.75	1.00
R630	R23	50c carmine	2.50	.20
R631	R23	55c carmine	3.50	2.00
a.		Horiz. pair, imperf. vert.	350.00	
R632	R23	80c carmine	6.00	2.00
		Nos. R620-R632 (13)	17.85	7.55

Size: 21 1/2x36 1/4mm

R633	R24	$1 carmine	4.00	.25
R634	R24	$1.10 carmine	7.00	2.25
a.		Horiz. pair, imperf. vert.	500.00	
b.		Imperf., pair	550.00	
R635	R24	$1.65 carmine	8.00	4.00
R636	R24	$2 carmine	6.00	.65
R637	R24	$2.20 carmine	10.00	6.00
R638	R24	$2.75 carmine	14.00	7.00
R639	R24	$3 carmine	8.00	3.00
R640	R24	$3.30 carmine	22.50	8.00
R641	R24	$4 carmine	16.00	7.50
R642	R24	$5 carmine	16.00	1.00
R643	R24	$10 carmine	35.00	1.75
R644	R24	$20 carmine	70.00	18.00

Size: 28 1/2x42mm

Perf. 12

Without Gum

R645	R25	$30 carmine	40.00	12.00
R646	R25	$50 carmine	75.00	25.00
R647	R25	$60 carmine	300.00	175.00
R648	R25	$100 carmine	35.00	12.00
R649	R25	$500 carmine	250.00	115.00
R650	R25	$1000 carmine	125.00	57.50
R651	R25	$2500 carmine	550.00	500.00
R652	R25	$5000 carmine	—	*1,500.*
R653	R25	$10,000 carmine	—	*1,500.*

Types of 1940 without Overprint

1954 Wmk. 191R *Perf. 11*

Size: 19x22mm

R654	R23	1c carmine	.15	.15
a.		Horiz. pair, imperf. vert.	—	
R655	R23	2c carmine	.15	.15
R656	R23	3c carmine	.15	.15
R657	R23	4c carmine	.15	.15
R658	R23	5c carmine	.15	.15
R659	R23	8c carmine	.25	.20
R660	R23	10c carmine	.25	.20
R661	R23	20c carmine	.50	.30
R662	R23	25c carmine	.60	.35
R663	R23	40c carmine	1.25	.60
R664	R23	50c carmine	1.65	.20
a.		Horiz. pair, imperf. vert	275.00	
R665	R23	55c carmine	1.50	1.25
R666	R23	80c carmine	2.25	1.75
		Nos. R654-R666 (13)	9.00	5.60

Size: 21 1/2x36 1/4mm

R667	R24	$1 carmine	1.50	.30
R668	R24	$1.10 carmine	3.25	2.50
R669	R24	$1.65 carmine	90.00	60.00
R670	R24	$2 carmine	1.75	.35
R671	R24	$2.20 carmine	4.50	3.75
R672	R24	$2.75 carmine	95.00	55.00
R673	R24	$3 carmine	3.00	2.00
R674	R24	$3.30 carmine	6.50	5.00
R675	R24	$4 carmine	4.00	3.50
R676	R24	$5 carmine	6.00	.45
R677	R24	$10 carmine	12.50	1.25
R678	R24	$20 carmine	27.50	5.75

Overprinted in Black "Series 1954"

Perf. 12

Size: 28 1/2x42mm

Without Gum

R679	R25	$30 carmine	30.00	12.00
R680	R25	$50 carmine	40.00	15.00
R681	R25	$60 carmine	65.00	20.00
R682	R25	$100 carmine	30.00	7.00
R683	R25	$500 carmine	—	75.00
R684	R25	$1000 carmine	150.00	55.00
R685	R25	$2500 carmine	—	175.00
R686	R25	$5000 carmine	—	850.00
R687	R25	$10,000 carmine	—	500.00

Overprinted in Black "Series 1955"
Without Gum

1955 Wmk. 191R *Perf. 12*

Size: 28 1/2x42mm

R688	R25	$30 carmine	40.00	11.50
R689	R25	$50 carmine	40.00	13.50
R690	R25	$60 carmine	70.00	24.00
R691	R25	$100 carmine	35.00	7.00
R692	R25	$500 carmine	—	125.00
R693	R25	$1000 carmine	—	35.00
R694	R25	$2500 carmine	—	130.00
R695	R25	$5000 carmine	*1,000.*	900.00
R696	R25	$10,000 carmine	—	600.00

Overprinted in Black
"Series 1956"
Without Gum

1956 Size: 28 1/2x42mm

R697	R25	$30 carmine	50.00	13.50
R698	R25	$50 carmine	55.00	17.00
R699	R25	$60 carmine	—	32.50
R700	R25	$100 carmine	50.00	12.50
R701	R25	$500 carmine	—	80.00
R702	R25	$1000 carmine	—	55.00
R703	R25	$2500 carmine	—	275.00
R704	R25	$5000 carmine	—	1,400.
R705	R25	$10,000 carmine	—	500.00

Overprinted in Black "Series 1957"
Without Gum

1957 Size: 28 1/2x42mm

R706	R25	$30 carmine	65.00	27.50
R707	R25	$50 carmine	50.00	24.00
R708	R25	$60 carmine	—	150.00
R709	R25	$100 carmine	45.00	12.50
R710	R25	$500 carmine	175.00	85.00
R711	R25	$1000 carmine	—	80.00
R712	R25	$2500 carmine	—	525.00
R713	R25	$5000 carmine	—	600.00
R714	R25	$10,000 carmine	—	450.00

Overprinted in Black "Series 1958"
Without Gum

1958 Size: 28 1/2x42mm

R715	R25	$30 carmine	75.00	20.00
R716	R25	$50 carmine	60.00	20.00
R717	R25	$60 carmine	—	25.00
R718	R25	$100 carmine	50.00	10.00
R719	R25	$500 carmine	125.00	55.00
R720	R25	$1000 carmine	—	67.50
R721	R25	$2500 carmine	—	750.00
R722	R25	$5000 carmine	—	1,750.
R723	R25	$10,000 carmine	—	900.00

Documentary Stamps and Type of 1940
Without Overprint
With Gum

1958 Size: 28 1/2x42mm

R724	R25	$30 carmine	35.00	7.00
a.		Vert. pair, imperf. horiz.	—	
R725	R25	$50 carmine	37.50	7.00
a.		Vert. pair, imperf. horiz.	—	
R726	R25	$60 carmine	75.00	20.00
R727	R25	$100 carmine	17.50	4.75
R728	R25	$500 carmine	80.00	25.00
R729	R25	$1000 carmine	50.00	20.00
a.		Vert. pair, imperf. horiz.		*600.00*
R730	R25	$2500 carmine	—	140.00
R731	R25	$5000 carmine	—	150.00
R732	R25	$10,000 carmine	—	125.00

Catalogue values for unused stamps in this section, from this point to the end of the section, are for Never Hinged items.

Internal Revenue Building, Washington, DC — R26

Giori Press Printing

1962, July 1 Unwmk. *Perf. 11*

R733	R26	10c vio bl & brt grn	1.10	.35

Centenary of Internal Revenue Service.

"Established 1862" Removed

1963

R734	R26	10c vio blue & brt green	3.25	.35

Documentary revenue stamps were no longer required after Dec. 31, 1967.

PROPRIETARY STAMPS

Stamps for use on proprietary articles were included in the first general issue of 1862-71. They are Nos. R3, R13, R14, R18, R22, R29, R31 and R38.

Washington — RB1

Various Frames and Sizes
Violet or Green Paper with Silk Threads

1871-74 Engr. *Perf. 12*

a. left column = Violet Paper (1871)

b. right column = Green Paper (1874)

RB1	RB1	1c green & blk	5.00	7.50
c.		Imperf.	80.00	
d.		Inverted center	*2,500.*	
RB2	RB1	2c green & blk	6.00	15.00
c.		Invtd. center, *violet*	*40,000.*	
d.		Invtd. center, *green*		8,500.
RB3	RB1	3c green & blk	15.00	45.00
c.		Sewing machine perf.	225.00	
d.		Inverted center	*16,000.*	
RB4	RB1	4c green & blk	10.00	15.00
c.		Inverted center	*22,500.*	
RB5	RB1	5c green & blk	130.00	140.00
c.		Inverted center	*80,000.*	
RB6	RB1	6c green & blk	35.00	85.00
RB7	RB1	10c green & blk ('73)	175.00	45.00
RB8	RB1	50c green & blk ('73)	500.00	900.00
RB9	RB1	$1 green & blk ('73)	*1,100.*	*3,750.*
RB10	RB1	$5 green & blk ('73)	*3,000.*	*27,500.*

Washington — RB2

Various Frames and Sizes
Green Paper

Wmk. 191R, Unwmkd. (Silk Paper)

1875-81

b. left column = Perf.

c. right column = Rouletted 6

RB11	RB2	1c green	.40	65.00
a.		Silk paper	1.90	
d.		Vert. pair, imperf btwn.		*250.00*
RB12	RB2	2c brown	1.40	80.00
a.		Silk paper	2.50	
RB13	RB2	3c orange	3.00	80.00
a.		Silk paper	12.50	
d.		Horiz. pair, imperf. btwn.		—
RB14	RB2	4c red brown	5.50	
a.		Silk paper	6.00	
RB15	RB2	4c red	4.50	125.00
RB16	RB2	5c black	90.00	*1,250.*
a.		Silk paper	110.00	
RB17	RB2	6c violet blue	20.00	225.00
a.		Silk paper	25.00	
RB18	RB2	6c violet	30.00	—
RB19	RB2	10c blue ('81)	300.00	

Many fraudulent roulettes exist.

Battleship — RB3

Rouletted 5 1/2

1898 Wmk. 191R Engr.

RB20	RB3	1/8c yellow green	.15	.15
a.		Vert. pair, imperf. horiz.	—	
RB21	RB3	1/4c brown	.15	.15
a.		1/4c red brown	.15	.15
b.		1/4c yellow brown	.15	.15
c.		1/4c orange brown	.15	.15
d.		1/4c bister	.15	.15
e.		Vert. pair, imperf. horiz.	—	—
f.		Printed on both sides	—	
RB22	RB3	3/8c deep orange	.15	.15
a.		Horiz. pair, imperf. vert.	11.00	
b.		Vert. pair, imperf. horiz.	—	
RB23	RB3	5/8c deep ultra	.15	.15
a.		Vert. pair, imperf. horiz.	60.00	
b.		Horiz. pair, imperf. btwn.	*250.00*	
RB24	RB3	1c dark green	1.00	.15
a.		Vert. pair, imperf. horiz.	*300.00*	
RB25	RB3	1 1/4c violet	.15	.15
a.		1 1/4c brown violet	.15	.15
b.		Vert. pair, imperf. btwn.	—	
RB26	RB3	1 7/8c dull blue	7.50	1.00
RB27	RB3	2c vio brown	.75	.20
a.		Horiz. pair, imperf. vert.	35.00	
RB28	RB3	2 1/2c lake	2.50	.15
a.		Vert. pair, imperf. horiz.	125.00	
RB29	RB3	3 3/4c olive gray	30.00	7.00
RB30	RB3	4c purple	7.50	.75
RB31	RB3	5c brown org	7.50	.75
a.		Vert. pair, imperf. horiz.	—	*300.00*
b.		Horiz. pair, imperf. vert.	—	*400.00*
		Nos. RB20-RB31 (12)	57.50	10.75

Hyphen Hole Perf. 7

RB20p	1/8c	.15	.15
RB21p	1/4c	.15	.20
g.	1/4c yellow brown	.15	.20
h.	1/4c orange brown	.15	.20
RB22p	3/8c	.25	.20
RB23p	5/8c	.25	.20
RB24p	1c	25.00	15.00
RB25p	1 1/4c	.20	.15
c.	1 1/4c brown violet	.20	.15
RB26p	1 7/8c	20.00	6.75
RB27p	2c	4.00	.30
RB28p	2 1/2c	2.50	.25
RB29p	3 3/4c	50.00	15.00
RB30p	4c	50.00	15.00
RB31p	5c	50.00	7.50

See note following No. R178.

RB4

RB5

Offset Printing

1914 Wmk. 190 *Perf. 10*

RB32	RB4	1/8c black	.20	.15
RB33	RB4	1/4c black	1.75	1.00
RB34	RB4	3/8c black	.20	.15
RB35	RB4	5/8c black	3.50	1.75
RB36	RB4	1 1/4c black	2.50	.80
RB37	RB4	1 7/8c black	35.00	15.00
RB38	RB4	2 1/2c black	7.50	2.50
RB39	RB4	3 1/8c black	80.00	50.00
RB40	RB4	3 3/4c black	35.00	20.00
RB41	RB4	4c black	50.00	27.50
RB42	RB4	4 3/8c black	*1,100.*	—
RB43	RB4	5c black	110.00	70.00
		Nos. RB32-RB41,RB43 (11)	325.65	188.85

Wmk. 191R

RB44	RB4	1/8c black	.20	.15
RB45	RB4	1/4c black	.20	.15
RB46	RB4	3/8c black	.60	.30
RB47	RB4	1/2c black	3.00	2.75
RB48	RB4	5/8c black	.20	.15
RB49	RB4	1c black	4.25	4.00
RB50	RB4	1 1/4c black	.35	.25
RB51	RB4	1 1/2c black	3.00	2.25
RB52	RB4	1 7/8c black	1.00	.60
RB53	RB4	2c black	5.00	4.00
RB54	RB4	2 1/2c black	1.25	1.00
RB55	RB4	3c black	4.00	2.75
RB56	RB4	3 1/8c black	5.00	3.00
RB57	RB4	3 3/4c black	11.00	7.50
RB58	RB4	4c black	.30	.20
RB59	RB4	4 3/8c black	14.00	8.00
RB60	RB4	5c black	3.00	2.50
RB61	RB4	6c black	55.00	40.00
RB62	RB4	8c black	17.50	11.00
RB63	RB4	10c black	11.00	7.00
RB64	RB4	20c black	22.50	17.50
		Nos. RB44-RB64 (21)	162.35	115.05

1919 *Perf. 11*

RB65	RB5	1c dark blue	.15	.15
RB66	RB5	2c dark blue	.15	.15
RB67	RB5	3c dark blue	1.00	.60
RB68	RB5	4c dark blue	1.00	.50
RB69	RB5	5c dark blue	1.25	.60
RB70	RB5	8c dark blue	14.00	9.00
RB71	RB5	10c dark blue	5.00	2.00
RB72	RB5	20c dark blue	7.50	3.00
RB73	RB5	40c dark blue	45.00	10.00
		Nos. RB65-RB73 (9)	75.05	26.00

FUTURE DELIVERY STAMPS

Issued to facilitate the collection of a tax upon each sale, agreement of sale or agreement to sell any products or merchandise at any exchange or board of trade, or other similar place for future delivery.

Documentary Stamps Nos. R228 to R250 Overprinted in Black or Red

FUTURE

DELIVERY

Offset Printing

1918-34 Wmk. 191R *Perf. 11*

Overprint Horizontal

(Lines 8mm apart)

RC1	R22	2c car rose	3.50	.15
RC2	R22	3c car rose ('34)	30.00	22.50
		Cut cancellation		12.50
RC3	R22	4c car rose	6.00	.15
RC3A	R22	5c car rose ('33)	75.00	5.00

118 UNITED STATES

RC4 R22 10c car rose 11.00 .15
a. Double overprint — 5.00
b. "FUTURE" omitted — 200.00
c. "DELIVERY FUTURE" 35.00
RC5 R22 20c car rose 15.00 .15
a. Double overprint 20.00
RC6 R22 25c car rose 35.00 .40
Cut cancellation .15
RC7 R22 40c car rose 40.00 .75
Cut cancellation .15
RC8 R22 50c car rose 8.50 .15
a. "DELIVERY" omitted — 100.00
RC9 R22 80c car rose 75.00 10.00
Cut cancellation 1.00
a. Double overprint 35.00
Cut cancellation 6.00
Nos. RC1-RC9 (10) 299.00 39.40

Overprint Vertical, Reading Up (Lines 2mm apart)

Engr.

RC10 R21 $1 green (R) 30.00 .25
Cut cancellation .15
a. Overprint reading down 275.00
b. Black overprint —
Cut cancellation 125.00
RC11 R21 $2 rose 35.00 .25
Cut cancellation .15
RC12 R21 $3 violet (R) 80.00 2.50
Cut cancellation .15
a. Overprint reading down — 50.00
RC13 R21 $5 dark blue (R) 60.00 .35
Cut cancellation .15
RC14 R21 $10 orange 80.00 .75
Cut cancellation .15
a. "DELIVERY FUTURE" 100.00
RC15 R21 $20 olive bis 150.00 4.00
Cut cancellation .50
Nos. RC10-RC15 (6) 435.00 8.10

Perf. 12

Overprint Horizontal (Lines 11 1/2mm apart)

Without Gum

RC16 R17 $30 ver, green numerals 70.00 3.50
Cut cancellation 1.25
a. Numerals in blue 60.00 3.50
Cut cancellation 1.50
b. As "a," imperf. 100.00
RC17 R19 $50 olive green 47.50 1.25
Cut cancellation .40
a. $50 olive bister 47.50 1.00
Cut cancellation .40
RC18 R19 $60 brown 70.00 2.25
Cut cancellation .75
a. Vert. pair, imperf. horiz. 400.00
RC19 R17 $100 yel green ('34) 80.00 27.50
Cut cancellation 7.00
RC20 R18 $500 blue, red numerals (R) 70.00 11.00
Cut cancellation 4.50
a. Numerals in orange — 50.00
Cut cancellation 11.00
RC21 R19 $1000 orange 85.00 5.50
Cut cancellation 1.50
a. Vert. pair, imperf. horiz. 900.00
Nos. RC16-RC21 (6) 422.50 51.00

See note after No. R227.

1923-24 Offset Printing *Perf. 11*

Overprint Horiz. (Lines 2mm apart)

RC22 R22 1c carmine rose 1.00 .20
RC23 R22 80c carmine rose 65.00 1.75
Cut cancellation .35

FUTURE

Documentary Stamps of 1917 Overprinted in Red or Black

DELIVERY

1925-34 Engr.

RC25 R21 $1 green (R) 27.50 .75
Cut cancellation .15
RC26 R21 $10 orange (Bk) ('34) 90.00 15.00
Cut cancellation 10.00

Overprinted like Nos. RC1-RC9

1928-29 Offset Printing *Perf. 10*

RC27 R22 10c carmine rose *1,500.*
RC28 R22 20c carmine rose *1,500.*

STOCK TRANSFER STAMPS

Issued to facilitate the collection of a tax on all sales or agreements to sell, or memoranda of sales or delivery of, or transfers of legal title to shares or certificates of stock.

STOCK

Documentary Stamps Nos. R228 to R259 Overprinted in Black or Red

TRANSFER

Offset Printing

1918-29 Wmk. 191R *Perf. 11*

Overprint Horiz. (Lines 8mm apart)

RD1 R22 1c car rose .85 .15
a. Double overprint — —
RD2 R22 2c car rose .20 .15
a. Double overprint — 5.00
Cut cancellation 2.50
RD3 R22 4c car rose .20 .15
a. Double overprint — 4.00
Cut cancellation 2.00
b. "STOCK" omitted 10.00
d. Overprint lines 10mm apart —
RD4 R22 5c car rose .25 .15
RD5 R22 10c car rose .25 .15
a. Double overprint 5.00
Cut cancellation 2.50
b. "STOCK" omitted —
RD6 R22 20c car rose .50 .15
a. Double overprint 6.00
b. "STOCK" double —
RD7 R22 25c car rose 1.50 .20
Cut cancellation .15
RD8 R22 40c car rose ('22) 1.25 .15
RD9 R22 50c car rose .65 .15
a. Double overprint —
RD10 R22 80c car rose 3.00 .30
Cut cancellation .15
Nos. RD1-RD10 (10) 8.65 1.70

Overprint Vertical, Reading Up (Lines 2mm apart)

Engr.

RD11 R21 $1 green (R) 70.00 20.00
Cut cancellation 3.00
a. Ovpt. reading down 125.00 20.00
Cut cancellation 7.50
RD12 R21 $1 green (Bk) 2.50 .25
a. Pair, one without ovpt. — 150.00
b. Ovptd. on back instead of face, inverted — 100.00
c. Ovpt. reading down — 6.00
d. $1 yellow green 2.75 .15
RD13 R21 $2 rose 2.50 .15
a. Ovpt. reading down 10.00
Cut cancellation 1.50
b. Vert. pair, imperf. horiz. 500.00
RD14 R21 $3 violet (R) 17.50 4.25
Cut cancellation .20
RD15 R21 $4 yellow brn 9.00 .15
Cut cancellation .15
RD16 R21 $5 dk blue (R) 6.00 .15
Cut cancellation .15
a. Ovpt. reading down 20.00 1.00
Cut cancellation .16
RD17 R21 $10 orange 16.00 .30
Cut cancellation .15
RD18 R21 $20 ol bis ('21) 75.00 20.00
Cut cancellation 3.00
Nos. RD11-RD18 (8) 198.50 45.25

1918 Without Gum *Perf. 12*

Overprint Horizontal (Lines 11 1/2mm apart)

RD19 R17 $30 ver, green numerals 17.50 4.50
Cut cancellation 1.00
a. Numerals in blue 55.00
RD20 R19 $50 olive green, *(Cleveland)* 110.00 55.00
Cut cancellation 20.00
RD21 R19 $60 brown 110.00 20.00
Cut cancellation 9.00
RD22 R17 $100 green 22.50 5.50
Cut cancellation 2.25
RD23 R18 $500 blue (R) 300.00 110.00
Cut cancellation 65.00
a. Numerals in orange 140.00
RD24 R19 $1000 orange 165.00 72.50
Cut cancellation 25.00

See note after No. R227.

1928-32 Offset Printing *Perf. 10*

Overprint Horiz. (Lines 8mm apart)

RD25 R22 2c carmine rose 2.50 .25
RD26 R22 4c carmine rose 2.50 .25
RD27 R22 10c carmine rose 2.00 .25
a. Inverted overprint *1,000.*
RD28 R22 20c carmine rose 3.00 .25
RD29 R22 50c carmine rose 3.50 .25

Overprint Vertical, Reading Up (Lines 2mm apart)

Engr.

RD30 R21 $1 green 30.00 .20
a. $1 yellow green — —
RD31 R21 $2 car rose 30.00 .15
a. Pair, one without overprint 200.00 175.00
RD32 R21 $10 orange 32.50 .35
Cut cancellation .15
Nos. RD25-RD32 (8) 106.00 1.95

STOCK

Overprinted Horiz. in Black

TRANSFER

1920-28 Offset Printing *Perf. 11*

RD33 R22 2c carmine rose 7.50 .70
RD34 R22 10c carmine rose 1.25 .30
b. Inverted overprint *1,500.*
RD35 R22 20c carmine rose 1.00 .20
a. Horiz. pair, one without overprint 175.00
d. Inverted overprint (perf. initials) —
RD36 R22 50c carmine rose 3.00 .20

Engr.

RD37 R21 $1 green 40.00 8.00
Cut cancellation .25
RD38 R21 $2 rose 35.00 8.00
Cut cancellation .25
Nos. RD33-RD38 (6) 87.75 17.40

Shifted overprints on the 10c, 20c and 50c result in "TRANSFER STOCK," "TRANSFER" omitted, "STOCK" omitted, pairs, one without overprint and other varieties.

Perf. 10

Offset Printing

RD39 R22 2c carmine rose 6.00 .50
RD40 R22 10c carmine rose 1.25 .50
RD41 R22 20c carmine rose 2.25 .25
Nos. RD39-RD41 (3) 9.50 1.25

Used values for Nos. RD42-RD372 are for copies which are neither cut nor perforated with initials. Copies with cut cancellations or perforated initials are valued in the Scott U.S. Specialized Catalogue.

SERIES 1940

Documentary Stamps of 1917-33 Overprinted in Black

STOCK TRANSFER

1940 *Perf. 11*

RD42 R22 1c rose pink 3.00 .45
a. "Series 1940" inverted — 225.00
RD43 R22 2c rose pink 3.00 .50
RD45 R22 4c rose pink 3.00 .20
RD46 R22 5c rose pink 3.50 .20
RD48 R22 10c rose pink 3.50 .20
RD49 R22 20c rose pink 7.50 .20
RD50 R22 25c rose pink 7.50 .60
RD51 R22 40c rose pink 5.00 .75
RD52 R22 50c rose pink 6.00 .25
RD53 R22 80c rose pink 90.00 50.00
Nos. RD42-RD53 (10) 132.00 53.35

Engr.

RD54 R21 $1 green 20.00 .35
RD55 R21 $2 rose 20.00 .60
RD56 R21 $3 violet 125.00 9.00
RD57 R21 $4 yel brown 45.00 1.00
RD58 R21 $5 dark blue 45.00 1.00
RD59 R21 $10 orange 100.00 6.00
RD60 R21 $20 olive bister 225.00 75.00
Nos. RD54-RD60 (7) 580.00 92.95

Stock Transfer Stamps of 1918 Handstamped in Blue "Series 1940"

1940 Without Gum *Perf. 12*

RD61 R17 $30 vermilion *900.* 550.
RD62 R19 $50 olive green *900.* 750.
a. Dbl. ovpt. (perf. initials canc.) *350.*
RD63 R19 $60 brown 1,150.
RD64 R17 $100 green 750. 550.
RD65 R18 $500 blue 2,200.
RD66 R19 $1000 orange 2,400.

Alexander Hamilton — ST1

Levi Woodbury — ST2 Thomas Corwin — ST3

Portraits (see R23-R25): 2c, Wolcott. 4c, Gallatin. 5c, Campbell. 10c, Crawford. 20c, Rush. 25c, Ingham. 40c, McLane. 50c, Duane. 80c, Taney. $2, Ewing. $3, Forward. $4, Spencer. $5, Bibb. $10, Walker. $20, Meredith. $50, Guthrie. $60, Cobb. $100, Thomas. $500, Dix. $1,000, Chase.

Overprinted in Black **SERIES 1940**

1940 Wmk. 191R *Perf. 11*

Various Portraits

Size: 19x22mm

RD67 ST1 1c brt green 9.00 2.75
RD68 ST1 2c brt green 5.50 1.40
RD70 ST1 4c brt green 10.00 3.75
RD71 ST1 5c brt green 6.00 1.40
a. Without overprint (cut canc.) 250.00
RD73 ST1 10c brt green 8.50 1.75
RD74 ST1 20c brt green 10.00 2.00
RD75 ST1 25c brt green 27.50 8.00
RD76 ST1 40c brt green 55.00 30.00
RD77 ST1 50c brt green 8.50 1.75
RD78 ST1 80c brt green 70.00 50.00
Nos. RD67-RD78 (10) 210.00 102.80

Size: 21 1/2x36 1/4mm

RD79 ST2 $1 brt green 30.00 3.50
a. Without overprint (perf. initials canc.) 225.00
RD80 ST2 $2 brt green 35.00 8.50
RD81 ST2 $3 brt green 55.00 10.00
RD82 ST2 $4 brt green 250.00 200.00
RD83 ST2 $5 brt green 50.00 12.50
RD84 ST2 $10 brt green 125.00 35.00
RD85 ST2 $20 brt green 450.00 70.00

Perf. 12

Without Gum

Size: 28 1/2x42mm

Various Frame Designs

RD86 ST3 $30 brt green — 140.00
RD87 ST3 $50 brt green 300.00 250.00
RD88 ST3 $60 brt green — 400.00
RD89 ST3 $100 brt green — 175.00
RD90 ST3 $500 brt green — 1,100.
RD91 ST3 $1000 brt green — 1,100.

Overprinted in Black "Series 1941" **SERIES 1941**

1941 Size: 19x22mm *Perf. 11*

RD92 ST1 1c brt green .65 .50
RD93 ST1 2c brt green .45 .25
RD95 ST1 4c brt green .40 .20
RD96 ST1 5c brt green .35 .15
RD98 ST1 10c brt green .75 .15
RD99 ST1 20c brt green 1.75 .25
RD100 ST1 25c brt green 1.75 .40
RD101 ST1 40c brt green 2.50 .75
RD102 ST1 50c brt green 3.75 .35
RD103 ST1 80c brt green 20.00 7.50
Nos. RD92-RD103 (10) 32.35 10.50

Size: 21 1/2x36 1/4mm

RD104 ST2 $1 brt green 11.00 .20
RD105 ST2 $2 brt green 12.50 .25
RD106 ST2 $3 brt green 19.00 1.50
RD107 ST2 $4 brt green 35.00 6.50
RD108 ST2 $5 brt green 35.00 .60
RD109 ST2 $10 brt green 75.00 4.00
RD110 ST2 $20 brt green 140.00 55.00
Nos. RD104-RD110 (7) 327.50 68.05

Perf. 12

Without Gum

Size: 28 1/2x42mm

RD111 ST3 $30 brt green 140.00 125.00
RD112 ST3 $50 brt green 240.00 175.00
RD113 ST3 $60 brt green 450.00 175.00
RD114 ST3 $100 brt green — 75.00
RD115 ST3 $500 brt green 875.00 *1,000.*
RD116 ST3 $1000 brt green — *1,100.*

Overprinted in Black "Series 1942"

1942 Size: 19x22mm *Perf. 11*

RD117 ST1 1c brt green .50 .30
RD118 ST1 2c brt green .40 .35
RD119 ST1 4c brt green 3.00 1.00
RD120 ST1 5c brt green .40 .15
a. Ovpt. inverted (cut cancel) 225.00
RD121 ST1 10c brt green 1.75 .15
RD122 ST1 20c brt green 2.00 .15
RD123 ST1 25c brt green 2.00 .15
RD124 ST1 40c brt green 4.00 .35
RD125 ST1 50c brt green 5.00 .20
RD126 ST1 80c brt green 17.50 5.25
Nos. RD117-RD126 (10) 36.55 8.05

Size: 21 1/2x36 1/4mm

RD127 ST2 $1 brt green 11.00 .35
RD128 ST2 $2 brt green 16.00 .35
RD129 ST2 $3 brt green 22.50 1.00
RD130 ST2 $4 brt green 35.00 17.50
RD131 ST2 $5 brt green 30.00 .35
a. Double overprint (perf. initials cancel) —
RD132 ST2 $10 brt green 60.00 7.50
RD133 ST2 $20 brt green 135.00 32.50
Nos. RD127-RD133 (7) 309.50 59.55

Perf. 12

Without Gum

Size: 28 1/2x42mm

RD134 ST3 $30 brt green 90.00 45.00
RD135 ST3 $50 brt green 150.00 90.00
RD136 ST3 $60 brt green — 110.00
RD137 ST3 $100 brt green — 77.50
RD138 ST3 $500 brt green — *8,000.*
RD139 ST3 $1000 brt green — 500.00

Overprinted in Black "Series 1943"

1943 Size: 19x22mm *Perf. 11*

RD140	ST1	1c	brt green	.40	.25
RD141	ST1	2c	brt green	.50	.40
RD142	ST1	4c	brt green	1.75	.20
RD143	ST1	5c	brt green	.50	.15
RD144	ST1	10c	brt green	1.00	.15
RD145	ST1	20c	brt green	1.75	.15
RD146	ST1	25c	brt green	3.50	.25
RD147	ST1	40c	brt green	3.50	.25
RD148	ST1	50c	brt green	3.50	.20
RD149	ST1	80c	brt green	12.50	4.50
			Nos. RD140-RD149 (10)	28.90	6.50

Size: 21½x36¼mm

RD150	ST2	$1	brt green	12.50	.15
RD151	ST2	$2	brt green	14.00	.35
RD152	ST2	$3	brt green	17.50	1.00
RD153	ST2	$4	brt green	35.00	15.00
RD154	ST2	$5	brt green	50.00	.35
RD155	ST2	$10	brt green	70.00	4.50
RD156	ST2	$20	brt green	125.00	35.00
			Nos. RD150-RD156 (7)	324.00	56.35

Perf. 12

Without Gum

Size: 28½x42mm

RD157	ST3	$30	brt green	200.00	100.00
RD158	ST3	$50	brt green	275.00	125.00
RD159	ST3	$60	brt green	—	300.00
RD160	ST3	$100	brt green	—	50.00
RD161	ST3	$500	brt green	—	425.00
RD162	ST3	$1000	brt green	—	250.00

Overprinted in Black "Series 1944"

Portraits: $2,500, William Windom. $5,000, C. J. Folger. $10,000, Walter Q. Gresham.

1944 Wmk. 191R *Perf. 11*

Size: 19x22mm

RD163	ST1	1c	brt green	.65	.60
RD164	ST1	2c	brt green	.45	.20
RD165	ST1	4c	brt green	.60	.25
RD166	ST1	5c	brt green	.50	.15
RD167	ST1	10c	brt green	.75	.15
RD168	ST1	20c	brt green	1.25	.20
RD169	ST1	25c	brt green	2.00	.30
RD170	ST1	40c	brt green	8.00	5.00
RD171	ST1	50c	brt green	4.50	.20
RD172	ST1	80c	brt green	7.50	4.50
			Nos. RD163-RD172 (10)	26.20	11.55

Size: 21½x36¼mm

RD173	ST2	$1	brt green	7.50	.40
RD174	ST2	$2	brt green	30.00	.60
RD175	ST2	$3	brt green	25.00	1.25
RD176	ST2	$4	brt green	30.00	5.00
RD177	ST2	$5	brt green	27.50	.90
RD178	ST2	$10	brt green	60.00	4.50
RD179	ST2	$20	brt green	100.00	8.00
			Nos. RD173-RD179 (7)	280.00	20.65

Perf. 12

Without Gum

Size: 28½x42mm

Bright Green

RD180	ST3	$30	125.00	60.00
RD181	ST3	$50	85.00	50.00
RD182	ST3	$60	150.00	100.00
RD183	ST3	$100	—	47.50
RD184	ST3	$500	—	400.00
RD185	ST3	$1000	—	—
		(cut cancel)		225.00
RD185A	ST3	$2500	—	—
RD185B	ST3	$5000	—	—
RD185C	ST3	$10,000	—	—
		(cut cancel)		*1,250.*

Overprinted in Black "Series 1945"

1945 Wmk. 191R *Perf. 11*

Size: 19x22mm

RD186	ST1	1c	brt green	.15	.15
RD187	ST1	2c	brt green	.25	.20
RD188	ST1	4c	brt green	.25	.20
RD189	ST1	5c	brt green	.25	.15
RD190	ST1	10c	brt green	.75	.35
RD191	ST1	20c	brt green	1.25	.30
RD192	ST1	25c	brt green	2.00	.35
RD193	ST1	40c	brt green	3.00	.20
RD194	ST1	50c	brt green	3.50	.25
RD195	ST1	80c	brt green	6.50	2.50
			Nos. RD186-RD195 (10)	17.90	4.65

Size: 21½x36¼mm

RD196	ST2	$1	brt green	12.50	.25
RD197	ST2	$2	brt green	17.50	.45
RD198	ST2	$3	brt green	30.00	.60
RD199	ST2	$4	brt green	30.00	2.50
RD200	ST2	$5	brt green	20.00	.50
RD201	ST2	$10	brt green	45.00	6.50
RD202	ST2	$20	brt green	70.00	8.00

Perf. 12

Without Gum

Size: 28½x42mm

Bright green

RD203	ST3	$30	90.00	60.00
RD204	ST3	$50	60.00	17.50
RD205	ST3	$60	150.00	125.00
RD206	ST3	$100	—	25.00
RD207	ST3	$500	—	500.00
RD208	ST3	$1000	—	550.00
RD208A	ST3	$2500	—	—
RD208B	ST3	$5000	—	—
RD208C	ST3	$10,000 cut canc.	—	*1,500.*

Overprinted in Black "Series 1946"

1946 Wmk. 191R *Perf. 11*

Size: 19x22mm

RD209	ST1	1c	brt green	.20	.15
	a.		Pair, one dated "1945"	*475.00*	
RD210	ST1	2c	brt green	.35	.15
RD211	ST1	4c	brt green	.30	.15
RD212	ST1	5c	brt green	.35	.15
RD213	ST1	10c	brt green	.75	.15
RD214	ST1	20c	brt green	1.50	.20
RD215	ST1	25c	brt green	1.50	.25
RD216	ST1	40c	brt green	3.50	.60
RD217	ST1	50c	brt green	4.50	.20
RD218	ST1	80c	brt green	9.00	6.00
			Nos. RD209-RD218 (10)	21.95	8.00

Size: 21½x36¼mm

RD219	ST2	$1	brt green	8.00	.50
RD220	ST2	$2	brt green	9.00	.50
RD221	ST2	$3	brt green	17.50	1.25
RD222	ST2	$4	brt green	17.50	5.50
RD223	ST2	$5	brt green	25.00	1.00
RD224	ST2	$10	brt green	50.00	2.50
RD225	ST2	$20	brt green	80.00	35.00
			Nos. RD219-RD225 (7)	207.00	46.25

Perf. 12

Without Gum

Size: 28½x42mm

RD226	ST3	$30	brt grn	70.00	35.00
RD227	ST3	$50	brt grn	55.00	40.00
RD228	ST3	$60	brt grn	125.00	82.50
RD229	ST3	$100	brt grn	77.50	35.00
RD230	ST3	$500	brt grn	—	165.00
RD231	ST3	$1000	brt grn	—	140.00
RD232	ST3	$2500	brt grn	—	—
			(cut cancel)		*5,750.*
RD233	ST3	$5000	brt grn	—	*5,500.*
RD234	ST3	$10,000	brt grn	—	—
			(cut cancel)		*2,000.*

Overprinted in Black "Series 1947"

1947 Wmk. 191R *Perf. 11*

Size: 19x22mm

RD235	ST1	1c	brt green	.65	.55
RD236	ST1	2c	brt green	.60	.50
RD237	ST1	4c	brt green	.50	.40
RD238	ST1	5c	brt green	.45	.35
RD239	ST1	10c	brt green	.60	.50
RD240	ST1	20c	brt green	1.10	.50
RD241	ST1	25c	brt green	1.75	.50
RD242	ST1	40c	brt green	3.00	.75
RD243	ST1	50c	brt green	4.00	.30
RD244	ST1	80c	brt green	15.00	10.00
			Nos. RD235-RD244 (10)	27.65	14.35

Size: 21½x36¼mm

RD245	ST2	$1	brt green	6.00	.50
RD246	ST2	$2	brt green	12.50	.75
RD247	ST2	$3	brt green	20.00	1.50
RD248	ST2	$4	brt green	32.50	6.00
RD249	ST2	$5	brt green	27.50	1.50
RD250	ST2	$10	brt green	45.00	5.00
RD251	ST2	$20	brt green	85.00	30.00
			Nos. RD245-RD251 (7)	228.50	45.25

Perf. 12

Without Gum

Size: 28½x42mm

RD252	ST3	$30	brt grn	60.00	40.00
RD253	ST3	$50	brt grn	125.00	82.50
RD254	ST3	$60	brt grn	150.00	125.00
RD255	ST3	$100	brt grn	—	35.00
RD256	ST3	$500	brt grn	—	250.00
RD257	ST3	$1000	brt grn	—	85.00
RD258	ST3	$2500	brt grn (cut canc.)	—	*350.00*
RD259	ST3	$5000	brt grn (cut canc.)	—	*300.00*
RD260	ST3	$10,000	brt grn (cut canc.)	—	55.00
	a.		Horiz. pair, imperf. vert. (cut canc.)		—

Overprinted in Black "Series 1948"

1948 Wmk. 191R *Perf. 11*

Size: 19x22mm

RD261	ST1	1c	brt green	.25	.25
RD262	ST1	2c	brt green	.25	.25
RD263	ST1	4c	brt green	.30	.30
RD264	ST1	5c	brt green	.25	.24
RD265	ST1	10c	brt green	.30	.25
RD266	ST1	20c	brt green	1.40	.35
RD267	ST1	25c	brt green	1.40	.40
RD268	ST1	40c	brt green	1.75	.75
RD269	ST1	50c	brt green	4.25	.30
RD270	ST1	80c	brt green	12.50	6.00
			Nos. RD261-RD270 (10)	22.65	9.09

Size: 21½x36¼mm

RD271	ST2	$1	brt green	8.50	.40
RD272	ST2	$2	brt green	12.50	.60
RD273	ST2	$3	brt green	15.00	3.75
RD274	ST2	$4	brt green	17.50	9.00
RD275	ST2	$5	brt green	25.00	2.50
RD276	ST2	$10	brt green	45.00	4.50
RD277	ST2	$20	brt green	75.00	18.00
			Nos. RD271-RD277 (7)	198.50	38.75

Perf. 12

Without Gum

Size: 28½x42mm

RD278	ST3	$30	brt grn	90.00	40.00
RD279	ST3	$50	brt grn	60.00	40.00
RD280	ST3	$60	brt grn	150.00	100.00
RD281	ST3	$100	brt grn	—	17.50
RD282	ST3	$500	brt grn	—	210.00
RD283	ST3	$1000	brt grn	—	100.00
RD284	ST3	$2500	brt grn	300.00	275.00
RD285	ST3	$5000	brt grn	—	250.00
RD286	ST3	$10,000	brt grn (cut canc.)	—	55.00

Overprinted in Black "Series 1949"

1949 Wmk. 191R *Perf. 11*

Size: 19x22mm

RD287	ST1	1c	brt green	.50	.45
RD288	ST1	2c	brt green	.50	.45
RD289	ST1	4c	brt green	.60	.50
RD290	ST1	5c	brt green	.60	.50
RD291	ST1	10c	brt green	1.30	.60
RD292	ST1	20c	brt green	2.10	.50
RD293	ST1	25c	brt green	3.00	.85
RD294	ST1	40c	brt green	5.50	1.50
RD295	ST1	50c	brt green	5.00	.25
RD296	ST1	80c	brt green	12.50	6.50
			Nos. RD287-RD296 (10)	31.60	12.10

Size: 21½x36¼mm

RD297	ST2	$1	brt green	10.00	.65
RD298	ST2	$2	brt green	15.00	.90
RD299	ST2	$3	brt green	32.50	4.50
RD300	ST2	$4	brt green	30.00	7.50
RD301	ST2	$5	brt green	40.00	2.00
RD302	ST2	$10	brt green	50.00	4.00
RD303	ST2	$20	brt green	115.00	15.00
			Nos. RD297-RD303 (7)	292.50	34.55

Perf. 12

Without Gum

Size: 28½x42mm

RD304	ST3	$30	brt grn	—	65.00
RD305	ST3	$50	brt grn	140.00	75.00
RD306	ST3	$60	brt grn	165.00	140.00
RD307	ST3	$100	brt grn	—	55.00
RD308	ST3	$500	brt grn	—	200.00
RD309	ST3	$1000	brt grn	—	80.00
RD310	ST3	$2500	brt grn (cut canc.)	—	*375.00*
RD311	ST3	$5000	brt grn (cut canc.)	—	*400.00*
RD312	ST3	$10,000	brt grn	—	300.00
	a.		Pair, one without ovpt. (cut cancel)		—

Overprinted in Black "Series 1950"

1950 Wmk. 191R *Perf. 11*

Size: 19x22mm

RD313	ST1	1c	brt green	.40	.35
RD314	ST1	2c	brt green	.40	.30
RD315	ST1	4c	brt green	.40	.35
RD316	ST1	5c	brt green	.40	.20
RD317	ST1	10c	brt green	2.00	.30
RD318	ST1	20c	brt green	2.75	.50
RD319	ST1	25c	brt green	4.00	.60
RD320	ST1	40c	brt green	4.75	.90
RD321	ST1	50c	brt green	7.50	.35
RD322	ST1	80c	brt green	9.50	5.00
			Nos. RD313-RD322 (10)	32.10	8.85

Size: 21½x36¼mm

RD323	ST2	$1	brt green	10.00	.40
RD324	ST2	$2	brt green	17.50	.75
RD325	ST2	$3	brt green	27.50	4.00
RD326	ST2	$4	brt green	35.00	7.50
RD327	ST2	$5	brt green	35.00	1.75
RD328	ST2	$10	brt green	80.00	5.00
RD329	ST2	$20	brt green	110.00	25.00
			Nos. RD323-RD329 (7)	315.00	44.40

Perf. 12

Without Gum

Size: 28½x42mm

RD330	ST3	$30	brt grn	80.00	60.00
RD331	ST3	$50	brt grn	75.00	70.00
RD332	ST3	$60	brt grn	—	110.00
RD333	ST3	$100	brt grn	—	35.00
	a.		Vert. pair, Imperf betwn.		—
RD334	ST3	$500	brt grn	—	165.00
RD335	ST3	$1000	brt grn	—	75.00
RD336	ST3	$2500	brt grn	—	*1,100.*
RD337	ST3	$5000	brt grn	—	650.00
RD338	ST3	$10,000	brt grn	—	450.00

Overprinted in Black "Series 1951"

1951 Wmk. 191R *Perf. 11*

Size: 19x22mm

RD339	ST1	1c	brt green	1.10	.35
RD340	ST1	2c	brt green	1.10	.30
RD341	ST1	4c	brt green	1.50	.50
RD342	ST1	5c	brt green	1.10	.35
RD343	ST1	10c	brt green	1.50	.30
RD344	ST1	20c	brt green	3.75	.90
RD345	ST1	25c	brt green	5.00	.90
RD346	ST1	40c	brt green	12.50	8.00
RD347	ST1	50c	brt green	8.50	.90
RD348	ST1	80c	brt green	15.00	10.00
			Nos. RD339-RD348 (10)	51.05	22.50

Size: 21½x36¼mm

RD349	ST2	$1	brt green	17.50	.80
RD350	ST2	$2	brt green	25.00	1.25
RD351	ST2	$3	brt green	35.00	10.00
RD352	ST2	$4	brt green	40.00	12.00
RD353	ST2	$5	brt green	50.00	2.50
RD354	ST2	$10	brt green	80.00	8.50
RD355	ST2	$20	brt green	125.00	17.50
			Nos. RD349-RD355 (7)	372.50	52.55

Perf. 12

Without Gum

Size: 28½x42mm

RD356	ST3	$30	brt grn	—	60.00
RD357	ST3	$50	brt grn	—	50.00
RD358	ST3	$60	brt grn	—	*600.00*
RD359	ST3	$100	brt grn	—	55.00
RD360	ST3	$500	brt grn	—	140.00
RD361	ST3	$1000	brt grn	—	75.00
RD362	ST3	$2500	brt grn	—	*1,100.*
RD363	ST3	$5000	brt grn	—	*1,250.*
RD364	ST3	$10,000	brt grn	—	120.00

Overprinted in Black "Series 1952"

1952 Wmk. 191R *Perf. 11*

Size: 19x22mm

RD365	ST1	1c	brt green	30.00	15.00
RD366	ST1	10c	brt green	30.00	15.00
RD367	ST1	20c	brt green	300.00	—
RD368	ST1	25c	brt green	400.00	—
RD369	ST1	40c	brt green	80.00	30.00

Size: 21½x36¼mm

RD370	ST2	$4	brt green	1,100.	550.
RD371	ST2	$10	brt green	*1,900.*	—
RD372	ST2	$20	brt green	*2,900.*	—

Stock Transfer stamps were discontinued in 1952.

See the Scott United States Specialized Catalogue for other categories of Revenue stamps.

Shop with Scott Publishing Co. 24 hours a day 7 days a week at
www.scottonline.com

HUNTING PERMIT STAMPS

The receipts of the sales of these "Migratory Bird Hunting" stamps help to maintain waterfowl life in the United States.

Catalogue values for unused stamps in this section are for Never Hinged items. Unused stamps with part or no gum sell for substantially less than the unused never hinged values.

Department of Agriculture

Used Values

Used value for No. RW1 is for stamp with handstamp or manuscript cancel, though technically it was illegal to deface the stamp. Beginning with No. RW2, the used value is for stamps with manuscript signature.

HP1

Various Designs
Inscribed "U. S. Department of Agriculture"
Engraved; Flat Plate Printing

1934		Unwmk.	Perf. 11	
		"Void after June 30, 1935"		
RW1	HP1	$1 blue	675.00	125.00
		Hinged	350.00	
		No gum	160.00	
a.		Imperf., pair		
b.		Vert. pair, imperf. horiz.	—	

1935		"Void after June 30, 1936"		
RW2		$1 Canvasback Ducks Taking to Flight	650.00	130.00
		Hinged	375.00	
		No gum	175.00	

1936		"Void after June 30, 1937"		
RW3		$1 Canada Geese in Flight	325.00	67.50
		Hinged	190.00	
		No gum	95.00	

1937		"Void after June 30, 1938"		
RW4		$1 Scaup Ducks Taking to Flight	275.00	52.50
		Hinged	150.00	
		No gum	75.00	

1938		"Void after June 30, 1939"		
RW5		$1 Pintail Drake and Duck Alighting	350.00	52.50
		Hinged	190.00	
		No gum	75.00	

Green-Winged Teal — HP2

Department of the Interior

Various Designs
Inscribed: "U. S. Department of the Interior"

1939		"Void after June 30, 1940"		
RW6	HP2	$1 chocolate	200.00	42.50
		Hinged	110.00	
		No gum	50.00	

1940		"Void after June 30, 1941"		
RW7		$1 Black Mallards	200.00	42.50
		Hinged	110.00	
		No gum	50.00	

1941		"Void after June 30, 1942"		
RW8		$1 Family of Ruddy Ducks	200.00	42.50
		Hinged	110.00	
		No gum	50.00	

1942		"Void after June 30, 1943"		
RW9		$1 Baldpates	200.00	42.50
		Hinged	110.00	
		No gum	50.00	

1943		"Void after June 30, 1944"		
RW10		$1 Wood Ducks	75.00	40.00
		Hinged	50.00	
		No gum	42.50	

1944		"Void after June 30, 1945"		
RW11		$1 White-fronted Geese	85.00	27.50
		Hinged	50.00	
		No gum	32.50	

1945		"Void after June 30, 1946"		
RW12		$1 Shoveller Ducks in Flight	60.00	25.00
		Hinged	35.00	
		No gum	27.50	

1946		"Void after June 30, 1947"		
RW13		$1 Redhead Ducks	45.00	13.00
		No gum	18.00	
a.		$1 bright rose pink		—

1947		"Void after June 30, 1948"		
RW14		$1 Snow Geese	45.00	14.00
		No gum	18.00	

1948		"Void after June 30, 1949"		
RW15		$1 Bufflehead Ducks in Flight	50.00	14.00
		No gum	21.00	

Goldeneye Ducks HP3

1949		"Void after June 30, 1950"		
RW16	HP3	$2 bright green	57.50	14.00
		No gum	22.50	

1950		"Void after June 30, 1951"		
RW17		$2 Trumpeter Swans in Flight	72.50	11.00
		No gum	25.00	

1951		"Void after June 30, 1952"		
RW18		$2 Gadwall Ducks	72.50	11.00
		No gum	25.00	

1952		"Void after June 30, 1953"		
RW19		$2 Harlequin Ducks	72.50	10.00
		No gum	25.00	

1953		"Void after June 30, 1954"		
RW20		$2 Blue-winged Teal	75.00	10.00
		No gum	25.00	

1954		"Void after June 30, 1955"		
RW21		$2 Ring-necked Ducks	75.00	9.50
		No gum	25.00	

1955		"Void after June 30, 1956"		
RW22		$2 Blue Geese	75.00	9.50
		No gum	25.00	

1956		"Void after June 30, 1957"		
RW23		$2 American Merganser	75.00	9.50
		No gum	25.00	

1957		"Void after June 30, 1958"		
RW24		$2 American Eiders	75.00	9.50
		No gum	25.00	
a.		Back inscription inverted		—

1958		"Void after June 30, 1959"		
RW25		$2 Canada Geese	72.50	9.00
		No gum	25.00	

Labrador Retriever Carrying Mallard Drake HP4

1959		Giori Press Printing		
		"Void after June 30, 1960"		
RW26	HP4	$3 blue, ocher & blk	92.50	9.50
		No gum	35.00	
a.		Back inscription inverted		—

Redhead Ducks HP5

1960		"Void after June 30, 1961"		
RW27	HP5	$3 red brn, dk bl & bister	80.00	9.50
		No gum	35.00	

1961		"Void after June 30, 1962"		
RW28		$3 Mallard Hen and Ducklings	82.50	9.50
		No gum	37.50	

Pintail Drakes Coming in for Landing HP6

1962		"Void after June 30, 1963"		
RW29	HP6	$3 dk bl, dk red brn & black	95.00	9.50
		No gum	55.00	

1963		"Void after June 30, 1964"		
RW30		$3 Pair of Brant landing	95.00	9.50
		No gum	55.00	

1964		"Void after June 30, 1965"		
RW31		$3 Hawaiian Nene Geese	95.00	9.50
		No gum	55.00	

1965		"Void after June 30, 1966"		
RW32		$3 3 Canvasback Drakes	92.50	9.50
		No gum	55.00	

Whistling Swans HP7

1966		"Void after June 30, 1967"		
RW33	HP7	$3 ultra, sl grn & blk	92.50	9.50
		No gum	50.00	

1967		"Void after June 30, 1968"		
RW34		$3 Old Squaw Ducks	100.00	9.50
		No gum	50.00	

1968		"Void after June 30, 1969"		
RW35		$3 Hooded Mergansers	57.50	8.50
		No gum	25.00	

MIGRATORY BIRD HUNTING STAMP
White-winged Scoters — HP8

1969		"Void after June 30, 1970"		
RW36	HP8	$3 gray, brn, indigo & brn red	57.50	7.00
		No gum	25.00	

1970		Litho. & Engr.		
		"Void after June 30, 1971"		
RW37		$3 Ross' Geese	57.50	7.00
		No gum	22.50	

1971		"Void after June 30, 1972"		
RW38		$3 3 Cinnamon Teal	40.00	7.00
		No gum	21.00	

1972		"Void after June 30, 1973"		
RW39		$5 Emperor Geese	25.00	7.00
		No gum	12.50	

1973		"Void after June 30, 1974"		
RW40		$5 Steller's Eiders	21.00	7.00
		No gum	12.00	

1974		"Void after June 30, 1975"		
RW41		$5 Wood Ducks	20.00	6.00
		No gum	9.50	

1975		"Void after June 30, 1976"		
RW42		$5 Weathered canvasback duck decoy and flying ducks	15.00	6.00
		No gum	8.00	

1-800-231-5926

Our Specialized Catalog picks up where all others leave off!

68 page catalog $3 refundable with order.

We Have It All!
Federal & State Stamps, Indian Reservation, Fishing, Foreign, Conservation, Prints, Frames and Decoys

Sam Houston Duck Company
A Specialized Catalogue

We offer New Issues and Subscription Services.

Sam Houston Duck Co.
P.O. Box 820087, Houston, TX 77282
281-493-6386 • www.samhoustonduck.com

UNITED STATES — CONFEDERATE STATES

1976 — Engr.
"Void after June 30, 1977"
RW43 $5 Family of Canada Geese   14.00 6.00
   No gum   7.50

1977 — Engr. & Litho.
"Void after June 30, 1978"
RW44 $5 Ross' Geese, pair   15.00 6.00
   No gum   7.50

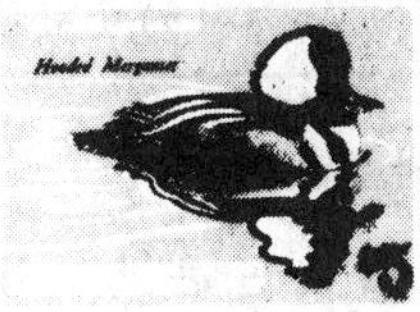

Hooded Merganser HP9

1978 — "Void after June 30, 1979"
RW45 HP9 $5 multicolored   12.50 6.00
   No gum   7.50

1979 — "Void after June 30, 1980"
RW46 $7.50 Green-winged teal   14.00 6.00
   No gum   8.00

1980 — "Void after June 30, 1981"
RW47 $7.50 Mallards   14.00 6.00
   No gum   8.00

1981 — "Void after June 30, 1982"
RW48 $7.50 Ruddy Ducks   14.00 6.00
   No gum   8.00

1982 — "Void after June 30, 1983"
RW49 $7.50 Canvasbacks   15.00 6.00
   No gum   8.00
   a. Orange & violet omitted

1983 — "Void after June 30, 1984"
RW50 $7.50 Pintails   15.00 6.00
   No gum   8.00

1984 — "Void after June 30, 1985"
RW51 $7.50 Widgeons   15.00 6.00
   No gum   8.00

1985 — "Void after June 30, 1986"
RW52 $7.50 Cinnamon Teal   14.00 6.00
   No gum   8.00

1986 — "Void after June 30, 1987"
RW53 $7.50 Fulvous Whistling Duck   15.00 6.00
   No gum   8.00
   a. Black omitted   3,750.

1987 — Perf. 11½x11
"Void after June 30, 1988"
RW54 $10 Redheads   15.00 9.00
   No gum   10.00

1988 — "Void after June 30, 1989"
RW55 $10 Snow Goose   16.00 9.00
   No gum   10.00

1989 — "Void after June 30, 1990"
RW56 $12.50 Lesser Scaups   19.00 10.00
   No gum   12.00

1990 — "Void after June 30, 1991"
RW57 $12.50 Black Bellied Whistling Duck   19.00 10.00
   No gum   12.00
   a. Back inscription omitted   425.00

The back inscription is on top of the gum so beware of copies with gum removed. Used examples of No. RW57a cannot exist.

King Eiders HP10

1991 — "Void after June 30, 1992"
RW58 HP10 $15 multicolored   22.50 11.00
   No gum   15.00
   a. Black (engr.) omitted   8,500.

1992 — "Void after June 30, 1993"
RW59 $15 Spectacled Eider   22.50 11.00
   No gum   15.00

1993 — "Void after June 30, 1994"
RW60 $15 Canvasbacks   22.50 11.00
   No gum   15.00
   a. Black (engr.) omitted   3,250.

1994 — "Void after June 30, 1995"
RW61 $15 Red-breasted mergansers   22.50 11.00
   No gum   15.00

1995 — "Void after June 30, 1996"
RW62 $15 Mallards   22.50 11.00
   No gum   15.00

1996 — "Void after June 30, 1997"
RW63 $15 Surf Scoters   22.50 11.00
   No gum   15.00

1997 — "Void after June 30, 1998"
RW64 $15 Canada Goose   22.50 11.00
   No gum   15.00

1998 — "Void after June 30, 1999"
RW65 $15 Barrow's Goldeneye   22.50 11.00
   Self-Adhesive
   Serpentine Die Cut
RW65A $15 Barrow's Goldeneye   22.50 11.00

#RW65 was sold in panes of 30, #RW65A in panes of 1.

CONFEDERATE STATES

ABERDEEN, MISS.

E1 / E1a

Handstamped
1XU1 E1   5c black   2,500.
1XU2 E1   10c (ms.) on 5c black   —

Abingdon, Va.

Handstamped
2XU1 E1a 2c black   11,000.
2XU2 E1a 5c black   850.
2XU3 E1a 10c black   2,200. 3,500.

No. 2XU1 is unique. The unused No. 2XU3 is a unique mint example, and the value represents the price realized in a 1997 auction sale..

Albany, Ga.

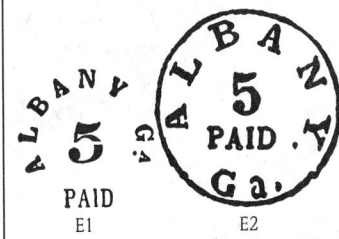

E1 / E2

Handstamped
3XU1 E1 5c greenish blue   700.
3XU2 E1 10c greenish blue   2,000.
3XU3 E1 10c on 5c grnsh blue   2,500.
3XU5 E2 5c greenish blue   —
3XU6 E2 10c greenish blue   2,250.

United States hunting permit stamps can be mounted in the Scott U.S. Federal and State Duck album.

Anderson Court House, S.C.

E1 / Two varieties — A1

Handstamped
4XU1 E1   5c black   1,500.
4XU2 E1   10c (ms.) black   2,500.

Athens, Ga.

Typo.
5X1 A1 5c purple (shades)   900. 950.
   a. Vertical tete beche pair   4,000.
5X2 A1 5c red   — 3,000.

Atlanta, Ga.

E1  / E2

E3

Handstamped
6XU1 E1 5c red   3,500.
6XU2 E1 5c black   175. 600.
6XU3 E1 10c on 5c black   1,500.
6XU4 E2 2c black   2,500.
6XU5 E2 5c black   1,500.
6XU6 E2 10c black   850.
6XU7 E2 10c on 5c black   2,500.
6XU8 E3 5c black   3,500.
6XU9 E3 10c black ("10" upright)   2,750.

Augusta, Ga.

E1

Handstamped
7XU1 E1 5c black
Provisional status questioned.

E1  / E1a

Austin, Miss.
Typo.
8XU1 E1 5c red, amber   20,000.
No. 8XU1 is unique.

Austin, Texas

Handstamped
9XU1 E1a 10c black   1,500.

Autaugaville, Ala.

E1  / E2

Handstamped
10XU1 E1 5c black   8,000.
10XU2 E2 5c black   12,000.

Baton Rouge, La.

A1  / A2

A3  / A4

Typeset
Ten varieties each of A1, A2 and A3
11X1 A1 2c green   5,000. 3,500.
   a. "McCcrmick"   8,000. 7,500.
11X2 A2 5c green & car   1,250. 1,100.
   a. "McCcrmick"   — 2,000.
11X3 A3 5c green & car   4,500. 1,750.
   a. "McCcrmick"   — 3,250.
11X4 A4 10c blue   6,000.

QUACK! QUACK!

If you are interested in...

STATE DUCK STAMPS

And Are Serious About Completing Your Collection... Michael Jaffe Stamps.. Can be Your Complete Duck Dealer!

Over 99% of all pictorial duck stamps always in stock at very competitive & attractive prices! Call for Complete Duck Catalog which lists all pictorial Duck Stamps, Hunter (agent) Stamps and Indian Reservation Stamps.

NEW ISSUE SERVICE!

Receive all the new State Duck Stamps without the hassle of trying to order them yourself. Automatically charged to your charge card as they come out. Only $1.75 over issue cost per stamp.

ALSO IN STOCK... ★ DUCK PRINTS
★ DUCK SOUVENIR CARDS
★ DUCK ALBUMS
★ FEDERAL DUCK STAMPS, MINT, USED, & UNUSED FOR FRAMING
★ DUCK FIRST DAY COVERS ★
SATISFACTION GUARANTEED ON EVERYTHING SOLD

MICHAEL JAFFE STAMPS INC.
P. O. Box 61484, Vancouver, WA 98666
Phone 360-695-6161 • FAX 360-695-1616
TOLL-FREE ORDER NUMBER 800-782-6770
email: mjaffe@brookmanstamps.com
web: www.brookmanstamps.com

ARA, SRS
Ducks Unlimited Sponsor

CONFEDERATE STATES

Beaumont, Tex.

A1 — BEAUMONT PAID 10 CENTS
A2 — BEAUMONT, TEXAS, PAID 10 CENTS POSTAGE

Typeset
Several varieties of A1

12X1	A1	10c black, *yellow*	4,500.
12X2	A1	10c black, *pink*	4,000.
12X3	A2	10c black, *yellow*, on cover	90,000.

Bridgeville, Ala.

Handstamped

13X1	A1	5c black & red	20,000.

Canton, Miss.

Handstamped

14XU1	E1	5c black	1,750.
14XU2	E1	10c (ms.) on 5c black	3,500.

Carolina City, N.C.

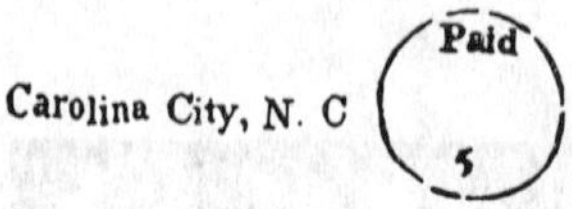

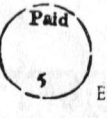

Handstamped

118XU1	E1	5c black	5,000.

Chapel Hill, N.C.

Handstamped

15XU1	E1	5c black	2,500.

Charleston, S.C.

Litho.

16X1	A1	5c blue	900.	750.

Typographed from Woodcut

16XU1	E1	5c blue	1,100.	1,750.
16XU2	E1	5c blue, *amber*	1,100.	1,750.
16XU3	E1	5c blue, *orange*	1,100.	1,750.
16XU4	E1	5c blue, *buff*	1,100.	1,750.
16XU5	E1	5c blue, *blue*	1,100.	1,750.
16XU6	E2	10c blue, *orange*		77,500.

Handstamped

16XU7	E2	10c black	3,000.

The No. 16XU6 used entire is unique; value based on 1997 auction realization.
No. 16XU7 is unique. It is a cut-out, not an entire. It may not have been mailed from Charleston and may not have paid postage.

Chattanooga, Tenn.

17XU2	E1	5c black	1,600.
17XU3	E1	5c on 2c black	3,250.

Christiansburg, Va.

Typeset. Impressed at top right.

99XU1	E1	5c black, *blue*	2,000.
99XU2	E1	5c blue	1,400.
99XU3	E1	5c black, *orange*	2,000.
99XU4	E1	5c green, on US envelope #U27	4,500.
99XU5	E1	10c blue	3,500.

Colaparchee, Ga.

Handstamped

119XU1	E1	5c black	3,500.

Columbia, S.C.

Handstamped

18XU1	E1	5c blue	500.	750.
18XU2	E1	5c black	600.	750.
18XU3	E1	10c on 5c blue		3,000.
18XU4	E2	5c blue (seal on front)		1,500.
	a.	Seal on back		700.
18XU5	E2	10c blue (seal on back)		2,000.

Circular Seal similar to E2, 27mm diameter

18XU6	E2	5c blue (seal on back)	2,500.

Columbia, Tenn.

Handstamped

113XU1	E1	5c red	3,500.

Columbus, Ga.

19XU1	E1a	5c blue	700.
19XU2	E1a	10c red	2,000.

Courtland, Ala.

Handstamped from Woodcut

103XU1	E1	5c black	—
103XU2	E1	5c red	10,000.

Provisional status of No. 103XU1 questioned.

Dalton, Ga.

Handstamped

20XU1	E1a	5c black	500.
	a.	Denomination omitted (5c rate)	650.
20XU2	E1a	10c black	700.
20XU3	E1a	10c (ms.) on 5c black	1,500.

Danville, Va.

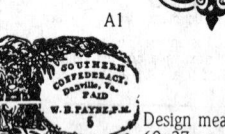

Design measures 60x37mm — E1

Wove Paper
Typeset

21X1	A1	5c red	5,500.
		Cut to shape	4,000.

Laid Paper

21X2	A1	5c red	6,500.

Two types: "SOUTHERN" in straight or curved line.

Typo.

21XU1	E1	5c black	5,500.
21XU2	E1	5c black, *amber*	5,500.
21XU3	E1	5c black, *dark buff*	5,250.

Handstamped

21XU4	E2	10c black	2,000.
21XU5	E1	10c blue	
21XU6	E3	10c black	2,750.

The existence of No. 21XU5 has been questioned.

Demopolis, Ala.

Handstamped. Signature in ms.

22XU1	E1	5c black ("Jno. Y. Hall")	2,000.
22XU2	E1	5c black ("J. Y. Hall")	2,000.
22XU3	E1	5c (ms.) black ("J. Y. Hall")	2,500.

Eatonton, Ga.

Handstamped

23XU1	E1	5c black	3,000.
23XU2	E1	5c + 5c black	1,250.

Emory, Va.

Handstamped on sheet margins of US 1857 1c stamps
Perf. 15 on Three Sides

24X1	A1	5c blue	— 3,500.

No. 24X1 exists with "5" above or below "PAID."

Handstamped

24XU1	E1	5c blue	2,000.
24XU2	E2	10c blue	4,400.

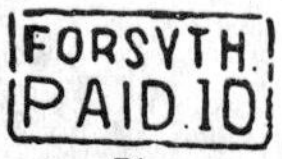

Fincastle, Va.

Typeset

104XU1	E1	10c black	20,000.

No. 104XU1 is unique.

CONFEDERATE STATES

Forsyth, Ga.

Handstamped
120XU1 E1a 10c black   1,350.

E1   A1

Franklin, N.C.
Typo.
25XU1 E1 5c blue, *buff*   30,000.
No. 25XU1 is unique.

Fredericksburg, Va.
Typeset. Ten varieties.
Thin Bluish Paper
26X1 A1 5c blue, *bluish*   250. 750.
26X2 A1 10c red (shades), *bluish*   900.

Gainesville, Ala.

E1   E2

Handstamped
27XU1 E1 5c black   5,000.
27XU2 E2 10c black   6,000.

Galveston, Tex.

E1

E2

Handstamped
98XU1 E1 5c black   500. 900.
98XU2 E1 10c black   1,750.
98XU3 E1 10c black   550. 2,400.
98XU4 E2 20c black   3,500.

Georgetown, S.C.

E1   Control

Handstamped
28XU1 E1 5c black   800.

Goliad, Tex.

A1   A2

Typeset
Several varieties of A1 and A2
29X1 A1 5c black   5,000.
29X2 A1 5c black, *gray*   4,500.
29X3 A1 5c black, *rose*   5,000.
29X4 A1 10c black   5,000.
29X5 A1 10c black, *rose*   5,000.
Type A1 stamps bear ms. control: "Clarke P.M."
29X6 A2 5c black, *gray*   7,000.
  a. "Goliad"   8,000.
29X7 A2 10c black, *gray*   5,000.
  a. "Goliad"   5,500.
29X8 A2 5c black, *dark blue*   6,000.
29X9 A2 10c black, *dark blue*   6,500.

Gonzales, Tex.

A1

30X1 A1 (5c) gold, *dark blue*   7,500.
No. 30X1 must bear double circle town cancel as validating control. All items of type A1 without this control are book labels.

Greensboro, Ala.

E1   E2

Handstamped
31XU1 E1 5c black   1,500.
31XU2 E1 10c black   2,750.
31XU3 E2 10c black   2,750.

Greensboro, N.C.

E1

Handstamped
32XU1 E1 10c red   1,250.

Greenville, Ala.

A1   A2

Typeset
33X1 A1 5c blue & red   22,500. 40,000.
33X2 A2 10c red & blue   40,000.
Two used examples each are known of Nos. 33X1-33X2. All are on covers, and the used values reflect this.

Greenville Court House, S.C.

PAID 5   E1   Control

Handstamped. Several Types.
34XU1 E1 5c black   1,800.
34XU2 E1 10c black   2,000.
34XU3 E1 20c (ms.) on 10c black   3,000.
Envelopes usually bear the black circle control on the back.

Greenwood Depot, Va.

A1

"PAID" Handstamped; value and signature ms.
Laid Paper
35X1 A1 10c black, *gray blue,* on cover   16,000.
Six examples are known of No. 35X1, all on covers. On only one cover is the stamp tied, and the catalogue value refers to this cover. Examples on cover but uncanceled are valued at $4,500.

Griffin, Ga.

E1

Handstamped
102XU1 E1 5c black   1,750.

Grove Hill, Ala.

A1   A1a

Typo.
36X1 A1 5c black, on cover   75,000.

Hallettsville, Tex.

Handstamped
Ruled Letter Paper
37X1 A1a 10c black, *gray blue,* on cover   15,000.

Hamburgh, S.C.

E1

Handstamped
112XU1 E1 5c black   2,000.

A1   A1a

Helena, Tex.
Typeset
Several varieties
38X1 A1 5c black, *buff*   7,500. 6,000.
38X2 A1 10c black, *gray*   5,000.

Hillsboro, N.C.

Handstamped
39X1 A1a 5c black, on cover   15,000.

Houston, Tex.

E1

Handstamped
40XU1 E1 5c red   — 700.
40XU2 E1 10c red   — 1,250.
40XU3 E1 10c black   2,000.
40XU4 E1 5c + 10c red   2,500.
40XU5 E1 10c + 10c red   2,500.
40XU6 E1 10c (ms.) on 5c red   3,000.

Huntsville, Tex.

E1   Control

Handstamped
92XU1 E1 5c black   2,500.
No. 92XU1 exists with "5" outside or within control circle.

I-U-KA

A1   E1

CONFEDERATE STATES

Independence, Tex.
Handstamped
41X1	A1	10c black, *buff*		3,250.
41X2	A1	10c black, *dull rose*		3,500.
41X3	A1	10c black, *buff* (small "10", "Pd" in ms.)		4,000.

No. 41X3 is known only cut to shape.

Iuka, Miss.
Handstamped
42XU1	E1	5c black		1,600.

Jackson, Miss.
Handstamped
43XU1	E1	5c black		500.
43XU2	E1	10c black		2,000.
43XU3	E1	10c on 5c black		2,750.
43XU4	E1	10c on 5c blue		2,750.

The 5c also exists on a lettersheet.

Jacksonville, Ala.
Handstamped
110XU1	E1a	5c black	—	1,500.

Jetersville, Va.
Handstamped ("5"); ms. ("AHA.")
Laid Paper
44X1	A1	5c black, vert. pair on cover, uncanceled		16,000.

Jonesboro, Tenn.
Handstamped
45XU1	E1	5c black		3,750.
45XU2	E1	5c dark blue		6,500.

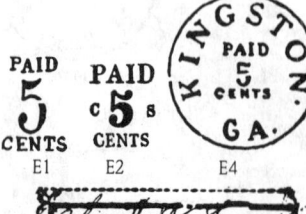

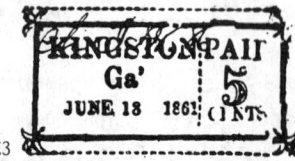

Kingston, Ga.
Typo. (E1-E3); Handstamped (E4)
46XU1	E1	5c black		2,000.
46XU2	E2	5c black		3,250.
a.	No "C" or "S" at sides of numeral			—
46XU3	E2	5c black, *amber*		2,750.
46XU4	E3	5c black		—
46XU5	E4	5c black		2,000.

Knoxville, Tenn.
Grayish White Laid Paper
47X1	A1	5c brick red	1,250.	900.
47X2	A1	5c carmine	1,750.	1,500.
47X3	A1	10c green, on cover		57,750.

The 5c has been reprinted in red, brown and chocolate on white and bluish wove and laid paper.
The No. 47X3 cover is unique. Value is based on 1997 auction sale.

Typo.
47XU1	E1	5c blue	750.	1,500.
47XU2	E1	5c blue, *orange*	750.	1,500.
47XU3	E1	10c red (cut to shape)		1,800.
47XU4	E1	10c red, *orange* (cut to shape)		1,800.

Handstamped
47XU5	E2	5c black	750.	1,500.
47XU6	E2	10c on 5c black		3,500.

Type E2 exists with "5" above or below "PAID."

La Grange, Tex.
Handstamped
48XU1	E1	5c black	—	2,000.
48XU2	E1	10c black		2,500.

Lake City, Fla.
Handstamped
96XU1	E1	10c black		2,000.

Envelopes have black circle control mark, or printed name of E.R. Ives, postmaster, on face or back.

Laurens Court House, S.C.
Handstamped
116XU1	E1	5c black	—	

Lenoir, N.C.
Handstamped from Woodcut
Paper has ruled lines in orange
49X1	A1	5c blue	3,250.	2,750.

Handstamped
49XU1	A1	5c black		3,500.
49XU2	A1	10c (5c + 5c) blue		3,500.
49XU3	E1	5c blue		2,500.
49XU4	E1	5c black		

The existence of No. 49XU4 has been questioned.

Lexington, Miss.
Handstamped
50XU1	E1	5c black		5,000.
50XU2	E1	10c black		5,000.

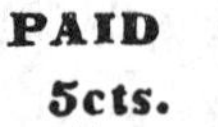

Liberty, Va.
Typeset. Laid Paper
74X1	A1	5c black		—

Two known on covers with Liberty, Va. postmark, one cover known with Salem, Va. postmark.

Limestone Springs, S.C.
Handstamped
121X1	A1a	5c black, on cover		4,000.

Stamps are round, square or rectangular. Covers are not postmarked.

Livingston, Ala.
Litho.
51X1	A1	5c blue		7,000.

Lynchburg, Va.
Stereotype from Woodcut
52X1	A1	5c blue (shades)	600.	1,000.

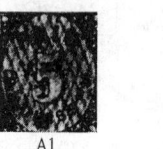

Typo.
52XU1	E1	5c black		1,500.
52XU2	E1	5c black, *amber*	650.	1,500.
52XU3	E1	5c black, *buff*		1,500.
52XU4	E1	5c black, *brown*	900.	1,500.

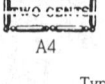

Macon, Ga.
Typeset. Wove Paper.
Several varieties of each. Ten of A2.
53X1	A1	5c blk, *lt blue green* (shades)	850.	600.
53X3	A2	5c black, *yellow*	2,500.	800.
53X4	A3	5c blk, *yel* (shades)	2,750.	1,250.
a.	Vertical tete beche pair			12,000.
53X5	A4	2c black, *gray green*		6,500.

Laid Paper
53X6	A2	5c black, *yellow*	3,000.	3,500.
53X7	A3	5c black, *yellow*	6,000.	
53X8	A1	5c blk, *lt blue green*	1,750.	2,000.

Handstamped
Two types of "PAID" and "5"
53XU1	E1	5c black	250.	500.

Marietta, Ga.
Handstamped
Two types of "PAID" and numerals
54XU1	E1	5c black		300.
54XU2	E1	10c on 5c black		1,750.
54XU3	E1	10c black		
54XU4	E2	5c black		2,000.

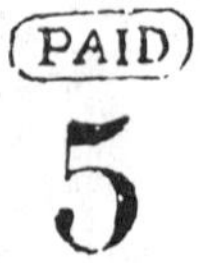

The existence of No. 54XU3 is questioned.

Marion, Va.
Handstamped Numeral within Typeset Frame
Wove Paper
55X1	A1	5c black		5,000.
55X2	A1	10c black	16,500.	8,000.

Bluish Laid Paper
55X3	A1	5c black		—

The 2c, 3c, 15c and 20c are believed to be bogus.

Memphis, Tenn.

CONFEDERATE STATES

Stereotype from Woodcut
56X1	A1	2c blue (shades)	80.	1,250.
56X2	A2	5c red (shades)	140.	175.
a.	Tete beche pair			1,500.
b.	Pair, one sideways	750.	—
c.	Pelure paper			

Typo.
56XU1	A2	5c red	2,500.
56XU2	A2	5c red, *amber*	2,500.
56XU3	A2	5c red, *orange*	2,250.

Micanopy, Fla.

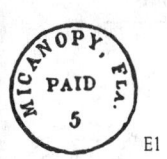

E1

105XU1	E1	5c black	11,500.
Handstamped

Milledgeville, Ga.

E1
E2 E3

Handstamped
57XU1	E1	5c black	250.
57XU2	E1	5c blue	800.
57XU3	E1	10c on 5c black	1,000.
57XU4	E2	10c black	225.	1,000.
57XU5	E3	10c black	700.

Mobile, Ala.

A1

Litho.
58X1	A1	2c black	1,500.	950.
58X2	A1	5c blue	275.	225.

Montgomery, Ala.

E1  E2  E3

Handstamped
59XU1	E1	5c red	750.
59XU2	E1	5c blue	400.	900.
59XU3	E1	10c red	800.
59XU4	E1	10c blue	900.
59XU5	E1	10c black	800.
59XU6	E1	10c on 5c red	2,750.

The 10c design is larger than the 5c.

59XU7	E2	2c blue	2,500.
59XU7A	E2	2c red	3,500.
59XU8	E2	5c black	2,250.
59XU9	E3	10c black	2,750.
59XU10	E3	10c red	1,500.

Mt. Lebanon, La.

A1

Woodcut, Design Reversed
60X1	A1	5c red brown, on cover	100,000.

No. 60X1 is unique.

Nashville, Tenn.

A1  A2

61X1	A1	3c carmine	150.
Typeset (5 varieties of 3c)

No. 61X1 was prepared by Postmaster McNish with the U.S. rate, but the stamp was never issued.

Stereotype from Woodcut
Gray Blue Ribbed Paper
61X2	A2	5c carmine (shades)	850.	500.
a.	Vertical tete beche pair			2,000.
61X3	A2	5c brick red	850.	450.
61X4	A2	5c gray (shades)	850.	625.
61X5	A2	5c violet brown	750.	475.
a.	Vertical tete beche pair	3,500.	2,500.
61X6	A2	10c green	3,000.	3,000.

Handstamped
61XU1	E1	5c blue	750.
61XU2	E1	5c + 10c blue	2,400.

New Orleans, La.

A1  A2

J.L.RIDDELL.P.M
Pd 5 CTS
N O.P.O

E1

Stereotype from Woodcut
62X1	A1	2c blue	150.	500.
a.	Printed on both sides		1,750.
62X2	A1	2c red (shades)	125.	1,000.
62X3	A2	2c brown, *white*	250.	150.
a.	Printed on both sides		1,750.
b.	5c ocher	650.	600.
62X4	A2	5c red brown, *bluish*	280.	175.
a.	Printed on both sides		2,750.
62X5	A2	5c yellow brown, *off white*	125.	225.
62X6	A2	5c red	—	7,500.
62X7	A2	5c red, *bluish*		10,000.

Handstamped
62XU1	E1	5c black	4,500.
62XU2	E1	10c black	12,500.

"J L. RIDDELL, P.M." omitted
62XU3	E1	2c black	9,500.

New Smyrna, Fla.

A1 A1a

Handstamped
63X1	A1	10c ("01") on 5c black	45,000.

No. 63X1 is unique.

Oakway, S.C.

Handstamped
115X1	A1a	5c black, on cover	—	66,000.

Two used examples of No. 115X1 are recorded, both on cover. Value represents 1997 auction sale realization for the cover on which the stamp is tied by manuscript "Paid."

E1  A1

Pensacola, Fla.
Handstamped
106XU1	E1	5c black	3,750.
106XU2	E1	10c (ms.) on 5c black	4,250.

Petersburg, Va.

Typeset (10 varieties)
65X1	A1	5c red (shades)	1,500.	450.

A1  A1a

Pittsylvania Court House, Va.
Typeset
Wove Paper
66X1	A1	5c red	6,000.	5,000.
	Octagonally cut		3,000.

Laid Paper
66X2	A1	5c red	6,500.
	Octagonally cut	5,500.

Pleasant Shade, Va.
Typeset (5 varieties)
67X1	A1a	5c blue	2,500.	5,000.

A1  E1

Port Lavaca, Tex.
Typeset
107X1	A1	10c black, on cover	25,000.

One example known. It is uncanceled on a postmarked cover.

Raleigh, N.C.

Handstamped
68XU1	E1	5c red	450.
68XU2	E1	5c blue	2,250.

A1  E1

Rheatown, Tenn.
Typeset. Three varieties.
69X1	A1	5c red	2,000.	2,750.
	Pen canceled		2,000.

Richmond, Tex.
Handstamped
70XU1	E1	5c red	1,500.
70XU2	E1	10c red	1,000.
70XU3	E1	10c on 5c red	5,000.
70XU4	E1	15c (ms.) on 10c red	5,000.

E1 E1a

Ringgold, Ga.
Handstamped
71XU1	E1	5c blue black	3,000.

Rutherfordton, N.C.

Handstamped; "Paid 5cts" in ms.
72X1	E1a	5c black, cut round, on cover (uncanceled)	25,000.

No. 72X1 is unique.

Salem, N.C.

E1 E2

"Paid 5" in Ms.
E1

"Paid 5" Handstamped
E2

Handstamped
73XU1	E1	5c black	1,150.
73XU2	E1	10c black	1,500.
73XU3	E2	5c black	1,500.
73XU4	E2	10c on 5c black	2,800.

Reprints exist on various papers. They either lack the "Paid" and value or have them counterfeited.

125

CONFEDERATE STATES

Salisbury, N.C.

E1 Typo.
Impressed at top left
75XU1 E1 5c black, *greenish* 5,000.

One example known with part of envelope torn away, leaving part of design missing. Illustration E1 partly suppositional.

San Antonio, Tex.

E1 E2 Control

Handstamped
76XU1 E1 10c black 275. 2,000.
76XU2 E2 10c black 2,500.

Black circle control mark is on front or back.

Savannah, Ga.

E1 Control
E2

Handstamped
101XU1 E1 5c black 225.
101XU2 E2 5c black 450.
101XU3 E1 10c black 600.
101XU4 E2 10c black 600.
101XU5 E1 10c on 5c black 1,500.
101XU6 E2 20c on 5c black 2,000.

Envelope must bear octagonal control mark. One example is known of No. 101XU6.

E1 E1a

Selma, Ala.
Handstamped; Signature in ms.
77XU1 E1 5c black 1,000.
77XU2 E1 10c black 2,500.
77XU3 E1 10c on 5c black 3,000.

Sparta, Ga.
93XU1 E1a 5c red — 1,000.
93XU2 E1a 10c red 2,250.

Spartanburg, S.C.

A1 A2

Handstamped on Ruled or Plain Wove Paper
78X1 A1 5c black 3,500.
 a. "5" omitted
78X2 A2 5c black, *bluish* 4,000.
78X3 A2 5c black, *brown* 4,000.

Most examples of Nos. 78X1-78X3 are cut round. Cut square examples in sound condition are worth much more.

Statesville, N.C.

E1

Handstamped
79XU1 E1 5c black 175. 450.
79XU2 E1 10c on 5c black 2,000.

Sumter, S.C.

E1

Handstamped
80XU1 E1 5c black 300.
80XU2 E1 10c black 300.
80XU3 E1 10c on 5c black 800.
80XU4 E1 2c (ms.) on 10c black 1,100.

Used examples of Nos. 80XU1-80XU2 are indistinguishable from handstamped "Paid" covers.

Talbotton, Ga.

E1 A1

Handstamped
94XU1 E1 5c black 750.
94XU2 E1 10c black 500.
94XU3 E1 10c on 5c black 2,000.

Tellico Plains, Tenn.
Typeset Laid Paper
81X1 A1 5c red 1,250. —
81X2 A1 10c red 2,500.

Thomasville, Ga.

PAID 5 E1

Control E2

Handstamped
82XU1 E1 5c black 500.
82XU2 E2 5c black 900.

Tullahoma, Tenn.

E1 Control

Handstamped
111XU1 E1 10c black 2,000.

Tuscumbia, Ala.

E1 E1a

Handstamped
83XU1 E1 5c black 250.
83XU2 E1 10c black 250.

Used examples of Nos. 83XU1-83XU2 are indistinguishable from handstamped "Paid" covers.

Tuscumbia, Ala.
Handstamped
84XU1 E1a 5c black 2,250.
84XU2 E1a 5c red 3,000.
84XU3 E1a 10c black 3,500.

See US Postmasters' Provisional No. 12XU1.

Union City, Tenn.

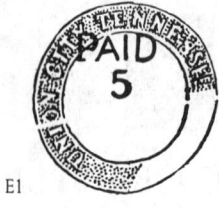

E1

The use of E1 to produce provisional envelopes is doubtful.

A1 A1a

Uniontown, Ala.
Typeset in settings of four (2x2)
Four varieties of each value
Laid Paper
86X1 A1 2c dk blue, *gray blue*,
        on cover —
86X2 A1 2c dark blue 5,500.

86X3 A1 5c green, *gray blue* 2,750. 2,000.
86X4 A1 5c green 2,750. 2,000.
86X5 A1 10c red, *gray blue*

Two examples known of No. 86X1, both on cover (drop letters), one uncanceled and one pen canceled.

Unionville, S.C.
Handstamped
Wove Paper with Blue Ruled Lines
87X1 A1a 5c black, *grayish*

Valdosta, Ga.

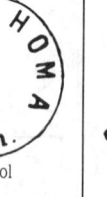

E1 Control

Handstamped
100XU1 E1 10c black 2,000.

The black control is usually on back of envelope.

Victoria, Tex.

A1 E1

Typeset
88X1 A1 5c red brown, *green* 4,000.
88X2 A1 10c red brown, *green* 5,000. 4,500.

Pelure Paper
88X3 A1 5c red brown, *green*
  ("10" in bold face
  type) 6,250. 6,250.

Walterborough, S.C.
Handstamped
108XU1 E1 10c black, *buff* 3,750.
108XU2 E1 10c carmine 3,500.

Warrenton, Ga.

E1

Handstamped
89XU1 E1 5c black 1,250.
89XU2 E1 10c (ms.) on 5c black 850.

E1 E1a

Washington, Ga.
Handstamped
117XU1 E1 10c black 2,000.

Weatherford, Tex.

Woodcut with "PAID" inserted in type.
Handstamped
| 109XU1 | E1a | 5c black | 2,000. |
| 109XU2 | E1a | 5c + 5c black | 11,000. |

No. 109XU2 is unique.

Winnsborough, S.C.

E1 — Control

Handstamped
| 97XU1 | E1 | 5c black | 1,500. |
| 97XU2 | E1 | 10c black | 2,000. |

Envelopes must bear black circle control on front or back.

Wytheville, Va.

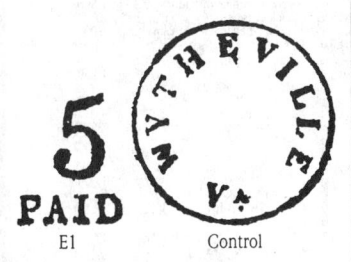

E1 — Control

Handstamped
| 114XU1 | E1 | 5c black | 900. |

For later additions, listed out of numerical sequence, see:

No. 74X1,	Liberty, Va.
No. 92XU1,	Huntsville, Tex.
No. 93XU1,	Sparta, Ga.
No. 94XU1,	Talbotton, Ga.
No. 96XU1,	Lake City, Fla.
No. 97XU1,	Winnsborough, S.C.
No. 98XU1,	Galveston, Tex.
No. 99XU1,	Christiansburg, Va.
No. 100XU1,	Valdosta, Ga.
No. 101XU1,	Savannah, Ga.
No. 102XU1,	Griffin, Ga.
No. 103XU1,	Courtland, Ala.
No. 104XU1,	Fincastle, Va.
No. 105XU1,	Micanopy, Fla.
No. 106XU1,	Pensacola, Fla.
No. 107X1,	Port Lavaca, Tex.
No. 108XU1,	Walterborough, S.C.
No. 109XU1,	Weatherford, Tex.
No. 110XU1,	Jacksonville, Ala.
No. 111XU1,	Tullahoma, Tenn.
No. 112XU1,	Hamburg, S.C.
No. 113XU1,	Columbia, Tenn.
No. 114XU1,	Wytheville, Va.
No. 115X1,	Oakway, S.C.
No. 116XU1,	Laurens Court House, S.C.
No. 117XU1,	Washington, Ga.
No. 118XU1,	Carolina City, N.C.
No. 119XU1,	Colaparchee, Ga.
No. 120XU1,	Forsyth, Ga.
No. 121XU1,	Limestone Springs, S.C.

GENERAL ISSUES

Jefferson Davis A1

Thomas Jefferson A2

1861   Unwmk.   Litho.   Imperf.

1	A1	5c green	225.00	150.00
		No gum	165.00	
a.		5c light green	225.00	150.00
		No gum	165.00	
b.		5c dark green	240.00	175.00
		No gum	175.00	
c.		5c olive green	260.00	175.00
		No gum	185.00	
2	A2	10c blue	280.00	190.00
		No gum	220.00	
a.		10c light blue	280.00	190.00
		No gum	220.00	
b.		10c dark blue	550.00	240.00
		No gum	425.00	
c.		10c indigo	2,750.	2,250.
		No gum	2,000.	
d.		Printed on both sides	—	
e.		10c greenish blue	475.00	300.00
		No gum	350.00	

The earliest printings of No. 2 were made by Hoyer & Ludwig, the later ones by J. T. Paterson & Co. Stamps of the later printings usually have a small colored dash below the lowest point of the upper left spandrel. See Nos. 4-5.

Andrew Jackson — A3

Jefferson Davis — A4

1862

3	A3	2c green	700.00	650.00
		No gum	550.00	
a.		2c bright yellow green	1,750.	—
		No gum	1,400.	
4	A1	5c blue	180.00	110.00
		No gum	135.00	
a.		5c dark blue	225.00	160.00
		No gum	160.00	
b.		5c light milky blue	270.00	200.00
		No gum	190.00	
5	A2	10c rose	1,250.	500.00
		No gum	950.00	
a.		10c carmine	2,800.	1,750.
		No gum	2,100.	

Typo.

6	A4	5c lt blue (London print)	10.00	27.50
		No gum	7.50	
7	A4	5c blue (local print)	13.00	20.00
		No gum	10.00	
a.		5c deep blue	14.00	30.00
		No gum	10.50	
b.		Printed on both sides	2,500.	850.00

No. 6 has fine, clear impression. No. 7 has coarser impression and the color is duller and often blurred.

Both 2c and 10c stamps, types A4 and A10, were privately printed in various colors.

Andrew Jackson — A5

1863   Engr.

8	A5	2c brown red	70.00	350.00
		No gum	55.00	
a.		2c pale red	90.00	450.00
		No gum	70.00	

Jefferson Davis
A6   A6a

Thick or Thin Paper

9	A6	10c blue	800.	525.
		No gum	625.	
a.		10c milky blue	800.	525.
		No gum	625.	
b.		10c gray blue	850.	625.
		No gum	650.	
10	A6a	10c blue (with frame line)	3,750.	1,250.
		No gum	3,000.	
a.		10c milky blue	3,750.	1,250.
		No gum	3,000.	
b.		10c greenish blue	4,250.	1,350.
		No gum	3,400.	
c.		10c dark blue	4,250.	1,350.
		No gum	3,400.	

Values of Nos. 10, 10a, 10b and 10c are for copies showing parts of lines on at least three sides. Stamps showing 4 complete lines sell for considerably more.

A7    A8

There are many slight differences between A7 and A8, the most noticeable being the additional line outside the ornaments at the corners of A8.

11	A7	10c blue	9.00	15.00
		No gum	7.50	
a.		10c milky blue	22.50	37.50
		No gum	19.00	
b.		10c dark blue	18.50	25.00
		No gum	15.00	
c.		10c greenish blue	17.50	17.50
		No gum	12.50	
d.		10c green	70.00	75.00
		No gum	60.00	
e.		Perforated	290.00	275.00
12	A8	10c blue	11.00	17.50
		No gum	9.00	
a.		10c milky blue	25.00	35.00
		No gum	20.00	
b.		10c light blue	11.00	17.50
		No gum	9.00	
c.		10c greenish blue	20.00	45.00
		No gum	16.50	
d.		10c dark blue	11.00	20.00
		No gum	9.00	
e.		10c green	90.00	110.00
		No gum	75.00	
f.		Perforated	290.00	275.00

The paper of Nos. 11 and 12 varies from thin hard to thick soft. The so-called laid paper is probably due to thick streaky gum.

George Washington A9

John C. Calhoun A10

13	A9	20c green	37.50	400.00
		No gum	27.50	
a.		20c yellow green	70.00	450.00
		No gum	47.50	
b.		20c dark green	65.00	500.00
		No gum	42.50	
c.		Diagonal half used as 10c on cover		2,000.
d.		Horiz. half used as 10c on cover		2,250.

1862   Typo.

14	A10	1c orange	90.00	
		No gum	70.00	
a.		1c deep orange	115.00	
		No gum	90.00	

The 1c was never put in use.

CANAL ZONE

kə-'nal 'zōn

LOCATION — A strip of land 10 miles wide, extending through the Republic of Panama, between the Atlantic and Pacific Oceans.

GOVT. — From 1904-79 a US Government Reservation; from 1979 under control of the Republic of Panama.

AREA — 552.8 sq. mi.

POP. — 41,800 (est. 1976)

The Canal Zone, site of the Panama Canal, was leased in perpetuity to the US for a cash payment of $10,000,000 and a yearly rental. Treaties between the two countries provided for transfer of control of this area to Panama in 1979, including the postal service.

100 Centavos = 1 Peso
100 Centesimos = 1 Balboa
100 Cents = 1 Dollar

Catalogue values for unused stamps in this country are for Never Hinged items, beginning with Scott 118 in the regular postage section and Scott C6 in the air post section.

Watermarks

Wmk. 190- "USPS" in Single-lined Capitals

Wmk. 191- Double-lined "USPS" in Capitals

Map of Panama — A1

Violet to Violet-blue Handstamp, "CANAL ZONE," on Panama Nos. 72-72c, 78 and 79

1904   Unwmk.   Perf. 12

1	A1	2c rose, both "PANAMA" up or down	550.00	425.00
a.		"CANAL ZONE" inverted	850.00	850.00
b.		"CANAL ZONE" double	2,000.	2,000.
c.		"CANAL ZONE" double, both inverted		
d.		"PANAMA" reading down and up	700.00	650.00
e.		As "d," "CANAL ZONE" inverted	6,500.	6,500.
f.		Vert. pair, "PANAMA" reading up on top 2c, down on other	2,000.	2,000.
2	A1	5c blue	225.00	175.00
a.		"CANAL ZONE" inverted	600.00	600.00
b.		"CANAL ZONE" double	2,250.	1,500.
c.		Pair, one without "CANAL ZONE"	5,000.	5,000.
d.		"CANAL ZONE" double, diagonal, running down to right	700.00	700.00
3	A1	10c yellow	375.00	225.00
a.		"CANAL ZONE" inverted	625.00	600.00
b.		"CANAL ZONE" double		12,500.
c.		Pair, one without "CANAL ZONE"	6,000.	5,000.
		Nos. 1-3 (3)	1,150.	825.00

On the 2c stamp "PANAMA" is normally about 13mm; on the 5c and 10c about 15mm.

Varieties of "PANAMA" overprint exist on the 2c with inverted "V" for "A," accent on "A," inverted "N," etc.

Counterfeit "CANAL ZONE" overprints exist.

US Nos. 300, 319, 304, 306 and 307 Overprinted in Black

CANAL ZONE   PANAMA

1904   Wmk. 191

4	A115	1c blue green	32.50	22.50
5	A129	2c carmine	30.00	25.00
a.		2c scarlet	32.50	25.00
6	A119	5c blue	100.00	65.00
7	A121	8c violet black	175.00	85.00
8	A122	10c pale red brown	150.00	90.00
		Nos. 4-8 (5)	487.50	287.50

Beware of fake overprints.

A2    A3

CANAL ZONE Regular Type

CANAL ZONE Antique Type

CANAL ZONE

Black Overprint on Stamps of Panama

1904-06 Unwmk.
9	A2	1c green	2.75	2.25
a.		"CANAL" in antique type	100.00	100.00
b.		"ZONE" in antique type	70.00	70.00
c.		Inverted overprint	—	2,250.
d.		Double overprint	1,250.	1,000.
10	A2	2c rose	4.50	2.50
a.		Inverted overprint	225.00	275.00
b.		"L" of "CANAL" sideways	2,500.	2,000.

Overprinted "CANAL ZONE" Black, "PANAMA" and Bar in Red on Panama Nos. 77-79 "PANAMA" 15mm long

11	A3	2c rose	7.50	5.00
a.		"ZONE" in antique type	175.00	175.00
b.		"PANAMA" inverted, bar at bottom	350.00	350.00
12	A3	5c blue	8.00	3.75
a.		"ZONE" in antique type	75.00	65.00
b.		"ZONE" in antique type	75.00	65.00
c.		"CANAL ZONE" double	600.00	600.00
d.		"PANAMA" ovpt. dbl.	1,050.	850.00
e.		"PANAMA" inverted, bar at bottom		1,000.
13	A3	10c yellow	22.50	12.50
a.		"CANAL" in antique type	200.00	200.00
b.		"ZONE" in antique type	175.00	160.00
c.		"PANAMA" ovpt. dbl.	600.00	600.00
d.		"PANAMA" overprint in red brown	27.50	27.50
		Nos. 11-13 (3)	38.00	21.25

With Added Surcharge in Red on Panama No. 81

8 cts

14	A3	8c on 50c bis brn	30.00	20.00
a.		"ZONE" in antique type	1,000.	1,000.
b.		"CANAL ZONE" invtd.	425.00	400.00
c.		Rose brown overprint	40.00	40.00
d.		As "c," "CANAL" in antique type	2,250.	
e.		As "c," "ZONE" in antique type	2,250.	
f.		As "c," "8 cts" double	850.00	
g.		As "c," "8" omitted	4,250.	

Panama No. 74 Overprinted "CANAL ZONE" in Regular Type in Black and Surch. Like No. 14 in Red. Both "PANAMA" Reading Up. "PANAMA" 13mm long.

1905
15	A3	8c on 50c bis brn	3,000.	4,500.
a.		"PANAMA" reading down & up	6,500.	—

On No. 15 with original gum the gum is almost always disturbed.

Panama Nos. 19 and 21 Surcharged in Black:

a. CANAL ZONE 1 ct.
b. CANAL ZONE 1 ct.
c. CANAL ZONE 1 ct.
d. CANAL ZONE 2 cts.

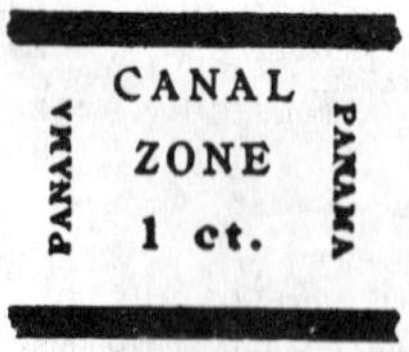

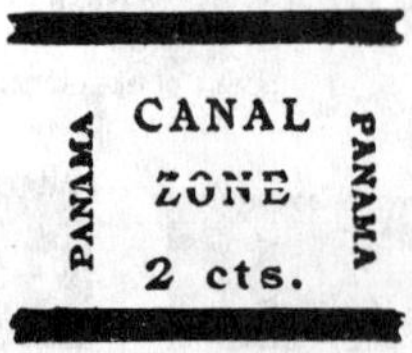

Canal Zone stamps can be mounted in the Scott U.S. Possessions album.

---

e. CANAL ZONE 2 cts.
f. CANAL ZONE 2 cts.

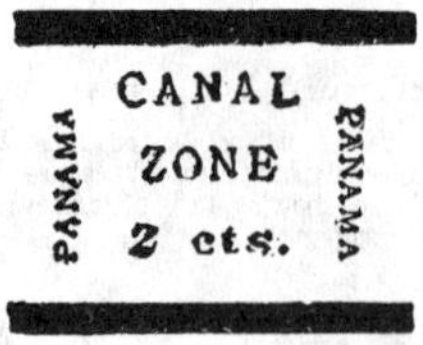

There were 3 printings of each denomination differing mainly in the relative position of the various parts of the surcharges. Varieties occur with invtd. "V" for the 3rd "A" in "PANAMA," "CA" spaced, "ZO" spaced, "2c" spaced, accents in various positions, and with bars shifted so that 2 bars appear on top or bottom of the stamp (either with or without the corresponding bar on top or bottom) and sometimes with only 1 bar at top or bottom.

1906
16	A4	1c on 20c vio, type a	1.90	1.60
a.		Surcharge type b	1.90	1.60
b.		Surcharge type c	2.00	1.60
c.		As #16, double surcharge		2,000.
17	A4	2c on 1p lake, type d	2.75	2.75
a.		Surcharge type e	2.75	2.75
b.		Surcharge type f	2.75	2.75

Panama No. 74 Overprinted "CANAL ZONE" in Regular Type in Black and Surcharged in Red

8 cts. (b)   **8 cts** (c)

Both "PANAMA" reading up
1905-06
18	A3 (b)	8c on 50c bis brn	55.00	50.00
a.		"ZONE" in antique type	200.00	180.00
b.		"PANAMA" down & up	175.00	160.00
19	A3 (c)	8c on 50c bis brn ('06)	55.00	45.00
a.		"CANAL" in antique type	210.00	180.00
b.		"ZONE" in antique type	210.00	180.00
c.		"8 cts." double	1,100.	1,100.
d.		"PANAMA" down & up	110.00	90.00

On Nos. 18-19 with original gum the gum is usually disturbed.

Panama No. 81 Overprinted "CANAL ZONE" in Regular Type in Black and Surcharged in Red Type "c" plus Period. "PANAMA" reading up and down

20	A3	8c on 50c bis brn	45.00	40.00
a.		"CANAL" in antique type	200.00	180.00
b.		"ZONE" in antique type	200.00	180.00
c.		"8 cts" omitted	750.00	750.00
d.		"8 cts" double		1,500.

Numerous minor varieties of all these surcharges exist. Nos. 14, 18, 19 and 20 exist without CANAL ZONE overprint but were not regularly issued.

Vasco Nunez de Balboa — A5
Francisco Hernandez de Cordoba — A6 
Justo Arosemena — A7 
Manuel J. Hurtado — A8 
Jose de Obaldia — A9

Stamps of Panama Ovptd. in Black
1906-07
Overprint Reading Up
21	A6	2c red & black	27.50	27.50
a.		"CANAL" only	4,000.	

Overprint Reading Down
22	A5	1c green & black	2.25	1.25
a.		Horiz. pair, imperf. btwn.	1,250.	1,250.
b.		Vert. pair, imperf. btwn.	1,750.	1,750.
c.		Vert. pair, imperf. horiz.	2,250.	1,750.
d.		Invtd. ovpt., reading up	550.00	550.00
e.		Double overprint	275.00	275.00
f.		Dbl. ovpt., one reading up	1,350.	1,350.
g.		Inverted center and ovpt. reading up	3,500.	2,750.
23	A6	2c red & black	3.25	1.40
a.		Horiz. pair, imperf. btwn.	1,750.	1,750.
b.		Vertical pair, one without overprint	1,750.	1,750.
c.		Double overprint	450.00	450.00
d.		Dbl. ovpt., one diagonal	750.00	750.00
e.		Pair, Nos. 23, 23d	1,750.	
f.		2c carmine red & black	5.00	2.75
g.		As "f," inverted center and overprint reading up		5,000.
h.		As "d," one "ZONE CANAL"	4,000.	
i.		"CANAL" double	3,250.	
24	A7	5c ultra & black	6.50	2.75
c.		Double overprint	450.00	350.00
d.		"CANAL" only	3,500.	
e.		"ZONE CANAL"	4,500.	
25	A8	8c purple & black	22.50	8.00
a.		Horizontal pair, imperf. between and at left margin	2,000.	—
26	A9	10c violet & black	20.00	8.00
a.		Dbl. ovpt., one reading up	3,250.	
b.		Overprint reading up	3,500.	
		Nos. 22-26 (5)	54.50	20.90

Nos. 22 to 25 occur with "CA" spaced.

Cordoba A11
Arosemena A12 
Hurtado — A13 
Jose de Obaldia — A14 

Overprint Reading Down
1909
27	A11	2c vermilion & black	12.50	6.50
a.		Horiz. pair, one without ovpt.	2,600.	
b.		Vert. pair, one without ovpt.	2,750.	
28	A12	5c deep blue & black	45.00	12.50
29	A13	8c violet & black	37.50	14.00
30	A14	10c violet & black	40.00	15.00
a.		Horiz. pair, one without ovpt.	2,400.	
b.		Vert. pair, one without ovpt.	2,600.	
		Nos. 27-30 (4)	135.00	48.00

Nos. 27-30 occur with "CA" spaced.
Do not confuse No. 27 with Nos. 39d or 53a.
For designs A11-A14 with overprints reading up, see Nos. 32-35, 39-41, 47-48, 53-54, 56-57.

Vasco Nunez de Balboa — A15    Type I

Black Overprint, Reading Up

Type I Overprint: "C" with serifs both top and bottom. "L" "Z" and "E" with slanting serif.

Compare Type I overprint with Types II to V illustrated before Nos. 38, 46, 52 and 55. Illustrations of Types I to V are considerably enlarged and do not show actual spacing between lines of overprint.

1909-10
31	A15	1c dk green & blk	4.00	1.60
a.		Inverted center and overprint reading down		15,000.
c.		Bklt. pane of 6 handmade, perf. margins	575.00	
32	A11	2c vermilion & blk	4.50	1.60
a.		Vert. pair, imperf. horiz	1,000.	1,000.
c.		Bklt. pane of 6, handmade, perf. margins	750.00	
d.		Double overprint		—
33	A12	5c dp blue & blk	15.00	4.00
a.		Double overprint	375.00	375.00

34	A13	8c violet & blk ('10)	11.00	5.25
a.		Vert. pair, one without ovpt.	1,500.	
35	A14	10c violet & black	50.00	20.00
		Nos. 31-35 (5)	84.50	32.45

See Nos. 38, 46, 52, 55.

A16    A17

Black Surcharge
1911
36	A16	10c on 13c gray	6.00	2.25
a.		"10 cts." inverted	250.00	250.00
b.		"10 cts." omitted	250.00	

1914
37	A17	10c gray	55.00	12.50

Type II: "C" with serif at top only. "L" and "E" with vertical serifs. "O" tilts to left

Black Overprint, Reading Up
1912-16
38	A15	1c green & blk ('13)	11.00	3.00
a.		Vert. pair, one without ovpt.	1,500.	1,500.
b.		Booklet pane of 6	600.00	
c.		As "b," handmade, perf. margins	1,000.	
39	A11	2c vermilion & blk	8.50	1.40
a.		Horiz. pair, right stamp without ovpt.	1,250.	
b.		Horiz. pair, left stamp without ovpt.	1,750.	
c.		Booklet pane of 6	500.00	
d.		Overprint reading down	175.00	
e.		As "d," inverted center	700.00	750.00
f.		As "e," booklet pane of 6 handmade, perf. margins	6,500.	
g.		As "e," handmade, perf. margins	1,000.	
h.		As #39, "CANAL" only		1,100.
40	A12	5c dp blue & blk	22.50	3.25
a.		With portrait of 2c		8,500.
41	A14	10c violet & blk ('16)	47.50	8.50
		Nos. 38-41 (4)	89.50	16.15

Map of Panama Canal — A18
Balboa Takes Possession of the Pacific Ocean — A19 
Gatun Locks — A20
Culebra Cut — A21

Blue Overprint, Type II
1915
42	A18	1c dark green & black	8.50	6.50
43	A19	2c carmine & black	10.00	4.25
44	A20	5c blue & black	11.00	5.75
45	A21	10c orange & black	22.50	11.00
		Nos. 42-45 (4)	52.00	27.50

Type III: Similar to Type I but letters appear thinner, particularly the lower bar of "L" "Z" and "E." Impressions are often light, rough and irregular

CANAL ZONE

Black Overprint, Reading Up
1915-20
46	A15	1c green & black	160.00	95.00
a.		Overprint reading down	375.00	
b.		Double overprint	300.00	
c.		"ZONE" double	4,250.	
d.		Dbl. ovpt., one "ZONE CANAL"	1,750.	
47	A11	2c orange ver & blk	3,000.	100.00
48	A12	5c dp blue & black	550.00	175.00
		Nos. 46-48 (3)	3,710.	370.00

S.S. "Panama" in Culebra Cut — A22

S.S. "Panama" in Culebra Cut — A23

S.S. "Cristobal" in Gatun Locks — A24

Blue Overprint, Type II
1917
49	A22	12c purple & black	17.50	5.50
50	A23	15c brt blue & black	55.00	22.50
51	A24	24c yel brown & black	45.00	14.00
		Nos. 49-51 (3)	117.50	42.00

Type IV: "C" thick at bottom, "E" with center bar same length as top and bottom bars

CANAL ZONE

Black Overprint, Reading Up
1918-20
52	A15	1c green & black	32.50	11.00
a.		Overprint reading down	175.00	
b.		Booklet pane of 6	650.00	
c.		Bklt. pane of 6, left vert. row of 3 without ovpt.	7,500.	
d.		Bklt. pane of 6, right vert. row of 3 with dbl. ovpt.	7,500.	
e.		Horiz. bklt. pane of 6, left stamp without overprint	3,000.	
f.		Horiz. bklt. pair, right stamp with dbl. overprint	3,000.	
53	A11	2c vermilion & blk	115.00	7.00
a.		Overprint reading down	150.00	150.00
b.		Horizontal pair, right stamp without overprint	2,000.	
c.		Booklet pane of 6	1,000.	
d.		Bklt. pane of 6, left vert. row of 3 without ovpt.	8,000.	
e.		Horiz. bklt. pair, left stamp without overprint	3,000.	4,500.
54	A12	5c dp blue & black ('20)	200.00	35.00
		Nos. 52-54 (3)	347.50	53.00

Normal spacing between words of overprint on Nos. 52 and 53 is 9 1/4mm. On No. 54 and the booklet printings of Nos. 52 and 53, the normal spacing is 9mm. Minor spacing varieties are known. No. 53e used is unique and is on cover.

Type V: Smaller block type 1 3/4mm high. "A" with flat top

CANAL ZONE

Black Overprint, Reading Up
1920-21
55	A15	1c lt green & black	22.50	3.50
a.		Overprint reading down	250.00	225.00
b.		Horiz. pair, right stamp without ovpt.	1,750.	
c.		Horiz. pair, left stamp without ovpt.	1,000.	
d.		"ZONE" only	2,750.	
e.		Booklet pane of 6	1,500.	
f.		"CANAL" double	1,250.	
56	A11	2c orange ver & blk	8.50	2.25
a.		Double overprint	575.00	
b.		Double overprint, one reading down	650.00	
c.		Horiz. pair, right stamp without ovpt.	1,500.	
d.		Horiz. pair, left stamp without ovpt.	1,000.	
e.		Vert. pair, one without overprint	1,500.	
f.		"ZONE" double	1,000.	
g.		Booklet pane of 6	850.00	
h.		"CANAL" double	1,000.	
57	A12	5c dp blue & black	325.00	55.00
a.		Horiz. pair, right stamp without ovpt.	2,500.	
b.		Horiz. pair, left stamp without ovpt.	2,500.	
		Nos. 55-57 (3)	356.00	60.75

Drydock at Balboa — A25

Ship in Pedro Miguel Locks — A26

Black Overprint, Type V
1920
58	A25	50c orange & black	275.00	160.00
59	A26	1b dk violet & blk	160.00	65.00

Jose Vallarino A27

The "Land Gate" A28

Bolivar's Tribute — A29

Municipal Building in 1821 and 1921 — A30

Statue of Balboa — A31

Tomas Herrera — A32

Jose de Fabrega — A33

Black or Red Overprint, Type V
1921
60	A27	1c green	3.75	1.40
a.		"CANAL" double	2,500.	
b.		Booklet pane of 6	900.00	
61	A28	2c carmine	3.00	1.50
a.		Overprint reading down	225.00	225.00
b.		Double overprint	900.00	
c.		Vert. pair, one without overprint	3,500.	
d.		"CANAL" double	1,900.	
f.		Booklet pane of 6	2,100.	
62	A29	5c blue (R)	11.00	4.50
a.		Overprint reading down (R)	60.00	
63	A30	10c violet	18.00	7.50
a.		Overprint reading down	100.00	
64	A31	15c light blue	47.50	17.50
65	A32	24c black brown	70.00	22.50
66	A33	50c black	150.00	100.00
		Nos. 60-66 (7)	303.25	154.90

Experts question the status of the 5c blue with a small type V overprint in red or black.

Black Overprint, Type III
1924
67	A27	1c green	500.	200.
a.		"ZONE CANAL" reading down	850.	
b.		"ZONE" reading down	1,900.	

Coat of Arms — A34

Black Overprint
1924
68	A34	1c dark green	11.00	4.50
69	A34	2c carmine	8.25	2.75

The 5c to 1b values were prepared but never issued. See listing in the Scott U.S. Specialized Catalogue.

US Nos. 551-554, 557, 562, 564-566, and 569-571 Overprinted in Red or Black

CANAL

Type A

ZONE

Letters "A" with Flat Tops

1924-25 Flat Plate Printing Perf. 11
70	A154	1/2c olive brown (R)	1.25	.75
71	A155	1c deep green	1.40	.90
a.		Inverted overprint	500.00	500.00
b.		"ZONE" inverted	350.00	325.00
c.		"CANAL" only	1,750.	
d.		"ZONE CANAL"	450.00	
e.		Booklet pane of 6	100.00	
72	A156	1 1/2c yellow brown	1.90	1.70
73	A157	2c carmine	7.50	1.70
a.		Booklet pane of 6	175.00	
74	A160	5c dark blue	19.00	8.50
75	A165	10c orange	45.00	22.50
76	A167	12c brown violet	35.00	32.50
a.		"ZONE" inverted	3,750.	3,000.
77	A168	14c dark blue	30.00	22.50
78	A169	15c gray	50.00	35.00
79	A172	30c olive brown	35.00	22.50
80	A173	50c lilac	75.00	45.00
81	A174	$1 violet brown	225.00	90.00
		Nos. 70-81 (12)	526.05	283.55

The space between the two lines of the overprint, on both type A and B, varies on some settings.

US Nos. 554, 555, 557, 562, 564-567, 569-571 and 623 Overprinted in Black or Red

CANAL

Type B

ZONE

Letters "A" with Sharp Pointed Tops

1925-26
84	A157	2c carmine	30.00	7.50
a.		"CANAL" ONLY	1,500.	
b.		"ZONE CANAL"	350.00	
c.		Horiz. pair, one without overprint	3,500.	
d.		Booklet pane of 6	175.00	
85	A158	3c violet	4.00	3.25
a.		"ZONE ZONE"	600.00	550.00
86	A160	5c dark blue	4.00	2.25
a.		"ZONE ZONE"	1,250.	
b.		"CANAL" inverted	950.00	
c.		Inverted overprint	500.00	
d.		Pair, one without overprint	3,250.	
e.		"ZONE" only	325.00	
f.		"ZONE" only	2,000.	
g.		Pair, one without ovpt., other ovpt. invtd.	2,250.	
h.		"CANAL" only	2,250.	
87	A165	10c orange	35.00	11.00
a.		"ZONE ZONE"	3,000.	
88	A167	12c brown violet	22.50	12.50
a.		"ZONE ZONE"	5,250.	
89	A168	14c dark blue	20.00	16.00
90	A169	15c gray	7.00	4.00
a.		"ZONE ZONE"	5,500.	
91	A187	17c black (R)	4.00	3.00
a.		"ZONE" only	900.00	
b.		"CANAL" only	1,700.	
c.		"ZONE CANAL"	175.00	
92	A170	20c carmine rose	7.25	3.25
a.		"CANAL" inverted	3,600.	
b.		"ZONE" inverted	3,850.	
c.		"ZONE CANAL"	3,600.	
93	A172	30c olive brown	5.00	4.00
94	A173	50c lilac	225.00	165.00
95	A174	$1 violet brown	125.00	60.00
		Nos. 84-95 (12)	488.75	291.75

Overprint Type B on US Sesquicentennial Stamp No. 627
1926
96	A188	2c carmine rose	4.50	3.75

On this stamp there is a space of 5mm between the two words of the overprint.

Overprint Type B on US Nos. 583, 584 and 591
1927 Rotary Press Printings Perf. 10
97	A157	2c carmine	42.50	11.00
a.		Pair, one without overprint	3,250.	
b.		Booklet pane of 6	650.00	
c.		"CANAL" only	2,000.	
d.		"ZONE" only	2,750.	
98	A158	3c violet	8.00	4.25
99	A165	10c orange	17.50	7.25
		Nos. 97-99 (3)	68.00	22.50

Overprint Type B on US Nos. 632, 634, 635, 637 and 642
Rotary Press Printings
1927-31 Perf. 11x10 1/2
100	A155	1c green	2.25	1.40
a.		Pair, one without overprint	3,000.	
101	A157	2c carmine	2.50	1.00
a.		Booklet pane of 6	175.00	
102	A158	3c violet	4.25	2.75
a.		Booklet pane of 6, handmade, perf. margins	6,500.	
103	A160	5c dark blue	30.00	10.00
104	A165	10c orange	17.50	10.00
		Nos. 100-104 (5)	56.50	25.15

Wet and Dry Printings

Canal Zone stamps printed by both the "wet" and "dry" process are Nos. 105, 108-109, 111-114, 117, 138-140, C21-C24, C26, J25, J27. Starting with Nos. 147 and C27, the Bureau of Engraving and Printing used the "dry" method exclusively. See note following US Scott 1029.

Maj. Gen. William Crawford Gorgas — A35

Maj. Gen. George Washington Goethals — A36

Gaillard Cut — A37

Maj. Gen. Harry Foote Hodges — A38

Lt. Col. David D. Gaillard — A39

Maj. Gen. William L. Sibert — A40

Jackson Smith — A41

Rear Adm. Harry H. Rousseau — A42

Col. Sydney B. Williamson — A43

J.C.S. Blackburn — A44

1928-40 Flat Plate Printing Perf. 11
105	A35	1c green	.15	.15
106	A36	2c carmine	.16	.15
a.		Booklet pane of 6	15.00	20.00
107	A37	5c blue ('29)	1.00	.40
108	A38	10c orange ('32)	.20	.20
109	A39	12c violet brown ('29)	.75	.60
110	A40	14c blue ('37)	.85	.85
111	A41	15c gray ('32)	.40	.35
112	A42	20c olive brown ('32)	.60	.20

CANAL ZONE

113 A43 30c brown black ('40) .80 .70
114 A44 50c lilac ('29) 1.50 .65
Nos. 105-114 (10) 6.41 4.25

For surcharges & overprints see #J21-J24, O1-O8.

United States Nos. 720 and 695
Overprinted type B

Rotary Press Printing
1933 Perf. 11x10½
115 A226 3c deep violet 2.75 .25
  b. "CANAL" only 2,600.
  c. Bklt. pane of 6, handmade, perf. margins 225.00
116 A168 14c dark blue 4.50 3.50
  a. "ZONE CANAL" 1,500.

Gen. George Washington Goethals — A45

Flat Plate Printing
1934, Aug. 15 Perf. 11
117 A45 3c deep violet .15 .15
  a. Booklet pane of 6 45.00 32.50
  b. As "a," handmade, perf. margins 225.00

20th anniv. of the Panama Canal opening. See No. 153.

Catalogue values for unused stamps in this section, from this point to the end of the section, are for Never Hinged items.

US Nos. 803 and 805 Overprinted in Black — **CANAL ZONE**

Rotary Press Printing
1939 Perf. 11x10½
118 A275 ½c deep orange .15 .15
119 A277 1½c bister brown .15 .15

Panama Canal Anniversary Issue

Balboa-Before A46
Balboa-After A47 
Gaillard Cut-Before A48 
Gaillard Cut-After A49 
Bas Obispo-Before A50 
Bas Obispo-After A51 
Gatun Locks-Before A52 
Gatun Locks-After A53 
Canal Channel-Before A54
Canal Channel-After A55
Gamboa-Before A56
Gamboa-After A57
Pedro Miguel Locks-Before A58
Pedro Miguel Locks-After A59
Gatun Spillway-Before A60
Gatun Spillway-After A61

Flat Plate Printing
1939, Aug. 15 Perf. 11
120 A46 1c yellow green .65 .30
121 A47 2c rose carmine .65 .35
122 A48 3c purple .65 .15
123 A49 5c dark blue 1.60 1.25
124 A50 6c red orange 3.00 3.00
125 A51 7c black 3.25 3.00
126 A52 8c green 4.75 3.50
127 A53 10c ultramarine 3.50 3.00
128 A54 11c blue green 8.00 8.50
129 A55 12c brown carmine 7.50 8.00
130 A56 14c dark violet 7.50 8.00
131 A57 15c olive green 10.00 6.00
132 A58 18c rose pink 10.00 8.50
133 A59 20c brown 12.50 7.50
134 A60 25c orange 17.50 17.50
135 A61 50c violet brown 22.50 6.00
Nos. 120-135 (16) 113.55 84.55

25th anniv. of the Panama Canal.

Maj. Gen. George W. Davis — A62
Gov. Charles E. Magoon — A63
Theodore Roosevelt — A64 
John F. Stevens — A65
John F. Wallace — A66 

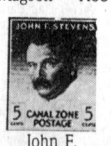

1946-49 Size: 19x22mm Perf. 11
136 A62 ½c bright red ('48) .40 .25
137 A63 1½c chocolate ('48) .40 .25
138 A64 2c rose carmine ('49) .15 .15
139 A65 5c deep blue .35 .20
140 A66 25c yellow green ('48) .85 .55
Nos. 136-140 (5) 2.15 1.40

See #155, 162, 164. For overprint see #O9.

Map of Biological Area and Coati-Mundi A67

1948, Apr. 17 Perf. 11
141 A67 10c black 1.10 .80

25th anniv. of the establishment of the Canal Zone Biological Area on Barro Colorado Is.

"Forty-niners" Arriving at Chagres — A68
Journey by "Bungo" to Las Cruces — A69 
Las Cruces Trail to Panama — A70 
Departure for San Francisco — A71

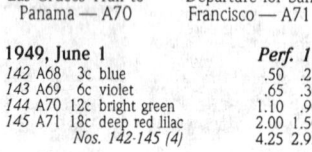

1949, June 1 Perf. 11
142 A68 3c blue .50 .25
143 A69 6c violet .65 .30
144 A70 12c bright green 1.10 .90
145 A71 18c deep red lilac 2.00 1.50
Nos. 142-145 (4) 4.25 2.95

Centenary of the California Gold Rush.

Workers in Culebra Cut — A72
Early Railroad Scene — A73 

1951, Aug. 15
146 A72 10c carmine 2.25 1.50

Contribution of West Indian laborers in the construction of the Canal.

1955, Jan. 28 Perf. 11
147 A73 3c violet .60 .50

Cent. of the completion of the Panama Railroad and the 1st transcontinental railroad trip in Americas.

Gorgas Hospital and Ancon Hill — A74

1957, Nov. 17
148 A74 3c black, blue green .40 .35

75th anniv. of Gorgas Hospital. Printed on two shades of blue green paper.

S.S. Ancon — A75

1958, Aug. 30 Engr. Unwmk.
149 A75 4c greenish blue .35 .30

Roosevelt Medal and Map — A76

1958, Nov. 15 Perf. 11
150 A76 4c brown .40 .30

Theodore Roosevelt (1858-1919).

Boy Scout Badge — A77
Administration Building — A78 

Giori Press Printing
1960, Feb. 8 Perf. 11
151 A77 4c dk blue, red & bister .45 .40

Boy Scouts of America, 50th anniv.

1960, Nov. 1 Engr. Perf. 11
152 A78 4c rose lilac .20 .15

Types of 1934, 1960 and 1946
Coil Stamps
1960-62 Perf. 10 Vert.
153 A45 3c deep violet .20 .15
Perf. 10 Horizontally
154 A78 4c deep rose lilac .20 .15
Perf. 10 Vertically
155 A65 5c deep blue .25 .20
Nos. 153-155 (3) .65 .50

Issue dates: 3c, 4c, 1960. 5c, Feb. 10, 1962.

Girl Scout Badge and Camp at Gatun Lake — A79

Giori Press Printing
1962, Mar. 12 Perf. 11
156 A79 4c blue, dk green & bister .40 .30

50th anniv. of Girl Scouts.

Thatcher Ferry Bridge and Map of Western Hemisphere A80

1962, Oct. 12
157 A80 4c black & silver .30 .25
  a. Silver (bridge) omitted 7,000.

Opening of the Thatcher Ferry Bridge, spanning the Panama Canal.

Goethals Memorial, Balboa — A81
Fort San Lorenzo — A82 

Giori Press Printing
1968-71 Perf. 11
158 A81 6c green & ultra .30 .30
159 A82 8c multicolored .35 .20

Issued: 6c, Mar. 15, 1968; 8c, July 14, 1971.

CANAL ZONE

Portrait Type of 1928-48
Coil Stamps
1975, Feb. 14   Engr.   Perf. 10 Vert.
160	A35	1c green	.15	.15
161	A38	10c orange	.70	.40
162	A66	25c yellow green	2.75	2.75
		Nos. 160-162 (3)	3.60	3.30

Dredge Cascadas A83

Giori Press Printing
1976, Feb. 23   Perf. 11
163	A83	13c multicolored	.35	.20
a.		Booklet pane of 4	3.00	—

Stevens Type of 1946
Rotary Press Printing
1977   Perf. 11x10½
Size: 19x22½mm
164	A65	5c deep blue	.60	.85
a.		Tagged	9.50	—

Towing Locomotive, Ship in Lock — A84

1978, Oct. 25   Engr.   Perf. 11
165	A84	15c dp green & blue green	.35	.20

AIR POST STAMPS

AIR MAIL

Nos. 105-106 Surcharged in Dark Blue

25 CENTS 25

Type I- Flag of "5" pointing up   **15**

Type II- Flag of "5" curved   **15**

Flat Plate Printing
1929   Unwmk.   Perf. 11
C1	A35	15c on 1c green, I	8.00	5.50
C2	A35	15c on 1c green, II	85.00	75.00
C3	A36	25c on 2c carmine	3.50	2.00
		Nos. C1-C3 (3)	96.50	82.50

AIR MAIL

Nos. 114 and 106 Surcharged

=10c

1929, Dec. 31
C4	A44	10c on 50c lilac	7.50	6.50
C5	A36	20c on 2c carmine	5.00	1.75
a.		Dropped "2" in surcharge	80.00	60.00

Catalogue values for unused stamps in this section, from this point to the end of the section, are for Never Hinged items.

Gaillard Cut — AP1

1931-49   Engr.
C6	AP1	4c red violet ('49)	.75	.70
C7	AP1	5c yellow green	.60	.15
C8	AP1	6c yellow brown ('46)	.75	.35
C9	AP1	10c orange	1.00	.35
C10	AP1	15c blue	1.25	.30
C11	AP1	20c red violet	2.00	.30
C12	AP1	30c rose lake ('41)	3.50	1.00
C13	AP1	40c yellow	3.50	1.10
C14	AP1	$1 black	8.50	1.90
		Nos. C6-C14 (9)	21.85	6.45

For overprints see Nos. CO1-CO14.

Douglas Plane over Sosa Hill — AP2

Planes and Map of Central America — AP3

Pan American Clipper and Scene near Fort Amador — AP4

Pan American Clipper at Cristobal Harbor — AP5

Pan American Clipper over Gaillard Cut — AP6

Pan American Clipper Landing — AP7

1939, July 15
C15	AP2	5c greenish black	3.75	2.25
C16	AP3	10c dull violet	3.00	2.25
C17	AP4	15c light brown	4.25	1.25
C18	AP5	25c blue	13.00	8.00
C19	AP6	30c rose carmine	12.00	6.75
C20	AP7	$1 green	35.00	22.50
		Nos. C15-C20 (6)	71.00	43.00

10th anniv. of Air Mail service and the 25th anniv. of the opening of the Panama Canal.

Globe and Wing — AP8

1951, July 16   Unwmk.   Perf. 11
C21	AP8	4c red violet	.75	.35
C22	AP8	6c brown	.50	.35
C23	AP8	10c red orange	.90	.35
C24	AP8	21c blue	7.50	4.00
C25	AP8	31c cerise	7.50	3.75
a.		Horiz. pair, imperf. vert.	1,000.	
C26	AP8	80c gray black	4.50	1.50
		Nos. C21-C26 (6)	21.65	10.20

1958, Aug. 16
C27	AP8	5c yellow green	1.00	.60
C28	AP8	7c olive	1.00	.45
C29	AP8	15c brown violet	3.75	2.75
C30	AP8	25c orange yellow	10.00	2.75
C31	AP8	35c dark blue	6.25	2.75
		Nos. C27-C31 (5)	22.00	9.30
		Nos. C21-C31 (11)	43.65	19.50

See No. C34.

Emblem of US Army Caribbean School — AP9

Giori Press Printing
1961, Nov. 21   Perf. 11
C32	AP9	15c red & dk blue	1.25	.75

Malaria Eradication Emblem and Mosquito AP10

1962, Sept. 24   Unwmk.   Perf. 11
C33	AP10	7c yellow & black	.45	.40

WHO drive to eradicate malaria.

Type of 1951
Rotary Press Printing
1963, Jan. 7   Perf. 10½x11
C34	AP8	8c carmine	.40	.30

Alliance Emblem AP11

Giori Press Printing
1963, Aug. 17   Unwmk.   Perf. 11
C35	AP11	15c gray, green & dk.ultra	1.10	.85

2nd anniv. of the Alliance for Progress, which aims to stimulate economic growth and raise living standards in Latin America.

Jet over Cristobal AP12

Designs: 8c, Gatun Locks. 15c, Madden Dam. 20c, Gaillard Cut. 30c, Miraflores Locks. 80c, Balboa.

1964, Aug. 15   Perf. 11
C36	AP12	6c green & black	.45	.35
C37	AP12	8c rose red & black	.45	.35
C38	AP12	15c blue & black	1.00	.75
C39	AP12	20c rose lilac & blk	1.50	1.00
C40	AP12	30c redsh brown & blk	2.25	2.25
C41	AP12	80c ol bister & black	3.75	3.00
		Nos. C36-C41 (6)	9.40	7.70

50th anniv. of the Panama Canal.

Seal and Jet Plane — AP13

1965, July 15   Unwmk.   Perf. 11
C42	AP13	6c green & black	.35	.30
C43	AP13	8c rose red & black	.30	.15
C44	AP13	15c blue & black	.50	.20
C45	AP13	20c lilac & black	.55	.30
C46	AP13	30c redsh brn & blk	.80	.30
C47	AP13	80c bister & black	2.00	.75
		Nos. C42-C47 (6)	4.50	2.00

1968-76
C48	AP13	10c dull orange & blk	.25	.15
a.		Booklet pane of 4 ('70)	4.25	—
C49	AP13	11c gray olive & blk	.25	.20
a.		Booklet pane of 4	3.50	—
C50	AP13	13c emerald & black	.80	.25
a.		Booklet pane of 4	6.00	—
C51	AP13	22c violet & black	.75	2.00
C52	AP13	25c pale yel green & blk	.60	.70
C53	AP13	35c salmon & black	.90	2.00
		Nos. C48-C53 (6)	3.55	5.30

Issued: 10c, 25c, 3/15/68; 11c, 9/24/71; 13c, 2/11/74; 22c, 35c, 5/10/76.

AIR POST OFFICIAL STAMPS

Officials and Air Post Officials were sold to the public only with a Balboa Heights, Canal Zone wavy line parcel post cancel while current. After being withdrawn from use, unused copies (except for Nos. CO8-CO12, O3 and O8) were sold at face value for three months beginning Jan. 2, 1952.

Used values are for the CTO copies, postally used copies being worth more.

OFFICIAL
Nos. C7, C9-C14 Overprinted in Black **PANAMA CANAL**

Two Types of Overprint
1941-42   Unwmk.   Perf. 11
"PANAMA CANAL" 19-20mm
CO1	AP1	5c yellow green	5.50	1.50
CO2	AP1	10c orange	8.50	2.00
CO3	AP1	15c blue	11.00	2.00
CO4	AP1	20c red violet	12.50	4.00
CO5	AP1	30c rose lake ('42)	17.50	5.00
CO6	AP1	40c yellow	17.50	7.50
CO7	AP1	$1 black	20.00	10.00
		Nos. CO1-CO7 (7)	92.50	32.00

Overprint varieties occur on Nos. CO1-CO7 and CO14: "O" over "N" of "PANAMA" (entire 3rd row). "O" broken at top (pos. 31). "O" over 2nd "A" of "PANAMA" (pos. 45). 1st "F" of "OFFICIAL" over 2nd "A" of "PANAMA" (pos. 50).

1941
"PANAMA CANAL" 17mm long
CO8	AP1	5c light green	—	160.00
CO9	AP1	10c orange	—	275.00
CO10	AP1	20c red violet	—	175.00
CO11	AP1	30c rose lake	—	65.00
CO12	AP1	40c yellow	—	180.00
		Nos. CO8-CO12 (5)		855.00

Same Overprint on No. C8
1947, Nov.
"PANAMA CANAL" 19-20mm long
CO14	AP1	6c yellow brown	12.50	5.00
a.		Inverted overprint	2,500.	

POSTAGE DUE STAMPS

Postage Due Stamps of the US Nos. J45a, J46a and J49a Overprinted in Black **CANAL ZONE**

1914, Mar.   Wmk. 190   Perf. 12
J1	D2	1c rose carmine	85.00	15.00
J2	D2	2c rose carmine	250.00	45.00
J3	D2	10c rose carmine	850.00	40.00
		Nos. J1-J3 (3)	1,185.	100.00

Castle Gate (See footnote) — D1

Statue of Columbus D2

Pedro J. Sosa D3

Blue Overprint, Type II, on Postage Due Stamps of Panama

1915   Unwmk.
J4	D1	1c olive brown	12.50	5.00
J5	D2	2c olive brown	200.00	17.50
J6	D3	10c olive brown	50.00	10.00
		Nos. J4-J6 (3)	262.50	32.50

The 1c was intended to show a gate of San Lorenzo Castle, Chagres. By error the stamp actually shows the main gate of San Geronimo Castle, Portobelo.

CANAL ZONE — CUBA

Surcharged in Red   CANAL **2** ZONE

J7	D1	1c on 1c olive brn	105.00 15.00
J8	D2	2c on 2c olive brn	25.00 7.00
J9	D3	10c on 10c olive brn	22.50 5.00
		Nos. J7-J9 (3)	152.50 27.00

Columbus Statue — D4
Capitol, Panama City — D5 

Carmine Surcharge

1919

J10	D4	2c on 2c olive brown	30.00 12.50
J11	D5	4c on 4c olive brown	35.00 15.00
a.		"ZONE" omitted	7,500.
b.		"4" omitted	7,500.

US Postage Due Stamps Nos. J61, J62b and J65b Overprinted in Black

CANAL

Type A

ZONE

Letters "A" with Flat Tops

1924   Perf. 11

J12	D2	1c carmine rose	110.00 27.50
J13	D2	2c deep claret	60.00 10.00
J14	D2	10c deep claret	250.00 50.00
		Nos. J12-J14 (3)	420.00 87.50

US Postage Stamps Nos. 552, 554 and 562 Overprinted Type A and additional Overprint in Red or Blue

POSTAGE DUE

1925

J15	A155	1c deep green	90.00 13.00
J16	A157	2c carmine (Bl)	22.50 7.00
J17	A165	10c orange	50.00 11.00
a.		"POSTAGE DUE" double	450.00
b.		"E" of "POSTAGE" missing	450.00
c.		As "a" and "b"	3,250.
		Nos. J15-J17 (3)	162.50 31.00

"CANAL ZONE" Type B Overprinted on US Nos. J61, J62, J65, J65a
Letters "A" with Sharp Pointed Tops

1925

J18	D2	1c carmine rose	8.00 3.00
a.		"ZONE ZONE"	1,250.
J19	D2	2c carmine rose	15.00 4.00
a.		"ZONE ZONE"	1,500.
J20	D2	10c carmine rose	150.00 20.00
a.		Pair, one without overprint	1,750.
b.		10c rose red	250.00 150.00
c.		As "b," double overprint	425.00 —
		Nos. J18-J20 (3)	173.00 27.00

No. 107 Surcharged in Black

POSTAGE DUE **10**

1929-30

J21	A37	1c on 5c blue	4.50 1.75
a.		"POSTAGE DUE" omitted	5,000.
J22	A37	2c on 5c blue	7.50 2.50
J23	A37	5c on 5c blue	7.50 2.75
J24	A37	10c on 5c blue	7.50 2.75
		Nos. J21-J24 (4)	27.00 9.75

On No. J23 the horizontal bars in the lower corners of the surcharge are omitted.

POSTAGE DUE 1 CENT   CANAL ZONE

Canal Zone Seal — D6

1932-41

J25	D6	1c claret	.15 .15
J26	D6	2c claret	.15 .20
J27	D6	5c claret	.35 .20
J28	D6	10c claret	1.40 1.50
J29	D6	15c claret ('41)	1.10 1.00
		Nos. J25-J29 (5)	3.15 3.05

The 1c and 5c are found in both "wet" and "dry" printings. (See note after US No. 1029.) The dry printings are in red violet.

OFFICIAL STAMPS

See note at beginning of Air Post Official Stamps.

Regular Issues of 1928-34 Overprinted in Black:

OFFICIAL PANAMA CANAL Type 1	OFFICIAL PANAMA CANAL Type 2

Type 1 - "PANAMA" 10mm long.
Type 1A - "PANAMA" 9mm long.

1941   Unwmk.   Perf. 11

O1	A35	1c yellow green (1)	2.25 .40
O2	A45	3c deep violet (1)	4.00 .75
O3	A37	5c blue (2)	1,000. 32.50
O4	A38	10c orange (1)	7.00 1.90
O5	A41	15c gray (1)	12.50 2.25
O6	A42	20c olive brown (1)	15.00 2.75
O7	A44	50c lilac (1)	37.50 5.50
O8	A44	50c rose lilac (1A)	625.00

Same Overprint on No. 139

1947

O9	A65	5c deep blue (1)	9.00 3.50

CUBA

'kyü–bə

LOCATION — The largest island of the West Indies; south of Florida.
GOVT. — socialist; under US military governor 1899-1902 and US provisional governor 1906-1909.
AREA — 44,206 sq. mi.
POP. — 9,710,000 (1981)
CAPITAL — Havana

Formerly a Spanish possession, Cuba's attempts to gain freedom led to US intervention in 1898. Under Treaty of Paris of that year, Spain relinquished the island to US trust. In 1902, a republic was established and Cuban Congress took over government from US military authorities.

100 Cents = 1 Dollar

Watermark

Wmk. 191- Double-lined "USPS" in Capitals

Values for Nos. 176-220 are for stamps in the grade of fine and in sound condition where such exist. Values for Nos. 221-J4 are for very fine examples.

King Alfonso XIII
A19   N2

United States Administration
Puerto Principe Issue
Issues of Cuba of 1898 and 1896 Surcharged:

HABILITADO **1** cent. (a)   HABILITADO **1** cents. (b)
HABILITADO **2** cents. (c)   HABILITADO **2** cents. (d)
HABILITADO **3** cents. (e)   HABILITADO **3** cents. (f)
HABILITADO **5** cents. (g)   HABILITADO **5** cents. (h)
HABILITADO **5** cents. (i)   HABILITADO **5** cents. (j)
HABILITADO **3** cents. (k)   HABILITADO **3** cents. (l)
HABILITADO **10** cents. (m)

Types a, c, d, e, f, g and h are 17½mm high, the others are 19½mm high.

Black Surcharge on #156-158, 160

1898-99

176	(a)	1c on 1m org brn	45. 30.
177	(b)	1c on 1m org brn	45. 35.
a.		Broken figure "1"	75. 65.
b.		Inverted surcharge	200.
d.		As "a," inverted	250.
178	(c)	2c on 2m org brn	22.50 18.
a.		Inverted surcharge	250. 50.
179	(d)	3c on 2m org brn	40. 35.
a.		Inverted surcharge	350. 100.
179B	(k)	3c on 1m org brn	300. 175.
c.		Double surcharge	1,500. 750.
179D	(l)	3c on 1m org brn	1,500. 675.
e.		Double surcharge	—
179F	(e)	3c on 2m org brn	1,500.

Value for No. 179F is for copies with minor faults.

179G	(f)	3c on 2m org brn	— 2,000.

Value for No. 179G is for copies with minor faults.

180	(e)	3c on 3m org brown	27.50 30.
a.		Inverted surcharge	100.
181	(h)	3c on 3m org brown	75. 75.
a.		Inverted surcharge	200.
182	(g)	5c on 1m org brown	700. 200.
a.		Inverted surcharge	500.
183	(h)	5c on 1m org brown	1,300. 500.
a.		Inverted surcharge	700.
184	(g)	5c on 2m org brown	750. 250.
185	(h)	5c on 2m org brown	1,500. 500.

186	(g)	5c on 3m org brown	165.
a.		Inverted surcharge	700.
187	(h)	5c on 3m org brown	400.
a.		Inverted surcharge	1,000.
188	(g)	5c on 5m org brown	70. 60.
a.		Inverted surcharge	400. 200.
b.		Double surcharge	—
189	(h)	5c on 5m org brown	350. 250.
a.		Inverted surcharge	400.
b.		Double surcharge	—

Values for Nos. 188, 189 are for the 1st printing. The 2nd printing was surcharged using a shiny ink.

189C	(i)	5c on 5m org brown	7,500.

Black Surcharge on No. P25

190	(g)	5c on ½m blue grn	250. 75.
a.		Inverted surcharge	500. 150.
b.		Pair, one without surch.	500.

Value for No. 190b is for pair with unsurcharged copy at right. Exists with unsurcharged stamp at left.

191	(h)	5c on ½m blue grn	300. 90.
a.		Inverted surcharge	200.
192	(i)	5c on ½m blue grn	550. 200.
a.		Dbl. surch., one diagonal	11,500.
193	(j)	5c on ½m blue grn	700. 300.

Red Surcharge on No. 161

196	(k)	3c on 1c black violet	60. 35.
a.		Inverted surcharge	300.
197	(l)	3c on 1c black violet	125. 55.
a.		Inverted surcharge	300.
198	(l)	5c on 1c black violet	20. 25.
b.		Vert. surch., reading up	3,500.
c.		Double surcharge	400. 600.
d.		Double invtd. surcharge	

No. 198b exists reading down.

199	(j)	5c on 1c black vio	50. 50.
a.		Inverted surcharge	250.
b.		Vertical surcharge	2,000.
c.		Double surcharge	1,000. 600.
200	(m)	10c on 1c black vio	20. 50.
a.		Broken figure "1"	40. 100.

Black Surcharge on Nos. P26-P30

201	(k)	3c on 1m blue green	350. 350.
a.		Inverted surcharge	450.
b.		"EENTS"	550. 450.
c.		As "b," inverted	850.
202	(l)	3c on 1m blue green	500. 400.
a.		Inverted surcharge	850.
203	(k)	3c on 2m blue green	850. 350.
a.		Inverted surcharge	1,250. 450.
b.		"EENTS"	850.
c.		As "a," inverted	950.
204	(l)	3c on 2m blue green	1,250. 600.
a.		Inverted surcharge	750.
205	(k)	3c on 3m blue green	900. 350.
a.		Inverted surcharge	500.
b.		"EENTS"	1,250. 450.
c.		As "b," inverted	700.
206	(l)	3c on 3m blue green	1,200. 550.
a.		Inverted surcharge	700.
211	(i)	5c on 1m blue green	1,800.
a.		"EENTS"	— 2,500.
212	(j)	5c on 1m blue green	2,250.
213	(i)	5c on 2m blue green	1,800.
a.		"EENTS"	— 1,900.
214	(j)	5c on 2m blue green	1,750.
215	(i)	5c on 3m blue green	500.
a.		"EENTS"	— 1,000.
216	(j)	5c on 3m blue green	— 1,000.
217	(i)	5c on 4m blue green	2,500. 900.
a.		Inverted surcharge	3,000. 1,500.
b.		"EENTS"	2,000.
c.		As "a," inverted	2,000.
218	(j)	5c on 4m blue green	1,250.
a.		Inverted surcharge	2,000.
219	(i)	5c on 8m blue green	2,500. 1,250.
a.		Inverted surcharge	1,500.
b.		"EENTS"	— 1,800.
c.		As "b," inverted	2,500.
220	(j)	5c on 8m blue green	2,000.
a.		Inverted surcharge	2,500.

CUBA

US Nos. 279, 267, 279B, 268, 281, 282C and 283 Surcharged in Black

1 c. de PESO.

1899   Wmk. 191   Perf. 12

221	A87	1c on 1c yellow green	5.25 .35
222	A88	2c on 2c reddish car, type III	10.00 .75
b.		2c on 2c vermilion, type III	10.00 .75
222A	A88	2c on 2c reddish car, type IV	5.75 .40
c.		2c on 2c vermilion, type IV	5.75 .40
d.		As #222A, inverted surcharge	3,500. 3,500.
223	A88	2½c on 2c reddish car, type III	5.00 .80
b.		2½c on 2c vermilion, type III	5.00 .80
223A	A88	2½c on 2c reddish car, type IV	3.50 .50
c.		2½c on 2c vermilion	3.50 .50
224	A89	3c on 3c purple	10.00 1.75
a.		"CUBA.A"	35.00 35.00
225	A91	5c on 5c blue	10.00 2.00
226	A94	10c on 10c br brn, type I	20.00 6.50
b.		"CUBA" omitted	4,000. 4,000.

CUBA — DANISH WEST INDIES

226A A94 10c on 10c brn, type II 6,000.
Nos. 221-226 (8) 69.50 13.05

The 2½c was sold and used as a 2 centavo stamp.

Excellent counterfeits of this and the preceding issue exist, especially inverted and double surcharges.

Issues of the Republic under US Military Rule

Statue of Columbus — A20
Royal Palms — A21 
"Cuba" — A22 
Ocean Liner — A23 
Cane Field — A24 

Wmk. U S-C (191C)

1899		Engr.	Perf. 12	
227	A20	1c yellow green	3.50	.15
228	A21	2c carmine	3.50	.15
a.		2c scarlet	3.50	.15
b.		Booklet pane of 6	2,000.	
229	A22	3c purple	3.50	.15
230	A23	5c blue	4.50	.20
231	A24	10c brown	11.00	.50
		Nos. 227-231 (5)	26.00	1.15

Unwatermarked stamps of designs A20-A24 were re-engraved and issued by the Cuban Republic. See Volume 2 for details of the re-engraving.

SPECIAL DELIVERY STAMPS

United States Administration

US No. E5 Surcharged in Red

CUBA.
10c.
de PESO

1899		Wmk. 191	Perf. 12	
E1	SD3	10c on 10c blue	130.00	100.00
a.		No period after "CUBA"	450.00	400.00

Issues of the Republic under US Military Rule

Special Delivery Messenger SD2

Inscribed: "Immediata"

1899		Wmk. 191C	Engr.	
E2	SD2	10c orange	45.00	15.00

POSTAGE DUE STAMPS

United States Administration

Postage Due Stamps of the US Nos. J38, J39, J41 and J42 Surcharged in Black Like Nos. 221-226A

1899		Wmk. 191	Perf. 12	
J1	D2	1c on 1c deep claret	45.00	5.25
J2	D2	2c on 2c deep claret	45.00	5.25
a.		Inverted surcharge	2,500.	
J3		5c on 5c deep claret	45.00	5.25
J4	D2	10c on 10c deep claret	27.50	2.50
		Nos. J1-J4 (4)	162.50	18.25

DANISH WEST INDIES

'dā-nish 'west 'in-dēs

LOCATION — Group of islands in the West Indies, lying east of Puerto Rico
GOVT. — Danish colony
AREA — 132 sq. mi.
POP. — 27,086 (1911)
CAPITAL — Charlotte Amalie

The US bought these islands in 1917 and they became the US Virgin Islands, using US stamps and currency.

100 Cents = 1 Dollar
100 Bit = 1 Franc (1905)

Watermarks

Wmk. 111- Small Crown 
Wmk. 112- Crown 
Wmk. 113- Crown 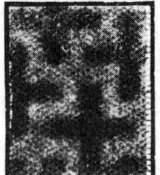
Wmk. 114- Multiple Crosses

Coat of Arms — A1

Yellowish Paper
Yellow Wavy-line Burelage, UL to LR

1856		Wmk. 111	Typo.	Imperf.
1	A1	3c dk car, brown gum	150.	185.
a.		3c dark carmine, yellow gum	160.	200.
b.		3c carmine, white gum	3,000.	3,000.

Reprint: 1981, carmine, back-printed across two stamps ("Reprint by Dansk Post og Telegrafmuseum 1978"), value, pair, $10.

White Paper
Yellow Wavy-line Burelage, UR to LL

1866				
2	A1	3c rose	50.00	40.00

No. 2 reprints unwatermarked: 1930 carmine, value $100. 1942 rose carmine, back-printed across each row ("Nytryk 1942 G. A. Hagemann Danmark og Dansk Vestindiens Friemaerker Bind 2"), value $50.

1872			Perf. 12½	
3	A1	3c rose	75.00	125.00

1873
Without Burelage

4	A1	4c dull blue	100.00	250.00
a.		Imperf., pair	600.00	—
b.		Horiz. pair, imperf. vert.	500.00	—

#4 reprints, unwatermarked, imperf.: 1930, ultramarine, value $100. 1942, blue back-printed like 1942 reprint of #2, value $50.

A2

Normal Frame
Inverted Frame 

The arabesques in the corners have a main stem and a branch. When the frame is in normal position, in the upper left corner the branch leaves the main stem half way between two little leaflets. In the lower right corner the branch starts at the foot of the second leaflet. When the frame is inverted the corner designs are, of course, transposed.

White Wove Paper, Varying from Thin to Thick

1874-79		Wmk. 112	Perf. 14x13½	
5	A2	1c green & brn red	17.50	10.00
a.		1c grn & rose lilac, thin paper	75.00	40.00
b.		1c grn & red violet, medium paper	40.00	40.00
c.		1c green & violet, thick paper	17.50	10.00
e.		Inverted frame	17.50	10.00
6	A2	3c blue & carmine	17.50	10.00
d.		Imperf., pair	300.00	
e.		Inverted frame	17.50	10.00
7	A2	4c brn & dull blue	15.00	15.00
		4c brown & ultramarine	250.00	200.00
c.		Diagonal half used as 2c on cover		100.00
d.		Inverted frame	1,500.	1,500.
8	A2	5c green & gray ('76)	20.00	15.00
b.		Inverted frame	20.00	15.00
9	A2	7c lilac & orange	20.00	35.00
a.		7c lilac & yellow	40.00	50.00
b.		Inverted frame	30.00	60.00
10	A2	10c blue & brn ('76)	20.00	10.00
b.		"cent.s"	25.00	17.50
c.		Inverted frame	20.00	10.00
11	A2	12c red lilac & yel green ('77)	22.50	37.50
a.		12c lilac & deep green	75.00	75.00
12	A2	14c lilac & green	350.00	500.00
a.		Inverted frame	2,000.	2,500.
13	A2	50c violet, thin paper ('79)	65.00	75.00
a.		50c gray violet, thick porous paper	100.00	150.00
		Nos. 5-13 (9)	547.50	707.50

The central element in the fan-shaped scrollwork at the outside of the lower left corner of Nos. 5a and 7b looks like an elongated diamond.

See Nos. 16-20. For surcharges see Nos. 14-15, 23-28, 40.

Nos. 9 and 13 Surcharged in Black

10 CENTS
1 CENT 1895

1887-95				
14	A2	1c on 7c lilac & org	50.00	90.00
a.		1c on 7c lilac & yellow	75.00	125.00
b.		Double surcharge	200.00	300.00
c.		Inverted frame	65.00	90.00
15	A2	10c on 50c violet, thin paper ('95)	20.00	50.00

Type of 1874-79

1896-1901			Perf. 13	
16	A2	1c green & red vio ('98)	8.00	8.00
a.		Normal frame	200.00	300.00
17	A2	3c blue & lake ('98)	8.00	8.00
a.		Normal frame	225.00	250.00
18	A2	4c bister & dull blue ('01)	9.00	9.00
a.		Diagonal half used as 2c on cover		25.00
b.		Inverted frame	35.00	30.00
c.		As "b," diagonal half used as 2c on cover		250.00

19	A2	5c green & gray	35.00	20.00
a.		Normal frame	600.00	900.00
20	A2	10c blue & brown ('01)	55.00	75.00
a.		Inverted frame	900.00	1,300.
b.		"cent.s"	60.00	95.00
		Nos. 16-20 (5)	115.00	120.00

Arms — A5

1900				
21	A5	1c light green	2.00	2.00
22	A5	5c light blue	8.00	12.00

See Nos. 29-30. For surcharges see Nos. 41-42.

Nos. 6, 17, 20 Surcharged:

2 CENTS 1902 c
8 Cents 1902 d

Surcharge "c" in Black

1902			Perf. 14x13½	
23	A2	2c on 3c blue & car	500.00	400.00
a.		"2" in date with straight tail	525.00	450.00
b.		Normal frame	2,500.	

Perf. 13

24	A2	2c on 3c blue & lake	8.00	12.50
a.		"2" in date with straight tail	15.00	20.00
b.		Dated "1901"	325.00	400.00
c.		Normal frame	150.00	175.00
d.		Dark green surcharge	1,250.	
e.		As "d" & "a"	1,500.	
f.		As "d" & "c"	6,000.	
25	A2	8c on 10c blue & brn	15.00	20.00
a.		"2" with straight tail	15.00	22.50
b.		On No. 20b	15.00	25.00
c.		Inverted frame	250.00	300.00

Only one copy of No. 24f can exist.

Surcharge "d" in Black

27	A2	2c on 3c blue & lake	8.00	17.00
a.		Normal frame	200.00	300.00
28	A2	8c on 10c blue & brn	7.00	7.00
a.		On No. 20b	9.00	9.00
b.		Inverted frame	200.00	250.00
		Nos. 23-28 (5)	538.00	456.50

1903			Wmk. 113	
29	A5	2c carmine	8.00	10.00
30	A5	8c brown	17.50	20.00

King Christian IX — A8
St. Thomas Harbor — A9 

1905		Typo.	Perf. 13	
31	A8	5b green	3.00	2.00
32	A8	10b red	4.00	2.00
33	A8	20b green & blue	10.00	8.00
34	A8	25b ultramarine	7.00	7.00
35	A8	40b red & gray	8.00	8.00
36	A8	50b yellow & gray	7.00	9.00

D.W.I. and Scandinavia
• Free Catalog • Stamps
• Postal History • Literature
• Want Lists Filled • Albums
• New Issue Service

CALL TOLL FREE
1-800-447-8267
(U.S. and CANADA)
or 336-376-9991
FAX 336-376-6750

Jay Smith
P.O. Box 650-X743
Snow Camp, NC 27349
email: info-x743@jaysmith.com

• The Scandinavia Specialist Since 1973 •

DANISH WEST INDIES — GUAM — HAWAII

Frame Typo., Center Engr.
Wmk. Two Crowns (113)
Perf. 12

37	A9	1fr green & blue	15.00	22.50
38	A9	2fr org red & brown	30.00	50.00
39	A9	5fr yellow & brown	75.00	150.00
		Nos. 31-39 (9)	159.00	

Favor cancels exist on #37-39. Value 25% less.

Nos. 18, 22, 30 Surcharged in Black **5 BIT 1905**

1905   **Wmk. 112**   *Perf. 13*
40	A2	5b on 4c bis & dull blue	9.00	17.50
a.	Inverted frame		30.00	45.00
41	A5	5b on 5c light blue	8.00	14.00

Wmk. 113
| 42 | A5 | 5b on 8c brown | 8.00 | 15.00 |
| | | Nos. 40-42 (3) | 25.00 | 46.50 |

Favor cancels exist on #40-42. Value 25% less.

Frederik VIII — A10    Christian X — A11

Frame Typo., Center Engr.
1907-08   **Wmk. 113**   *Perf. 13*
43	A10	5b green	1.50	1.00
44	A10	10b red	1.50	1.00
45	A10	15b violet & brown	3.50	3.50
46	A10	20b green & blue	30.00	15.00
47	A10	25b blue & dk blue	1.50	1.00
48	A10	30b claret & slate	40.00	35.00
49	A10	40b ver & gray	4.00	4.00
50	A10	50b yellow & brown	4.00	5.00
		Nos. 43-50 (8)	86.00	65.50

1915   **Wmk. 114**   *Perf. 14x14½*
51	A11	5b yellow green	2.00	5.00
52	A11	10b red	2.00	35.00
53	A11	15b lilac & red brown	2.00	35.00
54	A11	20b green & blue	2.00	35.00
55	A11	25b blue & dark blue	2.00	5.00
56	A11	30b claret & black	2.00	35.00
57	A11	40b orange & black	2.50	35.00
58	A11	50b yellow & brown	2.50	35.00
		Nos. 51-58 (8)	17.00	

Forged and favor cancellations exist.

POSTAGE DUE STAMPS

Royal Cipher, "Christian 9 Rex" — D1

1902   **Unwmk.**   **Litho.**   *Perf. 11½*
J1	D1	1c dark blue	5.00	10.00
J2	D1	4c dark blue	6.00	15.00
J3	D1	6c dark blue	25.00	45.00
J4	D1	10c dark blue	15.00	20.00
		Nos. J1-J4 (4)	51.00	90.00

There are five types of each value. On the 4c they may be distinguished by differences in the figures "4"; on the other values the differences are minute.

Used values of Nos. J1-J4 are for canceled copies. Uncanceled examples without gum have probably been used. Value 60% of unused.
Counterfeits of Nos. J1-J4 exist.

D2

1905-13   *Perf. 13*
J5	D2	5b red & gray	4.00	5.00
J6	D2	20b red & gray	10.00	12.50
J7	D2	30b red & gray	7.00	20.00
J8	D2	50b red & gray	9.00	9.00
a.	Perf. 14x14½ ('13)		35.00	110.00
b.	Perf. 11½		500.00	
	Nos. J5-J8 (4)		30.00	39.00

All values of this issue are known imperforate, but were not regularly issued.

Used values of Nos. J5-J8 are for canceled copies. Uncanceled examples without gum have probably been used. Value 60% of unused.
Counterfeits of Nos. J5-J8 exist.
Danish West Indies stamps were replaced by those of the US in 1917, after the US bought the islands.

GUAM
'gwäm

LOCATION — One of the Mariana Islands in the Pacific Ocean, about 1450 miles east of the Philippines
GOVT. — United States Possession
AREA — 206 sq. mi.
POP. — 9,000 (est. 1899)
CAPITAL — Agaña

Formerly a Spanish possession, Guam was ceded to the United States in 1898 following the Spanish-American War. Stamps overprinted "Guam" were superseded by the regular postage stamps of the United States in 1901.

100 Cents = 1 Dollar

US Nos. 279, 279B, 279Bc, 268, 280a, 281, 282, 272, 282C, 283, 284, 275, 275a, 276 and 276A
Overprinted in Black (1c-50c) or Red ($1)

GUAM

1899   **Wmk. 191**   *Perf. 12*
1	A87	1c deep green	20.00	25.00
2	A88	2c red, type IV	17.50	25.00
a.	2c rose carmine, type IV		22.50	30.00
3	A89	3c purple	125.00	175.00
4	A90	4c lilac brown	135.00	175.00
5	A91	5c blue	30.00	45.00
6	A92	6c lake	125.00	200.00
7	A93	8c violet brown	125.00	200.00
8	A94	10c brown, type I	45.00	55.00
9	A94	10c brown, type II	3,500.	—
10	A95	15c olive green	150.00	175.00
11	A96	50c orange	300.00	375.00
a.	50c red orange		500.00	
12	A97	$1 black, type I	350.00	400.00
13	A97	$1 black, type II	3,750.	
	Nos. 1-8,10-12 (11)		1,422.	1,850.

SPECIAL DELIVERY STAMP

United States No. E5 Overprinted in Red **GUAM**

1899   **Wmk. 191**   *Perf. 12*
| E1 | SD3 | 10c blue | 150.00 | 200.00 |

Guam Guard Mail stamps of 1930 are listed in the Scott Specialized United States Catalogue.

HAWAII
hə-'wä-yē

LOCATION — Group of 20 islands in the Pacific Ocean, about 2,000 miles southwest of San Francisco.
GOVT. — Former Kingdom and Republic
AREA — 6,435 sq. mi.
POP. — 150,000 (est. 1899)
CAPITAL — Honolulu

Until 1893 an independent kingdom, from 1893 to 1898 a republic, the Hawaiian Islands were annexed to the US in 1898. The Territory of Hawaii achieved statehood in 1959.

100 Cents = 1 Dollar

Values for Nos. 1-4 are for examples with minor damage that has been skillfully repaired.

A1    A2

A3

Pelure Paper
1851-52   **Unwmk.**   **Typeset**   *Imperf.*
1	A1	2c blue	660,000.	200,000.
2	A1	5c blue	45,000.	25,000.
3	A2	13c blue	22,500.	17,500.
4	A3	13c blue	40,000.	27,500.

Two varieties of each.
No. 1 unused is unique.

King Kamehameha III
A4   A5

Thick White Wove Paper
1853   *Engr.*
5	A4	5c blue	1,250.	950.
a.	Line through "Honolulu" (Pos. 2)		2,250.	1,250.
6	A5	13c dark red	600.	1,000.

See #8-9. See Special Printings section, #10-11.

A6

1857
| 7 | A6 | 5c on 13c dark red | 6,750. | 9,000. |

1857
Thin White Wove Paper
8	A4	5c blue	600.	575.
a.	Line through "Honolulu" (Pos. 2)		1,050.	1,000.
b.	Double impression		2,500.	3,500.

1861
Thin Bluish Wove Paper
| 9 | A4 | 5c blue | 350. | 250. |
| a. | Line through "Honolulu" (Pos. 2) | | 750. | 1,000. |

For Re-issues and Reprints of Types A4-A5 see Special Printings section.

Unused values for the Numeral stamps, Nos. 12-26, are for examples without gum.

A7

A8    A9

1859-62   **Typeset**
12	A7	1c lt blue, bluish white	7,500.	5,500.
a.	"1 Ce" omitted			15,000.
b.	"nt" omitted			
13	A7	2c lt blue, bluish white	6,000.	3,500.
a.	2c dark blue, bluish white	6,500.	3,750.
b.	Comma after "Cents"			
c.	No period after "Leta"			6,000.
14	A7	2c blk, grnsh blue ('62)	6,000.	3,500.
a.	"2-Cents."			

1863
15	A7	1c black, grayish	450.	1,000.
a.	Tete beche pair	3,500.	
b.	"NTER"		
c.	Period omitted after "Postage"	700.	
16	A7	2c black, grayish	800.	600.
a.	"2" at top of rectangle	3,500.	2,500.
b.	Printed on both sides		20,000.
c.	"NTER"	3,000.	3,000.
d.	2c black, grayish white	675.	575.
e.	Period omitted after "Cents"		
f.	Overlapping impressions		
g.	"TAGE."		
17	A7	2c dk blue, bluish	7,500.	6,500.
a.	"ISL"		
18	A7	2c black, blue gray	2,750.	4,500.

1864-65
19	A7	1c black	450.	1,000.
20	A7	2c black	600.	1,150.
21	A8	5c blue, blue ('65)	750.	550.
a.	Tete beche pair	7,500.	
b.	5c bluish black, grayish white	12,000.	
22	A9	5c blue, blue ('65)	500.	750.
a.	Tete beche pair	5,000.	
b.	5c blue, grayish white		
c.	Overlapping impressions		

1864   **Laid Paper**
23	A7	1c black	250.	2,000.
a.	HA instead of HAWAIIAN	2,500.	
b.	Tete beche pair	6,000.	
c.	Tete beche pair, #23, 23a	17,500.	
24	A7	2c black	250.	1,000.
a.	"NTER"	2,250.	
b.	"S" of "POSTAGE" omitted	1,000.	
c.	Tete beche pair	5,250.	

A10

1865   **Wove Paper**
25	A10	1c dark blue	250.	
a.	Double impression		
b.	With inverted impression of #21	6,500.	
26	A10	2c dark blue	250.	

Nos. 12 to 26 were typeset and were printed in settings of ten, each stamp differing from the others.

King Kamehameha IV — A11

1857
1861-63   *Litho.*
Horizontally Laid Paper
| 27 | A11 | 2c pale rose | 275. | 250. |
| a. | 2c carmine rose ('63) | 1,750. | 2,000. |

Vertically Laid Paper
| 28 | A11 | 2c pale rose | 275. | 150. |
| a. | 2c carmine rose ('63) | 275. | 325. |

For Re-issues and Reprints of Type A11 see Special Printings section.

Princess Victoria Kamamalu — A12    King Kamehameha IV — A13

King Kamehameha V
A14   A15

HAWAII

Mataio Kekuanaoa — A16

1864-86   Wove Paper   Engr.   Perf. 12

30	A12	1c purple ('86)	9.00	7.50
a.		1c mauve ('71)	35.00	15.00
b.		1c violet	15.00	10.00
31	A13	2c vermilion ('78)	15.00	9.00
a.		2c rose vermilion ('64)	35.00	12.50
b.		Half used as 1c on cover		8,500.
32	A14	5c blue ('66)	150.00	30.00
33	A15	6c yellow green ('71)	25.00	9.00
a.		6c bluish green ('78)		9.00
34	A16	18c dull rose ('71)	85.00	35.00
		Nos. 30-34 (5)	284.00	90.50

No. 32 has traces of rectangular frame lines surrounding the design. Nos. 39 and 52C have no such frame lines.

For overprints see #53, 58-60, 65, 66C, 71.

King David Kalakaua A17

Prince William Pitt Leleiohoku A18

1875

35	A17	2c brown	7.50	3.00
36	A18	12c black	55.00	27.50

See Nos. 38, 43, 46. For overprints see Nos. 56, 62-63, 66, 69.

Princess Likelike — A19

King David Kalakaua — A20

Queen Kapiolani — A21

Statue of King Kamehameha I — A22

King William Lunalilo A23

Queen Emma Kaleleonalani A24

1882

37	A19	1c blue	6.00	10.00
38	A17	2c lilac rose	125.00	45.00
39	A14	5c ultramarine	15.00	3.25
a.		Vert. pair, imperf. horiz.	4,250.	4,250.
40	A20	10c black	35.00	20.00
41	A21	15c red brown	55.00	25.00
		Nos. 37-41 (5)	236.00	103.25

1883-86

42	A19	1c green	2.75	1.90
43	A17	2c rose ('86)	4.00	1.00
a.		2c dull red	60.00	
44	A20	10c red brown ('84)	30.00	10.00
45	A20	10c vermilion	32.50	12.50
46	A18	12c red lilac	75.00	32.50
47	A22	25c dark violet	125.00	55.00
48	A23	50c red	150.00	82.50
49	A24	$1 rose red	225.00	135.00
		Maltese cross cancellation		75.00
		Nos. 42-49 (8)	644.25	330.40

Other fiscal cancellations exist on No. 49. For overprints see Nos. 54-55, 57, 61-61B, 64, 67-68, 70, 72-73.

For Reproduction and Reprint of the 2c see Special Printings section.

Queen Liliuokalani — A25

1890-91   Perf. 12

52	A25	2c dull violet ('91)	4.50	1.50
a.		Vert. pair, imperf. horiz.	3,750.	
52C	A14	5c deep indigo	105.00	135.00

Stamps of 1864-91 Overprinted in Red

Provisional GOVT. 1893

1893

53	A12	1c purple	7.50	12.50
a.		"189" instead of "1893"	400.00	
b.		No period after "GOVT"	200.00	200.00
54	A19	1c blue	6.00	12.50
a.		No period after "GOVT"	135.00	135.00
55	A19	1c green	1.50	3.00
a.		Pair, one without ovpt.	10,000.	
b.		Double overprint	600.00	450.00
56	A17	2c brown	10.00	20.00
a.		No period after "GOVT"	300.00	
57	A25	2c dull violet	1.50	1.25
a.		Inverted overprint	4,000.	3,500.
b.		Double overprint	850.00	650.00
c.		"18 3" instead of "1893"	600.00	500.00
58	A14	5c deep indigo	10.00	25.00
a.		No period after "GOVT"	225.00	250.00
59	A14	5c ultra	6.00	2.50
a.		Inverted overprint	1,250.	1,250.
b.		Double overprint	5,000.	
60	A15	6c green	15.00	25.00
a.		Double overprint	1,250.	
61	A20	10c black	9.00	15.00
a.		Double overprint	700.00	300.00
61B	A20	10c red brown	14,000.	30,000.
62	A18	12c black	9.00	17.50
a.		Double overprint	2,000.	
63	A18	12c red lilac	150.00	250.00
64	A22	25c dark violet	25.00	40.00
a.		No period after "GOVT"	300.00	300.00
		Nos. 53-61,62-64 (12)	250.50	424.25

Overprinted in Black

65	A13	2c vermilion	65.00	75.00
			250.00	250.00
66	A17	2c rose	1.25	2.25
a.			2,500.	
b.		No period after "GOVT"	50.00	60.00
66C	A15	6c green	14,000.	30,000.
67	A20	10c vermilion	15.00	30.00
68	A20	10c red brown	7.50	12.50
69	A18	12c red lilac	275.00	500.00
70	A21	15c red brown	20.00	30.00
		Double overprint	2,000.	
71	A16	18c dull rose	25.00	35.00
a.			350.00	
b.		Pair, one without ovpt.	2,500.	
c.		No period after "GOVT"	300.00	300.00
d.		"18 3" instead of "1893"	375.00	375.00
72	A23	50c red	60.00	90.00
b.		No period after "GOVT"	400.00	400.00
73	A24	$1 rose red	110.00	175.00
a.		No period after "GOVT"	425.00	400.00
		Nos. 65-66,67-73 (9)	578.75	949.75

Coat of Arms — A26

View of Honolulu — A27

Statue of Kamehameha I — A28

Stars and Palms — A29

S. S. "Arawa" — A30

Pres. Sanford Ballard Dole — A31

"CENTS" Added — A32

1894

74	A26	1c yellow	2.00	1.25
75	A27	2c brown	2.25	.60
76	A28	5c rose lake	4.00	1.50
77	A29	10c yellow green	6.00	4.50
78	A30	12c blue	12.50	17.50
79	A31	25c deep blue	12.50	17.50
		Nos. 74-79 (6)	39.25	42.85

1899

80	A26	1c dark green	1.50	1.25
81	A27	2c rose	1.35	1.00
a.		2c salmon	1.50	1.25
b.		Vert. pair, imperf. horiz.	4,500.	
82	A32	5c blue	5.50	3.00
		Nos. 80-82 (3)	8.35	5.25

OFFICIAL STAMPS

Lorrin Andrews Thurston — O1

1896   Unwmk.   Engr.   Perf. 12

O1	O1	2c green	35.00	17.50
O2	O1	5c black brown	35.00	17.50
O3	O1	6c deep ultra	35.00	17.50
O4	O1	10c bright rose	35.00	17.50
O5	O1	12c orange	35.00	17.50
O6	O1	25c gray violet	35.00	17.50
		Nos. O1-O6 (6)	210.00	105.00

Used values for Nos. O1-O6 are for copies canceled to order "FOREIGN OFFICE/HONOLULU H.I." in double circle without date.

The stamps of Hawaii were replaced by those of the United States.

SPECIAL PRINTINGS

Re-issues

1868   Ordinary White Wove Paper

10	A4	5c blue	25.00
a.		Line through "Honolulu" (Pos. 2)	50.00
11	A5	13c dull rose	250.00

Reprints:

5c. Originals have two small dots near the left side of the square in the upper right corner. These dots are missing in the reprints.

13c. The bottom of the 3 of 13 in the upper left corner is flattened in the originals and rounded in the reprints. The "t" of "Cts" on the left side is as tall as the "C" in the reprints, but shorter in the originals.

On August 19, 1892, the remaining supply of reprints was overprinted in black "REPRINT." The reprints (both with and without overprint) were sold at face value. See the Scott U.S. Specialized Catalogue.

1869   Engr.   Thin Wove Paper

29	A11	2c red	45.00

No. 29 was sold only at the Honolulu post office, at first without overprint and later with overprint "CANCELLED."

See note following No. 51.

Reproduction and Reprint
Yellowish Wove Paper

1886-89   Imperf.

50	A11	2c orange vermilion	150.00
51	A11	2c carmine ('89)	25.00

In 1885 the Postmaster General wished to have on sale complete sets of Hawaii's stamps as far back as type A11, but was unable to find either the stone from which Nos. 27 and 28, or the plate from which No. 29 was printed. He therefore sent a copy of No. 29 to the American Bank Note Co., with an order to engrave a new plate and print 10,000 stamps, of which 5000 were overprinted "Specimen" in blue.

The original No. 29 was printed in sheet of 15 (5x3), but the plate of these "Official Imitations" was made up of 50 stamps (10x5). Later, in 1887, the original die for No. 29 was discovered, and after retouching, a new plate was made and 37,500 stamps were printed. These, like the originals, were printed in sheets of 15. They were delivered during 1889 and 1890. In 1892 all remaining unsold in the Post Office were overprinted "Reprint."

No. 29 is red in color, and printed on very thin white wove paper. No. 50 is orange vermilion in color, on medium, white to buff paper. In No. 50 the vertical line on the left side of the portrait touches the horizontal line over the label "Elua Keneta", while in the other two varieties, Nos. 29 and 51, it does not touch the horizontal line by half a millimeter. In No. 51 there are three parallel lines on the left side of the King's nose, while in No. 29 and No. 50 there are no such lines. No. 51 is carmine in color and printed on thick, yellowish to buff wove paper.

It is claimed that both Nos. 50 and 51 were available for postage, although not made to fill a postal requirement.

Hawaii stamps can be mounted in the Scott U.S. Possessions album.

For all your stamp supply needs

www.scottonline.com

PHILIPPINES

ˌfi-lə-ˈpēnz

LOCATION — Group of 7,100 islands and islets in the Malay Archipelago, north of Borneo, in the North Pacific Ocean
GOVT. — US Admin., 1898-1946
AREA — 115,748 sq. mi.
POP. — 16,971,100 (est. 1941)
CAPITAL — Quezon City

The islands were ceded to the US by Spain in 1898. On Nov. 15, 1935, they were given their independence, subject to a transition period which ended July 4, 1946. On that date the Commonwealth became the "Republic of the Philippines."

100 Cents = 1 Dollar (1899)
100 Centavos = 1 Peso (1906)

Watermarks

Wmk. 191PI-Double-lined PIPS

Wmk. 190PI-Single-lined PIPS

Wmk. 257- Curved Wavy Lines

Issued under US Administration

Issues of the US Overprinted in Black

On No. 260

1899-1900 Unwmk. *Perf. 12*
212 A96 50c orange 400.00 250.00

On Nos. 279, 279d, 267, 268, 281, 282C, 283, 284, 275 and 275a

Wmk. 191
213 A87 1c yellow green 3.00 .60
a. Inverted overprint *13,500.*
214 A88 2c red, type IV 1.25 .60
a. 2c orange red, type IV ('01) 1.25 .60
b. Booklet pane of 6, red, type IV ('00) 300.00 *150.00*
c. 2c reddish car, type IV 1.90 .90
d. 2c rose car, type IV 2.25 1.10
215 A89 3c purple 5.75 1.25
216 A91 5c blue 5.50 .90
a. Inverted overprint *3,750.*
217 A94 10c brown, type I 17.50 4.00
217A A94 10c org brn, type II 200.00 32.50
218 A95 15c olive green 32.50 8.00
219 A96 50c orange 140.00 37.50
a. 50c red orange 275.00
Nos. 213-219 (8) 405.50 85.35

No. 216a is valued in the grade of fine.

On Nos. 280b, 282 and 272

1901
220 A90 4c orange brown 22.50 4.50
221 A92 6c lake 27.50 7.00
222 A93 8c violet brown 27.50 7.50
Nos. 220-222 (3) 77.50 19.00

On Nos. 276, 276A, 277a and 278

Red Overprint
223 A97 $1 black, type I 425. 240.
223A A97 $1 black, type II 2,250. 675.
224 A98 $2 dark blue 475. 250.
225 A99 $5 dark green 850. 650.

On Nos. 300-313 and shades

1903-04

Black Overprint
226 A115 1c blue green 4.00 .30
227 A116 2c carmine 7.50 1.10
228 A117 3c bright violet 67.50 12.50
229 A118 4c brown ('04) 75.00 22.50
a. 4c orange brown 75.00 20.00
230 A119 5c blue 11.00 1.00
231 A120 6c brnsh lake ('04) 80.00 22.50
232 A121 8c vio blk ('04) 40.00 12.50
233 A122 10c pale red brn ('04) 20.00 2.25
a. 10c red brown 25.00 3.00
b. Pair, one without ovpt. *1,500.*
234 A123 13c purple black 32.50 17.50
a. 13c brown violet 32.50 17.50
235 A124 15c olive green 60.00 15.00
236 A125 50c orange 130.00 35.00
Nos. 226-236 (11) 527.50 142.15

Red Overprint
237 A126 $1 black 450. 250.
238 A127 $2 dk blue ('04) 750. 750.
239 A128 $5 dk green ('04) 1,000. 900.

On Nos. 319, 319c in Black

1904
240 A129 2c carmine 5.50 2.25
a. Booklet pane of 6 *1,100.*
b. 2c scarlet 6.25 2.75

Jose Rizal — A40

Arms of Manila — A41

Designs: 4c, McKinley. 6c, Magellan. 8c, Miguel Lopez de Legaspi. 10c, Gen. Henry W. Lawton. 12c, Lincoln. 16c, Adm. William T. Sampson. 20c, Washington. 26c, Francisco Carriedo. 30c, Franklin.

Each Inscribed "Philippine Islands/United States of America"

1906, Sept. 8 Engr. Wmk. 191PI
241 A40 2c deep green .25 .15
a. 2c yellow green ('10) .40 .15
b. Booklet pane of 6 425.00
242 A40 4c carmine .30 .15
a. 4c carmine lake ('10) .60 .15
b. Booklet pane of 6 *600.00*
243 A40 6c violet 1.25 .20
244 A40 8c brown 2.50 .65
245 A40 10c blue 1.75 .20
246 A40 12c brown lake 5.00 2.00
247 A40 16c violet black 3.75 .20
248 A40 20c orange brown 4.00 .30
249 A40 26c violet brown 6.00 2.25
250 A40 30c olive green 4.75 1.50
251 A41 1p orange 27.50 7.00
252 A41 2p black 35.00 1.25
253 A41 4p dark blue 100.00 15.00
254 A41 10p dark green 225.00 70.00
Nos. 241-254 (14) 417.05 100.85

Change of Colors

1909-13 *Perf. 12*
255 A40 12c red orange 8.50 2.50
256 A40 16c olive green 3.50 .75
257 A40 20c yellow 7.50 1.25
258 A40 26c blue green 1.75 .75
259 A40 30c ultramarine 10.00 3.25
260 A41 1p pale violet 30.00 5.00
260A A41 2p vio brown ('13) 85.00 2.75
Nos. 255-260A (7) 146.25 16.25

1911 Wmk. 190PI *Perf. 12*
261 A40 2c green .65 .15
a. Booklet pane of 6 *475.00*
262 A40 4c carmine lake 2.50 .15
a. 4c carmine — —
b. Booklet pane of 6 *525.00*
263 A40 6c deep violet 2.00 .15
264 A40 8c brown 8.50 .45
265 A40 10c blue 3.25 .15
266 A40 12c orange 2.50 .45
267 A40 16c olive green 2.50 .15
268 A40 20c yellow 2.00 .15
a. 20c orange 2.00 .15
269 A40 26c blue green 3.00 .20
270 A40 30c ultramarine 3.50 .45
271 A41 1p pale violet 22.50 .55
272 A41 2p violet brown 27.50 .75
273 A41 4p deep blue 625.00 80.00
274 A41 10p deep green 225.00 25.00
Nos. 261-274 (14) 930.40 108.75

1914
275 A40 30c gray 10.00 .40

1914-23 *Perf. 10*
276 A40 2c green 1.75 .15
a. Booklet pane of 6 *400.00*
277 A40 4c carmine 1.75 .15
a. Booklet pane of 6 *400.00*
278 A40 6c light violet 37.50 9.00
a. 6c deep violet 42.50 6.00
279 A40 8c brown 40.00 10.00
280 A40 10c dark blue 25.00 .20
281 A40 16c olive green 75.00 4.50
282 A40 20c orange 22.50 .85
283 A40 30c gray 55.00 2.75
284 A41 1p pale violet 110.00 3.00
Nos. 276-284 (9) 368.50 30.60

1918-26 *Perf. 11*
285 A40 2c green 20.00 4.25
a. Booklet pane of 6 *650.00*
286 A40 4c carmine 25.00 2.50
a. Booklet pane of 6 *1,250.*
287 A40 6c deep violet 35.00 1.75
287A A40 8c light brown 200.00 25.00
288 A40 10c dark blue 52.50 1.50
289 A40 16c olive green 90.00 6.75
289A A40 20c orange 60.00 7.50
289C A40 30c gray 55.00 12.50
289D A41 1p pale violet 70.00 14.00
Nos. 285-289D (9) 607.50 75.75

1917-25 Unwmk. *Perf. 11*
290 A40 2c yellow green .15 .15
a. 2c dark green .15 .15
b. Vert. pair, imperf. horiz. *1,500.*
c. Horiz. pair, imperf. btwn. *1,500.* —
d. Vert. pair, imperf. btwn. *1,750.*
e. Booklet pane of 6 27.50
291 A40 4c carmine .15 .15
a. 4c light rose .15 .15
b. Booklet pane of 6 17.50 —
292 A40 6c deep violet .30 .15
a. 6c lilac .35 .15
b. 6c red violet .35 .15
c. Booklet pane of 6 *550.00* —
293 A40 8c yellow brown .20 .15
a. 8c orange brown .20 .15
294 A40 10c deep blue .20 .15
295 A40 12c red orange .30 .15
296 A40 16c light olive green 55.00 .25
a. 16c olive bister 55.00 .40
297 A40 20c orange yellow .30 .15
298 A40 26c green .45 .45
a. 26c blue green .55 .25
299 A40 30c gray .55 .15
300 A41 1p pale violet 27.50 1.00
a. 1p red lilac 27.50 1.00
b. 1p pale rose lilac 27.50 1.10
301 A41 2p violet brown 25.00 .75
302 A41 4p blue 22.50 .45
a. 4p dark blue 22.50 .45
Nos. 290-302 (13) 132.60 4.10

1923-26

Design: 16c, Adm. George Dewey.

303 A40 16c olive bister .90 .15
a. 16c olive green 1.30 .20
304 A41 10p deep green ('26) 45.00 5.00

See Nos. 326-353. For surcharges see Nos. 368-369, 450. For overprints see Nos. C1-C28, C36-C46, C54-C57, O5-O14.

Legislative Palace — A42

1926, Dec. 20 Unwmk. *Perf. 12*
319 A42 2c green & black .40 .25
a. Horiz. pair, imperf. btwn. *275.00*
b. Vert. pair, imperf. between *500.00*
320 A42 4c car & black .40 .35
a. Horiz. pair, imperf. btwn. *275.00*
b. Vert. pair, imperf. between *500.00*
321 A42 16c ol grn & black .75 .65
a. Horiz. pair, imperf. btwn. *350.00*
b. Vert. pair, imperf. between *550.00*
c. Double impression of center *575.00*
322 A42 18c lt brn & black .85 .50
a. Double impression of center *575.00*
b. Vert. pair, imperf. between *550.00*
323 A42 20c orange & black 1.20 .80
a. 20c orange & brown *500.00* —
b. Imperf., pair *450.00* *450.00*
c. As "a," imperf., pair *850.00*
d. Vert. pair, imperf. between *550.00*
324 A42 24c gray & black .85 .55
a. Vert. pair, imperf. between *550.00*
325 A42 1p rose lilac & blk 45.00 30.00
a. Vert. pair, imperf. between *625.00*
Nos. 319-325 (7) 49.45 33.10

Opening of the Legislative Palace.
For overprints see Nos. O1-O4.

Coil Stamp
Rizal Type of 1906

1928 *Perf. 11 Vertically*
326 A40 2c green 7.50 15.00

Types of 1906-23

1925-31 Unwmk. *Imperf.*
340 A40 2c yel grn ('31) .15 .15
a. green ('25) .25 .15
341 A40 4c car rose ('31) .15 .15
a. carmine ('25) .40 .20
342 A40 6c violet ('31) 1.00 1.00
a. deep violet ('25) 8.00 4.00
343 A40 8c brown ('31) .90 .90
a. yellow brown ('25) 6.00 3.00
344 A40 10c blue ('31) 1.00 1.00
a. deep blue ('25) 15.00 5.00
345 A40 12c dp orange ('31) 1.50 1.50
a. red orange ('25) 15.00 5.00
346 A40 16c olive green *(Dewey)* ('31) 1.10 1.10
a. bister green ('25) 12.50 4.00
347 A40 20c orange yel ('31) 1.10 1.10
a. yellow ('25) 12.50 4.00
348 A40 26c green ('31) 1.10 1.10
a. blue green ('25) 15.00 5.00
349 A40 30c light gray ('31) 1.25 1.25
a. gray ('25) 15.00 5.00
350 A41 1p lt violet ('31) 4.00 4.00
a. violet ('25) 70.00 30.00
351 A41 2p brn vio ('31) 10.00 10.00
a. violet brown ('25) 150.00 50.00
352 A41 4p blue ('31) 30.00 30.00
a. deep blue ('25) 700.00 300.00
353 A41 10p green ('31) 90.00 90.00
a. deep green ('25) 1,000. 500.00
Nos. 340-353 (14) 143.25 143.25
Nos. 340a-353a (14) 2,019. 915.35

Mount Mayon, Luzon — A43

Post Office, Manila — A44

Pier No. 7, Manila Bay A45

(See footnote) A46

Rice Planting — A47

Rice Terraces — A48

Baguio Zigzag — A49

1932, May 3 *Perf. 11*
354 A43 2c yellow green .40 .20
355 A44 4c rose carmine .35 .25
356 A45 12c orange .50 .50
357 A46 18c red orange 17.50 9.00
358 A47 20c yellow .65 .55
359 A48 24c deep violet 1.00 .65
360 A49 32c olive brown 1.00 .70
Nos. 354-360 (7) 21.40 11.85

The 18c vignette was intended to show Pagsanjan Falls in Laguna, central Luzon, and is so labeled. Through error, the stamp pictures Vernal Falls in Yosemite Natl. Park, CA.
For overprints see #C29-C35, C47-C51, C63.

Nos. 302, 302a Surcharged in Orange or Red

1932
368 A41 1p on 4p blue (O) 2.00 .45
a. 1p on 4p dark blue (O) 2.75 1.30
369 A41 2p on 4p dark blue (R) 3.50 .75
a. 2p on 4p blue (R) 3.50 .75

Baseball — A50

Tennis — A51

PHILIPPINES

Basketball — A52

1934, Apr. 14   Typo.   *Perf. 11½*
380	A50	2c yellow brown	1.50	.80
381	A51	6c ultramarine	.25	.20
382	A52	16c violet brown	.50	.50
a.		Vert. pair, imperf. between	1,250.	
		Vert. pair, imperf. horiz.	1,250.	

Tenth Far Eastern Championship Games.

Jose Rizal — A53
Woman and Carabao — A54 
La Filipina — A55 
Pearl Fishing — A56 
Fort Santiago — A57 
Salt Spring — A58 
Magellan's Landing, 1521 A59 
"Juan de la Cruz" A60 
Rice Terraces — A61 
"Blood Compact," 1565 — A62 
Barasoain Church, Malolos — A63 
Battle of Manila Bay, 1898 — A64 

Montalban Gorge — A65

George Washington — A66

1935, Feb. 15   Engr.   *Perf. 11*
383	A53	2c rose	.15	.15
384	A54	4c yellow green	.20	.15
385	A55	6c dark brown	.15	.15
386	A56	8c violet	.15	.15
387	A57	10c rose carmine	.15	.15
388	A58	12c black	.15	.15
389	A59	16c dark blue	.15	.15
390	A60	20c light olive green	.20	.15
391	A61	26c indigo	.25	.25
392	A62	30c orange red	.25	.25
393	A63	1p red orange & black	1.65	1.25
394	A64	2p bister brn & black	4.00	1.25
395	A65	4p blue & black	4.00	2.75
396	A66	5p green & black	8.00	2.00
		Nos. 383-396 (14)	19.45	8.95

For overprints see Nos. 411-424, 433-446, 463-466, 468, 472-474, 478-484, 485-494, C52-C53, O15-O36, O38, O40-O43, N2-N3, NO6. For surcharges see Nos. 449, N4-N9, N28, NO2-NO5.

Commonwealth Issues

The Temples of Human Progress A67

1935, Nov. 15
397	A67	2c carmine rose	.15	.15
398	A67	6c deep violet	.20	.15
399	A67	16c blue	.20	.15
400	A67	36c yellow green	.35	.30
401	A67	50c brown	.55	.55
		Nos. 397-401 (5)	1.45	1.30

Inauguration of the Philippine Commonwealth, Nov. 15th, 1935.

Jose Rizal — A68
President Manuel L. Quezon — A69 

1936, June 19   *Perf. 12*
402	A68	2c yellow brown	.15	.15
403	A68	6c slate blue	.15	.15
a.		Horiz. pair, imperf. vert.	1,350.	
404	A68	36c red brown	.50	.45
		Nos. 402-404 (3)	.80	.75

75th anniv. of the birth of Jose Rizal.

1936, Nov. 15   *Perf. 11*
408	A69	2c orange brown	.15	.15
409	A69	6c yellow green	.15	.15
410	A69	12c ultramarine	.15	.15
		Nos. 408-410 (3)	.45	.45

1st anniv. of the Commonwealth.
For overprints see Nos. 467, 475.

Nos. 383-396 Overprinted in Black

COMMON-WEALTH	COMMONWEALTH
a	b

1936-37   *Perf. 11*
411	A53	(a) 2c rose	.15	.15
a.		Booklet pane of 6	2.50	.65
412	A54	(b) 4c yel grn ('37)	.50	
413	A55	(a) 6c dark brown	.20	.15
414	A56	(b) 8c violet ('37)	.20	
415	A57	(b) 10c rose carmine	.20	.15
a.		"COMMONWEALT"		
416	A58	(b) 12c black ('37)	.20	.15
417	A59	(b) 16c dark blue	.20	.15
418	A60	(a) 20c lt ol grn ('37)	.65	.40
419	A61	(b) 26c indigo ('37)	.45	.35
420	A62	(b) 30c orange red	.35	.15
421	A63	(b) 1p red org & black	.65	.20
422	A64	(b) 2p bister brn & black ('37)	5.00	2.75
423	A65	(b) 4p blue & blk ('37)	17.50	3.00
424	A66	(b) 5p green & black ('37)	1.75	1.25
		Nos. 411-424 (14)	28.05	
		Nos. 411,413-424 (13)		9.05

Map of Philippines A70
Arms of Manila A71 

1937, Feb. 3
425	A70	2c yellow green	.15	.15
426	A70	6c light brown	.15	.15
427	A70	12c sapphire	.15	.15
428	A70	20c deep orange	.25	.15
429	A70	36c deep violet	.55	.40
430	A70	50c carmine	.65	.35
		Nos. 425-430 (6)	1.90	1.35

33rd Eucharistic Congress.

1937, Aug. 27   *Perf. 11*
431	A71	10p gray	4.25	2.00
432	A71	20p henna brown	2.25	1.40

For overprints see Nos. 495-496. For surcharges see Nos. 451, C58.

Nos. 383-396 Overprinted in Black

COMMON-WEALTH	COMMONWEALTH
a	b

1938-40   *Perf. 11*
433	A53	(a) 2c rose ('39)	.15	.15
a.		Booklet pane of 6	3.50	.65
b.		"WEALTH COMMON-"	4,000.	
c.		Hyphen omitted		
434	A54	(b) 4c yel grn ('40)	1.25	—
435	A55	(b) 6c dk brn ('39)	.15	.15
a.		6c golden brown	.15	
436	A56	(b) 8c violet ('39)	.15	.15
a.		"COMMONWEALT" (LR 31)	65.00	
437	A57	(b) 10c rose car ('39)	.15	.15
a.		"COMMONWEALT" (LR 31)		
438	A58	(b) 12c black ('40)	.15	.15
439	A59	(b) 16c dark blue	.15	.15
440	A60	(a) 20c lt ol grn ('39)	.15	.15
441	A61	(b) 26c indigo ('40)	.20	.20
442	A62	(b) 30c org red ('39)	1.40	.70
443	A63	(b) 1p red org & blk	.40	.20
444	A64	(b) 2p bis brn & blk	2.75	.75
445	A65	(b) 4p bl & blk ('40)	100.00	75.00
446	A66	(b) 5p grn & blk ('40)	4.50	2.75
		Nos. 433-446 (14)	111.55	
		Nos. 433,435-446 (13)		80.65

Overprint "b" measures 18½x1¾mm. No. 433b occurs in booklet pane, No. 433a, position 5; all copies are straight-edged, left and bottom.

Stamps of 1917-37 Surcharged in Red, Violet or Black

FIRST FOREIGN TRADE WEEK
2 CENTAVOS
MAY 21-27, 1939

FIRST FOREIGN TRADE WEEK
50 CENTAVOS **50**
MAY 21-27, 1939

FIRST FOREIGN TRADE WEEK
6 CENTAVOS **6**
MAY 21-27, 1939

1939, July 5
449	A54	2c on 4c yel green (R)	.15	.15
450	A40	6c on 26c blue grn (V)	.15	.15
a.		6c on 26c green	.65	.30
451	A71	50c on 20p henna brn (Bk)	1.00	1.00
		Nos. 449-451 (3)	1.30	1.30

Foreign Trade Week.

Triumphal Arch — A72
Malacanan Palace — A73 

1939, Nov. 15   *Perf. 11*
452	A72	2c yellow green	.15	.15
453	A72	6c carmine	.15	.15
454	A72	12c bright blue	.20	.15
		Nos. 452-454 (3)	.50	.45

For overprints see Nos. 469, 476.

1939, Nov. 15
455	A73	2c green	.15	.15
456	A73	6c orange	.15	.15
457	A73	12c carmine	.20	.15
		Nos. 455-457 (3)	.50	.45

#452-457 for 4th anniv. of the Commonwealth. For overprint see No. 470.

Quezon Taking Oath of Office — A74
Jose Rizal — A75 

1940, Feb. 8
458	A74	2c dark orange	.15	.15
459	A74	6c dark green	.15	.15
460	A74	12c purple	.25	.15
		Nos. 458-460 (3)	.55	.45

4th anniversary of Commonwealth.
For overprints see Nos. 471, 477.

Rotary Press Printing

1941, Apr. 14   *Perf. 11x10½*
Size: 19x22½mm
461	A75	2c apple green	.15	.15

Flat Plate Printing

1941-43   *Perf. 11*
Size: 18¾x22mm
462	A75	2c apple green ('43)	.15	.15
a.		2c pale apple green	.20	.15
b.		Bklt. pane of 6 (apple green, '43)	1.25	1.25
c.		Bklt. pane of 6 (pale apple green)	2.50	2.75

No. 462 was issued only in booklet panes and all copies have straight edges.
Further printings were made in 1942 and 1943 in different shades from the first supply of stamps sent to the islands.
For type A75 overprinted see Nos. 464, O37, O39, N1, NO1.

Philippine Stamps of 1935-41, Handstamped in Violet

VICTORY

1944   *Perf. 11, 11x10½*
463	A53	2c (#411)	260.00	95.00
a.		Booklet pane of 6	2,000.	
463B	A53	2c (#433)	1,200.	1,200.
464	A75	2c (#461)	2.50	2.25
465	A54	4c (#384)	25.00	25.00
466	A55	6c (#385)	1,500.	1,350.
467	A69	6c (#409)	110.00	85.00
468	A55	6c (#413)	650.00	600.00
469	A72	6c (#453)	135.00	110.00
470	A73	6c (#456)	600.00	550.00
471	A74	6c (#459)	160.00	160.00
472	A56	8c (#436)	15.00	20.00
473	A57	10c (#415)	110.00	75.00
474	A57	10c (#437)	135.00	110.00
475	A69	12c (#410)	400.00	175.00
476	A72	12c (#454)	3,500.	2,000.
477	A74	12c (#460)	190.00	135.00
478	A59	16c (#389)	700.00	
479	A59	16c (#417)	450.00	325.00
480	A59	16c (#439)	160.00	100.00
481	A60	20c (#440)	27.50	27.50
482	A62	30c (#420)	225.00	160.00
483	A62	30c (#442)	325.00	250.00
484	A63	1p (#443)	5,500.	4,000.

Nos. 463-484 are valued in the grade of fine to very fine.

Philippines stamps, U.S. issues, can be mounted in the Scott U.S. Possessions album.

PHILIPPINES

Types of 1935-37 Overprinted VICTORY

	COMMONWEALTH a	COMMONWEALTH b
1945		*Perf. 11*
485 A53 (a)	2c rose	.15 .15
486 A54 (b)	4c yellow green	.15 .15
487 A55 (a)	6c golden brown	.15 .15
488 A56 (b)	8c violet	.15 .15
489 A57 (b)	10c rose carmine	.15 .15
490 A58 (b)	12c black	.20 .15
491 A59 (b)	16c dark blue	.25 .15
492 A60 (a)	20c lt olive green	.30 .15
493 A62 (b)	30c orange red	.40 .35
494 A63 (b)	1p red org & black	1.10 .25

Nos. 431-432 Overprinted VICTORY in Black

495 A71	10p gray	40.00 13.50
496 A71	20p henna brown	35.00 15.00
	Nos. 485-496 (12)	78.00 30.30

Jose Rizal — A76

Rotary Press Printing

1946, May 28 *Perf. 11x10½*
497 A76 2c sepia .15 .15

For overprints see No. 503 (Philippines, Vol. 5) and No. O44.

Succeeding issues, released by the Philippine Republic on and after July 4, 1946, are listed in Vol. 5.

AIR POST STAMPS

Madrid-Manila Flight Issue

Regular Issue of 1917-26 Overprinted in Red or Violet

1926, May 13 Unwmk. *Perf. 11*
C1 A40	2c green (R)	7.50 3.50
C2 A40	4c carmine	10.00 4.25
a.	Inverted overprint	2,000. —
C3 A40	6c lilac (R)	47.50 14.00
C4 A40	8c org brown	47.50 14.00
C5 A40	10c deep blue (R)	47.50 14.00
C6 A40	12c red orange	47.50 25.00
C7 A40	16c lt olive green (Sampson)	1,750. 1,550.
C8 A40	16c ol bister (Sampson) (R)	3,250. 2,600.
C9 A40	16c olive green (Dewey)	55.00 25.00
C10 A40	20c orange yellow	55.00 25.00
C11 A40	26c blue green	55.00 27.50
C12 A40	30c gray	55.00 27.50
C13 A41	2p vio brown (R)	475.00 260.00
C14 A41	4p dark blue (R)	675.00 450.00
C15 A41	10p deep green	1,050. 625.00

Same Overprint on No. 269 Wmk. 190PI *Perf. 12*
C16 A40 26c blue green 2,400.

Same Overprint on No. 284 *Perf. 10*
C17 A41 1p pale violet 175.00 100.00

Flight of Spanish aviators Gallarza and Loriga from Madrid to Manila.

London-Orient Flight Issue

Regular Issue of 1917-25 Overprinted in Red

1928, Nov. 9 Unwmk. *Perf. 11*
C18 A40	2c green	.40 .25
C19 A40	4c carmine	.50 .40
C20 A40	6c violet	1.75 1.40
C21 A40	8c orange brown	1.90 1.60
C22 A40	10c deep blue	1.90 1.60
C23 A40	12c red orange	2.75 2.25
C24 A40	16c ol green (Dewey)	2.00 1.50
C25 A40	20c orange yellow	2.75 2.25
C26 A40	26c blue green	8.00 5.50
C27 A40	30c gray	8.00 5.50

Same Overprint on No. 271 Wmk. 190PI *Perf. 12*
C28 A41 1p pale violet 45.00 25.00
Nos. C18-C28 (11) 74.95 47.25

Flight from London to Manila.

Nos. 354-360 Overprinted ROUND-THE-WORLD FLIGHT VON GRONAU 1932

1932, Sept. 27 Unwmk. *Perf. 11*
C29 A43	2c yellow green	.40 .30
C30 A44	4c rose carmine	.40 .30
C31 A45	12c orange	.60 .50
C32 A46	18c red orange	3.50 3.25
C33 A47	20c yellow	1.75 1.50
C34 A48	24c deep violet	1.75 1.50
C35 A49	32c olive brown	1.75 1.50
	Nos. C29-C35 (7)	10.15 8.85

Visit of Capt. Wolfgang von Gronau on his round-the-world flight.

Regular Issue of 1917-25 Overprinted F. REIN MADRID-MANILA FLIGHT-1933

1933, Apr. 11
C36 A40	2c green	.40 .35
C37 A40	4c carmine	.45 .35
C38 A40	6c deep violet	.80 .75
C39 A40	8c orange brown	2.50 1.50
C40 A40	10c dark blue	2.25 1.00
C41 A40	12c orange	2.00 1.00
C42 A40	16c ol green (Dewey)	2.00 1.00
C43 A40	20c yellow	2.00 1.00
C44 A40	26c green	2.25 1.50
a.	26c blue green	3.00 1.80
C45 A40	30c gray	3.00 1.75
	Nos. C36-C45 (10)	17.65 10.20

Flight from Madrid to Manila of aviator Fernando Rein y Loring.

Stamp of 1917 Overprinted AIR MAIL

1933, May 26 Unwmk. *Perf. 11*
C46 A40 2c green .50 .40

Regular Issue of 1932 Overprinted AIR MAIL

C47 A44	4c rose carmine	.20 .15
C48 A45	12c orange	.30 .15
C49 A47	20c yellow	.30 .20
C50 A48	24c deep violet	.40 .25
C51 A49	32c olive brown	.50 .35
	Nos. C46-C51 (6)	2.20 1.50

Nos. 387 and 392 Overprinted in Gold P.I.-U.S. INITIAL FLIGHT December-1935

1935, Dec. 2
C52 A57 10c rose carmine .30 .20
C53 A62 30c orange red .50 .35

China Clipper flight from Manila to San Francisco, Dec. 2-5, 1935.

Regular Issue of 1917-25 Surcharged in Various Colors MANILA-MADRID ARNACAL FLIGHT-1936 2 CENTAVOS 2

1936, Sept. 6 *Perf. 11*
C54 A40	2c on 4c carmine (Bl)	.15 .15
C55 A40	6c on 12c red org (V)	.15 .15
C56 A40	16c on 26c blue green (Bk)	.25 .20
a.	16c on 26c green (Bk)	1.25 .70
	Nos. C54-C56 (3)	.55 .50

Manila-Madrid flight by aviators Antonio Arnaiz and Juan Calvo.

Regular Issue of 1917-37 Surcharged in Black or Red FIRST AIR MAIL EXHIBITION Feb 17 to 19, 1939 8 CENTAVOS 8

1939, Feb. 17
C57 A40 8c on 26c blue green .75 .40
a. 8c on 26c green 1.60 .10
C58 A71 1p on 10p gray (R) 3.00 2.25

1st Air Mail Exhib., Feb. 17-19, 1939.

Moro Vinta and Clipper — AP1

1941, June 30
C59 AP1	8c carmine	1.00 .60
C60 AP1	20c ultramarine	1.20 .45
C61 AP1	60c blue green	1.75 1.00
C62 AP1	1p sepia	.70 .50
	Nos. C59-C62 (4)	4.65 2.55

For overprint see No. NO7. For surcharges see Nos. N10-N11, N35-N36.

No. C47 Handstamped in VICTORY Violet

1944, Dec. 3 Unwmk. *Perf. 11*
C63 A44 4c rose carmine 1,600. 1,600.

SPECIAL DELIVERY STAMPS

US No. E5 Overprinted PHILIPPINES in Red

1901, Oct. 15 Wmk. 191 *Perf. 12*
E1 SD3 10c dark blue 110.00 100.00

Special Delivery Messenger SD2

1906 Engr. Wmk. 191PI
E2 SD2 20c ultramarine 30.00 7.50
b. 20c pale ultramarine 30.00 7.50

See Nos. E3-E6. For overprints see Nos. E7-E10, EO1.

Special Printing
Ovptd. in Red as #E1 on US #E6
1907
E2A SD4 10c ultramarine 2,250.

1911 Wmk. 190PI
E3 SD2 20c deep ultramarine 20.00 1.75

1916 *Perf. 10*
E4 SD2 20c deep ultra 175.00 50.00

1919 Unwmk. *Perf. 11*
E5 SD2 20c ultramarine .60 .20
a. 20c pale blue .75 .20
b. 20c dull violet .60 .20

Type of 1906 Issue
1925-31 *Imperf.*
E6 SD2 20c dull violet ('31) 20.00 17.50

Type of 1919 Overprinted in Black
1939 *Perf. 11*
E7 SD2 20c blue violet .25 .20

Nos. E5b and E7, Handstamped in Violet VICTORY

1944 *Perf. 11*
E8 SD2 20c (On #E5b) 700.00 500.00
E9 SD2 20c (On #E7) 190.00 150.00

Type SD2 Overprinted "VICTORY" As No. 486

1945
E10 SD2 20c blue violet .70 .55
a. "IC" close together 3.25 2.75

SPECIAL DELIVERY OFFICIAL STAMP

Type of 1906 Issue Overprinted O.B.

1931 Unwmk. *Perf. 11*
EO1 SD2 20c dull violet .65 .40
a. No period after "B" 20.00 15.00
b. Double overprint

POSTAGE DUE STAMPS

Postage Due Stamps of the US Nos. J38-J44 Overprinted in Black PHILIPPINES

1899, Aug. 16 Wmk. 191 *Perf. 12*
J1 D2	1c deep claret	5.75 1.25
J2 D2	2c deep claret	6.00 1.10
J3 D2	5c deep claret	15.00 2.25
J4 D2	10c deep claret	19.00 4.75
J5 D2	50c deep claret	200.00 90.00

No. J1 was used to pay regular postage Sept. 5-19, 1902.

1901, Aug. 31
J6 D2 3c deep claret 17.50 6.00
J7 D2 30c deep claret 225.00 95.00
Nos. J1-J7 (7) 488.25 200.35

Post Office Clerk — D3

1928, Aug. 21 Engr. Unwmk. *Perf. 11*
J8 D3	4c brown red	.15 .15
J9 D3	6c brown red	.15 .15
J10 D3	8c brown red	.15 .15
J11 D3	10c brown red	.15 .15
J12 D3	12c brown red	.15 .15
J13 D3	16c brown red	.15 .15
J14 D3	20c brown red	.15 .15
	Nos. J8-J14 (7)	1.05 1.05

For overprints see Nos. O16-O22, NJ1. For surcharge see No. J15.

No. J8 Surcharged in Blue 3 CVOS. 3

1937
J15 D3 3c on 4c brown red .20 .15

Nos. J8-J14 Handstamped in Violet VICTORY

1944
J16 D3	4c brown red	125.00 —
J17 D3	6c brown red	80.00 —
J18 D3	8c brown red	85.00 —
J19 D3	10c brown red	80.00 —
J20 D3	12c brown red	80.00 —
J21 D3	16c brown red	85.00 —
J22 D3	20c brown red	85.00 —
	Nos. J16-J22 (7)	620.00

PHILIPPINES

OFFICIAL STAMPS

Official Handstamped Overprints

"Officers purchasing stamps for government business may, if they so desire, overprint them with the letters "O.B." either in writing with black ink or by rubber stamps but in such a manner as not to obliterate the stamp that postmasters will be unable to determine whether the stamps have been previously used." C. M. Cotterman, Director of Posts, Dec. 26, 1905.

Beginning Jan. 1, 1906, all branches of the Insular Government used postage stamps to prepay postage instead of franking them as before. Some officials used manuscript, some utilized typewriting machines, some made press-printed overprints, but by far the larger number provided themselves with rubber stamps.

The majority of these read "O.B." but other forms were: "OFFICIAL BUSINESS" or "OFFICIAL MAIL" in 2 lines, with variations on many of these.

These "O.B." overprints are known on US 1899-1901 stamps; on 1903-06 stamps in red and blue; on 1906 stamps in red, blue, black, yellow and green.

"O.B." overprints were also made on the centavo and peso stamps of the Philippines, per order of May 25, 1907.

Beginning in 1926, the Bureau of Posts issued press-printed official stamps, but many government offices continued to handstamp ordinary postage stamps "O.B."

Regular Issue of 1926 Overprinted in Red — OFFICIAL

1926, Dec. 20 — Unwmk. — Perf. 12

O1	A42	2c green & black	2.25	1.00
O2	A42	4c carmine & black	2.25	1.20
a.	Vertical pair, imperf. between		750.00	
O3	A42	18c lt brown & black	7.00	4.00
O4	A42	20c orange & black	6.75	1.75
	Nos. O1-O4 (4)		18.25	7.95

Opening of the Legislative Palace.

Regular Issue of 1917-26 Overprinted — O. B.

1931 — Perf. 11

O5	A40	2c green	.15	.15
a.	No period after "B"		15.00	5.00
b.	No period after "O"		—	
O6	A40	4c carmine	.15	.15
a.	No period after "B"		15.00	5.00
O7	A40	6c deep violet	.20	.15
O8	A40	8c yellow brn	.20	.15
O9	A40	10c deep blue	.30	.15
O10	A40	12c red orange	.25	.15
a.	No period after "B"		32.50	
O11	A40	16c lt ol green (Dewey)	.25	.15
	16c olive bister		1.25	.20
O12	A40	20c orange yellow	.25	.15
a.	No period after "B"		22.50	15.00
O13	A40	26c green	.40	.30
	26c olive green		1.00	.65
O14	A40	30c gray	.30	.25
	Nos. O5-O14 (10)		2.45	1.75

Same Overprint on Nos. 383-392

1935

O15	A53	2c rose	.15	.15
a.	No period after "B"		15.00	5.00
O16	A54	4c yellow green	.15	.15
a.	No period after "B"		15.00	8.50
O17	A55	6c dark brown	.15	.15
a.	No period after "B"		20.00	17.50
O18	A56	8c violet	.15	.15
O19	A57	10c rose carmine	.20	.15
O20	A58	12c black	.20	.15
O21	A59	16c dark blue	.20	.15
O22	A60	20c lt olive green	.20	.15
O23	A61	26c indigo	.25	.20
O24	A62	30c orange red	.30	.25
	Nos. O15-O24 (10)		1.95	1.65

Same Overprint on Nos. 411 and 418

1937-38 — Perf. 11

O25	A53	2c rose	.15	.15
a.	No period after "B"		4.25	2.25
b.	Period after "B" raised (UL 4)			
O26	A60	20c lt olive green ('38)	.65	.50

Nos. 383-392 Overprinted in Black: O. B.

COMMONWEALTH — a — O. B. — b

1938-40

O27	A53(a)	2c rose	.15	.15
a.	Hyphen omitted		20.00	20.00
b.	No period after "B"		25.00	25.00
O28	A54(b)	4c yellow green	.15	.15
O29	A55(a)	6c dark brown	.15	.15
O30	A56(b)	8c violet	.15	.15
O31	A57(b)	10c rose carmine	.15	.15
a.	No period after "O"		30.00	30.00
O32	A58(b)	12c black	.15	.15
O33	A59(b)	16c dark blue	.20	.15
O34	A60(a)	20c lt ol green ('40)	.25	.25
O35	A61(b)	26c indigo	.30	.30
O36	A62(b)	30c orange red	.25	.25
	Nos. O27-O36 (10)		1.90	1.85

No. 461 Overprinted in Black — O. B.

1941, Apr. 14 — Unwmk. — Perf. 11x10½

O37	A75	2c apple green	.15	.15

Official Stamps Handstamped in Violet — VICTORY

1944 — Perf. 11, 11x10½

O38	A53	2c #O27	200.00	110.00
O39	A75	2c #O37	6.50	3.00
O40	A54	4c #O16	37.50	25.00
O40A	A55	6c #O29	4,250.	
O41	A57	10c #O31	135.00	
a.	No period after "O"			
O42	A60	20c #O22	6,000.	
O43	A60	20c #O26	1,550.	

No. 497 Overprinted Like No. O37 in Black

Perf. 11x10½

1946, June 19 — Unwmk.

O44	A76	2c sepia	.15	.15

OCCUPATION STAMPS

Issued under Japanese Occupation

Nos. 461, 438 and 439 Overprinted with Bars in Black

1942-43 — Unwmk. — Perf. 11x10½, 11

N1	A75	2c apple green	.15	.15
a.	Pair, one without overprint			
N2	A58	12c black ('43)	.15	.15
N3	A59	16c dark blue	5.00	3.75
	Nos. N1-N3 (3)		5.30	4.05

Nos. 435, 442, 443 and 423 Surcharged in Black

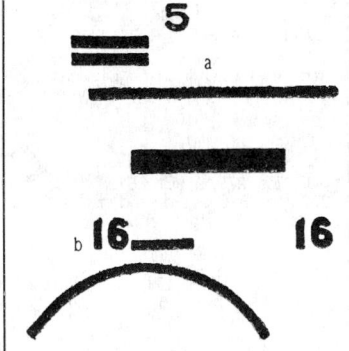

a — 5
b — 16
c — 50 CENTAVOS 50 — 1
d — ONE PESO

Perf. 11

N4	A55	5c on 6c golden brn	.15	.15
a.	Top bar shorter, thinner		.20	.20
b.	5c on 6c dark brown		.20	.20
c.	As "b" and"a"		.20	.20
N5	A62	16c on 30c orange red ('43)	.25	.25
N6	A63	50c on 1p red org & black ('43)	.60	.60
a.	Double surcharge		300.00	
N7	A65	1p on 4p blue & black ('43)	110.00	120.00
	Nos. N4-N7 (4)		111.00	121.00

On Nos. N4 and N4b, the top bar measures 1½x22½mm. On Nos. N4a and N4c, the top bar measures 1x21mm and the "5" is smaller and thinner.

No. 384 Surcharged in Black

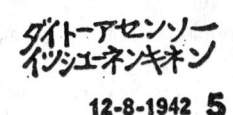

CONGRATULATIONS FALL OF BATAAN AND CORREGIDOR 1942 — 2

1942, May 18

N8	A54	2c on 4c yellow green	6.00	6.00

Japan's capture of Bataan and Corregidor. The American-Filipino forces finally surrendered May 7, 1942.

No. 384 Surcharged in Black

ダイトーアセンソー イツシューネンキネン 12-8-1942 5

1942, Dec. 8

N9	A54	5c on 4c yellow green	.50	.50

1st anniv. of the "Greater East Asia War."

Nos. C59 and C62 Surcharged in Black

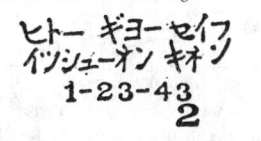

ヒトー ギヨーセイフ イツシューオン キネン 1-23-43 2

1943, Jan. 23

N10	AP1	2(c) on 8c carmine	.25	.25
N11	AP1	5c on 1p sepia	.50	.50

1st anniv. of the Philippine Executive Commission.

Nipa Hut — OS1
Rice Planting — OS2  
Mt. Mayon and Mt. Fuji — OS3 
Moro Vinta — OS4 

Engr., Typo. (2, 6, 25c)

1943-44 — Wmk. 257 — Perf. 13

N12	OS1	1c deep orange	.15	.15
N13	OS2	2c bright green	.15	.15
N14	OS1	4c slate green	.15	.15
N15	OS3	5c orange brown	.15	.15
N16	OS2	6c red	.15	.15
N17	OS3	10c blue green	.15	.15
N18	OS4	12c steel blue	1.00	1.00
N19	OS1	16c dark brown	.15	.15
N20	OS1	20c rose violet	1.25	1.25
N21	OS3	21c violet	.15	.15
N22	OS2	25c pale brown	.15	.15
N23	OS3	1p deep carmine	.75	.75
N24	OS4	2p dull violet	5.00	5.00
N25	OS4	5p dark olive	8.50	8.50
	Nos. N12-N25 (14)		17.85	17.85

For surcharges see Nos. NB5-NB7.

Map of Manila Bay Showing Bataan and Corregidor — OS5

1943, May 7 — Photo. — Unwmk.

N26	OS5	2c carmine red	.15	.15
N27	OS5	5c bright green	.25	.25

Fall of Bataan and Corregidor, 1st anniv.

No. 440 Surcharged in Black

Limbagan 1593-1943 — 12

1943, June 20 — Engr. — Perf. 11

N28	A60	12c on 20c lt olive green	.20	.20
a.	Double surcharge			

350th anniv. of the printing press in the Philippines. "Limbagan" is Tagalog for "printing press."

Rizal Monument, Filipina and Philippine Flag — OS6

1943, Oct. 14 — Photo. — Perf. 12

N29	OS6	5c light blue	.15	.15
a.	Imperf.		.15	.15
N30	OS6	12c orange	.15	.15
a.	Imperf.		.15	.15
N31	OS6	17c rose pink	.20	.20
a.	Imperf.		.20	.20
	Nos. N29-N31 (3)		.50	.50

"Independence of the Philippines." Japan granted "independence" Oct. 14, 1943, when the puppet republic was founded.

The imperforate stamps were issued without gum.

Jose Rizal — OS7
Rev. Jose Burgos — OS8 
Apolinario Mabini — OS9 

1944, Feb. 17 — Litho. — Perf. 12

N32	OS7	5c blue	.20	.20
a.	Imperf.		.15	.15
N33	OS8	12c carmine	.15	.15
a.	Imperf.		.15	.15
N34	OS9	17c deep orange	.15	.15
a.	Imperf.		.15	.15
	Nos. N32-N34 (3)		.50	.50

Nos. C60 and C61 Surcharged in Black

REPÚBLIKA NG PILIPINAS 5-7-44 5

1944, May 7 — Perf. 11

N35	AP1	5c on 20c ultra	.50	.35
N36	AP1	12c on 60c blue green	1.25	.85

Fall of Bataan and Corregidor, 2nd anniv.

PHILIPPINES — PUERTO RICO — RYUKYU ISLANDS

Jose P. Laurel — OS10

Without Gum
1945, Jan. 12   Litho.   Imperf.
N37	OS10	5c dull violet brown	.15	.15
N38	OS10	7c blue green	.15	.15
N39	OS10	20c chalky blue	.15	.15
		Nos. N37-N39 (3)	.45	.45

1st anniv. of the puppet Philippine Republic (Oct. 14, 1944). "S" stands for "sentimos."

OCCUPATION SEMI-POSTAL STAMPS

Woman, Farming and Cannery — OSP1

Unwmk.
1942, Nov. 12   Litho.   Perf. 12
NB1	OSP1	2c + 1c pale violet	.15	.15
NB2	OSP1	5c + 1c brt green	.25	.15
NB3	OSP1	16c + 2c orange	25.00	25.00
		Nos. NB1-NB3 (3)	25.40	25.30

Campaign to produce and conserve food. The surtax aided the Red Cross.

Souvenir Sheet

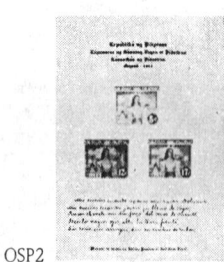

OSP2

Without Gum
1943, Oct. 14   Imperf.
NB4	OSP2	Sheet of 3	45.00	6.00

"Independence of the Philippines."
No. NB4 contains Nos. N29a-N31a. Lower inscription from Rizal's "Last Farewell." Sold for 2.50p.

Nos. N18, N20 and N21
Surcharged in Black

BAHÂ
1943
+21

1943, Dec. 8   Wmk. 257   Perf. 13
NB5	OS4	12c + 21c steel blue	.15	.15
NB6	OS1	20c + 36c rose violet	.15	.15
NB7	OS3	21c + 40c violet	.15	.15
		Nos. NB5-NB7 (3)	.45	.45

The surtax was for the benefit of victims of a Luzon flood.
"Baha" is Tagalog for "flood."

Souvenir Sheet

OSP3

Without Gum
1944, Feb. 9   Unwmk. Litho.   Imperf.
NB8	OSP3	Sheet of 3	5.00	3.00

No. NB8 contains Nos. N32a-N34a.
Sheet sold for 1p, surtax going to a fund for the care of heroes' monuments.

OCCUPATION POSTAGE DUE STAMP

No. J15 Ovptd. with Bar in Blue

1942, Oct. 14   Unwmk.   Perf. 11
NJ1	D3	3c on 4c brown red	35.00	20.00

On copies of No. J15, two lines were drawn in India ink with a ruling pen across "United States of America" by employees of the Short Paid Section of the Manila Post Office.
This was to make a provisional 3c postage due stamp which was used from Sept. 1, 1942, (when the letter rate was raised from 2c to 5c) until Oct. 14 when No. NJ1 went on sale.

OCCUPATION OFFICIAL STAMPS

Nos. 461, 413, 435, 435a and 442 Overprinted or Surcharged in Black with Bars and 公用 (K. P.)

1943-44   Unwmk.   Perf. 11x10½, 11
NO1	A75	2c apple green	.15	.15
a.		Double overprint	500.00	
NO2	A55	5c on 6c dk brown (#413, '44)	35.00	35.00
NO3	A55	5c on 6c gldn brn (No. 435a)	.15	.15
a.		Narrower spacing btwn. bars	.15	.15
b.		5c on 6c dark brown (#435)	.15	.15
c.		As "b," narrower spacing between bars	.15	.15
d.		Double surcharge		
NO4	A62	16c on 30c orange red	.30	.30
a.		Wider spacing between bars	.30	.30
		Nos. NO1-NO4 (4)	35.60	35.60

On Nos. NO3 and NO3b, the bar deleting "United States of America" is 9¾-10mm above the bar deleting "Common-". On Nos. NO3a and NO3c, the spacing is 8-8½mm.
On No. NO4 the center bar is 19mm long, 3½mm below the top bar and 6mm above the Japanese characters. On No. NO4a, the center bar is 20½mm long, 9mm below the top bar and 1mm above the Japanese characters.
"K. P." (Kagamitang Pampamahalaan) is Tagalog for "Official Business."

Nos. 435 and 435a Surcharged in Black

5
REPUBLIKA NG
PILIPINAS
(K. P.)

1944   Perf. 11
NO5	A55	5c on 6c golden brown	.15	.15
a.		5c on 6c dark brown	.15	.15

Nos. O34 and C62 Overprinted in Black

a   *Pilipinas*
    REPUBLIKA

b   K. P.
    REPUBLIKA NG PILIPINAS
    (K. P.)

NO6	A60(a)	20c lt olive green	.25	.25
NO7	AP1(b)	1p sepia	.65	.65

PUERTO RICO

ˌpwer-tə-ˈrē-(ˌ)kō

(Porto Rico)

LOCATION — Large island in the West Indies, east of Hispaniola
GOVT. — Former Spanish possession
AREA — 3,435 sq. mi.
POP. — 953,243 (1899)
CAPITAL — San Juan

The island was ceded to the US by the Treaty of 1898.
Spanish issues of 1855-73 used in both Puerto Rico and Cuba are listed as Cuba Nos. 1-4, 9-14, 18-21, 32-34, 35A-37, 39-41, 43-45, 47-49, 51-53, 55-57.
Spanish issues of 1873-1898 for Puerto Rico only are listed in Vol. 4 of this Catalogue.

100 Cents = 1 Dollar (1898)

Issued under US Administration
Ponce Issue

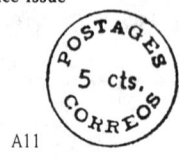

A11

1898   Unwmk.   Imperf.
200	A11	5c violet, *yellowish*		7,000.

The only way No. 200 is known used is hand-stamped on envelopes. Both unused stamps and used envelopes have a violet control mark.
Counterfeits exist of Nos. 200-201.

Coamo Issue

A12

1898   Unwmk.   Imperf.
201	A12	5c black	650.	1,050.

There are ten varieties in the setting (see the Scott United States Specialized Catalogue). The stamps bear the control mark "F. Santiago" in violet.

US Nos. 279, 279Bf, 281, 272 and 282C Overprinted in Black at 36 degree angle

PORTO RICO

1899   Wmk. 191   Perf. 12
210	A87	1c yellow green	5.00	1.40
a.		Ovpt. at 25 degree angle	7.50	2.25
211	A88	2c redsh car, type IV	4.25	1.25
a.		Ovpt. at 25 degree angle	5.50	2.25
212	A91	5c blue	9.00	2.50
213	A93	8c violet brown	27.50	17.50
a.		Ovpt. at 25 degree angle	32.50	18.50
c.		"PORTO RIC"	125.00	110.00
214	A94	10c brown, type I	17.50	6.00
		Nos. 210-214 (5)	63.25	28.65

Misspellings of the overprint, actually broken letters (PORTO RICU, PORTU RICO, FORTO RICO), are found on 1c, 2c, 8c and 10c.

US Nos. 279 and 279B Overprinted Diagonally in Black

PUERTO RICO

1900
215	A87	1c yellow green	6.00	1.40
216	A88	2c red, type IV	4.75	1.25
b.		Inverted overprint	8,250.	

POSTAGE DUE STAMPS

US Nos. J38, J39, J42 Overprinted like Nos. 210-214

1899   Wmk. 191   Perf. 12
J1	D2	1c deep claret	22.50	5.50
a.		Overprint at 25 degree angle	22.50	7.50
J2	D2	2c deep claret	11.00	6.00
a.		Overprint at 25 degree angle	15.00	7.00
J3	D2	10c deep claret	160.00	60.00
a.		Overprint at 25 degree angle	180.00	85.00
		Nos. J1-J3 (3)	193.50	71.50

Stamps of Puerto Rico were replaced by those of the US.

RYUKYU ISLANDS

LOCATION — Chain of 63 islands between Japan and Formosa, separating the East China Sea from the Pacific Ocean
GOVT. — Semi-autonomous under United States administration
AREA — 848 sq. mi.
POP. — 945,465 (1970)
CAPITAL — Naha, Okinawa

The Ryukyus were part of Japan until American forces occupied them in 1945. The islands reverted to Japan May 15, 1972.
Before the general issue of 1948, a number of provisional stamps were used. These included a mimeographed handstamped adhesive for Kume Island, and various current stamps of Japan handstamped with chops by the postmasters of Okinawa, Amami, Miyako and Yaeyama. Although authorized by American authorities, these provisionals were local in nature, so are omitted in the listings that follow. They are listed in the Scott United States Specialized Catalogue.

100 Sen = 1 Yen
100 Cents = 1 Dollar (1958)

Catalogue values for all unused stamps in this country are for Never Hinged items.

Watermark

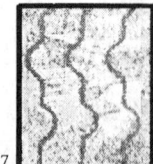

Wmk. 257

Cycad — A1   Lily — A2

Sailing Ship — A3    Farmer — A4

Wmk. 257
1949, July 18   Typo.   Perf. 13
Second Printing
1	A1	5s magenta	1.50	1.50
2	A2	10s yellow green	6.00	5.50
3	A1	20s yellow green	2.50	2.50
4	A3	30s vermilion	1.50	1.50
5	A2	40s magenta	1.50	1.50
6	A3	50s ultramarine	3.00	3.25
7	A4	1y ultramarine	6.00	5.50
		Nos. 1-7 (7)	22.00	21.25

First Printing
1948, July 1
1a	A1	5s magenta	2.50	3.50
2a	A2	10s yellow green	1.40	2.00
3a	A1	20s yellow green	1.40	2.00
4a	A3	30s vermilion	2.50	3.25
5a	A2	40s magenta	50.00	50.00
6a	A3	50s ultramarine	2.50	3.50
7a	A4	1y ultramarine	450.00	290.00
		Nos. 1a-7a (7)	510.30	354.25

First printing: thick yellow gum, dull colors, rough perforations, grayish paper.
Second printing: white gum, sharp colors, clean-cut perforations, white paper.

RYUKYU ISLANDS

Roof Tiles — A5

Ryukyu University — A6

Designs: 1y, Ryukyu girl. 2y, Shuri Castle. 3y, Guardian dragon. 4y, Two women. 5y, Sea shells.

Perf. 13x13½

1950, Jan. 21   Unwmk.   Photo.
8	A5	50s dark carmine rose	.20	.20
a.		White paper	.50	.50
9	A5	1y deep blue	2.50	2.00
10	A5	2y rose violet	11.00	6.00
11	A5	3y carmine rose	25.00	11.00
12	A5	4y grnsh gray	15.00	11.00
13	A5	5y blue green	7.50	5.00
		Nos. 8-13 (6)	61.20	35.20

No. 8a is on whiter paper with colorless gum. Issued Sept. 6, 1958.
No. 8 is on toned paper with yellowish gum.
For surcharges see Nos. 16-17.

1951, Feb. 12   Perf. 13½x13
14	A6	3y red brown	55.00	20.00

Opening of Ryukyu University, Feb. 12.

Pine Tree — A7

1951, Feb. 19   Perf. 13
15	A7	3y dark green	50.00	20.00

Reforestation Week, Feb. 18-24.

Nos. 8 and 10 Surcharged in Black

Three types of 10y surcharge:
I - Narrow-spaced rules, "10" normal spacing.
II - Wide-spaced rules, "10" normal spacing.
III - Rules and "10" both wide-spaced.

1952   Perf. 13x13½
16	A5	10y on 50s, type II	9.00	9.00
a.		Type I	35.00	35.00
b.		Type III	40.00	40.00
17	A5	100y on 2y rose vio	1,900.	1,200.

Surcharge forgeries are known of No. 17. Authentication by competent experts is recommended.

Dove, Bean Sprout and Map — A8

Madanbashi Bridge — A9

1952, Apr. 1   Perf. 13½x13
18	A8	3y deep plum	120.00	35.00

Establishment of the Government of the Ryukyu Islands (GRI), Apr. 1, 1952.

1952-53

Designs: 2y, Main Hall, Shuri Castle. 3y, Shurei Gate. 6y, Stone Gate, Sogenji temple, Naha. 10y, Benzaiten-do temple. 30y, Sonohan Utaki (altar) at Shuri Castle. 50y, Tamaudum (royal mausoleum), Shuri. 100y, Stone Bridge, Hosho Pond.

19	A9	1y red	.20	.20
20	A9	2y green	.25	.25
21	A9	3y aqua	.35	.35
22	A9	6y blue	1.75	1.75
23	A9	10y crimson rose	1.25	.90
24	A9	30y olive green	11.00	6.50
a.		30y light olive green ('58)	30.00	
25	A9	50y rose violet	15.00	8.25
26	A9	100y claret	20.00	6.25
		Nos. 19-26 (8)	51.05	24.45

Issued: 1y, 2y, 3y, 11/20/52; others, 1/20/53.

Reception at Shuri Castle — A10

Perry and American Fleet — A11

Perf. 13½x13, 13x13½

1953, May 26
27	A10	3y deep magenta	12.50	6.50
28	A11	6y dull blue	1.25	1.25

Centenary of the arrival of Commodore Matthew Calbraith Perry at Naha, Okinawa.

Chofu Ota and Pencil-shaped Matrix — A12

Shigo Toma and Pen — A13

1953, Oct. 1   Perf. 13½x13
29	A12	4y yellow brown	10.00	5.00

3rd Newspaper Week.

1954, Oct. 1
30	A13	4y blue	13.00	7.50

4th Newspaper Week.

Ryukyu Pottery A14

Noguni Shrine and Sweet Potato Plant A15

Designs: 15y, Lacquerware. 20y, Textile design.

1954-55   Photo.   Perf. 13
31	A14	4y brown	1.00	.60
32	A14	15y vermilion	4.00	2.00
33	A14	20y yellow orange	2.25	2.00
		Nos. 31-33 (3)	7.25	4.60

Issue dates: June 25, 1954, June 20, 1955.
For surcharges see Nos. C19, C21, C23.

1955, Nov. 26
34	A15	4y blue	11.00	7.00

350th anniv. of the introduction of the sweet potato to the Ryukyu Islands.

Stylized Trees — A16

Willow Dance — A17

1956, Feb. 18   Unwmk.
35	A16	4y bluish green	10.00	5.00

Arbor Week, Feb. 18-24.

1956, May 1   Perf. 13

Design: 8y, Straw hat dance. 14y, Dancer in warrior costume with fan.

36	A17	5y rose lilac	.90	.60
37	A17	8y violet blue	2.00	1.65
38	A17	14y reddish brown	3.00	2.00
		Nos. 36-38 (3)	5.90	4.25

For surcharges see Nos. C20, C22.

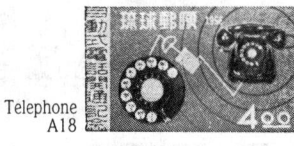

Telephone A18

1956, June 8
39	A18	4y violet blue	15.00	8.00

Establishment of dial telephone system.

Garland of Pine, Bamboo and Plum — A19

Map of Okinawa and Pencil Rocket — A20

1956, Dec. 1   Perf. 13½x13
40	A19	2y multicolored	2.00	1.50

New Year, 1957.

1957, Oct. 1   Photo.   Perf. 13½x13
41	A20	4y deep violet blue	.75	.75

7th annual Newspaper Week, Oct. 1-7.

Phoenix — A21

1957, Dec. 1   Unwmk.   Perf. 13
42	A21	2y multicolored	.25	.25

New Year, 1958.

Ryukyu Stamps — A22

1958, July 1   Perf. 13½
43	A22	4y multicolored	.80	.80

10th anniversary of first Ryukyu stamps.

Yen Symbol and Dollar Sign — A23

1958, Sept. 16   Typo.   Perf. 11
Without Gum
44	A23	½c orange	.90	.90
a.		Imperf., pair	1,000.	
b.		Horiz. pair, imperf. btwn.	100.00	
c.		Vert. pair, imperf. btwn.	150.00	
d.		Vert. strip of 4, imperf. btwn.	500.00	
45	A23	1c yellow green	1.40	1.40
a.		Horiz. pair, imperf. btwn.	150.00	
b.		Vert. pair, imperf. btwn.	110.00	
c.		Vert. strip of 3, imperf. btwn.	450.00	
d.		Vert. strip of 4, imperf. btwn.	500.00	
e.		Block of 4, imperf. btwn. vert & horiz.		
46	A23	2c dark blue	2.25	2.25
a.		Horiz. pair, imperf. btwn.	150.00	
b.		Vert. pair, imperf. btwn.	1,500.	
c.		Horiz. strip of 3, imperf. btwn.	300.00	
d.		Vert. strip of 4, imperf. btwn.	500.00	
47	A23	3c deep carmine	1.75	1.50
a.		Horiz. pair, imperf. btwn.	150.00	
b.		Vert. pair, imperf. btwn.	110.00	
c.		Vert. strip of 3, imperf. btwn.	300.00	
d.		Vert. strip of 4, imperf. btwn.	550.00	
e.		Block of 4, imperf. btwn. vert & horiz.		
48	A23	4c bright green	2.25	2.25
a.		Horiz. pair, imperf. btwn.	500.00	
b.		Vert. pair, imperf. btwn.	150.00	
49	A23	5c orange	4.25	3.75
a.		Horiz. pair, imperf. btwn.	150.00	
b.		Vert. pair, imperf. btwn.	750.00	
50	A23	10c aqua	5.75	4.75
a.		Horiz. pair, imperf. btwn.	200.00	
b.		Vert. pair, imperf. btwn.	150.00	
c.		Vert. strip of 3, imperf. btwn.	550.00	
51	A23	25c brt vio blue	8.00	6.00
a.		Gummed paper ('61)	9.50	8.50
b.		Horiz. pair, imperf. btwn.	1,400.	
c.		Vert. pair, imperf. btwn.		
d.		Vert. strip of 4, imperf. btwn.	600.00	
52	A23	50c gray	17.50	10.00
a.		Gummed paper ('61)	10.50	10.00
b.		Horiz. pair, imperf. btwn.	1,200.	
53	A23	$1 rose lilac	12.50	5.50
a.		Horiz. pair, imperf. btwn.	400.00	
b.		Vert. pair, imperf. btwn.	1,750.	
		Nos. 44-53 (10)	56.55	38.30

Printed locally. Perforation, paper and shade varieties exist.
Nos. 51a, 52a are on off-white paper and perf 10.3.

Gate of Courtesy — A24

1958, Oct. 15   Photo.   Perf. 13½
54	A24	3c multicolored	1.25	1.00

Restoration of Shureimon, Gate of Courtesy, on road leading to Shuri City.
Counterfeits exist.

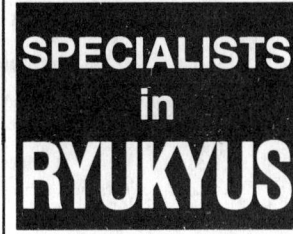

SPECIALISTS in RYUKYUS

We specialize in...
#44-53s,
postal stationery,
and
other rare items.

• • • • • •

PLEASE SEND $1.00 IN POSTAGE OR COIN FOR LISTS!

SHULL SERVICE
P.O. Box 15008
5910 Connecticut Ave.
Chevy Chase, MD 20825

Want lists serviced!

RYUKYU ISLANDS

Lion Dance
A25

Trees and Mountains
A26

1958, Dec. 10   Unwmk.   Perf. 13½
55   A25   1½c multicolored   .25   .20
New Year, 1959.

1959, Apr. 30   Litho.   Perf. 13½x13
56   A26   3c bl, yel grn, grn & red   .70   .60
"Make the Ryukyus Green" movement.

Yonaguni Moth
A27

1959, July 23   Photo.   Perf. 13
57   A27   3c multicolored   1.10   .90
Meeting of the Japanese Biological Education Society in Okinawa.

Hibiscus
A28

Toy (Yakaji)
A29

3c, Fish (Moorish idol). 8c, Sea shell (Phalium bandatum). 13c, Butterfly (Kallima Inachus Eucerca), denomination at left, butterfly going up. 17c, Jellyfish (Dactylometra pacifera Goette).

Inscribed 琉球郵便

1959, Aug. 10   Perf. 13x13½
58   A28   ½c multicolored   .20   .20
59   A28   3c multicolored   .75   .40
60   A28   8c lt ultra, blk & ocher 10.00 5.50
61   A28   13c lt bl, gray & org   2.50   1.75
62   A28   17c vio bl, red & yel   20.00   9.00
   Nos. 58-62 (5)   33.45 16.85

Four-character inscription measures 10x2mm on ½c; 12x3mm on 3c, 8c; 8½x2mm on 13c, 17c. See Nos. 76-80.

1959, Dec. 1   Litho.
63   A29   1½c gold & multi   .55   .38
New Year, 1960.

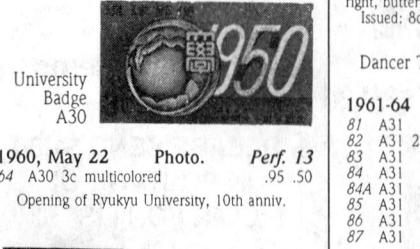

University Badge
A30

1960, May 22   Photo.   Perf. 13
64   A30   3c multicolored   .95   .50
Opening of Ryukyu University, 10th anniv.

Dancer — A31

Designs: Various Ryukyu Dances.

1960, Nov. 1   Photo.   Perf. 13
Dark Gray Background
65   A31   1c yellow, red & vio   1.25   .80
66   A31   2½c crimson, bl & yel   3.00   1.00
67   A31   5c dk blue, yel & red   .65   .50
68   A31   10c dk blue, yel & car   .80   .65
   Nos. 65-68 (4)   5.70   2.95
See Nos. 81-87, 220.

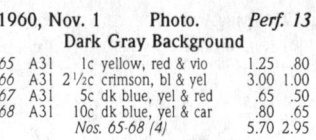

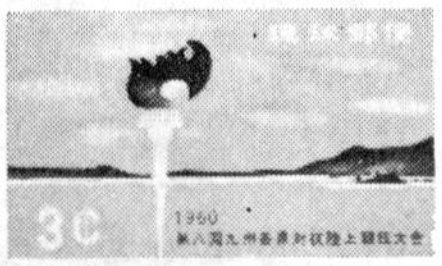

Torch and Nago Bay — A32

Runners at Starting Line — A33

1960, Nov. 8
72   A32   3c lt bl, grn & red   5.50   2.50
73   A33   8c orange & slate grn   .75   .75
8th Kyushu Inter-Prefectural Athletic Meet, Nago, Northern Okinawa, Nov. 6-7.

Little Egret and Rising Sun — A34

1960, Dec. 1   Unwmk.   Perf. 13
74   A34   3c reddish brown   5.50   2.50
National census.

Okinawa Bull Fight — A35

1960, Dec. 10   Perf. 13½
75   A35   1½c bis, dk bl & red brn 1.75   .65
New Year, 1961.

Type of 1959 With Japanese Inscription Redrawn:
琉球郵便

1960-61   Photo.   Perf. 13x13½
76   A28   ½c multicolored ('61)   .45   .45
77   A28   3c multicolored ('61)   .90   .35
78   A28   8c lt ultra, blk & ocher .90   .80
79   A28   13c blue, brn & red   1.10   .90
80   A28   17c violet bl, red & yel 15.00 6.00
   Nos. 76-80 (5)   18.35 8.50

Size of Japanese inscription on Nos. 78-80 is 10½x11½mm. On No. 79 the denomination is at right, butterfly going down.
Issued: 8c-17c, July 1; 3c, Aug. 23; ½c, Oct.

Dancer Type of 1960 with "RYUKYUS" Added in English

1961-64   Perf. 13
81   A31   1c multicolored   .15   .15
82   A31   2½c multicolored ('62)   .20   .15
83   A31   5c multicolored ('62)   .25   .25
84   A31   10c multicolored ('62)   .45   .40
84A   A31   20c multicolored ('64) 3.00   1.40
85   A31   25c multicolored ('62) 1.00   .90
86   A31   50c multicolored   2.50   1.40
87   A31 $1 multicolored   6.00   .25
   Nos. 81-87 (8)   13.55   4.90
Issue dates: 50c, $1, Sept. 1. 1c, Dec. 5. 25c, Feb. 1. 2½c, 5c, 10c, June 20. 20c, Jan. 20.

Pine Tree — A36

1961, May 1   Photo.   Perf. 13
88   A36   3c yellow green & red   1.50   1.25
"Make the Ryukyus Green" movement.

Naha, Steamer and Sailboat
A37

1961, May 20
89   A37   3c aqua   2.10   1.10
40th anniversary of Naha.

White Silver Temple — A38

Books and Bird — A39

1961, Oct. 1   Typo.   Perf. 11
90   A38   3c red brown   2.00   1.50
  a.   Horiz. pair, imperf. between 500.00
  b.   Vert. pair, imperf. between   600.00
Merger of townships Takamine, Kanegushiku and Miwa with Itoman.

1961, Nov. 12   Litho.   Perf. 13
91   A39   3c multicolored   1.10   .90
Issued for Book Week.

Rising Sun and Eagles — A40

Symbolic Steps, Trees and Government Building — A41

1961, Dec. 10   Photo.   Perf. 13½
92   A40   1½c gold, ver & blk   2.00   1.50
New Year, 1962.

1962, Apr. 1   Unwmk.   Perf. 13½
Design: 3c, Government Building.
93   A41   1½c multicolored   .60   .60
94   A41   3c brt green, red & gray   .80   .80
10th anniv. of the Government of the Ryukyu Islands (GRI).

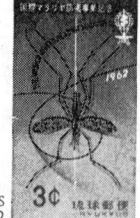

Anopheles Hyrcanus Sinensis — A42

8c, Malaria eradication emblem & Shurei gate.

1962, Apr. 7   Perf. 13½x13
95   A42   3c multicolored   .60   .60
96   A42   8c multicolored   .90   .75
WHO drive to eradicate malaria.

Dolls and Toys — A43

Linden or Sea Hibiscus — A44

1962, May 5   Litho.   Perf. 13½
97   A43   3c red, blk, bl & buff   1.10   .75
Issued for Children's Day.

1962, June 1   Photo.
Flowers: 3c, Indian coral tree. 8c, Iju (Schima liukiuensis Nakai). 13c, Touch-me-not (garden balsam). 17c, Shell flower (Alpinia speciosa).
98   A44   ½c multicolored   .15   .15
99   A44   3c multicolored   .35   .15
100   A44   8c multicolored   .40   .40
101   A44   13c multicolored   .60   .55
102   A44   17c multicolored   1.00   .80
   Nos. 98-102 (5)   2.50   2.05
See #107, 114 for 1½c and 15c flower stamps. For surcharge see No. 190.

Earthenware
A45

1962, July 5   Perf. 13½x13
103   A45   3c multicolored   3.50   2.50
Issued for Philatelic Week.

Japanese Fencing (Kendo)
A46

1962, July 25   Perf. 13
104   A46   3c multicolored   4.00   3.00
All-Japan Kendo Meeting, Okinawa, July 25.

Rabbit Playing near Water, Bingata Cloth Design — A47

Young Man and Woman, Stone Relief — A48

1962, Dec. 10   Perf. 13x13½
105   A47   1½c gold & multi   1.00   .80
New Year, 1963.

1963, Jan. 15   Photo.   Perf. 13½
106   A48   3c gold, black & blue   .90   .65
Issued for Adult Day.

Gooseneck Cactus
A49

Trees and Wooded Hills
A50

1963, Apr. 5   Perf. 13x13½
107   A49   1½c dk bl, grn, yel & pink   .15   .15

1963, Mar. 25   Perf. 13½x13
108   A50   3c ultra, green & red brn 1.00   .80
"Make the Ryukyus Green" movement.

Shop with Scott Publishing Co. 24 hours a day 7 days a week at www.scottonline.com

RYUKYU ISLANDS

Map of Okinawa — A51
Hawks over Islands — A52 

1963, Apr. 30   Unwmk.   Perf. 13½
109 A51 3c multicolored   1.25   1.00
Opening of the Round Road on Okinawa.

1963, May 10   Photo.
110 A52 3c multicolored   1.10   .95
Issued for Bird Day, May 10.

Shioya Bridge — A53

1963, June 5
111 A53 3c multicolored   1.10   .95
Opening of Shioya Bridge over Shioya Bay.

Tsuikin-wan Lacquerware Bowl — A54

1963, July 1   Unwmk.   Perf. 13½
112 A54 3c multicolored   3.00   2.50
Issued for Philatelic Week.

Map of Far East and JCI Emblem — A55

1963, Sept. 16   Photo.   Perf. 13½
113 A55 3c multicolored   .70   .50
Meeting of the Intl. Junior Chamber of Commerce (JCI), Naha, Okinawa, Sept. 16-19.

Mamaomoto A56
Site of Nakagusuku Castle A57 

1963, Oct. 15   Perf. 13x13½
114 A56 15c multicolored   2.00   .80

1963, Nov. 1   Perf. 13½x13
115 A57 3c multicolored   .70   .45
Protection of national cultural treasures.

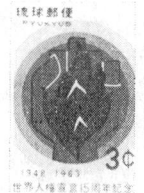

Flame — A58
Dragon (Bingata Pattern) — A59 

1963, Dec. 10   Perf. 13½
116 A58 3c red, dk bl & yel   .70   .45
15th anniversary of the Universal Declaration of Human Rights.

1963, Dec. 10   Photo.
117 A59 1½c multicolored   .60   .30
New Year, 1964.

Carnation A60
Pineapples and Sugar Cane A61 

1964, May 10   Perf. 13½
118 A60 3c blue, yel, blk & car   .40   .35
Issued for Mother's Day.

1964, June 1
119 A61 3c multicolored   .40   .35
Agricultural census.

Minsah Obi (Sash Woven of Kapok) — A62

1964, July 1   Unwmk.   Perf. 13½
120 A62 3c dp bl, rose pink & ocher   .55   .45
  a.   3c dp bl, dp car & ocher   .70   .60
Issued for Philatelic Week.

Girl Scout and Emblem — A63

1964, Aug. 31   Photo.
121 A63 3c multicolored   .40   .30
10th anniversary of Ryukyuan Girl Scouts.

Shuri Relay Station — A64
Parabolic Antenna and Map — A65 

1964, Sept. 1   Unwmk.   Perf. 13½
Black Overprint
122 A64 3c deep green   .65   .65
  a.   Figure "1" inverted   27.50 27.50
123 A65 8c ultra   1.25   1.25
Opening of the Ryukyu Islands-Japan microwave system carrying telephone and telegraph messages between the Ryukyus and Japan. Nos. 122-123 not issued without overprint.

Gate of Courtesy, Olympic Torch and Emblem — A66

1964, Sept. 7   Photo.   Perf. 13½x13
124 A66 3c ultra, yellow & red   .20   .15
Relaying of the Olympic torch on Okinawa en route to Tokyo.

"Naihanchi," Karate Stance — A67
"Makiwara," Strengthening Hands and Feet — A68 
"Kumite," Simulated Combat — A69 

1964-65   Photo.   Perf. 13½
125 A67 3c dull claret, yel & blk   .50   .30
126 A68 3c yellow & multi ('65)   .40   .30
127 A69 3c gray, red & blk ('65)   .40   .30
  Nos. 125-127 (3)   1.30   .90
Karate, Ryukyuan self-defense sport.
Issued: #125, 10/5; #126, 2/5; #127, 6/5.

Miyara Dunchi — A70
Snake and Iris (Bingata) — A71 

1964, Nov. 1   Perf. 13½
128 A70 3c multicolored   .25   .20
Protection of national cultural treasures. Miyara Dunchi was built as a residence by Miyara-pechin Toen in 1819.

1964, Dec. 10   Photo.
129 A71 1½c multicolored   .30   .20
New Year, 1965.

Boy Scouts — A72

1965, Feb. 6   Perf. 13½
130 A72 3c lt blue & multi   .45   .30
10th anniversary of Ryukyuan Boy Scouts.

Main Stadium, Onoyama A73

1965, July 1   Perf. 13x13½
131 A73 3c multicolored   .20   .20
Inauguration of the main stadium of the Onoyama athletic facilities.

Samisen of King Shoko — A74

1965, July 1   Photo.   Perf. 13½
132 A74 3c buff & multi   .45   .30
Issued for Philatelic Week.

Kin Power Plant — A75
ICY Emblem, Ryukyu Map — A76 

1965, July 1
133 A75 3c green & multi   .20   .20
Completion of Kin power plant.

1965, Aug. 24   Photo.   Perf. 13½
134 A76 3c multicolored   .20   .15
UN, 20th anniv.; Intl. Cooperation Year, 1964-65.

RYUKYU ISLANDS

SPECIAL OFFER
Scott Ryukyu Islands Album and Binder ($69.95) plus 117 all Different Mint Stamps ($40.70), a Total Scott Value of $110.65.

ONLY $83.00
Postpaid and Insured

CONSTANTLY BUYING!

JOHN B. HEAD
P.O. Drawer 7
Bethel, ME 04217

Phone 207-824-2462
Established 1955

Life #7482   1971   Charter #28

RYUKYU ISLANDS

Naha City Hall — A77

1965, Sept. 18   Unwmk.   Perf. 13½
135 A77 3c blue & multi   .20   .15
Completion of Naha City Hall.

Chinese Box Turtle A78

Horse (Bingata) A79

Turtles: No. 137, Hawksbill turtle (denomination at top, country name at bottom). No. 138, Asian terrapin (denomination and country name on top).

1965-66   Photo.   Perf. 13½
136 A78 3c gldn brn & multi   .30   .30
137 A78 3c black, yel & brn   .30   .30
138 A78 3c gray & multi   .30   .30
       Nos. 136-138 (3)   .90   .90

Issue dates: No. 136, Oct. 20, 1965. No. 137, Jan. 20, 1966. No. 138, Apr. 20, 1966.

1965, Dec. 10   Photo.   Perf. 13½
139 A79 1½c multicolored   .15   .15
  a. Gold omitted   1,200.   —

New Year, 1966.
There are 92 unused and 2 used examples of No. 139a known.

Noguchi's Okinawa Woodpecker A80

Sika Deer A81

1966   Photo.   Perf. 13½
140 A80 3c shown   .20   .20
141 A81 3c shown   .25   .25
142 A81 3c Dugong   .25   .25
       Nos. 140-142 (3)   .70   .70

Nature conservation.
Issued: #140, 2/15; #141, 3/15; #142, 4/20.

Ryukyu Bungalow Swallow — A82

1966, May 10   Photo.   Perf. 13½
143 A82 3c sky blue, blk & brn   .15   .15
4th Bird Week, May 10-16.

Lilies and Ruins A83

1966, June 23   Perf. 13x13½
144 A83 3c multicolored   .15   .15
Memorial Day, commemorating the end of the Battle of Okinawa, June 23, 1945.

University of the Ryukyus A84

1966, July 1
145 A84 3c multicolored   .15   .15
Transfer of the University of the Ryukyus from US authority to the Ryukyu Government.

Lacquerware, 18th Century — A85

Tile-Roofed House and UNESCO Emblem — A86

1966, Aug. 1   Perf. 13½
146 A85 3c gray & multi   .15   .15
Issued for Philatelic Week.

1966, Sept. 20   Photo.   Perf. 13½
147 A86 3c multicolored   .15   .15
UNESCO, 20th anniv.

Government Museum and Dragon Statue — A87

1966, Oct. 6
148 A87 3c multicolored   .15   .15
Completion of the GRI (Government of the Ryukyu Islands) Museum, Shuri.

Tomb of Nakasone-Tuimya Genga, Ruler of Miyako — A88

1966, Nov. 1   Photo.   Perf. 13½
149 A88 3c multicolored   .15   .15
Protection of national cultural treasures.

Ram in Iris Wreath (Bingata) A89

Clown Fish A90

1966, Dec. 10   Photo.   Perf. 13½
150 A89 1½c dk blue & multi   .15   .15
New Year, 1967.

1966-67
Fish: No. 152, Young boxfish (white numeral at lower left). No. 153, Forceps fish (pale buff numeral at lower right). No. 154, Spotted triggerfish (orange numeral). No. 155, Saddleback butterflyfish (carmine numeral, lower left).

151 A90 3c org red & multi   .20   .15
152 A90 3c org yel & multi ('67) .20   .15
153 A90 3c multi ('67)   .30   .25
154 A90 3c multi ('67)   .30   .25
155 A90 3c multi ('67)   .30   .25
       Nos. 151-155 (5)   1.30 1.05

Issue dates: #151, Dec. 20. #152, Jan. 10. #153, Apr. 10. #154, May 25. #155, June 10.

Tsuboya Urn — A91

Episcopal Miter — A92

1967, Apr. 20
156 A91 3c yellow & multi   .20   .20
Issued for Philatelic Week.

1967-68   Photo.   Perf. 13½
Seashells: No. 158, Venus comb murex. No. 159, Chiragra spider. No. 160, Green turban. No. 161, Euprotomus bulla.

157 A92 3c lt green & multi   .20   .15
158 A92 3c grnsh bl & multi   .20   .15
159 A92 3c emerald & multi   .25   .20
160 A92 3c lt blue & multi   .30   .20
161 A92 3c brt blue & multi   .60   .35
       Nos. 157-161 (5)   1.55 1.05

Issued: 1967, #157, July 20; #158, Aug. 30. 1968; #159, Jan. 18; #160, Feb. 20; #161, June 5.

Red-tiled Roofs and ITY Emblem — A93

1967, Sept. 11   Photo.   Perf. 13½
162 A93 3c multicolored   .20   .20
International Tourist Year.

Mobile TB Clinic — A94

1967, Oct. 13   Photo.   Perf. 13½
163 A94 3c lilac & multi   .20   .20
Anti-Tuberculosis Society, 15th anniv.

Hojo Bridge, Enkaku Temple, 1498 — A95

1967, Nov. 1
164 A95 3c blue grn & multi   .20   .20
Protection of national cultural treasures.

Monkey (Bingata) — A96

TV Tower and Map — A97

1967, Dec. 11   Photo.   Perf. 13½
165 A96 1½c silver & multi   .25   .20
New Year 1968.

1967, Dec. 22
166 A97 3c multicolored   .25   .20
Opening of Miyako and Yaeyama television stations.

Dr. Kijin Nakachi and Helper — A98

Pill Box (Inro) — A99

1968, Mar. 15   Photo.   Perf. 13½
167 A98 3c multicolored   .25   .20
120th anniv. of the first vaccination in the Ryukyu Islands, performed by Dr. Kijin Nakachi.

1968, Apr. 18
168 A99 3c gray & multi   .45   .45
Philatelic Week.

Young Man, Library, Book and Map of Ryukyu Islands — A100

1968, May 13
169 A100 3c multicolored   .30   .25
10th International Library Week.

Mailmen's Uniforms and Stamp of 1948 A101

1968, July 1   Photo.   Perf. 13x13½
170 A101 3c multicolored   .30   .25
1st Ryukyuan postage stamps, 20th anniv.

Main Gate, Enkaku Temple — A102

Photo. & Engr.
1968, July 15   Perf. 13½
171 A102 3c multicolored   .30   .25
Restoration of the main gate of the Enkaku Temple, built 1492-1495, and destroyed during WWII.

Old Man's Dance — A103

1968, Sept. 15   Photo.   Perf. 13½
172 A103 3c gold & multi   .30   .25
Issued for Old People's Day.

Mictyris Longicarpus A104

Crabs: No. 174, Uca dubia stimpson. No. 175, Baptozius vinosus. No. 176, Cardisoma carnifex. No. 177, Ocypode ceratophthalma pallas.

1968-69   Photo.   Perf. 13½
173 A104 3c blue, ocher & blk   .30   .25
174 A104 3c lt bl grn & multi   .35   .25
175 A104 3c lt green & multi   .35   .25

RYUKYU ISLANDS

176 A104 3c lt ultra & multi .45 .30
177 A104 3c lt ultra & multi .45 .30
 Nos. 173-177 (5) 1.90 1.35

Issued: #173, 10/10; #174, 2/5/69; #175, 3/5/69; #176, 5/15/69; #177, 6/2/69.

Saraswati Pavilion — A105

1968, Nov. 1   Photo.   Perf. 13½
178 A105 3c multicolored .30 .20

Restoration of the Saraswati Pavilion (in front of Enkaku Temple), destroyed during WWII.

Tennis Player A106

Cock and Iris (Bingata) A107

1968, Nov. 3   Photo.   Perf. 13½
179 A106 3c green & multi .40 .30

35th All-Japan East-West Men's Soft-ball Tennis Tournament, Naha City, Nov. 23-24.

1968, Dec. 10
180 A107 1½c orange & multi .25 .15

New Year, 1969.

Boxer — A108

Ink Slab Screen — A109

1969, Jan. 3
181 A108 3c gray & multi .40 .25

20th All-Japan Amateur Boxing Championships, University of the Ryukyus, Jan. 3-5.

1969, Apr. 17   Photo.   Perf. 13½
182 A109 3c salmon, indigo & red .40 .20

Philatelic Week.

Box Antennas and Map of Radio Link A110

Gate of Courtesy and Emblems A111

1969, July 1   Photo.   Perf. 13½
183 A110 3c multicolored .25 .20

Opening of the UHF (radio) circuit system between Okinawa and the outlying Miyako-Yaeyama Islands.

1969, Aug. 1   Photo.   Perf. 13½
184 A111 3c Prus bl, gold & ver .25 .20

22nd All-Japan Formative Education Study Conference, Naha, Aug. 1-3.

Tug of War Festival A112

Hari Boat Race A113

Izaiho Ceremony, Kudaka Island A114

Mortardrum Dance — A115

Sea God Dance A116

1969-70   Photo.   Perf. 13
185 A112 3c multicolored .30 .25
186 A113 3c multicolored .35 .25
187 A114 3c multicolored .35 .25
188 A115 3c multicolored ('70) .50 .35
189 A116 3c multicolored ('70) .50 .35
 Nos. 185-189 (5) 2.00 1.45

Folklore. Issue dates: #185, Aug. 1; #186, Sept. 5; #187, Oct. 3; #188, Jan. 20; #189, Feb. 27.

No. 99 Surcharged   改訂 ½¢

1969, Oct. 15   Photo.   Perf. 13½
190 A44 ½c on 3c multi .90 .90

Nakamura-ke Farm House, Built 1713-51 A117

1969, Nov. 1   Photo.   Perf. 13½
191 A117 3c multicolored .20 .15

Protection of national cultural treasures.

Statue of Kyuzo Toyama, Maps of Hawaiian and Ryukyu Islands — A118

1969, Dec. 5   Photo.   Perf. 13½
192 A118 3c lt ultra & multi .35 .35
 a. Without overprint 2,500.
 b. Wide-spaced bars 725.00

Ryukyu-Hawaii emigration led by Kyuzo Toyama, 70th anniversary.
The overprint - "1969" at lower left and bars across "1970" at upper right - was applied before No. 192 was issued.

Dog and Flowers (Bingata) A119

Sake Flask Made from Coconut A120

1969, Dec. 10
193 A119 1½c pink & multi .20 .15

New Year, 1970.

1970, Apr. 15   Photo.   Perf. 13½
194 A120 3c multicolored .25 .20

Philatelic Week.

Classic Opera Issue

"The Bell" (Shushin Kaneiri) — A121

Child and Kidnapper (Chunusudu) A122

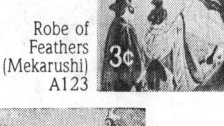

Robe of Feathers (Mekarushi) A123

Vengeance of Two Young Sons (Nidotichiuchi) A124

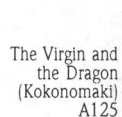

The Virgin and the Dragon (Kokonomaki) A125

1970   Photo.   Perf. 13½
195 A121 3c dull bl & multi .40 .40
196 A122 3c lt blue & multi .40 .40
197 A123 3c bluish grn & multi .40 .40
198 A124 3c dull bl grn & multi .40 .40
199 A125 3c multicolored .40 .40
 Nos. 195-199 (5) 2.00 2.00
 195a-199a, 5 sheets of 4 22.50 25.00

Issue dates: #195, Apr. 28. #196, May 29. #197, June 30. #198, July 30. #199, Aug. 25.

Underwater Observatory and Tropical Fish — A126

1970, May 22
200 A126 3c blue grn & multi .30 .25

Completion of the underwater observatory at Busena-Misaki, Nago.

Noboru Jahana (1865-1908), Politician A127

Map of Okinawa and People A128

Portraits: No. 202, Saion Gushichan Bunjaku (1682-1761), statesman. No. 203, Choho Giwan (1823-1876), regent and poet.

1970-71   Engr.   Perf. 13½
201 A127 3c rose claret .50 .30
202 A127 3c dull blue green .75 .55
203 A127 3c black .50 .30
 Nos. 201-203 (3) 1.75 1.15

Issued: #201, 9/25; #202, 12/22; #203, 1/2271.

1970, Oct. 1   Photo.
204 A128 3c red & multi .25 .15

Oct. 1, 1970 census.

Great Cycad of Une — A129

1970, Nov. 2   Photo.   Perf. 13½
205 A129 3c gold & multi .25 .20

Protection of national treasures.

Japanese Flag, Diet and Map of Ryukyus A130

Wild Boar and Cherry Blossoms (Bingata) A131

1970, Nov. 15   Photo.   Perf. 13½
206 A130 3c ultra & multi .80 .50

Citizens' participation in national administration according to Japanese law of Apr. 24, 1970.

1970, Dec. 10
207 A131 1½c multicolored .20 .20

New Year, 1971.

Low Hand Loom (Jibata) — A132

Farmer Wearing Palm Bark Raincoat and Kuba Leaf Hat — A133

Fisherman's Wooden Box and Scoop — A134

Designs: No. 209, Woman running a filature (reel). No. 211, Woman hulling rice with cylindrical "Shiri-ushi."

1971   Photo.   Perf. 13½
208 A132 3c lt blue & multi .30 .25
209 A132 3c pale grn & multi .30 .25
210 A133 3c lt blue & multi .35 .25
211 A132 3c yellow & multi .40 .30
212 A134 3c gray & multi .35 .25
 Nos. 208-212 (5) 1.70 1.30

Issue dates: #208, Feb. 16; #209, Mar. 16; #210, Apr. 30; #211, May 20; #212, June 15.

RYUKYU ISLANDS — UNITED NATIONS

Water Carrier (Taku) — A135

1971, Apr. 15   Photo.   Perf. 13½
213 A135 3c blue grn & multi   .35   .25
Philatelic Week.

Old and New Naha, and City Emblem A136

1971, May 20   Perf. 13
214 A136 3c ultra & multi   .25   .20
50th anniversary of Naha as a municipality.

Caesalpinia Pulcherrima — A137

Design: 2c, Madder (Sandanka).

1971   Photo.   Perf. 13
215 A137 2c gray & multi   .15   .15
216 A137 3c gray & multi   .20   .15
Issue dates: 2c, Sept. 30; 3c, May 10.

View from Mabuni Hill — A138

Mt. Arashi from Haneji Sea — A139

Yabuchi Island from Yakena Port — A140

1971-72
217 A138 3c green & multi   .20   .15
218 A139 3c blue & multi   .20   .15
219 A140 4c multi ('72)   .25   .15
    Nos. 217-219 (3)   .65   .45
Government parks. Issue dates: No. 217, July 30; No. 218, Aug. 30, 1971; No. 219, Jan. 20, 1972.

Dancer — A141

Deva King, Torinji Temple — A142

1971, Nov. 1   Photo.   Perf. 13
220 A141 4c Prus blue & multi   .20   .15

1971, Dec. 1
221 A142 4c dp blue & multi   .20   .20
Protection of national cultural treasures.

Rat and Chrysanthemums A143

Student Nurse A144

1971, Dec. 10
222 A143 2c brown org & multi   .20   .20
New Year 1972.

1971, Dec. 24
223 A144 4c lilac & multi   .20   .15
Nurses' training, 25th anniversary.

Birds on Seashore A145

Sun over Islands A147

Coral Reef — A146

1972   Photo.   Perf. 13
224 A145 5c brt blue & multi   .40   .25
225 A146 5c gray & multi   .40   .25
226 A147 5c ocher & multi   .40   .25
    Nos. 224-226 (3)   1.20   .75
Issued: #224, 4/14; #225, 3/30; #226, 3/21.

Dove, US and Japanese Flags — A148

1972, Apr. 17   Photo.   Perf. 13
227 A148 5c brt blue & multi   .60   .45
Ratification of the Reversion Agreement with US under which the Ryukyu Islands were returned to Japan.

Antique Sake Pot (Yushibin) — A149

1972, Apr. 20
228 A149 5c ultra & multi   .50   .35
Philatelic Week.
Ryukyu stamps were replaced by those of Japan after May 15, 1972.

AIR POST STAMPS

Dove and Map of Ryukyus — AP1

Perf. 13x13½
1950, Feb. 15   Unwmk.   Photo.
C1 AP1 8y bright blue   120.00 50.00
C2 AP1 12y green   35.00 20.00
C3 AP1 16y rose carmine   15.00 15.00
    Nos. C1-C3 (3)   170.00 85.00

Heavenly Maiden AP2

1951-54
C4 AP2 13y blue   2.50   1.50
C5 AP2 18y green   3.50   2.25
C6 AP2 30y cerise   6.00   1.75
C7 AP2 40y red violet   7.00   5.50
C8 AP2 50y yellow orange   9.00   6.50
    Nos. C4-C8 (5)   28.00 17.50
Issue dates: Oct. 1, 1951, Aug. 16, 1954.

Heavenly Maiden Playing Flute — AP3

1957, Aug. 1   Engr.   Perf. 13½
C9   AP3 15y blue green   8.00   3.50
C10 AP3 20y rose carmine   14.00   5.50
C11 AP3 35y yellow green   15.00   6.50
C12 AP3 45y reddish brown   16.00   8.00
C13 AP3 60y gray   18.00 10.00
    Nos. C9-C13 (5)   71.00 33.50

Same Surcharged in Brown Red or Light Ultramarine 改訂 9¢

1959, Dec. 20
C14 AP3 9c on 15y (BrR)   2.50   1.50
  a. Inverted surcharge   950.00
C15 AP3 14c on 20y (LU)   3.00   3.00
C16 AP3 19c on 35y (BrR)   8.00   5.00
C17 AP3 27c on 45y (LU)   17.50   6.00
C18 AP3 35c on 60y (BrR)   15.00   9.00
    Nos. C14-C18 (5)   46.00 24.50

改訂 9¢

Nos. 31-33, 36 and 38 Surcharged in Black, Brown, Red, Blue or Green

1960, Aug. 3   Photo.   Perf. 13
C19 A14 9c on 4y   3.00   1.00
  a. Surch. invtd. and transposed 15,000. 15,000.
  b. Invtd. surch. (legend only)   12,000.
  c. Surcharge transposed   1,500.
  d. Legend of surcharge only   4,000.
  e. Horiz. pair, one without surch. —
C20 A17 14c on 5y (Br)   3.50   1.75
C21 A14 19c on 15y (R)   2.50   1.50
C22 A17 27c on 14y (Bl)   9.00   2.75
C23 A14 35c on 20y (G)   6.00   3.75
    Nos. C19-C23 (5)   24.00 10.75

Nos. C19c and C19d are from a single sheet of 100 with surcharge shifted downward. Ten examples of No. C19c exist with "9c" also in bottom selvage. No. C19d is from the top row of the sheet. No. C19e is unique, pos. 100, caused by paper foldover.

Wind God — AP4

Designs: 9c, Heavenly Maiden (as on AP2). 14c, Heavenly Maiden (as on AP3). 27c, Wind God at right. 35c, Heavenly Maiden over treetops.

1961, Sept. 21   Photo.   Perf. 13½
C24 AP4 9c multicolored   .30   .20
C25 AP4 14c multicolored   .70   .60
C26 AP4 19c multicolored   .70   .70
C27 AP4 27c multicolored   3.00   .60
C28 AP4 35c multicolored   1.50   1.25
    Nos. C24-C28 (5)   6.20   3.35

Jet over Gate of Courtesy — AP5

Jet Plane — AP6

1963, Aug. 28   Perf. 13x13½
C29 AP5 5½c multicolored   .25   .25
C30 AP6 7c multicolored   .25   .25

SPECIAL DELIVERY STAMP

Dragon and Map of Ryukyus — SD1

Perf. 13x13½
1950, Feb. 15   Unwmk.   Photo.
E1 SD1 5y bright blue   30.00 16.00

UNITED NATIONS

yu-,nī-təd 'nā-shənz

LOCATION — Headquarters in New York City

United Nations stamps are used on UN official mail sent from UN Headquarters, NY, or from the UN Offices in Geneva, Switzerland, and Vienna, Austria to points throughout the world. They may be used on private correspondence sent through the UN post offices, and are valid only at the individual UN post offices.

UN mail is carried by the US, Swiss and Austrian postal systems.

The UN stamps issued for use in Geneva and Vienna are listed in separate sections at the end of the NY issues. They are denominated in centimes and francs, and are valid only in Geneva or Vienna. The UN stamps issued for use in New York, denominated in cents and dollars, are valid only in New York.

Letters bearing Nos. 170-174 provide an exception as they were carried by the Canadian postal system.

See Switzerland Nos. 7O1-7O39 in Volume 6 for stamps issued by the Swiss Government for official use of the UN European Office in Geneva.

The 1962 UN Temporary Executive Authority (UNTEA) overprints on stamps of Netherlands New Guinea are listed under West Irian in Volume 6.

Catalogue values for all unused stamps in this country are for Never Hinged items.

Stamps are inscribed in English, French or Spanish or are multi-lingual.

Watermark

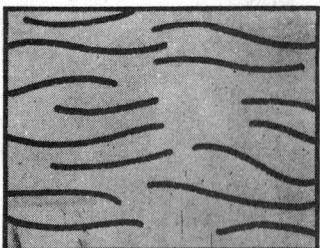

Wmk. 309- Wavy Lines

UNITED NATIONS

Peoples of the World — A1
UN Headquarters Building — A2 
"Peace, Justice, Security" — A3 
UN Flag — A4 
UN Children's Fund — A5 
World Unity — A6 

Perf. 13x12½, 12½x13, 12½x13½ (2c, 5c)

1951		Unwmk.	Engr. & Photo.	
1	A1	1c magenta	.15	.15
2	A2	1½c blue green	.15	.15
3	A3	2c purple	.15	.15
4	A4	3c magenta & blue	.15	.15
5	A5	5c blue	.15	.15
6	A1	10c chocolate	.25	.20
7	A4	15c violet & blue	.25	.20
8	A6	20c dark brown	.40	.20
9	A3	25c ol gray & blue	.40	.20
10	A2	50c indigo	2.50	1.50
11	A3	$1 red	1.60	.65
		Nos. 1-11 (11)	6.15	3.70

See Offices in Geneva Nos. 4, 14.

Veteran's War Memorial Building, San Francisco — A7

1952, Oct. 24   Engr.   Perf. 12
12   A7   5c blue   .15   .15
7th anniv. of the signing of the UN charter.

Globe and Encircled Flame — A8

1952, Dec. 10   Perf. 13½x14
13   A8   3c deep green   .15   .15
14   A8   5c blue   .25   .25
Fourth anniv. of the adoption of the Universal Declaration of Human Rights.

Refugee Family — A9

1953, Apr. 24   Perf. 12½x13
15   A9   3c dk red brn & rose brn   .15   .15
16   A9   5c indigo & blue   .30   .25
"Protection for Refugees."

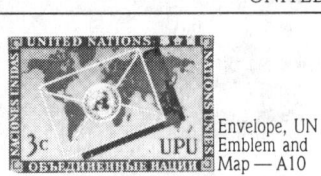

Envelope, UN Emblem and Map — A10

1953, June 12   Unwmk.   Perf. 13
17   A10   3c black brown   .15   .15
18   A10   5c dark blue   .65   .50
Issued to honor the UPU.

Gearwheels and UN Emblem — A11

1953, Oct. 24   Perf. 13x12½
19   A11   3c dark gray   .15   .15
20   A11   5c dark green   .40   .40
UN activities in the field of technical assistance.

Hands Reaching Toward Flame — A12
Ear of Wheat — A13 

1953, Dec. 10   Perf. 12½x13
21   A12   3c bright blue   .15   .15
22   A12   5c rose red   1.10   .50
Human Rights Day.

1954, Feb. 11
23   A13   3c dark green & yellow   .40   .20
24   A13   8c indigo & yellow   .85   .50
Issued to honor the FAO.

UN Emblem and Anvil — A14

1954, May 10   Perf. 12½x13
25   A14   3c brown   .15   .15
26   A14   8c magenta   1.40   .75
Honoring the ILO.

UN European Office, Geneva A15

1954, Oct. 25   Perf. 14
27   A15   3c dark blue violet   2.00   1.10
28   A15   8c red   .25   .25
UN Day.

Mother and Child — A16

1954, Dec. 10   Perf. 14
29   A16   3c red orange   7.00   2.00
30   A16   8c olive green   .25   .25
Human Rights Day.

Symbol of Flight — A17

1955, Feb. 9   Perf. 13½x14
31   A17   3c blue   1.75   .65
32   A17   8c rose carmine   .75   .75
International Civil Aviation Organization.

UNESCO Emblem A18

1955, May 11   Perf. 13½x14
33   A18   3c lilac rose   .15   .15
34   A18   8c light blue   .20   .20
Honoring the UN Educational, Scientific and Cultural Organization.

UN Charter A19

1955, Oct. 24   Perf. 13½x14
35   A19   3c deep plum   .90   .50
36   A19   4c dull green   .35   .20
37   A19   8c bluish black   .20   .20
    Nos. 35-37 (3)   1.45   .90
10th anniv. of the UN.

Souvenir Sheet
Wmk. 309   Imperf.
38   Sheet of 3   110.00   40.00
  a. A19 3c deep plum   10.00   1.50
  b. A19 4c dull green   10.00   1.50
  c. A19 8c bluish black   10.00   1.50

Two printings were made of No. 38. The first may be distinguished by the broken line of background shading on the 8c. It leaves a small white spot below the left leg of the "n" of "Unies." For the 2nd printing, the broken line was retouched, eliminating the white spot.

Hand Holding Torch — A20

1955, Dec. 9   Unwmk.   Perf. 14x13½
39   A20   3c ultra   .15   .15
40   A20   8c green   .20   .20
Human Rights Day, Dec. 10.

Symbols of Telecommunication — A21

1956, Feb. 17   Perf. 14
41   A21   3c turquoise blue   .15   .15
42   A21   8c deep carmine   .40   .30
Honoring the ITU.

Globe and Caduceus — A22

1956, Apr. 6   Perf. 14
43   A22   3c bright greenish blue   .15   .15
44   A22   8c golden brown   .30   .30
Honoring the World Health Organization.

General Assembly A23

1956, Oct. 24   Perf. 14
45   A23   3c dark blue   .15   .15
46   A23   8c gray olive   .15   .15
UN Day, Oct. 24.

Flame and Globe — A24

1956, Dec. 10   Perf. 14
47   A24   3c plum   .15   .15
48   A24   8c dark blue   .15   .15
Human Rights Day.

Weather Balloon — A25

1957, Jan. 28   Perf. 14
49   A25   3c violet blue   .15   .15
50   A25   8c dark carmine rose   .15   .15
Honoring the World Meteorological Organization.

Badge of UN Emergency Force — A26
UN Emblem and Globe — A27 

1957, Apr. 8   Perf. 14x12½
51   A26   3c light blue   .15   .15
52   A26   8c rose carmine   .15   .15
UN Emergency Force.

Re-engraved

1957, Apr.-May
53   A26   3c blue   .15   .15
54   A26   8c rose carmine   .35   .15

On Nos. 53-54 the background within and around the circles is shaded lightly, giving a halo effect. The letters are more distinct with a line around each letter.

1957, Oct. 24   Engr.   Perf. 12½x13
55   A27   3c orange brown   .15   .15
56   A27   8c dark blue green   .15   .15
Honoring the Security Council.

UNITED NATIONS

Flaming Torch — A28

1957, Dec. 10   *Perf. 14*
57   A28   3c red brown   .15   .15
58   A28   8c black   .15   .15

Human Rights Day.

Atom and UN Emblem A29

Central Hall, Westminster A30

1958, Feb. 10   *Perf. 12*
59   A29   3c olive   .15   .15
60   A29   8c blue   .15   .15

Honoring the International Atomic Energy Agency.

1958, Apr. 14   *Perf. 12*
61   A30   3c violet blue   .15   .15
62   A30   8c rose claret   .15   .15

Central Hall, Westminster, London, was the site of the first session of the UN General Assembly 1946.

UN Seal A31

Gearwheels A32

1958   *Perf. 13½x14*
63   A31   4c red orange   .15   .15
     Perf. 13x14
64   A31   8c bright blue   .15   .15

Issue dates: 4c, Oct. 24; 8c, June 2.

1958, Oct. 24   Engr.   *Perf. 12*
65   A32   4c dark blue green   .15   .15
66   A32   8c vermilion   .15   .15

Honoring the Economic and Social Council.

Hands Upholding Globe — A33

1958, Dec. 10   Unwmk.
67   A33   4c yellow green   .15   .15
68   A33   8c red brown   .15   .15

Human Rights Day and the 10th anniv. of the signing of the Universal Declaration of Human Rights.

New York City Building, Flushing Meadows A34

1959, Mar. 30   *Perf. 12*
69   A34   4c light lilac rose   .15   .15
70   A34   8c aqua   .15   .15

Site of many General Assembly meetings, 1946-50.

UN Emblems and Symbols of Agriculture, Industry and Trade — A35

Figure Adapted from Rodin's "Age of Bronze" — A36

1959, May 18   *Perf. 12*
71   A35   4c blue   .15   .15
72   A35   8c red orange   .20   .15

Honoring the UN Economic Commission for Europe.

1959, Oct. 23   Engr.   *Perf. 12*
73   A36   4c bright red   .15   .15
74   A36   8c dark olive green   .20   .15

Honor the Trusteeship Council.

World Refugee Year Emblem — A37

1959, Dec. 10   Unwmk.
75   A37   4c olive & red   .15   .15
76   A37   8c olive & brt greenish blue   .15   .15

World Refugee Year, July 1, 1959-June 30, 1960.

Chaillot Palace, Paris — A38

1960, Feb. 29   *Perf. 14*
77   A38   4c rose lilac & blue   .15   .15
78   A38   8c dull green & brown   .20   .15

Chaillot Palace in Paris was the site of General Assembly meetings in 1948 and 1951.

Map of Far East and Steel Beam — A39

1960, Apr. 11   Photo.   *Perf. 13x13½*
79   A39   4c dp cl, bl grn & dl yel   .15   .15
80   A39   8c ol green, blue & rose   .20   .15

Honoring the Economic Commission for Asia and the Far East (ECAFE).

Tree, FAO and UN Emblems — A40

1960, Aug. 29   *Perf. 13½*
81   A40   4c green, dk blue & org   .15   .15
   a.   Imperf., pair
82   A40   8c yel green, black & org   .15   .15

5th World Forestry Congress, Seattle, Wash., Aug. 29-Sept. 10.

UN Headquarters and Preamble to UN Charter — A41

1960, Oct. 24   Engr.   *Perf. 11*
83   A41   4c blue   .15   .15
84   A41   8c gray   .15   .15

Souvenir Sheet
Imperf
85   Sheet of 2   .50   .50
   a.   A41 4c blue   .25   .15
   b.   A41 8c gray   .25   .15

15th anniv. of the UN.

Block and Tackle — A42

Scales of Justice — A43

1960, Dec. 9   Photo.   *Perf. 13½x13*
86   A42   4c multicolored   .15   .15
87   A42   8c multicolored   .15   .15
   a.   Imperf., pair

Honoring the International Bank for Reconstruction and Development.
No. 86 exists imperf.

1961, Feb. 13   Unwmk.
88   A43   4c yel, org brn & blk   .15   .15
89   A43   8c yellow, green & black   .15   .15

Honoring the International Court of Justice. The design was taken from Raphael's "Stanze."
Nos. 88-89 exist imperf.

Seal of International Monetary Fund — A44

1961, Apr. 17   *Perf. 13x13½*
90   A44   4c bright bluish green   .15   .15
91   A44   7c fawn & yellow   .15   .15

Honoring the International Monetary Fund.
No. 90 exists imperf.

Abstract Group of Flags — A45

1961, June 5   *Perf. 11½*
92   A45   30c multicolored   .40   .15

See Offices in Geneva No. 10.

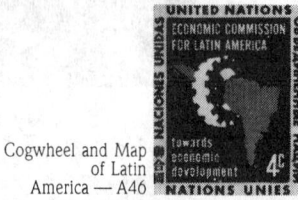

Cogwheel and Map of Latin America — A46

1961, Sept. 18   *Perf. 13½*
93   A46   4c blue, red & citron   .15   .15
94   A46   11c green, lilac & org ver   .30   .20

Honoring the Economic Commission for Latin America.

Africa House, Addis Ababa, and Map — A47

1961, Oct. 24   Photo.   *Perf. 11½*
95   A47   4c ultra, org, yel & brown   .15   .15
96   A47   11c emer, org, yel & brown   .25   .15

Honoring the Economic Commission for Africa.

Mother Bird Feeding Young and UNICEF Seal — A48

1961, Dec. 4   Unwmk.   *Perf. 11½*
97   A48   3c brown, gold, org & yel   .15   .15
98   A48   4c brown, gold, bl & emer   .15   .15
99   A48   13c deep green, gold, purple & pink   .20   .20
   Nos. 97-99 (3)   .50   .50

15th anniv. of the UN Children's Fund.

Family and Symbolic Buildings A49

1962, Feb. 28   Photo.   *Perf. 14½x14*
Central design multicolored
100   A49   4c bright blue   .15   .15
   a.   Black omitted
   b.   Yellow omitted   —
   c.   Brown omitted   —
101   A49   7c orange brown   .15   .15
   a.   Red omitted
   b.   Black omitted   —

UN program for housing and urban development.

"The World Against Malaria" — A50

1962, Mar. 30   *Perf. 14x14½*
Word frame in gray
102   A50   4c org, yel, green & black   .15   .15
103   A50   11c green, yel, brn & indigo   .25   .15

Honoring the WHO and to call attention to the international campaign to eradicate malaria from the world.

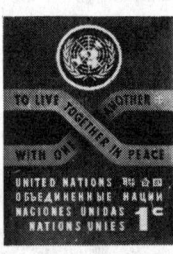

"Peace" — A51

UN Flag — A52

UNITED NATIONS

Hands Combining "UN" and Globe — A53

UN Emblem over Globe — A54

Photogravure; Engraved (5c)
1962, May 25   Perf. 14x14½
104 A51   1c ver, blue, black & gray   .15 .15
105 A52   3c lt green, Prus blue, yel & gray   .15 .15
    Perf. 12
    Size: 36½x23½mm
106 A53   5c dark carmine rose   .15 .15
    Perf. 12½
107 A54   11c dk & lt blue & gold   .25 .25
    Nos. 104-107 (4)   .70 .65
See #167 and UN Offices in Geneva #2, 6.

Flag at Half-mast and UN Headquarters A55

World Map Showing Congo A56

1962, Sept. 17   Unwmk.   Perf. 11½
108 A55   5c black, lt blue & blue   .15 .15
109 A55   15c black, gray ol & blue   .20 .20
1st anniv. of the death of Dag Hammarskjold, Secretary General of the UN 1953-61, in memory of those who died in the service of the UN.

1962, Oct. 24
110 A56   4c olive, org, black & yel   .15 .15
111 A56   11c bl grn, org, blk & yel   .20 .20
UN Operation in the Congo.

Globe in Universe and Palm Frond — A57

1962, Dec. 3   Engr.   Perf. 14x13½
112 A57   4c violet blue   .15 .15
113 A57   11c rose claret   .25 .15
Honoring the Committee on Peaceful Uses of Outer Space.

Development Decade Emblem — A58

    Perf. 11½
1963, Feb. 4   Unwmk.   Photo.
114 A58   5c pale grn, mar, dk blue & Prus blue   .15 .15
115 A58   11c yel, mar, dk blue & Prus blue   .20 .15
UN Development Decade and the UN Conference on the Application of Science and Technology for the Benefit of the Less Developed Areas, Geneva, Feb. 4-20.

Stalks of Wheat — A59

1963, Mar. 22   Perf. 11½
116 A59   5c ver, green & yellow   .15 .15
117 A59   11c ver, dp claret & yel   .25 .15
"Freedom from Hunger" campaign of the FAO.

Bridge over Map of New Guinea — A60

1963, Oct. 1   Unwmk.   Perf. 11½
118 A60   25c blue, green & gray   .45 .30
1st anniv. of the UN Temporary Executive Authority (UNTEA) in West New Guinea (West Irian).

General Assembly Building, New York — A61

1963, Nov. 4   Photo.   Perf. 13
119 A61   5c violet blue & multi   .15 .15
120 A61   11c green & multi   .20 .15
Since Oct. 1955 all sessions of the General Assembly have been held in the General Assembly Hall, UN Headquarters, N.Y.

Flame — A62

1963, Dec. 10   Perf. 13
121 A62   5c green, gold, red & yel   .15 .15
122 A62   11c car, gold, blue & yel   .20 .15
15th anniv. of the signing of the Universal Declaration of Human Rights.

Ships at Sea and IMCO Emblem — A63

1964, Jan. 13   Perf. 11½
123 A63   5c blue, ol, ocher & yel   .15 .15
124 A63   11c bl, dk grn, emer & yel   .20 .15
Honoring the Intergovernmental Maritime Consultative Organization.

Map of the World — A64

UN Emblem — A65

Three Men United Before Globe — A66

Stylized Globe and Weather Vane — A67

1964-71   Unwmk.   Photo.   Perf. 14
125 A64   2c lt bl, dk blue, org & yel green   .15 .15
    a. Perf. 13x13½ ('71)   .20 .15
    Perf. 11½
126 A65   7c dk bl, org brn & blk   .20 .15
127 A66   10c blue grn, ol grn & blk   .15 .15
128 A67   50c multicolored   .75 .45
    Nos. 125-128 (4)   1.30 .90
Dates of issue: 2c, 7c, 10c, May 29; 50c, Mar. 6, 1964. See UN Offices in Geneva Nos. 3, 12.

Arrows Showing Global Flow of Trade — A68

1964, June 15   Perf. 13
129 A68   5c black, red & yellow   .15 .15
130 A68   11c black, olive & yellow   .20 .15
UN Conference on Trade and Development, Geneva, Mar. 23-June 15.

Poppy Capsule and Hands — A69

1964, Sept. 21   Engr.   Perf. 12
131 A69   5c rose red & black   .15 .15
132 A69   11c emerald & black   .20 .15
International efforts and achievements in the control of narcotics.

Padlocked Atomic Blast — A70

"Education for Progress" — A71

Photogravure and Engraved
1964, Oct. 23   Perf. 11x11½
133 A70   5c dark red & dk brown   .15 .15
Signing of the nuclear test ban treaty pledging an end to nuclear explosions in the atmosphere, outer space and under water.

1964, Dec. 7   Photo.   Perf. 12½
134 A71   4c multicolored   .15 .15
135 A71   5c multicolored   .15 .15
136 A71   11c multicolored   .20 .15
    Nos. 134-136 (3)   .50 .45
UNESCO world campaign for universal literacy and for free compulsory primary education.

Progress Chart of Special Fund, Key and Globe A72

Leaves and View of Cyprus A73

    Perf. 13½x13
1965, Jan. 25   Unwmk.
137 A72   5c multicolored   .15 .15
138 A72   11c multicolored   .20 .15
    a. Black omitted (UN emblem on key)
Special Fund Program, which aims to speed economic growth and social advancement in low-income countries.

1965, Mar. 4   Photo.   Perf. 11½
139 A73   5c org, olive & black   .15 .15
140 A73   11c yel grn, blue grn & blk   .20 .15
UN Peace-keeping Force on Cyprus.

"From Semaphore to Satellite" — A74

1965, May 17   Unwmk.   Perf. 11½
141 A74   5c multicolored   .15 .15
142 A74   11c multicolored   .15 .15
Cent. of the ITU.

ICY Emblem — A75

1965, June 26   Engr.   Perf. 14x13½
143 A75   5c dark blue   .15 .15
144 A75   15c lilac rose   .20 .15
    Souvenir Sheet
145 A75   Sheet of 2, #143-144   .35 .30
20th anniv. of the UN and Intl. Cooperation Year.

"Peace" — A76

Opening Words, UN Charter — A77

UN Headquarters and Emblem — A78

UN Emblem — A79

UN Emblem — A80

1965-66   Photo.   Perf. 13½
146 A76   1c ver, bl, blk & gray   .15 .15
    Perf. 14
147 A77   15c ol bls, dull yel, blk & dp claret   .25 .15
    Perf. 12
148 A78   20c dk bl, bl, red & yel   .30 .20
    a. Yellow omitted
    Lithographed and Embossed
    Perf. 14
149 A79   25c lt bl & dk blue   .35 .20
    Photo.
    Perf. 11½
150 A80 $1 aqua & sapphire   1.75 1.50
    Nos. 146-150 (5)   2.80 2.20
Issue dates: 1c, 25c, Sept. 20, 1965. 15c, 20c, Oct. 25, 1965. $1, Mar. 25, 1966.
See UN Offices in Geneva Nos. 5, 9 and 11.

UNITED NATIONS

Fields and People
A81

Globe and Flags of UN Members
A82

1965, Nov. 29   Photo.   Perf. 12
151	A81	4c multicolored	.15	.15
152	A81	5c multicolored	.15	.15
153	A81	11c multicolored	.20	.15
		Nos. 151-153 (3)	.50	.45

Emphasize the importance of the world's population growth and its problems and to call attention to population trends and developments.

1966, Jan. 31   Photo.   Perf. 11½
| 154 | A82 | 5c multicolored | .15 | .15 |
| 155 | A82 | 15c multicolored | .20 | .15 |

World Federation of UN Associations.

WHO Headquarters, Geneva — A83

1966, May 26   Photo.   Perf. 12½x12
Granite Paper
| 156 | A83 | 5c multicolored | .15 | .15 |
| 157 | A83 | 11c multicolored | .20 | .15 |

WHO Headquarters, Geneva.

Coffee — A84

1966, Sept. 19   Perf. 13½x13
| 158 | A84 | 5c multicolored | .15 | .15 |
| 159 | A84 | 11c multicolored | .20 | .15 |

International Coffee Agreement of 1962.

UN Observer — A85

Children of Various Races — A86

1966, Oct. 24   Photo.   Perf. 11½
Granite Paper
| 160 | A85 | 15c multicolored | .25 | .15 |

Peace Keeping UN Observers.

1966, Nov. 28   Litho.   Perf. 13x13½
Designs: 5c, Children riding locomotive and tender. 11c, Children in open railroad car playing medical team.
161	A86	4c pink & multi	.15	.15
162	A86	5c pale green & multi	.15	.15
a.		Yellow omitted		
163	A86	11c ultra & multi	.20	.15
a.		Imperf., pair		—
b.		Dark blue omitted		
		Nos. 161-163 (3)	.50	.45

20th anniv. of UNICEF.

Hand Rolling up Sleeve and Chart Showing Progress — A87

1967, Jan. 23   Photo.   Perf. 12½
| 164 | A87 | 5c multicolored | .15 | .15 |
| 165 | A87 | 11c multicolored | .20 | .15 |

UN Development Program.

Type of 1962 and

UN Headquarters, New York and World Map — A88

1967   Photo.   Perf. 11½
| 166 | A88 | 1½c ultra, blk, org & ocher | .15 | .15 |

Size: 33x23mm
| 167 | A53 | 5c red brn, brn & org yel | .15 | .15 |

Issue dates: 1½c, Mar. 17; 5c, Jan. 23.
See UN Offices in Geneva No. 1.

Fireworks — A89

1967, Mar. 17   Perf. 14x14½
| 168 | A89 | 5c dark blue & multi | .15 | .15 |
| 169 | A89 | 11c brown lake & multi | .20 | .15 |

Honoring all nations which gained independence since 1945.

"Peace"
A90

UN Pavilion, EXPO '67
A91

Litho. & Engr.; Litho. (8c)
1967, Apr. 28   Perf. 11
170	A90	4c shown	.15	.15
171	A90	5c Justice	.15	.15
172	A91	8c shown	.15	.15
173	A90	10c Fraternity	.15	.15
174	A90	15c Truth	.20	.20
		Nos. 170-174 (5)	.80	.80

Montreal World's Fair, EXPO '67, Apr. 28-Oct. 27. Under special agreement with the Canadian Government Nos. 170-174 were valid for postage only on mail posted at the UN pavilion during the fair. The denominations are expressed in Canadian currency.

Luggage Tags and UN Emblem
A92

Unwmk.
1967, June 19   Litho.   Perf. 14
| 175 | A92 | 5c multicolored | .15 | .15 |
| 176 | A92 | 15c multicolored | .25 | .15 |

International Tourist Year, 1967.

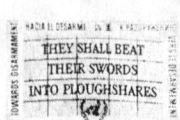

Quotation from Isaiah 2:4 — A93

1967, Oct. 24   Photo.
| 177 | A93 | 5c multicolored | .15 | .15 |
| 178 | A93 | 13c multicolored | .20 | .15 |

UN General Assembly's resolutions on general and complete disarmament and for suspension of nuclear and thermonuclear tests.

Art at UN Issue
Miniature Sheet

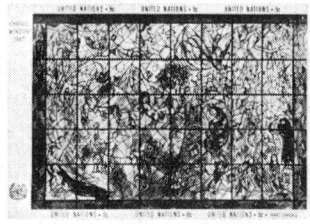

Memorial Window, by Marc Chagall — A94

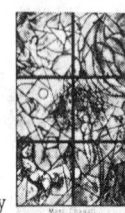

"The Kiss of Peace" by Marc Chagall — A95

Sizes: a, 41x46nn. b, 24x46mm. c, 41x33½mm. d, 36x33½mm. e, 29x33½mm. f, 41½x47mm.

1967, Nov. 17   Litho.   Rouletted 9
| 179 | A94 | Sheet of 6, a.-f. | .40 | .30 |

Perf. 12½x13½
| 180 | A95 | 6c multicolored | .15 | .15 |

No. 179 contains six 6c stamps, each rouletted on 3 sides, imperf. on fourth side. On Nos. 179a-179c, "United Nations. 6c" appears at top; on Nos. 179d-179f, at bottom. No. 179f includes name "Marc Chagall."

Globe and Major UN Organs — A96

1968, Jan. 16   Photo.   Perf. 11½
| 181 | A96 | 6c multicolored | .15 | .15 |
| 182 | A96 | 13c multicolored | .20 | .15 |

Honoring the UN Secretariat.

Statue by Henrik Starcke
A97

Factories and Chart
A98

Art at UN Issue
1968, Mar. 1   Photo.   Perf. 11½
| 183 | A97 | 6c blue & multi | .15 | .15 |
| 184 | A97 | 75c rose lake & multi | 1.10 | .85 |

The 6c is part of the "Art at UN" series. The 75c belongs to the definitive series. The 6c exists imperforate.
The Starcke statue represents mankind's search for freedom and happiness.
See UN Offices in Geneva No. 13.

1968, Apr. 18   Litho.   Perf. 12
| 185 | A98 | 6c multicolored | .15 | .15 |
| 186 | A98 | 13c multicolored | .20 | .15 |

UN Industrial Development Organization.

UN Headquarters — A99

1968, May 31   Litho.   Perf. 13½
| 187 | A99 | 6c multicolored | .15 | .15 |

Radarscope and Globes
A100

1968, Sept. 19   Photo.   Perf. 13x13½
| 188 | A100 | 6c green & multi | .15 | .15 |
| 189 | A100 | 20c lilac & multi | .30 | .20 |

World Weather Watch, a new weather system directed by the World Meterological Organization.

Human Rights Flame — A101

Books and UN Emblem — A102

Photogravure; Foil Embossed
1968, Nov. 22   Perf. 12½
| 190 | A101 | 6c brt bl, dp ultra & gold | .15 | .15 |
| 191 | A101 | 13c rose red, dk red & gold | .20 | .15 |

International Human Rights Year.

1969, Feb. 10   Litho.   Perf. 13½
| 192 | A102 | 6c yel green & multi | .15 | .15 |
| 193 | A102 | 13c bluish lilac & multi | .25 | .15 |

UN Institute for Training and Research (UNITAR).

UN Building, Santiago, Chile — A103

1969, Mar. 14   Litho.   Perf. 14
| 194 | A103 | 6c lt blue, vio bl & lt grn | .15 | .15 |
| 195 | A103 | 15c pink, cr & red brown | .25 | .20 |

The UN Building in Santiago, Chile is the seat of the UN Economic Commission for Latin America and of the Latin American Institute for Economic and Social Planning.

"UN" and UN Emblem
A104

UN Emblem and Scales of Justice
A105

1969, Mar. 14   Photo.   Perf. 13½
| 196 | A104 | 13c brt blue, black & gold | .20 | .15 |

See UN Offices in Geneva No. 7.

1969, Apr. 21   Photo.   Perf. 11½
Granite Paper
| 197 | A105 | 6c brt green, ultra & gold | .15 | .15 |
| 198 | A105 | 13c crim, lilac & gold | .20 | .15 |

20th anniv. session of the UN Intl. Law Commission.

UNITED NATIONS

Allegory of Labor, Emblems of UN and ILO — A106

1969, June 5   Photo.   Perf. 13
199 A106 6c blue, dp bl, yel & gold   .15 .15
200 A106 20c org ver, mag, yel & gold   .25 .20

"Labor and Development" and the 50th anniv. of the ILO.

Art at UN Issue

Ostrich, Tunisian Mosaic, 3rd Century — A107

Design: 13c, Pheasant.

1969, Nov. 21   Photo.   Perf. 14
201 A107 6c blue & multi   .15 .15
202 A107 13c red & multi   .20 .15

Art at UN Issue

Peace Bell, Gift of Japanese — A108

1970, Mar. 13   Photo.   Perf. 13½x13
203 A108 6c vio blue & multi   .15 .15
204 A108 25c claret & multi   .40 .25

Mekong River, Power Lines and Map of Delta — A109

1970, Mar. 13   Perf. 14
205 A109 6c dk blue & multi   .15 .15
206 A109 13c dp plum & multi   .20 .15

Lower Mekong Basin, Viet Nam, Development project under UN auspices.

"Fight Cancer" — A110

1970, May 22   Litho.   Perf. 14
207 A110 6c blue & black   .15 .15
208 A110 13c olive & black   .20 .15

Fight against cancer in connection with the 10th Intl. Cancer Congress of the International Union Against Cancer, Houston, Texas, May 22-29.

UN Emblem and Olive Branch — A111

UN Emblem — A112

1970, June 26   Photo.   Perf. 11½
209 A111 6c red, gold, dk & lt blue   .15 .15
210 A111 13c dk bl, gold, grn & red   .20 .15

Perf. 12½
211 A112 25c dk blue, gold & lt blue   .35 .25
Nos. 209-211 (3)   .70 .55

Souvenir Sheet
Imperf
212 Sheet of 3   .60 .60
  a. A111 6c multicolored   .15 .15
  b. A111 13c multicolored   .20 .15
  c. A112 25c multicolored   .30 .20

25th anniv. of the UN.

Scales, Olive Branch, Progress Symbol A113

Sea Bed, Fish, Underwater Research A114

1970, Nov. 20   Photo.   Perf. 13½
213 A113 6c gold & multi   .15 .15
214 A113 13c silver & multi .20 .15

Issued to publicize "Peace, Justice and Progress" in connection with the 25th anniv. of the UN.

Photogravure and Engraved
1971, Jan. 25   Perf. 13
215 A114 6c blue & multi   .15 .15

Peaceful uses of the sea bed. See Offices in Geneva No. 15.

Refugees, Sculpture by Kaare K. Nygaard — A115

Wheat and Globe — A116

1971, Mar. 12   Litho.   Perf. 13x12½
216 A115 6c brown, ocher & black   .15 .15
217 A115 13c ultra, grnsh blue & blk .20 .15

International support for refugees. See Offices in Geneva No. 16.

1971, Apr. 13   Photo.   Perf. 14
218 A116 13c brn red, gold & green   .20 .15

Publicizing the UN World Food Program. See Offices in Geneva No. 17.

UPU Headquarters, Bern — A117

1971, May 28   Photo.   Perf. 11½
219 A117 20c brown org & multi   .35 .20

Opening of new UPU Headquarters, Bern. See Offices in Geneva No. 18.

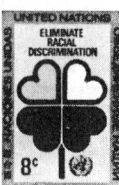

"Eliminate Racial Discrimination" — A118

A119

1971, Sept. 21   Photo.   Perf. 13½
220 A118 8c yel green & multi   .15 .15
221 A119 13c blue & multi   .20 .15

International Year Against Racial Discrimination. See Offices in Geneva Nos. 19-20.

UN Headquarters, New York — A120

UN Emblem and Symbolic Flags A121

1971, Oct. 22   Perf. 13½; 13 (60c)
222 A120 8c vio blue & multi   .15 .15
223 A121 60c ultra & multi   .75 .60

Maia by Pablo Picasso — A122

1971, Nov. 19   Photo.   Perf. 11½
224 A122 8c olive & multi   .15 .15
225 A122 21c ultra & multi   .30 .20

UN Intl. School. See Offices in Geneva No. 21.

Letter Changing Hands A123

1972, Jan. 5   Litho.   Perf. 14
226 A123 95c blue & multi   1.40 .95

"No More Nuclear Weapons" A124

1972, Feb. 14   Photo.   Perf. 13½x14
227 A124 8c dull rose, blk, bl & gray   .15 .15

To promote non-proliferation of nuclear weapons. See Offices in Geneva No. 23.

Proportions of Man (c. 1509), by Leonardo da Vinci A125

"Human Environment" A126

Lithographed and Engraved
1972, Apr. 7   Perf. 13x13½
228 A125 15c black & multi   .25 .20

World Health Day, Apr. 7. See Offices in Geneva No. 24.

Lithographed and Embossed
1972, June 5   Perf. 12½x14
229 A126 8c multicolored   .15 .15
230 A126 15c multicolored   .25 .20

UN Conference on Human Environment, Stockholm, June 5-16, 1972.

See Offices in Geneva Nos. 25-26.

"Europe" and UN Emblem A127

The Five Continents, by José Maria Sert A128

1972, Sept. 11   Litho.   Perf. 13x13½
231 A127 21c yel brown & multi   .35 .20

Economic Commission for Europe, 25th anniv. See Offices in Geneva No. 27.

Art at UN Issue
1972, Nov. 17   Photo.   Perf. 12x12½
232 A128 8c gold, brn & gldn brn   .15 .15
233 A128 15c gold, brn & blue grn   .30 .20

See Offices in Geneva Nos. 28-29.

Olive Branch and Broken Sword — A129

1973, Mar. 9   Litho.   Perf. 13½x13
234 A129 8c blue & multi   .15 .15
235 A129 15c lilac rose & multi   .35 .20

Disarmament Decade, 1970-79. Nos. 234-235 exist imperf. See Offices in Geneva Nos. 30-31.

Poppy Capsule and Skull — A130

Honeycomb — A131

1973, Apr. 13   Photo.   Perf. 13½
236 A130 8c multicolored   .15 .15
237 A130 15c multicolored   .35 .25

Fight against drug abuse. See Offices in Geneva No. 32.

1973, May 25   Photo.   Perf. 14
238 A131 8c olive bister & multi   .15 .15
239 A131 21c gray blue & multi   .40 .20

5th anniv. of the UN Volunteer Program. See UN Offices in Geneva No. 33.

Map of Africa with Namibia — A132

1973, Oct. 1   Photo.   Perf. 13½
240 A132 8c emerald & multi   .15 .15
241 A132 15c brt rose & multi   .35 .20

To publicize Namibia (South-West Africa), for which the UN General Assembly ended the mandate of South Africa and established the UN Council for Namibia to administer the territory until independence. See Offices in Geneva No. 34.

UN Emblem, Human Rights Flame — A133

UNITED NATIONS

1973, Nov. 16   Photo.   *Perf. 13½*
242 A133   8c dp carmine & multi   .15 .15
243 A133   21c blue green & multi   .35 .20

25th anniv. of the adoption and proclamation of the Universal Declaration of Human Rights. See Offices in Geneva Nos. 35-36.

ILO Headquarters, Geneva — A134

1974, Jan. 11   Photo.   *Perf. 14*
244 A134   10c ultra & multi   .20 .15
245 A134   21c blue green & multi   .35 .20

New Headquarters of Intl. Labor Organization. See Offices in Geneva Nos. 37-38.

Post Horn Encircling Globe — A135

1974, Mar. 22   Photo.   *Perf. 14*
246 A135   10c multicolored   .25 .15

Centenary of UPU. See Offices in Geneva Nos. 39-40.

Art at UN Issue

Peace Mural, by Candido Portinari — A136

1974, May 6   Photo.   *Perf. 14*
247 A136   10c gold & multi   .20 .15
248 A136   18c ultra & multi   .40 .30

See Offices in Geneva Nos. 41-42.

Dove and UN Emblem A137    UN Headquarters A138

Globe, UN Emblem, Flags — A139

1974, June 10   Photo.   *Perf. 14*
249 A137   2c dk bl & lt blue   .15 .15
250 A138   10c multicolored   .20 .15
251 A139   18c multicolored   .30 .20
     Nos. 249-251 (3)   .65 .50

Children of the World — A140    Law of the Sea — A141

1974, Oct. 18   Photo.   *Perf. 14*
252 A140   10c lt blue & multi   .20 .15
253 A140   18c lilac & multi   .40 .20

World Population Year. See Offices in Geneva Nos. 43-44.

1974, Nov. 22   Photo.   *Perf. 14*
254 A141   10c green & multi   .20 .15
255 A141   26c multicolored   .40 .25

UN General Assembly declared the sea bed common heritage of mankind, exempt from arms race. See Offices in Geneva No. 45.

Satellite and Globe — A142

1975, Mar. 14   Litho.   *Perf. 13*
256 A142   10c multicolored   .20 .15
257 A142   26c multicolored   .40 .25

Peaceful uses of outer space (meteorology, industry, fishing, communications). See Offices in Geneva Nos. 46-47.

Equality Between Men and Women — A143

1975, May 9   Litho.   *Perf. 15*
258 A143   10c multicolored   .20 .15
259 A143   18c multicolored   .40 .20

International Women's Year 1975. See Offices in Geneva Nos. 48-49.

UN Flag and "XXX" — A144

1975, June 26   Litho.   *Perf. 13*
260 A144   10c multicolored   .15 .15
261 A144   26c purple & multi   .50 .25

Souvenir Sheet
Imperf
262   Sheet of 2   .65 .20
   a.   A144 10c olive bister & multi   .20 .15
   b.   A144 26c purple & multi   .40 .15

30th anniv. of the UN. See Offices in Geneva Nos. 50-52.

Hand Reaching up over Map of Africa and Namibia — A145    Wild Rose Growing from Barbed Wire — A146

1975, Sept. 22   Photo.   *Perf. 13½*
263 A145   10c multicolored   .20 .15
264 A145   18c multicolored   .35 .20

"Namibia—United Nations direct responsibility." See note after No. 241. See Offices in Geneva Nos. 53-54.

1975, Nov. 21   Engr.   *Perf. 12½*
265 A146   13c ultramarine   .25 .15
266 A146   26c rose carmine   .50 .45

UN Peace-keeping Operations. See Offices in Geneva Nos. 55-56.

Symbolic Flags Forming Dove A147    UN Emblem A149

People of All Races A148

UN Flag — A150    Dove and Rainbow — A151

Perf. 13x13½, 13½x13, 14 (9c)
1976   Litho.; Photo. (9c)
267 A147   3c multicolored   .15 .15
268 A148   4c multicolored   .15 .15
269 A149   9c multicolored   .15 .15
270 A150   30c blue, emer & black   .40 .35
271 A151   50c multicolored   .70 .65
     Nos. 267-271 (5)   1.55 1.45

Issue dates: 9c, Nov. 19; others, Jan. 9. See Offices in Vienna No. 8.

Interlocking Bands — A152

1976, Mar. 12   Photo.   *Perf. 14*
272 A152   13c blue, green & black   .20 .15
273 A152   26c green & multi   .35 .30

World Federation of UN Association. See Offices in Geneva No. 57.

Cargo, Globe and Graph — A153    Houses Around Globe — A154

1976, Apr. 23   Photo.   *Perf. 11½*
274 A153   13c multicolored   .20 .15
275 A153   31c multicolored   .40 .30

UN Conference on Trade and Development (UNCTAD), Nairobi, Kenya, May 1976. See Offices in Geneva No. 58.

1976, May 28   Photo.   *Perf. 14*
276 A154   13c multicolored   .20 .15
277 A154   25c green & multi   .40 .30

Habitat, UN Conference on Human Settlements, Vancouver, Canada, May 31-June 11. See Offices in Geneva Nos. 59-60.

Magnifying Glass, Sheet of Stamps, UN Emblem — A155    Grain — A156

1976, Oct. 8   Photo.   *Perf. 11½*
278 A155   13c blue & multi   .20 .15
279 A155   31c green & multi   1.50 1.40

UN Postal Administration, 25th anniv. Sheets of 20. See Offices in Geneva #61-62.

1976, Nov. 19   Litho.   *Perf. 14½*
280 A156   13c multicolored   .25 .15

World Food Council. See Offices in Geneva No. 63.

WIPO Headquarters, Geneva A157

1977, Mar. 11   Photo.   *Perf. 14*
281 A157   13c citron & multi   .15 .15
282 A157   31c brt green & multi   .45 .30

World Intellectual Property Organization. See Geneva No. 64.

Drops of Water Falling into Funnel — A158

1977, Apr. 22   Photo.   *Perf. 13½x13*
283 A158   13c yellow & multi   .20 .15
284 A158   25c salmon & multi   .45 .25

UN Water Conf., Mar del Plata, Argentina, Mar. 14-25. See Offices in Geneva #65-66.

Burning Fuse Severed — A159

1977, May 27   Photo.   *Perf. 14*
285 A159   13c purple & multi   .15 .15
286 A159   31c dk blue & multi   .45 .30

UN Security Council. See Geneva #67-68.

"Combat Racism" A160

1977, Sept. 19   Litho.   *Perf. 13½x13*
287 A160   13c black & yellow   .15 .15
288 A160   25c black & vermilion   .40 .25

Fight against racial discrimination. See Geneva Nos. 69-70.

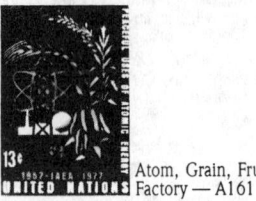

Atom, Grain, Fruit and Factory — A161

UNITED NATIONS

1977, Nov. 18 — Photo.
289 A161 13c yellow bister & multi .20 .15
290 A161 18c dull green & multi .35 .20

Peaceful uses of atomic energy. See Geneva Nos. 71-72.

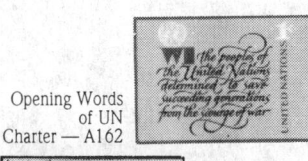

Opening Words of UN Charter — A162

"Live Together in Peace" — A163

People of the World — A164

1978, Jan. 27 — Litho. Perf. 14½
291 A162 1c gold, brown & red .15 .15
292 A163 25c multicolored .35 .30
293 A164 $1 multicolored 1.20 1.25
Nos. 291-293 (3) 1.70 1.70

See Offices in Geneva No. 73.

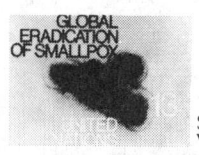

Smallpox Virus — A165

1978, Mar. 31 — Photo. Perf. 12x11½
294 A165 13c rose & black .15 .15
295 A165 31c blue & black .45 .40

Global eradication of smallpox. See Offices in Geneva Nos. 74-75.

Open Handcuff A166

Multicolored Bands and Clouds A167

1978, May 5 — Photo. Perf. 12
296 A166 13c multicolored .20 .15
297 A166 18c multicolored .30 .20

Liberation, justice and cooperation for Namibia. See Offices in Geneva No. 76.

1978, June 12 — Photo. Perf. 14
298 A167 13c multicolored .20 .15
299 A167 25c multicolored .40 .40

International Civil Aviation Organization for "Safety in the Air." See Offices in Geneva Nos. 77-78.

General Assembly A168

1978, Sept. 15 — Photo. Perf. 13½
300 A168 13c multicolored .20 .15
301 A168 18c multicolored .35 .25

See Offices in Geneva Nos. 79-80.

Hemispheres as Cogwheels A169

1978, Nov. 17 — Photo. Perf. 14
302 A169 13c multicolored .25 .15
303 A169 31c multicolored .60 .45

Technical Cooperation Among Developing Countries Conf., Buenos Aires, Argentina, Sept. 1978. See Offices in Geneva No. 81.

Hand Holding Olive Branch — A170

Tree of Various Races — A171

Globe, Dove with Olive Branch — A172

Birds and Globe — A173

1979, Jan. 19 — Photo. Perf. 14
304 A170 5c multicolored .15 .15
305 A171 14c multicolored .20 .15
306 A172 15c multicolored .30 .25
307 A173 20c multicolored .30 .25
Nos. 304-307 (4) .95 .80

UNDRO Against Fire and Water — A174

1979, Mar. 9 — Photo. Perf. 14
308 A174 15c multicolored .25 .20
309 A174 31c multicolored .35 .30

Office of the UN Disaster Relief Coordinator. See Offices in Geneva Nos. 82-83.

Child and ICY Emblem — A175

1979, May 4 — Photo. Perf. 14
310 A175 15c multicolored .20 .20
311 A175 31c multicolored .45 .40

International Year of the Child. See Offices in Geneva Nos. 84-85.

Map of Namibia, Olive Branch — A176

Scales and Sword of Justice — A177

1979, Oct. 5 — Litho. Perf. 13½
312 A176 15c multicolored .20 .20
313 A176 31c multicolored .40 .40

For a free and independent Namibia. See Offices in Geneva No. 86.

1979, Nov. 9 — Litho. Perf. 13x13½
314 A177 15c multicolored .20 .20
315 A177 20c multicolored .40 .35

Intl. Court of Justice, The Hague, Netherlands. See Offices in Geneva Nos. 87-88.

Graph of Economic Trends — A178

Key — A179

1980, Jan. 11 — Perf. 15x14½
316 A178 15c multicolored .20 .20
317 A179 31c multicolored .50 .35

New International Economic Order. See Offices in Geneva No. 89; Vienna No. 7.

Women's Year Emblems A180

1980, Mar. 7 — Litho. Perf. 14½x15
318 A180 15c multicolored .20 .20
319 A180 20c multicolored .30 .25

UN Decade for Women. See Offices in Geneva Nos. 90-91; Vienna Nos. 9-10.

UN Emblem and "UN" on Helmet A181

Arrows and UN Emblem A182

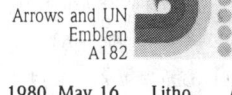

1980, May 16 — Litho. Perf. 14x13
320 A181 15c black & brt blue .25 .20
321 A182 31c multicolored .45 .40

UN Peace-keeping Operations. See Offices in Geneva No. 92; Vienna No. 11.

"35" and Flags — A183

Globe and Laurel — A184

1980, June 26 — Litho. Perf. 13
322 A183 15c multicolored .20 .20
323 A184 31c multicolored .40 .30

Souvenir Sheet
Imperf
324 Sheet of 2 .60 .45
 a. A183 15c multicolored .20
 b. A184 31c multicolored .40

35th anniv. of the UN. See Offices in Geneva Nos. 93-95; Vienna Nos. 12-14.

Flag of Turkey A185

1980, Sept. 26 — Litho. Perf. 12
Granite Paper
325 A185 15c shown .15 .15
326 A185 15c Luxembourg .15 .15
327 A185 15c Fiji .15 .15
328 A185 15c Viet Nam .15 .15
 a. Se-tenant block of 4 .75
329 A185 15c Guinea .15 .15
330 A185 15c Surinam .15 .15
331 A185 15c Bangladesh .15 .15
332 A185 15c Mali .15 .15
 a. Se-tenant block of 4 .75
333 A185 15c Yugoslavia .15 .15
334 A185 15c France .15 .15
335 A185 15c Venezuela .15 .15
336 A185 15c El Salvador .15 .15
 a. Se-tenant block of 4 .75
337 A185 15c Madagascar .15 .15
338 A185 15c Cameroon .15 .15
339 A185 15c Rwanda .15 .15
340 A185 15c Hungary .15 .15
 a. Se-tenant block of 4 .75
Nos. 325-340 (16) 2.40 2.40

Issued in 4 sheets of 16. Each sheet contains 4 blocks of 4 (Nos. 325-328, 329-332, 333-336, 337-340). A se-tenant block of 4 designs centers each sheet.
See #350-365, 374-389, 399-414, 425-440, 450-465, 477-492, 499-514, 528-543, 554-569, 690-697; 719-726.

Symbolic Flowers A186

Symbols of Progress A187

1980, Nov. 21 — Litho. Perf. 13½x13
341 A186 15c multicolored .30 .25
342 A187 20c multicolored .40 .35

Economic and Social Council (ECOSOC). See Offices in Geneva Nos. 96-97; Vienna Nos. 15-16.

Inalienable Rights of the Palestinian People A188

1981, Jan. 30 — Photo.
343 A188 15c multicolored .30 .25

See Offices in Geneva #98; Vienna #17.

Interlocking Puzzle Pieces — A189

Stylized Person — A190

1981, Mar. 6 — Photo.
344 A189 20c multicolored .35 .20
345 A190 35c multicolored .60 .40

Intl. Year of the Disabled. See Offices in Geneva Nos. 99-100; Vienna Nos. 18-19.

UNITED NATIONS

Divislava and Sebastocrator Kaloyan, Bulgarian Mural, 1259, Boyana Church, Sofia — A191

1981, Apr. 15 Photo. Perf. 11½
Granite Paper

| 346 | A191 | 20c multicolored | .30 | .30 |
| 347 | A191 | 31c multicolored | .45 | .40 |

See Offices in Geneva #101; Vienna #20.

Solar Energy — A192

Conference Emblem — A193

1981, May 29 Litho. Perf. 13

| 348 | A192 | 20c multicolored | .35 | .30 |
| 349 | A193 | 40c multicolored | .60 | .50 |

Conference on New and Renewable Sources of Energy, Nairobi, Aug. 10-21. See Offices in Geneva No. 102; Vienna No. 21.

Flag Type of 1980
1981, Sept. 25 Litho.
Granite Paper

350	A185	20c Djibouti	.25	.20
351	A185	20c Sri Lanka	.25	.20
352	A185	20c Bolivia	.25	.20
353	A185	20c Equatorial Guinea	.25	.20
a.		Se-tenant block of 4	1.25	
354	A185	20c Malta	.25	.20
355	A185	20c Czechoslovakia	.25	.20
356	A185	20c Thailand	.25	.20
357	A185	20c Trinidad & Tobago	.25	.20
a.		Se-tenant block of 4	1.25	
358	A185	20c Ukrainian SSR	.25	.20
359	A185	20c Kuwait	.25	.20
360	A185	20c Sudan	.25	.20
361	A185	20c Egypt	.25	.20
a.		Se-tenant block of 4	1.25	
362	A185	20c US	.25	.20
363	A185	20c Singapore	.25	.20
364	A185	20c Panama	.25	.20
365	A185	20c Costa Rica	.25	.20
a.		Se-tenant block of 4	1.25	
		Nos. 350-365 (16)	4.00	3.20

See note after No. 340.

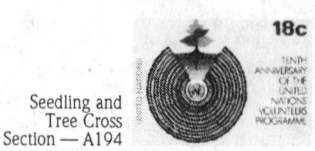

Seedling and Tree Cross Section — A194

"10" and Symbols of Progress — A195

1981, Nov. 13 Litho.

| 366 | A194 | 18c multicolored | .30 | .25 |
| 367 | A195 | 28c multicolored | .55 | .45 |

UN Volunteers Program, 10th anniv. See Offices in Geneva #103-104; Vienna #22-23.

United Nations Headquarters in New York stamps can be mounted in the Scott U.N. Singles and Postal Stationery album.

Respect for Human Rights — A196

Independence of Colonial Countries and People — A197

Second Disarmament Decade — A198

1982, Jan. 22 Perf. 11½x12

368	A196	17c multicolored	.30	.15
369	A197	28c multicolored	.50	.25
370	A198	40c multicolored	.80	.40
		Nos. 368-370 (3)	1.60	.80

10th Anniv. of UN Environment Program
A199   A200

1982, Mar. 19 Litho. Perf. 13½x13

| 371 | A199 | 20c multicolored | .30 | .25 |
| 372 | A200 | 40c multicolored | .75 | .65 |

See Offices in Geneva #107-108; Vienna #25-26.

UN Emblem and Olive Branch in Outer Space — A201

1982, June 11 Litho. Perf. 13 x 13½

| 373 | A201 | 20c multicolored | .55 | .45 |

Exploration and Peaceful Uses of Outer Space. See Offices in Geneva Nos. 109-110; Vienna No. 27.

Flag Type of 1980
1982, Sept. 24 Litho. Perf. 12
Granite Paper

374	A185	20c Austria	.25	.20
375	A185	20c Malaysia	.25	.20
376	A185	20c Seychelles	.25	.20
377	A185	20c Ireland	.25	.20
a.		Se-tenant block of 4	1.40	
378	A185	20c Mozambique	.25	.20
379	A185	20c Albania	.25	.20
380	A185	20c Dominica	.25	.20
381	A185	20c Solomon Islands	.25	.20
a.		Se-tenant block of 4	1.40	
382	A185	20c Philippines	.25	.20
383	A185	20c Swaziland	.25	.20
384	A185	20c Nicaragua	.25	.20
385	A185	20c Burma	.25	.20
a.		Se-tenant block of 4	1.40	
386	A185	20c Cape Verde	.25	.20
387	A185	20c Guyana	.25	.20
388	A185	20c Belgium	.25	.20
389	A185	20c Nigeria	.25	.20
a.		Se-tenant block of 4	1.40	
		Nos. 374-389 (16)	4.00	3.20

See note after No. 340.

Conservation and Protection of Nature — A202

1982, Nov. 19 Photo. Perf. 14

| 390 | A202 | 20c Leaf | .40 | .35 |
| 391 | A202 | 28c Butterfly | .55 | .50 |

See Offices in Geneva Nos. 111-112; Vienna Nos. 28-29.

World Communications Year — A203

World Communications Year — A204

1983, Jan. 28 Litho. Perf. 13

| 392 | A203 | 20c multicolored | .25 | .25 |
| 393 | A204 | 40c multicolored | .70 | .65 |

See Offices in Geneva #113; Vienna #30.

Safety at Sea
A205   A206

1983, Mar. 18 Litho. Perf. 14½

| 394 | A205 | 20c multicolored | .30 | .25 |
| 395 | A206 | 37c multicolored | .65 | .65 |

See Offices in Geneva #114-115; Vienna #31-32.

World Food Program A207

1983, Apr. 22 Engr. Perf. 13½

| 396 | A207 | 20c rose lake | .40 | .35 |

See Offices in Geneva #116; Vienna #33-34.

Trade and Development
A208   A209

1983, June 6 Litho. Perf. 14

| 397 | A208 | 20c multicolored | .35 | .25 |
| 398 | A209 | 28c multicolored | .70 | .65 |

See Offices in Geneva Nos. 117-118; Vienna Nos. 35-36.

Flag Type of 1980
1983, Sept. 23 Photo. Perf. 12
Granite Paper

399	A185	20c Great Britain	.25	.20
400	A185	20c Barbados	.25	.20
401	A185	20c Nepal	.25	.20
402	A185	20c Israel	.25	.20
a.		Se-tenant block of 4	1.50	
403	A185	20c Malawi	.25	.20
404	A185	20c Byelorussian SSR	.25	.20
405	A185	20c Jamaica	.25	.20
406	A185	20c Kenya	.25	.20
a.		Se-tenant block of 4	1.50	
407	A185	20c People's Republic of China	.25	.20
408	A185	20c Peru	.25	.20
409	A185	20c Bulgaria	.25	.20
410	A185	20c Canada	.25	.20
a.		Se-tenant block of 4	1.50	
411	A185	20c Somalia	.25	.20
412	A185	20c Senegal	.25	.20
413	A185	20c Brazil	.25	.20
414	A185	20c Sweden	.25	.20
a.		Se-tenant block of 4	1.50	
		Nos. 399-414 (16)	4.00	3.20

See note after No. 340.

35th Anniv. of the Universal Declaration of Human Rights
A210   A211
Photogravure and Engraved
1983, Dec. 9 Perf. 13½

| 415 | A210 | 20c Window Right | .30 | .25 |
| 416 | A211 | 40c Peace Treaty with Nature | .70 | .65 |

See Offices in Geneva #119-120, Vienna #37-38.

Intl. Population Conference A212

1984, Feb. 3 Litho. Perf. 14

| 417 | A212 | 20c multicolored | .30 | .25 |
| 418 | A212 | 40c multicolored | .65 | .60 |

See Offices in Geneva #121; Vienna #39.

Tractor Plowing A213

Rice Paddy A214

1984, Mar. 15 Litho. Perf. 14½

| 419 | A213 | 20c multicolored | .30 | .25 |
| 420 | A214 | 40c multicolored | .65 | .60 |

World Food Day, Oct. 16. See Offices in Geneva Nos. 122-123; Vienna Nos. 40-41.

Grand Canyon A215

Ancient City of Polonnaruwa, Sri Lanka — A216

1984, Apr. 18 Litho. Perf. 14

| 421 | A215 | 20c multicolored | .25 | .20 |
| 422 | A216 | 50c multicolored | .75 | .70 |

World Heritage (protection of world cultural and natural sites). See #601-602; Offices in Geneva #124-125, 211-212; Vienna #42-43, 125-126.

A217    A218

UNITED NATIONS

1984, May 29   Photo.   Perf. 11½
423 A217 20c multicolored   .45   .35
424 A218 50c multicolored   1.00   .85
Future for Refugees. See Offices in Geneva Nos. 126-127; Vienna Nos. 44-45.

Flag Type of 1980
1984, Sept. 21   Photo.   Perf. 12
Granite Paper
425 A185 20c Burundi   .55   .20
426 A185 20c Pakistan   .55   .20
427 A185 20c Benin   .55   .20
428 A185 20c Italy   .55   .20
  a.   Se-tenant block of 4   3.00
429 A185 20c Tanzania   .55   .20
430 A185 20c United Arab Emirates .55   .20
431 A185 20c Ecuador   .55   .20
432 A185 20c Bahamas   .55   .20
  a.   Se-tenant block of 4   3.00
433 A185 20c Poland   .55   .20
434 A185 20c Papua New Guinea   .55   .20
435 A185 20c Uruguay   .55   .20
436 A185 20c Chile   .55   .20
  a.   Se-tenant block of 4   3.00
437 A185 20c Paraguay   .55   .20
438 A185 20c Bhutan   .55   .20
439 A185 20c Central African Republic .55 .20
440 A185 20c Australia   .55   .20
  a.   Se-tenant block of 4   3.00
    Nos. 425-440 (16)   8.80   3.20
See note after No. 340.

Intl. Youth Year — A219

ILO Turin Center — A220

1984, Nov. 15   Litho.   Perf. 13½
441 A219 20c multicolored   .45   .30
442 A219 35c multicolored   1.00   .65
See Offices in Geneva #128; Vienna #46-47.

1985, Feb. 1   Engr.
443 A220 23c Turin Center emblem .65   .45
See Offices in Geneva #129-130; Vienna #48.

UN University A221

1985, Mar. 15   Photo.   Perf. 13½
444 A221 50c multicolored   1.25   .85
See Offices in Geneva #131-132; Vienna #49.

Peoples of the World — A222

Painting UN Emblem — A223

1985, May 10   Litho.   Perf. 14
445 A222 22c multicolored   .35   .30
446 A223 $3 multicolored   4.00   3.50
See Offices in Geneva #133-134; Vienna #50-51.

The Corner A224

Alvaro Raking Hay A225

Oil paintings (details) by American artist Andrew Wyeth.

1985, June 26   Photo.   Perf. 12x11½
447 A224 22c multicolored   .50   .35
448 A225 45c multicolored   1.00   .85

Souvenir Sheet
Imperf
449   Sheet of 2   1.65   1.10
  a.   A224 22c multicolored   .50   —
  b.   A225 45c multicolored   1.00   —
40th anniv. of the UN. No. 449 has multicolored margin with inscription and UN emblem. Size: 75x83mm. See Offices in Geneva Nos. 135-137; Vienna Nos. 52-54.

Flag Type of 1980
1985, Sept. 20   Photo.   Perf. 12
Granite Paper
450 A185 22c Grenada   .60   .50
451 A185 22c Federal Republic of Germany .60 .50
452 A185 22c Saudi Arabia   .60   .50
453 A185 22c Mexico   .60   .50
  a.   Se-tenant block of 4   3.25
454 A185 22c Uganda   .60   .50
455 A185 22c St. Thomas & Prince .60   .50
456 A185 22c USSR   .60   .50
457 A185 22c India   .60   .50
  a.   Se-tenant block of 4   3.25
458 A185 22c Liberia   .60   .50
459 A185 22c Mauritius   .60   .50
460 A185 22c Chad   .60   .50
461 A185 22c Dominican Republic   .60   .50
  a.   Se-tenant block of 4   3.25
462 A185 22c Sultanate of Oman   .60   .50
463 A185 22c Ghana   .60   .50
464 A185 22c Sierra Leone   .60   .50
465 A185 22c Finland   .60   .50
  a.   Se-tenant block of 4   3.25
    Nos. 450-465 (16)   9.60   8.00
See note after No. 340.

A226   A227

Photoravure and Engraved
1985, Nov. 22   Perf. 13½
466 A226 22c Asian child   .35   .30
467 A226 33c Breastfeeding   .65   .60
UNICEF Child Survival Campaign. See Offices in Geneva #138-139; Vienna #55-56.

1986, Jan. 31   Photo.   Perf. 11½
468 A227 22c Abstract Painting by Wosene Kosrof .60 .45
Africa in Crisis, campaign against hunger. See Offices in Geneva #140; Vienna #57.

Water Resources A228

1986, Mar. 14   Photo.   Perf. 13½
469 A228 22c Dam   1.60   1.25
470 A228 22c Irrigation   1.60   1.25
471 A228 22c Hygiene   1.60   1.25
472 A228 22c Well   1.60   1.25
  a.   Block of 4, #469-472   6.75   5.50
UN Development program. No. 472a has continuous design. See Offices in Geneva #141-144; Vienna #58-61.

Human Rights Stamp of 1954 — A229

Stamp collecting: 44c, Engraver.

1986, May 22   Engr.   Perf. 12½
473 A229 22c dk violet & brt blue .30   .30
474 A229 44c brown & emer green   .85   .80
See Offices in Geneva #146-147; Vienna #62-63.

Birds Nest in Tree — A230

Peace in Seven Languages A231

Photo. & Embossed
1986, June 20   Perf. 13½
475 A230 22c multicolored   .60   .45
476 A231 33c multicolored   1.50   1.25
Intl. Peace Year. See Offices in Geneva Nos. 148-149; Vienna Nos. 64-65.

Flag Type of 1980
1986, Sept. 19   Photo.   Perf. 12
Granite Paper
477 A185 22c New Zealand   .60   .45
478 A185 22c Lao PDR   .60   .45
479 A185 22c Burkina Faso   .60   .45
480 A185 22c Gambia   .60   .45
  a.   Se-tenant block of 4   3.25
481 A185 22c Maldives   .60   .45
482 A185 22c Ethiopia   .60   .45
483 A185 22c Jordan   .60   .45
484 A185 22c Zambia   .60   .45
  a.   Se-tenant block of 4   3.25
485 A185 22c Iceland   .60   .45
486 A185 22c Antigua & Barbuda   .60   .45
487 A185 22c Angola   .60   .45
488 A185 22c Botswana   .60   .45
  a.   Se-tenant block of 4   3.25
489 A185 22c Romania   .60   .45
490 A185 22c Togo   .60   .45
491 A185 22c Mauritania   .60   .45
492 A185 22c Colombia   .60   .45
  a.   Se-tenant block of 4   3.25
    Nos. 477-492 (16)   9.60   7.20
See note after No. 340.

Souvenir Sheet

World Federation of UN Associations, 40th Anniv. — A232

Designs: 22c, Mother Earth, by Edna Hibel, US. 33c, Watercolor by Salvador Dali (b. 1904), Spain. 39c, New Dawn, by Dong Kingman, US. 44c, Watercolor by Chaim Gross, US.

1986, Nov. 14   Litho.   Perf. 13x13½
493   Sheet of 4   4.50   1.65
  a.   A232 22c multicolored   .50   —
  b.   A232 33c multicolored   .80   —
  c.   A232 39c multicolored   .95   —
  d.   A232 44c multicolored   1.10   —
See Offices in Geneva #150; Vienna #66.

Trygve Halvdan Lie (1896-1968), 1st Secretary-General A233

Photogravure and Engraved
1987, Jan. 30   Perf. 13½
494 A233 22c multicolored   .85   .20
See Offices in Geneva #151; Vienna #67.

Intl. Year of Shelter for the Homeless A234

Perf. 13½x12½
1987, Mar. 13   Litho.
495 A234 22c Surveying, blueprint .45   .20
496 A234 44c Cutting lumber   1.40   .45
See Offices in Geneva #154-155; Vienna #68-69.

Fight Drug Abuse A235

1987, June 12   Litho.   Perf. 14½x15
497 A235 22c Construction   .65   .20
498 A235 33c Education   1.25   .35
See Offices in Geneva #156-157; Vienna #70-71.

Flag Type of 1980
1987, Sept. 18   Photo.   Perf. 12
Granite Paper
499 A185 22c Comoros   .60   .50
500 A185 22c Yemen PDR   .60   .50
501 A185 22c Mongolia   .60   .50
502 A185 22c Vanuatu   .60   .50
  a.   Se-tenant block of 4   3.25
503 A185 22c Japan   .60   .50
504 A185 22c Gabon   .60   .50
505 A185 22c Zimbabwe   .60   .50
506 A185 22c Iraq   .60   .50
  a.   Se-tenant block of 4   3.25
507 A185 22c Argentina   .60   .50
508 A185 22c Congo   .60   .50
509 A185 22c Niger   .60   .50
510 A185 22c St. Lucia   .60   .50
  a.   Se-tenant block of 4   3.25
511 A185 22c Bahrain   .60   .50
512 A185 22c Haiti   .60   .50
513 A185 22c Afghanistan   .60   .50
514 A185 22c Greece   .60   .50
  a.   Se-tenant block of 4   3.25
    Nos. 499-514 (16)   9.60   8.00
See note after No. 340.

UN Day — A236

Multinational people in various occupations.

1987, Oct. 23   Litho.   Perf. 14½x15
515 A236 22c multicolored   .50   .35
516 A236 39c multicolored   .75   .65
See Offices in Geneva #158-159; Vienna #74-75.

Immunize Every Child — A237

1987, Nov. 20   Litho.   Perf. 15x14½
517 A237 22c Measles   .85   .50
518 A237 44c Tetanus   2.00   1.50
See Offices in Geneva #160-161; Vienna #76-77.

UNITED NATIONS

Intl. Fund for Agricultural Development (IFAD) — A238

1988, Jan. 29   Litho.   *Perf. 13½*
519 A238 22c Fishing .55 .40
520 A238 33c Farming 1.10 .85
See Offices in Geneva #162-163; Vienna #78-79.

A239

1988, Jan. 29   Photo.   *Perf. 13½x14*
521 A239 3c multicolored ('88) .15 .15

Survival of the Forests A240

1988, Mar. 18   Litho.   *Perf. 14x15*
522 A240 25c multicolored 1.75 1.50
523 A240 44c multicolored 3.00 2.75
  a. Pair, #522-523 5.00 4.50
No. 523a has continuous design. See Offices in Geneva Nos. 165-166; Vienna Nos. 80-81.

Intl. Volunteer Day — A241

1988, May 6   *Perf. 13x14, 14x13*
524 A241 25c Education, vert. .55 .40
525 A241 50c Vocational training 1.25 1.00
See Offices in Geneva #167-168; Vienna #82-83.

Health in Sports A242

Perf. 13½x13, 13x13½
1988, June 17   Litho.
526 A242 25c Cycling, vert. .55 .45
527 A242 38c Marathon 1.40 1.10
See Offices in Geneva #169-170; Vienna #84-85.

Flag Type of 1980

1988, Sept. 16   Photo.   *Perf. 12*
Granite Paper
528 A185 25c Spain .60 .45
529 A185 25c St. Vincent & Grenadines .60 .45
530 A185 25c Ivory Coast .60 .45
531 A185 25c Lebanon .60 .45
  a. Se-tenant block of 4 3.25
532 A185 25c Yemen (Arab Republic) .60 .45
533 A185 25c Cuba .60 .45
534 A185 25c Denmark .60 .45
535 A185 25c Libya .60 .45
  a. Se-tenant block of 4 3.25

536 A185 25c Qatar .60 .45
537 A185 25c Zaire .60 .45
538 A185 25c Norway .60 .45
539 A185 25c German Democratic Republic .60 .45
  a. Se-tenant block of 4 3.25
540 A185 25c Iran .60 .45
541 A185 25c Tunisia .60 .45
542 A185 25c Samoa .60 .45
543 A185 25c Belize .60 .45
  a. Se-tenant block of 4 3.25
    Nos. 528-543 (16) 9.60 7.20
See note after No. 340.

A243   A244

1988, Dec. 9   Photo. & Engr.
544 A243 25c multicolored .60 .40
Souvenir Sheet
545 A243 $1 multicolored 1.75 1.40
Universal Declaration of Human Rights, 40th anniv.
See Offices in Geneva #171-172; Vienna #86-87.

1989, Jan. 27   Litho.   *Perf. 13x14*
546 A244 25c Energy and nature .75 .45
547 A244 45c Agriculture 1.50 1.00
World Bank. See Offices in Geneva Nos. 173-174; Vienna Nos. 88-89.

UN Peace-Keeping Force, 1988 Nobel Peace Prize Winner — A245

1989, Mar. 17   Litho.   *Perf. 14x13½*
548 A245 25c multicolored .55 .40
See Offices in Geneva #175, Vienna #90.

Aerial Photograph of New York Headquarters — A246

1989, Mar. 17   *Perf. 14½x14*
549 A246 45c multicolored .75 .60

World Weather Watch, 25th Anniv. (in 1988) — A247

Satellite photographs: 25c, Storm system off the East Coast, US. 36c, Typhoon Abby in the North-West Pacific.

1989, Apr. 21   Litho.   *Perf. 13x14*
550 A247 25c multicolored .80 .50
551 A247 36c multicolored 1.75 1.25
See Offices in Geneva #176-177; Vienna #91-92.

A248   A249

Photo. & Engr., Photo.
1989, Aug. 23   *Perf. 14*
552 A248 25c multicolored 2.75 .50
553 A249 90c multicolored 2.25 1.75
Offices in Vienna, 10th anniv. See Offices in Geneva Nos. 178-179; Vienna Nos. 93-94.

Flag Type of 1980

1989, Sept. 22   Photo.   *Perf. 12*
Granite Paper
554 A185 25c Indonesia .65 .55
555 A185 25c Lesotho .65 .55
556 A185 25c Guatemala .65 .55
557 A185 25c Netherlands .65 .55
  a. Se-tenant block of 4 3.50
558 A185 25c South Africa .65 .55
559 A185 25c Portugal .65 .55
560 A185 25c Morocco .65 .55
561 A185 25c Syrian Arab Republic .65 .55
  a. Se-tenant block of 4 3.50
562 A185 25c Honduras .65 .55
563 A185 25c Kampuchea .65 .55
564 A185 25c Guinea-Bissau .65 .55
565 A185 25c Cyprus .65 .55
  a. Se-tenant block of 4 3.50
566 A185 25c Algeria .65 .55
567 A185 25c Brunei .65 .55
568 A185 25c St. Kitts and Nevis .65 .55
569 A185 25c United Nations .65 .55
  a. Se-tenant block of 4 3.50
    Nos. 554-569 (16) 10.40 8.80
See note after No. 340.

Declaration of Human Rights, 40th Anniv. (in 1988) — A250

Paintings: 25c, *The Table of Universal Brotherhood*, by Jose Clemente Orozco. 45c, *Study for Composition II*, by Vassily Kandinsky.

1989, Nov. 17   Litho.   *Perf. 13½*
570 A250 25c multicolored .50 .50
571 A250 45c multicolored 1.00 .85
Printed in sheets of 12+12 se-tenant labels containing Articles 1 (25c) or 2 (45c) inscribed in English, French or German.
See Nos. 582-583, 599-600, 616-617, 627-628; Offices in Geneva Nos. 180-181, 193-194, 209-210, 224-225, 234-235; Vienna Nos. 95-96, 108-109, 123-124, 139-140, 150-151.

Intl. Trade Center — A251

1990, Feb. 2   Litho.   *Perf. 14½x15*
572 A251 25c multicolored 1.60 1.10
See Offices in Geneva #182; Vienna #97.

Fight AIDS Worldwide A252

Perf. 13½x12½
1990, Mar. 16   Litho.
573 A252 25c shown .65 .55
574 A252 40c Shadow over crowd 1.50 1.25
See Offices in Geneva #184-185; Vienna #99-100.

Medicinal Plants — A253

1990, May 4   Photo.   *Perf. 11½*
Granite Paper
575 A253 25c *Catharanthus roseus* .50 .45
576 A253 90c *Panax quinquefolium* 1.90 1.50
See Off. in Geneva #186-187; Vienna #101-102.

United Nations, 45th Anniv. A254

1990, June 26   Litho.   *Perf. 14½x13*
577 A254 25c shown .90 .70
578 A254 45c "45," emblem 2.75 .85
Souvenir Sheet
579   Sheet of 2, #577-578 7.50 2.00
See Off. in Geneva #188-189; Vienna #103-104.

Crime Prevention — A255

1990, Sept. 13   Photo.   *Perf. 14*
580 A255 25c Crimes of youth .90 .60
581 A255 36c Organized crime 2.25 1.00
See Off. in Geneva #191-192; Vienna #106-107.

Human Rights Type of 1989

Artwork: 25c, Fragment from the sarcophagus of Plotinus, c. 270 A.D. 45c, Combined Chambers of the High Court of Appeal by Charles Paul Renouard.

1990, Nov. 16   Litho.   *Perf. 13½*
582 A250 25c black, gray & tan .50 .35
583 A250 45c black & brown 1.00 .75
See Off. in Geneva #193-194; Vienna #108-109.
Printed in sheets of 12+12 se-tenant labels containing Articles 7 (25c) or 8 (45c) inscribed in English, French or German.

Economic Commission for Europe A256

1991, Mar. 15   Litho.   *Perf. 14*
584 A256 30c Two storks 1.10 .90
585 A256 30c Woodpecker, ibex 1.10 .90
586 A256 30c Capercaille, plover 1.10 .90
587 A256 30c Falcon, marmot 1.10 .90
  a. Block of 4, #584-587 4.50 3.75

Namibian Independence A257

1991, May 10   Litho.   *Perf. 14*
588 A257 30c Dunes, Namib Desert .75 .60
589 A257 50c Savanna 1.75 1.40
See Off. in Geneva #199-200; Vienna #114-115.

UNITED NATIONS

A258

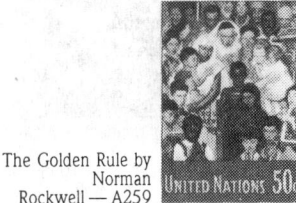

The Golden Rule by Norman Rockwell — A259

1991, Sept. 11   Litho.   Perf. 13½
590 A258 30c multicolored   .60   .55
Photo.   Perf. 12x11½
591 A259 50c multicolored   1.00 1.00

UN Headquarters, New York — A260

1991, May 10   Engr.   Perf. 13½
592 A260 $2 dark blue   3.00 2.50

Rights of the Child A261

1991, June 14   Litho.   Perf. 14½
593 A261 30c Children, globe   1.10   .50
594 A261 70c Houses, rainbow   2.50 1.50
See Off. in Geneva #203-204; Vienna #117-118.

Banning of Chemical Weapons A262

Design: 90c, Hand holding back chemical drums.

1991, Sept. 11   Litho.   Perf. 13½
595 A262 30c multicolored   1.00   .65
596 A262 90c multicolored   3.00 2.25
See Off. in Geneva #205-206; Vienna #119-120.

UN Postal Administration, 40th Anniv. — A263

1991, Oct. 24   Litho.   Perf. 14x15
597 A263 30c No. 1   1.10   .60
598 A263 40c No. 3   1.50 1.10
See Off. in Geneva #207-208; Vienna #121-122.

Human Rights Type of 1989
Artwork: 30c, The Last of England, by Ford Madox Brown. 50c, The Emigration to the East, by Tito Salas.

1991, Nov. 20   Litho.   Perf. 13½
599 A250 30c multicolored   .65   .30
600 A250 50c multicolored   1.10   .50
See Off. in Geneva #209-210; Vienna #123-124.

Printed in sheets of 12+12 se-tenant labels containing Articles 13 (30c) or 14 (50c) inscribed in English, French or German.

World Heritage Type of 1984
Designs: 30c, Uluru Natl. Park, Australia. 50c, The Great Wall of China.

1992, Jan. 24   Litho.   Perf. 13
Size: 35x28mm
601 A215 30c multicolored   .75   .60
602 A215 50c multicolored   1.50 1.00
See Off. in Geneva #211-212; Vienna #125-126.

Clean Oceans A264

1992, Mar. 13   Litho.   Perf. 14
603 A264 29c Ocean surface   .60   .55
604 A264 29c Ocean bottom   .60   .55
  a. Pair, #603-604   1.25 1.10
See Off. in Geneva #214-215; Vienna #127-128.
Printed in sheets of 12 containing 6 #604a.

Earth Summit A265

Designs: No. 605, Globe at LR. No. 606, Globe at LL. No. 607, Globe at UR. No. 608, Globe at UL.

1992, May 22   Photo.   Perf. 11½
605 A265 29c multicolored   .60   .50
606 A265 29c multicolored   .60   .50
607 A265 29c multicolored   .60   .50
608 A265 29c multicolored   .60   .50
  a. Block of 4, #605-608   2.50 2.00
See Off. in Geneva #216-219, Vienna #129-132.

Mission to Planet Earth — A266

Designs: No. 609, Satellites over city, sailboats, fishing boat. No. 610, Satellite over coast, passenger liner, dolphins, whale, volcano.

1992, Sept. 4   Photo.   Rouletted 8
Granite Paper
609 A266 29c multicolored   3.25   .60
610 A266 29c multicolored   3.25   .60
  a. Pair, #609-610   6.75 1.25
See Off. in Geneva #220-221; Vienna #133-134.

Science and Technology for Development A267

Design: 50c, Animal, man drinking.

1992, Oct. 2   Litho.   Perf. 14
611 A267 29c multicolored   .55   .45
612 A267 50c multicolored   .90   .70
See Off. in Geneva #222-223; Vienna #135-136.

UN University Building, Tokyo A268

UN Headquarters A269

Design: 40c, UN University Building, Tokyo, diff.

Perf. 14, 13½x13 (29c)
1992, Oct. 2   Litho.
613 A268 4c multicolored   .15   .15
614 A269 29c multicolored   .60   .55
615 A268 40c multicolored   .80   .75
  Nos. 613-615 (3)   1.55 1.45

Human Rights Type of 1989
Artwork: 29c, Lady Writing a Letter With her Maid, by Vermeer. 50c, The Meeting, by Ester Almqvist.

1992, Nov. 20   Litho.   Perf. 13½
616 A250 29c multicolored   .90   .55
617 A250 50c multicolored   1.25 1.00
See Off. in Geneva #224-225; Vienna #139-140.
Printed in sheets of 12+12 se-tenant labels containing Articles 19 (29c) and 20 (50c) inscribed in English, French or German.

Aging With Dignity — A270

Designs: 29c, Elderly couple, family. 52c, Old man, physician, woman holding fruit basket.

1993, Feb. 5   Litho.   Perf. 13
618 A270 29c multicolored   1.00   .90
619 A270 52c multicolored   1.75 1.00
See Off. in Geneva #226-227; Vienna #141-142.

Endangered Species A271

Designs: No. 620, Hairy-nosed wombat. No. 621, Whooping crane. No. 622, Giant clam. No. 623, Giant sable antelope.

1993, Mar. 3   Litho.   Perf. 13x12½
620 A271 29c multicolored   .60   .50
621 A271 29c multicolored   .60   .50
622 A271 29c multicolored   .60   .50
623 A271 29c multicolored   .60   .50
  a. Block of 4, #620-623   2.50 2.50
See Nos. 639-642, 657-660, 674-677, 700-703, 730-733; Offices in Geneva Nos. 228-231, 246-249, 264-267, 280-283, 298-301, 318-321; Vienna Nos. 143-146, 162-165, 180-183, 196-199; 214-217; 235-238.

Healthy Environment A272

Designs: 29c, Personal. 50c, Family.

1993, May 7   Litho.   Perf. 15x14½
624 A272 29c Man   .75   .45
625 A272 50c Family   1.25   .75
WHO, 45th anniv.
See Off. in Geneva #232-233; Vienna #147-148.

A273

1993, May 7   Litho.   Perf. 15x14
626 A273 5c multicolored   .15   .15

Human Rights Type of 1989
Artwork: 29c, Shocking Corn, by Thomas Hart Benton. 35c, The Library, by Jacob Lawrence.

1993, June 11   Litho.   Perf. 13½
627 A250 29c multicolored   1.00   .65
628 A250 35c multicolored   1.25   .80
See Off. in Geneva #234-235; Vienna #150-151.
Printed in sheets of 12 + 12 se-tenant labels containing Articles 25 (29c) and 26 (35c) inscribed in English, French or German.

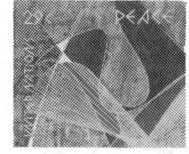

Intl. Peace Day — A274

Denomination at: No. 629, UL. No. 630, UR. No. 631, LL. No. 632, LR.

Rouletted 12½
1993, Sept. 21   Litho. & Engr.
629 A274 29c blue & multi   2.00   .75
630 A274 29c blue & multi   2.00   .75
631 A274 29c blue & multi   2.00   .75
632 A274 29c blue & multi   2.00   .75
  a. Block of 4, #629-632   9.00 7.00
See Off. in Geneva #236-239; Vienna #152-155.

Environment-Climate — A275

Designs: No. 633, Chameleon. No. 634, Palm trees, top of funnel cloud. No. 635, Bottom of funnel cloud, deer, antelope. No. 636, Bird of paradise.

1993, Oct. 29   Litho.   Perf. 14½
633 A275 29c multicolored   .70   .55
634 A275 29c multicolored   .70   .55
635 A275 29c multicolored   .70   .55
636 A275 29c multicolored   .70   .55
  a. Strip of 4, #633-636   3.00 2.25
See Off. in Geneva #240-243; Vienna #156-159.

Intl. Year of the Family — A276

Designs: 29c, Mother holding child, two children, woman. 45c, People tending crops.

1994, Feb. 4   Litho.   Perf. 13.1
637 A276 29c green & multi   1.25   .75
638 A276 45c blue & multi   2.00 1.10
See Off. in Geneva #244-245; Vienna #160-161.

Endangered Species Type of 1993
Designs: No. 639, Chimpanzee. No. 640, St. Lucia Amazon. No. 641, American crocodile. No. 642, Dama gazelle.

1994, Mar. 18   Litho.   Perf. 12.7
639 A271 29c multicolored   .60   .50
640 A271 29c multicolored   .60   .50
641 A271 29c multicolored   .60   .50
642 A271 29c multicolored   .60   .50
  a. Block of 4, #639-642   2.50 2.25
See Off. in Geneva #246-249; Vienna #162-165.

Ordering on-line is QUICK! EASY! CONVENIENT!
www.scottonline.com

UNITED NATIONS

Protection for Refugees — A277

1994, Apr. 29　Litho.　Perf. 14.3x14.8
643 A277 50c multicolored　　1.25　.70
See Offices in Geneva #250; Vienna #166.

Dove of Peace — A278

Sleeping Child, by Stanislaw Wyspianski A279

Mourning Owl, by Vanessa Isitt A280

1994, Apr. 29　Litho.　Perf. 12.9
644 A278 10c multicolored　　.20　.15
645 A279 19c multicolored　　.40　.35

Engr.
Perf. 13.1
646 A280 $1 red brown　　2.00　1.75

Intl. Decade for Natural Disaster Reduction A281

Earth viewed from space, outline map of: No. 647, North America. No. 648, Eurasia. No. 649, South America. No. 650, Australia and South Asia.

1994, May 27　Litho.　Perf. 13.9x14.2
647 A281 29c multicolored　　1.75　.60
648 A281 29c multicolored　　1.75　.60
649 A281 29c multicolored　　1.75　.60
650 A281 29c multicolored　　1.75　.60
　a.　Block of 4, #647-650　　8.00　3.00
See Off. in Geneva #251-254; Vienna #170-173.

Population and Development — A282

Designs: 29c, Children playing. 52c, Family with house, car, other possessions.

1994, Sept. 1　Litho.　Perf. 13.2x13.6
651 A282 29c multicolored　　.75　.60
652 A282 52c multicolored　　1.25　1.00
See Off. in Geneva #258-259; Vienna #174-175.

UNCTAD, 30th Anniv. — A283

1994, Oct. 28
653 A283 29c multicolored　　.60　.50
654 A283 50c multi, diff.　　1.00　.70
See Off. in Geneva #260-261; Vienna #176-177.

UN, 50th Anniv. — A284

Social Summit, Copenhagen — A285

1995, Jan. 1　Litho. & Engr.　Perf. 13.4
655 A284 32c multicolored　　1.25　.90
See Offices in Geneva #262; Vienna #178.

Perf. 13.6x13.9
1995, Feb. 3　Photo. & Engr.
656 A285 50c multicolored　　1.00　1.00
See Offices in Geneva #263; Vienna #179.

Endangered Species Type of 1993

Designs: No. 657, Giant armadillo. No. 658, American bald eagle. No. 659, Fijian/Tongan banded iguana. No. 660, Giant panda.

1995, Mar. 24　Litho.　Perf. 13x12 1/2
657 A271 32c multicolored　　.65　.55
658 A271 32c multicolored　　.65　.55
659 A271 32c multicolored　　.65　.55
660 A271 32c multicolored　　.65　.55
　a.　Block of 4, 657-660　　2.75　2.25
See Off. in Geneva #264-267; Vienna #180-183.

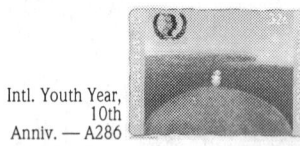

Intl. Youth Year, 10th Anniv. — A286

32c, Seated child. 55c, Children cycling.

1995, May 26　Litho.　Perf. 14.4x14.7
661 A286 32c multicolored　　.75　.45
662 A286 55c multicolored　　1.25　.85
See Off. in Geneva #268-269; Vienna #184-185.

UN, 50th Anniv. — A287

Designs: 32c, Hand with pen signing UN Charter, flags. 50c, Veterans' War Memorial, Opera House, San Francisco.

1995, June 26　Engr.　Perf. 13.3x13.6
663 A287 32c black　　.75　.45
664 A287 50c maroon　　1.10　.70

Souvenir Sheet
Litho. & Engr.
Imperf
665　Sheet of 2, #663-664　　2.50　2.00
　a.　A287 32c black　　1.00　.75
　b.　A287 50c maroon　　1.40　1.10
See Off. in Geneva #270-271; Vienna #186-187.

4th World Conference on Women, Beijing — A288

Designs: 32c, Mother and child. 40c, Seated woman, cranes flying above.

1995, Sept. 5　Photo.　Perf. 12
666 A288 32c multicolored　　.80　.40
Size: 28x50mm
667 A288 40c multicolored　　1.10　.50
See Off. in Geneva #273-274; Vienna #189-190.

UN Headquarters A289

1995, Sept. 5　Litho.　Perf. 15
668 A289 20c multicolored　　.40　.20

Miniature Sheet

United Nations, 50th Anniv. — A290

Designs: #669a-669 l, Various people in continuous design (2 blocks of six stamps with gutter between).

1995, Oct. 24　Litho.　Perf. 14
669　Sheet of 12　　9.00　5.00
　a.-l.　A290 32c any single　　.70　.40
670　Souvenir booklet　　10.00
　a.　A290 32c Booklet pane of 3, vert.
　　strip of 3 from UL of sheet　　2.50　2.50
　b.　A290 32c Booklet pane of 3, vert.
　　strip of 3 from UR of sheet　　2.50　2.50
　c.　A290 32c Booklet pane of 3, vert.
　　strip of 3 from LL of sheet　　2.50　2.50
　d.　A290 32c Booklet pane of 3, vert.
　　strip of 3 from LR of sheet　　2.50　2.50
See Off. in Geneva #275-276; Vienna #191-192.

WFUNA, 50th Anniv. — A291

1996, Feb. 2　Litho.　Perf. 13x13 1/2
671 A291 32c multicolored　　.65　.30
See Offices in Geneva #277; Vienna #193.

Mural, by Fernand Leger — A292

1996, Feb. 2　Litho.　Perf. 14 1/2x15
672 A292 32c multicolored　　.65　.30
673 A292 60c multi, diff.　　1.25　.60

Endangered Species Type of 1993

Designs: No. 674, Masdevallia veitchiana. No. 675, Saguaro cactus. No. 676, West Australian pitcher plant. No. 677, Encephalartos horridus.

1996, Mar. 14　Litho.　Perf. 12 1/2
674 A271 32c multicolored　　.65　.30
675 A271 32c multicolored　　.65　.30
676 A271 32c multicolored　　.65　.30
677 A271 32c multicolored　　.65　.30
　a.　Block of 4, #674-677　　2.75
See Off. in Geneva #280-283; Vienna #196-199.

City Summit (Habitat II) — A293

Designs: No. 678, Deer. No. 679, Man, child, dog sitting on hill, overlooking town. No. 680, People walking in park, city skyline. No. 681, Tropical park, Polynesian woman, boy. No. 682, Polynesian village, orchids, bird.

1996, June 3　Litho.　Perf. 14x13 1/2
678 A293 32c multicolored　　.70　.30
679 A293 32c multicolored　　.70　.30
680 A293 32c multicolored　　.70　.30
681 A293 32c multicolored　　.70　.30
682 A293 32c multicolored　　.70　.30
　a.　Strip of 5, #678-682　　3.50
See Off. in Geneva #284-288; Vienna #200-204.

Sport and the Environment — A294

1996 Summer Olympic Games, Atlanta, GA: 32c, Men's basketball, vert. 50c, Women's volleyball.

Perf. 14x14 1/2, 14 1/2x14
1996, July 19　　Litho.
683 A294 32c multicolored　　.65　.30
684 A294 50c multicolored　　1.00　.50
Souvenir Sheet
685 A294　Sheet of 2, #683-684　　1.90　1.65
See Off. in Geneva #289-291; Vienna #205-207.

Plea for Peace — A295

Designs: 32c, Doves. 60c, Stylized dove.

1996, Sept. 17　Litho.　Perf. 14 1/2x15
686 A295 32c multicolored　　.65　.30
687 A295 60c multicolored　　1.25　.60
See Off. in Geneva #292-293; Vienna #208-209.

UNICEF, 50th Anniv. — A296

Fairy Tales: 32c, Yeh-Shen, China. 60c, The Ugly Duckling, by Hans Christian Andersen.

1996, Nov. 20　Litho.　Perf. 14 1/2x15
688 A296 32c multicolored　　.65　.30
689 A296 60c multicolored　　1.25　.60
Panes of 8 + label.
See Off. in Geneva #294-295; Vienna #210-211.

Flag Type of 1980
1997, Feb. 12　Photo.　Perf. 12
Granite Paper
690 A185 32c Tadjikistan　　.65　.30
691 A185 32c Georgia　　.65　.30
692 A185 32c Armenia　　.65　.30
693 A185 32c Namibia　　.65　.30
　a.　Block of 4, #690-693　　2.60　1.20
694 A185 32c Liechtenstein　　.65　.30
695 A185 32c Republic of Korea　　.65　.30
696 A185 32c Kazakhstan　　.65　.30
697 A185 32c Latvia　　.65　.30
　a.　Block of 4, #694-697　　2.60　1.20
See note after No. 340.

Cherry Blossoms, UN Headquarters — A297

Peace Rose — A298

UNITED NATIONS

1997, Feb. 12   Litho.   *Perf. 14½*
698	A297	8c multicolored	.15	.15
699	A297	55c multicolored	1.10	.55

Endangered Species Type of 1993

Designs: No. 700, African elephant. No. 701, Major Mitchell's cockatoo. No. 702, Black-footed ferret. No. 703, Cougar.

1997, Mar. 13   Litho.   *Perf. 12½*
700	A271	32c multicolored	.65	.30
701	A271	32c multicolored	.65	.30
702	A271	32c multicolored	.65	.30
703	A271	32c multicolored	.65	.30
a.		Block of 4, #700-703	2.60	1.20

See Off. in Geneva #298-301; Vienna #214-217.

Earth Summit, 5th Anniv. — A299

Designs: No. 704, Sailboat. No. 705, Three sailboats. No. 706, Two people watching sailboat, sun. No. 707, Person, sailboat.
$1, Combined design similar to Nos. 704-707.

1997, May 30   Photo.   *Perf. 11.5*
Granite Paper
704	A299	32c multicolored	.65	.30
705	A299	32c multicolored	.65	.30
706	A299	32c multicolored	.65	.30
707	A299	32c multicolored	.65	.30
a.		Block of 4, #704-707	2.60	1.20

Souvenir Sheet
708	A299	$1 multicolored	2.00	2.00
a.		Ovptd. in sheet margin	2.00	2.00

See Off. in Geneva #302-306; Vienna #218-222.
No. 708 contains one 60x43mm stamp. Overprint in sheet margin of No. 708a reads "PACIFIC 97 / World Philatelic Exhibition / San Francisco, California / 29 May - 8 June 1997."

Transportation — A300

Ships: No. 709, Clipper ship. No. 710, Paddle steamer. No. 711, Ocean liner. No. 712, Hovercraft. No. 713, Hydrofoil.

1997, Aug. 29   Litho.   *Perf. 14x14½*
709	A300	32c multicolored	.65	.30
710	A300	32c multicolored	.65	.30
711	A300	32c multicolored	.65	.30
712	A300	32c multicolored	.65	.30
713	A300	32c multicolored	.65	.30
a.		Strip of 5, #709-713	3.25	1.50

See Off. in Geneva #307-311; Vienna #223-227.
No. 713a has continuous design.

Philately — A301

1997, Oct. 14   Litho.   *Perf. 13½x14*
714	A301	32c No. 473	.65	.30
715	A301	50c No. 474	1.00	.50

See Off. in Geneva #312-313; Vienna #228-229.

World Heritage Convention, 25th Anniv. — A302

Terracotta warriors of Xian: 32c, Single warrior. 60c, Massed warriors.
No. 718: a, like #716. b, like #717. c, like Geneva #314. d, like Geneva #315. e, like Vienna #230. f, like Vienna #231.

1997, Nov. 19   Litho.   *Perf. 13½*
716	A302	32c multicolored	.65	.30
717	A302	60c multicolored	1.25	.60
718		Souvenir booklet	3.75	
a.-f.		A302 8c any single	.15	.15
g.		Booklet pane of 4 #718a	.60	.60
h.		Booklet pane of 4 #718b	.60	.60
i.		Booklet pane of 4 #718c	.60	.60
j.		Booklet pane of 4 #718d	.60	.60
k.		Booklet pane of 4 #718e	.60	.60
l.		Booklet pane of 4 #718f	.60	.60

See Off. in Geneva #314-316; Vienna #230-232.

Flag Type of 1980

1998, Feb. 13   Photo.   *Perf. 12*
Granite Paper
719	A185	32c Micronesia	.65	.30
720	A185	32c Slovakia	.65	.30
721	A185	32c Democratic People's Republic of Korea	.65	.30
722	A185	32c Azerbaijan	.65	.30
a.		Block of 4, #719-722	2.60	
723	A185	32c Uzbekistan	.65	.30
724	A185	32c Monaco	.65	.30
725	A185	32c Czech Republic	.65	.30
726	A185	32c Estonia	.65	.30
a.		Block of 4, #723-726	2.60	

See note after No. 340.

A303

A304

A305

1998, Feb. 13   Litho.   *Perf. 14½x15*
727	A303	1c multicolored	.15	.15
728	A304	2c multicolored	.15	.15

Perf. 15x14½
729	A305	21c multicolored	.45	.20

Endangered Species Type of 1993

Designs: No. 730, Lesser galago. No. 731, Hawaiian goose. No. 732, Golden birdwing. No. 733, Sun bear.

1998, Mar. 13   Litho.   *Perf. 12½*
730	A271	32c multicolored	.65	.30
731	A271	32c multicolored	.65	.30
732	A271	32c multicolored	.65	.30
733	A271	32c multicolored	.65	.30
a.		Block of 4, #730-733	2.75	1.40

See Off. in Geneva #318-321; Vienna #235-238.

Intl. Year of the Ocean — A306

1998, May 20   Litho.   *Perf. 13x13½*
734	A306	Sheet of 12	7.50	4.00
a.-l.		32c any single	.60	.30

See Offices in Geneva #322; Vienna #239.

Rain Forests — A307

1998, June 19   Litho.   *Perf. 13x13½*
735	A307	32c Jaguar	.65	.30

Souvenir Sheet
736	A307	$2 like #735	4.00	2.00

See Off. in Geneva #323-324; Vienna #240-241.

U.N. Peacekeeping Forces, 50th Anniv. — A308

Designs: 33c, Commander with binoculars. 40c, Two soldiers on vehicle.

1998, Sept. 15   Photo.   *Perf. 12*
737	A308	33c multicolored	.65	.30
738	A308	40c multicolored	.80	.40

See Off. in Geneva #325-326; Vienna #242-243.

Universal Declaration of Human Rights, 50th Anniv. — A309

Stylized people: 32c, Carrying flag. 55c, Carrying pens.

1998, Oct. 27   Litho. & Photo.   *Perf. 13*
739	A309	32c multicolored	.65	.30
740	A309	55c multicolored	1.10	.55

See Off. in Geneva #327-328; Vienna #244-245.

Schönnbrun Palace, Vienna — A310

Designs: 33c, #743f, The Gloriette. 60c, #743b, Wall painting on fabric (detail), by Johann Wenzl Bergl, vert. No. 743a, Blue porcelain vase, vert. No. 743c, Porcelain stove, vert. No. 743d, Palace. No. 743e, Great Palm House (conservatory).

1998, Dec. 4   Litho.   *Perf. 14*
741	A310	33c multicolored	.65	.30
742	A310	60c multicolored	1.25	.65
743		Souvenir booklet	6.00	
a.-c.		A310 11c any single	.25	.25
d.-f.		A310 15c any single	.30	.30
g.		Booklet pane, 4 #743d	1.25	
h.		Booklet pane, 3 #743a	.75	
i.		Booklet pane, 3 #743b	.75	
j.		Booklet pane, 3 #743c	.75	
k.		Booklet pane, 4 #743e	1.25	
l.		Booklet pane, 4 #743f	1.25	

See Off. in Geneva #329-331; Vienna #246-248.

AIR POST STAMPS

Plane and Gull — AP1

UNITED NATIONS — OFFICES IN GENEVA, SWITZERLAND

Swallows and UN Emblem AP2

Unwmk.
1951, Dec. 14   Engr.   Perf. 14
C1	AP1	6c henna brown	.15	.15
C2	AP1	10c bright blue green	.15	.20
C3	AP2	15c deep ultra	.20	.25
a.		15c Prussian blue	100.00	
C4	AP2	25c gray black	.90	.35
		Nos. C1-C4 (4)	1.40	.95

The 6c, 15c and 25c exist imperforate.

Airplane Wing and Globe — AP3

1957, May 27   Perf. 12½x14
C5 AP3 4c maroon   .15 .15

1959, Feb. 9   Perf. 12½x13½
C6 AP3 5c rose red   .15 .15

UN Flag and Plane — AP4

1959, Feb. 9   Perf. 13½x14
C7 AP4 7c ultramarine   .15 .15

Outer Space — AP5

UN Emblem — AP6

"Flight Across Globe" — AP8

Bird of Laurel Leaves — AP7

Jet Plane and Envelope — AP9

1963-64   Photo.   Perf. 11½
| C8 | AP5 | 6c blk, blue & yel grn | .15 | .15 |
| C9 | AP6 | 8c yel, ol green & red | .15 | .15 |

Perf. 12½x12
C10 AP7 13c ultra, aqua, gray & car   .20 .20

Perf. 11½x12, 12x11½
C11 AP8 15c violet, buff, gray & pale grn ('64)   .35 .20
 a.   Gray omitted
C12 AP9 25c yel, org, gray, blue & red ('64)   .65 .30
 Nos. C8-C12 (5)   1.50 1.00

Dates of issue: 6c, 8c, 13c, June 17, 1963; 15c, 25c, May 1. See Offices in Geneva No. 8.

Jet Plane and UN Emblem — AP10

1968, Apr. 18   Litho.   Perf. 13
C13 AP10 20c multicolored   .30 .25

Wings, Envelopes and UN Emblem — AP11

1969, Apr. 21   Litho.
C14 AP11 10c org ver, org, yel & black   .20 .20

UN Emblem and Stylized Wing — AP12

Birds in Flight — AP13

Clouds AP14

"UN" and Plane — AP15

Lithograved and Engraved
1972, May 1   Perf. 13x13½
C15 AP12 9c lt blue, dark red & vio blue   .15 .15

Photo.   Perf. 14x13½
C16 AP13 11c blue & multi   .20 .15

Perf. 13½x14
C17 AP14 17c yel, red & orange   .25 .20

Perf. 13
C18 AP15 21c silver & multi   .30 .25
 Nos. C15-C18 (4)   .90 .75

Globe and Jet — AP16

Pathways Radiating from UN Emblem AP17

Bird in Flight, UN Headquarters AP18

Perf. 13, 12½x13 (18c)
1974, Sept. 16   Litho.
C19	AP16	13c multicolored	.20	.15
C20	AP17	18c multicolored	.25	.20
C21	AP18	26c blue & multi	.35	.30
		Nos. C19-C21 (3)	.80	.65

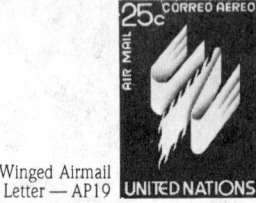

Winged Airmail Letter — AP19

Symbolic Globe and Plane — AP20

1977, June 27   Photo.   Perf. 14
| C22 | AP19 | 25c grnsh blue & multi | .35 | .25 |
| C23 | AP20 | 31c magenta | .40 | .30 |

OFFICES IN GENEVA, SWITZERLAND

For use only on mail posted at the Palais des Nations (UN European Office), Geneva. Inscribed in French unless otherwise stated.

100 Centimes = 1 Franc

Types of UN Issues 1961-69 and

UN European Office, Geneva — G1

Designs: 5c, UN Headquarters, New York, and world map. 10c, UN flag. 20c, Three men united before globe. 50c, Opening words of UN Charter. 60c, UN emblem over globe. 70c, "UN" and UN emblem. 75c, "Flight Across Globe." 80c, UN Headquarters and emblem. 90c, Abstract group of flags. 1fr, UN Emblem. 2fr, Stylized globe and weather vane. 3fr, Statue by Henrik Starcke. 10fr, "Peace, Justice, Security."

Perf. 13 (5c, 70c, 90c); Perf. 12½x12 (10c); Perf. 11½ (20c-60c, 3fr); Perf. 11½x12 (75c); Perf. 13½x14 (80c); Perf. 14 (1fr); Perf. 12x11½ (2fr); Perf. 12 (10fr)

Photogravure; Lithographed & Embossed (1fr); Engraved (10fr)
1969-70   Unwmk.
1	A88	5c purple & multi	.15	.15
a.		Green omitted	—	
2	A52	10c salmon & multi	.15	.15
3	A66	20c black & multi	.15	.15
4	G1	30c dk blue & multi	.15	.15
5	A77	50c ultra & multi	.20	.20
6	A54	60c dk brown, sal & gold	.25	.25
7	A104	70c red, black & gold	.25	.25
8	AP8	75c car rose & multi	.25	.25
9	A78	80c blue grn, red & yel	.30	.30
10	A45	90c blue & multi	.30	.30
11	A79	1fr lt & dk green	.30	.30
12	A67	2fr blue & multi	.65	.65
13	A97	3fr olive & multi	1.00	1.00
14	A3	10fr deep blue	3.25	3.25
		Nos. 1-14 (14)	7.35	7.35

The 20c, 80c and 90c are inscribed in French. The 75c and 10fr carry French inscription at top, English at bottom.
Issued: 60c, 10fr, 4/17/70; 70c, 80c, 90c, 2fr, 9/22/70; others, 10/4/69.

Sea Bed Type
Photogravure and Engraved
1971, Jan. 25   Perf. 13
15 A114 30c green & multi   .20 .20

Refugee Type
1971, Mar. 12   Litho.   Perf. 13x12½
16 A115 50c dp car, dp org & black   .20 .30

Food Program Type
1971, Apr. 13   Photo.   Perf. 14
17 A116 50c dk purple, gold & grn   .20 .30

UPU Headquarters Type
1971, May 28   Photo.   Perf. 11½
18 A117 75c green & multi   .30 .40

Eliminate Discrimination Types
1971, Sept. 21   Photo.   Perf. 13½
| 19 | A118 | 30c blue & multi | .20 | .20 |
| 20 | A119 | 50c multicolored | .30 | .30 |

Picasso Type
1971, Nov. 19   Photo.   Perf. 11½
21 A122 1.10fr carmine & multi   .75 .65

Palais des Nations, Geneva G2

1972, Jan. 5   Photo.   Perf. 11½
22 G2 40c olive & multi   .20 .20

Nuclear Weapons Type
1972, Feb. 14   Photo.   Perf. 13½x14
23 A124 40c yel green, blk, rose & gray   .25 .25

World Health Day Type
Lithographed and Engraved
1972, Apr. 7   Perf. 13x13½
24 A125 80c black & multi   .40 .40

Environment Type
Lithographed and Embossed
1972, June 5   Perf. 12½x14
| 25 | A126 | 40c multicolored | .20 | .20 |
| 26 | A126 | 80c multicolored | .45 | .45 |

ECE Type
1972, Sept. 11   Litho.   Perf. 13x13½
27 A127 1.10fr red & multi   1.00 .90

Art at UN Type
1972, Nov. 17   Photo.   Perf. 12x12½
| 28 | A128 | 40c gold, brown & red | .40 | .35 |
| 29 | A128 | 80c gold, brown & olive | .65 | .65 |

Disarmament Type
1973, Mar. 9   Litho.   Perf. 13½x13
| 30 | A129 | 60c violet & multi | .40 | .35 |
| 31 | A129 | 1.10fr olive & multi | .85 | .85 |

Nos. 30-31 exist imperf.

Drug Abuse Type
1973, Apr. 13   Photo.   Perf. 13½
32 A130 60c blue & multi   .45 .40

Volunteers Type
1973, May 25   Photo.   Perf. 14
33 A131 80c multicolored   .45 .45

Namibia Type
1973, Oct. 1   Photo.   Perf. 13½
34 A132 60c red & multi   .35 .35

Human Rights Type
1973, Nov. 16   Photo.   Perf. 13½
| 35 | A133 | 40c ultra & multi | .30 | .30 |
| 36 | A133 | 80c olive & multi | .50 | .50 |

ILO Headquarters Type
1974, Jan. 11   Photo.   Perf. 14
| 37 | A134 | 60c violet & multi | .50 | .45 |
| 38 | A134 | 80c brown & multi | .70 | .60 |

UPU Type
1974, Mar. 22   Photo.   Perf. 14
| 39 | A135 | 30c multicolored | .25 | .20 |
| 40 | A135 | 60c multicolored | .60 | .40 |

Art at UN Type
1974, May 6   Photo.   Perf. 14
| 41 | A136 | 60c dark red & multi | .40 | .40 |
| 42 | A136 | 1fr green & multi | .70 | .70 |

WPY Type
1974, Oct. 18   Photo.   Perf. 14
| 43 | A140 | 60c brt green & multi | .55 | .45 |
| 44 | A140 | 80c brown & multi | .70 | .60 |

Law of the Sea Type
1974, Nov. 22   Photo.   Perf. 14
45 A141 1.30fr blue & multi   .95 .95

Outer Space Type
1975, Mar. 14   Litho.   Perf. 13
| 46 | A142 | 60c multicolored | .50 | .35 |
| 47 | A142 | 90c multicolored | .75 | .55 |

UNITED NATIONS — OFFICES IN GENEVA, SWITZERLAND

IWY Type
1975, May 9   Litho.   *Perf. 15*
48 A143 60c multicolored .45 .40
49 A143 90c multicolored .65 .55

30th Anniv. Type
1975, June 26   Litho.   *Perf. 13*
50 A144 60c green & multi .45 .40
51 A144 90c violet & multi .65 .60

Souvenir Sheet
Imperf
52   Sheet of 2 .75 .75
   a. A144 60c green & multi .25 .25
   b. A144 90c violet & multi .50 .50

Namibia Type
1975, Sept. 22   Photo.   *Perf. 13½*
53 A145 50c multicolored .30 .30
54 A145 1.30fr multicolored 1.00 .70

Peace-keeping Operations Type
1975, Nov. 21   Engr.   *Perf. 12½*
55 A146 60c greenish blue .35 .35
56 A146 70c bright violet .65 .50

WFUNA Type
1976, Mar. 12   Photo.   *Perf. 14*
57 A152 90c multicolored 1.00 .65

UNCTAD Type
1976, Apr. 23   Photo.   *Perf. 11½*
58 A153 1.10fr multicolored 1.00 .80

Habitat Type
1976, May 28   Photo.   *Perf. 14*
59 A154 40c multicolored .25 .25
60 A154 1.50fr violet & multi .85 .85

UN Emblem, Post Horn and Rainbow — G3

1976, Oct. 8   Photo.   *Perf. 11½*
61 G3 80c tan & multi .60 .60
62 G3 1.10fr lt green & multi 1.90 1.90
Sheets of 20.

Food Council Type
1976, Nov. 19   Litho.   *Perf. 14½*
63 A156 70c multicolored .60 .55

WIPO Type
1977, Mar. 11   Photo.   *Perf. 14*
64 A157 80c red & multi .60 .55

Drop of Water and Globe — G4

1977, Apr. 22   Photo.   *Perf. 13½x13*
65 G4 80c ultra & multi .60 .50
66 G4 1.10fr dark car & multi .85 .75
UN Water Conference, Mar del Plata, Argentina, Mar. 14-25.

Hands Protecting UN Emblem — G5

1977, May 24   Photo.   *Perf. 14*
67 G5 80c blue & multi .60 .50
68 G5 1.10fr emerald & multi .85 .75
UN Security Council.

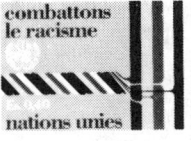

Colors of Five Races Spun into One Firm Rope — G6

1977, Sept. 19   Litho.   *Perf. 13*
69 G6 40c multicolored .25 .25
70 G6 1.10fr multicolored .65 .65
Fight against racial discrimination.

Atomic Energy Turning Partly into Olive Branch — G7

1977, Nov. 18   Photo.
71 G7 80c dark car & multi .50 .50
72 G7 1.10fr Prus blue & multi .75 .75
Peaceful uses of atomic energy.

"Tree" of Doves — G8

1978, Jan. 27   Litho.   *Perf. 14½*
73 G8 35c multicolored .15 .15

Globes with Smallpox Distribution — G9

1978, Mar. 31   Photo.   *Perf. 12x11½*
74 G9 80c yellow & multi .50 .50
75 G9 1.10fr lt green & multi .75 .75
Global eradication of smallpox.

Namibia Type
1978, May 5   Photo.   *Perf. 12*
76 A166 80c multicolored .75 .60

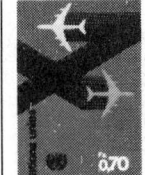

Jets and Flight Patterns — G10

1978, June 12   Photo.   *Perf. 14*
77 G10 70c multicolored .40 .30
78 G10 80c multicolored .75 .50
International Civil Aviation Organization for "Safety in the Air."

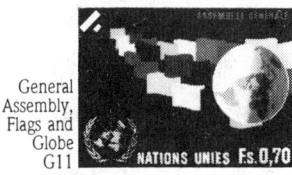

General Assembly, Flags and Globe — G11

1978, Sept. 15   Photo.   *Perf. 13½*
79 G11 70c multicolored .55 .55
80 G11 1.10fr multicolored .90 .60

Technical Cooperation Type
1978, Nov. 17   Photo.   *Perf. 14*
81 A169 80c multicolored .80 .55

Seismograph Recording Earthquake — G12

1979, Mar. 9   Photo.   *Perf. 14*
82 G12 80c multicolored .50 .50
83 G12 1.50fr multicolored .85 .85
Office of the UN Disaster Relief Coordinator (UNDRO).

Children and Rainbow — G13

1979, May 4   Photo.   *Perf. 14*
84 G13 80c multicolored .35 .35
85 G13 1.10fr multicolored .65 .65
International Year of the Child.

Namibia Type
1979, Oct. 5   Litho.   *Perf. 13½*
86 A176 1.10fr multicolored .50 .50

International Court of Justice, Scales — G14

1979, Nov. 9   Litho.   *Perf. 13x13½*
87 G14 80c multicolored .40 .40
88 G14 1.10fr multicolored .60 .60
International Court of Justice, The Hague, Netherlands.

Economic Order Type
1980, Jan. 11   *Perf. 15x14½*
89 A179 80c multicolored .75 .60

Women's Year Emblem — G15

1980, Mar. 7   Litho.   *Perf. 14½x15*
90 G15 40c multicolored .30 .30
91 G15 70c multicolored .75 .55
UN Decade for Women.

Peace-keeping Operations Type
1980, May 16   Litho.   *Perf. 14x13*
92 A181 1.10fr blue & green .80 .70

35th Anniv. Type and

Dove and "35" — G16

1980, June 26   Litho.   *Perf. 13*
93 G16 40c multicolored .35 .30
94 A183 70c multicolored .55 .50

Souvenir Sheet
Imperf
95   Sheet of 2 .75 .60
   a. G16 40c multicolored .25 —
   b. A183 70c multicolored .50 —
35th anniv. of the UN.

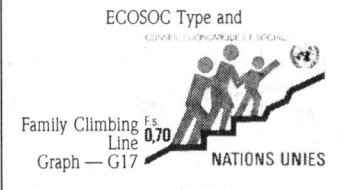

ECOSOC Type and

Family Climbing Line Graph — G17

1980, Nov. 21   Litho.   *Perf. 13½x13*
96 A186 40c multicolored .30 .25
97 G17 70c multicolored .60 .50

Palestinian Rights Type
1981, Jan. 30   Photo.
98 A188 80c multicolored .60 .60

Disabled Type of UN, Vienna
1981, Mar. 6   Photo.
99 A190 40c multicolored .25 .25
100 V4 1.50fr multicolored 1.00 1.00

Art Type
1981, Apr. 15   Photo.   *Perf. 11½*
101 A191 80c multicolored .75 .60

Energy Type
1981, May 29   Litho.   *Perf. 13*
102 A192 1.10fr multicolored .75 .75

Volunteers Program Type and Symbols of Science, Agriculture and Industry — G18

1981, Nov. 13   Litho.   *Perf. 13½x13*
103 A194 40c multicolored .45 .30
104 G18 80c multicolored .80 .55

Fight Against Apartheid — G19   Flower of Flags — G20

1982, Jan. 22   Photo.   *Perf. 11½x12*
105 G19 30c multicolored .20 .15
106 G20 1fr multicolored .70 .65

Human Environment — G21

1982, Mar. 19   Litho.   *Perf. 13½x13*
107 G21 40c multicolored .30 .15
108 A199 1.20fr multicolored 1.25 1.00

Outer Space Type and

Satellite Applications of Space Technology — G22

1982, June 11   Litho.   *Perf. 13x13½*
109 A201 80c multicolored .60 .45
110 G22 1fr multicolored .75 .60

Conservation and Protection of Nature
1982, Nov. 19   Photo.   *Perf. 14*
111 A202 40c Bird .45 .35
112 A202 1.50fr Reptile 1.10 .75

World Communications Year Type
1983, Jan. 28   Litho.   *Perf. 13*
113 A204 1.20fr multicolored 1.25 1.00

United Nations Offices in Geneva stamps can be mounted in the Scott U.N. Singles and Postal Stationery album.

UNITED NATIONS — OFFICES IN GENEVA, SWITZERLAND

Safety at Sea Type and

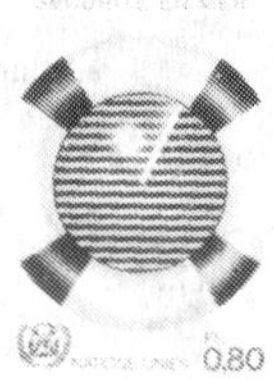

Life Preserver and Radar — G23

1983, Mar. 18	Litho.		*Perf. 14½*
114 A205	40c multicolored	.35	.35
115 A23	80c multicolored	.75	.75

World Food Program Type

1983, Apr. 22	Engr.		*Perf. 13½*
116 A207	1.50fr blue	1.25	1.00

Type of UN and

G24

1983, June 6	Litho.		*Perf. 14*
117 A208	80c multicolored	.50	.50
118 A24	1.10fr multicolored	.85	.85

35th Anniv. of the Universal Declaration of Human Rights

G25   G26

			Perf. 13½
1983, Dec. 9	Photo.		Engr.
119 G25	40c Homo Humus Humanitas	.45	.45
120 G26	1.20fr Right to Create	.95	.90

Intl. Population Conference Type

1984, Feb. 3	Litho.		*Perf. 14*
121 A212	1.20fr multicolored	1.00	.85

Fishing FAO — G27

Women Farm Workers, Africa — G28

1984, Mar. 15	Litho.		*Perf. 14½*
122 G27	50c multicolored	.35	.30
123 G28	80c multicolored	.65	.55

World Food Day.

Valletta, Malta — G29

Los Glaciares Natl. Park, Argentina — G30

1984, Apr. 18	Litho.		*Perf. 14*
124 G29	50c multicolored	.60	.60
125 G30	70c multicolored	.85	.80

World Heritage. See Nos. 211-212.

G31   G32

1984, May 29	Photo.		*Perf. 11½*
126 G31	35c multicolored	.35	.20
127 G32	1.50fr multicolored	1.25	.75

Refugees.

International Youth Year — G33

1984, Nov. 15	Litho.		*Perf. 13½*
128 G33	1.20fr multicolored	1.10	1.00

ILO Type of UN and

Turin Center — G34

1985, Feb. 1			Engr.
129 A220	80c Turin Center emblem	.60	.45
130 G34	1.20fr U Thant Pavilion	.90	.70

UN University Type

1985, Mar. 15	Photo.		*Perf. 13½*
131 A221	50c Farmer, discussion group	.55	.40
132 A221	80c As above	.90	.60

Postman — G35

Doves — G36

1985, May 10	Litho.		*Perf. 14*
133 G35	20c multicolored	.20	.15
134 G36	1.20fr multicolored	1.25	1.00

40th Anniv. Type

1985, June 26	Photo.		*Perf. 12x11½*
135 A224	50c multicolored	.55	.35
136 A225	70c multicolored	.80	.50

Souvenir Sheet
Imperf

137	Sheet of 2	2.00	1.10
a.	A224 50c multicolored	.65	
b.	A225 70c multicolored	.90	

UNICEF Child Survival Campaign
Photo. & Engr.

1985, Nov. 22			*Perf. 13½*
138 A226	50c Three girls	.50	.20
139 A226	1.20fr Infant drinking	1.10	1.00

Africa in Crisis Type

Abstract painting by Alemayehou Gabremedhin.

1986, Jan. 31	Photo.		*Perf. 11½*
140 A227	1.40fr Mother, hungry children	1.40	1.00

UN Development Program Type

1986, Mar. 14	Photo.		*Perf. 13½*
141 A228	35c Erosion control	2.00	1.50
142 A228	35c Logging	2.00	1.50
143 A228	35c Lumber transport	2.00	1.50
144 A228	35c Nursery	2.00	1.50
a.	Block of 4, #141-144	8.50	6.00

No. 144a has a continuous design.

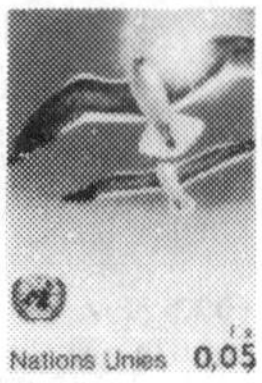

Doves and Sun — G37

1986, Mar. 14	Litho.		*Perf. 15x14½*
145 G37	5c multicolored	.15	.15

UN Stamp Collecting Type

Designs: 50c, UN Human Rights stamp. 80c, UN stamps.

1986, May 22	Engr.		*Perf. 12½*
146 A229	50c dk green & hn brn	.50	.40
147 A229	80c dk green & yel org	.90	.70

Flags and Globe as Dove — G38

Peace in French — G39

Photo. & Embossed

1986, June 20			*Perf. 13½*
148 G38	45c multicolored	.60	.45
149 G39	1.40fr multicolored	1.65	1.25

Intl. Peace Year.

WFUNA Anniv. Type
Souvenir Sheet

Designs: 35c, Abstract by Benigno Gomez, Honduras. 45c, Abstract by Alexander Calder (1898-1976), US. 50c, Abstract by Joan Miro (b. 1893), Spain. 70c, Sextet with Dove, by Ole Hamann, Denmark.

1986, Nov. 14	Litho.		*Perf. 13x13½*
150	Sheet of 4	4.25	2.00
a.	A232 35c multicolored	.55	—
b.	A232 45c multicolored	.75	—
c.	A232 50c multicolored	.95	—
d.	A232 70c multicolored	1.25	—

Trygve Lie Type
Photo. & Engr.

1987, Jan. 30			*Perf. 13½*
151 A233	1.40fr multicolored	1.25	1.00

Sheaf of Colored Bands, by Georges Mathieu — G40

Armillary Sphere, Palais des Nations — G41

Photo., Photo. & Engr. (No. 153)
Perf. 11½x12, 13½ (No. 153)

1987, Jan. 30			
152 G40	90c multicolored	.70	.60
153 G41	1.40fr multicolored	1.10	.90

Perf. 13½x12½

1987, Mar. 13			Litho.
154 A234	50c Construction	.60	.55
155 A234	90c Finishing interior	1.00	.90

Fight Drug Abuse Type

1987, June 12	Litho.		*Perf. 14½*
156 A235	80c Mother and child	.55	.55
157 A235	1.20fr Workers in rice paddy	.95	.95

UN Day Type

Designs: Multinational people in various occupations.

1987, Oct. 23	Litho.		*Perf. 14½x15*
158 A236	35c multicolored	.50	.50
159 A236	50c multicolored	.80	.75

Immunize Every Child Type

1987, Nov. 20	Litho.		*Perf. 15x14½*
160 A237	90c Whooping cough	1.40	1.00
161 A237	1.70fr Tuberculosis	2.50	1.15

IFAD Type

1988, Jan. 29	Litho.		*Perf. 13½*
162 A238	35c Flocks	.40	.35
163 A238	1.40fr Fruit	1.65	1.40

G42

1988, Jan. 29	Photo.		*Perf. 14*
164 G42	50c multicolored	.80	.70

Survival of the Forests Type

1988, Mar. 18	Litho.		*Perf. 14x15*
165 A240	50c Pine forest	1.75	1.50
166 A240	1.10fr as 50c	4.75	4.25
a.	Pair, #165-166	6.50	6.00

No. 166a has a continuous design.

Intl. Volunteer Day Type
Perf. 13x14, 14x13

1988, May 6			Litho.
167 A241	80c Agriculture, vert.	.95	.60
168 A241	90c Veterinary medicine	1.00	.70

Health in Sports Type
Perf. 13½x13, 13x13½

1988, June 17			Litho.
169 A242	50c Soccer, vert.	.50	.40
170 A242	1.40fr Swimming	1.50	1.25

Human Rights Declaration Anniv. Type

1988, Dec. 9	Photo. & Engr.		*Perf. 12*
171 A243	90c multicolored	.95	.85

Souvenir Sheet

172 A243	2fr multicolored	2.75	2.25

World Bank Type

1989, Jan. 27	Litho.		*Perf. 13x14*
173 A244	80c Telecommunications	1.00	.75
174 A244	1.40fr Industry	2.25	1.75

Peace-Keeping Force Type

1989, Mar. 17	Litho.		*Perf. 14x13½*
175 A245	90c multicolored	1.00	1.00

World Weather Watch Anniv. Type

Satellite photographs: 90c, Europe under the influence of Arctic air. 1.10fr, Surface temperatures of sea, ice and land surrounding the Kattegat between Denmark and Sweden.

1989, Apr. 21	Litho.		*Perf. 13x14*
176 A247	90c multicolored	1.25	1.00
177 A247	1.10fr multicolored	2.00	1.50

G43   G44

UNITED NATIONS — OFFICES IN GENEVA, SWITZERLAND

Photo. & Engr., Photo.
1989, Aug. 23 *Perf. 14*
178 G43 50c multicolored 1.10 .70
179 G44 2fr multicolored 3.50 2.50

Offices in Vienna, 10th anniv.

Human Rights Type of 1989
Paintings and sculpture: 35c, *Young Mother Sewing*, by Mary Cassatt. 80c, *The Unknown Slave*, sculpture by Albert Mangones.

1989, Nov. 17 Litho. *Perf. 13½*
180 A250 35c multicolored .40 .40
181 A250 80c multicolored 1.10 1.10

Printed in sheets of 12+12 se-tenant labels containing Articles 3 (35c) or 4 (80c) inscribed in French, German or English.

Intl. Trade Center Type
1990, Feb. 2 Litho. *Perf. 14½x15*
182 A251 1.50fr multicolored 2.50 2.00

G45

1990, Feb. 2 Photo. *Perf. 14x13½*
183 G45 5fr multicolored 5.00 4.00

Fight AIDS Worldwide G46a

G46

Perf. 13½x12½
1990, Mar. 16 Litho.
184 G46 50c multicolored 1.10 1.00
185 G46a 80c multicolored 1.75 .50

Medicinal Plants Type
1990, May 4 Photo. *Perf. 11½*
Granite Paper
186 A253 90c *Plumeria rubra* 1.25 .70
187 A253 1.40fr *Cinchona officinalis* 2.25 1.50

UN 45th Anniv. Type
"45," emblem and: 90c, Symbols of clean environment, transportation and industry. 1.10fr, Dove in silhouette.

1990, June 26 Litho. *Perf. 14½x13*
188 A254 90c multicolored 1.25 .45
189 A254 1.10fr multicolored 2.25 1.50

Souvenir Sheet
190 A254 Sheet of 2, #188-189 5.75 2.65

Crime Prevention Type
1990, Sept. 13 Photo. *Perf. 14*
191 A255 50c Official corruption 1.00 .70
192 A255 2fr Environmental crime 2.75 2.25

Human Rights Type of 1989
Paintings: 35c, *The Prison Courtyard* by Vincent Van Gogh. 90c, *Katho's Son Redeems the Evil Doer From Execution* by Albrecht Durer.

1990, Nov. 16 Litho. *Perf. 13½*
193 A250 35c multicolored .55 .25
194 A250 90c black & brown 1.50 .65

Printed in sheets of 12+12 se-tenant labels containing Articles 9 (35c) or 10 (90c) inscribed in French, German or English.

Economic Commission for Europe Type
1991, Mar. 15 Litho. *Perf. 14*
195 A256 90c Owl, gull 1.25 .60
196 A256 90c Bittern, otter 1.25 .60
197 A256 90c Swan, lizard 1.25 .60
198 A256 90c Great crested grebe 1.25 .60
a. Block of 4, #195-198 5.25 2.40

Namibian Independence Type
1991, May 10 Litho. *Perf. 14*
199 A257 70c Mountains 1.25 1.00
200 A257 90c Baobab tree 2.25 1.75

Ballots Filling Ballot Box — G47

UN Emblem — G48

1991, May 10 Litho. *Perf. 15x14½*
201 G47 80c multicolored 1.25 1.00
202 G48 1.50fr multicolored 2.50 2.00

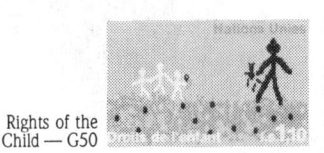

Rights of the Child — G50

Litho.
Perf. 14½
Perf. 15x14½
1991, June 14
203 G49 80c Hands holding infant 1.40 1.00
204 G50 1.10fr Children, flowers 2.00 1.50

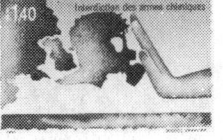

Banning of Chemical Weapons G52

1991, Sept. 11 Litho. *Perf. 13½*
205 G51 80c multicolored 1.50 1.00
206 G52 1.40fr multicolored 2.75 1.50

UN Postal Administration, 40th Anniv. Type
1991, Oct. 24 Litho. *Perf. 14x15*
207 A263 50c UN NY #7 .85 .70
208 A263 1.60fr UN NY #10 2.50 2.00

Human Rights Type of 1989
Artwork: 50c, *Early Morning in Ro...1925*, by Paul Klee. 90c, *The Marriage of Giovanni Arnolfini and Fiovanna Cenami*, by Jan Van Eyck.

1991, Nov. 20 Litho. *Perf. 13½*
209 A250 50c multicolored .85 .70
210 A250 90c multicolored 1.25 1.25

Printed in sheets of 12+12 se-tenant labels containing Articles 15 (50c) and 16 (90c) inscribed in French, German or English.

World Heritage Type of 1984
Designs: 50c, Sagarmatha Natl. Park, Nepal. 1.10fr, Stonehenge, United Kingdom.

1992, Jan. 24 *Perf. 13*
Size: 35x28mm
211 G29 50c multicolored 1.10 1.00
212 G29 1.10fr multicolored 2.50 1.65

G53

1992, Jan. 24 *Perf. 15x14½*
213 G53 3fr multicolored 3.50 3.00

Clean Oceans Type
1992, Mar. 13 Litho. *Perf. 14*
214 A264 80c Ocean surface, diff. 1.00 .75
215 A264 80c Ocean bottom, diff. 1.00 .75
a. Pair, #214-215 2.00 1.75

Printed in sheets of 12 containing 6 #215a.

Earth Summit Type
Designs: No. 216, Rainbow. No. 217, Faces shaped as clouds. No. 218, Two sailboats. No. 219, Woman with parasol, sailboat, flowers.

1992, May 22 Photo. *Perf. 11½*
216 A265 75c multicolored 1.10 .75
217 A265 75c multicolored 1.10 .75
218 A265 75c multicolored 1.10 .75
219 A265 75c multicolored 1.10 .75
a. Block of 4, #216-219 4.50 3.00

Mission to Planet Earth Type
Designs: No. 220, Space station. No. 221, Probes near Jupiter.

1992, Sept. 4 Photo. *Rouletted 8*
Granite Paper
220 A266 1.10fr multicolored 2.50 2.00
221 A266 1.10fr multicolored 2.50 2.00
a. Pair, #220-221 5.00 4.00

Science and Technology Type
Designs: 90c, Doctor, nurse. 1.60fr, Graduate seated before computer.

1992, Oct. 2 Litho. *Perf. 14*
222 A267 90c multicolored 1.40 .90
223 A267 1.60fr multicolored 2.50 1.75

Human Rights Type of 1989
Artwork: 50c, *The Oath of the Tennis Court*, by Jacques Louis David. 90c, *Rocking Chair I*, by Henry Moore.

1992, Nov. 20 Litho. *Perf. 13½*
224 A250 50c multicolored 1.00 .90
225 A250 90c multicolored 1.75 1.50

Printed in sheets of 12+12 se-tenant labels containing Articles 21 (50c) and 22 (90c) inscribed in French, German or English.

Aging With Dignity Type
Designs: 50c, Older man coaching soccer. 1.50fr, Older man working at computer terminal.

1993, Feb. 5 Litho. *Perf. 13*
226 A270 50c multicolored .80 .60
227 A270 1.50fr multicolored 2.50 1.75

Endangered Species Type
Designs: No. 228, Pongidae (gorilla). No. 229, Falco peregrinus (peregrine falcon). No. 230, Trichechus inunguis (Amazonian manatee). No. 231, Panthera uncia (snow leopard).

1993, Mar. 3 Litho. *Perf. 13x12½*
228 A271 80c multicolored 1.10 .90
229 A271 80c multicolored 1.10 .90
230 A271 80c multicolored 1.10 .90
231 A271 80c multicolored 1.10 .90
a. Block of 4, #228-231 4.50 4.00

Healthy Environment Type
1993, May 7 Litho. *Perf. 15x14½*
232 A272 60c Neighborhood 1.10 .70
233 A272 1fr Urban skyscrapers 2.50 1.50

Human Rights Type of 1989
Artwork: 50c, *Three Musicians*, by Pablo Picasso. 90c, *Voice of Space*, by Rene Magritte.

1993, June 11 Litho. *Perf. 13½*
234 A250 50c multicolored .75 .75
235 A250 90c multicolored 1.75 1.75

Printed in sheets of 12 + 12 se-tenant labels containing Article 27 (50c) and 28 (90c) inscribed in French, German or English.

Intl. Peace Day Type
Denomination at: No. 236, UL. No. 237, UR. No. 238, LL. No. 239, LR.

Rouletted 12½
1993, Sept. 21 Litho. & Engr.
236 A274 60c purple & multi 2.00 .90
237 A274 60c purple & multi 2.00 .90
238 A274 60c purple & multi 2.00 .90
239 A274 60c purple & multi 2.00 .90
a. Block of 4, #236-239 8.25 3.75

Environment-Climate Type
Designs: No. 240, Polar bears. No. 241, Whale sounding. No. 242, Elephant seal. No. 243, Penguins.

1993, Oct. 29 Litho. *Perf. 14½*
240 A275 1.10fr multicolored 1.50 1.25
241 A275 1.10fr multicolored 1.50 1.25
242 A275 1.10fr multicolored 1.50 1.25
243 A275 1.10fr multicolored 1.50 1.25
a. Strip of 4, #240-243 6.00 5.00

Intl. Year of the Family Type of 1993
Designs: 80c, Parents teaching child to walk. 1fr, Two women and child picking plants.

1994, Feb. 4 Litho. *Perf. 13.1*
244 A276 80c rose violet & multi 1.40 1.00
245 A276 1fr brown & multi 1.75 1.25

Endangered Species Type of 1993
Designs: No. 246, Mexican prairie dog. No. 247, Jabiru. No. 248, Blue whale. No. 249, Golden lion tamarin.

1994, Mar. 18 Litho. *Perf. 12.7*
246 A271 80c multicolored 1.10 .85
247 A271 80c multicolored 1.10 .85
248 A271 80c multicolored 1.10 .85
249 A271 80c multicolored 1.10 .85
a. Block of 4, #246-249 4.50 3.50

Protection for Refugees Type of 1994
Design: 1.20fr, Hand lifting figure over chasm.

1994, Apr. 29 Litho. *Perf. 14.3x14.8*
250 A277 1.20fr multicolored 2.75 2.25

Intl. Decade for Natural Disaster Reduction Type of 1994
Earth seen from space, outline map of: No. 251, North America. No. 252, Eurasia. No. 253, South America. No. 254, Australia and South Pacific region.

1994, May 27 Litho. *Perf. 13.9x14.2*
251 A281 60c multicolored 1.50 .50
252 A281 60c multicolored 1.50 .50
253 A281 60c multicolored 1.50 .50
254 A281 60c multicolored 1.50 .50
a. Block of 4, #251-254 6.50 2.00

Palais des Nations, Geneva G54

Creation of the World, by Oili Maki — G55

1994, Sept. 1 Litho. *Perf. 14.3x14.6*
255 G54 60c multicolored .75 .55
256 G55 80c multicolored 1.00 .70
257 G54 1.80fr multi, diff. 2.25 1.75

Population and Development Type of 1994
Designs: 60c, People shopping at open-air market. 80c, People on vacation crossing bridge.

1994, Sept. 1 Litho. *Perf. 13.2x13.6*
258 A282 60ç multicolored 1.25 .70
259 A282 80c multicolored 1.75 1.00

UNCTAD Type of 1994
1994, Oct. 28
260 A283 80c multi, diff. 1.25 1.00
261 A283 1fr multi, diff. 1.65 1.40
a. Grayish green omitted —

UN 50th Anniv. Type of 1995
1995, Jan. 1 Litho. & Engr. *Perf. 13.4*
262 A284 80c multicolored 1.40 1.25

UNITED NATIONS — OFFICES IN GENEVA, SWITZERLAND — OFFICES IN VIENNA, AUSTRIA

Social Summit Type of 1995
Perf. 13.6x13.9
1995, Feb. 3   Photo. & Engr.
263 A285 1fr multi, diff.   1.50 1.25

Endangered Species Type of 1993
Designs: No. 264, Crowned lemur, Lemur coronatus. No. 265, Giant Scops owl, Otus gurneyi. No. 266, Zetek's frog, Atelopus varius zeteki. No. 267, Wood bison, Bison bison athabascae.

1995, Mar. 24   Litho.   **Perf. 13x12½**
264 A271 80c multicolored   1.40 1.10
265 A271 80c multicolored   1.40 1.10
266 A271 80c multicolored   1.40 1.10
267 A271 80c multicolored   1.40 1.10
  a. Block of 4, 264-267   5.75 4.50

Intl. Youth Year Type of 1995
Designs: 80c, Farmer on tractor, fields at harvest time. 1fr, Couple standing by fields at night.

1995, May 26   Litho.   **Perf. 14.4x14.7**
268 A286 80c multicolored   1.40 1.10
269 A286 1fr multicolored   1.75 1.40

UN, 50th Anniv. Type of 1995
Designs: 60c, Like No. 663. 1.80fr, Like No. 664.

1995, June 26   Engr.   **Perf. 13.3x13.6**
270 A287 60c maroon   1.00 .60
271 A287 1.80fr green   3.25 1.75

Souvenir Sheet
Litho. & Engr.
Imperf
272 Sheet of 2, #270-271   4.25 4.25
  a. A287 60c maroon   1.00 1.00
  b. A287 1.80fr green   3.25 3.25

Conference on Women Type of 1995
Designs: 60c, Black woman, cranes flying above. 1fr, Women, dove.

1995, Sept. 5   Photo.   **Perf. 12**
273 A288 60c multicolored   1.50 .50
  Size: 28x50mm
274 A288 1fr multicolored   2.50 .85

UN People, 50th Anniv. Type of 1995
1995, Oct. 24   Litho.   **Perf. 14**
275 Sheet of 12   14.00 9.00
  a.-l. A290 30c any single   1.10 .70
276 Souvenir booklet   15.00
  a. A290 30c Booklet pane of 3, vert.
     strip of 3 from UL of sheet   3.75 3.50
  b. A290 30c Booklet pane of 3, vert.
     strip of 3 from UR of sheet   3.75 3.50
  c. A290 30c Booklet pane of 3, vert.
     strip of 3 from LL of sheet   3.75 3.50
  d. A290 30c Booklet pane of 3, vert.
     strip of 3 from LR of sheet   3.75 3.50

WFUNA, 50th Anniv. Type of 1996
1996, Feb. 2   Litho.   **Perf. 13x13½**
277 A291 80c multicolored   1.50 .65

The Galloping Horse Treading on a Flying Swallow, Chinese Bronzework, Eastern Han Dynasty (25-220 A.D.) — G56

Palais des Nations, Geneva G57

1996, Feb. 2   Litho.   **Perf. 14½x15**
278 G56 40c multicolored   .65 .30
279 G57 70c multicolored   1.10 .55

Endangered Species Type of 1993
Designs: No. 280, Paphiopedilum delenatii. No. 281, Pachypodium baronii. No. 282, Sternbergia lutea. No. 283, Darlingtonia californica.

1996, Mar. 14   Litho.   **Perf. 12½**
280 A271 80c multicolored   1.10 .65
281 A271 80c multicolored   1.10 .65
282 A271 80c multicolored   1.10 .65
283 A271 80c multicolored   1.10 .65
  a. Block of 4, #280-283   4.50 .65

City Summit Type of 1996
Designs: No. 284, Asian family. No. 285, Oriental garden. No. 286, Fruit, vegetable vendor, mosque. No. 287, Boys playing ball. No. 288, Couple reading newspaper.

1996, June 3   Litho.   **Perf. 14x13½**
284 A293 70c multicolored   .90 .30
285 A293 70c multicolored   .90 .30
286 A293 70c multicolored   .90 .30
287 A293 70c multicolored   .90 .30
288 A293 70c multicolored   .90 .30
  a. Strip of 5, #284-288   4.50

Sport and the Environment Type of 1996
Designs: 70c, Cycling, vert. 1.10fr, Sprinters.

Perf. 14x14½, 14½x14
1996, July 19   Litho.
289 A294 70c multicolored   1.25 .55
290 A294 1.10fr multicolored   1.75 .85

Souvenir Sheet
291 A294 Sheet of 2, #289-290   3.00 2.85

Plea for Peace Type of 1996
Designs: 90c, Tree filled with birds, vert. 1.10fr, Bouquet of flowers in rocket tail vase, vert.

1996, Sept. 17   Litho.   **Perf. 15x14½**
292 A295 90c multicolored   1.40 .70
293 A295 1.10fr multicolored   1.75 .85

UNICEF Type of 1996
Fairy Tales: 70c, The Sun and the Moon, South America. 1.80fr, Ananse, Africa.

1996, Nov. 20   Litho.   **Perf. 14½x15**
294 A296 70c multicolored   1.00 .55
295 A296 1.80fr multicolored   2.50 1.40

Panes of 8 + label.

UN Flag — G58

Palais des Nations Under Construction, by Massimo Campigli G59

1997, Feb. 12   Litho.   **Perf. 14½**
296 G58 10c multicolored   .15 .15
297 G59 1.10fr multicolored   1.50 .75

Endangered Species Type of 1993
Designs: No. 298, Ursus maritimus (polar bear). No. 299, Goura cristata (blue-crowned pigeon). No. 300, Amblyrhynchus cristatus (marine iguana). No. 703, Lama guanicoe (guanaco).

1997, Mar. 13   Litho.   **Perf. 12½**
298 A271 80c multicolored   1.10 .55
299 A271 80c multicolored   1.10 .55
300 A271 80c multicolored   1.10 .55
301 A271 80c multicolored   1.10 .55
  a. Block of 4, #298-301   4.50 2.25

Earth Summit Anniv. Type of 1997
Designs: No. 302, Person flying over mountain. No. 303, Mountain, person's face. No. 304, Person standing on mountain, sailboats. No. 305, Person, mountain, trees.
1.10fr, Combined design similar to Nos. 302-305.

1997, May 30   Photo.   **Perf. 11.5**
Granite Paper
302 A299 45c multicolored   .70 .30
303 A299 45c multicolored   .70 .30
304 A299 45c multicolored   .70 .30
305 A299 45c multicolored   .70 .30
  a. Block of 4, #302-305   2.80 1.20

Souvenir Sheet
306 A299 1.10fr multicolored   1.50 1.50

Transportation Type of 1997
Air transportation: No. 307, Zeppelin, Fokker trimotor. No. 308, Boeing 314 Clipper, Lockheed Constellation. No. 309, DeHavilland Comet. No. 310, Boeing 747, Illyushin jet. No. 311, Concorde.

1997, Aug. 29   Litho.   **Perf. 14x14½**
307 A300 70c multicolored   1.00 .50
308 A300 70c multicolored   1.00 .50
309 A300 70c multicolored   1.00 .50
310 A300 70c multicolored   1.00 .50
311 A300 70c multicolored   1.00 .50
  a. Strip of 5, #307-311   5.00 2.50

No. 311a has continuous design.

Philately Type of 1997
Designs: 70c, No. 146. 1.10fr, No. 147.

1997, Oct. 14   Litho.   **Perf. 13½x14**
312 A301 70c multicolored   1.00 .50
313 A301 1.10fr multicolored   1.50 .75

World Heritage Convention Type of 1997
Terracotta warriors of Xian: 45c, Single warrior. 70c, Massed warriors. No. 316a, like #716. No. 316b, like #717. No. 316c, like Geneva #314. No. 316d, like Geneva #315. No. 316e, like Vienna #230. No. 316f, like Vienna #231.

1997, Nov. 19   Litho.   **Perf. 13½**
314 A302 45c multicolored   .60 .30
315 A302 70c multicolored   1.00 .50
316 Souvenir booklet   3.75
  a.-f. A302 10c any single   .15 .15
  g. Booklet pane of 4 #316a   .60 .60
  h. Booklet pane of 4 #316b   .60 .60
  i. Booklet pane of 4 #316c   .60 .60
  j. Booklet pane of 4 #316d   .60 .60
  k. Booklet pane of 4 #316e   .60 .60
  l. Booklet pane of 4 #316f   .60 .60

Palais des Nations, Geneva G60

1998, Feb. 13   Litho.   **Perf. 14½x15**
317 G60 2fr multicolored   2.75 1.40

Endangered Species Type of 1993
Designs: No. 318, Macaca thibetana (short-tailed Tibetan macaque). No. 319, Phoenicopterus ruber (Caribbean flamingo). No. 320, Ornithoptera alexandrae (Queen Alexandra's birdwing). No. 321, Dama mesopotamica (Persian fallow deer).

1998, Mar. 13   Litho.   **Perf. 12½**
318 A271 80c multicolored   1.10 .55
319 A271 80c multicolored   1.10 .55
320 A271 80c multicolored   1.10 .55
321 A271 80c multicolored   1.10 .55
  a. Block of 4, #318-321   4.50 2.25

Intl. Year of the Ocean — G61

1998, May 20   Litho.   **Perf. 13x13½**
322 G61 Sheet of 12   8.00 4.50
  a.-l. 45c any single   .65 .35

Rain Forests Type of 1998
1998, June 19   **Perf. 13x13½**
323 A307 70c Orangutans   1.00 .50

Souvenir Sheet
324 A307 3fr like #323   4.00 2.00

Peacekeeping Type of 1998
Designs: 70c, Soldier with two children. 90c, Two soldiers, children.

1998, Sept. 15   Photo.   **Perf. 12**
325 A308 70c multicolored   1.00 .50
326 A308 90c multicolored   1.40 .70

Declaration of Human Rights Type of 1998
Designs: 90c, Stylized birds. 1.80fr, Stylized birds flying from hand.

Litho. & Photo.
1998, Oct. 27   **Perf. 13**
327 A309 90c multicolored   1.40 .70
328 A309 1.80fr multicolored   2.75 1.40

Schönnbrun Palace Type of 1998
Designs: 70c, #331b, Great Palm House. 1.10fr, #331d, Blue porcelain vase, vert. No. 331a, Palace. No. 331c, The Gloriette (archway). No. 331e, Wall painting on fabric (detail), by Johann Wenzl Bergl, vert. No. 331f, Porcelain stove, vert.

1998, Dec. 4   Litho.   **Perf. 14**
329 A310 70c multicolored   1.00 .50
330 A310 1.10fr multicolored   1.50 .75
331 Souvenir booklet   6.00
  a.-c. A310 10c any single   .15 .15
  d.-f. A310 30c any single   .45 .45
  g. Booklet pane, 4 #331a   .60
  h. Booklet pane, 3 #331d   1.40
  i. Booklet pane, 3 #331e   1.40
  j. Booklet pane, 3 #331f   1.40
  k. Booklet pane, 4 #331b   .60
  l. Booklet pane, 4 #331c   .60

OFFICES IN VIENNA, AUSTRIA

For use only on mail posted at the Vienna International Center for the UN and the International Atomic Energy Agency.

100 Groschen = 1 Schilling

Type of Geneva 1978, UN Types of 1961-72 and

Donaupark, Vienna — V1

Aerial View — V2

Perf. 11½
1979, Aug. 24   Photo.   Unwmk.
Granite Paper
1   G8   50g multicolored   .15 .15
2   A52   1s multicolored   .15 .15
3   V1   4s multicolored   .20 .20
4   AP13   5s multicolored   .25 .25
5   V2   6s multicolored   .35 .30
6   A45   10s multicolored   .50 .50
  Nos. 1-6 (6)   1.60 1.50

No. 6 has no frame.

Economic Order Type
1980, Jan. 11   Litho.   **Perf. 15x14½**
7   A178   4s multicolored   .70 .50

Dove Type
1980, Jan. 11   Litho.   **Perf. 13x13½**
8   A147   2.50s multicolored   .30 .20

Women's Year Emblem on World Map — V3

1980, Mar. 7   Litho.   **Perf. 14½x15**
9   V3   4s lt green & dk green   .40 .40
10   V3   6s bister brown   .70 .45

UN Decade for Women.

Peace-keeping Operations Type
1980, May 16   Litho.   **Perf. 14x13**
11   A182   6s multicolored   .50 .50

35th Anniv. Types of Geneva and UN
1980, June 26   Litho.   **Perf. 13**
12   G16   4s multicolored   .40 .25
13   A184   6s multicolored   .70 .45

UNITED NATIONS — OFFICES IN VIENNA, AUSTRIA

Souvenir Sheet
Imperf
14 Sheet of 2 .55 .55
a. G14 4s multicolored .20 —
b. A184 6s multicolored .35 —
35th anniv. of the UN.

ECOSOC Types of UN and Geneva
1980, Nov. 21 Litho. *Perf. 13½x13*
15 A187 4s multicolored .32 .20
16 G17 6s multicolored .55 .20

Palestinian Rights Type
1981, Jan. 30 Photo.
17 A188 4s multicolored .50 .45

Disabled Type of UN and

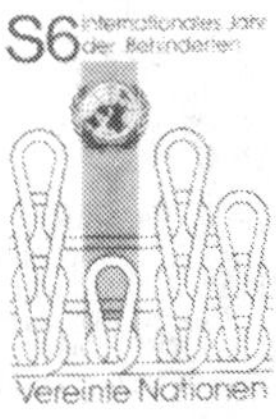

Interlocking Stitches — V4

1981, Mar. 6 Photo.
18 A189 4s multicolored .40 .35
19 V4 6s multicolored .60 .50

Art Type
1981, Apr. 15 Photo. *Perf. 11½*
20 A191 6s multicolored .75 .50

Energy Type
1981, May 29 Litho. *Perf. 13*
21 A193 7.50s multicolored .70 .50

Volunteers Program Types of UN and Geneva
1981, Nov. 13 Litho. *Perf. 13½x13*
22 A195 5s multicolored .55 .35
23 G18 7s multicolored 1.10 .65

"For a Better World" — V5

1982, Jan. 22 Photo. *Perf. 11½x12*
24 V5 3s multicolored .35 .20

Human Environment Types of UN and Geneva
1982, Mar. 19 Litho. *Perf. 13½x13*
25 A200 5s multicolored .45 .40
26 G21 7s multicolored .90 .55

Outer Space Type of Geneva
1982, June 11 Litho. *Perf. 13x13½*
27 G22 5s multicolored .70 .60

Conservation and Protection of Nature Type
1982, Nov. 19 Photo. *Perf. 14*
28 A202 5s Fish .50 .40
29 A202 7s Animal .70 .60

World Communications Year Type
1983, Jan. 28 Litho. *Perf. 13*
30 A203 4s multicolored .40 .40

Safety at Sea Types of Geneva and UN
1983, Mar. 18 Litho. *Perf. 14½*
31 G23 4s multicolored .45 .30
32 A206 6s multicolored .65 .55

World Food Program Type
1983, Apr. 22 Engr. *Perf. 13½*
33 A207 5s green .50 .35
34 A207 7s brown .70 .55

Trade and Development Types of Geneva and UN
1983, June 6 Litho. *Perf. 14*
35 G24 4s multicolored .45 .25
36 A209 8.50s multicolored .75 .65

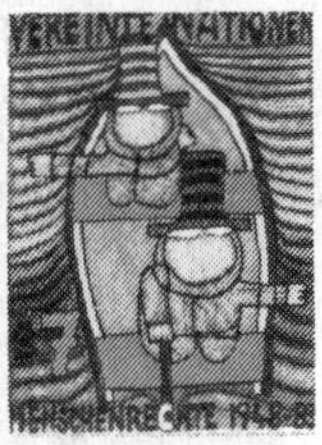

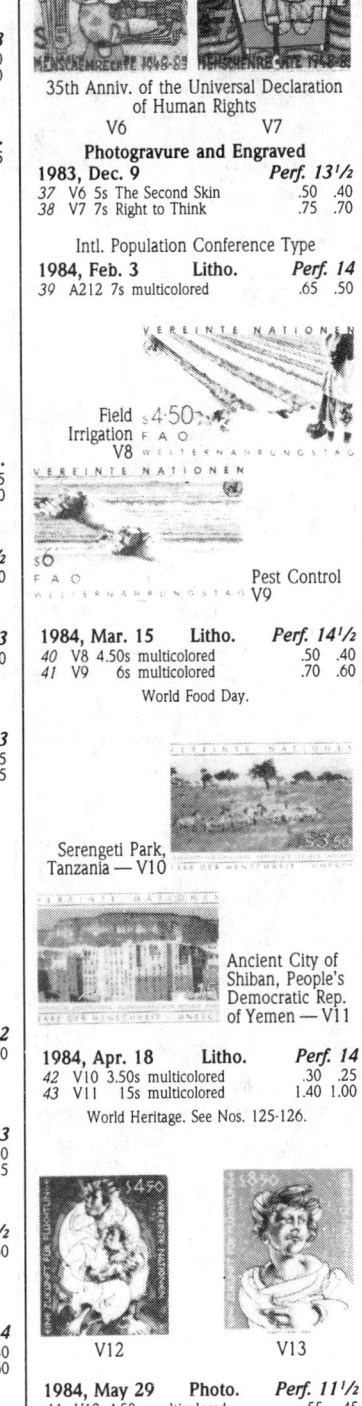

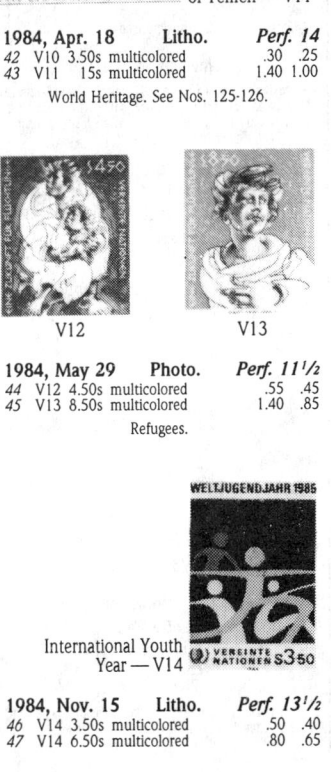

35th Anniv. of the Universal Declaration of Human Rights
V6 V7
Photogravure and Engraved
1983, Dec. 9 *Perf. 13½*
37 V6 5s The Second Skin .50 .40
38 V7 7s Right to Think .75 .70

Intl. Population Conference Type
1984, Feb. 3 Litho. *Perf. 14*
39 A212 7s multicolored .65 .50

Field Irrigation FAO — V8

Pest Control — V9

1984, Mar. 15 Litho. *Perf. 14½*
40 V8 4.50s multicolored .50 .40
41 V9 6s multicolored .70 .60
World Food Day.

Serengeti Park, Tanzania — V10

Ancient City of Shiban, People's Democratic Rep. of Yemen — V11

1984, Apr. 18 Litho. *Perf. 14*
42 V10 3.50s multicolored .30 .25
43 V11 15s multicolored 1.40 1.00
World Heritage. See Nos. 125-126.

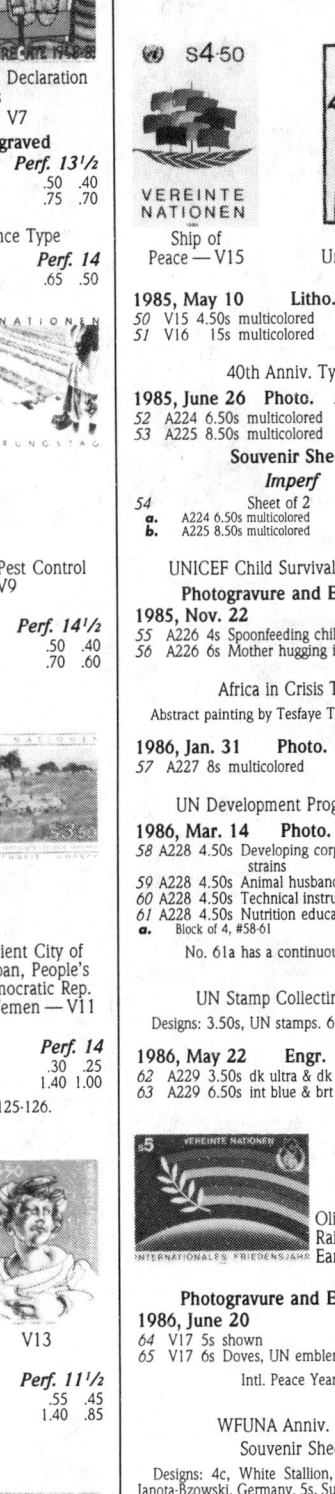

V12 V13

1984, May 29 Photo. *Perf. 11½*
44 V12 4.50s multicolored .55 .45
45 V13 8.50s multicolored 1.40 .85
Refugees.

International Youth Year — V14

1984, Nov. 15 Litho. *Perf. 13½*
46 V14 3.50s multicolored .50 .40
47 V14 6.50s multicolored .80 .65

ILO Type of Geneva
1985, Feb. 1 Engr. *Perf. 13½*
48 G34 7.50s U Thant Pavilion .85 .65

UN University Type
1985, Mar. 15 Photo. *Perf. 13½*
49 A221 8.50s Rural scene, scientist 1.00 .80

Ship of Peace — V15

Sharing Umbrella — V16

1985, May 10 Litho. *Perf. 14*
50 V15 4.50s multicolored .35 .30
51 V16 15s multicolored 2.50 2.25

40th Anniv. Type
1985, June 26 Photo. *Perf. 12x11½*
52 A224 6.50s multicolored 1.00 .55
53 A225 8.50s multicolored 1.50 1.00

Souvenir Sheet
Imperf
54 Sheet of 2 3.00 2.00
a. A224 6.50s multicolored .70 .60
b. A225 8.50s multicolored .90 .75

UNICEF Child Survival Campaign
Photogravure and Engraved
1985, Nov. 22 *Perf. 13½*
55 A226 4s Spoonfeeding children .90 .65
56 A226 6s Mother hugging infant 1.50 1.25

Africa in Crisis Type
Abstract painting by Tesfaye Tessema.
1986, Jan. 31 Photo. *Perf. 11½*
57 A227 8s multicolored .85 .70

UN Development Program Type
1986, Mar. 14 Photo. *Perf. 13½*
58 A228 4.50s Developing corp strains 1.65 .25
59 A228 4.50s Animal husbandry 1.65 .25
60 A228 4.50s Technical instruction 1.65 .25
61 A228 4.50s Nutrition education 1.65 .25
a. Block of 4, #58-61 6.75 1.00
No. 61a has a continuous design.

UN Stamp Collecting Type
Designs: 3.50s, UN stamps. 6.50s, Engraver.
1986, May 22 Engr. *Perf. 12½*
62 A229 3.50s dk ultra & dk brown .45 .35
63 A229 6.50s int blue & brt rose .90 .85

Olive Branch, Rainbow, Earth — V17

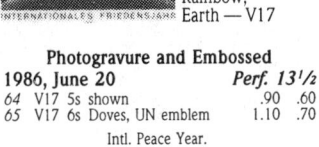

Photogravure and Embossed
1986, June 20 *Perf. 13½*
64 V17 5s shown .90 .60
65 V17 6s Doves, UN emblem 1.10 .70
Intl. Peace Year.

WFUNA Anniv. Type
Souvenir Sheet
Designs: 4c, White Stallion, by Elisabeth von Janota-Bzowski, Germany. 5s, Surrealistic landscape by Ernst Fuchs, Austria. 6s, Geometric abstract by Victor Vasarely (b. 1908), France. 7s, Mythological abstract by Wolfgang Hutter (b. 1928), Austria.
1986, Nov. 14 Litho. *Perf. 13½x13½*
66 Sheet of 4 4.25 4.00
a. A232 4s multicolored .75 .60
b. A232 5s multicolored .85 .70
c. A232 6s multicolored 1.00 .80
d. A232 7s multicolored 1.25 1.00

Trygve Lie Type
Photogravure and Engraved
1987, Jan. 30 *Perf. 13½*
67 A233 8s multicolored .90 .75

Shelter for the Homeless Type
Perf. 13½x12½
1987, Mar. 13 Litho.
68 A234 4s Family, homes .55 .40
69 A234 9.50s Entering home 1.25 1.10

Fight Drug Abuse Type
1987, June 12 Litho. *Perf. 14½x15*
70 A235 5s Soccer players .65 .50
71 A235 8s Family 1.00 .85

Donaupark, Vienna — V18

Peace Embracing the Earth — V19

1987, June 12 *Perf. 14½x15*
72 V18 2s multicolored .30 .25
73 V19 17s multicolored 1.75 1.50

UN Day Type
1987, Oct. 23 Litho. *Perf. 14½x15*
74 A236 5s multicolored .85 .65
75 A236 6s multicolored 1.00 1.00

Immunize Every Child Type
1987, Nov. 20 Litho. *Perf. 15x14½*
76 A237 4s Polio .90 .35
77 A237 9.50s Diphtheria 2.00 .75

IFAD Type
1988, Jan. 29 Litho. *Perf. 13½*
78 A238 4s Grains .75 .55
79 A238 6s Vegetables 1.10 .90

Survival of the Forests Type
Deciduous forest in fall.
1988, Mar. 18 Litho. *Perf. 14x15*
80 A240 4s multicolored 2.50 2.25
81 A240 5s multicolored 3.50 3.25
a. Pair, #80-81 6.00 6.00
No. 81a has a continuous design.

Intl. Volunteer Day Type
Perf. 13x14, 14x13
1988, May 6 Litho.
82 A241 6s Medical care, vert. .85 .70
83 A241 7.50s Construction 1.25 1.10

Health in Sports Type
Perf. 13½x13, 13x13½
1988, June 17 Litho.
84 A242 6s Skiing, vert. .85 .70
85 A242 8s Tennis 1.40 1.25

Human Rights Declaration Anniv. Type
1988, Dec. 9 Photo. & Engr. *Perf. 12*
86 A243 5s multicolored .75 .65
Souvenir Sheet
87 A243 11s multicolored 1.25 .50

World Bank Type
1989, Jan. 27 Litho. *Perf. 13x14*
88 A244 5.50s Transportation 1.25 .75
89 A244 8s Health care, education 1.90 1.75

Peace-Keeping Force Type
1989, Mar. 17 Litho. *Perf. 14x13½*
90 A245 6s multicolored .90 .80

World Weather Watch Anniv. Type
Designs: 4s, Helical cloud formation over Italy, the eastern Alps and parts of Yugoslavia. 9.50s, Rainfall in Tokyo, Japan.
1989, Apr. 21 Litho. *Perf. 13x14*
91 A247 4s multicolored 1.10 .75
92 A247 9.50s multicolored 2.50 2.25

UNITED NATIONS — OFFICES IN VIENNA, AUSTRIA

V20, V21

Photo. & Engr., Photo.
1989, Aug. 23   *Perf. 14*
93 V20 5s multicolored   4.50 .50
94 V21 7.50s multicolored   1.00 .70
Offices in Vienna, 10th anniv.

Human Rights Type
Paintings: 4s, *The Prisoners*, by Kathe Kollwitz. 6s, *Justice*, by Raphael.

1989, Nov. 17   Litho.   *Perf. 13½*
95 A250 4s multicolored   .65 .60
96 A250 6s multicolored   .90 .90
Printed in sheets of 12+12 se-tenant labels containing Articles 5 (4s) or 6 (6s) inscribed in German, English or French.

Intl. Trade Center Type
1990, Feb. 2   Litho.   *Perf. 14½x15*
97 A251 12s multicolored   1.50 1.25

Painting by Kurt Regschek — V22

1990, Feb. 2   Litho.   *Perf. 13x13½*
98 V22 1.50s multicolored   .30 .20

Fight AIDS Worldwide — V23

   Perf. 13½x12½   Litho.
99 V23 5s "AIDS"   1.00 .75
100 V23 11s Stylized figures, ink blot   2.50 2.00

Medicinal Plants Type
1990, May 4   Photo.   *Perf. 11½*
Granite Paper
101 A253 4.50s *Bixa orellana*   1.00 .75
102 A253 9.50s *Momordica charantia*   2.50 2.00

UN 45th Anniv. Type
"45" and emblem.

1990, June 26   Litho.   *Perf. 14½x13*
103 A254 7s multicolored   1.25 1.00
104 A254 9s multi, diff.   2.25 1.75

Souvenir Sheet
105 A254 Sheet of 2, #103-104   5.00 3.00

Crime Prevention Type
1990, Sept. 13   Photo.   *Perf. 14*
106 A255 6s Domestic violence   1.25 1.00
107 A255 8s Crime against cultural heritage   2.25 1.75

Human Rights Type of 1989
Paintings: 4.50s, Before the Judge by Sandor Bihari. 7s, Young Man Greeted by a Woman Writing a Poem by Suzuki Harunobu.

1990, Nov. 16   Litho.   *Perf. 13½*
108 A250 4.50s multicolored   .45 .40
109 A250 7s multicolored   1.40 1.00
Printed in sheets of 12+12 se-tenant labels containing Articles 11 (4.50s) or 12 (7s) inscribed in German, English or French.

Economic Commission for Europe Type
1991, Mar. 15   Litho.   *Perf. 14*
110 A256 5s Weasel, hoopoe   1.00 .75
111 A256 5s Warbler, swans   1.00 .75
112 A256 5s Badgers, squirrel   1.00 .75
113 A256 5s Fish   1.00 .75
   a. Block of 4, #110-113   4.25 4.00

Namibian Independence Type
1991, May 10   Litho.   *Perf. 14*
114 A257 6s Mountain, clouds   1.10 .75
115 A257 9.50s Dune, Namib Desert   2.50 2.00

V24

1991, May 10   Litho.   *Perf. 15x14½*
116 V24 20s multicolored   3.25 2.50

Rights of the Child — V26, V25

1991, June 14   Litho.   *Perf. 14½*
117 V25 7s Stick drawings   1.50 1.25
118 V26 9s Child, clock, fruit   2.00 1.65

Banning of Chemical Weapons — V28, V27

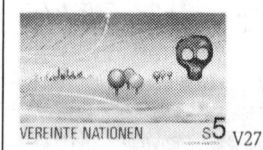

1991, Sept. 11   Litho.   *Perf. 13½*
119 V27 5s multicolored   1.25 .75
120 V28 10s multicolored   2.25 1.50

UN Postal Administration, 40th Anniv. Type
1991, Oct. 24   Litho.   *Perf. 14x15*
121 A263 5s UN NY No. 8   .85 .75
122 A263 8s UN NY No. 5   2.00 1.90

Human Rights Type of 1989
Artwork: 4.50s, Pre-columbian Mexican pottery, c. 600 A.D. 7s, Windows, 1912, by Robert Delaunay.

1991, Nov. 20   Litho.   *Perf. 13½*
123 A250 4.50s black & brown   .80 .75
124 A250 7s multicolored   1.40 1.25
Printed in sheets of 12+12 se-tenant labels containing Articles 17 (4.50s) and 18 (7s) inscribed in German, English or French.

World Heritage Type of 1984
Designs: 5s, Iguacu Natl. Park, Brazil. 9s, Abu Simbel, Egypt.

1992, Jan. 24   Litho.   *Perf. 13*
Size: 35x28mm
125 V10 5s multicolored   1.25 1.00
126 V10 9s multicolored   2.25 1.75

Clean Oceans Type
1992, Mar. 13   Litho.   *Perf. 14*
127 A264 7s Ocean surface, diff.   1.10 .60
128 A264 7s Ocean bottom, diff.   1.10 .60
   a. Pair, #127-128   2.25 1.20
Printed in sheets of 12 containing 6 #128a.

Earth Summit Type
1992, May 22   Photo.   *Perf. 11½*
129 A265 5.50s Man in space   1.25 1.00
130 A265 5.50s Sun   1.25 1.00
131 A265 5.50s Man fishing   1.25 1.00
132 A265 5.50s Sailboat   1.25 1.00
   a. Block of 4, #129-132   5.00 4.25

Mission to Planet Earth Type
Designs: No. 133, Satellite, person's mouth. No. 134, Satellite, person's ear.

1992, Sept. 4   Photo.   *Rouletted 8*
Granite Paper
133 A266 10s multicolored   2.75 1.00
134 A266 10s multicolored   2.75 1.00
   a. Pair, #133-134   5.50 2.00

Science and Technology Type
Designs: 5.50s, Woman emerging from computer screen. 7s, Green thumb growing flowers.

1992, Oct. 2   Litho.   *Perf. 14*
135 A267 5.50s multicolored   .80 .75
136 A267 7s multicolored   1.50 1.50

V29, Intl. Center, Vienna — V30

1992, Oct. 2   Litho.   *Perf. 13x13½*
137 V29 5.50s multicolored   1.00 .75
   Perf. 13½x13
138 V30 7s multicolored   1.50 1.50

Human Rights Type of 1989
Artwork: 6s, Les Constructeurs, by Fernand Leger. 10s, Sunday Afternoon on the Island of La Grande Jatte, by Georges Seurat.

1992, Nov. 20   Litho.   *Perf. 13½*
139 A250 6s multicolored   1.10 .85
140 A250 10s multicolored   1.90 1.50
Printed in sheets of 12+12 se-tenant labels containing Articles 23 (6s) and 24 (10s) inscribed in German, English or French.

Aging With Dignity Type
Designs: 5.50s, Elderly couple, family working in garden. 7s, Older woman teaching.

1993, Feb. 5   Litho.   *Perf. 13*
141 A270 5.50s multicolored   1.00 1.00
142 A270 7s multicolored   1.65 1.50

Endangered Species Type
Designs: No. 143, Equus grevyi (Grevy's zebra). No. 144, Spheniscus humboldti (Humboldt's penguins). No. 145, Varanus griseus (desert monitor). No. 146, Canis lupus (gray wolf).

1993, Mar. 3   Litho.   *Perf. 13x12½*
143 A271 7s multicolored   1.25 1.00
144 A271 7s multicolored   1.25 1.00
145 A271 7s multicolored   1.25 1.00
146 A271 7s multicolored   1.25 1.00
   a. Block of 4, #143-146   5.00 4.00

Healthy Environment Type
1993, May 7   Litho.   *Perf. 15x14½*
147 A272 6s Wave in ocean   1.40 .75
148 A272 10s Globe   2.25 1.50

V31

1993, May 7   Photo.   *Perf. 11½*
Granite Paper
149 V31 13s multicolored   2.50 2.25

Human Rights Type of 1989
Artwork: 5s, Lower Austrian Peasants' Wedding, by Ferdinand G. Waldmuller. 6s, Outback, by Sally Morgan.

1993, June 11   Litho.   *Perf. 13½*
150 A250 5s multicolored   1.25 .75
151 A250 6s multicolored   1.50 .50
Printed in sheets of 12 + 12 se-tenant labels containing Article 29 (5s) and 30 (6s) inscribed in German, English or French.

Intl. Peace Day Type
Denomination at: No. 152, UL. No. 153, UR. No. 154, LL. No. 155, LR.

1993, Sept. 21   *Rouletted 12½*   Litho. & Engr.
152 A274 5.50s green & multi   2.00 .90
153 A274 5.50s green & multi   2.00 .90
154 A274 5.50s green & multi   2.00 .90
155 A274 5.50s green & multi   2.00 .90
   a. Block of 4, #152-155   8.50 3.75

Environment-Climate Type
Designs: No. 156, Monkeys. No. 157, Bluebird, industrial pollution, volcano. No. 158, Volcano, nuclear power plant, tree stumps. No. 159, Cactus, tree stumps, owl.

1993, Oct. 29   Litho.   *Perf. 14½*
156 A275 7s multicolored   1.50 1.25
157 A275 7s multicolored   1.50 1.25
158 A275 7s multicolored   1.50 1.25
159 A275 7s multicolored   1.50 1.25
   a. Strip of 4, #156-159   6.00 5.00

Intl. Year of the Family Type of 1993
Designs: 5.50s, Adults, children holding hands. 8s, Two adults, child planting crops.

1994, Feb. 4   Litho.   *Perf. 13.1*
160 A276 5.50s blue green & multi   1.25 1.25
161 A276 8s red & multi   2.00 1.50

Endangered Species Type of 1993
Designs: No. 162, Ocelot. No. 163, White-breasted silver-eye. No. 164, Mediterranean monk seal. No. 165, Asian elephant.

1994, Mar. 18   Litho.   *Perf. 12.7*
162 A271 7s multicolored   1.40 1.25
163 A271 7s multicolored   1.40 1.25
164 A271 7s multicolored   1.40 1.25
165 A271 7s multicolored   1.40 1.25
   a. Block of 4, #162-165   5.75 5.00

Protection for Refugees Type of 1994
Design: 12s, Protective hands surround group of refugees.

1994, Apr. 29   Litho.   *Perf. 14.3x14.8*
166 A277 12s multicolored   2.00 1.50

V32, V33, 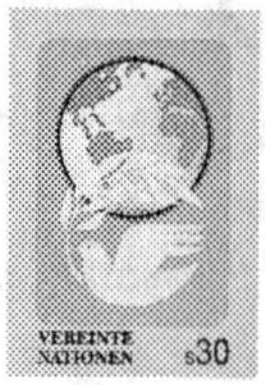 V34

1994, Apr. 29   Litho.   *Perf. 12.7*
167 V32 50g multicolored   .15 .15
168 V33 4s multicolored   .70 .50
169 V34 30s multicolored   5.00 4.00
   Nos. 167-169 (3)   5.85 4.65

Intl. Decade for Natural Disaster Reduction Type of 1994
Earth seen from space, outline map of: No. 170, North America. No. 171, Eurasia. No. 172, South America. No. 173, Australia and South Asia.

1994, May 27   Litho.   *Perf. 13.9x14.2*
170 A281 6s multicolored   1.75 .80
171 A281 6s multicolored   1.75 .80
172 A281 6s multicolored   1.75 .80
173 A281 6s multicolored   1.75 .80
   a. Block of 4, #170-173   7.00 3.50

Population and Development Type of 1994
Designs: 5.50s, Women teaching, running machine tool, coming home to family. 7s, Family on tropical island.

UNITED NATIONS — OFFICES IN VIENNA, AUSTRIA — ABU DHABI

1994, Sept. 1   Litho.   Perf. 13.2x13.6
| 174 | A282 | 5.50s multicolored | 1.25 | .75 |
| 175 | A282 | 7s multicolored | 1.50 | 1.25 |

UNCTAD Type of 1994
1994, Oct. 28
| 176 | A283 | 6s multi, diff. | 1.10 | .55 |
| 177 | A283 | 7s multi, diff. | 1.50 | .65 |

UN 50th Anniv. Type of 1995
1995, Jan. 1   Litho. & Engr.   Perf. 13.4
| 178 | A284 | 7s multicolored | 1.65 | .75 |

Social Summit Type of 1995
Perf. 13.6x13.9
1995, Feb. 3   Photo. & Engr.
| 179 | A285 | 14s multi, diff. | 2.50 | 1.50 |

Endangered Species Type of 1993
Designs: No. 180, Black rhinoceros, Diceros bicornis. No. 181, Golden conure, Aratinga guarouba. No. 182, Douc langur, Pygathrix nemaeus. No. 183, Arabian oryx, Oryx leucoryx.

1995, Mar. 24   Litho.   Perf. 13x12 1/2
180	A271	7s multicolored	1.25	1.25
181	A271	7s multicolored	1.25	1.25
182	A271	7s multicolored	1.25	1.25
183	A271	7s multicolored	1.25	1.25
a.		Block of 4, 180-183	5.00	5.00

Intl. Youth Year Type of 1995
Designs: 6s, Village in winter. 7s, Teepees.

1995, May 26   Litho.   Perf. 14.4x14.7
| 184 | A286 | 6s multicolored | 1.40 | 1.00 |
| 185 | A286 | 7s multicolored | 1.65 | 1.25 |

UN, 50th Anniv. Type of 1995
Designs: 7s, Like No. 663. 10s, Like No. 664.

1995, June 26   Engr.   Perf. 13.3x13.6
| 186 | A287 | 7s green | 1.40 | 1.25 |
| 187 | A287 | 10s black | 2.00 | 1.50 |

Souvenir Sheet
Litho. & Engr.
Imperf
188		Sheet of 2, #186-187	3.50	3.50
a.		A287 7s green	1.40	1.40
b.		A287 10s black	1.75	1.75

Conference on Women Type of 1995
Designs: 5.50s, Women amid tropical plants. 6s, Woman reading, swans on lake.

1995, Sept. 5   Photo.   Perf. 12
| 189 | A288 | 5.50s multicolored | 1.25 | .55 |

Size: 28x50mm
| 190 | A288 | 6s multicolored | 1.75 | .65 |

UN People, 50th Anniv. Type of 1995
1995, Oct. 24   Litho.   Perf. 14
191		Sheet of 12	16.00	11.00
a.-l.		A290 3s any single	1.25	.85
192		Souvenir booklet	16.00	
a.		A290 3s Booklet pane of 3, vert. strip of 3 from UL of sheet	3.75	3.00
b.		A290 3s Booklet pane of 3, vert. strip of 3 from UR of sheet	3.75	3.00
c.		A290 3s Booklet pane of 3, vert. strip of 3 from LL of sheet	3.75	3.00
d.		A290 3s Booklet pane of 3, vert. strip of 3 from LR of sheet	3.75	3.00

WFUNA, 50th Anniv. Type of 1996
Design: 7s, Harlequin holding dove.

1996, Feb. 2   Litho.   Perf. 13x13 1/2
| 193 | A291 | 7s multicolored | 1.35 | .65 |

UN Flag — V35
Abstract, by Karl Korab — V36 

1996, Feb. 2   Litho.   Perf. 15x14 1/2
| 194 | V35 | 1s multicolored | .20 | .15 |
| 195 | V36 | 10s multicolored | 2.00 | 1.00 |

Endangered Species Type of 1993
Designs: No. 196, Cypripedium calceolus. No. 197, Aztekium ritteri. No. 198, Euphorbia cremersii. No. 199, Dracula bella.

1996, Mar. 14   Litho.   Perf. 12 1/2
196	A271	7s multicolored	1.30	.65
197	A271	7s multicolored	1.30	.65
198	A271	7s multicolored	1.30	.65
199	A271	7s multicolored	1.30	.65
a.		Block of 4, #196-199	5.25	—

City Summit Type of 1996
Designs: No. 200, Arab family selling fruits, vegetables. No. 201, Woman beside stream, camels. No. 202, Woman carrying bundle on head, city skyline. No. 203, Woman threshing grain, yoke of oxen in field. No. 204, Native village, elephant.

1996, June 3   Litho.   Perf. 14x13 1/2
200	A293	6s multicolored	1.10	.30
201	A293	6s multicolored	1.10	.30
202	A293	6s multicolored	1.10	.30
203	A293	6s multicolored	1.10	.30
204	A293	6s multicolored	1.10	.30
a.		Strip of 5, #200-204	5.50	—

Sport and the Environment Type of 1996
Designs: 6s, Men's parallel bars (gymnastics), vert. 7s, Hurdles.

Perf. 14x14 1/2, 14 1/2x14
1996, July 19   Litho.
| 205 | A294 | 6s multicolored | 1.10 | .55 |
| 206 | A294 | 7s multicolored | 1.40 | .65 |

Souvenir Sheet
| 207 | A294 | Sheet of 2, #205-206 | 2.50 | 2.40 |

Plea for Peace Type of 1996
7s, Dove & butterflies. 10s, Stylized dove, diff.

1996, Sept. 17   Litho.   Perf. 14 1/2x15
| 208 | A295 | 7s multicolored | 1.25 | .65 |
| 209 | A295 | 10s multicolored | 1.90 | .95 |

UNICEF Type of 1996
Fairy Tales: 5.50s, Hansel and Gretel, by the Brothers Grimm. 8s, How Maui Stole Fire from the Gods, South Pacific.

1996, Nov. 20   Litho.   Perf. 14 1/2x15
| 210 | A296 | 5.50s multicolored | 1.00 | .50 |
| 211 | A296 | 8s multicolored | 1.50 | .75 |

Panes of 8 + label.

V37
Phoenixes Flying Down (Detail), by Sagenji Yoshida — V38 

1997, Feb. 12   Litho.   Perf. 14 1/2
| 212 | V37 | 5s multicolored | .85 | .40 |
| 213 | V38 | 6s multicolored | 1.00 | .50 |

Endangered Species Type of 1993
No. 214, Macaca sylvanus (Barbary macaque). No. 215, Anthropoides paradisea (blue crane). No. 216, Equus przewalskii (Przewalski horse). No. 217, Myrmecophaga tridactyla (giant anteater).

1997, Mar. 13   Litho.   Perf. 12 1/2
214	A271	7s multicolored	1.10	.55
215	A271	7s multicolored	1.10	.55
216	A271	7s multicolored	1.10	.55
217	A271	7s multicolored	1.10	.55
a.		Block of 4, #214-217	4.50	2.25

Earth Summit Anniv. Type of 1997
Designs: No. 218, Person running. No. 219, Hills, stream, trees. No. 220, Tree with orange leaves. No. 221, Tree with pink leaves. 11s, Combined design similar to Nos. 218-221.

1997, May 30   Photo.   Perf. 1.5
Granite Paper
218	A299	3.50s multicolored	.60	.30
219	A299	3.50s multicolored	.60	.30
220	A299	3.50s multicolored	.60	.30
221	A299	3.50s multicolored	.60	.30
a.		Block of 4, #218-221	2.50	1.25

Souvenir Sheet
| 222 | A299 | 11s multicolored | 1.75 | 1.75 |

Transportation Type of 1997
Ground transportation: No. 223, 1829 Rocket. 1901 Darraque. No. 224, Steam engine from Vladikawska Railway, trolley. No. 225, Double-decker bus. No. 226, 1950s diesel locomotive, semi-trailer. No. 227, High-speed train, electric car.

1997, Aug. 29   Litho.   Perf. 14x14 1/2
223	A300	7s multicolored	1.10	.55
224	A300	7s multicolored	1.10	.55
225	A300	7s multicolored	1.10	.55
226	A300	7s multicolored	1.10	.55
227	A300	7s multicolored	1.10	.55
a.		Strip of 5, #223-227	5.50	2.75

No. 227a has continuous design.

Philately Type of 1997
Designs: 6.50s, No. 62. 7s, No. 63.

1997, Oct. 14   Litho.   Perf. 13 1/2x14
| 228 | A301 | 6.50s multicolored | 1.00 | .50 |
| 229 | A301 | 7s multicolored | 1.10 | .55 |

World Heritage Convention Type of 1997
Terracotta warriors of Xian: 3s, Single warrior. 6s, Massed warriors. No. 232a, like #716. No. 232b, like #717. No. 232c, like Geneva #314. No. 232d, like Geneva #315. No. 232e, like Vienna #230. No. 232f, like Vienna #231.

1997, Nov. 19   Litho.   Perf. 13 1/2
230	A302	3s multicolored	.50	.25
231	A302	6s multicolored	1.00	.50
232		Souvenir booklet	4.00	
a.-f.		A302 1s any single	.15	.15
g.		Booklet pane of 4 #232a	.65	.65
h.		Booklet pane of 4 #232b	.65	.65
i.		Booklet pane of 4 #232c	.65	.65
j.		Booklet pane of 4 #232d	.65	.65
k.		Booklet pane of 4 #232e	.65	.65
l.		Booklet pane of 4 #232f	.65	.65

Japanese Peace Bell, Vienna — V39
Vienna Subway, Vienna Intl. Center — V40 

1998, Feb. 13   Litho.   Perf. 15x14 1/2
| 233 | V39 | 6.50s multicolored | 1.00 | .50 |
| 234 | V40 | 9s multicolored | 1.40 | .70 |

Endangered Species Type of 1993
Designs: No. 235, Chelonia mydas (green turtle). No. 236, Speotyto cunicularia (burrowing owl). No. 237, Trogonoptera brookiana (Rajah Brooke's birdwing). No. 238, Ailurus fulgens (lesser panda).

1998, Mar. 13   Litho.   Perf. 12 1/2
235	A271	7s multicolored	1.10	.55
236	A271	7s multicolored	1.10	.55
237	A271	7s multicolored	1.10	.55
238	A271	7s multicolored	1.10	.55
a.		Block of 4, #235-238	4.50	2.25

Intl. Year of the Ocean — V41

1998, May 20   Litho.   Perf. 13x13 1/2
| 239 | V41 | Sheet of 12 | 7.50 | 4.00 |
| a.-l. | | 3.50s any single | .60 | .35 |

Rain Forests Type of 1998
1998, June 19   Perf. 13x13 1/2
| 240 | A307 | 6.50s Ocelot | 1.00 | .50 |

Souvenir Sheet
| 241 | A307 | 12s like #240 | 3.50 | 1.75 |

Peacekeeping Type of 1998
Designs: 4s, Soldier passing out relief supplies. 7.50s, UN supervised voting.

1998, Sept. 15   Photo.   Perf. 12
| 242 | A308 | 4s multicolored | .70 | .35 |
| 243 | A308 | 7.50s multicolored | 1.30 | .65 |

Declaration of Human Rights Type of 1998
Designs: 4.50s, Stylized person. 7s, Gears.

Litho. & Photo.
1998, Oct. 27   Perf. 13
| 244 | A309 | 4.50s multicolored | .80 | .40 |
| 245 | A309 | 7s multicolored | 1.25 | .60 |

Schönnbrun Palace Type of 1998
Designs: 3.50s, #248d, Palace. 7s, #248c, Porcelain stove, vert. No. 248a, Blue porcelain vase, vert. No. 248b, Wall painting on fabric (detail), by Johann Wenzl Bergl, vert. No. 248e, Great Palm House (conservatory). No. 248f, The Gloriette (archway).

1998, Dec. 4   Litho.   Perf. 14
246	A310	3.50s multicolored	.60	.30
247	A310	7s multicolored	1.10	.55
248		Souvenir booklet	5.75	
a.-c.		A310 1s any single	.20	.20
d.-f.		A310 2s any single	.30	.30
g.		Booklet pane, 4 #248d	1.25	
h.		Booklet pane, 3 #248b	.60	
i.		Booklet pane, 3 #248c	.60	
j.		Booklet pane, 3 #248d	.60	
k.		Booklet pane, 3 #248e	1.25	
l.		Booklet pane, 4 #248f	1.25	

ABU DHABI
,ä–bü–'thä–bē

LOCATION — Arabia, on Persian Gulf
GOVT. — Sheikdom under British protection
POP. — 25,000 (estimated)
CAPITAL — Abu Dhabi

Abu Dhabi is one of six Persian Gulf sheikdoms to join the United Arab Emirates, which proclaimed its independence Dec. 2, 1971. See United Arab Emirates.

100 Naye Paise = 1 Rupee
1000 Fils = 1 Dinar (1966)

Catalogue values for all unused stamps in this country are for Never Hinged items.

Sheik Shakbut bin Sultan — A1
Palace — A2 

Designs: 40np, 50np, 75np, Gazelle. 5r, 10r, Oil rig and camels.

Perf. 14 1/2
1964, Mar. 30   Photo.   Unwmk.
1	A1	5np brt yellow green	.15	.15
2	A1	15np brown	.30	.15
3	A1	20np brt ultra	.40	.20
4	A1	30np red orange	.50	.25
5	A1	40np brt violet	.65	.35
6	A1	50np brown olive	.75	.35
7	A1	75np gray	1.25	.55

Engr.   Perf. 13x13 1/2
8	A2	1r light green	1.75	.75
9	A2	2r black	4.00	1.75
10	A2	5r carmine rose	10.00	4.75
11	A2	10r dark blue	22.50	12.00
		Nos. 1-11 (11)	42.25	21.25

For surcharges see Nos. 15-25.

Falcon Perched on Wrist — A3

40np, Falcon facing left. 2r, Falcon facing right.

ABU DHABI — ADEN

1965, Mar. 30   Photo.   Perf. 14½
12	A3	20np chlky blue & brn	2.75	.50
13	A3	40np ultra & brown	6.75	2.00
14	A3	2r brt blue grn & gray brn	30.00	15.00
		Nos. 12-14 (3)	39.50	17.50

Nos. 1-11 Surcharged

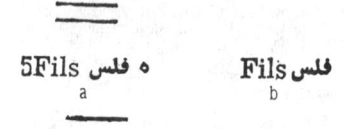

≡

5Fils ٥ فلس   Fils فلس
 a   b

100 Fils   ١٠٠ فلس
 c

1966, Oct. 1   Photo.   Perf. 14½
15	A1 (a)	5f on 5np	.20	.20
16	A1 (a)	15f on 15np	.65	.45
17	A1 (a)	20f on 20np	.90	.60
18	A1 (a)	30f on 30np	1.00	.75
19	A1 (b)	40f on 40np	1.75	1.00
20	A1 (b)	50f on 50np	7.50	9.00
21	A1 (b)	75f on 75np	9.00	9.00

Engr.   Perf. 13x13½
22	A2 (c)	100f on 1r	9.00	6.00
23	A2 (c)	200f on 2r	20.00	12.50
24	A2 (c)	500f on 5r	45.00	42.50
25	A2 (c)	1d on 10r	87.50	95.00
		Nos. 15-25 (11)	182.50	177.00

Overprint on No. 25 has "1 Dinar" on 1 line and 3 bars through old denomination.

Sheik Zaid bin Sultan al Nahayan — A4 ; A6

Dorcas Gazelle — A5

Designs: 5f, 15f, 20f, 35f, Crossed flags of Abu Dhabi. 200f, Falcon. 500f, 1d, Palace.

Engr.; Flags Litho.
1967, Apr. 1   Perf. 13x13½
26	A4	5f dull grn & red	.15	.15
27	A4	15f dk brown & red	.30	.20
28	A4	20f dk brown & red	.35	.25
29	A4	35f purple & red	.65	.45

Engr.
30	A4	40f green	.75	.55
31	A4	50f brown	1.00	.70
32	A4	60f blue	1.30	.80
33	A4	100f car rose	2.25	1.50

Litho.
34	A5	125f green & brn ol	2.75	1.90
35	A5	200f sky blue & brn	4.50	3.00
36	A5	500f org & brt pur	11.00	7.50
37	A5	1d green & vio bl	25.00	15.00
		Nos. 26-37 (12)	50.00	32.00

In 1969, the 15f was surcharged "25" in Arabic in black with a numbering machine.

1967, Aug. 6   Photo.   Perf. 14½x14
38	A6	40f Prussian green	1.40	1.10
39	A6	50f brown	1.40	.75
40	A6	60f blue	2.25	1.00
41	A6	100f carmine rose	4.00	1.90
		Nos. 38-41 (4)	9.05	4.75

Human Rights Flame and Sheik Zaid — A6a

Perf. 14½x14
1968, Apr. 1   Photo.   Unwmk.
42	A6a	35f peacock bl & gold	1.25	.60
43	A6a	60f dk blue & gold	2.00	.75
44	A6a	150f dk brown & gold	4.75	1.75
		Nos. 42-44 (3)	8.00	3.10

International Human Rights Year.

Sheik Zaid and Coat of Arms — A7

Perf. 14x14½
1968, Aug. 6   Photo.   Unwmk.
45	A7	5f green, sil, red & blk	.45	.15
46	A7	10f brn org, sil, red & blk	.70	.20
47	A7	100f lilac, gold, red & blk	4.25	1.50
48	A7	125f lt blue, gold, red & blk	6.00	2.25
		Nos. 45-48 (4)	11.40	4.10

Accession of Sheik Zaid, 2nd anniversary.

Abu Dhabi Airport — A8

5f, Buildings under construction and earth-moving equipment. 35f, New bridge and falcon. Each stamp shows different portrait of Sheik Zaid.

Perf. 12, 12½x13 (10f)
1969, Mar. 28   Litho.
Size: 5f, 35f, 59x34mm
49	A8	5f multicolored	1.00	.25
50	A8	10f multicolored	1.50	.60
51	A8	35f multicolored	6.00	2.50
		Nos. 49-51 (3)	8.50	3.35

Issued to publicize progress made in Abu Dhabi during preceding 2 years.

Sheik Zaid and Abu Dhabi Petroleum Co. — A9

Designs: 60f, Abu Dhabi Marine Areas drilling platform and helicopter. 125f, Zakum Field separator at night. 200f, Tank farm.

1969, Aug. 6   Litho.   Perf. 14x13½
52	A9	35f olive grn & multi	.65	.25
53	A9	60f yel brown & multi	1.25	.55
54	A9	125f multicolored	2.75	1.10
55	A9	200f red brown & multi	5.00	2.00
		Nos. 52-55 (4)	9.65	3.90

Accession of Sheik Zaid, 3rd anniversary.

Sheik Zaid — A10

Sheik Zaid and Stallion — A11

Designs: 5f, 25f, 60f, 90f, Oval frame around portrait. 150f, Gazelle and Sheik. 500f, Fort Jahili and Sheik. 1d, Grand Mosque and Sheik.

1970-71   Litho.   Perf. 14
56	A10	5f lt green & multi	.15	.15
57	A10	10f bister & multi	.30	.15
58	A10	25f lilac & multi	.65	.20
59	A10	35f violet & multi	.90	.30
60	A10	50f sepia & multi	1.50	.40
61	A10	60f violet & multi	1.75	.45
62	A10	70f rose red & multi	2.25	.60
63	A10	90f car rose & multi	2.50	.70
64	A11	125f multi ('71)	3.00	.85
65	A11	150f multi ('71)	3.50	1.00
66	A11	500f multi ('71)	11.00	3.50
67	A11	1d multi ('71)	22.50	6.50
		Nos. 56-67 (12)	50.00	14.80

For surcharge see No. 80.

Sheik Zaid and Mt. Fuji — A12

1970, Aug.   Litho.   Perf. 13½x13
68	A12	25f multicolored	1.75	1.00
69	A12	35f multicolored	2.00	1.25
70	A12	60f multicolored	3.75	1.75
		Nos. 68-70 (3)	7.50	4.00

Issued to publicize EXPO '70 International Exhibition, Osaka, Japan, Mar. 15-Sept. 13.

Abu Dhabi Airport — A13

Designs: 60f, Airport entrance. 150f, Aerial view of Abu Dhabi Town, vert.

Perf. 14x13½, 13½x14
1970, Sept. 22   Litho.
71	A13	25f multicolored	1.25	.50
72	A13	60f multicolored	4.00	1.25
73	A13	150f multicolored	7.25	3.00
		Nos. 71-73 (3)	12.50	4.75

Accession of Sheik Zaid, 4th anniversary.

Gamal Abdel Nasser — A14

1971, May 3   Litho.   Perf. 14
| 74 | A14 | 25f deep rose & blk | 2.75 | 2.00 |
| 75 | A14 | 35f rose violet & blk | 4.00 | 3.00 |

In memory of Gamal Abdel Nasser (1918-1970), President of UAR.

Scout Cars — A15

Designs: 60f, Patrol boat. 125f, Armored car in desert. 150f, Meteor jet fighters.

1971, Aug. 6   Litho.   Perf. 13
76	A15	35f multicolored	2.25	1.00
77	A15	60f multicolored	3.25	1.50
78	A15	125f multicolored	4.50	2.00
79	A15	150f multicolored	5.00	3.00
		Nos. 76-79 (4)	15.00	7.75

Accession of Sheik Zaid, 5th anniversary.

٥ فلس

No. 60 Surcharged in Green

5 Fils

1971, Dec. 8   Perf. 14
| 80 | A10 | 5f on 50f multi | 65.00 | 30.00 |

Dome of the Rock, Jerusalem — A16

Designs: Different views of Dome of the Rock.

1972, June 3   Perf. 13
81	A16	35f lt violet & multi	8.50	2.00
82	A16	60f lt violet & multi	12.50	2.50
83	A16	125f lilac & multi	24.00	5.50
		Nos. 81-83 (3)	45.00	10.00

Nos. 80-83 were issued after Abu Dhabi joined the United Arab Emirates Dec. 2, 1971. Stamps of UAE replaced those of Abu Dhabi. UAE Nos. 1-12 were used only in Abu Dhabi except the 10f and 25f which were issued later in Dubai and Sharjah.

ADEN

'ä-d°n

LOCATION — Southern Arabia
GOVT. — Former British colony and protectorate
AREA — 112,075 sq. mi.
POP. — 220,000 (est. 1964)
CAPITAL — Aden

Aden used India stamps before 1937.

In January, 1963, the colony of Aden (the port) and the sheikdoms and emirates of the Western Aden Protectorate formed the Federation of South Arabia. This did not include the Eastern Aden Protectorate with Kathiri and Qu'aiti States. Stamps of Aden, except those of Kathiri and Qu'aiti States, were replaced Apr. 1, 1965, by those of the Federation of South Arabia. See South Arabia, Vol. 1B, and People's Democratic Republic of Yemen, Vol. 5.

12 Pies = 1 Anna
16 Annas = 1 Rupee
100 Cents = 1 Shilling (1951)

Catalogue values for unused stamps in this country are for Never Hinged items, beginning with Scott 28 in the regular postage section and for all of the items in the states' sections.

Dhow — A1

Perf. 13x11 1/2

1937, Apr. 1 Engr. Wmk. 4

1	A1	1/2a lt green	1.65	1.25
2	A1	9p dark green	1.65	1.50
3	A1	1a black brown	1.65	.65
4	A1	2a red	1.65	1.65
5	A1	2 1/2a blue	1.50	.75
6	A1	3a carmine rose	4.25	5.75
7	A1	3 1/2a gray blue	3.00	1.75
8	A1	8a rose lilac	9.00	5.00
9	A1	1r brown	13.00	5.50
10	A1	2r orange yellow	22.50	14.00
11	A1	5r rose violet	50.00	57.50
12	A1	10r olive green	140.00	225.00
		Nos. 1-12 (12)	249.85	320.30
		Set, never hinged	325.00	

Common Design Types pictured following the introduction.

Coronation Issue
Common Design Type

1937, May 12 *Perf. 13 1/2x14*

13	CD302	1a black brown	.50	.75
14	CD302	2 1/2a blue	.75	1.40
15	CD302	3 1/2a gray blue	1.25	1.25
		Nos. 13-15 (3)	2.50	3.40
		Set, never hinged	3.25	

Aidrus Mosque — A2

Designs: 3/4a, 5r, Camel Corpsman. 1a, 2r, Aden Harbor. 1 1/2a, 1r, Adenese dhow. 2 1/2a, 8a, Mukalla. 3a, 14a, 10r, Capture of Aden, 1839.

1939-45 Engr. Wmk. 4 *Perf. 12 1/2*

16	A2	1/2a green	.25	.55
17	A2	3/4a brown violet	.60	1.25
18	A2	1a lt blue	.25	.25
19	A2	1 1/2a red	.50	.55
20	A2	2a dark brown	.25	.25
21	A2	2 1/2a brt ultra	.45	.30
22	A2	3a rose car & dk brn	.55	.25
23	A2	8a orange	.90	.40
23A	A2	14a lt bl & brn blk ('45)	1.10	1.00
24	A2	1r bright green	1.25	1.40
25	A2	2r rose vio & indigo	4.00	1.65
26	A2	5r dp ol & lake brn	10.00	6.50
27	A2	10r brt pur & brn	16.00	11.00
		Nos. 16-27 (13)	36.10	25.35
		Set, never hinged	55.00	

Catalogue values for unused stamps in this section, from this point to the end of the section, are for Never Hinged items.

Peace Issue
Common Design Type
Perf. 13 1/2x14

1946, Oct. 15 Engr. Wmk. 4

28	CD303	1 1/2a carmine	.15	.65
29	CD303	2 1/2a deep blue	.30	.30

Return to peace at end of World War II.

Silver Wedding Issue
Common Design Types

1949, Jan. 17 Photo. *Perf. 14x14 1/2*

30	CD304	1 1/2a scarlet	.40	.75

Engraved; Name Typographed
Perf. 11 1/2x11

31	CD305	10r purple	25.00	26.00

25th anniv. of the marriage of King George VI and Queen Elizabeth.

UPU Issue
Common Design Types
Surcharged with New Values in Annas and Rupees

Engr.; Name typo. on Nos. 33-34

1949, Oct. 10 *Perf. 13 1/2, 11x11 1/2*

32	CD306	2 1/2a on 20c dp ultra	.75	1.40
33	CD307	3a on 30c dp car	1.65	1.40
34	CD308	8a on 50c org	1.50	1.40
35	CD309	1r on 1sh blue	2.50	2.75
		Nos. 32-35 (4)	6.40	6.95

75th anniv. of the formation of the UPU.

Nos. 18 and 20-27 Surcharged with New Values in Black or Carmine

1951, Oct. 1 Wmk. 4 *Perf. 12 1/2*

36	A2	5c on 1a	.25	.40
37	A2	10c on 2a	.35	.45
38	A2	15c on 2 1/2a	.85	.95
a.		Double surcharge	650.00	
39	A2	20c on 3a	1.00	1.00
40	A2	30c on 8a (C)	1.00	1.00
41	A2	50c on 8a	1.00	.75
42	A2	70c on 14a	1.75	1.25
43	A2	1sh on 1r	.65	.75
44	A2	2sh on 2r	6.25	5.50
45	A2	5sh on 5r	15.00	11.00
46	A2	10sh on 10r	22.50	20.00
		Nos. 36-46 (11)	50.60	43.05

Surcharge on No. 40 includes 2 bars.

Coronation Issue
Common Design Type

1953, June 2 Engr. *Perf. 13 1/2x13*

47	CD312	15c dark green & black	.45	.35

Minaret — A10

Camel Transport — A11

15c, Crater. 25c, Mosque. 35c, Dhow. 50c, Map. 70c, Salt works. 1sh, Dhow building. 1sh, 25c, Colony Badge. 2sh, Aden Protectorate levy. 5sh, Crater Pass. 10sh, Tribesman. 20sh, Aden in 1572.

Perf. 12, 12x13 1/2 ('56)

1953-58 Engr. Wmk. 4

Size: 29x23, 23x29mm

48	A10	5c grn, perf. 12x13 1/2 ('56)	.15	.15
a.		Perf. 12	.15	.15
49	A11	10c orange	.15	.15
50	A11	15c blue green	.90	.50
51	A11	25c carmine	.60	.35
52	A10	35c ultra, perf. 12	1.75	1.75
a.		35c dp bl, perf. 12x13 1/2 ('58)	3.00	2.00
53	A10	50c blue, perf. 12	.15	.15
a.		Perf. 12x13 1/2 ('56)	.55	.15
54	A10	70c gray, perf. 12	.15	.15
a.		Perf. 12x13 1/2 ('56)	.60	.15
55	A11	1sh pur & sepia	.20	.15
55A	A11	1sh vio & black ('55)	1.10	.15
56	A10	1sh25c blk & lt blue ('56)	1.65	.50
57	A10	2sh car rose & sep	.90	.40
57A	A10	2sh car & black ('56)	4.25	.40
58	A10	5sh blue & sepia	.90	.40
58A	A10	5sh dk blue & blk ('56)	3.75	.50
59	A10	10sh olive & sepia	1.25	6.75
60	A10	10sh ol gray & blk ('54)	9.50	1.10

Size: 36 1/2x27mm
Perf. 13 1/2x13

61	A11	20sh rose vio & dk brn	4.75	8.50
61A	A11	20sh lt vio & blk ('57)	30.00	12.00
		Nos. 48-61A (18)	62.10	34.05

Various shades from two or more printings exist. No. 60 has heavier shading on tribesman's lower garment than No. 59.

See #66-75. For overprints see #63-64.

Type of 1953
Inscribed: "Royal Visit 1954"

1954, Apr. 27 *Perf. 12*

62	A11	1sh purple & sepia	.40	.40

Nos. 50 and 56 Overprinted in Red

تعديل
الدستور
١٩٥٩
No. 63

REVISED
CONSTITUTION
1959
No. 64

1959, Jan. 26 *Perf. 12, 12x13 1/2*

63	A11	15c dark blue green	.30	.30
64	A10	1sh25c black & light blue	.80	.80

Introduction of a revised constitution.

Freedom from Hunger Issue
Common Design Type
Perf. 14x14 1/2

1963, June 4 Photo. Wmk. 314

65	CD314	1sh25c green	1.50	.65

Types of 1953-57
Perf. 12x13 1/2, 12 (#67-69, 73)

1964-65 Engr. Wmk. 314

66	A10	5c green ('65)	.20	.25
67	A11	10c orange	.25	.15
68	A11	15c Prus green	.30	.25
69	A11	25c carmine	.50	.25
70	A10	35c dp blue	2.50	.75
71	A10	50c dull blue	2.50	.75
72	A10	70c gray	2.75	1.25
73	A11	1sh vio & black	2.75	1.25
74	A10	1sh25c blk & lt blue	5.50	7.25
75	A10	2sh car & blk ('65)	10.00	14.00
		Nos. 66-75 (10)	27.25	26.15

KATHIRI STATE OF SEIYUN

LOCATION — In Eastern Aden Protectorate
GOVT. — Sultanate
CAPITAL — Seiyun

Catalogue values for unused stamps in this section are for Never Hinged items.

Sultan Ja'far bin Mansur al Kathiri — A1

Seiyun — A2

Minaret at Tarim — A3

Designs: 2 1/2a, Mosque at Seiyun. 3a, Palace at Tarim. 8a, Mosque at Seiyun, horiz. 1r, South Gate, Tarim. 2r, Kathiri House. 5r, Mosque at Tarim.

1942 Engr. Wmk. 4 *Perf. 14*

1	A1	1/2a dark green	.15	.35
2	A1	3/4a copper brown	.15	.45
3	A1	1a deep blue	.20	.35

Perf. 13x11 1/2, 11 1/2x13

4	A2	1 1/2a dark car rose	.30	.40
5	A3	2a black brown	.30	.55
6	A3	2 1/2a deep blue	.60	1.00
7	A2	3a dk car rose & dull brn	.95	1.40
8	A2	8a orange red	.50	1.00
9	A3	1r green	1.40	1.65
10	A2	2r rose vio & dk blue	6.50	8.50
11	A3	5r gray green & fawn	16.00	12.50
		Nos. 1-11 (11)	27.05	28.15

For surcharges see Nos. 20-27.

Nos. 4, 6 Ovptd. in Black or Red:

VICTORY
ISSUE
8TH JUNE 1946
a

VICTORY
ISSUE
8TH JUNE
1946
b

Perf. 13x11 1/2, 11 1/2x13

1946, Oct. 15 Wmk. 4

12	A2 (a)	1 1/2a dark car rose	.15	.15
13	A3 (b)	2 1/2a deep blue (R)	.25	.25
a.		Inverted overprint	425.00	
b.		Double overprint	—	

Victory of the Allied Nations in WWII.

All examples of No. 13b have the 2nd overprint almost directly over the 1st.

Silver Wedding Issue
Common Design Types

1949, Jan. 17 Photo. *Perf. 14x14 1/2*

14	CD304	1 1/2a scarlet	.35	1.75

Engraved; Name Typo.
Perf. 11 1/2x11

15	CD305	5r green	11.00	10.00

25th anniv. of the marriage of King George VI and Queen Elizabeth.

UPU Issue
Common Design Types
Surcharged with New Values in Annas and Rupees

Engr.; Name Typo. on Nos. 17-18

1949, Oct. 10 *Perf. 13 1/2, 11x11 1/2*

16	CD306	2 1/2a on 20c dp ultra	.25	.50
17	CD307	3a on 30c dp car	1.00	.60
18	CD308	8a on 50c orange	.60	.75
19	CD309	1r on 1sh blue	1.10	1.10
		Nos. 16-19 (4)	2.95	2.95

75th anniv. of the formation of the UPU.

Nos. 3 and 5-11 Surcharged with New Values in Carmine or Black
Perf. 14, 13x11 1/2, 11 1/2x13

1951, Oct. 1 Engr. Wmk. 4

20	A1	5c on 1a (C)	.15	.20
21	A3	10c on 2a	.30	.20
22	A3	15c on 2 1/2a	.50	.50
23	A2	20c on 3a	.25	.50
24	A2	50c on 8a	.30	.25
25	A3	1sh on 1r	1.90	.70
26	A2	2sh on 2r	3.50	13.00
27	A3	5sh on 5r	12.50	27.50
		Nos. 20-27 (8)	19.40	42.85

Coronation Issue
Common Design Type

1953, June 2 *Perf. 13 1/2x13*

28	CD312	15c dk green & blk	.30	.25

Sultan Hussein A10

Qarn Adh Dhabi A11

Designs: 15c, Seiyun scene, horiz. 25c, Minaret at Tarim. 35c, Mosque at Seiyun. 50c, Palace at Tarim, horiz. 1sh, Mosque at Seiyun, horiz. 2sh, South Gate, Tarim. 5sh, Kathiri house, horiz. 10sh, Mosque entrance, Tarim.

1954, Jan. 15 Engr. *Perf. 12 1/2*

29	A10	5c dark brown	.15	.15
30	A10	10c deep blue	.15	.15

Perf. 13x11 1/2, 11 1/2x13

31	A11	15c dk blue green	.15	.15
32	A11	25c dk car rose	.15	.15
33	A11	35c deep blue	.15	.15
34	A11	50c dk car rose & dk brn	.15	.15
35	A11	1sh deep orange	.35	.30
36	A11	2sh gray green	1.00	.85
37	A11	5sh vio & dk blue	2.25	3.25
38	A11	10sh vio & yel brn	5.25	6.50
		Nos. 29-38 (10)	9.75	11.80

Perf. 11 1/2x13, 13x11 1/2

1964, July 1 Wmk. 314

Designs: 1sh25c, Seiyun, horiz. 1sh50c, View of Gheil Omer, horiz.

39	A11	70c black	.50	.35
40	A11	1sh25c bright green	.85	.60
41	A11	1sh50c purple	1.10	.80
		Nos. 39-41 (3)	2.45	1.75

QUAITI STATE OF SHIHR AND MUKALLA

LOCATION — In Eastern Aden Protectorate
GOVT. — Sultanate
CAPITAL — Mukalla

Catalogue values for unused stamps in this section are for Never Hinged items.

For all your stamp supply needs
www.scottonline.com

ADEN — Quaiti State of Shihr and Mukalla — AFARS AND ISSAS

Sultan Sir Saleh bin Ghalib al Qu'aiti — A1
Mukalla Harbor — A2 
Buildings at Shibam — A3 

Designs: 2a, Gateway of Shihr. 3a, Outpost of Mukalla. 8a, View of 'Einat. 1r, Governor's Castle, Du'an. 3r, Mosque in Hureidha. 5r, Meshhed.

1942		Engr.	Wmk. 4	Perf. 14	
1	A1	½a dark green		.50	.40
2	A1	¾a copper brown		.50	.30
3	A1	1a deep blue		.60	.55

Perf. 13x11½, 11½x13

4	A2	1½a dk car rose	.70	.40
5	A2	2a black brown	.75	.55
6	A3	2½a deep blue	.40	.30
7	A2	3a dk car rose & dl brn	.75	.40
8	A3	8a orange red	.50	.40
9	A2	1r green	1.65	1.40
10	A3	2r rose vio & dk blue	9.50	7.50
11	A3	5r gray green & fawn	13.00	10.00
		Nos. 1-11 (11)	28.85	22.20

For surcharges see Nos. 20-27.

Nos. 4, 6 Ovptd. in Black or Carmine like Kathiri Nos. 12-13

Perf. 11½x13, 13x11½

1946, Oct. 15
12	A2 (b)	1½a dk car rose	.15	.30
13	A3 (a)	2½a deep blue (C)	.25	.20

Victory of the Allied Nations in WWII.

Silver Wedding Issue
Common Design Types

1949, Jan. 17   Photo.   Perf. 14x14½
14	CD304	1½a scarlet	.45	1.75

Engraved; Name Typo.
Perf. 11½x11
15	CD305	5r green	12.00	10.50

25th anniv. of the marriage of King George VI and Queen Elizabeth.

UPU Issue
Common Design Types
Surcharged with New Values in Annas and Rupees

Engr.; Name Typo. on Nos. 17 and 18
1949, Oct. 10   Perf. 13½, 11x11½
16	CD306	2½a on 20c dp ultra	.15	.15
17	CD307	3a on 30c dp car	.50	.50
18	CD308	8a on 50c org	.65	.65
19	CD309	1r on 1sh blue	1.75	1.75
a.		Surcharge omitted	1,300.	
		Nos. 16-19 (4)	3.05	3.05

Nos. 3 and 5-11 Surcharged with New Values in Carmine or Black

Perf. 14, 13x11½, 11½x13

1951, Oct. 1   Engr.   Wmk. 4
20	A1	5c on 1a (C)	.15	.15
21	A2	10c on 2a	.15	.15
22	A3	15c on 2½a	.15	.15
23	A2	20c on 3a	.15	.15
24	A3	50c on 8a	.15	.15
25	A2	1sh on 1r	.30	.45
26	A3	2sh on 2r	4.50	7.50
27	A3	5sh on 5r	7.25	12.50
		Nos. 20-27 (8)	12.80	21.20

Coronation Issue
Common Design Type

1953, June 2   Engr.   Perf. 13½x13
28	CD312	15c dk blue & black	.45	.45

Qu'aiti State in Hadhramaut

Metal Work — A10
Fisheries — A11 

Designs: 10c, Mat making. 15c, Weaving. 25c, Pottery. 35c, Building. 50c, Date cultivation. 90c, Agriculture. 1sh25c, 10sh, Lime burning. 2sh, Dhow building. 5sh, Agriculture.

Perf. 11½x13, 13½x14

1955, Sept. 1   Engr.   Wmk. 4
29	A10	5c greenish blue	.15	.15
30	A10	10c black	.15	.15
31	A10	15c dk green	.15	.15
32	A10	25c carmine	.15	.15
33	A10	35c ultra	.20	.20
34	A10	50c red orange	.40	.40
35	A10	90c brown	.55	.55
36	A11	1sh purple & blk	.65	.65
37	A11	1sh25c red org & blk	.75	.75
38	A11	2sh dk blue & blk	1.40	1.40
39	A11	5sh green & blk	3.50	3.50
40	A11	10sh car & black	7.75	7.75
		Nos. 29-40 (12)	15.80	15.80

Types of 1955 with Portrait of Sultan Awadh Bin Saleh El-Qu'aiti
Design: 70c, Agriculture. Others as before.

1963, Oct. 20   Wmk. 314
41	A10	5c greenish blue	.15	.15
42	A10	10c black	.15	.15
43	A10	15c dark green	.15	.15
44	A10	25c carmine	.20	.15
45	A10	35c ultra	.30	.25
46	A10	50c red orange	.40	.35
47	A10	70c brown	.65	.60
48	A11	1sh purple & blk	.90	.85
49	A11	1sh25c red org & blk	1.25	1.10
50	A11	2sh dk blue & blk	1.90	1.75
51	A11	5sh green & blk	4.75	4.50
52	A11	10sh carmine & blk	10.50	10.00
		Nos. 41-52 (12)	21.30	20.00

AFARS AND ISSAS
French Territory of the
'ä-,fär(z) and ē-'sä(z)

LOCATION — East Africa
GOVT. — French Overseas Territory
AREA — 8,880 sq. mi.
POP. — 150,000 (est. 1974)
CAPITAL — Djibouti (Jibuti)

The French overseas territory of Somali Coast was renamed the French Territory of the Afars and Issas in 1967. It became the Djibouti Republic (which see) on June 27, 1977.

100 Centimes = 1 Franc

Catalogue values for all unused stamps in this country are for Never Hinged items.

Imperforates
Most stamps of Afars and Issas exist imperforate in issued and trial colors, and also in small presentation sheets in issued colors.

Grayheaded Kingfisher A48

1967   Engr.   Unwmk.   Perf. 13
310	A48	10fr Halcyon leucocephala	1.50	1.25
311	A48	15fr Haematopus ostralegus	2.00	1.50
312	A48	50fr Tringa nebularia	7.75	4.50
313	A48	55fr Coracias abyssinicus	9.50	5.25
314	A48	60fr Xerus rutilus	13.00	10.00
		Nos. 310-314 (5)	33.75	22.50

Issued: 10fr, 55fr, Aug. 21; 15fr, 50fr, 60fr, Sept. 25. See No. C50.

Soccer — A49

1967, Dec. 18   Engr.   Perf. 13
315	A49	25fr shown	1.90	1.50
316	A49	30fr Basketball	2.50	2.00

Common Design Types
Pictured in section at front of book.

WHO Anniversary Issue
Common Design Type

1968, May 4   Engr.   Perf. 13
317	CD126	15fr multicolored	1.25	1.00

20th anniv. of WHO.

Damerdjog Fortress — A50

Administration Buildings: 25fr, Ali Adde. 30fr, Dorra. 40fr, Assamo.

1968, May 17   Engr.   Perf. 13
318	A50	20fr slate, brn & emer	.90	.50
319	A50	25fr brt grn, bl & brn	.95	.50
320	A50	30fr brn ol, brn org & sl	1.10	.75
321	A50	40fr brn ol, sl & brt grn	2.00	1.50
		Nos. 318-321 (4)	4.95	3.25

Human Rights Year Issue
Common Design Type

1968, Aug. 10   Engr.   Perf. 13
322	CD127	10fr purple, ver & org	.75	.60
323	CD127	70fr green, pur & org	1.50	1.10

International Human Rights Year.

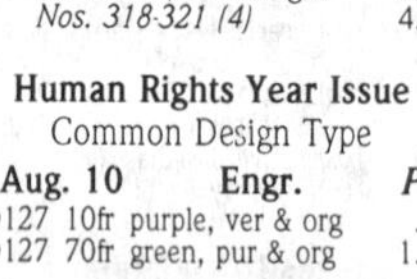

Radio-television Station, Djibouti — A52
High Commission Palace, Djibouti — A53 

Designs: 2fr, Justice Building. 5fr, Chamber of Deputies. 8fr, Great Mosque. 15fr, Monument of Free French Forces, vert. 40fr, Djibouti Post Office. 70fr, Residence of Gov. Léonce Lagarde at Obock. No. 332, Djibouti Harbormaster's Building. No. 333, Control tower, Djibouti Airport.

1968-70   Engr.   Perf. 13
324	A52	1fr dk red, sky bl & ind	.25	.15
325	A52	2fr green, bl & indigo	.25	.15
326	A52	5fr brn, sky bl & grn	.35	.20
327	A52	8fr choc, emer & gray	.40	.20
328	A52	15fr grn, sky bl & yel brn	3.00	2.00
329	A52	40fr green, brn & slate	2.00	1.00
330	A53	60fr multicolored	2.25	1.50
331	A53	70fr dl grn, gray & ol bis	3.00	1.50
332	A53	85fr multicolored	4.00	2.00
333	A52	85fr dk grn, bl & gray	4.50	2.50
		Nos. 324-333 (10)	20.00	11.20

Issue years: 1968 - 60fr; 1969 - 1fr-15fr, 70fr, 85fr; 1970 - 40fr, 85fr.

Locust — A54

Designs: 50fr, Pest control by helicopter. 55fr, Pest control by plane.

1969, Oct. 6   Engr.   Perf. 13
334	A54	15fr brn, grn & slate	2.50	1.00
335	A54	50fr dk grn, bl & ol brn	1.50	1.00
336	A54	55fr red brn, bl & brn	2.00	1.50
		Nos. 334-336 (3)	6.00	3.50

Campaign against locusts.

ILO Issue
Common Design Type

1969, Nov. 24   Engr.   Perf. 13
337	CD131	30fr orange, gray & lilac	1.25	.80

Afar Dagger in Ornamental Scabbard A56

1970, Apr. 3   Engr.   Perf. 13
338	A56	10fr yel grn, dk grn & org brn	.50	.35
339	A56	15fr grn, bl & org brn	.60	.35
340	A56	20fr yel grn, red & org brn	.80	.55
341	A56	25fr grn, plum & org brn	1.10	.55
		Nos. 338-341 (4)	3.00	1.80

See No. 364.

UPU Headquarters Issue
Common Design Type

1970, May 20   Engr.   Perf. 13
342	CD133	25fr brn, brt grn & choc	1.00	.60

Trapshooting A57
Motorboats A58 

Designs: 50fr, Steeplechase. 55fr, Sailboat, vert. 60fr, Equestrians.

1970   Engr.   Perf. 13
343	A57	30fr dp brn, yel grn & brt bl	1.65	.90
344	A58	48fr blue & multi	1.75	.90
345	A58	50fr cop red, bl & pur	2.25	1.25
346	A58	55fr red brn, bl & ol	1.75	1.25
347	A58	60fr ol, blk & red brn	2.75	1.75
		Nos. 343-347 (5)	10.15	6.05

Issued: 30fr, June 5; 48fr, Oct. 9; 50fr, 60fr, Nov. 6.

Automatic Ferry, Tadjourah A59

1970, Nov. 25
348	A59	48fr blue, brn & grn	2.25	1.40

Volcanic Geode — A60

AFARS AND ISSAS

Diabase and Chrysolite
A61

10fr, Doleritic basalt. 15fr, Olivine basalt.

1971		Photo.	Perf. 13	
349	A61	10fr black & multi	1.25	.50
350	A61	15fr black & multi	1.65	.50
351	A60	25fr black, crim & brn	3.50	1.50
352	A61	40fr black & multi	6.50	2.00
		Nos. 349-352 (4)	12.90	4.50

Issued: 10fr, 11/22; 15fr, 10/8; 25fr, 4/26; 40fr, 1/25.

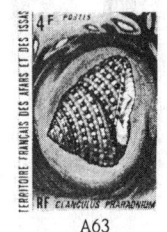

A62 A63

1971, July 1		Photo.	Perf. 12x12½	
353	A62	4fr Manta birostris	1.25	.50
354	A62	5fr Coryphaena hippurus	1.25	.50
355	A62	9fr Pristis pectinatus	2.50	1.50
		Nos. 353-355 (3)	5.00	2.50

See No. C60.

De Gaulle Issue
Common Design Type

Designs: 60fr, Gen. Charles de Gaulle, 1940. 85fr, Pres. de Gaulle, 1970.

1971, Nov. 9		Engr.	Perf. 13	
356	CD134	60fr dk vio bl & blk	2.00	1.50
357	CD134	85fr dk vio bl & blk	2.50	1.50

1972, Mar. 8		Photo.	Perf. 12½x13	

Shells: 4fr, Strawberry Top. 9fr, Cypraea pantherina. 20fr, Bull-mouth helmet. 50fr, Ethiopian volute.

358	A63	4fr olive & multi	1.25	.40
359	A63	9fr dk blue & multi	1.50	.60
360	A63	20fr dp green & multi	3.75	1.50
361	A63	50fr dp claret & multi	7.50	1.50
		Nos. 358-361 (4)	14.00	3.50

Shepherd — A64

Design: 10fr, Dromedary breeding.

1973, Apr. 11		Photo.	Perf. 13	
362	A64	9fr blue & multi	1.00	.30
363	A64	10fr blue & multi	1.00	.30

Afar Dagger — A65

1974, Jan. 29		Engr.	Perf. 13	
364	A65	30fr slate grn & dk brn	1.10	.65

For surcharge see No. 379.

Flamingos, Lake Abbe — A66

Designs: Flamingos and different views of Lake Abbe.

1974, Feb. 22		Photo.	Perf. 13	
370	A66	5fr multicolored	1.25	.30
371	A66	15fr multicolored	.60	.50
372	A66	50fr multicolored	1.90	1.25
		Nos. 370-372 (3)	3.75	2.05

Soccer Ball — A67

1974, May 24		Engr.	Perf. 13	
373	A67	25fr black & emerald	1.25	.80

World Cup Soccer Championship, Munich, June 13-July 7.

Letters Around UPU Emblem Oleo Chrysophylla
A68 A69

1974, Oct. 9		Engr.	Perf. 13	
374	A68	20fr multicolored	1.00	.50
375	A68	100fr multicolored	2.50	2.00

Centenary of Universal Postal Union.

1974, Nov. 22			Photo.	
376	A69	10fr shown	.75	.40
377	A69	15fr Ficus species	1.10	.60
378	A69	20fr Solanum adoense	2.25	1.00
		Nos. 376-378 (3)	4.10	2.00

Day Primary Forest.

No. 364 Surcharged with New Value and Two Bars in Red

1975, Jan. 1		Engr.	Perf. 13	
379	A65	40fr on 30fr multi	1.50	.90

Treasury — A70

Design: 25fr, Government buildings.

1975, Jan. 7		Engr.	Perf. 13	
380	A70	8fr blue, gray & red	.40	.30
381	A70	25fr red, blue & indigo	.75	.60

Ranella Spinosa — A71

Sea Shells: No. 382, Darioconus textile. No. 383, Murex palmarosa. 10fr, Conus sumatrensis. 15fr, Cypraea pulchra. No. 386, 45fr, Murex scolopax. No. 387, Cypraea exhusta. 55fr, Cypraea erythraensis. 60fr, Conus taeniatus.

1975-76		Engr.	Perf. 13	
382	A71	5fr blue grn & brn	1.25	.40
383	A71	5fr blue & multi ('76)	.90	.20
384	A71	10fr lilac, blk & brn	1.25	.40
385	A71	15fr blue, indigo & brn	1.25	.40
386	A71	20fr purple & lt brn	3.00	1.65
387	A71	20fr brt grn & multi ('76)	1.10	.40
388	A71	40fr green & brown	6.00	1.00
389	A71	45fr green, bl & bister	5.00	1.00
390	A71	55fr turq & multi ('76)	3.00	1.25
391	A71	60fr buff & sepia ('76)	6.00	1.75
		Nos. 382-391 (10)	29.75	8.65

Hypolimnas Misippus
A72

Butterflies: 40fr, Papilio nireus. 50fr, Acraea anemosa. 65fr, Holocerina smilax menieri. 70fr, Papilio demodocus. No. 397, Papilio dardanus. No. 398, Balachowsky gonimbrasca. 150fr, Vanessa cardui.

1975-76		Photo.	Perf. 13	
392	A72	25fr emerald & multi	1.90	1.00
393	A72	40fr yellow & multi	2.00	1.00
394	A72	50fr ultra & multi ('76)	2.25	1.50
395	A72	65fr olive & multi ('76)	3.25	1.50
396	A72	70fr violet & multi	4.25	2.00
397	A72	100fr blue & multi	5.50	2.00
398	A72	100fr Prus bl & multi ('76)	4.25	2.00
399	A72	150fr green & multi ('76)	6.00	2.00
		Nos. 392-399 (8)	29.40	13.00

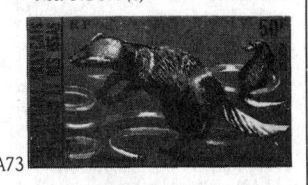

A73

	Perf. 13x12½, 12½x13			
1975-76			Photo.	
400	A73	10fr Hyaena hyaena	.55	.30
401	A73	15fr Cercopithecus aethiops	1.10	.50
402	A73	15fr Equus asinus somalicus	.90	.50
403	A73	30fr Dorcatragus megalotis	1.65	.90
404	A73	50fr Ichneumia albicauda	2.25	1.00
405	A73	60fr Hystrix galasta	2.75	1.25
406	A73	70fr Ictonyx striatus	4.00	1.75
407	A73	200fr Orycteropus afar	6.75	4.00
		Nos. 400-407 (8)	19.95	10.20

Issued: 10fr, 15fr, 30fr, 1976.

A74 A75

1975-76		Photo.	Perf. 12½x13	
413	A74	20fr Vidua macroura	1.25	.80
414	A74	25fr Psittacula krameri	1.25	.40
415	A74	50fr Cinnyris venustus	2.50	1.50
416	A74	60fr Ardea goliath	3.50	1.75
417	A74	100fr Scopus umbretta	4.50	2.50
418	A74	100fr Oena capensis	3.50	1.65
419	A74	300fr Platalea alba	9.00	4.00
		Nos. 413-419 (7)	25.50	12.60

Issued: 25fr, No. 418, 300fr, 1976.

1975, Dec. 19		Engr.	Perf. 13	
421	A75	20fr Palms	1.00	.40

Satellite and Alexander Graham Bell — A76

1976, Mar. 10		Engr.	Perf. 13	
422	A76	200fr dp bl, org & sl grn	4.00	2.25

Centenary of the first telephone call by Alexander Graham Bell, Mar. 10, 1876.

Basketball
A77

1976, July 7		Litho.	Perf. 12½	
423	A77	10fr shown	.45	.20
424	A77	15fr Bicycling	.60	.30
425	A77	40fr Soccer	1.10	.50
426	A77	60fr Running	1.40	.80
		Nos. 423-426 (4)	3.55	1.80

21st Olympic Games, Montreal, Canada, July 17-Aug. 1.

Pterois Radiata — A78

1976, Aug. 10		Photo.	Perf. 13x13½	
428	A78	45fr blue & multi	2.50	1.00

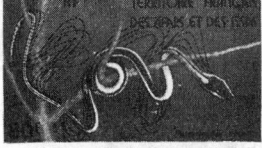

Psammophis Elegans — A79

Design: 70fr, Naja nigricollis, vert.

	Perf. 13x13½, 13½x13			
1976, Sept. 27			Photo.	
430	A79	70fr ocher & multi	2.75	1.50
431	A79	80fr emerald & multi	3.25	1.75

WANTED
MINT- NEVER HINGED

AFARS & ISSAS

• FRANCE AND ALL FRENCH AREAS!

Urgently needed MNH singles, sets, collections, accumulations, dealer stocks, etc.

PAYING TOP PRICES!

Let us know what you have or ship for our prompt 24 HOUR ANSWER!

GUY LESTRADE
2152 Lapiniere Blvd. Store 110
Brossard, QC, Canada J4W 1L9
Ph 450-656-7756
FAX: 450-656-7729
Email: glestrade@qmnet
www.guylestrade.com

AFARS AND ISSAS

Motorcyclist — A80

1977, Jan. 27 Litho. Perf. 12x12½
432 A80 200fr multicolored   5.25 2.75
Moto-Cross motorcycle race.

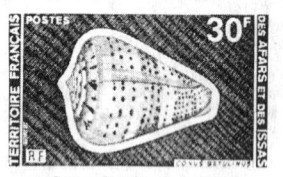

Conus Betulinus — A81

Sea Shells: 5fr, Cyprea tigris. 70fr, Conus striatus. 85fr, Cyprea mauritiana.

1977 Engr. Perf. 13
433 A81 5fr multicolored   .90 .50
434 A81 30fr multicolored   1.40 .60
435 A81 70fr multicolored   4.75 1.75
436 A81 85fr multicolored   5.00 2.00
  Nos. 433-436 (4)   12.05 4.85

Gaterin Gaterinus A82

1977, Apr. 15 Photo. Perf. 13x12½
437 A82 15fr shown   1.10 .40
438 A82 65fr Barracudas   3.25 1.10

AIR POST STAMPS

AP16   AP17

1967, Aug. 21 Unwmk. Engr. Perf. 13
C50 AP16 200fr Aquila rapax belisarius   15.00 7.50

1968 Engr. Perf. 13
48fr, Parachutists. 85fr, Water skier & skin diver.
C51 AP17 48fr brn ol, Prus bl & brn   2.75 1.50
C52 AP17 85fr dk brn, ol & Prus bl   3.75 2.50
  Issue dates: 48fr, Jan. 5; 85fr, Mar. 15.

Aerial Map of the Territory — AP18

1968, Nov. 15 Engr. Perf. 13
C53 AP18 500fr bl, dk brn & ocher   26.00 8.00

Buildings Type of Regular Issue
Designs: 100fr, Cathedral, vert. 200fr, Sayed Hassan Mosque, vert.

1969 Engr. Perf. 13
C54 A53 100fr multicolored   2.25 1.50
C55 A53 200fr multicolored   5.25 3.00
  Issue dates: 100fr, Apr. 4; 200fr, May 8.

Concorde Issue
Common Design Type

1969, Apr. 17
C56 CD129 100fr org red & olive   17.50 10.00

Arta Ionospheric Station — AP19

Japanese Sword Guard, Fish Design — AP20

1970, May 8 Engr. Perf. 13
C57 AP19 70fr multicolored   3.00 2.00

Gold embossed
1970, Oct. 26 Perf. 12½
200fr, Japanese sword guard, horse design.
C58 AP20 100fr multicolored   7.50 5.00
C59 AP20 200fr multicolored   9.50 5.50
  EXPO '70 International Exposition, Osaka, Japan, Mar. 15-Sept. 13.

Scarus vetula AP21

1971, July 1 Photo. Perf. 12½
C60 AP21 30fr black & multi   4.00 2.50

Djibouti Harbor AP22

1972, Feb. 3
C61 AP22 100fr blue & multi   4.00 2.25
  New Djibouti harbor.

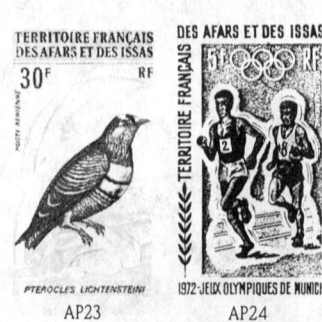

AP23   AP24

1972 Photo. Perf. 12½x13
C62 AP23 30fr Pterocles lichtensteini   1.90 1.40
C63 AP23 49fr Uppupa epops   4.50 2.50
C64 AP23 66fr Capella media   5.75 3.25
C65 AP23 500fr Francolinus ochropectus 24.00 9.00
  Nos. C62-C65 (4)   36.15 16.15
  Issue dates: #C65, Nov. 3, others Apr. 21.

1972, June 8 Engr. Perf. 13
Olympic Rings and: 5fr, Running. 10fr, Basketball. 55fr, Swimming, horiz. 60fr, Olympic torch and Greek frieze, horiz.
C66 AP24 5fr multicolored   .45 .30
C67 AP24 10fr multicolored   .55 .40
C68 AP24 55fr multicolored 1.75 1.10
C69 AP24 60fr multicolored 2.25 1.25
  Nos. C66-C69 (4)   5.00 3.05
20th Olympic Games, Munich, Aug. 26-Sept. 11.

Louis Pasteur — AP25

Design: 100fr, Albert Calmette and C. Guérin.

1972, Oct. 5 Engr. Perf. 13
C70 AP25 20fr multicolored 1.25 .50
C71 AP25 100fr multicolored 4.00 2.00
Pasteur, Calmette, Guerin, chemists and bacteriologists, benefactors of mankind.

1973, Jan. 15 Photo. Perf. 13
C72 AP26 30fr brown & multi 4.50 3.50
C73 AP26 200fr multicolored   8.00 6.00
Visit of Pres. Georges Pompidou of France, Jan. 15-17.

Map and Views of Territory — AP26

200fr, Woman and Mosque of Djibouti, vert.

AP27

1973, Feb. 26 Photo. Perf. 13x12½
C74 AP27 30fr Oryx beisa   2.00 1.00
C75 AP27 50fr Madogua saltiana 2.75 1.50
C76 AP27 66fr Felis caracal   3.75 2.00
  Nos. C74-C76 (3)   8.50 4.50
  See Nos. C94-C96.

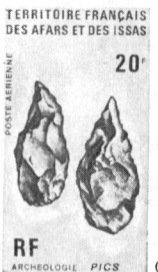

Celts — AP28

Various pre-historic flint tools. 40fr, 60fr, horiz.

1973 Perf. 13
C77 AP28 20fr yel grn, blk & brn   2.25 1.50
C78 AP28 40fr yellow & multi   2.75 2.00
C79 AP28 49fr lilac & multi   5.00 3.00
C80 AP28 60fr blue & multi   3.75 2.50
  Nos. C77-C80 (4)   13.75 9.00
  Issued: 20fr, 49fr, Mar. 16; 40fr, 60fr, Sept. 7.

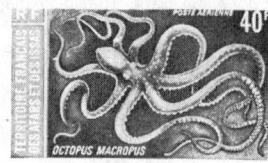

Octopus macropus — AP29

1973, Mar. 16
C81 AP29 40fr shown   3.00 1.00
C82 AP29 60fr Halicore dugong 5.00 2.50

AP30   AP31

Copernicus: 8fr, Nicolaus Copernicus, Polish astronomer. 9fr, William C. Roentgen, physicist, X-ray discoverer. No. C85, Edward Jenner, physician, discoverer of vaccination. No. C86, Marie Curie, discoverer of radium and polonium. 49fr, Robert Koch, physician and bacteriologist. 50fr, Clement Ader (1841-1925), French aviation pioneer. 55fr, Guglielmo Marconi, Italian electrical engineer, inventor. 85fr, Moliere, French playwright. 100fr, Henri Farman (1874-1937), French aviation pioneer. 150fr, Andre-Marie Ampere (1775-1836), French physicist. 250fr, Michelangelo Buonarroti (1475-1564), Italian sculptor, painter and architect.

1973-75 Engr. Perf. 13
C83 AP30   8fr multicolored   .65 .30
C84 AP30   9fr multicolored   1.00 .40
C85 AP30 10fr multicolored   .90 .40
C86 AP30 10fr multicolored   .75 .40
C87 AP30 49fr multicolored   3.25 1.65
C88 AP30 50fr multicolored   2.50 1.25
C89 AP30 55fr multicolored   1.90 1.00
C90 AP30 85fr multicolored   3.75 1.50
C91 AP30 100fr multicolored   3.75 2.00
C92 AP30 150fr multicolored   3.75 2.00
C93 AP30 250fr multicolored   6.50 1.50
  Nos. C83-C93 (11)   28.70 14.75
  Issued: 8fr, 85fr, 5/9/73; 9fr, #C85, 49fr, 10/12/73; 100fr, 1/29/74; 55fr, 3/22/74; #C86, 8/23/74; 150fr, 7/24/75; 250fr, 6/26/75; 50fr, 9/25/75.

Perf. 12½x13, 13x12½
1973, Dec. 12 Photo.
C94 AP31 20fr Papio anubis   1.25 .60
C95 AP31 50fr Genetta tigrina, horiz. 2.50 .90
C96 AP31 66fr Lapus habessinicus   4.00 1.50
  Nos. C94-C96 (3)   7.75 3.00

Spearfishing — AP32

1974, Apr. 14 Engr. Perf. 13
C97 AP32 200fr multicolored   7.50 4.50
No. C97 was prepared for release in Nov. 1972, for the 3rd Underwater Spearfishing Contest in the Red Sea. Dates were obliterated with a rectangle and the stamp was not issued without this obliteration.

Rock Carvings, Balho — AP33

1974, Apr. 26
C98 AP33 200fr carmine & slate   7.00 5.00

AFARS AND ISSAS — AFGHANISTAN

Lake Assal — AP34

Designs (Lake Assal): 50fr, Rock formations on shore. 85fr, Crystallized wood.

1974, Oct. 25   Photo.   *Perf. 13*
C99	AP34	49fr multicolored	1.25	.75
C100	AP34	50fr multicolored	1.75	1.00
C101	AP34	85fr multicolored	3.50	2.25
		Nos. C99-C101 (3)	6.50	4.00

Columba guinea — AP35

1975, May 23   Photo.   *Perf. 13*
C102	AP35	500fr multicolored	18.00	6.50

Djibouti Airport — AP36

1977, Mar. 1   Litho.   *Perf. 12*
C103	AP36	500fr multicolored	10.00	7.50

Opening of new Djibouti Airport.

Thomas A. Edison and Phonograph — AP37

Design: 75fr, Alexander Volta, electric train, lines and light bulb.

1977, May 5   Engr.   *Perf. 13*
C104	AP37	55fr multicolored	3.00	1.50
C105	AP37	75fr multicolored	4.50	2.50

Famous inventors: Thomas Alva Edison and Alexander Volta (1745-1827).

POSTAGE DUE STAMPS

Nomad's Milk Jug — D3

1969, Dec. 15   Engr.   *Perf. 14x13*   Unwmk.
J49	D3	1fr red brn, red lil & slate	.20	.20
J50	D3	2fr red brn, emer & slate	.20	.20
J51	D3	5fr red brn, bl & slate	.30	.30
J52	D3	10fr red brn, brn & slate	.80	.80
		Nos. J49-J52 (4)	1.50	1.50

AFGHANISTAN

af-'ga-nə-,stan

LOCATION — Central Asia, bounded by Iran, Russian Turkestan, Pakistan, Baluchistan and China
GOVT. — Republic
AREA — 251,773 sq. mi.
POP. — 17,150,000 (1984 est.)
CAPITAL — Kabul

Afghanistan changed from a constitutional monarchy to a republic in July 1973.

12 Shahi = 6 Sanar = 3 Abasi =
2 Krans = 1 Rupee Kabuli
60 Paisas = 1 Rupee (1921)
100 Pouls = 1 Rupee Afghani (1927)

Catalogue values for unused stamps in this country are for Never Hinged items, beginning with Scott 364 in the regular postage section, Scott B1 in the semi-postal section, Scott C7 in the airpost section, Scott O8 in officials section, and Scott RA6 in the postal tax section.

1871-78   A7   A8
Sanar.   Abasi.   6 Shahi.

1871-78   1871   1872
1 Rupee.   ½ Rupee.

1874   1876(A8)   1876 (A7)
1 Rupee.   Rupee.

1872   1874   1876 (A8)
                                  1877-78

From 1871 to 1892 and 1898 the Moslem year date appears on the stamp. Numerals as follows:

1	2	3	4	5
6	7	8	9	0

Until 1891 cancellation consisted of cutting or tearing a piece from the stamps. Such copies should not be considered as damaged.
Values are for cut square examples of good color. Cut to shape or faded copies sell for much less, particularly Nos. 2-10.
Nos. 2-108 are on laid paper of varying thickness except where wove is noted.
Until 1907 all stamps were issued ungummed.
The tiger's head on types A2 to A11 symbolizes the name of the contemporary amir, Sher (Tiger) Ali.

Kingdom of Kabul

Tiger's Head A2
(Both circles dotted)

1871   Unwmk.   Litho.   *Imperf.*
Dated "1288"
2	A2	1sh black	110.00	22.50
3	A2	1sa black	75.00	20.00
4	A2	1ab black	37.50	20.00
		Nos. 2-4 (3)	222.50	62.50

Thirty varieties of the shahi, 10 of the sanar and 5 of the abasi.
Similar designs without the tiger's head in the center are revenues.

A3
(Outer circle dotted)
Dated "1288"
5	A3	1sh black	175.00	35.00
6	A3	1sa black	75.00	22.50
7	A3	1ab black	37.50	22.50
		Nos. 5-7 (3)	287.50	80.00

Five varieties of each.

A4

1872   Toned Wove Paper
Dated "1289"
8	A4	6sh violet	850.	750.
9	A4	1rup violet	1,300.	1,100.

Two varieties of each. Date varies in location. Printed in sheets of 4 (2x2) containing two of each denomination.
Most used copies are smeared with a greasy ink cancel.

A4a

1873   White Laid Paper
Dated "1290"
10	A4a	1sh black	10.00	4.50
a.		Corner ornament missing	450.00	375.00
b.		Corner ornament retouched	60.00	25.00

15 varieties. Nos. 10a, 10b are the sixth stamp on the sheet.

A5

1873
11	A5	1sh black	2.25	2.00
11A	A5	1sh violet	500.00	

Sixty varieties of each.

A6   A7

1874
Dated "1291"
12	A5	1ab black	40.00	25.00
13	A5	½rup black	20.00	17.50
14	A5	1rup black	22.50	20.00
		Nos. 12-14 (3)	82.50	62.50

Five varieties of each.
Nos. 12-14 were printed on the same sheet. Se-tenant varieties exist.

1875
Dated "1292"
15	A6	1sa black	300.00	250.00
a.		Wide outer circle	600.00	
16	A6	1ab black	350.00	300.00
17	A6	1sa brown violet	22.50	22.50
a.		Wide outer circle	110.00	
18	A6	1ab brown violet	40.00	25.00

Ten varieties of the sanar, five of the abasi.
Nos. 15-16 and 17-18 were printed in the same sheets. Se-tenant pairs exist.

1876
Dated "1293"
19	A7	1sh black	300.00	150.00
20	A7	1sa black	375.00	200.00
21	A7	1ab black	600.00	325.00
22	A7	½rup black	375.00	200.00
23	A7	1rup black	550.00	200.00
24	A7	1sh violet	375.00	200.00
25	A7	1sa violet	350.00	200.00
26	A7	1ab violet	425.00	200.00
27	A7	½rup violet	90.00	55.00
28	A7	1rup violet	90.00	75.00

12 varieties of the shahi and 3 each of the other values.

A8

1876
Dated "1293"
29	A8	1sh gray	5.00	4.00
30	A8	1sa gray	7.50	4.00
31	A8	1ab gray	15.00	7.50
32	A8	½rup gray	17.50	10.00
33	A8	1rup gray	22.50	10.00
34	A8	1sh olive blk	125.00	
35	A8	1sa olive blk	175.00	
36	A8	1ab olive blk	350.00	
37	A8	½rup olive blk	250.00	
38	A8	1rup olive blk	275.00	
39	A8	1sh green	22.50	3.75
40	A8	1sa green	35.00	15.00
41	A8	1ab green	50.00	37.50
42	A8	½rup green	100.00	40.00
43	A8	1rup green	100.00	80.00
44	A8	1sh ocher	22.50	7.50
45	A8	1sa ocher	35.00	15.00
46	A8	1ab ocher	60.00	27.50
47	A8	½rup ocher	75.00	60.00
48	A8	1rup ocher	125.00	110.00
49	A8	1sh violet	22.50	5.50
50	A8	1sa violet	22.50	7.50
51	A8	1ab violet	35.00	10.00
52	A8	½rup violet	60.00	22.50
53	A8	1rup violet	75.00	35.00

12 varieties of the sanar, 6 of the abasi and 3 each of the ½ rupee and rupee.
24 varieties of the shahi, 4 of which show denomination written:

A9

AFGHANISTAN

1877
Dated "1294"

54	A9	1sh gray	3.50	2.25
55	A9	1sa gray	6.00	3.00
56	A9	1ab gray	9.00	6.00
57	A9	½rup gray	12.00	12.00
58	A9	1rup gray	12.00	12.00
59	A9	1sh black	10.00	
60	A9	1sa black	17.50	
61	A9	1ab black	42.50	
62	A9	½rup black	45.00	
63	A9	1rup black	45.00	
64	A9	1sh green	4.50	3.50
a.		Wove paper	12.00	
65	A9	1sa green	7.50	3.50
a.		Wove paper	16.00	12.00
66	A9	1ab green	10.00	10.00
a.		Wove paper	27.50	
67	A9	½rup green	14.00	14.00
a.		Wove paper	30.00	30.00
68	A9	1rup green	14.00	14.00
a.		Wove paper	30.00	30.00
69	A9	1sh ocher	3.50	2.00
70	A9	1sa ocher	10.00	3.50
71	A9	1ab ocher	17.50	16.00
72	A9	½rup ocher	30.00	30.00
73	A9	1rup ocher	30.00	30.00
74	A9	1sh violet	3.75	2.00
75	A9	1sa violet	7.50	2.75
76	A9	1ab violet	11.00	7.50
77	A9	½rup violet	17.50	14.00
78	A9	1rup violet	17.50	14.00

25 varieties of the shahi, 8 of the sanar, 3 of the abasi and 2 each of the ½rupee and rupee.

A10   A11

1878
Dated "1295"

79	A10	1sh gray	1.50	1.50
80	A10	1sa gray	1.75	1.75
81	A10	1ab gray	3.75	3.75
82	A10	½rup gray	10.00	7.50
83	A10	1rup gray	10.00	7.50
84	A10	1sh black	3.00	
85	A10	1sa black	3.00	
86	A10	1ab black	10.00	
87	A10	½rup black	20.00	
88	A10	1rup black	20.00	
89	A10	1sh green	21.00	20.00
90	A10	1sa green	3.00	3.00
91	A10	1ab green	11.00	10.00
92	A10	½rup green	21.00	17.50
93	A10	1rup green	21.00	17.50
94	A10	1sh ocher	10.00	3.00
95	A10	1sa ocher	3.00	2.25
96	A10	1ab ocher	11.00	10.00
97	A10	½rup ocher	21.00	21.00
98	A10	1rup ocher	16.00	16.00
99	A10	1sh violet	1.75	1.75
100	A10	1sa violet	1.75	1.75
101	A10	1ab violet	5.50	5.50
102	A10	½rup violet	21.00	17.50
103	A10	1rup violet	21.00	17.50
104	A11	1sh gray	2.00	1.75
105	A11	1sh black	90.00	
106	A11	1sh green	1.75	1.75
107	A11	1sh ocher	1.40	1.40
108	A11	1sh violet	2.00	1.75

40 varieties of the shahi, 30 of the sanar, 6 of the abasi and 2 each of the ½ rupee and 1 rupee.

The 1876, 1877 and 1878 issues were printed in separate colors for each main post office on the Peshawar-Kabul-Khulm (Tashkurghan) postal route. Some specialists consider the black printings to be proofs or trial colors.

There are many shades of these colors.

1ab, Type I (26mm) — A12
1ab, Type II (28mm) — A13

A14   A15

Dated "1298", numerals scattered through design

Handstamped, in watercolor

1881-90
Thin White Laid Batonne Paper

109	A12	1ab violet	1.75	1.10
109A	A13	1ab violet	3.50	2.50
110	A12	1ab black brn	3.50	1.75
111	A12	1ab rose	2.00	2.00
b.		Se-tenant with No. 111A	16.00	
111A	A13	1ab rose	2.50	2.00
112	A14	2ab violet	1.75	1.50
113	A14	2ab black brn	5.00	4.00
114	A14	2ab rose	3.00	3.00
115	A15	1rup violet	2.50	1.50
116	A15	1rup black brn	6.50	6.50
117	A15	1rup rose	3.00	3.00

Thin White Wove Batonne Paper

118	A12	1ab violet	6.50	4.00
119	A12	1ab vermilion	4.25	
120	A12	1ab rose		
121	A14	2ab violet		
122	A14	2ab vermilion	5.00	
122A	A14	2ab rose		
123	A15	1rup violet	8.25	
124	A15	1rup vermilion	6.50	
125	A15	1rup rose	8.25	

Thin White Laid Batonne Paper

126	A12	1ab brown org	2.50	2.50
126A	A13	1ab brn org (II)	3.50	3.50
127	A12	1ab carmine lake	2.50	2.50
a.		Laid paper		
128	A14	2ab brown org	2.50	2.50
129	A14	2ab carmine lake	3.00	3.00
130	A15	1rup brown org	10.00	10.00
131	A15	1rup car lake	4.25	4.25

Yellowish Laid Batonne Paper

132	A12	1ab purple		3.50
133	A12	1ab red	6.50	3.50

1884
Colored Wove Paper

133A	A13	1ab purple, yel (II)	17.50	17.50
134	A12	1ab purple, grn		
135	A12	1ab purple, blue	32.50	21.00
136	A12	1ab red, grn	37.50	
137	A12	1ab red, yel	1.75	
138	A12	1ab red, rose	6.00	
139	A14	2ab red, yel	6.00	
140	A14	2ab red, rose	5.50	
141	A14	2ab red, rose		
142	A14	2ab red, rose		
143	A15	1rup red, yel	6.50	6.50
145	A15	1rup red, rose	7.00	7.00

Thin Colored Ribbed Paper

146	A14	2ab red, yellow	3.00	
147	A15	1rup red, yellow	8.25	
148	A14	2ab lake, lilac	4.00	
149	A14	2ab lake, lilac	5.00	
150	A15	1rup lake, lilac	4.00	
151	A14	2ab lake, green	2.00	
152	A14	2ab lake, green	4.00	
153	A15	1rup lake, green	4.00	

1886-88
Colored Wove Paper

155	A12	1ab black, magenta	27.50	
156	A12	1ab claret brn, org	20.00	
156A	A12	1ab red, org	2.00	
156B	A14	2ab red, org	4.75	
156C	A15	1rup red, org	3.50	

Laid Batonné Paper

157	A12	1ab black, lavender	2.75	
158	A12	1ab cl brn, grn	6.50	
159	A12	1ab black, pink	17.50	
160	A14	2ab black, pink	35.00	
161	A15	1rup black, pink	20.00	

Laid Paper

162	A12	1ab black, pink	6.50	
163	A14	2ab black, pink	6.50	
164	A15	1rup black, pink	6.50	
165	A12	1ab brown, yel	6.50	
166	A14	2ab brown, yel	6.50	
167	A15	1rup brown, yel	6.50	
168	A12	1ab blue, grn	6.50	
169	A14	2ab blue, grn	6.50	
170	A15	1rup blue, grn	6.50	

1891
Colored Wove Paper

175	A12	1ab green, rose	22.50	
176	A15	1rup pur, grn batonne	22.50	

Nos. 109-176 fall into three categories:
1. Those regularly issued and in normal postal use from 1881 on, handstamped on thin white laid or wove paper in strip sheets containing 12 or more impressions of the same denomination arranged in two irregular rows, with the impressions often touching or overlappng.
2. The 1884 postal issues provisionally printed on smooth or ribbed colored wove paper as needed to supplement low stocks of the normal white paper stamps.
3. The "special" printings made in a range of colors on several types of laid or wove colored papers, most of which were never used for normal printings. These were produced periodically from 1886 to 1891 to meet philatelic demands. Although nominally valid for postage, most of the special printings were exported directly to fill dealers' orders, and few were ever postally used. Many of the sheets contained all three denominations with impressions separated by ruled lines. Sometimes different colors were used, so se-tenant multiples of denomination or color exist. Many combinations of stamp and paper colors exist besides those listed.

Various shades of each color exist.

Type A12 is known dated "1297."

Counterfeits, lithographed or typographed, are plentiful.

Kingdom of Afghanistan

A16   A17

A18

Dated "1309"
1891
Pelure Paper   Litho.

177	A16	1ab slate blue	.85	.85
a.		Tete beche pair	14.00	
178	A17	2ab slate blue	6.00	5.00
179	A18	1rup slate blue	12.25	10.00
		Nos. 177-179 (3)	19.10	15.85

Revenue stamps of similar design exist in various colors.

Nos. 177-179 were printed in panes on the same sheet, so se-tenant gutter pairs exist. Examples in black or red are proofs.

A Mosque Gate and Crossed Cannons (National Seal) — A19

Dated "1310" in Upper Right Corner
1892
Flimsy Wove Paper

180	A19	1ab black, green	2.00	1.60
181	A19	1ab black, orange	2.50	2.50
182	A19	1ab black, yellow	2.50	1.60
183	A19	1ab black, pink	2.50	1.60
184	A19	1ab black, lil rose	2.50	2.50
185	A19	1ab black, blue	4.25	3.50
186	A19	1ab black, salmon	2.50	2.00
187	A19	1ab black, magenta	2.50	2.50
188	A19	1ab black, violet	2.50	2.50
188A	A19	1ab black, scarlet	2.50	1.75

Many shades exist.

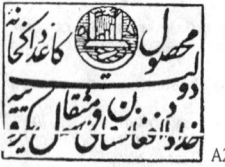

A20

A21

Undated
1894
Flimsy Wove Paper

189	A20	2ab black, green	6.50	6.50
190	A21	1rup black, green	10.00	10.00

24 varieties of the 2 abasi and 12 varieties of the rupee.

Nos. 189-190 and F3 were printed se-tenant in the same sheet. Pairs exist.

A21a

Dated "1316"
1898
Flimsy Wove Paper

191	A21a	2ab black, pink	2.50	
192	A21a	2ab black, magenta	2.50	
193	A21a	2ab black, yellow	1.10	
193A	A21a	2ab black, salmon	3.00	
194	A21a	2ab black, green	1.40	
195	A21a	2ab black, purple	1.75	
195A	A21a	2ab black, blue	17.50	
		Nos. 191-195A (7)	29.75	

Nos. 191-195A were not regularly issued. Genuinely used copies are scarce. No. 195A was found in remainder stocks and probably was never released.

A22   A23

A24

1907   Engr.   Imperf.
Medium Wove Paper

196	A22	1ab blue green	3.75	2.50
a.		1ab emerald	8.50	5.00
197	A22	1ab brt blue	10.00	10.00
198	A23	2ab deep blue	1.85	1.25
199	A24	1rup green	3.00	2.50
a.		1rup blue green	6.00	6.00

Zigzag Roulette 10

200	A22	1ab green	60.00	
201	A23	2ab blue	80.00	
201A	A24	1rup blue green	110.00	

1908   Perf. 12

202	A22	1ab green	10.00	6.25
203	A23	2ab deep blue	1.25	1.25
204	A24	1rup blue green	3.00	3.00
		Nos. 202-204 (3)	14.25	10.50

Twelve varieties of the 1 abasi, 6 of the 2 abasi, 4 of the 1 rupee.

Nos. 196-204 were issued in small sheets containing 3 or 4 panes. Gutter pairs, normal and tête bêche, exist.

A25   A26

A27

1909-19   Typo.   Perf. 12

205	A25	1ab ultra	.35	.25
a.		Imperf., pair	5.00	
206	A25	1ab red ('16)	.25	.15
a.		Imperf.		
207	A25	1ab rose ('18)	.25	.15
208	A26	2ab green	.50	.30
a.		Imperf., pair	3.00	
b.		Horiz. pair, imperf. btwn.		
208C	A26	2ab yellow ('16)	1.25	1.25
209	A26	2ab bis ('18-'19)	.90	.90
210	A27	1ab lilac brn	1.50	1.50
a.		1rup red brown	2.50	2.00
211	A27	1rup ol bis ('16)	1.50	1.50
		Nos. 205-211 (8)	6.50	6.00

A28

AFGHANISTAN

1913
212 A28 2pa drab brown ... 1.25 1.25
    a. 2pa red brown ... 1.25 1.25

No. 212 is inscribed "Tiket waraq dak" (Postal card stamps). It was usable only on postcards and not accepted for postage on letters.

Nos. 196-212 sometimes show letters of a papermaker's watermark, "Howard & Jones, London."

Royal Star — A29

1920, Aug. 24   *Perf. 12*
Size: 39x47mm
214 A29 10pa rose ... 20.00 12.00
215 A29 20pa red brown ... 45.00 18.00
216 A29 30pa green ... 90.00 60.00
  Nos. 214-216 (3) ... 155.00 90.00

Issued in sheets of two.

1921, Mar.
Size: 22½x28¼mm
217 A29 10pa rose ... .35 .15
    a. Perf. 11 ('27) ... .65 1.00
218 A29 20pa red brown ... 1.00 .50
219 A29 30pa yel green ... 1.00 .50
    a. Tete beche pair ... 6.00 5.50
    b. 30pa green ... 1.50 .75
    c. As "b," Tete beche pair ... 6.50 6.50
  Nos. 217-219 (3) ... 2.35 1.15

Two types of the 10pa, three of the 20pa.

Crest of King Amanullah — A32
A30   A32

1924, Feb. 26   *Perf. 12*
220 A30 10pa chocolate ... 10.00 6.00
    a. Tete beche pair ... 20.00 16.00

6th Independence Day.
Printed in sheets of four consisting of two tete beche pairs, and in sheets of two. Two types exist.

Some authorities believe that Nos. Q15-Q16 were issued as regular postage stamps.

1925, Feb. 26   *Perf. 12*
Size: 29x37mm
222 A32 10pa light brown ... 10.00 6.00

7th Independence Day.
Printed in sheets of 8 (two panes of 4).

1926, Feb. 28
Wove Paper
Size: 26x33mm
224 A32 10pa dark blue ... 1.40 1.40
    a. Imperf., pair ... 6.00
    b. Horiz. pair, imperf. btwn. ... 8.00
    c. Vert. pair, imperf. btwn. ... 8.00
    d. Laid paper ... 6.50 5.00

7th anniv. of Independence. Printed in sheets of 4, and in sheets of 8 (two panes of 4). Tete beche gutter pairs exist.

Tughra and Crest of Amanullah — A33

1927, Feb.
225 A33 10pa magenta ... 10.00 4.25
    a. Vertical pair, imperf. between ... 20.00
Dotted Background
226 A33 10pa magenta ... 5.50 4.25
    a. Horiz. pair, imperf. between ... 15.00

The surface of No. 226 is covered by a net of fine dots.
8th anniv. of Independence. Printed in sheets of 8 (two panes of 4). Tete beche gutter pairs exist.

National Seal — A34
A35 
A35a    A36 

1927, Oct.   *Imperf.*
227 A34 15p pink ... .35 .35
228 A35 30p Prus green ... .80 .40
229 A36 60p light blue ... 1.50 1.50
    a. Tete beche pair ... 4.50
  Nos. 227-229 (3) ... 2.65 2.25

1927-30   *Perf. 11, 12*
230 A34 15p pink ... .25 .15
231 A34 15p ultra ('29) ... .50 .30
232 A35 30p Prus green ... .35 .35
233 A35a 30p dp green ('30) ... .75 .70
234 A36 60p bright blue ... 1.50 1.00
    a. Tete beche pair ... 5.00
235 A36 60p black ('29) ... 1.40 .65
  Nos. 230-235 (6) ... 4.75 3.15

Nos. 230, 232 and 234 are usually imperforate on one or two sides.
No. 233 has been redrawn. A narrow border of pearls has been added and "30," in European and Arabic numerals, inserted in the upper spandrels.

Tughra and Crest of Amanullah — A37

1928, Feb. 27
236 A37 15p pink ... 2.00 2.00
    a. Tete beche pair ... 7.50
    b. Horiz. pair, imperf. vert. ... 6.00
    c. As "a," imperf. vert., block of 4 ... 10.00

9th anniv. of Independence. This stamp is always imperforate on one or two sides.
A 15p blue of somewhat similar design was prepared for the 10th anniv., but was not issued due to Amanullah's dethronement. Value, $15.

A38
A39    A40 
A41    A42 

1928-30   *Perf. 11, 12*
237 A38 2p dull blue ... 2.50 1.60
    a. Vertical pair, imperf. between
238 A38 2p lt rose ('30) ... .25 .25
239 A39 10p gray green ... .25 .15
    a. ... 5.00 5.00
    b. Vert. pair, imperf. horiz. ... .65
    c. Vert. pair, imperf. between ... 1.00
240   10p choc ('30) ... .50 .50
    a. 10p brown purple ('29) ... 10.00 2.50
241 A40 25p car rose ... .35 .25
242 A40 25p Prus green ('29) ... .75 .60
243 A41 40p ultra ... .40 .35
    a. Tete beche pair ... 5.00
244 A41 40p red rose ('29) ... 1.00 1.00
    a. Tete beche pair ... 7.00
    b. Vert. pair, imperf. horiz. ... 3.50
245 A42 50p red ... .30 .30
246 A42 50p dk blue ('29) ... 1.50 1.00
  Nos. 237-246 (10) ... 7.80 6.00

The sheets of these stamps are often imperforate at the outer margins.
Nos. 237-238 are newspaper stamps.

This handstamp was used for ten months by the Revolutionary Gov't in Kabul as a control mark on outgoing mail. It occasionally fell on the stamps but there is no evidence that it was officially used as an overprint. Unused copies were privately made.

Independence Monument — A46

Wmk. Large Seal in the Sheet
1931, Aug.   *Litho.*   *Perf. 12*
Laid Paper
Without Gum
262 A46 20p red ... 1.00 .60

13th Independence Day.

National Assembly Chamber — A47 
A48    A50 
National Assembly Building A49 
National Assembly Chamber A51

National Assembly Building — A52

1932   *Unwmk.*   *Typo.*   *Perf. 12*
Wove Paper
263 A47 40p olive ... 1.00 .40
264 A48 60p violet ... .65 .50
265 A49 80p dark red ... 1.00 .80
266 A50 1af black ... 10.00 4.25
267 A51 2af ultra ... 3.50 2.75
268 A52 3af gray green ... 4.25 3.50
  Nos. 263-268 (6) ... 20.40 12.20

Formation of the Natl. Council. Imperforate or perforated examples on ungummed chalky paper are proofs.
See Nos. 304-305.

Mosque at Balkh — A53
Kabul Fortress — A54 
Parliament House, Darul Funun — A55 
Parliament House, Darul Funun — A56 
Arch of Qalai Bist — A57 
Memorial Pillar of Knowledge and Ignorance — A58 
Independence Monument — A59 
Minaret at Herat — A60 
Arch of Paghman — A61 
Ruins at Balkh — A62

AFGHANISTAN

Minarets of Herat — A63
Great Buddha at Bamian — A64  

1932		Typo.	Perf. 12	
269	A53	10p brown	.50	.15
270	A54	15p dk brown	.60	.15
271	A55	20p red	.30	.15
272	A56	25p dk green	.75	.15
273	A57	30p red	.40	.30
274	A58	40p orange	.65	.35
275	A59	50p blue	.80	.35
a.		Tete beche pair	5.50	
276	A60	60p blue	1.50	.50
277	A61	80p violet	1.75	1.00
278	A62	1af dark blue	2.75	.60
279	A63	2af dk red violet	3.75	2.00
280	A64	3af claret	4.25	2.50
		Nos. 269-280 (12)	18.00	8.20

Counterfeits of types A53-A65 exist.
See Nos. 290-295, 298-299, 302-303.

Entwined 2's — A65

Two types:
Type I - Numerals shaded. Size about 21x29mm.
Type II - Numerals unshaded. Size about 21 3/4 x30mm.

1931-38			Perf. 12, 11x12	
281	A65	2p red brn (I)	.25	.15
282	A65	2p olive blk (I) ('34)	.25	.15
283	A65	2p grnsh gray (I) ('34)	.35	.15
283A	A65	2p black (I) ('36)	.35	.15
284	A65	2p salmon (II) ('38)	.25	.15
284A	A65	2p rose (I) ('38)	.25	.15
b.		Imperf., pair	3.00	
		Imperf		
285	A65	2p black (II) ('37)	.75	.15
286	A65	2p salmon (II) ('38)	.25	.15
		Nos. 281-286 (8)	2.70	1.20

The newspaper rate was 2 pouls.

A66
A67 

1932, Aug. Perf. 12
287 A66 1af Independence Monument 2.75 1.50
14th Independence Day.

1932, Oct. Typo.
1929 Liberation Monument, Kabul.
288 A67 80p red brown .85 .50

Arch of Paghman A68

1933, Aug.
289 A68 50p light ultra 1.25 1.25
15th Independence Day.

Royal Palace, Kabul — A69
Darrah-Shikari Pass, Hindu Kush — A70 

Types of 1932 and

1934-38		Typo.	Perf. 12	
290	A53	10p deep violet	.15	.15
291	A54	15p turq green	.20	.15
292	A55	20p magenta	.25	.15
293	A56	25p deep rose	.30	.15
294	A57	30p orange	.40	.20
295	A58	40p blue black	.75	.30
296	A69	45p dark blue	1.50	.15
297	A69	45p red ('38)	.50	.15
298	A59	50p orange	.30	.15
299	A60	60p purple	.85	.15
300	A70	75p red	1.00	.35
301	A70	75p dk blue ('38)	.60	.40
302	A61	80p brown vio	1.00	.50
303	A62	1af red violet	1.65	.15
304	A51	2af gray black	3.00	2.00
305	A52	3af ultra	5.00	3.00
		Nos. 290-305 (16)	17.45	9.80

Nos. 290, 292, 300, 304, 305 exist imperf.

Independence Monument — A71

1934, Aug. Litho. Without Gum
306 A71 50p pale green 2.50 1.25
a. Tete beche pair 10.00 3.50
16th year of Independence. Each sheet of 40 (4x10) included 4 tete beche pairs as lower half of sheet was inverted.

Independence Monument A74
Fireworks Display A75 

1935, Aug. 15 Laid Paper
309 A74 50p dark blue 1.25 1.25
17th year of Independence.

1936, Aug. 15 Wove Paper Perf. 12
310 A75 50p red violet 1.25 1.00
18th year of Independence.

Independence Monument and Nadir Shah — A76

1937
311 A76 50p vio & bis brn 1.00 .60
a. Imperf., pair 2.25
19th year of Independence.

Mohammed Nadir Shah A77
A78

1938 Perf. 11x12 Without Gum
315 A77 50p brt blue & sepia 5.00 2.50
a. Imperf. pair 20.00
20th year of Independence.

1939 Perf. 11, 12x11
317 A78 50p deep salmon 1.75 1.00
21st year of Independence.

National Arms A79

Parliament House, Darul Funun A80

Royal Palace, Kabul A81
Independence Monument A82 

Independence Monument and Nadir Shah — A83

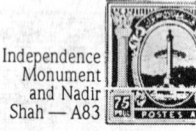

Mohammed Zahir Shah — A84

Mohammed Zahir Shah — A85

Perf. 11, 11x12, 12x11, 12
1939-61			Typo.	
318	A79	2p intense blk	.15	.15
318A	A79	2p brt pink ('61)	1.50	.15
319	A80	10p brt purple	.15	.15
320	A80	15p brt green	.15	.15
321	A80	20p red lilac	.15	.15
322	A81	25p rose red	1.00	.25
322A	A81	25p green ('41)	.50	.15
323	A81	30p orange	.20	.15
324	A81	40p dk gray	.20	.15
325	A82	45p brt carmine	.20	.15
326	A82	50p dp orange	.30	.20
327	A82	60p violet	.60	.20
328	A83	75p ultra	3.00	.15
328A	A83	75p red vio ('41)	.75	.30
328C	A83	75p brt red ('44)	3.00	3.00
328D	A83	75p chnt brn ('49)	4.00	3.00
329	A83	80p chocolate	.50	.50
a.		80p dull red violet (error)		
330	A84	1af brt red violet	1.50	.75
330A	A84	1af brt red vio ('44)	3.00	1.50
331	A85	2af copper red	1.75	.50
a.		2af dp rose red	2.50	1.35
332	A84	3af deep blue	3.75	1.60
		Nos. 318-332 (21)	26.35	14.25

Many shades exist in this issue.
On No. 332 the King faces slightly left.
No. 318A issued with and without gum.
See #795A-795B. For similar design see #907A.

Mohammed Nadir Shah — A86

1940, Aug. 23 Perf. 11
333 A86 50p gray green .75 .60
22nd year of Independence.

Independence Monument A87
Arch of Paghman A88 

1941, Aug. 23 Perf. 12
334 A87 15p gray green 8.00 2.75
335 A88 50p red brown 1.25 .85
23rd year of Independence.

Sugar Factory, Baghlan — A89

1942, Apr. Perf. 12
336 A89 1.25af blue (shades) 2.00 1.00
a. 1.25af ultra 2.00 1.00
In 1949, a 1.50af brown, type A89, was sold for 3af by the Philatelic Office, Kabul. It was not valid for postage. Value $3.50.

Independence Monument A90
Mohammed Nadir Shah and Arch of Paghman A91 

1942, Aug. 23 Perf. 12
337 A90 35p bright green 2.75 2.00
338 A91 125p chalky blue 1.40 1.10
24th year of Independence.

Independence Monument and Nadir Shah — A92
Mohammed Nadir Shah — A93 

Perf. 11x12, 12x11
1943, Aug. 25 Typo. Unwmk.
339 A92 35p carmine 18.00 6.00
340 A93 1.25af dark blue 3.00 1.75
25th year of Independence.

AFGHANISTAN

Tomb of Gohar Shad, Herat — A94

Ruins of Qalai Bist — A95

1944, May 1 — Perf. 12, 11x12
341	A94	35p orange	.50	.30
342	A95	70p violet	1.00	.60
a.		70p rose lilac	3.50	.75

A96 — A97

1944, Aug. — Perf. 12
343	A96	35p crimson	.80	.60
344	A97	1.25af ultra	1.40	1.10

26th year of Independence.

A98 — A99

1945, July
345	A98	35p dp red lil	.75	.65
346	A99	1.25af blue	1.75	1.50

27th year of Independence.

Mohammed Zahir Shah A100

Independence Monument A101

Mohammed Nadir Shah — A102

1946, July
347	A100	15p emerald	.45	.35
348	A101	20p dp red lilac	.70	.55
349	A102	125p blue	1.75	1.75
		Nos. 347-349 (3)	2.90	2.65

28th year of Independence.

Zahir Shah and Ruins of Qalai Bist — A103

A104 — A105

1947, Aug.
350	A103	15p yellow green	.30	.15
351	A104	35p plum	.40	.20
352	A105	125p deep blue	1.40	1.40
		Nos. 350-352 (3)	2.10	1.75

29th year of Independence.

Begging Child — A106

A107

1948, May Unwmk. Typo. Perf. 12
353	A106	35p yel green	3.00	2.00
354	A107	125p gray blue	3.00	2.25

Children's Day, May 29, 1948, and valid only on that day. Proceeds were used for Child Welfare.

A108 — A109

A110

1948, Aug.
355	A108	15p green	.20	.15
356	A109	20p magenta	.40	.15
357	A110	125p dark blue	.75	.70
		Nos. 355-357 (3)	1.35	1.00

30th year of Independence.

United Nations Emblem A111

1948, Oct. 24
358	A111	125p dk violet blue	7.00	7.00

UN, 3rd anniv. Valid one day only. Sheets of 9.

Maiwand Victory Column, Kandahar — A112

Zahir Shah and Ruins of Qalai Bist — A113

Independence Monument and Nadir Shah — A114

359	A112	25p green	.25	.15
360	A113	35p magenta	.35	.25
361	A114	1.25af blue	.90	.75
		Nos. 359-361 (3)	1.50	1.15

31st year of Independence.

> Catalogue values for unused stamps in this section, from this point to the end of the section, are for Never Hinged items.

Nadir Shah — A117

1950, Aug.
364	A117	35p red brown	.30	.30
365	A117	125p blue	.65	.65

32nd year of Independence.

Medical School and Nadir Shah A119

1950, Dec. 22 Typo. Perf. 12
Size: 38x25mm
367	A119	35p emerald	.60	.60

Size: 46x30mm
368	A119	1.25af deep blue	1.90	1.90
a.		1.25af black (error)	6.00	

19th anniv. of the founding of Afghanistan's Faculty of Medicine. On sale and valid for use on Dec. 22-28, 1950.

Minaret, Herat — A120

Zahir Shah — A121

Mosque of Khodja Abu Parsar, Balkh — A122

A123 — A124

20p, Buddha at Bamian. 40p, Ruined arch. 45p, Maiwand Victory onument. 50p, View of Kandahar. 60p, Ancient tower. 70p, Afghanistan flag. 80p, 1af, Profile of Zahir Shah in uniform.

Photogravure, Engraved, Engraved and Lithographed
Perf. 12, 12½, 13x12½, 13½
1951, Mar. 21 Unwmk.
Imprint: "Waterlow & Sons Limited, London"

369	A120	10p yellow & brn	.15	.15
370	A120	15p blue & brn	.15	.15
371	A120	20p black	5.00	2.75
372	A121	25p green	.15	.15
373	A122	30p cerise	.20	.15
374	A121	35p violet	.20	.15
375	A122	40p chestnut brn	.25	.15
376	A122	45p deep blue	.20	.15
377	A122	50p olive black	.45	.15
378	A120	60p black	1.50	.75
379	A122	70p dk grn, blk, red & grn	.25	.15
380	A123	75p cerise	.75	.35
381	A123	80p carmine & blk	.65	.35
382	A123	1af dp grn & vio	.45	.15
383	A124	1.25af rose lil & blk	5.00	.35
384	A124	2af ultra	1.10	.35
385	A124	3af ultra & blk	2.50	.90
		Nos. 369-385 (17)	18.95	7.50

Nos. 372, 374 and 381 to 385 are engraved, No. 379 is engraved and lithographed.
Imperfs. exist of the photogravure stamps.
See Nos. 445-451, 453, 552A-552D. For surcharges see Nos. B1-B2.

Arch of Paghman — A125

Nadir Shah and Independence Monument A126

Overprint in Violet

1951, Aug. 25 Perf. 13½x13, 13 Engr.
386	A125	35p dk green & blk	.60	.35
387	A126	1.25af deep blue	1.40	.85

Overprint reads "Sol 33 Istiqlal" or "33rd Year of Independence." Overprint measures about 11mm wide.
See Nos. 398-399B, 441-442.

Proposed Flag of Pashtunistan — A127

Design: 125p, Flag and Pashtunistan warrior.

1951, Sept. 2 Litho. Perf. 11½
388	A127	35p dull chocolate	.80	.65
389	A127	125p blue	2.00	1.75

Issued to publicize "Free Pashtunistan" Day.

Imperforates
From 1951 to 1958, quantities of nearly all locally-printed stamps were left imperforate and sold by the government at double face. From 1959 until March, 1964, many of the imperforates were sold for more than face value.

Avicenna — A128

1951, Nov. 4 Typo. Perf. 11½
390	A128	35p deep claret	.50	.35
391	A128	125p blue	1.40	1.10

20th anniv. of the founding of the natl. Graduate School of Medicine.

A129

AFGHANISTAN

Dove and UN Symbols — A130

1951, Oct. 24
| 392 | A129 | 35p magenta | 1.40 | 1.00 |
| 393 | A130 | 125p blue | 3.50 | 2.75 |

7th anniv. of the UN.

Amir Sher Ali Khan and Tiger Head Stamp — A131

Nos. 395, 397, Zahir Shah and stamp.

1951, Dec. 23   Litho.
394	A131	35p chocolate	.35	.35
395	A131	35p rose lilac	.35	.35
396	A131	125p ultra	.65	.60
a.		Cliche of 35p in plate of 125p	80.00	80.00
397	A131	125p aqua	.65	.60
		Nos. 394-397 (4)	2.00	1.90

76th anniv. of the UPU.

Stamps of 1951 Without Overprint
Perf. 13½x13, 13   Engr.

1952, Aug. 24
| 398 | A125 | 35p dk green & blk | 1.25 | 1.25 |
| 399 | A126 | 1.25af deep blue | 1.25 | 1.25 |

For overprints see #399A-399B, 441-442.

Same Overprinted in Violet

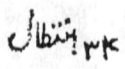

| 399A | A125 | 35p dk grn & blk | .60 | .40 |
| 399B | A126 | 1.25af deep blue | 1.60 | 1.00 |

#398-399B issued for 34th Independence Day.

Globe — A132

Perf. 11½   Unwmk.   Litho.
1952, Oct. 25
| 400 | A132 | 35p rose | .55 | .45 |
| 401 | A132 | 125p aqua | 1.10 | 1.00 |

Issued to honor the United Nations.

Symbol of Medicine — A134

Tribal Warrior, Natl. Flag — A135

1952, Nov.   Perf. 11½
| 403 | A134 | 35p chocolate | .40 | .35 |
| 404 | A134 | 125p violet blue | 1.10 | 1.10 |

21st anniv. of the natl. Graduate School of Medicine.
No. 404 is inscribed in French with white letters on a colored background.

1952, Sept. 1   Perf. 11
| 405 | A135 | 35p red | .30 | .30 |
| 406 | A135 | 125p dark blue | .60 | .60 |

No. 406 is inscribed in French "Pashtunistan Day, 1952."

Flags of Afghanistan & Pashtunistan A139

Badge of Pashtunistan A140

Perf. 10½x11, 11   Unwmk.
1953, Sept. 1
| 411 | A139 | 35p vermilion | .20 | .15 |
| 412 | A140 | 125p blue | .60 | .45 |

Issued to publicize "Free Pashtunistan" Day.

Nadir Shah and Flag Bearer — A141

A142

1953, Aug. 24   Perf. 11
| 413 | A141 | 35p green | .20 | .15 |
| 414 | A142 | 125p violet | .75 | .60 |

35th anniv. of Independence.

United Nations Emblem — A143

1953, Oct. 24
| 415 | A143 | 35p lilac | .60 | .60 |
| 416 | A143 | 125p violet blue | 1.50 | 1.20 |

United Nations Day, 1953.

Nadir Shah A144   A145

1953, Nov. 29
| 417 | A144 | 35p orange | .65 | .65 |
| 418 | A145 | 125p chalky blue | 1.50 | 1.50 |

22nd anniv. of the founding of the natl. Graduate School of Medicine.

Redrawn

35p. Original- Right character in second line of Persian inscription: ٣

Redrawn- Persian character: ٢

125p: Original- Inscribed "XXIII," "MADECINE" and "ANNIVERAIRE"
Redrawn- Inscribed "XXII," "MEDECINE" and "ANNIVERSAIRE"

1953
| 419 | A144 | 35p deep orange | 3.50 | |
| 420 | A145 | 125p chalky blue | 4.25 | |

Nadir Shah and Symbols of Independence A146

1954, Aug.   Typo.   Perf. 11
| 421 | A146 | 35p carmine rose | .35 | .30 |
| 422 | A146 | 125p violet blue | 1.00 | .80 |

36th year of Independence.

Raising Flag of Pashtunistan A147

1954, Sept.   Perf. 11½
| 423 | A147 | 35p chocolate | .35 | .30 |
| 424 | A147 | 125p blue | 1.00 | .80 |

Issued to publicize "Free Pashtunistan" Day.

UN Flag and Map — A148

1954, Oct. 24   Perf. 11
| 425 | A148 | 35p carmine rose | .65 | .65 |
| 426 | A148 | 125p dk violet blue | 2.00 | 2.00 |

9th anniv. of the United Nations.

UN Symbols — A149

Design: 125p, UN emblem & flags.

1955, June 26   Litho.   Perf. 11
Size: 26½x36mm
| 427 | A149 | 35p dark green | .45 | .40 |
Size: 28½x36mm
| 428 | A149 | 125p aqua | 1.10 | .90 |

10th anniv. of the UN charter.

Nadir Shah (center) and Brothers — A150

1929 Civil War Scene and Zahir Shah — A151

Tribal Elders' Council and Pashtun Flag — A152

1955, Aug.   Unwmk.   Perf. 11
429	A150	35p brt pink	.30	.30
430	A150	35p violet blue	.30	.30
431	A151	125p rose lilac	.90	.75
432	A151	125p light violet	.90	.75
		Nos. 429-432 (4)	2.40	2.10

37th anniv. of Independence.

1955, Sept. 5
| 433 | A152 | 35p orange brown | .20 | .20 |
| 434 | A152 | 125p yellow green | .90 | .65 |

Issued for "Free Pashtunistan" Day.

UN Flag — A153

A154

1955, Oct. 24   Unwmk.   Perf. 11
| 435 | A153 | 35p orange brown | .75 | .60 |
| 436 | A153 | 125p brt ultra | 1.40 | 1.10 |

10th anniv. of the United Nations.

1956, Aug.   Litho.
| 437 | A154 | 35p lt green | .25 | .20 |
| 438 | A154 | 140p lt violet blue | .90 | .75 |

38th year of Independence.

Jesh'n Exhibition Hall — A155

1956, Aug. 25
| 439 | A155 | 50p chocolate | .25 | .25 |
| 440 | A155 | 50p lt violet blue | .25 | .25 |

International Exposition at Kabul.
Of the 50p face value, only 35p paid postage. The remaining 15p went to the Exposition.

Nos. 398-399 Handstamped in Violet

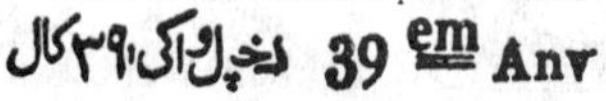

a   b

1957, Aug.   Engr.   Perf. 13½x13, 13
| 441 | A125 (a) | 35p dk green & blk | .40 | .20 |
| 442 | A126 (b) | 1.25af deep blue | .60 | .50 |

Arabic overprint measures 19mm.
39th year of independence.

Pashtunistan Flag — A156

1957, Sept. 1   Litho.   Perf. 11
| 443 | A156 | 50p pale lilac rose | .60 | .40 |
| 444 | A156 | 155p light violet | .90 | .75 |

Issued for "Free Pashtunistan" Day. French inscription on No. 444. 15p of each stamp went to the Pashtunistan Fund.

Types of 1951 and

Game of Buzkashi A157

Perf. 12, 12½, 12½x13, 13, 13x12, 13x12½, 13½x14
Photo., Engr., Engr.& Litho.
1957, Nov. 23   Unwmk.
Imprint: "Waterlow & Sons Limited, London"
445	A122	30p brown	.15	.15
446	A122	40p rose red	.20	.15
447	A122	50p yellow	.35	.15
448	A120	60p ultra	.40	.15
449	A123	75p brt violet	.50	.15
450	A123	80p violet & brn	.50	.15
451	A123	1af carmine & ultra	1.00	.15
452	A157	140p olive & dp claret	2.00	.50
453	A124	3af orange & blk	2.50	.50
		Nos. 445-453 (9)	7.60	2.05

No. 452 lacks imprint.

Nadir Shah and Flag-bearer A158

AFGHANISTAN

1958, Aug. 25   *Perf. 13½x14*
454 A158 35p dp yellow green   .20 .15
455 A158 140p brown   .55 .35
40th year of Independence.

Exposition Buildings — A159

1958, Aug. 23   *Litho.*   *Perf. 11*
456 A159 35p brt blue green   .15 .15
457 A159 140p vermilion   .50 .40
International Exposition at Kabul.

Pres. Celal Bayar of Turkey A160

Flags of UN and Afghanistan A161

1958, Sept. 13   *Unwmk.*
458 A160 50p lt blue   .20 .15
459 A160 100p brown   .35 .30
Visit of President Celal Bayar of Turkey.

1958, Oct. 24   *Photo.*   *Perf. 14x13½*
Flags in Original Colors
460 A161 50p dark gray   .60 .60
461 A161 100p green   1.10 .90
United Nations Day, Oct. 24.

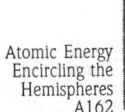

Atomic Energy Encircling the Hemispheres A162

1958, Oct. 20   *Perf. 13½x14*
462 A162 50p blue   .60 .35
463 A162 100p dp red lilac   .90 .55
Issued to promote Atoms for Peace.

UNESCO Building, Paris — A163

1958, Nov. 3
464 A163 50p dp yellow grn   .50 .40
465 A163 100p brown olive   .75 .60
UNESCO Headquarters in Paris opening, Nov. 3.

Globe and Torch — A164

Perf. 13½x14
1958, Dec. 10   *Unwmk.*
466 A164 50p lilac rose   .35 .35
467 A164 100p maroon   .65 .65
10th anniv. of the signing of the Universal Declaration of Human Rights.

Nadir Shah and Flags — A165

1959, Aug.   *Litho.*   *Perf. 11 Rough*
468 A165 35p light vermilion   .20 .20
469 A165 165p light violet   .65 .40
41st year of Independence.

Uprooted Oak Emblem — A166

1960, Apr. 7   *Perf. 11*
470 A166 50p deep orange   .15 .15
471 A166 165p blue   .35 .30
Issued to publicize World Refugee Year, July 1, 1959-June 30, 1960.
Two imperf. souvenir sheets exist. Both contain a 50p and a 165p, type A166, with marginal inscriptions and WRY emblem in maroon. On one sheet the stamps are in the colors of Nos. 470-471 (size 108x81mm). On the other, the 50p is blue and the 165p is deep orange (size 107x80mm). Value $4 each.
For surcharges see Nos. B35-B36.

Buzkashi A167

1960, May 4   *Perf. 11, Imperf.*
472 A167 25p rose red   .22 .15
473 A167 50p bluish green   .50 .35
  a.   Cliche of 25p in plate of 50p   20.00 20.00
See Nos. 549-550A.

Independence Monument — A168

1960, Aug.   *Perf. 11, 12*
474 A168 50p light blue   .15 .15
475 A168 175p bright pink   .40 .40
42nd Independence Day.

Globe and Flags — A169

1960, Oct. 24   *Litho.*   *Perf. 11, 12*
476 A169 50p rose lilac   .25 .20
477 A169 175p ultra   .75 .65
UN Day.
An imperf. souvenir sheet contains one each of Nos. 476-477 with marginal inscriptions ("La Journée des Nations Unies 1960" in French and Persian) and UN emblem in light blue. Size: 127x85½mm. Value $4.
This sheet was surcharged "+20ps" in 1962. Value $8.50.

Teacher Pointing to Globe — A170

1960, Oct. 23   *Perf. 11*
478 A170 50p brt pink   .20 .15
479 A170 100p brt green   .70 .45
Issued to publicize Teacher's Day.

Mohammed Zahir Shah — A171

1960, Oct. 15
480 A171 50p red brown   .30 .15
481 A171 150p dk car rose   .90 .30
Honoring the King on his 46th birthday.

Buzkashi A172

1960, Nov. 9   *Perf. 11*
482 A172 175p lt red brown   1.00 .40
See Nos. 551-552.

No. 482 Overprinted "1960" and Olympic Rings in Bright Green.

1960, Dec. 24
483 A172 175p red brown   2.00 1.75
  a.   Souv. sheet of 1, imperf.   8.50
17th Olympic Games, Rome, Aug. 25-Sept. 11.

Mir Wais — A173

1961, Jan. 5   *Unwmk.*   *Perf. 10½*
484 A173 50p brt rose lilac   .20 .15
485 A173 175p ultra   .60 .40
  a.   Souv. sheet of 2, #484-485, imperf.   2.00 2.00
Mir Wais (1665-1708), national leader.

No Postal Need
existed for the 1p-15p denominations issued with sets of 1961-63 (between Nos. 486 and 649, B37 and B65).
The lowest denomination actually used for non-philatelic postage in that period was 25p (except for the 2p newspaper rate for which separate stamps were provided).

Horse, Sheep and Camel — A174

#487, 175p, Rock partridge. 10p, 100p, Afghan hound. 15p, 150p, Grain & grasshopper, vert.

1961, Mar. 29   *Photo.*   *Perf. 13½x14*
486 A174 2p maroon & buff
487 A174 2p ultra & org
488 A174 5p brown & yel
489 A174 10p black & salmon
490 A174 15p blue grn & yel
491 A174 25p black & pink
492 A174 50p black & citron
493 A174 100p black & pink
494 A174 150p green & yel
495 A174 175p ultra & pink
    Nos. 486-495 (10)   2.00
Two souvenir sheets, perf. and imperf., contain 2 stamps, 1 each of #492-493. Value $2 each.

Afghan Fencing A175

Designs: No. 497, 5p, 25p, 50p, Wrestlers. 10p, 100p, Man with Indian clubs. 15p, 150p, Afghan fencing. 175p, Children skating.

1961, July 6   *Perf. 13½x14*
496 A175 2p green & rose lil
497 A175 2p brown & citron
498 A175 5p gray & rose
499 A175 10p blue & bister
500 A175 15p sl bl & dl lil
501 A175 25p black & dl bl
502 A175 50p sl grn & bis brn
503 A175 100p brown & bl grn
504 A175 150p brown & org yel
505 A175 175p black & blue
    Nos. 496-505 (10)   3.00
Issued for Children's Day.
A souvenir sheet exists, perf. and imperf., containing one each of Nos. 502-503. Value $4.50 each.
For surcharges see Nos. B37-B41.

Bande Amir Lakes — A176

1961, Aug. 7   *Photo.*   *Perf. 13½x14*
506 A176 3af brt blue   .35 .30
507 A176 10af rose claret   1.10 1.00

Nadir Shah — A177

Girl Scout — A178

1961, Aug. 23   *Perf. 14x13½*
508 A177 50p rose red & blk   .50 .40
509 A177 175p brt grn & org brn   1.00 .80
43rd Independence Day.
Two souvenir sheets, perf. and imperf., contain one each of Nos. 508-509. Value, each $2.50.

Perf. 14x13½
1961, July 23   *Unwmk.*
510 A178 50p dp car & dk gray   .40 .15
511 A178 175p dp grn & rose brn   .90 .40
Issued for Women's Day.
Two souvenir sheets exist, perf. and imperf., containing one each of Nos. 510-511. Value $3 each.

Exhibition Hall, Kabul — A179

1961, Aug. 23   *Perf. 13½x14*
512 A179 50p yel brn & yel grn   .15 .15
513 A179 175p blue & brn   .40 .30
International Exhibition at Kabul.

Pathan with Pashtunistan Flag — A180

1961, Aug. 31   *Photo.*   *Perf. 14x13½*
514 A180 50p blk, lil & red   .15 .15
515 A180 175p brn, grnsh bl & red   .35 .30
Issued for "Free Pashtunistan Day."
Souvenir sheets exist perf. and imperf. containing one each of Nos. 514-515. Value $2 each.

AFGHANISTAN

Assembly Building — A181

1961, Sept. 10   *Perf. 12*
516 A181 50p dk gray & brt grn .15 .15
517 A181 175p ultra & brn .45 .30
Anniv. of the founding of the Natl. Assembly. Souvenir sheets exist, perf. and imperf., containing one each of Nos. 516-517. Value $1 each.

Exterminating Anopheles Mosquito — A182

1961, Oct. 5   *Perf. 13½×14*
518 A182 50p blk & brn lil .50 .30
519 A182 175p maroon & brt grn 1.10 .50
Anti-Malaria campaign. Souvenir sheets exist, perf. and imperf., containing one each of Nos. 518-519. Value $4 each.

Zahir Shah — A183

1961, Oct. 15   *Perf. 13½*
520 A183 50p lilac & blue .15 .15
521 A183 175p emerald & red brn .40 .35
Issued to honor King Mohammed Zahir Shah on his 47th birthday. See Nos. 609-612.

Pomegranates A184

Fruit: No. 523, 5p, 25p, 50p, Grapes. 10p, 150p, Apples. 15p, 175p, Pomegranates. 100p, Melons.

1961, Oct. 16   *Perf. 13½×14*
Fruit in Natural Colors
522 A184 2p black
523 A184 2p green
524 A184 5p lilac rose
525 A184 10p lilac
526 A184 15p dk blue
527 A184 25p dull red
528 A184 50p purple
529 A184 100p brt blue
530 A184 150p brown
531 A184 175p olive gray
    Nos. 522-531 (10) 1.75
For Afghan Red Crescent Society. Souvenir sheets exist, perf. and imperf., containing one each of Nos. 528-529. Value $1.50 each.
For surcharges see Nos. B42-B46.

UN Headquarters, NY — A185

1961, Oct. 24   *Perf. 13½×14*
Vertical Borders in Emerald, Red and Black
532 A185 1p rose lilac
533 A185 2p slate
534 A185 3p brown
535 A185 4p ultra
536 A185 50p rose red
537 A185 75p gray
538 A185 175p brt green
    Nos. 532-538 (7) 1.50
16th anniv. of the UN. Souvenir sheets exist, perf. and imperf., containing one each of Nos. 536-538. Value $2 each.

Children Giving Flowers to Teacher — A186

People Raising UNESCO Symbol — A187

1961, Oct. 26   *Photo.*   *Perf. 12*
539 A186 2p multicolored
540 A186 5p multicolored
541 A186 10p multicolored
542 A186 15p multicolored
543 A186 25p multicolored
544 A186 50p multicolored
545 A186 100p multicolored
546 A186 150p multicolored
547 A186 175p multicolored
    Nos. 539-548 (10) 1.75
Issued for Teacher's Day. Souvenir sheets exist, perf. and imperf. containing one each of Nos. 545-546. Value, 2 sheets, $4.
For surcharges see Nos. B47-B51.

Buzkashi Types of 1960
1961-72   *Litho.*   *Perf. 10½, 11*
549 A167 25p violet .15 .15
   b. 25p brt vio, typo. ('72) .15 .15
549A A167 25p citron ('63) .20 .15
550 A167 50p blue .30 .15
550A A167 50p yel org ('69) .15 .15
551 A172 100p citron .45 .15
551A A172 150p orange ('64) .30 .15
552 A172 2af lt green 1.10 .45
    Nos. 549-552 (7) 2.65 1.35

Zahir Shah Types of 1951
Photo., Engr., Engr. & Litho.
1962   *Perf. 13×12, 13*
Imprint: "Thomas De La Rue & Co. Ltd."
552A A123 75p brt purple 1.10 .25
552B A123 1af car & ultra 1.40 .35
552C A124 2af blue 1.75 .75
552D A124 3af orange & blk 4.00 1.10
    Nos. 552A-552D (4) 8.25 2.45

1962, July 2   *Photo.*   *Perf. 14×13½*
553 A187 2p rose lil & brn
554 A187 2p ol bis & brn
555 A187 5p dp org & dk grn
556 A187 10p gray & mag
557 A187 15p blue & brn
558 A187 25p org yel & pur
559 A187 50p lt grn & pur
560 A187 75p brt cit & brn
561 A187 100p dp org & brn
    Nos. 553-561 (9) 1.60
15th anniv. of UNESCO. Souvenir sheets exist, perf. and imperf. One contains Nos. 558-559; the other contains Nos. 560-561. Value, $3 each.
For surcharges see Nos. B52-B60.

Ahmad Shah — A188

Afghan Hound — A189

1962, Feb. 24   *Photo.*   *Perf. 13½*
562 A188 50p red brn & gray .15 .15
563 A188 75p green & salmon .25 .20
564 A188 100p claret & bister .40 .30
    Nos. 562-564 (3) .80 .65
Ahmad Shah (1724-73), founded the Afghan kingdom in 1747 and ruled until 1773.

1962, Apr. 21   *Perf. 14×13½*
Designs: 5p, 75p, Afghan cock. 10p, 100p, Kondjid plant. 15p, 125p, Astrakhan skins.
565 A189 2p rose & brn
566 A189 2p lt green & brn
567 A189 5p dp rose & claret
568 A189 10p lt grn & sl grn
569 A189 15p blue grn & blk
570 A189 25p blue & brn
571 A189 50p gray & brn
572 A189 75p rose lil & lil
573 A189 100p gray & dl grn
574 A189 125p rose brn & blk
    Nos. 565-574 (10) 2.00
Agriculture Day. Perf. and imperf. souvenir sheets exist. Set of 4 sheets, value $4.

Athletes with Flag and Nadir Shah A190

Woman in National Costume A191

   Perf. 12
575 A190 25p multicolored .15 .15
576 A190 50p multicolored .20 .15
577 A190 75p multicolored .25 .15
    Nos. 575-577 (3) .60 .45
44th Independence Day.

1962, Aug. 30   *Perf. 11½×12*
578 A191 25p lilac & brn .15 .15
579 A191 50p green & brn .25 .15
    Nos. 578-579, C15-C16 (4) 1.85 1.15
Issued for Women's Day. A souvenir sheet exists containing one each of #578-579, C15-C16. Value $3.

Man and Woman with Flag — A192

Malaria Eradication Emblem and Swamp — A193

1962, Aug. 31   *Photo.*
580 A192 25p black, pale bl & red .15 .15
581 A192 50p black, grn & red .20 .15
582 A192 150p black, pink & red .45 .15
    Nos. 580-582 (3) .80 .45
Issued for "Free Pashtunistan Day."

1962, Sept. 5   *Perf. 14×13½*
583 A193 2p dk grn & ol gray
584 A193 2p dk green & sal
585 A193 5p red brn & ol
586 A193 10p red brn & brt grn
587 A193 15p red brn & gray
588 A193 25p brt bl & bluish grn
589 A193 50p red brn & rose lil
590 A193 75p black & blue
591 A193 100p black & brt pink
592 A193 150p black & bis brn
593 A193 175p black & orange
    Nos. 583-593 (11) 2.50
WHO drive to eradicate malaria. Perf. and imperf. souvenir sheets exist. Set of 4 sheets, value $6.50.
For surcharges see Nos. B61-B71.

National Assembly Building A194

   Perf. 10½, 11 (100p)
1962, Sept. 10   *Unwmk.*   *Litho.*
594 A194 25p lt green .35 .25
595 A194 50p blue .55 .35
596 A194 75p rose .70 .55
597 A194 100p violet 1.10 .90
598 A194 125p ultra 1.20 1.10
    Nos. 594-598 (5) 3.90 3.15
Establishment of the National Assembly.

Horse Racing — A195

Designs: 2p, Pole vaulting. 3p, Wrestling. 4p, Weight lifting. 5p, Soccer.

1962, Sept. 22   *Photo.*   *Perf. 12*
Black Inscriptions
599 A195 1p lt ol & red brn
600 A195 2p lt grn & red brn
601 A195 3p yellow & dk pur
602 A195 4p pale bl & grn
603 A195 5p bluish grn & dk brn
    Nos. 599-603, C17-C22 (11) 2.50
4th Asian Games, Djakarta, Indonesia. Two souvenir sheets exist. A perforated one contains a 125p blue, dark blue and brown stamp in horse racing design. An imperf. one contains a 2af buff, purple and black stamp in soccer design. Value, $3.50 each.

Runners A196

1p, 2p, Diver, vert. 4p, Peaches. 5p, Iris, vert.

   Perf. 11½×12, 12×11½
1962, Oct. 2   *Unwmk.*
604 A196 1p rose lil & brn
605 A196 2p blue & brn
606 A196 3p brt blue & lil
607 A196 4p ol gray & multi
608 A196 5p gray & multi
    Nos. 604-608, C23-C25 (8) 2.00
Issued for Children's Day.

King Type of 1961, Dated "1962"
1962, Oct. 15   *Perf. 13½*
Various Frames
609 A183 25p lilac rose & brn .15 .15
610 A183 50p orange brn & grn .15 .15
611 A183 75p blue & lake .15 .15
612 A183 100p green & red brn .30 .20
    Nos. 609-612 (4) .75 .65
Issued to honor King Mohammed Zahir Shah on his 48th birthday.

Grapes A197

1962, Oct. 16   *Perf. 12*
613 A197 1p shown
614 A197 2p Grapes
615 A197 3p Pears
616 A197 4p Wistaria
617 A197 5p Blossoms
    Nos. 613-617, C26-C28 (8) 1.00
For the Afghan Red Crescent Society.

AFGHANISTAN

UN Headquarters, NY and Flags of UN and Afghanistan — A198

1962, Oct. 24   Unwmk.
618 A198 1p multicolored
619 A198 2p multicolored
620 A198 3p multicolored
621 A198 4p multicolored
622 A198 5p multicolored
  Nos. 618-622, C29-C31 (8)   2.00

UN Day. Souvenir sheets exist. One contains a single 4af ultramarine stamp, perforated; the other, a 4af ocher stamp, imperf. Value, 2 sheets, $5.

Boy Scout — A199    Pole Vault — A200

1962, Oct. 18   Photo.   Perf. 12
623 A199 1p yel, dk grn & sal
624 A199 2p dl yel, slate & sal
625 A199 3p rose, blk & sal
626 A199 4p multicolored
  Nos. 623-626, C32-C35 (8)   2.25

Issued to honor the Boy Scouts.

1962, Oct. 25   Unwmk.   Perf. 12

3p, High jump. 4p, 5p, Different blossoms.
627 A200 1p lilac & dk grn
628 A200 2p yellow grn & brn
629 A200 3p bister & vio
630 A200 4p sal pink, grn & ultra
631 A200 5p yellow, grn & bl
  Nos. 627-631, C36-C37 (7)   1.25

Issued for Teacher's Day.

Rockets A201

1962, Nov. 29
632 A201 50p pale lil & dk bl   .45
633 A201 100p lt blue & red brn   .85

UN World Meteorological Day. A souvenir sheet contains one 5af pink and green stamp. Value $6.

Ansari Mausoleum, Herat — A202

   Perf. 13½
1963, Jan. 3   Unwmk.   Photo.
634 A202 50p purple & green   .15 .15
635 A202 75p gray & magenta   .20 .20
636 A202 100p orange brn & brn   .30 .30
  Nos. 634-636 (3)   .65 .65

Khwaja Abdullah Ansari, Sufi, religious leader and poet, on the 900th anniv. of his death.

Sheep — A203

Silkworm, Cocoons, Moth and Mulberry Branch A204

1963, Mar. 1   Perf. 12
637 A203 1p grnsh blue & blk
638 A203 2p yellow grn & blk
639 A203 3p lilac rose & blk
640 A204 4p gray, grn & brn
641 A204 5p red lil, grn & brn
  Nos. 637-641, C42-C44 (8)   2.25

Issued for the Day of Agriculture.

Rice — A205

Designs: 3p, Corn. 300p, Wheat emblem.

1963, Mar. 27   Unwmk.   Perf. 14
642 A205 2p gray, claret & grn   .15 .15
643 A205 3p green, yel & ocher   .15 .15
644 A205 300p dk blue & yel   .30 .30
  Nos. 642-644 (3)   .60 .60

FAO "Freedom from Hunger" campaign.

Meteorological Measuring Instrument A206

Designs: 3p, 10p, Weather station. 4p, 5p, Rockets in space.

1963, May 23   Photo.   Perf. 13½x14
645 A206 1p dp magenta & brn
646 A206 2p brt blue & brn
647 A206 3p red & brown
648 A206 4p orange & lilac
649 A206 5p green & dl vio
     Imperf
650 A206 10p red brn & grn
  Nos. 645-650, C46-C50 (11)   7.50

3rd UN World Meteorological Day, Mar. 23.

Independence Monument — A207

1963, Aug. 23   Litho.   Perf. 10½
651 A207 25p lt green   .15 .15
652 A207 50p orange   .15 .15
653 A207 150p rose carmine   .35 .20
  Nos. 651-653 (3)   .65 .50

45th Independence Day.

Pathans in Forest — A208

1963, Aug. 31   Unwmk.   Perf. 10½
654 A208 25p pale violet   .15 .15
655 A208 50p sky blue   .15 .15
655A A208 150p dull red brn   .45 .35
  Nos. 654-655A (3)   .75 .65

Issued for "Free Pashtunistan Day."

4th Asian Games, Djakarta A208a

Designs: 2p, 250p, 300p, Wrestling. 3p, 10p, Tennis. 4p, 500p, Javelin. 5p, 9af, Shot put.

1963, Sept. 3   Litho.   Perf. 12
656 A208a 2p rose vio & brn
656A A208a 3p olive grn & brn
656B A208a 4p blue & brn
656C A208a 5p yel grn & brn
656D A208a 10p lt bl grn & brn
656E A208a 300p yellow & vio
656F A208a 500p lt yel bis & brn
656G A208a 9af pale grn & vio
  Nos. 656-656G (8)   1.75
      Souvenir Sheets
656H A208a 250p lilac & vio
656I A208a 300p blue & blk

Nos. 656-656F are airmail. Nos. 656-656I exist imperf.

National Assembly Building A209

1963, Sept. 10   Perf. 11
657 A209 25p gray   .15 .15
658 A209 50p dull red   .15 .15
659 A209 75p brown   .20 .15
660 A209 100p olive   .30 .15
661 A209 125p lilac   .40 .20
  Nos. 657-661 (5)   1.20 .80

Issued to honor the National Assembly.

Balkh Gate A210

1963, Oct. 8
662 A210 3af choc (screened margins)   .40 .30
   a.   White margins   1.00 .35

In the original printing a halftone screen extended across the plate, covering the space between the stamps. A retouch removed the screen between the stamps (No. 662a).

Intl. Red Cross, Cent. A210a

4p, 5p, 200p, 3af, Nurse holding patient, vert. 10p, 4af, 6af, Crown Prince Ahmed Shah.

1963, Oct. 9   Perf. 13½
662B A210a 2p olive, blk & red
662C A210a 3p blue, blk & red
662D A210a 4p lt grn, blk & red
662E A210a 5p lt vio, blk & red
662F A210a 10p gray grn, red & blk
662G A210a 100p dull bl grn, red & blk
662H A210a 200p lt brn, blk & red
662I A210a 4af brt bl grn, red & blk
   m.   Souvenir sheet of 1
662J A210a 6af lt brn, red & blk
      Souvenir Sheet
662K A210a 3af dl blue, blk & red

Nos. 662G-662K are airmail. Nos. 662B-662K exist imperf.

Zahir Shah — A211    Kemal Ataturk — A212

1963, Oct. 15   Perf. 10½
663 A211 25p green   .15 .15
663A A211 50p gray   .15 .15
663B A211 75p carmine rose   .20 .15
663C A211 100p dull redsh brn   .30 .15
  Nos. 663-663C (4)   .80 .60

King Mohammed Zahir Shah, 49th birthday.

1963, Oct. 10   Perf. 10½
664 A212 1af blue   .15 .15
665 A212 3af rose lilac   .40 .35

25th anniv. of the death of Kemal Ataturk, president of Turkey.

Protection of Nubian Monuments A213

Designs: 5af, 7.50af, 10af, Ruins, vert.

   Perf. 12, Imperf. (150p, 250p, 10af)
1963, Nov. 16   Photo.
666 A213 100p lil rose & blk
666A A213 150p rose lil & blk
666B A213 200p brown & blk
666C A213 250p ultra & blk
666D A213 500p green & blk
666E A213 5af greenish blue & gray bl
666F A213 7.50af red brn & gray bl
666G A213 10af ver & gray bl

#666E-666G are airmail. #666D exists imperf.

Women's Day — A213a    Boy and Girl Scouts — A213c

A213b

1964, Jan. 5   Perf. 14x13½
667 A213a 2p multicolored
667A A213a 3p multicolored
667B A213a 4p multicolored
667C A213a 5p multicolored
667D A213a 10p multicolored

Exist imperf.

1964, Jan. 5   Perf. 13½x14, 14x13½
#668F-668G, 668K-668M, Girl with flag.
668 A213b 2p multi
668A A213b 3p multi
668B A213b 4p multi
668C A213b 5p multi
668D A213b 10p multi
668E A213c 2p multi
668F A213c 2af multi
668G A213c 2.50af multi
668H A213c 3af multi
668I A213c 4af multi
668J A213c 5af multi
668K A213c 1␣2af multi

181

AFGHANISTAN

Souvenir Sheets
668L	A213c	5af multi
668M	A213c	6af multi
668N	A213c	6af multi
668O	A213c	10af multi

Nos. 668E-668O are airmail. Nos 668-668K, 668N-668O exist imperf.

Children — A213d

1964, Jan. 22   *Perf. 12*
669	A213d	2p Playing ball
669A	A213d	3p like #669
669B	A213d	4p Swinging, jumping rope, vert.
669C	A213d	5p Skiing, vert.
669D	A213d	10p like #669
669E	A213d	200p like #669C
669F	A213d	300p like #669B

Nos. 669E-669F are airmail. All exist imperf.

Red Crescent Society — A213e

Designs: 100p, 200p, Pierre and Marie Curie, physicists. 2.50af, 7.50af Nurse examining child. 3.50af, 5af, Nurse and patients.

Perf. 14, Imperf. (#670A, 670C-670D)
1964, Feb. 8
670	A213e	100p multi
670A	A213e	100p multi
670B	A213e	200p multi
670C	A213e	2.50af multi
670D	A213e	3.50af multi
670E	A213e	5af multi
670F	A213e	7.50af multi

Nos. 670B-670D are airmail.

Teachers' Day — A213f

Flowers: 2p, 3p, 3af, 4af, Tulips. 4p, 5p, 3.50af, 6af, Flax. 10p, 1.50af, 2af, Iris.

Perf. 12, Imperf. (1.50af, 2af)
1964, Mar. 3
671	A213f	2p multicolored
671A	A213f	3p multicolored
671B	A213f	4p multicolored
671C	A213f	5p multicolored
671D	A213f	10p multicolored
671E	A213f	1.50af multicolored
671F	A213f	2af multicolored
671G	A213f	3af multicolored
671H	A213f	3.50af multicolored

Souvenir Sheets
671I	A213f	4af multicolored
671J	A213f	6af multi, imperf

#671E-671J are airmail. #671I-671D exist imperf.

A213g

UN Day: 5p, 10p, 2af, 3af, 4af, Doctor and nurse, vert.

1964, Mar. 9   *Perf. 14*
672	A213g	2p multicolored
672A	A213g	3p multicolored
672B	A213g	4p multicolored
672C	A213g	5p multicolored
672D	A213g	10p multicolored
672E	A213g	100p multicolored
672F	A213g	2af multicolored
672G	A213g	3af multicolored

Souvenir Sheets
672H	A213g	4af multi, imperf.
672I	A213g	5af multicolored

Nos. 672E-672G are airmail. Nos. 672-672G exist imperf.
For surcharges see Nos. B71A-B71J.

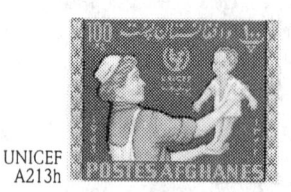

UNICEF A213h

Design: 5af, 7.50af, 10af, Children eating.

Perf. 14x13½, Imperf. (150p, 250p, 10af)
1964, Mar. 15
673	A213h	100p multicolored
673A	A213h	150p multicolored
673B	A213h	200p multicolored
673C	A213h	250p multicolored
673D	A213h	5af multicolored
673E	A213h	7.50af multicolored
673F	A213h	10af multicolored
	Nos. 673-673F (7)	10.00

Nos. 673D-673F are airmail.

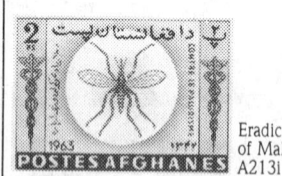

Eradication of Malaria A213i

Designs: 4p, 5p, 5af, 10af Spraying mosquitoes.

1964, Mar. 15   *Perf. 13½*
674	A213i	2p lt red brn & yel grn
674A	A213i	3p olive grn & buff
674B	A213i	4p dk vio & bl grn
674C	A213i	5p brn & grn
674D	A213i	2af Prus bl & ver
h.		Souvenir sheet of 1
674E	A213i	5af dk grn & lt red brn, imperf.
i.		Souv. sheet of 1, imperf.
674F	A213i	10af red brn & grnsh bl

674G A213i 10p on 4p Prus bl & rose

No. 674G not issued without surcharge. Nos. 674-674C, 674G exist imperf. Nos. 674D-674F are airmail.
Exists imperf.

"Tiger's Head" of 1878 — A214

1964, Mar. 22   *Photo.*   *Perf. 12*
675	A214	1.25af gold, grn & blk	.25	.15
676	A214	5af gold, rose car & blk	.55	.35

Issued to honor philately.

Unisphere and Flags — A215

1964, May 3   *Perf. 13½x14*
677	A215	6af crimson, gray & grn	.30	.20

New York World's Fair, 1964-65.

Hand Holding Torch — A216

1964, May 12   *Photo.*   *Perf. 14x13½*
678	A216	3.75af multicolored	.20	.20

1st UN Seminar on Human Rights in Kabul, May 1964. The denomination in Persian at right erroneously reads "3.25" but the stamp was sold and used as 3.75af.

Kandahar Airport A217

1964, Apr.   *Litho.*   *Perf. 10½, 11*
679	A217	7.75af dk red brown	.40	.20
680	A217	9.25af lt green	.50	.20
681	A217	10.50af lt green	.50	.30
682	A217	13.75af carmine rose	.70	.40
	Nos. 679-682 (4)		2.10	1.10

Inauguration of Kandahar Airport.

Snow Leopard A218

50p, Ibex, vert. 75p, Head of argali. 5af, Yak.

1964, June 25   *Photo.*   *Perf. 12*
683	A218	25p yellow & blue	.15	.15
684	A218	50p dl red & grn	.15	.15
685	A218	75p Prus bl & lil	.15	.15
686	A218	5af brt grn & dk brn	.30	.30
	Nos. 683-686 (4)		.75	.75

View of Herat — A219

Flag and Map of Afghanistan A220

Tourist publicity: 75p, Tomb of Queen Gowhar Shad, vert.

Perf. 13½x14, 14x13½
1964, July 12
687	A219	25p sepia & bl	.15	.15
688	A219	75p dp blue & buff	.15	.15
689	A220	3af red, blk & grn	.30	.15
	Nos. 687-689 (3)		.60	.45

Wrestling A221

25p, Hurdling, vert. 1af, Diving, vert. 5af, Soccer.

1964, July 26   *Perf. 12*
690	A221	25p ol bis, blk & car	.15	.15
691	A221	1af bl grn, blk & car	.15	.15
692	A221	3.75af yel grn, blk & car	.20	.20
693	A221	5af brn, blk & car	.30	.30
a.	Souv. sheet of 4, #690-693, imperf.		.90	.90
			.80	.80

18th Olympic Games, Tokyo, Oct. 10-25, 1964. No. 693a sold for 15af. The additional 5af went to the Afghanistan Olympic Committee.

Flag and Outline of Nadir Shah's Tomb — A222

1964, Aug. 24   *Photo.*
695	A222	25p multicolored	.15	.15
696	A222	75p multicolored	.15	.15

Independence Day. The stamps were printed with an erroneous inscription in upper left corner: "33rd year of independence." This was locally obliterated with a typographed gold bar.

Pashtunistan Flag — A223

Zahir Shah — A225

1964, Sept. 1   *Unwmk.*
697	A223	100p gold, blk, red, bl & grn	.15	.15

Issued for "Free Pashtunistan Day."

1964, Oct. 17   *Perf. 14x13½*
699	A225	1.25af gold & yel grn	.15	.15
700	A225	3.75af gold & rose	.20	.15
701	A225	50af gold & gray	2.00	1.75
	Nos. 699-701 (3)		2.35	2.05

King Mohammed Zahir Shah, 50th birthday.

Coat of Arms of Afghanistan and UN Emblem — A226

1964, Oct. 24   *Perf. 13½x14*
702	A226	5af gold, blk & dl bl	.20	.15

Issued for United Nations Day.

Emblem of Afghanistan Women's Association A227

1964, Nov. 9   *Photo.*   *Unwmk.*
703	A227	25p pink, dk bl & emer	.50	.25
704	A227	75p aqua, dk bl & emer	.75	.35
705	A227	1af sil, dk bl & emer	1.00	.50
	Nos. 703-705 (3)		2.25	1.10

Issued for Women's Day.

Poet Mowlana Nooruddin Abdul Rahman Jami (1414-1492) — A228

1964, Nov. 23   *Litho.*   *Perf. 11 Rough*
706	A228	1.50af blk, emer & yel	.85	.85

AFGHANISTAN

Woodpecker A229

Birds: 3.75af, Black-throated jay, vert. 5af, Impeyan pheasant, vert.

1965, Apr. 20   Photo.   Unwmk.   Perf. 13½x14, 14x13½
707	A229	1.25af multi	1.00	.50
708	A229	3.75af multi	1.75	.75
709	A229	5af multi	2.50	1.00
		Nos. 707-709 (3)	5.25	2.25

ITU Emblem, Old and New Communication Equipment A230

1965, May 17   Perf. 13½x14
| 710 | A230 | 5af lt bl, blk & red | .35 | .35 |

Cent. of the ITU.

"Red City," Bamian — A231

Designs: 3.75af, Ruins of ancient Bamian city. 5af, Bande Amir, mountain lakes.

1965, May 30   Perf. 13x13½
711	A231	1.25af pink & multi	.15	.15
712	A231	3.75af lt blue & multi	.20	.20
713	A231	5af yellow & multi	.30	.30
		Nos. 711-713 (3)	.65	.65

Issued for tourist publicity.

ICY Emblem A232

1965, June 25   Perf. 13½x13
| 714 | A232 | 5af multicolored | .25 | .25 |

International Cooperation Year, 1965.

ARIANA Air Lines Emblem and DC-3 — A233

Designs: 5af, DC-6 at right. 10af, DC-3 on top.

1965, July 15   Photo.   Unwmk.   Perf. 13½x14
715	A233	1.25af brt bl, gray & blk	.15	.15
716	A233	5af red lil, blk & bl	.30	.30
717	A233	10af bis, blk, bl gray & grn	.75	.75
a.		Souv. sheet of 3, #715-717, imperf.	1.00	1.00
		Nos. 715-717 (3)	1.20	1.20

10th anniv. of Afghan Air Lines, ARIANA.

Nadir Shah — A234

1965, Aug. 23   Perf. 14x13½
| 718 | A234 | 1af dl grn, blk & red brn | .25 | .15 |

For the 47th Independence Day.

Flag of Pashtunistan A235

1965, Aug. 31   Photo.   Unwmk.   Perf. 13½x14
| 719 | A235 | 1af multicolored | .25 | .15 |

Issued for "Free Pashtunistan Day."

Zahir Shah Signing Constitution — A236

1965, Sept. 11   Perf. 13x13½
| 720 | A236 | 1.50af brt grn & blk | .25 | .25 |

Promulgation of the new Constitution.

Zahir Shah and Oak Leaves — A237

1965, Oct. 14   Perf. 14x13½
| 721 | A237 | 1.25af blk, ultra & salmon | .15 | .15 |
| 722 | A237 | 6af blk, lt bl & rose lil | .40 | .35 |

King Mohammed Zahir Shah, 51st birthday.

Flags of UN and Afghanistan A238

1965, Oct. 24   Perf. 13½x14
| 723 | A238 | 5af multicolored | .20 | .20 |

Issued for United Nations Day.

Dappled Ground Gecko — A239

Designs: 4af, Caucasian agamid (lizard). 8af, Horsfield's tortoise.

1966, May 10   Photo.   Unwmk.   Perf. 13½x14
724	A239	3af tan & multi	.75	.35
725	A239	4af brt grn & multi	.85	.40
726	A239	8af violet & multi	1.50	.75
		Nos. 724-726 (3)	3.10	1.50

Soccer Player and Globe — A240

1966, July 31   Litho.   Perf. 14x13½
727	A240	2af rose red & blk	.60	.20
728	A240	6af violet bl & blk	1.10	.25
729	A240	12af bister brn & blk	2.25	.60
		Nos. 727-729 (3)	3.95	1.05

World Cup Soccer Championship, Wembley, England, July 11-30.

Cotton Flower and Boll — A241

5af, Silkworm. 7af, Farmer plowing with oxen.

1966, July 31   Perf. 13½x14
730	A241	1af multicolored	.50	.15
731	A241	5af multicolored	1.00	.30
732	A241	7af multicolored	1.40	.40
		Nos. 730-732 (3)	2.90	.85

Issued for the Day of Agriculture.

Independence Monument A242

1966, Aug. 23   Photo.   Perf. 13½x14
| 733 | A242 | 1af multicolored | .25 | .15 |
| 734 | A242 | 3af multicolored | .75 | .25 |

Issued to commemorate Independence Day.

Flag of Pashtunistan A243

1966, Aug. 31   Litho.   Perf. 11 Rough
| 735 | A243 | 1af bright blue | .50 | .15 |

"Free Pashtunistan Day."

Bagh-i-Bala Park Casino — A244

Tourist publicity: 2af, Map of Afghanistan. 8af, Tomb of Abd-er-Rahman. The casino on 4af is the former summer palace of Abd-er-Rahman near Kabul.

1966, Oct. 3   Photo.   Perf. 13½x14
736	A244	2af red & multi	.20	.15
737	A244	4af multicolored	.40	.30
738	A244	8af multicolored	.65	.60
a.		Souvenir sheet of 3, #736-738, imperf.	3.50	3.50
		Nos. 736-738 (3)	1.25	1.05

Zahir Shah — A245

UNESCO Emblem — A246

1966, Oct. 14   Perf. 14x13½
| 739 | A245 | 1af dk slate grn | .20 | .15 |
| 740 | A245 | 5af red brown | .50 | .25 |

King Mohammed Zahir Shah, 52nd birthday. See Nos. 760-761.

1967, Mar. 6   Litho.   Perf. 12
741	A246	2af multicolored	.60	.15
742	A246	6af multicolored	.75	.15
743	A246	12af multicolored	1.50	.30
		Nos. 741-743 (3)	2.85	.60

20th anniv. of UNESCO.

Zahir Shah and UN Emblem A247

1967   Photo.
| 744 | A247 | 5af multicolored | .40 | .15 |
| 745 | A247 | 10af multicolored | .75 | .30 |

UN Intl. Org. for Refugees, 20th anniv.

New Power Station — A248

Designs: 5af, Carpet, vert. 8af, Cement factory.

1967, Jan. 7   Photo.   Perf. 13½x14
746	A248	2af red lil & ol grn	.15	.15
747	A248	5af multicolored	.20	.15
748	A248	8af blk, dk bl & tan	.40	.25
		Nos. 746-748 (3)	.75	.55

Issued to publicize industrial development.

International Tourist Year Emblem — A249

Designs: 6af, International Tourist Year emblem and map of Afghanistan.

1967, May 11   Photo.   Perf. 12
749	A249	2af yel, blk & lt bl	.15	.15
750	A249	6af bis brn, blk & lt bl	.40	.20
a.		Souvenir sheet of 2, #749-750, imperf.	1.00	1.00

Intl. Tourist Year, 1967. No. 750a sold for 10af.

Power Dam, Dorunta A250

Macaque A251

6af, Sirobi Dam, vert. 8af, Reservoir at Jalalabad.

1967, July 2   Photo.   Perf. 12
751	A250	1af dk green & lil	.15	.15
752	A250	6af red brn & grnsh bl	.35	.35
753	A250	8af plum & dk bl	.50	.50
		Nos. 751-753 (3)	1.00	1.00

Progress in agriculture through electricity.

1967, July 28   Photo.   Perf. 12

Designs: 6af, Striped hyena, horiz. 12af, Persian gazelles, horiz.

754	A251	2af dull yel & indigo	.25	.15
755	A251	6af lt green & sepia	.70	.35
756	A251	12af lt bl & red brn	1.50	.75
		Nos. 754-756 (3)	2.45	1.25

AFGHANISTAN

Pashtun Dancers — A252

1967, Sept. 1 Photo. Perf. 12
757 A252 2af magenta & violet .50 .15
Issued for "Free Pashtunistan Day."

Retreat of British at Maiwand A253

Fireworks and UN Emblem A254

1967, Aug. 24
758 A253 1af dk brn & org ver .25 .15
759 A253 2af dk brn & brt pink .50 .15
Issued to commemorate Independence Day.

King Type of 1966

1967, Oct. 15 Photo. Perf. 14x13½
760 A245 2af brown red .15 .15
761 A245 8af dark blue .50 .25
Issued to honor King Mohammed Zahir Shah on his 53rd birthday.

1967, Oct. 24 Litho. Perf. 12
762 A254 10af violet bl & multi .65 .35
Issued for United Nations Day.

Greco-Roman Wrestlers A255

Said Jamalluddin Afghan A256

Design: 6af, Free style wrestlers.

1967, Nov. 20 Photo.
763 A255 4af ol grn & rose lil .50 .15
764 A255 6af dp carmine & brn .80 .20
a. Souvenir sheet of 2, #763-764, imperf. 5.00 5.00
1968 Olympic Games.

1967, Nov. 27
765 A256 1af magenta .15 .15
766 A256 5af brown .35 .20
Said Jamalluddin Afghan, politician (1839-97).

Bronze Vase, 11th-12th Centuries A257

WHO Emblem A258

Design: 7af, Bronze vase, Ghasnavide era, 11th-12th centuries.

1967, Dec. 23 Photo. Perf. 12
767 A257 3af lt green & brn .20 .15
768 A257 7af yel & slate grn .40 .30
a. Souvenir sheet of 2, #767-768, imperf. 2.50 2.50

1968, Apr. 7 Photo. Perf. 12
769 A258 2af citron & brt bl .15 .15
770 A258 7af rose & brt bl .30 .20
20th anniv. of the WHO.

Karakul — A259

1968, May 20 Photo. Perf. 12
771 A259 1af yellow & blk .25 .15
772 A259 6af lt blue & blk .70 .20
773 A259 12af ultra & dk brn 1.25 .40
Nos. 771-773 (3) 2.20 .75
Issued for the Day of Agriculture.

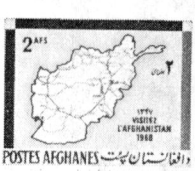

Map of Afghanistan A260

Victory Tower, Ghazni A261

Design: 16af, Mausoleum, Ghazni.

1968, June 3 Perf. 13½x14, 12
774 A260 2af red, blk, lt bl & grn .15 .15
775 A261 3af yel, dk brn & lt bl .20 .15
776 A261 16af pink & multi .95 .50
Nos. 774-776 (3) 1.30 .80
Issued for tourist publicity.

Cinereous Vulture — A262

Birds: 6af, Eagle owl. 7af, Greater flamingoes.

1968, July 3 Perf. 12
777 A262 1af sky blue & multi .75 .15
778 A262 6af yellow & multi 1.50 .20
779 A262 7af multicolored 1.75 .30
Nos. 777-779 (3) 4.00 .65

Game of "Pegsticking" A263

2af, Olympic flame & rings, vert. 12af, Buzkashi.

1968, July 20 Photo. Perf. 12
780 A263 2af multicolored .15 .15
781 A263 8af orange & multi .65 .30
782 A263 12af multicolored 1.00 .45
Nos. 780-782 (3) 1.80 .90
19th Olympic Games, Mexico City, Oct. 12-27.

Flower-decked Armored Car — A264

1968, Aug. 23
783 A264 6af multicolored .40 .20
Issued to commemorate Independence Day.

Flag of Pashtunistan A265

1968 Aug. 31 Photo. Perf. 12
784 A265 3af multicolored .25 .15
Issued for "Free Pashtunistan Day."

Zahir Shah — A266

Human Rights Flame — A267

1968, Oct. 14 Photo. Perf. 12
785 A266 2af ultra .15 .15
786 A266 8af brown .45 .30
King Mohammed Zahir Shah, 54th birthday.

1968, Oct. 24
787 A267 1af multicolored .15 .15
788 A267 2af violet, bis & blk .20 .15
789 A267 6af vio blk, bis & vio .40 .15
Nos. 787-789 (3) .75 .45

Souvenir Sheet
Imperf
790 A267 10af plum, bis & red org 1.50 1.50
International Human Rights Year.

Maolana Djalalodine Balkhi — A268

Kushan Mural — A269

1968, Nov. 26 Photo. Perf. 12
791 A268 4af dk green & mag .25 .15
Balkhi (1207-73), historian.

1969, Jan. 2
Design: 3af, Jug shaped like female torso.
792 A269 1af dk grn, mar & yel .25 .15
793 A269 3af violet, gray & mar .75 .15
a. Souv. sheet of 2, #792-793, imperf. 1.50 1.50
Archaeological finds at Bagram, 1st cent. B.C. to 2nd cent. A.D.

ILO Emblem A270

1969, Mar. 23 Photo. Perf. 12
794 A270 5af lt yel, lemon & blk .30 .20
795 A270 8af lt bl, grnsh bl & blk .50 .30
50th anniv. of the ILO.

Arms Type of 1939

1969, May (?) Typo.
795A A79 100p dark green .15 .15
795B A79 150p deep brown .25 .15
Nos. 795A-795B were normally used as newspaper stamps.

Badakhshan Scene — A271

Tourist Publicity: 2af, Map of Afghanistan. 7af, Three men on mules ascending the Pamir Mountains.

1969, July 6 Photo. Perf. 13½x14
796 A271 2af ocher & multi .20 .15
797 A271 4af multicolored .30 .15
798 A271 7af multicolored .75 .20
a. Souvenir sheet of 3, #796-798, imperf. 1.75 1.75
Nos. 796-798 (3) 1.25 .50
No. 798a sold for 15af.

Bust, from Hadda Treasure, 3rd-5th Centuries — A272

Zahir Shah and Queen Humeira — A273

Designs: 5af, Vase and jug. 10af, Statue of crowned woman. 5af and 10af from Bagram treasure, 1st-2nd centuries.

1969, Aug. 3 Photo. Perf. 14x13½
799 A272 1af olive grn & gold .15 .15
800 A272 5af purple & gold .20 .15
801 A272 10af dp blue & gold .40 .20
Nos. 799-801 (3) .75 .60

1969, Aug. 23 Perf. 12
802 A273 5af gold, dk bl & red brn .35 .20
803 A273 5af gold, dp lil & bl grn .65 .35
Issued to commemorate Independence Day.

Map of Pashtunistan and Rising Sun — A274

1969, Aug. 31 Typo. Perf. 10½
804 A274 2af lt blue & red .15 .15
Issued for "Free Pashtunistan Day."

Zahir Shah — A275

1969, Oct. 14 Photo. Perf. 12
Portrait in Natural Colors
805 A275 2af dk brown & gold .15 .15
806 A275 6af brown & gold .45 .20
King Mohammed Zahir Shah, 55th birthday.

UN Emblem and Flag of Afghanistan A276

1969, Oct. 24 Litho. Perf. 13½
807 A276 5af blue & multi .25 .15
Issued for United Nations Day.

ITU Emblem — A277

Wild Boar — A278

1969, Nov. 12
808 A277 6af ultra & multi .30 .20
809 A277 12af rose & multi .60 .35
Issued for World Telecommunications Day.

AFGHANISTAN

1969, Dec. 7 Photo. Perf. 12
1af, Long-tailed porcupine. 8af, Red deer.

810	A278	1af yellow & multi	.25	.20
811	A278	3af blue & multi	.75	.50
812	A278	8af pink & multi	2.00	1.00
		Nos. 810-812 (3)	3.00	1.70

Man's First Footprints on Moon, and Earth — A279

1969, Dec. 28 Perf. 13½x14
813	A279	1af yel grn & multi	.15	.15
814	A279	3af yellow & multi	.25	.15
815	A279	6af blue & multi	.40	.20
816	A279	8af red rose & multi	.65	.30
		Nos. 813-816 (4)	1.45	.80

Moon landing. See note after Algeria #427.

Anti-cancer Symbol — A280

Mirza Abdul Quader Bedel — A281

1970, Apr. 7 Photo. Perf. 14
| 817 | A280 | 2af dk grn & rose car | .15 | .15 |
| 818 | A280 | 6af dk bl & rose claret | .40 | .20 |

Issued to publicize the fight against cancer.

1970, May 6 Perf. 14x13½
| 819 | A281 | 5af multicolored | .25 | .15 |

Mirza Abdul Quader Bedel (1643-1720), poet.

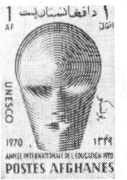

Education Year Emblem A282

Mother and Child A283

1970, June 7 Photo. Perf. 12
820	A282	1af black	.15	.15
821	A282	6af deep rose	.35	.20
822	A282	12af green	.75	.35
		Nos. 820-822 (3)	1.25	.70

International Education Year 1970.

1970, June 15 Perf. 13½
| 823 | A283 | 6af yellow & multi | .25 | .20 |

Issued for Mother's Day.

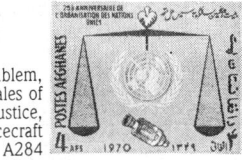

UN Emblem, Scales of Justice, Spacecraft A284

1970, June 26
| 824 | A284 | 4af yel, dk bl & dp bl | .20 | .15 |
| 825 | A284 | 6af pink, dk bl & brt bl | .35 | .20 |

25th anniversary of United Nations.

Mosque of the Amir of the two Swords, Kabul — A285

2af, Map of Afghanistan. 7af, Arch of Paghman.

1970, July 6 Perf. 12
Size: 30½x30½mm
| 826 | A285 | 2af lt bl, blk & citron | .15 | .15 |

Size: 36x26mm
827	A285	3af pink & multi	.20	.15
828	A285	7af yellow & multi	.40	.20
		Nos. 826-828 (3)	.75	.50

Issued for tourist publicity.

Zahir Shah Reviewing Troops A286

1970, Aug. 23 Photo. Perf. 13½
| 829 | A286 | 8af multicolored | .60 | .25 |

Issued to commemorate Independence Day.

Pathans — A287

1970, Aug. 31 Typo. Perf. 10½
| 830 | A287 | 2af ultra & red | .15 | .15 |

Issued for "Free Pashtunistan Day."

Quail — A288

4af, Golden eagle. 6af, Ringnecked pheasant.

1970, Sept. Photo. Perf. 12
831	A288	2af multicolored	.50	.25
832	A288	4af multicolored	1.00	.50
833	A288	6af multicolored	1.50	.75
		Nos. 831-833 (3)	3.00	1.50

Zahir Shah A289

Red Crescents A290

1970, Oct. 14 Photo. Perf. 14x13½
| 834 | A289 | 3af green & vio | .20 | .15 |
| 835 | A289 | 7af dk bl & vio brn | .60 | .25 |

King Mohammed Zahir Shah, 56th birthday.

1970, Oct. 16 Typo. Perf. 10½
| 836 | A290 | 2af black, gold & red | .15 | .15 |

Issued for the Red Crescent Society.

UN Emblem and Charter A291

1970, Oct. 24 Photo. Perf. 14
| 837 | A291 | 1af gold & multi | .15 | .15 |
| 838 | A291 | 5af gold & multi | .20 | .15 |

United Nations Day.

Tiger Heads of 1871 — A292

1970, Nov. 10 Perf. 12
839	A292	1af sal, lt grnsh bl & blk	.25	.15
840	A292	4af lt ultra, yel & blk	.50	.15
841	A292	12af lilac, lt bl & blk	.85	.35
		Nos. 839-841 (3)	1.60	.65

Cent. of the 1st Afghan postage stamps. The postal service was established in 1870, but the 1st stamps were issued in May, 1871.

Globe and Waves A293

1971, May 17 Photo. Perf. 13½
| 842 | A293 | 12af green, blk & bl | .60 | .35 |

3rd World Telecommunications Day.

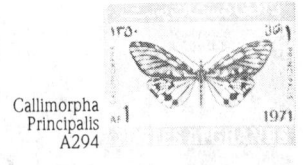

Callimorpha Principalis A294

Designs: 3af, Epizygaenella species. 5af, Parnassius autocrator.

1971, May 30 Perf. 13½x14
843	A294	1af vermilion & multi	1.00	.50
844	A294	3af yellow & multi	2.25	1.00
845	A294	5af ultra & multi	3.00	1.50
		Nos. 843-845 (3)	6.25	3.00

"UNESCO" and Half of Ancient Kushan Statue — A295

1971, June 26 Photo. Perf. 13½
| 846 | A295 | 6af ocher & vio | .40 | .20 |
| 847 | A295 | 10af lt blue & mar | .65 | .30 |

UNESCO-sponsored Intl. Kushani Seminar.

Tughra and Independence Monument — A296

1971, Aug. 23
| 848 | A296 | 7af rose red & multi | .40 | .20 |
| 849 | A296 | 9af red orange & multi | .65 | .30 |

Independence Day.

Pashtunistan Square, Kabul — A297

1971, Aug. 31 Typo. Perf. 10½
| 850 | A297 | 5af deep rose lilac | .27 | .15 |

"Free Pashtunistan Day."

Zahir Shah — A298

A299

1971, Oct. 14 Photo. Perf. 12½x12
| 851 | A298 | 9af lt green & multi | .40 | .30 |
| 852 | A298 | 17af yellow & multi | .75 | .55 |

King Mohammed Zahir Shah, 57th birthday.

1971, Oct. 16 Perf. 14x13½
Design: Map of Afghanistan, red crescent, various activities.
| 853 | A299 | 8af lt bl, red, grn & blk | .45 | .25 |

For Afghan Red Crescent Society.

Equality Year Emblem A300

1971, Oct. 24 Perf. 12
| 854 | A300 | 24af brt blue | 1.25 | .70 |

International Year Against Racial Discrimination and United Nations Day.

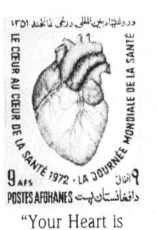

"Your Heart is your Health" — A301

Tulip — A302

1972, Apr. 7 Photo. Perf. 14
| 855 | A301 | 9af pale yellow & multi | .75 | .30 |
| 856 | A301 | 12af gray & multi | 1.50 | .35 |

World Health Day.

1972, June 5 Photo. Perf. 14
Designs: 10af, Rock partridge, horiz. 12af, Lynx, horiz. 18af, Allium stipitatum (flower).

857	A302	7af green & multi	.50	.25
858	A302	10af blue & multi	.75	.35
859	A302	12af lt green & multi	1.00	.35
860	A302	18af blue grn & multi	1.25	.60
		Nos. 857-860 (4)	3.50	1.55

Buddhist Shrine, Hadda A302a

185

AFGHANISTAN

Designs: 7af, Greco-Bactrian animal seal, 250 B.C. 9af, Greco-Oriental temple, Ai-Khanoum, 3rd-2nd centuries B.C.

1972, July 16 Photo. Perf. 12
861 A302a 3af brown & dl bl .50 .15
862 A302a 7af rose claret & dl grn .80 .20
863 A302a 9af green & lilac 1.10 .30
Nos. 861-863 (3) 2.40 .65
Tourist publicity.

King and Queen Reviewing Parade — A303

1972, Aug. 23 Photo. Perf. 13½
864 A303 25af gold & multi 4.00 1.00
Independence Day.
Used as a provisional in 1978 with king and queen portion removed.

Wrestling A304

1972, Aug. 26
865 A304 4af ol bis & multi .25 .15
866 A304 8af lt blue & multi .50 .25
867 A304 10af yel grn & multi .60 .30
868 A304 19af multicolored 1.25 .40
869 A304 21af lilac & multi 1.40 .45
a. Souv. sheet of 5, #865-869, imperf. 3.00 3.00
Nos. 865-869 (5) 4.00 1.55
20th Olympic Games, Munich, Aug. 26-Sept. 11.
No. 869a sold for 60af.

Pathan and View of Tribal Territory — A305

Zahir Shah — A306

1972, Aug. 31 Perf. 12½x12
870 A305 5af ultra & multi .25 .15
Pashtunistan day.

1972, Oct. 14 Photo. Perf. 14x13½
871 A306 7af gold, blk & Prus bl 1.50 .30
872 A306 14af gold, blk & lt brn 2.50 .50
58th birthday of King Mohammed Zahir Shah.

City Destroyed by Earthquake, Refugees — A307

1972, Oct. 16 Perf. 13½
873 A307 7af lt bl, red & blk .40 .20
For Afghan Red Crescent Society.

UN Emblem A308

1972, Oct. 24
874 A308 12af lt ultra & blk .65 .35
UN Economic Commission for Asia and the Far East (ECAFE), 25th anniv.

Ceramics A309

Designs: 9af, Leather coat, vert. 12af, Metal ware, vert. 16af, Inlaid artifacts.

1972, Dec. 10 Photo. Perf. 12
875 A309 7af gold & multi .40 .20
876 A309 9af gold & multi .55 .30
877 A309 12af gold & multi .70 .35
878 A309 16af gold & multi 1.00 .50
a. Souv. sheet of 4, #875-878, imperf. 2.25 2.25
Nos. 875-878 (4) 2.65 1.35
Handicraft industries. No. 878a sold for 45af.

WMO and National Emblems — A310

1973, Apr. 3 Photo. Perf. 14
879 A310 7af lt lil & dk grn .40 .20
880 A310 14af lt bl & dp claret .85 .45
Cent. of intl. meteorological cooperation.

Abu Rayhan al-Biruni — A311

Family — A312

1973, June 16 Photo. Perf. 13½
881 A311 10af multicolored .55 .30
Millennium of birth (973-1048), philosopher and mathematician.

1973, June 30 Photo. Perf. 13½
882 A312 9af orange & red lil .50 .30
Intl. Family Planning Fed., 21st anniv.

Republic

Impeyan Pheasant A313

Birds: 9af, Great crested grebe. 12af, Himalayan snow cock.

1973, July 29 Photo. Perf. 12x12½
883 A313 8af yellow & multi 1.25 .25
884 A313 9af blue & multi 1.75 .30
885 A313 12af multicolored 2.00 .75
Nos. 883-885 (3) 5.00 .90

Stylized Buzkashi Horseman A314

1973, Aug. Perf. 13½
886 A314 8af black .30 .25
Tourist publicity.

Fireworks A315

1973, Aug. 23 Photo. Perf. 12
887 A315 12af multicolored .45 .35
55th Independence Day.

Lake Abassine, Pashtunistan Flag — A316

1973, Aug. 31 Perf. 14x13½
888 A316 9af multicolored .50 .30
Pashtunistan Day.

Red Crescent — A317

1973, Oct. 16 Perf. 13½
889 A317 10af red, blk & gold .60 .30
Red Crescent Society.

Kemal Ataturk — A318

1973, Oct. 28 Litho. Perf. 10½
890 A318 1af blue .15 .15
891 A318 7af reddish brown .40 .20
50th anniversary of the Turkish Republic.

Human Rights Flame, Arms of Afghanistan A319

1973, Dec. 10 Photo. Perf. 12
892 A319 12af sil, blk & lt bl .45 .35
25th anniversary of the Universal Declaration of Human Rights.

Asiatic Black Bears — A320

1974, Mar. 26 Litho. Perf. 12
893 A320 5af shown .35 .15
894 A320 7af Afghan hound .50 .20
895 A320 10af Persian goat .70 .30
896 A320 12af Leopard .90 .35
a. Souv. sheet of 4, #893-896, imperf. 5.00 5.00
Nos. 893-896 (4) 2.45 1.00

Worker and Farmer A321

1974, May 1 Photo. Perf. 13½x12½
897 A321 9af rose red & multi .40 .25
International Labor Day, May 1.

Independence Monument and Arch — A322

1974, May 27 Photo. Perf. 12
898 A322 4af blue & multi .15 .15
899 A322 11af gold & multi .35 .35
56th Independence Day.

Arms of Afghanistan and Symbol of Cooperation A323

Pres. Mohammad Daoud Khan — A324

Designs: 5af, Flag of Republic of Afghanistan. 15af, Soldiers and coat of arms of the Republic.

1974, July 25 Perf. 13½x12½, 14
Sizes: 4af, 15af, 36x22mm; 5af, 7af, 36x26, 26x36mm
900 A323 4af multicolored .20 .15
901 A323 5af multicolored .25 .15
902 A324 7af green, brn & blk .30 .20
a. Souv. sheet of 2, #901-902, imperf. .70 .70
903 A323 15af multicolored .65 .40
a. Souv. sheet of 2, #900, 903, imperf. 1.00 1.00
Nos. 900-903 (4) 1.40 .90
1st anniv. of the Republic of Afghanistan.

Lesser Spotted Eagle — A325

AFGHANISTAN

Birds: 6af, White-fronted goose, ruddy shelduck and gray-lag goose. 11af, European coots and European crane.

1974, Aug. 6   Photo.   Perf. 13½x13
904	A325	1af car rose & multi	.25	.15
905	A325	6af blue & multi	.75	.20
906	A325	11af yellow & multi	1.50	.40
a.		Strip of 3, #904-906	1.00	1.00
		Nos. 904-906 (3)	2.50	.75

Flags of Pashtunistan and Afghanistan — A326

1974, Aug. 31   Photo.   Perf. 14
| 907 | A326 | 5af multicolored | .25 | .15 |

Pashtunistan Day.

Natl. Arms A326a

1974, Aug.   Typo.   Rough Perf. 11
| 907A | A326a | 100p green | | |

Coat of Arms — A327

1974, Oct. 9
| 908 | A327 | 7af gold, grn & blk | .25 | .20 |

Centenary of Universal Postal Union.

"un" and UN Emblem A328

1974, Oct. 24   Photo.   Perf. 14
| 909 | A328 | 5af lt ultra & dk bl | .25 | .15 |

United Nations Day.

Minaret of Jam — A329
Buddha, Hadda — A330

14af, Lady riding griffin, 2nd century, Bagram.

1975, May 5   Photo.   Perf. 13½
910	A329	7af multicolored	.25	.15
911	A330	14af multicolored	.60	.30
912	A330	15af multicolored	.65	.30
a.		Souvenir sheet of 3, #910-912, imperf.	3.50	3.50
		Nos. 910-912 (3)	1.50	.75

South Asia Tourism Year 1975.

New Flag of Afghanistan A331

1975, May 27   Photo.   Perf. 12
| 913 | A331 | 16af multicolored | .75 | .35 |

57th Independence Day.

Celebrating Crowd A332

1975, July 17   Photo.   Perf. 13½
| 914 | A332 | 9af blue & multi | .45 | .20 |
| 915 | A332 | 12af carmine & multi | .55 | .30 |

Second anniversary of the Republic.

Women's Year Emblems — A333

1975, Aug. 24   Photo.   Perf. 12
| 916 | A333 | 9af car, lt bl & blk | .30 | .20 |

International Women's Year 1975.

Pashtunistan Flag, Sun Rising Over Mountains A334
Mohammed Akbar Khan A335

1975, Aug. 31   Perf. 13½
| 917 | A334 | 10af multicolored | .30 | .25 |

Pashtunistan Day.

1976, Feb. 4   Photo.   Perf. 14
| 918 | A335 | 15af lt brown & multi | .45 | .35 |

Mohammed Akbar Khan (1816-1846), warrior son of Amir Dost Mohammed Khan.

Pres. Mohammad Daoud Khan
A336   A337

1974-78   Photo.   Perf. 14
919	A336	10af multi	.55	.20
920	A336	16af multi ('78)	2.00	.75
921	A336	19af multi	.75	.40
922	A336	21af multi	1.10	.45
923	A336	22af multi ('78)	3.00	1.60
924	A336	30af multi ('78)	4.00	2.25
925	A337	50af multi ('75)	2.25	1.10
926	A337	100af multi ('75)	4.50	2.00
		Nos. 919-926 (8)	18.15	8.75

Arms of Republic, Independence Monument — A338

1976, June 1   Photo.   Perf. 14
| 927 | A338 | 22af blue & multi | .65 | .45 |

58th Independence Day.

Flag Raising — A339

1976, July 17   Photo.   Perf. 14
| 928 | A339 | 30af multicolored | .90 | .75 |

Republic Day.

Mountain Peaks and Flag of Pashtunistan A340

1976, Aug. 31   Photo.   Perf. 14
| 929 | A340 | 16af multicolored | .50 | .40 |

Pashtunistan Day.

Coat of Arms — A340a

1976, Sept.   Litho.   Perf. 11 Rough
930	A340a	25p salmon	.25	.15
931	A340a	50p lt green	.25	.15
932	A340a	1af ultra	.25	.15
		Nos. 930-932 (3)	.75	.45

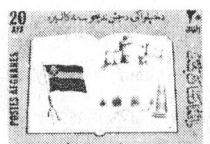

Flag and Views on Open Book — A341

1977, May 27   Photo.   Perf. 14
| 937 | A341 | 20af green & multi | .60 | .50 |

59th Independence Day.

Pres. Daoud and National Assembly — A342
President Taking Oath of Office — A343 

Designs: 10af, Inaugural address. 18af, Promulgation of Constitution.

1977, June 22
938	A342	7af multicolored	.65	.45
939	A343	8af multicolored	.70	.60
940	A343	10af multicolored	.90	.75
941	A342	18af multicolored	1.65	1.25
a.		Souvenir sheet of 4	3.00	3.00
		Nos. 938-941 (4)	3.90	3.05

Election of 1st Pres. and promulgation of Constitution. No. 941a contains 4 imperf. stamps similar to Nos. 938-941.

Jamalluddin Medal A344

1977, July 6   Photo.   Perf. 14
| 942 | A344 | 12af blue, blk & gold | .35 | .30 |

Sajo Jamalluddin Afghani, reformer, 80th death anniversary.

Afghanistan Flag over Crowd — A345

1977, July 17
| 943 | A345 | 22af multicolored | .65 | .55 |

Dancers, Fountain, Pashtunistan Flag — A346

1977, Aug. 31
| 944 | A346 | 30af multicolored | .90 | .75 |

Pashtunistan Day.

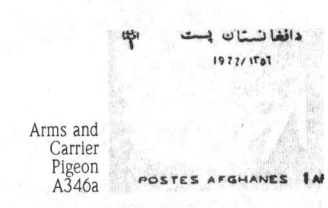

Arms and Carrier Pigeon A346a

1977, Oct. 30   Litho.   Perf. 11
| 944A | A346a | 1af black & blue | .15 | .15 |

Members of Parliament Congratulating Pres. Daoud — A347

1978, Feb. 5   Litho.   Perf. 14
| 945 | A347 | 20af multicolored | 1.75 | |

Election of first president, first anniversary.

Map of Afghanistan, UPU Emblem A348

1978, Apr. 1   Photo.   Perf. 14
| 946 | A348 | 10af green, blk & gold | .30 | .25 |

Afghanistan's UPU membership, 50th anniv.

AFGHANISTAN

Wall Telephone and Satellite Station — A349

1978, Apr. 12
947 A349 8af multicolored .25 .20
Afghanistan's ITU membership, 50th anniv.

Democratic Republic

Arrows Pointing to Crescent, Cross and Lion — A350

1978, July 6 Litho. Perf. 11 Rough
948 A350 3af black 1.00 .50
50th anniv. of Afghani Red Crescent Soc.

Khalq Party Emblem A350a

1978, Aug. Litho. Perf. 11
948A A350a 1af rose red & gold 1.25 .50
948B A350a 4af rose red & gold 1.75 .75

Qalai Bist Arch A351

1978, Aug. 19 Perf. 14
949 A351 16af Bamian Buddha 1.00 .40
949A A351 22af shown 1.25 .55
949B A351 30af Hazara Women 1.75 .90
Nos. 949-949B (3) 4.00 1.85

Men with Pashtunistan Flag — A352

Coat of Arms and Emblems — A353

1978, Aug. 31 Perf. 11 Rough
950 A352 7af ultra & red .20 .15
Pashtunistan Day.

1978, Sept. 8 Perf. 11
951 A353 20af rose red .60 .50
World Literacy Day.

A354

Perf. 11½ Rough
1978, Oct. 25 Litho. .55 .45
952 A354 18af light green
Hero of Afghanistan.

Khalq Party Flag — A355

1978, Oct. 19 Photo. Perf. 11½
953 A355 8af black, red & gold .25 .20
954 A355 9af black, red & gold .30 .20
"The mail serving the people."

Nour Mohammad Taraki — A356

1979, Jan. 1 Litho. Perf. 12
955 A356 12af multicolored .35 .15
Nour Mohammad Taraki, founder of People's Democratic Party of Afghanistan, installation as president.

Woman Breaking Chain — A357

1979, Mar. 8 Litho. Perf. 11
956 A357 14af red & ultra 1.50 .50
Women's Day. Inscribed "POSSTES."

Map of Afghanistan, Census Emblem A358

1979, Mar. 25 Litho. Perf. 12
957 A358 3af multicolored .75 .50
First comprehensive population census.

Farmers A359

1979, Mar. 21
958 A359 1af multicolored .50 .25
Agricultural advances.

Have you found a typo or other error in this catalogue? Inform the editors via our web site or e-mail

sctcat@
scottonline.com

Pres. Taraki Reading First Issue of Khalq — A360

1979, Apr. 11 Perf. 12½x12
959 A360 2af multicolored .25 .15
Khalq, newspaper of People's Democratic Republic of Afghanistan.

Pres. Noor Mohammad Taraki — A361

Plaza with Tank Monument and Fountain — A362

House where Revolution Started — A363

Designs: 50p, Taraki, tank. 12af, House where 1st Khalq Party Congress was held.

Perf. 12, 12½x12 (A362)
1979, Apr. 27 Litho.
959A A363 50p multicolored .15 .15
960 A361 4af multicolored .15 .15
961 A362 5af multicolored .25 .15
962 A363 6af multicolored .30 .25
963 A363 12af multicolored .50 .45
Nos. 959A-963 (5) 1.35 1.15
1st anniversary of revolution.

Carpenter and Blacksmith A364

1979, May 1 Perf. 12
964 A364 10af multicolored .30 .25
Int'l Labor Day.

Children, Flag and Map of Afghanistan — A366

1979, June 1 Litho. Perf. 12½x12
966 A366 16af multicolored 1.50 .75
International Year of the Child.

Doves Circling Asia in Globe A366a

1979 Litho. Perf. 11x10½
966A A366a 2af red & blue 1.00 .20

Armed Afghans, Kabul Memorial and Arch — A367

Pashtunistan Citizens, Flag — A368

1979, Aug. 19 Litho. Perf. 12
967 A367 30af multicolored 1.25 .75
60th independence day.

1979, Aug. 31
968 A368 9af multicolored .30 .20
Pashtunistan Day.

UPU Day — A369

1979, Oct. 9 Litho. Perf. 12
969 A369 15af multicolored .45 .38

Tombstone — A369a

1979, Oct. 25 Litho. Perf. 12½x12
969A A369a 22af multicolored 2.00 1.00

International Women's Day — A370

1980, Mar. 8 Litho. Perf. 12
970 A370 8af multicolored 3.00 3.00

Farmers' Day — A371

1980, Mar. 21 Litho. Perf. 11½x12
971 A371 2af multicolored .50 .25

AFGHANISTAN

Non-smoker and
Smoker — A372

1980, Apr. 7   *Perf. 11½*
972 A372 5af multicolored   .25 .15
Anti-smoking campaign; World Health Day.

Lenin, 110th
Birth
Anniversary
A373

1980, Apr. 22   *Perf. 12x12½*
973 A373 12af multicolored   .35 .30

People and
Fist on Map
of
Afghanistan
A374

1980, Apr. 27 Litho.   *Perf. 12½x12*
974 A374 1af multicolored   .25 .25
Saur Revolution, 2nd anniversary.

International
Workers'
Solidarity
Day — A375

1980, May 1
975 A375 9af multicolored   .30 .20

Wrestling,
Moscow '80
Emblem
A376

    Perf. 12x12½, 12½x12
1980, July 19
976 A376 3af Soccer, vert.   .60 .25
977 A376 6af shown   1.00 .45
978 A376 9af Buzkashi   1.65 .60
979 A376 10af Pegsticking   1.75 .75
    Nos. 976-979 (4)   5.00 2.05
22nd Summer Olympic Games, Moscow, July 19-Aug. 3.

61st Anniversary of Independence — A377

1980, Aug. 19 Litho.   *Perf. 12½x12*
980 A377 3af multicolored   .25 .15

Pashtunistan
Day — A378

1980, Aug. 30
981 A378 25af multicolored   .80 .65

Intl. UPU
Day — A379

1980, Oct. 9 Litho.   *Perf. 12½x12*
982 A379 20af multicolored   .60 .50

International
Women's
Day — A381

1981, Mar. 9 Litho.   *Perf. 12½x12*
984 A381 15af multicolored   .45 .40

Farmers' Day — A382

1981, Mar. 20 Litho.   *Perf. 12½x12*
985 A382 1af multicolored   .25 .25

Bighorn
Mountain Sheep
(Protected
Species) — A383

1981, Apr. 4   *Perf. 12x12½*
986 A383 12af multicolored   1.00 .75

Saur Revolution,
3rd Anniversary
A384

Intl. Workers'
Solidarity Day
A385

1981, Apr. 27   *Perf. 11*
987 A384 50p brown   .15 .15

1981, May 1   *Perf. 12½x12*
988 A385 10af multicolored   .30 .25

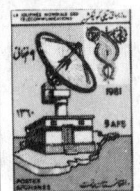

13th World
Telecommunications
Day — A387

1981, May 17 Litho.   *Perf. 12½x12*
990 A387 9af multicolored   .30 .20

Intl. Children's
Day — A388

1981, June 1   *Perf. 12x12½*
991 A388 15af multicolored   .45 .40

People's
Independence
Monument
62nd Anniv.
of Independence
A389

1981, Aug. 19
992 A389 4af multicolored   .15 .15

Pashtunistan
Day — A390

1981, Aug. 31 Litho.   *Perf. 12*
992A A390 2af multicolored   .25 .15

Intl. Tourism
Day — A391

1981, Sept. 27   *Perf. 12½x12*
993 A391 5af multicolored   .25 .15

World Food
Day — A392

1981, Oct. 16
995 A392 7af multicolored   .35 .15

Asia-Africa
Solidarity
Meeting
A393

1981, Nov. 18 Litho.   *Perf. 11*
996 A393 8af blue   .25 .20

Struggle
Against
Apartheid
A394

1300th Anniv. of
Bulgaria
A395

1981, Dec. 1   *Perf. 12½x12*
997 A394 4af multicolored   .30 .20

1981, Dec. 9   *Perf. 12x12½*
998 A395 20af multicolored   1.25 1.00

Buzkashi
Game
A395a

1980   *Photo.*   *Perf. 14*
998A A395a 50af multicolored   3.00 1.00
998B A395a 100af multicolored   6.00 2.00

Intl. Women's
Day — A396

1982, Mar. 8 Litho.   *Perf. 12*
999 A396 6af multicolored   .50 .25

Farmers'
Day — A397

1982, Mar. 21
1000 A397 4af multicolored   .25 .15

Rhubarb
Plant — A398

Saur Revolution,
4th
Anniv. — A399

Designs: Various local plants.

1982, Apr. 9 Litho.   *Perf. 12*
1001 A398 3af Judas trees   .25 .15
1002 A398 4af Rose of Sharon   .35 .15
1003 A398 16af shown   1.00 .40
    Nos. 1001-1003 (3)   1.60 .70

1982, Apr. 27
1004 A399 1af multicolored   .25 .15

George Dimitrov (1882-1947), First Prime Minister of Bulgaria — A400

AFGHANISTAN

Intl. Workers' Solidarity Day — A401

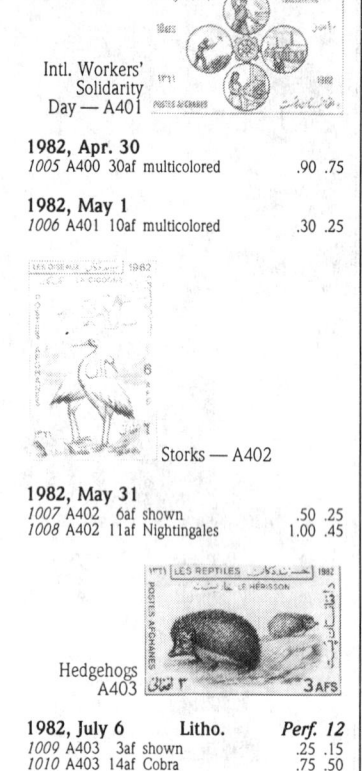

1982, Apr. 30
1005 A400 30af multicolored .90 .75

1982, May 1
1006 A401 10af multicolored .30 .25

Storks — A402

1982, May 31
1007 A402 6af shown .50 .25
1008 A402 11af Nightingales 1.00 .45

Hedgehogs A403

1982, July 6 Litho. *Perf. 12*
1009 A403 3af shown .25 .15
1010 A403 14af Cobra .75 .50
See Nos. 1020-1022.

63rd Anniv. of Independence A404

1982, Aug. 19
1011 A404 20af multicolored .60 .50

Pashtunistan Day — A405

1982, Aug. 31
1012 A405 32af multicolored 1.00 .80

World Tourism Day — A406

1982, Sept. 27 Litho. *Perf. 12*
1013 A406 9af multicolored .75 .50

UPU Day — A407

1982, Oct. 9
1014 A407 4af multicolored .50 .25

World Food Day — A408

1982, Oct. 16
1015 A408 9af multicolored .30 .20

37th Anniv. of UN — A409

1982, Oct. 24
1016 A409 15af multicolored .45 .40

ITU Plenipotentiaries Conference, Nairobi, Sept. — A410

1982, Oct. 26
1017 A410 8af multicolored .25 .20

TB Bacillus Centenary A411

Human Rights Declaration, 34th Anniv. A412

1982, Nov. 24 Litho. *Perf. 12*
1018 A411 7af multicolored .25 .20

1982, Dec. 10
1019 A412 5af multicolored .25 .15

Animal Type of 1982
1982, Dec. 16
1020 A403 2af Lions .25 .15
1021 A403 7af Donkeys .75 .20
1022 A403 12af Marmots, vert. 1.00 .25
Nos. 1020-1022 (3) 2.00 .60

Intl. Women's Day — A413

Mir Alicher Nawai Research Decade — A414

1983, Mar. 8
1023 A413 3af multicolored .25 .15

1983, Mar. 19
1024 A414 22af multicolored .70 .50

Farmers' Day — A415

1983, Mar. 21 Litho. *Perf. 12*
1025 A415 10af multicolored .30 .25

5th Anniv. of Saur Revolution A416

1983, Apr. 27 Litho. *Perf. 12*
1026 A416 15af multicolored 1.00 .50

Intl. Workers' Solidarity Day — A417

1983, May 1
1027 A417 2af multicolored .60 .50

World Communications Year — A418

1983, May 17
1028 A418 4af Modes of communication .25 .15
1029 A418 11af Building .75 .30

Intl. Children's Day — A419

1983, June 1 Litho. *Perf. 12*
1030 A419 25af multicolored 1.50 1.50

2nd Anniv. of National Front — A420

1983, June 15
1031 A420 1af multicolored .15 .15

Local Butterflies A421

Various butterflies. 9af, 13af vert.

1983, July 6
1032 A421 9af multicolored .55 .55
1033 A421 13af multicolored .80 .80
1034 A421 21af multicolored 1.25 1.25
Nos. 1032-1034 (3) 2.60 2.60

Struggle Against Apartheid — A422

1983, Aug. 1 Litho. *Perf. 12*
1035 A422 10af multicolored .60 .60

64th Anniv of Independence A423

1983, Aug. 19
1036 A423 6af multicolored .35 .35

Parliament House A423a

1983, Sept. Litho. *Perf. 12*
1036A A423a 50af shown 3.00 3.00
1036B A423a 100af Afghan Woman, Camel 6.00 6.00

A424

World Tourism Day — A425

1983, Sept. 27 Litho. *Perf. 12*
1037 A424 5af shown .30 .30
1038 A425 7af shown .45 .45
1039 A424 12af Golden statues .75 .75
1040 A425 16af Stone carving 1.00 1.00
Nos. 1037-1040 (4) 2.50 2.50

World Communications Year — A426

1983, Oct. 9 Litho. *Perf. 12*
1041 A426 14af Dish antenna, dove .85 .85
1042 A426 15af shown .90 .90

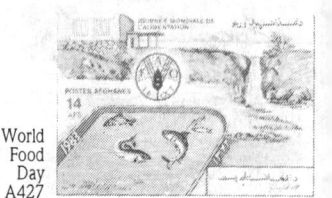

World Food Day A427

1983, Oct. 16 Litho. *Perf. 12*
1043 A427 14af multicolored .85 .85

Boxing A428

1983, Nov. 1 Litho. *Perf. 12*
1044 A428 1af Running .15 .15
1045 A428 18af shown 1.10 1.10
1046 A428 21af Wrestling 1.25 1.25
Nos. 1044-1046 (3) 2.50 2.50

AFGHANISTAN

Pashtunistan Day — A428a

1983, Nov. Litho. Perf. 12
1046A A428a 3af Pathans Waving Flag .20 .20

Handicrafts A429

1983, Nov. 22
1047 A429 2af Jewelry .15 .15
1048 A429 8af Stone ashtrays, dishes .50 .50
1049 A429 19af Furniture 1.10 1.10
1050 A429 30af Leather goods 1.90 1.90
Nos. 1047-1050 (4) 3.65 3.65

UN Declaration of Human Rights, 35th Anniv. A430

1983, Dec. 10 Litho. Perf. 12
1051 A430 20af multicolored 1.25 1.25

Kabul Polytechnical Institute, 20th Anniv. — A431

1983, Dec. 28 Perf. 12½x12
1052 A431 30af multicolored 1.90 1.90

1984 Winter Olympics A432

1984, Jan. Perf. 12
1053 A432 5af Figure skating .30 .30
1054 A432 9af Skiing .55 .55
1055 A432 11af Speed skating .65 .65
1056 A432 15af Hockey .90 .90
1057 A432 18af Biathlon 1.10 1.10
1058 A432 20af Ski jumping 1.25 1.25
1059 A432 22af Bobsledding 1.40 1.40
Nos. 1053-1059 (7) 6.15 6.15

Intl. Women's Day — A433

1984, Mar. 8
1060 A433 4af multicolored .25 .25

Farmers' Day — A434

Various agricultural scenes.

1984, Mar. 21 Litho. Perf. 12
1061 A434 2af multicolored .15 .15
1062 A434 4af multicolored .25 .25
1063 A434 7af multicolored .40 .40
1064 A434 9af multicolored .55 .55
1065 A434 15af multicolored .95 .95
1066 A434 18af multicolored 1.10 1.10
1067 A434 20af multicolored 1.25 1.25
Nos. 1061-1067 (7) 4.65 4.65

World Aviation Day — A435

1984, Apr. 12
1068 A435 5af Luna 1 .30 .30
1069 A435 8af Luna 2 .50 .50
1070 A435 11af Luna 3 .70 .70
1071 A435 17af Apollo 11 1.00 1.00
1072 A435 22af Soyuz 6 1.40 1.40
1073 A435 28af Soyuz 7 1.75 1.75
1074 A435 34af Soyuz 6, 7, 8 2.00 2.00
Nos. 1068-1074 (7) 7.65 7.65

Souvenir Sheet
Perf. 12x12½
1075 A435 25af S. Koroliov 1.50 1.50
No. 1075 contains one 30x41mm stamp.

Saur Revolution, 6th Anniv. A436

1984, Apr. 27 Perf. 12
1076 A436 3af multicolored .25 .25

65th Anniv. of Independence A437

1984, Aug. 19 Litho. Perf. 12
1077 A437 6af multicolored .40 .40

Pashto's and Balutchi's Day — A438

1984, Aug. 31
1078 A438 3af Symbolic sun, tribal terr. .25 .25

Wildlife A439

Perf. 12½x12, 12x12½
1984, May 5 Litho.
1079 A439 1af Cape hunting dog, vert. .15 .15
1080 A439 2af Argali sheep, vert. .15 .15
1081 A439 6af Przewalski's horse .40 .40
1082 A439 8af Wild boar, vert. .50 .50
1083 A439 17af Snow leopard 1.00 1.00
1084 A439 19af Tiger 1.25 1.25
1085 A439 22af Indian elephant, vert. 1.40 1.40
Nos. 1079-1085 (7) 4.85 4.85

19th UPU Congress, Hamburg A440

1984, June 18 Perf. 12x12½
1086 A440 25af German postman, 17th cent. 1.50 1.50
1087 A440 35af Postrider, 16th cent. 2.00 2.00
1088 A440 40af Carrier pigeon, letter 2.50 2.50
Nos. 1086-1088 (3) 6.00 6.00

Souvenir Sheet
1089 A440 50af Hamburg No. 3 in black 4.00 4.00
No. 1089 contains one 30x40mm stamp.

Natl. Aviation, 40th Anniv. A441

Soviet civil aircraft.

1984, June 29
1090 A441 1af Antonov AN-2 .15 .15
1091 A441 4af Ilyushin IL-12 .25 .25
1092 A441 9af Tupolev TU-104 .55 .55
1093 A441 11af Ilyushin IL-18 .60 .60
1094 A441 13af Tupolev TU-134 .80 .80
1095 A441 17af Ilyushin IL-62 1.00 1.00
1096 A441 21af Ilyushin IL-28 1.25 1.25
Nos. 1090-1096 (7) 4.60 4.60

Ettore Bugatti (1881-1947), Type 43, Italy — A442

Classic automobiles and their designers: 5af, Henry Ford, 1903 Model A, US. 8af, Rene Panhard (1841-1908), 1899 Landau, France. 11af, Gottlieb Daimler (1834-1900), 1935 Daimler-Benz, Germany. 12af, Carl Benz (1844-1929), 1893 Victoris, Germany. 15af, Armand Peugeot (1848-1915), 1892 Vis-a-Vis, France. 22af, Louis Chevrolet (1879-1941), 1925 Sedan, US.

1984, June 30
1097 A442 2af multicolored .15 .15
1098 A442 5af multicolored .30 .30
1099 A442 8af multicolored .50 .50
1100 A442 11af multicolored .70 .70
1101 A442 12af multicolored .75 .75
1102 A442 15af multicolored .90 .90
1103 A442 22af multicolored 1.40 1.40
Nos. 1097-1103 (7) 4.70 4.70

Qalai Bist Arch — A443

World Tourism Day: 2af, Ornamental buckled harness. 5af, Victory Monument and Memorial Arch, Kabul. 9af, Standing sculpture of Afghani ruler and attendants. 15af, Buffalo riders in snow. 19af, Camel driver, tent, camel in caparison. 21af, Horsemen playing buzkashi.

1984, Sept. 27
1104 A443 1af multicolored .15 .15
1105 A443 2af multicolored .15 .15
1106 A443 5af multicolored .30 .30
1107 A443 9af multicolored .55 .55
1108 A443 15af multicolored .60 .60
1109 A443 19af multicolored 1.10 1.10
1110 A443 21af multicolored 1.25 1.25
Nos. 1104-1110 (7) 4.10 4.10

UN World Food Day — A444

Fruit-bearing trees.

1984, Oct. 16
1111 A444 2af multicolored .15 .15
1112 A444 4af multicolored .25 .25
1113 A444 6af multicolored .40 .40
1114 A444 9af multicolored .55 .55
1115 A444 13af multicolored .80 .80
1116 A444 15af multicolored .90 .90
1117 A444 26af multicolored 1.65 1.65
Nos. 1111-1117 (7) 4.70 4.70

People's Democratic Party, 20th Anniv. A445

1985, Jan. 1
1118 A445 25af multicolored 1.50 1.50

Farmer's Day — A446

1985, Mar. 2
1119 A446 1af Oxen .15 .15
1120 A446 3af Mare, foal .20 .20
1121 A446 7af Brown horse .40 .40
1122 A446 8af White horse, vert. .50 .50
1123 A446 15af Sheep, sheepskins .90 .90
1124 A446 16af Shepherd, cattle, sheep 1.00 1.00
1125 A446 25af Family, camels 1.50 1.50
Nos. 1119-1125 (7) 4.65 4.65

Geologist's Day — A447

1985, Apr. 5
1126 A447 4af multicolored .25 .25

Lenin Leading Red Army, 1917, A448

Lenin and: 10af, Soviet Workers' Party deputies, Smolny. 15af, Revolutionaries, 1917, Leningrad. 50af, Portrait.

1985, Apr. 21 Perf. 12x12½
1127 A448 10af multicolored .60 .60
1128 A448 15af multicolored .90 .90
1129 A448 25af multicolored 1.50 1.50
Nos. 1127-1129 (3) 3.00 3.00

Souvenir Sheet
1130 A448 50af multicolored 4.00 4.00

Saur Revolution, 7th Anniv. — A449

1985, Apr. 27
1131 A449 21af multicolored 1.25 1.25

AFGHANISTAN

Berlin-Treptow Soviet War Memorial, Red Army at Siege of Berlin, 1945 — A450

Designs: 9af, Victorious Motherland monument, fireworks over Kremlin. 10af, Caecilienhof, site of Potsdam Treaty signing, flags of Great Britain, USSR and US.

1985, May 9   *Perf. 12½x12*
1132	A450	6af multicolored	.40	.40
1133	A450	9af multicolored	.55	.55
1134	A450	10af multicolored	.65	.65
		Nos. 1132-1134 (3)	1.60	1.60

End of World War II, defeat of Nazi Germany, 40th anniv.

INTELSAT, 20th Anniv. A451

Designs: 6af, INTELSAT satellite orbiting Earth. 9af, INTELSAT III. 10af, Rocket launch, Baikanur Space Center, vert.

Perf. 12x12½, 12½x12
1985, Apr. 6
1135	A451	6af multicolored	.40	.40
1136	A451	9af multicolored	.55	.55
1137	A451	10af multicolored	.60	.60
		Nos. 1135-1137 (3)	1.55	1.55

12th World Youth Festival, Moscow — A452

1985, May 5
1138	A452	7af Olympic stadium, Moscow	.50	.50
1139	A452	12af Festival emblem	.75	.75
1140	A452	13af Kremlin	.80	.80
1141	A452	18af Folk doll, emblem	1.10	1.10
		Nos. 1138-1141 (4)	3.15	3.15

Intl. Child Survival Campaign A453

1985, June 1
1142	A453	1af Weighing child	.15	.15
1143	A453	2af Immunization	.15	.15
1144	A453	4af Breastfeeding	.25	.25
1145	A453	5af Mother, child	.30	.30
		Nos. 1142-1145 (4)	.85	.85

Flowers A454

1985, July 5
1146	A454	2af Oenothera affinis	.15	.15
1147	A454	4af Erythrina crista-galli	.25	.25
1148	A454	8af Tillandsia aeranthos	.50	.50
1149	A454	13af Vinca major	.80	.80
1150	A454	18af Mirabilis jalapa	1.10	1.10
1151	A454	25af Cypella herbertii	1.50	1.50
1152	A454	30af Clytostoma callistegioides	1.90	1.90
		Nos. 1146-1152 (7)	6.20	6.20

Souvenir Sheet
Perf. 12½x11½
1153	A454	75af Sesbania punicea, horiz.	6.00	6.00

ARGENTINA '85.

1985, Aug. 19   *Perf. 12½x12½*
1154	A455	33af Mosque	2.00	2.00

Independence, 66th Anniv. A455

Pashto's and Balutchi's Day — A456

1985, Aug. 30
1155	A456	25af multicolored	1.50	1.50

UN Decade for Women A457

1985, Sept. 22
1156	A457	10af Emblems	.60	.60

World Tourism Day, 10th Anniv. A457a

1985, Sept. 27   *Litho.*   *Perf. 12*
1156A	A457a	1af Guldara Stupa	.15	.15
1156B	A457a	2af Mirwais Tomb, vert.	.15	.15
1156C	A457a	10af Statue of Bamyan, vert.	.60	.60
1156D	A457a	13af No Gumbad Mosque, vert.	.80	.80
1156E	A457a	14af Pule Kheshti Mosque	.85	.85
1156F	A457a	15af Bost Citadel	.90	.90
1156G	A457a	20af Ghazni Minaret, vert.	1.25	1.25
		Nos. 1156A-1156G (7)	4.70	4.70

Sports A457b

Perf. 12x12½, 12½x12
1985, Oct. 3   *Litho.*
1156H	A457b	1af Boxing	.15	.15
1156I	A457b	2af Volleyball	.15	.15
1156J	A457b	3af Soccer, vert.	.20	.20
1156K	A457b	12af Buzkashi	.90	.90
1156L	A457b	14af Weight lifting	1.00	1.00
1156M	A457b	18af Wrestling	1.25	1.25
1156N	A457b	25af Peg sticking	1.90	1.90
		Nos. 1156H-1156N (7)	5.55	5.55

World Food Day — A457c

1985, Oct. 16
1156O	A457c	25af multicolored	1.50	1.50

UN 40th Anniv. — A458

1985, Oct. 24   *Perf. 12½x12*
1157	A458	22af multicolored	1.40	1.40

Birds — A459

Perf. 12½x12, 12x12½
1985, Oct. 25
1158	A459	2af Jay	.15	.15
1159	A459	4af Plover, hummingbird	.25	.25
1160	A459	8af Pheasant	.50	.50
1161	A459	13af Hoopoe	.80	.80
1162	A459	18af Falcon	1.10	1.10
1163	A459	25af Partridge	1.50	1.50
1164	A459	30af Pelicans, horiz.	1.90	1.90
		Nos. 1158-1164 (7)	6.20	6.20

Souvenir Sheet
Perf. 12x12½
1165	A459	75af Parakeets	6.00	6.00

Mushrooms — A460

1985, June 10   *Litho.*   *Perf. 12½x12*
1165A	A460	3af Tricholomopsis rutilans	.20	.20
1166	A460	4af Boletus miniatoporus	.25	.25
1167	A460	7af Amanita rubescens	.45	.45
1168	A460	11af Boletus scaber	.65	.65
1169	A460	12af Coprinus atramentarius	.75	.75
1170	A460	18af Hypholoma	1.10	1.10
1171	A460	20af Boletus aurantiacus	1.25	1.25
		Nos. 1165A-1171 (7)	4.65	4.65

World Wildlife Fund — A461

1985, Nov. 25
1172	A461	2af Leopard, cubs	.15	.15
1173	A461	9af Adult's head	.55	.55
1174	A461	11af Adult	.70	.70
1175	A461	15af Cub	.90	.90
		Nos. 1172-1175 (4)	2.30	2.30

Motorcycle, Cent. — A462

Designs: Different makes and landmarks.

1985, Dec. 16
1176	A462	2af multicolored	.15	.15
1177	A462	4af multicolored	.25	.25
1178	A462	8af multicolored	.50	.50
1179	A462	13af multicolored	.75	.75
1180	A462	18af multicolored	1.00	1.00
1181	A462	25af multicolored	1.50	1.50
1182	A462	30af multicolored	1.75	1.75
		Nos. 1176-1182 (7)	5.90	5.90

Souvenir Sheet
Perf. 11½x12½
1183	A462	75af multicolored	6.00	6.00

People's Democratic Party, 21st Anniv. — A463

1986, Jan. 1   *Perf. 12½x12*
1184	A463	2af multicolored	.25	.25

27th Soviet Communist Party Congress — A464

1986, Mar. 31
1185	A464	25af Lenin	1.50	1.50

First Man in Space, 25th Anniv. — A465

Designs: 3af, Spacecraft. 7af, Soviet space achievement medal, vert. 9af, Rocket lift-off, vert. 11af, Yuri Gagarin, military decorations, vert. 13af, Gagarin, cosmonaut. 15af, Gagarin, politician. 17af, Gagarin wearing flight suit, vert.

Perf. 12½x12, 12x12½
1986, Apr. 12   *Litho.*
1186	A465	3af multicolored		
1187	A465	7af multicolored		
1188	A465	9af multicolored		
1189	A465	11af multicolored		
1190	A465	13af multicolored		
1191	A465	15af multicolored		
1192	A465	17af multicolored		
		Nos. 1186-1192 (7)	4.50	4.50

Loya Jirgah (Grand Assembly) of the People's Democratic Republic, 1st Anniv. A465a

1986, Apr. 23   *Litho.*   *Perf. 12½x12*
1192A	A465a	3af multicolored	.25	.25

AFGHANISTAN

Intl. Day of Labor
Solidarity — A465b

1986, May 1   *Perf. 12½x12*
1192B A465b 5af multicolored   .30 .30

Intl. Red
Crescent Day
A465c

1986, May 8   *Perf. 12x12½*
1192C A465c 7af multicolored   .45 .45

Intl. Children's
Day — A466

1986, June 1   *Perf. 12*
1193 A466 1af Mother, children, vert.   .15 .15
1194 A466 3af Mother, child, vert.   .25 .25
1195 A466 9af Children, map   .40 .40
    Nos. 1193-1195 (3)   .80 .80

World Youth
Day — A466a

1986, July 31   *Perf. 12x12½*
1195A A466a 15af multicolored   .90 .90

Pashtos' and
Baluchis'
Day — A467

1986, Aug. 31   *Perf. 12x12½*
1196 A467 4af multicolored   .25 .25

Intl. Peace
Year — A468

1986, Sept. 30 Photo.   *Perf. 12½x12*
1197 A468 12af black & Prus blue   .75 .75

A469

1986 World Cup Soccer Championships,
Mexico — A470

Various soccer plays.

1986, Apr. 15 Litho.   *Perf. 12*
1198 A469 3af multi, vert.
1199 A469 4af multicolored
1200 A469 7af multicolored
1201 A469 11af multi, vert.
1202 A469 12af multicolored
1203 A469 18af multi, vert.
1204 A469 20af multi, vert.
    Nos. 1198-1204 (7)   4.50 4.50

Souvenir Sheet
   Perf. 12½x12
1205 A470 75af multicolored   6.00 6.00

A471    A472

1986, Apr. 21   *Perf. 12½x12*
1206 A471 16af Lenin   1.00 1.00

1986, Apr. 27 Litho.   *Perf. 12½x12*
1207 A472 8af multicolored   .50 .50

Saur revolution, 8th anniv.

Natl. Independence,
67th Anniv. — A473

1986, Aug. 19 Litho.   *Perf. 12½x12*
1208 A473 10af multicolored   .65 .65

Literacy
Day — A474

1986, Sept. 18   *Perf. 12x12½*
1209 A474 2af multicolored   .25 .25

Dogs — A475 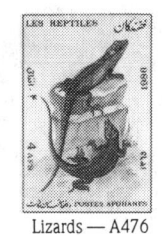   Lizards — A476

1986, May 19 Litho.   *Perf. 12x12½*
1210 A475 5af St. Bernard
1211 A475 7af Collie
1212 A475 8af Pointer
1213 A475 9af Golden retriever
1214 A475 11af German shepherd
1215 A475 15af Bulldog
1216 A475 20af Afghan hound
    Nos. 1210-1216 (7)   4.50 4.50

1986, July 7   *Perf. 12x12½, 12½x12*
1217 A476 3af Cobra
1218 A476 4af shown
1219 A476 5af Praying mantis
1220 A476 8af Beetle
1221 A476 9af Tarantula
1222 A476 10af Python
1223 A476 11af Scorpions
    Nos. 1217-1223 (7)   3.00 3.00
   Nos. 1217, 1219, 1221-1223 horiz.

STOCKHOLMIA '86 — A477

Ships.

1986, Aug. 28   *Perf. 12½x12*
1224 A477 4af multicolored
1225 A477 5af multicolored
1226 A477 6af multicolored
1227 A477 7af multicolored
1228 A477 8af multicolored
1229 A477 9af multicolored
1230 A477 11af multicolored
    Nos. 1224-1230 (7)   3.00 3.00

Souvenir Sheet
1231 A477 50af Galley   4.00 4.00

A479    A480

1986, Sept. 14   *Perf. 12*
1232 A479 3af lt blue, blk & olive
       gray   .25 .25

Reunion of Afghan tribes under the Supreme
Girgah.

1986, Oct. 25   *Perf. 12½x12*
1233 A480 3af black & brt ver   .25 .25

Natl. youth solidarity.

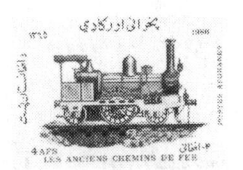

Locomotives — A481

1986, June 21   *Perf. 12½x12*
1234 A481 4af multicolored
1235 A481 5af multicolored
1236 A481 6af multicolored
1237 A481 7af multicolored
1238 A481 8af multicolored
1239 A481 9af multicolored
1240 A481 11af multicolored
    Nos. 1234-1240 (7)   3.00 3.00

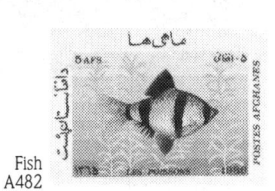

Fish
A482

Various fish.

1986, May 25
1241 A482 5af multicolored
1242 A482 7af multicolored
1243 A482 8af multicolored
1244 A482 9af multicolored
1245 A482 11af multicolored
1246 A482 15af multicolored
1247 A482 20af multicolored
    Nos. 1241-1247 (7)   4.50 4.50

Saur
Revolution,
9th Anniv.
A483

1987, Apr. 27   *Perf. 12*
1248 A483 3af multicolored   .25 .25

Natl.
Reconciliation
A484

1987, May 27   *Perf. 12x12½*
1249 A484 3af multicolored   .25 .25

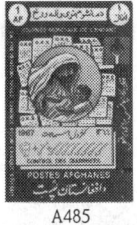

A485    A486

UN Child Survival
Campaign — A487

1987, June 1   *Perf. 12*
1250 A485 1af multicolored   .15 .15
1251 A486 5af multicolored   .30 .30
1252 A487 9af multicolored   .55 .55
    Nos. 1250-1252 (3)   1.00 1.00

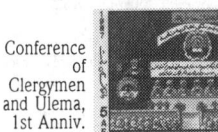

Conference
of
Clergymen
and Ulema,
1st Anniv.
A488

1987, June 30
1253 A488 5af multicolored   .30 .30

Butterflies — A489    A490

1987, July 3
1254 A489 7af multicolored
1255 A489 9af multi, diff.
1256 A489 10af multi, diff.
1257 A489 12af multi, diff.
1258 A489 15af multi, diff.
1259 A489 22af multi, diff.
1260 A489 25af multi, diff.
    Nos. 1254-1260 (7)   6.00 6.00
   10af, 15af and 22af horiz.

1987, Aug. 11
1261 A490 1af multicolored   .25 .25

1st election of local representatives for State Power and Administration.

Natl. Independence, 68th Anniv. — A490a

1987, Aug. 19
1261A A490a 3af multicolored   .25 .25

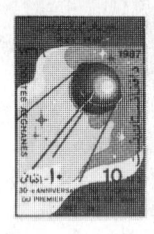

AFGHANISTAN

1st Artificial Satellite (Sputnik), 30th Anniv. — A491

1987, Oct. 4   Litho.   Perf. 12½x12
1262	A491	10af Sputnik		
1263	A491	15af Rocket launch		
1264	A491	25af Soyuz		
		Nos. 1262-1264 (3)	3.00	3.00

World Post Day — A492

1987, Oct. 9   Perf. 12x12½
| 1265 | A492 | 22af multicolored | 1.40 | 1.40 |

Intl. Communications and Transport Day — A493

1987, Oct. 24   Perf. 12½x12
| 1266 | A493 | 42af multicolored | 2.50 | 2.50 |

October Revolution in Russia, 70th Anniv. — A494

Mice — A495

1987, Nov. 7
| 1267 | A494 | 25af Lenin | 1.50 | 1.50 |

1987, Dec. 6   Perf. 12½x12, 12x12½
Various mice. Nos. 1269-1272 horiz.
1268	A495	2af multicolored		
1269	A495	4af multi, diff.		
1270	A495	8af multi, diff.		
1271	A495	16af multi, diff.		
1272	A495	20af multi, diff.		
		Nos. 1268-1272 (5)	3.00	3.00

Medicinal Plants — A496

Pashto's and Baluchis' Day — A497

1987, Nov. 11   Litho.   Perf. 12
1273	A496	3af Castor bean	.20	.20
1274	A496	6af Licorice	.35	.35
1275	A496	9af Chamomile	.55	.55
1276	A496	14af Datura	.80	.80
1277	A496	18af Dandelion	1.00	1.00
		Nos. 1273-1277 (5)	2.90	2.90

1987, Aug. 30
| 1278 | A497 | 4af multicolored | .25 | .25 |

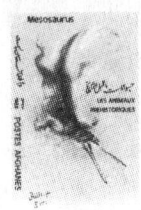

Dinosaurs A498

Pashtos' and Baluchis' Day A499

Perf. 12½x12, 12x12½
1988, June 6   Litho.
1279	A498	3af Mesosaurus	.20	.20
1280	A498	5af Styracosaurus	.30	.30
1281	A498	10af Uinatherium	.60	.60
1282	A498	15af Protoceratops	.90	.90
1283	A498	20af Stegosaurus	1.25	1.25
1284	A498	25af Ceratosaurus	1.50	1.50
1285	A498	30af Dinornis maximus	1.90	1.90
		Nos. 1279-1285 (7)	6.65	6.65
Nos. 1280-1283 horiz.

1988, Aug. 30   Perf. 12½x12
| 1286 | A499 | 23af multicolored | 1.40 | 1.40 |

Afghan-Soviet Joint Space Flight — A500

Valentina Tereshkova, 1st Woman in Space, 25th Anniv. — A501

1988, Aug. 30
| 1287 | A500 | 32af multicolored | 2.00 | 2.00 |

Perf. 12x12½, 12½x12
1988, Oct. 16
1288	A501	10af Portrait, rocket, horiz.	.60	.60
1289	A501	15af Lift-off, dove	.90	.90
1290	A501	25af Spacecraft, Earth, horiz.	1.50	1.50
		Nos. 1288-1290 (3)	3.00	3.00

Traditional Crafts — A502

Precious and Semiprecious Gems — A503

Perf. 12½x12, 12x12½
1988, Nov. 9   Litho.
1291	A502	2af Pitcher, bowls	.15	.15
1292	A502	4af Vases	.25	.25
1293	A502	5af Dress	.30	.30
1294	A502	9af Mats, napkins	.55	.55
1295	A502	15af Pocketbooks	.90	.90
1296	A502	23af Jewelry	1.40	1.40
1297	A502	50af Furniture	3.00	3.00
		Nos. 1291-1297 (7)	6.55	6.55
Nos. 1291-1292, 1294-1297 horiz.

1988, Dec. 5   Perf. 12½x12
1298	A503	13af Emeralds	.80	.80
1299	A503	37af Lapiz lazuli	2.25	2.25
1300	A503	40af Rubies	2.50	2.50
		Nos. 1298-1300 (3)	5.55	5.55

1988 Winter Olympics, Calgary — A504

1988, Dec. 25
1301	A504	2af Women's figure skating	.15	.15
1301A	A504	5af Skiing	.30	.30
1301B	A504	9af Bobsledding	.55	.55
1301C	A504	22af Biathlon	1.40	1.40
1301D	A504	37af Speed skating	2.25	2.25
Size: 80x60mm
| 1302 | A504 | 75af Ice hockey | 4.50 | 4.50 |
| | | Nos. 1301-1302 (6) | 9.15 | 9.15 |

A510

A511

A512

A513

A513a

Flowers — A514

Various flowering plants.

Perf. 12x12½, 12½x12
1988, Jan. 27   Litho.
1303	A510	3af multicolored	.15	.15
1304	A511	5af multicolored	.30	.30
1305	A511	7af multi, vert.	.40	.40
1306	A512	9af multicolored	.50	.50
1307	A513	12af multicolored	.75	.75
1308	A513a	15af multicolored	.90	.90
1309	A514	24af multicolored	1.50	1.50
		Nos. 1303-1309 (7)	4.50	4.50

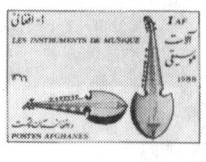

Traditional Musical Instruments A515

String and percussion instruments.

1988, Jan. 15   Litho.   Perf. 12
1310	A515	1af shown	.15	.15
1311	A515	3af drums	.20	.20
1312	A515	5af multi, diff.	.30	.30
1313	A515	15af multi, diff.	.90	.90
1314	A515	18af multi, diff.	1.10	1.10
1315	A515	25af multi, diff.	1.50	1.50
1316	A515	33af multi, diff.	2.00	2.00
		Nos. 1310-1316 (7)	6.15	6.15

Admission of Afghanistan to the ITU and UPU, 60th Anniv. — A516

1988, Apr. 13   Litho.   Perf. 12
| 1317 | A516 | 20af multicolored | 1.25 | 1.25 |

Saur Revolution, 10th Anniv. A517

1988, Apr. 23
| 1318 | A517 | 10af multicolored | .65 | .65 |

Fruit — A518

1988, July 18   Litho.   Perf. 12
1319	A518	2af Baskets, compote	.15	.15
1320	A518	4af Four baskets	.25	.25
1321	A518	7af Basket	.45	.45
1322	A518	8af Grapes, vert.	.50	.50
1323	A518	16af Market	1.00	1.00
1324	A518	22af Market, diff.	1.40	1.40
1325	A518	25af Vendor, vert.	1.50	1.50
		Nos. 1319-1325 (7)	5.25	5.25

AFGHANISTAN

Jawaharlal Nehru (1889-1964), 1st Prime Minister of Independent India — A519

1988, Nov. 14
| 1326 | A519 | 40af multicolored | 2.50 | 2.50 |

Natl. Independence, 69th Anniv. A520

1988, Aug. 1
| 1327 | A520 | 24af multicolored | 1.50 | 1.50 |

Intl. Red Cross and Red Crescent Organizations, 125th Annivs. — A521

1988, Sept. 26
| 1328 | A521 | 10af multicolored | .60 | .60 |

Natl. Reconciliation Institute, 2nd Anniv. — A522

1989, Jan. 4
| 1329 | A522 | 4af multicolored | .25 | .25 |

Chess A523

Boards, early matches and hand-made chessmen.

1989, Feb. 2   Litho.   *Perf. 12x12½*
1330	A523	2af Bishop	.15	.15
1331	A523	3af Queen	.20	.20
1332	A523	4af King (bust)	.25	.25
1333	A523	7af King, diff.	.40	.40
1334	A523	16af Knight	1.00	1.00
1335	A523	24af Pawn	1.50	1.50
1336	A523	45af Bishop, diff.	2.75	2.75
		Nos. 1330-1336 (7)	6.25	6.25

Paintings by Picasso — A524   Fauna — A525

Designs: 4af, *The Old Jew.* 6af, *The Two Mountebanks.* 8af, *Portrait of Ambrouse Vollar.* 22af, *Woman of Majorca.* 35af, *Acrobat on the Ball.* 75af, *Usine a Horta de Ebro.*

1989, Feb. 13   Litho.   *Perf. 12½x12*
1341	A524	4af multicolored	.25	.25
1342	A524	6af multicolored	.35	.35
1343	A524	8af multicolored	.50	.50
1344	A524	22af multicolored	1.40	1.40
1345	A524	35af multicolored	2.25	2.25

Size: 71x90mm
Imperf
| 1346 | A524 | 75af multicolored | 4.50 | 4.50 |
| | | Nos. 1341-1346 (6) | 9.25 | 9.25 |

1989, Feb. 20   Litho.   *Perf. 12½x12*
1347	A525	3af *Allactaga euphratica*	.15	.15
1348	A525	4af *Equus hemionus*	.25	.25
1349	A525	14af *Felis lynx*	.85	.85
1350	A525	35af *Gypaetus barbatus*	2.25	2.25
1351	A525	44af *Capra falconeri*	2.75	2.75

Size: 71x91mm
Imperf
| 1352 | A525 | 100af *Naja oxiana* | 6.00 | 6.00 |
| | | Nos. 1347-1352 (6) | 12.25 | 12.25 |

Intl. Women's Day — A526

1989, Mar. 8   *Perf. 12½x12*
| 1353 | A526 | 8af multicolored | .50 | .50 |

Restoration and Development of San'a, Yemen A527

1988, Dec. 27   Litho.   *Perf. 12*
| 1354 | A527 | 32af multicolored | 2.00 | 2.00 |

Agriculture Day — A528

1989, Mar. 21
1355	A528	1af Cattle	.15	.15
1356	A528	2af Old and new plows	.15	.15
1357	A528	3af Field workers	.20	.20
		Nos. 1355-1357 (3)	.50	.50

World Meteorology Day — A529

1989, Mar. 23
1358	A529	27af shown	1.65	1.65
1359	A529	32af Emblems	2.00	2.00
1360	A529	40af Weather station, balloon, vert.	2.50	2.50
		Nos. 1358-1360 (3)	6.15	6.15

Saur Revolution, 11th Anniv. A530

1989, Apr. 27
| 1361 | A530 | 20af multicolored | 1.25 | 1.25 |

Classic Automobiles — A531

1989, Dec. 30   Litho.   *Perf. 12½x12*
1362	A531	5af 1910 Duchs, Germany		
1363	A531	10af 1911 Ford, US		
1364	A531	20af 1911 Renault, France		
1365	A531	25af 1911, Russo-Balte, Russia		
1366	A531	30af 1926 Fiat, Italy		

Asia-Pacific Telecommunity, 10th Anniv. — A532

1989, Aug. 3   *Perf. 12*
| 1367 | A532 | 3af shown | | |
| 1368 | A532 | 27af Emblem, satellite dish | | |

Teacher's Day — A533

1989, May 30   Litho.   *Perf. 12*
| 1369 | A533 | 42af multicolored | 1.25 | |

French Revolution, Bicent. — A534

1989, July   Litho.   *Perf. 12*
| 1370 | A534 | 25af multicolored | .80 | |

Natl. Independence, 70th Anniv. A535

1989, Aug. 18   Litho.   *Perf. 12*
| 1371 | A535 | 25af multicolored | .80 | |

A536   Birds — A537

1989, Aug. 30
| 1372 | A536 | 3af multicolored | .15 | |

Pashtos' and Baluchis' Day.

1989, Dec. 5   Litho.   *Perf. 12*
1373	A537	3af *Platalea leucorodia*	.15	
1374	A537	5af *Porphyrio porhyrio*	.15	
1375	A537	10af *Botaurus stellaris*, horiz.	.30	
1376	A537	15af *Pelecanus onocrotalus*	.45	
1377	A537	20af *Netta rufina*	.60	
1378	A537	25af *Cygnus olor*	.75	
1379	A537	30af *Phalacrocorax carbo*, horiz.	.90	
		Nos. 1373-1379 (7)	3.30	

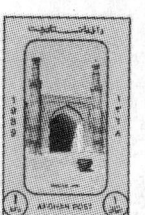

Tourism — A538   Mushrooms — A539

1989, Dec.
1380	A538	1af Mosque	.15	
1381	A538	2af Minaret	.15	
1382	A538	3af Buzkashi, horiz.	.15	
1383	A538	4af Jet over Hendo Kush, horiz.	.15	
		Nos. 1380-1383 (4)	.60	

1996, July 20   Litho.   *Perf. 12½x13*

Designs: 100af, *Suillus luteus.* 300af, *Russula virescens.* 400af, *Clitocybe inversa.* 500af, *Volvariella bombycina.* 600af, *Macrolepiota procera.* 800af, *Cystoderma cinnabarinum.* 4000af, *Lycoperdon umbrinum.*

1384	A539	100af multicolored	.25	
1385	A539	300af multicolored	.70	
1386	A539	400af multicolored	.95	
1387	A539	500af multicolored	1.10	
1388	A539	600af multicolored	1.40	
1389	A539	800af multicolored	1.75	
		Nos. 1384-1389 (6)	6.15	

Souvenir Sheet
| 1390 | A539 | 4000af multicolored | 5.25 | |

No. 1390 contains one 32x40mm stamp.

Bears A540

Designs: 500af, *Ursus americanus*, vert. 600af, *Ursus maritimus.* 800af, *Helarctos malayanus.* 900af, *Ursus arctos horribilis.* 1000af, *Ursus arctos pyreneicus*, vert. 4000af, *Ursus arctos syriacus*, vert.

Perf. 12½x13, 13x12½
1996, Aug. 15   Litho.
1391	A540	500af multicolored	.75	
1392	A540	600af multicolored	.90	
1393	A540	800af multicolored	1.25	
1394	A540	900af multicolored	1.40	
1395	A540	1000af multicolored	1.50	
		Nos. 1391-1395 (5)	5.80	

Souvenir Sheet
Perf. 13
| 1396 | A540 | 4000af multicolored | 6.15 | |

No. 1396 contains one 32x40mm stamp.

1998 World Cup Soccer Championships, France — A541

Various soccer players.

1996, Sept. 18   Litho.   *Perf. 13*
Background Color
1397	A541	500af green	.75	
1398	A541	600af purple	.90	
1399	A541	700af brown	1.00	

Size: 28x42mm
1400	A541	800af yellow	1.20	
1401	A541	900af blue	1.35	
1402	A541	1000af vermilion	1.50	
		Nos. 1397-1402 (6)	6.70	

Souvenir Sheet
Perf. 12½
| 1403 | A541 | 4000d multicolored | 6.00 | |

No. 1403 contains one 32x40mm stamp.

AFGHANISTAN

Silkworms — A542

Designs: 300af, Arctia caja. 400af, Sphinx ligustri. 500af, Zerynthia polyxema. 600af, Papilio machaon. 700af, Cerura vinula. 800af, Celerio euphorbiae. 3000af, Abraxes grossulariata.

1996, Oct. 7			Perf. 12½
1404	A542	300af multicolored	.45
1405	A542	400af multicolored	.60
1406	A542	500af multicolored	.75
1407	A542	600af multicolored	.90
1408	A542	700af multicolored	1.00
1409	A542	800af multicolored	1.20
		Nos. 1404-1409 (6)	4.90

Souvenir Sheet
Perf. 13
| 1410 | A542 | 3000af multicolored | 4.60 |

No. 1410 contains one 40x32mm stamp.

Domestic Cats — A543

Designs: 200af, American shorthair. 500af, Japanese bobtail. 600af, British shorthair. 800af, Devon rex. 1000af, Colorpoint shorthair. 1200af, Somali. 4000af, Sphinx.

1996		Litho.	Perf. 12½
1411	A543	200af multicolored	.30
1412	A543	500af multicolored	.75
1413	A543	600af multicolored	.90
1414	A543	800af multicolored	1.20
1415	A543	1000af multicolored	1.50
1416	A543	1200af multicolored	1.75
		Nos. 1411-1416 (6)	6.40

Souvenir Sheet
| 1417 | A543 | 3000af multicolored | 6.00 |

No. 1417 contains one 40x32mm stamp.

Horses A544

1996, Nov. 5			
1418	A544	200af Eohippus	.45
1419	A544	300af Miohippus	.65
1420	A544	400af Merychippus	.90
1421	A544	500af Pliohippus	1.10
1422	A544	600af Equus	1.30
		Nos. 1418-1422 (5)	4.40

Souvenir Sheet
Perf. 13
| 1423 | A544 | 3000af Trotter, sulky | 6.00 |

No. 1423 contains one 40x32mm stamp. Inscription on No. 1418 reads "Echippus."

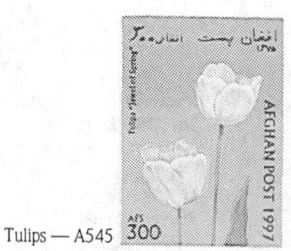

Tulips — A545

Designs: 300af, Jewel of Spring. 400af, Mrs. John Scheepers. 500af, Absalon. 600af, Queen of Sheba. 800af, Marlette. 1000af, Mary Housley. 3000af, Fosteriana Purissima.

1997		Litho.	Perf. 12½
1424	A545	300af multicolored	.45
1425	A545	400af multicolored	.60
1426	A545	500af multicolored	.70
1427	A545	600af multicolored	.90
1428	A545	800af multicolored	1.15
1429	A545	1000af multicolored	1.45
		Nos. 1424-1429 (6)	5.25

Souvenir Sheet
| 1430 | A545 | 3000af multicolored | 4.25 |

No. 1430 contains one 32x40mm stamp.

Llamas and Camels A546

Designs: 400af, Lama vicugna, vert. 600af, Lama guanicoe. 800af, Camelus dromedarius. 1000af, Lama guanicoe pacos, vert. 1200af, Lama guanicoe glama. 1500af, Camelus ferus bactrianus. 4000af, Camelus dromedarius, vert.

1997			
1431	A546	400af multicolored	.60
1432	A546	600af multicolored	.85
1433	A546	800af multicolored	1.15
1434	A546	1000af multicolored	1.45
1435	A546	1200af multicolored	1.70
1436	A546	1500af multicolored	2.20
		Nos. 1431-1436 (6)	7.95

Souvenir Sheet
| 1437 | A546 | 4000af multicolored | 5.75 |

No. 1437 contains one 32x40mm stamp.

Islamic Revolution, 4th Anniv. — A547

Design: 1500af, Farmer plowing beside stream.

1996		Litho.	Perf. 13
1438	A547	800af multicolored	1.50
1439	A547	1500af multicolored	3.00

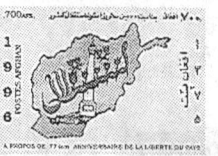

Independence, 77th Anniv. — A548

In Honor of Prophet Mohammed A549

1996			
1440	A548	700af multicolored	1.40
1441	A549	1500af multicolored	3.00

Domestic Cats A550

Designs: 30af, Norwegian forest. 50af, Ragdoll. 100af, Longhair Scottish fold. 200af, Oriental longhair. 300af, Manx. 500af, Sphinx. 1200af, Manx, diff.

1997			Perf. 12½
1442	A550	30af multicolored	.15
1443	A550	50af multicolored	.20
1444	A550	100af multicolored	.40
1445	A550	200af multicolored	.80
1446	A550	300af multicolored	1.25
1447	A550	500af multicolored	2.00
		Nos. 1442-1447 (6)	4.80

Souvenir Sheet
Perf. 13
| 1448 | A550 | 1200af multicolored | 4.50 |

No. 1448 contains one 40x32mm stamp.

Wildflowers A551

Designs: 50af, Nymphaea odorata. 100af, Nymphaea lotus. 200af, Aponogeton distachyus. 500af, Nymphaea capensis. 800af, Nymphaea rubra. 1000af, Pontederia cordata. 3000af, Nymphaea daubenyana, horiz.

1997		Litho.	Perf. 12½
1449	A551	50af multicolored	.15
1450	A551	100af multicolored	.15
1451	A551	200af multicolored	.25
1452	A551	500af multicolored	.65
1453	A551	800af multicolored	1.00
1454	A551	1000af multicolored	1.25
		Nos. 1449-1454 (6)	3.45

Souvenir Sheet
| 1455 | A551 | 3000af multicolored | 3.80 |

No. 1455 contains one 40x32mm stamp.

Early Sailing Ships — A552

Designs: 400af, Hanseatic cog. 600af, Northern Europe dromond. 800af, Venetian cargo ship. 1000af, Northern Europe merchant ship. 1200af, Ladia Russian war ship. 1500af, Genoa merchant ship. 4000af, Egyptian merchant ship.

1997		Litho.	Perf. 12½
1456	A552	400af multicolored	.45
1457	A552	600af multicolored	.70
a.		Pair, #1456-1457	1.15
1458	A552	800af multicolored	.95
1459	A552	1000af multicolored	1.15
a.		Pair, #1458-1459	2.10
1460	A552	1200af multicolored	1.40
1461	A552	1500af multicolored	1.75
a.		Pair, #1460-1461	3.15
		Nos. 1456-1461 (6)	6.40

Souvenir Sheet
| 1462 | A552 | 4000af multicolored | 4.60 |

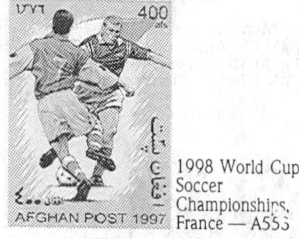

1998 World Cup Soccer Championships, France — A553

French flag, various soccer plays.

1997		Litho.	Perf. 12½
1463	A553	400af multicolored	.50
1464	A553	600af multicolored	.70
1465	A553	800af multicolored	.95
1466	A553	1000af multicolored	1.25
1467	A553	1200af multicolored	1.40
1468	A553	1500af multicolored	1.75
		Nos. 1463-1468 (6)	6.55

Souvenir Sheet
| 1469 | A553 | 4000af multicolored | 4.75 |

No. 1469 contains one 32x40mm stamp.

Mushrooms A554

Designs: 400af, Gomphidius glutinosus. 600af, Collybia fusipes. 800af, Stropharia aeruginosa. 1000af, Craterellus cornucopioides. 1200af, Guepinia helvelloides. 1500af, Ixocomus elegans. 4000af, Cantharellus cibarius.

1998		Litho.	Perf. 12½
1470	A554	400af multicolored	.45
1471	A554	600af multicolored	.70
1472	A554	800sh multicolored	.95
1473	A554	1000af multicolored	1.60
1474	A554	1200af multicolored	1.40
1475	A554	1500af multicolored	1.75
		Nos. 1470-1475 (6)	6.85

Souvenir Sheet
Perf. 13
| 1476 | A554 | 4000af multicolored | 4.60 |

No. 1476 contains one 40x32mm stamp.

Butterflies, Moths A556

Designs: 400af, Fabriciana adippe, vert. 600af, Nymphalis antiopa. 800af, Polygonia c-album. 1000af, Nymphalis polychloros. 1200af, Pararge aegeria. 1500af, Melitaea phoebe, vert. 4000af, Aglais urticae.

1998, July 3		Litho.	Perf. 12½	
1478	A556	400af multicolored	.50	.50
1479	A556	600af multicolored	.75	.75
1480	A556	800af multicolored	1.00	1.00
1481	A556	1000af multicolored	1.25	1.25
1482	A556	1200af multicolored	1.50	1.50
1483	A556	1500af multicolored	1.90	1.90
		Nos. 1478-1483 (6)	6.90	6.90

Souvenir Sheet
Perf. 13
| 1484 | A556 | 4000af multicolored | 4.75 | 4.75 |

No. 1484 contains one 40x32mm stamp.

A sheet of 9 stamps memorializing Princess Diana has been sold in the philatelic market. The editors do not believe that these stamps were sold in Afghanistan.

Ovis Vignei A557

World Wildlife Fund: a, 800af, Male. b, 1000af, Female nursing young. c, 1200af, Two males walking. d, 10,000af, Two males butting heads.

1998		Litho.	Perf. 12½	
1485	A557	Strip of 4, #a.-d.	7.00	7.00

SEMI-POSTAL STAMPS

Catalogue values for unused stamps in this section are for Never Hinged items.

AFGHANISTAN

No. 373 Surcharged in Violet

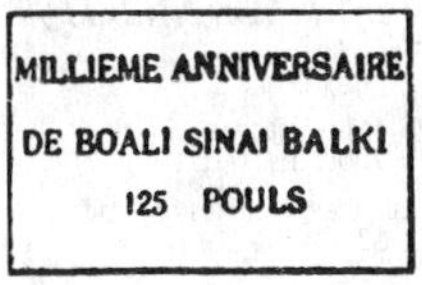

MILLIEME ANNIVERSAIRE
DE BOALI SINAI BALKI
125 POULS

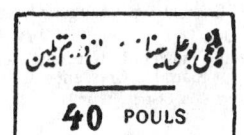

40 POULS

1952, July 12   Unwmk.   *Perf. 12½*
B1   A122   40p + 30p cerise   10.00   1.50
B2   A122   125p + 30p cerise   12.50   2.00

1000th anniv. of the birth of Avicenna.

Children at Play — SP1

1955, July 3   Typo.   *Perf. 11*
B3   SP1   35p + 15p dk green   .50   .35
B4   SP1   125p + 25p purple   1.00   .85

The surtax was for child welfare.

Amir Sher Ali Khan, Tiger Head Stamp and Zahir Shah — SP2

Children at Play — SP3

1955, July 2   Litho.
B5   SP2   35p + 15p carmine   .40   .30
B6   SP2   125p + 25p pale vio bl   .85   .55

85th anniv. of the Afghan post.

1956, June 20   Typo.
B7   SP3   35p + 15p brt vio bl   .75   .25
B8   SP3   140p + 15p dk org brn   1.25   .75

Issued for Children's Day. The surtax was for child welfare. No. B8 inscribed in French.

Pashtunistan Monument, Kabul — SP4

1956, Sept. 1   Litho.
B9   SP4   35p + 15p dp violet   .20   .20
B10   SP4   140p + 15p dk brown   .60   .60

"Free Pashtunistan" Day. The surtax aided the "Free Pashtunistan" movement.
No. B9 measures 30½x19½mm; No. B10, 29x19mm. On sale and valid for use only on Sept. 1-2.

Globe and Sun — SP5

Children on Seesaw — SP6

1956, Oct. 24   *Perf. 11*
B11   SP5   35p + 15p ultra   .65   .60
B12   SP5   140p + 15p red brown   1.25   1.00

Afghanistan's UN admission, 10th anniv.

1957, June 20   Unwmk.
B13   SP6   35p + 15p brt rose   .75   .25
B14   SP6   140p + 15p ultra   1.50   .90

Children's Day. Surtax for child welfare.

UN Headquarters and Emblems — SP7

1957, Oct. 24   *Perf. 11 Rough*
B15   SP7   35p + 15p red brown   .35   .20
B16   SP7   140p + 15p lt ultra   .65   .55

United Nations Day.

Swimming Pool and Children — SP8

1958, June 22   *Perf. 11*
B17   SP8   35p + 15p rose   .25   .20
B18   SP8   140p + 15p dl red brn   .75   .60

Children's Day. Surtax for child welfare.

Pashtunistan Flag — SP9

1958, Aug. 31
B19   SP9   35p + 15p lt blue   .20   .20
B20   SP9   140p + 15p red brown   .60   .60

Issued for "Free Pashtunistan Day."

Children Playing Tug of War — SP10

1959, June 23   *Perf. 11*
B21   SP10   35p + 15p brown vio   .50   .20
B22   SP10   165p + 15p brt pink   1.00   .60

Children's Day. Surtax for child welfare.

Pathans in Tribal Dance — SP11

1959, Sept.   Unwmk.   *Perf. 11 Rough*
B23   SP11   35p + 15p green   .50   .20
B24   SP11   165p + 15p orange   1.00   .60

Issued for "Free Pashtunistan Day."

Afghan Cavalryman with UN Flag — SP12

1959, Oct. 24   *Perf. 11 Rough*
B25   SP12   35p + 15p orange   .20   .15
B26   SP12   165p + 15p lt bl grn   .45   .40

Issued for United Nations Day.

Children — SP13

1960, Oct. 23   Litho.
B27   SP13   75p + 25p lt ultra   .75   .20
B28   SP13   175p + 25p lt green   1.50   .35

Children's Day. Surtax for child welfare.

Man with Spray Gun — SP14

1960, Sept. 6   *Perf. 11 Rough*
B29   SP14   50p + 50p orange   .80   1.00
B30   SP14   175p + 50p red brown   2.25   2.25

11th anniversary of the WHO malaria control program in Afghanistan.

SP15

1960, Sept. 1   Unwmk.
B31   SP15   50p + 50p rose   .25   .20
B32   SP15   175p + 50p dk blue   .55   .45

Issued for "Free Pashtunistan Day."

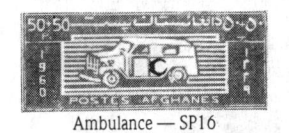

Ambulance — SP16

1960, Oct. 16   *Perf. 11*
Crescent in Red
B33   SP16   50p + 50p violet   .40   .30
B34   SP16   175p + 50p blue   .90   .75

Issued for the Red Crescent Society.

Nos. 470-471 Surcharged in Blue or Orange

1960, Dec. 31   Litho.   *Perf. 11*
B35   A166   50p + 25p dp org (Bl)   1.50   1.50
B36   A166   165p + 25p blue (O)   1.50   1.50

The souvenir sheets described after No. 471 were surcharged in carmine "+25 Ps" on each stamp. Value $5 each.
See general note after No. 485.

Nos. 496-500 Surcharged

UNICEF +25PS

1961   Unwmk.   Photo.   *Perf. 13½x14*
B37   A175   2p + 25p green & rose lil
B38   A175   2p + 25p brown & cit
B39   A175   5p + 25p gray & rose
B40   A175   10p + 25p blue & bis
B41   A175   15p + 25p sl bl & dl lil
     Nos. B37-B41 (5)   1.50

UNICEF. The same surcharge was applied to an imperf. souvenir sheet like that noted after No. 505. Value $4.50.

Nos. 522-526 Surcharged "+25PS" and Crescent in Red

1961, Oct. 16   *Perf. 13½x14*
B42   A184   2p + 25p black
B43   A184   2p + 25p green
B44   A184   5p + 25p lilac rose
B45   A184   10p + 25p lilac
B46   A184   15p + 25p dk blue
     Nos. B42-B46 (5)   2.00

Issued for the Red Crescent Society.

Nos. 539-543 Surcharged in Red: "UNESCO + 25PS"

1962   *Perf. 12*
B47   A186   2p + 25p multi
B48   A186   2p + 25p multi
B49   A186   5p + 25p multi
B50   A186   10p + 25p multi
B51   A186   15p + 25p multi
     Nos. B47-B51 (5)   1.50

UNESCO. The same surcharge was applied to the souvenir sheets mentioned after No. 548. Value, 2 sheets, $3.50.

Nos. 553-561 Surcharged: "Dag Hammarskjöld +20PS"

1962, Sept. 17   *Perf. 14x13½*
B52   A187   2p + 20p
B53   A187   2p + 20p
B54   A187   5p + 20p
B55   A187   10p + 20p
B56   A187   15p + 20p
B57   A187   25p + 20p
B58   A187   50p + 20p
B59   A187   75p + 20p
B60   A187   100p + 20p
     Nos. B52-B60 (9)   2.00

In memory of Dag Hammarskjold, Sec. Gen. of the UN, 1953-61. Perf. and imperf. souvenir sheets exist. Value, 2 sheets, $3.

Nos. 583-593 Surcharged "+15PS"

1963, Mar. 15   *Perf. 14x13½*
B61   A193   2p + 15p
B62   A193   2p + 15p
B63   A193   5p + 15p
B64   A193   10p + 15p
B65   A193   15p + 15p
B66   A193   25p + 15p
B67   A193   50p + 15p
B68   A193   75p + 15p
B69   A193   100p + 15p
B70   A193   150p + 15p
B71   A193   175p + 15p
     Nos. B61-B71 (11)   7.50

WHO drive to eradicate malaria.
Postally used copies of Nos. B37-B71 are uncommon and command a considerable premium over the values for unused copies.

Nos. 672-672G, 672I Surcharged in Various Positions

1964, Mar. 9
B71A   A213g   2p + 50p
B71B   A213g   3p + 50p
B71C   A213g   4p + 50p
B71D   A213g   5p + 50p
B71E   A213g   15p + 50p
B71F   A213g   100p + 50p
B71G   A213g   2af + 50p
B71H   A213g   3af + 50p

Souvenir Sheet
B71J   A213g   5af + 50p

Nos. B71E-B71G are airmail semi-postals.

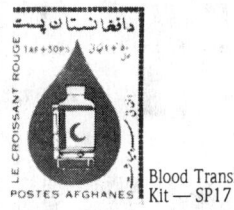

Blood Transfusion Kit — SP17

1964, Oct. 18   Litho.   *Perf. 10½*
B72   SP17   1af + 50p black & rose   .50   .15

Issued for the Red Crescent Society and Red Crescent Week, Oct. 18-24.

First Aid Station — SP18

1965, Oct.   Photo.   *Perf. 13½x14*
B73   SP18   1.50af + 50p multi   1.00   .50

Issued for the Red Crescent Society.

Children Playing — SP19

1966, Nov. 28   Photo.   *Perf. 13½x14*
B74   SP19   1af + 1af yel grn & cl   .35   .15
B75   SP19   3af + 2af yel & brn   .75   .20
B76   SP19   7af + 3af rose lil & grn   1.25   .40
     Nos. B74-B76 (3)   2.35   .75

Children's Day.

AFGHANISTAN

Nadir Shah Presenting Society Charter — SP20

1967   Photo.   Perf. 13x14
- B77 SP20 2af + 1af red & dk grn   .25   .15
- B78 SP20 5af + 1af lil rose & brn   .50   .25

Issued for the Red Crescent Society.

Vaccination SP21    **Red Crescent SP22**

1967, June 6   Photo.   Perf. 12
- B79 SP21 2af + 1af yellow & blk   .75   .15
- B80 SP21 5af + 2af pink & brn   1.00   .25

The surtax was for anti-tuberculosis work.

1967, Oct. 18   Photo.   Perf. 12
Crescent in Red
- B81 SP22 3af + 1af gray ol & blk   .50   .15
- B82 SP22 5af + 1af dl bl & blk   .75   .20

Issued for the Red Crescent Society.

Queen Humeira SP23    **Red Crescent SP24**

1968, June 14   Photo.   Perf. 12
- B83 SP23 2af + 2af red brown   .25   .20
- B84 SP23 7af + 2af dull green   .75   .50

Issued for Mother's Day.

1968, Oct. 16   Photo.   Perf. 12
- B85 SP24 4af + 1af yel, blk & red   .45   .25

Issued for the Red Crescent Society.

Red Cross, Crescent, Lion and Sun Emblems — SP25    **Mother and Child — SP26**

1969, May 5   Litho.   Perf. 14x13½
- B86 SP25 3af + 1af multicolored   .75   .20
- B87 SP25 5af + 1af multicolored   1.25   .30

League of Red Cross Societies, 50th anniv.

1969, June 14   Photo.   Perf. 12
- B88 SP26 1af + 1af yel org & brn   .25   .15
- B89 SP26 4af + 1af rose lil & pur   .40   .25
-    a. Souvenir sheet of 2   1.00   1.00

Mother's Day. No. B89a contains 2 imperf. stamps similar to Nos. B88-B89. Sold for 10af.

Red Crescent — SP27

1969, Oct. 16   Photo.   Perf. 12
- B90 SP27 6af + 1af multi   .75   .30

Issued for the Red Crescent Society.

UN and FAO Emblems, Farmer SP28

1973, May 24   Photo.   Perf. 13½
- B91 SP28 14af + 7af grnsh bl & lil   1.10   .75

World Food Program, 10th anniversary.

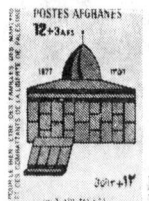

Dome of the Rock, Jerusalem — SP29

1977, Sept. 11   Photo.   Perf. 14
- B92 SP29 12af + 3af multi   1.50   .35

Surtax for Palestinian families and soldiers.

15 Cent. (lunar) of Islamic Pilgrimage (Hegira) — SP30

1981, Jan. 17   Litho.   Perf. 12½x12
- B93 SP30 13af + 2af multi   .45   .40

Red Crescent Aid Programs — SP31

1981, May 8   Perf. 12x12½
- B94 SP31 1af + 4af multi   1.00   1.00

Intl. Year of the Disabled — SP32

1981, Oct. 12   Perf. 12x12½
- B95 SP32 6af + 1af multi   .35   .25

AIR POST STAMPS

Plane over Kabul — AP1

		Perf. 12, 12x11, 11	
1939, Oct. 1		Typo.	Unwmk.
C1	AP1	5af orange	3.75 2.25
a.		Imperf., pair ('47)	22.50 22.50
b.		Horiz. pair, imperf. vert.	20.00
C2	AP1	10af blue	3.75 1.75
a.		10af lt bl	5.00 5.00
b.		Imperf., pair ('47)	22.50
c.		Horiz. pair, imperf. vert.	20.00
C3	AP1	20af emerald	7.50 5.00
a.		Imperf., pair ('47)	22.50
b.		Horiz. pair, imperf. vert.	20.00
c.		Vert. pair, imperf. horiz.	22.50
		Nos. C1-C3 (3)	15.00 9.00

These stamps come with clean-cut or rough perforations. Counterfeits exist.

1948, June 14   Perf. 12x11½
- C4 AP1 5af emerald   15.00   15.00
- C5 AP1 10af red orange   15.00   15.00
- C6 AP1 20af blue   15.00   15.00
-    Nos. C4-C6 (3)   45.00   45.00

Imperforates exist.

> Catalogue values for unused stamps in this section, from this point to the end of the section, are for Never Hinged items.

Plane over Palace Grounds, Kabul — AP2

1951-54   Engr.   Perf. 13½
Imprint: "Waterlow & Sons, Limited, London"
- C7 AP2 5af henna brn   2.50   .55
- C8 AP2 5af dp grn ('54)   3.50   .50
- C9 AP2 10af gray   4.00   1.40
- C10 AP2 20af dark blue   6.50   2.25

1957
- C11 AP2 5af ultra   .90   .35
- C12 AP2 10af dark vio   1.75   .75
-    Nos. C7-C12 (6)   19.15   5.80

See No. C38.

Ariana Plane over Hindu Kush — AP3

	Perf. 11, Imperf.	
1960-63	Litho.	Unwmk.
C13 AP3	75p light vio	.30 .30
C14 AP3	125p blue	.40 .45
	Perf. 10½, 11	
C14A AP3	5af citron ('63)	1.10 1.10
	Nos. C13-C14A (3)	1.80 1.85

Girl Scout — AP4

1962, Aug. 30   Photo.   Perf. 11½x12
- C15 AP4 100p ocher & brn   .60   .60
- C16 AP4 175p brt yel grn & brn   .85   .85

Women's Day. See #578-579 and note on souvenir sheet.

Sports Type of Regular Issue, 1962

Designs: 25p, 50p, Horse racing. 75p, 100p, Wrestling. 150p, Weight lifting. 175p, Soccer.

1962, Sept. 25   Unwmk.   Perf. 12
Black Inscriptions
- C17 A195 25p rose & red brn
- C18 A195 50p gray & red brn
- C19 A195 75p pale vio & dk grn
- C20 A195 100p gray ol & dk pur
- C21 A195 150p rose lil & grn
- C22 A195 175p sal & brn
-    Nos. C17-C22   2.25

Children's Day Type of Regular Issue

Perf. 11½x12, 12x11½
1962, Oct. 14   Unwmk.
- C23 A196 75p Runners
- C24 A196 150p Peaches
- C25 A196 200p Iris, vert.

A souvenir sheet contains one each of Nos. C23-C25. Value $2.50.

Red Crescent Type of Regular Issue

1962, Oct. 16   Perf. 12
Fruit and Flowers in Natural Colors; Carmine Crescent
- C26 A197 25p Grapes
- C27 A197 50p Pears
- C28 A197 100p Wistaria

Two souvenir sheets exist. One contains a 150p gray brown stamp in blossom design, the other a 200p gray stamp in wistaria design, imperf. Value, each $5.

UN Type of Regular Issue

1962, Oct. 24   Photo.
Flags in Original Colors, Black Inscriptions
- C29 A198 75p blue
- C30 A198 100p lt brn
- C31 A198 125p brt grn

Boy Scout Type of Regular Issue

1962, Oct. 25   Unwmk.   Perf. 12
- C32 A199 25p gray, blk, dl grn & sal
- C33 A199 50p grn, brn & sal
- C34 A199 75p bl grn, red brn & sal
- C35 A199 100p bl, slate & sal

Teacher's Day Type of Regular Issue

1962, Oct. 25
- C36 A200 100p Pole vault
- C37 A200 150p High jump

A souvenir sheet contains one 250p pink and slate green stamp in design of 150p. Value $2.50.

Type of 1951-54

1962   Engr.   Perf. 13½
Imprint: "Thomas De La Rue & Co. Ltd."
- C38 AP2 5af ultra   6.00   1.00

Agriculture Types of Regular Issue

1963, Mar. 1   Photo.   Unwmk.   Perf. 12
- C42 A204 100p dk car, grn & brn
- C43 A203 150p ocher & blk
- C44 A204 200p ultra, grn & brn

Hands Holding Wheat Emblem AP5

1963, Mar. 27   Photo.   Perf. 14
- C45 AP5 500p lil, lt brn & brn   1.75   .60

FAO "Freedom from Hunger" campaign. Two souvenir sheets exist. One contains a 1000p blue green, light brown and brown, type AP5, imperf. The other contains a 200p brown and green and 300p ultramarine, yellow and ocher in rice and corn designs, type A205. Values $6 and $2.50.

Meteorological Day Type of Regular Issue

Designs: 100p, 500p, Meteorological measuring instrument. 200p, 400p, Weather station. 300p, Rockets in space.

1963, May 23   Imperf.
- C46 A206 100p brn & bl

Perf. 13½x14
- C47 A206 200p brt grn & lil
- C48 A206 300p dk bl & rose
- C49 A206 400p bl & dl red brn
- C50 A206 500p car rose & gray grn

Nos. C47 and C50 printed se-tenant. Two souvenir sheets exist. One contains a 125p red and brown stamp in rocket design. The other contains a 100p blue and dull red brown in "rockets in space" design. Values $5 and $7.50.

AFGHANISTAN

Kabul International Airport — AP8

Perf. 12x11½
1964, Apr. Unwmk. Photo.
C57	AP8	10af red lil & grn	.55	.20
C58	AP8	20af dk grn & red lil	.80	.40
a.		Perf. 12 ('68)	5.00	3.00
C59	AP8	50af dk bl & grnsh bl	2.25	1.00
a.		Perf. 12 ('68)	8.00	5.00
		Nos. C57-C59 (3)	3.60	1.60

Inauguration of Kabul Airport Terminal. Nos. C58a-C59a are 36mm wide. Nos. C58-C59 are 35½mm wide.

Zahir Shah and Kabul Airport — AP9

Design: 100af, Zahir Shah and Ariana Plane.

1971 Photo. Perf. 12½x13½
C60	AP9	50af multi	10.00	8.00
C61	AP9	100af blk, red & grn	5.00	3.00

Remainders of No C60 were used, starting in 1978, with king's portrait removed.

REGISTRATION STAMPS

R1

Dated "1309"
1891 Unwmk. Litho. Imperf.
Pelure Paper
F1	R1	1r slate blue		2.00
a.		Tete beche pair		12.50

Genuinely used copies of No. F1 are rare. Counterfeit cancellations exist.

R2

Dated "1311"
1893 Thin Wove Paper
F2	R2	1r black, green		1.60

Genuinely used copies of No. F2 are rare. Counterfeit cancellations exist.

R3

Undated
1894
F3	R3	2ab black, green	8.00	10.00

12 varieties. See note below Nos. 189-190.

R4

Undated
1898-1900
F4	R4	2ab black, *deep rose*	4.00	4.00
F5	R4	2ab black, *lilac rose*	4.00	4.00
F6	R4	2ab black, *magenta*	6.00	4.00
F7	R4	2ab black, *salmon*	2.50	4.00
F8	R4	2ab black, *orange*	6.00	4.00
F9	R4	2ab black, *yellow*	2.50	4.00
F10	R4	2ab black, *green*	6.00	4.00
		Nos. F4-F10 (7)	31.00	28.00

Many shades of paper.
Nos. F4-F10 come in two sizes, measured between outer frame lines: 52x36mm, 1st printing; 46x33mm, 2nd printing. The outer frame line (not pictured) is 3-6mm from inner frame line.
Used on P.O. receipts.

OFFICIAL STAMPS

(Used only on interior mail.)

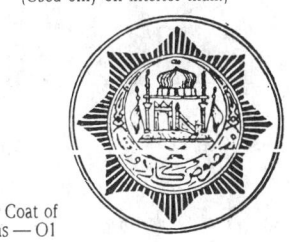

Coat of Arms — O1

1909 Unwmk. Typo. Perf. 12
Wove Paper
O1	O1	red	.75	1.00
a.		Carmine ('19?)	1.25	1.25

Later printings of No. O1 in scarlet, vermilion, claret, etc., on various types of paper, were issued until 1927.

Coat of Arms — O2

1939-68? Typo. Perf. 11, 12
O3	O2	15p emerald	.35	.15
O4	O2	30p ocher ('40)	.50	.50
O5	O2	45p dark carmine	.40	.35
O6	O2	50p brt car ('68)	.30	.30
a.		50p carmine rose ('55)	.50	.40
O7	O2	1af brt red violet	.80	.80
		Nos. O3-O7 (5)	2.35	2.10

Size of 50p, 24x31mm, others 22½x28mm.

Catalogue values for unused stamps in this section, from this point to the end of the section, are for Never Hinged items.

1964-65 Litho. Perf. 11
O8	O2	50p rose	.75	.75
a.		50p salmon ('65)	1.50	1.50

Stamps of this type are revenues.

PARCEL POST STAMPS

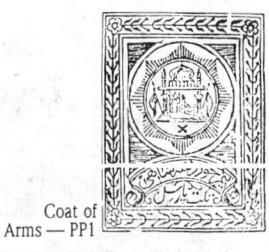

Coat of Arms — PP1

PP2

PP3

PP4

1909 Unwmk. Typo. Perf. 12
Q1	PP1	3sh bister	.85	1.00
a.		Imperf., pair	1.00	
Q2	PP2	1kr olive gray	1.10	1.25
a.		Imperf., pair	1.40	
Q3	PP3	1r orange	5.00	3.75
Q4	PP3	1r olive green	2.00	4.00
Q5	PP4	2r red	6.00	4.00
		Nos. Q1-Q5 (5)	14.95	14.00

1916-18
Q6	PP1	3sh green	5.00	2.50
Q7	PP2	1kr pale red	2.50	1.25
a.		1kr rose red ('18)	3.25	3.25
Q8	PP3	1r brown org	2.00	1.25
a.		1r deep brown ('18)	2.50	2.50
Q9	PP4	2r blue	5.00	3.00
		Nos. Q6-Q9 (4)	14.50	8.00

Nos. Q1-Q9 sometimes show letters of the papermaker's watermark "HOWARD & JONES LONDON."
Ungummed copies are remainders. They sell for one-third the price of mint examples.

Old Habibia College, Near Kabul — PP5

1921
Wove Paper
Q10	PP5	10pa chocolate	3.00	1.75
a.		Tete beche pair	6.25	
Q11	PP5	15pa light brn	4.50	2.50
a.		Tete beche pair	6.25	
Q12	PP5	30pa red violet	5.75	2.75
a.		Tete beche pair	8.75	
b.		Laid paper	15.00	7.50
Q13	PP5	1r brt blue	7.25	5.50
a.		Tete beche pair	20.00	
		Nos. Q10-Q13 (4)	20.50	12.50

Stamps of this issue are usually perforated on one or two sides only.
The laid paper of No. Q12b has a papermaker's watermark in the sheet.

PP6

PP7

PP8

1924-26
Wove Paper
Q15	PP6	5kr ultra ('26)	35.00	15.00
Q16	PP6	5r lilac	8.75	8.75

A 15r rose exists, but is not known to have been placed in use.

1928-29 Perf. 11, 11xImperf.
Q17	PP7	2r yellow orange	10.00	3.00
Q18	PP7	2r green ('29)	3.00	3.00
Q19	PP8	3r deep green	7.50	4.00
Q20	PP8	3r brown ('29)	5.00	5.00
		Nos. Q17-Q20 (4)	25.50	15.00

POSTAL TAX STAMPS

Aliabad Hospital near Kabul — PT1

Pierre and Marie Curie PT2

Perf. 12x11½, 12
1938, Dec. 22 Typo. Unwmk.
RA1	PT1	10p peacock grn	1.50	2.75
RA2	PT2	15p dull blue	1.50	2.75

Obligatory on all mail Dec. 22-28, 1938. The money was used for the Aliabad Hospital. See note with CD80.

Begging Child
PT3 PT4

1949, May 28 Typo. Perf. 12
RA3	PT3	35p red orange	1.60	1.60
RA4	PT4	125p ultra	2.50	2.00

United Nations Children's Day, May 28. Obligatory on all foreign mail on that date. Proceeds were used for child welfare.

The Scott Catalogue value is a retail value; that is, what you could expect to pay for the stamp in a grade of Very Fine. The value listed reflects recent actual dealer selling prices.

AFGHANISTAN — AGUERA, LA — AITUTAKI

Paghman Arch and UN Emblem — PT5

1949, Oct. 24
RA5 PT5 125p dk blue green 10.00 6.00
4th anniv. of the UN. Valid one day only. Issued in sheets of 9 (3x3).

> Catalogue values for unused stamps in this section, from this point to the end of the section, are for Never Hinged items.

Zahir Shah and Map of Afghanistan — PT6

1950, Mar. 30   Typo.
RA6 PT6 125p blue green 2.00 1.25
Return of Zahir Shah from a trip to Europe for his health. Valid for two weeks. The tax was used for public health purposes.

Hazara Youth — PT7

1950, May 28   Typo.   Perf. 11½
RA7 PT7 125p dk blue green 2.00 1.50
Tax for Child Welfare. Obligatory and valid only on May 28, 1950, on foreign mail.

Ruins of Qalai Bist and Globe — PT8

1950, Oct. 24
RA8 PT8 1.25af ultramarine 7.50 4.00
5th anniv. of the UN. Proceeds went to Afghanistan's UN Projects Committee.

Zahir Shah and Medical Center — PT9

1950, Dec. 22   Typo.   Perf. 11½
Size: 38x25mm
RA9 PT9 35p carmine 1.00 1.00
RA10 PT9 1.25af black 4.50 2.25
The tax was for the national Graduate School of Medicine.

> Shop with Scott Publishing Co. 24 hours a day 7 days a week at www.scottonline.com

Koochi Girl with Lamb — PT10

Kohistani Boy and Sheep — PT11

1951, May 28
RA11 PT10 35p emerald .... .75 .65
RA12 PT11 1.25af ultramarine .... .75 .65
The tax was for Child Welfare.

Distributing Gifts to Children — PT12

Qandahari Boys Dancing the "Attan" — PT13

1952, May 28   Litho.
RA13 PT12 35p chocolate .... .25 .25
RA14 PT13 125p violet .... .75 .75
The tax was for Child Welfare.

Soldier Receiving First Aid — PT14

1952, Oct.
RA15 PT14 10p light green .... .50 .35

Stretcher-bearers and Wounded — PT15

Soldier Assisting Wounded — PT16

1953, Oct.
RA16 PT15 10p yel grn & org red .... .50 .40
RA17 PT16 10p vio brn & org red .... .50 .40

Prince Mohammed Nadir — PT17

Map and Young Musicians — PT18

1953, May 28
RA18 PT17 35p orange yellow .... .20 .15
RA19 PT17 125p chalky blue .... .55 .55
No. RA19 is inscribed in French "Children's Day." The tax was for child welfare.

1954, May 28   Unwmk.   Perf. 11
RA20 PT18 35p purple .... .30 .15
RA21 PT18 125p ultra 1.10 1.10
No. RA21 is inscribed in French. The tax was for child welfare.

Red Crescent — PT19   PT20

1954, Oct. 17   Perf. 11½
RA22 PT19 20p blue & red .... .25 .20

1955, Oct. 18   Perf. 11
RA23 PT20 20p dull grn & car .... .50 .25

Zahir Shah and Red Crescent — PT21

1956, Oct. 18
RA24 PT21 20p lt grn & rose car .... .25 .20

Red Crescent Headquarters, Kabul — PT22

1957, Oct. 17
RA25 PT22 20p lt ultra & car .... .75 .50

Map and Crescent — PT23

1958, Oct.   Unwmk.   Perf. 11
RA26 PT23 25p yel grn & red .... .30 .30

PT24

1959, Oct. 17   Litho.   Perf. 11
RA27 PT24 25p lt violet & red .... .20 .15
The tax on Nos. RA15-RA17, RA22-RA27 was for the Red Crescent Society. Use of these stamps was required for one week.

AGUERA, LA

LOCATION — An administrative district in southern Rio de Oro on the northwest coast of Africa.
GOVT. — Spanish possession

AREA — Because of indefinite political boundaries, figures for area and population are not available.

100 Centimos = 1 Peseta

Type of 1920 Issue of Rio de Oro Overprinted **LA AGÜERA**

1920, June   Unwmk.   Perf. 13
1	A8	1c blue green	1.65	1.65
2	A8	2c olive brown	1.65	1.65
3	A8	5c deep green	1.65	1.65
4	A8	10c light red	1.65	1.65
5	A8	15c yellow	1.65	1.65
6	A8	20c lilac	1.65	1.65
7	A8	25c deep blue	1.65	1.65
8	A8	30c dark brown	1.65	1.65
9	A8	40c pink	1.65	1.65
10	A8	50c bright blue	4.50	4.00
11	A8	1p red brown	8.00	8.00
12	A8	4p dark violet	25.00	25.00
13	A8	10p orange	50.00	50.00
	Nos. 1-13 (13)		102.35	101.85

King Alfonso XIII — A2

1922, June   Typo.
14	A2	1c turquoise blue	.75	.75
15	A2	2c dark green	.75	.75
16	A2	5c blue green	.75	.75
17	A2	10c red	.75	.75
18	A2	15c red brown	.75	.75
19	A2	20c yellow	.75	.75
20	A2	25c deep blue	.75	.75
21	A2	30c dark brown	.75	.75
22	A2	40c rose red	1.00	1.00
23	A2	50c red violet	3.50	3.50
24	A2	1p rose	7.00	7.00
25	A2	4p violet	15.00	15.00
26	A2	10p orange	22.50	22.50
	Nos. 14-26 (13)		55.00	55.00

For later issues see Spanish Sahara.

AITUTAKI

ˌī-tə-ˈtäk-ē

LOCATION — One of the larger Cook Islands, in the South Pacific Ocean northeast of New Zealand
GOVT. — A dependency of the British dominion of New Zealand
AREA — 7 sq. mi.
POP. — 2,335 (1981)

The Cook Islands were attached to New Zealand in 1901. Stamps of Cook Islands were used in 1932-72.
Aitutaki acquired its own postal service in August 1972, though remaining part of Cook Islands.

12 Pence = 1 Shilling
100 Cents = 1 Dollar (1972)

> Catalogue values for unused stamps in this country are for Never Hinged items, beginning with Scott 37.

Watermark

Wmk. 61- Single-lined NZ and Star Close Together

AITUTAKI

Stamps of New Zealand Surcharged in Red or Blue:

AITUTAKI.	AITUTAKI.
Ava Pene.	Tai Pene.
a	b

1903		Engr.	Wmk. 61		Perf. 14	
1	A18(a)	½p green (R)			3.75	6.00
2	A35(b)	1p rose (Bl)			4.50	6.25

AITUTAKI.

Rua Pene Ma Te Ava.
c

AITUTAKI.	AITUTAKI.	AITUTAKI.
Toru Pene.	Ono Pene.	Tai Tiringi.
d	e	f

		Perf. 11		
3	A22(c)	2½p blue (R)	9.50	11.00
4	A23(d)	3p yellow brn (Bl)	12.00	14.00
5	A26(e)	6p red (Bl)	25.00	27.50
6	A29(f)	1sh scarlet (Bl)	55.00	80.00
a.		1sh orange red (Bl)	60.00	87.50

1911		Typo.		Perf. 14x15	
7	A41(a)	½p yellow grn (R)		1.00	2.25

		Engr. Perf. 14		
9	A22(c)	2½p deep blue (R)	7.50	16.00

AITUTAKI.	AITUTAKI.
Ono Pene.	Tai Tiringi.
g	h

1913-16			Typo.		
10	A42(b)	1p rose (Bl)		2.75	9.00
12	A41(g)	6p car rose (Bl) ('16)		37.50	85.00
13	A41(h)	1sh ver (Bl) ('14)		55.00	125.00

1916-17		Perf. 14x13½, 14x14½		
17	A45(g)	6p car rose (Bl)	10.00	22.50
18	A45(h)	1sh ver (Bl) ('17)	32.50	85.00
	Nos. 1-18 (13)		256.00	489.50

New Zealand Stamps of 1909-19 Overprinted in AITUTAKI. Red or Dark Blue

1917-20		Typo.	Perf. 14x15	
19	A43	½p yellow grn ('20)	.95	4.75
20	A42	1p car (Bl) ('20)	2.75	17.50
21	A47	1½p gray black	3.50	27.50
22	A47	1½p brown org ('19)	.80	6.50
23	A43	3p choc (Bl) ('19)	3.25	12.50

		Perf. 14x13½, 14x14½ Engr.		
24	A44	2½p dull blue ('18)	1.65	14.00
25	A45	3p vio brn (Bl) ('18)	1.75	16.00
26	A45	6p car rose (Bl)	4.50	17.00
27	A45	1sh vermilion (Bl)	11.00	25.00
	Nos. 19-27 (9)		30.15	140.75

Landing of Capt. Cook — A15

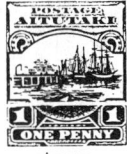

Avarua Waterfront — A16

Capt. James Cook — A17

Palm — A18

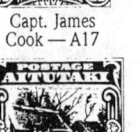

Houses at Arorangi — A19

Avarua Harbor — A20

1920		Engr.	Unwmk.		Perf. 14	
28	A15	½p green & black			3.25	22.50
29	A16	1p carmine & black			3.25	14.00
30	A17	1½p brown & blk			5.50	11.00
31	A18	3p dp blue & blk			2.00	12.00
32	A19	6p slate & red brn			6.25	15.00
33	A20	1sh claret & blk			9.00	24.00
	Nos. 28-33 (6)				29.25	98.50

Inverted centers, double frames, etc. are from printers waste.

Rarotongan Chief (Te Po) — A21

1926-27		Wmk. 61		Perf. 14	
34	A15	½p green & blk ('27)		2.00	8.00
35	A16	1p carmine & blk		5.00	6.00
36	A21	2½p blue & blk ('27)		7.00	45.00
	Nos. 34-36 (3)			14.00	59.00

Catalogue values for unused stamps in this section, from this point to the end of the section, are for Never Hinged items.

Cook Islands Nos. 199-200, 202, 205-206, 210, 212-213, 215-217 Overprinted *Aitutaki*

1972		Photo.	Unwmk.	Perf. 14x13½	
37	A34	½c gold & multi		.45	.70
38	A34	1c gold & multi		.80	1.25
39	A34	2½c gold & multi		5.25	6.00
40	A34	4c gold & multi		.75	.85
41	A34	5c gold & multi		6.00	7.00
42	A34	10c gold & multi		5.25	5.25
43	A34	20c gold & multi		.80	.90
44	A34	25c gold & multi		.80	.90
45	A34	50c gold & multi		4.00	2.75
46	A35	$1 gold & multi		6.00	6.00
47	A35	$2 gold & multi		1.10	.75
	Nos. 37-47 (11)			31.20	32.35

Overprint horizontal on Nos. 46-47. On $2, overprint is in capitals of different font; size: 21x3mm.
Issued: Nos. 37-46, Aug. 9; No. 47, Nov. 24.

Same Overprint Horizontal in Silver On Cook Islands Nos. 330-332

1972, Oct. 27			Perf. 13½	
48	A53	1c gold & multi	.15	.15
49	A53	5c gold & multi	.25	.25
50	A53	10c gold & multi	.40	.40
	Nos. 48-50 (3)		.80	.80

Fluorescence

Starting in 1972, stamps carry a "fluorescent security underprinting" in a multiple pattern of New Zealand's coat of arms with "Aitutaki" above, "Cook Islands" below and two stars at each side.

Silver Wedding Type of Cook Islands

1972, Nov. 20		Photo.	Perf. 13½	
		Size: 29x40mm		
51	A54	5c silver & multi	4.25	3.50
		Size: 66x40mm		
52	A54	15c silver & multi	2.00	1.65

25th anniversary of the marriage of Queen Elizabeth II and Prince Philip. Nos. 51-52 printed in sheets of 5 stamps and one label.

Flower Issue of Cook Islands Overprinted *Aitutaki*

1972, Dec. 11		Photo.	Perf. 14x13½	
53	A34	½c on #199	.15	.15
54	A34	1c on #200	.15	.15
55	A34	2½c on #202	.15	.15
56	A34	4c on #205	.15	.15
57	A34	5c on #206	.20	.20
58	A34	10c on #210	.30	.30
59	A34	20c on #212	.70	.70
60	A34	25c on #213	.90	.90
61	A34	50c on #215	1.75	1.75
62	A35	$1 on #217	3.75	3.75
	Nos. 53-62 (10)		8.20	8.20

See Nos. 73-76.

The Passion of Christ, by Mathias Grunewald — A22

Paintings: No. 63b, St. Veronica, by Rogier van der Weyden. No. 63c, Crucifixion, by Raphael. No. 63d, Resurrection, by della Francesca. No. 64a, Last Supper, by Master of Amiens. No. 64b, Condemnation of Christ, by Hans Holbein, the Elder. No. 64c, Crucifixion, by Rubens. No. 64d, Resurrection, by El Greco. No. 65a, Passion of Christ, by El Greco. No. 65b, St. Veronica, by Jakob Cornelisz. No. 65c, Crucifixion, by Rubens. No. 65d, Resurrection, by Dierik Bouts.

		Perf. 13½		
1973, Apr. 6		Photo.	Unwmk.	
63		Block of 4	.25	.25
a.-d.	A22	1c any single	.15	.15
64		Block of 4	.80	.80
a.-d.	A22	5c any single	.20	.20
65		Block of 4	1.90	1.90
a.-d.	A22	10c any single	.45	.45
	Nos. 63-65 (3)		2.95	2.95

Easter. Printed in blocks of 4 in sheets of 40. Design descriptions in top and bottom margins.

Coin Type of Cook Islands

Queen Elizabeth II Coins: 1c, Taro leaf. 2c, Pineapples. 5c, Hibiscus. 10c, Oranges. 20c, Fairy terns. 50c, Bonito. $1, Tangaroa, Polynesian god of creation, vert.

1973, May 14			Perf. 13x13½	
		Size: 37x24mm		
66	A55	1c dp car & multi	.15	.15
67	A55	2c blue & multi	.15	.15
68	A55	5c green & multi	.15	.15
		Size: 46x30mm		
69	A55	10c vio blue & multi	.15	.15
70	A55	20c green & multi	.30	.30
71	A55	50c dp car & multi	.70	.70
		Size: 32x54½mm		
72	A55	$1 blue, blk & sil	1.40	1.40
	Nos. 66-72 (7)		3.00	3.00

Cook Islands coinage commemorating silver wedding anniv. of Queen Elizabeth II.
Printed in sheets of 20 stamps and label showing Westminster Abbey.

Cook Islands Nos. 208, 210, 212 and 215 Overprinted Like Nos. 53-62 and: "TENTH ANNIVERSARY/ CESSATION/ OF/ NUCLEAR TESTING/ TREATY"

1973, July		Photo.	Perf. 14x13½	
73	A34	8c gold & multi	.15	.15
74	A34	10c gold & multi	.20	.20
75	A34	20c gold & multi	.50	.50
76	A34	50c gold & multi	1.10	1.10
	Nos. 73-76 (4)		1.95	1.95

Nuclear Test Ban Treaty, 10th anniv., protest against French nuclear testing on Mururoa Atoll.

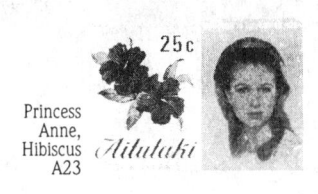

Princess Anne, Hibiscus A23

Design: 30c, Mark Phillips and hibiscus.

1973, Nov. 14		Photo.	Perf. 13½x14	
77	A23	25c gold & multi	.30	.30
78	A23	30c gold & multi	.40	.40
a.		Souvenir sheet of 2, #77-78	.80	.80

Wedding of Princess Anne and Capt. Mark Phillips.

Virgin and Child, by Il Perugino — A24

Paintings of the Virgin and Child by various masters.

1973, Dec.		Photo.	Perf. 13	
79		Block of 4	.25	.25
a.	A24	1c Van Dyck	.15	.15
b.	A24	1c Bartolommeo Montagna	.15	.15
c.	A24	1c Carlo Crivelli	.15	.15
d.	A24	1c Il Perugino	.15	.15
80		Block of 4	.75	.75
a.	A24	5c Cima da Conegliano	.15	.15
b.	A24	5c Memling	.15	.15
c.	A24	5c Veronese	.15	.15
d.	A24	5c Veronese	.15	.15
81		Block of 4	1.90	1.90
a.	A24	10c Raphael	.45	.45
b.	A24	10c Lorenzo Lotto	.45	.45
c.	A24	10c Del Colle	.45	.45
d.	A24	10c Memling	.45	.45
	Nos. 79-81 (3)		2.90	2.90

Christmas. Printed in blocks of 4 in sheets of 48. Design descriptions in margins.

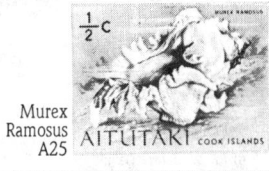

Murex Ramosus A25

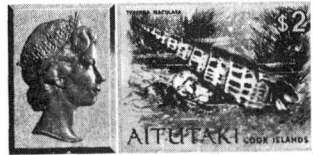

Terebra Maculata — A26

Pacific Shells: 1c, Nautilus macromphalus. 2c, Harpa major. 3c, Phalium strigatum. 4c, Cypraea talpa. 5c, Mitra stictica. 8c, Charonia tritonis. 10c, Murex triremis. 20c, Oliva sericea. 25c, Tritonalia rubeta. 60c, Strombus latissimus. $1, Biplex perca. $5, Cypraea hesitata.

1974-75		Photo.	Perf. 13	
82	A25	½c silver & multi	.50	.40
83	A25	1c silver & multi	.50	.40
84	A25	2c silver & multi	.50	.40
85	A25	3c silver & multi	.50	.40
86	A25	4c silver & multi	.50	.40
87	A25	5c silver & multi	.50	.40
88	A25	8c silver & multi	1.10	.50
89	A25	10c silver & multi	1.10	.50
90	A25	20c silver & multi	1.50	1.00
91	A25	25c silver & multi	1.75	1.00
92	A25	60c silver & multi	6.00	1.75
93	A25	$1 silver & multi	4.75	3.00

AITUTAKI

		Perf. 14		
94	A26	$2 silver & multi	7.50	4.25
95	A26	$5 silver & multi	27.50	16.00
		Nos. 82-95 (14)	54.20	30.40

Issued: #82-93, 1/31/74; $2, 1/20/75; $5, 2/28/75.
For overprints see Nos. O1-O16.

William Bligh and "Bounty" A27

1974, Apr. 11   Photo.   *Perf. 13*
Size: 38x22mm

96	A27	1c shown	.15	.15
97	A27	1c "Bounty" at sea	.15	.15
98	A27	5c Bligh and "Bounty" off Aitutaki	.45	.45
99	A27	5c Chart of Aitutaki, 1856	.45	.45
100	A27	8c James Cook and "Resolution"	.95	.95
101	A27	8c Maps of Aitutaki and Pacific Ocean	.95	.95
		Nos. 96-101,C1-C6 (12)	10.00	10.00

Capt. William Bligh (1754-1817), European discoverer of Aitutaki, Apr. 11, 1789. Stamps of same denomination printed se-tenant in sheets of 32.

Aitutaki Nos. 1 & 2 Map and UPU Emblem A28

Design: 50c, Aitutaki Nos. 4 and 28, map of Aitutaki and UPU emblem.

1974, July 15   Photo.   *Perf. 13½*

102	A28	25c blue & multi	.55	.55
103	A28	50c blue & multi	1.10	1.10
a.		Souvenir sheet of 2, #102-103	1.90	1.90

UPU, cent. Printed in sheets of 5 plus label showing UPU emblem.

A29   A30

Designs: Paintings of the Virgin and Child.

1974, Oct. 11   Photo.   *Perf. 13½*

104	A29	1c Van der Goes	.15	.15
105	A29	5c Giovanni Bellini	.15	.15
106	A29	8c Gerard David	.15	.15
107	A29	10c Antonello da Messina	.20	.20
108	A29	25c Joos van Cleve	.50	.50
109	A29	30c Maitre St. Catherine	.55	.55
a.		Souvenir sheet of 6, #104-109	2.00	2.00
		Nos. 104-109 (6)	1.70	1.70

Christmas. #104-109 printed in sheets of 15 stamps and corner label. See #B1-B6.

1974, Nov. 29   Photo.   *Perf. 14*

Designs: Churchill portraits.

110	A30	10c Dublin, Age 5	.15	.15
111	A30	25c As young man	.25	.15
112	A30	30c Inspecting troops, WWII	.35	.20
113	A30	50c Painting	.70	.40
114	A30	$1 Giving V sign	1.40	.80
a.		Souvenir sheet of 5, #110-114 + label, perf. 13½	4.50	3.75
		Nos. 110-114 (5)	2.85	1.70

Sir Winston Churchill (1874-1965). Nos. 110-114 printed in sheets of 5 stamps and corner label.

Emblem US & USSR Flags A31

Design: 50c, Icarus and Apollo Soyuz spacecraft.

1975, July 24   Photo.   *Perf. 13x14½*

115	A31	25c multicolored	.35	.35
116	A31	50c multicolored	.90	.90
a.		Souvenir sheet of 2	1.75	1.75

Apollo Soyuz space test project (Russo-American cooperation), launching July 15; link-up July 17. Nos. 115 and 116 each printed in sheets of 5 stamps and one label showing area of Apollo splashdowns. No. 116a contains one each of Nos. 115-116 with gold and black border and inscription.

Madonna and Child, by Pietro Lorenzetti — A32

Paintings: 7c, Adoration of the Kings, by Rogier van der Weyden. 15c, Madonna and Child, by Bartolommeo Montagna. 20c, Adoration of the Shepherds.

1975, Nov. 24   Photo.   *Perf. 14x13½*

117	A32	Strip of 3	.30	.30
a.		6c St. Francis	.15	.15
b.		6c Madonna and Child	.15	.15
c.		6c St. John the Evangelist	.15	.15
118	A32	Strip of 3	.30	.30
a.		7c One King	.15	.15
b.		7c Madonna and Child	.15	.15
c.		7c Two Kings	.15	.15
119	A32	Strip of 3	.75	.75
a.		15c St. Joseph	.25	.25
b.		15c Madonna and Child	.25	.25
c.		15c St. John the Baptist	.25	.25
120	A32	Strip of 3	1.25	1.25
a.		20c One Shepherd	.40	.40
b.		20c Madonna and Child	.40	.40
c.		20c Two Shepherds	.40	.40
d.		Souv. sheet of 12, #117-120, perf. 13½	3.50	3.50
		Nos. 117-120 (4)	2.60	2.60

Christmas. Nos. 117-120 printed in sheets of 30 (10 strips of 3).
For surcharges see Nos. B7-B10.

Descent from the Cross, detail — A33

Designs (Painting, Flemish School, 16th Century): 30c, Virgin Mary, disciple and body of Jesus. 35c, Mary Magdalene and disciple.

1976, Apr. 5   Photo.   *Perf. 13½*

121	A33	15c gold & multi	.15	.15
122	A33	30c gold & multi	.30	.30
123	A33	35c gold & multi	.70	.70
a.		Souvenir sheet of 3	1.65	1.65
		Nos. 121-123 (3)	1.15	1.15

Easter. No. 123a contains 3 stamps similar to Nos. 121-123, perf. 13, in continuous design without gold frames and white margins.

Declaration of Independence — A34

Paintings by John Trumbull: 35c, Surrender of Cornwallis at Yorktown. 50c, Washington's Farewell Address. a, "1976 BICENTENARY." b, "UNITED STATES." c, "INDEPENDENCE 1776."

1976, June 1   Photo.   *Perf. 13½*

124	A34	Strip of 3	1.50	1.50
a.-c.		30c any single	.50	.50
125	A34	Strip of 3	2.00	2.00
a.-c.		35c any single	.65	.65
126	A34	Strip of 3	2.75	2.75
a.-c.		50c any single	.90	.90
d.		Souvenir sheet of 9 (3x3)	6.25	6.25
		Nos. 124-126 (3)	6.25	6.25

American Bicentennial. Nos. 124-126 printed in sheets of 5 strips of 3 and 3-part corner label showing portrait of John Trumbull, commemorative inscription and portraits of Washington (30c), John Adams (35c) and Jefferson (50c). No. 126d contains 3 strips similar to Nos. 124-126.

Bicycling A35

Montreal Olympic Games Emblem and: 35c, Sailing. 60c, Field hockey. 70c, Running.

1976, July 15   Photo.   *Perf. 13x14*

127	A35	15c multicolored	.25	.25
128	A35	35c multicolored	.55	.55
129	A35	60c multicolored	.90	.90
130	A35	70c multicolored	1.10	1.10
a.		Souvenir sheet of 4	3.00	3.00
		Nos. 127-130 (4)	2.80	2.80

21st Olympic Games, Montreal, Canada, July 17-Aug. 1. Nos. 127-130 printed in sheets of 5 stamps and label showing coat of Arms and Montreal Olympic Games emblem. No. 130a contains 4 stamps similar to Nos. 127-130 with gold margin around each stamp.

Nos. 127-130a Overprinted Diagonally: "ROYAL VISIT JULY 1976"

1976, July 30

131	A35	15c multicolored	.20	.20
132	A35	35c multicolored	.55	.55
133	A35	60c multicolored	.75	.75
134	A35	70c multicolored	1.00	1.00
a.		Souvenir sheet of 4	3.00	3.00
		Nos. 131-134 (4)	2.50	2.50

Visit of Queen Elizabeth II to Montreal and official opening of the Games. Each stamp of No. 134a has diagonal overprint. Sheet margin has additional overprint: "ROYAL VISIT OF H.M. QUEEN ELIZABETH II/OFFICIALLY OPENED 17 JULY 1976."

Annunciation
A36   A37

Designs: Nos. 137-138, Angel appearing to the shepherds. Nos. 139-140, Nativity. Nos. 141-142, Three Kings.

1976, Oct. 18   *Perf. 13½x13*

135	A36	6c dk green & gold	.15	.15
136	A37	6c dk green & gold	.15	.15
137	A36	7c dk brown & gold	.15	.15
138	A37	7c dk brown & gold	.15	.15
139	A36	15c dk blue & gold	.20	.20
140	A37	15c dk blue & gold	.20	.20
141	A36	20c purple & gold	.25	.25
142	A37	20c purple & gold	.25	.25
a.		Souvenir sheet of 8	1.90	1.90
		Nos. 135-142 (8)	1.50	1.50

Christmas. Stamps of same denomination printed se-tenant in sheets of 50. No. 142a contains 8 stamps similar to Nos. 135-142 with white margin around each pair of stamps.

A. G. Bell and 1876 Telephone A38

Design: 70c, Satellite and radar.

1977, Mar. 3   Photo.   *Perf. 13½x13*

143	A38	25c rose & multi	.25	.25
144	A38	70c violet & multi	.85	.85
a.		Souvenir sheet of 2	1.65	1.65

Centenary of first telephone call by Alexander Graham Bell, Mar. 10, 1876. No. 144a contains a 25c in colors of 70c and 70c in colors of 25c.

Calvary (detail), by Rubens A39

Paintings by Rubens: 20c, Lamentation. 35c, Descent from the Cross.

1977, Mar. 31   Photo.   *Perf. 13½x14*

145	A39	15c gold & multi	.55	.55
146	A39	20c gold & multi	.70	.70
147	A39	35c gold & multi	1.00	1.00
a.		Souv. sheet of 3, #145-147, perf. 13	2.75	2.75
		Nos. 145-147 (3)	2.25	2.25

Easter, and 400th birth anniv. of Peter Paul Rubens (1577-1640), Flemish painter.

Capt. Bligh, "Bounty" and George III — A40

Designs: 35c, Rev. John Williams, George IV, First Christian Church. 50c, British flag, map of Aitutaki, Queen Victoria. $1, Elizabeth II and family on balcony after coronation.

1977, Apr. 21   *Perf. 13½*

148	A40	25c gold & multi	.20	.20
149	A40	35c gold & multi	.35	.35
150	A40	50c gold & multi	.50	.50
151	A40	$1 gold & multi	1.00	1.00
a.		Souvenir sheet of 4, #148-151	2.75	2.75
		Nos. 148-151 (4)	2.05	2.05

Reign of Queen Elizabeth II, 25th anniv.
For overprint and surcharge see Nos. O11, O15.

Annunciation
A41   A42

Designs: No. 154, Virgin, Child and ox. No. 155, Joseph and donkey (Nativity). No. 156, Three Kings. No. 157, Virgin and Child. No. 158, Joseph. No. 159, Virgin, Child and donkey (Flight into Egypt).

1977, Oct. 14   Photo.   *Perf. 13½x14*

152	A41	6c multicolored	.15	.15
153	A42	6c multicolored	.15	.15
154	A41	7c multicolored	.15	.15
155	A42	7c multicolored	.15	.15
156	A41	15c multicolored	.25	.25
157	A42	15c multicolored	.25	.25
158	A41	20c multicolored	.30	.30
159	A42	20c multicolored	.30	.30
a.		Souvenir sheet of 8, #152-159	1.65	1.65
		Nos. 152-159 (8)	1.70	1.70

Christmas. Stamps of same denomination printed se-tenant in sheets of 32.
For surcharges see Nos. B19-B26a.

Hawaiian Wood Figurine — A43

Designs: 50c, Talbot hunting dog, figure-head of "Resolution", horiz. $1, Temple figure.

1978, Jan. 19 Litho. *Perf. 13½*

160 A43 35c multicolored .55 .55
161 A43 50c multicolored .75 .75
162 A43 $1 multicolored 1.40 1.40
a. Souvenir sheet of 3, #160-162 3.00 3.00
Nos. 160-162 (3) 2.70 2.70

Bicentenary of Capt. Cook's arrival in Hawaii. Nos. 160-162 issued in sheets of 6.

Avignon Pietà, 15th Century A44

Paintings: 15c, Jesus Carrying Cross, by Simone di Martini. 35c, Christ at Emmaus, by Rembrandt.

1978, Mar. 17 Photo. *Perf. 13½x14*

163 A44 15c gold & multi .20 .20
164 A44 20c gold & multi .30 .30
165 A44 35c gold & multi .45 .45
a. Souvenir sheet of 3 1.40 1.40
Nos. 163-165 (3) .95 .95

Easter. No. 165a contains one each of Nos. 163-165, perf. 13½, and label showing Louvre, Paris. See Nos. B27-B29.

Elizabeth II — A45

Virgin and Child, by Dürer — A46

Souvenir Sheets

1978, June 15 Photo. *Perf. 13½x13*

166 Sheet of 6 2.75 2.75
a. A45 $1 Yale of Beaufort .25 .25
b. A45 $1 shown .25 .25
c. A45 $1 Ancestral statue .25 .25
d. Souvenir sheet of 6 1.50 1.50

25th anniv. of coronation of Queen Elizabeth II. No. 166 contains 2 each of Nos. 166a-166c, silver marginal inscription and coats of arms. No. 166d contains 2 strips of Nos. 166a-166c separated by horizontal slate green gutter showing Royal family on balcony, silver marginal inscription.

1978, Dec. 4 Photo. *Perf. 14½x13*

Designs: Various paintings of the Virgin and Child by Albrecht Dürer.

167 A46 15c multicolored .30 .30
168 A46 17c multicolored .35 .35
169 A46 30c multicolored .70 .70
170 A46 35c multicolored .90 .90
Nos. 167-170 (4) 2.25 2.25

Christmas; 450th death anniv. of Albrecht Dürer (1471-1528), German painter. Nos. 167-170 issued in sheets of 5 stamps and corner label. See No. B30.

Capt. Cook, by Nathaniel Dance — A47

Boy Holding Hibiscus, IYC Emblem — A48

Design: 75c, "Resolution" and "Adventure," by William Hodges.

1979, July 20 Photo. *Perf. 14x13½*

171 A47 50c multicolored 1.25 1.25
172 A47 75c multicolored 1.75 1.75
a. Souvenir sheet of 2, #171-172 3.00 3.00

Capt. James Cook (1728-1779), explorer, death bicentenary.

1979, Oct. 1 Photo. *Perf. 14x13½*

IYC Emblem and: 35c, Boy playing guitar. 65c, Boys in outrigger canoe.

173 A48 30c multicolored .30 .30
174 A48 35c multicolored .35 .35
175 A48 65c multicolored .70 .70
Nos. 173-175 (3) 1.35 1.35

See No. B31.

Aitutaki No. 102, Hill, Penny Black A49

Designs: Nos. 176, 178-179, 181, paintings of letter writers, Flemish School, 17th century.

1979, Nov. 14 Photo. *Perf. 13*

176 A49 50c Gabriel Metsu .55 .55
177 A49 50c shown .55 .55
178 A49 50c Jan Vermeer .55 .55
179 A49 65c Gerard Terborch .65 .65
180 A49 65c No. 103 (like No. 177) .65 .65
181 A49 65c Jan Vermeer .65 .65
Nos. 176-181 (6) 3.60 3.60

Souvenir Sheet

182 Sheet of 6 3.00 3.00
a. A49 30c like No. 176 .40 .40
b. A49 30c like No. 177 .40 .40
c. A49 30c like No. 178 .40 .40
d. A49 30c like No. 179 .40 .40
e. A49 30c like No. 180 .40 .40
f. A49 30c like No. 181 .40 .40

Sir Rowland Hill (1795-1879), originator of penny postage. Nos. 176-178 and 179-181 printed se-tenant in sheets of 9 (3x3).

Descent from the Cross, Detail — A50

Albert Einstein — A51

Easter: 30c, 35c, Descent from the Cross, by Quentin Metsys (details).

1980, Apr. 3 Photo. *Perf. 13x13½*

183 A50 20c multicolored .45 .45
184 A50 30c multicolored .65 .65
185 A50 35c multicolored .80 .80
Nos. 183-185 (3) 1.90 1.90

See No. B32.

1980, July 21 Photo. *Perf. 14*

186 A51 12c shown .55 .55
187 A51 12c Formula, atom structure .55 .55
188 A51 15c Portrait, diff. .65 .65
189 A51 15c Atomic blast .65 .65
190 A51 20c Portrait, diff. .90 .90
191 A51 20c Atomic blast, trees .90 .90
a. Souv. sheet of 6, #186-191, perf. 13 4.25 4.25
Nos. 186-191 (6) 4.20 4.20

Albert Einstein (1879-1955), theoretical physicist. Stamps of same denomination se-tenant.

A52

A53

1980, Sept. 26 Photo. *Perf. 14*

192 A52 6c Ancestral Figure, Aitutaki .15 .15
193 A52 6c God image staff, Rarotonga .15 .15
194 A52 6c Trade adze, Mangaia .15 .15
195 A52 6c Tangaroa carving, Rarotonga .15 .15
196 A52 12c Wooden image, Aitutaki .20 .20
197 A52 12c Hand club, Rarotonga .20 .20
198 A52 12c Carved mace, Mangaia .20 .20
199 A52 12c Fisherman's god, Rarotonga .20 .20
200 A52 15c Ti'i image, Aitutaki .20 .20
201 A52 15c Fisherman's god, diff. .20 .20
202 A52 15c Carved mace, Cook Islands .20 .20
203 A52 15c Tangaroa, diff. .20 .20
204 A52 20c Chief's headdress, Aitutaki .30 .30
205 A52 20c Carved mace, diff. .30 .30
206 A52 20c God image staff, diff. .30 .30
207 A52 20c like #195 .30 .30
a. Souvenir sheet of 16, #192-207 3.50
Nos. 192-207 (16) 3.40 3.40

Third South Pacific Arts Festival, Port Moresby, Papua New Guinea. Stamps of same denomination se-tenant.

1980, Nov. 21 Photo. *Perf. 13x13½*

Virgin and Child, Sculptures.

208 A53 15c 13th cent. .20 .20
209 A53 20c 14th cent. .30 .30
210 A53 25c 15th cent. .35 .35
211 A53 35c 15th cent., diff. .50 .50
Nos. 208-211 (4) 1.35 1.35

Christmas. See No. B33.

Mourning Virgin, by Pedro Roldan — A54

Sturnus Vulgaris — A55

Easter (Roldan Sculptures): 40c, Christ. 50c, Mourning St. John.

1981, Mar. 31 Photo. *Perf. 14*

212 A54 30c green & gold .40 .40
213 A54 40c brt purple & gold .50 .50
214 A54 50c dk blue & gold .65 .65
Nos. 212-214 (3) 1.55 1.55

See No. B34.

1981-82 *Perf. 14x13½, 13½x14*

215 A55 1c shown .25 .15
216 A55 1c Poephila gouldiae .25 .15
217 A55 2c Petroica multicolor .35 .15
218 A55 2c Pachycephala pectoralis .35 .15
219 A55 3c Falco peregrinus .40 .15
220 A55 3c Rhipidura rufifrous .40 .15
221 A55 4c Tyto alba .45 .15
222 A55 4c Padda oryzivora .45 .15
223 A55 5c Artamus leucorhynchus .50 .15
224 A55 5c Vini peruviana .50 .15
225 A55 6c Columba livia .60 .20
226 A55 6c Porphyrio porphyria .60 .20
227 A55 10c Geopelia striata .80 .35
228 A55 10c Lonchura castaneothorax .80 .35
229 A55 12c Acridotheres tristis .80 .40
230 A55 12c Egretta sacra .80 .40
231 A55 15c Diomeda melanophris .90 .45
232 A55 15c Numenius phaeopus .90 .45
233 A55 20c Gygis alba 1.00 .65
234 A55 20c Pluvialis dominica 1.00 .65
235 A55 25c Sula leucogaster 1.10 .80
236 A55 25c Anas superciliosa 1.10 .80
237 A55 30c Anas acuta 1.90 .90
238 A55 30c Fregata minor 1.90 .90
239 A55 35c Stercorarius pomarinus 2.00 1.10
240 A55 35c Conopoderas caffra 2.00 1.10
241 A55 40c Lalage maculosa 2.25 1.10
242 A55 40c Gallirallus philippensis 2.25 1.10
243 A55 50c Vini stepheni 2.50 1.50
244 A55 50c Diomedea epomophora 2.50 1.50
245 A55 70c Ptilinopus victor 5.00 2.00
246 A55 70c Erythrura cyaneovirens 5.00 2.00

Photo. *Perf. 13½*

Size: 35x47mm

246A A55 $1 Myiagra azureocapilla 6.00 4.00
246B A55 $2 Myiagra vanikorensis 10.00 8.00
246C A55 $4 Amandava amandava 17.00 13.00
246D A55 $5 Halcyon recurvirostris 18.00 16.00
Nos. 215-246D (36) 92.60 61.40

Issued: #215-230, 4/6; #231-238, 5/8; #239-246, 1/14/82; #246A-246B, 2/15/82.

Stamps of same denomination se-tenant. Nos. 231-246 horiz.

For surcharges and overprint see Nos. 293-306, 452-454, O40-O41.

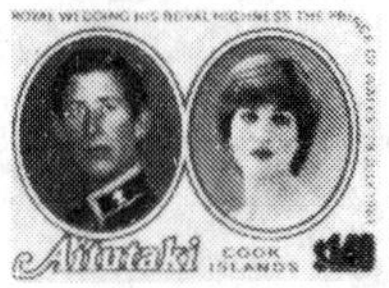

Prince Charles and Lady Diana — A56

Perf. 13x13½, 13½x13

1981, June 10 Photo.

247 A56 60c Charles, vert. .65 .65
248 A56 80c Lady Diana, vert. .85 .85
249 A56 $1.40 Shown 1.50 1.50
Nos. 247-249 (3) 3.00 3.00

Royal Wedding. Issued in sheets of 4.
For overprints and surcharges see Nos. 265-267, 307, 309, 355, 405-407, B35-B37.

1982 World Cup Soccer — A57

Designs: Various soccer players.

1981, Nov. 30 Photo. *Perf. 14*

250 A57 12c Pair, #250a-250b .40 .40
251 A57 15c Pair, #251a-251b .50 .50
252 A57 20c Pair, #252a-252b .65 .65
253 A57 25c Pair, #253a-253b .80 .80
Nos. 250-253 (4) 2.35 2.35

See No. B38.

Christmas A58

Rembrandt Etchings: 15c, Holy Family, 1632, vert. 30c, Virgin with Child, 1634, vert. 40c, Adoration of the Shepherds, 1654. 50c, Holy Family with Cat, 1644.

1981, Dec. 10 *Perf. 14*

254 A58 15c gold & dk brown .20 .20
255 A58 30c gold & dk brown .45 .45
256 A58 40c gold & dk brown .60 .60
257 A58 50c gold & dk brown .75 .75
Nos. 254-257 (4) 2.00 2.00

Souvenir Sheets

258 A58 80c + 5c like #254 .95 .95
259 A58 80c + 5c like #255 .95 .95
260 A58 80c + 5c like #256 .95 .95
261 A58 80c + 5c like #257 .95 .95

Nos. 258-261 have multicolored margins showing entire etching. Surtax on Nos. 258-261 was for local charities.

21st Birthday of Princess Diana — A59

1982, June 24 Photo. *Perf. 14*

262 A59 70c shown .75 .75
263 A59 $1 Wedding portrait 1.00 1.00
264 A59 $2 Diana, diff. 2.25 2.25
a. Souvenir sheet of 3, #262-264 4.50 4.50
Nos. 262-264 (3) 4.00 4.00

See #268-270a. For surcharges see #308, 310.

Nos. 247-249 Overprinted: "21 June 1982 PRINCE WILLIAM OF WALES" or "COMMEMORATING THE ROYAL BIRTH"

1982, July 13 *Perf. 13x13½,13½x13*

265 A56 60c multicolored 1.00 1.00
266 A56 80c multicolored 1.50 1.50
267 A56 $1.40 multicolored 2.50 2.50
Nos. 265-267 (3) 5.00 5.00

AITUTAKI

Nos. 262-264a Inscribed:
"ROYAL BIRTH 21 JUNE 1982
PRINCE WILLIAM OF WALES"

1982, Aug. 5   *Perf. 14*

268	A59	70c multicolored	1.10	1.10
269	A59	$1 multicolored	1.50	1.50
270	A59	$2 multicolored	3.00	3.00
a.		Souvenir sheet of 3	5.25	5.25
		Nos. 268-270 (3)	5.60	5.60

Christmas — A60

Madonna and Child Sculptures, 12th-15th Cent.

1982, Dec. 10   *Photo.*   *Perf. 13*

271	A60	18c multicolored	.25	.25
272	A60	36c multicolored	.55	.55
273	A60	48c multicolored	.75	.75
274	A60	60c multicolored	.90	.90
		Nos. 271-274 (4)	2.45	2.45

Souvenir Sheet

275		Sheet of 4	2.75	2.75
a.	A60	18c + 2c like 18c	.30	.30
b.	A60	36c + 2c like 36c	.55	.55
c.	A60	48c + 2c like 48c	.75	.75
d.	A60	60c + 2c like 60c	.90	.90

Surtax was for children's charities.

Commonwealth Day — A61

1983, Mar. 14   *Photo.*   *Perf. 13x13½*

276	A61	48c Bananas	1.25	1.25
277	A61	48c Ti'i statuette	1.25	1.25
278	A61	48c Boys canoeing	1.25	1.25
279	A61	48c Capt. William Bligh, Bounty	1.25	1.25
a.		Block of 4, #276-270	5.00	5.00

Scouting Year — A62

1983, Apr. 18   *Photo.*   *Perf. 14*

280	A62	36c Campfire	.55	.55
281	A62	48c Salute	.75	.75
282	A62	60c Hiking	.90	.90
		Nos. 280-282 (3)	2.20	2.20

Souvenir Sheet   *Perf. 13½*

283		Sheet of 3	3.00	3.00
a.	A62	36c + 3c like #280	.75	.75
b.	A62	48c + 3c like #281	.90	.90
c.	A62	60c + 3c like #282	1.25	1.25

Surtax was for benefit of Scouting.

Nos. 280-283 Overprinted:
"15th WORLD SCOUT JAMBOREE"

1983, July 11   *Photo.*   *Perf. 14*

284	A62	36c multicolored	.55	.55
285	A62	48c multicolored	.75	.75
286	A62	60c multicolored	.90	.90
		Nos. 284-286 (3)	2.20	2.20

Souvenir Sheet

287		Sheet of 3	3.00	3.00
a.	A62	36c + 3c like #284	.75	.75
b.	A62	48c + 3c like #285	.90	.90
c.	A62	60c + 3c like #286	1.25	1.25

A63    A64

Manned Flight Bicentenary: Modern sport balloons.

1983, July 22   *Photo.*   *Perf. 14x13*

288	A63	18c multicolored	.25	.25
289	A63	36c multicolored	.55	.55
290	A63	48c multicolored	.75	.75
291	A63	60c multicolored	.90	.90
		Nos. 288-291 (4)	2.45	2.45

Souvenir Sheet

292	A63	$2.50 multicolored	3.00	3.00

Nos. 233-246, 246D, 248-249, 263-264
Surcharged

1983, Sept. 22

293	A55	18c on 20c, #233	.90	.35
294	A55	18c on 20c, #234	.90	.35
295	A55	36c on 25c, #235	1.25	.70
296	A55	36c on 25c, #236	1.25	.70
297	A55	36c on 30c, #237	1.25	.70
298	A55	36c on 30c, #238	1.25	.70
299	A55	36c on 35c, #239	1.25	.70
300	A55	36c on 35c, #240	1.25	.70
301	A55	48c on 40c, #241	2.00	.95
302	A55	48c on 40c, #242	2.00	.95
303	A55	48c on 50c, #243	2.00	.95
304	A55	48c on 50c, #244	2.00	.95
305	A55	72c on 70c, #245	3.00	1.50
306	A55	72c on 70c, #246	3.00	1.50
307	A56	96c on 80c, #248	5.50	1.90
308	A59	96c on $1, #263	5.50	1.90
309	A56	$1.20 on $1.40, #249	6.50	2.50
310	A59	$1.20 on $2, #264	6.50	2.50

Size: 35x47mm

311	A55	$5.60 on $5, #246D	16.00	11.00
		Nos. 293-311 (19)	63.30	31.50

Nos. 293-306 printed in se-tenant pairs. Nos. 307-308, 310-311 vert.

1983, Sept. 29   *Photo.*   *Perf. 14*

312	A64	48c shown	.65	.65
313	A64	60c Communications satellite	.85	.85
314	A64	96c Global coverage	1.50	1.50
a.		Souvenir sheet of 3, #312-314	3.00	3.00
		Nos. 312-314 (3)	3.00	3.00

World Communications Year.

Christmas A65

Raphael Paintings.

1983, Nov. 21   *Photo.*   *Perf. 13½x14*

315	A65	36c Madonna of the Chair	.50	.50
316	A65	48c Alba Madonna	.65	.65
317	A65	60c Connestabile Madonna	.80	.80
		Nos. 315-317 (3)	1.95	1.95

Souvenir Sheet

318		Sheet of 3	2.50	2.50
a.	A65	36c + 3c like #315	.60	.60
b.	A65	48c + 3c like #316	.75	.75
c.	A65	60c + 3c like #317	.90	.90

1983, Dec. 15   *Imperf.*
Size: 46x46mm

319	A65	85c + 5c like #315	1.25	1.25
320	A65	85c + 5c like #316	1.25	1.25
321	A65	85c + 5c like #317	1.25	1.25
		Nos. 319-321 (3)	3.75	3.75

Surtax was for children's charities.

Local Birds — A66

1984   *Photo.*   *Perf. 14*

322	A66	2c as No. 216	.25	.25
323	A66	3c as No. 215	.25	.25
324	A66	5c as No. 217	.25	.25
325	A66	10c as No. 218	.25	.25
326	A66	12c as No. 220	.35	.35
327	A66	18c as No. 219	.45	.45
328	A66	24c as No. 221	.65	.65
329	A66	30c as No. 222	.75	.75
330	A66	36c as No. 223	.90	.90
331	A66	48c as No. 224	1.25	1.25
332	A66	50c as No. 225	.90	.90
333	A66	60c as No. 226	1.25	1.25
334	A66	72c as No. 227	1.50	1.50
335	A66	96c as No. 228	2.00	2.00
336	A66	$1.20 as No. 229	2.25	2.25
337	A66	$2.10 as No. 230	4.00	4.00
338	A66	$3 as No. 246A	5.75	5.75
339	A66	$4.20 as No. 246B	7.00	7.00
340	A66	$5.60 as No. 246C	7.50	7.50
341	A66	$9.60 as No. 246D	12.50	12.50
		Nos. 322-341 (20)	50.00	50.00

For overprints and surcharges see Nos. O17-O39.

1984 Summer Olympics — A67

1984, July 24   *Photo.*   *Perf. 13x13½*

342	A67	36c Javelin	.35	.35
343	A67	48c Shot put	.45	.45
344	A67	60c Hurdles	.55	.55
345	A67	$2 Handball	1.75	1.75
		Nos. 342-345 (4)	3.10	3.10

Souvenir Sheet

346		Sheet of 4	3.50	3.50
a.	A67	36c + 5c like #342	.40	.40
b.	A67	48c + 5c like #343	.50	.50
c.	A67	60c + 5c like #344	.60	.60
d.	A67	$2 + 5c like #345	1.75	1.75

Surtax was for benefit of local sports.

Nos. 342-345 Overprinted in Gold on Black with Winners' Names, Event, Nationality

1984, Aug. 21   *Photo.*   *Perf. 13x13½*

347	A67	36c multicolored	.35	.35
348	A67	48c multicolored	.45	.45
349	A67	60c multicolored	.55	.55
350	A67	$2 multicolored	1.75	1.75
		Nos. 347-350 (4)	3.10	3.10

Ausipex '84 — A68

1984, Sept. 14   *Photo.*   *Perf. 14*

351	A68	60c William Bligh, map	1.10	1.10
352	A68	96c Bounty, map	1.75	1.75
353	A68	$1.40 Stamps, map	2.50	2.50
		Nos. 351-353 (3)	5.35	5.35

Souvenir Sheet

354		Sheet of 3	5.50	5.50
a.	A68	60c + 5c like #351	1.10	1.10
b.	A68	96c + 5c like #352	1.65	1.65
c.	A68	$1.40 + 5c like #353	2.25	2.25

For overprint see No. 399.

No. 247 Surcharged with Black Bar and New Value in Gold and: "15.9.84 Birth/Prince Henry"

1984, Oct. 10   *Photo.*   *Perf. 13x13½*

355	A56	$3 multicolored	4.50	4.50

Issued in sheets of 4.

A69    A70

1984, Nov. 16   *Photo.*   *Perf. 13*

356	A69	36c Annunciation	.35	.35
357	A69	48c Nativity	.45	.45
358	A69	60c Epiphany	.55	.55
359	A69	96c Flight into Egypt	.90	.90
		Nos. 356-359 (4)	2.25	2.25

Souvenir Sheets   **Size: 45x53mm**   *Imperf*

360	A69	90c + 7c like #356	.90	.90
361	A69	90c + 7c like #357	.90	.90
362	A69	90c + 7c like #358	.90	.90
363	A69	90c + 7c like #359	.90	.90

Christmas.

1984, Dec. 10   *Photo.*   *Perf. 13½x14*

364	A70	48c Diana, Henry	.75	.75
365	A70	60c William, Henry	.90	.90
366	A70	$2.10 Family	2.75	2.75
		Nos. 364-366 (3)	4.40	4.40

Souvenir Sheet

367		Sheet of 3	4.50	4.50
a.	A70	96c + 7c like #364	1.40	1.40
b.	A70	96c + 7c like #365	1.40	1.40
c.	A70	96c + 7c like #366	1.40	1.40

Christmas, Birth of Prince Henry, Sept. 15. Surtax was for benefit of local children's charities.

Audubon Birth Bicentenary — A71

Illustrations of bird species by John J. Audubon.

1985, Mar. 22   *Litho.*   *Perf. 13*

368	A71	55c Gray kingbird	.80	.80
369	A71	65c Bohemian waxwing	.95	.95
370	A71	75c Summer tanager	1.25	1.25
371	A71	95c Cardinal	1.50	1.50
372	A71	$1.15 White-winged crossbill	1.75	1.75
		Nos. 368-372 (5)	6.25	6.25

Queen Mother, 85th Birthday A72

Photographs: 55c, Lady Elizabeth Bowes-Lyon, age 7. 65c, Engaged to the Duke of York, 75c, Duchess of York with daughter, Elizabeth. $1.30, Holding the infant Prince Charles. $3, Portrait taken on 63rd birthday.

1985-86   *Perf. 13½x13*

373	A72	55c multicolored	.50	.50
374	A72	65c multicolored	.60	.60
375	A72	75c multicolored	.65	.65
376	A72	$1.30 multicolored	1.25	1.25
a.		Souvenir sheet of 4, #373-376	3.25	3.25
		Nos. 373-376 (4)	3.00	3.00

Souvenir Sheet

377	A72	$3 multicolored	2.25	2.25

Nos. 373-376 printed in sheets of 4. Issued: #376a, 8/4/86; others, 6/14/85.

AITUTAKI

Intl. Youth Year — A73

Designs: 75c, The Calmady Children, by Thomas Lawrence (1769-1830). 90c, Madame Charpentier's Children, by Renoir (1841-1919). $1.40, Young Girls at Piano, by Renoir.

		1985, Sept. 16	Photo.	Perf. 13	
378	A73	75c multicolored		1.40	1.40
379	A73	90c multicolored		1.65	1.65
380	A73	$1.40 multicolored		2.75	2.75
		Nos. 378-380 (3)		5.80	5.80

Souvenir Sheet

381		Sheet of 3	3.75	3.75
a.		A73 75c + 10c like #378	.90	.90
b.		A73 90c + 10c like #379	1.10	1.10
c.		A73 $1.40 + 10c like #380	1.75	1.75

Surcharged for children's activities.

Adoration of the Magi, by Giotto di Bondone (1276-1337) — A74

		1985, Nov. 15	Photo.	Perf. 13½x13	
382	A74	95c multicolored		1.10	1.10
383	A74	95c multicolored		1.10	1.10
384	A74	$1.15 multicolored		1.40	1.40
385	A74	$1.15 multicolored		1.40	1.40
		Nos. 382-385 (4)		5.00	5.00

Souvenir Sheet
Imperf

386	A74	$6.40 multicolored	7.50	7.50

Christmas, return of Halley's Comet, 1985-86. Stamps of the same denomination se-tenant.

Halley's Comet A75

Designs: 90c, Halley's Comet, A.D. 684, wood engraving, Nuremberg Chronicles. $1.25, Sighting of 1066, Bayeux Tapestry, detail, c. 1092, France. $1.75, The Comet Inflicting Untold Disasters, 1456, Lucerne Chronicles, by Diebolt Schilling. $4.20, Melancolia I, engraving by Durer.

		1986, Feb. 25	Photo.	Perf. 13½x13	
387	A75	90c multicolored		1.00	1.00
388	A75	$1.25 multicolored		1.40	1.40
389	A75	$1.75 multicolored		2.00	2.00
		Nos. 387-389 (3)		4.40	4.40

Souvenir Sheets

390		Sheet of 3 + label	3.00	3.00
a.		A75 95c, like #387	1.00	1.00
b.		A75 95c, like #388	1.00	1.00
c.		A75 95c, like #389	1.00	1.00

Imperf

391	A75	$4.20 multicolored	4.75	4.75

Elizabeth II, 60th Birthday — A76

		1986, Apr. 21		Perf. 14
392	A76	95c Coronation portrait		1.10 1.10

Souvenir Sheet
Perf. 13½

393	A76	$4.20 Portrait, diff.	5.00	5.00

No. 392 printed in sheets of 5 with label picturing U.K. flag and Queen's flag for New Zealand.

Statue of Liberty, Cent. A77

		1986, June 27	Photo.	Perf. 14	
394	A77	$1 Liberty head		1.10	1.10
395	A77	$2.75 Statue		3.00	3.00

Souvenir Sheet
Perf. 13½

396		Sheet of 2	2.75	2.75
a.		A77 $1.25 like $1	1.25	1.25
b.		A77 $1.25 like $2.75	1.25	1.25

For surcharges see Nos B44, B49.

Wedding of Prince Andrew and Sarah Ferguson — A78

		1986, July 23		Perf. 14
397	A78	$2 multicolored		2.25 2.25

Souvenir Sheet
Perf. 13½

398	A78	$5 multicolored	5.75	5.75

No. 397 printed in sheets of 5 plus label picturing Westminster Abbey.
For surcharge see No. B48.

No. 354 Ovptd. with Gold Circle over AUSIPEX Emblem, Black and Gold STAMPEX '86 Emblem

		1986, Aug. 4	Photo.	Perf. 14
399		Sheet of 3		6.00 6.00
a.		A68 60c + 5c like #351		1.25 1.25
b.		A68 96c + 5c like #352		2.00 2.00
c.		A68 $1.40 + 5c like #353		2.75 2.75

STAMPEX '86, Adelaide, Aug. 4-10.

Christmas — A79

Paintings by Albrecht Durer: 75c, No. 404a, St. Anne with Virgin and Child. $1.35, No. 404b, Virgin and Child. $1.95, No. 404c, Adoration of the Magi. $2.75, No. 404d, Rosary Festivity.

		1986, Nov. 21	Litho.	Perf. 13½	
400	A79	75c multicolored		.80	.80
401	A79	$1.35 multicolored		1.50	1.50
402	A79	$1.95 multicolored		2.00	2.00
403	A79	$2.75 multicolored		3.00	3.00
		Nos. 400-403 (4)		7.30	7.30

Souvenir Sheet

404		Sheet of 4	7.00	7.00
a.-d.		A79 $1.65 any single	1.75	1.75

For surcharges see Nos. B39-B44, B46-B47, B50-B54.

Nos. 247-249 Surcharged in Gold and Black

		1987, Nov. 20		Perf. 13x12½	
405	A56	$2.50 on 60c No. 247		3.00	3.00
406	A56	$2.50 on 80c No. 248		3.00	3.00
407	A56	$2.50 on $1.40 No. 249		3.00	3.00
		Nos. 405-407 (3)		9.00	9.00

Issued in sheets of 4 with margin inscriptions overprinted with gold bar and "40th Anniversary of the Royal Wedding / 1947-1987" in black; "OVERPRINTED BY NEW ZEALAND GOVERNMENT PRINTER, / WELLINGTON, NOVEMBER 1987" at left.

A80

The Virgin with Garland, by Rubens — A81

Painting details.

		1987, Dec. 10	Photo.	Perf. 13x13½	
408	A80	70c UL		.90	.90
409	A80	85c UR		1.10	1.10
410	A80	$1.50 LL		2.00	2.00
411	A80	$1.85 LR		2.50	2.50
		Nos. 408-411 (4)		6.50	6.50

Souvenir Sheets

412		Sheet of 4	6.00	6.00
a.		A80 95c like No. 408	1.50	1.50
b.		A80 95c like No. 409	1.50	1.50
c.		A80 95c like No. 410	1.50	1.50
d.		A80 95c like No. 411	1.50	1.50

Perf. 13

413	A81	$6 multicolored	7.75	7.75

Christmas.

1988 Summer Olympics, Seoul — A82

Flags of Korea, Aitutaki, ancient and modern events, and Seoul Games emblem or $50 silver coin issued to commemorate the participation of Aitutaki athletes in the Olympics for the 1st time: 70c, No. 418a, Obverse of silver coin, chariot race, running. 85c, Emblem, running, soccer. 95c, Emblem, boxing, handball. $1.40, No. 418b, Reverse of coin, spearmen, women's tennis.

		1988, Aug. 22	Photo.	Perf. 14½x15	
414	A82	70c multicolored		.95	.95
415	A82	85c multicolored		1.10	1.10
416	A82	95c multicolored		1.25	1.25
417	A82	$1.40 multicolored		1.90	1.90
		Nos. 414-417 (4)		5.20	5.20

Souvenir Sheet

418		Sheet of 2	5.50	5.50
a.-b.		A82 $2 any single	2.75	2.75

Nos. 414-417 Ovptd. with Names of 1988 Olympic Gold Medalists

a. "FLORENCE GRIFFTH JOYNER / UNITED STATES / 100 M AND 200 M"
b. "GELINDO BORDIN / ITALY / MARATHON"
c. "HITOSHI SAITO / JAPAN / JUDO"
d. "STEFFI GRAF / WEST GERMANY / WOMEN'S TENNIS"

		1988, Oct. 10	Litho.	Perf. 14½x15	
419	A82 (a)	70c on No. 414		.95	.95
420	A82 (b)	85c on No. 415		1.10	1.10
421	A82 (c)	95c on No. 416		1.25	1.25
422	A82 (d)	$1.40 on No. 417		1.90	1.90
		Nos. 419-422 (4)		5.20	5.20

Griffith is spelled incorrectly on No. 419.

Christmas A83

Paintings by Rembrandt: 55c, Adoration of the Shepherds (detail), National Gallery, London. 70c, Holy Family, Alte Pinakothek, Munich. 85c, Presentation in the Temple, Kunsthalle, Hamburg. 95c, The Holy Family, Louvre, Paris. $1.15, Presentation in the Temple, diff., Mauritshuis, The Hague. $4.50, Adoration of the Shepherds (entire painting).

		1988, Nov. 2	Photo.	Perf. 13½	
423	A83	55c multicolored		.70	.70
424	A83	70c multicolored		.90	.90
425	A83	85c multicolored		1.10	1.10
426	A83	95c multicolored		1.25	1.25
427	A83	$1.15 multicolored		1.50	1.50
		Nos. 423-427 (5)		5.45	5.45

Souvenir Sheet
Perf. 14

428	A83	$4.50 multicolored	5.75	5.75

No. 428 contains one 52x34mm stamp.

A84

Mutiny on the Bounty, 200th Anniv. — A85

		1989, July 3	Photo.	Perf. 13½	
429	A84	55c Ship, Capt. Bligh		1.25	1.25
430	A84	65c Breadfruit		1.40	1.40
431	A84	75c Bligh, chart		1.65	1.65
432	A84	95c *Bounty* off Aitutaki		2.00	2.00
433	A84	$1.65 Christian, Bligh		3.75	3.75
		Nos. 429-433 (5)		10.05	10.05

Souvenir Sheet

434	A85	$4.20 Castaways	9.00	9.00

Discovery of Aitutaki by William Bligh, bicent.

1st Moon Landing, 20th Anniv. A86

Apollo 11 mission emblem, American flag, eagle, "The Eagle has landed" and: 75c, Astronaut standing on the lunar surface. $1.15, Conducting an experiment in front of the lunar module. $1.80, Carrying equipment. $6.40, Raising the flag.

		1989, July 28	Photo.	Perf. 13½x13	
435	A86	75c multicolored		.90	.90
436	A86	$1.15 multicolored		1.40	1.40
437	A86	$1.80 multicolored		2.25	2.25
		Nos. 435-437 (3)		4.55	4.55

Souvenir Sheet
Perf. 13½

438	A86	$6.40 multicolored	7.50	7.50

No. 438 contains one 42x31mm stamp.

AITUTAKI

Christmas — A87

Details from *Virgin in Glory*, by Titian: 70c, Virgin. 85c, Christ child. 95c, Angel. $1.25, Cherubs. $6, Entire painting.

1989, Nov. 20   Photo.   *Perf. 13½x13*
439	A87	70c multicolored	.90	.90
440	A87	85c multicolored	1.10	1.10
441	A87	95c multicolored	1.25	1.25
442	A87	$1.25 multicolored	1.65	1.65
		Nos. 439-442 (4)	4.90	4.90

Souvenir Sheet   *Perf. 13½*
443	A87	$6 multicolored	7.75	7.75

No. 443 contains one 45x60mm stamp.

World Environmental Protection — A88

Designs: a, Human comet, World Philatelic Programs emblem. b, Comet tail and "Protect The Endangered Earth!" $3, Human comet, emblem and inscription. (Illustration reduced.)

1990, Feb. 16   Photo.   *Perf. 13½x13*
444	A88	Pair	4.50	4.50
a.-b.		$1.75 any single	2.25	2.25

Souvenir Sheet
445	A88	$3 multicolored	4.00	4.00

No. 376a Ovptd. "Ninetieth / Birthday" in Black on Gold

Designs: 55c, Lady Elizabeth Bowes-Lyon, 1907. 65c, Lady Elizabeth engaged to Duke of York. 75c, As Duchess of York with daughter Elizabeth. $1.30, As Queen Mother with grandson.

1990, July 16   Litho.   *Perf. 13½x13*
446		Sheet of 4	4.00	4.00
a.	A72	55c multicolored	.65	.65
b.	A72	65c multicolored	.75	.75
c.	A72	75c multicolored	.90	.90
d.	A72	$1.30 multicolored	1.50	1.50

Christmas — A89

Paintings: 70c, Madonna of the Basket by Correggio. 85c, Virgin and Child by Morando. 95c, Adoration of the Child by Tiepolo. $1.75, Mystic Marriage of St. Catherine by Memling. $6, Donne Triptych by Memling.

1990, Nov. 28   Litho.   *Perf. 14*
447	A89	70c multicolored	.85	.85
448	A89	85c multicolored	1.00	1.00
449	A89	95c multicolored	1.10	1.10
450	A89	$1.75 multicolored	2.25	2.25
		Nos. 447-450 (4)	5.20	5.20

Souvenir Sheet
451	A89	$6 multicolored	7.50	7.50

Nos. 246A-246B Overprinted Birdpex '90

1990, Dec. 5   Photo.   *Perf. 13½*
452	A55	$1 multicolored	1.90	1.90
453	A55	$2 multicolored	3.75	3.75

Birdpex '90, 20 Intl. Ornithological Congress, New Zealand.

No. 246D Overprinted "COMMEMORATING 65TH BIRTHDAY OF H.M. QUEEN ELIZABETH II"

1991, Apr. 22   Photo.   *Perf. 13*
454	A55	$5 multicolored	6.25	6.25

Christmas — A90

Paintings: 80c, The Holy Family, by Mengs. 90c, Virgin and Child, by Fra Filippo Lippi. $1.05, Virgin and Child, by Durer. $1.75, Adoration of the Shepherds, by De La Tour. $6, The Holy Family, by Michelangelo.

1991, Nov. 13   Litho.   *Perf. 14*
455	A90	80c multicolored	.90	.90
456	A90	90c multicolored	1.10	1.10
457	A90	$1.05 multicolored	1.25	1.25
458	A90	$1.75 multicolored	2.00	2.00
		Nos. 455-458 (4)	5.25	5.25

Souvenir Sheet
459	A90	$6 multicolored	7.00	7.00

1992 Summer Olympics, Barcelona — A91

1992, July 29   Litho.   *Perf. 14*
460	A91	95c Hurdles	1.00	1.00
461	A91	$1.25 Weight lifting	1.40	1.40
462	A91	$1.50 Judo	1.75	1.75
463	A91	$1.95 Soccer	2.25	2.25
		Nos. 460-463 (4)	6.40	6.40

6th Festival of Pacific Arts, Rarotonga — A92

Canoes: 30c, Vaka Motu. 50c, Hamatafua. 95c, Alia Kalia Ndrua. $1.75, Hokule'a Hawaiian. $1.95, Tuamotu Pahi.

1992, Oct. 16   Litho.   *Perf. 14x15*
464	A92	30c multicolored	.35	.35
465	A92	50c multicolored	.55	.55
466	A92	95c multicolored	1.10	1.10
467	A92	$1.75 multicolored	2.00	2.00
468	A92	$1.95 multicolored	2.25	2.25
		Nos. 464-468 (5)	6.25	6.25

Overprinted "ROYAL VISIT"

1992, Oct. 16
469	A92	30c on #464	.35	.35
470	A92	50c on #465	.55	.55
471	A92	95c on #466	1.10	1.10
472	A92	$1.75 on #467	2.00	2.00
473	A92	$1.95 on #468	2.25	2.25
		Nos. 469-473 (5)	6.25	6.25

Christmas A93

Designs: Different details from Virgin's Nativity, by Guido Reni.

1992, Nov. 19   Litho.   *Perf. 13½*
474	A93	80c multicolored	.90	.90
475	A93	90c multicolored	1.10	1.10
476	A93	$1.05 multicolored	1.25	1.25
477	A93	$1.75 multicolored	1.90	1.90
		Nos. 474-477 (4)	5.15	5.15

Souvenir Sheet
478	A93	$6 like #476	6.50	6.50

No. 478 contains one 39x50mm stamp.

Discovery of America, 500th Anniv. — A94

Designs: $1.25, Columbus being blessed as he departs from Spain. $1.75, Map of Columbus' four voyages. $1.95, Columbus landing in New World.

1992, Dec. 11   *Perf. 14x15*
479	A94	$1.25 multicolored	1.40	1.40
480	A94	$1.75 multicolored	1.90	1.90
481	A94	$1.95 multicolored	2.25	2.25
		Nos. 479-481 (3)	5.55	5.55

Coronation of Queen Elizabeth II, 40th Anniv. — A95

Designs: a, Victoria, Edward VII. b, George V, George VI. c, Elizabeth II.

1993, June 4   Litho.   *Perf. 14*
482	A95	$1.75 Strip of 3, #a.-c.	6.00	6.00

Christmas — A96

Religious sculpture: 80c, Madonna and Child, by Nino Pisano. 90c, Virgin on Rosebush, by Luca Della Robbia. $1.15, Virgin with Child and St. John, by Juan Francisco Rustici. $1.95, Virgin with Child, by Michelangelo. $3, Madonna and Child, by Jacopo Della Quercia.

1993, Oct. 29   Litho.   *Perf. 14*
483	A96	80c multicolored	.90	.90
484	A96	90c multicolored	1.00	1.00
485	A96	$1.15 multicolored	1.25	1.25
486	A96	$1.95 multicolored	2.25	2.25

Size: 32x47mm   *Perf. 13½*
487	A96	$3 multicolored	3.50	3.50
		Nos. 483-487 (5)	8.90	8.90

1994 Winter Olympics, Lillehammer — A97

Designs: a, Ice hockey. b, Ski jumping. c, Cross-country skiing.

1994, Feb. 11   Litho.   *Perf. 14*
488	A97	$1.15 Strip of 3, #a.-c.	4.00	4.00

Flowers — A98

Hibiscus A98a

1994-97   Litho.   *Perf. 13½*
489	A98	5c Prostrate morning glory	.15	.15
490	A98	10c White frangipani	.15	.15
491	A98	15c Red hibiscus	.15	.15
492	A98	20c Yellow allamanda	.20	.20
493	A98	25c Royal poinciana	.25	.25
494	A98	30c White gardenia	.35	.35
495	A98	50c Pink frangipani	.55	.55
496	A98	80c Morning glory	.90	.90
497	A98	85c Yellow mallow	.95	.95
498	A98	90c Red coral tree	1.00	1.00
499	A98	$1 Cup of gold	1.10	1.10
500	A98	$2 Red cordia	2.25	2.25
501	A98a	$3 multicolored	3.75	3.75
502	A98a	$5 multicolored	6.25	6.25
503	A98a	$8 multicolored	10.00	10.00
		Nos. 489-503 (15)	28.00	28.00

Issued: 5c-90c, 2/17; $1, $2, 4/29; $3, $5, 11/18; $8, 11/21/97. This is an expanding set. Numbers may change.

First Manned Moon Landing, 25th Anniv. A99

Designs: No. 506, Astronauts Collins, Armstrong, Aldrin. No. 507, Splash down in South Pacific.

1994, July 20   Litho.   *Perf. 14*
506	A99	$2 multicolored	2.25	2.25
507	A99	$2 multicolored	2.25	2.25

Christmas — A100

Paintings: No. 508a, The Madonna of the Basket, by Corregio. b, Virgin & Child with Saints, by Hans Memling. c, The Virgin & Child with Flowers, by Dolci. d, Virgin & Child with Angels, by Bergognone.
No. 509a, The Adoration of the Kings, by Dosso. b, The Virgin & Child, by Bellini. c, The Virgin & Child, by Schiavone. d, Adoration of the Kings, by Dolci.

1994, Nov. 30   Litho.   *Perf. 14*
508	A100	85c Block of 4, #a.-d.	3.75	3.75
509	A100	90c Block of 4, #a.-d.	4.00	4.00

AITUTAKI

End of World War II, 50th Anniv. — A101

Designs: a, Battle of Britain, 1940. b, Battle of Midway, June 1942.

1995, Sept. 4 Litho. *Perf. 13½x13*
510 A101 $4 Pair, #a.-b. 10.50 10.50

No. 510 issued in sheets of 4 stamps.

Queen Mother, 95th Birthday A102

1995, Sept. 14 Litho. *Perf. 13x13½*
511 A102 $4 multicolored 5.25 5.25

UN, 50th Anniv. — A103

1995, Oct. 18 Litho. *Perf. 13½*
512 A103 $4.25 multicolored 5.50 5.50

Year of the Sea Turtle A104

1995, Dec. 1 Litho. *Perf. 14x13½*
513 A104 95c Green turtle 1.25 1.25
514 A104 $1.15 Leatherback turtle 1.50 1.50
515 A104 $1.50 Olive Ridley turtle 2.00 2.00
516 A104 $1.75 Loggerhead turtle 2.25 2.25
     Nos. 513-516 (4) 7.00 7.00

Queen Elizabeth II, 70th Birthday A105

1996, June 24 Litho. *Perf. 14*
517 A105 $4.50 multicolored 6.00 6.00

No. 517 was issued in sheets of 4.

Modern Olympic Games, Cent. A106

Designs: No. 518, Pierre de Coubertin, Olympic torch, parading athletes, 1896. No. 519, Modern sprinters, US flag, Atlanta, 1996.

1996, July 11 Litho. *Perf. 14*
518 A106 $2 multicolored 2.75 2.75
519 A106 $2 multicolored 2.75 2.75
  a. Pair, #518-519 5.50 5.50

Queen Elizabeth II and Prince Philip, 50th Wedding Anniv. A107

$2.50, Queen Elizabeth II, Prince Philip, Queen Mother, and King George VI. $6, like #520, close-up.

1997, Nov. 20 Litho. *Perf. 14*
520 A107 $2.50 multicolored 3.25 3.25

Souvenir Sheet
521 A107 $6 multicolored 7.75 7.75

No. 520 was issued in sheets of 4.

Diana, Princess of Wales (1961-97) — A108

1998, Apr. 15 Litho. *Perf. 14*
522 A108 $1 multicolored 1.25 1.25

Souvenir Sheet
523 A108 $4 like #522 4.75 4.75

No. 522 was issued in sheets of 5 + label. No. 523 is a continuous design.
For surcharge see No. B55.

SEMI-POSTAL STAMPS

Christmas Type of 1974

Designs: 1c+1c, like #104. 5c+1c, like #105. 8c+1c, like #106. 10c+1c, like #107. 25c+1c, like #108. 30c+1c, like #109.

1974, Dec. 2 Photo. *Perf. 13½*
B1 A29 1c + 1c multicolored .15 .15
B2 A29 5c + 1c multicolored .15 .15
B3 A29 8c + 1c multicolored .15 .15
B4 A29 10c + 1c multicolored .15 .15
B5 A29 25c + 1c multicolored .30 .30
B6 A29 30c + 1c multicolored .30 .30
     Nos. B1-B6 (6) 1.20 1.20

Surtax was for child welfare.

Nos. 117-120 Surcharged in Silver

1975, Dec. 19 Photo. *Perf. 14x13½*
B7 A32 Strip of 3 .30 .30
  a.-c. 6c+1c any single .15 .15
B8 A32 Strip of 3 .35 .35
  a.-c. 7c+1c any single .15 .15
B9 A32 Strip of 3 .90 .90
  a.-c. 15c+1c any single .30 .30
B10 A32 Strip of 3 1.25 1.25
  a.-c. 20c+1c any single .40 .40
     Nos. B7-B10 (4) 2.80 2.80

Christmas. The surtax was for children's activities during holiday season.

Nos. 135-142a Surcharged in Silver

1976, Nov. 19 Photo. *Perf. 13½x13*
B11 A36 6c + 1c multicolored .15 .15
B12 A37 6c + 1c multicolored .15 .15
B13 A36 7c + 1c multicolored .15 .15
B14 A37 7c + 1c multicolored .15 .15
B15 A36 15c + 1c multicolored .20 .20
B16 A37 15c + 1c multicolored .20 .20
B17 A36 20c + 1c multicolored .30 .30
B18 A37 20c + 1c multicolored .30 .30
  a. Souvenir sheet of 8 1.65 1.65
     Nos. B11-B18 (8) 1.60 1.60

Surtax was for child welfare. Stamps of No. B18a each surcharged 2c.

Nos. 152-159a Surcharged in Black

1977, Nov. 15 *Perf. 13½x14*
B19 A41 6c + 1c multicolored .15 .15
B20 A42 6c + 1c multicolored .15 .15
B21 A41 7c + 1c multicolored .15 .15
B22 A42 7c + 1c multicolored .15 .15
B23 A41 15c + 1c multicolored .20 .20
B24 A42 15c + 1c multicolored .20 .20
B25 A41 20c + 1c multicolored .30 .30
B26 A42 20c + 1c multicolored .30 .30
  a. Souvenir sheet of 8 1.65 1.65
     Nos. B19-B26 (8) 1.60 1.60

Surtax was for child welfare. Stamps of No. B26a each surcharged 2c.

Easter Type of 1978
Souvenir Sheets

Paintings: No. B27, like No. 163. No. B28, like No. 164. No. B29, like No. 165.

1978, Mar. 17 Photo. *Perf. 14*
B27 A44 50c + 5c multicolored .70 .70
B28 A44 50c + 5c multicolored .70 .70
B29 A44 50c + 5c multicolored .70 .70

Nos. B27-B29 contain one stamp 33x25mm.

Christmas Type of 1978
Souvenir Sheet

1978, Dec. 4 Photo. *Perf. 14½x13*
B30 Sheet of 4 2.25 2.25
  a. A46 15c + 2c like #167 .30 .30
  b. A46 17c + 2c like #168 .35 .35
  c. A46 30c + 2c like #169 .55 .55
  d. A46 35c + 2c like #170 .60 .60

Year of the Child Type
Souvenir Sheet

1979, Oct. 1 Photo. *Perf. 14x13½*
B31 Sheet of 3 1.40 1.40
  a. A48 30c + 3c like #173 .30 .30
  b. A48 35c + 3c like #174 .35 .35
  c. A48 65c + 3c like #175 .60 .60

Easter Type of 1980
Souvenir Sheet

Designs: No. B32 shows entire painting in continuous design. Nos. B32a-B32c similar to Nos. B183-185. Size of Nos. B32a-B32c: 25x50mm.

1980, Apr. 3 Photo. *Perf. 13x13½*
B32 Sheet of 3 1.40 1.40
  a. A50 20c + 2c multicolored .35 .35
  b. A50 30c + 2c multicolored .45 .45
  c. A50 35c + 2c multicolored .55 .55

Christmas Type of 1980
Souvenir Sheet

1980, Nov. 21 Photo. *Perf. 13x13½*
B33 Sheet of 4 1.40 1.40
  a. A53 15c + 2c like #208 .20 .20
  b. A53 20c + 2c like #209 .30 .30
  c. A53 25c + 2c like #210 .35 .35
  d. A53 35c + 2c like #211 .45 .45

Easter Type of 1981
Souvenir Sheet

1981, Mar. 31 Photo. *Perf. 13½*
B34 Sheet of 3 1.65 1.65
  a. A54 30c + 2c like #212 .35 .35
  b. A54 40c + 2c like #213 .50 .50
  c. A54 50c + 2c like #214 .65 .65

Nos. 247-249 Surcharged

1981, Nov. 23 Photo. *Perf. 13x13½*
B35 A56 60 + 5c multi .90 .90
B36 A56 80 + 5c multi 1.10 1.10
B37 A56 $1.40 + 5c multi 2.00 2.00
     Nos. B35-B37 (3) 4.00 4.00

Intl. Year of the Disabled. Surtax was for the handicapped.

Soccer Type of 1981
Souvenir Sheet

1981, Nov. 30 *Perf. 14*
B38 A57 Sheet of 8, multi 2.50 2.50

No. B38 contains stamps with 2c surtax similar to Nos. 250-253. Surtax was for local sports.

Nos. 400-404 Surcharged "NOVEMBER/21-24 1986/FIRST VISIT TO SOUTH/PACIFIC" and 10c in Silver

1986, Nov. 25 Litho. *Perf. 13½*
B39 A79 75c + 10c multi 1.25 1.25
B40 A79 $1.35 + 10c multi 2.00 2.00
B41 A79 $1.95 + 10c multi 3.00 3.00
B42 A79 $2.75 + 10c multi 4.00 4.00
     Nos. B39-B42 (4) 10.25 10.25

Souvenir Sheet
B43 Sheet of 4 13.00 13.00
  a.-d. A79 $1.65 +10c on #404a-404d 3.25 3.25

State visit of Pope John Paul II.
For surcharges see Nos. B51-B54.

Nos. 394-395, 397 and 400-403 Surcharged "HURRICANE RELIEF/ + 50c" in Silver or Black

1987, Apr. 29 Litho. *Perf. 13½, 14*
B44 A79 75c + 50c #400 2.00 2.00
B45 A77 $1 + 50c #394 (B) 2.50 2.50
B46 A79 $1.35 + 50c #401 3.00 3.00
B47 A79 $1.95 + 50c #402 3.25 3.25
B48 A78 $2 + 50c #397 3.25 3.25
B49 A77 $2.75 + 50c #395 (B) 4.25 4.25
B50 A79 $2.75 + 50c #403 4.25 4.25
     Nos. B44-B50 (7) 22.50 22.50

Nos. B39-B42 Surcharged "HURRICANE RELIEF / +50c" in Silver

1987, Apr. 29 Litho. *Perf. 13½*
B51 A79 75c + 50c No. B39 2.00 2.00
B52 A79 $1.35 + 50c No. B40 2.50 2.50
B53 A79 $1.95 + 50c No. B41 3.00 3.00
B54 A79 $2.75 + 50c No. B42 3.50 3.50
     Nos. B51-B54 (4) 11.00 11.00

Souvenir Sheet
No. 523 Surcharged
"CHILDREN'S/CHARITIES" in Silver

1998, Nov. 19 Litho. *Perf. 14*
B55 A108 $4 + $1 multicolored 6.25 6.25

AIR POST STAMPS

Capt. Bligh Type of 1974

1974, Sept. 9 Litho. *Perf. 13*
Size: 46x26mm
C1 A27 10c Bligh and "Bounty" .55 .55
C2 A27 10c "Bounty" at sea .55 .55
C3 A27 25c Bligh and "Bounty" 1.25 1.25
C4 A27 25c Chart, 1856 1.25 1.25
C5 A27 30c Cook and "Resolution" 1.65 1.65
C6 A27 30c Maps 1.65 1.65
     Nos. C1-C6 (6) 6.90 6.90

Stamps of same denomination printed se-tenant in sheets of 20. See note after No. 101.

OFFICIAL STAMPS

Nos. 83-90, 92-95, 150-151 Overprinted or Surcharged in Black, Silver or Gold O.H.M.S.

1978-79 Photo. *Perf. 13x13½*
O1 A25 1c multi .15 .15
O2 A25 2c multi .15 .15
O3 A25 3c multi .15 .15
O4 A25 4c multi (G) .15 .15
O5 A25 5c multi .15 .15
O6 A25 8c multi .15 .15
O7 A25 10c multi .15 .15
O8 A25 15c on 60c multi .20 .20
O9 A25 18c on 60c multi .25 .25
O10 A25 20c multi (G) .30 .30
O11 A40 50c multi .75 .70
O12 A25 60c multi .90 .80
O13 A25 $1 multi 1.40 1.25
O14 A26 $2 multi 3.00 2.75
O15 A40 $4 on $1 multi (S) 6.00 5.50
O16 A26 $5 multi 7.25 6.50
     Nos. O1-O16 (16) 21.10 19.25

Overprint on 4c, 20c, $1 diagonal.
Issued: #O14-O16, 2/20/79; others, 11/3/78.

Stamps of 1983-84 Ovptd. or Surcharged in Green O.H.M.S.

or Gold (#O29-O32) 75c

O.H.M.S.

1985, Aug. 9 *Perf. 14, 13x13½*
O17 A66 2c No. 322 .15 .15
O18 A66 5c No. 324 .15 .15
O19 A66 10c No. 325 .15 .15
O20 A66 12c No. 326 .15 .15
O21 A66 18c No. 327 .20 .20
O22 A66 20c on 24c No. 328 .20 .20
O23 A66 30c No. 329 .35 .35
O24 A66 40c on 36c No. 330 .45 .45
O25 A66 50c No. 332 .55 .55
O26 A66 65c on 48c No. 331 .65 .65
O27 A66 60c No. 333 .70 .70
O28 A66 60c on 72c No. 334 .75 .75
O29 A61 75c on 48c No. 276 .85 .85
O30 A61 75c on 48c No. 277 .85 .85
O31 A61 75c on 48c No. 278 .85 .85

AITUTAKI — AJMAN — ALAOUITES

O32	A61	75c on 48c No. 279	.85	.85
a.		Block of 4, Nos. O29-O32	3.50	3.50
O33	A66	80c on 96c No. 335	.90	.90
		Nos. O17-O33 (17)	8.75	8.75

Nos. 336-341, 246C-246D Overprinted or Surcharged Like Nos. O17-O28, O33 in Metallic Green or Blue

1986, Oct. 1   *Perf. 14*

O34	A66	$3 multi	3.00	3.00
O35	A66	$4.20 multi	4.25	4.25
O36	A66	$5.60 multi	5.75	5.75
O37	A66	$9.60 multi	10.00	10.00

1988-91   *Perf. 14*

O38	A66	$1.20 multi	1.50	1.50
O39	A66	$2.10 multi	2.50	2.50

Perf. 13½

O40	A55	$14 on $4 (B)	17.50	17.50
O41	A55	$18 on $5 (B)	22.50	22.50
		Nos. O34-O41 (8)	67.00	67.00

Issue dates: July 2, 1991. Others, June 15.

AJMAN

äj-'man

LOCATION — Oman Peninsula, Arabia, on Persian Gulf
GOVT. — Sheikdom under British Protection
AREA — 100 sq. mi.
POP. — 4,400
CAPITAL — Ajman

Ajman is one of six Persian Gulf sheikdoms to join the United Arab Emirates, which proclaimed its independence Dec. 2, 1971. See United Arab Emirates.

100 Naye Paise = 1 Rupee

> Catalogue values for all unused stamps in this country are for Never Hinged items.

Sheik Rashid bin Humaid al Naimi and Arab Stallion — A1

Designs: 2np, 50np, Regal angelfish. 3np, 70np, Camel. 4np, 1r, Angelfish. 5np, 1.50r, Green turtle. 10np, 2r, Jewelfish. 15np, 3r, White storks. 20np, 5r, White-eyed gulls. 30np, 10r, Lanner falcon. 40np as 1np.

1964   Photo. & Litho.   *Perf. 14*
Unwmk.
Size: 35x22mm

1	A1	1np gold & multi	.15	.15
2	A1	2np gold & multi	.15	.15
3	A1	3np gold & multi	.15	.15
4	A1	4np gold & multi	.15	.15
5	A1	5np gold & multi	.15	.15
6	A1	10np gold & multi	.15	.15
7	A1	15np gold & multi	.15	.15
8	A1	20np gold & multi	.15	.15
9	A1	30np gold & multi	.15	.15

Size: 42x27mm

10	A1	40np gold & multi	.20	.15
11	A1	50np gold & multi	.25	.15
12	A1	70np gold & multi	.25	.15
13	A1	1r gold & multi	.40	.15
14	A1	1.50r gold & multi	.50	.15
15	A1	2r gold & multi	.75	.15

Size: 53x33½mm

16	A1	3r gold & multi	1.00	.15
17	A1	5r gold & multi	1.50	.40
18	A1	10r gold & multi	3.25	.15
		Nos. 1-18 (18)	9.45	3.55

Issued: #1-9, 6/20; #10-15, 9/7; #16-18, 11/4.

Pres. and Mrs. John F. Kennedy with Caroline — A2

Pres. Kennedy: 10np, As a boy in football uniform. 15np, Diving. 50np, As navy lieutenant, receiving Navy and Marine Corps Medal from Capt. Frederic L. Conklin. 1r, Sailing with Jacqueline Kennedy. 2r, With Eleanor Roosevelt. 5r, With Lyndon B. Johnson and Hubert H. Humphrey. 10r, Portrait.

1964, Dec. 15   Photo.   *Perf. 13½x14*

19	A2	10np grn & red lil	.15	.15
20	A2	15np Prus bl & vio	.15	.15
21	A2	50np org brn & dk bl	.20	.15
22	A2	1r brn & Prus grn	.45	.15
23	A2	2r red lil & dp ol	.80	.15
24	A2	3r grn & red brn	1.25	.15
25	A2	5r vio & brn	1.90	.30
26	A2	10r dk bl & red brn	4.00	.70
		Nos. 19-26 (8)	8.90	1.95

John F. Kennedy (1917-63). A souvenir sheet contains one each of Nos. 23-26.

Runners at Start — A3

10np, 1.50r, Boxing. 25np, 2r, Judo. 50np, 5r, Gymnast on vaulting horse. 1r, 3r, Sailing yacht.

1965, Jan. 12   Photo.   *Perf. 13½x14*

27	A3	5np red brn, brt pink & Prus grn	.15	.15
28	A3	10np dk ol grn, bl gray & red brn	.15	.15
29	A3	15np dk vio, grn & sep	.15	.15
30	A3	25np bl sal pink & blk	.15	.15
31	A3	50np mar, bl & ind	.15	.15
32	A3	1r dk grn, lil & ultra	.35	.15
33	A3	1.50r lil, grn & brn	.55	.15
34	A3	2r red org, bis & dk bl	.75	.20
35	A3	3r dk brn, grnsh bl & lil	1.00	.25
36	A3	5r grn, yel & red brn	2.00	.40
		Nos. 27-36 (10)	5.40	1.90

18th Olympic Games, Tokyo, Oct. 10-25, 1964. A souvenir sheet contains four stamps similar to Nos. 33-36 in changed colors.

Stanley Gibbons Catalogue, 1865, US No. 1X2 — A4

Designs: 10np, Austria, Scarlet Mercury 1856. 15np, British Guiana 1c, 1856. 25np, Canada 12p, 1851. 50np, Hawaii 2c, 1851. 1r, Mauritius 2p, 1847. 3r, Switzerland, Geneva 10c, 1843. 5r, Tuscany 31, 1860. 5np, 15np, 50np and 3r show first edition of Stanley Gibbons Catalogue; 10np, 25np, 1r and 5r show 1965 Elizabethan Catalogue.

1965, May 6   Unwmk.   *Perf. 13*

37	A4	5np multi	.15	.15
38	A4	10np multi	.15	.15
39	A4	15np multi	.15	.15
40	A4	25np multi	.15	.15
41	A4	50np multi	.15	.15
42	A4	1r multi	.45	.15
43	A4	3r multi	.75	.20
a.		Souv. sheet of 4, #38-39, 42-43	2.00	
44	A4	5r multi	1.25	.30
a.		Souv. sheet of 4, #37, 40-41, 44	2.25	
		Nos. 37-44 (8)	3.20	1.40

Gibbons Catalogue Cent. Exhib., London, Feb. 17-20. Nos. 43a and 44a for 125th anniv. of 1st postage stamp. Sheets exist imperf.

Stamps of Ajman were replaced in 1972 by those of United Arab Emirates.

AIR POST STAMPS

Type of Regular Issue, 1964

Designs: 15np, Arab stallion. 25np, Regal angelfish. 35np, Camel. 50np, Angelfish. 75np, Green turtle. 1r, Jewelfish. 2r, White storks. 3r, White-eyed gulls. 5r, Lanner falcon.

1965   Photo. & Litho.   *Perf. 14*
Unwmk.
Size: 42x25½mm

C1	A1	15np silver & multi	.15	.15
C2	A1	25np silver & multi	.15	.15
C3	A1	35np silver & multi	.15	.15
C4	A1	50np silver & multi	.15	.15
C5	A1	75np silver & multi	.15	.15
C6	A1	1r silver & multi	.40	.15

Size: 53x33½mm

C7	A1	2r silver & multi	.75	.15
C8	A1	3r silver & multi	2.00	.20
C9	A1	5r silver & multi	3.25	.30
		Nos. C1-C9 (9)	7.15	1.55

Issue dates: #C1-C6, Nov. 15, C7-C9, Dec 18.

AIR POST OFFICIAL STAMPS

Type of Regular Issue, 1964

Designs: 75np, Jewelfish. 2r, White storks. 3r, White-eyed gulls. 5r, Lanner falcon.

1965, Dec. 18   Photo. & Litho.   *Perf. 14*
Unwmk.
Size: 42x25½mm

CO1	A1	75np gold & multi	.35	.15

Size: 53x33½mm

CO2	A1	2r gold & multi	1.00	.15
CO3	A1	3r gold & multi	1.50	.20
CO4	A1	5r gold & multi	3.00	.35
		Nos. CO1-CO4 (4)	5.85	.85

OFFICIAL STAMPS

Type of Regular Issue, 1964

25np, Arab stallion. 40np, Regal angelfish. 50np, Camel. 75np, Angelfish. 1r, Green turtle.

1965, Dec. 1   Photo. & Litho.   *Perf. 14*
Unwmk.
Size: 42x25½mm

O1	A1	25np gold & multi	.15	.15
O2	A1	40np gold & multi	.15	.15
O3	A1	50np gold & multi	.15	.15
O4	A1	75np gold & multi	.20	.15
O5	A1	1r multi	.25	.15
		Nos. O1-O5 (5)	.90	.75

ALAOUITES

'al-aủ-,witz

LOCATION — A division of Syria, in Western Asia
GOVT. — Under French Mandate
AREA — 2,500 sq. mi.
POP. — 278,000 (approx. 1930)
CAPITAL — Latakia

This territory became an independent state in 1924, although still administered under the French Mandate. In 1930 it was renamed Latakia and Syrian stamps overprinted "Lattaquie" superseded the stamps of Alaouites. For these and subsequent issues see Latakia and Syria.

100 Centimes = 1 Piaster

Issued under French Mandate
Stamps of France Surcharged:

ALAOUITES   ALAOUITES
0 P. 25   2 PIASTRES

العلويين   العلويين
١/٤ الغرش   غروش ٢

Nos. 1-6, 16-18   Nos. 7-15, 19-21

1925   Unwmk.   *Perf. 14x13½*

1	A16	10c on 2c vio brn	1.10	1.10
2	A22	25c on 5c green	.85	.85
3	A20	75c on 15c gray grn	1.50	1.50
4	A22	1p on 20c red brn	1.00	1.00
5	A22	1.25p on 25c blue	1.25	1.25
6	A22	1.50p on 30c red	4.50	4.50
7	A22	2p on 35c violet	1.00	1.00
8	A18	2p on 40c red & pale bl	2.00	2.00
9	A18	2p on 45c grn & bl	4.50	4.50
10	A18	3p on 60c vio & ultra	2.25	2.25
11	A20	3p on 60c lt vio	4.50	4.50
12	A20	4p on 85c vermilion	.80	.80
13	A18	5p on 1fr c & ol grn	1.25	1.25
14	A18	10p on 2fr org & pale bl	4.00	4.00
15	A18	25p on 5fr bl & buff	5.50	5.50
		Nos. 1-15 (15)	37.75	37.75

For overprints see Nos. C1-C4.

Same Surcharges on Pasteur Stamps of France

16	A23	50c on 10c green	.80	.80
17	A23	75c on 15c green	.80	.80
18	A23	1.50p on 30c red	1.00	1.00
19	A23	2p on 45c red	1.40	1.40
20	A23	2.50p on 50c blue	1.50	1.50
21	A23	4p on 75c blue	2.00	2.00
		Nos. 16-21 (6)	7.50	7.50

Stamps of Syria, 1925, Overprinted in Red, Black or Blue:

ALAOUITES   ALAOUITES
    العلويين
On A3, A5   On A4

1925, Mar. 1   *Perf. 12½, 13½*

25	A3	10c dk violet (R)	.30	.30
a.		Double overprint	15.00	15.00
26	A4	25c olive black (R)	.60	.60
a.		Inverted overprint	10.00	10.00
b.		Blue overprint	20.00	20.00
27	A4	50c yellow green	.45	.45
a.		Inverted overprint	10.00	10.00
b.		Blue overprint	20.00	20.00
c.		Red overprint	17.50	17.50
28	A4	75c brown orange	.50	.50
a.		Inverted overprint	9.00	9.00
29	A5	1p magenta	.75	.75
30	A4	1.25p deep green	.55	.55
a.		Red overprint	17.50	17.50
31	A4	1.50p rose red (Bl)	.55	.55
a.		Inverted overprint	10.00	10.00
b.		Black overprint	20.00	20.00
32	A4	2p dk brown (R)	.55	.55
a.		Blue overprint	25.00	25.00
33	A4	2.50p pck blue (R)	1.00	1.00
a.		Black overprint	25.00	25.00
34	A4	3p orange brown	.55	.55
a.		Inverted overprint	6.50	6.50
b.		Blue overprint	25.00	25.00
35	A4	5p violet	.70	.70
a.		Red overprint	25.00	25.00
36	A4	10p violet brown	1.00	1.00
37	A4	25p ultra (R)	2.50	2.50
		Nos. 25-37 (13)	10.00	10.00

For overprints see Nos. C5-C19.

Stamps of Syria, 1925, Surcharged in Black or Red:

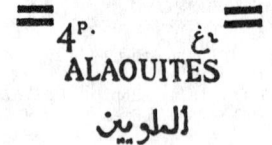

4P.
ALAOUITES
العلويين
Nos. 38-42

4P.50 ٤ ١/٢
Alaouites
العلويين
Nos. 43-45

1926

38	A4	3.50p on 75c brn org	.75	.60
a.		Surcharged on face and back	5.00	4.50
39	A4	4p on 25c ol blk (R)	1.00	.60
40	A4	6p on 2.50p pck bl (R)	.80	.60
41	A4	12p on 1.25p dp grn	.70	.60
a.		Inverted surcharge	10.00	10.00
42	A4	20p on 1.25p dp grn	1.25	1.10
43	A4	4.50p on 75c brn org	2.50	1.25
a.		Inverted surcharge	25.00	
44	A4	7.50p on 2.50p pck bl	2.00	1.25
45	A4	15p on 25p ultra	3.50	2.00
		Nos. 38-45 (8)	12.50	8.00

For overprint see No. C21.

Syria #199 Ovptd. like #25 in Red
1928

46	A3	5c on 10c dk violet	.30	.30
a.		Double surcharge	13.00	

Syria Nos. 178 and 174 Surcharged like Nos. 43-45 in Red
1928

47	A4	2p on 1.25p dp green	6.00	3.50
48	A4	4p on 25c olive black	3.25	2.50

For overprint see No. C20.

ALAOUITES

= 4P ٤٤ =
العلويين

49	A4	4p on 25c olive black	35.00	30.00
a.		Double impression		
		Nos. 46-49 (4)	44.55	36.30

AIR POST STAMPS

Nos. 8, 10, 13 & 14 with Additional Overprint in Black

طيارة   Avion

1925, Jan. 1   Unwmk.   Perf. 14x13½

C1	A18	2p on 40c	3.50	3.50
a.		Overprint reversed	60.00	
C2	A18	3p on 60c	5.25	5.25
a.		Overprint reversed	60.00	
C3	A18	5p on 1fr	3.50	3.50
C4	A18	10p on 2fr	3.50	3.50
		Nos. C1-C4 (4)	15.75	15.75

Nos. 32, 34, 35 & 36 With Additional Overprint in Green

AVION

1925, Mar. 1   Perf. 13½

C5	A4	2p dark brown	1.00	1.00
C6	A4	3p orange brown	1.00	1.00
C7	A4	5p violet	1.00	1.00
C8	A4	10p violet brown	1.00	1.00
		Nos. C5-C8 (4)	4.00	4.00

Nos. 32, 34, 35 & 36 With Additional Overprint in Red

1926, May 1

C9	A4	2p dark brown	1.40	1.40
C10	A4	3p orange brown	1.40	1.40
C11	A4	5p violet	1.40	1.40
C12	A4	10p violet brown	1.40	1.40
		Nos. C9-C12 (4)	5.60	5.60

No. C9 has the original overprint in black.
Double or inverted overprints, original or plane, are known on most of Nos. C9-C12. Value, $8-$10.
The red plane overprint was also applied to Nos. C5-C8. These are believed to have been essays, and were not regularly issued.

Nos. 27, 29, and 37 With Additional Overprint of Airplane in Red or Black

1929, June-July

C17	A4	50c yel grn (R)	.75	.75
a.		Plane overprint double	15.00	
b.		Plane ovpt. on face and back	11.00	
c.		Pair with plane overprint tete beche	35.00	
C18	A5	1p magenta (Bk)	2.75	2.75
C19	A4	25p ultra (R)	17.50	10.00
a.		Plane overprint inverted	60.00	60.00
		Nos. C17-C19 (3)	21.00	13.50

Nos. 47 and 45 With Additional Overprint of Airplane in Red

1929-30

C20	A4	2p on 1.25p ('30)	1.20	1.20
a.		Surcharge inverted	4.00	
b.		Double surcharge	3.50	
C21	A4	15p on 25p (Bk + R)	19.00	14.00
a.		Plane overprint inverted	35.00	35.00

POSTAGE DUE STAMPS

Postage Due Stamps of France, 1893-1920, Surcharged Like No. 1 (Nos. J1-J2) or No. 7 (Nos. J3-J5)

1925   Unwmk.   Perf. 14x13½

J1	D2	50c on 10c choc	1.90	1.90
J2	D2	1p on 20c ol grn	1.90	1.90
J3	D2	2p on 30c red	1.90	1.90
J4	D2	3p on 50c vio brn	1.90	1.90
J5	D2	5p on 1fr red brn, straw	1.90	1.90
		Nos. J1-J5 (5)	9.50	9.50

Postage Due Stamps of Syria, 1925, Overprinted Like No. 26 (Type D5) or No. 25 (Type D6) in Black, Blue or Red

1925   Perf. 13½

J6	D5	50c brown, yel	.60	.60
J7	D6	1p vio, rose (Bl)	.60	.60
a.		Black overprint	9.00	9.00
b.		Double overprint (Bk + Bl)	14.00	14.00
J8	D5	2p blk, blue (R)	1.00	1.00
J9	D5	3p blk, red org	1.40	1.40
J10	D5	5p blk, bl grn (R)	1.90	1.90
		Nos. J6-J10 (5)	5.50	5.50

The stamps of Alaouites were superseded in 1930 by those of Latakia.

ALBANIA
al-'bā-nē-ə

LOCATION — Southeastern Europe
GOVT. — Republic
AREA — 11,101 sq. mi.
POP. — 2,750,000 (1982 est.)
CAPITAL — Tirana

After the outbreak of World War I, the country fell into a state of anarchy when the Prince and all members of the International Commission left Albania. Subsequently General Ferrero in command of Italian troops declared Albania an independent country. A constitution was adopted and a republican form of government was instituted which continued until 1928 when, by constitutional amendment, Albania was declared to be a monarchy. The President of the republic, Ahmed Zogu, became king of the new state. Many unlisted varieties or surcharges and lithographed labels are said to have done postal duty in Albania and Epirus during this unsettled period.

In March 1939, Italy invaded Albania. King Zog fled but did not abdicate. The King of Italy acquired the crown.

Germany occupied Albania from September, 1943, until late 1944 when it became an independent state. The People's Republic began in January, 1946.

40 Paras = 1 Piaster = 1 Grossion
100 Centimes = 1 Franc (1917)
100 Qintar = 1 Franc
100 Qintar (Qindarka) = 1 Lek (1947)

Catalogue values for unused stamps in this country are for Never Hinged items, beginning with Scott 458 in the regular postage section, Scott B34 in the semi-postal section, and Scott C67 in the airpost section.

Watermarks

Wmk. 125- Lozenges

Wmk. 220- Double Headed Eagle

Stamps of Turkey Handstamped

SHQIPENIA

Handstamped on Issue of 1908
Perf. 12, 13½ and Compound

1913, June   Unwmk.

1	A19	2½pi violet brown	350.00	300.00

With Additional Overprint in Carmine

2	A19	10pa blue green	200.00	175.00

The eagle handstamp was applied to other Turkish stamps of 1908: 25pi green and 50 pi red brown. The 5pa ocher, Albania No. 4, was surcharged "2 paras." These three stamps were retained by officials. Values, $2,250, $5,500, $375.

Handstamped on Issue of 1909

4	A21	5pa ocher	175.00	175.00
5	A21	10pa blue green	175.00	100.00
6	A21	20pa car rose	140.00	100.00
7	A21	1pi ultra	125.00	100.00
8	A21	2pi blue black	225.00	175.00
10	A21	5pi dark violet	500.00	450.00
11	A21	10pi dull red	1,750.	1,750.

For surcharge see No. 19.

With Additional Overprint in Blue or Carmine

14	A21	20pa car rose (Bl)	350.00	350.00
15	A21	1pi brt blue (C)	700.00	650.00

Handstamped on Newspaper Stamp of 1911

17	A21	2pa olive green	140.00	125.00

Handstamped on Postage Due Stamp of 1908

18	A19	1pi black, dp rose	900.00	650.00

No. 18 was used for regular postage.

No. 6 Surcharged With New Value

19	A21	10pa on 20pa car rose	325.00	300.00

The overprint on #1-19 was handstamped and is found inverted, double, etc.
Nos. 6, 7 and 8 exist with the handstamp in red, blue or violet, but these varieties are not known to have been regularly issued.
Excellent counterfeits exist of Nos. 1 to 19.

A1

1913, July   Imperf.
Handstamped on White Laid Paper Without Eagle and Value

20	A1	(1pi) black	140.00	275.00
		Cut to shape	65.00	65.00
a.		Sewing machine perf.	200.00	175.00

1913, Aug.
Value Typewritten in Violet With Eagle

21	A1	10pa violet	8.00	6.00
22	A1	20pa red & black	9.00	7.50
23	A1	1gr black	9.00	9.00
24	A1	2gr blue & violet	10.00	8.50
25	A1	5gr violet & blue	14.00	12.00
26	A1	10gr blue	14.00	12.00
		Nos. 21-26 (6)	64.00	55.00

Nos. 21-26 exist with the eagle inverted or omitted and with numerous errors in the figures of value and the spelling of the word "grosh."

A2

Skanderbeg (George Castriota) — A3

1913, Nov.   Perf. 11½
Handstamped on White Laid Paper Eagle and Value in Black

27	A2	10pa green	3.00	2.00
b.		Eagle and value in green	25.00	
c.		10pa red (error)	20.00	20.00
d.		10pa violet (error)	20.00	20.00
29	A2	20pa red	4.00	3.00
b.		20pa green (error)	20.00	20.00
30	A2	30pa violet	4.00	3.00
a.		30pa ultra (error)	20.00	20.00
b.		30pa red (error)	20.00	20.00
31	A2	1gr ultramarine	5.00	4.00
a.		1gr green (error)	20.00	20.00
b.		1gr black (error)	20.00	20.00
c.		1gr violet (error)	20.00	20.00
33	A2	2gr black	8.00	7.00
a.		2gr violet (error)	20.00	20.00
b.		2gr black (error)	20.00	20.00
		Nos. 27-33 (5)	24.00	19.00

The stamps of this issue are known with eagle or value inverted or omitted.
1st anniv. of Albanian independence.

1913, Dec.   Typo.   Perf. 14

35	A3	2q orange brn & buff	1.00	1.00
36	A3	5q green & blue grn	1.00	1.00
37	A3	10q rose red	1.00	1.00
38	A3	25q dark blue	1.00	1.00
39	A3	50q violet & red	3.00	2.00
40	A3	1fr deep brown	7.00	6.00
		Nos. 35-40 (6)	14.00	12.00

For overprints and surcharges see Nos. 41-52, 105, J1-J9.

Nos. 35-40 Handstamped in Black or Violet

1914, Mar. 7

41	A3	2q orange brn & buff	20.00	18.00
42	A3	5q grn & bl grn (V)	20.00	18.00
43	A3	10q rose red	20.00	18.00
44	A3	25q dark blue (V)	20.00	18.00
45	A3	50q violet & red	20.00	18.00
46	A3	1fr deep brown	20.00	18.00
		Nos. 41-46 (6)	120.00	108.00

Issued to celebrate the arrival of Prince Wilhelm zu Wied on Mar. 7, 1914.

Nos. 35-40 Surcharged in Black:

5 PARA   a

1 GROSH   b

1914, Apr. 2

47	A3 (a)	5pa on 2q	1.10	1.10
48	A3 (a)	10pa on 5q	1.10	1.10
49	A3 (a)	20pa on 10q	2.00	1.50
50	A3 (b)	1gr on 25q	2.50	2.00
51	A3 (b)	2gr on 50q	2.50	2.00
52	A3 (b)	5gr on 1fr	13.00	11.00
		Nos. 47-52 (6)	22.20	18.70

For overprints see Nos. 105, J6-J9.

Inverted Surcharge

47a	A3 (a)	5pa on 2q	5.00	5.00
48a	A3 (a)	10pa on 5q	5.00	5.00
49a	A3 (a)	20pa on 10q	5.00	5.00
50a	A3 (b)	1gr on 25q	6.50	6.50
51a	A3 (b)	2gr on 50q	7.50	7.50
52a	A3 (b)	5gr on 1fr	21.00	21.00
		Nos. 47a-52b (6)	50.00	50.00

Ordering on-line is
QUICK!
EASY!
CONVENIENT!
www.scottonline.com

ALBANIA

Korce (Korytsa) Issues

A4

1914 Handstamped Imperf.
52A	A4	10pa violet & red	90.00	90.00	
c.		10pa black & red	90.00	90.00	
53	A4	25pa violet & red	90.00	90.00	
a.		25pa black & red	150.00	150.00	

Nos. 52A-53a originally were handstamped directly on the cover, so the paper varies. Later they were also produced in sheets; these are rarely found. Nos. 52A-53a were issued by Albanian military authorities.

A5  A6

1917 Typo. & Litho. Perf. 11½
54	A5	1c dk brown & grn	9.00	6.50	
55	A5	2c red & green	9.00	6.50	
56	A5	3c gray grn & grn	9.00	6.50	
57	A5	5c green & black	7.00	4.25	
58	A5	10c rose red & black	7.00	4.25	
59	A5	25c blue & black	7.00	4.25	
60	A5	50c violet & black	8.50	6.00	
61	A5	1fr brown & black	8.50	6.00	
		Nos. 54-61 (8)	65.00	44.25	

1917-18
62	A6	1c dk brown & grn	2.75	2.50	
63	A6	2c red & grn	2.75	2.50	
a.		"CTM" for "CTS"	30.00	30.00	
64	A6	3c black & green	2.75	2.50	
a.		"CTM" for "CTS"	30.00	30.00	
65	A6	5c green & black	2.75	2.75	
66	A6	10c dull red & black	2.75	2.75	
67	A6	50c violet & black	7.50	6.00	
68	A6	1fr red brn & black	10.00	8.00	
		Nos. 62-68 (7)	31.25	27.00	

Counterfeits abound of Nos. 54-68, 80-81.

No. 65 Surcharged in Red
QARKU / I / KORÇËS / 25 CTS

1918
80	A6	25c on 5c green & blk	55.00	45.00	

A7

1918
81	A7	25c blue & black	35.00	30.00	

General Issue

A8  A9

Handstamped in Rose or Blue — XVI MCMXIX

1919 Perf. 12½
84	A8	(2)q on 2h brown	4.25	4.25	
85	A8	5q on 16h green	4.25	4.25	
86	A8	10q on 8h rose (Bl)	4.25	4.25	
87	A8	25q on 64h blue	4.25	4.25	
88	A9	25q on 64h blue	200.00	200.00	
89	A8	50q on 32h violet	4.25	4.25	
90	A8	1fr on 1.28k org, bl	6.00	6.00	
		Nos. 84-90 (7)	227.25	227.25	

See Nos. J10-J13. Compare with types A10-A14. For overprints see Nos 91-104.

Handstamped in Rose or Blue

1919, Jan. 16
91	A8	(2)q on 2h brown	8.50	8.50	
92	A8	5q on 16h green	8.50	8.50	
93	A8	10q on 8h rose (Bl)	8.50	8.50	
94	A8	25q on 64h blue	26.00	26.00	
95	A9	25q on 64h blue	21.00	21.00	
96	A8	50q on 32h violet	8.50	8.50	
97	A8	1fr on 1.28k org, bl	4.50	4.50	
		Nos. 91-97 (7)	85.50	85.50	

Handstamped in Violet

1919
98	A8	(2)q on 2h brown	10.00	10.00	
99	A8	5q on 16h green	10.00	10.00	
100	A8	10q on 8h rose	10.00	10.00	
101	A8	25q on 64h blue	10.00	10.00	
102	A9	25q on 64h blue	100.00	90.00	
103	A8	50q on 32h violet	10.00	10.00	
104	A8	1fr on 1.28k org, bl	10.00	10.00	
		Nos. 98-104 (7)	160.00	150.00	

No. 50 Overprinted in Violet — SHKODER • 1919

1919 Perf. 14
105	A3	1gr on 25q blue	5.00	5.00	

A10  A11

1919, June 5 Perf. 11½, 12½
106	A10	10q on 2h brown	3.50	3.50	
107	A11	15q on 8h rose	3.50	3.50	
108	A11	20q on 16h green	3.50	3.50	
109	A10	25q on 64h blue	3.50	3.50	
110	A10	50q on 32h violet	3.50	3.50	
111	A11	1fr on 96h orange	3.50	3.50	
112	A10	2fr on 1.60k vio, buff	14.00	14.00	
		Nos. 106-112 (7)	35.00	35.00	

Nos. 106-108, 110 exist with inverted surcharge.

A12  A13

Black or Violet Surcharge

1919
113	A12	10q on 8h car	3.50	3.50	
114	A12	15q on 8h car (V)	3.50	3.50	
115	A13	20q on 16h green	3.50	3.50	
116	A13	25q on 35h violet	3.50	3.50	
117	A13	50q on 64h blue	9.25	9.25	
118	A13	1fr on 96h orange	4.75	4.75	
119	A12	2fr on 1.60k vio, buff	7.00	7.00	
		Nos. 113-119 (7)	35.00	35.00	

A14  A15

Overprinted in Blue or Black Without New Value

1920 Perf. 12½
120	A14	1q gray (Bl)	22.50	22.50	
121	A14	10q rose (Bk)	1.75	2.75	
a.		Double overprint	24.00	27.50	
122	A14	20q brown (Bl)	11.00	11.00	
123	A14	25q blue (Bk)	110.00	110.00	
124	A14	50q brown vio (Bk)	14.00	16.00	
		Nos. 120-124 (5)	159.25	162.25	

Counterfeit overprints exist of Nos. 120-128.

Surcharged with New Value
125	A14	2q on 10q rose (R)	4.25	4.25	
126	A14	5q on 10q rose (G)	4.25	4.25	
127	A14	25q on 10q rose (Bl)	4.25	4.25	
128	A14	50q on 10q rose (Br)	4.25	4.25	
		Nos. 125-128 (4)	17.00	17.00	

Stamps of type A14 (Portrait of the Prince zu Wied) were not placed in use without overprint or surcharge.

Post Horn Overprinted in Black

1920 Perf. 14x13
129	A15	2q orange	3.75	3.25	
130	A15	5q deep green	6.25	6.00	
131	A15	10q red	11.00	11.00	
132	A15	25q light blue	20.00	11.00	
133	A15	50q gray green	4.25	4.00	
134	A15	1fr claret	4.25	4.00	
		Nos. 129-134 (6)	49.50	39.25	

Type A15 was never placed in use without post horn or "Besa" overprint.

Stamps of Type A15 (No Post Horn) Overprinted — BESA

1921
135	A15	2q orange	3.25	3.25	
136	A15	5q deep green	4.50	4.50	
137	A15	10q red	7.75	7.75	
138	A15	25q light blue	17.50	14.00	
139	A15	50q gray green	5.75	5.75	
140	A15	1fr claret	4.75	4.75	
		Nos. 135-140 (6)	43.50	40.00	

For surcharge & overprints see #154, 156-157.

Stamps of these types, and with "TAKSE" overprint, were unauthorized and never placed in use. They are common.

Gjirokaster A18

Korcha — A19

Designs: 5q, Kanina. 10q, Berati. 25q, Bridge at Vezirit. 50q, Rozafat. 2fr, Dursit.

1923 Typo. Perf. 12½, 11½
147	A18	1q orange	.60	.60	
148	A18	5q yellow green	.50	.50	
149	A18	10q carmine	.50	.50	
150	A18	25q dark blue	.50	.50	
151	A18	50q dark green	.50	.50	
152	A19	1fr dark violet	.65	.65	
153	A19	2fr olive green	1.75	1.75	
		Nos. 147-153 (7)	5.00	5.00	

For overprints & surcharges see #158-185, B1-B8.

No. 135 Surcharged — Q 1

1922 Perf. 14x13
154	A15	1q on 2q orange	3.00	3.00	

Stamps of Type A15 (No Post Horn) Overprinted — BESA

1922
156	A15	5q deep green	3.00	2.50	
157	A15	10q red	3.00	2.50	

Nos. 147-151 Overprinted (top line in Black; diamond in Violet) — Mbledhje Kushtetuese TIRANE KALLNUER 1924

1924, Jan. Perf. 12½
158	A18	2q red orange	4.00	3.75	
159	A18	5q yellow green	4.00	3.75	
160	A18	10q carmine	4.00	3.75	
161	A18	25q dark blue	4.00	3.75	
162	A18	50q dark green	4.00	3.75	
		Nos. 158-162 (5)	20.00	18.75	

The words "Mbledhje Kushtetuese" are in taller letters on the 25q than on the other values. Opening of the Constituent Assembly.

No. 147 Surcharged — 1

1924
163	A18	1q on 2q red orange	2.25	2.25	

Nos. 163, 147-152 Overprinted — Triumf' i legalitetit 24 Dhetuer 1924

1924
164	A18	1q on 2q orange	1.75	2.50	
165	A18	2q orange	1.75	2.50	
166	A18	5q yellow green	1.75	2.50	
167	A18	10q carmine	1.75	2.50	
168	A18	25q dark blue	1.75	2.50	
169	A18	50q dark green	1.75	2.50	
170	A19	1fr dark violet	1.75	2.50	
		Nos. 164-170 (7)	12.25	17.50	

Issued to celebrate the return of the Government to the Capital after a revolution.

Nos. 163, 147-152 Overprinted — Republika Shqiptare 21 Kallnduer 1925

1925
171	A18	1q on 2q orange	1.75	2.50	
172	A18	2q orange	1.75	2.50	
173	A18	5q yellow green	1.75	2.50	
174	A18	10q carmine	1.75	2.50	
175	A18	25q dark blue	1.75	2.50	
176	A18	50q dark green	1.75	2.50	
177	A19	1fr dark violet	1.75	2.50	
		Nos. 171-177 (7)	12.25	17.50	

Proclamation of the Republic, Jan. 21, 1925. The date "1921" instead of "1925" occurs once in each sheet of 50.

Nos. 163, 147-153 Overprinted — Republika Shqiptare

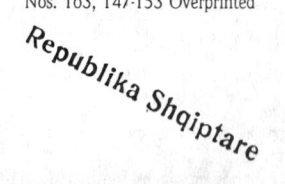

1925
178	A18	1q on 2q orange	.55	.75	
a.		Inverted overprint	7.00	7.00	
179	A18	2q orange	.55	.75	
180	A18	5q yellow green	.55	.75	
a.		Inverted overprint	7.00	7.00	
181	A18	10q carmine	.55	.75	
182	A18	25q dark blue	.55	.75	
183	A18	50q dark green	.55	.75	
184	A19	1fr dark violet	.65	.90	
185	A19	2fr olive green	.65	.90	
		Nos. 178-185 (8)	4.60	6.30	

ALBANIA

President Ahmed Zogu
A25   A26

1925   Perf. 13½, 13½x13

186	A25	1q orange	.15 .15
187	A25	2q red brown	.15 .15
188	A25	5q green	.15 .15
189	A25	10q rose red	.15 .15
190	A25	20q gray brown	1.50 1.50
191	A25	25q dark blue	.15 .15
192	A25	50q blue green	.55 .55
193	A26	1fr red & ultra	.95 .95
194	A26	2fr green & orange	.95 .95
195	A26	3fr brown & violet	1.50 1.50
196	A26	5fr violet & black	3.75 3.75
		Nos. 186-196 (11)	9.95 9.95

No. 193 in ultramarine and brown, and No. 194 in gray and brown were not regularly issued. Value, both $15.

For overprints & surcharges see #197-209, 238-248.

Nos. 186-196 Overprinted in Various Colors

1927

197	A25	1q orange (V)	.60 .40
198	A25	2q red brn (G)	.25 .15
199	A25	5q green (R)	1.25 .15
200	A25	10q rose red (Bl)	.25 .15
201	A25	20q gray brn (G)	7.50 7.50
202	A25	25q dk blue (R)	.60 .15
203	A25	50q blue grn (B)	.60 .15
204	A26	1fr red & ultra (Bk)	1.25 .15
205	A26	2fr green & org (Bk)	1.25 .15
206	A26	3fr brown & vio (Bk)	2.00 .55
207	A26	5fr violet & blk (Bk)	3.00 .95
		Nos. 197-207 (11)	18.55 10.45

No. 200 exists perf. 11.
For surcharges see Nos. 208-209, 238-240.

Nos. 200, 202 Surcharged in Black or Red

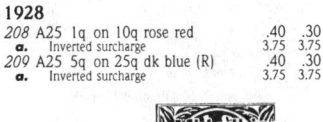

1928

208	A25	1q on 10q rose red	.40 .30
a.		Inverted surcharge	3.75 3.75
209	A25	5q on 25q dk blue (R)	.40 .30
a.		Inverted surcharge	3.75 3.75

King Zog I
A27   A28

Black Overprint

1928   Perf. 14x13½

210	A27	1q orange brown	2.25 2.25
211	A27	2q slate	2.25 2.25
212	A27	5q blue green	2.25 2.25
213	A27	10q rose red	2.25 2.25
214	A27	15q bister	12.00 12.00
215	A27	25q deep blue	1.75 1.75
216	A27	50q lilac rose	2.25 2.25

Red Overprint
Perf. 13½x14

217	A28	1fr blue & slate	2.50 2.50
		Nos. 210-217 (8)	27.50 27.50

Compare with types A29-A32.

A29   A30

Black or Red Overprint

1928   Perf. 14x13½

218	A29	1q orange brown	8.25 8.25
219	A29	2q slate (R)	8.25 8.25
220	A29	5q blue green	7.00 7.00
221	A29	10q rose red	4.50 4.50
222	A29	15q bister	4.75 4.75
223	A29	25q deep blue (R)	4.75 4.75
224	A29	50q lilac rose	5.25 5.25

Perf. 13½x14

225	A30	1fr blue & slate (R)	7.75 7.75
226	A30	2fr green & slate (R)	9.50 9.50
		Nos. 218-226 (9)	60.00 60.00

Proclamation of Ahmed Zogu as King of Albania.

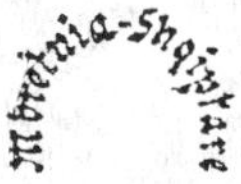

A31    A32

Black Overprint

1928   Perf. 14x13½

227	A31	1q orange brown	.35 .35
228	A31	2q slate	.35 .25
229	A31	5q blue green	2.25 .35
230	A31	10q rose red	.35 .25
231	A31	15q bister	9.00 8.00
232	A31	25q deep blue	.35 .25
233	A31	50q lilac rose	.60 .25

Perf. 13½x14

234	A32	1fr blue & slate	1.25 1.10
235	A32	2fr green & slate	1.25 1.25
236	A32	3fr dk red & ol bis	3.50 1.75
237	A32	5fr dull vio & gray	4.50 4.50
		Nos. 227-237 (11)	23.75 18.30

The overprint reads "Kingdom of Albania."

Nos. 203, 202, 200 Surcharged in Black

1929   Perf. 13½x13, 11½

238	A25	1q on 50q blue green	.35 .35
239	A25	5q on 25q dark blue	.35 .35
240	A25	15q on 10q rose red	.55 .50
		Nos. 238-240 (3)	1.25 1.20

Nos. 186-189, 191-194 Overprinted in Black or Red

1929   Perf. 11½, 13½

241	A25	1q orange	4.00 4.00
242	A25	2q red brown	4.00 4.00
243	A25	5q green	4.00 4.00
244	A25	10q rose red	4.00 4.00
245	A25	25q dark blue	4.00 4.00
246	A25	50q blue green (R)	4.75 4.75
247	A26	1fr red & ultra	7.00 7.00
248	A26	2fr green & orange	8.75 8.75
		Nos. 241-248 (8)	40.50 40.50

34th birthday of King Zog. The overprint reads "Long live the King."

Lake Butrinto — A33   **King Zog I** — A34

Zog Bridge — A35   **Ruin at Zog Manor** — A36

1930, Sept. 1   Photo.   Perf. 14, 14½   Wmk. 220

250	A33	1q slate	.15 .15
251	A33	2q orange red	.15 .15
252	A34	5q yellow green	.15 .15
253	A34	10q carmine	.15 .15
254	A34	15q dark brown	.15 .15
255	A34	25q dark ultra	.20 .15
256	A33	50q slate green	.30 .30
257	A35	1fr violet	.75 .75
258	A35	2fr indigo	.85 .85
259	A36	3fr gray green	1.90 1.90
260	A36	5fr orange brown	3.25 3.25
		Nos. 250-260 (11)	8.00 7.95

2nd anniversary of accession of King Zog I.
For overprints see Nos. 261-270, 299-309, J39.
For surcharges see Nos. 354-360.

Nos. 250-259 Overprinted in Black   **1 9 1 9 2 9 4—24Dhetuer—4**

1934, Dec. 24

261	A33	1q slate	2.00 2.00
262	A33	2q orange red	2.00 2.00
263	A34	5q yellow green	2.00 2.00
264	A34	10q carmine	2.00 2.00
265	A34	15q dark brown	2.00 2.00
266	A34	25q dark ultra	2.00 2.00
267	A33	50q slate green	2.00 2.00
268	A35	1fr violet	4.50 4.50
269	A35	2fr indigo	9.00 9.00
270	A36	3fr gray green	12.50 12.50
		Nos. 261-270 (10)	40.00 40.00

Tenth anniversary of the Constitution.

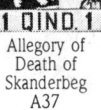

Allegory of Death of Skanderbeg — A37

Albanian Eagle in Turkish Shackles — A38

5q, 25q, 40q, 2fr, Eagle with wings spread.

1937   Unwmk.   Perf. 14

271	A37	1q brown violet	.15 .15
272	A38	2q brown	.15 .15
273	A38	5q lt green	.22 .22
274	A37	10q olive brown	.30 .30
275	A38	15q rose red	.38 .38
276	A38	25q blue	.70 .70
277	A37	50q deep green	.95 .95
278	A38	1fr violet	1.65 1.65
279	A38	2fr orange brown	4.25 4.25
		Nos. 271-279 (9)	8.75 8.75

Souvenir Sheet

280		Sheet of 3	13.00 12.00
a.	A37	20q red violet	2.50 2.50
b.	A38	30q olive brown	2.50 2.50
c.	A38	40q red	2.50 2.50

25th anniv. of independence from Turkey, proclaimed Nov. 26, 1912.

Queen Geraldine and King Zog — A40

1938   Perf. 14

281	A40	1q slate violet	.15 .15
282	A40	2q red brown	.15 .15
283	A40	5q green	.15 .15
284	A40	10q olive brown	.35 .35
285	A40	15q rose red	.50 .50
286	A40	25q blue	.85 .85
287	A40	50q Prus green	2.50 2.50
288	A40	1fr purple	5.25 5.25
		Nos. 281-288 (8)	9.90 9.90

Souvenir Sheet

289		Sheet of 4	18.00 18.00
a.	A40	20q dark red violet	1.75 1.75
b.	A40	30q brown olive	1.75 1.75

Wedding of King Zog and Countess Geraldine Apponyi, Apr. 27, 1938.
No. 289 contains 2 each of Nos. 289a, 289b.

Queen Geraldine — A42   **National Emblems** — A43

Designs: 10q, 25q, 30q, 1fr, King Zog.

1938

290	A42	1q dp red violet	.15 .15
291	A43	2q red orange	.15 .15
292	A42	5q deep green	.20 .20
293	A42	10q red brown	.20 .20
294	A42	15q deep rose	.55 .55
295	A42	25q deep blue	.70 .70
296	A43	50q gray black	1.75 1.75
297	A42	1fr slate green	6.00 6.00
		Nos. 290-297 (8)	9.70 9.70

Souvenir Sheet

298		Sheet of 3	18.00 18.00
b.	A43	20q Prussian green	2.00 2.00
c.	A42	30q deep violet	2.00 2.00

10th anniv. of royal rule. They were on sale for 3 days (Aug. 30-31, Sept. 1) only, during which their use was required on all mail.
No. 298 contains Nos. 294, 298b, 298c.

Issued under Italian Dominion

Nos. 250-260 Overprinted in Black   **Mbledhja Kushtetuëse 12-IV-1939 XVII**

1939   Wmk. 220   Perf. 14

299	A33	1q slate	.15 .15
300	A33	2q orange red	.15 .15
301	A34	5q yellow green	.15 .15
302	A34	10q carmine	.40 .40
303	A34	15q dark brown	.40 .40
304	A34	25q dark ultra	.60 .60
305	A33	50q slate green	.90 .90
306	A35	1fr violet	1.75 1.75
307	A35	2fr indigo	2.50 2.50
308	A36	3fr gray green	5.00 5.00
309	A36	5fr orange brown	7.00 7.00
		Nos. 299-309 (11)	19.00 19.00

Resolution adopted by the Natl. Assembly, Apr. 12, 1939, offering the Albanian Crown to Italy.

Native Costumes
A46   A47   A48

King Victor Emmanuel III
A49   A50

Native Costume A51   **Monastery** A52

Designs: 2fr, Bridge at Vezirit. 3fr, Ancient Columns. 5fr, Amphitheater.

1939   Unwmk.   Photo.   Perf. 14

310	A46	1q blue gray	.15 .15
311	A47	2q olive green	.15 .15
312	A48	3q golden brown	.15 .15
313	A49	5q green	.15 .15
314	A50	10q brown	.20 .15
315	A50	15q crimson	.25 .20
316	A50	25q sapphire	.40 .25
317	A50	30q brt violet	.55 .35
318	A51	50q dull purple	.70 .35
319	A49	65q red brown	1.00 1.00
320	A52	1fr myrtle green	1.25 1.25
321	A52	2fr brown lake	3.00 3.00
322	A52	3fr brown black	5.75 5.75
323	A52	5fr gray white	12.00 12.00
		Nos. 310-323 (14)	25.70 24.90

For overprints and surcharges see Nos. 331-353.

ALBANIA

King Victor Emmanuel III — A56

1942   Photo.
324	A56	5q green	.20	.20
325	A56	10q brown	.35	.35
326	A56	1r rose red	.55	.55
327	A56	25q blue	1.25	1.25
328	A56	65q red brown	1.90	1.90
329	A56	1fr myrtle green	3.50	3.50
330	A56	2fr gray violet	7.75	7.75
	Nos. 324-330 (7)	15.50	15.50

Conquest of Albania by Italy, 3rd anniv.

No. 311 Surcharged in Black   **1 QIND**

331	A47	1q on 2q olive green	1.00	1.00

Issued under German Administration

Stamps of 1939 Overprinted in Carmine or Brown   **14 Shtator 1943**

1943
332	A47	2q olive green	1.10	1.40
333	A48	3q golden brown	1.10	1.40
334	A49	5q green	1.10	1.40
335	A50	10q brown	1.10	1.40
336	A50	15q crimson (Br)	1.10	1.40
337	A50	25q sapphire	1.10	1.40
338	A50	30q brt violet	1.10	1.40
339	A49	65q red brown	1.25	2.25
340	A52	1fr myrtle green	7.75	10.00
341	A52	2fr brown lake	10.50	20.00
342	A52	3fr brown black	45.00	52.50

Surcharged with New Values
343	A48	1q on 3q gldn brn	1.10	1.40
344	A49	50q on 65q red brn	1.25	2.25
	Nos. 332-344 (13)	74.55	98.20

Proclamation of Albanian independence.
The overprint "14 Shtator 1943" on Nos. 324 to 328 is private and fraudulent.

Independent State

Nos. 312 to 317 and 319 to 321 Surcharged with New Value and Bars in Black or Carmine, and: **QEVERIJA DEMOKRAT. E SHQIPERISE 22-X-1944**

1945
345	A48	30q on 3q gldn brn	3.50	3.50
346	A49	40q on 5q green	3.50	3.50
347	A50	50q on 10q brown	3.50	3.50
348	A50	60q on 15q crimson	3.50	3.50
349	A50	80q on 25q saph (C)	3.50	3.50
350	A49	1fr on 30q brt vio	3.50	3.50
351	A49	2fr on 65q red brn	3.50	3.50
352	A52	3fr on 1fr myr grn	3.50	3.50
353	A52	5fr on 2fr brn lake	3.50	3.50
	Nos. 345-353 (9)	31.50	31.50

"DEMOKRATIKE" is not abbreviated on Nos. 352 and 353.

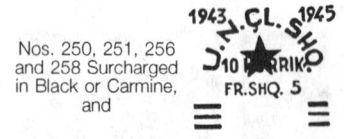

Nos. 250, 251, 256 and 258 Surcharged in Black or Carmine, and   **1943 J.N.ÇL. 1945 10 KORRIK FR.SHQ. 5**

1945   Wmk. 220
354	A33	30q on 1q slate	1.25	1.25
355	A33	60q on 1q slate	1.50	1.50
356	A33	80q on 1q slate	1.65	1.65
357	A33	1fr on 1q slate	2.50	2.50
358	A33	2fr on 2q org red	3.25	3.25
359	A33	3fr on 50q sl grn	8.50	8.50
360	A35	5fr on 2fr indigo	11.00	11.00
	Nos. 354-360 (7)	29.65	29.65

Albanian Natl. Army of Liberation, 2nd anniv.
The surcharge on No. 360 is condensed to fit the size of the stamp.

Country House, Labinot — A57

40q, 60q, Bridge at Berat. 1fr, 3fr, Permet.

1945, Nov. 28   Unwmk.   Typo.   Perf. 11
361	A57	20q bluish green	.20	.20
362	A57	30q deep orange	.40	.40
363	A57	40q brown	.40	.40
364	A57	60q red violet	.60	.60
365	A57	1fr rose red	1.25	1.25
366	A57	3fr dark blue	6.00	6.00
	Nos. 361-366 (6)	8.85	8.85

Counterfeits exist. See note after No. B33.
For overprints and surcharges see Nos. 367-378, 418-423, B28-B33.

Nos. 361 to 366 Overprinted in Black   **ASAMBLEJA KUSHTETUESE 10 KALLHUER 1946**

1946
367	A57	20q bluish green	.60	.60
368	A57	30q deep orange	.60	.60
369	A57	40q brown	.95	.95
370	A57	60q red violet	1.75	1.75
371	A57	1fr rose red	4.75	4.75
372	A57	3fr dark blue	7.50	7.50
	Nos. 367-372 (6)	16.15	16.15

Convocation of the Constitutional Assembly, Jan. 10, 1946.

People's Republic

Nos. 361 to 366 Overprinted in Black   **REPUBLIKA POPULLORE E SHQIPERISE**

1946
373	A57	20q bluish green	.75	.75
374	A57	30q deep orange	1.25	1.25
375	A57	40q brown	1.65	1.65
376	A57	60q red violet	2.75	2.75
377	A57	1fr rose red	5.00	5.00
378	A57	3fr dark blue	8.50	8.50
	Nos. 373-378 (6)	19.90	19.90

Proclamation of the Albanian People's Republic.
For surcharges see Nos. 418-423.

Globe, Dove and Olive Branch — A60

1946, Mar. 8   Perf. 11½, Imperf.   Typo.
Denomination in Black
379	A60	20q lilac & dull red	.15	.15
380	A60	40q dp lilac & dull red	.35	.35
381	A60	50q violet & dull red	.50	.50
382	A60	1fr lt blue & red	.80	.80
383	A60	2fr dk blue & red	1.65	1.65
	Nos. 379-383 (5)	3.45	3.45

International Women's Congress.

Athletes with Shot and Indian Club — A61

1946, Oct. 6   Perf. 11½   Litho.   Unwmk.
384	A61	1q grnsh black	6.00	6.00
385	A61	2q green	6.00	6.00
386	A61	5q brown	6.00	6.00
387	A61	10q crimson	6.00	6.00
388	A61	20q ultra	6.00	6.00
389	A61	40q rose violet	6.00	6.00
390	A61	1fr deep orange	10.00	10.00
	Nos. 384-390 (7)	46.00	46.00

Balkan Games, Tirana, Oct. 6-13.

Qemal Stafa — A62

1947, May 5   Perf. 12½x11½
391	A62	20q brn & yel brn	1.75	1.75
392	A62	28q dk green & blue	1.75	1.75
393	A62	40q brn blk & gray brn	3.00	3.00
a.	Souvenir sheet, #391-393	6.50	6.50
	Nos. 391-393 (3)	6.50	6.50

5th anniv. of the death of Qemal Stafa.

Young Railway Laborers A64

1947, May 16   Perf. 11½
395	A64	1q brn blk & gray brn	1.25	.60
396	A64	4q dk green & green	1.25	.60
397	A64	10q blk brn & bis brn	1.25	.60
398	A64	15q dk red & red	1.50	.60
399	A64	20q indigo & bl gray	2.00	.90
400	A64	28q dk blue & blue	3.00	.90
401	A64	40q brn vio & rose vio	7.75	4.25
402	A64	68q dk brn & org brn	12.00	7.75
	Nos. 395-402 (8)	30.00	16.20

Issued to publicize the construction of the Durres Elbasan Railway by Albanian youths.

Citizens Led by Hasim Zeneli — A65

Enver Hoxha and Vasil Shanto — A66

Vojo Kushi — A68

Inauguration of Vithkuq Brigade — A67

1947, July 10   Litho.
403	A65	16q brn org & red brn	3.25	3.25
404	A66	20q org brn & dk brn	3.25	3.25
405	A67	28q blue & dk blue	3.50	3.50
406	A68	40q lilac & dk brn	5.00	5.00
	Nos. 403-406 (4)	15.00	15.00

4th anniv. of the formation of Albania's army, July 10, 1943.

Conference Building Ruins, Peza — A69

Disabled Soldiers — A70

1947, Sept. 16
407	A69	2 l red violet	2.25	2.00
408	A69	2.50 l deep blue	2.25	2.00

Peza Conf., Sept. 16, 1942, 5th anniv.

1947, Nov. 17   Perf. 12½x11½
408A	A70	1 l red	3.50	3.50

Disabled War Veterans Cong., Nov. 14-20, 1947.

A71

A73

Designs: 2 l, Banquet. 2.50 l, Peasants rejoicing.

Perf. 11½x12½, 12½x11½
1947, Nov. 17   Unwmk.
409	A71	1.50 l dull violet	2.50	2.50
410	A71	2 l red	2.50	2.50
411	A71	2.50 l blue	2.50	2.50
412	A73	3 l rose red	2.50	2.50
	Nos. 409-412 (4)	10.00	10.00

Agrarian reform law of Nov. 17, 1946, 1st anniv.

Burning Farm Buildings A74

Designs: 2.50 l, Trench scene. 5 l, Firing line. 8 l, Winter advance. 12 l, Infantry column.

1947, Nov. 29   Perf. 11½x12½
413	A74	1.50 l red	1.65	1.65
414	A74	2.50 l rose brown	2.00	2.00
415	A74	5 l blue	2.50	2.50
416	A74	8 l purple	4.00	4.00
417	A74	12 l brown	6.00	6.00
	Nos. 413-417 (5)	16.15	16.15

3rd anniv. of Albania's liberation.

Nos. 373 to 378 Surcharged with New Value and Bars in Black

1948, Feb. 22   Perf. 11
418	A57	50 on 30q deep org	.25	.25
419	A57	1 l on 20q bluish grn	.50	.50
420	A57	2.50 l on 60q red vio	1.00	1.00
421	A57	3 l on 1fr rose red	1.25	1.25
422	A57	5 l on 3fr dark blue	2.25	2.25
423	A57	12 l on 40q brown	4.75	4.75
	Nos. 418-423 (6)	10.00	10.00

The two bars consist of four type squares each set close together.

Map, Train and Construction Workers A75

1948, June 1   Litho.   Perf. 11½
424	A75	50q dk car rose	1.10	.55
425	A75	1 l lt green & blk	1.25	.55
426	A75	1.50 l deep rose	1.25	.55
427	A75	2.50 l org brn & dk brn	1.25	.55
428	A75	5 l dull blue	2.00	1.10
429	A75	8 l salmon & dk brn	4.75	2.00
430	A75	12 l red vio & dk vio	6.50	2.25
431	A75	20 l olive gray	12.50	5.00
	Nos. 424-431 (8)	30.60	12.55

Issued to publicize the construction of the Durres-Tirana Railway.

ALBANIA

Design: 8 l, Battle scene.

Marching Soldiers A76

1948, July 10
432	A76	2.50 l yellow brown	1.25	1.25
433	A76	5 l dark blue	1.65	1.65
434	A76	8 l violet gray	3.25	3.25
		Nos. 432-434 (3)	6.15	6.15

5th anniv. of the formation of Albania's army.

Bricklayer, Flag, Globe and "Industry" A77

Map and Soldier A78

1949, May 1   Photo.   Perf. 12½x12
435	A77	2.50 l olive brown	.30	.30
436	A77	5 l blue	.70	.70
437	A77	8 l violet brown	1.10	1.10
		Nos. 435-437 (3)	2.10	2.10

Issued to publicize Labor Day, May 1, 1949.

1949, July 10   Unwmk.
438	A78	2.50 l brown	.50	.50
439	A78	5 l light ultra	.75	.75
440	A78	8 l brown orange	1.50	1.50
		Nos. 438-440 (3)	2.75	2.75

6th anniv. of the formation of Albania's army.

Enver Hoxha A79

Albanian Citizen and Spasski Tower, Kremlin A80

1949, Oct. 16   Engr.   Perf. 12½
441	A79	50q purple	.15	.15
442	A79	1 l dull green	.15	.15
443	A79	1.50 l car lake	.20	.15
444	A79	2.50 l brown	.30	.15
445	A79	5 l violet blue	.65	.15
446	A79	8 l sepia	1.10	.90
447	A79	12 l rose lilac	2.50	1.50
448	A79	20 l gray brown	5.00	2.50
		Nos. 441-448 (8)	10.05	5.65

1949, Sept. 10   Photo.   Perf. 12½x12
449	A80	2.50 l orange brown	.50	.50
450	A80	5 l deep ultra	1.00	1.00

Albanian-Soviet friendship.

Albanian Soldier and Flag A81

Battle Scene A82

1949, Nov. 29   Unwmk.   Perf. 12
451	A81	2.50 l brown	.25	.25
452	A82	3 l dark red	.50	.50
453	A81	5 l violet	.60	.60
454	A82	8 l black	1.65	1.65
		Nos. 451-454 (4)	3.00	3.00

Fifth anniversary of Albania's liberation.

Joseph V. Stalin — A83

Symbols of UPU and Postal Transport — A84

1949, Dec. 21
455	A83	2.50 l dark brown	.45	.55
456	A83	5 l violet blue	1.25	1.25
457	A83	8 l rose brown	2.00	2.25
		Nos. 455-457 (3)	3.70	4.05

70th anniv. of the birth of Joseph V. Stalin.

Canceled to Order
Beginning in 1950, Albania sold some issues in sheets canceled to order. Values in second column when much less than unused are for "CTO" copies. Postally used stamps are valued at slightly less than, or the same as, unused.

Catalogue values for unused stamps in this section, from this point to the end of the section, are for Never Hinged items.

1950, July 1   Photo.   Perf. 12x12½
458	A84	5 l blue	2.25	1.25
459	A84	8 l rose brown	3.25	1.75
460	A84	12 l sepia	4.00	2.25
		Nos. 458-460 (3)	9.50	5.25

75th anniv. (in 1949) of the UPU.

Sami Frasheri — A85

Arms and Albanian Flags — A86

Authors: 2.50 l, Andon Zako. 3 l, Naim Frasheri. 5 l, Kostandin Kristoforidhi.

1950, Nov. 5   Perf. 14
461	A85	2 l dark green	.70	.15
462	A85	2.50 l red brown	.95	.20
463	A85	3 l brown carmine	1.40	.25
464	A85	5 l deep blue	2.00	.60
		Nos. 461-464 (4)	5.05	1.20

"Jubilee of the Writers of the Renaissance."

1951, Jan. 11   Engr.   Perf. 14x13½
465	A86	2.50 l brown carmine	1.10	.25
466	A86	5 l deep blue	2.00	.50
467	A86	8 l sepia	3.00	1.00
		Nos. 465-467 (3)	6.10	1.75

5th anniv. of the formation of the Albanian People's Republic.

Skanderbeg A87

Enver Hoxha and Congress of Permet A88

1951, Mar. 1
468	A87	2.50 l brown	.75	.25
469	A87	5 l violet	1.50	.50
470	A87	8 l olive bister	2.50	1.00
		Nos. 468-470 (3)	4.75	1.75

483rd anniv. of the death of George Castriota (Skanderbeg).

1951, May 24   Photo.   Perf. 12
471	A88	2.50 l dark brown	.45	.20
472	A88	3 l rose brown	.70	.30
473	A88	5 l violet blue	1.10	.50
474	A88	8 l rose lilac	1.90	.80
		Nos. 471-474 (4)	4.15	1.80

Congress of Permet, 7th anniversary.

Child and Globe — A89

Weighing Baby — A90

1951, July 16
475	A89	2 l green	1.00	.30
476	A90	2.50 l brown	1.50	.40
477	A90	3 l red	2.00	.50
478	A89	5 l blue	3.00	.80
		Nos. 475-478 (4)	7.50	2.00

Intl. Children's Day, June 1, 1951.

Enver Hoxha and Birthplace of Albanian Communist Party — A91

1951, Nov. 8   Photo.   Perf. 14
479	A91	2.50 l olive brown	.30	.25
480	A91	3 l rose brown	.45	.35
481	A91	5 l dark slate blue	.70	.60
482	A91	8 l black	1.00	.85
		Nos. 479-482 (4)	2.45	2.05

Albanian Communist Party, 10th anniv.

Battle Scene — A92

1951, Nov. 28   Perf. 12x12½
483	A92	2.50 l brown	.40	.15
484	A92	5 l blue	.65	.40
485	A92	8 l brown carmine	1.40	.75
		Nos. 483-485 (3)	2.45	1.30

Albanian Communist Youth Org., 10th anniv.

Albanian Heroes (Haxhija, Lezhe, Giyebegej, Mezi and Dedej) — A93

Nos. 486-489 each show five "Heroes of the People"; No. 490 shows two (Stafa and Shanto).

1950, Dec. 25   Unwmk.   Perf. 14
486	A93	1 l dark green	.65	.15
487	A93	2.50 l purple	.80	.15
488	A93	3 l scarlet	.95	.25
489	A93	5 l brt blue	1.50	.35
490	A93	8 l olive brown	3.75	1.00
		Nos. 486-490 (5)	7.65	1.90

6th anniv. of Albania's liberation.

Tobacco Factory, Shkoder — A94

Composite, Lenin Hydroelectric Plant — A95

Designs: 1 l, Canal. 2.50 l, Textile factory. 3 l, "8 November" Cannery. 5 l, Motion Picture Studio, Tirana. 8 l, Stalin Textile Mill, Tirana. 20 l, Central Hydroelectric Dam.

1953, Aug. 1   Perf. 12x12½, 12½x12
491	A94	50q red brown	.15	.15
492	A94	1 l dull green	.15	.15
493	A94	2.50 l brown	.60	.15
494	A94	3 l rose brown	.85	.15
495	A94	5 l blue	1.25	.15
496	A94	8 l brown olive	2.25	.15
497	A95	12 l deep plum	3.50	.35
498	A95	20 l slate blue	6.25	.50
		Nos. 491-498 (8)	15.00	1.75

Liberation Scene — A96

1954, Nov. 29   Perf. 12x12½
499	A96	50q brown violet	.15	.15
500	A96	1 l olive green	.25	.15
501	A96	2.50 l yellow brown	.65	.15
502	A96	3 l carmine rose	.80	.15
503	A96	5 l gray blue	1.10	.15
504	A96	8 l rose brown	2.00	.55
		Nos. 499-504 (6)	4.95	1.30

10th anniversary of Albania's liberation.

School — A97

Pandeli Sotiri, Petro Nini Luarasi, Nuci Naci — A98

1956, Feb. 23   Unwmk.
505	A97	2 l rose violet	.35	.15
506	A98	2.50 l lt green	.50	.15
507	A98	5 l ultra	1.10	.20
508	A97	10 l brt grnsh blue	2.25	.35
		Nos. 505-508 (4)	4.20	.85

Opening of the 1st Albanian school, 70th anniv.

Flags — A99

Designs: 5 l, Labor Party headquarters, Tirana. 8 l, Marx and Lenin.

1957, June 1   Engr.   Perf. 11½x11
509	A99	2.50 l brown	.45	.15
510	A99	5 l lt violet blue	.90	.15
511	A99	8 l rose lilac	2.00	.20
		Nos. 509-511 (3)	3.35	.50

Albania's Labor Party, 15th anniv.

Congress Emblem A100

1957, Oct. 4   Unwmk.   Perf. 11½
512	A100	2.50 l gray brown	.50	.15
513	A100	3 l rose red	.70	.15
514	A100	5 l dark blue	.90	.15
515	A100	8 l green	1.65	.30
		Nos. 512-515 (4)	3.75	.75

4th Intl. Trade Union Cong., Leipzig, Oct. 4-15.

Lenin and Cruiser "Aurora" — A101

ALBANIA

1957, Nov. 7   Litho.   Perf. 10½

516	A101	2.50 l violet brown	.45	.15
517	A101	5 l violet blue	.95	.15
518	A101	8 l gray	1.25	.30
		Nos. 516-518 (3)	2.65	.60

40th anniv. of the Russian Revolution.

Albanian Fighter Holding Flag
A102

Naum Veqilharxhj
A103

1957, Nov. 28   Perf. 10½

519	A102	1.50 l magenta	.40	.15
520	A102	2.50 l brown	.60	.15
521	A102	5 l blue	1.00	.15
522	A102	8 l green	2.00	.30
		Nos. 519-522 (4)	4.00	.75

Proclamation of independence, 45th anniv.

1958, Feb. 1   Unwmk.

523	A103	2.50 l dark brown	.50	.15
524	A103	5 l violet blue	1.00	.15
525	A103	8 l rose lilac	2.00	.30
		Nos. 523-525 (3)	3.50	.60

160th anniv. of the birth of Naum Veqilharxhj, patriot and writer.

Luigi Gurakuqi
A104

Soldiers
A105

1958, Apr. 15   Photo.   Perf. 10½

526	A104	1.50 l dark green	.30	.15
527	A104	2.50 l brown	.40	.15
528	A104	5 l blue	.75	.15
529	A104	8 l sepia	1.50	.20
		Nos. 526-529 (4)	2.95	.65

Transfer of the ashes of Luigi Gurakuqi.

1958, July 10   Litho.

2.50 l, 11 l, Airman, sailor, soldier and tank.

530	A105	1.50 l blue green	.20	.15
531	A105	2.50 l dark red brown	.30	.15
532	A105	8 l rose red	.95	.15
533	A105	11 l bright blue	1.50	.25
		Nos. 530-533 (4)	2.95	.70

15th anniversary of Albanian army.

Cerciz Topulli and Mihal Grameno — A106

Buildings and Tree — A107

1958, July 1

534	A106	2.50 l dk olive bister	.35	.15
535	A107	3 l green	.45	.15
536	A106	5 l blue	.75	.15
537	A107	8 l red brown	1.25	.20
		Nos. 534-537 (4)	2.80	.65

50th anniversary, Battle of Mashkullore.

Ancient Amphitheater and Goddess of Butrinto — A108

1959, Jan. 25   Litho.   Perf. 10½

538	A108	2.50 l redsh brown	.65	.15
539	A108	6.50 l lt blue green	1.65	.15
540	A108	11 l dark blue	2.50	.40
		Nos. 538-540 (3)	4.80	.70

Cultural Monuments Week.

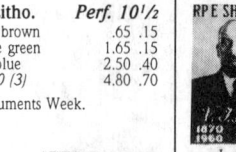

Frederic Joliot-Curie and World Peace Congress Emblem
A109

Basketball
A110

1959, July 1   Unwmk.

541	A109	1.50 l carmine rose	1.00	.20
542	A109	2.50 l rose violet	1.75	.30
543	A109	11 l blue	5.00	1.50
		Nos. 541-543 (3)	7.75	2.00

10th anniv. of the World Peace Movement.

1959, Nov. 20   Perf. 10½

Sports: 2.50 l, Soccer, 5 l, Runner. 11 l, Man and woman runners with torch and flags.

544	A110	1.50 l bright violet	.40	.15
545	A110	2.50 l emerald	.55	.15
546	A110	5 l carmine rose	1.50	.25
547	A110	11 l ultra	4.00	1.75
		Nos. 544-547 (4)	6.45	2.30

1st Albanian Spartacist Games.

Fighter and Flags
A111

Mother and Child, UN Emblem
A112

Designs: 2.50 l, Miner with drill standing guard. 3 l, Farm woman with sheaf of grain. 6.50 l, Man and woman in laboratory.

1959, Nov. 29

548	A111	1.50 l brt carmine	.50	.15
549	A111	2.50 l red brown	.70	.15
550	A111	3 l brt blue green	.90	.15
551	A111	6.50 l bright red	2.00	.25
a.		Souvenir sheet	6.00	6.00
		Nos. 548-551 (4)	4.10	.70

15th anniversary of Albania's liberation.
No. 551a contains one each of Nos. 548-551, imperf. and all in bright carmine. Inscribed ribbon frame of sheet and frame lines for each stamp are blue green.

1959, Dec. 5   Unwmk.

| 552 | A112 | 5 l lt grnsh blue | 3.00 | .55 |
| a. | | Miniature sheet | 3.00 | 3.00 |

10th anniv. (in 1958) of the signing of the Universal Declaration of Human Rights.
No. 552a contains one imperf. stamp similar to No. 552; ornamental border.

Woman with Olive Branch
A113

Alexander Moissi
A114

1960, Mar. 8   Litho.   Perf. 10½

| 553 | A113 | 2.50 l chocolate | .45 | .15 |
| 554 | A113 | 11 l rose carmine | 2.00 | .30 |

50th anniv. of Intl. Women's Day, Mar. 8.

1960, Apr. 20

| 555 | A114 | 3 l deep brown | .35 | .15 |
| 556 | A114 | 11 l Prus green | 1.40 | .25 |

80th anniversary of the birth of Alexander Moissi (Moisiu) (1880-1935), German actor.

Lenin
A115

School Building
A116

1960, Apr. 22

| 557 | A115 | 4 l Prus blue | 1.65 | .15 |
| 558 | A115 | 11 l lake | 3.50 | .20 |

90th anniversary of birth of Lenin.

1960, May 30   Litho.   Perf. 10½

| 559 | A116 | 5 l green | 1.25 | .20 |
| 560 | A116 | 6.50 l plum | 1.25 | .20 |

1st Albanian secondary school, 50th anniv.

Soldier on Guard Duty — A117

Liberation Monument, Tirana, Family and Policeman — A118

1960, May 12   Unwmk.   Perf. 10½

| 561 | A117 | 1.50 l carmine rose | .30 | .15 |
| 562 | A117 | 11 l Prus blue | 1.65 | .20 |

15th anniversary of the Frontier Guards.

1960, May 14

| 563 | A118 | 1.50 l green | .30 | .15 |
| 564 | A118 | 8.50 l brown | 1.65 | .25 |

15th anniversary of the People's Police.

Congress Site — A119

Pashko Vasa — A120

1960, Mar. 25

| 565 | A119 | 2.50 l sepia | .25 | .15 |
| 566 | A119 | 7.50 l dull blue | 1.00 | .25 |

40th anniversary, Congress of Louchnia.

1960, May 5

Designs: 1.50 l, Jani Vreto. 6.50 l, Sami Frasheri. 11 l, Page of statutes of association.

567	A120	1 l gray olive	.35	.15
568	A120	1.50 l brown	.50	.15
569	A120	6.50 l blue	1.10	.15
570	A120	11 l rose red	2.00	.20
		Nos. 567-570 (4)	3.95	.65

80th anniv. (in 1959) of the Association of Albanian Authors.

Albanian Fighter and Cannon
A121

TU-104 Plane, Clock Tower, Tirana, and Kremlin, Moscow
A122

1960, Aug. 2   Litho.   Perf. 10½

571	A121	1.50 l olive brown	.40	.15
572	A121	2.50 l maroon	.50	.15
573	A121	5 l dark blue	1.25	.20
		Nos. 571-573 (3)	2.15	.50

Battle of Viona (against Italian troops), 40th anniv.

1960, Aug. 18

574	A122	1 l redsh brown	.40	.15
575	A122	7.50 l brt grnsh blue	1.50	.25
576	A122	11.50 l gray	2.75	.60
		Nos. 574-576 (3)	4.65	1.10

TU-104 flights, Moscow-Tirana, 2nd anniv.

Rising Sun and Federation Emblem
A123

Ali Kelmendi
A124

1960, Nov. 10   Unwmk.   Perf. 10½

| 577 | A123 | 1.50 l ultra | .30 | .15 |
| 578 | A123 | 8.50 l red | 1.10 | .20 |

Intl. Youth Federation, 15th anniv.

1960, Dec. 5   Litho.   Perf. 10½

| 579 | A124 | 1.50 l pale gray grn | .30 | .15 |
| 580 | A124 | 11 l dull rose lake | .70 | .20 |

Ali Kelmendi, communist leader, 60th birthday.

Flags of Russia and Albania and Clasped Hands
A125

Marx and Lenin
A126

1961, Jan. 10   Unwmk.   Perf. 10½

| 581 | A125 | 2 l violet | .30 | .15 |
| 582 | A125 | 8 l dull red brown | .70 | .20 |

15th anniv. of the Albanian-Soviet Friendship Society.

1961, Feb. 13   Litho.

| 583 | A126 | 2 l rose red | .30 | .15 |
| 584 | A126 | 11 l violet blue | 1.10 | .20 |

Fourth Communist Party Congress.

Man from Shkoder
A127

Otter
A128

Costumes: 1.50 l, Woman from Shkoder. 6.50 l, Man from Lume. 11 l, Woman from Mirdite.

1961, Apr. 28   Perf. 10½

585	A127	1 l slate	.35	.15
586	A127	1.50 l dull claret	.60	.15
587	A127	6.50 l ultra	1.90	.20
588	A127	11 l red	3.25	.35
		Nos. 585-588 (4)	6.10	.85

1961, June 25   Unwmk.   Perf. 10½

Designs: 6.50 l, Badger. 11 l, Brown bear.

589	A128	2.50 l grayish blue	2.00	.25
590	A128	6.50 l blue green	4.50	.50
591	A128	11 l dark red brown	8.00	.85
		Nos. 589-591 (3)	14.50	1.60

ALBANIA

Dalmatian Pelicans A129

Cyclamen A130

1961, Sept. 30   *Perf. 14*
592	A129	1.50 l shown	2.00	.20
593	A129	7.50 l Gray herons	4.00	.40
594	A129	11 l Little egret	6.00	.60
		Nos. 592-594 (3)	12.00	1.20

1961, Oct. 27   *Litho.*
595	A130	1.50 l shown	2.00	.20
596	A130	8 l Forsythia	3.50	.20
597	A130	11 l Lily	4.50	.40
		Nos. 595-597 (3)	10.00	.75

Milosh G. Nikolla — A131

Flag with Marx and Lenin — A132

1961, Oct. 30   *Perf. 14*
598	A131	50q violet brown	.30	.15
599	A131	8.50 l Prus green	1.25	.25

50th anniv. of the birth of Milosh Gjergi Nikolla, poet.

1961, Nov. 8
600	A132	2.50 l vermilion	.50	.15
601	A132	7.50 l dull red brown	1.00	.25

20th anniv. of the founding of Albania's Communist Party.

Worker, Farm Woman and Emblem A133

Yuri Gagarin and Vostok 1 A134

1961, Nov. 23   *Unwmk.*   *Perf. 14*
602	A133	2.50 l violet blue	.50	.15
603	A133	7.50 l rose claret	1.00	.30

20th anniv. of the Albanian Workers' Party.

1962, Feb. 15   *Unwmk.*   *Perf. 14*
604	A134	50q blue	.35	.15
605	A134	4 l red lilac	1.65	.15
606	A134	11 l dk slate grn	3.25	.65
		Nos. 604-606 (3)	5.25	.95

1st manned space flight, made by Yuri A. Gagarin, Soviet astronaut, Apr. 12, 1961.
Nos. 604-606 were overprinted with an over-all yellow tint and with "POSTA AJRORE" (Air Mail) in maroon in 1962. Value, set $50.

Petro Nini Luarasi — A135

Malaria Eradication Emblem — A136

1962, Feb. 28
607	A135	50q Prus blue	.25	.15
608	A135	8.50 l olive gray	1.50	.25

50th anniv. (in 1961) of the death of Petro Nini Luarasi, Albanian patriot.

1962, Apr. 30   *Unwmk.*   *Perf. 14*
609	A136	1.50 l brt green	.15	.15
610	A136	2.50 l brown red	.15	.15
611	A136	10 l red lilac	.55	.25
612	A136	11 l blue	.90	.35
		Nos. 609-612 (4)	1.75	.90

WHO drive to eradicate malaria.
Souvenir sheets, perf. and imperf., contain one each of Nos. 609-612. Value $14.00 each. Nos. 609-612 imperf., value, set $14.00.

Camomile A137

Woman Diver A138

Medicinal plants.

1962, May 10
613	A137	50q shown	.20	.15
614	A137	8 l Linden	.75	.25
615	A137	11.50 l Garden sage	1.75	.50
		Nos. 613-615 (3)	2.70	.90

Value, imperf. set $12.

1962, May 31   *Perf. 14*

2.50 l, Pole vault. 3 l, Mt. Fuji & torch, horiz. 9 l, Woman javelin thrower. 10 l, Shot putting.

616	A138	50q brt grnsh bl & blk	.15	.15
617	A138	2.50 l gldn brn & sepia	.20	.15
618	A138	3 l blue & gray	.40	.15
619	A138	5 l rose car & dk brn	1.10	.45
620	A138	10 l olive & blk	1.25	.30
		Nos. 616-620 (5)	3.10	1.00

1964 Olympic Games, Tokyo. Value, imperf. set $25. A 15 l (like 3 l) exists in souv. sheet, perf. and imperf.

Globe and Orbits — A139

Dog Laika and Sputnik 2 — A140

Designs: 1.50 l, Rocket to the sun. 20 l, Lunik 3 photographing far side of the moon.

1962, June   *Unwmk.*   *Perf. 14*
621	A139	50q violet & org	.20	.15
622	A140	1 l blue grn & brn	.35	.15
623	A140	1.50 l yellow & ver	.50	.15
624	A139	20 l magenta & bl	3.50	.80
		Nos. 621-624 (4)	4.55	1.25

Russian space explorations.
#621-624 exist imperforate in changed colors.
Two miniature sheets exist, containing one 14-lek picturing Sputnik 1. The perforated 14-lek is yellow and brown; the imperf. red and brown.

Soccer Game, Map of South America — A141

2.50 l, 15 l, Soccer game and globe as ball.

1962, July   *Litho.*
625	A141	1 l org & dk pur	.15	.15
626	A141	2.50 l emer & bluish grn	.25	.15
627	A141	6.50 l lt brn & pink	.90	.15
628	A141	15 l bluish grn & mar	1.50	.35
		Nos. 625-628 (4)	2.80	.80

Issued to commemorate the World Soccer Championships, Chile, May 30-June 17.
Exist imperforate in changed colors.
Two miniature sheets exist, each containing a single 20-lek in design similar to A141. The perf. sheet is brown and green; the imperf., brown and orange.

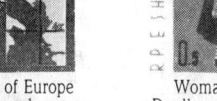

Map of Europe and Albania — A142

Woman of Dardhe — A143

Designs: 1 l, 2.50 l, Map of Adriatic Sea and Albania and Roman statue.

1962, Aug.
630	A142	50q multicolored	.40	.35
631	A142	1 l ultra & red	1.00	.80
632	A142	2.50 l blue & red	3.00	2.50
633	A142	11 l multicolored	6.00	5.00
		Nos. 630-633 (4)	10.40	8.65

Tourist propaganda. Imperforates in changed colors exist.
Miniature sheets containing a 7 l and 8 l stamp, perf. and imperf., exist.

1962, Sept.

Regional Costumes: 1 l, Man from Devoll. 2.50 l, Woman from Lunxheri. 14 l, Man from Gjirokaster.

635	A143	50q car, bl & pur	.15	.15
636	A143	1 l red brn & ocher	.35	.15
637	A143	2.50 l vio, yel grn & blk	.65	.15
638	A143	14 l red brn & pale grn	2.25	.50
		Nos. 635-638 (4)	3.20	.95

Value, imperf. set $18.

Chamois A144

Ismail Qemali A145

Animals: 1 l, Lynx, horiz. 1.50 l, Wild boar, horiz. 15 l, 20 l, Roe deer.

1962, Oct. 24   *Unwmk.*   *Perf. 14*
639	A144	50q sl grn & dk pur	.60	.15
640	A144	1 l orange & blk	1.10	.15
641	A144	1.50 l red brn & blk	1.50	.15
642	A144	15 l yel ol & red brn	7.75	1.00
		Nos. 639-642 (4)	10.95	1.45

Miniature Sheet

643	A144	20 l yel ol & red brn	15.00	15.00

Imperfs. in changed colors, value #639-642 $25, #643 $25.

1962, Dec. 28   *Litho.*

Designs: 1 l, Albania eagle. 16 l, Eagle over fortress formed by "RPSH."

644	A145	1 l red & red brn	.30	.15
645	A145	3 l org brn & blk	.55	.15
646	A145	16 l dk car rose & blk	3.50	.50
		Nos. 644-646 (3)	4.35	.80

50th anniv. of independence. Imperfs. in changed colors, value, set $12.50.

Monument of October Revolution A146

Henri Dunant, Cross, Globe and Nurse A147

1963, Jan. 5   *Unwmk.*   *Perf. 14*
647	A146	5 l shown	.50	.15
648	A146	10 l Lenin statue	1.25	.25

October Revolution (Russia, 1917), 45th anniv.

1963, Jan 25   *Unwmk.*   *Perf. 14*
649	A147	1.50 l rose lake, red & blk	.25	.15
650	A147	2.50 l lt bl, red & blk	.30	.15
651	A147	6 l emerald, red & blk	.75	.25
652	A147	10 l dull yel, red & blk	1.40	.35
		Nos. 649-652 (4)	2.70	.90

Cent. of the Geneva Conf., which led to the establishment of the Intl. Red Cross in 1864.
Imperfs. in changed colors, value, set $20.

Stalin and Battle of Stalingrad A148

Andrian G. Nikolayev A149

1963, Feb. 2
653	A148	8 l dk green & slate	4.00	.50

Battle of Stalingrad, 20th anniv. See #C67.

1963, Feb. 28   *Litho.*

Designs: 7.50 l, Vostoks 3 and 4 and globe, horiz. 20 l, Pavel R. Popovich. 25 l, Nikolayev, Popovich and globe with trajectories.

654	A149	2.50 l vio bl & sepia	.40	.15
655	A149	7.50 l lt blue & blk	.75	.15
656	A149	20 l violet & sepia	2.25	.70
		Nos. 654-656 (3)	3.40	1.00

Miniature Sheet

657	A149	25 l vio bl & sepia	12.00	12.00

1st group space flight of Vostoks 3 and 4, Aug. 11-15, 1962. Imperfs. in changed colors, value #654-656 $12, #657 $12.

"Albania" Decorating Police Officer — A150

Polyphylla Fullo — A151

1963, Mar. 20   *Unwmk.*   *Perf. 14*
658	A150	2.50 l crim, mag & blk	.40	.15
659	A150	7.50 l org ver, dk red & blk	1.40	.25

20th anniversary of the security police.

1963, Mar. 20

Beetles: 1.50 l, Lucanus cervus. 8 l, Procerus gigas. 10 l, Cicindela Albanica.

660	A151	50q ol grn & brn	.25	.15
661	A151	1.50 l blue & brn	.55	.15
662	A151	8 l dl rose & blk vio	2.75	1.10
663	A151	10 l brt citron & blk	3.00	1.25
		Nos. 660-663 (4)	6.55	2.65

1913 Stamp and Postmark — A152

Design: 10 l, Stamps of 1913, 1937 and 1962.

1963, May 5
664	A152	5 l yel, buff, bl & blk	.70	.25
665	A152	10 l car rose, grn & blk	1.40	.45

50th anniversary of Albanian stamps.

Boxer — A153

Crested Grebe — A154

ALBANIA

Designs: 3 l, Basketball baskets. 5 l, Volleyball. 6 l, Bicyclists. 9 l, Gymnast. 15 l, Hands holding torch, and map of Japan.

1963, May 25 — Perf. 13½
666	A153	2 l yel, blk & red brn	.25	.15
667	A153	3 l ocher, brn & bl	.35	.15
668	A153	5 l gray bl, red brn & brn	.60	.15
669	A153	6 l gray, dk gray & grn	.80	.25
670	A153	9 l rose, red brn & bl	1.50	.30
		Nos. 666-670 (5)	3.50	1.00

Miniature Sheet
671	A153	15 l lt bl, car, blk & brn	9.00	9.00

1964 Olympic Games in Tokyo. Value, imperfs. #666-670 $7.50, #671 $8.

1963, Apr. 20 — Litho. — Perf. 14
Birds: 3 l, Golden eagle. 6.50 l, Gray partridges. 11 l, Capercaillie.

672	A154	50q multicolored	.20	.15
673	A154	3 l multicolored	1.10	.25
674	A154	6.50 l multicolored	2.50	.55
675	A154	11 l multicolored	4.00	.85
		Nos. 672-675 (4)	7.80	1.80

Soldier and Building — A155

2.50 l, Soldier with pack, ship, plane. 5 l, Soldier in battle. 6 l, Soldier, bulldozer.

1963, July 10 — Unwmk. — Perf. 12
676	A155	1.50 l brick red, yel & blk	.30	.15
677	A155	2.50 l bl, ocher & brn	.40	.15
678	A155	5 l bluish grn, gray & blk	.90	.15
679	A155	6 l red brn, buff & bl	1.25	.25
		Nos. 676-679 (4)	2.85	.70

Albanian army, 20th anniversary.

Maj. Yuri A. Gagarin A156

Designs: 5 l, Maj. Gherman Titov. 7 l, Maj. Andrian G. Nikolayev. 11 l, Lt. Col. Pavel R. Popovich. 14 l, Lt. Col. Valeri Bykovski. 20 l, Lt. Valentina Tereshkova.

1963, July 30
Portraits in Yellow and Black
680	A156	3 l brt purple	.45	.15
681	A156	5 l dull blue	.65	.15
682	A156	6 l gray	.90	.15
683	A156	11 l deep claret	1.50	.35
684	A156	14 l blue green	2.25	.55
685	A156	20 l ultra	3.25	1.00
		Nos. 680-685 (6)	9.00	2.35

Man's conquest of space. Value, imperf. set $18.

Volleyball — A157

1963, Aug. 31 — Perf. 12x12½
686	A157	2 l shown	.15	.15
687	A157	3 l Weight lifting	.35	.15
688	A157	5 l Soccer	.65	.15
689	A157	7 l Boxing	.80	.25
690	A157	8 l Rowing	1.50	.30
		Nos. 686-690 (5)	3.45	1.00

European championships. Imperfs. in changed colors, value set $16.

Papilio Podalirius A158

1963, Sept. 29 — Litho.
Various Butterflies and Moths in Natural Colors
691	A158	1 l red	.15	.15
692	A158	2 l blue	.30	.15
693	A158	4 l dull lilac	.50	.25
694	A158	5 l pale green	.90	.40
695	A158	8 l bister	1.10	.55
696	A158	10 l light blue	1.65	.70
		Nos. 691-696 (6)	4.60	2.20

Oil Refinery, Cerrik — A159

Flag and Shield — A160

2.50 l, Food processing plant, Tirana, horiz. 30 l, Fruit canning plant. 50 l, Tannery, horiz.

1963, Nov. 15 — Unwmk. — Perf. 14
697	A159	2.50 l rose red, pnksh	.40	.15
698	A159	20 l slate grn, grnsh	1.40	.20
699	A159	30 l dull pur, grysh	3.25	.50
700	A159	50 l ocher, yel	3.50	.75
		Nos. 697-700 (4)	8.55	1.60

Industrial development in Albania.

1963, Nov. 24 — Perf. 12½x12
701	A160	2 l grnsh bl, blk, ocher & red	.35	.15
702	A160	8 l blue, blk, ocher & red	1.00	.50

1st Congress of Army Aid Assn.

Chinese, Caucasian and Negro Men — A161

1963, Dec. 10 — Perf. 12x11½
703	A161	3 l bister & blk	.50	.15
704	A161	5 l bister & ultra	.95	.20
705	A161	7 l bister & vio	1.50	.30
		Nos. 703-705 (3)	2.95	.65

15th anniv. of the Universal Declaration of Human Rights.

Slalom Ascent — A162

Lenin — A163

Designs: 50q, Bobsled, horiz. 6.50 l, Ice hockey, horiz. 12.50 l, Women's figure skating. No. 709A, Ski jumper.

1963, Dec. 25 — Perf. 14
706	A162	50q grnsh bl & blk	.15	.15
707	A162	2.50 l red, gray & blk	.30	.15
708	A162	6.50 l yel, blk & gray	.75	.20
709	A162	12.50 l red, blk & yel grn	1.75	.50
		Nos. 706-709 (4)	2.95	1.00

Miniature Sheet
709A	A162	12.50 l multi	4.25	4.25

9th Winter Olympic Games, Innsbruck, Jan. 29-Feb. 9, 1964. Imperfs. in changed colors, value #706-709 $25, #709A $30.

1964, Jan. 21 — Perf. 12½x12
710	A163	5 l gray & bister	.35	.15
711	A163	10 l gray & ocher	.65	.30

40th anniversary, death of Lenin.

Hurdling A164

Fish A165

Designs: 3 l, Track, horiz. 6.50 l, Rifle shooting, horiz. 8 l, Basketball.

Perf. 12½x12, 12x12½
1964, Jan. 30 — Litho.
712	A164	2.50 l pale vio & ultra	.30	.15
713	A164	3 l lt grn & red brn	.45	.15
714	A164	6.50 l blue & claret	.90	.20
715	A164	8 l lt blue & ocher	1.25	.20
		Nos. 712-715 (4)	2.90	.70

1st Games of the New Emerging Forces, GANEFO, Jakarta, Indonesia, Nov. 10-22, 1963.

1964, Feb. 26 — Unwmk. — Perf. 14
716	A165	50q Sturgeon	.15	.15
717	A165	1 l Gilthead	.15	.15
718	A165	1.50 l Striped mullet	.40	.15
719	A165	2.50 l Carp	.15	.15
720	A165	6.50 l Mackerel	1.65	.40
721	A165	10 l Lake Ohrid trout	3.00	.50
		Nos. 716-721 (6)	5.95	1.50

Wild Animals A166

1964, Mar. 28 — Perf. 12½x12
722	A166	1 l Red Squirrel	.15	.15
723	A166	1.50 l Beech marten	.15	.15
724	A166	2 l Red fox	.50	.15
725	A166	2.50 l Hedgehog	.55	.15
726	A166	3 l Hare	.65	.15
727	A166	5 l Jackal	1.10	.25
728	A166	7 l Wildcat	1.65	.35
729	A166	8 l Wolf	2.00	.50
		Nos. 722-729 (8)	6.75	1.85

Lighting Olympic Torch — A167

Designs: 5 l, Torch and globes. 7 l, 15 l, Olympic flag and Mt. Fuji. 10 l, National Stadium, Tokyo.

1964, May 18 — Perf. 12x12½
730	A167	3 l lt yel grn, yel & buff	.25	.15
731	A167	5 l red & vio blue	.35	.15
732	A167	7 l lt bl, ultra & yel	.55	.20
733	A167	10 l orange, bl & vio	.75	.25
		Nos. 730-733 (4)	1.90	.75

Miniature Sheet
734	A167	15 l lt bl, ultra & org	12.50	12.50

18th Olympic Games, Tokyo, Oct. 10-25, 1964. No. 734 contains one 49x62mm stamp. Imperfs. in changed colors, value #730-733 $11, #734 $14. See No. 745.

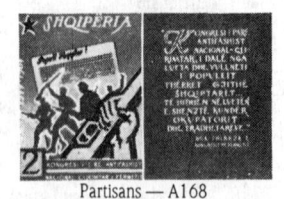

Partisans — A168

Perf. 12½x12
1964, May 24 — Unwmk.
735	A168	2 l orange, red & blk	.50	.15
736	A168	5 l multicolored	1.25	.15
737	A168	8 l red brn, blk & red	2.50	.20
		Nos. 735-737 (3)	4.25	.50

20th anniv. of the Natl. Anti-Fascist Cong. of Liberation, Permet, May 24, 1944. The label attached to each stamp, without perforations between, carries a quotation from the 1944 Congress.

Albanian Flag and Revolutionists A169

Full Moon A170

Perf. 12½x12
1964, June 10 — Litho. — Unwmk.
738	A169	2 l red & gray	.15	.15
739	A169	7.50 l lilac rose & gray	.60	.20

Albanian revolution of 1924, 40th anniv.

1964, June 27 — Perf. 12x12½
Designs: 5 l, New moon. 8 l, Half moon. 11 l, Waning moon. 15 l, Far side of moon.

740	A170	1 l purple & yel	.25	.15
741	A170	5 l violet & yel	.60	.15
742	A170	8 l blue & yel	1.10	.30
743	A170	11 l green & yel	1.75	.45
		Nos. 740-743 (4)	3.70	1.05

Miniature Sheet
Perf. 12 on 2 sides
744	A170	15 l ultra & yel	12.50	12.50

No. 744 contains one stamp, size: 35x36mm, perforated at top and bottom. Imperfs. in changed colors, value #740-743 $12.50, #744 $12.50.

No. 733 with Added Inscription: "Rimini 25-VI-64"

1964 — Perf. 12x12½
745	A167	10 l orange, bl & vio	3.50	3.00

"Toward Tokyo 1964" Phil. Exhib. at Rimini, Italy, June 25-July 6.

Wren — A171

Birds: 1 l, Penduline titmouse. 2.50 l, Green woodpecker. 3 l, Tree creeper. 4 l, Nuthatch. 5 l, Great titmouse. 6 l, Goldfinch. 18 l, Oriole.

1964, July 31 — Perf. 12x12½
746	A171	50q multi	.15	.15
747	A171	1 l orange & multi	.15	.15
748	A171	2.50 l multi	.25	.15
749	A171	3 l blue & multi	.35	.15
750	A171	4 l yellow & multi	.45	.15
751	A171	5 l blue & multi	.55	.15
752	A171	6 l lt vio & multi	.80	.30
753	A171	18 l pink & multi	2.25	.85
		Nos. 746-753 (8)	4.95	2.05

Running and Gymnastics A172

Sport: 2 l, Weight lifting, judo. 3 l, Equestrian, bicycling. 4 l, Soccer, water polo. 5 l, Wrestling, boxing. 6 l, Pentathlon, hockey. 7 l, Swimming, sailing. 8 l, Basketball, volleyball. 9 l, Rowing, canoeing. 10 l, Fencing, pistol shooting. 20 l, Three winners.

Perf. 12x12½
1964, Sept. 25 — Litho. — Unwmk.
754	A172	1 l lt bl, rose & multi	.15	.15
755	A172	2 l bis brn, bluish grn & vio	.15	.15
756	A172	3 l vio, red org & ol bis	.20	.15
757	A172	4 l grnsh bl, ol & ultra	.20	.15
758	A172	5 l grnsh bl, car & pale lil	.30	.15
759	A172	6 l dk bl, org & lt bl	.35	.15
760	A172	7 l dk bl, lt ol & org	.35	.15

ALBANIA

761	A172	8 l emerald, gray & yel	.50	.20
762	A172	9 l bl, yel & lil rose	.65	.30
763	A172	10 l brt grn, org brn & yel grn	1.65	.50
		Nos. 754-763 (10)	4.50	2.05

Miniature Sheet
Perf. 12

| 764 | A172 | 20 l violet & lemon | 10.00 | 5.00 |

18th Olympic Games, Tokyo, Oct. 10-25. No. 764 contains one stamp, size: 41x68mm. Imperfs. in changed colors, value #754-763 $12.50, #764 $12.50.

Arms of People's Republic of China — A173

Mao Tse-tung and Flag A174

1964, Oct. 1 *Perf. 11½x12, 12x11½*

| 765 | A173 | 7 l black, red & yellow | 2.00 | .30 |
| 766 | A174 | 8 l black, red & yellow | 3.00 | .40 |

People's Republic of China, 15th anniv.

Karl Marx A175

Jeronim de Rada A176

Designs: 5 l, St. Martin's Hall, London. 8 l, Friedrich Engels.

1964, Nov. 5 *Perf. 12x11½*

767	A175	2 l red, lt vio & blk	.55	.15
768	A175	5 l gray blk	1.10	.20
769	A175	8 l ocher, blk & red	2.25	.30
		Nos. 767-769 (3)	3.90	.65

Centenary of First Socialist International.

1964, Nov. 15 *Perf. 12½x11½*

| 770 | A176 | 7 l slate green | 1.10 | .30 |
| 771 | A176 | 8 l dull violet | 1.65 | .35 |

Birth of Jeronim de Rada, poet, 150th anniv.

Arms of Albania — A177

Factories A178

Designs: 3 l, Combine harvester. 4 l, Woman chemist. 10 l, Hands holding Constitution, hammer and sickle.

Perf. 11½x12, 12x11½

1964, Nov. 29

772	A177	1 l multicolored	.35	.15
773	A178	2 l red, yel & vio bl	.45	.15
774	A177	3 l red, yel & brn	.85	.15
775	A178	4 l red, yel & gray grn	1.00	.15
776	A177	10 l red, bl & blk	1.65	.45
		Nos. 772-776 (5)	4.30	1.05

20th anniversary of liberation.

Planet Mercury — A179

Planets: 2 l, Venus and rocket. 3 l, Earth, moon and rocket. 4 l, Mars and rocket. 5 l, Jupiter. 6 l, Saturn. 7 l, Uranus. 8 l, Neptune. 9 l, Pluto. 15 l, Solar system and rocket.

1964, Dec. 15 *Perf. 12x12½*

777	A179	1 l yellow & pur	.15	.15
778	A179	2 l multicolored	.15	.15
779	A179	3 l multicolored	.20	.15
780	A179	4 l multicolored	.25	.15
781	A179	5 l yel, dk pur & brn	.45	.15
782	A179	6 l lt grn, vio brn & yel	.60	.15
783	A179	7 l yellow & grn	.70	.20
784	A179	8 l yellow & vio	.85	.25
785	A179	9 l lt grn, yel & blk	1.25	.35
		Nos. 777-785 (9)	4.60	1.70

Miniature Sheet
Perf. 12 on 2 sides

| 786 | A179 | 15 l car, bl, yel & grn | 17.50 | 17.50 |

No. 786 contains one stamp, size: 62x51mm, perforated at top and bottom. Imperfs. in changed colors. Value #777-785, $15; #786, $17.50.

European Chestnut A180

Symbols of Industry A181

1965, Jan. 25 *Perf. 11½x12*

787	A180	1 l shown	.15	.15
788	A180	2 l Medlars	.25	.15
789	A180	3 l Persimmon	.50	.15
790	A180	4 l Pomegranate	.55	.15
791	A180	5 l Quince	.80	.20
792	A180	10 l Orange	1.65	.35
		Nos. 787-792 (6)	3.90	1.15

1965, Feb. 20

Designs: 5 l, Books, triangle and compass. 8 l, Beach, trees and hotel.

793	A181	2 l blk, car rose & pink	1.75	.40
794	A181	5 l yel, gray & blk	3.50	.85
795	A181	8 l blk, vio bl & lt bl	5.75	1.60
		Nos. 793-795 (3)	11.00	2.85

Professional trade associations, 20th anniv.

Water Buffalo A182

Various designs: Water buffalo.

1965, Mar. *Perf. 12x11½*

796	A182	1 l lt yel grn, yel & brn blk	.35	.15
797	A182	2 l lt bl, dk gray & blk	.85	.15
798	A182	3 l yellow, brn & grn	1.10	.15
799	A182	7 l brt grn, yel & brn blk	2.75	.35
800	A182	12 l pale lil, dk brn & ind	4.00	.65
		Nos. 796-800 (5)	9.05	1.45

Mountain View, Valbona — A183

1.50 l, Seashore. 3 l, Glacier and peak. 4 l, Gorge. 5 l, Mountain peaks. 9 l, Lake and hills.

1965, Mar. Litho. *Perf. 12*

801	A183	1.50 l multi	1.40	.15
802	A183	2.50 l multi	1.75	.20
803	A183	3 l multi, vert.	2.75	.25
804	A183	4 l multi, vert.	3.00	.40
805	A183	5 l multi	5.00	.50
806	A183	9 l multi	8.00	.75
		Nos. 801-806 (6)	21.90	2.25

Frontier Guard — A184

Small-bore Rifle Shooting, Prone — A185

1965, Apr. 25 Unwmk.

| 807 | A184 | 2.50 l lt blue & multi | .85 | .15 |
| 808 | A184 | 12.50 l lt ultra & multi | 3.50 | .90 |

20th anniversary of the Frontier Guards.

1965, May 10

Designs: 2 l, Rifle shooting, standing. 3 l, Target over map of Europe, showing Bucharest. 4 l, Pistol shooting. 15 l, Rifle shooting, kneeling.

809	A185	1 l lil, car rose, blk & brn	.15	.15
810	A185	2 l bl, blk, brn & vio bl	.35	.15
811	A185	3 l pink & car rose	.45	.15
812	A185	4 l bis, blk & vio brn	.60	.15
813	A185	15 l brt grn, brn & vio brn	2.25	.50
		Nos. 809-813 (5)	3.80	1.10

European Shooting Championships, Bucharest.

ITU Emblem, Old and New Communications Equipment — A186

Col. Pavel Belyayev — A187

1965, May 17 *Perf. 12½x12*

| 814 | A186 | 2.50 l brt grn, blk & lil rose | .50 | .15 |
| 815 | A186 | 12.50 l vio, blk & brt bl | 3.25 | .30 |

Centenary of the ITU.

1965, June 15 *Perf. 12*

Designs: 2 l, Voskhod II. 6.50 l, Lt. Col. Alexei Leonov. 20 l, Leonov floating in space.

816	A187	1.50 l lt blue & brn	.15	.15
817	A187	2 l dk bl, lt vio & lt ultra	.20	.15
818	A187	5 l lilac & brn	.70	.15
819	A187	20 l chlky bl, yel & blk	1.90	.35
		Nos. 816-819 (4)	2.95	.80

Miniature Sheet
Perf. 12 on 2 sides

| 820 | A187 | 20 l brt bl, org & blk | 6.00 | 6.00 |

Space flight of Voskhod II and 1st man walking in space, Lt. Col. Alexei Leonov. No. 820 contains one stamp, size: 51x59½mm, perforated at top and bottom. Imperf., brt grn background, value $6.

Marx and Lenin — A188

Mother and Child — A189

1965, June 21 *Perf. 12*

| 821 | A188 | 2.50 l dk brn, red & yel | .85 | .15 |
| 822 | A188 | 7.50 l sl grn, org ver & buff | 2.25 | .25 |

6th Conf. of Postal Ministers of Communist Countries, Peking, June 21-July 15.

Perf. 12½x12, 12x12½

1965, June 29 Litho. Unwmk.

Designs: 2 l, Pioneers. 3 l, Boy and girl at play, horiz. 4 l, Child on beach. 15 l, Girl with book.

823	A189	1 l brt bl, rose lil & blk	.15	.15
824	A189	2 l salmon, vio & blk	.35	.15
825	A189	3 l green, org & vio	.50	.15
826	A189	4 l multicolored	.70	.15
827	A189	15 l lil rose, brn & ocher	2.25	.40
		Nos. 823-827 (5)	3.95	1.00

Issued for International Children's Day.

Statue of Magistrate A190

Flowers A191

Designs: 1 l, Amphora. 2 l, Illyrian armor. 3 l, Mosaic, horiz. 15 l, Torso, Apollo statue.

1965, July 20 *Perf. 12*

828	A190	1 l ol, org & brn	.15	.15
829	A190	2 l gray grn, grn & brn	.25	.15
830	A190	3 l tan, brn, car & lil	.50	.15
831	A190	4 l green, bis & brn	.70	.20
832	A190	15 l gray & pale claret	1.75	.65
		Nos. 828-832 (5)	3.35	1.30

1965, Aug. 11 *Perf. 12½x12*

833	A191	1 l Fuchsia	.15	.15
834	A191	2 l Cyclamen	.30	.15
835	A191	3 l Tiger lily	.50	.15
836	A191	3.50 l Iris	.60	.15
837	A191	4 l Dahlia	.70	.15
838	A191	4.50 l Hydrangea	.80	.15
839	A191	5 l Rose	1.00	.20
840	A191	7 l Tulips	1.90	.30
		Nos. 833-840 (8)	5.95	1.40

Nos. 698-700 Surcharged New Value and Two Bars

1965, Aug. 16 *Perf. 14*

841	A159	5q on 30 l	.15	.15
842	A159	15q on 30 l	.30	.15
843	A159	25q on 50 l	.45	.15
844	A159	80q on 50 l	.90	.20
845	A159	1.10 l on 20 l	1.50	.30
846	A159	2 l on 20 l	2.75	.60
		Nos. 841-846 (6)	6.05	1.55

White Stork — A192

"Homecoming," by Bukurosh Sejdini — A193

Migratory Birds: 20q, Cuckoo. 30q, Hoopoe. 40q, European bee-eater. 50q, European nightjar. 1.50 l, Quail.

1965, Aug. 31 *Perf. 12*

847	A192	10q yellow, blk & gray	.20	.15
848	A192	20q brt pink, blk & dk bl	.35	.15
849	A192	30q violet, blk & bis	.65	.15
850	A192	40q emer, blk, yel & gray	1.40	.15
851	A192	50q ultra, brn & red brn	1.65	.25
852	A192	1.50 l bis, red brn & dp org	4.50	.75
		Nos. 847-852 (6)	8.75	1.60

1965, Sept. 26 Litho. *Perf. 12x12½*

853	A193	25q olive black	1.75	.15
854	A193	65q blue black	4.25	.35
855	A193	1.10 l black	6.50	.60
		Nos. 853-855 (3)	12.50	1.10

Second war veterans' meeting.

Hunting — A194

Oleander — A195

1965, Oct. 6 Litho. Unwmk.

856	A194	10q Capercaillie	.25	.15
857	A194	20q Deer	.40	.15
858	A194	30q Pheasant	.70	.20
859	A194	40q Mallards	1.10	.20
860	A194	50q Boar	1.25	.25
861	A194	1 l Rabbit	3.75	.55
		Nos. 856-861 (6)	7.45	1.50

1965, Oct. 26 *Perf. 12½x12*

Flowers: 20q, Forget-me-nots. 30q, Pink. 40q, White water lily. 50q, Bird's foot. 1 l, Corn poppy.

862	A195	10q brt bl, grn & car rose	.20	.15
863	A195	20q org red, bl, brn & grn	.40	.15
864	A195	30q vio, car rose & grn	.60	.15
865	A195	40q emerald, yel & blk	.80	.20
866	A195	50q org brn, yel & grn	1.00	.20
867	A195	1 l yel grn, blk & rose red	2.00	.70
		Nos. 862-867 (6)	5.00	1.55

Hotel Turizmi, Fier — A196

Freighter "Teuta" — A197

Buildings: 10q, Hotel, Peshkopi. 15q, Sanatorium, Tirana. 25q, Rest home, Pogradec. 65q, Partisan Sports Arena, Tirana. 80q, Rest home, Mali Dajt. 1.10 l, Culture House, Tirana. 1.60 l, Hotel Adriatik, Durres. 2 l, Migjeni Theater, Shkoder. 3 l, Alexander Moissi House of Culture, Durres.

1965, Oct. *Perf. 12x12½*

868	A196	5q blue & blk	.15	.15
869	A196	10q ocher & blk	.15	.15
870	A196	15q dull grn & blk	.15	.15
871	A196	25q violet & blk	.20	.15
872	A196	65q lt brn & blk	.70	.15
873	A196	80q yel grn & blk	.90	.15
874	A196	1.10 l lilac & blk	1.25	.20
875	A196	1.60 l lt vio bl & blk	1.90	.35
876	A196	2 l dull rose & blk	2.50	.50
877	A196	3 l gray & blk	4.00	.70
		Nos. 868-877 (10)	11.90	2.65

1965, Nov. 16

Ships: 20q, Raft. 30q, Sailing ship, 19th cent. 40q, Sailing ship, 18th cent. 50q, Freighter "Vlora." 1 l, Illyric galleys.

878	A197	10q brt grn & dk grn	.15	.15
879	A197	20q ol bis & dk grn	.20	.15
880	A197	30q lt & dp ultra	.35	.15
881	A197	40q vio & dp vio	.60	.20
882	A197	50q pink & dk red	.75	.20
883	A197	1 l bister & brn	1.50	.45
		Nos. 878-883 (6)	3.55	1.30

Brown Bear — A198

Basketball and Players — A199

Various Albanian bears. 50q, 55q, 60q, horiz.

1965, Dec. 7 *Perf. 11½x12*

884	A198	10q bister & dk brn	.30	.15
885	A198	20q pale brn & dk brn	.40	.15
886	A198	30q bis, dk brn & car	.65	.15
887	A198	35q pale brn & dk brn	.80	.15
888	A198	40q bister & dk brn	1.25	.20
889	A198	50q bister & dk brn	1.50	.20
890	A198	55q bister & dk brn	1.50	.30
891	A198	60q pale brn, dk brn & car	1.65	.45
		Nos. 884-891 (8)	8.05	1.75

1965, Dec. 15 Litho. *Perf. 12½x12*

Designs: 10q, Games' emblem (map of Albania and basket). 30q, 50q, Players with ball (diff. designs). 1.40 l, Basketball medal on ribbon.

892	A199	10q blue, yel & car	.15	.15
893	A199	20q rose lil, lt brn & blk	.35	.15
894	A199	30q bis, lt brn, red & blk	.45	.15
895	A199	50q lt grn, lt brn & blk	.95	.15
896	A199	1.40 l rose, blk, brn & yel	1.75	.50
		Nos. 892-896 (5)	3.65	1.10

7th Balkan Basketball Championships, Tirana, Dec. 15-19.

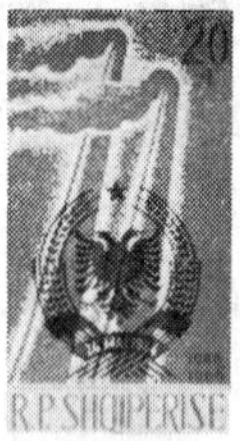

Arms of Republic and Smokestacks — A200

Designs (Arms and): 10q, Book. 30q, Wheat. 60q, Book, hammer and sickle. 80q, Factories.

1966, Jan. 11 Litho. *Perf. 11½x12*
Coat of Arms in Gold

897	A200	10q crimson & brn	.15	.15
898	A200	20q blue & vio bl	.15	.15
899	A200	30q org yel & brn	.35	.15
900	A200	60q yel grn & brt grn	.50	.20
901	A200	80q crimson & brn	1.10	.25
		Nos. 897-901 (5)	2.25	.90

Albanian People's Republic, 20th anniv.

Cow — A201

Perf. 12½x12, 12x12½
1966, Feb. 25

902	A201	10q shown	.20	.15
903	A201	20q Pig	.35	.15
904	A201	30q Ewe & lamb	.45	.15
905	A201	35q Ram	.65	.15
906	A201	40q Dog	.95	.15
907	A201	50q Cat, vert.	1.00	.15
908	A201	55q Horse, vert.	1.25	.25
909	A201	60q Ass, vert.	1.50	.30
		Nos. 902-909 (8)	6.35	1.45

Soccer Player and Map of Uruguay — A202

Andon Zako Cajupi — A203

5q, Globe in form of soccer ball. 15q, Player, map of Italy. 20q, Goalkeeper, map of France. 25q, Player, map of Brazil. 30q, Player, map of Switzerland. 35q, Player, map of Sweden. 40q, Player, map of Chile. 50q, Player, map of Great Britain. 70q, World Championship cup & ball.

1966, Mar. 20 Litho. *Perf. 12*

910	A202	5q gray & dp org	.15	.15
911	A202	10q lt brn, bl & vio	.15	.15
912	A202	15q cit, dk bl & brt bl	.15	.15
913	A202	20q org, vio bl & brt bl	.25	.15
914	A202	25q salmon & sepia	.30	.15
915	A202	30q lt yel grn & brn	.30	.15
916	A202	35q lt ultra & emer	.35	.15
917	A202	40q pink & brown	.55	.15
918	A202	50q pale grn, mag & rose red	.55	.15
919	A202	70q gray, brn, yel & blk	.70	.25
		Nos. 910-919 (10)	3.45	1.60

World Cup Soccer Championship, Wembley, England, July 11-30.

1966, Mar. 27 Unwmk.

920	A203	40q bluish blk	.50	.15
921	A203	1.10 l dark green	1.50	.15

Andon Zako Cajupi, poet, birth centenary .

Painted Lady — A204

WHO Headquarters, Geneva, and Emblem — A205

Designs: 20q, Blue dragonfly. 30q, Cloudless sulphur butterfly. 35q, 40q, Splendid dragonfly. 50q, Machaon swallow-tail. 55q, Sulphur butterfly. 60q, Whitemarbled butterfly.

1966, Apr. 21 Litho. *Perf. 11½x12*

922	A204	10q multicolored	.25	.15
923	A204	20q yellow & multi	.40	.15
924	A204	30q yellow & multi	.65	.15
925	A204	35q sky blue & multi	.80	.15
926	A204	40q multicolored	.85	.15
927	A204	50q rose & multi	1.10	.15
928	A204	55q multicolored	1.25	.15
929	A204	60q multicolored	2.00	.15
		Nos. 922-929 (8)	7.30	1.20

Perf. 12x12½, 12½x12
1966, May 3 Litho.

Designs (WHO Emblem and): 35q, Ambulance and stretcher bearers, vert. 60q, Albanian mother and nurse weighing infant, vert. 80q, X-ray machine and hospital.

930	A205	25q lt blue & blk	.30	.15
931	A205	35q salmon & ultra	.55	.15
932	A205	60q lt grn, bl & red	.90	.15
933	A205	80q yel, bl, grn & lt brn	1.25	.25
		Nos. 930-933 (4)	3.00	.70

Inauguration of the WHO Headquarters, Geneva.

Bird's Foot Starfish — A206

Designs: 25q, Starfish. 35q, Brittle star. 45q, Butthorn starfish. 50q, Starfish. 60q, Sea cucumber. 70q, Sea urchin.

1966, May 10 *Perf. 12x12½*

934	A206	15q multicolored	.25	.15
935	A206	25q multicolored	.45	.15
936	A206	35q multicolored	.65	.15
937	A206	45q multicolored	.90	.15
938	A206	50q multicolored	1.10	.20
939	A206	60q multicolored	1.25	.20
940	A206	70q multicolored	1.90	.35
		Nos. 934-940 (7)	6.50	1.35

Luna 10 — A207

30q, 80q, Trajectory of Luna 10, earth & moon.

1966, June 10 *Perf. 12x12½*

941	A207	20q blue, yel & blk	.35	.15
942	A207	30q yel grn, blk & bl	.45	.15
943	A207	70q vio, yel & blk	.90	.20
944	A207	80q yel, vio, grn & blk	1.25	.20
		Nos. 941-944 (4)	2.95	.70

Launching of the 1st artificial moon satellite, Luna 10, Apr. 3, 1966.

Jules Rimet Cup and Soccer — A208

Designs: Various scenes of soccer play.

1966, July 12 Litho. *Perf. 12x12½*
Black Inscriptions

945	A208	10q ocher & lilac	.15	.15
946	A208	20q lt blue & cit	.15	.15
947	A208	30q brick red & Prus bl	.25	.15
948	A208	35q lt ultra & rose	.30	.15
949	A208	40q yel grn & lt red brn	.35	.15
950	A208	50q lt red brn & yel grn	.60	.15
951	A208	55q rose lil & yel grn	.65	.15
952	A208	60q dp rose & ocher	1.25	.25
		Nos. 945-952 (8)	3.70	1.30

World Cup Soccer Championship, Wembley, England, July 11-30.

Water Level Map of Albania — A209

30q, Water measure & fields. 70q, Turbine & pylon. 80q, Hydrological decade emblem.

1966, July *Perf. 12½x12*

953	A209	20q brick red, blk & org	.30	.15
954	A209	30q emer, blk & lt brn	.50	.15
955	A209	70q brt violet & blk	1.10	.25
956	A209	80q brt bl, org, yel & blk	1.25	.30
		Nos. 953-956 (4)	3.15	.85

Hydrological Decade (UNESCO), 1965-74.

Greek Turtle — A210

Designs: 15q, Grass snake. 25q, European pond turtle. 30q, Wall lizard. 35q, Wall gecko. 45q, Emerald lizard. 50q, Slowworm. 90q, Horned viper (or sand viper).

1966, Aug. 10 Litho. *Perf. 12½x12*

957	A210	10q gray & multi	.15	.15
958	A210	15q yellow & multi	.20	.15
959	A210	25q ultra & multi	.30	.15
960	A210	30q multicolored	.45	.20
961	A210	35q multicolored	.60	.20
962	A210	45q multicolored	.70	.25
963	A210	50q orange & multi	.80	.30
964	A210	90q lilac & multi	1.75	.55
		Nos. 957-964 (8)	4.95	1.95

Persian Cat A211

Cats: 10q, Siamese, vert. 15q, European tabby, vert. 25q, Black kitten. 60q, 65q, 80q, Various Persians.

Perf. 12x12½, 12½x12
1966, Sept. 20 Litho.

965	A211	10q multicolored	.15	.15
966	A211	15q blk, sepia & car	.25	.15
967	A211	25q blk, dk & lt brn	.30	.15
968	A211	45q blk, org & yel	.60	.15
969	A211	60q blk, brn & yel	.75	.20
970	A211	65q multicolored	.90	.20
971	A211	80q blk, gray & yel	1.50	.30
		Nos. 965-971 (7)	4.45	1.30

Pjeter Budi, Writer — A212

ALBANIA

1966, Oct. 5   Perf. 12x12½
972	A212	25q buff & slate grn	.25 .15
973	A212	1.75 l gray & dull claret	1.75 .45

UNESCO Emblem — A213

Designs (UNESCO Emblem and): 15q, Open book, rose and school. 25q, Male folk dancers. 1.55 l, Jug, column and old building.

1966, Oct. 20   Litho.   Perf. 12
974	A213	5q lt gray & multi	.15 .15
975	A213	15q dp blue & multi	.25 .15
976	A213	25q gray & multi	.50 .15
977	A213	1.55 l multi	2.00 .50
		Nos. 974-977 (4)	2.90 .95

20th anniv. of UNESCO.

Hand Holding Book with Pictures of Marx, Engels, Lenin and Stalin — A214

Hammer and Sickle, Party Emblem in Sunburst — A215

Designs: 25q, Map of Albania, hammer and sickle, symbols of agriculture and industry. 65q, Symbolic grain and factories. 95q, Fists holding rifle, spade, axe, sickle and book.

1966, Nov. 1   Litho.   Perf. 11½x12
978	A214	15q vermilion & gold	.35 .15
979	A214	25q multicolored	.55 .15
980	A214	65q brn, brn org & gold	1.25 .15
981	A214	95q yellow & multi	1.90 .35
		Nos. 978-981 (4)	4.05 .80

Albanian Communist Party, 5th Cong.

1966, Nov. 8

Designs: 25q, Partisan and sunburst. 65q, Steel worker and blast furnace. 95q, Combine harvester, factories, and pylon.

982	A215	15q orange & multi	.30 .15
983	A215	25q red & multi	.40 .15
984	A215	65q multicolored	1.10 .15
985	A215	95q blue & multi	1.50 .35
		Nos. 982-985 (4)	3.30 .80

25th anniv. of the founding of the Albanian Workers Party.

Russian Wolfhound — A216

Dogs: 15q, Sheep dog. 25q, English setter. 45q, English springer spaniel. 60q, Bulldog. 65q, Saint Bernard. 80q, Dachshund.

1966   Litho.   Perf. 12½x12
986	A216	10q green & multi	.20 .15
987	A216	15q multicolored	.30 .15
988	A216	25q lilac & multi	.40 .15
989	A216	45q rose & multi	.75 .15
990	A216	60q brown & multi	1.00 .40
991	A216	65q ultra & multi	1.10 .45
992	A216	80q blue grn & multi	1.50 .50
		Nos. 986-992 (7)	5.25 2.15

Ndre Mjeda — A217

Proclamation — A218

1966   Perf. 12½x12
993	A217	25q brt bl & dk brn	.50 .15
994	A217	1.75 l brt grn & dk brn	2.00 .65

Birth Centenary of the priest Ndre Mjeda.

1966   Perf. 11½x12, 12x11½

Designs: 10q, Banner, man and woman holding gun and axe, horiz. 1.85 l, man with axe and banner and partisan with gun.

995	A218	5q lt brn, red & blk	.15 .15
996	A218	10q red, blk, gray & bl	.20 .15
997	A218	1.85 l red, blk & salmon	1.50 .30
		Nos. 995-997 (3)	1.85 .60

25th anniv. of the Albanian Communist Party.

Golden Eagle — A219

Birds of Prey: 15q, European sea eagle. 25q, Griffon vulture. 40q, Common sparrowhawk. 50q, Osprey. 70q, Egyptian vulture. 90q, Kestrel.

1966, Dec. 20   Litho.   Perf. 11½x12
998	A219	10q gray & multi	.20 .15
999	A219	15q multicolored	.25 .15
1000	A219	25q citron & multi	.45 .15
1001	A219	40q multicolored	.80 .20
1002	A219	50q multicolored	.95 .15
1003	A219	70q yellow & multi	1.40 .45
1004	A219	90q multicolored	1.90 .45
		Nos. 998-1004 (7)	5.95 1.70

Hake — A220

Fish: 15q, Red mullet. 25q, Opah. 40q, Atlantic wolf fish. 65q, Lumpfish. 80q, Swordfish. 1.15 l, Shorthorn sculpin.

1967, Jan.   Photo.   Perf. 12x11½   Fish in Natural Colors
1005	A220	10q blue	.15 .15
1006	A220	15q lt yellow grn	.25 .15
1007	A220	25q Prus blue	.35 .15
1008	A220	40q emerald	.85 .20
1009	A220	65q brt blue grn	.95 .25
1010	A220	80q blue	1.40 .35
1011	A220	1.15 l brt green	1.75 .60
		Nos. 1005-1011 (7)	5.70 1.85

White Pelican — A221

Designs: Various groups of pelicans.

1967, Feb. 22   Litho.   Perf. 12
1012	A221	10q pink & multi	.15 .15
1013	A221	15q pink & multi	.25 .15
1014	A221	25q pink & multi	.55 .15
1015	A221	50q pink & multi	1.00 .15
1016	A221	2 l pink & multi	3.75 .75
		Nos. 1012-1016 (5)	5.70 1.35

Camellia — A222

Flowers: 10q, Chrysanthemum. 15q, Hollyhock. 25q, Flowering Maple. 35q, Peony. 65q, Gladiolus. 80q, Freesia. 1.15 l, Carnation.

Unwmk.

1967, Apr. 12   Litho.   Perf. 12   Flowers in Natural Colors
1017	A222	5q pale brown	.15 .15
1018	A222	10q lt lilac	.15 .15
1019	A222	15q gray	.25 .15
1020	A222	25q ultra	.40 .15
1021	A222	35q lt blue	.70 .15
1022	A222	65q lt blue grn	1.00 .15
1023	A222	80q lt bluish gray	1.50 .25
1024	A222	1.15 l dull yellow	2.00 .40
		Nos. 1017-1024 (8)	6.15 1.55

A223

Rose — A224

Design: Congress emblem and power station.

1967, Apr. 24   Litho.   Perf. 12
1025	A223	25q multi	.25 .15
1026	A223	1.75 l multi	2.25 .45

Cong. of the Union of Professional Workers, Tirana, Apr. 24.

1967, May 15   Perf. 12x12½

Various Roses in Natural Colors.

1027	A224	5q blue gray	.15 .15
1028	A224	10q brt blue	.15 .15
1029	A224	15q rose violet	.20 .15
1030	A224	25q lemon	.35 .15
1031	A224	35q brt grnsh blue	.45 .15
1032	A224	65q gray	.85 .15
1033	A224	80q brown	1.10 .25
1034	A224	1.65 l gray green	2.50 .45
		Nos. 1027-1034 (8)	5.75 1.60

Seashore, Bregdet Borsh — A225

Views: 15q, Buthrotum, vert. 25q, Shore, Fshati Piqeras. 45q, Shore, Bregdet. 50q, Shore, Bregdet Himare. 65q, Ship, Sarande (Santi Quaranta). 80q, Shore, Dhermi. 1 l, Sunset, Bregdet, vert.

Perf. 12x12½, 12½x12

1967, June 10
1035	A225	15q multicolored	.20 .15
1036	A225	20q multicolored	.25 .15
1037	A225	30q multicolored	.30 .15
1038	A225	45q multicolored	.80 .15
1039	A225	50q multicolored	.90 .15
1040	A225	65q multicolored	1.25 .20
1041	A225	80q multicolored	1.40 .25
1042	A225	1 l multicolored	1.90 .35
		Nos. 1035-1042 (8)	7.00 1.55

Fawn — A226

Roe Deer: 20q, Stag, vert. 25q, Doe, vert. 30q, Young stag and doe. 35q, Doe and fawn. 40q, Young stag, vert. 65q, Stag and doe, vert. 70q, Running stag and does.

Perf. 12½x12, 12x12½

1967, July 20   Litho.
1043	A226	15q multicolored	.35 .15
1044	A226	20q multicolored	.35 .15
1045	A226	25q multicolored	.55 .15
1046	A226	30q multicolored	.65 .15
1047	A226	40q multicolored	.80 .15
1048	A226	65q multicolored	1.00 .15
1049	A226	65q multicolored	1.65 .30
1050	A226	70q multicolored	1.65 .35
		Nos. 1043-1050 (8)	7.00 1.55

Man and Woman from Madhe — A227

Regional Costumes: 20q, Woman from Zadrimes. 25q, Dancer and drummer, Kukesit. 45q, Woman spinner, Dardhes. 50q, Farm couple, Mysegese. 65q, Dancer with tambourine, Tirana. 80q, Man and woman, Dropullit. 1 l, Piper, Laberise.

1967, Aug. 25   Perf. 12
1051	A227	15q tan & multi	.15 .15
1052	A227	20q lt yellow grn	.20 .15
1053	A227	25q multicolored	.20 .15
1054	A227	45q sky blue & multi	.35 .20
1055	A227	50q lemon & multi	.55 .25
1056	A227	65q pink & multi	.60 .35
1057	A227	80q multi	.80 .40
1058	A227	1 l gray & multi	1.10 .55
		Nos. 1051-1058 (8)	3.95 2.20

Fighters and Newspaper — A228

Designs: 75q, Printing plant, newspapers and microphone. 2 l, People holding newspaper.

1967, Aug. 25   Perf. 12½x12
1059	A228	25q multicolored	.40 .15
1060	A228	75q pink & multi	.85 .15
1061	A228	2 l multicolored	2.25 .35
		Nos. 1059-1061 (3)	3.50 .65

Issued for the Day of the Press.

Street Scene, by Kolë Idromeno — A229

Hakmarrja Battalion, by Sali Shijaku — A230

Designs: 20q, David, fresco by Onufri, 16th century, vert. 45q, Woman's head, ancient mosaic, vert. 50q, Men on horseback from 16th century icon, vert. 65q, Farm Women, by Zef Shoshi. 80q, Street Scene, by Vangjush Mio. 1 l, Bride, by Kolë Idromeno, vert.

Perf. 12, 12x12½, (A230)

1967, Oct. 25   Litho.
1062	A229	15q multicolored	.40 .15
1063	A229	20q multicolored	.45 .15
1064	A230	25q multicolored	.55 .15
1065	A229	45q multicolored	1.10 .15
1066	A229	50q multicolored	1.40 .15
1067	A230	65q multicolored	1.65 .15
1068	A230	80q multicolored	1.90 .25
1069	A230	1 l multicolored	2.50 .30
		Nos. 1062-1069 (8)	9.95 1.45

ALBANIA

Lenin at Storming of Winter Palace — A231

Rabbit — A232

Designs: 15q, Lenin and Stalin, horiz. 50q, Lenin and Stalin addressing meeting. 1.10 l, Storming of the Winter Palace, horiz.

1967, Nov. 7		Perf. 12
1070 A231 15q red & multi	.25	.15
1071 A231 25q slate grn & blk	.55	.15
1072 A231 50q brn, blk & brn vio	.85	.15
1073 A231 1.10 l lilac, gray & blk	2.75	.25
Nos. 1070-1073 (4)	4.40	.70

50th anniv. of the Russian October Revolution.

1967, Nov. 25

Designs: Various hares and rabbits. The 15q, 25q, 35q, 40q and 1 l are horizontal.

1074 A232 15q orange & multi	.20	.15
1075 A232 20q brt yel & multi	.20	.15
1076 A232 25q lt brn & multi	.25	.15
1077 A232 35q multicolored	.35	.15
1078 A232 40q yellow & multi	.65	.15
1079 A232 50q pink & multi	.75	.15
1080 A232 65q multicolored	1.25	.30
1081 A232 1 l lilac & multi	2.00	.45
Nos. 1074-1081 (8)	5.65	1.65

University, Torch and Book — A233

1967	Litho.	Perf. 12
1082 A233 25q multi	.25	.15
1083 A233 1.75 l multi	1.40	.30

10th anniv. of the founding of the State University, Tirana.

Coat of Arms and Soldiers A234

Designs: 65q, Arms, Factory, grain, flag, gun and radio tower. 1.20 l, Arms and hand holding torch.

1967		Perf. 12x11½
1084 A234 15q multi	.20	.15
1085 A234 65q multi	.55	.15
1086 A234 1.20 l multi	1.00	.15
Nos. 1084-1086 (3)	1.75	.45

25th anniversary of the Democratic Front.

Turkey — A235

Designs: 20q, Duck. 25q, Hen. 45q, Rooster. 50q, Guinea fowl. 65q, Goose, horiz. 80q, Mallard, horiz. 1 l, Chicks, horiz.

Perf. 12x12½, 12½x12		
1967, Nov. 25		Photo.
1087 A235 15q gold & multi	.25	.15
1088 A235 20q gold & multi	.25	.15
1089 A235 25q gold & multi	.30	.15
1090 A235 45q gold & multi	.50	.15
1091 A235 50q gold & multi	.75	.15
1092 A235 65q gold & multi	.95	.20
1093 A235 80q gold & multi	1.75	.30
1094 A235 1 l gold & multi	2.25	.40
Nos. 1087-1094 (8)	7.00	1.65

Skanderbeg A236

Designs: 10q, Arms of Skanderbeg. 25q, Helmet and sword. 30q, Kruje Castle. 35q, Petreles Castle. 65q, Berati Castle. 80q, Skanderbeg addressing national chiefs. 90q, Battle of Albulenes.

1967, Dec. 10   Litho.   Perf. 12x12½
Medallion in Bister and Dark Brown

1095 A236 10q gold & violet	.15	.15
1096 A236 15q gold & rose car	.15	.15
1097 A236 25q gold & vio bl	.20	.15
1098 A236 30q gold & dk blue	.25	.15
1099 A236 35q gold & maroon	.35	.15
1100 A236 65q gold & green	.60	.15
1101 A236 80q gold & gray brn	.95	.15
1102 A236 90q gold & ultra	1.75	.20
Nos. 1095-1102 (8)	4.40	1.25

500th anniv. of the death of Skanderbeg (George Castriota), national hero.

Ice Hockey — A237

Designs: 15q, 2 l, Winter Olympics emblem. 30q, Women's figure skating. 50q, Slalom. 80q, Downhill skiing. 1 l, Ski jump.

1967-68

1103 A237 15q multicolored	.15	.15
1104 A237 25q multicolored	.15	.15
1105 A237 30q multicolored	.15	.15
1106 A237 50q multicolored	.30	.15
1107 A237 80q multicolored	.60	.20
1108 A237 1 l multicolored	.85	.25
Nos. 1103-1108 (6)	2.20	1.05

Miniature Sheet
Imperf

1109 A237 2 l red, gray & brt bl ('68)	6.00	6.00

10th Winter Olympic Games, Grenoble, France, Feb. 6-18.
Nos. 1103-1108 issued Dec. 29, 1967.

Skanderbeg Monument, Kruje — A238

Designs: 10q, Skanderbeg monument, Tirana. 15q, Skanderbeg portrait, Uffizi Galleries, Florence. 25q, engraved portrait of Gen. Tanush Topia. 35q, Portrait of Gen. Gjergj Arianti, horiz. 65q, Portrait bust of Skanderbeg by O. Paskali. 80q, Title page of "The Life of Skanderbeg." 90q, Skanderbeg battling the Turks, painting by S. Rrota, horiz.

Perf. 12x12½, 12½x12
1968, Jan. 17   Litho.

1110 A238 10q multicolored	.15	.15
1111 A238 15q multicolored	.25	.15
1112 A238 25q blk, yel & lt bl	.35	.15
1113 A238 30q multicolored	.40	.15
1114 A238 35q lt vio, pink & blk	.65	.15
1115 A238 65q multicolored	1.00	.15
1116 A238 80q pink, blk & yel	1.25	.20
1117 A238 90q beige & multi	1.75	.25
Nos. 1110-1117 (8)	5.80	1.35

500th anniv. of the death of Skanderbeg (George Castriota), national hero.

Carnation A239

1968, Feb. 15   Perf. 12
Various Carnations in Natural Colors

1118 A239 15q green	.15	.15
1119 A239 20q dk brown	.15	.15
1120 A239 25q brt blue	.15	.15
1121 A239 50q gray olive	.30	.15
1122 A239 80q bluish gray	.75	.15
1123 A239 1.10 l violet gray	1.00	.25
Nos. 1118-1123 (6)	2.50	1.00

"Electrification" A240

65q, Farm tractor, horiz. 1.10 l, Cow & herd.

1968, Mar. 5   Litho.   Perf. 12

1124 A240 25q multi	.25	.15
1125 A240 65q multi	.70	.15
1126 A240 1.10 l multi	1.00	.20
Nos. 1124-1126 (3)	1.95	.50

Fifth Farm Cooperatives Congress.

Goat A241

Various goats. 15q, 20q, 25q are vertical.

Perf. 12x12½, 12½x12
1968, Mar. 25

1127 A241 15q multi	.15	.15
1128 A241 20q multi	.15	.15
1129 A241 25q multi	.20	.15
1130 A241 30q multi	.30	.15
1131 A241 40q multi	.40	.15
1132 A241 50q multi	.45	.15
1133 A241 80q multi	.80	.20
1134 A241 1.40 l multi	2.00	.35
Nos. 1127-1134 (8)	4.45	1.45

Zef N. Jubani — A242

Physician and Hospital — A243

1968, Mar. 30   Perf. 12

1135 A242 25q yellow & choc	.25	.15
1136 A242 1.75 l lt violet & blk	1.10	.30

Sesquicentennial of the birth of Zef N. Jubani, writer and scholar.

Perf. 12½x12, 12x12½
1968, Apr. 7   Litho.

Designs (World Health Organization Emblem and): 65q, Hospital and microscope, horiz. 1.10 l, Mother feeding child.

1137 A243 25q green & claret	.15	.15
1138 A243 65q black, yel & bl	.55	.15
1139 A243 1.10 l black & dp org	.80	.20
Nos. 1137-1139 (3)	1.50	.50

20th anniv. of WHO.

Scientist A244

Women: 15q, Militia member. 60q, Farm worker. 1 l, Factory worker.

1968, Apr. 14   Perf. 12

1140 A244 15q ver & dk red	.35	.15
1141 A244 25q blue grn & grn	.50	.15
1142 A244 60q dull yel & brn	.80	.15
1143 A244 1 l lt vio & vio	2.00	.30
Nos. 1140-1143 (4)	3.65	.75

Albanian Women's Organization, 25th anniv.

Karl Marx — A245

Designs: 25q, Marx lecturing to students. 65q, "Das Kapital," "Communist Manifesto" and marching crowd. 95q, Full-face portrait.

1968, May 5   Litho.   Perf. 12

1144 A245 15q gray, dk bl & bis	.25	.15
1145 A245 25q brn vio, dk brn & dl yel	.50	.15
1146 A245 65q gray, blk, brn & car	1.25	.20
1147 A245 95q gray, ocher & blk	2.00	.35
Nos. 1144-1147 (4)	4.00	.85

Karl Marx, 150th birth anniversary.

Heliopsis — A246

Flowers: 20q, Red flax. 25q, Orchid. 30q, Gloxinia. 40q, Turk's-cap lily. 80q, Amaryllis. 1.40 l, Red magnolia.

1968, May 10   Perf. 12x12½

1148 A246 15q gold & multi	.15	.15
1149 A246 20q gold & multi	.15	.15
1150 A246 25q gold & multi	.15	.15
1151 A246 30q gold & multi	.15	.15
1152 A246 40q gold & multi	.45	.15
1153 A246 80q gold & multi	.55	.15
1154 A246 1.40 l gold & multi	.85	.30
Nos. 1148-1154 (7)	2.45	1.20

Proclamation of Prizren A247

25q, Abdyl Frasheri. 40q, House in Prizren.

1968, June 10   Litho.   Perf. 12

1155 A247 25q emerald & blk	.20	.15
1156 A247 40q multicolored	.45	.15
1157 A247 85q yellow & multi	.85	.25
Nos. 1155-1157 (3)	1.50	.55

League of Prizren against the Turks, 90th anniv.

ALBANIA

Shepherd, by A. Kushi — A248

Paintings from Tirana Art Gallery: 20q, View of Tirana, by V. Mio, horiz. 25q, Mountaineer, by G. Madhi. 40q, Refugees, by A. Buza. 80q, Guerrillas of Shahin Matrakut, by S. Xega. 1.50 l, Portrait of an Old Man, by S. Papadhimitri. 1.70 l, View of Scutari, by S. Rrota. 2.50 l, Woman in Scutari Costume, by Z. Colombi.

1968, June 20   Perf. 12x12½
1158	A248	15q gold & multi	.15	.15
1159	A248	20q gold & multi	.20	.15
1160	A248	25q gold & multi	.25	.15
1161	A248	40q gold & multi	.45	.15
1162	A248	80q gold & multi	.75	.15
1163	A248	1.50 l gold & multi	1.25	.25
1164	A248	1.70 l gold & multi	1.50	.50
		Nos. 1158-1164 (7)	4.55	1.50

Miniature Sheet   Perf. 12½xImperf.

1165 A248 2.50 l multi   2.00 .90
No. 1165 contains one stamp, size: 50x71mm.

Soldier and Guns — A249

Designs: 25q, Sailor and warships. 65q, Aviator and planes, vert. 95q, Militiamen and woman.

1968, July 10   Litho.   Perf. 12
1166	A249	15q multicolored	.30	.15
1167	A249	25q multicolored	.45	.15
1168	A249	65q multicolored	1.25	.15
1169	A249	95q multicolored	2.50	.20
		Nos. 1166-1169 (4)	4.50	.65

25th anniversary of the People's Army.

Squid — A250

Designs: 20q, Crayfish. 25q, Whelk. 50q, Crab. 70q, Spiny lobster. 80q, Shore crab. 90q, Norway lobster.

1968, Aug. 20
1170	A250	15q multicolored	.15	.15
1171	A250	20q multicolored	.20	.15
1172	A250	25q multicolored	.25	.15
1173	A250	50q multicolored	.45	.15
1174	A250	70q multicolored	.70	.25
1175	A250	80q multicolored	.90	.30
1176	A250	90q multicolored	1.25	.35
		Nos. 1170-1176 (7)	3.90	1.50

Women's Relay Race — A251

Sport: 20q, Running. 25q, Women's discus. 30q, Equestrian. 40q, High jump. 50q, Women's hurdling. 80q, Soccer. 1.40 l, Woman diver. 2 l, Olympic stadium.

1968, Sept. 23   Photo.   Perf. 12
1177	A251	15q multicolored	.15	.15
1178	A251	20q multicolored	.15	.15
1179	A251	25q multicolored	.15	.15
1180	A251	30q multicolored	.20	.15
1181	A251	40q multicolored	.25	.15
1182	A251	50q multicolored	.35	.15
1183	A251	80q multicolored	.55	.15
1184	A251	1.40 l multicolored	.95	.35
		Nos. 1177-1184 (8)	2.75	1.40

Souvenir Sheet   Perf. 12½ Horizontally

1185 A251 2 l multicolored   2.25 .75

19th Olympic Games, Mexico City, Oct. 12-27. No. 1185 contains one rectangular stamp, size: 64x54mm. Value of imperfs., #1177-1184 $7, #1185 $5.

Enver Hoxha — A252

1968, Oct. 16   Litho.   Perf. 12
1186	A252	25q blue gray	.35	.15
1187	A252	35q rose brown	.50	.20
1188	A252	80q violet	.90	.35
1189	A252	1.10 l brown	1.10	.50
		Nos. 1186-1189 (4)	2.85	1.20

Souvenir Sheet   Imperf

1190 A252 1.50 l rose red, bl vio & gold   55.00 40.00

60th birthday of Enver Hoxha, First Secretary of the Central Committee of the Communist Party of Albania.

Book and Pupils — A253

1968, Nov. 14   Photo.
1191	A253	15q maroon & slate grn	.45	.15
1192	A253	85q gray olive & sepia	2.75	.20

60th anniv. of the Congress of Monastir, Nov. 14-22, 1908, which adopted a unified Albanian alphabet.

Waxwing — A254

Birds: 20q, Rose-colored starling. 25q, Kingfishers. 50q, Long-tailed tits. 80q, Wallcreeper. 1.10 l, Bearded tit.

1968, Nov. 15   Litho.
Birds in Natural Colors
1193	A254	15q lt blue & blk	.15	.15
1194	A254	20q bister & blk	.15	.15
1195	A254	25q pink & blk	.30	.15
1196	A254	50q lt yel grn & blk	.35	.15
1197	A254	80q bis brn & blk	.80	.20
1198	A254	1.10 l pale green & blk	1.00	.25
		Nos. 1193-1198 (6)	2.75	1.05

Mao Tse-tung — A255

1968, Dec. 26   Litho.   Perf. 12½x12
1199	A255	25q gold, red & blk	.40	.15
1200	A255	1.75 l gold, red & blk	2.00	.30

75th birthday of Mao Tse-tung, Chairman of the Communist Party of the People's Republic of China.

Adem Reka and Crane — A256

Portraits: 10q, Pjeter Lleshi and power lines. 15q, Mohammed Shehu and Myrteza Kepi. 25q, Shkurte Vata and women railroad workers. 65q, Agron Elezi, frontier guard. 80q, Ismet Bruçaj and mountain road. 1.30 l, Fuat Cela, blind revolutionary.

1969, Feb. 10   Litho.   Perf. 12x12½
1201	A256	5q multicolored	.15	.15
1202	A256	10q multicolored	.15	.15
1203	A256	15q multicolored	.15	.15
1204	A256	25q multicolored	.15	.15
1205	A256	65q multicolored	.40	.15
1206	A256	80q multicolored	.75	.15
1207	A256	1.30 l multicolored	1.25	.20
		Nos. 1201-1207 (7)	3.00	1.10

Issued to honor a contemporary heroine and heroes.

Meteorological Instruments A257

Designs: 25q, Water gauge. 1.60 l, Radar, balloon and isobars.

1969, Feb. 25   Perf. 12
1208	A257	15q multicolored	.25	.15
1209	A257	25q ultra, org & blk	.45	.15
1210	A257	1.60 l rose vio, yel & blk	2.50	.25
		Nos. 1208-1210 (3)	3.20	.55

20th anniv. of Albanian hydrometeorology.

Partisans, 1944, by F. Haxmiu — A258

Paintings: 5q, Student Revolutionists, by P. Mele, vert. 65q, Steel Mill, by C. Ceka. 80q, Reconstruction, by V. Kilica. 1.10 l, Harvest, by N. Jonuzi. 1.15 l, Terraced Landscape, by S. Kaceli. 2 l, Partisans' Meeting.

Perf. 12x12½, 12½x12
1969, Apr. 25   Litho.
Size: 31½x41½mm
1211 A258 5q buff & multi   .15 .15
Size: 51½x30½mm
1212 A258 25q buff & multi   .15 .15
Size: 40½x32mm
1213 A258 65q buff & multi   .35 .15
Size: 51½x30½mm
1214	A258	80q buff & multi	.65	.15
1215	A258	1.10 l buff & multi	.70	.15
1216	A258	1.15 l buff & multi	.95	.20
		Nos. 1211-1216 (6)	2.95	.95

Miniature Sheet   Imperf
Size: 111x90mm
1217 A258 2 l ocher & multi   1.75 1.75

Leonardo da Vinci, Self-portrait A259

Designs (after Leonardo da Vinci): 35q, Lilies. 40q, Design for a flying machine, horiz. 1 l, Portrait of Beatrice. No. 1222, Portrait of a Noblewoman. No. 1223, Mona Lisa.

Perf. 12x12½, 12½x12
1969, May 2   Litho.
1218	A259	25q gold & sepia	.20	.15
1219	A259	35q gold & sepia	.40	.15
1220	A259	40q gold & sepia	.45	.15
1221	A259	1 l gold & multi	1.25	.20
1222	A259	2 l gold & multi	2.25	.55
		Nos. 1218-1222 (5)	4.55	1.20

Miniature Sheet   Imperf
1223 A259 2 l gold & multi   3.25 2.25

Leonardo da Vinci (1452-1519), painter, sculptor, architect and engineer.

First Congress Meeting Place — A260

Designs: 1 l, Albanian coat of arms. 2.25 l, Two partisans with guns and flag.

1969, May 24   Perf. 12
1224	A260	25q lt grn, blk & red	.35	.15
1225	A260	2.25 l multi	2.50	.85

Souvenir Sheet
1226 A260 1 l gold, bl, blk & red   30.00 12.50

25th anniversary of the First Anti-Fascist Congress of Permet, May 24, 1944.

Albanian Violet — A261

Designs: Violets and Pansies.

1969, June 30   Litho.   Perf. 12x12½
1227	A261	5q gold & multi	.15	.15
1228	A261	10q gold & multi	.15	.15
1229	A261	15q gold & multi	.15	.15
1230	A261	20q gold & multi	.20	.15
1231	A261	25q gold & multi	.35	.15
1232	A261	80q gold & multi	.50	.30
1233	A261	1.95 l gold & multi	1.40	.65
		Nos. 1227-1233 (7)	2.90	1.70

Plum, Fruit and Blossoms — A262

ALBANIA

Designs: Blossoms and Fruits.

1969, Aug. 10   Litho.   *Perf. 12*

1234	A262	10q shown	.15	.15
1235	A262	15q Lemon	.20	.15
1236	A262	25q Pomegranate	.30	.15
1237	A262	50q Cherry	.60	.15
1238	A262	80q Peach	.95	.20
1239	A262	1.20 l Apple	1.75	.35
		Nos. 1234-1239 (6)	3.95	1.15

Basketball — A263

Designs: 10q, 80q, 2.20 l, Various views of basketball game. 25q, Hand aiming ball at basket and map of Europe, horiz.

1969, Sept. 15   Litho.   *Perf. 12*

1240	A263	10q multi	.15	.15
1241	A263	15q buff & multi	.15	.15
1242	A263	25q blue & multi	.25	.15
1243	A263	80q multi	.65	.15
1244	A263	2.20 l multi	1.65	.50
		Nos. 1240-1244 (5)	2.85	1.10

16th European Basketball Championships, Naples, Italy, Sept. 27-Oct. 5.

Runner — A264

Designs: 5q, Games' emblem. 10q, Woman gymnast. 20q, Pistol shooting. 25q, Swimmer at start. 80q, Bicyclist. 95q, Soccer.

1969, Sept. 30

1245	A264	5q multicolored	.15	.15
1246	A264	10q multicolored	.15	.15
1247	A264	15q multicolored	.15	.15
1248	A264	20q multicolored	.30	.15
1249	A264	25q multicolored	.40	.15
1250	A264	80q multicolored	.80	.15
1251	A264	95q multicolored	1.25	.20
		Nos. 1245-1251 (7)	3.20	1.10

Second National Spartakiad.

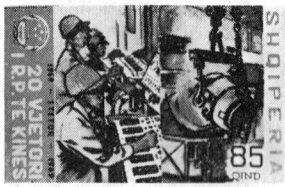

Electronic Technicians, Steel Ladle — A265

Designs: 25q, Mao Tse-tung with microphones, vert. 1.40 l, Children holding Mao's red book, vert.

1969, Oct. 1   Litho.   *Perf. 12*

1252	A265	25q multi	.40	.15
1253	A265	85q multi	1.00	.15
1254	A265	1.40 l multi	1.65	.30
		Nos. 1252-1254 (3)	3.05	.60

People's Republic of China, 20th anniv.

Enver Hoxha — A266

Designs: 80q, Pages from Berat resolution. 1.45 l, Partisans with flag.

1969, Oct. 20   Litho.   *Perf. 12*

1255	A266	25q multicolored	.20	.15
1256	A266	80q gray & multi	.50	.15
1257	A266	1.45 l ocher & multi	.80	.30
		Nos. 1255-1257 (3)	1.50	.60

25th anniv. of the 2nd reunion of the Natl. Antifascist Liberation Council, Berat.

Soldiers — A267

Designs: 30q, Oil refinery. 35q, Combine harvester. 45q, Hydroelectric station and dam. 55q, Militia woman, man and soldier. 1.10 l, Dancers and musicians.

1969, Nov. 29

1258	A267	25q multi	.25	.15
1259	A267	30q multi	.25	.15
1260	A267	35q multi	.25	.15
1261	A267	45q multi	.30	.15
1262	A267	55q multi	.80	.15
1263	A267	1.10 l multi	1.65	.15
		Nos. 1258-1263 (6)	3.50	.90

25th anniv. of the socialist republic.

Joseph V. Stalin, (1879-1953), Russian Political Leader — A268

1969, Dec. 21   Litho.   *Perf. 12*

1264	A268	15q lilac	.15	.15
1265	A268	25q slate blue	.20	.15
1266	A268	1 l brown	.75	.15
1267	A268	1.10 l violet blue	1.25	.20
		Nos. 1264-1267 (4)	2.35	.65

Head of Woman — A269

Greco-Roman Mosaics: 25q, Geometrical floor design, horiz. 80q, Bird and tree, horiz. 1.10 l, Floor with birds and grapes, horiz. 1.20 l, Fragment with corn within oval design.

1969, Dec. 25   *Perf. 12½x12*

1268	A269	15q gold & multi	.15	.15
1269	A269	25q gold & multi	.15	.15
1270	A269	80q gold & multi	.45	.15
1271	A269	1.10 l gold & multi	.70	.15
1272	A269	1.20 l gold & multi	.95	.30
		Nos. 1268-1272 (5)	2.40	.90

Cancellation of 1920 — A270

1970, Jan. 21   Litho.   *Perf. 12*

1273	A270	25q red, gray & blk	.20	.15
1274	A270	1.25 l dk grn, yel & blk	1.25	.15

Congress of Louchnia, 50th anniversary.

Worker, Student and Flag — A271

1970, Feb. 11   *Perf. 12½x12*

1275	A271	25q red & multi	.20	.15
1276	A271	1.75 l red & multi	1.25	.25

Vocational organizations in Albania, 25th anniv.

Turk's-cap Lily — A272

Lilies: 5q, Cernum, vert. 15q, Madonna, vert. 25q, Royal, vert. 1.10 l, Tiger. 1.15 l, Albanian.

Perf. 11½x12, 12x11½

1970, Mar. 10   Litho.

1277	A272	5q multi	.15	.15
1278	A272	15q multi	.15	.15
1279	A272	25q multi	.30	.15
1280	A272	80q multi	.75	.15
1281	A272	1.10 l multi	1.10	.15
1282	A272	1.15 l multi	1.40	.25
		Nos. 1277-1282 (6)	3.85	1.00

Lenin A273

Designs (Lenin): 5q, Portrait, vert. 25q, As volunteer construction worker. 95q, Addressing crowd. 1.10 l, Saluting, vert.

1970, Apr. 22   Litho.   *Perf. 12*

1283	A273	5q multi	.15	.15
1284	A273	15q multi	.15	.15
1285	A273	25q multi	.20	.15
1286	A273	95q multi	.60	.15
1287	A273	1.10 l multi	1.10	.15
		Nos. 1283-1287 (5)	2.20	.75

Centenary of birth of Lenin (1870-1924).

Frontier Guard A274

1970, Apr. 25

1288	A274	25q multi	.45	.15
1289	A274	1.25 l multi	2.50	.20

25th anniversary of Frontier Guards.

Soccer Players — A275

Designs: 5q, Jules Rimet Cup and globes. 10q, Aztec Stadium, Mexico City. 25q, Defending goal. 65q, 80q, No. 1296, Two soccer players in various plays. No. 1297, Mexican horseman and volcano Popocatepetl.

1970, May 15   Litho.   *Perf. 12½x12*

1290	A275	5q multicolored	.15	.15
1291	A275	10q multicolored	.15	.15
1292	A275	15q multicolored	.15	.15
1293	A275	25q lt green & multi	.25	.15
1294	A275	65q pink & multi	.30	.15
1295	A275	80q lt blue & multi	.55	.15
1296	A275	2 l yellow & multi	1.50	.25
		Nos. 1290-1296 (7)	2.95	1.15

Souvenir Sheet

Perf 12 x Imperf

1297 A275   2 l multicolored   2.25   .80

World Soccer Championships for the Jules Rimet Cup, Mexico City, May 31-June 21, 1970. No. 1297 contains one large horizontal stamp. Nos. 1290-1297 exist imperf.

UPU Headquarters and Monument, Bern — A276

1970, May 30   Litho.   *Perf. 12½x12*

1298	A276	25q ultra, gray & blk	.15	.15
1299	A276	1.10 l orange, buff & blk	.65	.15
1300	A276	1.15 l green, gray & blk	.90	.25
		Nos. 1298-1300 (3)	1.70	.60

Inauguration of the new UPU Headquarters in Bern.

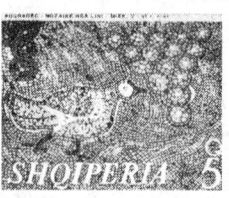

Bird and Grapes Mosaic A277

Mosaics, 5th-6th centuries, excavated near Pogradec: 10q, Waterfowl and grapes. 20q, Bird and tree stump. 25q, Bird and leaves. 65q, Fish. 2.25 l, Peacock, vert.

Perf. 12½x12, 12x12½

1970, July 10

1301	A277	5q multi	.15	.15
1302	A277	10q multi	.15	.15
1303	A277	20q multi	.20	.15
1304	A277	25q multi	.30	.15
1305	A277	65q multi	.55	.15
1306	A277	2.25 l multi	1.75	.35
		Nos. 1301-1306 (6)	3.10	1.10

Fruit Harvest and Dancers A278

Designs: 25q, Contour-plowed fields and conference table. 80q, Cattle and newspapers. 1.30 l, Wheat harvest.

1970, Aug. 28   Litho.   *Perf. 12x11½*

1307	A278	15q brt violet & blk	.15	.15
1308	A278	25q dp blue & blk	.20	.15
1309	A278	80q dp brown & blk	.60	.15
1310	A278	1.30 l org brn & blk	.90	.15
		Nos. 1307-1310 (4)	1.85	.60

25th anniv. of the agrarian reform law.

Attacking Partisans — A279

Designs: 25q, Partisans with horses and flag. 1.60 l, Partisans.

1970, Sept. 3   *Perf. 12*

1311	A279	15q org brn & blk	.15	.15
1312	A279	25q brn, yel & blk	.15	.15
1313	A279	1.60 l dp grn & blk	1.25	.30
		Nos. 1311-1313 (3)	1.55	.60

50th anniversary of liberation of Vlona.

ALBANIA

Miners, by Nexhmedin Zajmi — A280

Paintings from the National Gallery, Tirana: 5q, Bringing in the Harvest, by Isuf Sulovari, vert. 15q, The Activists, by Dhimitraq Trebicka, vert. 65q, Instruction of Partisans, by Hasan Nallbani. 95q, Architectural Planning, by Vilson Kilica. No. 1319, Woman Machinist, by Zef Shoshi, vert. No. 1320, Partisan Destroying Tank, by Sali Shijaku, vert.

1970, Sept. 25   Perf. 12½x12, 12x12½   Litho.
1314	A280	5q multicolored	.15	.15
1315	A280	15q multicolored	.15	.15
1316	A280	25q multicolored	.20	.15
1317	A280	65q multicolored	.25	.15
1318	A280	95q multicolored	.45	.15
1319	A280	2 l multicolored	1.75	.30
		Nos. 1314-1319 (6)	2.95	1.05

Miniature Sheet
Imperf
1320	A280	2 l multicolored	1.50	.95

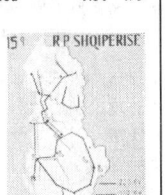

Electrification Map of Albania — A281

Designs: 25q, Light bulb, hammer and sickle emblem, map of Albania and power graph. 80q, Linemen at work. 1.10 l, Use of electricity on the farm, in home and business.

1970, Oct. 25   Litho.   Perf. 12
1321	A281	15q multi	.15	.15
1322	A281	25q multi	.15	.15
1323	A281	80q multi	.70	.15
1324	A281	1.10 l multi	1.00	.15
		Nos. 1321-1324 (4)	2.00	.60

Albanian village electrification completion.

Friedrich Engels — A282

Designs: 1.10 l, Engels as young man. 1.15 l, Engels addressing crowd.

1970, Nov. 28   Litho.   Perf. 12x12½
1325	A282	25q bister & dk bl	.20	.15
1326	A282	1.10 l bister & dp claret	.60	.20
1327	A282	1.15 l bister & dk ol grn	.70	.25
		Nos. 1325-1327 (3)	1.50	.60

150th anniv. of the birth of Friedrich Engels (1820-95), German socialist, collaborator with Karl Marx.

Ludwig van Beethoven — A283

Designs: 5q, Birthplace, Bonn. 25q, 65q, 1.10 l, various portraits. 1.80 l, Scene from Fidelio, horiz.

1970, Dec. 16   Litho.   Perf. 12
1328	A283	5q dp plum & gold	.15	.15
1329	A283	15q brt rose lil & sil	.15	.15
1330	A283	25q green & gold	.15	.15
1331	A283	65q magenta & sil	.30	.15
1332	A283	1.10 l dk blue & gold	.60	.25
1333	A283	1.80 l black & sil	1.40	.45
		Nos. 1328-1333 (6)	2.75	1.30

Ludwig van Beethoven (1770-1827), composer.

Coat of Arms A284

Designs: 25q, Proclamation. 80q, Enver Hoxha reading proclamation. 1.30 l, Young people and proclamation.

1971, Jan. 11   Litho.   Perf. 12
1334	A284	15q lt bl, gold, blk & red	.15	.15
1335	A284	25q rose lil, blk, gold & gray	.20	.15
1336	A284	80q emerald, blk & gold	.55	.15
1337	A284	1.30 l yel org, blk & gold	.85	.25
		Nos. 1334-1337 (4)	1.75	.70

Declaration of the Republic, 25th anniv.

"Liberty" A285    **Black Men A286**

Designs: 50q, Women's brigade. 65q, Street battle, horiz. 1.10 l, Execution, horiz.

Perf. 12x11½, 11½x12
1971, Mar. 18   Litho.
1338	A285	25q dk bl & bl	.15	.15
1339	A285	50q slate green	.35	.15
1340	A285	65q dk brn & chestnut	.50	.15
1341	A285	1.10 l purple	.75	.15
		Nos. 1338-1341 (4)	1.75	.60

Centenary of the Paris Commune.

1971, Mar. 21   Perf. 12x12½
1.10 l, Men of 3 races. 1.15 l, Black protest.
1342	A286	50q blk & bis brn	.60	.15
1343	A286	1.10 l blk & rose car	.60	.15
1344	A286	1.15 l blk & ver	.70	.15
		Nos. 1342-1344 (3)	1.45	.45

Intl. year against racial discrimination.

Tulip — A287

Designs: Various tulips.

1971, Mar. 25
1345	A287	5q multi	.15	.15
1346	A287	10q yellow & multi	.15	.15
1347	A287	15q pink & multi	.15	.15
1348	A287	20q lt blue & multi	.15	.15
1349	A287	25q multi	.25	.15
1350	A287	80q multi	.50	.15
1351	A287	1 l multi	.75	.20
1352	A287	1.45 l citron & multi	1.10	.25
		Nos. 1345-1352 (8)	3.20	1.35

Perf. 11½x12, 12x11½
1971, May 15   Litho.
Art Works by Dürer: 15q, Three peasants. 25q, Dancing peasant couple. 45q, The bagpiper. 65q, View of Kalkrebut, horiz. 2.40 l, View of Trent, horiz. 2.50 l, Self-portrait.
1353	A288	10q black & pale grn	.15	.15
1354	A288	15q black & pale lil	.15	.15
1355	A288	25q black & pale bl	.25	.15
1356	A288	45q black & pale rose	.40	.15
1357	A288	65q black & multi	.60	.15
1358	A288	2.40 l black & multi	2.25	.35
		Nos. 1353-1358 (6)	3.80	1.10

Miniature Sheet
Imperf
1359	A288	2.50 l multi	3.00	.80

Albrecht Dürer (1471-1528), German painter and engraver.

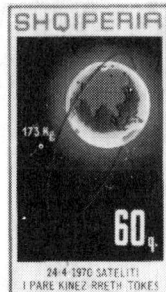

Satellite Orbiting Globe — A289

Designs: 1.20 l, Government Building, Tirana, and Red Star emblem. 2.20 l, like 60q, 2.50 l, Flag of People's Republic of China forming trajectory around globe.

1971, June 10   Litho.   Perf. 12x12½
1360	A289	60q purple & multi	.40	.15
1361	A289	1.20 l ver & multi	1.00	.25
1362	A289	2.20 l green & multi	1.60	.45

Imperf
1363	A289	2.50 l vio blk & multi	2.50	.90
		Nos. 1360-1363 (4)	5.50	1.75

Space developments of People's Republic of China.

Mao Tse-tung — A290

Designs: 1.05 l, House where Communist Party was founded, horiz. 1.20 l, Peking crowd with placards, horiz.

1971, July 1   Perf. 12x12½, 12x12½
1364	A290	25q silver & multi	.30	.15
1365	A290	1.05 l silver & multi	.95	.15
1366	A290	1.20 l silver & multi	1.25	.25
		Nos. 1364-1366 (3)	2.50	.55

50th anniv. of Chinese Communist Party.

Crested Titmouse — A291

1971, Aug. 15   Litho.   Perf. 12½x12
1367	A291	5q shown	.15	.15
1368	A291	10q European serin	.15	.15
1369	A291	15q Linnet	.15	.15
1370	A291	25q Firecrest	.15	.15
1371	A291	45q Rock thrush	.40	.15
1372	A291	60q Blue tit	.60	.25
1373	A291	2.40 l Chaffinch	2.00	.60
a.		Block of 7, #1367-1373 + label	3.00	3.00

Continuous design with bird's nest label at upper left.

Olympic Rings and Running — A292

Designs (Olympic Rings and): 10q, Hurdles. 15q, Canoeing. 25q, Gymnastics. 80q, Fencing. 1.05 l, Soccer. 2 l, Runner at finish line. 3.60 l, Diving, women's.

1971, Sept. 15
1374	A292	5q green & multi	.15	.15
1375	A292	10q multicolored	.15	.15
1376	A292	15q blue & multi	.15	.15
1377	A292	25q violet & multi	.15	.15
1378	A292	80q multi	.35	.15
1379	A292	1.05 l multicolored	.45	.15
1380	A292	3.60 l multicolored	2.50	.50
		Nos. 1374-1380 (7)	3.90	1.40

Souvenir Sheet
Imperf
1381	A292	2 l brt blue & multi	2.50	.75

20th Olympic Games, Munich, Aug. 26-Sept. 10, 1972.

Workers with Flags — A293

Designs: 1.05 l, Party Headquarters, Tirana, and Red Star. 1.20 l, Rifle, star, flag and "VI," vert.

1971, Nov. 1   Perf. 12
1382	A293	25q gold, sil, red & bl	.20	.15
1383	A293	1.05 l gold, sil, red & bl	.65	.15
1384	A293	1.20 l gold, sil, red & blk	.80	.25
		Nos. 1382-1384 (3)	1.65	.55

6th Congress of Workers' Party.

Factories and Workers A294

Designs: 80q, "XXX" and flag, vert. 1.55 l, Enver Hoxha and flags.

1971, Nov. 8
1385	A294	15q gold, sil, lil & yel	.20	.15
1386	A294	80q gold, sil & red	.70	.15
1387	A294	1.55 l gold, sil, red & brn	1.40	.25
		Nos. 1385-1387 (3)	2.30	.55

30th anniversary of Workers' Party.

Construction Work, by M. Fushekati — A295

Contemporary Albanian Paintings: 5q, Young Man, by R. Kuci, vert. 25q, Partisan, by D. Jukniu, vert. 80q, Fliers, by S. Kristo. 1.20 l, Girl in Forest, by A. Sadikaj. 1.55 l, Warriors with Spears and Shields, by S. Kamberi. 2 l, Freedom Fighter, by I. Lulani.

Perf. 12x12½, 12½x12
1971, Nov. 20
1388	A295	5q gold & multi	.15	.15
1389	A295	15q gold & multi	.15	.15
1390	A295	25q gold & multi	.15	.15
1391	A295	80q gold & multi	.40	.15
1392	A295	1.20 l gold & multi	.90	.20
1393	A295	1.55 l gold & multi	1.10	.25
		Nos. 1388-1393 (6)	2.85	1.05

Miniature Sheet
Imperf
1394	A295	2 l gold & multi	2.25	.70

223

ALBANIA

Young Workers' Emblem — A296

1971, Nov. 23   Perf. 12x12½
| 1395 | A296 | 15q lt blue & multi | .15 | .15 |
| 1396 | A296 | 1.35 l grnsh gray & multi | 1.10 | .25 |

Albanian Young Workers' Union, 30th anniv.

"Halili and Hajria" Ballet — A297

Scenes from "Halili and Hajria" Ballet: 10q, Brother and sister. 15q, Hajria before Sultan Suleiman. 50q, Hajria and husband. 80q, Execution of Halili. 1.40 l, Hajria killing her husband.

1971, Dec. 27   Perf. 12½x12
1397	A297	5q silver & multi	.15	.15
1398	A297	10q silver & multi	.15	.15
1399	A297	15q silver & multi	.15	.15
1400	A297	50q silver & multi	.45	.15
1401	A297	80q silver & multi	.70	.15
1402	A297	1.40 l silver & multi	1.10	.35
		Nos. 1397-1402 (6)	2.70	1.10

Albanian ballet Halili and Hajria after drama by Kol Jakova.

Biathlon and Olympic Rings — A298

Designs (Olympic Rings and): 10q, Sledding. 15q, Ice hockey. 20q, Bobsledding. 50q, Speed skating. 1 l, Slalom. 2 l, Ski jump. 2.50 l, Figure skating, pairs.

1972, Feb. 10
1403	A298	5q lt olive & multi	.15	.15
1404	A298	10q lt violet & multi	.15	.15
1405	A298	15q multicolored	.15	.15
1406	A298	20q pink & multi	.15	.15
1407	A298	50q lt blue & multi	.30	.15
1408	A298	1 l ocher & multi	.75	.20
1409	A298	2 l lilac & multi	1.50	.35
		Nos. 1403-1409 (7)	3.15	1.30

Souvenir Sheet
Imperf
| 1410 | A298 | 2.50 l blue & multi | 2.25 | .50 |

11th Winter Olympic Games, Sapporo, Japan, Feb. 3-13.

Wild Strawberries A299

Wild Fruits and Nuts: 10q, Blackberries. 15q, Hazelnuts. 20q, Walnuts. 25q, Strawberry-tree fruit. 30q, Dogwood berries. 2.40 l, Rowan berries.

1972, Mar. 20   Litho.   Perf. 12
1411	A299	5q lt grn & multi	.15	.15
1412	A299	10q yellow & multi	.15	.15
1413	A299	15q lt vio & multi	.15	.15
1414	A299	20q pink & multi	.20	.15
1415	A299	25q multi	.25	.15
1416	A299	30q multi	.35	.15
1417	A299	2.40 l multi	1.75	.45
		Nos. 1411-1417 (7)	3.00	1.35

"Your Heart is your Health" — A300   Worker and Student — A301

World Health Day: 1.20 l, Cardiac patient and electrocardiogram.

1972, Apr. 7   Perf. 12x12½
| 1418 | A300 | 1.10 l multicolored | .55 | .15 |
| 1419 | A300 | 1.20 l rose & multi | .70 | .25 |

Perf. 11½x12½
1972, Apr. 24   Litho.

7th Trade Union Cong., May 8: 2.05 l, Assembly Hall, dancers and emblem.
| 1420 | A301 | 25q multi | .25 | .15 |
| 1421 | A301 | 2.05 l blue & multi | 1.50 | .40 |

Qemal Stafa A302

Designs: 15q, Memorial flame. 25q, Monument "Spirit of Defiance," vert.

1972, May 5   Perf. 12½x12, 12x12½
1422	A302	15q gray & multi	.15	.15
1423	A302	25q sal rose, blk & gray	.15	.15
1424	A302	1.90 l dull yel & blk	1.10	.30
		Nos. 1422-1424 (3)	1.40	.60

30th anniversary of the murder of Qemal Stafa and of Martyrs' Day.

Camellia — A303

Designs: Various camellias.

1972, May 10   Perf. 12x12½
Flowers in Natural Colors
1425	A303	5q lt blue & blk	.15	.15
1426	A303	10q citron & blk	.15	.15
1427	A303	15q grnsh gray & blk	.15	.15
1428	A303	25q pale sal & blk	.15	.15
1429	A303	45q gray & blk	.30	.15
1430	A303	50q sal pink & blk	.45	.15
1431	A303	2.50 l bluish gray & blk	1.90	.75
		Nos. 1425-1431 (7)	3.25	1.65

High Jump — A304

Designs (Olympic and Motion Emblems and): 10q, Running. 15q, Shot put. 20q, Bicycling. 25q, Pole vault. 50q, Hurdles, women's. 5q, Hockey. 2 l, Swimming. 2.50 l, Diving, women's.

1972, June 30   Litho.   Perf. 12½x12
1432	A304	5q multicolored	.15	.15
1433	A304	10q lt brn & multi	.15	.15
1434	A304	15q lt lil & multi	.15	.15
1435	A304	20q multicolored	.15	.15
1436	A304	25q lt vio & multi	.15	.15
1437	A304	50q lt grn & multi	.40	.15
1438	A304	75q multicolored	.80	.15
1439	A304	2 l multicolored	1.50	.30
		Nos. 1432-1439 (8)	3.45	1.35

Miniature Sheet
Imperf
| 1440 | A304 | 2.50 l multi | 1.50 | .85 |

20th Olympic Games, Munich, Aug. 26-Sept. 11. Nos. 1432-1439 each issued in sheets of 8 stamps and one label (3x3) showing Olympic rings in gold.

Autobus A305

Designs: 25q, Electric train. 80q, Ocean liner Tirana. 1.05 l, Automobile. 1.20 l, Trailer truck.

1972, July 25   Litho.   Perf. 12
1441	A305	15q org brn & multi	.15	.15
1442	A305	25q gray & multi	.15	.15
1443	A305	80q dp grn & multi	.40	.15
1444	A305	1.05 l multi	.55	.15
1445	A305	1.20 l multi	.65	.15
		Nos. 1441-1445 (5)	1.90	.75

Arm Wrestling A306

Folk Games: 10q, Piggyback ball game. 15q, Women's jumping. 25q, Rope game (srum). 90q, Leapfrog. 2 l, Women throwing pitchers.

1972, Aug. 18
1446	A306	5q multi	.15	.15
1447	A306	10q lt bl & multi	.15	.15
1448	A306	15q rose & multi	.15	.15
1449	A306	25q lt bl & multi	.15	.15
1450	A306	90q ocher & multi	.65	.15
1451	A306	2 l lt grn & multi	1.25	.25
		Nos. 1446-1451 (6)	2.50	1.00

1st National Festival of People's Games.

Mastheads — A307

30th Press Day: 25q, Printing press. 1.90 l, Workers reading paper.

1972, Aug. 25
1452	A307	15q lt bl & blk	.15	.15
1453	A307	25q red, grn & blk	.20	.15
1454	A307	1.90 l lt vio & blk	1.25	.35
		Nos. 1452-1454 (3)	1.60	.65

Map of Peza Area, Memorial Tablet A308

1972, Sept. 16
1455	A308	15q shown	.20	.15
1456	A308	25q Guerrillas with flag	.30	.15
1457	A308	1.90 l Peza Conference memorial	1.75	.35
		Nos. 1455-1457 (3)	2.25	.65

30th anniversary, Conference of Peza.

Partisans, by Sotir Capo — A309

Paintings: 10q, Woman, by Ismail Lulani, vert. 15q, "Communists," by Lec Shkreli, vert. 20q, View of Nendorit, 1941, by Sali Shijaku, vert. 50q, Woman with Sheaf, by Zef Shoshi, vert. 1 l, Landscape with Children, by Dhimitraq Trebicka. 2 l, Women on Bicycles, by Vilson Kilica. 2.30 l, Folk Dance, by Abdurrahim Buza.

Perf. 12½x12, 12x12½
1972, Sept. 25   Litho.
1458	A309	5q gold & multi	.15	.15
1459	A309	10q gold & multi	.15	.15
1460	A309	15q gold & multi	.15	.15
1461	A309	20q gold & multi	.15	.15
1462	A309	50q gold & multi	.35	.15
1463	A309	1 l gold & multi	.70	.15
1464	A309	2 l gold & multi	1.50	.35
		Nos. 1458-1464 (7)	3.15	1.25

Miniature Sheet
Imperf
| 1465 | A309 | 2.30 l gold & multi | 2.00 | .80 |

No. 1465 contains one 41x68mm stamp.

Congress Emblem — A310

Design: 2.05 l, Young worker with banner.

1972, Oct. 23   Litho.   Perf. 12
| 1466 | A310 | 25q silver, red & gold | .15 | .15 |
| 1467 | A310 | 2.05 l silver & multi | 1.65 | .45 |

Union of Working Youth, 6th Congress.

Hammer and Sickle — A311   Ismail Qemali — A312

Design: 1.20 l, Lenin as orator.

1972, Nov. 7   Litho.   Perf. 11½x12
| 1468 | A311 | 1.10 l multi | .55 | .20 |
| 1469 | A311 | 1.20 l multi | .60 | .25 |

55th anniv. of the Russian October Revolution.

Perf. 12x11½, 11½x12
1972, Nov. 29

Designs: 15q, Albanian fighters, horiz. 65q, Rally, horiz. 1.25 l, Coat of arms.
1470	A312	15q red, brt bl & blk	.15	.15
1471	A312	25q yel, blk & red	.20	.15
1472	A312	65q red, sal & blk	.50	.15
1473	A312	1.25 l dl red & blk	.95	.15
		Nos. 1470-1473 (4)	1.80	.70

60th anniv. of independence.

Cock, Mosaic A313

Mosaics, 2nd-5th centuries, excavated near Buthrotium and Apollonia: 10q, Bird, vert. 15q, Partridges, vert. 25q, Warrior's legs. 45q, Nymph riding dolphin, vert. 50q, Fish, vert. 2.50 l, Warrior with helmet.

Perf. 12½x12, 12x12½
1972, Dec. 10
1474	A313	5q silver & multi	.15	.15
1475	A313	10q silver & multi	.15	.15
1476	A313	15q silver & multi	.15	.15
1477	A313	25q silver & multi	.15	.15
1478	A313	45q silver & multi	.20	.15

ALBANIA

1479	A313	50q silver & multi	.30	.15
1480	A313	2.50 l silver & multi	1.25	.40
		Nos. 1474-1480 (7)	2.35	1.30

Nicolaus Copernicus — A314

Designs: 10q, 25q, 80q, 1.20 l, Various portraits of Copernicus. 1.60 l, Heliocentric solar system.

1973, Feb. 19   Litho.   Perf. 12x12½

1481	A314	5q lilac rose & multi	.15	.15
1482	A314	10q dull olive & multi	.15	.15
1483	A314	25q multicolored	.20	.15
1484	A314	80q lt violet & multi	.60	.15
1485	A314	1.20 l blue & multi	.85	.25
1486	A314	1.60 l gray & multi	1.25	.35
		Nos. 1481-1486 (6)	3.20	1.20

500th anniversary of the birth of Nicolaus Copernicus (1473-1543), Polish astronomer.

Flowering Cactus — A315

Designs: Various flowering cacti.

1973, Mar. 25   Litho.   Perf. 12

1487	A315	10q multicolored	.15	.15
1488	A315	15q multicolored	.15	.15
1489	A315	20q beige & multi	.15	.15
1490	A315	25q gray & multi	.20	.15
1491	A315	30q beige & multi	.30	.15
1492	A315	65q gray & multi	.75	.15
1493	A315	80q multicolored	.95	.15
1494	A315	2 l multicolored	2.50	.30
a.		Block of 8, #1487-1494	5.00	3.00
		Nos. 1487-1494 (8)	5.15	1.35

Guard and Factories A316

Design: 1.80 l, Guard and guards with prisoner.

1973, Mar. 20   Litho.   Perf. 12½x12

1495	A316	25q ultra & blk	.30	.15
1496	A316	1.80 l dk red & multi	1.40	.40

30th anniv. of the State Security Branch.

Common Tern A317

Sea Birds: 15q, White-winged black terns, vert. 25q, Black-headed gull, vert. 45q, Great black-headed gull. 80q, Slender-billed gull, vert. 2.40 l, Sandwich terns.

Perf. 12½x12, 12x12½
1973, Apr. 30

1497	A317	5q gold & multi	.15	.15
1498	A317	15q gold & multi	.15	.15
1499	A317	25q gold & multi	.30	.15
1500	A317	45q gold & multi	.35	.15
1501	A317	80q gold & multi	.80	.20
1502	A317	2.40 l gold & multi	2.50	.50
		Nos. 1497-1502 (6)	4.25	1.30

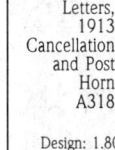

Letters, 1913 Cancellation and Post Horn A318

Design: 1.80 l, Mailman, 1913 cancel.

1973, May, 5   Litho.   Perf. 12x11½

1503	A318	25q red & multi	.40	.15
1504	A318	1.80 l red & multi	2.50	.50

60th anniversary of Albanian stamps.

Farmer, Worker, Soldier A319

Design: 25q, Woman and factory, vert.

1973, June 4   Perf. 12

1505	A319	25q carmine rose	.25	.15
1506	A319	1.80 l yel, dp org & blk	1.50	.45

7th Congress of Albanian Women's Union.

Creation of General Staff, by G. Madhi — A320

Designs: 40q, "August 1949," sculpture by Sh. Haderi, vert. 60q, "Generation after Generation," sculpture by H. Dule, vert. 80q, "Defend Revolutionary Victories," by M. Fushekati.

1973, July 10   Litho.   Perf. 12½x12

1507	A320	25q gold & multi	3.25	.15
1508	A320	40q gold & multi	5.00	.15
1509	A320	60q gold & multi	7.50	.25
1510	A320	80q gold & multi	9.25	.25
		Nos. 1507-1510 (4)	25.00	.80

30th anniversary of the People's Army.

"Electrification," by S. Hysa — A321

Albanian Paintings: 10q, Woman Textile Worker, by N. Nallbani. 15q, Gymnasts, by M. Fushekati. 50q, Aviator, by F. Stamo. 80q, Fascist Prisoner, by A. Lakuriqi. 1.20 l, Workers with Banner, by P. Mele. 1.30 l, Farm Woman, by Zef Shoshi. 2.05 l, Battle of Tenda, by F. Haxhiu. 10q, 50q, 80q, 1.20 l, 1.30 l, vertical.

Perf. 12½x12, 12x12½
1973, Aug. 10

1511	A321	5q gold & multi	.15	.15
1512	A321	10q gold & multi	.15	.15
1513	A321	15q gold & multi	.15	.15
1514	A321	50q gold & multi	.25	.15
1515	A321	80q gold & multi	.55	.15
1516	A321	1.20 l gold & multi	.90	.15
1517	A321	1.30 l gold & multi	.95	.20
		Nos. 1511-1517 (7)	3.10	1.10

Souvenir Sheet
Imperf

1518	A321	2.05 l multi	2.25	.65

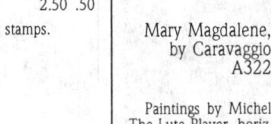

Mary Magdalene, by Caravaggio A322

Paintings by Michelangelo da Caravaggio: 10q, The Lute Player, horiz. 15q, Self-portrait. 50q, Boy Carrying Fruit and Flowers. 80q, Still Life, horiz. 1.20 l, Narcissus. 1.30 l, Boy Peeling Apple. 2.05 l, Man with Feathered Hat.

Perf. 12x12½, 12½x12
1973, Sept. 28

1519	A322	5q gold & multi	.15	.15
1520	A322	10q gold & multi	.15	.15
1521	A322	15q gold, blk & gray	.15	.15
1522	A322	50q gold & multi	.25	.15
1523	A322	80q gold & multi	.60	.15
1524	A322	1.20 l gold & multi	.80	.25
1525	A322	1.30 l gold & multi	.90	.25
		Nos. 1519-1525 (7)	3.00	1.25

Souvenir Sheet
Imperf

1526	A322	2.05 l multi	3.75	.60

Michelangelo da Caravaggio (Merisi; 1573?-1609), Italian painter. No. 1526 contains one stamp, size: 63x73mm.

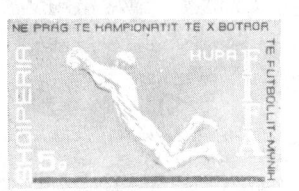

Soccer — A323

Designs: 5q-1.25 l, Various soccer scenes. 2.05 l, Ball in goal and list of cities where championships were held.

1973, Oct. 30   Litho.   Perf. 12½x12

1527	A323	5q multi	.15	.15
1528	A323	10q multi	.15	.15
1529	A323	15q multi	.15	.15
1530	A323	20q multi	.15	.15
1531	A323	25q multi	.20	.15
1532	A323	90q multi	.65	.15
1533	A323	1.20 l multi	.95	.15
1534	A323	1.25 l multi	1.10	.20
		Nos. 1527-1534 (8)	3.50	1.25

Minature Sheet
Imperf

1535	A323	2.05 l multi	2.00	.60

World Soccer Cup, Munich 1974.

Weight Lifter — A324

Designs: Various stages of weight lifting. 1.20 l, 1.60 l, horiz.

1973, Oct. 30   Litho.   Perf. 12

1536	A324	5q multi	.15	.15
1537	A324	10q multi	.15	.15
1538	A324	25q multi	.20	.15
1539	A324	90q multi	.55	.20
1540	A324	1.20 l multi	.45	.15
1541	A324	1.60 l multi	.95	.15
		Nos. 1536-1541 (6)	2.45	.95

Weight Lifting Championships, Havana, Cuba.

Ballet — A325   Harvester Combine — A326

Designs: 5q, Cement factory, Kavaje. 10q, Ali Kelmendi truck factory and tank cars, horiz. 25q, "Communication." 35q, Skiers and hotel, horiz. 60q, Resort, horiz. 80q, Mountain lake. 1 l, Mao Tse-tung textile mill. 1.20 l, Steel workers. 2.40 l, Welder and pipe. 3 l, Skanderbeg Monument, Tirana. 5 l, Roman arches, Durres.

Perf. 12½x12, 12x12½
1973-74   Litho.

1543	A325	5q gold & multi	.15	.15
1544	A325	10q gold & multi	.15	.15
1545	A325	15q gold & multi	.15	.15
1545A	A326	20q gold & multi	.15	.15
1546	A326	25q gold & multi	.20	.15
1547	A326	35q gold & multi	.20	.15
1548	A326	60q gold & multi	.35	.15
1549	A326	80q gold & multi	.50	.15
1549A	A326	1 l gold & multi	.45	.15
1549B	A326	1.20 l gold & multi	.75	.15
1549C	A326	2.40 l gold & multi	1.50	.35
1550	A326	3 l gold & multi	1.75	.35
1551	A326	5 l gold & multi	2.75	.60
		Nos. 1543-1551 (13)	9.05	2.80

Issue dates: Nos. 1545-1546, 1549-1550, Dec. 5, 1973; others, 1974.

Mao Tse-tung — A327

80th birthday of Mao Tse-tung: 1.20 l, Mao Tse-tung addressing crowd.

1973, Dec. 26   Perf. 12

1552	A327	85q gold, red & sepia	.80	.15
1553	A327	1.20 l gold, red & sepia	1.25	.20

Old Man and Dog, by Gericault — A328

Paintings by Jean Louis André Theodore Gericault: 10q, Horse's Head. 15q, Male Model. 25q, Head of Black Man. 1.20 l, Self-portrait. 2.05 l, Raft of the Medusa, horiz. 2.20 l, Battle of the Giants.

Perf. 12x12½, 12½x12
1974, Jan. 18   Litho.

1554	A328	10q gold & multi	.15	.15
1555	A328	15q gold & multi	.15	.15
1556	A328	20q gold & multi	.15	.15
1557	A328	25q gold & blk	.25	.15
1558	A328	1.20 l gold & multi	.90	.15
1559	A328	2.20 l gold & multi	1.75	.35
		Nos. 1554-1559 (6)	3.35	1.10

Souvenir Sheet
Imperf

1560	A328	2.05 l gold & multi	1.50	.45

No. 1560 contains one 87x78mm stamp.

For all your stamp supply needs

www.scottonline.com

ALBANIA

Lenin, by Pandi Mele — A329

Designs: 25q, Lenin with Sailors on Cruiser Aurora, by Dhimitraq Trebicka, horiz. 1.20 l, Lenin, by Vilson Kilica.

1974, Jan. 21   Perf. 12½x12, 12x12½
1561	A329	25q gold & multi	.20 .15
1562	A329	60q gold & multi	.50 .15
1563	A329	1.20 l gold & multi	1.10 .25
		Nos. 1561-1563 (3)	1.80 .55

50th anniv. of the death of Lenin.

Swimming Duck, Mosaic — A330

Designs: Mosaics from the 5th-6th Centuries A.D., excavated near Buthrotium, Pogradec and Apollonia.

1974, Feb. 20   Litho.   Perf. 12½x12
1564	A330	5q shown	.15 .15
1565	A330	10q Bird and flower	.15 .15
1566	A330	15q Vase and grapes	.15 .15
1567	A330	25q Duck	.20 .15
1568	A330	40q Donkey and bird	.30 .15
1569	A330	2.50 l Sea horse	1.50 .35
		Nos. 1564-1569 (6)	2.45 1.10

Soccer — A331

Various scenes from soccer. 2.05 l, World Soccer Cup & names of participating countries.

1974, Apr. 25   Litho.   Perf. 12½x12
1570	A331	10q gold & multi	.15 .15
1571	A331	15q gold & multi	.15 .15
1572	A331	20q gold & multi	.15 .15
1573	A331	25q gold & multi	.15 .15
1574	A331	40q gold & multi	.30 .15
1575	A331	80q gold & multi	.55 .15
1576	A331	1 l gold & multi	.85 .25
1577	A331	1.20 l gold & multi	1.10 .35
		Nos. 1570-1577 (8)	3.40 1.50

Souvenir Sheet
Imperf
1578 A331 2.05 l gold & multi   2.50 .90

World Cup Soccer Championship, Munich, June 13-July 7. No. 1578 contains one stamp (60x60mm) with simulated perforations. Nos. 1570-1577 exist imperf, No. 1578 with simulated perfs omitted.

Arms of Albania, Soldier — A332

Design: 1.80 l, Soldier and front page of 1944 Congress Book.

1974, May 24   Litho.   Perf. 12
1579	A332	25q multicolored	.20 .15
1580	A332	1.80 l multicolored	1.25 .25

30th anniversary of the First Anti-Fascist Liberation Congress of Permet.

Medicinal Plants — A333

40q, 80q, 2.20 l, horiz.

1974, May 5   Perf. 12x12½
1581	A333	10q Bittersweet	.15 .15
1582	A333	15q Arbutus	.15 .15
1583	A333	20q Lilies of the valley	.15 .15
1584	A333	25q Autumn crocus	.20 .15
1585	A333	40q Borage	.25 .15
1586	A333	80q Soapwort	.85 .15
1587	A333	2.20 l Gentian	1.90 .40
		Nos. 1581-1587 (7)	3.65 1.30

Revolutionaries with Albanian Flag — A334

1.80 l, Portraits of 5 revolutionaries, vert.

Perf. 12½x12, 12x12½
1974, June 10
1588	A334	25q red, blk & lil	.15 .15
1589	A334	1.80 l yel, red & blk	.80 .25

50th anniversary Albanian Bourgeois Democratic Revolution.

European Redwing — A335

Designs: Songbirds; Nos. 1597-1600 vert.

Perf. 12½x12, 12x12½
1974, July 15   Litho.
1594	A335	10q shown	.15 .15
1595	A335	15q European robin	.15 .15
1596	A335	20q Greenfinch	.15 .15
1597	A335	25q Bullfinch	.15 .15
1598	A335	40q Hawfinch	.35 .15
1599	A335	80q Blackcap	.85 .15
1600	A335	2.20 l Nightingale	1.90 .45
		Nos. 1594-1600 (7)	3.70 1.40

Globe — A336

Cent. of UPU: 1.20 l, UPU emblem. 2.05 l, Jet over globe.

1974, Aug. 25   Litho.   Perf. 12x12½
1601	A336	85q green & multi	.80 .15
1602	A336	1.20 l vio & ol grn	1.25 .20

Miniature Sheet
Imperf
1603 A336 2.05 l blue & multi   12.00 12.00

Widows, by Sali Shijaku — A337

Albanian Paintings: 15q, Drillers, by Danish Jukniu, vert. 20q, Workers with Blueprints, by Clirim Ceka. 25q, Call to Action, by Spiro Kristo, vert. 40q, Winter Battle, by Sabaudin Xhaferi. 80q, Comrades, by Clirim Ceka, vert. 1 l, Aiding the Partisans, by Guri Madhi. 1.20 l, Teacher with Pupils, by Kleo Nini Brezat. 2.05 l, Comrades in Arms, by Guri Madhi.

Perf. 12½x12, 12x12½
1974, Sept. 25
1604	A337	10q silver & multi	.15 .15
1605	A337	15q silver & multi	.15 .15
1606	A337	20q silver & multi	.20 .15
1607	A337	25q silver & multi	.20 .15
1608	A337	40q silver & multi	.40 .15
1609	A337	80q silver & multi	.75 .15
1610	A337	1 l silver & multi	.95 .15
1611	A337	1.20 l silver & multi	1.00 .20
		Nos. 1604-1611 (8)	3.80 1.25

Miniature Sheet
Imperf
1612 A337 2.05 l silver & multi   2.00 .40

Crowd on Tien An Men Square A338

Design: 1.20 l, Mao Tse-tung, vert.

1974, Oct. 1   Perf. 12
1613	A338	85q gold & multi	.80 .15
1614	A338	1.20 l gold & multi	1.25 .15

25th anniversary of the proclamation of the People's Republic of China.

Women's Volleyball A339

Designs (Spartakiad Medal and): 15q, Women hurdlers. 20q, Women gymnasts. 25q, Mass exercises in Stadium. 40q, Weight lifter. 80q, Wrestlers. 1 l, Military rifle drill. 1.20 l, Soccer.

1974, Oct. 9   Perf. 12x12½
1615	A339	10q multi	.15 .15
1616	A339	15q multi	.15 .15
1617	A339	20q multi	.15 .15
1618	A339	25q gray & multi	.15 .15
1619	A339	40q multi	.15 .15
1620	A339	80q multi	.45 .15
1621	A339	1 l multi	.50 .15
1622	A339	1.20 l tan & multi	.60 .20
		Nos. 1615-1622 (8)	2.30 1.25

National Spartakiad, Oct. 9-17.

View of Berat — A340

Designs: 80q, Enver Hoxha addressing Congress, bas-relief, horiz. 1 l, Hoxha and leaders leaving Congress Hall.

Perf. 12x12½, 12½x12
1974, Oct. 20   Litho.
1623	A340	25q rose car & blk	.30 .15
1624	A340	80q yel, brn & blk	.60 .15
1625	A340	1 l dp lilac & blk	.90 .15
		Nos. 1623-1625 (3)	1.80 .45

30th anniversary of 2nd Congress of Berat.

Anniversary Emblem, Factory Guards A341

35q, Chemical industry. 50q, Agriculture. 80q, Arts. 1 l, Atomic diagram & computer. 1.20 l, Youth education. 2.05 l, Crowd & History Book.

1974, Nov. 29   Litho.   Perf. 12½x12
1626	A341	25q green & multi	.15 .15
1627	A341	35q ultra & multi	.15 .15
1628	A341	50q brown & multi	.25 .15
1629	A341	80q multicolored	.40 .15
1630	A341	1 l violet & multi	.45 .15
1631	A341	1.20 l multicolored	.50 .15
		Nos. 1626-1631 (6)	1.90 .95

Miniature Sheet
Imperf
1632 A341 2.05 l gold & multi   2.00 .50

30th anniv. of liberation from Fascism.

Artemis, from Apolloni — A342

1974, Dec. 25   Photo.   Perf. 12x12½
1633	A342	10q shown	.15 .15
1634	A342	15q Zeus statue	.15 .15
1635	A342	20q Poseidon statue	.15 .15
1636	A342	25q Illyrian helmet	.15 .15
1637	A342	40q Amphora	.20 .15
1638	A342	80q Agrippa	.50 .15
1639	A342	1 l Demosthenes	.60 .15
1640	A342	1.20 l Head of Bilia	.70 .20
		Nos. 1633-1640 (8)	2.60 1.25

Miniature Sheet
Imperf
1641 A342 2.05 l Artemis & amphora   2.00 .60

Archaeological discoveries in Albania.

Workers and Factories A343

Design: 25q, Handshake, tools and book, vert.

1975, Feb. 11   Litho.   Perf. 12
1642	A343	25q brown & multi	.15 .15
1643	A343	1.80 l yellow & multi	1.10 .30

Albanian Trade Unions, 30th anniversary.

Chicory A344

1975, Feb. 15
1644	A344	5q shown	.15 .15
1645	A344	10q Houseleek	.15 .15
1646	A344	15q Columbine	.15 .15
1647	A344	20q Anemone	.15 .15

ALBANIA

1648	A344	25q Hibiscus	.15	.15
1649	A344	30q Gentian	.15	.15
1650	A344	35q Hollyhock	.15	.15
1651	A344	2.70 l Iris	1.20	.40
		Nos. 1644-1651 (8)	2.25	1.45

Protected flowers.

Jesus, from Doni Madonna — A345

Works by Michelangelo: 10q, Slave, sculpture. 15q, Head of Dawn, sculpture. 20q, Awakening Giant, sculpture. 25q, Cumaenian Sybil, Sistine Chapel. 30q, Lorenzo di Medici, sculpture. 1.20 l, David, sculpture. 2.05 l, Self-portrait. 3.90 l, Delphic Sybil, Sistine Chapel.

1975, Mar. 20   Litho.   Perf. 12x12½

1652	A345	5q gold & multi	.15	.15
1653	A345	10q gold & multi	.15	.15
1654	A345	15q gold & multi	.15	.15
1655	A345	20q gold & multi	.15	.15
1656	A345	25q gold & multi	.15	.15
1657	A345	30q gold & multi	.15	.15
1658	A345	1.20 l gold & multi	.35	.20
1659	A345	3.90 l gold & multi	1.50	.50
		Nos. 1652-1659 (8)	2.75	1.60

Miniature Sheet
Imperf

| 1660 | A345 | 2.05 l gold & multi | 1.10 | .50 |

Michelangelo Buonarroti (1475-1564), Italian sculptor, painter and architect.

Two-wheeled Cart — A346

Albanian Transportation of the Past: 5q, Horseback rider. 15q, Lake ferry. 20q, Coastal threemaster. 25q, Phaeton. 3.35 l, Early automobile on bridge.

1975, Apr. 15   Litho.   Perf. 12½x12

1661	A346	5q bl grn & multi	.15	.15
1662	A346	10q ol & multi	.15	.15
1663	A346	15q lil & multi	.15	.15
1664	A346	20q multi	.15	.15
1665	A346	25q multi	.15	.15
1666	A346	3.35 l ocher & multi	1.50	.50
		Nos. 1661-1666 (6)	2.25	1.25

Guard at Frontier Stone — A347

Guardsman and Militia — A348

1975, Apr. 25   Perf. 12

| 1667 | A347 | 25q multi | .15 | .15 |
| 1668 | A348 | 1.80 l multi | 1.10 | .20 |

30th anniversary of Frontier Guards.

Posting Illegal Poster — A349

Designs: 60q, Partisans in battle. 1.20 l, Partisan killing German soldier, and Albanian coat of arms.

1975, May 9   Perf. 12½x12

1669	A349	25q multi	.15	.15
1670	A349	60q multi	.25	.15
1671	A349	1.20 l red & multi	.75	.25
		Nos. 1669-1671 (3)	1.15	.55

30th anniversary of victory over Fascism.

European Widgeons — A350

Waterfowl: 10q, Red-crested pochards. 15q, White-fronted goose. 20q, Northern pintails. 25q, Red-breasted merganser. 30q, Eider ducks. 35q, Whooper swan. 2.70 l, Shovelers.

1975, June 15   Litho.   Perf. 12

1672	A350	5q brt blue & multi	.15	.15
1673	A350	10q yel grn & multi	.15	.15
1674	A350	15q brt rose lil & multi	.15	.15
1675	A350	20q bl grn & multi	.15	.15
1676	A350	25q multicolored	.15	.15
1677	A350	30q multicolored	.15	.15
1678	A350	35q orange & multi	.15	.15
1679	A350	2.70 l multi	1.65	.35
		Nos. 1672-1679 (8)	2.70	1.40

Shyqyri Kanapari, by Musa Qarri — A351

Albanian Paintings: 10q, Woman Saving Children in Sea, by Agim Faja. 15q, "November 28, 1912" (revolution), by Petrit Ceno, horiz. 20q, "Workers Unite," by Sali Shijaku. 25q, The Partisan Shota Galica, by Ismail Lulani. 30q, Victorious Resistance Fighters, 1943, by Nestor Jonuzi. 80q, Partisan Couple in Front of Red Flag, by Vilson Halimi. 2.05 l, Dancing Procession, by Abdurahim Buza. 2.25 l, Republic Day Celebration, by Fatmir Haxhiu, horiz.

Perf. 12x12½, 12½x12
1975, July 15   Litho.

1680	A351	5q gold & multi	.15	.15
1681	A351	10q gold & multi	.15	.15
1682	A351	15q gold & multi	.15	.15
1683	A351	20q gold & multi	.15	.15
1684	A351	25q gold & multi	.15	.15
1685	A351	30q gold & multi	.20	.15
1686	A351	80q gold & multi	.35	.15
1687	A351	2.25 l gold & multi	1.25	.30
		Nos. 1680-1687 (8)	2.55	1.35

Miniature Sheet
Imperf

| 1688 | A351 | 2.05 l gold & multi | 1.65 | .50 |

Nos. 1680-1687 issued in sheets of 8 stamps and gold center label showing palette and easel.

Farmer Holding Reform Law — A352

Design: 2 l, Produce and farm machinery.

1975, Aug. 28   Perf. 12

| 1689 | A352 | 15q multicolored | .15 | .15 |
| 1690 | A352 | 2 l multicolored | 1.10 | .35 |

Agrarian reform, 30th anniversary.

Alcynonium Palmatum — A353

Corals: 10q, Paramuricea chamaeleon. 20q, Coralium rubrum. 25q, Eunicella covalini. 3.70 l, Cladocora cespitosa.

1975, Sept. 25   Litho.   Perf. 12

1691	A353	5q blue, ol & blk	.15	.15
1692	A353	10q blue & multi	.15	.15
1693	A353	20q blue & multi	.15	.15
1694	A353	25q blue & blk	.20	.15
1695	A353	3.70 l blue & blk	2.00	.50
		Nos. 1691-1695 (5)	2.65	1.10

Bicycling — A354

Designs (Montreal Olympic Games Emblem and): 10q, Canoeing. 15q, Fieldball. 20q, Basketball. 25q, Water polo. 30q, Hockey. 1.20 l, Pole vault. 2.05 l, Fencing. 2.15 l, Montreal Olympic Games emblem and various sports.

1975, Oct. 20   Litho.   Perf. 12½

1696	A354	5q multi	.15	.15
1697	A354	10q multi	.15	.15
1698	A354	15q multi	.15	.15
1699	A354	20q multi	.15	.15
1700	A354	25q multi	.15	.15
1701	A354	30q multi	.15	.15
1702	A354	1.20 l multi	.40	.15
1703	A354	2.05 l multi	.85	.25
		Nos. 1696-1703 (8)	2.15	1.30

Miniature Sheet
Imperf

| 1704 | A354 | 2.15 l org & multi | 2.75 | 1.75 |

21st Olympic Games, Montreal, July 18-Aug. 8, 1976. Nos. 1696-1703 exist imperf.

Power Lines Leading to Village — A355

Designs: 25q, Transformers and insulators. 80q, Dam and power station. 85q, Television set, power lines, grain and cogwheel.

1975, Oct. 25   Perf. 12½x12½

1705	A355	15q ultra & yel	.15	.15
1706	A355	25q brt vio & pink	.15	.15
1707	A355	80q lt grn & gray	.40	.15
1708	A355	85q ocher & brn	.40	.15
		Nos. 1705-1708 (4)	1.10	.60

General electrification, 5th anniversary.

Child, Rabbit and Teddy Bear Planting Tree — A356

Fairy Tales: 10q, Mother fox. 15q, Ducks in school. 20q, Little pigs building house. 25q, Animals watching television. 30q, Rabbit and bear at work. 35q, Working and playing ants. 2.70 l, Wolf in sheep's clothes.

1975, Dec. 25   Litho.   Perf. 12½x12

1709	A356	5q black & multi	.15	.15
1710	A356	10q black & multi	.15	.15
1711	A356	15q black & multi	.15	.15
1712	A356	20q black & multi	.15	.15
1713	A356	25q black & multi	.15	.15
1714	A356	30q black & multi	.15	.15
1715	A356	35q black & multi	.20	.15
1716	A356	2.70 l black & multi	1.25	.30
		Nos. 1709-1716 (8)	2.35	1.35

Arms, People, Factories — A357

Design: 1.90 l, Arms, government building, celebrating crowd.

1976, Jan. 11   Litho.   Perf. 12

| 1717 | A357 | 25q gold & multi | .15 | .15 |
| 1718 | A357 | 1.90 l gold & multi | .85 | .25 |

30th anniversary of proclamation of Albanian People's Republic.

Ice Hockey, Olympic Games Emblem — A358

Designs: 10q, Speed skating. 15q, Biathlon. 50q, Ski jump. 1.20 l, Slalom. 2.15 l, Figure skating, pairs. 2.30 l, One-man bobsled.

1976, Feb. 4

1719	A358	5q silver & multi	.15	.15
1720	A358	10q silver & multi	.15	.15
1721	A358	15q silver & multi	.15	.15
1722	A358	50q silver & multi	.25	.15
1723	A358	1.20 l silver & multi	.60	.15
1724	A358	2.30 l silver & multi	1.40	.35
		Nos. 1719-1724 (6)	2.70	1.10

Miniature Sheet
Perf. 12 on 2 sides x Imperf.

| 1725 | A358 | 2.15 l silver & multi | 1.90 | .80 |

12th Winter Olympic Games, Innsbruck, Austria, Feb. 4-15.

Meadow Saffron — A359

Medicinal Plants: 10q, Deadly night-shade. 15q, Yellow gentian. 20q, Horse chestnut. 70q, Shield fern. 80q, Marshmallow. 2.30 l, Thorn apple.

1976, Apr. 10   Litho.   Perf. 12x12½

1726	A359	5q black & multi	.15	.15
1727	A359	10q black & multi	.15	.15
1728	A359	15q black & multi	.15	.15

ALBANIA

1729	A359	20q black & multi	.15	.15
1730	A359	70q black & multi	.25	.15
1731	A359	80q black & multi	.45	.15
1732	A359	2.30 l black & multi	1.25	.35
		Nos. 1726-1732 (7)	2.55	1.25

Bowl and Spoon — A360

15q, Flask, vert. 20q, Carved handles, vert. 25q, Pistol and dagger. 80q, Wall hanging, vert. 1.20 l, Earrings and belt buckle. 1.40 l, Jugs, vert.

1976 Litho. Perf. 12½x12, 12x12½

1733	A360	10q lilac & multi	.15	.15
1734	A360	15q gray & multi	.15	.15
1735	A360	20q multi	.15	.15
1736	A360	25q car & multi	.15	.15
1737	A360	80q yellow & multi	.35	.15
1738	A360	1.20 l multi	.50	.15
1739	A360	1.40 l tan & multi	.65	.25
		Nos. 1733-1739 (7)	2.00	1.15

Natl. Ethnographic Conf., Tirana, June 28.
For surcharge see No. 1873.

Founding of Cooperatives, by Zef Shoshi — A361

Paintings: 10q, Going to Work, by Agim Zajmi, vert. 25q, Crowd Listening to Loudspeaker, by Vilson Kilica. 40q, Woman Welder, by Sabaudin Xhaferi, vert. 50q, Factory, by Isuf Sulovari, vert. 1.20 l, 1942 Revolt, by Lec Shkreli, vert. 1.60 l, Coming Home from Work, by Agron Dine. 2.05 l, Honoring a Young Pioneer, by Andon Lakuriqi.

Perf. 12½x12, 12x12½

1976, Aug. 8 Litho.

1740	A361	5q gold & multi	.15	.15
1741	A361	10q gold & multi	.15	.15
1742	A361	25q gold & multi	.15	.15
1743	A361	40q gold & multi	.15	.15
1744	A361	50q gold & multi	.15	.15
1745	A361	1.20 l gold & multi	.50	.15
1746	A361	1.60 l gold & multi	.75	.30
		Nos. 1740-1746 (7)	2.00	1.20

Miniature Sheet
Perf. 12 on 2 sides x Imperf.

| 1747 | A361 | 2.05 l gold & multi | 1.10 | .45 |

Red Flag, Agricultural Symbols — A362

Enver Hoxha, Partisans and Albanian Flag — A363

Design: 1.20 l, Red flag and raised pickax.

1976, Nov. 1

1748	A362	25q multi	.20	.15
1749	A362	1.20 l multi	.80	.20

7th Workers Party Congress.

1976, Oct. 28 Perf. 12x12½

1.90 l, Demonstrators with Albanian flag.

1750	A363	25q multi	.15	.15
1751	A363	1.90 l multi	1.00	.30

Anti-Fascist demonstrations, 35th anniv.

Attacking Partisans, Meeting House — A364

Designs (Red Flag and): 25q, Partisans, pickax and gun. 80q, Workers, soldiers, pickax and gun. 1.20 l, Agriculture and industry. 1.70 l, Dancers, symbols of science and art.

1976, Nov. 8 Litho. Perf. 12x12½

1752	A364	15q gold & multi	.15	.15
1753	A364	25q gold & multi	.15	.15
1754	A364	80q gold & multi	.30	.15
1755	A364	1.20 l gold & multi	.50	.15
1756	A364	1.70 l gold & multi	1.00	.20
		Nos. 1752-1756 (5)	2.10	.80

35th anniv. of 1st Workers Party Cong.

Young Workers and Track A365

Design: 1.25 l, Young soldiers and Albanian flag.

1976, Nov. 23 Perf. 12

1757	A365	80q yellow & multi	.55	.15
1758	A365	1.25 l carmine & multi	.75	.20

Union of Young Communists, 35th anniv.

"Cuca e Maleve" Ballet A366

Designs: Scenes from ballet "Mountain Girl."

1976, Dec. 14 Perf. 12

1759	A366	10q gold & multi	.15	.15
1760	A366	15q gold & multi	.15	.15
1761	A366	20q gold & multi	.15	.15
1762	A366	25q gold & multi	.15	.15
1763	A366	80q gold & multi	.55	.15
1764	A366	1.20 l gold & multi	.75	.20
1765	A366	1.40 l gold & multi	.95	.25
		Nos. 1759-1765 (7)	2.85	1.20

Miniature Sheet
Perf. 12 on 2 sides x Imperf.

| 1766 | A366 | 2.05 l gold & multi | 1.75 | .45 |

Bashtoves Castle A367

Albanian Castles: 15q, Gjirokastres. 20q, Ali Pash Tepelenes. 25q, Petreles. 80q, Beratit. 1.20 l, Durresit. 1.40 l, Krujes.

1976, Dec. 30 Litho. Perf. 12

1767	A367	10q black & dull bl	.15	.15
1768	A367	15q black & grn	.15	.15
1769	A367	20q black & gray	.15	.15
1770	A367	25q black & brn	.15	.15
1771	A367	80q black & rose	.40	.15
1772	A367	1.20 l black & vio	.45	.15
1773	A367	1.40 l black & brn red	.90	.15
		Nos. 1767-1773 (7)	2.35	1.05

Skanderbeg's Shield and Spear — A368

Skanderbeg's Weapons: 80q, Helmet, sword and scabbard. 1 l, Halberd, quiver with arrows, crossbow and spear.

1977, Jan. 28 Litho. Perf. 12

1774	A368	15q silver & multi	.50	.15
1775	A368	80q silver & multi	2.25	.20
1776	A368	1 l silver & multi	3.25	.25
		Nos. 1774-1776 (3)	6.00	.60

Skanderbeg (1403-1468), national hero.

Ilia Oiqi, Messenger in Storm — A369

Modern Heroes: 10q, Ilia Dashi, sailor in battle. 25q, Fran Ndue Ivanaj, fisherman in storm. 80q, Zeliha Allmetaj, woman rescuing child. 1 l, Ylli Zaimi, rescuing goats from flood. 1.90 l, Isuf Plloci, fighting forest fire.

1977, Feb. 28 Litho. Perf. 12x12½

1777	A369	5q brown & multi	.15	.15
1778	A369	10q ultra & multi	.15	.15
1779	A369	25q blue & multi	.15	.15
1780	A369	80q ocher & multi	.50	.15
1781	A369	1 l brown & multi	.80	.15
1782	A369	1.90 l brown & multi	1.40	.20
		Nos. 1777-1782 (6)	3.15	.95

Polyvinylchloride Plant, Vlore — A370

6th Five-year plan: 25q, Naphtha fractioning plant, Balish. 65q, Hydroelectric station and dam, Fjerzes. 1 l, Metallurgical plant and blast furance, Elbasan.

1977, Mar. 29 Litho. Perf. 12½x12

1783	A370	15q silver & multi	.15	.15
1784	A370	25q silver & multi	.30	.15
1785	A370	65q silver & multi	.65	.15
1786	A370	1 l silver & multi	1.10	.15
		Nos. 1783-1786 (4)	2.20	.60

Qerime Halil Galica — A371

Victory Monument, Tirana — A372

Design: 1.25 l, Qerime Halil Galica "Shota" and father Azem Galica.

1977, Apr. 20 Litho. Perf. 12

1787	A371	80q dark red	.65	.15
1788	A371	1.25 l gray blue	1.10	.15

"Shota" Galica, communist fighter.

1977, May 5 Litho. Perf. 12

Designs (Red Star and): 80q, Clenched fist, Albanian flag. 1.20 l, Bust of Qemal Stafa and poppies.

1789	A372	25q multi	.30	.15
1790	A372	80q multi	.90	.15
1791	A372	1.20 l multi	1.50	.20
		Nos. 1789-1791 (3)	2.70	.50

35th anniversary of Martyrs' Day.

Physician Visiting Farm, Mobile Clinic — A373

Designs: 10q, Cowherd and cattle ranch. 20q, Militia woman helping with harvest, rifle and combine. 80q, Modern village, highway and power lines. 2.95 l, Tractor and greenhouses.

1977, June 18

1792	A373	5q multi	.15	.15
1793	A373	10q multi	.15	.15
1794	A373	20q multi	.15	.15
1795	A373	80q multi	.40	.15
1796	A373	2.95 l multi	2.50	.40
		Nos. 1792-1796 (5)	3.35	1.00

"Socialist transformation of the villages."

Armed Workers, Flag and Factory — A374

1.80 l, Workers with proclamation and flags.

1977, June 20

1797	A374	25q multi	.20	.15
1798	A374	1.80 l multi	1.25	.20

9th Labor Unions Congress.

Kerchief Dance — A375

Designs: Various folk dances.

1977, Aug. 20 Litho. Perf. 12

1799	A375	5q multi	.15	.15
1800	A375	10q multi	.15	.15
1801	A375	15q multi	.15	.15
1802	A375	25q multi	.15	.15
1803	A375	80q multi	.30	.15
1804	A375	1 l multi	.60	.20
1805	A375	1.55 l multi	.75	.20
		Nos. 1799-1805 (7)	2.25	1.20

Miniature Sheet
Perf. 12 on 2 sides x Imperf.

| 1806 | A375 | 2.05 l multi | 1.25 | .40 |

See Nos. 1836-1840, 1884-1888.

Attack A376

Designs: 25q, Enver Hoxha addressing Army. 80q, Volunteers and riflemen. 1 l, Volunteers, hydrofoil patrolboat and MiG planes. 1.90 l, Volunteers and Albanian flag.

1977, July 10 Litho. Perf. 12

1807	A376	15q gold & multi	.15	.15
1808	A376	25q gold & multi	.15	.15
1809	A376	80q gold & multi	.45	.15
1810	A376	1 l gold & multi	.70	.15
1811	A376	1.90 l gold & multi	1.25	.25
		Nos. 1807-1811 (5)	2.70	.85

"One People-One Army."

Armed Workers, Article 3 of Constitution A377

Design: 1.20 l, Symbols of farming and fertilizer industry, Article 25 of Constitution.

1977, Oct.

1812	A377	25q red, gold & blk	.25	.15
1813	A377	1.20 l red, gold & blk	.95	.20

New Constitution.

ALBANIA

Picnic — A378

Film Frames: 15q, Telephone lineman in winter. 25q, Two men and a woman. 80q, Workers. 1.20 l, Boys playing in street. 1.60 l, Harvest.

1977, Oct. 25	Litho.	Perf. 12½x12
1814 A378	10q blue green	.15 .15
1815 A378	15q multi	.15 .15
1816 A378	25q black	.15 .15
1817 A378	80q multi	.55 .15
1818 A378	1.20 l deep claret	.95 .15
1819 A378	1.60 l multi	1.25 .20
Nos. 1814-1819 (6)		3.20 .95

Albanian films.

Farm Workers in Field, by V. Mio A379

Paintings by V. Mio: 10q, Landscape in Snow. 15q, Grazing Sheep under Walnut Tree in Spring. 25q, Street in Korce. 80q, Horseback Riders on Mountain Pass. 1 l, Boats on Shore. 1.75 l, Tractors Plowing Fields. 2.05 l, Self-portrait.

1977, Dec. 25	Litho.	Perf. 12½x12
1820 A379	5q gold & multi	.15 .15
1821 A379	10q gold & multi	.15 .15
1822 A379	15q gold & multi	.15 .15
1823 A379	25q gold & multi	.15 .15
1824 A379	80q gold & multi	.40 .15
1825 A379	1 l gold & multi	.45 .15
1826 A379	1.75 l gold & multi	.80 .15
Nos. 1820-1826 (7)		2.25 1.05

Miniature Sheet
Imperf.; Perf. 12 Horiz. between Vignette and Value Panel

| 1827 A379 | 2.05 l gold & multi | 2.00 .35 |

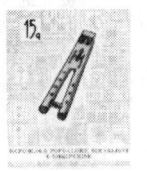

Pan Flute — A380

Albanian Flag, Monument and People — A381

Folk Musical Instruments: 25q, Single-string goat's-head fiddle. 80q, Woodwind. 1.20 l, Drum. 1.70 l, Bagpipe. Background shows various woven folk patterns.

1978, Jan. 20		Perf. 12x12½
1828 A380	15q multi	.15 .15
1829 A380	25q multi	.25 .15
1830 A380	80q multi	.70 .15
1831 A380	1.20 l multi	1.10 .15
1832 A380	1.70 l multi	1.50 .20
Nos. 1828-1832 (5)		3.70 .80

1978		Perf. 12½x12, 12x12½

Designs: 25q, Ismail Qemali and fighters, horiz. 1.65 l, People dancing around Albanian flag, horiz.

1833 A381	15q multi	.20 .15
1834 A381	25q multi	.25 .15
1835 A381	1.65 l multi	1.50 .20
Nos. 1833-1835 (3)		1.95 .50

65th anniversary of independence.

Folk Dancing Type of 1977
Designs: Various dances.

1978, Feb. 15	Litho.	Perf. 12
1836 A375	5q multi	.15 .15
1837 A375	15q multi	.15 .15
1838 A375	80q multi	.35 .15
1839 A375	1 l multi	.50 .15
1840 A375	2.30 l multi	1.00 .25
Nos. 1836-1840 (5)		2.15 .85

Nos. 1836-1840 have white background around dancers, Nos. 1799-1805 have pinkish shadows.

Tractor Drivers, by Dhimitraq Trebicka A382

Working Class Paintings: 80q, Steeplejack, by Spiro Kristo. 85q, "A Point in the Discussion," by Skender Milori. 90q, Oil rig crew, by Anesti Cini, vert. 1.60 l, Metal workers, by Ramadan Karanxha. 2.20 l, Political discussion, by Sotiraq Sholla.

1978, Mar. 25	Litho.	Perf. 12
1841 A382	25q multi	.15 .15
1842 A382	80q multi	.35 .15
1843 A382	85q multi	.35 .15
1844 A382	90q multi	.40 .15
1845 A382	1.60 l multi	.80 .15
Nos. 1841-1845 (5)		2.05 .85

Miniature Sheet
Perf. 12 on 2 sides x Imperf.

| 1846 A382 | 2.20 l multi | 1.75 .40 |

Woman with Rifle and Pickax A383

1.95 l, Farm & Militia women, industrial plant.

1978, June 1	Litho.	Perf. 12
1847 A383	25q gold & red	.25 .15
1848 A383	1.95 l gold & red	1.40 .25

8th Congress of Women's Union.

Children and Flowers — A384

Designs: 10q, Children with rifle, ax, book and flags. 25q, Dancing children in folk costume. 1.80 l, Children in school.

1978, June 1	Litho.	
1849 A384	5q multi	.15 .15
1850 A384	10q multi	.15 .15
1851 A384	25q multi	.25 .15
1852 A384	1.80 l multi	1.50 .20
Nos. 1849-1852 (4)		2.05 .65

International Children's Day.

Spirit of Skanderbeg as Conqueror — A385

Designs: 10q, Battle at Mostar Bridge. 80q, Marchers and Albanian flag. 1.20 l, Riflemen in winter battle. 1.65 l, Abdyl Frasheri (1839-1892). 2.20 l, Rifles, scroll and pen, League building. 2.60 l, League headquarters, Prizren.

1978, June 10	Litho.	Perf. 12
1853 A385	10q multi	.15 .15
1854 A385	25q multi	.15 .15
1855 A385	80q multi	.25 .15
1856 A385	1.20 l multi	.55 .15
1857 A385	1.65 l multi	.85 .20
1858 A385	2.60 l multi	1.00 .30
Nos. 1853-1858 (6)		2.95 1.10

Miniature Sheet
Perf. 12 on 2 sides x Imperf.

| 1859 A385 | 2.20 l multi | 2.00 .35 |

Centenary of League of Prizren.

Guerrillas and Flag, 1943 — A386

Designs: 25q, Soldier, sailor, airman, militiaman, horiz. 1.90 l, Members of armed forces, civil guards, and Young Pioneers.

1978, July 10		Perf. 11½x12½
1860 A386	5q multi	.15 .15
1861 A386	25q multi	.45 .15
1862 A386	1.90 l multi	3.25 .20
Nos. 1860-1862 (3)		3.85 .50

35th anniversary of People's Army.

Woman with Machine Carbine — A387

Kerchief Dance — A388

Designs: 25q, Man with target rifle, horiz. 95q, Man shooting with telescopic sights, horiz. 2.40 l, Woman target shooting with pistol.

Perf. 12½x12, 12x12½

1978, Sept. 20	Litho.	
1863 A387	25q black & yel	.15 .15
1864 A387	80q orange & blk	.35 .15
1865 A387	95q red & blk	.50 .15
1866 A387	2.40 l carmine & blk	1.10 .30
Nos. 1863-1866 (4)		2.10 .75

32nd National Rifle-shooting Championships, Sept. 20.

1978, Oct. 6		Perf. 12

Designs: 15q, Musicians. 25q, Fiddler with single-stringed instrument. 80q, Dancers, men. 1.20 l, Saber dance. 1.90 l, Singers, women.

1867 A388	10q multi	.15 .15
1868 A388	15q multi	.15 .15
1869 A388	25q multi	.15 .15
1870 A388	80q multi	.30 .15
1871 A388	1.20 l multi	.60 .15
1872 A388	1.90 l multi	.95 .25
Nos. 1867-1872 (6)		2.30 1.00

National Folklore Festival.
See Nos. 2082-2085, 2289-2290.

No. 1736 Surcharged with New Value, 2 Bars and "RICCIONE 78"

1978	Litho.	Perf. 12½x12
1873 A360	3.30 l on 25q multi	5.00 1.10

Riccione 78 Philatelic Exhibition.

Enver Hoxha — A389

1978, Oct. 16	Litho.	Perf. 12x12½
1874 A389	80q red & multi	.30 .15
1875 A389	1.20 l red & multi	.45 .15
1876 A389	2.40 l red & multi	.90 .25
Nos. 1874-1876 (3)		1.65 .55

Miniature Sheet
Perf. 12½ on 2 sides x Imperf.

| 1877 A389 | 2.20 l red & multi | 1.75 .40 |

70th birthday of Enver Hoxha, First Secretary of Central Committee of the Communist Party of Albania.

Woman and Wheat — A390

Designs: 25q, Woman with egg crates. 80q, Shepherd and sheep. 2.60 l, Milkmaid and cows.

1978, Dec. 15		Perf. 12x12½
1878 A390	15q multicolored	.20 .15
1879 A390	25q multicolored	.35 .15
1880 A390	80q multicolored	.90 .15
1881 A390	2.60 l multicolored	2.50 .50
Nos. 1878-1881 (4)		3.95 .95

Dora d'Istria — A391

Tower House — A392

Design: 1.10 l, Full portrait of Dora d'Istria, author; birth sesquicentennial.

1979, Jan. 22	Litho.	Perf. 12
1882 A391	80q lt grn & blk	.70 .15
1883 A391	1.10 l vio brn & blk	.80 .15

Costume Type of 1977
Designs: Various folk dances.

1979, Feb. 25		
1884 A375	15q multi	.15 .15
1885 A375	25q multi	.15 .15
1886 A375	80q multi	.40 .15
1887 A375	1.20 l multi	.50 .15
1888 A375	1.40 l multi	.75 .25
Nos. 1884-1888 (5)		1.95 .85

#1884-1888 have white background. Denomination in UL on #1885, in UR on #1802; LL on #1886, UL on #1803.

1979, Mar. 20		

Traditional Houses: 15q, Stone gallery house, horiz. 80q, House with wooden galleries, horiz. 1.20 l, Galleried tower house. 1.40 l, 1.90 l, Tower houses, diff.

1889 A392	15q multi	.15 .15
1890 A392	25q multi	.15 .15
1891 A392	80q multi	.40 .15
1892 A392	1.20 l multi	.50 .15
1893 A392	1.40 l multi	.75 .25
Nos. 1889-1893 (5)		1.95 .85

Miniature Sheet
Perf. 12 on 2 sides x imperf.

| 1894 A392 | 1.90 l multi | 1.50 .40 |

See Nos. 2015-2018.

Soldier, Factories, Wheat A393

1.65 l, Soldiers, workers and coat of arms.

1979, May 14	Litho.	Perf. 12
1895 A393	25q multi	.45 .15
1896 A393	1.65 l multi	2.00 .20

Congress of Permet, 35th anniversary.

Albanian Flag — A394

1979, June 4		
1897 A394	25q multi	.50 .15
1898 A394	1.65 l multi	2.50 .20

5th Congress of Albanian Democratic Front.

ALBANIA

Vasil Shanto,
(1913-44)
A395

Alexander Moissi,
(1880-1935),
Actor — A396

Design: 25q, 90q, Qemal Stafa (1921-42).

1979
1899	A395	15q multi	.15	.15
1900	A395	25q multi	.20	.15
1901	A395	60q multi	.60	.15
1902	A396	80q multi	.80	.15
1903	A395	90q multi	.80	.15
1904	A396	1.10 l multi, diff.	1.00	.40
		Nos. 1899-1904 (6)	3.55	.95

Shanto and Stafa, anti-Fascist fighters.
Issued: type A396, Apr. 2; type A395, May 5.
For similar design see A410.

Winter Campaign, by Arben
Basha — A397

Paintings of Military Scenes by: 25q, Ismail Lulani. 80q, Myrteza Fushekati. 1.20 l, Muhamet Deliu. 1.40 l, Jorgji Gjikopulli. 1.90 l, Fatmir Haxhiu.

1979, July 15   Litho.   Perf. 12½x12
1905	A397	15q multi	.15	.15
1906	A397	25q multi	.15	.15
1907	A397	80q multi	.35	.15
1908	A397	1.20 l multi	.60	.15
1909	A397	1.40 l multi	.65	.25
		Nos. 1905-1909 (5)	1.90	.85

Miniature Sheet
Perf. 12 on 2 sides x Imperf.
| 1910 | A397 | 1.90 l multi | 1.75 | .40 |

Athletes
Surrounding Flag
A398

Literary Society
Headquarters
A399

1979, Oct. 1   Litho.   Perf. 12
1911	A398	15q shown	.15	.15
1912	A398	25q Shooting	.15	.15
1913	A398	80q Dancing	.25	.15
1914	A398	1.20 l Soccer	.50	.15
1915	A398	1.40 l High jump	.65	.25
		Nos. 1911-1915 (5)	1.70	.85

Liberation Spartakiad, 35th anniversary.

1979, Oct. 12

Albanian Literary Society Centenary: 25q, Seal and charter. 80q, Founder. 1.55 l, 1879 Headquarters. 1.90 l, Founders.

1916	A399	25q multi	.15	.15
1917	A399	80q multi	.40	.15
1918	A399	1.20 l multi	.60	.15
1919	A399	1.55 l multi	.75	.20
		Nos. 1916-1919 (4)	1.90	.65

Miniature Sheet
Perf. 12½ on 2 sides x Imperf.
| 1920 | A399 | 1.90 l multi | 2.00 | .40 |

Congress Statute,
Coat of
Arms — A400

1979, Oct. 20   Photo.   Perf. 12x12½
| 1921 | A400 | 25q multi | .50 | .15 |
| 1922 | A400 | 1.65 l multi | 2.50 | .25 |

2nd Congress of Berat, 35th anniversary.

Children Entering
School,
Books — A401

1979   Litho.   Perf. 12½x12
1923	A401	5q shown	.15	.15
1924	A401	10q Communications	.15	.15
1925	A401	15q Steel workers	.15	.15
1926	A401	20q Dancers, instruments	.15	.15
1927	A401	25q Newspapers, radio, television	.20	.15
1928	A401	60q Textile worker	.40	.15
1929	A401	80q Armed forces	.55	.15
1930	A401	1.20 l Industry	.80	.20
1931	A401	1.60 l Transportation	1.00	.30
1932	A401	2.40 l Agriculture	1.50	.35
1932A	A401	3 l Medicine	1.90	.50
		Nos. 1923-1932A (11)	6.95	2.40

Workers and
Factory
A402

Worker, Red Flag and: 80q, Hand holding sickle and rifle. 1.20 l, Red star and open book. 1.55 l, Open book and cogwheel.

1979, Nov. 29
1933	A402	25q multi	.15	.15
1934	A402	80q multi	.20	.15
1935	A402	1.20 l multi	.50	.15
1936	A402	1.55 l multi	.60	.15
		Nos. 1933-1936 (4)	1.45	.60

35th anniversary of independence.

Joseph Stalin — A403

Design: 1.10 l, Stalin on dais, horiz.

1979, Dec. 21   Litho.   Perf. 12
| 1937 | A403 | 80q red & dk bl | .75 | .15 |
| 1938 | A403 | 1.10 l red & dk bl | 1.00 | .20 |

Joseph Stalin (1879-1953), birth centenary.

Fireplace and
Pottery,
Korcar
A404

Home Furnishings: 80q, Cupboard bed, dagger, pistol, ammunition pouch, Shkodar. 1.20 l, Stool, pot, chair, Mirdit. 1.35 l, Chimney, dagger, jacket, Gjirokaster.

1980, Feb. 27   Litho.   Perf. 12
1939	A404	25q multi	.15	.15
1940	A404	80q multi	.35	.15
1941	A404	1.20 l multi	.55	.20
1942	A404	1.35 l multi	.60	.30
		Nos. 1939-1942 (4)	1.65	.80

See Nos. 1985-1988.

Pipe, Painted
Flask — A405

1980, Mar. 4
1943	A405	25q shown	.15	.15
1944	A405	80q Leather handbags	.35	.15
1945	A405	1.20 l Carved eagle, embroidered rug	.55	.20
1946	A405	1.35 l Lace	.60	.30
		Nos. 1943-1946 (4)	1.65	.80

Prof. Aleksander
Xhuvanit Birth
Centenary — A406

1980, Mar. 14
| 1947 | A406 | 80q multi | .55 | .15 |
| 1948 | A406 | 1 l multi | .70 | .20 |

Revolutionaries on Horseback — A407

Insurrection at Kosove, 70th Anniversary: 1 l, Battle scene.

1980, Apr. 4
| 1949 | A407 | 60q red & black | .60 | .15 |
| 1950 | A407 | 1 l red & black | .75 | .20 |

Soldiers and Workers Laboring to Aid the
Stricken Populations, by D. Jukinui and I.
Lulani — A408

1980, Apr. 15   Litho.   Perf. 12½
| 1951 | A408 | 80q lt blue & multi | .60 | .15 |
| 1952 | A408 | 1 l lt blue grn & multi | .75 | .20 |

Lenin, 110th Birth
Anniversary — A409

1980, Apr. 22
| 1953 | A409 | 80q multi | .90 | .15 |
| 1954 | A409 | 1 l multi | 1.10 | .20 |

Misto Mame
and Ali Demi,
War Martyrs
A410

War Martyrs: 80q, Sadik Staveleci, Vojo Kusji, Hoxhi Martini. 1.20 l, Bule Naipi, Persefoni Kokedhima. 1.35 l, Ndoc Deda, Hydajet Lezha, Naim Gyylbegu, Ndoc Mazi, Ahmed Haxha.

1980, May 5
1955	A410	25q multi	.15	.15
1956	A410	80q multi	.40	.15
1957	A410	1.20 l multi	.55	.20
1958	A410	1.35 l multi	.70	.30
		Nos. 1955-1958 (4)	1.80	.80

See Nos. 2012A-2012D, 2025-2028, 2064-2067, 2122-2125, 2171-2174, 2207-2209.

Scene from
"Mirela"
A411

1980, June 7
1959	A411	15q shown	.15	.15
1960	A411	25q The Scribbler	.15	.15
1961	A411	80q Circus Bears	.35	.15
1962	A411	2.40 l Waterdrops	1.00	.35
		Nos. 1959-1962 (4)	1.65	.80

Carrying Iron Castings in the Enver Hoxha
Tractor Combine, by S. Shijaku and M.
Fushekati — A412

Paintings (Gallery of Figurative Paintings, Tirana): 80q, The Welder, by Harilla Dhima. 1.20 l, Steel Erectors, by Petro Kokushta. 1.35 l, Pandeli Lena, 1.80 l Communists, by Vilson Kilica.

1980, July 22
1963	A412	25q multi	.15	.15
1964	A412	80q multi	.35	.15
1965	A412	1.20 l multi	.50	.15
1966	A412	1.35 l multi	.65	.25
		Nos. 1963-1966 (4)	1.65	.70

Souvenir Sheet
| 1967 | A412 | 1.80 l multi | 1.40 | .40 |

Gate, Parchment
Miniature, 11th
Cent. — A413

Bas reliefs of the Middle Ages: 80q, Eagle, 13th cent. 1.20 l, Heraldic lion, 14th cent. 1.35 l, Pheasant, 14th cent.

1980, Sept. 27   Litho.   Perf. 12
1968	A413	25q gold & blk	.15	.15
1969	A413	80q gold & blk	.25	.15
1970	A413	1.20 l gold & blk	.45	.15
1971	A413	1.35 l gold & blk	.55	.25
		Nos. 1968-1971 (4)	1.40	.70

Divjaka
National
Park — A414

1980, Nov. 6   Photo.
1972	A414	80q shown	.50	.15
1973	A414	1.20 l Lura	.85	.25
1974	A414	1.60 l Thethi	1.10	.25
		Nos. 1972-1974 (3)	2.45	.65

Souvenir Sheet
Perf. 12½
| 1975 | A414 | 1.80 l Llogara Park | 2.00 | .75 |

ALBANIA

Citizens, Flag and Arms of Albania — A415

1981, Jan. 11   Litho.   Perf. 12
1976 A415   shown   .50 .15
1977 A415 1 l People's Party Headquarters, Tirana   .75 .25

35th anniversary of the Republic.

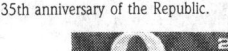

Child's Bed — A416

1981, Mar. 20   Litho.   Perf. 12
1978 A416   25q shown   .15 .15
1979 A416   80q Wooden bucket, brass bottle   .35 .20
1980 A416 1.20 l Shoes   .55 .25
1981 A416 1.35 l Jugs   .60 .30
   Nos. 1978-1981 (4)   1.65 .90

A417 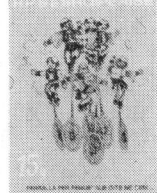   A419

1981, Apr. 20
1982 A417   80q Soldiers   .40 .20
1983 A417   1 l Sword combat   .60 .25

Souvenir Sheet
Perf. 12½ Vert.
1984 A417 1.80 l Soldier with pistol   1.25 .80

Battle of Shtimje centenary.

Home Furnishings Type of 1980

1981, Feb. 25   Litho.   Perf. 12
1985 A404   25q House interior, Labara   .15 .15
1986 A404   80q Labara, diff.   .35 .20
1987 A404 1.20 l Mat   .55 .25
1988 A404 1.35 l Dibres   .55 .30
   Nos. 1985-1988 (4)   1.60 .90

1981, June   Perf. 12

Designs: Children's circus.
1989 A419   15q multi   .15 .15
1990 A419   25q multi   .15 .15
1991 A419   80q multi   .35 .20
1992 A419 2.40 l multi   1.00 .60
   Nos. 1989-1992 (4)   1.65 1.10

Soccer Players A420

1982 World Cup Soccer Elimination Games: Various soccer players.

1981, Mar. 31   Litho.   Perf. 12
1993 A420   25q multi   .25 .15
1994 A420   80q multi   1.90 .40
1995 A420 1.20 l multi   2.75 .65
1996 A420 1.35 l multi   3.50 .80
   Nos. 1993-1996 (4)   8.40 2.00

Allies, by S. Hysa A421

Paintings: 80q, Warriors, by A. Buza. 1.20 l, Rallying to the Flag, Dec. 1911, by A. Zajmi, vert. 1.35 l, My Flag is My Heart, by L. Cefa, vert. 1.80 l, Circling the Flag in a Common Cause, by N. Vasia.

1981, July 10   Perf. 12½x12
1997 A421   25q multi   .15 .15
1998 A421   80q multi   .35 .20
1999 A421 1.20 l multi   .50 .25
2000 A421 1.35 l multi   .55 .30
   Nos. 1997-2000 (4)   1.55 .90

Souvenir Sheet
2001 A421 1.80 l multi   1.40 .85

No. 2001 contains one stamp, size: 55x55mm.

Rifleman A422

1981, Aug. 30   Perf. 12
2002 A422   25q shown   .15 .15
2003 A422   80q Weight lifting   .40 .20
2004 A422 1.20 l Volleyball   .55 .25
2005 A422 1.35 l Soccer   .65 .35
   Nos. 2002-2005 (4)   1.75 .95

Albanian Workers' Party, 8th Congress A423

1981, Nov. 1
2006 A423 80q Flag, star   .30 .20
2007 A423 1 l Flag, hammer & sickle   .40 .25

Albanian Workers' Party, 40th Anniv. — A424    Communist Youth Org., 40th Anniv. — A425

1981, Nov. 8
2008 A424 80q Symbols of industrialization   .35 .25
2009 A424 2.80 l Fist, emblem   1.25 .70

Souvenir Sheet
2010 A424 1.80 l Enver Hoxha, Memoirs   2.00 .85

1981, Nov. 23
2011 A425 80q Star, ax, map   .65 .20
2012 A425 1 l Flags, star   .85 .25

War Martyrs Type of 1980

Portraits: 25q, Perlat Rexhepi (1919-42) and Branko Kadia (1921-42). 80q, Xheladin Beqiri (1908-44) and Hajdar Dushi (1916-44). 1.20 l, Koci Bako (1905-41), Vasil Laci (1923-41) and Mujo Ulqinaku (1898-1939). 1.35 l, Mine Peza (1875-1942) and Zoja Cure (1920-44).

1981, May 5   Litho.   Perf. 12
2012A A410   25q silver & multi   .20 .15
2012B A410   80q gold & multi   .75 .40
2012C A410 1.20 l silver & multi   1.25 .55
2012D A410 1.35 l gold & multi   1.40 .60
   Nos. 2012A-2012D (4)   3.60 1.70

Fan S. Noli, Writer, Birth Centenary — A426

1982, Jan. 6   Litho.   Perf. 12
2013 A426   80q lt ol grn & gold   .40 .20
2014 A426 1.10 l lt red brn & gold   .60 .25

Traditional Houses Type of 1979

1982, Feb.   Perf. 12½x12
2015 A392   25q Bulqize   .30 .20
2016 A392   80q Lebush   .35 .20
2017 A392 1.20 l Bicaj   .55 .30
2018 A392 1.55 l Klos   .80 .40
   Nos. 2015-2018 (4)   2.00 1.10

TB Bacillus Centenary A428

1982, Mar. 24   Perf. 12
2019 A428   80q Globe   1.00 .25
2020 A428 1.10 l Koch   1.40 .35

Albanian League House, Prizren, by K. Buza A429

Kosova Landscapes: 25q, Castle at Prizrenit, by G. Madhi. 1.20 l, Mountain Gorge at Rogove, by K. Buza. 1.55 l, Street of the Hadhji at Zekes, by G. Madhi. 25q, 1.20 l, 1.55 l vert.

1982, Apr. 15   Perf. 12x12½, 12½x12   Litho.
2021 A429   25q multi   .20 .15
2022 A429   80q multi   .50 .15
2023 A429 1.20 l multi   .70 .20
2024 A429 1.55 l multi   1.00 .30
   Nos. 2021-2024 (4)   2.40 .80

War Martyr Type of 1980

Designs: 25q, Hibe Palikuqi, Liri Gero. 80q, Mihal Duri, Kajo Karafili. 1.20 l, Fato Dudumi, Margarita Tutulani, Shejnaze Juka. 1.55 l, Memo Meto, Gjok Doci.

1982, May   Perf. 12
2025 A410   25q multi   .15 .15
2026 A410   80q multi   .35 .20
2027 A410 1.20 l multi   .60 .30
2028 A410 1.55 l multi   .85 .45
   Nos. 2025-2028 (4)   1.95 1.10

Loading Freighter A430

Children's Paintings.

1982, June 15   Perf. 12½x12
2029 A430   15q shown   .15 .15
2030 A430   80q Forest   .55 .20
2031 A430 1.20 l City   .90 .30
2032 A430 1.65 l Park   1.25 .45
   Nos. 2029-2032 (4)   2.85 1.10

9th Congress of Trade Unions A431

1982, June 6   Litho.   Perf. 12
2033 A431   80q Workers, factories   .80 .20
2034 A431 1.10 l Emblem, flag   1.10 .25

Alpine Village Festival, by Danish Jukniu A432

Industrial Development Paintings: 80q, Hydroelectric Station Builders, by Ali Miruku. 1.20 l, Steel Workers, by Clirim Ceka. 1.55 l, Oil drillers, by Pandeli Lena. 1.90 l, Trapping the Furnace, by Jorgji Gjikopulli.

1982, July   Perf. 12½
2035 A432   25q multi   .15 .15
2036 A432   80q multi   .50 .15
2037 A432 1.20 l multi   .75 .20
2038 A432 1.55 l multi   1.00 .30
   Nos. 2035-2038 (4)   2.40 .80

Souvenir Sheet
Perf. 12
2039 A432 1.90 l multi   1.65 .40

No. 2039 contains one 54x48mm stamp.

Communist Party Newspaper "Voice of the People," 40th Anniv. — A432a

1982, Aug. 25   Litho.   Perf. 12
2039A A432a   80q Newspapers
2039B A432a 1.10 l Paper, press

40th Anniv. of Democratic Front — A433

1982, Sept. 16   Perf. 12
2040 A433   80q Glory to the Heroes of Peza Monument   .80 .20
2041 A433 1.10 l Marchers   1.10 .25

8th Youth Congress — A434    Handmade Shoulder Bags — A435

1982, Oct. 4
2042 A434   80q multi   .80 .20
2043 A434 1.10 l multi   1.10 .25

1982, Nov.
2044 A435   25q Rug, horiz.   .15 .15
2045 A435   80q shown   .40 .15
2046 A435 1.20 l Wooden pots, bowls, horiz.   .60 .20
2047 A435 1.55 l Jug   .80 .30
   Nos. 2044-2047 (4)   1.95 .80

70th Anniv. of Independence A436

1982, Nov. 28
2048 A436   20q Ishamil Qemali   .15 .15
2049 A436 1.20 l Partisans   .60 .20
2050 A436 2.40 l Partisans, diff.   1.25 .40
   Nos. 2048-2050 (3)   2.00 .75

Souvenir Sheet
2051 A436 1.90 l Independence Monument, Tirana   1.65 .40

Dhermi Beach A437

ALBANIA

1982, Dec. 20

2052	A437	25q	shown	.15	.15
2053	A437	50q	Sarande	.50	.20
2054	A437	1.20 l	Ksamil	.75	.25
2055	A437	1.55 l	Lukove	1.00	.35
		Nos. 2052-2055 (4)		2.40	.95

Handkerchief Dancers — A438

Folkdancers.

1983, Feb. 20   Litho.   *Perf. 12*

2056	A438	25q	shown	.15	.15
2057	A438	80q	With kerchief, drum	.40	.20
2058	A438	1.20 l	With guitar, flute, tambourine	.60	.25
2059	A438	1.55 l	Women	.80	.35
		Nos. 2056-2059 (4)		1.95	.95

Karl Marks — A439    A440

1983, Mar. 14   Litho.   *Perf. 12*

2060	A439	80q multi		1.10	.20
2061	A439	1.10 l multi		1.50	.25

Karl Marx (1818-83).

1983, Apr. 20

2062	A440	80q	Electricity generation	.40	.20
2063	A440	1.10 l	Gas & oil production	.55	.25

Energy development.

War Martyr Type of 1980

Designs: 25q, Asim Zeneli (1916-43), Nazmi Rushiti (1919-42). 80q, Shyqyri Ishmi (1922-42), Shyqyri Alimerko (1923-43), Myzafer Asqeriu (1918-42). 1.20 l, Oybra Sokoli (1924-44), Qeriba Derri (1905-44), Ylbere Bilibashi (1928-44). 1.55 l, Themo Vasi (1915-43), Abaz Shehu (1905-42).

1983, May 5   Litho.   *Perf. 12*

2064	A410	25q multi		.15	.15
2065	A410	80q multi		.40	.20
2066	A410	1.20 l multi		.60	.25
2067	A410	1.55 l multi		.80	.35
		Nos. 2064-2067 (4)		1.95	.95

Women's Union, 9th Congress — A441

1983, June 1   Litho.   *Perf. 12x12½*

2068	A441	80q red & gold		.85	.20
2069	A441	1.10 l blue & gold		1.10	.25

Bicycling A442

1983, June 20   *Perf. 12*

2070	A442	25q	shown	.15	.15
2071	A442	80q	Chess	.40	.20
2072	A442	1.20 l	Gymnastics	.60	.25
2073	A442	1.55 l	Wrestling	.80	.35
		Nos. 2070-2073 (4)		1.95	.95

40th Anniv. of People's Army — A443

1983, July 10

2074	A443	20q	Armed services	.15	.15
2075	A443	1.20 l	Soldier, gun barrels	.85	.25
2076	A443	2.40 l	Factory guard, crowd	1.65	.50
		Nos. 2074-2076 (3)		2.65	.90

Sunny Day, by Myrteza Fushekati A444

Paintings: 80q, Messenger of the Grasp, by Niko Progi. 1.20 l, 29 November 1944, by Harilla Dhimo. 1.55 l, Fireworks, by Pandi Mele. 1.90 l, Partisan Assault, by Sali Shijaku and M. Fushekati.

1983, Aug. 28   Litho.   *Perf. 12½x12*

2077	A444	25q multi	.15	.15
2078	A444	80q multi	.40	.20
2079	A444	1.20 l multi	.60	.25
2080	A444	1.55 l multi	.80	.35
		Nos. 2077-2080 (4)	1.95	.95

Souvenir Sheet
Perf. 12

2081	A444	1.90 l multi	4.00	.50

Folklore Festival Type of 1978

Gjirokaster Folklore Festival: folkdances.

1983, Oct. 6   Litho.   *Perf. 12*

2082	A388	25q	Sword dance	.15	.15
2083	A388	80q	Kerchief dance	.50	.20
2084	A388	1.20 l	Shepherd flautists	.75	.25
2085	A388	1.55 l	Garland dance	1.00	.35
		Nos. 2082-2085 (4)		2.40	.95

World Communications Year — A446

1983, Nov. 10

2086	A446	60q multi	.40	.15
2087	A446	1.20 l multi	.85	.25

75th Birthday of Enver Hoxha — A447

1983, Oct. 16   Litho.   *Perf. 12½*

2088	A447	80q multi	.40	.20
2089	A447	1.20 l multi	.60	.25
2090	A447	1.80 l multi	.90	.40
		Nos. 2088-2090 (3)	1.90	.85

Souvenir Sheet
Perf. 12

2091	A447	1.90 l multi	1.40	.50

The Right to a Joint Triumph, by J. Keraj A448

Era of Skanderbeg in Figurative Art: 80q, The Heroic Center of the Battle of Krujes, by N. Bakalli. 1.20 l, The Rights of the Enemy after our Triumph, by N. Progri. 1.55 l, The Discussion at Lezhes, by B. Ahmeti. 1.90 l, Victory over the Turks, by G. Madhi.

1983, Dec. 10   *Perf. 12½x12*

2092	A448	25q multi	.20	.15
2093	A448	80q multi	.60	.20
2094	A448	1.20 l multi	.90	.25
2095	A448	1.55 l multi	1.25	.35
		Nos. 2092-2095 (4)	2.95	.95

Souvenir Sheet
Perf. 12

2096	A448	1.90 l multi	2.25	.50

Greco-Roman Ruins of Illyria — A449

1983, Dec. 28   *Perf. 12*

2097	A449	80q Amphitheater, Buthroxtum	.65	.20
2098	A449	1.20 l Colonnade, Apollonium	.95	.25
2099	A449	1.80 l Vaulted gallery, amphitheater at Epidamnus	1.40	.40
		Nos. 2097-2099 (3)	3.00	.85

Archeological Discoveries A450

Designs: Apollo, 3rd cent. 25q, Tombstone, Korce, 3rd cent. 80q, Apollo, diff. 1st cent. 1.10 l, Earthenware pot (child's head), Tren, 1st cent. 1.20 l, Man's head, Dyrrah, 2.20 l, Eros with Dolphin, statue Bronze Dyrrah, 3rd cent.

1984, Feb. 25   *Perf. 12x12½*

2100	A450	15q multi	.15	.15
2101	A450	25q multi	.15	.15
2102	A450	80q multi	.40	.20
2103	A450	1.10 l multi	.55	.20
2104	A450	1.20 l multi	.60	.25
2105	A450	2.20 l multi	1.10	.50
		Nos. 2100-2105 (6)	2.95	1.45

Clock Towers — A451

1984, Mar. 30   *Perf. 12*

2106	A451	15q	Gjirokaster	.15	.15
2107	A451	25q	Kavaje	.15	.15
2108	A451	80q	Elbasan	.40	.20
2109	A451	1.10 l	Tirana	.55	.20
2110	A451	1.20 l	Peqin	.60	.25
2111	A451	2.20 l	Kruje	1.10	.50
		Nos. 2106-2111 (6)		2.95	1.45

40th Anniv. of Liberation A452

1984, Apr. 20   Litho.   *Perf. 12*

2112	A452	15q	Student & microscope	.15	.15
2113	A452	25q	Guerrilla with flag	.15	.15
2114	A452	80q	Children with flag	.40	.20
2115	A452	1.10 l	Soldier	.55	.20
2116	A452	1.20 l	Workers with flag	.60	.25
2117	A452	2.20 l	Militia at dam	1.10	.50
		Nos. 2112-2117 (6)		2.95	1.45

Children — A453

1984, May   Litho.   *Perf. 12*

2118	A453	15q	Children reading	.15	.15
2119	A453	25q	Young pioneers	.25	.15
2120	A453	60q	Gardening	.60	.20
2121	A453	2.80 l	Kite flying	2.75	.60
		Nos. 2118-2121 (4)		3.75	1.05

War Martyr Type of 1980

Designs: 15q, Manush Almani, Mustafa Matohiti, Kastriot Muco. 25q, Zaho Koka, Reshit Collaku, Maliq Muco. 1.20 l, Lefter Talo, Tom Kola, Fuat Babani. 2.20 l, Myslysm Shyri, Dervish Hexali, Skender Caci.

1984, May 5   Litho.   *Perf. 12*

2122	A410	15q multi	.15	.15
2123	A410	25q multi	.15	.15
2124	A410	1.20 l multi	.95	.30
2125	A410	1.55 l multi	1.75	.60
		Nos. 2122-2125 (4)	3.00	1.20

A454    A455

1984, May 24   Litho.   *Perf. 12*

2126	A454	80q	Enver Hoxha	.80	.20
2127	A454	1.10 l	Resistance fighter	1.25	.30

40th anniv. of Permet Congress.

1984, June 12   Litho.   *Perf. 12*

2128	A455	15q	Goalkeeper	.15	.15
2129	A455	25q	Referee	.20	.15
2130	A455	1.20 l	Map of Europe	.90	.45
2131	A455	2.20 l	Field diagram	1.75	.90
		Nos. 2128-2131 (4)		3.00	1.65

European soccer championships.

Freedom Came, by Myrteza Fushekati A456

Paintings, Tirana Gallery of Figurative Art: 25q, Morning, by Zamir Mati, vert. 80q, My Darling, by Agim Zajmi, vert. 2.60 l, For the Partisans, by Arben Basha. 1.90 l, Eagle, by Zamir Mati, vert.

1984, June 12   *Perf. 12½*

2132	A456	15q multi	.15	.15
2133	A456	25q multi	.25	.15
2134	A456	80q multi	.80	.25
2135	A456	2.60 l multi	2.75	.80
		Nos. 2132-2135 (4)	3.95	1.35

Souvenir Sheet
Perf. 12 Horiz.

2136	A456	1.90 l multi	3.00	.60

Flora — A457

ALBANIA

1984, Aug. 20   Litho.   *Perf. 12*
2137	A457	15q Moraceae L.	.35	.15
2138	A457	25q Plantaginaceae L.	.60	.15
2139	A457	1.20 l Hypericaceae L.	2.75	.60
2140	A457	2.20 l Leontopodium alpinum	5.25	1.10
		Nos. 2137-2140 (4)	8.95	2.00

AUSIPEX '84, Melbourne, Sept. 21-30 — A458

1984, Sept. 21   Litho.   *Perf. 12 Horiz.*
2141	A458	1.90 l Sword dancers, emblem	1.50	.75

A459    A460

Forestry, logging, UNFAO emblem.

1984, Sept. 25   *Perf. 12*
2142	A459	15q Beech trees, transport	.15	.15
2143	A459	25q Pine forest, logging cable	.20	.15
2144	A459	1.20 l Firs, sawmill	.90	.45
2145	A459	2.20 l Forester clearing woods	1.75	.90
		Nos. 2142-2145 (4)	3.00	1.65

1984, Oct. 13   *Perf. 12½*
2146	A460	1.20 l View of Gjirokaster	2.00	.45

EURPHILA '84, Rome.

5th National Spartakiad — A461

1984, Oct. 19   *Perf. 12*
2147	A461	15q Soccer	.15	.15
2148	A461	25q Women's track & field	.20	.15
2149	A461	80q Weight lifting	.60	.30
2150	A461	2.20 l Pistol shooting	1.75	.90
		Nos. 2147-2150 (4)	2.70	1.50

Souvenir Sheet
Perf. 12 Horiz.
2151	A461	1.90 l Opening ceremony, red flags	2.00	.75

November 29 Revolution, 40th Anniv. A462

1984, Nov. 29   *Perf. 12*
2152	A462	80q Industrial reconstruction	1.25	.30
2153	A462	1.10 l Natl. flag, partisans	1.65	.40

Souvenir Sheet
Perf. 12 Horiz.
2154	A462	1.90 l Gen. Enver Hoxha reading 1944 declaration	2.00	.75

Archaeological Discoveries from Illyria — A463

Designs: 15q, Iron Age water container. 80q, Terra-cotta woman's head, 6th-7th cent. B.C. 1.20 l, Aphrodite, bust, 3rd cent. B.C. 1.70 l, Nike, A.D. 1st-2nd cent. bronze statue.

1985, Feb. 25   *Perf. 12x12½*
2155	A463	15q multi	.15	.15
2156	A463	80q multi	.80	.40
2157	A463	1.20 l multi	1.10	.55
2158	A463	1.70 l multi	1.75	.85
		Nos. 2155-2158 (4)	3.80	1.95

Hysni Kapo (1915-1980), Natl. Labor Party Leader — A464

1985, Mar. 4   *Perf. 12*
2159	A464	90q red & blk	.85	.45
2160	A464	1.10 l chlky bl & blk	1.10	.55

OLYMPHILEX '85, Lausanne A465

1985, Mar. 18
2161	A465	25q Women's track & field	.25	.15
2162	A465	60q Weight lifting	.60	.30
2163	A465	1.20 l Soccer	1.10	.55
2164	A465	1.50 l Women's pistol shooting	1.25	.65
		Nos. 2161-2164 (4)	3.20	1.65

Johann Sebastian Bach — A466

1985, Mar. 31
2165	A466	80q Portrait, manuscript	2.00	.40
2166	A466	1.20 l Eisenach, birthplace	3.00	.55

Gen. Enver Hoxha (1908-1985) A467

1985, Apr. 11   *Perf. 12½*
2167	A467	80q multicolored	.80	.40

Souvenir Sheet
Imperf
2168	A467	1.90 l multicolored	2.00	1.00

Natl. Frontier Guards, 40th Anniv. A468

1985, Apr. 25   *Perf. 12*
2169	A468	25q Guardsman, family	.35	.15
2170	A468	80q At frontier post	1.10	.40

War Martyrs Type of 1980

Cameo portraits: 25q, Mitro Xhani (1916-44), Nimete Progonati (1929-44), Kozma Nushi (1909-44). 40q, Ajet Xhindoli (1922-43), Mustafa Kacaci (1903-44), Estref Caka Osaja (1919-44). 60q, Celo Sinani (1929-44), Lt. Ambro Andoni (1920-44), Meleq Gosnishti (1913-44). 1.20 l, Thodhori Mastora (1920-44), Fejzi Micoli (1919-45), Hysen Cino (1920-44).

1985, May 5
2171	A410	25q multi	.25	.15
2172	A410	40q multi	.40	.20
2173	A410	60q multi	.60	.30
2174	A410	1.20 l multi	1.25	.55
		Nos. 2171-2174 (4)	2.50	1.20

Victory over Fascism A469

Designs: 25q, Rifle, red flag, inscribed May 9. 80q, Hand holding rifle, globe, broken swastika.

1985, May 9
2175	A469	25q multi	.65	.15
2176	A469	80q multi	2.00	.40

End of World War II, 40th anniv.

Primary School, by Thoma Malo A470

Paintings, Tirana Gallery of Figurative Art: 80q, The Heroes, by Hysen Devolli, vert. 90q, In Our Days, by Angjelin Dodmasej, vert. 1.20 l, Going Off to Sow, by Ksenofon Dilo. 1.90 l, Foundry Workers, by Mikel Gurashi.

1985, June 25   *Perf. 12½*
2177	A470	25q multi	.25	.15
2178	A470	80q multi	.80	.40
2179	A470	90q multi	.85	.45
2180	A470	1.20 l multi	1.10	.55
		Nos. 2177-2180 (4)	3.00	1.55

Souvenir Sheet
Perf. 12 Horiz.
2181	A470	1.90 l multi	2.00	1.00

Basketball Championships, Spain — A471

Fruits — A472

Various plays.

1985, July 20   Litho.   *Perf. 12*
2182	A471	25q dull bl & blk	.25	.15
2183	A471	80q dull grn & blk	.80	.40
2184	A471	1.20 l dl vio & blk	1.10	.60
2185	A471	1.60 l dl rose & blk	1.50	.75
		Nos. 2182-2185 (4)	3.65	1.90

1985, Aug. 20
2186	A472	25q Oranges	.25	.15
2187	A472	80q Plums	.80	.40
2188	A472	1.20 l Apples	1.10	.60
2189	A472	1.60 l Cherries	1.50	.75
		Nos. 2186-2189 (4)	3.65	1.90

Architecture A473

1985, Sept. 20
2190	A473	25q Kruja	.25	.15
2191	A473	80q Gjirokastra	.80	.40
2192	A473	1.20 l Berati	1.10	.60
2193	A473	1.60 l Shkodera	1.50	.75
		Nos. 2190-2193 (4)	3.65	1.90

Natl. Folk Theater Festival — A474

Various scenes from folk plays.

1985, Oct. 6
2194	A474	25q multi	.25	.15
2195	A474	80q multi	.80	.40
2196	A474	1.20 l multi	1.10	.60
2197	A474	1.60 l multi	1.50	.75

Size: 56x82mm
Imperf
2198	A474	1.90 l multi	3.50	1.90
		Nos. 2194-2198 (5)	7.15	3.80

Socialist People's Republic, 40th Anniv. A475

1986, Jan. 11   Litho.   *Perf. 12½*
2199	A475	25q Natl. crest, vert.	.70	.15
2200	A475	80q Proclamation, 1946	2.25	.40

A476    A477

Designs: 25q, Dam, River Drin, Melgun. 80q, Bust of Enver Hoxha, dam power house.

1986, Feb. 20   *Perf. 12*
2201	A476	25q multi	1.25	.15
2202	A476	80q multi	3.75	.40

Enver Hoxha hydro-electric power station, Koman.

1986, Mar. 20   Litho.   *Perf. 12*

Flowers.
2203	A477	25q Gymnospermium shqipetarum	.35	.15
2204	A477	1.20 l Leucojum valentinum	1.90	.60
	a.	Pair, #2203-2204	2.25	1.00

No. 2204a sold only in booklets of 2; exists imperf.

ALBANIA

A478

Famous Men — A479

Designs: 25q, Maxim Gorky, Russian author. 80q, Andre Marie Ampere, French physicist. 1.20 l, James Watt, English inventor of modern steam engine. 2.40 l, Franz Liszt, Hungarian composer.

1986, Apr. 20
2205		Strip of 4	4.40	2.20
a.	A478	25q dull red brown	.25	.15
b.	A478	80q dull violet	.75	.40
c.	A478	1.20 l dull blue green	1.10	.60
d.	A478	2.40 l dull lilac rose	2.25	.90

Size: 88x72mm
Imperf
2206	A479	1.90 l multi	1.75	.88

No. 2206 has central area picturing Gorky, Ampere, Watt and Liszt, perf. 12½.

War Martyrs Type of 1980

Portraits: 25q, Ramiz Aranitasi (1923-43), Inajete Dumi (1924-44) and Laze Nuro Ferraj (1897-1944). 80q, Dine Kalenja (1919-44), Kozma Naska (1921-44), Met Hasa (1929-44) and Fahri Ramadani (1920-44). 1.20 l, Hiqmet Buzi (1927-44), Bajram Tusha (1922-42), Mumin Selami (1923-42) and Hajrfdin Bylyshi (1923-42).

1986, May 5 Perf. 12
2207	A410	30q multi	.65	.15
2208	A410	80q multi	2.25	.40
2209	A410	1.20 l multi	3.00	.55
	Nos. 2207-2209 (3)		5.90	1.10

A480

1986 World Cup Soccer Championships, Mexico — A481

1986, May 31 Litho. Perf. 12
2210	A480	25q Globe, world cup	.25	.15
2211	A480	1.20 l Player, soccer ball	1.25	.60

Size: 97x64mm
Imperf
2212	A481	1.90 l multi	1.75	.90
	Nos. 2210-2212 (3)		3.25	1.65

No. 2212 has central label, perf. 12½.

Shop with Scott Publishing Co. 24 hours a day 7 days a week at www.scottonline.com

Transportation Workers' Day, 40th Anniv. — A482

1986, Aug. 10 Litho. Perf. 12
2213	A482	1.20 l multi	3.00	.60

Prominent Albanians A483

Designs: 30q, Naim Frasheri (1846-1900), poet. 60q, Ndre Mjeda (1866-1937), poet. 90q, Petro Nini Luarasi (1865-1911), poet, journalist. 1 l, Andon Zako Cajupi (1866-1930), poet. 1.20 l, Millosh Gjergj Nikolla Migjeni (1911-1938), novelist. 2.60 l, Urani Rumbo (1884-1936), educator.

1986, Sept. 20 Litho. Perf. 12
2214	A483	30q multi	.30	.15
2215	A483	60q multi	.60	.30
2216	A483	90q multi	.90	.45
2217	A483	1 l multi	.95	.50
2218	A483	1.20 l multi	1.10	.60
2219	A483	2.60 l multi	2.50	1.25
	Nos. 2214-2219 (6)		6.35	3.25

Albanian Workers' Party, 9th Congress, Tirana A484

1986, Nov. 3 Litho. Perf. 12
2220	A484	30q multi	1.90	.25

A485 A486

Albanian Workers' Party, 45th Anniv.: 30q, Handstamp, signature of Hoxha. 1.20 l, Marx, Engels, Lenin and Stalin, party building.

1986, Nov. 8
2221	A485	30q multi	.60	.15
2222	A485	1.20 l multi	2.25	.60

1986, Nov. 29 Perf. 12x12½
Statue of Mother Albania.
2223	A486	10q peacock blue	.15	.15
2224	A486	20q henna brn	.20	.15
2225	A486	30q vermilion	.30	.15
2226	A486	50q dk olive bis	.50	.25
2227	A486	60q lt olive grn	.60	.30
2228	A486	80q rose	.80	.40
2229	A486	90q ultra	.90	.45
2230	A486	1.20 l green	1.10	.60
2231	A486	1.60 l red vio	1.50	.75
2232	A486	2.20 l myrtle grn	2.00	1.10
2233	A486	3 l brn org	2.75	1.40
2234	A486	6 l yel bister	5.50	2.25
	Nos. 2223-2234 (12)		16.30	7.95

For surcharges see Nos. 2435-2439.

Artifacts A487

Designs: 30q, Head of Aesoulapius, 5th cent. B.C. Byllis, marble. 80q, Aphrodite, 3rd cent. B.C., Fier, terracotta. 1 l, Pan, 3rd-2nd cent, B.C., Byllis, bronze. 1.20 l, Jupiter, A.D. 2nd cent., Tirana, limestone.

1987, Feb. 20
2235	A487	30q multi	.30	.15
2236	A487	80q multi	.75	.40
2237	A487	1 l multi	.95	.45
2238	A487	1.20 l multi	1.10	.60
	Nos. 2235-2238 (4)		3.10	1.60

1st Albanian School, Cent. — A488

Famous Men — A489

Gun, quill pen, book of the alphabet and: 30q, Monument, vert. 80q, School, Korca. 1.20 l, Students.

1987, Mar. 7 Perf. 12
2239	A488	30q multi	.35	.15
2240	A488	80q multi	.85	.40
2241	A488	1.20 l multi	1.25	.60
	Nos. 2239-2241 (3)		2.45	1.15

1987, Apr. 20

Designs: 30q, Victor Hugo, French author. 80q, Galileo Galilei, Italian mathematician, philosopher. 90q, Charles Darwin, British biologist. 1.30 l, Miguel Cervantes, Spanish novelist.

2242	A489	30q multi	.30	.15
2243	A489	80q multi	.75	.40
2244	A489	90q multi	.90	.45
2245	A489	1.30 l multi	1.25	.80
	Nos. 2242-2245 (4)		3.20	1.80

World Food Day — A490

10th Trade Unions Cong. — A491

1987, May 20
2246	A490	30q Forsythia europaea	.30	.15
2247	A490	90q Moltkia doerfleri	.85	.45
2248	A490	2.10 l Wulfenia baldacii	2.00	1.00
	Nos. 2246-2248 (3)		3.15	1.60

1987, June 25
2249	A491	1.20 l multi	2.25	.60

Sowing, by Bujar Asllani — A492

Paintings in the Eponymous Museum, Tirana: 30q, The Sustenance of Industry, by Myrteza Fushekati, vert. 80q, The Gifted Partisan, by Skender Kokobobo, vert. 1.20 l, At the Forging Block, by Clirim Ceka.

Perf. 12x12½, 12½x12
1987, July 20 Litho.
2250	A492	30q multi	.30	.15
2251	A492	80q multi	.80	.40
2252	A492	1 l shown	1.00	.50
2253	A492	1.20 l multi	1.25	.60
	Nos. 2250-2253 (4)		3.35	1.65

A493

OLYMPHILEX '87, Rome, Aug. 29-Sept. 6 — A494

Illustration A494 reduced.

1987, Aug. 29 Litho. Perf. 12½
2254	A493	30q Hammer throw	.30	.15
2255	A493	90q Running	.90	.45
2256	A493	1.10 l Shot put	1.25	.60

Size: 85x60mm
2257	A494	1.90 l Runner, globe	2.00	1.00
	Nos. 2254-2257 (4)		4.45	2.20

Famous Men — A495

Designs: 30q, Themistokli Germenji (1871-1917), author, politician. 80q, Bajram Curri (1862-1925), founder of the Albanian League. 90q, Aleks Stavre Drenova (1872-1947), poet. 1.30 l, Gjerasim D. Qiriazi (1861-1894), teacher, journalist.

1987, Sept. 30 Perf. 12
2258	A495	30q multi	.30	.15
2259	A495	80q multi	.80	.40
2260	A495	90q multi	.90	.45
2261	A495	1.30 l multi	1.30	.65
	Nos. 2258-2261 (4)		3.30	1.65

Albanian Labor Party Congress, Tirana A496

1987, Oct. 22 Litho. Perf. 12
2262	A496	1.20 l multi	1.90	.60

Natl. Independence, 75th Anniv. — A497

Postal Administration, 75th Anniv. — A498

1987, Nov. 27
2263	A497	1.20 l State flag	1.90	.60

1987, Dec. 5
2264	A498	90q P.O. emblem	2.00	.45
2265	A498	1.20 l State seal	2.50	.60

ALBANIA

Art & Literature — A499

WHO, 40th Anniv. — A500

Portraits: 30q, Lord Byron (1788-1824), English Poet. 1.20 l, Eugene Delacroix (1798-1863), French painter.

1988, Mar. 10
| 2266 | A499 | 30q org brn & blk | 1.00 | .15 |
| 2267 | A499 | 1.20 l pale vio & blk | 4.00 | .60 |

1988, Apr. 7
| 2268 | A500 | 90q multi | 2.00 | .45 |
| 2269 | A500 | 1.20 l multi | 2.50 | .60 |

Flowers — A501

1988, May 20
Booklet Stamps
2270	A501	30q *Sideritis raeseri*	.75	.15
2271	A501	90q *Lunaria telekiana*	2.25	.45
2272	A501	2.10 l *Sanguisorba albanica*	5.50	1.10
a.	Bklt. pane of 3, plus label		8.50	
	Nos. 2270-2272 (3)		8.50	1.70

10th Women's Federation Congress A502

1988, June 6
| 2273 | A502 | 90q blk, red & dark org | 2.50 | .45 |

European Soccer Championships — A503

Various athletes.
1.90 l, Goalie designs of Nos. 2274-2276.

1988, June 10
2274	A503	30q multicolored	.30	.15
2275	A503	80q multicolored	.80	.40
2276	A503	1.20 l multicolored	1.25	.60

Size: 79x68mm
Imperf
| 2277 | A503 | 1.90 l multicolored | 1.90 | .95 |
| | Nos. 2274-2277 (4) | | 4.25 | 2.10 |

Migjeni (1911-1938), Poet — A507

1988, Aug. 26 *Litho.* *Perf. 12*
| 2285 | A507 | 90q silver & brown | 2.50 | .50 |

Ballads — A508

1988, Sept. 5
2286	A508	30q Dede Skurra	1.00	.15
2287	A508	90q Omeri Iri	3.00	.50
2288	A508	1.20 l Gjergj Elez Alia	4.00	.65
	Nos. 2286-2288 (3)		8.00	1.30

Folklore Festival Type of 1978
1988, Oct. 6
| 2289 | A388 | 30q Kerchief Dance | 1.25 | .15 |
| 2290 | A388 | 1.20 l Dancers with raised arm | 4.75 | .65 |

Enver Hoxha Museum A510

Perf. 12x12½, 12½x12
1988, Oct. 16 *Litho.*
| 2291 | A510 | 90q Portrait, vert. | 1.10 | .35 |
| 2292 | A510 | 1.20 l shown | 1.40 | .50 |

Enver Hoxha (1908-1985), Communist leader.

Locomotives, Map Showing Rail Network — A512

1989, Feb. 28 *Litho.* *Perf. 12½x12*
2295	A512	30q 1947	.20	.15
2296	A512	90q 1949	.65	.35
2297	A512	1.20 l 1978	.85	.40
2298	A512	1.80 l 1985	1.25	.65
2299	A512	2.40 l 1988	1.65	.85
	Nos. 2295-2299 (5)		4.60	2.40

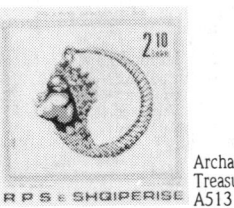

Archaeological Treasures A513

30q, Illyrian grave. 90q, Warrior on horseback.

1989, Mar. 10 *Litho.* *Perf. 12*
2300	A513	30q blk & tan	.20	.15
2301	A513	90q blk & dl grn	.65	.35
2302	A513	2.10 l shown	1.50	.75
	Nos. 2300-2302 (3)		2.35	1.25

Folklore — A514

1989, Apr. 5 *Litho.* *Perf. 12x12½*
2303	A514	30q multicolored	.20	.15
2304	A514	80q multi, diff.	.55	.30
2305	A514	1 l multi, diff.	.70	.35
2306	A514	1.20 l multi, diff.	.85	.45
	Nos. 2303-2306 (4)		2.30	1.25

Flowers — A515    Famous People — A516

Designs: 30q, *Aster albanicus*. 90q, *Orchis x papariosti*. 2.10 l, *Orchis albanica*.

1989, May 10 *Perf. 12*
2307	A515	30q multicolored	.20	.15
2308	A515	90q multicolored	.65	.35
2309	A515	2.10 l multicolored	1.50	.75
	Nos. 2307-2309 (3)		2.35	1.25

1989, June 3

Designs: 30q, Johann Strauss the Younger (1825-1899), composer. 80q, Marie Curie (1867-1834), chemist. 1 l, Federico Garcia Lorca (1898-1936), poet. 1.20 l, Albert Einstein (1879-1955), physicist.

2310	A516	30q gold & blk brn	.20	.15
2311	A516	80q gold & blk brn	.60	.30
2312	A516	1 l gold & blk brn	.75	.35
2313	A516	1.20 l gold & blk brn	.85	.45
	Nos. 2310-2313 (4)		2.40	1.25

6th Congress of Albanian Democratic Front A517

1989, June 26
| 2314 | A517 | 1.20 l multicolored | 1.50 | .65 |

French Revolution, Bicent. — A518

90q, Storming of the Bastille. 1.20 l, Statue.

1989, July 7 *Litho.* *Perf. 12½*
| 2315 | A518 | 90q multicolored | .75 | .40 |
| 2316 | A518 | 1.20 l shown | 1.00 | .50 |

Illyrian Ship — A519

1989, July 25 *Perf. 12*
2317	A519	30q shown	.25	.15
2318	A519	80q Caravel	.60	.30
2319	A519	90q 3-masted schooner	.65	.35
2320	A519	1.30 l Modern cargo ship	1.00	.50
	Nos. 2317-2320 (4)		2.50	1.30

A520    A521

Famous Men: 30q, Pjeter Bogdani (1625-1689), writer. 80q, Gavril Dara (1826-1889), poet. 90q, Thimi Mitko (1820-1890), writer. 1.30 l, Kole Idromeno (1860-1939), painter.

1989, Aug. 30 *Litho.* *Perf. 12*
2321	A520	30q multicolored	.30	.15
2322	A520	80q multicolored	.80	.40
2323	A520	90q multicolored	.90	.45
2324	A520	1.30 l multicolored	1.25	.65
	Nos. 2321-2324 (4)		3.25	1.65

1989, Sept. 29
| 2325 | A521 | 90q shown | .70 | .35 |
| 2326 | A521 | 1.20 l Workers | .95 | .50 |

First Communist International, 125th anniv.

Spartakiad Games — A522

1989, Oct. 27 *Perf. 12x12½*
2327	A522	30q Gymnastics	.20	.15
2328	A522	80q Soccer	.55	.30
2329	A522	1 l Cycling	.70	.35
2330	A522	1.20 l Running	.85	.45
	Nos. 2327-2330 (4)		2.30	1.25

Miniature Sheet

45th Anniv. of Liberation — A523

1989, Nov. 29 *Perf. 12x12½*
2331	Sheet of 4		2.50	1.25
a.	A523 30q Revolutionary		.20	.15
b.	A523 80q "45"		.55	.30
c.	A523 1 l Coat of arms		.70	.35
d.	A523 1.20 l Workers		.85	.45

Rupicapra Rupicapra — A524

1990, Mar. 15 *Perf. 12*
2332	A524	10q Two adults	.15	.15
2333	A524	30q Adult, kid	.30	.15
2334	A524	80q Adult	.80	.40
2335	A524	90q Adult head	.90	.45
a.	Block of 4, #2332-2335		2.10	1.10

World Wildlife Fund.

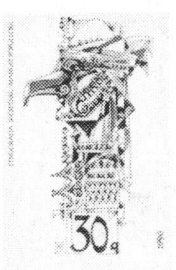

Tribal Masks — A525

1990, Apr. 4 *Perf. 12x12½*
2336	A525	30q shown	.30	.15
2337	A525	90q multi, diff.	.95	.50
2338	A525	1.20 l multi, diff.	1.25	.65
2339	A525	1.80 l multi, diff.	1.90	.95
	Nos. 2336-2339 (4)		4.40	2.25

ALBANIA

Mushrooms A526

1990, Apr. 28 Litho. Perf. 12
2340	A526	30q Amanita caesarea	.25	.15
2341	A526	90q Lepiota procera	.75	.40
2342	A526	1.20 l Boletus edulis	1.00	.50
2343	A526	1.80 l Clathrus cancelatus	1.50	.75
		Nos. 2340-2343 (4)	3.50	1.80

First Postage Stamp, 150th Anniv. A527

1990, May 6 Perf. 12
2344	A527	90q shown	.95	.50
2345	A527	1.20 l Post rider	1.25	.60
2346	A527	1.80 l Carriage	1.75	.95
a.		Bklt. pane of 3, #2344-2346 + label	4.25	
		Nos. 2344-2346 (3)	3.95	2.05

World Cup Soccer, Italy — A528

1990, June Litho. Perf. 12
2347	A528	30q multicolored	.50	.25
2348	A528	90q multi, diff.	1.40	.75
2349	A528	1.20 l multi, diff.	2.00	1.00

Size: 80x63mm
Imperf
| 2350 | A528 | 3.30 l multi, diff. | 5.30 | 2.65 |
| | | Nos. 2347-2350 (4) | 9.20 | 4.65 |

Vincent Van Gogh, Death Cent. A529

Self portraits and: 30q, Details from various paintings. 90q, Woman in field. 2.10 l, Asylum. 2.40 l, Self-portrait.

1990, July 27
2351	A529	30q multicolored	.50	.25
2352	A529	90q multicolored	1.40	.75
2353	A529	2.10 l multicolored	3.50	1.75

Size: 87x73mm
Imperf
| 2354 | A529 | 2.40 l multicolored | 1.90 | .95 |
| | | Nos. 2351-2354 (4) | 7.30 | 3.70 |

Albanian Folklore — A530

Scenes from medieval folktale of "Gjergj Elez Alia": 30q, Alia lying wounded. 90q, Alia being helped onto horse. 1.20 l, Alia fighting Bajloz. 1.80 l, Alia on horseback over severed head of Bajloz.

1990, Aug. 30 Perf. 12½x12
2355	A530	30q multicolored	.50	.25
2356	A530	90q multicolored	1.40	.70
2357	A530	1.20 l multicolored	2.00	.95
2358	A530	1.80 l multicolored	3.00	1.50
		Nos. 2355-2358 (4)	6.90	3.40

Founding of Berat, 2400th Anniv. A531

Designs: 30q, Xhamia E Plumbit. 90q, Kisha E Shen Triadhes. 1.20 l, Ura E Beratit. 1.80 l, Onufri-Piktor Mesjetar. 2.40 l, Nikolla-Piktor Mesjetar.

1990, Sept. 20 Perf. 12½
2359		Block of 5 + 4 labels	4.25	2.10
a.	A531	30q multi	.20	.15
b.	A531	90q multi	.65	.30
c.	A531	1.20 l multi	.70	.35
d.	A531	1.80 l multi	1.25	.65
e.	A531	2.40 l multi	1.40	.70

No. 2359 was sold in souvenir folders for 9.90 l.

Illyrian Heroes — A532

1990, Oct. 20 Perf. 12
2360	A532	30q Pirroja	.50	.25
2361	A532	90q Teuta	1.40	.70
2362	A532	1.20 l Bato	2.00	.95
2363	A532	1.80 l Bardhyli	3.00	1.50
		Nos. 2360-2363 (4)	6.90	3.40

Intl. Literacy Year — A533

1990, Oct. 30
| 2364 | A533 | 90q lt bl & multi | 1.40 | .70 |
| 2365 | A533 | 1.20 l pink & multi | 2.00 | .95 |

Albanian Horseman by Eugene Delacroix A534

Designs: 1.20 l, Albanian Woman by Camille Corot. 1.80 l, Skanderbeg by unknown artist.

1990, Nov. 30 Perf. 12x12½
2366	A534	30q multicolored	.50	.25
2367	A534	1.20 l multicolored	1.90	.95
2368	A534	1.80 l multicolored	3.00	1.50
		Nos. 2366-2368 (3)	5.40	2.70

Isa Boletini (1864-1916), Freedom Fighter — A535

1991, Jan. 23 Litho. Perf. 12x12½
| 2369 | A535 | 90q Portrait | .65 | .30 |
| 2370 | A535 | 1.20 l shown | .90 | .45 |

Pierre Auguste Renoir (1841-1919), Painter — A537

Paintings: 30q, Girl Reading, 1876, vert. 90q, The Swing, 1876, vert. 1.20 l, Boating Party, 1868-1869. 1.80 l, Flowers and grapes, 1878. 3 l, Self-portrait.

1991, Feb. 25 Perf. 12½x12
2373	A537	30q multicolored	.20	.15
2374	A537	90q multicolored	.65	.30
2375	A537	1.20 l multicolored	.90	.45
2376	A537	1.80 l multicolored	1.25	.65

Size: 95x75mm
Imperf
| 2377 | A537 | 3 l multicolored | 4.75 | 2.50 |
| | | Nos. 2373-2377 (5) | 7.75 | 4.05 |

Flowers — A538

1991, Mar. 30 Perf. 12
2378	A538	30q Cistus albanicus	.50	.25
2379	A538	90q Trifolium pilczii	1.40	.75
2380	A538	1.80 l Lilium albanicum	3.00	1.50
		Nos. 2378-2380 (3)	4.90	2.50

Legend of Rozafa — A539

Various scenes from legend.

1991, Sept. 30 Litho. Perf. 12x12½
2381	A539	30q multicolored	.50	.25
2382	A539	90q multicolored	1.40	.70
2383	A539	1.20 l multicolored	2.00	.95
2384	A539	1.80 l multicolored	3.00	1.50
		Nos. 2381-2384 (4)	6.90	3.40

Wolfgang Amadeus Mozart, Death Bicent. — A540

1991, Oct. 5 Litho. Perf. 12
2385	A540	90q Conducting	.70	.35
2386	A540	1.20 l Portrait	.90	.45
2387	A540	1.80 l Playing piano	1.40	.70

Size: 89x70mm
Imperf
| 2388 | A540 | 3 l Medal, score | 4.00 | 4.00 |
| | | Nos. 2385-2388 (4) | 7.00 | 5.50 |

Airplanes A541

Designs: 30q, Glider, Otto Lilienthal, 1896. 80q, Avion III, Clement Ader, 1897. 90q, Flyer, Wright Brothers, 1903. 1.20 l, Concorde. 1.80 l, Tupolev 114. 2.40 l, Dornier 31 E.

1992, Jan. 27 Litho. Perf. 12½x12
2389	A541	30q multicolored	.50	.25
2390	A541	80q multicolored	1.25	.65
2391	A541	90q multicolored	1.40	.70
2392	A541	1.20 l multicolored	2.00	1.00
2393	A541	1.80 l multicolored	3.00	1.50
2394	A541	2.40 l multicolored	4.00	2.00
		Nos. 2389-2394 (6)	12.15	6.05

No. 2393 misidentifies a Tupolev 144.

Explorers A542

1992, Jan. 10
2395	A542	30q Bering	.50	.25
2396	A542	90q Columbus	1.40	.70
2397	A542	1.80 l Magellan	3.00	1.50
		Nos. 2395-2397 (3)	4.90	2.45

1992 Winter Olympics, Albertville A543

1992, Feb. 15 Litho. Perf. 12½
2398	A543	30q Ski jumping	.25	.15
2399	A543	90q Cross country skiing	.70	.35
2400	A543	1.20 l Pairs figure skating	.95	.50
2401	A543	1.80 l Luge	1.40	.70
		Nos. 2398-2401 (4)	3.30	1.70

Participation of Albania in Conference on Security and Cooperation in Europe, Berlin (1991) — A544

1992, Mar. 31 Litho. Perf. 12½x12
2402	A544	90q shown	.95	.95
2403	A544	1.20 l Flags, map	1.25	1.25
a.		Pair, #2402-2403	2.25	2.25

Dated 1991. Issued in sheets containing 2 #2403a, 3 each #2402-2403 + 2 labels.

Albanian Admission to CEPT A545

ALBANIA

1992, Apr. 25   Litho.   Perf. 12½
2404 A545 90q Envelopes, CEPT
               emblem   .90   .90
2405 A545 1.20 l shown   1.25 1.25
  a.   Pair, #2404-2405   2.25 2.25
Issued in sheets containing 2 #2405a, 3 each #2404-2405 and 2 labels.

Martyrs' Day — A546

1992, May 5   Perf. 12x12½
2406 A546 90q Freedom flame,
               vert.   1.00 1.00
  Perf. 12½x12
2407 A546 4.10 l Flowers   4.50 4.50

European Soccer Championships, Sweden '92 — A547

Various stylized designs of soccer plays.

1992, June 10   Litho.   Perf. 12
2408 A547 30q green & lt grn   .15   .15
2409 A547 90q blue & pink   .25   .25
2410 A547 10.80 l henna & tan   3.00 3.00
  Size: 90x70mm
  Imperf
2411 A547 5 l tan, lt green & pink   1.40 1.40
  Nos. 2408-2411 (4)   4.80 4.80

1992 Summer Olympics, Barcelona A548

1992, June 14   Litho.   Perf. 12
2412 A548 30q Tennis   .35   .35
2413 A548 90q Baseball   1.00 1.00
2414 A548 1.80 l Table tennis   2.00 2.00
  Size: 90x70mm
  Imperf
2415 A548 5 l Torch bearer   1.45 1.45
  Nos. 2412-2415 (4)   4.80 4.80

United Europe A549

1992, July 10   Litho.   Perf. 12
2416 A549 1.20 l multicolored   .90   .45

Horses A550

1992, Aug. 10   Litho.   Perf. 12
2417 A550 30q Native   .15   .15
2418 A550 90q Nonius   .25   .25
2419 A550 1.20 l Arabian, vert.   .35   .35
2420 A550 10.60 l Haflinger, vert.   2.75 2.75
  Nos. 2417-2420 (4)   3.50 3.50

Discovery of America, 500th Anniv. A551

Map of North and South America and: 60q, Columbus, sailing ships. 3.20 l, Columbus meeting natives.

1992, Aug. 20
2421 A551 60q blk, bl & gray   .25   .25
2422 A551 3.20 l blk, brn & gray   1.25 1.25
  Size: 90x70mm
  Imperf
2423 A551 5 l Map, Columbus

A552   A553

Mother Theresa, infant.

1992, Oct. 4   Litho.   Perf. 12x12½
2424 A552 40q fawn   .15   .15
2425 A552 60q brown   .15   .15
2426 A552 1 l violet   .15   .15
2427 A552 1.80 l gray   .25   .25
2428 A552 2 l red   .30   .30
2429 A552 2.40 l green   .35   .35
2430 A552 3.20 l blue   .50   .50
2431 A552 5.60 l rose violet   1.00 1.00
2432 A552 7.20 l olive   1.05 1.05
2433 A552 10 l orange brown   1.50 1.50
  Nos. 2424-2433 (10)   5.40 5.40
See Nos. 2472-2476.

1993, Apr. 25   Litho.   Perf. 12
2434 A553 16 l multicolored   2.50 2.50
Visit of Pope John Paul II.

Nos. 2223-2226, 2229 Surcharged

1993, May 2   Litho.   Perf. 12x12½
2435 A486 3 l on 10q   .60   .60
2436 A486 6.50 l on 20q   1.25 1.25
2437 A486 13 l on 30q   2.50 2.50
2438 A486 20 l on 90q   4.00 4.00
2439 A486 30 l on 50q   5.75 5.75
  Nos. 2435-2439 (5)   14.10 14.10

Lef Nosi (1873-1945), Minister of Posts — A554

1993, May 5   Litho.   Perf. 12
2440 A554 6.50 l olive brown & bister   .90   .90
First Albanian postage stamps, 80th anniv.

Europa A555

Contemporary paintings by: 3 l, A. Zajmi, vert. 7 l, E. Hila. 20 l, B. Ahmeti-Peizazh.

1993, May 28   Litho.   Perf. 12
2441 A555 3 l multicolored   .55   .55
2442 A555 7 l multicolored   1.25 1.25
2443 A555 20 l multicolored   3.75 3.75
  Nos. 2441-2443 (3)   5.55 5.55

1993 Mediterranean Games, France A556

1993, June 20   Litho.   Perf. 12
2444 A556 3 l Running   .55   .55
2445 A556 16 l Kayaking   3.00 3.00
2446 A556 21 l Cycling   3.75 3.75
  Size: 111x78mm
  Imperf
2447 A556 20 l Mediterranean map   3.50 3.50
  Nos. 2444-2447 (4)   10.80 10.80

Frang Bardhi, Author, 350th Death Anniv. — A557

1993, Aug. 20   Litho.   Perf. 12x12½
2448 A557 6.50 l shown   1.10 1.10
  Size: 89x101mm
  Imperf
2449 A557 20 l Writing at desk   3.50 3.50

A558   A559

1994, July 17   Litho.   Perf. 12
2450 A558 42 l shown   1.50 1.50
2451 A558 68 l Mascot, ball, US map   2.50 2.50
1994 World Cup Soccer Championships, US.

1994, Dec. 31   Litho.   Perf. 14
European Inventors, Discoveries: 50 l, Gjovalin Gjadri, engineer. 100 l, Karl von Ghega, Austrian engineer. 150 l, Sketch of road project.
2452 A559 50 l multicolored   2.00 2.00
2453 A559 100 l multicolored   4.00 4.00
  Size: 50x70mm
  Imperf
2454 A559 150 l multicolored   6.00 6.00
  Nos. 2452-2454 (3)   12.00 12.00
Europa (#2454).

Ali Pasa of Tepelene (Lion of Janina) (1744-1822) A560

1995, Jan. 28   Perf. 14
2455 A560 60 l shown   2.50 2.50
  Size: 70x50mm
2456 A560 100 l Tepelene Palace   4.00 4.00

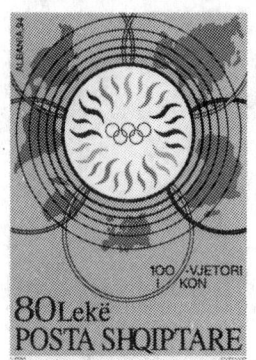

Intl. Olympic Committee, Cent. — A561

1995, Feb. 2   Imperf.
2457 A561 80 l multicolored   3.25 3.25

Karl Benz (1844-1929), Automobile Pioneer — A562

Designs: 5 l, Automobile company emblem, Benz. 10 l, Modern Mercedes Benz automobile. 60 l, First four-wheel Benz 1886 motor car. 125 l, Pre-war Mercedes touring car.

1995, Jan. 21   Litho.   Perf. 14
2458 A562 5 l multicolored   .15   .15
2459 A562 10 l multicolored   .30   .30
2460 A562 60 l multicolored   1.65 1.65
2461 A562 125 l multicolored   3.50 3.50
  Nos. 2458-2461 (4)   5.60 5.60

Liberation, 50th Anniv. (in 1994) A563

1995, Jan. 28   Litho.   Perf. 14
2462 A563 50 l black, gray & red   2.00 2.00
Dated 1994.

Miniature Sheet

Albania '93 — A564

Composers: a, 3 l, Wagner. b, 6.50 l, Grieg. c, 11 l, Gounod. d, 20 l, Tchaikovsky.

1995, Jan. 26   Perf. 12
2463 A564 Sheet of 4, #a.-d.   2.00 2.00

Veskopoja Academy, 250th Anniv. — A565

Buildings of Veskopoja.

1995, Feb. 2
2464 A565 42 l multicolored   1.50 1.50
2465 A565 68 l multicolored   2.50 2.50
  a.   Pair, #2464-2465   4.00 4.00

ALBANIA

Bleta
Apricula — A566

Peace &
Freedom — A567

1995, Aug. 20   Litho.   Perf. 12
2466 A566 5 l On flower   .20   .20
2467 A566 10 l Honeycomb, bee   .40   .40
2468 A566 25 l Emerging from cell
                 of honeycomb   1.00 1.00
       Nos. 2466-2468 (3)   1.60 1.60

1995, Aug. 10   Perf. 13½x14
Stylized hands reaching for: 50 l, Olive branch. 100 l, Peace dove. 150 l, Stylized person.
2469 A567 50 l multicolored   1.50 1.50
2470 A567 100 l multicolored   3.25 3.25
       Size: 80x60mm
       Imperf
2471 A567 150 l multicolored   4.75 4.75
       Nos. 2469-2471 (3)   9.50 9.50

Europa.

Mother Teresa Type of 1992
1994-95   Litho.   Perf. 12x12½
2472 A552   5 l violet   .25   .25
2473 A552 18 l orange   .85   .85
2474 A552 20 l rose lilac   .95   .95
2475 A552 25 l green   1.10 1.10
2476 A552 60 l olive   2.75 2.75
       Nos. 2472-2476 (5)   5.90 5.90
Issued: 20 l, 1994; 60 l, 1995; others, 7/94.

Arctic
Explorers — A568

Designs: a, Fridtjof Nansen (1861-1930), Norway. b, James Cook (1728-79), England. c, Roald Amundsen (1872-1928), Norway. d, Robert F. Scott (1872-1928), Great Britain.

1995, Sept. 14   Litho.   Perf. 13½x14
2477 A568 25 l Block of 4, #a.-d. 4.25 4.25

UN, 50th
Anniv.
A569

1995, Sept. 14   Litho.   Perf. 14x13½
2478 A569   2 l shown   .15   .15
2479 A569 100 l like #2478, flags
              streaming to right 4.25 4.25

Poets — A570

1995   Perf. 13½x14
2480 A570 25 l Pol Elyar   1.10 1.10
2481 A570 50 l Sergej Esnin   2.25 2.25
   a. Pair, #2480-2481   3.50 3.50

Entry into
Council of
Europe
A571

Designs: 25 l, Doves flying from headquarters, Strasbourg. 85 l, Albanian eagle over map of Europe.

1995   Perf. 14x13½
2482 A571 25 l multicolored   1.10 1.10
2483 A571 85 l multicolored   3.75 3.75

Jan Kukuzeli,
Composer
A572

Stylized figure: 18 l, Writing. 20 l, Holding hand to head. 100 l, Holding up scroll of paper.

1995, Oct. 17   Perf. 13½x14
2484 A572 18 l multicolored   .85   .85
2485 A572 20 l multicolored   .95   .95
       Size: 74x74mm
2486 A572 100 l multicolored   4.50 4.50
       Nos. 2484-2486 (3)   6.30 6.30

World Tourism
Organization, 20th
Anniv. — A573

Stylized designs: 18 l, Church, saint holding scroll. 20 l, City, older buildings. 42 l, City, modern buildings.

1995, Oct. 17
2487 A573 18 l multicolored   1.00 1.00
2488 A573 20 l multicolored   1.10 1.10
2489 A573 42 l multicolored   2.50 2.50
       Nos. 2487-2489 (3)   4.60 4.60

Fables of Jean
de la Fontaine
(1621-95)
A574

Designs: 2 l, Raptor, turtle, wolf, goose, mouse, lion, rats. 3 l, Crow, goose, dog, foxes. 25 l, Insect, doves, frogs. 60 l, Drawings of Da la Fontaine, animals, birds.

1995, Aug. 20   Litho.   Perf. 14x13½
2490 A574   2 l multicolored   .15   .15
2491 A574   3 l multicolored   .15   .15
2492 A574 25 l multicolored   .95   .95
       Imperf
       Size: 73x56mm
2493 A574 60 l multicolored 2.70 2.70
       Nos. 2490-2493 (4)   3.95 3.95

Folklore Festival,
Berat — A575

Motion Pictures,
Cent. — A576

Stylized designs: 5 l, Men's choir. 50 l, Costumed woman seated in chair.

1995, Oct. 17   Litho.   Perf. 13½x14
2494 A575   5 l multicolored   .20   .20
2495 A575 50 l multicolored 2.25 2.25

1995, Nov. 17
2496 A576 10 l Louis Lumiere .45   .45
2497 A576 85 l Auguste Lumiere 3.75 3.75
   a. Pair, #2496-2497   4.20 4.20

Elvis Presley
(1935-77)
A577

1995, Nov. 20   Litho.   Perf. 14x13½
2498 A577   3 l orange & multi .15   .15
2499 A577 60 l green & multi 2.50 2.50

A578

A579

1995, Nov. 25   Perf. 13½x14
2500 A578 10 l 1925 Bank notes .45 .45
2501 A578 25 l 1995 Bank notes 1.10 1.10
National Bank, 70th anniv.

1995, Nov. 27   Litho.   Perf. 13½x14
2502 A579   5 l shown   .20   .20
2503 A579 50 l Maiden planting tree 2.25 2.25
Democracy, 5th anniv.

A580

Mother
Teresa — A581

Designs: 25 l, Soccer ball, British flag, map of Europe, stadium. 100 l, Soccer ball, player.

1996, June 4   Perf. 14
2504 A580 25 l multicolored   1.10 1.10
2505 A580 100 l multicolored   4.50 4.50
Euro '96, European Soccer Championships, Great Britain.

1996, May 5   Perf. 13½x14
2506 A581 25 l blue & multi   1.10 1.10
2507 A581 100 l red & multi   4.50 4.50
       Size: 52x74mm
       Imperf
2508 A581 150 l Mother Teresa,
              diff.   6.75 6.75
       Nos. 2506-2508 (3)   12.35 12.35
Europa. For overprint see No. 2551.

GSM Cellular
Telephone
Transmission
A582

Designs: 10 l, Satellite transmitting signals. 60 l, Uses for cellular telephone, vert.

Perf. 13x13½, 13½x13
1996, Aug. 1   Litho.
2509 A582 10 l multicolored   .45   .45
2510 A582 60 l multicolored   2.50 2.50

1996 Summer
Olympic Games,
Atlanta — A583

Stylized designs.

1996, Aug. 3   Litho.   Perf. 13x14
2511 A583   5 l Runners   .20   .20
2512 A583 25 l Throwers   1.00 1.00
2513 A583 60 l Jumpers   2.40 2.40
       Size: 52x37mm
       Imperf
2514 A583 100 l Emblem, US flag 4.00 4.00
       Nos. 2511-2514 (4)   7.60 7.60

Gottfried Wilhelm Leibniz (1646-1716),
Mathematician — A584

85 l, René Descartes (1596-1650), mathematician.

1996, Sept. 20   Litho.   Perf. 14
2515 A584 10 l multicolored   .40   .40
2516 A584 85 l multicolored 3.50 3.50

Paintings by
Francisco
Goya (1746-
1828)
A585

Designs: 10 l, The Naked Maja. 60 l, Dona Isabel Cobos de Porcel. 100 l, Self portrait.

1996, Sept. 25   Perf. 14x13½
2517 A585 10 l multicolored   .40   .40
2518 A585 60 l multicolored 2.50 2.50
       Souvenir Sheet
2519 A585 100 l multicolored 4.00 4.00

Religious
Engravings — A586

UNICEF, 50th
Anniv. — A587

Designs: a, 5 l, Book cover showing crucifixion, angels. b, 25 l, Medallion of crucifixion. c, 85 l, Book cover depicting life of Christ.

1996, Nov. 5   Perf. 13x13½
2520 A586 Block of 3, #a.-c. + label 4.75 4.75

1996, Nov. 11   Perf. 13½
Children's paintings: 5 l, Fairy princess. 10 l, Doll, sun. 25 l, Sea life. 50 l, House, people.
2521 A587   5 l multicolored   .20   .20
2522 A587 10 l multicolored   .45   .45
2523 A587 25 l multicolored 1.10 1.10
2524 A587 50 l multicolored 2.25 2.25
       Nos. 2521-2524 (4)   4.00 4.00

ALBANIA

Gjergj Fishta (1871-1940), Writer, Priest
A588

Omar Khayyam
A589

1996, Dec. 20 — Perf. 13½x14
2525 A588 10 l shown .40 .40
2526 A588 60 l Battle scene, portrait 2.50 2.50

1997, Mar. 6 — Perf. 14
2527 A589 20 l shown .70 .70
2528 A589 50 l Portrait, diff. 1.75 1.75

A590

A591

1997, Mar. 20 — Perf. 14x14½
2529 A590 20 l Portrait .70 .70
2530 A590 60 l Printing press 2.15 2.15
   a. Pair, #2529-2530 2.85 2.85
Johannes Gutenberg (1397?-1468).

1997, May 5   Litho.   Perf. 13x14
The Azure Eye (Stories and Legends): 30 l, Dragon on rock looking at warrior, donkey. 100 l, Dragon drinking water from pond, warrior.
2531 A591 30 l multicolored 1.20 1.20
2532 A591 100 l multicolored 4.00 4.00
Europa.

A592

A593

1997, Apr. 10 — Perf. 14
2533 A592 10 l Pelicanus Crispus .40 .40
2534 A592 80 l Pelicans, diff. 3.00 3.00
   a. Pair, #2533-2534 3.40 3.40
No. 2534a is a continuous design.

1997, June 25   Litho.   Perf. 14
2535 A593 10 l black & dark brown .40 .40
2536 A593 60 l black & blue black 1.00 1.00

Souvenir Sheet
2537 A593 80 l gray brown 2.90 2.90
Faik Konica (1875-1942), writer and politician.
No. 2537 contains one 22x26mm stamp.

A594

Skanderbeg — A595

1997 Mediterranean Games, Bari: 20 l, Man running. 30 l, Woman running, 3-man canoe. 100 l, Man breaking finish line, silhouettes of man and woman.

1997, June 13
2538 A594 20 l Man running .75 .75
2539 A594 30 l Woman running, canoe 1.10 1.10

Size: 52x74mm
Imperf
2540 A594 100 l multicolored 3.60 3.60

1997, Aug. 25   Litho.   Perf. 13
2541 A595 5 l red brn & red .20 .20
2542 A595 10 l dp ol & ol .40 .40
2543 A595 20 l dp green & grn .80 .80
2544 A595 25 l dp mag & red lil 1.00 1.00
2545 A595 30 l dk violet & vio 1.20 1.20
2546 A595 50 l black 2.00 2.00
2547 A595 60 l brown & lt brn 2.40 2.40
2548 A595 80 l dk brown & brn 3.20 3.20
2549 A595 100 l dk red brown & red brn 3.90 3.90
2550 A595 110 l dark blue 4.30 4.30
   Nos. 2541-2550 (10) 19.40 19.40

No. 2507 Ovptd. in Silver
"HOMAZH / 1910-1997"

1997 — Perf. 13½x14
2551 A581 100 l red & multi 6.50 6.50

Religious Manuscripts — A596

Albanian Codex: a, 10 l, 11th cent. b, 25 l, 6th cent. c, 60 l, 6th cent., diff.

1997, Nov. 15   Litho.   Perf. 13x14
2552 A596 Block of 3, #a.-c. + label 3.50 3.50
See No. 2575.

Post and Telecommunications
Administration, 85th Anniv. — A597

1997, Dec. 4 — Perf. 13½
2553 A597 10 l multi .40 .40
2554 A597 30 l multi, diff. 1.10 1.10

A598

A599

1998, Mar. 25   Litho.   Perf. 14
2555 A598 30 l red brown & multi .75 .75
2556 A598 100 l tan & multi 2.75 2.75
   a. Pair, #2555-2556 3.50 3.50
Nikete Dardani, musician.

1998, Apr. 15
Legends of Pogradecit: a, 30 l, Old man seated at table. b, 50 l, Three Graces. c, 60 l, Two women, fountain. d, 80 l, Iceman.
2557 A599 Block of 4, #a.-d. 5.50 5.50

A600

A601

1998, May 5   Litho.   Perf. 13x14
2558 A600 60 l shown 1.50 1.50
2559 A600 100 l multi, diff. 2.50 2.50

Size: 50x72mm
Imperf
2560 A600 150 l multi, diff. 3.75 3.75
Europa (folk festivals).

1998, June 10   Litho.   Perf. 13½x13
Albanian League of Prizren, 120th anniv.: a, 30 l, Abdyl Frasheri. b, 50 l, Sulejman Vokshi. c, 60 l, Iljaz Pashe Dibra. d, 80 l, Ymer Prizreni.
2561 A601 Block of 4, #a.-d. 5.50 5.50

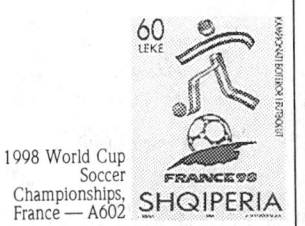

1998 World Cup Soccer Championships, France — A602

Perf. 13½
1998, June 10
Stylized soccer players.
2562 A602 60 l multicolored 1.50 1.50
2563 A602 100 l multicolored 2.50 2.50

Size: 50x73mm
Imperf
2564 A602 120 l Mascot 3.00 3.00

European Youth Greco-Roman Wrestling Championships, Albania — A603

1998, July 5 — Perf. 13½
2565 A603 30 l shown .75 .75
2566 A603 60 l Wrestlers, diff. 1.50 1.50
   a. Pair, #2565-2566 2.25 2.25

Eqerem Cabej (1908-1980), Albanian Etymologist — A604

1998, Aug. 7 — Perf. 14
2567 A604 60 l yel brn & multi 1.50 1.50
2568 A604 80 l brown red & multi 2.00 2.00
   a. Pair, #2567-2568 3.50 3.50

Paul Gauguin (1848-1903)
A605

Paintings (details): 60 l, The Vision after the Sermon. 80 l, Ea Haere Ia Oe.
120 l, Stylized design to resemble self-portrait.

1998, Sept. 10 — Perf. 13½
2569 A605 60 l multicolored 1.50 1.50
2570 A605 80 l multicolored 2.00 2.00
   a. Pair, #2569-2570 3.50 3.50

Size: 50x73mm
Imperf
2571 A605 120 l multicolored 3.00 3.00

Epitaph of Gllavenica, 14th Cent. Depiction of Christ
A606

Designs: 30 l, Entire cloth showing artwork. 80 l, Closer view.
100 l, Upper portion of cloth, vert.

1998, Oct. 5 — Perf. 14½x14
2572 A606 30 l multicolored .75 .75
2573 A606 80 l multicolored 2.00 2.00

Souvenir Sheet
Perf. 13
2574 A606 100 l multicolored 2.50 2.50
No. 2574 contains one 25x29mm stamp.

Religious Manuscripts Type of 1997
Illustrations from Purple Codex, Gold Codex: a, 30 l, Manuscript, columns on sides, arched top. b, 50 l, Manuscript cover with embossed pictures of icons. c, 80 l, Manuscript picturing cathedral, birds.

1998, Oct. 15 — Perf. 13x14
2575 A596 Block of 3, #a.-c. + label 3.90 3.90

Mikel Koliqi (1902-97), First Albanian Cardinal — A607

1998, Nov. 28 — Perf. 14
2576 A607 30 l shown .75 .75
2577 A607 100 l Portrait, facing 2.50 2.50
   a. Pair, #2576-2577 3.25 3.25

ALBANIA & EASTERN EUROPE

Bulgaria

Czechoslovakia

Hungary

Poland

Romania

Russia & Assoc. Territories

WANTLISTS INVITED

Lists available on request at 50¢ for each country.

R.J.B. Mail Sales
25958 Genesee Trail Rd.
#424
Golden, CO 80401

ALBANIA

Mother Teresa (1910-97) — A608

Diana, Princess of Wales (1961-97) — A609

Perf. 14x13½, 13½x14

1998, Sept. 5   Photo.
2578	A608	60 l With child, horiz.	1.50	.75
2579	A608	100 l shown	2.50	1.25

See Italy Nos. 2254-2255.

1998   Litho.   *Perf. 13½*
2580	A609	60 l shown	1.50	.75
2581	A609	100 l With Mother Teresa	2.50	1.25

SEMI-POSTAL STAMPS

Nos. 148-151 Surcharged in Red and Black

1924, Nov. 1
B1	A18	5q + 5q yel grn	5.00	6.50
B2	A18	10q + 5q carmine	5.00	6.50
B3	A18	25q + 5q dark blue	5.00	6.50
B4	A18	50q + 5q dark grn	5.00	6.50
		Nos. B1-B4 (4)	20.00	26.00

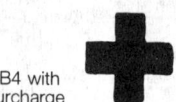

Nos. B1 to B4 with Additional Surcharge in Red and Black

+ 5 qind.

1924
B5	A18	5q + 5q + 5q yel grn	5.00	6.50
B6	A18	10q + 5q + 5q car	5.00	6.50
B7	A18	25q + 5q + 5q dk bl	5.00	6.50
B8	A18	50q + 5q + 5q dk grn	5.00	6.50
		Nos. B5-B8 (4)	20.00	26.00

Issued under Italian Dominion

Nurse and Child — SP1

    Unwmk.

1943, Apr. 1   Photo.   *Perf. 14*
B9	SP1	5q + 5q dark grn	.25	.25
B10	SP1	10q + 10q olive brn	.25	.25
B11	SP1	15q + 10q rose red	.35	.35
B12	SP1	25q + 15q saphire	.50	.50
B13	SP1	30q + 20q violet	.60	.60
B14	SP1	50q + 25q dk org	.75	.75
B15	SP1	65q + 10q grnsh blk	1.10	1.10
B16	SP1	1fr + 40q chestnut	2.50	2.50
		Nos. B9-B16 (8)	6.30	6.30

The surtax was for the control of tuberculosis. For surcharges see Nos. B24-B27.

Issued under German Administration

War Victims — SP2

1944, Sept. 22
B17	SP2	5q + 5(q) dp grn	2.10	2.75
B18	SP2	10q + 5(q) dp brn	2.10	2.75
B19	SP2	15q + 5(q) car lake	2.10	2.75
B20	SP2	25q + 10(q) dp blue	2.10	2.75
B21	SP2	1fr + 50q dk olive	2.10	2.75
B22	SP2	2fr + 1(fr) purple	2.10	2.75
B23	SP2	3fr + 1.50(fr) dk org	2.10	2.75
		Nos. B17-B23 (7)	14.70	19.25

Surtax for victims of World War II.

Independent State

Nos. B9 to B12 Surcharged in Carmine

1945, May 4   Unwmk.   *Perf. 14*
B24	SP1	30q +15q on 5q+5q	1.75	1.75
B25	SP1	50q +25q on 10q+10q	1.75	1.75
B26	SP1	1fr +50q on 15q+10q	5.00	5.00
B27	SP1	2fr +1fr on 25q+15q	8.75	8.75
		Nos. B24-B27 (4)	17.25	17.25

The surtax was for the Albanian Red Cross.

People's Republic

Nos. 361 to 366 Overprinted in Red (cross) and Surcharged in Black

1946, July 16   *Perf. 11*
B28	A57	20q + 10q bluish grn	6.50	6.50
B29	A57	30q + 15q dp org	6.50	6.50
B30	A57	40q + 20q brown	6.50	6.50
B31	A57	60q + 30q red vio	6.50	6.50
B32	A57	1fr + 50q rose red	6.50	6.50
B33	A57	3fr + 1.50fr dk bl	6.50	6.50
		Nos. B28-B33 (6)	39.00	39.00

To honor and benefit the Congress of the Albanian Red Cross.
Counterfeits: lithographed, dull gum. Genuine: typographed, shiny gum.

Catalogue values for unused stamps in this section, from this point to the end of the section, are for Never Hinged items.

SP3    SP4

First Aid and Red Cross: 25q+5q, Nurse carrying child on stretcher. 65q+25q, Symbolic blood transfusion. 80q+40q, Mother and child.

1967, Dec. 1   Litho.   *Perf. 11½x12*
B34	SP3	15q + 5q blk, red & brn	.90	.45
B35	SP3	25q + 5q multi	1.00	.60
B36	SP3	65q + 25q multi	3.00	.65
B37	SP3	80q + 40q multi	5.00	1.50
		Nos. B34-B37 (4)	9.90	3.20

6th congress of the Albanian Red Cross.

1996, Aug. 5   Litho.   *Perf. 13½x13*
B38	SP4	50 l +10 l multi	2.50	2.50

Albanian Red Cross, 75th anniv.

AIR POST STAMPS

Airplane Crossing Mountains AP1

    Wmk. 125

1925, May 30   Typo.   *Perf. 14*
C1	AP1	5q green	.50	.50
C2	AP1	10q rose red	.50	.50
C3	AP1	25q deep blue	.450	
C4	AP1	50q dark green	1.00	1.00
C5	AP1	1fr dk vio & blk	1.90	1.90
C6	AP1	2fr ol grn & vio	3.00	3.00
C7	AP1	3fr brn org & dk grn	5.25	5.25
		Nos. C1-C7 (7)	16.65	12.65

Nos. C1-C7 exist imperf.
For overprint see Nos. C8-C28.

Nos. C1-C7 Overprinted **Rep. Shqiptare**

1927, Jan. 18
C8	AP1	5q green	3.00	3.00
a.		Dbl. overprint, one invtd.	35.00	
C9	AP1	10q rose red	3.00	3.00
a.		Inverted overprint	30.00	
b.		Dbl. overprint, one invtd.	35.00	
C10	AP1	25q deep blue	1.60	1.60
C11	AP1	50q dark grn	1.60	1.60
a.		Inverted overprint	30.00	
C12	AP1	1fr dk vio & blk	1.60	1.60
a.		Inverted overprint	30.00	
b.		Double overprint	30.00	
C13	AP1	2fr ol grn & vio	1.60	1.60
C14	AP1	3fr brn org & dk grn	2.75	2.75
		Nos. C8-C14 (7)	15.15	15.15

Nos. C1-C7 Overprinted **REP. SHQYPTARE / Fluturim' i I-ar / Vlonë--Brindisi / 21. IV. 1928**

1928, Apr. 21
C15	AP1	5q green	1.25	1.25
a.		Inverted overprint	20.00	
C16	AP1	10q rose red	1.25	1.25
C17	AP1	25q deep blue	1.25	1.25
C18	AP1	50q dark green	1.25	1.25
C19	AP1	1fr dk vio & blk	18.00	18.00
C20	AP1	2fr ol grn & vio	18.00	18.00
C21	AP1	3fr brn org & dk grn	18.00	18.00
		Nos. C15-C21 (7)	59.00	59.00

First flight across the Adriatic, Valona to Brindisi, Apr. 21, 1928.
The variety "SHQYRTARE" occurs once in the sheet for each value. Value 3 times normal.

Nos. C1-C7 Overprinted in Red Brown **Mbr. Shqiptare**

1929, Dec. 1
C22	AP1	5q green	3.25	3.25
C23	AP1	10q rose red	3.25	3.25
C24	AP1	25q deep blue	3.50	3.50
C25	AP1	50q dark grn	15.00	17.50
C26	AP1	1fr dk vio & blk	150.00	165.00
C27	AP1	2fr ol grn	150.00	165.00
C28	AP1	3fr brn org & dk grn	150.00	165.00
		Nos. C22-C28 (7)	475.00	522.50

Excellent counterfeits exist.

King Zog and Airplane over Tirana — AP2

AP3

1930, Oct. 8   Photo.   Unwmk.
C29	AP2	5q yellow green	.30	.30
C30	AP2	15q rose red	.40	.40
C31	AP2	20q slate blue	.55	.55
C32	AP2	50q olive green	.75	.75
C33	AP3	1fr dark blue	1.65	1.65
C34	AP3	2fr olive brown	5.25	5.25
C35	AP3	3fr purple	7.00	7.00
		Nos. C29-C35 (7)	15.90	15.90

For overprints and surcharges see Nos. C36-C45.

Nos. C29-C35 Overprinted **TIRANE-ROME / 6 KORRIK 1931**

1931, July 6
C36	AP2	5q yellow grn	1.75	1.75
a.		Double overprint	65.00	
C37	AP2	15q rose red	1.75	1.75
C38	AP2	20q slate blue	1.75	1.75
C39	AP2	50q olive grn	1.75	1.75
C40	AP3	1fr dark blue	14.00	14.00
C41	AP3	2fr olive brn	14.00	14.00
C42	AP3	3fr purple	14.00	14.00
a.		Inverted overprint	175.00	
		Nos. C36-C42 (7)	49.00	49.00

1st air post flight from Tirana to Rome.
Only a very small part of this issue was sold to the public. Most of the stamps were given to the Aviation Company to help provide funds for conducting the service.

Issued under Italian Dominion

Nos. C29-C30 Overprinted in Black **Mbledhja Kushtetuëse / 12-IV-1939 / XVII**

1939, Apr. 19   Unwmk.   *Perf. 14*
C43	AP2	5q yel green	.75	.75
C44	AP2	15q rose red	.75	.75

No. C32 With Additional Surcharge
C45	AP2	20q on 50q ol grn	1.50	1.50
a.		Inverted overprint		
		Nos. C43-C45 (3)	3.00	3.00

See note after No. 309.

King Victor Emmanuel III and Plane over Mountains AP4

1939, Aug. 4   Photo.
C46	AP4	20q brown	12.00	4.00

Shepherds AP5

Map of Albania Showing Air Routes — AP6

Designs: 20q, Victor Emmanuel III and harbor view. 50q, Woman and river valley. 1fr, Bridge at Vezirit. 2fr, Ruins. 3fr, Women waving to plane.

1940, Mar. 20   Unwmk.
C47	AP5	5q green	.25	.25
C48	AP6	15q rose red	.25	.25
C49	AP5	20q deep blue	.25	.25
C50	AP6	50q brown	.65	.65
C51	AP5	1fr myrtle green	1.25	1.50
C52	AP6	2fr brown black	4.25	5.00
C53	AP6	3fr rose violet	12.50	14.00
		Nos. C47-C53 (7)	19.40	21.90

People's Republic

Vuno-Himare AP12

Albanian Towns: 1 l, 10 l, Rozafat-Shkoder. 2 l, 20 l, Keshtjelle-Butrinto.

ALBANIA — ALEXANDRETTA

1950, Dec. 15 Engr. Perf. 12½x12

C54	AP12	50q gray black	.25	.25
C55	AP12	1 l red brown	.25	.25
C56	AP12	2 l ultra	.45	.45
C57	AP12	5 l deep green	.95	.95
C58	AP12	10 l deep blue	2.25	2.25
C59	AP12	20 l purple	5.75	5.75
		Nos. C54-C59 (6)	9.90	9.90

Nos. C56-C58 Surcharged with New Value and Bars in Red or Black

1952-53

C60	AP12	50q on 2 l (R)	40.00	40.00
C61	AP12	50q on 5 l	10.00	5.00
C62	AP12	2.50 l on 5 l (R)	60.00	60.00
C63	AP12	2.50 l on 10 l	10.00	5.00
		Nos. C60-C63 (4)	120.00	110.00

Issued: #C60, C62, 12/26/52; #C61, C63, 3/14/53.

Catalogue values for unused stamps in this section, from this point to the end of the section, are for Never Hinged items.

Banner with Lenin, Map of Stalingrad and Tanks — AP13

1963, Feb. 2 Litho. Perf. 14

C67	AP13	7 l grn & dp car	3.00	.60

20th anniversary, Battle of Stalingrad.

Sputnik and Sun — AP14

Designs: 3 l, Lunik 4. 5 l, Lunik 3 photographing far side of the Moon. 8 l, Venus space probe. 12 l, Mars 1.

1963, Oct. 31 Unwmk. Perf. 12

C68	AP14	2 l org, yel & blk	.25	.30
C69	AP14	3 l multi	.50	.30
C70	AP14	5 l rose lil, yel & blk	.90	.45
C71	AP14	8 l multi	1.25	.85
C72	AP14	12 l blue & org	2.25	2.50
		Nos. C68-72 (5)	5.15	4.40

Russian interplanetary explorations.

Nos. C68 and C71 Overprinted: "Riccione 23-8-1964"

1964, Aug. 23

C73	AP14	2 l org, yel & blk	8.00	3.50
C74	AP14	8 l multicolored	12.00	5.25

Intl. Space Exhib. in Riccione, Italy.

Plane over Berati AP15

1975, Nov. 25 Litho. Perf. 12

C75	AP15	20q multi	.15	.15
C76	AP15	40q Gjirokaster	.15	.15
C77	AP15	60q Sarande	.20	.15
C78	AP15	90q Durres	.50	.15
C79	AP15	1.20 l Kruje	.75	.15
C80	AP15	2.40 l Boga	1.65	.35
C81	AP15	4.05 l Tirana	2.50	.70
		Nos. C75-C81 (7)	5.90	1.80

SPECIAL DELIVERY STAMPS

Issued under Italian Dominion

King Victor Emmanuel III — SD1

1940 Unwmk. Photo. Perf. 14

E1	SD1	25q bright violet	.40	.40
E2	SD1	50q red orange	1.25	1.50

Issued under German Administration

No. E1 Overprinted in Carmine

14 Shtator 1943

1943

E3	SD1	25q bright violet	15.00	17.50

Proclamation of Albanian independence.

POSTAGE DUE STAMPS

Nos. 35-39 Handstamped in Various Colors

T Taksë

1914, Feb. 23 Unwmk. Perf. 14

J1	A3	2q org brn & buff (Bl)	6.00	1.65
J2	A3	5q green (R)	6.00	2.50
J3	A3	10q rose red (Bl)	8.00	1.65
J4	A3	25q dark blue (R)	10.00	1.65
J5	A3	50q vio & red (Bk)	14.00	5.00
		Nos. J1-J5 (5)	44.00	12.45

The two parts of the overprint are handstamped separately. Stamps exist with one or both handstamps inverted, double, omitted or in wrong color.

Nos. 48-51 Overprinted in Black

TAKSË

1914, Apr. 16

J6	A3 (a)	10pa on 5q green	2.75	2.25
J7	A3 (a)	20pa on 10q rose red	2.75	2.25
J8	A3 (b)	1gr on 25q blue	2.75	2.25
J9	A3 (b)	2gr on 50q vio & red	2.75	2.25
		Nos. J6-J9 (4)	11.00	9.00

Same Design as Regular Issue of 1919, Overprinted

TAXE

1919, Feb. 10 Perf. 11½, 12½

J10	A8	(4)q on 4h rose	5.00	4.50
J11	A8	(10)q on 10k red, grn	5.00	4.50
J12	A8	20q on 2k org, gray	5.00	4.50
J13	A8	50q on 5k brn, yel	5.00	4.50
		Nos. J10-J13 (4)	20.00	18.00

Fortress at Scutari — D3

D5

Post Horn Overprinted in Black

1920, Apr. 1 Perf. 14x13

J14	D3	4q olive green	.40	.40
J15	D3	10q rose red	.85	.85
J16	D3	20q bister brn	.85	.85
J17	D3	50q black	2.00	2.00
		Nos. J14-J17 (4)	4.10	4.10

1922 Perf. 12½, 11½

Background of Red Wavy Lines

J23	D5	4q black, red	1.00	1.00
J24	D5	10q black, red	1.00	1.00
J25	D5	20q black, red	1.00	1.00
J26	D5	50q black, red	1.00	1.00
		Nos. J23-J26 (4)	4.00	4.00

Same Overprinted in White

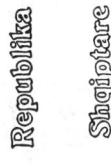

1925

J27	D5	4q black, red	1.00	1.00
J28	D5	10q black, red	1.00	1.00
J29	D5	20q black, red	1.00	1.00
J30	D5	50q black, red	1.00	1.00
		Nos. J27-J30 (4)	4.00	4.00

The 10q with overprint in gold was a trial printing. It was not put in use.

D7

Coat of Arms — D8

Overprinted "QINDAR" in Red

1926, Dec. 24 Perf. 13½x13

J31	D7	10q dark blue	.25	.20
J32	D7	20q green	.50	.40
J33	D7	30q red brown	.80	.60
J34	D7	50q dark brown	1.25	1.00
		Nos. J31-J34 (4)	2.80	2.20

Wmk. Double Headed Eagle (220)

1930, Sept. 1 Photo. Perf. 14, 14½

J35	D8	10q dark blue	4.75	4.75
J36	D8	20q rose red	1.25	1.25
J37	D8	30q violet	1.25	1.25
J38	D8	50q dark green	1.50	1.50
		Nos. J35-J38 (4)	8.75	8.75

Nos. J36-J38 exist with overprint "14 Shtator 1943" (see Nos. 332-344) which is private and fraudulent on these stamps.

No. 253 Overprinted **Taksë**

1936 Perf. 14

J39	A34	10q carmine	3.50	4.75

Issued under Italian Dominion

Coat of Arms — D9

1940 Unwmk. Photo. Perf. 14

J40	D9	4q red orange	22.50	18.00
J41	D9	10q bright violet	22.50	18.00
J42	D9	20q brown	22.50	18.00
J43	D9	30q dark blue	22.50	18.00
J44	D9	50q carmine rose	22.50	18.00
		Nos. J40-J44 (5)	112.50	90.00

ALEXANDRETTA

,a-lig-(,)zan-'dre-tə

LOCATION — A political territory in northern Syria, bordering on Turkey
GOVT. — French mandate
AREA — 10,000 sq. mi. (approx.)
POP. — 270,000 (approx.)

Included in the Syrian territory mandated to France under the Versailles Treaty, the name was changed to Hatay in 1938. The following year France returned the territory to Turkey in exchange for certain concessions. See Hatay.

100 Centimes = 1 Piaster

Stamps of Syria, 1930-36, Overprinted or Surcharged in Black or Red:

Sandjak d'Alexandrette (a)
D'ALEXANDRETTE (b)
Sandjak d'Alexandrette (c)

Sandjak d'Alexandrette 2P,50 (d)

POSTES Sandjak d'Alexandrette 12P,50 (e)

1938 Unwmk. Perf. 12x12½

1	A6 (a)	10c vio brn	.40	.40
2	A6 (a)	20c brn org	.50	.50

Perf. 13½

3	A9 (b)	50c vio (R)	.50	.50
4	A10 (b)	1p bis brn	.60	.60
5	A9 (b)	2p dk vio (R)	.80	.80
6	A13 (b)	3p yel grn (R)	1.75	1.75
7	A10 (b)	4p yel org	1.75	1.75
8	A16 (b)	6p grnsh blk (R)	2.00	2.00
9	A18 (b)	25p vio brn	6.50	6.50
10	A15 (c)	75c org red	.60	.60
11	A10 (d)	2.50p on 4p yel org	1.00	1.00
12	AP2 (e)	12.50p on 15p org red	3.00	3.00
		Nos. 1-12 (12)	19.40	19.40

Issue dates: #1-9, Apr. 14, #10-12, Sept. 2.

Nos. 4, 7, 10-12 Overprinted in Black

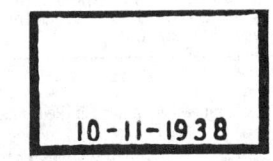

10-11-1938

1938, Nov. 10

13	A10	75c	30.00	30.00
14	A10	1p	20.00	18.00
15	A10	2.50p on 4p	12.50	11.00
16	A10	4p	15.00	13.50
17	AP2	12.50p on 15p	30.00	30.00
		Nos. 13-17 (5)	107.50	102.50

Death of Kemal Ataturk, pres. of Turkey.

AIR POST STAMPS

Air Post Stamps of Syria, 1937, Overprinted Type "b" in Red or Black

1938, Apr. 14 Unwmk. Perf. 13

C1	AP14	½p dark vio (R)	.75	.75
C2	AP15	1p black (R)	.35	.35
C3	AP14	2p blue grn (R)	1.50	1.50
C4	AP15	3p deep ultra	1.75	1.75
C5	AP14	5p rose lake	4.50	4.50
C6	AP15	10p red brown	5.00	5.00
C7	AP15	15p lake brown	5.75	5.75
C8	AP15	25p dk blue (R)	7.50	7.50
		Nos. C1-C8 (8)	27.10	27.10

POSTAGE DUE STAMPS

Postage Due Stamps of Syria, 1925-31, Ovptd. Type "b" in Black or Red

1938, Apr. 14 Unwmk. Perf. 13½

J1	D5	50c brown, yel	1.00	.80
J2	D6	1p violet, rose	1.25	1.10
J3	D5	2p blk, blue (R)	1.75	1.60
J4	D5	3p blk, red org	3.50	3.25
J5	D5	5p blk, bl grn (R)	5.50	5.00
J6	D7	8p blk, gray bl (R)	6.00	5.00
		Nos. J1-J6 (6)	19.00	16.75

On No. J2, the overprint is vertical, reading up, other denominations, horizontal.

Stamps of Alexandretta were discontinued in 1938 and replaced by those of Hatay.

Have you found a typo or other error in this catalogue? Inform the editors via our web site or e-mail

sctcat@ scottonline.com

ALGERIA

al-'jir-ē-ə

LOCATION — North Africa
GOVT. — Republic
AREA — 919,595 sq. mi.
POP. — 21,463,000 (1984 est.)
CAPITAL — Algiers

The former French colony of Algeria became an integral part of France on Sept. 1, 1958, when French stamps replaced Algerian stamps. Algeria became an independent country July 3, 1962.

100 Centimes = 1 Franc
100 Centimes = 1 Dinar (1964)

Catalogue values for unused stamps in this country are for Never Hinged items, beginning with Scott 109 in the regular postage section, Scott B27 in the semi-postal section, Scott C1 in the airpost section, Scott CB1 in the airpost semi-postal section, and Scott J25 in the postage due section.

Stamps of France Overprinted in Red, Blue or Black:

ALGÉRIE   ALGÉRIE
   a   b

ALGÉRIE   ALGÉRIE
   c   d

1924-26   Unwmk.   Perf. 14x13½

1	A16(a)	1c dk gray (R)	.15	.15
2	A16(a)	2c violet brn	.15	.15
3	A16(a)	3c orange	.15	.15
4	A16(a)	4c yel brn (Bl)	.15	.15
5	A22(a)	5c orange (Bl)	.15	.15
6	A16(a)	5c green ('25)	.15	.15
7	A23(a)	10c green	.15	.15
b.		Booklet pane of 10	1.50	
8	A22(a)	10c green ('25)	.50	.15
9	A20(a)	15c slate grn	.15	.15
10	A23(a)	15c green ('25)	.15	.15
11	A22(a)	15c red brn (Bl) ('26)	.15	.15
12	A22(a)	20c red brn (Bl)	.15	.15
13	A22(a)	25c blue (R)	.15	.15
a.		Booklet pane of 10	3.00	
14	A22(a)	30c red (Bl)	.15	.15
15	A22(a)	30c cerise ('25)	.50	.15
16	A22(a)	30c lt bl (R) ('25)	.15	.15
a.		Booklet pane of 10	2.00	
17	A22(a)	35c violet	.15	.15
18	A18(b)	40c red & pale bl	.15	.15
19	A18(b)	40c ol brn (R) ('25)	.75	.20
20	A18(b)	45c grn & bl (R)	.25	.15
21	A23(a)	45c red (Bl) ('25)	.30	.15
22	A23(a)	50c blue (R)	.15	.15
23	A23(a)	60c lt violet	.15	.15
a.		Inverted overprint	250.00	
24	A20(a)	65c rose (Bl)	.15	.15
25	A23(a)	75c blue (R)	.25	.15
a.		Double overprint	65.00	
26	A20(a)	80c ver ('26)	.40	.15
27	A20(a)	85c ver (Bl)	.25	.15
28	A18(b)	1fr cl & ol grn	1.00	.15
29	A22(a)	1.05fr ver ('26)	.55	.25
30	A18(c)	2fr org & pale bl	.40	.30
31	A18(b)	3fr vio & bl ('26)	3.00	.55
32	A18(d)	5fr bl & buff (R)	4.00	1.00
		Nos. 1-32 (32)	19.00	9.35

No. 15 was issued precanceled only. Values for precanceled stamps in first column are for those which have not been through the post and have original gum. Values in second column are for postally used, gumless stamps.
For surcharges see Nos. 75, P1.

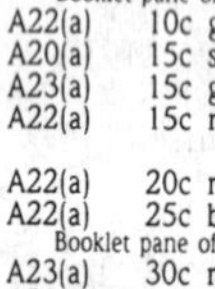

Street in Kasbah, Algiers — A1 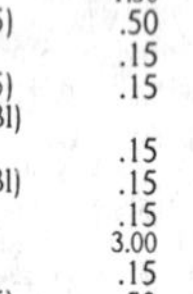
Mosque of Sidi Abder-Rahman — A2

La Pêcherie Mosque — A3
Marabout of Sidi Yacoub — A4 

1926-39   Typo.   Perf. 14x13½

33	A1	1c olive	.15	.15
34	A1	2c red brown	.15	.15
35	A1	3c orange	.15	.15
36	A1	5c blue green	.15	.15
37	A1	10c brt violet	.15	.15
a.		Booklet pane of 10	3.25	
38	A2	15c orange brn	.15	.15
39	A2	20c green	.15	.15
40	A2	20c deep rose	.15	.15
41	A2	25c blue grn	.15	.15
42	A2	25c blue ('27)	.40	.15
43	A2	25c vio bl ('39)	.15	.15
44	A2	30c blue	.25	.15
45	A2	30c bl grn ('27)	.80	.30
46	A2	35c dp violet	1.00	.65
47	A2	40c olive green	.15	.15
a.		Booklet pane of 10	2.25	
48	A3	45c violet brn	.25	.20
49	A3	50c blue	.25	.15
a.		Booklet pane of 10	3.50	
50	A3	50c dk red ('30)	.15	.15
a.		Booklet pane of 10	4.75	
51	A3	60c yellow grn	.15	.15
52	A3	65c blk brn ('27)	1.25	.85
53	A1	65c ultra ('38)	.15	.15
a.		Booklet pane of 10	1.75	
54	A3	75c carmine	.30	.25
55	A3	75c blue ('29)	2.25	.15
56	A3	80c orange red	.45	.25
57	A3	90c red ('27)	5.00	2.75
58	A4	1fr gray grn & red brn	.65	.20
59	A3	1.05fr lt brown	.55	.30
60	A3	1.10fr mag ('27)	5.00	1.75
61	A4	1.25fr dk bl & ultra	1.00	.80
62	A4	1.50fr dk bl & ultra ('27)	2.25	.15
63	A4	2fr Prus bl & blk brn	1.90	.20
64	A4	3fr violet & org	3.25	.65
65	A4	5fr red & violet	6.00	2.00
66	A4	10fr ol brn & rose ('27)	40.00	20.00
67	A4	20fr vio & grn ('27)	5.00	4.00
		Nos. 33-67 (35)	80.00	38.00

Type A4, 50c blue and rose red, inscribed "CENTENAIRE-ALGERIE" is France No. 255.
See design A24. For stamps and types surcharged see Nos. 68-74, 131, 136, 187, B1-B13, J27, P2.

Stamps of 1926 Surcharged with New Values

1927

68	A2	10c on 35c dp violet	.15	.15
69	A2	25c on 30c blue	.15	.15
70	A2	30c on 25c blue grn	.15	.15
71	A3	65c on 60c yel grn	.75	.15
72	A3	90c on 80c org red	.50	.20
73	A1	1.10fr on 1.05fr lt brn	.30	.15
74	A4	1.50fr on 1.25fr dk bl & ultra	1.25	.45
		Nos. 68-74 (7)	3.25	1.60

Bars cancel the old value on #68, 69, 73, 74.

No. 4 Surcharged 5c

1927

| 75 | A16 | 5c on 4c yellow brown | .75 | .25 |

Bay of Algiers — A5

1930, May 4   Engr.   Perf. 11, 12½

| 78 | A5 | 10fr red brown | 9.50 | 7.50 |
| a. | | Imperf., pair | 25.00 | |

Cent. of Algeria and for Intl. Phil. Exhib. of North Africa, May, 1930.
One copy of No. 78 was sold with each 10fr admission.

Travel across the Sahara — A6

Arch of Triumph, Lambese — A7

Admiralty Building, Algiers — A8

Kings' Tombs near Touggourt — A9

El-Kebir Mosque, Algiers — A10

Oued River at Colomb-Bechar A11

Sidi Bon Medine Cemetery at Tlemcen A13

View of Ghardaia A12

1936-41   Engr.   Perf. 13

79	A6	1c ultra	.15	.15
80	A11	2c dk violet	.15	.15
81	A7	3c dk blue grn	.15	.15
82	A12	5c red violet	.15	.15
83	A8	10c emerald	.15	.15
84	A9	15c red	.15	.15
85	A13	20c dk blue grn	.15	.15
86	A10	25c rose vio	.32	.15
87	A12	30c yellow grn	.28	.15
88	A9	40c brown vio	.15	.15
89	A13	45c deep ultra	.65	.40
90	A8	50c red	.40	.15
91	A6	65c red brn	2.50	1.75
92	A6	65c rose car ('37)	.35	.15
93	A6	70c red brn ('39)	.15	.15
94	A11	75c slate bl	.18	.15
95	A7	90c henna brn	.65	.45
96	A10	1fr brown	.18	.15
97	A8	1.25fr lt violet	.35	.18
98	A8	1.25fr car rose ('39)	.30	.15
99	A11	1.50fr turq blue	.90	.18
99A	A11	1.50fr rose ('40)	.35	.15
100	A12	1.75fr henna brn	.15	.15
101	A7	2fr dk brown	.15	.15
102	A6	2.25fr yellow grn	8.00	6.50
103	A12	2.50fr dk ultra ('41)	.28	.26
104	A13	3fr magenta	.26	.15
105	A10	3.50fr pck blue	1.90	1.40
106	A8	5fr slate blue	.28	.15
107	A11	10fr henna brn	.32	.20
108	A9	20fr turq blue	.60	.35
		Nos. 79-108 (31)	20.70	14.82

See Nos. 124-125, 162.
Nos. 82 and 100 with surcharge "E. F. M. 30frs" (Emergency Field Message) were used in 1943 to pay cable tolls for US and Canadian servicemen. For other surcharges see Nos. 122, B27.

Catalogue values for unused stamps in this section, from this point to the end of the section, are for Never Hinged items.

Algerian Pavilion — A14

1937   Perf. 13

109	A14	40c brt green	.40	.35
110	A14	50c rose carmine	.25	.15
111	A14	1.50fr blue	.60	.25
112	A14	1.75fr brown black	.65	.45
		Nos. 109-112 (4)	1.90	1.25

Paris International Exposition.

Constantine in 1837 — A15

1937

113	A15	65c deep rose	.30	.15
114	A15	1fr brown	3.25	.50
115	A15	1.75fr blue green	.25	.20
116	A15	2.15fr red violet	.20	.15
		Nos. 113-116 (4)	4.00	1.00

Taking of Constantine by the French, cent.

Ruins of a Roman Villa — A16

1938

117	A16	30c green	.50	.30
118	A16	65c ultra	.15	.15
119	A16	75c rose violet	.55	.40
120	A16	3fr carmine rose	1.40	1.40
121	A16	5fr yellow brown	2.25	2.25
		Nos. 117-121 (5)	4.85	4.50

Centenary of Philippeville.

1938

122	A8	25c on 50c red	.15	.15
a.		Double surcharge	35.00	30.00
b.		Inverted surcharge	20.00	18.00

Types of 1936
1939
Numerals of Value on Colorless Background

| 124 | A7 | 90c henna brown | .15 | .15 |
| 125 | A10 | 2.25fr blue green | .20 | .20 |

For surcharge see No. B38.

American Export Liner Unloading Cargo — A17

1939

126	A17	20c green	.65	.65
127	A17	40c red violet	.65	.50
128	A17	90c brown black	.35	.20
129	A17	1.25fr rose	2.25	.80
130	A17	2.25fr ultra	.65	.60
		Nos. 126-130 (5)	4.55	2.75

New York World's Fair.

Type of 1926, Surcharged in Black

Two types of surcharge:
I - Bars 6mm
II - Bars 7mm

1939-40   Perf. 14x13½

131	A1	1fr on 90c crimson (I)	.15	.15
a.		Booklet pane of 10		
b.		Double surcharge (I)	35.00	
c.		Inverted surcharge (I)	22.50	
d.		Pair, one without surch. (I)	800.00	
e.		Type II ('40)	1.50	.15
f.		Inverted surcharge (II)	27.50	
g.		Pair, one without surch. (II)	800.00	

ALGERIA

View of Algiers — A18

1941   **Typo.**
132 A18   30c ultra   .15 .15
133 A18   70c sepia   .15 .15
134 A18   1fr carmine rose   .15 .15
    Nos. 132-134 (3)   .45 .45
    See No. 163.

Marshal Pétain
A19   A20

1941   **Engr.**   **Perf. 13**
135 A19   1fr dark blue   .30 .15
For stamp and type surcharged see #B36-B37.

No. 53 Surcharged in Black with New Value and Bars

1941   **Perf. 14x13½**
136 A1   50c on 65c ultra   .30 .15
  a.   Booklet pane of 10   21.00
  b.   Inverted surcharge   21.00
  c.   Pair, one without surch.   52.50

1942   **Perf. 14x13**
137 A20   1.50fr orange red   .15 .15
Four other denominations of type A20 exist (4, 5, 10, 20fr), but were not placed in use.

Constantine   Oran
A21   A22

Arms of Algiers — A23

Engraver's Name at Lower Left

1942-43   **Photo.**   **Perf. 12**
138 A21   40c dark vio ('43)   .15 .15
139 A22   60c rose ('43)   .15 .15
140 A21   1.20fr yel grn ('43)   .15 .15
141 A23   1.50fr car rose   .15 .15
142 A22   2fr sapphire   .20 .15
143 A21   2.40fr rose ('43)   .15 .15
144 A23   3fr sapphire   .20 .15
145 A21   4fr blue ('43)   .15 .15
146 A22   5fr yel grn ('43)   .15 .15
    Nos. 138-146 (9)   1.45 1.35
For type surcharged see No. 166.

Imperforates
Nearly all of Algeria Nos. 138-285, B39-B96, C1-C12 and CB1-CB3 exist imperforate. See note after France No. 395.

Without Engraver's Name

1942-45   **Typo.**   **Perf. 14x13½**
147 A23   10c dull brn vio ('45)   .15 .15
148 A22   30c dp bl grn ('45)   .15 .15
149 A21   40c dull brn vio ('45)   .15 .15
150 A22   60c rose ('45)   .15 .15
151 A21   70c deep bl ('45)   .15 .15
152 A23   80c dk bl grn ('43)   .22 .22
153 A21   1.20fr bl grn ('45)   .20 .15
154 A23   1.50fr brt rose ('43)   .15 .15
155 A22   2fr dp blue ('45)   .20 .15
156 A21   2.40fr rose ('45)   .30 .15
157 A23   3fr dp blue ('45)   .15 .15
158 A22   4.50fr brown vio   .20 .15
    Nos. 147-158 (12)   2.17 1.94
For surcharge see No. 190.

La Pêcherie Mosque — A24

1942   **Typo.**
159 A24   50c dull red   .15 .15
  a.   Booklet pane of 10   2.75

1942   **Photo.**   **Perf. 12**
160 A24   40c gray green   .15 .15
161 A24   50c red   .15 .15

Types of 1936-41, Without "RF"

1942   **Engr.**   **Perf. 13**
162 A11   1.50fr rose   .30 .15

    Typo.   **Perf. 14x13½**
163 A18   30c ultra   .15 .15

"One Aim Alone - Victory"
A25   A26

1943   **Litho.**   **Perf. 12**
164 A25   1.50fr deep rose   .15 .15
165 A26   1.50fr dark blue   .15 .15

Type of 1942-3 Surcharged with New Value in Black

1943   **Photo.**
166 A22   2fr on 5fr red orange   .15 .15
  a.   Surcharge omitted   140.00

Summer Palace, Algiers — A27

1944, Dec. 1   **Litho.**
167 A27   15fr slate   .80 .80
168 A27   20fr lt blue grn   .60 .40
169 A27   50fr dk carmine   .60 .50
170 A27   100fr deep blue   1.50 1.25
171 A27   200fr dull bis brn   2.50 1.40
    Nos. 167-171 (5)   6.00 4.35

Marianne   Gallic Cock
A28   A29

1944-45
172 A28   10c gray   .15 .15
173 A28   30c red violet   .15 .15
174 A29   40c rose car ('45)   .15 .15
175 A28   50c red   .15 .15
176 A28   80c emerald   .15 .15
177 A29   1fr green ('45)   .15 .15
178 A28   1.20fr rose lilac   .15 .15
179 A28   1.50fr dark blue   .15 .15
  a.   Double impression   20.00
180 A29   2fr red   .15 .15
  a.   Double impression   22.50
181 A29   2fr dk brown ('45)   .15 .15
182 A28   2.40fr rose red   .15 .15
183 A28   3fr purple   .15 .15
184 A29   4fr ultra ('45)   .15 .15
185 A28   4.50fr olive blk   .30 .25
186 A29   10fr grnsh blk ('45)   .50 .35
    Nos. 172-186 (15)   2.75 2.55

No. 38 Surcharged in Black   **0f.30**

1944   **Perf. 14x13½**
187 A2   30c on 15c orange brn   .15 .15
  a.   Inverted surcharge   10.00 4.00
This stamp exists precanceled only. See note below No. 32.

No. 154 Surcharged "RF" and New Value

1945
190 A23   50c on 1.50fr brt rose   .15 .15
  a.   Inverted surcharge   15.00

Stamps of France, 1944, Overprinted Type "a" of 1924 in Black

1945-46
191 A99   80c yellow grn   .15 .15
192 A99   1fr grnsh blue   .15 .15
193 A99   1.20fr violet   .15 .15
194 A99   2fr violet brown   .25 .15
195 A99   2.40fr carmine rose   .25 .15
196 A99   3fr orange   .15 .15
    Nos. 191-196 (6)   1.20 .90

Same Overprint on Stamps of France, 1945-47, in Black, Red or Carmine

1945-47
197 A145   40c lilac rose   .15 .15
198 A145   50c violet bl (R)   .15 .15
199 A145   60c brt ultra (R)   .25 .15
200 A146   1fr rose red   .20 .15
201 A146   1.50fr rose lilac ('47)   .15 .15
202 A147   2fr myr grn (R) ('46)   .15 .15
203 A147   3fr deep rose   .15 .15
204 A147   4.50fr ultra (C) ('47)   .55 .15
205 A147   5fr lt green ('46)   .15 .15
206 A147   10fr ultra   .50 .20
    Nos. 197-206 (10)   2.40 1.60

Same Overprint on France No. 383 and New Value Surcharged in Black

1946
207 A99   2fr on 1.50fr henna brn   .15 .15
  a.   Without "2F"   110.00

Same Overprint on France Nos. 562 and 564, in Carmine or Blue

1947
208 A153   10c dp ultra & blk (C)   .25 .25
209 A155   50c brown, yel & red (Bl)   .30 .30

Constantine   Algiers
A30   A31

Arms of Oran — A32

    Perf. 14x13½

1947-49   **Unwmk.**   **Typo.**
210 A30   10c dk grn & brt red   .15 .15
211 A31   50c black & orange   .15 .15
212 A32   1fr ultra & yellow   .15 .15
213 A30   1.30fr blk & grnsh bl   .55 .35
214 A31   1.50fr pur & org brn   .15 .15
215 A32   2fr blk & brt grn   .15 .15
216 A30   2.50fr blk & brt red   .35 .30
217 A31   3fr vio brn & grn   .15 .15
218 A32   3.50fr lt grn & rose lil   .15 .15
219 A30   4fr dk brn & brt grn   .15 .15
220 A31   4.50fr ultra & scar   .15 .15
221 A31   5fr blk & grnsh bl   .15 .15
222 A32   6fr brown & scarlet   .22 .15
223 A32   8fr choc & ultra ('48)   .20 .15
224 A30   10fr car & choc ('48)   .35 .15
225 A31   15fr black & red ('49)   .35 .15
    Nos. 210-225 (16)   3.52 2.75

See Nos. 274-280, 285.

Peoples of the World — A33

1949, Oct. 24   **Engr.**   **Perf. 13**
226 A33   5fr green   1.25 1.00
227 A33   15fr scarlet   1.25 1.00
228 A33   25fr ultra   2.75 1.75
    Nos. 226-228 (3)   5.25 4.75
75th anniv. of the UPU.

Grapes   Apollo of
A34   Cherchell
            A35

Designs: 25fr, Dates. 40fr, Oranges and lemons.

1950, Feb. 25
229 A34   20fr multicolored   1.25 .35
230 A34   25fr multicolored   1.40 .40
231 A34   40fr multicolored   2.75 .80
    Nos. 229-231 (3)   5.40 1.55

1952   **Unwmk.**   **Perf. 13**
Designs: 12fr, 18fr, Isis statue, Cherchell. 15fr, 20fr, Child with eagle.
240 A35   10fr gray black   .25 .15
241 A35   12fr orange brn   .35 .15
242 A35   15fr deep blue   .25 .15
243 A35   18fr rose red   .35 .25
244 A35   20fr deep green   .35 .15
245 A35   30fr deep blue   .65 .35
    Nos. 240-245 (6)   2.20 1.20

War Memorial,   Fossilized
Algiers — A38   Nautilus — A39

Phonolite Dike — A40

1952, Apr. 11
246 A38   12fr dark green   .50 .35
Issued to honor the French Africa Army.

1952, Aug. 11
247 A39   15fr brt crimson   .85 .60
248 A40   30fr deep ultra   .90 .65
19th Intl. Geological Cong., Algiers, Sept. 8-15.

French and Algerian Soldiers and Camel — A41

1952, Nov. 30
249 A41   12fr chestnut brown   1.00 .60
50th anniv. of the establishment of the Sahara Companies.

Eugène Millon — A42

Values quoted in this catalogue are for stamps graded Very Fine and with no faults. An illustrated guide to grade is provided in the "Catalogue Information" section of the Introduction.

ALGERIA

François C. Maillot — A43

Oranges — A44

Portrait: 50fr, Alphonse Laveran.

1954, Jan. 4	Unwmk.	Engr.	Perf. 13
250 A42 25fr dk grn & choc		1.10	.18
251 A43 40fr org brn & brn car		1.75	.60
252 A42 50fr ultra & indigo		1.75	.22
Nos. 250-252 (3)		4.60	1.00

Military Health Service.

1954, May 8
253 A44 15fr indigo & blue .70 .40

3rd Intl. Cong. on Agronomy, Algiers, 1954.

Type of France, 1954 Overprinted type "a" in Black
Unwmk.

1954, June 6	Engr.	Perf. 13
254 A240 15fr rose carmine	.55	.45

Liberation of France, 10th anniversary.

Darguinah Hydroelectric Works A45

Patio of Bardo Museum A46

1954, June 19
255 A45 15fr lilac rose .65 .45

Opening of Darguinah hydroelectric works.

1954	Typo.	Perf. 14x13½
257 A46 12fr red brn & brn org	.60	.25
258 A46 15fr dk blue & blue	.60	.25

See Nos. 267-271.

Type of France, 1954, Overprinted type "a" in Carmine

1954	Engr.	Perf. 13
260 A247 12fr dark green	.50	.45

150th anniv. of the 1st Legion of Honor awards at Camp de Boulogne.

St. Augustine — A47

1954, Nov. 11
261 A47 15fr chocolate .75 .65

1600th anniv. of the birth of St. Augustine.

Aesculapius Statue and El Kattar Hospital, Algiers — A48

1955, Apr. 3	Unwmk.	Perf. 13
262 A48 15fr red	.50	.35

Issued to publicize the 30th French Congress of Medicine, Algiers, April 3-6, 1955.

Chenua Mountain and View of Tipasa — A49

1955, May 31
263 A49 50fr brown carmine .50 .20

2000th anniv. of the founding of Tipasa.

Type of France, 1955 Overprinted type "a" in Red

1955, June 13
264 A251 30fr deep ultra .60 .45

Rotary Intl., 50th anniv.

Marianne A50

Great Kabylia Mountains A51

1955, Oct. 3	Typo.	Perf. 14x13½	Unwmk.
265 A50 15fr carmine		.40	.25

See No. 284.

1955, Dec. 17	Engr.	Perf. 13
266 A51 100fr indigo & ultra	2.00	.20

Bardo Type of 1954, "Postes" and "Algerie" in White

1955-57	Unwmk.	Typo.	Perf. 14x13½
267 A46 10fr dk brown & lt brown		.25	.15
268 A46 12fr red brn & brn org ('56)		.20	.15
269 A46 18fr crimson & ver ('57)		.45	.20
270 A46 20fr grn & yel grn ('57)		.35	.25
271 A46 25fr purple & brt purple		.50	.15
Nos. 267-271 (5)		1.75	.90

Marshal Franchet d'Esperey A52

1956, May 25	Engr.	Perf. 13
272 A52 15fr sapphire & indigo	.70	.60

Birth cent. of Marshal Franchet d'Esperey.

Marshal Jacques Leclerc — A53

1956, Nov. 29
273 A53 15fr red brown & sepia .50 .50

Death of Marshal Leclerc.
For type surcharged see No. B90.

Type of 1947-49 and 
Arms of Bône — A54

1956-58	Typo.	Perf. 14x13½
274 A54 1fr green & ver	.15	.15
275 A54 2fr ver & ultra ('58)	.35	.20
276 A54 3fr ultra & emer ('58)	.35	.15
277 A54 5fr ultra & yellow	.15	.15
278 A31 6fr red & grn ('57)	.35	.25
279 A54 10fr dp cl & emer ('58)	.40	.25
280 A54 12fr ultra & red ('58)	.40	.25
Nos. 274-280 (7)	2.15	1.40

Nos. 275 and 279 are inscribed "Republique Francaise." See No. 285.

View of Oran — A55

1956-58	Engr.	Perf. 13
281 A55 30fr dull purple	.45	.18
282 A55 35fr car rose ('58)	.75	.45

Electric Train Crossing Bridge — A56

1957, Mar. 25
283 A56 40fr dk blue grn & emer .60 .18

Marianne Type of 1955 Inscribed "Algerie" Vertically
Perf. 14x13½

1957, Dec. 2	Typo.	Unwmk.
284 A50 20fr ultra	.40	.15

Arms Type of 1947-49 Inscribed "Republique Francaise"

1958, July
285 A31 6fr red & green 10.00 10.00

Independent State
France Nos. 939, 968, 945-946 and 1013 Overprinted "EA" and Bars, Handstamped or Typographed, in Black or Red

1962, July 2		
286 A336 10c brt green	.25	.20
a. Typographed overprint	.30	.20
287 A349 25c lake & gray	.20	.15
a. Handstamped overprint	.25	.15
288 A339 45c brt vio & ol gray	3.50	3.00
a. Handstamped overprint	15.00	10.00
289 A339 50c sl grn & lt claret	5.00	3.00
a. Handstamped overprint	15.00	12.00
290 A372 1fr dk bl, sl & bis	2.75	1.00
a. Handstamped overprint	4.00	1.50
Nos. 286-290 (5)	11.70	7.35

Post offices were authorized to overprint their stock of these 5 French stamps. The size of the letters was specified as 3x6mm each, but various sizes were used. The post offices had permission to make their own rubber stamps. Typography, pen or pencil were also used. Many types exist. Colors of handstamped overprints include black, red, blue, violet. "EA" stands for Etat Algérien.

Mosque, Tlemcen — A57

Roman Gates of Lodi, Médéa — A58

Designs: 5c, Kerrata Gorge. 10c, Dam at Foum el Gherza. 95c, Oil field, Hassi Messaoud.

1962, Nov. 1	Engr.	Perf. 13
291 A57 5c Prus grn, grn & choc	.15	.15
292 A57 10c ol blk & dk bl	.15	.15
293 A57 25c sl grn, brn & ver	.40	.15
294 A57 95c dk bl, blk & bis	1.50	.55
295 A58 1fr green & blk	1.50	1.10
Nos. 291-295 (5)	3.70	2.10

The designs of Nos. 291-295 are similar to French issues of 1959-61 with "Republique Algerienne" replacing "Republique Francaise."

Flag, Rifle, Olive Branch — A59

Design: Nos. 300-303, Broken chain and rifle added to design A59.

1963, Jan. 6	Litho.	Perf. 12½
Flag in Green and Red		
296 A59 5c bister brown	.15	.15
297 A59 10c blue	.15	.15
298 A59 25c vermilion	1.00	.15
299 A59 95c violet	.90	.45
300 A59 1fr green	.75	.15
301 A59 2fr brown	2.00	.45
302 A59 5fr lilac	3.00	1.25
303 A59 10fr gray	11.50	7.00
Nos. 296-303 (8)	19.45	9.75

Nos. 296-299 for the successful revolution and Nos. 300-303 the return of peace.

Men of Various Races, Wheat Emblem and Globe — A60

1963, Mar. 21	Engr.	Perf. 13
304 A60 25c maroon, dl grn & yel	.28	.22

FAO "Freedom from Hunger" campaign.

Map of Algeria and Emblems — A61

Physicians from 13th Century Manuscript — A62

1963, July 5	Unwmk.	Perf. 13
305 A61 25c bl, dk brn, grn & red	.40	.15

1st anniv. of Algeria's independence.

1963, July 29		Engr.
306 A62 25c brn red, grn & bis	1.00	.35

2nd Congress of the Union of Arab physicians.

Orange and Blossom A63

Scales and Scroll A64

1963		Perf. 14x13
307 A63 8c gray grn & org	.65	.65
308 A63 20c slate & org red	.75	.75
309 A63 40c grnsh bl & org	1.00	1.00
310 A63 55c ol grn & org red	2.00	2.00
Nos. 307-310 (4)	4.40	4.40

Nos. 307-310 issued precanceled only. See note below No. 32.

1963, Oct. 13	Unwmk.	Perf. 13
311 A64 25c blk, grn & rose red	.42	.28

Issued to honor the new constitution.

Guerrillas A65

Centenary Emblem A66

1963, Nov. 1
312 A65 25c dk brn, yel grn & car .55 .25

9th anniversary of Algerian revolution.

1963, Dec. 8	Photo.	Perf. 12
313 A66 25c lt vio bl, yel & dk red	.55	.28

Centenary of International Red Cross.

ALGERIA

UNESCO Emblem, Scales and Globe — A67

Workers — A68

Industrial & Agricultural Symbols — A73

Gas Flames and Pipes — A74

1963, Dec. 16   Unwmk.   Perf. 12
314 A67 25c lt blue & blk   .55 .25
15th anniv. of the Universal Declaration of Human Rights.

1964, May 1   Engr.   Perf. 13
315 A68 50c dull red, red org & bl   .90 .50
Issued for the Labor Festival.

Map of Africa and Flags — A69

1964, May 25   Unwmk.   Perf. 13
316 A69 45c blue, orange & car   .55 .28
Africa Day on the 1st anniv. of the Addis Ababa charter on African unity.

Ramses II Battling the Hittites (from Abu Simbel) — A70

Design: 30c, Two statues of Ramses II.

1964, June 28   Engr.   Perf. 13
317 A70 20c choc, red & vio bl   .55 .32
318 A70 30c brn, red & grnsh bl   .65 .40
UNESCO world campaign to save historic monuments in Nubia.

A71   A72

5, 25, 85c, Tractors. 10, 30, 65c, Men working with lathe. 12, 15, 45c, Electronics center & atom symbol. 20, 50, 95c, Draftsman & bricklayer.

1964-65   Typo.   Perf. 14x13½
319 A71 5c red lilac   .15 .15
320 A71 10c brown   .15 .15
321 A71 12c emerald ('65)   .38 .15
322 A71 15c dk blue ('65)   .25 .15
323 A71 20c yellow   .42 .15
324 A71 25c red   .50 .15
325 A71 30c purple ('65)   .42 .15
326 A71 45c rose car   .50 .18
327 A71 50c ultra   .62 .15
328 A71 65c orange   .80 .18
329 A71 85c green   1.40 .22
330 A71 95c car rose   1.75 .26
   Nos. 319-330 (12)   7.34 2.04
For surcharges see Nos. 389, 424.

1964, Aug. 30   Engr.   Perf. 13
331 A72 85c Communications tower   1.50 .75
Inauguration of the Hertzian cable telephone line Algiers-Annaba.

1964, Sept. 26   Typo.   Perf. 13½x14
332 A73 25c lt ultra, yel & red   .60 .45
1st Intl. Fair at Algiers, Sept. 26-Oct. 11.

1964, Sept. 27
333 A74 30c violet, blue & yel   .45 .35
Arzew natural gas liquification plant opening.

Planting Trees A75

Children and UNICEF Emblem A76

1964, Nov. 29   Unwmk.
334 A75 25c slate grn, yel & car   .28 .20
National reforestation campaign.

1964, Dec. 13   Perf. 13½x14
335 A76 15c pink, vio bl & lt grn   .25 .20
Issued for Children's Day.

Decorated Camel Saddle — A77

1965, May 29   Typo.   Perf. 13½x14
336 A77 20c blk, red, emer & brn   .22 .15
Handicrafts of Sahara.

ICY Emblem A78

1965, Aug. 29   Engr.   Perf. 13
337 A78 30c blk, mar & bl grn   .45 .32
338 A78 60c blk, brt bl & bl grn   .85 .38
International Cooperation Year, 1965.

ITU Emblem A79

1965, Sept. 19
339 A79 60c purple, emer & buff   .45 .30
340 A79 95c dk brn, mar & buff   .65 .35
Cent. of the ITU.

Book, Grain, Cogwheel and UNESCO Emblem — A84

Design: 60c, Grain, cogwheel, book and UNESCO emblem.

Musicians A80

Miniatures by Mohammed Racim: 60c, Two female musicians. 5d, Algerian princess and antelope.

1965, Dec. 27   Photo.   Perf. 11½
341 A80 30c multicolored   .70 .55
342 A80 60c multicolored   1.10 .70
343 A80 5d multicolored   8.00 5.25
   Nos. 341-343 (3)   9.80 6.50

Bulls, Painted in 6000 B.C. A81

Wall Paintings from Tassili-N-Ajjer, c. 6000 B.C.: No. 345, Shepherd, vert. 2d, Fleeing ostriches. 3d, Two girls, vert.

1966, Jan. 29   Photo.   Perf. 11½
344 A81 1d brn, bis & red brn   2.75 1.90
345 A81 1d gray, blk, ocher & dk brn   2.75 1.90
346 A81 2d brn, ocher & red brn   6.50 3.00
347 A81 3d buff, blk, ocher & red   8.00 4.25
   Nos. 344-347 (4)   20.00 11.05
See Nos. 365-368.

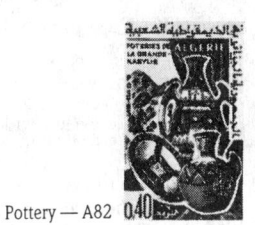

Pottery — A82

Handicrafts from Great Kabylia: 50c, Weaving, woman at loom, horiz. 70c, Jewelry.

1966, Feb. 26   Engr.   Perf. 13
348 A82 40c Prus bl, brn red & blk   .28 .22
349 A82 50c dk red, ol & ocher   .38 .28
350 A82 70c vio bl, blk & red   .65 .40
   Nos. 348-350 (3)   1.31 .90

Weather Balloon, Compass Rose and Anemometer A83

1966, Mar. 23   Engr.   Unwmk.
351 A83 1d claret, brt bl & grn   .85 .38
World Meteorological Day.

1966, May 2   Typo.   Perf. 13x14
352 A84 30c yellow bis & blk   .22 .20
353 A84 60c dk red, gray & blk   .40 .22
Literacy as basis for development.

WHO Headquarters, Geneva A85

1966, May 30   Engr.   Perf. 13
354 A85 30c multicolored   .35 .30
355 A85 60c multicolored   .70 .40
Inauguration of the WHO Headquarters, Geneva.

Algerian Scout Emblem — A86

Arab Jamboree Emblem — A87

1966, July 23   Photo.   Perf. 12x12½
356 A86 30c multicolored   .65 .50
357 A87 1d multicolored   1.75 1.25
No. 356 commemorates the 30th anniv. of the Algerian Mohammedan Boy Scouts. No. 357, the 7th Arab Boy Scout Jamboree, held at Good Daim, Libya, Aug. 12.

Map of Palestine and Victims A88

Abd-el-Kader A89

1966, Sept. 26   Typo.   Perf. 10½
358 A88 30c red & black   .80 .40
Deir Yassin Massacre, Apr. 9, 1948.

1966, Nov. 2   Photo.   Perf. 11½
359 A89 30c multicolored   .38 .15
360 A89 95c multicolored   1.10 .35
Transfer from Damascus to Algiers of the ashes of Abd-el-Kader (1807?-1883), Emir of Mascara. See Nos. 382-387.

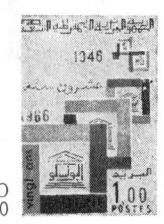

UNESCO Emblem — A90

1966, Nov. 19   Typo.   Perf. 10½
361 A90 1d multicolored   1.00 .35
20th anniv. of UNESCO.

ALGERIA

Horseman — A91

Miniatures by Mohammed Racim: 1.50d, Woman at her toilette. 2d, The pirate Barbarossa in front of the Admiralty.

1966, Dec. 17   Photo.   Perf. 11½
Granite Paper
362	A91	1d multicolored	3.25	1.40
363	A91	1.50d multicolored	4.25	2.00
364	A91	2d multicolored	7.00	3.50
		Nos. 362-364 (3)	14.50	6.90

Wall Paintings Type of 1966

Wall Paintings from Tassili-N-Ajjer, c. 6000 B.C.: 1d, Cow. No. 366, Antelope. No. 367, Archers. 3d, Warrior, vert.

1967, Jan. 28   Photo.   Perf. 11½
365	A81	1d brn, bis & dl vio	2.75	1.90
366	A81	2d brn, ocher & red brn	5.00	3.25
367	A81	2d brn, yel & red brn	5.00	3.25
368	A81	3d blk, gray, yel & red brn	7.75	5.00
		Nos. 365-368 (4)	20.50	13.40

Bardo Museum — A92

La Kalaa Minaret — A93

Design: 1.30d, Ruins at Sedrata.

1967, Feb. 27   Photo.   Perf. 13
369	A92	35c multicolored	.20	.15
370	A93	95c multicolored	.45	.28
371	A92	1.30d multicolored	.75	.40
		Nos. 369-371 (3)	1.40	.83

Moretti and International Tourist Year Emblem — A94

Design: 70c, Tuareg riding camel, Tassili, and Tourist Year Emblem, vert.

1967, Apr. 29   Litho.   Perf. 14
372	A94	40c multi	.50	.22
373	A94	70c multi	1.00	.35

International Tourist Year, 1967.

Spiny-tailed Agamid — A95

Designs: 20c, Ostrich, vert. 40c, Slender-horned gazelle, vert. 70c, Fennec.

1967, June 24   Photo.   Perf. 11½
374	A95	5c bister & blk	.60	.50
375	A95	20c ocher, blk & pink	1.25	.80
376	A95	40c ol bis, blk & red brn	2.00	1.00
377	A95	70c gray, blk & dp grn	3.50	2.00
		Nos. 374-377 (4)	7.35	4.30

Dancers — A96

Typographed and Engraved
1967, July 4   Perf. 10½
378	A96	50c gray vio, yel & blk	.45	.32

National Youth Festival.

Map of the Mediterranean and Sport Scenes — A97

1967, Sept. 2   Typo.   Perf. 10½
379	A97	30c black, red & blue	.25	.20

Issued to publicize the 5th Mediterranean Games, Tunis, Sept. 8-17.

Skiers — A98

Olympic Emblem and Sports — A99

1967, Oct. 21   Engr.   Perf. 13
380	A98	30c brt blue & ultra	.32	.20
381	A99	95c brn org, pur & brt grn	.80	.52

Issued to publicize the 10th Winter Olympic Games, Grenoble, Feb. 6-18, 1968.

Abd-el-Kader Type of 1966
Lithographed, Photogravure
1967-71   Perf. 13½, 11½
382	A89	5c dull pur ('68)	.15	.15
383	A89	10c green	.85	.35
383A	A89	10c sl grn (litho., '69)	.15	.15
383B	A89	25c orange ('71)	.18	.15
384	A89	30c black ('68)	.50	.20
385	A89	30c lt violet ('68)	.75	.30
386	A89	50c rose claret	.65	.18
387	A89	70c violet blue	.85	.22
		Nos. 382-387 (8)	4.08	1.70

No. 383, 50c and 70c, issued Nov. 13, 1967, are on granite paper, photo. The 5c, No.383A, 25c and 30c are litho., perf. 13½; others, perf. 11½.

The three 1967 stamps (No. 383, 50c, 70c) have numerals thin, narrow and close together; the Arabic inscription at lower right is 2mm high. The 5 litho. stamps are redrawn, with numerals thicker and spaced more widely; Arabic at lower right 3mm high.

Boy Scouts Holding Jamboree Emblem — A100

1967, Dec. 23   Engr.   Perf. 13
388	A100	1d multicolored	1.00	.80

12th Boy Scout World Jamboree, Farragut State Park, Idaho, Aug. 1-9.

No. 324 Surcharged
1967   Typo.   Perf. 14x13½
389	A71	30c on 25c red	.50	.20

Mandolin — A101

1968, Feb. 17   Photo.   Perf. 12½x13
390	A101	30c shown	.35	.22
391	A101	40c Lute	.40	.25
392	A101	1.30d Rebec	1.40	.65
		Nos. 390-392 (3)	2.15	1.12

Nememcha Rug — A102

Algerian Rugs: 70c, Guergour. 95c, Djebel-Amour. 1.30d, Kalaa.

1968, Apr. 13   Photo.   Perf. 11½
393	A102	30c multi	.75	.75
394	A102	70c multi	1.50	1.50
395	A102	95c multi	2.00	2.00
396	A102	1.30d multi	2.50	2.50
		Nos. 393-396 (4)	6.75	6.75

Human Rights Flame — A103

1968, May 18   Typo.   Perf. 10½
397	A103	40c blue, red & yel	.40	.28

International Human Rights Year, 1968.

WHO Emblem — A104

1968, May 18
398	A104	70c blk, lt bl & yel	.55	.28

20th anniv. of the WHO.

Welder — A105

Athletes, Olympic Flame and Rings — A106

1968, June 15   Engr.   Perf. 13
399	A105	30c gray, brn & ultra	.25	.18

Algerian emigration to Europe.

Perf. 12½x13, 13x12½
1968, July 4   Photo.

50c, Soccer player. 1d, Mexican pyramid, emblem, Olympic flame, rings & athletes, horiz.

400	A106	30c green, red & yel	.35	.28
401	A106	50c rose car & multi	.60	.32
402	A106	1d dk grn, org, brn & red	1.10	.65
		Nos. 400-402 (3)	2.05	1.25

19th Olympic Games, Mexico City, Oct. 12-27.

Scouts and Emblem — A107

Barbary Sheep — A108

1968, July 4   Perf. 13
403	A107	30c multicolored	.50	.18

8th Arab Boy Scout Jamboree, Algiers, 1968.

1968, Oct. 19   Photo.   Perf. 11½
404	A108	40c shown	.48	.25
405	A108	1d Red deer	1.25	.60

Hunting Scenes, Djemila — A109

"Industry" — A110

Design: 95c, Neptune's chariot, Timgad, horiz. Both designs are from Roman mosaics.

Perf. 12½x13, 13x12½
1968, Nov. 23   Photo.
406	A109	40c gray & multi	.35	.22
407	A109	95c gray & multi	.85	.50

1968, Dec. 14   Perf. 11½

Designs: No. 409, Miner with drill. 95c, "Energy" (circle and rays).

408	A110	30c dp orange & sil	.25	.18
409	A110	30c brown & multi	.25	.18
410	A110	95c silver, red & blk	.75	.35
		Nos. 408-410 (3)	1.25	.71

Issued to publicize industrial development.

Opuntia Ficus Indica — A111

Flowers: 40c, Carnations. 70c, Roses. 95c, Bird-of-paradise flower.

ALGERIA

1969, Jan. Photo. *Perf. 11½*
Flowers in Natural Colors
411	A111	25c pink & blk	.52	.25
412	A111	40c yellow & blk	.65	.32
413	A111	70c gray & blk	1.25	.45
414	A111	95c brt blue & blk	2.00	.80
		Nos. 411-414 (4)	4.42	1.82

See Nos. 496-499.

Irrigation Dam at Djorf Torba-Oued Guir — A112

Design: 1.50d, Truck on Highway No. 51 and camel caravan.

1969, Feb. 22 Photo. *Perf. 11½*
| 415 | A112 | 30c multi | .24 | .18 |
| 416 | A112 | 1.50d multi | 1.25 | .65 |

Public works in the Sahara.

Mail Coach — A113

1969, Mar. 22 Photo. *Perf. 11½*
| 417 | A113 | 1d multicolored | 1.10 | .60 |

Issued for Stamp Day, 1969.

Capitol, Timgad — A114

Design: 1d, Septimius Temple, Djemila, horiz.

1969, Apr. 5 Photo. *Perf. 13x12½*
| 418 | A114 | 30c gray & multi | .35 | .18 |
| 419 | A114 | 1d gray & multi | .85 | .35 |

Second Timgad Festival, Apr. 4-8.

ILO Emblem — A115   Arabian Saddle — A116

1969, May 24 Photo. *Perf. 11½*
| 420 | A115 | 95c dp car, yel & blk | 1.00 | .38 |

50th anniv. of the ILO.

1969, June 28 Photo. *Perf. 12x12½*
Algerian Handicrafts: 30c, Bookcase. 60c, Decorated copper plate.

Granite Paper
421	A116	30c multicolored	.28	.20
422	A116	60c multicolored	.55	.25
423	A116	1d multicolored	1.00	.45
		Nos. 421-423 (3)	1.83	.90

0,20
No. 321 Surcharged

1969 Typo. *Perf. 14x13½*
| 424 | A71 | 20c on 12c emerald | .22 | .15 |

Pan-African Culture Festival Emblem — A117   African Development Bank Emblem — A118

1969, July 19 Photo. *Perf. 12½*
| 425 | A117 | 30c multicolored | .32 | .18 |

Issued to commemorate the First Pan-African Culture Festival, Algiers, July 21-Aug. 1.

1969, Aug. 23 Typo. *Perf. 10½*
| 426 | A118 | 30c dull blue, yel & blk | .32 | .20 |

5th anniversary of the African Development Bank.

Astronauts and Landing Module on Moon — A119

Perf. 12½x11½
1969, Aug. 23 Photo.
| 427 | A119 | 50c gold & multi | .60 | .35 |

Man's 1st landing on the moon, July 20, 1969. US astronauts Neil A. Armstrong and Col. Edwin E. Aldrin, Jr., with Lieut. Col. Michael Collins piloting Apollo 11.

Algerian Women, by Dinet — A120

1.50d, The Watchmen, by Etienne Dinet.

1969, Nov. 29 Photo. *Perf. 14½*
| 428 | A120 | 1d multi | 1.75 | .90 |
| 429 | A120 | 1.50d multi | 2.75 | 1.40 |

Mother and Child — A121

1969, Dec. 27 Photo. *Perf. 11½*
| 430 | A121 | 30c multicolored | .32 | .24 |

Issued to promote mother and child protection.

Agricultural Growth Chart, Tractor and Dam — A122

Designs: 30c, Transportation and development. 50c, Abstract symbols of industrialization.

1970, Jan. 31 Photo. *Perf. 12½*
Size: 37x23mm
| 431 | A122 | 25c dk brn, yel & org | .16 | .15 |

Litho. *Perf. 14*
Size: 49x23mm
| 432 | A122 | 30c blue & multi | .24 | .18 |

Photo. *Perf. 12½*
Size: 37x23mm
| 433 | A122 | 50c rose lilac & blk | .28 | .20 |
| | | Nos. 431-433 (3) | .68 | .53 |

Four-Year Development Plan.

Old and New Mail Delivery — A123   Spiny Lobster — A124

1970, Feb. 28 Photo. *Perf. 11½*
Granite Paper
| 434 | A123 | 30c multicolored | .28 | .18 |

Issued for Stamp Day.

1970, Mar. 28
Designs: 40c, Mollusks. 75c, Retepora cellulosa. 1d, Red coral.
435	A124	30c ocher & multi	.35	.18
436	A124	40c multicolored	.50	.22
437	A124	75c ultra & multi	.90	.35
438	A124	1d lt blue & multi	1.25	.48
		Nos. 435-438 (4)	3.00	1.23

Oranges, EXPO '70 Emblem — A125

Designs (EXPO '70 Emblem and): 60c, Algerian pavilion. 70c, Grapes.

1970, Apr. 25 Photo. *Perf. 12½x12*
439	A125	30c lt blue, grn & org	.50	.15
440	A125	60c multicolored	.65	.18
441	A125	70c multicolored	1.00	.32
		Nos. 439-441 (3)	2.15	.65

EXPO '70 International Exhibition, Osaka, Japan, Mar. 15-Sept. 13, 1970.

Olives, Oil Bottle — A126   Saber — A127

1970, May 16 Photo. *Perf. 12½x12*
| 442 | A126 | 1d yellow & multi | 1.00 | .65 |

Olive Year, 1969-1970.

Common Design Types pictured following the introduction.

UPU Headquarters Issue
Common Design Type
1970, May 30 *Perf. 13*
Size: 36x26mm
| 443 | CD133 | 75c multicolored | .50 | .40 |

1970, June 27 Photo. *Perf. 12½*
Designs: 40c, Guns, 18th century, horiz. 1d, Pistol, 18th century, horiz.
444	A127	40c yellow & multi	.65	.22
445	A127	75c red & multi	.80	.40
446	A127	1d multicolored	1.25	.50
		Nos. 444-446 (3)	2.70	1.12

Map of Arab Countries and Arab League Flag — A128

Typographed and Engraved
1970, July 25 *Perf. 10½*
| 447 | A128 | 30c grn, ocher & lt bl | .30 | .20 |

25th anniversary of the Arab League.

Lenin — A129

1970, Aug. 29 Litho. *Perf. 11½x12*
| 448 | A129 | 30c brown & buff | .25 | .20 |

Lenin (1870-1924), Russian communist leader.

Exhibition Hall and Algiers Fair Emblem — A130

1970, Sept. 11 Engr. *Perf. 14x13½*
| 449 | A130 | 60c lt olive green | .40 | .30 |

New Exhibition Hall for Algiers International Fair.

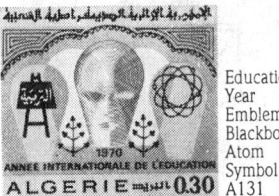

Education Year Emblem, Blackboard, Atom Symbol — A131

Koran Page — A132

1970, Oct. 24 Photo. *Perf. 14*
| 450 | A131 | 30c pink, blk, gold & lt bl | .22 | .18 |
| 451 | A132 | 3d multicolored | 2.50 | 1.50 |

Issued for International Education Year.

Great Mosque, Tlemcen — A133

Design: 40c, Ketchaoua Mosque, Algiers, vert. 1d, Mosque, Sidi-Okba, vert.

ALGERIA

1970-71   Litho.   Perf. 14
456 A133 30c multicolored .22 .15
457 A133 40c sepia & lemon ('71) .25 .15
458 A133 1d multicolored .65 .28
    Nos. 456-458 (3) 1.12 .58

Symbols of the Arts — A134

1970, Dec. 26   Photo.   Perf. 13x12½
459 A134 1d grn, lt grn & org .80 .45

Main Post Office, Algiers A135

1971, Jan. 23   Perf. 11½
460 A135 30c multicolored .32 .20
Stamp Day, 1971.

Hurdling A136

1971, Mar. 7   Photo.   Perf. 11½
461 A136 20c lt blue & slate .25 .20
462 A136 40c lt ol grn & slate .35 .35
463 A136 75c salmon pink & slate .65 .50
    Nos. 461-463 (3) 1.25 1.05
Mediterranean Games, Izmir, Turkey, Oct. 1971.

Symbolic Head — A137

1971, Mar. 27   Perf. 12½
464 A137 60c car rose, blk & sil .32 .20
Intl. year against racial discrimination.

Emblem and Technicians A138

1971, Apr. 24   Photo.   Perf. 12½x12
465 A138 70c claret, org & bluish blk .40 .30
Founding of the Institute of Technology.

Woman from Aurès — A139

Regional Costumes: 70c, Man from Oran. 80c, Man from Algiers. 90c, Woman from Amour Mountains.

1971, Oct. 16   Perf. 11½
466 A139 50c gold & multi 1.50 .65
467 A139 70c gold & multi 1.65 1.00
468 A139 80c gold & multi 2.25 1.10
469 A139 90c gold & multi 2.50 1.25
    Nos. 466-469 (4) 7.90 4.00
See Nos. 485-488, 534-537.

UNICEF Emblem, Birds and Plants — A140

1971, Dec. 6   Perf. 11½
470 A140 60c multicolored .55 .32
25th anniv. of UNICEF.

Lion of St. Mark A141

Design: 1.15d, Bridge of Sighs, Venice, vert.

1972, Jan. 24   Litho.   Perf. 12
471 A141 80c multi .60 .32
472 A141 1.15d multi .90 .52
UNESCO campaign to save Venice.

Javelin A142    Book and Book Year Emblem A143

Designs: 25c, Bicycling, horiz. 60c, Wrestling. 1d, Gymnast on rings.

1972, Mar. 25   Photo.   Perf. 11½
473 A142 25c maroon & multi .30 .20
474 A142 40c ocher & multi .35 .25
475 A142 60c ultra & multi .40 .40
476 A142 1d rose & multi 1.00 .50
    Nos. 473-476 (4) 2.05 1.35
20th Olympic Games, Munich, Aug. 26-Sept. 11.

1972, Apr. 15
477 A143 1.15d bister, brn & red .65 .48
International Book Year 1972.

Mailmen A144    Flowers A145

1972, Apr. 22
478 A144 40c gray & multi .25 .15
Stamp Day 1972.

1972, May 27
479 A145 50c Jasmine .65 .28
480 A145 60c Violets .75 .35
481 A145 1.15d Tuberose 1.50 .55
    Nos. 479-481 (3) 2.90 1.18

Olympic Stadium, Chéraga — A146

1972, June 10
482 A146 50c gray, choc & grn .60 .32

New Day, Algerian Flag — A147

1972, July 5
483 A147 1d green & multi .65 .42
10th anniversary of independence.

Festival Emblem — A148    Mailing a Letter — A149

1972, July 5   Litho.   Perf. 10½
484 A148 40c grn, dk brn & org .22 .15
1st Arab Youth Festival, Algiers, July 5-11.

Costume Type of 1971
Regional Costumes: 50c, Woman from Hoggar. 60c, Kabyle woman. 70c, Man from Mzab. 90c, Woman from Tlemcen.

1972, Nov. 18   Photo.   Perf. 11½
485 A139 50c gold & multi .80 .70
486 A139 60c gold & multi 1.10 .90
487 A139 70c gold & multi 1.25 1.10
488 A139 90c gold & multi 1.75 1.25
    Nos. 485-488 (4) 4.90 3.95

1973, Jan. 20   Photo.   Perf. 11
489 A149 40c orange & multi .40 .20
Stamp Day.

Ho Chi Minh, Map of Viet Nam — A150

1973, Feb. 17   Photo.   Perf. 11½
490 A150 40c multicolored .75 .50
To honor the people of Viet Nam.

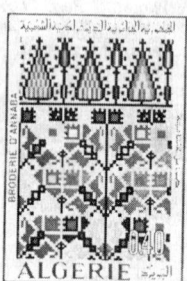

Embroidery from Annaba — A151

Designs: 60c, Tree of Life pattern from Algiers. 80c, Constantine embroidery.

1973, Feb. 24
491 A151 40c gray & multi .75 .40
492 A151 60c blue and multi 1.00 .60
493 A151 80c dk red, gold & blk 1.50 .80
    Nos. 491-493 (3) 3.25 1.80

Stylized Globe and Wheat — A152

1973, Mar. 26   Photo.   Perf. 11½
494 A152 1.15d brt rose lil, org & grn .75 .50
World Food Program, 10th anniversary.

Soldier and Flag A153

1973, Apr. 23   Photo.   Perf. 14x13½
495 A153 40c multicolored .25 .18
Honoring the National Service.

Flower Type of 1969
Flowers: 30c, Opuntia ficus indica. 40c, Roses. 1d, Carnations. 1.15d, Bird-of-paradise flower.

1973, May 21   Photo.   Perf. 11½
Flowers in Natural Colors
496 A111 30c pink & blk .40 .18
497 A111 40c gray & blk .50 .25
498 A111 1d yellow & multi .90 .40
499 A111 1.15d multi 1.25 .50
    Nos. 496-499 (4) 3.05 1.28
For overprints and surcharges see #518-519, 531.

OAU Emblem — A154

1973, May 28   Photo.   Perf. 12½x13
500 A154 40c multicolored .40 .20
Org. for African Unity, 10th anniv.

Desert and Fruitful Land, Farmer and Family A155

1973, June 18   Perf. 11½
501 A155 40c gold & multi .50 .40
Agricultural revolution.

ALGERIA

Map of Africa, Scout Emblem — A156

1973, July 16   Litho.   Perf. 10½
502 A156 80c purple   1.00 .50
24th Boy Scout World Conference (1st in Africa), Nairobi, Kenya, July 16-21.

Algerian PTT Emblem — A157

1973, Aug. 6   Perf. 14
503 A157 40c blue & orange   .22 .15
Adoption of new emblem for Post, Telegraph and Telephone System.

Conference Emblem — A158

Perf. 13½x12½
1973, Sept. 5   Photo.
504 A158 40c dp rose & multi   .18 .15
505 A158 80c blue grn & multi   .52 .26
4th Summit Conference of Non-aligned Nations, Algiers, Sept. 5-9.

Port of Skikda A159

1973, Sept. 29   Photo.   Perf. 11½
506 A159 80c ocher, blk & ultra   .48 .25
New port of Skikda.

Young Workers — A160

1973, Oct. 22   Photo.   Perf. 13
507 A160 40c multicolored   .22 .15
Voluntary work service.

Arms of Algiers A161

1973, Dec. 22   Photo.   Perf. 13
508 A161 2d gold & multi   1.60 1.10
Millennium of Algiers.

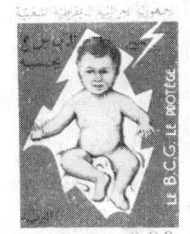

Infant — A162

1974, Jan. 7   Litho.   Perf. 10½x11
509 A162 80c orange & multi   .60 .35
Fight against tuberculosis.

Man and Woman, Industry and Transportation A163

1974, Feb. 18   Photo.   Perf. 11½
510 A163 80c multicolored   .48 .20
Four-year plan.

A164

1974, Feb. 25   Photo.   Perf. 11½
511 A164 1.50d multi   1.10 .65
Millennium of the birth of abu-al-Rayhan al-Biruni (973-1048), philosopher and mathematician.

Map and Colors of Algeria, Tunisia, Morocco A165

1974, Mar. 4   Photo.   Perf. 13
512 A165 40c gold & multi   .28 .20
Maghreb Committee for Coordination of Posts and Telecommunications.

Hand Holding Rifle A166

1974, Mar. 25   Perf. 11½
513 A166 80c red & black   .30 .20
Solidarity with the struggle of the people of South Africa.

Mother and Children A167

1974, Apr. 8   Perf. 13½
514 A167 85c multicolored   .35 .22
Honoring Algerian mothers.

Village A168

Designs: 80c, Harvest. 90c, Tractor and sun. Designs after children's drawings.

1974, June 15
Size: 45x26mm
515 A168 70c multicolored   .40 .18
Size: 48x33mm
516 A168 80c multicolored   .48 .28
517 A168 90c multicolored   .60 .42
  Nos. 515-517 (3)   1.48 .88

Nos. 498-499 Overprinted "FLORALIES/1974"

1974, June 22   Photo.   Perf. 11½
518 A111 1d multi   .65 .35
519 A111 1.15d multi   .70 .40
1974 Flower Show.

Stamp Vending Machine — A169

1974, Oct. 7   Photo.   Perf. 13
520 A169 80c multicolored   .42 .20
Stamp Day 1974.

UPU Emblem and Globe — A170

1974, Oct. 14   Perf. 14
521 A170 80c multicolored   .50 .28
Centenary of Universal Postal Union.

"Revolution" — A171

Soldiers and Mountains — A172

Raising New Flag — A173

Design: 1d, Algerian struggle for independence (people, sun and fields).

1974, Nov. 4   Photo.   Perf. 14
522 A171 40c multicolored   .28 .18
523 A172 70c multicolored   .40 .22
524 A173 95c multicolored   .48 .22
525 A171 1d multicolored   .60 .28
  Nos. 522-525 (4)   1.76 .90
20th anniv. of the start of the revolution.

"Horizon 1980" — A174

Ewer and Basin — A175

1974, Nov. 23   Photo.   Perf. 13
526 A174 95c ocher, dk red & blk   .55 .25
10-year development plan, 1971-1980.

1974, Dec. 21   Perf. 11½
527 A175 50c shown   .22 .15
528 A175 60c Coffee pot   .28 .20
529 A175 95c Sugar bowl   .45 .30
530 A175 1d Bath tub   .50 .35
  Nos. 527-530 (4)   1.45 1.00
17th century Algerian copperware.

No. 497 Surcharged with New Value and Heavy Bar

1975, Jan. 4
531 A111 50c on 40c multi   .50 .40

Mediterranean Games' Emblem — A176

1975, Jan. 27   Perf. 13½
532 A176 50c purple, yel & grn   .28 .18
533 A176 1d orange, bl & mar   .60 .22
Mediterranean Games, Algiers, 1975.

Costume Type of 1971

Regional Costumes: No. 534, Woman from Hoggar. No. 535, Woman from Algiers. No. 536, Woman from Oran. No. 537, Man from Tlemcen.

1975, Feb. 22   Photo.   Perf. 11½
534 A139 1d gold & multi   .90 .80
535 A139 1d gold & multi   .90 .80
536 A139 1d gold & multi   .90 .80
537 A139 1d gold & multi   .90 .80
  Nos. 534-537 (4)   3.60 3.20

Map of Arab Countries, ALO Emblem A177

1975, Mar. 10   Litho.   Perf. 10½x11
538 A177 50c red brown   .25 .15
Arab Labor Organization, 10th anniversary.

Blood Transfusion A178

1975, Mar. 15   Perf. 14
539 A178 50c car rose & multi   .32 .18
Blood donation and transfusions.

ALGERIA

Post Office, Al-
Kantara
A179

Policeman and Map
of Algeria
A180

1975, May 10   Photo.   Perf. 11½
Granite Paper
540 A179 50c multicolored   .25   .15
Stamp Day 1975.

1975, June 1   Photo.   Perf. 13
541 A180 50c multicolored   .75   .40
Natl. Security and 10th Natl. Police Day.

Ground
Receiving
Station
A181

Designs: 1d, Map of Algeria with locations of radar sites, transmission mast and satellite. 1.20d, Main and subsidiary stations.

1975, June 28   Photo.   Perf. 13
542 A181   50c blue & multi   .28   .15
543 A181   1d blue & multi   .55   .20
544 A181   1.20d blue & multi   .60   .22
     Nos. 542-544 (3)   1.43   .57
National satellite telecommunications network.

Revolutionary with
Flag — A182

1975, Aug. 20   Photo.   Perf. 11½
545 A182 1d multicolored   .50   .25
August 20th Revolutionary Movement (Skikda), 20th anniversary.

Swimming and
Games'
Emblem
A183

Perf. 13x13½, 13½x13
1975, Aug. 23   Photo.
546 A183   25c shown   .15   .15
547 A183   50c Judo, map   .25   .18
548 A183   70c Soccer, vert.   .48   .22
549 A183   1d Running, vert.   .55   .25
550 A183   1.20d Handball, vert. .70   .38
  a. Souv. sheet of 5, #546-550, perf 13 4.50 4.50
     Nos. 546-550 (5)   2.13 1.18
7th Mediterranean Games, Algiers, 8/23-9/46.
No. 550a sold for 4.50d. Exists imperf., same value.

Setif, Guelma,
Kherrata — A184

1975   Litho.   Perf. 13½x14
551 A184   5c orange & blk   .15   .15
552 A184 10c emerald & brn   .15   .15
553 A184 25c dl blue & blk   .15   .15
554 A184 30c lemon & blk   .15   .15
555 A184 50c brt grn & blk   .22   .15
556 A184 70c fawn & blk   .35   .15
557 A184   1d vermilion & blk   .50   .25
     Nos. 551-557 (7)   1.67 1.15
30th anniv. of victory in World War II.
Issue dates: 50c, 1d, Nov. 3; others, Dec. 17.
For surcharge see No. 611.

Map of
Maghreb and
APU Emblem
A185

1975, Nov. 20   Photo.   Perf. 11½
558 A185 1d multicolored   .55   .28
10th Cong. of Arab Postal Union, Algiers.

Mosaic, Bey
Constantine's
Palace — A186

Dey-Alger Palace — A187

Famous buildings: 2d, Prayer niche, Medersa Sidi-Boumediene, Tlemcen.

1975, Dec. 22
559 A186   1d lt blue & multi   .60   .22
560 A186   2d buff & multi   1.10   .60
561 A187 2.50d buff & blk   1.60   .90
     Nos. 559-561 (3)   3.30 1.72

Al-Azhar
University
A188

Perf. 11½x12½
1975, Dec. 29   Litho.
562 A188 2d multicolored   1.10   .60
Millennium of Al-Azhar University.

Red-billed
Firefinch — A189

Birds: 1.40d, Black-headed bush shrike, horiz. 2d, Blue tit. 2.50d, Blackbellied sandgrouse, horiz.

1976, Jan. 24   Photo.   Perf. 11½
563 A189   50c multi   .35   .18
564 A189 1.40d multi   .85   .55
565 A189   2d multi   1.10   .65
566 A189 2.50d multi   1.50   .90
     Nos. 563-566 (4)   3.80 2.28
See Nos. 595-598.

Telephones 1876
and 1976 — A190

Map of Africa
with Angola and
its Flag — A191

1976, Feb. 23   Photo.   Perf. 13½x13
567 A190 1.40d rose, dk & lt bl .65   .38
Centenary of first telephone call by Alexander Graham Bell, Mar. 10, 1876.

1976, Feb. 23   Perf. 11½
568 A191 50c brown & multi   .25   .15
Algeria's solidarity with the People's Republic of Angola.

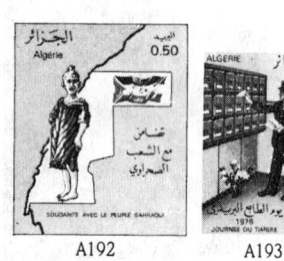

A192   A193

Sahraoui flag and child, map of former Spanish Sahara.

1976, Mar. 15   Photo.   Perf. 11½
569 A192 50c multicolored   .25   .15
Algeria's solidarity with Sahraoui Arab Democratic Republic, former Spanish Sahara.

1976, Mar. 22
570 A193 1.40d Mailman   .60   .32
Stamp Day 1976.

Microscope,
Slide with TB
Bacilli,
Patients
A194

1976, Apr. 26   Perf. 13x13½
571 A194 50c multicolored   .40   .20
Fight against tuberculosis.

"Setif, Guelma,
Kherrata" — A195

1976, May 24   Photo.   Perf. 13½x13
572 A195 50c blue & yellow   .35   .15
 a.   Booklet pane of 6   4.75
 b.   Booklet pane of 10   4.00
No. 572 was issued in booklets only.

Ram's Head over
Landscape — A196

People Holding
Torch, Map of
Algeria — A197

1976, June 17   Photo.   Perf. 11½
573 A196 50c multicolored   .40   .20
Livestock breeding.

1976, June 29   Photo.   Perf. 14x13½
574 A197 50c multicolored   .25   .15
National Charter.

Palestine Map and
Flag — A198

Map of
Africa — A199

1976, July 12   Perf. 11½
Granite Paper
575 A198 50c multicolored   2.00 1.00
Solidarity with the Palestinians.

1976, Oct. 3   Litho.   Perf. 10½x11
576 A199 2d dk blue & multi   1.00   .50
2nd Pan-African Commercial Fair, Algiers.

Blind
Brushmaker
A200

The
Blind,
by
Dinet
A201

1976, Oct. 23   Photo.   Perf. 14½
577 A200 1.20d blue & multi   .65   .35
578 A201 1.40d gold & multi   1.50   .75
Rehabilitation of the blind.

ALGERIA

"Constitution 1976" — A202

1976, Nov. 19   Photo.   *Perf. 11½*
579 A202 2d multicolored   1.00 .55
New Constitution.

Soldiers Planting Seedlings — A203

1976, Nov. 25   Litho.   *Perf. 12*
580 A203 1.40d multicolored   .75 .35
Green barrier against the Sahara.

Ornamental Border and Inscription A204

1976, Dec. 18   Photo.   *Perf. 11½*
Granite Paper
581 A204 2d multicolored   1.25 .75
Re-election of Pres. Houari Boumediene.
See No. 627.

Map with Charge Zones and Dials A205

People and Buildings A206

1977, Jan. 22   *Perf. 13*
582 A205 40c silver & multi   .28 .15
Inauguration of automatic national and international telephone service.

1977, Jan. 29   Photo.   *Perf. 11½*
583 A206 60c on 50c multi   .35 .18
2nd General Population and Buildings Census. No. 583 was not issued without the typographed red brown surcharge, date, and bars.

Sahara Museum, Uargla — A207

1977, Feb. 12   Litho.   *Perf. 14*
584 A207 60c multicolored   .35 .20

El-Kantara Gorge — A208

Perf. 12½x13½
1977, Feb. 19   Photo.
585 A208 20c green & yellow   .15 .15
   a.   Bklt. pane, 3 #585, 4 #586 + label   8.00
   b.   Bklt. pane, 5 #585, 2 #587 + label   6.50
586 A208 60c brt lilac & yel   .18 .15
587 A208 1d brown & yellow   .40 .15
   Nos. 585-587 (3)   .73 .45

National Assembly — A209

1977, Feb. 27   *Perf. 11½*
588 A209 2d multicolored   1.00 .60

People and Flag — A210

Soldier and Flag — A211

Perf. 13½, 11½ (3d)
1977, Mar. 12   Photo.
589 A210 2d multicolored   1.25 .40
590 A211 3d multicolored   1.75 .65
Solidarity with the peoples of Zimbabwe (Rhodesia), 2d; Namibia, 3d.

Winter, Roman Mosaic — A212

The Seasons from Roman Villa, 2nd century A.D.: 1.40d, Fall. 2d, Summer. 3d, Spring.

1977, Apr. 21   Photo.   *Perf. 11½*
Granite Paper
591 A212 1.20d multi   .95 .52
592 A212 1.40d multi   1.25 .52
593 A212 2d multi   1.65 .95
594 A212 3d multi   2.50 1.65
   a.   Souv. sheet of 4, #591-594, perf., imperf.   10.00 10.00
   Nos. 591-594 (4)   6.35 3.64
No. 594a sold for 8d.

Bird Type of 1976
Birds: 60c, Tristram's warbler. 1.40d, Moussier's redstart, horiz. 2d, Temminck's horned lark, horiz. 3d, Eurasian hoopoe.

1977, May 21   Photo.   *Perf. 11½*
595 A189 60c multi   .75 .22
596 A189 1.40d multi   1.25 .40
597 A189 2d multi   1.75 .65
598 A189 3d multi   2.50 1.10
   Nos. 595-598 (4)   6.25 2.37

Horseman — A213
Design: 5d, Attacking horsemen, horiz.

1977, June 25   Photo.   *Perf. 11½*
599 A213 2d multicolored   1.65 .75
600 A213 5d multicolored   3.50 2.00

Flag Colors, Games Emblem — A214

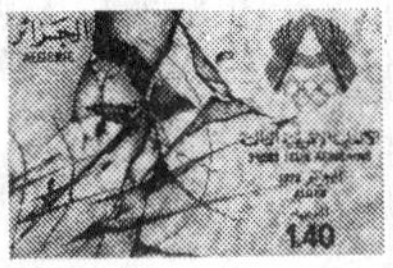

Wall Painting, Games Emblem A215

1977, Sept. 24   Photo.   *Perf. 11½*
601 A214 60c multi   .35 .22
602 A215 1.40d multi   .80 .45
3rd African Games, Algiers 1978.

Village and Tractor A216

1977, Nov. 12   *Perf. 14x13*
603 A216 1.40d multi   .90 .65
Socialist agricultural village.

Almohades Dirham, 12th Century — A217

Ancient Coins: 1.40d, Almohades coin, 12th century. 2d, Almoravides dinar, 11th century.

1977, Dec. 17   Photo.   *Perf. 11½*
604 A217 60c ultra, sil & blk   .50 .35
605 A217 1.40d green, gold & brn   1.10 .50
606 A217 2d red brn, gold & brn   1.50 .90
   Nos. 604-606 (3)   3.10 1.75

Flowering Trees — A218

1978, Feb. 11   Photo.   *Perf. 11½*
607 A218 60c Cherry   .35 .24
608 A218 1.20d Peach   .85 .50
609 A218 1.30d Almond   .85 .50
610 A218 1.40d Apple   .90 .55
   Nos. 607-610 (4)   2.95 1.79

No. 555 Surcharged with New Value and Bar
1978, Feb. 11   Litho.   *Perf. 13½x14*
611 A184 60c on 50c   .50 .16

Children with Traffic Signs and Car — A219

1978, Apr. 29   Photo.   *Perf. 11½*
612 A219 60c multicolored   .28 .15
Road safety and protection of children.

Sports and Games Emblems A220

Designs (Games Emblem and): 60c, Rower, vert. 1.20d, Flag colors, vert. 1.30d, Fireworks, vert. 1.40d, Map of Africa and dancers, vert.

1978, July 13   Photo.   *Perf. 11½*
613 A220 40c multi   .18 .15
614 A220 60c multi   .28 .18
615 A220 1.20d multi   .60 .28
616 A220 1.30d multi   .60 .35
617 A220 1.40d multi   .65 .35
   Nos. 613-617 (5)   2.31 1.31
3rd African Games, Algiers, July 13-28.

TB Patient Returning to Family A221

1978, Oct. 5   Photo.   *Perf. 13½x14*
618 A221 60c multicolored   .35 .16
Anti-tuberculosis campaign.

Holy Kaaba — A222

1978, Oct. 28   Photo.   *Perf. 11½*
619 A222 60c multicolored   .28 .15
Pilgrimage to Mecca.

National Servicemen Building Road — A223

1978, Nov. 4
620 A223 60c multicolored   .28 .15
African Unity Road from El Goleah to In Salah, inauguration.

For all your stamp supply needs
www.scottonline.com

ALGERIA

Fibula
A224

Pres. Boumediene
A225

Jewelry: 1.35d, Pendant. 1.40d, Ankle ring.

1978, Dec. 21   Photo.   Perf. 12x11½
621 A224 1.20d multi .... .65   .28
622 A224 1.35d multi .... .70   .28
623 A224 1.40d multi 1.10 1.10
         Nos. 621-623 (3) 2.45 1.66

1979, Jan. 7   Photo.   Perf. 12x11½
624 A225 60c green, red & brown .... .28   .15
Houari Boumediene, pres. of Algeria 1965-1978.

Torch and
Books
A226

1979, Jan. 27   Photo.   Perf. 11½
625 A226 60c multicolored .... .28   .18
Natl. Front of Liberation Party Cong.

Pres. Boumediene
A227

1979, Feb. 4   Photo.   Perf. 11½
626 A227 1.40d multi .... .65   .28
40 days after death of Pres. Houari Boumediène.

Ornamental Type of 1976
Proclamation of new President.

1979, Feb. 10
627 A204 2d multicolored .... 1.00   .35
Election of Pres. Chadli Bendjedid.

A229

A230

1979, Apr. 18   Photo.   Perf. 11½
628 A229 60c multicolored .... .28   .15
Sheik Abdul-Hamid Ben Badis (1889-1940).

1979, May 19   Photo.   Perf. 13½x14
Designs: 1.20d, Telephone dial, map of Africa.
1.40d, Symbolic Morse key and waves.
629 A230 1.20d multi .... .55   .22
630 A230 1.40d multi .... .60   .22
Telecom '79 Exhib., Geneva, Sept. 20-26.

Harvest, IYC
Emblem — A231

Design: 1.40d, Dancers and IYC emblem, vert.

Perf. 11½x11, 11x11½
1979, June 21
631 A231 60c multi .... .40   .20
632 A231 1.40d multi .... .60   .45
International Year of the Child.

A232

A233

1979, Oct. 20   Photo.   Perf. 11½
633 A232 1.40d Nuthatch .... .90   .40

1979, Nov. 1   Photo.   Perf. 12½
Designs: 1.40d, Flag, soldiers and workers. 3d, Revolutionaries and emblem.
634 A233 1.40d multi .... .90   .22
         Size: 37x48mm
         Perf. 11½
635 A233 3d multi .... 2.25   .65
November 1 revolution, 25th anniversary.

Hegira, 1500
Anniv.
A234

1979, Dec. 2   Photo.   Perf. 11½
636 A234 3d multicolored .... 1.25   .65

Camels, Lion,
Men and
Slave — A235

Dionysian Procession (Setif Mosaic): 1.35d, Elephants, tigers and women. Men in tiger-drawn cart. No. 639a has continuous design.

1980, Feb. 16   Photo.   Perf. 11½
         Granite Paper
637 A235 1.20d multi .... .55   .22
638 A235 1.35d multi .... .60   .35
639 A235 1.40d multi .... .65   .55
  a. Strip of 3, #637-639 .... 1.80 1.25

Science Day — A236

1980, Apr. 19   Photo.   Perf. 12
640 A236 60c multicolored .... .28   .20

Dam and
Workers — A237

1980, June 17   Photo.   Perf. 11½
641 A237 60c multicolored .... .28   .15
Extraordinary Congress of the National Liberation Front Party.

Olympic
Sports,
Moscow '80
Emblem
A238

1980, June 28
642 A238 50c Flame, rings, vert. .... .22   .15
643 A238 1.40d shown .... .65   .35
22nd Summer Olympic Games, Moscow, July 19-Aug. 3.

20th Anniversary of OPEC — A239

Perf. 11x10½, 10½x11
1980, Sept. 15   Engr.
644 A239 60c Men holding OPEC
             emblem, vert. .... .28   .15
645 A239 1.40d shown .... .65   .35

Aures
Valley
A240

1980, Sept. 25   Litho.   Perf. 13½x14
646 A240 50c shown .... .22   .15
647 A240 1d El Oued Oasis .... .40   .18
648 A240 1.40d Tassili Rocks .... .60   .22
649 A240 2d View of Algiers .... .90   .40
         Nos. 646-649 (4) .... 2.12   .95
World Tourism Conf., Manila, Sept. 27.

Avicenna (980-1037),
Philosopher and
Physician
A241

1980, Oct. 25   Photo.   Perf. 12
650 A241 2d multicolored .... 1.50   .75

Ruins
of El
Asnam
A242

1980, Nov. 13   Photo.   Perf. 12
651 A242 3d multicolored .... 1.25   .45
Earthquake relief.

Crown
A243

1980, Dec. 20   Photo.   Perf. 12
         Granite Paper
652 A243 60c Necklace, vert. .... .28   .18
653 A243 1.40d Earrings, bracelet,
             vert. .... .60   .28
654 A243 2d shown .... .80   .45
         Nos. 652-654 (3) .... 1.68   .91
See Nos. 705-707.

1980-1984 Five-Year
Plan — A244

1981, Jan. 29   Litho.   Perf. 14
655 A244 60c multicolored .... .25   .15

Basket Weaving — A245

1981, Feb. 19   Photo.   Perf. 12½
         Granite Paper
656 A245 40c shown .... .20   .15
657 A245 60c Rug weaving .... .28   .15
658 A245 1d Coppersmith .... .40   .18
659 A245 1.40d Jeweler .... .60   .32
         Nos. 656-659 (4) .... 1.48   .80

Cedar
Tree — A246

Arbor Day: 1.40d, Cypress tree, vert.

1981, Mar. 19   Photo.   Perf. 12
         Granite Paper
660 A246 60c multi .... .30   .15
661 A246 1.40d multi .... .60   .32

ALGERIA

Mohamed Bachir el Ibrahimi (1869-1965)
A247

Children Going to School — A248

1981, Apr. 16
Granite Paper
| 662 | A247 | 60c multicolored | .25 | .15 |
| 663 | A248 | 60c multicolored | .25 | .15 |

Science Day.

12th International Hydatidological Congress, Algiers — A249

1981, Apr. 23 Perf. 14x13½
664 A249 2d multicolored .80 .32

13th World Telecommunications Day — A250

1981, May 14 Photo. Perf. 14x13½
665 A250 1.40d multi .60 .20

Disabled People and Hand Offering Flower A251

Perf. 12½x13, 13x12½
1981, June 20 Litho.
| 666 | A251 | 1.20d Symbolic globe, vert. | .55 | .18 |
| 667 | A251 | 1.40d shown | .60 | .18 |

Intl. Year of the Disabled.

Papilio Machaon A252

1981, Aug. 20 Photo. Perf. 11½
Granite Paper
668	A252	60c shown	.25	.15
669	A252	1.20d Rhodocera rhamni	.55	.20
670	A252	1.40d Charaxes jasius	.60	.25
671	A252	2d Papilio podalirius	.80	.40
		Nos. 668-671 (4)	2.20	1.00

Monk Seal — A253

1981, Sept. 17 Perf. 14x13½
| 672 | A253 | 60c shown | .25 | .15 |
| 673 | A253 | 1.40d Macaque | .60 | .35 |

World Food Day — A254

Cave Drawings of Tassili — A255

1981, Oct. 16 Photo. Perf. 14x14½
674 A254 2d multicolored .65 .35

1981, Nov. 21 Perf. 11½
Designs: Various cave drawings. 1.60d, 2d horiz.
675	A255	60c multi	.30	.15
676	A255	1d multi	.50	.18
677	A255	1.60d multi	.75	.32
678	A255	2d multi	.90	.40
		Nos. 675-678 (4)	2.45	1.05

Galley, 17-18th Cent. A256

1981, Dec. 17 Photo. Perf. 11½
| 679 | A256 | 60c shown | .40 | .18 |
| 680 | A256 | 1.60d Ship, diff. | .90 | .35 |

1982 World Cup Soccer A257

Designs: Various soccer players.
Perf. 13x12½, 12½x13
1982, Feb. 25 Litho.
| 681 | A257 | 80c multi, vert. | .35 | .15 |
| 682 | A257 | 2.80d multi | 1.10 | .50 |

TB Bacillus Centenary — A258

1982, Mar. 20 Photo. Perf. 14½x14
683 A258 80c multi .35 .15

Painted Stand A259

1982, Apr. 24 Photo. Perf. 11½
Granite Paper
| 684 | A259 | 80c Mirror, vert. | .35 | .18 |
| 685 | A259 | 2d shown | .80 | .40 |

Size: 48x33mm
| 686 | A259 | 2.40d Chest | 1.00 | .55 |
| | | Nos. 684-686 (3) | 2.15 | 1.13 |

Djamaael Djadid Mosque, Algiers — A260

1982, May 15 Litho. Perf. 14
687	A260	80c shown	.35	.15
688	A260	2.40d Sidi Boumediene Mosque, Tlemcen	1.00	.50
689	A260	3d Garden of Dey, Algiers	1.25	.55
		Nos. 687-689 (3)	2.60	1.20

See Nos. 731-734, 745-747, 774, 778-783.

Callitris Articulata A261

Independence, 20th Anniv. A262

Designs: Medicinal plants.

1982, May 27 Photo. Perf. 11½
Granite Paper
690	A261	50c shown	.20	.15
691	A261	80c Artemisia herba-alba	.25	.15
692	A261	1d Ricinus communis	.50	.20
693	A261	2.40d Thymus fontanesii	.90	.45
		Nos. 690-693 (4)	1.85	.95

1982, July 5
Granite Paper
694	A262	50c Riflemen	.20	.15
695	A262	80c Soldiers, horiz.	.32	.18
696	A262	2d Symbols, citizens, horiz.	.80	.45
		Nos. 694-696 (3)	1.32	.78

Souvenir Sheet
697 A262 5d Emblem 2.00 2.00

No. 697 contains one 32x39mm stamp.

Soummam Congress A263

1982, Aug. 20 Litho.
698 A263 80c Congress building .35 .15

Scouting Year — A264

1982, Oct. 21 Photo.
Granite Paper
699 A264 2.80d multi 1.10 .45

Palestinian Child — A265

Chlamydotis Undulata — A266

1982, Nov. 25 Litho. Perf. 10½
700 A265 1.60d multi 2.00 .75

Perf. 15x14, 14x15
1982, Dec. 23 Photo.
Protected birds. 50c, 2d horiz.
701	A266	50c Geronticus eremita	.40	.15
702	A266	80c shown	.65	.18
703	A266	2d Aguila rapax	1.25	.40
704	A266	2.40d Gypaetus barbatus	1.75	.45
		Nos. 701-704 (4)	4.05	1.18

Jewelry Type of 1980
1983, Feb. 10 Perf. 11½
Granite Paper
705	A243	50c Picture frame	.18	.15
706	A243	1d Flaska	.38	.28
707	A243	2d Brooch, horiz.	.75	.45
		Nos. 705-707 (3)	1.31	.88

A267

A268

1983, Mar. 17 Photo.
Granite Paper
| 708 | A267 | 80c Abies numidica, vert. | .32 | .15 |
| 709 | A267 | 2.80d Acacia raddiana | 1.10 | .60 |

Intl. Arbor Day.

Perf. 12x12½, 12½x12
1983, Apr. 21 Photo.
Various minerals. 1.20d, 2.40d horiz.
Granite Paper
710	A268	70c multi	.28	.15
711	A268	80c multi	.32	.20
712	A268	1.20d multi	.50	.30
713	A268	2.40d multi	1.00	.60
		Nos. 710-713 (4)	2.10	1.25

30th Anniv. of Intl. Customs Cooperation Council A269

1983, May 14 Photo. Perf. 11½
Granite Paper
714 A269 80c multi .35 .18

Emir Abdelkader Death Centenary — A270

1983, May 22 Photo. Perf. 12
Granite Paper
715 A270 4d multi 1.60 .75

A271

A272

Local mushrooms.

1983, July 21 Perf. 14x15
716	A271	50c Amanita muscaria	.20	.15
717	A271	80c Amanita phalloides	.32	.18
718	A271	1.40d Pleurotus eryngii	.55	.35
719	A271	2.80d Tefezia leonis	1.00	.60
		Nos. 716-719 (4)	2.07	1.28

1983, Sept. 1 Photo. Perf. 11½
720 A272 80c multi .35 .15

ibn-Khaldun, historian, philosopher.

ALGERIA

World Communications Year — A273

1983, Sept. 22   *Perf. 11½x12½*   Litho.
721 A273   80c Post Office, Algiers   .35   .15
722 A273   2.40d Telephone, circuit box   1.00   .38

Goat and Tassili Mountains — A274

1983, Oct. 20   Litho.   *Perf. 12½x13*
723 A274   50c shown   .20   .15
724 A274   80c Tuaregs in native costume   .32   .18
725 A274   2.40d Animals, rock painting   1.00   .40
726 A274   2.80d Rock formation   1.00   .60
Nos. 723-726 (4)   2.52   1.33

Sloughi Dog — A275

    Perf. 14x14½, 14½x14
1983, Nov. 24   Photo.
727 A275   80c shown   .60   .40
728 A275   2.40d Sloughi, horiz.   1.50   .75

Natl. Liberation Party, 5th Congress — A276

1983, Dec. 19   Photo.   *Perf. 11½*
729 A276   80c Symbols of development   .35   .22

Souvenir Sheet
730 A276   5d Emblem   3.00   2.50
No. 730 contains one 32x38mm stamp.

View Type of 1982
1984, Jan. 26   Litho.   *Perf. 14*
731 A260   10c View of Oran, 1830   .15   .15
732 A260   1d Sidi Abderahman and Taalibi Mosques   .40   .18
733 A260   2d Bejaia, 1830   .80   .35
734 A260   4d Constantine, 1830   1.75   .60
Nos. 731-734 (4)   3.10   1.28
See Nos. 745-747, 781, 783.

Pottery A278

    Perf. 11½x12, 12x11½
1984, Feb. 23   Photo.
    Granite Paper
735 A278   80c Jug, vert.   .35   .22
736 A278   1d Platter   .40   .22
737 A278   2d Oil lamp, vert.   .80   .45
738 A278   2.40d Pitcher   1.00   .60
Nos. 735-738 (4)   2.55   1.49

Fountains of Old Algiers — A279

1984 Summer Olympics — A280

Various fountains.

1984, Mar. 22   Photo.   *Perf. 11½*
    Granite Paper
739 A279   50c multi   .20   .15
740 A279   80c multi   .38   .20
741 A279   2.40d multi   1.00   .60
Nos. 739-741 (3)   1.58   .95

1984, May 19   Photo.   *Perf. 11½*
    Granite Paper
742 A280   1d multi   .45   .28

Brown Stallion — A281

1984, June 14   Photo.   *Perf. 11½*
    Granite Paper
743 A281   80c shown   .35   .18
744 A281   2.40d White mare   1.00   .60

View Type of 1982
1984   Litho.   *Perf. 14*
745   A260   5c Mustapha Pacha   .15   .15
746   A260   20c Bab Azzoun   .15   .15
746A A260   30c Algiers   .15   .15
746B A260   40c Kolea   .15   .15
746C A260   50c Algiers   .15   .15
747   A260   70c Mostaganem   .32   .15
Nos. 745-747 (6)   1.07   .90
Issued: #745, 746, 747, 7/19; #746A-746C, 10/20.

Lute — A282

Native musical instruments.

1984, Sept. 22   Litho.   *Perf. 15x14*
748 A282   80c shown   .22   .15
749 A282   1d Drum   .28   .15
750 A282   2.40d Fiddle   .65   .35
751 A282   2.80d Bagpipe   .70   .40
Nos. 748-751 (4)   1.85   1.05

30th Anniv. of Algerian Revolution — A284

1984, Nov. 3   Photo.   *Perf. 11½x12*
757 A284   80c Partisans   .22   .15

Souvenir Sheet
758 A284   5d Algerian flags, vert.   2.00   1.00

M'Zab Valley A285

1984, Dec. 15   *Perf. 15x14, 14x15*
759 A285   80c Map of valley   .22   .15
760 A285   2.40d Town of M'Zab, vert.   .65   .32

18th and 19th Century Metalware — A286

1985, Jan. 26   Photo.   *Perf. 11½*
761 A286   80c Coffee pot   .22   .15
762 A286   2d Bowl, horiz.   .50   .25
763 A286   2.40d Covered bowl   .65   .32
Nos. 761-763 (3)   1.37   .72

Fish — A287

1985, Feb. 23   Photo.   *Perf. 15x14*
764 A287   50c Thunnus thynnus   .15   .15
765 A287   80c Sparus aurata   .20   .15
766 A287   2.40d Epinephelus guaza   .60   .30
767 A287   2.80d Mustelus mustelus   .65   .35
Nos. 764-767 (4)   1.60   .95

National Games — A288

1985, Mar. 28   *Perf. 11½x12*
    Granite Paper
768 A288   80c Doves, emblem   .20   .15

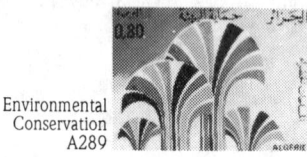

Environmental Conservation A289

1985, Apr. 25   *Perf. 13½*
769 A289   80c Stylized trees   .20   .15
770 A289   1.40d Stylized waves   .38   .20

View Type of 1982 and

The Casbah — A290   **View of Constantine — A290a**

Street Scene in Algiers — A290b

Designs: 2.50d, Djamaael Djadid Mosque, Algiers. 2.90d, like #746. 5d, like #746A. 1.50d, like #746B. 4.20d, like #764.

    Perf. 13½x12½, 13 (#774, 4.20d),
    Perf. 13½x14 (#775)
    Perf. 14½x14 (2d)
    Photo., Litho. (2d, 6.20d, 7.50d, #775)
1985-94
771 A290   20c dk blue & buff   .15   .15
772 A290   80c sage grn & buff   .20   .15
773 A290a   1d dk olive grn   .50   .25
   a.   Bklt. pane of 5 + label   2.50
774 A290   1.50d dull red   .55   .30
775 A290b   1.50d red brown & brn   .25   .15
   a.   Booklet pane of 6   1.50
776 A290b   2d dk blue & lt blue   .15   .15
   a.   Booklet pane of 5 + label   .95
777 A290   2.40d chestnut & buff   .60   .30
   a.   Bklt. pane of 5 (20c, 3 80c, 2.40d) + label   1.40
778 A260   2.50d bluish green   .98   .50
779 A260   2.90d slate   1.15   .50
780 A260   4.20d gray green   1.60   .80
781 A260   5d deep bister & black   1.95   .98
    Perf. 14
782 A260   6.20d like #731   1.05   .52
783 A260   7.50d like #745   1.30   .65
Nos. 771-783 (13)   10.43   5.53
Nos. 771-772, 777 issued only in booklet panes.
Issued: 20c, 80c, 2.40d, 6/1/85; 1d, 1/26/89; 2.50d, 2.90d, 5d, 2/23/89; #774, 4.20d, 3/21/91; #775, 5/20/92; 6.20d, 7.50d, 4/22/92; 2d, 10/21/93; #776a, 10/21/94.
See No. 1010.

UN, 40th Anniv. — A291   **Natl. Youth Festival — A292**

1985, June 26   Photo.   *Perf. 14*
784 A291   1d Dove, emblem, 40   .25   .15

1985, July 5   Litho.   *Perf. 13½*
785 A292   80c multicolored   .20   .15

Intl. Youth Year — A293

1985, July 5
786 A293   80c Silhouette, globe, emblem, vert.   .20   .15
787 A293   1.40d Doves, globe   .38   .20

World Map, OPEC — A294

1985, Sept. 14   Photo.   *Perf. 12½x13*
788 A294   80c multicolored   .20   .15
Organization of Petroleum Exporting Countries, 25th anniv.

Family Planning A295   **El-Meniaa Township A296**

1985, Oct. 3   Litho.   *Perf. 14*
789 A295   80c Mother and sons   .20   .15
790 A295   1.40d Weighing infant   .38   .18
791 A295   1.70d Breast-feeding   .45   .22
Nos. 789-791 (3)   1.03   .55

1985, Oct. 24   Engr.   *Perf. 13*
792 A296   80c Chetaibi Bay, horiz.   .55   .25
793 A296   2d shown   .50   .25
794 A296   2.40d Bou Noura Town, horiz.   .65   .32
Nos. 792-794 (3)   1.35   .72

ALGERIA

The Palm Grove, by N. Dinet — A297

1985, Nov. 21   Photo.   Perf. 11½x12
Granite Paper
795 A297 2d multi .... .50 .25
796 A297 3d multi, diff. .... .70 .40

Tapestries A298
Various designs.

1985, Dec. 19
Granite Paper
797 A298 80c multi .... .20 .15
798 A298 1.40d multi .... .38 .20
799 A298 2.40d multi .... .60 .32
800 A298 2.80d multi .... .70 .40
Nos. 797-800 (4) 1.88 1.07

Wildcats A299

Perf. 12x11½, 11½x12
1986, Jan. 23
Granite Paper
801 A299 80c Felis margarita .... .55 .15
802 A299 1d Felis caracal .... .70 .15
803 A299 2d Felis sylvestris .... 1.40 .80
804 A299 2.40d Felis serval, vert. .... 1.90 .95
Nos. 801-804 (4) 4.55 2.05

UN Child Survival Campaign — A300
Algerian General Worker's Union, 30th Anniv. — A301 

1986, Feb. 13   Litho.   Perf. 13½
805 A300 80c Oral vaccine .... .20 .15
806 A300 1.40d Mother, child, sun .... .40 .18
807 A300 1.70d Three children .... .45 .22
Nos. 805-807 (3) .... 1.05 .55

1986, Feb. 24   Perf. 12½
Granite Paper
808 A301 2d multi .... .50 .25

National Charter — A302
Natl. Day of the Disabled — A303 

1986, Mar. 6   Photo.   Perf. 11½
Granite Paper
809 A302 4d multi .... 1.50 .55

1986, Mar. 15   Perf. 12½x13
810 A303 80c multi .... .20 .15

A304    A305

1986, Apr. 17   Litho.   Perf. 14x15
811 A304 80c multi .... .20 .15
Anti-Tuberculosis campaign.

1986, Apr. 24   Perf. 14
812 A305 2d Soccer ball, sombrero .50 .25
813 A305 2.40d Soccer players .... .65 .32
1986 World Cup Soccer Championships, Mexico.

Inner Courtyards — A306
Blood Donation Campaign — A307 

1986, May 15   Photo.   Perf. 11½
Granite Paper
814 A306 80c multi .... .20 .15
815 A306 2.40d multi, diff. .... .65 .32
816 A306 3d multi, diff. .... .80 .40
Nos. 814-816 (3) .... 1.65 .87

1986, June 26   Litho.   Perf. 13½
817 A307 80c multi .... .22 .15

Southern District Radio Communication Inauguration — A308

1986, July   Perf. 13
818 A308 60c multi .... .16 .15

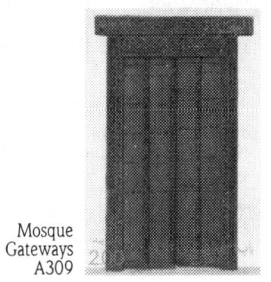

Mosque Gateways A309

1986, Sept. 27   Photo.   Perf. 12x11½
Granite Paper
819 A309 2d Door .... .50 .25
820 A309 2.40d Ornamental arch .... .65 .32

Intl. Peace Year — A310

1986, Oct. 16   Perf. 13½x14½
Photo.
821 A310 2.40d multi .... .65 .32

Folk Dancing A311

1986, Nov. 22   Litho.   Perf. 14x13½
822 A311 80c Woman, scarf .... .22 .15
823 A311 2.40d Woman, diff. .... .65 .32
824 A311 2.80d Man, sword .... .70 .40
Nos. 822-824 (3) .... 1.57 .87

Flowers — A312

1986, Dec. 18   Photo.   Perf. 14
825 A312 80c Narcissus tazetta .... .22 .15
826 A312 1.40d Iris unguicularis .... .40 .20
827 A312 2.40d Capparis spinosa .... .65 .32
828 A312 2.80d Gladiolus segetum .... .70 .40
Nos. 825-828 (4) 1.97 1.07
See Nos. 936-938.

Abstract Paintings by Mohammed Issia Khem A313

Perf. 11½x12, 12x11½
1987, Jan. 29   Litho.
829 A313 2d Man and woman, vert. .65 .35
830 A313 5d Man and books .... 1.60 .80

Jewelry from Aures A314

1987, Feb. 27   Photo.   Perf. 12
Granite Paper
831 A314 1d Earrings .... .35 .16
832 A314 1.80d Bracelets .... .60 .30
833 A314 2.90d Nose rings .... 1.00 .50
834 A314 3.30d Necklace .... 1.10 .55
Nos. 831-834 (4) 3.05 1.51
Nos. 831-833 vert.

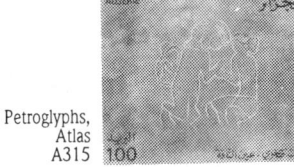

Petroglyphs, Atlas A315

1987, Mar. 26   Litho.   Perf. 12x11½
Granite Paper
835 A315 1d Man and woman .... .35 .16
836 A315 2.90d Goat .... 1.00 .50
837 A315 3.30d Horse, bull .... 1.10 .60
Nos. 835-837 (3) 2.45 1.26

Syringe as an Umbrella — A316

1987, Apr. 7   Perf. 11½
Granite Paper
838 A316 1d multi .... .35 .16
Child Immunization Campaign, World Health Day.

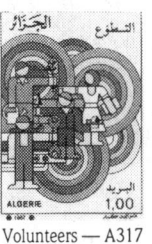

Volunteers — A317
Third General Census — A318 

1987, Apr. 23   Perf. 10½
839 A317 1d multi .... .35 .16

1987, May 21   Perf. 13½
840 A318 1d multi .... .35 .16

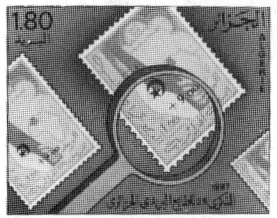

Algerian Postage, 25th Anniv. — A319
War Orphans' Fund label (1fr + 9fr) of 1962.

1987, July 5   Photo.   Perf. 11½x12
Granite Paper
841 A319 1.80d multi .... .60 .32

A320   A321

1987, July 5
Granite Paper
842 A320 1d multi .... .35 .16
Souvenir Sheet
843 A321 5d multi 1.60 1.60
Natl. independence, 25th anniv.

Amateur Theater Festival, Mostaganem A322

1987, July 20   Perf. 12x11½
Granite Paper
844 A322 1d Actors on stage .... .35 .16
845 A322 1.80d Theater .... .60 .32
a. Pair, #844-845 .... 1.00 .50
No. 845a has continuous design.

ALGERIA

Mediterranean Games, Latakia — A323

1987, Aug. 6 Perf. 13x12½, 12½x13
846 A323 1d Discus .35 .16
847 A323 2.90d Tennis, vert. 1.00 .50
848 A323 3.30d Team handball 1.10 .55
 Nos. 846-848 (3) 2.45 1.21

Birds — A324

1987   Litho.   Perf. 13½
849 A324 1d Phoenicopterus ruber roseus .50 .25
850 A324 1.80d Porphyrio porphyrio .90 .50
851 A324 2.50d Elanus caeruleus 1.25 .65
852 A324 2.90d Milvus milvus 1.50 .75
 Nos. 849-852 (4) 4.15 2.15

Agriculture — A325

1987, Nov. 26   Litho.
853 A325 1d Planting .35 .16
854 A325 1d Reservoir .35 .16
855 A325 1d Harvesting crop, vert. .35 .16
856 A325 1d Produce, vert. .35 .16
 Nos. 853-856 (4) 1.40 .64

African Telecommunications Day — A326

1987, Dec. 7   Perf. 10½
857 A326 1d multi .35 .16

Transportation A327

1987, Dec. 18 Litho. Perf. 10½x11
858 A327 2.90d shown 1.00 .50
859 A327 3.30d Diesel train 1.10 .55

Algerian Universities A328

Various campuses.

 Perf. 10½x11, 11x10½
1987, Dec. 26
860 A328 1d shown .35 .16
861 A328 2.50d multi, diff. .80 .40
862 A328 2.90d multi, diff. 1.00 .50
863 A328 3.30d multi, diff., vert. 1.10 .55
 Nos. 860-863 (4) 3.25 1.61

Intl. Rural Development Fund, 10th Anniv. A329

1988, Jan. 27   Perf. 10½x11
864 A329 1d multi .50 .25

Autonomy of State-owned Utilities — A330

1988, Feb. 27 Litho. Perf. 11x10½
865 A330 1d multi .50 .25

Intl. Women's Day — A331    **Arab Scouts, 75th Anniv. — A332**

1988, Mar. 10 Litho. Perf. 11x10½
866 A331 1d multi .50 .25

1988, Apr. 7 Litho. Perf. 10½
867 A332 2d multi .95 .48

1988 Summer Olympics, Seoul — A333    **Hot Springs — A334**

1988, July 23 Litho. Perf. 10½
868 A333 2.90d multi 1.40 .70

1988, July 16
869 A334 1d shown .50 .25
870 A334 2.90d Caverns, horiz. 1.40 .70
871 A334 3.30d Gazebo, fountain, horiz. 1.60 .80
 Nos. 869-871 (3) 3.50 1.75

World Wildlife Fund — A335

Barbary apes, *Macaca sylvanus*.

1988, Sept. 17 Litho. Perf. 10½
872 A335 50c Adult .25 .15
873 A335 90c Family .45 .22
874 A335 1d Close-up, vert. .50 .25
875 A335 1.80d Seated on branch, vert. .90 .45
 Nos. 872-875 (4) 2.10 1.07

Intl. Literacy Day — A336    **WHO, 40th Anniv. — A337**

1988, Sept. 10   Photo.   Perf. 10½
876 A336 2.90d multi 1.40 .70

1988, Oct. 15
877 A337 2.90d multi 1.40 .70

Fight Apartheid A338

1988, Nov. 19 Litho. Perf. 10½x11
878 A338 2.50d multi 1.20 .60

Natl. Front Congress — A339

1988, Nov. 29   Perf. 11x10½
879 A339 1d multi .50 .25

Agriculture A340

1988, Dec. 24   Perf. 10½
880 A340 1d Irrigation .50 .25
881 A340 1d Orchard, fields, livestock .50 .25

Natl. Goals — A342    **Airports — A343**

1989, Mar. 9   Litho.   Perf. 11½
Granite Paper
886 A342 1d shown .50 .25
887 A342 1d Ancient fort .50 .25
888 A342 1d Telecommunications .50 .25
889 A342 1d Modern buildings .50 .25
 Nos. 886-889 (4) 2.00 1.00
 Nos. 887-889 horiz.

 Perf. 10½x11, 11x10½
1989, Mar. 23
890 A343 2.90d Oran Es Senia, horiz. 1.25 .70
891 A343 3.30d Tebessa, horiz. 1.50 .80
892 A343 5d shown 2.25 1.25
 Nos. 890-892 (3) 5.00 2.75

Development of the South A344

1989, Apr. 24   Litho.   Perf. 13½
893 A344 1d Irrigation .45 .25
894 A344 1.80d Building .90 .45
895 A344 2.50d Fossil fuel extraction, vert. 1.25 .60
 Nos. 893-895 (3) 2.60 1.30

Eradicate Locusts A345

1989, May 25   Perf. 10½
896 A345 1d multi .50 .25

National Service — A346

1989, May 11   Litho.   Perf. 13½
897 A346 2d multicolored .78 .40

1st Moon Landing, 20th Anniv. A347

4d, Astronaut, lunar module, Moon's surface.

1989, July 23 Litho. Perf. 13½
898 A347 2.90d shown 1.00 .55
899 A347 4d multi, vert. 1.40 .75

Interparliamentary Union, Cent. — A348

1989, Sept. 4   Perf. 10½
900 A348 2.90d gold, brt rose lil & blk 1.10 .55

Produce A349

1989, Sept. 23   Litho.   Perf. 11½
Granite Paper
901 Strip of 3 4.00 2.00
 a. A349 2d multi, diff. .75 .40
 b. A349 3d multi, diff. 1.10 .55
 c. A349 5d shown 2.00 1.00

ALGERIA

Fish — A350

1989, Oct. 27   Litho.   *Perf. 13½*
902 A350 1d *Sarda sarda* .35 .20
903 A350 1.80d *Zeus faber* .60 .35
904 A350 2.90d *Pagellus bogaraveo* 1.00 .55
905 A350 3.30d *Xiphias gladius* 1.10 .65
    Nos. 902-905 (4) 3.05 1.75

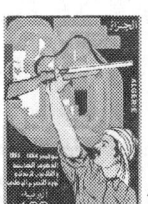

Algerian Revolution, 35th Anniv. — A351

1989, Nov. 4   Litho.   *Perf. 13½*
906 A351 1d multicolored .40 .20

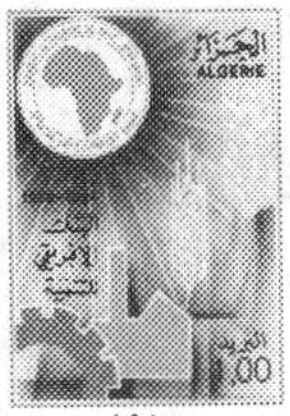

African Development Bank, 25th Anniv. A352

Mushrooms A353

1989, Nov. 18   *Perf. 10½*
907 A352 1d multicolored .40 .20

1989, Dec. 16   *Perf. 13½*
908 A353 1d *Boletus satanas* .35 .20
909 A353 1.80d *Psalliota xanthoderma* .60 .35
910 A353 2.90d *Lepiota procera* 1.00 .55
911 A353 3.30d *Lactarius deliciosus* 1.10 .65
    Nos. 908-911 (4) 3.05 1.75

A354 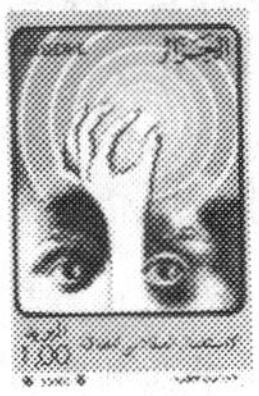   A355

1990, Jan. 18   Litho.   *Perf. 10½*
912 A354 1d multicolored .40 .20
Pan-African Postal Union, 10th anniv.

1990, Feb. 22   Litho.   *Perf. 14*
913 A355 1d Energy conservation .25 .15

A356    A357

1990, Mar. 2   Photo.   *Perf. 11½*
914 A356 3d multicolored .65 .30
African Soccer Championships.

1990, May 17   Litho.   *Perf. 13½*
917 A357 2.90d shown .75 .40
918 A357 5d Trophy 1.25 .65
World Cup Soccer Championships, Italy.

Rural Electrification A358

1990, June 21
919 A358 2d multicolored .50 .25

Youth A359

Youth Holding Rainbow — A360

1990, July 6   *Perf. 13½*
920 A359 2d multicolored .50 .25
921 A360 3d multicolored .75 .35

Maghreb Arab Union — A361

1990   *Perf. 14x13½*
922 A361 1d multicolored .38 .20

Vocations — A362

1990, Apr. 26   Litho.   *Perf. 12½*
923 A362 2d Craftsmen .75 .40
924 A362 2.90d Auto mechanics 1.15 .60
925 A362 3.30d Deep sea fishing 1.25 .65
    Nos. 923-925 (3) 3.15 1.65

Organization of Petroleum Exporting Countries (OPEC), 30th Anniv. A363

1990   *Perf. 13½*
926 A363 2d multicolored .75 .40

Savings Promotion — A364

1990, Oct. 31   Litho.   *Perf. 14*
927 A364 1d multicolored .35 .20

Namibian Independence A365

1990, Nov. 8
928 A365 3d multicolored 1.10 .60

A366    A367

Farm animals.

1990, Nov. 29   *Perf. 13½*
929 A366 1d Duck .35 .20
930 A366 2d Rabbit, horiz. .65 .40
931 A366 2.90d Turkey 1.00 .60
932 A366 3d Rooster, horiz. 1.00 .60
    Nos. 929-932 (4) 3.00 1.80

1990, Dec. 11
933 A367 1d multicolored .35 .20
Anti-French Riots, 30th anniv.

A368    A369

1990, Dec. 20   *Perf. 14*
934 A368 1d multicolored .35 .20
Fight against respiratory diseases.

1991, Feb. 24   Litho.   *Perf. 13½*
935 A369 1d multicolored .35 .15
Constitution, 2nd anniv.

Flower Type of 1986
1991, May 23   Litho.   *Perf. 13½*
Size: 26x36mm
936 A312 2d *Jasminum fruticans* .60 .30
937 A312 4d *Dianthus crinitus* 1.10 .65
938 A312 5d *Cyclamen africanum* 1.50 .85
    Nos. 936-938 (3) 3.20 1.80

Children's Drawings A370

1991, June 3   Litho.   *Perf. 13½*
939 A370 3d shown 1.00 .50
940 A370 4d Children playing 1.25 .65

Maghreb Arab Union Summit — A371

1991, June 10
941 A371 1d multicolored .30 .15

Geneva Convention on Refugees, 40th Anniv. A372

   Perf. 14½x13½
1991, July 28   Litho.
942 A372 3d multicolored 1.00 .50

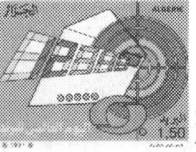

Postal Service A373

1991, Oct. 12   *Perf. 14*
943 A373 1.50d shown .55 .25
944 A373 4.20d Expo emblem, vert. 1.50 .75
Telecom '91, 6th World Forum and Exposition on Telecommunications, Geneva, Switzerland (No. 944).

Butterflies A374

1991, Nov. 21   Litho.   *Perf. 11½*
Granite Paper
945 A374 2d *Zerynthia rumina* .30 .15
946 A374 4d *Melitaea didyma* .65 .30
947 A374 6d *Vanessa atalanta* 1.00 .50
948 A374 7d *Nymphalis polychloros* 1.10 .55
    Nos. 945-948 (4) 3.05 1.50

A375    A376

1991, Dec. 21   *Perf. 12*
Granite Paper
949 A375 3d Necklace .45 .25
950 A375 4d Jewelry of Southern Tuaregs .60 .30
951 A375 5d Brooch .75 .40
952 A375 7d Rings, horiz. 1.00 .55
    Nos. 949-952 (4) 2.80 1.50

1992, Mar. 8   Litho.   *Perf. 14*
953 A376 1.50d Algerian Women .20 .15

ALGERIA

Gazelles A377

Designs: 1.50d, Gazella dorcas. 6.20d, Gazella cuvieri. 8.60d, Gazella dama.

1992, May 13			Perf. 14½x13
954 A377	1.50d multicolored	.25	.15
955 A377	6.20d multicolored	.95	.50
956 A377	8.60d multicolored	1.25	.65
Nos. 954-956 (3)		2.45	1.30

1992 Summer Olympics, Barcelona A379

1992, June 24	Litho.	Perf. 14
958 A379 6.20d Runners		1.10 .55

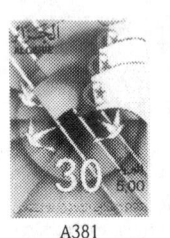

A381  A382

1992, July 7	Litho.	Perf. 14
960 A381 5d multicolored		.90 .45

Independence, 30th anniv.

1992, Sept. 23   Litho.   Perf. 14
Designs: Medicinal plants.

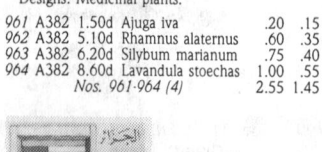

961 A382	1.50d Ajuga iva	.20	.15
962 A382	5.10d Rhamnus alaternus	.60	.35
963 A382	6.20d Silybum marianum	.75	.40
964 A382	8.60d Lavandula stoechas	1.00	.55
Nos. 961-964 (4)		2.55	1.45

Post Office Modernization A383

1992, Oct. 10	Litho.	Perf. 14
965 A383 1.50d multicolored		.20 .15

Marine Life — A384

Designs: 1.50d, Hippocampus hippocampus. 2.70d, Caretta caretta. 6.20d, Muraena helena. 7.50d, Palinurus elephas.

1992, Dec. 23			
966 A384	1.50d multicolored	.20	.15
967 A384	2.70d multicolored	.35	.20
968 A384	6.20d multicolored	.85	.40
969 A384	7.50d multicolored	1.00	.50
Nos. 966-969 (4)		2.40	1.25

Pres. Mohammad Boudiaf (1919-92) A385

1992, Nov. 3	Litho.	Perf. 11½
Granite Paper		
970 A385 2d green & multi		.30 .15
971 A385 8.60d blue & multi		1.10 .55

Coins A386

1992, Dec. 16   Litho.   Perf. 11½
Granite Paper

972 A386	1.50d Numidia, 2nd cent. BC	.20	.15
973 A386	2d Dinar, 14th cent.	.30	.15
974 A386	5.10d Dinar, 11th cent.	.65	.35
975 A386	6.20d Abdelkader, 19th cent.	.85	.40
Nos. 972-975 (4)		2.00	1.05

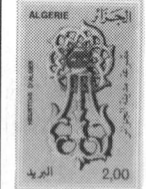

Door Knockers — A387    Flowering Trees — A388

1993, Feb. 17	Litho.	Perf. 14
976 A387	2d Algiers	.30 .15
977 A387	5.60d Constantine	.75 .40
978 A387	8.60d Tlemcen	1.10 .60
Nos. 976-978 (3)		2.15 1.15

Perf. 12x11½, 11½x12
1993, Mar. 17
Granite Paper

979 A388	4.50d Neflier (medlar), horiz.	.55	.30
980 A388	8.60d Cognassier (quince)	1.10	.60
981 A388	11d Abricotier (apricot)	1.40	.75
Nos. 979-981 (3)		3.05	1.65

Natl. Coast Guard Service, 20th Anniv. A389

1993, Apr. 3	Litho.	Perf. 14
982 A389 2d multicolored		.30 .15

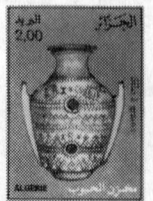

Traditional Grain Processing — A390

1993, May 19	Litho.	Perf. 14
983 A390	2d Container	.25 .15
984 A390	5.60d Millstone	.75 .40
985 A390	8.60d Press	1.10 .55
Nos. 983-985 (3)		2.10 1.10

Royal Mausoleums A391

1993, June 16	Litho.	Perf. 14
986 A391	8.60d Mauretania	1.10 .60
987 A391	12d El Khroub	1.65 .80

Ports — A392

1993, Oct. 20	Litho.	Perf. 14x13½
988 A392	2d Annaba	.25 .15
989 A392	8.60d Arzew	1.10 .55

Varanus Griseus A393

Design: 2d, Chamaeleo vulgaris, vert.

Perf. 13½x14, 14x13½
1993, Nov. 20

| 990 A393 | 2d multicolored | .25 .15 |
| 991 A393 | 8.60d multicolored | 1.10 .55 |

Tourism A394

1993, Dec. 18	Litho.	Perf. 14x13½
992 A394	2d Tipaza	.20 .15
993 A394	8.60d Kerzaz	.80 .40

A395    Chahid Day — A396

1994, Jan. 2		Perf. 13½x14
994 A395 2d multicolored		.20 .15

SONATRACH (Natl. Society for Research, Transformation, and Commercialization of Hydrocarbons), 30th anniv.

1994, Feb. 18	Litho.	Perf. 13½x14
995 A396 2d multicolored		.20 .15

1994 World Cup Soccer Championships, US — A397

1994, Mar. 16		Perf. 14x13½
996 A397 8.60d multicolored		.80 .40

A398    Ancient Petroglyphs — A399

Orchids: 5.60d, Orchis simia lam. 8.60d, Ophrys lutea cavan. 11d, Ophrys apifera huds.

1994, Apr. 20	Litho.	Perf. 11½
Granite Paper		
997 A398	5.60d multicolored	.55 .30
998 A398	8.60d multicolored	.85 .40
999 A398	11d multicolored	1.10 .55
Nos. 997-999 (3)		2.50 1.25

1994, May 21	Litho.	Perf. 13x14
1000 A399	3d Inscriptions	.35 .20
1001 A399	10d Man on horse	1.25 .60

A400    A401

1994, June 25
1002 A400 12d multicolored   1.25 .65
Intl. Olympic Committee, cent.

1994, July 13
1003 A401 3d multicolored   .35 .20
World Population Day.

Views of Algiers Type of 1992
Design: 3d, like #775.

1994, July 13	Litho.	Perf. 14
1010 A290b 3d dk blue & lt blue		.35 .18

This is an expanding set. Number may change.

Jewelry from Saharan Atlas Region A402

Perf. 13½x14, 14x13½
1994, Oct. 18   Litho.

1019 A402	3d Fibules, vert.	.15 .15
1020 A402	5d Belt	.25 .15
1021 A402	12d Bracelets	.55 .28
Nos. 1019-1021 (3)		.95 .58

A403    A404

1994, Nov. 3   Litho.   Perf. 13½x14
1022 A403 3d multicolored   .38 .18
Algerian Revolution, 40th anniv.

1994, Nov. 16   Litho.   Perf. 13½x14
| 1023 A404 | 3d Ladybugs | .15 .15 |
| 1024 A404 | 12d Beetles | .55 .28 |

ALGERIA

Fight Against AIDS — A405

1994, Dec. 1   Litho.   *Perf. 14x13½*
1025 A405 3d multicolored   .38   .18

Folk Dances — A406

Minerals — A407

1994, Dec. 17   Litho.   *Perf. 13½x14*
1026 A406 3d Algeroise   .15   .15
1027 A406 10d Constantinoise   .50   .25
1028 A406 12d Alaoui   .55   .28
     Nos. 1026-1028 (3)   1.20   .68

1994, Sept. 21
1029 A407 3d Gres lite-erode   .15   .15
1030 A407 5d Cipolin   .25   .15
1031 A407 10d Marne a turitella   .50   .25
     Nos. 1029-1031 (3)   .90   .55

World Tourism Organization, 20th Anniv. A408

1995, Jan. 28   Litho.   *Perf. 14x13½*
1032 A408 3d multicolored   .35   .20

Honey Bees — A409

Flowers — A410

     Perf. 13½x14, 14x13½
1995, Feb. 22
1033 A409 3d shown   .35   .20
1034 A409 13d On flower, horiz.   1.50   .75

1995, Mar. 29   Photo.   *Perf. 11½*
     Granite Paper
1035 A410 3d Dahlias   .35   .20
1036 A410 10d Zinnias   1.10   .55
1037 A410 13d Lilacs   1.50   .75
     Nos. 1035-1037 (3)   2.95   1.50

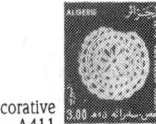

Decorative Stonework — A411

Various patterns.

1995, Apr. 19   *Perf. 14*
1039 A411 3d brown   .35   .20
1040 A411 4d green   .45   .25
1041 A411 5d deep claret   .55   .30
     Nos. 1039-1041 (3)   1.35   .75

This is an expanding set. Numbers may change.

End of World War II, 50th Anniv. A413

1995, May 3   *Perf. 14x13½*
1048 A413 3d multicolored   .35   .20

Souvenir Sheet

VE Day, 50th Anniv. — A414

Illustration reduced.

1995, May 10   Litho.   *Perf. 13½x14*
1049 A414 13d multicolored   1.65   .85

Volleyball, Cent. — A415

Environmental Protection — A416

1995, June 14
1050 A415 3d multicolored   .40   .20

1995, June 5
1051 A416 3d Air, water pollution   .40   .20
1052 A416 13d Air pollution   1.65   .85

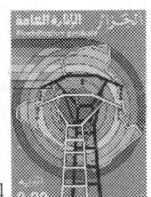

General Electrification — A417

1995, July 5   Litho.   *Perf. 13½x14*
1053 A417 3d multicolored   .45   .20

UN, 50th Anniv. A418

1995, Oct. 24   *Perf. 14x13½*
1054 A418 13d multicolored   2.00   1.00

Pottery — A419

1995, Nov. 14   Litho.   *Perf. 14*
10d, Pot, Lakhdaria. 20d, Pitcher, Aokas. 21d, Jar, Larbaa Nath Iraten. 30d, Vase, Ouadhia.

1055 A419 10d dark brown   1.50   .75
1056 A419 20d dull maroon   3.00   1.50
1057 A419 21d golden brown   3.25   1.65
1058 A419 30d dark rose brown   4.50   2.25
     Nos. 1055-1058 (4)   12.25   6.15

Aquatic Birds — A420

1995, Dec. 20   Litho.   *Perf. 14x13½*
1059 A420 3d Tadorna tadorna   .45   .20
1060 A420 5d Gallinago gallinago   .75   .35

1996 Summer Olympics, Atlanta A421

1996, Jan. 24   Litho.   *Perf. 14x13½*
1061 A421 20d multicolored   3.00   1.50

Touareg Leather Crafts — A422

     Perf. 14x13½, 13½x14
1996, Feb. 14   Litho.
1062 A422 5d shown   .75   .40
1063 A422 16d Saddle bag, vert.   2.40   1.20

Pasteur Institute of Algeria — A423

1996, Mar. 20   Litho.   *Perf. 13½x14*
1064 A423 5d multicolored   .75   .40

Youm El Ilm — A424

Designs: 16d, Dove, stylus, vert. 23d, Open book showing pencil, stylus, compass, satellite in earth orbit, vert.

     Perf. 14x13½, 13½x14
1996, Apr. 16   Litho.
1065 A424 5d multicolored   .75   .40
1066 A424 16d multicolored   2.40   1.20
1067 A424 23d multicolored   3.50   3.50
     Nos. 1065-1067 (3)   6.65   5.10

Minerals A425

Mineral, region: 10d, Iron, Djebel-Ouenza. 20d, Gold, Tirek-Amesmessa.

1996, May 6   Litho.   *Perf. 14x13½*
1068 A425 10d multicolored   .35   .20
1069 A425 20d multicolored   .75   .35

Butterflies A426

Designs: 5d, Pandoriana pandora. 10d, Coenonympha pamphilus. 20d, Cynthia cardui. 23d, Melanargia galathea.

1996, June 12   Litho.   *Perf. 11½*
     Granite Paper
1070 A426 5d multicolored   .20   .15
1071 A426 10d multicolored   .35   .20
1072 A426 20d multicolored   .65   .35
1073 A426 23d multicolored   .85   .40
     Nos. 1070-1073 (4)   2.05   1.10

Civil Protection A427

Designs: 5d, Giving medical aid, ambulance. 23d, Prevention of natural disasters, vert.

     Perf. 14x13½, 13½x14
1996, Oct. 9   Litho.
1074 A427 5d multicolored   .20   .15
1075 A427 23d multicolored   .85   .40

World Day Against Use of Illegal Drugs — A428

1996, June 26   Litho.   *Perf. 14x13½*
1076 A428 5d multicolored   .20   .15

UNICEF, 50th Anniv. — A429

Stylized designs: 5d, Two children, wreath, pencils, flowers. 10d, Five children, pencil, key, flower, flag, hypodermic.

1996, Nov. 20   Litho.   *Perf. 13½x14*
1077 A429 5d multicolored   .20   .15
1078 A429 10d multicolored   .35   .20

4th General Census A430

1997, Feb. 12   Litho.   *Perf. 14x13½*
1079 A430 5d multicolored   .20   .15

ALGERIA

A431

A432

1997, Feb. 27   Perf. 13½x14
1080 A431 5d multicolored   .20   .15

Protest at Ouargla, 35th anniv.

1996, Dec. 18   Litho.   Perf. 13½x14

Interior Courts of Algerian Dwellings: 5d, Palace of Hassan Pasha. 10d, Khedaouj El-Amia, Algiers. 20d, Palace of Light. 30d, Abdellatif Villa.

1081	A432	5d multicolored	.20	.15
1082	A432	10d multicolored	.35	.20
1083	A432	20d multicolored	.70	.35
1084	A432	30d multicolored	1.10	.55
		Nos. 1081-1084 (4)	2.35	1.25

Paintings by Ismail Samson (1934-88) A433

20d, Woman with Pigeons. 30d, Interrogation.

1996, Dec. 25   Perf. 14
1085 A433 20d multicolored   .70   .35
1086 A433 30d multicolored   1.10   .55

Victory Day, 35th Anniv. A434

1997, Mar. 19   Perf. 14x13½
1087 A434 5d multicolored   .20   .15

Flowers — A435

Designs: 5d, Ficaria verna. 16d, Lonicera arborea. 23d, Papaver rhoeas.

1997, Apr. 23   Litho.   Perf. 13½x14
1088 A435 5d multicolored   .20   .15
1089 A435 16d multicolored   .55   .30
1090 A435 23d multicolored   .80   .40
    Nos. 1088-1090 (3)   1.55   .85

World Day to Stop Smoking — A436    Legislative Elections — A437

1997, May 31   Litho.   Perf. 13½x14
1091 A436 5d multicolored   .20   .15

1997, June 4
1092 A437 5d multicolored   .20   .15

Scorpions A438

Designs: 5d, Buthus occitanus tunetanus. 10d, Androctonus australis hector.

1997, June 18   Perf. 14x13½
1093 A438 5d multicolored   .20   .15
1094 A438 10d multicolored   .35   .20

Natl. Independence, 35th Anniv. — A439

Designs: 5d, Crowd celebrating, flags. 10d, Doves, broken chain, "35," flag.

1997, July 5   Litho.   Perf. 14x13½
1095 A439 5d multicolored   .20   .15

Souvenir Sheet
Perf. 14
1096 A439 10d multicolored   .35   .20
No. 1096 contains one 30x40mm stamp.

A440    A441

Wood Carvings: 5d, Inscription, Nedroma Mosque. 23d, Door, Ketchaoua Mosque.

1997, Jan. 15   Litho.   Perf. 13½x14
1097 A440 5d multicolored   .20   .15
1098 A440 23d multicolored   .80   .40

1997, Aug. 17   Litho.   Perf. 13½x14
1099 A441 5d multicolored   .20   .15

Moufdi Zakaria (1908-77), poet.

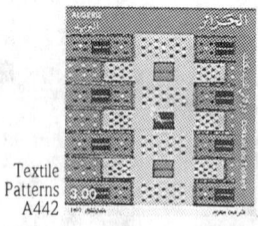

Textile Patterns A442

1997, Sept. 17   Litho.   Perf. 14
1100 A442 3d Dokkali   .15   .15
1101 A442 5d Tellis   .20   .15
1102 A442 10d Bou-Taleb   .35   .20
1103 A442 20d Ddil   .70   .35
    Nos. 1100-1103 (4)   1.40   .85

Natl. Police Force, 25th Anniv. A443

1997, Oct. 6   Perf. 14x13½
1104 A443 5d multicolored   .20   .15

Express Mail Service A444

1997, Oct. 9
1105 A444 5d multicolored   .20   .15

Local Elections — A445

1997, Oct. 23   Perf. 13½x14
1106 A445 5d multicolored   .20   .15

Lighthouses A446

Perf. 14x13½, 13½x14
1997, Nov. 5   Litho.
1107 A446 5d Tenes   .20   .15
1108 A446 10d Cape Caxine, vert.   .35   .20

New Airpost Service, 1st Anniv. A447

1997, Nov. 17   Perf. 14x13½
1109 A447 5d multicolored   .20   .15

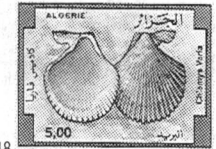

Shells — A448

Designs: 5d, Chlamys varia. 10d, Bolinus brandaris. 20d, Hinia reticulata, vert.

Perf. 14x13½, 13½x14
1997, Dec. 17   Litho.
1110 A448 5d multicolored   .20   .15
1111 A448 10d multicolored   .35   .20
1112 A448 20d multicolored   .70   .35
    Nos. 1110-1112 (3)   1.25   .70

A449    A450

1997, Dec. 25   Perf. 14x13½
1113 A449 5d multicolored   .20   .15

Election of the Natl. Council.

1997, Dec. 30   Litho.   Perf. 13½x14

Completion of Government Reforms: a, Natl. flag, people, book, ballot box. b, People, open book, torch. c, Ballot box. d, Flag, rising sun, flower. e, Ballots, building, flag.

1114 A450 5d Strip of 5, #a.-e.   .85   .45

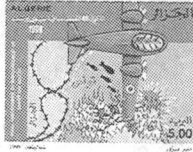

Bombing of Sakiet Sidi Youcef, 40th Anniv. A451

1998, Feb. 8   Litho.   Perf. 14x13½
1115 A451 5d multicolored   .20   .15

National Archives A452

1998, Feb. 16
1116 A452 5d multicolored   .20   .15

SEMI-POSTAL STAMPS

Regular Issue of 1926 Surcharged in Black or Red

+10ᶜ

1927   Unwmk.   Perf. 14x13½

B1	A1	5c +5c bl grn	.50	.50
B2	A1	10c +10c lilac	.50	.50
B3	A2	15c +15c org brn	.50	.50
B4	A2	20c +20c car rose	.50	.50
B5	A2	25c +25c bl grn	.50	.50
B6	A2	30c +30c lt bl	.50	.50
B7	A2	35c +35c dp vio	.55	.55
B8	A2	40c +40c ol grn	.60	.60
B9	A3	50c +50c dp bl (R)	.60	.60
a.		Double surcharge	200.00	200.00
B10	A3	80c +80c red org	.60	.60
B11	A4	1fr +1fr gray grn & red brn	.65	.65
B12	A4	2fr +2fr Prus bl & blk brn	15.00	15.00
B13	A4	5fr +5fr red & vio	21.00	21.00
		Nos. B1-B13 (13)	42.00	42.00

The surtax was for the benefit of wounded soldiers. Government officials speculated in this issue.

Railroad Terminal, Oran — SP1

Ruins at Djemila SP2   Mosque of Sidi Abd-er-Rahman SP3

Designs: 10c+10c, Rummel Gorge, Constantine. 15c+15c, Admiralty Buildings, Algiers. 25c+25c, View of Algiers. 30c+30c, Trajan's Arch, Timgad. 40c+40c, Temple of the North, Djemila. 75c+75c Mansourah Minaret, Tlemcen. 1f+1f, View of Ghardaia. 1.50f+1.50f, View of Tolga. 2f+2f, Tuareg warriors. 3f+3f, Kasbah, Algiers.

1930   Engr.   Perf. 12½

B14	SP1	5c +5c orange	5.00	5.00
B15	SP1	10c +10c ol grn	5.00	5.00
B16	SP1	15c +15c dk brn	5.00	5.00
B17	SP1	25c +25c black	5.00	5.00
B18	SP1	30c +30c dk red	5.00	5.00
B19	SP1	40c +40c ap grn	5.00	5.00
B20	SP2	50c +50c ultra	5.00	5.00
B21	SP2	75c +75c red pur	5.00	5.00
B22	SP2	1fr +1fr org red	5.00	5.00
B23	SP2	1.50fr +1.50f deep ultra	5.00	5.00
B24	SP2	2fr +2fr dk car	5.00	5.00
B25	SP2	3fr +3fr dk grn	5.00	5.00

ALGERIA

B26 SP3 5fr +5fr grn & car 12.00 12.00
  a. Center inverted 450.00
  Nos. B14-B26 (13) 72.00 72.00

Centenary of the French occupation of Algeria. The surtax on the stamps was given to the funds for the celebration.

Nos. B14-B26 exist imperf. Value, set in pairs, $350.

> Catalogue values for unused stamps in this section, from this point to the end of the section, are for Never Hinged items.

No. 102 Surcharged in Red

1918 - 11 Nov. - 1938
0.65 + 0.35

1938 *Perf. 13*
B27 A6 65c +35c on 2.25fr yel grn .50 .40

20th anniversary of Armistice.

René Caillié, Charles Lavigerie and Henri Duveyrier — SP14

1939 *Engr.*
B28 SP14 30c +20c dk bl grn 1.00 .60
B29 SP14 90c +60c car rose 1.25 .65
B30 SP14 2.25fr +75c ultra 6.75 6.25
B31 SP14 5fr +5fr brn blk 14.00 14.00
  Nos. B28-B31 (4) 23.00 21.50

Pioneers of the Sahara.

French and Algerian Soldiers — SP15

1940 *Photo.* *Perf. 12*
B32 SP15 1fr +1fr bl & car .50 .40
B33 SP15 1fr +2fr brn rose & blk .50 .40
B34 SP15 1fr +4fr dp grn & red .70 .60
B35 SP15 1fr +9fr brn & car 1.00 1.00
  Nos. B32-B35 (4) 2.70 2.40

The surtax was used to assist the families of mobilized men.

Type of Regular Issue, 1941 Surcharged in Carmine +4ᶠ

1941 *Engr.* *Perf. 13*
B36 A19 1fr +4fr black .20 .20

No. 135 Surcharged in Carmine SECOURS NATIONAL +4ᶠ

B37 A19 1fr +4fr dark blue .20 .20

The surtax was for National Relief.

No. 124 Surcharged in Black "+60c"

1942
B38 A7 90c +60c henna brn .15 .15
  a. Double surcharge 55.00

The surtax was used for National Relief. The stamp could also be used as 1.50 francs for postage.

Mother and Child — SP16

1943, Dec. 1 *Litho.* *Perf. 12*
B39 SP16 50c +4.50fr brt pink .50 .25
B40 SP16 1.50fr +8.50fr lt grn .50 .25
B41 SP16 3fr +12fr dp bl .50 .25
B42 SP16 5fr +15fr vio brn .50 .25
  Nos. B39-B42 (4) 2.00 1.00

The surtax was for the benefit of soldiers and prisoners of war.

Planes over Fields — SP17

1945, July 2 *Unwmk.* *Engr.* *Perf. 13*
B43 SP17 1.50fr +3.50fr lt ultra, red org & blk .25 .25

The surtax was for the benefit of Algerian airmen and their families.

France No. B192 Overprinted Type "a" of 1924 in Black

1945
B44 SP146 4fr +6fr dk vio brn .25 .20

The surtax was for war victims of the P.T.T.

Overprinted in Blue on Type of France, 1945

1945, Oct. 15
B45 SP150 2fr +3fr dk brn .40 .40

For Stamp Day.

Overprinted in Blue on Type of France, 1946

1946, June 29
B46 SP160 3fr +2fr red .45 .45

For Stamp Day.

Children Playing by Stream — SP18

Girl — SP19

Athlete — SP20

Repatriated Prisoner and Bay of Algiers — SP21

1946, Oct. 2 *Engr.* *Perf. 13*
B47 SP18 3fr +17fr dark grn .65 .65
B48 SP19 4fr +21fr red .65 .65
B49 SP20 8fr +27fr rose lilac 2.75 2.75
B50 SP21 10fr +35fr dark blue .70 .70
  Nos. B47-B50 (4) 4.75 4.75

Type of France, 1947, Overprinted type "a" of 1924 in Carmine

1947, Mar. 15
B51 SP172 4.50fr +5.50fr dp ultra .40 .40

For Stamp Day.

Same on Type of France, 1947, Surcharged Like No. B36 in Carmine

1947, Nov. 13
B52 A173 5fr +10fr dk Prus grn .55 .40

Type of France, 1948, Overprinted in Dark Green — f

1948, Mar. 6
B53 SP176 6fr +4fr dk grn .45 .45

For Stamp Day.

Type of France, 1948, Overprinted type "a" of 1924 in Blue and New Value

1948, May
B54 A176 6fr +4fr red .35 .35

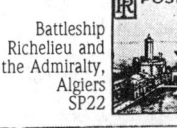

Battleship Richelieu and the Admiralty, Algiers — SP22

Aircraft Carrier Arromanches — SP23

1949, Jan. 15 *Unwmk.* *Engr.* *Perf. 13*
B55 SP22 10fr +15fr dp blue 4.50 4.50
B56 SP23 18fr +22fr red 4.50 4.50

The surtax was for naval charities.

Type of France, 1949, Overprinted in Blue — g

1949, Mar. 26
B57 SP180 15fr +5fr lilac rose 1.10 1.10

For Stamp Day, Mar. 26-27.

Type of France, 1950, Overprinted type "f" in Green

1950, Mar. 11
B58 SP183 12fr +3fr blk brn 1.10 1.10

For Stamp Day, Mar. 11-12.

Foreign Legionary — SP24

1950, Apr. 30
B59 SP24 15fr +5fr dk grn 1.10 1.10

Charles de Foucauld and Gen. J. F. H. Laperrine — SP25

1950, Aug. 21 *Unwmk.* *Perf. 13*
B60 SP25 25fr +5fr brn ol & brn blk 3.00 3.00

50th anniversary of the presence of the French in the Sahara.

Emir Abd-el-Kader and Marshal T. R. Bugeaud — SP26

1950, Aug. 21
B61 SP26 40fr +10fr dk brn & blk brn 3.00 3.00

Unveiling of a monument to Emir Abd-el-Kader at Cacheron.

Col. Colonna d'Ornano and Fine Arts Museum, Algiers — SP27

1951, Jan. 11
B62 SP27 15fr +5fr blk brn, vio brn & red brn .65 .65

Death of Col. Colonna d'Ornano, 10th anniv.

Type of France, 1951, Overprinted type "a" of 1924 in Black

1951, Mar. 10
B63 SP186 12fr +3fr brown .85 .85

For Stamp Day.

Type of France, 1952, Overprinted type "g" in Dark Blue

1952, Mar. 8 *Unwmk.* *Perf. 13*
B64 SP190 12fr +3fr dk bl 1.25 1.25

For Stamp Day.

French Military Medal — SP28

1952, July 5 *Unwmk.* *Engr.* *Perf. 13*
B65 SP28 15fr +5fr grn, yel & brn 1.25 1.25

Centenary of the creation of the French Military Medal.

Type of France 1952, Surcharged type "g" and Surtax in Black

1952, Sept. 15
B66 A222 30fr +5fr dp ultra 1.25 1.25

10th anniv. of the defense of Bir-Hakeim.

View of El Oued — SP29

Design: 12fr+3fr, View of Bou-Noura.

1952, Nov. 15 *Engr.*
B67 SP29 8fr +2fr ultra & red 1.10 1.10
B68 SP29 12fr +3fr red 1.90 1.90

The surtax was for the Red Cross.

Type of France, 1953, Overprinted type "a" of 1924 in Black

1953, Mar. 14 *Engr.*
B69 SP193 12fr +3fr purple 1.00 .90

For Stamp Day. Surtax for Red Cross.

Victory of Cythera — SP30

1953, Dec. 18 *Unwmk.* *Perf. 13*
B70 SP30 15fr +5fr blk brn & brn .60 .60

The surtax was for army welfare work.

Type of France, 1954, Overprinted type "a" of 1924 in Black

1954, Mar. 20 *Unwmk.* *Perf. 13*
B71 SP196 12fr +3fr scarlet .65 .65

For Stamp Day.

ALGERIA

Soldiers and Flags — SP31

Foreign Legionary — SP32

1954, Mar. 27
B72 SP31 15fr +5fr dk brn .50 .50
The surtax was for old soldiers.

1954, Apr. 30
B73 SP32 15fr +5fr dk grn 1.00 1.00
The surtax was for the welfare fund of the Foreign Legion.

Nurses and Verdun Hospital, Algiers — SP33

Design: 15fr+5fr, J. H. Dunant & ruins at Djemila.

1954, Oct. 30
B74 SP33 12fr +3fr indigo & red 1.75 1.75
B75 SP33 15fr +5fr pur & red 2.00 2.00
The surtax was for the Red Cross.

Earthquake Victims and Ruins — SP34

First Aid — SP35

Design: #B80-B81, Removing wounded.

1954, Dec. 5
B76 SP34 12fr +4fr dk vio brn 1.00 1.00
B77 SP34 15fr +5fr dp bl 1.00 1.00
B78 SP35 18fr +6fr lil rose 1.75 1.75
B79 SP35 20fr +7fr violet 1.75 1.75
B80 SP35 25fr +8fr rose brn 2.00 2.00
B81 SP35 30fr +10fr brt bl grn 2.00 2.00
Nos. B76-B81 (6) 9.50 9.50
The surtax was for victims of the Orleansville earthquake disaster of September 1954.

Type of France, 1955, Overprinted type "a" of 1924 in Black

1955, Mar. 19
B82 SP199 12fr +3fr dp ultra 1.00 1.00
For Stamp Day, Mar. 19-20.

Women and Children SP36

Cancer Victim SP37

1955, Nov. 5
B83 SP36 15fr +5fr blue & indigo .60 .60
The tax was for war victims.

1956, Mar. 3 Unwmk. Perf. 13
B84 SP37 15fr +5fr dk brn .50 .50
The surtax was for the Algerian Cancer Society. The male figure in the design is Rodin's "Age of Bronze."

Type of France, 1956, Overprinted type "a" of 1924 in Black

1956, Mar.
B85 SP202 12fr +3fr red .45 .45
For Stamp Day, Mar. 17-18.

Foreign Legion Rest Home — SP38

1956, Apr. 29
B86 SP38 15fr +5fr dk bl grn 1.25 1.25
Honoring the French Foreign Legion.

Type of France, 1957, Overprinted type "f" in Black

1957, Mar. 16 Engr. Perf. 13
B87 SP204 12fr +3fr dull purple .70 .70
For Stamp Day and to honor the Maritime Postal Service.

Fennec SP39

Design: 15fr+5fr, Stork flying over roofs.

1957, Apr. 6
B88 SP39 12fr +3fr red brn & red 3.75 3.75
B89 SP39 15fr +5fr sepia & red 3.75 3.75
The surtax was for the Red Cross.

Type of Regular Issue, 1956 Surcharged in Dark Blue **18 JUIN 1940 +5F**

1957, June 18
B90 A53 15fr +5fr scar & rose red .95 .95
17th anniv. of General de Gaulle's appeal for a Free France.

The Giaour, by Delacroix — SP40

On the Banks of the Oued, by Fromentin SP41

Design: 35fr+10fr, Dancer, by Chasseriau.

1957, Nov. 30 Unwmk. Engr. Perf. 13
B91 SP40 15fr +5fr dk car 3.75 3.75
B92 SP41 20fr +5fr grn 3.75 3.75
B93 SP40 35fr +10fr dk bl 3.75 3.75
Nos. B91-B93 (3) 11.25 11.25
Surtax for army welfare organizations.

Type of France Overprinted type "f" in Blue

1958, Mar. 15 Unwmk. Perf. 13
B94 SP206 15fr +5fr org brn .75 .75
For Stamp Day.

Ordering on-line is QUICK! EASY! CONVENIENT!
www.scottonline.com

Bird-of-Paradise Flower — SP42

Arms & Marshal's Baton — SP43

1958, June 14 Engr. Perf. 13
B95 SP42 20fr +5fr grn, org & vio 2.25 2.25
The surtax was for Child Welfare.

1958, July 20
B96 SP43 20fr +5fr ultra, car & grn 1.00 1.00
Marshal de Lattre Foundation.

Independent State

Clasped Hands, Wheat, Olive Branch — SP44

Burning Books — SP45

1963, May 27 Unwmk. Perf. 13
B97 SP44 50c +20c sl grn, brt grn & car .80 .60
Surtax for the Natl. Solidarity Fund.

1965, June 7 Engr. Perf. 13
B98 SP45 20c +5c ol grn, red & blk .50 .40
Issued to commemorate the burning of the Library of Algiers, June 7, 1962.

Soldiers and Woman Comforting Wounded Soldier — SP46

1966, Aug. 20 Photo. Perf. 11½
B99 SP46 30c +10c multi 1.25 .70
B100 SP46 95c +10c multi 1.75 1.10
Day of the Moudjahid (Moslem volunteers).

Red Crescent, Boy and Girl — SP47

1967, May 27 Litho. Perf. 14
B101 SP47 30c +10c brt grn, brn & car .45 .35
Algerian Red Crescent Society.

Flood Victims — SP48

Design: 95c+25c, Rescuing flood victims.

1969, Nov. 15 Typo. Perf. 10½
B102 SP48 30c +10c dl bl, sal & blk .45 .35
Litho.
B103 SP48 95c +25c multi 1.00 .65

Red Crescent Flag — SP49

1971, May 17 Engr. Perf. 10½
B104 SP49 30c +10c slate grn & car .35 .28
Algerian Red Crescent Society.

Intl. Children's Day — SP50

1989, June 1 Litho. Perf. 10½x11
B105 SP50 1d +30c multi .65 .48
Surtax for child welfare.

Solidarity with Palestinians SP51

1990, Dec. 9 Litho. Perf. 10½x11
B106 SP51 1d +30c multi .50 .30

Natl. Solidarity with Education — SP52

1995, Sept. 20 Litho. Perf. 13x14
B107 SP52 3d +50c multi .50 .25

AIR POST STAMPS

Catalogue values for unused stamps in this section are for Never Hinged items.

Plane over Algiers Harbor — AP1

Two types of 20fr:
Type I - Monogram "F" without serifs. "POSTE" indented 3mm.
Type II - Monogram "F" with serifs. "POSTE" indented 4½mm.

Unwmk.

1946, June 20 Engr. Perf. 13
C1 AP1 5fr red .15 .15
C2 AP1 10fr deep blue .15 .15
C3 AP1 15fr deep green .40 .15
C4 AP1 20fr brown (II) .20 .15
C4A AP1 20fr brown (I) 100.00 65.00
C5 AP1 25fr violet .45 .15
C6 AP1 40fr gray black .55 .15
Nos. C1-C4,C5-CC6 (6) 1.90 .90
For surcharges see Nos. C7, CB1-CB2.

ALGERIA — ALLENSTEIN

No. C1 Surcharged in Black — 10%

1947, Jan. 18
C7 AP1 (4.50fr) on 5fr red .15 .15

Storks over Mosque — AP2

Plane over Village — AP3

1949-53
C8	AP2	50fr green	2.00	.25
C9	AP3	100fr brown	1.75	.25
C10	AP2	200fr bright red	4.00	3.00
C11	AP3	500fr ultra ('53)	14.00	10.00
		Nos. C8-C11 (4)	21.75	13.50

Beni Bahdel Dam — AP4

1957, July 1 Unwmk. Perf. 13
C12 AP4 200fr dark red 3.25 .75

Caravelle over Ghardaia — AP5

Designs: 2d, Caravelle over El Oued. 5d, Caravelle over Tipasa.

1967-68 Engr. Perf. 13
C13	AP5	1d lil, org brn & emer	1.00	.50
C14	AP5	2d brt bl, org brn & emer	2.50	1.25
C15	AP5	5d brt bl, grn & org brn ('68)	6.00	2.75
		Nos. C13-C15 (3)	9.50	4.50

Plane over Casbah, Algiers — AP6

Designs: 3d, Plane over Oran. 4d, Plane over Rhumel Gorge.

1971-72 Photo. Perf. 12½
C16	AP6	2d grysh blk & multi	1.65	.80
C17	AP6	3d violet & blk	2.50	1.40
C18	AP6	4d blk & multi	3.25	1.75
		Nos. C16-C18 (3)	7.40	3.95

Issued: 2d, 6/12/71; 3d, 4d, 2/28/72.

Storks and Plane — AP7

1979, Mar. 24 Photo. Perf. 11½
C19 AP7 10d multi 4.00 1.60

Plane Approaching Coastal City — AP8

1991, Apr. 26 Litho. Perf. 13½
| C20 | AP8 | 10d shown | 3.00 | 1.50 |
| C21 | AP8 | 20d Plane over city | 6.00 | 3.00 |

Plane Over Djidjelli Corniche — AP9

1993, Sept. 25 Engr. Perf. 13½x14
C22 AP9 50d blue, green & brown 6.25 3.25

AIR POST SEMI-POSTAL STAMPS

Catalogue values for unused stamps in this section are for Never Hinged items.

No. C2 Surcharged in Carmine

‡ 18 Juin 1940 +10 Fr.

1947, June 18 Perf. 13
CB1 AP1 10fr +10fr deep blue .70 .60

7th anniv. of Gen. Charles de Gaulle's speech in London, June 18, 1940.

‡ No. C1 Surcharged 18 JUIN 1940 in Blue +10 Fr.

1948, June 18
CB2 AP1 5fr +10fr red .70 .60

8th anniv. of Gen. Charles de Gaulle's speech in London, June 18, 1940.

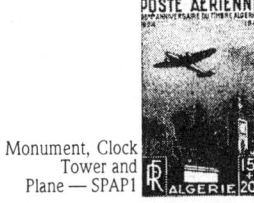

Monument, Clock Tower and Plane — SPAP1

1949, Nov. 10 Engr. Unwmk.
CB3 SPAP1 15fr +20fr dk brn 3.50 3.50

25th anniv. of Algeria's 1st postage stamps.

POSTAGE DUE STAMPS

D1  *D2*

Perf. 14x13½
1926-27 Typo. Unwmk.
J1	D1	5c light blue	.15	.15
J2	D1	10c dk brn	.15	.15
J3	D1	20c olive grn	.15	.15
J4	D1	25c car rose	.35	.35
J5	D1	30c rose red	.15	.15
J6	D1	45c blue grn	.50	.50
J7	D1	50c brn vio	.15	.15
J8	D1	60c green ('27)	1.25	.30
J9	D1	1fr red brn, *straw*	.15	.15
J10	D1	2fr lil rose ('27)	.15	.15
J11	D1	3fr deep blue ('27)	.15	.15
		Nos. J1-J11 (11)	3.30	2.35

See Nos. J25-J26, J28-J32. For surcharges, see Nos. J18-J20.

1926-27
J12	D2	1c olive grn	.15	.15
J13	D2	10c violet	.40	.20
J14	D2	30c bister	.25	.20
J15	D2	60c dull red	.20	.20
J16	D2	1fr brt vio ('27)	11.00	1.75
J17	D2	2fr lt bl ('27)	7.50	.65
		Nos. J12-J17 (6)	19.50	3.15

See note below France No. J51. For surcharges, see Nos. J21-J24.

Stamps of 1926 Surcharged

1927
J18	D1	60c on 20c olive grn	.90	.25
J19	D1	2fr on 45c blue grn	1.10	.65
J20	D1	3fr on 25c car rose	.75	.25
		Nos. J18-J20 (3)	2.75	1.15

Recouvrement Stamps of 1926 Surcharged — 10c

1927-32
J21	D2	10c on 30c bis ('32)	2.25	1.50
J22	D2	1fr on 1c olive grn	.65	.60
J23	D2	1fr on 60c dl red ('32)	11.00	.22
J24	D2	2fr on 10c violet	6.25	6.25
		Nos. J21-J24 (4)	20.15	8.57

Catalogue values for unused stamps in this section, from this point to the end of the section, are for Never Hinged items.

Type of 1926, Without "R F"

1942 Typo. Perf. 14x13½
| J25 | D1 | 30c dark red | .15 | .15 |
| J26 | D1 | 2fr magenta | .18 | .18 |

Type of 1926 Surcharged in Red — T 0.50

1944 Perf. 14x13½
J27	A2	50c on 20c yel grn	.15	.15
a.		Inverted surcharge	3.50	
b.		Double surcharge	9.50	

No. J27 was issued precanceled only. See note after No. 32.

Type of 1926

1944 Litho. Perf. 12
J28	D1	1.50fr brt rose lilac	.28	.22
J29	D1	2fr greenish blue	.28	.22
J30	D1	5fr rose carmine	.28	.22
		Nos. J28-J30 (3)	.84	.66

Type of 1926

1947 Typo. Perf. 14x13½
J32 D1 5fr green .60 .45

France Nos. J80-J81 Overprinted Type "a" of 1925 in Carmine or Black

1947
| J33 | D5 | 10c sepia (C) | .15 | .15 |
| J34 | D5 | 30c bright red violet | .15 | .15 |

D3

1947-55 Unwmk. Engr. Perf. 14x13
J35	D3	20c red	.15	.15
J36	D3	60c ultra	.22	.20
J37	D3	1fr dk org brn	.15	.15
J38	D3	1.50fr dull green	.40	.38
J39	D3	2fr red	.15	.15
J40	D3	3fr violet	.15	.15
J41	D3	5fr ultra ('49)	.15	.15
J42	D3	6fr black	.20	.18
J43	D3	10fr lil rose	.20	.15
J44	D3	15fr ol grn ('55)	.45	.45
J45	D3	20fr brt grn	.22	.15
J46	D3	30fr red org ('55)	.40	.38
J47	D3	50fr indigo ('51)	.95	.95
J48	D3	100fr brt bl ('53)	4.00	3.50
		Nos. J35-J48 (14)	7.79	7.09

Independent State

France Nos. J93-J97 Overprinted "EA" in Black like Nos. 286-290

Perf. 14x13½
1962, July 2 Typo. Unwmk.

Handstamped Overprint
J49	D6	5c bright pink	2.25	1.60
J50	D6	10c red orange	2.25	1.40
J51	D6	20c olive bister	2.25	1.40
J52	D6	50c dark green	3.00	2.75
J53	D6	1fr deep green	4.25	4.00
		Nos. J49-J53 (5)	14.00	11.15

Typographed Overprint
J49a	D6	5c bright pink	6.00	6.00
J50a	D6	10c red orange	6.00	6.00
J51a	D6	20c olive bister	5.50	5.50
J52a	D6	50c dark green	14.00	14.00
J53a	D6	1fr deep green	25.00	25.00
		Nos. J49a-J53a (5)	56.50	56.50

See note after No. 290.

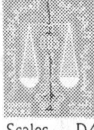

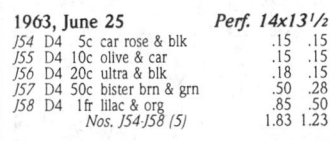

Scales — D4  *Grain — D5*

1963, June 25 Perf. 14x13½
J54	D4	5c car rose & blk	.15	.15
J55	D4	10c olive & car	.15	.15
J56	D4	20c ultra & blk	.18	.15
J57	D4	50c brown brn & grn	.50	.50
J58	D4	1fr lilac & org	.85	.50
		Nos. J54-J58 (5)	1.83	1.23

#J58 Surcharged with New Value & 3 Bars

1968, Mar. 28 Typo. Perf. 14x13½
J59 D4 60c on 1fr lilac & org .40 .28

1972-93 Litho. Perf. 13½x14
J60	D5	10c bister	.15	.15
J61	D5	20c deep brown	.15	.15
J62	D5	40c orange	.20	.15
J63	D5	50c dk vio blue	.22	.15
J64	D5	80c dk olive gray	.38	.15
J65	D5	1d green	.42	.15
J66	D5	2d blue	.95	.42
J67	D5	3d violet	.45	.22
J68	D5	4d lilac rose	.58	.28
		Nos. J60-J68 (9)	3.50	1.92

Issued: 3d, 4d, 1/21/93; others, 10/21/72.

NEWSPAPER STAMPS

Nos. 1 and 33 Surcharged in Red — ½ centime

1924-26 Unwmk. Perf. 14x13½
P1	A16	½c on 1c dk gray	.15	.15
a.		Triple surcharge	87.50	
P2	A1	½c on 1c olive ('26)	.15	.15

ALLENSTEIN

ˈa-lən-ˌshtīn

LOCATION — In East Prussia
AREA — 4,457 sq. mi.
POP. — 540,000 (estimated 1920)
CAPITAL — Allenstein

Allenstein, a district of East Prussia, held a plebiscite in 1920 under the Versailles Treaty, voting to join Germany rather than Poland. Later that year, Allenstein became part of the German Republic.

100 Pfennig = 1 Mark

PLÉBISCITE

Stamps of Germany, 1906-20, Overprinted

OLSZTYN ALLENSTEIN

Perf. 14, 14½, 14x14½, 14½x14

1920			Wmk. 125	
1	A16	5pf green	.15	.15
2	A16	10pf carmine	.15	.15
3	A22	15pf dk vio	.15	.15
4	A22	15pf vio brn	6.50	6.50
5	A16	20pf bl vio	.15	.15
6	A16	30pf org & blk, *buff*	.40	.25
7	A16	40pf lake & blk	.30	.20
8	A16	50pf pur & blk, *buff*	.30	.20
9	A16	75pf grn & blk	.30	.20
10	A17	1m car rose	.85	.80
a.		Double overprint	375.00	600.00
11	A17	1.25m green	.70	.70
a.		Double overprint	475.00	1,000.
12	A17	1.50m yel brn	.70	.90
13	A21	2.50m lilac rose	1.40	4.00
14	A19	3m blk vio	1.75	1.75
a.		Double overprint	350.00	925.00
b.		Inverted overprint	375.00	600.00
		Nos. 1-14 (14)	13.80	16.10

Overprinted

TRAITÉ DE VERSAILLES
COMMISSION D'ADMINISTRATION ET DE PLÉBISCITE
ART. 94 ET 95
OLSZTYN-ALLENSTEIN

15	A16	5pf green	.15	.25
16	A16	10pf carmine	.15	.25
17	A22	15pf dark vio	.15	.15
18	A22	15pf vio brn	30.00	30.00
19	A16	20pf blue vio	.15	.15
20	A16	30pf org & blk, *buff*	.40	.35
21	A16	40pf lake & blk	.40	.35
22	A16	50pf pur & blk, *buff*	.15	.15
23	A16	75pf grn & blk	.15	.15
24	A17	1m car rose	.75	.75
a.		Inverted overprint	550.00	750.00
25	A17	1.25m green	.70	.70
26	A17	1.50m yel brn	.70	.70
27	A21	2.50m lilac rose	1.50	2.50
28	A19	3m blk vio	1.25	1.25
a.		Inverted overprint	350.00	550.00
b.		Double overprint	325.00	550.00
		Nos. 15-28 (14)	36.60	37.70

The 40pf carmine rose (Germany No. 124) exists with this oval overprint, but it is doubtful whether it was regularly issued. Value $250.

ANDORRA

an-'dòr-ə

LOCATION — On the southern slope of the Pyrenees Mountains between France and Spain.
GOVT. — Co-principality
AREA — 179 sq. mi.
POP. — 26,500 (1976)
CAPITAL — Andorre-la-Vieille

Andorra is subject to the joint control of France and the Spanish Bishop of Urgel and pays annual tribute to both. The country has no monetary unit of its own, the peseta and franc both being in general use.

100 Centimos = 1 Peseta
100 Centimes = 1 Franc

Catalogue values for unused stamps in the Spanish Administration for this country are for Never Hinged items, beginning with Scott 50 in the regular postage section and Scott C2 in the airpost section; for the French Administration of this country, Never Hinged items begin at Scott 78 for regular postage, Scott B1 for the semi-postal section, Scott C1 for the airpost section, and Scott J21 for the postage due section.

SPANISH ADMINISTRATION

A majority of the Spanish Andorra stamps issued to about 1950 are poorly centered. The very fine examples that are valued will be fairly well centered. Poorly centered stamps sell for less.

Stamps of Spain, 1922-26, Overprinted in Red or Black

CORREOS ANDORRA

Perf. 14, 13½x12½, 12½x11½

1928			Unwmk.	
1	A49	2c olive green	.55	.55

Control Numbers on Back

2	A49	5c car rose (Bk)	.65	.65
3	A49	10c green	.65	.65
4	A49	15c slate blue	2.25	2.00
5	A49	20c violet	2.25	2.00
6	A49	25c rose red (Bk)	2.25	2.00
7	A49	30c black brown	10.00	6.75
8	A49	40c deep blue	10.00	4.75
9	A49	50c orange (Bk)	10.00	6.75
10	A49a	1p blue blk	12.00	10.00
11	A49a	4p lake (Bk)	85.00	70.00
12	A49a	10p brown (Bk)	140.00	100.00
		Nos. 1-12 (12)	275.60	206.10

Counterfeit overprints exist.

La Vall — A1
St. Julia de Loria — A3 
St. Juan de Caselles — A2
St. Coloma — A4
General Council — A5 

1929, Nov. 25		Engr.	Perf. 14	
13	A1	2c olive green	1.00	.50

Control Numbers on Back

14	A2	5c carmine lake	2.00	1.25
15	A3	10c yellow green	2.00	2.00
16	A4	15c slate green	2.00	2.00
17	A3	20c violet	2.00	2.00
18	A4	25c carmine rose	6.00	6.00
19	A1	30c olive brown	65.00	65.00
20	A2	40c dark blue	5.00	3.00
21	A3	50c deep orange	5.00	4.00
22	A3	1p slate	12.00	12.00
23	A5	4p deep rose	65.00	65.00
24	A5	10p bister brown	65.00	65.00
		Nos. 13-24 (12)	232.00	227.75

Nos. 13-24, 26, 28, 32 exist imperforate.

1931-38		Perf. 11½		
13a	A1	2c	4.00	1.50

Control Numbers on Back

14a	A2	5c	7.00	6.00
15a	A3	10c	7.00	3.50
16a	A4	15c	20.00	14.00
17a	A3	20c	10.00	8.00
18a	A4	25c	6.00	4.50
19a	A1	30c ('33)	85.00	60.00
20a	A2	40c ('35)	10.00	7.50
22a	A5	1p ('38)	25.00	16.00
b.		Control number omitted	1,400.	

Without Control Numbers

1936-43		Perf. 11½x11		
25	A1	2c red brown ('37)	2.50	1.00
26	A2	5c dark brown	2.50	1.00
27	A3	10c blue green	10.00	4.50
a.		10c yellow green	80.00	65.00
28	A4	15c green ('37)	6.25	4.00
29	A3	20c violet	8.00	4.00
30	A4	25c deep rose ('37)	4.00	4.00
31	A1	30c carmine	4.00	2.75
31A	A2	40c dark blue	600.00	400.00
32	A1	45c rose red ('37)	4.00	1.00

33	A3	50c deep orange	8.75	4.00
34	A1	60c deep blue ('37)	6.00	4.00
35	A5	4p deep rose ('43)	40.00	40.00
36	A5	10p bister brn ('43)	50.00	50.00
		Nos. 25-31,32-36 (12)	146.00	121.25

Edelweiss — A6
Provost — A7 
Coat of Arms — A8 
Plaza of Ordino — A9 
Chapel of Meritxell — A10 
Map — A11 

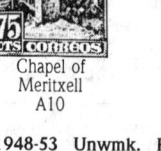

1948-53	Unwmk.	Photo.	Perf. 12½	
37	A6	2c dark olive grn ('51)	.40	.70
38	A6	5c deep orange ('53)	.40	.70
39	A6	10c deep blue ('53)	.45	.70

		Engr.	Perf. 9½x10	
40	A7	20c brown vio	6.50	3.00
41	A7	25c org, perf. 12½ ('53)	4.75	2.25
42	A8	30c dk slate grn	8.50	3.50
43	A9	50c deep green	10.00	5.00
44	A10	75c dark blue	15.00	5.00
45	A9	90c dp car rose	6.50	4.00
46	A10	1p brt orange ver	10.00	5.00
47	A8	1.35c dk blue vio	6.50	6.00

		Perf. 10		
48	A11	4p ultra ('53)	10.00	10.00
49	A11	10p dk violet brn ('51)	21.00	10.00
		Nos. 37-49 (13)	100.00	55.85

Catalogue values for unused stamps in this section, from this point to the end of the section, are for Never Hinged items.

Bridge of St. Anthony — A12
Madonna of Meritxell, 8th Century — A13 

1963-64	Unwmk.	Engr.	Perf. 13	
50	A12	25c dk gray & sepia	.20	.15
51	A12	70c dk sl grn & brn blk	.20	.15
52	A12	1p slate & dull pur	.30	.15
53	A12	2p violet & dull pur	.30	.15
54	A12	2.50p rose claret	.80	.60
55	A12	3p blk & grnsh gray	1.40	.60
56	A12	5p dk brn & choc	2.00	1.10
57	A13	6p sepia & car	3.00	1.10
		Nos. 50-57 (8)	8.20	4.00

Issued: 25c-2p, 7/20/63; 2.50p-6p, 2/29/64.

Narcissus — A14
Encamp Valley — A15 

1966, June 10		Engr.	Perf. 13	
58	A14	50c shown	.20	.15
59	A14	1p Pinks	.20	.15
60	A14	5p Jonquils	1.10	.15
61	A14	10p Hellebore	2.50	.65
		Nos. 58-61 (4)	4.00	1.50

Common Design Types pictured following the introduction.

Europa Issue 1972
Common Design Type

1972, May 2		Photo.	Perf. 13	
		Size: 25½x38mm		
62	CD15	8p multicolored	125.00	80.00

1972, July 4		Photo.	Perf. 13	

Tourist publicity: 1.50p, Massana (village). 2p, Skiing on De La Casa Pass. 5p, Pessons Lake, horiz.

63	A15	1p multicolored	.20	.15
64	A15	1.50p multicolored	.70	.55
65	A15	2p multicolored	1.75	.55
66	A15	5p multicolored	2.25	.90
		Nos. 63-66 (4)	4.90	2.15

Butterfly Stroke — A16

Design: 2p, Volleyball, vert.

1972, Oct.		Photo.	Perf. 13	
67	A16	2p lt blue & multi	.20	.15
68	A16	5p multicolored	.30	.20

20th Olympic Games, Munich, Aug. 26-Sept. 11.

St. Anthony Singers — A17

1972, Dec. 5		Photo.	Perf. 13	
69	A17	1p shown	.15	.15
70	A17	1.50p Les Caramelles (boys' choir)	.15	.15
71	A17	2p Nativity scene	.15	.15
72	A17	5p Man holding giant cigar, vert	.50	.15
73	A17	8p Hermit of Meritxell, vert	.70	.35
74	A17	15p Marratxa dancers	1.65	.50
		Nos. 69-74 (6)	3.30	1.45

Andorran customs. No. 71 is for Christmas.

Europa Issue 1973
Common Design Type and

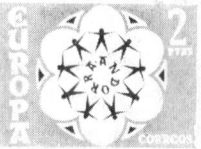

Symbol of Unity — A18

1973, Apr. 30		Photo.	Perf. 13	
75	A18	2p ultra, red & blk	.20	.15
		Size: 37x25mm		
76	CD16	8p tan, red & blk	.70	.30

ANDORRA

Nativity — A19

Virgin of Ordino — A20

Christmas: 5p, Adoration of the Kings. Designs are from altar panels of Meritxell Parish Church.

1973, Dec. 14   Photo.   *Perf. 13*
77 A19 2p multicolored   .15 .15
78 A19 5p multicolored   .65 .40

1974, Apr. 29   Photo.   *Perf. 13*
Europa: 8p, Les Banyes Cross.
79 A20 2p multicolored   1.10 .40
80 A20 8p slate & brt blue   3.50 1.10

Cupboard — A21

Crowns of Virgin and Child of Roser — A22

1974, July 30   Photo.   *Perf. 13*
81 A21 10p multicolored   1.65 .50
82 A22 25p dark red & multi   4.00 1.65

UPU Monument, Bern — A23

1974, Oct. 9   Photo.   *Perf. 13*
83 A23 15p multicolored   1.25 .55
Centenary of Universal Postal Union.

Nativity A24

Christmas: 5p, Adoration of the Kings.

1974, Dec. 4   Photo.   *Perf. 13*
84 A24 2p multicolored   .50 .20
85 A24 5p multicolored   1.75 .45

Mail Delivery, Andorra, 19th Century — A25

12th Century Painting, Ordino Church — A26

1975, Apr. 4   Photo.   *Perf. 13*
86 A25 3p multicolored   .30 .15
Espana 75 International Philatelic Exhibition, Madrid, Apr. 4-13.

1975, Apr. 28   Photo.   *Perf. 13*
Design: 12p, Christ in Glory, 12th century Romanesque painting, Ordino church.
87 A26 3p multicolored   1.25 .35
88 A26 12p multicolored   2.25 .60

Urgel Cathedral and Document — A27

1975, Oct. 4   Photo.   *Perf. 13*
89 A27 7p multicolored   .90 .50
Millennium of consecration of Urgel Cathedral, and Literary Festival 1975.

Nativity, Ordino A28

Christmas: 7p, Adoration of the Kings, Ordino.

1975, Dec. 3   Photo.   *Perf. 13*
90 A28 3p multicolored   .20 .15
91 A28 7p multicolored   .40 .25

Caldron and CEPT Emblem — A29

Slalom and Montreal Olympic Emblem — A30

Europa: 12p, Chest and CEPT emblem, horiz.

1976, May 3   Photo.   *Perf. 13*
92 A29 3p bister & multi   .20 .15
93 A29 12p yellow & multi   .60 .15

1976, July 9   Photo.   *Perf. 13*
Design: 15p, One-man canoe and Montreal Olympic emblem, horiz.
94 A30 7p multicolored   .20 .15
95 A30 15p multicolored   .40 .25
21st Olympic Games, Montreal, Canada, July 17-Aug. 1.

Nativity A31

Christmas: 25p, Adoration of the Kings. Wall paintings in La Massana Church.

1976, Dec. 7   Photo.   *Perf. 13*
96 A31 3p multicolored   .15 .15
97 A31 25p multicolored   .40 .25

View of Ansalonge A32

Europa: 12p, Xuclar, valley, mountains.

1977, May 2   Litho.   *Perf. 13*
98 A32 3p multicolored   .15 .15
99 A32 12p multicolored   .45 .25

Cross of Terme — A33

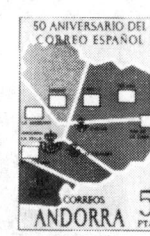

Map of Post Offices — A34

Christmas: 12p, Church of St. Miguel d'Engolasters.

1977, Dec. 2   Photo.   *Perf. 13x12½*
100 A33 5p multicolored   .30 .25
101 A33 12p multicolored   .70 .50

Souvenir Sheet

Designs: 10p, Mail delivery. 20p, Post Office, 1928. 25p, Andorran coat of arms.

1978, Mar. 31   Photo.   *Perf. 13x13½*
102   Sheet of 4   .85 .85
 a. A34 5p multicolored   .15 .15
 b. A34 10p multicolored   .15 .15
 c. A34 20p multicolored   .25 .25
 d. A34 25p multicolored   .30 .30
Spanish postal service in Andorra, 50th anniv.

La Vall — A35

Europa: 12p, St. Juan de Caselles.

1978, May 2   *Perf. 13*
103 A35 5p multicolored   .15 .15
104 A35 12p multicolored   .25 .15

Crown, Bishop's Mitre and Staff — A36

1978, Sept. 24   Photo.   *Perf. 13*
105 A36 5p brown, car & yel   .35 .15
700th anniversary of the signing of treaty establishing Co-Principality of Andorra.

Holy Family — A37

Young Woman — A38

Christmas: 25p, Adoration of the Kings. Both designs after frescoes in the Church of St. Mary d'Encamp.

1978, Dec. 5   Photo.   *Perf. 13*
106 A37 5p multicolored   .15 .15
107 A37 25p multicolored   .35 .20

1979, Feb. 14   Photo.   *Perf. 13*
Designs: 5p, Young man. 12p, Bridegroom and bride riding mule.
108 A38 3p multicolored   .15 .15
109 A38 5p multicolored   .15 .15
110 A38 12p multicolored   .20 .15
   Nos. 108-110 (3)   .50 .45

Old Mail Truck A39

Europa: 12p, Stampless covers of 1846 & 1854.

1979, Apr. 30   Engr.   *Perf. 13*
111 A39 5p yel grn & dk blue   .15 .15
112 A39 12p dk red & violet   .25 .15

Children Holding Hands A40

1979, Oct. 18   Photo.   *Perf. 13*
113 A40 19p multicolored   .35 .20
International Year of the Child.

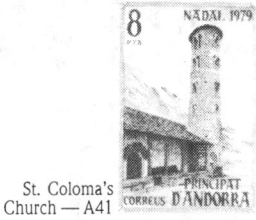

St. Coloma's Church — A41

Christmas: 25p, Agnus Dei roundel, St. Coloma's Church.

1979, Nov. 28   Photo.   *Perf. 13½*
114 A41 8p multicolored   .15 .15
115 A41 25p multicolored   .35 .25

Bishop Pere d'Arg A42

Bishops of Urgel: 5p, Josep Caixal. 13p, Joan Benlloch.

1979, Dec. 27   Engr.
116 A42 1p dk blue & brown   .15 .15
117 A42 5p rose lake & purple   .15 .15
118 A42 13p brown & dk green   .20 .15
   Nos. 116-118 (3)   .50 .45
See Nos. 132-133, 159, 175, C4.

Antoni Fiter, Magistrate — A43

Europa: 19p, Francesc Cairat, magistrate.

1980, Apr. 28   Photo.   *Perf. 13x13½*
119 A43 8p bister, blk & brn   .15 .15
120 A43 19p lt green & blk   .30 .20

Boxing, Moscow '80 Emblem A44

ANDORRA

1980, July 23 Photo. Perf. 13½x13
121	A44	5p Downhill skiing	.15	.15
122	A44	8p shown	.15	.15
123	A44	50p Target shooting	.70	.50
		Nos. 121-123 (3)	1.00	.80

12th Winter Olympic Games, Lake Placid, NY, Feb. 12-24 (5p); 22nd Summer Olympic Games, Moscow, July 19-Aug. 3.

Nativity A45

1980, Dec. 12 Litho. Perf. 13
| 124 | A45 | 10p Nativity, vert. | .15 | .15 |
| 125 | A45 | 22p shown | .35 | .20 |

Christmas 1980.

Children Dancing at Santa Anna Feast — A46

Europa: 30p, Going to church on Aplec de la Verge de Canolich Day.

1981, May 7 Photo. Perf. 13
| 126 | A46 | 12p multicolored | .15 | .15 |
| 127 | A46 | 30p multicolored | .40 | .25 |

50th Anniv. of Police Force — A47

1981, July 2 Photo. Perf. 13½x13
| 128 | A47 | 30p multicolored | .40 | .20 |

Intl. Year of the Disabled A48

1981, Oct. 8 Photo. Perf. 13½
| 129 | A48 | 50p multicolored | .65 | .30 |

Christmas 1981 — A49

Designs: Encamp Church retable.

1981, Dec. 3 Photo. Perf. 13½
| 130 | A49 | 12p Nativity | .15 | .15 |
| 131 | A49 | 30p Adoration | .40 | .20 |

Bishops of Urgel Type of 1979

1981, Dec. 12 Engr. Perf. 13½
| 132 | A42 | 7p Salvador Casanas | .15 | .15 |
| 133 | A42 | 20p Josep de Boltas | .30 | .15 |

Natl. Arms — A51

1982, Feb. 17 Photo. Perf. 13x13½
134	A51	1p bright pink	.15	.15
135	A51	3p bister brown	.15	.15
136	A51	7p red orange	.15	.15
137	A51	12p lake	.15	.15
138	A51	15p ultra	.20	.15
139	A51	20p blue green	.25	.15
140	A51	30p crimson rose	.35	.15

Perf. 13½x12½
1982, Sept. 30 Engr.
Size: 25½x30½mm
141	A51	50p dark green	.80	.20
142	A51	100p dark blue	1.65	.50
		Nos. 134-142 (9)	3.85	1.75

For type A51 without "PTA" see #192-198.

Europa 1982 — A52

1982, May 12 Photo. Perf. 13
| 143 | A52 | 14p New Reforms, 1866, vert. | .20 | .15 |
| 144 | A52 | 33p Reform of Institutions, 1981 | .45 | .25 |

1982 World Cup — A53

Designs: Various soccer players.

1982, June 13 Photo. Perf. 13x13½
145	A53	14p multicolored	.45	.45
146	A53	33p multicolored	1.00	1.00
a.		Pair, #145-146 + label	1.50	1.50

A54   A55

Anniversaries: 9p, Permanent Spanish and French delegations, cent. 14p, 50th anniv. of Andorran stamps. 23p, St. Francis of Assisi (1182-1226). 33p, Anyos Pro-Vicarial District membership centenary (Relacio sobre la Vall de Andorra titlepage).

1982, Sept. 7 Engr. Perf. 13
147	A54	9p dk blue & brown	.15	.15
148	A54	14p black & green	.50	.20
149	A54	23p dk blue & brown	.30	.15
150	A54	33p black & olive grn	.60	.45
		Nos. 147-150 (4)	1.55	.95

Perf. 13x13½, 13½x13
1982, Dec. 9 Photo.
Christmas: 14p, Madonna and Child, Andorra la Vieille Church, vert. 33p, El Tio de Nadal (children in traditional costumes striking hollow tree).
| 151 | A55 | 14p multicolored | .20 | .15 |
| 152 | A55 | 33p multicolored | .45 | .25 |

Europa 1983 A56

1983, June 7 Photo. Perf. 13
| 153 | A56 | 16p La Cortinada Church, architect, 12th cent. | .20 | .15 |
| 154 | A56 | 38p Water mill, 16th cent. | .55 | .40 |

Local Mushrooms — A57

1983, July 20 Photo. Perf. 13x12½
| 155 | A57 | 16p Lactarius sanguifluus | 1.25 | .50 |

See Nos. 165, 169, 172.

Universal Suffrage, 50th Anniv. A58

Photogravure and Engraved
1983, Sept. 6 Perf. 13
| 156 | A58 | 10p multicolored | .15 | .15 |

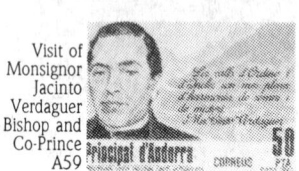

Visit of Monsignor Jacinto Verdaguer Bishop and Co-Prince A59

1983, Sept. 6
| 157 | A59 | 50p multicolored | .80 | .45 |

Christmas 1983 — A60

Saint Cerni de Nagol, Romanesque fresco, Church of San Cerni de Nagol.

1983, Nov. 24 Photo. Perf. 13½
| 158 | A60 | 16p multicolored | .30 | .15 |

Bishops of Urgel Type of 1979

1983, Dec. 7 Engr. Perf. 13
| 159 | A42 | 26p Joan J. Laguarda Fenollera | .35 | .20 |

1984 Winter Olympics A62

1984, Feb. 17 Litho. Perf. 13½x14
| 160 | A62 | 16p Ski jumping | .35 | .15 |

ESPANA '84 — A63

1984, Apr. 27 Photo. Perf. 13
| 161 | A63 | 26p Emblems | .35 | .15 |

Europa (1959-84) A64

1984, May 5 Engr.
| 162 | A64 | 16p brown | .25 | .15 |
| 163 | A64 | 38p blue | .60 | .35 |

1984 Summer Olympics A65

1984, Aug. 9 Litho. Perf. 13½x14
| 164 | A65 | 40p Running | .60 | .35 |

Mushroom Type of 1983
1984, Sept. 27 Photo. Perf. 13x12½
| 165 | A57 | 11p Morchella esculenta | 10.00 | 1.50 |

Christmas 1984 — A66

1984, Dec. 6 Photo. Perf. 13½
| 166 | A66 | 17p Nativity carving | .30 | .15 |

Europa 1985 A67

18p, Mossen Enric Arfany, composer, natl. hymn score. 45p, Musician Playing Viol, Romanesque fresco detail, La Cortinada Church, vert.

1985, May 3 Engr. Perf. 13½
| 167 | A67 | 18p dk vio, grn & chocolate | .25 | .15 |
| 168 | A67 | 45p green & chocolate | .75 | .25 |

Mushroom Type of 1983
Perf. 13½x12½
1985, Sept. 19 Photo.
| 169 | A57 | 30p Gyromitra esculenta | .50 | .25 |

Pal Village — A68

1985, Nov. 7 Engr. Perf. 13½
| 170 | A68 | 17p brt ultra & dk blue | .30 | .15 |

Christmas 1985 — A69

Fresco: Angels Playing Trumpet and Psaltery, St. Bartholomew Chapel.

1985, Dec. 11 Photo. Perf. 13½x13
| 171 | A69 | 17p multicolored | .30 | .15 |

Mushroom Type of 1983
Perf. 13½x12½
1986, Apr. 10 Photo.
| 172 | A57 | 30p Marasmius oreades | .50 | .25 |

Europa 1986 — A70

ANDORRA

1986, May 5   Engr.   *Perf. 13*
173 A70 17p Water   .25 .15
174 A70 45p Soil and air   .70 .25

Bishops of Urgel Type of 1979

1986, Sept. 11   Engr.   *Perf. 13½*
175 A42 35p Justi Guitart   .50 .20

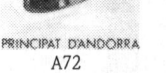

A72 — Santa Roma de Les Bons Church bell.
A73

1986, Dec. 11   Litho.   *Perf. 14*
176 A72 19p multicolored   .30 .15

Christmas.

1987, Mar. 27   Photo.   *Perf. 14*
177 A73 48p multicolored   .70 .40

Visit of the co-princes: the Bishop of Urgel and president of France, September 26, 1986.

Europa 1987 — A74

Modern architecture: 19p, Meritxell Sanctuary interior. 48p, Sanctuary exterior, vert.

1987, May 15   Engr.   *Perf. 14x13½*
178 A74 19p dark blue & brown   .25 .15
179 A74 48p dark blue & brown   .70 .25

Souvenir Sheet

1992 Summer Olympics, Barcelona — A75

20p, House of the Valleys. 50p, Bell tower, Chapel of the Archangel Michael, and torch-bearer.

1987, July 20   Photo.   *Perf. 14*
180   Sheet of 2   4.00 4.00
   a. A75 20p multicolored   1.10 1.10
   b. A75 50p multicolored   2.75 2.75

Local Mushrooms — A76

1987, Sept. 11   *Perf. 13½x12½*
181 A76 100p Boletus edulis   1.40 .60

Christmas — A77

Design: Detail from a Catalan manuscript, De Nativitat, by R. Llull.

1987, Nov. 18   Litho.   *Perf. 14*
182 A77 20p multicolored   .30 .15

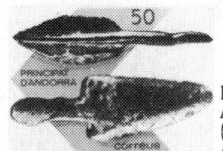

Lance and Arrowhead (Bronze Age) — A78

1988, Mar. 25   Photo.   *Perf. 14*
183 A78 50p multicolored   .75 .30

Europa 1988 — A79

Pyrenean Mastiff — A80

Transport and communications: 20p, Les Bons, a medieval road. 45p, Trader and pack mules, early 20th cent.

1988, May 5   Engr.   *Perf. 14x13½*
184 A79 20p dark blue & dark red   .25 .15
185 A79 45p dark blue & dark red   .60 .25

1988, July 26   Litho.   *Perf. 14x13½*
186 A80 20p multicolored   .30 .15

Bishop of Urgel and Seigneur of Caboet Confirming Co-Principality, 700th Anniv. — A81

1988, Oct. 24   Litho.   *Perf. 14x13½*
187 A81 20p gold, blk & int blue   .30 .15

Christmas 1988 — A82

1988, Nov. 30   Litho.   *Perf. 14x13½*
188 A82 20p multicolored   .30 .15

Arms Type of 1982 Without "PTA"

1988, Dec. 2   Photo.   *Perf. 13x13½*
192 A51 20p brt blue green   .30 .15

Size: 25x30½mm
Engr.

194 A51 50p grnsh black   .75 .30
196 A51 100p dark blue   1.50 .50
198 A51 500p dark brown   7.75 2.50
   Nos. 192-198 (4)   10.30 3.45

This is an expanding set. Numbers will change if necessary.

Europa 1989 — A83

Perf. 14x13½, 13½x14
1989, May 8   Litho. & Engr.
200 A83 20p Leapfrog, vert.   .30 .15
201 A83 45p Tug of war   .60 .25

Santa Roma Church, Les Bons — A84

Perf. 13½x14
1989, June 20   Litho. & Engr.
202 A84 50p blk, dp blue & grn blue   .65 .25

Anniv. Emblem — A85

Christmas — A86

1989, Oct. 26   Litho.   *Perf. 14x13½*
203 A85 20p multicolored   .30 .15

Intl. Red Cross and Red Crescent societies, 125th anniv.; Year for the Protection of Human Life.

1989, Dec. 1
204 A86 20p The Immaculate Conception   .30 .15

Europa 1990 — A87

Post offices.

Perf. 13½x14, 14x13½
1990, May 17   Photo.
205 A87 20p shown   .30 .15
206 A87 50p Post office, vert.   .70 .30

Gomphidius Rutilus — A88

1990, June 21   Litho.   *Perf. 13x13½*
207 A88 45p multicolored   .70 .35

Plandolit House — A89

Christmas — A90

Perf. 13x12½
1990, Oct. 17   Litho. & Engr.
208 A89 20p brown & org yel   .35 .15

1990, Nov. 26   Litho.   *Perf. 14x13½*
209 A90 25p lake, brn & bister   .40 .20

4th Games of the Small European States — A91

1991, Apr. 29   Photo.   *Perf. 13½x14*
210 A91 25p Discus   .40 .20
211 A91 45p High jump, runner   .75 .35

Europa — A92

Perf. 14x13½, 13½x14
1991, May 10   Litho.
212 A92 25p Olympus-1 satellite   .45 .20
213 A92 55p Olympus-1, horiz.   .95 .45

A93

Christmas — A94

1991, Sept. 20   Litho.   *Perf. 13x12½*
214 A93 45p Macrolepiota Procera   .70 .35

1991, Nov. 29   Photo.   *Perf. 14x13½*
215 A94 25p multicolored   .40 .20

Woman Carrying Water Pails — A95

1992, Feb. 14   Photo.   *Perf. 13½x14*
216 A95 25p multicolored   .40 .20

Discovery of America, 500th Anniv. — A96

Perf. 14x13½, 13½x14
1992, May 8   Photo.
217 A96 27p Santa Maria, vert.   .50 .20
218 A96 45p King Ferdinand   .80 .35

Europa.

1992 Summer Olympics, Barcelona — A97

1992, July 22   Photo.   *Perf. 13½x14*
219 A97 27p Kayak   .65 .30

Nativity Scene, by Fra Angelico — A98

1992, Nov. 18   Photo.   *Perf. 14*
220 A98 27p multicolored   .50 .20

ANDORRA

Natl. Automobile Museum — A99

1992, Sept. 10   Litho. & Engr.   Perf. 13½x14
221 A99 27p 1894 Benz   .50   .30

Cantharellus Cibarius — A100

1993, Mar. 25   Photo.   Perf. 13½x14
222 A100 28p multicolored   .65   .30

Contemporary Paintings — A101

Europa: 28p, Upstream, by John Alan Morrison. 45p, Rhythm, by Angel Calvente, vert.

1993, May 20   Litho.   Perf. 13½x14, 14x13½
223 A101 28p multicolored   .65   .30
224 A101 45p multicolored   1.10   .50

A102    A103

1993, Sept. 23   Litho.   Perf. 14
225 A102 28p multicolored   .70   .30

Art and Literature Society, 25th anniv.

1993, Nov. 25   Litho. & Engr.   Perf. 14x13½
226 A103 28p Christmas   .70   .30

Souvenir Sheet

Constitution, 1st Anniv. — A104

1994, Mar. 14   Photo.   Perf. 14
227 A104 29p multicolored   .75   .75

Sir Alexander Fleming (1881-1955), Co-discoverer of Penicillin — A105

1994, May 6   Photo.   Perf. 13½x14
228 A105 29p Portrait   .75   .75
229 A105 55p AIDS virus   1.50   1.50

Europa.

Hygrophorus Gliocyclus — A106

1994, Sept. 27   Photo.   Perf. 14
230 A106 29p multicolored   .75   .75

Christmas — A107

1994, Nov. 29   Photo.   Perf. 14x13½
231 A107 29p multicolored   .75   .75

Nature Conservation in Europe — A108

1995, Mar. 23   Photo.   Perf. 14
232 A108 30p Farm in valley   .80   .80
233 A108 60p Stone fence, valley   1.65   1.65

Europa — A109

1995, May 8   Photo.   Perf. 14
234 A109 60p multicolored   1.65   1.65

Christmas — A110

1995, Nov. 8   Photo.   Perf. 14
235 A110 30p Flight to Egypt   .80   .80

Entrance Into Council of Europe — A111

1995, Nov. 10
236 A111 30p multicolored   .80   .80

Mushrooms — A112

1996, Apr. 30   Photo.   Perf. 14
237 A112 30p Ramaria aurea   .80   .80
238 A112 60p Tuber melanosporum   1.65   1.65

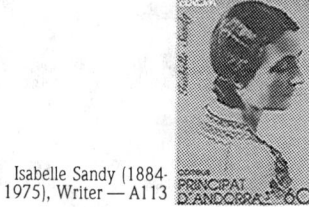

Isabelle Sandy (1884-1975), Writer — A113

1996, May 7
239 A113 60p brown & violet   1.75   1.75

Europa.

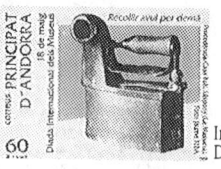

Intl. Museum Day — A114

Design: Antique coal-heated iron.

1996, Sept. 12   Photo.   Perf. 14
240 A114 60p multicolored   .95   .95

Christmas — A115

The Annunciation, by Andrew Martin, 1753, St. Eulalia d'Encamp Church.

1996, Nov. 26   Photo.   Perf. 14
241 A115 30p multicolored   .45   .45

Museums of Andorra — A116

Early bicycles designed by: 32p, Karl Drais, 1818. 65p, Pierre Michaux, 1861.

1997, Apr. 28   Photo.   Perf. 14
242 A116 32p multicolored   .45   .45
243 A116 65p multicolored   .90   .90

See Nos. 248-249.

A117    UNESCO — A118

Europa (Stories and Legends): Hikers watching family of bears crossing over river on fallen tree.

1997, May 6   Photo.   Perf. 14
244 A117 65p multicolored   .90   .90

1997, Sept. 30   Photo.   Perf. 14
245 A118 32p multicolored   .45   .45

> Andorra, Spanish Administration, stamps can be mounted in the annually supplemented Scott Spain and Spanish Andorra album.

Christmas — A119

1997, Nov. 25   Photo.   Perf. 14
246 A119 32p multicolored   .45   .45

1998 Winter Olympic Games, Nagano — A120

1998, Feb. 23   Photo.   Perf. 14
247 A120 35p Slalom skier   .45   .45

Museums of Andorra Type of 1997

Early bicycles: 35p, Kangaroo, 1878. 70p, Hirondelle, 1889.

1998, Apr. 24   Photo.   Perf. 13½x14
248 A116 35p multicolored   .45   .45
249 A116 70p multicolored   .90   .90

Harlequins, Canillas Carnival — A121

1998, May 22   Photo.   Perf. 14
250 A121 70p multicolored   .95   .95

Europa.

Manual Digest, 250th Anniv. — A122

1998, Sept. 30   Photo.   Perf. 14
251 A122 35p multicolored   .50   .50

Inauguration of the Postal Museum of Andorra — A123

1998, Nov. 19   Photo.   Perf. 14
252 A123 70p multicolored   1.00   1.00

Christmas — A124

1998, Nov. 26
253 A124 35p multicolored   .50   .50

ANDORRA

AIR POST STAMPS

AP1

Unwmk.
1951, June 27 Engr. Perf. 11
C1 AP1 1p dark violet brown 22.50 5.00

Catalogue values for unused stamps in this section, from this point to the end of the section, are for Never Hinged items.

AP2

AP3

Litho. & Engr.
1983, Oct. 20 Perf. 13
C2 AP2 20p brown & bis brn .30 .20
  Jaime Sansa Nequi, Episcopal Church official.

1984, Oct. 25 Photo. Perf. 13
C3 AP3 20p multicolored .35 .25
  Pyrenees Art Center.

Bishops of Urgel Type of 1979
1985, June 13 Engr. Perf. 13½
C4 A42 20p Ramon Iglesias .35 .20

SPECIAL DELIVERY STAMPS

Special Delivery Stamp of Spain, 1905 Overprinted

CORREOS
ANDORRA

1928 Unwmk. Perf. 14
Without Control Number on Back
E1 SD1 20c red 62.50 65.00
With Control Number on Back
E2 SD1 20c pale red 45.00 50.00

Eagle over Mountain Pass — SD2

1929 Perf. 14
With Control Number on Back
E3 SD2 20c scarlet 20.00 20.00
  a. Perf. 11½ 300.00

1937 Perf. 11½x11
Without Control Number on Back
E4 SD2 20c red 7.50 6.50

Arms and Squirrel — SD3

1949 Unwmk. Engr. Perf. 10x9½
E5 SD3 25c red 4.00 4.00

FRENCH ADMINISTRATION

Stamps and Types of France, 1900-1929, Overprinted **ANDORRE**

Perf. 14x13½

1931, June 16 Unwmk.
1	A16	1c gray	.55	.55
a.		Double overprint	950.00	950.00
2	A16	2c red brown	.60	.60
3	A16	3c orange	.60	.60
4	A16	5c green	1.00	1.00
5	A16	10c lilac	1.50	1.50
6	A22	15c red brown	3.00	3.00
7	A22	20c red violet	4.00	4.00
8	A22	25c yellow brn	4.00	4.00
9	A22	30c green	4.00	4.00
10	A22	40c ultra	6.75	6.75
11	A25	45c lt violet	7.25	7.25
12	A20	50c vermilion	6.25	6.25
13	A20	65c gray green	10.00	10.00
14	A20	75c rose lilac	13.00	13.00
15	A20	90c red	17.50	17.50
16	A20	1fr dull blue	18.00	18.00
17	A22	1.50fr light blue	25.00	25.00

Overprinted **ANDORRE**

18	A18	2fr org & pale bl	17.00	17.00
19	A18	3fr brt vio & rose	60.00	60.00
20	A18	5fr dk bl & buff	100.00	100.00
21	A18	10fr grn & red	175.00	175.00
22	A18	20fr mag & grn	250.00	250.00
		Nos. 1-22 (22)	725.00	725.00

See No. P1 for ½c on 1c gray.
Nos. 9, 15 and 17 were not issued in France without overprint.

Chapel of Meritxell A50

Bridge of St. Anthony A51

St. Miguel d'Engolasters A52

Gorge of St. Julia A53

Old Andorra — A54

1932-43 Engr. Perf. 13
23	A50	1c gray blk	.30	.25
24	A50	2c violet	.40	.40
25	A50	3c brown	.30	.30
26	A50	5c blue green	.40	.40
27	A51	10c dull lilac	.65	.60
28	A50	15c deep red	1.00	1.00
29	A51	20c lt rose	6.25	4.50
30	A52	25c brown	2.25	2.25
31	A51	25c brn car ('37)	4.50	6.50
32	A51	30c emerald	1.75	1.50
33	A51	40c ultra	5.00	4.25
34	A51	40c brn blk ('39)	.65	.60
35	A51	45c lt red	6.00	5.00
36	A51	45c bl grn ('39)	3.00	2.50
37	A52	50c lilac rose	6.50	5.00
38	A51	50c lt vio ('39)	3.00	2.50
38A	A51	50c grn ('40)	1.40	1.40
39	A51	55c lt vio ('38)	9.50	6.00
40	A51	60c yel brn ('38)	.60	.50
41	A52	65c yel grn	35.00	35.00
42	A51	65c blue ('38)	6.50	5.50
43	A51	70c red ('39)	1.30	1.00
44	A52	75c violet	3.25	2.50
45	A51	75c ultra ('39)	2.50	2.25
46	A51	80c green ('38)	13.00	9.50
46A	A53	80c bl grn ('40)	.25	.30
47	A53	90c deep rose	3.25	2.25
48	A53	90c dk grn ('39)	2.25	2.25
49	A53	1fr blue grn	9.50	6.00
50	A53	1fr scarlet ('38)	15.00	15.00
51	A53	1fr dp ultra ('39)	.25	.25
51A	A53	1.20fr brt vio ('42)	.25	.25
52	A50	1.25fr rose car ('33)	35.00	25.00
52A	A50	1.25fr rose ('38)	3.00	1.40
52B	A53	1.30fr sepia ('40)	.25	.25
53	A54	1.50fr ultra	8.25	7.50
53A	A50	1.50fr crim ('40)	.25	.25
54	A53	1.75fr violet ('33)	80.00	80.00
55	A53	1.75fr dk red ('38)	30.00	22.50
56	A53	2fr red violet	3.75	3.50
56A	A50	2fr rose red ('40)	1.00	.65
56B	A50	2fr dk bl grn ('42)	.25	.25
57	A50	2.15fr dk vio ('38)	40.00	27.50
58	A50	2.25fr ultra ('39)	4.00	3.00
58A	A50	2.40fr red ('42)	.25	.20
59	A50	2.50fr gray blk ('39)	4.00	3.00
59A	A50	2.50fr dp ultra ('40)	1.30	1.25
60	A53	3fr orange brn	3.75	3.50
60A	A53	3fr red brn ('40)	.30	.25
60B	A50	4fr sl bl ('42)	.30	.25
60C	A50	4.50fr dp vio ('42)	.75	.75
61	A54	5fr brown	.40	.35
62	A54	10fr violet	.45	.40
62B	A54	15fr dp ultra ('42)	.50	.50
63	A54	20fr rose lake	.50	.40
63A	A51	50fr turq bl ('43)	1.00	.50
		Nos. 23-63A (56)	365.00	310.50

A 20c ultra exists. Value $12,500.

No. 37 Surcharged with Bars and New Value in Black

1935, Sept. 25
64	A52	20c on 50c lil rose	13.00	11.00
a.		Double surcharge	2,000.	

Coat of Arms
A55   A56

1936-42 Perf. 14x13
65	A55	1c black ('37)	.15	.15
66	A55	2c blue	.15	.15
67	A55	3c brown	.15	.15
68	A55	5c rose lilac	.15	.15
69	A55	10c ultra ('37)	.15	.15
70	A55	15c red violet	.55	.55
71	A55	20c emerald ('37)	.15	.15
72	A55	30c cop red ('38)	.30	.30
72A	A55	30c blk brn ('42)	.15	.15
73	A55	35c Prus grn ('38)	30.00	30.00
74	A55	40c cop red ('42)	.15	.15
75	A55	50c Prus grn ('42)	.15	.15
76	A55	60c turq bl ('42)	.15	.15
77	A55	70c vio ('42)	.15	.15
		Nos. 65-77 (14)	32.50	32.50

Catalogue values for unused stamps in this section, from this point to the end of the section, are for Never Hinged items.

1944
78	A56	10c violet	.15	.15
79	A56	30c deep magenta	.15	.15
80	A56	40c dull blue	.15	.15
81	A56	50c orange red	.15	.15
82	A56	60c black	.15	.15
83	A56	70c brt red violet	.15	.15
84	A56	80c blue green	.15	.15
		Nos. 78-84 (7)	1.05	1.05

See No. 114.

St. Jean de Caselles A57

La Maison des Vallees — A58

Old Andorra A59

Provost A60

1944-47 Perf. 13
85	A57	1fr brown violet	.30	.15
86	A57	1.20fr blue	.15	.15
87	A57	1.50fr red	.30	.15
88	A57	2fr dk blue grn	.15	.15
89	A58	2.40fr rose red	.25	.20
90	A58	2.50fr rose red ('46)	4.00	1.40
91	A58	3fr sepia	.15	.15
92	A58	4fr ultra	.30	.15
93	A59	4.50fr brown blk	.30	.15
94	A58	4.50fr dk bl grn ('47)	6.50	3.50
95	A59	5fr ultra	.25	.20
96	A59	5fr Prus grn ('46)	.50	.30
97	A59	6fr rose car ('45)	.35	.15
98	A59	10fr Prus green	.15	.15
99	A59	10fr ultra ('46)	.25	.15
100	A60	15fr rose lilac	.60	.25
101	A60	20fr deep blue	.65	.45
102	A60	25fr lt rose red ('46)	4.00	2.25
103	A60	40fr dk green ('46)	4.00	3.00
104	A60	50fr sepia	1.90	1.10
		Nos. 85-104 (20)	25.05	14.15

1948-49
105	A58	4fr lt blue grn	.70	.70
106	A59	6fr violet brn	.35	.35
107	A59	8fr indigo	1.00	1.00
108	A59	12fr bright red	.75	.75
109	A59	12fr blue grn ('49)	.85	.75
110	A59	15fr crimson ('49)	.45	.45
111	A60	18fr deep blue	2.50	1.50
112	A60	20fr dark violet	2.00	1.65
113	A60	25fr ultra ('49)	1.40	1.10
		Nos. 105-113 (9)	10.00	8.25

1949-51 Perf. 14x13, 13
114	A56	1fr deep blue	.75	.55
115	A57	3fr red ('51)	4.50	4.00
116	A57	4fr sepia	2.00	2.00
117	A58	5fr emerald	2.25	2.25
118	A58	5fr purple ('51)	4.50	4.50
119	A58	6fr blue grn ('51)	3.50	3.25
120	A58	8fr brown	1.00	.70
121	A59	15fr blk brn ('51)	5.00	4.00
122	A59	18fr rose red ('51)	13.00	7.00
123	A60	30fr ultra ('51)	20.00	7.00
		Nos. 114-123 (10)	56.50	35.25

Les Escaldres Spa — A61

St. Coloma Belfry — A62

Designs: 15fr-25fr, Gothic cross. 30fr-75fr, Village of Les Bons.

1955-58 Unwmk. Engr. Perf. 13
124	A61	1fr dk gray bl	.18	.15
125	A61	2fr dp green	.18	.15
126	A61	3fr red	.18	.15
127	A61	5fr chocolate	.18	.15
128	A62	6fr dk bl grn	.45	.38
129	A62	8fr rose brown	.45	.45
130	A62	10fr brt violet	.70	.55
131	A62	12fr indigo	.75	.60
132	A61	15fr red	1.00	.85
133	A61	18fr blue grn	1.00	.85
134	A61	20fr dp purple	1.65	1.50
135	A61	25fr sepia	2.00	1.50
136	A62	30fr deep blue	24.00	16.00
137	A62	35fr Prus bl ('57)	9.00	6.75
138	A62	40fr dk green	25.00	18.00
139	A62	50fr cerise	3.00	2.25
140	A62	65fr purple ('58)	8.50	5.75
141	A62	70fr chestnut ('57)	6.00	5.75
142	A62	75fr violet blue	40.00	32.50
		Nos. 124-142 (19)	124.22	94.28

Issued: 35fr, 70fr, 8/19; 65fr, 2/10; others, 2/15.

ANDORRA

Coat of Arms — A63

Gothic Cross, Meritxell — A64

Designs: 65c, 85c, 1fr, Pond of Engolasters.

1961, June 19 Typo. Perf. 14x13
143	A63	5c brt green & blk	.15	.15
144	A63	10c red, pink & blk	.15	.15
145	A63	15c blue & black	.15	.15
146	A63	20c yellow & brown	.20	.20

Engr. Perf. 13
147	A64	25c violet, bl & grn	.25	.25
148	A64	30c mar, ol grn & brn	.30	.30
149	A64	45c indigo, bl & grn	13.00	6.50
150	A64	50c pur, lt brn & ol grn	1.00	1.00
151	A64	65c bl, ol & brn	17.50	14.00
152	A64	85c rose lil, vio bl & brn	17.50	14.00
153	A64	1fr grnsh bl, ind & brn	1.00	1.00
		Nos. 143-153 (11)	51.20	37.70

See Nos. 161-166A.

Imperforates
Most stamps of Andorra, French Administration, from 1961 onward exist imperforate in issued and trial colors, and also in small presentation sheets in issued colors.

Telstar and Globe Showing Andover and Pleumeur-Bodou — A65

1962, Sept. 29 Engr.
154	A65	50c ultra & purple	1.35	1.35

1st television connection of the US and Europe through the Telstar satellite, July 11-12.

"La Sardane" A66

Charlemagne Crossing Andorra — A67

1fr, Louis le Debonnaire giving founding charter.

1963, June 22 Unwmk. Perf. 13
155	A66	20c lil rose, cl & ol grn	3.50	3.50
156	A67	50c sl grn & dk car rose	6.00	6.00
157	A67	1fr red brn, ultra & dk grn	9.50	9.50
		Nos. 155-157 (3)	19.00	19.00

Old Andorra Church and Champs-Elysées Palace — A68

1964, Jan. 20 Engr.
158	A68	25c blk, grn & vio brn	1.20	.75

"PHILATEC," Intl. Philatelic and Postal Techniques Exhib., Paris, June 5-21, 1964.

Bishop of Urgel and Seigneur of Caboet Confirming Co-Principality, 1288 — A69

Design: 60c, Napoleon re-establishing Co-principality, 1806.

1964, Apr. 25 Engr. Perf. 13
159	A69	60c dk brn, red brn & sl grn	12.50	12.50
160	A69	1fr brt bl, org brn & blk	12.50	12.50

Arms Type of 1961

1964, May 16 Typo. Perf. 14x13
161	A63	1c dk blue & gray	.15	.15
162	A63	2c black & orange	.15	.15
163	A63	12c purple, emer & yel	.30	.30
164	A63	18c black, lil & pink	.30	.30
		Nos. 161-164 (4)	.90	.90

Scenic Type of 1961

Designs: 40c, 45c, Gothic Cross, Meritxell. 60c, 90c, Pond of Engolasters.

1965-71 Engr. Perf. 13
165	A64	40c dk brn, org brn & sl grn	.50	.50
165A	A64	45c vio bl, ol bis & slate	1.00	.75
166	A64	60c org brn & dk brn	.60	.60
166A	A64	90c ultra, bl grn & bister	.50	.50
		Nos. 165-166A (4)	2.60	2.35

Issued: 40c, 60c, Apr. 24, 1965. 45c, June 13, 1970. 90c, Aug. 28, 1971.

Syncom Satellite over Pleumeur-Bodou Station — A70

Andorra House, Paris — A71

1965, May 17 Unwmk.
167	A70	60c dp car, lil & bl	4.00	3.25

Cent. of the ITU.

1965, June 5
168	A71	25c dk bl, org brn & ol gray	.90	.75

Ski Lift — A72

Design: 25c, Chair lift, vert.

1966, Apr. 2 Engr. Perf. 13
169	A72	25c brt bl, grn & dk brn	1.00	.80
170	A72	40c mag, brt ultra & sep	1.40	1.25

Winter sports in Andorra.

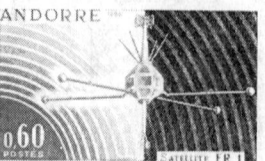

FR-1 Satellite — A73

1966, May 7 Perf. 13
171	A73	60c brt bl, grn & dk grn	1.50	1.50

Issued to commemorate the launching of the scientific satellite FR-1, Dec. 6, 1965.

Common Design Types
pictured following the introduction.

Europa Issue, 1966
Common Design Type

1966, Sept. 24 Engr. Perf. 13
Size: 21½x35½mm
172	CD9	60c brown	3.00	2.25

Folk Dancers, Sculpture by Josep Viladomat A74

Telephone Encircling the Globe A75

1967, Apr. 29 Engr. Perf. 13
173	A74	30c ol grn, dp grn & slate	.60	.45

Cent. (in 1966) of the New Reform, which reaffirmed and strengthened political freedom in Andorra.

Europa Issue, 1967
Common Design Type

1967, Apr. 29 Size: 22x36mm
174	CD10	30c bluish blk & lt bl	1.75	1.50
175	CD10	60c dk red & brt pink	2.75	2.00

1967, Apr. 29
176	A75	60c dk car, vio & blk	1.25	1.00

Automatic telephone service.

Injured Father at Home — A76

1967, Sept. 23 Engr. Perf. 13
177	A76	2.30fr ocher, dk red brn & brn red	8.00	4.50

Introduction of Social Security System.

Jesus in Garden of Gethsemane A77

Designs (from 16th century frescoes in La Maison des Vallees): 30c, The Kiss of Judas. 60c, The Descent from the Cross (Pieta).

1967, Sept. 23
178	A77	25c black & red brn	.50	.40
179	A77	30c purple & red lilac	.75	.50
180	A77	60c indigo & Prus blue	1.40	.90
		Nos. 178-180 (3)	2.65	1.80

See Nos. 185-187.

Downhill Skier — A78

1968, Jan. 27 Engr. Perf. 13
181	A78	40c org, ver & red lil	.75	.60

10th Winter Olympic Games, Grenoble, France, Feb. 6-18.

Europa Issue, 1968
Common Design Type

1968, Apr. 27 Engr. Perf. 13
Size: 36x22mm
182	CD11	30c gray & brt bl	5.00	3.00
183	CD11	60c brown & lilac	7.50	3.75

High Jump — A79

1968, Oct. 12 Engr. Perf. 13
184	A79	40c brt blue & brn	1.20	1.00

19th Olympic Games, Mexico City, Oct. 12-27.

Fresco Type of 1967
Designs (from 16th century frescoes in La Maison des Vallees): 25c, The Scourging of Christ. 30c, Christ Carrying the Cross. 60c, The Crucifixion. (All horiz.)

1968, Oct. 12
185	A77	25c dk grn & gray grn	.60	.60
186	A77	30c dk brown & lilac	1.00	1.00
187	A77	60c dk car & vio brn	1.40	1.40
		Nos. 185-187 (3)	3.00	3.00

Europa Issue, 1969
Common Design Type

1969, Apr. 26 Engr. Perf. 13
188	CD12	40c rose car, gray & dl bl	6.00	2.50
189	CD12	70c indigo, dl red & ol	9.00	5.00

10th anniv. of the Conf. of European Postal and Telecommunications Administrations.

Kayak on Isère River A80

Drops of Water and Diamond A80a

1969, Aug. 2 Engr. Perf. 13
190	A80	70c dk sl grn, ultra & ind	2.25	2.25

Intl. Canoe & Kayak Championships, Bourg-Saint-Maurice, Savoy, July 31-Aug. 6.

1969, Sept. 27 Engr. Perf. 13
191	A80a	70c blk, dp ultra & grnsh bl	4.50	4.50

European Water Charter.

St. John, the Woman and the Dragon — A81

The Revelation (From the Altar of St. John, Caselles): 40c, St. John Hearing Voice from Heaven on Patmos. 70c, St. John and the Seven Candlesticks.

1969, Oct. 18
192	A81	30c brn, dp pur & brn red	.65	.65
193	A81	40c gray, dk brn & ol	1.00	1.00
194	A81	70c dk red, maroon & brt rose lilac	1.75	1.75
		Nos. 192-194 (3)	3.40	3.40

See Nos. 199-201, 207-209, 214-216.

ANDORRA

Field Ball — A82

Shot Put — A83

1970, Feb. 21 Engr. *Perf. 13*
195 A82 80c multi 1.75 1.25

Issued to publicize the 7th International Field Ball Games, France, Feb. 26-Mar. 8.

Europa Issue, 1970
Common Design Type

1970, May 2 Engr. *Perf. 13*
Size: 36x22mm
196 CD13 40c orange 4.00 2.00
197 CD13 80c violet blue 8.00 4.00

1970, Sept. 11 Engr. *Perf. 13*
198 A83 80c bl & dk brn 1.25 1.00

1st European Junior Athletic Championships, Colombes, France, Sept. 11-13.

Altar Type of 1969

The Revelation (from the Altar of St. John, Caselles): 30c, St. John recording angel's message. 40c, Angel erecting column symbolizing faithful in heaven. 80c, St. John's trial in kettle of boiling oil.

1970, Oct. 24
199 A81 30c dp car, dk brn & brt pur .75 .75
200 A81 40c violet & slate grn .90 .90
201 A81 80c ol, dk bl & car rose 1.75 1.75
Nos. 199-201 (3) 3.40 3.40

Ice Skating — A84

1971, Feb. 20 Engr. *Perf. 13*
202 A84 80c dk red, red lil & pur 2.25 1.50

World Figure Skating Championships, Lyons, France, Feb. 23-28.

Capercaillie — A85

Nature protection: No. 204, Brown bear.

1971, Apr. 24 Photo. *Perf. 13*
203 A85 80c multicolored 3.25 2.25
  Engr.
204 A85 80c blue, grn & brn 3.25 2.25

Europa Issue, 1971
Common Design Type

1971, May 8 Engr. *Perf. 13*
Size: 35½x22mm
205 CD14 50c rose red 5.50 3.00
206 CD14 80c lt blue green 8.50 4.00

Altar Type of 1969

The Revelation (from the Altar of St. John, Caselles): 30c, St. John preaching, Rev. 1:3. 50c, "The Sign of the Beast . . ." Rev. 16:1-2. 90c, The Woman, Rev. 17:1.

1971, Sept. 18
207 A81 30c dl grn, ol & brt grn .75 .75
208 A81 50c rose car, org & ol brn 1.00 1.00
209 A81 90c blk, dk pur & bl 1.60 1.60
Nos. 207-209 (3) 3.35 3.35

Europa Issue 1972
Common Design Type

1972, Apr. 29 Photo. *Perf. 13*
Size: 21½x37mm
210 CD15 50c brt mag & multi 5.00 3.00
211 CD15 90c multicolored 7.00 4.50

Golden Eagle — A86

1972, May 27 Engr.
212 A86 60c dk grn, olive & plum 3.50 2.00

Nature protection.

Shooting — A87

1972, July 8
213 A87 1fr dk purple 1.75 1.40

20th Olympic Games, Munich, Aug. 26-Sept. 11.

Altar Type of 1969

The Revelation (from the Altar of St. John, Caselles): 30c, St. John, bishop and servant. 50c, Resurrection of Lazarus. 90c, Angel with lance and nails.

1972, Sept. 16 Engr. *Perf. 13*
214 A81 30c dk ol, gray & red lil .75 .75
215 A81 50c vio blue & slate 1.10 1.10
216 A81 90c dk Prus bl & sl grn 1.75 1.75
Nos. 214-216 (3) 3.60 3.60

De Gaulle as Coprince of Andorra — A88

90c, De Gaulle in front of Maison des Vallées.

1972, Oct. 23 Engr. *Perf. 13*
217 A88 50c violet blue 1.25 1.25
218 A88 90c dk carmine 1.75 1.75
  a. Pair, #217-218 + label 3.00 3.00

Visit of Charles de Gaulle to Andorra, 5th anniv. See Nos. 399-400.

Europa Issue 1973
Common Design Type

1973, Apr. 28 Photo. *Perf. 13*
Size: 36x22mm
219 CD16 50c violet & multi 5.50 2.75
220 CD16 90c dk red & multi 8.50 3.00

Virgin of Canolich — A89

1973, June 16 Engr. *Perf. 13*
221 A89 1fr ol, Prus bl & vio 1.65 1.65

Lily — A90

Blue Titmouse — A91

Designs: 45c, Iris. 50c, Columbine. 65c, Tobacco. No. 226, Pinks. No. 227, Narcissuses.

1973-74 Photo. *Perf. 13*
222 A90 30c car rose & multi .40 .40
223 A90 45c yel grn & multi .25 .25
224 A90 50c buff & multi 1.40 1.40
225 A90 65c gray & multi .40 .40
226 A90 90c ultra & multi .85 .85
227 A90 90c grnsh bl & multi .75 .75
Nos. 222-227 (6) 4.05 4.05

See Nos. 238-240.

1973-74 Photo. *Perf. 13*

Nature protection: 60c, Citril finch and mistletoe. 80c, Eurasian bullfinch. 1fr, Lesser spotted woodpecker.

228 A91 60c buff & multi 3.25 3.00
229 A91 80c gray & multi 2.25 2.00
230 A91 90c gray & multi 2.25 2.00
231 A91 1fr yel grn & multi 2.25 2.00
Nos. 228-231 (4) 10.00 9.00

Europa Issue 1974

Virgin of Pal — A92

Design: 90c, Virgin of Santa Coloma. Statues are polychrome 12th century carvings by rural artists.

1974, Apr. 27 Engr. *Perf. 13*
232 A92 50c multicolored 5.00 3.75
233 A92 90c multicolored 10.00 5.00

Arms of Andorra and Cahors Bridge — A93

Mail Box, Chutes and Globe — A94

1974, Aug. 24 Engr. *Perf. 13*
234 A93 1fr blue, vio & org 1.00 .60

First anniversary of meeting of the co-princes of Andorra: Pres. Georges Pompidou of France and Msgr. Juan Marti Alanis, Bishop of Urgel.

1974, Oct. 5 Engr. *Perf. 13*
235 A94 1.20fr multi 1.25 1.10

Centenary of Universal Postal Union.

Coronation of St. Marti, 16th Century — A95

Europa: 80c, Crucifixion, 16th cent., vert.

Perf. 11½x13, 13x11½
1975, Apr. 26 Photo.
236 A95 80c gold & multi 4.25 3.00
237 A95 1.20fr gold & multi 5.75 3.50

Flower Type of 1973

Designs: 60c, Gentian. 80c, Anemone. 1.20fr, Autumn crocus.

1975, May 10 Photo. *Perf. 13*
238 A90 60c olive & multi .35 .35
239 A90 80c brt rose & multi .75 .75
240 A90 1.20fr green & multi .80 .80
Nos. 238-240 (3) 1.90 1.90

Abstract Design — A96

1975, June 7 Engr. *Perf. 13*
241 A96 2fr bl, magenta & emer 1.75 1.75

ARPHILA 75 International Philatelic Exhibition, Paris, June 6-16.

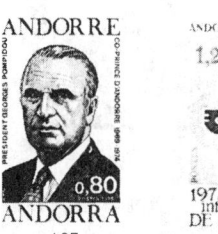

A97

A98

1975, Aug. 23 Engr. *Perf. 13*
242 A97 80c violet bl & blk .80 .80

Georges Pompidou (1911-74), pres. of France and co-prince of Andorra (1969-74).

1975, Nov. 8 Engr. *Perf. 13*
243 A98 1.20fr Costume, IWY Emblem 1.25 1.00

International Women's Year.

Skier and Snowflake — A99

1976, Jan. 31 Engr. *Perf. 13*
244 A99 1.20fr multicolored 1.25 1.00

12th Winter Olympic Games, Innsbruck, Austria, Feb. 4-15.

Telephone and Satellite — A100

1976, Mar. 20 Engr. *Perf. 13*
245 A100 1fr multicolored .80 .80

Centenary of first telephone call by Alexander Graham Bell, Mar. 10, 1876.

Catalan Forge — A101

Europa: 1.20fr, Lacemaker.

ANDORRA

1976, May 8   Engr.   *Perf. 13*
246 A101   80c multi   1.50   1.10
247 A101   1.20fr multi   2.50   1.65

Thomas Jefferson — A102
Trapshooting — A103 

1976, July 3   Engr.   *Perf. 13*
248 A102   1.20fr multi   1.10   .90

American Bicentennial.

1976, July 17   Engr.   *Perf. 13*
249 A103   2fr multi   1.75   1.25

21st Olympic Games, Montreal, Canada, July 17-Aug. 1.

Meritxell Sanctuary and Old Chapel — A104

1976, Sept. 4   Engr.   *Perf. 13*
250 A104   1fr multi   1.00   .80

Dedication of rebuilt Meritxell Church, Sept. 8, 1976.

Apollo — A105
Ermine — A106 

Design: 1.40fr, Morio butterfly.

1976, Oct. 16   Photo.   *Perf. 13*
251 A105   80c black & multi   1.75   1.25
252 A105   1.40fr salmon & multi   2.25   1.65

Nature protection.

1977, Apr. 2   Photo.   *Perf. 13*
253 A106   1fr vio bl, gray & blk   1.50   1.50

Nature protection.

St. Jean de Caselles — A107
Manual Digest, 1748, Arms of Andorra — A108 

Europa: 1.40fr, Sant Vicens Castle.

1977, Apr. 30   Engr.   *Perf. 13*
254 A107   1fr multi   1.75   .90
255 A107   1.40fr multi   2.25   1.40

1977, June 11   Engr.   *Perf. 13*
256 A108   80c grn, bl & brn   .80   .70

Establishment of Institute of Andorran Studies.

St. Romanus of Caesarea — A109

1977, July 23   Engr.   *Perf. 12½x13*
257 A109   2fr multi   1.25   1.00

Design from altarpiece in Church of St. Roma de les Bons.

General Council Chamber — A110
Guillem d'Arény Plandolit — A111 

1977, Sept. 24   Engr.   *Perf. 13*
258 A110   1.10fr multi   2.25   1.10
259 A111   2fr car & dk brn   1.50   1.10

Andorran heritage. Guillem d'Arény Plandolit started Andorran reform movement in 1866.

Squirrel — A112
Flag and Valira River Bridge — A113 

1978, Mar. 18   Engr.   *Perf. 13*
260 A112   1fr multi   .95   .55

1978, Apr. 8
261 A113   80c multi   .60   .55

Signing of the treaty establishing the Co-Principality of Andorra, 700th anniv.

Pal Church — A114

Europa: 1.40fr, Charlemagne's Castle, Charlemagne on horseback, vert.

1978, Apr. 29   Engr.   *Perf. 13*
262 A114   1fr multi   2.00   1.65
263 A114   1.40fr multi   3.00   2.25

Virgin of Sispony — A115

1978, May 20   Engr.   *Perf. 12x13*
264 A115   2fr multi   1.25   1.00

Visura Tribunal — A116

1978, June 24   Engr.   *Perf. 13*
265 A116   1.20fr multi   .80   .50

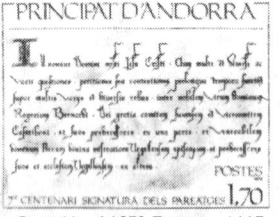

Preamble of 1278 Treaty — A117

1978, Sept. 2   Engr.   *Perf. 13x12½*
266 A117   1.70fr multi   .85   .50

700th anniversary of the signing of treaty establishing Co-Principality of Andorra.

Pyrenean Chamois — A118
White Partridges — A119 

1979, Mar. 26   Engr.   *Perf. 13*
267 A118   1fr multi   .50   .35

1979, Apr. 9   Photo.   *Perf. 13*
268 A119   1.20fr multi   .75   .60

Nature protection. See Nos. 288-289.

French Mailman, 1900 — A120

Europa: 1.70fr, 1st French p.o. in Andorra.

1979, Apr. 28   Engr.   *Perf. 13*
269 A120   1.20fr multi   1.10   .90
270 A120   1.70fr multi   1.65   1.10

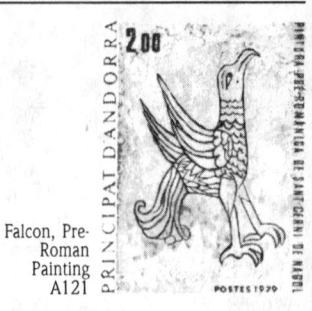

Falcon, Pre-Roman Painting — A121

1979, June 2   Engr.   *Perf. 12½x13*
271 A121   2fr multi   1.00   .75

A122
A123 

Child with Lambs, Church, IYC emblem.

1979, July 7   Photo.   *Perf. 13*
272 A122   1.70fr multi   .80   .50

International Year of the Child.

1979, Sept. 29   Engr.   *Perf. 13*
273 A123   2fr multi   1.00   .75

700th anniversary of Co-Principality of Andorra.

Judo Hold — A124
Farm House, Cortinada — A125 

1979, Nov. 24   Engr.   *Perf. 13*
274 A124   1.30fr multi   .80   .45

World Judo Championships, Paris, Dec. 1979.

1980, Jan. 26   Engr.   *Perf. 13*
275 A125   1.10fr multi   .50   .45

Cross-Country Skiing — A126

1980, Feb. 9
276 A126   1.80fr ultra & lil rose   1.50   .90

13th Winter Olympic Games, Lake Placid, NY, Feb. 12-24.

Have you found a typo or other error in this catalogue?

Inform the editors via our web site or e-mail

sctcat@
scottonline.com

ANDORRA

A128
A129 

1980, Aug. 30 Engr. *Perf. 13*
278 A128 1.20fr multi .55 .35
World Bicycling championships.

1980, Apr. 26 Engr. *Perf. 13*
Europa: 1.30fr, Charlemagne (742-814). 1.80fr, Napoleon I (1769-1821).
279 A129 1.30fr multi .50 .35
280 A129 1.80fr gray grn & brn .80 .55

Pyrenees Lily — A130

1980 Photo.
281 A130 1.10fr Dog-toothed violet .50 .30
282 A130 1.30fr shown .55 .35
Nature protection. Issue dates: 1.10fr, June 21, 1.30fr, May 17.

De La Vall House, 400th Anniversary of Restoration A131

1980, Sept. 6 Engr.
283 A131 1.40fr multi .50 .35

Angel, Church of St. Cerni de Nagol, Pre-Romanesque Fresco — A132

1980, Oct. 27 *Perf. 13x12½*
284 A132 2fr multi 1.00 .70

Bordes de Mereig Mountain Village A133

1981, Mar. 21 Engr. *Perf. 13*
285 A133 1.40fr bl gray & dk brn .50 .40

Europa Issue 1981

Ball de l'Ossa, Winter Game A134

1981, May 16 Engr.
286 A134 1.40fr shown .65 .45
287 A134 2fr El Contrapas dance .80 .60

Bird Type of 1979

1981, June 20 Photo.
288 A119 1.20fr Phylloscopus bonelli .60 .30
289 A119 1.40fr Tichodroma muraria .60 .40

World Fencing Championship, Clermont-Ferrand, July 2-13 — A135

1981, July 4 Engr.
290 A135 2fr bl & blk .70 .40

St. Martin, 12th Cent. Tapestry — A136

1981, Sept. 5 Engr. *Perf. 12x13*
291 A136 3fr multi 1.10 .80

Intl. Drinking Water Decade A137

Intl. Year of the Disabled A138

1981, Oct. 17 *Perf. 13*
292 A137 1.60fr multi .60 .40

1981, Nov. 7
293 A138 2.30fr multi .80 .70

Europa 1982 — A139

1982, May 8 Engr. *Perf. 13*
294 A139 1.60fr Creation of Andorran govt., 1982 .60 .40
295 A139 2.30fr Land Council, 1419 .90 .55

1982 World Cup — A140

Designs: Various soccer players. Nos. 296-297 se-tenant with label showing natl. arms.

1982, June 12 Engr. *Perf. 13*
296 A140 1.60fr red & dk brn .60 .45
297 A140 2.60fr red & dk brn .90 .65

Souvenir Sheet

No. 52 — A141

1982, Aug. 21 Engr.
298 A141 5fr blk & rose car 1.60 1.60
1st Andorran Stamp Exhib., Aug. 21-Sept. 19.

Horse, Roman Wall Painting — A142

1982, Sept. 4 Photo. *Perf. 13x12½*
299 A142 3fr multi 1.10 .90

Wild Cat — A143

1982, Oct. 9 Engr. *Perf. 13*
300 A143 1.80fr shown .90 .50
301 A143 2.60fr Pine trees 1.00 .65

TB Bacillus Centenary A144

St. Thomas Aquinas (1225-74) A145

1982, Nov. 13
302 A144 2.10fr Koch, lungs .75 .60

1982, Dec. 4
303 A145 2fr multi .80 .60

Manned Flight Bicentenary A146

1983, Feb. 26 Engr.
304 A146 2fr multi .75 .60

Nature Protection A147

1983, Apr. 16 Engr. *Perf. 13*
305 A147 1fr Birch trees .40 .20
306 A147 1.50fr Trout .60 .40
See Nos. 325-326.

Europa 1983 — A148

Catalane Gold Works.

1983, May 7 Engr. *Perf. 13*
307 A148 1.80fr Exterior .70 .45
308 A148 2.60fr Interior .90 .60

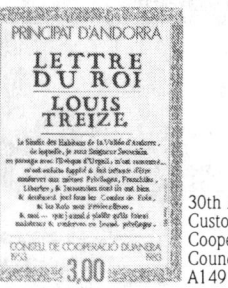

30th Anniv. of Customs Cooperation Council A149

1983, May 14
309 A149 3fr Letter of King Louis XIII 1.25 .80

First Arms of Valleys of Andorra A150

1983, Sept. 3 Engr. *Perf. 13*
310 A150 5c olive grn & red .15 .15
311 A150 10c grn & olive grn .15 .15
312 A150 20c brt pur & red .15 .15
313 A150 30c brn vio & red .15 .15
314 A150 40c dk bl & ultra .15 .15
315 A150 50c gray & red .15 .15
316 A150 1fr deep magenta .30 .20
317 A150 2fr org red & red brn .75 .35
318 A150 5fr dk brn & red 1.40 .85
Nos. 310-318 (9) 3.35 2.30
See Nos. 329-335, 380-385, 464-465.

Painting, Cortinada Church A151

1983, Sept. 24 *Perf. 12x13*
319 A151 4fr multi 1.50 1.00

Plandolit House — A152

1983, Oct. 15 Photo. *Perf. 13*
320 A152 1.60fr dp ultra & brn .50 .35

1984 Winter Olympics A153

1984, Feb. 18 Engr.
321 A153 2.80fr multicolored 1.00 .70

Pyrenees Region Work Community (Labor Org.) — A154

1984, Apr. 28 Engr. *Perf. 13*
322 A154 3fr brt blue & sepia 1.00 .65

ANDORRA

Europa (1959-84) A155

1984, May 5 Engr.
323 A155 2fr brt grn 1.00 .50
324 A155 2.80fr rose car 1.25 .75

Nature Protection Type of 1983
1984, July 7 Perf. 13
325 A147 1.70fr Chestnut tree .65 .40
326 A147 2.10fr Walnut tree .80 .50

Pyrenees Art Center A155a

1984, Sept. 7 Engr.
327 A155a 3fr multi 1.10 .80

Romanesque Fresco, Church of St. Cerni de Nagol A156

1984, Nov. 17 Perf. 12x13
328 A156 5fr multi 1.75 1.25

First Arms Type of 1983
1984-87 Engr. Perf. 13
329 A150 1.90fr emerald .65 .15
330 A150 2.20fr red orange .75 .15
  a. Bklt. pane. 2 #329, 6 #330 6.25
331 A150 3fr bl grn & red brn .75 .45
332 A150 4fr brt org & brn 1.15 .85
333 A150 10fr brn org & blk 2.50 1.50
334 A150 15fr grn & dk grn 4.25 3.25
335 A150 20fr brt bl & red brn 5.25 3.00
  Nos. 329-335 (7) 15.30 9.35

Nos. 329-330 issued in booklets only.
Issued: 3fr, 20fr, 12/1/84; 10fr, 2/9/85; 4fr, 15fr, 4/19/86; 1.90fr, 2.20fr, 3/28/87.

Saint Julia Valley A157

1985, Apr. 13 Engr.
336 A157 2fr multi .80 .45

Europa 1985 — A158

Intl. Youth Year — A159

1985, May 4 Engr.
337 A158 2.10fr Le Val D'Andorre .95 .55
338 A158 3fr Instruments 1.40 .75

1985, June 8 Engr.
339 A159 3fr multi .90 .60

Wildlife Conservation A160

1985, Aug. 3 Photo.
340 A160 1.80fr Anas platyrhynchos .65 .40
341 A160 2.20fr Carduelis carduelis .85 .45

Two Saints, Medieval Fresco in St. Cerni de Nagol Church A161

1985, Sept. 14 Engr. Perf. 12½x13
342 A161 5fr multi 1.50 1.10

Postal Museum Inauguration — A162

1986, Mar. 22 Engr. Perf. 13
343 A162 2.20fr like No. 269 .80 .15

Europa 1986 A163

1986, May 3 Engr. Perf. 13
344 A163 2.20fr Ansalonga .90 .35
345 A163 3.20fr Isard 1.50 .50

1986 World Cup Soccer Championships, Mexico — A164

1986, June 14
346 A164 3fr multi .85 .15

Angonella Lake — A165

1986, June 28
347 A165 2.20fr multi .65 .15

Manual Digest Frontispiece, 1748 A166

1986, Sept. 6 Engr.
348 A166 5fr chnt brn, gray ol & blk 1.65 .30

Intl. Peace Year — A167

1986, Sept. 29
349 A167 1.90fr bl gray & grnsh bl .65 .15

A168   A169

1986, Oct. 18 Engr. Perf. 13½x13
350 A168 1.90fr St. Vicenc D'Enclar .80 .15

1987, Mar. 27 Litho. Perf. 12½x13
351 A169 2.20fr Contemporary natl. coat of arms 1.75 .15
Visit of the French co-prince.

Europa 1987 — A170

1987, May 2 Engr. Perf. 13
352 A170 2.20fr Meritxell Sanctuary 1.00 .30
353 A170 3.40fr Pleta D'Ordino 1.50 .50

Ransol Village — A171

1987, June 13 Photo.
354 A171 1.90fr multicolored 1.00 .15

Nature A172

1987, July 4
355 A172 1.90fr Cavall rogenc 1.10 .15
356 A172 2.20fr Graellsia isabellae 1.40 .15

Aryalsu, Romanesque Painting, La Cortinada Church A173

Perf. 12½x13
1987, Sept. 5 Litho. & Engr.
357 A173 5fr multi 2.00 .35

Hiker Looking at Map — A174

1987, Sept. 19 Engr. Perf. 13
358 A174 2fr olive, grn & dark brn vio .80 .15

Medieval Iron Key, La Cortinada A175

1987, Oct. 17 Litho.
359 A175 3fr multi 1.10 .20

Andorran Coat of Arms — A176

Booklet Stamp
1988, Feb. 6 Engr. Perf. 13
360 A176 2.20fr red .80 .20
  a. Bklt. pane of 10 8.00
See Nos. 388-389B.

Shoemaker's Last from Roc de l'Oral — A177

1988, Feb. 13 Photo.
361 A177 3fr multi 1.25 .30

Rugby — A178

1988, Mar. 19 Engr. Perf. 13½x13
362 A178 2.20fr emer grn, Prus grn & brn .95 .20

Europa 1988 — A179   Hot Springs, Escaldes — A180

Transport and communication: 2.20fr, Broadcast tower. 3.60fr, Computer graphics.

1988, May 2 Engr. Perf. 13
363 A179 2.20fr multicolored .90 .20
364 A179 3.60fr multicolored 1.40 .35

1988, May 14 Engr.
365 A180 2.20fr Prus blue, org brn & emer .85 .15

Tor D'Ansalonga Farmhouse, Ansalonga Pass — A181

1988, June 13 Engr.
366 A181 2fr multi .75 .15

ANDORRA

Sheepdog — A182

1988, July 2   Photo.
367 A182   2fr shown   .90   .20
368 A182   2.20fr Hare   1.10   .20

Roman Fresco, 8th Cent., St. Steven's Church, Andorre-La-Vieille — A183

1988, Sept. 3   Engr.   Perf. 13x12½
369 A183   5fr multicolored   1.75   .40

French Revolution, Bicent. — A184

1989, Jan. 1   Litho.   Perf. 13
370 A184   2.20fr red & vio bl   .85   .15

Poble de Pal Village A185

1989, Mar. 4   Engr.   Perf. 13
371 A185   2.20fr indigo & lilac   .80   .15

Europa 1989 — A186

Children's games.

1989, June 9   Engr.   Perf. 13
372 A186   2.20fr Human tower   .80   .15
373 A186   3.60fr The handkerchief   1.40   .30

Red Cross — A187

1989, May 6
374 A187   3.60fr multi   1.25   .25

Visigothic- Merovingian Age Cincture from a Column, St. Vicenc D'Anclar — A188

1989, June 3   Photo.
375 A188   3fr multi   1.00   .20

Wildlife A189

1989, Sept. 18   Engr.   Perf. 13
376 A189   2.20fr Wild boar   .90   .20
377 A189   3.60fr Newt   1.40   .40

Scene of Salome from the Retable of St. Michael of Mosquera, Encamp — A190

1989, Oct. 16   Perf. 13x13½
378 A190   5fr multi   1.50   .30

La Margineda Bridge A191

1990, Feb. 26   Engr.   Perf. 13
379 A191   2.30fr multi   .80   .15

Tourism.

Arms Types of 1983 and 1988

1990-93   Engr.   Perf. 13
380 A150   2.10fr green   .80   .15
381 A150   2.20fr green   1.50   .50
382 A150   2.30fr vermilion   .85   .20
383 A150   2.40fr green   .90   .30
384 A150   2.50fr vermilion   1.75   .35
385 A150   2.80fr vermilion   1.00   .30
Nos. 380-385 (6)   6.80   2.00

Booklet Stamps
Perf. 13
386 A176   2.30fr red   .85   .20
   a. Booklet pane of 5   4.25
387 A176   2.50fr vermilion   1.70   .55
   a. Booklet pane of 5   8.50
388 A176   2.80fr red   1.00   .30
   c. Booklet pane of 5   5.00
Nos. 386-388 (3)   3.55   1.05

Issued: 2.20fr, #384, 10/28/91; #387, 10/21/91; 2.40fr, 2.80fr, 8/9/93; 2.10fr, 2.30fr, 1990.

Llorts Mines A193

1990, Apr. 21   Engr.   Perf. 12½x13
390 A193   3.20fr multicolored   1.25   .25

Europa A194

Designs: 2.30fr, Early post office. 3.20fr, Modern post office.

1990, May 5   Perf. 13
391 A194   2.30fr blk & scar   .95   .20
392 A194   3.20fr scar & vio   1.40   .25

Otter A195

1990, May 25   Perf. 12x13
393 A195   2.30fr Roses, vert.   .95   .20
394 A195   3.20fr shown   1.40   .25

Censer of St. Roma of Les Bons A196

1990, June 25   Perf. 12½x13
395 A196   3fr multicolored   1.10   .30

Tobacco Drying Sheds, Les Bons A197

1990, Sept. 15   Engr.   Perf. 12½x13
396 A197   2.30fr multi   .85   .20

St. Coloma (Detail) A198

1990, Oct. 8   Perf. 12½x13
397 A198   5fr multi   2.00   .75

Coin from Church of St. Eulalia d'Encamp A199

1990, Oct. 27   Litho.   Perf. 13
398 A199   3.20fr multi   1.10   .40

De Gaulle Type of 1972 Dated 1990

1990, Oct. 23   Engr.   Perf. 13
399 A88   2.30fr vio bl   1.00   .35
400 A88   3.20fr dk car   1.40   .55
   a. Pair, #399-400 + label   2.40   .85

Birth centenary of De Gaulle.

4th Games of the Small European States — A200

1991, Apr. 8   Photo.   Perf. 13
401 A200   2.50fr multicolored   .90   .30

Chapel of St. Roma Dels Vilars — A201

1991, Mar. 9   Engr.   Perf. 13
402 A201   2.50fr multicolored   .90   .30

Europa — A202

Perf. 13x12½, 12½x13
1991, Apr. 27
403 A202   2.50fr TV satellite   .90   .30
404 A202   3.50fr Telescope, horiz.   1.25   .45

Bottles from Tombs of St. Vincenc d'Enclar A203

1991, May 11   Photo.   Perf. 13
405 A203   3.20fr multicolored   1.25   .40

Farm Animals A204

1991, June 22   Engr.   Perf. 13
406 A204   2.50fr Sheep   .90   .30
407 A204   3.50fr Cow   1.25   .40

Petanque World Championships — A205

1991, Sept. 14   Engr.   Perf. 13
408 A205   2.50fr multicolored   .90   .30

Wolfgang Amadeus Mozart, Death Bicent. A206

1991, Oct. 5
409 A206   3.40fr multicolored   1.40   .45

Virgin and Child of St. Julia and St. Germa A207

1991, Nov. 16   Engr.   Perf. 12½x13
410 A207   5fr multicolored   2.00   .65

ANDORRA

1992 Winter Olympics, Albertville — A208

1992, Feb. 10	Litho.		Perf. 13
411	A208	2.50fr Slalom skiing	.95 .30
412	A208	3.40fr Figure skating	1.25 .40
a.		Pair, #411-412 + label	2.25 .70

Church of St. Andrew of Arinsal A209

1992, Mar. 21	Engr.		Perf. 12x13
413	A209	2.50fr black & tan	1.10 .35

Discovery of America, 500th Anniv. A210

1992, Apr. 25			Perf. 13
414	A210	2.50fr Columbus' fleet	.90 .30
415	A210	3.40fr Landing in New World	1.25 .40

Europa.

1992 Summer Olympics, Barcelona A211

European Globeflower A212

1992, June 8	Litho.		Perf. 13
416	A211	2.50fr Kayaking	1.00 .35
417	A211	3.40fr Shooting	1.40 .45
a.		Pair, #416-417 + label	2.40 .80

1992, July 6

Design: 3.40fr, Vulture, horiz.

| 418 | A212 | 2.50fr multicolored | 1.00 .35 |
| 419 | A212 | 3.40fr multicolored | 1.40 .45 |

Martyrdom of St. Eulalia A213

1992, Sept. 14	Photo.		Perf. 13
420	A213	4fr multicolored	1.65 .55

Andorra, French Administration, stamps can be mounted in the annually supplemented Scott Monaco and French Andorra album.

Sculpture by Mauro Staccioli A214

1992, Oct. 5	Engr.		Perf. 12½x13
421	A214	5fr multicolored	2.00 .70

Ordino Arcalis '91.

Tempest in a Tea Cup, by Dennis Oppenheim — A215

1992, Nov. 14	Engr.		Perf. 13x12½
422	A215	5fr multicolored	2.00 .70

Skiing in Andorra — A216

Ski resorts: No. 423: a, 2.50fr, Soldeu El Tarter. b, 3.40fr, Arinsal.
No. 424: a, 2.50fr, Pas de la Casa-Grau Roig. b, 2.50fr, Ordino Arcalis. c, 3.40fr, Pal.

1993, Mar. 13	Litho.		Perf. 13
423	A216	Pair, #a.-b. + label	2.25 .75
424	A216	Strip of 3, #a.-c.	3.25 1.00

Sculptures — A217

Europa: 2.50fr, "Estructures Autogeneradores," by Jorge du Bon, vert. 3.40fr, Sculpture, "Fisicromia per Andorra," by Carlos Cruz-Diez.

1993, May 15	Engr.		Perf. 12½x13
425	A217	2.50fr multicolored	1.00 .35
		Litho.	Perf. 14x13½
426	A217	3.40fr multicolored	1.40 .45

Butterflies A218

1993, June 28	Litho.		Perf. 13
427	A218	2.50fr Polymmatus icarus	.95 .30
428	A218	4.20fr Nymphalidae	1.50 .50

Tour de France Bicycle Race — A219

1993, July 20	Litho.		Perf. 13
429	A219	2.50fr multicolored	.90 .30

Andorra School, 10th Anniv. A220

1993, Sept. 20	Litho.		Perf. 13
430	A220	2.80fr multicolored	1.00 .35

Un Lloc Paga, by Michael Warren A221

1993, Oct. 18	Engr.		Perf. 12½x13
431	A221	5fr blue & black	1.75 .60

Sculpture, by Erik Dietman A222

1993, Nov. 8	Engr.		Perf. 12½x13
432	A222	5fr multicolored	1.75 .60

1994 Winter Olympics, Lillehammer A223

1994, Feb. 21	Litho.		Perf. 13
433	A223	3.70fr multicolored	1.25 .45

1st Anniversary of the Constitution — A224

Designs: 2.80fr, Monument, by Emili Armengol. 3.70fr, Stone tablet with inscription.

1994, Mar. 15	Litho.		Perf. 13
434	A224	2.80fr multicolored	1.00 .35
435	A224	3.70fr multicolored	1.40 .48
a.		Pair, #434-435 + label	2.40 .85

European Discoveries A225

Europa: 2.80fr, Discovery of AIDS virus. 3.70fr, Radio diffusion.

1994, May 9	Litho.		Perf. 13
436	A225	2.80fr multicolored	1.10 .35
437	A225	3.70fr multicolored	1.50 .50

1994 World Cup Soccer Championships, US — A226

1994, June 20			
438	A226	3.70fr multicolored	1.50 .50

Tourist Sports — A227

#439, Mountain climbing. #440, Fishing. #441, Horseback riding. #442, Mountain biking.

1994, July 11			
439	A227	2.80fr multicolored	1.10 .35
440	A227	2.80fr multicolored	1.10 .35
a.		Pair, #439-440 + label	2.20 .70
441	A227	2.80fr multicolored	1.10 .35
442	A227	2.80fr multicolored	1.10 .35
a.		Pair, #441-442 + label	2.20 .70
		Nos. 439-442 (4)	4.40 1.40

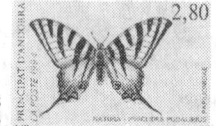

Butterflies A228

1994, Sept. 5	Litho.		Perf. 13
443	A228	2.80fr Iphiclides podalirus	1.10 .35
444	A228	4.40fr Aglais urticae	1.75 .60

A229

A230

1994, Oct. 22	Litho.		Perf. 13
445	A229	2.80fr multicolored	1.25 .42

Meeting of the Co-Princes, 1st anniv.

1995, Feb. 27	Litho.		Perf. 13
446	A230	2.80fr multicolored	1.25 .40

European Nature Conservation Year

1995 World Cup Rugby Championships — A231

1995, Apr. 24	Litho.		Perf. 13
447	A231	2.80fr multicolored	1.25 .40

ANDORRA

Peace & Freedom A232

Europa: 2.80fr, Dove with olive branch. 3.70fr, Flock of doves.

1995, May 2
448 A232 2.80fr multicolored 1.25 .40
449 A232 3.70fr multicolored 1.65 .50

Caritas in Andorra, 15th Anniv. A233

1995, May 15 Litho. *Perf. 13*
450 A233 2.80fr multicolored 1.25 1.00

Caldea Health Spa — A234

1995, June 26 Litho. *Perf. 13*
451 A234 2.80fr multicolored 1.25 1.00

Ordino Natl. Auditorium A235

1995, July 10 Litho. & Engr.
452 A235 3.70fr black & buff 1.65 1.25

Virgin of Meritxell — A236

1995, Sept. 11 Litho. *Perf. 14*
453 A236 4.40fr multicolored 1.90 1.50

Protection of Nature A237

Butterflies: 2.80fr, Papallona llimonera, vert. 3.70fr, Papallona melanargia galathea.

1995, Sept. 25 *Perf. 13*
454 A237 2.80fr multicolored 1.25 1.00
455 A237 3.70fr multicolored 1.65 1.25

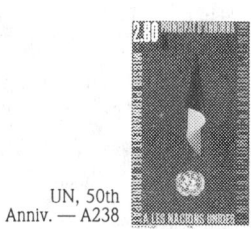

UN, 50th Anniv. — A238

1995, Oct. 21 Litho. *Perf. 13*
456 A238 2.80fr Flag, emblem 1.25 1.00
457 A238 3.70fr Emblem, "50," flag 1.65 1.25
 a. Pair, #456-457 + label 3.00 3.00

Andorra's Entrance into Council of Europe A239

1995, Nov. 4
458 A239 2.80fr multicolored 1.25 1.00

World Skiing Championships, Ordino Arcalis — A240

1996, Jan. 29 Litho. *Perf. 13*
459 A240 2.80fr multicolored 1.25 1.25

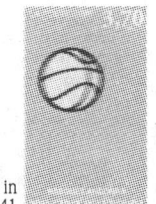

Basketball in Andorra — A241

1996, Jan. 29 Litho. *Perf. 13*
460 A241 3.70fr multicolored 1.65 1.65

Our Lady of Meritxell Special School, 25th Anniv. A242

1996, Feb. 17 Litho. *Perf. 13*
461 A242 2.80fr multicolored 1.20 1.20

Songbirds A243

1996, Mar. 25
462 A243 3fr Pit riog 1.30 1.30
463 A243 3.80fr Mallarenga carbonera 1.65 1.65

First Arms Type of 1983
1996, Apr. 17 Engr. *Perf. 13*
464 A150 2.70fr green 1.20 1.20
465 A150 3fr red 1.30 1.30

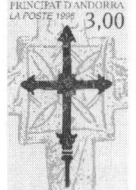

Cross of St. James d'Engordany — A244

1996, Apr. 20 Litho.
466 A244 3fr multicolored 1.30 1.30

Censar of St. Eulalia d'Encamp A245

1996, Apr. 20
467 A245 3.80fr multicolored 1.70 1.70

Europa — A246    Chess — A247

1996, May 6
468 A246 3fr Ermessenda de Castellbo 1.30 1.30

1996, June 8 Litho. *Perf. 13*
469 A247 4.50fr multicolored 2.00 2.00

1996 Summer Olympic Games, Atlanta A248

1996, June 29 Litho. *Perf. 13*
470 A248 3fr multicolored 1.25 1.25

Arms of the Community of Canillo — A249

Serpentine Die Cut 7 Vert.
1996, June 10 Litho.
Self-Adhesive
471 A249 (3fr) multicolored 1.75 1.75

Natl. Children's Choir, 5th Anniv. A250

1996, Sept. 14 *Perf. 13*
472 A250 3fr multicolored 1.30 1.30

Livestock Fair — A251

1996, Oct. 26 Engr. *Perf. 12x13*
473 A251 3fr multicolored 1.25 1.25

Churches A252

#474, St. Romá de Les Bons. #475, St. Coloma.

1996, Nov. 16 Litho. *Perf. 13*
474 A252 6.70fr multicolored 2.80 2.80
475 A252 6.70fr multicolored 2.80 2.80

A253    A254

1997, Jan. 7 Litho. *Perf. 13*
476 A253 3fr multicolored 1.25 1.25
 Pres. Francois Mitterrand (1916-96).

Sawtooth Die Cut 7 Vert. x Straight Die Cut
1997, Feb. 24 Litho.
Self-Adhesive
477 A254 (3fr) Arms of Encamp 1.25 1.25
 a. Booklet pane of 10 12.50

By its nature, No. 477a is a complete booklet. The peelable paper backing serves as a booklet cover.

A255    A256

1997, Mar. 22 *Perf. 13*
478 A255 3fr Volleyball 1.25 1.25

1997, May 12 Litho. *Perf. 13*
479 A256 3fr "The White Lady" 1.25 1.25
 Europa (Stories and Legends).

Oreneta Cuablanca A257

1997, May 31 Litho. *Perf. 13*
480 A257 3.80fr multicolored 1.60 1.60

Paintings of Mills — A258

1997, Sept. 15 Litho. *Perf. 13*
481 A258 3fr Cal Pal, vert. 1.15 1.15
482 A258 4.50fr Mas d'en Sole 1.70 1.70

Religious Artifacts A259

Designs: 3fr, Monstrance of St. Iscle and St. Victoria. 15.50fr, Altar piece of St. Pierre d'Alxirivall.

1997, Oct. 27
483 A259 3fr multicolored 1.15 1.15
484 A259 15.50fr multicolored 5.75 5.75
 a. Pair, #483-484 + label 6.90 6.90

ANDORRA

Legends — A260

Designs: No. 485, Legend of Meritxell. No. 486, The cross of seven arms. 3.80fr, The fountain of Esmelicat.

1997, Nov. 22		Litho.		Perf. 13
485	A260	3fr multicolored	1.10	1.10
486	A260	3fr multicolored	1.10	1.10
487	A260	3.80fr multicolored	1.40	1.40
a.		Strip of 3, #485-487	3.60	3.60

Monaco Intl. Philatelic Exhibition — A261

1997, Nov. 28		Litho.		Perf. 13
488	A261	3fr Chapel of St. Miguel d'Engolasters	1.10	1.10

Happy Anniversary A262

1998 Winter Olympic Games, Nagano A263

1998, Jan. 3		Litho.		Perf. 13
489	A262	3fr Juggling candles	1.10	1.10

1998, Feb. 14				
490	A263	4.40fr multicolored	1.75	1.75

Arms of Ordino — A264

Serpentine Die Cut Vert.

1998, Mar. 7			Litho.
		Booklet Stamp	
		Self-Adhesive	
491	A491	(3fr) multicolored	1.10 1.10
a.		Booklet pane of 10	11.00
		Complete booklet, #491a	11.00

Mesa de Vila Church — A265

1998, Mar. 28			Perf. 13
492	A265	4.50fr multicolored	1.70 1.70

Rotary Club of Andorra, 20th Anniv. A265a

1998, Apr. 11			
493	A265a	3fr multicolored	1.10 1.10

Finch A266

1998		Litho.		Perf. 13
494	A266	3.80fr multicolored	1.40	1.40

1998 World Cup Soccer Championships, France — A267

1998, June 6		Litho.		Perf. 13
495	A267	3fr multicolored	1.10	1.10

For overprint see No. 499.

Music Festival A268

1998, June 20		Litho.		Perf. 13
496	A268	3fr multicolored	1.10	1.10

Europa.

Expo '98, Lisbon A269

1998, July 6			
497	A269	5fr multicolored	1.75 1.75

Chalice, House of the Valleys — A270

1998, Sept. 19		Litho.		Perf. 13
498	A270	4.50fr multicolored	1.60	1.60

No. 495 Ovptd. "FINAL / FRANCA/BRASIL / 3-0"

1998, Nov. 16			
499	A267	3fr multicolored	1.10 1.10

Early Maps of Andorra A271

1998, Nov. 16				
500	A271	3fr 1717, vert.	1.10	1.10
501	A271	15.50fr 1777	5.75	5.75

SEMI-POSTAL STAMP

Catalogue values for unused stamps in this section are for Never Hinged items.

Virgin of St. Coloma — SP1

1964, July 25		Unwmk.	Engr.	Perf. 13
B1	SP1	25c + 10c multi	22.00	22.00

The surtax was for the Red Cross.

AIR POST STAMPS

Catalogue values for unused stamps in this section are for Never Hinged items.

Chamois AP1

1950, Feb. 20		Unwmk.	Engr.	Perf. 13
C1	AP1	100fr indigo	65.00	45.00

East Branch of Valira River — AP2

1955-57				
C2	AP2	100fr dark green	8.50	6.50
C3	AP2	200fr cerise	17.50	14.00
C4	AP2	500fr deep blue ('57)	90.00	65.00
		Nos. C2-C4 (3)	116.00	85.50

D'Inclès Valley — AP3

1961-64		Unwmk.		Perf. 13
C5	AP3	2fr red, ol gray & claret	1.00	.65
C6	AP3	3fr bl, mar & slate grn	1.25	1.25
C7	AP3	5fr rose lil & red org	2.00	1.75
C8	AP3	10fr bl grn & slate grn	3.75	3.50
		Nos. C5-C8 (4)	8.00	7.15

Issued: 10fr, 4/25/64; others, 6/19/61.

POSTAGE DUE STAMPS

Postage Due Stamps of France, 1893-1931, Overprinted
ANDORRE

On Stamps of 1893-1926

1931-33		Unwmk.		Perf. 14x13½
J1	D2	5c blue	1.00	1.00
J2	D2	10c brown	1.00	1.00
J3	D2	30c rose red	.40	.40
J4	D2	50c violet brn	1.00	1.00
J5	D2	60c green	10.00	10.00
J6	D2	1fr red brn, *straw*	.50	.50
J7	D2	2fr brt violet	6.00	6.00
J8	D2	3fr magenta	1.10	1.10
		Nos. J1-J8 (8)	21.00	21.00

On Stamps of 1927-31

J9	D4	1c olive grn	1.25	1.25
J10	D4	10c rose	2.75	2.75
J11	D4	60c red	16.00	16.00
J12	D4	1fr Prus grn ('32)	65.00	65.00
J13	D4	1.20fr on 2fr bl	50.00	50.00
J14	D4	2fr ol brn ('33)	140.00	140.00
J15	D4	5fr on 1fr vio	65.00	65.00
		Nos. J9-J15 (7)	340.00	340.00

D5    D6

1935-41				Typo.
J16	D5	1c gray grn	2.25	1.75
J17	D6	5c lt bl ('37)	3.75	4.50
J18	D6	10c brn ('41)	3.00	4.50
J19	D6	2fr vio ('41)	6.00	3.25
J20	D6	5fr red org ('41)	11.00	3.25
		Nos. J16-J20 (5)	26.00	16.75

Catalogue values for unused stamps in this section, from this point to the end of the section, are for Never Hinged items.

Wheat Sheaves — D7

1943-46			Perf. 14x13½
J21	D7	10c sepia	1.00 1.00
J22	D7	30c brt red vio	1.50 1.50
J23	D7	50c blue grn	1.75 1.75
J24	D7	1fr brt ultra	.80 .80
J25	D7	1.50fr rose red	5.75 5.75
J26	D7	2fr turq blue	1.50 1.50
J27	D7	3fr brown org	2.75 2.75
J28	D7	4fr dp vio ('45)	4.50 4.50
J29	D7	5fr brt pink	4.50 4.50
J30	D7	10fr red org ('45)	5.75 5.75
J31	D7	20fr olive brn ('46)	6.00 6.00
		Nos. J21-J31 (11)	35.80 35.80

Inscribed: "Timbre Taxe"

1946-53			
J32	D7	10c sepia ('46)	1.10 1.10
J33	D7	1fr ultra	.75 .75
J34	D7	2fr turq blue	1.00 1.00
J35	D7	3fr orange brn	2.00 2.00
J36	D7	4fr violet	2.75 2.75
J37	D7	5fr brt pink	1.75 1.75
J38	D7	10fr red orange	2.75 2.75
J39	D7	20fr olive brn	6.25 6.25
J40	D7	50fr dk green ('50)	16.50 16.50
J41	D7	100fr dp green ('53)	87.50 87.50
		Nos. J32-J41 (10)	122.35 122.35

Inscribed: "Timbre Taxe"

1961, June 19			Perf. 14x13½
J42	D7	5c rose pink	3.00 3.00
J43	D7	10c red orange	6.00 6.00
J44	D7	20c olive	9.00 9.00
J45	D7	50c dark slate green	15.00 15.00
		Nos. J42-J45 (4)	33.00 33.00

D8    D9

1964-71		Typo.	Perf. 14x13½
J46	D8	5c Centaury ('65)	.15 .15
J47	D8	10c Gentian ('65)	.15 .15
J48	D8	15c Corn poppy	.15 .15
J49	D8	20c Violets ('71)	.15 .15
J50	D8	30c Forget-me-not	.15 .15
J51	D8	40c Columbine ('71)	.20 .20
J52	D8	50c Clover ('65)	.30 .30
		Nos. J46-J52 (7)	1.25 1.25

1985, Oct. 21			Engr.	Perf. 13
J53	D9	10c Holly	.15	.15
J54	D9	20c Blueberries	.15	.15
J55	D9	30c Raspberries	.15	.15
J56	D9	40c Bilberries	.20	.15
J57	D9	50c Blackberries	.20	.15
J58	D9	1fr Broom	.35	.30

J59 D9 2fr Rosehips .65 .35
J60 D9 3fr Nightshade 1.00 .60
J61 D9 4fr Nabiu 1.40 .75
J62 D9 5fr Strawberries 1.75 .95
Nos. J53-J62 (10) 6.00 3.70

NEWSPAPER STAMP

France No. P7 Overprinted

ANDORRE

1931 Unwmk. *Perf. 14x13½*
P1 A16 ½c on 1c gray .75 .75

ANGOLA

aŋ-'gō-lə

LOCATION — S.W. Africa between Zaire and Namibia.
GOVT. — Republic
AREA — 481,351 sq. mi.
POP. — 7,108,000 (1983 est.)
CAPITAL — Luanda

Angola was a Portuguese overseas territory until it became independent November 11, 1975, as the People's Republic of Angola.

1000 Reis = 1 Milreis
100 Centavos = 1 Escudo (1913, 1954)
100 Centavos = 1 Angolar (1932)
10 Lweys = 1 Kwanza (1977)

Catalogue values for unused stamps in this country are for Never Hinged items, beginning with Scott 328 in the regular postage section, Scott C26 in the airpost section, Scott J31 in the postage due section, and Scott RA7 in the postal tax section.

Watermark

Wmk. 232- Maltese Cross

Portuguese Crown — A1

Perf. 12½, 13½

1870-77 Typo. Unwmk.
1 A1 5r black 3.00 1.10
a. Perf. 13½ 9.00 3.25
2 A1 10r yellow 22.50 10.00
3 A1 20r bister 3.50 2.00
a. Perf. 13½ 65.00 50.00
4 A1 25r red 10.00 3.00
a. 25r rose 10.00 2.00
c. 25r rose, perf. 14 225.00 75.00
d. Perf. 13½ 20.00 8.00
5 A1 40r blue ('77) 150.00 75.00
6 A1 50r green 50.00 15.00
a. Perf. 13½ 225.00 65.00
7 A1 100r lilac 3.00 2.00
a. Perf. 12½ 8.00 4.00
8 A1 200r orange ('77) 3.00 2.00
a. Perf. 12½ 4.00 1.65
9 A1 300r choc ('77) 3.00 3.00
a. Perf. 12½ 10.00 4.75

1881-85
10 A1 10r green ('83) 4.00 1.50
a. Perf. 12½ 20.00 2.25
11 A1 20r carmine rose ('85) 9.00 5.00
12 A1 25r violet ('85) 4.00 2.00
a. Perf. 13½ 6.00 2.75
13 A1 40r buff ('82) 5.00 2.00
a. Perf. 12½ 6.00 2.00
15 A1 50r blue 14.00 1.65
a. Perf. 13½ 20.00 1.65
Nos. 10-15 (5) 36.00 12.15

Two types of numerals are found on #2, 11, 13, 15.

The cliche of 40r in plate of 20r error, was discovered before the stamps were issued. All copies were defaced by a blue pencil mark.

In perf. 12½, Nos. 1-4, 4a and 6, as well as 7a, were printed in 1870 on thicker paper and 1875 on normal paper. Stamps of the earlier printing sell for 2 to 5 times more than those of the 1875 printing.

Some reprints of the 1870-85 issues are on a smooth white chalky paper, ungummed and perf. 13½.

Other reprints of these issues are on thin ivory paper with shiny white gum and clear-cut perf. 13½.

King Luiz — A2

King Carlos — A3

1886 Embossed *Perf. 12½*
16 A2 5r black 3.50 3.25
a. Perf. 13½ 11.50 8.50
17 A2 10r green 3.50 3.00
a. Perf. 13½ 13.00 7.25
18 A2 20r rose 10.00 6.25
a. Perf. 13½ 12.50 6.50
19 A2 25r red violet 7.50 1.50
20 A2 40r chocolate 8.00 5.00
21 A2 50r blue 10.50 2.00
22 A2 100r yellow brn 14.00 6.00
23 A2 200r gray violet 18.00 9.00
24 A2 300r orange 20.00 11.00
Nos. 16-24 (9) 95.00 47.00

For surcharges see #61-69, 172-174, 208-210.

Reprints of 5r, 20r & 100r have cleancut perf. 13½.

Perf. 11½, 12½, 13½

1893-94 Typo.
25 A3 5r yellow 1.00 .85
26 A3 10r redsh violet 2.00 .90
27 A3 15r chocolate 2.75 1.25
28 A3 20r lavender 2.75 1.25
29 A3 25r green 1.25 1.00
a. Perf. 12½ 4.00 2.00
30 A3 50r light blue 3.25 1.25
a. Perf. 13½ 5.00 2.75
31 A3 75r carmine 6.00 3.50
a. Perf. 11½ 8.00 6.25
32 A3 80r lt green 6.75 3.50
33 A3 100r brown, *buff* 6.75 3.50
a. Perf. 11½ 50.00 32.50
34 A3 150r car, *rose* 12.00 9.00
35 A3 200r dk blue, *lt bl* 14.00 11.00
36 A3 300r dk blue, *sal* 14.00 11.00
Nos. 25-36 (12) 72.50 48.00

For surcharges see Nos. 70-81, 175-179, 213-216, 234.

No. P1 Surcharged in Blue

1894, Aug.
37 N1 25r on 2½r brown 80.00 22.50

King Carlos — A5

1898-1903 *Perf. 11½*
Name and Value in Black except 500r
38 A5 2½r gray .15 .15
39 A5 5r orange .15 .15
40 A5 10r yellow grn .15 .15
41 A5 15r violet brn 1.50 .70
42 A5 15r gray green ('03) .65 .50
43 A5 20r gray violet .25 .20
44 A5 25r sea green 1.00 .40
45 A5 25r car ('03) .50 .15
46 A5 50r blue 1.65 .35
47 A5 50r brown ('03) 3.00 2.00
48 A5 65r dull blue ('03) 9.00 7.00
49 A5 75r rose 4.50 1.65
50 A5 75r red violet ('03) 1.25 .90
51 A5 80r violet 5.25 1.75
52 A5 100r dk blue, *blue* .90 .65
53 A5 115r org brn, *pink* ('03) 8.00 6.00
54 A5 130r brn, *straw* ('03) 8.00 6.00
55 A5 150r brn, *straw* 8.00 5.00
56 A5 200r red vio, *pink* 2.25 1.00
57 A5 300r dk blue, *rose* 3.25 3.25
58 A5 400r dull bl, *straw* ('03) 2.50 2.25
59 A5 500r blk & red, *bl* ('01) 2.75 2.75
60 A5 700r vio, *yelsh* ('01) 14.00 10.00
Nos. 38-60 (23) 78.65 52.95

For surcharges and overprints see Nos. 83-102, 113-117, 159-171, 181-183, 217-218, 221-225.

Stamps of 1886-94 Surcharged in Black or Red

65 RÉIS

Two types of surcharge:
I - 3mm between numeral and REIS.
II - 4½mm spacing.

1902 *Perf. 12½*
61 A2 65r on 40r choc 4.50 3.50
62 A2 65r on 300r org, I 4.50 3.50
a. Type II 32.50 25.00
63 A2 115r on 10r green 3.75 3.25
a. Inverted surcharge
b. Perf. 13½ 18.00 17.00
64 A2 115r on 200r gray vio 3.50 2.75
65 A2 130r on 50r blue 5.75 4.75
66 A2 130r on 100r brown 4.00 3.00
67 A2 400r on 20r rose 60.00 30.00
a. Perf. 13½ 60.00 45.00
68 A2 400r on 25r violet 8.50 6.00
69 A2 400r on 5r black (R) 6.75 6.25
a. Double surcharge
Nos. 61-69 (9) 101.25 63.00

For surcharges see Nos. 172-174, 208-210.

Perf. 11½, 12½, 13½
70 A3 65r on 5r yel, I 4.00 2.75
a. Type II 10.00 10.00
71 A3 65r on 10r red vio, I 3.25 2.25
a. Type II 13.00 5.25
b. Perf. 11½, type I 8.75 5.25
c. Perf. 11½, type II 3.50 2.50
72 A3 65r on 20r lav 4.00 2.75
a. Type II 6.50 6.00
73 65r on 25r green 3.00 2.25
a. Perf. 11½ 9.25 7.25
74 A3 115r on 80r lt grn 5.25 4.00
75 A3 115r on 100r brn, *buff* 5.25 3.25
a. Perf. 13½ 9.25 6.50
76 A3 115r on 150r car, *rose* 8.00 5.25
a. Perf. 13½ 10.00 6.00
77 A3 130r on 15r choc 2.75 2.00
78 A3 130r on 75r carmine 3.00 2.25
a. Perf. 13½ 14.00 11.50
79 A3 130r on 300r dk bl, *sal* 8.25 6.00
80 A3 400r on 50r lt bl 3.25 2.75
81 A3 400r on 200r bl, *bl* 3.25 3.25
a. Perf. 13½ 21.00 8.75
82 N1 400r on 2½r brn 1.10 1.10
a. Type II 2.50 2.25
Nos. 70-82 (13) 54.35 39.85

For surcharges see #175-180, 211-216, 234-235.

Reprints of Nos. 65, 67, 68 and 69 have clean-cut perforation 13½.

Stamps of 1898 Overprinted — a

PROVISORIO

1902 *Perf. 11½*
83 A5 15r brown 1.00 .60
84 A5 25r sea green .85 .35
85 A5 50r blue 1.50 .85
86 A5 75r rose 2.75 2.00
Nos. 83-86 (4) 6.10 3.80

For surcharge see No. 116.

No. 48 Surcharged in Black

50 RÉIS

1905
87 A5 50r on 65r dull blue 2.75 1.25

For surcharge see No. 183.

Stamps of 1898-1903 Overprinted in Carmine or Green — b

REPUBLICA

1911
88 A5 2½r gray .15 .15
89 A5 5r orange yel .15 .15
90 A5 10r light green .22 .20
91 A5 15r gray green .25 .20
92 A5 20r gray violet .25 .20
93 A5 25r car (G) .25 .15
94 A5 50r brown 1.50 .90
95 A5 75r lilac 2.50 2.50
96 A5 100r dk blue, *bl* 2.50 2.50
97 A5 115r org brn, *pink* .90 .60
98 A5 130r brn, *straw* .90 .60
99 A5 200r red lil, *pnksh* .90 .60
100 A5 400r dull bl, *straw* 1.25 .65
101 A5 500r blk & red, *bl* 1.10 .65
102 A5 700r violet, *yelsh* 1.25 .70
Nos. 88-102 (15) 14.07 10.75

Inverted and double overprints of Nos. 88-102 were made intentionally.

For surcharges see Nos. 217-218, 221-222, 224.

King Manuel II — A6

Ceres — A7

Overprinted in Carmine or Green

1912 *Perf. 11½x12*
103 A6 2½r violet .22 *.32*
104 A6 5r black .25 *.40*
105 A6 10r gray green .35 .30
106 A6 20r carmine (G) .35 .30
107 A6 25r violet brown .35 .30
108 A6 50r dk blue .60 .50
109 A6 75r bister brown .65 *.65*
110 A6 100r brown, *lt green* 1.65 .70
111 A6 200r dk green, *salmon* 1.10 .70
112 A6 300r black, *azure* 1.10 .70
Nos. 103-112 (10) 6.62 4.87

For surcharges see Nos. 219-220, 226-227.

No. 91 Surcharged with New Values as

5

1912, June *Perf. 11½*
113 A5 2½r on 15r gray green 2.25 2.25
114 A5 5r on 15r gray green 1.75 1.50
115 A5 10r on 15r gray green 1.75 1.50
Nos. 113-115 (3) 5.75 5.25

Inverted and double surcharges of Nos. 113-115 were made intentionally.

Nos. 86 and 50 Surcharged "25" in Black and Overprinted in Violet — c

REPUBLICA

1912
116 A5 25r on 75r rose 65.00 50.00
117 A5 25r on 75r red violet 2.75 1.50
a. "REUPBLICA" 27.50 25.00
b. "25" omitted 27.50 25.00
c. "REPUBLICA" omitted 27.50 25.00

1914-26 Typo. *Perf. 12x11½, 15x14*
Name and Value in Black
118 A7 ¼c olive brown .15 *.15*
a. Inscriptions inverted 6.00
119 A7 ½c black .15 *.15*
120 A7 1c blue green .15 *.15*
121 A7 1c yel grn ('22) .15 .15
122 A7 1½c lilac brown .15 .15
123 A7 2c carmine .15 .15
124 A7 2c gray ('25) .30 *1.00*
125 A7 2½c lt violet .15 .15
126 A7 3c orange ('21) .15 *.60*
127 A7 4c dull rose ('21) .15 .15
128 A7 4½c gray ('21) .15 *.80*
130 A7 5c blue .15 .15
131 A7 6c lilac ('21) .15 .15
132 A7 7c ultra ('21) .15 .15
133 A7 7½c yellow brn .15 .15
134 A7 8c slate .15 .15
135 A7 10c orange brn .20 .15
136 A7 12c olive brn ('21) .35 .22
137 A7 12c dp green ('25) .20 .15
138 A7 15c plum .40 .15
139 A7 15c brown rose ('21) .15 .15
140 A7 20c yel green .25 .15
141 A7 24c ultra ('25) 1.10 .75
142 A7 25c choc ('25) 1.10 .75
143 A7 30c brown, *green* 1.25 *2.00*
144 A7 30c gray grn ('21) .65 .15
145 A7 40c brown, *pink* 3.00 2.00
146 A7 40c turq blue ('21) .60 .15
147 A7 50c orange, *sal* 6.00 4.25
148 A7 50c lt violet ('25) 1.00 .15
149 A7 60c dk blue ('21) .55 .15
150 A7 60c dp rose ('26) 40.00 40.00
151 A7 80c pink ('22) 1.25 .15

152 A7 1e green, *blue* 3.00 2.25
153 A7 1e rose ('22) 1.50 .15
154 A7 1e dp blue ('25) 3.00 3.00
155 A7 2e dk violet ('22) 1.25 .50
156 A7 5e buff ('25) 15.00 2.25
157 A7 10e pink ('25) 22.50 10.00
158 A7 20e pale turq ('25) 50.00 35.00
Nos. 118-158 (40) 156.85 108.97

Two kinds of paper, chalky-surfaced paper and ordinary, were used for Nos. 118-120, 122-123, 125, 130, 133-135, 138 and 140. Those on coated paper sell unused for 10 to 40 times the values listed; used for about 5 to 20 times.

All but #143, 145, 147 come perf 12x11½. All but #124, 137, 141-142, 146, 148, 151, 153-154, 156-158 come perf 15x14.

For surcharges see Nos. 228-229, 236-239.

Stamps of 1898-1903 Overprinted type "c" in Red or Green

On Stamps of 1898-1903

1914 *Perf. 11½, 12*
159 A5 10r yel green (R) 3.25 2.50
160 A5 15r gray green (R) 3.25 2.50
161 A5 20r gray violet (G) .80 .80
163 A5 75r red violet (G) .80 .80
164 A5 100r blue, *blue* (R) 1.25 1.25
165 A5 115r org brn, *pink* (R) *60.00*
167 A5 200r red vio, *pnksh* (G) .90 .50
169 A5 400r dl bl, *straw* (R) 40.00 30.00
170 A5 500r blk & red, *bl* (R) 5.00 3.00
171 A5 700r vio, *yelsh* (G) 15.00 12.00

Inverted and double overprints were made intentionally. No. 165 was not regularly issued. Red overprints on the 20r, 75r, 200r were not regularly issued. The 130r was not regularly issued without surcharge (No. 225).

On Nos. 63-65, 74-76, 78-79, 82

Perf. 11½, 12½, 13½
172 A2 115r on 10r (R) 30.00 20.00
a. Perf. 13½ 30.00 20.00
173 A2 115r on 200r (R) 35.00 20.00
174 A2 130r on 50r (R) 35.00 20.00
175 A3 115r on 80r (R) 100.00 75.00
176 A3 115r on 100r (R) 250.00 150.00
177 A3 115r on 150r (G) 165.00 125.00
178 A3 130r on 75r (G) 1.75 1.65
179 A3 130r on 300r (R) 4.00 3.25
a. Perf. 12½ 7.00 4.50
180 N1 400r on 2½r (R) .40 .40
a. Perf. 11½ 1.65 1.25
Nos. 172-180 (9) 621.15 415.30

Overprinted PROVISORIO

On Stamps of 1902

Perf. 11½, 12
181 A5 50r blue (R) .90 .60
182 A5 75r rose (G) 2.75 2.00

On No. 87

183 A5 50r on 65r dull blue (R) 2.50 2.50
Nos. 181-183 (3) 6.15 5.10

Inverted and double surcharges of Nos. 181-183 were made intentionally.

Common Design Types pictured following the introduction.

Vasco da Gama Issue of Various Portuguese Colonies

Common Design Types CD20-CD27 Surcharged

REPUBLICA
ANGOLA
¼ C.

On Stamps of Macao

1913 *Perf. 12½ to 16*
184 ¼c on ½a blue grn 4.00 4.00
185 ½c on 1a red 3.00 3.00
186 1c on 2a red violet 3.00 3.00
187 2½c on 4a yel green 2.00 2.00
188 5c on 8a dk blue 2.00 2.00
189 7½c on 12a vio brn 5.50 5.50
190 10c on 16a bister brn 4.00 4.00
191 15c on 24a bister 4.00 4.00
Nos. 184-191 (8) 27.50 27.50

On Stamps of Portuguese Africa

Perf. 14 to 15
192 ¼c on 2½r blue grn .75 .75
193 ½c on 5r red .75 .75
194 1c on 10r red violet .75 .75
195 2½c on 25r yel grn .75 .75
196 5c on 50r dk blue .75 .75
197 7½c on 75r vio brn 2.50 2.50
198 10c on 100r bister brn 1.25 1.25
199 15c on 150r bister 1.75 1.75
Nos. 192-199 (8) 9.25 9.25

On Stamps of Timor

200 ¼c on ½a blue grn 2.00 2.00
201 ½c on 1a red 2.00 2.00
202 1c on 2a red vio 2.00 2.00
203 2½c on 4a yel grn 2.00 2.00
204 5c on 8a dk blue 2.00 2.00
205 7½c on 12a vio brn 3.00 3.00
206 10c on 16a bis brn 2.00 2.00
207 15c on 24a bister 2.00 2.00
Nos. 200-207 (8) 17.00 17.00
Nos. 184-207 (24) 53.75 53.75

Provisional Issue of 1902 Overprinted in Carmine

REPUBLICA

1915 *Perf. 11½, 12½, 13½*
208 A2 115r on 10r green 1.00 *2.00*
209 A2 115r on 200r gray vio .90 *2.00*
210 A2 130r on 100r brown .70 *2.00*
211 A3 115r on 80r lt green 1.10 *2.00*
212 A3 115r on 100r brn, *buff* .90 *2.00*
a. Perf. 11½ 17.00 *17.00*
213 A3 115r on 150r car, *rose* 1.75 *2.00*
214 A3 130r on 15r choc .65 *2.00*
a. Perf. 12½ 7.00 7.00
215 A3 130r on 75r carmine 1.50 *1.75*
216 A3 130r on 300r dk bl, *sal* 1.10 *1.75*
Nos. 208-216 (9) 9.60 *17.50*

Stamps of 1911-14 Surcharged in Black:

½ C.

½ C. d e

On Stamps of 1911

1919 *Perf. 11½*
217 A5 (d) ½c on 75r red lilac 1.50 *2.00*
218 A5 (d) 2½c on 100r blue, *grysh* 1.75 *2.00*

On Stamps of 1912

Perf. 11½x12
219 A6 (e) ½c on 75r bis brn .65 *.65*
220 A6 (e) 2½c on 100r brn, *lt grn* .85 .40

On Stamps of 1914

221 A5 (d) ½c on 75r red lil .65 .40
222 A5 (d) 2½c on 100r bl, *grysh* .70 .60
Nos. 217-222 (6) 6.10 *6.05*

Inverted and double surcharges were made for sale to collectors.

Nos. 163, 98 and Type of 1914 Surcharged with New Values and Bars in Black

1921
223 A5 (c) 00.5c on 75r *350.00 350.00*
224 A5 (b) 4c on 130r (#98) .70 *.70*
225 A5 (c) 4c on 130r brn, *straw* 2.75 2.50

Nos. 109 and 108 Surcharged with New Values and Bars in Black

226 A6 00.5c on 75c .85 .85
227 A6 1c on 50r .75 .65

Nos. 133 and 138 Surcharged with New Values and Bars in Black

228 A7 00.5c on 7½c .70 .60
229 A7 04c on 15c 1.10 1.10
Nos. 224-229 (6) 6.85 6.40

The 04c surcharge exists on the 15c brown rose, perf 12x11½, No. 139.

Nos. 81-82 Surcharged

República

40 C.

1925 *Perf. 12½*
234 A3 40c on 400r on 200r bl, *bl* .80 .65
a. Perf. 13½ 3.25 2.25
235 N1 40c on 400c on 2½r brn .60 .60
a. Perf. 13½ .60 .60

Nos. 150-151, 154-155 Surcharged

70 C.

1931 *Perf. 11½*
236 A7 50c on 60c deep rose 1.10 .80
237 A7 70c on 80c pink 2.25 1.00
238 A7 70c on 1e deep blue 2.00 1.10
239 A7 1.40e on 2e dark violet 2.00 1.10
Nos. 236-239 (4) 7.35 4.00

Ceres — A14

Perf. 12x11½

1932-46 **Typo.** **Wmk. 232**
243 A14 1c bister brn .15 .15
244 A14 5c dk brown .15 .15
245 A14 10c dp violet .15 .15
246 A14 15c black .15 .15
247 A14 20c gray .25 .15
248 A14 30c myrtle grn .25 .15
249 A14 35c yel grn ('46) 4.50 2.00
250 A14 40c dp orange .25 .15
251 A14 45c lt blue .85 .65
252 A14 50c lt brown .15 .15
253 A14 60c olive grn .30 .15
254 A14 70c orange brn .65 .15
255 A14 80c emerald .25 .15
256 A14 85c rose 2.00 2.00
257 A14 1a claret .65 .18
258 A14 1.40a dk blue 4.50 1.10
258A A14 1.75a dk blue ('46) 6.00 1.10
259 A14 2a dull vio 2.25 .35
260 A14 5a pale yel grn 3.00 .50
261 A14 10a olive bis 10.00 .90
262 A14 20a orange 17.50 2.00
Nos. 243-262 (21) 53.95 12.43

For surcharges see Nos. 263-267, 271-273, 294A-300, J31-J36.

Surcharged with New Value and Bars

5½mm between bars and new value.

1934
263 A14 10c on 45c lt bl 1.25 .70
264 A14 20c on 85c rose 1.10 .70
265 A14 30c on 1.40a dk bl 1.10 .70
266 A14 70c on 2a dl vio 1.50 1.10
267 A14 80c on 5a pale yel grn 2.25 1.00
Nos. 263-267 (5) 7.20 4.20

See Nos. 294A-300.

Nos. J26, J30 Surcharged in Black

CORREIOS
5
CENTAVOS

1935 **Unwmk.** *Perf. 11½*
268 D2 5c on 6c lt brown .90 .60
269 D2 30c on 50c gray .90 .60
270 D2 40c on 50c gray .90 .60
Nos. 268-270 (3) 2.70 1.80

No. 255 Surcharged in Black

0,15 Cent.

1938 **Wmk. 232** *Perf. 12x11½*
271 A14 5c on 80c emerald .40 *1.00*
272 A14 10c on 80c emerald .50 *1.75*
273 A14 15c on 80c emerald .65 *2.50*
Nos. 271-273 (3) 1.55 *5.25*

Vasco da Gama Issue

Common Design Types

Engr.; Name & Value Typo. in Black

Perf. 13½x13

1938, July 26 **Unwmk.**
274 CD34 1c gray green .15 .15
275 CD34 5c orange brn .15 .15
276 CD34 10c dk carmine .15 .15
277 CD34 15c dk violet brn .15 .15
278 CD34 20c slate .20 .15
279 CD35 30c rose violet .25 .15
280 CD35 35c brt green .35 .20
281 CD35 40c brown .25 .15
282 CD35 50c brt red vio .25 .15
283 CD36 60c gray black .35 .15
284 CD36 70c brown vio .30 .15
285 CD36 80c orange .30 .15
286 CD36 1a red .30 .15
287 CD37 1.75a blue .85 .30
288 CD37 2a brown car 1.50 .30
289 CD37 5a olive grn 3.00 .30
290 CD38 10a blue vio 6.50 .60
291 CD38 20a red brown 15.00 1.10
Nos. 274-291 (18) 30.00 4.60

For surcharges see Nos. 301-304.

Marble Column and Portuguese Arms with Cross — A20

1938, July 29 *Perf. 12½*
292 A20 80c blue green 1.00 .95
293 A20 1.75a deep blue 5.00 1.00
294 A20 20a dk red brown 14.00 11.00
Nos. 292-294 (3) 20.00 12.95

Visit of the President of Portugal to this colony in 1938.

Stamps of 1932 Surcharged with New Value and Bars

8mm between bars and new value.

1941-45 **Wmk. 232** *Perf. 12x11½*
294A A14 5c on 80c emer ('45) .22 .20
295 A14 10c on 45c lt blue .65 .55
296 A14 15c on 45c lt blue 1.00 .70
297 A14 20c on 85c rose .65 .55
298 A14 35c on 85c rose .65 .55
299 A14 50c on 1.40a dk blue .65 .55
300 A14 60c on 1a claret 5.75 4.00
Nos. 294A-300 (7) 9.57 7.10

Nos. 285 to 287 Surcharged with New Values and Bars in Black or Red

1945 **Unwmk.** *Perf. 13½x13*
301 CD36 5c on 80c org .28 .20
302 CD36 50c on 1a red .60 .20
303 CD37 50c on 1.75a bl (R) .42 .20
304 CD37 50c on 1.75a bl .60 .20
Nos. 301-304 (4) 1.90 .80

Sao Miguel Fort, Luanda — A21

John IV — A22

Designs: 10c, Our Lady of Nazareth Church, Luanda. 50c, Salvador Correia de Sa e Bene vides. 1a, Surrender of Luanda. 1.75a, Diogo Cao. 2a, Manuel Cerveira Pereira. 5a, Stone Cliffs, Yelala. 10a, Paulo Dias de Novais. 20a, Massangano Fort.

Perf. 14½

1948, May **Unwmk.** **Litho.**
305 A21 5c dk violet .15 .15
306 A21 10c dk brown .25 .20
307 A22 30c blue grn .15 .15
308 A22 50c vio brown .15 .15
309 A21 1a carmine .32 .15
310 A22 1.75a slate blue .65 .20
311 A22 2a green .65 .20
312 A21 5a gray black 1.00 .32
313 A22 10a rose lilac 2.00 .35
314 A21 20a gray blue 5.00 1.10
a. Sheet of 10, #305-314 40.00 40.00
Nos. 305-314 (10) 10.32 2.97

300th anniv. of the restoration of Angola to Portugal. No. 314a sold for 42.50a.

Lady of Fatima Issue

Common Design Type

1948, Dec.
315 CD40 50c carmine .65 .50
316 CD40 3a ultra 2.00 1.00
317 CD40 6a red orange 7.00 2.50
318 CD40 9a dp claret 17.00 3.00
Nos. 315-318 (4) 26.65 7.00

Our Lady of the Rosary at Fatima, Portugal.

Chiumbe River — A24

Black Rocks — A25

ANGOLA

Designs: 50c, View of Luanda. 2.50a, Sa da Bandeira. 3.50a, Mocamedes. 15a, Cubal River. 50a, Duke of Bragança Falls.

1949		Unwmk.	Perf. 13½	
319	A24	20c dk slate blue	.15	.15
320	A25	40c black brown	.15	.15
321	A24	50c rose brown	.15	.15
322	A24	2.50a blue violet	1.10	.25
323	A24	3.50a slate gray	1.10	.25
323A	A24	15a dk green	8.25	1.50
324	A24	50a dp green	22.50	3.75
		Nos. 319-324 (7)	33.40	6.20

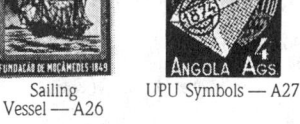

Sailing Vessel — A26

UPU Symbols — A27

1949, Aug.			Perf. 14	
325	A26	1a chocolate	4.00	.32
326	A26	4a dk Prus green	10.00	.85

Centenary of founding of Mocamedes.

1949, Oct.				
327	A27	4a dk grn & lt grn	3.50	1.50

75th anniv. of the UPU.

Catalogue values for unused stamps in this section, from this point to the end of the section, are for Never Hinged items.

Stamp of 1870 — A28

1950, Apr. 2			Perf. 11½x12	
328	A28	50c yellow green	.80	.25
329	A28	1a fawn	.80	.25
330	A28	4a black	3.25	.70
a.		Sheet of 3, #328-330	7.50	7.50
		Nos. 328-330 (3)	4.85	1.20

Angola's first philatelic exhibition, marking the 80th anniversary of Angola's first stamps.

No. 330a contains Nos. 328, 329 (inverted), 330, perf. 11½ and sold for 6.50a. All copies carry an oval exhibition cancellation in the margin but the stamps were valid for postage.

Holy Year Issue
Common Design Types

1950, May			Perf. 13x13½	
331	CD41	1a dull rose vio	.32	.15
332	CD42	4a black	3.00	.32

Dark Chanting Goshawk A31

European Bee Eater A32

10c, Racquet-tailed roller. 15c, Bateleur eagle. 50c, Giant kingfisher. 1a, Yellow-fronted barbet. 1.50a, Openbill (stork). 2a, Southern ground hornbill. 2.50a, African skimmer. 3a, Shikra. 3.50a, Denham's bustard. 4a, African golden oriole. 4.50a, Long-tailed shrike. 5a, Red-shouldered glossy starling. 6a, Sharp-tailed glossy starling. 7a, Red-shouldered widow bird. 10a, Half-colored kingfisher. 12.50a, White-crowned shrike. 15a, White-winged babbling starling. 20a, Yellow-billed hornbill. 25a, Amethyst starling. 30a, Orange-breasted shrike. 40a, Secretary bird. 50a, Rosy-faced lovebird.

Photogravure and Lithographed
1951		Unwmk.	Perf. 11½	
Birds in Natural Colors				
333	A31	5c lt blue	.20	.50
334	A31	10c aqua	.20	.15
335	A32	15c salmon pink	.30	1.00
336	A32	20c pale yellow	.50	.22
337	A31	50c gray blue	.30	.15
338	A31	1a lilac	.30	.15
339	A31	1.50a gray buff	.40	.15
340	A31	2a cream	.40	.15
341	A32	2.50a gray	.40	.15
342	A32	3a lemon yel	.40	.18
343	A31	3.50a lt gray	.40	.18
344	A31	4a rose buff	1.25	.18
345	A32	4.50a rose lilac	1.25	.20
346	A31	5a green	6.25	.20
347	A31	6a blue	6.25	.55
348	A31	7a orange	6.25	.75
349	A31	10a lilac rose	40.00	1.10
350	A32	12.50a slate gray	8.50	1.75
351	A31	15a pale olive	8.50	1.75
352	A31	20a pale bis brn	45.00	4.50
353	A31	25a lilac rose	25.00	2.50
354	A32	30a pale salmon	25.00	3.00
355	A31	40a yellow	50.00	3.75
356	A31	50a turquoise	110.00	14.00
		Nos. 333-356 (24)	337.05	37.21

Holy Year Extension Issue
Common Design Type

1951, Oct.		Litho.	Perf. 14	
357	CD43	4a orange	1.25	.50

Sheets contain alternate vertical rows of stamps and labels bearing quotations from Pope Pius XII or the Patriarch Cardinal of Lisbon.

Medical Congress Issue
Common Design Type

Design: Medical examination

1952, June			Perf. 13½	
358	CD44	1a vio blue & brn blk	.40	.20

Head of Christ — A35

1952, Oct.		Unwmk.	Perf. 13	
359	A35	10c dk blue & buff	.15	.15
360	A35	50c dk ol grn & ol gray	.20	.15
361	A35	2a rose vio & cream	1.25	.15
		Nos. 359-361 (3)	1.60	.45

Exhibition of Sacred Missionary Art, Lisbon, 1951.

Leopard A36

Sable Antelope A37

Animals: 20c, Elephant. 30c, Eland. 40c, African crocodile. 50c, Impala. 1a, Mountain zebra. 1.50a, Sitatunga. 2a, Black rhinoceros. 2.50a, Gemsbok. 2.50a, Lion. 3a, Buffalo. 3.50a, Springbok. 4a, Brindled gnu. 5a, Hartebeest. 7a, Wart hog. 10a, Defassa waterbuck. 12.50a, Hippopotamus. 15a, Greater kudu. 20a, Giraffe.

1953, Aug. 15			Perf. 12½	
362	A36	5c multicolored	.15	.15
363	A37	10c multicolored	.15	.15
364	A37	20c multicolored	.15	.15
365	A37	30c multicolored	.15	.15
366	A36	40c multicolored	.15	.15
367	A37	50c multicolored	.15	.15
368	A37	1a multicolored	.20	.15
369	A37	1.50a multicolored	.15	.15
370	A36	2a multicolored	.18	.15
371	A37	2.30a multicolored	.24	.15
372	A37	2.50a multicolored	.30	.15
373	A36	3a multicolored	.30	.15
374	A37	3.50a multicolored	.18	.15
375	A37	4a multicolored	6.00	.24
376	A37	5a multicolored	.32	.15
377	A37	7a multicolored	.75	.24
378	A37	10a multicolored	1.25	.20
379	A37	12.50a multicolored	4.00	1.65
380	A37	15a multicolored	4.00	1.25
381	A37	20a multicolored	5.00	.35
		Nos. 362-381 (20)	23.77	6.03

Stamp of Portugal and Arms of Colonies — A38

1953, Nov.		Photo.	Perf. 13	
Stamp and Arms Multicolored				
382	A38	50c gray & dark gray	.55	.32

Cent. of Portugal's 1st postage stamps.

Map and Plane — A39

Typographed and Lithographed
1954, May 27			Perf. 13½	
383	A39	35c multicolored	.15	.15
384	A39	4.50e multicolored	.70	.30

Visit of Pres. Francisco H C. Lopes.

Sao Paulo Issue
Common Design Type

1954			Litho.	
385	CD46	1e bister & gray	.32	.20

Map of Angola — A41

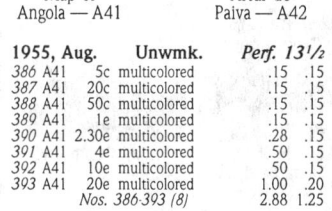

Artur de Paiva — A42

1955, Aug.		Unwmk.	Perf. 13½	
386	A41	5c multicolored	.15	.15
387	A41	20c multicolored	.15	.15
388	A41	50c multicolored	.15	.15
389	A41	1e multicolored	.15	.15
390	A41	2.30e multicolored	.28	.15
391	A41	4e multicolored	.50	.15
392	A41	10e multicolored	.50	.15
393	A41	20e multicolored	1.00	.20
		Nos. 386-393 (8)	2.88	1.25

For overprints see Nos. 593, 598, 604.

1956, Oct. 9			Perf. 13½x12½	
394	A42	1e blk, dk bl & ocher	.20	.15

Cent. of the birth of Col. Artur de Paiva.

Man of Malange — A43

Jose M. Antunes — A44

Various Costumes in Multicolor; Inscriptions in Black Brown

1957, Jan. 1		Photo.	Perf. 11½	
Granite Paper				
395	A43	5c gray	.15	.15
396	A43	10c orange yel	.15	.15
397	A43	15c lt blue grn	.15	.15
398	A43	20c pale rose vio	.15	.15
399	A43	30c brt rose	.15	.15
400	A43	40c blue gray	.15	.15
401	A43	50c pale olive	.15	.15
402	A43	80c lt violet	.15	.15
403	A43	1.50e buff	1.00	.15
404	A43	2.50e lt yel grn	1.00	.15
405	A43	4e salmon	.50	.15
406	A43	10e salmon pink	1.00	.25
		Nos. 395-406 (12)	4.70	1.90

1957, Apr.			Perf. 13½	
407	A44	1e aqua & brown	.65	.20

Birth cent. of Father Jose Maria Antunes.

Fair Emblem, Globe and Arms — A45

1958, July		Litho.	Perf. 12x11½	
408	A45	1.50e multicolored	.25	.15

World's Fair, Brussels, Apr. 17-Oct. 19.

Tropical Medicine Congress Issue
Common Design Type

Design: Securidaca longipedunculata.

1958, Dec. 15			Perf. 13½	
409	CD47	2.50e multicolored	1.10	.70

Medicine Man — A47

Welwitschia Mirabilis — A48

Designs: 1.50e, Early government doctor. 2.50e, Modern medical team.

1958, Dec. 18			Perf. 11½x12	
410	A47	1e blue blk & brown	.20	.15
411	A47	1.50e gray, blk & brown	.50	.20
412	A47	2.50e multicolored	.75	.40
		Nos. 410-412 (3)	1.45	.75

75th anniversary of the Maria Pia Hospital, Luanda.

1959, Oct. 1		Litho.	Perf. 14½	
Various Views of Plant and Various Frames				
413	A48	1.50e lt brown, grn & blk	.55	.45
414	A48	2.50e multicolored	.85	.50
415	A48	5e multicolored	1.10	.75
416	A48	10e multicolored	2.75	1.00
		Nos. 413-416 (4)	5.25	2.70

Centenary of discovery of Welwitschia mirabilis, desert plant.

Map of West Africa, c. 1540, by Jorge Reinel — A49

1960, June 25			Perf. 13½	
417	A49	2.50e multicolored	.20	.15

500th anniv. of the death of Prince Henry the Navigator.

Distributing Medicines — A50

Girl of Angola — A51

1960, Oct.		Litho.	Perf. 14½	
418	A50	2.50e multicolored	.30	.15

10th anniv. of the Commission for Technical Cooperation in Africa South of the Sahara (C.C.T.A).

1961, Nov. 30		Unwmk.	Perf. 13	

Various portraits.

419	A51	10c multicolored	.15	.15
420	A51	15c multicolored	.15	.15
421	A51	30c multicolored	.15	.15
422	A51	40c multicolored	.15	.15
423	A51	60c multicolored	.15	.15
424	A51	1.50e multicolored	.15	.15
425	A51	2e multicolored	.60	.15
426	A51	2.50e multicolored	.85	.15
427	A51	3e multicolored	2.00	.20
428	A51	4e multicolored	.90	.20
429	A51	5e multicolored	.70	.20
430	A51	7.50e multicolored	.90	.45
431	A51	10e multicolored	.70	.25
432	A51	15e multicolored	.65	.40

ANGOLA

432A	A51	25e multicolored	1.90	.65
432B	A51	50e multicolored	3.25	1.00
		Nos. 419-432B (16)	13.35	4.55

Sports Issue
Common Design Type

Sports: 50c, Flying. 1e, Rowing. 1.50e, Water polo. 2.50e, Hammer throwing. 4.50e, High jump. 15e, Weight lifting.

1962, Jan. 18   *Perf. 13½*
Multicolored Design

433	CD48	50c lt blue	.15	.15
434	CD48	1e olive bister	.70	.15
435	CD48	1.50e salmon	.32	.15
436	CD48	2.50e lt green	.40	.15
437	CD48	4.50e pale blue	.32	.25
438	CD48	15e yellow	1.50	.65
		Nos. 433-438 (6)	3.39	1.50

For overprint see No. 608.

Anti-Malaria Issue
Common Design Type

Design: Anopheles funestus.

1962, April   Litho.   *Perf. 13½*

439	CD49	2.50e multicolored	.60	.32

Gen. Norton de Matos — A54

Locusts — A56

1962, Aug. 8   Unwmk.   *Perf. 14½*

440	A54	2.50e multicolored	.30	.15

50th anniv. of the founding of Nova Lisboa.

1963, June 2   Litho.   *Perf. 14*

447	A56	2.50e multicolored	.40	.20

15th anniv. of the Intl. Anti-Locust Organ.

Arms of Luanda A57

Vila de Santo Antonio do Zaire — A58

Coats of Arms (Provinces and Cities): 10c, Massangano. 15c, Sanza-Pombo. 25c, Ambriz. 30c, Muxima. 40c, Ambrizete. 50c, Carmona. 60c, Catete. 70c, Quibaxe. No. 458, Maquelo do Zombo. 1e, Salazar. 1.20e, Bembe. No. 461, Malanje. No. 462, Caxito. 1.80e, Dondo. 2e, Henrique de Carvalho. No. 465, Moçamedes. No. 466, Damba. 3e, Novo Redondo. 3.50e, S. Salvador do Congo. 4e, Cuimba. 5e, Luso. 6.50e, Negage. 7e, Quitexe. 7.50e, S. Filipe de Benguela. 8e, Mucaba. 9e, 31 de Janeiro. 10e, Lobito. 11e, Nova Caipemba. 12.50e, Gabela. 14e, Songo. 15e Sá da Bandeira. 17e, Quimbele. 17.50e, Silva Porto. 20e, Nova Lisboa. 22.50e, Cabinda. 25e, Noqui. 30e, Serpa Pinto. 35e, Santa Cruz. 50e, General Freire.

1963   *Perf. 13½*
Arms in Original Colors; Red and Violet Blue Inscriptions

448	A57	5c tan	.15	.15
449	A57	10c lt blue	.15	.15
450	A58	15c salmon	.15	.15
451	A58	20c olive	.15	.15
452	A58	25c lt blue	.15	.15
453	A57	30c buff	.15	.15
454	A58	40c gray	.15	.15
455	A57	50c lt green	.15	.15
456	A58	60c brt yellow	.15	.15
457	A58	70c dull rose	.15	.15
458	A57	1e pale lilac	.30	.15
459	A58	1e dull yellow	.20	.15
460	A58	1.20e rose	.15	.15
461	A57	1.50e pale salmon	.60	.15
462	A58	1.50e lt green	.40	.15
463	A58	1.80e yel olive	.22	.15
464	A57	2e lt yel green	.30	.15
465	A57	2.50e lt gray	1.50	.15
466	A58	2.50e dull blue	1.25	.15
467	A57	3e yel olive	.42	.15
468	A57	3.50e gray	.50	.15
469	A58	4e citron	.35	.15
470	A57	5e citron	.40	.25
471	A58	6.50e tan	.40	.25
472	A58	7e rose lilac	.42	.25
473	A57	7.50e pale lilac	.55	.30
474	A58	8e lt aqua	.45	.30
475	A58	9e yellow	.60	.30
476	A57	10e dp salmon	.70	.35
477	A58	11e dull yel grn	.70	.55
478	A57	12.50e pale blue	.90	.45
479	A58	14e lt gray	.90	.45
480	A57	15e lt blue	1.00	.45
481	A58	17e pale blue	1.10	.70
482	A57	17.50e dull yellow	1.50	1.00
483	A57	20e lt aqua	1.50	.70
484	A57	22.50e gray	1.50	1.00
485	A58	25e citron	1.50	1.00
486	A57	30e yellow	2.00	1.35
487	A58	35e grysh blue	2.00	1.50
488	A58	50e dp yellow	3.00	1.25
		Nos. 448-488 (41)	28.81	15.27

Pres. Américo Rodrigues Thomaz — A59

1963, Sept. 16   Litho.

489	A59	2.50e multicolored	.50	.30

Visit of the President of Portugal.

Airline Anniversary Issue
Common Design Type

1963, Oct. 5   Unwmk.   *Perf. 14½*

490	CD50	1e lt blue & multi	.25	.15

Cathedral of Sá da Bandeira A61

Malange Cathedral A62

Churches: 20c, Landana. 30c, Luanda Cathedral. 40c, Gabela. 50c, St. Martin's Chapel, Baia dos Tigres. 1.50e, St. Peter, Chibia. 2e, Church of Our Lady, Benguela. 2.50e, Church of Jesus, Luanda. 3e, Camabatela. 3.50e, Mission, Cabinda. 4e, Vila Folgares. 4.50e, Church of Our Lady, Lobito. 5e, Church of Cabinda. 7.50e, Cacuso Church, Malange. 10e, Lubango Mission. 12.50e, Huila Mission. 15e, Church of Our Lady, Luanda Island.

1963, Nov. 1   Litho.
Multicolored Design and Inscription

491	A61	10c gray blue	.15	.15
492	A61	20c pink	.15	.15
493	A61	30c lt blue	.15	.15
494	A61	40c tan	.15	.15
495	A61	50c lt green	.15	.15
496	A62	1e buff	.15	.15
497	A61	1.50e lt vio blue	.15	.15
498	A62	2e pale rose	.15	.15
499	A61	2.50e gray	.15	.15
500	A62	3e buff	.18	.15
501	A61	3.50e olive	.22	.15
502	A62	4e buff	.22	.20
503	A62	4.50e pale blue	.40	.22
504	A61	5e tan	.50	.22
505	A62	7.50e gray	.60	.32
506	A61	10e dull yellow	.75	.40
507	A62	12.50e bister	1.00	.80
508	A62	15e pale gray vio	2.50	.70
		Nos. 491-508 (18)	7.72	4.51

National Overseas Bank Issue
Common Design Type

Design: Antonio Teixeira de Sousa.

1964, May 16   *Perf. 13½*

509	CD51	2.50e multicolored	.40	.22

Commerce Building and Arms of Chamber of Commerce A64

1964, Nov.   Litho.   *Perf. 12*

510	A64	1e multicolored	.15	.15

Luanda Chamber of Commerce centenary.

ITU Issue
Common Design Type

1965, May 17   Unwmk.   *Perf. 14½*

511	CD52	2.50e gray & multi	.70	.25

Plane over Luanda Airport — A65

Harquebusier, 1539 — A66

1965, Dec. 3   Litho.   *Perf. 13*

512	A65	2.50e multicolored	.22	.15

25th anniv. of DTA, Direccao dos Transportes Aereos.

1966, Feb. 25   Litho.   *Perf. 14½*

50c, Harquebusier, 1539. 1e, Harquebusier, 1640. 1.50e, Infantry officer, 1777. 2e, Standard bearer, infantry, 1777. 2.50e, Infantry soldier, 1777. 3e, Cavalry officer, 1783. 4e, Cavalry soldier, 1783. 4.50e, Infantry officer, 1807. 5e, Infantry soldier, 1807. 6e, Cavalry officer, 1807. 8e, Cavalry soldier, 1807. 9e, Infantry soldier, 1873.

513	A66	50c multicolored	.15	.15
514	A66	1e multicolored	.15	.15
515	A66	1.50e multicolored	.15	.15
516	A66	2e multicolored	.15	.15
517	A66	2.50e multicolored	.20	.15
518	A66	3e multicolored	.20	.15
519	A66	4e multicolored	.40	.25
520	A66	4.50e multicolored	.40	.25
521	A66	5e multicolored	.60	.18
522	A66	6e multicolored	.75	.50
523	A66	8e multicolored	1.25	.85
524	A66	9e multicolored	1.50	1.00
		Nos. 513-524 (12)	5.90	3.93

National Revolution Issue
Common Design Type

Design: St. Paul's Hospital and Commercial and Industrial School.

1966, May 28   Litho.   *Perf. 12*

525	CD53	1e multicolored	.20	.15

Emblem of Holy Ghost Society — A68

1966   Litho.   *Perf. 13*

526	A68	1e blue & multi	.15	.15

Centenary of the Holy Ghost Society.

Navy Club Issue
Common Design Type

Designs: 1e, Mendes Barata and cruiser Dom Carlos I. 2.50e, Capt. Augusto de Castilho and corvette Mindelo.

1967, Jan. 31   Litho.   *Perf. 13*

527	CD54	1e multicolored	.38	.15
528	CD54	2.50e multicolored	.65	.18

Fatima Basilica — A70

Angola Map, Manuel Cerveira Pereira — A71

1967, May 13   Litho.   *Perf. 12½x13*

529	A70	50c multicolored	.15	.15

50th anniv. of the apparition of the Virgin Mary to 3 shepherd children at Fatima.

1967, Aug. 15   Litho.   *Perf. 12½x13*

530	A71	50c multicolored	.15	.15

350th anniv. of the founding of Benguela.

Administration Building, Carmona — A72

1967   Litho.   *Perf. 12*

531	A72	1e multicolored	.15	.15

50th anniv. of the founding of Carmona.

Military Order of Valor — A73

Our Lady of Hope — A74

Designs: 50c, Ribbon of the Three Orders. 1.50e, Military Order of Avis. 2e, Military Order of Christ. 2.50e, Military Order of St. John of Espada. 3e, Order of the Empire. 4e, Order of Prince Henry. 5e, Order of Benemerencia. 10e, Order of Public Instruction. 20e, Order for Industrial and Agricultural Merit.

1967, Oct. 31   *Perf. 14*

532	A73	50c lt gray & multi	.15	.15
533	A73	1e lt green & multi	.15	.15
534	A73	1.50e yellow & multi	.15	.15
535	A73	2e multicolored	.15	.15
536	A73	2.50e multicolored	.15	.15
537	A73	3e lt olive & multi	.18	.15
538	A73	4e gray & multi	.20	.15
539	A73	5e multicolored	.25	.15
540	A73	10e lilac & multi	.40	.25
541	A73	20e lt blue & multi	1.00	.52
		Nos. 532-541 (10)	2.78	1.97

1968, Apr. 22   Litho.   *Perf. 14*

Designs: 1e, Belmonte Castle, horiz. 1.50e, St. Jerome's Convent. 2.50e, Cabral's Armada.

542	A74	50c yellow & multi	.15	.15
543	A74	1e gray & multi	.25	.15
544	A74	1.50e lt blue & multi	.40	.15
545	A74	2.50e buff & multi	.60	.15
		Nos. 542-545 (4)	1.40	.60

500th anniv. of the birth of Pedro Alvares Cabral, navigator who took possession of Brazil for Portugal.

Francisco Inocencio de Souza Coutinho — A75

1969, Jan. 7   Litho.   *Perf. 14*

546	A75	2e multicolored	.25	.20

Founding of Novo Redondo, 200th anniv.

ANGOLA

Admiral Coutinho Issue
Common Design Type
Design: Adm. Gago Coutinho and his first ship.

1969, Feb. 17   Litho.   *Perf. 14*
547 CD55 2.50e multicolored   .30 .15

Compass Rose A77

Portal of St. Jeronimo's Monastery A79

1969, Aug. 29   Litho.   *Perf. 14*
548 A77 1e multicolored   .15 .15

500th anniv. of the birth of Vasco da Gama (1469-1524), navigator.

Administration Reform Issue
Common Design Type

1969, Sept. 25   Litho.   *Perf. 14*
549 CD56 1.50e multicolored   .15 .15

1969, Dec. 1   Litho.   *Perf. 14*
550 A79 3e multicolored   .20 .15

500th anniv. of the birth of King Manuel I.

Angolasaurus Bocagei — A80

Fossils and Minerals: 1e, Ferrometeorite. 1.50e, Dioptase crystals. 2e, Gondwanidium. 2.50e, Diamonds. 3e, Estromatolite. 3.50e, Procarcharodon megalodon. 4e, Microceratodus angolensis. 4.50e, Moscovite. 5e, Barite. 6e, Nostoceras. 10e, Rotula orbiculus angolensis.

1970, Oct. 31   Litho.   *Perf. 13*
551 A80 50c tan & multi   .15 .15
552 A80 1e multicolored   .15 .15
553 A80 1.50e multicolored   .15 .15
554 A80 2e multicolored   .20 .15
555 A80 2.50e lt gray & multi   .20 .15
556 A80 3e multicolored   .20 .15
557 A80 3.50e blue & multi   .30 .15
558 A80 4e lt gray & multi   .30 .15
559 A80 4.50e gray & multi   .30 .15
560 A80 5e gray & multi   .30 .15
561 A80 6e pink & multi   .60 .20
562 A80 10e lt blue & multi   .75 .32
   Nos. 551-562 (12)   3.60 2.02

Marshal Carmona Issue
Common Design Type

1970, Nov. 15   Litho.   *Perf. 14*
563 CD57 2.50e multicolored   .22 .15

Arms of Malanje, Cotton Boll and Field — A82

1970, Nov. 20   *Perf. 13*
564 A82 2.50e multicolored   .22 .15

Centenary of the municipality of Malanje.

Mail Ships and Angola No. 1 — A83

4.50e, Steam locomotive and Angola No. 4.

1970, Dec. 1   *Perf. 13½*
565 A83 1.50e multicolored   .30 .15
566 A83 4.50e multicolored   .65 .22

Cent. of stamps of Angola. See No. C36. For overprint see No. 616B.

Map of Africa, Diagram of Seismic Tests — A84

Galleon on Congo River — A85

1971, Aug. 22   Litho.   *Perf. 13*
567 A84 2.50e multicolored   .15 .15

5th Regional Conference of Soil and Foundation Engineers, Luanda, Aug. 22-Sept. 5.

1972, May 25   Litho.   *Perf. 13*
568 A85 1e emerald & multi   .15 .15

4th centenary of the publication of The Lusiads by Luiz Camoens.

Olympic Games Issue
Common Design Type

1972, June 20   *Perf. 14x13½*
569 CD59 50c multicolored   .15 .15

Lisbon-Rio de Janeiro Flight Issue
Common Design Type

1972, Sept. 20   Litho.   *Perf. 13½*
570 CD60 1e multicolored   .15 .15

WMO Centenary Issue
Common Design Type

1973, Dec. 15   Litho.   *Perf. 13*
571 CD61 1e dk gray & multi   .15 .15

Radar Station A89

1974, June 25   Litho.   *Perf. 13*
572 A89 2e multicolored   .22 .15

Establishment of satellite communications network via Intelsat among Portugal, Angola and Mozambique.
For overprint see No. 616A.

Harpa Doris — A90

Designs: Sea shells.

1974, Oct. 25   Litho.   *Perf. 12x12½*
573 A90 25c shown   .15 .15
574 A90 30c Murex melanamathos   .15 .15
575 A90 50c Venus foliaceo lamellosa   .15 .15
576 A90 70c Lathyrus filosus   .15 .15
577 A90 1e Cymbium cisium   .18 .15
578 A90 1.50e Cassis tesselata   .18 .15
579 A90 2e Cypraea stercoraria   .18 .15
580 A90 2.50e Conus prometheus   .18 .18
581 A90 3e Strombus latus   .18 .18
582 A90 3.50e Tympanotonus fuscatus   .18 .18
583 A90 4e Cardium costatum   .25 .20
584 A90 5e Natica fulminea   .25 .20
585 A90 6e Lyropecten nodosus   .30 .20
586 A90 7e Tonna galea   .75 .25
587 A90 10e Donax rugosus   .90 .30
588 A90 25e Cymatium trigonum   1.50 .40
589 A90 30e Olivancilaria acuminata   2.50 .75
590 A90 35e Semifusus morio   2.50 .75
591 A90 40e Clavatula lineata   3.00 1.00
592 A90 50e Solarium granulatum   4.00 1.50
   Nos. 573-592 (20)   17.63 7.14

For overprints see Nos. 605-607, 617-630.

No. 386 Overprinted in Blue: "1974 / FILATELIA / JUVENIL"

1974, Dec. 21   Litho.   *Perf. 13½*
593 A41 5c multicolored   .15 .15

Youth philately.

Republic

Star and Hand Holding Rifle — A91

1975, Nov. 11   Litho.   *Perf. 13x13½*
594 A91 1.50e red & multi   .15 .15

Independence in 1975.

Diquiche Mask — A92

Design: 3e, Bui ou Congolo mask.

1976, Feb. 6   *Perf. 13½*
595 A92 50c lt blue & multi   .15 .15
596 A92 3e multicolored   .20 .15

Workers — A93

President Agostinho Neto — A94

1976, May 1   Litho.   *Perf. 12*
597 A93 1e red & multi   .15 .15

International Workers' Day.

No. 392 Overprinted Bar and: "DIA DO SELO / 15 Junho 1976 / REP. POPULAR / DE"

1976, June 15   Litho.   *Perf. 13½*
598 A41 10e multicolored   .40 .25

Stamp Day.

1976, Nov. 11   Litho.   *Perf. 13*
599 A94 50c yel & dk brown   .15 .15
600 A94 2e lt gray & plum   .15 .15
601 A94 3e gray & indigo   .15 .15
602 A94 5e buff & brown   .20 .15
603 A94 10e tan & sepia   .40 .15
   a. Souv. sheet of 1, imperf.   2.00 1.25
   Nos. 599-603 (5)   1.05 .75

First anniversary of independence.

Nos. 393, 588-589, 592 Overprinted with Bar over Republica Portuguesa and: "REPUBLICA POPULAR DE"

1977, Feb. 9   *Perf. 13½, 12x12½*
604 A41 20e multicolored   1.25 .25
605 A90 25e multicolored   1.75 .35
606 A90 30e multicolored   2.50 .50
607 A90 50e multicolored   4.00 .75
   Nos. 604-607 (4)   9.50 1.85

Overprint in 3 lines on No. 604, in 2 lines on others.

No. 438 Overprinted with Bar over Republica Portuguesa and: "S. Silvestre / 1976 / Rep. Popular / de"

1976, Dec. 31   *Perf. 13½*
608 CD48 15e multicolored   3.50 .25

Child and WHO Emblem — A95

Map of Africa, Flag of Angola — A96

1977   Litho.   *Perf. 10½*
609 A95 2.50k blk & lt blue   .15 .15

Campaign for vaccination against poliomyelitis.

Anti-Apartheid Emblem — A97

1979, June 20   Litho.   *Perf. 13½*
611 A97 1k multicolored   .15 .15

Anti-Apartheid Year.

Human Rights Emblem — A98

Child Flowers, Globe, IYC Emblem — A99

1979, June 15   Litho.   *Perf. 13½*
612 A98 2.50k multicolored   .15 .15

Declaration of Human Rights, 30th anniv. (in 1975).

1980, May 1   Litho.   *Perf. 14x14½*
613 A99 3.50k multicolored   .15 .15

International Year of the Child (1979).

Running, Moscow '80 Emblem A100

5th Anniv. of Independence A101

1980, Dec. 15   Litho.   *Perf. 13½*
614 A100 9k shown   .32 .15
615 A100 12k Swimming, horiz.   .40 .20

22nd Summer Olympic Games, Moscow, July 19-Aug. 3.

1980, Nov. 11
616 A101 5.50k multicolored   .15 .15

Nos. 572, 566 Overprinted with Bar and: "REPUBLICA POPULAR / DE"

1980-81   Litho.   *Perf. 13½x13*
616A A89 2e multi (bar only)   .50
616B A83 4.50e multicolored   1.00

Issue dates: 2e, May 17, 1981, 4.50e, June 15. See No. C37.

Nos. 577-580, 582-591 Overprinted with Black Bar over "Republica Portuguesa"

1981, June 15   Litho.   *Perf. 12x12½*
617 A90 1e multicolored
618 A90 1.50e multicolored
619 A90 2e multicolored

ANGOLA

620 A90	2.50e multicolored		
621 A90	3.50e multicolored		
622 A90	4e multicolored		
623 A90	5e multicolored		
624 A90	6e multicolored		
625 A90	7e multicolored		
626 A90	10e multicolored		
627 A90	25e multicolored		
628 A90	30e multicolored		
629 A90	35e multicolored		
630 A90	40e multicolored		
	Nos. 617-630 (14)	15.00	8.00

Man Walking with Canes, Tchibinda Ilunga Statue — A102

1981, Sept. 5 Litho. Perf. 13½

631 A102	9k multicolored	.32	.20

Turipex '81 tourism exhibition.

M.P.L.A. Workers' Party Congress — A103

1980, Dec. 23 Litho. Perf. 14

632 A103	50 l Millet	.15	.15
633 A103	5k Coffee	.20	.15
634 A103	7.50k Sunflowers	.25	.15
635 A103	13.50k Cotton	.40	.20
636 A103	14k Oil	.45	.25
637 A103	16k Diamonds	.45	.25
	Nos. 632-637 (6)	1.90	1.15

People's Power — A104

Natl. Heroes' Day — A105

1980, Nov. 11

638 A104	40k lt blue & blk	1.25	.40

1980, Sept. 17 Perf. 14x13½

639 A105	4.50k Former Pres. Neto	.15	.15
640 A105	50k Neto, diff.	1.50	.65

Soweto Uprising, 5th Anniv. A106

1981

641 A106	4.50k multicolored	.20	.15

2nd Central African Games A107

1981, Sept. 3 Litho. Perf. 13½

642 A107	50 l Bicycling, tennis	.15	.15
643 A107	5k Judo, boxing	.20	.15
644 A107	6k Basketball, volleyball	.22	.15
645 A107	10k Handball, soccer	.40	.25
	Nos. 642-645 (4)	.97	.70

Souvenir Sheet
Imperf

646 A107	15k multicolored		2.00

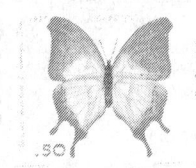

Charaxes Kahldeni A108

1982, Feb. 26 Litho. Perf. 13½

647 A108	50 l shown	.15	.15
648 A108	1k Abantis zambesiaca	.15	.15
649 A108	5k Catacroptera cloanthe	.20	.15
650 A108	9k Myrina ficedula, vert.	.40	.15
651 A108	10k Colotis danae	.40	.15
652 A108	15k Acraea acrita	.52	.25
653 A108	100k Precis hierta	2.75	1.25
a.	Souvenir sheet	2.00	1.00
	Nos. 647-653 (7)	4.57	2.25

No. 653a contains Nos. 647-653, imperf., and sold for 30k (stamps probably not valid individually).

5th Anniv. of UN Membership A109

5.50k, The Silence of the Night, by Musseque Catambor. 7.50k, Cotton picking, Catete.

1982, Sept. 22 Litho.

654 A109	5.50k multicolored	.20	.15
655 A109	7.50k multicolored	.25	.15

20th Anniv. of Engineering Laboratory A110

1982, Dec. 21 Litho. Perf. 14

656 A110	9k Lab	.25	.15
657 A110	13k Worker, vert.	.40	.20
658 A110	100k Equipment, vert.	3.25	1.25
	Nos. 656-658 (3)	3.90	1.60

Local Flowers A111

1983, Feb. 18 Perf. 13½

659 A111	5k Dichrostachys glomerata	.15	.15
660 A111	12k Amblygonocarpus obtusangulus	.40	.15
661 A111	50k Albizzia versicolor	2.00	.65
	Nos. 659-661 (3)	2.55	.95

Women's Org., First Congress — A112

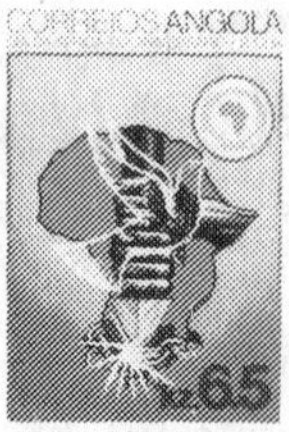

Africa Day — A113

1983 Litho. Perf. 13½

662 A112	20k multicolored	.80	.80

1983, June 30 Perf. 13

663 A113	6.5k multi	.25	.25

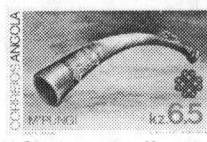

World Communications Year — A114

1983, June 30 Litho. Perf. 13½

664 A114	6.5k M'pungi	.25	.25
665 A114	12k Mondu	.40	.40

BRASILIANA '83 Stamp Exhibition, Rio de Janeiro, July 29-Aug. 7 — A115

Crop-eating insects.

1983, July 29 Litho. Perf. 13

666 A115	4.5k Antestiopsis lineaticollis	.18	.18
667 A115	6.5k Stephanoderes hampei ferr.	.25	.25
668 A115	10k Zonocerus variegatus	.40	.40
	Nos. 666-668 (3)	.83	.83

25th Anniv. of Economic Commission for Africa A116

1983, Aug. 2

669 A116	10k Map, emblem	.40	.40

185th Anniv. of Post Office A117

1983, Dec. 7 Litho. Perf. 13½

670 A117	50 l Mail collection, vert.	.15	.15
671 A117	3.5k Unloading mail plane	.15	.15
672 A117	5k Sorting mail	.20	.20
673 A117	15k Mailing letter, vert.	.60	.60
674 A117	30k Post office box delivery	1.25	1.25
a.	Min. sheet of 3, #671-672, 674	4.00	4.00
	Nos. 670-674 (5)	2.35	2.35

No. 674a sold for 100k.

Local Butterflies A118

1984, Jan. 20 Litho. Perf. 13½

675 A118	50 l Parasa karschi	.15	.15
676 A118	1k Diaphone angolensis	.15	.15
677 A118	3.5k Choeropasis jucunda	.15	.15
678 A118	6.5k Hespagarista rendalli	.25	.25
679 A118	15k Euchromia guineensis	.60	.60
680 A118	17.5k Mazuca roseistriga	.70	.70
681 A118	20k Utetheisa callima	.85	.85
	Nos. 675-681 (7)	2.85	2.85

A119

A120

1984, Apr. 11 Litho. Perf. 13½

682 A119	30k multicolored	1.25	1.25

First Natl. Worker's Union Congress, Apr. 11-16.

1984, Oct. 24 Litho. Perf. 13½

Local birds.

683 A120	10.50k Bucorvos leadbeateri	.45	.40
684 A120	14k Gypohicax angolensis	.55	.50
685 A120	16k Ardea goliath	.60	.50
686 A120	19.50k Pelicanus onocrotalus	.80	.75
687 A120	22k Platelea alba	.90	.90
688 A120	26k Balearica pavonnia	1.00	1.00
	Nos. 683-688 (6)	4.30	4.05

Local Animals A121

1984, Nov. 12

689 A121	1k Tragelephus strepsicerus	.15	.15
690 A121	4k Antidorcas marsupialis angolerusis	.15	.15
691 A121	5k Pan troglodytes	.20	.20
692 A121	10k Sycerus caffer	.40	.40
693 A121	15k Hippotragus niger variani	.60	.60
694 A121	20k Orycteropus afer	.80	.80
695 A121	25k Crocuta crocuta	1.00	1.00
	Nos. 689-695 (7)	3.30	3.30

Angolese Monuments A122

1985, Feb. 21 Litho. Perf. 13½

696 A122	5k San Pedro da Barra	.22	.22
697 A122	12.5k Nova Oeiras	.55	.55
698 A122	18k M'Banza Kongo	.80	.80
699 A122	26k Massangano	1.10	1.10
700 A122	39k Escravatura Museum	1.65	1.65
	Nos. 696-700 (5)	4.32	4.32

United Workers' Party, 25th Anniv. A123

1985, May Litho. Perf. 12

701 A123	77k XXV, red flags	1.50	1.50

Printed in sheets of 5.

A124

A125

1985, May

702 A124	1k Flags	.15	.15
703 A124	11k Oil drilling platform, Cabinda	.22	.22
704 A124	57k Conference	1.10	1.10
a.	Strip of 3, #702-704	1.40	1.40

Southern African Development Council, 5th anniv.

Lithographed and Typographed

1985, July 5 Perf. 11

Medicinal plants.

705 A125	1k Lonchocarpus sericeus	.15	.15
706 A125	4k Gossypium	.15	.15
707 A125	11k Cassia occidentalis	.22	.22
708 A125	25.50k Gloriosa superba	.50	.50
709 A125	55k Cochlospermum angolensis	1.10	1.10
	Nos. 705-709 (5)	2.12	2.12

ARGENTINA '85 exhibition.

ANGOLA

5th Natl. Heroes Day — A126

Natl. flag and: 10.50k, Portrait of Agostinho Neto, party leader. 36.50k, Neto working.

1985   Litho.   Perf. 13½
710	A126	10.50k multicolored	.20	.20
711	A126	36.50k multicolored	.70	.70

Ministerial Conference of Non-Aligned Countries, Luanda A127

1985, Sept. 4   Photo.   Perf. 11
712	A127	35k multicolored	1.50	1.50

UN, 40th Anniv. A128

1985, Oct. 29   Litho.   Perf. 11
713	A128	12.50k multicolored	.55	.55

Industry and Natural Resources A129

1985, Nov. 11
714	A129	50 l Cement Factory	.15	.15
715	A129	5k Logging	.22	.22
716	A129	7k Quartz	.30	.30
717	A129	10k Iron mine	.42	.42
a.		Souvenir sheet of 4, #714-717, imperf.	1.00	1.00
		Nos. 714-717 (4)	1.09	1.09

Natl. independence, 10th anniv.

2nd Natl. Workers' Party Congress (MPLA) A130

1985, Nov. 28   Perf. 13½
718	A130	20k multicolored	.85	.85

Demostenes de Almeida Clington Races, 30th Anniv. — A131

Various runners.

1985, Dec. 13
719	A131	50 l multicolored	.15	.15
720	A131	5k multicolored	.22	.22
721	A131	6.50k multicolored	.28	.28
722	A131	10k multicolored	.42	.42
		Nos. 719-722 (4)	1.07	1.07

1986 World Cup Soccer Championships, Mexico — A132

Map, soccer field and various plays.

1986, May 6   Litho.   Perf. 11½x11
723	A132	50 l multi	.15	.15
724	A132	3.50k multi	.15	.15
725	A132	5k multi	.22	.22
726	A132	7k multi	.30	.30
727	A132	10k multi	.42	.42
728	A132	18k multi	.85	.85
		Nos. 723-728 (6)	2.09	2.09

Struggle Against Portugal, 25th Anniv. A133

1986, May 6   Perf. 11x11½
729	A133	15k multicolored	.65	.65

First Man in Space, 25th Anniv. A134

1986, Aug. 21   Litho.   Perf. 11x11½
730	A134	50 l Skylab, US	.15	.15
731	A134	1k Spacecraft	.15	.15
732	A134	5k A. Leonov space-walking	.22	.22
733	A134	10k Lunokhod on Moon	.42	.42
734	A134	13k Apollo-Soyuz link-up	.60	.60
		Nos. 730-734 (5)	1.54	1.54

Admission of Angola to UN, 10th Anniv. — A135

1986, Dec. 1   Litho.   Perf. 11x11½
735	A135	22k multi	.90	.90

Liberation Movement, 30th Anniv. — A136

1986, Dec. 3   Perf. 11½x11
736	A136	Strip of 3	.65	.65
a.-c.		5k any single	.20	.20

Angolese at work, fighting and: No. 736a, "1956." No. 736b, Congress emblem, "1980." No. 736c, Labor Party emblem, "1985."

Agostinho Neto University, 10th Anniv. A137

1986, Dec. 30   Litho.   Perf. 11x11½
737	A137	50 l Mathematics	.15	.15
738	A137	1k Law	.15	.15
739	A137	10k Medicine	.45	.45
		Nos. 737-739 (3)	.75	.75

Tribal Hairstyles — A138

1987, Apr. 15   Litho.   Perf. 11½x11
740	A138	1k Ouioca	.15	.15
741	A138	1.50k Luanda	.15	.15
742	A138	5k Humbe	.15	.15
743	A138	7k Muila	.15	.15
744	A138	20k Muila, diff.	.45	.45
745	A138	30k Dilolo	.70	.70
		Nos. 740-745 (6)	1.75	1.75

Landscapes — A139    Lenin — A140

Perf. 11½x12, 12x11½

1987, July 7   Litho.
746	A139	50 l Pambala Shore	.15	.15
747	A139	1.50k Dala Waterfalls	.15	.15
748	A139	3.50k Black Stones	.15	.15
749	A139	5k Cuango River	.15	.15
750	A139	10k Launda coast	.22	.22
751	A139	20k Hills of Leba	.50	.50
		Nos. 746-751 (6)	1.32	1.32

Nos. 746-747, 749 and 751 horiz.

1987, Nov. 25   Perf. 12x12½
752	A140	15k multi	.58	.58

October Revolution, Russia, 70th anniv.

2nd Congress of the Organization of Angolan Women (OMA) — A141

1988, May 30   Litho.   Perf. 13x13½
753	A141	2k shown	.15	.15
754	A141	10k Soldier, nurse, technician, student	.35	.35

Victory Carnival, 10th Anniv. — A142

Various carnival scenes.

1988, June 15   Litho.   Perf. 13½x13
755	A142	5k shown	.16	.16
756	A142	10k multi, diff.	.32	.32

Augusto N'Gangula (1956-1968), Youth Pioneer Killed by Portuguese Colonial Army — A143

Agostinho Neto Pioneers' Organization (OPA), 25th Anniv. — A144

1989, Oct. 2   Litho.   Perf. 12x11½
757	A143	12k multicolored	.40	.40
758	A144	15k multicolored	.48	.48

Pioneer Day.

10th Natl. Soccer Championships, Benguela, May 1 — A145

1989, Oct. 16
759	A145	5k shown	.16	.16
760	A145	5k Luanda, 3 years	.16	.16
761	A145	5k Luanda, 5 years	.16	.16
		Nos. 759-761 (3)	.48	.48

Intl. Fund for Agricultural Development, 10th Anniv. — A146

1990, Feb. 15   Litho.   Perf. 11½x12
762	A146	10k multicolored	.70	.70

Ingombotas' Houses A147

Architecture: 2k, Alta Train Station. 5k, National Museum of Anthropology. 15k, Ana Joaquina Palace. 23k, Iron Palace. 36k, Meteorological observatory, vert. 50k, People's Palace.

Perf. 12x11½, 11½x12

1990, Feb. 20
763	A147	1k shown	.15	.15
764	A147	2k multicolored	.15	.15
765	A147	5k multicolored	.32	.32
766	A147	15k multicolored	.98	.98
767	A147	23k multicolored	1.50	1.50
768	A147	36k multicolored	2.30	2.30
769	A147	50k multicolored	3.25	3.25
		Nos. 763-769 (7)	8.65	8.65

Luanda and Benguela Railways A148

Various maps and locomotives.

1990, Mar. 1   Perf. 12x11½
770	A148	5k shown	.35	.35
771	A148	12k Garrat T (left)	.80	.80
772	A148	12k Garrat T (right)	.80	.80
a.		Pair, #771-772	1.60	1.60
773	A148	14k Mikado	.95	.95
		Nos. 770-773 (4)	2.90	2.90

Souvenir Sheet
774	A148	25k Diesel electric	2.35	2.35

No. 772a has a continuous design.

ANGOLA

Southern Africa Development Coordinating Conf. (SADCC), 10th Anniv. — A149

1990, Apr. 1   *Litho.*   *Perf. 14*
775	A149	5k shown	1.25	1.25
776	A149	9k Floating oil rig	2.50	2.50

Pan-African Postal Union (PAPU), 10th Anniv. — A150

1990, Apr. 6
777	A150	4k shown	.75	.75
778	A150	10k Simulated stamp, map	1.50	1.50

Paintings by Raul Indipwo — A151

1990, Apr. 24
779	A151	6k *Tres Gracas*	.42	.42
780	A151	9k *Muxima*, vert.	.65	.65

Stamp World London 90.

Hippotragus Niger Variani, Adult Male and Female — A152

1990, May 9   *Perf. 14x13½*
781	A152	5k Adult male	.35	.35
782	A152	5k shown	.35	.35
783	A152	5k Adult female	.35	.35
784	A152	5k Female, calf	.35	.35
		Nos. 781-784 (4)	1.40	1.40

World Wildlife Fund. Various combinations available in blocks or strips of four.

Rosa de Porcelana — A153

1990, June 2   *Litho.*   *Perf. 14*
785	A153	5k shown	.35	.35
786	A153	8k Cravo burro	.56	.56
787	A153	10k Alamandra	.70	.70
		Nos. 785-787 (3)	1.61	1.61

Souvenir Sheet
788	A153	40k Hibiscus	2.70	2.70

Belgica '90.

Angola stamps can be mounted in the Scott annually supplemented Portugal album.

Miniature Sheet

Intl. Literacy Year — A154

Various animals and forest scenes.

1990, July 26   *Litho.*   *Perf. 14*
789		Sheet of 30	2.25	2.25
a.		A154 1k any single	.15	.15
790	A154	5k Zebra	.35	.35
791	A154	5k Butterfly	.35	.35
792	A154	5k Horse	.35	.35
a.		Block of 3, #790-792 + label	1.05	1.05

People's Assembly, 10th Anniv. — A155

1990, Nov. 11   *Perf. 14*
793	A155	10k multicolored	.70	.70

3rd Natl. Labor Congress — A156

1990   *Litho.*   *Perf. 13½*
794	A156	14k multicolored	1.35	1.35

War of Independence, 30th Anniv. — A157

Uniforms.

1991, Feb. 28   *Litho.*   *Perf. 14*
795	A157	6k Machete, 1961	.42	.42
a.		Perf. 13½ vert.	.42	.42
796	A157	6k Rifle, 1962-63	.42	.42
a.		Perf. 13½ vert.	.42	.42
797	A157	6k Rifle, 1968	.42	.42
a.		Perf. 13½ vert.	.42	.42
798	A157	6k Automatic rifle, 1972	.42	.42
a.		Perf. 13½ vert.	.42	.42
b.		Bklt. pane of 4, #795a-798a	1.70	
		Nos. 795-798 (4)	1.68	1.68

Musical Instruments A158

Designs: a, Marimba. b, Mucupela. c, Ngoma la Txina. d, Kissange.

Tourism A159

1991, Apr. 5   *Litho.*   *Perf. 14*
799	A158	6k Block or strip of 4, #799a-799d	1.70	1.70

Designs: 3k, Iona National Park. 7k, Kalandula Waterfalls. 35k, Lobito Bay. 60k, Weltwitschia Mirabilis plant.

1991, June 25   *Litho.*   *Perf. 14*
800	A159	3k multi	.15	.15
801	A159	7k multi	.24	.24
802	A159	35k multi	1.15	1.15
803	A159	60k multi	2.00	2.00
		Nos. 800-803 (4)	3.54	3.54

Dogs — A160

1991, July 5   *Litho.*   *Perf. 14*
804	A160	5k Kabir of dembos	.16	.16
805	A160	7k Ombua	.24	.24
806	A160	11k Kabir massongo	.38	.38
807	A160	12k Kawa tchowe	.40	.40
		Nos. 804-807 (4)	1.18	1.18

1992 Summer Olympics, Barcelona — A161

1991, July 26   *Perf. 13*
808	A161	4k Judo	.15	.15
809	A161	6k Sailing	.20	.20
810	A161	10k Running	.35	.35
811	A161	100k Swimming	3.35	3.35
		Nos. 808-811 (4)	4.05	4.05

Navigation Aids — A162

1991, Nov. 8   *Litho.*   *Perf. 12*
812	A162	5k Quadrant	.16	.16
813	A162	15k Astrolabe	.52	.52
814	A162	20k Cross-staff	.70	.70
815	A162	50k Portolano	1.75	1.75
		Nos. 812-815 (4)	3.13	3.13

Iberex '91.

Rays — A163

1992, Mar. 30   *Litho.*   *Perf. 14*
816	A163	40k Myliobatis aquila	.15	.15
817	A163	50k Aetobatus narinari	.18	.18
818	A163	66k Manta birostris	.24	.24
819	A163	80k Raja miraletus	.30	.30
		Nos. 816-819 (4)	.87	.87

Souvenir Sheet
Perf. 13½
820	A163	25k Manta birostris, diff.	.15	.15

Quioca Masks — A164

1992, Apr. 30   *Litho.*   *Perf. 13½*
821	A164	60k Kalelwa	.22	.22
822	A164	100k Mukixe Wa Kino	.38	.38
823	A164	150k Cikunza	.55	.55
824	A164	250k Mukixi Wa Mbwesu	.92	.92
		Nos. 821-824 (4)	2.07	2.07

See Nos. 854-857, 868-871, 883-886, 895-898.

Medicinal Plants — A165

Designs: 200k, Pteroxylon obliquum. 300k, Spondias mombin. 500k, Parinari curatellifolia. 600k, Cochlospermum angolense.

1992, May 8   *Perf. 14*
825	A165	200k brown & pale yel	.75	.75
826	A165	300k brown & pale yel	1.10	1.10
827	A165	500k brown & pale yel	1.85	1.85
828	A165	600k brown & pale yel	2.20	2.20
a.		Block or strip of 4, #825-828	5.90	5.90

Evangelization of Angola, 500th Anniv. — A166

1992, May 10   *Perf. 13½*
829	A166	150k King, missionaries	.55	.55
830	A166	420k Ruins of M'banza Congo	1.55	1.55
831	A166	470k Maxima Church	1.75	1.75
832	A166	500k Faces of people	1.90	1.90
		Nos. 829-832 (4)	5.75	5.75

Traditional Houses — A167

Perf. 14, 13½ Vert. (#832A)
1992, May 22
832A	A167	150k Dimbas	1.25	1.25
b.		Bklt. pane of 4, #832A, 833a-835a	5.00	
833	A167	330k Cokwe	1.25	1.25
a.		Perf. 13½ vert.	1.25	1.25
834	A167	360k Mbali	1.35	1.35
a.		Perf. 13½ vert.	1.35	1.35
835	A167	420k Ambwelas	1.55	1.55
a.		Perf. 13½ vert.	1.55	1.55
836	A167	500k Upper Zambezi	1.90	1.90
		Nos. 832A-836 (5)	7.30	7.30

Expo '92, Seville.

Agapornis Roseicollis A168

ANGOLA

1992, June 2   *Perf. 12x11½*
837 A168 150k Two birds on branch .55 .55
838 A168 200k Birds feeding .75 .75
839 A168 250k Hand holding bird .92 .92
840 A168 300k Bird on perch 1.10 1.10
    a. Strip of 4, #837-840 3.35 3.35

Expo '92, Seville.

Souvenir Sheet

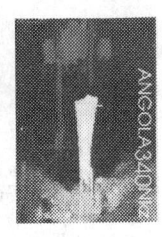

Visit of Pope John Paul II to Angola — A169

Abstract paintings: a, 340k, The Crucifixion. b, 370k, The Resurrection.

1992, June 4   *Litho.*   *Perf. 13½*
841 A169 Sheet of 2, #a.-b. + 2 labels 1.80 1.80

1992 Summer Olympics, Barcelona A170

1992, July 30   *Perf. 14*
842 A170 120k Hurdles .32 .32
843 A170 180k Cycling .50 .50
844 A170 240k Roller hockey .65 .65
845 A170 360k Basketball 1.00 1.00
    Nos. 842-845 (4) 2.47 2.47

Native Fishing — A171

1992, Aug. 5   *Perf. 11½x12*
846 A171 65k Building traps .18 .18
847 A171 90k Using nets .25 .25
848 A171 100k Laying traps .28 .28
849 A171 120k Fisherman in boats .32 .32
    Nos. 846-849 (4) 1.03 1.03

Souvenir Sheet

Discovery of America, 500th Anniv. — A172

1992, Sept. 18   *Litho.*   *Perf. 12*
850 A172 500k multicolored 1.35 1.35

Genoa '92.

First Free Elections in Angola — A173

Designs: 120k, People voting. 150k, Map, ballot box, peace doves. 200k, People, dove, hand dropping ballot into ballot box.

1992, Oct. 27   *Litho.*   *Perf. 11½x12*
851 A173 120k multicolored .32 .32
852 A173 150k multicolored .42 .42
853 A173 200k multicolored .55 .55
    Nos. 851-853 (3) 1.29 1.29

Quioca Mask Type of 1992

1992, Nov. 6   *Perf. 13½*
854 A164 72k Cihongo .28 .28
855 A164 80k Mbwasu .30 .30
856 A164 120k Cinhanga .45 .45
857 A164 210k Kalewa .80 .80
    Nos. 854-857 (4) 1.83 1.83

Inauguration of Express Mail Service A174

1992, Dec. 14   *Litho.*   *Perf. 12x11½*
858 A174 450k Truck 1.05 1.05
859 A174 550k Airplane 1.25 1.25

Meteorological Instruments — A175

1993, Mar. 23   *Litho.*   *Perf. 11½x12*
860 A175 250k Weather balloon .58 .58
861 A175 470k Actinometer 1.10 1.10
862 A175 500k Rain gauge 1.15 1.15
    Nos. 860-862 (3) 2.83 2.83

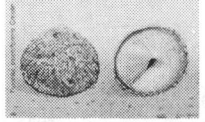

Seashells A176

1993, Apr. 6   *Perf. 12x11½*
863 A176 210k Trochita trochiformis .48 .48
864 A176 330k Strombus latus .75 .75
865 A176 400k Aporrhais pesgallinae .95 .95
866 A176 500k Fusos aff. albinus 1.15 1.15
    Nos. 863-866 (4) 3.33 3.33

Souvenir Sheet
867 A176 1000k Pusionella nifat 2.30 2.30

Quioca Art Type of 1992

1993, June 7   *Litho.*   *Perf. 12*
868 A164 72k Men with vehicles .15 .15
869 A164 210k Cavalier .45 .45
870 A164 420k Airplane .90 .90
871 A164 600k Men carrying stretcher 1.25 1.25
    Nos. 868-871 (4) 2.75 2.75

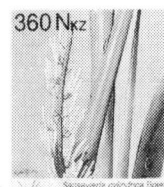

Flowering Plants — A177

1993, June 28   *Perf. 11½x12*
872 A177 360k Sansevieria cylindrica .75 .75
873 A177 400k Euphorbia tirucalli .85 .85
874 A177 500k Opuntia ficus-indica 1.05 1.05
875 A177 600k Dracaena aubryana 1.25 1.25
    Nos. 872-875 (4) 3.90 3.90

Souvenir Sheet

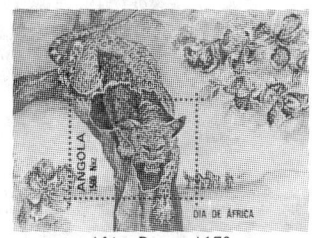

Africa Day — A178

1993, May 31   *Perf. 12*
876 A178 1500k Leopard 3.15 3.15

Tribal Pipes — A179

1993, Aug. 16   *Litho.*   *Perf. 11½x12*
877 A179 72k Vimbundi .15 .15
878 A179 200k Vimbundi, diff. .42 .42
879 A179 420k Mutopa .88 .88
880 A179 600k Pexi 1.25 1.25
    Nos. 877-880 (4) 2.70 2.70

Souvenir Sheet

Union of Portuguese Speaking Capitals — A180

1993, July 30   *Perf. 12x11½*
881 A180 1500k multicolored 3.15 3.15

Turtles — A181

Designs: a, 180k, Chelonia mydas (b). b, 450k, Eretmochelys imbricata. c, 550k, Dermochelys coriacea. d, 630k, Caretta caretta.

1993, July 9   *Litho.*   *Perf. 12½x12*
882 A181 Block of 4, #a.-d. 3.50 3.50

Quioca Art Type of 1992

1993, Sept. 1   *Litho.*   *Perf. 12*
883 A164 300k Leopard .65 .65
884 A164 600k Malhado 1.25 1.25
885 A164 800k Birds 1.65 1.65
886 A164 1000k Chickens 2.00 2.00
    Nos. 883-886 (4) 5.55 5.55

Mushrooms — A182    A183

1993, Dec. 5   *Litho.*   *Perf. 12*
887 A182 300k Tricholoma georgii .55 .55
    a. Perf. 11½ vert. .55 .55
888 A182 500k Amanita phalloides .95 .95
    a. Perf. 11½ vert. .95 .95
889 A182 600k Amanita vaginata 1.10 1.10
    a. Perf. 11½ vert. 1.10 1.10
890 A182 1000k Macrolepiota procera 1.90 1.90
    a. Perf. 11½ vert. 1.90 1.90
    b. Booklet pane of 4, #887a-890a 4.50
    Nos. 887-890 (4) 4.50 4.50

1994, Jan. 10   *Litho.*   *Perf. 12*
Natl. Culture Day: 500k, Cinganji, wood carving of dancer. 1000k, Ohunya yo soma, staff with woman's face. 1200k, Ongende, sculpture of man on donkey. 2200k, Upi, corn pestle.
891 A183 500k multicolored .45 .45
892 A183 1000k multicolored .90 .90
893 A183 1200k multicolored 1.10 1.10
894 A183 2200k multicolored 2.00 2.00
    Nos. 891-894 (4) 4.45 4.45

Hong Kong '94.

Quioca Art Type of 1992

1994, Feb. 21   *Litho.*   *Perf. 12*
895 A164 500k Bird on flower .32 .32
896 A164 2000k Plant with roots 1.30 1.30
897 A164 2500k Feto 1.65 1.65
898 A164 3000k Plant 2.00 2.00
    Nos. 895-898 (4) 5.27 5.27

Social Responsibilities of AIDS — A184

Designs: 500k, Mass of people. 1000k, Witchdoctor receiving AIDS through needle, people being educated. 3000k, Stylized man, woman.

1994, May 5   *Perf. 12*
899 A184 500k multicolored .32 .32
900 A184 1000k multicolored .65 .65
901 A184 3000k multicolored 2.00 2.00
    Nos. 899-901 (3) 2.97 2.97

1994 World Cup Soccer Championships, US — A185

1994, June 17   *Perf. 14*
902 A185 500k Large arrows, small ball .32 .32
903 A185 700k Small arrows, large ball .45 .45
904 A185 2200k Ball in goal 1.50 1.50
905 A185 2500k Ball, foot 1.65 1.65
    Nos. 902-905 (4) 3.92 3.92

Dinosaurs A186

1994, Aug. 16   *Litho.*   *Perf. 12*
906 A186 1000k Brachiosaurus .15 .15
907 A186 3000k Spinosaurus .55 .55
908 A186 5000k Ouranosaurus .90 .90
909 A186 10,000k Lesothosaurus 1.90 1.90
    Nos. 906-909 (4) 3.50 3.50

Souvenir Sheet
910 A186 19,000k Lesothosaurus, map of Africa 3.50 3.50

PHILAKOREA '94, SINGPEX '94. No. 910 contains one 44x34mm stamp.

Tourism
A187

1994, Sept. 27   Litho.   Perf. 12x11½
911	A187	2000k Birds	.18	.18
912	A187	4000k Wild animals	.35	.35
913	A187	8000k Native women	.75	.75
914	A187	10,000k Native men	.90	.90
		Nos. 911-914 (4)	2.18	2.18

Post Boxes — A188

Designs: 5000k, Letters, bundled mail wall box. 7500k, Wall box for letters. 10,000k, Pillar box. 21,000k, Multi-function units.

1994, Oct. 7   Perf. 14½
915	A188	5000k multicolored	.45	.45
916	A188	7500k multicolored	.70	.70
917	A188	10,000k multicolored	.90	.90
918	A188	21,000k multicolored	1.90	1.90
		Nos. 915-918 (4)	3.95	3.95

Cotton Pests — A189

Insects: 5000k, Heliothis armigera. 6000k, Bemisia tabasi. 10,000k, Dysdercus. 27,000k, Spodoptera exigua.

1994, Nov. 11   Litho.   Perf. 14
919	A189	5000k multicolored	.45	.45
920	A189	6000k multicolored	.55	.55
921	A189	10,000k multicolored	.95	.95
922	A189	27,000k multicolored	2.50	2.50
		Nos. 919-922 (4)	4.45	4.45

Intl. Olympic Committee, Cent. — A190

1994, Dec. 15
| 923 | A190 | 27,000k multicolored | 2.75 | 2.75 |

Tribal Culture A191

Designs: 10,000k. Rubbing sticks to start fire. 15,000k, Extracting sap from tree. 20,000k, Smoking tribal pipe. 25,000k, Shooting bow & arrow. 28,000k, Mothers, children. 30,000k, Cave art.

1995, Jan. 6   Litho.   Perf. 14
924	A191	10,000k multicolored	.42	.42
925	A191	15,000k multicolored	.65	.65
926	A191	20,000k multicolored	.85	.85
927	A191	25,000k multicolored	1.00	1.00
928	A191	28,000k multicolored	1.10	1.10
929	A191	30,000k multicolored	1.25	1.25
		Nos. 924-929 (6)	5.27	5.27

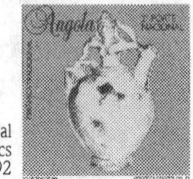

Traditional Ceramics A192

Designs: No. 930, Pitcher with bust of a woman as stopper. No. 931, Cone-shaped vase. No. 932, Bird-shaped vase. No. 933, Pitcher with bust of a man as stopper.

1995, Jan. 2   Litho.   Perf. 14½
930	A192	(2) 2nd class natl.		
931	A192	(1) 1st class natl.		
932	A192	(2) 2nd class intl.		
933	A192	(1) 1st class intl.		
		Nos. 930-933 (4)	3.25	

Rotary Intl., 90th Anniv. A193

a, Immunizing boy against polio. b, Medical examination. c, Immunizing girl against polio. No. 936, Dove over map.

1995, Feb. 23   Litho.   Perf. 14
934		Strip of 3	2.25	2.25
a.-c.	A193	27,000k any single	.75	.75
935		Strip of 3	2.25	2.25
a.-c.	A193	27,000k any single	.75	.75

Souvenir Sheet
| 936 | A193 | 81,000k multicolored | 4.00 | 4.00 |
| a. | | English inscription | 4.00 | 4.00 |

No. 934 has Portuguese inscriptions. No. 935 has English inscriptions. Both were issued in sheets of 9 stamps.
No. 936 contains Portuguese inscription in sheet margin.

Rotary Intl., 90th Anniv. — A194

Illustration reduced.

Litho. & Embossed
1995, Feb. 23   Perf. 11½x12
| 937 | A194 | 81,000k gold | | |

World Telecommunications Day — A195

Designs: No. 938, 1957 Sputnik 1. No. 939, Shuttle, Intelsat satellite.

1995   Litho.   Perf. 14
938	A195	27,000k multicolored	1.50	1.50
939	A195	27,000k multicolored	1.50	1.50
a.		Souvenir sheet, #938-939	3.00	3.00

Independence, 20th Anniv. — A196

1995, Nov. 11   Litho.   Perf. 14
| 940 | A196 | 2900k multicolored | 1.50 | 1.50 |

4th World Conference on Women, Beijing — A197

Designs: 375k, Women working in fields. 1106k, Woman teaching, girls with book. 1265k, Woman in industry, career woman. 2900k, Woman in native headdress, vert.
1500k, Native mother, children, vert.

1996, Jan. 29   Litho.   Perf. 14
941	A197	375k multicolored	.15	.15
942	A197	1106k multicolored	.40	.40
943	A197	1265k multicolored	.45	.45
944	A197	2900k multicolored	1.00	1.00
		Nos. 941-944 (4)	2.00	2.00

Souvenir Sheet
| 945 | A197 | 1500k multicolored | .50 | .50 |

UN Assistance Programs A198

Designs: 200k, Boy, highlift moving supplies. 1265k, Supply ship arriving. No. 948, Two high lifts. No. 949, Tractor-trailer traveling past vultures, native girl.
No. 950, Man, ship.

1996   Litho.   Perf. 14
946	A198	200k multicolored	.15	.15
947	A198	1265k multicolored	.50	.50
948	A198	2583k multicolored	1.00	1.00
949	A198	2583k multicolored	1.00	1.00
		Nos. 946-949 (4)	2.65	2.65

Souvenir Sheet
| 950 | A198 | 1265k multicolored | .50 | .50 |

Flora and Fauna A199

1500k, Verdant hawkmoth. 4400k, Water lily. 5100k, Panther toad. 6000k, African wild dog.
1500k: a, Western honey buzzard. b, Bateleur. c, Common kestrel.
4400k: d, Red-crested turaco. e, Giraffe. f, Elephant.
5100k: g, Hippopotamus. h, Cattle egret. i, Lion.
6000k: j, Helmeted turtle. k, African pygmy goose. l, Egyptian plover.
12,000k, Spotted hyena.

1996, Apr. 20   Litho.   Perf. 14
| 951-954 | A199 | Set of 4 | 1.00 | 1.00 |
| 955 | A199 | Sheet of 12, #a.-l. | 4.00 | 4.00 |

Souvenir Sheet
| 956 | A199 | 12,000k multicolored | .80 | .80 |

Sheets of 12

Birds — A200

Fowl: No. 957a, California quail. b, Greater prairie chicken. c, Painted quail. d, Golden pheasant. e, Roulroul partridge. f, Ceylon sourfowl. g, Himalayan snowcock. h, Temminicks tragopan. i, Lady Amherst's pheasant. j, Great curassow. k, Red-legged partridge. l, Impeyan pheasant.
Hummingbirds: No. 958a, Anna's. b, Blue-throated. c, Broad-tailed. d, Costa's. e, White-eared. f, Calliope. g, Violet-crowned. h, Rufous. i, Crimson topaz. j, Broad-billed. k, Frilled coquette. l, Ruby-throated.

No. 959, Ring-necked pheasant. No. 960, Racquet-tail hummingbird.

1996, Apr. 20
| 957-958 | A200 | 5500k #a.-l., each | 4.25 | 4.25 |

Souvenir Sheets
| 959-960 | A200 | 12,000k each | .80 | .80 |

Lubrapex '96 A201

Wild animals: a, 180k, Lions attacking zebra. b, 450k, Zebras, lions, diff. c, 180k, Zebras grazing, lions stalking. d, 450k, Panthera leo. e, 550k, Cheetah. f, 630k, Cheetah running. g, 550k, Cheetah chasing antilope. h, 630k, Cheetah attacking antelope. i, 180k, Antilope (gnu) being attacked by wild dogs. j, 450k, Antelope, wild dogs. k, 180k, Pack of wild dogs. l, 450k, Licaon pictus. m, 550k, Panthera pardus. n, 630k, Oryx. o, 550k, Oryx, diff. p, 630k, Leopard attacking oryx.

1996, Apr. 27
| 961 | A201 | Sheet of 16, #a.-p. | 6.00 | 6.00 |

Sheets of 6

Ships A202

Designs: No. 962a, Styrbjorn, Sweden, 1789. b, Constellation, US, 1797. c, Taureau, France, 1865. d, Bomb Ketch, France, 1682. e, Sardegna, Italy, 1881. f, HMS Glasgow, England, 1867.
No. 963a, Essex, US, 1812. b, HMS Inflexible, England, 1881. c, HMS Minotaur, England, 1863. d, Napoleon, France, 1854. e, Sophia Amalia, Denmark, 1650. f, Massena, France, 1887.
No. 964, HMS Tremendous, England, 1806, vert. No. 965, Royal Prince, England, 1666.

1996, May 4
| 962-963 | A202 | 6000k #a.-f., each | 2.50 | 2.50 |

Souvenir Sheets
| 964-965 | A202 | 12,000k each | .80 | .80 |

UN, 50th Anniv. (in 1995) A203

Designs: No. 966, Boys pumping water. No. 967, Man, woman with girl.
8000k, Unloading supplies from ship.

1996, Apr. 27   Litho.   Perf. 14
| 966 | A203 | 3500k multicolored | 1.00 | 1.00 |
| 967 | A203 | 3500k multicolored | 1.00 | 1.00 |

Souvenir Sheet
| 968 | A203 | 8000k multicolored | 1.00 | 1.00 |

Sonangol, 20th Anniv. A204

Face in traditional mask, costume, native birds, and: No. 969, Oil derricks. No. 970, Oil storage tanks, ship. 2500k, Refinery equipment. 5000k, Cargo shipment, jet.

1996, May 12
969	A204	1000k multicolored	.15	.15
970	A204	1000k multicolored	.15	.15
971	A204	2500k multicolored	.25	.25
972	A204	5000k multicolored	.55	.55
		Nos. 969-972 (4)	1.10	1.10

ANGOLA

Brapex '96
A205

#973, Slaves in hold. #974, Slaves fleeing ship as it's overturned. #975, Slave boats approaching ship. #976, Slaves talking with captain.
50,000k, like #975.

1996, Oct. 19	Litho.		Perf. 14
973	A205	20,000k multicolored	1.30 1.30
974	A205	20,000k multicolored	1.30 1.30
975	A205	30,000k multicolored	1.90 1.90
976	A205	30,000k multicolored	1.90 1.90
		Nos. 973-976 (4)	6.40 6.40

Souvenir Sheet

977	A205	50,000k multicolored	3.20 3.20

Churches — A206

Designs: 5,000k, Mission, Huila. No. 979, Church of the Nazarene. No. 980, Church of Our Lady of Pó Pulo. 25,000k, St. Adriáo Church.

1996, Dec. 6	Litho.		Perf. 14
978	A206	5,000k multicolored	.30 .30
979	A206	10,000k multicolored	.65 .65
980	A206	15,000k multicolored	.65 .65
981	A206	25,000k multicolored	1.60 1.60
		Nos. 978-981 (4)	3.20 3.20

1996 Summer Olympic Games, Atlanta
A207

1996, Dec. 9			
982	A207	5,000k Handball, vert.	.30 .30
983	A207	10,000k Swimming	.65 .65
984	A207	25,000k Track & field, vert.	1.60 1.60
985	A207	35,000k Shooting	2.25 2.25
		Nos. 982-985 (4)	4.80 4.80

Souvenir Sheet

986	A207	65,000k Basketball	4.00 4.00

MPLA (Liberation Movement), 40th Anniv. — A208

1996, Dec. 10	Litho.		Perf. 14
987	A208	30,000k Dolphins, map	1.80 1.80

Trains A209

Trains A209a

No. 988: a, AVE, Spain. b, Bullet Train, Japan. c, GM F7 Warbonnet, US. d, Deltic, Great Britain. e, Eurostar, France/Great Britain. f, ETR 450, Italy.
No. 989: a, Class E1300, Morocco. b, ICE, Germany. c, X2000, Sweden. d, TGV Duplex, France.
No. 989E: f, Steam engine. g, Garrat. h, General Electric.
No. 990, Canadian Pacific 4-4-0, Canada. No. 991, Via Rail Canadian, Canada.

1997, May 29	Litho.		Perf. 14

Sheets of 6, 4 or 3

988	A209	100,000k #a.-f.	6.00 6.00
989	A209	140,000k #a.-d.	6.00 6.00
989E	A209a	250,000k Sheet of 3, #f.-h.	5.75 5.75

Souvenir Sheets
Perf. 13½

990-991	A209	110,000k each	4.00 4.00

Nos. 990-991 contain one 38x50 or 50x38mm stamp, respectively.
PACIFIC 97.

Horses A210

No. 992: a, Thoroughbred. b, Palomino, appaloosa. c, Arabians. d, Arabian colt. e, Thoroughbred colt. f, Mustang. g, Mustang, diff. h, Furioso.
No. 993: a, Thoroughbred. b, Arabian, palomino. c, Arabian, chincoteague. d, Pintos. e, Przewalski's horse. f, Thoroughbred colt. g, Arabians. h, New forest pony.
No. 994: a, Selle Francais. b, Fjord. c, Percheron. d, Italian heavy draft. e, Shagya Arab. f, Avelignese. g, Czechoslovakian warmblood. h, New forest pony.
215,000k, Thoroughbreds. 220,000k, Thoroughbreds, diff.

1997, July 5	Litho.		Perf. 14

Sheets of 8

992	A210	100,000k #a.-h.	4.00 4.00
993	A210	120,000k #a.-h.	5.00 5.00
994	A210	140,000k #a.-h.	5.50 5.50

Souvenir Sheets

995	A210	215,000k multicolored	4.00 4.00
996	A210	220,000k multicolored	4.00 4.00

PACIFIC 97.

1998 World Cup Soccer Championships, France — A211

Winners holding World Cup trophy: No. 997: a, Uruguay, 1930. b, Germany, 1954. c, Brazil, 1970. d, Argentina, 1986. e, Brazil, 1994.
Winning team pictures: No. 998a, Germany, 1954. b, Uruguay, 1958. c, Italy, 1938. d, Brazil, 1962. e, Brazil, 1970. f, Uruguay, 1930.
220,000k, Angolan team members standing. 250,000k, 1997 Angolan team picture.

1997, July 5	Litho.		Perf. 14

Sheets of 5 or 6

997	A211	100,000k #a.-e. + label	5.00 5.00
998	A211	100,000k #a.-f.	6.00 6.00

Souvenir Sheets

999	A211	220,000k multicolored	3.60 3.60
1000	A211	250,000k multicolored	4.00 4.00

ENSA (Security System), 20th Anniv. — A212

"Star" emblem, and stylized protection of "egg:" #1001, Industry. #1002, Recreation. #1003, Homes, shelters. #1004, Accident prevention. 350,000k, Emblem.

1998	Litho.		Perf. 13½
1001-1004	A212	240,000k Set of 4	7.50 7.50

Souvenir Sheet
Perf. 13½x13

1005	A212	350,000k multicolored	2.75 2.75

No. 1005 contains one 60x40mm stamp.

GURN (Natl. Unity & Reconciliation Government), 1st Anniv. — A213

Emblem, portion of country map and: 100,000k, a, Sea, swordfish, ships, oil derrick. b, Sea, ships, swordfish. c, Sea, swordfish, ships, mining car on railroad track. d, Sea, power lines.
200,000k: e, Train on track, antelope. f, Mining cars on track, tractor pulling cart. g, Railroad track across rivers, tractor plowing. h, Power lines. i, UR corner of map, crystals. j, Train on track. k, Elephant, tree. l, Trunk of tree, bottom edge of map.

1998

1006	A213	Sheet of 12, #a.-l.	15.00 15.00

Souvenir Sheet

Education in Angola — A214

Illustration reduced.

1998

1007	A214	400,000k multicolored	3.25 3.25

Diana, Princess of Wales (1961-97) — A215

Various portraits, color of sheet margin: No. 1008, pale green. No. 1009, pale yellow.
400,000k, Wearing protective clothing.

1998, May 21	Litho.		Perf. 14

Sheets of 6

1008-1009	A215	100,000k #a.-f., each	4.75 4.75

Souvenir Sheet

1010	A215	400,000k multicolored	3.25 3.25

See No. 1028.

Expo '98, Lisbon A216

Marine life: No. 1011, 100,000k, Anemones. No. 1012, 100,000k, Sea urchin. No. 1013, 100,000k, Sea horses. No. 1014, 100,000k, Coral (Caravela). No. 1015, 240,000k, Sea slug. No. 1016, 240,000k, Worms (Tunicados).

1998, May 21			Perf. 13½
1011-1016	A216	Set of 6	7.00 7.00

Butterflies — A217

No. 1017: a, Metamorpha stelene. b, Papilio glaucus. c, Danaus plexippus. d, Catonephele numilli. e, Plebejus argus. f, Hypolimnas bolina.
No. 1018: a, Terinos terpander. b, Bematistes aganice. c, Hebomoia glaucippe. d, Colias eurytheme. e, Pereute leucodrosime. f, Lycaena dispar.
No. 1019, horiz.: a, Dynastor napolean. b, Zeuxidia amethystus. c, Battus philenor. d, Phoebis philea. e, Danaus chrysippus. f, Glaucopsyche alexis.
No. 1020, Euphaedra neophron. No. 1021, Thecla betulae, horiz. No. 1022, Uraneis ucubis, armillaria staminea.

1998, May 21			Perf. 14

Sheets of 6

1017-1019	A217	120,000k #a.-f., each	6.00 6.00

Souvenir Sheets

1020-1022	A217	250,000k each	4.00 4.00

Cats and Dogs A218

Cats: No. 1023a, British tortoiseshell. b, Chinchilla. c, Russian blue. d, Black Persian (longhair). e, British red tabby. f, Birman.
Dogs: No. 1024a, West Highland terrier. b, Irish setter. c, Dachshund. d, St. John water dog. e, Shetland sheep dog. f, Dalmatian.
No. 1025, Turkish van (swimming cat). No. 1026, Labrador retriever.

1998, May 21	Litho.		Perf. 14x13½

Sheets of 6

1023-1024	A218	140,000k #a.-f., each	6.75 6.75

Souvenir Sheets

1025-1026	A218	500,000k each	4.00 4.00

Wild Animals A219

100,000k: a, Panthera leo. b, Hippopotamus amphibius. c, Loxodonta africana. d, Giraffa camelopardalis.
220,000k: e, Syncerus caffer-caffer. f, Gorilla gorilla. g, Ceratotherim simum. h, Oryx gazella.

1998, July 24	Litho.		Perf. 14
1027	A219	Sheet of 8, #a.-h.	10.00 10.00

Diana, Princes of Wales Type of 1998

Pictures showing Diana's campaign to ban land mines: a, With girl. b, With two boys. c, Wearing protective clothing.

1998, Aug. 31	Litho.		Perf. 14
1028	A215	150,000k Strip of 3, #a.-c.	4.75 4.75

No. 1028 was issued in sheets of 6 stamps.

Ordering on-line is QUICK! EASY! CONVENIENT!
www.scottonline.com

ANGOLA

Intl. Year of the Ocean — A220

Marine life: No. 1029a, Pagurites. b, Callinectes marginatus. c, Thais forbesi. d, Ostrea tulipa. e, Balanus amohitrite. f, Uca tangeri.
No. 1030: a, Littorina angulifera. b, Semifusus morio. c, Thais coronata. d, Cerithium atratum (red branch). e, Ostrea tulipa. f, Cerithium atratum (green branch).
No. 1031, Goniopsis, horiz. No. 1032, Unidentified shell.

1998, Sept. 4   **Sheets of 6**
1029	A220	100,000k #a.-f.	3.00	3.00
1030	A220	170,000k #a.-f.	5.00	5.00

Souvenir Sheets
1031-1032	A220	300,000k each	4.00	4.00

Souvenir Sheet

Battle Against Polio in Angola — A221

Illustration reduced.

1998, Aug. 28   **Litho.**   **Perf. 13½**
1033	A221	500,000k multicolored	2.50	2.50

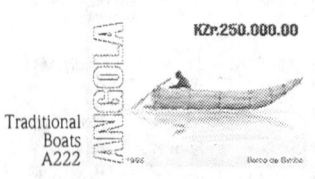

Traditional Boats A222

Designs: No. 1034, 250,000k, Boat, Bimba. No. 1035, 250,000k, Canoe with sail, Ndongo. 500,000k, Constructing boat, Ndongo.

1998, Sept. 4   **Perf. 14**
1034-1036	A222	Set of 3	5.00	5.00

Titanic A223

Views of Titanic: a, Under tow. b, Stern. c, Starboard side at night. d, At dock.

1998, Sept. 4
1037	A223	350,000k Sheet of 4, #a.-d.	7.00	7.00

No. 1037c is 76x30mm. No. 1037d is 38x61mm.

Angolan Food A224

Various vegetables, fruits: #1038, 100,000k, 4 fruits. #1039, 100,000k, Squash sliced in half. #1040, 120,000k, Ears of corn. #1041, 120,000k, Green beans. #1042, 140,000k, Fruit with red seeds sliced in half. #1043, 140,000k, Sliced bananas.

1998
1038-1043	A224	Set of 6	5.50	5.50

Portugal '98.

SEMI-POSTAL STAMPS

Angolan Red Cross — SP1

1991, Sept. 19   **Litho.**   **Perf. 14**
B1	SP1	20k +5k Mother and child	.85	.85
B2	SP1	40k +5k Zebra and foal	1.50	1.50

AIR POST STAMPS

Common Design Type
Perf. 13½x13

1938, July 26   **Engr.**   **Unwmk.**
Name and Value in Black
C1	CD39	10c scarlet	.15	.15
C2	CD39	20c purple	.25	.15
C3	CD39	50c orange	.15	.15
C4	CD39	1a ultra	.38	.15
C5	CD39	2a lilac brn	.85	.15
C6	CD39	3a dk green	2.25	.25
C7	CD39	5a red brown	3.25	.35
C8	CD39	9a rose carmine	4.25	1.10
C9	CD39	10a magenta	5.50	1.10
		Nos. C1-C9 (9)	17.03	3.55

No. C7 exists with overprint "Exposicao Internacional de Nova York, 1939-1940" and Trylon and Perisphere.

AP2    Planes Circling Globe — AP3

1947, Aug.   **Litho.**   **Perf. 10½**
C10	AP2	1a red brown	6.25	1.65
C11	AP2	2a yellow grn	6.25	1.65
C12	AP2	3a orange	8.00	1.65
C13	AP2	3.50a orange	10.00	4.00
C14	AP2	5a olive grn	90.00	15.00
C15	AP2	6a rose	90.00	17.50
C16	AP2	9a red	275.00	200.00
C17	AP2	10a green	175.00	60.00
C18	AP2	20a blue	175.00	60.00
C19	AP2	50a black	400.00	200.00
C20	AP2	100a yellow	750.00	600.00
		Nos. C10-C20 (11)	1,985.	1,161.

1949, May 1   **Photo.**   **Perf. 11½**
C21	AP3	1a henna brown	.15	.15
C22	AP3	2a red brown	.40	.15
C23	AP3	3a plum	.65	.15
C24	AP3	6a dull green	2.00	.40
C25	AP3	9a violet brown	3.00	1.00
		Nos. C21-C25 (5)	6.20	1.85

> Catalogue values for unused stamps in this section, from this point to the end of the section, are for Never Hinged items.

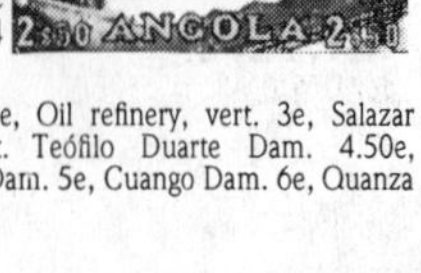

Cambambe Dam — AP4

Designs: 1.50e, Oil refinery, vert. 3e, Salazar Dam. 4e, Capt. Teófilo Duarte Dam. 4.50e, Craveiro Lopes Dam. 5e, Cuango Dam. 6e, Quanza River Bridge. 7e, Capt. Teófilo Duarte Bridge. 8.50e, Oliveira Salazar Bridge. 12.50e, Capt. Silva Carvalho Bridge.

Perf. 11½x12, 12x11½
1965, July 12   **Litho.**   **Unwmk.**
C26	AP4	1.50e multicolored	1.00	.15
C27	AP4	2.50e multicolored	.60	.15
C28	AP4	3e multicolored	1.00	.15
C29	AP4	4e multicolored	.40	.15
C30	AP4	4.50e multicolored	.40	.15
C31	AP4	5e multicolored	.65	.20
C32	AP4	6e multicolored	.65	.20
C33	AP4	7e multicolored	1.00	.20
C34	AP4	8.50e multicolored	1.25	.55
C35	AP4	12.50e multicolored	1.50	.65
		Nos. C26-C35 (10)	8.45	2.55

Stamp Centenary Type
Design: 2.50e, Boeing 707 jet & Angola #2.

1970, Dec. 1   **Litho.**   **Perf. 13½**
C36	A83	2.50e multicolored	.45	.15
a.		Souv. sheet of 3, #565-566, C36	2.50	2.50

No. C36a sold for 15e.

No. C36 Overprinted with Bar and: "REPUBLICA POPULAR / DE"

1980, June 15   **Litho.**   **Perf. 13½**
C37	A83	2.50e multicolored		.15

POSTAGE DUE STAMPS

D1    D2

1904   **Unwmk.**   **Typo.**   **Perf. 11½x12**
J1	D1	5r yellow grn	.25	.15
J2	D1	10r slate	.25	.15
J3	D1	20r yellow brn	.35	.32
J4	D1	30r orange	.60	.60
J5	D1	50r gray brown	.60	.60
J6	D1	60r red brown	4.00	2.50
J7	D1	100r lilac	1.75	1.65
J8	D1	130r dull blue	1.75	1.65
J9	D1	200r carmine	4.00	3.00
J10	D1	500r gray violet	4.00	3.00
		Nos. J1-J10 (10)	17.55	13.62

Postage Due Stamps of 1904 Overprinted in Carmine or Green

1911
J11	D1	5r yellow grn	.20	.20
J12	D1	10r slate	.20	.20
J13	D1	20r yellow brn	.20	.20
J14	D1	30r orange	.30	.30
J15	D1	50r gray brown	.30	.30
J16	D1	60r red brown	.60	.60
J17	D1	100r lilac	.60	.60
J18	D1	130r dull blue	.60	.60
J19	D1	200r carmine (G)	.60	.60
J20	D1	500r gray violet	.70	.70
		Nos. J11-J20 (10)	4.30	4.30

1921   **Perf. 11½**
J21	D2	½c yellow green	.15	.15
J22	D2	1c slate	.15	.15
J23	D2	2c orange brown	.15	.15
J24	D2	3c orange	.15	.15
J25	D2	5c gray brown	.15	.15
J26	D2	6c lt brown	.15	.15
J27	D2	10c red violet	.15	.15
J28	D2	13c dull blue	.20	.20
J29	D2	20c carmine	.20	.20
J30	D2	50c gray	.20	.20
		Nos. J21-J30 (10)	1.65	1.65

For surcharges see Nos. 268-270.

> Catalogue values for unused stamps in this section, from this point to the end of the section, are for Never Hinged items.

Stamps of 1932 Surcharged in Black

PORTEADO
10
Centavos

1948   **Wmk. 232**   **Perf. 12x11½**
J31	A14	10c on 20c gray	.20	.20
J32	A14	20c on 30c myrtle grn	.20	.20
J33	A14	30c on 50c lt brown	.45	.45
J34	A14	40c on 1a claret	.45	.45
J35	A14	50c on 2a dull vio	.90	.45
J36	A14	1a on 5a pale yel grn	1.25	1.00
		Nos. J31-J36 (6)	3.45	2.75

Common Design Type
Photogravure and Typographed
1952   **Unwmk.**   **Perf. 14**
Numeral in Red, Frame Multicolored
J37	CD45	10c red brown	.15	.15
J38	CD45	30c olive green	.15	.15
J39	CD45	50c chocolate	.15	.15
J40	CD45	1a dk vio blue	.15	.15
J41	CD45	2a red brown	.20	.20
J42	CD45	5a black brown	.32	.32
		Nos. J37-J42 (6)	1.12	1.12

NEWSPAPER STAMP

N1

Perf. 11½, 12½, 13½
1893   **Typo.**   **Unwmk.**
P1	N1	2½r brown	1.00	.70

No. P1 was also used for ordinary postage. For surcharges see Nos. 37, 82, 180, 235.

POSTAL TAX STAMPS

Pombal Issue
Common Design Types
1925, May 8   **Unwmk.**   **Perf. 12½**
RA1	CD28	15c lilac & black	.32	.25
RA2	CD29	15c lilac & black	.32	.25
RA3	CD30	15c lilac & black	.32	.25
		Nos. RA1-RA3 (3)	.96	.75

"Charity" PT1   Coat of Arms PT2

1929   **Litho.**   **Perf. 11**
Without Gum
RA4	PT1	50c dark blue	2.00	.70

1939   **Without Gum**   **Perf. 10½**
RA5	PT2	50c turq green	1.75	.15
RA6	PT2	1a red	3.25	1.50

A 1.50a, type PT2, was issued for fiscal use.

> Catalogue values for unused stamps in this section, from this point to the end of the section, are for Never Hinged items.

Old Man — PT3    Mother and Child — PT4

ANGOLA — ANGRA — ANGUILLA

Designs: 1e, Boy. 1.50e, Girl.
Imprint: "Foto-Lito-E.G.A.-Luanda"

1955	Unwmk.	Perf. 13

Heads in dark brown

RA7	PT3	50c dk ocher	.15	.15
RA8	PT3	1e orange ver	.75	.40
RA9	PT3	1.50e brt yel grn	.50	.25
		Nos. RA7-RA9 (3)	1.40	.80

A 2.50e, type PT3 showing an old woman, was issued for revenue use.
See Nos. RA16, RA19-RA21, RA25-RA27.

No. RA7 Surcharged with New Values and two Bars in Red or Black

1957-58

Head in dark brown

RA11	PT3	10c on 50c dk ocher (R)	.25	.25
RA12	PT3	10c on 50c dk ocher ('58)	.20	.20
RA13	PT3	30c on 50c dk ocher	.22	.22
		Nos. RA11-RA13 (3)	.67	.67

1959	Litho.	Perf. 13

Design: 30c, Boy and girl.

RA14	PT4	10c orange & blk	.15	.15
RA15	PT4	30c slate & blk	.15	.15

Type of 1955 Redrawn

Design: 1e, Boy.

1961, Nov.		Perf. 13
RA16	PT3	1e salmon pink & dk brn	.20	.20

Denomination in italics.

Yellow, White and Black Men — PT5

1962, July 1	Typo.	Perf. 10½

Without Gum

RA17	PT5	50c multicolored	.65	.65
RA18	PT5	1e multicolored	.32	.32

Issued for the Provincial Settlement Committee (Junta Provincial do Povoamento). The tax was used to promote Portuguese settlement in Angola, and to raise educational and living standards of recent immigrants.
Denominations higher than 1e were used for revenue purposes.

Head Type of 1955
Without Imprint

Designs: 50c, Old man. 1e, Boy. 1.50e, Girl.

1964-65	Litho.	Perf. 11½

Heads in dark brown

RA19	PT3	50c orange	.15	.15
RA20	PT3	1e dull red org ('65)	.20	.20
RA21	PT3	1.50e yel grn ('65)	.25	.25
		Nos. RA19-RA21 (3)	.60	.60

No. RA20 is second redrawing of 1e, with bolder lettering and denomination in gothic. Space between "Assistencia" and denomination on RA19-RA21 is ½mm; on 1955 issue space is 2mm.

Map of Angola, Industrial and Farm Workers — PT6

1965, Sept. 1	Litho.	Perf. 13
RA22	PT6	50c multicolored	.35	.15
RA23	PT6	1e multicolored	.35	.25

The 2e was used for revenue purposes.

Head Type of 1955
Imprint: "I.N.A." or "INA" (1e)

Designs: 50c, Old man. 1e, Boy. 1.50e, Girl.

1966

Heads in dark brown

RA25	PT3	50c dull orange	.15	.15
RA26	PT3	1e dull brick red	.15	.15
RA27	PT3	1.50e lt yel grn	.32	.15
		Nos. RA25-RA27 (3)	.62	.45

Woman Planting Tree — PT7

1972	Litho.	Perf. 13
RA28	PT7	50c shown	.15	.15
RA29	PT7	1e Workers	.15	.15
RA30	PT7	2e Produce	.20	.20
		Nos. RA28-RA30 (3)	.50	.50

POSTAL TAX DUE STAMPS

Pombal Issue
Common Design Types

1925, May 8	Unwmk.	Perf. 12½
RAJ1	CD28	30c lilac & black	.50	1.25
RAJ2	CD29	30c lilac & black	.50	1.25
RAJ3	CD30	30c lilac & black	.50	1.25
		Nos. RAJ1-RAJ3 (3)	1.50	3.75

See note after Portugal No. RAJ4.

ANGRA

'aŋ-grə

LOCATION — An administrative district of the Azores, consisting of the islands of Terceira, Sao Jorge and Graciosa.
GOVT. — A district of Portugal
AREA — 275 sq. mi.
POP. — 70,000 (approx.)
CAPITAL — Angra do Heroismo

1000 Reis = 1 Milreis

King Carlos
A1 A2

1892-93	Typo.	Unwmk.	Perf. 12½
1	A1	5r yellow	3.00	1.30
a.		Perf. 11½	6.50	4.00
b.		Perf. 13½	2.75	1.30
2	A1	10r redsh violet	3.00	1.30
a.		Perf. 13½	3.75	2.00
3	A1	15r chocolate	3.50	2.00
a.		Perf. 13½	3.75	2.00
4	A1	20r lavender	3.75	2.00
a.		Perf. 13½	3.75	2.00
5	A1	25r green	4.00	.50
a.		Perf. 13½	7.00	.90
b.		Perf. 13½	5.00	.90
7	A1	50r blue	7.75	3.00
a.		Perf. 13½	10.00	4.50
8	A1	75r carmine	9.00	3.50
9	A1	80r yellow green	10.00	7.00
10	A1	100r brown, yel, perf. 13½ ('93)	35.00	10.00
a.		Perf. 12½	140.00	95.00
11	A1	150r car, rose ('93)	50.00	25.00
a.		Perf. 13½	60.00	37.50
12	A1	200r dk blue, bl ('93)	50.00	25.00
a.		Perf. 13½	60.00	37.50
13	A1	300r dk blue, sal ('93)	50.00	25.00
a.		Perf. 13½	60.00	37.50

Reprints of 50r, 150r, 200r and 300r, made in 1900, are perf. 11½ and ungummed. Value, each $7.50. Reprints of all values, made in 1905, have shiny white gum and clean-cut perf. 13½.

1897-1905		Perf. 11½

Name and Value in Black except Nos. 26 and 35

14	A2	2½r gray	.65	.35
15	A2	5r orange	.65	.35
a.		Diagonal half used as 2½r on cover		22.50
16	A2	10r yellow grn	.70	.40
17	A2	15r brown	8.50	3.50
18	A2	15r gray grn ('99)	.90	.45
19	A2	20r gray violet	1.50	.90
20	A2	25r sea green	2.75	.90
21	A2	25r car rose ('99)	.70	.40
22	A2	50r dark blue	5.00	1.25
23	A2	50r ultra ('05)	12.50	8.00
24	A2	65r slate bl ('98)	1.00	.40
25	A2	75r rose	3.00	1.00
26	A2	75r gray brn & car, straw ('05)	16.00	19.00
27	A2	80r violet	1.50	1.00
28	A2	100r dk blue, bl	2.50	1.25
29	A2	115r org brn, pink ('98)	2.50	1.40
30	A2	130r gray brn, straw ('98)	2.50	1.40
31	A2	150r lt brn, straw	2.50	1.40
32	A2	180r sl, pnksh ('98)	3.00	2.00
33	A2	200r red vio, pnksh	5.00	2.75
34	A2	300r blue, rose	7.50	4.00
35	A2	500r blk & red, bl	16.00	10.00
a.		Perf. 12½	21.00	12.50
		Nos. 14-35 (22)	96.85	62.10

Azores stamps were used in Angra from 1906 to 1931, when they were superseded by those of Portugal.

ANGUILLA

aŋ-,gwi-lə

LOCATION — In the West Indies southeast of Puerto Rico
GOVT. — British territory
AREA — 60 sq. mi.
POP. — 6,500 (est. 1980)
CAPITAL — The Valley

Anguilla separated unilaterally from the Associated State of St. Kitts-Nevis-Anguilla in 1967, formalized in 1980 following direct United Kingdom intervention some years before. A British Commissioner exercises executive authority.

100 Cents = 1 Dollar

Catalogue values for all unused stamps in this country are for Never Hinged items.

St. Kitts-Nevis Nos. 145-160 Overprinted

Independent
Anguilla
On Type A14

Independent
Anguilla
On Type A15

1967, Sept. 4	Photo.	Wmk. 314	Perf. 14
1	A14	½c blue & dk brn	25.00	22.50
2	A15	1c multicolored	25.00	7.00
3	A15	2c multicolored	25.00	2.00
4	A15	3c multicolored	25.00	5.00
5	A15	4c multicolored	25.00	6.00
6	A15	5c multicolored	100.00	20.00
7	A15	6c multicolored	50.00	10.00
8	A15	10c multicolored	25.00	7.50
9	A14	15c multicolored	55.00	12.00
10	A15	20c multicolored	85.00	20.00
11	A15	25c multicolored	70.00	22.50
12	A15	50c multicolored	2,000.	500.00
13	A14	60c multicolored	2,500.	900.00
14	A14	$1 multicolored	1,600.	425.00
15	A15	$2.50 multicolored	1,600.	325.00
16	A14	$5 multicolored	1,300.	325.00
		Nos. 1-16 (16)	9,510.	2,609.

Counterfeit overprints exist.

Mahogany Tree, The Quarter — A1

Designs: 2c, Sombrero Lighthouse. 3c, St. Mary's Church. 4c, Valley Police Station. 5c, Old Plantation House, Mt. Fortune. 6c, Valley Post Office. 10c, Methodist Church, West End. 15c, Wall-Blake Airport. 20c, Plane over Sandy Ground. 25c, Island Harbor. 40c, Map of Anguilla. 60c, Hermit crab and starfish. $1, Hibiscus. $2.50, Coconut harvest. $5, Spiny lobster.

1967-68	Litho.	Perf. 12½x13
		Unwmk.
17	A1	1c orange & multi	.15	.15
18	A1	2c gray green & blk	.15	.15
19	A1	3c emerald & blk	.15	.15
20	A1	4c brt blue & blk	.15	.15
21	A1	5c lt blue & multi	.15	.15
22	A1	6c ver & black	.15	.15
23	A1	10c multicolored	.15	.15
24	A1	15c multicolored	.15	.15
25	A1	20c multicolored	.20	.20
26	A1	25c multicolored	.30	.30
27	A1	40c blue & multi	.45	.45
28	A1	60c yellow & multi	.65	.65
29	A1	$1 lt green & multi	1.25	1.25
30	A1	$2.50 multicolored	3.25	3.25
31	A1	$5 multicolored	6.00	6.00
		Nos. 17-31 (15)	13.30	13.30

Issued: 1c, 5c, 10c, 20c, 25c, 40c, 11/27/67; 3c, 4c, 15c, 60c, $1, $5, 2/10/68; 2c, 6c, $2.50, 3/21/68.
For overprints see Nos. 53-67, 78-82.

Sailboats
A2

Designs: 15c, Boat building. 25c, Schooner Warspite. 40c, Yacht Atlantic Star.

1968, May 11		Perf. 14
32	A2	10c rose & multi	.30	.30
33	A2	15c olive & multi	.50	.50
34	A2	25c lilac rose & multi	.75	.75
35	A2	40c dull blue & multi	1.25	1.25
		Nos. 32-35 (4)	2.80	2.80

Purple-throated Carib — A3

Girl Guide Badge — A4

Anguillan Birds: 15c, Bananaquit. 25c, Blacknecked stilt, horiz. 40c, Royal tern, horiz.

1968, July 8		
36	A3	10c dull yel & multi	.45	.30
37	A3	15c yel green & multi	.60	.40
38	A3	25c multicolored	1.75	.95
39	A3	40c multicolored	2.00	1.65
		Nos. 36-39 (4)	4.80	3.30

		Perf. 13x13½, 13½x13

1968, Oct. 14		

Designs: 10c, Girl Guide badge, horiz. 25c, Badge and Headquarters, horiz. 40c, Merit Badges.

40	A4	10c lt green & multi	.20	.20
41	A4	15c lt blue & multi	.25	.25
42	A4	25c multicolored	.55	.55
43	A4	40c multicolored	.75	.75
		Nos. 40-43 (4)	1.75	1.75

Anguillan Girl Guides, 35th anniversary.

Three Kings — A5

Christmas: 10c, Three Kings seeing Star, vert. 15c, Holy Family, vert. 40c, Shepherds seeing Star. 50c, Holy Family and donkey.

1968, Nov. 18		
44	A5	1c lilac rose & black	.15	.15
45	A5	10c blue & black	.15	.15
46	A5	15c brown & black	.30	.30
47	A5	40c brt ultra & black	.80	.80
48	A5	50c green & black	1.10	1.10
		Nos. 44-48 (5)	2.50	2.50

ANGUILLA

Bagging Salt — A6

Salt Industry: 15c, Packing salt. 40c, Salt pond. 50c, Loading salt.

1969, Jan. 4			Perf. 13	
49	A6	10c red & multi	.15	.15
50	A6	15c lt blue & multi	.20	.20
51	A6	40c emerald & multi	.55	.55
52	A6	50c purple & multi	.65	.65
		Nos. 49-52 (4)	1.55	1.55

Nos. 17-31 Overprinted: "INDEPENDENCE/JANUARY, 1969"

1969, Jan. 9			Perf. 12½x13	
53	A1	1c orange & multi	.15	.15
54	A1	2c gray green & blk	.15	.15
55	A1	3c emerald & blk	.15	.15
56	A1	4c brt blue & blk	.15	.15
57	A1	5c lt blue & multi	.15	.15
58	A1	6c vermilion & blk	.15	.15
59	A1	10c multicolored	.15	.15
60	A1	15c multicolored	.20	.20
61	A1	20c multicolored	.25	.25
62	A1	25c multicolored	.35	.35
63	A1	40c blue & multi	.50	.50
64	A1	60c yellow & multi	.70	.70
65	A1	$1 lt green & multi	1.25	1.25
66	A1	$2.50 multicolored	3.00	3.00
67	A1	$5 multicolored	6.25	6.25
		Nos. 53-67 (15)	13.55	13.55

Crucifixion, School of Quentin Massys — A7

Easter: 40c, The Last Supper, ascribed to Roberti.

1969, Mar. 31		Litho.	Perf. 13½	
68	A7	25c multicolored	.35	.35
69	A7	40c multicolored	.65	.65

Amaryllis A8

1969, June 10			Perf. 14	
70	A8	10c shown	.20	.20
71	A8	15c Bougainvillea	.35	.35
72	A8	40c Hibiscus	.80	.80
73	A8	50c Cattleya orchid	1.10	1.10
		Nos. 70-73 (4)	2.45	2.45

Turban and Star Shells — A9

Sea Shells: 15c, Spiny oysters. 40c, Scotch, royal and smooth bonnets. 50c, Triton trumpet.

1969, Sept. 22				
74	A9	10c multicolored	.35	.35
75	A9	15c multicolored	.50	.50
76	A9	40c multicolored	1.10	1.10
77	A9	50c multicolored	1.50	1.50
		Nos. 74-77 (4)	3.45	3.45

Nos. 17, 25-28 Overprinted "CHRISTMAS 1969" and Various Christmas Designs

1969, Oct. 27			Perf. 12½x13	
78	A1	1c orange & multi	.15	.15
79	A1	20c multicolored	.35	.25
80	A1	25c multicolored	.45	.45
81	A1	40c blue & multi	.85	.75
82	A1	60c yellow & multi	2.00	1.85
		Nos. 78-82 (5)	3.80	2.85

Red Goatfish A10

Designs: 15c, Blue-striped grunts. 40c, Mutton grouper. 50c, Banded butterfly-fish.

1969, Dec. 1			Perf. 14	
83	A10	10c multicolored	.25	.25
84	A10	15c multicolored	.40	.40
85	A10	40c multicolored	1.25	1.25
86	A10	50c multicolored	1.50	1.50
		Nos. 83-86 (4)	3.40	3.40

Morning Glory — A11

1970, Feb. 23				
87	A11	10c shown	.20	.20
88	A11	15c Blue petrea	.35	.35
89	A11	40c Hibiscus	1.25	1.25
90	A11	50c Flamboyant	1.65	1.65
		Nos. 87-90 (4)	3.45	3.45

The Way to Calvary, by Tiepolo — A12

Easter: 20c, Crucifixion, by Masaccio, vert. 40c, Descent from the Cross, by Rosso Fiorentino, vert. 60c, Jesus Carrying the Cross, by Murillo.

1970, Mar. 26			Perf. 13½	
91	A12	10c multicolored	.15	.15
92	A12	20c multicolored	.25	.25
93	A12	40c multicolored	.50	.50
94	A12	60c multicolored	.70	.70
		Nos. 91-94 (4)	1.60	1.60

Anguilla Map, Scout Badge A13

Designs: 15c, Cub Scouts practicing first aid. 40c, Monkey bridge. 50c, Scout Headquarters, The Valley, and Lord Baden-Powell.

1970, Aug. 10			Perf. 13	
95	A13	10c multicolored	.25	.25
96	A13	15c multicolored	.35	.35
97	A13	40c multicolored	.90	.90
98	A13	50c multicolored	1.10	1.10
		Nos. 95-98 (4)	2.60	2.60

Anguilla Boy Scouts, 40th anniversary.

Boat Building A14

Designs: 2c, Road construction. 3c, Blowing Point dock. 4c, Radio announcer. 5c, Cottage Hospital extension. 6c, Valley secondary school. 10c, Hotel extension. 15c, Sandy Ground. 20c, Supermarket and movie house. 25c, Bananas and mangoes. 40c, Wall-Blake airport. 60c, Sandy Ground jetty. $1, Administration building. $2.50, Cow and calf. $5, Sandy Hill Bay.

1970, Nov. 23			Litho.	Perf. 14
99	A14	1c multicolored	.15	.15
100	A14	2c multicolored	.15	.15
101	A14	3c multicolored	.15	.15
102	A14	4c multicolored	.15	.15
103	A14	5c multicolored	.15	.15
104	A14	6c multicolored	.15	.15
105	A14	10c multicolored	.20	.20
106	A14	15c multicolored	.25	.25
107	A14	20c multicolored	.30	.30
108	A14	25c multicolored	.35	.35
109	A14	40c multicolored	.60	.60
110	A14	60c multicolored	.90	.90
111	A14	$1 multicolored	1.50	1.50
112	A14	$2.50 multicolored	3.50	3.50
113	A14	$5 multicolored	7.25	7.25
		Nos. 99-113 (15)	15.75	15.75

Adoration of the Shepherds, by Guido Reni — A15

Christmas: 20c, Virgin and Child, by Benozzo Gozzoli. 25c, Nativity, by Botticelli. 40c, Santa Margherita Madonna, by Mazzola. 50c, Adoration of the Kings, by Tiepolo.

1970, Dec. 11			Perf. 13½	
114	A15	1c multicolored	.15	.15
115	A15	20c multicolored	.30	.30
116	A15	25c multicolored	.35	.35
117	A15	40c multicolored	.55	.55
118	A15	50c multicolored	.60	.60
		Nos. 114-118 (5)	1.95	1.95

Angels Weeping over the Dead Christ, by Guercino — A16

Easter: 10c, Ecce Homo, by Correggio, vert. 15c, Christ Appearing to St. Peter, by Carracci, vert. 50c, The Supper at Emmaus, by Caravaggio.

1971, Mar. 29				
119	A16	10c pink & multi	.15	.15
120	A16	15c lt blue & multi	.25	.25
121	A16	40c yel green & multi	.60	.60
122	A16	50c violet & multi	.70	.70
		Nos. 119-122 (4)	1.70	1.70

Hypolimnas Misippus A17

Butterflies: 15c, Junonia lavinia. 40c, Agraulis vanillae. 50c, Danaus plexippus.

1971, June 21			Perf. 14x14½	
123	A17	10c multicolored	.80	.80
124	A17	15c multicolored	1.10	1.10
125	A17	40c multicolored	2.00	2.00
126	A17	50c multicolored	2.50	2.50
		Nos. 123-126 (4)	6.40	6.40

Magnanime and Aimable in Battle — A18

Ships: 15c, HMS Duke and Agamemnon against Glorieux. 25c, HMS Formidable and Namur against Ville de Paris. 40c, HMS Canada. 50c, HMS St. Albans and wreck of Hector.

1971, Aug. 30			Litho.	Perf. 14
127	A18	10c multicolored	.35	.35
128	A18	15c multicolored	.60	.60
129	A18	25c multicolored	1.25	1.25
130	A18	40c multicolored	2.00	2.00
131	A18	50c multicolored	2.75	2.75
a.		Strip of 5, #127-131	7.25	7.25

West Indies sea battles.

Ansidei Madonna, by Raphael — A19

Christmas: 25c, Mystic Nativity, by Botticelli. 40c, Virgin and Child, School of Seville, inscribed Murillo. 50c, Madonna of the Iris, ascribed to Dürer.

1971, Nov. 29			Perf. 14x13½	
132	A19	20c green & multi	.30	.30
133	A19	25c blue & multi	.35	.35
134	A19	40c lilac rose & multi	.60	.60
135	A19	50c violet & multi	.75	.75
		Nos. 132-135 (4)	2.00	2.00

Map of Anguilla and St. Maarten, by Jefferys, 1775 — A20

Jesus Buffeted, Stained-glass Window — A21

Maps of Anguilla by: 15c, Samuel Fahlberg, 1814. 40c, Thomas Jefferys, 1775, horiz. 50c, Capt. E. Barnett, 1847, horiz.

Perf. 14x13½, 13½x14

1972, Jan. 24				
136	A20	10c lt blue & multi	.20	.20
137	A20	15c lt green & multi	.35	.35
138	A20	40c lt orange & multi	.90	.90
139	A20	50c lt ultra & multi	1.10	1.10
		Nos. 136-139 (4)	2.55	2.55

1972, Mar. 14			Perf. 14x13½	

Easter (19th cent. Stained-glass Windows, Bray Church): 15c, Jesus Carrying the Cross. 25c, Crucifixion. 40c, Descent from the Cross. 50c, Burial.

140	A21	10c multicolored	.20	.20
141	A21	15c multicolored	.30	.30
142	A21	25c multicolored	.45	.45
143	A21	40c multicolored	.90	.90
144	A21	50c multicolored	1.00	1.00
a.		Strip of 5, #140-144	3.00	3.00

Spear Fishing A22

Sandy Ground A23

ANGUILLA

1972-75			Perf. 13½
145	A22	1c shown	.15 .15
146	A23	2c Loblolly tree, vert.	.15 .15
147	A23	3c shown	.15 .15
148	A23	4c Ferry, Blowing Point, vert.	.15 .15
149	A23	5c Agriculture	.15 .15
150	A23	6c St. Mary's Church, vert.	.15 .15
151	A23	10c St. Gerard's Church	.20 .20
152	A22	15c Cottage Hospital	.30 .30
153	A23	20c Public Library	.35 .35
154	A23	25c Sunset, Blowing Point	.50 .50
155	A22	40c Boat building	.75 .75
156	A22	60c Hibiscus	1.25 1.25
157	A23	$1 Man-o-war bird	2.50 2.50
158	A23	$2.50 Frangipani	5.75 5.75
159	A23	$5 Brown pelican	11.00 11.00
160	A22	$10 Green-back turtle	27.50 27.50
		Nos. 145-160 (16)	51.00 51.00

Issued: $10, 5/20/75; others 10/30/72.
For overprints see Nos. 229-246.

Common Design Types pictured following the introduction.

Silver Wedding Issue, 1972
Common Design Type

Design: Queen Elizabeth II, Prince Philip, schooner and dolphin.

1972, Nov. 20	Photo.		Perf. 14x14½ Wmk. 314
161	CD324	25c olive & multi	1.50 1.50
162	CD324	40c maroon & multi	1.75 1.75

Flight into Egypt — A24

1972, Dec. 4	Litho.		Unwmk. Perf. 13½
163	A24	1c shown	.15 .15
164	A24	20c Star of Bethlehem	.30 .30
165	A24	25c Nativity	.35 .35
166	A24	40c Three Kings	.55 .55
167	A24	50c Adoration of the Kings	.80 .80
a.		Vert. strip of 4, #164-167	2.25 2.25
		Nos. 163-167 (5)	2.15 2.15

Christmas.

Betrayal of Jesus — A25

1973, Mar. 26			
168	A25	1c shown	.15 .15
169	A25	10c Man of Sorrow	.15 .15
170	A25	20c Jesus Carrying Cross	.25 .25
171	A25	25c Crucifixion	.30 .30
172	A25	40c Descent from Cross	.50 .50
173	A25	50c Resurrection	.70 .70
a.		Souvenir sheet of 6	2.25 2.25
b.		Vert. strip of 5, #169-173	2.00 2.00
		Nos. 168-173 (6)	2.05 2.05

Easter. #173a contains 6 stamps similar to #168-173 with bottom panel in lilac rose.

Santa Maria A26

1973, Sept. 10			
174	A26	1c shown	.15 .15
175	A26	20c Old West Indies map	.55 .55
176	A26	40c Map of voyages	1.40 1.40
177	A26	70c Sighting land	2.25 2.25
178	A26	$1.20 Columbus landing	4.75 4.75
a.		Souvenir sheet of 6, #174-178	10.00 10.00
b.		Horiz. strip of 4, #175-178	9.00 9.00
		Nos. 174-178 (5)	9.10 9.10

Discovery of West Indies by Columbus.

Princess Anne's Wedding Issue
Common Design Type

1973, Nov. 14	Wmk. 314		Perf. 13½
179	CD325	60c blue grn & multi	.35 .35
180	CD325	$1.20 lilac & multi	.65 .65

Wedding of Princess Anne and Capt. Mark Phillips, Nov. 14, 1973.

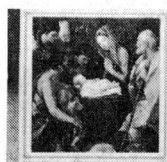

Adoration of the Shepherds, by Guido Reni — A27

Paintings: 10c, Virgin and Child, by Filippino Lippi. 20c, Nativity, by Meester Van de Brunswijkse Diptiek. 25c, Madonna of the Meadow, by Bellini. 40c, Virgin and Child, by Cima. 50c, Adoration of the Kings, by Geertgen Tot Sint Jans.

1973, Dec. 2			Unwmk.
181	A27	1c multicolored	.15 .15
182	A27	10c multicolored	.15 .15
183	A27	20c multicolored	.20 .20
184	A27	25c multicolored	.25 .25
185	A27	40c multicolored	.45 .45
186	A27	50c multicolored	.60 .60
a.		Souvenir sheet of 6, #181-186	1.90 1.90
b.		Horiz. strip of 5, #182-186	1.90 1.90
		Nos. 181-186 (6)	1.80 1.80

Christmas.

Crucifixion, by Raphael — A28

Easter (Details from Crucifixion by Raphael): 15c, Virgin Mary and St. John. 20c, The Two Marys. 25c, Left Angel. 40c, Right Angel. $1, Christ on the Cross.

1974, Mar. 30			
187	A28	1c lilac & multi	.15 .15
188	A28	15c gray & multi	.15 .15
189	A28	20c salmon & multi	.20 .20
190	A28	25c yel green & multi	.25 .25
191	A28	40c orange & multi	.30 .30
192	A28	$1 lt blue & multi	.80 .80
a.		Souvenir sheet of 6, #187-192	1.75 1.75
b.		Vert. strip of 5, #188-192	1.75 1.75
		Nos. 187-192 (6)	1.85 1.85

Churchill Making Victory Sign — A29

Designs: 20c, Roosevelt, Churchill, American and British flags. 25c, Churchill broadcasting during the war. 40c, Blenheim Palace. 60c, Churchill Statue and Parliament. $1.20, Chartwell.

1974, June 24			
193	A29	10c multicolored	.15 .15
194	A29	20c multicolored	.20 .20
195	A29	25c multicolored	.25 .25
196	A29	40c multicolored	.35 .35
197	A29	60c multicolored	.55 .55
198	A29	$1.20 multicolored	1.25 1.25
a.		Souvenir sheet of 6, #193-198	2.75 2.75
b.		Horiz. strip of 5, #194-198	2.75 2.75
		Nos. 193-198 (6)	2.75 2.75

Sir Winston Spencer Churchill (1874-1965).

UPU Emblem, Map of Anguilla — A30

1974, Aug. 27			
199	A30	1c black & ultra	.15 .15
200	A30	20c black & orange	.15 .15
201	A30	25c black & yellow	.15 .15
202	A30	40c black & brt lilac	.30 .30
203	A30	60c black & lt green	.40 .40
204	A30	$1.20 black & blue	.70 .70
a.		Souvenir sheet of 6, #200-204	2.50 2.50
b.		Horiz. strip of 5, #200-204	1.75 1.75
		Nos. 199-204 (6)	1.85 1.85

UPU, centenary. No. 204a contains one each of Nos. 199-204 with second row (40c, 60c, $1.20) perf. 15 at bottom.

Fishermen Seeing Star — A31

Christmas: 20c, Nativity. 25c, King offering gift. 40c, Star over map of Anguilla. 60c, Family looking at star. $1.20, Two angels with star and "Peace."

1974, Dec. 16	Litho.		Perf. 14½
205	A31	1c brt blue & multi	.15 .15
206	A31	10c dull grn & multi	.15 .15
207	A31	25c gray & multi	.15 .15
208	A31	40c car & multi	.35 .35
209	A31	60c dp blue & multi	.50 .50
210	A31	$1.20 ultra & multi	.80 .80
a.		Souvenir sheet of 6, #205-210	2.75 2.75
b.		Horiz. strip of 5, #206-210	2.00 2.00
		Nos. 205-210 (6)	2.10 2.10

Virgin Mary, St. John, Mary Magdalene — A32

Paintings from Isenheim Altar, by Matthias Grunewald: 10c, Crucifixion. 15c, John the Baptist. 20c, St. Sebastian and Angels. $1, Burial of Christ, horiz. $1.50, St. Anthony, the Hermit.

1975, Mar. 25			Perf. 13½
211	A32	1c multicolored	.15 .15
212	A32	10c multicolored	.15 .15
213	A32	15c multicolored	.15 .15
214	A32	20c multicolored	.15 .15
215	A32	$1 multicolored	.60 .60
216	A32	$1.50 multicolored	1.00 1.00
a.		Souvenir sheet of 6	2.50 2.50
b.		Horiz. strip of 5, #212-216	2.25 2.25
		Nos. 211-216 (6)	2.20 2.20

Easter. No. 216a contains 6 stamps similar to Nos. 211-216 with simulated perforations.

Statue of Liberty, N.Y. Skyline A33

Designs: 10c, Capitol, Washington, D.C. 15c, Congress voting independence. 20c, Washington, map and his battles. $1, Boston Tea Party. $1.50, Bicentennial emblem, historic U.S. flags.

1975, Nov. 10			
217	A33	1c multicolored	.15 .15
218	A33	10c multicolored	.15 .15
219	A33	15c multicolored	.15 .15
220	A33	20c multicolored	.20 .20
221	A33	$1 multicolored	.95 .95
222	A33	$1.50 multicolored	1.40 1.40
a.		Souvenir sheet of 6	3.50 3.50
b.		Horiz. strip of 5, #218-222	3.00 3.00
		Nos. 217-222 (6)	3.00 3.00

American Bicentennial. No. 222a contains one each of Nos. 217-222 with second row (20c, $1, $1.50) perf. 15 at bottom.

Virgin and Child with St. John, by Raphael — A34

Paintings, Virgin and Child by: 10c, Cima. 15c, Dolci. 20c, Durer. $1, Bellini. $1.50, Botticelli.

1975, Dec. 8			Perf. 14x13½
223	A34	1c ultra & multi	.15 .15
224	A34	10c Prus blue & multi	.15 .15
225	A34	15c plum & multi	.15 .15
226	A34	20c car rose & multi	.15 .15
227	A34	$1 brt grn & multi	.85 .85
228	A34	$1.50 blue grn & multi	1.25 1.25
a.		Souvenir sheet of 6, #223-228	3.00 3.00
b.		Horiz. strip of 5, #224-228	2.75 2.75
		Nos. 223-228 (6)	2.70 2.70

Christmas.

Nos. 145-146, 148, 150-160 Overprinted "NEW CONSTITUTION 1976"

1976	Litho.		Perf. 13½
229	A22	1c #145	.15 .15
230	A22	2c on 1c #145	.15 .15
231	A23	2c #146	.85 .85
232	A22	3c on 40c #155	.15 .15
233	A23	4c #148	.15 .15
234	A23	5c on 40c #155	.15 .15
235	A23	6c #150	.15 .15
236	A23	10c on 20c #153	.15 .15
237	A23	10c #151	1.10 1.10
238	A22	15c #152	.15 .15
239	A23	20c #153	.25 .25
240	A23	25c #154	.30 .30
241	A22	40c #155	.45 .45
242	A22	60c #156	.70 .70
243	A23	$1 #157	1.10 1.10
244	A23	$2.50 #158	2.50 2.50
245	A23	$5 #159	5.00 5.00
246	A22	$10 #160	12.00 12.00
		Nos. 229-246 (18)	25.45 25.45

Flowering Trees — A35

1976, Feb. 16			Perf. 13½x14
247	A35	1c Almond	.15 .15
248	A35	10c Clusia rosea	.15 .15
249	A35	15c Calabash	.15 .15
250	A35	20c Cordia	.20 .20
251	A35	$1 Papaya	.85 .85
252	A35	$1.50 Flamboyant	1.25 1.25
a.		Souvenir sheet of 6, #247-252	3.00 3.00
b.		Horiz. strip of 5, #248-252	2.50 2.50
		Nos. 247-252 (6)	2.75 2.75

The Three Marys — A36

Designs: 10c, Crucifixion. 15c, Two soldiers. 20c, Annunciation. $1, Altar tapestry, 1470, Monastery of Rheinau, Switzerland, horiz. $1.50, "Noli me Tangere" (Jesus and Mary Magdalene). Designs of vertical stamps show details from tapestry shown on $1 stamp.

ANGUILLA

1976, Apr. 5 Perf. 14x13½, 13½x14
253	A36	1c multicolored	.15	.15
254	A36	10c multicolored	.15	.15
255	A36	15c multicolored	.15	.15
256	A36	20c multicolored	.20	.20
257	A36	80c multicolored	.80	.80
258	A36	$1.50 multicolored	1.10	1.10
a.		Souvenir sheet of 6	2.75	2.75
b.		Horiz. strip of 5, #254-258	2.50	2.50
		Nos. 253-258 (6)	2.55	2.55

Easter. No. 258a contains 6 stamps similar to Nos. 253-258 with simulated perforations.

Le Desius and La Vaillante Approaching Anguilla — A37

Sailing Ships: 3c, Sailboat leaving Anguilla for Antigua to get help. 15c, HMS Lapwing in battle with frigate Le Desius and brig La Vaillante. 25c, La Vaillante aground off St. Maarten. $1, Lapwing. $1.50, Le Desius burning.

1976, Nov. 8 Litho. Perf. 13½x14
259	A37	1c multicolored	.15	.15
260	A37	3c multicolored	.15	.15
261	A37	15c multicolored	.30	.30
262	A37	25c multicolored	.50	.50
263	A37	$1 multicolored	2.25	2.25
264	A37	$1.50 multicolored	3.25	3.25
a.		Souvenir sheet of 6, #259-264	6.75	6.75
b.		Strip of 5, #260-264	6.50	6.50
		Nos. 259-264 (6)	6.60	6.60

Bicentenary of Battle of Anguilla between French and British ships.

Christmas Carnival — A38

Children's Paintings: 3c, 3 children dreaming of Christmas gifts. 15c, Caroling. 25c, Candlelight procession. $1, Going to Church on Christmas Eve. $1.50, Airport, coming home for Christmas.

1976, Nov. 22
265	A38	1c multicolored	.15	.15
266	A38	3c multicolored	.15	.15
267	A38	15c multicolored	.15	.15
268	A38	25c multicolored	.20	.15
269	A38	$1 multicolored	.70	.65
270	A38	$1.50 multicolored	1.00	.70
a.		Souvenir sheet of 6, #265-270	2.25	1.75
b.		Strip of 5, #266-270	2.25	1.75
		Nos. 265-270 (6)	2.35	1.90

Christmas. For overprints and surcharges see Nos. 305-310a.

Prince Charles and HMS Minerva, 1973 — A39

Designs: 40c, Prince Philip landing at Road Bay, 1964. $1.20, Homage to Queen at Coronation. $2.50, Coronation regalia and map of Anguilla.

1977, Feb. 9
271	A39	25c multicolored	.15	.15
272	A39	40c multicolored	.20	.20
273	A39	$1.20 multicolored	.55	.55
274	A39	$2.50 multicolored	1.10	1.10
a.		Souvenir sheet of 4, #271-274	2.00	2.00
		Nos. 271-274 (4)	2.00	2.00

25th anniv. of reign of Queen Elizabeth II.

Anguilla stamps can be mounted in the annual Scott Anguilla supplement.

Yellow-crowned Night Heron — A40

Designs: 2c, Great barracuda. 3c, Queen conch. 4c, Spanish bayonet (Yucca). 5c, Trunkfish. 6c, Cable and telegraph building. 10c, American sparrow hawk. 15c, Ground orchids. 20c, Parlorfish. 22c, Lobster fishing boat. 35c, Boat race. 50c Sea bean (flowers). $1, Sandy Island with palms. $2.50, Manchineel (fruit). $5, Ground lizard. $10, Red-billed tropic bird.

1977-78 Litho. Perf. 13½x14
275	A40	1c multicolored	.15	.15
276	A40	2c multicolored	.15	.15
277	A40	3c multicolored	.15	.15
278	A40	4c multicolored	.15	.15
279	A40	5c multicolored	.15	.15
280	A40	6c multicolored	.15	.15
281	A40	10c multicolored	.15	.15
282	A40	15c multicolored	.15	.15
283	A40	20c multicolored	.25	.25
284	A40	22c multicolored	.30	.30
285	A40	35c multicolored	.50	.50
286	A40	50c multicolored	.65	.65
287	A40	$1 multicolored	1.40	1.40
288	A40	$2.50 multicolored	3.25	3.25
289	A40	$5 multicolored	6.50	6.50
290	A40	$10 multicolored	13.00	13.00
		Nos. 275-290 (16)	27.05	27.05

Issued: #275-280, 290, 4/18/77; others 2/20/78.

For overprints and surcharges see Nos. 319-324, 337-342, 387-390, 402-404, 407-415, 417-423.

Crucifixion, by Quentin Massys — A41

Easter (Paintings): 3c, Betrayal of Christ, by Ugolino. 22c, Way to Calvary, by Ugolino. 30c, The Deposition, by Ugolino. $1, Resurrection, by Ugolino. $1.50, Crucifixion, by Andrea del Castagno.

1977, Apr. 25
291	A41	1c multicolored	.15	.15
292	A41	3c multicolored	.15	.15
293	A41	22c multicolored	.15	.15
294	A41	30c multicolored	.20	.20
295	A41	$1 multicolored	.70	.70
296	A41	$1.50 multicolored	1.00	1.00
a.		Souvenir sheet of 6, #291-296	2.50	2.50
b.		Strip of 5, #292-296	2.25	2.25
		Nos. 291-296 (6)	2.35	2.35

Nos. 271-274, 274b Overprinted: "ROYAL VISIT/TO WEST INDIES"

1977, Oct. 26 Litho. Perf. 13½x14
297	A39	25c multicolored	.15	.15
298	A39	40c multicolored	.20	.20
299	A39	$1.20 multicolored	.60	.60
300	A39	$2.50 multicolored	1.25	1.25
a.		Souvenir sheet of 4	2.50	2.50
		Nos. 297-300 (4)	2.20	2.20

Visit of Queen Elizabeth II to West Indies.

Suzanne Fourment in Velvet Hat, by Rubens — A42

Rubens Paintings: 40c, Helena Fourment with her Children. $1.20, Rubens with his wife. $2.50, Marchesa Brigida Spinola-Doria.

1977, Nov. 1 Perf. 14x13½
301	A42	25c black & multi	.15	.15
302	A42	40c black & multi	.20	.20
303	A42	$1.20 multicolored	.75	.75
304	A42	$2.50 black & multi	1.50	1.50
a.		Souvenir sheet of 4, #301-304	3.00	3.00
		Nos. 301-304 (4)	2.60	2.60

Peter Paul Rubens, 400th birth anniv. Nos. 301-304 printed in sheets of 5 stamps and blue label with Rubens' portrait.

Nos. 265-270b Overprinted 1977 and Surcharged

1977, Nov. 7 Perf. 13½x14
305	A38	1c multicolored	.15	.15
306	A38	5c on 3c multi	.15	.15
307	A38	12c on 15c multi	.15	.15
308	A38	18c on 25c multi	.15	.15
309	A38	$1 multicolored	.65	.65
310	A38	$2.50 on $1.50 multi	1.75	1.75
a.		Souvenir sheet of 6, #305-310	3.25	1.75
b.		Strip of 5, #306-310	3.00	3.00
		Nos. 305-310 (6)	3.00	3.00

Christmas. Stamps and souvenir sheets have "1976" and old denomination obliterated with variously shaped rectangles.

Nos. 301-304a Ovptd. in Gold: "EASTER 1978"

1978, Mar. 6 Perf. 14x13½
311	A42	25c black & multi	.15	.15
312	A42	40c black & multi	.25	.25
313	A42	$1.20 black & multi	.65	.65
314	A42	$2.50 black & multi	1.40	1.40
a.		Souvenir sheet of 4, #311-314	2.75	2.75
		Nos. 311-314 (4)	2.45	2.45

Buckingham Palace A43

Designs: 50c, Coronation procession. $1.50, Royal family on balcony. $2.50, Royal coat of arms.

1978, Apr. 6 Perf. 14
315	A43	22c multicolored	.15	.15
316	A43	50c multicolored	.15	.15
317	A43	$1.50 multicolored	.45	.45
318	A43	$2.50 multicolored	.70	.70
a.		Souvenir sheet of 4, #315-318	1.65	1.65
		Nos. 315-318 (4)	1.45	1.45

25th anniv. of coronation of Queen Elizabeth II. #315-318 each exist in a booklet pane of 2.

Nos. 284-285 and 288 Ovptd. and Surcharged: "VALLEY / SECONDARY / SCHOOL / 1953-1978"

1978, Aug. 14 Perf. 13½x14
319	A40	22c multicolored	.25	.25
320	A40	35c multicolored	.35	.35
321	A40	$1.50 on $2.50 multi	1.50	1.50
		Nos. 319-321 (3)	2.10	2.10

Valley Secondary School, 25th anniv. Surcharge on No. 321 includes heavy bar over old denomination.

Nos. 286-287, 289 Ovptd. and Surcharged: "ROAD / METHODIST / CHURCH / 1878-1978"

1978, Aug. 14
322	A40	50c multicolored	.45	.45
323	A40	$1 multicolored	.85	.85
324	A40	$1.20 on $5 multi	1.10	1.10
		Nos. 322-324 (3)	2.40	2.40

Road Methodist Church, centenary. Surcharge on No. 324 includes heavy bar over old denomination.

Mother and Child A44

Christmas: 12c, Christmas masquerade. 18c, Christmas dinner. 22c, Serenade. $1, Star over manger. $2.50, Family going to church.

1978, Dec. 11 Litho. Perf. 13½
325	A44	5c multicolored	.15	.15
326	A44	12c multicolored	.15	.15
327	A44	18c multicolored	.15	.15
328	A44	22c multicolored	.15	.15
329	A44	$1 multicolored	.60	.45
330	A44	$2.50 multicolored	1.40	1.25
a.		Souvenir sheet of 6, #325-330	2.75	2.00
		Nos. 325-330 (6)	2.60	2.30

Type A44 in Changed Colors with IYC Emblem and Inscription.

1979, Jan. 15 Litho. Perf. 13½
331	A44	5c multicolored	.15	.15
332	A44	12c multicolored	.15	.15
333	A44	18c multicolored	.15	.15
334	A44	22c multicolored	.15	.15
335	A44	$1 multicolored	.65	.65
336	A44	$2.50 multicolored	1.40	1.40
a.		Souvenir sheet of 4, #331-336	3.00	3.00
		Nos. 331-336 (6)	2.65	2.65

Intl. Year of the Child. For overprint, see No. 416.

Nos. 275-278, 280-281 Surcharged

1979, Feb. 8 Litho. Perf. 13½x14
337	A40	12c on 2c multi	.45	.45
338	A40	14c on 4c multi	.50	.50
339	A40	18c on 3c multi	.75	.75
340	A40	25c on 6c multi	1.25	1.25
341	A40	38c on 10c multi	1.75	1.75
342	A40	40c on 1c multi	2.00	2.00
		Nos. 337-342 (6)	6.70	6.70

Valley Methodist Church A45

Church Interiors: 12c, St. Mary's Anglican Church, The Valley. 18c, St. Gerard's Roman Catholic Church, The Valley. 22c, Road Methodist Church. $1.50, St. Augustine's Anglican Church, East End. $2.50, West End Methodist Church.

1979, Mar. 30 Litho. Perf. 14
343	A45	5c multicolored	.15	.15
344	A45	12c multicolored	.15	.15
345	A45	18c multicolored	.15	.15
346	A45	22c multicolored	.15	.15
347	A45	$1.50 multicolored	.70	.70
348	A45	$2.50 multicolored	1.25	1.25
a.		Souvenir sheet of 6	2.50	2.50
b.		Strip of 6, #343-348	2.50	2.50

Easter. No. 348a contains Nos. 343-348 in 2 horizontal rows of 3.

US No. C3a A46

Designs: No. 350, Cape of Good Hope #1. No. 351, Penny Black. No. 352, Germany #C36. No. 353, US #245. No. 354, Great Britain #93.

1979, Apr. 23 Litho. Perf. 14
349	A46	1c multicolored	.15	.15
350	A46	12c multicolored	.15	.15
351	A46	22c multicolored	.15	.15
352	A46	35c multicolored	.15	.15
353	A46	$1.50 multicolored	.65	.65
354	A46	$2.50 multicolored	1.10	1.10
a.		Souvenir sheet of 6, #349-353	2.50	2.50
		Nos. 349-354 (6)	2.35	2.35

Sir Rowland Hill (1795-1879), originator of penny postage.

Wright's Flyer A — A47

History of Aviation: 12c, Louis Bleriot landing at Dover, 1909. 18c, Vickers Vimy, 1919. 22c, Spirit of St. Louis, 1927. $1.50, LZ127 Graf Zeppelin, 1928. $2.50, Concorde, 1979.

1979, May 21 Litho. Perf. 14
355	A47	5c multicolored	.15	.15
356	A47	12c multicolored	.15	.15
357	A47	18c multicolored	.15	.15
358	A47	22c multicolored	.15	.15
359	A47	$1.50 multicolored	1.00	1.00
360	A47	$2.50 multicolored	1.50	1.50
a.		Souvenir sheet of 6, #355-360	3.00	3.00
		Nos. 355-360 (6)	3.10	3.10

ANGUILLA

Map of Anguilla, Map and View of Sombrero Island — A48

Map of Anguilla, Map and View of: 12c, Anguillita Island. 18c, Sandy Island. 25c, Prickly Pear Cays. $1, Dog Island. $2.50, Scrub Island.

1979		Litho.		Perf. 14	
361	A48	5c multicolored		.15	.15
362	A48	12c multicolored		.15	.15
363	A48	18c multicolored		.15	.15
364	A48	25c multicolored		.15	.15
365	A48	$1 multicolored		.45	.45
366	A48	$2.50 multicolored		1.25	1.25
a.		Souvenir sheet of 6, #361-366		2.75	2.75
		Nos. 361-366 (6)		2.30	2.30

Anguilla's Outer Islands.

Red Poinsettia — A49

1979, Oct. 22		Litho.		Perf. 14½	
367	A49	22c shown		.15	.15
368	A49	35c Kalanchoe		.20	.15
369	A49	$1.50 Cream poinsettia		.85	.70
370	A49	$2.50 White poinsettia		1.50	1.10
a.		Souvenir sheet of 4, #367-370		3.25	2.25
		Nos. 367-370 (4)		2.70	2.10

Christmas.

Booths and Frames — A50

50c, Earls Court Exhibition Hall. $1.50, Penny Black, Great Britain #2. $2.50, Exhibition emblem.

1979, Dec. 10		Litho.		Perf. 13, 14½	
371	A50	35c multicolored		.15	.15
372	A50	50c multicolored		.20	.20
373	A50	$1.50 multicolored		.75	.75
374	A50	$2.50 multicolored		1.25	1.25
a.		Souvenir sheet of 4, #371-374		2.50	2.50
		Nos. 371-374 (4)		2.35	2.35

London 1980 Intl. Stamp Exhibition, May 6-14, 1980.

Lake Placid and Olympic Rings — A51

Olympic Rings and: 18c, Ice Hockey. 35c, Figure skating. 50c, Bobsledding. $1, Ski jump. $2.50, Luge.

1980, Jan.		Litho.		Perf. 13½, 14½	
375	A51	5c multicolored		.15	.15
376	A51	18c multicolored		.15	.15
377	A51	35c multicolored		.15	.15
378	A51	50c multicolored		.20	.20
379	A51	$1 multicolored		.40	.40
380	A51	$2.50 multicolored		1.00	1.00
a.		Souvenir sheet of 6, #375-380		2.50	2.50
		Nos. 375-380 (6)		2.05	2.05

13th Winter Olympic Games, Lake Placid, NY, Feb. 12-24.

Salt Field — A52

1980, Apr. 14		Litho.		Perf. 14	
381	A52	5c shown		.15	.15
382	A52	12c Tallying salt		.15	.15
383	A52	18c Unloading salt flats		.15	.15
384	A52	22c Storage pile		.15	.15
385	A52	$1 Bagging and grinding		.45	.45
386	A52	$2.50 Loading onto boats		1.10	1.10
a.		Souvenir sheet of 6, #381-386		2.25	2.25
		Nos. 381-386 (6)		2.15	2.15

Salt industry.

Nos. 281, 288 Overprinted: "50th Anniversary / Scouting 1980"

1980, Apr. 16				Perf. 13½x14	
387	A40	10c multicolored		.15	.15
388	A40	$2.50 multicolored		2.00	2.00

Nos. 283, 289 Overprinted: "75th Anniversary / Rotary 1980" and Rotary Emblem

1980, Apr. 16				Perf. 13½x14	
389	A40	20c multicolored		.15	.15
390	A40	$5 multicolored		3.75	3.75

Rotary International, 75th anniversary.

Big Ben, Great Britain #643, London 1980 Emblem — A53

Designs: $1.50, Canada #756. $2.50, Statue of Liberty, US #1632.

1980, May					
391	A53	50c multicolored		.25	.25
392	A53	$1.50 multicolored		.85	.85
393	A53	$1.40 multicolored		1.40	1.40
a.		Souvenir sheet of 3, #391-393		2.75	2.75
		Nos. 391-393 (3)		2.50	2.50

London 1980 International Stamp Exhibition, May 6-14.

Queen Mother Elizabeth, 80th Birthday — A54

1980, Aug. 4		Litho.		Perf. 14	
394	A54	35c multicolored		.20	.20
395	A54	50c multicolored		.30	.30
396	A54	$1.50 multicolored		.90	.90
397	A54	$3 multicolored		1.75	1.75
a.		Souvenir sheet of 4, #394-397		3.25	3.25
		Nos. 394-397 (4)		3.15	3.15

Pelicans — A55

1980, Nov. 10		Litho.		Perf. 14	
398	A55	5c shown		.15	.15
399	A55	22c Great gray herons		.20	.20
400	A55	$1.50 Swallows		1.65	1.65
401	A55	$3 Hummingbirds		3.25	3.25
a.		Souvenir sheet of 4, #398-401		8.00	8.00
		Nos. 398-401 (4)		5.25	5.25

Christmas. For overprints see #405-406.

Nos. 275, 278, 280-290, 334, 400-401 Overprinted: "SEPARATION 1980"

Perf. 13½x14, 14 (A55)

1980, Dec. 18					Litho.	
402	A40	1c #275			.15	.15
403	A40	2c on 4c #278			.15	.15
404	A40	5c on 15c #282			.15	.15
405	A55	5c on $1.50 #400			.15	.15
406	A55	5c on $3 #401			.15	.15
407	A40	10c #281			.15	.15
408	A40	12c on $1 #287			.15	.15
409	A40	14c on $2.50 #288			.15	.15
410	A40	15c #282			.15	.15
411	A40	18c on $5 #289			.15	.15
412	A40	20c #283			.20	.20
413	A40	22c #284			.20	.20
414	A40	25c on 15c #282			.20	.20
415	A40	35c #285			.25	.25
416	A44	38c on 22c #334			.30	.30
417	A40	40c on 1c #275			.30	.30
418	A40	50c #286			.40	.40
419	A40	$1 #287			.65	.65
420	A40	$2.50 #288			1.50	1.50
421	A40	$5 #289			3.00	3.00
422	A40	$10 #290			6.75	6.75
423	A40	$10 on 6c #280			6.75	6.75
		Nos. 402-423 (22)			22.00	22.00

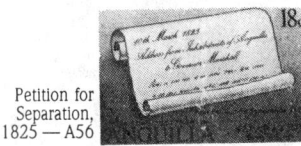

Petition for Separation, 1825 — A56

1980, Dec. 18				Perf. 14	
424	A56	18c shown		.15	.15
425	A56	22c Referendum ballot, 1967		.15	.15
426	A56	35c Airport blockade, 1967		.25	.25
427	A56	50c Anguilla flag		.35	.35
428	A56	$1 Separation celebration, 1980		.65	.65
a.		Souvenir sheet of 5, #424-428		1.60	1.60
		Nos. 424-428 (5)		1.55	1.55

Separation from St. Kitts-Nevis.

Nelson's Dockyard, by R. Granger Barrett — A57

Ship Paintings: 35c, Agamemnon, Vanguard, Elephant, Captain and Victory, by Nicholas Pocock. 50c, Victory, by Monamy Swaine. $3, Battle of Trafalgar, by Clarkson Stanfield. $5, Lord Nelson, by L.F. Abbott and Nelson's arms.

1981, Mar. 2		Litho.		Perf. 14	
429	A57	22c multicolored		.30	.30
430	A57	35c multicolored		.45	.45
431	A57	50c multicolored		.65	.65
432	A57	$3 multicolored		3.50	3.50
		Nos. 429-432 (4)		4.90	4.90

Souvenir Sheet

| 433 | A57 | $5 multicolored | 3.75 | 3.75 |

Lord Horatio Nelson (1758-1805), 175th death anniversary (1980).

Minnie Mouse — A58

Easter: Various Disney characters in Easter outfits.

1981, Mar. 30		Litho.		Perf. 13½	
434	A58	1c multicolored		.15	.15
435	A58	2c multicolored		.15	.15
436	A58	3c multicolored		.15	.15
437	A58	5c multicolored		.15	.15
438	A58	7c multicolored		.15	.15
439	A58	9c multicolored		.15	.15
440	A58	10c multicolored		.15	.15
441	A58	$2 multicolored		1.65	1.65
442	A58	$3 multicolored		2.25	2.25
		Nos. 434-442 (9)		4.95	4.95

Souvenir Sheet

| 443 | A58 | $5 multicolored | 4.75 | 4.75 |

Prince Charles, Lady Diana, St. Paul's Cathedral — A59

1981, June 15		Litho.		Perf. 14	
444	A59	5c shown		.15	.15
a.		Souvenir sheet of 2		.30	.30
b.		Wmk. 380		.30	.30
c.		Booklet pane of 4 #444b		1.25	1.25
445	A59	$2.50 Althorp		.80	.80
a.		Souvenir sheet of 2		1.65	1.65
446	A59	$3 Windsor Castle		1.00	1.00
a.		Souvenir sheet of 2		2.00	2.00
b.		Wmk. 380		2.00	2.00
c.		Booklet pane of 4 #446b		8.00	8.00
		Nos. 444-446 (3)		1.95	1.95

Souvenir Sheet

| 447 | A59 | $5 Buckingham Palace | 2.00 | 2.00 |

Royal Wedding. Nos. 444a-446a contain stamps in different colors.

Boys Climbing Tree — A60

1981		Litho.		Perf. 14	
448	A60	5c shown		.15	.15
449	A60	10c Boys sailing boats		.15	.15
450	A60	15c Children playing instruments		.15	.15
451	A60	$3 Children with animals		2.25	2.25
		Nos. 448-451 (4)		2.70	2.70

Souvenir Sheet

| 452 | A60 | $4 Boys playing soccer, vert. | 3.75 | 3.75 |

UNICEF, 35th anniv.
Issued: 5c-15c, July 31; $3-$4, Sept. 30.

"The Children were Nestled all Snug in their Beds" — A61

Christmas: Scenes from Walt Disney's The Night Before Christmas.

1981, Nov. 2		Litho.		Perf. 13½	
453	A61	1c multicolored		.15	.15
454	A61	2c multicolored		.15	.15
455	A61	3c multicolored		.15	.15
456	A61	5c multicolored		.15	.15
457	A61	7c multicolored		.15	.15
458	A61	10c multicolored		.15	.15
459	A61	12c multicolored		.15	.15
460	A61	$2 multicolored		1.75	1.75
461	A61	$3 multicolored		2.75	2.75
		Nos. 453-461 (9)		5.55	5.55

Souvenir Sheet

| 462 | A61 | $5 multicolored | 4.75 | 4.75 |

Red Grouper — A62

1982, Jan. 1		Litho.		Perf. 14	
463	A62	1c shown		.15	.15
464	A62	5c Ferries, Blowing Point		.15	.15
465	A62	10c Racing boats		.15	.15
466	A62	15c Majorettes		.15	.15

ANGUILLA

467 A62	20c Launching boat, Sandy Hill	.20	.20
468 A62	25c Coral	.25	.25
469 A62	30c Little Bay cliffs	.30	.30
470 A62	35c Fountain Cave	1.00	.60
471 A62	40c Sandy Isld.	.40	.40
472 A62	45c Landing, Sombrero	.45	.45
473 A62	50c on 45c, #472	.50	.50
474 A62	60c Seine fishing	2.00	1.00
475 A62	75c Boat race, Sandy Ground	.75	.75
476 A62	$1 Bagging lobster, Island Harbor	2.00	1.00
477 A62	$5 Pelicans	10.00	7.50
478 A62	$7.50 Hibiscus	10.00	7.50
479 A62	$10 Queen triggerfish	13.00	10.00
	Nos. 463-479 (17)	41.45	30.95

For overprints and surcharges see Nos. 507-510, 546A-546D, 578-582, 606-608, 640-647.

Easter — A63

Princess Diana, 21st Birthday — A64

Designs: Butterflies on flowers.

1982, Apr. 5
480 A63	10c Zebra, anthurium	.15	.15
481 A63	35c Caribbean buckeye	.35	.35
482 A63	75c Monarch, allamanda	.75	.75
483 A63	$3 Red rim, orchid	3.00	3.00
	Nos. 480-483 (4)	4.25	4.25

Souvenir Sheet
| 484 A63 | $5 Flambeau, amaryllis | 3.50 | 3.50 |

1982, May 17

Designs: Portraits, 1961-1981.
485 A64	10c 1961	.15	.15
486 A64	30c 1968	.20	.20
487 A64	40c 1970	.25	.25
488 A64	60c 1974	.40	.40
489 A64	$2 1981	1.40	1.40
490 A64	$3 1981	2.00	2.00
a.	Souvenir sheet of 6, #485-490	4.50	4.50
	Nos. 485-490 (6)	4.40	4.40

Souvenir Sheet
| 491 A64 | $5 1981 | 3.75 | 3.75 |

For overprints see Nos. 639A-639G.

1982 World Cup — A65

Designs: Various Disney characters playing soccer.

1982, Aug. 3   Litho.   Perf. 11
492 A65	1c multicolored	.15	.15
493 A65	3c multicolored	.15	.15
494 A65	4c multicolored	.15	.15
495 A65	5c multicolored	.15	.15
496 A65	7c multicolored	.15	.15
497 A65	9c multicolored	.15	.15
498 A65	10c multicolored	.15	.15
499 A65	$2.50 multicolored	2.25	2.25
500 A65	$3 multicolored	2.75	2.75
	Nos. 492-500 (9)	6.05	6.05

Souvenir Sheet   Perf. 14
| 501 A65 | $5 multicolored | 5.50 | 5.50 |

Scouting Year — A66

1982, July 5
502 A66	10c Pitching tent	.15	.15
503 A66	35c Marching band	.30	.30
504 A66	75c Sailing	.65	.65
505 A66	$3 Flag bearers	2.50	2.50
	Nos. 502-505 (4)	3.60	3.60

Souvenir Sheet
| 506 A66 | $5 Camping | 4.00 | 4.00 |

Nos. 465, 474-475, 477 Overprinted: "COMMONWEALTH / GAMES 1982"

1982, Oct. 18   Litho.   Perf. 14
507 A62	15c multicolored	.15	.15
508 A62	60c multicolored	.45	.45
509 A62	75c multicolored	.55	.55
510 A62	$5 multicolored	3.75	3.75
	Nos. 507-510 (4)	4.90	4.90

12th Commonwealth Games, Brisbane, Australia, Sept. 30-Oct. 9.

Christmas — A67

Scenes from Walt Disney's Winnie the Pooh.

1982, Nov. 29
511 A67	1c multicolored	.15	.15
512 A67	2c multicolored	.15	.15
513 A67	3c multicolored	.15	.15
514 A67	5c multicolored	.15	.15
515 A67	7c multicolored	.15	.15
516 A67	10c multicolored	.15	.15
517 A67	12c multicolored	.15	.15
518 A67	20c multicolored	.15	.15
519 A67	$5 multicolored	6.00	4.00
	Nos. 511-519 (9)	7.20	5.20

Souvenir Sheet
| 520 A67 | $5 multicolored | 7.00 | 4.50 |

Commonwealth Day (Mar. 14) — A68

1983, Feb. 28   Litho.   Perf. 14
521 A68	10c Carnival procession	.15	.15
522 A68	35c Flags	.30	.30
523 A68	75c Economic cooperation	.65	.65
524 A68	$2.50 Salt pond	2.00	2.00
	Nos. 521-524 (4)	3.10	3.10

Souvenir Sheet
| 525 A68 | $5 Map showing Commonwealth | 4.00 | 4.00 |

Easter — A69

Ten Commandments.

1983, Mar. 31   Litho.   Perf. 14
526 A69	1c multicolored	.15	.15
527 A69	2c multicolored	.15	.15
528 A69	3c multicolored	.15	.15
529 A69	10c multicolored	.15	.15
530 A69	35c multicolored	.25	.25
531 A69	60c multicolored	.45	.45
532 A69	75c multicolored	.55	.55
533 A69	$2 multicolored	1.50	1.50
534 A69	$2.50 multicolored	1.75	1.75
535 A69	$5 multicolored	3.75	3.75
	Nos. 526-535 (10)	8.85	8.85

Souvenir Sheet
| 536 A69 | $5 Moses Taking Tablets | 4.00 | 4.00 |

Local Turtles and World Wildlife Fund Emblem — A70

1983, Aug. 10   Litho.   Perf. 13½
537 A70	10c Leatherback	.30	.30
538 A70	35c Hawksbill	.95	.95
539 A70	75c Green	2.25	2.25
540 A70	$1 Loggerhead	3.25	3.25
	Nos. 537-540 (4)	6.75	6.75

Souvenir Sheet
| 541 A70 | $5 Leatherback, diff. | 5.75 | 5.75 |

1983, Aug. 10   Litho.   Perf. 12
537a A70	10c Leatherback	.40	.40
538a A70	35c Hawksbill	1.40	1.40
539a A70	75c Green	3.00	3.00
540a A70	$1 Loggerhead	4.00	4.00
	Nos. 537a-540a (4)	8.80	8.80

Manned Flight Bicentenary — A71

1983, Aug. 22   Perf. 14
542 A71	10c Montgolfiere, 1783	.15	.15
543 A71	60c Blanchard & Jeffries, 1785	.45	.45
544 A71	$1 Giffard's airship, 1852	.75	.75
545 A71	$2.50 Lilienthal's glider, 1890	1.75	1.75
	Nos. 542-545 (4)	3.10	3.10

Souvenir Sheet
| 546 A71 | $5 Wright Brothers' plane, 1909 | 3.75 | 3.75 |

Nos. 465, 471, 476-477 Overprinted: 150TH ANNIVERSARY / ABOLITION OF SLAVERY ACT

1983, Oct. 24   Litho.   Perf. 14
546A A62	10c Racing boats	.15	.15
546B A62	40c Sandy Isld	.35	.35
546C A62	$1 Bagging lobster, Island Harbor	.90	.90
546D A62	$5 Pelicans	4.50	4.50
	Nos. 546A-546D (4)	5.90	5.90

Jiminy Cricket — A72

Designs: Various Disney productions.

1983, Nov. 14   Perf. 13½
547 A72	1c shown	.15	.15
548 A72	2c Jiminy Cricket, kettle	.15	.15
549 A72	3c Jiminy Cricket, toys	.15	.15
550 A72	4c Mickey and Morty	.15	.15
551 A72	5c Scrooge McDuck	.15	.15
552 A72	6c Minnie and Goofy	.15	.15
553 A72	10c Goofy and Elf	.15	.15
554 A72	$2 Scrooge McDuck, diff.	1.75	1.75
555 A72	$3 Disney characters	2.75	2.75
	Nos. 547-555 (9)	5.55	5.55

Souvenir Sheet
| 556 A72 | $5 Scrooge McDuck | 4.50 | 4.50 |

Boys' Brigade Centenary — A73

1983, Sept. 12   Litho.   Perf. 14
557 A73	10c Anguilla company, banner	.15	.15
558 A73	$5 Marching with drummer	3.75	3.75
a.	Souvenir sheet of 2, #557-558	3.85	3.85

1984 Olympics, Los Angeles — A74

Mickey Mouse Competing in Decathlon.

1984, Feb. 20   Litho.   Perf. 14
559 A74	1c 100-meter run	.15	.15
560 A74	2c Long jump	.15	.15
561 A74	3c Shot put	.15	.15
562 A74	4c High jump	.15	.15
563 A74	5c 400-meter run	.15	.15
564 A74	6c Hurdles	.15	.15
565 A74	10c Discus	.15	.15
566 A74	$1 Pole vault	.95	.95
567 A74	$4 Javelin	3.75	3.75
	Nos. 559-567 (9)	5.75	5.75

Souvenir Sheet
| 568 A74 | $5 1500-meter run | 5.50 | 5.50 |

1984, Apr. 24   Perf. 12½x12
559a A74	1c	.15	.15
560a A74	2c	.15	.15
561a A74	3c	.15	.15
562a A74	4c	.15	.15
563a A74	5c	.15	.15
564a A74	6c	.15	.15
565a A74	10c	.15	.15
566a A74	$1	.95	.95
567a A74	$4	3.75	3.75
	Nos. 559a-567a (9)	5.75	5.75

Souvenir Sheet
| 568a A74 | $5 With Olympic rings emblem | 5.50 | 5.50 |

Nos. 559a-567a inscribed with Olympic rings emblem. Printed in sheets of 5 plus label.

Easter — A75

Ceiling and Wall Frescoes, La Stanze della Segnatura, by Raphael (details).

1984, Apr. 19   Litho.   Perf. 13½x14
569 A75	10c Justice	.15	.15
570 A75	25c Poetry	.20	.20
571 A75	35c Philosophy	.25	.25
572 A75	40c Theology	.30	.30
573 A75	$1 Abraham & Paul	.75	.75
574 A75	$2 Moses & Matthew	1.50	1.50
575 A75	$3 John & David	2.25	2.25
576 A75	$4 Peter & Adam	3.00	3.00
	Nos. 569-576 (8)	8.40	8.40

Souvenir Sheet
| 577 A75 | $5 Astronomy | 3.75 | 3.75 |

Nos. 463, 469, 477-479 Surcharged

1984   Litho.   Perf. 14
578 A62	25c on $7.50 #478	.20	.20
579 A62	35c on 30c #469	.30	.30
580 A62	60c on 1c #463	.50	.50
581 A62	$2.50 on $5 #477	2.00	2.00
582 A62	$2.50 on $10 #479	2.00	2.00
	Nos. 578-582 (5)	5.00	5.00

Issue dates: 25c, May 17, others, Apr. 24.

ANGUILLA

Ausipex '84
A76

Australian stamps.

1984, July 16		Litho.	Perf. 13½	
583	A76	10c No. 2	.15	.15
584	A76	75c No. 18	.55	.55
585	A76	$1 No. 130	.80	.80
586	A76	$2.50 No. 178	2.00	2.00
		Nos. 583-586 (4)	3.50	3.50

Souvenir Sheet

587	A76	$5 Nos. 378, 379	3.75	3.75

Slavery Abolition Sesquicentennial — A77

Abolitionists and Vignettes: 10c, Thomas Fowell Buxton, planting sugar cane. 25c, Abraham Lincoln, cotton field. 35c, Henri Christophe, armed slave revolt. 60c, Thomas Clarkson, addressing Anti-Slavery Society. 75c, William Wilberforce, slave auction. $1, Olaudah Equiano, slave raid on Benin coast. $2.50, General Gordon, slave convoy in Sudan. $5, Granville Sharp, restraining ship captain from boarding slave.

1984, Aug. 1			Perf. 12	
588	A77	10c multicolored	.15	.15
589	A77	20c multicolored	.20	.20
590	A77	35c multicolored	.25	.25
591	A77	60c multicolored	.40	.40
592	A77	75c multicolored	.50	.50
593	A77	$1 multicolored	.75	.75
594	A77	$2.50 multicolored	1.75	1.75
595	A77	$5 multicolored	3.50	3.50
a.		Miniature sheet of 8, #588-595	7.75	7.75
		Nos. 588-595 (8)	7.50	7.50

For overprints see Nos. 688-695a.

Christmas — A78

Various Disney characters and celebrations.

		Perf. 14, 12½x12 ($2)	Litho.	
596	A78	1c multicolored	.15	.15
597	A78	2c multicolored	.15	.15
598	A78	3c multicolored	.15	.15
599	A78	5c multicolored	.15	.15
600	A78	10c multicolored	.15	.15
601	A78	10c multicolored	.15	.15
602	A78	$1 multicolored	.80	.80
603	A78	$2 multicolored	1.65	1.65
604	A78	$4 multicolored	3.25	3.25
		Nos. 596-604 (9)	6.60	6.60

Souvenir Sheet

605	A78	$5 multicolored	4.25	4.25

Nos. 464-465, 477 Overprinted or Surcharged: "U.P.U. CONGRESS / HAMBURG 1984"

1984, Aug. 13				
606	A62	5c #464	.15	.15
607	A62	20c on 10c #465	.15	.15
608	A62	$5 #477	4.00	4.00
		Nos. 606-608 (3)	4.30	4.30

Intl. Civil Aviation Org., 40th Anniv.
A79

1984, Dec. 3		Litho.	Perf. 14	
609	A79	60c Icarus, by Hans Erni	.45	.45
610	A79	75c Sun Princess, by Sadiou Diouf	.55	.55
611	A79	$2.50 Anniv. emblem, vert.	1.75	1.75
		Nos. 609-611 (3)	2.75	2.75

Souvenir Sheet

612	A79	$5 Map of the Caribbean	3.75	3.75

Audubon Birth Bicent. — A80

Queen Mother 85th Birthday — A81

Illustrations by artist and naturalist J. J. Audubon (1785-1851).

1985, Apr. 30		Litho.	Perf. 14	
613	A80	10c Hirundo rustica	.15	.15
614	A80	60c Mycteria americana	.45	.45
615	A80	75c Sterna dougallii	.55	.55
616	A80	$5 Pandion haliaetus	3.75	3.75
		Nos. 613-616 (4)	4.90	4.90

Souvenir Sheets

617	A80	$4 Vireo solitarus, horiz.	3.00	3.00
618	A80	$4 Piranga ludoviciana, horiz.	3.00	3.00

1985, July 2				

Photographs: 10c, Visiting the children's ward at King's College Hospital. $2, Inspecting Royal Marine Volunteer Cadets at Deal. $3, Outside Clarence House in London. $5, In an open carriage at Ascot.

619	A81	10c multicolored	.15	.15
620	A81	$2 multicolored	1.25	1.25
621	A81	$3 multicolored	1.90	1.90
		Nos. 619-621 (3)	3.30	3.30

Souvenir Sheet

622	A81	$5 multicolored	3.75	3.75

Nos. 619-621 printed in sheetlets of 5.

Birds
A82

1985-86		Litho.	Perf. 13½x14	
623	A82	5c Brown pelican	.15	.15
624	A82	10c Turtle dove	.15	.15
625	A82	15c Man-o-war	.15	.15
626	A82	20c Antillean crested hummingbird	.15	.15
627	A82	25c White-tailed tropicbird	.35	.35
628	A82	30c Caribbean elaenia	.35	.35
629	A82	35c Black-whiskered vireo	.35	.35
629A	A82	35c Lesser Antillean bullfinch ('86)	.45	.45
630	A82	40c Yellow-crowned night heron	.55	.55
631	A82	45c Pearly-eyed thrasher	.70	.70
632	A82	50c Laughing bird	.80	.80
633	A82	65c Brown booby	.80	.80
634	A82	80c Gray kingbird	1.50	1.50
635	A82	$1 Audubon's shearwater	2.00	2.00
636	A82	$1.35 Roseate tern	2.00	2.00
637	A82	$2.50 Bananaquit	4.00	4.00
638	A82	$5 Belted kingfisher	4.25	4.25
639	A82	$10 Green heron	8.50	8.50
		Nos. 623-639 (18)	27.20	27.20

Issued: 25c, 65c, $1.35, $5, 7/22; 45c, 50c, 80c, $1, $10, 9/30; 5c-20c, 30c, #629, 40c, $2.50, 11/11; #629A, 3/10.

For overprints and surcharges see Nos. 678-682, 713-716, 723-739, 750-753, 764-767.

Nos. 485-491 Overprinted "PRINCE HENRY / BIRTH 15.9.84."

1985, Oct. 31		Litho.	Perf. 14	
639A	A64	10c multicolored	.15	.15
639B	A64	30c multicolored	.20	.20
639C	A64	45c multicolored	.30	.30
639D	A64	60c multicolored	.45	.45
639E	A64	$2 multicolored	1.50	1.50
639F	A64	$3 multicolored	2.25	2.25
h.		Souv. sheet of 6, #639A-639F	4.80	4.80
		Nos. 639A-639F (6)	4.85	4.85

Souvenir Sheet

639G	A64	$5 multicolored	3.75	3.75

Nos. 464, 469 and 477 Ovptd. with Anniversary Emblem and "GIRL GUIDES 75th ANNIVERSARY / 1910-1985"

1985, Oct. 14		Litho.	Perf. 14	
640	A62	5c multicolored	.15	.15
641	A62	20c multicolored	.20	.20
642	A62	75c multicolored	.55	.55
643	A62	$5 multicolored	3.75	3.75
		Nos. 640-643 (4)	4.65	4.65

Nos. 465 and 470 Overprinted or Surcharged with Organization Emblem and "80th ANNIVERSARY ROTARY 1985."

1985, Nov. 18				
644	A62	10c multicolored	.15	.15
645	A62	35c on 30c multi	.25	.25

Nos. 476, 469 Surcharged or Ovptd. with Emblem, Text and "INTERNATIONAL YOUTH YEAR"

1985, Nov. 18				
646	A62	$1 multicolored	.75	.75
647	A62	$5 on 30c multi	3.75	3.75

Brothers Grimm — A83

Christmas: Disney characters in Hansel and Gretel.

1985, Nov. 11		Litho.	Perf. 14	
648	A83	5c multicolored	.15	.15
649	A83	50c multicolored	.40	.40
650	A83	90c multicolored	.70	.70
651	A83	$4 multicolored	3.25	3.25
		Nos. 648-651 (4)	4.50	4.50

Souvenir Sheet

652	A83	$5 multicolored	4.50	4.50

Mark Twain (1835-1910), Author — A84

Disney characters in Huckleberry Finn.

1985, Nov. 11				
653	A84	10c multicolored	.15	.15
654	A84	60c multicolored	.60	.60
654A	A84	$1 multicolored	1.00	1.00
655	A84	$3 multicolored	3.25	3.25
		Nos. 653-655 (4)	5.00	5.00

Souvenir Sheet

656	A84	$5 multicolored	4.50	4.50

Christmas. No. 654A printed in sheets of 8.

Statue of Liberty Centennial
A85

1985, Nov. 25				
657	A85	10c Danmark, Denmark	.15	.15
658	A85	20c Eagle, USA	.20	.20
659	A85	60c Amerigo Vespucci, Italy	.50	.50
660	A85	75c Sir Winston Churchill, G.B.	.60	.60
661	A85	$2 Nippon Maru, Japan	1.65	1.65
662	A85	$2.50 Gorch, Germany	1.90	1.90
		Nos. 657-662 (6)	5.00	5.00

Souvenir Sheet

663	A85	$5 Statue of Liberty, vert.	3.75	3.75

Easter — A86

Stained glass windows.

1986, Mar. 27		Litho.	Perf. 14	
664	A86	10c multicolored	.15	.15
665	A86	25c multicolored	.20	.20
666	A86	45c multicolored	.35	.35
667	A86	$4 multicolored	3.00	3.00
		Nos. 664-667 (4)	3.70	3.70

Souvenir Sheet

668	A86	$5 multi, horiz.	4.00	4.00

A87

Halley's Comet
A88

Designs: 5c, Johannes Hevelius (1611-1687), Mayan temple observatory. 10c, US Viking probe landing on Mars, 1976. 60c, Theatri Cosmicum (detail), 1668. $4, Sighting, 1835. $5, Comet over Anguilla.

1986, Mar. 24				
669	A87	5c multicolored	.15	.15
670	A87	10c multicolored	.15	.15
671	A87	60c multicolored	.45	.45
672	A87	$4 multicolored	3.00	3.00
		Nos. 669-672 (4)	3.75	3.75

Souvenir Sheet

673	A88	$5 multicolored	3.75	3.75

Queen Elizabeth II, 60th Birthday
Common Design Type

1986, Apr. 21				
674	CD339	20c Inspecting guards, 1946	.15	.15
675	CD339	$2 Garter Ceremony, 1985	1.50	1.50
676	CD339	$3 Trooping the color	2.25	2.25
		Nos. 674-676 (3)	3.90	3.90

Souvenir Sheet

677	CD339	$5 Christening, 1926	3.75	3.75

Nos. 623, 631, 635, 637 and 639 Ovptd. "AMERIPEX 1986"

1986, May 22			Perf. 13½x14	
678	A82	5c multicolored	.15	.15
679	A82	45c multicolored	.35	.35
680	A82	$1 multicolored	.75	.75
681	A82	$2.50 multicolored	1.85	1.85
682	A82	$10 multicolored	7.50	7.50
		Nos. 678-682 (5)	10.60	10.60

Wedding of Prince Andrew and Sarah Ferguson — A89

ANGUILLA

1986, July 23   Litho.   *Perf. 14, 12*
683	A89	10c Couple	.15	.15
684	A89	35c Andrew	.25	.25
685	A89	$2 Sarah	1.50	1.50
686	A89	$3 Couple, diff.	2.25	2.25
		Nos. 683-686 (4)	4.15	4.15

Souvenir Sheet
687	A89	$6 Westminster Abbey	4.50	4.50

Nos. 588-595 Ovptd. "INTERNATIONAL / YEAR OF / PEACE"

1986, Sept. 29   Litho.   *Perf. 12*
688	A77	10c multicolored	.20	.20
689	A77	25c multicolored	.30	.30
690	A77	35c multicolored	.35	.35
691	A77	60c multicolored	.55	.55
692	A77	75c multicolored	.70	.70
693	A77	$1 multicolored	.90	.90
694	A77	$2.50 multicolored	2.00	2.00
695	A77	$5 multicolored	4.00	4.00
a.		Miniature sheet of 8, #688-695	9.00	9.00
		Nos. 688-695 (8)	9.00	9.00

Ships — A90

1986, Nov. 29   Litho.   *Perf. 14*
696	A90	10c Trading Sloop	.15	.15
697	A90	45c Lady Rodney	.35	.35
698	A90	80c West Derby	.65	.65
699	A90	$3 Warspite	2.40	2.40
		Nos. 696-699 (4)	3.55	3.55

Souvenir Sheet
700	A90	$6 Boat Race Day, vert.	4.50	4.50

Christmas.

Discovery of America, 500th Anniv. (in 1992) — A91

Dragon Tree — A92

Designs: 5c, Christopher Columbus, astrolabe. 10c, Aboard ship. 35c, Santa Maria. 80c, Ferdinand, Isabella, horiz. $4, Indians. No. 707, Caribbean manatee, horiz.

1986, Dec. 22
701	A91	5c multicolored	.15	.15
702	A91	10c multicolored	.15	.15
703	A91	35c multicolored	.30	.30
704	A91	80c multicolored	.65	.65
705	A91	$4 multicolored	3.25	3.25
		Nos. 701-705 (5)	4.50	4.50

Souvenir Sheets
706	A92	$5 shown	4.00	4.00
707	A92	$5 multicolored	4.00	4.00

Butterflies A93

1987, Apr. 14   Litho.   *Perf. 14*
708	A93	10c Monarch	.15	.15
709	A93	80c White peacock	.65	.65
710	A93	$1 Zebra	.80	.80
711	A93	$2 Caribbean buckeye	1.65	1.65
		Nos. 708-711 (4)	3.25	3.25

Souvenir Sheet
712	A93	$6 Flambeau	4.50	4.50

Easter.

Nos. 629A, 631, 634 and 639 Ovptd. with CAPEX '87 Emblem in Red

1987, May 25   Litho.   *Perf. 13½x14*
713	A82	35c on No. 629A	.25	.25
714	A82	45c on No. 631	.35	.35
715	A82	80c on No. 634	.60	.60
716	A82	$10 on No. 639	7.50	7.50
		Nos. 713-716 (4)	8.70	8.70

Separation from St. Kitts and Nevis, 20th Anniv. — A94

Designs: 10c, Old goose iron, electric iron. 35c, Old East End School, Albena Lake-Hodge Comprehensive College. 45c, Old market place, People's Market. 80c, Old ferries and modern ferry at Blowing Point. $1, Old and new cable and wireless offices. $2, Public meeting at Burrowes Park, House of Assembly.

1987, May 25   *Perf. 14*
717	A94	10c multicolored	.15	.15
718	A94	35c multicolored	.25	.25
719	A94	45c multicolored	.35	.35
720	A94	80c multicolored	.60	.60
721	A94	$1 multicolored	.75	.75
722	A94	$2 multicolored	1.50	1.50
a.		Souvenir sheet of 6, #717-722	3.50	3.50
		Nos. 717-722 (6)	3.60	3.60

Nos. 623, 625-628, 629A-639 Ovptd. "20 YEARS OF PROGRESS / 1967-1987" in Red or Surcharged in Red & Black

1987, Sept. 4   Litho.   *Perf. 13½x14*
723	A82	5c No. 623	.15	.15
724	A82	10c on 15c No. 625	.15	.15
725	A82	15c No. 625	.15	.15
726	A82	20c No. 626	.15	.15
727	A82	25c No. 627	.20	.20
728	A82	30c No. 628	.20	.20
729	A82	35c No. 629A	.25	.25
730	A82	40c No. 630	.25	.25
731	A82	45c No. 631	.30	.30
732	A82	50c No. 632	.30	.30
733	A82	65c No. 633	.45	.45
734	A82	80c No. 634	.55	.55
735	A82	$1 No. 635	.70	.70
736	A82	$1.35 No. 636	.90	.90
737	A82	$2.50 No. 637	1.75	1.75
738	A82	$5 No. 638	3.50	3.50
739	A82	$10 No. 639	6.75	6.75
		Nos. 723-739 (17)	16.70	16.70

Cricket World Cup A95

Various action scenes.

1987, Oct. 5   *Perf. 14*
740	A95	10c multicolored	.15	.15
741	A95	35c multicolored	.30	.30
742	A95	45c multicolored	.40	.40
743	A95	$2.50 multicolored	2.00	2.00
		Nos. 740-743 (4)	2.85	2.85

Souvenir Sheet
744	A95	$6 multicolored	4.50	4.50

Sea Shells, Crabs A96

1987, Nov. 2
745	A96	10c West Indian top shell	.15	.15
746	A96	35c Ghost crab	.30	.30
747	A96	50c Spiny Caribbean vase	.40	.40
748	A96	$2 Great land crab	1.60	1.60
		Nos. 745-748 (4)	2.45	2.45

Souvenir Sheet
749	A96	$6 Queen conch	4.75	4.75

Christmas.

Nos. 629A, 635-636 and 639 Ovptd. "40TH WEDDING ANNIVERSARY / H.M. QUEEN ELIZABETH II / H.R.H. THE DUKE OF EDINBURGH" in Scarlet

1987, Dec. 14   Litho.   *Perf. 13½x14*
750	A82	35c multicolored	.30	.30
751	A82	$1 multicolored	.75	.75
752	A82	$1.35 multicolored	1.00	1.00
753	A82	$10 multicolored	7.50	7.50
		Nos. 750-753 (4)	9.55	9.55

Easter (Lilies) — A97

1988 Summer Olympics, Seoul — A98

1988, Mar. 28   Litho.   *Perf. 14*
754	A97	30c Crinum erubescens	.30	.30
755	A97	45c Hymenocallis caribaea	.40	.40
756	A97	$1 Crinum macowanii	.90	.90
757	A97	$2.50 Hemerocallis fulva	2.25	2.25
		Nos. 754-757 (4)	3.85	3.85

Souvenir Sheet
758	A97	$6 Lilium longiflorum	5.25	5.25

1988, July 25   Litho.   *Perf. 14*
759	A98	35c 4x100-Meter relay	.30	.30
760	A98	45c Windsurfing	.35	.35
761	A98	50c Tennis	.40	.40
762	A98	80c Basketball	.60	.60
		Nos. 759-762 (4)	1.65	1.65

Souvenir Sheet
763	A98	$6 Women's 200 meters	4.50	4.50

Nos. 629A, 634-635 and 637 Ovptd. "H.R.H. PRINCESS / ALEXANDRA'S / VISIT NOVEMBER 1988"

1988, Dec. 14   Litho.   *Perf. 13½x14*
764	A82	35c multicolored	.30	.30
765	A82	80c multicolored	.60	.60
766	A82	$1 multicolored	.75	.75
767	A82	$2.50 multicolored	1.90	1.90
		Nos. 764-767 (4)	3.55	3.55

Marine Life A99

1988, Dec. 5   Litho.   *Perf. 14*
768	A99	35c Common sea fan	.30	.30
769	A99	80c Coral crab	.60	.60
770	A99	$1 Grooved brain coral	.75	.75
771	A99	$1.60 Old wife	1.20	1.20
		Nos. 768-771 (4)	2.85	2.85

Souvenir Sheet
772	A99	$6 West Indies spiny lobster	4.50	4.50

Christmas.

Lizards A100

1989, Feb. 20   Litho.   *Perf. 13½x14*
773	A100	45c Wood slave	.35	.35
774	A100	80c Slippery back	.60	.60
775	A100	$2.50 Iguana	1.75	1.75
		Nos. 773-775 (3)	2.70	2.70

Souvenir Sheet
776	A100	$6 Tree lizard	4.50	4.50

Easter — A101

Paintings: 35c, Christ Crowned with Thorns, by Hieronymous Bosch (c. 1450-1516). 80c, Christ Bearing the Cross, by David. $1, The Deposition, by David. $1.60, Pieta, by Rogier van der Weyden (1400-1464). $6, Crucified Christ with the Virgin Mary and Saints, by Raphael.

1989, Mar. 23   Litho.   *Perf. 14x13½*
777	A101	35c multicolored	.30	.30
778	A101	80c multicolored	.60	.60
779	A101	$1 multicolored	.75	.75
780	A101	$1.60 multicolored	1.20	1.20
		Nos. 777-780 (4)	2.85	2.85

Souvenir Sheet
781	A101	$6 multicolored	4.50	4.50

University of the West Indies, 40th Anniv. — A102

1989, Apr. 24   Litho.   *Perf. 14x13½*
782	A102	$5 Coat of arms	3.75	3.75

Nos. 634-636 and 638 Ovptd. "20th / ANNIVERSARY / MOON / LANDING"

1989, July 3   Litho.   *Perf. 13½X14*
783	A82	80c multicolored	.60	.60
784	A82	$1 multicolored	.75	.75
785	A82	$1.35 multicolored	1.00	1.00
786	A82	$5 multicolored	3.75	3.75
		Nos. 783-786 (4)	6.10	6.10

Christmas — A103

Well-known and historic houses.

1989, Dec. 4   Litho.   *Perf. 13½x14*
787	A103	5c Lone Star, 1930	.15	.15
788	A103	35c Whitehouse, 1906	.30	.30
789	A103	45c Hodges House	.35	.35
790	A103	80c Warden's Place	.60	.60
		Nos. 787-790 (4)	1.40	1.40

Souvenir Sheet
791	A103	$6 Wallblake House, 1787	4.50	4.50

Fish A104

1990, Apr. 2   Litho.   *Perf. 13½x14*
792	A104	5c Blear eye	.15	.15
793	A104	10c Redman	.15	.15
794	A104	15c Speckletail	.15	.15
795	A104	25c Grunt	.15	.15
796	A104	30c Amber jack	.20	.20
797	A104	35c Red hind	.25	.25
798	A104	40c Goatfish	.30	.30
799	A104	45c Old wife	.35	.35
800	A104	50c Butter fish	.40	.40
801	A104	65c Shell fish	.50	.50
802	A104	80c Yellowtail snapper	.60	.60
803	A104	$1 Katy	.75	.75

ANGUILLA

804	A104	$1.35 Mutton grouper	1.00	1.00
805	A104	$2.50 Doctor fish	1.90	1.90
806	A104	$5 Angelfish	3.75	3.75
807	A104	$10 Barracuda	7.50	7.50
		Nos. 792-807 (16)	18.10	18.10

Nos. 792-793, 797 exist inscribed 1992. For overprints and surcharge see #821-824, 849.

Easter — A105

1990, Apr. 2   Perf. 14x13½

811	A105	35c Last Supper	.25	.25
812	A105	45c Trial	.35	.35
813	A105	$1.35 Calvary	1.00	1.00
814	A105	$2.50 Empty tomb	1.90	1.90
		Nos. 811-814 (4)	3.50	3.50

Souvenir Sheet

815	A105	$6 The Resurrection	4.50	4.50

See Nos. 834-838.

Cape of Good Hope #7 — A106

Stamps of Great Britain and exhibition emblem: 25c, #1, vert. 50c, #2, vert. $2.50, #93. $6, #1-2.

1990, Apr. 30   Perf. 14

816	A106	25c multicolored	.20	.20
817	A106	50c multicolored	.35	.35
818	A106	$1.50 shown	1.10	1.10
819	A106	$2.50 multicolored	1.90	1.90
		Nos. 816-819 (4)	3.55	3.55

Souvenir Sheet

820	A106	$6 multicolored	4.50	4.50

Stamp World London '90, Penny Black 150th anniv.

Nos. 803-806 Overprinted:
 a. EXPO '90
 b. 1990 INTERNATIONAL / LITERACY YEAR
 c. WORLD CUP FOOTBALL / CHAMPIONSHIPS 1990
 d. 90TH BIRTHDAY / H.M. THE QUEEN MOTHER

1990, Sept. 24   Litho.   Perf. 13½x14

821	A104(a)	$1 Katy	.75	.75
822	A104(b)	$1.35 Mutton grouper	1.00	1.00
823	A104(c)	$2.50 Doctor fish	1.90	1.90
824	A104(d)	$5 Angelfish	3.75	3.75
		Nos. 821-824 (4)	7.40	7.40

Christmas — A107

Birds.

1990, Dec. 3   Perf. 14

825	A107	10c Laughing gull	.20	.20
826	A107	35c Brown booby	.35	.35
827	A107	$1.50 Bridled tern	1.40	1.40
828	A107	$3.50 Brown pelican	3.50	3.50
		Nos. 825-828 (4)	5.45	5.45

Souvenir Sheet

829	A107	$6 Least tern	7.00	7.00

Flags A108

1991, Nov. 5   Litho.   Perf. 13½x14

830	A108	50c Mermaid	.40	.40
831	A108	80c New Anguilla official	.60	.60
832	A108	$1 Three dolphins	.75	.75
833	A108	$5 Governor's official	3.75	3.75
		Nos. 830-833 (4)	5.50	5.50

Nos. 811-815 Inscribed or Overprinted "1991"

1991, Apr. 30   Litho.   Perf. 14x13½

834	A105	35c like #811	.25	.25
835	A105	45c like #812	.35	.35
836	A105	$1.35 like #813	1.00	1.00
837	A105	$2.50 like #814	1.90	1.90
		Nos. 834-837 (4)	3.50	3.50

Souvenir Sheet

838	A105	$6 like #815	7.75	7.75

Easter. "1990" obliterated by black bar in souvenir sheet margin.

Christmas — A109

Perf. 14x13½, 13½x14

1991, Dec.   Litho.

839	A109	5c Angel, vert.	.15	.15
840	A109	35c Santa, vert.	.25	.25
841	A109	80c shown	.60	.60
842	A109	$1 Palm trees, poinsettias	.75	.75
		Nos. 839-842 (4)	1.75	1.75

Souvenir Sheet

843	A109	$5 Homes, holly	3.75	3.75

Easter A110

Designs: 35c, Church, angels holding palms, vert. 45c Church, angels singing, vert. 80c, Village. $1, People going to church, vert. $5, People at beach, sailboats.

1992   Litho.   Perf. 14

844	A110	35c multicolored	.30	.30
845	A110	45c multicolored	.40	.40
846	A110	80c multicolored	.70	.70
847	A110	$1 multicolored	.85	.85
848	A110	$5 multicolored	4.25	4.25
		Nos. 844-848 (5)	6.50	6.50

No. 796 Surcharged $1.60

1992, June 10   Litho.   Perf. 13½x14

849	A104	$1.60 on 30c #796	1.40	1.40

No. 849 inscribed "1992."

Independence, 25th Anniv. — A111

1992, Aug. 10   Litho.   Perf. 14

850	A111	80c Official seal, flag	.60	.60
851	A111	$1 Official seal	.70	.70
852	A111	$1.60 Flags, airport	1.25	1.25
853	A111	$2 First seal	1.40	1.40
		Nos. 850-853 (4)	3.95	3.95

Souvenir Sheet

854	A111	$10 #1, 8-11, 15-16	8.50	8.50

No. 854 contains one 85x85mm stamp.

Sailboat Racing A112

Designs: 20c, On course. 35c, Stylized boat poster. 45c, Start of race. No. 858, Blue Bird, 1971, vert. No. 859, Construction plans for Blue Bird, vert. $1, Stylized boat poster, diff. $6, Like Nos. 855 & 857.

Perf. 13½x14, 14x13½

1992, Oct. 12   Litho.

855	A112	20c multicolored	.15	.15
856	A112	35c multicolored	.25	.25
857	A112	45c multicolored	.35	.35
858	A112	80c multicolored	.55	.55
859	A112	80c multicolored	.55	.55
a.		Pair, #858-859	1.10	1.10
860	A112	$1 multicolored	.70	.70
		Nos. 855-860 (6)	2.55	2.55

Souvenir Sheet

861	A112	$6 multicolored	4.55	4.55

No. 861 contains one 96x31mm stamp.

Discovery of America, 500th Anniv. A113

1992, Dec. 15   Litho.   Perf. 14

862	A113	80c Landfall	.70	.70
863	A113	$1 Columbus, vert.	.85	.85
864	A113	$2 Fleet	1.65	1.65
865	A113	$3 Pinta	2.50	2.50
		Nos. 862-865 (4)	5.70	5.70

Souvenir Sheet

866	A113	$6 Map of voyage, vert.	5.00	5.00

Christmas A114

Various Christmas trees and: 20c, Mucka Jumbie on stilts. 70c, Masquerading house to house. $1.05, Christmas baking, old oven style. $2.40, $5, Collecting presents.

1992, Dec. 7

867	A114	20c multicolored	.15	.15
868	A114	70c multicolored	.60	.60
869	A114	$1.05 multicolored	.90	.90
870	A114	$2.40 multicolored	2.00	2.00
		Nos. 867-870 (4)	3.65	3.65

Souvenir Sheet

871	A114	$5 Sheet of 1 + 3 labels	4.25	4.25

Labels on No. 871 are similar to Nos. 867-869, but without denomination.

Easter — A115

Children's drawings: 20c, Kite flying. 45c, Cliff top village service. 80c, Morning devotion on Sombrero. $1.50, Hilltop church service. $5, Good Friday kites.

1993, Mar. 29   Litho.   Perf. 14

872	A115	20c multicolored	.15	.15
873	A115	45c multicolored	.40	.40
874	A115	80c multicolored	.65	.65
875	A115	$1.50 multicolored	1.25	1.25
		Nos. 872-875 (4)	2.45	2.45

Souvenir Sheet

876	A115	$5 multicolored	4.25	4.25

No. 876 contains one 42x56mm stamp.

Native Industries A116

1993, June 23   Litho.   Perf. 14

877	A116	20c Salt	.15	.15
878	A116	80c Tobacco	.65	.65
879	A116	$1 Cotton	.80	.80
880	A116	$2 Sugar cane	1.60	1.60
		Nos. 877-880 (4)	3.20	3.20

Souvenir Sheet

881	A116	$6 Fishing	4.75	4.75

Coronation of Queen Elizabeth II, 40th Anniv. — A117

Designs: 80c, Lord Great Chamberlain presents the spurs of chivalry. $1, The benediction. $2, Queen Elizabeth II, coronation photograph. $3, St. Edward's Crown. $6, Queen, Prince Philip in Gold State Coach.

1993, Aug. 16   Litho.   Perf. 14

882	A117	80c multicolored	.65	.65
883	A117	$1 multicolored	.80	.80
884	A117	$2 multicolored	1.65	1.65
885	A117	$3 multicolored	2.50	2.50
		Nos. 882-885 (4)	5.60	5.60

Souvenir Sheet

886	A117	$6 multicolored	4.75	4.75

Anguilla Carnival — A118

1993, Aug. 23   Litho.   Perf. 14

887	A118	20c Pan musician	.15	.15
888	A118	45c Pirates	.35	.35
889	A118	80c Stars	.65	.65
890	A118	$1 Playing mas	.80	.80
891	A118	$2 Masqueraders	1.65	1.65
892	A118	$3 Commandos	2.50	2.50
		Nos. 887-892 (6)	6.10	6.10

Souvenir Sheet

893	A118	$5 Carnival fantasy	4.00	4.00

Christmas — A119   Mail Delivery — A120

Traditional Christmas customs: 20c, Mucka Jumbies. 35c, Serenaders. 45c, Baking. $3, Five-fingers Christmas tree. $4, Mucka Jumbies and serenaders.

ANGUILLA — ANJOUAN

1993, Dec. 7   Litho.   *Perf. 14x13½*

894	A119	20c multicolored	.20	.20
895	A119	35c multicolored	.30	.30
896	A119	45c multicolored	.40	.40
897	A119	$3 multicolored	2.50	2.50
		Nos. 894-897 (4)	3.40	3.40

Souvenir Sheet
Perf. 14

| 898 | A119 | $4 multicolored | 3.50 | 3.50 |

No. 898 contains one 54x42mm stamp.

1993, Feb. 11   Litho.   *Perf. 14*

Designs: 20c, Traveling Branch mail van, Sandy Ground, horiz. 45c, Mail boat, Betsy R, The Forest. 80c, Old post office, horiz. $1, Mail by jeep, Island Harbor. $4, New post office, 1993, horiz.

899	A120	20c multicolored	.20	.20
900	A120	45c multicolored	.40	.40
901	A120	80c multicolored	.70	.70
902	A120	$1 multicolored	.85	.85
903	A120	$4 multicolored	3.50	3.50
		Nos. 899-903 (5)	5.65	5.65

Royal Visits — A121    Easter — A122

1994, Feb. 18

904	A121	45c Princess Alexandra	.35	.35
905	A121	50c Princess Alice	.45	.45
906	A121	80c Prince Philip	.70	.70
907	A121	$1 Prince Charles	.85	.85
908	A121	$2 Queen Elizabeth II	1.65	1.65
a.		Souvenir sheet of 4, #904-908	4.00	4.00
		Nos. 904-908 (5)	4.00	4.00

1994, Apr. 6   Litho.   *Perf. 14x15*

Stained glass windows: 20c, Crucifixion. 45c, Empty tomb. 80c, Resurrection. $3, Risen Christ with disciples.

909	A122	20c multicolored	.20	.20
910	A122	45c multicolored	.40	.40
911	A122	80c multicolored	.75	.75
912	A122	$3 multicolored	2.75	2.75
		Nos. 909-912 (4)	4.10	4.10

Christmas — A123

Designs: 20c, Adoration of the shepherds. 30c, Magi, shepherds. 35c, The Annunciation. 45c, Nativity Scene. $2.40, Flight into Egypt.

1994, Nov. 22   Litho.   *Perf. 14*

913	A123	20c multicolored	.20	.20
914	A123	30c multicolored	.30	.30
915	A123	35c multicolored	.35	.35
916	A123	45c multicolored	.45	.45
917	A123	$2.40 multicolored	2.50	2.50
		Nos. 913-917 (5)	3.80	3.80

1994 World Cup Soccer Championships, US — A124

Soccer player and: 20c, Pontiac Silverdome, Detroit. 70c, Foxboro Stadium, Boston. $1.80, RFK Memorial Stadium, Washington. $2.40, Soldier Field, Chicago. $6, Two players.

1994, Oct. 3   Litho.   *Perf. 13½x14*

918	A124	20c multicolored	.20	.20
919	A124	70c multicolored	.65	.65
920	A124	$1.80 multicolored	1.65	1.65
921	A124	$2.40 multicolored	1.90	1.90
		Nos. 918-921 (4)	4.40	4.40

Souvenir Sheet

| 922 | A124 | $6 multicolored | 5.50 | 5.50 |

Easter A125

Turtle dove: 45c, One on tree branch. 50c, One on nest, one on branch. $5, Mother with young.

1995, Apr. 10   Litho.   *Perf. 14*

923	A125	20c multicolored	.20	.20
924	A125	45c multicolored	.40	.40
925	A125	50c multicolored	.45	.45
926	A125	$5 multicolored	4.75	4.75
		Nos. 923-926 (4)	5.80	5.80

UN, 50th Anniv. A126

Secretaries general and: 20c, Trygve Lie (1946-53), general assembly. 80c, UN flag, UN headquarters with "50" (no portrait). $1, Dag Hammarskjold (1953-61), charter, U Thant (1961-71). $5, UN complex, New York, vert. (no portrait).

1995, June 26   *Perf. 13½x14, 14x13½*   Litho.

927	A126	20c multicolored	.20	.20
928	A126	80c multicolored	.75	.75
929	A126	$1 multicolored	.95	.95
930	A126	$5 multicolored	4.75	4.75
		Nos. 927-930 (4)	6.65	6.65

Caribbean Development Bank, 25th Anniv. — A127

Designs: 45c, Emblem, map of Anguilla. $5, Local headquarters along waterfront.

1995, Aug. 15   Litho.   *Perf. 13½x14*

931	A127	45c multicolored	.45	.45
932	A127	$5 multicolored	5.00	5.00
a.		Pair, #931-932	5.45	5.45

Whales A128

Perf. 13½x14, 14x13½

1995, Nov. 24   Litho.

933	A128	20c Blue whale	.20	.20
934	A128	45c Right whale, vert.	.40	.40
935	A128	$1 Sperm whale	.90	.90
936	A128	$5 Humpback whale	4.25	4.25
		Nos. 933-936 (4)	5.75	5.75

Christmas A129

1995, Dec. 12   *Perf. 14½*

937	A129	10c Palm tree	.15	.15
938	A129	25c Fish net floats	.20	.20
939	A129	45c Sea shells	.40	.40
940	A129	$5 Fish	4.25	4.25
		Nos. 937-940 (4)	5.00	5.00

Corals — A130

1996, June 21   Litho.   *Perf. 14x14½*

941	A130	20c Deep water gorgonia	.20	.20
942	A130	80c Common sea fan	.70	.70
943	A130	$5 Venus sea fern	4.25	4.25
		Nos. 941-943 (3)	5.15	5.15

A131    A132

1996 Summer Olympic Games, Atlanta: 20c, Running. 80c, Javelin, wheelchair basketball. $1, High jump. $3.50, Olympic torch, Greek, US flags.

1996, Dec. 12   Litho.   *Perf. 14*

944	A131	20c multicolored	.15	.15
945	A131	80c multicolored	.65	.65
946	A131	$1 multicolored	.80	.80
947	A131	$3.50 multicolored	2.75	2.75
		Nos. 944-947 (4)	4.35	4.35

1996, Dec. 12

Battle for Anguilla, bicent.: 60c, Sandy Hill Fort, HMS Lapwing. 75c, French troops destroy church, horiz. $1.50, HMS Lapwing defeats Valiant, Decius, horiz. $4, French troops land, Rendezvous Bay.

948	A132	60c multicolored	.50	.50
949	A132	75c multicolored	.60	.60
950	A132	$1.50 multicolored	1.25	1.25
951	A132	$4 multicolored	3.25	3.25
		Nos. 948+951 (1)	3.25	3.25

Fruits and Nuts A133

1997, Apr. 30   Litho.   *Perf. 14*

952	A133	10c Gooseberry	.15	.15
953	A133	20c West Indian cherry	.20	.20
954	A133	40c Tamarind	.35	.35
955	A133	50c Pomme-surette	.40	.40
956	A133	60c Sea almond	.50	.50
957	A133	75c Sea grape	.65	.65
958	A133	80c Banana	.65	.65
959	A133	$1 Genip	.85	.85
960	A133	$1.10 Coco plum	.90	.90
961	A133	$1.25 Pope	1.00	1.00
962	A133	$1.50 Papaya	1.25	1.25
963	A133	$2 Sugar apple	1.75	1.75
964	A133	$3 Soursop	2.50	2.50
965	A133	$4 Pomegrante	3.25	3.25
966	A133	$5 Cashew	4.25	4.25
967	A133	$10 Mango	8.25	8.25
		Nos. 952-967 (16)	26.90	26.90

Iguanas A134

World Wildlife Fund: a, 20c, Baby iguanas emerging from eggs, juvenile iguana. b, 50c, Adult on rock. c, 75c, Two iguanas on tree limbs. d, $3, Adult up close, adult on tree branch.

1997, Oct. 13   Litho.   *Perf. 13½x14*

| 968 | A134 | Strip of 4, #a.-d. | 4.00 | 4.00 |

Diana, Princess of Wales (1961-67) — A135

Designs: a, 15c, In red & white. b, $1, In yellow. c, $1.90, Wearing tiara. d, $2.25, Wearing blouse with Red Cross emblem.

1998, Apr. 14   Litho.   *Perf. 14*

| 969 | A135 | Strip of 4, #a.-d. | 4.00 | 4.00 |

No. 969 was issued in sheets of 16 stamps.

Fountain Cavern Carvings A136

Designs: 30c, Rainbow Deity (Juluca). $1.25, Lizard. $2.25, Solar Chieftan. $2.75, Creator.

1998   *Perf. 14x14½*

970	A136	30c multicolored	.25	.25
971	A136	$1.25 multicolored	1.10	1.10
972	A136	$2.25 multicolored	1.90	1.90
973	A136	$2.75 multicolored	2.25	2.25
		Nos. 970-973 (4)	5.50	5.50

ANJOUAN

'an-jü-wän

LOCATION — One of the Comoro Islands in the Mozambique Channel between Madagascar and Mozambique.
GOVT. — Former French colony.
AREA — 89 sq. mi.
POP. — 20,000 (approx. 1912)
CAPITAL — Mossamondu
See Comoro Islands.

100 Centimes = 1 Franc

Navigation and Commerce — A1

Perf. 14x13½

1892-1907   Typo.   Unwmk.

Name of Colony in Blue or Carmine

1	A1	1c black, *blue*	.85	.80
2	A1	2c brown, *buff*	1.25	1.10
3	A1	4c claret, *lav*	2.00	1.50
4	A1	5c green, *grnsh*	3.50	3.00
5	A1	10c blk, *lavender*	4.25	2.50
6	A1	10c red ('00)	17.50	12.50
7	A1	15c blue, quadrille paper	4.25	3.25
8	A1	15c gray, *lt gray* ('00)	9.00	6.50
9	A1	20c red, *green*	4.50	3.25
10	A1	25c black, *rose*	5.00	4.75
11	A1	25c blue ('00)	8.00	8.00
12	A1	30c brn, *bister*	12.50	10.00
13	A1	35c blk, *yel* ('06)	5.75	4.50

14	A1	40c red, *straw*	24.00	15.00
15	A1	45c blk, *gray grn* ('07)	80.00	77.50
16	A1	50c car, *rose*	25.00	17.00
17	A1	50c brn, *az* ('00)	16.00	9.00
18	A1	75c vio, *orange*	25.00	15.00
19	A1	1fr brnz grn, *straw*	55.00	42.50
		Nos. 1-19 (19)	303.35	237.65

Perf. 13½x14 stamps are counterfeits.

Issues of 1892-1907 Surcharged in Black or Carmine

05   10

1912
20	A1	5c on 2c brn, *buff*	.50	.50
21	A1	5c on 4c cl, *lav* (C)	.50	.50
22	A1	5c on 15c blue (C)	.50	.50
23	A1	5c on 20c red, *green*	.50	.50
24	A1	5c on 25c blk, *rose* (C)	.50	.50
25	A1	5c on 30c brn, *bis* (C)	.50	.50
26	A1	10c on 40c red, *straw*	.70	.70
27	A1	10c on 45c black, *gray green* (C)	.85	.85
28	A1	10c on 50c car, *rose*	1.90	1.90
29	A1	10c on 75c vio, *org*	1.35	1.35
30	A1	10c on 1fr brnz grn, *straw*	1.35	1.35
		Nos. 20-30 (11)	9.15	9.15

Nos. 21-23, 30 exist in pairs, one without surcharge. Value $550 each.

Two spacings between the surcharged numerals are found on Nos. 20-30.

Nos. 20-30 were available for use in Madagascar and the Comoro archipelago.

The stamps of Anjouan were superseded by those of Madagascar, and in 1950 by those of Comoro Islands.

ANNAM AND TONKIN
a-'nam and 'tän-'kin

LOCATION — In French Indo-China bordering on the China Sea on the east and Siam on the west.
GOVT. — French Protectorate
AREA — 97,503 sq. mi.
POP. — 14,124,000 (approx. 1890)
CAPITAL — Annam: Hue; Tonkin: Hanoi

For administrative purposes, the Protectorates of Annam, Tonkin, Cambodia, Laos and the Colony of Cochin-China were grouped together and were known as French Indo-China.

100 Centimes = 1 Franc

Catalogue values for unused stamps are for examples without gum as most stamps were issued in that condition.

Stamps of French Colonies, 1881-86 Handstamped Surcharged in Black:

A & T   A & T
1   5

Perf. 14x13½
1888, Jan. 21   Unwmk.
1	A9	1c on 2c brn, *buff*	22.50	20.00
a.		Inverted surcharge	100.00	100.00
b.		Sideways surcharge	100.00	100.00
2	A9	1c on 4c claret, *lav*	17.50	14.00
a.		Inverted surcharge	100.00	100.00
b.		Double surcharge	125.00	125.00
c.		Sideways surcharge	100.00	100.00
3	A9	5c on 10c blk, *lav*	17.50	15.00
a.		Inverted surcharge	100.00	100.00
b.		Double surcharge	125.00	125.00

Hyphen between "A" and "T"
7	A9	1c on 2c brn, *buff*	220.00	200.00
a.		Inverted surcharge	450.00	
8	A9	1c on 4c claret, *lav*	350.00	350.00
9	A9	5c on 10c blk, *lav*	160.00	160.00

A 5c on 2c was prepared but not issued. Value $6,500.

In these surcharges there are different types of numerals and letters.

There are numerous other errors in the placing of the surcharges, including double one inverted, double both inverted, one double one sideways, pair #1, 7, and pair one without surcharge. Such varieties command substantial premiums.

These stamps were superseded in 1892 by those of Indo-China.

ANTIGUA
an-'tēg-(w)ə

LOCATION — In the West Indies, southeast of Puerto Rico
GOVT. — Independent state
AREA — 171 sq. mi.
POP. — 74,000 (est. 1981)
CAPITAL — St. John's

Antigua was one of the presidencies of the former Leeward Islands colony until becoming a Crown Colony in 1956. It became an Associated State of the United Kingdom in 1967 and an independent nation on November 1, 1981, taking the name of Antigua and Barbuda.

Antigua stamps were discontinued in 1890 and resumed in 1903. In the interim, stamps of Leeward Islands were used. Between 1903-1956, stamps of Antigua and Leeward Islands were used concurrently.

12 Pence = 1 Shilling
20 Shillings = 1 Pound
100 Cents = 1 Dollar (1951)

Catalogue values for unused stamps in this country are for Never Hinged items, beginning with Scott 96.

Watermarks

Wmk. 5- Star

Values for unused stamps are for examples with original gum as defined in the catalogue introduction. Any exceptions will be noted. Very fine examples of Nos. 1-8, 11, 18-20 will have perforations touching the design on at least one frameline due to the narrow spacing of the stamps on the plates. Stamps with perfs clear of the framelines on all four sides are extremely scarce and will command higher prices.

Queen Victoria
A1   A2

Rough Perf. 14-16
1862   Engr.   Unwmk.
1	A1	6p blue green	1,000.	650.
a.		Perf. 11-13	5,250.	
b.		Perf. 11-13x14-16	2,750.	
c.		Perf. 11-13 compound with 14-16	3,000.	

There is a question whether Nos. 1a-1c ever did postal duty.
Values for No. 1 are for stamps with perfs. cutting into the design. Values for No. 1b are for copies without gum.

1863-67   Wmk. 5
2	A1	1p lilac rose	110.00	32.50
a.		Vert. pair, imperf. btwn.	15,000.	
3	A1	1p vermilion ('67)	375.00	27.50
a.		Horiz. pair, imperf. btwn.	16,000.	
4	A1	6p green	350.00	30.00
a.		6p yellow green	3,750.	70.00
b.		Pair, imperf. between		
c.		6p dark green	375.00	30.00

1872   Wmk. 1   Perf. 12½
5	A1	1p lake	100.00	27.50
6	A1	1p vermilion	125.00	27.50
7	A1	6p blue green	550.00	11.00
		Nos. 5-7 (3)	775.00	66.00

1873-79   Perf. 14
8	A1	1p lake	95.00	12.50
a.		Half used as ½p on cover		2,500.

Typo.
9	A2	2½p red brown ('79)	600.00	175.00
10	A2	4p blue ('79)	300.00	18.00

Engr.
11	A1	6p blue green ('76)	300.00	13.50

1882-86   Typo.   Wmk. 2
12	A2	½p green	2.75	10.00
13	A2	2½p red brown	125.00	47.50
14	A2	2½p ultra ('86)	8.25	12.00
15	A2	4p blue	275.00	18.00
16	A2	4p brown org ('86)	2.25	3.25
17	A2	1sh violet ('86)	175.00	125.00

Engr.
18	A1	1p carmine ('84)	1.25	3.00
19	A1	6p deep green	60.00	125.00

No. 18 was used for a time in St. Christopher and is identified by the "A12" cancellation.

1884   Perf. 12
20	A1	1p rose red	50.00	17.00

Seal of the Colony — A3
King Edward VII — A4 

1903   Typo.   Wmk. 1   Perf. 14
21	A3	½p blue grn & blk	2.75	3.75
a.		Bluish paper ('09)	85.00	85.00
22	A3	1p car & black	4.50	.90
a.		Bluish paper ('09)	85.00	85.00
23	A3	2p org brn & vio	5.50	22.50
24	A3	2½p ultra & black	7.50	12.00
25	A3	3p ocher & gray green	8.75	18.00
26	A3	6p black & red vio	26.00	45.00
27	A3	1sh violet & ultra	32.50	45.00
28	A3	2sh pur & gray green	55.00	75.00
29	A3	2sh6p red vio & blk	20.00	45.00
30	A4	5sh pur & gray green	65.00	90.00
		Nos. 21-30 (10)	227.50	357.15

The 2½p, 1sh and 5sh exist on both ordinary and chalky paper.

1908-15   Wmk. 3
31	A3	½p green	2.00	3.25
32	A3	1p carmine	3.50	1.75
a.		1p scarlet ('15)	4.00	2.75
33	A3	2p org brn & dull vio ('12)	3.25	22.50
34	A3	2½p ultra	7.75	14.00
35	A3	3p ocher & grn ('12)	5.50	16.00
36	A3	6p blk & red vio ('11)	6.25	30.00
37	A3	1sh vio & ultra	14.00	62.50
38	A3	2sh vio & green ('12)	55.00	70.00
		Nos. 31-38 (8)	97.25	220.00

Nos. 33, 35-38 are on chalky paper.
For overprints see Nos. MR1-MR3.

George V — A6
St. John's Harbor — A7 

1913
41	A6	5sh violet & green	70.00	95.00

1921-29   Wmk. 4
42	A7	½p green	.80	.20
43	A7	1p rose red	.75	.20
44	A7	1p dp violet ('23)	1.75	1.40
45	A7	1½p orange ('22)	1.50	6.50
46	A7	1½p rose red ('26)	2.50	1.75
47	A7	1½p fawn ('29)	1.60	.55
48	A7	2p gray	1.10	.75
49	A7	2½p ultra	3.00	5.00
50	A7	2½p orange ('23)	1.25	16.00

Chalky Paper
51	A7	3p violet, *yel* ('25)	3.50	8.00
52	A7	6p vio & red vio	2.75	5.75
53	A7	1sh black, *emer* ('29)	5.75	7.50
54	A7	2sh vio & ultra, *blue* ('27)	9.50	45.00
55	A7	2sh6p blk & red, *blue* ('27)	16.00	21.00
56	A7	3sh grn & vio ('22)	22.50	65.00
57	A7	4sh blk & red ('22)	45.00	50.00
		Nos. 42-57 (16)	119.25	234.60

Wmk. 3
Chalky Paper
58	A7	3p violet, *yel*	3.25	10.00
59	A7	4p black & red, *yel* ('22)	1.40	4.75
60	A7	1sh black, *emerald*	3.50	6.50
61	A7	2sh vio & ultra, *bl*	9.25	17.50
62	A7	2sh6p blk & red, *bl*	12.00	40.00
63	A7	5sh grn & red, *yel* ('22)	8.00	35.00
64	A7	£1 vio & black, *red* ('22)	225.00	250.00
		Nos. 58-64 (7)	262.40	363.75

Old Dockyard, English Harbour — A8
Govt. House, St. John's — A9 

Nelson's "Victory," 1805 — A10
Sir Thomas Warner's Ship, 1632 — A11  

Perf. 12½
1932, Jan. 27   Engr.   Wmk. 4
67	A8	½p green	1.60	4.75
68	A8	1p scarlet	2.25	3.50
69	A8	1½p lt brown	2.50	4.00
70	A9	2p gray	3.25	14.00
71	A9	2½p ultra	3.25	8.00
72	A9	3p orange	4.00	11.00
73	A10	6p violet	9.00	22.50
74	A10	1sh olive green	15.00	22.50
75	A10	2sh6p claret	35.00	45.00
76	A11	5sh red brn & black	95.00	110.00
		Nos. 67-76 (10)	170.85	245.25

Tercentenary of the colony.

Common Design Types pictured following the introduction.

Silver Jubilee Issue
Common Design Type
1935, May 6   Perf. 13½x14
77	CD301	1p car & blue	1.60	1.50
78	CD301	1½p gray blk & ultra	2.10	1.25
79	CD301	2½p ultra & brn	4.25	4.00
80	CD301	1sh brt vio & ind	8.00	12.50
		Nos. 77-80 (4)	15.95	19.25

Coronation Issue
Common Design Type
1937, May 12   Perf. 11x11½
81	CD302	1p carmine	.30	.30
82	CD302	1½p brown	.40	.40
83	CD302	2½p deep ultra	1.00	1.00
		Nos. 81-83 (3)	1.70	1.70
		Set, never hinged	2.25	

English Harbour — A14
Nelson's Dockyard — A15 

Fort James — A16
St. John's Harbor — A17

ANTIGUA

1938-48 Engr. Perf. 12½
84	A14	½p green	.20	.60
85	A15	1p red	1.40	1.40
86	A15	1½p brown violet	2.00	.45
87	A14	2p dark gray	.15	.45
88	A15	2½p deep ultra	.35	.65
89	A17	3p orange	.30	.60
90	A17	6p purple	.60	.60
91	A17	1sh red brn & blk	1.90	.70
92	A16	2sh6p deep claret	15.00	6.25
93	A17	5sh olive green	10.00	5.75
94	A15	10sh red vio ('48)	11.00	21.00
95	A16	£1 Prus blue ('48)	17.00	27.50
		Nos. 84-95 (12)	59.90	65.95
		Set, never hinged	80.00	

See Nos. 107-113, 115-116, 118-121, 136-142, 144-145.
For overprint see Nos. 125-126.

Catalogue values for unused stamps in this section, from this point to the end of the section, are for Never Hinged items.

Peace Issue
Common Design Type
1946, Nov. 1 Wmk. 4 Perf. 13½x14
96	CD303	1½p brown	.30	.30
97	CD303	3p deep orange	.35	.35

Silver Wedding Issue
Common Design Types
1949, Jan. 3 Photo. Perf. 14x14½
| 98 | CD304 | 2½p bright ultra | .30 | .55 |

Engraved; Name Typographed
Perf. 11½x11
| 99 | CD305 | 5sh dk brown olive | 7.50 | 9.00 |

UPU Issue
Common Design Types
Perf. 13½, 11x11½
1949, Oct. 10 Wmk. 4
Engr.; Name Typo. on 3p and 6p
100	CD306	2½p deep ultra	.15	.15
101	CD307	3p orange	.55	.55
102	CD308	6p purple	1.10	1.10
103	CD309	1sh red brown	1.25	1.25
		Nos. 100-103 (4)	3.05	3.05

University Issue
Common Design Types
Perf. 14x14½
1951, Feb. 16 Engr. Wmk. 4
| 104 | CD310 | 3c chocolate & blk | .35 | .35 |
| 105 | CD311 | 12c purple & blk | 1.00 | 1.00 |

Coronation Issue
Common Design Type
1953, June 2 Perf. 13½x13
| 106 | CD312 | 2c dk green & blk | .50 | .50 |

Types of 1938 with Portrait of Queen Elizabeth II

Martello Tower — A24

Perf. 13x13½, 13½x13
1953-56 Wmk. 4
107	A16	½c dk red brn ('56)	.15	.15
108	A14	1c gray	.15	.15
109	A15	2c deep green	.15	.15
110	A15	3c yellow & blk	.20	.15
111	A14	4c rose red (shades)	1.00	.15
112	A15	5c dull vio & blk	1.90	.40
113	A16	6c orange	1.50	.15
114	A24	8c deep blue	1.65	.15
115	A17	12c violet	1.65	.15
116	A17	24c chocolate & blk	1.90	.15
117	A24	48c dp bl & rose lil	5.75	.60
118	A16	60c claret	6.00	.50
119	A17	$1.20 olive green	1.50	.50
120	A15	$2.40 magenta	6.25	8.50
121	A16	$4.80 greenish blue	10.50	12.50
		Nos. 107-121 (15)	40.25	24.15

See #143. For overprint see #125-126.

West Indies Federation
Common Design Type
Perf. 11½x11
1958, Apr. 22 Engr. Wmk. 314
122	CD313	3c green	.35	.20
123	CD313	6c blue	.90	.35
124	CD313	12c carmine rose	1.65	.75
		Nos. 122-124 (3)	2.90	1.30

Nos. 110 and 115 Overprinted in Red or Black: "Commemoration Antigua Constitution 1960"
Perf. 13x13½, 13½x13
1960, Jan. 1 Wmk. 4
| 125 | A15 | 3c yellow & black | .15 | .15 |
| 126 | A17 | 12c violet (Blk) | .20 | .20 |

Constitutional reforms effective Jan. 1, 1960.

Lord Nelson and Nelson's Dockyard A26

Perf. 11½x11
1961, Nov. 14 Wmk. 314
| 127 | A26 | 20c brown & lilac | .60 | .40 |
| 128 | A26 | 30c dk blue & green | 1.00 | .60 |

Completion of the restoration of Lord Nelson's headquarters, English Harbour.

Stamp of 1862 and Royal Mail Steam Packet in English Harbour
A27

1962, Aug. 1 Engr. Perf. 13
129	A27	3c dull green & pur	.15	.15
130	A27	10c dull green & ultra	.20	.20
131	A27	12c dull green & blk	.30	.30
132	A27	50c dull grn & brn org	1.50	1.50
		Nos. 129-132 (4)	2.15	2.15

Centenary of first Antigua postage stamp.

Freedom from Hunger Issue
Common Design Type
Perf. 14x14½
1963, June 4 Photo. Wmk. 314
| 133 | CD314 | 12c green | .40 | .40 |

Red Cross Centenary Issue
Common Design Type
1963, Sept. 2 Litho. Perf. 13
| 134 | CD315 | 3c black & red | .15 | .15 |
| 135 | CD315 | 12c ultra & red | 1.10 | 1.10 |

Types of 1938-53 with Portrait of Queen Elizabeth II
Perf. 13x13½, 13½x13
1963-65 Engr. Wmk. 314
136	A16	½c brown ('65)	.30	.30
137	A14	1c gray ('65)	.30	.30
138	A15	2c deep green	.15	.15
139	A15	3c orange yel & blk	.20	.20
140	A14	4c brown red	.35	.35
141	A15	5c dull vio & black	.35	.35
142	A16	6c orange	.40	.40
143	A24	8c deep blue	.45	.45
144	A17	12c violet	.85	.85
145	A17	24c choc & black	1.75	1.75
		Nos. 136-145 (10)	5.10	5.10

For surcharge see No. 152.

Shakespeare Issue
Common Design Type
Perf. 14x14½
1964, Apr. 23 Photo. Wmk. 314
| 151 | CD316 | 12c red brown | .35 | .35 |

No. 144 Surcharged with New Value and Bars
Perf. 13½x13
1965, Apr. 1 Wmk. 314
| 152 | A17 | 15c on 12c violet | .35 | .35 |

ITU Issue
Common Design Type
Perf. 11x11½
1965, May 17 Litho. Wmk. 314
| 153 | CD317 | 2c blue & ver | .15 | .15 |
| 154 | CD317 | 50c orange & vio bl | 1.75 | 1.75 |

Intl. Cooperation Year Issue
Common Design Type
1965, Oct. 25 Perf. 14½
| 155 | CD318 | 4c blue grn & claret | .15 | .15 |
| 156 | CD318 | 15c lt vio & green | .70 | .70 |

Churchill Memorial Issue
Common Design Type
1966, Jan. 24 Photo. Perf. 14
Design in Black, Gold and Carmine Rose
157	CD319	½c bright blue	.15	.15
158	CD319	4c green	.20	.20
159	CD319	25c brown	.85	.70
160	CD319	35c violet	1.40	1.10
		Nos. 157-160 (4)	2.60	2.15

Royal Visit Issue
Common Design Type
1966, Feb. 4 Litho. Perf. 11x12
Portraits in Black
| 161 | CD320 | 6c violet blue | 1.25 | .90 |
| 162 | CD320 | 15c dark car rose | 2.00 | 1.10 |

World Cup Soccer Issue
Common Design Type
1966, July 1 Wmk. 314 Perf. 14
| 163 | CD321 | 6c multicolored | .15 | .15 |
| 164 | CD321 | 35c multicolored | .65 | .65 |

WHO Headquarters Issue
Common Design Type
1966, Sept. 20 Perf. 14
| 165 | CD322 | 2c multicolored | .15 | .15 |
| 166 | CD322 | 15c multicolored | .75 | .75 |

Nelson's Dockyard A35

Designs: 1c, Old post office, St. John's. 2c, Health Center. 3c, Teachers' Training College. 4c, Martello Tower, Barbuda. 5c, Ruins of officers quarters, Shirley Heights. 6c, Government House, Barbuda. 10c, Princess Margaret School. 15c, Air terminal. 25c, General post office. 35c, Clarence House. 50c, Government House. 75c, Administration building. $1, Court House, St. John's. $2.50, Magistrates' Court. $5, St. John's Cathedral.

Perf. 11½x11
1966, Nov. 1 Engr. Wmk. 314
167	A35	½c green & blue	.15	.15
168	A35	1c purple & rose	.15	.15
169	A35	2c slate & org	.15	.15
170	A35	3c rose red & blk	.15	.15
171	A35	4c dull vio & brn	.15	.15
172	A35	5c vio bl & olive	.15	.15
a.		Booklet pane of 4	.40	
173	A35	6c dp org & pur	.15	.15
174	A35	10c brt grn & rose red	.20	.20
a.		Booklet pane of 4 ('68)	1.00	
175	A35	15c brn & blue	.25	.25
a.		Booklet pane of 4 ('68)	1.25	
176	A35	25c slate & brn	.45	.45
177	A35	35c dp rose & sep	.60	.60
178	A35	50c green & black	.90	.90
179	A35	75c Prus bl & vio blue	1.10	1.10
180	A35	$1 dp rose & olive	1.50	1.50
181	A35	$2.50 black & rose	3.75	3.75
182	A35	$5 ol grn & dl vio	7.75	7.75
		Nos. 167-182 (16)	17.55	17.55

For surcharge see No. 231.

1969 Perf. 13½
167a	A35	½c	.15	.15
168a	A35	1c	.15	.15
169a	A35	2c	.15	.15
170a	A35	3c	.15	.15
171a	A35	4c	.15	.15
172b	A35	5c	.15	.15
173a	A35	6c	.15	.15
174b	A35	10c	.20	.20
175b	A35	15c	.30	.30
176a	A35	25c	.50	.50
177a	A35	35c	.60	.60
178a	A35	50c	.95	.95
180a	A35	$1	2.00	2.00
181a	A35	$2.50	5.50	5.50
182a	A35	$5	19.00	19.00
		Nos. 167a-182a (15)	30.10	30.10

UNESCO Anniversary Issue
Common Design Type
1966, Dec. 1 Litho. Perf. 14
183	CD323	4c "Education"	.15	.15
184	CD323	25c "Science"	.40	.40
185	CD323	$1 "Culture"	2.00	2.00
		Nos. 183-185 (3)	2.55	2.55

Independent State

Flag of Antigua, Spiny Lobster, Maps of Antigua and Barbuda
A37

Designs: 15c, 35c, Flag of Antigua. 25c, Flag and Premier's Office Building.

1967, Feb. 27 Photo. Perf. 14
186	A37	4c multicolored	.15	.15
187	A37	15c multicolored	.15	.15
188	A37	25c multicolored	.25	.25
189	A37	35c multicolored	.30	.30
		Nos. 186-189 (4)	.85	.85

Antigua's independence, Feb. 27, 1967.

Gilbert Memorial Church, Antigua — A38

Designs: 25c, Nathaniel Gilbert's House. 35c, Map of the Caribbean and Central America.

Perf. 14x13½
1967, May 18 Photo. Wmk. 314
190	A38	4c brt red & black	.15	.15
191	A38	25c emerald & black	.30	.30
192	A38	35c ultra & black	.40	.40
		Nos. 190-192 (3)	.85	.85

Attainment of autonomy by the Methodist Church in the Caribbean and the Americas, and the opening of headquarters near St. John's, Antigua, May 1967.

Antiguan and British Royal Arms — A39

1967, July 21 Perf. 14½x14
| 193 | A39 | 15c dark green & multi | .20 | .20 |
| 194 | A39 | 35c deep blue & multi | .45 | .45 |

Granting of a new coat of arms to the State of Antigua; 300th anniv. of the Treaty of Breda.

Sailing Ship, 17th Century A40

Design: 6c, 35c, Map of Barbuda from Jan Blaeu's Atlas, 1665.

Perf. 11½x11
1967, Dec. 14 Engr. Wmk. 314
195	A40	4c dark blue	.15	.15
196	A40	6c deep plum	.15	.15
197	A40	25c green	.30	.30
198	A40	35c black	.50	.50
		Nos. 195-198 (4)	1.10	1.10

Resettlement of Barbuda, 300th anniv.

Dow Hill Antenna — A41

ANTIGUA

Designs: 15c, Antenna and rocket blasting off. 25c, Nose cone orbiting moon. 50c, Re-entry of space capsule.

1968, Mar. 29   Photo.   Perf. 14½x14   Wmk. 314

199	A41	4c dk blue, org & black	.15	.15
200	A41	15c dk blue, org & black	.15	.15
201	A41	25c dk blue, org & black	.25	.25
202	A41	50c dk blue, org & black	.45	.45
		Nos. 199-202 (4)	1.00	1.00

Dedication of the Dow Hill tracking station in Antigua for the NASA Apollo project.

Beach and Sailfish A42

Designs: ½c, 50c, Limbo dancer, flames and dancing girls. 15c, Three girls on a beach and water skier. 35c, Woman scuba diver, corals and fish.

1968, July 1   Photo.   Perf. 14

203	A42	½c red & multi	.15	.15
204	A42	15c sky blue & multi	.20	.20
205	A42	25c blue & multi	.30	.30
206	A42	35c brt blue & multi	.35	.35
207	A42	50c multicolored	.60	.60
		Nos. 203-207 (5)	1.60	1.60

Issued for tourist publicity.

St. John's Harbor, 1768 A43

St. John's Harbor: 15c, 1829. 25c, Map of deep-sea harbor, 1968. 35c, Dock, 1968. 2c, Like $1.

Engr. & Litho.; Engr. ($1)
1968, Oct. 31   Wmk. 314   Perf. 13

208	A43	2c dp car & lt blue	.15	.15
209	A43	15c sepia & yel grn	.20	.20
210	A43	25c dk blue & yel	.40	.40
211	A43	35c dp green & sal	.45	.45
212	A43	$1 black	1.50	1.50
		Nos. 208-212 (5)	2.70	2.70

Opening of St. John's deep-sea harbor.

Mace and Parliament A44

Mace and: 15c, Mace bearer. 25c, House of Representatives, interior. 50c, Antigua coat of arms and great seal.

1969, Feb. 3   Photo.   Perf. 12½

213	A44	4c crimson & multi	.15	.15
214	A44	15c crimson & multi	.20	.20
215	A44	25c crimson & multi	.30	.30
216	A44	50c crimson & multi	.60	.60
		Nos. 213-216 (4)	1.25	1.25

300th anniversary of Antigua Parliament.

CARIFTA Cargo — A45

Design: 4c, 15c, Ship, plane and trucks, horiz.

Perf. 13½x13, 13x13½
1969, Apr. 14   Litho.   Wmk. 314

217	A45	4c blk & brt lilac rose	.15	.15
218	A45	15c blk & brt grnsh blue	.20	.20
219	A45	25c bister & black	.20	.20
220	A45	35c tan & black	.35	.35
		Nos. 217-220 (4)	.90	.90

1st anniv. of CARIFTA (Caribbean Free Trade Area).

Map of Redonda Island A46

25c, View of Redonda from the sea & seagulls.

1969, Aug. 1   Photo.   Perf. 13x13½

221	A46	15c ultra & multi	.25	.25
222	A46	25c multicolored	.40	.40
223	A46	50c salmon & multi	1.10	1.10
		Nos. 221-223 (3)	1.75	1.75

Centenary of Redonda phosphate industry.

Adoration of the Kings, by Guglielmo Marcillat A47

Christmas: 10c, 50c, Holy Family, by anonymous German artist, 15th century.

1969, Oct. 15   Litho.   Perf. 13x14

224	A47	6c bister brn & multi	.15	.15
225	A47	10c fawn & multi	.15	.15
226	A47	35c gray olive & multi	.35	.35
227	A47	50c gray blue & multi	.60	.60
		Nos. 224-227 (4)	1.25	1.25

Arms of Antigua — A48

Coil Stamps
Perf. 14½x14
1970, Jan. 30   Photo.   Wmk. 314

228	A48	5c bright blue	.15	.15
229	A48	10c bright green	.20	.20
230	A48	25c deep magenta	.45	.45
		Nos. 228-230 (3)	.80	.80

No. 176 Surcharged 20¢

1970, Jan. 2   Engr.   Perf. 11½x11

231	A35	20c on 25c slate & brown	.35	.15

Sikorsky S-38 A49

Aircraft: 20c, Dornier DO-X. 35c, Hawker Siddeley 748. 50c, Douglas C-124C Globemaster II. 75c, Vickers VC 10.

1970, Feb. 16   Litho.   Perf. 14½

232	A49	5c brt green & multi	.15	.15
233	A49	20c ultra & multi	.35	.35
234	A49	35c blue grn & multi	.60	.60
235	A49	50c blue & multi	.90	.90
236	A49	75c vio blue & multi	1.50	1.50
		Nos. 232-236 (5)	3.50	3.50

40th anniversary of air service.

Dickens and Scene from "Pickwick Papers" A50

Charles Dickens (1812-1870), English novelist and Scene from: 5c, "Nicholas Nickleby." 35c, "Oliver Twist." $1, "David Copperfield."

Wmk. 314
1970, May 19   Litho.   Perf. 14

237	A50	5c olive & sepia	.15	.15
238	A50	20c aqua & sepia	.25	.20
239	A50	35c violet & sepia	.30	.30
240	A50	$1 scarlet & sepia	1.00	.80
		Nos. 237-240 (4)	1.70	1.45

Carib Indian and War Canoe — A51

Ships: 1c, Columbus and "Niña." 2c, Sir Thomas Warner's arms and sailing ship. 3c, Viscount Hood and "Barfleur." 4c, Sir George Rodney and "Formidable." 5c, Capt. Horatio Nelson and "Boreas." 6c, King William IV and "Pegasus." 10c, Blackbeard (Edward Teach) and pirate ketch. 15c, Capt. Cuthbert Collingwood and "Pelican." 20c, Admiral Nelson and "Victoria." 25c, Paddle steamer "Solent" and Steam Packet Company emblem. 35c, King George V and corvette "Canada." 50c, Cruiser "Renown" and royal badge. 75c, S.S. "Federal Maple" and maple leaf. $1, Racing yacht "Sol-Quest" and Gallant 53 class emblem. $2.50, Missile destroyer "London" and her emblem. $5, Tug "Pathfinder" and arms of Antigua.

Wmk. 314 Sideways
1970, Aug. 19   Litho.   Perf. 14

241	A51	½c ocher & multi	.15	.15
242	A51	1c Prus bl & multi	.15	.15
243	A51	2c yel grn & multi	.15	.15
244	A51	3c ol bis & multi	.15	.15
245	A51	4c bl gray & multi	.15	.15
246	A51	5c fawn & multi	.20	.15
247	A51	6c rose lil & multi	.20	.15
248	A51	10c brn org & multi	.25	.15
249	A51	15c ultra & multi	.40	.25
250	A51	20c ol grn & multi	.35	.20
251	A51	25c olive & multi	.40	.20
252	A51	35c dull red brn & multi	.70	.35
253	A51	50c lt brn & multi	.95	.55
254	A51	75c beige & multi	1.25	.75
255	A51	$1 Prus green & multi	1.90	1.10
256	A51	$2.50 gray & multi	5.50	2.75
257	A51	$5 yel & multi	12.50	7.00
		Nos. 241-257 (17)	25.35	14.35

1972-74   Wmk. 314 Upright

241a	A51	½c	.15	.15
242a	A51	1c	.15	.15
244a	A51	3c	.15	.15
245a	A51	4c	.15	.15
246a	A51	5c	.15	.15
247a	A51	6c	.15	.15
248a	A51	10c	.20	.20
249a	A51	15c	1.60	1.25
254a	A51	75c	3.25	1.60
255a	A51	$1	3.60	1.60
256a	A51	$2.50	6.00	7.50
257a	A51	$5	6.75	10.50
		Nos. 241a-257a (12)	22.30	22.20

For surcharge see No. 368.

1975, Jan. 21   Wmk. 373

257b	A51	$5 yellow & multi	13.00	13.00

Nativity, by Albrecht Dürer — A52

Private, 4th West India Regiment, 1804 — A53

Christmas: 10c, 50c, Adoration of the Magi, by Albrecht Dürer.

Dickens and Scene from "Pickwick Papers" A50

Engr. & Litho.
1970, Oct. 28   Perf. 13½x14

258	A52	3c brt grnsh blue & blk	.15	.15
259	A52	10c pink & plum	.15	.15
260	A52	35c brick red & black	.35	.35
261	A52	50c lilac & violet	.60	.60
		Nos. 258-261 (4)	1.25	1.25

Perf. 14x13½
1970, Dec. 1   Litho.   Wmk. 314

Military Uniforms: ½c, Drummer Boy, 4th King's Own Regiment, 1759. 20c, Grenadier Company Officer, 60th Regiment, The Royal American, 1809. 35c, Light Company Officer, 93rd Regiment, The Sutherland Highlanders, 1826-1834. 75c, Private, 3rd West India Regiment, 1851.

262	A53	½c lake & multi	.15	.15
263	A53	10c brn org & multi	.40	.40
264	A53	20c Prus grn & multi	.70	.70
265	A53	35c dl pur & multi	1.40	1.40
266	A53	75c dk ol grn & multi	3.75	3.75
a.		Souv. sheet of 5, #262-266 + label	8.25	8.25
		Nos. 262-266 (5)	6.40	6.40

See #274-278, 283-287, 307-311, 329-333.

Market Woman Voting — A54

Voting by: 20c, Businessman. 35c, Mother (and child). 50c, Workman.

Perf. 14½x14
1971, Feb. 1   Photo.   Wmk. 314

267	A54	5c brown	.15	.15
268	A54	20c olive black	.15	.15
269	A54	35c rose magenta	.20	.20
270	A54	50c violet blue	.35	.35
		Nos. 267-270 (4)	.85	.85

Adult suffrage, 20th anniversary.

Last Supper, from The Small Passion, by Dürer — A55

Woodcuts by Albrecht Dürer: 35c, Crucifixion from Eichstaff Missal. 75c, Resurrection from The Great Passion.

Perf. 14x13½
1971, Apr. 7   Litho.   Wmk. 314

271	A55	5c gray, red & black	.15	.15
272	A55	35c gray, violet & black	.25	.25
273	A55	75c gray, gold & black	.55	.55
		Nos. 271-273 (3)	.95	.95

Easter.

Military Uniform Type of 1970

Military Uniforms: ½c, Private, Suffolk Regiment, 1704. 10c, Grenadier, South Staffordshire, 1751. 20c, Fusilier, Royal Northumberland, 1778. 35c, Private, Northamptonshire, 1793. 75c, Private, East Yorkshire, 1805.

1971, July 12   Litho.   Wmk. 314

274	A53	½c gray grn & multi	.15	.15
275	A53	10c bluish blk & multi	.30	.30
276	A53	20c dk pur & multi	.50	.50
277	A53	35c dk ol & multi	1.10	1.10
278	A53	75c brown & multi	2.50	2.50
a.		Souvenir sheet of 5, #274-278 + label	7.25	7.25
		Nos. 274-278 (5)	4.55	4.55

Antigua stamps can be mounted in the annual Scott Antigua supplement.

Virgin and Child, by Veronese — A56

Christmas: 5c, 50c, Adoration of the Shepherds, by Bonifazio Veronese.

1971, Oct. 4 *Perf. 14x13½*

279 A56	3c multicolored		.15	.15
280 A56	5c multicolored		.15	.15
281 A56	35c multicolored		.45	.45
282 A56	50c multicolored		.70	.70
	Nos. 279-282 (4)		1.45	1.45

Uniform Type of 1970

Military Uniforms: ½c, Officer, King's Own Borderers Regiment, 1815. 10c, Sergeant, Buckinghamshire Regiment, 1837. 20c, Private, South Hampshire Regiment, 1853. 35c, Officer, Royal Artillery, 1854. 75c, Private, Worcestershire Regiment, 1870.

1972, July 1

283 A53	½c ol brn & multi	.15	.15
284 A53	10c dp grn & multi	.35	.35
285 A53	20c brt vio & multi	.70	.70
286 A53	35c mar & multi	1.40	1.40
287 A53	75c dk vio bl & multi	3.00	3.00
a.	Souvenir sheet of 5, #283-287 + label	8.00	8.00
	Nos. 283-287 (5)	5.60	5.60

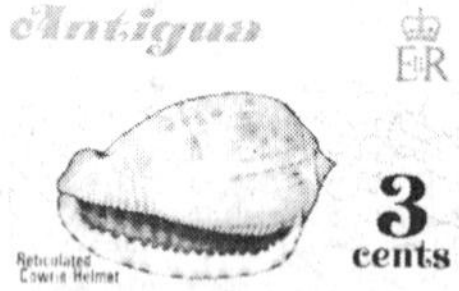

Reticulated Helmet Cowrie A57

Sea Shells: 5c, Measled cowrie. 35c, West Indian fighting conch. 50c, Hawkwing conch.

1972, Aug. 1 *Perf. 14½x14*

288 A57	3c multicolored	.15	.15
289 A57	5c ver & multi	.35	.35
290 A57	35c lt vio & multi	1.40	1.40
291 A57	50c rose red & multi	2.25	2.25
	Nos. 288-291 (4)	4.15	4.15

St. John's Cathedral, 1745-1843 A58

Christmas: 50c, Interior of St. John's. 75c, St. John's rebuilt.

1972, Nov. 6 **Litho.** *Perf. 14*

292 A58	35c org brn & multi	.35	.35
293 A58	50c vio & multi	.60	.60
294 A58	75c multicolored	1.00	1.00
a.	Souv. sheet of 3, #292-294, perf. 15	3.25	3.25
	Nos. 292-294 (3)	1.95	1.95

Silver Wedding Issue, 1972

Common Design Type

1972, Nov. 20 **Photo.** *Perf. 14x14½*

295 CD324	20c ultra & multi	.25	.25
296 CD324	35c steel bl & multi	.40	.40

Map of Antigua, Batsman Driving Ball — A60

Designs: 35c, Batsman and wicketkeeper. $1, Emblem of Rising Sun Cricket Club.

1972, Dec. 15 *Perf. 13½x14*

297 A60	5c multicolored	.25	.25
298 A60	35c multicolored	1.10	1.10
299 A60	$1 multicolored	2.75	2.75
a.	Souvenir sheet of 3, #297-299	5.00	5.00
	Nos. 297-299 (3)	4.10	4.10

Rising Sun Cricket Club, St. John's, 50th anniv.

Map of Antigua and Yacht — A61

1972, Dec. 29 *Perf. 14½*

300 A61	35c shown	.30	.30
301 A61	50c Racing yachts	.35	.35
302 A61	75c St. John's G.P.O.	.65	.65
303 A61	$1 Statue of Liberty	1.00	1.00
a.	Souvenir sheet of 2, #301, 303	2.50	2.50
	Nos. 300-303 (4)	2.30	2.30

Opening of Antigua and Barbuda Information Office in New York City.

Window with Episcopal Coat of Arms — A62

Stained glass windows from Cathedral of St. John: 35c, Crucifixion. 75c, Arm of Rt. Rev. D.G. Davis, 1st bishop of Antigua.

1973, Apr. 16 **Litho.** *Perf. 13½*

304 A62	5c yellow & multi	.15	.15
305 A62	35c brt lilac & multi	.25	.25
306 A62	75c blue & multi	.55	.55
	Nos. 304-306 (3)	.95	.95

Easter.

Uniform Type of 1970

Military Uniforms: ½c, Private, Col. Zacharia Tiffin's Regiment, 1701. 10c, Private, 63rd Regiment, 1759. 20c, Officer, 35th Sussex Regiment, 1828. 35c, Private, 2nd West India Regiment, 1853. 75c, Sergeant, Princess of Wales Regiment, Hertfordshire, 1858.

Perf. 14x13½

1973, July 1 **Wmk. 314**

307 A53	½c dp ultra & multi	.15	.15
308 A53	10c rose lilac & multi	.20	.20
309 A53	20c gray & multi	.40	.40
310 A53	35c multicolored	.70	.70
311 A53	75c multicolored	1.75	1.75
a.	Souvenir sheet of 5	4.00	4.00
	Nos. 307-311 (5)	3.20	3.20

No. 311a contains one each of Nos. 307-311 and label with coat of arms and date.

Butterfly Costumes — A63

Designs: 20c, Carnival revelers. 35c, Costumed group. 75c, Carnival Queen.

Perf. 13½x14

1973, July 30 **Unwmk.**

312 A63	5c multicolored	.15	.15
313 A63	20c multicolored	.20	.20
314 A63	35c multicolored	.35	.35
315 A63	75c multicolored	.90	.90
a.	Souvenir sheet of 4, #312-315	2.00	2.00
	Nos. 312-315 (4)	1.60	1.60

Carnival, July 29-Aug. 7.

Virgin of the Porridge, by David — A64

Christmas: 5c, Adoration of the Kings, by Stomer. 20c, Virgin of the Grand Duke, by Raphael. 35c, Nativity with God the Father and Holy Ghost, by Tiepolo. $1, Madonna and Child, by Murillo.

Perf. 14½

1973, Oct. 15 **Photo.** **Unwmk.**

316 A64	3c brt blue & multi	.15	.15
317 A64	5c emerald & multi	.15	.15
318 A64	20c gold & multi	.25	.25
319 A64	35c violet & multi	.45	.45
320 A64	$1 red & multi	1.25	1.25
a.	Souvenir sheet of 5, #316-320	3.00	3.00
	Nos. 316-320 (5)	2.25	2.25

Princess Anne and Mark Phillips A65

Design: $2, different border.

1973, Nov. 14 **Litho.** *Perf. 13½*

321 A65	35c dull ultra & multi	.20	.20
322 A65	$2 yel grn & multi	1.00	1.00
a.	Souvenir sheet of 2, #321-322	1.25	1.25

Wedding of Princess Anne and Capt. Mark Phillips.

Nos. 321-322 were issued in sheets of 5 plus label.

Nos. 321-322 and 322a Overprinted Vertically: "HONEYMOON / VISIT / DECEMBER 16th / 1973"

1973, Dec. 15 **Litho.** *Perf. 13½*

323 A65	35c multicolored	.20	.20
324 A65	$2 multicolored	1.00	1.00
a.	Souvenir sheet of 2, #323-324	1.60	1.60

Visit of Princess Anne and Mark Phillips to Antigua, Dec. 16. Same overprint in sheet margins of Nos. 323-324 and 324a.

Arms of Antigua and U.W.I. A66

Designs: 20c, Dancers. 35c, Antigua campus. 75c, Chancellor Sir Hugh Wooding.

1974, Feb. 18 **Wmk. 314**

325 A66	5c multicolored	.15	.15
326 A66	20c multicolored	.15	.15
327 A66	35c multicolored	.30	.30
328 A66	75c multicolored	.55	.55
	Nos. 325-328 (4)	1.15	1.15

University of the West Indies, 24th anniv.

Uniform Type of 1970

Military Uniforms: ½c, Officer, 59th Foot, 1797. 10c, Gunner, Royal Artillery, 1800. 20c, Private, 1st West India Regiment, 1830. 35c, Officer, Gordon Highlanders, 1843. 75c, Private, Royal Welsh Fusiliers, 1846.

1974, May 1 *Perf. 14x13½*

329 A53	½c dull grn & multi	.15	.15
330 A53	10c ocher & multi	.15	.15
331 A53	20c multicolored	.35	.35
332 A53	35c gray bl & multi	.55	.55
333 A53	75c dk gray & multi	1.25	1.25
a.	Souvenir sheet of 5, #329-333	3.00	3.00
	Nos. 329-333 (5)	2.45	2.45

English Mailman and Coach, Helicopter — A67

UPU, Cent.: 1c, English bellman, 1846; Orinoco mailboat, 1851; telecommunications satellite. 2c, English mailtrain guard, 1852; Swiss post passenger bus, 1906; Italian hydrofoil. 5c, Swiss messenger, 16th century; Wells Fargo coach, 1800; Concorde. 20c, German position, 1820; Japanese mailmen, 19th century; carrier pigeon. 35c, Contemporary Antiguan mailman; radar station; aquaplane. $1, Medieval French courier; American train, 1884; British Airways jet.

1974, July 15 **Litho.** *Perf. 14½*

334 A67	½c multicolored	.15	.15
335 A67	1c multicolored	.15	.15
336 A67	2c multicolored	.15	.15
337 A67	5c multicolored	.15	.15
338 A67	20c multicolored	.35	.30
339 A67	35c multicolored	.75	.55
340 A67	$1 multicolored	1.75	1.40
a.	Souvenir sheet of 7, #334-340 + label, perf. 13	3.50	3.50
	Nos. 334-340 (7)	3.45	2.85

For surcharges see Nos. 365-367.

Traditional Steel Band A68

Carnival 1974 (Steel Bands): 5c, Traditional players, vert. 35c, Modern steel band. 75c, Modern players, vert.

1974, Aug. 1, **Wmk. 314** *Perf. 14*

341 A68	5c rose red, dk red & blk	.15	.15
342 A68	20c ocher, brn & blk	.15	.15
343 A68	35c yel grn, grn & blk	.30	.30
344 A68	75c dl bl, dk bl & blk	.55	.55
a.	Souvenir sheet of 4, #341-344	1.50	1.50
	Nos. 341-344 (4)	1.15	1.15

Soccer — A69

Designs: Games' emblem and soccer.

1974, Sept. 23 **Unwmk.** *Perf. 14½*

345 A69	5c multicolored	.15	.15
346 A69	35c multicolored	.30	.30
347 A69	75c multicolored	.65	.65
348 A69	$1 multicolored	.90	.90
a.	Souvenir sheet of 4	2.25	2.25
	Nos. 345-348 (4)	2.00	2.00

World Cup Soccer Championship, Munich, June 13-July 7. Nos. 345-348 issued in sheets of 5 plus label showing Soccer Cup. No. 348a contains one each of Nos. 345-348, perf. 13½, and 2 labels.

For overprints and surcharges see Nos. 361-364.

Winston Churchill (1874-1965) at Harrow A70

Designs: 35c, St. Paul's during bombing and Churchill portrait. 75c, Churchill's coat of arms and catafalque. $1, Churchill during Boer war, warrant for arrest and map of his escape route.

1974, Oct. 20 **Unwmk.** *Perf. 14½*

349 A70	5c multicolored	.15	.15
350 A70	35c multicolored	.30	.30
351 A70	75c multicolored	.70	.70
352 A70	$1 multicolored	.85	.85
a.	Souvenir sheet of 4, #349-352	2.00	2.00
	Nos. 349-352 (4)	2.00	2.00

Virgin and Child, by Giovanni Bellini — A71

ANTIGUA

Christmas: Paintings of the Virgin and Child.

1974, Nov. 18   Litho.   Perf. 14½

353	A71	½c shown	.15	.15
354	A71	1c Raphael	.15	.15
355	A71	2c Van der Weyden	.15	.15
356	A71	3c Giorgione	.15	.15
357	A71	5c Andrea Mantegna	.15	.15
358	A71	20c Alvise Vivarini	.25	.25
359	A71	35c Bartolommeo Montagna	.40	.40
360	A71	75c Lorenzo Costa	.85	.85
a.		Souvenir sheet of 4, #357-360, perf. 13½	1.60	1.60
		Nos. 353-360 (8)	2.25	2.25

Nos. 346-348 Overprinted and No. 344 Surcharged and Overprinted: "EARTHQUAKE / RELIEF"

1974, Oct. 16   Litho.   Perf. 14½, 14

361	A69	35c multicolored	.20	.15
362	A69	75c multicolored	.60	.50
363	A69	$1 multicolored	.80	.65
364	A68	$5 on 75c multi	4.00	3.50
		Nos. 361-364 (4)	5.60	4.80

Earthquake of Oct. 8, 1974.

Nos. 338-340 and 254a Surcharged with New Value and Two Bars

1974-75   Wmk. 314   Perf. 14½

365	A67	50c on 20c	.50	.50
366	A67	$2.50 on 35c	2.25	2.25
367	A67	$5 on $1	4.50	4.50

Perf. 14

368	A51	$10 on 75c	8.75	8.75
		Nos. 365-368 (4)	16.00	16.00

Carib War Canoe, English Harbour — A72

Designs (Nelson's Dockyard): 15c, Raising ship, 1770. 35c, Lord Nelson and "Boreas." 50c, Yachts arriving for Sailing Week, 1974. $1, "Anchorage" in Old Dockyard, 1970.

1975, Mar. 17   Unwmk.   Perf. 14½

369	A72	5c multicolored	.15	.15
370	A72	15c multicolored	.35	.35
371	A72	35c multicolored	.60	.60
372	A72	50c multicolored	.90	.90
373	A72	$1 multicolored	1.75	1.75
		Nos. 369-373 (5)	3.75	3.75

Souvenir Sheet
Perf. 13½

| 373A | A72 | Sheet of 5, #369-373 | 4.50 | 4.50 |

Stamps in No. 373A are 43x28mm.

Lady of the Valley Church A73

Churches of Antigua: 20c, Gilbert Memorial. 35c, Grace Hill Moravian. 50c, St. Phillip's. $1, Ebenezer Methodist.

1975, May 19   Litho.   Perf. 14½

374	A73	5c multicolored	.15	.15
375	A73	20c multicolored	.15	.15
376	A73	35c multicolored	.25	.25
377	A73	50c multicolored	.40	.40
378	A73	$1 multicolored	.70	.70
a.		Souvenir sheet of 3, #376-378, perf. 13½	2.00	2.00
		Nos. 374-378 (5)	1.65	1.65

Antigua, Senex's Atlas, 1721, and Hevelius Sextant, 1640 — A74

Maps of Antigua: 20c, Jeffery's Atlas, 1775, and 18th century engraving of ship. 35c, Barbuda and Antigua, 1775 and 1975. $1, St. John's and English Harbour, 1973.

1975, July 21   Wmk. 314

379	A74	5c multicolored	.15	.15
380	A74	20c multicolored	.40	.40
381	A74	35c multicolored	.65	.65
382	A74	$1 multicolored	1.90	1.90
a.		Souvenir sheet of 4, #379-382	3.25	3.25
		Nos. 379-382 (4)	3.10	3.10

Bugler and Sunset — A75

Nordjamb 75 Emblem and: 20c, Black and white Scouts, tents and flags. 35c, Lord Baden-Powell and tents. $2, Dahomey dancers.

Unwmk.
1975, Aug. 26   Litho.   Perf. 14

383	A75	15c multicolored	.25	.25
384	A75	20c multicolored	.35	.35
385	A75	35c multicolored	.50	.50
386	A75	$2 multicolored	2.25	2.25
a.		Souvenir sheet of 4, #383-386	4.25	4.25
		Nos. 383-386 (4)	3.35	3.35

Nordjamb 75, 14th Boy Scout Jamboree, Lillehammer, Norway, July 29-Aug. 7.

Eurema Elathea — A76

Butterflies: 1c, Danaus plexippus. 2c, Phoebis philea. 5c, Marpesia petreus thetys. 20c, Eurema proterpia. 35c, Papilio polydamas. $2, Vanessa cardui.

1975, Oct. 30   Litho.   Perf. 14

387	A76	½c multicolored	.15	.15
388	A76	1c multicolored	.15	.15
389	A76	2c multicolored	.15	.15
390	A76	5c multicolored	.15	.15
391	A76	20c multicolored	.50	.40
392	A76	35c multicolored	.90	.75
393	A76	$2 multicolored	4.50	3.50
a.		Miniature sheet of 4, #390-393	6.75	6.75
		Nos. 387-393 (7)	6.50	5.25

Virgin and Child, by Correggio — A77

Christmas: Virgin and Child paintings.

1975, Nov. 17   Unwmk.

394	A77	½c shown	.15	.15
395	A77	1c El Greco	.15	.15
396	A77	2c Durer	.15	.15
397	A77	3c Antonello	.15	.15
398	A77	5c Bellini	.15	.15
399	A77	10c Durer	.15	.15
400	A77	35c Bellini	.45	.45
401	A77	$2 Durer	1.90	1.90
a.		Souvenir sheet of 4, #398-401	3.25	3.25
		Nos. 394-401 (8)	3.25	3.25

West Indies Team — A78

Designs: 5c, Batsman I.V.A. Richards and cup, vert. 35c, Bowler A.M.E. Roberts and cup, vert.

1975, Dec. 15   Litho.   Perf. 14

402	A78	5c multicolored	.20	.15
403	A78	35c multicolored	.90	.75
404	A78	$2 multicolored	3.50	3.50
		Nos. 402-404 (3)	4.60	4.40

World Cricket Cup, victory of West Indies team.

Antillean Crested Hummingbird A79

Irrigation System, Diamond Estate — A80

Designs: 1c, Imperial parrot. 2c, Zenaida dove. 3c, Loggerhead kingbird. 4c, Red-necked pigeon. 5c, Rufous-throated solitaire. 6c, Orchid tree. 10c, Bougainvillea. 15c, Geiger tree. 20c, Flamboyant. 25c, Hibiscus. 35c, Flame of the Woods. 50c, Cannon at Fort James. 75c, Premier's Office. $1, Potworks Dam. $5, Government House. $10, Coolidge International Airport.

1976, Jan. 19   Litho.   Perf. 15

405	A79	½c multicolored	.15	.15
406	A79	1c multicolored	.15	.15
407	A79	2c multicolored	.15	.15
408	A79	3c multicolored	.15	.15
409	A79	4c multicolored	.15	.15
410	A79	5c multicolored	.15	.15
411	A79	6c multicolored	.15	.15
412	A79	10c multicolored	.15	.15
413	A79	15c multicolored	.15	.15
414	A79	20c multicolored	.20	.20
415	A79	25c multicolored	.25	.25
416	A79	35c multicolored	.25	.25
417	A79	50c multicolored	.35	.35
418	A79	75c multicolored	.50	.50
419	A79	$1 multicolored	.70	.70

Perf. 13½x14

420	A80	$2.50 rose & multi	1.50	1.50
421	A80	$5 lilac & multi	3.25	3.25
422	A80	$10 multicolored	6.75	6.75
		Nos. 405-422 (18)	15.00	15.00

In 1978 Nos. 405-422 were reissued with "1978" centered below design.
For overprints, see Nos. 607-617.

Privates, Clark's Illinois Regiment — A81

Designs: 1c, Riflemen, Pennsylvania Militia. 2c, Decorated American powder horn. 5c, Water bottle of Maryland troops. 35c, "Liberty Tree" and "Rattlesnake" flags. $1, American privateer Montgomery. $2.50, Congress Flag. $5, Continental Navy sloop Ranger.

1976, Mar. 17   Litho.   Perf. 14½

423	A81	½c multicolored	.15	.15
424	A81	1c multicolored	.15	.15
425	A81	2c multicolored	.15	.15
426	A81	5c multicolored	.15	.15
427	A81	35c multicolored	.35	.35
428	A81	$1 multicolored	1.00	1.00
429	A81	$5 multicolored	4.25	4.25
		Nos. 423-429 (7)	6.20	6.20

Souvenir Sheet
Perf. 13

| 430 | A81 | $2.50 multicolored | 3.50 | 3.50 |

American Bicentennial.

High Jump, Olympic Rings — A82

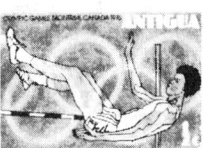

Olympic Rings and: 1c, Boxing. 2c, Pole vault. 15c, Swimming. 30c, Running. $1, Bicycling. $2, Shot put.

1976, July 12   Litho.   Perf. 14½

431	A82	½c yellow & multi	.15	.15
432	A82	1c purple & multi	.15	.15
433	A82	2c emerald & multi	.15	.15
434	A82	15c brt blue & multi	.15	.15
435	A82	30c olive & multi	.30	.30
436	A82	$1 orange & multi	.75	.75
437	A82	$2 red & multi	1.50	1.50
		Souvenir sheet of 4	3.00	3.00
		Nos. 431-437 (7)	3.15	3.15

21st Olympic Games, Montreal, Canada, July 17-Aug. 1. No. 437a contains one each of Nos. 434-437, perf. 13½.

Water Skiing A83

Water Sports: 1c, Sailfish sailing. 2c, Snorkeling. 20c, Deep-sea fishing. 50c, Scuba diving. $2, Swimming.

1976, Aug. 26   Perf. 14

438	A83	½c yel grn & multi	.15	.15
439	A83	1c sepia & multi	.15	.15
440	A83	2c gray & multi	.15	.15
441	A83	20c multicolored	.15	.15
442	A83	50c brt vio & multi	.40	.40
443	A83	$2 lt gray & multi	1.25	1.25
a.		Souvenir sheet of 3, #441-443	2.50	2.50
		Nos. 438-443 (6)	2.25	2.25

French Angelfish — A84

1976, Oct. 4   Litho.   Perf. 13½x14

444	A84	15c shown	.25	.25
445	A84	30c Yellowfish grouper	.40	.40
446	A84	50c Yellowtail snappers	.75	.75
447	A84	90c Shy hamlet	1.25	1.25
		Nos. 444-447 (4)	2.65	2.65

The Annunciation A85

Christmas: 10c, Flight into Egypt. 15c, Three Kings. 50c, Shepherds and star. $1, Kings presenting gifts to Christ Child.

1976, Nov. 15   Litho.   Perf. 14

448	A85	8c multicolored	.15	.15
449	A85	10c multicolored	.15	.15
450	A85	15c multicolored	.15	.15
451	A85	50c multicolored	.35	.35
452	A85	$1 multi	.65	.65
		Nos. 448-452 (5)	1.45	1.45

Mercury and UPU Emblem A86

Designs: 1c, Alfred Nobel, symbols of prize categories. 10c, Viking spacecraft. 50c, Vivi Richards (batsman) and Andy Roberts (bowler). $1, Alexander G. Bell, telephones, 1876 and 1976. $2, Schooner Freelance.

1976, Dec. 28   Litho.   Perf. 14

453	A86	½c multicolored	.15	.15
454	A86	1c multicolored	.15	.15
455	A86	10c multicolored	.15	.15
456	A86	50c multicolored	.65	.65
457	A86	$1 multicolored	1.00	1.00
458	A86	$2 multicolored	1.75	1.75
a.		Souvenir sheet of 4, #455-458	4.25	4.25
		Nos. 453-458 (6)	3.85	3.85

Special 1976 Events: UN Postal Admin., 25th anniv. (½c); Nobel Prize, 75th anniv. (1c); Viking Space Mission to Mars (10c); World Cricket Cup

ANTIGUA

victory (50c); Telephone cent. ($1); Operation Sail, American Bicent. ($2).

Royal Family — A87

Designs: 30c, Elizabeth II and Prince Philip touring Antigua. 50c, Queen enthroned. 90c, Queen wearing crown. $2.50, Queen and Prince Charles. $5, Queen and Prince Philip.

1977, Feb. 7			Perf. 13½x14	
459 A87	10c multicolored		.15	.15
460 A87	30c multicolored		.15	.15
461 A87	50c multicolored		.25	.25
462 A87	90c multicolored		.50	.50
463 A87	$2.50 multicolored		1.25	1.25
Nos. 459-463 (5)			2.30	2.30

Souvenir Sheet

| 464 | $5 multicolored | | 3.00 | 3.00 |

25th anniv. of the reign of Queen Elizabeth II.
Nos. 459-463 were printed in sheets of 40. Sheets of 5 plus label, perf. 12, probably were not sold by the Antigua Post Office.
A booklet of self-adhesive stamps contains one pane of six rouletted and die cut 50c stamps in design of 90c, and one pane of one die cut $5. Stamps have changed colors. Panes have marginal inscriptions.
For overprints see Nos. 477-482.

Scouts Camping A88

Boy Scout Emblem and: 1c, Scouts on hike. 2c, Rock climbing. 10c, Cutting logs. 30c, Map and compass reading. 50c, First aid. $2, Scouts on raft.

1977, May 23	Litho.		Perf. 14	
465 A88	½c multicolored		.15	.15
466 A88	1c multicolored		.15	.15
467 A88	2c multicolored		.15	.15
468 A88	10c multicolored		.15	.15
469 A88	30c multicolored		.30	.30
470 A88	50c multicolored		.50	.50
471 A88	$2 multicolored		1.75	1.75
a.	Souvenir sheet of 3, #469-471		3.00	3.00
Nos. 465-471 (7)			3.15	3.15

Caribbean Boy Scout Jamboree, Jamaica.

Carnival Queen Holding Horseshoe — A89

Designs: 30c, Carnival Queen in feather costume. 50c, Butterfly costume. 90c, Carnival Queen with ornaments. $1, Carnival King and Queen.

1977, July 18	Litho.		Perf. 14	
472 A89	10c multicolored		.15	.15
473 A89	30c multicolored		.20	.20
474 A89	50c multicolored		.30	.30
475 A89	90c multicolored		.55	.55
476 A89	$1 multicolored		.60	.60
a.	Souvenir sheet of 4, #473-476		1.90	1.90
Nos. 472-476 (5)			1.80	1.80

21st Summer Carnival.

Nos. 459-464 Overprinted: "ROYAL VISIT / 28th OCTOBER 1977"

1977, Oct. 17			Litho.	
477 A87	10c multicolored		.15	.15
478 A87	30c multicolored		.15	.15
479 A87	50c multicolored		.20	.20

Perf. 13½x14, 12

480 A87	90c multicolored		.40	.40
481 A87	$2.50 multicolored		1.10	1.10
Nos. 477-481 (5)			2.00	2.00

Souvenir Sheet

| 482 A87 | $5 multicolored | | 2.75 | 2.75 |

Visit of Queen Elizabeth II, Oct. 28.

Virgin and Child, by Cosimo Tura — A90

Virgin and Child by: 1c, $2, Carlo Crivelli (different). 2c, 25c, Lorenzo Lotto (different). 8c, Jacopo da Pontormo. 10c, Tura.

1977, Nov. 15	Litho.		Perf. 14	
483 A90	½c multicolored		.15	.15
484 A90	1c multicolored		.15	.15
485 A90	2c multicolored		.15	.15
486 A90	8c multicolored		.15	.15
487 A90	10c multicolored		.15	.15
488 A90	25c multicolored		.15	.15
489 A90	$2 multicolored		1.50	1.50
a.	Souvenir sheet of 4, #486-489		1.75	1.75
Nos. 483-489 (7)			2.40	2.40

Christmas.

Pineapple A91

10th anniv. of Statehood: 15c, Flag of Antigua. 50c, Police band. 90c, Prime Minister V. C. Bird. $2, Coat of Arms.

1977, Dec. 28	Litho.		Perf. 13x13½	
490 A91	10c multicolored		.15	.15
491 A91	15c multicolored		.15	.15
492 A91	50c multicolored		.40	.40
493 A91	90c multicolored		.75	.75
494 A91	$2 multicolored		1.60	1.60
a.	Souv. sheet of 4, #491-494, perf. 14		2.75	2.75
Nos. 490-494 (5)			3.05	3.05

Wright Glider III, 1902 — A92

Designs: 1c, Flyer I in air, 1903. 2c, Weight and derrick launch system and Wright engine, 1903. 10c, Orville Wright, vert. 50c, Flyer III, 1905. 90c, Wilbur Wright, vert. $2, Wright Model B, 1910. $2.50, Flyer I, 1903, on ground.

1978, Mar. 28			Perf. 14	
495 A92	½c multicolored		.15	.15
496 A92	1c multicolored		.15	.15
497 A92	2c multicolored		.15	.15
498 A92	10c multicolored		.15	.15
499 A92	50c multicolored		.35	.35
500 A92	90c multicolored		.60	.60
501 A92	$2 multicolored		1.40	1.40
Nos. 495-501 (7)			2.95	2.95

Souvenir Sheet

| 502 A92 | $2.50 multicolored | | 2.00 | 2.00 |

1st powered flight by Wright brothers, 75th anniv.

Sunfish Regatta A93

Sailing Week 1978: 50c, Fishing and work boat race. 90c, Curtain Bluff race. $2, Powerboat rally. $2.50, Guadeloupe-Antigua race.

1978, Apr. 29	Litho.		Perf. 14½	
503 A93	10c multicolored		.15	.15
504 A93	50c multicolored		.40	.40
505 A93	90c multicolored		.75	.75
506 A93	$2 multicolored		1.60	1.60
Nos. 503-506 (4)			2.90	2.90

Souvenir Sheet

| 507 A93 | $2.50 multicolored | | 2.40 | 2.40 |

Elizabeth II and Prince Philip — A94

Designs: 30c, Coronation. 50c, State coach. 90c, Elizabth II and Archbishop. $2.50, Elizabeth II. $5, Elizabeth II, Prince Philip, Prince Charles and Princess Anne as children.

1978, June 2	Litho.		Perf. 14, 12	
508 A94	10c multicolored		.15	.15
509 A94	30c multicolored		.15	.15
510 A94	50c multicolored		.20	.20
511 A94	90c multicolored		.40	.40
512 A94	$2.50 multicolored		1.10	1.10
Nos. 508-512 (5)			2.00	2.00

Souvenir Sheet

| 513 A94 | $5 multicolored | | 2.25 | 2.25 |

25th anniv. of coronation of Queen Elizabeth II.
Nos. 508-512 were printed in sheets of 50 (2 panes of 25), perf. 14, and in sheets of 3 plus label, perf. 12, with frames in changed colors.

Glass Coach A95

Royal Coaches: 50c, Irish state coach. $5, Coronation coach.

1978, June 2	Litho.		Imperf.	
514	Souvenir booklet		5.50	
a.	A95 Bklt. pane of 6 (3 each 25c and 50c)		1.65	
b.	A95 Bklt. pane of 1 ($5)		3.50	

25th anniversary of coronation of Queen Elizabeth II. No. 514 contains 2 booklet panes printed on peelable paper backing showing royal processions.

Soccer — A96

Purple Wreath — A97

Designs: Various soccer scenes. Stamps in souvenir sheet horizontal.

1978, Aug. 18	Litho.		Perf. 15	
515 A96	10c multicolored		.15	.15
516 A96	15c multicolored		.15	.15
517 A96	$3 multicolored		2.75	2.75
Nos. 515-517 (3)			3.05	3.05

Souvenir Sheet

518	Sheet of 4		3.25	3.25
a.	A96 25c multicolored		.25	.25
b.	A96 30c multicolored		.30	.30
c.	A96 50c multicolored		.50	.50
d.	A96 $2 multicolored		2.00	2.00

11th World Cup Soccer Championship, Argentina, June 1-25.

1978, Oct.	Litho.		Perf. 14	
519 A97	25c shown		.20	.20
520 A97	50c Sunflowers		.45	.45
521 A97	90c Frangipani		.80	.80
522 A97	$2 Passionflower		1.65	1.65
Nos. 519-522 (4)			3.10	3.10

Souvenir Sheet

| 523 A97 | $2.50 Red hibiscus | | 2.50 | 2.50 |

St. Ildefonso Receiving Chasuble, by Rubens A98

Christmas: 25c, Flight of St. Barbara, by Rubens. $2, Holy Family, by Sebastiano del Piombo. $4, Annunciation, by Rubens.

1978, Oct. 30			Perf. 14	
524 A98	8c multicolored		.15	.15
525 A98	25c multicolored		.15	.15
526 A98	$2 multicolored		1.50	1.50
Nos. 524-526 (3)			1.80	1.80

Souvenir Sheet

| 527 A98 | $4 multicolored | | 4.00 | 4.00 |

Antigua No. 2 — A99

Crucifixion, by Durer — A100

Designs: 50c, Great Britain Penny Black, 1840. $1, Woman posting letter in pillar box, and coach. $2, Mail train, ship, plane and Concorde. $2.50, Rowland Hill.

1979, Feb. 12	Litho.		Perf. 14	
528 A99	25c multicolored		.15	.15
529 A99	50c multicolored		.20	.20
530 A99	$1 multicolored		.40	.40
531 A99	$2 multicolored		.85	.85
Nos. 528-531 (4)			1.60	1.60

Souvenir Sheet

| 532 A99 | $2.50 multicolored | | 1.40 | 1.40 |

Sir Rowland Hill (1795-1879), originator of penny postage.
Nos. 528-531 were printed in sheets of 50 (2 panes of 25), perf. 14, and in sheets of 5 plus label, perf. 12, with frames in changed colors.
For overprints see Nos. 571A-571D.

| 1979, Mar. 15 | | | | |

Designs (after Dürer): 10c, Deposition. $2.50, Crucifixion. $4, Man of Sorrows.

533 A100	10c multicolored		.15	.15
534 A100	50c multicolored		.30	.30
535 A100	$4 multicolored		2.25	2.25
Nos. 533-535 (3)			2.70	2.70

Souvenir Sheet

| 536 A100 | $2.50 multicolored | | 1.65 | 1.65 |

Easter.

Child Playing with Sailboat — A101

IYC emblem, child's hand holding toy: 50c, Rocket. 90c, Automobile. $2, Train. $5, Plane.

ANTIGUA

1979, Apr. 9		Litho.	Perf. 14	
537	A101	25c multicolored	.15	.15
538	A101	50c multicolored	.30	.30
539	A101	90c multicolored	.60	.60
540	A101	$2 multicolored	1.40	1.40
		Nos. 537-540 (4)	2.45	2.45

Souvenir Sheet

541	A101	$5 multicolored	4.00	4.00

International Year of the Child.

Yellowjacks — A102

Sport Fish: 50c, Bluefin tunas. 90c, Sailfish. $2.50, Barracuda. $3, Wahoos.

1979, May		Litho.	Perf. 14½	
542	A102	30c multicolored	.25	.25
543	A102	50c multicolored	.40	.40
544	A102	90c multicolored	.70	.70
545	A102	$3 multicolored	2.25	2.25
		Nos. 542-545 (4)	3.60	3.60

Souvenir Sheet

546	A102	$2.50 multicolored	2.00	2.00

Capt. Cook and his Birthplace at Marton — A103

Holy Family — A104

Capt. James Cook (1728-1779) and: 50c, HMS Endeavour. 90c, Marine timekeeper. $2.50, HMS Resolution. $3, Landing at Botany Bay.

1979, July 2		Litho.	Perf. 14	
547	A103	25c multicolored	.20	.20
548	A103	50c multicolored	.35	.35
549	A103	90c multicolored	.60	.60
550	A103	$3 multicolored	2.00	2.00
		Nos. 547-550 (4)	3.15	3.15

Souvenir Sheet

551	A103	$2.50 multicolored	2.25	2.25

1979, Oct. 1		Litho.	Perf. 14	

Stained-glass Windows: 25c, Flight into Egypt. 50c, Shepherd and star. $3, Angel with trumpet. $4, Three Kings offering gifts.

552	A104	8c multicolored	.15	.15
553	A104	25c multicolored	.15	.15
554	A104	50c multicolored	.25	.25
555	A104	$4 multicolored	2.00	2.00
		Nos. 552-555 (4)	2.55	2.55

Souvenir Sheet
Perf. 12x12½

556	A104	$3 multicolored	2.00	2.00

Christmas.

Javelin, Olympic Rings — A105

1980, Feb. 7		Litho.	Perf. 14	
557	A105	10c shown	.15	.15
558	A105	25c Running	.20	.20
559	A105	$1 Pole vault	.65	.65
560	A105	$2 Hurdles	1.40	1.40
		Nos. 557-560 (4)	2.40	2.40

Souvenir Sheet

561	A105	$3 Boxing, horiz.	1.75	1.75

22nd Summer Olympic Games, Moscow, July 19-Aug. 3.

Disney Characters and IYC Emblem — A106

Designs: Transportation scenes. ½c, 2c, 3c, 4c, 5c, $1, $2.50, horiz.

1980, Mar. 24		Litho.	Perf. 11	
562	A106	½c Mickey, plane	.15	.15
563	A106	1c Donald, car	.15	.15
564	A106	2c Goofy driving taxi	.15	.15
565	A106	3c Mickey, Minnie in sidecar	.15	.15
566	A106	4c Huey, Dewey and Louie	.15	.15
567	A106	5c Grandma Duck	.15	.15
568	A106	10c Mickey in jeep	.15	.15
569	A106	$1 Chip and Dale sailing	1.00	1.00
570	A106	$4 Donald on train	4.00	4.00
		Nos. 562-570 (9)	6.05	6.05

Souvenir Sheet

571	A106	$2.50 Goofy in glider	5.50	5.50

Nos. 528-531 in Changed Colors
Overprinted "LONDON 1980"

1980, May 6		Litho.	Perf. 12	
571A	A99	25c multicolored	.20	.20
571B	A99	50c multicolored	.35	.35
571C	A99	$1 multicolored	.60	.60
571D	A99	$4 multicolored	1.40	1.40
		Nos. 571A-571D (4)	2.55	2.55

London '80 Intl. Stamp Exhib., May 6-14.

Birth of Venus, by Botticelli — A106a

Designs: 10c, David, by Donatello, vert. 50c, Reclining Couple, sarcophagus, Cerveteri. 90c, The Garden of Earthly Delights, by Hieronymus Bosch. $1, Portinari Altarpiece, by Hugo van der Goes. $4, Eleanora of Toledo and her Son Giovanni de Medici, by Bronzino, vert. $5, The Holy Family, by Rembrandt.

Perf. 13½x14, 14x13½

1980, June 23			Litho.	
572	A106a	10c multicolored	.15	.15
573	A106a	30c multicolored	.15	.15
574	A106a	50c multicolored	.25	.25
575	A106a	90c multicolored	.45	.45
576	A106a	$1 multicolored	.50	.50
577	A106a	$4 multicolored	2.75	2.75
		Nos. 572-577 (6)	4.25	4.25

Souvenir Sheet
Perf. 14

578	A106a	$5 multicolored	3.75	3.75

Anniversary Emblem, Intl. Headquarters, Evanston, IL — A107

1980, July 21		Litho.	Perf. 14	
579	A107	3c shown	.20	.20
580	A107	50c Antigua club banner	.35	.35
581	A107	90c Map of Antigua	.60	.60
582	A107	$3 Paul. P. Harris, emblem	2.00	2.00
		Nos. 579-582 (4)	3.15	3.15

Souvenir Sheet

583	A107	$5 Emblems, Antigua flags	3.00	3.00

Rotary International, 75th anniv.

Queen Mother Elizabeth, 80th Birthday — A108

1980, Sept. 15				
584	A108	10c multicolored	.15	.15
585	A108	$2.50 multicolored	1.65	1.65

Souvenir Sheet
Perf. 12

586	A108	$3 multicolored	1.75	1.75

Ringed Kingfisher — A109

1980, Nov. 3		Litho.	Perf. 14	
587	A109	10c shown	.15	.15
588	A109	30c Plain pigeon	.45	.30
589	A109	$1 Green-throated carib	1.10	.80
590	A109	$2 Black-necked stilt	2.50	1.75
		Nos. 587-590 (4)	4.20	3.00

Souvenir Sheet

591	A109	$2.50 Roseate tern	3.50	3.50

Sleeping Beauty and the Prince — A110

Christmas: Various scenes from Walt Disney's Sleeping Beauty. $4 vert.

1980, Dec. 23		Perf. 11, 13½x14 ($4)		
592	A110	½c multicolored	.15	.15
593	A110	1c multicolored	.15	.15
594	A110	2c multicolored	.15	.15
595	A110	4c multicolored	.15	.15
596	A110	8c multicolored	.15	.15
597	A110	10c multicolored	.15	.15
598	A110	25c multicolored	.25	.25
599	A110	$2 multicolored	1.75	1.75
600	A110	$2.50 multicolored	2.25	2.25
		Nos. 592-600 (9)	5.15	5.15

Souvenir Sheet

601	A110	$4 multicolored	3.25	3.25

Sugar-cane Railway Diesel Locomotive No. 15 — A111

1981, Jan. 12			Perf. 14	
602	A111	25c shown	.15	.15
603	A111	50c Narrow-gauge steam locomotive	.40	.40
604	A111	90c Diesels #1, #10	.75	.75
605	A111	$3 Hauling sugar-cane	2.25	2.25
		Nos. 602-605 (4)	3.55	3.55

Souvenir Sheet

606	A111	$2.50 Sugar factory, train yard	1.90	1.90

Nos. 411-412, 414-422 Overprinted:
"INDEPENDENCE 1981"

1981, Mar. 31				Litho.
607	A79	6c multicolored	.15	.15
608	A79	15c multicolored	.15	.15
609	A79	20c multicolored	.15	.15
610	A79	25c multicolored	.20	.20
611	A79	35c multicolored	.20	.20
612	A79	50c multicolored	.35	.35
613	A79	75c multicolored	.55	.55
614	A79	$1 multicolored	.65	.65
615	A80	$2.50 multicolored	1.50	1.50
616	A80	$5 multicolored	3.50	3.50
617	A80	$10 multicolored	6.75	6.75
		Nos. 607-617 (11)	14.15	14.15

Pipes of Pan, by Picasso — A112

Paintings by Pablo Picasso (1881-1973): 50c, Seated Harlequin. 90c, Paulo as Harlequin. $4, Mother and Child. $5, Three Musicians.

1981, May 5		Litho.	Perf. 14	
618	A112	10c multicolored	.15	.15
619	A112	50c multicolored	.35	.35
620	A112	90c multicolored	.60	.60
621	A112	$4 multicolored	2.50	2.50
		Nos. 618-621 (4)	3.60	3.60

Souvenir Sheet
Perf. 14x14½

622	A112	$5 multicolored	3.25	3.25

Royal Wedding Issue
Common Design Type

1981, June 16		Litho.	Perf. 14	
623	CD331	25c Couple	.15	.15
624	CD331	50c Glamis Castle	.25	.25
625	CD331	$4 Charles	2.00	2.00
		Nos. 623-625 (3)	2.40	2.40

Souvenir Sheet

626	CD331	$5 Glass coach	2.50	2.50
627	CD331	Booklet	9.00	
a.		Pane of 6 (2x25c, 2x$1, 2x$2), Charles	5.00	
b.		Pane of 1, $5, Couple	5.00	

No. 627 contains imperf., self-adhesive stamps.
Nos. 623-625 also printed in sheets of 5 plus label, perf. 12 in changed colors.
For surcharges see Nos. 792, 795, 802, 805.

Campfire Sing — A113

1981, Oct. 28		Litho.	Perf. 15	
628	A113	10c Irene Joshua	.15	.15
629	A113	50c shown	.40	.40
630	A113	90c Sailing	.70	.70
631	A113	$2.50 Milking cow	1.90	1.90
		Nos. 628-631 (4)	3.15	3.15

Souvenir Sheet

632	A113	$5 Flag raising	3.75	3.75

Girl Guides, 50th anniv.

Independence — A114    A115

1981, Nov. 1		Litho.	Perf. 15	
633	A114	10c Arms	.15	.15
634	A114	50c Flag	.35	.35
635	A114	90c Prime Minister Bird	.60	.60
636	A114	$2.50 St. John's Cathedral, horiz.	1.75	1.75
		Nos. 633-636 (4)	2.85	2.85

Souvenir Sheet

637	A114	$5 Map	3.25	3.25

No. 637 contains one 41x41mm stamp.

1981, Nov. 16

Christmas (Virgin and Child Paintings by): 8c, Holy Night, by Jacques Stella (1596-1657). 30c Julius Schnorr von Carolfeld (1794-1872). $1, Alonso Cano (1601-1667). $3, Lorenzo de Credi

ANTIGUA

(1459-1537). $5, Holy Family, by Pieter von Avoni (1600-1652).

638	A115	8c	multicolored	.15	.15
639	A115	30c	multicolored	.25	.25
640	A115	$1	multicolored	.75	.75
641	A115	$3	multicolored	2.25	2.25
		Nos. 638-641 (4)		3.40	3.40

Souvenir Sheet

| 642 | A115 | $5 | multicolored | | 3.25 | 3.25 |

Intl. Year of the Disabled — A116

1981, Dec. 1   Litho.   Perf. 15

643	A116	10c	Swimming	.15	.15
644	A116	50c	Discus	.35	.35
645	A116	90c	Archery	.60	.60
646	A116	$2	Baseball	1.40	1.40
		Nos. 643-646 (4)		2.50	2.50

Souvenir Sheet

| 647 | A116 | $4 | Basketball | | 3.00 | 3.00 |

1982 World Cup Soccer — A117

Designs: Various soccer players.

1982, Apr. 15   Litho.   Perf. 14

648	A117	10c	multicolored	.15	.15
649	A117	50c	multicolored	.35	.35
650	A117	90c	multicolored	.60	.60
651	A117	$4	multicolored	2.75	2.75
		Nos. 648-651 (4)		3.85	3.85

Souvenir Sheet

| 652 | A117 | $5 | multicolored | | 3.75 | 3.75 |

Also issued in sheetlets of 5 + label in changed colors, perf. 12.

A118    A119

1982, June 17   Litho.   Perf. 14½

653	A118	10c	A-300 Airbus	.15	.15
654	A118	50c	Hawker-Siddeley 748	.40	.40
655	A118	90c	De Havilland Twin Otter DCH6	.70	.70
656	A118	$2.50	Britten-Norman Islander	1.75	1.75
		Nos. 653-656 (4)		3.00	3.00

Souvenir Sheet

| 657 | A118 | $5 | Jet, horiz. | | 3.50 | 3.50 |

Coolidge Intl. Airport opening.

1982, June 28   Litho.   Perf. 14½

658	A119	10c	Cordia, vert.	.15	.15
659	A119	50c	Golden spotted mongoose	.40	.40
660	A119	90c	Corallita, vert.	.70	.70
661	A119	$3	Bulldog bats	2.25	2.25
		Nos. 658-661 (4)		3.50	3.50

Souvenir Sheet

| 662 | A119 | $5 | Caribbean monk seals | | 3.75 | 3.75 |

Charles Darwin's death centenary.

Shop with Scott Publishing Co. 24 hours a day 7 days a week at www.scottonline.com

---

Princess Diana Issue
Common Design Type

1982, July 1   Litho.   Perf. 14½x14

663	CD332	90c	Greenwich Palace	.60	.60
664	CD332	$1	Wedding	.65	.65
665	CD332	$4	Diana	2.50	2.50
		Nos. 663-665 (3)		3.75	3.75

Souvenir Sheet

| 666 | CD332 | $5 | Diana, diff. | | 3.75 | 3.75 |

For overprints and surcharges see Nos. 672-675, 797, 799, 803, 806.

Scouting Year — A120

Designs: Independence Day celebration.

1982, July 15   Perf. 14

667	A120	10c	Decorating buildings	.15	.15
668	A120	50c	Helping woman	.40	.40
669	A120	90c	Princess Margaret	.70	.70
670	A120	$2.20	Cub Scout giving directions	1.75	1.75
		Nos. 667-670 (4)		3.00	3.00

Souvenir Sheet

| 671 | A120 | $5 | Baden-Powell | | 3.75 | 3.75 |

Nos. 663-666 Overprinted: "ROYAL BABY / 21.6.82"

1982, Aug. 30   Litho.   Perf. 14½x14

672	CD332	90c	multicolored	.70	.70
673	CD332	$1	multicolored	.75	.75
674	CD332	$4	multicolored	3.00	3.00
		Nos. 672-674 (3)		4.45	4.45

Souvenir Sheet

| 675 | CD332 | $5 | multicolored | | 3.50 | 3.50 |

For surcharges see Nos. 798, 800, 804, 807.

Roosevelt Driving by "The Little White House" — A121

1982, Sept. 20   Perf. 15

676	A121	10c	shown	.15	.15
677	A121	25c	Washington as blacksmith	.20	.20
678	A121	45c	Churchill, Roosevelt, Stalin	.35	.35
679	A121	60c	Washington crossing Delaware, vert.	.45	.45
680	A121	$1	Roosevelt on train, vert.	.75	.75
681	A121	$3	Roosevelt, vert.	2.25	2.25
		Nos. 676-681 (6)		4.15	4.15

Souvenir Sheets

| 682 | A121 | $4 | Washington, vert. | 3.00 | 3.00 |
| 683 | A121 | $4 | Eleanor and Franklin | 3.00 | 3.00 |

George Washington's 250th birth anniv. and Franklin D. Roosevelt's birth centenary.

Christmas — A122

Raphael Paintings.

1982, Nov.   Litho.   Perf. 14

684	A122	10c	Annunciation	.15	.15
685	A122	30c	Adoration of the Magi	.20	.20
686	A122	$1	Presentation at the Temple	.75	.75
687	A122	$4	Coronation of the Virgin	2.75	2.75
		Nos. 684-687 (4)		3.85	3.85

Souvenir Sheet

| 688 | A122 | $5 | Marriage of the Virgin | | 3.50 | 3.50 |

500th Birth Anniv. of Raphael — A123

1983, Jan. 28   Litho.   Perf. 14½

689	A123	45c	Galatea taking Reins of Dolphins, vert.	.35	.35
690	A123	50c	Sea Nymphs carried by Tritons, vert.	.40	.40
691	A123	60c	Winged Angel Steering Dolphins	.45	.45
692	A123	$4	Cupids Shooting Arrows	2.75	2.75
		Nos. 689-692 (4)		3.95	3.95

Souvenir Sheet

| 693 | A123 | $5 | Galatea | | 3.25 | 3.25 |

A124

1983, Mar. 14   Perf. 14

694	A124	25c	Pineapple crop	.20	.20
695	A124	45c	Carnival	.30	.30
696	A124	60c	Tourists, sailboat	.40	.40
697	A124	$3	Control Tower	2.00	2.00
		Nos. 694-697 (4)		2.90	2.90

Commonwealth Day.

World Communications Year — A125

1983, Apr. 5   Litho.   Perf. 14

698	A125	15c	TV screen, camera	.15	.15
699	A125	50c	Police radio, car	.40	.40
700	A125	60c	Long distance phone call	.45	.45
701	A125	$3	Dish antenna, planets	2.25	2.25
		Nos. 698-701 (4)		3.25	3.25

Souvenir Sheet

| 702 | A125 | $5 | Comsat satellite | | 3.75 | 3.75 |

Imperforates
Quantities of imperforates of Nos. 745-749, 755-759, 819, 821, 810, 811, 815, 909, 935, 936, 961 and possibly others, became available when the printer was liquidated.

Bottlenose Dolphin — A126

1983, May 9   Litho.   Perf. 15

703	A126	15c	shown	.15	.15
704	A126	50c	Finback whale	.35	.35
705	A126	60c	Bowhead whale	.40	.40
706	A126	$3	Spectacled porpoise	2.00	2.00
		Nos. 703-706 (4)		2.90	2.90

Souvenir Sheet

| 707 | A126 | $5 | Unicorn whale | | 3.50 | 3.50 |

Cashew Nut — A127

1983, July 11   Perf. 14

708	A127	1c	shown	.15	.15
709	A127	2c	Passion fruit	.15	.15
710	A127	3c	Mango	.15	.15
711	A127	5c	Grapefruit	.15	.15
712	A127	10c	Pawpaw	.15	.15
713	A127	15c	Breadfruit	.15	.15
714	A127	20c	Coconut	.15	.15
715	A127	25c	Oleander	.20	.20

716	A127	30c	Banana	.25	.25
717	A127	40c	Pineapple	.30	.30
718	A127	45c	Cordcia	.35	.35
719	A127	50c	Cassia	.40	.40
720	A127	60c	Poui	.45	.45
721	A127	$1	Frangipani	.75	.75
722	A127	$2	Flamboyant	1.50	1.50
723	A127	$2.50	Lemon	1.75	1.75
724	A127	$5	Lignum vitae	3.75	3.75
725	A127	$10	Arms	7.50	7.50
		Nos. 708-725 (18)		18.25	18.25

1985   Perf. 12½x12

708a	A127	1c		.15	.15
709a	A127	2c		.15	.15
710a	A127	3c		.15	.15
711a	A127	5c		.15	.15
712a	A127	10c		.15	.15
713a	A127	15c		.15	.15
714a	A127	20c		.15	.15
715a	A127	25c		.20	.20
716a	A127	30c		.25	.25
717a	A127	40c		.30	.30
718a	A127	45c		.35	.35
719a	A127	50c		.45	.45
720a	A127	60c		.50	.50
721a	A127	$1		.80	.80
722a	A127	$2		1.65	1.65
723a	A127	$2.50		1.90	1.90
724a	A127	$5		4.00	4.00
725a	A127	$10		8.00	8.00
		Nos. 708a-725a (18)		19.45	19.45

Issue dates: $2-$5, Dec. Others Mar.

Manned Flight Bicentenary — A128

1983, Aug. 15   Perf. 15

726	A128	30c	Dornier DoX	.20	.20
727	A128	50c	Supermarine S-6B	.35	.35
728	A128	60c	Curtiss F9C, USS Akron	.40	.40
729	A128	$4	Pro Juventute balloon	2.75	2.75
		Nos. 726-729 (4)		3.70	3.70

Souvenir Sheet

| 730 | A128 | $5 | Graf Zeppelin | | 3.25 | 3.25 |

Christmas — A129

Raphael Paintings: 10c, 30c, $1, $4, Sybils and Angels details. $5, Vision of Ezekiel.

1983, Oct. 4   Litho.   Perf. 14

731	A129	10c	Angel flying with scroll	.15	.15
732	A129	30c	Angel, diff.	.30	.30
733	A129	$1	Inscribing tablet	.30	.30
734	A129	$4	Angel showing tablet	3.25	3.25
		Nos. 731-734 (4)		4.00	4.00

Souvenir Sheet

| 735 | A129 | $5 | multicolored | | 3.75 | 3.75 |

Methodist Church, Anniv. — A130    1984 Olympics, Los Angeles — A131

Designs: 15c, John Wesley founder of Methodism. 50c, Nathaniel Gilbert, Antiguan founder. 60c, St. John's Methodist Church Steeple. $3, Ebenezer Methodist Church.

1983, Nov.   Litho.   Perf. 14

736	A130	15c	multicolored	.15	.15
737	A130	50c	multicolored	.40	.40
738	A130	60c	multicolored	.45	.45
739	A130	$3	multicolored	2.25	2.25
		Nos. 736-739 (4)		3.25	3.25

ANTIGUA

1984, Jan. Litho. Perf. 15
740 A131 25c Discus .20 .20
741 A131 50c Gymnastics .40 .40
742 A131 90c Hurdling .70 .70
743 A131 $3 Bicycling 2.25 2.25
Nos. 740-743 (4) 3.55 3.55
Souvenir Sheet
744 A131 $5 Volleyball, horiz. 3.75 3.75

Booker Vanguard A132

1984, June 4 Litho. Perf. 15
745 A132 45c shown .35 .35
746 A132 50c Canberra .40 .40
747 A132 60c Yachts .45 .45
748 A132 $4 Fairwind 3.00 3.00
Nos. 745-748 (4) 4.20 4.20
Souvenir Sheet
749 A132 $5 Man-of-war, vert. 3.75 3.75

Local Flowers — A133

US Presidents — A134

1984, June 25 Litho. Perf. 15
755 A133 15c multicolored .15 .15
756 A133 50c multicolored .40 .40
757 A133 60c multicolored .45 .45
758 A133 $3 multicolored 2.25 2.25
Nos. 755-758 (4) 3.25 3.25
Souvenir Sheet
759 A133 $5 multicolored 3.75 3.75

1984, July 18 Litho. Perf. 14
760 A134 10c Lincoln .15 .15
761 A134 20c Truman .15 .15
762 A134 30c Eisenhower .20 .20
763 A134 40c Reagan .30 .30
764 A134 90c Lincoln, diff. .70 .70
765 A134 $1.10 Truman, diff. .85 .85
766 A134 $1.50 Eisenhower, diff. 1.15 1.15
767 A134 $2 Reagan, diff. 1.50 1.50
Nos. 760-767 (8) 5.00 5.00

Slavery Abolition Sesquicentennial A135

1984, Aug. 1
768 A135 40c Moravian Mission .30 .30
769 A135 50c Antigua Courthouse, 1823 .40 .40
770 A135 60c Sugar cane planting .45 .45
771 A135 $3 Boiling House, Delaps' Estate 2.25 2.25
Nos. 768-771 (4) 3.40 3.40
Souvenir Sheet
772 A135 $5 Willoughby Bay 3.75 3.75

Song Birds — A136

1984, Aug. 15 Perf. 15
773 A136 40c Rufous-sided towhee .30 .30
774 A136 50c Parula warbler .40 .40
775 A136 60c House wren .45 .45
776 A136 $2 Ruby-crowned kinglet 1.50 1.50
777 A136 $3 Yellow-shafted flicker 2.25 2.25
Nos. 773-777 (5) 4.90 4.90
Souvenir Sheet
778 A136 $5 Yellow-breasted chat 3.75 3.75

AUSIPEX '84 — A137

The Blue Dancers, by Degas — A137a

1984, Sept. 21 Perf. 15
779 A137 $1 Grass skiing .75 .75
780 A137 $5 Australian rules football 3.75 3.75
Souvenir Sheet
781 A137 $5 Boomerang 3.75 3.75

1984, Oct. Litho. Perf. 15
Paintings by Correggio: 25c, Virgin and Infant with Angels and Cherubs. 60c, The Four Saints. 90c, Saint Catherine. $3, The Campori Madonna. #790, St. John the Baptist.
Paintings by Degas: 50c, The Pink Dancers. 70c, Two Dancers. $4, Dancers at the Bar. #791, Folk Dancers.

782 A137a 15c multicolored .15 .15
783 A137a 25c multicolored .20 .20
784 A137a 50c multicolored .40 .40
785 A137a 60c multicolored .45 .45
786 A137a 70c multicolored .50 .50
787 A137a 90c multicolored .65 .65
788 A137a $3 multicolored 2.25 2.25
789 A137a $4 multicolored 3.00 3.00
Nos. 782-789 (8) 7.60 7.60
Souvenir Sheets
790 A137a $5 multicolored 3.75 3.75
791 A137a $5 multi, horiz. 3.75 3.75

Nos. 623-626, 663-666, 672-675, 694-697 Surcharged in Black or Gold

1984, June Perf. 14, 14½x14
792 CD331 $2 on 25c #623 1.50 1.50
793 CD334 $2 on 25c #694 1.50 1.50
794 CD334 $2 on 45c #695 1.50 1.50
795 CD331 $2 on 50c #624 1.50 1.50
796 CD334 $2 on 60c #696 1.50 1.50
797 CD332 $2 on 90c #663 (G) 1.50 1.50
798 CD332 $2 on 90c #672 (G) 1.50 1.50
799 CD332 $2 on $1 #664 (G) 1.50 1.50
800 CD332 $2 on $1 #673 (G) 1.50 1.50
801 CD334 $2 on $3 #697 1.50 1.50
802 CD331 $2 on $4 #625 1.50 1.50
803 CD332 $2 on $4 #665 (G) 1.50 1.50
804 CD332 $2 on $4 #674 (G) 1.50 1.50
Nos. 792-804 (13) 19.50 19.50
Souvenir Sheets
805 CD331 $2 on $5 #626 1.50 1.50
806 CD332 $2 on $5 #666 1.50 1.50
807 CD332 $2 on $5 #675 1.50 1.50

Nos. 797-800, 803-804 exist with silver surcharge.

Christmas 1984 and 50th Anniv. of Donald Duck — A138

Scenes from various Donald Duck comics.

1984, Nov. Litho. Perf. 11
808 A138 1c multicolored .15 .15
809 A138 2c multicolored .15 .15
810 A138 3c multicolored .15 .15
811 A138 4c multicolored .15 .15
812 A138 5c multicolored .15 .15
813 A138 10c multicolored .15 .15
814 A138 $1 multicolored 1.00 1.00
815 A138 $2 multicolored 1.90 1.90
816 A138 $5 multicolored 5.00 5.00
Nos. 808-816 (9) 8.80 8.80
Souvenir Sheets Perf. 14
817 A138 $5 multi, horiz. 5.00 5.00
818 A138 $5 Donald on beach 5.00 5.00

20th Century Leaders A139

1984, Nov. 19 Litho. Perf. 15
819 A139 60c John F. Kennedy (1917-1963), vert. .50 .50
820 A139 60c Winston Churchill (1874-1965), vert. .50 .50
821 A139 60c Mahatma Gandhi (1869-1948), vert. .50 .50
822 A139 60c Mao Tse-Tung (1883-1976), vert. .50 .50
823 A139 $1 Kennedy in Berlin .80 .80
824 A139 $1 Churchill in Paris .80 .80
825 A139 $1 Gandhi in Great Britain .80 .80
826 A139 $1 Mao in Peking .80 .80
Nos. 819-826 (8) 5.20 5.20
Souvenir Sheet
827 A139 $5 Flags of Great Britain, India, China, USA 3.75 3.75

Statue of Liberty Centennial A140

1985, Jan. 7
828 A140 25c Torch on display, 1885 .15 .15
829 A140 30c Restoration, 1984-1986, vert. .20 .20
830 A140 50c Bartholdi supervising construction, 1876 .30 .30
831 A140 90c Statue on Liberty Island .65 .65
832 A140 $1 Dedication Ceremony, 1886, vert. .70 .70
833 A140 $3 Operation Sail, 1976, vert. 2.00 2.00
Nos. 828-833 (6) 4.00 4.00
Souvenir Sheet
834 A140 $5 Port of New York 3.75 3.75

Traditional Scenes A141

1985, Jan. 21
835 A141 15c Ceramics, Arawak pot shard .15 .15
836 A141 50c Tatooing, body design .40 .40
837 A141 60c Harvesting Manioc, god Yocahu .45 .45
838 A141 $3 Caribs in battle, war club 2.25 2.25
Nos. 835-838 (4) 3.25 3.25
Souvenir Sheet
839 A141 $5 Tainos worshiping 3.75 3.75

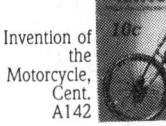

Invention of the Motorcycle, Cent. A142

1985, Mar. 7 Perf. 14
840 A142 10c Triumph 2HP Jap, 1903 .15 .15
841 A142 30c Indian Arrow, 1949 .25 .25
842 A142 60c BMW R100RS, 1976 .45 .45
843 A142 $4 Harley Davidson Model II, 1916 3.00 3.00
Nos. 840-843 (4) 3.85 3.85
Souvenir Sheet
844 A142 $5 Laverda Jota, 1975 3.75 3.75

John J. Audubon, 200th Birth Anniv. A143

1985, Mar. 25 Perf. 14
845 A143 90c Horned grebe .70 .70
846 A143 $1 Least petrel .75 .75
847 A143 $1.50 Great blue heron 1.10 1.10
848 A143 $3 Double-crested cormorant 2.25 2.25
Nos. 845-848 (4) 4.80 4.80
Souvenir Sheet
849 A143 $5 White-tailed tropic bird, vert. 3.75 3.75

See Nos. 910-914.

Butterflies A144

1985, Apr. 16 Perf. 14
850 A144 30c Polygrapha cyanea .20 .20
851 A144 60c Leodonta dysoni .50 .50
852 A144 95c Junea doraete .85 .85
853 A144 $4 Prepona xenagoras 3.50 3.50
Nos. 850-853 (4) 5.05 5.05
Souvenir Sheet
854 A144 $5 Caerois gerdrudtus 4.25 4.25

Cessna 172 — A145

1985, Apr. 30
855 A145 30c shown .20 .20
856 A145 90c Fokker DVII .60 .60
857 A145 $1.50 Spad VII 1.00 1.00
858 A145 $3 Boeing 747 1.90 1.90
Nos. 855-858 (4) 3.70 3.70
Souvenir Sheet
859 A145 $5 Twin Otter, Coolidge Intl. Airport 3.75 3.75

40th anniv. of the ICAO. Nos. 855, 858-859 show the ICAO and UN emblems.

Maimonides (1135-1204), Judaic Philosopher and Physician — A146

1985, June 17 Litho. Perf. 14
860 A146 $2 yellow green 2.00 2.00
Souvenir Sheet
861 A146 $5 deep brown 4.00 4.00

Intl. Youth Year A147

1985, July 1
862 A147 25c Agriculture .20 .20
863 A147 50c Hotel management .35 .35
864 A147 60c Environmental studies .50 .50
865 A147 $3 Windsurfing 2.25 2.25
Nos. 862-865 (4) 3.30 3.30
Souvenir Sheet
866 A147 $5 Youths, national flag 3.75 3.75

Queen Mother, 85th Birthday — A148

ANTIGUA

Designs: 90c, $1, Attending a church service. No. 867A, $1.50, Touring the London Gardens, children in a sandpit. $2.50, $3, Photograph (1979). $5, With Prince Edward at the wedding of Prince Charles and Lady Diana Spencer.

Perf. 14, 12x12½ (90c, $1, $3)

1985, July 15

866A	A148	90c multi ('86)	.65	.65
867	A148	$1 multi	.75	.75
867A	A148	$1 multi ('86)	.75	.75
868	A148	$1.50 multi	1.10	1.10
869	A148	$2.50 multi	1.75	1.75
869A	A148	$3 multi ('86)	2.00	2.00
		Nos. 866A-869A (6)	7.00	7.00

Souvenir Sheet

870	A148	$5 multicolored	3.50	3.50

Nos. 866A, 867A, 869A issued in sheets of 5 plus label on Jan. 13, 1986.

Marine Life — A149

Johann Sebastian Bach — A150

1985, Aug. 1 *Perf. 14*

871	A149	15c Fregata magnificens	.15	.15
872	A149	45c Diploria labyrinthiformis	.40	.40
873	A149	60c Oreaster reticulatus	.50	.50
874	A149	$3 Gymnothorax moringa	2.25	2.25
		Nos. 871-874 (4)	3.30	3.30

Souvenir Sheet

875	A149	$5 Acropora palmata	3.75	3.75

1985, Aug. 26 *Litho. Perf. 14*

876	A150	25c Bass trombone	.15	.15
877	A150	50c English horn	.30	.30
878	A150	$1 Violino piccolo	.65	.65
879	A150	$3 Bass rackett	1.90	1.90
		Nos. 876-879 (4)	3.00	3.00

Souvenir Sheet

880	A150	$5 Portrait	3.25	3.25

Girl Guides, 75th Anniv. A151

Public service and growth-oriented activities.

1985, Sept. 10

881	A151	15c Public service	.15	.15
882	A151	45c Guides meeting	.40	.40
883	A151	60c Lord and Lady Baden-Powell	.50	.50
884	A151	$3 Nature study	2.25	2.25
		Nos. 881-884 (4)	3.30	3.30

Souvenir Sheet

885	A151	$5 Barn swallow	3.75	3.75

State Visit of Elizabeth II, Oct. 24 A152

1985, Oct. 24 *Litho. Perf. 14½*

886	A152	60c National flags	.45	.45
887	A152	$1 Elizabeth II, vert.	.75	.75
888	A152	$4 HMY Britannia	3.00	3.00
		Nos. 886-888 (3)	4.20	4.20

Souvenir Sheet

889	A152	$5 Map of Antigua	3.75	3.75

Mark Twain A153

Disney characters in Roughing It.

1985, Nov. 4 *Perf. 14*

890	A153	25c Cowboys and Indians	.20	.20
891	A153	50c Canoeing	.40	.40
892	A153	$1.10 Pony Express	.90	.90
893	A153	$1.50 Buffalo hunt in Missouri	1.25	1.25
894	A153	$2 Nevada silver mine	1.75	1.75
		Nos. 890-894 (5)	4.50	4.50

Souvenir Sheet

895	A153	$5 Stagecoach on Kansas plains	4.50	4.50

Jacob and Wilhelm Grimm, Fabulists and Philologists — A154

Disney characters in Spindle, Shuttle and Needle.

1985, Nov. 11

896	A154	30c multicolored	.25	.25
897	A154	60c multicolored	.55	.55
898	A154	70c multicolored	.60	.60
899	A154	$1 multicolored	.90	.90
900	A154	$3 multicolored	2.75	2.75
		Nos. 896-900 (5)	5.05	5.05

Souvenir Sheet

900A	A154	$5 multicolored	4.50	4.50

UN 40th Anniv. A155

Stamps of UN and portraits: 40c, No. 18 and Benjamin Franklin. $1, No. 391 and George Washington Carver, agricultural chemist. $3, No. 299 and Charles Lindbergh. $5, Marc Chagall, artist, vert.

1985, Nov. 18 *Perf. 13½x14*

901	A155	40c multicolored	.30	.30
902	A155	$1 multicolored	.75	.75
903	A155	$3 multicolored	2.25	2.25
		Nos. 901-903 (3)	3.30	3.30

Souvenir Sheet
Perf. 14x13½

904	A155	$5 multicolored	3.75	3.75

Christmas — A156

Religious paintings: 10c, Madonna and Child, by De Landi. 25c, Madonna and Child, by Bonaventura Berlingheiri (d. 1244). 60c, The Nativity, by Fra Angelico (1400-1455). $4, Presentation in the Temple, by Giovanni di Paolo Grazia (c.1403-1482). $5, The Nativity, by Antoniazzo Romano.

1985, Dec. 30 *Perf. 15*

905	A156	10c multicolored	.15	.15
906	A156	25c multicolored	.20	.20
907	A156	60c multicolored	.45	.45
908	A156	$4 multicolored	3.00	3.00
		Nos. 905-908 (4)	3.80	3.80

Souvenir Sheet

909	A156	$5 multicolored	3.75	3.75

Audubon Type of 1985

Illustrations of North American ducks.

1986, Jan. 6 *Perf. 12½x12*

910	A143	60c Mallard	.45	.45
911	A143	90c Dusky duck	.65	.65
912	A143	$1.50 Common pintail	1.10	1.10
913	A143	$3 Widgeon	2.25	2.25
		Nos. 910-913 (4)	4.45	4.45

Souvenir Sheet
Perf. 14

914	A143	$5 Common eider	3.75	3.75

1986 World Cup Soccer Championships, Mexico — A157

1986, Mar. 17 *Litho. Perf. 14*

915	A157	30c shown	.25	.25
916	A157	60c Heading the ball	.45	.45
917	A157	$1 Referee	.75	.75
918	A157	$4 Goal	3.00	3.00
		Nos. 915-918 (4)	4.45	4.45

Souvenir Sheet

919	A157	$5 Action	3.75	3.75

Nos. 916-917 vert.
For overprints see Nos. 963-967.

A158

Halley's Comet A159

Designs: 5c, Edmond Halley, Greenwich Observatory. 10c, Me 163B Komet. German WWII fighter plane. 60c, Montezuma sighting comet, 1517. $4, Pocahontas saving Capt. John Smith's life, 1607 sighting as sign for Powhattan Indians to raid Jamestown. $5, Comet over Antigua.

1986, Mar. 24

920	A158	5c multicolored	.15	.15
921	A158	10c multicolored	.15	.15
922	A158	60c multicolored	.45	.45
923	A158	$4 multicolored	3.00	3.00
		Nos. 920-923 (4)	3.75	3.75

Souvenir Sheet

924	A159	$5 multicolored	3.75	3.75

For overprints see Nos. 973-977.

Queen Elizabeth II, 60th Birthday
Common Design Type

1986, Apr. 21

925	CD339	60c Wedding, 1947	.45	.45
926	CD339	$1 Trooping the color	.75	.75
927	CD339	$4 Visiting Scotland	3.00	3.00
		Nos. 925-927 (3)	4.20	4.20

Souvenir Sheet

928	CD339	$5 Held by Queen Mary, 1927	3.75	3.75

Boats — A160

1986, May 15

929	A160	30c Tugboat	.25	.25
930	A160	60c Fishing boat	.45	.45
931	A160	$1 Sailboat 2056	.75	.75
932	A160	$4 Lateen-rigged sailboat	3.00	3.00
		Nos. 929-932 (4)	4.45	4.45

Souvenir Sheet

933	A160	$5 Boatbuilding	3.75	3.75

AMERIPEX '86 — A161

American trains.

1986, May 22 *Perf. 15*

934	A161	25c Hiawatha	.20	.20
935	A161	50c Grand Canyon	.40	.40
936	A161	$1 Powhattan Arrow	.75	.75
937	A161	$3 Empire State	2.25	2.25
		Nos. 934-937 (4)	3.60	3.60

Souvenir Sheet

938	A161	$5 Daylight	3.75	3.75

Wedding of Prince Andrew and Sarah Ferguson
Common Design Type

1986, July 23 *Perf. 14*

939	CD340	45c Couple	.35	.35
940	CD340	60c Prince Andrew	.45	.45
941	CD340	$4 Princes Andrew, Philip	3.00	3.00
		Nos. 939-941 (3)	3.80	3.80

Souvenir Sheet

942	CD340	$5 Couple, diff.	3.50	3.50

Conch Shells — A162

1986, Aug. 6 *Litho. Perf. 15*

943	A162	15c Say fly-specked cerith	.15	.15
944	A162	45c Gmelin smooth scotch bonnet	.35	.35
945	A162	60c Linne West Indian crown conch	.45	.45
946	A162	$3 Murex ciboney	2.25	2.25
		Nos. 943-946 (4)	3.20	3.20

Souvenir Sheet

947	A162	$5 Atlantic natica	3.75	3.75

Flowers A163

1986, Aug. 25 *Litho. Perf. 15*

948	A163	10c Water lily	.15	.15
949	A163	15c Queen of the night	.15	.15
950	A163	50c Cup of gold	.40	.40
951	A163	60c Beach morning glory	.45	.45
952	A163	70c Golden trumpet	.55	.55
953	A163	$1 Air plant	.75	.75
954	A163	$3 Purple wreath	2.25	2.25
955	A163	$4 Zephyr lily	3.00	3.00
		Nos. 948-955 (8)	7.70	7.70

Souvenir Sheets

956	A163	$4 Dozakie	3.00	3.00
957	A163	$5 Four o'clock	3.75	3.75

ANTIGUA

Fungi — A164

1986, Sept. 15
958	A164	10c Hygrocybe occidentalis scarletina	.15	.15
959	A164	50c Trogia buccinalis	.35	.35
960	A164	$1 Collybia subpruinosa	.75	.75
961	A164	$4 Leucocoprinus brebissonii	3.00	3.00
		Nos. 958-961 (4)	4.25	4.25

Souvenir Sheet
| 962 | A164 | $5 Pyrrhoglossum pyrrhum | 3.75 | 3.75 |

Nos. 915-919 Ovptd. "WINNERS Argentina 3 W. Germany 2" in Gold in 2 or 3 lines

1986, Sept. 15 *Perf. 14*
963	A157	30c multicolored	.20	.20
964	A157	60c multicolored	.45	.45
965	A157	$1 multicolored	.75	.75
966	A157	$4 multicolored	3.00	3.00
		Nos. 963-966 (4)	4.40	4.40

Souvenir Sheet
| 967 | A157 | $5 multicolored | 3.75 | 3.75 |

Automobile, Cent. A165

Carl Benz and classic automobiles.

1986, Oct. 20
968	A165	10c 1933 Auburn Speedster	.15	.15
968A	A165	15c 1986 Mercury Sable	.15	.15
969	A165	50c 1959 Cadillac	.40	.40
970	A165	60c 1950 Studebaker	.45	.45
970A	A165	70c 1939 Lagonda V-12	.50	.50
970B	A165	$1 1930 Adler Standard	.75	.75
970C	A165	$3 1956 DKW	2.25	2.25
971	A165	$4 1936 Mercedes 500K	3.00	3.00
		Nos. 968-971 (8)	7.65	7.65

Souvenir Sheets
| 972 | A165 | $5 1921 Mercedes Knight | 3.75 | 3.75 |
| 972A | A165 | $5 1896 Daimler | 3.75 | 3.75 |

Nos. 920-924 Ovptd. with Halley's Comet Emblem in Black or Silver

1986, Oct. 22 Litho. *Perf. 14*
973	A158	5c multicolored	.15	.15
974	A158	10c multicolored	.15	.15
975	A158	60c multicolored	.45	.45
976	A158	$4 multicolored	3.00	3.00
		Nos. 973-976 (4)	3.75	3.75

Souvenir Sheet
| 977 | A159 | $5 multicolored (S) | 3.75 | 3.75 |

Christmas — A166

Disney characters as children.

1986, Nov. 4 *Perf. 11*
978	A166	25c Mickey	.20	.20
979	A166	30c Mickey, Minnie	.20	.20
980	A166	40c Aunt Matilda, Goofy	.30	.30
981	A166	60c Goofy, Pluto	.45	.45
982	A166	70c Pluto, Donald, Daisy	.55	.55
983	A166	$1.50 Stringing popcorn	1.10	1.10
984	A166	$3 Grandma Duck, Minnie	2.25	2.25
985	A166	$4 Donald, Pete	3.00	3.00
		Nos. 978-985 (8)	8.05	8.05

Souvenir Sheets *Perf. 14*
| 986 | A166 | $5 Playing with presents | 3.75 | 3.75 |
| 987 | A166 | $5 Reindeer | 3.75 | 3.75 |

Nos. 985 printed in sheets of 8.

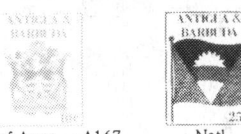

Coat of Arms — A167

Natl. Flag — A168

1986, Nov. 25 Litho. *Perf. 14x14½*
| 988 | A167 | 10c bright blue | .15 | .15 |
| 989 | A168 | 25c orange | .20 | .20 |

Marc Chagall (1887-1985), Artist — A169

Designs: No. 990, The Profile, 1957. No. 991, Portrait of the Artist's Sister, 1910. No. 992, Bride with Fan, 1911. No. 993, David in Profile, 1914. No. 994, Fiancee with Bouquet, 1977. No. 995, Self-portrait with Brushes, 1909. No. 996, The Walk, 1973. No. 997, Candles, 1938. No. 998, Fall of Icarus, 1975. No. 999, Myth of Orpheus, 1977.

1987, Mar. 30 Litho. *Perf. 13½x14*
990	A169	10c multicolored	.15	.15
991	A169	30c multicolored	.20	.20
992	A169	40c multicolored	.30	.30
993	A169	45c multicolored	.45	.45
994	A169	90c multicolored	.70	.70
995	A169	$1 multicolored	.75	.75
996	A169	$3 multicolored	2.25	2.25
997	A169	$4 multicolored	3.00	3.00

Size: 110x95mm *Imperf*
998	A169	$5 multicolored	3.75	3.75
999	A169	$5 multicolored	3.75	3.75
		Nos. 990-999 (10)	15.30	15.30

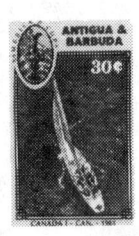

America's Cup A171

1987, Feb. 5 *Perf. 15*
1000	A170	30c Canada I, 1981	.25	.25
1001	A170	60c Gretel II, 1970	.45	.45
1002	A170	$1 Sceptre, 1958	.75	.75
1003	A170	$3 Vigilant, 1893	2.25	2.25
		Nos. 1000-1003 (4)	3.70	3.70

Souvenir Sheet
| 1004 | A171 | $5 Australia II, Liberty, 1983 | 3.75 | 3.75 |

Fish, World Wildlife Fund A172

Marine Birds A173

1987, Feb. 23 Litho. *Perf. 14*
1005	A172	15c Bridled burrfish	.15	.15
1006	A172	30c Brown noddy	.25	.25
1007	A172	40c Nassau grouper	.30	.30
1008	A173	50c Laughing gull	.40	.40
1009	A172	60c French angelfish	.50	.50
1010	A172	$1 Porkfish	.80	.80
1011	A173	$2 Royal tern	1.65	1.65
1012	A173	$3 Sooty tern	2.50	2.50
		Nos. 1005-1012 (8)	6.55	6.55

Souvenir Sheets
| 1013 | A172 | $5 Banded butterfly fish | 4.00 | 4.00 |
| 1014 | A173 | $5 Brown booby | 4.00 | 4.00 |

The 30c, 50c, $2, $3 and Nos. 1013-1014 do not picture the WWF emblem.
For overprints see Nos. 1137-1139A.

Statue of Liberty, Cent. A174

Photographs by Peter B. Kaplan.

1987, Apr. 20 *Perf. 14*
1015	A174	15c Lee Iacocca	.15	.15
1016	A174	30c Statue at dusk	.25	.25
1017	A174	45c Crown, head	.35	.35
1018	A174	50c Iacocca, torch	.40	.40
1019	A174	60c Crown observatory	.50	.50
1020	A174	90c Interior restoration	.70	.70
1021	A174	$1 Head	.80	.80
1022	A174	$2 Statue at sunset	1.65	1.65
1023	A174	$3 Men on scaffold, flag	2.50	2.50
1024	A174	$4 Statue at night	4.00	4.00
		Nos. 1015-1024 (10)	11.30	11.30

Nos. 1015-1018, 1021-1022, 1024 vert.

A175

Transportation Innovations — A175a

1987, Apr. 19 *Perf. 15*
1025	A175	10c Spirit of Australia, 1978	.15	.15
1026	A175a	15c Siemens' Electric locomotive, 1879	.15	.15
1027	A175	30c USS Triton, 1960	.25	.25
1028	A175a	50c Trevithick, 1801	.40	.40
1029	A175	60c USS New Jersey, 1942	.45	.45
1030	A175a	70c Draisine bicycle, 1818	.50	.50
1031	A175	90c SS United States, 1952	.70	.70
1032	A175a	$1.50 Cierva C-4, 1923	1.10	1.10
1033	A175a	$2 Curtiss NC-4, 1919	1.50	1.50
1034	A175	$3 Queen Elizabeth II, 1969	2.25	2.25
		Nos. 1025-1034 (10)	7.45	7.45

Reptiles and Amphibians A176

1987, June 15 *Perf. 14*
1035	A176	30c Eleutherodactylus martinicensis	.25	.25
1036	A176	60c Thecadactylus bapicauda	.50	.50
1037	A176	$1 Anolis bimaculatus leachi	.75	.75
1038	A176	$3 Geochelone carbonaria	2.25	2.25
		Nos. 1035-1038 (4)	3.75	3.75

Souvenir Sheet
| 1039 | A176 | $5 Ameiva griswoldi | 3.75 | 3.75 |

Entertainers — A177

1987, May 11
1040	A177	15c Grace Kelly	.15	.15
1041	A177	30c Marilyn Monroe	.30	.30
1042	A177	45c Orson Welles	.45	.45
1043	A177	50c Judy Garland	.50	.50
1044	A177	60c John Lennon	.60	.60
1045	A177	$1 Rock Hudson	1.00	1.00
1046	A177	$2 John Wayne	2.00	2.00
1047	A177	$3 Elvis Presley	3.00	3.00
		Nos. 1040-1047 (8)	8.00	8.00

No. 1047 Overprinted

1987, Sept. 9 Litho. *Perf. 14*
| 1047A | A177 | $3 multicolored | 3.00 | 3.00 |

1988 Summer Olympics, Seoul A178

1987, Mar. 23
1048	A178	10c Basketball	.15	.15
1049	A178	60c Fencing	.50	.50
1050	A178	$1 Women's gymnastics	.75	.75
1051	A178	$3 Soccer	2.25	2.25
		Nos. 1048-1051 (4)	3.65	3.65

Souvenir Sheet
| 1052 | A178 | $5 Boxing glove | 3.75 | 3.75 |

16th World Scout Jamboree, Australia, 1987-88 A179

1987, Nov. 2 Litho. *Perf. 15*
1053	A179	10c Campfire, red kangaroo	.15	.15
1054	A179	60c Kayaking, blue-winged kookaburra	.45	.45
1055	A179	$1 Obstacle course, ring-tailed rock wallaby	.75	.75
1056	A179	$3 Field kitchen, koalas	2.25	2.25
		Nos. 1053-1056 (4)	3.60	3.60

Souvenir Sheet
| 1057 | A179 | $5 Flags | 3.75 | 3.75 |

US Constitution Bicent. A180

Designs: 15c, Virginia House of Burgesses exercising right of freedom of speech. 45c, Connecticut state seal. 60c, Delaware state seal. $4, Gouverneur Morris (1752-1816), principal writer of the Constitution, vert. $5, Roger Sherman (1721-1793), jurist and statesman, vert.

ANTIGUA

1987, Nov. 16　Litho.　Perf. 14
1058	A180	15c multicolored	.15	.15
1059	A180	45c multicolored	.35	.35
1060	A180	60c multicolored	.50	.50
1061	A180	$4 multicolored	3.00	3.00
		Nos. 1058-1061 (4)	4.00	4.00

Souvenir Sheet
| 1062 | A180 | $5 multicolored | 3.75 | 3.75 |

Christmas — A181

A182

Paintings: 45c, Madonna and Child, by Bernardo Daddi (1290-1355). 60c, Joseph, detail from The Nativity, by Sano Di Pietro (1406-1481). $1, Mary, detail from Di Pietro's The Nativity. $4, Music-making Angel, by Melozzo Da Forli (1438-1494). $5, The Flight into Egypt, by Di Pietro.

1987, Dec. 1
1063	A181	45c multicolored	.30	.30
1064	A181	60c multicolored	.45	.45
1065	A181	$1 multicolored	.75	.75
1066	A181	$4 multicolored	3.00	3.00
		Nos. 1063-1066 (4)	4.50	4.50

Souvenir Sheet
| 1067 | A181 | $5 multicolored | 3.75 | 3.75 |

1988, Feb. 8　Litho.　Perf. 14
1068	A182	25c Wedding portrait	.15	.15
1069	A182	60c Elizabeth II, c. 1970	.45	.45
1070	A182	$2 Christening of Charles, 1948	1.50	1.50
1071	A182	$3 Elizabeth II, c. 1980	2.25	2.25
		Nos. 1068-1071 (4)	4.35	4.35

Souvenir Sheet
| 1072 | A182 | $5 Royal family, c. 1951 | 3.75 | 3.75 |

40th wedding anniv. of Queen Elizabeth II and Prince Philip.

Tropical Birds A183

1988, Mar. 1
1073	A183	10c Great blue heron, vert.	.15	.15
1074	A183	15c Ringed kingfisher	.15	.15
1075	A183	50c Bananaquit	.40	.40
1076	A183	60c Purple gallinule	.45	.45
1077	A183	70c Blue-hooded euphonia	.55	.55
1078	A183	$1 Caribbean parakeet, vert.	.80	.80
1079	A183	$3 Troupial	2.25	2.25
1080	A183	$4 Hummingbird	3.00	3.00
		Nos. 1073-1080 (8)	7.75	7.75

Souvenir Sheets
| 1081 | A183 | $5 Roseate flamingo, vert. | 3.75 | 3.75 |
| 1082 | A183 | $5 Brown pelicans, vert. | 3.75 | 3.75 |

Salvation Army — A184

1988, Mar. 7
1083	A184	25c Day-care, Antigua	.20	.20
1084	A184	30c Penicillin inoculation, Indonesia	.25	.25
1085	A184	40c Day-care Center, Bolivia	.30	.30
1086	A184	45c Rehabilitation, India	.35	.35
1087	A184	50c Training the blind, Kenya	.40	.40
1088	A184	60c Infant care, Ghana	.45	.45
1089	A184	$1 Job training, Zambia	.75	.75
1090	A184	$2 Food distribution, Sri Lanka	1.50	1.50
		Nos. 1083-1090 (8)	4.20	4.20

Souvenir Sheet
| 1091 | A184 | $5 General Eva Burrows | 3.75 | 3.75 |

A185

Discovery of America, 500th Anniv. (in 1992) A186

Anniv. emblem and: 10c, Fleet. 30c, View of fleet in harbor from Paino Indian village. 45c, Caravel anchored in harbor, Paino village. 60c, Columbus, 3 Indians in canoe. 90c, Indian, parrot, Columbus. $1, Columbus in longboat. $3, Spanish guard, fleet in harbor. $4, Ships under full sail. No. 1100, Stone cross given to Columbus by Queen Isabella. No. 1101, Gold exelente.

1988, Mar. 14　Litho.　Perf. 14
1092	A185	10c multicolored	.15	.15
1093	A185	30c multicolored	.20	.20
1094	A185	45c multicolored	.35	.35
1095	A185	60c multicolored	.45	.45
1096	A185	90c multicolored	.70	.70
1097	A185	$1 multicolored	.75	.75
1098	A185	$3 multicolored	2.25	2.25
1099	A185	$4 multicolored	3.00	3.00
		Nos. 1092-1099 (8)	7.85	7.85

Souvenir Sheets
| 1100 | A186 | $5 multicolored | 3.75 | 3.75 |
| 1101 | A186 | $5 multicolored | 3.75 | 3.75 |

Paintings by Titian — A187

Details: 30c, Bust of Christ. 40c, Scourging of Christ. 45c, Madonna in Glory with Saints. 50c, The Averoldi Polyptych. $1, Christ Crowned with Thorns. $2, Christ Mocked. $3, Christ and Simon of Cyrene. $4, Crucifixion with Virgin and Saints. No. 1110, Ecce Homo. No. 1111, Noli Me Tangere.

1988, Apr. 11　Litho.　Perf. 13½x14
1102	A187	30c shown	.20	.20
1103	A187	40c multicolored	.30	.30
1104	A187	45c multicolored	.35	.35
1105	A187	50c multicolored	.40	.40
1106	A187	$1 multicolored	.75	.75
1107	A187	$2 multicolored	1.50	1.50
1108	A187	$3 multicolored	2.25	2.25
1109	A187	$4 multicolored	3.00	3.00
		Nos. 1102-1109 (8)	8.75	8.75

Souvenir Sheets
| 1110 | A187 | $5 multicolored | 3.75 | 3.75 |
| 1111 | A187 | $5 multicolored | 3.75 | 3.75 |

Sailing Week A188

1988, Apr. 18　　Perf. 15
1112	A188	30c Canada I, 1980	.20	.20
1113	A188	60c Gretel II, Australia, 1970	.50	.50
1114	A188	$1 Sceptre, GB, 1958	.80	.80
1115	A188	$3 Vigilant, US, 1893	2.25	2.25
		Nos. 1112-1115 (4)	3.75	3.75

Souvenir Sheet
| 1116 | A188 | $5 Australia II, 1983 | 3.75 | 3.75 |

Walt Disney Animated Characters and Epcot Center, Walt Disney World — A189

1988, May 3　Perf. 14x13½, 13½x14
1116A	A189	1c like 25c	.15	.15
1116B	A189	2c like 30c	.15	.15
1116C	A189	3c like 40c	.15	.15
1116D	A189	4c like 60c	.15	.15
1116E	A189	5c like 70c	.15	.15
1116F	A189	10c like $1.50	.15	.15
1117	A189	25c The Living Seas	.20	.20
1118	A189	30c World of Motion	.20	.20
1119	A189	40c Spaceship Earth	.30	.30
1120	A189	60c Universe of Energy	.45	.45
1121	A189	70c Journey to Imagination	.60	.60
1122	A189	$1.50 The Land	1.10	1.10
1123	A189	$3 Communicore	2.25	2.25
1124	A189	$4 Horizons	3.00	3.00
		Nos. 1116A-1124 (14)	9.00	9.00

Souvenir Sheets
| 1125 | A189 | $5 Epcot Center | 3.75 | 3.75 |
| 1126 | A189 | $5 The Contemporary Resort Hotel | 3.75 | 3.75 |

30c, 40c, $1.50, $3 and No. 1126 are vert.

Flowering Trees
A190　　A191

1988, May 16　　Perf. 14
1127	A190	10c Jacaranda	.15	.15
1128	A190	30c Cordia	.25	.25
1129	A190	50c Orchid tree	.40	.40
1130	A190	90c Flamboyant	.70	.70
1131	A190	$1 African tulip tree	.75	.75
1132	A190	$2 Potato tree	1.50	1.50
1133	A190	$3 Crepe myrtle	2.25	2.25
1134	A190	$4 Pitch apple	3.00	3.00
		Nos. 1127-1134 (8)	9.00	9.00

Souvenir Sheets
| 1135 | A191 | $5 Cassia | 3.75 | 3.75 |
| 1136 | A191 | $5 Chinaberry | 3.75 | 3.75 |

Nos. 1011-1012, 1014 and 1013 Ovptd. in Black for Philatelic Exhibitions

a　Praga '88

b　INDEPENDENCE 40

c　FINLANDIA 88

d　OLYMPHILEX '88

1988, May 9　Litho.　Perf. 14
| 1137 | A173 | (a) $2 multicolored | 1.50 | 1.50 |
| 1138 | A173 | (b) $3 multicolored | 2.25 | 2.25 |

Souvenir Sheets
| 1139 | A173 | (c) $5 multicolored | 3.75 | 3.75 |
| 1139A | A172 | (d) $5 multicolored | 3.75 | 3.75 |

1988 Summer Olympics, Seoul A192

1988, June 10
1140	A192	40c Gymnastic rings, vert.	.30	.30
1141	A192	60c Weight lifting, vert.	.45	.45
1142	A192	$1 Water polo	.75	.75
1143	A192	$3 Boxing	2.25	2.25
		Nos. 1140-1143 (4)	3.75	3.75

Souvenir Sheet
| 1144 | A192 | $5 Torch-bearer, vert. | 3.75 | 3.75 |

Butterflies A193

1988-90　Litho.　Perf. 14
1145	A193	1c Monarch	.15	.15
1146	A193	2c Jamaican clearwing	.15	.15
1147	A193	3c Yellow-barred ringlet	.15	.15
1148	A193	5c Cracker	.15	.15
1149	A193	10c Jamaican mestra	.15	.15
1150	A193	15c Mimic	.15	.15
1151	A193	20c Silver spot	.15	.15
1152	A193	25c Zebra	.20	.20
1153	A193	30c Fiery sulphur	.20	.20
1154	A193	40c Androgeus swallowtail	.30	.30
1155	A193	45c Giant brimstone	.35	.35
1156	A193	50c Orbed sulphur	.35	.35
1157	A193	60c Blue-backed skipper	.45	.45
1158	A193	$1 Common white skipper	.75	.75
1159	A193	$2 Baracoa skipper	1.50	1.50
1160	A193	$2.50 Mangrove skipper	1.90	1.90
1161	A193	$5 Silver king	3.75	3.75
1161A	A193	$10 Pygmy skipper	7.50	7.50
1162	A193	Parides lycimenes	15.00	15.00
		Nos. 1145-1162 (19)	33.30	33.30

Issued: $20, Feb. 19, 1990; others, Aug. 29. This is an expanding set. Numbers will change if necessary.

John F. Kennedy A194

1988, Nov. 22　Litho.　Perf. 14
1162A	A194	1c like 30c	.15	.15
1162B	A194	2c like $4	.15	.15
1162C	A194	3c like $1	.15	.15
1162D	A194	4c like 60c	.15	.15
1163	A194	30c First family	.20	.20
1164	A194	60c Motorcade, Mexico	.45	.45
1165	A194	$1 Funeral procession	.75	.75
1166	A194	$4 Aboard PT109	3.00	3.00
		Nos. 1162A-1166 (8)	5.00	5.00

Souvenir Sheet
| 1167 | A194 | $5 Taking Oath of Office | 3.75 | 3.75 |

Miniature Sheet

Christmas, Mickey Mouse 60th Anniv. — A195

Walt Disney characters: No. 1168a, Morty and Ferdie. No. 1168b, Goofy. No. 1168c, Chip-n-Dale. No. 1168d, Huey and Dewey. No. 1168e, Minnie Mouse. No. 1168f, Pluto. No. 1168g, Mickey Mouse. No. 1168h, Donald Duck and Louie. No. 1169, Goofy driving Mickey and Minnie in a horse-drawn carriage. No. 1170, Characters on roller skates, caroling.

ANTIGUA

1988, Dec. 1   *Perf. 13½x14, 14x13½*

1168	A195	Sheet of 8	6.00	6.00
a.-h.		$1 any single	.75	.75

Souvenir Sheets

1169	A195	$7 multicolored	5.25	5.25
1170	A195	$7 multi, horiz.	5.25	5.25

1988, Dec. 1   *Litho.*   *Perf. 14*

1171	A195	10c like No. 1168e	.15	.15
1172	A195	25c like No. 1168f	.20	.20
1173	A195	30c like No. 1168g	.25	.25
1174	A195	70c like No. 1168h	.50	.50
		Nos. 1171-1174 (4)	1.10	1.10

Arawak Indian Whip Dance — A196

UPAE and discovery of America emblems and: a, Five adults. b, Eight adults. c, Seven adults. d, Three adults, three children.

1989, May 16   *Litho.*   *Perf. 14*

1175		Strip of 4	4.50	4.50
a.-d.	A196	$1.50 any single	1.10	1.10

Souvenir Sheet

1176	A196	$6 Arawak chief	4.50	4.50

Discovery of America 500th anniv. (in 1992), pre-Columbian societies and customs.

Jet Flight, 50th Anniv. A197

Various jet aircraft.

1989, May 29   *Litho.*   *Perf. 14x13½*

1177	A197	10c DeHavilland Comet 4	.15	.15
1178	A197	30c Messerschmitt Me262	.20	.20
1179	A197	40c Boeing 707	.30	.30
1180	A197	60c Canadair F-86 Sabre	.45	.45
1181	A197	$1 Lockheed F-104 Starfighter	.75	.75
1182	A197	$2 McDonnell Douglas DC-10	1.50	1.50
1183	A197	$3 Boeing 747	2.25	2.25
1184	A197	$4 McDonnell F-4 Phantom	3.00	3.00
		Nos. 1177-1184 (8)	8.60	8.60

Souvenir Sheets

1185	A197	$7 Grumman F-14 Tomcat	5.25	5.25
1186	A197	$7 Concorde	5.25	5.25

Caribbean Cruise Ships A198

1989, June 20   *Litho.*   *Perf. 14*

1187	A198	25c TSS *Festivale*	.20	.20
1188	A198	45c M.S. *Southward*	.30	.30
1189	A198	50c M.S. *Sagafjord*	.40	.40
1190	A198	60c MTS *Daphne*	.45	.45
1191	A198	75c M.V. *Cunard Countess*	.55	.55
1192	A198	90c M.S. *Song of America*	.70	.70
1193	A198	$3 M.S. *Island Princess*	2.25	2.25
1194	A198	$4 S.S. *Galileo*	3.00	3.00
		Nos. 1187-1194 (8)	7.85	7.85

Souvenir Sheets

1195	A198	$6 S.S. *Norway*	4.50	4.50
1196	A198	$6 S.S. *Oceanic*	4.50	4.50

Paintings by Hiroshige — A199

Designs: 25c, *Fish Swimming by Duck Half submerged in Stream*. 45c, *Crane and Wave*. 50c, *Sparrows and Morning Glories*. 60c, *Crested Blackbird and Flowering Cherry*. $1, *Great Knot Sitting among Water Grass*. $2, *Goose on a Bank of Water*. $3, *Black Paradise Flycatcher and Blossoms*. $4, *Sleepy Owl Perched on a Pine Branch*. No. 1205, *Bullfinch Flying Near a Clematis Branch*. No. 1206, *Titmouse on a Cherry Branch*.

1989, July 3   *Perf. 14x13½*

1197	A199	25c multicolored	.20	.20
1198	A199	45c multicolored	.35	.35
1199	A199	50c multicolored	.40	.40
1200	A199	60c multicolored	.45	.45
1201	A199	$1 multicolored	.75	.75
1202	A199	$2 multicolored	1.50	1.50
1203	A199	$3 multicolored	2.25	2.25
1204	A199	$4 multicolored	3.00	3.00
		Nos. 1197-1204 (8)	8.90	8.90

Souvenir Sheets

1205	A199	$5 multicolored	3.75	3.75
1206	A199	$5 multicolored	3.75	3.75

Hirohito (1901-1989) and enthronement of Akihito as emperor of Japan.

PHILEXFRANCE '89 — A200

Walt Disney characters, French landmarks: 1c, Helicopter over the Seine. 2c, Arc de Triomphe. 3c, Painting Notre Dame Cathedral. 4c, Entrance to the Metro. 5c, Fashion show. 10c, Follies. No. 1213, Shopping stalls on the Seine. $6, Sidewalk cafe, Left Bank. No. 1215, Hot air balloon *Ear Force One*. No. 1216, Dining.

1989, July 7   *Perf. 14x13½*

1207	A200	1c multicolored	.15	.15
1208	A200	2c multicolored	.15	.15
1209	A200	3c multicolored	.15	.15
1210	A200	4c multicolored	.15	.15
1211	A200	5c multicolored	.15	.15
1212	A200	10c multicolored	.15	.15
1213	A200	$5 multicolored	3.75	3.75
1214	A200	$6 multicolored	4.50	4.50
		Nos. 1207-1214 (8)	9.15	9.15

Souvenir Sheets

1215	A200	$5 multicolored	3.75	3.75
1216	A200	$5 multicolored	3.75	3.75

1990 World Cup Soccer Championships, Italy — A201

Natl. flag, various actions of a defending goalie.

1989, Aug. 21   *Perf. 14*

1217	A201	15c multicolored	.15	.15
1218	A201	25c multicolored	.20	.20
1219	A201	$1 multicolored	.75	.75
1220	A201	$4 multicolored	3.00	3.00
		Nos. 1217-1220 (4)	4.10	4.10

Souvenir Sheets

1221	A201	$5 2 players, horiz.	3.75	3.75
1222	A201	$5 3 players, horiz.	3.75	3.75

For overprints see Nos. 1344-1349.

Mushrooms A202

1989, Oct. 12   *Litho.*   *Perf. 14*

1223	A202	10c Lilac fairy helmet	.15	.15
1224	A202	25c Rough psathyrella, vert.	.20	.20
1225	A202	50c Golden tops	.40	.40
1226	A202	60c Blue cap, vert.	.45	.45
1227	A202	75c Brown cap, vert.	.55	.55
1228	A202	$1 Green gill, vert.	.75	.75
1229	A202	$3 Red pinwheel	2.25	2.25
1230	A202	$4 Red chanterelle	3.00	3.00
		Nos. 1223-1230 (8)	7.75	7.75

Souvenir Sheets

1231	A202	$6 Slender stalk	4.50	4.50
1232	A202	$6 Paddy straw mushroom	4.50	4.50

Nos. 1224, 1226-1228, 1231 vert.

Wildlife A203

1989, Oct. 19   *Litho.*   *Perf. 14*

1233	A203	25c Hutia	.20	.20
1234	A203	45c Caribbean monk seal	.35	.35
1235	A203	60c Mustache bat, vert.	.45	.45
1236	A203	$4 Manatee, vert.	3.00	3.00
		Nos. 1233-1236 (4)	4.00	4.00

Souvenir Sheet

1237	A203	$5 West Indies giant rice rat	3.75	3.75

American Philatelic Soc. Emblem, Stamps on Stamps and Walt Disney Characters Promoting Philately A204

Designs: 1c, Israel #150, printing press. 2c, Italy #1238, first day cancel. 3c, US #143L4, Pony Express recruits. 4c, Denmark #566, early radio broadcast. 5c, German Democratic Republic #702, television. 10c, Great Britain #1, stamp collector. $4, Japan #1414, integrated circuits. $6, Germany #B667, boom box. No. 1246, US #1355, C3a, and Jenny biplane over Disneyland, horiz. No. 1247, US #940, 1421 and stamps for the wounded.

1989, Nov. 2   *Perf. 13½x14, 14x13½*

1238	A204	1c multicolored	.15	.15
1239	A204	2c multicolored	.15	.15
1240	A204	3c multicolored	.15	.15
1241	A204	4c multicolored	.15	.15
1242	A204	5c multicolored	.15	.15
1243	A204	10c multicolored	.15	.15
1244	A204	$4 multicolored	3.00	3.00
1245	A204	$6 multicolored	4.50	4.50
		Nos. 1238-1245 (8)	8.40	8.40

Souvenir Sheets

1246	A204	$5 multicolored	3.75	3.75
1247	A204	$5 multicolored	3.75	3.75

Locomotives and Walt Disney Characters — A205

Perf. 14x13½, 13½x14

1989, Nov. 17

1248	A205	25c John Bull, 1831	.20	.20
1249	A205	45c Atlantic, 1832	.35	.35
1250	A205	50c William Crook's, 1861	.40	.40
1251	A205	60c Minnetonka, 1869	.45	.45
1252	A205	$1 Thatcher Perkins, 1863	.75	.75
1253	A205	$2 Pioneer, 1848	1.50	1.50
1254	A205	$3 Peppersass, 1869	2.25	2.25
1255	A205	$4 Gimbels Flyer	3.00	3.00
		Nos. 1248-1255 (8)	8.90	8.90

Souvenir Sheets

1256	A205	$6 #6100 Class S-1 & 1835 Thomas Jefferson	4.50	4.50
1257	A205	$6 Jupiter & #119	4.50	4.50

New York World's Fair, 50th anniv., and World Stamp Expo '89, Washington, DC.

1st Moon Landing, 20th Anniv. A206

1989, Nov. 24   *Litho.*   *Perf. 14*

1258	A206	10c Apollo 11 liftoff	.15	.15
1259	A206	45c Aldrin walking on Moon	.35	.35
1260	A206	$1 *Eagle* ascending from Moon	.75	.75
1261	A206	$4 Recovery after splashdown	3.00	3.00
		Nos. 1258-1261 (4)	4.25	4.25

Souvenir Sheet

1262	A206	$5 Armstrong	3.75	3.75

Nos. 1258-1259 and 1262, vert.

Souvenir Sheet

Smithsonian Institution, Washington, DC — A207

1989, Nov. 17   *Litho.*   *Perf. 14*

1263	A207	$4 multicolored	3.00	3.00

World Stamp Expo '89.

Christmas — A208

Religious paintings: 10c, *The Small Cowper Madonna*. 25c, *Madonna of the Goldfinch*. 30c, *The Alba Madonna*. 50c, *Bologna Altarpiece* (attendant). 60c, *Bologna Altarpiece* (heralding angel). 70c, *Bologna Altarpiece* (archangel). $4, *Bologna Altarpiece* (saint holding ledger). No. 1271, *Madonna of Foligno*. No. 1272, *The Marriage of the Virgin*. No. 1273, *Bologna Altarpiece* (Madonna and Child).
Bologna Altarpiece by Giotto. Other paintings by Raphael.

1989, Dec. 11   *Litho.*   *Perf. 14*

1264	A208	10c multicolored	.15	.15
1265	A208	25c multicolored	.20	.20
1266	A208	30c multicolored	.25	.25
1267	A208	50c multicolored	.35	.35
1268	A208	60c multicolored	.45	.45
1269	A208	70c multicolored	.50	.50
1270	A208	$4 multicolored	3.00	3.00
1271	A208	$5 multicolored	3.75	3.75
		Nos. 1264-1271 (8)	8.65	8.65

Souvenir Sheets

1272	A208	$5 multicolored	3.75	3.75
1273	A208	$5 multicolored	3.75	3.75

ANTIGUA

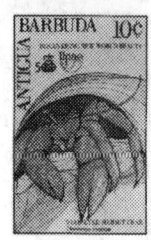

America Issue — A210

UPAE, discovery of America 500th anniv. emblems and marine life: 10c, Star-eyed hermit crab. 20c, Spiny lobster. 25c, Magnificent banded fanworm. 45c, Cannonball jellyfish. 60c, Red-spiny sea star. $2, Peppermint shrimp. $3, Coral crab. $4, Branching fire coral. No. 1283, Common sea fan. No. 1284, Portuguese man-of-war.

1990, Mar. 26	**Litho.**		**Perf. 14**	
1275	A210	10c multicolored	.15	.15
1276	A210	20c multicolored	.15	.15
1277	A210	25c multicolored	.20	.20
1278	A210	45c multicolored	.35	.35
1279	A210	60c multicolored	.45	.45
1280	A210	$2 multicolored	1.50	1.50
1281	A210	$3 multicolored	2.25	2.25
1282	A210	$4 multicolored	3.00	3.00
		Nos. 1275-1282 (8)	8.05	8.05
		Souvenir Sheets		
1283	A210	$5 multicolored	3.75	3.75
1284	A210	$5 multicolored	3.75	3.75

1990, Apr. 17			**Perf. 14**	
1285	A211	15c Vanilla mexicana	.15	.15
1286	A211	45c Epidendrum ibaguense	.35	.35
1287	A211	50c Epidendrum secundum	.40	.40
1288	A211	60c Maxillaria conferta	.45	.45
1289	A211	$1 Oncidium altissimum	.75	.75
1290	A211	$2 Spiranthes lanceolata	1.50	1.50
1291	A211	$3 Tonopsis utriculariodes	2.25	2.25
1292	A211	$5 Epidendrum nocturnum	3.75	3.75
		Nos. 1285-1292 (8)	9.60	9.60
		Souvenir Sheets		
1293	A211	$6 Octomeria graminifolia	4.50	4.50
1294	A211	$6 Rodrigueizia lanceolata	4.50	4.50

EXPO '90, Osaka.

Fish A212

1990, May 21			**Perf. 14**	
1295	A212	10c Flamefish	.15	.15
1296	A212	15c Coney	.15	.15
1297	A212	50c Squirrelfish	.40	.40
1298	A212	60c Sergeant major	.45	.45
1299	A212	$1 Yellowtail snapper	.75	.75
1300	A212	$2 Rock beauty	1.50	1.50
1301	A212	$3 Spanish hogfish	2.25	2.25
1302	A212	$4 Striped parrotfish	3.00	3.00
		Nos. 1295-1302 (8)	8.65	8.65
		Souvenir sheets		
1303	A212	$5 Blackbar soldierfish	3.75	3.75
1304	A212	$5 Foureye butterflyfish	3.75	3.75

Victoria and Elizabeth II — A213

1990, May 3	**Litho.**		**Perf. 15x14**	
1305	A213	45c green	.35	.35
1306	A213	60c bright rose	.45	.45
1307	A213	$5 bright ultra	3.75	3.75
		Nos. 1305-1307 (3)	4.55	4.55
		Souvenir Sheet		
1308	A213	$6 black	4.50	4.50

Penny Black, 150th anniv.

Royal Mail Transport A214

Designs: 50c, Steam packet *Britannia*, 1840. 75c, Railway mail car, 1892. $4, *Centaurus* seaplane, 1938. $6, Subway, 1927.

1990, May 3			**Perf. 13½**	
1309	A214	50c red & deep green	.40	.40
1310	A214	75c red & vio brn	.60	.60
1311	A214	$4 red & brt ultra	3.00	3.00
		Nos. 1309-1311 (3)	4.00	4.00
		Souvenir Sheet		
1312	A214	$6 red & black	4.50	4.50

Stamp World London '90.

Miniature Sheet

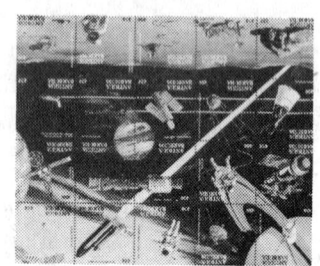

Space Achievements — A215

Designs: a, *Voyager 2* passing Saturn. b, *Pioneer 11* photographing Saturn. c, Manned maneuvering unit. d, *Columbia* space shuttle. e, Splashdown of Apollo 10 command module. f, *Skylab*. g, Ed White space walking, Gemini 4 mission. h, Apollo module, Apollo-Soyuz mission. i, Soyuz module, Apollo-Soyuz mission. j, *Mariner 1* passing Venus. k, Gemini 4 module. l, *Sputnik*. m, Hubble Space Telescope. n, X-15 rocket plane. o, Bell X-1 breaking sound barrier. p, Astronaut, Apollo 17 mission. q, American lunar rover. r, Lunar module, Apollo 14 mission. s, First men on the Moon, Apollo 11 mission. t, Lunokhod, Soviet lunar rover.

1990, June 11	**Litho.**		**Perf. 14**	
1313	A215	Sheet of 20	6.75	6.75
	a.-t.	45c any single	.30	.30

Mickey Production Studios — A216

Walt Disney characters in Hollywood: 45c, Minnie Mouse reading script. 50c, Director Mickey Mouse, take 1 of Minnie. 60c, Make-up artist Daisy Duck. $1, Clarabelle as Cleopatra. $2, Mickey, Goofy, Donald Duck. $3, Goofy destroying set. $4, Mickey, Donald editing film. No. 1322, Mickey directs surfing film. No. 1323, Minnie, Daisy, Clarabelle in musical.

1990, Sept. 3	**Litho.**		**Perf. 14x13½**	
1314	A216	25c shown	.20	.20
1315	A216	45c multicolored	.35	.35
1316	A216	50c multicolored	.40	.40
1317	A216	60c multicolored	.45	.45
1318	A216	$1 multicolored	.75	.75
1319	A216	$2 multicolored	1.50	1.50
1320	A216	$3 multicolored	2.25	2.25
1321	A216	$4 multicolored	3.00	3.00
		Nos. 1314-1321 (8)	8.90	8.90
		Souvenir Sheets		
1322	A216	$5 multicolored	3.75	3.75
1323	A216	$5 multicolored	3.75	3.75

A217 **A218**

1990, Aug. 27	**Litho.**		**Perf. 14**	
1324	A217	15c multicolored	.15	.15
1325	A217	35c multi, diff.	.30	.30
1326	A217	75c multi, diff.	.55	.55
1327	A217	$3 multi, diff.	2.25	2.25
		Nos. 1324-1327 (4)	3.25	3.25
		Souvenir Sheet		
1328	A217	$6 multi, diff.	4.50	4.50

Queen Mother, 90th birthday.

1990, Oct. 1	**Litho.**		**Perf. 14**	
1329	A218	50c 20-Kilometer Walk	.35	.35
1330	A218	75c Triple jump	.55	.55
1331	A218	$1 10,000 meter run	.75	.75
1332	A218	$5 Javelin	3.75	3.75
		Nos. 1329-1332 (4)	5.40	5.40
		Souvenir Sheet		
1333	A218	$6 Opening ceremony, Los Angeles, 1984	4.50	4.50

1992 Summer Olympics, Barcelona.

Intl. Literacy Year A219

Walt Disney characters in scenes from books by Charles Dickens: 15c, Huey and Dewey, Christmas Stories. 45c, Donald Duck, Bleak House. 50c, Dewey, Bad Pete, Oliver Twist. 60c, Daisy Duck, Old Curiosity Shop. $1, Little Nell. $2, Scrooge McDuck, Pickwick Papers. $3, Mickey and Minnie Mouse, Dombey and Son. $5, Minnie, Our Mutual Friend. No. 1342, Mickey and friends, David Copperfield. No. 1343, Pinocchio, Oliver Twist.

1990, Oct. 15	**Litho.**		**Perf. 14**	
1334	A219	15c multicolored	.15	.15
1335	A219	45c multicolored	.35	.35
1336	A219	50c multicolored	.40	.40
1337	A219	60c multicolored	.45	.45
1338	A219	$1 multicolored	.75	.75
1339	A219	$2 multicolored	1.50	1.50
1340	A219	$3 multicolored	2.25	2.25
1341	A219	$5 multicolored	3.75	3.75
		Nos. 1334-1341 (8)	9.60	9.60
		Souvenir Sheets		
1342	A219	$6 multicolored	4.50	4.50
1343	A219	$6 multicolored	4.50	4.50

Winners Nos. 1217-1222 Overprinted
West Germany 1
Argentina 0

1990, Nov. 11				
1344	A201	15c multicolored	.15	.15
1345	A201	25c multicolored	.20	.20
1346	A201	$1 multicolored	.75	.75
1347	A201	$4 multicolored	3.00	3.00
		Nos. 1344-1347 (4)	4.10	4.10
		Souvenir Sheets		
1348	A201	$5 on #1221	3.75	3.75
1349	A201	$5 on #1222	3.75	3.75

Overprint on Nos. 1348-1349 is 32x13mm.

Birds — A220

1990, Nov. 19				
1350	A220	10c Pearly-eyed thrasher	.15	.15
1351	A220	25c Purple-throated carib	.20	.20
1352	A220	50c Common yellow-throat	.35	.35
1353	A220	60c American kestrel	.45	.45
1354	A220	$1 Yellow-bellied sapsucker	.75	.75
1355	A220	$2 Purple gallinule	1.50	1.50
1356	A220	$3 Yellow-crowned night heron	2.25	2.25
1357	A220	$4 Blue-hooded euphonia	3.00	3.00
		Nos. 1350-1357 (8)	8.65	8.65
		Souvenir Sheets		
1358	A220	$6 Brown pelican	4.50	4.50
1359	A220	$6 Frigate bird	4.50	4.50

Christmas — A221

Paintings: 25c, Madonna and Child with Saints by del Piombo. 30c, Virgin and Child with Angels by Grunewald, vert. 40c, Holy Family and a Shepherd by Titian. 60c, Virgin and Child by Fra Filippo Lippi, vert. $1, Jesus, St. John and Two Angels by Rubens. $2, Adoration of the Shepherds by Catena. $4, Adoration of the Magi by Giorgione. $5, Virgin and Child Adored by a Warrior by Catena. No. 1368, Allegory of the Blessings of Jacob by Rubens, vert. No. 1369, Adoration of the Magi by Fra Angelico, vert.

		Perf. 14x13½, 13½x14		
1990, Dec. 10			**Litho.**	
1360	A221	25c multicolored	.20	.20
1361	A221	30c multicolored	.25	.25
1362	A221	40c multicolored	.30	.30
1363	A221	60c multicolored	.45	.45
1364	A221	$1 multicolored	.75	.75
1365	A221	$2 multicolored	1.50	1.50
1366	A221	$4 multicolored	3.00	3.00
1367	A221	$5 multicolored	3.75	3.75
		Nos. 1360-1367 (8)	10.20	10.20
		Souvenir Sheets		
1368	A221	$6 multicolored	4.50	4.50
1369	A221	$6 multicolored	4.50	4.50

Peter Paul Rubens (1577-1640), Painter — A222

Entire paintings or different details from: 25c, Rape of the Daughters of Leucippus. 45c, $2, $4, Bacchanal. 50c, $1, $3, Rape of the Sabine Women. 60c, Battle of the Amazons. No. 1378, Rape of Hippodameia. No. 1379, Battle of the Amazons.

1991, Jan. 21	**Litho.**		**Perf. 14**	
1370	A222	25c multicolored	.20	.20
1371	A222	45c multicolored	.35	.35
1372	A222	50c multicolored	.40	.40
1373	A222	60c multicolored	.45	.45
1374	A222	$1 multicolored	.75	.75
1375	A222	$2 multicolored	1.50	1.50
1376	A222	$3 multicolored	2.25	2.25
1377	A222	$4 multicolored	3.00	3.00
		Nos. 1370-1377 (8)	8.90	8.90
		Souvenir Sheets		
1378	A222	$6 multicolored	4.50	4.50
1379	A222	$6 multicolored	4.50	4.50

World War II Milestones A223

Designs: 10c, US troops enter Germany, Sept. 11, 1944. 15c, All axis forces surrender in North Africa, May 12, 1943. 25c, US troops invade Kwajalein, Jan. 31, 1944. 45c, Roosevelt and Churchill meet in Casablanca, Jan. 14, 1943. 50c,

ANTIGUA

Marshal Badoglio signs agreement with allies, Sept. 1, 1943. $1, Mountbatten appointed Supreme Allied Commander, Southeast Asia Command, Nov. 22, 1940. $2, Major Greek tactical victory, Koritza, Oct. 25, 1943. $4, Britain and USSR sign mutual assistance pact, July 12, 1941. $5, Operation Torch, Nov. 8, 1942. No. 1389, Japanese attack on Pearl Harbor, Dec. 7, 1941. No. 1390, American bombing attack on Schweinfurt, Oct. 14, 1943.

1991, Mar. 11   Litho.   Perf. 14

1380	A223	10c multicolored	.15	.15
1381	A223	15c multicolored	.15	.15
1382	A223	25c multicolored	.20	.20
1383	A223	45c multicolored	.35	.35
1384	A223	50c multicolored	.40	.40
1385	A223	$1 multicolored	.75	.75
1386	A223	$2 multicolored	1.50	1.50
1387	A223	$4 multicolored	3.00	3.00
1388	A223	$5 multicolored	3.75	3.75
		Nos. 1380-1388 (9)	10.25	10.25

Souvenir Sheets

| 1389 | A223 | $6 multicolored | 4.50 | 4.50 |
| 1390 | A223 | $6 multicolored | 4.50 | 4.50 |

Cog Railways of the World — A224

Designs: 25c, Prince Regent, Middleton Colliery, 1812. 30c, Snowdon Mountain Railway, Wales. 40c, 1st Railcar at Hell Gate, Manitou and Pike's Peak Railway. 60c, PNKA Rack Railway, Amberawa, Java. $1, Green Mountain Railway, Mt. Desert Island, Maine, 1883. $2, Cog locomotive, Pike's Peak, 1891. $4, Vitznau-Rigi Cog Railway, Lake Lucerne. $5, Leopoldina Railway, Brazil. No. 1399, Electric Cog Donkey Engines, Panama Canal. No. 1400, Gornergratbahn, 1st electric cog railway in Switzerland, vert.

1991, Mar. 18   Litho.   Perf. 14

1391	A224	25c multicolored	.20	.20
1392	A224	30c multicolored	.25	.25
1393	A224	40c multicolored	.30	.30
1394	A224	60c multicolored	.45	.45
1395	A224	$1 multicolored	.75	.75
1396	A224	$2 multicolored	1.50	1.50
1397	A224	$4 multicolored	3.00	3.00
1398	A224	$5 multicolored	3.75	3.75
		Nos. 1391-1398 (8)	10.20	10.20

Souvenir Sheets

| 1399 | A224 | $6 multicolored | 4.50 | 4.50 |
| 1400 | A224 | $6 multicolored | 4.50 | 4.50 |

Butterflies — A225

1991, Apr. 15   Litho.   Perf. 14

1401	A225	10c Zebra	.15	.15
1402	A225	35c Southern daggertail	.25	.25
1403	A225	50c Red anartia	.40	.40
1404	A225	75c Malachite	.55	.55
1405	A225	$1 Polydamas swallowtail	.75	.75
1406	A225	$2 Orion	1.50	1.50
1407	A225	$4 Mimic	3.00	3.00
1408	A225	$5 Cracker	3.75	3.75
		Nos. 1401-1408 (8)	10.35	10.35

Souvenir Sheets
Caterpillars

| 1409 | A225 | $6 Monarch, vert. | 4.50 | 4.50 |
| 1410 | A225 | $6 Painted lady, vert. | 4.50 | 4.50 |

Voyages of Discovery — A226

Designs: 10c, Hanno, Phoenicia, c. 450 B.C. 15c, Pytheas, Greece, 325 B.C. 45c, Eric the Red, Viking, A.D. 985. 60c, Leif Erikson, Viking, A.D. 1000. $1, Scylax, Greece, A.D. 518. $2, Marco Polo, A.D. 1259. $4, Queen Hatsheput, Egypt, 1493 B.C. $5, St. Brendan, Ireland, 500 A.D. No. 1419, Columbus, bareheaded. No. 1420, Columbus, wearing hat.

1991, Apr. 22

1411	A226	10c multicolored	.15	.15
1412	A226	15c multicolored	.15	.15
1413	A226	45c multicolored	.35	.35
1414	A226	60c multicolored	.45	.45
1415	A226	$1 multicolored	.75	.75
1416	A226	$2 multicolored	1.50	1.50
1417	A226	$4 multicolored	3.00	3.00
1418	A226	$5 multicolored	3.75	3.75
		Nos. 1411-1418 (8)	10.10	10.10

Souvenir Sheets

| 1419 | A226 | $6 multicolored | 4.50 | 4.50 |
| 1420 | A226 | $6 multicolored | 4.50 | 4.50 |

Discovery of America, 500th anniv. (in 1992).

Paintings by Vincent Van Gogh — A227

Designs: 5c, Portrait of Camille Roulin. 10c, Portrait of Armand Roulin. 15c, Young Peasant Woman with Straw Hat Sitting in the Wheat. 25c, Portrait of Adeline Ravoux. 30c, The Schoolboy (Camille Roulin). 40c, Portrait of Doctor Gachet. 50c, Portrait of a Man. 75c, Two Children. $2, Portrait of Postman Joseph Roulin. $3, The Seated Zouave. $4, L'arlesienne: Madame Ginoux with Books. No. 1432, Self Portrait, November/December 1888. No. 1433, Flowering Garden. No. 1434, Farmhouse in Provence. $6, The Bridge at Trinquetaille.

1991, May 13   Perf. 13½

1421	A227	5c multicolored	.15	.15
1422	A227	10c multicolored	.15	.15
1423	A227	15c multicolored	.15	.15
1424	A227	25c multicolored	.20	.20
1425	A227	30c multicolored	.25	.25
1426	A227	40c multicolored	.30	.30
1427	A227	50c multicolored	.35	.35
1428	A227	75c multicolored	.55	.55
1429	A227	$2 multicolored	1.50	1.50
1430	A227	$3 multicolored	2.25	2.25
1431	A227	$4 multicolored	3.00	3.00
1432	A227	$5 multicolored	3.75	3.75
		Nos. 1421-1432 (12)	12.60	12.60

Size: 102x76mm
Imperf

1433	A227	$5 multicolored	3.75	3.75
1434	A227	$5 multicolored	3.75	3.75
1435	A227	$6 multicolored	4.50	4.50

Phila Nippon '91 — A228

Walt Disney characters demonstrating Japanese martial arts: 10c, Mickey as champion sumo wrestler, vert. 15c, Goofy using tonfa. 45c, Ninja Donald in full field dress. 60c, Mickey using weapon in kung fu, vert. $1, Goofy tries kendo, vert. $2, Mickey, Donald demonstrating special technique of aikido. $4, Mickey flips Donald with judo throw. $5, Mickey demonstrates yabusame (target shooting from running horse), vert. No. 1444, Mickey using karate. No. 1445, Mickey demonstrating tamashiwara (powerbreaking), vert.

Perf. 13½x14, 14x13½
1991, June 29   Litho.

1436	A228	10c multicolored	.15	.15
1437	A228	15c multicolored	.15	.15
1438	A228	45c multicolored	.35	.35
1439	A228	60c multicolored	.45	.45
1440	A228	$1 multicolored	.75	.75
1441	A228	$2 multicolored	1.50	1.50
1442	A228	$4 multicolored	3.00	3.00
1443	A228	$5 multicolored	3.75	3.75
		Nos. 1436-1443 (8)	10.10	10.10

Souvenir Sheets

| 1444 | A228 | $6 multicolored | 4.50 | 4.50 |
| 1445 | A228 | $6 multicolored | 4.50 | 4.50 |

Royal Family Birthday, Anniversary
Common Design Type

1991, July 8   Litho.   Perf. 14

1446	CD347	10c multicolored	.15	.15
1447	CD347	15c multicolored	.15	.15
1448	CD347	20c multicolored	.15	.15
1449	CD347	40c multicolored	.30	.30
1450	CD347	$1 multicolored	.75	.75
1451	CD347	$2 multicolored	1.50	1.50
1452	CD347	$4 multicolored	3.00	3.00
1453	CD347	$5 multicolored	3.75	3.75
		Nos. 1446-1453 (8)	9.75	9.75

Souvenir Sheets

| 1454 | CD347 | $4 Elizabeth, Philip | 3.00 | 3.00 |
| 1455 | CD347 | $4 Charles, Diana, sons | 3.00 | 3.00 |

10c, 40c, $1, $5, No. 1455, Charles and Diana, 10th wedding anniversary. Others, Queen Elizabeth II, 65th birthday.

Walt Disney Characters Playing Golf — A229

Designs: 10c, Daisy Duck teeing off. 15c, Goofy using 3-Wood. 45c, Mickey using 3-Iron. 60c, Mickey missing ball using 6-Iron. $1, Donald trying 8-Iron to get out of pond. $2, Minnie using 9-Iron. $4, Donald digging hole with sand wedge. $5, Goofy trying new approach with putter. No. 1464, Grandma Duck using pitching wedge. No. 1465, Mickey cheering Minnie as she uses her 5-Wood, horiz.

Perf. 13½x14, 14x13½
1991, Aug. 7   Litho.

1456	A229	10c multicolored	.15	.15
1457	A229	15c multicolored	.15	.15
1458	A229	45c multicolored	.35	.35
1459	A229	60c multicolored	.45	.45
1460	A229	$1 multicolored	.75	.75
1461	A229	$2 multicolored	1.50	1.50
1462	A229	$4 multicolored	3.00	3.00
1463	A229	$5 multicolored	3.75	3.75
		Nos. 1456-1463 (8)	10.10	10.10

Souvenir Sheets

| 1464 | A229 | $6 multicolored | 4.50 | 4.50 |
| 1465 | A229 | $6 multicolored | 4.50 | 4.50 |

1992 Summer Olympics, Barcelona — A230

Archie Comics, 50th anniv.: 10c, Moose receiving gold medal. 25c, Archie, Veronica, Mr. Lodge, polo match, horiz. 40c, Archie & Betty, fencing. 60c, Archie, women's volleyball. $1, Archie, tennis. $2, Archie, marathon race. $4, Archie, judging women's gymnastics, horiz. $5, Archie, Betty, Veronica, basketball. No. 1474, Archie, soccer. No. 1475, Archie, Betty, baseball, horiz.

Perf. 13½x14, 14x13½
1991, Aug. 19

1466	A230	10c multicolored	.15	.15
1467	A230	25c multicolored	.20	.20
1468	A230	40c multicolored	.30	.30
1469	A230	60c multicolored	.45	.45
1470	A230	$1 multicolored	.75	.75
1471	A230	$2 multicolored	1.50	1.50
1472	A230	$4 multicolored	3.00	3.00
1473	A230	$5 multicolored	3.75	3.75
		Nos. 1466-1473 (8)	10.10	10.10

Souvenir Sheets

| 1474 | A230 | $6 multicolored | 4.50 | 4.50 |
| 1475 | A230 | $6 multicolored | 4.50 | 4.50 |

Charles de Gaulle, Birth Cent. — A231

Charles de Gaulle: 10c, and Pres. Kennedy, families, 1961. 15c, and Pres. Roosevelt, 1945, vert. 45c, and Chancellor Adenauer, 1962, vert. 60c, Liberation of Paris, 1944, vert. $1, Crossing the Rhine, 1945. $2, In Algiers, 1944. $4, and Pres. Eisenhower, 1960. $5, Returning from Germany, 1968, vert. No. 1484, and Churchill at Casablanca, 1943. No. 1485, and Citizens.

1991, Sept. 10   Litho.   Perf. 14

1476	A231	10c multicolored	.15	.15
1477	A231	15c multicolored	.15	.15
1478	A231	35c multicolored	.35	.35
1479	A231	60c multicolored	.45	.45
1480	A231	$1 multicolored	.75	.75
1481	A231	$2 multicolored	1.50	1.50
1482	A231	$4 multicolored	3.00	3.00
1483	A231	$5 multicolored	3.75	3.75
		Nos. 1476-1483 (8)	10.10	10.10

Souvenir Sheets

| 1484 | A231 | $6 multicolored | 4.50 | 4.50 |
| 1485 | A231 | $6 multicolored | 4.50 | 4.50 |

Independence, 10th Anniv. — A232

Designs: 10c, Island maps, government building. $6, Old P. O., St. Johns, #1 & #635.

1991, Oct. 28

| 1486 | A232 | 10c multicolored | .15 | .15 |

Souvenir Sheet

| 1487 | A232 | $6 multicolored | 4.50 | 4.50 |

No. 1487 contains one 50x38mm stamp.

Miniature Sheet

Attack on Pearl Harbor, 50th Anniv. A233

Designs: No. 1488a, Bow of Nimitz class carrier, Ticonderoga class cruiser. b, Tourist boat to Arizona Memorial. c, USS Arizona Memorial. d, Aircraft salute to missing men. e, White tern. f, Japanese Kate torpedo bombers. g, Japanese Zero fighters. h, Battleship row in flames. i, USS Nevada breaking out. j, Zeros returning to carriers.

1991, Dec. 9   Perf. 14½x15

| 1488 | A233 | $1 Sheet of 10, #a.-j. | 7.50 | 7.50 |

Inscription for No. 1488f incorrectly describes torpedo bombers as Zekes.

3rd Antigua Methodist Cub Scout Pack, 60th Anniv. A234

Designs: $2, Lord Robert Baden-Powell, scouts, vert. $3.50, Scouts around campfire. $5, Antigua & Barbuda flag, Jamboree emblem, vert.

1991, Dec. 9   Perf. 14

1489	A234	75c multicolored	.60	.60
1490	A234	$1.50 multicolored	1.50	1.50
1491	A234	$3.50 multicolored	2.75	2.75
		Nos. 1489-1491 (3)	4.85	4.85

Souvenir Sheet

| 1492 | A234 | $5 multicolored | 3.75 | 3.75 |

17th World Scout Jamboree, Korea.

ANTIGUA

Wolfgang Amadeus Mozart, Death Bicent. — A235

Portrait of Mozart and: $1.50, Scene from opera, Don Giovanni. $4, St. Peter's Cathedral, Salzburg.

1991, Dec. 9

| 1493 | A235 | $1.50 multicolored | 1.10 | 1.10 |
| 1494 | A235 | $4 multicolored | 3.00 | 3.00 |

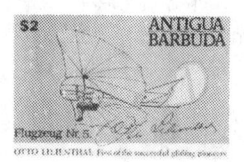

Anniversaries and Events — A236

Designs: $2, Otto Lilienthal's glider No. 5. $2.50, Locomotive cab, vert.

1991, Dec. 9   Litho.   *Perf. 14*

| 1495 | A236 | $2 multicolored | 1.50 | 1.50 |
| 1496 | A236 | $2.50 multicolored | 1.90 | 1.90 |

First glider flight, cent. (No. 1495). Trans-Siberian Railway, cent. (No. 1496). Numbers have been reserved for additional values in this set.

Brandenburg Gate, Bicent. — A237

Designs: 25c, Demonstrators in autos, German flag. $2, Statue. $3, Portions of decorative frieze.

1991, Dec. 9   Litho.   *Perf. 14*

1499	A237	25c multicolored	.20	.20
1500	A237	$2 multicolored	1.50	1.50
1501	A237	$3 multicolored	2.25	2.25
		Nos. 1499-1501 (3)	3.95	3.95

Souvenir Sheet

| 1502 | A237 | $4 multicolored | 3.00 | 3.00 |

Christmas — A238

Paintings by Fra Angelico: 10c, The Annunciation. 30c, Nativity. 40c, Adoration of the Magi. 60c, Presentation in the Temple. $1, Circumcision. $3, Flight into Egypt. $4, Massacre of the Innocents. $5, Christ Teaching in the Temple. No. 1511, Adoration of the Magi, diff. No. 1512, Adoration of the Magi (Cook Tondo).

1991, Dec. 12   *Perf. 12*

1503	A238	10c multicolored	.15	.15
1504	A238	30c multicolored	.25	.25
1505	A238	40c multicolored	.30	.30
1506	A238	60c multicolored	.45	.45
1507	A238	$1 multicolored	.75	.75
1508	A238	$3 multicolored	2.25	2.25
1509	A238	$4 multicolored	3.00	3.00
1510	A238	$5 multicolored	3.75	3.75
		Nos. 1503-1510 (8)	10.90	10.90

Souvenir Sheets

| 1511 | A238 | $6 multicolored | 4.50 | 4.50 |
| 1512 | A238 | $6 multicolored | 4.50 | 4.50 |

Queen Elizabeth II's Accession to the Throne, 40th Anniv.
Common Design Type
Queen Elizabeth II and various island scenes.

1992, Feb. 6   Litho.   *Perf. 14*

1513	CD348	10c multicolored	.15	.15
1514	CD348	30c multicolored	.20	.20
1515	CD348	$1 multicolored	.75	.75
1516	CD348	$5 multicolored	3.75	3.75
		Nos. 1513-1516 (4)	4.85	4.85

Souvenir Sheets

| 1517 | CD348 | $6 Beach | 4.50 | 4.50 |
| 1518 | CD348 | $6 Flora | 4.50 | 4.50 |

Mushrooms — A239

1992   Litho.   *Perf. 14*

1519	A239	10c Amanita caesarea	.15	.15
1520	A239	15c Collybia fusipes	.15	.15
1521	A239	30c Boletus aereus	.20	.20
1522	A239	40c Laccaria amethystina	.30	.30
1523	A239	$1 Russula virescens	.75	.75
1524	A239	$2 Tricholoma auratum	1.50	1.50
1525	A239	$4 Calocybe gambosa	3.00	3.00
1526	A239	$5 Panus tigrinus	3.75	3.75
		Nos. 1519-1526 (8)	9.80	9.80

Souvenir Sheet

| 1527 | A239 | $6 Auricularia auricula | 4.50 | 4.50 |
| 1528 | A239 | $6 Clavariadelphus truncatus | 4.50 | 4.50 |

Issued: 10c, 30c, $1, $5, #1528, May 18; others, Mar.

Disney Characters at Summer Olympics, Barcelona — A240

Designs: 10c, Mickey presenting gold medal to mermaid for swimming. 15c, Dewey and Huey watching Louie in kayak. 30c, Uncle McScrooge, Donald yachting. 50c, Donald, horse trying water polo. $1, Big Pete weight lifting. $2, Donald, Goofy fencing. $4, Mickey, Donald playing volleyball. $5, Goofy vaulting over horse. No. 1537, Mickey playing basketball, horiz. No. 1538, Minnie Mouse on uneven parallel bars, horiz. No. 1539, Mickey, Goofy, and Donald judging Minnie's floor exercise, horiz. No. 1540, Mickey running after soccer ball.

1992, Mar. 16   *Perf. 13*

1529	A240	10c multicolored	.15	.15
1530	A240	15c multicolored	.15	.15
1531	A240	30c multicolored	.20	.20
1532	A240	50c multicolored	.40	.40
1533	A240	$1 multicolored	.75	.75
1534	A240	$2 multicolored	1.50	1.50
1535	A240	$4 multicolored	3.00	3.00
1536	A240	$5 multicolored	3.75	3.75
		Nos. 1529-1536 (8)	9.90	9.90

Souvenir Sheets

| 1537-1540 | A240 | $6 each | 4.50 | 4.50 |

Dinosaurs — A241

1992, Apr. 6   *Perf. 14*

1541	A241	10c Pteranodon	.15	.15
1542	A241	15c Brachiosaurus	.15	.15
1543	A241	30c Tyrannosaurus rex	.20	.20
1544	A241	50c Parasaurolophus	.40	.40
1545	A241	$1 Deinonychus	.75	.75
1546	A241	$2 Triceratops	1.50	1.50
1547	A241	$4 Protoceratops	3.00	3.00
1548	A241	$5 Stegosaurus	3.75	3.75
		Nos. 1541-1548 (8)	9.90	9.90

Souvenir Sheets

| 1549 | A241 | $6 Apatosaurus | 4.50 | 4.50 |
| 1550 | A241 | $6 Allosaurus | 4.50 | 4.50 |

Nos. 1541-1544 are vert.

Easter — A242

Paintings: 10c, Supper at Emmaus, by Caravaggio. 15c, The Vision of St. Peter, by Francisco de Zurbaran. 30c, $1, Christ Driving the Money Changers from the Temple, by Tiepolo (detail on $1). 40c, Martyrdom of St. Bartholomew (detail), by Jusepe de Ribera. $2, Crucifixion (detail), by Albrecht Altdorfer. $4, $5, The Deposition (diff. detail), by Fra Angelico. No. 1559, Crucifixion, by Albrecht Altdorfer, vert. No. 1560, The Last Supper, by Vicente Juan Masip.

1992   *Perf. 14x13½*

1551	A242	10c multicolored	.15	.15
1552	A242	15c multicolored	.15	.15
1553	A242	30c multicolored	.20	.20
1554	A242	40c multicolored	.30	.30
1555	A242	$1 multicolored	.75	.75
1556	A242	$2 multicolored	1.50	1.50
1557	A242	$4 multicolored	3.00	3.00
1558	A242	$5 multicolored	3.75	3.75
		Nos. 1551-1558 (8)	9.80	9.80

Souvenir Sheet
Perf. 13½x14

| 1559 | A242 | $6 multicolored | 4.50 | 4.50 |
| 1560 | A242 | $6 multicolored | 4.50 | 4.50 |

Spanish Art — A243

Designs: 10c, The Miracle at the Well, by Alonso Cano. 15c, The Poet Luis de Gongora y Argote, by Velazquez. 30c, The Painter Francisco Goya, by Vincente Lopez Portana. 40c, Maria de Las Nieves Michaela Fourdiniere, by Luis Paret y Alcazar. $1, Charles III Eating before His Court, by Paret y Alcazar, horiz. $2, A Rain Shower in Granada, by Antonio Munoz Degrain, horiz. $4, Sarah Bernhardt, by Santiago Rusinol y Prats. $5, The Hermitage Garden, by Joaquin Mir Trinxet. No. 1569, Olympus: Battle with the Giants, by Francisco Bayeu y Subias. No. 1570, The Ascent of Monsieur Boucle's Montgolfier Balloon in the Gardens of Aranjuez, by Antonio Carnicero.

1992, May 11

1561	A243	10c multicolored	.15	.15
1562	A243	15c multicolored	.15	.15
1563	A243	30c multicolored	.20	.20
1564	A243	40c multicolored	.30	.30
1565	A243	$1 multicolored	.75	.75
1566	A243	$2 multicolored	1.50	1.50
1567	A243	$4 multicolored	3.00	3.00
1568	A243	$5 multicolored	3.75	3.75

Size: 120x95mm
Imperf

1569	A243	$6 multicolored	4.50	4.50
1570	A243	$6 multicolored	4.50	4.50
		Nos. 1561-1570 (10)	18.80	18.80

Granada '92.

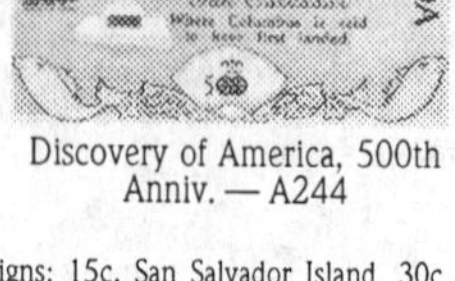

Discovery of America, 500th Anniv. — A244

Designs: 15c, San Salvador Island. 30c, Martin Alonzo Pinzon, captain of Pinta. 40c, Columbus, signature, coat of arms. $1, Pinta. $2, Nina. $4, Santa Maria. No. 1577, Sea monster. No. 1578, Map, sailing ship.

1992, May 25   Litho.   *Perf. 14*

1571	A244	15c multicolored	.15	.15
1572	A244	30c multicolored	.20	.20
1573	A244	40c multicolored	.30	.30
1574	A244	$1 multicolored	.75	.75
1575	A244	$2 multicolored	1.50	1.50
1576	A244	$4 multicolored	3.00	3.00
		Nos. 1571-1576 (6)	5.90	5.90

Souvenir Sheets

| 1577 | A244 | $6 multicolored | 4.50 | 4.50 |
| 1578 | A244 | $6 multicolored | 4.50 | 4.50 |

World Columbian Stamp Expo '92, Chicago.

Hummel Figurines — A245

Wanderers: 15c, No. 1587a, Boy sitting on rock pointing to flower in cap. 30c, No. 1587b, Girl sitting on fence. 40c, No. 1587c, Boy holding binoculars. 50c, No. 1587d, Boy carrying umbrella. $1, No. 1588a, Two boys looking up at direction marker. $2, No. 1588b, Boy carrying basket on back, walking with stick. $4, No. 1588c, Two girls, goat. $5, No. 1588d, Boy carrying walking stick.

1993, Jan. 6   Litho.   *Perf. 14*

1579	A245	15c multicolored	.15	.15
1580	A245	30c multicolored	.20	.20
1581	A245	40c multicolored	.30	.30
1582	A245	50c multicolored	.40	.40
1583	A245	$1 multicolored	.75	.75
1584	A245	$2 multicolored	1.50	1.50
1585	A245	$4 multicolored	3.00	3.00
1586	A245	$5 multicolored	3.75	3.75
		Nos. 1579-1586 (8)	10.05	10.05

Souvenir Sheet

| 1587 | A245 | $1.50 Sheet of 4, #a.-d. | 4.50 | 4.50 |
| 1588 | A245 | $1.50 Sheet of 4, #a.-d. | 4.50 | 4.50 |

Hummingbirds and Flowers — A246

Designs: 10c, Antillean crested, wild plantain. 25c, Green mango, parrot's plantain. 45c, Purple-throated carib, lobster claws. 60c, Antillean mango, coral plant. $1, Vervain, cardinal's guard. $2, Rufous breasted hermit, heliconia. $4, Blue-headed, red ginger. $5, Green-throated carib, ornamental banana. No. 1597, Bee, jungle flame. No. 1598, Western streamertails, bignonia.

1992, Aug. 10   Litho.   *Perf. 14*

1589	A246	10c multicolored	.15	.15
1590	A246	25c multicolored	.20	.20
1591	A246	45c multicolored	.35	.35
1592	A246	60c multicolored	.45	.45
1593	A246	$1 multicolored	.75	.75
1594	A246	$2 multicolored	1.50	1.50
1595	A246	$4 multicolored	3.00	3.00
1596	A246	$5 multicolored	3.75	3.75
		Nos. 1589-1596 (8)	10.15	10.15

Souvenir Sheets

| 1597 | A246 | $6 multicolored | 6.75 | 6.75 |
| 1598 | A246 | $6 multicolored | 6.75 | 6.75 |

Genoa '92.

Discovery of America, 500th Anniv. — A247

1992   Litho.   *Perf. 14½*

| 1599 | A247 | $1 Coming ashore | .75 | .75 |
| 1600 | A247 | $2 Natives, ships | 1.50 | 1.50 |

Organization of East Caribbean States.

ANTIGUA

Souvenir Sheet

Madison Square Garden, NYC — A248

1992		Litho.		Perf. 14
1601	A248	$6 multicolored	5.00	5.00

Postage Stamp Mega-Event, Jacob Javits Center, New York City.

Elvis Presley (1935-1977) A249

Various pictures of Elvis Presley.

1992			Perf. 13½x14
1602	A249	$1 Sheet of 9, #a.-i.	7.00 7.00

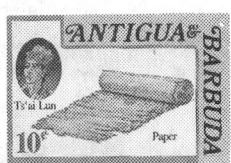

Inventors and Pioneers A250

Designs: 10c, Ts'ai Lun, paper. 25c, Igor I. Sikorsky, 4-engine airplane. 30c, Alexander Graham Bell, telephone. 40c, Johannes Gutenberg, printing press. 60c, James Watt, steam engine. $1, Anton van Leeuwenhoek, microscope. $4, Louis Braille, Braille printing. $5, Galileo, telescope. No. 1607, Phonograph. No. 1608, Steamboat.

1992, Oct. 19		Litho.		Perf. 14
1603	A250	10c multicolored	.15	.15
1604	A250	25c multicolored	.20	.20
1605	A250	30c multicolored	.25	.25
1605A	A250	40c multicolored	.40	.40
1605B	A250	60c multicolored	.45	.45
1605C	A250	$1 multicolored	.75	.75
1605D	A250	$4 multicolored	3.00	3.00
1606	A250	$5 multicolored	3.75	3.75
		Nos. 1603-1606 (8)	8.95	8.95

Souvenir Sheet

| 1607 | A250 | $6 multicolored | 4.50 | 4.50 |
| 1608 | A250 | $6 multicolored | 4.50 | 4.50 |

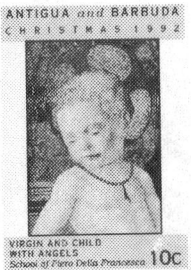

Christmas A251

Details from Paintings: 10c, Virgin and Child with Angels, by School of Piero Della Francesca. 25c, Madonna Degli Alberelli, by Giovanni Bellini. 30c, Madonna and Child with St. Anthony Abbot and St. Sigismund, by Neroccio di Landi. 40c, Madonna and the Grand Duke, by Raphael. 60c, The Nativity, by George de la Tour. $1, Holy Family, by Jacob Jordaens. $4, Madonna and Child Enthroned, by Margaritone. $5, Madonna and Child on a Curved Throne, by Byzantine artist. No. 1617, Madonna and Child, by Domenico Ghirlandaio (both names misspelled). No. 1618, The Holy Family, by Pontormo.

1992			Perf. 13½x14
1609	A251	10c multicolored	.15 .15
1610	A251	25c multicolored	.20 .20
1611	A251	30c multicolored	.25 .25
1612	A251	40c multicolored	.30 .30
1613	A251	60c multicolored	.45 .45
1614	A251	$1 multicolored	.75 .75
1615	A251	$4 multicolored	3.00 3.00
1616	A251	$5 multicolored	3.75 3.75
		Nos. 1609-1616 (8)	8.85 8.85

Souvenir Sheet

| 1617 | A251 | $6 multicolored | 4.50 4.50 |
| 1618 | A251 | $6 multicolored | 4.50 4.50 |

A252

A253

Anniversaries and Events: 10c, Cosomonauts. 40c, Graf Zeppelin, Goodyear blimp. 45c, Right Rev. Daniel C. Davis, St. John's Cathedral. 75c, Konrad Adenauer. $1, Bus Mosbacher, Weatherly. $1.50, Rain forest. No. 1625, Felis tigris. No. 1626, Flag, emblems, plant. No. 1627, Women acting on stage. $2.25, Women carrying baskets of food on their heads. $3, Lions Club emblem, club member. No. 1630, West German, NATO flags. No. 1631, China's Long March Booster Rocket. No. 1632, Dr. Hugo Eckener. No. 1633, The Hindenburg. No. 1634, Brandenburg Gate, German flag. No. 1635, Monarch butterfly. No. 1636, Hermes Shuttle, Columbus Space Station.

1992		Litho.		Perf. 14
1619	A252	10c multicolored	.15	.15
1620	A252	40c multicolored	.30	.30
1621	A253	45c multicolored	.35	.35
1622	A252	75c multicolored	.60	.60
1623	A252	$1 multicolored	.75	.75
1624	A252	$1.50 multicolored	1.10	1.10
1625	A252	$2 multicolored	1.50	1.50
1626	A253	$2 multicolored	1.50	1.50
1627	A253	$2 multicolored	1.50	1.50
1628	A252	$2.25 multicolored	1.75	1.75
1629	A252	$3 multicolored	2.25	2.25
1630	A252	$4 multicolored	3.00	3.00
1631	A252	$4 multicolored	3.00	3.00
1632	A252	$6 multicolored	4.50	4.50
		Nos. 1619-1632 (14)	22.25	22.25

Souvenir Sheets

| 1633-1636 | A252 | $6 each | 4.50 4.50 |

Intl. Space Year (#1619, 1631, 1636). Count Zeppelin, 75th anniv. of death (#1620, 1632-1633). Diocese of Northeast Caribbean and Aruba District, 150th anniv. (#1621). Konrad Adenauer, 25th anniv. of death (#1622, 1630, 1634). 1962 winner of America's Cup (#1623). Earth Summit, Rio (#1624-1625, 1635). Inter-American Institute for Cooperation on Agriculture, 50th anniv. (#1626). Cultural Development, 40th anniv. (#1627). WHO Intl. Conf. on Nutrition, Rome (#1628). Lions Club, 75th anniv. (#1629).

Issued: #1619, 1621-1623, 1626-1631, 1634, 1636, Nov.; #1624-1625, 1635, Dec. 14.

Euro Disney, Paris — A254

Disney characters: 10c, Golf course. 25c, Davy Crockett Campground. 30c, Cheyenne Hotel. 40c, Santa Fe Hotel. $1, New York Hotel. $2, In car, map showing location. $4, Pirates of the Caribbean. $5, Adventureland. No. 1645, Mickey Mouse on map with star, vert. No. 1646, Roof turret at entrance, Mickey Mouse in uniform. No. 1646A, Mickey Mouse, colored spots on poster, vert. No. 1646B, Mickey on poster, vert., diff.

1992-93		Litho.	Perf. 14x13½
1637	A254	10c multicolored	.15 .15
1638	A254	25c multicolored	.20 .20
1639	A254	30c multicolored	.25 .25
1640	A254	40c multicolored	.30 .30
1641	A254	$1 multicolored	.75 .75
1642	A254	$2 multicolored	1.50 1.50
1643	A254	$4 multicolored	3.00 3.00
1644	A254	$5 multicolored	3.75 3.75
		Nos. 1637-1644 (8)	9.90 9.90

Souvenir Sheets
Perf. 13½x14

| 1645-1646B | A254 | $6 each | 4.50 4.50 |

Issue dates: Nos. 1638-1639, 1642-1643, 1646-1646B, Feb. 22, 1993. Others, Dec. 1992.

Miniature Sheets

Louvre Museum, Bicent. A255

Details or entire paintings, by Peter Paul Rubens: No. 1647a, Destiny of Marie de' Medici. b, Birth of Marie de'Medici. c, Marie's Education. d, Destiny of Marie de'Medici, diff. e, Henry IV Receives the Portrait. f, The Meeting at Lyons. g, The Marriage. h, The Birth of Louis XIII.

No. 1648a, The Capture of Juliers. b, The Exchange of Princesses. c, The Happiness of the Regency. d, The Majority of Louis XIII. e, The Flight from Blois. f, The Treaty of Angouleme. g, The Peace of Angers. h, The Queen's Reconciliation with Her Son.

$6, Helene Fourment Au Carosse.

1993, Mar. 22		Litho.	Perf. 12
1647	A255	$1 Sheet of 8, #a.-h. + label	6.00 6.00
1648	A255	$1 Sheet of 8, #a.-h. + label	6.00 6.00

Souvenir Sheet
Perf. 14½

| 1649 | A255 | $6 multicolored | 4.50 4.50 |

No. 1649 contains one 55x88mm stamp.

Flowers — A256

1993, Mar. 15		Litho.	Perf. 14
1650	A256	15c Cardinal's guard	.15 .15
1651	A256	25c Giant granadilla	.20 .20
1652	A256	30c Spider flower	.25 .25
1653	A256	40c Gold vine	.30 .30
1654	A256	$1 Frangipani	.75 .75
1655	A256	$2 Bougainvillea	1.50 1.50
1656	A256	$4 Yellow oleander	3.00 3.00
1657	A256	$5 Spicy jatropha	3.75 3.75
		Nos. 1650-1657 (8)	9.90 9.90

Souvenir Sheets

| 1658 | A256 | $6 Bird lime tree | 4.50 4.50 |
| 1659 | A256 | $6 Fairy lily | 4.50 4.50 |

Endangered Species — A257

Designs: No. 1660a, St. Lucia parrot. b, Cahow. c, Swallow-tailed kite. d, Everglades kite. e, Imperial parrot. f, Humpback whale. g, Puerto Rican pigeon. h, St. Vincent parrot. i, Puerto Rican parrot. j, Leatherback turtle. k, American crocodile. l, Hawksbill turtle.

No. 1662, West Indian manatee.

1993, Apr. 5			
1660	A257	$1 Sheet of 12, #a.-l.	9.00 9.00

Souvenir Sheets

| 1661 | A257 | $6 like #1660f | 4.50 4.50 |
| 1662 | A257 | $6 multicolored | 4.50 4.50 |

Philatelic Publishing Personalities — A258

Portrait, stamp: No. 1663, J. Walter Scott (1842-1919), US "#C3a," Antigua #1. No. 1664, Theodore Champion, France #8, Antigua #1. No. 1665, E. Stanley Gibbons (1856-1913), cover of his first price list and catalogue, Antigua #1. No. 1666, Hugo Michel (1866-1944), Bavaria #1, Antigua #1. No. 1667, Alberto (1877-1944) and Giulio (1902-1987) Bolaffi, Sardinia #1, Great Britain #3. No. 1668, Richard Borek (1874-1947), Brunswick #24, Bavaria #1.

Front pages, Mekeel's Weekly Stamp News: No. 1669a, Jan. 7, 1890. b, Feb. 12, 1993.

1993, June 14			
1663	A258	$1.50 multicolored	1.10 1.10
1664	A258	$1.50 multicolored	1.10 1.10
1665	A258	$1.50 multicolored	1.10 1.10
1666	A258	$1.50 multicolored	1.10 1.10
1667	A258	$1.50 multicolored	1.10 1.10
1668	A258	$1.50 multicolored	1.10 1.10
		Nos. 1663-1668 (6)	6.60 6.60

Souvenir Sheet

| 1669 | A258 | $3 Sheet of 2, #a.-b. | 4.50 4.50 |

Mekeel's Weekly Stamp News, cent. (in 1891; #1669).

Miniature Sheets

Coronation of Queen Elizabeth II, 40th Anniv. — A259

Coronation: 1670a, 30c, Official photograph. b, 40c, Crown of Queen Elizabeth, the Queen Mother. c, $2, Dignataries attending ceremony. d, $4, Queen, Prince Edward.

$6, Portrait, by Denis Fildes.

First decade, 1953-1963: No. 1671a, Wedding photograph of Princess Margaret and Antony Armstrong-Jones. b, Queen opening Parliament, Prince Philip. c, Queen holding infant. d, Royal family. e, Queen Elizabeth II, formal portrait. f, Queen, Charles de Gaulle. g, Queen, Pope John XXIII. h, Queen inspecting troops.

Second decade, 1963-1973: No. 1672a, Investiture of Charles as Prince of Wales. b, Queen opening Parliament, Prince Philip, diff. c, Queen holding infant, diff. d, Queen, Prince Philip, children. e, Wearing blue robe, diadem. f, Prince Philip, Queen seated. g, Prince Charles, Queen at microphone. h, Queen conversing, model airplane.

Third decade, 1973-1983: No. 1673a, Wedding photograph of Prince Charles and Princess Diana. b, Queen opening Parliament, Prince Philip, diff. c, Princess Diana with infant. d, Princess Anne with infant. e, Portrait of Queen. f, Queen waving, Prince Philip. g, Queen, Pope John Paul II. h, Wedding portrait of Mark Phillips and Princess Anne.

Fourth decade, 1983-1993: No. 1674a, Wedding photograph of Sarah Ferguson and Prince Andrew. b, Queen opening Parliament, Prince Philip, diff. c, Princess Diana holding infant, diff. d, Sarah Ferguson, infant. e, Queen wearing blue dress. f, Queen waving from carriage, Prince Philip. g, Queen wearing military uniform. h, Queen Mother.

1993, June 2		Litho.	Perf. 13½x14
1670	A259	Sheet, 2 each #a.-d.	10.00 10.00

Sheets of 8

1671	A259	$1 #a.-h. + label	6.00 6.00
1672	A259	$1 #a.-h. + label	6.00 6.00
1673	A259	$1 #a.-h. + label	6.00 6.00
1674	A259	$1 #a.-h. + label	6.00 6.00

Souvenir Sheet
Perf. 14

| 1675 | A259 | $6 multicolored | 4.50 4.50 |

No. 1675 contains one 28x42mm stamp.

ANTIGUA

Wedding of Japan's Crown Prince Naruhito and Masako Owada — A260

Cameo photos of couple and: 40c, Crown Prince. $3, Princess.
$6, Princess wearing white coat, vert.

1993, Aug. 16   Litho.   Perf. 14
| 1676 | A260 | 40c multicolored | .30 | .30 |
| 1677 | A260 | $3 multicolored | 2.25 | 2.25 |

Souvenir Sheet
| 1678 | A260 | $6 multicolored | 4.50 | 4.50 |

Picasso (1881-1973) — A261

Paintings: 30c, Cat and Bird, 1939. 40c, Fish on a Newspaper, 1957. $5, Dying Bull, 1934. $6, Woman with a Dog, 1953.

1993, Aug. 16   Litho.   Perf. 14
1679	A261	30c multicolored	.25	.25
1680	A261	40c multicolored	.30	.30
1681	A261	$5 multicolored	4.00	4.00
	Nos. 1679-1681 (3)		4.55	4.55

Souvenir Sheet
| 1682 | A261 | $6 multicolored | 4.50 | 4.50 |

Copernicus (1473-1543) — A262

Designs: 40c, Astronomical devices. $4, Photograph of supernova. $5, Copernicus.

1993, Aug. 16
| 1683 | A262 | 40c multicolored | .30 | .30 |
| 1684 | A262 | $4 multicolored | 3.25 | 3.25 |

Souvenir Sheet
| 1685 | A262 | $6 multicolored | 3.75 | 3.75 |

Willy Brandt (1913-1992), German Chancellor — A263

Designs: 30c, Helmut Schmidt, George Leber, Brandt. $4, Brandt, newspaper headlines. $6, Brandt at Warsaw Ghetto Memorial, 1970.

1993, Aug. 16
| 1686 | A263 | 30c multicolored | .25 | .25 |
| 1687 | A263 | $4 multicolored | 3.25 | 3.25 |

Souvenir Sheet
| 1688 | A263 | $6 multicolored | 4.50 | 4.50 |

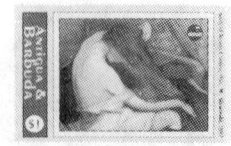

Polska '93 — A264

Paintings: $1, Study of a Woman Combing Her Hair, by Wladyslaw Slewinski, 1897. $3, Artist's Wife with Cat, by Konrad Kryzanowski, 1912. $6, General Confusion, by S. I. Witkiewicz, 1930, vert.

1993, Aug. 16
| 1689 | A264 | $1 multicolored | .80 | .80 |
| 1690 | A264 | $3 multicolored | 2.50 | 2.50 |

Souvenir Sheet
| 1691 | A264 | $6 multicolored | 4.50 | 4.50 |

Inauguration of Pres. William J. Clinton — A265

Designs: $5, Pres. Clinton driving car. $6, Pres. Clinton, inauguration ceremony, vert.

1993, Aug. 16
| 1692 | A265 | $5 multicolored | 4.00 | 4.00 |

Souvenir Sheet
| 1693 | A265 | $6 multicolored | 4.50 | 4.50 |

No. 1693 contains one 43x57mm stamp.

1994 Winter Olympics, Lillehammer, Norway — A266

Designs: 15c, Irina Rodnina, Alexei Ulanov, gold medalists, pairs figure skating, 1972. $5, Alberto Tomba, gold medal, giant slalom, 1988, 1992. $6, Yvonne van Gennip, Andrea Ehrig, gold, bronze medalists, speedskating, 1988.

1993, Aug. 16
| 1694 | A266 | 15c multicolored | .15 | .15 |
| 1695 | A266 | $5 multicolored | 4.00 | 4.00 |

Souvenir Sheet
| 1696 | A266 | $6 multicolored | 4.50 | 4.50 |

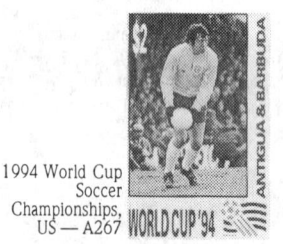

1994 World Cup Soccer Championships, US — A267

English soccer players: No. 1697, Gordon Banks. No. 1698, 1709, Bobby Moore. No. 1699, Peter Shilton. No. 1700, Nobby Stiles. No. 1701, Bryan Robson. No. 1702, Geoff Hurst. No. 1703, Gary Lineker. No. 1704, Bobby Charlton. No. 1705, Martin Peters. No. 1706, John Barnes. No. 1707, David Platt. No. 1708, Paul Gascoigne. No. 1710, Player holding 1990 Fair Play Winners Trophy.

1993, July 30   Litho.   Perf. 14
| 1697-1708 | A267 | $2 Set of 12 | 18.00 | 18.00 |

Souvenir Sheets
| 1709 | A267 | $6 multicolored | 4.50 | 4.50 |
| 1710 | A267 | $6 multicolored | 4.50 | 4.50 |

Nos. 1697-1708 issued in sheets of five plus label identifying player.

Aviation Anniversaries — A268

Designs: 30c, Dr. Hugo Eckener, Dr. Wm. Beckers, zeppelin over Lake George, NY. No. 1712, Chicago Century of Progress Exhibition seen from zeppelin. No. 1713, George Washington, Blanchard's balloon, vert. No. 1714, Gloster E.28/39, first British jet plane. $4, Pres. Wilson watching take-off of first scheduled air mail plane. No. 1716, Hindenburg over Ebbets Field, Brooklyn, NY, 1937. No. 1717, Gloster Meteor in combat. No. 1718, Eckener, vert. No. 1719, Alexander Hamilton, Pres. Washington, John Jay, gondola of Blanchard's balloon. No. 1720, PBY-5.

1993, Oct. 11
1711	A268	30c multicolored	.20	.20
1712	A268	40c multicolored	.30	.30
1713	A268	40c multicolored	.30	.30
1714	A268	40c multicolored	.30	.30
1715	A268	$4 multicolored	3.00	3.00
1716	A268	$5 multicolored	3.75	3.75
1717	A268	$5 multicolored	3.75	3.75
	Nos. 1711-1717 (7)		11.60	11.60

Souvenir Sheets
1718	A268	$6 multicolored	4.50	4.50
1719	A268	$6 multicolored	4.50	4.50
1720	A268	$6 multicolored	4.50	4.50

Dr. Hugo Eckener, 125th anniv. of birth (#1711-1712, 1716, 1718). First US balloon flight, bicent. (#1713, 1715, 1719). Royal Air Force, 75th anniv. (#1714, 1717, 1720).
No. 1720 contains one 57x43mm stamp.

Mickey Mouse Movie Posters — A269

Nos. 1721-1729: 10c, The Musical Farmer, 1932. 15c, Little Whirlwind, 1941. 30c, Pluto's Dream House, 1940. 40c, Gulliver Mickey, 1934. 50c, Alpine Climbers, 1936. $1, Mr. Mouse Takes a Trip, 1940. $2, The Nifty Nineties, 1941. $4, Mickey Down Under, 1948. $5, The Pointer, 1939.
#1730, The Simple Things, 1953. #1731, The Prince and the Pauper, 1990.

1993, Oct. 25   Litho.   Perf. 13½x14
| 1721-1729 | A269 | Set of 9 | 12.00 | 12.00 |

Souvenir Sheets
| 1730-1731 | A269 | $6 each | 4.50 | 4.50 |

St. John's Lodge #492, 150th Anniv. A270

Designs: 10c, W.K. Heath, Grand Inspector 1961-82, vert. 30c, Present Masonic Hall. 40c, 1st Masonic Hall. 60c, J.L.E. Jeffery, Grand Inspector 1953-61, vert.

1993, Aug. 16   Litho.   Perf. 14
| 1732-1735 | A270 | Set of 4 | 1.10 | 1.10 |

First Ford Engine and Benz's First 4-Wheel Car, Cent. A271

Designs: 30c, Lincoln Continental. 40c, 1914 Mercedes racing car. $4, 1966 Ford GT40. $5, 1954 Mercedes Benz gull wing coupe, street version. No. 1740, Mustang emblem. No. 1741, US #1286A, Germany #471.

1993, Oct. 11   Litho.   Perf. 14
| 1736-1739 | A271 | Set of 4 | 7.00 | 7.00 |

Souvenir Sheets
| 1740-1741 | A271 | $6 each | 4.50 | 4.50 |

Christmas — A272

Nos. 1742-1750, Disney characters in The Nutcracker: 10c, 15c, 20c, 30c, 40c, 50c, 60c, $3, $6. 1751, Minnie and Mickey. No. 1752, Mickey, vert.

1993, Nov. 8   Perf. 14x13½, 13½x14
| 1742-1750 | A272 | Set of 9 | 8.50 | 8.50 |

Souvenir Sheets
| 1751-1752 | A272 | $6 each | 4.50 | 4.50 |

Fine Art — A273

Paintings by Rembrandt: No. 1753, 15c, Hannah and Samuel. 30c, Isaac & Rebecca (The Jewish Bride). 40c, Jacob Wrestling with the Angel. $5, Moses with the Tablets of the Law.
Paintings by Matisse: No. 1754, 15c, Guitarist. 60c, Interior with a Goldfish Bowl. $1, Portrait of Mlle. Yvonne Landsberg. $4, The Toboggan, Plate XX from Jazz. No. 1761, The Blinding of Samson by the Philistines, by Rembrandt. No. 1762, The Three Sisters, by Matisse.

1993, Nov. 22   Perf. 13½x14
| 1753-1760 | A273 | Set of 8 | 9.00 | 9.00 |

Souvenir Sheets
| 1761-1762 | A273 | $6 each | 4.50 | 4.50 |

A274

Hong Kong '94 — A275

Stamps, fishing boats at Shau Kei Wan: No. 1763, Hong Kong #370, bow of boat. No. 1764, Stern of boat, #1300.
Museum of Qin figures, Shaanxi Province, Tomb of Qin First Emperor: No. 1765a, Inside museum. b, Cavalryman, horse. c, Warriors in battle formation. d, Painted bronze horses, chariot. e, Pekingese dog (not antiquity). f, Chin warrior figures, horses.

1994, Feb. 18   Litho.   Perf. 14
1763	A274	40c multicolored	.30	.30
1764	A274	40c multicolored	.30	.30
a.	Pair, #1763-1764		.60	.60

Miniature Sheet
| 1765 | A275 | 40c Sheet of 6, #a.-f. | 1.75 | 1.75 |

Nos. 1763-1764 issued in sheets of 5 pairs. No. 1764a is a continuous design.
New Year 1994 (Year of the Dog) (#1765e).

Hong Kong '94 — A276

Disney characters: 10c, Mickey's "Pleasure Junk." 15c, Mandarin Minnie. 30c, Donald, Daisy journey by house boat. 50c, Mickey, Birdman of Mongkok. $1, Pluto encounters a good-luck dog. $2, Minnie, Daisy celebrate Bun Festival. $4, Goofy, the noodle maker. $5, Goofy pulls Mickey in a rickshaw.

ANTIGUA

No. 1774, Mickey celebrating New Year with Dragon Dance, horiz. No. 1775, View of Hong Kong Harbor, horiz.

1994, Feb. 18   Litho.   Perf. 13½x14
1766-1773 A276 Set of 8   10.00 10.00

Souvenir Sheets
Perf. 14x13½
1774-1775 A276 $5 each   3.75 3.75

Miniature Sheets of 8

Sierra Club, Cent. — A277

No. 1776: a, Bactrian camel, emblem UR. b, Bactrian camel, emblem UL. c, African elephant, emblem UL. d, African elephant, emblem UR. e, Leopard, blue background. f, Leopard, emblem UR. g, Leopard, emblem UL. h, Club emblem.
No. 1777: a, Sumatran rhinoceros, lying on ground. b, Sumatran rhinoceros, looking straight ahead. c, Ring-tailed lemur standing. d, Ring-tailed lemur sitting on branch. e, Red-fronted brown lemur on branch. f, Red-fronted brown lemur. g, Red-fronted brown lemur, diff.
No. 1778, Sumatran rhinoceros, horiz. No. 1779, Ring-tailed lemur, horiz. No. 1780, Bactrian camel, horiz. No. 1781, African elephant, horiz.

1994, Mar. 1   Litho.   Perf. 14
1776 A277 $1.50 #a.-h.   9.00 9.00
1777 A277 $1.50 #a.-g, #1776h   9.00 9.00

Souvenir Sheets
1778-1781 A277 $1.50 each   1.10 1.10

Miniature Sheets

New Year 1994 (Year of the Dog) A278

Small breeds of dogs: No. 1782a, West highland white terrier. b, Beagle. c, Scottish terrier. d, Pekingese. e, Dachshund. f, Yorkshire terrier. g, Pomeranian. h, Poodle. i, Shetland sheepdog. j, Pug. k, Shih tzu. l, Chihuahua.
Large breeds of dogs: No. 1783a, Mastiff. b, Border collie. c, Samoyed. d, Airedale terrier. e, English setter. f, Rough collie. g, Newfoundland. h, Weimaraner. i, English springer spaniel. j, Dalmatian. k, Boxer. l, Old English sheepdog.
No. 1784, Welsh corgi. No. 1785, Labrador retriever.

1994, Apr. 5   Perf. 14
1782 A278 50c Sheet of 12, #a.-l.   4.50 4.50
1783 A278 75c Sheet of 12, #a.-l.   6.75 6.75

Souvenir Sheets
1784-1785 A278 $6 each   4.50 4.50

Orchids — A279    Butterflies — A280

Designs: 10c, Spiranthes lanceolata. 20c, Ionopsis utricularioides. 30c, Tetramicra canaliculata. 50c, Oncidium picturatum. $1, Epidendrum difforme. $2, Epidendrum ciliare. $4, Epidendrum ibaguense. $5, Epidendrum nocturnum.
No. 1794, Encyclia cochleata. No. 1795, Rodriguezia lanceolata.

1994, Apr. 11   Perf. 14
1786-1793 A279 Set of 8   10.00 10.00

Souvenir Sheets
1794-1795 A279 $6 each   4.50 4.50

1994, June 27   Perf. 14
Designs: 10c, Monarch. 15c, Florida white. 30c, Little sulphur. 40c, Troglodyte. $1, Common longtail skipper. $2, Caribbean buckeye. $4, Polydamas swallowtail. $5, Zebra.
#1804, Cloudless sulphur. #1805, Hanno blue.

1796-1803 A280 Set of 8   10.00 10.00

Souvenir Sheets
1804-1805 A280 $6 each   4.50 4.50

Miniature Sheet of 9

Marine Life — A281

Designs: No. 1806a, Bottlenose dolphin. b, Killer whale (a). c, Spinner dolphin (b). d, Ocean sunfish (a). e, Caribbean reef shark, short fin pilot whale (d, f). f, Butterfly fish. g, Moray eel. h, Trigger fish. i, Red lobster (h).
#1807, Blue marlin, horiz. #1808, Sea horse.

1994, July 21   Litho.   Perf. 14
1806 A281 50c a.-i.   3.50 3.50

Souvenir Sheets
1807-1808 A281 $6 each   4.50 4.50

Intl. Year of the Family A282

1994, Aug. 4
1809 A282 90c multicolored   .70   .70

D-Day, 50th Anniv. A283

Designs: 40c, Short Sunderland attacks U-boat. $2, Lockheed P-38 Lightning attacks train. $3, B-26 Marauders of 9th Air Force.
$6, Hawker Typhoon Fighter Bombers.

1994, Aug. 4
1810-1812 A283 Set of 3   4.25 4.25

Souvenir Sheet
1813 A283 $6 multicolored   4.50 4.50

A284

Intl. Olympic Committee, Cent. — A285

Designs: 50c, Edwin Moses, US, hurdles, 1984. $1.50, Steffi Graf, Germany, tennis, 1988. $6, Johann Olav Koss, Norway, speed skating, 1994.

1994, Aug. 4
1814 A284 50c multicolored   .40   .40
1815 A284 $1.50 multicolored   1.10 1.10

Souvenir Sheet
1816 A285 $6 multicolored   4.50 4.50

English Touring Cricket, Cent. A286

35c, M.A. Atherton, England, Wisden Trophy. 75c, I.V.A. Richards, Leeward Islands, vert. $1.20, R.B. Richardson, Leeward Islands, Wisden Trophy. $3, First English team, 1895.

1994, Aug. 4
1817-1819 A286 Set of 3   1.75 1.75

Souvenir Sheet
1820 A286 $3 multicolored   2.25 2.25

Miniature Sheets of 6

First Manned Moon Landing, 25th Anniv. A287

No. 1821: a, Edwin E. Aldrin, Jr. b, First footprint on Moon. c, Neil A. Armstrong. d, Aldrin descending to lunar surface. e, Aldrin deploys ALSET. f, Aldrin, US flag, Tranquility Base.
No. 1822: a, Scientific research, Tranquility Base. b, Plaque on Moon. c, Eagle ascending to docking. d, Command module in lunar orbit. e, US No. C76 made from die carried to Moon. f, Pres. Nixon, Apollo 11 crew.
$6, Armstrong, Aldrin, Postmaster General Blount.

1994, Aug. 4
1821-1822 A287 $1.50 #a.-f.   6.75 6.75

Souvenir Sheet
1823 A287 $6 multicolored   4.50 4.50

A288

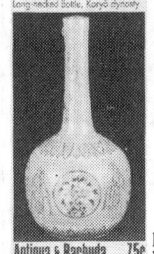

PHILAKOREA '94 — A289

Designs: 40c, Entrance bridge, Songgwangsa Temple. 90c, Song-op Folk Village, Cheju. $3, Panoramic view, Port Sogwip'o.
Ceramics, Koryo & Choson Dynasties: No. 1827a, Long-necked bottle. b, Jar. c, Jar, diff. d, Ewer in form of bamboo shoot. e, Jar, diff. f, Pear-shaped bottle. g, Porcelain jar with dragon design. h, Porcelain jar with bonsai design.
$4, Ox, ox herder, vert.

1994, Aug. 4   Perf. 14, 13½ (#1827)
1824-1826 A288 Set of 3   3.50 3.50

Miniature Sheet of 8
1827 A289 75c #a.-h.   6.00 6.00

Souvenir Sheet
1828 A288 $4 multicolored   3.00 3.00

Miniature Sheets of 8

Stars of Country & Western Music — A290

No. 1829: a, Patsy Cline. b, Tanya Tucker. c, Dolly Parton. d, Anne Murray. e, Tammy Wynette. f, Loretta Lynn. g, Reba McEntire. h, Skeeter Davis.
No. 1830a, Travis Tritt. b, Dwight Yoakam. c, Billy Ray Cyrus. d, Alan Jackson. e, Garth Brooks. f, Vince Gill. g, Clint Black. h, Eddie Rabbit.
No. 1831: a, Hank Snow. b, Gene Autry. c, Jimmie Rogers. d, Ernest Tubb. e, Eddy Arnold. f, Willie Nelson. g, Johnny Cash. h, George Jones.
No. 1832, Kitty Wells, horiz. No. 1833, Hank Williams, Sr. No. 1834, Hank Williams, Jr.

1994, Aug. 18   Litho.   Perf. 14
1829-1831 A290 75c #a.-h., each   4.50 4.50

Souvenir Sheets
1832-1834 A290 $6 each   4.50 4.50

1994 World Cup Soccer Championships, US — A291

Designs: 15c, Hugo Sanchez, Mexico. 35c, Juergen Klinsman, Germany. 65c, Antigua player. $1.20, Cobi Jones, US. $4, Roberto Baggio, Italy. $5, Bwalya Kalusha, Zambia.
No. 1841, FIFA World Cup Trophy, vert. No. 1842, Maldive Islands player, vert.

1994, Sept. 19
1835-1840 A291 Set of 6   8.50 8.50

Souvenir Sheets
1841-1842 A291 $6 each   4.50 4.50

Order of the Caribbean Community — A292

First award recipients: 65c, Sir Shridath Ramphal, statesman, Guyana. 90c, William Demas, economist, Trinidad & Tobago. $1.20, Derek Walcott, writer, St. Lucia.

1994, Sept. 26
1843-1845 A292 Set of 3   2.00 2.00

Herman E. Sieger (1902-54) A293

Design: Germany #C35, Graf Zeppelin, Sieger.

1994   Litho.   Perf. 14
1846 A293 $1.50 multicolored   1.25 1.25

Birds A294

Designs: 10c, Magnificent frigate birds. 15c, Bridled quail dove. 30c, Magnificent frigate bird hatchling. 40c, Purple-throated carib, vert. No. 1851, $1, Antigua broad-wing hawk, vert. No. 1852, $1, Magnificent frigate bird, vert. $3, Magnificent frigate bird, white head. $4, Yellow warbler.
No. 1855, West Indian Whistling duck. No. 1856, Magnificent frigate bird, diff., vert.

1994, Dec. 12   Litho.   Perf. 14
1847-1854 A294 Set of 8   7.50 7.50

Souvenir Sheets
1855-1856 A294 $6 each   4.50 4.50

World Wildlife Fund (#1847, 1849, 1852-1853).

ANTIGUA

Christmas A295

Paintings of Madonnas: 15c, The Virgin and Child by the Fireside, by Robert Campin. 35c, The Reading Madonna, by Giorgione. 40c, Madonna and Child, by Giovanni Bellini. 45c, The Litta Madonna, by da Vinci. 65c, The Virgin and Child Under the Apple Tree, by Lucas Cranach the Elder. 75c, Madonna and Child, by Master of the Female Half-Lengths. $1.20, An Allegory of the Church, by Alessandro Allori. $5, Madonna and Child Wreathed with Flowers, by Jacob Jordaens.
No. 1865, The Virgin Enthroned with Child, by Bohemian Master. No. 1866, Madonna and Child with (painting's) Commissioners, by Palma Vecchio.

1994, Dec. 12				**Perf. 13½x14**
1857-1864	A295	Set of 8		6.75 6.75
	Souvenir Sheets			
1865-1866	A295	$6 each		4.50 4.50

Birds — A296

Designs: 15c, Magnificent frigate bird. 25c, Blue-hooded euphonia. 35c, Meadowlark. 40c, Red-billed tropic bird. 45c, Greater flamingo. 60c, Yellow-faced grassquit. 65c, Yellow-billed cuckoo. 70c, Purple-throated carib. 75c, Bananaquit. 90c, Painted bunting. $1.20, Red-legged honeycreeper. $2, Jacana. $5, Greater antillean bullfinch. $10, Caribbean elaenia. $20, Trembler.

1994				**Perf. 14½x14**
1867	A296	15c multicolored	.15	.15
1868	A296	25c multicolored	.20	.20
1869	A296	35c multicolored	.25	.25
1870	A296	40c multicolored	.60	.60
1871	A296	45c multicolored	.35	.35
1872	A296	60c multicolored	.45	.45
1873	A296	65c multicolored	.45	.45
1874	A296	70c multicolored	.50	.50
1875	A296	75c multicolored	.55	.55
1876	A296	90c multicolored	.70	.70
1877	A296	$1.20 multicolored	.90	.90
1878	A296	$2 multicolored	1.50	1.50
1879	A296	$5 multicolored	4.50	4.50
1880	A296	$10 multicolored	7.50	7.50
1881	A296	$20 multicolored	15.00	15.00
	Nos. 1867-1881 (15)		33.60	33.60

Prehistoric Animals — A297

Designs, vert: 15c, Pachycephalosaurus. 20c, Afrovenator. 65c, Centrosaurus. 90c, Pentaceratops. $1.20, Tarbosaurus. $5, Styracosaur.
No. 1888a, Kronosaur. b, Ichthyosaur. c, Plesiosaur. d, Archelon. e, Two tyrannosaurs. f, One tyrannosaur. g, One parasaurolophus. h, Two parasaurolophuses. i, Oviraptor. j, Protoceratops with eggs. k, Pteranodon, protoceratops. l, Protoceratops.
#1889, Carnotaurus. #1890, Corythosaurus.

1995, May 15		**Litho.**		**Perf. 14**
1882-1887	A297	Set of 6		6.25 6.25
	Miniature Sheet of 12			
1888	A297	75c #a.-l.		6.75 6.75
	Souvenir Sheets			
1889-1890	A297	$6 each		4.50 4.50

1996 Summer Olympics, Atlanta — A298

Gold medalists: 15c, Al Oerter, US, discus. 20c, Greg Louganis, US, diving. 65c, Naim Suleymanoglu, Turkey, weight lifting. 90c, Louise Ritter, US, high jump. $1.20, Nadia Comaneci, Romania, gymnastics. $5, Olga Boldarenko, USSR, 10,000-meter run.
No. 1897, Lutz Hessilch, Germany, 1000-meter sprint cycling, vert. No. 1898, US team, eight-oared shell, 800-, 1500-meters.

1995, June 6		**Litho.**		**Perf. 14**
1891-1896	A298	Set of 6		6.00 6.00
	Souvenir Sheets			
1897-1898	A298	$6 each		4.50 4.50

Miniature Sheets of 6 or 8

End of World War II, 50th Anniv. A299

No. 1899: a, Chiang Kai-Shek. b, Gen. MacArthur. c, Gen. Chennault. d, Brigadier Orde C. Wingate. e, Gen. Stillwell. f, Field Marshall William Slim.
No. 1900: a, Map of Germany showing battle plan. b, Tanks, infantry advance. c, Red Army at gates of Berlin. d, German defenses smashed. e, Airstrikes on Berlin. f, German soldiers give up. g, Berlin falls to Russians. h, Germany surrenders.
$3, Plane, ship, Adm. Chester Nimitz. $6, Gen. Konev at command post outside Berlin, vert.

1995, July 20				
1899	A299	$1.20 #a.-f. + label	5.50	5.50
1900	A299	$1.20 #a.-h. + label	7.25	7.25
	Souvenir Sheets			
1901	A299	$3 multicolored	2.25	2.25
1902	A299	$6 multicolored	4.50	4.50

UN, 50th Anniv. — A300

FAO, 50th Anniv. — A301

No. 1903: a, 75c, Earl of Halifax, signatures. b, 90c, Virginia Gildersleeve. c, $1.20, Harold Stassen. $6, Franklin D. Roosevelt.

1995, July 20		**Litho.**		**Perf. 14**
1903	A300	Strip of 3, #a.-c.	2.25	2.25
	Souvenir Sheet			
1904	A300	$6 multicolored	4.50	4.50
	No. 1903 is a continuous design.			

1995, July 20

Street market scene: No. 1905a, 75c, Two women, bananas. b, 90c, Women, crates, produce. c, $1.20, Women talking, one with box of food on head.
$6, Tractor.

1905	A301	Strip of 3, #a.-c.	2.25	2.25
	Souvenir Sheet			
1906	A301	$6 multicolored	4.50	4.50
	No. 1905 is a continuous design.			

Rotary Intl., 90th Anniv. — A302

1995, July 20				
1907	A302	$5 shown	3.75	3.75
	Souvenir Sheet			
1908	A302	$6 Natl. flag, Rotary emblem	4.50	4.50

Queen Mother, 95th Birthday A303

No. 1909: a, Drawing. b, White & dark pink hat. c, Formal portrait. d, Blue green hat, dress.
No. 1910, Light blue dress, pearls.

1995, July 20				**Perf. 13½x14**
1909	A303	$1.50 Strip or block of 4, #a.-d.	4.50	4.50
	Souvenir Sheet			
1910	A303	$6 multicolored	4.50	4.50
	No. 1909 was issued in sheets of 2 each.			

Miniature Sheet of 12

Ducks — A304

No. 1911: a, Ring-necked duck. b, Ruddy duck. c, Green-winged teal (d). d, Wood duck. e, Hooded merganser (f). f, Lesser scaup (g). g, West Indian tree duck (h, k, l). h, Fulvous whistling duck (l). i, Bahama pintail. j, Shoveler (i). k, Masked duck (l). l, American widgeon.
$6, Blue-winged teal.

1995, Aug. 31		**Litho.**		**Perf. 14**
1911	A304	75c #a.-l.	6.75	6.75
	Souvenir Sheet			
1912	A304	$6 multicolored	4.50	4.50

Bees A305

Designs: 90c, Mining bee. $1.20, Solitary bee. $1.65, Leaf-cutter. $1.75, Honey bee.
$6, Solitary mining bee.

1995, Sept. 7				
1913-1916	A305	Set of 4	4.25	4.25
	Souvenir Sheet			
1917	A305	$6 multicolored	4.50	4.50

Miniature Sheet of 12

Domestic Cats A306

Designs: a, Somali. b, Persian. c, Devon rex. d, Turkish angora. e, Himalayan. f, Maine coon. g, Nonpedigree. h, American wirehair. i, British shorthair. j, American curl. k, Black nonpedigree. l, Birman.
$6, Siberian, vert.

1995, Sept. 7				
1918	A306	45c #a.-l.	4.00	4.00
	Souvenir Sheet			
1919	A306	$6 multicolored	4.50	4.50

Miniature Sheet

Tourism A307

Stylized paintings depicting: a, Caring. b, Marketing. c, Working. d, Enjoying life.

1995, July 31		**Litho.**		**Perf. 14**
1920	A307	$2 Sheet of 4, #a.-d.	6.00	6.00

Greenbay Moravian Church, 150th Anniv. — A308

20c, 1st structure, wood & stone. 60c, 1st stone, concrete building, 3/67. 75c, $2, Present structure. 90c, John A. Buckley, 1st minister of African descent. $1.20, John Ephraim Knight, longest serving minister. $6, Front of present structure.

1995, Sept. 4				
1921-1926	A308	Set of 6	4.25	4.25
	Souvenir Sheet			
1927	A308	$6 multicolored	4.50	4.50

Miniature Sheet of 12

Flowers — A309

No. 1928: a, Narcissus. b, Camellia. c, Iris. d, Tulip. e, Poppy. f, Peony. g, Magnolia. h, Oriental lily. i, Rose. j, Pansy. k, Hydrangea. l, Azaleas.
$6, Bird of paradise, calla lily.

1995, Sept. 7				
1928	A309	75c #a.-l.	6.75	6.75
	Souvenir Sheet			
1929	A309	$6 multicolored	4.50	4.50

1995 Boy Scout Jamboree, Holland A310

Tents: No. 1930a, Explorer. b, Camper. c, Wall. No. 1931a, Trail tarp. b, Miner's. c, Voyager.

ANTIGUA

No. 1932, Scout with camping equipment, vert.
No. 1933, Scout making camp fire.

1995, Oct. 5
1930-1931 A310 $1.20 Strip of 3,
 #a.-c, each 2.75 2.75
Souvenir Sheets
1932-1933 A310 $6 each 4.50 4.50
For overprints see Nos. 1963-1966.

Trains — A311

Designs: 35c, Gabon. 65c, Canadian. 75c, US. 90c, British high-speed. $1.20, French high-speed. No. 1939, American high-speed (Amtrak).
No. 1940: a, Australian diesel. b, Italian high-speed. c, Thai diesel. d, US steam. e, South African steam. f, Natal steam. g, US war train. h, British steam. i, British steam, diff.
No. 1941, Australian diesel, vert. No. 1942, Asian steam, vert.

1995, Oct. 23   Litho.   Perf. 14
1934-1939 A311 Set of 6 7.50 7.50
Miniature Sheet
1940 A311 $1.20 Sheet of 9, #a.-i. 8.25 8.25
Souvenir Sheets
1941-1942 A311 $6 each 4.50 4.50
Miniature Sheet

Birds — A312

No. 1943: a, Purple-thoated carib. b, Antillean crested hummingbird. c, Bananaquit (d). d, Mangrove cuckoo. e, Troupial. f, Green-throated carib (e, g). g, Yellow warbler (h). h, Blue-hooded Euphonia. i, Scally-breasted thrasher. j, Burrowing owl (i). k, Caribbean crackle (k). l, Adelaide's warbler.
$6, Purple gallinule.

1995
1943 A312 75c Sheet of 12, #a.-l. 6.75 6.75
Souvenir Sheet
1944 A312 $6 multicolored 4.50 4.50
Miniature Sheets of 9

Nobel Prize Fund Established, Cent. — A313

Recipients: No. 1945a, S.Y. Agnon, literature, 1966. b, Kipling, literature, 1907. c, Aleksandr Solzhenitsyn, literature, 1970. d, Jack Steinberger, physics, 1988. e, Andrei Sakharov, peace, 1975. f, Otto Stern, physics, 1943. g, Steinbeck, literature, 1962. h, Nadine Gordimer, literature, 1991. i, Faulkner, literature, 1949.
No. 1946: a, Hammarskjold, peace, 1961. b, Georg Wittig, chemistry, 1979. c, Wilhelm Ostwald, chemistry, 1909. d, Koch, physiology or medicine, 1945. e, Karl Ziegler, chemistry, 1963. f, Fleming, physiology or medicine, 1945. g, Hermann Staudinger, chemistry, 1953. h, Manfred Eigen, chemistry, 1967. i, Arno Penzias, physics, 1978.
No. 1947, Elie Wiesel, peace, 1986, vert. No. 1948, Dalai Lama, peace, 1989, vert.

1995, Nov. 8
1945-1946 A313 $1 #a.-i. + label,
 each 6.75 6.75
Souvenir Sheets
1947-1948 A313 $6 each 4.50 4.50

Christmas A314

Details or entire paintings: 15c, Rest on the Flight into Egypt, by Veronese. 35c, Madonna with The Child, by Van Dyck. 65c, Sacred Conversation Piece, by Veronese. 75c, Vision of Saint Anthony, by Van Dyck. 90c, The Virgin and the Infant, by Van Eyck. No. 1954, The Immaculate Conception, by Tiepolo.
$5, Christ Appearing to His Mother, by Van Der Weyden. No. 1956, Infant Jesus and the Young St. John, by Murillo.

1995, Dec. 18   Litho.   Perf. 13½x14
1949-1954 A314 Set of 6 6.75 6.75
Souvenir Sheets
1955 A314 $5 multicolored 3.75 3.75
1956 A314 $6 multicolored 4.50 4.50
Miniature Sheet

Elvis Presley (1935-77) A315

Nos. 1957-1958, Various portraits depicting Presley's life.

1995, Dec. 8   Perf. 14
1957 A315 $1 Sheet of 9, #a.-i. 6.75 6.75
Souvenir Sheet
1958 A315 $6 multicolored 4.50 4.50

John Lennon (1940-80), Entertainer — A316

45c, 50c, 65c, 75c, Various portraits of Lennon.

1995, Dec. 8
1959-1962 A316 Set of 4 1.75 1.75
Souvenir Sheet
1962A A316 $6 like 75c 4.50 4.50
Nos. 1959-1962 were each issued in miniature sheets of 16.
No. 1962A has a continuous design.

Nos. 1930-1933 Ovptd.

1995, Dec. 14
1963-1964 A310 $1.20 Strip of 3,
 #a.-c., each 2.75 2.75
Souvenir Sheets
1965-1966 A310 $6 each 4.50 4.50
Size and location of overprint varies.

Mushrooms A317

Designs: No. 1967a, Hygrophoropsis aurantiaca. b, Hygrophorus bakerensis. c, Hygrophorus conicus. d, Hygrophorus miniatus.
No. 1968a, Suillus brevipes. b, Suillus luteus. c, Suillus granulatus. d, Suillus caerulescens.
No. 1969, Conocybe filaris. No. 1970, Hygrocybe flavescens.

1996, Apr. 22   Litho.   Perf. 14
1967-1968 A317 75c Strip of 4, #a.-
 d., each 2.25 2.25
Souvenir Sheets
1969-1970 A317 $6 each 4.50 4.50
#1967-1968 were each issued in sheets of 12 stamps.

Sailing Ships A318

Designs: 15c, Resolution. 25c, Mayflower. 45c, Santa Maria. No. 1970D, 75c, Aemilia, Holland, 1630. No. 1970E, 75c, Sovereign of the Seas, England, 1637. 90c, HMS Victory, England, 1765.
Battleships: No. 1971: a, Aemila, Holland, 1630. b, Sovereign of the Seas, England, 1637. c, Royal Louis, France, 1692. d, HMS Royal George, England, 1715. e, Le Protecteur, France, 1761. f, HMS Victory, England, 1765.
Ships of exploration: No. 1972: a, Santa Maria. b, Victoria. c, Golden Hinde. d, Mayflower. e, Griffin. f, Resolution.
No. 1973, Grande Hermine. No. 1974, USS Constitution, 1797.

1996, Apr. 25
1970A-1970F A318 Set of 6 2.50 2.50
Sheets of 6
1971 A318 $1.20 #a.-f. 5.50 5.50
1972 A318 $1.50 #a.-f. 6.75 6.75
Souvenir Sheets
1973-1974 A318 $6 each 4.50 4.50

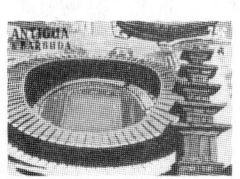

1996 Summer Olympics, Atlanta — A319

Designs: 65c, Florence Griffith Joyner, women's track, vert. 75c, Olympic Stadium, Seoul, 1988. 90c, Allison Jolly, yachting. $1.20, 2000m Tandem cyclying.
Medalists: No. 1979a, Wolfgang Nordwig, pole vault. b, Shirley Strong, women's 100m hurdles. c, Sergei Bubka, pole vault. d, Filbert Bayi, 3000m steeplechase. e, Victor Saneyev, triple jump. f, Silke Renk, women's javelin. g, Daley Thompson, decathlon. h, Bob Richards, pole vault. i, Parry O'Brien, shot put.
Diving medalists: No. 1980a, Ingrid Kramer, women's platform. b, Kelly McCormick, women's springboard. c, Gary Tobian, men's springboard. d, Greg Louganis, men's diving. e, Michelle Mitchell, women's platform. f, Zhou Jihong, women's platform. g, Wendy Wyland, women's platform. h, Xu Yanmei, women's platform. i, Fu Mingxia, women's platform.
$5, Bill Toomey, decathlon. $6, Mark Lenzi, men's springboard.

1996, May 6
1975-1978 A319 Set of 4 2.50 2.50
Sheets of 9
1979-1980 A319 90c #a.-i., each 6.25 6.25
Souvenir Sheets
1981 A319 $5 multicolored 3.75 3.75
1982 A319 $6 multicolored 4.50 4.50

Sea Birds A320

Designs: No. 1983a, Black skimmer. b, Black-capped petrel. c, Sooty tern. d, Royal tern.
No. 1984a, Pomarina jaegger. b, White-tailed tropicbird. c, Northern gannet. d, Laughing gull.
$5, Great frigatebird. $6, Brown pelican.

1996, May 13
1983-1984 A320 75c Vert. strip of 4,
 #a.-d., each 2.25 2.25
Souvenir Sheets
1985 A320 $5 multicolored 3.75 3.75
1986 A320 $6 multicolored 4.50 4.50
Nos. 1983-1984 were each issued in sheets of 12 stamps with each strip in sheet having a different order.

Disney Characters In Scenes from Jules Verne's Science Fiction Novels — A321

Designs: 1c, Around the World in Eighty Days. 2c, Journey to the Center of the Earth. 5c, Michel Strogoff. 10c, From the Earth to the Moon. 15c, Five Weeks in a Balloon. 20c, Around the World in Eighty Days, diff. $1, The Mysterious Island. $2, From the Earth to the Moon, diff. $3, Captain Grant's Children. $5, Twenty Thousand Leagues Under the Sea.
No. 1997, Twenty Thousand Leagues Under the Sea, diff. No. 1998, Journey to the Center of the Earth, diff.

1996, June 6   Litho.   Perf. 14x13½
1987-1996 A321 Set of 10 8.75 8.75
Souvenir Sheets
1997-1998 A321 $6 each 4.50 4.50

Bruce Lee (1940-73), Martial Arts Expert — A322

Various portraits.

1996, June 13   Perf. 14
1999 A322 75c Sheet of 9, #a.-i. 5.25 5.25
Souvenir Sheet
2000 A322 $5 multicolored 3.75 3.75
China '96 (#1999).

Queen Elizabeth II, 70th Birthday A323

Designs: a, In blue dress, pearls. b, Carrying bouquet of flowers. c, In uniform.
$6, Painting as younger woman.

ANTIGUA

1996, July 17   Perf. 13½x14
2001 A323 $2 Strip of 3, #a.-c.   4.50 4.50
Souvenir Sheet
2002 A323 $6 multicolored   4.50 4.50
No. 2001 was issued in sheets of 9 stamps.

Traditional Cavalry — A324

a, Ancient Egyptian. b, 13th cent. English. c, 16th cent. Spanish. d, 18th cent. Chinese. $6, 19th cent. French.

1996, July 24   Litho.   Perf. 14
2003 A324 60c Block of 4, #a.-d.   1.75 1.75
Souvenir Sheet
2004 A324 $6 multicolored   4.50 4.50
No. 2003 was issued in sheets of 16 stamps.

A325    A326

UNICEF, 50th Anniv.: 75c, Girl. 90c, Children. $1.20, Woman holding baby. $6, Girl, diff.

1996, July 30
2005-2007 A325 Set of 3   2.00 2.00
Souvenir Sheet
2008 A325 $6 multicolored   4.50 4.50

1996, July 30
Site, flower: 75c, Tomb of Zachariah, verbascum sinuatum. 90c, Pool of Siloam, hyacinthus orientalis. $1.20, Hurva Synagogue, ranunculus asiaticus.
$6, Model of Herod's Temple.
2009-2011 A326 Set of 3   2.25 2.25
Souvenir Sheet
2012 A326 $6 multicolored   4.50 4.50
Jerusalem, 3000th anniv.

Radio, Cent. — A327

Entertainers: 65c, Kate Smith. 75c, Dinah Shore. 90c, Rudy Vallee. $1.20, Bing Crosby.
$6, Jo Stafford.

1996, July 30
2013-2016 A327 Set of 4   2.75 2.75
Souvenir Sheet
2017 A327 $6 multicolored   4.50 4.50

The lack of a value for a listed item does not necessarily indicate rarity.

Christmas A328

Details or entire paintings, by Filippo Lippi: 60c, Madonna Enthroned. 90c, Adoration of the Child and Saints. $1, Annunciation. $1.20, Birth of the Virgin. $1.60, Adoration of the Child. $1.75, Madonna and Child.
No. 2024, Madonna and Child, diff. No. 2025, Circumcision.

1996, Nov. 25   Perf. 13½x14
2018-2023 A328   Set of 6   5.25 5.25
Souvenir Sheets
2024-2025 A328 $6 each   4.50 4.50

Disney Pals A329

Designs: 1c, Goofy, Wilbur. 2c, Donald, Goofy. 5c, Donald, Panchito, Jose Carioca. 10c, Mickey, Goofy. 15c, Dale, Chip. 20c, Pluto, Mickey. $1, Daisy, Minnie at ice cream shop. $2, Daisy, Minnie. $3, Gus Goose, Donald.
No. 2035, Donald, vert. No. 2036, Goofy.

1997, Feb. 17   Litho.   Perf. 14x13½
2026-2034 A329   Set of 9   5.00 5.00
Souvenir Sheets
Perf. 13½x14, 14x13½
2035-2036 A329 $6 each   4.50 4.50

Salute to Broadway A330

Stars, show: No. 2037: a, Robert Preston, The Music Man. b, Michael Crawford, Phantom of the Opera. c, Zero Mostel, Fiddler on the Roof. d, Patti Lupone, Evita. e, Raul Julia, Threepenny Opera. f, Mary Martin, South Pacific. g, Carol Channing, Hello Dolly. h, Yul Brynner, The King and I. i, Julie Andrews, My Fair Lady.
$6, Mickey Rooney, Sugar Babies.

1997   Perf. 14
2037 A330 $1 Sheet of 9, #a.-i.   6.80 6.80
Souvenir Sheet
2038 A330 $6 multicolored   4.50 4.50

Butterflies — A331

Designs: 90c, Charaxes porthos. $1.20, Aethiopana honorifis. $1.60, Charaxes hadrianus. $1.75, Precis westermanni.
No. 2043: a, Charaxes protoclea. b, Byblia ilithyia. c, Black-headed tchagra (bird). d, Charaxes nobilis. e, Pseudacraea boisduvali. f, Charaxes smaragdalis. g, Charaxes lasti. h, Pseudacraea poggei. i, Graphium colonna.
No. 2044a, Carmine bee-eater (bird). b, Pseudacraea eurytus. c, Hypolimnas monteironis. d, Charaxes anticlea. e, Graphium leonidas. f, Graphium illyris. g, Nepheronia argia. h, Graphium policenes. i, Papilio dardanus.
No. 2045, Euxanthe tiberius, horiz. No. 2046, Charaxes lactitinctus, horiz. No. 2047, Euphaedra neophron.

1997, Mar. 10
2039-2042 A331 Set of 4   4.00 4.00
Sheets of 9
2043-2044 A331 $1.10 #a.-i., each   7.50 7.50
Souvenir Sheets
2045-2047 A331 $6 each   4.50 4.50

UNESCO, 50th Anniv. — A332

World Heritage Sites: 60c, Convent of the Companions of Jesus, Morelia, Mexico. 90c, Fortress, San Lorenzo, Panama, vert. $1, Canaima Natl. Park, Venezuela, vert. $1.20, Huascarán Natl. Park, Peru, vert. $1.60, Church of San Francisco, Guatemala, vert. $1.75, Santo Domingo, Dominican Republic, vert.
No. 2054, vert: a-c, Guanajuato, Mexico. d, Jesuit missions of the Chiquitos, Bolivia. e, Huascarán Natl. Park, Peru. f, Jesuit missions, La Santisima, Paraguay. g, Cartagena, Colombia. h, Old Havana fortification, Cuba.
No. 2055: a, Tikal Natl. Park, Guatemala. b, Rio Platano Reserve, Honduras. c, Ruins of Copán, Honduras. d, Church of El Carmen, Antigua, Guatemala. e, Teotihuacán, Mexico.
No. 2056, Teotihuacán, Mexico, diff. No. 2057, Tikal Natl. Park, Guatemala, diff.

1997, Apr. 10   Litho.   Perf. 14
2048-2053 A332 Set of 6   5.25 5.25
Sheets of 8 or 5
2054 A332 $1.10 #a.-h. + label   6.75 6.75
2055 A332 $1.65 #a.-e. + label   6.25 6.25
Souvenir Sheets
2056-2057 A332 $6 each   4.50 4.50

Fauna — A333

No. 2058: a, Red bishop. b, Yellow baboon. c, Superb starling. d, Ratel. e, Hunting dog. f, Serval.
No. 2059: a, Okapi. b, Giant forest squirrel. c, Masked weaver. d, Common genet. e, Yellow-billed stork. f, Red-headed agama.
No. 2060, Malachite kingfisher. No. 2061, Gray crowned crane. No. 2062, Bat-eared fox.

1997, Apr. 24
2058 A333 $1.20 Sheet of 6, #a.-f.   5.50 5.50
2059 A333 $1.65 Sheet of 6, #a.-f.   7.50 7.50
Souvenir Sheets
2060-2062 A333 $6 each   4.50 4.50

Charlie Chaplin (1889-1977), Comedian, Actor A334

Various portraits.

1997, Feb. 24   Litho.   Perf. 14
2063 A334 $1 Sheet of 9, #a.-i.   6.75 6.75
Souvenir Sheet
2064 A334 $6 multicolored   4.50 4.50

Paul P. Harris (1868-1947), Founder of Rotary, Intl. — A335

Designs: $1.75, Service above self, James Grant, Ivory Coast, 1994, portrait of Harris.
$6, Group study exchange, New Zealand.

1997, June 12   Litho.   Perf. 14
2065 A335 $1.75 multicolored   1.25 1.25
Souvenir Sheet
2066 A335 $6 multicolored   4.50 4.50

Heinrich von Stephan (1831-97) A336

Portrait of Von Stephan and: No. 2067: a, Kaiser Wilhelm I. b, UPU emblem. c, Pigeon Post.
$6, Von Stephan, Basel messenger, 1400's.

1997, June 12
2067 A336 $1.75 Sheet of 3, #a.-c.   4.00 4.00
Souvenir Sheet
2068 A336 $6 multicolored   4.50 4.50
PACIFIC 97.

Queen Elizabeth II, Prince Philip, 50th Wedding Anniv. A337

No. 2069: a, Queen. b, Royal arms. c, Queen, Prince in royal attire. d, Queen, King riding in open carriage. e, Balmoral Castle. f, Prince Philip.
$6, Early portrait of Queen, King in royal attire.

1997, June 12
2069 A337 $1 Sheet of 6, #a.-f.   4.50 4.50
Souvenir Sheet
2070 A337 $6 multicolored   4.50 4.50

Grimm's Fairy Tales A338

Scenes from "Cinderella:" No. 2071: a, Mother, stepsisters. b, Cinderella, fairy godmother. c, Cinderella, Prince Charming.
$6, Prince trying shoe on Cinderella.

1997, June 13   Perf. 13½x14
2071 A338 $1.75 Sheet of 3, #a.-c.   4.00 4.00
Souvenir Sheet
2072 A338 $6 multicolored   4.50 4.50

ANTIGUA

Chernobyl Disaster, 10th Anniv. — A339

Designs: $1.65, UNESCO. $2, Chabad's Children of Chernobyl.

1997, June 12
2073	A339	$1.65 multicolored	1.25	1.25
2074	A339	$2 multicolored	1.50	1.50

Mushrooms A340

Designs: 45c, Marasmius rotula. 65c, Cantharellus cibarius. 70c, Lepiota cristata. 90c, Auricularia mesenterica. $1, Pholiota alnicola. $1.65, Leccinum aurantiacum.
No. 2081: a, Entoloma serrulatum. b, Panaeolus sphinctrinus. c, Volvariella bombycina. d, Conocybe percincta. e, Pluteus cervinus. f, Russula foetens.
No. 2082, Panellus serotinus. No. 2083, Amanita cothurnata.

1997, Aug. 12 Litho. Perf. 14
2075-2080	A340	Set of 6	4.00	4.00

Sheets of 6
2081	A340	$1.75 #a.-f.	8.00	8.00

Souvenir Sheets
2082-2083	A340	$6 each	4.50	4.50

Orchids — A341

Designs: 45c, Odontoglossum cervantesii. 65c, Medford star. 75c, Motes resplendent. 90c, Debutante. $1, Apple blossom. $2, Dendrobium.
No. 2090: a, Angel lace. b, Precious stones. c, Orange theope butterfly. d, Promenaea xanthina. e, Lycaste macrobulbon. f, Amesiella philippinensis. g, Machu Picchu. h, Zuma urchin.
No. 2091: a, Sophia Martin. b, Dogface butterfly. c, White mink purple. d, Showgirl. e, Mem. Dorothy Bertsch. f, Black II. g, Leeanum. h, Paphiopedilum macranthum.
No. 2092, Seine. No. 2093, Paphiopedilum gratrixianum.

1997, Aug. 19 Litho. Perf. 14
2084-2089	A341	Set of 6	4.25	4.25

Sheets of 8
2090-2091	A341	$1.65 #a.-h., each	5.00	5.00

Souvenir Sheets
2092-2093	A341	$6 each	4.50	4.50

1998 World Cup Soccer Championships, France — A342

Designs: 60c, Maradona, Argentina, 1986. 75c, Fritzwalter, W. Germany, 1954. 90c, Zoff, Italy, 1982. $1.20, Moore, England, 1966. $1.65, Alberto, Brazil, 1970. $1.75, Matthäus, W. Germany.
No. 2100, vert: a, Ademir, Brazil, 1950. b, Eusebio, Portugal, 1966. c, Fontaine, France, 1958. d, Schillaci, Italy, 1990. e, Leonidas, Brazil, 1938. f, Stabile, Argentina, 1930. g, Nejedly, Czechoslovakia, 1934. h, Muller, W. Germany, 1970.
No. 2101, Players, W. Germany, 1990. No. 2102, Bebeto, Brazil, vert.

1997, Oct. 6 Litho. Perf. 14
2094-2099	A342	Set of 6	6.00	6.00

Sheet of 8 + Label
2100	A342	$1 #a.-h.	6.00	6.00

Souvenir Sheets
2101-2102	A342	$6 each	4.50	4.50

Domestic Animals A343

Dogs: No. 2103: a, Dachshund. b, Staffordshire terrier. c, Sharpei. d, Beagle. e, Norfolk terrier. f, Golden retriever.
Cats: No. 2104: a, Scottish fold. b, Japanese bobtail. c, Tabby manx. d, Bicolor American shorthair. e, Sorrel abyssinian. f, Himalayan blue point.
No. 2105, Siberian husky, vert. No. 2106, Red tabby American shorthair kitten, vert.

1997, Oct. 27 Litho. Perf. 14

Sheets of 6
2103-2104	A343	$1.65 #a.-f., each	7.50	7.50

Souvenir Sheets
2105-2106	A343	$6 each	4.50	4.50

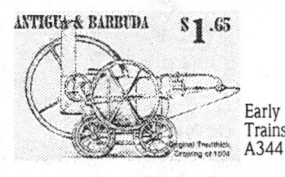

Early Trains A344

No. 2107: a, Original Trevithick drawing, 1804. b, "Puffing Billy," William Hedley, 1860. c, Crampton locomotive, Northern Railway, France, 1858. d, Twenty-five ton locomotive, Lawrence Machine Shop, 1860's. e, First locomotive "Mississippi," built in England. f, "Coppernob," locomotive by Edward Bury, Furness Railway.
No. 2108: a, "Jenny Lind," by David Joy for E.B. Wilson. b, "Atlantic" type locomotive, by Schenectady Locomotive Works, 1899. c, British built tank engine, Japan, by Kisons of Leeds, 1881. d, Express freight locomotive, 4-8-2 type, Pennsylvania Railroad. e, Four-cylinder locomotive, by Karl Golsdorf, Austria. f, "E" series 0-10-0 locomotive, produced by Lugansk Works, Russia, 1930.
No. 2109, "Patente" George Stephenson, 1843. No. 2110, Brunel's Trestle, Lynher River.

1997, Nov. 10

Sheets of 6
2107-2108	A344	$1.65 #a.-f., each	7.50	7.50

Souvenir Sheets
2109-2110	A344	$6 each	4.50	4.50

Christmas A345

Entire paintings or details: 15c, The Angel Leaving Tobias and His Family, by Rembrandt. 25c, The Resurrection, by Martin Knoller. 60c, Astronomy, by Raphael. 75c, Music-making Angel, by Melozzo da Forli. 90c, Amor, by Parmigianino. $1.20, Madonna and Child with Saints John the Baptist, Anthony, Stephen and Jerome, by Rosso Fiorentino.
No. 2117, The Portinari Altarpiece, by Hugo Van Der Goes. No. 2118, The Wedding of Tobiolo, by Gianantonio and Francesco Guardi.

1997, Dec. 2 Litho. Perf. 14
2111-2116	A345	Set of 6	5.25	5.25

Souvenir Sheets
2117-2118	A345	$6 each	4.50	4.50

Diana, Princess of Wales (1961-97) — A346

Various portraits, color of sheet margin: No. 2119, Pale green. No. 2120, Pale pink. No. 2121, With her sons (in margin). No. 2122, With Pope John Paul II (in margin).

1998, Jan. 19 Litho. Perf. 14

Sheets of 6
2119-2120	A346	$1.65 #a.-f., each	7.50	7.50

Souvenir Sheets
2121-2122	A346	$6 each	4.50	4.50

Fish A347

Designs: 75c, Yellow damselfish. 90c, Barred hamlet. $1, Jewelfish. $1.20, Bluehead wrasse. $1.50, Queen angelfish. $1.75, Queen triggerfish.
No. 2129: a, Jack-knife fish. b, Cuban hogfish. c, Sergeant major. d, Neon goby. e, Jawfish. f, Flamefish.
No. 2130: a, Rock beauty. b, Yellowtail snapper. c, Creole wrasse. d, Slender filefish. e, Squirrel fish. f, Fairy basslet.
No. 2131, Black-capped gramma. No. 2132, Porkfish.

1998, Feb. 19
2123-2128	A347	Set of 6	5.50	5.50

Sheets of 6
2129-2130	A347	$1.65 #a.-f., each	7.50	7.50

Souvenir Sheets
2131-2132	A347	$6 each	4.50	4.50

Cedar Hall Moravian Church, 175th Anniv. A348

Designs: 20c, First church, manse, 1822-40. 45c, Cedar Hall School, 1840. 75c, Hugh A. King, former minister. 90c, Present structure. $1.20, Water tank, 1822. $2, Former manse demolished, 1978. $6, Present structure, diff.

1998, Mar. 16 Litho. Perf. 14
2133-2138	A348	Set of 6	4.25	4.25

Souvenir Sheet
2139	A348	$6 multicolored	4.50	4.50

No. 2139 contains one 50x37mm stamp.

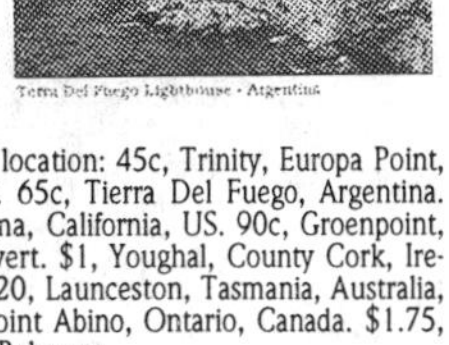

Lighthouses A349

Lighthouse, location: 45c, Trinity, Europa Point, Gibraltar, vert. 65c, Tierra Del Fuego, Argentina. 75c, Point Loma, California, US. 90c, Groenpoint, South Africa, vert. $1, Youghal, County Cork, Ireland, vert. $1.20, Launceston, Tasmania, Australia, vert. $1.65, Point Abino, Ontario, Canada. $1.75, Great Inagua, Bahamas.
$6, Capa Hatteras, North Carolina, US, vert.

1998, Apr. 20
2140-2147	A349	Set of 8	6.50	6.50

Souvenir Sheet
2148	A349	$6 multicolored	4.50	4.50

Winnie the Pooh — A350

No. 2149: a, Pooh, Tigger in January. b, Pooh, Piglet in February. c, Piglet in March. d, Tigger, Pooh, Piglet in April. e, Kanga, Roo in May. f, Pooh, Owl in June.
No. 2150: a, Pooh, Eeyore, Tigger, Piglet in July. b, Pooh, Piglet in August. c, Christopher Robin in September. d, Eeyore in October. e, Pooh, Rabbit in November. f, Pooh, Piglet in December.
No. 2151, Pooh, Rabbit holding blanket, Spring. No. 2152, Pooh holding hand to mouth, Summer. No. 2153, Pooh holding rake, Fall. No. 2154, Eeyore, Pooh, Winter.

1998, May 11 Litho. Perf. 13½x14

Sheets of 6
2149-2150	A360	$1 #a.-f., each	4.50	4.50

Souvenir Sheet
2151-2154	A350	$6 each	4.50	4.50

Thomas Oliver Robinson Memorial High School, Cent. A351

Designs: 20c, $6, Nellie Robinson (1880-1972), founder, vert. 45c, School picture, 1985. 65c, Former building, 1930-49. 75c, Students with present headmistress, Natalie Hurst. 90c, Ina Loving (1908-96), educator, vert. $1.20, Present building, 1950.

1998, July 23 Litho. Perf. 14
2155-2160	A351	Set of 6	3.25	3.25

Souvenir Sheet
2161	A351	$6 multicolored	4.50	4.50

No. 2161 is a continuous design.

Intl. Year of the Ocean A352

Marine life, "20,000 Leagues Under the Sea:" No. 2162: a, Spotted eagle ray. b, Manta ray. c, Hawksbill turtle. d, Jellyfish. e, Queen angelfish. f, Octopus. g, Emperor angelfish. h, Regal angelfish. i, Porkfish. j, Raccoon butterfly fish. k, Atlantic barracuda. l, Sea horse. m, Nautilus. n, Trumpet fish. o, White tip shark. p, Spanish galleon. q, Black tip shark. r, Long-nosed butterfly fish. s, Green moray eel. t, Captain Nemo. u, Treasure chest. v, Hammerhead shark. w, Divers. x, Lion fish. y, Clown fish.
Wildlife and birds: No. 2163: a, Maroon tailed conure. b, Cocoi heron. c, Common tern. d, Rainbow lorikeet. e, Saddleback butterfly fish. f, Goatfish, cat shark. g, Blue shark, stingray. h, Majestic snapper. i, Nassau grouper. j, Black-cap gramma, blue tang. k, Stingrays. l, Stingrays, giant starfish.
#2164, Fiddler ray. #2165, Humpback whale.

1998, Aug. 17
2162	A352	40c Sheet of 25, #a.-y.	7.50	7.50
2163	A352	75c Sheet of 12, #a.-l.	6.75	6.75

Souvenir Sheets
2164-2165	A352	$6 each	4.50	4.50

Ships A353

ANTIGUA — ARGENTINA

No. 2166: a, Savannah. b, Viking ship. c, Greek warship.
No. 2167: a, Clipper. b, Dhow. c, Fishing cat.
No. 2168, Dory, vert. No. 2169, Baltimore clipper. No. 2170, English warship, 13th cent.

1998, Aug. 18   Perf. 14x14½
Sheets of 3
2166-2167 A353 $1.75 #a.-c., each   4.00 4.00
Souvenir Sheets
Perf. 14
2168-2170 A353 $6 each   4.50 4.50

CARICOM, 25th Anniv. A354

1998, Aug. 20   Litho.   Perf. 13½
2171 A354 $1 multicolored   .75 .75

Antique Automobiles A355

No. 2172: a, 1911 Torpedo. b, 1913 Mercedes 22. c, 1920 Rover. d, 1956 Mercedes Benz. e, 1934 Packard V12. f, 1924 Opel.
Fords: No. 2173: a, 1896. b, 1903 Model A. c, 1928 Model T. d, 1922 Model T. e, 1929 Blackhawk. f, 1934 Sedan. #2174, 1908. #2175, 1929.

1998, Sept. 1   Perf. 14
Sheets of 6
2172-2173 A355 $1.65 #a.-f., each   7.50 7.50
Souvenir Sheets
2174-2175 A355 $6 each   4.50 4.50
Nos. 2174-2175 each contain one 60x40mm stamp.

Aircraft A356

No. 2176: a, NASA Space Shuttle. b, Saab Grippen. c, Eurofighter EF2000. d, Sukhoi SU 27. e, Northrop B-2. f, Lockheed F-117 Nighthawk.
No. 2177: a, Lockheed-Boeing General Dynamics Yf-22. b, Dassault-Breguet Rafale BO 1. c, MiG 29. d, Dassault-Breguet Mirage 2000D. e, Rockwell B-1B Lancer. f, McDonnell-Douglas C-17A.
No. 2178, Sukhoi SU 35. No. 2179, F18 Hornet.

1998, Sept. 21
Sheets of 6
2176-2177 A356 $1.65 #a.-f., each   7.50 7.50
Souvenir Sheets
2178-2179 A356 $6 each   4.50 4.50

Famous People of the 20th Cent. — A357
Diana, Princess of Wales (1961-97) — A358 

Inventors and their inventions: No. 2180: a, Rudolf Diesel (1858-1913). b, Internal combustion, diesel engines. c, Zeppelin war balloon, Intrepid. d, Ferdinand von Zeppelin (1838-1917). e, Wilhelm Conrad Röntgen (1845-1923). f, X-ray machine. g, Saturn rocket. h, Wernher von Braun (1912-77).
No. 2181: a, Carl Benz (1844-1929). b, Internal combustion engine, automobile. c, Atomic bomb. d, Albert Einstein. e, Leopold Godowsky, Jr. (1901-83) and Leopold Damrosch Mannes (1899-1964). f, Kodachrome film. g, First turbo jet airplane. h, Hans Pabst von Ohain (1911-98).

No. 2182, Hans Geiger (1882-1945), inventor of the Geiger counter. No. 2183, William Shockley (1910-89), developer of transistors.

1998, Nov. 10   Litho.   Perf. 14
Sheets of 8
2180-2181 A357 $1 #a.-h., each   6.00 6.00
Souvenir Sheets
2182-2183 A357 $6 each   4.50 4.50
Nos. 2180b-2180c, 2180f-2180g, 2181b-2181c, 2181f-2181g are 53x38mm.

1998, Nov. 18
2184 A358 $1.20 multicolored   .90 .90
No. 2184 was issued in sheets of 6.

Gandhi — A359
Picasso — A360 

Portraits: 90c, Up close, later years. $1, Seated with hands clasped. $1.20, Up close, early years. $1.65, Primary school, Rajkot, age 7. $6, Wwith stick, walking with boy (in margin).

1998, Nov. 18
2185-2188 A359 Set of 4   2.75 2.75
Souvenir Sheet
2189 A359 $6 multicolored   2.25 2.25

1998, Nov. 18
Paintings: $1.20, Figures on the Seashore, 1931, horiz. $1.65, Three Figures Under a Tree, 1907. $1.75, Two Women Running on the Beach, 1922, horiz.
$6, Bullfight, 1900, horiz.
2190-2192 A360 Set of 3   3.50 3.50
Souvenir Sheet
2193 A360 $6 multicolored   4.50 4.50

1998 World Scouting Jamboree, Chile A361

90c, Handshake. $1, Scouts hiking. $1.20, Sign. $6, Lord Baden-Powell.

1998, Oct. 8   Litho.   Perf. 14
2194-2196 A361 Set of 3   2.50 2.50
Souvenir Sheet
2197 A361 $6 multicolored   4.50 4.50

Organization of American States, 50th Anniv. A362

1998, Nov. 18   Perf. 13½
2198 A362 $1 multicolored   .75 .75

Enzo Ferrari (1898-1988), Automobile Manufacturer — A363

No. 2199: a, Top view of Dino 246 GT-GTS. b, Front view of Dino 246 GT-GTS. c, 1977 365 GT4 BB.
$6, Dino 246 GT-GTS.

1998, Nov. 18   Perf. 14
2199 A363 $1.75 Sheet of 3, #a.-c.   4.00 4.00
Souvenir Sheet
2200 A363 $6 multicolored   4.50 4.50
No. 2200 contains one 92x35mm stamp.

Royal Air Force, 80th Anniv. A364

No. 2201: a, McDonnell Douglas Phantom FGR1. b, Sepecat Jaguar GR1A. c, Panavia Tornado F3. d, McDonnell Douglas Phantom FGR2.
No. 2202, Eurofighter 2000, Hurricane. No. 2203, Hawk, biplane.

1998, Nov. 18
2201 A364 $1.75 Sheet of 4, #a.-d.   4.00 4.00
Souvenir Sheets
2202-2203 A364 $6 each   4.50 4.50

Sea Birds A365

Designs: 15c, Brown pelican. 25c, Dunlin. 45c, Atlantic puffin. 90c, Pied cormorant.
No. 2208: a, King eider. b, Inca tern. c, Dovekie. d, Ross's bull. e, Brown noddy. f, Marbled murrelet. g, Northern gannet. h, Razorbill. i, Long-tailed jaeger. j, Black guillemot. k, Whimbrel. l, Oystercatcher.
No. 2209, Rhynchops niger. No. 2210, Diomedea exulans.

1998, Nov. 24
2204-2207 A365 Set of 4   1.25 1.25
2208 A365 75c Sheet of 12, #a.-l.   6.75 6.75
Souvenir Sheets
2209-2210 A365 $6 each   4.50 4.50

Christmas A366

Dogs with Christmas decorations: 15c, Border collie. 25c, Dalmatian. 65c, Weimaraner. 75c, Scottish terrier. 90c, Long-haired dachshund. $1.20, Golden retriever. $2, Pekingese.
No. 2218, Dalmatian, diff. No. 2219, Jack Russell terrier.

1998, Dec. 10
2211-2217 A366 Set of 7   4.50 4.50
Souvenir Sheet
2218-2219 A366 $6 each   4.50 4.50

WAR TAX STAMPS

No. 31 and Type A3 Overprinted in Black or Red   **WAR STAMP**

1916-18   Wmk. 3   Perf. 14
MR1 A3 ½p green   .45 1.10
MR2 A3 ½p green (R) ('17)   .75 .75
MR3 A3 1½p orange ('18)   .45 .65
   Nos. MR1-MR3 (3)   1.65 2.50

ARGENTINA

,är-jən-'tē-nə

LOCATION — In South America
GOVT. — Republic
AREA — 1,084,120 sq. mi.
POP. — 27,949,480 (1980)
CAPITAL — Buenos Aires

100 Centavos = 1 Peso (1858, 1992)
100 Centavos = 1 Austral (1985)

Catalogue values for unused stamps in this country are for Never Hinged items, beginning with Scott 587 in the regular postage section, Scott B12 in the semi-postal section, Scott C59 in the airpost section, Scott CB1 in the airpost semi-postal section and Scott O79 in the officials section.

Watermarks

Wmk. 84- Italic RA

Wmk. 85- Small Sun, 4½mm 
Wmk. 86- Large Sun, 6mm

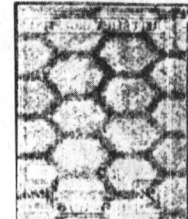

Wmk. 87- Honeycomb

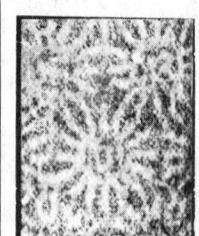

Wmk. 88- Multiple Suns

Wmk. 89- Large Sun

In this watermark the face of the sun is 7mm in diameter, the rays are heavier than in the large sun watermark of 1896-1911 and the watermarks are placed close together, so that parts of several frequently appear on one stamp. This paper was intended to be used for fiscal stamps and is usually referred to as "fiscal sun paper."

Wmk. 90- RA in Sun

ARGENTINA

In 1928 watermark 90 was slightly modified, making the diameter of the Sun 9mm instead of 10mm. Several types of this watermark exist.

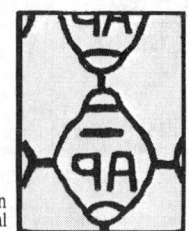

Wmk. 205- AP in Oval

The letters "AP" are the initials of "AHORRO POSTAL." This paper was formerly used exclusively for Postal Savings stamps.

Wmk. 287- Double Circle and Letters in Sheet

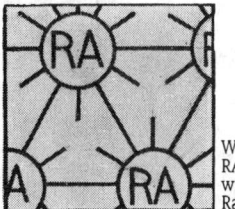

Wmk. 288- RA in Sun with Straight Rays

Wmk. 365- Argentine Arms, "Casa de Moneda de la Nacion" & "RA" Multiple

Values for Unused
Unused values for Nos. 5-17 are for examples without gum. Examples with original gum command higher prices. Unused values of Nos. 1-4B and stamps after No. 17 are for examples with original gum as defined in the catalogue introduction.

Argentine Confederation

Symbolical of the Argentine Confederation
A1   A2

1858, May 1   Unwmk.   Litho.   Imperf.

1	A1	5c red	1.50	24.00
a.		Colon after "5"	1.75	32.50
b.		Colon after "V"	1.75	32.50
2	A1	10c green	2.50	55.00
f.		Diagonal half used as 5c on cover		800.00
3	A1	15c blue	16.00	150.00
c.		One-third used as 5c on cover		6,500.
		Nos. 1-3 (3)	20.00	229.00

There are nine varieties of Nos. 1, 2 and 3. Counterfeits and forged cancellations of Nos. 1-3 are plentiful.

1860, Jan.

4	A2	5c red	3.25	70.00
4A	A2	10c green	7.00	
4B	A2	15c blue	25.00	
		Nos. 4-4B (3)	35.25	

Nos. 4A and 4B were never placed in use. Some compositions of Nos. 4-4B contain 8 different types across the sheet. Other settings exist with minor variations. Counterfeits and forged cancellations of Nos. 4-4B are plentiful.

Argentine Republic

Seal of the Republic — A3

Broad "C" in "CENTAVOS," Accent on "U" of "REPUBLICA"

1862, Jan. 11

5	A3	5c rose	40.00	37.50
a.		5c rose lilac	87.50	35.00
6	A3	10c green	140.00	65.00
b.		Diagonal half used as 5c on cover		4,750.
7	A3	15c blue	275.00	225.00
a.		Without accent on "U"	7,000.	3,000.
b.		Tete beche pair	100,000.	100,000.
i.		15c ultramarine	425.00	325.00
j.		Diagonal third used as 5c on cover		5,000.

Only one used example of No. 7b is known. It has faults. Two unused examples are known. One is sound with origonal gum, the other is in a block, without gum, and has tiny faults.

Broad "C" in "CENTAVOS," No Accent on "U"

1863

7C	A3	5c rose	18.00	21.00
d.		5c rose lilac	100.00	110.00
e.		Worn plate (rose)	200.00	52.50
7F	A3	10c yellow green	350.00	140.00
g.		10c olive green	500.00	250.00
k.		10c green, ribbed paper	425.00	200.00
l.		Worn plate (green)	325.00	150.00
m.		Worn plate (olive green)	425.00	165.00

Narrow "C" in "CENTAVOS," No Accent on "U"

1864

7H	A3	5c rose red	160.00	32.50

The so-called reprints of 10c and 15c are counterfeits. They have narrow "C" and straight lines in shield. Nos. 7C and 7H have been extensively counterfeited.

Rivadavia Issue

Bernardino Rivadavia
A4   A5

Rivadavia — A6

1864-67   Engr.   Wmk. 84   Imperf.
Clear Impressions

8	A4	5c brown rose	1,300.	160.
a.		5c orange red ('67)	1,500.	160.
9	A5	10c green	2,000.	1,200.
10	A6	15c blue	7,250.	4,000.

Perf. 11½
Dull to Worn Impressions

11	A4	5c brown rose ('65)	30.00	12.00
11B	A4	5c lake	77.50	17.50
12	A5	10c green	80.00	30.00
a.		Half used as 5c on cover		1,100.
b.		Horiz. pair, imperf vert.		1,750.
13	A6	15c blue	275.00	110.00

1867-72   Unwmk.   Imperf.

14	A4	5c carmine ('72)	250.	65.
15	A4	5c rose	200.	100.
15A	A5	10c green	4,000.	4,000.
16	A6	15c blue	2,250.	1,750.

Nos. 15A-16 issued without gum.

1867   Perf. 11½

17	A4	5c carmine	350.00	150.00

Nos. 14, 15 and 17 exist with part of papermaker's wmk. "LACROIX FRERES."

Rivadavia
A7

Manuel Belgrano
A8

Jose de San Martin — A9

Groundwork of Horizontal Lines

1867-68   Perf. 12

18	A7	5c vermilion	200.00	10.00
18A	A8	10c green	30.00	4.50
b.		Diag. half used as 5c on cover		750.00
19	A9	15c blue	65.00	15.00

Groundwork of Crossed Lines

20	A7	5c vermilion	10.50	.65
21	A9	15c blue	92.50	12.00

See Nos. 27, 33-34, 39 and types A19, A33, A34, A37. For surcharges and overprints see Nos. 30-32, 41-42, 47-51, O6-O7, O26.

Gen. Antonio G. Balcarce
A10

Mariano Moreno
A11

Carlos Maria de Alvear — A12

Gervasio Antonio Posadas — A13

Cornelio Saavedra — A14

1873

22	A10	1c purple	5.00	2.00
a.		1c gray violet	6.25	2.00
23	A11	4c brown	4.75	.40
a.		4c red brown	17.00	2.00
24	A12	30c orange	100.00	15.00
a.		Vert. pair, imperf horiz.	4,000.	
25	A13	60c black	100.00	4.75
26	A14	90c blue	25.00	2.25
		Nos. 22-26 (5)	234.75	24.40

For overprints see Nos. O5, O12-O14, O19-O21, O25, O29.

1873   Laid Paper

27	A8	10c green	200.00	20.00

Nos. 18, 18A Surcharged in Black

Nos. 30-31    No. 32

1877, Feb.   Wove Paper

30	A7	1c on 5c vermilion	47.50	15.00
a.		Inverted surcharge	350.00	200.00
31	A7	2c on 5c vermilion	92.50	60.00
a.		Inverted surcharge	700.00	500.00
32	A8	8c on 10c green	125.00	30.00
b.		Inverted surcharge	500.00	425.00
		Nos. 30-32 (3)	265.00	105.00

Varieties also exist with double and triple surcharges, surcharge on reverse, 8c on No. 27, all made clandestinely from the original cliches of the surcharges.
Forgeries of these surcharges include the inverted and double varieties.

1876-77   Rouletted

33	A7	5c vermilion	150.00	60.00
34	A7	8c lake ('77)	25.00	.35

ARGENTINA-ALL LATIN AMERICA-SPAIN
West Europe Topicals ...And much more !!!
The most interesting Philatelic Auction from Argentina
Three differents by year, + 5000 lots each
Bilingual Catalogues (English & Spanish) and
Binumeral (Scott & Yvert) - **Free upon request**
Visa, Mastercard and checks are accepted
Juan N. Simona
TE/FAX: 54-2281-497281 or 497346, 24 hrs. a day
E-mail : simonafilatelia@simonafilatelia.com.ar
Http : \\ www.simonafilatelia.com.ar
C.C.40-7311 Chillar(Buenos Aires)Argentina

ARGENTINA

Belgrano A17
Dalmacio Vélez Sarsfield A18 
San Martín — A19 

1878   *Rouletted*
35	A17	16c green	8.00	1.10
36	A18	20c blue	10.00	3.00
37	A19	24c blue	17.00	3.00
		Nos. 35-37 (3)	35.00	7.10

See No. 56. For overprints see Nos. O9-O10, O15-O17, O22, O28.

Vicente Lopez — A20
Alvear — A21 

1877-80   *Perf. 12*
38	A20	2c yellow green	4.25	.90
39	A7	8c lake ('80)	4.25	.35
a.		8c brown lake	27.50	.35
40	A21	25c lake ('78)	22.50	6.00
		Nos. 38-40 (3)	31.00	7.25

For overprints see Nos. O4, O11, O18, O24.

No. 18 Surcharged in Black

½ (PROVISORIO)   Large "P" Wide "V"
½ (PROVISORIO)   Small/ "P" Narrow "V"

1882
41	A7	½c on 5c ver	1.50	1.50
a.		Double surcharge	80.00	80.00
b.		Inverted surcharge	20.00	20.00
c.		"PROVISORIO" omitted	80.00	80.00
d.		Fraction omitted	50.00	
e.		"PROVISOBIO"	30.00	30.00
f.		Pair, one without surcharge	200.00	
g.		Small "P" in "PROVISORIO"	2.50	2.50
h.		As "a," small "P" in "PROVISORIO"	32.50	32.50
i.		As "b," small "P" in "PROVISORIO"	40.00	40.00
j.		As "d," small "P" in "PROVISORIO"	15.00	15.00

Perforated across Middle of Stamp
42	A7	½c on 5c ver	3.00	3.00
a.		"PROVISORIQ"	40.00	40.00
b.		Large "P" in "PROVISORIO"	30.00	22.50

A23

1882   *Typo.*   *Perf. 12*
43	A23	½c brown	1.40	.80
a.		Imperf., pair	40.00	40.00
44	A23	1c red, perf. 14	3.50	1.00
a.		Perf. 12	9.00	4.25
45	A23	12c ultra	55.00	8.75
a.		Perf. 14	45.00	8.75

Engr.
46	A23	12c grnsh blue, perf. 14	125.00	11.00
		Nos. 43-46 (4)	184.90	21.85

See type A29. For overprints see Nos. O2, O8, O23, O27.

No. 21 Surcharged in Red:

1884 ½ (a)   **1c 1884** (b)   **CUATRO Centavos 1884** (c)

1884   *Engr.*   *Perf. 12*
47	A9 (a)	½c on 15c blue	2.00	1.50
a.		Groundwork of horiz. lines	100.00	80.00
b.		Inverted surcharge	27.50	20.00
48	A9 (b)	1c on 15c blue	16.00	13.00
a.		Groundwork of horiz. lines	10.00	6.00
b.		Inverted surcharge	80.00	55.00
c.		Double surcharge	40.00	32.50
d.		Triple surcharge	350.00	

Nos. 20-21 Surcharged in Black
49	A7	½c on 5c ver	4.00	3.00
a.		Inverted surcharge	150.00	110.00
b.		Date omitted	150.00	
c.		Pair, one without surcharge	375.00	
d.		Double surcharge	550.00	
50	A9 (a)	½c on 15c blue	10.00	8.00
a.		Groundwork of horiz. lines	30.00	25.00
b.		Inverted surcharge	70.00	55.00
c.		Pair, one without surcharge	325.00	
51	A7 (c)	4c on 5c ver	10.00	6.00
a.		Inverted surcharge	25.00	20.00
b.		Double surcharge	325.00	200.00
c.		Pair, one without surcharge but with "4" in manuscript	550.00	350.00
d.		Pair, one without surcharge	250.00	
		Nos. 47-51 (5)	42.00	31.50

A29

1884-85   *Engr.*   *Perf. 12*
52	A29	½c red brown	.90	.45
a.		Horiz. pair, imperf vert.	300.00	250.00
53	A29	1c rose red	5.25	.45
a.		Horiz. pair, imperf vert.	300.00	250.00
54	A29	12c grnsh blue ('85)	30.00	1.25
a.		12c deep blue	25.00	1.25
b.		Horiz. pair, imperf vert.	300.00	250.00
		Nos. 52-54 (3)	36.15	2.15

For overprints see Nos. O1, O3, O9.

San Martin Type of 1878

1887   *Engr.*
56	A19	24c blue	17.50	1.40

Justo Jose de Urquiza A30
Lopez A31 
Miguel Juarez Celman — A32 
Rivadavia (Large head) — A33 
Rivadavia (Small head) A34 
Domingo F. Sarmiento A35 
Nicolas Avellaneda A36 
San Martin A37 

Julio A. Roca A37a
Belgrano A37b 
Manuel Dorrego — A38 
Moreno — A39 
Bartolome Mitre — A40 

CINCO CENTAVOS.
A33 - Shows collar on left side only.
A34 - Shows collar on both sides. Lozenges in background larger and clearer than in A33.

1888-90   *Litho.*   *Perf. 11½*
57	A30	½c blue	.50	.45
b.		Vert. pair, imperf. horiz.	120.00	65.00
c.		Horiz. pair, imperf. vert.	120.00	65.00
58	A31	2c yellow green	9.25	6.00
b.		Vert. pair, imperf. horiz.	200.00	
59	A32	3c blue green	1.75	.60
b.		Vert. pair, imperf. horiz.	80.00	
c.		Horiz. pair, imperf. btwn.	100.00	
d.		Vert. pair, imperf. btwn.	25.00	
60	A33	5c carmine	8.00	.75
b.		Vert. pair, imperf. horiz.	100.00	
61	A34	5c carmine	11.00	1.25
b.		Vert. pair, imperf. horiz.	400.00	
62	A35	6c red	25.00	15.00
b.		Vert. pair, imperf. horiz.	80.00	
c.		Perf. 12	52.50	42.50
63	A36	10c brown	15.00	1.10
64	A37	15c orange	15.00	1.65
d.		Vert. pair, imperf. between	600.00	
64A	A37a	20c green	12.00	1.25
64B	A37b	25c purple	15.00	1.65
65	A38	30c chocolate	21.00	2.50
b.		30c reddish chocolate brown	400.00	80.00
c.		Horiz. pair, imperf. between	400.00	325.00
66	A39	40c slate, perf. 12	25.00	3.00
a.		Perf. 11½	80.00	16.00
b.		Horiz. pair, imperf. btwn. (#66)	600.00	
67	A40	50c blue	100.00	8.75
		Nos. 57-67 (13)	258.50	43.45

In this issue there are several varieties of each value, the difference between them being in the relative position of the head to the frame.

Imperf., Pairs
57a	A30	½c	75.00	60.00
58a	A31	2c	55.00	
59a	A32	3c	35.00	25.00
61a	A34	5c	100.00	
62a	A35	6c	55.00	
63a	A36	10c	55.00	
64c	A37	15c	200.00	
65a	A38	30c	275.00	200.00

Urquiza A41
Velez Sarsfield A42 
Miguel Juarez Celman A43  
Rivadavia (Large head) A44 

Sarmiento A45
Juan Bautista Alberdi A46 

1888-89   *Engr.*   *Perf. 11½, 11½x12*
68	A41	½c ultra	.30	.15
a.		Vert. pair, imperf. horiz.	30.00	
b.		Imperf., pair	30.00	
69	A42	1c brown	.85	.15
a.		Vert. pair, imperf. horiz.	65.00	
b.		Vert. pair, imperf. btwn.	—	
c.		Imperf., pair	30.00	
d.		Horiz. pair, imperf. btwn.	100.00	
70	A43	3c blue green	2.50	.70
71	A44	3c rose	2.75	.15
a.		Imperf., pair	40.00	
72	A45	6c blue black	1.40	.55
b.		Perf. 11½x12	12.50	3.00
73	A46	12c blue	5.50	1.75
a.		Imperf., pair	30.00	
b.		bluish paper	8.00	2.00
c.		Perf. 11½	8.25	3.25
		Nos. 68-73 (6)	13.30	3.45

#69-70 exist with papermakers' watermarks.
See No. 77, types A50, A61. For surcharges see Nos. 83-84.

Jose Maria Paz A48
Santiago Derqui A49 
Rivadavia (Small head) A50 
Avellaneda A51 
Moreno A53 
Mitre A54 
Posadas — A55 

1890   *Engr.*   *Perf. 11½*
75	A48	¼c green	.15	.15
76	A49	2c violet	.85	.15
a.		2c purple	.85	.15
b.		2c slate	1.25	.30
c.		Horiz. pair, imperf. btwn.	25.00	
d.		Imperf., pair	35.00	
e.		Perf. 11½x12	5.00	.25
77	A50	5c carmine	1.90	.15
a.		Imperf., pair	50.00	25.00
b.		Perf. 11½x12	50.00	.30
c.		Vert. pair, imperf. btwn.	75.00	60.00
d.		Horiz. pair, imperf. btwn.	75.00	60.00
78	A51	10c brown	1.65	.25
b.		Imperf., pair	150.00	
c.		Vert. pair, imperf. btwn.	225.00	
80	A53	40c olive green	5.00	.80
a.		Imperf., pair	40.00	
b.		Horiz. pair, imperf. btwn.		250.00
81	A54	50c orange	4.00	.80
a.		Imperf., pair	60.00	
b.		Perf. 11½x12	4.25	1.10
82	A55	60c black	15.00	2.75
a.		Imperf., pair		
b.		Vert. pair, imperf. btwn.	125.00	100.00
		Nos. 75-82 (7)	28.55	5.05

Type A50 differs from type A44 in having the head smaller, the letters of "Cinco Centavos" not as tall, and the curved ornaments at sides close to the first and last letters of "Republica Argentina."

Lithographed Surcharge on No. 73 in Black or Red

¼

1890 *Perf. 11½x12*

83	A46	¼c on 12c blue	.40	.40
a.		Perf. 11½	35.00	25.00
b.		Double surcharge	75.00	35.00
c.		Inverted surcharge	80.00	
84	A46	¼c on 12c blue (R)	.40	.40
a.		Double surcharge	52.50	52.50
b.		Perf. 11½	7.00	2.00

Surcharge is different on #83 and 84.

Nos. 83-84 exist as pairs, one without surcharge. These were privately produced.

Rivadavia A57

Jose de San Martin A58

Gregorio Araoz de Lamadrid — A59

Admiral Guillermo Brown — A60

1891 **Engr.** *Perf. 11½*

85	A57	8c carmine rose	1.25	.20
a.		Imperf., pair	75.00	
86	A58	1p deep blue	40.00	5.75
87	A59	5p ultra	200.00	16.00
88	A60	20p green	300.00	45.00
		Nos. 85-88 (4)	541.25	66.95

A 10p brown and a 50p red were prepared but not issued. Values: 10p $1,500 for fine, 50p $1,000 with rough or somewhat damaged perfs.

Velez Sarsfield — A61

"Santa Maria," "Nina" and "Pinta" — A62

1890 *Perf. 11½*

89	A61	1c brown	.80	.40
b.		Horiz. pair, imperf. btwn.		*550.00*

Type A61 is a re-engraving of A42. The figure "1" in each upper corner has a short horizontal serif instead of a long one pointing downward. In type A61 the first and last letters of "Correos y Telegrafos" are closer to the curved ornaments below than in type A42. Background is of horizontal lines (crosshatching on No. 69).

1892, Oct. 12 **Wmk. 85** *Perf. 11½*

90	A62	2c light blue	6.00	3.00
a.		Double impression	190.00	
91	A62	5c dark blue	8.50	5.00

Discovery of America, 400th anniv. Counterfeits of Nos. 90-91 are litho.

Rivadavia A63

Belgrano A64

San Martin — A65

Perf. 11½, 12 and Compound

1892-95 **Wmk. 85**

92	A63	½c dull blue	.30	.15
a.		½c bright ultra	50.00	25.00
93	A63	1c brown	.35	.15
94	A63	2c green	.35	.15
95	A63	3c orange ('95)	1.00	.15
96	A63	5c carmine	1.50	.15
b.		5c green (error)	350.00	350.00
98	A64	10c carmine rose	10.00	.40
99	A64	12c deep blue ('93)	7.00	.40
100	A64	16c gray	12.50	.55
101	A64	24c gray brown	12.50	.55
b.		Perf. 12	25.00	7.00
102	A64	50c blue green	18.00	.55
b.		Perf. 12	25.00	2.75
103	A65	1p lake ('93)	10.00	.70
a.		1p red brown	17.50	5.00
104	A65	2p dark green	21.00	2.25
a.		Perf. 12	77.50	27.50
105	A65	5p dark blue	38.00	2.75
		Nos. 92-105 (13)	132.50	8.90

The high values of this and succeeding issues are frequently punched with the word "INUTILIZADO," parts of the letters showing on each stamp. These punched stamps sell for only a small fraction of the catalogue values.

Reprints of No. 96b have white gum. The original stamp has yellowish gum. Value $125.

Imperf., Pairs

92b	A63	½c	55.00	—
93a	A63	1c	55.00	—
94a	A63	2c	25.00	—
96a	A63	5c	25.00	—
98a	A64	10c	55.00	—
99a	A64	12c	55.00	—
100a	A64	16c	55.00	—
101a	A64	24c	55.00	—
102a	A64	50c	55.00	—
103b	A65	1p	60.00	—
105a	A65	5p	140.00	—

Nos. 102a, 103b and 105a exist only without gum; the other imperfs are found with or without gum, and values are the same for either condition.

Vertical Pairs, Imperf. Between

92c	A63	½c	125.00	
93b	A63	1c	100.00	
94b	A63	2c	50.00	
95a	A63	3c	250.00	
96c	A63	5c	45.00	50.00
98b	A64	10c	100.00	
99b	A64	12c	100.00	

Horizontal Pairs, Imperf. Between

93c	A63	1c	110.00	
94c	A63	2c	55.00	
96d	A63	5c	55.00	45.00
98c	A64	10c	110.00	

1896-97 **Wmk. 86**

106	A63	½c slate	.50	.15
a.		½c gray blue	.50	.15
b.		½c indigo	.50	.15
107	A63	1c brown	.50	.15
108	A63	2c yellow green	.60	.15
109	A63	3c orange	.60	.15
110	A63	5c carmine	.60	.15
a.		Imperf., pair	100.00	
111	A64	10c carmine rose	8.00	.15
112	A64	12c deep blue	4.00	.15
a.		Imperf., pair	—	
113	A64	16c gray	10.00	.80
114	A64	24c gray brown	10.50	1.25
a.		Imperf., pair	100.00	—
115	A64	30c orange ('97)	10.00	.60
116	A64	50c blue green	10.00	.60
117	A64	80c dull violet	18.00	.80
118	A65	1p lake	25.00	.75
119	A65	1p20c black ('97)	10.00	3.50
120	A65	2p dark green	15.00	7.00
121	A65	5p dark blue	90.00	10.00
a.		Perf. 12	325.00	90.00
		Nos. 106-121 (16)	213.30	26.35

Vertical Pairs, Imperf. Between

106c	A63	½c	200.00	
107a	A63	1c	125.00	
108a	A63	2c	125.00	
109a	A63	3c	200.00	
110b	A63	5c	125.00	125.00
112b	A64	12c	125.00	100.00

Horizontal Pairs, Imperf. Between

107b	A63	1c	125.00	
108b	A63	2c	125.00	
110c	A63	5c	125.00	80.00
111a	A64	10c	125.00	
112c	A64	12c	125.00	

Allegory, Liberty Seated
A66 A67

Perf. 11½, 12 and Compound

1899-1903

122	A66	½c yellow brown	.15	.15
123	A66	1c green	.20	.15
124	A66	2c slate	.20	.15
125	A66	3c orange ('01)	.85	.15
126	A66	4c yellow ('03)	1.50	.20
127	A66	5c carmine rose	.20	.15
128	A66	6c black ('03)	1.00	.40
129	A66	10c dark green	1.50	.30
130	A66	12c dull blue	1.00	.30
131	A66	12c olive grn ('01)	1.00	.50
132	A66	15c sea green ('01)	2.75	.50
132B	A66	15c dull blue ('01)	3.00	.50
133	A66	16c orange	7.50	3.75
134	A66	20c claret	2.00	.15
135	A66	24c violet	3.50	.70
136	A66	30c rose	7.50	.40
137	A66	30c vermilion ('01)	3.75	.40
a.		30c scarlet	50.00	2.50
138	A66	50c brt blue	4.75	.40
139	A67	1p bl & blk, perf. 11½	14.00	.65
a.		Center inverted	*1,500.*	*525.00*
b.		Perf. 12	250.00	125.00
140	A67	5p orange & blk	57.50	7.00
		Punch cancellation		1.50
a.		Center inverted	*2,750.*	—
141	A67	10p green & blk	50.00	9.25
		Punch cancellation		1.75
a.		Center inverted	*3,500.*	
		Punch cancellation		675.00
142	A67	20p red & black	200.00	21.00
		Punch cancellation		1.75
a.		Center invtd.(punch cancel)		*2,000.*
		Nos. 122-142 (22)	363.85	47.35

Imperf., Pairs

122a	A66	½c	30.00	
123a	A66	1c	45.00	
124a	A66	2c	15.00	
125a	A66	3c	250.00	
127a	A66	5c	15.00	
128a	A66	6c	45.00	
129a	A66	10c	45.00	
132a	A66	15c	45.00	

Vertical Pairs, Imperf. Between

122b	A66	½c	10.00	10.00
123b	A66	1c	10.00	10.00
124b	A66	2c	5.00	5.00
125b	A66	3c	200.00	150.00
126a	A66	4c	250.00	200.00
127b	A66	5c	5.00	3.00
128b	A66	6c	12.00	10.00
129b	A66	10c	75.00	
132c	A66	15c	12.00	10.00

Horizontal Pairs, Imperf. Between

122c	A66	½c	30.00	20.00
123c	A66	1c	50.00	20.00
124c	A66	2c	10.00	5.00
125c	A66	3c	220.00	150.00
126b	A66	4c	275.00	
127c	A66	5c	10.00	5.00
128c	A66	6c	17.50	10.00
129c	A66	10c	17.50	10.00
132d	A66	15c	35.00	20.00
138a	A66	50c	165.00	

River Port of Rosario A68

1902, Oct. 26 *Perf. 11½, 11½x12*

143	A68	5c deep blue	4.50	2.50
a.		Imperf., pair	95.00	
b.		Vert. pair, imperf. btwn.	95.00	
c.		Horiz. pair, imperf. btwn.	75.00	

Completion of port facilities at Rosario.

San Martin
A69 A70

Perf. 13½, 13½x12½

1908-09 **Typo.**

144	A69	½c violet	.15	.15
145	A69	1c brnsh buff	.20	.15
146	A69	2c chocolate	.55	.15
147	A69	3c green	.70	.30
148	A69	4c redsh violet	1.40	.30
149	A69	5c carmine	.30	.15
150	A69	6c olive bister	.80	.25
151	A69	10c gray green	1.50	.15
152	A69	12c yellow buff	.40	.40
153	A69	12c dk blue ('09)	1.25	.15
154	A69	15c apple green	1.75	.85
155	A69	20c ultra	1.25	.15
156	A69	24c red brown	3.25	.60
157	A69	30c dull rose	5.00	.60
158	A69	50c black	4.75	.40
159	A70	1p sl bl & pink	11.00	1.75
		Nos. 144-159 (16)	34.25	6.50

The 1c blue was not issued. Value $250.

Wmk. 86 appears on ½, 1, 6, 20, 24 and 50c. Other values have similar wmk. with wavy rays.

Stamps lacking wmk. are from outer rows printed on sheet margin.

Pyramid of May — A71

Nicolas Rodriguez Pena and Hipolito Vieytes — A72

Meeting at Pena's Home — A73

Designs: 3c, Miguel de Azcuenaga (1754-1833) and Father Manuel M. Alberti (1763-1811). 4c, Viceroy's house and Fort Buenos Aires. 5c, Cornelio Saavedra (1759-1829). 10c, Antonio Luis Beruti (1772-1842) and French distributing badges. 12c, Congress building. 20c, Juan Jose Castelli (1764-1812) and Domingo Matheu (1765-1831). 24c, First council. 30c, Manuel Belgrano (1770-1820) and Juan Larrea (1782-1847). 50c, First meeting of republican government, May 25, 1810. 1p, Mariano Moreno (1778-1811) and Juan Jose Paso (1758-1833). 5p, Oath of the Junta. 10p, Centenary Monument. 20p, Jose Francisco de San Martin (1778-1850).

Inscribed "1810 1910"
Various Frames

1910, May 1 **Engr.** *Perf. 11½*

160	A71	½c bl & gray bl	.30	.15
161	A72	1c blue grn & blk	.30	.15
b.		Horiz. pair, imperf. btwn.	*65.00*	
162	A73	2c olive & gray	.20	.15
163	A72	3c green	.70	.15
164	A73	4c dk blue & grn	.70	.25
165	A71	5c carmine	.40	.15
166	A73	10c yel brn & blk	1.75	.20
167	A73	12c brt blue	1.40	.25
168	A72	20c gray brn & blk	3.25	.35
169	A73	24c org brn & bl	1.75	.90
170	A72	30c lilac & blk	1.75	.65
171	A71	50c carmine & blk	4.50	.90
172	A72	1p brt blue	10.00	3.50
173	A73	5p orange & vio	70.00	30.00
		Punch cancel		2.50
174	A71	10p orange & blk	90.00	65.00
		Punch cancel		3.00
175	A71	20p dp blue & ind	150.00	90.00
		Punch cancel		4.50
		Nos. 160-175 (16)	337.00	192.75

Centenary of the republic.

Center Inverted

160a	A71	½c	*750.00*
161a	A72	1c	*750.00*
162a	A73	2c	*800.00*
164a	A73	4c	*500.00*
167a	A73	12c	*650.00*
171a	A71	50c	*650.00*
173a	A73	5p	*650.00*

Domingo F. Sarmiento A87

Agriculture A88

1911, May 15 **Typo.** *Perf. 13½*

176	A87	5c gray brn & blk	.75	.50

Domingo Faustino Sarmiento (1811-88), pres. of Argentina, 1868-74.

Wmk. 86, without Face

1911 **Engr.** *Perf. 12*

Size: 19x25mm

177	A88	5c vermilion	.40	.15
178	A88	12c deep blue	5.00	.20
		Set value		.25

Wmk. 86, with Face

1911 **Typo.** *Perf. 13½x12½*

Size: 18x23mm

179	A88	½c violet	.15	.15
180	A88	1c brown ocher	.15	.15
181	A88	2c chocolate	.20	.15
a.		Perf. 13½	4.25	1.75
b.		Imperf., pair	*26.00*	
182	A88	3c green	.40	.15
183	A88	4c brown violet	.35	.25
184	A88	10c gray green	.50	.15
185	A88	20c ultra	4.25	1.00
186	A88	24c red brown	5.25	3.50
187	A88	30c claret	1.75	.50
188	A88	50c black	8.00	.85
		Nos. 179-188 (10)	21.00	6.85

The 5c dull red is a proof. In this issue Wmk. 86 comes: straight rays (4c, 20c, 24c) and wavy rays (2c). All other values exist with both forms.

Wmk. 87 (Horiz. or Vert.)

1912-14 *Perf. 13½x12½*

189	A88	½c violet	.15	.15
190	A88	1c ocher	.15	.15
191	A88	2c chocolate	.30	.15
192	A88	3c green	.60	.15
193	A88	4c brown violet	.60	.15
194	A88	5c red	.15	.15

ARGENTINA

195	A88	10c deep green	1.40	.15
196	A88	12c deep blue	1.40	.15
197	A88	20c ultra	8.00	.70
198	A88	24c red brown	3.25	1.65
199	A88	30c claret	8.00	.60
200	A88	50c black	5.00	.60
		Nos. 189-200 (12)	29.00	4.75

See Nos. 208-212. For overprints see Nos. OD1-OD8, OD47-OD54, OD102-OD108, OD146-OD152, OD183-OD190, OD235-OD241, OD281-OD284, OD318-OD323.

Perf. 13½

189a	A88	½c	.80	.25
190a	A88	1c	.80	.25
191a	A88	2c	.80	.15
192a	A88	3c	35.00	16.00
193a	A88	4c	1.65	.70
194a	A88	5c	.30	.15
196a	A88	12c	3.25	.80
197a	A88	20c	5.00	.70
		Nos. 189a-197a (8)	47.60	19.00

A89

1912-13   Perf. 13½

201	A89	1p dull bl & rose	6.00	1.00
		Punch cancel		.30
202	A89	5p slate & ol grn	19.00	6.00
		Punch cancel		.60
203	A89	10p violet & blue	75.00	9.00
		Punch cancel		1.40
204	A89	20p blue & claret	175.00	60.00
		Punch cancel		2.00
		Nos. 201-204 (4)	275.00	76.00

1915   Unwmk.   Perf. 13½x12½

208	A88	1c ocher	.50	.15
209	A88	2c chocolate	.50	.15
212	A88	5c red	.50	.15
		Nos. 208-212 (3)	1.50	.45

Only these denominations were printed on paper without watermark.

Other stamps of the series are known unwatermarked but they are from the outer rows of sheets the other parts of which are watermarked.

Francisco Narciso de Laprida — A90

Declaration of Independence — A91

Jose de San Martin   A92   A92a

Perf. 13½, 13½x12½

1916, July 9   Litho.   Wmk. 87

215	A90	½c violet	.20	.15
216	A90	1c buff	.25	.15

Perf. 13½x12½

217	A90	2c chocolate	.20	.15
218	A90	3c green	.45	.15
219	A90	4c red violet	.65	.15

Perf. 13½

220	A91	5c red	.30	.15
a.		Imperf., pair	40.00	
221	A91	10c gray green	1.50	.15
222	A92	12c blue	.65	.15
223	A92	20c ultra	1.00	.25
224	A92	24c red brown	1.65	.75
225	A92	30c claret	1.65	.35
226	A92	50c gray black	3.25	.45
227	A92a	1p slate bl & red	9.25	4.00
a.		Imperf., pair	325.00	.50
228	A92a	5p black & gray grn	110.00	40.00
		Punch cancel		3.25
229	A92a	10p violet & blue	110.00	75.00
		Punch cancel		2.50
230	A92a	20p dull blue & cl	165.00	67.50
		Punch cancel		1.00
a.		Imperf., pair	650.00	
		Nos. 215-230 (16)	406.00	189.50

Cent. of Argentina's declaration of independence of Spain, July 9, 1816.

The watermark is either vert. or horiz. on Nos. 215-220, 232; only vert. on No. 221, and only horiz. on Nos. 223-230.
For overprints see #OD9, OD55-OD56, OD109, OD153, OD191-OD192, OD285, OD324.

A93    A94

A94a

Juan Gregorio Pujol — A95

1917   Perf. 13½, 13½x12½

231	A93	½c violet	.20	.15
232	A93	1c buff	.25	.15
233	A93	2c brown	.25	.15
234	A93	3c lt green	.75	.15
235	A93	4c red violet	.80	.40
236	A93	5c red	.25	.15
a.		Imperf., pair	14.00	
237	A93	10c gray green	1.50	.15

Perf. 13½

238	A94	12c blue	1.00	.15
239	A94	20c ultra	1.50	.20
240	A94	24c red brown	4.50	2.00
241	A94	30c claret	4.50	.60
242	A94	50c gray black	4.00	.60
243	A94a	1p slate bl & red	4.00	.35
244	A94a	5p black & gray grn	20.00	3.00
		Punch cancel		1.50
245	A94a	10p violet & blue	47.50	9.25
246	A94a	20p dull blue & cl	77.50	15.00
		Punch cancel		.80
a.		Center inverted	1,200.	875.00
		Nos. 231-246 (16)	168.50	32.45

The watermark is either vert. or horiz. on Nos. 231-236, 238; only vert. on No. 237, and only horiz. on Nos. 239-246.

1918, June 15   Litho.   Perf. 13½

247	A95	5c bister & gray	.70	.25

Cent. of the birth of Juan G. Pujol (1817-61), lawyer and legislator.

Perf. 13½, 13½x12½

1918-19   Unwmk.

248	A93	½c violet	.15	.15
249	A93	1c buff	.15	.15
a.		Imperf., pair	14.00	
250	A93	2c brown	.15	.15
251	A93	3c lt green	.25	.15
252	A93	4c red violet	.25	.15
253	A93	5c red	.15	.15
254	A93	10c gray green	1.10	.15

Perf. 13½

255	A94	12c blue	1.25	.15
256	A94	20c ultra	1.65	.15
257	A94	24c red brown	2.00	.50
258	A94	30c claret	2.50	.40
259	A94	50c gray black	5.50	.25
		Nos. 248-259 (12)	15.10	2.40

The stamps of this issue sometimes show letters of papermakers' watermarks.
There were two printings, in 1918 and 1923, using different ink and paper.

Perf. 13½, 13½x12½

1920   Wmk. 88

264	A93	½c violet	.20	.15
265	A93	1c buff	.25	.15
266	A93	2c brown	.25	.15
267	A93	3c green	1.50	.30
268	A93	4c red violet	2.00	1.25
269	A93	5c red	.40	.15
270	A93	10c gray green	3.25	.15

Perf. 13½

271	A94	12c blue	1.75	.15
272	A94	20c ultra	2.50	.15
274	A94	30c claret	8.25	.70
275	A94	50c gray black	5.00	.90
		Nos. 264-275 (11)	25.35	4.20

See #292-300, 304-307A, 310-314, 318, 322.
For overprints see Nos. OD10-OD20, OD57-OD71, OD74, OD110-OD121, OD154-OD159, OD161-OD162, OD193-OD207, OD209-OD211, OD242-OD252, OD254-OD255, OD286-OD290, OD325-OD328, OD330.

Perf. 13½, 13½x12½

1920   Wmk. 89

292	A93	½c violet	2.00	.75
293	A93	1c buff	5.00	.75
294	A93	2c brown	3.00	.75
297	A93	5c red	4.00	.50
298	A93	10c gray green	4.00	.40

Belgrano's Mausoleum — A96

Creation of Argentine Flag — A97

Gen. Manuel Belgrano — A98

1920, June 18   Perf. 13½

280	A96	2c red	.35	.20
a.		Perf. 13½x12½	.35	.20
281	A97	5c rose & blue	.40	.15
282	A98	12c green & blue	.75	.75
		Nos. 280-282 (3)	1.50	1.10

Belgrano (1770-1820), Argentine general, patriot and diplomat.

Gen. Justo Jose de Urquiza — A99

Bartolome Mitre — A100

1920, Nov. 11

283	A99	5c gray blue	.25	.15

Gen. Justo Jose de Urquiza (1801-70), pres. of Argentina, 1854-60. See No. 303.

1921, June 26   Unwmk.

284	A100	2c violet brown	.25	.20
285	A100	5c light blue	.25	.15

Bartolome Mitre (1821-1906), pres. of Argentina, 1862-65.

Allegory, Pan-America — A101

1921, Aug. 25   Perf. 13½

286	A101	3c violet	.55	.30
287	A101	5c blue	.80	.15
288	A101	10c vio brown	1.40	.35
289	A101	12c rose	2.00	.75
		Nos. 286-289 (4)	4.75	1.55

Inscribed "Buenos Aires-Agosto de 1921" — A102

Inscribed "Republica Argentina" — A103

1921, Oct.   Perf. 13½x12½

290	A102	5c rose	.30	.15
a.		Perf. 13½	1.25	.15
291	A103	5c rose	1.50	.15
a.		Perf. 13½	2.50	.15

1st Pan-American Postal Cong., Buenos Aires, Aug., 1921.

See Nos. 308-309, 319. For overprints see Nos. OD72, OD160, OD208, OD253, OD329.

Perf. 13½

299	A94	12c blue	3,000.	125.00
300	A94	20c ultra	12.00	.75
		Nos. 292-298,300 (6)	30.00	3.90

1920

303	A99	5c gray blue	350.00	225.00

Perf. 13½, 13½x12½

1922-23   Wmk. 90

304	A93	½c violet	.15	.15
305	A93	1c buff	.15	.15
306	A93	2c brown	.15	.15
307	A93	3c green	.45	.15
307A	A93	4c red violet	3.75	1.00
308	A102	5c rose	2.25	.15
309	A103	5c red	1.50	.15
310	A93	10c gray green	4.75	.30

Perf. 13½

311	A94	12c blue	.85	.15
312	A94	20c ultra	1.25	.15
313	A94	24c red brown	9.25	4.50
314	A94	30c claret	5.50	.50
		Nos. 304-314 (12)	30.00	7.65

Paper with Gray Overprint RA in Sun
Perf. 13½, 13½x12½

1922-23   Unwmk.

318	A93	2c brown	3.00	1.00
319	A103	5c red	2.00	.70

Perf. 13½

322	A94	20c ultra	15.00	1.50
		Nos. 318-322 (3)	20.00	2.80

San Martín   A104   A105
With Period after Value

1923, May   Litho.   Wmk. 90

323	A104	½c red violet	.20	.20
324	A104	1c buff	.30	.15
325	A104	2c dark brown	.30	.15
326	A104	3c lt green	.30	.20
327	A104	4c red brown	.30	.20
328	A104	5c red	.30	.15
329	A104	10c dull green	2.50	.15
330	A104	12c deep blue	.40	.15
331	A104	20c ultra	1.00	.15
332	A104	24c lt brown	2.50	1.50
333	A104	30c claret	7.75	.60
334	A104	50c black	4.00	.35

Without Period after Value
Wmk. 87   Perf. 13½

335	A105	1p blue & red	4.00	.15
336	A105	5p gray lilac & grn	16.00	1.75
		Punch cancel		.60
337	A105	10p claret & blue	55.00	10.50
		Punch cancel		1.00
338	A105	20p slate & brn lake	90.00	30.00
		Punch cancel		.60
a.		Center inverted		
		Nos. 323-338 (16)	184.85	46.35

Nos. 335-338 and 353-356 canceled with round or oval killers in purple (revenue cancellations) sell for one-fifth to one-half as much as postally used copies.
For overprints see Nos. 399-404.

Design of 1923
Without Period after Value
Perf. 13½, 13½x12½

1923-24   Litho.   Wmk. 90

340	A104	½c red violet	.15	.15
341	A104	1c buff	.15	.15
342	A104	2c dk brown	.15	.15
343	A104	3c green	.15	.15
a.		Imperf., pair	8.00	
344	A104	4c red brown	.40	.15
345	A104	5c red	.15	.15
346	A104	10c dull green	.30	.15
347	A104	12c deep blue	.50	.15
348	A104	20c ultra	.40	.15
349	A104	24c lt brown	1.65	.70
350	A104	25c purple	.80	.15
351	A104	30c claret	1.65	.15
352	A104	50c black	1.65	.15
353	A105	1p blue & red	4.00	.15
		Punch cancel		.20
354	A105	5p dk violet & grn	15.00	.75
		Punch cancel		.20
355	A105	10p claret & blue	32.50	3.25
		Punch cancel		.20
356	A105	20p slate & lake	47.50	7.50
		Punch cancel		.20
		Nos. 340-356 (17)	105.35	14.15

ARGENTINA

1931-33 Typographed

343b	A104	3c		1.40	.25
345a	A104	5c		2.50	.15
346a	A104	10c		4.00	.20
347a	A104	12c		8.50	1.50
348a	A104	20c		32.50	1.65
350a	A104	25c		20.00	.75
351a	A104	30c		15.00	.40
	Nos. 343b-351a (7)			83.90	4.90

The typographed stamps were issued only in coils and have a rough impression with heavy shading about the eyes and nose. Nos. 343 and 346 are known without watermark.

Nos. 341-345, 347-349, 351a may be found in pairs, one with period.

See note after No. 338. See Nos. 362-368. For overprints see Nos. OD21-OD33, OD75-OD87, OD122-OD133, OD163-OD175, OD212-OD226, OD256-OD268, OD291-OD304, OD331-OD345.

Rivadavia — A106

1926, Feb. 8 — Perf. 13½
357 A106 5c rose .40 .15

Presidency of Bernardino Rivadavia, cent.

Rivadavia A108 
San Martin A109

General Post Office, 1926 — A110
General Post Office, 1826 — A111 

1926, July 1 — Perf. 13½x12½
358 A108 3c gray green .15 .15
359 A109 5c red .15 .15

Perf. 13½
360 A110 12c deep blue .90 .20
361 A111 25c chocolate 1.65 .15
  a. "1326" for "1826" 6.00 .75
  Nos. 358-361 (4) 2.85 .65

Centenary of the Post Office.
For overprints see Nos. OD34, OD88, OD134, OD227-OD228, OD269, OD305, OD346.

Type of 1923-31 Issue Without Period after Value
1927 Wmk. 205 Perf. 13½x12½
362 A104 ½c red violet .25 .25
  a. Pelure paper 1.75 1.75
363 A104 1c buff .25 .25
364 A104 2c dark brown .25 .15
  a. Pelure paper .35 .15
365 A104 5c red .30 .15
  a. Period after value 3.50 1.90
  b. Pelure paper .40 .20
366 A104 10c dull green 4.50 2.25
367 A104 20c ultra 18.00 2.25

Perf. 13½
368 A105 1p blue & red 35.00 7.00
  Nos. 362-368 (7) 58.55 12.30

Arms of Argentina and Brazil — A112

Wmk. RA in Sun (90)
1928, Aug. 27 — Perf. 12½x13
369 A112 5c rose red 1.00 .25
370 A112 12c deep blue 1.50 .50

Cent. of peace between the Empire of Brazil and the United Provinces of the Rio de la Plata.

Allegory, Discovery of the New World A113 
"Spain" and "Argentina" A114

"America" Offering Laurels to Columbus — A115

1929, Oct. 12 Litho. Perf. 13½
371 A113 2c lilac brown .85 .25
372 A114 5c light red .85 .15
373 A115 12c dull blue 2.00 .75
  Nos. 371-373 (3) 3.70 1.15

Discovery of America by Columbus, 437th anniv.

Spirit of Victory Attending Insurgents A116
March of the Victorious Insurgents A117 

Perf. 13½x12½ (A116), 12½x13 (A117)
1930
374 A116 ½c violet gray .15 .15
375 A116 1c myrtle green .20 .20
376 A116 2c dull violet .25 .15
377 A116 3c green .30 .25
378 A116 4c violet .25 .25
379 A116 5c rose red .15 .15
380 A116 10c gray black .70 .35
381 A117 12c dull blue .50 .25
382 A117 20c ocher .50 .25
383 A117 24c red brown 2.25 1.50
384 A117 25c green 2.50 1.50
385 A117 30c deep violet 4.50 2.00
386 A117 50c black 6.25 2.50
387 A117 1p sl bl & red 11.00 4.00
388 A117 2p black & org 22.50 10.00
389 A117 5p dull grn & blk 65.00 40.00
390 A117 10p dp red brn & dull blue 90.00 42.50
391 A117 20p yel grn & dl bl 225.00 100.00
392 A117 50p dk grn & vio 600.00 450.00
  Nos. 374-390 (17) 207.00 112.00

Revolution of 1930.
Nos. 387-392 with oval (parcel post) cancellation sell for less.
For overprint see No. 405.

1931 Perf. 12½x13
393 A117 ½c red violet .15 .15
394 A117 1c gray black 1.25 .50
395 A117 3c green .60 .30
396 A117 4c red brown .35 .25
397 A117 5c red .15 .15
  a. Plane omitted, top left corner 3.00 1.65
398 A117 10c dull green 1.25 .30
  Nos. 393-398 (6) 3.75 1.65

Revolution of 1930.

Stamps of 1924-25 Overprinted in Red or Green

-6-
Septiembre
1930 - 1931

1931, Sept. 6 Perf. 13½, 13½x12½
399 A104 3c green .20 .20
400 A104 10c dull green .60 .60
401 A104 30c claret (G) 3.25 3.25
402 A104 50c black 3.25 3.25

Overprinted in Blue
1930
Septiembre
6
1931

403 A105 1p blue & red 3.75 3.25
404 A105 5p dk violet & grn 70.00 20.00

No. 388 Overprinted in Blue
6 Septiembre 1931

Perf. 12½x13
405 A117 2p black & orange 13.00 9.00
  Nos. 399-405 (7) 94.05 39.55

1st anniv. of the Revolution of 1930.
See Nos. C30-C34.

Refrigeration Compressor — A118

Perf. 13½x12½
1932, Aug. 29 Litho.
406 A118 3c green .40 .25
407 A118 10c scarlet 1.25 .15
408 A118 12c gray blue 3.25 1.25
  Nos. 406-408 (3) 4.90 1.65

6th Intl. Refrigeration Congress.

Port of La Plata — A119 
Pres. Julio A. Roca — A120

Municipal Palace — A121

Cathedral of La Plata — A122

Dardo Rocha — A123

Perf. 13½x13, 13x13½ (10c)
1933, Jan.
409 A119 3c green & dk brn .35 .30
410 A120 10c orange & dk vio .50 .20
411 A121 15c dk blue & dp blue 3.50 1.75
412 A122 20c violet & yel brn 1.65 1.00
413 A123 30c dk grn & vio brn 14.00 5.50
  Nos. 409-413 (5) 20.00 8.75

50th anniv. of the founding of the city of La Plata, Nov. 19th, 1882.

Christ of the Andes — A124

Buenos Aires Cathedral A125

1934, Oct. 1 Perf. 13x13½, 13½x13
414 A124 10c rose & brown .70 .20
415 A125 15c dark blue 1.40 .45

32nd Intl. Eucharistic Cong., Oct. 10-14.

"Liberty" with Arms of Brazil and Argentina A126
Symbolical of "Peace" and "Friendship" A127 

1935, May 15 Perf. 13x13½
416 A126 10c red .85 .25
417 A127 15c blue 1.65 .50

Visit of Pres. Getulio Vargas of Brazil.

Belgrano A128 
Sarmiento A129

Urquiza A130 
Louis Braille A131

San Martin A132 
Brown A133

Moreno A134 
Alberdi A135

Nicolas Avellaneda A136 
Rivadavia A137

Mitre A138 
Bull (Cattle Breeding) A139

Martin Güemes A140
Agriculture A141

ARGENTINA

Merino Sheep (Wool) — A142

Sugar Cane A143

Oil Well (Petroleum) A144

Map of South America A145, A146

Fruit A147

Iguacu Falls (Scenic Wonders) A148

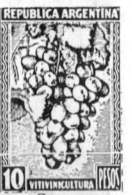

Grapes (Vineyards) A149

Cotton A150

Two types of A140:
Type I - Inscribed Juan Martin Guemes.
Type II - Inscribed Martin Güemes.

Perf. 13, 13½x13, 13x13½
1935-51   Litho.   Wmk. 90

418	A128	½c red violet	.15	.15
419	A129	1c buff	.15	.15
a.		Typo.	.15	.15
420	A130	2c dark brown	.15	.15
421	A131	2½c black ('39)	.15	.15
422	A132	3c green	.15	.15
423	A132	3c lt gray ('39)	.15	.15
424	A134	3c lt gray ('46)	.15	.15
425	A133	4c lt gray	.15	.15
426	A133	4c sage green ('39)	.15	.15
427	A134	5c yel brn, typo.	.15	.15
a.		Tete beche pair, typo.	4.50	2.25
b.		Booklet pane of 8, typo.		
c.		Booklet pane of 4, typo.		
d.		Litho.	1.40	.15
428	A135	6c olive green	.20	.15
429	A136	8c orange ('39)	.15	.15
430	A137	10c car, typo.	.30	.15
431	A137	10c brown ('42)	.15	.15
a.		Typo.	.40	
432	A138	12c brown	.20	.15
433	A138	12c red ('39)	.15	.15
434	A139	15c slate bl ('36)	.85	.15
435	A139	15c pale ultra ('39)	.50	.15
436	A140	15c lt gray bl (II) ('42)	37.50	1.75
437	A140	20c lt ultra (I)	.60	.15
438	A140	20c lt ultra (II) ('36)		
439	A140	20c bl gray (II) ('39)	.35	.15
439A	A139	20c dk bl & pale bl, ('42) 22x33mm	.85	.15
440	A139	20c blue ('51)	.15	.15
a.		Typo.	.15	.15
441	A141	25c carmine ('36)	.20	.15
442	A142	30c org brn ('36)	.50	.15
443	A143	40c dk violet ('36)	.40	.15
444	A144	50c red & org ('36)	.35	.15
445	A145	1p brn blk & lt bl ('36)	17.00	.70
446	A146	1p brn blk & lt bl ('37)	7.00	.15
a.		Chalky paper	42.50	.85
447	A147	2p brn lake & dk ultra ('36)	.85	.15
448	A148	5p ind & ol grn	6.00	.30
449	A149	10p brn lake & blk	35.00	1.95
450	A150	20p bl grn & brn ('36)	47.50	7.50
		Nos. 418-450 (34)	158.60	16.55

See Nos. 485-500, 523-540, 659, 668. For overprints see Nos. O37-O41, O43-O51, O53-O56, O58-O78, O108, O112, OD35-OD46, OD89-OD101, OD135-OD145, OD176-OD182C, OD229-OD234F, OD270-OD280, OD306-OD317, OD347-OD357.

No. 439A exists with attached label showing medallion. Value $42.50 unused, $22.50 used.

Souvenir Sheet

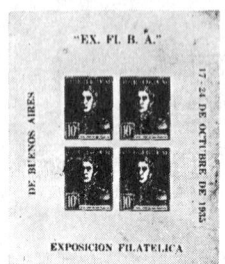

A151

Without Period after Value
1935, Oct. 17   Litho.   Imperf.

452	A151	Sheet of 4	52.50	30.00
a.		10c dull green	7.00	4.00

Phil. Exhib. at Buenos Aires, Oct. 17-24, 1935. The stamps were on sale during the 8 days of the exhibition only. Sheets measure 83x101mm.

Plaque — A152

1936, Dec. 1   Perf. 13x13½
453	A152	10c rose	.50	.25

Inter-American Conference for Peace.

Domingo Faustino Sarmiento A153

"Presidente Sarmiento" A154

1938, Sept. 5

454	A153	3c sage green	.20	.15
455	A153	5c red	.20	.15
456	A153	15c deep blue	.60	.15
457	A153	50c orange	1.75	1.00
		Nos. 454-457 (4)	2.75	1.45

50th anniv. of the death of Domingo Faustino Sarmiento, pres., educator and author.

1939, Mar. 16
458	A154	5c greenish blue	.35	.15

Final voyage of the training ship "Presidente Sarmiento."

Allegory of the UPU — A155

Coat of Arms — A157

Post Office, Buenos Aires — A156

Iguacu Falls — A158

Bonete Hill, Nahuel Huapi Park — A159

Allegory of Modern Communications A160

Argentina, Land of Promise A161

Lake Frias, Nahuel Huapi Park — A162

Perf. 13x13½, 13½x13
1939, Apr. 1   Photo.

459	A155	5c rose carmine	.15	.15
460	A156	15c grnsh black	.40	.25
461	A157	20c brt blue	.40	.15
462	A158	25c dp blue grn	.85	.40
463	A159	50c brown	1.65	.65
464	A160	1p brown violet	1.90	.80
465	A161	2p magenta	8.75	5.25
466	A162	5p purple	35.00	16.00
		Nos. 459-466 (8)	49.10	23.65

Universal Postal Union, 11th Congress.

Souvenir Sheets

A163

A164

1939, May 12   Wmk. 90   Imperf.

467	A163	Sheet of 4	6.00	4.25
a.		5c rose carmine (A155)	1.25	.75
b.		20c bright blue (A157)	1.25	.75
c.		25c deep blue green (A158)	1.25	.75
d.		50c brown (A159)	1.25	.75
468	A164	Sheet of 4	6.00	4.25

Issued in four forms:
a.	Unsevered horizontal pair of sheets, type A163 at left, A164 at right	15.00	15.00
b.	Unsevered vertical pair of sheets, type A163 at top, A164 at bottom	15.00	15.00
c.	Unsevered block of 4 sheets, type A163 at left, A164 at right	52.50	52.50
d.	Unsevered block of 4 sheets, type A163 at top, A164 at bottom	52.50	52.50

11th Cong. of the UPU and the Argentina Intl. Phil. Exposition (C.Y.T.R.A.).
No. 468 contains Nos. 467a-467d.

Family and New House — A165

Perf. 13½x13
1939, Oct. 2   Litho.   Wmk. 90
469	A165	5c bluish green	.25	.15

1st Pan-American Housing Congress.

Bird Carrying Record — A166

Head of Liberty and Arms of Argentina — A167

Record and Winged Letter — A168

1939, Dec. 11   Photo.   Perf. 13

470	A166	1.18p indigo	15.00	7.00
471	A167	1.32p bright blue	15.00	7.00
472	A168	1.50p dark brown	50.00	27.50
		Nos. 470-472 (3)	80.00	41.50

These stamps were issued for the recording and mailing of flexible phonograph records.

Map of the Americas — A169

1940, Apr. 14   Perf. 13x13½
473	A169	15c ultramarine	.40	.15

50th anniv. of the Pan American Union.

Souvenir Sheet

Reproductions of Early Argentine Stamps — A170

Wmk. RA in Sun (90)
1940, May 25   Litho.   Imperf.

474	A170	Sheet of 5	9.50	5.50
a.		5c dark blue (Corrientes A2)	1.10	.70
b.		5c red (Argentina A1)	1.10	.70

ARGENTINA

c. 5c dark blue (Cordoba #1) 1.10 .70
d. 5c red (Argentina A3) 1.10 .70
e. 10c dark blue (Buenos Aires A1) 1.10 .70

100th anniv. of the first postage stamp.

General Domingo French and Colonel Antonio Beruti — A171

1941, Feb. 20   *Perf. 13½x13*
475 A171 5c dk gray blue & lt blue   .32 .15

Issued in honor of General French and Colonel Beruti, patriots.

Marco M. de Avellaneda A172

Statue of Gen. Julio Roca A173

1941, Oct. 3   *Perf. 13x13½*
476 A172 5c dull slate blue   .32 .15

Marco M. de Avellaneda, (1814-41), Army leader and martyr.

1941, Oct. 19   *Photo.*   *Wmk. 90*
477 A173 5c dark olive green   .32 .15

Dedication of a monument to Lt. Gen. Julio Argentino Roca (1843-1914).

Carlos Pellegrini and Bank of the Nation — A174

1941, Oct. 26   *Perf. 13½x13*
478 A174 5c brown carmine   .32 .15

Founding of the Bank of the Nation, 50th anniv.

Gen. Juan Lavalle — A175

1941, Dec. 5   *Perf. 13x13½*
479 A175 5c bright blue   .32 .15

Gen. Juan Galo de Lavalle (1797-1841).

National Postal Savings Bank — A176

1942, Apr. 5   *Litho.*   *Perf. 13½x13*
480 A176 1c pale olive   .20 .15

Jose Manuel Estrada — A177

1942, July 13   *Perf. 13x13½*
481 A177 5c brown violet   .32 .15

Jose Estrada (1842-1894), writer and diplomat.

No. 481 exists with label, showing medallion, attached. Value, pair $10.

Types of 1935-51
Perf. 13, 13x13½, 13½x13
1942-50   *Litho.*   *Wmk. 288*
485 A128 ½c brown violet 4.75 1.00
486 A129 1c buff ('50) .15 .15
487 A130 2c dk brown ('50) .15 .15
488 A132 3c lt gray 16.00 1.25
489 A134 3c lt gray ('49) .16 .15
490 A137 10c red brown ('49) .20 .15
491 A138 12c red .20 .15
492 A140 15c lt gray blue (II) .28 .15
493 A143 20c dk sl bl & pale bl 1.25 .15
494 A141 25c dull rose .60 .15
495 A142 30c orange brn ('49) 1.25 .15
496 A143 40c violet ('49) 8.00 .15
497 A144 50c red & org ('49) 8.00 .18
498 A146 1p brn blk & lt bl 6.50 .18
 ('49)
499 A147 2p brn lake & bl 13.00 .75
 ('49)
500 A148 5p ind & ol grn 50.00 4.50
 ('49)
Nos. 485-500 (16) 110.49 9.36

No. 493 measures 22x33mm.

Post Office, Buenos Aires — A178

Proposed Columbus Lighthouse — A179

Inscribed: "Correos y Telegrafos."

1942, Oct. 5   *Litho.*   *Perf. 13*
503 A178 35c lt ultra 2.75 .15
See Nos. 541-543.

1942, Oct. 12   *Wmk. 288*
504 A179 15c dull blue 3.00 .15
Wmk. 90
505 A179 15c dull blue 60.00 5.00

450th anniv. of the discovery of America by Columbus.

Jose C. Paz — A180

Books and Argentine Flag — A181

1942, Dec. 15   *Wmk. 288*
506 A180 5c dark gray .35 .15

Cent. of the birth of Jose C. Paz, statesman and founder of the newspaper La Prensa.

1943, Apr. 1   *Litho.*   *Perf. 13*
507 A181 5c dull blue .18 .15

1st Book Fair of Argentina.

Arms of Argentina Inscribed "Honesty, Justice, Duty" — A182

1943-50   *Wmk. 288*   *Perf. 13*
Size: 20x26mm
508 A182 5c red ('50) 2.50 .15
Wmk. 90
509 A182 5c red .22 .15
 a. 5c dull red, unsurfaced paper 3.00 .15
510 A182 15c green .70 .15
Perf. 13x13½
Size: 22x33mm
511 A182 20c dark blue 1.10 .15
Nos. 508-511 (4) 4.52 .60

Change of political organization, June 4, 1943.

Independence House, Tucuman A183

Liberty Head and Savings Bank A184

1943-51   *Wmk. 90*   *Perf. 13*
512 A183 5c blue green .90 .15
Wmk. 288
513 A183 5c blue green ('51) .35 .15

Restoration of Independence House.

1943, Oct. 25   *Wmk. 90*
514 A184 5c violet brown .15 .15
Wmk. 288
515 A184 5c violet brown 37.50 3.00

1st conference of National Postal Savings.

Port of Buenos Aires in 1800 — A185

1943, Dec. 11   *Wmk. 90*
516 A185 5c gray black .15 .15

Day of Exports.

Warship, Merchant Ship and Sailboat A186

Arms of Argentine Republic A187

1944, Jan. 31   *Perf. 13*
517 A186 5c blue .18 .15

Issued to commemorate Sea Week.

1944, June 4
518 A187 5c dull blue .15 .15

1st anniv. of the change of political organization in Argentina.

St. Gabriel A188

Cross at Palermo A189

1944, Oct. 11
519 A188 3c yellow green .15 .15
520 A189 5c deep rose .15 .15

Fourth national Eucharistic Congress.

Allegory of Savings A190

Reservists A191

1944, Oct. 24
521 A190 5c gray .15 .15

20th anniv. of the National Savings Bank.

1944, Dec. 1
522 A191 5c blue .15 .15

Day of the Reservists.

Types of 1935-51
Perf. 13x13½, 13½x13
1945-47   *Litho.*   *Unwmk.*
523 A128 ½c brown vio ('46) .15 .15
524 A129 1c yellow brown .15 .15
525 A130 2c sepia .15 .15
526 A132 3c lt gray (San Martin) .42 .15
527 A134 3c lt gray (Moreno) .15 .15
 ('46)
528 A135 6c olive grn ('47) .18 .15
529 A137 10c brown ('46) 1.25 .15
530 A140 15c lt gray bl (II) .75 .15
531 A139 20c dk sl bl & pale bl 1.25 .15
532 A141 25c dull rose .45 .15
533 A142 30c orange brown .35 .15
534 A143 40c violet 1.25 .15
535 A144 50c red & orange 1.25 .15
536 A146 1p brown blk & lt bl 1.65 .15
537 A147 2p brown lake & bl 8.00 .22
538 A148 5p ind & ol grn ('46) 45.00 2.50
539 A149 10p dp cl & int blk 5.50 .90
540 A150 20p bl grn & brn ('46) 5.75 .90
Nos. 523-540 (18) 73.65 6.62

No. 531 measures 22x33mm.

Post Office Type Inscribed:
"Correos y Telecommunicaciones"
1945   *Unwmk.*   *Perf. 13x13½*
541 A178 35c lt ultra 1.25 .15
Wmk. 90
542 A178 35c lt ultra 1.25 .15
Wmk. 288
543 A178 35c lt ultra .35 .15
Nos. 541-543 (3) 2.85 .45

Bernardino Rivadavia A192   A193

Mausoleum of Rivadavia A194

Perf. 13½x13
1945, Sept. 1   *Litho.*   *Unwmk.*
544 A192 3c blue green .15 .15
545 A193 5c rose .15 .15
546 A194 20c blue .28 .15
Nos. 544-546 (3) .58 .45

Cent. of the death of Bernardino Rivadavia, Argentina's first president.

No. 546 exists with mute label attached. The pair sells for four times the price of the single stamp.

San Martin A195

Monument to Army of the Andes, Mendoza A196

For all your stamp supply needs
www.scottonline.com

ARGENTINA

1945-46   Wmk. 90   Typo. or Litho.
547 A195 5c carmine .... .15 .15
   a. Litho. ('46) .... .15 .15
Wmk. 288
548 A195 5c carmine, litho. 120.00 20.00
Unwmk.
549 A195 5c carmine ('46) .... .52 .15
   a. Litho. ('46) .... .20 .15
For overprints see Nos. O42, O57.

1946, Jan. 14   Litho.   Perf. 13½x13
550 A196 5c violet brown .... .15 .15
Issued to honor the Unknown Soldier of the War for Independence.

A197
A198 

1946, Apr. 12
551 A197 5c Franklin D. Roosevelt ..... .15 .15

1946, June 4   Perf. 13x13½
Liberty Administering Presidential Oath.
552 A198 5c blue .... .15 .15
Inauguration of Pres. Juan D. Perón, 6/4/46.

Argentina Receiving Popular Acclaim A199

1946, Oct. 17   Perf. 13½x13
553 A199 5c rose violet .... .16 .15
554 A199 10c blue green .... .24 .15
555 A199 15c dark blue .... .48 .18
556 A199 50c red brown .... .70 .30
557 A199 1p carmine rose .... 1.40 .70
   Nos. 553-557 (5) 2.98 1.48
First anniversary of the political organization change of Oct. 17, 1945.

Coin Bank and World Map — A200

1946, Oct. 31   Unwmk.
558 A200 30c dk rose car & pink ..... .60 .15
Universal Day of Savings, October 31, 1946.

Argentine Industry A201
International Bridge Connecting Argentina and Brazil A202 

1946, Dec. 6   Perf. 13½x13
559 A201 5c violet brown .... .15 .15
Day of Argentine Industry, Dec. 6.

1947, May 21   Litho.   Perf. 13½x13
560 A202 5c green .... .15 .15
Opening of the Argentina-Brazil International Bridge, May 21, 1947.

Map of Argentine Antarctic Claims — A203
Justice — A204 

1947-49   Unwmk.   Perf. 13x13½
561 A203 5c violet & lilac .... .35 .15
562 A203 20c dk car rose & rose ..... .70 .15
Wmk. 90
563 A203 20c dk car rose & rose ..... 2.00 .20
Wmk. 288
564 A203 20c dk car rose & rose ('49) 2.00 .15
   Nos. 561-564 (4) .... 5.05 .65
1st Argentine Antarctic mail, 43rd anniv.

1947, June 4   Unwmk.
565 A204 5c brn vio & pale yel ...... .15 .15
1st anniversary of the Peron government.

Icarus Falling — A205

1947, Sept. 25   Perf. 13½x13
566 A205 15c red violet .... .15 .15
Aviation Week.

Training Ship Presidente Sarmiento — A206

1947, Oct. 5   Perf. 13½x13
567 A206 5c blue .... .18 .15
50th anniv. of the launching of the Argentine training frigate "Presidente Sarmiento."

Cervantes and Characters from Don Quixote — A207

Perf. 13½x13
1947, Oct. 12   Photo.   Wmk. 90
568 A207 5c olive green .... .15 .15
400th anniv. of the birth of Miguel de Cervantes Saavedra, playwright and poet.

Gen. Jose de San Martin — A208

Perf. 13½x13
1947-49   Unwmk.   Litho.
569 A208 5c dull green .... .15 .15
Wmk. 288
570 A208 5c dull green ('49) .... .15 .15
Transfer of the remains of Gen. Jose de San Martin's parents.

School Children — A209
Statue of Araucanian Indian — A210 

1947-49   Unwmk.   Perf. 13x13½
571 A209 5c green .... .15 .15
Wmk. 90
574 A209 20c brown .... .35 .15
Wmk. 288
575 A209 5c green ('49) .... .35 .15
   Nos. 571-575 (3) .... .85 .45
Argentine School Crusade for World Peace.

1948, May 21   Wmk. 90
576 A210 25c yellow brown .... .30 .15
American Indian Day, Apr. 19.

Cap of Liberty — A211
Manual Stop Signal — A212 

1948, July 16
577 A211 5c ultra .... .15 .15
Revolution of June 4, 1943, 5th anniv.

1948, July 22
578 A212 5c chocolate & yellow ...... .15 .15
Traffic Safety Day, June 10.

Post Horn and Oak Leaves — A213
Argentine Farmers — A214 

1948, July 22   Unwmk.
579 A213 5c lilac rose .... .15 .15
200th anniversary of the establishment of regular postal service on the Plata River.

Perf. 13½x13
1948, Sept. 20   Wmk. 288
580 A214 10c red brown .... .15 .15
Agriculture Day, Sept. 8, 1948.

Liberty and Symbols of Progress — A215

Perf. 13½x13
1948, Nov. 23   Photo.   Wmk. 287
581 A215 25c red brown .... .18 .15
3rd anniversary of President Juan D. Peron's return to power, October 17, 1945.

Souvenir Sheets

A216

15c, Mail coach. 45c, Buenos Aires in 18th cent. 55c, 1st train, 1857. 85c, Sailing ship, 1767.

1948, Dec. 21   Unwmk.   Imperf.
582 A216 Sheet of 4 .... 3.00 3.00
   a. 15c dark green .... .45 .45
   b. 45c orange brown .... .45 .45
   c. 55c lilac brown .... .45 .45
   d. 85c ultramarine .... .45 .45

A217

Designs: 85c, Domingo de Basavilibaso (1709-75). 1.05p, Postrider. 1.20p, Sailing ship, 1798. 1.90p, Courier in the Andes, 1772.

583 A217 Sheet of 4 .... 14.00 11.00
   a. 85c brown 3.00 2.50
   b. 1.05p dark green 3.00 2.50
   c. 1.20p dark blue 3.00 2.50
   d. 1.90p red brown 3.00 2.50
200th anniversary of the establishment of regular postal service on the Plata River.

Winged Wheel — A218

Perf. 13½x13
1949, Mar. 1   Wmk. 288
584 A218 10c blue .... .22 .15
Railroad nationalization, 1st anniv.

Liberty A219

1949, June 20   Engr.   Wmk. 90
585 A219 1p red & red violet .... .42 .15
Ratification of the Constitution of 1949.

Allegory of the UPU A220

1949, Nov. 19
586 A220 25c dk grn & yel grn .... .22 .15
75th anniv. of the UPU.

> Catalogue values for unused stamps in this section, from this point to the end of the section, are for Never Hinged items.

ARGENTINA

Gen. Jose de San Martin — A221

San Martin at Boulogne sur Mer A222

Mausoleum of San Martin — A223

Designs: 20c, 50c, 75c, Different Portraits of San Martin. 1p, House where San Martin died.

Engr., Photo. (25c, 1p, 2p)
1950, Aug. 17   Wmk. 90   Perf. 13½
587	A221	10c indigo & dk pur	.15	.15
588	A221	20c red brn & dk brn	.15	.15
589	A222	25c brown	.15	.15
590	A221	50c dk green & ind	.42	.15
591	A221	75c choc & dk grn	.42	.15
a.		Souv. sheet of 4, #587, 588, 590, 591, imperf.	1.25	.80
592	A222	1p dark green	.85	.25
593	A223	2p dp red lilac	.70	.35
		Nos. 587-593 (7)	2.84	1.35

Death cent. of General Jose de San Martin.

Map Showing Antarctic Claims — A224

1951, May 21   Litho.   Perf. 13x13½
594 A224 1p choc & lt blue .70 .15

For overprint see No. O52.

Pegasus and Train A225

Communications Symbols — A226

Design: 25c, Ship and dolphin.

1951, Oct. 17   Photo.   Perf. 13½
595	A225	5c dark brown	.15	.15
596	A225	25c Prus green	.24	.15
597	A226	40c rose brown	.28	.15
		Nos. 595-597 (3)	.67	.45

Close of Argentine Five Year Plan.

Woman Voter and "Argentina" A227

1951, Dec. 14   Perf. 13½x13
598 A227 10c brown violet .15 .15

Granting of women's suffrage.

Eva Peron
A228   A229

Litho. or Engraved (#605)
1952, Aug. 26   Wmk. 90   Perf. 13
599	A228	1c orange brown	.15	.15
600	A228	5c gray	.15	.15
601	A228	10c rose lilac	.15	.15
602	A228	20c rose pink	.15	.15
603	A228	25c dull green	.15	.15
604	A228	40c dull violet	.15	.15
605	A228	45c deep blue	.15	.15
606	A228	50c dull brown	.15	.15

Photo.
607	A229	1p dark brown	.26	.15
608	A229	1.50p deep green	1.50	.15
609	A229	2p brt carmine	.45	.15
610	A229	3p indigo	.75	.15
		Nos. 599-610 (12)	4.16	1.80

For overprints see Nos. O79-O85.

Inscribed: "Eva Peron"
1952-53   Perf. 13x13½
611	A229	1p dark brown	.30	.15
612	A229	1.50p deep green	1.10	.15
613	A229	2p brt car ('53)	1.10	.15
614	A229	3p indigo	2.75	.15

Engr.
Perf. 13½x13
Size: 30x40mm
615	A229	5p red brown	2.75	.35
616	A229	10p red	7.00	1.40
617	A229	20p green	11.00	4.00
618	A228	50p ultra	20.00	10.00
		Nos. 611-618 (8)	46.00	16.35

For overprints see Nos. O86-O93.

Indian Funeral Urn — A230

1953, Aug. 28   Photo.   Perf. 13x13½
619 A230 50c blue green .18 .15

Founding of Santiago del Estero, 400th anniv.

Rescue Ship "Uruguay" A231

1953, Oct. 8   Perf. 13½
620 A231 50c ultra .85 .15

50th anniv. of the rescue of the Antarctic expedition of Otto C. Nordenskjold.

Planting Argentine Flag in the Antarctic — A232

1954, Jan. 20   Engr.   Perf. 13½x13
621 A232 1.45p blue 1.25 .15

50th anniv. of Argentina's 1st antarctic p.o. and the establishing of the La Hoy radio p.o. in the South Orkneys.

Wired Communications A233

Television A234

Perf. 13x13½, 13½x13
1954, Apr.   Photo.   Wmk. 90
622	A233	1.50p shown	.35	.25
623	A233	3p Radio	1.10	.28
624	A234	5p shown	1.40	.55
		Nos. 622-624 (3)	2.85	1.08

Intl. Plenipotentiary Conf. of Telecommunications, Buenos Aires, 1952.

Pediment, Buenos Aires Stock Exchange A235

1954, July 13   Perf. 13½x13
625 A235 1p dark green .28 .15

Cent. of the establishment of the Buenos Aires Stock Exchange.

Eva Peron — A236

1954   Wmk. 90
626 A236 3p dp car rose 1.25 .25

Wmk. 288
627 A236 3p dp car rose 225.00 40.00

2nd anniv. of the death of Eva Peron.

Jose de San Martin A237

Wheat A238

Industry A238a

Eva Peron Foundation Building A239

Cliffs of Humahuaca A240

Gen. Jose de San Martin — A241

Designs: 50c, Buenos Aires harbor. 1p, Cattle ranch (Ganaderia). 3p, Nihuil Dam. 5p, Iguacu Falls, vert. 20p, Mt. Fitz Roy, vert.

Perf. 13½, 13x13½ (80c), 13½x13 (#639, 641-642)
Engraved (#632, 638-642),
Photogravure (#634-637)
1954-59   Wmk. 90
628	A237	20c brt red, typo.	.15	.15
629	A237	20c red, litho. ('55)	.60	.15
630	A237	40c red, litho. ('56)	.16	.15
631	A237	40c brt red, typo. ('55)	.25	.15
632	A239	50c blue ('56)	.15	.15
633	A239	50c bl, litho. ('59)	.16	.15
634	A238	80c brown	.22	.15
635	A239	1p brown ('58)	.26	.15
636	A238a	1.50p ultra ('55)	.20	.15
637	A239	2p dk rose lake	.32	.15
638	A239	3p violet brn ('56)	.32	.15
639	A240	5p gray grn ('55)	5.25	.15
a.		Perf. 13½	6.50	.15
640	A240	10p yel grn ('55)	3.75	.15
641	A240	20p dull vio ('55)	7.75	.15
a.		Perf. 13½	9.50	.15
642	A241	50p ultra & ind ('53)	7.75	.15
a.		Perf. 13½	7.75	.15
		Nos. 628-642 (15)	27.29	2.25

See Nos. 699-700. For similar designs inscribed "Republica Argentina" see Nos. 823-827, 890, 935, 937, 940, 990, 995, 1039, 1044, 1048.
For overprints see Nos. O94-O106, O142, O153-O157.

Allegory — A242

1954, Aug. 26   Typo.   Perf. 13½
643 A242 1.50p slate black .65 .15

Cent. of the establishment of the Buenos Aires Grain Exchange.

Argentina stamps can be mounted in the Scott annual Argentina supplement.

ARGENTINA

Clasped Hands and Congress Medal — A243

1955, Mar. 21   Photo.   Perf. 13½x13
644 A243 3p red brown   .80 .15
Issued to publicize the National Productivity and Social Welfare Congress.

Allegory of Aviation — A244

Argentina Breaking Chains — A245

1955, June 18   Wmk. 90   Perf. 13½
645 A244 1.50p olive gray   .65 .15
Commercial aviation in Argentina, 25th anniv.

1955, Oct. 16   Litho.
647 A245 1.50p olive green   .32 .15
Liberation Revolution of Sept. 16, 1955.

Army Navy and Air Force Emblems A246

Perf. 13½x13
1955, Dec. 31   Photo.   Wmk. 90
648 A246 3p blue   .42 .15
"Brotherhood of the Armed Forces."

A247    A248

1956, Feb. 3   Perf. 13½
649 A247 1.50p Justo Jose de Urquiza   .28 .15
Battle of Caseros, 104th anniversary.

1956, July 28   Engr.   Perf. 13½x13
650 A248 2p Coin and die   .28 .15
75th anniversary of the Argentine Mint.

1856 Stamp of Corrientes A249

Juan G. Pujol — A250

Design: 2.40p, Stamp of 1860-78.

1956, Aug. 21
651 A249 40c dk grn & blue   .15 .15
652 A249 2.40p brn & lil rose   .30 .15

Photo.
653 A250 4.40p brt blue   .65 .18
 a. Souv. sheet of 3, #651-653, imperf.   2.25 2.00
    Nos. 651-653 (3)   1.10 .48
Centenary of Argentine postage stamps. No. 653a for the Argentine stamp cent. and Philatelic Exhib. for the Cent. of Corrientes Stamps, Oct. 12-21. The 4.40p is photo., the other two stamps and border litho. Colors of 40c and 2.40p differ slightly from engraved stamps.

Felling Trees, La Pampa A251

Maté Herb and Gourd, Misiones A252

Design: 1p, Cotton plant and harvest, Chaco.

1956, Sept. 1   Perf. 13½
654 A251 50c ultra   .15 .15
655 A251 1p magenta   .18 .15
656 A252 1.50p green   .22 .15
    Nos. 654-656 (3)   .55 .45
Elevation of the territories of La Pampa, Chaco and Misiones to provinces.

"Liberty" A253

Florentino Ameghino A254

Perf. 13½
1956, Sept. 15   Wmk. 90   Photo.
657 A253 2.40p lilac rose   .30 .15
1st anniv. of the Revolution of Liberation.

1956, Nov. 30
658 A254 2.40p brown   .30 .15
Issued to honor Florentino Ameghino (1854-1911), anthropologist.
For overprint see No. O110.

Adm. Brown Type of 1935-51
1956   Litho.   Perf. 13
Two types:
I. Bust touches upper frame line of name panel at bottom.
II. White line separates bust from frame line.
Size: 19½-20½x26-27mm
659 A133 20c dull purple (I)   .18 .15
 a. Type II   .18 .15
 b. Size 19½x25¼mm (I)   .15 .15
For overprint see No. O108.

Benjamin Franklin A255

1956, Dec. 22   Photo.   Perf. 13½
660 A255 40c intense blue   .30 .15
250th anniv. of the birth of Benjamin Franklin.

Frigate "Hercules" A256

Guillermo Brown A257

1957, Mar. 2
661 A256 40c brt blue   .15 .15
662 A257 2.40p gray black   .35 .15
    Nos. 661-662, C63-C65 (5)   1.05 .75
Admiral Guillermo (William) Brown (1777-1857), founder of the Argentine navy.

Roque Saenz Pena (1851-1914) A258

Church of Santo Domingo, 1807 A259

1957, Apr. 1
663 A258 4.40p grnsh gray   .45 .15
Roque Saenz Pena, pres. 1910-14.
For overprint see No. O111.

1957, July 6   Wmk. 90
664 A259 40c brt blue green   .15 .15
150th anniv. of the defense of Buenos Aires.

"La Portena" — A260

1957, Aug. 31   Wmk. 90   Perf. 13½
665 A260 40c pale brown   .18 .15
Centenary of Argentine railroads.

Esteban Echeverria A261

"Liberty" A262

1957, Sept. 2   Perf. 13x13½
666 A261 2p claret   .22 .15
Esteban Echeverria (1805-1851), poet.
For overprint see No. O109.

1957, Sept. 28   Perf. 13½
667 A262 40c carmine rose   .15 .15
Constitutional reform convention.

Portrait Type of 1935-51
1957, Oct. 28   Litho.   Perf. 13½
Size: 16½x22mm
668 A128 5c Jose Hernandez   .15 .15
For overprint see No. O112.

Oil Derrick and Hands Holding Oil — A263

Perf. 13½
1957, Dec. 21   Wmk. 90   Photo.
669 A263 40c bright blue   .18 .15
50th anniv. of the national oil industry.

Museum, La Plata — A264

1958, Jan. 11
670 A264 40c dark gray   .15 .15
City of La Plata, 75th anniversary.

A265    A266

40c, Locomotive & arms of Argentina & Bolivia.
1p, Map of Argentine-Bolivian boundary & plane.

1958, Apr. 19   Wmk. 90   Perf. 13½
671 A265 40c slate & dp car   .28 .15
672 A266 1p dark brown   .28 .15
Argentine-Bolivian friendship. No. 671 for the opening of the Jacuiba-Santa Cruz railroad; No. 672, the exchange of presidential visits.

Symbols of the Republic A267

Flag Monument A268

1958, Apr. 30   Photo. & Engr.
673 A267 40c multicolored   .15 .15
674 A267 1p multicolored   .16 .15
675 A267 2p multicolored   .25 .15
    Nos. 673-675 (3)   .56 .45
Transmission of Presidential power.

1958, June 21   Litho.   Wmk. 90
676 A268 40c blue & violet bl   .15 .15
1st anniv. of the Flag Monument of Rosario.

ARGENTINA

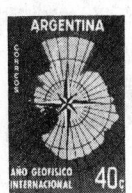

Map of Antarctica — A269

Stamp of Cordoba and Mail Coach — A270

1958, July 12   *Perf. 13½*
677 A269 40c car rose & blk   .48 .18
International Geophysical Year, 1957-58.

1958, Oct. 18
678 A270 40c pale blue & slate   .15 .15
     Nos. 678,C72-C73 (3)   .60 .45
Centenary of Cordoba postage stamps.

"Slave" by Michelangelo and UN Emblem — A271

Engraved and Lithographed
1959, Mar. 14   Wmk. 90   *Perf. 13½*
679 A271 40c violet brn & gray   .15 .15
10th anniv. (in 1958) of the signing of the Universal Declaration of Human Rights.

Orchids and Globe — A272

1959, May 23   Photo.   *Perf. 13½*
680 A272 1p dull claret   .22 .15
1st International Horticulture Exposition.

Pope Pius XII — A273

William Harvey — A274

1959, June 20   Engr.   *Perf. 13½*
681 A273 1p yellow & black   .18 .15
Pope Pius XII, 1876-1958.

1959, Aug. 8   Litho.   Wmk. 90
1p, Claude Bernard. 1.50p, Ivan P. Pavlov.
682 A274 50c green   .15 .15
683 A274 1p dark red   .15 .15
684 A274 1.50p brown   .22 .15
     Nos. 682-684 (3)   .52 .45
21st Intl. Cong. of Physiological Sciences, Buenos Aires.

Type of 1958 and

Domestic Horse A275

Jose de San Martin A276

Tierra del Fuego — A277

Inca Bridge, Mendoza A278

Ski Jumper A279

Mar del Plata A280

Designs: 10c, Cayman. 20c, Llama. 50c, Puma. No. 690, Sunflower. 3p, Zapata Slope, Catamarca. 12p, 23p, 25p, Red Quebracho tree. 20p, Nahuel Huapi Lake. 22p, "Industry" (cogwheel and factory).
Two overall paper sizes for 1p, 5p:
I - 27x37½mm or 37½x27mm.
II - 27x39mm or 39x27mm.

Perf. 13x13½
1959-70   Litho.   Wmk. 90
685 A275 10c slate green   .15 .15
686 A275 20c dl red brn ('61)   .15 .15
687 A275 50c bister ('60)   .15 .15
688 A275 50c bis, typo. ('60)   .18 .15
689 A275 1p rose red   .15 .15
     Perf. 13½
690 A278 1p brn, photo., I ('61)   .15 .15
    a. Paper II ('69)   .18 .15
690B A278 1p brown, I   .65 .15
691 A276 2p rose red ('61)   .25 .15
692 A276 2p red, typo. (19½ x 26mm) ('61)   .32 .15
    a. Redrawn (19½ x 25mm)   4.75 .15
693 A277 3p dk bl, photo. ('60)   .16 .15
694 A276 4p red, typo ('62)   .18 .15
694A A276 4p red ('62)   .38 .15
695 A277 2p gray brn, photo., I   .38 .15
    e. 5p dark brown, paper II ('70)   6.25 .15
695A A276 8p ver ('65)   1.25 .15
695B A276 8p red, typo. ('65)   .32 .15
695C A276 10p ver ('66)   .65 .15
695D A276 10p red, typo. ('66)   .48 .15

     Photo.
696 A278 10p lt red brn ('60)   .48 .15
697 A278 12p dk brn vio ('62)   .80 .15
697A A278 12p dk brn, litho. ('64)   8.00 .15
698 A278 20p Prus grn ('60)   2.75 .15
698A A276 20p red, typo. ('67)   .25 .15
699 A238a 22p ultra ('62)   1.50 .15
700 A238a 22p ultra, litho. ('62)   24.00 .15
701 A278 23p green ('65)   4.75 .15
702 A278 25p dp vio ('66)   1.25 .15
703 A278 25p pur, litho. ('66)   6.25 .15
704 A279 100p blue ('61)   5.00 .15
705 A280 300p dp ultra ('62)   2.75 .15
     Nos. 685-705 (29)   63.73 4.35

See Nos. 882-887, 889, 892, 923-925, 928-930, 938, 987-989, 991.
For overprints and surcharges see Nos. 1076, C82-C83, O113-O118, O122-O124, O126-O141, O143-O145, O163.
The 300p remained on sale as a 3p stamp after the 1970 currency exchange.

Symbolic Sailboat — A281

Child Playing with Doll — A282

1959, Oct. 3   Litho.   *Perf. 13½*
706 A281 1p blk, red & bl   .15 .15
Red Cross sanitary education campaign.

1959, Oct. 17
707 A282 1p red & blk   .15 .15
Issued for Mother's Day, 1959.

Buenos Aires 1p Stamp of 1859 — A283

1959, Nov. 21   Wmk. 90   *Perf. 13½*
708 A283 1p gray & dk bl   .15 .15
Issued for the Day of Philately.

Bartolomé Mitre and Justo José de Urquiza A284

1959, Dec. 12   Photo.   *Perf. 13½*
709 A284 1p purple   .15 .15
Treaty of San Jose de Flores, centenary.

WRY Emblem A285

Abraham Lincoln A286

1960, Apr. 7   Litho.   Wmk. 90
710 A285 1p bister & car   .15 .15
711 A285 4.20p apple grn & dp claret   .32 .20
World Refugee Year, July 1, 1959-June 30, 1960.
See No. B25.

1960, Apr. 14   Photo.   *Perf. 13½*
712 A286 5p ultra   .42 .18
Sesquicentennial (in 1959) of the birth of Abraham Lincoln.

Cornelio Saavedra and Cabildo, Buenos Aires — A287

"Cabildo" and: 2p, Juan José Paso. 4.20p, Manuel Alberti and Miguel Azcuénaga. 10.70p, Juan Larrea and Domingo Matheu.

     Perf. 13½
1960, May 28   Wmk. 90   Photo.
713 A287 1p rose lilac   .15 .15
714 A287 2p bluish grn   .15 .15
715 A287 4.20p gray & grn   .24 .15
716 A287 10.70p gray & ultra   .45 .20
     Nos. 713-716 (6)   1.49 .95
150th anniversary of the May Revolution.
Souvenir sheets are Nos. C75a and C76a.

Luis Maria Drago — A288

Juan Bautista Alberdi — A289

1960, July 8
717 A288 4.20p brown   .22 .15
Ccentenary of the birth of Dr. Luis Maria Drago, statesman and jurist.

1960, Sept. 10   Wmk. 90   *Perf. 13½*
718 A289 1p green   .15 .15
150th anniversary of the birth of Juan Bautista Alberdi, statesman and philosopher.

Map of Argentina and Antarctic Sector — A290

Caravel and Emblem — A291

1960, Sept. 24   Litho.   *Perf. 13½*
719 A290 5p violet   .85 .22
National census of 1960.

1960, Oct. 1   Photo.
720 A291 1p dk olive grn   .15 .15
721 A291 5p brown   .45 .15
     Nos. 720-721,C78-C79 (4)   1.15 .60
8th Congress of the Postal Union of the Americas and Spain.

Virgin of Luján, Patroness of Argentina A292

Argentine Boy Scout Emblem A293

1960, Nov. 12   Wmk. 90   *Perf. 13½*
722 A292 1p dark blue   .15 .15
First Inter-American Marian Congress.

1961, Jan. 17   Litho.
723 A293 1p car rose & blk   .28 .15
International Patrol Encampment of the Boy Scouts, Buenos Aires.

"Shipment of Cereals," by Quinquela Martin A294

1961, Feb. 11   Photo.   *Perf. 13½*
724 A294 1p red brown   .28 .15
Export drive: "To export is to advance."

ARGENTINA

Naval Battle of San Nicolás — A295
Mariano Moreno by Juan de Dios Rivera — A296 

1961, Mar. 2   *Perf. 13½*
725 A295 2p gray   .28 .15
Naval battle of San Nicolas, 150th anniv.

1961, Mar. 25   *Perf. 13½*
726 A296 2p blue   .15 .15
Mariano Moreno (1778-1811), writer, politician, member of the 1810 Junta.

Emperor Trajan Statue — A297
Rabindranath Tagore — A298 

1961, Apr. 11
727 A297 2p slate green   .15 .15
Visit of Pres. Giovanni Gronchi of Italy to Argentina, April 1961.

1961, May 13   Photo.   *Perf. 13½*
728 A298 2p purple, *grysh*   .15 .15
Centenary of the birth of Rabindranath Tagore, Indian poet.

San Martin Statue, Madrid — A299

1961, May 24   Wmk. 90
729 A299 1p olive gray   .15 .15
Unveiling of a statue of General José de San Martin in Madrid.

Manuel Belgrano — A300

1961, June 17   *Perf. 13½*
730 A300 2p violet blue   .15 .15
Erection of a monument by Hector Rocha, to General Manuel Belgrano in Buenos Aires.

Explorers, Sledge and Dog Team — A301

1961, Aug. 19   Photo.   Wmk. 90
731 A301 2p black   .70 .22
10th anniversary of the General San Martin Base, Argentine Antarctic.

Spanish Conquistador and Sword — A302
Sarmiento Statue by Rodin, Buenos Aires — A303 

1961, Aug. 19   Litho.
732 A302 2p red & blk   .15 .15
First city of Jujuy, 400th anniversary.

1961, Sept. 9   Photo.
733 A303 2p violet   .15 .15
Domingo Faustino Sarmiento (1811-88), political leader and writer.

Symbol of World Town Planning A304

1961, Nov. 25   Litho.   *Perf. 13½*
734 A304 2p ultra & yel   .15 .15
World Town Planning Day, Nov. 8.

Manuel Belgrano Statue, Buenos Aires A305
Grenadier, Flag and Regimental Emblem A306 

1962, Feb. 24   Photo.
735 A305 2p Prus blue   .15 .15
150th anniversary of the Argentine flag.

1962, Mar. 31   Wmk. 90   *Perf. 13½*
736 A306 2p carmine rose   .15 .15
150th anniversary of the San Martin Grenadier Guards regiment.

Mosquito and Malaria Eradication Emblem — A307

1962, Apr. 7   Litho.
737 A307 2p vermilion & blk   .15 .15
WHO drive to eradicate malaria.

Church of the Virgin of Luján — A308
Bust of Juan Jufrè — A309 

1962, May 12   *Perf. 13½*
738 A308 2p org brn & blk   .15 .15
75th anniversary of the pontifical coronation of the Virgin of Lujan.

1962, June 23   Photo.
739 A309 2p Prus blue   .15 .15
Founding of San Juan, 4th cent.

"Soaring into Space" A310
Juan Vucetich A311 

1962, Aug. 18   Litho.   *Perf. 13½*
740 A310 2p maroon, blk & bl   .15 .15
Argentine Air Force, 50th anniversary.

1962, Oct. 6   Photo.   Wmk. 90
741 A311 2p green   .15 .15
Juan Vucetich (1864-1925), inventor of the Argentine system of fingerprinting.

Domingo F. Sarmiento A312
February 20th Monument, Salta A313 

Design: 4p, Jose Hernandez.

1962-66   Photo.   *Perf. 13½*
742   A312 2p deep green   .65 .15
  Litho.
742A A312 2p lt green ('64)   .55 .15
  Photo.
742B A312 4p dull red ('65)   .45 .15
  Litho.
742C A312 4p rose red ('66)   .60 .15
  Nos. 742-742C (4)   2.25 .60
See No. 817-819. For overprints see Nos. O119-O121, O125, O149.

1963, Feb. 23   Photo.   Wmk. 90
743 A313 2p dark green   .15 .15
150th anniversary of the Battle of Salta, War of Independence.

Gear Wheels — A314

1963, Mar. 16   Litho.   *Perf. 13½*
744 A314 4p gray, blk & brt rose   .15 .15
Argentine Industrial Union, 75th anniv.

National College, Buenos Aires — A315
Child Draining Cup — A316 

1963, Mar. 16   Wmk. 90
745 A315 4p dull org & blk   .18 .15
National College of Buenos Aires, cent.

1963, Apr. 6
746 A316 4p multicolored   .15 .15
FAO "Freedom from Hunger" campaign.

Frigate "La Argentina," 1817, by Emilio Biggeri — A317

1963, May 18   Photo.
747 A317 4p bluish green   .28 .15
Issued for Navy Day, May 17.

Seat of 1813 Assembly and Official Seal — A318

1963, July 13   Litho.   *Perf. 13½*
748 A318 4p lt blue & blk   .15 .15
150th anniversary of the 1813 Assembly.

Battle of San Lorenzo, 1813 A319

1963, Aug. 24
749 A319 4p grn & blk, *grnsh*   .20 .15
Sesquicentennial of the Battle of San Lorenzo.

Queen Nefertari Offering Papyrus Flowers, Abu Simbel — A320

1963, Sept. 14   *Perf. 13½*
750 A320 4p ocher, blk & bl grn   .28 .15
Campaign to save the historic monuments in Nubia.

Government House, Buenos Aires A321

1963, Oct. 12   Wmk. 90   *Perf. 13½*
751 A321 5p rose & brown   .16 .15
Inauguration of President Arturo Illia.

"Science" A322
Francisco de las Carreras, Supreme Court Justice A323 

1963, Oct. 16   Litho.
752 A322 4p org brn, bl & blk   .15 .15
10th Latin-American Neurosurgery Congress.

1963, Nov. 23   Photo.   *Perf. 13½*
753 A323 5p bluish green   .15 .15
Centenary of judicial power.

ARGENTINA

Blackboards — A324

1963, Nov. 23   Litho.
754 A324 5p red, blk & bl   .15 .15
Issued to publicize "Teachers for America" through the Alliance for Progress program.

Kemal Atatürk — A325

"Payador" by Juan Carlos Castagnino — A326

1963, Dec. 28   Photo.   Perf. 13½
755 A325 12p dark gray   .28 .15
25th anniversary of the death of Kemal Atatürk, president of Turkey.

1964, Jan. 25   Litho.
756 A326 4p ultra, blk & lt bl   .32 .15
Fourth National Folklore Festival.

Maps of South Georgia, South Orkney and South Sandwich Islands — A327

1964, Feb. 22   Wmk. 90   Perf. 13½
Size: 33x22mm
757 A327 2p lt & dk bl & bister   1.25 .24
Size: 30x40mm
758 A327 4p lt & dk bl & ol grn   1.75 .30
Nos. 757-758,C92 (3)   4.75 1.24
60th anniversary of Argentina's claim to Antarctic territories.

Jorge Newbery in Cockpit — A328

1964, Feb. 23   Photo.
759 A328 4p deep green   .16 .15
Newbery, aviator, 50th death anniv.

John F. Kennedy — A329

José Brochero by José Cuello — A330

1964, Apr. 14   Engr.   Wmk. 90
760 A329 4p claret & dk bl   .35 .15
President John F. Kennedy (1917-63).

1964, May 9   Photo.   Perf. 13½
761 A330 4p light sepia   .16 .15
50th anniversary of the death of Father Jose Gabriel Brochero.

Soldier of Patricios Regiment — A331

1964, May 29   Litho.   Wmk. 90
762 A331 4p blk, ultra & red   .38 .20
Issued for Army Day. Later Army Day stamps, inscribed "Republica Argentina," are of type A340a.

Pope John XXIII — A332

1964, June 27   Engr.
763 A332 4p orange & blk   .22 .15
Issued in memory of Pope John XXIII.

University of Cordoba Arms — A333

Pigeons and UN Building, NYC — A334

1964, Aug. 22   Litho.   Wmk. 90
764 A333 4p blk, ultra & yel   .15 .15
350th anniv. of the University of Cordoba.

1964, Oct. 24   Perf. 13½
765 A334 4p dk blue & lt blue   .15 .15
Issued for United Nations Day.

Joaquin V. Gonzalez — A335

Julio Argentino Roca — A336

1964, Nov. 14   Photo.
766 A335 4p dk rose carmine   .15 .15
Centenary (in 1963) of the birth of Joaquin V. Gonzalez, writer.

1964, Dec. 12   Perf. 13½
767 A336 4p violet blue   .15 .15
General Julio A. Roca, (1843-1914), president of Argentina, (1880-86, 1898-1904).

Market at Montserrat Square, by Carlos Morel — A337

1964, Dec. 19   Photo.
768 A337 4p sepia   .30 .18
19th century Argentine painter Carlos Morel.

Icebreaker General San Martin — A338

Girl with Piggy Bank — A339

Design: 2p, General Belgrano Base, Antarctica.

1965   Perf. 13½
769 A338 2p dull purple   .42 .15
770 A338 4p ultra   .48 .15
Issued to publicize the national territory of Tierra del Fuego, Antarctic and South Atlantic Isles.
Issue dates: 4p, Feb. 27; 2p, June 5.

1965, Apr. 3   Litho.
771 A339 4p red org & blk   .15 .15
National Postal Savings Bank, 50th anniv.

Sun and Globe — A340

1965, May 29
772 A340 4p blk, org & dl bl   .24 .15
Nos. 772,C98-C99 (3)   1.66 .85
International Quiet Sun Year, 1964-65.

Hussar of Pueyrredon Regiment — A340a

Ricardo Rojas (1882-1957) — A341

1965, June 5   Wmk. 90   Perf. 13½
773 A340a 8p dp ultra, blk & red   .48 .18
Issued for Army Day. See Nos. 796, 838, 857, 893, 944, 958, 974, 1145.

1965, June 26   Photo.
Portraits: No. 775, Ricardo Guiraldes (1886-1927). No. 776, Enrique Larreta (1873-1961). No. 777, Leopoldo Lugones (1874-1938). No. 778, Roberto J. Payro (1867-1928).
774 A341 8p brown   .35 .16
775 A341 8p brown   .35 .16
776 A341 8p brown   .35 .16
777 A341 8p brown   .35 .16
778 A341 8p brown   .35 .16
Nos. 774-778 (5)   1.75 .80
Issued to honor Argentine writers. Printed setenant in sheets of 100 (10x10); 2 horizontal rows of each design with Guiraldes in top rows and Rojas in bottom rows.

Hipolito Yrigoyen — A342

1965, July 3   Litho.
779 A342 8p pink & black   .20 .15
Hipolito Yrigoyen (1852-1933), president of Argentina 1916-22, 1928-30.

Children Looking Through Window — A343

1965, July 24   Photo.
780 A343 8p salmon & blk   .24 .15
International Seminar on Mental Health.

Child's Funerary Urn and 16th Century Map — A344

1965, Aug. 7   Litho.
781 A344 8p lt grn, dk red, brn & ocher   .32 .15
City of San Miguel de Tucuman, 400th anniv.

Cardinal Cagliero — A345

Dante Alighieri — A346

1965, Aug. 21   Photo.
782 A345 8p violet   .20 .15
Juan Cardinal Cagliero (1839-1926), missionary to Argentina and Bishop of Magida.

1965, Sept. 16   Wmk. 90   Perf. 13½
783 A346 8p light ultra   .28 .15
Dante Alighieri (1265-1321), Italian poet.

Clipper "Mimosa" and Map of Patagonia — A347

1965, Sept. 25   Litho.
784 A347 8p red & black   .28 .15
Centenary of Welsh colonization of Chubut, and the founding of the city of Rawson.

Map of Buenos Aires, Cock and Compass Emblem of Federal Police — A348

1965, Oct. 30   Photo.   Perf. 13½
785 A348 8p carmine rose   .32 .15
Issued for Federal Police Day.

ARGENTINA

Child's Drawing of Children — A349

1965, Nov. 6   Litho.   Wmk. 90
786   A349   8p lt yel grn & blk   .28   .15
Public education law, 81st anniversary.

Church of St. Francis, Catamarca A350

Ruben Dario A351

1965, Dec. 8
787   A350   8p org yel & red brn   .20   .15
Brother Mamerto de la Asuncion Esquiu, preacher, teacher and official of 1885 Provincial Constitutional Convention.

Litho. and Photo.

1965, Dec. 22   Perf. 13½
788   A351   15p bl vio, gray   .20   .15
Ruben Dario (pen name of Felix Ruben Garcia Sarmiento, 1867-1916), Nicaraguan poet, newspaper correspondent and diplomat.

"The Orange Seller" A352

Pueyrredon Paintings: No. 790, "Stop at the Grocery Store." No. 791, "Landscape at San Fernando" (sailboats). No. 792, "Bathing Horses at River Plata."

1966, Jan. 29   Photo.   Perf. 13½
789   A352   8p bluish green   .70   .40
790   A352   8p bluish green   .70   .40
791   A352   8p bluish green   .70   .40
792   A352   8p bluish green   .70   .40
   a.   Block of 4, #789-792 + 2 labels   2.80   1.60
Prilidiano Pueyrredon (1823-1870), painter.

Sun Yat-sen, Flags of Argentina and China — A353

1966, Mar. 12   Wmk. 90   Perf. 13½
793   A353   8p dk red brown   .70   .22
Dr. Sun Yat-sen (1866-1925), founder of the Republic of China.

Souvenir Sheet

Rivadavia Issue of 1864 — A354

Wmk. 90

1966, Apr. 20   Litho.   Imperf.
794   A354   Sheet of 3   .95   .95
   a.   4p gray & red brown   .15   .15
   b.   5p gray & green   .15   .15
   c.   8p gray & dark blue   .16   .16
2nd Rio de la Plata Stamp Show, Buenos Aires, Mar. 16-24.

People of Various Races and WHO Emblem A355

1966, Apr. 23   Perf. 13½
795   A355   8p brown & blk   .28   .15
Opening of the WHO Headquarters, Geneva.

Soldier Type of 1965
Army Day: 8p, Cavalryman, Guemes Infernal Regiment.

1966, May 28   Litho.
796   A340a   8p multicolored   .55   .30

Coat of Arms — A356

Arms: a, Buenos Aires. b, Federal Capital. c, Catamarca. d, Cordoba. e, Corrientes. f, Chaco. g, Chubut. h, Entre Rios. i, Formosa. j, Jujuy. k, La Pampa. l, La Rioja. m, Mendoza. n, Misiones. o, Neuquen. p, Salta. q, San Juan. r, San Luis. s, Santa Cruz. t, Santa Fe. u, Santiago del Estero. v, Tucuman. w, map of Rio Negro. x, map of Tierra del Fuego, Antarctica. y, South Atlantic Islands.

1966, July 30   Wmk. 90   Perf. 13½
797   Sheet of 25   40.00
   a.-y.   A356   10p black & multi   1.00   .65
150th anniv. of Argentina's Declaration of Independence.

Three Crosses, Caritas Emblem — A357

1966, Sept. 10   Perf. 13½
798   A357   10p ol grn, blk & lt bl   .22   .15
Caritas, charity organization.

Hilario Ascasubi (1807-75) — A358

Portraits: #800, Estanislao del Campo (1834-80). #801, Miguel Cane (1851-1905). #802, Lucio V. Lopez (1848-94). #803, Rafael Obligado (1851-1920). #804, Luis Agote (1868-1954), M.D. #805, Juan B. Ambrosetti (1865-1917), naturalist and archaeologist. #806, Miguel Lillo (1862-1931), botanist and chemist. #807, Francisco P. Moreno (1852-1919), naturalist and paleontologist. #808, Francisco J. Muñiz (1795-1871), physician.

1966   Photo.   Wmk. 90
799   A358   10p dk blue green   .42   .35
800   A358   10p dk blue green   .42   .35
801   A358   10p dk blue green   .42   .35
802   A358   10p dk blue green   .42   .35
803   A358   10p dk blue green   .42   .35
804   A358   10p deep violet   .42   .35
805   A358   10p deep violet   .42   .35
806   A358   10p deep violet   .42   .35
807   A358   10p deep violet   .42   .35
808   A358   10p deep violet   .42   .35
   Nos. 799-808 (10)   4.20   3.50
Nos. 799-803 issued Sept. 17 to honor Argentine writers. Printed se-tenant in sheets of 100 (10x10); 2 horizontal rows of each portrait. Nos. 804-808 issued Oct. 22 to honor Argentine scientists; 2 horizontal rows of each portrait. Scientists set has value at upper left, frame line with rounded corners.

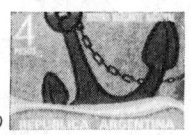

Anchor — A359

1966, Oct. 8   Litho.
809   A359   4p multicolored   .22   .15
Argentine merchant marine.

Flags and Map of the Americas — A360

Argentine National Bank — A361

1966, Oct. 29   Perf. 13½
810   A360   10p gray & multi   .24   .15
7th Conference of American Armies.

1966, Nov. 5   Photo.
811   A361   10p brt blue green   .20   .15
75th anniv. of the Argentine National Bank.

La Salle Monument and College, Buenos Aires — A362

1966, Nov. 26   Litho.   Perf. 13½
812   A362   10p brown org & blk   .20   .15
75th anniv. of the Colegio de la Salle, Buenos Aires, and to honor Saint Jean Baptiste de la Salle (1651-1719), educator.

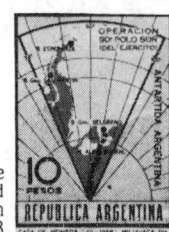

Map of Argentine Antarctica and Expedition Route — A363

1966, Dec. 10   Wmk. 90
813   A363   10p multicolored   .70   .45
1965 Argentine Antarctic expedition, which planted the Argentine flag on the South Pole. See No. 851.

Juan Martin de Pueyrredon A364

Gen. Juan de Las Heras A365

1966, Dec. 17   Photo.   Perf. 13½
814   A364   10p dull red brn   .18   .15
Issued to honor Juan Martin de Pueyrredon (1777-1850), Governor of Cordoba and of the United Provinces of the River Plata.

1966, Dec. 17   Engr.
815   A365   10p black   .18   .15
Issued to honor Gen. Juan Gregorio de Las Heras (1780-1866), Peruvian field marshal and aide-de-camp to San Martin.

Inscribed "Republica Argentina"
Types of 1955-61 and

Guillermo Brown — A366

Trout Leaping in National Park — A366a

Designs: 6p, Jose Hernandez. 50p, Gen. Jose de San Martin. 500p, Red deer in forest.

Two overall paper sizes for 6p, 50p (No. 827) and 90p:
I - 27x37½mm
II - 27x39mm

1965-68   Wmk. 90   Photo.   Perf. 13½
817   A366   6p rose red, litho, I ('67)   1.25   .15
818   A366   6p rose red ('67)   2.25   .15
819   A366   6p brn, 15x22mm ('68)   .15   .15
823   A238a   43p dk car rose   6.25   .15
824   A238a   45p brn ('66)   4.25   .15
825   A238a   45p brn, litho ('67)   7.00   .15
826   A241   50p dk bl, 29x40mm   7.00   .15
827   A241   50p dk bl, 22x31½mm, I ('67)   4.75   .15
   a.   Paper II   2.75   .15
828   A366   90p ol bis, I ('67)   3.00   .15
   a.   Paper II   12.00   .15

Engr.
829   A495   500p yellow grn ('66)   1.40   .28
829A   A366a   1,000p vio bl ('68)   5.50   1.25
   Nos. 817-829A (11)   42.80   2.88

The 500p and 1,000p remained on sale as 5p and 10p stamps after the 1970 currency exchange. See Nos. 888, 891, 939, 941, 992, 1031, 1040, 1045-1047. For surcharge and overprints see Nos. 1077, O153-O158, O162.

Pre-Columbian Pottery — A367

1967, Feb. 18   Litho.   Perf. 13½
830   A367   10p multicolored   .28   .15
20th anniv. of UNESCO.

ARGENTINA

"The Meal" by Fernando Fader — A368

1967, Feb. 25   Photo.   Wmk. 90
831 A368 10p red brown   .28 .15
Issued in memory of the Argentine painter Fernando Fader (1882-1935).

Col. Juana Azurduy de Padilla (1781-1862), Soldier — A369

Schooner "Invencible," 1811 — A370

Famous Argentine Women: #833, Juana Manuela Gorriti, writer. #834, Cecilia Grierson (1858-1934), physician. #835, Juana Paula Manso (1819-75), writer and educator. #836, Alfonsina Storni (1892-1938), writer and educator.

1967, May 13   Photo.   Perf. 13½
832 A369 6p dark brown   .32 .20
833 A369 6p dark brown   .32 .20
834 A369 6p dark brown   .32 .20
835 A369 6p dark brown   .32 .20
836 A369 6p dark brown   .32 .20
    Nos. 832-836 (5)   1.60 1.00
Printed se-tenant in sheets of 100 (10x10); 2 horizontal rows of each portrait.

1967, May 20   Litho.
837 A370 20p multicolored   .85 .35
Issued for Navy Day.

Soldier Type of 1965
Army Day: 20p, Highlander (Arribeños Corps).

1967, May 27
838 A340a 20p multicolored   .70 .28

Souvenir Sheet

Manuel Belgrano and José Artigas — A371

1967, June 22   Imperf.
839 A371   Sheet of 2   .40 .40
    a.   6p gray & brown   .15 .15
    b.   22p brown & gray   .24 .24
Third Rio de la Plata Stamp Show, Montevideo, Uruguay, June 18-25.

Peace Dove and Valise — A372

PADELAI Emblem — A373

1967, Aug. 5   Litho.   Perf. 13½
840 A372 20p multicolored   .22 .15
Issued for International Tourist Year 1967.

1967, Aug. 12   Litho.
841 A373 20p multicolored   .22 .15
75th anniv. of the Children's Welfare Association (Patronato de la Infancia-PADELAI).

Stagecoach and Modern City — A374

1967, Sept. 23   Wmk. 90   Perf. 13½
842 A374 20p rose, yel & blk   .26 .15
Centenary of Villa Maria, Cordoba.

San Martin by Ibarra — A375

"Battle of Chacabuco" by P. Subercaseaux — A376

1967, Sept. 30   Litho.
843 A375 20p blk brn & pale yel   .55 .15
Engr.
844 A376 40p blue black   .85 .20
Battle of Chacabuco, 150th anniversary.

Exhibition Rooms — A377

1967, Oct. 11   Photo.
845 A377 20p blue gray   .20 .15
Government House Museum, 10th anniv.

Pedro L. Zanni, Fokker and 1924 Flight Route — A378

1967, Oct. 21   Litho.   Perf. 13½
846 A378 20p multicolored   .28 .15
Issued for Aviation Week and to commemorate the 1924 flight of the Fokker seaplane "Province of Buenos Aires" from Amsterdam, Netherlands, to Osaka, Japan.

Training Ship General Brown, by Emilio Biggeri — A379

1967, Oct. 28   Wmk. 90
847 A379 20p multicolored   .85 .35
Issued to honor the Military Naval School.

Ovidio Lagos and Front Page — A380

St. Barbara — A381

1967, Nov. 11   Photo.
848 A380 20p sepia   .15 .15
Centenary of La Capital, Rosario newspaper.

1967, Dec. 2   Perf. 13½
849 A381 20p rose red   .28 .15
St. Barbara, patron saint of artillerymen.

Portrait of his Wife, by Eduardo Sivori — A382

1968, Jan. 27   Photo.   Perf. 13½
850 A382 20p blue green   .28 .15
Eduardo Sivori (1847-1918), painter.

Antarctic Type of 1966 and

Admiral Brown Scientific Station — A383

Planes over Map of Antarctica — A384

6p, Map showing radio-postal stations 1966-67.

1968, Feb. 17   Litho.   Wmk. 90
851 A363 6p multicolored   .45 .18
852 A383 20p multicolored   .60 .24
853 A384 40p multicolored   1.00 .30
    Nos. 851-853 (3)   2.05 .72
Issued to publicize Argentine research projects in Argentine Antarctica.

The Annunciation, by Leonardo da Vinci — A385

Man in Wheelchair and Factory — A386

1968, Mar. 23   Photo.   Perf. 13½
854 A385 20p lilac rose   .20 .15
Issued for the Day of the Army Communications System and its patron saint, Gabriel.

1968, Mar. 23   Litho.
855 A386 20p green & black   .20 .15
Day of Rehabilitation of the Handicapped.

Children and WHO Emblem — A387

1968, May 11   Wmk. 90   Perf. 13½
856 A387 20p dk vio bl & ver   .20 .15
20th anniv. of WHO.

Soldier Type of 1965
Army Day: 20p, Uniform of First Artillery Regiment "General Iriarte."

1968, June 8   Litho.
857 A340a 20p multicolored   .75 .24

Frigate "Libertad," Painting by Emilio Biggeri — A388

1968, June 15   Wmk. 90
858 A388 20p multicolored   .75 .24
Issued for Navy Day.

Guillermo Rawson and Old Hospital — A389

1968, July 20   Photo.   Perf. 13½
859 A389 6p olive bister   .16 .15
Cent. of Rawson Hospital, Buenos Aires.

Student Directing Traffic for Schoolmates — A390

1968, Aug. 10   Litho.   Perf. 13½
860 A390 20p lt bl, blk, buff & car   .15 .15
Traffic safety and education.

ARGENTINA

O'Higgins Joining San Martin at Battle of Maipu, by P. Subercaseaux — A391

1968, Aug. 15			Engr.
861	A391	40p bluish black	.65 .30

Sesquicentennial of the Battle of Maipu.

Osvaldo Magnasco (1864-1920), Lawyer, Professor of Law and Minister of Justice — A392

1968, Sept. 7		Photo.	Perf. 13½
862	A392	20p brown	.22 .15

Grandmother's Birthday, by Patricia Lynch — A393

The Sea, by Edgardo Gomez — A394

1968, Sept. 21			Litho.
863	A393	20p multicolored	.24 .15
864	A394	20p multicolored	.24 .15
		Set value	.16

The designs were chosen in a competition among kindergarten and elementary school children.

Mar del Plata at Night — A395

1968, Oct. 19		Litho.	Perf. 13½
865	A395	20p black, ocher & bl	.22 .15
		Nos. 865,C113-C114 (3)	1.27 .61

4th Plenary Assembly of the Intl. Telegraph and Telephone Consultative Committee, Mar del Plata, Sept. 23-Oct. 25.

Frontier Gendarme A396

Patrol Boat A397

1968, Oct. 26			
866	A396	20p multicolored	.30 .15
867	A397	20p blue, vio bl & blk	.30 .15

No. 866 honors the Gendarmery; No. 867 the Coast Guard.

Aaron de Anchorena and Pampero Balloon — A398

1968, Nov. 2			Photo.
868	A398	20p blue & multi	.32 .15

22nd Aeronautics and Space Week.

St. Martin of Tours, by Alfredo Guido — A399

1968, Nov. 9			Litho.
869	A399	20p lilac & dk brn	.20 .15

St. Martin of Tours, patron saint of Buenos Aires.

Municipal Bank Emblem — A400

1968, Nov. 16			
870	A400	20p multicolored	.20 .15

90th anniv. of the Buenos Aires Municipal Bank.

Anniversary Emblem A401

1968, Dec. 14	Wmk. 90		Perf. 13½
871	A401	20p car rose & dk grn	.20 .15

25th anniversary of ALPI (Fight Against Polio Association).

Shovel and State Coal Fields Emblem A402

Pouring Ladle and Army Manufacturing Emblem A403

1968, Dec. 21			Litho.
872	A402	20p orange, bl & blk	.26 .15
873	A403	20p dl vio, dl yel & blk	.26 .15

Issued to publicize the National Coal and Steel industry at the Rio Turbio coal fields and the Zapla blast furnaces.

Woman Potter, by Ramon Gomez Cornet — A404

1968, Dec. 21		Photo.	Perf. 13½
874	A404	20p carmine rose	.48 .40

Centenary of the Witcomb Gallery.

View of Buenos Aires and Rio de la Plata by Ulrico Schmidl A405

1969, Feb. 8		Litho.	Wmk. 90
875	A405	20p yellow, blk & ver	.48 .35

Ulrico Schmidl (c. 1462-1554) who wrote "Journey to the Rio de la Plata and Paraguay."

Types of 1955-67

Designs: 50c, Puma. 1p, Sunflower. 3p, Zapata Slope, Catamarca. 5p, Tierra del Fuego. 6p, José Hernandez. 10p, Inca Bridge, Mendoza. 50p, José de San Martin. 90p, Guillermo Brown. 100p, Ski jumper.

	Photo.; Litho. (50c, 3p, 10p)		
1969-70		Wmk. 365	Perf. 13½
882	A275	50c bister ('70)	.70 .15
883	A277	5p brown	1.25 .15
884	A279	100p blue	26.00 1.40
		Unwmk.	
885	A278	1p brown ('70)	.65 .15
886	A277	3p dk blue ('70)	.65 .15
a.	Wmk. 90		5.25 .35
887	A277	5p brown ('70)	.75 .15
888	A366	6p red brn, 15x22mm ('70)	1.25 .15
889	A278	50p dull red ('70)	.52 .15
a.	Wmk. 90		475.00 47.50
890	A241	50p dk bl, 22x31½mm ('70)	1.75 .15
891	A366	9p ol brn, 22x32mm ('70)	3.50 .18
892	A279	100p blue ('70)	9.00 .30
		Nos. 882-892 (11)	46.02 3.08

For surcharges see Nos. 1076-1077.

Soldier Type of 1965

Army Day: 20p, Sapper (gastador) of Buenos Aires Province, 1856.

	Perf. 13½		
1969, May 31		Wmk. 365	Litho.
893	A340a	20p multicolored	.85 .35

Frigate Hercules, by Emilio Biggeri — A406

1969, May 31			
894	A406	20p multicolored	1.00 .28

Issued for Navy Day.

"All Men are Equal" A407

ILO Emblem A408

1969, June 28			Wmk. 90
895	A407	20p black & ocher	.20 .15

International Human Rights Year.

1969, June 28		Litho.	Wmk. 365
896	A408	20p lt green & multi	.20 .15

50th anniv. of the ILO.

Pedro N. Arata (1849-1922), Chemist — A409

Radar Antenna, Balcarce Station and Satellite — A410

Portraits: No. 898, Miguel Fernandez (1883-1950), zoologist. No. 899, Ángel P. Gallardo (1867-1934), biologist. No. 900, Cristobal M. Hicken (1875-1933), botanist. No. 901, Eduardo Ladislao Holmberg, M.D. (1852-1937), natural scientist.

1969, Aug. 9		Wmk. 365	Perf. 13½
897	A409	6p Arata	.42 .15
898	A409	6p Fernandez	.42 .15
899	A409	6p Gallardo	.42 .15
900	A409	6p Hicken	.42 .15
901	A409	6p Holmberg	.42 .15
		Nos. 897-901 (5)	2.10 .75

Argentine scientists. See No. 778 note.

1969, Aug. 23			Wmk. 99
902	A410	20p yellow & blk	.28 .15

Communications by satellite through Intl. Telecommunications Satellite Consortium (INTELSAT). See No. C115.

Nieuport 28, Flight Route and Map of Buenos Aires Province A411

1969, Sept. 13		Litho.	Wmk. 90
903	A411	20p multicolored	.28 .15

50th anniv. of the first Argentine airmail service from El Palomar to Mar del Plata, flown Feb. 23-24, 1919, by Capt. Pedro L. Zanni.

Military College Gate and Emblem A412

1969, Oct. 4		Wmk. 365	Perf. 13½
904	A412	20p multicolored	.28 .15

Cent. of the National Military College, El Palomar (Greater Buenos Aires).

Gen. Angel Pacheco A413

La Farola, Logotype of La Prensa A414

1969, Nov. 8		Photo.	Wmk. 365
905	A413	20p deep green	.22 .15

Gen. Angel Pacheco (1795-1869).

1969, Nov. 8		Litho.	Perf. 13½

#907, Bartolomé Mitre & La Nacion logotype.

| 906 | A414 | 20p orange, yel & blk | .70 .22 |
| 907 | A414 | 20p brt green & blk | .70 .22 |

Cent. of newspapers La Prensa and La Nacion.

ARGENTINA

Julian Aguirre — A415

Musicians: No. 909, Felipe Boero. No. 910, Constantino Gaito. No. 911, Carlos Lopez Buchardo. No. 912, Alberto Williams.

1969, Dec. 6   **Wmk. 365**   **Perf. 13½**   **Photo.**
908	A415	6p Aguirre	.55	.30
909	A415	6p Boero	.55	.30
910	A415	6p Gaito	.55	.30
911	A415	6p Buchardo	.55	.30
912	A415	6p Williams	.55	.30
		Nos. 908-912 (5)	2.75	1.50

Argentine musicians. See No. 778 note.

Lt. Benjamin Matienzo and Nieuport Plane A416

1969, Dec. 13   **Litho.**
913 A416 20p multicolored   .55 .35

23rd Aeronautics and Space Week.

High Power Lines and Map A417

Design: 20p, Map of Santa Fe Province and schematic view of tunnel.

1969, Dec. 13
914 A417 6p multicolored   .50 .15
915 A417 20p multicolored   1.00 .15

Completion of development projects: 6p for the hydroelectric dams on the Limay and Neuquen Rivers, the 20p the tunnel under Rio Grande from Sante Fe to Parana.

Lions Emblem A418

1969, Dec. 20   **Wmk. 365**   **Perf. 13½**
916 A418 20p black, emer & org   .60 .24

Argentine Lions Intl. Club, 50th anniv.

Madonna and Child, by Raul Soldi — A419

1969, Dec. 27   **Litho.**
917 A419 20p multicolored   .70 .28

Christmas 1969.

Manuel Belgrano, by Jean Gericault — A420

The Creation of the Flag, Bas-relief by Jose Fioravanti — A421

1970, July 4   **Unwmk.**   **Perf. 13½**   **Photo.**
918 A420 20c deep brown   .35 .15

                Litho.   **Perf. 12½**
919 A421 50c bister, blk & bl   .85 .50

Gen. Manuel Belgrano (1770-1820), Argentine patriot.

San Jose Palace A422

1970, Aug. 9   **Litho.**   **Perf. 13½**
920 A422 20c yellow grn & multi   .22 .15

Cent. of the death of Gen. Justo Jose de Urquiza (1801-70), pres. of Argentina, 1854-60.

Schooner "Juliet" A423

1970, Aug. 8   **Unwmk.**
921 A423 20c multicolored   1.00 .40

Issued for Navy Day.

Receiver of 1920 and Waves A424

1970, Aug. 29
922 A424 20c lt blue & multi   .30 .15

50th anniv. of Argentine broadcasting.

Types of 1955-67 Inscribed "Republica Argentina" and Types A425, A426

Belgrano A425   Lujan Basilica A426

Designs: 1c, Sunflower. 3c, Zapata Slope, Catamarca. 5c, Tierra del Fuego. 8c, No. 931, Belgrano. 10c, Inca Bridge, Mendoza. 25c, 50c, 70c, Jose de San Martin. 65c, 90c, 1.20p, San Martin. 1p, Ski jumper. 1.15p, 1.80p, Adm. Brown.

1970-73   **Photo.**   **Unwmk.**   **Perf. 13½**
923	A278	1c dk green ('71)	.15	.15
924	A277	3c car rose ('71)	.15	.15
925	A277	5c blue ('71)	.15	.15
926	A425	6c deep blue	.15	.15
927	A425	8c green ('72)	.15	.15
928	A278	10c dull red ('71)	.38	.15
929	A278	10c brn, litho. ('71)	.52	.15
930	A278	10c orange brn ('72)	.45	.15
931	A278	10c brown ('73)	.20	.15
932	A426	18c yel & dk brn, litho ('73)	.20	.15
933	A425	25c brown ('71)	.32	.15
934	A425	50c scarlet ('72)	1.25	.15
935	A241	65c brn, 22x31½mm, paper II ('71)	.65	.15
936	A425	70c dk blue ('73)	.32	.15
937	A241	90c emer, 22x31½mm ('72)	3.25	.15
938	A279	1p brn, 22½x29½mm ('71)	1.90	.15
939	A366	1.15p dk bl, 22½x32mm	1.10	.15
940	A241	1.20p org, 22x31½mm ('71)	1.10	.15
941	A366	1.80p brown ('73)	1.10	.15
		Nos. 923-941 (19)	13.49	2.85

The imprint "Casa de Moneda de la Nacion" (in capitals) appears on 3c, 5c, Nos. 928-929; 65c, 90c, 1p, 1.20p.
On type A425 only the 6c is inscribed "Ley 18.188" below denomination.
Fluorescent paper was used in printing the 25c, 50c, and 70c. The 3c, 5c, 8c, No. 931 and 65c were issued on both ordinary and fluorescent paper.
See Nos. 987-996, 1032-1038, 1042-1043, 1089-1107. For overprint and surcharge see Nos. 1010, 1078.

Soldier Type of 1965
20c, Galloping messenger of Field Army, 1879.

1970, Oct. 17   **Litho.**   **Perf. 13½**
944 A340a 20c multicolored   .80 .26

Dome of Cathedral of Cordoba — A430

1970, Nov. 7   **Unwmk.**
945 A430 50c gray & blk   .80 .15

Bishopric of Tucuman, 400th anniv. See #C131.

People Around UN Emblem — A431

1970, Nov. 7
946 A431 20c tan & multi   .20 .15

25th anniversary of the United Nations.

State Mint and Medal A432

1970, Nov. 28   **Unwmk.**   **Perf. 13½**
947 A432 20c gold, grn & blk   .20 .15

inauguration of the State Mint Building, 25th anniversary.

St. John Bosco and Dean Funes College A433

1970, Dec. 19   **Litho.**
948 A433 20c olive & blk   .20 .15

Honoring the work of the Salesian Order in Patagonia.

Nativity, by Horacio Gramajo Gutierrez — A434

1970, Dec. 19
949 A434 20c multicolored   .55 .35

Christmas 1970.

Argentine Flag, Map of Argentine Antarctica — A435

1971, Feb. 20   **Litho.**   **Perf. 13½**
950 A435 20c multicolored   1.25 .50

Argentine South Pole Expedition, 5th anniv.

Phosphorescent Sorting Code and Albert Einstein — A436

1971, Apr. 30   **Unwmk.**   **Perf. 13½**
951 A436 25c multicolored   .48 .30

Electronics in postal development.

Symbolic Road Crossing A437

1971, May 29   **Litho.**
952 A437 25c blue & blk   .25 .18

Inter-American Regional Meeting of the Intl. Federation of Roads, Buenos Aires, Mar. 28-31.

Elias Alippi — A438

Actors: No. 954, Juan Aurelio Casacuberta. No. 955, Angelina Pagano. No. 956, Roberto Casaux. No. 957, Florencio Parravicini. See No. 778 note.

1971, May 29   **Litho.**
953	A438	15c Alippi	.35	.20
954	A438	15c Casacuberta	.35	.20
955	A438	15c Pagano	.35	.20

ARGENTINA

956	A438	15c Casaux	.35 .20
957	A438	15c Parravicini	.35 .20
		Nos. 953-957 (5)	1.75 1.00

Soldier Type of 1965
Army Day, May 29: Artilleryman, 1826.

1971, July 3   Unwmk.   *Perf. 13½*
958   A340a   25c multicolored   1.25 .50

Bilander "Carmen," by Emilio Biggeri — A439

1971, July 3
959   A439   25c multicolored   1.25 .25
Navy Day

Peruvian Order of the Sun — A440

1971, Aug. 28
960   A440   31c multicolored   .32 .15
Sesquicentennial of Peru's independence.

Güemes in Battle, by Lorenzo Gigli — A441

No. 962, Death of Güemes, by Antonio Alice.

1971, Aug. 28   Size: **39x29mm**
961   A441   25c multicolored   .48 .30

Size: **84x29mm**
962   A441   25c multicolored   .48 .30

Sesquicentennial of the death of Martin Miguel de Güemes, leader in Gaucho War, Governor and Captain General of Salta Province.

Stylized Tulip — A442

1971, Sept. 18
963   A442   25c tan & multi   .26 .15
3rd Intl. and 8th Natl. Horticultural Exhib.

Father Antonio Saenz, by Juan Gut — A443

1971, Sept. 18
964   A433   25c gray & multi   .26 .15
Sesquicentennial of University of Buenos Aires, and to honor Father Antonio Saenz, first Chancellor and Rector.

Fabricaciones Militares Emblem — A444

1971, Oct. 16   Unwmk.   *Perf. 13½*
965   A444   25c brn, gold, bl & blk   .26 .15
30th anniv. of military armament works.

Cars and Trucks — A445

Design: 65c, Tree converted into paper.

1971, Oct. 16
966   A445   25c dull bl & multi   .52 .20
967   A445   65c green & multi   1.25 .50
     Nos. 966-967,C134 (3)   2.37 .94
Nationalized industries.

Luis C. Candelaria and his Plane, 1918 — A446

1971, Nov. 27
968   A446   25c multicolored   .25 .18
25th Aeronautics and Space Week.

Observatory and Nebula of Magellan — A447

1971, Nov. 27
969   A447   25c multicolored   .25 .15
Cordoba Astronomical Observatory, cent.

Christ in Majesty — A448

1971, Dec. 18   Litho.
970   A448   25c blk & multi   .25 .15
Christmas 1971. Design is from a tapestry by Horacio Butler in Basilica of St. Francis, Buenos Aires.

Mother and Child, by J. C. Castagnino — A449

1972, May 6   Unwmk.   *Perf. 13½*
971   A449   25c fawn & black   .25 .18
25th anniv. (in 1971) of UNICEF.

Mailman's Bag — A450

1972, Sept. 2   Litho.   *Perf. 13½*
972   A450   25c lemon & multi   .16 .15
Bicentenary of appointment of first Argentine mailman.

Adm. Brown Station, Map of Antarctica — A451

1972, Sept. 2
973   A451   25c blue & multi   .70 .35
10th anniv. (in 1971) of Antarctic Treaty.

Soldier Type of 1965
Army Day: 25c, Sergeant, Negro and Mulatto Corps, 1806-1807.

1972, Sept. 23
974   A340a   25c multicolored   .75 .35

Brigantine "Santisima Trinidad" — A452

1972, Sept. 23
975   A452   25c multicolored   .75 .35
Navy Day. See No. 1006.

A453   A454

1972, Sept. 30   Litho.   *Perf. 13½*
976   A453   45c Oil pump   .90 .20
50th anniv. of the organ. of the state oil fields (Yacimientos Petroliferos Fiscales).

1972, Sept. 30
977   A454   25c Sounding balloon   .25 .15
Cent. of Natl. Meteorological Service.

Trees and Globe — A455

1972, Oct. 14   *Perf. 13x13½*
978   A455   25c bl, blk & lt bl   .70 .20
7th World Forestry Congress, Buenos Aires, Oct. 4-18.

Arms of Naval School, Frigate "Presidente Sarmiento" — A456

1972, Oct. 14
979   A456   25c gold & multi   .65 .35
Centenary of Military Naval School.

Early Balloon and Plane, Antonio de Marchi — A457   Bartolomé Mitre — A458

1972, Nov. 4   *Perf. 13½*
980   A457   25c multicolored   .26 .20
Aeronautics and Space Week, and in honor of Baron Antonio de Marchi (1875-1934), aviation pioneer.

1972, Nov. 4   Engr.
981   A458   25c dark blue   .16 .15
Pres. Bartolome Mitre (1821-1906), writer, historian, soldier.

Flower and Heart — A459

1972, Dec. 2   Litho.   *Perf. 13½*
982   A459   90c lt bl, ultra & blk   .60 .35
"Your heart is your health," World Health Day.

"Martin Fierro," by Juan C. Castignano — A460   "Spirit of the Gaucho," by Vicente Forte — A461

1972, Dec. 2   Litho.   *Perf. 13½*
983   A460   50c multicolored   .32 .20
984   A461   90c multicolored   .65 .35
Intl. Book Year 1972, and cent. of publication of the poem, Martin Fierro, by Jose Hernandez (1834-86).

Iguacu Falls and Tourist Year Emblem — A462

1972, Dec. 16   *Perf. 13x13½*
985   A462   45c multicolored   .28 .15
Tourism Year of the Americas.

ARGENTINA

King, Wood Carving, 18th Century — A463

1972, Dec. 16 **Perf. 13½**
986 A463 50c multicolored .50 .25
Christmas 1972.

Types of 1955-73 Inscribed "Republica Argentina" and

Moon Valley, San Juan Province — A463a

Designs: 1c, Sunflower. 5c, Tierra del Fuego. 10c, Inca Bridge, Mendoza. 50c, Lujan Basilica. 65c, 22.50p, San Martin. 1p, Ski jumper. 1.15p, 4.50p, Guillermo Brown. 1.80p, Manuel Belgrano.

Litho.; Photo. (1c, 65c, 1p)
Perf. 13½, 12½ (1.80p)
1972-75 **Wmk. 365**
987 A278 1c dk green .16 .15
988 A277 5c dark blue .16 .15
989 A278 10c bister brn .16 .15
989A A426 50c dull pur ('75) .16 .15
990 A241 65c gray brown 3.25 .15
991 A279 1p brown 1.40 .15
992 A366 1.15p dk gray bl 1.40 .15
993 A425 1.80p blue ('75) .16 .15
994 A366 4.50p green ('75) .65 .15
995 A241 22.50p vio bl ('75) 1.40 .15
996 A463a 50p multi ('75) 2.75 .32
Nos. 987-996 (11) 11.65 1.82

Paper size of 1c is 27½x39mm; others of 1972, 37x27, 27x37mm.
Size of 22.50p, 50p: 26½x38½mm.
See Nos. 1050, 1108.

Cock (Symbolic of Police) — A464

First Coin of Bank of Buenos Aires — A465

1973, Feb. 3 **Litho.** **Unwmk.**
997 A464 50c lt green & multi .30 .15
Sesqui. of Federal Police of Argentina.

1973, Feb. 3 **Perf. 13½**
998 A465 50c purple, yel & brn .15 .15
Sesquicentennial of the Bank of Buenos Aires Province.

DC-3 Planes Over Antarctica A466

1973, Apr. 28 **Litho.** **Perf. 13½**
999 A466 50c lt blue & multi 1.50 .60
10th anniversary of Argentina's first flight to the South Pole.

Rivadavia's Chair, Argentine Arms and Colors — A467

1973, May 19 **Litho.** **Perf. 13½**
1000 A467 50c multicolored .25 .15
Inauguration of Pres. Hector J. Campora, May 25, 1973.

San Martin, by Gil de Castro — A468

San Martin and Bolivar A469

1973, July 7 **Litho.** **Perf. 13½**
1001 A468 50c lt green & multi .35 .15
1002 A469 50c yellow & multi .35 .15
Gen. San Martin's farewell to the people of Peru and his meeting with Simon Bolivar at Guayaquil July 26-27, 1822.

Eva Peron A470

1973, July 26 **Perf. 13½**
1003 A470 70c black, org & bl .20 .15
Maria Eva Duarte de Peron (1919-1952), political leader.

House of Viceroy Sobremonte, by Hortensia de Virgilion — A471

1973, July 28 **Perf. 13x13½**
1004 A471 50c blue & multi .20 .15
400th anniversary of the city of Cordoba.

Woman, by Lino Spilimbergo A472

New and Old Telephones A473

1973, Aug. 28 **Litho.** **Perf. 13½**
1005 A472 70c multicolored .70 .15
Philatelists' Day. See Nos. B60-B61.

Ship Type of 1972
Navy Day: 70c, Frigate "La Argentina."

1973, Oct. 27 **Litho.** **Perf. 13½**
1006 A452 70c multicolored .60 .35

1973, Oct. 27
1007 A473 70c brt blue & multi .40 .20
25th anniv. of natl. telecommunications system.

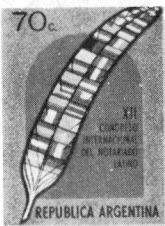

Plume Made of Flags of Participants A474

1973, Nov. 3 **Perf. 13½**
1008 A474 70c yellow bis & multi .25 .15
12th Cong. of Latin Notaries, Buenos Aires.

No. 940 Overprinted

TRANSMISION DEL MANDO PRESIDENCIAL
12 OCTUBRE 1973

1973, Nov. 30 **Photo.**
1010 A241 1.20p orange .85 .20
Assumption of presidency by Juan Peron, Oct. 12.

Virgin and Child, Window, La Plata Cathedral — A476

Christmas: 1.20p, Nativity, by Bruno Venier, b. 1914.

1973, Dec. 15 **Litho.** **Perf. 13½**
1011 A476 70c gray & multi .35 .18
1012 A476 1.20p black & multi .70 .35

The Lama, by Juan Batlle Planas — A477

Paintings: 50c, Houses in Boca District, by Eugenio Daneri, horiz. 90c, The Blue Grotto, by Emilio Pettoruti, horiz.

1974, Feb. 9 **Litho.** **Perf. 13½**
1013 A477 50c multicolored .28 .15
1014 A477 70c multicolored .35 .20
1015 A477 90c multicolored .60 .28
Nos. 1013-1015,B64 (4) 1.51 .85
Argentine painters.

Mar del Plata A478

1974, Feb. 9
1016 A478 70c multicolored .28 .15
Centenary of Mar del Plata.

Weather Symbols A479

Justo Santa Maria de Oro A480

1974, Mar. 23 **Litho.** **Perf. 13½**
1017 A479 1.20p multicolored .35 .20
Cent. of intl. meteorological cooperation.

1974, Mar. 23
1018 A480 70c multicolored .20 .15
Bicentenary of the birth of Brother Justo Santa Maria de Oro (1772-1836), theologian, patriot, first Argentine bishop.

Belisario Roldan (1873-1922), Writer — A481

1974, June 29 **Photo.** **Unwmk.**
1019 A481 70c bl & brn .20 .15

Poster with Names of OAS Members A482

1974, June 29 **Litho.**
1020 A482 1.38p multicolored .18 .15
Organization of American States, 25th anniv.

ENCOTEL Emblem — A483

1974, Aug. 10 **Litho.** **Perf. 13**
1021 A483 1.20p blue, gold & blk .42 .15
ENCOTEL, Natl. Post and Telegraph Press.

Flags of Argentina, Bolivia, Brazil, Paraguay, Uruguay — A484

1974, Aug. 16 **Perf. 13½**
1022 A484 1.38p multicolored .22 .15
6th Meeting of Foreign Ministers of Rio de la Plata Basin Countries.

The values of stamps in less than very fine condition generally are less than catalogue value.

ARGENTINA

El Chocon Hydroelectric Complex, Limay River — A485

Somisa Steel Mill, San Nicolas — A486

Gen. Belgrano Bridge, Chaco-Corrientes — A487

Perf. 13½, 13x13½ (4.50p)
1974, Sept. 14
1023	A485	70c multicolored	.40	.18
1024	A486	1.20p multicolored	.60	.35
1025	A487	4.50p multicolored	2.00	.52
	Nos. 1023-1025 (3)		3.00	1.05

Development projects.

Brigantine Belgrano, by Emilio Biggeri A488

1974, Oct. 26   Litho.   Perf. 13½
| 1026 | A488 | 1.20p multicolored | .60 | .30 |

Departure into exile in Chile of General San Martin, Sept. 22, 1822.

Alberto R. Mascias and Bleriot Plane — A489

1974, Oct. 26   Unwmk.
| 1027 | A489 | 1.20p multicolored | .50 | .25 |

Air Force Day, Aug. 10, and to honor Alberto Roque Garcias (1878-1951), aviation pioneer.
Exists with wmk. 365.

Hussar, 1812, by Eleodoro Marenco — A490

1974, Oct. 26
| 1028 | A490 | 1.20p multicolored | .50 | .25 |

Army Day.

Post Horn and Flags A491

1974, Nov. 23   Unwmk.   Perf. 13½
| 1029 | A491 | 2.65p multicolored | .85 | .20 |

Centenary of Universal Postal Union.
Exists with wmk. 365.

Franciscan Monastery A492

1974, Nov. 23   Litho.
| 1030 | A492 | 1.20p multicolored | .40 | .15 |

400th anniversary, city of Santa Fe.

Trout Type of 1968
1974   Engr.   Unwmk.
| 1031 | A366a | 1000p vio bl | 3.25 | .80 |

Due to a shortage of 10p stamps a quantity of this 1,000p was released for use as 10p.

Types of 1954-73 Inscribed "Republica Argentina" and

Red Deer in Forest — A495

Congress Building A497

Designs: 30c, 60c, 1.80p, Manuel Belgrano. 50c, Lujan Basilica. No. 1036, 2p, 6p, San Martin (16x22½mm). 2.70p, 7.50p, 22.50p, San Martin (22x31½mm). 4.50p, 13.50p, Guillermo Brown. 10p, Leaping trout.

1974-76   Unwmk.   Photo.   Perf. 13½
1032	A425	30c brown vio	.15	.15
1033	A426	50c blk & brn red	.15	.15
1034	A426	50c bister & bl	.15	.15
1035	A425	60c ocher	.15	.15
1036	A425	1.20p red	.30	.15
1037	A425	1.80p deep blue	.15	.15
1038	A425	2p dark purple	.20	.15
1039	A241	2.70p dk bl, 22x31½mm	.24	.15
1040	A366	4.50p green	.85	.15
1041	A495	5p yellow green	.40	.15
1042	A425	6p red orange	.20	.15
1043	A425	6p emerald	.20	.15
1044	A241	7.50p grn, 22x31½mm	.85	.15
1045	A366a	10p violet blue	1.00	.15
1046	A366	13.50p scar, 16x22½mm	.85	.15
1047	A366	13.50p scar, 22x31½mm	.85	.15
1048	A241	22.50p dp bl, 22x31½mm	.75	.15
1049	A497	30p yel & dk red brn	1.10	.15
1050	A463a	50p multicolored	1.50	.15
	Nos. 1032-1050 (19)		10.04	2.85

Nos. 1033-1035, 1037-1038, 1042-1044, 1046-1048 issued in 1976, No. 1050 in 1976.
Fluorescent paper was used in printing No. 1036, 2p, Nos. 1044 and 1047. The 30p was issued on both ordinary and fluorescent paper.
See No. 829. For type of A495 overprinted see No. 1144.

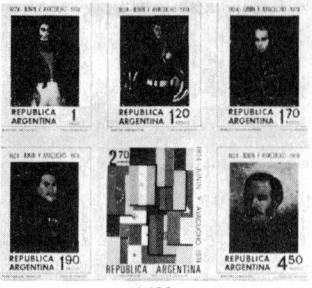

Miniature Sheet

A498

1974, Dec. 7   Litho.   Perf. 13½
1052	A498	Sheet of 6	3.50	2.75
a.		1p Mariano Necochea	.25	
b.		1.20p Jose de San Martin	.25	
c.		1.70p Manuel Isidoro Suarez	.35	
d.		1.90p Juan Pascual Pringles	.42	
e.		2.70p Latin American flags	.65	
f.		4.50p Jose Felix Bogado	1.10	

Sesqui. of Battles of Junin and Ayacucho.

Dove, by Vito Campanella A499

St. Anne, by Raul Soldi — A500

1974, Dec. 21   Litho.   Perf. 13½
| 1053 | A499 | 1.20p multicolored | .48 | .18 |
| 1054 | A500 | 2.65p multicolored | .75 | .30 |

Christmas 1974.

Boy Looking at Stamp — A501

1974, Dec. 21
| 1055 | A501 | 1.70p black & yel | .38 | .15 |

World Youth Philately Year.

Space Monsters, by Raquel Forner A502

Argentine modern art: 4.50p, Dream, by Emilio Centurion.

1975, Feb. 22   Litho.   Perf. 13½
| 1056 | A502 | 2.70p multi | .90 | .26 |
| 1057 | A502 | 4.50p multi | 1.75 | .40 |

Indian Woman and Cathedral, Catamarca — A503

Tourist Publicity: #1059, Carved chancel and street scene. #1060, Grazing cattleand monastery yard. #1061, Painted pottery and power station. #1062, Farm cart and colonial mansion. #1063, Perito Moreno glacier and spinning mill. #1064, Lake Lapataia and scientific surveyor. #1065, Los Alerces National Park and oil derrick.

1975   Litho.   Unwmk.   Perf. 13½
1058	A503	1.20p shown	.25	.15
1059	A503	1.20p Jujuy	.25	.15
1060	A503	1.20p Salta	.25	.15
1061	A503	1.20p Santiago del Estero	.25	.15
1062	A503	1.20p Tucuman	.25	.15
1063	A503	6p Santa Cruz	.50	.15
1064	A503	6p Tierra del Fuego	.50	.15
1065	A503	6p Chubut	.50	.15
	Nos. 1058-1065 (8)		2.75	1.20

Issue dates: 1.20p, Mar. 8; 6p, Dec. 20.

"We Have Been Inoculated" A504

1975, Apr. 26   Unwmk.   Perf. 13½
| 1066 | A504 | 2p multi | .45 | .22 |

Children's inoculation campaign (child's painting).

Hugo A. Acuña and South Orkney Station — A505

Designs: No. 1068, Francisco P. Moreno and Lake Nahuel Huapi. No. 1069, Lt. Col. Luis Piedra Buena and cutter, Luisito. No. 1070, Ensign José M. Sobral and Snow Hill House. No. 1071, Capt. Carlos M. Moyano and Cerro del Toro (mountain).

1975, June 28   Litho.   Perf. 13
1067	A505	2p grnsh bl & multi	.26	.15
1068	A505	2p yel grn & multi	.26	.15
1069	A505	2p lt vio & multi	.26	.15
1070	A505	2p gray bl & multi	.26	.15
1071	A505	2p pale grn & multi	.26	.15
	Nos. 1067-1071 (5)		1.30	.75

Pioneers of Antarctica.

Frigate "25 de Mayo" A506

1975, Sept. 27   Unwmk.   Perf. 13½
| 1072 | A506 | 6p multi | .42 | .22 |

Navy Day 1975.

Eduardo Bradley and Balloon — A507

1975, Sept. 27   Wmk. 365
| 1073 | A507 | 6p multi | .42 | .22 |

Air Force Day.

ARGENTINA

Declaration of Independence, by Juan M. Blanes — A508

1975, Oct. 25
1074 A508 6p multi .32 .15
Sesquicentennial of Uruguay's declaration of independence.

Flame A509

1975, Oct. 17 Unwmk.
1075 A509 6p gray & multi .32 .15
Loyalty Day, 30th anniversary of Pres. Peron's accession to power.

Nos. 886, 891 and 932 Surcharged

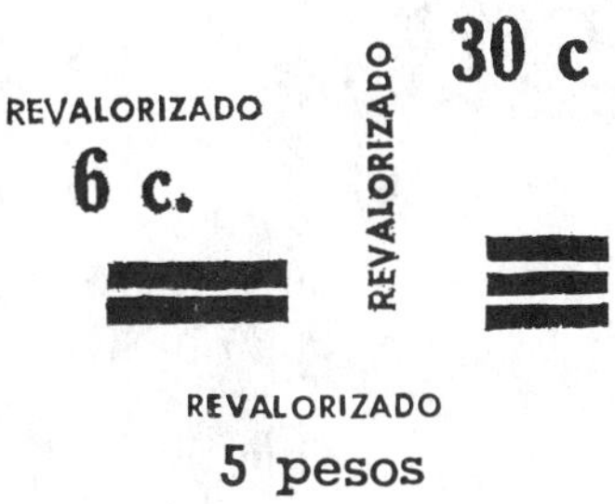

1975 Lithographed, Photogravure
1076 A277 6c on 3p .15 .15
1077 A366 30c on 90p .15 .15
1078 A426 5p on 18c .35 .18
Nos. 1076-1078 (3) .65 .48
Issued: 6c, 10/30; 30c, 11/20; 5p, 10/24. The 6c also exists on No. 886a.

International Bridge, Flags of Argentina and Uruguay — A510

1975, Oct. 25 Litho. Wmk. 365
1081 A510 6p multi .35 .18
Opening of bridge connecting Colon, Argentina, and Paysandu, Uruguay.

Post Horn, Surcharged A511

1975, Nov. 8
1082 A511 10p on 20c multi .45 .15
Introduction of postal code. Not issued without surcharge.

Nurse Holding Infant A512

1975, Dec. 13 Litho. Perf. 13½
1083 A512 6p multi .45 .15
Children's Hospital, centenary.

Nativity, Nueva Pompeya Church — A513

1975, Dec. 13 Litho. Unwmk.
1084 A513 6p multi .30 .18
Christmas 1975.

Types of 1970-75 and

Church of St. Francis, Salta — A515

Designs: 3p, No. 1099, 60p, 90p, Manuel Belgrano. 12p, 15p, 20p, 30p, No. 1100, 100p, 110p, 120p, 130p, San Martin. 15p, 70p, Guillermo Brown. 300p, Moon Valley (lower inscriptions italic). 500p, Adm. Brown Station, Antarctica.

1976-78 Photo. Unwmk. Perf. 13½
1089 A425 3p slate .15 .15
1090 A425 12p rose red .25 .15

Perf. 12½x13
Litho. Wmk. 365
1091 A425 12p rose red .20 .15
1092 A425 12p emerald .20 .15

Perf. 13½
Photo. Unwmk.
1093 A425 12p emer ('77) .20 .15
1094 A425 15p rose red .20 .15
1095 A425 15p vio bl ('77) .20 .15
1097 A425 20p rose red ('77) .35 .15
1098 A425 30p rose red ('77) .35 .15
1099 A425 40p dp grn .52 .15
1100 A425 40p rose red ('77) .35 .15
1101 A425 60p dk bl ('77) .70 .20
1102 A425 70p dk bl ('77) .85 .20
1103 A425 90p emer ('77) 1.00 .28
1104 A425 100p red .75 .24
1105 A425 110p rose red ('78) .52 .18
1106 A425 120p rose red ('78) .60 .20
1107 A425 130p rose red ('78) .70 .24

Litho.
1108 A463a 300p multi 3.50 1.50
1109 A515 500p multi ('77) 8.25 1.40
1110 A515 1000p multi ('77) 10.00 2.00
Nos. 1089-1110 (21) 29.84 8.09

Fluorescent paper was used in printing both 12p rose red, 15p rose red, 20p, 30p, 40p rose red, 100p, 110p, 120p, 130p. No. 1099 and the 300p were issued on both ordinary and fluorescent paper. 300p and 500p exist with wmk. 365.
See Nos. B73-B74.

A516

1976 Photo. Unwmk. Perf. 13½
1112 A516 12c gray & blk .15 .15
1113 A516 50c gray & grn .15 .15
1114 A516 1p red & blk .15 .15
1115 A516 4p bl & blk .15 .15
1116 A516 5p org & blk .15 .15
1117 A516 6p dp brn & blk .15 .15
1118 A516 10p gray & vio bl .22 .15
1119 A516 27p lt grn & blk .52 .15
1120 A516 30p lt bl & blk .90 .15
1121 A516 45p yel & blk .90 .15
1122 A516 50p dl grn & blk 1.25 .15
1123 A516 100p brt grn & red 1.65 .25

Perf. 13x12½
1976 Litho. Wmk. 365
1124 A516 5p org & blk .20 .15
1125 A516 27p lt grn & blk .52 .15
1126 A516 45p yel & blk 1.25 .15
Nos. 1112-1126 (15) 8.31 2.35

The 1p, 6p, 10p, 50p and No. 1116 were issued on both ordinary and fluorescent paper.

Jet and Airlines Emblem — A517

Perf. 13x13½
1976, Apr. 24 Litho. Unwmk.
1130 A517 30p bl, lt bl & dk bl 1.00 .20
Argentine Airlines, 25th anniversary.

Frigate Heroina and Map of Falkland Islands — A518

1976, Apr. 26
1131 A518 6p multi 1.00 .40
Argentina's claim to Falkland Islands.

Louis Braille — A519

Perf. 13½
1976, May 22 Engr. Wmk. 365
1132 A519 19.70 dp bl .28 .15
Sesquicentennial of the invention of the Braille system of writing for the blind by Louis Braille (1809-1852).

Private, 7th Infantry Regiment — A520

1976, May 29 Litho. Unwmk.
1133 A520 12p multi .38 .18
Army Day.

Schooner Rio de la Plata, by Emilio Biggeri A521

1976, June 19
1134 A521 12p multi .38 .18
Navy Day.

Dr. Bernardo Houssay A522

Argentine Nobel Prize Winners: 15p, Luis F. Leloir, chemistry, 1970. 20p, Carlos Saavedra Lamas, peace, 1936. Bernardo Houssay, medicine and physiology, 1947.

1976, Aug. 14 Litho. Perf. 13½
1135 A522 10p org & blk .22 .15
1136 A522 15p yel & blk .32 .16
1137 A522 20p ocher & blk .45 .22
Nos. 1135-1137 (3) .99 .53

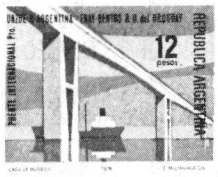

Rio de la Plata International Bridge A523

1976, Sept. 18 Litho. Perf. 13½
1138 A523 12p multi .28 .15
Inauguration of International Bridge connecting Puerte Unzue, Argentina, and Fray Bentos, Uruguay.

Pipelines and Cooling Tower, Gen. Mosconi Plant A524

1976, Nov. 20 Litho. Perf. 13½
1139 A524 28p multi .42 .20

Pablo Teodoro Fels and Bleriot Monoplane, 1910 A525

1976, Nov. 20
1140 A525 15p multi .32 .15
Air Force Day.

Nativity A526

1976, Dec. 18 Litho. Perf. 13½
1141 A526 20p multi .65 .28
Christmas. Painting by Edith Chiapetto.

Water Conference Emblem — A527

1977, Mar. 19 Litho. Perf. 13½
1142 A527 70p multi .70 .25
UN Water Conf., Mar del Plata, Mar. 14-25.

ARGENTINA

Dalmacio Velez Sarsfield — A528

1977, Mar. 19   Engr.
1143 A528 50p blk & red brn .70 .28

Dalmacio Velez Sarsfield (1800-1875), author of Argentine civil code.

Red Deer Type of 1974 Surcharged

1977, July 30   Photo.   Perf. 13½
1144 A495 100p on 5p brn 1.40 .35

Sesquicentennial of Uruguayan postal service. Not issued without surcharge.

Soldier, 16th Lancers — A529

1977, July 30
1145 A529 30p multi .40 .20

Army Day.

Schooner Sarandi, by Emilio Biggeri — A530

1977, July 30
1146 A530 30p multi .42 .22

Navy Day.

Soccer Games' Emblem — A531

70p, Argentina '78 emblem, flags & soccer field.

1977, May 14
1147 A531 30p multi .40 .18
1148 A531 70p multi .85 .42

11th World Cup Soccer Championship, Argentina, June 1-25, 1978.

The Visit, by Horacio Butler — A532

Consecration, by Miguel P. Caride — A533

1977, Mar. 26   Litho.
1149 A532 50p multi .52 .25
1150 A533 70p multi .65 .38

Argentine artists.

Sierra de la Ventana — A534

Views: No. 1152, Civic Center, Santa Rosa. No. 1153, Skiers, San Martin de los Andes. No. 1154, Boat on Lake Fonck, Rio Negro.

1977, Oct. 8   Litho.   Perf. 13x13½
1151 A534 30p multi .32 .16
1152 A534 30p multi .32 .16
1153 A534 30p multi .32 .16
1154 A534 30p multi .32 .16
    Nos. 1151-1154 (4) 1.28 .64

Guillermo Brown, by R. del Villar — A535

1977, Oct. 8   Perf. 13½
1155 A535 30p multi .38 .22

Adm. Guillermo Brown (1777-1857), leader in fight for independence, bicentenary of birth.

Jet — A536

Double-decker, 1926 — A537

1977   Litho.   Perf. 13½
1156 A536 30p multi .24 .15
1157 A537 40p multi .32 .20

50th anniversary of military plane production (30p); Air Force Day (40p).
Issue dates: 30p, Dec. 3; 40p, Nov. 26.

Adoration of the Kings — A538

1977, Dec. 17
1158 A538 100p multi 1.00 .28

Christmas 1977.

Historic City Hall, Buenos Aires — A539

Chapel of Rio Grande Museum, Tierra del Fuego — A540

Designs: 5p, 20p, La Plata Museum. 10p, Independence Hall, Tucuman. 40p, City Hall, Salta, vert. No. 1165, City Hall, Buenos Aires. 100p, Columbus Theater, Buenos Aires. 200p, flag Monument, Rosario. 280p, 300p, Chapel of Rio Grande Museum, Tierra del Fuego. 480p, 520p, 800, Ruins of Jesuit Mission Church of San Ignacio, Misiones. 500p, Candonga Chapel, Cordoba. 1000p, G.P.O., Buenos Aires. 2000p, Civic Center, Bariloche, Rio Negro.

Three types of 10p: I. Nine vertical window bars; small imprint "E. MILIAVACA Dib." II. Nine bars; large imprint "E. MILIAVACA DIB." III. Redrawn; 5 bars; large imprint.

1977-81   Photo.   Unwmk.   Perf. 13½
Size: 32x21mm, 21x32mm

1159 A540 5p gray & blk .15 .15
1160 A540 10p lt ultra & blk, I .15 .15
   a.   Type II .15 .15
1161 A540 10p lt bl & blk, III .15 .15
1162 A540 20p citron & blk, litho. .15 .15
1163 A540 40p gray bl & blk .24 .15
1164 A539 50p yel & blk .28 .15
1165 A540 50p citron & blk .16 .15
1166 A540 100p org & blk, litho. .35 .15
   a.   Wmk. 365 92.50 24.00
1167 A540 100p red org & blk .15 .15
1168 A540 100p turq & blk .15 .15
1169 A539 200p lt bl & blk .48 .24
1170 A540 280p rose & blk 14.00 .20
1171 A540 300p lemon & blk .95 .15
1172 A540 480p org & blk 1.75 .24
1173 A540 500p yel grn & blk 1.75 .20
1174 A540 520p org & blk 1.75 .30
1175 A540 800p rose lil & blk 2.25 .32
1176 A540 1000p lem bis & blk 2.50 .38
1177 A540 1000p gold & blk, 40x29mm 3.75 .38
1178 A540 2000p multi 2.25 .38
    Nos. 1159-1178 (20) 33.36 4.29

#1161, 1163, 1165, 1167, 1169, 1171, 1173, 1176, 1177 were issued on both ordinary and fluorescent paper. No. 1174 was issued only on fluorescent paper. All others were issued only on ordinary paper.
Issued: #1164, 5/30/77; 280p, 12/15/77; #1160, 3/14/78; 480p, 5/22/78; 5p, 7/25/78; 20p, 500p, 9/8/78; #1166, 9/20/78; #1177, 9/28/78; 520p, 9/30/78; 300p, 10/5/78; 40p, 12/1/78; #1161/79; #1165, 1/8/79; 800p, 3/20/79; #1167, 4/25/79; 200p, 6/23/79; #1176, 12/15/79; 2000p, 6/25/80; #1168, 5/26/81.

For overprints see Nos. 1253, 1315.

Soccer Games' Emblem — A544

1978, Feb. 10   Photo.   Perf. 13½
1179 A544 200p yel grn & bl .85 .28

11th World Cup Soccer Championship, Argentina, June 1-25. Exists with wmk. 365.

View of El Rio, Rosario — A545

Designs (Argentina '78 Emblem and): 100p, Rio Tercero Dam, Cordoba. 150p, Cordillera Mountains, Mendoza. 200p, City Center, Mar del Plata. 300p, View of Buenos Aires.

1978, May 6   Litho.   Perf. 13
1180 A545 50p multi .16 .15
1181 A545 100p multi .32 .15
1182 A545 150p multi .50 .16
1183 A545 200p multi .50 .24
1184 A545 300p multi 1.10 .32
    Nos. 1180-1184 (5) 2.58 1.02

Sites of 11th World Cup Soccer Championship, June 1-25.

Children — A546

1978, May 20
1185 A546 100p multi .35 .15

50th anniversary of Children's Institute.

Labor Day, by B. Quinquela Martin — A547

Design: No. 1187, Woman's torso, sculpture by Orlando Pierri.

1978, May 20   Perf. 13½
1186 A547 100p multi .35 .15
1187 A547 100p multi .35 .15

Argentina, Hungary, France, Italy and Emblem — A548

Stadium A549

Teams and Argentina '78 Emblem: 200p, Poland, Fed. Rep. of Germany, Tunisia, Mexico. 300p, Austria, Spain, Sweden, Brazil. 400p, Netherlands, Iran, Peru, Scotland.

1978   Litho.   Perf. 13
1188 A548 100p multi .32 .15
1189 A548 200p multi .65 .15
1190 A548 300p multi .95 .25
1191 A548 400p multi 1.25 .30
    Nos. 1188-1191 (4) 3.17 .85

Souvenir Sheet
Lithographed and Engraved
Perf. 13½
1192 A549 700p buff & blk 2.50 1.40

11th World Cup Soccer Championship, Argentina, June 1-25. Issued: Nos. 1188-1191, June 6, No. 1192, June 3.

ARGENTINA

Stadium Type of 1978 Inscribed in Red: "ARGENTINA / CAMPEON"

Lithographed and Engraved

1978, Sept. 2   *Perf. 13½*
1193 A549 1000p bufl, blk & red   3.25   1.40

Argentina's victory in 1978 Soccer Championship. No. 1193 has margin similar to No. 1192 with Rimet Cup emblem added in red.

Young Tree Nourished by Old Trunk, UN Emblem — A550

1978 Sept. 2   **Litho.**
1194 A550 100p multi   .35   .22

Technical Cooperation among Developing Countries Conf., Buenos Aires, Sept. 1978.

Emblems of Buenos Aires and Bank — A551

1978, Sept. 16
1195 A551 100p multi   .35   .22

Bank of City of Buenos Aires, centenary.

General Savio and Steel Production — A552

1978, Sept. 16
1196 A552 100p multi   .35   .22

Gen. Manuel N. Savio (1892-1948), general manager of military heavy industry.

San Martin — A553

1978, Oct.   **Engr.**
1197 A553 2000p grnsh blk   6.25   1.10

1979   **Wmk. 365**
1198 A553 2000p grnsh blk   4.75   .35

Gen Jose de San Martin (1778-1850), soldier and statesman. See No. 1292.

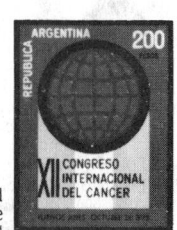

Globe and Argentine Flag — A554

1978, Oct. 7   **Litho.**   *Perf. 13½*
1199 A554 200p multi   .70   .28

12th Intl. Cancer Cong., Buenos Aires, Oct. 5-11.

Chessboard, Queen and Pawn — A555

1978, Oct. 7
1200 A555 200p multi   2.00   .65

23rd National Chess Olympics, Buenos Aires, Oct. 25-Nov. 12.

Correct Positioning of Stamps — A557

Design: 50p, Use correct postal code number.

1978   **Photo.**   *Perf. 13½*
1201 A557 20p ultra   .15   .15
1203 A557 50p carmine   .22   .15

No. 1201 issued on both ordinary and fluorescent paper.

A558   A559

1978-82   **Photo.**   *Perf. 13½*
1204 A558 150p bl & ultra   .35   .15
1205 A558 180p bl & ultra   .45   .15
1206 A558 200p bl & ultra   .32   .15
1207 A559 240p ol bis & bl ('79)   .38   .15
1208 A559 260p blk & lt bl ('79)   .42   .15
1209 A559 290p blk & lt bl ('79)   .45   .15
1210 A559 310p mag & bl ('79)   .50   .18
1211 A559 350p ver & bl ('79)   .65   .20
1212 A559 450p ultra & bl   .52   .18
1213 A559 600p grn & bl ('80)   .70   .24
1214 A559 700p blk & bl ('80)   .70   .24
1215 A559 800p red & bl ('81)   .65   .15
1216 A559 1100p gray & bl ('81)   .90   .15
1217 A559 1500p blk & bl ('81)   .35   .15
1218 A559 1700p grn & bl ('82)   .45   .15
    Nos. 1204-1218 (15)   7.79   2.54

No. 1204 issued on fluorescent and ordinary paper. No. 1206 issued only on fluorescent paper. For overprint see No. 1338.

Balsa "24" — A561

Ships: 200p, Tug Legador. 300p, River Parana tug No. 34. 400p, Passenger ship Ciudad de Parana.

1978, Nov. 4   **Litho.**   *Perf. 13½*
1220 A561 100p multi   .24   .15
1221 A561 200p multi   .48   .20
1222 A561 300p multi   .70   .30
   a.   Pair, #1221-1222   1.20
1223 A561 400p multi   .95   .40
   a.   Pair, #1220, 1223   1.20
    Nos. 1220-1223 (4)   2.37   1.05

20th anniversary of national river fleet. Issued on fluorescent paper.

View and Arms of Bahia Blanca — A562

1978, Nov. 25   **Litho.**   *Perf. 13½*
1224 A562 20p multi   .48   .15

Sesquicentennial of Bahia Blanca.

"Spain," (Queen Isabella and Columbus) by Arturo Dresco — A563

1978, Nov. 25
1225 A563 300p multi   2.75   .30

Visit of King Juan Carlos and Queen Sofia of Spain to Argentina, Nov. 26.

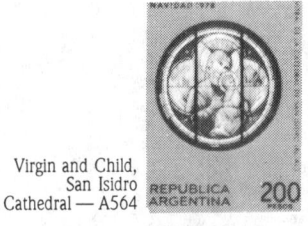

Virgin and Child, San Isidro Cathedral — A564

1978, Dec. 16
1226 A564 200p gold & multi   .55   .28

Christmas 1978.

Slope at Chacabuco, by Pedro Subercaseaux — A565

Painting: 1000p, The Embrace of Maipu (San Martin and O'Higgins), by Pedro Subercaseaux, vert.

1978, Dec. 16   **Litho.**   *Perf. 13½*
1227 A565 500p multi   1.00   .26
1228 A565 1000p multi   2.00   .40

José de San Martin, 200th birth anniversary.

Adolfo Alsina — A566

Design: No. 1230, Mariano Moreno.

1979, Jan. 20
1229 A566 200p lt bl & blk   .30   .15
1230 A566 200p yel red & blk   .30   .15

Adolfo Alsina (1828-1877), political leader, vice-president; Mariano Moreno (1778-1811), lawyer, educator, political leader.

Argentina No. 37 and UPU Emblem — A567

1979, Jan. 20
1231 A567 200p multi   .22   .15

Centenary of Argentina's UPU membership.

Still-life, by Carcova — A568

Painting: 300p, The Laundresses, by Faustino Brughetti.

1979, Mar. 3
1232 A568 200p multi   .45   .15
1233 A568 300p multi   .60   .20

Ernesto de la Carcova (1866-1927) and Faustino Brughetti (1877-1956), Argentine painters.

A569   A570

1979, Mar. 3
1234 A569 200p Balcarce Earth station   .55   .25

Third Inter-American Telecommunications Conference, Buenos Aires, March 5-9.

1979
1235 A570 30p Stamp collecting   .15   .15

Printed on ordinary and fluorescent paper.

European Olive — A571   Laurel and Regimental Emblem — A572

1979, June 2   **Litho.**   *Perf. 13½*
1236 A571 100p shown   .26   .15
1237 A571 200p Tea   .55   .26
1238 A571 300p Sorghum   .85   .40
1239 A571 400p Common flax   1.10   .55
    Nos. 1236-1239 (4)   2.76   1.36

1979, June 9
1240 A572 200p gold & multi   .42   .22

Founding of Subteniente Berdina Village in memory of Sub-lieutenant Rodolfo Hernan Berdina, killed by terrorists in 1975.

15-Cent Minimum Value
The minimum catalogue value is 15 cents. Separating se-tenant pieces into individual stamps does not increase the value of the stamps since demand for the separated stamps may be small.

ARGENTINA

"75" and Automobile Club Emblem A573

1979, June 9
1241 A573 200p gold & multi .40 .20
Argentine Automobile Club, 75th anniv.

Exchange Building and Emblem A574

1979, June 9
1242 A574 200p bl, blk & gold .40 .20
Grain Exchange, 125th anniversary.

Cavalry Officer, 1817 — A575

1979, July 7 Litho. Perf. 13½
1243 A575 200p multi 1.00 .30
Army Day.

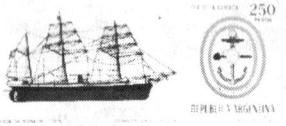

Corvette Uruguay and Navy Emblem — A576

#1245, Hydrographic service ship & emblem.

1979 Perf. 13
1244 A576 250p multi .85 .35
1245 A576 250p multi .85 .35
Navy Day; Cent. of Naval Hydrographic Service. Issued: #1244, July 28; #1245, July 7.

Tree and Man — A577

1979, July 28 Perf. 13½
1246 A577 250p multi .60 .22
Protection of the Environment Day, June 5.

"Spad" Flying over Andes, and Vicente Almandos Almonacid A578

1979, Aug. 4
1247 A578 250p multi .70 .22
Air Force Day.

Gen. Julio A. Roca Occupying Rio Negro, by Juan M. Blanes A579

1979, Aug. 4
1248 A579 250p multi .70 .22
Conquest of Rio Negro Desert, centenary.

Rowland Hill — A580

1979, Sept. 29 Litho. Perf. 13½
1249 A580 300p gray red & blk .55 .22
Sir Rowland Hill (1795-1879), originator of penny postage.

Viedma Navarez Monument A581

1979, Sept. 29
1250 A581 300p multi .60 .22
Viedma and Carmen de Patagones towns, bicentenary.

Pope Paul VI — A582

Design: No. 1252, Pope John Paul I.

1979, Oct. 27 Engr. Perf. 13½
1251 A582 500p black 1.00 .28
1252 A582 500p sepia 1.00 .28

No. 1169 Overprinted in Red: "75 ANIV. / SOCIEDAD/ FILATELICA / DE ROSARIO"

1979, Nov. 10 Photo. Perf. 13½
1253 A539 200p lt bl & blk .60 .20
Rosario Philatelic Society, 75th anniversary.

A583

A584

1979, Nov. 10 Litho.
1254 A583 300p multi .70 .28
Frontier resettlement.

1979, Dec. 1 Litho. Perf. 13½
1255 A584 300p multi .70 .28
Military Geographic Institute centenary.

Christmas 1979 A585

1979, Dec. 1
1256 A585 300p multi .55 .22

General Mosconi Birth Centenary — A586

1979, Dec. 15 Engr. Perf. 13½
1257 A586 1000p blk & bl 1.50 .24

Rotary Emblem and Globe A587

1979, Dec. 29 Litho.
1258 A587 300p multi 1.75 .35
Rotary International, 75th anniversary.

Child and IYC Emblem — A588

Family, by Pablo Menicucci A589

1979, Dec. 29
1259 A588 500p lt bl & sepia .75 .15
1260 A589 1000p multi 1.50 .22
International Year of the Child.

Microphone, Waves, ITU Emblem — A590

1980, Mar. 22 Litho. Perf. 13x13½
1261 A590 500p multi .95 .26
Regional Administrative Conference on Broadcasting by Hectometric Waves for Area 2, Buenos Aires, Mar. 10-29.

Guillermo Brown — A591

1980 Engr. Perf. 13½
1262 A591 5000p black 4.50 .15
See No. 1372.

Argentine Red Cross Centenary A592

1980, Apr. 19 Litho. Perf. 13½
1263 A592 500p multi .52 .20

OAS Emblem — A593

1980, Apr. 19
1264 A593 500p multi .55 .22
Day of the Americas, Apr. 14.

Dish Antennae, Balcarce A594

1980, Apr. 26 Litho. & Engr.
1265 A594 300p shown .38 .20
1266 A594 300p Hydroelectric Station, Salto Grande .38 .20
1267 A594 300p Bridge, Zarate-Brazo Largo .38 .20
Nos. 1265-1267 (3) 1.14 .60

Capt. Hipolito Bouchard, Frigate "Argentina" — A595

1980, May 31 Litho. Perf. 13x13½
1268 A595 500p multicolored .70 .28
Navy Day.

ARGENTINA

"Villarino," San Martin, by Theodore Gericault — A596

1980, May 31
1269 A596 500p multicolored .70 .28

Return of the remains of Gen. Jose de San Martin to Argentina, centenary.

Buenos Aires Gazette, 1810, Signature A597

1980, June 7 *Perf. 13½*
1270 A597 500p multicolored .55 .22

Journalism Day.

Miniature Sheet

Coaches in Victoria Square — A598

1980 June 14
1271 Sheet of 14 9.00 9.00
  a. A598 500p any single .60 .60

Buenos Aires, 400th anniv. No. 1271 shows ceramic mural of Victoria Square by Rodolfo Franco in continuous design. See No. 1285.

Gen. Pedro Aramburu — A599

1980, July 12 Litho. *Perf. 13½*
1272 A599 500p yel & blk .55 .22

Gen. Pedro Eugenio Aramburu (1903-1970), provisional president, 1955.

Army Day A600

1980, July 12
1273 A600 500p multicolored .85 .28

Gen. Juan Gregorio de Las Heras — A601

Gen. Juan Gregorio de Las Heras (1780-1866), Hero of 1817 War of Independence — A601

Grandees of Argentina Bicentenary: No. 1275, Rivadavia. No. 1276, Brig. Gen Jose Matias Zapiola (1780-1874), naval commander and statesman.

1980, Aug. 2 Litho. *Perf. 13½*
1274 A601 500p tan & blk .55 .22
1275 A601 500p multicolored .55 .22
1276 A601 500p lt lilac & blk .55 .22
  Nos. 1274-1276 (3) 1.65 .66

Avro "Gosport" Biplane, Maj. Francisco de Artega — A602

1980, Aug. 16 *Perf. 13*
1277 A602 500p multicolored .70 .22

Air Force Day. Artega (1882-1930) was first director of Military Aircraft Factory where Avro "Gosport" was built (1927).

University of La Plata, 75th Anniversary A603

1980, Aug. 16 *Perf. 13½*
1278 A603 500p multi .55 .22

Souvenir Sheets

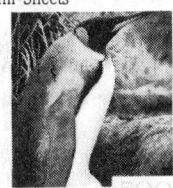

Emperor Penguin — A604

South Orkneys Argentine Base A605   A606

No. 1279 (A604): a, shown. b, Bearded penguin. c, Adelie penguins. d, Papua penguins. e, Sea elephants. f, A605 shown. g, A606 shown. h, Fur seals. i, Giant petrels. j, Blue-eyed cororants. k, Stormy petrels. m, Anarctic doves.

1980, Sept. 27 Litho. *Perf. 13½*
1279 Sheet of 12 11.00 11.00
  a.-m. A604 500p, any single .75 .60
1280 Sheet of 12 11.00 11.00
  a. A605 500p Puerto Soledad .75 .60
  b. A606 500p Different view .75 .60

75th anniv. of Argentina's presence in the South Orkneys and 150th anniv. of political and military command in the Falkland Islands. Nos. 1279-1280 each contain 12 stamps (4x3) with landscape designs in center of sheets. Silhouettes of Argentine exploration ships in margins. #1280 contains #1279a-1279e, 1279h-1279m, 1280a-1280b.

Anti-smoking Campaign — A608

1980, Oct. 11
1282 A608 700p multi .90 .22

National Census — A609

1980, Sept.
1283 A609 500p blk & bl 1.00 .20

Madonna and Child (Congress Emblem) A610

1980, Oct. 1 Litho.
1284 A610 700p multi .85 .15

National Marian Cong., Mendoza, Oct. 8-12

Mural Type of 1980
Miniature Sheet

1980, Oct. 25
1285 Sheet of 14 9.00 9.00
  a. A598 500p, any single .60 .50

Buenos Aires, 400th anniv./Buenos Aires '80 Stamp Exhib., Oct. 24-Nov. 2. No. 1285 shows ceramic mural Arte bajo la Ciudad by Alfredo Guido in continuous design.

Technical Military Academy, 50th Anniversary A611

Amateur Radio Operation A612

1980, Nov. 1
1286 A611 700p multi .75 .15

1980, Nov. 1
1287 A612 700p multi .75 .15

Medal — A613   Lujan Cathedral Floor Plan — A614

1980, Nov. 29 Litho. *Perf. 13½*
1288 A613 700p multi .75 .25
1289 A614 700p olive & brn .75 .25

Christmas 1980. 150th anniv. of apparition of Holy Virgin to St. Catherine Laboure, Paris (No. 1288), 350th anniv. of apparition at Lujan.

150th Death Anniversary of Simon Bolivar — A615

1980, Dec. 13
1290 A615 700p multi .75 .25

Soccer Gold Cup Championship, Montevideo, 1980 — A616

1981, Jan. 3 Litho.
1291 A616 1000p multi 1.10 .25

San Martin Type of 1978

1981, Jan. 20 Engr. *Perf. 13½*
1292 A553 10,000p dark blue 7.25 .16

Landscape in Lujan, by Marcos Tiglio A617

Paintings: No. 1304, Expansion of Light along a Straight Line, by Miguel Angel Vidal, vert.

1981, Apr. 11 Litho.
1303 A617 1000p multi .85 .30
1304 A617 1000p multi .85 .30

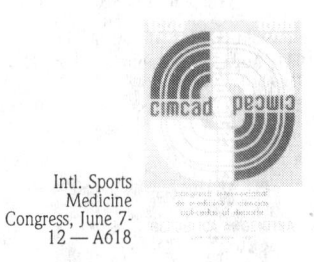

Intl. Sports Medicine Congress, June 7-12 — A618

1981, June 6 Litho. *Perf. 13½*
1305 A618 1000p bl & dk brn .75 .20

Esperanza Base, Antarctica A619

Cargo Plane, Map of Vice-Commodore Marambio Island — A620

Perf. 13½, 13x13½ (No. 1308)
1981, June 13
1306 A619 1000p shown 1.40 .42
1307 A619 2000p Almirante Irizar 2.50 .55
1308 A620 2000p shown 2.50 .85
  Nos. 1306-1308 (3) 6.40 1.82

Antarctic Treaty 20th anniv.

Antique Pistols (Military Club Centenary) A621

1981, June 27 *Perf. 13½*
1309 A621 1000p Club building .80 .15
1310 A621 2000p shown .80 .15

ARGENTINA

Gen. Juan A. Alvarez de Arenales (1770-1831) A622

Famous Men: No. 1312, Felix G. Frias (1816-1881), writer. No. 1313, Jose E. Uriburu (1831-1914), statesman.

1981, Aug. 8	Litho.	Perf. 13½
1311 A622 1000p multi		.70 .15
1312 A622 1000p multi		.70 .15
1313 A622 1000p multi		.70 .15
Nos. 1311-1313 (3)		2.10 .45

Naval Observatory Centenary — A623

1981, Aug. 15   Litho.   Perf. 13x13½
1314 A623 1000p multi   .75 .24

No. 1176 Overprinted in Red: "50 ANIV. DE LA ASOCIACION / FILATELICA Y NUMISMATICA / DE BAHIA BLANCA"

1981, Aug. 15   Photo.   Perf. 13½
1315 A540 1000p lem & blk   1.90 .25

50th anniv. of Bahia Blanca Philatelic and Numismatic Society.

St. Cayetano, Stained-glass Window, Buenos Aires — A624

1981, Sept. 5   Litho.   Perf. 13½
1316 A624 1000p multi   .70 .15

St. Cayetano, founder of Teatino Order, 500th birth anniv.

Pablo Castaibert (1883-1909) and his Monoplane (Air Force Day) — A625

1981, Sept. 5   Perf. 13x13½
1317 A625 1000p multi   .65 .15

Intl. Year of the Disabled A626

1981, Sept. 10   Perf. 13½
1318 A626 1000p multi   .65 .15

22nd Latin-American Steelmakers' Congress, Buenos Aires, Sept. 21-23 — A627

1981, Sept. 19
1319 A627 1000p multi   .65 .15

Army Regiment No. 1 (Patricios), 175th Anniv. — A628

1981, Oct. 10   Litho.   Perf. 13½
1320 A628 1500p Natl. arms   .45 .15
1321 A628 1500p shown   .45 .15
  a.   Pair, #1320-1321   .90 .30

A629   A630

San Martin as artillery Captain in Battle of Bailen, 1808.

1981, Oct. 5
1322 Sheet of 8 + 4 labels   4.75 1.75
  a. A629 1000p multi   .35 .18
  b. A629 1500p multi   .52 .18

Espamer '81 Intl. Stamp Exhib. (Americas, Spain, Portugal), Buenos Aires, Nov. 13-22.
No. 1322 contains 2 each se-tenant pairs with label between.

1981, Oct. 5
1323 A630 1000p multi   2.25 .32

Anti-indiscriminate whaling.

Espamer '81 Emblem and Ship — A631

1981
1324 A631 1300p multi   .55 .16

No. 1324 Overprinted in Blue: "CURSO SUPERIOR DE ORGANIZACIONES DE FILATELICOS-UPAE-BUENOS AIRES-1981"

1981, Nov. 7   Photo.   Perf. 13½
1325 A631 1300p multi   1.25 .18

Postal Administration philatelic training course.

Soccer Players — A632

Designs: Soccer players.

1981, Nov. 13		Litho.
1326 Sheet of 4 + 2 labels		7.25 7.25
a. A632 1000p multi		.25 .25
b. A632 3000p multi		.65 .65
c. A632 5000p multi		1.10 1.10
d. A632 15,000p multi		3.25 3.25

Espamer '81.

"Peso" Coin Centenary A633

1981, Nov. 21
1327 A633 2000p Patacon, 1881   .38 .15
1328 A633 3000p Argentine Oro, 1881 .60 .15

Christmas 1981 — A634

1981, Dec. 12
1329 A634 1500p multi   .85 .24

Traffic Safety A635

1981, Dec. 19		Litho.
1330 A635 1000p Observe traffic lights, vert.		.75 .38
1331 A635 2000p Drive carefully, vert.		.75 .38
1332 A635 3000p Cross at white lines		.75 .38
1333 A635 4000p Don't shine head- lights		1.50 .38
Nos. 1330-1333 (4)		3.75 1.52

Francisco Luis Bernardez, Ciuda Laura — A636

Writers and title pages from their works: 2000p, Lucio V. Mansilla, Excursion a los indios ranqueles. 3000p, Conrado Nale Roxlo, El Grillo. 4000p, Victoria Ocampo, Sur.

1982, Mar. 20		Litho.
1334 A636 1000p shown		.60 .20
1335 A636 2000p multi		.85 .20
1336 A636 3000p multi		1.25 .28
1337 A636 4000p multi		1.75 .28
Nos. 1334-1337 (4)		4.45 .96

No. 1218 Overprinted: "LAS / MALVINAS / SON/ ARGENTINAS"

1982, Apr. 17   Photo.   Perf. 13½
1338 A559 1700p green & blue   .48 .20

Argentina's claim on Falkland Islds.

Robert Koch — A637

American Airforces Commanders' 22nd Conf. — A638

1982, Apr. 17   Litho.   Wmk. 365
1339 A637 2000p multi   .48 .25

TB bacillus centenary and 25th Intl. Tuberculosis Conference.

1982, Apr. 17
1340 A638 2000p multi   .70 .28

Stone Carving, City Founder's Signature (Don Hernando de Lerma) A639

1982, Apr. 17
1341 A639 2000p multi   .70 .28

Souvenir Sheet
1342 A639 5000p multi   2.00 2.00

City of Salta, 400th anniv. No. 1342 contains one 43x30mm stamp.

Naval Center Centenary — A640

1982, Apr. 24   Perf. 13x13½
1343 A640 2000p multi   .70 .28

Chorisia Speciosa — A641

1982	Unwmk.	Photo.	Perf. 13½
1344 A641	200p	Zinnia peruviana	.15 .15
1345 A641	300p	Ipomoea purpurea	.15 .15
1346 A641	400p	Tillandsia aeranthos	.15 .15
1347 A641	500p	shown	.15 .15
1348 A641	800p	Oncidium bifolium	.15 .15
1349 A641	1000p	Erythrina crista-galli	.15 .15
1350 A641	2000p	Jacaranda mimosi-folia	.22 .15
1351 A641	3000p	Bauhinia candicans	.32 .15
1352 A641	5000p	Tecoma stans	.52 .15
1353 A641	10,000p	Tabebuia ipe	1.10 .22
1354 A641	20,000p	Passiflora coerulea	2.25 .35
1355 A641	30,000p	Aristolochia littoralis	3.25 .52
1356 A641	50,000p	Oxalis enneaphylla	5.25 .70
Nos. 1344-1356 (13)			13.81 3.14

Nos. 1344-1346, 1348-1350 issued on fluorescent paper. Nos. 1353-1356 issued on ordinary paper. Others issued on both fluorescent and ordinary paper.

Issue dates: 500p, 2000p, 5000p, 10,000p, May 22. 200p, 300p, 1000p, 20,000p, Sept. 25. 400p, 800p, 30,000p, 50,000p, Dec. 4. 3000p, Dec. 18.
See Nos. 1429-1443A, 1515-1527, 1683-1691.
For overprint see No. 1382.

ARGENTINA

10th Death Anniv. of Gen. Juan C. Sanchez — A641a

1982, May 29 Litho. Wmk. 365
1364 A641a 5000p grn & blk .90 .28

Luis Venet, First Commander — A641b

1982, June 12
1365 A641b 5000p org & blk 1.10 .45
 Size: 83x28mm
1366 A641b 5000p Map .75 .30
 a. Pair, Nos. 1365-1366 2.00 2.00

153rd Anniv. of Malvinas Political and Military Command District.

Visit of Pope John Paul II — A641c

1982, June 12
1367 A641c 5000p multi 1.75 .55

Organ Grinder, by Aldo Severi (b. 1928) — A641d

3000p, Still Life, by Santiago Cogorno (b. 1915).

1982, July 3 Wmk. 365
1368 A641d 2000p shown .26 .20
1369 A641d 3000p multi .40 .20

Guillermo Brown Type of 1980 and:

Jose de San Martin — A641e

1982 Litho. and Engr.
 Unwmk. Perf. 13½
1372 A591 30,000p blk & bl 3.25 .65
1376 A641e 50,000p sepia & car 6.50 .85
Issue dates: 30,000p, June; 50,000p, July.

Scouting Year A641f

1982, Aug. 7 Litho. Wmk. 365
1380 A641f 5000p multi 1.25 .15

Alconafta Fuel Campaign A641g

1982, Aug. 7 Wmk. 365
1381 A641g 2000p multi .32 .15

No. 1352 Overprinted: "50 ANIVERSARIO SOCIEDAD FILATELICA DE TUCUMAN"

1982, Aug. 7 Photo. Unwmk.
1382 A641 5000p multi 1.50 1.25

Rio III Central Nuclear Power Plant, Cordoba A642

 Perf. 13½
1982, Sept. 4 Litho. Wmk. 365
1383 A642 2000p shown .30 .15
1384 A642 2000p Control room .30 .15

Namibia Day — A643

1982, Sept. 4
1385 A643 5000p Map .75 .15

Formosa Cathedral A644

Churches and Cathedrals of the Northeast: 2000p, Our Lady of Itati, Corrientes, vert. 3000p, Resistencia Cathedral, Chaco, vert. 10,000p, St. Ignatius Church ruins, Misiones.

1982, Sept. 18 Litho. & Engr.
1386 A644 2000p dk grn & blk .24 .15
1387 A644 3000p dk brn & brn .35 .15
1388 A644 5000p dk bl & brn .60 .20
1389 A644 10,000p dp org & blk 1.10 .35
 Nos. 1386-1389 (4) 2.29 .85

Tension Sideral, by Mario Alberto Agatiello — A645

Sculpture (Espamer '81 and Juvenex '82 Exhibitions): 3000p, Sugerencia II, by Eduardo Mac Entyre. 5000p, Storm, by Carlos Silva.

1982, Oct. 2 Litho. Perf. 13½
1390 A645 2000p multi .24 .15
1391 A645 3000p multi .45 .15
1392 A645 5000p multi .60 .18
 Nos. 1390-1392 (3) 1.29 .48

Sante Fe Bridge A646

1982, Oct. 16 Litho. & Engr.
1393 A646 2000p bl & blk .38 .15

2nd Southern Cross Games, Santa Fe and Rosario, Nov. 26-Dec. 5.

10th World Men's Volleyball Championship — A647

1982, Oct. 16 Litho. Wmk. 365
1394 A647 2000p multi .24 .15
1395 A647 5000p multi .48 .18

Los Andes Newspaper Centenary A648

Design: Army of the Andes Monument, Hill of Glory, Mendoza.

1982, Oct. 30
1396 A648 5000p multi .50 .18

A649    A650

1982, Oct. 30 Wmk. 365
1397 A649 5000p Signs .55 .22

50th Anniv. of Natl. Roads, Administration.

1982, Nov. 20 Litho.

La Plata City Cent.: No. 1400: a, Cathedral, diff. b, Head, top. c, Observatory. d, City Hall, diff. e, Head, bottom. f, University.

1398 A650 5000p Cathedral .75 .15
1399 A650 5000p City Hall .75 .15
1400 Sheet of 6 2.25 1.00
 a.-f. A650 2500p any single .28 .15

Well, Natl. Hydrocarbon Congress Emblem — A651

1982, Nov. 20
1401 A651 5000p multi .50 .20

Oil Discovery, Comodoro Rivadavia, 75th anniv.

Jockey Club of Buenos Aires Centenary — A652    Christmas 1982 — A653

#1403, Carlos Pellegrini, first president.

1982, Dec. 4 Litho.
1402 A652 5000p Emblem .52 .15
1403 A652 5000p multi .52 .15

1982, Dec. 18 Perf. 13½
1404 A653 3000p St. Vincent de Paul 1.50 .15
 Size: 29x38mm
1405 A653 5000p St. Francis of Assisi 1.25 .15

Pedro B. Palacios (1854-1917), Writer — A654

Writers: 2000p, Leopoldo Marechal (1900-1970). 3000p, Delfina Bunge de Galvez (1881-1952). 4000p, Manuel Galvez (1882-1962). 5000p, Evaristo Carriego (1883-1912).

1983, Mar. 26 Litho. Perf. 13½
1406 A654 1000p multi .15 .15
1407 A654 2000p multi .22 .15
1408 A654 3000p multi .32 .15
1409 A654 4000p multi .42 .15
1410 A654 5000p multi .55 .18
 a. Strip of 5, #1406-1410 1.75 1.00

Recovery of the Malvinas (Falkland Islands) — A655

1983, Apr. 9 Litho. Perf. 13½
1411 A655 20,000p Map, flag .60 .30

Telecommunications Systems — A656

1983, Apr. 16 Wmk. 365
1412 A656 5000p SITRAM .75 .15
1413 A656 5000p RED ARPAC .75 .15

ARGENTINA

Naval League Emblem — A657

1983, May 14   Litho.   Perf. 13½
1414 A657 5000p multi   .35 .15
Navy Day and 50th anniv. of Naval League.

Allegory, by Victor Rebuffo — A658

1983, May 14
1415 A658 5000p multi   .35 .15
Natl. Arts Fund, 25th Anniv.

75th Anniv. of Colon Opera House, Buenos Aires — A659

1983, May 28   Wmk. 365
1416 A659 5000p Main hall   .70 .15
1417 A659 10000p Stage   1.00 .15

Protected Species A660

1983, July 2   Litho.   Perf. 13½
1418 A660 1p Chrysocyon brachy-
             urus   .32 .15
1419 A660 1.50p Ozotocerus bezoar-
             ticus   .48 .15
1420 A660 2p Myrmecophaga
             tridactyla   .55 .15
1421 A660 2.50p Leo onca   .65 .16
             Nos. 1418-1421 (4) 2.00 .61

City of Catamarca, 300th Anniv. — A661

Foundation of the City of Catamarca, by Luis Varela Lezana (1900-1982).

1983, July 16   Litho.   Perf. 13½
1422 A661 1p multi   .32 .15

Mamerto Esquiu (1826-1883) A662

1983, July 16
1423 A662 1p multi   .32 .15

Bolivar, by Herrera Toro — A663

Bolivar, Engraving by Kepper — A664

Perf. 13 (A663), 13½ (A664)
1983   Unwmk.
1424 A663   1p multi   .30 .15
1425 A664   2p black   .60 .15
1426 A664 10p San Martin   3.00 1.50
             Nos. 1424-1426 (3) 3.90 1.80
Issue dates: 1p, 2p, July 23. 10p, Aug. 20.
See Nos. 1457-1462B.

Gen. Toribio de Luzuriaga (1782-1842) A665

1983, Aug. 20   Litho.   Perf. 13½
1427 A665 1p multi   .30 .15

50th Anniv. of San Martin National Institute A666

1983, Aug. 20   Engr.   Unwmk.
1428 A666 2p sepia   .60 .16

Flower Type of 1982 in New Currency
1983-85   Photo.   Perf. 13½
1429 A641   5c like #1347   .15 .15
1430 A641 10c like #1349   .15 .15
1431 A641 20c like #1350   .15 .15
1432 A641 30c like #1351   .15 .15
1433 A641 40c Eichhornia cras-
             sipes   .15 .15
1434 A641 50c like #1352   .15 .15
1435 A641   1p like #1353   .15 .15
1435A A641 1.80p Mutisia retusa .15 .15
1436 A641   2p like #1354   .22 .15
1437 A641   3p like #1355   .32 .15
1438 A641   5p like #1356   .55 .20
1439 A641 10p Alstroemeria
             aurantiaca   1.10 .80
1440 A641 20p like #1345   .55 .16
1441 A641 30p Embothrium
             coccineum   3.50 2.50
1442 A641 50p like #1346   1.10 .40

1443 A641 100p like #1348   1.65 .48
1443A A641 300p Cassia carnaval .80 .24
             Nos. 1429-1443A (17) 10.99 6.28
Issue Dates: 20p, Aug. 27, 1984; 50p, Oct. 19, 1984; 100p, Dec. 1984; 300p, June 15, 1985.
Nos. 1429, 1433, 1435A issued on fluorescent paper. Nos. 1443, 1443A issued on ordinary paper. Others issued on both ordinary and fluorescent paper.
For overprint and surcharge see #1489, 1530.

Intl. Rotary South American Regional Conference, Buenos Aires, Sept. 25-28 — A667

1983, Sept. 24   Litho.
1444 A667 1p multi   .55 .24

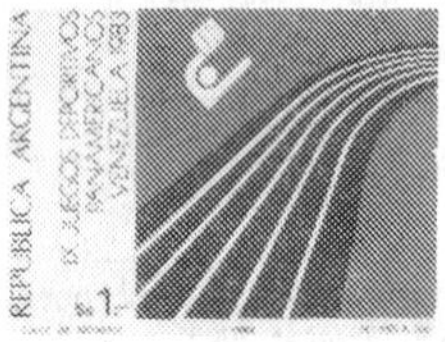

9th Pan American Games, Caracas, Aug. 13-28 A668

1983, Sept. 24
1445 A668 1p Track   .32 .15
1446 A668 2p Emblem   .65 .28

World Communications Year — A669

1983, Oct. 8   Perf. 13½
1447 A669 2p multi   .60 .24

Squash Peddler by Antonio Berni (1905-1981) A670

2p, Figure in Yellow by Luis Seoane (1910-79).

1983, Oct. 15   Perf. 13½
1448 A670 1p multi   .32 .15
1449 A670 2p multi   .52 .22

World Communications Year — A671

Designs: 1p, Wagon, 18th cent. 2p, Post chaise, 19th cent. 4p, Steam locomotive, 1857. 5p, Tramway, 1910.

1983, Nov. 19   Litho.   Perf. 13½
1450 A671 1p multi   .15 .15
1451 A671 2p multi   .24 .15
1452 A671 4p multi   .50 .20
1453 A671 5p multi   .65 .26
             Nos. 1450-1453 (4) 1.54 .76

A672

A673

1983, Nov. 26   Litho.   Perf. 12½x12
1454 A672 2p General Post Office .42 .18
World Communications Year.

1983, Dec. 10   Photo.   Perf. 13½
1455 A673 2p Coin, 1813   .30 .18
Return to elected government.

Eudyptes Crestatus A674

Designs: b, Diomedea exulans. c, Diomedea melanophris. d, Eudyptes chrysolophus. e, Luis Piedra Buena. f, Carlos Maria Moyano. g, Luis Py. h, Augusto Lasserre. i, Phoebetria palpebrata. j, Hydrurga leptonyx. k, Lobodon carcinophagus. l, Leptonychotes weddelli.

1983, Dec. 10   Litho.
1456   Sheet of 12   4.50 2.25
 a.-l. A674 2p any single   .35 .15
Southern pioneers and fauna. Margin depicts various airplanes and emblems.

Bolivar Type of 1983
Famous men: 10p, Angel J. Carranza (1834-99), historian. No. 1458, 500p, Guillermo Brown. No. 1459, Estanislao del Campo (1834-80), poet. 30p, Jose Hernandez (1834-86), author. 40p, Vicente Lopez y Planes (1784-1856), poet and patriot. 50p, San Martin. 200p, Belgrano.

1983-85   Litho. & Engr.   Perf. 13½
1457 A664   10p pale bl & dk bl .15 .15
1458 A664   20p dk bl & blk   2.75 1.40
1459 A664   20p dl brn ol & ol
              blk   .15 .15
1460 A664   30p pale bl & bluish
              blk   .15 .15
1461 A664   40p lt bl grn & blk .18 .15
1462 A664   50p Prus & choc   1.10 .24
1462A A664 200p int bl & blk   3.00 .95
1462B A664 500p brn & int bl   1.50 .32
             Nos. 1457-1462B (8) 8.98 3.51
Issue dates: #1458, Oct. 6, 1983. 10p, #1459, 30p, 40p, Mar. 23, 1985. 50p, Apr. 23, 1985. 200p, Nov. 2, 1985. 500p, May 2, 1985.

Christmas 1983 A675

Nativity Scenes: 2p, Tapestry, by Silke. 3p, Stained-glass window, San Carlos de Bariloche's Wayn Church, vert.

1983, Dec. 17   Litho.   Perf. 13½
1463 A675 2p multi   .30 .15
1464 A675 3p multi   .55 .28

ARGENTINA

Centenary of El Dia Newspaper — A676

1984, Mar. 24   Litho.
1465 A676 4p Masthead, printing roll   .38   .20

Alejandro Carbo Teachers' College Centenary A677

1984, June 2   Litho.   Perf. 13½
1466 A677 10p Building   .42   .22

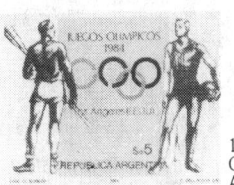

1984 Olympics A678

#1468, Weightlifting, discus, shot put. #1469, Javelin, fencing. #1470, Bicycling, swimming.

1984, July 28   Litho.   Perf. 13½
1467 A678 5p shown   .22   .15
1468 A678 5p multicolored   .22   .15
1469 A678 10p multicolored   .45   .22
1470 A678 10p multicolored   .45   .22
    Nos. 1467-1470 (4)   1.34   .74

Rosario Stock Exchange Centenary A679

1984, Aug. 11
1471 A679 10p multicolored   .45   .22

Wheat A680

1984, Aug. 11
1472 A680 10p shown   .48   .24
1473 A680 10p Corn   .48   .24
1474 A680 10p Sunflower   .48   .24
    Nos. 1472-1474 (3)   1.44   .72

18th FAO Regional Conference for Latin America and Caribbean (No. 1472); 3rd Natl. Corn Congress (No. 1473); World Food Day (No. 1474).

Wildlife Protection A681

1984, Sept. 22   Litho.   Perf. 13½
1475 A681 20p Hippocamelus bisulcus   .40   .15
1476 A681 20p Vicugna vicugna   .40   .15
1477 A681 20p Aburria jacutinga   .40   .15

1478 A681 20p Mergus octosetaceus   .40   .15
1479 A681 20p Podiceps gallardoi   .40   .15
    Nos. 1475-1479 (5)   2.00   .75

First Latin American Theater Festival, Cordoba, Oct. — A682

1984, Oct. 13   Litho.   Perf. 13½
1480 A682 20p Mask   .25   .15

Intl. Eucharistic Congress, 50th Anniv. A683

Design: Apostles' Communion, by Fra Angelico.

1984, Oct. 13
1481 A683 20p multicolored   .30   .15

Glaciares Natl. Park (UNESCO World Heritage List) A684

1984, Nov. 17   Litho.
1482 A684 20p Sea   .25   .15
1483 A684 30p Glacier   .42   .15

City of Puerto Deseado Centenary A685

1984, Nov. 17   Perf. 13½
1484 A685 20p shown   .30   .15
1485 A685 20p Ushuaia centenary   .30   .15

Childrens' Paintings, Christmas 1984 A686

1984, Dec. 1   Litho.   Perf. 13½
1486 A686 20p Diego Aguero   .32   .15
1487 A686 30p Leandro Ruiz   .60   .15
1488 A686 50p Maria Castillo, vert.   .60   .15
    Nos. 1486-1488 (3)   1.52   .45

No. 1439 Overprinted

1984, Dec. 1   Photo.   Perf. 13½
1489 A641 10p multicolored   .26   .22
    Buenos Aires Philatelic Center, 50th anniv.

Vista Del Jardin Zoologico, by Fermin Eguia — A687

Paintings: No. 1491, El Congreso Iluminado, by Francisco Travieso. No. 1492, Galpones (La Boca), by Marcos Borio.

1984, Dec. 15   Perf. 13½
1490 A687 20p multi   .28   .15
1491 A687 20p multi, vert.   .28   .15
1492 A687 20p multi, vert.   .28   .15
    Nos. 1490-1492 (3)   .84   .45

Gen. Martin Miguel de Guemes (1785-1821) — A688

1985, Mar. 23   Litho.   Perf. 13½
1493 A688 30p multicolored   .26   .15

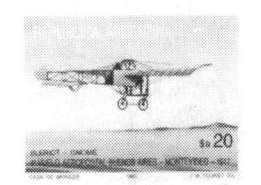

ARGENTINA '85 Exhibition — A689

First airmail service from: 20p, Buenos Aires to Montevideo, 1917. 40p, Cordoba to Villa Dolores, 1925. 60p, Bahia Blanca to Comodoro Rivadavia, 1929. 80p, Argentina to Germany, 1934. 100p, naval service to the Antarctic, 1952.

1985, Apr. 27
1494 A689 20p Bleriot Gnome   .16   .15
1495 A689 40p Junker F-13L   .32   .15
1496 A689 60p Latte 25   .50   .20
1497 A689 80p L.Z. 127 Graf Zeppelin   .65   .30
1498 A689 100p Consolidated PBY Catalina   .85   .40
    Nos. 1494-1498 (5)   2.48   1.20

Central Bank, 50th Anniv. A690

1985, June 1
1499 A690 80p Bank Bldg., Buenos Aires   .55   .18

Jose A. Ferreyra (1889-1943), Director of Munequitas Portenas A691

Famous directors and their films: No. 1501, Leopoldo Torre Nilsson (1924-1978), scene from Martin Fierro.

1985, June 1
1500 A691 100p shown   .60   .18
1501 A691 100p multi   .60   .18

Carlos Gardel (1890-1935), Entertainer — A692

Paintings: No. 1502, Gardel playing the guitar on stage, by Carlos Alonso (b. 1929). No. 1503, Gardel in a wide-brimmed hat, by Hermegildo Sabat (b. 1933). No. 1504, Portrait of Gardel in an ornamental frame, by Aldo Severi (b. 1928) and Martiniano Arce (b. 1939).

1985, June 15
1502 A692 200p multi   .95   .45
1503 A692 200p multi   .95   .45
1504 A692 200p multi   .95   .45
    Nos. 1502-1504 (3)   2.85   1.35

The Arrival, by Pedro Figari A693

A Halt on the Plains, by Prilidiano Pueyrredon — A693a

Oil paintings (details): 30c, The Wagon Square, by C. B. de Quiros. Ilustration A693a is reduced.

1985, July 6   Litho.   Perf. 13½
1505 A693 20c multi   1.00   .24
1506 A693 30c multi   1.25   .24

Souvenir Sheet
Perf. 12
1507 A693a Sheet of 2   2.50   2.50
  a. 20c Pilgrims, vert.   .30   .30
  b. 30c Wagon   .40   .40

ARGENTINA '85. No. 1507 contains 2 30x40mm stamps. See No. 1542.

Buenos Aires to Montevideo, 1917 Teodoro Fels Flight A694

Historic flight covers: #1509, Villa Dolores to Cordoba, 1925. #1510, Buenos Aires to France, 1929 St. Exupery flight. #1511, Buenos Aires to Bremerhaven, 1934 Graf Zeppelin flight. #1512, First Antarctic flight, 1952.

1985, July 13   Perf. 12x12½
1508 A694 10c emer & multi   .40   .15
1509 A694 10c ultra & multi   .40   .15
1510 A694 10c lt choc & multi   .40   .15
1511 A694 10c chnt & multi   .40   .15
1512 A694 10c ap grn & multi   .40   .15
    Nos. 1508-1512 (5)   2.00   .75

ARGENTINA '85.

Illuminated Fruit, by Fortunato Lacamera (1887-1951) — A695

Paintings: 20c, Woman with Bird, by Juan del Prete, vert.

1985, Sept. 7   Perf. 13½
1513 A695 20c multi   .85   .30
1514 A695 30c multi   1.00   .30

Flower Types of 1982-85

Designs: 1a, Begonia micranthera var. hieronymi. 5a, Gymnocalycium bruchii.

1985-88   Photo.   Perf. 13½
1515 A641 ½c like #1356   .15   .15
1516 A641 1c like #1439   .15   .15
1517 A641 2c like #1345   .15   .15
1518 A641 3c like #1441   .15   .15
1519 A641 5c like #1346   .22   .15
1520 A641 10c like #1348   .35   .15
1521 A641 20c like #1347   .70   .16
1522 A641 30c like #1443A   1.10   .25
1523 A641 50c like #1344   1.75   .35
1524 A641 1a multi   3.50   .15
1525 A641 2a like #1351   .38   .15
1526 A641 5a multi   6.75   3.00

353

ARGENTINA

Size: 15x23mm
1527	A641	8½c like #1349	.32	.15
		Nos. 1515-1527 (13)	15.67	5.61

Issue dates: ½c, 1c, Dec. 16. 2c, 8½c, 30c, Sept. 18. 3c, 5c, 10c, 50c, 1a, Sept. 7. 20c, Oct. 17. 5a, Mar. 21, 1987. 2a, Dec. 5, 1988.

No. 1435 Surcharged
1986, Nov. 4   Photo.   Perf. 13½
1530	A641	10c on 1p No. 1435	.15	.15

Folk Musical Instruments A699

1985, Sept. 14   Litho.   Perf. 13½
1531	A699	20c Frame drum	.55	.22
1532	A699	20c Long flute	.55	.22
1533	A699	20c Jew's harp	.55	.22
1534	A699	20c Pan flutes	.55	.22
1535	A699	20c Musical bow	.55	.22
		Nos. 1531-1535 (5)	2.75	1.10

Juan Bautista Alberdi (1810-1884), Historian, Politician A700

Famous men: Nicolas Avellaneda (1836-1885), President in 1874. 30c, Fr. Luis Beltran (1784-1827), military and naval engineer. 40c, Ricardo Levene (1885-1959), historian, author.

1985, Oct. 5
1536	A700	10c multi	.22	.15
1537	A700	20c multi	.45	.22
1538	A700	30c multi	.65	.32
1539	A700	40c multi	1.10	.45
		Nos. 1536-1539 (4)	2.42	1.14

Type of 1985 and

Skaters A701

Deception, by J. H. Rivoira A702

1985, Oct. 19   Litho.   Perf. 13½
1540	A701	20c multi	.35	.32
1541	A702	30c multi	.50	.48

Size: 147x75mm
Imperf
1542	A693a	1a multi	1.90

IYY. No. 1542 is inscribed in silver with the UN 40th anniversary and IYY emblems.

Shop with Scott Publishing Co. 24 hours a day 7 days a week at www.scottonline.com

Provincial Views — A703

Designs: No. 1543, Rock Window, Buenos Aires. No. 1544, Forclaz Windmill, Entre Rios. No. 1545, Lake Potrero de los Funes, San Luis. No. 1546, Mission church, north-east province. No. 1547, Penguin colony, Punta Tombo, Chubut. No. 1548, Water Mirrors, Cordoba.

1985, Nov. 23   Perf. 13½
1543	A703	10c multi	.26	.25
1544	A703	10c multi	.26	.25
1545	A703	10c multi	.26	.25
1546	A703	10c multi	.26	.25
1547	A703	10c multi	.26	.25
1548	A703	10c multi	.26	.25
		Nos. 1543-1548 (6)	1.56	1.50

Christmas 1985 — A704

Designs: 10c, Birth of Our Lord, by Carlos Cortes. 20c, Christmas, by Hector Viola.

1985, Dec. 7
1549	A704	10c multi	.24	.18
1550	A704	20c multi	.48	.45

Natl. Campaign for the Prevention of Blindness A705

1985, Dec. 7
1551	A705	10c multi	.24	.18

Rio Gallegos City, Cent. — A716

1985, Dec. 21   Litho.   Perf. 13½
1552	A716	10c Church	.24	.18

Natl. Grape Harvest Festival, 50th Anniv. A717

1986, Mar. 15
1553	A717	10c multi	.24	.18

Historical Architecture in Buenos Aires — A718

Designs: No. 1554, Valentin Alsina House, Italian Period, 1860-70. No. 1555, House on Cerrito Street, French influence, 1880-1900. No. 1556, House on the Avenida de Mayo y Santiago del Estero, Art Nouveau, 1900-10. No. 1557, Customs Building, academic architecture, 1900-15. No. 1558, Isaac Fernandez Blanco Museum, house of architect Martin Noel, natl. restoration, 1910-30. Nos. 1554-1556 vert.

1986, Apr. 19
1554	A718	20c multi	.40	.30
1555	A718	20c multi	.40	.30
1556	A718	20c multi	.40	.30
1557	A718	20c multi	.40	.30
1558	A718	20c multi	.40	.30
		Nos. 1554-1558 (5)	2.00	1.50

Antarctic Bases, Pioneers and Fauna — A719

Designs: a, Base, Jubany. b, Arctocephalus gazella. c, Otaria byronica. d, Gen. Belgrano Base. e, Daption capensis. f, Diomedia melanophris. g, Apterodytes patagonica. h, Macronectes giganteus. i, Hugo Alberto Acuna (1885-1953). j, Spheniscus magellanicus. k, Gallinago gallinage. l, Capt. Agustin del Castillo (1855-89).

1986, May 31
1559		Sheet of 12	9.00	9.00
a.-l.	A719	10c any single	.75	.75

Famous People — A720

Statuary, Buenos Aires — A721

#1560, Dr. Alicia Moreau de Justo, human rights activist. #1561, Dr. Emilio Ravignani (1886-1954), historian. #1562, Indira Gandhi.

1986, July 5   Litho.   Perf. 13½
1560	A720	10c multi	.40	.22
1561	A720	10c multi	.40	.22
1562	A720	30c multi	1.25	.65
		Nos. 1560-1562 (3)	2.05	1.09

1986, July 5

Designs: 20c, Fountain of the Nereids, by Dolores Lola Mora (1866-1936). 30c, Lamenting at Work, by Rogelio Yrurtia (1879-1950), horiz.

1563	A721	20c multi	.52	.45
1564	A721	30c multi	.80	.65

Famous Men — A722

Designs: No. 1565, Francisco N. Laprida (1786-1829), politician. No. 1566, Estanislao Lopez (1786-1838), brigadier general. No. 1567, Francisco Ramirez (1786-1821), general.

1986, Aug. 9   Litho.   Perf. 13
1565	A722	20c dl yel, brn & blk	.42	.38
1566	A722	20c dl yel, brn & blk	.42	.38
1567	A722	20c dl yel, brn & blk	.42	.38
		Nos. 1565-1567 (3)	1.26	1.14

Fr. Ceferino Namuncura (1886-1905) A723

1986, Aug. 30   Perf. 13½
1568	A723	20c multi	.60	.40

Miniature Sheets

Natl. Team Victory, 1986 World Cup Soccer Championships, Mexico — A724

Designs: No. 1569a-1569d, Team. Nos. 1569e-1569h, Shot on goal. Nos. 1570a-1570d, Action close-up. Nos. 1570e-1570h, Diego Maradona holding soccer cup.

1986, Nov. 8   Litho.   Perf. 13½
1569	A724	Sheet of 8	9.25	12.00
a.-h.		75c any single	1.15	1.50
1570	A724	Sheet of 8	9.25	12.00
a.-h.		75c any single	1.15	1.50

San Francisco (Cordoba), Cent. A725

1986, Nov. 8
1571	A725	20c Municipal Building	.50	.45

Trelew City (Chubut), Cent. A726

1986, Nov. 22   Litho.   Perf. 13½
1572	A726	20c Old railroad station, 1865	.50	.45

Mutualism Day A727

1986, Nov. 22
1573	A727	20c multi	.60	.45

ARGENTINA

Christmas
A728

Designs: 20c, Naif retable, by Aniko Szabo (b. 1945). 30c, Everyone's Tree, by Franca Delacqua (b. 1947).

1986, Dec. 13	Litho.	Perf. 13½
1574 A728 20c multicolored	.50	.35
1575 A728 30c multicolored	.60	.35

Santa Rosa de Lima, 400th Birth Anniv. — A729

Rio Cuarto Municipal Building — A730

1986, Dec. 13
1576 A729 50c multicolored   1.75 .75

1986, Dec. 20
1577 A730 20c shown   .40 .25
1578 A730 20c Court Building, Cordoba   .40 .25

Rio Cuarto City, bicent. Court Building, Cordoba, 50th anniv.

Antarctic Treaty, 25th Anniv. — A731

1987, Mar. 7	Litho.	Perf. 13½
1579 A731 20c Marine biologist	.35	.20
1580 A731 30c Ornithologist	.60	.25

Souvenir Sheet
Perf. 12
1581   Sheet of 2   1.00 .50
   a.   A731 20c like No. 1579   .40 .20
   b.   A731 30c like No. 1580   .55 .25

No. 1581 contains 2 stamps, size: 40x50mm.

Natl. Mortgage Bank, Cent. A732

1987, Mar. 21		Perf. 13½
1582 A732 20c multicolored		.65 .45

Natl. Cooperative Associations Movement — A733

1987, Mar. 21
1583 A733 20c multicolored   .65 .45

Second State Visit of Pope John Paul II — A734

1987, Apr. 4	Engr., Litho. (No. 1585)	Perf. 13½
1584 A734 20c shown		.35 .25
1585 A734 80c Papal blessing		1.40 .70

Souvenir Sheet
Perf. 12
1586 A734 1a like 20c   2.25 2.25

No. 1586 contains one 40x50mm stamp.

Intl. Peace Year A735

30c, Pigeon, abstract sculpture by Victor Kaniuka.

1987, Apr. 11		Litho.
1587 A735 20c multicolored		.35 .20
1588 A735 30c multicolored		.55 .35

Low Handicap World Polo Championships A736

Design: Polo Players, painting by Alejandro Moy.

1987, Apr. 11
1589 A736 20c multicolored   .75 .20

Miniature Sheet

ICOM '86 — A737

Designs: a, Emblem. b, Family crest, National History Museum, Buenos Aires. c, St. Bartholomew, Enrique Larreta Museum of Spanish Art, Buenos Aires. d, Zoomorphic club, Patagonian Museum, San Carlos de Bariloche. e, Supplication, anthropomorphic sculpture, Natural Sciences Museum, La Plata. f, Wrought iron lattice from the house of J. Urquiza, president of the Confederation of Argentina, Entre Rios History Museum, Parana. g, St. Joseph, 18th cent. wood figurine, Northern History Museum, Salta. h, Funerary urn, Provincial Archaeological Museum, Santiago del Estero.

1987, May 30
1590   Sheet of 8   3.50 3.50
   a.-h.   A737 25c any single   .40 .30

Intl. Council of Museums, 14th general conf.

Natl. College of Monserrat, Cordoba, 300th Anniv. — A738

1987, July 4		Imperf.
1591 A738 1a multicolored		1.40 1.40

Monserrat '87 Philatelic Exposition.

Fight Drug Abuse A739

Design: The Proportions of Man, by da Vinci.

1987, Aug. 15   Perf. 13½
1592 A739 30c multicolored   .45 .20

Famous Men A740

Portraits and quotations: 20c, Jorge Luis Borges (1899-1986), writer. 30c, Armando Discepolo (1887-1971), playwright. 50c, Carlos A. Pueyrredon (1887-1962), professor, Legion of Honor laureate.

1987, Aug. 15
1593 A740 20c multicolored   .30 .15
1594 A740 30c multicolored   .50 .25
1595 A740 50c multicolored   .75 .35
   Nos. 1593-1595 (3)   1.55 .75

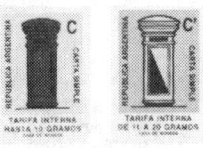

Pillar Boxes
A741   A742

1987	Photo.	Perf. 13½
1596 A741 (30c) yel, blk & dark red		.80 .30
1597 A742 (33c) lt blue grn, blk & yel		.85 .35

Issue dates: (30c), June 8; (33c), July 13.

The Sower, by Julio Vanzo A743

1987, Sept. 12
1598 A743 30c multicolored   .35 .15

Argentine Agrarian Federation, 75th anniv.

10th Pan American Games, Indianapolis, Aug. 7-25 — A744

1987, Sept. 26
1599 A744 20c Basketball   .25 .20
1600 A744 30c Rowing   .35 .20
1601 A744 50c Yachting   .55 .20
   Nos. 1599-1601 (3)   1.15 .60

Children Playing Doctor, WHO Emblem A745

1987, Oct. 7
1602 A745 30c multi   .35

Vaccinate every child campaign.

Heroes of the Revolution A746

Signing of the San Nicolas Accord, 1852, by Rafael del Villar A747

Independence anniversaries and historic events: No. 1603, Maj.-Col. Ignacio Alvarez Thomas (1787-1857). No. 1604, Col. Manuel Crispulo Bernabe Dorrego (1787-1829). No. 1606, 18th cent. Spanish map of the Falkland Isls., administered by Jacinto de Altolaguirre.

1987, Oct. 17
1603 A746 25c shown   .30 .20
1604 A746 25c multi   .30 .20
1605 A747 50c shown   .55 .30
1606 A747 50c multi   .55 .30
   Nos. 1603-1606 (4)   1.70 1.00

Museum established in the House of the San Nicholas Accord, 50th anniv. (#1605); Jacinto de Altolaguirre (1754-1787), governor the Malvinas Isls. for the King of Spain (#1606).

Celedonio Galvan Moreno, 1st Director A748

1987, Nov. 21
1607 A748 50c multicolored   .55 .40

Postas Argentinas magazine, 50th anniv.

ARGENTINA

LRA National Radio, Buenos Aires, 50th Anniv. — A749

1987, Nov. 21
1608 A749 50c multicolored .55 .40

Natl. Philatelic Society, Cent. A750

1987, Nov. 21
1609 A750 1a Jose Marco del Pont 1.10 .55

Christmas A751

Tapestries: 50c, *Navidad*, by Alisia Frega. 1a, *Vitral*, by Silvina Trigos.

1987, Dec. 5
1610 A751 50c multicolored .55 .20
1611 A751 1a multicolored 1.10 .55

Natl. Parks — A752

1987, Dec. 19 *Perf. 13x13½*
1612 A752 50c Baritu .55 .35
1613 A752 50c Nahuel Huapi .55 .35
1614 A752 50c Rio Pilcomayo .55 .35
1615 A752 50c Tierra del Fuego .55 .35
1616 A752 50c Iguacu .55 .35
  Nos. 1612-1616 (5) 2.75 1.75
See Nos. 1647-1651, 1715-1719, 1742-1746.

Landscapes in Buenos Aires Painted by Jose Cannella A753

1988-89 *Litho.* *Perf. 13½*
1617 A753 5a Caminito 2.00 1.10
1618 A753 10a Viejo Almacen 4.00 2.25
1618A A753 10a like No. 1618 1.05 .50
1618B A753 50a like No. 1617 1.05 .50
  c. Wmk 365 120.00
  Nos. 1617-1618B (4) 8.10 4.35
No. 1618 inscribed "Viejo Almacen"; No. 1618A inscribed "El Viejo Almacen."
Issue dates: 5a, #1618, 3/15; #1618A, 10/20; 50a, 5/30/89.
For overprint see No. 1635.

Minstrel in a Tavern, by Carlos Morel A754

Paintings: No. 1620, Interior of Curuzu, by Candido Lopez.

1988, Mar. 19 *Litho.* *Perf. 13½*
1619 A754 1a shown .60 .30
1620 A754 1a multicolored .60 .30
See Nos. 1640-1641.

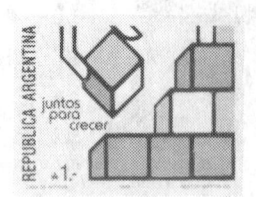

Argentine-Brazilian Economic Cooperation and Integration Program for Mutual Growth — A755

1988, Mar. 19
1621 A755 1a multicolored .50 .25

Cities of Alta Gracia and Corrientes, 400th Annivs. A756

1988, Apr. 9 *Litho.* *Perf. 13½*
1622 A756 1a Alta Gracia Church .75 .40
1623 A756 1a Chapel of St. Anne, Corrientes .75 .40

Labor Day — A757

Grain Carriers, a tile mosaic by Alfredo Guido, Line D of Nueve de Julio station, Buenos Aires subway: a, (UL). b, (UR). c, (LL). d, (LR).

1988, May 21
1624 A757 Block of 4 2.00 2.00
  a.-d. 50c any single .50 .50

1988 Summer Olympics, Seoul — A758

1988, July 16 *Litho.* *Perf. 13½*
1625 A758 1a Running .30 .15
1626 A758 2a Soccer .75 .30
1627 A758 3a Field hockey 1.10 .50
1628 A758 4a Tennis 1.40 .65
  Nos. 1625-1628 (4) 3.55 1.60

Mendoza Bank, Cent. A759

Natl. Gendarmerie, Cent. — A760

1988, Aug. 13
1629 A759 2a multicolored .65 .45
1630 A760 2a multicolored .65 .45

Sarmiento and Cathedral School to the North, Buenos Aires A761

1988, Sept. 10 *Litho.* *Perf. 13½*
1631 A761 3a multicolored .65 .45
Domingo Faustino Sarmiento (1811-1888), educator, politician.

St. Cayetano, Patron of Workers — A762

El Amor, by Antonio Berni, Pacific Gallery, Buenos Aires — A763

1988, Sept. 10 *Litho.*
1632 A762 2a multicolored .45 .45
1633 A762 3a Our Lady of Carmen, Cuyo .70 .70

Souvenir Sheet
Perf. 12
1634 A763 5a multicolored 1.00 1.00
Liniers Philatelic Circle and the Argentine Western Philatelic Institution (IFADO), 50th annivs.
No. 1634 contains one 40x30mm stamp.

No. 1617 Ovptd. with Congress Emblem and:
"XXI CONGRESO DE LA SOCIEDAD INTERNACIONAL DE UROLOGIA"

1988, Oct. 29 *Litho.* *Perf. 13½*
1635 A753 5a multicolored 3.50 .40
21st Congress of the Intl. Urology Soc.

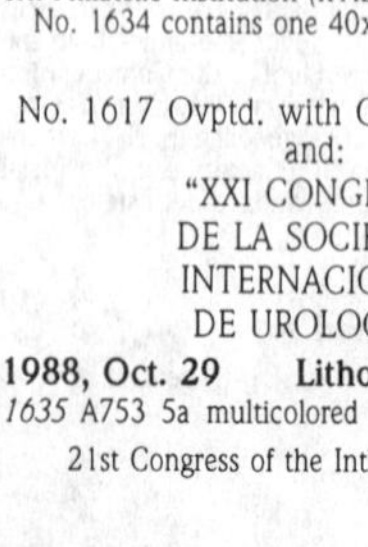

Tourism A763a

1988, Nov. 1 *Litho.* *Perf. 13½*
1635A A763a 3a Purmamarca, Jujuy .50 .25
Size: 28½x38mm
1635B A763a 20a Ushuaia 3.35 1.65

Buenos Aires Subway, 75th Anniv. A764

1988, Dec. 17 *Litho.* *Perf. 13½*
1636 A764 5a Train, c. 1913 1.10 .55

Christmas A765

Frescoes in Ucrania Cathedral, Buenos Aires: No. 1637, *Virgin Patron*. No. 1638, *Virgin of Tenderness*.

1988, Dec. 17
1637 A765 5a multicolored 1.25 .50
1638 A765 5a multicolored 1.25 .50

St. John Bosco (1815-1888), Educator, and Church in Ushuala — A766

1989, Apr. 8 *Litho.* *Perf. 13½*
1639 A766 5a multicolored .30 .20
Dated 1988.

Art Type of 1988

Paintings: No. 1640, *Blancos*, by Fernando Fader (1882-1935). No. 1641, *Rincon de los Areneros*, by Justo Lynch (1870-1953).

1989, Apr. 8
1640 A754 5a multicolored .50 .15
1641 A754 5a multicolored .50 .15

Holy Week A767

Sculpture and churches: No. 1642, *The Crown of Thorns*, Calvary of Tandil, and Church of Our Lady Carmelite, Tandil. No. 1643, *Jesus the Nazarene* and Metropolitan Cathedral, Buenos Aires. No. 1644, *Jesus Encounters His Mother* (scene of the crucifixion), La Quebrada Village, San Luis. No. 1645, *Our Lady of Sorrow* and Church of Humahuaca, Jujuy.

1989, Apr. 22 *Litho.* *Perf. 13½*
1642 A767 2a multicolored .20 .15
1643 A767 2a multicolored .20 .15
1644 A767 3a multicolored .30 .20
1645 A767 3a multicolored .30 .20
  Nos. 1642-1645 (4) 1.00 .70

Printed in sheets of 16+4 labels containing blocks of 4 of each design. Labels picture Jesus's arrival in Jerusalem (Palm Sunday).

ARGENTINA

Prevent Alcoholism — A768

1989, Apr. 22
1646 A768 5a multicolored .30 .20

Natl. Park Type of 1987

1989, May 6 Perf. 13x13½
1647 A752 5a Lihue Calel .70 .15
1648 A752 5a El Palmar .70 .15
1649 A752 5a Calilegua .70 .15
1650 A752 5a Chaco .70 .15
1651 A752 5a Los Glaciares .70 .15
Nos. 1647-1651 (5) 3.50 .75

Admission of Argentina to the ITU, Cent. A769

1989, May 6 Perf. 13½
1652 A769 10a multicolored .45 .20

World Model Aircraft Championships — A770

1989, May 27 Litho. Perf. 13½
1653 A770 5a F1A glider .20 .15
1654 A770 5a F1B rubber band motor .20 .15
1655 A770 10a F1C gas motor .35 .20
Nos. 1653-1655 (3) .75 .50

French Revolution, Bicent. — A771

Designs: 10a, "All men are born free and equal." 15a, French flag and *La Marianne*, by Gandon. 25a, *Liberty Guiding the People*, by Delacroix.

1989, July 1 Litho. Perf. 13½
1656 A771 10a shown .15 .15
1657 A771 15a multicolored .15 .15

Souvenir Sheet
Perf. 12
1658 A771 25a multicolored .25 .15

No. 1658 contains one 40x30mm stamp.

The Republic, a Bronze Bust in the Congreso de la Nacion, Buenos Aires — A772

1989, Aug. 12 Litho. Perf. 13½
1659 A772 300a on 50a multi .75 .50

Peaceful transition of power (presidential office). Not issued without surcharge.

Immigration to Argentina — A773

1989, Aug. 19 Perf. 13½
1660 A773 150a S.S. *Weser*, 1889 .65 .35
1661 A773 200a Immigrant hotel, 1889 .75 .45

Souvenir Sheet
Perf. 12
1662 Sheet of 2 1.65 1.65
a. A773 150a like No. 1660 .65 .35
b. A773 200a like No. 1661 .75 .45

No. 1662 contains 40c30mm stamps.

Famous Men A774

Designs: No. 1663, Fr. Guillermo Furlong (1889-1974), historian, and title page of *The Jesuits*. No. 1664, Dr. Gregorio Alvarez (1889-1986), physician, and title page of *Canto a Chos Malal*. 200a, Brig.-Gen. Enrique Martinez (1789-1870) and lithograph *La Batalla de Maipu*, by Teodoro Gericault.

1989, Oct. 7 Litho. Perf. 13½
1663 A774 150a multicolored .35 .20
1664 A774 150a multicolored .35 .20
1665 A774 200a multicolored .35 .20
Nos. 1663-1665 (3) 1.05 .60

America Issue — A775

Emblem of the Postal Union of the Americas and Spain (PUAS) and pre-Columbian art from Catamarca Province: 200a, Wooden mask from Atajo, Loma Morada. 300a, Urn of the Santa Maria Culture (Phase 3) from Punta de Balastro, Santa Maria Department.

1989, Oct. 14
1666 A775 200a multicolored .50 .35
1667 A775 300a multicolored .75 .50

Federal Police Week — A776

Children's drawings: No. 1668, Diego Molinari, age 13. No. 1669, Carlos Alberto Sarago, age 8. No. 1670, Roxana Andrea Osuna, age 7. No. 1671, Pablo Javier Quaglia, age 9.

1989, Oct. 28 Litho. Perf. 13½
1668 A776 100a multi .25 .15
1669 A776 100a multi .25 .15
1670 A776 150a multi .40 .20
1671 A776 150a multi .40 .20
Nos. 1668-1671 (4) 1.30 .70

Battle of Vuelta de Obligado, 1845 — A777

(Illustration reduced.)

1989, Dec. 2 Litho. Perf. 13x13½
1672 A777 300a multicolored .40 .20

Paintings A778

Cristo de los Cerros, Sculpture by Chipo Cespedes — A779

1989, Dec. 2 Perf. 13½
1673 A778 200a Gato Frias .35 .20
1674 A778 200a Maria Carballido .35 .20
1675 A779 300a shown .35 .20
Nos. 1673-1675 (3) 1.05 .60

Christmas.

Buenos Aires Port, Cent. — A780

(Illustration reduced.)

1990, Mar. 3 Litho. Perf. 13½
1676 A780 Strip of 4 7.50 2.50
a.-d. 200a any single 1.25 .65

Aconcagua Intl. Fair, Mendoza — A781

Design: Aconcagua mountain, Los Horcones Lagoon and fair emblem.
(Illustration reduced.)

1990, Mar. 3
1677 A781 Pair 2.00 1.00
a.-b. 500a any single 1.00 .50

Natl. Savings and Insurance Fund, 75th Anniv. A782

1990, May 5 Litho. Perf. 13½
1678 A782 1000a multicolored .35 .20

1990 World Cup Soccer Championships, Italy — A783

Designs: a, Athlete's torso (striped jersey). b, Athlete's torso (solid jersey). c, Players' feet, soccer ball. d, Player (knee to waist).

1990, May 5
1679 Sheet of 4 5.00 5.00
a.-d. A783 2500a multicolored 1.00 1.00

Carlos Pellegrini, Commercial High School Founder, Cent. — A784

1990, June 2 Litho. Perf. 13½
1680 A784 2000a multicolored .30 .20

Youth Against Drugs A785

1990, June 2
1681 A785 2000a multicolored .30 .20

Intl. Literacy Year A786

1990, July 14 Litho. Perf. 13½
1682 A786 2000a multicolored .30 .20

Flower Type of 1982 in New Currency

1989-90 Photo. Perf. 13½
1683 A641 10a like #1433 .15 .15
1684 A641 20a like #1435A .15 .15
1685 A641 50a like #1354 .15 .15
1686 A641 100a like #1439 .20 .15
1687 A641 300a like #1345 .40 .20
1688 A641 500a like #1441 .65 .35
1689 A641 1000a like #1355 .15 .15
1690 A641 5000a like #1349 1.00 .70
1691 A641 10,000a like #1350 1.50 1.00
Nos. 1683-1691 (9) 4.35 3.00

Issued: 20a, 100a, 300a, 500a, 8/1/89; 10a, 8/24/89; 50a, 8/30/89; 1000, 3/8/90; 5000a, 4/6/90; 10,000a, 7/2/90.

ARGENTINA

World Basketball Championships A787

1990, Aug. 11   Litho.   Perf. 13½
1703 A787 2000a multicolored   2.00 1.50

Souvenir Sheet
Perf. 12
1704 A787 5000a Jump ball   3.75 2.75

Postal Union of the Americas and Spain, 14th Congress A788

1990, Sept. 15   Litho.   Perf. 13½
1705 A788 3000a Arms, seal   1.50   .75
1706 A788 3000a Sailing ships   1.50   .75
1707 A788 3000a Modern freighter   1.50   .75
1708 A788 3000a Van, cargo plane   1.50   .75
  Nos. 1705-1708 (4)   6.00 3.00

America Issue A789

1990, Oct. 13
1709 A789 3000a Iguacu Falls,
                hamelia erecta   1.50   .60
1710 A789 3000a Puerto Deseado,
                elephant seal   1.50   .60

Natl. Parks Type of 1987

1990, Oct. 27   Perf. 13x13½
1715 A752 3000a Lanin   1.50   .65
1716 A752 3000a Laguna Blanca   1.50   .65
1717 A752 3000a Perito Moreno   1.50   .65
1718 A752 3000a Puelo   1.50   .65
1719 A752 3000a El Rey   1.50   .65
  Nos. 1715-1719 (5)   7.50 3.25

Stamp Day A790

1990, Oct. 27   Perf. 13½
1720 A790 3000a multicolored   1.50   .60

Salvation Army, Cent. A793

Designs: No. 1722, Natl. University of the Littoral, Santa Fe, cent.

1990, Dec. 1   Litho.   Perf. 13½
1721 A793 3000a multicolored   1.75 1.00
1722 A793 3000a multicolored   1.75 1.00
  a.   Pair, #1721-1722 + label   3.75 2.25

Miniature Sheets

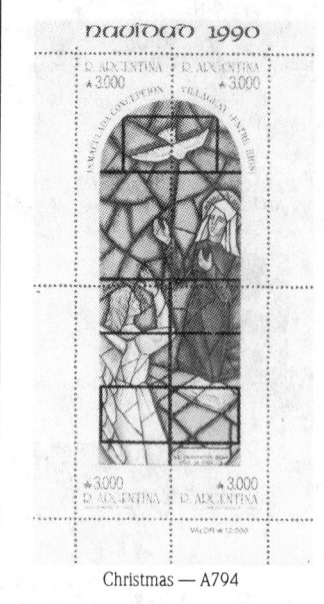

Christmas — A794

Stained glass windows: No. 1723, The Immaculate Conception. No. 1724, The Nativity. No. 1725, Presentation of Jesus at the Temple.

1990, Dec. 1   Perf. 13½x13
Sheets of 4
1723 A794 3000a #a.-d.   6.00 6.00
1724 A794 3000a #a.-d.   6.00 6.00
1725 A794 3000a #a.-d.   6.00 6.00

Landscapes A795

Paintings: No. 1726, Los Sauces, by Atilio Malinverno. No. 1727, Paisaje, by Pio Collivadino, vert.

1991, May 4   Litho.   Perf. 13½
1726 A795 4000a multicolored   1.00   .85
1727 A795 4000a multicolored   1.00   .85

Return of Remains of Juan Manuel de Rosas (1793-1877) A796

1991, June 1   Litho.   Perf. 13½
1728 A796 4000a multicolored   1.00   .85

Swiss Confederation, 700th Anniv. — A797

1991, Aug. 3   Litho.   Perf. 13½
1729 A797 4000a multicolored   .95   .80

Miniature Sheet

Cartoons — A798

Designs: a, Hernan, the Corsair by Jose Luis Salinas. b, Don Fulgencio by Lino Palacio. c, Medical Rules of Salerno by Oscar Esteban Conti. d, Buenos Aires Undershirt by Alejandro del Prado. e, Girls! by Jose A.G. Divito. f, Langostino by Eduardo Carlos Ferro. g, Mafalda by Joaquin Salvador Lavoro. h, Mort Cinder by Alberto Breccia.

1991, Aug. 3
1730 A798 4000a Sheet of 8, #a.-h.   7.75 7.50

City of La Rioja, 400th Anniv. — A799

1991, Sept. 14   Litho.   Perf. 13½
1731 A799 4000a multicolored   1.00   .85

First Balloon Flight over the Andes, 75th Anniv. — A800

Illustration reduced.

1991, Sept. 14
1732 A800 4000a multicolored   1.00   .85

America Issue A801

Designs: No. 1733, Magellan's caravel, Our Lady of Victory. No. 1734, Ships of Juan Diaz de Solis.

1991, Nov. 9   Litho.   Perf. 13½
1733 A801 4000a multicolored   1.00   .80
1734 A801 4000a multicolored   1.00   .80

Anniversaries — A802

Designs: a, J. Enrique Pestalozzi, founder of newspaper, Daily Argentinian. b, Leandro N. Alem, founder of Radical People's Party. c, Man with rifle, emblem of Argentine Federal Shooting Club. d, Dr. Nicasio Etchepareborda, emblem of College of Odontology. e, Dalmiro Huergo, emblem of Graduate School of Economics.

1991, Nov. 30
1735 A802 4000a Strip of 5, #a.-e.   5.00 4.00

Christmas — A803

Stained glass windows from Our Lady of Lourdes Basilica, Buenos Aires: Nos. 1736a-1736b, Top and bottom portions of Virgin of the Valley, Catamarca. Nos. 1736c-1736d, Top and bottom portions of Virgin of the Rosary of the Miracle, Cordoba.

1991, Nov. 30
1736 A803 4000a Block of 4, #a.-d.   5.00 3.50

Famous Men A804

Designs: a, Gen. Juan de Lavalle (1797-1841), Peruvian medal of honor. b, Brig. Gen. Jose Maria del Rosario Siriaco Paz (1791-1854), medal. c, Marco Manuel de Avellaneda (1813-1841), lawyer. d, Guillermo Enrique Hudson (1841-1922), author.

1991, Dec. 14   Litho.   Perf. 13½
1737 A804 4000a Block of 4, #a.-d.   5.00 3.50

Birds — A805

1991, Dec. 28
1738 A805 4000a Pterocnemia pennata   1.25   .85
1739 A805 4000a Morphnu guianensis   1.25   .85
1740 A805 4000a Ara chloroptera   1.25   .85
  Nos. 1738-1740 (3)   3.75 2.55

Miniature Sheet

Arbrafex '92, Argentina-Brazil Philatelic Exhibition — A806

Traditional costumes: a, Gaucho, woman. b, Gaucho, horse. c, Gaucho in store. d, Gaucho holding lariat.

1992   Litho.   Perf. 13½
1741 A806 38c Sheet of 4, #a.-d.   3.00 3.00

Natl. Parks Type of 1987

1992, Apr. 4   Litho.   Perf. 13x13½
1742 A752 38c Alerces   .75   .55
1743 A752 38c Formosa Nature Reserve   .75   .55
1744 A752 38c Petrified Forest   .75   .55
1745 A752 38c Arrayanes   .75   .55
1746 A752 38c Laguna de los
               Pozuelos   .75   .55
  Nos. 1742-1746 (5)   3.75 2.75

ARGENTINA

Mushrooms — A807

1992-94		Photo.	Perf. 13½	
1748	A807	10c Psilocybe cubensis	.20	.15
1749	A807	25c Coprinus atramentarius	.50	.35
a.		Wmk. 365	30.00	30.00
1750	A807	38c like #1748	.75	.55
1751	A807	48c like #1749	.95	.65
1752	A807	50c Suillus granulatus	1.00	.70
1753	A807	51c Morchella esculenta	1.00	.70
1754	A807	61c Amanita muscaria	1.25	.85
1755	A807	68c Coprinus comatus	1.25	.85
1756	A807	1p like #1754	2.00	1.40
1757	A807	1.25p like #1752	2.50	1.75
1758	A807	1.77p Stropharia oerugninosa	3.50	2.50
1759	A807	2p like #1753	4.00	2.75
		Nos. 1748-1759 (12)	18.90	13.20

No. 1758 not issued without overprint "Centro Filatelico de Neuquen y Rio Negro 50th Aniversario."

Issued: 38c, 4/4/92; 48c, 51c, 61c, 8/1/92; 1.77p, 11/7/92; 25c, 50c, 8/17/93; 1p, 2p, 8/26/93; 10c, 1/11/94; 68c, 1.25p, 10/10/92; #1749a, 1997.

See design A838.

Falkland Islands War, 10th Anniv. A808

1992, May 2		Litho.	Perf. 13½	
1767	A808	38c Pucara 1A-58	.75	.55
1768	A808	38c Cruiser Gen. Belgrano	.75	.55
1769	A808	38c Soldier and truck	.75	.55
		Nos. 1767-1769 (3)	2.25	1.65

Miniature Sheet

Preserve the Environment A809

a, Deer. b, Geese. c, Butterflies. d, Whale.

1992, June 6		Litho.	Perf. 12	
1770	A809	38c Sheet of 4, #a.-d.	3.00	3.00

Paintings by Florencio Molina Campos A810

1992, June 6			Perf. 13½	
1771	A810	38c A La Sombra	.75	.55
1772	A810	38c Tileforo Areco, vert.	.75	.55

Famous Men A811

Designs: No. 1773, Gen. Lucio N. Mansilla (1792-1871). No. 1774, Jose Manuel Estrada (1842-1894), writer. No. 1775, Brig. Gen. Jose I. Garmendia (1842-1915).

1992, July 4		Litho.	Perf. 13½	
1773	A811	38c multicolored	.75	.55
1774	A811	38c multicolored	.75	.55
1775	A811	38c multicolored	.75	.55
		Nos. 1773-1775 (3)	2.25	1.65

Fight Against Drugs — A812

1992, Aug. 1			Perf. 13½x13	
1776	A812	38c multicolored	.75	.55

Col. Jose M. Calaza, 140th Birth Anniv. A813

1992, Sept. 5		Litho.	Perf. 13½	
1777	A813	38c multicolored	.75	.55

Discovery of America, 500th Anniv. — A814

Designs: a, Columbus, castle, ship. b, Native drawings, Columbus.

1992, Oct. 10		Litho.	Perf. 13½	
1778	A814	38c Pair, #a.-b.	1.50	1.50

Argentine Film Posters — A815

1992, Nov. 7		Litho.	Perf. 13½	
1779	A815	38c Dios Se Lo Pague, 1948	.75	.55
1780	A815	38c Las Aguas Bajan Turbias, 1952	.75	.55
1781	A815	38c Un Guapo Del 900, 1960	.75	.55
1782	A815	38c La Tregua, 1974	.75	.55
1783	A815	38c La Historia Oficial, 1984	.75	.55
		Nos. 1779-1783 (5)	3.75	2.75

Christmas — A816

1992, Nov. 28				
1784	A816	38c multicolored	.75	.55

Miniature Sheet

Iberoprenfil '92 — A817

Lighthouses: a, Punta Mogotes. b, Rio Negro. c, San Antonio. d, Cabo Blanco.

1992, Dec. 5				
1785	A817	38c Sheet of 4, #a.-d.	3.00	3.00

Fight Against AIDS
A818   A819

1992, Dec. 12		Litho.	Perf. 13½	
1786	A818	10c multicolored	.20	.15
1787	A819	26c multicolored	.55	.40

Intl. Space Year A820

1992, Dec. 19				
1788	A820	38c multicolored	.75	.55

Souvenir Sheet

Miraculous Lord Crucifix, 400th Anniv. of Arrival in America — A821

1992, Dec. 26			Perf. 12	
1789	A821	76c multicolored	1.50	1.50

Jujuy City, 400th Anniv. — A822

1993, Apr. 24		Litho.	Perf. 13½	
1790	A822	38c multicolored	.75	.55

Argentina Soccer Assoc., Cent. A823

1993, Mar. 27				
1791	A823	38c multicolored	.75	.55

Souvenir Sheet

Intl. Philatelic Exhibitions — A824

Designs: a, 38c, City Hall, Poznan, Poland. b, 48c, Statue of Christ the Redeemer, Rio de Janeiro, Brazil. c, 76c, Royal Palace, Bangkok, Thailand.

1993, May 8		Litho.	Perf. 12	
1792	A824	Sheet of 3, #a.-c.	3.25	3.25

Polska '93 (#1792a), Brasiliana '93 (#1792b), Bangkok '92 (#1792c).

Luis C. Candelaria's Flight Over Andes Mountains, 75th Anniv. — A825

1993, June 26		Litho.	Perf. 13x13½	
1793	A825	38c multicolored	.75	.55

Illustration reduced.

Order of San Martin, 50th Anniv. — A826

National History Academy, Cent. — A827

1993, May 29			Perf. 13½	
1794	A826	38c multicolored	.75	.55
1795	A827	38c multicolored	.75	.55

ARGENTINA

Armed Forces Memorial Day — A828

1993, June 12
1796 A828 38c National Gendarmerie .75 .55
1797 A828 38c Coast Guard .75 .55

Paintings A829

#1798, Old House, by Norberto Russo. #1799, Pa'las Casas, by Adriana Zaefferer.

1993, Aug. 14 Litho. Perf. 13½
1798 A829 38c multicolored .75 .55
1799 A829 38c multicolored .75 .55

Pato — A830

1993, Aug. 28 Litho. Perf. 12
1800 A830 1p multicolored 2.00 1.40

Nut-Bearing Trees — A831

#1801, Enterolobium contortisiliquum. #1802, Prosopis alba. #1803, Magnolia grandiflora. #1804, Erythrina falcata. Illustration reduced.

1993, Sept. 25 Litho. Perf. 13x13½
1801 A831 75c multicolored 1.50 1.00
1802 A831 75c multicolored 1.50 1.00
1803 A831 1.50p multicolored 3.00 2.00
1804 A831 1.50p multicolored 3.00 2.00
Nos. 1801-1804 (4) 9.00 6.00

America Issue A832

Whales: 50c, Eubalaena australis. 75c, Cephalorhynchus commersonii.

1993, Oct. 9 Perf. 13½
1805 A832 50c multicolored 1.00 .70
1806 A832 75c multicolored 1.50 1.10

Miniature Sheet

Christmas, New Year — A833

Denomination at: a, UL. b, UR. c, LL. d, LR.

1993, Dec. 4 Litho. Perf. 13½
1807 A833 75c Sheet of 4, #a.-d. 6.00 6.00

Cave of the Hands, Santa Cruz — A834

1993, Dec. 18
1808 A834 1p multicolored 2.00 1.40

New Emblem, Argentine Postal Service — A835

Illustration reduced.

1994, Jan. 8 Perf. 11½
1809 A835 75c multicolored 1.50 1.00

A836

1994 World Cup Soccer Championships, US — A837

Players from: 25c, Germany, 1990. 50c, Brazil, 1970. 75c, 1.50p, Argentina, 1986. 1p, Italy, 1982.

1994, June 11 Perf. 13½
1810 A836 25c multicolored .50 .15
1811 A836 50c multicolored 1.00 .70
1812 A836 75c multicolored 1.50 1.00
1813 A836 1p multicolored 2.00 1.40
Nos. 1810-1813 (4) 5.00 3.25

Souvenir Sheet
Perf. 12
1814 A836 1.50p multicolored 3.00 3.00

No. 1814 contains one 40x50mm stamp with continuous design.
Nos. 1810-1813 issued in sheets containing a block of 4 of each stamp + 4 labels.

1994, July 23 Perf. 13½

Drawings of championships by: No. 1815, Julian Lisenberg. No. 1816, Matias Taylor, vert. No. 1817, Torcuato S. Gonzalez Agote, vert. No. 1818, Maria Paula Palma.

1815 A837 75c multicolored 1.50 1.00
1816 A837 75c multicolored 1.50 1.00
1817 A837 75c multicolored 1.50 1.00
1818 A837 75c multicolored 1.50 1.00
Nos. 1815-1818 (4) 6.00 4.00

A838

Molothrus Badius — A838a

1994-95 Litho. Perf. 13½
1819 A838 10c like #1748 .20 .15
1820 A838 25c like #1749 .50 .35
1823 A838 50c like #1752 1.00 .70
1828 A838 1p like #1754 2.00 1.40
1832 A838 2p like #1753 4.00 2.75
1835 A838a 9.40p multicolored 19.00 13.00
Nos. 1819-1835 (6) 26.70 18.35

See design A807.
Issued: 10c, 25c, 50c, 1p, 2p, 6/14/94; 9.40p, 4/12/95.
This is an expanding set. Numbers may change.

Wildlife of Falkland Islands A839

Designs: 25c, Melanodera melanodera. 50c, Pygoscelis papua. 75c, Tachyeres brachypterus. 1p, Mirounga leonina.

1994, Aug 6
1839 A839 25c multicolored .50 .35
1840 A839 50c multicolored 1.00 .70
1841 A839 75c multicolored 1.50 1.00
1842 A839 1p multicolored 2.00 1.40
Nos. 1839-1842 (4) 5.00 3.45

City of San Luis, 400th Anniv. — A840

1994, Aug. 20
1843 A840 75c multicolored 1.50 1.00

Province of Tierra del Fuego, Antarctica and South Atlantic Islands — A841

1994, Aug. 20
1844 A841 75c multicolored 1.50 1.00

Argentine Inventors — A842

Designs: No. 1845, Ladislao Jose Biro (1899-1985), ball point pen. No. 1846, Raul Pateras de Pescara (1890-1966), helicopter. No. 1847, Quirino Cristiani (1896-1984), animated drawings. No. 1848, Enrique Finochietto (1881-1948), surgical instruments.

1994, Oct. 1
1845 A842 75c multicolored 1.50 1.00
1846 A842 75c multicolored 1.50 1.00
1847 A842 75c multicolored 1.50 1.00
1848 A842 75c multicolored 1.50 1.00
a. Block of 4, #1845-1848 6.00 6.00

Issued in sheets containing 4 #1848a + 4 labels.

UNICEF Christmas A843

1994, Nov. 26 Litho. Perf. 11½
1849 A843 50c shown 1.00 .70
1850 A843 75c Bell, bulb, star, diff. 1.50 1.00

Take Care of Our Planet A844

Children's paintings: No. 1851, Boy, girl holding earth, vert. No. 1852, Children outdoors, vert. No. 1853, World as house. No. 1854, People around "world" table.

1994, Dec. 3 Perf. 13½
1851 A844 25c multicolored .50 .35
1852 A844 25c multicolored .50 .35
1853 A844 50c multicolored 1.00 .70
1854 A844 50c multicolored 1.00 .70
Nos. 1851-1854 (4) 3.00 2.10

Christmas — A845

1994, Dec. 10
1855 A845 50c Annunciation 1.00 .70
1856 A845 75c Madonna & Child 1.50 1.00

Nos. 1855-1856 each issued in sheets of 20 + 5 labels.

12th Pan American Games, Mar del Plata A846

1995 Litho. Perf. 13½
1857 A846 75c Running 1.50 1.00
1858 A846 75c Cycling 1.50 1.00
1859 A846 75c Diving 1.50 1.00
1860 A846 1.25p Gymnastics, vert. 2.50 1.75
1861 A846 1.25p Soccer, vert. 2.50 1.75
Nos. 1857-1861 (5) 9.50 6.50

Issued: No. 1857, 2/18; others, 3/11.

ARGENTINA

Natl. Constitution — A847

Design: 75c, Natl. Congress Dome, woman from statue The Republic Triumphant.

1995, Apr. 8
1862 A847 75c multicolored ... 1.50 1.00

21st Intl. Book Fair — A848

Illustration reduced.

1995, Apr. 8
1863 A848 75c multicolored ... 1.50 1.00

Birds A849

1995 Litho. Perf. 13½
1876 A849 5p Carduelis magellanica ... 10.00 7.00
1880 A849 10p Zonotrichia capensis ... 20.00 14.00

Issued: 5p, 10p, 5/23/95. This is an expanding set. Numbers may change.

A850

1995, Mar. 25 Litho. Die Cut
Self-Adhesive
1883A A850 25c multicolored ... .50 .35
1884 A850 75c multicolored ... 1.50 1.00
a. Booklet pane, 2 #1883A, 6 #1884 ... 12.50
  Complete booklet, #1884a ... 12.50
b. Booklet pane, 4 #1883A, 12 #1884 ... 25.00
  Complete booklet, #1884b ... 25.00

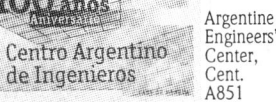

Argentine Engineers' Center, Cent. A851

1995, June 3 Perf. 13½
1885 A851 75c multicolored ... 1.50 1.00

Jose Marti (1853-95) — A852

#1887, Antonio Jose de Sucre (1795-1830).

1995, Aug. 12 Litho. Perf. 13½
1886 A852 1p multicolored ... 2.00 1.40
1887 A852 1p multicolored ... 2.00 1.40

Fauna — A853

1995, Sept. 1 Litho. Perf. 13½
1888 A853 5c Ostrich ... .15 .15
1889 A853 25c Penguin ... .50 .35
1890 A853 50c Toucan ... 1.00 .70
1891 A853 75c Condor ... 1.50 1.00
1892 A853 1p Owl ... 2.00 1.40
1893 A853 2p Bigua ... 4.00 2.75
1894 A853 2.75p Tero ... 5.50 3.75
Booklet Stamps
Perf. 13½ on 2 or 3 Sides
1895 A853 25c Alligator ... .50 .35
1896 A853 50c Fox ... 1.00 .70
1897 A853 75c Anteater ... 1.50 1.00
1898 A853 75c Deer ... 1.50 1.00
1899 A853 75c Whale ... 1.50 1.00
a. Booklet pane, 1 each Nos. 1889-1891, 1895-1899 ... 9.00
  Complete booklet, #1899a ... 9.00
Nos. 1888-1899 (12) ... 20.65 14.15

See No. 1958.

Native Heritage — A854

a, Cave drawings, shifting sands. b, Stone mask. c, Anthropomorphous vessel. d, Woven textile.

1995, Sept. 9
1900 A854 75c Block of 4, #a.-d. ... 6.00 6.00

Sunflower, Postal Service Emblem — A855

1995, Oct. 7
1901 A855 75c multicolored ... 1.50 1.00

Juan D. Peron (1895-1974) — A856

1995, Oct. 7
1902 A856 75c lt ol bis & dk bl ... 1.50 1.00

Miniature Sheet

Anniversaries — A857

Annivs: a, UN, 50th. b, ICAO, 50th (in 1994). c, FAO, 50th. d, ILO, 75th (in 1994).

1995, Oct. 14 Perf. 12
1903 A857 75c Sheet of 4, #a.-d. ... 6.00 6.00

Christmas and New Year — A858

Designs: Nos. 1904, 1908, Christmas tree, presents. No. 1905, "1996." No. 1906, Champagne glasses. No. 1907, Present.

1995, Nov. 25 Litho. Perf. 13½
1904 A858 75c multicolored ... 1.50 1.00
Booklet Stamps
Perf. 13½ on 1 or 2 Sides
1905 A858 75c multicolored ... 1.50 1.00
1906 A858 75c multicolored ... 1.50 1.00
1907 A858 75c multicolored ... 1.50 1.00
1908 A858 75c multicolored ... 1.50 1.00
a. Booklet pane, #1905-1908 + label ... 6.00
  Complete booklet, #1908a ... 6.00
Nos. 1904-1908 (5) ... 7.50 5.00

No. 1908a is a continuous design. Ribbon extends from edge to edge on #1908 and stops at edge of package on #1905.

Miniature Sheet

Motion Pictures, Cent. — A859

Black and white film clips, director: a, The Battleship Potemkin, Sergei Eisenstein (Soviet Union). b, Casablanca, Michael Curtiz (US). c, Bicycle Thief, Vittorio De Sica (Italy). d, Limelights, Charles Chaplin (England). e, The 400 Blows, Francois Truffaut (France). f, Chronicle of the Lonely Child, Leonardo Favio (Argentina).

1995, Dec. 2 Perf. 13½
1909 A859 75c Sheet of 6, #a.-f. ... 9.00 9.00

The Sky — A860

1995, Dec. 16 Perf. 13½ on 3 Sides
Booklet Stamps
1910 A860 25c Dirigible ... .50 .35
1911 A860 25c Kite ... .50 .35
1912 A860 25c Hot air balloon ... .50 .35
1913 A860 50c Balloons ... 1.00 .70
1914 A860 50c Paper airplane ... 1.00 .70
1915 A860 75c Airplane ... 1.50 1.00
1916 A860 75c Helicopter ... 1.50 1.00
1917 A860 75c Parachute ... 1.50 1.00
a. Booklet pane, #1910-1917 + label ... 8.00
  Complete booklet, No. 1917a ... 8.00

Nos. 1910-1917 do not appear in Scott number order in No. 1917a, which has a continuous design.

America Issue A861

Postal vehicles from Postal and Telegraph Museum: No. 1918, Horse and carriage. No. 1919, Truck.

1995, Dec. 16 Perf. 13½
1918 A861 75c multicolored ... 1.50 1.00
1919 A861 75c multicolored ... 1.50 1.00

Olympic Games, Cent. A862

1996, Mar. 30 Litho. Perf. 13½
1920 A862 75c Running ... 1.50 1.00
1921 A862 1p Discus ... 2.00 1.40

Physicians A863

Designs: a, Francisco J. Muniz (1795-1871). b, Ricardo Gutierrez (1838-96). c, Ignacio Pirovano (1844-95). d, Esteban L. Maradona (1895-1995).

1996, Apr. 20 Litho. Perf. 12
1922 A863 50c Sheet of 4, #a.-d. ... 4.00 4.00
a.-d. Any single ... 1.00 1.00

Jerusalem, 3000th Anniv. — A864

7th cent. mosaic maps of city, denomination at: No. 1923, LL. No. 1924, LR.

1996, May 18 Litho. Perf. 13½
1923 A864 75c multicolored ... 1.50 1.00
1924 A864 75c multicolored ... 1.50 1.00
a. Pair, #1923-1924 ... 3.00 3.00

No. 1924a is a continuous design and was issued in sheets of 8 + 4 labels.

Endangered Fauna — A865

1996, June 15 Litho. Perf. 13½
1925 A865 75c Capybara ... 1.50 1.00
1926 A865 75c Guanaco ... 1.50 1.00
a. Pair, #1925-1926 ... 3.00 3.00

America Issue.

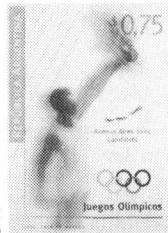

Summer Olympic Games — A866

Designs: 75c, Torch bearer, Buenos Aires, candidate for 2004 Games. 1p, Men's eight with coxswain, Atlanta, 1996.

1996, July 6
1927 A866 75c multicolored ... 1.50 1.00
1928 A866 1p multicolored ... 2.00 1.40

ARGENTINA

National Parks — A867

Wildlife, national park: No. 1929, Mountain turkey, Diamante. No. 1930, Parrot, San Antonio Nature Reserve. No. 1931, Deer, Otamendi Natl. Reserve. No. 1932, Rabbit, El Leoncito Nature Reserve.
Illustration reduced.

1996, Aug. 24   Litho.   Perf. 13x13½
1929	A867	75c multicolored	1.50	1.00
1930	A867	75c multicolored	1.50	1.00
1931	A867	75c multicolored	1.50	1.00
1932	A867	75c multicolored	1.50	1.00
	Nos. 1929-1932 (4)		6.00	4.00

Central Post Office, Buenos Aires — A868

1996, Oct. 5   Litho.   Die Cut
Self-Adhesive
Size: 25x35mm
| 1933 | A868 | 75c multicolored | 1.50 | 1.50 |

Vignette of No. 1933 is broken by circular and rectangular die cut areas to guard against reuse. See Nos. 1983-1984.

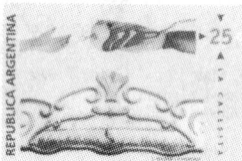

Carousel Figures — A869

#1934, Hand-carved decorative ornaments. #1935, Child on carousel horse. #1936, Carousel. #1937, Heads of horses. #1938, Child in airplane. #1939, Carousel pig. #1940, Boy in car.

1996, Oct. 5   Perf. 13½ Horiz.
Booklet Stamps
1934	A869	25c multicolored	.50	.50
1935	A869	25c multicolored	.50	.50
1936	A869	25c multicolored	.50	.50
1937	A869	50c multicolored	1.00	1.00
1938	A869	50c multicolored	1.00	1.00
1939	A869	50c multicolored	1.00	1.00
1940	A869	75c multicolored	1.50	1.50
a.	Booklet pane, #1934-1940		6.00	
	Complete booklet, #1940a		6.00	

Sequence of stamps in No. 1940a: No. 1940, 1934, 1937, 1935, 1938, 1936, 1939.

Port Belgrano Naval Base, Cent. — A870

Designs: 25c, LST "San Antonio." 50c, Corvette *Rosales*. 75c, Destroyer *Hercules*. 1p, Aircraft carrier, "25th of May."

1996-97   Litho.   Perf. 13½
1941	A870	25c multicolored	.50	.50
1942	A870	50c multicolored	1.00	1.00
1943	A870	75c multicolored	1.50	1.50
1944	A870	1p multicolored	2.00	2.00
	Nos. 1941-1944 (4)		5.00	5.00

Issued: 25c, 1p, 10/5/96; 50c, 75c, 2/1/97.

Christmas A871

Tapestries: 75c, Nativity, by Gladys Angelica Rinaldi, vert. 1p, Candles, by Norma Bonet de Maekawa.

1996, Nov. 30   Litho.   Perf. 13½
| 1945 | A871 | 75c multicolored | 1.50 | 1.50 |
| 1946 | A871 | 1p multicolored | 2.00 | 2.00 |

Exploration of Antarctica — A872

Designs: 75c, Melchior Base. 1.25p, icebreaker ARA Alte. Irizar.

1996, Nov. 30
| 1947 | A872 | 75c multicolored | 1.50 | 1.50 |
| 1948 | A872 | 1.25p multicolored | 2.50 | 2.50 |

National Gallery, Cent. — A873

Paintings of women by: 75c, Paul Gauguin, vert. No. 1950, Edouard Monet, vert. No. 1951, Amedeo Modigiliani, vert. 1.25p, Pablo Picasso.

1996, Dec. 14
1949	A873	75c multicolored	1.50	1.50
1950	A873	1p multicolored	2.00	2.00
1951	A873	1p multicolored	2.00	2.00
1952	A873	1.25p multicolored	2.50	2.50
	Nos. 1949-1952 (4)		8.00	8.00

Mining Industry — A874

1997, Feb. 1   Litho.   Perf. 13½
| 1953 | A874 | 75c Granite | 1.50 | 1.50 |
| 1954 | A874 | 1.25p Borax | 2.50 | 2.50 |

Traditional Costumes — A875

1997, Feb. 22   Litho.   Perf. 13½
| 1955 | A875 | 75c multicolored | 1.50 | 1.50 |

America issue.

Repatriation of the Curved Sword of Gen. San Martin, Cent. — A876

1997, Mar. 15   Litho.   Perf. 13½
| 1956 | A876 | 75c multicolored | 1.50 | 1.50 |

29th Youth Rugby World Championships — A877

1997, Mar. 22
| 1957 | A877 | 75c multicolored | 1.50 | 1.50 |

Fauna Type of 1995
1997, Feb. 22   Litho.   Perf. 13½
| 1958 | A853 | 10c Reddish sandpiper | .20 | .20 |

Buenos Aires-Rio de Janeiro Regatta, 50th Anniv. — A879

1997, Apr. 5   Litho.   Perf. 13½
| 1960 | A879 | 75c Fortuna II | 1.50 | 1.50 |

Natl. History Museum, Cent. A880

1997, May 17
| 1961 | A880 | 75c multicolored | 1.50 | 1.50 |

La Plata Natl. University, Cent. — A881

1997, May 17
| 1962 | A881 | 75c multicolored | 1.50 | 1.50 |

Lighthouses A882

Designs: a, Cabo Virgenes. b, Isla Pingüino. c, San Juan de Salvamento. d, Punta Delgada.

1997, May 31
| 1963 | A882 | 75c Sheet of 4, #a.-d. | 6.00 | 6.00 |

Ramón J. Cárcano (1860-1946), Developer of Postal and Telegraph System A883

1997, May 31
| 1964 | A883 | 75c multicolored | 1.50 | 1.50 |

Buenos Aires, Candidate for 2004 Summer Olympics — A884

1997, June 21
| 1965 | A884 | 75c multicolored | 1.50 | 1.50 |

First Electric Tram in Buenos Aires, Cent. A885

Designs: a, Lacroze Suburban Service Tram Co, 1912. b, Lacroze Urban Service Tram Co., 1927. c, Anglo Argentina Tram Co., 1930. d, Buenos Aires City Transportation Corp., 1942. e, Military Manufacture Tram, 1956. f, South Electric Tram, 1908.

1997, July 12
Sheet of 6
| 1966 | A885 | 75c #a.-f. + 2 labels | 9.00 | 9.00 |

Monument to Joaquín V. González (1863-1923), La Rioja — A886

1997, Aug. 9
| 1967 | A886 | 75c multicolored | 1.50 | 1.50 |

Musicians and Composers A887

Paintings: No. 1968, Alberto Ginastera (1916-83), by Carlos Nine. No. 1969, Astor Piazzolla (1921-92), by Carlos Alonso. No. 1970, Anibal Troilo (1914-75), by Hermenegildo Sabat. No. 1971, Atahualpa Yupanqui (b. 1908), by Luis Scafati.

1997, Aug. 9
1968	A887	75c multicolored	1.50	1.50
1969	A887	75c multicolored	1.50	1.50
1970	A887	75c multicolored	1.50	1.50
1971	A887	75c multicolored	1.50	1.50
	Nos. 1968-1971 (4)		6.00	6.00

ARGENTINA

Argentine Authors — A888

Designs: No. 1972, Jorge Luis Borges (1899-1986), maze. No. 1973, Julio Cortázar (1914-84), hop scotch game.

1997, Aug. 30   Litho.   Perf. 13
1972 A888 1p multicolored   2.00 2.00
1973 A888 1p multicolored   2.00 2.00

Women's Political Rights Law, 50th Anniv. A889

1997, Sept. 6   Litho.   Perf. 13½
1974 A889 75c Eva Perón   1.50 1.50

Mercosur (Common Market of Latin America) A890

1997, Sept. 27   Litho.   Perf. 13½
1975 A890 75c multicolored   1.50 1.50

See Bolivia #1019, Brazil #2646, Paraguay #2564, Uruguay #1681.

Launching of Frigate President Sarmiento, Cent. A891

No. 1976, Painting of ship by Hugo Leban. No. 1977: a, Ship. b, Ship's figurehead, vert.

1997, Oct. 4
1976 A891 75c multicolored   1.50 1.50

Souvenir Sheet
Perf. 12
1977 A891 75c Sheet of 2, #a.-b.   3.00 3.00

No. 1977 contains two 40x30mm stamps.

Ernesto "Che" Guevara (1928-67) A892

1997, Oct. 18
1978 A892 75c multicolored   1.50 1.50

Ecology on Stamps — A893

Children's drawings: No. 1979, Animal, by J. Chiapparo, vert. No. 1980, Vicuna, by L.L. Portal, vert. No. 1981, Seal, by A. Lloren. No. 1982, Bird in flight, by J. Saccone.

1997, Nov. 8   Litho.   Perf. 13½
1979 A893 50c multicolored   1.00 1.00
1980 A893 50c multicolored   1.00 1.00
1981 A893 75c multicolored   1.50 1.50
1982 A893 75c multicolored   1.50 1.50
     Nos. 1979-1982 (4)   5.00 5.00

Central Post Office, Buenos Aires, Type of 1996

1997, July 24   Litho.   Die Cut
Self-Adhesive
Size: 23x35mm
1983 A868 25c multicolored   .50 .50
1984 A868 75c multicolored   1.50 1.50
   a. Booklet pane, 2 #1983, 6 #1984   10.00
     Complete booklet, #1984a   10.00

Nos. 1983-1984 are broken at both the top and bottom of each stamp by three lines of wavy die cutting.

Christmas — A893a

Nativity scene tapestries by: #1984B, 1984G, Mary José. #1984C, Elena Aguilar. #1984D, Silvia Pettachi. #1984E, Ana Escobar. #1984F, Alejandra Martinez. #1984H, Nidia Martinez.

1997, Nov. 22   Litho.   Perf. 13½
1984B A893a 75c multicolored   1.50 1.50

Booklet Stamps
Self-Adhesive
Size: 44x27mm
Die Cut
1984C A893a 25c multicolored   .50 .50
1984D A893a 25c multicolored   .50 .50
1984E A893a 50c multicolored   1.00 1.00
1984F A893a 50c multicolored   1.00 1.00
1984G A893a 75c multicolored   1.50 1.50
1984H A893a 75c multicolored   1.50 1.50
   i. Booklet pane, #1984C-1984H   6.00

Nos. 1984C-1984H are broken at upper right by three die cut chevrons.

Mother Teresa (1910-97) A893b

1997, Dec. 27
1984J A893b 75c multicolored   1.50 1.50

Dr. Bernardo A. Houssay (1887-1971), 1947 Nobel Prize Winner in Medicine — A894

1998, Jan. 31   Litho.   Perf. 13½
1985 A894 75c multicolored   1.50 1.50

First Ascension of Mount Aconcagua, Cent. — A895

Illustration reduced.

1998, Feb. 14   Perf. 12
1986 A895 1.25p multicolored   2.50 2.50

Founding of San Martin de los Andes, Cent. A896

1998, Mar. 14   Litho.   Perf. 13½
1987 A896 75c multicolored   1.50 1.50

Regimental Quarters of Gen. San Martin's Mounted Grenadiers A897

Designs: a, Statue. b, Large jar with painting of San Martin. c, Regimental seal. d, Regimental quarters.

1998, Mar. 21   Litho.   Perf. 13½
1988 A897 75c Block of 4, #a.-d.   6.00 6.00

Protection of the Ozone A898

1998, Mar. 28   Litho.   Perf. 13½
1989 A898 75c multicolored   1.50 1.50

America Issue — A899

Letter carriers: #1990, Wearing white uniform. #1991, Carrying letter bag with shoulder strap.

1998, Apr. 4
1990 A899 75c multicolored   1.50 1.50
1991 A899 75c multicolored   1.50 1.50

Characters from Stories by Maria Elena Walsh — A900

#1992, El Reino Del Reves. #1993, Zoo Loco. #1994, Dailan Kifki. #1995, Manuelita.

1998, Apr. 17   Litho.   Die Cut
Booklet Stamps
Self-Adhesive
1992 A900 75c multicolored   1.50 1.50
1993 A900 75c multicolored   1.50 1.50
1994 A900 75c multicolored   1.50 1.50
1995 A900 75c multicolored   1.50 1.50
   a. Complete booklet, #1992-1995   6.00

Historic Chapels A901

#1996, San Pedro de Fiambalá, Catamarca. #1997, Huacalera, Jujuy. #1998, Santo Domingo, La Rioja. #1999, Tumbaya, Jujuy.

1998, Apr. 25   Litho.   Perf. 13x13½
1996 A901 75c multicolored   1.50 1.50
1997 A901 75c multicolored   1.50 1.50
1998 A901 75c multicolored   1.50 1.50
1999 A901 75c multicolored   1.50 1.50
     Nos. 1996-1999 (4)   6.00 6.00

White Helmets, A Commitment to Humanity — A902

1998, May 23   Litho.   Perf. 13½
2000 A902 1p multicolored   2.00 2.00

1998 World Cup Soccer Championships, France — A903

Stylized players representing: a, Argentina. b, Croatia. c, Jamaica. d, Japan.

1998, May 30
2001 A903 75c Block of 4, #a.-d.   6.00 6.00

ARGENTINA

Journalist's Day — A904

1998, June 20
2002 A904 75c multicolored 1.50 1.50

Creation of Argentine Postal System, 250th Anniv. — A905

a, Corrientes design A2, peso coin. b, Building, post box.

1998, June 27
2003 A905 75c Pair, #a.-b. 3.00 3.00

Ruins, Mission St. Ignacio — A906

1998, July 25 Litho. Perf. 13½
2005 A906 75c multicolored 1.50 1.50
Mercosur.

Cattle A907

1998, Aug. 1
2006 A907 25c Brahman .50 .50
2007 A907 25c Aberdeen-Angus .50 .50
2008 A907 50c Hereford 1.00 1.00
2009 A907 50c Criolla 1.00 1.00
2010 A907 75c Holland-Argentina 1.50 1.50
2011 A907 75c Shorthorn 1.50 1.50
 Nos. 2006-2011 (6) 6.00 6.00

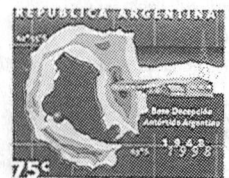

Deception Island Base, Antarctica, 50th Anniv. — A908

1998, Aug. 15 Litho. Perf. 14½
2012 A908 75c multicolored 1.50 1.50

State of Israel, 50th Anniv. A909

1998, Sept. 5 Litho. Perf. 13½
2013 A909 75c multicolored 1.50 1.50

Argentine-Japan Friendship Treaty, Cent. — A910

1998, Oct. 3
2014 A910 75c multicolored 1.50 1.50

Post Office Building, Buenos Aires, 70th Anniv. — A911

Designs: No. 2015, Building, clock, tile. No. 2016, Column ornamentation, tile, bench.

1998, Oct. 3
2015 A911 75c multicolored 1.50 1.50
2016 A911 75c multicolored 1.50 1.50
 a. Pair, #2015-2016 3.00 3.00

SEMI-POSTAL STAMPS

Samuel F. B. Morse — SP1 
Globe — SP2

Landing of Columbus — SP5
Map of Argentina — SP6 

Designs: 10c+5c, Alexander Graham Bell. 25c+15c, Rowland Hill.

Wmk. RA in Sun (90)
1944, Jan. 5 Litho. Perf. 13
B1 SP1 3c +2c lt vio & sl bl .35 .25
B2 SP2 5c +5c dl red & sl bl .65 .20
B3 SP1 10c +5c org & slate bl 1.25 .70
B4 SP1 25c +15c red brn & sl bl 1.75 1.10
B5 SP5 1p +50c lt grn & sl bl 8.00 7.25
 Nos. B1-B5 (5) 12.00 9.50
The surtax was for the Postal Employees Benefit Association.

1944, Feb. 17 Wmk. 90 Perf. 13
B6 SP6 5c +10c ol yel & slate .75 .50
B7 SP6 5c +50c vio brn & slate 3.25 2.00
B8 SP6 5c +1p ol org & slate 9.00 6.50
B9 SP6 5c +20p dp bl & slate 22.50 15.00
 Nos. B6-B9 (4) 35.50 24.00
The surtax was for the victims of the San Juan earthquake.

Souvenir Sheets

National Anthem and Flag — SP7

Illustration reduced.

1944, July 17 Imperf.
B10 SP7 5c +1p vio brn & lt bl 1.90 1.90
B11 SP7 5c +50p bl blk & lt bl 350.00 250.00
Surtax for the needy in the provinces of La Rioja and Catamarca.

Catalogue values for unused stamps in this section, from this point to the end of the section, are for Never Hinged items.

Stamp Designing — SP8

1950, Aug. 26 Photo. Perf. 13½
B12 SP8 10c +10c violet .24 .24
 Nos. B12,CB1-CB5 (6) 20.42 15.61
Argentine Intl. Philatelic Exhibition, 1950.

Poliomyelitis Victim — SP9

1956, Apr. 14 Perf. 13½x13
B13 SP9 20c +30c slate .30 .15
The surtax was for the poliomyelitis fund. Head in design is from Correggio's "Antiope," Louvre.

Stamp of 1858 and Mail Coach on Raft — SP10

Designs: 2.40p+1.20p, Album, magnifying glass and stamp of 1858. 4.40p+2.20p, Government seat of Confederation, Parana.

1958, Mar. 29 Litho. Perf. 13½
B14 SP10 40c +20c brt grn & dl pur .32 .24
B15 SP10 2.40p +1.20p ol gray & bl .40 .26
B16 SP10 4.40p +2.20p lt bl & dp claret .60 .40
 Nos. B14-B16,CB8-CB12 (8) 5.84 4.66
Surtax for Intl. Centennial Philatelic Exhibition, Paraná, Entre Rios, Apr. 19-27.

View of Flooded Land — SP11

1958, Oct. 4 Photo. Perf. 13½
B17 SP11 40c +20c brown .15 .15
 Nos. B17,CB13-CB14 (3) 1.20 1.10
The surtax was for flood victims in the Buenos Aires district.

Child Receiving Blood — SP12
Runner — SP13 

1958, Dec. 20 Litho. Wmk. 90
B18 SP12 1p +50c blk & rose red .20 .15
The surtax went to the Anti-Leukemia Foundation.

1959, Sept. 5 Perf. 13½
Designs: 50c+20c, Basketball players, vert. 1p+50c, Boxers, vert.
B19 SP13 20c +10c emer & blk .20 .16
B20 SP13 50c +20c yel & blk .15 .15
B21 SP13 1p +50c mar & blk .20 .16
 Nos. B19-B21,CB15-CB16 (5) 1.55 1.21
3rd Pan American Games, Chicago, Aug. 27-Sept. 7, 1959.

Condor — SP14

Birds: 50c+20c, Fork-tailed flycatchers. 1p+50c, Magellanic woodpecker.

1960, Feb. 6
B22 SP14 20c +10c dk bl .15 .15
B23 SP14 50c +20c dp vio bl .15 .15
B24 SP14 1p +50c brn & buff .20 .15
 Nos. B22-B24,CB17-CB18 (5) 1.25 1.00
The surtax was for child welfare work. See Nos. B30, CB29.

Souvenir Sheet

Uprooted Oak Emblem — SP15

1960, Apr. 7 Wmk. 90 Imperf.
B25 SP15 Sheet of 2 1.25 1.25
 a. 1p +50c bister & carmine .55 .55
 b. 4.20p + 2.10p apple grn & dp claret .55 .55
WRY, July 1, 1959-June 30, 1960.
The surtax was for aid to refugees.

ARGENTINA

ARGENTINA Jacaranda — SP16

Flowers: 1p+1p, Passionflower. 3p+3p, Orchid. 5p+5p, Tabebuia.

1960, Dec. 3   Photo.   Perf. 13½
B26	SP16	50c +50c deep blue	.15	.15
B27	SP16	1p +1p bluish grn	.15	.15
B28	SP16	3p +3p henna brn	.32	.22
B29	SP16	5p +5p dark brn	.52	.35
	Nos. B26-B29 (4)	1.14	.87

"TEMEX 61" (Intl. Thematic Exposition). For overprints see Nos. B31-B34.

Type of 1960
Bird: 4.20p+2.10p, Blue-eyed shag.

1961, Feb. 25   Wmk. 90   Perf. 13½
B30 SP16 4.20p +2.10p chestnut brn   .48   .32

Surtax for child welfare work. See #CB29.

Nos. B26-B29 Overprinted in Black, Brown, Blue or Red: "14 DE ABRIL DIA DE LAS AMERICAS"

1961, Apr. 15
B31	SP16	50c +50c deep blue	.15	.15
B32	SP16	1p +1p bluish grn (Brn)	.15	.15
B33	SP16	3p +3p henna brn (Bl)	.32	.25
B34	SP16	5p +5p dk brn (R)	.52	.42
	Nos. B31-B34 (4)	1.14	.97

Day of the Americas, Apr. 14.

Cathedral, Cordoba — SP17
Stamp of 1862 — SP18

Flight into Egypt, by Ana Maria Moncalvo — SP19

Design: 10p+10p, Cathedral, Buenos Aires.

Perf. 13½
1961, Oct. 21   Wmk. 90   Photo.
B35	SP17	2p +2p rose claret	.22	.15
B36	SP18	3p +3p green	.32	.18
B37	SP17	10p +10p brt blue	.90	.52
a.		Souvenir sheet of 3	1.75	1.10
	Nos. B35-B37 (3)	1.44	.85

1962 International Stamp Exhibition. No. B37a contains three imperf. stamps similar to Nos. B35-B37 in dark blue.

1961, Dec. 16   Litho.
B38	SP19	2p +1p lilac & blk brn	.15	.15
B39	SP19	10p +5p light & deep claret	.52	.35

The surtax was for child welfare.

Chalk-browed Mockingbird — SP20
Soccer — SP21

Design: 12p+6p, Rufous-collared sparrow.

1962, Dec. 29   Perf. 13½
B40	SP20	4p +2p bis, brn & bl grn	.90	.60
B41	SP20	12p +6p gray, yel, grn & brn	1.50	1.10

The surtax was for child welfare. See Nos. B44, B47, B48-B50, CB32, CB35-CB36.

1963, May 18   Perf. 13½
B42	SP21	4p +2p multi	.22	.15
B43	SP21	12p +6p Horsemanship	.45	.35
a.		Dark carmine (jacket) omitted		
	Nos. B42-B43,CB31 (3)	1.22	1.00

4th Pan American Games, Sao Paulo.

Bird Type of 1962
Design: Vermilion flycatcher.

1963, Dec. 21   Litho.
B44 SP20 4p +2p blk, red, org & grn   .60   .28

The surtax was for child welfare. See No. CB32.

Fencers — SP22

Design: 4p+2p, National Stadium, Tokyo, horiz.

1964, July 18   Wmk. 90   Perf. 13½
B45	SP22	4p +2p red, ocher & brn	.16	.15
B46	SP22	12p +6p bl grn & blk	.40	.32
	Nos. B45-B46,CB33 (3)	1.06	.97

18th Olympic Games, Tokyo, Oct. 10-25, 1964. See No. CB33.

Bird Type of 1962
Design: Red-crested cardinal.

1964, Dec. 23   Litho.
B47 SP20 4p +2p dk bl, red & grn   .60   .30

The surtax was for child welfare. See #CB35.

Bird Type of 1962
Inscribed "R. ARGENTINA"
Designs: 8p+4p, Lapwing. 10p+5p, Scarlet-headed marshbird, horiz. 20p+10p, Amazon kingfisher.

1966-67   Perf. 13½
B48	SP20	8p +4p blk, ol, brt grn & red	.80	.35
B49	SP20	10p +5p blk, bl, org & grn	.80	.55
B50	SP20	20p +10p blk, yel, bl & pink	.40	.35
	Nos. B48-B50,CB36,CB38-CB39 (6)	4.30	3.25

The surtax was for child welfare. Issue dates: 8p+4p, Mar. 26, 1966. 10p+5p, Jan. 14, 1967. 20p+10p, Dec. 23, 1967.

Grandmother's Birthday, by Patricia Lynch; Lions Emblem — SP23

Perf. 12½x13½
1968, Dec. 14   Litho.   Wmk. 90
B51 SP23 40p +20p multi   .45   .38

1st Lions Intl. Benevolent Phil. Exhib. Surtax for the Children's Hospital Benevolent Fund.

White-faced Tree Duck — SP24

1969, Sept. 20   Wmk. 365   Perf. 13½
B52 SP24 20p +10p multi   .48   .35

Surtax for child welfare. See No. CB40.

Slender-tailed Woodstar (Hummingbird) SP25

1970, May 9   Wmk. 365   Perf. 13½
B53 SP25 20c +10c multi   .45   .40

The surtax was for child welfare. See Nos. CB41, B56-B59, B62-B63.

Dolphinfish — SP26

1971, Feb. 20   Unwmk.   Perf. 12½
Size: 75x15mm
B54 SP26 20c +10c multi   .52   .45

Surtax for child welfare. See No. CB42.

Children with Stamps, by Mariette Lydis — SP27

1971, Dec. 18   Litho.   Perf. 13½
B55 SP27 1p + 50p multi   .48   .32

2nd Lions Intl. Solidarity Stamp Exhib.

Bird Type of 1970
Birds: 25c+10c, Saffron finch. 65c+30c, Rufous-bellied thrush, horiz.

1972, May 6   Unwmk.   Perf. 13½
B56	SP25	25c + 10c multi	.32	.20
B57	SP25	65c + 30c multi	.45	.32

Surtax was for child welfare.

Bird Type of 1970
Birds: 50c+25c, Southern screamer (chaja). 90c+45c, Saffron-cowled blackbird, horiz.

1973, Apr. 28
B58	SP25	50c + 25c multi	.48	.32
B59	SP25	90c + 45c multi	.70	.48

Surtax was for child welfare.

Painting Type of Regular Issue
Designs: 15c+15c, Still Life, by Alfredo Guttero, horiz. 90c+90c, Nude, by Miguel C. Victorica, horiz.

1973, Aug. 28   Litho.   Perf. 13½
B60	A472	15c + 15c multi	.28	.18
B61	A472	90c + 90c multi	1.00	.70

Bird Type of 1970
Birds: 70c+30p, Blue seed-eater. 1.20p+60c, Hooded siskin.

1974, May 11   Litho.   Perf. 13½
B62	SP25	70c + 30c multi	.50	.35
B63	SP25	1.20p + 60c multi	.75	.42

Surtax was for child welfare.

Painting Type of 1974
Design: 70c+30c, The Lama, by Juan Batlle Planas.

1974, May 11   Litho.   Perf. 13½
B64 A477 70c + 30c multi   .28   .22

PRENFIL-74 UPU, Intl. Exhib. of Phil. Periodicals, Buenos Aires, Oct. 1-12.

Plushcrested Jay — SP28

Designs: 13p+6.50p, Golden-collared macaw. 20p+10p, Begonia. 40p+20p, Teasel.

1976, June 12   Litho.   Perf. 13½
B65	SP28	7p + 3.50p multi	.20	.15
B66	SP28	13p + 6.50p multi	.32	.20
B67	SP28	20p + 10p multi	.48	.32
B68	SP28	40p + 20p multi	.95	.48
	Nos. B65-B68 (4)	1.95	1.15

Argentine philately.

Telegraph, Communications Satellite — SP29

Designs: 20p+10p, Old and new mail trucks. 60p+30p, Old, new packet boats. 70p+35p, Biplane and jet.

1977, July 16   Litho.   Perf. 13½
B69	SP29	10p + 5p multi	.30	.20
B70	SP29	20p + 10p multi	.50	.60
B71	SP29	60p + 30p multi	1.00	.85
B72	SP29	70p + 35p multi	1.25	.85
	Nos. B69-B72 (4)	3.05	2.50

Surtax was for Argentine philately. No. B70 exists with wmk. 365.

Church of St. Francis Type, 1977, Inscribed: "EXPOSICION ARGENTINA '77"

1977, Aug. 27
B73 A515 160p + 80p multi   2.50   2.00

Surtax was for Argentina '77 Philatelic Exhibition. Issued in sheets of 4.

No. B73 Overprinted with Soccer Cup Emblem

1978, Feb. 4   Litho.   Perf. 13½
B74	A515	160p + 80p multi	4.50	4.25
a.		Souvenir sheet of 4	20.00	19.00

11th World Cup Soccer Championship, Argentina, June 1-25.

Spinus Magellanicus SP30

Birds: #B76, Variable seedeater. #B77, Yellow thrush. #B78, Pyrocephalus rubineus. #B79, Great kiskadee.

ARGENTINA

1978, Aug. 5	Litho.	Perf. 13½
B75 SP30 50p + 50p multi	.90	.60
B76 SP30 100p + 100p multi	1.10	.90
B77 SP30 150p + 150p multi	1.40	1.25
B78 SP30 200p + 200p multi	1.75	1.75
B79 SP30 500p + 500p multi	8.50	7.25
Nos. B75-B79 (5)	13.65	11.75

ARGENTINA '78, Inter-American Philatelic Exhibition, Buenos Aires, Oct. 27-Nov. 5. Nos. B75-B79 issued in sheets of 4 with marginal inscriptions commemorating Exhibition and 1978 Soccer Championship.

Caravel "Magdalena," 16th Century — SP31

Sailing Ships: 500+500p, 3 master "Rio de la Plata," 17th cent. 600+600p, Corvette "Descubierta," 18th cent. 1500+1500p, Naval Academy yacht "A.R.A. Fortuna," 1979.

1979, Sept. 8	Litho.	Perf. 13½
B80 SP31 400p +400p multi	4.00	2.75
B81 SP31 500p +500p multi	4.75	2.50
B82 SP31 600p +600p multi	6.00	3.25
B83 SP31 1500p +1500p multi	15.00	8.00
Nos. B80-B83 (4)	29.75	16.00

Buenos Aires '80, International Philatelic Exhibition, Oct. 24-Nov. 2, 1980. Issued in sheets of 4.

Purmamarca Church — SP32

Churches: 200p + 100p, Molinos. 300p + 150p, Animana. 400p + 200p, San Jose de Lules.

1979, Nov. 3	Litho.	Perf. 13½
B84 SP32 100p + 50p multi	.25	.15
B85 SP32 200p + 100p multi	.45	.15
B86 SP32 300p + 150p multi	.60	.18
B87 SP32 400p + 200p multi	.90	.24
Nos. B84-B87 (4)	2.20	.72

Buenos Aires No. 3, Exhibition and Society Emblems — SP33

Argentine Stamps: 750p+750p, type A580. 1000p+1000p, No. 91. 2000p+2000p, type A588.

1979, Dec. 15	Litho.	Perf. 13½
B88 SP33 250p + 250p multi	.90	.70
B89 SP33 750p + 750p multi	2.25	1.75
B90 SP33 1000p + 1000p multi	3.00	2.50
B91 SP33 2000p + 2000p multi	6.00	5.00
Nos. B88-B91 (4)	12.15	9.95

PRENFIL '80, Intl. Philatelic Literature and Publications Exhib., Buenos Aires, Nov. 7-16, 1980.

Minuet, by Carlos E. Pellegrini SP34

Paintings: 700p+350p, Media Cana, by Carlos Morel. 800p+400p, Cielito, by Pellegrini. 1000p+500p, El Gato, by Juan Leon Palliere.

1981, July 11	Litho.	Perf. 13½
B92 SP34 500p + 250p multi	.70	.35
B93 SP34 700p + 350p multi	1.00	.70
B94 SP34 800p + 400p multi	1.10	.90
B95 SP34 1000p + 500p multi	1.40	1.25
Nos. B92-B95 (4)	4.20	3.20

Espamer '81 Intl. Stamp Exhib. (Americas, Spain, Portugal), Buenos Aires, Nov. 13-22.

Canal, by Beatrix Bongliani (b. 1933) SP35

Tapestries: 1000p+500p, Shadows, by Silvia Sieburger, vert. 2000p+1000p, Interpretation of a Rectangle, by Silke R. de Haupt, vert. 4000p+2000p, Tilcara, by Tana Sachs.

1982, July 31	Litho.	Perf. 13½
B96 SP35 1000p + 500p multi	.20	.20
B97 SP35 2000p + 1000p multi	.40	.40
B98 SP35 3000p + 1500p multi	.60	.60
B99 SP35 4000p + 2000p multi	.80	.80
Nos. B96-B99 (4)	2.00	2.00

Boy Playing Marbles — SP36

1983, July 2	Litho.	Perf. 13½
B100 SP36 20c + 10c shown	.20	.15
B101 SP36 30c + 15c Jumping rope	.45	.16
B102 SP36 50c + 25c Hopscotch	.85	.20
B103 SP36 1p + 50c Flying kites	1.10	.48
B104 SP36 2p + 1p Spinning top	1.65	.65
Nos. B100-B104 (5)	4.25	1.64

Surtax was for natl. philatelic associations. See Nos. B106-B110.

Compass, 15th Cent. SP37

ARGENTINA '85 Intl. Stamp Show: b, Arms of Spain, Argentina. c, Columbus' arms. d-f, Columbus' arrival at San Salvador Island. Nos. B105d-B105f in continuous design; ships shown on singles range in size, left to right, from small to large. Surtax was for exhibition.

1984, Apr. 28	Litho.	Perf. 13½
B105 Block of 6	3.75	3.75
a.-f. SP37 5p + 2.50p, any single	.52	.26

Children's Game Type of 1983

1984, July 7	Litho.	Perf. 13½
B106 SP36 2p + 1p Blind Man's Buff	.15	.15
B107 SP36 3p + 1.50p The Loop	.30	.24
B108 SP36 4p + 2p Leap Frog	.35	.30
B109 SP36 5p + 2.50p Rolling the loop	.45	.35
B110 SP36 6p + 3p Ball Mold	.55	.45
Nos. B106-B110 (5)	1.80	1.49

Butterflies SP38

1985, Nov. 9	Litho.	Perf. 13½
B111 SP38 5c + 2c Rothschildia jacobaeae	.75	.20
B112 SP38 10c + 5c Heliconius erato phyllis	.75	.40
B113 SP38 20c + 10c Precis evarete hilaris	1.00	.75
B114 SP38 25c + 13c Cyanopepla pretiosa	1.50	1.00
B115 SP38 40c + 20c Papilio androgeus	2.00	1.50
Nos. B111-B115 (5)	6.00	3.85

Children's Drawings SP39

1986, Aug. 30		Litho.
B116 SP39 5c + 2c N. Pastor	.15	.15
B117 SP39 10c + 5c T. Valleistein	.30	.30
B118 SP39 20c + 10c J.M. Flores	.60	.60
B119 SP39 25c + 13c M.E. Pezzuto	.75	.75
B120 SP39 40c + 20c E. Diehl	1.10	1.10
Nos. B116-B120 (5)	2.90	2.90

Surtax for natl. philatelic associations.

Miniature Sheets

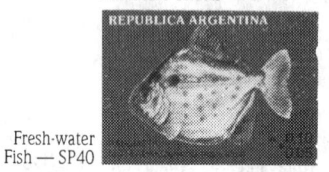

Fresh-water Fish — SP40

No. B121: a, Metynnis maculatus. b, Cynolebias nigripinnis. c, Leporinus solarii. d, Aphyocharax rathbuni. e, Corydoras aeneus. f, Thoracocharax securis. g, Cynolebias melanotaenia. h, Cichlasoma facetum.
No. B122: a, Tetragonopterus argenteus. b, Hemigrammus caudovittatus. c, Astyanax bimaculatus. d, Gymnocorymbus ternetzi. e, Hoplias malabaricus. f, Aphyocharax rubripinnis. g, Apistogramma agassizi. h, Pyrrhulina rachoviana.

1987, June 27		
B121 Sheet of 8	2.00	1.75
a.-h. SP40 10c +5c, any single	.25	.20
B122 Sheet of 8	4.00	3.50
a.-h. SP40 20c +10c, any single	.50	.40

PRENFIL '88, Intl. Philatelic Literature and Media Exhibition, Buenos Aires, Nov. 25-Dec. 2 — SP41

Locomotives and railroad car: No. B123, Yatay locomotive, 1888. No. B124, FCCA electric passenger car, 1914. No. B125, B-15 locomotive, 1942. No. B126, GT-22 No. 200 locomotive, 1988.

1988, June 4	Litho.	Perf. 13½
B123 SP41 1a +50c multi	.65	.50
B124 SP41 1a +50c multi	.65	.50
B125 SP41 1a +50c multi	.65	.50
B126 SP41 1a +50c multi	.65	.50
Nos. B123-B126 (4)	2.60	2.00

Nos. B123-B125 each issued in sheets of 4.

Horses SP42

Paintings: No. B127, The Waiting, by Gustavo Solari. No. B128, Mare and Foal, by E. Castro. No. B129, Saint Isidor, by Castro. No. B130, At Lagoon's Edge, by F. Romero Carranza. No. B131, Under the Tail, by Castro.

1988, Oct. 29	Litho.	Perf. 13½
B127 SP42 2a +1a multi	.70	.50
B128 SP42 2a +1a multi	.70	.50
B129 SP42 2a +1a multi	.70	.50
B130 SP42 2a +1a multi	.70	.50
B131 SP42 2a +1a multi	.70	.50
Nos. B127-B131 (5)	3.50	2.50

PRENFIL '88 — SP43

Covers of philatelic magazines.

1988, Nov. 26	Litho.	Perf. 13½
B132 SP43 1a +1a Cronaca Filatelica, Italy	.40	.30
B133 SP43 1a +1a CO-FI, Brazil	.40	.30
B134 SP43 1a +1a References de la Poste, France	.40	.30
B135 SP43 2a +2a Postas Argentinas	.65	.50
Nos. B132-B135 (4)	1.85	1.40

Souvenir Sheet

ARBRAPEX '88 — SP44

Designs: No. B136a, Candel Delivery at San Ignacio, by Leonie Matthis, Cornelio Saavedra Museum, Buenos Aires. No. B136b, Immaculate Conception, a statue in the Isaac Fernandez Blanco Museum, Buenos Aires.

1988, Nov. 26		Perf. 12
B136 SP44 Sheet of 2	1.60	1.25
a. 2a +2a multi	.65	.50
b. 3a +3a multi	.95	.70

Fish SP45

#B137, Diplomystes viedmensis. #B138, Haplochiton taeniatus. #B139, Percichthys trucha. #B140, Galaxias platei. #B141, Salmo fario.

1989, June 24	Litho.	Perf. 13½
B137 SP45 10a +5a multi	.25	.20
B138 SP45 10a +5a multi	.25	.20
B139 SP45 10a +5a multi	.25	.20
B140 SP45 10a +5a multi	.25	.20
B141 SP45 10a +5a multi	.25	.20
Nos. B137-B141 (5)	1.25	1.00

Printed in sheets of 4.

Discovery of America 500th Anniv. (in 1992) and ESPAMER '90 — SP46

Documents and chronicles: No. B142, Columbus's coat of arms, Book of Privileges title page. No. B143, Illustration from New Chronicle and Good Government, by Guaman Poma de Ayala. No. B144, Illustration from Discovery and Conquest of Peru, by Pedro de Cieza de Leon. No. B145, Illustration from Travel to the River Plate, by Ulrico Schmidl.

1989, Sept. 16	Litho.	Perf. 13½
Yellow, Rose Violet & Black		
B142 SP46 100a +50a	.90	.80
B143 SP46 150a +50a	.90	.80
B144 SP46 200a +100a	.90	.80
B145 SP46 250a +100a	.90	.80
Nos. B142-B145 (4)	3.60	3.20

ARGENTINA

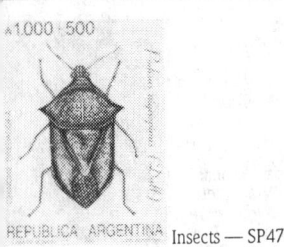

Insects — SP47

Designs: No. B146, *Podisus nigrispinus.* No. B147, *Adalia bipunctata.* No. B148, *Nabis punctipennis.* No. B149, *Hippodamia convergens.* No. B150, *Calleida suturalis.*

1990, June 30	Litho.		Perf. 13½	
B146	SP47	1000a +500a multi	1.00	.85
B147	SP47	1000a +500a multi	1.00	.85
B148	SP47	1000a +500a multi	1.00	.85
B149	SP47	1000a +500a multi	1.00	.85
B150	SP47	1000a +500a multi	1.00	.85
	Nos. B146-B150 (5)		5.00	4.25

Printed in sheets of 4.

Souvenir Sheet

First Natl. Exposition of Aerophilately — SP48

Designs: a, Lieut. Marcos A. Zar, Macchi seaplane. b, Capt. Antonio Parodi, Ansaldo SVA biplane. (Illustration reduced).

1990, July 14	Litho.		Perf. 12	
B151	Sheet of 2		6.00	6.00
a.	SP48 2000a +2000a multi		3.00	2.50
b.	SP48 3000a +3000a multi		3.00	2.50

Souvenir Sheet

1992 Summer Olympics, Barcelona SP49

Designs: a, Shot put. b, High jump. c, Hurdles. d, Pole vault.

1990, Dec. 15	Litho.		Perf. 13½	
B152	Sheet of 4		9.00	9.00
a.-d.	SP49 2000a +2000a multi		2.25	2.25

Espamer '91 Philatelic Exhibition.
See No. B155.

Souvenir Sheet

Discovery of America, 500th Anniv. (in 1992) — SP50

Voyage of Alesandro Malaspina, 1789-1794: a, Sailing ship. b, Malaspina. c, Indian, hut. d, Indian, horse, artist drawing.

1990, Oct. 13	Litho.		Perf. 13½	
B153	Sheet of 4		6.00	6.00
a.-d.	SP50 2000a +1000a, any single		1.50	1.50

Espamer '91, Buenos Aires.

Souvenir Sheet

Race Cars and Drivers — SP51

Designs: a, Juan Manuel Fangio. b, Juan Manuel Bordeu. c, Carlos Alberto Reutemann. d, Oscar and Juan Galvez.

1991	Litho.		Perf. 13½	
B154	SP51	Sheet of 4	4.75	4.75
a.-d.		2500a +2500a, any single	1.25	1.25

Espamer '91.

Souvenir Sheet

1992 Summer Olympics Type of 1990

Women's gymnastics routines: a, Floor exercise. b, Uneven parallel bars. c, Balance beam. d, Rhythmic gymnastics.

1991, June 29	Litho.		Perf. 13½	
B155	Sheet of 4		4.75	4.75
a.-d.	SP49 2500a +2500a, any single		1.25	1.25

Espamer '91.

Iberoprenfil '92 SP52

Designs: No. B156, Castor missile. No. B157, Satellite LUSAT 1.

1991, Dec. 28	Litho.		Perf. 13½	
B156	SP52	4000a +4000a multi	2.00	1.75
B157	SP52	4000a +4000a multi	2.00	1.75

Dinosaurs — SP53

1992, May 2	Litho.		Perf. 13½	
B158	SP53	38c +38c Carnotaurus	1.50	1.50
B159	SP53	38c +38c Amargasaurus	1.50	1.50

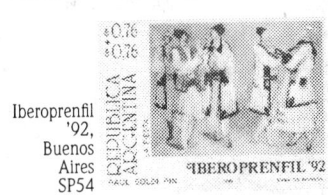

Iberoprenfil '92, Buenos Aires SP54

Paintings by Raul Soldi (b. 1905): No. B160, The Fiesta. No. B161, Church of St. Anne of Glew.

1992, Sept. 5	Litho.		Perf. 13½	
B160	SP54	76c +76c multi	3.00	3.00
B161	SP54	76c +76c multi	3.00	3.00

Parafil '92 — SP55

1992, Nov. 21	Litho.		Perf. 13½	
B162	SP55	76c +76c multi	3.00	3.00

2nd Argentine-Paraguayan Philatelic Exhibition, Buenos Aires.

Souvenir Sheet

Birds — SP56

a, Egretta thula. b, Amblyramphus holosericeus. c, Paroaria coronata. d, Chloroceryle amazona.

1993, July 17	Litho.		Perf. 13½	
B163	SP56	38c +38c Sheet of 4	6.00	6.00

Souvenir Sheet

Latin American Air Post Philatelic Exhibition — SP57

Designs: a, 25c+25c, Antoine de Saint-Exupery (1940-44), pilot, author. b, 75c+75c, "The Little Prince," vert. Illustration reduced.

1995, June 3	Litho.		Perf. 12	
B164	SP57	Sheet of 2, #a.-b.	4.00	4.00

For overprint see No. B180.

Souvenir Sheet

Exploration of Antarctica SP58

75c+25c, Transport ship ARA Bahia Aguirre.
1.25p+75c, Argentine Air Force Hercules C-130.

1995, July 8				
B165	SP58	Sheet of 2, #a.-b.	6.00	6.00

Aerofila '96 SP59

Historic airplanes, pilots: No. B166, "Plus ultra," Ramón Franco Bahamonde (1896-1938). No. B167, 14 Bis, Alberto Santos-Dumont (1873-1932). No. B168, Spirit of St. Louis, Charles A. Lindbergh (1902-1974). No. B169, Buenos Aires, Eduardo A. Olivero (1896-1966).

1996, July 13	Litho.		Perf. 13½	
B166	SP59	25c +25c multi	1.00	1.00
B167	SP59	25c +25c multi	1.00	1.00
B168	SP59	50c +50c multi	2.00	2.00
B169	SP59	50c +50c multi	2.00	2.00
	Nos. B166-B169 (4)		6.00	6.00

Ceramic Murals from Buenos Aires Subway — SP60

1996, Sept. 21	Litho.		Perf. 13½	
B170	SP60	1p +50c Dragon	3.00	3.00
B171	SP60	1.50p +1p Bird	5.00	5.00

MEVIFIL '97, 1st Intl. Exhibition of Audio-Visual and Philatelic Information Media — SP61

Designs: No. B172, France Type A1. No. B173, Spain Type A3. No. B174, Argentina Type A4. No. B175, Buenos Aires Type A1.

1997, May 10	Litho.		Perf. 13½	
B172	SP61	50c +50c multi	2.00	2.00
B173	SP61	50c +50c multi	2.00	2.00
B174	SP61	50c +50c multi	2.00	2.00
B175	SP61	50c +50c multi	2.00	2.00
a.	Block of 4, #B172-B175		8.00	8.00

Issued in sheets of 16 stamps + 4 labels.

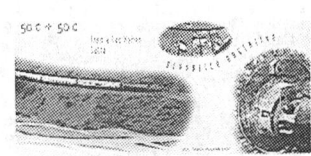

Trains — SP62

Designs: No. B176, Las Nubes (Train to the Clouds), Salta. No. B177, Historical train, Buenos Aires. No. B178, Old Patagonian Express, Rio Negro-Chubut. No. B179, Southern Fueguino Railway, Tierra Del Fuego.
Illustration reduced.

1997, Sept. 6	Litho.		Perf. 13	
B176	SP62	50c +50c multi	2.00	2.00
B177	SP62	50c +50c multi	2.00	2.00
B178	SP62	50c +50c multi	2.00	2.00
B179	SP62	50c +50c multi	2.00	2.00
	Nos. B176-B179 (4)		8.00	8.00

No. B164 Ovptd. in Red Violet in Sheet Margin:
1927 70th 1997
ANIVERSARIO/AEROPOSTA/ARGENTINA

1997, Sept. 27	Litho.		Perf. 12	
B180	SP57	Sheet of 2, #a.-b.	4.00	4.00

AIR POST STAMPS

Airplane Circles the Globe — AP1

Eagle — AP2

ARGENTINA

Wings Cross the Sea — AP3

Condor on Mountain Crag — AP4

Perforations of Nos. C1-C37 vary from clean-cut to rough and uneven, with many skipped perfs.

Perf. 13x13½, 13½x13
1928, Mar. 1   Litho.   Wmk. 90

C1	AP1	5c lt red	1.25	.50
C2	AP1	10c Prus blue	2.25	1.00
C3	AP2	15c lt brown	2.25	.80
C4	AP1	18c lilac gray	3.00	2.75
a.		18c brown lilac	3.25	2.75
b.		Double impression	375.00	
C5	AP2	20c ultra	2.25	.80
C6	AP2	24c deep blue	3.50	2.75
C7	AP3	25c brt violet	3.50	1.50
C8	AP3	30c rose red	5.25	1.00
C9	AP4	35c rose	3.50	1.00
C10	AP1	36c bister brn	2.50	1.50
C11	AP2	50c gray black	4.00	.50
C12	AP2	54c chocolate	3.50	2.00
C13	AP2	72c yellow grn	4.75	2.00
a.		Double impression	300.00	
C14	AP2	90c dk brown	9.00	1.75
C15	AP3	1p slate bl & red	11.00	.65
C16	AP3	1.08p rose & dk bl	16.00	4.50
C17	AP3	1.26p dull vio & grn	20.00	8.00
C18	AP4	1.80p blue & lil rose	20.00	8.00
C19	AP4	3.60p gray & blue	42.50	19.00
		Nos. C1-C19 (19)	160.00	60.00

The watermark on No. C4a is larger than on the other stamps of this set, measuring 10mm across Sun.

Zeppelin First Flight
Air Post Stamps of 1928 Overprinted in Blue

1930, May

C20	AP2	20c ultra	10.00	5.00
C21	AP4	50c gray black	20.00	10.00
a.		Inverted overprint	475.00	
C22	AP3	1p slate bl & red	21.00	10.00
a.		Inverted overprint	650.00	
C23	AP4	1.80p blue & lil rose	55.00	25.00
C24	AP4	3.60p gray & blue	150.00	70.00
		Nos. C20-C24 (5)	256.00	120.00

Overprinted in Green

C25	AP2	20c ultra	10.00	6.00
C26	AP4	50c gray black	12.50	9.00
C27	AP3	90c dark brown	10.00	6.00
C28	AP3	1p slate bl & red	20.00	12.50
C29	AP4	1.80p blue & lil rose	600.00	400.00
a.		Thick paper	850.00	
		Nos. C25-C29 (5)	652.50	433.50

Air Post Stamps of 1928 Overprinted in Red or Blue

1930

6 Septiembre -1931-   6 de Septiembre 1930 — 1931
On AP1-AP2   On AP3-AP4

1931

C30	AP1	18c lilac gray	2.00	1.50
C31	AP2	72c yellow green	14.00	10.50
C32	AP3	90c dark brown	14.00	10.50
C33	AP4	1.80p bl & lil rose (Bl)	30.00	22.50
C34	AP4	3.60p gray & blue	57.50	40.00
		Nos. C30-C34 (5)	117.50	85.00

1st anniv. of the Revolution of 1930.

Zeppelin Issue
Nos. C1, C4, C4a, C14 Overprinted in Blue or Red

GRAF ZEPPELIN 1932   GRAF ZEPPELIN 1932
On AP1   On AP3

1932, Aug. 4

C35	AP1	5c lt red (Bl)	3.00	2.00
C36	AP1	18c lilac gray (R)	12.50	9.00
a.		18c brown lilac (R)	100.00	60.00
C37	AP3	90c dark brown (R)	32.50	26.00
		Nos. C35-C37 (3)	48.00	37.00

Plane and Letter — AP5

Mercury — AP6

Plane in Flight — AP7

Perf. 13½x13, 13x13½
1940, Oct. 23   Photo.   Wmk. 90

C38	AP5	30c deep orange	5.00	.15
C39	AP6	50c dark brown	7.50	.20
C40	AP5	1p carmine	1.75	.15
C41	AP7	1.25p deep green	.50	.15
C42	AP5	2.50p bright blue	1.25	.20
		Nos. C38-C42 (5)	16.00	.85

Plane and Letter — AP8

Mercury and Plane — AP9

Perf. 13½x13, 13x13½
1942, Oct. 6   Litho.   Wmk. 90

C43	AP8	30c orange	.15	.15
C44	AP9	50c dull brn & buff	.40	.15

See Nos. C49-C52, C57, C61.

Plane over Iguaçu Falls — AP10

Plane over the Andes — AP11

Perf. 13½x13
1946, June 10   Unwmk.

C45	AP10	15c dull red brn	.25	.15
C46	AP11	25c gray green	.15	.15

See Nos. C53-C54.

Allegory of Flight — AP12

Astrolabe — AP13

Perf. 13½x13, 13x13½
1946, Sept. 25   Litho.   Unwmk.
Surface-Tinted Paper

C47	AP12	15c sl grn, pale grn	.55	.15
C48	AP13	60c vio brn, ocher	.55	.35

Types of 1942
1946-48   Unwmk.   *Perf. 13½x13*

C49	AP8	30c orange	1.40	.15
C50	AP9	50c dull brn & buff	2.50	.15
C51	AP8	1p carmine ('47)	1.25	.15
C52	AP8	2.50p brt blue ('48)	5.50	.75
		Nos. C49-C52 (4)	10.65	1.20

Types of 1946
1948   Wmk. 90

C53	AP10	15c dull red brn	.15	.15
C54	AP11	25c gray green	.25	.15

Atlas (National Museum, Naples) — AP14

Map of Argentine Republic, Globe and Caliper — AP15

Perf. 13½x13, 13x13½
1948-49   Photo.   Wmk. 288

C55	AP14	45c dk brown ('49)	.35	.20
C56	AP15	70c dark green	.50	.25

4th Pan-American Reunion of Cartographers, Buenos Aires, Oct.-Nov., 1948.

Mercury Type of 1942
1949   Litho.   *Perf. 13x13½*

C57	AP9	50c dull brn & buff	.40	.15

Marksmanship Trophy — AP16

1949, Nov. 4   Photo.

C58	AP16	75c brown	.75	.20

World Rifle Championship, 1949.

Catalogue values for unused stamps in this section, from this point to the end of the section, are for Never Hinged items.

Douglas DC-3 and Condor AP17

Perf. 13x13½
1951, June 20   Wmk. 90

C59	AP17	20c dk olive grn	.20	.15

10th anniversary of the State air lines.

Douglas DC-6 and Condor — AP18

1951, Oct. 17   *Perf. 13½*

C60	AP18	20c blue	.20	.15

End of Argentine 5-year Plan.

Plane-Letter Type of 1942
1951   Litho.   *Perf. 13½x13*

C61	AP8	1p carmine	.40	.15

Jesus by Leonardo da Vinci (detail, "Virgin of the Rocks") — AP19

Perf. 13½x13
1956, Sept. 29   Photo.   Wmk. 90

C62	AP19	1p dull purple	.35	.15

Issued to express the gratitude of the children of Argentina to the people of the world for their help against poliomyelitis.

Battle of Montevideo AP20

Leonardo Rosales and Tomas Espora — AP21

Guillermo Brown — AP22

AP23

1957, Mar. 2   *Perf. 13½*

C63	AP20	60c blue gray	.15	.15
C64	AP21	1p brt pink	.15	.15
C65	AP22	2p brown	.25	.15
		Nos. C63-C65 (3)	.55	.45

Cent. of the death of Admiral Guillermo Brown, founder of the Argentine navy.

1957, Aug. 16

Map of Americas and Arms of Buenos Aires.

C66	AP23	2p rose violet	.42	.20

Issued to publicize the Inter-American Economic Conference in Buenos Aires.

AP24    AP25

1957, Aug. 31   Wmk. 90   *Perf. 13½*

C67	AP24	60c Modern jlcomotive	.15	.15

Centenary of Argentine railroads.

1957, Sept. 14

C68	AP25	1p Globe, Flag, Compass Rose	.20	.15
C69	AP25	2p Key	.30	.15

1957 International Congress for Tourism.

Birds Carrying Letters — AP26

1957, Nov. 6

C70	AP26	1p bright blue	.15	.15

Issued for Letter Writing Week, Oct. 6-12.

ARGENTINA

Early Plane — AP27

1958, May 31   *Perf. 13½*
C71 AP27 2p maroon   .20 .15
50th anniversary of the Argentine Aviation Club.

Stamp Anniv. Type

Designs: 80c, Stamp of Buenos Aires and view of the Plaza de la Aduana. 1p, Stamp of 1858 and "The Post of Santa Fe."

1958   Litho.   *Perf. 13½*
C72 A270 80c pale bis & sl bl   .20 .15
C73 A270 1p red org & dk bl   .25 .15
Centenary of the first postage stamps of Buenos Aires and the Argentine Confederation.
Issue dates: 80c, Oct. 18; 1p, Aug. 23.

Comet Jet over World Map AP29

1959, May 16   *Perf. 13½*
C74 AP29 5p black & olive   .35 .15
Inauguration of jet flights by Argentine Airlines.

Type of Regular Issue, 1960.

"Cabildo" and: 1.80p, Mariano Moreno. 5p, Manuel Belgrano and Juan Jose Castelli.

Perf. 13½
1960, May 28   Wmk. 90   Photo.
C75 A287 1.80p red brown   .15 .15
    a. Souvenir sheet of 3   .65 .40
C76 A287 5p buff & purple   .35 .15
    a. Souvenir sheet of 3   1.25 .80

Souvenir sheets are imperf. No. C75a contains one No. C75 and 1p and 2p resembling Nos. 713-714; stamps in reddish brown. No. C76a contains one No. C76 and 4.20p and 10.70p resembling Nos. 715-716; stamps are in green.

Symbolic of New Provinces — AP30

1960, July 8   Litho.
C77 AP30 1.80p dp car & blue   .15 .15
Elevation of the territories of Chubut, Formosa, Neuquen, Rio Negro and Santa Cruz to provinces.

Type of Regular Issue, 1960

1960, Oct. 1   Photo.   *Perf. 13½*
C78 A291 1.80p rose lilac   .15 .15
C79 A291 10.70p brt grnsh blue   .40 .15

UNESCO Emblem AP31

1962, July 14   Litho.
C80 AP31 13p ocher & brown   .40 .25
15th anniv. of UNESCO.

Mail Coach — AP32

1962, Oct. 6   Wmk. 90   *Perf. 13½*
C81 AP32 5.60p gray brn & blk   .20 .15
Mailman's Day, Sept. 14, 1962.

No. 695 and Type of 1959 Surcharged in Green

AEREO 5 60 PESOS

1962, Oct. 31   Photo.
C82 A277 5.60p on 5p brown   .30 .15
C83 A277 18p on 5p brn, grnsh   1.00 .20

UPAE Emblem AP33 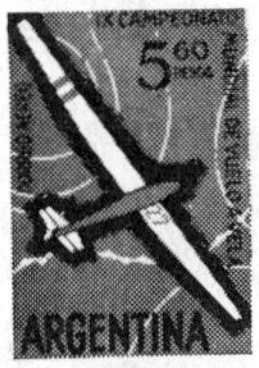   Skylark AP34

1962, Nov. 24   Photo.   *Perf. 13½*
C84 AP33 5.60p dark blue   .20 .15
50th anniv. of the founding of the Postal Union of the Americas and Spain, UPAE.

1963, Feb. 9   Litho.
Design: 11p, Super Albatros.
C85 AP34 5.60p blue & black   .20 .15
C86 AP34 11p blue, blk & red   .30 .15
9th World Gliding Championships.

Symbolic Plane — AP35

1963-65   Wmk. 90   *Perf. 13½*
C87 AP35 5.60p dk pur, car & brt grn   .40 .15
C88 AP35 7p black & bis ('64)   .55 .15
C88A AP35 7p black & bis ('65)   4.00 .55
C89 AP35 11p blk, dk pur & grn   .55 .25
C90 AP35 18p dk pur, red & vio bl   1.10 .35
C91 AP35 21p brown, red & gray   1.40 .55
    Nos. C87-C91 (6)   8.00 2.00

"Argentina" reads down on No. C88, up on No. C88A. See Nos. C101-C104, C108-C111, C123-C126, C135-C141. For overprint and surcharges see Nos. C96, C146-C150.

Type of Regular Issue, 1964

18p, Map of Falkland Islands (Islas Malvinas).

1964, Feb. 22   *Perf. 13½*
Size: 33x22mm
C92 A327 18p lt & dk bl & ol grn   1.75 .70

UPU Monument, Bern, and UN Emblem — AP36

1964, May 23   Engr.   *Perf. 13½*
C93 AP36 18p red & dk brown   .52 .25
15th UPU Cong., Vienna, Austria, May-June 1964.

Discovery of America, Florentine Woodcut — AP37

1964, Oct. 10   Litho.
C94 AP37 13p tan & black   .35 .30
Day of the Race, Columbus Day.

Lt. Matienzo Base, Antarctica AP38

1965, Feb. 27   Photo.   *Perf. 13½*
C95 AP38 11p salmon pink   .52 .15
Issued to publicize the national territory of Tierra del Fuego, Antarctic and South Atlantic Isles.

No. C88A Overprinted in Silver:
"PRIMERS / JORNADAS FILATELICAS / RIOPLATENSES"

1965, Mar. 17   Litho.
C96 AP35 7p black & bister   .24 .15
1st Rio de la Plata Stamp Show, sponsored jointly by the Argentine and Uruguayan Philatelic Associations, Montevideo, Mar. 19-28.

ITU Emblem — AP39    Ascending Rocket — AP40

1965, May 11   Wmk. 90   *Perf. 13½*
C97 AP39 18p slate, blk & red   .42 .22
Centenary of the ITU.

1965, May 29   Photo.   *Perf. 13½*
Design: 50p, Earth with trajectories and magnetic field, horiz.
C98 AP40 18p vermilion   .42 .20
C99 AP40 50p dp violet blue   1.00 .50
6th Symposium on Space Research, held in Buenos Aires, and to honor the Natl. Commission of Space Research.

Type of 1963-65 Inscribed "Republica Argentina" Reading Down

1965, Oct. 13   Litho.   Wmk. 90
C101 AP35 12p dk car rose & brn   1.40 .20
C102 AP35 15p vio blue & dk red   .85 .26
C103 AP35 27.50p dk bl grn & gray   1.40 .40
C104 AP35 30.50p dk brown & dk bl   2.00 .60
    Nos. C101-C104 (4)   5.65 1.46

Argentine Antarctica Map and Centaur Rocket — AP41

1966, Feb. 19   *Perf. 13½*
C105 AP41 27.50p blue, blk & dp org   1.00 .75
Launchings of sounding balloons and of a Gamma Centaur rocket in Antarctica during February, 1965.

Sea Gull and Southern Cross AP42

1966, May 14   *Perf. 13½*
C106 AP42 12p Prus blue, blk & red   .32 .15
50th anniv. of the Naval Aviation School.

Blériot Plane Flown by Fels, 1917 — AP43

1967, Sept. 2   Litho.   *Perf. 13½*
C107 AP43 26p olive, bl & blk   .26 .15
Flight by Theodore Fels from Buenos Aires to Montevideo, Sept. 2, 1917, allegedly the 1st intl. airmail flight.

Type of 1963-65 Inscribed "Republica Argentina" Reading Down

1967, Dec. 20   *Perf. 13½*
C108 AP35 26p brown   .60 .22
C109 AP35 40p violet   4.50 .30
C110 AP35 68p blue green   3.00 .45
C111 AP35 78p ultra   1.25 .60
    Nos. C108-C111 (4)   9.35 1.57

Vito Dumas and Ketch "Legh II" AP44

1968, July 27   Litho.   Wmk. 90
C112 AP44 68p bl, blk, red & vio bl   .65 .40
Issued to commemorate Vito Dumas's one-man voyage around the world in 1943.

Type of Regular Issue and Assembly Emblem AP45

Design: 40p, Globe and map of South America.

1968, Oct. 19   Litho.   *Perf. 13½*
C113 A395 40p brt pink, lt bl & blk   .40 .16
C114 AP45 68p bl, lt bl, gold & blk   .65 .30
4th Plenary Assembly of the Intl. Telegraph and Telephone Consultative Committee, Mar del Plata, Sept. 23-Oct. 25.

Radar Antenna, Balcarce Station — AP46

Perf. 13½
1969, Aug. 23   Wmk. 90   Photo.
C115 AP46 40p blue gray   .70 .22
Communications by satellite through Intl. Telecommunications Consortium (INTELSAT).

ARGENTINA

Atucha Nuclear Center AP47

1969, Dec. 13   Litho.   Wmk. 365
C116 AP47 26p blue & multi   1.40   .80
Completion of Atucha Nuclear Center.

Type of 1963-65 Inscribed "Republica Argentina" Reading Down

1969-71   Perf. 13½
C123 AP35 40p violet   5.00   .32
C124 AP35 68p dk blue grn ('70)   2.00   .60
                   Unwmk.
C125 AP35 26p yellow brn ('71)   .32   .20
C126 AP35 40p violet ('71)   2.75   .40
  Nos. C123-C126 (4)   10.07 1.52

Old Fire Engine and Fire Brigade Emblem AP48

1970, Aug. 8   Litho.   Unwmk.
C128 AP48 40c green & multi   .55   .28
Centenary of the Fire Brigade.

Education Year Emblem — AP49

1970, Aug. 29   Perf. 13½
C129 AP49 68c blue & blk   .42   .25
Issued for International Education Year.

Fleet Leaving Valparaiso, by Antonio Abel AP50

1970, Oct. 17   Litho.   Perf. 13½
C130 AP50 26c multicolored   1.00   .35
150th anniv. of the departure for Peru of the liberation fleet from Valparaiso, Chile.

Sumampa Chapel AP51

1970, Nov. 7   Photo.
C131 AP51 40c multicolored   .95   .35
Bishopric of Tucuman, 400th anniversary.

Buenos Aires Planetarium AP52

1970, Nov. 28   Litho.   Perf. 13½
C132 AP52 40c multicolored   .60   .26

Jorge Newbery and Morane Saulnier Plane AP53

1970, Dec. 19
C133 AP53 26c bl, blk, yel & grn   .38   .25
24th Aeronautics and Space Week.

Industries Type of Regular Issue
Design: 31c, Refinery.

1971, Oct. 16   Litho.   Perf. 13½
C134 A445 31c red, blk & yel   .60   .24

Type of 1963-65 Inscribed "Republica Argentina" Reading Down

1971-74   Unwmk.
C135 AP35 45c brown   3.25   .15
C136 AP35 68c red   .48   .15
C137 AP35 70c vio blue ('73)   .80   .15
C138 AP35 90c emerald ('73)   1.90   .15
C139 AP35 1.70p blue ('74)   .48   .25
C140 AP35 1.95p emerald ('74)   .48   .30
C141 AP35 2.65p dp claret ('74)   .48   .40
  Nos. C135-C141 (7)   7.87 1.55

Fluorescent paper was used for Nos. C135-C136, C138-C141. The 70c was issued on both papers.

Don Quixote, Drawing by Ignacio Zuloaga — AP54

1975, Apr. 26   Photo.   Perf. 13½
C145 AP54 2.75p yellow, blk & red   .60   .35
Day of the Race and for Espana 75 Intl. Philatelic Exhibition, Madrid, Apr. 4-13.

No. C87 Surcharged **100 PESOS**

1975, Sept. 15   Litho.   Wmk. 90
C146 AP35 9.20p on 5.60p   .90   .18
C147 AP35 19.70p on 5.60p   1.25   .45
C148 AP35 100p on 5.60p   5.50 2.25
  Nos. C146-C148 (3)   7.65 2.88

No. C87 Surcharged **REVALORIZADO 9.20 PESOS**

1975, Oct. 15
C149 AP35 9.20p on 5.60p   .70   .30
C150 AP35 19.70p on 5.60p   1.25   .60

Argentine State Airline, 50th Anniv. AP55

1990, Sept. 15   Litho.   Perf. 13½
C151 AP55 2500a Junkers JU52-3M   1.25   .90
C152 AP55 2500a Grumman SA-16   1.25   .90
C153 AP55 2500a Fokker F-27   1.25   .90
C154 AP55 2500a Fokker F-28   1.25   .90
  Nos. C151-C154 (4)   5.00 3.60

AIR POST SEMI-POSTAL STAMPS

Catalogue values for unused stamps in this section are for Never Hinged items.

Philatelic Exhibition Type

Designs: 45c+45c, Stamp engraving. 70c+70c, Proofing stamp die. 1p+1p, Sheet of stamps. 2.50p+2.50p, The letter. 5p+5p, Gen. San Martin.

1950, Aug. 26   Perf. 13½   Photo.   Wmk. 90
CB1 SP8 45c + 45c violet bl   .38   .24
CB2 SP8 70c + 70c dark brown   .55   .38
  a. Souv. sheet of 3, #B12, CB1, CB2, imperf.   3.00 3.00
CB3 SP8 1p + 1p cerise   1.50 1.50
CB4 SP8 2.50p + 2.50p ol gray   8.50 6.00
CB5 SP8 5p + 5p dull green   9.25 7.25
  Nos. CB1-CB5 (5)   20.18 15.37

Argentine Intl. Philatelic Exhib., 1950.

Pieta by Michelangelo SPAP2

1951, Dec. 22   Perf. 13½x13
CB6 SPAP2 2.45p +7.55p grnsh blk   21.00 14.00
Surtax as for the Eva Peron Foundation.

Flower and Child's Head — SPAP3   Stamp of 1858 — SPAP4

1958, Mar. 15   Perf. 13½
CB7 SPAP3 1p +50c deep claret   .28   .28
Surtax for National Council for Children.

1958, Mar. 29   Litho.   Wmk. 90
CB8 SPAP4 1p + 50c gray ol & bl   .40   .32
CB9 SPAP4 2p + 1p rose lilac & vio   .52   .42
CB10 SPAP4 3p + 1.50p green & brown   .60   .52
CB11 SPAP4 5p + 2.50p gray ol & car rose   1.00   .85
CB12 SPAP4 10p + 5p gray ol & brn   2.00 1.65
  Nos. CB8-CB12 (5)   4.52 3.76

The surtax was for the Intl. Centennial Philatelic Exhibition, Buenos Aires, Apr. 19-27.

Type of Semi-Postal Issue, 1958
Designs: 1p+50c, Flooded area. 5p+2.50p, House and truck under water.

1958, Oct. 4   Photo.   Perf. 13½
CB13 SP11 1p + 50c dull purple   .25   .20
CB14 SP11 5p + 2.50p grnsh blue   .80   .75

The surtax was for victims of a flood in the Buenos Aires district.

Type of Semi-Postal Issue, 1959

1959, Sept. 5   Litho.   Perf. 13½
CB15 SP13 2p + 1p Rowing   .40   .26
CB16 SP13 3p + 1.50p Woman diver   .60   .48

Type of Semi-Postal Issue, 1960
Birds: 2p+1p, Rufous tinamou. 3p+1.50p, Rhea.

1960, Feb. 6   Perf. 13½
CB17 SP14 2p + 1p rose car & sal   .30   .20
CB18 SP14 3p + 1.50p slate green   .45   .35

The surtax was for child welfare work.
See No. CB29.

Buenos Aires Market Place, 1810 — SPAP5   Seibo, National Flower — SPAP6

6p+3p, Oxcart water carrier. 10.70p+5.30p, Settlers landing. 20p+10p, The Fort.

1960, Aug. 20   Photo.   Wmk. 90
CB19 SPAP5 2 + 1p rose brown   .16   .15
CB20 SPAP5 6 + 3p gray   .35   .24
CB21 SPAP5 10.70 + 5.30p blue   .60   .35
CB22 SPAP5 20 + 10p bluish grn   1.00   .85
  Nos. CB19-CB22 (4)   2.11 1.59

Inter-American Philatelic Exhibition EFIMAYO 1960, Buenos Aires, Oct. 12-24, held to for the sesquicentennial of the May Revolution of 1910. For overprints see Nos. CB25-CB28.

1960, Sept. 10   Perf. 13½
10.70p+5.30p, Copihue, Chile's national flower.
CB23 SPAP6 6 + 3p lilac rose   .35   .28
CB24 SPAP6 10.70 + 5.30p vermilion   .52   .42

The surtax was for earthquake victims in Chile.

Nos. CB19-CB22 Overprinted: "DIA DE LAS NACIONES UNIDAS 24 DE OCTUBRE"

1960, Oct. 8
CB25 SPAP5 2 + 1p rose brown   .20   .15
CB26 SPAP5 6 + 3p gray   .32   .28
CB27 SPAP5 10.70 + 5.30p blue   .48   .42
CB28 SPAP5 20 + 10p bluish green   .85   .75
  Nos. CB25-CB28 (4)   1.85 1.60

United Nations Day, Oct. 24, 1960.

Type of Semi-Postal Issue, 1960
Design: Emperor penguins.

1961, Feb. 25   Photo.   Wmk. 90
CB29 SP14 1.80p + 90c gray   .32   .20
The surtax was for child welfare work.

Type of Semi-Postal Issue, 1962

Stamp of 1862 — SPAP7   Crutch, Olympic Torch and Rings — SPAP8

1962, May 19   Litho.
CB30 SPAP7 6.50p + 6.50p Prus bl & grnsh bl   .70   .65

Opening of the "Argentina 62" Philatelic Exhibition, Buenos Aires, May 19-29.

Type of Semi-Postal Issue, 1963

1963, May 18   Wmk. 90   Perf. 13½
CB31 SP21 11p + 5p Bicycling   .55   .50

Type of Semi-Postal Issue, 1962

1963, Dec. 21   Perf. 13½
CB32 SP20 11p + 5p Great kiskadee   .70   .60

The surtax was for child welfare.

Type of Semi-Postal Issue, 1964

1964, July 18   Litho.
CB33 SP22 11p + 5p Sailboat   .50   .50

1964, Sept. 19   Litho.   Perf. 13½
CB34 SPAP8 18p + 9p bluish grn, blk, red & yel .60   .60

13th "Olympic" games for the handicapped, Tokyo, 1964.

Bird Type of Semi-Postal Issue, 1962

1964, Dec. 23   Litho.   Wmk. 90
CB35 SP20 18p + 9p Chilean swallow   .90   .75

The surtax was for child welfare.

ARGENTINA

Bird Type of Semi-Postal Issue, 1962, Inscribed "R. ARGENTINA"

Design: Rufous ovenbird.

1966, Mar. 26 Perf. 13½
CB36 SP20 27.50p + 12.50p bl, ocher, yel & grn .80 .70

The surtax was for child welfare.

Coat of Arms — SPAP9

1966, June 25 Litho. Perf. 13½
CB37 SPAP9 10p + 10p yellow & multi 1.75 1.40

ARGENTINA '66 Philatelic Exhibition held in connection with the sesquicentennial celebration of the Declaration of Independence, Buenos Aires, July 16-23. The surtax was for the Exhibition. Issued in sheets of 4.

Bird Type of Semi-Postal Issue, 1962, Inscribed "R. ARGENTINA"

Designs: 15p+7p, Blue and yellow tanager. 26p+13p, Toco toucan.

1967 Litho. Wmk. 90
CB38 SP20 15p + 7p blk, bl, grn & yel 1.00 .90
CB39 SP20 26p + 13p blk, org, yel & bl .50 .40

The surtax was for child welfare.
Issue dates: 15p+7p, Jan. 14. 26p+13p, Dec. 23.

Bird Type of Semi-Postal Issue, 1969

Design: 26p+13p, Lineated woodpecker.

1969, Sept. 20 Wmk. 365 Perf. 13½
CB40 SP24 26p + 13p multi .48 .40

The surtax was for child welfare.

Bird Type of Semi-Postal Issue, 1970

Design: 40c+20c, Chilean flamingo.

1970, May 9 Litho. Wmk. 365
CB41 SP25 40c + 20c multi .45 .40

The surtax was for child welfare.

Fish Type of Semi-Postal Issue, 1971

Design: Pejerrey (atherinidae family).

1971, Feb. 20 Unwmk. Perf. 12½
Size: 75x15mm
CB42 SP26 40c + 20c lt blue & multi .40 .40

The surtax was for child welfare.

OFFICIAL STAMPS

Regular Issues Overprinted in Black

1884-87 Unwmk. Perf. 12, 14
O1 A29 ½c brown 12.00 10.00
O2 A23 1c red 8.00 6.00
  b. Perf. 12 40.00 30.00
O3 A29 1c red .50 .35
  b. Double overprint 35.00 35.00
O4 A20 2c green .50 .35
  b. Double overprint 35.00 35.00
O5 A11 4c brown .50 .35
O6 A7 8c lake .50 .35
O7 A8 10c green 40.00 25.00
O8 A23 12c ultra (#45) 6.50 4.00
  a. Perf. 14 325.00 125.00
O9 A29 12c grnsh blue .80 .60
O10 A19 24c blue 1.00 .85
O11 A21 25c lake 16.00 12.50
O12 A12 30c orange 32.50 20.00
O13 A13 60c black 20.00 12.50

O14 A14 90c blue 20.00 15.00
  b. Double overprint 50.00 45.00
  Nos. O1-O14 (14) 158.80 107.85

Inverted Overprint
O1a A29 ½c 16.00 12.00
O2a A23 1c Perf. 14 50.00 40.00
  c. Perf. 12 32.50 30.00
O3a A29 1c 1.50 1.00
O4a A20 2c 65.00 40.00
O5a A11 4c 40.00 32.50
O6a A7 8c 60.00 60.00
O8b A23 12c Perf. 12 12.50 —
O9a A29 12c 125.00 65.00
O10a A19 24c 2.75 1.65
O13a A13 60c 90.00 50.00
O14a A14 90c 50.00 40.00

1884 Rouletted
O15 A17 16c green 1.75 1.00
  a. Double overprint 15.00 —
  b. Inverted overprint 125.00 —
O16 A18 20c blue 8.00 7.00
  a. Inverted overprint 60.00 60.00
O17 A19 24c blue 1.25 1.00
  a. Inverted overprint 4.00 2.50
  b. Double ovpt. one inverted 250.00 —
  Nos. O15-O17 (3) 11.00 9.00

Overprinted Diagonally in Red
1885 Perf. 12
O18 A20 2c green 2.00 1.50
  a. Inverted overprint 40.00 32.50
O19 A11 4c brown 2.00 1.25
  a. Inverted overprint 40.00 30.00
  b. Double overprint 50.00 —
O20 A13 60c black 20.00 16.00
O21 A14 90c blue 200.00 150.00

1885 Rouletted
O22 A19 24c blue 17.50 12.50

On all of these stamps, the overprint is found reading both upwards and downwards. Counterfeits exist of No. O21 overprint and others.

Regular Issues Handstamped Horizontally in Black **OFICIAL**

1884 Perf. 12, 14
O23 A23 1c red 50.00 17.00
  a. Perf. 12 150.00 100.00
O24 A20 2c green, diagonal overprint 25.00 15.00
  a. Horizontal overprint 150.00 125.00
O25 A11 4c brown 10.00 7.50
O26 A7 8c lake 10.00 10.00
O27 A23 12c ultra 27.50 20.00

Overprinted Diagonally
O28 A19 24c bl, rouletted 20.00 14.00
O29 A13 60c black 15.00 10.00

Counterfeit overprints exist.

Liberty Head — O1

Perf. 11½, 12 and Compound
1901, Dec. 1 Engr.
O31 O1 1c gray .20 .15
  b. Vert. pair, imperf. horiz. 50.00
  c. Horiz. pair, imperf. vert. 50.00
O32 O1 2c orange brown .30 .20
O33 O1 5c red .40 .20
  b. Vert. pair, imperf. horiz. 50.00
O34 O1 10c dark green .45 .20
O35 O1 30c dark blue 4.00 1.00
O36 O1 50c orange 1.65 1.00
  Nos. O31-O36 (6) 7.00 2.75

Imperf, Pairs
O31a O1 1c 40.00
O32a O1 2c 40.00
O33a O1 5c 50.00
O34a O1 10c 40.00
O35a O1 30c 65.00
O36a O1 50c 50.00

Regular Stamps of 1935-51 Overprinted in Black

SERVICIO OFICIAL c

Perf. 13x13½, 13½x13, 13
1938-54 Wmk. RA in Sun (90)
O37 A129 1c buff ('40) .15 .15
O38 A130 2c dk brn ('40) .15 .15
O39 A132 3c grn ('39) .15 .15
O40 A132 3c lt gray ('39) .15 .15
O41 A134 5c yel brn .15 .15
O42 A195 5c car ('53) .15 .15
O43 A137 10c carmine .15 .15
O44 A137 10c brn ('39) .15 .15

O45 A140 15c lt gray bl, type II ('47) .15 .15
O46 A139 15c slate blue .50 .15
O47 A139 15c pale ultra ('39) .15 .15
O48 A139 20c blue ('53) .30 .15
O49 A141 25c carmine .15 .15
  a. Overprint 11mm .20 .15
O49B A143 40c dk violet .90 .15
O50 A144 50c red & org .15 .15
  a. Overprint 11mm .25 .15
O51 A146 1p brn blk & lt bl ('40) .20 .15
O52 A224 1p choc & lt bl ('51) .20 .15
  a. Overprint 11mm .20 .15
O53 A147 2p brn lake & dk ultra (ovpt. 11mm) ('54) .70 .15
  Nos. O37-O53 (18) 4.60 2.70

Overprinted in Black on Stamps and Types of 1945-47

Perf. 13x13½, 13½x13
1945-46 Unwmk.
O54 A130 2c sepia 2.75 .40
O55 A134 3c lt gray 2.25 .30
O56 A134 5c yel brn .65 .15
O57 A195 5c dp car .15 .15
O58 A137 10c brown .15 .15
  a. Double overprint
O59 A140 15c lt gray bl, type II .15 .15
O61 A141 25c dull rose .15 .15
O62 A144 50c red & org .55 .15
O63 A146 1p brn blk & lt bl .15 .15
O64 A147 2p brn lake & bl .40 .15
O65 A148 5p ind & ol grn .15 .15
O66 A149 10p dp cl & int blk .45 .15
O67 A150 20p lt grn & brn 1.00 .30
  Nos. O54-O67 (13) 8.95 2.50

Overprinted in Black on Stamps and Types of 1942-50

Perf. 13, 13x13½
1944-51 Wmk. 288
O73 A134 3c lt gray 1.10 .50
O74 A134 5c yellow brown .25 .15
O75 A137 10c red brown .15 .15
O76 A140 15c lt gray bl, type II .25 .15
O77 A144 50c red & org (overprint 11 mm) 1.50 .50
O78 A146 1p brn blk & lt bl (overprint 11mm) 1.75 .35
  Nos. O73-O78 (6) 5.00 1.80

Catalogue values for unused stamps in this section, from this point to the end of the section, are for Never Hinged items.

Nos. 600-606 Overprinted in Black

SERVICIO OFICIAL d

1953 Wmk. 90 Perf. 13
O79 A228 5c gray .15 .15
O80 A228 10c rose lilac .15 .15
O81 A228 20c rose pink .15 .15
O82 A228 25c dull green .15 .15
O83 A228 40c dull violet .15 .15
O84 A228 45c deep blue .20 .15
O85 A228 50c dull broen .15 .15

Nos. 611-617 Overprinted Type "e" in Blue

Perf. 13x13½, 13½x13
O86 A229 1p dk brown .15 .15
O87 A229 1.50p dp green .30 .15
O88 A229 2p brt carmine .20 .15
O89 A229 3p indigo .55 .25

Size: 30x40mm
O90 A229 5p red brown .55 .45
O91 A228 10p red 2.75 1.75
O92 A229 20p green 30.00 20.00
  Nos. O79-O92 (14) 35.60 23.95

No. 612 Overprinted Type "f" in Blue
O93 A229 1.50p dp grn 1.00 .30

Regular Issues of 1954-59 Variously Overprinted in Black or Blue

S. OFICIAL   SERVICIO OFICIAL
  g   h

Perf. 13½, 13x13½, 13½x13
1955-61 Litho. Wmk. 90
O94 A237(c) 20c red (#629) .15 .15
O95 A237(d) 20c red (#629) .15 .15
O96 A237(d) 40c red, ovpt. 15mm (#630) .15 .15

Engr.
O97 A239(g) 50c bl (#632) .15 .15

Photo.
O98 A239(h) 1p brn (#635) .15 .15
O99 A239(e) 1p brn (Bl, #635) .15 .15
O100 A239(e) 1p brn (Bk, #635) .15 .15

Engr.
O101 A239(h) 3p vio brn (#638) .15 .15
O102 A240(h) 5p gray grn (#639) .30 .15
O103 A240(h) 10p yel grn (#640) .45 .15
O104 A240(f) 20p dl vio (#641) .75 .30
O105 A240(h) 20p dl vio (#641) .75 .25
O106 A241(i) 50p ultra & ind (#642) 1.10 .20
  Nos. O94-O106 (13) 4.55 2.25

The overprints on Nos. O99-O100 and O103-O104 are horizontal; that on No. O109 is vertical. On No. O106 overprint measures 23mm.
Issue dates: No. O102, 1957. Nos. O97, O101, O103, O105, 1958. Nos. O98-O99, O104, 1959. No. O100, 1960. No. O106, 1961.

No. 659 Overprinted Type "d"

1957 Wmk. 90 Litho. Perf. 13
O108 A133 20c dl pur (ovpt. 15mm) .15 .15

Nos. 666, 658 and 663 Variously Overprinted

1957 Photo. Perf. 13x13½, 13½
O109 A261(g) 2p claret .20 .15
O110 A254(e) 2.40p brown .20 .15
O111 A258(c) 4.40p grnsh gray .25 .15
  Nos. O109-O111 (3) .65 .45

Nos. 668, 685-687, 690-691, 693-705, 742, 742C and Types of 1959-65 Overprinted in black, Blue or Red Types "e," "g," or

S. OFICIAL   **S. OFICIAL**
  i   j

S. OFICIAL   **S. OFICIAL**   **S. OFICIAL**
  k   m   n

Lithographed; Photogravure
1960-68 Perf. 13x13½, 13½
O112 A128(g) 5c buff (vert. ovpt.) .15 .15
O113 A275(j) 10c sl grn .15 .15
O114 A275(j) 20c dl red brn .15 .15
O115 A275(j) 50c bister .15 .15
O116 A278(k) 1p brn .15 .15
O117 A278(j) 1p brn, photo. (vert. ovpt.) .20 .15
O117A A278(j) 1p brn, litho., (down) .20 .15
O118 A276(j) 2p rose red .15 .15
O119 A312(m) 2p dp grn (down) .25 .15
O120 A312(j) 2p brt grn (up) .15 .15
O121 A312(j) 2p grn litho. (down) .25 .15
O122 A277(e) 3p dk bl (horiz.) .20 .15
O123 A277(j) 3p dk blue .20 .15
O124 A276(j) 4p red, litho. .20 .15
O125 A312(j) 4p rose red, litho. (down) .20 .15
O126 A277(e) 5p brn (Bl) (horiz.) .25 .15
O127 A277(e) 5p brn (Bk) (horiz.) .25 .15
O128 A277(j) 5p sepia .15 .15
O129 A277(e) 5p sepia (horiz. ovpt.) .15 .15
O130 A278(j) 8p red .20 .15
O131 A278(i) 10p lt red brn .45 .15
O132 A276(j) 10p vermilion .20 .15
O133 A278(j) 10p brn car (up) .20 .15
O134 A278(m) 12p dk brn vio .35 .15
O135 A278(k) 20p Prus grn .50 .15
O136 A278(j) 20p Prus grn (up) .40 .15
O137 A278(m) 20p red, litho. .35 .15
O138 A276(m) 20p red, litho. .35 .15
O139 A278(j) 23p grn (vert. ovpt.) .50 .15
O140 A278(j) 25p dp vio, photo. (R) (up) .50 .15
O141 A278(j) 25p pur, litho. (R) (down) .50 .15
O142 A241(n) 50p dk blue 1.10 .15
O143 A279(m) 100p bl (horiz. ovpt.) 1.10 .35

O144 A279(m) 100p blue (up) 1.10 .35
O145 A280(m) 300p dp violet 2.25 .60
Nos. O112-O145 (35) 13.50 6.10

The "m" overprint measures 15½mm on 2p; 14½mm on 12p, 100p and 300p; 13mm on 20p.
Issue dates: Nos. O122, O127, O135, 1961. Nos. O122-O114, O116, O118, 1962. No. O124, 1963. Nos. O119, O134, O143, 1964. Nos. O117, O125, O130, O139, O144, 1965. Nos. O120, O128, O132-O133, O136, O140, O142, O145, 1966. Nos. O121, O129, O137-O138, O141, 1967. No. O117A, 1968.

Nos. 699, 823-825, 827-829, and Type of 1962 Overprinted in Black or Red Types "j," "m," or "o"

o **SERVICIO OFICIAL**

Inscribed: "Republica Argentina"

Litho., Photo., Engr.

1964-67 Wmk. 90 *Perf. 13½*

O149 A312(j) 6p rose red (down) .25 .15
O153 A238a(m) 22p ultra .50 .15
O154 A238a(j) 43p dk car rose (down) .75 .15
O155 A238a(j) 45p brn, photo. (up) .75 .15
O156 A238a(j) 45p brn, litho. (up) 1.10 .20
O157 A241(j) 50p dk bl (up) (R) 2.25 .15
O158 A366(j) 90p ol bis (up) 2.75 .20
O162 A495(o) 500p yel grn 3.50 .80
Nos. O149-O162 (8) 11.85 1.95

Issued: No. O153, 1964; No. O155, 1966; Nos. O149, O156-O162, 1967.

Type of 1959-67 Ovptd. Type "j"

1969 Litho. Wmk. 365 *Perf. 13½*

O163 A276 20p vermilion .20 .15

OFFICIAL DEPARTMENT STAMPS

Regular Issues of 1911-37 Overprinted in Black

M. A. Type I **M. A.** Type II

Ministry of Agriculture (M. A.)

Type I

1913-37

On Stamp of 1911

OD1 A88 2c #181 .15 .15

On Stamps of 1912-14

OD2 A88 1c #190 .15 .15
OD3 A88 2c #191 .15 .15
OD4 A88 5c #194 .30 .15
OD5 A88 12c #196 .15 .15
Nos. OD2-OD5 (4) .75 .60

On Stamps of 1915-16

OD6 A88 1c #208 .15 .15
OD7 A88 2c #209 .15 .15
OD8 A88 5c #212 .15 .15
OD9 A91 5c #220 .15 .15
Nos. OD6-OD9 (4) .60 .60

On Stamp of 1917

OD10 A94 12c #238 .30 .15

On Stamps of 1918-19

OD11 A93 1c #249 .15 .15
OD12 A93 2c #250 .15 .15
OD13 A93 5c #253 .15 .15
OD14 A94 12c #255 .15 .15
OD15 A94 20c #256 .15 .15
Nos. OD10-OD15 (6) 1.05 .90

On Stamps of 1920

OD16 A93 1c #265 .30 .25
OD17 A93 2c #266 .50 .25
OD18 A93 5c #269 .20 .15
Nos. OD16-OD18 (3) 1.00 .65

On Stamps of 1922-23

OD19 A94 12c #311 1.00 .40
OD20 A94 20c #312 25.00

On Stamps of 1923

OD21 A104 1c #324 .15 .15
OD22 A104 2c #325 .25 .15
OD23 A104 5c #328 .15 .15
OD24 A104 12c #330 .15 .15
OD25 A104 20c #331 .15 .15
Nos. OD21-OD25 (5) .85 .75

On Stamps of 1923-31

OD26 A104 1c #341 .15 .15
OD27 A104 2c #342, I .15 .15
a. Type II 1.50 .75
OD28 A104 3c #343 .15 .15
OD29 A104 5c #345, II .15 .15
a. Type I .15 .15
OD30 A104 10c #346, II .15 .15
a. Type I .15 .15
OD31 A104 12c #347 .15 .15
OD32 A104 20c #348, I .15 .15
a. Type II .15 .15
OD33 A104 30c #351 .15 .15
Nos. OD26-OD33 (8) 1.20 1.20

On Stamp of 1926

OD34 A110 12c #360 .15 .15

Type II

On Stamps of 1935-37

OD35 A129 1c #419 .15 .15
OD36 A130 2c #420 .15 .15
OD37 A132 3c #422 .15 .15
OD38 A134 5c #427 .15 .15
OD39 A137 10c #430 .15 .15
OD40 A139 15c #434 .50 .15
OD41 A140 20c #437 .30 .15
OD42 A140 20c #438 .20 .15
OD43 A141 25c #441 .25 .15
OD44 A142 30c #442 .15 .15
OD45 A145 1p #445 2.50 1.50
OD46 A146 1p #446 .50 .25
Nos. OD35-OD46 (12) 5.15 3.25

Ministry of War (M. G.)

Type I

On Stamp of 1911

OD47 A88 2c #181 .15 .15

On Stamps of 1912-14

OD48 A88 1c #190 .15 .15
OD49 A88 2c #191 .75 .15
OD50 A88 5c #194 .15 .15
OD51 A88 12c #196 .15 .15
Nos. OD48-OD51 (4) 1.20 .60

On Stamps of 1915-16

OD52 A88 1c #208 6.00 .75
OD53 A88 2c #209 .60 .15
OD54 A88 5c #212 .75 .15
OD55 A91 5c #220 1.00 .25
OD56 A92 12c #222 1.00 .35
Nos. OD52-OD56 (5) 9.35 1.65

On Stamps of 1917

OD57 A93 1c #232 .30 .15
OD58 A93 2c #233 .40 .15
OD59 A93 5c #236 .30 .15
OD60 A94 12c #238 .60 .15
Nos. OD57-OD60 (4) 1.60 .60

On Stamps of 1918-19

OD61 A93 1c #249 .15 .15
OD62 A93 2c #250 .15 .15
OD63 A93 5c #253 .15 .15
OD64 A94 12c #255 .40 .15
OD65 A94 20c #256 1.25 .15
Nos. OD61-OD65 (5) 2.10 .75

On Stamps of 1920

OD66 A93 2c #266 .40 .15
OD67 A93 5c #269 .40 .15
OD68 A94 12c #271 .35 .15
Nos. OD66-OD68 (3) 1.15 .45

On Stamp of 1920

OD69 A94 12c #299 2.00 .25

On Stamps of 1922-23

OD70 A93 1c #305 .75 .15
OD71 A93 2c #306 1.50 .45
OD72 A103 5c #309 .75 .15
OD73 A94 20c #312 .30 .15
Nos. OD70-OD73 (4) 3.30 .90

On Stamp of 1922-23

OD74 A93 2c #318 5.00 .50

On Stamps of 1923

OD75 A104 1c #324 .15 .15
OD76 A104 2c #325 .15 .15
OD77 A104 5c #328 .15 .15
OD78 A104 12c #330 .15 .15
OD79 A104 20c #331 1.00 .15
Nos. OD75-OD79 (5) 1.60 .75

On Stamps of 1923-31

OD80 A104 1c #341 1.25 .45
OD81 A104 2c #342 .20 .15
OD82 A104 3c #343, I .15 .15
a. Type II .40 .15
OD83 A104 5c #345, I .15 .15
a. Type II .20 .15
OD84 A104 10c #346, II .15 .15
a. Type I .60 .15
OD85 A104 20c #348, I .15 .15
a. Type II .40 .15
OD86 A104 30c #351, II .20 .15
a. Type I 1.00 .15
OD87 A105 1p #353 2.00 .30
Nos. OD80-OD87 (8) 4.25 1.65

On Stamp of 1926

OD88 A109 5c #359 .60 .15

Type II

On Stamps of 1935-37

OD89 A129 1c #419 .15 .15
OD90 A130 2c #420 .15 .15
OD91 A132 3c #422 .15 .15
OD92 A134 5c #427 .15 .15
OD93 A137 10c #430 .15 .15
OD94 A139 15c #434 .25 .15
OD95 A140 20c #437 1.00 .15
OD96 A140 20c #438 .25 .15
OD97 A141 25c #441 .15 .15
OD98 A142 30c #442 .15 .15
OD99 A144 50c #444 .25 .15
OD100 A145 1p #445 1.25 .50
OD101 A146 1p #446 .50 .25
Nos. OD89-OD101 (13) 4.55 2.40

Ministry of Finance (M. H.)

Type I

On Stamp of 1911

OD102 A88 2c #181 .15 .15

On Stamps of 1912-14

OD103 A88 1c #190 .15 .15
OD104 A88 2c #191 .15 .15
OD105 A88 5c #194 .20 .15
OD106 A88 12c #196 .15 .15
Nos. OD103-OD106 (4) .65 .60

On Stamps of 1915-16

OD107 A88 2c #209 .15 .15
OD108 A88 5c #212 .15 .15
OD109 A91 5c #220 .15 .15
Nos. OD107-OD109 (3) .45 .45

On Stamps of 1917

OD110 A93 2c #233 .15 .15
OD111 A93 5c #236 1.25 .15
OD112 A94 12c #238 .15 .15
Nos. OD110-OD112 (3) 1.55 .45

On Stamps of 1918-19

OD113 A93 2c #250 25.00
OD114 A93 5c #253 .20 .15
OD115 A94 12c #255 .45 .15
OD116 A94 20c #256 .45 .15

On Stamps of 1920

OD117 A93 1c #265 .75 .45
OD118 A93 2c #266 1.25 .45
OD119 A93 5c #269 .30 .15
OD120 A94 12c #271 .60 .20
Nos. OD117-OD120 (4) 2.90 1.25

On Stamp of 1922-23

OD121 A94 20c #312 12.50 2.50

On Stamps of 1923

OD122 A104 1c #324 .75 .40
OD123 A104 2c #325 .15 .15
OD124 A104 5c #328 .15 .15
OD125 A104 12c #330 .15 .15
OD126 A104 20c #331 .15 .15
Nos. OD122-OD126 (5) 1.35 1.00

On Stamps of 1923-31

OD127 A104 3c #343 7.00 1.50
OD128 A104 5c #345 .15 .15
OD129 A104 10c #346 .15 .15
OD130 A104 12c #347 7.00 3.75
OD131 A104 20c #348, I .15 .15
a. Type II .35 .15
OD132 A104 30c #351 .25 .15
OD133 A105 1p #353 .40 .15
Nos. OD127-OD133 (7) 15.10 6.00

On Stamp of 1926

OD134 A110 12c #360 12.50 12.50

Type II

On Stamps of 1935-37

OD135 A129 1c #419 .15 .15
OD136 A130 2c #420 .15 .15
OD137 A132 3c #422 .15 .15
OD138 A134 5c #427 .15 .15
OD139 A137 10c #430 .15 .15
OD140 A139 15c #434 .45 .15
OD141 A140 20c #437 .15 .15
OD142 A140 20c #438 .15 .15
OD143 A142 30c #442 .15 .15
OD144 A145 1p #445 2.00 1.00
OD145 A146 1p #446 .50 .25
Nos. OD135-OD145 (11) 4.15 2.60

Ministry of the Interior (M. I.)

Type I

On Stamp of 1911

OD146 A88 2c #181 .25 .15

On Stamps of 1912-14

OD147 A88 1c #190 .15 .15
OD148 A88 2c #191 .15 .15
OD149 A88 5c #194 .15 .15
OD150 A88 12c #196 .15 .15
Nos. OD146-OD150 (5) .85 .75

On Stamps of 1915-17

OD151 A88 2c #209 .80 .30
OD152 A88 5c #212 .75 .15
OD153 A91 5c #220 .60 .15
OD154 A93 5c #236 1.50 .15
Nos. OD151-OD154 (4) 3.65 .75

On Stamps of 1918-19

OD155 A93 2c #250 .15 .15
OD156 A93 5c #253 .15 .15

On Stamps of 1920

OD157 A93 1c #265 3.75 1.25
OD158 A93 5c #269 .75 .35

On Stamps of 1922-23

OD159 A93 2c #306 12.50 12.50
OD160 A103 5c #309 3.50 1.25
OD161 A94 12c #311 1.25 .40
OD162 A94 20c #312 1.25 .40
Nos. OD159-OD162 (4) 18.50 14.55

On Stamps of 1923

OD163 A104 1c #324 .15 .15
OD164 A104 2c #325 .15 .15
OD165 A104 5c #328 .15 .15
OD166 A104 12c #330 2.00 2.00
OD167 A104 20c #331 .75 .15
Nos. OD163-OD167 (5) 3.20 2.60

On Stamps of 1923-31

OD168 A104 1c #341 .15 .15
OD169 A104 2c #342 .15 .15
OD170 A104 3c #343, II .15 .15
a. Type I 1.25 .30
OD171 A104 5c #345, I .15 .15
a. Type II .15 .15
OD172 A104 10c #346, II .15 .15
OD173 A104 12c #347 .30 .15
OD174 A104 20c #348, II .15 .15
a. Type I .75 .15
OD175 A104 30c #351 .15 .15
Nos. OD168-OD175 (8) 1.35 1.20

Type II

On Stamps of 1935-37

OD176 A129 1c #419 .15 .15
OD177 A130 2c #420 .15 .15
OD178 A132 3c #422 .15 .15
OD178A A134 5c #427 .15 .15
OD179 A137 10c #430 .15 .15
OD180 A139 15c #434 .30 .15
OD181 A140 20c #437 .75 .15
OD182 A140 20c #438 .20 .15
OD182A A142 30c #442 .15 .15
OD182B A145 1p #445 2.00 1.00
OD182C A146 1p #446 .50 .25
Nos. OD176-OD182C (11) 4.65 2.60

Ministry of Justice and Instruction (M. J. I.)

Type I

On Stamp of 1911

OD183 A88 2c #181 1.25 .15

On Stamps of 1912-14

OD184 A88 1c #190 1.50 .15
OD185 A88 2c #191 1.00 .15
OD186 A88 5c #194 .45 .15
OD187 A88 12c #196 .45 .15
Nos. OD184-OD187 (4) 3.40 .60

On Stamps of 1915-17

OD188 A88 1c #208 .30 .15
OD189 A88 2c #209 .30 .15
OD190 A88 5c #212 1.00 .15
OD191 A91 5c #220 .25 .15
OD192 A92 12c #222 .75 .15
Nos. OD188-OD192 (5) 2.60 .75

On Stamps of 1917

OD193 A93 1c #232 .25 .15
OD194 A93 2c #233 .75 .15
OD195 A93 5c #236 .25 .15
OD196 A94 12c #238 17.50 5.00
Nos. OD193-OD196 (4) 18.75 5.45

On Stamps of 1918-19

OD197 A93 1c #249 .15 .15
OD198 A93 2c #250 .15 .15
OD199 A93 5c #253 .15 .15
OD200 A94 12c #255 .20 .15
OD201 A94 20c #256 .50 .15
Nos. OD197-OD201 (5) 1.15 .75

On Stamps of 1920

OD202 A93 1c #265 .25 .15
OD203 A93 2c #266 .20 .15
OD204 A93 5c #269 .20 .15
OD205 A94 12c #271 .40 .15
Nos. OD202-OD205 (4) 1.05 .60

On Stamps of 1922-23

OD206 A93 1c #305 .25 .15
OD207 A93 2c #306 1.50 .50
OD208 A103 5c #309 .25 .15
OD209 A94 12c #311 10.00 1.75
OD210 A94 20c #312 1.50 .30
Nos. OD206-OD210 (5) 13.50 2.85

On Stamp of 1922-23

OD211 A93 2c #318 2.50 2.50

On Stamps of 1923

OD212 A104 1c #324 .15 .15
OD213 A104 2c #325 .15 .15
OD214 A104 5c #328 .15 .15
OD215 A104 12c #330 .15 .15
OD216 A104 20c #331 .50 .15
Nos. OD212-OD216 (5) 1.10 .75

On Stamps of 1923-31

OD217 A104 ½c #340 2.00 .75
OD218 A104 1c #341, I .15 .15
a. Type II .15 .15
OD219 A104 2c #342 .15 .15
OD220 A104 3c #343, I .15 .15
a. Type II .15 .15
OD221 A104 5c #345, I .15 .15
a. Type II .15 .15
OD222 A104 10c #346, II .15 .15
a. Type I .30 .15
OD223 A104 12c #347, I .15 .15
a. Type II .30 .15

OD224	A104	20c #348, I	.15	.15
a.		Type II	.15	.15
OD225	A104	30c #351	.15	.15
OD226	A105	1p #353	.40	.50
		Nos. OD217-OD226 (10)	3.60	2.45

On Stamps of 1926

OD227	A109	5c #359	.15	.15
OD228	A110	12c #360	.20	.15

Type II

On Stamps of 1935-37

OD229	A129	1c #419	.15	.15
OD230	A130	2c #420	.15	.15
OD231	A132	3c #422	.15	.15
OD232	A134	5c #427	.15	.15
OD233	A137	10c #430	.15	.15
OD234	A139	15c #434	.45	.15
OD234A	A140	20c #437	.15	.15
OD234B	A140	20c #438	.20	.15
OD234C	A141	25c #441	.15	.15
OD234D	A142	30c #442	.15	.15
OD234E	A145	1p #445	1.00	.60
OD234F	A146	1p #446	.30	.20
		Nos. OD229-OD234F (12)	3.15	2.30

Ministry of Marine
(M. M.)
Type I

On Stamp of 1911

OD235	A88	2c #181	.20	.15

On Stamps of 1912-14

OD236	A88	1c #190	.15	.15
OD237	A88	2c #191	.15	.15
OD238	A88	5c #194	2.00	.15
OD239	A88	12c #196	.15	.15
		Nos. OD236-OD239 (4)	2.45	.60

On Stamps of 1915-16

OD240	A88	2c #209	.60	.15
OD241	A88	5c #212	.40	.15

On Stamps of 1917

OD242	A93	1c #232	.15	.15
OD243	A93	2c #233	.15	.15
OD244	A93	5c #236	.15	.15
		Nos. OD242-OD244 (3)	.45	.45

On Stamps of 1918-19

OD245	A93	1c #249	.15	.15
OD246	A93	2c #250	.15	.15
OD247	A93	5c #253	.25	.15
OD248	A94	12c #255	.25	.15
OD249	A94	20c #256	3.00	.35
		Nos. OD245-OD249 (5)	3.80	.95

On Stamps of 1920

OD250	A93	1c #265	.15	.15
OD251	A93	2c #266	.20	.15
OD252	A93	5c #269	.25	.15
		Nos. OD250-OD252 (3)	.60	.45

On Stamps of 1922-23

OD253	A103	5c #309	1.00	.15
OD254	A94	12c #311	7.00	7.00
OD255	A94	20c #312	7.00	1.50
		Nos. OD253-OD254 (2)	8.00	7.15

On Stamps of 1923

OD256	A104	1c #324	.15	.15
OD257	A104	2c #325	.15	.15
OD258	A104	5c #328	.35	.15
OD259	A104	12c #330	.65	.15
OD260	A104	20c #331	.65	.15
		Nos. OD256-OD260 (5)	1.95	.75

On Stamps of 1923-31

OD261	A104	1c #341	.75	.25
OD262	A104	2c #342	.15	.15
OD263	A104	3c #343	.60	.20
OD264	A104	5c #345, I	.15	.15
a.		Type II	.60	.15
OD265	A104	10c #346	.60	.15
OD266	A104	20c #348, II	.60	.15
a.		Type I	.75	.15
OD267	A104	30c #351	1.00	.15
OD268	A105	1p #353	11.00	3.00
		Nos. OD261-OD268 (8)	14.85	4.20

On Stamp of 1926

OD269	A109	5c #359	.50	.15

Type II

On Stamps of 1935-37

OD270	A129	1c #419	.15	.15
OD271	A130	2c #420	.15	.15
OD272	A132	3c #422	.15	.15
OD273	A134	5c #427	.15	.15
OD274	A137	10c #430	.25	.15
OD275	A139	15c #434	.30	.15
OD276	A140	20c #437	.40	.15
OD277	A140	20c #438	.30	.15
OD278	A142	30c #442	.25	.15
OD279	A145	1p #445	3.25	1.00
OD280	A146	1p #446	.75	.25
		Nos. OD270-OD280 (11)	6.10	2.60

Ministry of Public Works
(M. O. P.)
Type I

On Stamp of 1911

OD281	A88	2c #181	.30	.15

On Stamps of 1912-14

OD282	A88	1c #190	.30	.15
OD283	A88	5c #194	.15	.15
OD284	A88	12c #196	1.50	.35
		Nos. OD282-OD284 (3)	1.95	.65

On Stamps of 1916-19

OD285	A91	5c #220	10.00	1.00
OD286	A94	12c #238	25.00	
OD287	A94	20c #256	25.00	

On Stamps of 1920

OD288	A93	2c #266	6.00	2.50
OD289	A93	5c #269	2.00	.15
OD290	A94	12c #271	20.00	6.00
		Nos. OD288-OD290 (3)	28.00	8.65

On Stamps of 1923

OD291	A104	1c #324	.40	.15
OD292	A104	2c #325	.30	.15
OD293	A104	5c #328	.40	.15
OD294	A104	12c #330	.60	.15
OD295	A104	20c #331	1.00	.15
		Nos. OD291-OD295 (5)	2.70	.75

On Stamps of 1923-31

OD296	A104	1c #341	.15	.15
OD297	A104	2c #342	.15	.15
OD298	A104	3c #343	.15	.15
OD299	A104	5c #345, I	.15	.15
a.		Type II	.15	.15
OD300	A104	10c #346	.15	.15
OD301	A104	12c #347	9.00	1.25
OD302	A104	20c #348, I	.15	.15
a.		Type II	2.50	.50
OD303	A104	30c #351	.40	.15
OD304	A105	1p #353	20.00	6.00
		Nos. OD296-OD304 (9)	30.30	8.30

On Stamp of 1926

OD305	A109	5c #359	.60	.15

Type II

On Stamps of 1935-37

OD306	A129	1c #419	.15	.15
OD307	A130	2c #420	.15	.15
OD308	A132	3c #422	.15	.15
OD309	A134	5c #427	.15	.15
OD310	A137	10c #430	.30	.15
OD311	A139	15c #434	.60	.15
OD312	A140	20c #437	.75	.15
OD313	A140	20c #438	.15	.15
OD314	A142	30c #442	.15	.15
OD315	A144	50c #444	.15	.15
OD316	A145	1p #445	2.00	1.00
OD317	A146	1p #446	.50	.25
		Nos. OD306-OD317 (12)	5.20	2.75

Ministry of Foreign Affairs and Religion
(M. R. C.)
Type I

On Stamp of 1911

OD318	A88	2c #181	5.00	1.25

On Stamps of 1912-14

OD319	A88	1c #190	.15	.15
OD320	A88	2c #191	.15	.15
OD321	A88	5c #194	.40	.15
OD322	A88	12c #196	1.50	.25
		Nos. OD319-OD322 (4)	2.20	.70

On Stamps of 1915-19

OD323	A88	5c #212	.40	.15
OD324	A91	5c #220	.15	.15
OD325	A94	20c #256	2.00	.75
		Nos. OD323-OD325 (3)	2.55	1.05

On Stamps of 1920

OD326	A93	1c #265	.40	.15
OD327	A93	5c #269	.15	.15

On Stamps of 1922-23

OD328	A93	2c #306	9.00	3.50
OD329	A103	5c #309	27.50	
OD330	A93	10c #311	22.50	
		Nos. OD328-OD330 (3)	59.00	

On Stamps of 1923

OD331	A104	1c #324	.15	.15
OD332	A104	2c #325	.15	.15
OD333	A104	5c #328	.15	.15
OD334	A104	12c #330	.15	.15
OD335	A104	20c #331	.15	.15
		Nos. OD331-OD335 (5)	.75	.75

On Stamps of 1923-31

OD336	A104	½c #340	1.00	.50
OD337	A104	1c #341	.15	.15
OD338	A104	2c #342	.15	.15
OD339	A104	3c #343	.15	.15
OD340	A104	5c #345	.15	.15
OD341	A104	10c #346, II	.15	.15
a.		Type I	1.50	.15
OD342	A104	12c #347	.15	.15
OD343	A104	20c #348, I	.15	.15
a.		Type II	.15	.15
OD344	A104	30c #351, I	.15	.15
a.		Type II	.15	.15
OD345	A105	1p #353	.40	.20
		Nos. OD336-OD346 (11)	2.75	2.05

On Stamp of 1926

OD346	A110	12c #360	.15	.15

Type II

On Stamps of 1935-37

OD347	A129	1c #419	.15	.15
OD348	A130	2c #420	.15	.15
OD349	A132	3c #422	.15	.15
OD350	A134	5c #427	.15	.15
OD351	A137	10c #430	.15	.15
OD352	A139	15c #434	.15	.15
OD353	A140	20c #437	.15	.15
OD354	A140	20c #438	.15	.15
OD355	A142	30c #442	.15	.15
OD356	A145	1p #445	2.50	1.25
OD357	A146	1p #446	1.00	.50
		Nos. OD347-OD357 (11)	4.85	3.10

BUENOS AIRES

The central point of the Argentine struggle for independence. At intervals Buenos Aires maintained an independent government but after 1862 became a province of the Argentine Republic.

8 Reales = 1 Peso

> Values of Buenos Aires Nos. 1-8 vary according to condition. Quotations are for fine copies. Very fine to superb specimens sell at much higher prices, and inferior or poor copies sell at reduced values, depending on the condition of the individual specimen.
> Nos. 1-8 were issued without gum.

Steamship — A1

1858 Unwmk. Typo. *Imperf.*

1	A1	1 (in) pesos lt brn	*350.*	*250.*
2	A1	2 (dos) pesos blue	175.	140.
b.		Diagonal half used as 1p on cover		*7,500.*
3	A1	3 (tres) pesos grn	1,500.	*750.*
a.		3p dark green	1,800.	*825.*
4	A1	4 (cuatro) pesos ver	4,750.	*1,750.*
a.		Half used as 2p on cover		*15,000.*
5	A1	5 (cinco) pesos org	4,250.	*1,400.*
a.		5p ocher	4,250.	*1,400.*
b.		5p olive yellow	4,250.	*1,400.*

Issued: #2-5, Apr. 29; #1, Oct. 26.

1858, Oct. 26

6	A1	4 (cuatro) reales brown	250.	200.
a.		4r gray brown	250.	200.
b.		4r yellow brown	250.	200.

1859, Jan. 1

7	A1	1 (in) pesos blue	165.	225.
a.		1p indigo	200.	250.
b.		Impression on reverse of stamp in blue	*3,000.*	
c.		Double impression	250.	300.
d.		Tete beche pair		*65,000.*
e.		Half used as 4r on cover		*7,500.*
8	A1	1 (to) pesos blue	350.	225.

Nos. 1, 2, 3 and 7 have been reprinted on very thick, hand-made paper. The same four stamps and No. 8 have been reprinted on thin, hard, white wove paper.

Counterfeits of Nos. 1-8 are plentiful.

Liberty Head — A2

1859, Sept. 3

9	A2	4r green, *bluish*	250.00	160.00
10	A2	1p blue	35.00	17.50
11	A2	2p vermilion	350.00	150.00
a.		2p red	300.00	125.00

Both clear and rough impressions of these stamps may be found. They have generally been called Paris and Local prints, respectively, but the opinion now obtains that the differences are due to the impression and that they do not represent separate issues. Values are for fine impressions. Rough or blurred impressions sell for less.

Many shades exist of Nos. 1-11.

1862, Oct. 4

12	A2	1p rose	200.00	100.00
13	A2	2p blue	350.00	75.00

All three values have been reprinted in black, brownish black, blue and red brown on thin hard white paper. The 4r has also been reprinted in green on bluish paper.

Values are for fine impressions. Rough or blurred impressions sell for less.

CORDOBA

A province in the central part of the Argentine Republic.

100 Centavos = 1 Peso

Arms of Cordoba — A1

Unwmk.

1858, Oct. 28 Litho. *Imperf.*

Laid Paper

1	A1	5c blue	125.	
2	A1	10c black	*2,500.*	

Cordoba stamps were printed on laid paper, but stamps from edges of the sheets sometimes do not show any laid lines and appear to be on wove paper. Counterfeits are plentiful.

CORRIENTES

The northeast province of the Argentine Republic.

1 Real M(oneda) C(orriente) =
12½ Centavos M.C. = 50 Centavos
100 Centavos Fuertes = 1 Peso Fuerte

> Nos. 1-2 were issued without gum. Nos. 3-8 were issued both with and without gum (values the same).

Ceres

A1 A2

Unwmk.

1856, Aug. 21 Typo. *Imperf.*

1	A1	1r black, *blue*	85.00	*115.00*

No. 1 used is valued with pen cancellation.

Pen Stroke Through "Un Real"

1860, Feb. 8

2	A1	(3c) black, *blue*	350.00	*175.00*

No. 2 used is valued with pen cancellation.

1860-78

3	A2	(3c) black, *blue*	9.50	*30.00*
4	A2	(2c) blk, *yel grn* ('64)	37.50	37.50
a.		(2c) black, *blue green*	92.50	110.00
5	A2	(2c) blk, *yel* ('67)	7.50	*19.00*
6	A2	(3c) blk, *dk bl* ('71)	3.00	*19.00*
7	A2	(3c) blk, *rose red* ('76)	100.00	50.00
a.		(3c) black, *lil rose* ('75)	135.00	80.00
8	A2	(3c) blk, *dk rose* ('79)	8.00	*32.50*
a.		(3c) black, *red vio* ('77)	60.00	35.00
		Nos. 3-8 (6)	165.50	188.00

Pen canceled examples of Nos. 3-8 sell for much less.

Printed from settings of 8 varieties, 3 or 4 impressions constituting a sheet. Some impressions were printed inverted and tete beche pairs may be cut from adjacent impressions.

From Jan. 1 to Feb. 24, 1864, No. 4 was used as a 5 centavos stamp but copies so used can only be distinguished when they bear dated cancellations.

The reprints show numerous spots and small defects which are not found on the originals. They are printed on gray blue, dull blue, gray green, dull orange and light magenta papers.

ARMENIA

är–'mē–nē–ə

LOCATION — South of Russia bounded by Georgia, Azerbaijan, Iran and Turkey
GOVT. — Republic
AREA — 11,306 sq. mi.
POP. — 3,300,000 (1989)
CAPITAL — Yerevan

With Azerbaijan and Georgia, Armenia made up the Transcaucasian Federation of Soviet Republics.

Stamps of Armenia were replaced in 1923 by those of Transcaucasian Federated Republics.

With the breakup of the Soviet Union on Dec. 26, 1991, Armenia and ten former Soviet republics established the Commonwealth of Independent States.

100 Kopecks = 1 Ruble
100 Luma = 1 Dram (1993)

Catalogue values for unused stamps in this country are for Never Hinged items, beginning with Scott 430 in the regular postage section.

Counterfeits abound of all overprinted and surcharged stamps.

Watermark

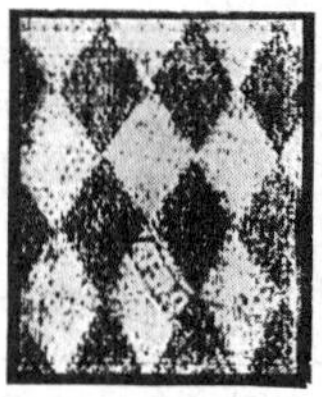

Diamonds — Wmk. 171

Perforations
Perforations are the same as the basic Russian stamps.

National Republic
Russian Stamps of 1902-19 Handstamped

Thirteen types exist of both framed and unframed overprints. The device is the Armenian "H," initial of Hayasdan (Armenia). Inverted and double overprints are found.

Surcharged **K 60 K**

Type I - Without periods.
Type II - Periods after 1st "K" and "60."

Black Surcharge

1919 Unwmk. *Perf. 14x14½*

1 A14 60k on 1k orange (II) 2.50 .40
a. Imperf. (I) 1.00 .24
b. Imperf. (II) 1.00 .24

Violet Surcharge

2 A14 60k on 1k orange (II) .50 .50

Handstamped in Violet — a

Perf.

6 A15 4k carmine 2.00 2.00
7 A14 5k claret, imperf. 7.50 7.50
a. Perf. 5.00 5.00
9 A14 10k on 7k lt blue 5.00 1.25
10 A11 15k red brn & bl 3.00 .25
11 A8 20k blue & car 2.00 1.00
13 A11 35k red brn & grn 3.50 3.50
14 A8 50k violet & green 3.50 3.50
15 A14 60k on 1k orange (II) 2.00 2.00
a. Imperf. (I) 1.90 2.00
b. Imperf. (II) 8.50 9.00
18 A13 5r dk bl, grn & pale bl 3.50 4.25
a. Imperf. 1.00 1.00
19 A12 7r dk green & pink 1.75 2.00
20 A13 10r scarlet, yel & gray 1.75 2.00

Handstamped in Black

31 A14 2k green, imperf. 1.00 .15
a. Perf. 5.00 4.25
32 A14 3k red, imperf. 1.00 .20
a. Perf. 5.00 2.00
33 A15 4k carmine .15 .20
34 A14 5k claret 1.00 .20
a. Imperf. 5.00 5.00
36 A15 10k dark blue 2.00 .65
37 A14 10k on 7k lt blue .50 .15
38 A11 15k red brn & bl .50 .15
a. Imperf. 3.00 3.00
39 A8 20k blue & car 1.00 .20
40 A11 25k green & gray vio 1.00 .20
41 A11 35k red brn & grn 1.00 .15
42 A8 50k violet & green 1.00 .15
43 A14 60k on 1k orange (II) 2.50 2.50
43A A11 70k brown & org 1.00 .30
b. Imperf. .50 .30
44 A9 1r pale brn, dk brn & org 1.50 .30
a. Imperf. .50 .50
45 A12 3½r mar & lt grn, imperf. 5.00 .65
a. Perf. 5.00 .85
46 A13 5r dk bl, grn & pale bl .60 .65
a. Imperf. 6.00 1.00
47 A12 7r dk green & pink 6.00 1.10
48 A13 10r scar, yel & gray 50.00 1.00

Handstamped in Violet — c

Unwmk. *Perf.*
Wove Paper

62 A14 2k green, imperf. .40 .40
a. Perf. 4.50 4.50
63 A14 3k red, imperf. .25 .25
a. Perf. 3.00 2.75
64 A15 4k carmine .50 .50
65 A14 5k claret 3.00 .40
a. Imperf. 3.00 .60
67 A15 10k dark blue 1.00 .85
68 A14 10k on 7k lt bl 1.00 .65
69 A11 15k red brn & bl 2.50 2.50
70 A8 20k blue & car .40 .40
71 A11 25k grn & gray vio 1.00 1.00
72 A11 35k red brn & grn 1.50 1.50
73 A8 50k violet & grn .50 .50
74 A14 60k on 1k org (II) 2.50 2.00
a. Imperf. (I) 1.65 1.65
b. Imperf. (II) 2.00 2.00
75 A9 1r pale brn, dk brn & org .60 .60
a. Imperf. 1.50 1.50
76 A12 3½r mar & lt grn, imperf. .75 .75
a. Perf. 1.00 1.00
77 A13 5r dk bl, grn & pale bl, imperf. 5.00 5.00
a. Perf. 4.00 4.00
78 A12 7r dk green & pink 7.50 7.50
79 A13 10r scar, yel & gray 2.25 1.90

Imperf

85 A11 70k brown & org 5.00 2.00

Handstamped in Black
Perf.

90 A14 1k orange 10.00 4.50
a. Imperf. 10.00 6.00
91 A14 2k green, imperf. 1.00 .15
a. Perf. 7.50 2.50
92 A14 3k red, imperf. 1.00 .20
a. Perf. 10.00 2.75
93 A15 4k carmine .50 .50
94 A14 5k claret 1.00 .15
a. Imperf. 3.00 .60
95 A14 7k light blue 15.00 15.00
96 A15 10k dark blue 12.00 12.00
97 A14 10k on 7k lt bl .15 .15
98 A11 15k red brn & bl .20 .15
99 A8 20k blue & car .15 .15
100 A11 25k grn & gray vio .50 .20
101 A11 35k red brn & grn .20 .15
102 A8 50k violet & grn .20 .15
102A A14 60k on 1k org, imperf. (I) .30 .30
b. Imperf. (II) .50 .50
c. Perf. (II) 2.50 1.25
103 A9 1r pale brn, dk brn & org 1.00 1.00
a. Imperf. .75 .75
104 A12 3½r maroon & lt grn 4.00 .50
a. Imperf. 5.00 .30
105 A13 5r dk bl, grn & pale bl 2.50 2.50
a. Imperf. 2.50 2.50
106 A12 7r dk green & pink 3.00 2.50
107 A13 10r scar, yel & gray 7.00 3.50

Imperf

113 A11 70k brown & org 1.00 .25

Handstamped in Violet or Black:

f

g

Violet Surcharge, Type f

1920 *Perf.*

120 A14 3r on 3k red, imperf. .85 .85
a. Perf. 2.50 2.50
121 A14 5r on 3k red 3.75 3.25
122 A15 5r on 4k car 10.00 8.00
123 A14 5r on 5k claret, imperf. 10.00 10.00
a. Perf. 10.00 8.00
124 A15 5r on 10k dk blue 10.00 8.00
125 A14 5r on 10k on 7k lt bl 10.00 8.00
126 A8 5r on 20k bl & car

Imperf

127 A14 5r on 2k green 7.00 7.00
128 A11 5r on 35k red brn & grn 7.00 7.00

Black Surcharge, Type f or Type g (#130)
Perf.

130 A14 1r on 1k orange .50 .50
a. Imperf. .75 .75
131 A14 3r on 3k red .15 .15
a. Imperf. .15 .15
132 A15 3r on 4k carmine 3.00 3.00
133 A14 5r on 2k green, imperf. .15 .15
a. Perf. 2.00 2.00
134 A14 5r on 3k red 5.00 5.00
a. Imperf. 2.50 2.50
135 A15 5r on 4k carmine .40 .40
a. Imperf. 4.75 4.75
136 A14 5r on 5k claret .50 .50
a. Imperf. .50 .50
137 A14 5r on 7k lt blue 2.00 2.00
138 A15 5r on 10k dk blue .50 .50
139 A14 5r on 10k on 7k lt bl .50 .50
140 A11 5r on 14k bl & rose 2.00 2.00
141 A11 5r on 15k red brn & blue .50 .50
a. Imperf. 2.00 2.00
142 A8 5r on 20k bl & car .50 .50
a. Imperf. 10.00 10.00
143 A11 5r on 20k on 14k bl & rose 12.00 12.00
144 A11 5r on 25k grn & gray vio 12.00 12.00

Black Surcharge, Type g or Type f (#148A, 151)

145 A14 10r on 1k org, imperf. .90 .90
a. Perf. 225.00 225.00
146 A14 10r on 3k red 175.00 175.00
147 A14 10r on 5k claret 15.00 15.00
a. Imperf. 6.00
148 A8 10r on 20k bl & car 15.00 15.00
148A A11 10r on 25k grn & gray vio 8.00 8.00
149 A11 10r on 25k grn & gray vio 5.00 5.00
a. Imperf. 8.00 8.00
150 A11 10r on 35k red brn & grn .50 .50
151 A8 10r on 50k brn vio & grn 1.75 1.75
152 A8 10r on 50k brn vio & grn .45 .45
152A A11 10r on 70k brn & org, imperf. 3.00 3.00
b. Perf. 200.00 200.00
152C A8 25r on 20k bl & car 4.00 4.00
153 A11 25r on 25k grn & gray vio 2.00 2.00
154 A11 25r on 35k red brn & grn 2.00 2.00
a. Imperf. 3.50 3.50
155 A8 25r on 50k vio & grn 4.00 4.00
a. Imperf. 5.00 5.00
156 A11 25r on 70k brn & org 8.00 8.00
a. Imperf. 5.00 5.00
157 A9 50r on 1r pale brn, dk brn & org, imperf. 1.00 1.00
a. Perf. 5.00 5.00
158 A13 50r on 5r dk bl, grn & lt bl 10.00 10.00
a. Imperf. 10.00 10.00
159 A12 100r on 3½r mar & lt grn 7.00 7.00
a. Imperf. 7.00 7.00
160 A13 100r on 5r dk bl, grn & pale bl 10.00 10.00
a. Imperf. 7.00 7.00
161 A12 100r on 7r dk grn & pink 10.00 10.00
a. Imperf. 35.00 35.00
162 A13 100r on 10r scar, yel & gray 10.00 10.00

Wmk. Wavy Lines (168)
Perf. 11½
Vertically Laid Paper

163 A12 100r on 3½r blk & gray 100.00 100.00
164 A12 100r on 7r blk & yel 100.00 100.00

1920 Unwmk. *Imperf.*
Wove Paper

166 A14 (g) 1r on 60k on 1k org (I) 12.00 12.00
168 A14 (f) 5r on 1k orange 9.00 9.00
173 A11 (f) 5r on 35k red brn & grn 2.50 2.50
177 A11 (g) 50r on 70k brn & org 5.00 5.00
179 A12 (g) 50r on 3½r mar & lt grn 2.00 2.00
181 A9 (g) 100r on 1r pale brn, dk brn & org 4.00 4.00

Romanov Issues Surcharged Type g or Type f (#185-187, 190)
On Stamps of 1913

1920 *Perf. 13½*

184 A16 1r on 1k brn org 10.00 10.00
185 A18 3r on 3k rose red 15.00 15.00
186 A19 5r on 4k dull red 10.00 10.00
187 A22 5r on 14k blue grn 60.00 60.00
187A A19 10r on 4k dull red 30.00
187B A26 10r on 35k gray vio & dk grn
187C A19 25r on 4k dull red 10.00 10.00
188 A26 25r on 35k gray vio & dk grn 2.75 2.75
189 A28 25r on 70k yel grn & brn 2.75 2.75
190 A31 50r on 3r dk violet 2.00 2.00
190A A16 100r on 1k brn org 100.00 100.00
190B A17 100r on 2k green 100.00 100.00
191 A30 100r on 2r brown 10.50 10.50
192 A31 100r on 3r dk vio 10.50 10.50

On Stamps of 1915, Type g
Thin Cardboard
Inscriptions on Back
Perf. 12

193 A21 100r on 10k blue 3.00
194 A23 100r on 15k brown 3.00
195 A24 100r on 20k ol grn 3.00

On Stamps of 1916, Type f
Perf. 13½

196 A20 5r on 10k on 7k brown 5.00 5.00
197 A22 5r on 20k on 14k bl grn 8.00 8.00

Surch. Type f or Type g (#204-205A, 207-207C, 210-211) over Type c
Type c in Violet
Perf.

200 A15 5r on 4k carmine 1.00 1.00
201 A15 5r on 10k dk blue 1.00 1.00
202 A11 5r on 15k red brn & bl 2.00 2.00
203 A8 5r on 20k blue & car 1.75 1.75
204 A11 10r on 25k grn & gray vio 1.50 1.50
205 A11 10r on 35k red brn & grn 3.00 3.00
205A A8 10r on 50k brn vio & grn 3.50 3.50
206 A8 25r on 50k brn vio & grn 150.00 150.00
207 A9 50r on 1r pale brn, dk brn & org, imperf. 3.50 3.50
a. Perf. 25.00 25.00
207B A12 100r on 3½r mar & lt grn 30.00
207C A12 100r on 7r dk grn & pink 9.00

Imperf

208 A14 5r on 2k green 25.00 25.00
209 A14 5r on 5k claret 25.00 25.00
210 A11 25r on 70k brn & org 5.50 5.50
211 A13 100r on 5r dk bl, grn & pale bl 1.00 1.00

Surcharged Type g or Type f (212-213, 215, 219-219A, 221-222) over Type c
Type c in Black
Perf.

212 A14 5r on 7k lt bl 150.00 150.00
213 A14 5r on 10k on 7k lt bl 5.00 5.00
214 A11 5r on 15k red brn & bl .50 .50
215 A8 5r on 20k blue & car 3.00 3.00
215A A11 10r on 5r on 25k grn & gray vio 5.00 5.00
216 A11 10r on 35k red brn & grn .50 .50
217 A8 10r on 50k brn vio & grn 1.00 1.00
217A A9 50r on 1r pale brn, dk brn & org 1.00 1.00
b. Imperf. 1.10 1.10
217C A12 100r on 3½r mar & lt grn 1.50 1.50
218 A13 100r on 5r dk bl, grn & pale bl 10.00 10.00
a. Imperf. 1.75 1.75
219 A12 100r on 7r dk grn & pink 15.00 15.00
219A A13 100r on 10r scar, yel & gray 10.00 10.00

Imperf

220 A14 1r on 60k on 1k org (I) 20.00 20.00
221 A14 5r on 2k green .80 .80
222 A14 5r on 5k claret 3.00 3.00
223 A11 10r on 70k brn & org 2.00 2.00
224 A11 25r on 70k brn & org 2.00 2.00

ARMENIA

Surcharged Type g or Type f (#233) over Type a
Type a in Violet
Imperf

231	A9	50r on 1r pale brn, dk brn & org	140.00	140.00
232	A13	100r on 5r dk bl, grn & pale bl	10.50	

Type a in Black
Perf.

233	A8	5r on 20k blue & car	.80	.80
233A	A11	10r on 25k grn & gray vio	55.00	55.00
234	A11	10r on 35k red brn & grn	.90	.90
235	A12	100r on 3½r mar & lt grn	1.25	1.25
a.		Imperf.	1.50	1.50

Imperf

237	A14	5r on 2k green	125.00	125.00
237A	A11	10r on 70k brn & org		

Surcharged Type a and New Value
Type a in Violet
Perf.

238	A11	10r on 15k red brn & blue	.80	.80

Type a in Black

239	A8	5r on 20k blue & car	3.00	3.00
239A	A8	10r on 20k blue & car	3.00	3.00
239B	A8	10r on 50k brn red & grn	7.50	

Imperf

240	A12	100r on 3½r mar & lt grn	1.90	1.90

Surcharged Type c and New Value
Type c in Black

1920 *Perf.*

241	A15	5r on 4k red	1.75	1.75
242	A11	5r on 15k red brn & bl	1.00	1.00
243	A8	10r on 20k blue & car	1.75	1.75
243A	A11	10r on 25k grn & gray vio	1.00	1.00
244	A11	10r on 35k red brn & grn	1.00	1.00
a.		With additional surch. "5r"	1.50	1.50
245	A12	100r on 3½r mar & lt grn	1.50	1.50

Imperf

247	A14	3r on 3k red	4.75	4.75
248	A14	5r on 2k green	.30	.30
249	A9	50r on 1r pale brn, dk brn & org	.90	.90

Type c in Violet

249A	A14	5r on 2k green	6.50	

Postal Savings Stamps Surcharged

A1 A2 A3

Perf. 14½x15
Wmk. 171

250	A1	60k on 1k red & buff	50.00	50.00
251	A2	1r on 1k red & buff	5.00	5.00
252	A3	5r on 5k green & buff	7.25	7.25
253	A3	5r on 10k brown & buff	30.00	3.00

Russian Semi-Postal Stamps of 1914-18 Surcharged with Armenian Monogram and New Values like Regular Issues
On Stamps of 1914
Unwmk. *Perf.*

255	SP5	25r on 1k red brn & dk grn, *straw*	60.00	60.00
256	SP6	25r on 3k mar & gray grn, *pink*	60.00	60.00
257	SP7	50r on 7 dk brn & dk grn, *buff*	20.00	20.00
258	SP5	100r on 1k red brn & dk grn, *straw*	25.00	25.00
259	SP6	100r on 3k mar & gray grn, *pink*	25.00	25.00
260	SP7	100r on 7k dk brn & dk grn, *buff*	25.00	25.00

On Stamps of 1915-19

261	SP5	25r on 1k org brn & gray	75.00	75.00
262	SP6	25r on 3k car & gray	30.00	30.00
263	SP8	50r on 10k dk bl & brn	25.00	25.00
264	SP5	100r on 1k org brn & gray	3.25	3.50
265	SP8	100r on 10k dk bl & brn	3.25	3.50

These surcharged semi-postal stamps were used for ordinary postage.

A set of 10 stamps in the above designs, and in a third design showing a woman quilling, was prepared in 1920, but not issued. Value of set, $4. Exist with "SPECIMEN" overprint and imperf. Reprints exist.

Soviet Socialist Republic

Hammer and Sickle — A7
Mythological Monster — A8 
Symbols of Soviet Republics on Designs from old Armenian Manuscripts — A9 
Ruined City of Ani — A10 
Mythological Monster — A11 
Armenian Soldier — A12  
Soviet Symbols, Armenian Designs — A14 
Mythological Monster — A13 
Mt. Alagöz and Plain of Shirak A15 
Fisherman on River Aras — A16 
Post Office in Erevan and Mt. Ararat A17 
Ruin in City of Ani — A18 
Street in Erevan — A19 
Lake Sevan and Sevan Monastery A20 
Mythological Subject from old Armenian Monument — A21 
Mt. Ararat A22 

1921 *Unwmk.* *Perf. 11½, Imperf.*

278	A7	1r gray green	.30	
279	A8	2r slate gray	.30	
280	A9	3r carmine	.30	
281	A10	5r dark brown	.30	
282	A11	25r gray	.30	.20
283	A12	50r red	.15	
284	A13	100r orange	.15	
285	A14	250r dark blue	.15	
286	A15	500r brown vio	.15	
287	A16	1000r sea green	.25	
288	A17	2000r bister	.30	
289	A18	5000r dark brown	.30	
290	A19	10,000r dull red	.30	
291	A20	15,000r slate blue	.30	
292	A21	20,000r lake	.30	
293	A22	25,000r gray blue	.65	
294	A22	25,000r brown olive	5.50	
		Nos. 278-294 (17)		

Except the 25r, Nos. 278-294 were not regularly issued and used. Counterfeits exist.
For surcharges see Nos. 347-390.

Russian Stamps of 1909-17 Surcharged

Wove Paper
Lozenges of Varnish on Face

1921, Aug. *Perf. 13½*

295	A9	5000r on 1r	10.00
296	A12	5000r on 3½r	10.00
297	A13	5000r on 5r	10.00
298	A12	5000r on 7r	10.00
299	A13	5000r on 10r	10.00
		Nos. 295-299 (5)	50.00

Nos. 295-299 were not officially issued. Counterfeits abound.

Mt. Ararat and Soviet Star A23
A24
Soviet Symbols — A25 
Crane — A26 
Peasant — A27  
Harpy — A28 
Peasant Sowing — A29 
Soviet Symbols — A30 
Forging — A31 
Plowing A32 

1922 *Perf. 11½*

300	A23	50r green & red	.35
301	A24	300r slate bl & buff	.40
302	A25	400r blue & pink	.40
303	A26	500r vio & pale lil	.40
304	A27	1000r dull bl & pale bl	.40
305	A28	2000r black & gray	.65
306	A29	3000r black & grn	.65
307	A30	4000r black & lt brn	.65
308	A31	5000r black & dull red	.55
309	A32	10,000r black & pale rose	.55
a.		Tête bêche pair	35.00
		Nos. 300-309 (10)	5.00

Nos. 300-309 were not issued without surcharge. Stamps of types A23 to A32, printed in other colors than Nos. 300 to 309, are essays.

Nos. 300-309 with Handstamped Surcharge of New Values in Rose, Violet or Black

1922

310	10,000 on 50r (R)	8.50	11.00
311	10,000 on 50r (V)	8.50	11.00
312	10,000 on 50r	8.50	11.00
313	15,000 on 300r (R)	8.50	14.00

ARMENIA

314	15,000 on 300r (V)		8.50	14.00
315	15,000 on 300r		8.50	14.00
316	25,000 on 400r (V)		8.50	14.00
317	25,000 on 400r		8.50	14.00
318	30,000 on 500r (R)		10.00	17.00
319	30,000 on 500r (V)		10.00	17.00
320	30,000 on 500r		10.00	17.00
321	50,000 on 1000r (R)		8.50	14.00
322	50,000 on 1000r (V)		8.50	14.00
323	50,000 on 1000r		8.50	14.00
324	75,000 on 3000r		11.00	17.00
325	100,000 on 2000r (R)		20.00	20.00
326	100,000 on 2000r (V)		20.00	20.00
327	100,000 on 2000r		20.00	20.00
328	200,000 on 4000r (V)		22.50	22.50
329	200,000 on 4000r		22.50	22.50
330	300,000 on 5000r (V)		30.00	45.00
331	300,000 on 5000r		30.00	45.00
332	500,000 on 10,000r (V)		30.00	30.00
333	500,000 on 10,000r		30.00	30.00
	Nos. 310-333 (24)		359.50	471.00

Goose — A33

Armenian Woman at Well — A35

Armenian Village Scene — A34

Mt. Ararat — A36

Mt. Ararat A37

New Values in Gold Kopecks, Handstamped Surcharge in Black

1922 — *Imperf.*

334	A33	1(k) on 250r rose	12.50	12.50
335	A33	1(k) on 250r gray	20.00	20.00
336	A34	2(k) on 500r rose	8.00	8.00
337	A34	2(k) on 500r gray	8.00	8.00
338	A35	4(k) on 1000r rose	8.00	8.00
339	A35	4(k) on 1000r gray	15.00	15.00
340	A36	5(k) on 2000r gray	8.00	8.00
341	A36	10(k) on 4000r rose	8.00	8.00
342	A37	15(k) on 5000r rose	52.50	52.50
343	A37	20(k) on 5000r gray	8.00	8.00
	Nos. 334-343 (10)		148.00	148.00

Nos. 334-343 were issued for postal tax purposes.
Nos. 334-343 exist without surcharge but are not known to have been issued in that condition. Counterfeits exist of both sets.

Regular Issue of 1921 Handstamped with New Values in Black or Red Short, Thick Numerals

1922 — *Imperf.*

347	A8	2(k) on 2r (R)	50.00	50.00
350	A11	4(k) on 25r (R)	30.00	30.00
353	A13	10(k) on 100r (R)	20.00	20.00
354	A14	15(k) on 250r	10.00	10.00
355	A15	20(k) on 500r	15.00	15.00
a.		With "k" written in red	10.00	10.00
357	A22	50(k) on 25,000r bl (R)	12.00	12.00
358	A22	50(k) on 25,000r brn ol (R)	9.00	9.00
359	A22	50(k) on 25,000r brn ol		
	Nos. 347-358 (7)		146.00	146.00

Perf. 11½

360	A7	1(k) on 1r, imperf.	25.00	25.00
a.	Perf.		15.00	15.00
361	A7	1(k) on 1r (R)	35.00	35.00
a.	Imperf.		40.00	40.00
362	A8	2(k) on 2r, imperf.	40.00	40.00
a.	Perf.		40.00	40.00
363	A15	2(k) on 500r	35.00	35.00
a.	Imperf.		50.00	50.00
364	A15	2(k) on 500r (R)	9.00	9.00
365	A11	4(k) on 25r, imperf.	25.00	25.00
a.	Perf.		25.00	25.00
366	A12	5(k) on 50r, imperf.	1.75	1.75
a.	Perf.		2.50	2.50
367	A13	10(k) on 100r	20.00	20.00
a.	Imperf.		20.00	20.00
368	A21	35(k) on 20,000r, imperf.	50.00	50.00
a.	With "k" written in violet		50.00	50.00
b.	Perf.		65.00	65.00
c.	As "a," perf.		65.00	65.00
d.	With "kop" written in violet, imperf.			
	Nos. 360-368 (9)		240.75	240.75

Manuscript Surcharge in Red
Perf. 11½

371	A14	1k on 250r dk bl	40.00	40.00

Handstamped in Black or Red Tall, Thin Numerals
Imperf

377	A11	4(k) on 25r (R)	4.25	4.25
379	A13	10(k) on 100r	10.00	10.00
380	A15	20(k) on 500r	6.00	6.00
381	A22	50k on 25,000r bl	75.00	75.00
a.	Surcharged "50" only		50.00	50.00
382	A22	50k on 25,000r bl (R)	12.00	12.00
382A	A22	50k on 25,000r brn ol	24.00	24.00
	Nos. 377-382A (6)		131.25	131.25

On Nos. 381, 382 and 382A the letter "k" forms part of the surcharge.

Perf. 11½

383	A7	1(k) on 1r (R)	50.00	50.00
a.	Imperf.			
384	A14	1(k) on 250r	1.75	1.75
385	A15	2(k) on 500r	8.00	8.00
a.	Imperf.		20.00	20.00
386	A15	2(k) on 500r (R)	20.00	20.00
387	A9	3(k) on 3r	20.00	20.00
a.	Imperf.		20.00	20.00
388	A21	3(k) on 20,000r, imperf.	10.00	10.00
a.	Perf.		50.00	50.00
389	A11	4(k) on 25r	2.50	2.50
a.	Imperf.		4.25	4.25
390	A12	5(k) on 50r, imperf.	10.00	10.00
a.	Perf.		10.00	10.00
	Nos. 383-390 (8)		122.25	122.25

Catalogue values for unused stamps in this section, from this point to the end of the section, are for Never Hinged items.

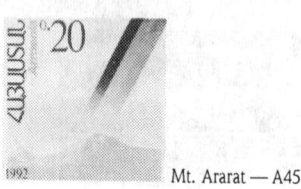

Mt. Ararat — A45

a, 20k. b, 2r. c, 5r.

1992, May 28 Litho. *Perf. 14*
430 A45 Strip of 3, #a.-c. 3.00 3.00

Souvenir Sheet
431 A45 7r Eagle & Mt. Ararat 30.00 30.00

AT & T Communications System in Armenia — A45a

1992, July 1 Litho. *Perf. 13x13½*
431A A45a 50k multicolored 3.00 3.00

A46

A47

1992 Summer Olympics, Barcelona: a, 40k, Ancient Greek wrestlers. b, 3.60r, Boxing. c, 5r, Weight lifting. d, 12r, Gymnastics.

1992, July 25 Litho. *Perf. 14*
432 A46 Strip of 4, #a.-d. 3.00 3.00

1992-93 Litho. *Perf. 14½, 15x14½*

20k, Natl. flag. 1r, Goddess Waroubini, Orgov radio telescope. 2r, Yerevan Airport. No. 436, Goddess Anahit. No. 437, Runic message, 7th cent B.C. 5r, UPU emblem. 20r, Silver cup.

433	A47	20k multicolored	.15	.15
434	A47	1r gray green	.15	.15
435	A47	2r blue	.30	.30
436	A47	3r brown	.50	.50
437	A47	3r bronze	.15	.15
438	A47	5r brown black	.75	.75
439	A47	20r gray	.15	.15
	Nos. 433-439 (7)		2.15	2.15

No. 435 is airmail. See Nos. 464-471, 521-524.
Issued: #436, 20k, 2r, 5r, 8/25/92; others, 5/12/93.

Religious Artifacts — A50

Yerevan '93 — A52

David of Sassoun, by Hakop Kojoian — A50a

Scenic Views — A51

1993, May 23 Litho. *Perf. 14*

448	A50	40k Marker	.15	.15
449	A50	80k Gospel page	.25	.25
450	A50	3.60r Bas-relief, 13th cent.	1.00	1.00
451	A50	5r Icon of the Madonna	1.65	1.65
	Nos. 448-451 (4)		3.05	3.05

Souvenir Sheet
Perf. 14x13½
451A A50a 12r multicolored 6.00 6.00

1993, May 24 *Perf. 14*

Designs (illustration reduced): 40k, Garni Canyon, vert. 80k, Shaki Waterfall, Zangezur, vert. 3.60r, Arpa River Canyon, vert. 5r, Lake Sevan. 12r, Mount Aragats.

452	A51	40k multicolored	.15	.15
453	A51	80k multicolored	.15	.15
454	A51	3.60r multicolored	.50	.50
455	A51	5r multicolored	.65	.65
456	A51	12r multicolored	1.65	1.65
	Nos. 452-456 (5)		3.10	3.10

1993, May 25 *Perf. 14½*
457 A52 10r multicolored .50 .50
a. Min. sheet of 6 + 2 labels 4.25

For surcharges see Nos. 485-486.

Souvenir Sheet

Noah's Descent from Mt. Ararat, by Hovhannes Aivazovsky — A52

1993, May 24 Litho. *Perf. 14½*
458 A52 7r multicolored 2.50 2.50

Religious Relics, Echmiadzin — A53

Designs: 3r, Wooden panel, descent from cross, 9th cent. 5r, Gilded silver reliquary for Holy Cross of Khotakerats. 12r, Cross depicting right hand of St. Karapet, 14th cent. 30r, Reliquary for arm of St. Thaddeus the Apostle, 17th cent. 50r, Gilded silver vessel for consecrated ointment, 1815.

1994, Aug. 4 Litho. *Perf. 14x14½*

459	A53	3d multicolored	.15	.15
460	A53	5d multicolored	.15	.15
461	A53	12d multicolored	.30	.30
462	A53	30d multicolored	.80	.80
463	A53	50d multicolored	1.25	1.25
	Nos. 459-463 (5)		2.65	2.65

Artifacts and Landmarks Type of 1993

Gods of Van (Urartu): 10 l, Shivini, god of the sun. 50 l, Tayshaba, god of elements. 10d, Khaldi, supreme god.
25d, Natl. arms.

1994 *Perf. 14½*

464	A47	10 l black & brown	.15	.15
465	A47	50 l black & red brown	.15	.15
469	A47	10d black & gray	.50	.50
471	A47	25d red & bister	1.25	1.25
	Nos. 464-471 (4)		2.05	2.05

Issued: 10 l, 50 l, 10d, 25d, 8/4/94.
This is an expanding set. Numbers may change.

A54

1994, Dec. 31 Litho. *Perf. 14½x14*
479 A54 16d No. 1a .45 .45

First Armenian postage stamp, 75th anniv.

A54a

A54b

1994, Dec. 30 Litho. *Perf. 14x14½*
480 A54a 30d Early printing press .50 .50
First Armenian periodical, 170th anniv.

1994, Dec. 30 Litho. *Perf. 14x14½*
481 A54b 30d Natl. arms, stadium .55 .55
Natl. Olympic Committee.

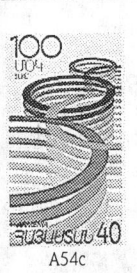

ARMENIA

A54c
A54d 

1994, Dec. 30 Litho. *Perf. 14x14½*
482 A54c 40d Olympic rings .75 .75
Intl. Olympic Committee, Cent.

1994, Dec. 31 Litho. *Perf. 14x14½*
483 A54d 50d multi + label .85 .85
Ervand Otian (1869-1926)

A54e

1994, Dec. 31 Litho. *Perf. 14½x14*
484 A54e 50d multi + label .85 .85
Levon Shant (1869-1951).

No. 457 Surcharged in Blue or Red Brown

a   b

1994, Sept. 10 Litho. *Perf. 14*
485 A52(a) 40d on 10r (Bl) 1.65 1.65
486 A52(b) 40d on 10r (RB) 1.65 1.65
Yerevan '94.

A55    A56

Christianity in Armenia: 60d, Cross, 10th-11th cent. No. 488, Kings Abgar & Trdat, 1836. No. 489, St. Bartholomew, St. Thaddeus. 80d, St. Gregory, the Illuminator. 90d, Baptism of the Armenian people, 1892. 400d, Plan of Echmiadzin, c. 1660, engr. by Jakob Peeters.

1995, Apr. 3 Litho. *Perf. 14x15*
487 A55 60d multicolored .55 .55
488 A55 70d multicolored .65 .65
489 A55 70d multicolored .65 .65
490 A55 80d multicolored .75 .75
491 A55 90d multicolored .85 .85
Nos. 487-491 (5) 3.45 3.45
Souvenir Sheet
492 A55 400d multicolored 4.00 4.00
Nos. 488-489 are 45x44mm.

1995, Apr. 3
493 A56 150d gray & black 1.25 1.25
Vazgen I (1908-94), Catholikos of All Armenians.

Armenia Fund — A57

1995, Apr. 27 *Perf. 15x14*
494 A57 90d multicolored .80 .80

UN, 50th Anniv. A58

1995, Apr. 28
495 A58 90d multicolored .80 .80

Cultural Artifacts — A59

Designs: 30d, Black polished pottery, 14th-13th cent. B.C. 60d, Silver cup, 5th cent. B.C. 130d, Gohar carpet, 1700 A.D.

1995, Apr. 27 *Perf. 15x14*
496 A59 30d multicolored .30 .30
497 A59 60d multicolored .50 .50
498 A59 130d multicolored 1.25 1.25
Nos. 496-498 (3) 2.05 2.05

Birds — A60

1995, Apr. 27 *Perf. 14*
499 A60 40d Milvus milvus .50 .50
500 A60 60d Aquila chrysaetos .75 .75

End of World War II, 50th Anniv. A61

Designs: No. 501, P. Kitsook, 408th Armenian Rifle Division. No. 502, A. Sargissin, N. Safarian, 89th Taman Armenian Triple Order-Bearer Division. No. 503, B. Chernikov, N. Tavartkeladze, V. Penkovsky, 76th Armenian Alpine Rifle Red Banner (51st Guards) Division. No. 504, S. Zakian, H. Babayan, I. Lyudnikov, 390th Armenian Rifle Division. No. 505, A. Vasillian, M. Dobrovolsky, Y. Grechany, G. Sorokin, 409th Armenian Rifle Division.
No. 506, vert.: a, Marshal Hovhannes Baghramian. b, Adm. Hovhannes Issakov. c, Marshal Hamazasp Babajanian. d, Marshal Sergey Khoudyakov.
No. 507: Return of the Hero, by Mariam Aslamazian.

1995, Sept. 30 Litho. *Perf. 15x14*
501 A61 60d multicolored .35 .35
502 A61 60d multicolored .35 .35
503 A61 60d multicolored .35 .35
504 A61 60d multicolored .35 .35
505 A61 60d multicolored .35 .35
Nos. 501-505 (5) 1.75 1.75
Miniature Sheet *Perf. 15x14½*
506 A61 60d Sheet of 4, #a.-d. 1.50 1.50
Souvenir Sheet *Perf. 15x14*
507 A61 300d multicolored 2.00 2.00

Authors A62

Designs: No. 508, Ghevond Alishan (1820-1901). No. 509, Gregor Artsruni (1845-92), vert. No. 510, Franz Werfel (1890-1945).

1995, Oct. 5 Litho. *Perf. 15x14*
508 A62 90d blue & black .75 .75
509 A62 90d multicolored .75 .75
510 A62 90d blue & maroon .75 .75
Nos. 508-510 (3) 2.25 2.25
Nos. 508-510 issued with se-tenant label.

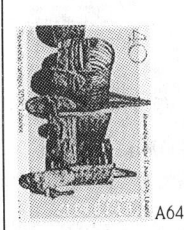

A64

Prehistoric artifacts: 40d, Four-wheeled carriages, 15th cent. BC, horiz. 60d, Bronze model of geocentric solar system, 11-10th cent. BC. 90d, Tombstone, Red Tufa, 7-6th cent. BC.

1995, Dec. 5 *Perf. 14½x15, 15x14½*
512 A64 40d multicolored .25 .25
513 A64 60d multicolored .40 .40
514 A64 90d multicolored .60 .60
Nos. 512-514 (3) 1.25 1.25

A65

Christianity in Armenia — A66

Views of Yerevan: 60d, Brandy distillery, wine cellars. 80d, Abovian Street. 90d, Sports and concert complex. 100d, Baghramian Avenue. 120d, Republic Square.
400d, Panoramic photograph of Yerevan.

1995, Dec. 5 *Perf. 15x14*
515 A65 60d salmon & black .35 .35
516 A65 80d pale orange & black .45 .45
517 A65 90d buff & black .50 .50
Size: 61x24mm
518 A65 100d pale yellow bis & blk .60 .60
519 A65 120d dull orange & black .75 .75
Nos. 515-519 (5) 2.65 2.65
Souvenir Sheet
520 A66 400d multicolored 3.00 3.00

No. 464 Surcharged in Green, Red, Blue Violet, or Red Brown

1996, Mar. 30 Litho. *Perf. 14½*
521 A47 40d on 10l (G) 1.00 1.00
522 A47 100d on 10l (R) 2.50 2.50
523 A47 150d on 10l (BV) 3.50 3.50
524 A47 200d on 10l (RB) 5.00 5.00
Nos. 521-524 (4) 12.00 12.00

Alexsandre Griboyedov (1795-1829), Writer — A67

1996, Apr. 24 Litho. *Perf. 14x14½*
525 A67 90d multicolored .70 .70
No. 525 is printed se-tenant with label.

Khrimian Hayrik (1820-1907), Catholicos of All Armenians A68

1996, Apr. 30 *Perf. 14½x14*
526 A68 90d brown & blue .70 .70
No. 526 is printed se-tenant with label.

Admiral Lazar Serbryakov (1795-1862) A69

1996, Apr. 30
527 A69 90d multicolored .70 .70
No. 527 is printed se-tenant with label.

Armenian Red Cross, 75th Anniv. — A70

1996, May 3 *Perf. 14x14½*
528 A70 60d multicolored .45 .45

Motion Pictures, Cent. A71

1996, May 3 *Perf. 14½x14*
529 A71 60d multicolored .45 .45

Endangered Fauna — A72

1996, May 3 *Perf. 14*
530 A72 40d Carpa aegagrus .30 .30
531 A72 60d Panthera pardus .45 .45

Armenia stamps can be mounted in the annual Scott Commonwealth of Independent States supplement.

ARMENIA

1996 Summer Olympics, Atlanta — A73

Modern Olympic Games, Cent. — A74

Designs: a, 40d, Cyclist. b, 60d, Athletic event. c, 90d, Wrestling.

1996, July 25
532 A73 Strip of 3, #a.-c.   1.25   1.25

1996, July 25   *Perf. 14x14½*
533 A74 60d multicolored   .45   .45

Fridtjof Nansen (1861-1930), Arctic Explorer — A75

1996, May 20   Litho.   *Perf. 14x14½*
534 A75 90d multicolored   .60   .60

32nd Chess Olympiad, Yerevan — A76

#535, Petrosian-Botvinnik, World Championship match, Moscow, 1963. #536, Kasparov-Karpov, World Championship Match, Leningrad, 1986. #537, G. Kasparian, first prize winner, Contest of the Shakhmati v SSSR magazine, 1939. #538, 32nd Chess Olympiad, Yerevan.

1996, Sept. 15   Litho.   *Perf. 14*
535 A76 40d multicolored   .35   .35
536 A76 40d multicolored   .35   .35
537 A76 40d multicolored   .35   .35
538 A76 40d multicolored   .35   .35
  a. Booklet pane, #535-538   1.50
    Complete booklet, 2 #538a   3.00
  Nos. 535-538 (4)   1.40   1.40

No. 538a issued 9/24.

Tigran Petrosian, World Chess Champion, Chess House, Yerevan — A77

1996, Sept. 20   *Perf. 14x15*
539 A77 90d multicolored   .75   .75

Capra Aegagrus A78

World Wildlife Fund: 70d, Two running. 100d, One standing. 130d, One holding head down. 350d, Two facing forward.

1996, Oct. 20   Litho.   *Perf. 14½x14*
540 A78 70d multicolored   .40   .40
541 A78 100d multicolored   .50   .50
542 A78 130d multicolored   .75   .75
543 A78 350d multicolored   2.00   2.00
  a. Block of 4, #540-543   3.75   3.75
  b. Booklet pane, 2 #543a   7.50
    Complete booklet, #543b   7.50

Issued in sheets of 16 stamps.

Christianity in Armenia, 1700th Anniv. — A79

Armenian churches: No. 544, St. Catherine Church, St. Petersburg, 1780. No. 545, Church of the Holy Mother, Kishinev, 1803. No. 546, Church of the Holy Mother, Samarkand, 1903. No. 547, Armenian Church, Lvov, 1370. No. 548, St. Hripsime Church, Yalta, 1913.
500d, Church of St. Gevorg of Etchmiadzin, Tbilisi, 1805.

1996   Litho.   *Perf. 14x15*
544 A79 100d multicolored   .50   .50
545 A79 100d multicolored   .50   .50
546 A79 100d multicolored   .50   .50
547 A79 100d multicolored   .50   .50
548 A79 100d multicolored   .50   .50
  Nos. 544-548 (5)   2.50   2.50

Souvenir Sheet
549 A79 500d multicolored   2.50   2.50

First Armenian Printing Press, Etchmiadzin, 225th Anniv. — A80

1997, Mar. 26   Litho.   *Perf. 15x14*
550 A80 70d multicolored   .35   .35

Armenian Entertainers A81

#551, Folk singer, Jivani (1846-1909). #552, Arno Babajanian (1921-83), composer, vert.

1997, Mar. 26   *Perf. 15x14, 14x15*
551 A81 90d multicolored   .45   .45
552 A81 90d multicolored   .45   .45

Paintings from Natl. Gallery of Armenia A82

#553, "One of my Dreams," by Eghishe Tadevossian. #554, "Countryside," by Gevorg Bashinjaghian. #555, "Portrait of Natalia Tehumian," by Hakob Hovnatanian. #556, "Salomé," by Vardges Sureniants.

1997, May 28   Litho.   *Perf. 15x14*
553 A82 150d multi   .70   .70
554 A82 150d multi   .70   .70
555 A82 150d multi, vert.   .70   .70
556 A82 150d multi, vert.   .70   .70
  Nos. 553-556 (4)   2.80   2.80

See Nos. 573-575.

Rouben Mamulian (1897-1987), Motion Picture Director — A83

1997, Oct. 8   Litho.   *Perf. 15x14*
557 A83 150d multicolored   .70   .70

Moscow '97, World Philatelic Exhibition — A84

1997, Oct. 17   *Perf. 14x15*
558 A84 170d St. Basil's Cathedral   .80   .80

Eghishe Charents (1897-1937), Poet — A85

1997, Oct. 19   *Perf. 14x15*
559 A85 150d multicolored   .70   .70

A86    A87

Europa (Stories and Legends): 170d, Hayk, the Progenitor of the Armenians. 250d, Vahagn, the Dragon Slayer.

1997, Oct. 18   *Perf. 14x15*
560 A86 170d multicolored   .80   .80
561 A86 250d multicolored   1.15   1.15

1997, Dec. 19   Litho.   *Perf. 14*
562 A87 40d Iris lycotis   .20   .20
563 A87 170d Iris elegantissima   .85   .85

Religious Buildings — A88    Christmas — A89

#564, San Lazzaro, the Mekhitarian Congregation, Venice. #565, St. Gregory the Illuminator Cathedral, Anthelias. #566, St. Khach Armenian Church, Rostov upon Don. #567, St. James Monastery, Jerusalem. #568, Nercissian School, Tbilisi. 500d, Lazarian Seminary, Moscow.

1997, Dec. 22   *Perf. 15x14, 14x15*
564 A88 100d multi, horiz.   .50   .50
565 A88 100d multi   .50   .50
566 A88 100d multi   .50   .50
567 A88 100d multi, horiz.   .50   .50

Size: 60x21mm
568 A88 100d multi, horiz.   .50   .50
  Nos. 564-568 (5)   2.50   2.50

Souvenir Sheet
569 A88 500d multicolored   2.50   2.50

Christianity in Armenia, 1700th anniv. (in 2001).

1997, Dec. 26   *Perf. 14x15*
570 A89 40d multicolored   .25   .25

Diana, Princess of Wales (1961-97) A90

1998, Apr. 8   Litho.   *Perf. 15x14*
571 A90 250d multicolored   1.00   1.00

No. 571 was issued in sheets of 5 + label.

Karabakh Movement, 10th Anniv. — A91

1998, Feb. 20   Litho.   *Perf. 13½x14*
572 A91 250d multicolored   1.00   1.00

Paintings from Natl. Gallery of Armenia Type of 1997

#573, "Tartar Women's Dance," by Alexander Bazhbeouk-Melikian. #574, "Family. Generations," by Yervand Kochar. #575, "Spring in Our Yard," by Haroutiun Kalents.

1998, Feb. 21   *Perf. 15x14, 14x15*
573 A82 150d multi   .65   .65
574 A82 150d multi, vert.   .65   .65
575 A82 150d multi, vert.   .65   .65
  Nos. 573-575 (3)   1.95   1.95

National Holidays and Festivals A93

Europa: 170d, Couple jumping over fire, Trndez. 250d, Girls taking part in traditional ceremony, Ascension Day.

1998, June 24   Litho.   *Perf. 15x14*
577 A93 170d multicolored   .80   .80
578 A93 250d multicolored   1.25   1.25

Butterflies A94    National Costumes A95

1998, June 26   *Perf. 14*
579 A94 170d Papilio alexanor   .80   .80
580 A94 250d Rethera komarovi   1.25   1.25

1998, July 16   Litho.   *Perf. 14x13½*
581 A95 170d Ayrarat   .75   .75
582 A95 250d Vaspurakan   1.10   1.10

Ordering on-line is
QUICK!
EASY!
CONVENIENT!
www.scottonline.com

ARMENIA — ARUBA

AIR POST STAMPS

AP1,  AP2

Design: 90d, Artiom Katsian (1886-1943), world record holding pilot on range and altitude in 1909.

1995, Dec. 5   *Litho.*   *Perf. 14x15*
C1   AP1   90d multicolored   .75   .75

1996, Apr. 30   *Litho.*   *Perf. 14x14½*
C2   AP2   90d multicolored   .70   .70

Nelson Stepanian (1913-44), WWII fighter ace.

ARUBA
ə-'rü–bə

LOCATION — West Indies, north of Venezuela
AREA — 78 sq. mi.
POP. — 67,014

On Jan. 1, 1986 Aruba, formerly part of Netherlands Antilles, achieved a separate status within the Kingdom of the Netherlands.

100 Cents = 1 Gulden

> Catalogue values for all unused stamps in this country are for Never Hinged items.

Traditional House — A1

1986-87   *Litho.*   *Unwmk.*   *Perf. 14x13*
1	A1	5c shown	.15	.15
2	A1	15c King William III Tower	.15	.15
3	A1	20c Loading crane	.15	.15
4	A1	25c Lighthouse	.20	.20
5	A1	30c Snake	.25	.25
6	A1	35c Owl	.30	.30
7	A1	45c Shell	.40	.40
8	A1	55c Frog	.50	.50
9	A1	60c Water skier	.55	.55
10	A1	65c Net fishing	.60	.60
11	A1	75c Music box	.70	.70
12	A1	85c Pre-Columbian bisque pot	.75	.75
13	A1	90c Bulb cactus	.80	.80
14	A1	100c Grain	.85	.85
15	A1	150c Watapana tree	1.40	1.40
16	A1	250c Aloe plant	2.25	2.25
		Nos. 1-16 (16)	10.00	10.00

Issue dates: 5c, 30c, 60c, 150c, Jan. 1. 15c, 35c, 65c, 250c, Feb. 5. 20c, 45c, 75c, 100c, Apr. 7, 1987. 25c, 55c, 85c, 90c, July 17, 1987.

Independence — A2

1986, Jan. 1   *Perf. 14x13, 13x14*
18	A2	25c Map	.20	.20
19	A2	45c Coat of arms, vert.	.35	.35
20	A2	55c Natl. anthem, vert.	.45	.45
21	A2	100c Flag	.75	.75
		Nos. 18-21 (4)	1.75	1.75

Intl. Peace Year — A3

1986, Aug. 29   *Litho.*   *Perf. 14x13*
22	A3	60c shown	.45	.45
23	A3	100c Barbed wire	.75	.75

Princess Juliana and Prince Bernhard, 50th Wedding Anniv. — A4

1987, Jan. 7   *Photo.*   *Perf. 13x14*
| 24 | A4 | 135c multicolored | 1.25 | 1.25 |

State Visit of Queen Beatrix and Prince Claus of the Netherlands — A5

1987, Feb. 16   *Litho.*   *Perf. 14x13*
25	A5	55c shown	.50	.50
26	A5	60c Prince William-Alexander	.50	.50

Tourism — A6

1987, June 5   *Litho.*
27	A6	60c Beach and sea	.90	.90
28	A6	100c Rock and cacti	1.50	1.50

Aloe Vera Plant — A7    Coins — A8

1988, Jan. 27   *Litho.*   *Perf. 13x14*
29	A7	45c Field	.50	.50
30	A7	65c Plant	.65	.65
31	A7	100c Harvest	1.10	1.10
		Nos. 29-31 (3)	2.25	2.25

1988, Mar. 16   *Litho.*   *Perf. 13x14*
32	A8	25c 25-cent	.30	.30
33	A8	55c 50-cent	.65	.65
34	A8	65c 5 and 10-cent	.80	.80
35	A8	150c 1-florin	1.90	1.90
		Nos. 32-35 (4)	3.65	3.65

Love Issue — A9    A10

1988, May 4
36	A9	70c shown	.75	.75
37	A9	135c Seashells, coastal scenery	1.40	1.40

1988, Aug. 24
38	A10	35c shown	.40	.40
39	A10	100c Emblems	1.10	1.10

Aruba, the 162nd member of the Intl. Olympic Committee (35c), 1988 Summer Olympics, Seoul (100c).

Carnival — A11

1989, Jan. 5   *Perf. 14x13*
40	A11	45c Two children	.45	.45
41	A11	60c Girl	.60	.60
42	A11	100c Entertainer	1.00	1.00
		Nos. 40-42 (3)	2.05	2.05

Maripampun, *Omphalophalmum Rubrum* — A12

1989, Mar. 16   *Litho.*   *Perf. 14x13*
43	A12	35c Leaves	.35	.35
44	A12	55c Pods	.55	.55
45	A12	200c Blossom	1.90	1.90
		Nos. 43-45 (3)	2.80	2.80

New Year 1990 — A13    UPU — A14

Dande band members playing instruments or singing: 25c, Violin, tambor, cuatro, marimba. 70c, Lead singer, guitar. 150c, Accordion, urri, guitar.

1989, Nov. 16   *Litho.*   *Perf. 13x14*
46	A13	25c multicolored	.25	.25
47	A13	70c multicolored	.70	.70
48	A13	150c multicolored	1.50	1.50
		Nos. 46-48 (3)	2.45	2.45

1989, June 8   *Litho.*   *Perf. 13x14*
| 49 | A14 | 250c multicolored | 2.50 | 2.50 |

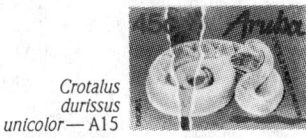

Crotalus durissus unicolor — A15

1989, Aug. 24   *Perf. 14x13*
50	A15	45c shown	.50	.50
51	A15	55c multi, diff.	.60	.60
52	A15	60c multi, diff.	.70	.70
		Nos. 50-52 (3)	1.80	1.80

Species in danger of extinction.

Man Living in Harmony with Nature — A16

1990, Feb. 7   *Perf. 13x14, 14x13*
53	A16	45c The land	.50	.50
54	A16	55c shown	.60	.60
55	A16	100c The sea	1.10	1.10
		Nos. 53-55 (3)	2.20	2.20

Environmental protection. #53, 55 horiz.

Marine Life — A17

Designs: 60c, Giant caribbean anemone, Pederson's cleaning shrimp. 70c, Queen angelfish, red and orange coral. 100c, Banded coral shrimp, fire sponge, yellow boring sponge.

1990, Apr. 4   *Litho.*   *Perf. 14x13*
56	A17	60c multicolored	.70	.70
57	A17	70c multicolored	.80	.80
58	A17	100c multicolored	1.10	1.10
		Nos. 56-58 (3)	2.60	2.60

A18    A19

1990, May 30   *Litho.*   *Perf. 13x14*
59	A18	35c multicolored	.30	.30
60	A18	200c Character trademark	1.75	1.75

World Cup Soccer Championships, Italy.

1990, Sept. 12
61	A19	45c Tools	.50	.50
62	A19	60c Stone figure	.65	.65
63	A19	100c Jar	1.10	1.10
		Nos. 61-63 (3)	2.25	2.25

Archeological discoveries.

Landscapes A20

1991, Jan. 31   *Litho.*   *Perf. 14x13*
64	A20	55c Seashore	.60	.60
65	A20	65c Desert	.70	.70
66	A20	100c Cactus, ocean view	1.10	1.10
		Nos. 64-66 (3)	2.40	2.40

Working Women — A21 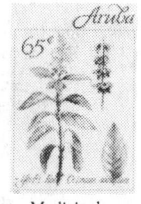   Medicinal Plants — A22

Designs: 35c, Taking care of others. 70c, Housewife. 100c, Women in society.

1991, Mar. 28   *Litho.*   *Perf. 13x14*
67	A21	35c multicolored	.40	.40
68	A21	70c multicolored	.85	.85
69	A21	100c multicolored	1.25	1.25
		Nos. 67-69 (3)	2.50	2.50

Style of inscriptions varies.

1991, May 29
70	A22	65c Ocimum sanctum	.70	.70
71	A22	75c Jatropha gossypifolia	.80	.80
72	A22	95c Croton flavens	1.00	1.00
		Nos. 70-72 (3)	2.50	2.50

A23    A24

Aruban Handicrafts: 35c, Fish net, wood hook, wooden needle. 250c, Straw hat, hat block.

1991, July 31   *Litho.*   *Perf. 13x14*
73	A23	35c lt bl, dk bl & blk	.40	.40
74	A23	250c pink, lil rose & blk	2.75	2.75

ARUBA

1991, Nov. 29 Litho. *Perf. 13x14*
75	A24	35c Toucan	.40	.40
76	A24	70c People shaking hands	.75	.75
77	A24	100c Windmill	1.10	1.10
		Nos. 75-77 (3)	2.25	2.25

Welcome to Aruba.

Aruba Postal Service, Cent. — A25

Designs: 60c, Government decree, 1892, vert. 75c, First post office. 80c, Current post office.

Perf. 13x14, 14x13
1992, Jan. 31 Litho.
78	A25	60c multicolored	.65	.65
79	A25	75c multicolored	.85	.85
80	A25	80c multicolored	.90	.90
		Nos. 78-80 (3)	2.40	2.40

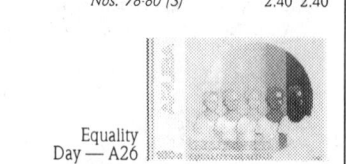

Equality Day — A26

1992, Mar. 25 Litho. *Perf. 14x13*
| 81 | A26 | 100c People of five races | 1.00 | 1.00 |
| 82 | A26 | 100c Woman, man, scales | 1.00 | 1.00 |

Discovery of America, 500th Anniv. — A27

1992, July 30 Litho. *Perf. 13x14*
83	A27	30c Columbus	.35	.35
84	A27	40c Sailing ship	.45	.45
85	A27	50c Natives, map	.55	.55
		Nos. 83-85 (3)	1.35	1.35

Natural Bridges in Aruba — A28

Designs: 70c, Seroe Colorado Bridge, south coast. 80c, Natural Bridge, north coast.

1992, Nov. 30 Litho. *Perf. 14x13*
| 86 | A28 | 70c multicolored | .85 | .85 |
| 87 | A28 | 80c multicolored | .90 | .90 |

A29 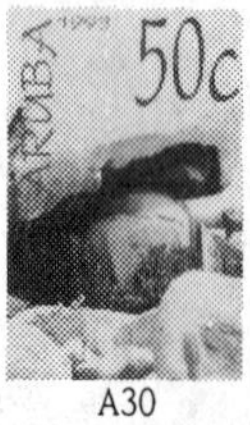 A30

1993, Jan. 29 Litho. *Perf. 13x14*
| 88 | A29 | 200c multicolored | 2.50 | 2.50 |

Express mail service.

1993, Mar. 31 Litho. *Perf. 13x14*

Various rock formations found in Districts of Ayo and Casibari.

89	A30	50c multicolored	.65	.65
90	A30	60c multicolored	.75	.75
91	A30	100c multicolored	1.25	1.25
		Nos. 89-91 (3)	2.65	2.65

Folklore — A31    Sailing Sports — A32

40c, String instruments, drum. 70c, Traditional music & games. 80c, Dera Gai song lyrics.

1993, May 28 Litho. *Perf. 13x14*
92	A31	40c multicolored	.50	.50
93	A31	70c multicolored	.85	.85
94	A31	80c multicolored	1.00	1.00
		Nos. 92-94 (3)	2.35	2.35

1993, July 30 Litho. *Perf. 13x14*
95	A32	50c Sailboating	.60	.60
96	A32	65c Land sailing	.80	.80
97	A32	75c Wind surfing	.95	.95
		Nos. 95-97 (3)	2.35	2.35

Iguana Iguana — A33

Perf. 14x13, 13x14
1993, Sept. 1 Litho.
98	A33	35c Young	.45	.45
99	A33	60c Almost grown	.75	.75
100	A33	100c Mature, vert.	1.25	1.25
		Nos. 98-100 (3)	2.45	2.45

Burrowing Owl — A34

Perf. 14x13, 13x14
1994, Jan. 28 Litho.
101	A34	5c Two adults	.15	.15
102	A34	10c Two adults, young	.15	.15
103	A34	35c Adult with prey, vert.	.45	.45
104	A34	40c Adult, vert.	.50	.50
		Nos. 101-104 (4)	1.25	1.25

World Wildlife Fund.

A35  A36

Intl. Olympic Committee, Cent.: 90c, Baron Pierre de Coubertin (1863-1937), founder of modern Olympics.

1994, Mar. 29 Litho. *Perf. 13x14*
| 105 | A35 | 50c multicolored | .65 | .65 |
| 106 | A35 | 90c multicolored | 1.10 | 1.10 |

1994, July 7 Litho. *Perf. 13x14*
| 107 | A36 | 65c shown | .80 | .80 |
| 108 | A36 | 150c Mascot, soccer ball | 1.90 | 1.90 |

1994 World Cup Soccer Championships, US.

Wild Fruit — A37

Designs: 40c, Malpighia punicifolia. 70c, Cordia sebestena. 85c, Pithecellobium unguis-cati. 150c, Coccoloba uvifera.

1994, Sept. 28 Litho. *Perf. 13x14*
109	A37	40c multicolored	.50	.50
110	A37	70c multicolored	.90	.90
111	A37	85c multicolored	1.10	1.10
112	A37	150c multicolored	1.90	1.90
		Nos. 109-112 (4)	4.40	4.40

Architectural Landmarks A38

Designs: 35c, Government building, 1888. 60c, Ecury residence, 1929, vert. 100c, Protestant Church, 1846, vert.

1995, Jan. 27 Litho. *Perf. 14x13*
| 113 | A38 | 35c multicolored | .45 | .45 |

Perf. 13x14
114	A38	60c multicolored	.75	.75
115	A38	100c multicolored	1.25	1.25
		Nos. 113-115 (3)	2.45	2.45

UN, 50th Anniv. — A39    Interpaso Horses — A40

Designs: 30c, Flags, sea, UN emblem, dove, text from UN charter. 200c, World with flags, doves, UN emblem.

1995, Mar. 29 Litho. *Perf. 13x14*
| 116 | A39 | 30c multicolored | .35 | .35 |
| 117 | A39 | 200c multicolored | 2.25 | 2.25 |

1995, May 26 *Perf. 14x13, 13x14*

Designs: 25c, 10-time champion Casanova II, ribbons, horiz. 75c, Paso Fino, horiz. 80c, Horse doing figure 8. 90c, Girl on horse.

118	A40	25c multicolored	.25	.25
119	A40	75c multicolored	.85	.85
120	A40	80c multicolored	.90	.90
121	A40	90c multicolored	1.00	1.00
		Nos. 118-121 (4)	3.00	3.00

Vegetables — A41

1995, July 28 Litho. *Perf. 13x14*
122	A41	25c Vigna sinensis	.30	.30
123	A41	50c Cucumis anguria	.55	.55
124	A41	70c Hibiscus esculentus	.80	.80
125	A41	85c Cucurbita moschata	.95	.95
		Nos. 122-125 (4)	2.60	2.60

Turtles — A42

1995, Sept. 27 Litho. *Perf. 14x13*
126	A42	15c Hawksbill	.15	.15
127	A42	50c Green	.55	.55
128	A42	95c Loggerhead	1.00	1.00
129	A42	100c Leatherback	1.10	1.10
		Nos. 126-129 (4)	2.80	2.80

Separate Status, 10th Anniv. — A43

Statesmen and politicians: No. 130, Jan Hendrik Albert Eman (1887-1957). No. 131, Juan Enrique Irausquin (1904-62). No. 132, Cornelis Albert Eman (1916-67). No. 133, Gilberto Francois Croes (1938-85).

1996, Jan. 1 Litho. *Perf. 13x14*
130	A43	100c multicolored	1.10	1.10
131	A43	100c multicolored	1.10	1.10
132	A43	100c multicolored	1.10	1.10
133	A43	100c multicolored	1.10	1.10
		Nos. 130-133 (4)	4.40	4.40

The 1986 date on No. 133 is in error.

America Issue — A44

National dresswear: 65c, Woman wearing long, full dress, apron, vert. 70c, Man wearing hat, bow tie, white shirt, black pants, vert. 100c, Couple dancing.

Perf. 13x14, 14x13
1996, Mar. 25 Litho.
134	A44	65c multicolored	.75	.75
135	A44	70c multicolored	.80	.80
136	A44	100c multicolored	1.10	1.10
		Nos. 134-136 (3)	2.65	2.65

1996 Summer Olympic Games, Atlanta A45

1996, May 28 Litho. *Perf. 14x13*
| 137 | A45 | 85c Runners | 1.10 | 1.10 |
| 138 | A45 | 130c Cyclist | 1.65 | 1.65 |

A46  A47

Famous Women: No. 139, Livia (Mimi) Ecury (1920-91), nurse. No. 140, Lolita Euson (1914-94), poet. No. 141, Laura Wernet-Paskel (1911-62), teacher.

1996, Sept. 27 Litho. *Perf. 13x14*
139	A46	60c multicolored	.70	.70
140	A46	60c multicolored	.70	.70
141	A46	60c multicolored	.70	.70
		Nos. 139-141 (3)	2.10	2.10

1997, Jan. 23 Litho. *Perf. 13x14*

Year of Papiamento 1997: 50c, Sign promoting use of Papiamento language, children playing on beach, people in water, boat. 140c, "Papiamento," sunrise.

| 142 | A47 | 50c multicolored | .55 | .55 |
| 143 | A47 | 140c multicolored | 1.65 | 1.65 |

Mailman on Bicycle, 1936-57 — A48

America issue: 70c, Mailman handing mail to woman, jeep, 1957-88. 80c, Mailman on motor scooter placing mail in mailbox, 1995.

1997, Mar. 27 Litho. *Perf. 14x13*
144	A48	60c multicolored	.70	.70
145	A48	70c multicolored	.80	.80
146	A48	80c multicolored	.90	.90
		Nos. 144-146 (3)	2.40	2.40

ARUBA

Aruban Architectrue A49

Designs: 30c, Decorated cunucu house. 65c, Steps with "popchi's." 100c, Arends's Building, vert.

1997, May 22   Litho.   Perf. 14x13
| 147 | A49 | 30c multicolored | .40 | .40 |
| 148 | A49 | 65c multicolored | .80 | .80 |

Perf. 13x14
| 149 | A49 | 100c multicolored | 1.25 | 1.25 |
| | | Nos. 147-149 (3) | 2.45 | 2.45 |

Marine Life — A50

Designs: a, Marlin jumping out of water, lighthouse. b, Dolphin jumping out of water, trees, plants on beach. c, Iguana on rock, beach. d, Dolphin, fish. e, Two dolphins, fish. f, Fish, turtles, owl on beach. g, Various fish among coral. h, Diver, shipwreck, fish, coral. i, Various fish.

1997, May 29   Litho.   Perf. 12½x13
| 150 | A50 | 90c Sheet of 9, #a.-i. | 10.00 | 10.00 |

PACIFIC 97.

Cruise Tourism — A51

Designs: 35c, Ship at pier, tourists walking toward ship. 50c, Ship with gangway lowered, tourists. 150c, Ship out to sea, small boat.

1997, July 24   Litho.   Perf. 14x13
151	A51	35c multicolored	.40	.40
152	A51	50c multicolored	.55	.55
153	A51	150c multicolored	1.70	1.70
		Nos. 151-153 (3)	2.65	2.65

Aruban Wild Flowers — A52

50c, Erythrina velutina. 60c, Cordia dentata. 70c, Tabebuia billbergii. 130c, Guaiacum officinale.

1997, Sept. 25
154	A52	50c multicolored	.55	.55
155	A52	60c multicolored	.70	.70
156	A52	70c multicolored	.80	.80
157	A52	130c multicolored	1.45	1.45
		Nos. 154-157 (4)	3.50	3.50

Fort Zoutman, Bicent. — A53

1998, Jan. 13   Litho.   Perf. 14x13
| 158 | A53 | 30c sepia & multi | .35 | .35 |
| 159 | A53 | 250c gray & multi | 3.00 | 3.00 |

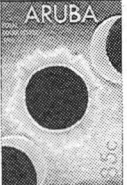

Total Solar Eclipse, 1998 — A54

1998, Feb. 26   Litho.   Perf. 13x14
| 160 | A54 | 85c shown | 1.10 | 1.10 |
| 161 | A54 | 100c Map, track of eclipse | 1.25 | 1.25 |

Native Birds — A55

50c, Mimus gilvus. 60c, Falco sparverius. 70c, Icterus icterus. 150c, Coereba flaveola.

1998, July 10   Perf. 14x13, 13x14   Litho.
162	A55	50c multi	.55	.55
163	A55	60c multi, vert.	.70	.70
164	A55	70c multi, vert.	.80	.80
165	A55	150c multi	1.75	1.75
		Nos. 162-165 (4)	3.80	3.80

World Stamp 1998 — A56

1998, Sept. 8   Litho.   Perf. 14x13
| 166 | A56 | 225c multicolored | 2.50 | 2.50 |

SEMI-POSTAL STAMPS

Surtax for child welfare organizations unless otherwise stated.

Solidarity SP1

1986, May 7   Litho.   Perf. 14x13
B1	SP1	30c + 10c shown	.30	.30
B2	SP1	35c + 15c Three ropes	.40	.40
B3	SP1	60c + 25c One rope	.60	.60
		Nos. B1-B3 (3)	1.30	1.30

Surtax for social and cultural projects.

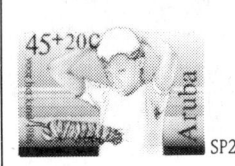

SP2

1986, Oct. 29   Litho.   Perf. 14x13
B4	SP2	45c + 20c Boy, caterpillar	.70	.70
B5	SP2	70c + 25c Boy, cocoon	1.00	1.00
B6	SP2	100c + 40c Girl, butterfly	1.50	1.50
		Nos. B4-B6 (3)	3.20	3.20

Christmas SP3

1987, Oct. 27   Litho.   Perf. 14x13
B7	SP3	25c +10c Boy on beach	.35	.35
B8	SP3	45c +20c Drawing Christmas tree	.70	.70
B9	SP3	70c +30c Child, creche figures	1.10	1.10
		Nos. B7-B9 (3)	2.15	2.15

Solidarity SP4

YMCA emblem in various geometric designs.

1988, Aug. 3   Litho.   Perf. 14x13
B10	SP4	45c +20c shown	.70	.70
B11	SP4	60c +25c multi, diff.	.90	.90
B12	SP4	100c +50c multi, diff.	1.65	1.65
		Nos. B10-B12 (3)	3.25	3.25

11th YMCA world council. Surtax for social and cultural projects.

Children's Toys — SP5

1988, Oct. 26   Perf. 13x14
B13	SP5	45c +20c Jacks	.70	.70
B14	SP5	70c +30c Top	1.10	1.10
B15	SP5	100c +50c Kite	1.65	1.65
		Nos. B13-B15 (3)	3.45	3.45

Children — SP6

1989, Oct. 26   Perf. 14x13
B16	SP6	45c +20c Baby spoon	.65	.65
B17	SP6	60c +30c Chasing a ball	.85	.85
B18	SP6	100c +50c Adult & child holding hands	1.50	1.50
		Nos. B16-B18 (3)	3.00	3.00

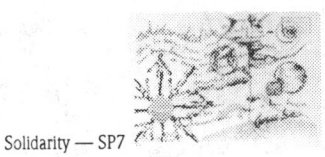

Solidarity — SP7

1990, July 25
| B19 | SP7 | 55c +25c shown | 1.10 | 1.10 |
| B20 | SP7 | 100c +50c Family, house | 2.00 | 2.00 |

Surtax for social and cultural projects.

SP8    SP9

Christmas song.

1990, Oct. 24   Litho.   Perf. 13x14
B21	SP8	45c +20c Wind surfboards	.75	.75
B22	SP8	60c +30c shown	1.00	1.00
B23	SP8	100c +50c Kites, lizard	1.75	1.75
		Nos. B21-B23 (3)	3.50	3.50

1991, Oct. 25   Litho.   Perf. 13x14

Literacy: 45c+25c, Discovery of reading. 60c+35c, Pointing to letter. 100c+50c, Child reading.

B24	SP9	45c +25c multi	.75	.75
B25	SP9	60c +35c multi	1.00	1.00
B26	SP9	100c +50c multi	1.65	1.65
		Nos. B24-B26 (3)	3.40	3.40

Solidarity SP10

55c+30c, Girl scouts, flag & emblem. 100c+50c, Hand holding cancer fund emblem, people.

1992, May 27   Litho.   Perf. 14x13
| B27 | SP10 | 55c +30c multi | .90 | .90 |
| B28 | SP10 | 100c +50c multi | 1.65 | 1.65 |

Surtax for social and cultural projects.

Postal Services of Aruba, Cent. — SP11

Designs: 50c+30c, Heart. 70c+35c, Airplane, letters. 100c+55c, Pigeon with letter in beak, vert.

1992, Oct. 30   Litho.   Perf. 14x13
| B29 | SP11 | 50c +30c multi | 1.00 | 1.00 |
| B30 | SP11 | 70c +35c multi | 1.40 | 1.40 |

Perf. 13x14
| B31 | SP11 | 100c +50c multi | 2.00 | 2.00 |
| | | Nos. B29-B31 (3) | 4.40 | 4.40 |

Youth Foreign Study Programs SP12

Abstract designs of: 50c+30c, Landscapes. 75c+40c, Young man, scenes of other countries, vert. 100c+50c, Integrating cultures.

1993, Oct. 27   Perf. 14x13, 13x14
B32	SP12	50c +30c multi	1.00	1.00
B33	SP12	75c +40c multi	1.40	1.40
B34	SP12	100c +50c multi	1.90	1.90
		Nos. B32-B34 (3)	4.30	4.30

Intl. Year of the Family — SP13

Designs: 50c+35c, Family seated, reading, studying. 100c+50c, Family playing in front of house.

1994, May 30   Litho.   Perf. 14x13
| B35 | SP13 | 50c +35c multi | 1.10 | 1.10 |
| B36 | SP13 | 100c +50c multi | 1.90 | 1.90 |

Surtax for social and cultural projects.

SP14

Designs: 50c+30c, Children on anchor with umbrella. 80c+35c, Children inside Sun. 100c+50c, Child riding owl.

1994, Oct. 27   Litho.   Perf. 14x13
B37	SP14	50c +30c multi	1.00	1.00
B38	SP14	80c +35c multi	1.40	1.40
B39	SP14	100c +50c multi	1.90	1.90
		Nos. B37-B39 (3)	4.30	4.30

SP15    SP16

Children's drawings: 50c+25c, Children with balloons, house. 70c+35c, Three people with picnic basket on sunny day. 100c+50c, People gardening on sunny day.

1995, Oct. 26   Litho.   Perf. 13x14
B40	SP15	50c +25c multi	.85	.85
B41	SP15	70c +35c multi	1.25	1.25
B42	SP15	100c +50c multi	1.65	1.65
		Nos. B40-B42 (3)	3.75	3.75

1996, July 26   Litho.   Perf. 13x14

El Sol Naciente Lodge, 75th Anniv.: 60c+30c, Masonic emblems. 100c+ 50c, Columns, terrestrial and celestial globes.

| B43 | SP16 | 60c +30c multi | 1.10 | 1.10 |
| B44 | SP16 | 100c +50c multi | 1.90 | 1.90 |

Surtax for social and cultural projects.

SP17

Cartoons: 50c+25c, Mother, baby rabbit waiting at school bus stop. 70c+35c, Mother, baby owl, outside school. 100c+50c, Children flying kite.

1996, Oct. 24 Litho. *Perf. 14x13*

B45	SP17	50c +25c multi	.95	.95
B46	SP17	70c +35c multi	1.25	1.25
B47	SP17	100c +50c multi	1.90	1.90
		Nos. B45-B47 (3)	4.10	4.10

SP18

Designs: 50c+25c, Girl sitting among aloe plants. 70c+35c, Boy, butterfly, cactus, vert. 100c+50c, Girl swimming under water, fish, coral.

Perf. 14x13, 13x14

1997, Oct. 23 Litho.

B48	SP18	50c +25c multi	.85	.85
B49	SP18	70c +35c multi	1.25	1.25
B50	SP18	100c +50c multi	1.65	1.65
		Nos. B48-B50 (3)	3.75	3.75

SP19

Service Organizations: 60c+30c, Globe, emblem of Lions Intl., wheelchair balanced on map of Aruba. 100c+50c, Child reading book, emblem of Rotary Intl., woman in rocking chair.

1998, May 29 Litho. *Perf. 14x13*

B51	SP19	60c +30c multi	1.20	1.20
B52	SP19	100c +50c multi	2.00	2.00

SP20

Designs: 50c+25c, Girl performing traditional ribbon dance. 80c+40c, Boy playing a cuarta. 100c+50c, Two boys playing basketball.

1998, Oct. 22 Litho. *Perf. 13x14*

B53	SP20	50c +25c multi	.85	.85
B54	SP20	80c +40c multi	1.25	1.25
B55	SP20	100c +50c multi	1.75	1.75
		Nos. B53-B55 (3)	3.85	3.85

ASCENSION

ə-'sen(t)-shən

LOCATION — An island in the South Atlantic Ocean, 900 miles from Liberia
GOVT. — A part of the British Crown Colony of St. Helena
AREA — 34 sq. mi.
POP. — 1,625 (1982)

In 1922 Ascension was placed under the administration of the Colonial Office and annexed to the British Crown Colony of St. Helena. The only post office is at Georgetown.

12 Pence = 1 Shilling
20 Shillings = 1 Pound
100 Pence = 1 Pound (1971)

Ascension stamps can be mounted in the Scott British Africa album.

Catalogue values for unused stamps in this country are for Never Hinged items, beginning with Scott 50.

Stamps and Types of St. Helena, 1912-22 Overprinted in Black or Red

ASCENSION

1922 Wmk. 4 *Perf. 14*

1	A9	½p green & blk	3.00	*9.00*
2	A10	1p green	4.00	*9.50*
3	A10	1½p rose red	13.00	*40.00*
4	A9	2p gray & blk	11.00	*10.00*
5	A9	3p ultra	10.50	*12.50*
6	A10	8p dl vio & blk	21.00	*35.00*
7	A10	2sh ultra & blk, *blue*	67.50	*90.00*
8	A10	3sh vio & blk	110.00	*120.00*

Wmk. 3

9	A9	1sh blk, *gray grn* (R)	22.50	*35.00*
		Nos. 1-9 (9)	262.50	*361.00*

Seal of Colony — A3

1924-27 Typo. Wmk. 4 *Perf. 14*

Chalky Paper

10	A3	½p black & gray	2.25	*9.25*
11	A3	1p green & blk	3.50	*5.50*
12	A3	1½p rose red	5.00	*20.00*
13	A3	2p bluish gray & gray	6.50	4.50
14	A3	3p ultra	4.25	*9.25*
15	A3	4p blk & gray, *yel*	35.00	*62.50*
16	A3	5p ol & lil ('27)	9.00	*16.00*
17	A3	6p rose lil & gray	40.00	*67.50*
18	A3	8p violet & gray	9.50	*32.50*
19	A3	1sh brown & gray	15.00	*37.50*
20	A3	2sh ultra & gray, *blue*	50.00	*72.50*
21	A3	3sh blk & gray, *blue*	70.00	*77.50*
		Nos. 10-21 (12)	250.00	*414.50*

View of Georgetown A4

Map of Ascension — A5

Sooty Tern Breeding Colony A9

Designs: 1½p, Pier at Georgetown. 3p, Long Beach. 5p, Three Sisters. 5sh, Green Mountain.

1934, July 2 Engr.

23	A4	½p violet & blk	.75	.75
24	A5	1p lt grn & blk	1.50	1.10
25	A4	1½p red & black	1.50	2.10
26	A5	2p org & black	1.50	*2.40*
27	A4	3p ultra & blk	1.50	1.40
28	A4	5p blue & black	1.90	*3.00*
29	A5	8p dk brn & blk	3.50	*4.50*
30	A9	1sh carmine & blk	15.00	6.00
31	A5	2sh6p violet & blk	30.00	*45.00*
32	A4	5sh brown & blk	52.50	*65.00*
		Nos. 23-32 (10)	109.65	*131.25*

Common Design Types pictured following the introduction.

Silver Jubilee Issue

Common Design Type

1935, May 6 *Perf. 11x12*

33	CD301	1½p car & dk blue	2.75	*4.25*
34	CD301	2p blk & ultra	8.25	*18.00*
35	CD301	5p ind & grn	12.50	*20.00*
36	CD301	1sh brn vio & indigo	17.50	*22.50*
		Nos. 33-36 (4)	41.00	*64.75*

25th anniv. of the reign of King George V.

Coronation Issue

Common Design Type

1937, May 19 *Perf. 13½x14*

37	CD302	1p deep green	.20	.20
38	CD302	2p deep orange	.80	.80
39	CD302	3p bright ultra	1.00	1.00
		Nos. 37-39 (3)	2.00	2.00
		Set, never hinged	3.00	

Georgetown A11

Designs: 1p, 2p, 4p, Green Mountain. 1½p, 2sh6p, Pier at Georgetown. 3p, 5sh, Long Beach. 6p, 10sh, Three Sisters.

1938-49 *Perf. 13½*

Center in Black

40	A11	½p violet, perf. 13 ('44)	.30	*1.40*
		Never hinged	.65	
a.		Perf. 13½	1.40	1.00
		Never hinged	3.00	
41	A11	1p green	18.00	7.50
		Never hinged	37.50	
41A	A11	1p org yel, perf. 13 ('42)	.20	*.55*
		Never hinged	.45	
b.		Perf. 14 ('49)	.30	*15.00*
		Never hinged	.65	
c.		Perf. 13½	6.00	*8.50*
		Never hinged	13.50	
42	A11	1½p red, perf. 13 ('44)	.35	*.75*
		Never hinged	.75	
a.		Perf. 14 ('49)	1.40	*12.00*
		Never hinged	2.75	
b.		Perf. 13½	1.50	1.40
		Never hinged	3.25	
43	A11	2p orange, perf. 13 ('44)	.35	.40
		Never hinged	.75	
a.		Perf. 14 ('49)	2.00	*32.50*
		Never hinged	3.00	
b.		Perf. 13½	1.65	1.00
		Never hinged	3.25	
44	A11	3p ultra	50.00	25.00
		Never hinged	95.00	
44A	A11	3p black, perf. 13 ('44)	.30	*.80*
		Never hinged	.65	
c.		Perf. 13 ½('40)	7.50	.90
		Never hinged	14.00	
44B	A11	4p ultra, perf. 13 ('44)	2.00	*2.75*
		Never hinged	4.00	
d.		Perf. 13½	5.50	3.00
		Never hinged	10.50	
45	A11	6p gray blue	4.00	1.00
		Never hinged	8.25	
a.		Perf. 13 ('44)	4.00	4.00
		Never hinged	8.25	

Perf. 13

46	A11	1sh dk brown ('44)	3.25	2.00
		Never hinged	4.50	
a.		Perf. 13½	5.75	1.40
		Never hinged	11.50	
47	A11	2sh6p car ('44)	15.00	*30.00*
		Never hinged	32.50	
a.		Perf. 13½	20.00	7.00
		Never hinged	37.50	
48	A11	5sh yel brn ('44)	22.50	25.00
		Never hinged	45.00	
a.		Perf. 13½	52.50	7.00
		Never hinged	100.00	
49	A11	10sh red vio ('44)	42.50	*52.50*
		Never hinged	62.50	
a.		Perf. 13½	52.50	40.00
		Never hinged	110.00	

See Nos. 54-56.

Catalogue values for unused stamps in this section, from this point to the end of the section, are for Never Hinged items.

Peace Issue

Common Design Type

Perf. 13½x14

1946, Oct. 21 Engr. Wmk. 4

50	CD303	2p deep orange	.25	.25
51	CD303	4p deep blue	.30	.30

Silver Wedding Issue

Common Design Types

1948, Oct. 20 Photo. *Perf. 14x14½*

52	CD304	3p black	.50	.50

Engraved; Name Typographed

Perf. 11½x11

53	CD305	10sh red violet	40.00	*40.00*

Type of 1938

Designs: 1p, Three Sisters. 1½p, Georgetown Pier. 2p, Green Mountain.

1949, June 1 Engr. Wmk. 4 *Perf. 13*

54	A11	1p green & black	.30	.30

Perf. 14

55	A11	1½p lilac rose & blk	.35	.35
a.		Perf. 13	.50	.50
b.		1½p carmine & black	6.00	4.75
56	A11	2p red & black	.50	.50
		Nos. 54-56 (3)	1.15	1.15

Issue date: No. 55a, Feb. 25, 1953.

UPU Issue

Common Design Types

Engr.; Name Typo. on Nos. 58, 59

1949, Oct. 10 *Perf. 13½, 11x11½*

57	CD306	3p rose carmine	1.25	1.10
58	CD307	4p indigo	3.00	2.50
59	CD308	6p olive	3.25	3.00
60	CD309	1sh slate	6.25	6.00
		Nos. 57-60 (4)	13.75	12.60

Coronation Issue

Common Design Type

1953, June 2 Engr. *Perf. 13½x13*

61	CD312	3p gray & black	1.50	1.50

Reservoir A16

Designs: 1p, Map of Ascension. 1½p, Georgetown. 2p, Map showing Ascension between South America and Africa and cable lines. 2½p, Mountain road. 3p, Yellow-billed tropic bird. 4p, Longfinned tuna. 6p, Waves. 7p, Young green turtles. 1sh, Land crab. 2sh6p, Sooty tern (wideawake). 5sh, Perfect Crater. 10sh, View from Northwest.

1956, Nov. 19 Wmk. 4 *Perf. 13*

Center in Black

62	A16	½p brown	.15	.15
63	A16	1p lilac rose	.35	.30
64	A16	1½p orange	.35	.25
65	A16	2p carmine	.55	.35
66	A16	2½p orange brown	.65	.55
67	A16	3p blue	.90	.50
68	A16	4p turq blue	.85	.85
69	A16	6p dark blue	1.10	1.10
70	A16	7p olive	1.40	1.40
71	A16	1sh scarlet	1.90	1.50
72	A16	2sh6p brown violet	19.00	11.00
73	A16	5sh bright green	25.00	16.00
74	A16	10sh purple	50.00	30.00
		Nos. 62-74 (13)	102.20	63.95

Brown Booby — A17

Birds: 1½p, Black tern. 2p, Fairy tern. 3p, Red-billed tropic bird in flight. 4½p, Brown noddy. 6p, Sooty tern. 7p, Frigate bird. 10p, Blue-faced booby. 1sh, Yellow-billed tropic bird. 1sh6p, Red-billed tropic bird. 2sh6p, Madeiran storm petrel. 5sh, Red-footed booby (brown phase). 10sh, Frigate birds. £1, Red-footed booby (white phase).

Perf. 14x14½

1963, May 23 Photo. Wmk. 314

75	A17	1p multicolored	.15	.15
a.		Booklet pane of 4	.30	
76	A17	1½p multicolored	.15	.15
a.		Booklet pane of 4	.50	
b.		Blue omitted	70.00	
77	A17	2p multicolored	.15	.15
a.		Booklet pane of 4	1.10	
78	A17	3p multicolored	.20	.15
a.		Booklet pane of 4	1.25	
79	A17	4½p multicolored	.25	.20
80	A17	6p multicolored	.35	.25
a.		Booklet pane of 4	3.25	
81	A17	7p multicolored	.35	.30
82	A17	10p multicolored	.50	.40
83	A17	1sh multicolored	.55	.50
84	A17	1sh6p multicolored	1.10	1.00
a.		Booklet pane of 4	6.25	
85	A17	2sh6p multicolored	2.75	2.50
86	A17	5sh multicolored	5.50	5.00
87	A17	10sh multicolored	12.50	10.00
88	A17	£1 multicolored	22.50	20.00
		Nos. 75-88 (14)	47.00	40.75

ASCENSION

Freedom from Hunger Issue
Common Design Type
1963, June 4　　　　　　　Wmk. 314
89　CD314　1sh6p car rose　　　3.00　2.50

Red Cross Centenary Issue
Common Design Type
1963, Sept. 2　　Litho.　　*Perf. 13*
90　CD315　3p black & red　　　.90　.90
91　CD315　1sh6p ultra & red　　6.00　6.00

ITU Issue
Common Design Type
　　　　　　　　Perf. 11x11½
1965, May 17　　Litho.　　Wmk. 314
92　CD317　3p mag & violet　　　.60　.60
93　CD317　6p grnsh bl & brn org　1.60　1.60

Intl. Cooperation Year Issue
Common Design Type
1965, Oct. 25　Wmk. 314　*Perf. 14½*
94　CD318　1p bl grn & claret　　.40　.30
95　CD318　6p lt vio & green　　1.60　1.50

Churchill Memorial Issue
Common Design Type
1966, Jan. 24　　Photo.　　*Perf. 14*
Design in Black, Gold and Carmine Rose
96　CD319　1p bright blue　　　.35　.25
97　CD319　3p green　　　　　1.25　.85
98　CD319　6p brown　　　　　1.60　1.40
99　CD319　1sh6p violet　　　　5.00　4.00
　　Nos. 96-99 (4)　　　　　　8.20　6.50

World Cup Soccer Issue
Common Design Type
1966, July 1　　Litho.　　*Perf. 14*
100　CD321　3p multicolored　　　.70　.55
101　CD321　6p multicolored　　1.40　2.25

WHO Headquarters Issue
Common Design Type
1966, Sept. 20　　Litho.　　*Perf. 14*
102　CD322　3p multicolored　　1.25　1.00
103　CD322　1sh6p multicolored　3.25　3.00

Apollo Satellite Station, Ascension — A18

Wmk. 314
1966, Nov. 7　　Photo.　　*Perf. 14*
104　A18　4p purple & black　　.15　.15
105　A18　8p blue grn & blk　　.15　.15
106　A18　1sh3p brn ol & blk　　.30　.20
107　A18　2sh6p brt grnsh blue & black　　　　　.60　.40
　　Nos. 104-107 (4)　　　　　1.20　.90

Opening of the Apollo communications satellite-earth station, part of the US Apollo program.

UNESCO Anniversary Issue
Common Design Type
1967, Jan. 3　　Litho.　　*Perf. 14*
108　CD323　3p "Education"　　.70　.65
109　CD323　6p "Science"　　　2.00　1.75
110　CD323　1sh6p "Culture"　　5.00　5.00
　　Nos. 108-110 (3)　　　　　7.70　7.40

BBC Emblem A19

Photo.; Gold Impressed
1967, Dec. 1　Wmk. 314　*Perf. 14½*
111　A19　1p ultra & gold　　　.15　.15
112　A19　3p dk green & gold　.15　.15
113　A19　6p brt purple & gold　.20　.20
114　A19　1sh6p brt red & gold　.50　.50
　　Nos. 111-114 (4)　　　　　1.00　1.00

Opening of the British Broadcasting Company's South Atlantic Relay Station on Ascension Island.

Human Rights Flame and Chain — A20

　　　　　　　Perf. 14½x14
1968, July 8　　Litho.　　Wmk. 314
115　A20　6p org, car & blk　　.20　.15
116　A20　1sh6p gray, mag & blk　.30　.25
117　A20　2sh6p brt grn, plum & blk　.60　.50
　　Nos. 115-117 (3)　　　　　1.10　.90

International Human Rights Year.

Blackfish A21

Fish: No. 119, Sailfish. 6p, Oldwife. 8p, Leather jacks. 1sh6p, Yellowtails. 1sh9p, Tuna. 2sh3p, Mako sharks. 2sh11p, Rock hind (jack).

　　　　　Perf. 13x12½
1968-69　　Wmk. 314　　Litho.
118　A21　4p brt grnsh bl & blk　.25　.20
119　A21　4p red & multi　　　.30　.25
120　A21　6p yel olive & multi　.40　.35
121　A21　8p brt rose lil & multi　.55　.40
122　A21　1sh6p brown & multi　1.75　1.40
123　A21　1sh9p emer & multi　1.00　.85
124　A21　2sh3p ocher & multi　1.60　1.10
125　A21　2sh11p dp org & multi　3.25　2.00
　　Nos. 118-125 (8)　　　　　9.10　6.55

Issue dates: No. 119, 6p, 1sh6p, 2sh11p, Mar. 3, 1969; others, Oct. 23, 1968.
See Nos. 130-133.

Arms of R.N.S. Rattlesnake — A22

Coats of Arms of Royal Naval Ships: 9p, Weston. 1sh9p, Undaunted. 2sh3p, Eagle.

　　　　　　Perf. 14x14½
1969, Oct. 1　　Photo.　　Wmk. 314
126　A22　4p multicolored　　.25　.25
127　A22　9p multicolored　　.50　.50
128　A22　1sh9p multicolored　1.25　1.25
129　A22　2sh3p multicolored　1.75　1.75
　　a.　Min. sheet of 4, #126-129　6.75　5.75
　　Nos. 126-129 (4)　　　　3.75　3.75

See Nos. 134-137, 152-159, 166-169.

Fish Type of 1968
Deep-sea fish: 4p, Wahoo. 9p, Coalfish. 1sh9p, Dolphinfishes. 2sh3p, Soldierfish.

1970, Apr. 6　　Litho.　　*Perf. 14*
130　A21　4p bluish grn & multi　.55　.35
131　A21　9p org & multi　　　.90　.60
132　A21　1sh9p ultra & multi　1.75　1.40
133　A21　2sh3p gray & multi　3.25　2.00
　　Nos. 130-133 (4)　　　　6.45　4.35

Naval Arms Type of 1969
4p, Penelope. 9p, Carlisle. 1sh6p, Amphion. 2sh6p, Magpie.

　　　　　Perf. 12½x12
1970, Sept. 7　　Photo.　　Wmk. 314
134　A22　4p ultra, gold & blk　.25　.25
135　A22　9p lt bl, blk, gold & red　.50　.50
136　A22　1sh6p grnsh bl, gold & blk　1.25　1.25
137　A22　2sh6p lt grnsh bl, gold & blk　2.00　2.00
　　a.　Miniature sheet of 4, #134-137　7.50　6.00
　　Nos. 134-137 (4)　　　　4.00　4.00

Decimal Currency Issue

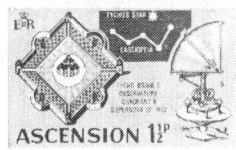

Tycho Brahe's Observatory, Quadrant and Supernova, 1572 — A23

Man into Space: ½p, Chinese rocket, 1232, vert. 1p, Medieval Arab astronomers, vert. 2p, Galileo, his telescope and drawing of moon, 1609. 2½p, Isaac Newton, telescope and apple. 3½p, Harrison's chronometer and ship, 1735. 4½p, First American manned orbital flight (Project Mercury, 1962, vert.). 5p, Reflector of Palomar telescope and ring nebula in Lyra, Messier 57. 7½p, Jodrell Bank telescope. 10p, Mariner 7, 1969, and telescopic view of Mars. 12½p, Sputnik 2 and dog Laika, 1957. 25p, Astronaut walking in space, 1965 (Gemini 4; vert.). 50p, US astronauts and moon landing module, 1969. £1, Future space research station.

1971, Feb. 15　　Litho.　　*Perf. 14½*
138　A23　½p multicolored　　.15　.15
　　a.　Booklet pane of 4　　　.50
139　A23　1p multicolored　　.15　.15
　　a.　Booklet pane of 4　　　.75
140　A23　1½p multicolored　　.20　.20
　　a.　Booklet pane of 4　　　1.00
141　A23　2p multicolored　　.20　.20
　　a.　Booklet pane of 4　　　1.90
142　A23　2½p multicolored　　.35　.35
　　a.　Booklet pane of 4　　　2.50
143　A23　3½p multicolored　　.45　.45
　　a.　Booklet pane of 4　　　3.50
144　A23　4½p multicolored　　.60　.60
145　A23　5p multicolored　　.65　.65
146　A23　7½p multicolored　　.75　.75
147　A23　10p multicolored　　1.00　1.00
148　A23　12½p multicolored　1.40　1.40
149　A23　25p multicolored　　2.50　2.50
150　A23　50p multicolored　　5.25　5.25
151　A23　£1 multicolored　　10.00　10.00
　　Nos. 138-151 (14)　　　23.65　23.65

For overprints see Nos. 189-191.

Arms of H.M.S. Phoenix — A24 　　Course of Quest — A25

Coats of Arms of Royal Naval Ships: 4p, Milford. 9p, Pelican. 15p, Oberon.

1971, Nov. 15　Photo.　*Perf. 13½x13*
152　A24　2p gold & multi　　.20　.20
153　A24　4p gold & multi　　.40　.40
154　A24　9p gold & multi　　1.10　1.10
155　A24　15p gold & multi　　2.25　2.25
　　a.　Souvenir sheet of 4, #152-155　7.00　7.00
　　Nos. 152-155 (4)　　　　3.95　3.95

Naval Arms Type of 1969
1½p, Lowestoft. 3p, Auckland. 6p, Nigeria. 17½p, Bermuda.

1972, May 22　　Litho.　　*Perf. 14x14½*
156　A22　1½p bl, gold & blk　.20　.20
157　A22　3p grnsh bl, gold & blk　.45　.45
158　A22　6p grn, gold, blk & bl　.90　.90
159　A22　17½p lil, gold, blk & red　2.75　2.75
　　a.　Miniature sheet of 4, #156-159　5.00　5.00
　　Nos. 156-159 (4)　　　　4.30　4.30

1972, Aug. 2　　　　　*Perf. 14*
Designs: 4p, Shackleton and "Quest", horiz. 7½p, Shackleton's cabin and Quest in pack ice, horiz. 11p, Shackleton statue, London, and memorial cairn, South Georgia.
160　A25　2½p multicolored　　.30　.30
161　A25　4p multicolored　　.50　.50
162　A25　7½p multicolored　　1.00　1.00
163　A25　11p multicolored　　1.65　1.65
　　a.　Souvenir sheet of 4, #160-163　4.25　4.25
　　Nos. 160-163 (4)　　　　3.45　3.45

Sir Ernest Henry Shackleton (1874-1922), explorer of Antarctica.

Silver Wedding Issue, 1972
Common Design Type
Design: Queen Elizabeth II, Prince Philip, land crab and shark.

1972, Nov. 20　Photo.　*Perf. 14x14½*
164　CD324　2p violet & multi　.15　.15
165　CD324　16p car rose & multi　.75　.75

Naval Arms Type of 1969
2p, Birmingham. 4p, Cardiff. 9p, Penzance. 13p, Rochester.

1973, May 28　　Litho.　　Wmk. 314
166　A22　2p blue & multi　　.60　.42
167　A22　4p yel grn & multi　1.50　1.10
168　A22　9p lt blue & multi　3.00　2.25
169　A22　13p violet & multi　4.25　3.75
　　a.　Min. sheet of 4, #166-169　18.00　18.00
　　Nos. 166-169 (4)　　　　9.35　7.52

Turtles — A26

1973, Aug. 28　　　　　*Perf. 13½*
170　A26　4p Green　　　　1.65　1.10
171　A26　9p Loggerhead　　3.25　2.25
172　A26　12p Hawksbill　　5.25　3.50
　　Nos. 170-172 (3)　　　10.15　6.85

Light Infantry Marine Sergeant, 1900 — A27

Uniforms (Royal Marines): 6p, Private, 1816. 12p, Officer, Light Infantry, 1880. 20p, Color Sergeant, Artillery, 1910.

1973, Oct. 31　　　　　*Perf. 14½*
173　A27　2p multicolored　　.50　.50
174　A27　6p lt green & multi　1.75　1.75
175　A27　12p lt blue & multi　3.50　3.50
176　A27　20p lt lilac & multi　6.00　6.00
　　Nos. 173-176 (4)　　　11.75　11.75

Departure of the Royal Marines from Ascension, 50th anniv.

Princess Anne's Wedding Issue
Common Design Type
1973, Nov. 14　　　　　*Perf. 14*
177　CD325　2p ocher & multi　.15　.15
178　CD325　18p multicolored　.65　.65

Letter and UPU Emblem A29

UPU Cent.: 9p, Emblem and Mercury.

　　　　　　　　Perf. 14½
1974, Mar. 27　　Litho.　　Wmk. 314
179　A29　2p multicolored　　.20　.20
180　A29　9p vio blue & multi　.70　.70

Young Churchill and Blenheim Palace A30

25p, Churchill and UN Headquarters, NYC.

1974, Nov. 30　　Litho.　　Unwmk.
181　A30　5p slate grn & multi　.20　.20
182　A30　25p purple & multi　.80　.80
　　a.　Souvenir sheet of 2, #181-182　2.00　1.75

Sir Winston Churchill (1874-1965).

ASCENSION

Skylab over Photograph of Ascension Taken by Skylab — A31

Skylab Space Station: 18p, Command module and photo of Ascension from Skylab 4.

1975, Mar. 20   Wmk. 314   Perf. 14½
183	A31	2p multicolored	.15	.15
184	A31	18p multicolored	1.00	1.00

US Air Force C-141A Starlifter — A32

Aircraft: 5p, Royal Air Force C-130 Hercules. 9p, Vickers VC-10. 24p, U.S. Air Force C-5A Galaxy.

Perf. 13½x14
1975, June 19   Litho.   Wmk. 314
185	A32	2p multicolored	.25	.25
186	A32	5p multicolored	.60	.60
187	A32	9p multicolored	1.10	1.10
188	A32	24p multicolored	3.00	3.00
a.		Souvenir sheet of 4, #185-188	10.00	10.00
		Nos. 185-188 (4)	4.95	4.95

Wideawake Airfield, Ascension Island.

APOLLO-SOYUZ LINK 1975
Nos. 144, 148-149 Overprinted

1975, Aug.   Litho.   Perf. 14½
189	A23	4½p multicolored	.20	.20
190	A23	12½p multicolored	.40	.40
191	A23	25p multicolored	.95	.95
		Nos. 189-191 (3)	1.55	1.55

Apollo Soyuz space test project (Russo-American cooperation), launching July 15; link-up, July 17.

HMS Peruvian and Zenobia Arriving Oct. 22, 1815 — A33

Designs: 5p, Water Supply, Dampiers Drip. 9p, First Landing, Oct. 1815. 15p, The Garden on Green Mountain. All designs after paintings by Isobel McManus.

1975, Oct. 22   Wmk. 373   Perf. 14½
192	A33	2p lt blue & multi	.15	.15
193	A33	5p lt blue & multi	.30	.20
194	A33	9p red & multi	.45	.40
195	A33	15p red & multi	.90	.75
		Nos. 192-195 (4)	1.80	1.50

British occupation, 160th anniv.

Canaries — A34

Designs: 2p, Fairy tern, vert. 3p, Waxbills. 4p, Black noddy, vert. 5p, Brown noddy. 6p, Common mynah. 7p, Madeira storm petrels, vert. 8p, Sooty terns. 9p, White booby, vert. 10p, Red-footed booby. 15p, Red-throated francolin, vert. 18p, Brown booby, vert. 25p, Red-billed bo'sun bird. 50p, Yellow-billed bo'sun bird. £1, Ascension frigatebird, vert. £2, Boatswain Island Bird Sanctuary and birds.

Perf. 14x14½, 14½x14
1976, Apr. 26   Litho.   Wmk. 373
Size: 35x27mm, 27x35mm
196	A34	1p multicolored	.15	.15
197	A34	2p multicolored	.15	.15
198	A34	3p multicolored	.15	.15
199	A34	4p multicolored	.15	.15
200	A34	5p multicolored	.20	.15
201	A34	6p multicolored	.20	.15
202	A34	7p multicolored	.25	.20
203	A34	8p multicolored	.30	.20
204	A34	9p multicolored	.40	.25
205	A34	10p multicolored	.45	.25
206	A34	15p multicolored	.65	.40
207	A34	18p multicolored	.85	.50
208	A34	25p multicolored	1.25	.65
209	A34	50p multicolored	2.25	1.25
210	A34	£1 multicolored	3.25	2.75

Perf. 13½
Size: 46x33mm
211	A34	£2 multicolored	6.50	5.25
		Nos. 196-211 (16)	17.15	12.60

Great Britain Type A1 with Ascension Cancel — A35

9p, Ascension No. 1, vert. 25p, Freighter Southampton Castle.

1976, May 4   Perf. 13½x14, 14x13½
212	A35	5p lt brn, car & blk	.15	.15
213	A35	9p gray grn, grn & blk	.30	.30
214	A35	25p blue & multi	.95	.95
a.		Souvenir sheet of 3	2.25	2.25
		Nos. 212-214 (3)	1.40	1.40

Festival of Stamps 1976. #214a contains one each of Ascension #214, St. Helena #297 and Tristan da Cunha #208.

US Base — A36

Designs: 9p, NASA Station, Devil's Ashpit. 25p, Viking satellite landing on Mars.

Perf. 13½
1976, July 4   Litho.   Wmk. 373
215	A36	8p black & multi	.40	.40
216	A36	9p black & multi	.50	.50
217	A36	25p black & multi	1.10	1.10
		Nos. 215-217 (3)	2.00	2.00

American Bicentennial. No. 215 also for the 20th anniv. of Bahamas Long Range Proving Ground (extension) Agreement.

Queen in Coronation Coach — A37

Designs: 8p, Prince Philip on Ascension Island, 1957, vert. 12p, Queen leaving Buckingham Palace in coronation coach.

Perf. 14x13½, 13½x14
1977, Feb. 7   Litho.   Wmk. 373
218	A37	8p multicolored	.20	.20
219	A37	12p multicolored	.30	.25
220	A37	25p multicolored	.60	.55
		Nos. 218-220 (3)	1.10	1.00

Reign of Queen Elizabeth II, 25th anniv.

Water Pipe in Tunnel — A38

Designs: 5p, Breakneck Valley wells. 12p, Break tank in pipe line, horiz. 25p, Dam & reservoir, horiz.

1977, June 27   Litho.   Perf. 14½
221	A38	3p multicolored	.15	.15
222	A38	8p multicolored	.20	.20
223	A38	12p multicolored	.50	.50
224	A38	25p multicolored	1.00	1.00
		Nos. 221-224 (4)	1.85	1.85

Water supplies constructed by Royal Marines, 1832 and 1881.

Mars Bay Site, 1877 — A39

Designs: 8p, Mars Bay and instrument sites. 12p, Prof. and Mrs. Gill before their tent. 25p, Map of Ascension.

Perf. 13½x14
1977, Oct. 3   Litho.   Wmk. 373
225	A39	3p multicolored	.15	.15
226	A39	8p multicolored	.30	.25
227	A39	12p multicolored	.50	.45
228	A39	25p multicolored	1.00	.85
		Nos. 225-228 (4)	1.95	1.70

Centenary of visit of Prof. David Gill (1843-1914), astronomer, to Ascension.

Elizabeth II Coronation Anniversary Issue
Souvenir Sheet
Common Design Types
Unwmk.

1978, May 21   Litho.   Perf. 15
229		Sheet of 6	2.50	2.50
a.	CD326	25p Lion of England	.40	.40
b.	CD327	25p Elizabeth II	.40	.40
c.	CD328	25p Green turtle	.40	.40

No. 229 contains 2 se-tenant strips of Nos. 229a-229c, separated by horizontal gutter with commemorative and descriptive inscriptions and showing central part of coronation procession with coach.

East Crater (Broken Tooth) — A40

Volcanoes: 5p, Hollands Crater (Hollow Tooth). 12p, Bears Back. 15p, Green Mountain. 25p, Two Boats village.

1978, Sept. 4   Litho.   Perf. 14½
230	A40	3p multicolored	.15	.15
231	A40	5p multicolored	.15	.15
232	A40	12p multicolored	.45	.45
233	A40	15p multicolored	.55	.55
234	A40	25p multicolored	.90	.90
a.		Souvenir sheet, 2 each #230-234	4.50	4.50
b.		Strip of 5, #230-234	2.25	2.25

No. 234b shows panoramic view of volcanic terrain.

Resolution — A41

Capt. Cook's voyages: 8p, Cook's chronometer. 12p, Green turtle. 25p, Cook after Flaxman/Wedgwood medallion.

Litho.; Litho. & Engr. (25p)
1979, Jan. 8   Perf. 11
235	A41	3p multicolored	.15	.15
236	A41	8p multicolored	.30	.25
237	A41	12p multicolored	.55	.40
238	A41	25p multicolored	1.10	.85
		Nos. 235-238 (4)	2.10	1.65

St. Mary's Church, Georgetown — A42

Designs: 12p, Old map of Ascension Island. 50p, Ascension, by Rembrandt.

Perf. 14½
1979, May 24   Litho.   Wmk. 373
239	A42	8p multicolored	.15	.15
240	A42	12p multicolored	.25	.25
241	A42	50p multicolored	.95	.95
		Nos. 239-241 (3)	1.35	1.35

Ascension Day.

Landing Cable at Comfortless Cove — A43

Eastern Telegraph Co., 80th anniv.: 8p, Cable Ship Anglia. 12p, Map showing cables across the Atlantic, vert. 15p, Cable-laying ship. 25p, Cable and earth station.

1979, Sept. 15
242	A43	3p rose car & black	.15	.15
243	A43	8p dk yel grn & black	.20	.20
244	A43	12p yel bister & black	.30	.30
245	A43	15p violet & black	.35	.35
246	A43	25p deep org & black	.55	.55
		Nos. 242-246 (5)	1.55	1.55

Ascension No. 1 — A44

1979, Dec. 17   Wmk. 373   Perf. 14
247	A44	3p shown	.15	.15
248	A44	8p No. 73	.15	.15
249	A44	12p No. 14	.20	.20
250	A44	50p Hill portrait, vert.	.85	.85
		Nos. 247-250 (4)	1.35	1.35

Sir Rowland Hill (1795-1879), originator of penny postage.

Anogramma Ascensionis — A45

1980, Feb. 18   Litho.   Perf. 14½
251	A45	3p shown	.15	.15
252	A45	6p Xiphopteris ascensionense	.15	.15
253	A45	8p Sporobolus caespitosus	.20	.20
254	A45	15p Sporobolus durus, vert.	.25	.25
255	A45	18p Dryopteris ascensionis, vert.	.40	.40
256	A45	24p Marattia purpurascens, vert.	.50	.50
		Nos. 251-256 (6)	1.65	1.65

17th Century Bottle Post, London 1980 Emblem — A46

1980, May 1   Wmk. 373   Perf. 14
257	A46	8p shown	.15	.15
258	A46	12p 36-gun frigate, 19th century	.25	.25
259	A46	15p "Garth Castle," 1863	.30	.30
260	A46	50p "St. Helena," Lockheed C141	.85	.85
a.		Souvenir sheet of 4, #257-260	2.00	2.00
		Nos. 257-260 (4)	1.55	1.55

London 1980 Intl. Stamp Exhib., May 6-14.

ASCENSION

Queen Mother Elizabeth Birthday
Common Design Type

1980, Aug. 11   Litho.   Perf. 14
261 CD330 15p multicolored   .40   .40

Lubbock's Yellowtail — A47

1980, Sept. 15   Litho.   Perf. 13½x14
262 A47   3p shown   .15   .15
263 A47 10p Resplendent angelfish .30   .30
264 A47 25p Hedgehog butterflyfish .70   .70
265 A47 40p Marmalade razorfish 1.10 1.10
    Nos. 262-265 (4)   2.25 2.25

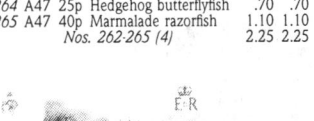

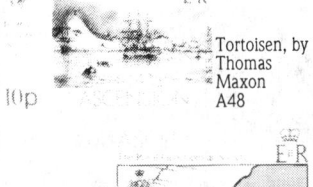

Tortoisen, by Thomas Maxon — A48

Map of South Atlantic Ridge and Continental Drift — A49

15p, Wideawake Fair, by Linton Palmer, 1866.

1980, Nov. 17   Perf. 13½, 14 (60p)
266 A48 10p multicolored   .20   .20
267 A48 15p multicolored   .35   .35
268 A49 60p multicolored 1.25 1.25
    Nos. 266-268 (3)   1.80 1.80

Royal Geographical Soc., 50th anniv.

Green Mountain Farm, 1881 — A50

Designs: 15p, Two Boats, 1881. 20p, Green Mountain and Two Boats farms, 1981. 30p, Green Mountain Farm, 1981.

1981, Feb. 15   Litho.   Perf. 14
269 A50 12p multicolored   .20   .20
270 A50 15p multicolored   .30   .30
271 A50 20p multicolored   .35   .35
272 A50 30p multicolored   .65   .65
    Nos. 269-272 (4)   1.50 1.50

Cable and Wireless Earth Station — A51

1981, Apr. 27   Litho.   Perf. 14
273   Sheet of 10   3.75 3.75
  a. A51 15p multicolored   .35   .35

Flight of Columbia space shuttle. Gutter contains story of Ascension and space shuttle; margin shows craft and dish antenna.

Poinsettia A52

1981, May 11   Wmk. 373   Perf. 13½
274 A52   1p shown   .15   .15
275 A52   2p Clusterered wax flower .15   .15
276 A52   3p Kolanchoe, vert. .15   .15
277 A52   4p Yellow pops   .15   .15
278 A52   5p Camel's foot creeper .15   .15
279 A52   8p White oleander   .20   .20
280 A52 10p Ascension lily, vert. .25   .25
281 A52 12p Coral plant, vert. .30   .30
282 A52 15p Yellow allamanda   .40   .40
283 A52 20p Ascension euphorbia .50   .50
284 A52 30p Flame of the forest, vert. .85   .85
285 A52 40p Bougainvillea   1.00 1.00
    Size: 42x53mm
286 A52 50p Solanum   1.25 1.25
287 A52 £1 Ladies petticoat 2.75 2.75
288 A52 £2 Red hibiscus   5.25 5.25
    Nos. 274-288 (15)   13.50 13.50

Nos. 275-276, 280, 282-283 and 287 also inscribed 1982.
For overprints see Nos. 321-322.

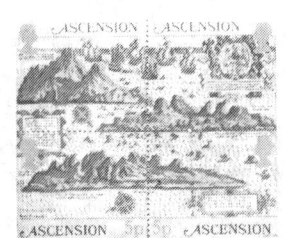

Linschoten's Map of Ascension, 1599 (Illustration reduced) — A53

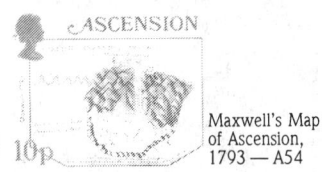

Maxwell's Map of Ascension, 1793 — A54

Designs: Old maps of Ascension.

1981, May 22   Perf. 14½
289 A53   Sheet of 4   .60   .60
  a.-d.   5p any single   .15   .15
290 A54 10p shown   .25   .25
291 A54 12p Maxwell, 1793, diff. .35   .35
292 A54 15p Eckberg & Chapman, 1811 .40   .40
293 A54 40p Campbell, 1819   1.10 1.10
    Nos. 289-293 (5)   2.70 2.70

Royal Wedding Issue
Common Design Type

1981, July 22   Wmk. 373   Perf. 14
294 CD331 10p Bouquet   .20   .20
295 CD331 15p Charles   .30   .30
296 CD331 50p Couple   1.00 1.00
    Nos. 294-296 (3)   1.50 1.50

Nos. 294-296 each se-tenant with label.

Man Shining Cannon — A55

1981, Sept. 14   Litho.   Perf. 14
297 A55   5p shown   .15   .15
298 A55 10p Mountain climbing   .20   .20
299 A55 15p First aid treatment .35   .35
300 A55 40p Duke of Edinburgh   .80   .80
    Nos. 297-300 (4)   1.50 1.50

Duke of Edinburgh's Awards, 25th anniv.

Scouting Year — A56

1982, Feb. 22   Litho.   Perf. 14
301 A56 10p Parallel rope walking .25   .25
302 A56 15p 1st Ascension scout flag .40   .40
303 A56 25p Radio operators   .55   .55
304 A56 40p Baden-Powell   .75   .75
  a.   Souvenir sheet of 4   2.25 2.25
          Nos. 301-304 (4)   1.95 1.95

No. 304a contains stamps in designs of Nos. 301-304 (30x30mm, perf. 14½, diamond-shape).

Sesquicentennial of Charles Darwin's Visit — A57

1982, Apr. 19
305 A57 10p Portrait   .25   .25
306 A57 12p Pistols   .35   .35
307 A57 15p Rock crab   .40   .40
308 A57 40p Beagle   1.10 1.10
    Nos. 305-308 (4)   2.10 2.10

40th Anniv. of Wideawake Airfield — A58

1982, June 15   Litho.   Perf. 14
309 A58   5p Fairey Swordfish   .60   .60
310 A58 10p North American B25C Mitchell .80   .80
311 A58 15p Boeing EC-135N Aria 1.10 1.10
312 A58 50p Lockheed Hercules 1.65 1.65
    Nos. 309-312 (4)   4.15 4.15

Princess Diana Issue
Common Design Type
Perf. 14½x14

1982, July 1   Wmk. 373
313 CD333 12p Arms   .30   .30
314 CD333 15p Diana   .40   .40
315 CD333 25p Wedding   .60   .60
316 CD333 50p Portrait   1.25 1.25
    Nos. 313-316 (4)   2.55 2.55

Christmas and 50th Anniv. of BBC Overseas Broadcasting — A59

Anniv. Emblem and: 5p, Bush House (London headquarters). 10p, Atlantic relay station. 25p, Lord Reith, first director general. 40p, King George V delivering Christmas address, 1932.

1982, Dec. 20   Litho.   Perf. 14
317 A59   5p multicolored   .15   .15
318 A59 10p multicolored   .30   .30
319 A59 25p multicolored   .70   .70
320 A59 40p multicolored   1.10 1.10
    Nos. 317-320 (4)   2.25 2.25

Nos. 282-283 Overprinted: "1st PARTICIPATION / COMMONWEALTH GAMES 1982"

1982   Litho.   Perf. 13½
321 A52 15p multicolored   .40   .40
322 A52 20p multicolored   .50   .50

12th Commonwealth Games, Brisbane, Australia, Sept. 30-Oct. 9.

A60

1983, Mar. 1   Perf. 14
323 A60   7p Marasmius echinosphaerus .25   .25
324 A60 12p Chlorophyllum molybdites .45   .45
325 A60 15p Leucocoprinus cepaestipes .55   .55
326 A60 20p Lycoperdon marginatum .75   .75
327 A60 50p Marasmiellus distantifolius 1.75 1.75
    Nos. 323-327 (5)   3.75 3.75

View of Georgetown A61

1983, May 12   Litho.   Perf. 14
328 A61   7p shown   .30   .30
329 A61 15p Farm, Green Mountain .30   .30
330 A61 20p Boatswain Bird Isld. .45   .45
331 A61 60p Telemetry Hill   1.10 1.10
    Nos. 328-331 (4)   2.15 2.15

See Nos. 359-362.

Manned Flight Bicentenary — A62

Military Aircraft.

1983, Aug. 1   Wmk. 373   Perf. 14
332 A62 12p Wessex Five helicopter .75   .75
333 A62 15p Vulcan B2   .85   .85
334 A62 20p Nimrod MR2P   1.00 1.00
335 A62 60p Victor K2   1.75 1.75
    Nos. 332-335 (4)   4.35 4.35

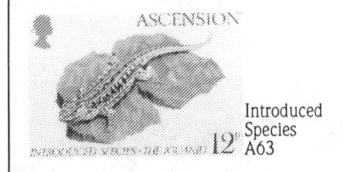

Introduced Species A63

1983, Sept.   Litho.   Wmk. 373
336 A63 12p Iguanid   .30   .30
337 A63 15p Rabbit   .40   .40
338 A63 20p Cat   .50   .50
339 A63 60p Donkey   1.50 1.50
    Nos. 336-339 (4)   2.70 2.70

Tellina Antonii Philippi A64

1983, Nov. 28   Litho.   Perf. 14½
340 A64   7p shown   .20   .20
341 A64 12p Nodipecten nodosus .35   .35
342 A64 15p Cypraea lurida oceanica .45   .45
343 A64 20p Nerita ascensionis gmelin .60   .60
344 A64 50p Micromelo undatus 1.50 1.50
    Nos. 340-344 (5)   3.10 3.10

St. Helena Colony, 150th Anniv. — A65

Designs: First issue inscribed Ascension instead of overprinted.

ASCENSION

1984, Jan. 10 Litho. Perf. 14
345	A65	12p No. 3	.30	.30
346	A65	15p No. 4	.40	.40
347	A65	20p No. 6	.50	.50
348	A65	60p No. 9	1.50	1.50
		Nos. 345-348 (4)	2.70	2.70

Souvenir Sheet

Visit of Prince Andrew — A66

1984, Apr. 10 Perf. 14½x14
349		Sheet of 2	2.25	2.25
a.	A66	12p Andrew	.25	.25
b.	A66	70p In naval uniform	1.75	1.75

Lloyd's List Issue
Common Design Type

1984, May 28
351	CD335	12p Naval semaphore	.25	.25
352	CD335	15p "Southampton Castle"	.35	.35
353	CD335	20p Pier Head	.45	.45
354	CD335	70p Dane	1.50	1.50
		Nos. 351-354 (4)	2.55	2.55

1984 Coins and Wildlife A67

1984, June Perf. 14
355	A67	12p One penny, yellowfin tuna	.45	.45
356	A67	15p Two pence, donkeys	.60	.60
357	A67	20p Fifty pence, green turtle	.70	.70
358	A67	70p One pound, sooty terns	1.75	1.75
		Nos. 355-358 (4)	3.50	3.50

View Type of 1983

1984, Oct. Litho. Wmk. 373
359	A61	12p Devil's Riding School	.25	.25
360	A61	15p St. Mary's Church	.35	.35
361	A61	20p Two Boats Village	.50	.50
362	A61	70p Ascension Isld.	1.75	1.75
		Nos. 359-362 (4)	2.85	2.85

Trees — A68

1985, Mar. 8 Litho. Perf. 14½x14
363	A68	7p Bermuda cypress	.50	.50
364	A68	12p Norfolk Island pine	.55	.55
365	A68	15p Screwpine	.65	.65
366	A68	20p Eucalyptus	.80	.80
367	A68	65p Spore tree	2.00	2.00
		Nos. 363-367 (5)	4.50	4.50

Military Firearms A69

Large guns and insignia: 12p, Thirty-two pounder small bore muzzle loader, c. 1820; Royal Marines hat plate, c. 1816. 15p, Seven-inch rifled muzzle loader, c. 1866; royal cipher. 20p, Seven-pounder rifled muzzle loader, c. 1877; Royal Artillery badge. 70p, HMS Hood 5.5-inch gun; ship crest.

1985, July 21 Wmk. 373 Perf. 14½
368	A69	12p multicolored	.65	.65
369	A69	15p multicolored	.75	.75
370	A69	20p multicolored	.80	.80
371	A69	70p multicolored	2.25	2.25
		Nos. 368-371 (4)	4.45	4.45

Queen Mother 85th Birthday
Common Design Type

Designs: 12p, With Duke of York, Balmoral, 1924. 15p, With Princes Andrew and Edward. 20p, At Ascot. 70p, Christening of Prince Henry, Windsor Castle. 75p, Leaving the QEII, 1968.

Perf. 14½x14

1985, June 7 Wmk. 384
372	CD336	12p multicolored	.25	.25
373	CD336	15p multicolored	.30	.30
374	CD336	20p multicolored	.40	.40
375	CD336	70p multicolored	1.40	1.40
		Nos. 372-375 (4)	2.35	2.35

Souvenir Sheet
376	CD336	75p multicolored	1.65	1.50

Intl. Youth Year, Girl Guides 75th Anniv. — A70

1985, Oct. 4 Wmk. 373
377	A70	12p Guides' banner	.65	.65
378	A70	15p First aid	.75	.75
379	A70	20p Camping	.85	.85
380	A70	70p Lady Baden-Powell	2.50	2.50
		Nos. 377-380 (4)	4.75	4.75

Wildflowers A71  — Halley's Comet A72

Wmk. 384

1985, Dec. 6 Litho. Perf. 14
381	A71	12p Clerodendrum fragrans	.40	.40
382	A71	15p Shell ginger	.45	.45
383	A71	20p Cape daisy	.60	.60
384	A71	70p Ginger lily	1.75	1.75
		Nos. 381-384 (4)	3.20	3.20

1986, Mar. 7

Designs: 12p, Newton's reflector telescope. 15p, Edmond Halley, Old Greenwich Observatory. 20p, Short's Gregorian telescope, comet, 1759. 70p, ICE space probe, Ascension satellite tracking station.

385	A72	12p multicolored	.55	.55
386	A72	15p multicolored	.65	.65
387	A72	20p multicolored	.70	.70
388	A72	70p multicolored	2.00	2.00
		Nos. 385-388 (4)	3.90	3.90

Queen Elizabeth II 60th Birthday
Common Design Type

Designs: 7p, Infant photograph, 1926. 15p, 1st worldwide Christmas broadcast, 1952. 20p, Garter Ceremony, Windsor Castle, 1983. 35p, Royal Tour, New Zealand, 1981. £1, Visiting Crown Agents' offices, 1983.

1986, Apr. 21 Perf. 14x14½
389	CD337	7p scarlet, blk & sil	.15	.15
390	CD337	15p ultra, blk & sil	.25	.25
391	CD337	20p green & multi	.35	.35
392	CD337	35p violet & multi	.65	.65
393	CD337	£1 rose vio & multi	1.75	1.75
		Nos. 389-393 (5)	3.15	3.15

For overprints see Nos. 431-435.

AMERIPEX '86 — A73

1986, May 22 Perf. 14½
394	A73	12p No. 183	.35	.35
395	A73	15p No. 260	.45	.45
396	A73	20p No. 215	.55	.55
397	A73	70p No. 310	2.00	2.00
		Nos. 394-397 (4)	3.35	3.35

Souvenir Sheet
398	A73	75p Statue of Liberty, New York Harbor	2.25	2.25

Statue of Liberty, cent.

Royal Wedding Issue, 1986
Common Design Type

Designs: 15p, Couple kissing. 35p, Andrew in navy uniform, helicopter.

Wmk. 384

1986, July 23 Litho. Perf. 14
399	CD338	15p multicolored	.45	.45
400	CD338	35p multicolored	1.00	1.00

Ships A74

1986, Oct. 14 Wmk. 384 Perf. 14½
401	A74	1p Ganymede, c. 1811	.15	.15
402	A74	2p Kangaroo, c. 1811	.15	.15
403	A74	4p Trinculo, c. 1811	.15	.15
404	A74	5p Daring, c. 1811	.15	.15
405	A74	9p Thais, c. 1811	.30	.30
406	A74	10p Pheasant, 1819	.35	.35
407	A74	15p Myrmidon, 1819	.45	.45
408	A74	18p Atholl, 1825	.55	.55
409	A74	20p Medina, 1830	.60	.60
410	A74	25p Saracen, 1840	.80	.80
411	A74	30p Hydra, c. 1845	.90	.90
412	A74	50p Sealark, 1840	1.40	1.40
413	A74	70p Rattlesnake, 1868	1.90	1.90
414	A74	£1 Penelope, 1889	3.00	3.00
415	A74	£2 Monarch, 1897	6.00	6.00
		Nos. 401-415 (15)	16.85	16.85

For surcharges see Nos. 502-504.

Edible Bush Fruits A75

1987, Jan. 29 Perf. 14
416	A75	12p Cape gooseberry	.35	.35
417	A75	15p Prickly pear	.45	.45
418	A75	20p Guava	.60	.60
419	A75	70p Loquat	2.00	2.00
		Nos. 416-419 (4)	3.40	3.40

1st Manned Space Flight, 25th Anniv. — A76
Military Uniforms, 1815-20 — A77 

1987, Mar. 30
420	A76	15p Ignition	.45	.45
421	A76	18p Lift-off	.55	.55
422	A76	25p Reentry	.70	.70
423	A76	£1 Splashdown	3.00	3.00
		Nos. 420-423 (4)	4.70	4.70

Souvenir Sheet
424	A76	70p Friendship 7 capsule	2.25	2.25

1987, June 29

Designs: a, Captains in full dress, 1st landing on Ascension. b, Surgeon and sailors at campsite. c, Seaman returning from Dampier's Drip with water supply. d, Midshipman at lookout post. e, Commander and surveyor.

425		Strip of 5	4.00	4.00
a.-e.	A77	25p multicolored	.80	.80

See Nos. 458, 474, 482, 507.

Butterflies A78

1987, Aug. 10 Perf. 14½
426	A78	15p Painted lady	.60	.60
427	A78	18p Monarch	.75	.75
428	A78	25p Diadem	1.00	1.00
429	A78	£1 Long-tailed blue	3.75	3.75
		Nos. 426-429 (4)	6.10	6.10

See Nos. 436-439, 459-462.

Birds — A79

Designs: a, Ascension frigatebirds (males). b, Brown booby, frigatebird, white boobies. c, Frigatebird, white booby. d, Ascension frigatebirds (females). e, Adult frigatebird feeding young.

1987, Oct. 8 Wmk. 373 Perf. 14
430		Strip of 5	6.00	6.00
a.-e.	A79	25p any single	1.25	1.25

No. 430 has continuous design.
See No. 453.

Nos. 389-393 Ovptd. "40TH WEDDING ANNIVERSARY" in Silver
Perf. 14x14½

1987, Dec. 9 Litho. Wmk. 384
431	CD337	7p scar, blk & sil	.20	.20
432	CD337	15p ultra, blk & sil	.40	.40
433	CD337	20p green & multi	.60	.60
434	CD337	35p violet & multi	1.00	1.00
435	CD337	£1 rose vio & multi	2.75	2.75
		Nos. 431-435 (5)	4.95	4.95

40th wedding anniv. of Queen Elizabeth II and Prince Philip.

Insects Type of 1987

1988, Jan. 18 Perf. 14½
436	A78	15p Field cricket	.60	.60
437	A78	18p Bush cricket	.75	.75
438	A78	25p Ladybug	1.00	1.00
439	A78	£1 Burnished brass moth	4.00	4.00
		Nos. 436-439 (4)	6.35	6.35

Capt. William Bate (d. 1838), 1st Garrison Commander and Colonial Founder of Ascension A80

Designs: 9p, Bate's Memorial, St. Mary's Church. 15p, Commodore's Cottage, Cross Hill. 18p, North East or Bate's Cottage, 1833. 25p, Landmarks on map. 70p, Bate and 3 soldiers.

1988, Apr. 14 Litho. Perf. 14
440	A80	9p multicolored	.35	.35
441	A80	15p multicolored	.55	.55
442	A80	18p multicolored	.65	.65
443	A80	25p multicolored	.90	.90
444	A80	70p multicolored	2.25	2.25
		Nos. 440-444 (5)	4.70	4.70

For all your stamp supply needs
www.scottonline.com

ASCENSION

Australia Bicentennial Emblem and Ships Named HMS Resolution — A81

1988, June 23	Litho.	Perf. 14
445 A81 9p 3-Masted squarerigger, 1667		.35 .35
446 A81 18p 3-Masted squarerigger, 1772		.65 .65
447 A81 25p Navy cruiser, 1892		.90 .90
448 A81 65p Battleship, 1916		2.25 2.25
Nos. 445-448 (4)		4.15 4.15

Australia bicentennial.

Nos. 445-448 Overprinted

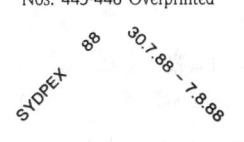

SYDPEX '88 30.7.88 – 7.8.88

1988, July 30	Wmk. 384 Litho.	Perf. 14
449 A81 9p multicolored		.35 .35
450 A81 18p multicolored		.65 .65
451 A81 25p multicolored		.90 .90
452 A81 65p multicolored		2.25 2.25
Nos. 449-452 (4)		4.15 4.15

SYDPEX '88, July 30-Aug. 7.

Bird Type of 1987

Behaviors of the wideawake tern, Sterna fuscata: a, Two adults, flock overhead. b, Nesting (two birds). c, Nesting (three birds). d, Adult and young. e, Tern flapping its wings.

1988, Aug. 15		Perf. 14
453 Strip of 5		6.00 6.00
a.-e. A79 25p any single		1.25 1.25

No. 453 has continuous design.

Lloyds of London, 300th Anniv.
Common Design Type

Designs: 8p, Lloyd's Coffee House, Tower Street, 1688. 18p, Cable ship Alert, horiz. 25p, Satellite recovery in space, horiz. 65p, Ship Good Hope Castle on fire off Ascension, 1973.

1988, Oct. 17	Wmk. 373 Litho.	Perf. 14
454 CD341 8p multicolored		.30 .30
455 CD341 18p multicolored		.60 .60
456 CD341 25p multicolored		.85 .85
457 CD341 65p multicolored		2.25 2.25
Nos. 454-457 (4)		4.00 4.00

Military Uniforms Type of 1987

Uniforms of the Royal Marines: a, Marines arrive in Ascension (marines), 1821. b, Semaphore station (officer, marine), 1829. c, Octagonal tank (sergeant), 1831. d, Water pipe tunnel (officers), 1833. e, Constructing barracks (officer), 1834.

1988, Nov. 21		
458 Strip of 5		5.00 5.00
a.-e. A77 25p multicolored		1.00 1.00

Insect Type of 1987

1989, Jan. 16	Litho. Wmk. 384	Perf. 14½
459 A78 15p Plume moth		.60 .60
460 A78 18p Green bottle		.70 .70
461 A78 25p Weevil		.95 .95
462 A78 £1 Paper wasp		3.75 3.75
Nos. 459-462 (4)		6.00 6.00

Land Crabs, Gecarcinus Lagostoma — A82

1989, Apr. 17		
463 A82 15p multi		.50 .50
464 A82 18p multi, diff.		.65 .65
465 A82 25p multi, diff.		.90 .90
466 A82 £1 multi, diff.		3.50 3.50
Nos. 463-466 (4)		5.55 5.55

Miniature Sheet

467 Sheet of 4		5.50 5.50
a. A82 15p like No. 463		.50 .50
b. A82 18p like No. 464		.65 .65
c. A82 25p like No. 465		.85 .85
d. A82 £1 like No. 466		3.50 3.50

Vignettes of Nos. 467a-467d do not have frame.

Moon Landing, 20th Anniv.
Common Design Type

Apollo 7: 15p, Tracking Station, Ascension Is. 18p, Launch, Cape Kennedy. 25p, Mission emblem. 70p, Expended Saturn IVB stage. £1, Lunar landing profile for the Apollo 11 mission.

1989, July 20		Perf. 14x13½
Size of Nos. 469-470: 29x29mm		
468 CD342 15p multicolored		.45 .45
469 CD342 18p multicolored		.55 .55
470 CD342 25p multicolored		.75 .75
471 CD342 70p multicolored		2.10 2.10
Nos. 468-471 (4)		3.85 3.85

Souvenir Sheet

| 472 CD342 £1 multicolored | | 3.00 3.00 |

Souvenir Sheet

A83

1989, July 7		Perf. 14x13½
473 A83 75p Emblems, No. 60		2.50 2.50

Miniature Sheet

World Stamp Expo '89, Washington, DC, and PHILEXFRANCE '89, Paris — A84

The Statue of Liberty and scenes from the centenary celebrations, 1986: a, Operation Sail. b, Face. c, Upper body. d, Three crown points. e, Ships in harbor, view of lower Manhattan. f, Ship in port, New York City.

1989, Aug. 21		Wmk. 373
474 Sheet of 6		2.75 2.75
a.-f. A84 15p any single		.45 .45

Devil's Ashpit Tracking Station A85

1989, Sept. 30	Wmk. 384	Perf. 14
475 Sheet, 5 each #a.-b.		6.75 6.75
a. A85 18p shown		.55 .55
b. A85 25p US space shuttle launch		.80 .80

Termination of NASA tracking operations, begun in 1965, at the station.

Shells and Mollusks A86

1989, Nov. 6	Wmk. 384 Litho.	Perf. 14
476 A86 8p Strombus latus		.30 .30
477 A86 18p Tonna galea		.65 .65
478 A86 25p Harpa doris		.85 .85
479 A86 £1 Charonia variegata		3.25 3.25
Nos. 476-479 (4)		5.05 5.05

Donkeys — A87

1989, Nov. 17	Litho. Wmk. 384	
Perf. 14 on 3 Sides		
Booklet Stamps		
480 A87 18p shown		.50 .50
a. Booklet pane of 6		3.00
481 A87 25p Green turtle		.75 .75
a. Booklet pane of 4		3.00

No. 480a sold for £1.

Military Type of 1987

Royal Navy equipment, c. 1815-1820: a, Seaman's pistol, hat, cutlass. b, Midshipman's belt buckle, button, sword, hat. c, Surgeon's hat, sword, instrument chest. d, Captain's hat, telescope, sword. e, Admiral's epaulet, megaphone, hat, pocket.

1990, Feb. 12	Litho.	Perf. 14
482 Strip of 5		4.75 4.75
a.-e. A77 25p any single		.95 .95

World Wildlife Fund — A88

Frigate birds (Fregata aquila): 9p, Family group. 10p, Chick. 11p, Male in flight. 15p, Female and immature in flight.

	Perf. 14½x14	
1990, Mar. 5	Litho. Wmk. 373	
483 A88 9p multicolored		.60 .60
484 A88 10p multicolored		.65 .65
485 A88 11p multicolored		.70 .70
486 A88 15p multicolored		.95 .95
Nos. 483-486 (4)		2.90 2.90

Great Britain Nos. 1-2 — A89

Exhibition emblem and: 18p, Early Ascension cancellations. 25p, Unloading mail at Wideawake Airfield. £1, Main P.O., Royal Mail van.

1990, May 3	Litho.	Perf. 14
487 A89 9p shown		.30 .30
488 A89 18p multicolored		.60 .60
489 A89 25p multicolored		.85 .85
490 A89 £1 multicolored		3.25 3.25
Nos. 487-490 (4)		5.00 5.00

Penny Black 150th anniv., Stamp World London '90.

Queen Mother, 90th Birthday
Common Design Types

1990, Aug. 4	Wmk. 384	Perf. 14x15
491 CD343 25p Portrait, 1940		.85 .85

	Perf. 14½	
492 CD344 £1 King, Queen with soldiers		3.25 3.25

Garth Castle, 1910 — A90

Designs: 18p, RMS St. Helena, 1982. 25p, Launching new RMS St. Helena, 1989. 70p, Duke of York launching new RMS St. Helena. £1, New RMS St. Helena.

	Perf. 14½	
1990, Sept. 13	Litho. Wmk. 373	
493 A90 9p multicolored		.35 .35
494 A90 18p multicolored		.65 .65
495 A90 25p multicolored		.90 .90
496 A90 70p multicolored		2.50 2.50
Nos. 493-496 (4)		4.40 4.40

Souvenir Sheet

| 497 A90 £1 multicolored | | 3.50 3.50 |

See St. Helena Nos. 535-539, Tristan da Cunha Nos. 482-486.

Christmas — A91

Sculpture (8p) and paintings of Madonna and Child by: 8p, Felici. 18p, Unknown artist. 25p, Gebhard. 65p, Gritti.

1990, Oct. 24		Perf. 14
498 A91 8p multicolored		.30 .30
499 A91 18p multicolored		.65 .65
500 A91 25p multicolored		.90 .90
501 A91 65p multicolored		3.25 3.25
Nos. 498-501 (4)		5.10 5.10

Nos. 410, 412 & 414 Ovptd. in Silver BRITISH FOR 175 YEARS

1991, Feb. 5	Wmk. 384	Perf. 14½
502 A74 25p on #410		1.00 1.00
503 A74 50p on #412		2.00 2.00
504 A74 £1 on #414		4.00 4.00
Nos. 502-504 (3)		7.00 7.00

Elizabeth & Philip, Birthdays
Common Design Types

1991, June 18		
505 CD345 25p multicolored		.80 .80
506 CD346 25p multicolored		.80 .80
a. Pair, #505-506 + label		1.60 1.60

Military Uniforms Type of 1987

Royal Marines Equipment 1821-1844: a, Officer's shako, epaulettes, belt plate, button. b, Officer's cap, sword, epaulettes, belt plate. c, Drum Major's shako with cords, staff. d, Sergeant's shako, chevrons, belt plate, canteen. e, Drummer's drum, sticks, shako.

1991, Aug. 1	Wmk. 373	Perf. 14
507 A77 25p Strip of 5, #a.-e.		4.00 4.00

Atlantic Relay Station, 25th Anniv. A92

Designs: 15p, BBC Atlantic relay station. 18p, English Bay transmitters. 25p, Satellite receiving station, vert. 70p, Antenna support tower, vert.

1991, Sept. 17	Wmk. 384	Perf. 14½
508 A92 15p multicolored		.50 .50
509 A92 18p multicolored		.60 .60
510 A92 25p multicolored		.85 .85
511 A92 70p multicolored		2.50 2.50
Nos. 508-511 (4)		4.45 4.45

ASCENSION

Christmas — A93

Designs: 8p, St. Mary's Church, exterior. 18p, St. Mary's Church, interior. 25p, Grotto of Our Lady of Ascension, exterior. 65p, Grotto of Our Lady of Ascension, interior.

1991, Oct. 1   *Perf. 14*
512	A93	8p multicolored	.30	.30
513	A93	18p multicolored	.60	.60
514	A93	25p multicolored	.85	.85
515	A93	65p multicolored	2.25	2.25
		Nos. 512-515 (4)	4.00	4.00

Fish — A94

Wmk. 373
1991, Dec. 10   *Litho.*   *Perf. 14*
516	A94	1p Blackfish	.15	.15
517	A94	2p Five finger	.15	.15
518	A94	4p Resplendent angelfish	.15	.15
519	A94	5p Silver fish	.15	.15
520	A94	9p Gurnard	.30	.30
521	A94	10p Blue dad	.35	.35
522	A94	15p Cunning fish	.50	.50
523	A94	18p Grouper	.60	.60
524	A94	20p Moray eel	.65	.65
525	A94	25p Hardback soldierfish	.85	.85
526	A94	30p Blue marlin	1.00	1.00
527	A94	50p Wahoo	1.65	1.65
528	A94	70p Yellowfin tuna	2.25	2.25
529	A94	£1 Blue shark	3.25	3.25
530	A94	£2.50 Bottlenose dolphin	8.50	8.50
		Nos. 516-530 (15)	20.50	20.50

Queen Elizabeth II's Accession to the Throne, 40th Anniv.
Common Design Type
Wmk. 373
1992, Feb. 6   *Litho.*   *Perf. 14*
531	CD349	9p multicolored	.30	.30
532	CD349	15p multicolored	.50	.50
533	CD349	18p multicolored	.60	.60
534	CD349	25p multicolored	.85	.85
535	CD349	70p multicolored	2.25	2.25
		Nos. 531-535 (5)	4.50	4.50

Discovery of America, 500th Anniv. — A95

Wmk. 373
1992, Feb. 18   *Litho.*   *Perf. 14*
536	A95	9p STV Eye of the Wind	.30	.30
537	A95	18p STV Soren Larsen	.60	.60
538	A95	25p Pinta, Santa Maria, & Nina	.85	.85
539	A95	70p Columbus, Santa Maria	2.25	2.25
		Nos. 536-539 (4)	4.00	4.00

World Columbian Stamp Expo '92, Chicago and Genoa '92 Intl. Philatelic Exhibitions.

Wideawake Airfield, 50th Anniv. — A96

Wmk. 373
1992, May 5   *Litho.*   *Perf. 14*
540	A96	15p Control tower	.50	.50
541	A96	18p Nose hangar	.60	.60
542	A96	25p Construction work	.85	.85
543	A96	70p Laying fuel pipeline	2.25	2.25
		Nos. 540-543 (4)	4.20	4.20

Ascension's Participation in Falkland Islands' Liberation, 10th Anniv. — A97

#548a, 15p + 3p like #544. b, 18p + 4p like #545. c, 25p + 5p like #546. d, 65p + 13p like #547.

Wmk. 373
1992, June 12   *Litho.*   *Perf. 14*
544	A97	15p Nimrod Mk.2	.50	.50
545	A97	18p VC10	.60	.60
546	A97	25p Wessex HU Mk.5 helicopter	.85	.85
547	A97	65p Vulcan B2	2.25	2.25
		Nos. 544-547 (4)	4.20	4.20

Souvenir Sheet
548	A97	Sheet of 4, #a.-d.	5.00	5.00

Surtax for Soldiers', Sailors' and Airmen's Families Association.

Christmas — A98

Wmk. 384
1992, Oct. 13   *Litho.*   *Perf. 14*
549	A98	8p multicolored	.30	.30
550	A98	18p multicolored	.70	.70
551	A98	25p multicolored	.95	.95
552	A98	65p multicolored	2.50	2.50
		Nos. 549-552 (4)	4.45	4.45

Children's drawings: 8p, Snowman, rocks, candle. 18p, Underwater Santa, Christmas tree. 25p, Hello, bells. 65p, Nativity Scene, angel.

Yellow Canary — A99

Perf. 14½
1993, Jan. 12   *Litho.*   **Wmk. 373**
553	A99	15p Singing male	.45	.45
554	A99	18p Adult male, female	.55	.55
555	A99	25p Young calling for food	.80	.80
556	A99	70p Mixed flock	2.25	2.25
		Nos. 553-556 (4)	4.05	4.05

Royal Air Force, 75th Anniv.
Common Design Type

Designs: 9p, Sopwith Snipe. No. 558, Supermarine Southampton. 30p, Avro Anson. 70p, Vickers Wellington 1C.

No. 561a, Westland Lysander. b, Gloster Meteor. c, DeHavilland Comet. d, British Aerospace Nimrod.

Wmk. 373
1993, Apr. 1   *Litho.*   *Perf. 14*
557	CD350	20p multicolored	.60	.60
558	CD350	25p multicolored	.70	.70
559	CD350	30p multicolored	.85	.85
560	CD350	70p multicolored	2.25	2.25
		Nos. 557-560 (4)	4.40	4.40

Souvenir Sheet
561	CD350	25p Sheet of 4, #a.-d.	3.00	3.00

South Atlantic Cable Company, 25th Anniv. — A100

Designs: 20p, Map showing cable route. 25p, Cable ship laying cable. 30p, Map of Ascension. 70p, Cable ship off Ascension.

Perf. 14x14½
1993, June 8   *Litho.*   **Wmk. 384**
562	A100	20p multicolored	.60	.60
563	A100	25p multicolored	.75	.75
564	A100	30p multicolored	.90	.90
565	A100	70p multicolored	2.00	2.00
		Nos. 562-565 (4)	4.25	4.25

Flowers — A101

Perf. 14x14½
1993, Aug. 3   *Litho.*   **Wmk. 384**
566	A101	20p Lantana camara	.60	.60
567	A101	25p Moonflower	.75	.75
568	A101	30p Hibiscus	.90	.90
569	A101	70p Frangipani	2.00	2.00
		Nos. 566-569 (4)	4.25	4.25

Christmas — A102

Designs: 12p, Child mailing Christmas card. 20p, Mail loaded onto Tristar. 25p, Plane in flight. 30p, Mail unloaded at Wideawake Airfield. 65p, Child reading card, Georgetown.

Perf. 14½x14
1993, Oct. 19   *Litho.*   **Wmk. 373**
570	A102	12p multicolored	.35	.35
571	A102	20p multicolored	.60	.60
572	A102	25p multicolored	.75	.75
573	A102	30p multicolored	.90	.90
574	A102	65p multicolored	2.00	2.00
	a.	Souvenir sheet of 5, #570-574	4.60	4.60
		Nos. 570-574 (5)	4.60	4.60

Stamps from No. 574a show a continuous design, while Nos. 570-574 have white borders on sides.

Prehistoric Aquatic Reptiles — A103

1994, Jan. 25   **Wmk. 373**   *Perf. 14*
575	A103	12p Ichthyosaurus	.35	.35
576	A103	20p Metriorhynchus	.60	.60
577	A103	25p Mosasaurus	.75	.75
578	A103	30p Elasmosaurus	.90	.90
579	A103	65p Plesiosaurus	1.90	1.90
		Nos. 575-579 (5)	4.50	4.50

Ovptd. with Hong Kong '94 Emblem
1994, Feb. 18
580	A103	12p on #575	.35	.35
581	A103	20p on #576	.60	.60
582	A103	25p on #577	.75	.75
583	A103	30p on #578	.90	.90
584	A103	65p on #579	1.90	1.90
		Nos. 580-584 (5)	4.50	4.50

Green Turtle — A104

Designs: 20p, Four on beach. 25p, Crawling in sand. No. 587, Crawling from sea. 65p, Swimming. No. 589a, Side view, crawling from sea. b, Digging nest. c, Hatchlings heading to sea. d, Digging nest, diff.

1994, Mar. 22
585	A104	20p multicolored	.60	.60
586	A104	25p multicolored	.75	.75
587	A104	30p multicolored	.90	.90
588	A104	65p multicolored	1.90	1.90
		Nos. 585-588 (4)	4.15	4.15

Souvenir Sheet
589	A104	30p Sheet of 4, #a.-d.	3.50	3.50

Civilian Ships — A105

Ships serving during Falkland Islands War, 1982: 20p, Tug Yorkshireman. 25p, Minesweeper support ship RMS St. Helena. 30p, Oil tanker British ESK. 65p, Cruise liner Uganda, hospital ship.

1994, June 14
590	A105	20p multicolored	.60	.60
591	A105	25p multicolored	.75	.75
592	A105	30p multicolored	.90	.90
593	A105	65p multicolored	1.90	1.90
		Nos. 590-593 (4)	4.15	4.15

Sooty Tern — A106

1994, Aug. 16
594	A106	20p Chick	.60	.60
595	A106	25p Juvenile	.75	.75
596	A106	30p Brooding adult	.90	.90
597	A106	65p Displaying male	1.90	1.90
		Nos. 594-597 (4)	4.15	4.15

Souvenir Sheet
598	A106	£1 Dread	3.00	3.00

Christmas — A107

Donkeys: 12p, Mare with foal. 20p, Young adult. 25p, Foal. 30p, Adult, egrets. 65p, Adult.

1994, Oct. 11   *Perf. 14x14½*
599	A107	12p multicolored	.40	.40
600	A107	20p multicolored	.60	.60
601	A107	25p multicolored	.75	.75
602	A107	30p multicolored	.95	.95
603	A107	65p multicolored	2.00	2.00
		Nos. 599-603 (5)	4.70	4.70

Flowers — A108

Designs: 20p, Leonurus japonicus, vert. 25p, Periwinkle. 30p, Four o'clock, vert. 65p, Blood flower.

1995, Jan. 10   *Perf. 14*
604	A108	20p multicolored	.60	.60
605	A108	25p multicolored	.75	.75
606	A108	30p multicolored	.95	.95
607	A108	65p multicolored	2.00	2.00
		Nos. 604-607 (4)	4.30	4.30

ASCENSION

Island Scenes, c. 1895
A109

Designs: 12p, Horse-drawn wagon, Two Boats, Green Mountain. 20p, Island stewards' store. 25p, Royal Navy headquarters, barracks. 30p, Police office. 65p, Pier head.

1995, Mar. 7   Wmk. 384   Perf. 14½
608	A109	12p sepia	.35	.35
609	A109	20p sepia	.60	.60
610	A109	25p sepia	.75	.75
611	A109	30p sepia	.90	.90
612	A109	65p sepia	2.00	2.00
		Nos. 608-612 (5)	4.60	4.60

End of World War II, 50th Anniv.
Common Design Types

Designs: 20p, 5.5-inch guns taken from HMS Hood, 1941. 25p, Fairey Swordfish, first aircraft to land at Ascension. 30p, HMS Dorsetshire patrolling South Atlantic. 65p, HMS Devonshire patrolling South Atlantic.
£1, Reverse of War Medal, 1939-45.

1995, May 8   Wmk. 373   Perf. 14
613	CD351	20p multicolored	.60	.60
614	CD351	25p multicolored	.75	.75
615	CD351	30p multicolored	.90	.90
616	CD351	65p multicolored	2.00	2.00
		Nos. 613-616 (4)	4.25	4.25

Souvenir Sheet
617	CD352	£1 multicolored	3.00	3.00

Butterflies — A110

1995, Sept. 1   Wmk. 384
618	A110	20p Long-tailed blue	.60	.60
619	A110	25p Painted lady	.75	.75
620	A110	30p Diadem	.90	.90
621	A110	65p African monarch	2.00	2.00
		Nos. 618-621 (4)	4.25	4.25

Souvenir Sheet
622	A110	£1 Red admiral	3.00	3.00

Singapore '95 (#622).

Christmas A111

Designs based on children's drawings: 12p, Santa on boat. 20p, Santa on wall. 25p, Santa in chimney. 30p, Santa on dolphin. 65p, South Atlantic run.

1995, Oct. 10   Wmk. 373
623	A111	12p multicolored	.35	.35
624	A111	20p multicolored	.60	.60
625	A111	25p multicolored	.75	.75
626	A111	30p multicolored	.90	.90
627	A111	65p multicolored	2.00	2.00
		Nos. 623-627 (5)	4.60	4.60

Mollusks A112

12p, Cypraea lurida. 25p, Cypraea spurca. 30p, Harpa doris. 65p, Umbraculum umbraculum.

1996, Jan. 10   Litho.   Perf. 14
628	A112	12p multicolored	.35	.35
629	A112	25p multicolored	.75	.75
630	A112	30p multicolored	.90	.90
631	A112	65p multicolored	2.00	2.00
a.		Strip of 4, #628-631	4.00	4.00

Queen Elizabeth II, 70th Birthday
Common Design Type

Various portraits of Queen, scenes of Ascension: 20p, St. Marys Church. 25p, The Residency. 30p, Roman Catholic Grotto. 65p, The Exiles Club.

Perf. 13½
1996, Apr. 22   Litho.   Wmk. 384
632	CD354	20p multicolored	.65	.65
633	CD354	25p multicolored	.80	.80
634	CD354	30p multicolored	1.00	1.00
635	CD354	65p multicolored	2.00	2.00
		Nos. 632-635 (4)	4.45	4.45

CAPEX '96 A113

Island transport: 20p, US Army Jeep. 25p, 1924 Citreon 7.5HP two seater. 30p, 1930 Austin Ten-four Tourer. 65p, Series 1 Land Rover.

Wmk. 384
1996, June 8   Litho.   Perf. 14
636	A113	20p multicolored	.65	.65
637	A113	25p multicolored	.80	.80
638	A113	30p multicolored	1.00	1.00
639	A113	65p multicolored	2.00	2.00
		Nos. 636-639 (4)	4.45	4.45

Birds and Their Young — A114

Designs: 1p, Madeiran storm petrel. 2p, Red-billed tropicbird. 4p, Indian mynah. 5p, House sparrow. 7p, Common waxbill. 10p, White tern. 12p, Francolin. 15p, Brown noddy. 20p, Yellow canary. 25p, Black noddy. 30p, Red-footed booby. 40p, Yellow-billed tropicbird. 65p, Brown booby. £1, Masked booby. £2, Sooty tern. £3, Ascension frigate bird.

Wmk. 373
1996, Aug. 12   Litho.   Perf. 13
640	A114	1p multicolored	.15	.15
641	A114	2p multicolored	.15	.15
642	A114	4p multicolored	.15	.15
643	A114	5p multicolored	.15	.15
644	A114	7p multicolored	.20	.20
645	A114	10p multicolored	.30	.30
646	A114	12p multicolored	.35	.35
647	A114	15p multicolored	.45	.45
648	A114	20p multicolored	.60	.60
649	A114	25p multicolored	.70	.70
650	A114	30p multicolored	.90	.90
651	A114	40p multicolored	1.10	1.10
652	A114	65p multicolored	1.90	1.90
a.		Sheet of 1, perf. 14	2.10	2.10
653	A114	£1 multicolored	3.00	3.00
a.		Souvenir sheet of 1	3.25	3.25
654	A114	£2 multicolored	6.00	6.00
655	A114	£3 multicolored	9.00	9.00
		Nos. 640-655 (16)	25.10	25.10

No. 652a for Hong Kong '97. Issued 2/3/97.
No. 653a for return of Hong Kong to China. Issued 7/1/97.

BBC Atlantic Relay Station, 30th Anniv.
A115

Various views of relay station: 20p, 25p, Towers. 30p, Towers, buildings. 65p, Satellite dish, towers, beach.

1996, Sept. 9   Wmk. 384   Perf. 14
656	A115	20p multicolored	.65	.65
657	A115	25p multicolored	.80	.80
658	A115	30p multicolored	1.00	1.00
659	A115	65p multicolored	2.00	2.00
		Nos. 656-659 (4)	4.45	4.45

Christmas A116

Santa Claus: 12p, On satellite dish. 20p, Playing golf. 25p, By beach. 30p, On RAF Tristar. 65p, Aboard RMS St. Helena.

Perf. 14x14½
1996, Sept. 23   Litho.   Wmk. 373
660	A116	12p multicolored	.40	.40
661	A116	20p multicolored	.65	.65
662	A116	25p multicolored	.80	.80
663	A116	30p multicolored	1.00	1.00
664	A116	65p multicolored	2.00	2.00
		Nos. 660-664 (5)	4.85	4.85

UNICEF, 50th anniv.

A117   A118

Perf. 14½
1997, Jan. 7   Litho.   Wmk. 373
665	A117	20p Date palm	.65	.65
666	A117	25p Mauritius hemp	.80	.80
667	A117	30p Norfolk Island pine	1.00	1.00
668	A117	65p Dwarf palm	2.00	2.00
		Nos. 665-668 (4)	4.45	4.45

Hong Kong '97.

Perf. 14½
1997, Apr. 1   Litho.   Wmk. 373

Flag, ship or aircraft: 12p, Great Britain Red Ensign, tanker Maserk Ascension. 25p, RAF Ensign, Tristar. 30p, NASA emblem, Space Shuttle Atlantis. 65p, Royal Navy White Ensign, HMS Northumberland.

669	A118	12p multicolored	.40	.40
670	A118	25p multicolored	.80	.80
671	A118	30p multicolored	.95	.95
672	A118	65p multicolored	2.00	2.00
		Nos. 669-672 (4)	4.15	4.15

Herbs A119

Designs: a, Solanum sodomaeum. b, Ageratum conyzoides. c, Leonurus sibricus. d, Cerastium vulgatum. e, Commelina diffusa.

Perf. 14x14½
1997, June 7   Litho.   Wmk. 373
673	A119	30p Strip of 5, #a.-e.	5.00	5.00

A120    Birds — A121

Queen Elizabeth II and Prince Philip, 50th Wedding Anniv.: No. 674, Queen Elizabeth II. No. 675, Prince Philip playing polo. No. 676, Queen petting horse. No. 677, Prince Philip. No. 678, Prince Philip, Queen Elizabeth II. No. 679, Prince Harry, Prince William riding horses.

£1.50, Queen Elizabeth, Prince Philip riding in open carriage.

Perf. 13½
1997, July 10   Litho.   Wmk. 384
674	A120	20p multicolored	.65	.65
675	A120	20p multicolored	.65	.65
a.		Pair, #674-675	1.30	1.30
676	A120	25p multicolored	.85	.85
677	A120	25p multicolored	.85	.85
a.		Pair, #676-677	1.70	1.70
678	A120	30p multicolored	1.00	1.00
679	A120	30p multicolored	1.00	1.00
a.		Pair, #678-679	2.00	2.00
		Nos. 674-679 (6)	5.00	5.00

Souvenir Sheet
680	A120	£1.50 multicolored	4.75	4.75

Perf. 14 on 3 Sides
1997, Sept. 1   Litho.   Wmk. 373
Booklet Stamps
681	A121	15p like #644	.50	.50
682	A121	35p like #648	1.10	1.10
a.		Booklet pane, 2 ea #681-682	3.25	
		Complete booklet, #682a	3.25	

Game Fish — A122

Perf. 14x14½
1997, Sept. 3   Litho.   Wmk. 373
683	A122	12p Black marlin	.40	.40
684	A122	20p Atlantic sailfish	.65	.65
685	A122	25p Swordfish	.80	.80
686	A122	30p Wahoo	.95	.95
687	A122	£1 Yellowfin tuna	3.25	3.25
		Nos. 683-687 (5)	6.05	6.05

A123    A124

St. Mary's Church (Christmas): 15p, Interior view. 35p, Stained glass window, Madonna and Child. 40p, Stained glass window, Falklands, 1982. 50p, Stained glass window.

Wmk. 384
1997, Oct. 1   Litho.   Perf. 14
688	A123	15p multicolored	.50	.50
689	A123	35p multicolored	1.10	1.10
690	A123	40p multicolored	1.25	1.25
691	A123	50p multicolored	1.75	1.75
		Nos. 688-691 (4)	4.60	4.60

Wmk. 373
1998, Feb. 10   Litho.   Perf. 14

Insects: 15p, Cactoblastis cactorum. 35p, Teleonemia scrupulosa. 40p, Neltumius arizonensis. 50p, Algarobius prosopis.

692	A124	15p multicolored	.50	.50
693	A124	35p multicolored	1.10	1.10
694	A124	40p multicolored	1.30	1.30
695	A124	50p multicolored	1.60	1.60
		Nos. 692-695 (4)	4.50	4.50

Diana, Princess of Wales (1961-97)
Common Design Type

Designs: a, In polka-dotted dress. b, In yellow blouse. c, With longer hair style. d, Holding flowers.

Perf. 14½x14
1998, Mar. 31   Litho.   Wmk. 373
696	CD355	35p Sheet of 4, #a.-d.	5.25	5.25

No. 696 sold for £1.40 + 20p, with surtax from international sales being donated to the Princess Diana Memorial Fund and surtax from national sales being donated to designated local charity.

Royal Air Force, 80th Anniv.
Common Design Type of 1993
Re-inscribed

15p, Fairey Fawn. 35p, Vickers Vernon. 40p, Supermarine Spitfire F-22. 50p, Bristol Britannia C2.

No. 701: a, Blackburn Kangaroo. b, SE5a. c, Curtiss Kittyhawk III. d, Boeing Fortress II (B-17).

ASCENSION — AUSTRALIAN STATES — NEW SOUTH WALES

Wmk. 384
1998, Apr. 1   **Litho.**   *Perf. 14*
697	CD350	15p multicolored	.70	.70
698	CD350	35p multicolored	1.65	1.65
699	CD350	40p multicolored	1.90	1.90
700	CD350	50p multicolored	2.25	2.25
	Nos. 697-700 (4)		6.50	6.50

Souvenir Sheet
701	CD350	50p Sheet of 4, #a.-d.	6.75	6.75

Birds — A125
Island Sports — A126 

Wmk. 373
1998, June 15   **Litho.**   *Perf. 14*
702	A125	15p Swallow	.50	.50
703	A125	25p House martin	.80	.80
704	A125	35p Cattle egret	1.10	1.10
705	A125	40p Swift	1.25	1.25
706	A125	50p Allen's gallinule	1.60	1.60
	Nos. 702-706 (5)		5.25	5.25

Wmk. 373
1998, Aug. 17   **Litho.**   *Perf. 14*
707	A126	15p Cricket	.50	.50
708	A126	35p Golf	1.10	1.10
709	A126	40p Soccer	1.25	1.25
710	A126	50p Trapshooting	1.60	1.60
	Nos. 707-709 (3)		2.85	2.85

Christmas A127

Designs: 15p, Children's nativity play. 35p, Santa arriving on Ascension. 40p, Santa arriving at a party. 50p, Carol singers.

Wmk. 373
1998, Oct. 1   **Litho.**   *Perf. 14*
711	A127	15p multicolored	.50	.50
712	A127	35p multicolored	1.10	1.10
713	A127	40p multicolored	1.25	1.25
714	A127	50p multicolored	1.60	1.60
	Nos. 711-714 (4)		4.45	4.45

POSTAGE DUE STAMPS

Outline Map of Ascension — D1

1986   **Litho.**   *Perf. 15x14*
J1	D1	1p beige & brown	.15	.15
J2	D1	2p orange & brown	.15	.15
J3	D1	5p org ver & brn	.15	.15
J4	D1	7p violet & black	.20	.20
J5	D1	10p ultra & black	.25	.25
J6	D1	25p pale green & blk	.60	.60
	Nos. J1-J6 (6)		1.50	1.50

AUSTRALIAN STATES

NEW SOUTH WALES

'nü saúth 'wā(ə)lz

LOCATION — Southeast coast of Australia in the South Pacific Ocean
GOVT. — British Crown Colony
AREA — 309,432 sq. mi.
POP. — 1,500,000 (estimated, 1900)

CAPITAL — Sydney

In 1901 New South Wales united with five other British colonies to form the Commonwealth of Australia. Stamps of Australia are now used.

12 Pence = 1 Shilling
20 Shillings = 1 Pound

Watermarks

Wmk. 12- Crown and Single-lined A
Wmk. 13- Large Crown and Double-lined A 
Wmk. 49- Double-lined Numerals Corresponding with the Value 
Wmk. 50- Single-lined Numeral 
Wmk. 51- Single-lined Numeral 
Wmk. 52- Single-lined Numeral 
Wmk. 53- 5/- 
Wmk. 54- Small Crown and NSW 
Wmk. 55- Large Crown and NSW 
Wmk. 56- NSW 
Wmk. 57- 5/- NSW in Diamond 
Wmk. 58- 20/- NSW in Circle 
Wmk. 70- V and Crown 
Wmk. 199- Crown and A in Circle 

Values for unused stamps are for examples with original gum as defined in the catalogue introduction except for Nos. 1-20 which are rarely found with gum and are valued without gum. Very fine examples of Nos. 35-100, F3-F5, J1-J10 and O1-O40 will have perforations touching the framelines or design on one or more sides due to the narrow spacing of the stamps on the plates and imperfect perforation methods. Stamps with perfs clear of the design on all four sides are scarce and will command higher prices.

Seal of the Colony
A1   A2

A1 has no clouds. A2 has clouds added to the design, except in pos. 15.

1850   Unwmk.   Engr.   *Imperf.*
1	A1	1p red, *yelsh wove*	4,000.	400.
b.		1p red, *bluish wove*	4,000.	350.
2	A2	1p red, *yelsh wove*	2,500.	275.
b.		1p red, *yellowish laid*	4,000.	450.
c.		1p red, *bluish wove*	2,500.	275.
e.		1p red, *bluish laid*		
f.		Hill unshaded	4,250.	450.
g.		No clouds	4,250.	450.
h.		No trees	4,250.	450.

Twenty-five varieties.
Stamps from early impressions of the plate sell at considerably higher prices.
No. 1 was reproduced by the collotype process in a souvenir sheet distributed at the London International Stamp Exhibition 1950. The paper is white.

Plate I — A3    Plate II — A4

Plate I: Vertically lined background.
Plate I re-touched: Lines above and below "POSTAGE" and "TWO PENCE" deepened. Outlines of circular band around picture also deepened.
Plate II (First re-engraving of Plate I): Horizontally lined background; the bale on the left side is dated and there is a dot in the star in each corner.
Plate II retouched: Dots and dashes added in lower spandrels.

Plate I
Late (worn plate) Impressions
3	A3	2p blue, *yelsh wove*	1,600.	150.
a.		Early impressions	4,500.	350.

Twenty-four varieties.

Plate I, Retouched
4	A3	2p blue, *yelsh wove*	2,750.	250.

Twelve varieties.

Plate II
Late (worn plate) Impressions
5	A4	2p blue, *yelsh wove*	1,750.	175.
a.		2p blue, *bluish wove*	1,750.	175.
b.		2p blue, *grayish wove*	1,750.	175.
c.		"CREVIT" omitted	—	350.
d.		Pick and shovel omitted	—	275.
e.		No whip	3,250.	225.
h.		Early impressions	4,000.	225.

Plate II, Retouched
5F	A4	2p blue, *bluish wove*	2,250.	200.
g.		No whip		275.
i.		"CREVIT" omitted		375.

Eleven varieties.

Plate III — A5    Plate IV — A6

Plate III (Second re-engraving of Plate I): The bale is not dated and, with the exception of Nos. 7, 10 and 12, it is single-lined. There are no dots in the stars.
Plate IV (Third re-engraving of Plate I): The bale is double-lined and there is a circle in the center of each star.

1850-51
6	A5	2p blue, *grayish wove*	2,100.	175.
a.		Fan with 6 segments	—	350.
b.		Double-lined bale	—	350.
c.		No whip	—	250.
7	A6	2p blue, *bluish wove* ('51)	2,250.	150.
a.		2p ultra, *white laid*	2,750.	150.
b.		2p blue, *grayish wove*	2,250.	150.
c.		Fan with 6 segments	—	200.
d.		No clouds	—	200.

Twenty-four varieties.

Plate V — A7    A8

Plate V (Fourth re-engraving of Plate I): There is a pearl in the fan-shaped ornament below the central design.

1850-51
8	A7	2p blue, *grayish wove* ('51)	2,250.	165.
a.		2p ultra, *white laid*	3,250.	275.
b.		Fan with 6 segments	—	250.
c.		Pick and shovel omitted	—	250.
9	A8	3p green, *bluish wove*	2,250.	200.
a.		3p green, *yellowish wove*	3,750.	225.
b.		3p green, *yellowish laid*	4,500.	400.
c.		3p green, *bluish laid*	4,500.	400.
d.		No whip	2,500.	300.

Twenty-four varieties of #8, twenty-five of #9.

Queen Victoria
A9   A10

TWO PENCE
Plate I - Background of wavy lines.
Plate II - Stars in corners.
Plate III (Plate I re-engraved) - Background of crossed lines.

SIX PENCE
Plate I - Background of fine lines.
Plate II (Plate I re-engraved) - Background of coarse lines.

1851   **Yellowish Wove Paper**
10	A9	1p carmine	1,650.	250.00
b.		No leaves to right of "SOUTH"	3,250.	365.00
c.		Two leaves to right of "SOUTH"	3,250.	425.00
d.		"WALE"	3,250.	425.00
11	A9	2p ultra, Plate I	750.00	90.00

NEW SOUTH WALES

1852		Bluish Laid Paper		
12	A9	1p carmine	3,000.	400.
a.		No leaves to right of "SOUTH"		500.
b.		Two leaves to right of "SOUTH"		600.
c.		"WALE"		600.

1852-55 Bluish or Grayish Wove Paper

13	A9	1p red	750.00	125.00
a.		1p carmine	1,000.	140.00
b.		No leaves to right of "SOUTH"		200.00
c.		Two leaves to right of "SOUTH"		250.00
d.		"WALE"		200.00
14	A9	2p blue, Plate I	300.00	27.50
a.		2p ultramarine	325.00	27.50
b.		2p slate	425.00	27.50
15	A10	2p blue, Plate II ('53)	900.00	87.50
a.		"WAEES"	2,300.	450.00
16	A9	2p blue, Plate III ('55)	425.00	55.00
17	A9	3p green	900.00	140.00
a.		3p emerald	1,300.	100.00
b.		"WACES"	2,300.	325.00
18	A9	6p brown, Plate I	2,000.	250.00
a.		6p black brown	2,000.	225.00
b.		"WALLS"	4,250.	425.00
19	A9	6p brown, Plate II	2,000.	250.00
a.		6p bister brown	2,000.	225.00
20	A9	8p yellow ('53)	3,600.	550.00
a.		8p orange	3,600.	550.00
b.		No leaves to right of "SOUTH"		900.00

The plates of the 1, 2, 3 and 8p each contained 50 varieties and those of the 6p 25 varieties.

The 2p, plate II, 6p, plate II, and 8p have been reprinted on grayish blue wove paper. The reprints of the 2p have the spandrels and background much worn. Most of the reprints of the 6p have no floreate ornaments to the right and left of "South". On all the values the wreath has been retouched.

Type of 1851 and:

A11,  A12,  A13,  A14

1854-55 Wmk. 49

23	A9	1p orange	125.00	13.00
a.		No leaves to right of "SOUTH"	275.00	60.00
b.		Two leaves to right of "SOUTH"	400.00	100.00
c.		"WALE"	400.00	125.00
24	A9	2p blue	100.00	10.00
a.		2p ultramarine	100.00	10.00
25	A9	3p green	150.00	25.00
a.		"WACES"		80.00
b.		Watermarked "2"		500.00

Value for No. 25b is for copy with the design cut into.

26	A11	5p green	800.00	375.00
27	A12	6p sage green	425.00	32.50
28	A12	6p brown	450.00	30.00
a.		Watermarked "8"	1,650.	85.00
29	A12	6p gray	325.00	30.00
a.		Watermarked "8"	1,650.	80.00
30	A13	8p orange ('55)	4,750.	1,000.
a.		8p yellow	4,750.	1,000.
31	A14	1sh pale red brown	650.00	75.00
a.		1sh red	650.00	75.00
b.		Watermarked "2"	2,000.	150.00

See Nos. 38-42, 56, 58, 65, 67.

Nos. 38-42 exist with wide margins. Copies with perforations trimmed are often offered as Nos. 26, 30, and 30a.

A15,  A16

1856

32	A15	1p red	90.00	16.00
a.		1p orange	90.00	16.00
b.		Printed on both sides		2,250.
33	A15	2p blue	110.00	5.00
a.		Watermarked "1"		5,000.
b.		Watermarked "5"	550.00	25.00
c.		Watermarked "8"		
34	A15	3p green	750.00	80.00
a.		3p yellow green	725.00	75.00
b.		Watermarked "2"		4,000.
		Nos. 32-34 (3)	950.00	101.00

The two known copies of No. 33c are in museums. Both are used.

The 1p has been reprinted in orange on paper watermarked Small Crown and NSW, and the 2p in deep blue on paper watermarked single lined "2". These reprints are usually overprinted "SPECIMEN."

See Nos. 34C-37, 54, 63, 90.

1859 Litho.

| 34C | A15 | 2p light blue | | 625.00 |

1860-63 Engr. Wmk. 49 Perf. 13

35	A15	1p red	55.00	8.00
a.		1p orange	100.00	15.00
b.		Perf. 12x13		2,000.
c.		Perf. 12	90.00	15.00
36	A15	2p blue, perf. 12	100.00	9.00
a.		Watermarked "1"		3,500.
c.		Perf. 12x13	2,600.	250.00
37	A15	3p blue green	50.00	8.00
a.		3p yellow green	50.00	8.00
b.		3p deep green	45.00	10.00
c.		Watermarked "6"	60.00	10.50
d.		Perf. 12	600.00	45.00
38	A11	5p dark green	40.00	12.50
a.		5p yellow green	50.00	21.00
b.		Perf. 12	165.00	42.50
39	A12	6p brown, perf. 12	275.00	45.00
a.		6p gray, perf. 12	275.00	45.00
40	A12	6p violet	55.00	3.00
a.		6p aniline lilac	950.00	150.00
b.		Watermarked "5"	360.00	30.00
c.		Watermarked "12"	240.00	20.00
e.		Perf. 12	275.00	25.00
41	A13	8p yellow	140.00	40.00
a.		8p orange	150.00	35.00
b.		Perf. 12	2,100.	550.00
42	A14	1sh rose	65.00	8.00
a.		1sh carmine	55.00	5.75
c.		Perf. 12	400.00	50.00
		Nos. 35-42 (8)	780.00	133.50

1864 Wmk. 50 Perf. 13

| 43 | A15 | 1p red | 45.00 | 15.00 |

1861-80 Wmk. 53 Perf. 13

44	A16	5sh dull violet	250.00	40.00
a.		5sh purple	225.00	30.00
b.		5sh dull violet, perf. 12	1,650.	400.00
c.		5sh purple, perf. 12	250.00	50.00
d.		5sh purple, perf. 12	250.00	42.50
e.		5sh purple, perf. 12x10	450.00	65.00

See No. 101. For overprint see No. O11.
Reprints are perf. 10 and overprinted "REPRINT" in black.

A17,  A18

1862-65 Typo. Unwmk. Perf. 13

45	A17	1p red ('65)	72.50	20.00
a.		Perf. 14	72.50	55.00
46	A18	2p blue	30.00	2.50
a.		Perf. 14	60.00	17.50

1863-64 Wmk. 50 Perf. 13

47	A17	1p red	21.00	.90
a.		Watermarked "2"	95.00	10.50
48	A18	2p blue	10.00	.35
a.		Watermarked "1"	135.00	5.00

1862 Wmk. 49 Perf. 13

49	A18	2p blue	50.00	8.50
a.		Watermarked "5"	135.00	18.00
b.		Perf. 12x13	600.00	
c.		Perf. 12	165.00	16.00

See Nos. 52-53, 61-62, 70-76.

A19,  A20

1867, Sept. Wmk. 51, 52 Perf. 13

50	A19	4p red brown	30.00	3.25
a.		Imperf.		
51	A20	10p lilac	11.00	3.50
a.		Imperf.		
b.		Horiz. pair, imperf. between	600.00	

See Nos. 55, 64, 91, 97, 117, 129.

A21,  A22,  A23

Typo.; Engr. (3p, 5p, 8p)
1871-84 Wmk. 54 Perf. 13

52	A17	1p red	4.50	.15
a.		Perf. 10	400.00	15.00
b.		Perf. 13x10	15.00	.20
c.		Horiz. pair imperf. between		
53	A18	2p blue	7.00	.20
a.		Imperf.		
b.		Horiz. pair, imperf. vert.		800.00
c.		Perf. 10	400.00	21.00
d.		Perf. 13x10	4.50	.20
e.		Perf. 10x12		30.00
f.		Perf. 11x12		
54	A15	3p green ('74)	21.00	1.75
a.		Perf. 11	225.00	150.00
b.		Perf. 12	500.00	250.00
c.		Perf. 10x12	175.00	35.00
d.		Perf. 12x11	135.00	50.00
e.		Perf. 10	70.00	4.50
f.		Perf. 13x10	135.00	13.00
55	A19	4p red brown ('77)	40.00	5.00
a.		Imperf.	300.00	50.00
b.		Perf. 13x10	75.00	2.50
56	A11	5p dk grn, perf. 10 ('84)	15.00	7.50
a.		Imperf.		
b.		Perf. 12	325.00	135.00
c.		Perf. 10x12	24.00	9.00
d.		Perf. 13x10		
57	A21	6p lilac ('72)	35.00	.75
a.		Imperf.		
b.		Perf. 13x10	50.00	1.75
c.		Perf. 10	325.00	9.00
58	A13	8p yellow ('77)	90.00	16.00
a.		Imperf.		
b.		Perf. 10	325.00	21.00
c.		Perf. 13x10	225.00	18.00
59	A22	9p on 10p red brown, perf. 12 (Bk)	14.00	3.00
a.		Double surcharge, blk & bl	195.00	
b.		Perf. 10x12	375.00	300.00
c.		Perf. 10	12.00	3.25
d.		Perf. 12x11	18.00	5.75
e.		Perf. 11x12	18.00	5.75
f.		Perf. 13	24.00	2.75
g.		Perf. 11	40.00	7.25
h.		Perf. 10x11	50.00	12.00
60	A23	1sh black ('76)	75.00	1.50
a.		Imperf.		
b.		Perf. 10x12	275.00	3.25
c.		Perf. 10	550.00	12.00
		Nos. 52-60 (9)	301.50	35.85

The surcharge on #59 measures 15mm.
See #66, 68. For overprints see #O1-O10.

Typo.; Engr. (3p, 5p, 8p)
1882-91 Wmk. 55 Perf. 11x12

61	A17	1p red	5.00	.15
a.		Perf. 10	9.00	.15
b.		Perf. 10x13	120.00	5.00
c.		Perf. 10x12	325.00	85.00
d.		Perf. 12x11		150.00
e.		Perf. 10x11	600.00	150.00
f.		Perf. 11		200.00
g.		Perf. 13		135.00
62	A18	2p blue	5.00	.20
a.		Perf. 10	12.00	.20
b.		Perf. 13x10	90.00	2.50
c.		Perf. 13	600.00	135.00
d.		Perf. 12x10	325.00	70.00
e.		Perf. 11		135.00
f.		Perf. 12x11		135.00
g.		Perf. 11x10	600.00	135.00
h.		Perf. 12		275.00
63	A15	3p green	4.75	.35
a.		Imperf., pair	200.00	
b.		Vert. pair, imperf. btwn.	225.00	
c.		Imperf. vert., pair		
d.		Double impression		
e.		Perf. 10	7.25	.35
f.		Perf. 11	7.25	.35
g.		Perf. 12	8.00	.35
h.		Perf. 12x11	8.00	.40
i.		Perf. 10x12	210.00	12.50
m.		Perf. 10x11	20.00	1.25
n.		Perf. 12x10	100.00	3.50
64	A19	4p red brown	27.50	1.40
a.		Perf. 10	27.50	1.65
b.		Perf. 10x12		150.00
c.		Perf. 12		40.00
65	A11	5p dk blue green	7.25	.70
a.		Imperf., pair	225.00	
b.		Perf. 11	13.00	.75
c.		Perf. 10	13.00	.80
d.		Perf. 10x12	13.00	.80
f.		5p green, perf. 12x11	7.50	.75
g.		5p green, perf. 11x10	42.50	2.00
h.		5p green, perf. 12x10	75.00	3.25
i.		5p green, perf. 10x11	35.00	3.75
j.		5p green, perf. 11		3.75
66	A21	6p lilac, perf. 10	30.00	.75
a.		Horiz. pair, imperf. between		825.00
b.		Perf. 10x12	30.00	1.25
c.		Perf. 11x12	32.50	1.25
d.		Perf. 12	95.00	2.75
e.		Perf. 11x10	60.00	.75
f.		Perf. 11	95.00	6.00
g.		Perf. 10x13		325.00
67	A13	8p yellow, perf. 10	100.00	15.00
a.		Perf. 11	90.00	13.00
b.		Perf. 12	120.00	18.00
c.		Perf. 10x12	100.00	20.00
68	A23	1sh black	60.00	.75
a.		Perf. 10x13		12.00
b.		Perf. 10	55.00	.75
c.		Perf. 11	225.00	12.00
d.		Perf. 10x12		
		Nos. 61-68 (8)	239.50	19.30

Nos. 63 and 65 exist with two types of watermark 55 - spacings of 1mm or 2mm between crown and NSW.

See No. 90. For surcharges and overprints see Nos. 92-94, O12-O19.

The 1, 2, 4, 6, 8p and 1sh have been reprinted on paper watermarked Large Crown and NSW. The 1, 2, 4p and 1sh are perforated 11x12, the 6p is perforated 10 and the 8p 11. All are overprinted "REPRINT," the 1sh in red and the others in black.

1886-87 Typo. Wmk. 56 Perf. 11x12
Bluish Revenue Stamp Paper

70	A17	1p scarlet	11.00	2.50
a.		Perf. 10	18.00	4.50
71	A18	2p dark blue	15.00	4.50
a.		Perf. 10	65.00	9.00

For overprint, see No. O20.

A24

Perf. 12 (#73-75), 12x10 (#72, 75A) and Compound
1885-86 "POSTAGE" in Black

72	A24	5sh green & vio	450.00	65.00
a.		Perf. 10		
73	A24	10sh rose & vio	1,250.	240.00
74	A24	£1 rose & vio	2,750.	1,000.
a.		Perf. 13		2,100.

"POSTAGE" in Blue
Bluish Paper

75	A24	10sh rose & vio	175.00	35.00
b.		Perf. 10	750.00	165.00

NEW SOUTH WALES

	c. Perf. 12x11	375.00	150.00

White Paper

75A	A24 £1 rose & vio	3,750.	1,750.

For overprints, see Nos. O21-O23.
The 5sh with black overprint and the £1 with blue overprint have been reprinted on paper watermarked NSW. They are perforated 12x10 and are overprinted "REPRINT" in black.

1894 — White Paper, "POSTAGE" in Blue

76	A24 10sh rose & violet	175.00	30.00
a.	Double overprint		

See No. 108B.

View of Sydney — A25
Emu — A26 
Captain Cook — A27 
Victoria and Coat of Arms — A28 
Lyrebird A29 
Kangaroo A30 

1888-89 — Wmk. 55 — Perf. 11x12

77	A25 1p violet	3.50	.15
a.	Perf. 12	4.50	.15
b.	Perf. 12x11½	16.00	.15
78	A26 2p blue	3.00	.15
a.	Imperf., pair	125.00	
b.	Perf. 12	7.50	.15
c.	Perf. 12x11½	13.00	.15
79	A27 4p brown	9.00	.75
a.	Perf. 12x11½	15.00	.75
b.	Perf. 12	15.00	.75
c.	Perf. 11	450.00	135.00
d.	Imperf.		
80	A28 6p carmine rose	22.50	1.25
a.	Perf. 12	15.00	1.25
b.	Perf. 12x11½	35.00	1.75
81	A29 8p red violet	11.00	.75
a.	Perf. 12	9.00	1.50
b.	Perf. 12x11½	12.00	1.50
82	A30 1sh vio brown ('89)	14.00	.75
a.	Imperf., pair	725.00	
b.	Perf. 12x11½	16.00	.75
c.	Perf. 12	24.00	.75
	Nos. 77-82 (6)	63.00	3.80

First British settlement in Australia, cent.
For overprints see Nos. O24-O29.

1888 — Wmk. 56 — Perf. 11x12

83	A25 1p violet	11.00	1.40
84	A26 2p blue	65.00	6.75

See #104B-106C, 113-115, 118, 125-127, 130.

Map of Australia — A31
Governors Capt. Arthur Phillip (above) and Lord Carrington — A32 

1888-89 — Wmk. 53 — Perf. 10

85	A31 5sh violet ('89)	240.00	55.00
86	A32 20sh ultra	375.00	175.00

See #88, 120. For overprints see #O30-O31.

1890 — Wmk. 57 — Perf. 10

87	A31 5sh violet	200.00	17.50
a.	Perf. 11	200.00	22.50
b.	Perf. 10x11	225.00	17.50
c.	Perf. 12	360.00	25.00

Perf. 11x12 — Wmk. 58

88	A32 20sh ultra	225.00	75.00
a.	Perf. 11	250.00	57.50
b.	Perf. 10	250.00	77.50
c.	Perf. 12	350.00	135.00

For overprints see Nos. O32-O33.

"Australia" A33
Victoria A37 

1890, Dec. 22 — Wmk. 55 — Perf. 11x12

89	A33 2½p ultra	2.00	.38
a.	Perf. 12	11.50	.38
b.	Perf. 12x11½	67.50	50.00

For overprint see No. O35.

Type of 1856
1891 — Engr. — Wmk. 52 — Perf. 10

90	A15 3p green	10.00	15.00
a.	Double impression		

Type of 1867
1893 — Typo. — Perf. 11

91	A20 10p lilac	15.00	6.00
a.	Perf. 10	16.00	7.50
b.	Perf. 11x10 or 10x11	24.00	12.00
c.	Perf. 12x11	175.00	24.00

Types of 1862-84 Surcharged in Black:

SEVEN-PENCE

Halfpenny a
HALFPENNY b

1891, Jan. 5 — Wmk. 55 — Perf. 11x12

92	A17(a) ½p on 1p gray	1.25	1.25
a.	Imperf.		
b.	Surcharge omitted		
c.	Double surcharge		
93	A21(b) 7½p on 6p brown	3.50	1.65
a.	Perf. 12	3.50	1.25
b.	Perf. 11	3.50	1.25
c.	Perf. 12	4.25	1.75
d.	Perf. 10x12	4.25	1.75
94	A23(b) 12½p on 1sh red	7.00	4.00
a.	Perf. 12x11½	4.75	4.00
b.	Perf. 10	7.00	4.00
c.	Perf. 11	4.75	4.00
d.	Perf. 12	5.50	4.00
	Nos. 92-94 (3)	11.75	6.90

For overprints see Nos. O34, O36-O37.

1892

95	A37 ½p slate	1.25	.15
a.	Perf. 12x11½	1.25	.15
b.	Perf. 12	1.25	.15
c.	Perf. 10	27.50	.90
d.	Perf. 10x12	150.00	10.50
e.	Perf. 11	165.00	9.00

See #102, 109, 121. For overprint see #O38.

Types of 1867-71
1897 — Perf. 11x12

96	A22 9p on 10p red brn (Bk)	8.00	3.25
a.	9p on 10p org brn (Bk)	8.00	3.25
b.	Surcharge omitted	125.00	
c.	Double surcharge	125.00	100.00
d.	Perf. 11	11.00	7.50
e.	Perf. 12	9.00	7.50
97	A20 10p violet	12.00	5.50
a.	Perf. 12x11½	12.00	5.50
b.	Perf. 11	13.00	6.00
c.	Perf. 12	13.00	6.00

The surcharge on No. 96 measures 13½mm.
For overprints see Nos. O39-O40.

Seal A38
Victoria A39 
A40 

ONE PENNY:

Die I - The first pearl in the crown at the left is merged into the arch, the shading under the fleur-de-lis is indistinct, and the "s" of "WALES" is open.
Die II - The first pearl is circular, the vertical shading under the fleur-de-lis is clear, and the "s" of "WALES" not so open.

2½ PENCE:
Die I - There are 12 radiating lines in the star on the Queen's breast.
Die II - There are 16 radiating lines in the star. The eye is nearly full of color.

1897 — Perf. 12

98	A38 1p rose red (II)	2.50	.15
a.	Die II, perf. 11x12	3.00	.15
b.	Imperf., pair	75.00	
c.	Imperf. horiz., pair	600.00	
d.	Die II, perf. 12x11½	4.50	.15
e.	Die II, perf. 12	7.50	.60
f.	Die II, perf. 12x11½	2.00	.15
g.	Die II, perf. 11x12	3.00	.15
99	A39 2p deep blue	2.25	.15
a.	Perf. 11x12	2.75	.15
b.	Perf. 12x11½	2.75	.15
100	A40 2½p dp purple (II)	4.25	1.10
a.	Die II, perf. 12x11	6.50	1.10
b.	Die II, perf. 11	7.50	1.90
c.	Die II, perf. 11½x12	10.50	1.10
d.	Die II, perf. 11x12	4.25	1.10
e.	Die II, perf. 11½x12	8.00	1.10
	Nos. 98-100 (3)	9.00	1.40

Sixtieth year of Queen Victoria's reign.
See Nos. 103-104, 110-112, 122-124.

Type of 1861
1897 — Engr. — Wmk. 53 — Perf. 11

101	A16 5sh red violet	75.00	15.00
a.	Horiz. pair, imperf. btwn.	3,000.	
b.	Perf. 11x12 or 12x11	75.00	17.00
c.	Perf. 12	90.00	15.00

Perf. 12x11½, 11½x12
1899, Oct. — Typo. — Wmk. 55

HALF PENNY:
Die I - Narrow "H" in "HALF."

102	A37 ½p blue green (I)	1.00	.15
a.	Imperf., pair	60.00	45.00
103	A39 2p ultra	1.25	.15
a.	Imperf., pair	55.00	
104	A40 2½p dk blue (II)	2.50	.38
a.	Imperf., pair	90.00	
104B	A27 4p org brown	9.00	.50
a.	Imperf. pair	300.00	
105	A28 6p emerald	37.50	3.25
a.	Imperf., pair	235.00	
106	A28 6p orange	11.00	.75
a.	6p yellow	14.00	.75
b.	Imperf., pair	195.00	
106C	A29 8p magenta	9.00	2.00
	Nos. 102-106C (7)	71.25	7.18

Lyrebird A41
"Australia" A42 

1903 — Perf. 12x11½

107	A41 2sh6p blue green	42.50	14.00

See Nos. 119, 131.

1903 — Wmk. 70 — Perf. 12½

108	A42 9p org brn & ultra	10.00	2.75
a.	Perf. 11	750.00	425.00

See No. 128.

Type of 1885-86
1904 — Wmk. 56 — Perf. 11
Chalky Paper
"POSTAGE" in Blue

108B	A24 10sh brt rose & violet	175.00	25.00
c.	Perf. 12x11	140.00	25.00
d.	Perf. 12	140.00	25.00

The watermark (NSW) of No. 108B is 20x7mm, with rounded angles in "N" and "W." On No. 75, the watermark is 21x7mm, with sharp angles in the "N" and "W."

HALF PENNY:
Die II - Wide "H" in "HALF."

Perf. 11, 11x12½, 12x11½ and Compound
1905-06 — Wmk. 12

109	A37 ½p blue grn (II)	1.25	.40
a.	½p blue green (I)	2.75	.40
b.	Booklet pane of 12		
110	A38 1p car rose (I)	1.25	.15
a.	Booklet pane of 6		
b.	Booklet pane of 12		
111	A39 2p deep ultra	1.50	.15
112	A40 2½p dk blue (II)	2.50	.40
113	A27 4p org brown	8.25	.75

114	A28 6p orange	10.00	.75
a.	6p yellow	8.50	.75
b.	Perf. 11	250.00	
115	A29 8p magenta	11.00	1.50
117	A20 10p violet	12.50	2.25
118	A30 1sh vio brown	11.00	.75
119	A41 2sh6p blue green	27.50	12.00

Wmk. 199

120	A32 20sh ultra	200.00	75.00
	Nos. 109-115, 117-120 (11)	286.75	94.20

1906-07 — Wmk. 13

121	A37 ½p green (I)	10.00	2.00
122	A38 1p rose (II)	6.00	1.50
123	A39 2p ultra	6.00	1.50
124	A40 2½p blue (II)	70.00	
125	A27 4p org brown	15.00	10.00
126	A28 6p orange	40.00	25.00
127	A29 8p red violet	50.00	30.00
128	A42 9p org brn & ultra, perf. 12x12½ ('06)	8.00	2.00
a.	Perf. 11	65.00	55.00
129	A20 10p violet	100.00	
130	A30 1sh vio brown	50.00	20.00
131	A41 2sh6p blue green	100.00	75.00
	Nos. 121-131 (11)	455.00	
	Nos. 121-123, 125-128, 130-131 (9)		167.00

Portions of some of the sheets on which the above are printed show the watermark "COMMONWEALTH OF AUSTRALIA." Stamps may also be found from portions of the sheet without watermark.

SEMI-POSTAL STAMPS

Allegory of Charity
SP1 SP2

Illustrations reduced.

1897, June — Wmk. 55 — Perf. 11

B1	SP1 1p (1sh) green & brown	35.00	25.00
B2	SP2 2½p (2sh6p) rose, bl & gold	225.00	250.00

Diamond Jubilee of Queen Victoria.
The difference between the postal and face values of these stamps was donated to a fund for a home for consumptives.

REGISTRATION STAMPS

Queen Victoria — R1

1856, Jan. 1 — Unwmk. — Engr. — Imperf.

F1	R1 (6p) orange & blue	600.00	75.00
F2	R1 (6p) red & blue	575.00	75.00
a.	Frame printed on back	2,750.	1,350.

1860 — Perf. 12, 13

F3	R1 (6p) orange & blue	280.00	30.00
F4	R1 (6p) red & blue	265.00	30.00

Nos. F1 to F4 exist also on paper with papermaker's watermark in sheet.

1863 — Wmk. 49

F5	R1 (6p) red & blue	75.00	15.00

Fifty varieties.

Nos. F1-F2 were reprinted on thin white wove unwatermarked paper and on thick yellowish wove unwatermarked paper; the former are usually overprinted "SPECIMEN." No. F4 was reprinted on thin white wove unwatermarked paper; perf. 10 and overprinted "REPRINT" in black.

NEW SOUTH WALES — QUEENSLAND

POSTAGE DUE STAMPS

D1

Perf. 10, 11, 11½, 12 and Compound
1891-92 Typo. Wmk. 55

J1	D1	½p green, perf 10	3.25	1.50
J2	D1	1p green	4.00	.75
a.		Perf. 12	20.00	3.75
J3	D1	2p green	5.00	.75
a.		Perf. 10x12	17.00	4.00
J4	D1	3p green	10.00	2.50
J5	D1	4p green	10.00	.75
J6	D1	6p green, perf 10	15.00	2.25
J7	D1	8p green, perf 10	70.00	10.00
J8	D1	5sh green, perf 10	165.00	25.00
a.		Perf. 11	225.00	85.00
J9	D1	10sh green, perf 12x10	225.00	50.00
a.		Perf. 10	365.00	
J10	D1	20sh green, perf 12x10	300.00	
a.		Perf. 10	350.00	70.00
b.		Perf. 12		
		Nos. J1-J10 (10)	807.25	93.50

Nos. J1-J5 exist on both ordinary and chalky paper.
Used values for Nos. J8-J10 are for c-t-o copies.

OFFICIAL STAMPS

Regular Issues Overprinted **O S** in Black or Red

Perf. 10, 11, 12, 13 and Compound
1879-80 Wmk. 54

O1	A17	1p red	9.25	1.50
a.		Perf. 10	325.00	40.00
b.		Perf. 10x13	22.50	4.50
O2	A18	2p blue	15.00	3.50
a.		Perf. 11x12		250.00
b.		Perf. 10	250.00	40.00
O3	A15	3p green (R)		300.00
O4	A15	3p green	225.00	65.00
a.		Watermarked "6"		500.00
b.		Double overprint		
O5	A19	4p red brown	225.00	11.50
a.		Perf. 10	300.00	14.00
O6	A11	5p dark green	24.00	13.00
O7	A21	6p lilac	300.00	10.00
b.		Perf. 10x13		65.00
O8	A13	8p yellow (R)	1,000.	200.00
O9	A13	8p yellow		22.50
a.		Perf. 10	375.00	115.00
O10	A23	1sh black (R)	300.00	11.00
a.		Perf. 10		16.00
b.		Perf. 10x13		30.00

1880 Wmk. 53

O11	A16	5sh lilac, perf. 11	265.00	75.00
a.		Double overprint		
b.		Perf. 10	375.00	150.00
c.		Perf. 12x10	325.00	130.00
d.		Perf. 10x12	465.00	82.50

1881 Wmk. 55

O12	A17	1p red	6.00	.75
a.		Perf. 10x13		225.00
O13	A18	2p blue	6.50	1.00
a.		Perf. 10x13	360.00	100.00
O14	A15	3p green	6.00	1.65
a.		Double overprint		
b.		Perf. 12	240.00	130.00
c.		Perf. 11		
O15	A19	4p red brown	11.00	2.25
a.		Perf. 10x12		90.00
b.		Perf. 12	360.00	225.00
O16	A11	5p dark green	12.00	5.00
a.		Perf. 12	100.00	
b.		Perf. 10x12	400.00	130.00
O17	A21	6p lilac	22.50	4.00
a.		Perf. 12		60.00
b.		Perf. 11x12	72.50	16.00
O18	A13	8p yellow	27.50	9.50
a.		Double overprint		
b.		Perf. 12	240.00	50.00
O19	A23	1sh black (R)	27.50	3.25
a.		Double overprint		
b.		Perf. 10x13		70.00
c.		Perf. 11		
		Nos. O12-O19 (8)	119.00	27.40

Beware of other red overprints on watermark 55 stamps.

1881 Wmk. 56

O20	A17	1p red	32.50	10.00

1887-90

O21	A24	10sh on #75		350.00
O22	A24	£1 on #75A	3,250.	3,250.

No. 75 Overprinted **O S**

1889

O23	A24	10sh rose & vio	1,950.	600.00
a.		Perf. 10	3,500.	2,250.

Overprinted **O S**

1888-89 Wmk. 55

O24	A25	1p violet	1.50	.15
a.		Overprinted "O" only		
O25	A26	2p blue	1.50	.15
O26	A27	4p red brown	6.00	1.50
O27	A28	6p carmine	8.00	2.00
O28	A29	8p red lilac	14.00	4.00
O29	A30	1sh vio brown	14.00	2.00
a.		Double overprint		
		Nos. O24-O29 (6)	45.00	9.80

Wmk. 53

O30	A31	5sh violet (R)	700.00	450.00
O31	A32	20sh ultra	1,250.	

1890 Wmk. 57

O32	A31	5sh violet	150.00	60.00
a.		Perf. 12	625.00	

Wmk. 58

O33	A32	20sh ultra	2,000.	

Centenary of the founding of the Colony (Nos. O24-O33).

1891 Wmk. 55

O34	A17(a)	½p on 1p gray & black	47.50	14.00
a.		Double overprint		
O35	A33	2½p ultra	7.00	3.25
O36	A21(b)	7½p on 6p brn & black	35.00	12.00
O37	A23(b)	12½p on 1sh red & black	60.00	32.50
		Nos. O34-O37 (4)	149.50	61.75

1892

O38	A37	½p gray	5.50	4.00

1894 Wmk. 54

O39	A22	9p on 10p red brn	300.00	350.00

Wmk. 52

O40	A20	10p lilac, perf. 10	225.00	200.00
a.		Perf. 11x10	350.00	325.00

The official stamps became obsolete on Dec. 31, 1894. In Aug., 1895, sets of 32 varieties of "O.S." stamps, together with some envelopes and postal cards, were placed on sale at the Sydney post office at £2 per set. These sets contained most of the varieties listed above and a few which are not known in the original issues. An obliteration consisting of the letters G.P.O. or N.S.W. in three concentric ovals was lightly applied to the center of each block of four stamps. It is understood that the earlier stamps and many of the overprints were reprinted to make up these sets.

QUEENSLAND

'kwēnz-ˌland

LOCATION — Northeastern part of Australia
GOVT. — British Crown Colony
AREA — 670,500 sq. mi.
POP. — 498,129 (1901)
CAPITAL — Brisbane

Originally a part of New South Wales, Queensland was constituted a separate colony in 1859. It was one of the six British Colonies that united in 1901 to form the Commonwealth of Australia.

12 Pence = 1 Shilling
20 Shillings = 1 Pound

Values for unused stamps are for examples with original gum as defined in the catalogue introduction. Very fine examples of Nos. 4-73, 84-125, 128-140, and F1-F3b will have perforations touching the design on at least one or more sides due to the narrow spacing of the stamps on the plates. Stamps with perfs clear of the design on all four sides are scarce and will command higher prices.

Watermarks

Wmk. 5- Small Star
Wmk. 6- Large Star 
Wmk. 12- Crown and Single-lined A 
Wmk. 13- Crown and Double-lined A 
Wmk. 65- "Queensland Postage Stamps" in Sheet in Script Capitals 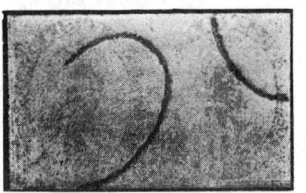 
Wmks. 66 & 67- "Queensland" in Large Single-lined Roman Capitals in the Sheet and Short-pointed Star to Each Stamp (Stars Vary Slightly in Size and Shape)
Wmk. 68- Crown and Q 
Wmk. 69- Large Crown and Q 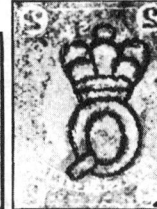

There are two varieties of the watermark 68, differing slightly in the position and shape of the crown and the tongue of the "Q."

Wmk. 70- V and Crown

Queen Victoria — A1

1860, Nov. 1 Engr. Wmk. 6 Imperf.

1	A1	1p deep rose	3,000.	750.
2	A1	2p deep blue	6,250.	2,250.
3	A1	6p deep green	4,250.	750.

Clean-Cut Perf. 14 to 16

4	A1	1p deep rose	1,750.	225.
5	A1	2p deep blue	475.	100.
6	A1	6p deep green	475.	60.

Clean-Cut Perf. 14 to 16
1860-61 Wmk. 5

6A	A1	2p blue	525.00	100.00
b.		Horiz. pair, imperf. vert.		875.00
6D	A1	3p brown ('61)	275.00	50.00
6E	A1	6p deep green	550.00	50.00
6F	A1	1sh gray violet	475.00	65.00

Regular Perf. 14

6H	A1	1p rose	125.00	35.00
6I	A1	2p deep blue	325.00	35.00

Rough Perf. 14 to 16

7	A1	1p deep rose	80.00	35.00
8	A1	2p blue	90.00	35.00
9	A1	3p brown ('61)	55.00	30.00
a.		Horiz. pair, imperf. vert.		2,000.
10	A1	6p deep green	150.00	25.00
a.		6p yellow green	200.00	25.00
11	A1	1sh dull violet	400.00	85.00

Thick Yellowish Paper
Square Perf. 12½ to 13
1862-67 Unwmk.

12	A1	1p Indian red	325.00	70.00
13	A1	1p orange ('63)	60.00	15.00
a.		Perf. 13, round holes ('67)	60.00	15.00
b.		Imperf.		
c.		Imperf., pair		525.00
14	A1	2p deep blue	40.00	17.00
a.		2p pale blue	90.00	30.00
b.		Perf. 13, round holes ('67)	90.00	30.00
c.		Imperf., pair		500.00
e.		Horiz. pair, imperf. between		900.00
f.		Vert. pair, imperf. between	1,200	
15	A1	3p brown ('63)	55.00	30.00
a.		Imperf.		
b.		Perf. 13, round holes ('67)		
16	A1	6p yellow grn ('63)	80.00	15.00
a.		6p green	125.00	25.00
b.		Perf. 13, round holes ('67)	125.00	25.00
c.		Imperf. pair		500.00
d.		Imperf., pair		950.00
17	A1	1sh gray ('63)	125.00	50.00
b.		Imperf. horizontally		
c.		Horiz. pair, imperf. between		950.00
d.		Perf. 13, round holes ('67)		

White Wove Paper
1865 Wmk. 5 Rough Perf. 13

18	A1	1p orange	55.00	20.00
a.		Horiz. pair, imperf. vert.	425.00	
19	A1	2p blue	50.00	16.00
a.		Vert. pair, imperf. horiz.	900.00	
b.		Half used as 1p on cover		2,000.
20	A1	6p yellow green	135.00	24.00
		Nos. 18-20 (3)	240.00	60.00

Perf. 13, Round Holes
1866 Wmk. 65

21	A1	1p orange vermilion	160.00	25.00
22	A1	2p blue	55.00	18.00
b.		Diagonal half used as 1p on cover		

1866 Unwmk. Litho. Perf. 13

23	A1	4p lilac	90.00	18.00
a.		4p slate	140.00	20.00
24	A1	5sh pink	225.00	50.00
b.		Vert. pair, imperf between		725.00

Wmk. 66, 67
1868-74 Engr. Perf. 13

25	A1	1p orange ('71)	45.00	5.00
26	A1	2p blue	45.00	1.90
27	A1	3p grnsh brn ('71)	85.00	2.50
a.		3p brown	87.50	3.50
b.		3p olive brown	87.50	3.50
28	A1	4p yel green ('71)	125.00	8.50
a.		6p deep green	175.00	11.00
30	A1	1sh grnsh gray ('72)	375.00	40.00
31	A1	1sh violet ('74)	200.00	20.00

Perf. 12

32	A1	1p orange	275.00	30.00
33	A1	2p blue		37.50
34	A1	3p brown	275.00	110.00
35	A1	6p deep green	900.00	42.50
36	A1	1sh violet		37.50

Perf. 13x12

36A	A1	1p orange		250.00
37	A1	2p blue	1,500.	100.00
37A	A1	3p brown		1,250.

The reprints are perforated 13 and the colors differ slightly from those of the originals.

QUEENSLAND

1868-75		Wmk. 68		Perf. 13	
38	A1	1p orange		45.00	5.00
39	A1	1p rose ('74)		50.00	9.00
40	A1	2p blue		35.00	2.50
b.		Imperf., pair		315.00	
41	A1	3p brown ('75)		65.00	14.00
42	A1	6p yel green ('69)		100.00	7.50
a.		6p apple green		135.00	10.00
b.		6p deep green		125.00	10.00
43	A1	1sh violet ('75)		150.00	26.00
		Nos. 38-43 (6)		445.00	64.00

No. 40 exists in vert. pair, imperf. btwn.

1876-78			Perf. 12	
44	A1	1p orange	35.00	3.00
a.		Imperf.	300.00	
45	A1	1p rose	45.00	11.00
46	A1	2p blue	22.50	1.50
a.		Imperf.		
47	A1	3p brown	60.00	10.00
48	A1	6p yellow green	125.00	5.00
a.		6p apple green	135.00	4.75
b.		6p deep green	135.00	4.75
49	A1	1sh violet	42.50	5.00
		Nos. 44-49 (6)	330.00	35.50

#44, 49 exist in vertical pairs, imperf. between.

		Perf. 13x12		
49B	A1	1p orange	165.00	
49C	A1	2p blue	1,800.	200.00
49D	A1	4p yellow		
49E	A1	6p deep green	200.00	

The reprints are perforated 12 and are in paler colors than the originals.

1879		Unwmk.	Perf. 12	
50	A1	6p pale emerald	200.00	25.00
a.		Horiz. pair, imperf. vert.	650.00	

A2  A3

1875-81		Litho.	Wmk. 68	Perf. 13	
50B	A1	4p yellow ('75)		800.00	42.50
			Perf. 12		
51	A1	4p buff ('76)		600.00	22.50
a.		4p yellow		600.00	22.50
52	A1	2sh pale blue ('81)		55.00	12.00
a.		2sh deep blue		67.50	12.00
b.		Imperf.			
53	A2	2sh6p lt red ('81)		110.00	30.00
54	A1	5sh orange brn ('81)		150.00	27.50
a.		5sh fawn		150.00	27.50
55	A1	10sh brown ('81)		325.00	110.00
a.		Imperf., pair		550.00	
56	A1	20sh rose ('81)		650.00	90.00
		Nos. 50B-56 (7)		2,690.	334.50

Nos. 53-56, 62-64, 74-83 with pen (revenue) cancellations removed are often offered as unused.

1879-81		Typo.	Wmk. 68	Perf. 12	
57	A3	1p rose red		9.50	1.50
a.		1p red orange		9.50	1.75
b.		1p brown orange		30.00	5.50
c.		"QOENSLAND"		110.00	32.50
d.		Imperf.			
e.		Vert. pair, imperf. horiz.			90.00
58	A3	2p gray blue		22.50	.70
a.		2p deep ultra		27.50	.80
b.		Imperf.			
c.		"PENGE"			70.00
d.		"TW" joined		25.00	1.10
e.		Vert. pair, imperf. horiz.		450.00	
59	A3	4p orange yellow		100.00	10.00
a.		Imperf.			
60	A3	6p yellow green		55.00	5.00
a.		Imperf.			
61	A3	1sh pale violet ('81)		50.00	5.00
a.		1sh deep violet		45.00	3.75
		Nos. 57-61 (5)		237.00	22.20

The stamps of type A3 were electrotyped from plates made up of groups of four types, differing in minor details. Two dies were used for the 1p and 2p, giving eight varieties for each of those values. Nos. 59-60 exist imperf. vertically.
For surcharge see No. 65.

Moire on Back

1878-79			Unwmk.	
62	A3	1p brown org ('79)	400.00	60.00
a.		"QOENSLAND"		2,000.
63	A3	2p deep ultra ('79)	500.00	30.00
a.		"PENGE"	4,750.	725.00
64	A1	1sh red violet	100.00	47.50
		Nos. 62-64 (3)	1,000.	137.50

No. 57b Surcharged Vertically in Black **Half-penny**

1881			Wmk. 68	
65	A3	½p on 1p brn org	175.00	95.00
a.		"QOENSLAND"	1,000.	825.00

A4  A5

1882-83		Typo.	Perf. 12	
66	A4	1p pale red	5.75	.20
a.		1p rose	5.75	.20
b.		Imperf.	30.00	30.00
67	A4	2p gray blue	9.00	.20
a.		2p deep ultra	9.00	.20
b.		Imperf.		
68	A4	4p yellow ('83)	20.00	1.00
a.		"PENGE"	125.00	45.00
b.		Imperf., pair		150.00
69	A4	6p yellow green	10.00	.70
70	A4	1sh violet ('83)	12.00	1.00
		Nos. 66-70 (5)	56.75	3.10

There are eight minor varieties of the 1p, twelve of the 2p and four each of the other values. On the 1p there is a period after "PENNY." On all values the lines of shading on the neck extend from side to side.
Compare design A4 with A6, A10, A11, A15, A16.

1883			Perf. 9½x12	
71	A4	1p rose	160.00	25.00
72	A4	2p gray blue	350.00	55.00
73	A4	1sh pale violet	225.00	30.00
		Nos. 71-73 (3)	735.00	110.00

Beware of faked perfs.
See Nos. 94, 95, 100.

Wmk. 68 Twice Sideways

1882-85		Engr.	Thin Paper	Perf. 12	
74	A5	2sh ultra		60.00	18.00
75	A5	2sh6p vermilion		50.00	22.50
76	A5	5sh car rose ('85)		50.00	25.00
77	A5	10sh brown		95.00	42.50
78	A5	£1 dark green ('83)		165.00	55.00
		Nos. 74-78 (5)		420.00	163.00

The 2sh, 5sh and £1 exist imperf.
There are two varieties of the watermark on Nos. 74-78, as in the 1879-81 issue.
Copies with revenue cancels sell for $3.25-6.50.

1886	Thick Paper	Wmk. 69	Perf. 12	
79	A5	2sh ultra	100.00	35.00
80	A5	2sh6p vermilion	40.00	22.50
81	A5	5sh car rose	37.50	30.00
82	A5	10sh dark brown	100.00	40.00
83	A5	£1 dark green	175.00	60.00
		Nos. 79-83 (5)	452.50	187.50

High value stamps with cancellations removed are offered as unused.
Copies with revenue cancels sell for $3.25-6.50.
See Nos. 126-127, 141-144.

A6

Redrawn

1887-89		Typo.	Wmk. 68	Perf. 12	
84	A6	1p orange		4.50	.20
a.		Imperf., pair		40.00	60.00
85	A6	2p gray blue		9.00	.20
a.		2p deep ultra		11.50	.24
86	A6	2sh red brown ('89)		65.00	20.00
			Perf. 9½x12		
88	A6	2p deep ultra		250.00	110.00
		Nos. 84-88 (4)		328.50	130.40

The 1p has no period after the value.
In the redrawn stamps the shading lines on the neck are not completed at the left, leaving an irregular white line along that side.
Variety "LA" joined exists on Nos. 84-86, 88, 90, 91, 93, 97, 98, 102.
On No. 88 beware of faked perfs.

A7  A8

1890-92			Perf. 12½, 13	
89	A7	½p green	4.50	.32
90	A6	1p orange red	3.00	.15
91	A6	2p gray blue	5.00	.15
92	A8	2½p rose carmine	11.00	.35
93	A6	3p brown ('92)	9.00	2.00
94	A4	4p orange	15.00	1.25
a.		4p yellow	16.00	1.25
b.		"PENGE"	65.00	27.50
95	A6	6p green	11.00	2.00
96	A6	2sh red brown	40.00	8.25
		Nos. 89-96 (8)	98.50	14.47

The ½p and 3p exist imperf.

1895	Wmk. 69	Perf. 12½, 13		
		Thick Paper		
98	A6	1p orange	3.50	.50
99	A6	2p gray blue	3.50	.50
		Perf. 12		
100	A4	1sh pale violet	17.00	3.75
		Nos. 98-100 (3)	24.00	4.75

A9  A10

Moiré on Back

1895	Unwmk.	Perf. 12½, 13		
101	A9	½p green	1.90	1.90
a.		Without moire	55.00	
102	A6	1p orange	2.25	2.25
a.		"PE" missing		
		Wmk. 68		
103	A9	½p green	2.25	.35
a.		½p deep green	1.65	.35
b.		Printed on both sides	60.00	
104	A10	1p orange	2.50	.15
105	A10	2p gray blue	3.25	.25
		Wmk. 69		
		Thick Paper		
106	A9	½p green	1.90	1.90

1895-96	Unwmk.	Thin Paper		
	Crown and Q Faintly Impressed			
107	A9	½p green	2.75	.80
108	A10	1p orange	4.00	1.10
108A	A6	2p gray blue	11.00	

A11  A12

A13

1895-96		Wmk. 68		
109	A11	1p red	8.50	.16
110	A12	2½p rose	9.00	1.75
111	A13	5p violet brown	11.00	1.75
111A	A11	6p yellow green		

A14  A15

A16  A17

A18  A19

TWO PENCE:
Type I - Point of bust does not touch frame.
Type II - First redrawing. The top of the crown, the chignon and the point of the bust touch the frame. The forehead is completely shaded.
Type III - Second redrawing. The top of crown does not touch the frame, though the chignon and the point of the bust do. The forehead and the bridge of the nose are not shaded.

1897-1900			Perf. 12½, 13	
112	A14	½p deep green	3.50	2.00
a.		Perf. 12		150.00
113	A15	1p red	1.50	.15
a.		Perf. 12	1.75	.20
114	A16	2p gray blue (I)	2.00	.15
a.		Perf. 12		6.00
115	A17	2½p rose	17.00	6.25
116	A17	2½p violet, blue	8.50	.70
117	A15	3p brown	8.00	.70
118	A15	4p bright yellow	8.00	.70
119	A18	5p violet brown	7.50	1.25
120	A15	6p yellow green	9.00	.70
121	A19	1sh lilac	13.00	1.65
a.		1sh light violet	16.00	1.65
122	A19	2sh turq blue	32.50	6.00
		Nos. 112-122 (11)	110.50	20.25

1898		Serrated Roulette 13		
123	A15	1p scarlet	5.00	2.00
a.		Serrated and perf. 13	6.00	3.00
b.		Serrated in black	10.00	10.00
c.		Serrated without color and in black	9.00	9.00
d.		Same as "b," and perf. 13	85.00	
e.		Same as "c," and perf. 13	110.00	

Queen Victoria — A20

1899		Typo.	Perf. 12, 12½, 13	
124	A20	½p blue green	1.00	.25

Unwatermarked stamps are proofs.

"Australia" — A21

NINE PENCE:
Type I- "QUEENSLAND" 18x1½mm.
Type II- "QUEENSLAND" 17½x1¼mm.

1903		Wmk. 70	Perf. 12½	
125	A21	9p org brn & ultra, type I	13.00	3.50
a.		9p org brn & ultra, type II	12.00	3.00

See No. 128.

Type of 1882

		Perf. 12, 12½, 13		
1906		Litho.		Wmk. 68
126	A5	5sh rose	150.00	82.50
127	A5	£1 dark green	500.00	150.00

1907		Typo.	Wmk. 13	Perf. 12½
128	A21	9p yel brn & ultra, type I	15.00	3.00
a.		9p yel brn & ultra, type II	27.50	4.25
b.		Perf. 11, type II		240.00

1907		Wmk. 68	Perf. 12½, 13	
129	A16	2p ultra, type II	9.00	1.25
129A	A18	5p dark brown	9.00	1.90
b.		5p olive brown	9.00	1.90

1907-09			Wmk. 12	
130	A20	½p deep green	1.25	.30
131	A15	1p red	1.25	.15
a.		Imperf., pair	200.00	
132	A16	2p ultra, type II	7.50	.15
133	A16	2p ultra, type III	2.25	.15
134	A15	3p pale brown	10.00	1.00
135	A15	4p bright yellow	12.00	2.75
136	A15	4p gray black ('09)	12.00	1.65
137	A18	5p brown	8.50	1.65
a.		5p olive brown	10.50	3.25
138	A15	6p yellow green	12.00	2.50
139	A19	1sh violet	15.00	3.75
140	A19	2sh turquoise bl	35.00	9.00

QUEENSLAND — SOUTH AUSTRALIA

Wmk. 12 Sideways
Litho.
141	A5	2sh6p deep orange	50.00	37.50
142	A5	5sh rose	55.00	37.50
143	A5	10sh dark brown	100.00	35.00
144	A5	£1 blue green	225.00	135.00
		Nos. 130-144 (15)	546.75	268.05

SEMI-POSTAL STAMPS

Queen Victoria, Colors and Bearers — SP1

SP2

Perf. 12, 12½
1900, June 19 — **Wmk. 68**
B1	SP1	1p red lilac	80.00	90.00
B2	SP2	2p deep violet	200.00	210.00

These stamps were sold at 1sh and 2sh respectively. The difference was applied to a patriotic fund in connection with the Boer War.

REGISTRATION STAMPS

R1

Clean-Cut Perf. 14 to 16
1861 — **Wmk. 5** — **Engr.**
F1	R1	(6p) olive yellow	400.00	75.00
a.		Horiz. pair, imperf. vert.	4,500.	

Rough Perf. 14 to 16
F2	R1	(6p) dull yellow	50.00	35.00

1864 — **Perf. 12½ to 13**
F3	R1	(6p) golden yellow	80.00	40.00
a.		Imperf.		
b.		Double impression	900.00	

The reprints are watermarked with a small truncated star and perforated 12.

SOUTH AUSTRALIA
'sau̇th ȯ-'strāl-yə

LOCATION — Central part of southern Australia
GOVT. — British Colony
AREA — 380,070 sq. mi.
POP. — 358,346 (1901)
CAPITAL — Adelaide

South Australia was one of the six British colonies that united in 1901 to form the Commonwealth of Australia.

12 Pence = 1 Shilling
20 Shillings = 1 Pound

South Australia stamps can be mounted in the Scott Australia album.

Values for unused stamps are for examples with original gum as defined in the catalogue introduction. Very fine examples of Nos. 10-60 and O1-O60 will have perforations slightly cutting into the framelines or design on one or more sides due to the narrow spacing of the stamps on the plates. Stamps with perfs clear on all sides are scarce to rare and will command higher to substantially higher prices.

Watermarks

Wmk. 6- Star with Long Narrow Points
Wmk. 7- Star with Short Broad Points 
Wmk. 70- Crown and V  
Wmk. 72- Crown and SA 
Wmk. 73- Crown and SA, Letters Close 
Wmk. 74- Crown and Single-lined A 

Queen Victoria — A1

1855-56 — **Engr.** — **Wmk. 6** — **Imperf.**
London Print
1	A1	1p dark green	2,750.	375.
2	A1	2p dull carmine	600.	80.
3	A1	6p deep blue	2,500.	150.
4	A1	1sh violet ('56)	4,500.	

No. 4 was never put in use. Nos. 1 and 3 without watermark are proofs.

1856-59 — **Local Print**
5	A1	1p deep yel grn ('58)	6,000.	550.00
a.		1p yellow green ('58)		550.00
6	A1	2p blood red	1,500.	80.00
a.		Printed on both sides		
b.		2p orange red ('56)	—	90.00
7	A1	2p pale red ('57)	700.00	60.00
a.		Printed on both sides		650.00
8	A1	6p slate blue ('57)	2,500.	175.00
9	A1	1sh orange ('57)	4,750.	350.00
b.		1sh red orange	—	375.00

1858-59 — **Rouletted**
10	A1	1p yellow grn ('59)	475.00	45.00
a.		Horiz. pair, imperf. between		
b.		1p pale yellow green	500.00	50.00
11	A1	2p pale red ('59)	125.00	22.50
a.		Printed on both sides		
12	A1	6p slate blue	375.00	35.00
13	A1	1sh orange ('59)	1,250.	35.00
c.		Printed on both sides		1,400.

See Nos. 14-16, 19-20, 25-26, 28-29, 32, 35-36, 41-43, 47, 51-52, 69-70, 73, 113, 118. For overprints see Nos. O1-O2, O5, O7, O9, O11-O13, O17, O20, O27, O30, O32, O39-O40, O42, O52, O76, O85.

A2  — A3

Surcharge on #22-24, 34, 49-50

TEN PENCE

1860-69 — **Rouletted**
14	A1	1p dull blue green	45.00	22.50
a.		1p deep green	250.00	65.00
b.		1p bright green	250.00	65.00
15	A1	1p sage green	72.50	27.50
16	A1	2p vermilion ('62)	50.00	4.00
a.		Horiz. pair, imperf. btwn.	700.00	350.00
b.		Rouletted and perf. all around		700.00
c.		Printed on both sides		500.00
18	A2	4p dull violet ('67)	75.00	17.00
19	A1	6p grnsh blue ('63)	65.00	3.75
20	A1	6p dull blue	85.00	3.75
a.		6p sky blue	125.00	6.50
b.		6p Prussian blue	750.00	50.00
c.		Horiz. pair, imperf. between		850.00
d.		6p ultramarine	60.00	3.75
e.		Horiz. pair, imperf. btwn. (#20f)	—	425.00
f.		6p indigo blue	—	60.00
g.		Rouletted and perf. all around (#20f)	—	350.00
21	A3	9p gray lilac ('69)	55.00	9.00
b.		Double impression		
c.		Rouletted and perf. all around	1,750.	275.00
22	A3	10p on 9p red orange (Bl) ('66)	125.00	25.00
23	A3	10p on 9p yel (Bl) ('67)	165.00	21.00
24	A3	10p on 9p yel (Blk) ('69)	1,300.	32.50
a.		Inverted surcharge	—	2,750.
c.		Printed on both sides	—	1,100.
d.		Rouletted x perf. 10		
24E	A1	1sh red brown	135.00	13.00
f.		Vert. pair, imperf. btwn.		1,250.
25	A1	1sh lake brown ('65)	135.00	13.00
a.		Horiz. pair, imperf. btwn.		425.00
26	A1	1sh brown ('63)	140.00	16.00
a.		1sh chestnut ('64)	150.00	11.00
27	A2	2sh carmine ('67)	165.00	27.50
a.		Horiz. pair, imperf. btwn.		1,000.

There are six varieties of the surcharge "TEN PENCE" in this and subsequent issues.
Nos. 16b, 20g, 21c, 28a, 32c, 33a are rouletted remainders that were later perforated.
See Nos. 31, 33, 46, 48, 53, 63, 68, 72, 74, 112, 113B, 119-120. For overprints see Nos. O4, O6, O8, O10, O16, O18, O21, O26, O29, O31, O33, O37-O38, O41B, O43, O53. For surcharges see Nos. 34, 44-45, 49-50, 59, 67, 71, O19, O28, O36, O41. Compare with design A6a.

1867-72 — **Perf. 11½ to 12½xRoulette**
28	A1	1p blue green	225.00	32.50
a.		Rouletted and perf. all around		650.00
29	A1	1p yellow green	140.00	20.00
31	A2	4p dull violet ('68)	1,500.	110.00
a.		4p purple ('69)	—	110.00
32	A1	6p Prus blue	450.00	21.00
b.		6p sky blue	500.00	17.50
c.		Printed on both sides		
d.		Rouletted and perf. all around		300.00
e.		6p indigo blue ('69)	475.00	25.00
33	A3	9p gray lilac ('72)		275.00
34	A3	10p on 9p yel (Bl) ('68)	800.00	35.00
a.		Printed on both sides	—	500.00
35	A1	1sh chestnut ('68)	275.00	30.00
36	A1	1sh lake brown ('69)	275.00	25.00

#44-45 — **3-PENCE**

Perf. 10, 11½, 12½ and Compound
1867-74
41	A1	1p yellow green	45.00	17.50
42	A1	1p blue green	60.00	12.50
a.		Printed on both sides		
43	A1	2p vermilion		1,250.
44	A2	3p on 4p dp bl (Blk) ('70)	60.00	5.50
a.		3p on 4p ultra, black surcharge	125.00	5.50
b.		Surcharge omitted	20,000.	5,000.
c.		Double surcharge		4,500.
d.		Surcharged on both sides		3,250.
45	A2	3p on 4p sl bl (Red) ('70)	425.00	32.50
46	A2	4p dull violet	60.00	9.00

47	A1	6p dark blue	90.00	8.00
a.		6p sky blue	350.00	9.25
b.		Imperf. vert., pair		
48	A3	9p red lilac ('72)	47.50	5.00
a.		9p violet	115.00	5.50
b.		9p red violet	115.00	5.50
c.		Printed on both sides		350.00
49	A3	10p on 9p yel (Bl) ('68)	1,500.	26.00
50	A3	10p on 9p yel (Blk) ('69)	150.00	21.00
51	A1	1sh deep brown	150.00	12.00
52	A1	1sh red brown	100.00	12.00
a.		1sh chestnut	125.00	12.50
53	A2	2sh carmine	60.00	7.50
a.		Printed on both sides		400.00
b.		Horiz. pair, imperf. vert.		

See Nos. 67, O14, O28, O36.

A6  — A6a

1868 — **Typo.** — **Wmk. 72** — **Rouletted**
54	A6a	2p orange red	65.00	4.00
a.		Imperf.		
b.		Printed on both sides		275.00
c.		Horiz. pair, imperf. btwn.		275.00

1869 — **Perf. 11½ to 12½xRoulette**
55	A6a	2p orange red		150.00

1870 — **Perf. 10xRoulette**
56	A6a	2p orange red	350.00	30.00

Perf. 10, 11½, 12½ and Compound
1868-75
57	A6	1p blue green ('75)	24.00	4.50
58	A6a	2p orange red	13.00	1.00
a.		Printed on both sides		200.00
b.		Horiz. pair, imperf. vert.		

Engr.
59	A3	10p on 9p yellow (Bl)		1,500.

1869 — **Typo.** — **Wmk. 6** — **Rouletted**
60	A6a	2p orange red	65.00	11.50
a.		Imperf.		
b.		Printed on both sides		

Perf. 11½ to 12½xRoulette
61	A6a	2p orange red		125.00

Perf. 11½ to 12½
61B	A6a	2p orange red		

See Nos. 62, 64-66, 97-98, 105-106, 115-116, 133-134, 145-146. For overprints see Nos. O3, O22-O25, O34-O35, O44-O47, O55-O56, O62-O63, O68-O69, O74, O78-O79. For surcharges see Nos. 75, O49.

1871 — **Wmk. 70** — **Perf. 10**
62	A6a	2p orange red	75.00	16.00

Engr.
63	A2	4p dull violet	2,250.	350.00
a.		Printed on both sides		

Copies of the 4p from edge of sheet sometimes lack watermark.

Perf. 10, 11½, 12½ and Compound
1876-80 — **Typo.** — **Wmk. 73**
64	A6	1p green	6.00	.50
65	A6	2p orange	4.25	.50
66	A6a	2p blood red ('80)	225.00	7.50
		Nos. 64-66 (3)	235.25	8.50

See #97-98, 105-106, 115-116, 133-134, 145-146.

HALF-PENNY — No. 75
8 PENCE — No. 71

1876-84 — **Engr.** — **Wmk. 7**
67	A2	3p on 4p ultra (Blk)	65.00	17.50
a.		3p on 4p deep blue		15.00
b.		Double surcharge		1,500.
68	A2	4p reddish violet	50.00	5.50
a.		4p dull violet	60.00	9.00
69	A1	6p deep blue	65.00	4.50
a.		Horiz. pair, imperf. vert.		
b.		Imperf.		
70	A1	6p pale ultra ('84)	40.00	2.25
71	A3	8p on 9p bister brn	65.00	7.50
a.		8p on 9p yellow brown	57.50	2.50
b.		8p on 9p gray brown ('80)	52.50	4.00
d.		Double surcharge		380.00
72	A3	9p rose lilac	10.00	5.50
a.		Printed on both sides		300.00

396 SOUTH AUSTRALIA

73 A1 1sh red brown 37.50 3.25
a. 1sh brown 40.00 2.50
b. Horiz. pair, imperf. btwn. 300.00
74 A2 2sh carmine 35.00 4.50
a. Horiz. pair, imperf. vert. 400.00
b. Imperf., pair

For overprint see No. O41.

1882 Wmk. 73 *Perf. 10*

Black Surcharge

75 A6 ½p on 1p green 10.50 4.00

A9

A10

A11

A12

Perf. 10, 11½, 12½ and Compound

1883-90 Typo.

76 A9 ½p chocolate brown 2.25 .25
a. ½p red brown ('89) 2.25 .25
b. ½p bister brown 3.50 .25
78 A10 3p deep green ('86) 6.50 .75
a. 3p olive green ('90) 11.00 1.50
79 A11 4p violet ('90) 7.75 1.75
80 A12 6p blue ('87) 7.75 1.00
Nos. 76-80 (4) 24.25 3.75

See Nos. 96, 100-101, 104, 108-109, 111. For overprints see Nos. O50-O51, O54, O58, O60-O61, O64, O66-O67, O71, O73, O75, O81-O82. For surcharges see Nos. 94-95, 99, O48, O57, O59.

A13

1886-96 *Perf. 10, 11½ to 12½*

81 A13 2sh6p violet 27.50 6.50
82 A13 5sh rose 40.00 16.00
83 A13 10sh green 100.00 25.00
84 A13 15sh buff 200.00 140.00
85 A13 £1 blue 165.00 60.00
86 A13 £2 red brown 475.00 150.00
87 A13 50sh rose red 600.00 200.00
88 A13 £3 olive green 825.00
89 A13 £4 lemon 1,000.
90 A13 £5 gray 2,700.
90A A13 £5 brown ('96) 2,600.
91 A13 £10 bronze 3,000. 700.00
92 A13 £15 silver 6,500.
93 A13 £20 lilac 8,250.

For overprints see Nos. O83-O84.

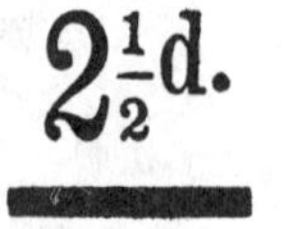

#94, 99

#95

Perf. 10, 11½x12½ and Compound

1891

Brown Surcharge

94 A11 2½p on 4p green 8.00 1.40
a. "½" nearer the "2" 30.00 20.00
b. Pair, imperf. between 375.00
c. Fraction bar omitted 90.00 80.00

Carmine Surcharge

95 A12 5p on 6p red brown 17.00 6.00
a. No period after "D" 165.00

See #99. For overprints see #O48, O57, O59.

Many stamps of the issues of 1855-91 have been reprinted; they are all on paper watermarked Crown and SA, letters wide apart, and are overprinted "REPRINT."

1893 Typo. *Perf. 15*

96 A9 ½p brown 3.00 .18
a. Horiz. pair, imperf. between 125.00
b. Pair, perf. 12 between and perf. 15 around 195.00 50.00

97 A6 1p green 3.50 .20
98 A6a 2p orange 6.50 .15
a. Vert. pair, imperf. between 225.00
99 A11 2½p on 4p green 12.00 1.65
a. "½" nearer the "2" 40.00 35.00
b. Fraction bar omitted
100 A11 4p gray violet 13.00 2.00
101 A12 6p blue 32.50 4.25
Nos. 96-101 (6) 70.50 8.43

Kangaroo, Palm — A16

Coat of Arms — A17

1894, Mar. 1

102 A16 2½p blue violet 13.00 1.50
103 A17 5p dull violet 15.00 2.50

See Nos. 107, 110, 117, 135-136, 147, 151. For overprints see Nos. O65, O70, O72, O80.

1895-97 *Perf. 13*

104 A9 ½p pale brown 3.00 .25
105 A6 1p green 5.25 .50
a. Vert. pair, imperf. between
106 A6a 2p orange 4.25 .15
107 A16 2½p blue violet 7.50 .32
108 A10 3p olive green ('97) 5.00 .30
109 A11 4p bright violet 6.50 .32
110 A17 5p dull violet 7.00 .32
111 A12 6p blue 8.00 .38
Nos. 104-111 (8) 46.50 2.54

Some authorities regard the so-called redrawn 1p stamps with thicker lettering (said to have been issued in 1897) as impressions from a new or cleaned plate.

Perf. 11½, 12½, Clean-Cut, Compound

1896 Engr. Wmk. 7

112 A3 9p lilac rose 12.50 6.50
113 A1 1sh dark brown 26.00 5.50
a. Horiz. pair, imperf. vert.
c. Vert. pair, imperf. btwn. 180.00
113B A2 2sh carmine 32.50 8.00
Nos. 112-113B (3) 71.00 20.00

Adelaide Post Office — A18

1899 Typo. Wmk. 73 *Perf. 13*

114 A18 ½p yellow green 1.75 .25
115 A6 1p carmine 3.00 .20
a. 1p scarlet 2.75 .50
116 A6a 2p purple 2.25 .25
117 A16 2½p dark blue 7.00 .75
Nos. 114-117 (4) 14.00 1.45

See #132, 144. For overprint see #O77.

Perf. 11½, 12½

1901 Engr. Wmk. 72

118 A1 1sh dark brown 24.00 16.00
a. 1sh red brown 24.00 10.00
b. Horiz. pair, imperf. vert.
119 A2 2sh carmine 27.50 15.00

1902

120 A3 9p magenta 20.00 20.00

A19

A20

Perf. 11½, 12½ and Compound

1902-03 Typo. Wmk. 73

121 A19 3p olive green 4.75 .75
122 A19 4p red orange 7.50 1.50
123 A19 6p blue green 6.50 1.50
124 A19 8p ultra (value 19mm long) 8.50 2.25
124A A19 8p ultra (value 16½mm long) ('03) 13.00 3.00
b. "EIGNT" 900.00 3,000.
125 A19 9p claret 8.50 2.25
a. Pair, imperf. between 300.00
126 A19 10p org buff 11.00 3.50
127 A19 1sh brown ('03) 12.00 3.00
a. Horiz. or vert. pair, imperf. btwn. 700.00
128 A19 2sh6p purple 32.50 9.00
129 A19 5sh rose 75.00 52.50
130 A19 10sh green ('03) 110.00 65.00
131 A19 £1 blue 275.00 150.00
Nos. 121-131 (12) 564.25 294.25

1904 *Perf. 12x11½*

132 A18 ½p yellow green 3.00 .60
133 A6 1p rose 6.50 .60
134 A6a 2p purple 6.50 .60
135 A16 2½p dark blue 14.00 1.50
136 A17 5p dull violet 11.00 1.75
Nos. 132-136 (5) 41.00 5.05

1904-08 *Perf. 12 and 12x11½*

137 A20 6p blue green 8.25 1.75
138 A20 8p ultra ('06) 11.50 2.25
139 A20 9p claret 8.00 1.65
139A A20 10p org buff ('07) 20.00 5.25
b. Pair, imperf. between 325.00 225.00
140 A20 1sh brown 12.00 2.00
a. Pair, imperf. between 250.00
141 A20 2sh6p purple ('05) 55.00 8.25
142 A20 5sh scarlet 55.00 32.50
142B A20 10sh green ('08) 140.00 125.00
143 A20 £1 deep blue 200.00 140.00
Nos. 137-143 (9) 509.75 318.65

See Nos. 148-150, 152-157.

1906-12 Wmk. 74

144 A18 ½p green 1.50 .15
145 A6 1p carmine 1.50 .15
146 A6a 2p purple 2.50 .15
a. Horiz. pair, imperf. between
147 A16 2½p dk blue ('11) 10.50 1.50
148 A20 3p ol grn (value 19mm long) 6.50 1.25
a. Horiz. pair, imperf. between
149 A20 3p ol grn (value 17mm long) ('09) 8.50 1.50
150 A20 4p red orange 9.75 1.75
151 A17 5p dull vio ('08) 8.50 2.00
152 A20 6p blue grn ('07) 7.50 1.10
a. Vert. pair, imperf. between 240.00
153 A20 8p ultra ('09) 15.00 5.50
154 A20 9p claret 15.00 3.00
a. Vert. pair, imperf. between 195.00
b. Horiz. pair, imperf. between 225.00
155 A20 1sh brown 11.00 3.00
a. Pair, imperf. between 175.00
156 A20 2sh6p purple ('09) 32.50 10.50
157 A20 5sh lt red ('12) 82.50
Nos. 144-157 (14) 212.75 31.55

OFFICIAL STAMPS

For Departments

Regular Issues Overprinted in Red, Black or Blue:

A. (Architect), A. G. (Attorney General), A. O. (Audit Office), B. D. (Barracks Department), B. G. (Botanical Gardens), B. M. (Bench of Magistrates), C. (Customs), C. D. (Convict Department), C. L. (Crown Lands), C. O. (Commissariat Officer), C. S. (Chief Secretary), C. Sgn. (Colonial Surgeon), C. P. (Commissioner of Police), C. T. (Commissioner of Titles), D. B. (Destitute Board), D. R. (Deed Registry), E. (Engineer), E. B. (Education Board),

G. P. (Government Printer), G. S. (Government Storekeeper), G. T. (Goolwa Tramway), G. F. (Gold Fields), H. (Hospital), H. A. (House of Assembly), I. A. (Immigration Agent), I. E. (Intestate Estates), I. S. (Inspector of Sheep), L. A. (Lunatic Asylum), L. C. (Legislative Council), L. L. (Legislative Library), L. T. (Land Titles), M. (Military), M. B. (Marine Board), M. R. (Manager of Railways), M. R. G. (Main Roads Gambierton), N. T. (Northern Territory),

O. A. (Official Assignee), P. (Police), P. A. (Protector of Aborigines), P. O. (Post Office), P. S. (Private Secretary), P. W. (Public Works), R. B. (Road Board), R. G. (Registrar General of Births, &c.), S. (Sheriff), S. C. (Supreme Court), S.G. (Surveyor General), S. M. (Stipendiary Magistrate), S. T. (Superintendent of Telegraph), T. (Treasurer), T. R. (Titles Registry), V. (Volunteers), V. A. (Valuator), V. N. (Vaccination), W. (Waterworks).

1868-74 Wmk. 6 *Rouletted*

O1 A1 1p green
O2 A1 2p pale red
O3 A6a 2p vermilion
O4 A2 4p dull violet
O5 A1 6p slate blue
O6 A3 9p gray lilac
O7 A1 1sh brown
O8 A2 2sh carmine

Perf. 11½ to 12½ x Roulette

O9 A1 1p green
O10 A2 4p dull violet
O11 A1 6p blue
O12 A1 1sh brown

Perf. 10, 11½, 12½ and Compound

O13 A1 1p green
O14 A2 3p on 4p slate blue (Red)
O16 A2 4p dull violet
O17 A1 6p deep blue
O18 A3 9p violet
O19 A3 10p on 9p yellow (Blk)
O20 A1 1sh brown
O21 A2 2sh carmine

Rouletted

Wmk. 72

O22 A6a 2p orange

Perf. 10 x Roulette

O23 A6a 2p orange

Perf. 10, 11½, 12½ and Compound

O24 A6a 2p orange

Wmk. 70

Perf. 10

O25 A6a 2p orange
O26 A2 4p dull violet

For General Use

Overprinted in Black **O.S.**

Perf. 10, 11½, 12½ and Compound

1874 Wmk. 6

O27 A1 1p green — 450.00
a. Printed on both sides
O28 A2 3p on 4p ultra 150.00
a. No period after "S" 375.00
O29 A2 4p dull violet 27.50 9.50
a. Inverted overprint
b. No period after "S" 25.00
c. Perf. 10 1,650. 400.00
O30 A1 6p deep blue 55.00 9.50
a. No period after "S" 22.50
O31 A3 9p violet 250.00 60.00
a. No period after "S" 300.00
O32 A1 1sh red brown 55.00 16.00
a. Double overprint 27.50
b. No period after "S" 110.00 40.00
O33 A2 2sh carmine 67.50 14.00
a. Double overprint
b. No period after "S" 32.50

1874-75 Wmk. 72

O34 A6 1p blue green 100.00 27.50
a. Inverted overprint
O35 A6a 2p orange 14.00 1.40

1876-86 Wmk. 7

O36 A2 3p on 4p ultra
O37 A2 4p dull violet 100.00 17.00
O38 A2 4p reddish vio 37.50 3.00
a. Double overprint
b. Inverted overprint
c. Dbl. ovpt., one inverted
O39 A1 6p dark blue 62.50 5.00
a. Double overprint 37.50
b. Inverted overprint
O40 A1 6p ultramarine 57.50 4.50
a. Double overprint
b. Inverted overprint
O41 A3 8p on 9p yel brn 425.00 125.00
a. Double overprint 750.00
O41B A3 9p violet 4,000.
O42 A1 1sh red brown 45.00 5.00
a. Inverted overprint 150.00 75.00
b. Double overprint
O43 A2 2sh carmine 110.00 8.00
a. Double overprint 70.00
b. Inverted overprint 75.00

1880-91 Wmk. 73

O44 A6 1p blue green 11.00 .50
a. Inverted overprint 22.50
b. Double overprint 35.00 20.00
c. Dbl. ovpt., one inverted
O45 A6 1p yellow green 12.00 .50
O46 A6a 2p orange 11.00 .25
a. Inverted overprint 10.00
b. Double overprint 70.00 25.00
c. Overprinted sideways
d. Dbl. ovpt., one inverted
e. Dbl. ovpt., both inverted 57.50
O47 A6a 2p blood red 52.50 5.00
O48 A11 2½p on 4p green 35.00 9.50
a. "½" nearer the "2" 75.00
b. Double overprint
c. Pair, one without ovpt.
Nos. O44-O48 (5) 121.50 15.75

1882-90 *Perf. 10*

O49 A6 ½p on 1p green 25.00 8.00
a. Inverted overprint
O50 A11 4p violet 21.00 1.90
O51 A12 6p blue 12.00 1.25
a. Double overprint
Nos. O49-O51 (3) 58.00 11.15

Overprinted in Black **O.S.**

Perf. 10, 11½, 12½ and Compound

1891 Wmk. 7

O52 A1 1sh red brown 42.50 3.50
O53 A2 2sh carmine 100.00 10.00
a. Double overprint

1891-95		**Wmk. 73**		
O54	A9	½p brown	12.00	2.50
O55	A6	1p blue green	12.00	.30
	a.	Double overprint	80.00	
O56	A6a	2p orange	12.00	.30
O57	A11	2½p on 4p green	45.00	2.75
	a.	"½" nearer the "2"	52.50	18.00
	b.	Inverted overprint	100.00	
O58	A11	4p violet	17.50	1.25
O59	A12	5p on 6p red brn	55.00	.80
O60	A12	6p blue	9.75	.75
		Nos. O54-O60 (7)	163.25	10.35
1893				**Perf. 15**
O61	A9	½p brown	15.00	1.75
O62	A6	1p green	11.00	.30
O63	A6a	2p orange	12.00	.15
	a.	Inverted overprint		18.00
	b.	Double overprint		32.50
O64	A11	4p gray violet	65.00	1.75
	a.	Double overprint		21.00
O65	A17	5p dull violet	80.00	4.50
O66	A12	6p blue	20.00	.70
		Nos. O61-O66 (6)	203.00	9.15
1896				**Perf. 13**
O67	A9	½p brown	12.50	1.75
	a.	Triple overprint		
O68	A6	1p green	16.00	.15
O69	A6a	2p orange	11.00	.15
O70	A16	2½p blue violet	60.00	1.40
O71	A11	4p brt violet	65.00	1.75
	a.	Double overprint	30.00	40.00
O72	A17	5p dull violet	60.00	4.25
O73	A12	6p blue	25.00	.90
		Nos. O67-O73 (7)	249.50	10.35

On No. O67a, one overprint is upright, two sideways.

Same Overprint in Dark Blue

1891-95				**Perf. 10**
O74	A6	1p green	150.00	15.00
O75	A12	6p blue		

Black Overprint
Perf. 11½, 12½, Clean-Cut

1897				**Wmk. 7**
O76	A1	1sh brown	40.00	4.50
	a.	Double overprint		

Overprinted in Black O. S.

1900		**Wmk. 73**		**Perf. 13**
O77	A18	½p yellow green	10.00	1.75
O78	A6	1p carmine rose	11.50	.15
	a.	Inverted overprint		
	b.	Double overprint		
O79	A6a	2p purple	11.50	.15
	a.	Inverted ovpt.	40.00	
O80	A16	2½p dark blue	82.50	1.40
	a.	Inverted overprint		30.00
O81	A11	4p violet	65.00	.70
	a.	Inverted overprint	125.00	
O82	A12	6p blue	20.00	.70
		Nos. O77-O82 (6)	200.50	4.85
1901				**Perf. 10**
O83	A13	2sh6p violet	2,000.	2,000.
O84	A13	5sh rose	2,250.	2,250.

On Nos. O77-O82 the letters "O.S." are 11½mm apart; on Nos. O83-O84, 14½mm apart.

Overprinted in Black O.S.

1903		**Wmk. 72**		**Perf. 11½, 12½**
O85	A1	1sh red brown	40.00	25.00

Many of the official stamps are found with one or both the periods after "O.S." missing. This occurs more often in the later than in the earlier issues.

TASMANIA

taz-'mā-nē-ə

LOCATION — An island off the southeastern coast of Australia
GOVT. — British Colony
AREA — 26,215 sq. mi.
POP. — 172,475 (1901)
CAPITAL — Hobart

Tasmania was one of the six British colonies that united in 1901 to form the Commonwealth of Australia. The island was originally named Van Diemen's Land by its discoverer, Abel Tasman, the present name having been adopted in 1853. Stamps of Australia are now used.

12 Pence = 1 Shilling
20 Shillings = 1 Pound

Watermarks

Wmk. 6- Large Star
Wmk. 49- Double-lined Numeral 
Wmk. 75- Double-lined Numeral 
Wmk. 50- Single-lined "2" 
Wmk. 51- Single-lined "4" 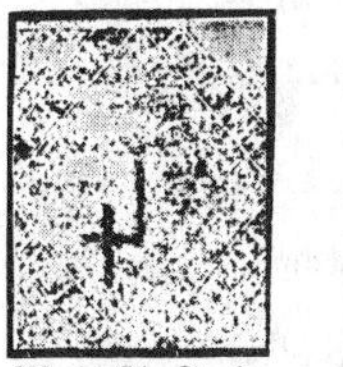
Wmk. 52- Single-lined "10" 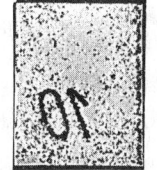
Wmk. 70- V and Crown 
Wmk. 13- Crown & Double-lined A 
Wmk. 76- TAS 
Wmk. 77- TAS 
Wmk. 78- Multiple TAS 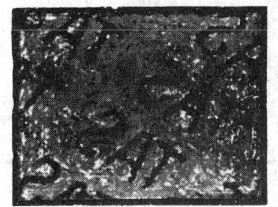

Values for unused stamps are for examples with original gum as defined in the catalogue introduction except for Nos. 1-2a and 10 which are valued without gum as few examples exist with any remaining original gum. Very fine examples of Nos. 17-75a will have perforations touching the design on one or more sides due to the narrow spacing of the stamps on the plates. Stamps with perfs clear of the design on all four sides are scarce and command higher prices.

Queen Victoria
A1   A2

1853, Nov. 1 Unwmk. Engr.				**Imperf.**
1	A1	1p blue	3,250.	750.00
2	A2	4p red orange	2,000.	300.00
	a.	4p yellow orange	2,250.	300.00
		Cut to shape		15.00

Twenty-four varieties of each.
The 4p on vertically laid paper is believed to be a proof. Value, unused, $6,250.

The reprints are made from defaced plates and show marks across the face of each stamp. They are on thin and thick, unwatermarked paper and thin cardboard; only the first are perforated. Nearly all the reprints of Tasmania may be found with and without the overprint "REPRINT."

Nos. 1-47A with pen or revenue cancellations sell for a small fraction of the price of postally used specimens. Copies are found with pen cancellation removed.

Queen Victoria — A3

1855		**Wmk. 6**		**Wove Paper**
4	A3	1p dark carmine	6,000.	825.00
5	A3	2p green	1,800.	500.00
	a.	2p deep green	1,800.	600.00
6	A3	4p deep blue	1,250.	85.00
1856-57				**Unwmk.**
7	A3	1p pale red	6,000.	500.00
8	A3	2p emerald ('57)	7,250.	700.00
9	A3	4p blue ('57)	650.00	85.00
1856				**Pelure Paper**
10	A3	1p brown red	3,000.	600.00
1857				**Wmk. 49, 75**
11	A3	1p carmine	80.00	15.00
	a.	1p orange red	85.00	15.00
	b.	1p brown red	275.00	17.00
	c.	Double impression		165.00
12	A3	2p sage green	130.00	42.50
	a.	2p yellow green	250.00	55.00
	b.	2p green		30.00
13	A3	4p pale blue	100.00	13.00
	b.	Printed on both sides		
		Nos. 11-13 (3)	310.00	

See #17-19, 23-25, 29-31, 35-37, 39-41, 45-47A.

A4    A4a

1858				
14	A4	6p gray lilac	125.00	50.00
	a.	6p red violet	600.00	150.00
	b.	Double impression		200.00
15	A4	6p blue gray	325.00	70.00
16	A4a	1sh vermilion	500.00	55.00
		Nos. 14-16 (3)	950.00	175.00

No. 15 watermarked large star was not regularly issued.

1864				**Rouletted**
17	A3	1p carmine	375.00	125.00
	a.	1p brick red		180.00
18	A3	2p yellow grn	375.00	
19	A3	4p blue		180.00
21	A4	6p gray lilac	225.00	
22	A4a	1sh vermilion	625.00	
1864-69				**Perf. 10**
23	A3	1p brick red	50.00	19.00
	a.	1p carmine	50.00	19.00
	b.	1p orange red	50.00	19.00
24	A3	2p yellow green	275.00	65.00
	a.	2p sage green	375.00	150.00
25	A3	4p blue	125.00	9.00
	a.	Double impression		100.00
26	A4	6p lilac	140.00	12.50
	a.	6p red lilac	375.00	55.00
27	A4	6p slate blue	190.00	20.00
28	A4a	1sh vermilion	100.00	17.50
	a.	Horiz. pair, imperf. vert.		
		Nos. 23-28 (6)	880.00	143.00
1864-69				**Perf. 12, 12½**
29	A3	1p carmine	24.00	6.00
	a.	1p orange red	40.00	16.00
	b.	1p brick red	42.50	22.50
	c.	Double impression		
	d.	Wmkd. "2"		950.00
		As "d.," pen cancel		125.00
30	A3	2p yellow green	130.00	35.00
	a.	2p dark green	200.00	35.00
	b.	2p sage green	250.00	100.00
31	A3	4p blue	65.00	11.00
		Perf. 11½, 12½		
32	A4	6p red lilac	25.00	11.00
	a.	6p purple	75.00	21.00
	b.	6p violet	110.00	17.50
	d.	Horiz. pair, imperf. vert.		
	e.	Double impression		100.00
33	A4	6p slate blue, perf. 12½	250.00	65.00
34	A4a	1sh vermilion	90.00	27.50
	a.	Double impression		165.00
	b.	Horiz. pair, imperf. vert.		
		Nos. 29-34 (6)	584.00	155.50

The reprints are on unwatermarked paper, perforated 11½, and on thin cardboard, imperforate and perforated.

Pin-perf. 5½ to 9½, 13½ to 14½

1867				
35	A3	1p carmine	350.00	77.50
36	A3	2p yellow green	275.00	
37	A3	4p blue	165.00	
38	A4	6p gray	150.00	
38A	A4	6p red lilac	450.00	
38B	A4a	1sh vermilion		

Oblique Roulette

39	A3	1p carmine	675.00	275.00
40	A3	2p yellow green	400.00	
41	A3	4p blue	325.00	
42	A4	6p gray	550.00	
43	A4	6p red lilac	575.00	
44	A4a	1sh vermilion	750.00	
1868				**Serrate Perf. 19**
45	A3	1p carmine	225.00	100.00
46	A3	2p yellow green	175.00	
47	A3	4p blue	650.00	110.00
47A	A3	6p purple	500.00	

Queen Victoria — A5

1870-71 Typo. Wmk. 50				**Perf. 11½**
48	A5	2p blue green	35.00	3.25
	a.	Imperf., pair		
	b.	Perf. 12	45.00	5.00
	d.	2p blue green	80.00	6.50
	e.	As "d," perf. 12	40.00	5.00

See Nos. 49-75, 98, 108-109.

Wmk. 51

49	A5	1p rose ('71)	60.00	20.00
	a.	Imperf., pair	600.00	215.00
50	A5	4p blue	725.00	300.00

Wmk. 52

51	A5	1p rose	40.00	9.00
	a.	Imperf. pair	265.00	250.00
	c.	Perf. 11½	1,000.	
52	A5	10p black	20.00	6.00
	a.	Imperf. pair	120.00	
	b.	Perf. 11½	25.00	20.00

The reprints are on unwatermarked paper. The 4p has also been reprinted on thin cardboard, imperf and perf.

1871-76		**Wmk. 76**		**Perf. 11½**
53	A5	1p rose	4.50	.60
	a.	Imperf.		
	c.	Perf. 12	65.00	
53B	A5	1p vermilion ('73)	250.00	95.00
54	A5	2p deep green ('72)	12.00	.60
	a.	2p yellow green	120.00	1.25
	b.	2p green	45.00	.60
	c.	Imperf. pair		120.00
	d.	2p green, perf. 12	450.00	135.00
	e.	Double impression		
55	A5	3p brown	37.50	4.50
	a.	3p purple brown	37.50	4.50
	b.	As "a," imperf. pair		325.00
56	A5	3p red brown ('71)	37.50	4.50
	a.	3p indian red	35.00	4.50
	b.	Imperf. pair	120.00	
	c.	Vert. pair, imperf. horiz.		
	d.	Perf. 12	85.00	21.00
57	A5	4p dull yellow ('76)	40.00	7.50
	a.	Perf. 12	225.00	15.00

TASMANIA — VICTORIA

58	A5 9p blue	20.00	7.50
a.	Imperf. pair	120.00	
b.	Perf. 12	40.00	40.00
59	A5 5sh bright violet	125.00	25.00
a.	Imperf.		
b.	Horiz. pair, imperf. vert.		
c.	Perf. 12	175.00	150.00
	Pen cancel		.30
	Nos. 53-59 (8)	526.50	145.20

The reprints are on unwatermarked paper, the 5sh has also been reprinted on thin cardboard; all are perforated.

1878   Wmk. 77   Perf. 14

60	A5 1p rose	4.50	.60
61	A5 2p deep green	4.50	.60
62	A5 8p violet brown	15.00	4.50
	Nos. 60-62 (3)	24.00	5.70

The 8p has been reprinted on thin unwatermarked paper, perforated 11½.

1880-83   Perf. 12, 11½

63	A5 3p indian red, perf. 12	9.00	2.00
a.	Imperf. pair	85.00	
b.	Horiz. pair, imperf. between	600.00	
c.	Perf. 11½	10.50	3.00
64	A5 4p lem, perf. 11½ ('83)	40.00	7.50
a.	4p olive yellow, perf. 11½	10.00	21.00
b.	Printed on both sides	210.00	
c.	Imperf.		
d.	4p deep yellow, perf. 12	75.00	22.50

Type of 1871 Surcharged in Black **Halfpenny**

1889   Perf. 14

65	A5 ½p on 1p carmine	9.00	1.75
a.	"al" sideways in surcharge	825.00	500.00

No. 65 has been reprinted on thin cardboard, perforated 12, with the surcharge "Halfpenny" 19mm long.

1889-96   Perf. 11½

66	A5 ½p red orange	2.25	.70
a.	½p yellow orange	2.25	.70
b.	Perf. 12	2.00	.85
67	A5 1p dull red	8.25	2.00
a.	1p vermilion	5.00	2.00
68	A5 2½p car. perf. 12	8.25	3.25
a.	1p pink, perf. 12	27.50	5.00
b.	1p salmon rose, perf. 12	8.25	3.25
c.	Imperf. pair	92.50	92.50

Perf. 12

69	A5 4p bister ('96)	18.00	8.25
70	A5 9p chalky bl ('96)	10.00	3.25
	Nos. 66-70 (5)	46.75	17.45

1891   Wmk. 76   Perf. 11½

71	A5 ½p orange	16.00	8.25
a.	½p brown orange	16.00	8.25
b.	Imperf. pair	75.00	
c.	Perf. 12	35.00	9.25
72	A5 1p salmon rose	21.00	11.50
a.	1p carmine, perf. 12	40.00	20.00
73	A5 4p ol bis, perf. 12	15.00	6.50
	Nos. 71-73 (3)	52.00	26.25

See Nos. 98, 108-109.

Surcharged in Black **d. 2½**

1891   Wmk. 77   Perf. 11½
Surcharge 14mm High

74	A5 2½ on 9p lt blue	6.00	6.50
a.	Dbl. surcharge, one invtd.	210.00	200.00
b.	Imperf. pair	135.00	

Perf. 12
Surcharge 15mm High

75	A5 2½ on 9p lt blue	5.50	5.00
a.	Surcharged in blue		

No. 74 has been reprinted on thin unwatermarked paper, imperforate. There is also a reprint on thin cardboard, in deep ultramarine, with surcharge 16½mm high, and perforated 12.

A8    A9

1892-99   Typo.   Perf. 14

76	A8 ½p orange & vio	.85	.35
77	A9 2½p magenta	2.50	.65
78	A8 5p pale bl & brn	3.50	1.40
79	A8 6p blue vio & blk	3.50	1.50
80	A8 10p red brn & grn ('99)	6.75	5.50
81	A8 1sh rose & green	4.50	1.50
82	A8 2sh6p brown & blue	25.00	8.00
83	A8 5sh brn vio & red	37.50	17.00
84	A8 10sh brt vio & brn	75.00	45.00
85	A8 £1 green & yel	475.00	225.00
	Nos. 76-85 (10)	634.10	305.90

No. 80 shows the numeral on white tablet. See Nos. 99, 110-111.

Lake Marion A10   Mt. Wellington A11

View of Hobart — A12    Tasman's Arch — A13

Spring River, Port Davey — A14    Russell Falls — A15

Mt. Gould and Lake St. Clair — A16

Dilston Falls — A17

1899-1900   Engr.   Wmk. 78   Perf. 14

86	A10 ½p dark green	5.00	1.75
87	A11 1p carmine	5.00	.60
88	A12 2p violet	5.50	.45
89	A13 2½p dark blue	11.00	5.00
90	A14 3p dark brown	8.50	1.75
91	A15 4p ocher	16.00	2.25
92	A16 5p ultramarine	16.00	7.50
93	A17 6p lake	20.00	6.50
	Nos. 86-93 (8)	87.00	25.80

See Nos. 94-97, 102-107, 114-117.

Perf. 11, 12½, 11x12½

1902-03   Litho., Typo.   Wmk. 70

94	A10 ½p green	2.25	.30
95	A11 1p carmine	5.50	.15
96	A11 1p dull red	5.00	.20
97	A12 2p violet	3.25	.15
98	A5 9p blue	9.00	3.00
a.	9p ultramarine	225.00	
b.	9p indigo	90.00	
c.	Perf. 11	7.25	3.50
99	A8 1sh rose & green	12.00	3.75
	Perf. 11	27.50	27.50
	Nos. 94-99 (6)	37.00	7.55

Nos. 94, 97 are litho., Nos. 96, 98-99 typo. No. 95 was printed both ways.

No. 78 Surcharged in Black **1½d**

1904   Wmk. 77   Perf. 14

100	A8 1½p on 5p blue & brn	1.75	1.25

Perf. 11, 12, 12½ and Compound

1905-08   Typo.   Wmk. 13

102	A10 ½p dull green	2.00	.15
a.	Booklet pane of 12		
103	A11 1p carmine	2.00	.15
a.	Booklet pane of 18		
104	A12 2p violet	3.50	.15
105	A14 3p dark brown	7.00	2.00
106	A15 4p ocher	13.00	2.25
107	A17 6p lake	40.00	5.00
108	A5 8p violet brown	19.00	5.00
109	A5 9p blue	8.00	3.00
110	A8 1sh rose & green	13.00	2.50
111	A8 10sh brt vio & brn	100.00	62.50
a.	Perf. 11	175.00	
	Nos. 102-111 (10)	207.50	82.70

Nos. 104-107 also printed litho.

1911   Redrawn

114	A12 2p bright violet	3.50	.30
115	A15 4p dull yellow	16.00	8.00
116	A17 6p lake	17.00	8.00
	Nos. 114-116 (3)	36.50	16.30

The redrawn 2p measures 33½x25mm instead of 32½x24½mm. There are many slight changes in the clouds and other parts of the design.

The 4p is much lighter, especially the waterfall and trees above it. This appears to be a new or cleaned plate rather than a redrawn one.

In the redrawn 6p there are more colored lines in the waterfall and the river and more white dots in the trees.

No. 114 Surcharged in Red **ONE PENNY**

1912

117	A12 1p on 2p bright violet	.85	.50

VICTORIA

vik-'tōr-ē-ə

LOCATION — In the extreme southeastern part of Australia
GOVT. — British Colony
AREA — 87,884 sq. mi.
POP. — 1,201,341 (1901)
CAPITAL — Melbourne

Victoria was one of the six former British colonies which united on Jan. 1, 1901, to form the Commonwealth of Australia.

12 Pence = 1 Shilling
20 Shillings = 1 Pound

Unused values for Nos. 1-16 are for stamps without gum as these stamps are seldom found with original gum. Otherwise, unused values are for stamps with original gum as defined in the catalogue introduction.

Very fine examples of all rouletted, perforated and serrate perforated stamps from Nos. 9-109 and F2 will have roulettes, perforations or serrate perforations touching the design. Examples clear on four sides range from scarce to rare and will command higher prices.

Watermarks

Wmk. 6- Large Star    Wmk. 80

Wmk. 50    Wmk. 80a

Wmk. 81    Wmk. 139

Wmk. 49   Wmk. 75

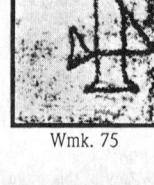

Wmk. 70- V and Crown    Wmk. 13- Crown & Double-lined A

Queen Victoria A1   Victoria on Throne A2

1850   Litho.   Unwmk.   Imperf.

1	A1 1p dull red	875.00	90.00
a.	1p vermilion	600.00	125.00
2	A1 1p rose	375.00	75.00
a.	1p pink	400.00	85.00
3	A1 3p blue	600.00	45.00
a.	3p light blue	550.00	45.00
4	A1 3p indigo	625.00	50.00
	Nos. 1-4 (4)	2,475.00	260.00

Nos. 1-4 exist with and without frame line.

THREE TYPES OF 2p:
Type I - Border, two sets of nine wavy lines crisscrossing. Background, 22 groups of wavy triple lines below "VICTORIA".
Type II - Border, same. Background, 15 groups of wavy triple lines below "VICTORIA."
Type III - Border, two sets of five wavy lines crisscrossing. Background, same as type II.

5	A1 2p lilac, I	3,000.	300.00
a.	2p brn lilac, I	3,750.	325.00
6	A1 2p brn lilac, II	1,000.	90.00
a.	2p gray lilac, II	1,000.	90.00
7	A1 2p brn lilac, III	875.00	80.00
a.	2p gray lilac, III	875.00	90.00
b.	Value omitted, III		2,500.
8	A1 2p yel brn, III	650.00	55.00

Rouletted 7

9	A1 1p vermilion		2,250.
10	A1 3p blue		140.00
a.	3p deep blue	1,600.	190.00

Perf. 12

12	A1 3p blue	2,000.	125.00
a.	3p deep blue	2,000.	125.00

1852   Engr.   Imperf.

14	A2 2p reddish brown	160.00	35.00

#14 was reprinted on paper with watermark 70, imperf. & perf. 12½, overprinted "REPRINT."

1854   Litho.

15	A2 2p gray brown	220.00	35.00
16	A2 2p brown lilac	200.00	30.00
	2p red lilac	250.00	35.00

Fifty varieties.

VICTORIA

A3, A4

1854-58   *Typo.*
17   A3   6p orange   175.00   25.00
   a.   6p red orange   225.00   27.50
See Nos. 19-20, 22-24A, 26-28

Lithographed
18   A4   1sh blue   450.00   20.00
See Nos. 21, 25.

Typographed
19   A3   2sh green   1,100.   125.00

1857-58   *Rouletted 7, 9½*
20   A3   6p orange   525.00   60.00

Lithographed
21   A4   1sh blue   1,500.   90.00

Typographed
22   A3   2sh green ('58)   4,000.   225.00

Small Serrate Perf. 19
23   A3   6p orange   1,200.   100.00

Large Serpentine Perf. 10½
24   A3   6p orange   800.00   55.00

Serrate x Serpentine Perf.
24A   A3   6p orange   125.00

1859   *Litho.*   *Perf. 12*
25   A4   1sh blue   180.00   14.00

Typographed
26   A3   2sh green   260.00   37.50

1861   *Wmk. "SIX PENCE" (80)*
27   A3   6p black   260.00   50.00

Wmk. Single-lined "2" (50)
1864   *Perf. 12, 13*
28   A3   2sh blue, *green*   250.00   8.50

A5

Wmk. Large Star (6)
1856, Oct.   *Engr.*   *Imperf.*
29   A5   1p green   125.00   30.00

1858   *Rouletted 5½-6½*
30   A5   6p blue   125.00   7.00

Nos. 29 and 30 have been reprinted on paper watermarked V and Crown. They are imperforate and overprinted "REPRINT."

A6, A7

1857-61   *Typo.*   *Imperf.*
31   A6   1p yellow green   100.00   15.00
   a.   Printed on both sides   900.00
32   A6   4p vermilion   275.00   15.00
   a.   Printed on both sides   900.00
33   A6   4p rose   200.00   11.50

Rouletted 7 to 9½
34   A6   1p yellow green   325.00   125.00

35   A6   4p rose   525.00   40.00

Perf. 12
36   A6   1p yellow green   600.00   325.00

Unwmk.   *Imperf.*
37   A6   1p blue green   300.00   15.00
38   A6   2p lilac   240.00   15.00
39   A6   4p rose   500.00   40.00

Copies of No. 39 printed in dull carmine on thin paper are regarded as printer's waste and of little value. They are also found printed on both sides.

Rouletted 7 to 9½
40   A6   1p blue green   300.00   10.00
   a.   1p yellow green   400.00   32.50
   b.   Horiz. pair, imperf. btwn.   1,000.
41   A6   2p lilac   1,200.   32.50
42   A6   4p rose   300.00   8.00
   a.   Horiz. pair, imperf. btwn.   1,000.

Perf. 12
43   A6   1p blue green   160.00   10.00
   a.   1p yellow green   200.00   15.00
   b.   Horiz. pair, imperf. btwn.   650.00
44   A6   2p lilac   90.00
45   A6   4p rose   180.00   5.00
   b.   Vert. pair, imperf. btwn.

Serrate Perf. 19
45A   A6   2p lilac   600.00   250.00

Laid Paper
Imperf
46   A6   4p rose   600.00   22.50

Rouletted 5 to 7
47   A6   2p dark lilac   200.00   8.00
   a.   2p brown lilac   225.00   8.00
   b.   2p violet   150.00   5.00
48   A6   4p rose   160.00   5.25

Perf. 12
49   A6   2p lilac   240.00   14.00
50   A6   4p rose   150.00   11.00

Wove Paper
1860   *Wmk. Value in Words (80)*
51   A6   1p yellow green   60.00   8.00
   a.   Wmk. "FOUR PENCE" (error)   2,000.
52   A6   2p gray lilac   140.00   7.50
   a.   2p brown lilac   400.00   24.00

Wmk. "THREE PENCE" (80)
53   A6   2p gray lilac   240.00   10.00

Single-lined "2" (50)
54   A6   2p lilac   160.00   16.00
   a.   2p gray lilac   160.00   16.00
   b.   2p brown lilac   160.00   16.00
   c.   As "b," wmkd. single-lined "6"   4,500.

1860   *Unwmk.*   *Laid Paper*
56   A7   3p deep blue   360.00   45.00

Wmk. Value in Words (80)
Perf. 11½ to 12
1860-62   *Wove Paper*
57   A7   3p blue   175.00   10.00
58   A7   3p claret   175.00   35.00
   a.   Perf. 13   190.00   40.00
59   A7   4p rose   175.00   4.50
60   A7   6p orange   3,000.   325.00
61   A7   6p black   250.00   8.00

Wmk. "FIVE SHILLINGS" (80)
62   A7   4p rose   1,500.   20.00

Wmk. Single-lined "4" (80a)
1863   *Imperf.*
63   A7   4p rose   —   135.00

Rouletted
64   A7   4p rose   2,400.   200.00

Perf. 11½ to 12
65   A7   4p rose   100.00   8.00

1863   *Unwmk.*   *Perf. 12*
66   A7   4p rose   450.00   10.50

A8, A9

1861-63   *Wmk. 80*   *Perf. 11½ to 12*
67   A8   1p green   90.00   9.00
68   A9   6p black   175.00   7.50

Wmk. Double-lined "1" (139)
69   A8   1p green   200.00   13.00

Wmk. Single-lined Figures (50)
70   A8   1p green   45.00   6.50
71   A9   6p black   175.00   6.50

The 1p and 6p of 1861-63 are known on paper without watermark but were probably impressions on the margins of watermarked sheets.

A10, A11, A12, A13

Wmk. Single-lined Figures (50, 80a, 81)
1863-67   *Perf. 11½ to 13*
74   A10   1p green   70.00   4.00
   a.   Double impression   900.00
75   A10   2p gray lilac   75.00   4.00
   a.   2p violet   50.00   2.75
76   A10   4p rose   110.00   3.00
   a.   Double impression   900.00
77   A11   6p blue   87.50   3.00
78   A10   8p orange   300.00   50.00
79   A12   10p brn, *rose*   150.00   4.50
80   A13   1sh blue, *blue*   150.00   3.00
     Nos. 74-80 (7)   942.50   71.50

See Nos. 81-82, 84-96, 99-101, 108-112, 115-119, 124-126, 144, 188. Compare type A11 with type A54.

A14

Wmk. Double-lined "1" (139)
81   A10   1p green   95.00   5.00
82   A10   2p gray lilac   250.00   8.00
83   A14   3p lilac   200.00   35.00
84   A11   6p blue   65.00   6.00
     Nos. 81-84 (4)   610.00   54.00

See Nos. 97, 113, 155, 186. Compare type A14 with type A51.

Wmk. Double-lined "2" (49)
85   A11   6p blue   3,250.

Wmk. Single-lined "4" (80a)
86   A10   1p green   150.00   11.00
87   A10   2p gray lilac   200.00   7.00
88   A11   6p blue   1,500.

Wmk. Double-lined "4" (75)
89   A10   1p green   1,300.   145.00
90   A10   2p gray lilac   200.00   6.00
91   A10   4p rose   225.00   7.00
92   A11   6p blue   325.00   18.00

Wmk. Single-lined "6" (50)
93   A10   1p green   250.00   10.00
94   A10   2p gray lilac   225.00   5.75

Wmk. Single-lined "8" (50)
95   A10   1p green   200.00   15.00
96   A10   2p gray lilac   250.00   6.50
97   A14   3p lilac   200.00   30.00
99   A12   10p slate   400.00   120.00

Wmk. "SIX PENCE" (80)
100   A10   1p green   750.00   21.00
101   A11   6p blue   350.00   15.00

All values of the 1864-67 series except the 3p and 8p are known on unwatermarked paper. They are probably varieties from watermarked sheets which have been so placed on the printing press that some of the stamps escaped the watermark.

One copy of the 2p gray lilac, type A10, is reported to exist with only "PENCE" of watermark 80 showing. Some believe this is part of the "SIX PENCE" watermark.

1870   *Wmk. "THREE PENCE" (80)*
108   A11   6p blue   225.00   6.25

Wmk. "FOUR PENCE" (80)
109   A11   6p blue   500.00   40.00

A15

1867-78   *Wmk. (70)*   *Perf. 11½ to 13*
110   A10   1p green   60.00   2.00
111   A10   2p lilac   85.00   3.25
   a.   2p gray lilac   62.50   2.00
112   A10   2p lilac, *lilac*   90.00   3.00
113   A14   3p red lilac   300.00   18.00
   a.   3p lilac   350.00   20.00
114   A14   3p orange   22.50   2.00
   a.   3p yellow   62.50   2.00
115   A10   4p rose   90.00   3.50
116   A11   6p blue   25.00   2.50
117   A11   6p ultra   27.50   2.50
   a.   6p lilac blue   62.50   2.25
118   A10   8p brn, *rose*   125.00   5.00
119   A13   1sh bl, *blue*   250.00   10.00
120   A15   5sh bl, *yel*   1,700.   450.00
121   A15   5sh bl & rose   160.00   15.00
   a.   Without blue line under crown   140.00   15.00
122   A15   5sh ultra & rose   175.00   20.00

See #126, 144, 188. For surcharge see #124.
For additional stamps of type A15, see No. 191. Compare type A15 with type A58.

A16, A19

1870   *Perf. 13*
123   A16   2p lilac   40.00   2.00
   a.   Perf. 12   40.00   1.25

No. 110 Surcharged in ½ ½
Red   **HALF**

1873, July 19   *Perf. 13, 12*
124   A10   ½p on 1p green   35.00   10.00

9   9
No. 79 Surcharged in
Blue   **NINEPENCE**

1871   *Wmk. Single-lined "10" (81)*
125   A12   9p on 10p brn, *rose*   350.00   11.00
   a.   Double surcharge   1,200.

If you are a Collector of Victoria
Call the experts: *LIANE & SERGIO SISMONDO*
"THE CLASSIC COLLECTOR"
Visit our website: www.sismondostamps.com
BUYING, SELLING, APPRAISALS.
RARE AND CLASSIC STAMPS, POSTAL HISTORY, PROOFS.

10035 Carousel Center Drive
Syracuse, NY 13290-0001
Ph. 315-422-2331, Fax 315-422-2956
P.O. Box 6277, Station J,
Ottawa, Canada K2A 1T4.
Ph. 613-722-1621, Fax: 613-728-7305
e-mail: sismondo@dreamscape.com

VICTORIA

1873-78   Typo.
| 126 | A10 | 8p brown, *rose* ('78) | 125.00 | 6.50 |
| 127 | A19 | 9p brown, *rose* | 125.00 | 6.50 |

For additional stamps of type A19, see Nos. 128-129, 174-175. Compare type A19 with type A55.

1875   Wmk. V and Crown (70)
| 128 | A19 | 9p brown, *rose* | 140.00 | 11.00 |

No. 128 Surcharged in Black

8d   8d

EIGHTPENCE

1876
| 129 | A19 | 8p on 9p brn, *rose* | 175.00 | 14.00 |

1873-81   Perf. 13, 12
130	A21	½p rose ('74)	5.50	.35
131	A21	½p rose, *rose* ('78)	20.00	8.00
132	A22	1p grn ('75)	15.00	.50
133	A22	1p grn, *gray* ('78)	90.00	60.00
134	A22	1p grn, *yel* ('78)	60.00	15.00
135	A23	2p violet	15.00	.25
136	A23	2p vio, *grnsh* ('78)	125.00	15.00
137	A23	2p vio, *buff* ('78)	125.00	15.00
137A	A23	2p vio, *lil* ('78)		340.00
138	A24	1sh bl, *bl* ('76)	55.00	4.00
139	A25	2sh bl, *grn* ('81)	175.00	20.00

See Nos. 140, 156A-159, 184, 189-190. Compare type A21 with type A46, A24 with A56, A25 with A57.

1878   Double-lined Outer Oval
140	A23	2p violet	20.00	.25
a.		Imperf., pair		
b.		Pair, imperf. btwn.		400.00

1881-83   Perf. 12½
141	A26	1p green ('83)	14.00	.90
142	A27	2p brown	27.50	.25
143	A27	2p lilac	12.00	.15
144	A10	4p car rose	200.00	2.75
145	A28	4p car rose	30.00	1.50
		Nos. 141-145 (5)	283.50	5.55

See Nos. 156, 185, 187. Compare type A26 with type A47, A27 with A49, A28 with A52.

1884-86
146	A29	½p rose	6.00	.40
147	A30	1p green	6.00	.20
148	A31	2p violet	4.75	.15
a.		2p lilac rose	10.50	.16
		3p ocher	6.50	
149	A30	3p bister	8.00	.50
150	A32	4p magenta	32.50	2.25
a.		4p violet (error)	4,000.	400.00
151	A30	6p gray blue	42.50	1.40
		6p ultramarine	35.00	1.40
152	A33	8p rose, *rose*	22.50	4.50
153	A34	1sh blue, *yel*	47.50	3.25
154	A33	2sh olive, *grn*	22.50	2.00
		Nos. 146-154 (9)	192.25	14.65

See Nos. 177-178, 192A. Compare types A31-A32 with types A37-A38.

Nos. 114, 145, 138-139 Overprinted "STAMP / DUTY" Vertically in Blue or Black

1885
155	A14	3p orange (Bl)	60.00	21.00
156	A28	4p car rose (Bl)	50.00	12.50
156A	A24	1sh bl, *bl* (Bl)		1,250.
157	A24	1sh bl, *bl* (Bk)	95.00	22.50
158	A25	2sh bl, *grn* (Bk)	75.00	20.00
		Nos. 155-156,157-158 (4)	280.00	76.00

Reprints of 4p and 1sh have brighter colors than originals. They lack the overprint "REPRINT."

1886-87   Perf. 12½
159	A35	½p lilac	16.00	3.00
160	A35	½p rose	4.50	.15
160A	A35	½p scarlet	5.00	.15
161	A36	1p green	5.00	.15
162	A37	2p violet	3.00	.15
a.		2p red lilac	2.00	.15
b.		Imperf.		
163	A38	4p red	6.00	.60
164	A39	6p blue	7.50	.40
165	A39	6p ultra	7.50	.15
166	A40	1sh lilac brown	22.50	1.50
		Nos. 159-166 (9)	77.00	6.25

See No. 180.

Southern Cross A43   **Queen Victoria** A44

1889
| 167 | A41 | 1sh6p blue | 110.00 | 62.50 |
| 168 | A41 | 1sh6p orange | 15.00 | 4.00 |

1890-95   Perf. 12½
169	A42	1p org brn	2.25	.15
a.		1p chocolate brown	2.75	.15
170	A42	1p yel brn	2.00	.15
171	A42	1p brn org, *pink* ('91)	1.65	.50
172	A43	2½p brn red, *yel*	6.00	.50
173	A44	5p choc ('91)	7.00	.50
174	A19	9p green ('92)	20.00	5.00
175	A19	9p rose red	13.00	1.50
		9p red ('95)	13.00	1.50
176	A40	1sh deep claret	15.00	.50
a.		1sh red brown	13.00	.38
b.		1sh maroon	20.00	1.00
177	A33	2sh yel grn	25.00	10.00
178	A33	2sh emerald	20.00	5.00
		Nos. 169-178 (10)	111.90	24.80

In 1891 many stamps of the early issues were reprinted. They are on paper watermarked V and Crown, perforated 12, 12½, and overprinted "REPRINT."

See Nos. 181, 183, 192. Compare type A43 with type A50, A44 with A53.

1897
| 179 | A45 | 1½p yellow green | 4.00 | 1.75 |

See No. 182. Compare type A45 with type A48.

1899
180	A35	½p emerald	5.00	.20
181	A42	1p brt rose	4.00	.15
182	A45	1½p red, *yel*	2.75	1.50
183	A43	2½p dark blue	6.50	1.25
		Nos. 180-183 (4)	18.25	3.10

1901
184	A21	½p blue green	1.90	.50
a.		"VICTCRIA"	65.00	25.00
185	A27	2p violet	4.50	.15
186	A14	3p brown org	14.00	1.50
187	A28	4p bister	25.00	5.00
188	A11	6p emerald	9.00	2.75
189	A24	1sh orange yel	30.00	10.00
190	A25	2sh blue, *rose*	40.00	11.00
191	A15	5sh rose red & bl	60.00	20.00
		Nos. 184-191 (8)	184.40	50.90

1901
| 192 | A42 | 1p olive green | 6.50 | 5.00 |
| 192A | A30 | 3p sage green | 21.00 | 12.00 |

Nos. 192-192A were available for postal use until June 30, 1901, and thereafter restricted to revenue use.

1901   Perf. 11, 12½ and Compound
193	A46	½p blue green	1.50	.15
194	A47	1p rose red	1.25	.15
a.		1p rose	1.25	.15
195	A48	1½p red, *yellow*	2.25	.50
a.		Perf. 11	50.00	32.50
196	A49	2p violet	2.75	.15
197	A50	2½p blue	3.25	.15
198	A51	3p brown org	6.00	.30
199	A52	4p bister	6.00	.35
200	A53	5p chocolate	5.25	.25
201	A54	6p emerald	8.00	.50
202	A55	9p rose	10.00	.75
203	A56	1sh org yel	11.50	.75
204	A57	2sh blue, *rose*	21.00	2.25
205	A58	5sh rose red & bl	65.00	12.50
a.		5sh carmine & blue	65.00	9.00
		Nos. 193-205 (13)	143.75	18.75

See Nos. 209-229, 232.

King Edward VII A59   A60

1901-05
206	A59	£1 deep rose	300.00	125.00
a.		Perf. 11 ('05)	325.00	140.00
208	A60	£2 dk blue ('02)	750.00	275.00
a.		Perf. 11 ('05)	850.00	600.00

See Nos. 230-231.

1903   Redrawn
| 209 | A56 | 1sh yellow | 15.00 | 1.40 |
| a. | | 1sh orange | 13.00 | 1.40 |

No. 209 has the network lighter than No. 203. In the latter the "P" and "E" of "POSTAGE" are in a position more nearly horizontal than on No. 209.

Perf. 11, 12x12½, 12½, 12½x11
1905-10   Wmk. 13
218	A46	½p blue green	1.25	.60
219	A47	1p rose red	1.00	.15
a.		1p carmine rose	2.00	.15
220	A49	2p violet	3.25	.15
a.		2p purple	3.25	.15
221	A50	2½p blue	3.50	.25
222	A51	3p brown org	4.50	.30
a.		3p dull yellow	5.25	.15
223	A52	4p bister	6.50	.40
224	A53	5p chocolate	6.00	.32
225	A54	6p emerald	8.25	.48
226	A55	9p orange brown	10.00	1.10
a.		9p brown rose	13.00	1.10
227	A55	9p car rose	10.00	1.10
228	A56	1sh yellow ('08)	10.00	1.00
229	A58	5sh orange red & ultra	62.50	12.50
a.		5sh rose red & ultra	70.00	12.50
230	A59	£1 pale red ('07)	325.00	110.00
a.		£1 rose ('10)	325.00	100.00
231	A60	£2 dull blue	750.00	300.00
		Nos. 218-229 (12)	126.75	18.35

No. 220 Surcharged in ONE PENNY Red

1912, July 1
| 232 | A49 | 1p on 2p violet | .32 | .20 |

VICTORIA — WESTERN AUSTRALIA

POSTAL-FISCAL STAMPS

On Jan. 1, 1884, all postage and fiscal stamps were made available for either purpose. Therefore all stamps inscribed "Stamp Duty" on hand at that date or issued thereafter can be considered as postage stamps.

Values for used are for postally canceled.

PF5
PF6
PF7
PF8
PF9
PF10
Coat of Arms — PF11

Wmk. V and Crown (70)
1884-96   Typo.   Perf. 12½

AR1	PF5	1sh6p rose	150.00	15.00
AR2	PF6	2sh bl, grn	150.00	12.00
AR3	PF7	2sh6p orange	150.00	30.00
AR4	PF8	3sh bister	87.50	15.00

Lithographed

AR5	PF8	3sh vio, bl	275.00	30.00
AR6	PF9	4sh orange	85.00	5.75
a.		4sh vermilion	85.00	5.75

Typographed

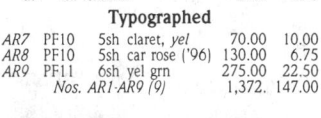

AR7	PF10	5sh claret, yel	70.00	10.00
AR8	PF10	5sh car rose ('96)	130.00	6.75
AR9	PF11	6sh yel grn	275.00	22.50
		Nos. AR1-AR9 (9)	1,372.	147.00

PF12
PF13
PF14
PF15
PF16
PF17
PF18
PF19

AR10	PF12	10sh brown	250.00	100.00
AR11	PF12	10sh gray grn	240.00	17.50

Lithographed

AR12	PF13	15sh lilac		250.00

Typographed

AR13	PF13	15sh pale brn	500.00	150.00

Lithographed

AR14	PF14	£1 org, yel	500.00	47.50
AR15	PF15	£1 5sh pink	1,350.	90.00
AR16	PF16	£1 10sh ol grn	1,000.	22.50
AR17	PF17	35sh violet		250.00
		Revenue cancellation		

Typographed

AR18	PF18	£2 blue	1,200.	65.00
AR19	PF19	45sh gray lilac	2,000.	250.00

PF20
PF21

Litho.

AR20	PF20	£5 rose		200.00

Typographed

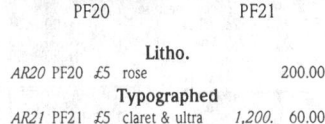

AR21	PF21	£5 claret & ultra	1,200.	60.00

SEMI-POSTAL STAMPS

SP1

Queen Victoria and Figure of Charity — SP2

Wmk. V and Crown (70)
1897, Oct.   Typo.   Perf. 12½

B1	SP1	1p deep blue	15.00	18.00
B2	SP2	2½p red brown	110.00	110.00

These stamps were sold at 1sh and 2sh6p respectively. The premium was given to a charitable institution.

Victoria Cross — SP3

Scout Reporting — SP4

1900

B3	SP3	1p brown olive	70.00	70.00
B4	SP4	2p emerald	140.00	140.00

These stamps were sold at 1sh and 2sh respectively. The premium was given to a patriotic fund in connection with the South African War.

REGISTRATION STAMPS

R1

1854, Dec. 1   Typo.   Unwmk.   *Imperf.*

F1	R1	1sh rose & blue	1,000.	100.00

1857   *Rouletted 7*

F2	R1	1sh rose & blue	5,000.	150.00

LATE FEE STAMP

LF1

1855, Jan. 1   Typo.   Unwmk.   *Imperf.*

I1	LF1	6p lilac & green	650.00	150.00

POSTAGE DUE STAMPS

D1

Wmk. V and Crown (70)
1890   Typo.   Perf. 12½

J1	D1	½p claret & blue	2.00	1.65
J2	D1	1p claret & blue	3.25	1.25
J3	D1	2p claret & blue	5.00	1.50
J4	D1	4p claret & blue	6.00	1.75
J5	D1	5p claret & blue	5.50	1.65
J6	D1	6p claret & blue	6.25	1.50
J7	D1	10p claret & blue	60.00	32.50
J8	D1	1sh claret & blue	35.00	5.00
J9	D1	2sh claret & blue	92.50	42.50
J10	D1	5sh claret & blue	140.00	90.00
		Nos. J1-J10 (10)	355.50	179.30

1891

J11	D1	½p lake & blue	2.50	2.00
J12	D1	1p brown red & blue	4.25	1.25
J13	D1	2p brown red & blue	4.25	.90
J14	D1	4p lake & blue	6.50	4.50
		Nos. J11-J14 (4)	17.50	8.65

1894

J15	D1	½p bl grn & rose	1.65	1.40
J16	D1	1p bl grn & rose	.70	.35
J17	D1	2p bl grn & rose	1.50	.30
J18	D1	4p bl grn & rose	3.50	1.25
J19	D1	5p bl grn & rose	4.00	2.25
J20	D1	6p bl grn & rose	4.00	2.50
J21	D1	10p bl grn & rose	10.00	8.50
J22	D1	1sh bl grn & rose	5.00	2.75
J23	D1	2sh green & rose	60.00	20.00
J24	D1	5sh green & rose	100.00	35.00
		Nos. J15-J24 (10)	190.35	74.30

1906   *Wmk. 13*

J25	D1	½p yel grn & rose	1.65	1.65
J26	D1	1p yel grn & rose	3.00	.65
J27	D1	2p yel grn & rose	6.50	1.50
J28	D1	4p yel grn & rose	13.00	10.00
		Nos. J25-J28 (4)	24.15	13.80

A 5p with wmk. 13 exists but was not issued.

WESTERN AUSTRALIA

ˈwes-tərn o-ˈstrāl-yə

LOCATION — Western part of Australia, occupying about a third of that continent
GOVT. — British Colony
AREA — 975,920 sq. mi.
POP. — 184,124 (1901)
CAPITAL — Perth

Western Australia was one of the six British colonies that united on January 1, 1901, to form the Commonwealth of Australia.

12 Pence = 1 Shilling
20 Shillings = 1 Pound

Unused values for Nos. 1-10 are for stamps without gum as these stamps are seldom found with original gum. Otherwise, unused values are for stamps with original gum as defined in the catalogue introduction.

Very fine examples of all rouletted and perforated stamps from Nos. 6-34 have roulettes or perforations touching the design. Examples clear on all four sides range from scarce to rare and will command higher prices.

Watermarks

Wmk. 82- Swan

Wmk. 83- Crown and W A

Wmk. 70- V and Crown

Wmk. 13- Crown & Double-lined A

Western Australia stamps can be mounted in the Scott Australia album.

WESTERN AUSTRALIA — AUSTRALIA

Wmk. 74 -
Crown and
Single-lined A

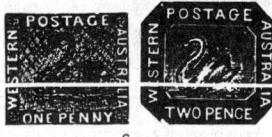

Swan
A1   A2

1854-57   Engr.   Wmk. 82   Imperf.
1   A1   1p black   750.   190.

Litho.
2   A2   2p brown, red ('57)   1,300.   425.
a.   2p brown, deep red ('57)   1,500.   475.
b.   Printed on both sides   1,500.   750.

See Nos. 4, 6-7, 9, 14-39, 44-52, 54, 59-61. For surcharges see Nos. 41, 55-56.

A3   A4

3   A3   4p blue   275.   150.
a.   Frame inverted   60,000.
     As "a," cut to shape   16,000.
b.   4p slate blue   1,000.   575.
4   A2   6p bronze ('57)   3,000.   600.
5   A4   1sh pale brown   400.   225.
a.   1sh dark brown   500.   375.
b.   1sh dark red brown   800.   500.
c.   1sh pale red brown   1,800.

Engraved
Rouletted
6   A1   1p black   1,750.   500.

Lithographed
7   A2   2p brown, red ('57)   3,250.   1,200.
a.   Printed on both sides
8   A3   4p blue   1,400.   600.
9   A2   6p bronze ('57)   3,500.   1,000.
10   A4   1sh brown   2,000.   700.

The 2p, 4p and 6p are known with pin-perforation but this is believed to be unofficial.

1860   Engr.   Imperf.
14   A1   2p vermilion   100.00   87.50
a.   2p pale orange   95.00   60.00
15   A1   4p blue   185.00   800.00
16   A1   6p dull green   1,100.   600.00

Rouletted
17   A1   2p vermilion   600.00   200.00
a.   2p pale orange   600.00   200.00
18   A1   4p deep blue   2,500.   —
19   A1   6p dull green   400.00

1861   Clean-Cut Perf. 14 to 16
20   A1   1p rose   330.00   80.00
a.   Imperf.
21   A1   2p blue   70.00   25.00
a.   Imperf., pair
b.   Horiz. pair, imperf. vert.
22   A1   4p vermilion   265.00   150.00
a.   Imperf.
23   A1   6p purple brn   175.00   35.00
a.   Imperf.
24   A1   1sh green   300.00   45.00
a.   Imperf.

Rough Perf. 14 to 16
24B   A1   1p rose   200.00   27.50
24C   A1   6p pur brn, bluish   750.00   50.00
24D   A1   1sh deep green   1,200.   350.00

Perf. 14
25   A1   1p rose   140.00   45.00
25A   A1   2p blue   70.00   30.00
25B   A1   4p vermilion   200.00   85.00

Unwmk.   Perf. 13
26   A1   1p lake   40.00   5.50
28   A1   6p violet   90.00   32.50

1865-79   Wmk. 1   Perf. 12½
29   A1   1p bister   40.00   2.00
30   A1   1p yel ocher   60.00   5.50
31   A1   2p yellow   45.00   .60
a.   2p lilac (error) ('79)   7,500.   3,750.
32   A1   4p carmine   50.00   5.50
a.   Double impression   6,000.
33   A1   6p violet   62.50   6.00
a.   6p lilac   130.00   6.00
b.   6p red lilac   120.00   6.00
c.   Double impression
34   A1   1sh bright green   85.00   10.50
a.   1sh sage green   140.00   18.00
   Nos. 29-34 (6)   342.50   30.10

1872-78   Perf. 14
35   A1   1p bister   50.00   2.00
36   A1   1p yellow ocher   40.00   .48
37   A1   2p yellow   40.00   .40
38   A1   4p carmine   200.00   65.00
39   A1   6p lilac   80.00   4.00
   Nos. 35-39 (5)   410.00   71.88

A5   A8

1872   Typo.
40   A5   3p red brown   26.00   3.75
a.   3p brown   26.00   3.75

See #53, 92. For surcharges see #57, 69-72A.

No. 31 Surcharged **ONE PENNY**
in Green

1875   Engr.   Perf. 12½
41   A1   1p on 2p yellow   200.00   45.00
a.   Pair, one without surcharge
b.   "O" of "ONE" omitted
c.   Triple surcharge

Forged surcharges exist.

1882   Wmk. 2   Perf. 12
44   A1   1p ocher yellow   85.00   1.65
46   A1   2p yellow   110.00   1.10
47   A1   4p carmine   160.00   27.50
48   A1   6p pale violet   275.00   27.50
   Nos. 44-48 (4)   630.00   57.75

1882   Perf. 14
49   A1   1p ocher yellow   14.00   .20
50   A1   2p yellow   18.00   .20
51   A1   4p carmine   72.50   11.50
52   A1   6p pale violet   80.00   2.50
a.   6p violet   47.50   2.50

Typographed
53   A5   3p red brown   8.50   .70
a.   3p brown   12.50   .45
   Nos. 49-53 (5)   193.00   15.10

1883   Engr.   Perf. 12x14
54   A1   1p ocher yellow   1,650.   300.00

Nos. 44 and 49 Surcharged in Red **½**

1884   Perf. 12
55   A1   ½p on 1p ocher yel   9.00   12.00

Perf. 14
56   A1   ½p on 1p ocher yel   13.00   15.00

No. 40 Surcharged in Green **1d.**

1885   Typo.   Wmk. 1
57   A5   1p on 3p red brown   27.50   8.50
a.   1p on 3p brown   12.00   6.00
b.   "1" with straight top   27.50   11.00

Wmk. Crown and C A (2)
1885   Typo.   Perf. 14
58   A8   ½p green   2.00   .15
      See No. 89.

1888   Engr.
59   A1   1p rose   12.00   .70
60   A1   2p slate   30.00   2.00
61   A1   4p red brown   82.50   18.00
   Nos. 59-61 (3)   124.50   20.70

A9   A10

A11   A12

1890-93   Typo.
62   A9   1p carmine rose   6.50   .15
63   A10   2p slate   10.00   .15
64   A11   2½p blue   6.00   .80
65   A12   4p orange brown   6.00   .80
66   A12   5p bister   8.25   1.00
67   A12   6p violet   14.00   .80
68   A12   1sh olive green   16.00   2.25
   Nos. 62-68 (7)   66.75   5.95

See Nos. 73-74, 76, 80, 90, 94.

Nos. 40 and 53a **ONE PENNY**
Surcharged in Green

1893   Wmk. Crown and C C (1)
69   A5   1p on 3p red brown   9.50   5.00
a.   1p on 3p brown   8.00   3.25
b.   Double surcharge   725.00

Wmkd. Crown and C A (2)
70   A5   1p on 3p brown   40.00   9.00

Nos. 40a and 53a **Half-penny**
Surcharged in Green

1895   Wmk. Crown and C C (1)
71   A5   ½p on 3p brown   7.00   3.00
a.   Double surcharge   700.00

Green and Red Surcharge
72   A5   ½p on 3p yellow   125.00

Wmk. Crown and C A (2)
72A   A5   ½p on 3p brown   75.00

After the supply of paper watermarked Crown and C C was exhausted, No. 72A was printed. Ostensibly this was to provide samples for Postal Union distribution, but a supply for philatelic demands was also made.

Types of 1890-93 and

A15

1899-1901   Typo.   Wmk. 83
73   A9   1p carmine rose   3.50   .15
74   A10   2p yellow   9.00   .15
75   A15   2½p blue ('01)   6.00   .20
   Nos. 73-75 (3)   18.50   .50

A16   A17

A18   A19

A20   A21

A22   Southern Cross — A23

Queen Victoria
A24   A25

Perf. 12½, 12x12½
1902-05   Wmk. 70
76   A9   1p carmine rose   6.50   .15
a.   1p salmon
b.   Perf. 11   100.00   5.00
   Perf. 12½x11   180.00
77   A16   2p yellow   3.25   .20
a.   Perf. 11   125.00   5.50
b.   Perf. 12½x11   220.00
79   A17   4p orange brn   6.00   .80
a.   Perf. 11   375.00   110.00
80   A12   5p olive bis ('05)   72.50   40.00
a.   Perf. 11   45.00   21.00
81   A18   8p pale yel grn   20.00   2.75
82   A19   9p orange   27.50   4.00
a.   Perf. 11   60.00   40.00
83   A20   10p red   27.50   5.50
84   A21   2sh red (shades), yel   42.50   8.25
a.   Perf. 11   125.00   55.00
85   A22   2sh6p dk bl, rose   40.00   7.75
86   A23   5sh blue green   70.00   19.00
87   A24   10sh violet   175.00   60.00
88   A25   £1 brown org   475.00   225.00
   Nos. 76-88 (12)   965.75   373.40

Perf. 12½, 12x12½
1905-12   Wmk. 13
89   A8   ½p dp green ('10)   2.25   .35
90   A9   1p rose   3.00   .20
e.   Perf. 11   13.00   2.50
f.   Perf. 12½x11   200.00   82.50
91   A16   2p yellow   3.00   .15
a.   Perf. 11   11.00   4.50
b.   Perf. 12½x11   230.00   95.00
92   A5   3p brown   6.50   .40
a.   Perf. 11   12.00   2.75
b.   Perf. 12½x11   265.00   82.50
93   A17   4p orange brn   8.00   1.50
a.   4p bister brown   8.00   1.50
b.   Perf. 11   465.00   90.00
94   A12   5p olive bis   10.00   .70
a.   Perf. 11   25.00   8.50
95   A18   8p pale yel grn ('12)   16.00   17.00
96   A19   9p orange   21.00   3.00
a.   Perf. 11   65.00   55.00
97   A20   10p red orange   21.00   10.00
98   A23   5s blue green   140.00   40.00
   Nos. 89-98 (10)   230.75   73.30

For surcharge see No. 103.

A26   A27

1906-07   Wmk. 83   Perf. 14
99   A26   6p bright violet   18.00   .70
100   A27   1sh olive green   25.00   6.00

1912   Wmk. 74   Perf. 11½x12
101   A26   6p bright violet   11.00   3.00
102   A27   1sh gray green   22.50   9.00
a.   Perf. 12½

No. 91 Surcharged **ONE PENNY**

1912   Wmk. 13   Perf. 12½
103   A16   1p on 2p yellow   .75   .40

Stamps of Western Australia were replaced by those of Australia.

AUSTRALIA

ȯ-ˈstrāl-yə

LOCATION — Oceania, south of Indonesia, bounded on the west by the Indian Ocean
GOVT. — Self-governing dominion of the British Commonwealth
AREA — 2,967,909 sq. mi.
POP. — 15,276,100 (est. 1982)
CAPITAL — Canberra

AUSTRALIA

Australia includes the former British colonies of New South Wales, Victoria, Queensland, South Australia, Western Australia and Tasmania.

12 Pence = 1 Shilling
20 Shillings = 1 Pound
100 Cents = 1 Dollar (1966)

Catalogue values for unused stamps in this country are for Never Hinged items, beginning with Scott 197 in the regular postage section, Scott C6 in the air post section, Scott J71 in the postage due section, and all of the Australian Antarctic Territory.

Watermarks

Wmk. 8- Wide Crown and Wide A

Wmk. 9- Wide Crown and Narrow A

Wmk. 10- Narrow Crown and Narrow A

Wmk. 11- Multiple Crown and A

Wmk. 12- Crown and Single-lined A

Wmk. 13- Large Crown and Double-lined A

Wmk. 55- Large Crown and NSW

Wmk. 203- Small Crown and A Multiple

Wmk. 228- Small Crown and C of A Multiple

Kangaroo and Map — A1

1913 Typo. Wmk. 8 Perf. 11½, 12

1	A1	½p yellow green	5.00 1.75
2	A1	1p carmine	6.75 .50
d.		Wmkd. sideways	800.00 210.00
3	A1	2p gray	22.50 4.00
4	A1	2½p dark blue	25.00 8.50
5	A1	3p olive bister	40.00 4.50
6	A1	4p orange	45.00 18.00
7	A1	5p orange brown	40.00 25.00
8	A1	6p ultra	45.00 13.00
9	A1	9p purple	40.00 20.00
10	A1	1sh blue green	45.00 12.50
11	A1	2sh brown	150.00 75.00
12	A1	5sh yellow & gray	250.00 140.00
13	A1	10sh pink & gray	600.00 425.00
		Never hinged	725.00
14	A1	£1 ultra & brown	1,300. 1,000.
		Never hinged	1,500.
15	A1	£2 dp rose & blk	2,250. 1,400.
		Nos. 1-12 (12)	714.25 322.75
		Set, never hinged	1,300.

On No. 4 "2½d" is colorless in solid blue background.
See Nos. 38-59, 96-102, 121-129, 206.

King George V
A2

Kookaburra (Kingfisher)
A3

1913-14 Unwmk. Engr. Perf. 11

17	A2	1p carmine	4.25 4.25
		Never hinged	5.75
a.		Vert. pair, imperf. between	2,000.
18	A3	6p lake brown ('14)	70.00 35.00
		Never hinged	150.00

See No. 95.

A4

ONE PENNY
Die I - Normal die, having outside the oval band with "AUSTRALIA" a white line and a heavy colored line.
Die Ia - As die I with a small white spur below the right serif at foot of the "1" in left tablet.
Die II - A heavy colored line between two white lines back of the emu's neck. A white scratch crossing the vertical shading lines at the lowest point of the bust.

TWO PENCE
Die I - The numeral "2" is thin. The upper curve is 1mm. across and a very thin line connects it with the foot of the figure.

Have You Got The Complete Picture?

Don't Believe Everything You Read

Unlike other catalogs, the two volume Stanley Gibbons British Commonwealth book lists a staggering 37 different 6d 'Kangaroos', 27 in blue and 10 in brown, including different dies, important plate flaws, official perfins and overprints and inverted watermarks. Used prices range from £1.50 to £1000, so the additional information given in the Stanley Gibbons catalog could raise a very ordinary stamp to a quite exceptional one.

Stanley Gibbons Set The Standards

With all these extra facts, figures and extensive footnotes, combined with the unique knowledge that Stanley Gibbons is the only major publisher whose catalog represents the companies price list, you can rest assured that Stanley Gibbons catalogs will provide you with the complete picture.

If You Collect British Commonwealth You Need This Catalogue

Volume 1 GB & A-I Countries $46.00
Volume 2 J-Z Countries $46.00
SAVE $10
Special Offer Plus FREE P&P $82.00

To Order, Or For Information Of Other Products Complete & Fax The Coupon Below. Alternatively, Email, Phone Or Write To Stanley Gibbons.

FAX YOUR ORDER ON (011) 44 1425 470247
OR EMAIL sales@stangib.demon.co.uk

PLEASE SEND: Vat No. 239 088341

Item	Description	QTY	Price	Total
$2811(99)	British Commonwealth Part 1 (Countries A-I inc. GB)		$46.00	
$2811(99)	British Commonwealth Part 1 (Countries J-Z)		$46.00	
$2811/2812(99)	Two Volume Set Offer (Special Set Offer)		$82.00	

P&P FREE
Total $

☐ Please find my cheque/postal order enclosed
☐ I authorise you to charge my ☐ Mastercard ☐ Visa ☐ Diners ☐ Amex
Card No: ☐☐☐☐ ☐☐☐☐ ☐☐☐☐ ☐☐☐☐
Expiry Date: ☐☐ SG Account No: M☐☐☐☐☐☐
Signature: _____ Date: _____
Name: (Mr/Mrs/Miss/Ms) _____
Address: _____
_____
_____
Zip code: _____ Tel No: _____

☐ Please also send me a copy of your Stanley Gibbons Mail Order Colour Brochure

To: **STANLEY GIBBONS PUBLICATIONS**
5, Parkside, Christchurch Road, Ringwood, Hants, England BH24 3SH
Tel: 011 44 1425 472363 Fax: 011 44 1425 470247 e.mail sales@stangib.demon.co.uk

STANLEY GIBBONS
SCOTTS/99

AUSTRALIA

OUR PRICES ARE LOWER & OUR SERVICE IS BETTER FOR:
1. AUSTRALIA & TERRITORIES
2. AUSTRALIAN STATES
3. NEW ZEALAND 4. SOUTH PACIFIC IS.

Please Write, Phone or Fax for your FREE copy of one of the above LISTS. Want Lists are welcome.
Member ASDA (Aust.) & APS.

PITTWATER PHILATELIC SERVICE
P.O. Box 478, Avalon Beach, NSW 2107, AUSTRALIA
Phone +61-2-9974-5707 • Fax+61-2-9974-1177

Die II - The "2" is thicker than in die I. The top curve is 1½mm across and a strong white line connects it with the foot of the figure. There are thin vertical lines across the ends of the groups of short horizontal lines at each side of "TWO PENCE."

THREE PENCE
Die I - The ends of the thin horizontal lines in the background run into the solid color of the various parts of the design. The numerals are thin and the letters of "THREE PENCE" are thin and irregular.
Die II - The oval about the portrait, the shields with the numerals, etc., are outlined by thin white lines which separate them from the horizontal background lines. The numerals are thick and the letters of "THREE PENCE" are heavy and regular.

FIVE PENCE
Die I - The top of the flag of the "5" is slightly curved.
Die II - The top of the flag of the "5" is flat. There are thin white vertical lines across the ends of the short horizontal lines at each side of "FIVE PENCE."

1914-24	Typo.	Wmk. 9	Perf. 14	
19	A4	½p emerald ('15)	2.50	.40
a.		Thin "½" at right	1,400.	700.00
20	A4	½p orange ('23)	2.50	1.25
21	A4	1p red (I)	4.25	.15
a.		1p carmine rose (I)	8.25	.80
b.		1p red (Ia)	375.00	4.75
c.		1p carmine (II) ('18)	60.00	30.00
		Never hinged	95.00	
22	A4	1p vio (I) ('22)	3.50	.60
a.		1p red violet	5.50	1.50
		Never hinged	8.00	
23	A4	1p green (I) ('24)	3.50	.20
24	A4	1½p choc ('18)	5.00	.20
a.		1½p red brown	5.50	.20
		Never hinged	12.00	
b.		1½p black brown	4.50	.25
		Never hinged	6.75	
25	A4	1½p emerald ('23)	2.75	.15
26	A4	1½p scarlet ('24)	2.00	.15
27	A4	2p brn org (I) ('20)	5.00	.25
a.		2p orange (I) ('20)	6.50	.30
		Never hinged	19.00	
b.		Booklet pane of 6		
28	A4	2p red (I) ('22)	5.00	.15
29	A4	2p red brn (I) ('24)	15.00	3.75
30	A4	3p ultra (I) ('24)	25.00	2.25
31	A4	4p orange ('15)	17.00	2.25
a.		4p yellow	110.00	13.00
32	A4	4p violet ('21)	17.50	13.00
33	A4	4p lt ultra ('22)	37.50	4.50
34	A4	4p ol bis ('24)	27.50	4.00
35	A4	4½p violet ('24)	22.50	4.00
36	A4	5p org brn (I) ('15)	18.00	3.00
37	A4	1sh4p lt blue ('20)	65.00	19.00
		Nos. 19-37 (19)	281.00	59.25
		Set, never hinged	675.00	

See Nos. 60-76, 113-120, 124.

1915			Perf. 11½, 12	
38	A1	2p gray	42.50	11.00
		Never hinged	95.00	
39	A1	2½p dark blue	42.50	15.00
		Never hinged	140.00	
40	A1	6p ultra	125.00	19.00
		Never hinged	275.00	
41	A1	9p violet	125.00	32.50
		Never hinged	275.00	
42	A1	1sh blue green	125.00	20.00
		Never hinged	325.00	
43	A1	2sh brown	375.00	87.50
		Never hinged	900.00	
44	A1	5sh yellow & gray	700.00	165.00
		Never hinged	1,500.	
		Nos. 38-44 (7)	1,535.	350.00

1915-24			Wmk. 10	
45	A1	2p gray	20.00	5.00
46	A1	2½p dark blue	20.00	7.50
a.		"1" of fraction omitted	10,000.	3,500.
47	A1	3p olive bister	17.00	3.00
48	A1	6p ultra	45.00	7.00
a.		6p chalky blue	65.00	7.00
49	A1	6p yel brn ('23)	20.00	1.75
50	A1	9p violet	35.00	4.50
a.		9p lilac	30.00	4.50
51	A1	1sh blue grn ('16)	35.00	2.50
		Wmkd. sideways ('20)	72.50	72.50
52	A1	2sh brown ('16)	150.00	15.00
53	A1	2sh vio brn ('24)	50.00	20.00
54	A1	5sh yel & gray ('18)	180.00	80.00
a.		Wmkd. sideways	3,000.	2,500.
55	A1	10sh brt pink & gray ('17)	400.00	150.00
		Never hinged	750.00	
		Wmkd. sideways	5,000.	3,000.
56	A1	£1 ultra & brn ('16)	1,250.	700.00
a.		£1 ultra & brn org ('16)	1,300.	700.00
b.		Wmkd. sideways	5,000.	2,000.
57	A1	£1 gray ('24)	450.00	275.00
		Never hinged	825.00	
58	A1	£2 dp rose & blk ('19)	2,250.	1,250.
59	A1	£2 rose & vio brn ('24)	1,750.	1,200.
		Nos. 45-54 (10)	572.00	146.25
		Set, never hinged	1,300.	

		Perf. 14, 14½, 14½x14		
1918-23			Wmk. 11	
60	A4	½p emerald	3.00	1.00
		Never hinged	4.25	
a.		Thin "½" at right	110.00	45.00
61	A4	1p rose (I)	20.00	9.00
		Never hinged	27.50	
62	A4	1p dl grn (I) ('24)	4.75	4.75
		Never hinged	7.00	
63	A4	1½p choc ('19)	5.00	1.00
		Never hinged	11.00	
a.		1½p red brown ('19)	8.00	1.00
		Never hinged	12.50	
		Nos. 60-63 (4)	32.75	15.75

1924			Unwmk.	Perf. 14
64	A4	1p green (I)	4.25	3.75
		Never hinged	5.50	
65	A4	1½p carmine	4.25	3.00
		Never hinged	6.75	

		Perf. 14, 13½x12½		
1926-30			Wmk. 203	
66	A4	½p orange	1.40	1.00
a.		Perf. 14 ('27)	5.25	5.25
		Never hinged	6.75	
67	A4	1p green (I)	1.50	.40
a.		1p green (Ia)	47.50	60.00
		Never hinged	65.00	
b.		Perf. 14	2.75	.45
		Never hinged	4.50	
68	A4	1½p rose red ('27)	2.75	.15
c.		Perf. 14 ('26)	6.00	.65
		Never hinged	12.00	
69	A4	1½p red brn ('30)	4.00	2.00
70	A4	2p red brn (I) ('28)	7.00	4.00
a.		Perf. 14 ('27)	24.00	16.00
		Never hinged	40.00	
71	A4	2p red (II) ('30)	4.00	.20
a.		2p red (I) ('30)	5.00	1.65
		Never hinged	12.00	
c.		Unwmkd. (II) ('31)	1,500.	1,000.
72	A4	3p ultra (I)	22.50	2.25
a.		3p ultra (II) ('29)	14.00	1.00
		Never hinged	30.00	
b.		Perf. 14	17.50	4.50
		Never hinged	37.50	
73	A4	4p ol bis ('29)	16.00	.80
a.		Perf. 14 ('28)	42.50	22.50
		Never hinged	85.00	
74	A4	4½p dk vio ('27)	17.00	3.75
a.		Perf. 13½x12½ ('28)	47.50	13.00
		Never hinged	67.50	
75	A4	5p brn buff (II) ('30)	16.00	.95
76	A4	1sh4p pale turq bl ('28)	85.00	20.00
a.		Perf. 14 ('27)	125.00	67.50
		Never hinged	300.00	
		Nos. 66-76 (11)	177.15	35.50
		Set, never hinged	275.00	

For surcharges & overprints see #106-107, O3-O4.

Parliament House, Canberra — A5

1927, May 9		Unwmk. Engr.	Perf. 11	
94	A5	1½p brown red	.45	.20
		Never hinged	.85	
a.		Vert. pair, imperf. btwn.	2,750.	2,500.

Opening of Parliament House at Canberra.

Melbourne Exhibition Issue
Kookaburra Type of 1914

1928, Oct. 29				
95	A3	3p deep blue	3.75	3.00
		Never hinged	5.25	
a.		Pane of 4	110.00	135.00
		Never hinged	175.00	

No. 95a was issued at the Melbourne Intl. Phil. Exhib. No marginal inscription. Printed in sheets of 60 stamps (15 panes). No. 95 was printed in sheets of 120 and issued Nov. 2 throughout Australia.

Kangaroo-Map Type of 1913
Perf. 11½, 12

1929-30			Wmk. 203	Typo.
96	A1	6p brown	21.00	3.00
		Never hinged	27.50	
97	A1	9p violet	30.00	4.00
		Never hinged	70.00	
98	A1	1sh blue green	27.50	2.25
		Never hinged	65.00	
99	A1	2sh red brown	60.00	9.00
		Never hinged	140.00	
100	A1	5sh yel & gray	190.00	60.00
		Never hinged	325.00	
101	A1	10sh pink & gray	325.00	250.00
		Never hinged	575.00	
102	A1	£2 dl red & blk ('30)	1,800.	425.00
		Nos. 96-102 (7)	2,453.	753.25

For overprint see No. O5.

Black Swan — A6    Capt. Charles Sturt — A7

1929, Sept. 28		Unwmk. Engr.	Perf. 11	
103	A6	1½p dull red	.75	.75
		Never hinged	1.40	

Centenary of Western Australia.

1930, June 2				
104	A7	1½p dark red	.40	.15
		Never hinged	.45	
105	A7	3p dark blue	3.50	3.00
		Never hinged	6.00	

Capt. Charles Sturt's exploration of the Murray River, cent.

FIVE

Nos. 68 and 74a surcharged

PENCE

1930		Wmk. 203	Perf. 13½x12½	
106	A4	2p on 1½p rose red	.75	.25
		Never hinged	1.50	
107	A4	5p on 4½p dark violet	5.00	5.00
		Never hinged	10.00	

"Southern Cross" over Hemispheres A8

Perf. 11, 11½

1931, Mar. 19			Unwmk.	
111	A8	2p dull red	.75	.15
		Never hinged	1.10	
112	A8	3p blue	4.75	3.25
		Never hinged	8.00	
		Nos. 111-112, C2 (3)	13.00	10.90

Trans-oceanic flights (1928-1930) of Sir Charles Edward Kingsford-Smith (1897-1935).
See #C3 for similar design. For overprints see #CO1, O1-O2.

Types of 1913-23 Issues
Perf. 13½x12½

1931-36			Typo.	Wmk. 228
113	A4	½p orange ('32)	2.50	1.65
		Never hinged	3.00	
114	A4	1p green (I)	1.00	.15
		Never hinged	1.90	
115	A4	1½p red brn ('36)	6.00	4.50
		Never hinged	7.25	
116	A4	2p red (II)	1.75	.15
		Never hinged	2.50	
117	A4	3p ultra (II) ('32)	17.50	.30
		Never hinged	21.00	
118	A4	4p ol bis ('33)	16.00	.45
		Never hinged	26.00	
120	A4	5p brn buff (II) ('32)	12.00	.30
		Never hinged	20.00	

Perf. 11½, 12; 13½x12½ (1sh4p)

121	A1	6p yel brn ('36)	16.00	11.00
		Never hinged	20.00	
122	A1	9p violet ('32)	11.00	1.75
		Never hinged	35.00	
124	A4	1sh4p lt blue ('32)	47.50	6.00
		Never hinged	135.00	
125	A1	2sh red brn ('35)	4.00	.90
		Never hinged	6.00	
126	A1	5sh yel & gray ('32)	125.00	18.00
127	A1	10sh pink & gray ('32)	325.00	100.00
128	A1	£1 gray ('35)	450.00	165.00
129	A1	£2 dl rose & blk ('34)	2,000.	350.00
		Nos. 113-129 (15)	3,035.	660.15

For redrawn 2sh see No. 206. For overprints see Nos. O6-O11.

Sydney Harbor Bridge — A9

1932, Mar. 14		Unwmk. Engr.	Perf. 11	
130	A9	2p red	1.90	.50
		Never hinged	2.25	

IF YOU COLLECT...
AUSTRALIA
... you need our bimonthly pricelists, featuring Australia, Canada, Great Britain, Ireland, Newfoundland, New Zealand and United States.
Call 800-842-5305 (USA) or 800-437-8036 (Canada) to request our mailings, or write...
THE PERF GAUGE
P.O. Box 2648
Inverness, FL 34451-2648
ALWAYS BUYING!

AUSTRALIA

131	A9 3p blue	4.00	3.00
	Never hinged	6.75	
132	A9 5sh gray green	350.00	200.00
	Never hinged	575.00	

Wmk. 228
Perf. 10½
Typo.

133	A9 2p red	1.65	.80
	Never hinged	2.75	

Opening of the Sydney Harbor Bridge on Mar. 19, 1932.
Value for 5sh, used, is for CTO copies.
For overprints see Nos. O12-O13.

Kookaburra A14

Male Lyrebird A16

1932, June 1   **Perf. 13½x12½**

139	A14 6p light brown	15.00	.50
	Never hinged	25.00	

1932, Feb. 15   **Unwmk.**   **Perf. 11**
Size: 21½x25mm

141	A16 1sh green	37.50	.75
	Never hinged	75.00	

See #175, 300. For overprint see #O14.

Yarra Yarra Tribesman, Yarra River and View of Melbourne — A17

Perf. 10½
1934, July 2   **Engr.**   **Wmk. 228**

142	A17 2p vermilion	1.10	.30
	Never hinged	1.75	
a.	Perf. 11½	3.75	.75
	Never hinged	6.50	
143	A17 3p blue	2.75	2.50
	Never hinged	5.25	
a.	Perf. 11½	4.25	2.50
	Never hinged	6.50	
144	A17 1sh black	40.00	16.00
	Never hinged	67.50	
a.	Perf. 11½	40.00	20.00
	Never hinged	72.50	
	Nos. 142-144 (3)	43.85	18.80

Centenary of Victoria.

Merino Sheep — A18

1934, Nov. 1   **Perf. 11½**

147	A18 2p copper red	2.50	.20
	Never hinged	3.50	
148	A18 3p dark blue	8.50	4.50
	Never hinged	12.00	
149	A18 9p dark violet	35.00	25.00
	Never hinged	67.50	
	Nos. 147-149 (3)	46.00	29.70

Capt. John Macarthur (1767-1834), "father of the New South Wales woolen industry."
There are two types of the 2p.

Cenotaph in Whitehall, London — A19

George V on His Charger "Anzac" — A20

1935, Mar. 18   **Perf. 13½x12½**

150	A19 2p red	.65	.15
	Never hinged	.90	

Perf. 11

151	A19 1sh black	40.00	25.00
	Never hinged	70.00	

Anzacs' landing at Gallipoli, 20th anniv.

1935, May 2   **Perf. 11½**

152	A20 2p red	.40	.15
	Never hinged	.70	
153	A20 3p blue	3.00	2.25
	Never hinged	7.50	
154	A20 2sh violet	37.50	30.00
	Never hinged	70.00	
	Nos. 152-154 (3)	40.90	32.40

25th anniv. of the reign of King George V.

Amphitrite Joining Cables between Australia and Tasmania — A21

1936, Apr. 1

157	A21 2p red	.35	.15
		.45	
158	A21 3p dark blue	3.25	2.00
		4.75	

Australia/Tasmania telephone link.

Proclamation Tree and View of Adelaide, 1936 — A22

1936, Aug. 3

159	A22 2p red	.40	.15
		1.10	
160	A22 3p dark blue	3.25	3.25
	Never hinged	5.00	
161	A22 1sh green	12.00	6.00
		20.00	
	Nos. 159-161 (3)	15.65	9.40

Centenary of South Australia.

Gov. Arthur Phillip at Sydney Cove — A23

1937, Oct. 1   **Perf. 13x13½**

163	A23 2p red	.90	.15
	Never hinged	1.90	
164	A23 3p ultra	2.75	1.65
	Never hinged	4.50	
165	A23 9p violet	16.00	11.00
	Never hinged	25.00	
	Nos. 163-165 (3)	19.65	12.80

150th anniversary of New South Wales.

Kangaroo A24

Queen Elizabeth A25

King George VI A26   A27

Koala — A28

Merino Sheep — A29

Kookaburra (Kingfisher) A30

Platypus A31

Queen Elizabeth and King George VI in Coronation Robes
A32   A33

King George VI and Queen Elizabeth — A34

Two Types of A25 and A26:
Type I - Highlighted background. Lines around letters of Australia Postage and numerals of value.
Type II - Background of heavy diagonal lines without the highlighted effect. No lines around letters and numerals.

Perf. 13½x14, 14x13½
1937-46   **Engr.**   **Wmk. 228**

166	A24 ½p org, perf. 15x14 ('42)	.15	.15
a.	Perf. 13½x14 ('38)	.70	.25
	Never hinged	1.25	
167	A25 1p emerald (I)	.20	.15
168	A26 1½p dull red brn (II)	3.00	1.75
a.	Perf. 15x14 ('41)	4.25	3.50
	Never hinged	6.25	
169	A26 2p scarlet (I)	.30	.15
170	A27 3p dp ultra, thin paper ('38)	12.00	.80
a.	3p ultramarine	12.00	.60
	Never hinged	30.00	
171	A28 4p grn, perf. 15x14 ('42)	.85	.15
a.	Perf. 13½x14 ('38)	2.50	.90
	Never hinged	5.00	
172	A29 5p pale rose vio, perf. 14x15 ('46)	1.25	.50
a.	Perf. 14x13½ ('38)	2.50	.55
	Never hinged	4.00	
173	A30 6p vio brn, perf. 15x14 ('42)	.60	.15
a.	Perf. 13½x14	5.25	.85
	Never hinged	15.00	
b.	6p chocolate, perf. 15x14	1.00	.15
	Never hinged	1.50	
174	A31 9p sep, perf. 14x15 ('43)	1.75	.15
a.	Perf. 14x13½ ('38)	3.75	.90
	Never hinged	7.25	
175	A16 1sh gray grn, perf. 15x14 ('41)	1.10	.15
a.	Perf. 13½x14	17.00	2.00
	Never hinged	47.50	
176	A27 1sh4p magenta ('38)	1.50	.50

Perf. 13½

177	A32 5sh dl red brn ('38)	5.00	2.50
178	A33 10sh dl gray vio ('38)	30.00	13.00
179	A34 £1 bl gray ('38)	60.00	27.50
	Nos. 166-179 (14)	117.70	47.60
	Set, never hinged	200.00	

No. 175 measures 17½x21½mm.
See #223A, 293, 295, 298, 300. For surcharge & overprints see #190, M1, M4-M5, M7.

1938-42   **Perf. 15x14**

180	A25 1p emerald (II)	.55	.25
181	A25 1p dl red brn (II) ('41)	.50	.15
181B	A26 1½p bl grn (II) ('41)	.60	.15
182	A26 2p scarlet (II)	.60	.15
182B	A26 2p red vio (II) ('41)	.20	.15

183	A27 3p dk ultra ('40)	12.00	.60
183A	A27 3p dk vio brn ('42)	.20	.15
	Nos. 180-183A (7)	14.65	1.60
	Set, never hinged	35.00	

No. 183 differs from Nos. 170-170a in the shading lines on the king's left eyebrow which go downward, left to right, instead of the reverse. Also, more of the left epaulette shows.
For surcharges & overprint see #188-189, M3.

Coil Perforation

A special perforation was applied to stamps intended for use in coils to make separation easier. It consists of small and large holes (2 small, 10 large, 2 small) on the stamps' narrow side. Some of the stamps so perforated were sold in sheets.
This coil perforation may be found on Nos. 166, 181, 182, 182B, 193, 215, 223A, 231, 257, 315-316, 319, 319a and others.

For Australia & the Entire British Commonwealth Pre-1960

Aron R. Halberstam Philatelists, Ltd.
POB 150168, Van Brunt Station
Brooklyn, NY 11215-0168
Tel: 718-788-3978
Fax: 718-965-3099
Toll Free: 800-343-1303

Call or write for our Free Price List, or send us your Want Lists.

VISA   MasterCard   AMERICAN EXPRESS
Accepted on all orders.

We are also eager buyers of better Commonwealth collections and singles or sets. Let us know what you have to offer.

PTS   APS   ASDA

FREE PRICE LIST
AUSTRALASIA & SOUTH PACIFIC
12,000 prices — includes every Scott Number, Postal Stationery, Back of Book, etc.
Also important Auctions & Postal Bid Sales
Write, Fax or E-mail me today!

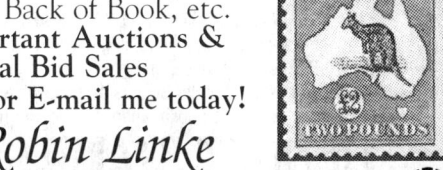

Robin Linke
181 Jersey Street Wembley Western Australia 6014
Tel: +61-8-9387-5327   Fax: +61-8-9387-1646
Email: linke@inf.net.au • Website:http://www.inf.net.au/~linke

AUSTRALIA

Nurse, Sailor, Soldier
and Aviator — A35

Perf. 13½x13
1940, July 15   Engr.   Wmk. 228
184 A35   1p green   1.00   .15
     Never hinged   2.00
185 A35   2p red   1.00   .15
     Never hinged   2.00
186 A35   3p ultra   4.00   3.00
     Never hinged   7.00
187 A35   6p chocolate   12.50   10.00
     Never hinged   21.00
     Nos. 184-187 (4)   18.50   13.30

Australia's participation in WWII.

No. 182 Surcharged in Blue   2½d

1941, Dec. 10   Perf. 15x14
188 A26   2½p on 2p red   .20   .15
     Never hinged   .25

No. 183 Surcharged in Blue and Yellow   3½d

189 A27   3½p on 3p dk ultra   .40   .35
     Never hinged   .50

No. 172a Surcharged in Purple   5½d

Perf. 14x13½
190 A29   5½p on 5p pale rose violet   3.25   3.25
     Never hinged   4.00
     Nos. 188-190 (3)   3.85   3.75

Queen Elizabeth A36   A37
King George VI A38   A39  
George VI and Blue Wrens — A40 
Emu — A41 

1942-44   Engr.   Perf. 15x14
191 A36   1p brown vio ('43)   .15   .15
192 A37   1½p green   .20   .15
193 A38   2p lt rose vio ('44)   .15   .15
194 A39   2½p red   .20   .15
195 A40   3½p ultramarine   .20   .15
196 A41   5½p indigo   .35   .15
     Nos. 191-196 (6)   1.25   .90
     Set, never hinged   1.75

See #224-225. For overprint see #M2.

Catalogue values for unused stamps in this section, from this point to the end of the section, are for Never Hinged items.

Duke and Duchess of Gloucester — A42

1945, Feb. 19   Engr.   Perf. 14½
197 A42   2½p brown red   .15   .15
198 A42   3½p bright ultra   .25   .25
199 A42   5½p indigo   .25   .25
     Nos. 197-199 (3)   .65   .65

Inauguration of the Duke of Gloucester as Governor General.

Official Crest and Inscriptions — A43

Dove and Australian Flag A44

Angel of Peace; "Motherhood" and "Industry" A45

1946, Feb. 18   Wmk. 228   Perf. 14½
200 A43   2½p carmine   .20   .15
201 A44   3½p deep ultra   .20   .15
202 A45   5½p deep yellow green   .40   .35
     Nos. 200-202 (3)   .80   .75

End of WWII. See #1456-1458.

Sir Thomas Mitchell and Map of Queensland — A46

1946, Oct. 14
203 A46   2½p dark carmine   .15   .15
204 A46   3½p deep ultra   .20   .15
205 A46   1sh olive green   .80   .35
     Nos. 203-205 (3)   1.15   .75

Sir Thomas Mitchell's exploration of central Queensland, cent.

Kangaroo-Map Type of 1913 Redrawn

1945, Dec.   Typo.   Perf. 11½
206 A1   2sh dk red brown   4.50   1.65

The R and A of AUSTRALIA are separated at the base and there is a single line between the value tablet and "Two Shillings." On No. 125 the tail of the R touches the A, while two lines appear between value tablet and "Two Shillings." There are many other minor differences in the design.

For overprint see No. M6.

John Shortland — A47
Pouring Steel — A48 
Loading Coal — A49 

1947, Sept.   Engr.   Perf. 14½x14
207 A47   2½p brown red   .30   .15

Perf. 14½
208 A48   3½p deep blue   .25   .30
209 A49   5½p deep green   .35   .30
     Nos. 207-209 (3)   .90   .75

150th anniv. of the discovery of the Hunter River estuary, site of Newcastle by Lieut. John Shortland. By error the 2½p shows his father, Capt. John Shortland.

Princess Elizabeth — A50

Perf. 14x14½
1947, Nov. 20   Wmk. 228
210 A50   1p brown violet   .20   .15

See No. 215.

Hereford Bull A51
Crocodile A52 

1948, Feb. 16   Perf. 14½
211 A51   1sh3p violet brown   1.90   .70
212 A52   2sh chocolate   2.50   .15

See No. 302.

William J. Farrer — A53

Design: No. 214, Ferdinand von Mueller.

1948   Perf. 14½x14
213 A53   2½p red   .20   .15
214 A53   2½p dark red   .20   .15

William J. Farrer (1845-1906), wheat researcher, and Ferdinand von Mueller (1825-1896), German-born botanist.

Issue dates: #213, July 12. #214, Sept. 13.

Elizabeth Type of 1947
1948, Aug.   Unwmk.   Perf. 14x14½
215 A50   1p brown violet   .15   .15

Scout in Uniform — A55
Arms of Australia — A56 

1948, Nov. 15   Engr.   Wmk. 228
216 A55   2½p brown red   .20   .15

Pan-Pacific Scout Jamboree, Victoria, Dec. 29, 1948 to Jan. 9, 1949. See No. 249.

1949-50   Wmk. 228   Perf. 14x13½
218 A56   5sh dark red   4.00   .15
219 A56   10sh red violet   21.00   .40
220 A56   £1 deep blue   35.00   3.25
221 A56   £2 green ('50)   140.00   15.00
     Nos. 218-221 (4)   200.00   18.80

Henry Lawson A57
Outback Mail Carrier and Plane A58 

Perf. 14½x14
1949, June 17   Unwmk.
222 A57   2½p rose brown   .15   .15

Henry Hertzberg Lawson (1867-1922), author and poet.

1949, Oct. 10
223 A58   3½p violet blue   .25   .15

UPU, 75th anniv.

Types of 1938, 1942-44 & A59

Aborigine A59
John Forrest A60 

1948-50   Unwmk.   Perf. 14½x14
223A A24   ½p orange ('49)   .15   .15
224 A37   1½p green ('49)   .25   .15
225 A38   2p lt rose violet   .30   .15
     Wmk. 228
226 A59   8½p dark brown ('50)   .50   .35
     Nos. 223A-226 (4)   1.20   .80

Issue dates: 2p, Dec., ½p, Sept., 1½p, Aug. 29, 8½p, Aug. 14.
See Nos. 248, 303.

1949, Nov. 28   Wmk. 228
227 A60   2½p brown red   .15   .15

Forrest (1847-1918), explorer & statesman.

New South Wales A61
Victoria A62 

First stamp designs.

Perf. 14½x14
1950, Sept. 27   Unwmk.
228 A61   2½p rose brown   .25   .15
229 A62   2½p rose brown   .25   .15
   a.   Pair, #228-229   .65   .40

Cent. of Australian adhesive postage stamps. Issued in sheets of 160 stamps containing alternate copies of Nos. 228 and 229.

"G'Day," if you collect:

AUSTRALIA & AUSTRALIA STATES

...THEN OUR POSTAL BID SALES ARE FOR YOU!

We regularly offer thousands of interesting lots and as your 'greenback' buys well over $1.50 Aussie, there's some great buys to be made. Fair Dinkum! Our catalogues are free to regular bidders and available now, so why not write, or fax now, for your complimentary copy of our next catalogue.

BUDGET STAMP SALES

G.P.O. Box 4131, Melbourne, Victoria 3001, AUSTRALIA
Phone/Fax (24 hour) direct +61-3-9650-7748

AUSTRALIA

Elizabeth A63
George VI A64 
A65 
A66 

1950-51 Engr. Unwmk.
230	A63	1½p deep green	.30	.15
231	A63	2p yellow grn ('51)	.20	.15
232	A64	2½p violet brn ('51)	.20	.15
233	A64	3p dull green ('51)	.30	.15
		Nos. 230-233 (4)	1.00	.60

Issue dates: 1½p, June 19, 2p, Mar. 28, 2½p, May 23, 3p, Nov. 14.

1950-52   Wmk. 228
234	A64	2½p red	.15	.15
235	A64	3p red ('51)	.15	.15
236	A65	3½p red brown ('51)	.30	.15
237	A65	4½p scarlet ('52)	.40	.35
238	A65	6½p choc ('52)	.30	.15
238A	A65	6½p blue green ('52)	.40	.15
239	A66	7½p deep blue ('51)	.45	.15
		Nos. 234-239 (7)	2.15	1.55

Issued: 2½p, 4/12; 3p, 2/28; 7½p, 10/31; 3½p, 11/28; 4½p, #238, 2/20; #238A, 4/9.

Sir Edmund Barton A67
Duke of York Opening First Federal Parliament A68 

Designs: No. 241, Sir Henry Parkes. 1sh6p, Parliament House, Canberra.

1951, May 1   Engr.   Perf. 14½x14   Unwmk.
240	A67	3p carmine	.40	.15
241	A67	3p carmine	.40	.15
a.		Pair, #240, 241	.80	.65
242	A68	5½p deep blue	.40	.15
243	A68	1sh6p red brown	1.25	.90
		Nos. 240-243 (4)	2.45	1.85

Founding of the Commonwealth of Australia, 50th anniv.

Edward Hammond Hargraves A69
King George VI A70 

Design: No. 245, Charles Joseph Latrobe (1801-1875), first governor of Victoria.

1951, July 2
244	A69	3p rose brown	.25	.15
245	A69	3p rose brown	.25	.15
a.		Pair, #244, 245	.65	.65

Discovery of gold in Australia, cent. (No. 244); Establishment of representative government in Victoria, cent. (No. 245). Sheets contain alternate rows of Nos. 244 and 245.

1952, Mar. 19   Wmk. 228   Perf. 14½
247	A70	1sh½p slate blue	1.65	.25

Aborigine Type of 1950 Redrawn
Size: 20½x25mm
248	A59	2sh6p dark brown	3.25	.25

Portrait as on A59; lettering altered and value repeated at lower left. See No. 303.

Scout Type of 1948 Dated "1952-53"
Perf. 14x14½
1952, Nov. 19   Wmk. 228
249	A55	3½p red brown	.20	.15

Pan-Pacific Scout Jamboree, Greystanes, Dec. 30, 1952, to Jan. 9, 1953.

Modern Dairy, Butter Production — A71

Perf. 14½
1953, Feb. 11   Unwmk.   Typo.
250	A71	3p shown	.75	.15
251	A71	3p Wheat	.75	.15
252	A71	3p Beef	.75	.15
a.		Strip of 3, #250-252	6.50	6.50
253	A71	3½p shown	.75	.15
254	A71	3½p Wheat	.75	.15
255	A71	3½p Beef	.75	.15
a.		Strip of 3, #253-255	4.50	4.50
		Nos. 250-255 (6)	4.50	4.50

Both the 3p and 3½p were printed in panes of 50 stamps: 17 Butter, 17 Wheat and 16 Beef. The stamps were issued to encourage food production.

Queen Elizabeth II — A72

Perf. 14½x14
1953-54   Unwmk.   Engr.
256	A72	1p purple	.15	.15
256A	A72	2½p deep blue ('54)	.25	.15
257	A72	3p dark green	.15	.15

Wmk. 228
258	A72	3½p dark red	.25	.15
258B	A72	6½p orange ('54)	.90	.15
		Nos. 256-258B (5)	1.80	.75

Issue dates: 3½p, Apr. 21. 3p, June 17. 1p, Aug. 19. 2½p, 6½p, June 23.
See Nos. 292 and 296.

Coronation Issue

Queen Elizabeth II A73

1953, May 25   Unwmk.
259	A73	3½p rose red	.25	.15
260	A73	7½p violet	.70	.45
261	A73	2sh dull green	2.25	1.10
		Nos. 259-261 (3)	3.20	1.70

Boy and Girl with Calf — A74

1953, Sept. 3   Perf. 14½
262	A74	3½p dp green & red brn	.25	.15

Official establishment of Young Farmers' Clubs, 25th anniv.

Lieut. Gov. David Collins A75 
Tasmania Stamp of 1853 A77

Sullivan Cove, Hobart A76

#264, Lieut. Gov. William Paterson (facing left).

1953, Sept. 23   Perf. 14½x14
263	A75	3½p red brown	.35	.15
264	A75	3½p red brown	.35	.15
a.		Pair, #263-264	1.25	1.10
265	A76	2sh green	4.25	3.25
		Nos. 263-265 (3)	4.95	3.55

Settlement in Tasmania, 150th anniv. Sheets contain alternate rows of Nos. 263 and 264.

1953, Nov. 11   Perf. 14½
266	A77	3p red	.20	.15

Tasmania's first postage stamps, cent.

Elizabeth II and Duke of Edinburgh — A78

Elizabeth II — A79
Telegraph Pole and Key — A80 

1954, Feb. 2   Perf. 14½x14, 14x14½
267	A78	3½p rose red	.20	.15
268	A78	3½p purple	.35	.75
269	A78	2sh green	1.50	1.00
		Nos. 267-269 (3)	2.05	1.90

Visit of Queen Elizabeth II and the Duke of Edinburgh, 1954.

1954, Apr. 7   Engr.   Perf. 14
270	A80	3½p dark red	.25	.15

Inauguration of the telegraph in Australia, cent.

Red Cross and Globe — A81
Swan — A82 

1954, June 9   Perf. 14½x14
271	A81	3½p deep blue & red	.20	.15

Australian Red Cross Society.

1954, Aug. 2   Unwmk.   Perf. 14½
274	A82	3½p black	.20	.15

Western Australia's first postage stamp, cent.

Diesel and Early Steam Locomotives A83

1954, Sept. 13   Perf. 14x14½
275	A83	3½p red brown	.20	.15

Centenary of Australian railroads.

Have you found a typo or other error in this catalogue? Inform the editors via our web site or e-mail
sctcat@scottonline.com

Antarctic Flora and Fauna and Map A84
Olympic Circles and Arms of Melbourne A85 

1954, Nov. 17   Perf. 14
276	A84	3½p black	.20	.15

Australia's interest in the Antarctic continent.

1954, Dec. 1
277	A85	2sh dark blue	2.00	1.50

16th Olympic Games to be held in Melbourne Nov.-Dec. 1956. See No. 286.

Globe, Flags and Rotary Emblem — A86

1955, Feb. 23   Perf. 14x14½
278	A86	3½p carmine	.20	.15

Rotary International, 50th anniv.

Elizabeth II — A87
Top of US Monument, Canberra — A88 

1955, Mar. 9   Wmk. 228   Perf. 14½
279	A87	1sh½p dk gray blue	3.50	.25

See No. 301.

1955, May 4   Unwmk.   Perf. 14x14½
280	A88	3½p deep ultra	.20	.15

Friendship between Australia and the US.

Cobb and Company Mail Coach — A89

1955, July 6   Perf. 14½x14
281	A89	3½p dark brown	.20	.15
282	A89	2sh brown	2.50	1.90

Pioneers of Australia's coaching era.

World Map, YMCA Emblem A90

Engr. and Typo.
1955, Aug. 10   Perf. 14
283	A90	3½p Prus green & red	.20	.15

Centenary of YMCA.

AUSTRALIA

Florence Nightingale and
Modern Nurse — A91

Queen
Victoria — A92

1955, Sept. 21   Engr.   Perf. 14x14½
284 A91 3½p red violet   .20 .15
Centenary of Florence Nightingale's work in the Crimea and of the founding of modern nursing.

1955, Oct. 17   Perf. 14½
285 A92 3½p green   .20 .15
South Australia's first postage stamps, cent.

Olympic Type of 1954
1955, Nov. 30   Unwmk.   Perf. 14
286 A85 2sh deep green   2.25 1.50
16th Olympic Games at Melbourne, Nov. 22-Dec. 8, 1956.

Queen Victoria, Queen Elizabeth II and Badges of Victoria, New South Wales and Tasmania
A93

1956, Sept. 26   Perf. 14½x14
287 A93 3½p brown carmine   .25 .15
Centenary of responsible government in Victoria, New South Wales and Tasmania.

Melbourne
Coat of
Arms — A94

Southern Cross,
Olympic
Torch — A95

Collins Street,
Melbourne
A96

Design: 2sh, Melbourne across Yarra River.

1956, Oct. 31   Engr.   Perf. 14½, 14
288 A94 4p dark carmine   .20 .15
289 A95 7½p ultramarine   .55 .45
Photo.
Perf. 14x14½
290 A96 1sh multicolored   .75 .45
Perf. 12x11½
Granite Paper
291 A96 2sh multicolored   1.40 1.00
   Nos. 288-291 (4)   2.90 2.05
16th Olympic Games, Melbourne, 11/22-12/8.
A lithographed souvenir sheet incorporating reproductions of Nos. 288-291 in reduced size was of private origin and not postally valid.

Types of 1938-55 and

Queen Elizabeth II — A97

Perf. 14½x14, 14x15, 15x14, 14½
1956-57   Engr.   Unwmk.
292 A72 3½p dark red   1.00 .15
293 A28 4p green   1.65 .15
294 A97 4p claret ('57)   .30 .15
   a. Booklet pane of 6 ('57)   7.50
295 A30 6p brown violet   2.75 .15
296 A72 6½p orange   1.75 .15
297 A97 7½p violet ('57)   3.00 .40
298 A31 9p sepia   9.00 .55
299 A97 10p gray blue ('57)   2.75 .15
300 A16 1sh gray green   6.00 .30
301 A87 1sh7p redsh brn ('57)   4.50 .30
302 A52 2sh chocolate   12.00 .25
303 A59 2sh6p brown ('57)   9.00 .25
   Nos. 292-303 (12)   53.70 2.95

No. 300 measures 17½x21½mm. No. 303 measures 20½x25mm and is the redrawn type of 1952.
Issued: 3½p, 7/2; 2sh, 7/21; #293, 6p, 8/18; 6½p, Sept. 9p, 1sh, 12/13; 2sh6p, 1/30; 10p, 3/6; #294, 1sh7p, 3/13; 7½p, 11/13.

South Australia Coat of
Arms — A99

1957, Apr. 17   Unwmk.   Perf. 14½
304 A99 4p brown red   .20 .15
Centenary of responsible government in South Australia.

Caduceus and
Map of Australia
A100

1957, Aug. 21   Perf. 14½x14
305 A100 7p violet blue   .60 .15
Royal Flying Doctor Service of Australia.

Star of
Bethlehem and
Praying
Child — A101

1957, Nov. 6   Engr.
306 A101 3½p dull rose   .25 .15
307 A101 4p pale purple   .25 .15
Christmas.

Canberra War
Memorial,
Sailor and
Airman
A102

Design: No. 309, As No. 308 with soldier and service woman. Printed in alternate rows in sheet.

1958, Feb. 10   Unwmk.
308 A102 5½p brown carmine   1.25 .75
309 A102 5½p brown carmine   1.25 .75
   a. Pair, #308-309   3.50 3.50

Sir Charles Kingsford-
Smith and "Southern
Cross" — A103

1958, Aug. 27   Perf. 14x14½
310 A103 8p brt violet blue   1.00 .90
1st air crossing of the Tasman Sea, 30th anniv.
See New Zealand No. 321.

Broken Hill Mine
A104

Nativity
A105

1958, Sept. 10   Perf. 14½x14
311 A104 4p brown   .25 .15
Broken Hill mining field, 75th anniv.

1958, Nov. 5   Perf. 14½x15
312 A105 3½p dark red   .15 .15
313 A105 4p dark purple   .25 .15
Christmas.

A106   A107   A109

A108   A110

Platypus
A111

Tasmanian
Tiger
A112

Flannel Flower
A113

Aboriginal Stockman
Cutting Out a Steer
A114

Designs: 3p, Queen Elizabeth II facing right. 6p, Banded anteater. 8p, Tiger cat. 9p, Kangaroos. 11p, Rabbit bandicoot. 1sh6p, Christmas bells (flower). 2sh3p, Wattle (flower). 2sh5p, Banksia (flower). 3sh, Waratah (flower).

FIVE PENCE
Die I - Four short lines inside "5" at right of ball; six short lines left of ball; full length line above ball is seventh from bottom. Odd numbered horizontal rows in each sheet are in Die I.
Die II - Five short lines inside "5" at right of ball; seven at left; full length line above ball is eighth from bottom. Even numbered horizontal rows in each sheet are in Die II.

Perf. 14½x14, 14x14½, 14½
1959-64   Engr.   Unwmk.
314 A106 1p dull violet   .25 .15
315 A107 2p red brown   .35 .15
316 A108 3p bluish green   .25 .15
317 A108 3½p dark green   .45 .15
318 A109 4p carmine   .35 .15
   a. Booklet pane of 6   25.00
319 A110 5p dark blue (I)   .65 .15
   a. 5p dark blue (II)   .65 .15
   b. Booklet pane of 6 ('60)   12.00
320 A111 6p chocolate   .65 .15
321 A111 8p red brown   .60 .15
322 A111 9p brown black   2.50 .20
323 A111 11p dark blue   .95 .15
324 A111 1sh slate green   3.75 .15
325 A112 1sh2p dk purple   1.50 .20
326 A113 1sh6p red, yellow   2.50 .60
327 A113 2sh dark blue   2.50 .15
328 A113 2sh3p green, yel   2.50 .20
328A A113 2sh3p yellow grn   7.50 1.00
329 A113 2sh5p brown, yellow   8.75   .40
330 A113 3sh crimson   3.50 .35
Wmk. 228
331 A114 5sh red brown   25.00 1.00
   Nos. 314-331 (19)   64.50 5.60

Issued: 1p, 4p, 2/2; 3½p, 3/18; 2sh, 4/8; 3p, 5/20; 3sh, 7/15; 1sh, #328, 9/9; 5p, 10/1; 9p, 10/21; 1sh6p, 2/3/60; 2sh5p, 3/16/60; 8p, 5/11/60; 6p, 9/30/60; 11p, 5/3/61; 5sh, 7/26/61; 2p, 1sh2p, 3/21/62; #328A, 10/28/64.

Luminescent Printings
Paper with an orange red phosphorescence (surface coating), was used for some printings of the Colombo Plan 1sh, No. 340, the Churchill 5p, No. 389, and several regular postage stamps. These include 2p, 3p, 6p, 8p, 9p, 11p, 1sh2p, 1sh6p and 2sh3p (Nos. 315, 316, 365, 367, 321, 368, 323, 325, 369, 328A).
Stamps printed only on phosphorescent paper include the Monash 5p, Hargrave 5p, ICY 2sh3p and Christmas 5p (Nos. 388, 390-393) and succeeding commemoratives; the 2sh, 2sh6p and 3sh regular birds (Nos. 370, 372, 373); and most of the regular series in decimal currency.
Ink with a phosphorescent content was used in printing most of the 5p red, No. 366, almost all of the 5p red booklets, No. 366a, most of the decimal 4c regular, No. 397, and its booklet pane, No. 397a, and all of No. 398.

Postmaster
Isaac Nichols
Boarding Vessel
to Receive
Mail — A115

1959, Apr. 22   Perf. 14½x14
332 A115 4p dark gray blue   .25 .15
First post office, Sydney, 150th anniv.

Parliament House,
Brisbane, and Queensland
Arms — A116

1959, June 5   Perf. 14x14½
333 A116 4p dk green & violet   .25 .15
Cent. of Queensland self-government.

Approach of the
Magi — A117

1959, Nov. 4   Perf. 15x14½
334 A117 5p purple   .25 .15
Christmas.

Girl Guide and
Lord Baden-
Powell — A118

1960, Aug. 18   Perf. 14½x14
335 A118 5p dark blue   .30 .15
50th anniversary of the Girl Guides.

The Overlanders by
Sir Daryl
Lindsay — A119

Melbourne Cup
and Archer, 1861
Winner — A120

1960, Sept. 21   Perf. 14½
336 A119 5p lilac rose   .30 .15
Exploration of Australia's Northern Territory, cent.

1960, Oct. 12   Unwmk.
337 A120 5p sepia   .30 .15
Centenary of the Melbourne Cup.

AUSTRALIA

Queen Victoria
A121

Open Bible and Candle
A122

1960, Nov. 2   Engr.   Perf. 14½
338 A121 5p dark green   .20 .15
Centenary of the first Queensland stamps.

1960, Nov. 9   Unwmk.
339 A122 5p maroon   .20 .15
Christmas; beginning of 350th anniv. year of the publication of the King James translation of the Bible.

Colombo Plan Emblem — A123

1961, June 30   Perf. 14x14½
340 A123 1sh red brown   .75 .15
Colombo Plan for the peaceful development of South East Asia countries, 10th anniv.

Dame Nellie Melba, by Sir Bertram Mackennal — A124

1961, Sept. 20   Perf. 14½
341 A124 5p deep blue   .30 .15
Dame Nellie Melba, singer, birth cent.

Page from Book of Hours, 15th Century — A125

John McDouall Stuart — A126

1961, Nov. 8   Perf. 14½x14
342 A125 5p reddish brown   .30 .15
Christmas; end of the 350th anniv. year of the publication of the King James translation of the Bible.

1962, July 25   Unwmk.   Perf. 14½
345 A126 5p carmine   .30 .15
First south-north crossing of Australia by John McDouall Stuart, cent.

Nurse and Rev. Flynn's Grave — A127

1962, Sept. 5   Photo.   Perf. 13½
346 A127 5p multicolored   .30 .15
a.   Red omitted   275.00
Australian Inland Mission founded by Rev. John Flynn, 50th anniv.

Woman and Globe — A128

Madonna and Child — A129

1962, Sept. 26   Engr.   Perf. 14x14½
347 A128 5p dark green   .30 .15
World Conf. of the Associated Country Women of the World, Melbourne, Oct. 2-12.

1962, Oct. 17   Perf. 14½
348 A129 5p deep violet   .30 .15
Christmas.

View of Perth and Kangaroo Paw — A130

Arms of Perth — A131

1962, Nov. 1   Photo.   Perf. 14
349 A130 5p multicolored   .30 .15
a.   Red omitted   450.00

Perf. 14½x14
350 A131 2sh3p emer, blk, red & ultra   4.00 4.00
British Empire and Commonwealth Games, Perth, Nov. 22-Dec. 1.

Elizabeth II — A132

Elizabeth II and Prince Philip — A133

1963, Feb. 18   Engr.   Perf. 14½
351 A132 5p dark green   .30 .15
352 A133 2sh3 red brown   4.00 4.00
Visit of Elizabeth II and Prince Philip.

Walter Burley Griffin and Arms of Canberra A134

Red Cross Centenary Emblem A135

1963, Mar. 8   Unwmk.   Perf. 14½x14
353 A134 5p dark green   .35 .15
50th anniv. of Canberra; Walter Burley Griffin, American architect, who laid out plan for Canberra.

1963, May 8   Photo.   Perf. 13½x13
354 A135 5p dk blue, red & gray   .35 .15
Centenary of the International Red Cross.

Explorers Blaxland, Lawson and Wentworth Looking West from Mt. York — A136

1963, May 28   Engr.   Perf. 14½x14
355 A136 5p dark blue   .30 .15
1st crossing of the Blue Mts., 150th anniv.

Globe, Ship, Plane and Map of Australia A137

1963, Aug. 28   Unwmk.
356 A137 5p red   .35 .15
Importance of exports to Australian economy.

Elizabeth II — A138

Black-backed Magpie and Eucalyptus — A139

Abel Tasman and Ship A144

George Bass, Whaleboat A145

Designs: 6p, Yellow-tailed thornbill, horiz. 1sh6p, Galah on tree stump. 2sh, Golden whistler. 2sh5p, Blue wren and bracken fern. 2sh6p, Scarlet robin, horiz. 3sh, Straw-necked ibis. 5sh, William Dampier and "Roebuck" sailing ship. 7sh6p, Capt. James Cook. 10sh, Matthew Flinders and three-master "Investigator." £2, Admiral Philip Parker King.

1963-65   Unwmk.   Engr.   Perf. 15x14
365 A138 5p green   .25 .15
a.   Booklet pane of 6 ('64)   20.00
b.   Pair, imperf. btwn.   3.75 3.75
366 A138 5p red   .25 .15
a.   Booklet pane of 6   25.00

Photo.   Perf. 13½
367 A139 6p multicolored   .45 .15
a.   Vert. pair, imperf. btwn.
368 A139 9p multicolored   2.50 1.90
369 A139 1sh6p multicolored   1.25 1.10
370 A139 2sh multicolored   2.50 .30
371 A139 2sh5p multicolored   8.25 2.25
372 A139 2sh6p multicolored   3.75 1.50
a.   Red omitted   1,000.
373 A139 3sh multicolored   2.50 1.25

Engr.   Perf. 14½x14, 14½x15
374 A144 4sh violet blue   3.75 .55

Wmk. 228
375 A145 5sh red brown   5.25 1.25
376 A144 7sh6p olive green   24.00 15.00
377 A144 10sh deep claret   30.00 7.25
378 A145 £1 purple   50.00 22.50
379 A145 £2 brown black   100.00 90.00
Nos. 365-379 (15)   234.70 145.30

No. 365a was printed in sheets of 288 which were sold intact by the Philatelic Bureau. These sheets have been broken to obtain pairs and blocks which are imperf. between (see No. 365b).
Issued: #365, 4sh, 10/9/63; 10sh, £1, 2/26/64; 9p, 1sh6p, 2sh5p, 3/11/64; 6p, 8/19/64; 7sh6p, £2, 8/26/64; 5sh, 11/25/64; 2sh, 2sh6p, 3sh, 4/21/65; #366, 6/30/65.
See Nos. 400-401, 406-417.

Star of Bethlehem — A146

1963, Oct. 25   Unwmk.   Perf. 14½
380 A146 5p blue   .20 .15
Christmas.

Cable Around World and Under Sea — A147

1963, Dec. 3   Photo.   Perf. 13½
381 A147 2sh3p gray, ver, blk & blue   6.00 4.25
Opening of the Commonwealth Pacific (telephone) cable service (COMPAC).
See New Zealand No. 364.

Bleriot 60 Plane, 1914 — A148

1964, July 1   Engr.   Perf. 14½x14
382 A148 5p olive green   .20 .15
383 A148 2sh3p red   5.25 4.25
50th anniv. of the first air mail flight in Australia; Maurice Guillaux, aviator.

Child Looking at Nativity Scene — A149

1964, Oct. 21   Photo.   Perf. 13½
384 A149 5p bl, blk, red & buff   .20 .15
a.   Red omitted   375.00
b.   Black omitted   375.00
Christmas.

"Simpson and His Donkey" by Wallace Anderson — A150

1965, Apr. 14   Engr.   Perf. 14x14½
385 A150 5p olive bister   .20 .15
386 A150 8p dark blue   1.25 .90
387 A150 2sh3p rose claret   4.50 4.00
Nos. 385-387 (3)   5.95 5.05
50th anniv. of the landing of the Australian and New Zealand Army Corps (ANZAC) at Gallipoli, Turkey, Apr. 25, 1915. Private John Simpson Kirkpatrick saved the lives of many wounded soldiers. The statue erected in his honor stands in front of Melbourne's Shrine of Remembrance.

Radio Mast and Satellite Orbiting Earth A151

Winston Churchill A152

AUSTRALIA

1965, May 10 Photo. *Perf. 13½*
388 A151 5p multicolored .20 .15
  a. Black ("5d" and pylon) omitted 650.00
ITU, cent.

1965, May 24
389 A152 5p lt blue, gray & blk .25 .15
Sir Winston Spencer Churchill (1874-1965), statesman and WWII leader.
See New Zealand No. 371.

John Monash and Transmission Tower — A153

Lawrence Hargrave and Sketch for 1902 Seaplane — A154

1965, June 23 Photo. *Perf. 13½*
390 A153 5p red, yel, blk & lt brn .25 .15
Birth cent. of General Sir John Monash (1865-1931), soldier, Vice-Chancellor of University of Melbourne and chairman of the Victoria state electricity commission.

1965, Aug. 4 Unwmk. *Perf. 13½*
391 A154 5p multicolored .25 .15
  a. Purple (5d) omitted 190.00
50th anniv. of the death of Lawrence Hargrave (1850-1915), aviation pioneer.

ICY Emblem A155

Nativity A156

1965, Sept. 1 Photo. *Perf. 13½*
392 A155 2sh3p lt blue & green 2.75 2.50
International Cooperation Year.

1965, Oct. 20 Unwmk. *Perf. 13½*
393 A156 5p multicolored .30 .15
  a. Gold omitted 300.00
  b. Ultramarine omitted 325.00
Christmas.

Types of 1963-65 and

Elizabeth II — A157

Humbug Fish — A158

Designs: No. 400, Yellow-tailed thornbill, horiz. 6c, blue-faced honeyeater, horiz. 8c, Coral fish. 9c, Hermit crab. 10c Anemone fish. 13c, Red-necked avocet. 15c, Galah on tree stump. 20c, Golden whistler. 24c Azure kingfisher, horiz. 25c, Scarlet robin, horiz. 30c Straw-necked ibis. 40c Abel Tasman and ship. 50c, William Dampier and "Roebuck" sailing ship. 75c, Capt. James Cook. $1, Matthew Flinders and three-master "Investigator." $2, George Bass and whaleboat. $4, Admiral Philip Parker King.

Perf. 14½x14 (A157); 13½ (A158, A139)
Engr. (A157), Photo. (A158, A139)
1966-71
394 A157 1c red brown .25 .15
395 A157 2c olive green .50 .15
396 A157 3c Prus green .65 .15
397 A157 4c red .15 .15
    Booklet pane of 5 + label 30.00
398 A157 5c on 4c red ('67) .75 .15
    Booklet pane of 5 + label 5.50
399 A157 5c dk blue ('67) 1.00 .15
  a. Booklet pane of 5 + label 11.00
  b. Booklet pane of 10 55.00
400 A139 5c lt grn, blk, brn & yel .20 .15
    Booklet pane of 10 45.00
401 A139 6c gray, blk, lem & bl .55 .25
401A A157 6c orange ('70) .15 .15
402 A158 7c brn, ver, blk & gray 1.00 .15
402A A157 7c dp rose lilac ('71) .20 .15
403 A158 8c multicolored 1.10 .15
404 A158 9c multicolored 1.50 .15
405 A158 10c lt brn, blk, org & bl 1.10 .25
406 A139 13c lt bl grn, blk, gray & red 2.00 .50
  a. Red omitted 400.00
407 A139 15c lt grn, blk, gray & rose 3.50 .40
  a. Gray omitted 1,500.
408 A139 20c pink, blk, yel & gray 5.75 .15
  a. Yellow omitted 350.00
409 A139 24c tan, blk, vio bl & org 1.10 .55
410 A139 25c gray, grn, blk & red 3.75 .15
  a. Red omitted 750.00
411 A139 30c lt grn, buff, blk & red 19.00 .40
  a. Red omitted 575.00

Engr.
Perf. 14½x14, 14½x15
412 A144 40c violet blue 13.50 .30
413 A145 50c brown red 17.00 .15
414 A144 75c olive green 1.00 1.00
415 A144 $1 deep claret 2.50 .30
  a. Perf 15x14 75.00 15.00
416 A145 $2 purple 7.50 1.10
417 A145 $4 sepia 5.50 4.50
Nos. 394-417 (26) 91.20 11.80

No. 398 issued in booklets only.
Booklet panes Nos. 399b and 400a were issued for the use of "Australian Defence Forces," as the covers read, in Viet Nam.
Issued: #398, 399, 9/29/67; #401A, 9/28/70; #402A, 10/1/71; #415a, 1973; others, 2/14/66.

Coil Stamps
1966-67 Photo. *Perf. 15 Horiz.*
418 A157 3c emerald, blk & buff .40 .35
419 A157 4c org red, blk & buff .60 .15
420 A157 5c blue, black & buff .75 .15
Nos. 418-420 (3) 1.75 .65
Issued: 5c, Sept. 29, 1967; others, Feb. 14, 1966.

Rescue — A159

1966 July 6 Photo. *Perf. 13½*
421 A159 4c blue, ultra & black .25 .15
Royal Life Saving Society, 75th anniv.

Adoration of the Shepherds A160

1966, Oct. 19 Photo. *Perf. 13½*
422 A160 4c olive & black .25 .15
Christmas.

Dutch Sailing Ship, 17th Century A161

Hands Reaching for Bible A162

1966, Oct. 24 Photo. *Perf. 13½*
423 A161 4c bl, blk, dp org & gold .25 .15
350th anniv. of Dirk Hartog's discovery of the Australian west coast, and his landing on the island named after him.

1967, Mar. 7 Photo. *Perf. 13½*
424 A162 4c multicolored .25 .15
British and Foreign Bible Soc., 150th anniv.

Combination Lock and Antique Keys — A163

1967, Apr. 5 Photo. *Perf. 13½*
425 A163 4c emerald, blk & lt blue .25 .15
150th anniv. of banking in Australia (Bank of New South Wales).

Lions Intl., 50th Anniv. — A164

1967, June 7 Photo. *Perf. 13½*
426 A164 4c ultra, black & gold .25 .15

YWCA Emblems and Flags — A165

1967, Aug. 21 Photo. *Perf. 13½*
427 A165 4c dk blue, lt bl & lilac .25 .15
World Council Meeting of the YWCA, Monash University, Victoria, Aug. 14-Sept. 1.

Seated Women Symbolizing Obstetrics and Gynecology, Female Symbol A166

1967, Sept. 20 Photo. *Perf. 13½*
428 A166 4c lilac, dk blue & blk .25 .15
5th World Congress of Gynecology and Obstetrics, Sydney, Sept. 23-30.

Gothic Arches and Christmas Bell Flower — A167

Cross, Stars of David and Yin Yang Forming Mandala — A168

1967 Photo. *Perf. 13½*
429 A167 5c multicolored .25 .15
430 A168 25c multicolored 2.25 2.25
Christmas.
Issue dates: 5c, Oct. 18; 25c, Nov. 27.

Satellite Orbiting Earth — A169

Satellite and Antenna, Moree, N.S.W. — A170

Design: 20c, World weather map connecting Washington, Moscow and Melbourne, and computer and teleprinter tape spools.

1968, Mar. 20 Photo. *Perf. 13½*
431 A169 5c dull yel, red, bl & dk blue .25 .15
432 A169 20c blue, blk & red 3.00 3.00
433 A170 25c Prus blue, blk & lt green 3.50 3.50
Nos. 431-433 (3) 6.75 6.65
Use of satellites for weather observations and communications.

Kangaroo Paw, Western Australia A171

Sturt's Desert Rose, Northern Territory A171a

State Flowers: 13c, Pink heath, Victoria. 15c, Tasmanian blue gum, Tasmania. 20c, Sturt's desert pea, South Australia. 25c, Cooktown orchid, Queensland. 30c, Waratah, New South Wales.

1968, July 10 Photo. *Perf. 13½*
Flowers in Natural Colors
434 A171 6c bister & dk brn .30 .20
435 A171 13c lt grnsh blue .40 .15
436 A171 15c dk brn & yel 1.50 .25
437 A171 20c lemon & black 5.25 .15
438 A171 25c light ultra 3.75 .15
439 A171 30c chocolate 1.10 .15
Nos. 434-439 (6) 12.30 1.05

Coil Stamps
1970-75 Photo. *Perf. 14½ Horiz.*
Designs: 5c, Golden wattle, national flower. 7c, 10c, Sturt's desert pea.
439A A171a 2c dk grn & multi .20 .15
  i. Lettering and value bolder .20 .15
439B A171a 4c gray & multi .50 .40
439C A171a 5c gray & multi .20 .15
439D A171a 6c gray & multi 1.10 .50
  h. Green omitted 300.00
439E A171a 7c blk, red & grn .35 .15
  f. Green omitted 150.00
439G A171a 10c blk, red & grn .30 .15
Nos. 439A-439G (6) 2.65 1.50
Issued: 4c, 5c, 4/27; 6c, 10/28; 2c, 7c, 10/1/71; 10c, 1/15/75; #439Ai, 11/73.

Soil Testing Through Chemistry and by Computer A172

Hippocrates and Hands Holding Hypodermic A173

1968, Aug. 6 Photo. *Perf. 13½*
440 A172 5c multicolored .25 .15
441 A173 5c multicolored .25 .15
9th Intl. Congress of Soil Science, University of Adelaide, Aug. 6-16 (No. 440); General Assembly of World Medical Associations, Sydney, Aug. 6-9 (No. 441). Nos. 440-441 printed in sheets of 100 in two separate panes of 50 connected by a gutter. Each sheet contains 10 gutter pairs.

Runner and Aztec Calendar Stone A174

Symbolic House and Money A175

Design: 25c, Aztec calendar stone and Mexican flag, horiz.

AUSTRALIA

1968, Oct. 2

| 442 | A174 | 5c multicolored | .20 | .15 |
| 443 | A174 | 25c multicolored | 2.25 | 2.00 |

19th Olympic Games, Mexico City, Oct. 12-27. Nos. 442-443 printed in sheets of 100 in two separate panes of 50 connected by a gutter. Each sheet contains 10 gutter pairs.

1968, Oct. 16

| 444 | A175 | 5c multicolored | .25 | .15 |

11th Triennial Congress of the Intl. Union of Building Societies and Savings Associations, Sydney, Oct. 20-27.

View of Bethlehem and Church Window — A176

1968, Oct. 23 Photo. Perf. 13½

| 445 | A176 | 5c lt bl, red, grn & gold | .20 | .15 |
| a. | | Red omitted | 350.00 | |

Christmas.

Edgeworth David (1858-1934), Geologist A177

Sir Edmund Barton (1849-1920) A178

Reginald C. and John R. Duigan, Aviators — A179

Famous Australians: No. 447, Caroline Chisholm (1808-1877), social worker and reformer. No. 448, Albert Namatjira (1902-1959), aborigine, artist. No. 449, Andrew Barton (Banjo) Paterson (1864-1941), poet and writer.

1968, Nov. 6 Engr. Perf. 15x14

446	A177	5c green, *greenish*	1.25	.15
a.		Booklet pane of 5 + label	6.25	
447	A177	5c purple, *pink*	1.25	.15
a.		Booklet pane of 5 + label	6.25	
448	A177	5c dark brown, *buff*	1.25	.15
a.		Booklet pane of 5 + label	6.25	
449	A177	5c indigo, *lt blue*	1.25	.15
a.		Booklet pane of 5 + label	6.25	
		Nos. 446-449 (4)	5.00	.60

1969, Oct. 22 Engr. Perf. 15x14

Prime Ministers: No. 451, Alfred Deakin (1856-1919). No. 452, John C. Watson (1867-1941). No.453, Sir George H. Reid (1845-1918).

450	A178	5c indigo, *greenish*	1.25	.15
a.		Booklet pane of 5 + label	6.25	
451	A178	5c indigo, *greenish*	1.25	.15
a.		Booklet pane of 5 + label	6.25	
452	A178	5c indigo, *greenish*	1.25	.15
a.		Booklet pane of 5 + label	6.25	
453	A178	5c indigo, *greenish*	1.25	.15
a.		Booklet pane of 5 + label	6.25	
		Nos. 450-453 (4)	5.00	.60

1970, Nov. 16 Engr. Perf. 15x14

Famous Australians: No. 455, Lachlan Macquarie (1761-1824), Governor of New South Wales. No. 456, Adam Lindsay Gordon (1833-1870), poet. No. 457, Edward John Eyre (1815-1901), explorer.

454	A179	6c dark blue	1.25	.15
a.		Booklet pane of 5 + label	6.25	
455	A179	6c dark brown, *salmon*	1.25	.15
a.		Booklet pane of 5 + label	6.25	
456	A179	6c magenta, *brt pink*	1.25	.15
a.		Booklet pane of 5 + label	6.25	
457	A179	6c brown red, *salmon*	1.25	.15
a.		Booklet pane of 5 + label	6.25	
		Nos. 454-457 (4)	5.00	.60

Nos. 446-457 were issued in booklet panes only; all stamps have 1 or 2 straight edges.

Macquarie Lighthouse — A180

Perf. 14½x13½

1968, Nov. 27 Engr.

| 458 | A180 | 5c indigo, *buff* | .35 | .15 |

Macquarie Lighthouse, Outer South Head, Sydney, 150th anniv.

Surveyor George W. Goyder and Assistants, 1869; Building in Darwin, 1969 — A181

1969, Feb. 5 Photo. Perf. 13½

| 459 | A181 | 5c black brn & dull yel | .20 | .15 |

First permanent settlement of the Northern Territory of Australia, cent.

Melbourne Harbor Scene — A182

1969, Feb. 26 Photo. Perf. 13½

| 460 | A182 | 5c dull blue & multi | .20 | .15 |

6th Biennial Conference of the Intl. Assoc. of Ports and Harbors, Melbourne, March 3-8.

Overlapping Circles — A183

1969, June 5 Photo. Perf. 13½

| 461 | A183 | 5c gray, vio bl, bl & gold | .20 | .15 |

ILO, 50th anniv.

Sugar Cane — A184

Designs (Primary industries): 15c, Eucalyptus (timber). 20c, Wheat. 25c, Ram, ewe and lamb (wool).

1969, Sept. 17 Perf. 13½x13

462	A184	7c blue & multi	.75	.75
463	A184	15c emerald & multi	3.75	3.50
464	A184	20c org brn & multi	1.40	.60
465	A184	25c gray, black & yel	1.25	.70
		Nos. 462-465 (4)	7.15	5.55

Nativity — A185  Tree of Life — A186

Perf. 13½x13, 13x13½

1969, Oct. 15 Photo.

| 466 | A185 | 5c multicolored | .20 | .15 |
| 467 | A186 | 25c multicolored | 2.75 | 2.75 |

Christmas.

Vickers Vimy Flown by Ross Smith, England to Australia A187

Designs: No. 469, B.E. 2E plane, automobile and spectators. No. 470, Ford truck and surveyors Lieuts. Hudson Fysh and P.J. McGinness.

1969, Nov. 12 Perf. 13x13½

468	A187	5c bl, blk, cop red & ol	.60	.35
469	A187	5c bl, blk, cop red & ol	.60	.35
470	A187	5c cop red, black & ol	.60	.35
a.		Strip of 3, #468-470	3.50	3.00
		Nos. 468-470 (3)	1.80	1.05

50th anniv. of the first England to Australia flight by Capt. Ross Smith and Lieut. Keith Smith. Nos. 468-470 are printed se-tenant with various combinations possible.

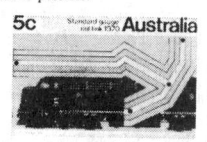

Diesel Locomotive and New Track Linking Melbourne, Sydney and Brisbane with Perth — A188

1970, Feb. 11 Photo. Perf. 13x13½

| 471 | A188 | 5c multicolored | .25 | .15 |

Completion of the standard gauge railroad between Sydney and Perth.

EXPO '70 Australian Pavilion A189

Design: 20c, Southern Cross and Japanese inscription: "From the country of the south with warm feeling."

1970, Mar. 16 Photo. Perf. 13x13½

| 472 | A189 | 5c bl, blk, red & brnz | .25 | .15 |
| 473 | A189 | 20c red & black | 1.00 | .45 |

EXPO '70 Intl. Exhib., Osaka, Japan, Mar. 15-Sept. 13.

Queen Elizabeth II and Prince Philip — A190

Australian Flag — A191

1970, Mar. 31

| 474 | A190 | 5c yel bister & black | .25 | .15 |
| 475 | A191 | 30c vio blue & multi | 2.25 | 2.00 |

Visit of Queen Elizabeth II, Prince Philip and Princess Anne to Australia.

Steer, Alfalfa and Native Spear Grass — A192

1970, Apr. 13 Photo. Perf. 13x13½

| 476 | A192 | 5c emerald & multi | .25 | .20 |

11th Intl. Grasslands Congress, Surfers Paradise, Queensland, Apr. 13-23.

Capt. James Cook and "Endeavour" — A193

Designs: No. 478, Sextant and "Endeavour." No. 479, "Endeavour," landing party and kangaroo. No. 480, Daniel Charles Solander, Sir Joseph Banks, Cook, map and botanical drawing. No. 481, Cook taking possession with Union Jack; "Endeavour" and coral. 30c, Cook, "Endeavour," sextant, kangaroo and aborigines.

1970, Apr. 20 Perf. 13½x13

Size: 24x35½mm

477	A193	5c org brn & multi	.50	.15
478	A193	5c org brn & multi	.50	.15
479	A193	5c org brn & multi	.50	.15
480	A193	5c org brn & multi	.50	.15
481	A193	5c org brn & multi	.50	.15
a.		Strip of 5, #477-481	2.50	2.50

Size: 62x29mm

482	A193	30c org brn & multi	3.50	3.50
a.		Souv. sheet of 6, #477-482, imperf.	11.00	11.00
		Nos. 477-482 (6)	6.00	4.25

Cook's discovery and exploration of the eastern coast of Australia, 200th anniv.

No. 481a has continuous design.

No. 482a with brown marginal overprint "Souvenir Sheet ANPEX 1970..." is of private origin.

Snowy Mountains Hydroelectric Project — A194

Designs: 8c, Ord River hydroelectric project (dam, cotton plant and boll). 9c, Bauxite and aluminum production (mine, conveyor belt and aluminum window frame). 10c, Oil and natural gas (offshore drilling rig and pipelines).

1970, Aug. 31 Photo. Perf. 13x13½

483	A194	7c multicolored	1.65	.40
484	A194	8c multicolored	.25	.15
485	A194	9c multicolored	.25	.15
486	A194	10c multicolored	1.10	.15
		Nos. 483-486 (4)	3.25	.85

Australian economic development.

Flame Symbolizing Democracy and Freedom of Speech — A195

1970, Oct. 2 Photo. Perf. 13½x13

| 487 | A195 | 6c green & multi | .25 | .15 |

16th Commonwealth Parliamentary Assoc. Conference, Canberra, Oct. 2-9.

Herd of Illawarra Shorthorns and Laboratory A196

1970, Oct. 7 Perf. 13x13½

| 488 | A196 | 6c multicolored | .25 | .15 |

18th Intl. Dairy Cong., Sydney, Oct. 12-16.

Australia stamps can be mounted in the Scott Australia album.

AUSTRALIA

Madonna and Child, by William Beasley — A197

UN Emblem, Dove and Symbols — A198

1970, Oct. 14   *Perf. 13½x13*
489 A197 6c multicolored   .25   .15
Christmas.

1970, Oct. 19
490 A198 6c blue & multi   .25   .15
25th anniversary of the United Nations.

Qantas Boeing 707, and Avro 504 — A199

Design: 30c, Sunbeam Dyak powered Avro 504 on ground and Qantas Boeing 707 in the air.

1970, Nov. 2   *Perf. 13x13½*
491 A199 6c multicolored   .20   .15
492 A199 30c multicolored   1.40   1.40
Qantas, Australian overseas airlines, 50th anniv.

Japanese Noh Actor, Australian Dancer and Chinese Opera Character — A200

Designs: 15c, Chinese pipe and trumpet, Australian aboriginal didgeridoo, Thai fiddle, Indian double oboe and Tibetan drums. 20c, Red Sea dhow, Chinese junk, Australian lifeguard's surfboard, Malaysian and South Indian river boats.

1971, Jan. 6   *Photo.*   *Perf. 13½x13*
493 A200 7c multicolored   .60   .15
494 A200 15c multicolored   1.50   1.10
495 A200 20c multicolored   1.50   .80
Nos. 493-495 (3)   3.60   2.05

Link between Australia and Asia; 28th Intl. Congress of Orientalists, Canberra, Jan. 6-12.

Southern Cross — A201

1971, Apr. 21   *Photo.*   *Perf. 13½x13*
496 A201 6c multicolored   .25   .15
Australian Natives Assoc., cent.

Symbolic Market Graphs — A202

Rotary Emblem — A203

1971, May 5   *Perf. 13½x13*
497 A202 6c silver & multi   .25   .15
Centenary of Sydney Stock Exchange.

1971, May 17   *Perf. 13x13½*
498 A203 6c multicolored   .25   .15
First Intl. Rotary Convention held in Australia, Sydney, May 16-20.

DH-9A, Australian Mirage Jet Fighters — A204

RSPCA Centenary — A205

1971, June 9   *Perf. 13½x13*
499 A204 6c multicolored   .35   .15
Royal Australian Air Force, 50th anniv.

1971, July 5   *Photo.*   *Perf. 13½x13*

Designs: 12c, Man and lamb (animal science). 18c, Kangaroo (fauna conservation). 24c, Seeing eye dog (animals' aid to man).

500 A205 6c blk, brown & org   .25   .15
501 A205 12c blk, dk grn & yel   .75   .15
502 A205 18c brown & multi   .95   .30
503 A205 24c blue & multi   1.25   .50
Nos. 500-503 (4)   3.20   1.10

Royal Society for Prevention of Cruelty to Animals in Australia, cent.

Longnecked Tortoise, Painted on Bark — A206

Aboriginal Art: 25c, Mourners' body paintings, Warramunga tribe. 30c, Cave painting, Western Arnhem Land, vert. 35c, Graveposts, Bathurst and Melville Islands, vert.

Perf. 13x13½, 13½x13
1971, Sept. 29
504 A206 20c multicolored   .65   .25
505 A206 25c multicolored   .65   .45
506 A206 30c multicolored   .90   .35
507 A206 35c multicolored   .65   .40
Nos. 504-507 (4)   2.85   1.45

Three Kings and Star — A207

1971, Oct. 13   *Photo.*   *Perf. 13½x13*
508 Block of 7   50.00
a. A207 7c brt grn, dk bl (Kings) & lil   9.00   .30
b. A207 7c lil. red brn, grn & dk bl   6.25   .15
c. A207 7c red brown & lilac   1.75   .15
d. A207 7c lilac, red brn & brt grn   2.75   .15
e. A207 7c red brown & dark blue   3.00   .15
f. A207 7c lilac, green & dk blue   20.00   1.40
g. A207 7c brt grn, dk bl & lilac (Kings)   3.50   .15

Christmas. Nos. 508a-508g printed se-tenant in sheets of 50. Each sheet contains 2 green crosses formed by 4 No. 508g and three No. 508a.

Andrew Fisher (1862-1928) — A208

Cameo Brooch — A209

Prime Ministers: No. 515, Joseph Cook (1860-1947). No. 516, William Morris Hughes (1864-1952). No. 517, Stanley Melbourne Bruce (1883-1967).

1972, Mar. 8   *Engr.*   *Perf. 15x14*
514 A208 7c dark blue   .75   .15
   a. Booklet pane of 5 + label   4.00
515 A208 7c dark red   .75   .15
   a. Booklet pane of 5 + label   4.00
516 A208 7c dark red   .75   .15
   a. Booklet pane of 5 + label   4.00
517 A208 7c dark red   .75   .15
   a. Booklet pane of 5 + label   4.00
Nos. 514-517 (4)   3.00   .60

Nos. 514-517 were issued in booklets only; all stamps have one or two straight edges.

1972, Apr. 18   *Photo.*   *Perf. 13½*
518 A209 7c multicolored   .25   .15
Country Women's Assoc., 50th anniv.

Apple and Banana — A210

1972, June 14
519 A210 20c shown   1.50   1.50
520 A210 25c Rice   2.25   2.25
521 A210 30c Fish   2.25   2.25
522 A210 35c Cattle   5.25   5.25
Nos. 519-522 (4)   11.25   11.25

Worker in Sheltered Workshop — A211

18c, Amputee assembling electrical circuit, horiz. 24c, Boy wearing Toronto splint, playing ball.

1972, Aug. 2   *Perf. 13½x13*
523 A211 12c green & brown   .25   .15
524 A211 18c orange & olive   1.25   .20
525 A211 24c brown & ultra   .50   .20
Nos. 523-525 (3)   2.00   .55

Rehabilitation of the handicapped.

Overland Telegraph Line — A212

1972, Aug. 22   *Photo.*   *Perf. 13x13½*
526 A212 7c dk red, blk & lemon   .25   .15
Centenary of overland telegraph line.

Athlete, Olympic Rings — A213

1972, Aug. 28   *Perf. 13½x13*
527 A213 7c shown   .15   .15
528 A213 7c Swimming   .15   .15
529 A213 7c Rowing   .15   .15
530 A213 35c Equestrian   4.50   4.00
Nos. 527-530 (4)   4.95   4.45

20th Olympic Games, Munich, Aug. 26-Sept. 11.

Abacus, Numerals, Computer Circuits — A214

1972, Oct. 16   *Photo.*   *Perf. 13½x13*
531 A214 7c multicolored   .20   .15
10th Intl. Congress of Accountants.

19th Cent. Combine Harvester — A215

Perf. 13½x13, 13x13½
1972, Nov. 15   *Photo.*
532 A215 5c Pioneer family, vert.   .15   .15
533 A215 10c Water pump, vert.   .45   .15
534 A215 15c shown   .30   .15
535 A215 40c Pioneer house   .65   .15
536 A215 50c Cobb & Co. coach   1.10   .20
537 A215 60c Early Morse key, vert.   1.00   .45
538 A215 80c Paddle-wheel steamer   1.10   .45
Nos. 532-538 (7)   4.75   1.70

Australian pioneer life.

Jesus and Children — A216

Dove, Cross and "Darkness into Light" — A217

Metric Conversion, Mass — A218

Perf. 14½x14, 13½x13
1972, Nov. 29
539 A216 7c tan & multi   .35   .15
540 A217 35c blue & multi   9.00   9.00
Christmas.

1973, Mar. 7   *Photo.*   *Perf. 14x14½*

Metric conversion: No. 542, Temperature, horiz. No. 543, Length. No. 544, Volume.

541 A218 7c pale vio & multi   .80   .15
542 A218 7c yellow & multi   .80   .15
543 A218 7c yel green & multi   .80   .15
544 A218 7c brt rose & multi   .80   .15
Nos. 541-544 (4)   3.20   .60

Conversion to metric system.

Stylized Caduceus and Laurel — A219

1973, Apr. 4   *Photo.*   *Perf. 14½x14*
545 A219 7c dk bl, emer & lil rose   .25   .15
WHO, 25th anniv.

Dame Mary Gilmore, Writer — A220

Shipping Industry — A221

Famous Australians: No. 547, William Charles Wentworth, explorer. No. 548, Sir Isaac Isaacs, lawyer, first Australian-born Governor-General. No. 549, Marcus Clarke, writer.

Engr. & Litho.
1973, May 16   *Perf. 15x14*
546 A220 7c bister & black   1.25   .15
547 A220 7c bister & black   1.25   .15
548 A220 7c black & violet   1.25   .15
549 A220 7c black & violet   1.25   .15
   a. Block of 4, #546-549   5.00   1.00

1973, June 6   *Photo.*   *Perf. 13½x13*

Designs: 25c, Iron ore and steel. 30c, Truck convoy (beef road). 35c, Aerial mapping.

550 A221 20c ultra & multi   2.25   1.65
551 A221 25c red & multi   1.90   1.90
552 A221 30c ol brn & multi   2.50   2.50
553 A221 35c olive & multi   3.50   3.50
Nos. 550-553 (4)   10.15   9.55

Australian economic development.

AUSTRALIA

Banded Coral Shrimp A222

Chrysoprase A223

Helichrysum Thomsonii A223a

Wombat A224

Radio Astronomy A225

Red Gums of the Far North, by Hans Heysen — A226

Coming South (Immigrants), by Tom Roberts — A226a

Paintings: $1, Sergeant of Light Horse, by George Lambert. No. 575, On the Wallaby Track. $4, Shearing the Rams, by Tom Roberts. No. 577, McMahon's Point, by Arthur Streeton. No. 578, Mentone.

Perf. 14x15, 15x14 (A222, A223, A223a); Perf. 14x14½ (A224); Perf. 13x13½ (A225, A226, $1)

1973-84			Photo.	
554	A222	1c shown	.15	.15
555	A222	2c Fiddler crab	.15	.15
556	A222	3c Coral crab	.15	.15
557	A222	4c Mauve stinger	.15	.15
558	A223	6c shown	.15	.15
559	A223	7c Agate	.15	.15
560	A223	8c Opal	.15	.15
561	A223	9c Rhodonite	.15	.15
562	A223	10c Star sapphire ('74)	.15	.15
563	A225	11c Atomic absorption spectrophotometry ('75)	.55	.25
564	A223a	18c shown ('75)	.50	.15
565	A224	20c shown ('74)	.40	.15
566	A224	24c shown ('75)	1.00	.40
567	A224	25c Spiny anteater ('74)	1.25	.35
568	A224	30c Brushtail possum ('74)	.70	.20
569	A225	33c Immunology ('75)	1.00	1.00
570	A223a	45c Callistemon teretifolius, horiz. ('75)	.65	.25
571	A225	48c Oceanography ('75)	1.75	1.10
572	A224	75c Feather-tailed glider ('74)	1.25	.75
573	A226a	$1 multi ('74)	1.50	.25
574	A226	$2 shown ('74)	2.75	.30
575	A226	$2 multi ('81)	2.50	.30
576	A226	$4 multi ('74)	5.00	2.25

Litho.
Perf. 14½
577	A226a	$5 multi ('79)	7.00	2.00
578	A226	$5 multi ('84)	6.00	1.25
579	A226a	$10 shown ('77)	12.00	3.25
		Nos. 554-579 (26)	47.15	15.55

Issued: 1c-9c, 7/11; 20c, 25c, 30c, 75c, 2/13; $1, #574, $4, 4/24; 10c, 10/16; 11c, 24c, 33c, 48c, 5/14; 18c, 45c, 8/27; $10, 10/19; #577, 3/14; #575, 6/17; #578, 4/4.

No. 560 Surcharged in Red = 9c

Perf. 15x14
| 580 | A223 | 9c on 8c multi ('74) | .20 | .15 |

Hand Protecting Playing Children A227

1973, Sept. 5 Photo. Perf. 13x13½
| 581 | A227 | 7c bis brn, grn & plum | .25 | .15 |

50th anniv. of Legacy, an ex-servicemen's organization concerned with the welfare of widows and children of servicemen.

Baptism of Christ A228

The Good Shepherd A229

1973, Oct. 3 Perf. 14x14½
| 582 | A228 | 7c gold & multi | .30 | .15 |
| a. | Perf. 14x15 | | 4.00 | .60 |

Perf. 13½
| 583 | A229 | 30c gold & multi | 3.75 | 3.75 |

Christmas.

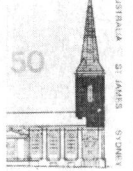

Buchanan's Hotel, Townsville — A230

St. James' Church, Sydney — A231

Designs: 7c, Opera House, Sydney. 40c, Como House, Melbourne.

1973, Oct. 17 Photo. Perf. 14½x14
584	A230	7c lt blue & ultra	.40	.15
a.	Perf. 15x14		4.00	.80
585	A230	10c bister & black	.60	.35

Perf. 13x13½, 13½x13
586	A230	40c dl pink, gray & blk	.75	.75
587	A231	50c gray & multi	2.00	1.50
		Nos. 584-587 (4)	3.75	2.75

Australian architecture; opening of the Sydney Opera House, Oct. 14, 1973 (No. 584).

Radio and Gramophone Speaker A232

1973, Nov. 21 Photo. Perf. 13½x13
| 588 | A232 | 7c dull blue, blk & brn | .25 | .15 |

Broadcasting in Australia, 50th anniv.

Supreme Court Judge on Bench A233

Australian Football A234

1974, May 15 Photo. Perf. 14x14½
| 589 | A233 | 7c multicolored | .25 | .15 |

150th anniv. of the proclamation of the Charter of Justice in New South Wales and Van Diemen's Land (Australia's Third Charter).

1974, July 24 Photo. Perf. 14x14½
590	A234	7c shown	.35	.15
591	A234	7c Cricket	.35	.15
592	A234	7c Golf	.35	.15
593	A234	7c Surfing	.35	.15
594	A234	7c Tennis	.35	.15
595	A234	7c Bowls, horiz.	.35	.15
596	A234	7c Rugby, horiz.	.35	.15
		Nos. 590-596 (7)	2.45	1.05

Carrier Pigeon — A235

Designs: 30c, Carrier pigeons, vert.

1974, Oct. 9 Photo. Perf. 14½x14
| 597 | A235 | 7c multicolored | .25 | .15 |
| a. | Perf. 15x14 | | .75 | .15 |

Perf. 13½x13
| 598 | A235 | 30c multicolored | 1.00 | 1.00 |

UPU, cent. A booklet containing a strip of 5 each of Nos. 597-598 was produced and sold for $4 Australian by the National Stamp Week Promotion Council with government approval.

William Charles Wentworth A236

Adoration of the Kings, by Dürer A237

Typo. & Litho.
1974, Oct. 9 Perf. 14x15
| 599 | A236 | 7c bister & black | .35 | .15 |
| a. | Perf. 14x14½ | | .90 | .25 |

Sesquicentennial of 1st Australian independent newspaper. W. C. Wentworth and Dr. Robert Wardell were the editors and the "A" is type from masthead of "The Australian."

1974, Nov. 13 Engr. Perf. 14x14½
Christmas: 35c, Flight into Egypt, by Albrecht Dürer.
| 600 | A237 | 10c buff & black | .22 | .15 |
| 601 | A237 | 35c buff & black | .90 | .90 |

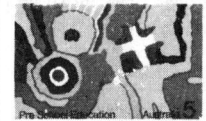

Pre-school Education A238

Correspondence Schools A239

Science Education A240

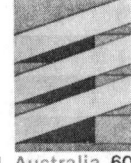

Advanced Education — A241

Perf. 13x13½, 13½x13
1974, Nov. 20 Photo.
602	A238	5c multicolored	.25	.15
603	A239	11c multicolored	.35	.25
604	A240	15c multicolored	.40	.30
605	A241	60c multicolored	1.00	.95
		Nos. 602-605 (4)	2.00	1.65

"Avoid Pollution" A242

"Road Safety" A243

Design: No. 607, "Avoid bush fires."

1975, Jan. 29 Photo. Perf. 14½x14
606	A242	10c multicolored	.30	.15
a.	Perf. 15x14		7.50	3.75
607	A242	10c multicolored	.30	.15
a.	Perf. 15x14		1.50	1.00

Perf. 14x14½
| 608 | A243 | 10c multicolored | .30 | .15 |
| | | Nos. 606-608 (3) | .90 | .45 |

Environmental dangers.

Symbols of Womanhood, Sun, Moon A244

Joseph B. Chifley (1885-1951) A245

1975, Mar. 12 Photo. Perf. 14x14½
| 609 | A244 | 10c dk vio blue & grn | .25 | .15 |

International Women's Year.

1975, Mar. 26
610	A245	10c shown	.20	.15
611	A245	10c John Curtin, 1885-1945	.20	.15
612	A245	10c Arthur W. Fadden, 1895-1973	.20	.15
613	A245	10c Joseph A. Lyons, 1879-1939	.20	.15
614	A245	10c Earle Page, 1880-1963	.20	.15
615	A245	10c John H. Scullin, 1876-1953	.20	.15
		Nos. 610-615 (6)	1.20	.90

Australian Prime Ministers.

Australian Postal Commission A246

Design: No. 617, Australian Telecommunications Commission.

1975, July 1 Photo. Perf. 14½x14
| 616 | A246 | 10c red, black & gray | .40 | .20 |
| a. | Perf. 15x14 | | .50 | .15 |

AUSTRALIA

617	A246 10c yel, black & gray	.40	.20
a.	Pair, #616-617	.95	.75
b.	Perf. 15x14	.50	.15
c.	Pair, #616a, 617b	1.25	1.00

Formation of Australian Postal and Telecommunications Commissions. Printed checkerwise.

Edith Cowan, Judge and Legislator A247

Truganini, Last Tasmanian Aborigine A248

Portraits: No. 619, Louisa Lawson (1848-1920), journalist. No. 620, Ethel Florence (Henry Handel) Richardson (1870-1946), novelist. No. 621, Catherine Spence (1825-1910), teacher, journalist, voting reformer. No. 622, Emma Constance Stone (1856-1902), first Australian woman physician.

1975, Aug. 6   Photo.   Perf. 14x14½

618	A247 10c olive grn & multi	.30	.30
a.	Perf. 14x15	.35	.35
619	A247 10c yel bister & multi	.30	.30
a.	Perf. 14x15	.35	.35
620	A248 10c olive & multi	.30	.30
a.	Perf. 14x15	.35	.35
621	A248 10c gray & multi	.30	.30
a.	Perf. 14x15	.35	.35
622	A247 10c violet & multi	.30	.30
a.	Perf. 14x15	.35	.35
623	A248 10c brown & multi	.30	.30
a.	Perf. 14x15	.35	.35
	Nos. 618-623 (6)	1.80	1.80

Famous Australian women.

Spirit House (PNG) and Sydney Opera House — A249

Bird in Flight and Southern Cross — A250

1975, Sept. 16   Photo.   Perf. 13½

624	A249 18c multicolored	.40	.15
625	A250 25c multicolored	.75	.55

Papua New Guinea independence, Sept. 16, 1975.

Adoration of the Kings — A251

"The Light Shineth in the Darkness" — A252

1975, Oct. 29   Photo.   Perf. 14½x14

626	A251 15c multicolored	.30	.15
627	A252 45c silver & multi	1.50	1.50

Christmas.

Australian Coat of Arms — A253

Two Types of A253:
Type I — Kangaroo: eye is dot, right paw has 1 toe, left foot has 1 toe. Emu: feet have 1 toe.
Type II — Kangaroo: eye is line, right paw has 3 toes, left foot has 2 toes. Emu: feet have 2 toes.
Other differences exist.

1976, Jan. 5   Photo.   Perf. 14½x14

628	A253 18c multicolored, type I	.40	.15
a.	Type II	.75	.25

"Williams' Coffin" Telephone, 1878 — A254

1976, Mar. 10   Photo.   Perf. 13½

| 629 | A254 18c buff & multi | .35 | .15 |

Centenary of first telephone call by Alexander Graham Bell, Mar. 10, 1876.

John Oxley — A255

Designs: Australian explorers.

1976, June 9   Photo.   Perf. 13½

630	A255 18c shown	.25	.15
631	A255 18c Hamilton Hume and William Hovell	.25	.15
632	A255 18c John Forrest	.25	.15
633	A255 18c Ernest Giles	.25	.15
634	A255 18c Peter Warburton	.25	.15
635	A255 18c William Gosse	.25	.15
	Nos. 630-635 (6)	1.50	.90

Survey Rule, Graph, Punched Tape — A256

1976, June 15   Perf. 15x14

| 636 | A256 18c multicolored | .30 | .15 |

Commonwealth Scientific and Industrial Research Organization, 50th anniv.

Soccer Goalkeeper A257

Olympic Rings and: No. 638, Woman gymnast, vert. 25c, Woman diver, vert. 40c, Bicycling.

Perf. 13x13½, 13½x13

1976, July 14   Photo.

637	A257 18c multicolored	.30	.15
638	A257 18c multicolored	.30	.15
639	A257 25c multicolored	.45	.40
640	A257 40c multicolored	.65	.50
	Nos. 637-640 (4)	1.70	1.20

21st Olympic Games, Montreal, Canada, July 17-Aug. 1.

Richmond Bridge, Tasmania A258

Mt. Buffalo, Victoria A259

Designs: 25c, Broken Bay, New South Wales. 35c, Wittenoom Gorge, Western Australia. 70c, Barrier Reef, Queensland. 85c, Ayers Rock, Northern Territory.

Perf. 14½x14, 14x14½

1976, Aug. 25   Photo.

641	A258 5c multicolored	.25	.15
642	A258 15c multicolored	.45	.20
643	A258 35c multicolored	.40	.30
644	A259 50c multicolored	.65	.25
645	A258 70c multicolored	.80	.35
646	A258 85c multicolored	1.25	1.00
	Nos. 641-646 (6)	3.80	2.25

Blamire Young and Australia No. 59 — A260

1976, Sept. 27   Photo.   Perf. 13½

| 647 | A260 18c apple green & multi | .35 | .15 |

Miniature Sheet

648		Sheet of 4	1.65	1.50
a.	A260 18c yellow & dark brown	.35	.35
b.	A260 18c rose, dk brown & yel	.35	.35
c.	A260 18c blue, dk brn, rose & yel	.35	.35

Natl. Stamp Week, Sept. 27-Oct. 3. Blamire Young (1862-1935), designer of Australia's 1st issue. No. 648 shows different stages of 4-color printing. The 4th stamp in sheet is identical with No. 647.

John Oxley — A255

Virgin and Child, after Simone Cantarini A261

Holly, Toy Koala, Christmas Tree and Decoration, Partridge A262

1976, Nov. 1   Photo.   Perf. 14½x14

| 649 | A261 15c brt car & lt blue | .30 | .20 |

Perf. 13½

| 650 | A262 45c multicolored | .80 | .75 |

Christmas.

John Gould (1804-1881) Ornithologist A263

Violinists A264

Famous Australians: No. 652, Thomas Laby (1880-1946), nuclear scientist. No. 653, Sir Baldwin Spencer (1860-1929), anthropologist (aborigines). No. 654, Griffith Taylor (1880-1963), geographer and arctic explorer.

1976, Nov. 10   Perf. 15x14

651	A263 18c shown	.30	.15
652	A263 18c Laby	.30	.15
653	A263 18c Spencer	.30	.15
654	A263 18c Taylor	.30	.15
	Nos. 651-654 (4)	1.20	.60

1977, Jan. 19   Photo.   Perf. 14x14½

655	A264 20c shown	.35	.20
656	A264 30c Dramatic scene	.40	.20
657	A264 40c Dancer	.70	.40
658	A264 60c Opera singer	.90	.20
	Nos. 655-658 (4)	2.35	1.00

Performing arts in Australia.

Elizabeth II A265

Wicket Keeper, Slip Fieldsman A266

Design: 45c, Elizabeth II and Prince Philip.

1977, Feb. 2

659	A265 18c multicolored	.30	.15
660	A265 45c multicolored	.75	.75

Reign of Queen Elizabeth II, 25th anniv.

1977, Mar. 9   Photo.   Perf. 13½

Cricket match, 19th century: No. 662, Umpire and batsman. No. 663, Two fieldsmen. No. 664, Batsman and umpire. No. 665, Bowler and fieldsman. 45c, Batsman facing bowler.

661	A266 18c gray & multi	.35	.25
662	A266 18c gray & multi	.35	.25
663	A266 18c gray & multi	.35	.25
664	A266 18c gray & multi	.35	.25
665	A266 18c gray & multi	.35	.25
a.	Strip of 5, #661-665	2.00	2.00
666	A266 45c gray & multi	.90	.90
	Nos. 661-666 (6)	2.65	2.15

Parliament House, Canberra A267

1977, Apr. 13   Perf. 14½x14

| 667 | A267 18c multicolored | .40 | .15 |

Parliament House, Canberra, 50th anniv.

Trade Union Workers A268

1977, May 9   Photo.   Perf. 13

| 668 | A268 18c multicolored | .35 | .15 |

Australian Council of Trade Unions (ACTU), 50th anniv.

Surfing Santa — A269

Virgin and Child — A270

1977, Oct. 31   Photo.   Perf. 14x14½

| 669 | A269 15c multicolored | .35 | .15 |

Perf. 13½x13

| 670 | A270 45c multicolored | .75 | .75 |

Christmas.

Australian Flag — A271

1978, Jan. 26   Photo.   Perf. 13x13½

| 671 | A271 18c multicolored | .35 | .15 |

Australia Day, 190th anniversary of first permanent settlement in New South Wales.

Harry Hawker and Sopwith "Camel" A272

Australian Aviators and their Planes: No. 673, Bert Hinkler and Avro Avian. No. 674, Charles Kingsford-Smith and Fokker "Southern Cross." No. 675, Charles Ulm and "Southern Cross."

1978, Apr. 19   Litho.   Perf. 15½

672	A272 18c ultra & multi	.30	.15
673	A272 18c blue & multi	.30	.15
674	A272 18c orange & multi	.30	.15

AUSTRALIA

675	A272 18c yellow & multi	.30	.15
	Souv. sheet, 2 each #674-675, imperf.	1.65	1.65
	Nos. 672-675 (4)	1.20	.60

No. 675a for 50th anniv. of first Trans-Pacific flight from Oakland, Cal., to Brisbane.

Beechcraft Baron Landing — A273

1978, May 15   Photo.   Perf. 13½

676	A273 18c multicolored	.30	.20

Royal Flying Doctor Service, 50th anniv.

Illawarra Flame Tree — A274

Sturt's Desert Rose, Map of Australia — A275

Australian trees: 25c, Ghost gum. 40c, Grass tree. 45c, Cootamundra wattle.

1978, June 1

677	A274 18c multicolored	.20	.15
678	A274 25c multicolored	.60	.60
679	A274 40c multicolored	.70	.70
680	A274 45c multicolored	.65	.65
	Nos. 677-680 (4)	2.15	2.10

1978, June 19   Litho.   Perf. 15½

681	A275 18c multicolored	.35	.15

Establishment of Government of the Northern Territory.

Hooded Dotterel — A276

Australian birds: 20c, Little grebe. 25c, Spurwing Plover. 30c, Pied oystercatcher. 55c, Lotus bird.

1978   Photo.   Perf. 13½

682	A276 5c multicolored	.15	.15
683	A276 20c multicolored	.25	.15
684	A276 25c multicolored	.35	.15
685	A276 30c multicolored	.40	.30
686	A276 55c multicolored	.70	.50
	Nos. 682-686 (5)	1.85	1.25

Issued: Nos. 683, 686, July 3; others, July 17. See Nos. 713-718, 732-739, 768.

Australia No. 95 on Album Page — A277

Virgin and Child, by Simon Marmion — A278

1978, Sept. 25   Litho.   Perf. 15½

687	A277 20c multicolored	.35	.15
a.	Miniature sheet of 4	1.65	1.65

National Stamp Week; 50th anniv. of Melbourne Intl. Phil. Exhib., Oct. 1928.

1978

Paintings from National Gallery, Victoria: 15c, Virgin and Child, after Van Eyck. 55c, Holy Family, by Perino del Vaga.

Perf. 15

688	A278 15c multicolored	.20	.15
689	A278 25c multicolored	.50	.50
690	A278 55c multicolored	.80	.80
	Nos. 688-690 (3)	1.50	1.45

Christmas. Issued: 25c, Oct. 3; others, Nov. 1.

Tulloch — A279

Race horses: 35c, Bernborough, vert. 50c, Phar Lap, vert. 55c, Peter Pan.

Perf. 15x14, 14x15

1978, Oct. 18   Photo.

691	A279 20c multicolored	.25	.15
692	A279 35c multicolored	.50	.50
693	A279 50c multicolored	.75	.75
694	A279 55c multicolored	.75	.75
	Nos. 691-694 (4)	2.25	2.15

Australian horse racing.

Flag Raising at Sydney Cove — A280

1979, Jan. 26   Litho.   Perf. 15½

695	A280 20c multicolored	.35	.15

Australia Day, Jan. 26.

Passenger Steamer Canberra A281

Ferries and Murray River Steamers: 35c, M.V. Lady Denman. 50c, P.S. Murray River Queen. 55c, Hydrofoil Curl Curl.

1979, Feb. 14   Photo.   Perf. 13½

696	A281 20c multicolored	.30	.15
697	A281 35c multicolored	.50	.40
698	A281 50c multicolored	.75	.65
699	A281 55c multicolored	.85	.85
	Nos. 696-699 (4)	2.40	2.05

Port Campbell — A282

Designs: Australian National Parks.

1979, Apr. 9   Litho.   Perf. 15½

700	A282 20c shown	.30	.15
701	A282 20c Uluru	.30	.15
702	A282 20c Royal	.30	.15
703	A282 20c Flinders Ranges	.30	.15
704	A282 20c Namburg	.30	.15
a.	Strip of 5, #700-704	1.50	
705	A282 20c Girraween, vert.	.30	.15
706	A282 20c Mount Field, vert.	.30	.15
a.	Pair, #705-706	.60	
	Nos. 700-706 (7)	2.10	1.05

Double Fairlie — A283

Australian steam locomotives: 35c, Puffing Billy. 50c, Pichi Richi. 55c, Zig Zag.

Perf. 13½, 15x14 (20c)

1979, May 16   Photo.

707	A283 20c multicolored	.35	.15
708	A283 35c multicolored	.65	.40
709	A283 50c multicolored	.90	.75
710	A283 55c multicolored	.95	.95
	Nos. 707-710 (4)	2.85	2.25

"Black Swan" — A284

1979, June 6   Photo.   Perf. 13½

711	A284 20c multicolored	.35	.20

150th anniversary of Western Australia.

Children Playing, IYC Emblem A285

1979, Aug. 13   Litho.   Perf. 13½x13

712	A285 20c multicolored	.30	.20

International Year of the Child.

Bird Type of 1978

Australian birds: 1c, Zebra finch. 2c, Crimson finch. 15c, Forest kingfisher, vert. 20c, Eastern yellow robin. 40c, Lovely wren, vert. 50c, Flame robin, vert.

1979, Sept. 17   Photo.   Perf. 13½

713	A276 1c multicolored	.15	.15
714	A276 2c multicolored	.15	.15
715	A276 15c multicolored	.30	.15
716	A276 20c multicolored	.30	.15
717	A276 40c multicolored	.50	.20
718	A276 50c multicolored	.70	.20
	Nos. 713-718 (6)	2.10	1.00

Christmas Letters, Flag-wrapped Parcels A286

Trout Fishing A287

Christmas: 15c, Nativity, icon. 55c, Madonna and Child, by Buglioni.

1979   Litho.   Perf. 13

719	A286 15c multicolored	.15	.15
720	A286 25c multicolored	.30	.30
721	A286 55c multicolored	.90	.90
	Nos. 719-721 (3)	1.35	1.35

Issue dates: 25c, Sept. 24. Others, Nov. 1.

1979, Oct. 24   Photo.   Perf. 14x14½

Sport fishing: 35c, Angler. 50c, Black marlin fishing. 55c, Surf fishing.

722	A287 20c multicolored	.25	.15
723	A287 35c multicolored	.45	.45
724	A287 50c multicolored	.70	.45
725	A287 55c multicolored	.75	.70
	Nos. 722-725 (4)	2.15	1.75

Matthew Flinders, Map of Australia A288

1980, Jan. 23   Litho.   Perf. 13½

726	A288 20c multicolored	.30	.15

Australia Day, Jan. 28.

Dingo — A289

1980, Feb. 20   Litho.   Perf. 13½x13

727	A289 20c shown	.30	.20
728	A289 25c Border collie	.35	.35
729	A289 35c Australian terrier	.60	.40
730	A289 50c Australian cattle dog	.80	.70
731	A289 65c Australian kelpie	.65	.65
	Nos. 727-731 (5)	2.70	2.30

Bird Type of 1978

Perf. 13½, 14x15 (22c), 13x12½ (28c, 60c)

1980   Litho., Photo. (22c)

732	A276 10c Golden-shoulder parrot, vert.	.15	.15
a.	Perf. 14½x14	1.25	.50
733	A276 22c White-tailed kingfisher, vert.	.30	.15
734	A276 28c Rainbow bird, vert.	.45	.15
735	A276 35c Regent bower bird, vert.	.45	.20
736	A276 45c Masked woodswallow	.95	.20
a.	Perf. 14x14½	4.00	2.00
737	A276 60c King parrot, vert.	.75	.25
738	A276 80c Rainbow pitta	1.00	.40
739	A276 $1 Western magpie, vert.	1.25	.30
	Nos. 732-739 (8)	5.30	1.80

Issued: #733, 734, 737, Mar. 31; others, July 1.

Queen Elizabeth II, 54th Birthday — A290

1980, Apr. 21   Litho.   Perf. 13x13½

740	A290 22c multicolored	.35	.15

Wanderer A291

High Court Building, Canberra A292

1980, May 7   Litho.   Perf. 13x13½

741	Strip of 5	1.75	1.50
a.	A291 22c shown	.30	.15
b.	A291 22c Stealing sheep	.30	.15
c.	A291 22c Squatter on horseback	.30	.15
d.	A291 22c Three troopers	.30	.15
e.	A291 22c Wanderer's ghost	.30	.15

"Waltzing Matilda", poem by Andrew Barton Patterson (1864-1941). No. 741 in continuous design.

1980, May 19

742	A292 22c multicolored	.35	.15

Opening of High Court of Australia Building, Canberra, May 26.

Salvation Army Officers — A294

Perf. 13x13½, 13½x13

1980, Aug. 11

747	A294 22c shown	.30	.15
748	A294 22c St. Vincent de Paul Society, vert.	.30	.15
749	A294 22c Meals on Wheels, vert.	.30	.15
750	A294 22c "Life. Be in it." (Joggers, bicyclists)	.30	.15
	Nos. 747-750 (4)	1.20	.60

AUSTRALIA

Mailman c. 1900 — A295

Holy Family, by Prospero Fontana — A296

1980, Sept. 29   Litho.   Perf. 13x13½
751	A295	22c Mailbox	.35	.15
752	A295	22c shown	.35	.15
753	A295	22c Mail truck	.35	.15
754	A295	22c Mailman, mailbox	.35	.15
755	A295	22c Mailman, diff.	.35	.15
a.		Souvenir sheet of 3	1.25	1.00
b.		Strip of 5, #751-755	1.75	1.00

Natl. Stamp Week, Sept. 29-Oct. 5. #755a contains stamps similar to #751, 753, 755.

1980   Perf. 13x13½
Christmas: 15c, Virgin Enthroned, by Justin O'Brien. 60c, Virgin and Child, by Michael Zuern the Younger, 1680.
756	A296	15c multicolored	.25	.15
757	A296	28c multicolored	.45	.45
758	A296	60c multicolored	.90	.65
		Nos. 756-758 (3)	1.60	1.25

Issued: 15c, 60c, Nov. 3; 28c, Oct. 1.

CA-6 Wackett Trainer, 1941 — A297

Designs: Australian military training planes.

1980, Nov. 19   Perf. 13½x14
759	A297	22c shown	.30	.25
760	A297	40c Winjeel, 1955	.60	.60
761	A297	45c Boomerang, 1944	.65	.50
762	A297	60c Nomad, 1975	1.00	.60
		Nos. 759-762 (4)	2.55	1.95

Bird Type of 1978

1980, Nov. 17   Litho.   Perf. 13½
| 768 | A276 | 18c Spotted catbird, vert. | .35 | .15 |

Flag on Map of Australia A298

1981, Jan. 21
| 771 | A298 | 22c multicolored | .35 | .15 |

Australia Day, Jan. 21.

Jockey Darby Munro (1913-1966), by Tony Rafty — A299

Australian sportsmen (Caricatures by Tony Rafty): 35c, Victor Trumper (1877-1915), cricket batsman. 55c, Norman Brookes (1877-1968), tennis player. 60c, Walter Lindrum (1898-1960), billiards player.

1981, Feb. 18   Perf. 14x13½
772	A299	22c multicolored	.25	.15
773	A299	35c multicolored	.45	.45
774	A299	55c multicolored	.65	.65
775	A299	60c multicolored	.75	.75
		Nos. 772-775 (4)	2.10	2.00

Australia No. C2 and Cover — A300

Perf. 13x13½, 13½x13
1981, Mar. 25   Litho.
| 776 | A300 | 22c Australia No. C2, vert. | .30 | .25 |
| 777 | A300 | 60c shown | .90 | .80 |

Australia-United Kingdom official airmail service, 50th anniv.

Map of Australia, APEX Emblem A301

1981, Apr. 6   Photo.   Perf. 13x13½
| 778 | A301 | 22c multicolored | .30 | .15 |

50th anniv. of APEX (young men's service club).

Queen Elizabeth's Personal Flag of Australia A302

1981, Apr. 21   Perf. 13
| 779 | A302 | 22c multicolored | .35 | .15 |

Queen Elizabeth II, 55th birthday.

License Inspected, Forrest Creek, by S.T. Gill — A303

Gold Rush Era (Sketches by S.T. Gill): No. 781, Puddling. No. 782, Quality of Washing Stuff. No. 783, Diggers on Route to Deposit Gold.

1981, May 20   Photo.   Perf. 13x13½
780	A303	22c multicolored	.30	.15
781	A303	22c multicolored	.30	.15
782	A303	22c multicolored	.30	.15
783	A303	22c multicolored	.30	.15
		Nos. 780-783 (4)	1.20	.60

Lace Monitor — A303a

Tasmanian Tiger — A304

Two Types of A304:
Type I - Indistinct line at right of ear, stripes even with base of tail.
Type II - Heavy line at right of ear, stripes longer.

1981-83   Litho.
784	A303a	1c shown	.15	.15
785	A303a	3c Corroboree frog	.15	.15
786	A304	5c Queensland hairy-nosed wombat, vert.	.15	.15
787	A303a	15c Eastern snake-necked tortoise	.20	.15
788	A304	24c shown, type I	.35	.15
a.		Type II	.35	.15
789	A304	25c Greater bilby, vert.	.35	.15
790	A303a	27c Blue Mountains tree frog	.40	.20
791	A304	30c Bridled nail-tailed wallaby, vert.	.40	.20
792	A303a	40c Smooth knob-tailed gecko	.55	.25
793	A304	50c Leadbeater's opossum	.85	.40
794	A304	55c Stick-nest rat, vert.	.85	.40
795	A303a	65c Yellow-faced whip snake	1.00	.45
796	A303a	70c Crucifix toad	1.10	.55
797	A303a	75c Eastern water dragon	1.10	.55
798	A303a	85c Centralian blue-tongued lizard	1.25	.65
799	A303a	90c Freshwater crocodile	1.40	.70
800	A303a	95c Thorny devil	1.50	.75
		Nos. 784-800 (17)	11.75	6.00

Perfs: 1c, 70c, 85c, 95c, 13½; 15c, 27c, 40c, 50c, 65c, 75c, 90c, 12½x13; 5c, 25c, 30c, 55c, 13x12½; 24c, 13x13½.

Issued: 24c, 7/1/81; 5c, 25c, 30c, 50c, 55c, 7/15/81; 3c, 27c, 65c, 75c, 4/19/82; 15c, 40c, 90c, 6/16/82. 1c, 70c, 85c, 95c, 2/2/83.

1982-84   Perf. 14x14½, 14½x14
785a	A303a	3c ('84)	.30	.15
786a	A304	5c ('84)	.90	.15
787a	A303a	15c ('84)	.70	.25
789a	A304	25c ('83)	1.10	.20
790a	A303a	27c	.75	.25
792a	A303a	40c ('84)	2.00	.30
793a	A304	50c ('83)	1.25	.40
795a	A303a	65c ('84)	1.40	.60
797a	A303a	75c ('84)	1.50	.80
		Nos. 785a-797a (9)	9.90	3.10

Prince Charles and Lady Diana — A305

1981, July 29   Litho.   Perf. 13
| 804 | A305 | 24c multicolored | .40 | .15 |
| 805 | A305 | 60c multicolored | 1.15 | .75 |

Royal Wedding.

Cortinarius Cinnabarinus A306

Intl. Year of the Disabled A307

Designs: Fungi.

1981, Aug. 19   Litho.   Perf. 13
806	A306	24c shown	.35	.15
807	A306	35c Coprinus comatus	.50	.50
808	A306	55c Armillaria luteo-obubalina	.95	.80
809	A306	60c Cortinarius austro-venetus	1.10	1.00
		Nos. 806-809 (4)	2.90	2.45

1981, Sept. 16   Perf. 14x13½
| 810 | A307 | 24c multicolored | .40 | .15 |

Christmas Bush for His Adorning A308

Globe A309

Christmas (Carols by William James and John Wheeler): 30c, The Silver Stars are in the Sky. 60c, Noeltime.

1981   Litho.   Perf. 13x13½
811	A308	18c multicolored	.35	.15
812	A308	30c multicolored	.50	.35
813	A308	60c multicolored	1.25	1.00
		Nos. 811-813 (3)	2.10	1.50

Issue dates: 30c, Sept. 28; others, Nov. 2.

1981, Sept. 30
| 814 | A309 | 24c multicolored | .35 | .15 |
| 815 | A309 | 60c multicolored | 1.00 | .90 |

Commonwealth Heads of Government Meeting, Melbourne, Sept. 30-Oct. 7.

Yacht — A310

1981, Oct. 14   Litho.   Perf. 13x13½
816	A310	24c Ocean racer	.45	.15
817	A310	35c Lightweight sharpie	.60	.60
818	A310	55c 12-Meter	.90	.60
819	A310	60c Sabot	1.10	1.00
		Nos. 816-819 (4)	3.05	2.35

Australia Day, Jan. 26 — A311

1982, Jan. 20   Litho.   Perf. 13x13½
| 820 | A311 | 24c multicolored | .40 | .15 |

Sperm Whale — A312

Perf. 13x13½, 13½x13
1982, Feb. 17
821	A312	24c shown	.35	.15
822	A312	35c Southern right whale, vert.	.60	.60
823	A312	55c Blue whale, vert.	.90	.75
824	A312	60c Humpback whale	1.00	1.00
		Nos. 821-824 (4)	2.85	2.50

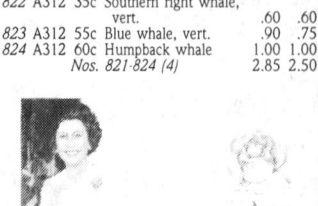

Elizabeth II, 56th Birthday — A313

Roses — A314

1982, Apr. 21   Perf. 13½
| 825 | A313 | 27c multicolored | .40 | .15 |

1982, May 19   Perf. 13x13½
826	A314	27c Marjorie Atherton	.40	.30
827	A314	40c Imp	.65	.60
828	A314	65c Minnie Watson	1.00	1.00
829	A314	75c Satellite	1.10	.75
		Nos. 826-829 (4)	3.15	2.85

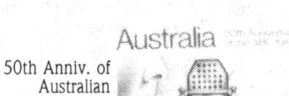

50th Anniv. of Australian Broadcasting Commission A315

1982, June 16   Perf. 13½x13
830	A315	27c Announcer, microphone	.45	.25
831	A315	27c Emblem	.45	.25
a.		Pair, #830-831	.90	.50

#830-831 se-tenant in continuous design.

Alice Springs Post Office, 1872 — A316

1982, Aug. 4   Perf. 13½x14, 14x13½
832	A316	27c shown	.35	.15
833	A316	27c Kingston, 1869	.35	.15
834	A316	27c York, 1893	.35	.15
835	A316	27c Flemington, 1890, vert.	.35	.15
836	A316	27c Forbes, 1881, vert.	.35	.15
837	A316	27c Launceston, 1889, vert.	.35	.15
838	A316	27c Rockhampton, 1892, vert.	.35	.15
		Nos. 832-838 (7)	2.45	1.05

AUSTRALIA

Christmas — A317

1st Australian Christmas cards, 1881. 21c, horiz.

1982		Litho.		Perf. 14½	
839	A317	21c multicolored		.35	.15
840	A317	35c multicolored		.60	.30
841	A317	75c multicolored		1.25	1.10
		Nos. 839-841 (3)		2.20	1.55

Issue dates: 35c, Sept. 15; others, Nov. 1.

12th Commonwealth Games, Brisbane, Sept. 30-Oct. 9 — A318

1982, Sept. 22		Litho.	Perf. 14x14½	
842	A318	27c Archery	.45	.15
843	A318	27c Boxing	.45	.15
844	A318	27c Weightlifting	.45	.15
a.		Souvenir sheet of 3, #842-844	1.50	1.40
845	A318	75c Pole vault	.90	.90
		Nos. 842-845 (4)	2.25	1.35

Natl. Stamp Week — A319

1982, Sept. 27		Perf. 13x13½	
846	A319 27c No. 132	.40	.15

A320  A321

Design: Gurgurr (Moon Spirit), Bark Painting by Yirawala Gunwinggu Tribe.

1982, Oct. 12		Perf. 14½	
847	A320 27c multicolored	.40	.15

Opening of Natl. Gallery, Canberra.

	Perf. 12½x13½		
1982, Nov. 17		**Photo.**	

Designs: Various eucalypts (gum trees).

848	A321	1c Pink-flowered marri	.15	.15
849	A321	2c Gungurru	.15	.15
850	A321	3c Red-flowering gum	1.00	.55
851	A321	10c Tasmanian blue gum	1.00	.60
852	A321	27c Forrest's marlock	.75	.50
a.		Bklt. pane of 9 + label (#850-851, 2 #848-849, 3 #852)	5.00	
b.		Bklt. pane (2 each #848-849, 852)	2.10	
		Nos. 848-852 (5)	3.05	1.95

Nos. 848-852 issued in booklets only.

Mimi Spirits Singing and Dancing, by David Milaybuma A322

Aboriginal Bark Paintings: Music and dance of the Mimi Spirits, Gunwinggu Tribe.

1982, Nov. 17		Litho.	Perf. 13½x14	
853	A322	27c shown	.40	.25
854	A322	40c Lofty Nabardayal	.65	.65
855	A322	65c Jimmy Galareya	1.00	.75
856	A322	75c Dick Nguleingulei Murrumurru	1.10	1.00
		Nos. 853-856 (4)	3.15	2.65

Historic Fire Engines A323

1983, Jan. 12		Perf. 13½x14	
857	A323	27c Shand Mason Steam, 1891	.40	.25
858	A323	40c Hotchkiss, 1914	.65	.65
859	A323	65c Ahrens-Fox PS2, 1929	1.00	1.00
860	A323	75c Merryweather Manual, 1851	1.10	1.00
		Nos. 857-860 (4)	3.15	2.90

Australia Day — A324

1983, Jan. 26		Litho.	Perf. 14½	
861	A324	27c Sirius	.45	.25
862	A324	27c Supply	.45	.25
a.		Pair, #861-862	.90	.75

A325  A326

1983, Feb. 2		Perf. 14x13½	
863	A325 27c multicolored	.40	.15

Australia-New Zealand Closer Economic Relationship agreement (ANZCER).

1983, Mar. 9		Litho.	Perf. 14½	
864	A326	27c Equality, dignity	.45	.20
865	A326	27c Social justice, cooperation	.45	.20
866	A326	27c Liberty, freedom	.45	.20
867	A326	75c Peace, harmony	1.25	1.25
		Nos. 864-867 (4)	2.60	1.85

Commonwealth day.

Queen Elizabeth II, 57th Birthday A327

1983, Apr. 20		Perf. 14½	
868	A327 27c Britannia	.40	.15

World Communications Year — A328

1983, May 18		Litho.	Perf. 13½x14	
869	A328 27c multicolored	.45	.15

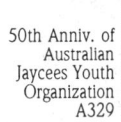

50th Anniv. of Australian Jaycees Youth Organization A329

1983, June 8			
870	A329 27c multicolored	.40	.15

St. John Ambulance Cent. — A330  **Regent Skipper — A331**

1983, June 8		Perf. 13½x14	
871	A330 27c multicolored	.40	.15

1983		Perf. 13½, 14½x14 (30c)	
872	A331	4c shown	.15	.15
873	A331	10c Cairn's birdwing	.15	.15
874	A331	20c Macleay's swallowtail	.30	.15
875	A331	27c Ulysses	.45	.15
875A	A331	30c Chlorinda hairstreak	.50	.15
876	A331	35c Blue tiger	.55	.20
877	A331	45c Big greasy	.60	.20
878	A331	60c Wood white	.85	.30
879	A331	80c Amaryllis azure	1.00	.40
880	A331	$1 Sword grass brown	1.25	.15
		Nos. 872-880 (10)	5.80	2.00

Issue dates: 30c, Oct. 24; others, June 15.

The Sentimental Bloke, by C.J. Dennis, 1909 — A332

Folktale scenes: a, The bloke. b, Doreen - the intro. c, The stror at coot. d, Hitched. e, The mooch of life.

1983, Aug. 3		Perf. 14½	
881	Strip of 5	2.25	1.50
a.-e.	A332 27c multi, any single	.45	.30

Kookaburra Bird Wearing Santa Hat — A333

1983		Litho.	Perf. 13½x14	
882	A333	24c Nativity	.35	.35
883	A333	35c multicolored	.50	.35
884	A333	85c Holiday beach scene	1.25	.60
		Nos. 882-884 (3)	2.10	1.30

Christmas. Issued: #883, 9/14; #882, 884, 11/2.

Inland Explorers — A334

Clay sculptures by Dianne Quinn: No. 885, Ludwig Leichhardt (1813-48). No. 886, William John Wills (1834-61), Robert O'Hara Burke (1821-61). No. 887, Paul Edmund de Strzelecki (1797-1873). No. 888, Alexander Forrest (1849-1901).

1983, Sept. 26		Perf. 14½	
885	A334 30c multicolored	.40	.15
886	A334 30c multicolored	.40	.15
887	A334 30c multicolored	.40	.15
888	A334 30c multicolored	.40	.15
	Nos. 885-888 (4)	1.60	.60

Australia Day — A335

1984, Jan. 26		Litho.	Perf. 13½x14	
889	A335 30c Cooks' Cottage	.40	.15

50th Anniv. of Official Air Mail Service — A336

Designs: Pilot Charles Ulm (1898-1934); his plane, "Faith in Australia," and different flight covers.

1984, Feb. 22		Litho.	Perf. 13½	
890	A336	45c Australia-New Zealand	1.00	.60
891	A336	45c Australia-Papua New Guinea	1.00	.60
a.		Pair, #890-891	2.00	1.75

Thomson, 1898 — A337

Australian-made vintage cars: b, Tarrant, 1906. c, Australian Six, 1919. d, Summit, 1923. e, Chic, 1924.

1984, Mar. 14		Perf. 14½	
892	Strip of 5	2.25	1.50
a.-e.	A337 30c any single	.45	.25

Queen Elizabeth II, 58th Birthday — A338

1984, Apr. 18		Perf. 14½	
893	A338 30c multicolored	.40	.15

Clipper Ships — A339

	Perf. 14x13½, 13½x14		
1984, May 23			
894	A339	30c Cutty Sark, 1869, vert.	.35	.30
895	A339	45c Orient, 1853	.55	.55
896	A339	75c Sobraon, 1866	.90	.90
897	A339	85c Thermopylae, 1868, vert.	1.10	1.10
		Nos. 894-897 (4)	2.90	2.85

Freestyle Skiing — A340 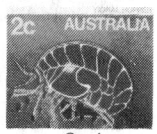 **Coral Hopper — A341**

1984, June 6		Litho.	Perf. 14½	
898	A340	30c shown	.50	.20
899	A340	30c Slalom, horiz.	.50	.20
900	A340	30c Cross-country, horiz.	.50	.20
901	A340	30c Downhill	.50	.20
		Nos. 898-901 (4)	2.00	.80

	Perf. 13½, 14x14½ (30c, 33c)	
1984-86		**Litho.**
902	A341	2c shown	.15	.15
903	A341	3c Jimble	.15	.15
904	A341	5c Tasseled anglerfish	.15	.15
905	A341	10c Stonefish	.15	.15
906	A341	20c Red handfish	.25	.15
907	A341	25c Orange-tipped cowrie	.45	.25
908	A341	30c Choat's wrasse	.55	.25
909	A341	33c Leafy sea dragon	.45	.20
910	A341	40c Red velvet fish	.55	.25
911	A341	45c Texile cone shell	.65	.30
912	A341	50c Blue-lined surgeonfish	.90	.50
913	A341	55c Bennett's nudibranch	1.00	.50
914	A341	60c Lionfish	.85	.40
915	A341	65c Stingray	.95	.40
916	A341	70c Blue-ringed octopus	1.00	.50

AUSTRALIA

917 A341 80c Pineapple fish 1.15 .55
918 A341 85c Regal angelfish 1.50 .95
919 A341 90c Crab-eyed goby 1.20 .55
920 A341 $1 Crown of thorns starfish 1.50 .60
Nos. 902-920 (19) 13.55 6.95

Issued: 2c, 25c, 30c, 50c, 55c, 85c, June 18; 5c, 20c, 40c, 80c, 90c, June 12, 1985; 3c, 10c, 45c, 60c, 65c, 70c, $1, June 11, 1986.

1984 Summer Olympics A342

Event stages.

Perf. 13½x14, 14x13½
1984, July 25   **Litho.**
922 A342 30c Start (facing down) .45 .20
923 A342 30c Competing (facing right) .45 .20
924 A342 30c Finish, vert. .45 .20
Nos. 922-924 (3) 1.35 .60

Ausipex '84 — A343 / Christmas — A344

Designs: No. 926a, Victoria #3. b, New South Wales #1. c, Tasmania #1. d, South Australia #1. e, Western Australia #1. f, Queensland #3.

1984   **Perf. 14½**
925 A343 30c No. 2 .45 .15

Souvenir Sheet
926 Sheet of 7 3.50 3.00
a.-f. A343 30c any single .50 .20

#926 contains #925, 926a-926f. Issue dates: #925, Aug. 22; #926, Sept. 21.

1984   **Litho.**   **Perf. 14x13½**
927 A344 24c Angel and Child .30 .25
928 A344 30c Veiled Virgin and Child .35 .25
929 A344 40c Angel .50 .40
930 A344 50c Three Kings .65 .45
931 A344 85c Madonna and Child 1.10 1.00
Nos. 927-931 (5) 2.90 2.35

Stained-glass windows. Issue dates: 40c, Sept. 17; others, Oct. 30.

European Settlement Bicentenary A345 / Settlement of Victoria Sesquicentenary A346

Design: No. 932, Bicentennial Emblem.
Rock paintings: No. 933, Stick figures, Cobar Region, New South Wales. No. 934, Bunjil's Cave, Grampians, Western Victoria. No. 935, Quinkan Gallery, Cape York, Queensland. No. 936, Wandjina Spirit and Snake Babies, Gibb River, Western Australia. No. 937, Rock Python, Western Australia. No. 938, Silver Barramundi, Kakadu Natl. Park, Northern Territory. 85c, Rock Possum, Kakadu Natl. Park.

1984, Nov. 7   **Litho.**   **Perf. 14½**
932 A345 30c multicolored .45 .25
933 A345 30c multicolored .45 .25
934 A345 30c multicolored .45 .25
935 A345 30c multicolored .45 .25
936 A345 30c multicolored .45 .25
937 A345 30c multicolored .45 .25
938 A345 30c multicolored .45 .25
939 A345 85c multicolored 1.25 .60
Nos. 932-939 (8) 4.40 2.35

1984, Nov. 19
940 A346 30c Helmeted honeyeater .45 .20
941 A346 30c Leadbeater's possum .45 .20
a. Pair, #940-941 .90

Australia Day — A347

1985, Jan. 25   **Litho.**
942 A347 30c Musgrave Ranges, by Sidney Nolan .45 .20
943 A347 30c The Walls of China, by Russell Drysdale .45 .20
a. Pair, #942-943 .90

Intl. Youth Year — A348

1985, Feb. 13   **Litho.**   **Perf. 14x13½**
944 A348 30c multicolored .40 .15

Royal Victorian Volunteer Artillery — A349 / District Nursing Service Centenary — A350

Colonial military uniforms: b, Western Australian Pinjarrah Cavalry. c, New South Wales Lancers. d, New South Wales Contingent to the Sudan. e, Victorian Mounted Rifles.

1985, Feb. 25   **Perf. 14½**
945 Strip of 5 2.25 2.00
a.-e. A349 33c any single .45 .15

1985, Mar. 13
946 A350 33c multicolored .40 .15

Australian Cockatoo A351

Perf. 14 Horiz. on 1 or 2 sides
1985, Mar. 13
947 A351 1c apple grn, yel & buff .50 .50
948 A351 33c apple grn, yel, & lt grnsh blue .45 .20
a. Bklt. pane, 1 #947, 3 #948 2.75

Issued in booklets only.

A352 / A353

1985, Apr. 10   **Perf. 13**
949 A352 33c Abel Tasman, explorer .55 .30
950 A352 33c The Eendracht .55 .30
951 A352 33c William Dampier .55 .30
952 A352 90c Globe and hand 1.50 .90
a. Souvenir sheet of 4, #949-952 3.50 2.00
Nos. 949-952 (4) 3.15 1.80

1985, Apr. 22   **Perf. 14x13½**
953 A353 33c Queen's Badge, Order of Australia .45 .15

Queen Elizabeth II, 59th birthday.

A354 / A356

1985, May 15   **Litho.**   **Perf. 14x13**
954 A354 33c Soil .45 .30
955 A354 50c Air .65 .50
956 A354 80c Water 1.00 .70
957 A354 90c Energy 1.10 .90
Nos. 954-957 (4) 3.20 2.40

Environmental conservation.

1985, July 17   **Litho.**   **Perf. 14½**
Illustrations from classic children's books: a, Elves & Fairies, by Annie Rentoul. b, The Magic Pudding, text and illustrations by Norman Lindsay. c, Ginger Meggs, by James Charles Bancks. d, Blinky Bill, by Dorothy Wall. e, Snugglepot and Cuddlepie, by May Gibbs.

960 Strip of 5 2.25 1.25
a.-e. A356 33c any single .40 .20

Electronic Mail — A357

1985, Sept. 18   **Litho.**
961 A357 33c multicolored .40 .15

Christmas A358

1985, Sept. 18   **Litho.**
962 A358 45c multicolored .45 .35

See Nos. 967-970.

Coastal Shipwrecks A359

Salvaged antiquities: 33c, Astrolabe from Batavia, 1629. 50c, German beardman (Bellarmine) jug from Vergulde Draeck, 1656. 90c, Wooden bobbins from Batavia, and scissors from Zeewijk, 1727. $1, Silver buckle from Zeewijk.

1985, Oct. 2   **Litho.**   **Perf. 13**
963 A359 33c multicolored .50 .20
964 A359 50c multicolored .75 .75
965 A359 90c multicolored 1.40 1.25
966 A359 $1 multicolored 1.50 1.00
Nos. 963-966 (4) 4.15 3.20

Christmas Type of 1985
Illustrations by Scott Hartshorne.

1985, Nov. 1   **Litho.**   **Perf. 14**
967 A358 27c Angel with trumpet .30 .15
968 A358 33c Angel with bells .40 .25
969 A358 55c Angel with star .70 .65
970 A358 90c Angel with ornament 1.10 1.10
Nos. 967-970 (4) 2.50 2.15

Australia Day — A360 / AUSSAT — A361

1986, Jan. 24   **Litho.**   **Perf. 14½**
971 A360 33c Aboriginal painting .40 .15

1986, Jan. 24
Various communications satellites.
972 A361 33c multicolored .35 .15
973 A361 80c multicolored 1.15 .75

South Australia, Sesquicent. A362

1986, Feb. 12   **Perf. 13½x14**
974 A362 33c Sailing ship Buffalo .50 .15
975 A362 33c City Sign, sculpture by O.H. Hajek .50 .15
a. Pair, #974-975 1.00 .60

Cook's New Holland Expedition A363

1986, Mar. 12   **Perf. 13**
976 A363 33c Hibiscus merankensis .45 .30
977 A363 33c Banksia serrata .45 .30
978 A363 50c Dillenia alata .70 .70
979 A363 90c Corria reflexa 1.10 .85
980 A363 90c Parkinson 1.25 1.00
981 A363 90c Banks 1.25 1.25
Nos. 976-981 (6) 5.20 4.50

Australian bicentennial. Sydney Parkinson (d. 1775), artist. Sir Joseph Banks (1743-1820), naturalist.

Halley's Comet A364 / Elizabeth II, 60th Birthday A365

1986, Apr. 9   **Perf. 14x13½**
982 A364 33c Radio telescope, trajectory diagram .45 .15

1986, Apr. 21   **Perf. 14½**
983 A365 33c multicolored .45 .15

Horses — A366

1986, May 21
984 A366 33c Brumbies .45 .25
985 A366 80c Stock horse mustering 1.10 .65
986 A366 90c Show-jumping 1.25 .95
987 A366 $1 Australian pony 1.40 .95
Nos. 984-987 (4) 4.20 2.80

AUSTRALIA

Click Go the Shears,
Folk Song — A366a

Lines from the song: b, Old shearer stands. c, Ringer looks around. d, Boss of the board. e, Tarboy is there. f, Shearing is all over.

1986, July 21   Litho.   Perf. 14½
987A   Strip of 5   2.75   1.50
 b.-f.   A366a 33c, any single   .55   .15

Amalgamated Shearers' Union, predecessor of the Australian Workers' Union, cent.

Australia Bicentennial A367

Settling of Botany Bay penal colony: No. 988, King George III, c. 1767, by A. Ramsay. No. 989, Lord Sydney, secretary of state, 1783-1789, by Gilbert Stuart. No. 990, Capt. Arthur Phillip, 1st penal colony governor, by F. Wheatley, 1786. $1, Capt. John Hunter, governor, 1795-1800, by W. B. Bennett, 1815.

1986, Aug. 6   Litho.   Perf. 13
988   A367 33c multicolored   .50   .30
989   A367 33c multicolored   .50   .30
990   A367 33c multicolored   .50   .30
991   A367 $1 multicolored   1.50   1.00
     Nos. 988-991 (4)   3.00   1.90

Wildlife — A368

Alpine Wildflowers — A369

Designs: a, Red kangaroo. b, Emu. c, Koala. d, Kookaburra. e, Platypus.

1986, Aug. 13   Perf. 14½x14
992   Strip of 5   2.00   1.25
 a.-e. A368 36c any single   .40   .15

Rouletted 9½ Vert. on 1 or 2 sides
1986, Aug. 25
Booklet Stamps
993   A369 3c Royal bluebell   .45   .45
994   A369 5c Alpine marsh marigold 1.00   1.00
995   A369 25c Mount Buffalo sunray 1.00   .75
996   A369 36c Silver snow daisy   .90   .20
 a.   Bklt. pane, #993, #994, 2 #996   3.25
 b.   Bklt. pane, #993, #995, 2 #996   3.25
     Nos. 993-996 (4)   3.35   2.40

Orchids — A370

America's Cup Triumph '83 — A371

1986, Sept. 18   Perf. 14½
997   A370 36c Elythranthera emarginata .60   .15
998   A370 55c Dendrobium nindii   1.00   .60
999   A370 90c Caleana major   1.65   1.00
1000 A370 $1 Thelymitra variegata   1.75   1.10
     Nos. 997-1000 (4)   5.00   2.85

1986, Sept. 26   Perf. 14x13½
1001 A371 36c Australia II crossing finish line .60   .25
1002 A371 36c Trophy   .60   .25
1003 A371 36c Boxing kangaroo   .60   .25
     Nos. 1001-1003 (3)   1.80   .75

Intl. Peace Year — A372

1986, Oct. 22   Litho.   Perf. 14x13½
1004 A372 36c multicolored   .50   .15

Christmas A373

Kindergarten nativity play: No. 1005, Holy Family, vert. No. 1006, Three Kings, vert. No. 1007, Angels. No. 1008a, Angels, peasants. No. 1008b, Holy Family, angels, vert. No. 1008c, Shepherd, angels, vert. No. 1008d, Three Kings. No. 1008e, Shepherds.

1986, Nov. 3   Litho.
1005 A373 30c multicolored   .50   .15
 a.   Perf 14x13½   1.00   .50
1006 A373 34c multicolored   .60   .25
1007 A373 60c multicolored   1.00   .65
     Nos. 1005-1007 (3)   2.10   1.05

Souvenir Sheet
1008   Sheet of 5   2.50   2.50
 a.-e. A373 30c any single   .50   .50

Perfs: Nos. 1005-1006, 1008c, 15x14½; Nos. 1007, 1008a 1008e, 14½x15; No. 1008b, 15x14½x15x15; 1008d, 14½x15x14x14½.

Australia Day — A374

1987, Jan. 23   Litho.   Perf. 13½x14
1009 A374 36c Flag, circuit board   .45   .15
1010 A374 36c Made in Australia campaign emblem .45   .15

America's Cup — A375

Fruits — A376

Views of yachts racing.

1987, Jan. 28   Perf. 15x14½
1011 A375 36c multicolored   .50   .20
1012 A375 55c multicolored   .80   .55
1013 A375 90c multicolored   1.40   .90
1014 A375 $1 multicolored   1.65   .95
     Nos. 1011-1014 (4)   4.35   2.60

1987, Feb. 11   Perf. 14x13½
1015 A376 36c Melons, grapes   .55   .30
1016 A376 65c Tropical fruit   1.00   .60
1017 A376 90c Pears, apples, oranges 1.40   .90
1018 A376 $1 Berries, peaches   1.50   .95
     Nos. 1015-1018 (4)   4.45   2.75

Agricultural Shows — A377

1987, Apr. 10   Litho.   Perf. 14x13½
1019 A377 36c Livestock   .55   .15
1020 A377 65c Produce   1.00   .60
1021 A377 90c Carnival   1.40   .95
1022 A377 $1 Farmers   1.50   .95
     Nos. 1019-1022 (4)   4.45   2.60

Queen Elizabeth II, 61st Birthday A378

1987, Apr. 21   Perf. 13½x14
1023 A378 36c multicolored   .45   .15

First Fleet Leaving England — A379

Continuous design: No. 1024a, Convicts awaiting transportation. b, Capt. Arthur Phillip, Mrs. Phillip, longboat on shore. c, Sailors relaxing and working. d, Longboats heading from and to fleet. 4e, Fleet in harbor.
No. 1025a, Longboat approaching Tenerife, The Canary Isls. b, Fishing in Tenerife Harbor. $1, Fleet, dolphins.

1987   Perf. 13
1024   Strip of 5   4.00   4.00
 a.-e. A379 36c any single   .80   .20
1025   Pair   1.00   1.00
 a.-b. A379 36c any single   .50   .20
1026 A379 $1 multicolored   1.50   1.50
     Nos. 1024-1026 (3)   6.50   6.50

Australia bicent.; departure of the First Fleet, May 13, 1787; arrival at Tenerife, June 1787. Issued: #1024, May 13; #1025-1026, June 3.

1987, Aug. 6

First Fleet arrives at Rio de Janeiro, Aug. 1787: a, Whale, storm in the Atlantic. b, Citrus grove. c, Market. d, Religious procession. e, Fireworks over harbor.

1027   Strip of 5   2.25   2.25
 a.-e. A379 37c any single   .45   .15

No. 1027 has a continuous design.

1987, Oct. 13

First Fleet arrives at Cape of Good Hope, Oct. 1787: No. 1028a, British officer surveys livestock and supplies, Table Mountain. No. 1028b, Ships anchored in Table Bay. No. 1029, Fishermen pull in nets as the Fleet approaches the Cape.

1028   Pair   .90   .90
 a.-b. A379 37c any single   .45   .20
1029 A379 $1 multicolored   1.25   .50

No. 1028 has a continuous design.

1988, Jan. 26

Arrival of the First Fleet, Sydney Cove, Jan. 1788: a, Five aborigines on shore. b, Four aborigines on shore. c, Kangaroos. d, White cranes. e, Flag raising.

1030   Strip of 5   2.75   2.75
 a.-e. A379 37c any single   .55   .20

Printed se-tenant in a continuous design.

The Early Years: Sydney Cove and Parramatta Colonies — A380

Details from panorama "View of Sydney from the East Side of the Cove," 1808, painted by convict artist John Eyre to illustrate The Present Picture of New South Wales, published in London in 1811, and paintings in British and Australian museums: a, Government House, 1790, Sydney, by midshipman George Raper. b, Government Farm, Parramatta, 1791, attributed to the Port Jackson Painter. c, Parramatta Road, 1796, attributed to convict artist Thomas Watling. d, The Rocks and Sydney Cove, 1800, an aquatint engraving by Edward Dayes. e, Sydney Hospital, 1803, by George William Evans, an explorer and surveyor-general of New South Wales. Printed se-tenant in a continuous design.

1988, Apr. 13   Litho.   Perf. 13
1031   Strip of 5   3.00   3.00
 a.-e. A380 37c any single   .60   .20

Australia Bicentennial.

The Man from Snowy River, 1890, Ballad by A.B. Paterson — A381

Fauna — A382

Excerpts: a, At the station. b, Mountain bred. c, Terrible descent. d, At their heels. e, Brought them back.

1987, June 24   Perf. 14x13½
1034   Strip of 5   2.75   2.75
 a.-e. A381 36c any single   .55   .30

Printed se-tenant in a continuous design.

1987, July 1   Perf. 14½x14

Designs: a, Possum. b, Cockatoo. c, Wombat. d, Rosella. e, Echidna.

1035   Strip of 5   2.25   2.25
 a.-e. A382 37c any single   .45   .15

Printed se-tenant in a continuous design.

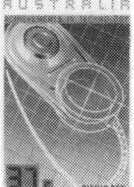

Technology — A383

1987, Aug. 19   Perf. 14½
1036 A383 37c Bionic ear   .40   .15
1037 A383 53c Microchips   .55   .30
1038 A383 63c Robotics   .70   .35
1039 A383 68c Zirconia ceramics   .75   .35
     Nos. 1036-1039 (4)   2.40   1.15

Children A384

1987, Sept. 16
1040 A384 37c Crayfishing   .45   .15
1041 A384 55c Cat's cradle   .65   .30
1042 A384 90c Eating meat pies   1.00   .45
1043 A384 $1 Playing with a joey   1.25   .50
     Nos. 1040-1043 (4)   3.35   1.40

Christmas A385

Carolers: a, Woman, two girls. b, Man, two girls. c, Four children. d, Man, two women, boy. e, Six youths. 37c, three women, two men. Nos. 1044a-1044e are vert.

AUSTRALIA

1987, Nov. 2   Litho.   Perf. 14½
1044   Strip of 5   2.00 2.00
a.-e.   A385 30c any single   .40   .15

Perf. 13½x14
1045 A385 37c multicolored   .45   .20
1046 A385 63c shown   .80   .30
       Nos. 1044-1046 (3)   3.25 2.50

Carols by Candlelight, Christmas Eve, Sidney Myer Bowl, Melbourne.

Aboriginal Crafts — A386

Designs: 3c, Spearthrower, Western Australia. 15c, Shield, New South Wales. No. 1049, Basket, Queensland. No. 1050, Bowl, Central Australia. No. 1051, Belt, Northern Territory.

Perf. 15½ Horiz.
1987, Oct. 13   Photo.
1047 A386 3c multicolored   1.25 1.25
1048 A386 15c multicolored   1.90 1.25
1049 A386 37c multicolored   1.10   .35
   a.   Bkt. pane, 2 each #1047, #1049   4.50
1050 A386 37c multicolored   1.25   .35
1051 A386 37c multicolored   1.25   .35
   a.   Bkt. pane, 1 #1048, 3 #1050, 2
         #1051   9.00
       Nos. 1047-1051 (5)   6.75 3.55

Issued only in booklets.

Caricature of Australian Koala and American Bald Eagle — A387

1988, Jan. 26   Perf. 13
1052 A387 37c multicolored   .55   .15

Australia bicentennial. See No. 1086 and US No. 2370.

Living Together — A388

Cartoons.

1988   Perf. 14
1053 A388   1c Religion   .15   .15
1054 A388   2c Industry   .15   .15
1055 A388   3c Local government   .15   .15
1056 A388   4c Trade unions   .15   .15
1057 A388   5c Parliament   .15   .15
1058 A388 10c Transportation   .15   .15
1059 A388 15c Sports   .20   .15
1060 A388 20c Commerce   .30   .15
1061 A388 25c Housing   .35   .15
1062 A388 30c Welfare   .45   .15
1063 A388 55c Postal services   .55   .20
   a.   Booklet pane of 10   5.50
1063B A388 39c Tourism   .55   .20
   c.   Booklet pane of 10   5.50
1064 A388 40c Recreation   .60   .20
1065 A388 45c Health   .70   .25
1066 A388 50c Mining   .75   .30
1067 A388 53c Primary industry   .80   .30
1068 A388 55c Education   .85   .30
1069 A388 60c Armed Forces   .95   .35
1070 A388 65c Police   1.00   .35
1071 A388 65c Telecommunica-
             tions   1.00   .35
1072 A388 68c The media   1.10   .40
1073 A388 70c Science and tech-
             nology   1.10   .40
1074 A388 75c Visual arts   1.10   .45
1075 A388 80c Performing arts   1.25   .45
1076 A388 90c Banking   1.40   .50
1077 A388 95c Law   1.50   .55
1078 A388 $1 Rescue and emer-
             gency services   1.50   .55
       Nos. 1053-1078 (27)   18.90 7.60

Issued: 1c, 2c, 3c, 5c, 30c, 40c, 55c, 60c, 63c, 65c, 68c, 75c, 95c, 3/16; 39c, 9/28; others, 2/17.

Queen Elizabeth II, 62nd Birthday A389

1988, Apr. 21   Perf. 14½
1079 A389 37c multicolored   .60   .20

EXPO '88, Brisbane, Apr. 30-Oct. 30 — A390

1988, Apr. 29   Perf. 13
1080 A390 37c multicolored   .60   .20

Opening of Parliament House, Canberra A391

1988, May 9   Perf. 14½
1081 A391 37c multicolored   .60   .20

Australia Bicentennial A392

Designs: No. 1082, Colonist, clipper ship. No. 1083, British and Australian parliaments, Queen Elizabeth II. No. 1084, Cricketer W.G. Grace. No. 1085, John Lennon (1940-1980), William Shakespeare (1564-1616) and Sydney Opera House. #1083a, 1085a have continuous design picturing flag of Australia.

1988, June 21   Litho.   Perf. 13
1082 A392 37c multicolored   .80   .20
1083 A392 37c multicolored   .80   .20
   a.   Pair, #1082-1083   1.75   .75
1084 A392 $1 multicolored   2.25   .55
1085 A392 $1 multicolored   2.25   .55
   a.   Pair, #1084-1085   4.75 2.50
       Nos. 1082-1085 (4)   6.10 1.50

See Great Britain Nos. 1222-1225.

Caricature Type of 1988

Design: Caricature of an Australian koala and New Zealand kiwi.

1988, June 21   Litho.   Perf. 13½
1086 A387 37c multicolored   .60   .20

Australia bicentennial. See New Zealand No. 907.

"Dream" Lore on Art of the Desert — A393

Aboriginal paintings from Papunya Settlement in the Flinders University Art Museum: 37c, Bush Potato Country, by Turkey Tolsen Tjupurrula with by David Corby Tjapaltjarri. 55c, Courtship Rejected, by Limpi Puntungka Tjapangati. 90c, Medicine Story, anonymous. $1, Ancestor Dreaming, by Tim Leura Tjapaltjarri.

1988, Aug. 1   Litho.   Perf. 13
1087 A393 37c multicolored   .60   .20
1088 A393 55c multicolored   .90   .75
1089 A393 90c multicolored   1.50   .50
1090 A393 $1 multicolored   1.65   .55
       Nos. 1087-1090 (4)   4.65 2.00

1988 Summer Olympics, Seoul — A394

1988, Sept. 14   Perf. 14½
1091 A394 37c Basketball   .60   .20
1092 A394 65c Running   1.10   .90
1093 A394 $1 Rhythmic gymnastics   1.65   .55
       Nos. 1091-1093 (3)   3.35 1.65

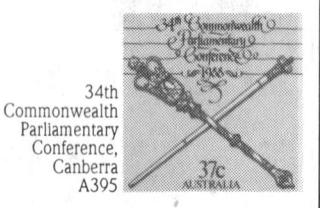

34th Commonwealth Parliamentary Conference, Canberra A395

1988, Sept. 19
1094 A395 37c Scepter and mace   .60   .20

Works in the Contemporary Decorative Arts Collection at the Natl. Gallery — A396

Roulette 9 Horiz.
1988, Sept. 28   Litho.
1095 A396 2c "Australian Fetish,"
             by Peter Tully   2.50 2.50
1096 A396 5c Vase by Colin Levy   2.50 2.50
1097 A396 39c Teapot by Frank Bau-
             er   .75   .35
   a.   Bkt. pane of 3 (2c, 2 39c)   4.50
   b.   Bkt. pane of 6 (5c, 5 39c)   6.25
       Nos. 1095-1097 (3)   5.75 5.35

Nos. 1095-1097 issued in booklets only.

Views — A397

1988, Oct. 17   Photo.   Perf. 13
1098 A397 39c The Desert   .65   .25
1099 A397 55c The Top End   .90   .30
1100 A397 65c The Coast   1.10   .40
1101 A397 70c The Bush   1.10   .40
       Nos. 1098-1101 (4)   3.75 1.35

Christmas A398

Children's design contest winning drawings: 32c, Nativity scene, by Danielle Hush, age 7. 39c, Koala wearing a Santa hat, by Kylie Courtney, age 6. 63c, Cockatoo wearing a Santa hat, by Benjamin Stevenson, age 10.

1988, Oct. 31   Perf. 13½x13
1102 A398 32c multicolored   .55   .15
1103 A398 39c multicolored   .65   .20
1104 A398 63c multicolored   1.10   .55
       Nos. 1102-1104 (3)   2.30   .90

Sir Henry Parkes (1815-1896), Advocate of the Federation of the Six Colonies — A399

1989, Jan. 25   Litho.   Perf. 14x13½
1105 A399 39c multicolored   .70   .15

Australia Day.

Sports — A400

1989, Feb. 13   Perf. 14x14½
1106 A400   1c Bowls   .15   .15
   a.   Perf. 13½x14 ('90)   .15   .15
1107 A400   2c Bowling   .15   .15
   a.   Perf. 13x13½ ('91)   .15   .15
1108 A400   3c Football   .15   .15
1109 A400 39c Fishing   .70   .15
   a.   Booklet pane of 10   7.00
   d.   Perf. 13x13½ on 3 sides ('90)   .70   .20
   e.   Booklet pane of 10, #1109d   7.00
1109B A400 41c Cycling   .60   .20
   c.   Booklet pane of 10   6.25
1110 A400 55c Kite-flying   .95   .30
1111 A400 70c Cricket   1.25   .40
1112 A400 $1.10 Golf   1.95   .65

1990-94
1114 A400   5c Kayaking, canoeing   .15   .15
   a.   Perf. 13x13½   .15   .15
1115 A400 10c Windsurfing   .15   .15
   a.   Perf. 13x13½   .30   .15
1116 A400 20c Tennis   .30   .15
   a.   Perf. 13x13½   .30   .30
1117 A400 65c Rock climbing   1.00   .35
   a.   Perf. 13x13½   1.00 1.00
1118 A400 $1 Running   1.50   .50
   a.   Perf. 13x13½   3.75 2.00

Issued: #1114a, 1115a, 1116a, 1117a, 1118, 1/17/90; #1118a, 1/91; #1115, 1117, 2/92; #1116, 7/93; #1114, 3/94.

1990, Aug. 27
1119 A400 43c Skateboarding   .65   .15
   a.   Booklet pane of 10   6.75

Perf. 13½
1120 A400 $1.20 Hang-gliding   1.90   .50

1991, Aug. 22   Perf. 14x14½
1121 A400 75c Netball   1.10   .40
1122 A400 80c Squash   1.25   .40
1123 A400 85c Diving   1.25   .40
1124 A400 90c Soccer   1.40   .45
       Nos. 1106-1124 (19)   16.55 5.80

For self-adhesive stamps see #1185-1186.
This is an expanding set. Numbers will change when completed.

Botanical Gardens — A401

Designs: $2, Nooroo, New South Wales. $5, Mawarra, Victoria. $10, Palm House, Adelaide Botanical Garden. $20, A View of the Artist's House and Garden in Mills Plains, Van Diemen's Land by John Glover.

1989   Litho. & Engr.   Perf. 14
1132 A401 $2 multicolored   3.00 1.00
   a.   Perf. 14x13½ ('91)   3.00 1.00
1133 A401 $5 multicolored   7.75 2.50
   a.   Perf. 14x13½   8.50 2.50
1134 A401 $10 multicolored   15.00 4.25

Perf. 14½x14
1135 A401 $20 multicolored   27.50 8.00
       Nos. 1132-1135 (4)   53.25 15.75

Issued: $10, 4/12; $2, $5, 9/13; $20, 8/15.

AUSTRALIA

Sheep — A402

1989, Feb. 27   *Perf. 13½x14*
1136	A402	39c Merino	.70	.20
1137	A402	39c Poll Dorset	.70	.20
1138	A402	85c Polwarth	1.50	.50
1139	A402	$1 Corriedale	1.75	.75
		Nos. 1136-1139 (4)	4.65	1.65

World Sheep and Wool Congress, Tasmania, Feb. 27-Mar. 6.

Queen Elizabeth II, 63rd Birthday — A403

1989, Apr. 21   *Litho.*   *Perf. 14½*
| 1140 | A403 | 39c Statue by John Dowie | .65 | .20 |

Colonial Australia A404

Pastoral Era: a, Immigrant ship in port, c. 1835. b, Pioneer's hut, wool bales in dray. c, Squatter's homestead. d, Shepherds. e, Explorers.

1989, May 10
| 1141 | | Strip of 5 | 3.25 | 1.10 |
| a.-e. | A404 | 39c any single | .65 | .20 |

Stars of Stage and Screen — A405

Performers and directors: 39c, Gladys Moncrieff and Roy Rene, the stage, 1920's. 85c, Charles Chauvel and Chips Rafferty, talking films. $1, Nellie Stewart and James Cassius Williamson, the stage, 1890's. $1.10, Lottie Lyell and Raymond Longford, silent films.

1989, July 12   *Litho.*   *Perf. 14½*
1142	A405	39c multicolored	.60	.20
a.		Perf. 14x13½ ('90)	6.50	6.50
1143	A405	85c multicolored	1.25	1.00
1144	A405	$1 multicolored	1.50	.50
1145	A405	$1.10 multicolored	1.65	.55
		Nos. 1142-1145 (4)	5.00	2.25

Impressionist Paintings A406

Paintings by Australian artists: No. 1146, *Impression for Golden Summer*, by Sir Arthur Streeton. No. 1147, *All on a Summer's Day*, by Charles Conder, vert. No. 1148, *Petit Dejeuner*, by Frederick McCubbin. No. 1149, *Impression*, by Tom Roberts.

Perf. 13½x14, 14x13½
1989, Aug. 23   *Litho.*
1146	A406	41c shown	.60	.20
1147	A406	41c multicolored	.60	.20
1148	A406	41c multicolored	.60	.20
1149	A406	41c multicolored	.60	.20
		Nos. 1146-1149 (4)	2.40	.80

The Urban Environment — A407

1989, Sept. 1   *Perf. 15½*
Booklet Stamps
1150	A407	41c Freeways	.70	.70
1151	A407	41c Architecture	.70	.70
1152	A407	41c Commuter train	.70	.70
a.		Bklt. pane of 7, 2 each #1150, 1152 and 3 #1151	5.00	
		Nos. 1150-1152 (3)	2.10	2.10

No. 1152a sold for $3.

Australian Youth Hostels, 50th Anniv. A408

1989, Sept. 13   *Perf. 14½*
| 1153 | A408 | 41c multicolored | .65 | .20 |

Street Cars — A409

Designs: No. 1154, Horse-drawn tram, Adelaide, 1878. No. 1155, Steam tram, Sydney, 1884. No. 1156, Cable car, Melbourne, 1886. No. 1157, Double-deck electric tram, Hobart, 1893. No. 1158, Combination electric tram, Brisbane, 1901.

1989, Oct. 11   *Litho.*   *Perf. 13½x14*
1154	A409	41c multicolored	.65	.20
1155	A409	41c multicolored	.65	.20
1156	A409	41c multicolored	.65	.20
a.		Perf. 14½ on 3 sides	1.30	1.30
b.		Booklet pane of 10, #1156a	13.00	
1157	A409	41c multicolored	.65	.20
1158	A409	41c multicolored	.65	.20
		Nos. 1154-1158 (5)	3.25	1.00

Purchase of booklet containing No. 1156b included STAMPSHOW '89 admission ticket and a Melbourne one-day transit pass. Sold for $8.

Christmas — A410
Radio Australia, 50th Anniv. — A411

Illuminations: 36c, Annunciation, from the Nicholai Joseph Foucault Book of Hours, c. 1510-20. 41c, Annunciation to the Shepherds, from the Wharncliffe Hours, c. 1475. 80c, Adoration of the Magi, from Parisian Book of Hours, c. 1490-1500.

1989, Nov. 1   *Perf. 14x13½*
| 1159 | A410 | 36c multicolored | .55 | .15 |
| a. | | Booklet pane of 10 | 5.50 | |

Perf. 15x14½
1160	A410	41c multicolored	.65	.20
1161	A410	80c multicolored	1.25	.55
		Nos. 1159-1161 (3)	2.45	.90

1989, Nov. 1   *Perf. 14x13½*
| 1162 | A411 | 41c multicolored | .65 | .20 |

Australia Day — A412
Special Occasions — A413

1990, Jan. 17   *Litho.*   *Perf. 15x14½*
| 1163 | A412 | 41c Golden wattle | .65 | .20 |

1990, Feb. 7   *Perf. 14x13½*
1164	A413	41c Thinking of You	.65	.20
a.		Booklet pane of 10	6.50	
b.		Perf. 14½ on 3 sides	.65	.15
c.		Booklet pane of 10, #1164b	6.50	

See No. 1193.

Women Practicing Medicine in Australia, Cent. A414

1990, Feb. 7   *Perf. 14½x15*
| 1165 | A414 | 41c Constance Stone | .65 | .20 |

Dr. Constance Stone, Australia's first woman doctor.

A415   A416

Fauna of the High Country.

1990, Feb. 21   *Perf. 14x13½*
1166	A415	41c Greater glider	.65	.15
1167	A415	65c Spotted-tailed quoll	1.00	.55
1168	A415	70c Mountain pygmy-possum	1.10	.60
1169	A415	80c Brush-tailed rock-wallaby	1.25	.70
		Nos. 1166-1169 (4)	4.00	2.00

1990, Mar. 14
1170	A416	41c Quit smoking	.65	.20
1171	A416	41c Don't drink and drive	.65	.20
1172	A416	41c Eat right	.65	.20
1173	A416	41c Medical check-ups	.65	.20
		Nos. 1170-1173 (4)	2.60	.80

Community health.

A417   A418

Scenes from WW II, 1940-41: #1174, Anzacs at the front. #1175, Women working in factories, aircraft at the ready. 65c, Veterans and memorial parade. $1, Helicopters picking up wounded, cemetery. $1.10, Anzacs reading mail from home, 5 women watching departure of 2 ships.

1990, Apr. 12   *Litho.*   *Perf. 14½*
1174	A417	41c shown	.65	.20
1175	A417	41c multicolored	.65	.20
1176	A417	65c multicolored	1.00	.55
1177	A417	$1 multicolored	1.50	.65
1178	A417	$1.10 multicolored	1.75	.70
		Nos. 1174-1178 (5)	5.55	2.30

Australia and New Zealand Army Corps (ANZAC).

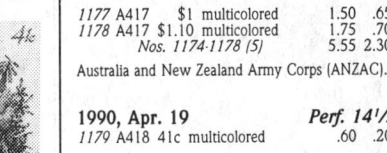

1990, Apr. 19   *Perf. 14½*
| 1179 | A418 | 41c multicolored | .60 | .20 |

Penny Black, 150th Anniv. A419

Stamps on stamps: a, New South Wales #44. b, South Australia #4. c, Tasmania #2. d, Victoria #120. e, Queensland #111A. f, Western Australia #3a.

1990, May 1   *Perf. 13½x14*
1180		Block of 6	3.75	1.25
a.-f.	A419	41c any single	.60	.20
g.		Souvenir sheet of 6	3.75	3.75

The Gold Rush — A420

a, Off to the diggings. b, The diggings. c, Panning for gold. d, Commissioner's tent. e, Gold escort.

1990, May 16   *Perf. 13*
| 1181 | | Strip of 5 | 3.00 | 2.50 |
| a.-e. | A420 | 41c any single | .60 | .20 |

Cooperation in Antarctic Research A421

1990, June 13   *Litho.*   *Perf. 14½x14*
1182	A421	41c Glaciology	.60	.20
1183	A421	$1.10 Krill (marine biology)	1.65	.55
a.		Min. sheet of 2, #1182-1183	2.25	2.25

See Russia Nos. 5902-5903. For overprint see No. 1198.

Colonial Australia A422

Boom Time: a, Land boom. b, Building boom. c, Investment boom. d, Retail boom. e, Factory boom.

1990, July 12   *Litho.*   *Perf. 13*
| 1184 | | Strip of 5 | 3.25 | 2.50 |
| a.-e. | A422 | 41c any single | .65 | .25 |

Sports Type of 1989

1990-91   *Typo.*   *Die Cut Perf. 11½*
Self-Adhesive
1185	A400	41c Cycling	.75	.65
1186	A400	43c Skateboarding	.70	.15
a.		Litho.	.70	.15

Blue background has large dots on No. 1186 and smaller dots on No. 1186a. No. 1186 is on waxed paper backing printed with 0 to 4 koalas. No. 1186a is on plain paper backing printed with one kangaroo.

Issued: 41c, 5/16; #1186, 8/27; #1186a, 1991. This is an expanding set. Numbers will change if necessary.

AUSTRALIA

Salmon Gums by Robert Juniper — A423

Design: 43c, The Blue Dress by Brian Dunlop.

1990, Sept. 3   Litho.   Perf. 15½ Vert.
Booklet Stamps
1191	A423	28c multicolored	.45	.30
a.		Perf. 14½ vert.	.45	.30
1192	A423	43c multicolored	.65	.50
a.		Bklt. pane, #1191, 4 #1192	3.25	
b.		Perf. 14½ vert.	.65	.50
c.		Booklet pane, #1191a, 4 #1192b	3.25	

Thinking Of You Type
1990, Sept. 3   Perf. 14½
1193	A413	43c multicolored	.65	.15
a.		Booklet pane of 10	6.75	

Christmas A424

1990, Oct. 31   Litho.   Perf. 14½
1194	A424	38c Kookaburras	.60	.20
a.		Booklet pane of 10	6.25	
1195	A424	43c Nativity, vert.	.70	.20
1196	A424	80c Opossum	1.40	.60
		Nos. 1194-1196 (3)	2.70	1.00

Local Government in Australia, 150th Anniv. — A425

1990, Oct. 31
1197	A425	43c Town Hall, Adelaide	.70	.20

No. 1183a Ovptd. in Gold

WORLD STAMP EXHIBITION
24 AUG - 2 SEPT 1990

1990   Litho.   Perf. 14½x14
1198	A421	Miniature sheet of 2	3.75	3.75

Overprint applied to sheet margin only.

Flags — A426

1991, Jan. 10   Litho.   Perf. 14½
1199	A426	43c National flag	.70	.20
1200	A426	90c White ensign	1.40	.55
1201	A426	$1 Air Force ensign	1.50	.65
1202	A426	$1.20 Red ensign	1.75	.75
		Nos. 1199-1202 (4)	5.35	2.15

Australia Day.

Water Birds A427

1991, Feb. 14
1203	A427	43c Black swan	.70	.20
1204	A427	43c Black-necked stork, vert.	.70	.20
1205	A427	85c Cape Barren goose, vert.	1.25	1.00
1206	A427	$1 Chestnut teal	1.50	.55
		Nos. 1203-1206 (4)	4.15	1.95

Women's Wartime Services, 50th Anniv. A428

50th Anniversaries: No. 1208, Siege of Tobruk. $1.20, Australian War Memorial, Canberra.

1991, Mar. 14   Litho.   Perf. 14½
1207	A428	43c shown	.70	.20
1208	A428	43c multicolored	.70	.20
1209	A428	$1.20 multicolored	1.75	.70
		Nos. 1207-1209 (3)	3.15	1.10

Queen Elizabeth II's 65th Birthday — A429

1991, Apr. 11   Litho.   Perf. 14½
1210	A429	43c multicolored	.70	.20

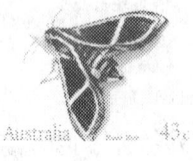

Insects A430

1991, Apr. 11
1211	A430	43c Hawk moth	.70	.20
1212	A430	43c Cotton harlequin bug	.70	.20
1213	A430	80c Leichhardt's grasshopper	1.25	.60
1214	A430	$1 Jewel beetle	1.50	.70
		Nos. 1211-1214 (4)	4.15	1.70

Australian Photography, 150th Anniv. — A431

Designs: No. 1215a, Bondi, by Max Dupain, 1939. No. 1215b, Gears for the Mining Industry, Vickers Ruwolt Melbourne, by Wolfgang Sievers, 1967. 70c, Wheel of Youth, by Harold Cazneaux, 1929. $1.20, Teacup Ballet, by Olive Cotton, 1935.

1991, May 13   Litho.   Perf. 14½
1215		Pair	1.40	.40
a.-b.		A431 43c any single	.70	.20
1216	A431	70c blk, olive & claret	1.10	.50
1217	A431	$1.20 blk, gray & Prus bl	1.75	.75
		Nos. 1215-1217 (3)	4.25	1.65

Golden Days of Radio — A432

Pets — A433

1991, June 13   Litho.   Perf. 14½
1218	A432	43c Music & variety shows	.65	.20
1219	A432	43c Soap operas	.65	.20
1220	A432	85c Quiz shows	1.25	1.25
1221	A432	$1 Children's stories	1.50	.60
		Nos. 1218-1221 (4)	4.05	2.30

1991, July 25   Litho.   Perf. 14½
1222	A433	43c Puppy	.65	.20
1223	A433	43c Kitten	.65	.20
1224	A433	70c Pony	1.10	.40
1225	A433	$1 Cockatoo	1.50	.60
		Nos. 1222-1225 (4)	3.90	1.40

George Vancouver (1757-1798) and Edward John Eyre (1815-1901), Explorers — A434

1991, Sept. 26   Litho.   Perf. 14½
1226	A434	$1.05 multicolored	1.60	.55
a.		Souvenir sheet of 1	1.60	1.60
b.		As "a," overprinted in gold	2.75	2.75

Vancouver's visit to Western Australia, 200th anniv. and Eyre's journey to Albany, Western Australia, 150th anniv.

No. 1226b overprinted in sheet margin with show emblem and: "PHILANIPPON / WORLD STAMP / EXHIBITION / TOKYO / 16-24 NOV 1991" followed by Japanese inscription. Issue date: #1226b, Nov. 16.

Australian Literature of the 1890's A435

Designs: 43c, Seven Little Australians by Ethel Turner. 75c, On Our Selection by Steele Rudd. $1, Clancy of the Overflow by A.B. "Banjo" Paterson, vert. $1.20, The Drover's Wife by Henry Lawson, vert.

1991, Oct. 10
1227	A435	43c multicolored	.65	.20
1228	A435	75c multicolored	1.10	.50
1229	A435	$1 multicolored	1.60	.65
1230	A435	$1.20 multicolored	1.90	.80
		Nos. 1227-1230 (4)	5.25	2.15

Christmas A436

1991, Nov. 1
1231	A436	38c Shepherd	.60	.20
a.		Booklet pane of 20	12.00	
1232	A436	43c Baby Jesus	.65	.20
1233	A436	90c Wise man, camel	1.40	.45
		Nos. 1231-1233 (3)	2.65	.85

Thinking of You — A437

1992, Jan. 2   Litho.   Perf. 14½x15
1234	A437	45c Wildflowers	.70	.25
a.		Booklet pane of 10	7.00	

Threatened Species — A438

Designs: No. 1235a, Parma wallaby. b, Ghost bat. c, Long-tailed dunnart. d, Little pygmy possum. e, Dusky hopping mouse. f, Squirrel glider.

1992, Jan. 2   Litho.   Perf. 14x14½
1235		Block of 6	4.00	3.50
a.-f.		A438 45c any single	.65	.25

Die Cut
Perf. 11½
Self-Adhesive
1241	A438	45c like #1235a	.65	.25
a.		Typo.	.65	.25
1242	A438	45c like #1235b	.65	.25
a.		Typo.	.65	.25
1243	A438	45c like #1235c	.65	.25
a.		Typo.	.65	.25
1244	A438	45c like #1235d	.65	.25
a.		Typo.	.65	.25
1245	A438	45c like #1235e	.65	.25
a.		Typo.	.65	.25
1246	A438	45c like #1235f	.65	.25
a.		Typo.	.65	.25
b.		Bklt. pane, 2 each #1241-1244, 1 each #1245-1246	6.25	
c.		Pane of 5, #1242-1246	3.25	
d.		Strip of 6, #1241-1246	4.00	
e.		Strip of 6, #1241a-1246a	4.00	
f.		#1246c overprinted	4.00	
g.		As "f," no die cutting	190.00	

Litho. stamps are sharper in appearance than typo. stamps, most notably on the black lettering. Nos. 1246b and 1246c have tagging bars which make the right portion of the stamps appear toned.

No. 1246f - overprinted in Gold on sheet margin of No. 1246c with emblem of "WORLD COLUMBIAN / STAMP EXPO '92 / MAY 22-31, 1992 - CHICAGO." Issued in May.

See Nos. 1271-1293, 1406-1417.

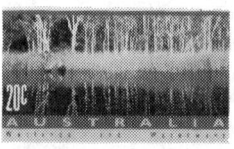

Wetlands — A439

Perf. 14½ Horiz.
1992, Jan. 2   Booklet Stamps   Photo.
1247	A439	20c Noosa River, Queensland	.55	.45
a.		Perf. 14 horiz.	.55	
1248	A439	45c Lake Eildon, Victoria	.55	.45
a.		Bklt. pane, 1 #1247, 4 #1248	2.75	
		Complete booklet, #1248a	2.75	
b.		Perf. 14 horiz.	.55	
c.		Bklt. pane, 1 #1247a, 4 #1248b	2.75	
		Complete booklet, #1248c	2.75	

Sailing Ships A440

Perf. 14½x15, 15x14½
1992, Jan. 15   Litho.
1249	A440	45c Young Endeavour	.70	.20
1250	A440	45c Britannia, vert.	.70	.20
1251	A440	$1.05 Akarana, vert.	1.60	.60
1252	A440	$1.20 John Louis	1.75	.70
a.		Sheet of 4, #1249-1252	4.75	4.75
b.		As "a," overprinted	5.50	5.50
c.		As "a," overprinted	7.50	7.50
		Nos. 1249-1252 (4)	4.75	1.70

Australia Day. Discovery of America, 500th anniv. (No. 1252a).

Overprint in gold on sheet margin of No. 1252b contains emblem and "WORLD COLUMBIAN / STAMP EXPO '92 / MAY 22-31, 1992-CHICAGO." No. 1252b issued in May.

Overprint in gold on sheet margin of No. 1252c contains emblem and "GENOVA '92 / 18-27 SEPTEMBER." No. 1252c issued in Sept.

Australian Battles, 1942 — A441

AUSTRALIA

1992, Feb. 19   Litho.   *Perf. 14½*
1253	A441	45c Bombing of Darwin	.65	.20
1254	A441	75c Milne Bay	1.00	.60
1255	A441	75c Kokoda Trail	1.00	.60
1256	A441	$1.05 Coral Sea	1.50	.80
1257	A441	$1.20 El Alamein	1.70	.95
		Nos. 1253-1257 (5)	5.85	3.15

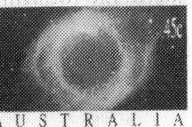

Intl. Space Year — A442

1992, Mar. 19
1258	A442	45c Helix Nebula	.65	.20
1259	A442	$1.05 The Pleiades	1.50	.65
1260	A442	$1.20 Spiral Galaxy NGC 2997	1.60	.70
a.		Sheet of 3, #1258-1260	3.75	3.75
b.		As "a," overprinted	5.00	5.00
		Nos. 1258-1260 (3)	3.75	1.55

Overprint on sheet margin of No. 1260b contains emblem of "WORLD COLUMBIAN / STAMP EXPO '92 / MAY 22-31, 1992-CHICAGO." No. 1260b issued in May.

Queen Elizabeth II, 66th Birthday A443

1992, Apr. 9   *Perf. 14x14½*
1261	A443	45c Wmk. 228 & #258	.65	.20

Vineyard Regions A444

Designs: No. 1262, Hunter Valley New South Wales. No. 1263, North Eastern Victoria. No. 1264, Barossa Valley South Australia. No. 1265, Coonawarra South Australia. No. 1266, Margaret River Western Australia.

1992, Apr. 9
1262	A444	45c multicolored	.65	.20
1263	A444	45c multicolored	.65	.20
1264	A444	45c multicolored	.65	.20
1265	A444	45c multicolored	.65	.20
1266	A444	45c multicolored	.65	.20
		Nos. 1262-1266 (5)	3.25	1.00

Land Care — A445

Designs: a, Salt action. b, Farm planning. c, Erosion control. d, Tree planting. e, Dune care.

1992, June 11   Litho.   *Perf. 14½x14*
1267	Strip of 5	3.25	2.25
a.-e.	A445 45c Any single	.60	.20

1992 Summer Olympics and Paralympics, Barcelona A446

1992, July 2   *Perf. 14½*
1268	A446	45c Cycling	.60	.20
1269	A446	$1.20 Weight lifting	1.75	.60
1270	A446	$1.20 High jump	1.75	.60
		Nos. 1268-1270 (3)	4.10	1.40

Threatened Species Type of 1992

1992-96   Litho.   *Perf. 14x14½*
1271	A438	30c Saltwater crocodile	.40	.15
1272	A438	35c Echidna	.50	.20
1273	A438	40c Platypus	.55	.20
1274	A438	45c Kangaroo	.65	.20
1275	A438	45c Adult kangaroo with joey	.65	.20
1276	A438	45c Two adult kangaroos	.65	.20
a.		Sheet of 3, #1274-1276	2.10	1.00
1277	A438	45c Four koalas	.65	.20
1278	A438	45c Koala walking	.65	.20
1279	A438	45c Koala in tree	.65	.20
a.		Block of 6, #1274-1279	4.00	1.40
b.		Souvenir sheet of 6, #1274-1279	4.00	4.00
1280	A438	50c Koala	.70	.25
1281	A438	60c Common brushtail possum	.85	.30
1282	A438	70c Kookaburra	.95	.35
1283	A438	85c Pelican	1.25	.40
1284	A438	90c Eastern gray kangaroo	1.25	.40
1285	A438	95c Common wombat	1.40	.45
1286	A438	$1.20 Pink cockatoo	1.65	.55
1287	A438	$1.35 Emu	1.85	.60
		Nos. 1271-1287 (17)	15.40	5.10

PHILAKOREA '94 (#1279b).

No. 1276a inscribed in sheet margin with "CHINA '96 - 9th Asian International Exhibition" in Chinese and English and exhibition emblems.

Issued: 35c, 50c, 60c, 95c, 8/13; 40c, 70c, 90c, $1.20, 8/12/93; 30c, 85c, $1.35, 3/10/94; 45c, 5/12/94; #1279b, 8/94; #1276a, 5/18/96.

1996   Litho.   *Perf. 14x14½*
1274a	A438	45c brown panel	.60	.20
b.		Bright orange panel	.60	
1275a	A438	45c brown panel	.60	.20
b.		Bright orange panel	.60	
1276b	A438	45c brown panel	.60	.20
c.		Bright orange panel	.60	
1277a	A438	45c brown panel	.60	.20
b.		Bright orange panel	.60	
1278a	A438	45c brown panel	.60	.20
b.		Bright orange panel	.60	
1279c	A438	45c brown panel	.60	.20
d.		Block of 6, #1274a-1275a, 1276b, 1277a-1278a, 1279c	4.00	1.40
e.		Bright orange panel	.60	
f.		Block of 6, #1274b-1275b, 1276c, 1277b-1278b, 1279e	4.00	1.40

Australia and denomination are orange, and date is 1½mm long on No. 1279a. Date is 1mm long on Nos. 1279d and 1279f. No. 1279d comes from 2 Koala printing. No. 1279f comes from 3 Koala printing.

Die Cut Perf. 11

1994, May 12   Litho.
Self-Adhesive
1288	A438	45c like #1280	.65	.20
1289	A438	45c like #1281	.65	.20
1290	A438	45c like #1282	.65	.20
1291	A438	45c like #1282A	.65	.20
1292	A438	45c like #1282B	.65	.20
1293	A438	45c like #1282C	.65	.20
a.		Bklt. pane, #1290, 1293, 2 each #1288-1289, 1291-1292	6.50	
b.		Strip of 6, #1288-1293	4.00	

Opening of Sydney Harbor Tunnel, August 29 — A447

Sydney Harbor Bridge and Tunnel: a, Left side. b, Right side.

1992, Aug. 28   Litho.   *Perf. 14½*
1296	A447	45c Pair, #a.-b.	1.25	.45
c.		Pair, #d.-e., perf 15½	1.25	.45

Buildings in Western Australia Goldfield Towns — A448

Designs: No. 1297, Warden's Courthouse, Coolgardie. No. 1298, Post Office, Kalgoorlie. $1.05, York Hotel, Kalgoorlie. $1.20, Town Hall, Kalgoorlie.

1992, Sept. 17   Litho.   *Perf. 14x14½*
1297	A448	45c multicolored	.60	.20
1298	A448	45c multicolored	.60	.20
1299	A448	$1.05 multicolored	1.40	.50
1300	A448	$1.20 multicolored	1.65	.60
		Nos. 1297-1300 (4)	4.25	1.50

Sheffield Shield Cricket Competition, Cent. — A449

Cricket match, 1890s: 45c, Bowler. $1.20, Batsman, wicket keeper.

1992, Oct. 15   Litho.   *Perf. 14½*
1301	A449	45c multicolored	.60	.20
1302	A449	$1.20 multicolored	1.60	.55

Christmas A450

Designs: 40c, Children dressed as Mary and Joseph with baby carriage. 45c, Boy jumping from bed Christmas morning. $1, Boy and girl singing Christmas carol.

1992, Oct. 30   Litho.   *Perf. 14x14½*
1303	A450	40c multicolored	.55	.55
a.		Booklet pane of 20	11.00	
1304	A450	45c multicolored	.60	.20
1305	A450	$1 multicolored	1.25	.45
		Nos. 1303-1305 (3)	2.40	1.20

Watercolor Paintings by Albert Namatjira A451

Designs: No. 1306a, Ghost Gum, Central Australia. b, Across the Plain to Mount Giles.

1993, Jan. 14   Litho.   *Perf. 14x15*
1306	A451	45c Pair, #a.-b.	1.25	.40

Australia Day.

Dreamings A452

Aboriginal paintings: 45c, Wild Onion Dreaming, by Pauline Nakamarra Woods. 75c, Yam Plants, by Jack Wunuwun, vert. 85c, Goose Egg Hunt, by George Milpurrurru, vert. $1, Kalumpiwarra-Ngulalintji, by Rover Thomas.

Perf. 14x14½, 14½x14

1993, Feb. 4   Litho.
1307	A452	45c red & multi	.65	.20
1308	A452	75c org yel & multi	1.00	.30
1309	A452	85c buff & multi	1.10	.35
1310	A452	$1 salmon & multi	1.25	.45
		Nos. 1307-1310 (4)	4.00	1.30

World Heritage Sites in Australia — A453

1993, Mar. 4   Litho.   *Perf. 14½x14*
1311	A453	45c Uluru (Ayers Rock)	.65	.20
1312	A453	85c Fraser Island	1.10	.40
1313	A453	95c Shark Bay	1.25	.40
1314	A453	$2 Kakadu	2.50	.85
		Nos. 1311-1314 (4)	5.50	1.85

See Nos. 1485-1488.

World War II Ships A454

Designs: 45c, Cruiser HMAS Sydney II. 85c, Corvette HMAS Bathurst. $1.05, Destroyer HMAS Arunta. $1.20, Hospital Ship Centaur.

1993, Apr. 7   Litho.   *Perf. 14x14½*
1315	A454	45c multicolored	.65	.20
1316	A454	85c multicolored	1.10	.35
1317	A454	$1.05 multicolored	1.40	.60
1318	A454	$1.20 multicolored	1.60	.65
		Nos. 1315-1318 (4)	4.75	1.80

A455   A456

1993, Apr. 7   *Perf. 14½x14*
1319	A455	45c multicolored	.65	.20

Queen Elizabeth II, 67th birthday.

1993, May 7   Litho.   *Perf. 14½x14*

Designs based on 19th century trade union banners: No. 1320, Baker, shoe maker. No. 1321, Stevedore, seamstresses. $1, Blacksmith, telephone operator, cook. $1.20, Carpenters.

1320	A456	45c multicolored	.60	.20
1321	A456	45c multicolored	.60	.20
1322	A456	$1 multicolored	1.25	.55
1323	A456	$1.20 multicolored	1.50	.65
		Nos. 1320-1323 (4)	3.95	1.60

Working life in the 1890s.

Trains — A457

Designs: No. 1324, Centenary Special, Tasmania. No. 1325, Spirit of Progress. No. 1326, Western Endeavour. No. 1327, Silver City Comet. No. 1328, Kuranda Tourist Train. No. 1329, The Ghan.

1993, June 1   *Perf. 14x14½*
1324	A457	45c multicolored	.60	.20
1325	A457	45c multicolored	.60	.20
1326	A457	45c multicolored	.60	.20
1327	A457	45c multicolored	.60	.20
1328	A457	45c multicolored	.60	.20
1329	A457	45c multicolored	.60	.20
a.		Block of 6, #1324-1329	3.75	2.75

Die Cut Perf. 12x11½
Self-Adhesive
1330	A457	45c like No. 1324	.60	.20
1331	A457	45c like No. 1325	.60	.20
1332	A457	45c like No. 1326	.60	.20
1333	A457	45c like No. 1327	.60	.20
1334	A457	45c like No. 1328	.60	.20
1335	A457	45c like No. 1329	.60	.20
a.		Strip of 6, #1330-1335	3.75	
b.		Bklt. pane of 10, #1332, 1335, 2 each #1330-1331, 1333-1334	6.00	

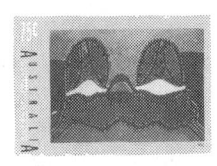

Aboriginal Art — A458

Aboriginal paintings: 45c, Black Cockatoo Feather, by Fiona Foley, vert. 75c, Ngarrgooroon Country, by Hector Jandany. $1, Ngak Ngak, by Ginger Riley. $1.05, Untitled work, by Robert Cole, vert.

Perf. 14½x14, 14x14½

1993, July 1   Litho.
1336	A458	45c henna brown & multi	.60	.20
1337	A458	75c brown & multi	1.00	.30

1338 A458 $1 gray & multi 1.25 .55
1339 A458 $1.05 olive & multi 1.40 .60
Nos. 1336-1339 (4) 4.25 1.65

Dame Enid Lyons, MP, and Sen. Dorothy Tangney
A459

Design: No. 1340, Stylized globe, natl. arms, Inter-Parliamentary Conference emblem.

1993, Sept. 2 Litho. *Perf. 14½*
1340 A459 45c multicolored .60 .20
1341 A459 45c multicolored .60 .20
a. Pair, #1340-1341 1.20 .40

90th Inter-Parliamentary Union Conference (#1340). First women in Australian Federal Parliament, 50th anniv. (#1341). Nos. 1340-1341 printed in panes of 25 with 16 #1340 and 9 #1341. Panes with 16 #1341 and 9 #1340 were issued Nov. 19, but were available only through Philatelic Agency.

A460

A461

Dinosaurs: No. 1342, 1348, Ornithocheirus, horiz. No. 1343, 1349, Leaellynasaura. No. 1344, Allosaurus. No. 1345, Timimus. No. 1346, Muttaburrasaurus. No. 1347, Minmi, horiz.

1993, Oct. 1 *Perf. 14x14½, 14½x14*
1342 A460 45c multicolored .60 .20
1343 A460 45c multicolored .60 .20
1344 A461 45c multicolored .60 .20
1345 A461 45c multicolored .60 .20

Size: 29x50mm

1346 A461 75c multicolored .95 .35
1347 A461 $1.05 multicolored 1.40 .60
a. Souvenir sheet of 6, #1342-1347 4.75 4.75
b. As "a," overprinted 5.50 5.50
c. As "a," overprinted 5.50 5.50
Nos. 1342-1347 (6) 4.75 1.75

Self-Adhesive

Die Cut Perf. 11½

1348 A460 45c multicolored .60 .20
1349 A460 45c multicolored .60 .20
a. Bklt. pane, 5 each #1348-1349 6.00

Overprint in gold on sheet margin of No. 1347b contains "BANGKOK 1993" show emblem and "WORLD PHILATELIC / EXHIBITION / BANGKOK 1-10 OCTOBER 1993."

Overprint in gold on sheet margin of No. 1347c contains dinosaur and "Sydney / STAMP & COIN / SHOW / 15-17 October 1993."

Christmas — A462

1993, Nov. 1 Litho. *Perf. 14½x14*
1354 A462 40c Goodwill .50 .15
a. Booklet pane of 20 10.50
1355 A462 45c Joy .60 .20
1356 A462 $1 Peace 1.25 .45
Nos. 1354-1356 (3) 2.35 .80

Australia Day — A463

Landscape paintings: 45c, Shoalhaven River Bank-Dawn, by Arthur Boyd. 85c, Wimmera (from Mt. Arapiles), by Sir Sidney Nolan. $1.05, Lagoon, Wimmera, by Nolan. $2, White Cockatoos in Paddock with Flame Trees, by Boyd, vert.

Perf. 14½x14, 14x14½

1994, Jan. 13 Litho.
1357 A463 45c multicolored .65 .20
1358 A463 85c multicolored 1.25 .40
1359 A463 $1.05 multicolored 1.50 .50
1360 A463 $2 multicolored 3.00 1.00
Nos. 1357-1360 (4) 6.40 2.10

See Nos. 1418-1421, 1476-1479, 1572-1574.

Royal Life Saving Society, Cent.
A464

1994, Jan. 20 Litho. *Perf. 14x14½*
1361 A464 45c Vigilance .65 .20
1362 A464 45c Education .65 .20
1363 A464 95c Drill 1.40 .45
1364 A464 $1.20 Fitness 1.75 .55
Nos. 1361-1364 (4) 4.45 1.40

Die Cut Perf. 11½

Self-Adhesive

1365 A464 45c like #1361 .85 .20
1366 A464 45c like #1362 .85 .20
a. Pair, #1365-1366 1.75
b. Booklet pane, 5 #1366a 8.75

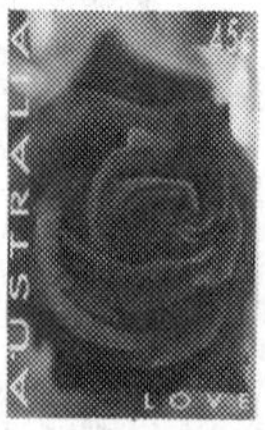

Thinking of You — A465

1994, Feb. 3 Litho. *Perf. 14½x14*
1367 A465 45c Rose .60 .20
1368 A465 45c Tulips .60 .20
1369 A465 45c Poppies .60 .20
a. Pair, #1368-1369 1.25 .40
b. Booklet pane, 5 #1369a 6.25
Nos. 1367-1369 (3) 1.80 .60

A466

A467

1994, Apr. 8 Litho. *Perf. 14½*
1370 A466 45c multicolored .65 .20

Queen Elizabeth II, 68th birthday.

1994, Apr. 8 *Perf. 14½x14*
1371 A467 95c multicolored 1.25 .45

Opening of Friendship Bridge, Thailand-Laos.

Intl. Year of the Family — A468

Children's paintings of their families: 45c, Bobbie Lea Blackmore. 75c, Kathryn Teoh. $1, Maree McCarthy.

1994, Apr. 14 Litho. *Perf. 14x14½*
1372 A468 45c multicolored .65 .20
1373 A468 75c multicolored 1.10 .35
1374 A468 $1 multicolored 1.50 .50
Nos. 1372-1374 (3) 3.25 1.05

Australian Women's Right to Vote, Cent. — A469

1994, June 9 Litho. *Perf. 14x14½*
1375 A469 45c multicolored .65 .20

Bunyips Folklore Creatures
A470

Types of Bunyips: No. 1376, Aboriginal legend. No. 1377, Nature Spirit. 90c, Berkeley's Creek. $1.35, Natural history.

1994, July 14 Litho. *Perf. 14x14½*
1376 A470 45c multicolored .65 .20
1377 A470 45c multicolored .65 .20
a. Pair, #1376-1377 1.25 .40
1378 A470 90c multicolored 1.25 .40
1379 A470 $1.35 multicolored 2.00 .65
Nos. 1376-1379 (4) 4.55 1.45

World War II Prime Ministers
A471

Designs: a, Robert Menzies. b, Arthur Fadden. c, John Curtin. d, Francis (Frank) Forde. e, Joseph Benedict (Ben) Chifley.

1994, Aug. 11
1380 Strip of 5 3.25 1.10
a.-e. A471 45c any single .65 .20

Aviation Pioneers — A472

Designs: No. 1381, Lawrence Hargrave, box kites. No. 1382, Ross and Keith Smith, Vickers Vimy. $1.35, Ivor McIntyre, Stanley Globe, Fairey IIID A10-3 seaplane. $1.80, Freda Thompson, DeHavilland Moth Major.

1994, Aug. 29 Engr. *Perf. 12*
1381 A472 45c multicolored .65 .20
1382 A472 45c multicolored .65 .20
1383 A472 $1.35 multicolored 2.00 .65
1384 A472 $1.80 multicolored 2.50 .85
Nos. 1381-1384 (4) 5.80 1.90

First England-Australia flight within 30-day time span (#1382). First aerial circumnavigation of Australia (#1383). First woman to fly solo from England-Australia (#1384).

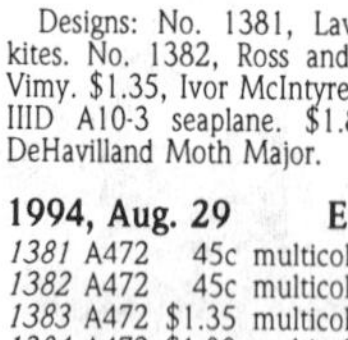

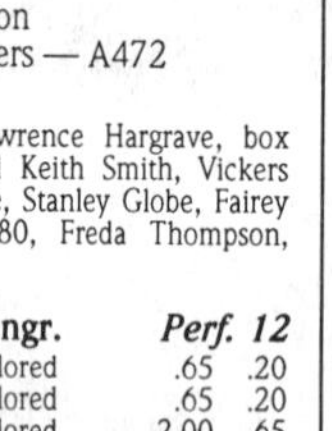

Australian Zoo Animals
A473 A474

Perf. 14x14½, 14½x14

1994, Sept. 28 Litho.
1385 A473 45c Scarlet macaw .65 .20
1386 A473 45c Cheetah, vert. .65 .20
1387 A474 45c Fijian crested iguana .65 .20
1388 A474 45c Orangutan .65 .20

Size: 50x30mm

Perf. 14½x14

1389 A473 $1 Asian elephant 1.50 1.50
a. Souv. sheet of 5, #1385-1389, perf. 14½ 4.25 4.25
b. As "a," ovptd. 6.00 6.00
c. As "a," ovptd. 6.00 6.00
d. As "a," ovptd. 6.00 6.00
e. As "a," ovptd. 6.00 6.00
Nos. 1385-1389 (5) 4.10 2.30

Self-Adhesive

Die Cut Perf. 11½

1390 A473 45c like #1385 1.00 .25
1391 A473 45c like #1386 1.00 .25
a. Booklet pane, 6 #1390, 4 #1391 10.00

Overprint in gold on sheet margin:

No. 1389b, show emblem and "Brisbane Stamp Show Zoos / October 21-23, 1994."

No. 1389c, show emblem and "SYDNEY / STAMP / AND / COIN / SHOW / 30/9/94 TO 2/10/94."

No. 1389d, show emblem and "Stampshow '94 Melbourne October 27-30 / National/State Centennial Exhibition 1894-1994."

No. 1389e, show emblem and "STAMP SHOW 94 / Fremantle Convention Centre / 5-6 November 1994."

Christmas
A475

Details from Adoration of the Magi, by Giovanni Toscani: 40c, Madonna and Child, vert. 45c, One of Magi, horse and groom. $1, Joseph receiving frankincense from Magi. $1.80, Entire painting.

1994, Oct. 31 Litho. *Perf. 14½x14*
1392 A475 40c multicolored .60 .20
a. Booklet pane of 20 12.00
Complete booklet, #1392a 12.00

Perf. 14x14½

1393 A475 45c multicolored .70 .25
1394 A475 $1 multicolored 1.60 .40

Size: 50x30mm

1395 A475 $1.80 multicolored 2.75 .80
Nos. 1392-1395 (4) 5.65 1.65

50th Sydney-Hobart Yacht Race — A476

Designs: a, Yachts bow-on, Sydney Opera House, Harbor Bridge. b, Two yachts abeam.

1994, Oct. 31 *Perf. 14½*
1396 Pair 1.40 .50
a.-b. A476 45c any single .70 .25

Self-Adhesive

Die Cut Perf. 11½

1397 A476 45c like #1396a 1.10 .25
1397A A476 45c like #1396b 1.10 .25

A477

1994, Nov. 2 Litho. *Die Cut Perf. 17*

Self-Adhesive

Booklet Stamps

Background Color

1398 A477 45c bluish green .70 .25
1399 A477 45c blue .70 .25
1400 A477 45c purple .70 .25
1401 A477 45c yellow green .70 .25
1402 A477 45c pale yellow green .70 .25
1403 A477 45c pale red brown .70 .25
1404 A477 45c rose .70 .25
1405 A477 45c orange yellow .70 .25
a. Booklet pane of 20 14.00
Nos. 1398-1405 (8) 5.60 2.00

No. 1405a contains 3 each #1399, 1401, 1403, 1405 and 2 each #1398, 1400, 1402, 1404. No. 1405a was sold in ATM machines, at the Natl. Philatelic Center, and Australian Philatelic Bureau.

Threatened Species Type of 1992

1994, Aug. Litho. *Die Cut Perf. 11½*

Self-Adhesive

Size: 53x31mm

1406	A438	45c like #1235a	.70	.35
1407	A438	45c like #1235b	.70	.35
1408	A438	45c like #1235c	.70	.35
1409	A438	45c like #1235d	.70	.35
1410	A438	45c like #1235e	.70	.35
1411	A438	45c like #1235f	.70	.35
a.		Strip of 6, #1406-1411	4.25	
		Nos. 1406-1411 (6)	4.20	2.10

Nos. 1406-1411 have computer-generated denomination and inscription "NPC" at bottom. Inscriptions "AUSTRALIA," animal name and "THREATENED SPECIES" appear beside design instead of above and below it as on No. 1235.

No. 1411a was issued with "PHILA KOREA" CODE.

Die Cut Perf. 11

1994, Nov. 17 Litho.

Self-Adhesive

Size: 40x27mm

1412	A438	45c like #1280	.70	.25
1413	A438	45c like #1282B	.70	.25
1414	A438	45c like #1282	.70	.25
1415	A438	45c like #1282A	.70	.25
1416	A438	45c like #1281	.70	.25
1417	A438	45c like #1282C	.70	.25
		Nos. 1412-1417 (6)	4.20	1.50

Nos. 1412-1417 have computer-generated denominations and location codes printed at bottom of each stamp. They differ from Nos. 1280-1282C in size and location of inscriptions.

Nos. 1412-1417 can be printed with denominations from 45c-$100. We have listed the 45c value with the NPC (National Philatelic Center) code which is available through the Australian Philatelic Bureau.

Nos. 1412-1417 were issued with "SINGAPORE '95" code on Sept. 1, 1995.

Australia Day Type of 1994

Paintings: No. 1418, Back Verandah, by Russell Drysdale. No. 1419, Skull Springs Country, by Guy Grey-Smith. $1.05, Outcamp, by Robert Juniper. $1.20, Kite Flying, by Ian Fairweather.

1995, Jan. 12 Litho. *Perf. 15x14½*

1418	A463	45c multicolored	.70	.25
1419	A463	45c multicolored	.70	.25
1420	A463	$1.05 multicolored	1.60	.40
1421	A463	$1.20 multicolored	1.75	.45
		Nos. 1418-1421 (4)	4.75	1.35

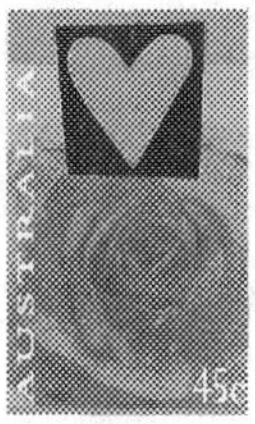

St. Valentine's Day — A478

Various designs: a, Red heart. b, Red & gold heart. c, Gold heart.

1995, Feb. 6 Litho. *Perf. 14½x14*

1422		Strip of 3	2.10	.75
a.-c.	A478	45c any single	.70	.25

See No. 1480.

Endeavour A479

#1423: a, Captain Cook's Endeavour. b, Replica.

1995, Feb. 9 Litho. *Perf. 14x14½*

1423		Pair	1.40	.50
a.-b.	A479	45c any single	.70	.25

Booklet Stamps

Size: 44x26mm

Perf. 14 Horiz.

1424	A479	20c like #1423a	.30	.15
1425	A479	45c like #1423b	.70	.25
a.		Booklet pane, 1 #1424, 4 #1425	3.25	
		Complete booklet, #1425a	3.25	

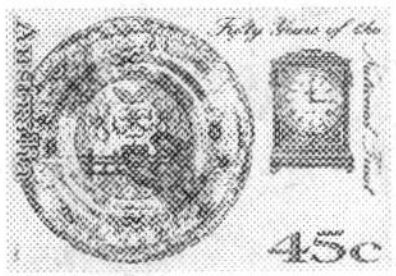

Natl. Trust, 50th Anniv. — A480

Designs: No. 1426a, Coalport plate, Regency style bracket clock. No. 1426b, 15th-16th cent. x-frame Italian style chair, 19th cent. Steiner doll. $1, Advance Australia teapot, neo-classical parian-ware statuette. $2, China urn, silver bowl.

1995, Mar. 16 Engr. *Perf. 14x14½*

1426		Pair	1.40	.50
a.-b.	A480	45c any single	.70	.25
1427	A480	$1 red brown & blue	1.50	.50
1428	A480	$2 blue & green	3.00	1.00
		Nos. 1426-1428 (3)	5.90	2.00

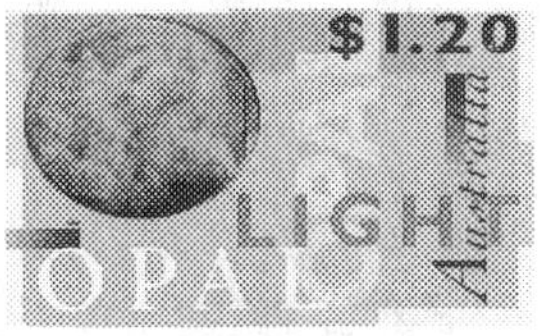

Opals — A481

1995, Apr. 5 Litho. *Perf. 14½x14*

1429	A481	$1.20 Light opal	1.75	.90
1430	A481	$2.50 Black opal	3.75	1.90

Nos. 1429-1430 each contain a holographic image. Soaking in water may affect the hologram.

See Nos. 1554-1555.

A482

A483

1995, Apr. 20 Litho. *Perf. 14½*

1431	A482	45c multicolored	.65	.20

Queen Elizabeth II, 69th birthday.

1995, Apr. 20 Litho. *Perf. 14½x14*

Famous Australians from World War II.

1432	A483	45c Sir Edward Dunlop	.65	.25
1433	A483	45c Mrs. Jessie Vasey	.65	.25
1434	A483	45c Tom Derrick	.65	.25
1435	A483	45c Rawdon Hume Middleton	.65	.25
a.		Block of 4, #1432-1435	2.60	1.00

Self-Adhesive

Die Cut Perf. 11½

1436	A483	45c like #1432	.65	.20
1437	A483	45c like #1433	.65	.20
1438	A483	45c like #1434	.65	.20
1439	A483	45c like #1435	.65	.20
a.		Booklet pane, 4 #1436, 2 each #1437-1439	6.50	
b.		Strip of 4, #1436-1439	3.00	
		Nos. 1432-1439 (8)	5.20	1.80

See Nos. 1452-1455.

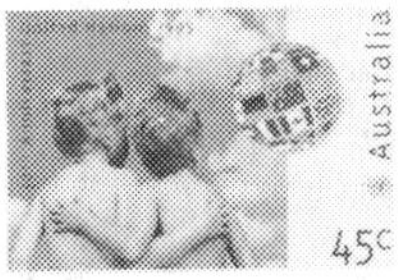

UN, 50th Anniv. A484

1995, May 11 Litho. *Perf. 14x14½*

1440	A484	45c + label, multi	.65	.20
a.		Block of 4 + 4 labels	2.75	.90

No. 1440 was issued se-tenant with label in blocks of 4 + 4 labels in four designs. In alternating rows, labels appear on left or right side of stamp.

A485

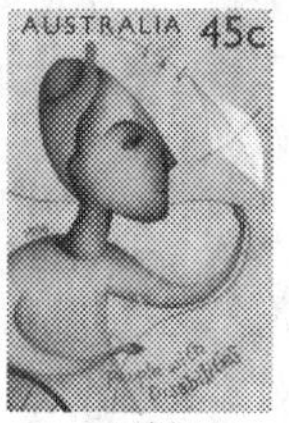

A486

Poster, scene from: No. 1441, The Story of the Kelly Gang, 1906. No. 1442, On Our Selection, 1932. No. 1443, Jedda, 1955. No. 1444, Picnic at Hanging Rock, 1970s. No. 1445, Strictly Ballroom, 1992.

1995, June 8 Litho. *Perf. 14½x14*

1441	A485	45c multicolored	.65	.25
1442	A485	45c multicolored	.65	.25
1443	A485	45c multicolored	.65	.25
1444	A485	45c multicolored	.65	.25
1445	A485	45c multicolored	.65	.25
a.		Strip of 5, #1441-1445	3.25	1.25

Self-Adhesive

Die Cut Perf. 11½

1446	A485	45c like #1441	.65	.20
1447	A485	45c like #1442	.65	.20
1448	A485	45c like #1443	.65	.20
1449	A485	45c like #1444	.65	.20
1450	A485	45c like #1445	.65	.20
a.		Strip of 5, #1446-1450	3.50	
b.		Booklet pane, 2 each #1446-1450	6.50	

Motion Pictures, cent.

By its nature No. 1450b constitutes a complete booklet. The peelable backing serves as a booklet cover.

1995, July 13 Litho. *Perf. 14½x14*

People with Disabilities: No. 1451a, Person flying kite from wheelchair. b, Blind person playing violin, guide dog.

1451		Pair	1.25	.95
a.-b.	A486	45c any single	.60	.20

Famous Australians from World War II Type of 1995

1995, Aug. 10 Litho. *Perf. 14½x14*

1452	A483	45c Leon Goldsworthy	.65	.25
1453	A483	45c Len Waters	.65	.25
1454	A483	45c Ellen Savage	.65	.25
1455	A483	45c Percy Collins	.65	.25
a.		Block of 4, #1452-1455	2.60	2.25

Peace Types of 1946

Perf. 14x14½, 14½x14

1995, Aug. 10 Engr.

1456	A43	45c red brown	.65	.20
1457	A45	45c dark green	.65	.20
1458	A44	$1.50 dark blue	2.25	2.00
		Nos. 1456-1458 (3)	3.55	2.40

End of World War II, 50th anniv.

Wildlife A487

Designs: a, Koalas. b, Pandas.

1995, Sept. 1 Litho. *Perf. 14*

1459		Pair	1.25	.95
a.-b.	A487	45c any single	.60	.20
c.		Souv. sheet #1459a, perf. 11x11½	.60	.60
d.		Souv. sheet #1459b, perf. 11x11½	.60	.60
e.		#1459c Ovptd. in sheet margin	1.00	1.00
f.		#1459d Ovptd. in sheet margin	1.00	1.00

Overprints read: No. 1459e: "AUSTRALIAN STAMP EXHIBITION." No. 1459f: "INTERNATIONAL STAMP & COIN EXPO. / BEIJING '95."

Issued: No. 1459f, 9/14/95.

See People's Republic of China Nos. 2597-2598.

Australian Medical Discoveries A488

Designs: No. 1461a, Joseph Slattery, Thomas Lyle, Walter Filmer, x-ray pioneers. No. 1461b, Jean Macnamara, Macfarlane Burnet, viruses and immunology. No. 1461C, Fred Hollows, eye care, vert. $2.50, Howard Florey, co-discoverer of penicillin, vert.

Perf. 14x14½, 14½x14

1995, Sept. 7

1461		Pair	1.25	.95
a.-b.	A488	45c any single	.60	.20
1461C	A488	45c multicolored	.60	.20
1461D	A488	$2.50 multicolored	3.75	1.50
		Nos. 1461-1461D (3)	5.60	2.65

No. 1461D exists in sheetlets of 10.

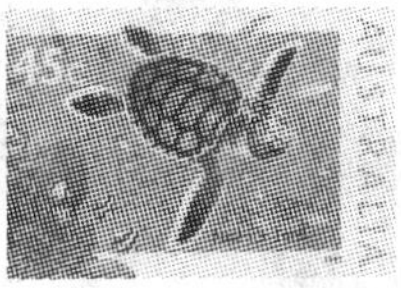

The World Down Under A489

Designs: Nos. 1462a, 1465a, Flatback turtle. Nos. 1462b, 1465b, Flame angelfish, nudibranch. Nos. 1463a, 1465c, Potato cod, giant maori wrasse. Nos. 1463b, 1465d, Giant trevally. Nos. 1464a, 1465e, Black marlin. Nos. 1464b, 1465f, Mako & tiger sharks.

1995, Oct. 3 Litho. *Perf. 14x14½*

1462		Pair	1.25	.80
a.-b.	A489	45c any single	.60	.20
1463		Pair	1.25	.80
a.-b.	A489	45c any single	.60	.20
1464		Pair	1.25	.80
a.-b.	A489	45c any single	.60	.20
		Nos. 1462-1464 (3)	3.75	2.40

Miniature Sheet of 6

1465	A489	45c #a.-f.	4.00	3.75
g.		Ovptd. in sheet margin	4.50	
h.		Ovptd. in sheet margin	4.50	
i.		Ovptd. in sheet margin	4.50	
j.		Ovptd. in sheet margin	4.50	
k.		Ovptd. in sheet margin	4.50	

Nos. 1462-1464 have pale blue border on three sides. No. 1465 is a continuous design and does not have the pale border. Fish on No. 1465 are printed with additional phosphor ink producing a glow-in-the-dark effect under ultraviolet light.

Overprints in gold in sheet margin of No. 1465 include show emblems and text:

No. 1465g: "ADELAIDE / STAMP AND / COLLECTIBLES / FAIR / 14/10/95 - / 15/10/95."

No. 1465h: "SYDNEY / CENTREPOINT 95 / STAMPSHOW."

No. 1465i: "Brisbane Stamp Show / 20-22 October 1995."

No. 1465j: "Melbourne Stamp & Coin Fair / 27-29 October 1995."

No. 1465k: "Swanpex WA / 28-29 October 1995."

Booklet Stamps

Self-Adhesive

Die Cut Perf. 11½

1466	A489	45c like #1462a	.65	.20
1467	A489	45c like #1462b	.65	.20
1468	A489	45c like #1463a	.65	.20
1469	A489	45c like #1463b	.65	.20
1470	A489	45c like #1464a	.65	.20
1471	A489	45c like #1464b	.65	.20
a.		Booklet pane, #1470-1471, 2 each #1466-1469	6.50	
b.		Strip of 6, #1466-1471	4.50	

By its nature, No. 1471a constitutes a complete booklet. The peelable backing serves as a booklet cover.

Christmas — A490

Stained glass windows, Our Lady Help of Christians Church, Melbourne: 40c, Madonna and Child. 45c, Angel carrying banner. $1, Three rejoicing angels.

1995, Nov. 1 Litho. *Perf. 14½x14*

1472	A490	40c multicolored	.60	.30
1473	A490	45c multicolored	.65	.30
1474	A490	$1 multicolored	1.50	.75
		Nos. 1472-1474 (3)	2.75	1.35

Booklet Stamp

Self-Adhesive

Die Cut Perf. 11½

1475	A490	40c multicolored	.60	.30
a.		Booklet pane of 20	12.00	

Madonna and Child on No. 1475 are printed with additional phosphor ink giving parts of the stamp a rough texture.

By its nature, No. 1475a constitutes a complete booklet. The peelable backing serves as a booklet cover, which also contains 20 labels. The complete

AUSTRALIA

booklet is available with backing showing two different advertisements.

Australia Day Type of 1994

Paintings by Australian women: 45c, West Australian Banksia, by Margaret Preston, vert. 85c, The Babe is Wise, by Lina Bryans, vert. $1, The Bridge in Curve, by Grace Cossington Smith. $1.20, Beach Umbrellas, by Vida Lahey.

1996, Jan. 16 — Perf. 14x14½, 14½x14 Litho.

1476	A463	45c multicolored	.65	.20
1477	A463	85c multicolored	1.25	.40
1478	A463	$1 multicolored	1.50	.50
1479	A463	$1.20 multicolored	1.75	.60
		Nos. 1476-1479 (4)	5.15	1.70

Heart and Roses A491

1996, Jan. 30 — Perf. 14x14½

1480	A491	45c gold & multi	.65	.20

See No. 1422.

Military Aviation A492

#1481, Firefly, Sea Fury. #1482, Beaufighter, Kittyhawk. #1483, Hornet. #1484, Kiowa.

1996, Feb. 26 — Litho. Perf. 14x14½

1481	A492	45c multicolored	.70	.20
1482	A492	45c multicolored	.70	.20
1483	A492	45c multicolored	.70	.20
1484	A492	45c multicolored	.70	.20
a.		Block of 4, #1481-1484	2.80	2.50

Australian World Heritage Sites Type of 1993

Designs: 45c, Tasmanian Wilderness. 75c, Willandra Lakes. 95c, Fossil Cave, Naracoorte. $1, Lord Howe Island.

1996, Mar. 14 — Litho. Perf. 14½x14

1485	A453	45c multicolored	.70	.20
1486	A453	75c multicolored	1.25	.40
1487	A453	95c multicolored	1.40	.45
1488	A453	$1 multicolored	1.50	.50
		Nos. 1485-1488 (4)	4.85	1.55

Indonesian Bear Cuscus — A493

Design: No. 1489, Australian Spotted Cuscus.

1996, Mar. 22

1489	A493	45c multicolored	.70	.20
1490	A493	45c multicolored	.70	.20
a.		Pair, Nos. 1489-1490	1.40	.95
b.		Souvenir sheet, No. 1490a	1.40	1.40

No. 1490a has continuous design.
nO. 1490B exists overprinted "WORLD PHILATELIC YOUTH EXHIBITION / PAMERAN FILATELI REMAJA DUNIA / INDONESIA '96." These were sold at the show, but apparently were never sold by the philatelic agency.
See Indonesia Nos. 1640-1642.

Queen Elizabeth II, 70th Birthday A494

Perf. 14x14½

1996, Apr. 11 — Litho. & Engr.

1491	A494	45c multicolored	.70	.20

North Melbourne Kangaroos A495

Brisbane Bears A496

Geelong Cats — A509

Hawthorn Hawks — A510

1996, Apr. 23 — Litho. Perf. 14½x14

1492	A495	45c multicolored	.70	.50
1493	A496	45c multicolored	.70	.50
1494	A497	45c multicolored	.70	.50
1495	A498	45c multicolored	.70	.50
1496	A499	45c multicolored	.70	.50
1497	A500	45c multicolored	.70	.50
1498	A501	45c multicolored	.70	.50
1499	A502	45c multicolored	.70	.50
1500	A503	45c multicolored	.70	.50
1501	A504	45c multicolored	.70	.50
1502	A505	45c multicolored	.70	.50
1503	A506	45c multicolored	.70	.50
1504	A507	45c multicolored	.70	.50
1505	A508	45c multicolored	.70	.50
1506	A509	45c multicolored	.70	.50
1507	A510	45c multicolored	.70	.50
a.		Min. sheet of 16, #1492-1507	11.25	

Sydney Swans — A497

Carlton Blues — A498

Adelaide Crows — A499

Fitzroy Lions — A500

Richmond Tigers — A501

St. Kilda Saints — A502

Melbourne Demons — A503

Collingwood Magpies — A504

Fremantle Dockers — A505

Footscray Bulldogs — A506

West Coast Eagles — A507

Essendon Bombers — A508

Booklet Stamps
Self-Adhesive
Serpentine Die Cut 11½

1508	A495	45c multicolored	.70	.20
a.		Booklet pane of 10	7.00	
1509	A496	45c multicolored	.70	.20
a.		Booklet pane of 10	7.00	
1510	A497	45c multicolored	.70	.20
a.		Booklet pane of 10	7.00	
1511	A498	45c multicolored	.70	.20
a.		Booklet pane of 10	7.00	
1512	A499	45c multicolored	.70	.20
a.		Booklet pane of 10	7.00	
1513	A500	45c multicolored	.70	.20
a.		Booklet pane of 10	7.00	
1514	A501	45c multicolored	.70	.20
a.		Booklet pane of 10	7.00	
1515	A502	45c multicolored	.70	.20
a.		Booklet pane of 10	7.00	
1516	A503	45c multicolored	.70	.20
a.		Booklet pane of 10	7.00	
1517	A504	45c multicolored	.70	.20
a.		Booklet pane of 10	7.00	
1518	A505	45c multicolored	.70	.20
a.		Booklet pane of 10	7.00	
1519	A506	45c multicolored	.70	.20
a.		Booklet pane of 10	7.00	
1520	A507	45c multicolored	.70	.20
a.		Booklet pane of 10	7.00	
1521	A508	45c multicolored	.70	.20
a.		Booklet pane of 10	7.00	
1522	A509	45c multicolored	.70	.20
a.		Booklet pane of 10	7.00	
1523	A510	45c multicolored	.70	.20
a.		Booklet pane of 10	7.00	

By their nature, Nos. 1508a-1523a are complete booklets. The peelable paper backing serves as a booklet cover.
Australian Football League, cent.

Flora and Fauna — A511

Designs: 5c, Leadbeater's possum. 10c, Powerful owl. 20c, Saltwater crocodile, Kangkong flower. 25c, Northern dwarf tree frog, red lily. No. 1528, Little kingfisher. No. 1529, Jacana. No. 1530, Jabiru. No. 1531, Brolga. $1, Big greasy butterfly, water lily. $2, Blackwood wattle. $5, Mountain ash, fern. $10, Kakadu Wetlands during lightning storm, great egret, red lily.

1996-97 — Litho. Perf. 14x14½

1524	A511	5c multicolored	.15	.15
1525	A511	10c multicolored	.15	.15
1526	A511	20c multicolored	.30	.15
1527	A511	25c multicolored	.40	.15
1528	A511	45c multicolored	.70	.20
1529	A511	45c multicolored	.70	.20
1530	A511	45c multicolored	.70	.20
1531	A511	45c multicolored	.70	.20
a.		Block of 4, #1528-1531	2.80	.80
b.		Souvenir sheet of 2, #1530-1531	1.20	
1532	A511	$1 multicolored	1.60	.40
1533	A511	$2 multicolored	3.25	1.00

Size: 30x50mm

1534	A511	$5 multicolored	8.00	2.60
1535	A511	$10 multicolored	15.00	4.00
a.		Souvenir sheet of 1	15.00	4.00
b.		As "a," ovptd. in sheet margin	15.00	4.00
		Nos. 1524-1535 (12)	31.65	9.40

Booklet Stamps
Self-Adhesive
Serpentine Die Cut 11½

1536	A511	45c like #1529	.70	.20
1537	A511	45c like #1528	.70	.20
1538	A511	45c like #1531	.70	.20
1539	A511	45c like #1530	.70	.20
a.		Booklet pane, 3 ea #1536, #1538, 2 ea #1537, #1539	7.00	
b.		Strip of 4, #1536-1539	2.80	

No. 1531b is inscribed in sheet margin with Shanghai '97 emblem and "International Stamp & Coin Exposition Shanghai '97" in Chinese and English.
No. 1538b overprinted in silver in sheet margin with PACIFIC 97 emblem and "Australia Post Exhibition Sheet No. 4."
By its nature No. 1539a is a complete booklet. The peelable backing serves as a booklet cover.
Issued: 5c, 10c, $2, $5, 5/9/96; 20c, 25c, $1, $10, #1538a, 4/10/97; #1528-1531, 1536-1539, 6/2/97; #1531b, 11/17/97.

Modern Olympic Games, Cent. A512

#1540, Edwin Flack, 1st Australian gold medalist, runners. #1541, Fanny Durack, 1st Australian woman gold medalist, swimmers. $1.05, Paralympics, Atlanta.

Perf. 14x14½

1996, June 6 — Litho. & Engr.

1540	A512	45c multicolored	.70	.20
1541	A512	45c multicolored	.70	.20
a.		Pair, #1540-1541	1.40	.65
1542	A512	$1.05 multicolored	1.60	1.00
		Nos. 1540-1542 (3)	3.00	1.40

Transfer of Olympic Flag from Atlanta to Sydney A513

1996, July 22 — Litho.

1543	A513	45c multicolored	.70	.20

Issued in sheets of 10.

Children's Book Council, 50th Anniv. — A514

Covers from "Book of the Year" books: No. 1544, "Animalia." No. 1545, "Greetings from Sandy Beach." No. 1546, "Who Sank the Boat?" No. 1547, "John Brown, Rose and the Midnight Cat."

1996, July 4 — Litho. Perf. 14x14½

1544	A514	45c multicolored	.70	.45
1545	A514	45c multicolored	.70	.45
1546	A514	45c multicolored	.70	.45
1547	A514	45c multicolored	.70	.45
a.		Block of 4, #1544-1547	2.80	2.50

Serpentine Die Cut 11½
Self-Adhesive

1548	A514	45c like #1544	.70	.20
1549	A514	45c like #1546	.70	.20
1550	A514	45c like #1547	.70	.20
1551	A514	45c like #1545	.70	.20
a.		Booklet pane, 4 #1548, 2 each #1549-1551	7.00	
b.		Strip of 4, #1548-1551	2.80	

By its nature, No. 1551a is a complete booklet. The peelable paper backing serves as a booklet cover.

National Council of Women, Cent. — A515

Designs: 45c, Margaret Windeyer (1866-1939), honorary life president. $1, Rose Scott (1847-1925), founding executive member.

1996, Aug. 8 Litho. *Perf. 14½x14*
1552 A515 45c claret & yellow .70 .20
1553 A515 $1 blue & yellow 1.50 1.50

Gems Type of 1995

1996, Sept. 5 Litho. *Perf. 14½x14*
1554 A481 45c Pearl .70 .20
1555 A481 $1.20 Diamond 1.90 1.90

No. 1555 contains a round foil design. Soaking in water may affect the design.

Arts Councils in Regional Australia A516

Silhouettes of performing artists, outdoor scene: 20c, Ballet dancer, violinist, field, bales, trees. 45c, Violinist, hand holding flower, dancer, tree in field.

1996, Sept. 12 Litho. *Perf. 14 Horiz.*
Booklet Stamps
1556 A516 20c multicolored .30 .15
1557 A516 45c multicolored .70 .20
a. Booklet pane, 1 #1556, 4 #1557 3.25
Complete booklet, #1557a 3.25

Pets
A517 A518

1996-97 *Perf. 14x14½, 14½x14*
1558 A517 45c Cockatoo .70 .20
1559 A517 45c Ducks, vert. .70 .20
1560 A517 45c Dog, cat, vert. .70 .20
a. Pair, #1559-1560 1.40 .80
1561 A518 45c Dog, puppy .70 .20
1562 A518 45c Kittens .70 .20
a. Pair, #1561-1562 1.40 .80

Size: 29x49mm
1563 A518 45c Pony, horse .70 .20
a. Souvenir sheet, #1558-1563 4.25 4.25
b. As "a," ovptd. 4.25 4.25
c. As "a," ovptd. 4.25 4.25
d. As "a," ovptd. 4.25 4.25
e. As "a," ovptd. 4.25 4.25
f. As "a," ovptd. 4.25 4.25
g. As "a," ovptd. 4.25 4.25
h. As "a," ovptd. 4.25 4.25
Nos. 1558-1563 (6) 4.20 1.20

Self-Adhesive
Serpentine Die Cut 11½
1564 A518 45c like #1561 .70 .20
1565 A518 45c like #1562 .70 .20
a. Bklt. pane, 6 #1564, 4 #1565 7.00

No. 1563a is a continuous design.

Overprints in gold on sheet margin: No. 1563b, show emblem and "10TH ASIAN INTERNATIONAL PHILATELIC EXHIBITION 1996" in Chinese and English. No. 1563c, pets emblem and, "ASDA CENTREPOINT '96 STAMP AND COIN SHOW / 5-7 October 1996." No. 1563d, pets emblem and "ST PETERS STAMP & COLLECTIBLE FAIR / 12-13 OCTOBER 1996." No. 1563e, pets emblem and "MELBOURNE '96 NATIONAL PHILATELIC EXHIBITION / 17-20 OCTOBER 1996." No. 1563f, pets emblem and "QUEENSLAND SPRING STAMP AND COIN SHOW / 25-27 OCTOBER 1996." No. 1563g, pets emblem and "SWANPEX '96 / 26-27 OCTOBER 1996." No. 1563h: Hong Kong '97 emblem and "11TH ASIAN INTERNATIONAL STAMP EXHIBITION / 12-16 FEBRUARY 1997."

By its nature, No. 1565a is a complete booklet. The peelable paper backing serves as a booklet cover.

Issued: Nos. 1558-1563, 1563a, 1564-1465, 10/1/96; Nos. 1563b-1563g, 10/3/96; No. 1563h, 2/12/97.

Baron Ferdinand von Mueller (1825-96), Botanist — A519

1996, Oct. 9 *Perf. 14*
1566 A519 $1.20 multicolored 1.90 1.00

See Germany No. 1949.

Christmas — A520

1996, Nov. 1 *Perf. 14½x14*
1567 A520 40c Madonna and Child .65 .20
1568 A520 45c Wise man .70 .20
1569 A520 $1 Shepherd boy, lamb 1.50 .30
Nos. 1567-1569 (3) 2.85 .70

Self-Adhesive
Serpentine Die Cut 12
1570 A520 40c like #1567 .65 .20
a. Booklet pane of 20 13.00

By its nature, No. 1570a is a complete booklet. The peelable paper backing serves as a booklet cover.

Exploration of Australian Coast & Christmas Island by Willem de Vlamingh, 300th Anniv. — A521

Portrait of a Dutch Navigator, by Jan Verkolje.

1996, Nov. 1 *Perf. 14x14½*
1571 A521 45c multicolored .70 .20
a. Pair, #1571 & Christmas Is. #404 1.40 .80

Australia Day Type of 1994

Paintings: 85c, Landscape '74, by Fred Williams. 90c, The Balcony 2, by Brett Whiteley. $1.20, Fire Haze at Gerringong, by Lloyd Rees.

1997, Jan. 16 Litho. *Perf. 14½x14*
1572 A463 85c multicolored 1.25 .40
1573 A463 90c multicolored 1.40 .45
1574 A463 $1.20 multicolored 1.90 .60
Nos. 1572-1574 (3) 4.55 1.45

A522 A523

Sir Donald Bradman, cricketer.

1997, Jan. 23 Litho. *Perf. 14½*
1575 A522 45c Portrait .70 .20
1576 A522 45c At bat .70 .20
a. Pair, No. 1575-1576 1.40 .80

See Nos. 1634-1646.

1997, Jan. 29 *Perf. 14½x14*
1577 A523 45c Rose .70 .20

Serpentine Die Cut 11½
Booklet Stamp
Self-Adhesive
1578 A523 45c like #1577 .70 .20
a. Booklet pane of 10 7.00

Greetings. By its nature, No. 1578a is a complete booklet. The peelable paper backing, which also contains 12 labels, serves as a booklet cover.

Classic Cars — A524

#1579, 1934 Ford Coupe Utility. #1580, 1948 GMH Holden 48-215 (FX). #1581, 1958 Austin Lancer. #1582, 1962 Chrysler Valiant R Series.

1997, Feb. 27 Litho. *Perf. 14x14½*
1579 A524 45c multicolored .70 .20
a. Booklet pane of 4 2.80
1580 A524 45c multicolored .70 .20
a. Booklet pane of 4 2.80
1581 A524 45c multicolored .70 .20
a. Booklet pane of 4 2.80
1582 A524 45c multicolored .70 .20
a. Booklet pane of 4 2.80
b. Block of 4, #1579-1582 2.80 1.60
Complete booklet, #1579a, 1580a, 1581a, 1582a 16.00

Complete booklet contains 2 postal cards and 16 self-adhesive labels.

Serpentine Die Cut 12
Booklet Stamps
Self-Adhesive
1583 A524 45c like #1579 .70 .20
1584 A524 45c like #1580 .70 .20
1585 A524 45c like #1581 .70 .20
1586 A524 45c like #1582 .70 .20
a. Booklet pane of 10, 2 ea #1583, 1585, 3 ea #1584, 1586 7.00
b. Strip of 4, #1583-1586 2.80

By its nature, No. 1586a is a complete booklet. The peelable backing serves as a booklet cover. The backing for No. 1586b is inscribed with a 3x8mm black vertical box and "SNP CAMBEC."

Circuses in Australia, 150th Anniv. — A525

#1591, Queen of the Arena, May Wirth (1894-1978). #1592, Wizard of the Wire, Con Colleano (1899-1973). #1593, Clowns. #1594, Tumblers.

1997, Mar. 13 Litho. *Perf. 14½x14*
1591 A525 45c multicolored .70 .20
1592 A525 45c multicolored .70 .20
1593 A525 45c multicolored .70 .20
1594 A525 45c multicolored .70 .20
a. Block of 4, #1591-1594 2.80 1.60

Queen Elizabeth II, 71st Birthday, 50th Wedding Anniv. — A526

1997, Apr. 17 Engr. *Perf. 14x14½*
1595 A526 45c Design A50 .70 .20

A527 A528

1997, Apr. 17 *Perf. 14½x14*
1596 A527 45c multicolored .70 .20

Lions Clubs of Australia, 50th anniv.

1997, May 8 Litho. *Perf. 14½x14*

Dolls and Teddy Bears: No. 1597, Doll wearing red hat. No. 1598, Bear standing. No. 1599, Doll wearing white dress holding teddy bear. No. 1600, Doll in brown outfit. No. 1601, Teddy bear seated.

1597 A528 45c multicolored .70 .20
1598 A528 45c multicolored .70 .20
1599 A528 45c multicolored .70 .20
1600 A528 45c multicolored .70 .20
1601 A528 45c multicolored .70 .20
a. Strip of 5, #1597-1601 3.50 2.00

Emergency Services A529

#1602, Disaster victim evacuated. #1603, Police rescue hiker. $1.05, Rapid response saves home. $1.20, Ambulance dash saves life.

1997, July 10 Litho. *Perf. 14x14½*
1602 A529 45c multicolored .70 .20
1603 A529 45c multicolored .70 .20
a. Pair, #1602-1603 1.40 .40
1604 A529 $1.05 multicolored 1.60 .50
1605 A529 $1.20 multicolored 1.80 .55
Nos. 1602-1605 (4) 4.80 1.45

Arrival of Merino Sheep in Australia, Bicent. A530

Designs: No. 1606, George Peppin, Junior (1827-76), breeder, Merino sheep. No. 1607, "Pepe" chair, uses of wool.

1997, Aug. 7 Litho. *Perf. 14x14½*
1606 A530 45c multicolored .70 .20
1607 A530 45c multicolored .70 .20
a. Pair, #1606-1607 1.40 .80

Scenes from "The Dreaming," Animated Stories for Children A531

Designs: 45c, Dumbi the Owl. $1, The Two Willy-Willies. $1.20, How Brolga Became a Bird. $1.80, Tuggan-Tuggan.

1997, Aug. 21 *Perf. 14½*
1608 A531 45c multicolored .70 .20
1609 A531 $1 multicolored 1.50 .40
1610 A531 $1.20 multicolored 1.75 .45
1611 A531 $1.80 multicolored 2.75 .70
Nos. 1608-1611 (4) 6.70 1.75

Prehistoric Animals — A532

Designs: No. 1612, Rhoetosaurus brownei. No. 1613, Mcnamaraspis kaprios. No. 1614, Ninjemys oweni. No. 1615, Paracyclotosaurus davidi. No. 1616, Woolungasaurus glendowerensis.

1997, Sept. 4 Litho. *Perf. 14½x14*
1612 A532 45c multicolored .65 .20
1613 A532 45c multicolored .65 .20
1614 A532 45c multicolored .65 .20
1615 A532 45c multicolored .65 .20
1616 A532 45c multicolored .65 .20
a. Strip of 5, #1612-1616 3.25 2.00

Printed in sheets of 10 stamps.

AUSTRALIA

Nocturnal Animals
A533 A534

1997, Oct. 1   Litho.   Perf. 14½x14, 14x14½

1617	A533	45c Barking owl	.65	.20
1618	A533	45c Spotted-tailed quoll	.65	.20
a.		Pair, #1617-1618	1.30	.80
1619	A534	45c Platypus	.65	.20
1620	A534	45c Brown antechinus	.65	.20
1621	A534	45c Dingo	.65	.20
a.		Strip of 3, #1619-1621	2.00	1.25

Size: 49x29mm

1622	A534	45c Yellow-bellied glider	.65	.20
a.		Souvenir sheet, #1617-1622	4.00	4.00
		Nos. 1617-1622 (6)	3.90	1.20

No. 1622a is printed with additional phosphor ink revealing a glow-in-the-dark spider and web under ultraviolet light.

Size: 21x32mm
Serpentine Die Cut Perf. 11½
Self-Adhesive

1623	A533	45c like #1617	.65	.20
1624	A533	45c like #1618	.65	.20
a.		Booklet pane, 5 each #1623-1624	6.50	
b.		Pair, #1623-1624	1.30	

By its nature No. 1624a is a complete booklet. The peelable paper backing serves as a booklet cover.

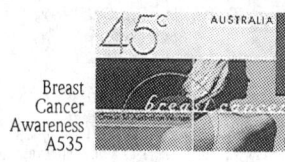

Breast Cancer Awareness — A535

1997, Oct. 27   Litho.   Perf. 14x14½

| 1625 | A535 | 45c multicolored | .65 | .20 |

Christmas — A536

Children in Christmas Nativity pageant: 40c, Angels. 45c, Mary holding Baby Jesus. $1, Three Wise Men.

1997, Nov. 3

1626	A536	40c multicolored	.60	.20
1627	A536	45c multicolored	.65	.20
1628	A536	$1 multicolored	1.40	.45
		Nos. 1626-1628 (3)	2.65	.85

Booklet Stamps
Serpentine Die Cut Perf. 11½
Self-Adhesive

| 1629 | A536 | 40c multicolored | .60 | .20 |
| a. | | Booklet pane of 20 | 12.00 | |

By its nature No. 1629a is a complete booklet. The peelable paper backing serves as a booklet cover, which also contains 20 labels.

Maritime Heritage — A537

1998, Jan. 15   Litho.   Perf. 14½x14

1630	A537	45c Flying Cloud	.60	.20
a.		Sheet of 10	6.00	2.00
1631	A537	85c Marco Polo	1.15	.35
1632	A537	$1 Chusan	1.30	.40
1633	A537	$1.20 Heather Belle	1.60	.50
		Nos. 1630-1633 (4)	4.65	1.45

Australia '99 (#1630a). Issued: #1630a, 6/17/98.

Legends Type of 1997

Olympians: No. 1634: a, Betty Cuthbert. b, Cuthbert running. c, Herb Elliott. d, Elliott running. e, Dawn Fraser. f, Fraser swimming. g, Marjorie Jackson. h, Jackson running. i, Murray Rose. j, Rose swimming. k, Shirley Strickland. l, Strickland clearing hurdle.

1998, Jan. 21   Perf. 14x14½

Size: 34x27mm

| 1634 | | Sheet of 12 | 7.25 | 2.50 |
| a.-l. | | A522 any single | .60 | .20 |

Booklet Stamps
Self-Adhesive
Serpentine Die Cut 11½
Size: 34x25mm

1635	A522	45c like #1634a	.60	.20
1636	A522	45c like #1634b	.60	.20
1637	A522	45c like #1634c	.60	.20
1638	A522	45c like #1634d	.60	.20
1639	A522	45c like #1634e	.60	.20
1640	A522	45c like #1634f	.60	.20
1641	A522	45c like #1634g	.60	.20
1642	A522	45c like #1634h	.60	.20
1643	A522	45c like #1634i	.60	.20
1644	A522	45c like #1634j	.60	.20
1645	A522	45c like #1634k	.60	.20
1646	A522	45c like #1634l	.60	.20
a.		Booklet pane of 12, #1635-1646	7.25	

By its nature, No. 1646a is a complete booklet. The peelable backing serves as a booklet cover.

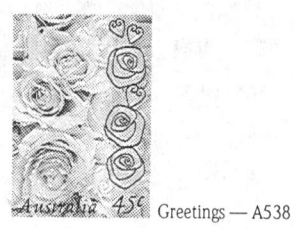

Greetings — A538

1998, Feb. 12   Litho.   Perf. 14½x14

| 1647 | A538 | 45c Champagne roses | .60 | .15 |

Booklet Stamp
Self-Adhesive
Serpentine Die Cut 11½

| 1648 | A538 | 45c like #1647 | .60 | .15 |
| a. | | Booklet pane of 10 | 6.00 | |

By its nature No. 1648a is a complete booklet. The peelable paper backing, which contains 12 labels, serves as a booklet cover.

Queen Elizabeth II, 72nd Birthday — A539

1998, Apr. 9   Litho.   Perf. 14x14½

| 1649 | A539 | 45c multicolored | .60 | .20 |

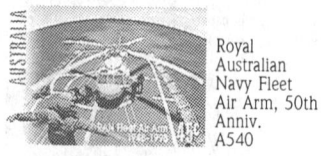

Royal Australian Navy Fleet Air Arm, 50th Anniv. — A540

1998, Apr. 9

| 1650 | A540 | 45c multicolored | .60 | .20 |

Farming in Australia — A541

Designs: No. 1651, Sheep for producing wool. No. 1652, Sheaves of wheat. No. 1653, Herding cattle on horseback. No. 1654, Harvesting sugar cane. No. 1655, Dairy cattle, man on motorcycle.

1998, Apr. 21

1651	A541	45c multicolored	.60	.20
1652	A541	45c multicolored	.60	.20
1653	A541	45c multicolored	.60	.20
1654	A541	45c multicolored	.60	.20
1655	A541	45c multicolored	.60	.20
a.		Strip of 5, #1651-1655	3.00	1.00

Booklet Stamps
Self-Adhesive
Serpentine Die Cut 11½
Size: 37x25mm

1656	A541	45c like #1651	.60	.20
1657	A541	45c like #1652	.60	.20
1658	A541	45c like #1653	.60	.20
1659	A541	45c like #1654	.60	.20
1660	A541	45c like #1655	.60	.20
a.		Booklet pane, 2 each #1656-1660	6.00	

The peelable backing of No. 1660a serves as a booklet cover.

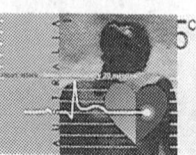

Heart Health — A542

1998, May 4   Litho.   Perf. 14x14½

| 1661 | A542 | 45c multicolored | .60 | .20 |

Rock and Roll in Australia — A543

a, "The Wild One," by Johnny O'Keefe, 1958. b, "Oh Yeah Uh Huh," by Col Joye and the Joye Boys, 1959. c, "He's My Blonde-headed Stompie Wompie Real Gone Surfer Boy," by Little Pattie, 1963. d, "Shakin' All Over," by Normie Rowe, 1965. e, "She's So Fine," by The Easybeats, 1965. f, "The Real Thing," by Russell Morris, 1969. g, "Turn Up Your Radio," by The Masters Apprentices, 1970. h, "Eagle Rock," by Daddy Cool, 1971. i, "Most People I Know Think That I'm Crazy," by Billy Thorpe & the Aztecs, 1972. j, "Horror Movie," by Skyhooks, 1974. k, "It's a Long Way to the Top," by AC/DC, 1975. l, "Howzat," by Sherbet, 1976.

1998, May 26

| 1662 | | Sheet of 12 | 7.25 | 2.50 |
| a.-l. | | 45c any single | .60 | .20 |

Coil Stamps
Self-Adhesive
Serpentine Die Cut 11½
Size: 37x25mm

1663	A543	45c like #1662a	.60	.20
1664	A543	45c like #1662b	.60	.20
1665	A543	45c like #1662c	.60	.20
1666	A543	45c like #1662d	.60	.20
1667	A543	45c like #1662e	.60	.20
1668	A543	45c like #1662f	.60	.20
1669	A543	45c like #1662g	.60	.20
1670	A543	45c like #1662h	.60	.20
1671	A543	45c like #1662i	.60	.20
1672	A543	45c like #1662j	.60	.20
1673	A543	45c like #1662k	.60	.20
1674	A543	45c like #1662l	.60	.20
a.		Strip of 12 + label	7.25	

Endangered Birds — A544

World Wildlife Fund: #1675, Helmeted honeyeater. #1676, Orange-bellied parrot. #1677, Red-tailed black cockatoo. #1678, Gouldian finch.

1998, June 25   Perf. 14x14½

1675	A544	5c multicolored	.15	.15
1676	A544	5c multicolored	.15	.15
a.		Pair, #1675-1676	.15	.15
1677	A544	45c multicolored	.60	.20
1678	A544	45c multicolored	.60	.20
a.		Pair, #1677-1678	1.20	.40

Performing and Visual Arts — A545

Young people: No. 1679, Playing French horn. No. 1680, Dancing.

1998, July 16   Litho.   Perf. 14x14½

1679	A545	45c multicolored	.60	.20
1680	A545	45c multicolored	.60	.20
a.		Pair, #1679-1680	1.20	.40

Orchids — A546

Designs: 45c, Phalaenopsis rosenstromii. 85c, Arundina graminifolia. $1, Grammatophyllum speciosum. $1.20, Dendrobium phalaenopsis.

1998, Aug. 6   Litho.   Perf. 14½x14

1681	A546	45c multicolored	.60	.20
1682	A546	85c multicolored	1.00	.35
1683	A546	$1 multicolored	1.25	.40

FROM AUSTRALIA'S BEST KNOWN STAMP DEALER... EXCELLENT STOCKS OF...

AUSTRALIA
Australian Antarctic
Cocos • Christmas
Norfolk • Nauru
Pitcairn • P.N.G.
New Guinea • New Zealand
and Pacific
AT COMPETITIVE PRICES!

- BIG SAVINGS on Complete COUNTRY and YEAR COLLECTIONS
- WANT LISTS (Scott Numbers) welcome. All items guaranteed.

BUYING & SELLING

YOU CANNOT AFFORD TO DEAL WITH ANYONE BUT...

MAX STERN & CO.
234 Flinders Street (Port Phillip Arcade)
Box 997H, G.P.O. Melbourne,
3001, AUSTRALIA
Phone (in Australia) 3-96546751
Phone (outside Australia) 61396546751
FAX 61-3-9650-7192
Email: maxstern@netspace.net.au
Website: http://www.netspace.net.au/~maxstern
AGENTS FOR THE U.S. POSTAL SERVICE IN AUSTRALIA AND NEW ZEALAND
American Stamp Dealers' Association Member since 1948.
Hon. Life Member A.S.D.A. Australia

For all your stamp supply needs
www.scottonline.com

AUSTRALIA

1684 A546 $1.20 multicolored 1.50 .50
  a. Souvenir sheet, #1681-1684 4.50 1.50
  Nos. 1681-1684 (4) 4.35 1.45
  See Singapore Nos. 858-861b.

The Teapot of Truth, by Cartoonist Michael Leunig — A547

Designs: No. 1685, Angel carrying teapot, bird with flower. No. 1686, Birds perched on heart-shaped vine. No. 1687, Characters using their tea into cup. $1, Stylized family. $1.20, Stylized teapot with face and legs.

1998, Aug. 13   Perf. 14x14½
1685 A547 45c multicolored .60 .20
  a. Booklet pane of 4 2.50
1686 A547 45c multicolored .60 .20
  a. Booklet pane of 4 2.50
1687 A547 45c multicolored .60 .20
  a. Booklet pane of 4 2.50

Size: 30x25mm
1688 A547 $1 multicolored 1.25 .40
  a. Booklet pane of 2 2.50
1689 A547 $1.20 multicolored 1.50 .50
  a. Booklet pane of 2 3.00
  Complete booklet, #1685a, 1686a, 1687a, 1688a, 1689a, 1 postal card & 16 self-adhesive labels 14.00
  Nos. 1685-1689 (5) 4.55 1.50

A548   A549

Butterflies,
1998, Sept. 3   Litho.   Perf. 14½x14
1690 A548 45c Red lacewing .55 .20
1691 A548 45c Dull oakblue .55 .20
1692 A548 45c Meadow argus .55 .20
1693 A548 45c Ulysses .55 .20
1694 A548 45c Common red-eye .55 .20
  a. Strip of 5, #1690-1694 2.75 1.00

Self-Adhesive
Serpentine Die Cut 11½
1695 A548 45c like #1690 .55 .20
1696 A548 45c like #1691 .55 .20
1697 A548 45c like #1692 .55 .20
1698 A548 45c like #1693 .55 .20
1699 A548 45c like #1694 .55 .20
  a. Strip of 5, #1695-1699 2.75

1998, Sept. 10
#1700, Sextant, map of Bass Strait. #1701, Telescope, map of Van Diemen's Land (Tasmania).
1700 A549 45c multicolored .55 .20
1701 A549 45c multicolored .55 .20
  a. Pair, #1700-1701 1.10 .40
Circumnavigation of Tasmania by George Bass (1771-c. 1803) and Matthew Flinders (1774-1814), bicent.

Marine Life
A550   A551

#1702, Fiery squid. #1703, Manta ray. #1704, Bottlenose dolphin. #1705, Weedy seadragon. #1706, Southern right whale. #1707, White pointer shark.

Perf. 14½x14, 14x14½
1998, Oct. 1   Litho.
1702 A550 45c multi .55 .20
1703 A550 45c multi, horiz. .55 .20
1704 A551 45c multi .55 .20

1705 A551 45c multi .55 .20
  a. Pair, #1704-1705 1.10 .40
Size: 50x30mm
1706 A551 45c multi, horiz. .55 .20
1707 A551 45c multi .55 .20
  a. Souvenir sheet, #1702-1707 3.30 1.20
  Nos. 1702-1707 (5) 4.55 1.50

Booklet Stamps
Self-Adhesive
Serpentine Die Cut Perf. 11½
1708 A551 45c like #1704 .55 .20
1709 A551 45c like #1705 .55 .20
  a. Booklet pane, 5 each #1708-1709 5.50
No. 1709a is a complete booklet. The peelable paper backing serves as a booklet cover.
Nos. 1708-1709 also exist in coils.

Universal Declaration of Human Rights, 50th Anniv. — A552

1998, Oct. 22   Litho.   Perf. 14½x14
1712 A552 45c multicolored .60 .20

Christmas — A553

40c, Magi. 45c, Nativity. $1, Journey to Bethlehem.

1998, Nov. 2   Perf. 14x14½
1713 A553 40c multicolored .50 .20
1714 A553 45c multicolored .60 .20
1715 A553 $1 multicolored 1.25 .45
  Nos. 1713-1715 (3) 2.35 .85

Booklet Stamp
Self-Adhesive
Serpentine Die Cut Perf. 11½
1716 A553 40c multicolored .50 .20
  a. Booklet pane of 20 10.00
No. 1716a is a complete booklet.

AIR POST STAMPS

Airplane over Bush Lands — AP1

Unwmk.
1929, May 20   Engr.   Perf. 11
C1 AP1 3p deep green 7.50 3.00
  Never hinged 12.50
  a. Booklet pane of 4 ('30) 125.00

Kingsford-Smith Type of 1931
1931, Mar. 19
C2 A8 6p gray violet 7.50 7.50
  Never hinged 12.50

AP3

1931, Nov. 4
C3 AP3 6p olive brown 15.00 9.00
  Never hinged 22.50
For overprint see No. CO1.

Mercury and Hemispheres — AP4

1934, Dec. 1   Perf. 11
C4 AP4 1sh6p violet brown 30.00 1.75
  Never hinged 75.00

Perf. 13x13½
1937, Oct. 22   Wmk. 228
C5 AP4 1sh6p violet brown 7.50 .25
  Never hinged 12.50

Catalogue values for unused stamps in this section, from this point to the end of the section, are for Never Hinged items.

Mercury and Globe — AP5

1949, Sept. 1   Perf. 14½
C6 AP5 1sh6p sepia 1.75 .15

1956, Dec. 6   Unwmk.
C7 AP5 1sh6p sepia 16.00 .85

Super-Constellation over Globe — AP6

1958, Jan. 6   Perf. 14½x14
C8 AP6 2sh dark violet blue 2.50 1.75
Inauguration of Australian "Round the World" air service.

AIR POST OFFICIAL STAMP

No. C3 Overprinted **O S**

Perf. 11, 11½
1931, Nov. 17   Unwmk.
CO1 AP3 6p olive brown 25.00 30.00
  Never hinged 40.00
Issued primarily for official use, but to prevent speculation, a quantity was issued for public distribution.

POSTAGE DUE STAMPS

Very fine examples of Nos. J1-J38 will have perforations touching the design on one or more sides due to the narrow spacing of the stamps on the plates. Stamps with perfs clear of the design on all four sides are scarce and will command higher prices.

D1   D2

1902 Typo.   Wmk. 55   Perf. 11½, 12
J1 D1 ½p emerald 8.25 9.50
J2 D1 1p emerald 16.00 6.50
  a. Perf. 11 600.00 250.00
J3 D1 2p emerald 20.00 7.75
J4 D1 3p emerald 30.00 10.00
J5 D1 4p emerald 35.00 10.00
J6 D1 6p emerald 45.00 19.00

J7 D1 8p emerald 125.00 110.00
J8 D1 5sh emerald 250.00 82.50
  Nos. J1-J8 (8) 529.25 255.25
The 1p, 2p and 4p, type D1, exist also in perforations compounding 11 with 11½ & 12.

Perf. 11½, 12, 11 and 11 Compound with 11½, 12
1902-04
J9 D2 ½p emerald 7.25 8.25
  a. Perf. 11 82.50 65.00
J10 D2 1p emerald 4.50 2.75
  a. Perf. 11 110.00 37.50
J11 D2 2p emerald 15.00 3.50
J12 D2 3p emerald 55.00 8.75
J13 D2 4p emerald 50.00 6.00
J14 D2 5p emerald 50.00 16.00
  a. Perf. 11 125.00 32.50
J15 D2 6p emerald 72.50 18.00
J16 D2 8p emerald 125.00 40.00
J17 D2 10p emerald 87.50 15.00
J18 D2 1sh emerald 57.50 14.00
  a. Perf. 11 175.00 45.00
J19 D2 2sh emerald 110.00 25.00
J20 D2 5sh emerald 225.00 22.50
  a. Perf. 11 375.00 150.00
J21 D2 10sh emerald 2,750. 1,050.
J22 D2 20sh emerald 4,000. 1,900.
  Nos. J9-J20 (12) 859.25 179.75

Perf. 11½, 12 Compound with 11
1906   Wmk. 12
J23 D2 ½p emerald 14.00 10.00
J24 D2 1p emerald 30.00 5.50
  a. Perf. 11 650.00 250.00
J25 D2 2p emerald 50.00 10.00
J26 D2 3p emerald 375.00 300.00
J27 D2 4p emerald 77.50 27.50
  a. Perf. 11 900.00 400.00
J28 D2 6p emerald 140.00 75.00
  Nos. J23-J28 (6) 686.50 375.50

1907   Wmk. 13   Perf. 11½x11
J29 D2 ½p emerald 45.00 45.00
J30 D2 1p emerald 72.50 45.00
J31 D2 2p emerald 165.00 100.00
J32 D2 4p emerald 225.00 125.00
J33 D2 6p emerald 325.00 140.00
  Nos. J29-J33 (5) 832.50 455.00

D3   D4

Perf. 11, 11½x11 (1sh, 5sh)
1908-09   Wmk. 12
J34 D3 1sh emer ('09) 125.00 16.00
J35 D3 2sh emerald 1,100. 500.00
J36 D3 5sh emerald 225.00 52.50
J37 D3 10sh emerald 1,900. 1,750.
J38 D3 20sh emerald 5,250. 5,000.

Perf. 11, 12x12½, 12½, 14
1909   Wmk. 13
J39 D4 ½p green & car 8.75 3.75
J40 D4 1p green & car 11.00 1.65
J41 D4 2p green & car 14.00 1.90
J42 D4 3p green & car 22.50 6.50
J43 D4 4p green & car 25.00 3.75
J44 D4 6p green & car 22.50 3.50
J45 D4 1sh green & car 22.50 2.75
J46 D4 2sh green & car 82.50 14.00
J47 D4 5sh green & car 82.50 14.00
J48 D4 10sh green & car 350.00 300.00
J49 D4 £1 green & car 550.00 325.00
  Nos. J39-J49 (11) 1,191. 676.55

1922-25   Wmk. 10   Perf. 14, 11
J50 D4 ½p grn & car ('23) 6.50 1.75
J51 D4 1p green & car 6.50 1.90
J52 D4 1½p yellow green & rose ('25) 3.75 3.75
J53 D4 2p green & car 8.00 3.75
J54 D4 3p green & car 15.00 2.75
J55 D4 4p green & car 19.00 2.25
J56 D4 6p green & car 22.50 13.00
  Nos. J50-J56 (7) 81.25 28.65

1931-37   Wmk. 228   Perf. 11, 14
J57 D4 ½p yel green & rose ('34) 10.00 9.00
J58 D4 1p yel grn & rose 4.00 .75
J59 D4 2p yel grn & rose 4.00 .75
J60 D4 3p yel grn & rose ('37) 125.00 42.50
J61 D4 4p yel grn & rose ('34) 20.00 2.00
J62 D4 6p yel grn & rose ('36) 350.00 300.00
J63 D4 1sh yel grn & rose ('34) 50.00 17.50
  Nos. J57-J63 (7) 563.00 372.50

AUSTRALIA

D5

Engraved; Value Typo.
1938   Perf. 14½x14
J64	D5	½p green & car	.75	1.25
J65	D5	1p green & car	5.00	.50
J66	D5	2p green & car	4.50	.50
J67	D5	3p green & car	15.00	3.50
J68	D5	4p green & car	4.50	.25
J69	D5	6p green & car	45.00	17.50
J70	D5	1sh green & car	20.00	7.50
		Nos. J64-J70 (7)	94.75	31.00

Catalogue values for unused stamps in this section, from this point to the end of the section, are for Never Hinged items.

Type of 1938
Value Tablet Redrawn

Original   Redrawn

Pence denominations: "D" has melon-shaped center in redrawn tablet. The redrawn 3p differs slightly, having semi-melon-shaped "D" center, with vertical white stroke half filling it.
1sh. 1938: Numeral "1" narrow, with six background lines above.
1sh. 1947: Numeral broader, showing more white space around dotted central ornament. Three lines above.

1946-57   Wmk. 228
J71	D5	½p grn & car ('56)	2.50	1.40
J72	D5	1p grn & car ('47)	1.25	.25
J73	D5	2p green & car	.75	1.00
J74	D5	3p green & car	4.00	.35
J75	D5	4p grn & car ('52)	5.00	.50
J76	D5	5p grn & car ('48)	7.50	1.25
J77	D5	6p grn & car ('47)	7.50	.65
J78	D5	7p grn & car ('53)	5.00	3.00
J79	D5	8p grn & car ('57)	12.50	11.50
J80	D5	1sh grn & car ('47)	12.50	1.25
		Nos. J71-J80 (10)	58.50	21.15

1953-54
White Tablet, Carmine Numeral
J81	D5	1sh grn & car ('54)	9.00	5.00
J82	D5	2sh green & car	12.50	10.00
J83	D5	5sh green & car	17.50	2.50
		Nos. J81-J83 (3)	39.00	17.50

Issued: 2sh, 5sh, Aug. 26; 1sh, Feb. 17.

Redrawn Type of 1947-57
Two Types of Some Pence Values:
Type I - Background lines touch numeral, "D" and period.
Type II - Lines do not touch numeral, etc.
Second engraving of 1sh has sharper and thicker lines.
The ½p type II has 7 dots under the "2."
The 8p type II has distinct lines in centers of "8" and between "8" and "D."

Engr.; Value Typo.
1958-60   Unwmk.   Perf. 14½x14
J86	D5	½p grn & car (II)	2.50	1.10
a.		Six dots under the "2"	3.75	.95
J87	D5	1p grn & car (II)	2.50	.40
a.		Type I	3.25	.40
J88	D5	3p grn & car (II)	2.50	.75
J89	D5	4p grn & car (I)	5.00	4.00
a.		Type II ('59)	12.00	3.00
J90	D5	5p grn & car (II)	11.00	6.00
a.		Type II ('59)	70.00	22.50
J91	D5	6p grn & car (II)	6.50	1.75
J92	D5	8p grn & car (II)	10.00	15.00
a.		Indistinct lines	15.00	15.00
J93	D5	10p grn & car (II)	7.50	3.25

White Tablet, Carmine Numeral
J94	D5	1sh green & car	8.50	2.50
a.		2nd redrawing ('60)	9.00	.60
J95	D5	2sh grn & car	26.00	5.50
		Nos. J86-J95 (10)	82.00	40.25

Issued: 1sh, 9/8/58; 10p, 12/9/59; 2sh, 3/8/60; 3p, 6p, 5/25/60; others, 2/27/58.

MILITARY STAMPS

Nos. 166, 191, 183A, 173, 175, 206 and 177 Overprinted in Black:

B.C.O.F.   B.C.O.F.   B.C.O.F.
JAPAN   JAPAN   JAPAN
1946   1946   1946
a   b   c

Perf. 14½x14, 15x14, 11½, 13½x13
1946-47   Wmk. 228
M1	A24(a)	½p orange	2.75	2.75
M2	A36(b)	1p brown vio	2.25	2.25
a.		Blue overprint	100.00	67.50
M3	A27(b)	3p dk vio brn	2.00	.75
M4	A30(a)	6p brn violet	5.00	5.00
M5	A16(a)	1sh gray green	7.50	7.50
M6	A1 (c)	2sh dk red brn	22.50	22.50
M7	A32(c)	5sh dl red brn	110.00	100.00
		Nos. M1-M7 (7)	152.00	140.75

"B.C.O.F." stands for "British Commonwealth Occupation Force."
Forged overprints of Nos. M6-M7 exist.
Issued: #M1-M3, 10/11/46; #M4-M7, 5/8/47.

OFFICIAL STAMPS

Perforated Initials
In 1913-31, postage stamps were perforated "OS" for federal official use. This catalogue does not list varieties with perforated initials.

Overprinted Official stamps are comparatively more difficult to find well centered than the basic issues on which they are printed. This is because poorly centered sheets were purposely chosen to be overprinted.

Overprinted   **O S**

On Regular Issue of 1931
1931, May 4   Unwmk.   Perf. 11, 11½
O1	A8	2p dull red	60.00	22.50
O2	A8	3p blue	175.00	35.00

These stamps were issued primarily for official use but to prevent speculation a quantity was issued for public distribution.
Used values are for cto copies.
Counterfeit overprints exist.

On Regular Issues of 1928-32
1932   Wmk. 203   Perf. 13½x12½
O3	A4	2p red (II)	10.00	.90
O4	A4	4p olive bister	30.00	6.00

Perf. 11½, 12
O5	A1	6p brown	67.50	35.00

1932-33   Wmk. 228   Perf. 13½x12½
O6	A4	½p orange	6.00	1.25
a.		Inverted overprint	3,000.	1,500.
O7	A4	1p green (I)	2.00	.75
O8	A4	2p red (II)	5.00	.60
a.		Inverted overprint		2,250.
O9	A4	3p ultra (II) ('33)	14.00	7.50
O10	A4	5p brown buff	42.50	21.00
a.		Wmk. 203		—

Perf. 11½, 12
O11	A1	6p yellow brown	35.00	25.00
a.		Inverted overprint		—
		Nos. O6-O11 (6)	104.50	56.10

1932   Unwmk.   Perf. 11, 11½
O12	A9	2p red	5.50	4.50
O13	A9	3p blue	18.00	18.00
O14	A16	1sh gray green	55.00	32.50
		Nos. O12-O14 (3)	78.50	55.00

AUSTRALIAN ANTARCTIC TERRITORY

Catalogue values for all unused stamps in this section are for Never Hinged items.

All stamps are also valid for postage in Australia.

Edgeworth David, Douglas Mawson and A.F. McKay (1908-09 South Pole Expedition) — A1

Australian Explorers and Map of Antarctica — A2

Designs: 8p, Loading weasel (snow truck). 1sh, Dog team and iceberg, vert. 2sh3p, Emperor penguins and map, vert.

Perf. 14½, 14½x14, 14x14½
1957-59   Engr.   Unwmk.
L1	A1	5p brown	.50	.15
L2	A2	8p dark blue	2.25	1.25
L3	A2	1sh dark green	4.00	2.10
L4	A2	2sh ultra ('57)	3.50	.35
L5	A2	2sh3p green	12.00	6.00
		Nos. L1-L5 (5)	22.25	9.85

Nos. L1 and L2 were printed as 4p and 7p stamps and surcharged typographically in black and dark blue before issuance.
Sizes of stamps: No. L2, 34x21mm; Nos. L3, L5, 21x34mm; No. L4, 43½x25½mm.

1961, July 5   Perf. 14½
L6	A1	5p dark blue	1.10	.20

The denomination on No. L6 is not within a typographed circle, but is part of the engraved design.

Sir Douglas Mawson A3

Lookout and Iceberg A4

1961, Oct. 18
L7	A3	5p dark green	.70	.20

50th anniv. of the 1911-14 Australian Antarctic Expedition.

Perf. 13½x13, 13x13½
1966-68   Photo.   Unwmk.
Designs: 1c, Aurora australis and camera dome. 2c, Banding penguins. 5c, Branding of elephant seals. 7c, Measuring snow strata. 10c, Wind gauges. 15c, Weather balloon. 20c, Helicopter. 25c, Radio operator. 50c, Ice compression tests. $1, "Mock sun" (parahelion) and dogs. 20c, 25c, 50c and $1 horizontal.

L8	A4	1c multicolored	.55	.30
L9	A4	2c multicolored	1.00	.45
L10	A4	4c multicolored	1.10	.45
L11	A4	5c multicolored	1.75	1.25
L12	A4	7c multicolored	.55	.35
L13	A4	10c multicolored	2.50	.90
L14	A4	15c multicolored	3.25	3.25
L15	A4	20c multicolored	7.00	4.00
L16	A4	25c multicolored	4.00	4.25
L17	A4	50c multicolored	21.00	8.00
L18	A4	$1 multicolored	27.50	18.00
		Nos. L8-L18 (11)	70.20	41.20

Issued: 5c, 9/25/68; others, 9/28/66.
Nos. L8-L18 are on phosphorescent helecon paper. Fluorescent orange is one of the colors used in printing the 10c, 15c, 20c and 50c.

Sastrugi Snow Formation — A5

1971, June 23   Photo.   Perf. 13x13½
L19	A5	6c shown	.55	.55
L20	A5	30c Pancake ice	6.00	6.00

10th anniv. of the Antarctic Treaty pledging peaceful uses of and scientific cooperation in Antarctica.

Capt. Cook, Sextant, Azimuth Compass — A6

Design: 35c, Chart of Cook's circumnavigation of Antarctica, and "Resolution."

1972, Sept. 13   Photo.   Perf. 13x13½
L21	A6	7c bister & multi	2.00	.95
L22	A6	35c buff & multi	5.50	6.00

Bicentenary of Capt. James Cook's circumnavigation of Antarctica.

Plankton and Krill Shrimp — A7

Mawson's D.H. Gipsy Moth, 1931 — A8

Food Chain (Essential for Survival): 7c, Adelie penguin feeding on krill shrimp. 9c, Leopard seal pursuing fish, horiz. 10c, Killer whale hunting seals, horiz. 20c, Wandering albatross, horiz. $1, Sperm whale attacking giant squid.
Explorers' Aircraft: 8c, Rymill's DH Fox Moth returning to Barry Island. 25c, Hubert Wilkins Lockheed Vega, horiz. 30c, Lincoln Ellsworth's Northrop Gamma. 35c, Lars Christensen's Avro

---

ANTARCTICA!

Buying & Selling
Stamps, Covers & Ephemera
Free price list upon request.
Internationally competitive prices.
Diverse range of material from Britain (BAT), France (FSAT), Australia (AAT), NZ (Ross Dependency), US, USSR, Argentina, Chile, Japan, Korea, China, Belgium, RSA, Germany, Norway, etc., plus many wonderful topical areas represented.

Antarctic Philatelic Exchange
1208A-280 Simcoe St., Toronto, Ontario, M5T 2Y5, Canada
(416) 593-7849   jporter@interlog.com   www.interlog.com/~jporter
Member: APS, ASPP, GBPPHS, NZAS, RSAAS

AUSTRALIA — AUSTRIA

Avian and Framnes Mountains, horiz. 50c, Richard Byrd's Ford Tri-Motor dropping US flag over South Pole.

Perf. 13½x13, 13x13½

L23	A7	1c multicolored	.15 .15
L24	A8	5c multicolored	.15 .15
L25	A7	7c multicolored	1.40 .60
L26	A8	8c multicolored	.30 .30
L27	A7	9c multicolored	.25 .25
L28	A7	10c multicolored	3.00 1.25
L29	A7	20c multicolored	.35 .35
L30	A8	25c multicolored	.35 .35
L31	A8	30c multicolored	.35 .35
L32	A8	35c multicolored	.30 .45
L33	A8	50c multicolored	1.25 .85
L34	A7	$1 multicolored	2.25 .85
		Nos. L23-L34 (12)	10.10 5.90

Adm. Byrd, Plane, Mountains — A9

Design: 20c, Adm. Byrd, Floyd Bennett tri-motored plane, map of Antarctica.

1979, June 20 Litho. Perf. 15½

L35	A9	20c multicolored	.50 .50
L36	A9	55c multicolored	1.00 .95

50th anniv. of first flight over South Pole by Richard Byrd (1888-1957).

"S.Y. Nimrod" A10

2c, 5c, 22c, 25c, 40c, 55c, $1 are vertical. No. L41 actually pictures the S.S. Morning.

Perf. 13½x13, 13x13½

1974-81 Litho.

L37	A10	1c S.Y. Aurora	.15 .15
L38	A10	2c R.Y. Penola	.15 .15
L39	A10	5c M.V. Thala Dan	.15 .15
L40	A10	10c H.M.S. Challenger	.15 .15
L41	A10	15c shown	.95 .95
L42	A10	15c S.Y. Nimrod, stern view	.25 .20
L43	A10	20c R.R.S. Discovery II	.30 .30
L44	A10	22c R.Y.S. Terra Nova	.30 .30
L45	A10	25c S.S. Endurance	.40 .35
L46	A10	30c S.S. Fram	.50 .50
L47	A10	35c M.S. Nella Dan	.45 .45
L48	A10	40c M.S. Kista Dan	.50 .50
L49	A10	45c L'Astrolabe	.55 .55
L50	A10	50c S.S. Norvegia	.70 .70
L51	A10	55c S.Y. Discovery	.80 .80
L52	A10	$1 H.M.S. Resolution	1.25 .65
		Nos. L37-L52 (16)	7.55 6.85

A11   A12

1982, May 5 Litho. Perf. 14x13½

L53	A11	27c Mawson, landscape	.35 .35
L54	A11	75c Mawson, map	1.25 1.25

Sir Douglas Mawson (1882-1958), explorer.

1983, Apr. 6 Litho. Perf. 14½

Local Wildlife: a, Light-mantled sooty albatross. b, Macquarie Isld. shags. c, Elephant seals. d, Royal penguins. e, Antarctic prions.

L55		Strip of 5, multi	2.25 2.25
a.-e.		A12 27c, any single	.45 .45

Australian Antarctic Territory stamps can be mounted in the Scott Australia Dependencies album.

12th Antarctic Treaty Consultative Meeting, Canberra, Sept. 13-27 — A13

1983, Sept. 7 Litho. Perf. 14½

L56	A13	27c multicolored	.40 .40

South Magnetic Pole Expedition, 75th Anniv. — A14

1984, Jan. 16

L57	A14	30c Prismatic compass	.40 .40
L58	A14	85c Aneroid barometer	1.25 1.25

Dog Team, Mawson Station — A15

1984-87 Litho. Perf. 14½x15

L60	A15	2c Summer afternoon	.15 .15
L61	A15	5c shown	.15 .15
L62	A15	10c Evening	.15 .15
L63	A15	15c Prince Charles Mts.	.20 .20
L64	A15	20c Morning	.30 .30
L65	A15	25c Sea ice, iceberg	.40 .40
L66	A15	30c Mt. Coates	.50 .50
L67	A15	33c Iceberg Alley, Mawson	.50 .50
L68	A15	36c Winter evening	.50 .50
L69	A15	45c Brash ice, vert.	.65 .65
L70	A15	60c Midwinter shadows	.85 .85
L71	A15	75c Coastline	1.10 1.10
L72	A15	85c Landing field	1.35 1.35
L73	A15	90c Pancake ice, vert.	1.25 1.25
L74	A15	$1 Emperor penguins, Auster Rookery	1.50 1.50
		Nos. L60-L74 (15)	9.55 9.55

Issued: 5, 25, 30, 75, 85c, 7/18/84; 15, 33, 45, 90c, $1, 8/7/85; 2, 10, 20, 36, 60c, 3/11/87.

A16   A17

1986, Sept. 17 Litho. Perf. 14x13½

L75	A16	36c multicolored	.55 .55

Antarctic Treaty, 25th anniv.

1988, July 20 Litho. Perf. 13

Environment, Conservation and Technology: a, Hour-glass dolphins and the Nella Dan. b, Emperor penguins and Davis Station. c, Crabeater seal and helicopters. d, Adelie penguins and snow-ice transport vehicle. e, Gray-headed albatross and photographer.

L76		Strip of 5	3.10 1.20
a.-e.		A17 37c any single	.60 .20

Paintings by Sir Sidney Nolan (b. 1917) — A18

1989, June 14 Litho. Perf. 14x13½

L77	A18	39c Antarctica	.65 .65
L78	A18	39c Iceberg Alley	.65 .65
L79	A18	60c Glacial Flow	1.00 1.00
L80	A18	80c Frozen Sea	1.35 1.35
		Nos. L77-L80 (4)	3.65 3.65

Aurora Australis A19

Design: $1.20, Research ship Aurora Australis.

1991, June 20 Litho. Perf. 14½

L81	A19	43c multicolored	.65 .20
L82	A19	$1.20 multicolored	1.90 .65

Antarctic Treaty, 30th anniv. (No. L81).

Regional Wildlife A20

Perf. 14x14½, 14½x14

1992-93 Litho.

L83	A20	45c Adelie penguin	.60 .25
L84	A20	75c Elephant seal	.95 .35
L85	A20	85c Northern giant petrel	1.10 .40
L86	A20	95c Weddell seal	1.25 .45
L86A	A20	$1 Royal penguins	1.25 .50
L87	A20	$1.20 Emperor penguin, vert.	1.50 .60
L88	A20	$1.40 Fur seals	1.65 .70
L89	A20	$1.50 King penguins, vert.	1.90 .75
		Nos. L83-L89 (8)	10.20 4.00

Issued: $1, $1.40, $1.50, 1/14/93; others, 5/14/92.

The Last Huskies A21

1994, Jan. 13 Litho. Perf. 14½

L90	A21	45c Dog up close, vert.	.65 .20
L91	A21	75c Sled team	1.10 .35
L92	A21	85c Dog seated, vert.	1.25 .40
L93	A21	$1.05 Three dogs	1.50 .50
		Nos. L90-L93 (4)	4.50 1.45

Whales & Dolphins A22

1995, June 15 Litho. Perf. 14½

L94	A22	45c Humpback whale	.65 .20
L95	A22	45c Hourglass dolphin, vert.	.65 .20
L96	A22	45c Minke whale, vert.	.65 .20
a.		Pair, #L95-L96	1.30 .45
L97	A22	$1 Killer whale	1.40 .50
a.		Souvenir sheet of 4, #L94-L97	3.50 3.50
b.		As "a," overprinted	3.50 3.50
c.		As "a," overprinted	3.50 3.50
		Nos. L94-L97 (4)	3.35 1.10

No. L97b is overprinted in gold in sheet margin with Singapore '95 emblem and: "Australia Post Exhibition Sheet No. 2," and, in both Chinese and English, with "Singapore 95 World Stamp Exhibition."
No. L97c is overprinted in gold in sheet margin with exhibition emblem, "Australian Post Exhibition Sheet No. 3" and "CAPEX '96 WORLD PHILATELIC EXHIBITION / EXPOSITION PHILATELIQUE MONDIALE"

Issued: #L97b, 9/1/95; #L97c, 6/15/96.

Landscapes, by Christian Clare Robertson — A23

#L98, Rafting sea ice. #L99, Shadow on the Plateau. $1, Ice cave. $1.20, Twelve Lake.

1996, May 16 Litho. Perf. 14½x14

L98	A23	45c multicolored	.70 .25
L99	A23	45c multicolored	.70 .25
a.		Pair, Nos. L98-L99	1.40 .50
L100	A23	$1 multicolored	1.60 .60
L101	A23	$1.20 multicolored	1.90 .60
		Nos. L98-L101 (4)	4.90 1.60

Australian Natl. Antarctic Research Expeditions, 50th Anniv. A24

Designs: No. L102, Apple field huts. No. L103, Inside an apple hut. 95c, Summer surveying. $1.05, Sea ice research. $1.20, Remote field camp.

1997, May 15 Litho. Perf. 14x14½

L102	A24	45c multicolored	.70 .20
L103	A24	45c multicolored	.70 .20
a.		Pair, #L102-L103	1.40 .40
L104	A24	95c multicolored	1.50 .45
L105	A24	$1.05 multicolored	1.65 .50
L106	A24	$1.20 multicolored	1.90 .55
		Nos. L102-L106 (5)	6.45 1.90

Modes of Transportation A25

Designs: No. L107, Snowmobile. No. L108, Ship, "Aurora Australis." $1, Helicopter airlifting a four-wheel drive ATV, vert. $2, Antarctic Hagglunds (rubber-tracked vehicles with fiberglass cabins), vert.

Perf. 14x14½, 14½x14

1998, Mar. 5 Litho.

L107	A25	45c multicolored	.60 .20
L108	A25	45c multicolored	.60 .20
a.		Pair, #L107-L108	1.20 .40
L109	A25	$1 multicolored	1.30 .45
L110	A25	$2 multicolored	2.60 .90
		Nos. L107-L110 (4)	5.10 1.75

AUSTRIA

ȯs-trē-ə

LOCATION — Central Europe
GOVT. — Republic
AREA — 32,376 sq. mi.
POP. — 7,555,338 (1981)
CAPITAL — Vienna

Before 1867 Austria was an absolute monarchy, which included Hungary and Lombardy-Venetia. In 1867 the Austro-Hungarian Monarchy was established, with Austria and Hungary as equal partners. After World War I, in 1918, the different nationalities established their own states and only the German-speaking parts remained, forming a republic under the name "Deutschosterreich" (German Austria), which name was shortly again changed to "Austria." In 1938 German forces occupied Austria, which became part of the German Reich.

Have you found a typo or other error in this catalogue?

Inform the editors via our web site or e-mail

sctcat@
scottonline.com

After the liberation by Allied troops in 1945, an independent republic was re-established.

60 Kreuzer = 1 Gulden
100 Neu-Kreuzer = 1 Gulden (1858)
100 Heller = 1 Krone (1899)
100 Groschen = 1 Schilling (1925)

Catalogue values for unused stamps in this country are for Never Hinged items, beginning with Scott 432 in the regular postage section, Scott B165 in the semi-postal section, Scott C47 in the airpost section, Scott J175 in the postage due section, and Scott 4N1 in the AMG section.

Unused stamps without gum sell for about one-third or less of the values quoted.

Watermarks

Wmk. 91 - "BRIEF-MARKEN" In Double-lined Capitals Across the Middle of the Sheet

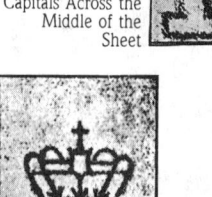

Wmk. 140 - Crown

Issues of the Austrian Monarchy (including Hungary)

Coat of Arms — A1

NINE KREUZER

Type I. One heavy line around coat of arms center. On the 9kr the top of "9" is about on a level with "Kreuzer" and not near the top of the label. Each cliche has the "9" in a different position.

Type IA. As type I, but with 1¼mm between "9" and "K."

Type II. One heavy line around coat of arms center. On the 9kr the top of "9" is much higher than the top of the word "Kreuzer" and nearly touches the top of the label.

Type III. As type II, but with two, thinner, lines around the center.

Wmk. K.K.H.M. in Sheet or Unwmk.

1850 Typo. *Imperf.*

The stamps of this issue were at first printed on a rough hand-made paper, varying in thickness and having a watermark in script letters K.K.H.M., the initials of Kaiserlich Königliches Handels-Ministerium (Imperial and Royal Ministry of Commerce), vertically in the gutter between the panes. Parts of these letters show on margin stamps in the sheet. From 1854 a thick, smooth machine-made paper without watermark was used.

Thin to Thick Paper

1	A1	1kr yellow	950.00	70.00
a.		Printed on both sides	*1,900.*	130.00
b.		1kr orange	1,100.	100.00
c.		1kr brown orange	1,900.	375.00
2	A1	2kr black	950.00	60.00
a.		Ribbed paper	—	*1,600.*
b.		2kr gray black	1,100.	70.00
d.		Half used as 1kr on cover		*25,000.*
3	A1	3kr red	350.00	3.00
a.		Ribbed paper	*1,900.*	95.00
b.		Laid paper	—	*9,000.*
c.		Printed on both sides		*7,500.*
4	A1	6kr brown	550.00	4.25
a.		Ribbed paper		*1,300.*
c.		Diagonal half used as 3kr on cover		*10,000.*
5	A1	9kr blue, type II	700.00	3.00
a.		9kr blue, type I	*1,150.*	7.50
b.		9kr blue, type IA	*13,500.*	*1,000.*
c.		Laid paper, type III		*6,750.*
d.		Printed on both sides, type II		*7,500.*

1854 Machine-made Paper, Type III

1d	A1	1kr yellow	*800.00*	70.00
2c	A1	2kr black	*725.00*	55.00
3e	A1	3kr red	*275.00*	2.10
f.		3kr red, type I	*2,100.*	27.50
4b	A1	6kr brown	*450.00*	3.50
5e	A1	9kr blue	*525.00*	2.25

In 1852-54, Nos. 1 to 5, rouletted 14, were used in Tokay and Homonna. A 12kr blue exists, but was not issued.

The reprints are type III in brighter colors, some on paper watermarked "Briefmarken" in the sheet.

For similar design see Lombardy-Venetia A1.

Emperor Franz Josef
A2 A3 A4

A5 A6

1858-59 Embossed *Perf. 14½*

Two Types of Each Value.

Type I. Loops of the bow at the back of the head broken, except the 2kr. In the 2kr, the "2" has a flat foot, thinning to the right. The frame line in the UR corner is thicker than the line below. In the 5kr the top frame line is unbroken.

Type II. Loops complete. Wreath projects further at top of head. In the 2kr, the "2" has a more curved foot of uniform thickness, with a shading line in the upper and lower curves. The frame line UR is thicker than the line below. In the 5kr the top frame line is broken.

6	A2	2kr yellow, type II	675.00	42.50
a.		2kr yellow, type I	1,700.	350.00
b.		2kr orange, type II	1,800.	225.00
c.		Half used as 1kr on cover		*25,000.*
7	A3	3kr black, type II	*1,900.*	175.00
a.		3kr black, type I	1,100.	225.00
8	A3	3kr green, type II ('59)	925.00	125.00
9	A4	5kr red, type II	225.00	.85
a.		5kr red, type I	350.00	11.50
b.		5kr red, type II with type I frame	400.00	20.00
10	A5	10kr brown, type II	550.00	2.50
a.		10kr brown, type I	625.00	27.50
b.		Half used as 5kr on cover		*10,000.*
11	A6	15kr blue, type II	525.00	1.75
a.		Type I	1,050.	12.50
b.		Half used as 7kr on cover		—

The reprints are of type II and are perforated 10½, 11, 12, 12½ and 13. There are also imperforate reprints of Nos. 6 to 8.

For similar designs see Lombardy-Venetia A2-A6.

Franz Josef — A7

Coat of Arms — A8

1860-61 Embossed *Perf. 14*

12	A7	2kr yellow	300.00	25.00
a.		Half used as 1kr on cover		*12,500.*
13	A7	3kr green	275.00	22.50
14	A7	5kr red	175.00	.75
15	A7	10kr brown	275.00	1.75
a.		Half used as 5kr on cover		*5,500.*
16	A7	15kr blue	275.00	1.00

The reprints are perforated 9, 9½, 10, 10½, 11, 11½, 12, 12½, 13 and 13½. There are also imperforate reprints of the 2 and 3kr.

For similar design see Lombardy-Venetia A7. For overprints see Poland Nos. J11-J12.

1863

17	A8	2kr yellow	450.00	80.00
a.		Half used as 1kr on cover		*12,500.*
18	A8	3kr green	350.00	75.00
19	A8	5kr rose	300.00	7.00
20	A8	10kr blue	775.00	8.25
21	A8	15kr yellow brown	950.00	10.00

For similar design see Lombardy-Venetia A1.

Wmk. 91, or, before July 1864, Unwmkd.

1863-64 *Perf. 9½*

22	A8	2kr yellow ('64)	125.00	10.00
a.		Half used as 1kr on cover		*12,500.*
23	A8	3kr green ('64)	125.00	10.00
24	A8	5kr rose	45.00	.40
25	A8	10kr blue	140.00	2.50
a.		Half used as 5kr on cover		*11,000.*
26	A8	15kr yellow brown	140.00	1.50
		Nos. 22-26 (5)	575.00	24.40

The reprints are perforated 10½, 11½, 13 and 13½. There are also imperforate reprints of the 2 and 3kr.

Issues of Austro-Hungarian Monarchy

From 1867 to 1871 the independent postal administrations of Austria and Hungary used the same stamps.

A9

A10

5 kr:

Type I. In arabesques in lower left corner, the small ornament at left of the curve nearest the figure "5" is short and has three points at bottom.

Type II. The ornament is prolonged within the curve and has two points at bottom. The corresponding ornament at top of the lower left corner does not touch the curve (1872).

Type III. Similar to type II but the top ornament is joined to the curve (1881). Two different printing methods were used for the 1867-74 issues. The first produced stamps on which the hair and whiskers were coarse and thick, from the second they were fine and clear.

1867-72 Wmk. 91 Typo. *Perf. 9½*

Coarse Print

27	A9	2kr yellow	85.00	1.75
a.		Half used as 1kr on cover		*12,500.*
28	A9	3kr green	80.00	2.00
29	A9	5kr rose, type I	55.00	.20
a.		5kr rose, type II	50.00	.20
b.		Perf. 10½, type II	125.00	
c.		Cliché of 3kr in plate of 5kr		*52,500.*
30	A9	10kr blue	165.00	2.25
a.		Half used as 5kr on cover		*15,000.*
31	A9	15kr brown	140.00	4.25
32	A9	25kr lilac	20.00	12.50
a.		25kr gray lilac	20.00	15.00
b.		25kr brown violet	125.00	32.50

Perf. 12

33	A10	50kr light brown	27.50	*90.00*
a.		50kr pale red brown	275.00	100.00
b.		50kr brownish rose	325.00	175.00
c.		Pair, imperf. btwn., vert. or horizontal	700.00	*1,000.*

Issues for Austria only

1874-80 *Perf. 9½*

Fine Print

34	A9	2kr yellow ('76)	7.00	.75
35	A9	3kr green ('76)	32.50	.50
36	A9	5kr rose, type III	10.00	.20
37	A9	10kr blue ('75)	67.50	.40
38	A9	15kr brown ('77)	5.00	4.00
39	A9	25kr gray lil ('78)	1.10	*110.00*

Perf. 9

34a	A9	2kr	175.00	40.00
35a	A9	3kr	140.00	20.00
36a	A9	5kr	50.00	2.25
37a	A9	10kr	275.00	25.00
38a	A9	15kr	350.00	70.00

Perf. 10½

34b	A9	2kr	40.00	2.75
35b	A9	3kr	60.00	1.75
36b	A9	5kr	9.00	.75
37b	A9	10kr	140.00	2.25
38b	A9	15kr	175.00	16.00

Perf. 12

34c	A9	2kr	175.00	87.50
35c	A9	3kr	150.00	14.00
36c	A9	5kr	35.00	3.25
37c	A9	10kr	325.00	90.00
38c	A9	15kr	425.00	125.00
40	A10	50kr brown ('80)	16.00	*100.00*

Perf. 13

34d	A9	2kr	200.00	200.00
35d	A9	3kr	140.00	25.00
36d	A9	5kr	70.00	12.50
37d	A9	10kr	175.00	60.00
38d	A9	15kr	425.00	275.00
40a	A10	50kr	20.00	*110.00*

Various compound perforations exist.

Values are for stamps that do not show the watermark. Stamps showing the watermark often sell for more.

For similar designs see Offices in the Turkish Empire A1-A2.

A11

Perf. 9, 9½, 10, 10½, 11½, 12, 12½

1883

Inscriptions in Black

41	A11	2kr brown	5.50	.50
42	A11	3kr green	4.75	.30
43	A11	5kr rose	11.00	.25
a.		Vert. pair, imperf. btwn.	250.00	350.00
44	A11	10kr blue	4.25	.35
45	A11	20kr gray	55.00	3.25
46	A11	50kr red lilac	300.00	52.50

The last printings of Nos. 41-46 are watermarked "ZEITUNGS-MARKEN" instead of "BRIEF-MARKEN." Values are for stamps that do not show watermark. Stamps with watermarks that are identifiable as being from "BRIEF-MARKEN" sheets often sell for slightly more, while those with watermarks identifying stamps from "ZEITUNGS-MARKEN" sheets often sell for considerably more.

The 5kr has been reprinted in a dull red rose, perforated 10½.

For similar design see Offices in the Turkish Empire A3.

For surcharges see Offices in the Turkish Empire Nos. 15-19.

A12

A13

Perf. 9 to 13½, also Compound

1890-96 Unwmk.

Granite Paper

Numerals in black, Nos. 51-61

51	A12	1kr dark gray	1.25	.25
a.		Pair, imperf. between	160.00	350.00
52	A12	2kr light brown	.25	.25
53	A12	3kr gray green	.40	.25
a.		Pair, imperf. between	175.00	425.00
54	A12	5kr rose	.40	.25
a.		Pair, imperf. between	160.00	325.00
55	A12	10kr ultramarine	.75	.25
a.		Pair, imperf. between	200.00	425.00
56	A12	12kr claret	2.00	.35
a.		Pair, imperf. between	—	—
57	A12	15kr lilac	1.25	.35
a.		Pair, imperf. between	200.00	425.00
58	A12	20kr olive green	30.00	2.00
59	A12	24kr gray blue	2.00	1.25
a.		Pair, imperf. between	225.00	425.00
60	A12	30kr dark brown	2.50	.65
61	A12	50kr violet	5.00	7.50

Engr.

62	A13	1gld dark blue	1.50	2.25
63	A13	1gld pale lilac ('96)	35.00	3.50
64	A13	2gld carmine	3.50	12.50
65	A13	2gld gray green ('96)	15.00	27.50
		Nos. 51-65 (15)	100.80	59.10

Nearly all values of the 1890-1907 issues are found with numerals missing in one or more corners, some with numerals printed on the back.

For surcharges see Offices in the Turkish Empire Nos. 20-25, 28-31.

A14

Perf. 9 to 13½, also Compound

1891 Typo.

Numerals in black

66	A14	20kr olive green	2.25	.25
67	A14	24kr gray blue	4.50	.75
68	A14	30kr brown	2.25	.25
a.		Pair, imperf. between	225.00	350.00
b.		Perf. 9	100.00	32.50
69	A14	50kr violet	2.75	.40
		Nos. 66-69 (4)	11.75	1.65

For surcharges see Offices in the Turkish Empire Nos. 26-27.

A15

A16

A17

A18

Perf. 10½ to 13½ and Compound

1899

Without Varnish Bars

Numerals in black, Nos. 70-82

70	A15	1h lilac	.55	.15
b.		Imperf.	55.00	100.00
c.		Perf. 10½	15.00	4.50
d.		Numerals inverted	375.00	950.00
71	A15	2h dark gray	2.50	.50
72	A15	3h bister brown	5.00	.15
b.		"3" in lower right corner sideways		*1,100.*
73	A15	5h blue green	7.25	.15
c.		Perf. 10½	10.50	2.75
74	A15	6h orange	.40	.15
75	A16	10h rose	8.00	.15
b.		Perf. 10½	300.00	125.00
76	A16	20h brown	.60	.20
77	A16	25h ultramarine	50.00	.30
78	A16	30h red violet	14.50	2.25
b.		Horiz. pair, imperf. btwn.	275.00	—
80	A17	40h green	25.00	2.50
81	A17	50h gray blue	16.00	3.50
b.		All four "50's" parallel		*1,600.*
82	A17	60h brown	35.00	1.00
b.		Horiz. pair, imperf. btwn.	275.00	—
c.		Perf. 10½	50.00	1.50

Engr.

83	A18	1k carmine rose	2.25	.20
a.		1k carmine	5.00	.20
b.		Vert. pair, imperf. btwn.	275.00	300.00
84	A18	2k gray lilac	45.00	.40
a.		Vert. pair, imperf. btwn.	275.00	500.00
85	A18	4k gray green	4.00	10.00
		Nos. 70-85 (15)	216.05	21.60

For surcharges see Offices in Crete Nos. 1-7, Offices in the Turkish Empire Nos. 32-45.

1901 **With Varnish Bars**

70a	A15	1h lilac	1.75	.40
71a	A15	2h dark gray	1.75	.35
72a	A15	3h bister brown	.35	.15
73a	A15	5h blue green	.20	.15
74a	A15	6h orange	.20	.15
75a	A16	10h rose	.25	.15
76a	A16	20h brown	.65	.15
77a	A16	25h ultra	.85	.20
78a	A16	30h red violet	1.75	.90
79	A17	35h green	.85	.40
80a	A17	40h green	1.65	3.25
81a	A17	50h gray blue	4.00	6.75
82a	A17	60h brown	2.00	.65
		Nos. 70a-78a,79,80a-82a (13)	16.25	13.65

The diagonal yellow bars of varnish were printed across the face to prevent cleaning.

A19

A20

A21

Perf. 12½ to 13½ and Compound

1905-07 **Typo.**

Colored Numerals

Without Varnish Bars

86	A19	1h lilac	.20	*.35*
87	A19	2h dark gray	.20	.20
88	A19	3h bister brown	.20	.15
89	A19	5h dk blue green	8.50	.15
90	A19	5h yellow grn ('06)	.40	.15
91	A19	6h deep orange	.40	.15
92	A20	10h carmine ('06)	.45	.15
93	A20	12h violet ('07)	1.00	.65
94	A20	20h brown ('06)	2.75	.15
95	A20	25h ultra ('06)	3.50	.35
96	A20	30h red violet ('06)	6.00	.25

Black Numerals

97	A20	10h carmine	10.50	.15
98	A20	20h brown	35.00	1.75
99	A20	25h ultra	32.50	1.75
100	A20	30h red violet	52.50	1.50

White Numerals

101	A21	35h green	2.25	.25
102	A21	40h deep violet	2.25	.75
103	A21	50h dull blue	2.75	2.25
104	A21	60h yellow brown	2.75	.60
105	A21	72h rose	2.75	1.60
		Nos. 86-105 (20)	166.85	13.30

For surcharges see Offices in Crete #8-14.

1904

With Varnish Bars

86a	A19	1h lilac	.50	*.90*
87a	A19	2h dark gray	1.60	.55
88a	A19	3h bister brown	1.75	.15
89a	A19	5h dk blue green	3.50	.15
91a	A19	6h deep orange	6.00	.30
97a	A20	10h carmine	2.00	.15
98a	A20	20h brown	27.50	.75
99a	A20	25h ultra	32.50	.75
100a	A20	30h red violet	40.00	1.50
101a	A21	35h green	32.50	.60
102a	A21	40h deep violet	30.00	3.50
103a	A21	50h dull blue	30.00	7.00
104a	A21	60h yellow brown	35.00	1.10
105a	A21	72h rose	1.10	1.10
		Nos. 86a-105a (14)	243.95	18.50

Stamps of the 1901, 1904 and 1905 issues perf. 9 or 10½, also compound with 12½, were not sold at any post office, but were supplied only to some high-ranking officials. This applies also to the contemporary issues of Austrian Offices Abroad.

Karl VI — A22

Franz Josef — A23

Schönbrunn Castle — A24

Franz Josef — A25

Designs: 2h, Maria Theresa. 3h, Joseph II. 5h, 10h, 25h, Franz Josef. 6h, Leopold II. 12h, Franz I. 20h, Ferdinand I. 30h, Franz Josef as youth. 35h, Franz Josef in middle age. 60h, Franz Josef on horseback. 1k, Franz Josef in royal robes. 5k, Hofburg, Vienna.

1908-13 **Typo.** *Perf. 12½*

110	A22	1h gray black	.25	.15
111	A22	2h blue violet ('13)	.20	*.45*
a.		2h violet	.25	.15
112	A22	3h magenta	.20	.15
113	A22	5h yellow green	.20	.15
a.		Booklet pane of 6	25.00	
114	A22	6h buff	.60	.60
b.		6h orange brown ('13)	1.50	1.25
115	A22	10h rose	.20	.15
a.		Booklet pane of 6	75.00	
116	A22	12h scarlet	1.25	.80
117	A22	20h chocolate	1.65	.20
118	A22	25h ultra ('13)	1.40	.25
a.		25h deep blue	2.50	.25
119	A22	30h olive green	3.75	.25
120	A22	35h slate	2.25	.15

Engr.

121	A23	50h dark green	.65	.25
a.		Vert. pair, imperf. btwn.	190.00	*275.00*
b.		Horiz. pair, imperf. btwn.	190.00	*275.00*
122	A23	60h deep carmine	.35	.15
a.		Vert. pair, imperf. btwn.	275.00	*325.00*
b.		Horiz. pair, imperf. btwn.	275.00	*325.00*
123	A23	72h dk brown ('13)	1.75	.30
124	A23	1k purple	12.00	.20
a.		Vert. pair, imperf. btwn.	190.00	*275.00*
b.		Horiz. pair, imperf. btwn.	190.00	*275.00*
125	A24	2k lake & olive grn	18.00	.35
126	A24	5k bister & dk vio	35.00	4.00
127	A25	10k blue, bis & dp brn	165.00	50.00
		Nos. 110-127 (18)	244.70	58.55
		Set, never hinged	540.00	

Definitive set issued for the 60th year of the reign of Emperor Franz Josef.

The 1h-35h exist on both ordinary (1913) and chalk-surfaced (1908) paper.

All values exist imperforate. They were not sold at any post office, but presented to a number of high government officials. This applies also to all imperforate stamps of later issues, including semi-postals, etc., and those of the Austrian Offices Abroad.

Litho. forgeries of No. 127 exist.

For overprint and surcharge see #J47-J48. For similar designs see Offices in Crete A5-A6, Offices in the Turkish Empire A16-A17.

Birthday Jubilee Issue

Similar to 1908 Issue, but designs enlarged by labels at top and bottom bearing dates "1830" and "1910"

1910 **Typo.**

128	A22	1h gray black	4.00	*6.25*
129	A22	2h violet	5.00	*7.75*
130	A22	3h magenta	4.50	*6.75*
131	A22	5h yellow green	.20	.20
132	A22	6h buff	2.50	*5.00*
133	A22	10h rose	.20	.20
134	A22	12h scarlet	3.00	*6.50*
135	A22	20h chocolate	5.50	*6.25*
136	A22	25h deep blue	1.25	1.25
137	A22	30h olive green	3.25	*4.50*
138	A22	35h slate	3.25	*4.50*

Engr.

139	A23	50h dark green	4.50	*8.00*
140	A23	60h deep carmine	4.50	*8.00*
141	A23	1k purple	4.50	*9.00*
142	A24	2k lake & ol grn	125.00	*190.00*
143	A24	5k bister & dk vio	92.50	*150.00*
144	A25	10k blue, bis & dp brn	175.00	*275.00*
		Nos. 128-144 (17)	438.65	*689.15*
		Set, never hinged	736.00	

80th birthday of Emperor Franz Josef.

All values exist imperforate.

Litho. forgeries of Nos. 142-144 exist.

Austrian Crown — A37

Franz Josef — A38

Coat of Arms

A39 A40

1916-18 **Typo.**

145	A37	3h brt violet	.15	.15
146	A37	5h lt green	.15	.15
a.		Booklet pane of 6	14.00	
b.		Booklet pane of 4 + 2 labels	27.50	
147	A37	6h deep orange	.25	*.65*
148	A37	10h magenta	.15	.15
a.		Booklet pane of 6	27.50	
149	A37	12h light blue	.30	*1.10*
150	A38	15h rose red	.40	.15
a.		Booklet pane of 6	15.00	
151	A38	20h chocolate	3.25	.15
152	A38	25h blue	5.00	.40
153	A38	30h slate	4.50	.65
154	A39	40h olive green	.15	.15
155	A39	50h blue green	.20	.15
156	A39	60h deep blue	.15	.15
157	A39	80h orange brown	.15	.15
158	A39	90h red violet	.15	.15
159	A39	1k car, *yel* ('18)	.30	.20

Engr.

160	A40	2k dark blue	.55	.20
161	A40	3k claret	9.00	.90
162	A40	4k deep green	1.75	1.75
163	A40	10k deep violet	21.00	30.00
		Nos. 145-163 (19)	47.55	37.35
		Set, never hinged	107.00	

Stamps of type A38 have two varieties of the frame. Stamps of type A40 have various decorations about the shield.

Nos. 145-163 exist imperf. Value, set $400.

1917 **Ordinary Paper**

164	A40	2k light blue	.75	.50
165	A40	3k carmine rose	10.00	.75
166	A40	4k yellow green	1.10	1.10
167	A40	10k violet	90.00	70.00
		Nos. 164-167 (4)	101.85	72.35
		Set, never hinged	232.00	

Nos. 164-167 exist imperf. Value, set $250.

See Nos. 172-175 (granite paper). For overprints and surcharges see Nos. 181-199, C1-C3, J60-J63, N1-N5, N10-N19, N33-N37, N42-N51. Western Ukraine 2-7, 11-15, 19-28, 57-58, 85-89, 94-103, N3-N14, NJ13.

Emperor Karl I — A42

1917-18 **Typo.**

168	A42	15h dull red	.15	.15
a.		Booklet pane of 6	14.00	
169	A42	20h dk green ('18)	.20	.15
a.		20h green ('17)	.55	.20
170	A42	25h blue	.70	.15
171	A42	30h dull violet	.75	.15
		Nos. 168-171 (4)	1.80	.60
		Set, never hinged	5.80	

Nos. 168-171 exist imperf. Value, set $40.

For overprints and surcharges see Nos. N6-N9, N20, N38-N41, N52, N64. Western Ukraine 1, 8, 16-18, 90-93, N15-N18.

1918-19 **Engr.**

Granite Paper

172	A40	2k light blue	.20	*.45*
a.		Perf. 11½	450.00	*525.00*
		Never hinged, #172a	750.00	
173	A40	3k carmine rose	.25	*1.10*
174	A40	4k yellow green ('19)	4.00	*13.50*
175	A40	10k lt violet ('19)	7.50	*16.00*
		Nos. 172-175 (4)	11.95	*31.05*
		Set, never hinged	17.35	

Issues of the Republic

Austrian Stamps of 1916-18 Overprinted

Deutschösterreich

1918-19 **Unwmk.** *Perf. 12½*

181	A37	3h bright violet	.15	.15
182	A37	5h light green	.15	.15
183	A37	6h deep orange	.15	.15
184	A37	10h magenta	.15	.15
185	A37	12h light blue	.25	*1.25*
186	A42	15h dull red	.20	*1.00*
187	A42	20h deep green	.15	.15
188	A42	25h blue	.15	.15
189	A42	30h dull violet	.15	.15
190	A39	40h olive green	.15	.15
191	A39	50h deep green	.45	*1.10*

If you are a Collector of Austria

Call the experts: ***LIANE & SERGIO SISMONDO***

"THE CLASSIC COLLECTOR"

Visit our website:www.sismondostamps.com

BUYING, SELLING, APPRAISALS.

RARE AND CLASSIC STAMPS, POSTAL HISTORY, PROOFS.

10035 Carousel Center Drive
Syracuse, NY 13290-0001
Ph. 315-422-2331, Fax 315-422-2956
P.O. Box 6277, Station J,
Ottawa, Canada K2A 1T4.
Ph. 613-722-1621, Fax: 613-728-7305
e-mail:sismondo@dreamscape.com

AUSTRIA

★ AUSTRIA ★

GERMANY • GERMAN STATES • COLONIES • WWI • WWII
OCCUPATIONS • DANZIG • SAAR • LOCALS
III REICH • FEDERAL REPUBLIC • BERLIN • DDR

FRANCE, AUSTRIA, SWITZERLAND, LIECHTENSTEIN

FREE - Send for our new extensive Price Lists from #1 to date.
Mint & Used Singles, Sets, Errors, Varieties, Booklets, Combinations,
Inflation Sheets, Covers plus individual Year Sets. Want lists filled,
you want it, we have it. Unlimited stock at your disposal.

JOSEPH EDER
P.O. Box 5517, Hamden, CT 06518
Tel. (203) 281-0742 • Fax (203) 230-2410
Email: jeder@nai.net

WE ALSO BUY!

192	A39	60h deep blue	.45	1.75
193	A39	80h orange brown	.15	.15
a.		Inverted overprint	200.00	
		Never hinged, #193a	275.00	
194	A39	90h red violet	.15	.45
195	A39	1k carmine, yel	.15	.25

Granite Paper

196	A40	2k light blue	.15	.15
a.		Pair, imperf. between	225.00	
		Never hinged, #196a	325.00	
b.		Perf. 11½	65.00	62.50
		Never hinged, #196b	100.00	
197	A40	3k carmine rose	.30	.75
198	A40	4k yellow green	.80	1.90
a.		Perf. 11½	16.00	25.00
		Never hinged, #198a	37.50	
199	A40	10k deep violet	7.25	17.50
		Nos. 181-199 (19)	11.50	27.45
		Set, never hinged	19.70	

Nos. 181, 182, 184, 187-191, 194, 197 and 199 exist imperforate.

Post Horn — A43

Coat of Arms — A44

Allegory of New Republic — A45

1919-20 Typo. Perf. 12½
Ordinary Paper

200	A43	3h gray	.15	.15
201	A44	5h yellow green	.15	.15
202	A44	5h gray ('20)	.15	.15
203	A43	6h orange	.15	.45
204	A44	10h deep rose	.15	.15
205	A44	10h red ('20)	.15	.15
a.		Thick grayish paper ('20)	.15	.15

FREE PRICE LISTS
FOR AUSTRIA, GERMANY, AND ALL RELATED STATES

Extensive price lists include something for everyone from beginners to specialists. Prices are reasonable, quality is high.

"Discounts are available for larger orders."

R. SCHNEIDER
P.O. BOX 23049, BELLEVILLE, IL 62223
Phone 618-277-8543, FAX 618-277-1050
http://www.RSchneiderStamps.com

206	A43	12h grnsh blue	.15	.65
207	A43	15h bister ('20)	.20	.55
a.		Thick grayish paper ('20)	.15	.15
208	A45	20h dark green	.15	.15
a.		20h yellow green	.15	.15
b.		As "a", thick grysh paper ('20)	.50	2.00
209	A44	25h blue	.15	.15
210	A43	25h violet ('20)	.15	.15
211	A45	30h dark brown	.15	.15
212	A45	40h violet	.15	.15
213	A45	40h lake ('20)	.15	.15
214	A45	45h olive green	.20	.60
215	A45	50h dark blue	.15	.15
a.		Thick grayish paper ('20)	.25	.55
216	A43	60h olive green ('20)	.15	.15
217	A44	1k carmine, yel	.15	.15
218	A44	1k light blue ('20)	.15	.15
		Nos. 200-218 (19)	2.95	4.50
		Set, never hinged	3.65	

All values exist imperf. (For regularly issued imperfs, see Nos. 227-235.)

For overprints and surcharge see Nos. B11-B19, B30-B38, J102, N21, N27, N53, N58, N65, N71.

Parliament Building — A46

1919-20 Engr. Perf. 12½, 11½
Granite Paper

219	A46	2k vermilion & blk	.25	.55
a.		Center inverted	3,500.	
220	A46	2½k olive bis ('20)	.15	.25
221	A46	3k blue & blk brn	.15	.15
222	A46	4k carmine & blk	.15	.15
a.		Center inverted	1,750.	1,400.
223	A46	5k black ('20)	.15	.15
a.		Perf. 11½x12½	45.00	67.50
224	A46	7½k plum	.20	.35
a.		Perf. 11½	110.00	160.00
b.		Perf. 11½x12½	75.00	125.00
225	A46	10k olive grn & blk brn	.20	.35
a.		Perf. 11½x12½	125.00	175.00
b.		Perf. 11½	14.50	25.00
226	A46	20k lilac & red ('20)	.15	.45
a.		Center inverted	10,500.	6,250.
b.		Perf. 11½	62.50	110.00
		Nos. 219-226 (8)	1.40	2.40
		Set, never hinged	2.00	

A number of values exist imperforate between. Values, $300 to $400 a pair.

See No. 248. For overprints and surcharge see Nos. B23-B29, B43-B49, N30, N60, N74.

1920 Typo. Imperf.
Ordinary Paper

227	A44	5h yellow green	.15	.45
228	A44	5h gray	.15	.15
229	A44	10h deep rose	.15	.15
230	A44	10h red	.15	.15
231	A44	15h bister	.15	.15
232	A43	25h violet	.15	.15
233	A45	30h dark brown	.15	.15
234	A45	40h violet	.15	.15
235	A43	60h olive green	.15	.15
		Nos. 227-235 (9)	1.35	1.65
		Set, never hinged	1.35	

Arms
A47   A48

1920-21 Typo. Perf. 12½
Ordinary Paper

238	A47	80h rose	.15	.15
239	A47	1k black brown	.15	.15
241	A47	1½k green ('21)	.15	.15
242	A47	2k blue	.15	.15
243	A48	3k yel grn & dk grn ('21)	.15	.25
244	A48	4k red & claret ('21)	.15	.15
245	A48	5k vio & claret ('21)	.15	.15
246	A48	7½k yellow & brown ('21)	.15	.25
247	A48	10k ultra & blue ('21)	.15	.20
		Nos. 238-247 (9)	1.35	1.60
		Set, never hinged	1.35	

Nos. 238-245, 247 exist on white paper of good quality and on thick grayish paper of inferior quality; No. 246 only on white paper.

For overprints and surcharges see Nos. B20-B22, B39-B42, N22-N23, N31, N54-N55, N61-N62, N66-N67.

1921 Engr.

248	A46	50k dk violet, yel	.35	.80
		Never hinged	.60	
a.		Perf. 11½	15.00	50.00
		Never hinged	25.00	

Symbols of Agriculture A49

Symbols of Labor and Industry A50

1922-24 Typo. Perf. 12½

250	A49	½k olive bister	.15	.60
251	A50	1k brown	.15	.15
252	A50	2k cobalt blue	.15	.15
253	A50	2½k orange brown	.15	.15
254	A50	4k dull violet	.15	1.00
255	A50	5k gray green	.15	.15
256	A49	7½k gray violet	.15	.15
257	A50	10k claret	.15	.15
258	A49	12½k gray green	.15	.15
259	A49	15k bluish green	.15	.15
260	A49	20k dark blue	.15	.15
261	A49	25k claret	.15	.15
262	A50	30k pale gray	.15	.15
263	A50	45k pale red	.15	.15
264	A50	50k orange brown	.15	.15
265	A50	60k yellow green	.15	.15
266	A50	75k ultramarine	.15	.15
267	A50	80k yellow	.15	.15
268	A49	100k gray	.15	.15
269	A49	120k brown	.15	.15
270	A49	150k orange	.15	.15
271	A49	160k light green	.15	.15
272	A49	180k red	.15	.15
273	A49	200k pink	.15	.15
274	A49	240k dark violet	.15	.15
275	A49	300k light blue	.15	.15
276	A49	400k deep green	.85	.15
a.		400k gray green	.85	.30
277	A49	500k yellow	.20	.15
278	A49	600k slate	.20	.15
279	A50	700k brown ('24)	.70	.15
280	A49	800k violet ('24)	.80	1.50
281	A50	1000k violet ('23)	.55	.20
282	A50	1200k car rose ('23)	.35	.45
283	A50	1500k orange ('24)	1.00	.20
284	A50	1600k slate ('23)	2.75	2.75
285	A50	2000k deep blue ('23)	3.50	1.50
286	A50	3000k lt blue ('23)	11.00	1.75
287	A50	4000k dk bl, bl ('24)	5.00	2.10
		Nos. 250-287 (38)	30.80	16.25
		Set, never hinged	90.00	

Nos. 250-287 exist imperf. Value, set $500.
For overprints and surcharges see #N24-N26, N28-N29, N32, N56, N59, N63, N68-N70, N72-N73.

Symbols of Art and Science — A51

1922-24 Engr. Perf. 12½

288	A51	20k dark brown	.15	.15
a.		Perf. 11½	1.10	1.25
		Never hinged, #288a	1.65	
289	A51	25k blue	.15	.15
a.		Perf. 11½	1.00	2.50
		Never hinged, #289a	1.90	
290	A51	50k brown red	.15	.15
a.		Perf. 11½	2.25	3.50
		Never hinged, #290a	3.75	
b.		Vert. pair, imperf. btwn.	200.00	250.00
		Never hinged	250.00	
291	A51	100k deep green	.15	.15
a.		Perf. 11½	5.50	8.00
		Never hinged, #291a	8.00	
b.		Vert. pair, imperf. btwn.	—	375.00
292	A51	200k dark violet	.15	.15
a.		Perf. 11½	8.00	13.50
		Never hinged, #292a	12.00	
b.		Vert. pair, imperf. btwn.	300.00	
		Never hinged	375.00	
293	A51	500k dp orange	.20	1.00
294	A51	1000k blk vio, yel	.15	.15
a.		Perf. 11½	160.00	250.00
		Never hinged, #294a	400.00	
b.		Vert. pair, imperf. btwn.	250.00	
		Never hinged	300.00	
c.		Horiz. pair, imperf. btwn.	300.00	
		Never hinged	375.00	
295	A51	2000k olive grn, yel	.15	.15
a.		Vert. pair, imperf. btwn.	275.00	
		Never hinged	325.00	
296	A51	3000k claret brn ('23)	8.00	.65
297	A51	5000k gray black ('23)	1.50	1.50

Granite Paper

298	A51	10,000k red brown ('24)	3.25	4.00
		Nos. 288-298 (11)	14.00	8.20
		Set, never hinged	34.80	

On Nos. 281-287, 291-298 "kronen" is abbreviated to "k" and transposed with the numerals.
Nos. 288-298 exist imperf. Value, set $375.

Numeral A52

Fields Crossed by Telegraph Wires A53

White-Shouldered Eagle — A54

Church of Minorite Friars — A55

1925-27 Typo. Perf. 12

303	A52	1g dark gray	.20	.15
304	A52	2g claret	.35	.15
305	A52	3g scarlet	.70	.15
306	A52	4g grnsh blue ('27)	1.10	.15
307	A52	5g brown orange	1.50	.15
308	A52	6g ultramarine	1.25	.15
309	A52	7g chocolate	1.50	.15
310	A52	8g yellow green	5.75	.15
311	A53	10g orange	.35	.15
313	A53	15g red lilac	.35	.15
314	A53	16g dark blue	.35	.15
315	A53	18g olive green	1.10	.55
316	A54	20g dark violet	.35	.15
317	A54	24g carmine	.70	.40
318	A54	30g dark brown	.55	.15
319	A54	40g ultramarine	1.10	.15
320	A54	45g yellow brown	1.25	.15
321	A54	50g gray	1.50	.25
322	A54	80g turquoise blue	3.25	4.50

AUSTRID

Perf. 12½
Engr.
323	A55	1s deep green	15.00	1.40
a.		1s light green	200.00	8.25
		Never hinged, #323a	625.00	
324	A55	2s brown rose	6.25	10.00
		Nos. 303-324 (21)	44.45	19.35
		Set, never hinged	137.50	

#303-305, 307-324 exist imperf. Value, set $400.
For type A52 surcharged see Nos. B118.

Güssing — A56
National Library, Vienna — A57

Designs: 15g, Hochosterwitz. 16g, 20g, Durnstein. 18g, Traunsee. 24g, Salzburg. 30g, Seewiesen. 40g, Innsbruck. 50g, Worthersee. 60g, Hohenems. 2s, St. Stephen's Cathedral, Vienna.

1929-30   Typo.   Perf. 12½
Size: 25½x21½mm
326	A56	10g brown orange	.90	.15
327	A56	10g bister ('30)	.90	.15
328	A56	15g violet brown	.70	1.25
329	A56	16g dark gray	.25	.15
330	A56	18g blue green	.40	.45
331	A56	20g dark gray ('30)	.40	.15
332	A56	24g maroon	4.25	6.00
333	A56	24g lake ('30)	6.50	.45
334	A56	30g dark violet	4.25	.15
335	A56	40g dark blue	7.25	.15
336	A56	50g gray violet ('30)	27.50	.20
337	A56	60g olive green	22.50	.25

Engr.
Size: 21x26mm
338	A57	1s black brown	5.25	.25
a.		Horiz. pair, imperf. btwn.	225.00	
		Never hinged	300.00	
b.		Vert. pair, imperf. btwn.	225.00	
		Never hinged	300.00	
339	A57	2s dark green	9.25	8.75
a.		Horiz. pair, imperf. btwn.	225.00	
		Never hinged	300.00	
		Nos. 326-339 (14)	90.30	18.50
		Set, never hinged	288.90	

Type of 1929-30 Issue
Designs: 12g, Traunsee. 64g, Hohenems.

1932   Perf. 12
Size: 21x16½mm
340	A56	10g olive brown	.80	.15
341	A56	12g blue green	1.50	.15
342	A56	18g blue green	1.40	2.10
343	A56	20g dark gray	1.10	.15
344	A56	24g carmine rose	5.25	.15
345	A56	24g dull violet	3.50	.15
346	A56	30g dark violet	17.50	.15
347	A56	30g carmine rose	4.25	.15
a.		Vert. pair, imperf. btwn.	40.00	
		Never hinged. #347a	50.00	
348	A56	40g dark blue	19.00	.90
349	A56	40g dark violet	6.25	.30
350	A56	50g gray violet	24.00	.30
351	A56	50g dull blue	5.75	.15
352	A56	60g gray green	52.50	2.50
353	A56	64g gray green	12.00	.30
		Nos. 340-353 (14)	154.80	7.75
		Set, never hinged	504.00	

For overprints and surcharges see Nos. B87-B92, B119-B121.

Burgenland A67
Tyrol A68

Costumes of various districts: 3g, Burgenland. 4g, 5g, Carinthia. 6g, 8g, Lower Austria. 12g, 20g, Upper Austria. 24g, 25g, Salzburg. 30g, 35g, Styria. 45g, Tyrol. 60g, Vorarlberg bridal couple. 64g, Vorarlberg. 1s, Viennese family. 2s, Military.

1934-35   Typo.   Perf. 12
354	A67	1g dark violet	.15	.15
355	A67	3g scarlet	.15	.15
356	A67	4g olive green	.15	.15
357	A67	5g red violet	.15	.15
358	A67	6g ultramarine	.20	.25
359	A67	8g green	.15	.15
360	A67	12g dark brown	.15	.15
361	A67	20g yellow brown	.15	.15
362	A67	24g grnsh blue	.15	.15
363	A67	25g violet	.20	.25
364	A67	30g maroon	.15	.15
365	A67	35g rose carmine	.30	.45

Perf. 12½
366	A68	40g slate gray	.40	.25
367	A68	45g brown red	.35	.15
368	A68	60g ultramarine	.60	.35
369	A68	64g brown	.75	.15
370	A68	1s deep violet	.90	.55
371	A68	2s dull green	35.00	65.00

Designs Redrawn
Perf. 12 (6g), 12½ (2s)
372	A67	6g ultra ('35)	.15	.15
373	A68	2s emerald ('35)	3.25	5.25
		Nos. 354-373 (20)	43.45	74.15
		Set, never hinged	108.00	

The design of No. 358 looks as though the man's ears were on backwards, while No. 372 appears correctly.
On No. 373 there are seven feathers on each side of the eagle instead of five.
Nos. 354-373 exist imperf. Value, set $375.
For surcharges see Nos. B128-B131.

Dollfuss Mourning Issue

Engelbert Dollfuss — A85

1934-35   Engr.   Perf. 12½
374	A85	24g greenish black	.40	.30
		Never hinged	1.25	
375	A85	24g indigo ('35)	.75	.70
		Never hinged	2.50	

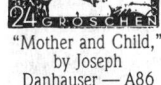

"Mother and Child," by Joseph Danhauser — A86
"Madonna and Child," after Painting by Dürer — A87

1935, May 1
376	A86	24g dark blue	.40	.20
		Never hinged	1.00	
a.		Vert. pair, imperf. btwn.	200.00	
		Never hinged	250.00	
b.		Horiz. pair, imperf. btwn.	190.00	
		Never hinged	225.00	

Mother's Day. Nos. 376-377 exist imperf. Value, each $150.

1936, May 5   Photo.
377	A87	24g violet blue	.15	.30
		Never hinged	.55	

Mother's Day.

Farm Workers — A88

Design: 5s, Factory workers.

1936, June   Engr.   Perf. 12½
378	A88	3s red orange	12.50	17.50
		Never hinged	24.00	
379	A88	5s brown black	30.00	42.50
		Never hinged	45.00	

Nos. 378-379 exist imperf. Value, set $210.

Engelbert Dollfuss — A90
Mother and Child — A91

1936, July 25
380	A90	10s dark blue	675.00	800.00
		Never hinged	900.00	

Second anniv. of death of Engelbert Dollfuss, chancellor. Exists imperf. Value, $1,750.

1937, May 5   Photo.   Perf. 12
381	A91	24g henna brown	.20	.25
		Never hinged	.55	

Mother's Day. Exists imperf. Value, $140.

S.S. Maria Anna — A92

1937, June 9
382	A92	12g red brown	.60	.35
383	A92	24g deep blue	.60	.35
384	A92	64g dark green	.60	.80
		Nos. 382-384 (3)	1.80	1.50
		Set, never hinged	5.00	

Cent. of steamship service on Danube River. Exist imperf. Value, set $350.

First Locomotive, "Austria" — A95

Designs: 25g, Modern steam locomotive. 35g, Modern electric train.

1937, Nov. 22
385	A95	12g black brown	.20	.15
386	A95	25g dark violet	.65	1.00
387	A95	35g brown red	1.65	2.25
		Nos. 385-387 (3)	2.50	3.40
		Set, never hinged	6.90	

Centenary of Austrian railways. Exist imperf. Value, set $90.

Rose and Zodiac Signs — A98

1937   Engr.   Perf. 13x12½
388	A98	12g dark green	.15	.15
389	A98	24g dark carmine	.15	.15
		Set, never hinged	.30	

For Use in Vienna, Lower Austria and Burgenland
Germany Nos. 509-511 and 511B
Overprinted in Black

a   b

Austria

WE BUY & SELL!

Comprehensive Stock!
Top Quality
at Realistic Prices!
Prompt Service!
Satisfaction Guaranteed!

FREE PRICE LIST: Complete Year Sets • Sets & Singles • Offices • Occupation • Bosnia • Covers • Proofs • Specialized Material *Want lists invited! Good stock of Classics!*

WE BUY! Sell to a knowledgeable specialist for Top Prices!

Save 10%!
Complete Run 1958-1998
Purchase the complete run of Austria Year Sets from 1958-1998 and save 10%!
Regularly $810.10   10% Off! $729.00

Henry Gitner Philatelists, Inc.

Philately-The Quiet Excitement!
P.O. Box 3077-S, Middletown, NY 10940
Tel: 914-343-5151 Fax: 914-343-0068
Toll Free: 1-800-947-8267
E-mail: hgitner@hgitner.com
http://www.hgitner.com

AUSTRIA

1945   Unwmk.   Perf. 14
390	A115(a)	5pf dp yellow green	.15	.20
391	A115(b)	6pf purple	.15	.20
392	A115(a)	8pf red	.15	.20
393	A115(b)	12pf carmine	.15	.20
		Nos. 390-393 (4)	.60	.80
		Set, never hinged	.60	

Nos. 390-393 exist with overprint inverted or double.

German No. 507, the 3pf, with overprint "a" was prepared, not issued, but sold to collectors after the definitive Republic issue had been placed in use. Value $30, hinged, $60, never hinged.

German Semi-Postal Stamps, #B207, B209, B210, B283 Surcharged in Black

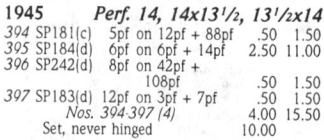

c   **ÖSTERREICH 5 Pf.**

d   **ÖSTERREICH 8 Pf.**

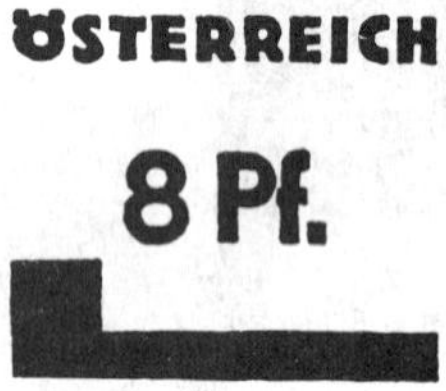

1945   Perf. 14, 14x13½, 13½x14
394	SP181(c)	5pf on 12pf + 88pf	.50	1.50
395	SP184(d)	6pf on 14pf + 86pf	2.50	11.00
396	SP242(d)	8pf on 42pf + 108pf	.50	1.50
397	SP183(d)	12pf on 3pf + 7pf	.50	1.50
		Nos. 394-397 (4)	4.00	15.50
		Set, never hinged	10.00	

The surcharges are spaced to fit the stamps.

Stamps of Germany, Nos. 509 to 511, 511B, 519 and 529 Overprinted

e   Österreich (on bars)   f   Österreich

1945   Typo.   Perf. 14
Size: 18½x22½mm
398	A115(e)	5pf dp yellow green	.25	.45
399	A115(f)	5pf dp yellow green	4.00	7.75
400	A115(e)	6pf purple	.15	.35
401	A115(e)	8pf red	.15	.35
402	A115(e)	12pf carmine	.20	.35

Engr.
Size: 21½x26mm
403	A115(e)	30pf olive green	6.25	10.00
a.		Thin bar at bottom	15.00	17.50
a.		Never hinged	25.00	
404	A118(e)	42pf brt green	15.00	32.50
a.		Thin bar at bottom	15.00	27.50
a.		Never hinged	25.00	
		Nos. 398-404 (7)	26.00	51.75
		Set, never hinged	55.00	

On Nos. 403a and 404a, the bottom bar of the overprint is 2½mm wide, and, as the overprint was applied in two operations, "Österreich" is usually not exactly centered in its diagonal slot. On Nos. 403 and 404, the bottom bar is 3mm wide, and "Österreich" is always well centered.

Germany Nos. 524-527 (the 1m, 2m, 3m and 5m), overprinted with vertical bars and "Österreich" similar to "e" and "f", were prepared, not issued, but sold to collectors after the definitive Republic issue had been placed in use. Value for set, $70 hinged, $150 ever hinged.

Counterfeits exist of Nos. 403-404, 403a-404a and 1m-5m overprints.

For Use in Styria

Stamps of Germany Nos. 506 to 511, 511A, 511B, 514 to 523 and 529 Overprinted in Black

Österreich

1945   Unwmk.   Typo.   Perf. 14
Size: 18½x22½mm
405	A115	1pf gray black	1.50	3.00
406	A115	3pf lt brown	1.50	3.00
407	A115	4pf slate	5.00	10.00
408	A115	5pf dp yellow grn	1.00	2.00
409	A115	6pf purple	.20	.30
410	A115	8pf red	.75	1.65
411	A115	10pf dark brown	1.50	3.25
412	A115	12pf carmine	.15	.30

Engr.
413	A115	15pf brown lake	.75	1.75
414	A115	16pf pck green	14.00	18.00
415	A115	20pf blue	2.75	5.25
416	A115	24pf orange brown	10.00	18.00

Size: 22½x26mm
417	A115	25pf brt ultra	1.00	2.75
418	A115	30pf olive green	1.00	2.00
419	A115	40pf red violet	1.25	2.25
420	A118	42pf brt green	2.00	3.50
421	A115	50pf myrtle green	1.40	3.50
422	A115	60pf dk red brown	2.25	4.75
423	A115	80pf indigo	2.00	3.75
		Nos. 405-423 (19)	50.00	89.00
		Set, never hinged	110.00	

Overprinted on Nos. 524-527
Perf. 12½, 14
424	A116	1m dk slate grn	7.50	20.00
a.	Perf. 12½		100.00	
425	A116	2m violet	7.50	25.00
a.	Perf. 14		12.00	45.00
426	A116	3m copper red	25.00	55.00
a.			125.00	
427	A116	5m dark blue	225.00	525.00
a.			575.00	
		Nos. 424-427 (4)	265.00	
		Set, never hinged	450.00	

On the preceding four stamps the innermost vertical lines are 10½mm apart; on the pfennig values 6½mm apart.

Counterfeits exist of Nos. 405-427 overprints.

Germany Nos. 524 to 527 Overprinted in Black

Österreich

Perf. 14
428	A116	1m dk slate grn	10.50	22.50
429	A116	2m violet	10.50	27.50

Perf. 12½
430	A116	3m copper red	21.00	60.00
431	A116	5m dark blue	140.00	450.00
a.	Perf. 14		600.00	
		Nos. 428-431 (4)	182.00	
		Set, never hinged	375.00	

On the preceding four stamps, "Österreich" is thinner, measuring 16mm. On the previous set of 23 values it measures 18mm.

Counterfeits exist of Nos. 428-431 overprints.

Catalogue values for unused stamps in this section, from this point to the end of the section, are for Never Hinged items.

For Use in Vienna, Lower Austria and Burgenland

Coat of Arms
A99   A100

Typographed or Lithographed
1945, July 3   Unwmk.   Perf. 14x13½
Size: 21x25mm
432	A99	3pf brown	.15	.15
433	A99	4pf slate	.15	.15
434	A99	5pf dark green	.15	.15
435	A99	6pf deep violet	.15	.15
436	A99	8pf orange brown	.15	.15
437	A99	10pf deep brown	.15	.15
438	A99	12pf rose carmine	.15	.15
439	A99	15pf orange red	.15	.15
440	A99	16pf dull blue green	.15	.35

Perf. 14
Size: 24x28½mm
441	A99	20pf light blue	.15	.15
442	A99	24pf orange	.15	.15
443	A99	25pf dark blue	.15	.15
444	A99	30pf deep gray grn	.15	.15
445	A99	38pf ultramarine	.15	.15
446	A99	40pf brt red vio	.15	.15
447	A99	42pf sage green	.15	.15
448	A99	50pf blue green	.15	.60
449	A99	60pf maroon	.15	.15
450	A99	80pf dull lilac	.15	.15

Engr.   Perf. 14x13½
451	A100	1m dark green	.15	.60
452	A100	2m dark purple	.15	.60
453	A100	3m dark violet	.15	.60
454	A100	5m brown red	.15	.60
		Nos. 432-454 (23)	3.45	5.95

Nos. 432, 433, 437, 439, 440, 443, 446, 448, 449 are typographed. Nos. 434, 435, 441, 442 are lithographed; the other values exist both ways.
For overprint see No. 604.

For General Use

Lermoos, Winter Scene — A101
The Prater Woods, Vienna — A105  
Hochosterwitz, Carinthia A106 
Lake Constance A110 
Dürnstein, Lower Austria A124 

Designs: 4g, Eisenerz surface mine. 5g, Leopoldsberg, near Vienna. 6g, Hohensalzburg, Salzburg Province. 12g, Wolfgang See, near Salzburg. 15g, Forchtenstein Castle, Burgenland. 16g, Gesäuse Valley. 24g, Höldrichs Mill, Lower Austria. 25g, Oetz Valley Outlet, Tyrol. 30g, Neusiedler Lake, Burgenland. 35g, Belvedere Palace, Vienna. 38g, Langbath Lake. 40g, Mariazell, Styria. 42g, Traunkirchen. 45g, Hartenstein Castle. 50g, Silvretta Mountains, Vorarlberg. 60g, Railroad viaducts near Semmering. 70g, Waterfall of Bad-Gastein, Salzburg. 80g, Kaiser Mountains, Tyrol. 90g, Wayside Shrine, Tragöss, Styria. 2s, St. Christof am Arlberg, Tyrol. 3s, Heiligenblut, Carinthia. 5s, Schönbrunn, Vienna.

1945-46   Photo.   Perf. 14x13½
455	A101	3g sapphire	.15	.15
456	A101	4g dp orange ('46)	.15	.15
457	A101	5g dk carmine rose	.15	.15
458	A101	6g dk slate green	.15	.15
459	A105	8g golden brown	.15	.15
460	A106	10g dark green	.15	.15
461	A106	12g dark brown	.15	.15
462	A106	15g dk slate bl ('46)	.15	.15
463	A106	16g chnt brn ('46)	.15	.15

Perf. 13½x14
464	A110	20g dp ultra ('46)	.15	.15
465	A110	24g dp yellow grn ('46)	.15	.15
466	A110	25g gray black ('46)	.15	.15
467	A110	30g dark red	.15	.15
468	A110	35g brown red ('46)	.15	.15
469	A110	38g brown olive ('46)	.15	.15
470	A110	40g gray	.15	.15
471	A110	42g brown orange ('46)	.15	.15
472	A110	45g dark blue ('46)	.15	.25
473	A110	50g dark blue	.15	.15
474	A110	60g dark violet	.15	.15
	Imperf., pair		50.00	60.00
475	A110	70g Prus blue ('46)	.15	.25
476	A110	80g brown	.15	.40
477	A110	90g Prussian green	1.10	1.10
478	A124	1s dk red brn ('46)	.75	.75
479	A124	2s blue gray ('46)	2.75	2.75

480	A124	3s dk slate grn ('46)	.75	.80
481	A124	5s dark red ('46)	1.50	1.75

See Nos. 486-488, 496-515. For overprints and surcharges see Nos. 492-493, B166, B280, B287.

No. 461 Overprinted in Carmine

1946, Sept. 26
482	A106	12g dark brown	.15	.20

Meeting of the Soc. for Cultural and Economic Relations with the USSR, Vienna, Sept. 26-29.

City Hall Park, Vienna   A128
Hochosterwitz, Carinthia   A129 

1946-47   Perf. 14x13½
Photo.   Unwmk.
483	A128	8g deep plum	.15	.15
484	A128	8g olive brown	.15	.15
a.		8g dark olive green	.15	.15
485	A129	10g dk brn vio ('47)	.15	.15

Perf. 13½x14
486	A110	30g blue gray ('47)	.15	.15
487	A110	50g brown violet ('47)	.25	.25
488	A110	60g violet blue ('47)	2.00	1.10
		Nos. 483-488 (6)	2.85	1.95

See No. 502.

Franz Grillparzer — A130
Franz Schubert — A131 

1947   Engr.   Perf. 14x13½
489	A130	18g chocolate	.15	.15

Photo.
490	A130	18g dk violet brn	.15	.15

Death of Grillparzer, dramatic poet, 75th anniv.
A second printing of No. 490 on thicker paper has a darker frame and clearer delineation of the portrait.
Issue dates: #489, Feb. 10; #490, Mar. 31.

1947, Mar. 31   Engr.
491	A131	12g dark green	.15	.15

150th birth anniv. of Franz Schubert, musician and composer.

Nos. 469 and 463 Surcharged in Brown

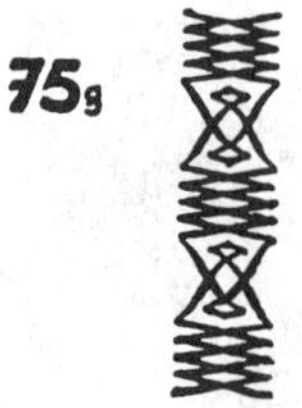

75g   **$1.40**

1947, Sept. 1   Photo.   Perf. 14
492	A110	75g on 38g brown ol	.20	.80
493	A106	1.40s on 16g chnt brn	.15	.15

The surcharge on No. 493 varies from brown to black brown.

AUSTRIA

Symbols of Global Telegraphic Communication — A132

1947, Nov. 5   Engr.   Perf. 14x13½
495 A132   40g dark violet   .15 .15
Centenary of the telegraph in Austria.

Scenic Type of 1946

1946, Aug.   Photo.   Perf. 13½x14
496 A124   1s dark brown   1.25   .50
497 A124   2s dark blue   7.00   2.75
498 A124   3s dark slate green   2.25   .75
499 A124   5s dark red   32.50   8.00
    Nos. 496-499 (4)   43.00   12.00

On Nos. 478 to 481 the upper and lower panels show a screen effect. On Nos. 496 to 499 the panels appear to be solid color.

Scenic Types of 1945-46

1947-48   Photo.   Perf. 14x13½
500 A101   3g bright red   .15 .15
501 A101   5g bright red   .15 .15
502 A129   10g bright red   .15 .15
503 A106   15g brt red ('48)   1.40 1.25
    Perf. 13½x14
504 A110   20g bright red   .50 .15
505 A110   30g bright red   .75 .15
506 A110   40g bright red   .75 .15
507 A110   50g bright red   1.00 .15
508 A110   60g brt red ('48)   6.50 1.25
509 A110   70g brt red ('48)   3.50 .15
510 A110   80g brt red ('48)   3.50 .15
511 A110   90g brt red ('48)   3.75 .25
512 A124   1s dark violet   .80 .15
513 A124   2s dark violet   1.10 .20
514 A124   3s dk violet ('48)   9.00 1.00
515 A124   5s dk violet ('48)   11.00 1.50
    Nos. 500-515 (16)   44.00 6.95

Carl Michael Ziehrer (1843-1922), Composer — A133

#517, Adalbert Stifter (1805-68), novelist. #518, Anton Bruckner (1824-96), composer. 60g, Friedrich von Amerling (1803-87), painter.

1948-49   Engr.
516 A133   20g dull green   .35 .20
517 A133   40g chocolate   5.00 2.50
518 A133   40g dark green   5.00 4.00
519 A133   60g rose brown   .65 .30
    Nos. 516-519 (4)   11.00 7.00

Issue dates: 20g, Jan. 21, No. 517, Sept. 6, No. 518, Sept. 3, 1949, 60g, Jan. 26.

Vorarlberg, Montafon Valley — A134
Costume of Vienna, 1850 — A135

Designs (Austrian Costumes): 3g, Tyrol, Inn Valley. 5g, Salzburg, Pinzgau. 10g, Styria, Salzkammergut. 15g, Burgenland, Lutzmannsburg. 25g, Vienna, 1850. 30g, Salzburg, Pongau. 40g, Vienna, 1840. 45g, Carinthia, Lesach Valley. 50g, Vorarlberg, Bregenzer Forest. 60g, Carinthia, Lavant Valley. 70g, Lower Austria, Wachau. 75g, Styria, Salzkammergut. 80g, Styria, Enns Valley. 90g, Central Styria. 1s, Tyrol, Puster Valley. 1.20s, Lower Austria, Vienna Woods. 1.40s, Upper Austria, Inn District. 1.45s, Wilten. 1.50s, Vienna, 1853. 1.60s, Vienna, 1830. 1.70s, East Tyrol, Kals. 2s, Upper Austria. 2.20s, Ischl, 1820. 2.40s, Kitzbuhel. 2.50s, Upper Steiermark, 1850. 2.70s, Little Walser Valley. 3s, Burgenland. 3.50s, Lower Austria, 1850. 4.50s, Gail Valley. 5s, Ziller Valley. 7s, Steiermark, Sulm Valley.

    Perf. 14x13½
1948-52   Unwmk.   Photo.
520 A134   3g gray ('50)   .60 .50
521 A134   5g dark green ('49)   .25 .15
522 A134   10g deep blue   .25 .15
523 A134   15g brown   .60 .15
524 A134   20g yellow green   .20 .15
525 A134   25g brown ('49)   .20 .15
526 A134   30g dk car rose   2.50 .15
527 A134   30g dk violet ('50)   .60 .15
528 A134   40g violet   2.50 .15
529 A134   40g green ('49)   .20 .15
530 A134   45g violet blue   2.25 .40
531 A134   50g orange brn ('49)   .60 .15
532 A134   60g scarlet   .20 .15
533 A134   70g brt blue grn ('49)   .20 .15
534 A134   75g blue   3.75 .40
535 A134   80g carmine rose ('49)   .35 .15
536 A134   90g brown vio ('49)   22.50 .30
537 A134   1s ultramarine   4.00 .15
538 A134   1s rose red ('50)   62.50 .15
539 A134   1s dk green ('51)   .20 .15
540 A134   1.20s violet ('49)   .40 .15
541 A134   1.40s brown   2.50 .15
542 A134   1.45s dk carmine ('51)   1.00 .15
543 A134   1.50s ultra ('51)   .60 .15
544 A134   1.60s orange red ('49)   .20 .15
545 A134   1.70s violet blue ('50)   2.50 .55
546 A134   2s blue green   .40 .15
547 A134   2.20s slate ('52)   4.75 .15
548 A134   2.40s blue ('51)   1.00 .15
549 A134   2.50s brown ('52)   4.50 .15
550 A134   2.70s dk brown ('51)   .45 .45
551 A134   3s brown car ('49)   1.90 .15
552 A134   3.50s dull grn ('51)   9.75 .15
553 A134   4.50s brown vio ('51)   .60 .40
554 A134   5s dark red vio   1.00 .15
555 A134   7s olive ('52)   1.50 .15
    Engr.
556 A135   10s gray ('50)   27.50 5.00
    Nos. 520-556 (37)   165.00 12.35

In 1958-59, 21 denominations of this set were printed on white paper, differing from the previous grayish paper with yellowish gum.

Pres. Karl Renner — A136

1948, Nov. 12   Perf. 14x13½
557 A136   1s deep blue   1.90 1.10
Founding of the Austrian Republic, 30th anniv. See Nos. 573, 636.

Franz Gruber and Josef Mohr — A137

1948, Dec. 18   Perf. 13½x14
558 A137   60g red brown   4.25 4.00
130th anniv. of the hymn "Silent Night, Holy Night".

Symbolical of Child Welfare — A138
Johann Strauss, the Younger — A139

1949, May 14   Photo.   Perf. 14x13½
559 A138   1s bright blue   11.50 1.25
1st year of activity of UNICEF in Austria.

1949   Engr.
30g, Johann Strauss, the elder. #561, Johann Strauss, the younger. #562, Karl Millöcker.
560 A139   30g violet brown   2.25 1.65
561 A139   1s dark blue   2.75 1.10
562 A139   1s dark blue   12.00 6.25
    Nos. 560-562 (3)   17.00 9.00

Johann Strauss, the elder (1804-49), Johann Strauss, the younger (1825-99), and Karl Millöcker (1842-1899), composers. See #574.

Esperanto Star, Olive Branches — A140
St. Gebhard — A141

1949, June 25   Photo.
563 A140   20g blue green   1.00 .50
Austrian Esperanto Congress at Graz.

1949, Aug. 6   Engr.
564 A141   30g dark violet   1.50 1.25
St. Gebhard (949-995), Bishop of Vorarlberg.

Letter, Roses and Post Horn — A142

UPU, 75th Anniv.: 60g, Plaque. 1s, "Austria," wings and monogram.

1949, Oct. 8   Perf. 13½x14
565 A142   40g dark green   3.75 1.65
566 A142   60g dk carmine   3.75 1.65
567 A142   1s dk violet blue   6.50 4.75
    Nos. 565-567 (3)   14.00 8.05

Moritz Michael Daffinger — A143
Andreas Hofer — A144

30g, Alexander Girardi. #569, Daffinger. #570, Hofer. #571, Josef Madersperger.

1950   Unwmk.   Perf. 14x13½
568 A144   30g dark blue   1.50 .75
569 A143   60g red brown   6.00 3.25
570 A144   60g dark violet   10.50 6.50
571 A144   60g purple   4.50 2.25
    Nos. 568-571 (4)   22.50 12.75

Alexander Girardi (1850-1918), actor; Moritz Michael Daffinger (1790-1849), painter; Andreas Hofer (1767-1810), patriot; Josef Madersperger (1768-1850), inventor.
Issue dates: 30g, Dec. 5; No. 569, Jan. 25; No. 570, Feb. 20; No. 571, Oct. 2.

Austrian Stamp of 1850 — A146

1950, May 20   Perf. 14½
572 A146   1s black, straw   1.65 .90
Centenary of Austrian postage stamps.

Renner Type of 1948, Frame and Inscriptions Altered

1951, Mar. 3
573 A136   1s black, straw   1.40 .20
In memory of Pres. Karl Renner, 1870-1950.

Strauss Type of 1949
Portrait: 60g, Joseph Lanner.

1951, Apr. 12
574 A139   60g dk blue green   3.50 1.10
150th birth anniv. of Joseph Lanner, composer.

Martin Johann Schmidt — A147
Boy Scout Emblem — A148

1951, June 28   Engr.   Perf. 14x13½
575 A147   1sh brown red   4.50 2.00
150th death anniv. of Martin Johann Schmidt, painter.

1951, Aug. 3   Engr. and Litho.
576 A148   1sh dk grn, ocher & pink   3.50 2.75
7th World Scout Jamboree, Bad Ischl-St. Wolfgang, Aug. 3-13, 1951.

Wilhelm Kienzl A149
Josef Schrammel A150

Design: 1s, Karl von Ghega.

1951-52   Engr.   Unwmk.
577 A149   1s deep green ('52)   6.50 1.10
578 A149   1.50s indigo   3.00 .90
579 A150   1.50s violet blue ('52)   6.50 1.10
    Nos. 577-579 (3)   16.00 3.10

Ghega (1802-60), civil engineer; Kienzl (1857-1941), composer; Schrammel (1852-95), composer. See #582.
Issued: 1s, Mar. 2; #578, Oct. 3; #579, Mar. 3.

Breakfast Pavilion, Schönbrunn A151

1952, May 24   Perf. 13½x14
580 A151   1.50s dark green   5.75 1.00
Vienna Zoological Gardens, 200th anniv.

Globe as Dot Over "i" — A152
School Girl — A153

1952, July 1   Perf. 14x13½
581 A152   1.50s dark blue   5.00 .65
Formation of the Intl. Union of Socialist Youth Camp, Vienna, July 1-10, 1952.

AUSTRIA

Type Similar to A150
Portrait: 1s, Nikolaus Lenau.

1952, Aug. 13
582 A150 1s deep green   6.00 1.10

Nikolaus Lenau, pseudonym of Nikolaus Franz Niembsch von Strehlenau (1802-50), poet.

1952, Sept. 6
583 A153 2.40s dp violet blue   9.00 1.75

Issued to stimulate letter-writing between Austrian and foreign school children.

Hugo Wolf — A154
Pres. Theodor Körner — A155 

1953, Feb. 21 Engr.   Perf. 14x13½
587 A154 1.50s dark blue   6.00 .70

Hugo Wolf, composer, 50th death anniv.

1953, Apr. 24
588 A155 1.50s dk violet blue   6.00 .70

80th birthday of Pres. Theodor Körner. See Nos. 591, 614.

State Theater, Linz, and Masks — A156

1953, Oct. 17 Perf. 13½x14
589 A156 1.50s dark gray   14.00 1.50

State Theater at Linz, 150th anniv.

Child and Christmas Tree — A157
Karl von Rokitansky — A158 

1953, Nov. 30 Perf. 14x13½
590 A157 1s dark green   1.40 .20

See No. 597.

Type Similar to A155
Portrait: 1.50s, Moritz von Schwind.

1954, Jan. 21   Perf. 14x13½
591 A155 1.50s purple   12.00 1.10

Moritz von Schwind, painter, 150th birth anniv.

1954, Feb. 19
592 A158 1.50s purple   14.00 1.40

Karl von Rokitansky, physician, 150th birth anniv. See No. 595.

Esperanto Star and Wreath — A159

Engr. and Photo.
1954, June 5   Perf. 13½x14
593 A159 1s dk brown & emer   4.50 .20

Esperanto movement in Austria, 50th anniv.

A160
A161 

1954, Aug. 4 Engr.   Perf. 14x13½
594 A160 1s dark blue green   10.00 1.65

300th birth anniv. of Johann Michael Rottmayr von Rosenbrunn, painter.

Type Similar to A158
Portrait: 1.50s, Carl Auer von Welsbach.

1954, Aug. 4
595 A158 1.50s violet blue   30.00 1.50

25th death anniv. of Carl Auer von Welsbach (1858-1929), chemist.

1954, Oct. 2   Unwmk.
596 A161 1s brown   2.25 .18

2nd Intl. Congress for Catholic Church Music, Vienna, Oct. 4-10, 1954.

Christmas Type of 1953
1954, Nov. 30
597 A157 1s dark blue   2.75 .25

Arms of Austria and Official Publication A162

1954, Dec. 18   Engr.
598 A162 1s salmon & black   2.25 .20

Austria's State Printing Plant, 150th anniv., and Wiener Zeitung, government newspaper, 250th year of publication.

Parliament Building A163

Designs: 1s, Western railroad station, Vienna. 1.45s, Letters forming flag. 1.50s, Public housing, Vienna. 2.40s, Limberg dam.

1955, Apr. 27   Perf. 13½x14
599 A163 70g rose violet   1.50 .20
600 A163 1s deep ultra   5.50 .20
601 A163 1.45s scarlet   8.25 1.65
602 A163 1.50s brown   17.50 .20
603 A163 2.40s dk blue green   8.25 3.20
  Nos. 599-603 (5)   41.00 5.25

10th anniv. of Austria's liberation.

Type of 1945 Overprinted in Blue   STAATSVERTRAG 1955

1955, May 15   Perf. 14x13½
604 A100 2s blue gray   2.00 .20

Signing of the state treaty with the US, France, Great Britain and Russia, May 15, 1955.

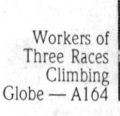

Workers of Three Races Climbing Globe — A164

1955, May 20   Perf. 13½x14
605 A164 1s indigo   2.00 1.65

4th congress of the Intl. Confederation of Free Trade Unions, Vienna, May.

Burgtheater, Vienna — A165

Design: 2.40s, Opera House, Vienna.

1955, July 25
606 A165 1.50s light sepia   3.00 .20
607 A165 2.40s dark blue   4.00 1.25

Re-opening of the Burgtheater and Opera House in Vienna.

Symbolic of Austria's Desire to Join the UN — A166

1955, Oct. 24   Unwmk.
608 A166 2.40s green   14.00 1.40

Tenth anniversary of UN.

Wolfgang Amadeus Mozart — A167
Symbolic of Austria's Joining the UN — A168 

1956, Jan. 21   Perf. 14x13½
609 A167 2.40s slate blue   3.75 .50

200th birth anniv. of Wolfgang Amadeus Mozart, composer.

1956, Feb. 20
610 A168 2.40s chocolate   11.00 1.10

Austria's admission to the UN.

Globe Showing Energy of the Earth — A169

1956, May 8   Perf. 13½x14
611 A169 2.40s deep blue   10.00 1.40

Fifth Intl. Power Conf., Vienna, June 17-23.

Map of Europe and City Maps — A170
J.B. Fischer von Erlach — A171 

Photo. and Typo.
1956, June 8   Perf. 14x13½
612 A170 1.45s lt grn blk & red   2.50 .50

23rd Intl. Housing and Town Planning Congress, Vienna, July 22-28.

1956, July 20   Engr.
613 A171 1.50s brown   1.25 1.10

300th birth anniv. of Johann Bernhard Fischer von Erlach, architect.

Körner Type of 1953
1957, Jan. 11
614 A155 1.50s gray black   1.50 1.25

Death of Pres. Theodor Körner.

Dr. Julius Wagner-Jauregg A172
Anton Wildgans A173 

1957, Mar. 7   Perf. 14x13½
615 A172 2.40s brn violet   3.25 1.25

Birth cent. of Dr. Julius Wagner-Jauregg, psychiatrist.

1957, May 3   Unwmk.
616 A173 1s violet blue   .30 .15

Anton Wildgans, poet, 25th death anniv.

Old and New Postal Motor Coach — A174

1957, June 14   Perf. 13½x14
617 A174 1s black, yellow   .30 .15

Austrian Postal Motor Coach Service, 50th anniv.

Gasherbrum II and Glacier A175

1957, July 27
618 A175 1.50s gray blue   .35 .15

Austrian Karakorum Expedition, which climbed Mount Gasherbrum II on July 7, 1956.

A176
A177 

Designs: 20g, Farmhouse at Mörbisch. 50g, Heiligenstadt, Vienna. 1s, Mariazell. 1.40s, County seat, Klagenfurt. 1.50s, Rabenhof Building, Erdberg, Vienna. 1.80s, The Mint, Hall, Tyrol. 2s, Christkindl Church. 3.40s, Steiner Gate, Krems. 4s, Vienna Gate, Hainburg. 4.50s, Schwechat Airport, Vienna. 5.50s, Chur Gate, Feldkirch. 6s, County seat, Graz. 6.40s, "Golden Roof," Innsbruck. 10s, Heidenreichstein Castle.

1957-61   Litho.   Perf. 14x13½
    Size: 20x25mm
618A A176 20g violet blk ('61)   .15 .15
619 A176 50g bluish black ('59) .15 .15
    Engr.
620 A176 1s chocolate   1.25 .15
    Typo.
621 A176 1s chocolate   1.75 .15
    Litho.
622 A176 1s choc ('59)   .90 .15
622A A176 1.40s brt greenish bl ('60)   .30 .15
623 A176 1.50s rose lake ('58)   .50 .15
624 A176 1.80s brt ultra ('60)   .30 .15
625 A176 2s dull blue ('58)   6.00 .15
626 A176 3.40s yel grn ('60)   .90 .20
627 A176 4s brt red lil ('60)   .75 .15
627A A176 4.50s dl green ('60)   1.00 .50
628 A176 5.50s grnsh gray ('60) .55 .20
629 A176 6s brt vio ('60)   1.00 .15
629A A176 6.40s brt blue ('60)   1.00 .90
    Engr.
    Size: 22x28mm
630 A177 10s dk bl grn   3.00 .45
    Nos. 618A-630 (16)   19.50 4.50

Of the three 1s stamps above, Nos. 620 and 621 have two names in imprint (designer H. Strohofer, engraver G. Wimmer). No. 622 has only Strohofer's name.

AUSTRIA

Values for Nos. 618A-624, 626-630 are for stamps on white paper. Most denominations also come on grayish paper with yellowish gum.
See Nos. 688-702.

1960-65   Photo.   Perf. 14½x14
Size: 17x21mm
630A A176 50g slate ('64)   .15 .15
630B A176 1s chocolate   .15 .15
Size: 17x21mm
630C A176 1.50s dk car ('65)   .20 .15
      Nos. 630A-630C (3)   .50 .45
Nos. 630A-630C issued in sheets and coils.

Graukogel, Badgastein — A180

1958, Feb. 1   Engr.   Perf. 14x13½
631 A180 1.50s dark blue   .25 .15
Intl. Ski Federation Alpine championships, Badgastein, Feb. 2-7.

Plane over Map of Austria — A181

1958, Mar. 27   Perf. 13½x14
632 A181 4s red   .45 .15
Re-opening of Austrian Airlines.

Mother and Daughter A182
Walther von der Vogelweide A183 

1958, May 8   Unwmk.   Perf. 14x13½
633 A182 1.50s dark blue   .25 .15
Issued for Mother's Day.

1958, July 17   Litho. and Engr.
634 A183 1.50s multicolored   .25 .15
3rd Austrian Song Festival, Vienna, July 17-20.

Oswald Redlich — A184
Giant "E" on Map — A185 

1958, Sept. 17   Engr.
635 A184 2.40s ultramarine   .45 .15
Prof. Oswald Redlich (1858-1944), historian, birth cent.

Renner Type of 1948
1958, Nov. 12
636 A136 1.50s deep green   .45 .25
Austrian Republic, 40th anniv.

1959, Mar. 9
637 A185 2.40s emerald   .35 .20
Idea of a United Europe.

Cigarette Machine and Trademark of Tobacco Monopoly — A186
Archduke Johann — A187 

1959, May 8   Unwmk.   Perf. 13½
638 A186 2.40s dark olive bister .30 .15
Austrian tobacco monopoly, 175th anniv.

1959, May 11   Perf. 14x13½
639 A187 1.50s deep green   .25 .20
Archduke Johann of Austria, military leader and humanitarian, death cent.

Capercaillie A188
Joseph Haydn A189 

1959, May 20   Engr.
640 A188 1s rose violet   .30 .15
641 A188 1.50s blue violet   .65 .15
642 A188 2.40s dk bl green   .45 .35
643 A188 3.50s dark brown   .35 .20
      Nos. 640-643 (4)   1.75 .85
Congress of the Intl. Hunting Council, Vienna, May 20-24.

1959, May 30   Unwmk.
644 A189 1.50s violet brown   .45 .20
Joseph Haydn, composer, 150th death anniv.

Coat of Arms, Tyrol A190
Antenna, Zugspitze A191 

1959, June 13   Perf. 14x13½
645 A190 1.50s rose red   .25 .15
Fight for liberation of Tyrol, 150th anniv.

1959, June 19   Perf. 13½
646 A191 2.40s dk bl grn   .30 .15
Inauguration of Austria's relay system.

Field Ball Player A192
Orchestral Instruments A193 

1s, Runner. 1.80s, Gymnast on vaulting horse. 2s, Woman hurdler. 2.20s, Hammer thrower.

1959-70   Engr.   Perf. 14x13½
647   A192 1s lilac   .20 .15
648   A192 1.50s blue green   .50 .20
648A A192 1.80s carmine ('62)   .45 .35
648B A192 2s rose lake ('70)   .25 .15
648C A192 2.20s bluish blk ('67) .25 .15
      Nos. 647-648C (5)   1.65 1.00

1959, Aug. 19   Perf. 14x13½
649 A193 2.40s dull bl & blk   .30 .15
World tour of the Vienna Philharmonic Orchestra.

Family Fleeing over Mountains A194

1960, Apr. 7   Engr.   Perf. 13½x14
650 A194 3s Prussian green   .65 .25
WRY, July 1, 1959-June 30, 1960.

President Adolf Schärf — A195

1960, Apr. 20   Perf. 13½x14
651 A195 1.50s gray olive   .65 .15
Pres. Adolf Scharf, 70th birthday.

Young Hikers and Hostel — A196

1960, May 20   Perf. 13½x14
652 A196 1s carmine rose   .25 .15
Youth hiking; youth hostel movement.

Anton Eiselsberg — A197
Gustav Mahler — A198 

Litho. and Engr.
1960, June 20   Perf. 14x13½
653 A197 1.50s buff & dk brn   .70 .15
Dr. Anton Eiselsberg, surgeon, birth cent.

1960, July 7   Engr.
654 A198 1.50s chocolate   .70 .15
Gustav Mahler, composer, birth cent.

Jakob Prandtauer, Melk Abbey — A199
Gross Glockner Mountain Road — A200 

1960, July 16   Unwmk.
655 A199 1.50s red brown   .70 .15
Jakob Prandtauer, architect, 300th birth anniv.

1960, Aug. 3
656 A200 1.80s dark blue   .70 .50
Gross Glockner Mountain Road, 25th anniv.

Ionic Capital — A201

1960, Aug. 29   Perf. 14x13½
657 A201 3s black   1.40 .75
Europa: Idea of a United Europe.

Griffen, Carinthia A202

1960, Oct. 10   Engr.   Perf. 13½x14
658 A202 1.50s slate green   .30 .15
40th anniv. of the plebiscite which kept Carinthia with Austria.

Flame and Broken Chain — A203

1961, May 8   Unwmk.   Perf. 14x13½
659 A203 1.50s scarlet   .30 .15
Victims in Austria's fight for freedom.

First Austrian Mail Plane, 1918 — A204

1961, May 15   Perf. 13½x14
660 A204 5s violet blue   .70 .30
Airmail Phil. Exhib., LUPOSTA 1961, Vienna, May.

Austria stamps can be mounted in the Scott annually supplemented Austria album.

AUSTRIA

Transportation by Road, Rail and Waterway — A205
Mountain Mower, by Albin Egger-Lienz — A206 

Engraved and Typographed
1961, May 29   *Perf. 13½*
661 A205 3s rose red & olive   .45 .30
13th European Conference of Transportation ministers, Vienna, May 29-31.

1961, June 12   Engr.   *Perf. 13½x14*
Designs: 1.50s, The Kiss, by August von Pettenkofen. 3s, Girl, by Anton Romako. 5s, Ariadne's Triumph, by Hans Makart.

Inscriptions in Red Brown
662 A206 1s rose lake   .15 .15
663 A206 1.50s dull violet   .25 .25
664 A206 3s olive green   .75 .70
665 A206 5s blue violet   .45 .40
     Nos. 662-665 (4)   1.60 1.50
Society of Creative Artists, Künstlerhaus, Vienna, cent.

Sonnblick Mountain and Observatory A207
Mercury and Globe A208 

1961, Sept. 1   *Perf. 14x13½*
666 A207 1.80s violet blue   .40 .30
Sonnblick meteorological observatory, 75th anniv.

1961, Sept. 18
667 A208 3s black   .70 .40
Intl. Banking Congress, Vienna, Sept. 1961. English inscription listing UN financial groups.

Coal Mine Shaft — A209

Designs: 1.50s, Generator. 1.80s, Iron blast furnace. 3s, Pouring steel. 5s, Oil refinery.

1961, Sept. 15   Engr.   *Perf. 14x13½*
668 A209 1s black   .20 .15
669 A209 1.50s green   .25 .20
670 A209 1.80s dark car rose   .55 .40
671 A209 3s bright lilac   .70 .55
672 A209 5s blue   .90 .70
     Nos. 668-672 (5)   2.60 2.00
15th anniversary of nationalized industry.

Arms of Burgenland A210
Franz Liszt A211 

1961, Oct. 9   Engr. and Litho.
673 A210 1.50s blk, yel & dk red   .35 .15
Burgenland as part of the Austrian Republic, 40th anniv.

1961, Oct. 20   Engr.
674 A211 3s dark brown   .55 .40
Franz Liszt, composer, 150th birth anniv.

Parliament A212

1961, Dec. 18   *Perf. 13½x14*
675 A212 1s brown   .20 .15
Austrian Bureau of Budget, 200th anniv.

Kaprun-Mooserboden Reservoir — A213

Hydroelectric Power Plants: 1.50s, Ybbs-Persenbeug dam and locks. 1.80s, Lünersee dam and reservoir. 3s, Grossraming dam. 4s, Bisamberg transformer plant. 6.40s, St. Andrä power plant.

1962, Mar. 26   Unwmk.
676 A213 1s violet blue   .15 .15
677 A213 1.50s red lilac   .25 .20
678 A213 1.80s green   .40 .35
679 A213 3s brown   .40 .35
680 A213 4s rose red   .40 .35
681 A213 6.40s gray   1.25 1.10
     Nos. 676-681 (6)   2.85 2.50
Nationalization of the electric power industry, 15th anniv.

Johann Nestroy A214
Friedrich Gauermann A215 

1962, May 25   *Perf. 14x13½*
682 A214 1s violet   .20 .15
Johann Nepomuk Nestroy, Viennese playwright, author and actor, death cent.

1962, July 6   Engr.
683 A215 1.50s intense blue   .20 .15
Friedrich Gauermann (1807-1862), landscape painter, death cent.

Scout Emblem and Handshake — A216

1962, Oct. 5
684 A216 1.50s dark green   .35 .20
Austria's Boy Scouts, 50th anniv.

Lowlands Forest A217

1.50s, Deciduous forest. 3s, Fir & larch forest.

1962, Oct. 12   *Perf. 13½x14*
685 A217 1s greenish gray   .20 .15
686 A217 1.50s reddish brown   .25 .25
687 A217 3s dk slate green   .90 .70
     Nos. 685-687 (3)   1.35 1.10

Buildings Types of 1957-61

Designs: 30g, City Hall, Vienna. 40g, Porcia Castle, Spittal on the Drau. 60g, Tanners' Tower, Wels. 70g, Residence Fountain, Salzburg. 80g, Old farmhouse, Pinzgau. 1s, Romanesque columns, Millstatt Abbey. 1.20s, Kornmesser House, Bruck on the Mur. 1.30s, Schatten Castle, Feldkirch, Vorarlberg. 2s, Dragon Fountain, Klagenfurt. 2.20s, Beethoven House, Vienna. 2.50s, Danube Bridge, Linz. 3s, Swiss Gate, Vienna. 3.50s, Esterhazy Palace, Eisenstadt. 8s, City Hall, Steyr. 20s, Melk Abbey.

1962-70   Litho.   *Perf. 14x13½*
     Size: 20x25mm
688 A176 30g greenish gray   .50 .15
689 A176 40g rose red   .15 .15
690 A176 60g violet brown   .35 .15
691 A176 70g dark blue   .25 .15
692 A176 80g yellow brown   .35 .15
693 A176 1s brown ('70)   .20 .15
694 A176 1.20s red lilac   .40 .15
695 A176 1.30s green ('67)   .15 .15
696 A176 2s dk blue ('68)   .25 .15
697 A176 2.20s green   1.40 .15
698 A176 2.50s violet   .80 .15
699 A176 3s bright blue   .65 .15
700 A176 3.50s rose carmine   .80 .15
701 A176 8s claret ('65)   1.00 .15
     Perf. 13½
     Size: 28x36½mm
702 A177 20s rose claret ('63)   2.50 .35
     Nos. 688-702 (15)   9.75 2.45
Values for Nos. 688-702 are for stamps on white paper. Some denominations also come on grayish paper with yellowish gum.

Electric Locomotive and Train of 1837 A218

Lithographed and Engraved
1962, Nov. 9   *Perf. 13½x14*
703 A218 3s buff & black   .90 .40
125th anniversary of Austrian railroads.

Postilions and Postal Clerk, 1863 — A219
Hermann Bahr — A220 

1963, May 7   Photo.   *Perf. 14x13½*
704 A219 3s dk brn & citron   .70 .40
First Intl. Postal Conference, Paris, cent.

Lithographed and Engraved
1963, July 19   *Perf. 14x13½*
705 A220 1.50s blue & black   .25 .15
Centenary of birth of Hermann Bahr, poet.

St. Florian Statue, Kefermarkt, Contemporary and Old Fire Engines — A221

1963, Aug. 30   Unwmk.
706 A221 1.50s brt rose & blk   .25 .15
Austrian volunteer fire brigades, cent.

Factory, Flag and "ÖGB" on Map of Austria A222

1963, Sept. 23   Litho.   *Perf. 13½x14*
707 A222 1.50s gray, red & dk brn   .25 .15
5th Congress of the Austrian Trade Union Federation (ÖGB), Sept. 23-28.

Arms of Austria and Tyrol — A223

1963, Sept. 27   Unwmk.
708 A223 1.50s tan, blk, red & yel   .25 .15
Tyrol's union with Austria, 600th anniv.

Prince Eugene of Savoy — A224
Centenary Emblem — A225 

1963, Oct. 18   Engr.   *Perf. 14x13½*
709 A224 1.50s violet   .25 .15
Prince Eugene of Savoy (1663-1736), Austrian general, 300th birth anniv.

1963, Oct. 25   Engr. and Photo.
710 A225 3s blk, sil & red   .50 .20
Intl. Red Cross, cent.

AUSTRIA

Slalom A226

Sports: 1.20s, Biathlon (skier with rifle). 1.50s, Ski jump. 1.80s, Women's figure skating. 2.20s, Ice hockey. 3s, Tobogganing. 4s, Bobsledding.

Photo. and Engr.
1963, Nov. 11 Perf. 13½x14
711	A226	1s multi	.15	.15
712	A226	1.20s multi	.15	.15
713	A226	1.50s multi	.20	.15
714	A226	1.80s multi	.25	.15
715	A226	2.20s multi	.40	.25
716	A226	3s multi	.30	.20
717	A226	4s multi	.55	.35
		Nos. 711-717 (7)	2.00	1.40

9th Winter Olympic Games, Innsbruck, Jan. 29-Feb. 9, 1964.

Baroque Creche by Josef Thaddäus Stammel — A227

1963, Nov. 29 Engr. Perf. 14x13½
718 A227 2s dark Prus green .25 .15

Flowers A228

1964, Apr. 17 Litho. Perf. 14
719	A228	1s Nasturtium	.15	.15
720	A228	1.50s Peony	.20	.15
721	A228	1.80s Clematis	.25	.15
722	A228	2.20s Dahlia	.35	.20
723	A228	3s Morning glory	.40	.25
724	A228	4s Hollyhock	.50	.35
		Nos. 719-724 (6)	1.85	1.25

Vienna Intl. Garden Show, Apr. 16-Oct. 11.

St. Mary Magdalene and Apostle — A229

Pallas Athena and National Council Chamber — A230

1964, May 21 Engr. Perf. 13½
725 A229 1.50s bluish black .25 .15

Romanesque art in Austria. The 12th century stained-glass window is from the Weitensfeld Church, the bust of the Apostle from the portal of St. Stephen's Cathedral, Vienna.

Engr. and Litho.
1964, May 25 Perf. 14x13½
726 A230 1.80s black & emer .30 .15

2nd Parliamentary and Scientific Conf., Vienna.

The Kiss, by Gustav Klimt A231

1964, June 5 Litho. Perf. 13½
727 A231 3s multicolored .35 .25

Re-opening of the Vienna Secession, a museum devoted to early 20th century art (art nouveau).

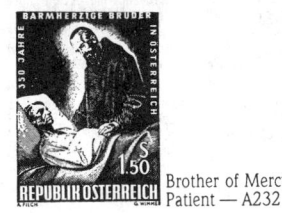

Brother of Mercy and Patient — A232

1964, June 11 Engr. Perf. 14x13½
728 A232 1.50s dark blue .25 .15

Brothers of Mercy in Austria, 350th anniv.

"Bringing the News of Victory at Kunersdorf" by Bernardo Bellotto A233

"The Post in Art": 1.20s, Changing Horses at Relay Station, by Julius Hörmann. 1.50s, The Honeymoon Trip, by Moritz von Schwind. 1.80s, After the Rain, by Ignaz Raffalt. 2.20s, Mailcoach in the Mountains, by Adam Klein. 3s, Changing Horses at Bavarian Border, by Friedrich Gauermann. 4s, Postal Sleigh (Truck) in the Mountains, by Adalbert Pilch. 6.40s, Saalbach Post Office, by Adalbert Pilch.

1964, June 15 Perf. 13½x14
729	A233	1s rose claret	.15	.15
730	A233	1.20s sepia	.15	.15
731	A233	1.50s violet blue	.15	.15
732	A233	1.80s brt violet	.15	.15
733	A233	2.20s black	.25	.15
734	A233	3s dl car rose	.30	.20
735	A233	4s slate green	.35	.20
736	A233	6.40s dull claret	.80	.45
		Nos. 729-736 (8)	2.25	1.60

15th UPU Cong., Vienna, May-June 1964.

Workers — A234

1964, Sept. 4 Perf. 14x13½
737 A234 1s black .15 .15

Centenary of Austrian Labor Movement.

Common Design Types pictured following the introduction.

Europa Issue, 1964
Common Design Type
1964, Sept. 14 Litho. Perf. 12
Size: 21x36mm
738 CD7 3s dark blue .50 .15

Emblem of Radio Austria and Transistor Radio Panel A235

1964, Oct. 1 Photo. Perf. 13½
739 A235 1s black brn & red .15 .15

Forty years of Radio Austria.

A236 A237

Litho. and Engr.
1964, Oct. 12 Perf. 14x13½
740 A236 1.50s Old printing press .15 .15

6th Congress of the Intl. Graphic Federation, Vienna, Oct. 12-17.

Typo. and Engr.
1965, Apr. 20 Perf. 12
741 A237 1.50s bluish black .20 .15

Pres. Adolf Schärf and Scharf Student Center.

Dr. Adolf Schärf (1890-1965), Pres. of Austria (1957-65).

Ruins and New Buildings — A238

1965, Apr. 27 Engr. Perf. 14x13½
742 A238 1.80s carmine lake .20 .15

Twenty years of reconstruction.

Oldest Seal of Vienna University — A239

St. George, 16th Century Wood Sculpture — A240

Photo. and Engr.
1965, May 10 Perf. 14x13½
743 A239 3s gold & red .35 .20

University of Vienna, 600th anniv.

1965, May 17 Engr.
744 A240 1.80s bluish black .25 .15

Art of the Danube Art School, 1490-1540, exhibition, May-Oct. 1965. The stamp background shows an engraving by Albrecht Altdorfer.

ITU Emblem, Telegraph Key and TV Antenna — A241

Ferdinand Raimund — A242

1965, May 17 Unwmk.
745 A241 3s violet blue .35 .20

ITU, cent.

1965 Engr. Perf. 14x13½

Portraits: No. 746, Dr. Ignaz Philipp Semmelweis. No. 747, Bertha von Suttner. No. 749, Ferdinand Georg Waldmüller.

746	A242	1.50s violet	.30	.15
747	A242	1.50s bluish black	.30	.15
748	A242	3s dark brown	.55	.15
749	A242	3s greenish blk	.55	.20
		Nos. 746-749 (4)	1.70	.65

Semmelweis (1818-65), who discovered the cause of puerperal fever and introduced antisepsis into obstetrics (#746). 60th anniv. of the awarding of the Nobel Prize for Peace to von Suttner (1843-1914), pacifist and author (#747). Raimund (1790-1836), actor and playwright (#748). Waldmüller (1793-1865), painter (#749).

Issue dates: No. 746, Aug. 13; No. 747, Dec. 1; No. 748, June 1; No. 749, Aug. 23.

Dancers with Tambourines A243

Red Cross and Strip of Gauze A244

Design: 1.50s, Male gymnasts with practice bars.

1965, July 20 Photo. and Engr.
| 750 | A243 | 1.50s gray & black | .20 | .15 |
| 751 | A243 | 3s bister & blk | .35 | .25 |

4th Gymnaestrada, intl. athletic meet, Vienna, July 20-24.

1965, Oct. 1 Litho. Perf. 14x13½
752 A244 3s black & red .35 .15

20th Intl. Red Cross Conference, Vienna.

Austrian Flag and Eagle with Mural Crown — A245

Austrian Flag, UN Headquarters and Emblem — A246

1965, Oct. 7 Photo. and Engr.
753 A245 1.50s gold, red & blk .15 .15

50th anniv. of the Union of Austrian Towns.

Lithographed and Engraved
1965, Oct. 25 Unwmk. Perf. 12
754 A246 3s blk, brt bl & red .45 .15

Austria's admission to the UN, 10th anniv.

AUSTRIA

University of Technology, Vienna — A247

1965, Nov. 8   Engr.   Perf. 13½x14
755 A247 1.50s violet   .15   .15
Vienna University of Technology, 150th anniv.

Map of Austria with Postal Zone Numbers — A248

1966, Jan. 14   Photo.   Perf. 12
756 A248 1.50s yel, red & blk   .15   .15
Introduction of postal zone numbers, Jan. 1, 1966.

PTT Building, Emblem and Churches of Sts. Maria Rotunda and Barbara A249

Maria von Ebner Eschenbach A250

Lithographed and Engraved
1966, Mar. 4   Perf. 14x13½
757 A249 1.50s blk, *dull yellow*   .15   .15
Headquarters of the Post and Telegraph Administration, cent.

1966, Mar. 11   Engr.
758 A250 3s plum   .35   .15
50th death anniv. of Maria von Ebner Eschenbach (1830-1916), novelist and poet.

Ferris Wheel, Prater — A251

1966, Apr. 19   Engr.   Perf. 14x13½
759 A251 1.50s slate green   .15   .15
Opening of the Prater (park), Vienna, to the public by Emperor Joseph II, 200th anniv.

A252    A253

1966, May 6   Unwmk.   Perf. 12
760 A252 3s dark brown   .35   .15
Josef Hoffmann (1870-1956), architect, 10th death anniv.

Photo. and Engr.
1966, May 27   Perf. 14
761 A253 1.50s Wiener Neustadt Arms   .15   .15
Wiener Neustadt Art Exhib., centered around the time and person of Frederick III (1440-93).

Austrian Eagle and Emblem of National Bank A254

1966, May 27   Perf. 14
762 A254 3s gray grn, dk brn & dk green .35   .15
Austrian National Bank, 150th anniv.

Puppy — A255    A256

Litho. and Engr.
1966, June 16   Perf. 12
763 A255 1.80s yellow & black   .25   .15
120th anniv. of the Vienna Humane Society.

1966, Aug. 17   Litho.   Perf. 13½
Alpine Flowers: 1.50s, Columbine. 1.80s, Turk's cap. 2.20s, Wulfenia carinthiaca. 3s, Globeflowers. 4s, Fire lily. 5s, Pasqueflower.

Flowers in Natural Colors
764 A256 1.50s dark blue   .15   .15
765 A256 1.80s dark blue   .25   .15
766 A256 2.20s dark blue   .35   .20
767 A256 3s dark blue   .50   .30
768 A256 4s dark blue   .50   .35
769 A256 5s dark blue   .50   .35
  Nos. 764-769 (6)   2.25 1.50

Fair Building A257

1966, Aug. 26   Engr.   Perf. 13½x13
770 A257 3s violet blue   .35   .15
First International Fair at Wels.

Peter Anich, Map, Globe and Books — A258

Sick Worker and Health Emblem — A259

1966, Sept. 1   Perf. 14x13½
771 A258 1.80s black   .20   .15
Peter Anich (1723-1766), Tirolean cartographer and farmer, 200th death anniv.

1966, Sept. 19   Engr. and Litho.
772 A259 3s black & vermilion   .35   .15
15th Occupational Medicine Congress, Vienna, Sept. 19-24.

Theater Collection: "Eunuchus" by Terence from a 1496 Edition A260

Designs: 1.80s, Map Collection: Title page of Geographia Blavania (Cronus, Hercules and celestial sphere). 2.20s, Picture Archive and Portrait Collection: View of Old Vienna after a watercolor by Anton Stutzinger. 3s, Manuscript Collection: Illustration from the 15th century "Livre du Cuer d'Amours Espris" of the Duke René d'Anjou.

Photogravure and Engraved
1966, Sept. 28   Perf. 13½x14
773 A260 1.50s multicolored   .15   .15
774 A260 1.80s multicolored   .20   .15
775 A260 2.20s multicolored   .25   .20
776 A260 3s multicolored   .30   .20
  Nos. 773-776 (4)   .90   .70
Austrian National Library.

Young Girl A261   Strawberries A262

Litho. and Engr.
1966, Oct. 3   Perf. 14x13½
777 A261 3s light blue & black   .35   .15
"Save the Child" society, 10th anniv.

1966, Nov. 25   Photo.   Perf. 13½x13
778 A262 50g shown   .20   .15
779 A262 1s Grapes   .20   .15
780 A262 1.50s Apple   .20   .15
781 A262 1.80s Blackberries   .25   .20
782 A262 2.20s Apricots   .25   .20
783 A262 3s Cherries   .35   .25
  Nos. 778-783 (6)   1.45 1.10

Coat of Arms of University of Linz — A263

Ice Skater, 1866 — A264

Photo. and Engr.
1966, Dec. 9   Perf. 14x13½
784 A263 3s multi   .35   .15
Inauguration of the University of Linz, Oct. 8, 1966.

Photo. and Engr.
1967, Feb. 3   Perf. 14x13½
785 A264 3s pale bl & dk bl   .35   .15
Centenary of Vienna Ice Skating Club.

Ballet Dancer — A265    Karl Schönherr — A266

1967, Feb. 15   Engr.   Perf. 11½x12
786 A265 3s deep claret   .35   .15
  a. Perf. 12   1.25 1.10
"Blue Danube" waltz by Johann Strauss, cent.

1967, Feb. 24   Engr.   Perf. 14x13½
787 A266 3s gray brown   .35   .15
Dr. Karl Schönherr (1867-1943), poet, playwright and physician.

Ice Hockey Goalkeeper A267

Photogravure and Engraved
1967, Mar. 17   Perf. 13½x14
788 A267 3s pale grn & dk bl   .35   .15
Ice Hockey Championships, Vienna, Mar. 18-29.

Violin, Organ and Laurel — A268

1967, Mar. 28   Engr.   Perf. 13½
789 A268 3.50s indigo   .40   .15
Vienna Philharmonic Orchestra, 125th anniv.

Motherhood, Watercolor by Peter Fendi A269

1967, Apr. 28   Litho.   Perf. 14
790 A269 2s multicolored   .25   .15
Mother's Day.

Gothic Mantle Madonna — A270

1967, May 19   Engr.   Perf. 13½x14
791 A270 3s slate   .35   .15
"Austrian Gothic," art exhibition, Krems, 1967. The Gothic wood carving is from Frauenstein in Upper Austria.

Medieval Gold Cross — A271

Swan, Tapestry by Oscar Kokoschka — A272

AUSTRIA

Litho. and Engr.

1967, June 9   **Perf. 13½**
792 A271 3.50s Prus grn & multi   .40 .15
Salzburg Treasure Chamber; exhibition at Salzburg Cathedral, June 12-Sept. 15.

1967, June 9   **Photo.**
793 A272 2s multicolored   .25 .15
Nibelungen District Art Exhibition, Pöchlarn, celebrating the 700th anniversary of Pöchlarn as a city. The design is from the border of the Amor and Psyche tapestry at the Salzburg Festival Theater.

View and Arms of Vienna — A273

Engraved and Photogravure

1967, June 12   **Perf. 13x13½**
794 A273 3s black & red   .35 .15
10th Europa Talks, "Science and Society in Europe," Vienna, June 13-17.

Prize Bull "Mucki" A274

1967, Aug. 28   **Engr.**   **Perf. 13½**
795 A274 2s deep claret   .35 .15
Centenary of the Ried Festival and the Agricultural Fair.

Potato Beetle — A275

Engraved and Photogravure

1967, Aug. 29   **Perf. 13½x14**
796 A275 3s black & multi   .35 .15
6th Intl. Congress for Plant Protection, Vienna.

First Locomotive Used on Brenner Pass — A276

1967, Sept. 23   **Photo.**   **Perf. 12**
797 A276 3.50s tan & slate grn   .45 .15
Centenary of railroad over Brenner Pass.

Christ in Glory — A277

1967, Oct. 9   **Perf. 13½**
798 A277 2s multicolored   .25 .15
Restoration of the Romanesque (11th century) frescoes in the Lambach monastery church.

Main Gate to Fair, Prater, Vienna — A278

1967, Oct. 24   **Photo.**   **Perf. 13½x14**
799 A278 2s choc & buff   .25 .15
Congress of Intl. Trade Fairs, Vienna, Oct., 1967.

Medal Showing Minerva and Art Symbols A279

Frankfurt Medal for Reformation, 1717 A280

Litho. & Engr.

1967, Oct. 25   **Perf. 13½**
800 A279 2s dk brn, dk bl & yel   .25 .15
Vienna Academy of Fine Arts, 275th anniv. The medal was designed by Georg Raphael Donner (1693-1741) and is awarded as an artist's prize.

1967, Oct. 31   **Engr.**   **Perf. 14x13½**
801 A280 3.50s blue black   .40 .15
450th anniversary of the Reformation.

Mountain Range and Stone Pines A281

1967, Nov. 7   **Perf. 13½**
802 A281 3.50s green   .40 .15
Centenary of academic study of forestry.

Land Survey Monument, 1770 — A282

St. Leopold, Window, Heiligenkreuz Abbey — A283

1967, Nov. 7   **Photo.**
803 A282 2s olive black   .25 .15
150th anniversary of official land records.

1967, Nov. 15   **Engr. & Photo.**
804 A283 1.80s multicolored   .25 .15
Margrave Leopold III (1075-1136), patron saint of Austria.

Tragic Mask and Violin — A284

Nativity from 15th Century Altar — A285

1967, Nov. 17   **Perf. 13½**
805 A284 3.50s bluish lil & blk   .40 .15
Academy of Music and Dramatic Art, 150th anniv.

1967, Nov. 27   **Engr.**   **Perf. 14x13½**
806 A285 2s green   .25 .15
Christmas. The design shows the late Gothic carved center panel of the altar in St. John's Chapel in Nonnberg Convent, Salzburg.

Innsbruck Stadium, Alps and FISU Emblem — A286

Camillo Sitte — A287

1968, Jan. 22   **Engr.**   **Perf. 13½**
807 A286 2s dark blue   .25 .15
Winter University Games under the auspices of FISU (Fédération Internationale du Sport Universitaire), Innsbruck, Jan. 21-28.

1968, Apr. 17   **Perf. 13½**
808 A287 2s black brown   .25 .15
125th birth anniv. of Camillo Sitte (1843-1903), architect and city planner.

Mother and Child — A288

1968, May 7
809 A288 2s slate green   .25 .15
Mother's Day.

Cup and Serpent Emblem — A289

1968, May 7   **Photo.**
810 A289 3.50s dp plum, gray & gold   .40 .15
Bicentenary of the Veterinary College.

Bride with Lace Veil — A290

1968, May 24   **Engr.**   **Perf. 12**
811 A290 3.50s blue black   .40 .15
Embroidery industry of Vorarlberg, cent.

Horse Race A291

1968, June 4   **Perf. 13½**
812 A291 3.50s sepia   .40 .20
Centenary of horse racing at Freudenau, Vienna.

Dr. Karl Landsteiner A292

Peter Rosegger A293

1968, June 14   **Perf. 14x13½**
813 A292 3.50s dark blue   .40 .20
Birth cent. of Dr. Karl Landsteiner (1868-1943), pathologist, discoverer of the four main human blood types.

1968, June 26
814 A293 2s slate green   .25 .15
50th death anniv. of Peter Rosegger (1843-1918), poet and writer.

Angelica Kauffmann, Self-portrait A294

Bronze Statue of Young Man, 1st Century B.C. A295

1968, July 15   **Engr.**   **Perf. 14x13½**
815 A294 2s intense black   .25 .15
"Angelica Kauffmann and her Contemporaries," art exhibitions, Bregenz, July 28-Oct. 13, and Vienna, Oct. 22, 1968-Jan. 6, 1969.

1968, July 15   **Litho. & Engr.**
816 A295 2s grnsh gray & blk   .25 .15
20 years of excavations on Magdalene Mountain, Carinthia.

Bishop, Romanesque Bas-relief — A296

1968, Sept. 20   **Engr.**   **Perf. 14x13½**
817 A296 2s blue gray   .25 .15
Graz-Seckau Bishopric, 750th anniv.

AUSTRIA

Koloman
Moser — A297

Human Rights
Flame — A298

Engr. & Photo.
1968, Oct. 18   Perf. 12
818 A297 2s black brn & ver   .25 .15
50th death anniv. of Koloman Moser (1868-1918), stamp designer and painter.

1968, Oct. 18   Photo.   Perf. 14x13½
819 A298 1.50s gray, dp car & dk
           green   .30 .15
International Human Rights Year.

A299   A300

Designs: No. 820, Pres. Karl Renner and States' arms. No. 821, Coats of arms of Austria and Austrian states. No. 822, Article I of Austrian Constitution and States' coats of arms.

Engr. & Photo.
1968, Nov. 11   Perf. 13½
820 A299 2s black & multi   .35 .30
821 A299 2s black & multi   .35 .30
822 A299 2s black & multi   .35 .30
       Nos. 820-822 (3)   1.05 .90
50th anniversary of Republic of Austria.

1968, Nov. 29   Engr.   Perf. 14x13½
Crèche, Memorial Chapel, Oberndorf-Salzburg.
823 A300 2s slate green   .25 .15
Christmas; 150th anniv. of "Silent Night, Holy Night" hymn.

Angels, from Last Judgment by Troger (Röhrenbach-Greillenstein Chapel) — A301

Baroque Frescoes: No. 825, Vanquished Demons, by Paul Troger, Altenburg Abbey. No. 826, Sts. Peter and Paul, by Troger, Melk Abbey. No. 827, The Glorification of Mary, by Franz Anton Maulpertsch, Maria Treu Church, Vienna. No. 828, St. Leopold Carried into Heaven, by Maulpertsch, Ebenfurth Castle Chapel. No. 829, Symbolic figures from The Triumph of Apollo, by Maulpertsch, Halbthurn Castle.

Engr. & Photo.
1968, Dec. 11   Perf. 13½x14
824 A301 2s multicolored   .30 .30
825 A301 2s multicolored   .30 .30
826 A301 2s multicolored   .30 .30
827 A301 2s multicolored   .30 .30
828 A301 2s multicolored   .30 .30
829 A301 2s multicolored   .30 .30
       Nos. 824-829 (6)   1.80 1.80

St. Stephen — A302

Statues in St. Stephen's Cathedral, Vienna: No. 831, St. Paul. No. 832, Mantle Madonna. No. 833, St. Christopher. No. 834, St. George and the Dragon. No. 835, St. Sebastian.

1969, Jan. 28   Engr.   Perf. 13½
830 A302 2s black   .30 .30
831 A302 2s rose claret   .30 .30
832 A302 2s gray violet   .30 .30
833 A302 2s slate blue   .30 .30
834 A302 2s slate green   .30 .30
835 A302 2s dk red brn   .30 .30
       Nos. 830-835 (6)   1.80 1.80
500th anniversary of Diocese of Vienna.

Parliament
and Pallas
Athena
Fountain,
Vienna
A303

1969, Apr. 8   Engr.   Perf. 13½
836 A303 2s greenish black   .25 .15
Interparliamentary Union Conf., Vienna, 4/7-13.

Europa Issue, 1969
Common Design Type
1969, Apr. 28   Photo.   Perf. 12
837 CD12 2s gray grn, brick red &
           blue   .25 .15

Council of Europe
Emblem — A304

1969, May 5
838 A304 3.50s gray, ultra, blk & yel .45 .25
20th anniversary of Council of Europe.

Frontier
Guards — A305

Engr. & Photo.
1969, May 14   Perf. 12
839 A305 2s sepia & red   .25 .15
Austrian Federal Army.

Don Giovanni, by
Mozart — A306

Cent. of Vienna Opera House: a, Don Giovanni, Mozart. b, Magic Flute, Mozart. c, Fidelio, Beethoven. d, Lohengrin, Wagner. e, Don Carlos, Verdi. f, Carmen, Bizet. g, Rosencavalier, Richard Strauss. h, Swan Lake, Ballet by Tchaikovsky.

1969, May 23   Perf. 13½
840 A306 Sheet of 8   4.00 4.00
a.-h.   2s, any single   .35 .35
Centenary of Vienna Opera House.
No. 840 contains 8 stamps arranged around gold and red center label showing Opera House. Printed in sheets containing 4 Nos. 840 with wide gutters between.

A307   A308

Gothic armor of Maximilian I.

1969, June 4   Engr.
841 A307 2s bluish black   .25 .15
Emperor Maximilian I Exhibition, Innsbruck, May 30-Oct. 5.

1969, June 16   Photo.   Perf. 13½
Oldest Municipal Seal of Vienna.
842 A308 2s tan, red & black   .25 .15
19th Cong. of the Intl. Org. of Municipalities, Vienna, June 1969.

A309   A310

Girl's head and village house.

Engraved and Photogravure
1969, June 16   Perf. 13½x14
843 A309 2s yel grn & sepia   .25 .15
20th anniv. of the Children's Village Movement in Austria (SOS Villages).

1969, Aug. 22   Photo.   Perf. 13x13½
Hands holding wrench, and UN emblem.
844 A310 2s deep green   .25 .15
ILO, 50th anniv.

A311   A312

Austria's flag and shield circling the world.

Engraved and Lithographed
1969, Aug. 22   Perf. 14x13½
845 A311 3.50s slate & red   .40 .20
Year of Austrians Living Abroad, 1969.

Engraved and Photogravure
1969, Sept. 26   Perf. 13½
Etchings: No. 846, Young Hare, by Dürer. No. 847, El Cid Killing a Bull, by Francisco de Goya. No. 848, Madonna with the Pomegranate, by Raphael. No. 849, The Painter, by Peter Brueghel. No. 850, Rubens' Son Nicolas, by Rubens. No. 851, Self-portrait, by Rembrandt. No. 852, Lady Reading, by Francois Guerin. No. 853, Wife of the Artist, by Egon Schiele.

Gray Frame, Buff Background
846 A312 2s black & brown   .30 .30
847 A312 2s black   .30 .30
848 A312 2s black   .30 .30
849 A312 2s black   .30 .30
850 A312 2s black & salmon   .30 .30
851 A312 2s black   .30 .30
852 A312 2s black & salmon   .30 .30
853 A312 2s black   .30 .30
       Nos. 846-853 (8)   2.40 2.40
Etching collection in the Albertina, Vienna, 200th anniv.

President Franz
Jonas — A313

1969, Oct. 3
854 A313 2s gray & vio blue   .25 .15
70th birthday of Franz Jonas, Austrian Pres.

Post Horn,
Globe and
Lightning
A314

1969, Oct. 17   Perf. 13½x14
855 A314 2s multicolored   .25 .15
Union of Postal and Telegraph employees, 50th anniv.

Savings Box,
about 1450
A315

Madonna, by
Albin Egger-Lienz
A316

1969, Oct. 31   Photo.   Perf. 13x13½
856 A315 2s silver & slate green .25 .15
The importance of savings.

Engr. & Photo.
1969, Nov. 24   Perf. 12
857 A316 2s dp claret & pale yel .25 .15
Christmas.

Josef
Schöffel — A317

St. Klemens M.
Hofbauer — A318

1970, Feb. 6   Engr.   Perf. 14x13½
858 A317 2s dull purple   .25 .15
60th death anniv. of Josef Schöffel, (1832-1910), who saved the Vienna Woods.

Engraved and Photogravure
1970, Mar. 13   Perf. 14x13½
859 A318 2s dk brn & lt tan   .25 .15
150th death anniv. St. Klemens Maria Hofbauer (1751-1820); Redemptorist preacher in Poland and Austria, canonized in 1909.

AUSTRIA

Chancellor Leopold Figl
A319

Belvedere Palace, Vienna
A320

1970, Apr. 27   Engr.   Perf. 13½
860 A319 2s dark olive gray   .25 .15
861 A320 2s dark rose brown   .25 .15
25th anniversary of Second Republic.

A321   A322

1970, May 19   Engr.   Perf. 13½
862 A321 2s Krimml waterfalls   .30 .15
European Nature Conservation Year, 1970.

Litho. & Engr.
1970, June 5   Perf. 13½
St. Leopold on oldest seal of Innsbruck University.
863 A322 2s red & black   .30 .15
Leopold Franzens University, Innsbruck, 300th anniv.

Organ, Great Hall, Music Academy — A323

Photo. & Engr.
1970, June 5   Perf. 14
864 A323 2s gold & deep claret   .25 .15
Vienna Music Academy Building, cent.

Tower Clock, 1450-1550
A324

The Beggar Student, by Carl Millöcker
A325

Old Clocks from Vienna Horological Museum: #866, Lyre clock, 1790-1815. #867, Pendant clock 1600-50. #868, Pendant watch, 1800-30. #869, Bracket clock, 1720-60. #870, French column clock, 1820-50.

1970
865 A324 1.50s buff & sepia   .25 .25
866 A324 1.50s greenish & grn   .25 .25
867 A324 2s pale bl & dk bl   .30 .30
868 A324 2s pale rose & lake   .30 .30
869 A324 3.50s buff & brown   .50 .50
870 A324 3.50s pale lil & brn vio   .50 .50
  Nos. 865-870 (6)   2.10 2.10
Issued: #865, 867, 869, 6/22; others, 10/23.

1970   Photo & Engr.   Perf. 13½
Operettas: No. 872, Fledermaus, by Johann Strauss. No. 873, The Dream Waltz, by Oscar Strauss. No. 874, The Bird Seller, by Carl Zeller. No. 875, The Merry Widow, by Franz Lehar. No. 876, Two Hearts in Three-quarter Time, by Robert Stolz.
871 A325 1.50s pale grn & grn   .25 .25
872 A325 1.50s yel & vio blue   .25 .25
873 A325 2s pale rose & vio brn   .30 .30
874 A325 2s pale grn & sep   .30 .30
875 A325 3.50s pale bl & ind   .50 .50
876 A325 3.50s beige & slate   .50 .50
  Nos. 871-876 (6)   2.10 2.10
Issued: #871, 873, 875, 7/3; others 9/11.

Bregenz Festival Stage — A326

1970, July 23   Photo.
877 A326 3.50s dark blue & buff   .40 .20
25th anniversary of Bregenz Festival.

Salzburg Festival Emblem — A327

1970, July 27   Perf. 14
878 A327 3.50s blk, red, gold & gray   .40 .20
50th anniversary of Salzburg Festival.

A328   A329

1970, Aug. 31   Engr.
879 A328 3.50s dark gray   .45 .20
13th General Assembly of the World Veterans Federation, Aug. 28-Sept. 4. The head of St. John is from a sculpture showing the Agony in the Garden in the chapel of the Parish Church in Ried. It is attributed to Thomas Schwanthaler (1634-1702).

1970, Sept. 16   Perf. 14x13½
880 A329 2s chocolate   .25 .15
Thomas Koschat (1845-1914), Carinthian composer of songs.

Mountain Scene
A330

1970, Sept. 16   Photo.   Perf. 14x13½
881 A330 2s vio bl & pink   .25 .15
Hiking and mountaineering in Austria.

Alfred Cossmann
A331

Arms of Carinthia
A332

1970, Oct. 2   Engr.   Perf. 14x13½
882 A331 2s dark brown   .25 .15
Alfred Cossmann (1870-1951), engraver.

1970, Oct. 2   Photo. & Engr.   Perf. 14
883 A332 2s ol, red, gold, blk & sil   .25 .15
Carinthian plebiscite, 50th anniversary.

UN Emblem — A333

1970, Oct. 23   Litho.   Perf. 14x13½
884 A333 3.50s lt blue & blk   .50 .20
25th anniversary of the United Nations.

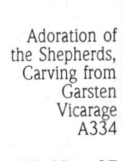

Adoration of the Shepherds, Carving from Garsten Vicarage
A334

1970, Nov. 27   Engr.   Perf. 13½x14
885 A334 2s dk violet blue   .25 .15
Christmas.

Karl Renner — A335

Beethoven, by Georg Waldmüller — A336

1970, Dec. 14   Engr.   Perf. 14x13½
886 A335 2s deep claret   .25 .15
Karl Renner (1870-1950), Austrian Pres., birth cent.

1970, Dec. 16   Photo. & Engr.   Perf. 13½
887 A336 3.50s black & buff   .50 .20
Ludwig van Beethoven (1770-1827), composer, birth bicentenary.

Enrica Handel-Mazzetti
A337

1971, Jan. 11   Engr.   Perf. 14x13½
888 A337 2s sepia   .25 .15
Birth cent. of Enrica von Handel-Mazzetti (1871-1955), novelist and poet.

"Watch Out for Kinder!"
A338

1971, Feb. 18   Photo.   Perf. 13½
889 A338 2s blk, red brn & brt grn   .25 .15
Traffic safety.

Saltcellar, by Benvenuto Cellini
A339

Art Treasures: 1.50s, Covered vessel, made of prase, gold and precious stones, Florentine, 1580. 2s, Emperor Joseph I, ivory statue by Matthias Steinle, 1693.

Photo. & Engr.
1971, Mar. 22   Perf. 14
890 A339 1.50s gray & slate grn   .20 .15
891 A339 2s gray & deep plum   .25 .20
892 A339 3.50s gray, blk & bister   .55 .35
  Nos. 890-892 (3)   1.00 .70

Emblem of Austrian Wholesalers' Organization
A340

1971, Apr. 16   Photo.   Perf. 13½
893 A340 3.50s multicolored   .45 .20
Intl. Chamber of Commerce, 23rd Congress, Vienna, Apr. 17-23.

Jacopo de Strada, by Titian — A341

Paintings in Vienna Museum: 2s, Village Feast, by Peter Brueghel, the Elder. 3.50s, Young Venetian Woman, by Albrecht Dürer.

1971, May 6   Engr.   Perf. 13½
894 A341 1.50s rose lake   .25 .15
895 A341 2s greenish black   .25 .20
896 A341 3.50s deep brown   .50 .35
  Nos. 894-896 (3)   1.00 .70

Seal of Paulus of Franchenfordia, 1380 — A342

Photo. & Engr.
1971, May 6   Perf. 13½x14
897 A342 3.50s dk brn & bister   .40 .20
Congress commemorating the centenary of the Austrian Notaries' Statute, May 5-8.

AUSTRIA

St. Matthew — A343

August Neilreich — A344

1971, May 27 Perf. 12½x13½
898 A343 2s brt rose lil & brn .25 .15
Exhibition of "1000 Years of Art in Krems." The statue of St. Matthew is from the Lentl Altar, created about 1520 by the Master of the Pulkau Altar.

1971, June 1 Engr. Perf. 14x13½
899 A344 2s brown .25 .15
August Neilreich (1803-71), botanist.

Singer with Lyre — A345

Photo. & Engr.
1971, July 1 Perf. 13½x14
900 A345 4s lt bl, vio bl & gold .50 .30
Intl. Choir Festival, Vienna, July 1-4.

Coat of Arms of Kitzbuhel — A346

1971, Aug. 23 Perf. 14
901 A346 2.50s gold & multi .35 .15
700th anniversary of the town of Kitzbuhel.

Vienna Stock Exchange — A347

1971, Sept. 1 Engr. Perf. 13½x14
902 A347 4s reddish brown .55 .20
Bicentenary of the Vienna Stock Exchange.

First and Latest Exhibition Halls — A348

1971, Sept. 6 Photo. Perf. 13½x13
903 A348 2.50s dp rose lilac .35 .15
Vienna Intl. Fair, 50th anniv.

Trade Union Emblem — A349

Arms of Burgenland — A350

1971, Sept. 20 Perf. 14x13½
904 A349 2s gray, buff & red .25 .15
Austrian Trade Union Assoc., 25th anniv.

1971, Oct. 1
905 A350 2s dk bl, gold, red & blk .25 .15
50th anniv. of Burgenland joining Austria.

Marcus Car — A351

1971, Oct. 1 Photo. & Engr. Perf. 14
906 A351 4s pale green & blk .50 .25
Austrian Automobile, Motorcycle and Touring Club, 75th anniv.

Europa Bridge — A352

1971, Oct. 8 Engr. Perf. 14x13½
907 A352 4s violet blue .50 .25
Opening of highway over Brenner Pass.

Styria's Iron Mountain — A353

Designs: 2s, Austrian Nitrogen Products, Ltd., Linz. 4s, United Austrian Iron and Steel Works, Ltd. (VÖEST), Linz Harbor.

1971, Oct. 15 Perf. 13½
908 A353 1.50s reddish brown .25 .15
909 A353 2s bluish black .30 .20
910 A353 4s dk slate grn .45 .35
  Nos. 908-910 (3) 1.00 .70
25 years of nationalized industry.

High-speed Train on Semmering — A354

Trout Fisherman — A355

1971, Oct. 21 Perf. 14
911 A354 2s claret .25 .15
Inter-city rapid train service.

1971, Nov. 15 Perf. 13½
912 A355 2s dark red brn .25 .15

Erich Tschermak-Seysenegg — A356

Infant Jesus as Savior, by Dürer — A357

Photo. & Engr.
1971, Nov. 15 Perf. 14x13½
913 A356 2s pale ol & dk pur .25 .15
Birth cent. of Dr. Erich Tschermak-Seysenegg (1871-1962), botanist.

1971, Nov. 26 Perf. 13½
914 A357 2s gold & multi .25 .15
Christmas.

Franz Grillparzer, by Moritz Daffinger — A358

Fountain, Main Square, Friesach — A359

Perf. 14x13½
1972, Jan. 21 Litho. & Engr.
915 A358 2s buff, gold & blk .30 .15
Death cent. of Franz Grillparzer (1791-1872), dramatic poet.

1972, Feb. 23 Engr. Perf. 14x13½
Designs: 2s, Fountain, Heiligenkreuz Abbey. 2.50s, Leopold Fountain, Innsbruck.
916 A359 1.50s rose lilac .25 .15
917 A359 2s brown .25 .20
918 A359 2.50s olive .30 .25
  Nos. 916-918 (3) .80 .60

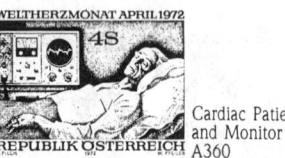

Cardiac Patient and Monitor — A360

1972, Apr. 11 Perf. 13½x14
919 A360 4s violet brown .55 .25
World Health Day.

A361

A362

Design: St. Michael's Gate, Royal Palace, Vienna.
1972, Apr. 11 Perf. 14x13½
920 A361 4s violet blue .55 .25
Conference of European Post and Telecommunications Ministers, Vienna, Apr. 11-14.

1972, May 5 Photo. & Engr. Perf. 14
921 A362 2s Sculpture, Gurk Cathedral .30 .15
900th anniv. of Gurk (Carinthia) Diocese. The design is after the central column supporting the sarcophagus of St. Hemma in Gurk Cathedral.

City Hall, Congress Emblem — A363

1972, May 23 Litho. & Engr.
922 A363 4s red, blk & yel .55 .20
9th Intl. Congress of Public and Cooperative Economy, Vienna, May 23-25.

Power Line in Carnic Alps — A364

Designs: 2.50s, Power Station, Semmering. 4s, Zemm Power Station (lake in Zillertaler Alps).
1972, June 28 Perf. 13½x12
923 A364 70g gray & violet .15 .15
924 A364 2.50s gray & red brn .30 .30
925 A364 4s gray & slate .45 .45
  Nos. 923-925 (3) .90 .90
Nationalization of the power industry, 25th anniv.

Runner with Olympic Torch — A365

St. Hermes, by Conrad Laib — A366

Engr. & Photo.
1972, Aug. 21 Perf. 14x13½
926 A365 2s sepia & red .25 .15
Olympic torch relay from Olympia, Greece, to Munich, Germany, passing through Austria.

1972, Aug. 21 Engr.
927 A366 2s violet brown .25 .15
Exhibition of Late Gothic Art, Salzburg.

Pears — A367

1972, Sept. Perf. 14
928 A367 2.50s dk blue & multi .30 .15
World Congress of small plot Gardeners, Vienna, Sept. 7-10.

Souvenir Sheet

Spanish Walk — A368

1972, Sept. 12 Perf. 13½
929 A368 Sheet of 6 2.75 2.75
  a. 2s Spanish walk .25 .25
  b. 2s Piaffe .25 .25
  c. 2.50s Levade .32 .32
  d. 2.50s On long rein .32 .32
  e. 4s Capriole .52 .52
  f. 4s Courbette .52 .52
400th anniv. of the Spanish Riding School in Vienna.

AUSTRIA

Arms of University
of Agriculture
A369

Church and Old
University
A370

Photo. & Engr.
1972, Oct. 17 Perf. 14x13½
930 A369 2s black & multi .25 .15
University of Agriculture, Vienna, cent.

1972, Nov. 7 Engr.
931 A370 4s red brown .55 .20
Paris Lodron University, Salzburg, 350th anniv.

Carl Michael
Ziehrer — A371

1972, Nov. 14
932 A371 2s rose claret .25 .15
50th death anniv. of Carl Michael Ziehrer (1843-1922), composer.

Virgin and
Child, Wood,
1420-30
A372

Photo. & Engr.
1972, Dec. 1 Perf. 13½
933 A372 2s olive & chocolate .25 .15
Christmas.

Racing
Sleigh, 1750
A373

Designs: 2s, Coronation landau, 1824. 2.50s, Imperial state coach, 1763.

1972, Dec. 12
934 A373 1.50s pale gray & brn .20 .15
935 A373 2s pale gray & sl grn .30 .15
936 A373 2.50s pale gray & plum .35 .25
Nos. 934-936 (3) .85 .55
Collection of historic state coaches and carriages in Schönbrunn Palace.

Map of Austrian
Telephone
System — A374

1972, Dec. 14 Photo. Perf. 14
937 A374 2s yellow & blk .25 .15
Completion of automation of Austrian telephone system.

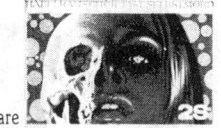

"Drugs are
Death" — A375

1973, Jan. 26 Photo. Perf. 13½x14
938 A375 2s scarlet & multi 1.50 .45
Fight against drug abuse.

Alfons
Petzold — A376

Theodor
Körner — A377

1973, Jan. 26 Engr. Perf. 14x13½
939 A376 2s reddish brn .25 .15
50th death anniv. of Alfons Petzold (1882-1923), poet.

Photo. & Engr.
1973, Apr. 24 Perf. 14x13½
940 A377 2s gray & deep claret .25 .15
Theodor Korner (1873-1957), Austrian Pres., birth cent.

Douglas DC-9 — A378

1973, May 14 Perf. 13½x14
941 A378 2s vio bl & rose red .30 .15
First intl. airmail service, Vienna to Kiev, Mar. 31, 1918, 55th anniv.; Austrian Aviation Corporation, 50th anniv.; Austrian Airlines, 15th anniv.

Otto
Loewi — A379

"Support" — A380

1973, June 4 Engr. Perf. 14x13½
942 A379 4s deep violet .55 .20
Birth cent. of Otto Loewi (1873-1961), pharmacologist, winner of 1936 Nobel prize.

1973, June 25
943 A380 2s dark blue .25 .15
Federation of Austrian Social Insurance Institutes, 25th anniv.

Europa Issue 1973

Post Horn and
Telephone — A381

1973, July 9 Photo. Perf. 14
944 A381 2.50s ocher, blk & yel .30 .15

Dornbirn Fair
Emblem
A382

1973, July 27 Perf. 13½x14
945 A382 2s multicolored .30 .15
Dornbirn Trade Fair, 25th anniversary.

Hurdles — A383

Leo Slezak — A384

1973, Aug. 13 Engr. Perf. 14x13½
946 A383 4s gray olive .50 .20
23rd Intl. Military Pentathlon Championships, Wiener Neustadt, Aug. 13-18.

1973, Aug. 17 Perf. 14
947 A384 4s dark brown .50 .20
Leo Slezak (1873-1946), operatic tenor.

Gate, Vienna Hofburg,
and ISI
Emblem — A385

Photogravure and Engraved
1973, Aug. 20 Perf. 14x13½
948 A385 2s gray, dk brn & ver .25 .15
39th Congress of Intl. Statistical Institute, Vienna, Aug. 20-30.

Tegetthoff off
Franz Josef
Land, by Julius
Prayer — A386

1973, Aug. 30 Engr. Perf. 13½x14
949 A386 2.50s Prussian grn .30 .15
Discovery of Franz Josef Land by an Austrian North Pole expedition, cent.

Academy of
Science, by
Canaletto
A387

1973, Sept. 4
950 A387 2.50s violet .30 .15
Intl. meteorological cooperation, cent.

Arms of Viennese
Tanners
A388

Max Reinhardt
A389

Photo. & Engr.
1973, Sept. 4 Perf. 14
951 A388 4s red & multi .55 .20
13th Congress of the Intl. Union of Leather Chemists' Societies, Vienna, Sept. 1-7.

1973, Sept. 7 Engr. Perf. 13x13½
952 A389 2s rose magenta .25 .15
Max Reinhardt (1873-1943), theatrical director and stage manager.

Trotter
A390

1973, Sept. 28 Perf. 13½
953 A390 2s green .30 .15
Centenary of Vienna Trotting Association.

Ferdinand
Hanusch — A391

1973, Sept. 28 Perf. 14x13½
954 A391 2s rose brown .25 .15
50th death anniv. of Ferdinand Hanusch (1866-1923), secretary of state.

Police Radio
Operator
A392

1973, Oct. 2 Perf. 13½x14
955 A392 4s violet blue .50 .20
50th anniv. of Intl. Criminal Police Org. (INTERPOL).

Josef Petzval's
Photographic
Lens — A393

1973, Oct. 8 Litho. & Engr. Perf. 14
956 A393 2.50s blue & multi .30 .15
EUROPHOT Photographic Cong., Vienna.

Emperor's
Spring, Hell
Valley — A394

Photo. & Engr.
1973, Oct. 23 Perf. 13½x14
957 A394 2s sepia, blue & red .25 .15
Vienna's first mountain spring water supply system, cent.

Since 1867, American stamp collectors have been using the Scott Catalogue to identify their stamps and Scott Albums to house their collections.

Almsee, Upper Austria — A395

Hofburg and Prince Eugene Statue, Vienna — A395a

Designs: 50g, Farmhouses, Zillertal, Tirol. 1s, Kahlenbergerdorf. 1.50s, Bludenz, Vorarlberg. 2s, Inn Bridge, Alt Finstermunz. 2.50s, Murau, Styria. 3s, Bischofsmütze, Salzburg. 3.50s, Easter Church, Oberwart. 4.50s, Windmill, Retz. 5s, Aggstein Castle, Lower Austria. 6s, Lindauer Hut, Vorarlberg. 6.50s, Holy Cross Church, Villach, Carinthia. 7s, Falkenstein Castle, Carinthia. 7.50s, Hohensalzburg. 8s, Votive column, Reiteregg, Styria. 10s, Lake Neusiedl, Burgenland. 11s, Old Town, Enns. 16s, Openair Museum, Bad Tatzmannsdorf. 20s, Myra waterfalls.

Photo. & Engr.
1973-78   Perf. 13½x14
Size: 23x29mm
Type A395

958	50g gray & slate green	.15	.15
959	1s brn & dk brown	.15	.15
960	1.50s rose & brown	.25	.15
961	2s gray bl & dk blue	.30	.15
962	2.50s vio & dp violet	.35	.15
963	3s lt ultra & vio blue	.45	.15
963A	3.50s dl org & brown	.50	.15
964	4s brt lil & pur	.55	.15
965	4.50s brt grn & bl green	.60	.15
966	5s lilac & vio	.65	.15
967	6s dp rose & dk violet	.80	.15
968	6.50s bl grn & indigo	.90	.15
969	7s sage grn & sl green	.95	.15
970	7.50s lil rose & claret	1.00	.25
971	8s dl red & dp brown	1.10	.20
972	10s gray grn & dk green	1.40	.20
973	11s ver & dk carmine	1.65	.15
974	16s bister & brown	2.25	.60
975	20s ol bis & ol grn	2.75	1.25

Type A395a

| 976 | 50s gray vio & vio bl | 6.75 | 2.50 |
| Nos. 958-976 (20) | | 23.50 | 7.10 |

Issue dates: 1974, Nos. 960-963. 1975, Nos. 958-959, 967, 976. 1976, Nos. 965, 971, 973. 1977, Nos. 968, 970, 974-975. 1978, No. 963A. See Nos. 1100-1109.

Nativity — A396

Pregl — A397

1973, Nov. 30   Perf. 14
977 A396 2s multicolored   .30   .15
Christmas. Design from 14th century stained-glass window.

1973, Dec. 12   Engr.   Perf. 14x13½
978 A397 4s deep blue   .50   .20
50th anniv. of the awarding of the Nobel prize for chemistry to Fritz Pregl (1869-1930).

Shop with Scott Publishing Co. 24 hours a day 7 days a week at www.scottonline.com

Telex Machine A398

Hofmannsthal A399

1974, Jan. 14   Photo.   Perf. 14x13½
979 A398 2.50s ultramarine   .30   .15
50th anniversary of Radio Austria.

1974, Feb. 1   Engr.   Perf. 14
980 A399 4s violet blue   .50   .20
Birth cent. of Hugo Hofmannsthal (1874-1929), poet and playwright.

Anton Bruckner and Bruckner House A400

1974, Mar. 22   Engr.   Perf. 14
981 A400 4s brown   .50   .20
Founding of Anton Bruckner House (concert hall), Linz, and birth of Anton Bruckner (1824-1896), composer, 150th anniv.

Vegetables A401

Photo. & Engr.
1974, Apr. 18   Perf. 14
982 A401 2s shown   .30   .20
983 A401 2.50s Fruits   .35   .30
984 A401 4s Flowers   .50   .50
Nos. 982-984 (3)   1.15   1.00
Intl. Garden Show, Vienna, Apr. 18-Oct. 14.

Seal of Judenburg A402

Karl Kraus A403

1974, Apr. 24   Photo.   Perf. 14x13½
985 A402 2s plum & multi   .30   .15
750th anniversary of Judenburg.

1974, Apr. 6   Engr.
986 A403 4s dark red   .50   .20
Karl Kraus (1874-1936), poet and satirist, birth cent.

St. Michael, by Thomas Schwanthaler — A404

1974, May 3
987 A404 2.50s slate green   .30   .15
Exhibition of the works by the Schwanthaler Family of sculptors, (1633-1848), Reichersberg am Inn, May 3-Oct. 13.

A405

A406

Europa: King Arthur, from tomb of Maximilian I

1974, May 8   Perf. 13½
988 A405 2.50s ocher & slate blue   .30   .15

Photo. & Engr.
1974, May 17   Perf. 14x13½
De Dion Bouton motor tricycle.
989 A406 2s gray & vio brn   .30   .15
Austrian Automobile Assoc., 75th anniv.

Satyr's Head, Terracotta A407

1974, May 22   Perf. 13½x14
990 A407 2s org brn, gold & blk   .30   .15
Exhibition, "Renaissance in Austria," Schallaburg Castle, May 22-Nov. 14.

Road Transport Union Emblem A408

Maulbertsch, Self-portrait A409

1974, May 24   Photo.   Perf. 14x13½
991 A408 4s deep orange & blk   .50   .20
14th Congress of the Intl. Road Transport Union, Innsbruck.

1974, June 7   Engr.   Perf. 14x13½
992 A409 2s violet brown   .25   .15
Franz Anton Maulbertsch (1724-96), painter, 250th birth anniv.

Gendarmes, 1824 and 1974 — A410

1974, June 7   Photo.   Perf. 13½x14
993 A410 2s red & multi   .25   .15
125th anniversary of Austrian gendarmery.

Fencing A411

Photo. & Engr.
1974, June 14   Perf. 13½
994 A411 2.50s red org & blk   .30   .15

Transportation Symbols — A412

St. Virgil, Sculpture from Nonntal Church — A413

1974, June 18   Photo.   Perf. 14x13½
995 A412 4s lt ultra & multi   .50   .20
European Conference of Transportation Ministers, Vienna, June 18-21.

1974, June 28   Engr.   Perf. 13½x14
996 A413 2s violet blue   .25   .15
Consecration of the Cathedral of Salzburg by Scotch-Irish Bishop Feirgil (St. Virgil), 1200th anniv. Salzburg was a center of Christianization in the 8th century.

Franz Jonas and Austrian Eagle — A414

1974, June 28
997 A414 2s black   .25   .15
Jonas (1899-1974), Austrian Pres., 1965-1974.

Franz Stelzhamer — A415

Diver — A416

1974, July 12   Engr.   Perf. 14x13½
998 A415 2s indigo   .25   .15
Franz Stelzhamer (1802-1874), poet who wrote in Upper Austrian vernacular, death cent.

Photo. & Engr.
1974, Aug. 16   Perf. 13x13½
999 A416 4s blue & sepia   .50   .20
13th European Swimming, Diving and Water Polo Championships, Vienna, Aug. 18-25.

Ferdinand Ritter von Hebra — A417

1974, Sept. 10   Engr.   Perf. 14x13½
1000 A417 4s brown   .50   .20
30th Meeting of the Assoc. of German-speaking Dermatologists, Graz, Sept. 10-14. Dr. von Hebra (1816-1880) was a founder of modern dermatology.

AUSTRIA

Arnold Schönberg A418

1974, Sept. 13   *Perf. 13½x14*
1001 A418 2.50s purple   .30 .15
Schönberg (1874-1951), composer.

Radio Station, Salzburg A419

1974, Oct. 1   Photo.   *Perf. 13½x14*
1002 A419 2s multicolored   .25 .15
50th anniversary of Austrian broadcasting.

Edmund Eysler (1874-1949), Composer — A420

1974, Oct. 4   Engr.   *Perf. 14x13½*
1003 A420 2s dark olive   .25 .15

Mailman, Mail Coach and Train, UPU Emblem A421

4s, Mailman, jet, truck, 1974, & UPU emblem.

1974, Oct. 9   Photo.   *Perf. 13½*
1004 A421 2s deep claret & lil   .25 .15
1005 A421 4s dark blue & gray   .50 .20
Centenary of Universal Postal Union.

Gauntlet Protecting Rose — A422

1974, Oct. 23   Photo.   *Perf. 13½x14*
1006 A422 2s multicolored   .25 .15
Environment protection.

Austrian Sports Pool Emblem A423

1974, Oct. 23   Photo.   *Perf. 13½x14*
1007 A423 70g multicolored   .15 .15
Austrian Sports Pool (lottery), 25th anniv.

Carl Ditters von Dittersdorf A424

Virgin and Child, Wood, c. 1600 A425

1974, Oct. 24   Engr.   *Perf. 14x13½*
1008 A424 2s Prussian green   .25 .15
Von Dittersdorf (1739-1799), composer.

1974, Nov. 29   Photo. & Engr.
1009 A425 2s brown & gold   .35 .15
Christmas.

A426   A427

1974, Dec. 18
1010 A426 4s gray & black   .55 .20
Franz Schmidt (1874-1939), composer.

Photo. & Engr.
1975, Jan. 24   *Perf. 13½*
1011 A427 2.50s St. Christopher   .40 .15
European Architectural Heritage Year. The design shows part of a wooden figure from central panel of the retable in the Kefermarkt Church, 1490-1497.

Safety Belt and Skeleton Arms — A428

Stained Glass Window, Vienna City Hall — A429

1975, Apr. 1   Photo.   *Perf. 14x13½*
1012 A428 70g violet & multi   .15 .15
Introduction of obligatory use of automobile safety belts.

1975, Apr. 2   *Perf. 14*
1013 A429 2.50s multicolored   .30 .15
11th meeting of the Council of European Municipalities, Vienna, Apr. 2-5.

Austria as Mediator — A430

Forest — A431

1975, May 2   Litho.   *Perf. 14*
1014 A430 2s blk & bister   .30 .15
2nd Republic of Austria, 30th anniv.

1975, May 6   Engr.
1015 A431 2s green   .35 .15
National forests, 50th anniversary.

High Priest, by Michael Pacher — A432

Gosaukamm Funicular — A433

Europa Issue 1975
Photo. & Engr.
1975, May 27   *Perf. 14x13½*
1016 A432 2.50s black & multi   .40 .15
Design is detail from painting "The Marriage of Joseph and Mary," by Michael Pacher (c. 1450-1500).

1975, June 23   *Perf. 14x13½*
1017 A433 2s slate & red   .30 .15
4th Intl. Funicular Cong., Vienna, June 23-27.

Josef Misson and Mühlbach am Manhartsberg A434

1975, June 27   *Perf. 13½x14*
1018 A434 2s choc & redsh brn   .25 .15
Josef Misson (1803-1875), poet who wrote in Lower Austrian vernacular, death cent.

Setting Sun and "P" — A435

1975, Aug. 27   Litho.   *Perf. 14x13½*
1019 A435 1.50s org, blk & bl   .20 .15
Austrian Assoc. of Pensioners 25th anniv. meeting, Vienna, Aug. 1975.

Ferdinand Porsche A436

Photo. & Engr.
1975, Sept. 3   *Perf. 13½x14*
1020 A436 1.50s gray & purple   .25 .15
Ferdinand Porsche (1875-1951), engineer, developer of Porsche and Volkswagen cars, birth cent.

Leo Fall (1873-1925), Composer — A437

1975, Sept. 16   Engr.   *Perf. 14x13½*
1021 A437 2s violet   .25 .15

Judo Throw — A438

Heinrich Angeli — A439

1975, Oct. 20   Photo.   *Perf. 14x13½*
1022 A438 2.50s gold & multi   .30 .15
10th World Judo Championships, Vienna, Oct. 20-26.

1975, Oct. 21   Engr.   *Perf. 14x13½*
1023 A439 2s rose lake   .30 .15
Heinrich Angeli (1840-1925), painter, 50th death anniv.

Johann Strauss and Dancers A440

Photo. & Engr.
1975, Oct. 24   *Perf. 13½x14*
1024 A440 4s ocher & sepia   .55 .20
Johann Strauss (1825-1899), composer.

Stylized Musician Playing a Viol — A441

Symbolic House — A442

1975, Oct. 30   *Perf. 14x13½*
1025 A441 2.50s silver & vio bl   .35 .15
Vienna Symphony Orchestra, 75th anniv.

1975, Oct. 31   Photo.
1026 A442 2s multicolored   .25 .15
Austrian building savings societies, 50th anniv.

Fan with "Hanswurst" Scene, 18th Century A443

1975, Nov. 14   Photo.   *Perf. 13½x14*
1027 A443 1.50s green & multi   .20 .15
Salzburg Theater bicentenary.

Virgin and Child, from 15th Century Altar A444

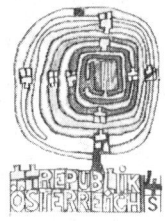

"The Spiral Tree," by Hundertwasser A445

AUSTRIA

Photo. & Engr.
1975, Nov. 28 Perf. 13x13½
1028 A444 2s gold & dull purple .25 .15
Christmas.

Photo., Engr. & Typo.
1975, Dec. 11 Perf. 13½x14
1029 A445 4s multicolored .65 .25
Austrian modern art. Friedenstreich Hundertwasser is the pseudonym of Friedrich Stowasser (b. 1928).

Old Burgtheater — A446

No. 1030b, Grand staircase, new Burgtheater.

Perf. 14 (pane), 13½x14 (stamps)
1976, Apr. 8 Engr.
1030 Pane of 2 + label 1.10 1.10
 a. A446 3s violet blue .30 .30
 b. A446 3s deep brown .30 .30
Bicentenary of Vienna Burgtheater. Label (head of Pan) and inscription in vermilion.

Dr. Robert Barany (1876-1936), Winner of Nobel Prize for Medicine, 1914 — A447

Photo. & Engr.
1976, Apr. 22 Perf. 14x13½
1031 A447 3s blue & brown .45 .15

Ammonite — A448

1976, Apr. 30 Photo. Perf. 13½x14
1032 A448 3s red & multi .45 .15
Vienna Museum of Natural History, Centenary Exhibition.

Carinthian Dukes' Coronation Chair — A449

Siege of Linz, 17th Century Etching — A450

Photo. & Engr.
1976, May 6 Perf. 14x13½
1033 A449 3s grnsh blk & org .45 .15
Millennium of Carinthia.

1976, May 14
1034 A450 4s blk & gray grn .55 .20
Upper Austrian Peasants' War, 350th anniv.

Skittles — A451

1976, May 14 Perf. 13½x14
1035 A451 4s black & org .55 .20
11th World Skittles Championships, Vienna.

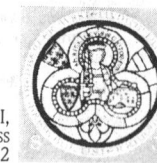

Duke Heinrich II, Stained-glass Window — A452

1976, May 14 Perf. 14
1036 A452 3s multicolored .45 .15
Babenberg Exhibition, Lilienfeld.

St. Wolfgang, from Pacher Altar — A453

1976, May 26 Engr. Perf. 13½
1037 A453 6s bright violet .75 .40
Intl. Art Exhibition at St. Wolfgang.

Europa Issue 1976

Tassilo Cup, Kremsmunster, 777 — A454

Photo. & Engr.
1976, Aug. 13 Perf. 14x13½
1038 A454 4s ultra & multi .60 .20

Timber Fair Emblem — A455

Constantin Economo, M.D. — A456

1976, Aug. 13 Photo.
1039 A455 3s green & multi .35 .15
Austrian Timber Fair, Klagenfurt, 25th anniv.

1976, Aug. 23 Engr.
1040 A456 3s dark red brown .35 .15
Dr. Economo (1876-1931), neurologist.

Administrative Court, by Salomon Klein — A457

1976, Oct. 25 Engr. Perf. 13½x14
1041 A457 6s deep brown .80 .30
Austrian Central Administrative Court, cent.

Souvenir Sheet

Coats of Arms of Austrian Provinces — A458

Millennium of Austria: a, Lower Austria. b, Upper Austria. c, Styria. d, Carinthia. e, Tyrol. f, Voralberg. g, Salzburg. h, Burgenland. i, Vienna.

Photo. & Engr.
1976, Oct. 25 Perf. 14
1042 Sheet of 9 3.00 3.00
 a.-i. A458 2s any single .30 .30

"Cancer" A459

1976, Nov. 17 Photo. Perf. 14x13½
1043 A459 2.50s multicolored .35 .15
Fight against cancer.

UN Emblem and Bridge — A460

1976, Nov. 17
1044 A460 3s blue & gold .45 .15
UN Industrial Development Org. (UNIDO), 10th anniv.

Punched Tape, Map of Europe — A461

1976, Nov. 17 Perf. 14
1045 A461 1.50s multicolored .15 .15
Austrian Press Agency (APA), 30th anniv.

Viktor Kaplan, Kaplan Turbine — A462

Photo. & Engr.
1976, Nov. 26 Perf. 13½x14
1046 A462 2.50s multicolored .35 .15
Viktor Kaplan (1876-1934), inventor of Kaplan turbine, birth centenary.

Nativity, by Konrad von Friesach, c. 1450 A463

1976, Nov. 26 Perf. 13½
1047 A463 3s multicolored .40 .15
Christmas.

Augustin, the Piper — A464

Photo. & Engr.
1976, Dec. 29 Perf. 13½
1048 A464 6s multicolored .75 .25
Modern Austrian art.

Rainer Maria Rilke (1875-1926), Poet A465

Vienna City Synagogue A466

1976, Dec. 29 Engr. Perf. 14x13½
1049 A465 3s deep violet .40 .15

1976, Dec. 29 Photo. Perf. 13½
1050 A466 1.50s multicolored .20 .15
Sesquicentennial of Vienna City Synagogue.

Nikolaus Joseph von Jacquin (1727-1817), Botanist — A467

1977, Feb. 16 Engr. Perf. 14x13½
1051 A467 4s chocolate .55 .20

Oswald von Wolkenstein (1377-1445), Poet — A468

Photo. & Engr.
1977, Feb. 16 Perf. 14
1052 A468 3s multicolored .35 .15

Handball A469

1977, Feb. 25 Photo. Perf. 13½x14
1053 A469 1.50s multicolored .15 .15
World Indoor Handball Championships, Austria, Feb. 5-Mar. 6.

AUSTRIA

A470  A471

1977, Apr. 12   Engr.   *Perf. 14x13½*
1054 A470 6s dk violet blue   .70   .25
Alfred Kubin (1877-1959), illustrator and writer.

1977, Apr. 22   Engr.   *Perf. 13½*
Designs: 2.50s, Great Spire, St. Stephen's Cathedral. 3s, Heathen Tower and Frederick's Gable. 4s, Interior view with Albertinian Choir.
1055 A471 2.50s dark brown   .35   .15
1056 A471 3s dark blue   .40   .25
1057 A471 4s rose lake   .50   .35
Nos. 1055-1057 (3)   1.25   .75
Restoration and re-opening of St. Stephen's Cathedral, Vienna, 25th anniversary.

Fritz Hermanovsky-Orlando (1877-1954), Poet and Artist — A472

1977, Apr. 29   Photo. & Engr.   *Perf. 13½x14*
1058 A472 6s Prus green & gold   .70   .25

IAEA Emblem A473    Arms of Schwanenstadt A474

1977, May 2   Photo.   *Perf. 14*
1059 A473 3s brt bl, lt bl & gold   .35   .15
Intl. Atomic Energy Agency (IAEA), 20th anniv.

1977, June 10   Photo.   *Perf. 14x13½*
1060 A474 3s dk brown & multi   .35   .15
Town of Schwanenstadt, 350th anniv.

Europa Issue 1977

Attersee, Upper Austria — A475

1977, June 10   Engr.   *Perf. 14*
1061 A475 6s olive green   .90   .30

Globe, by Vincenzo Coronelli, 1688 — A476

1977, June 29   Photo. & Engr.   *Perf. 14*
1062 A476 3s black & buff   .35   .15
5th Intl. Symposium of the Coronelli World Fed. of Friends of the Globe, Austria, June 29-July 3.

Kayak Race — A477

1977, July 15   Photo.   *Perf. 13½x14*
1063 A477 4s multicolored   .50   .20
3rd Kayak Slalom White Water Race on Lieser River, Spittal.

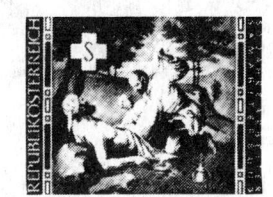

The Good Samaritan, by Francesco Bassano — A478

1977, Sept. 16   Photo. & Engr.
1064 A478 1.50s brown & red   .20   .15
Workers' Good Samaritan Org., 50th anniv.

Papermakers' Coat of Arms — A479    Man with Austrian Flag Lifting Barbed Wire — A480

1977, Oct. 10   *Perf. 14x13½*
1065 A479 3s multicolored   .35   .15
17th Conf. of the European Committee of Pulp and Paper Technology (EUCEPA), Vienna.

1977, Nov. 3   *Perf. 14*
1066 A480 2.50s slate & red   .35   .15
Honoring the martyrs for Austria's freedom.

"Austria," First Steam Locomotive in Austria — A481

Designs: 2.50s, Steam locomotive 214. 3s, Electric locomotive 1044.

1977, Nov. 17   Photo. & Engr.   *Perf. 13½*
1067 A481 1.50s multicolored   .20   .15
1068 A481 2.50s multicolored   .40   .15
1069 A481 3s multicolored   .45   .20
Nos. 1067-1069 (3)   1.05   .50
140th anniversary of Austrian railroads.

A482  A483

Virgin and Child, wood statue, Mariastein, Tyrol.

1977, Nov. 25   *Perf. 14x13½*
1070 A482 3s multicolored   .30   .15
Christmas.

1977, Dec. 2   *Perf. 13½x14*
The Danube Maiden, by Wolfgang Hutter.
1071 A483 6s multicolored   .75   .20
Modern Austrian art.

Egon Friedell (1878-1938), Writer and Historian A484

1978, Jan. 23   Photo. & Engr.
1072 A484 3s lt blue & blk   .40   .15

Subway Train — A485

1978, Feb. 24   Photo.   *Perf. 13½x14*
1073 A485 3s multicolored   .45   .15
New Vienna subway system.

Biathlon Competition A486

1978, Feb. 28   Photo. & Engr.
1074 A486 4s multicolored   .45   .20
Biathlon World Championships, Hochfilzen, Tyrol, Feb. 28-Mar. 5.

Leopold Kunschak (1871-1953), Political Leader — A487

1978, Mar. 13   Engr.   *Perf. 14x13½*
1075 A487 3s violet blue   .40   .15

Coyote, Aztec Feather Shield — A488

1978, Mar. 13   Photo.   *Perf. 13½x14*
1076 A488 3s multicolored   .40   .15
Ethnographical Museum, 50th anniv. exhibition.

Alpine Farm, Woodcut by Suitbert Lobisser — A489

1978, Mar. 23   Engr.   *Perf. 13½*
1077 A489 3s dark brown, buff   .40   .15
Lobisser (1878-1943), graphic artist.

Capercaillie, Hunting Bag, 1730, and Rifle, 1655 — A490

1978, Apr. 28   Photo. & Engr.   *Perf. 13½*
1078 A490 6s multicolored   .75   .35
Intl. Hunting Exhibition, Marchegg.

Europa Issue 1978

Riegersburg, Styria — A491

1978, May 3   Engr.
1079 A491 6s deep rose lilac   .75   .35

Parliament, Vienna, and Map of Europe — A492    Admont Pietà, c. 1410 — A493

1978, May 3   Photo.   *Perf. 14x13½*
1080 A492 4s multicolored   .45   .20
3rd Interparliamentary Conference for European Cooperation and Security, Vienna.

1978, May 26   Photo. & Engr.
1081 A493 2.50s ocher & black   .25   .15
Gothic Art in Styria Exhibition, St. Lambrecht, 1978.

Ort Castle, Gmunden — A494

1978, June 9
1082 A494 3s multicolored   .30   .15
700th anniversary of Gmunden City.

Child with Flowers and Fruit — A495    Lehar and his Home, Bad Ischl — A496

AUSTRIA

Photo. & Engr.
1978, June 30   Perf. 14x13½
1083 A495 6s gold & multi   .85 .35
25 years of Social Tourism.

1978, July 14 Engr.   Perf. 14x13½
1084 A496 6s slate   .75 .30
International Lehar Congress, Bad Ischl. Franz Lehar (1870-1948), operetta composer.

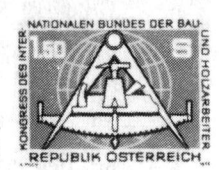

Congress Emblem — A497

1978, Aug. 21 Photo.   Perf. 13½x14
1085 A497 1.50s black, red & yel   .20 .15
Cong. of Intl. Fed. of Building Construction and Wood Workers, Vienna, Aug. 20-24.

Ottokar of Bohemia and Rudolf of Hapsburg — A498

1978, Aug. 25   Photo. & Engr.
1086 A498 3s multicolored   .35 .15
Battle of Dürnkrut and Jedenspeigen (Marchfeld), which established Hapsburg rule in Austria, 700th anniversary.

First Documentary Reference to Villach, "ad pontem uillah" — A499

1978, Sept. 8 Litho.   Perf. 13½x14
1087 A499 3s multicolored   .35 .15
1100th anniversary of Villach, Carinthia.

Seal of Graz, 1440 — A500
Emperor Maximilian Fishing — A501 

Photo. & Engr.
1978, Sept. 13   Perf. 14x13½
1088 A500 4s multicolored   .50 .25
850th anniversary of Graz.

1978, Sept. 15   Perf. 14x13½
1089 A501 4s multicolored   .50 .20
World Fishing Championships, Vienna, Sept. 1978.

"Aid to the Handicapped" — A502

1978, Oct. 2 Photo.   Perf. 13½x14
1090 A502 6s orange brn & blk   .75 .30

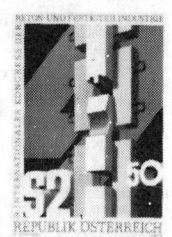

Symbolic Column — A503

1978, Oct. 9 Photo.   Perf. 13½
1091 A503 2.50s orange, blk & gray   .30 .15
9th Intl. Congress of Concrete and Prefabrication Industries, Vienna, Oct. 8-13.

Grace, by Albin Egger-Lienz — A504

1978, Oct. 27   Perf. 13½x14
1092 A504 6s multicolored   .75 .30
European Family Congress, Vienna, Oct. 26-29.

Lise Meitner (1878-1968), Physicist, and Atom Symbol — A505

1978, Nov. 7 Engr.   Perf. 14x13½
1093 A505 6s dark violet   .75 .30

Viktor Adler, by Anton Hanak — A506

Photo. & Engr.
1978, Nov. 10   Perf. 13½x14
1094 A506 3s vermilion & black   .40 .15
Viktor Adler (1852-1918), leader of Social Democratic Party, 60th death anniversary.

Franz Schubert, by Josef Kriehuber — A507
Virgin and Child, Wilhering Church — A508 

1978, Nov. 17 Engr.   Perf. 14
1095 A507 6s reddish brown   .65 .35
Franz Schubert (1797-1828), composer.

Perf. 12½x13½
1978, Dec. 1   Photo. & Engr.
1096 A508 3s multicolored   .35 .15
Christmas.

Archduke Johann Shelter, Grossglockner — A509

1978, Dec. 6   Perf. 13½x14
1097 A509 1.50s gold & dk vio bl   .20 .15
Austrian Alpine Club, centenary.

A510   A511

Adam, by Rudolf Hausner.

1978, Dec. 6 Photo.   Perf. 13½x14
1098 A510 6s multicolored   .75 .35
Modern Austrian art.

1978, Dec. 6   Perf. 14x13½
1099 A511 6s Bound Hands   .75 .30
Universal Declaration of Human Rights, 30th anniv.

Type of 1973
Designs: 20g, Freistadt, Upper Austria. 3s, Bishofsmutze, Salzburg. 4.20s, Hirschegg, Kleinwalsertal. 5.50s, Peace Chapel, Stoderzinken. 5.60s, Riezlern, Kleinwalsertal. 9s, Asten Carinthia. 12s, Kufstein Fortress. 14s, Weiszsee, Salzburg.

Photo. & Engr.
1978-83   Perf. 13½x14
Size: 23x29mm
1100 A395 20g vio bl & dk bl   .15 .15
Size: 17x21mm
1102 A395 3s lt ultra & vio bl   .45 .15
Size: 23x29mm
1104 A395 4.20s blk & grysh bl   .55 .15
1105 A395 5.50s lilac & pur   .75 .20
1106 A395 5.60s yel grn & ol grn   .75 .20
1107 A395   9s rose & car   1.25 .45
1108 A395 12s ocher & vio brn   1.75 .15
1109 A395 14s lt green & green   2.00 .20
Nos. 1100-1109 (8)   7.65 1.65

Issued: 3s, 12/7/78; 4.20s, 6/22/79; 20g, 6/27/80; 12s, 10/3/80; 14s, 1/27/82; 5.50s, 5.60s, 7/1/82; 9s, 2/9/83.

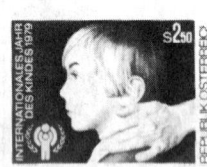

Child and IYC Emblem — A512

Photo. & Engr.
1979, Jan. 16   Perf. 14
1110 A512 2.50s dk blue, blk & brn   .30 .15
International Year of the Child.

CCIR Emblem — A513

1979, Jan. 16 Photo.   Perf. 13½x14
1111 A513 6s multicolored   .75 .30
Intl. Radio Consultative Committee (CCIR) of the ITU, 50th anniv.

Air Rifle, Air Pistol and Club Emblem — A514

Photo. & Engr.
1979, Mar. 7   Perf. 13½
1112 A514 6s multicolored   .75 .30
Austrian Shooting Club, cent., and European Air Rifle and Air Pistol Championships, Graz.

Figure Skater — A515

1979, Mar. 7 Photo.   Perf. 14x13½
1113 A515 4s multicolored   .55 .25
World Ice Skating Championships, Vienna.

Steamer Franz I — A516

Designs: 2.50s, Tugboat Linz. 3s, Passenger ship Theodor Körner.

1979, Mar. 13 Engr.   Perf. 13½
1114 A516 1.50s violet blue   .20 .15
1115 A516 2.50s sepia   .30 .15
1116 A516   3s magenta   .35 .20
Nos. 1114-1116 (3)   .85 .50
1st Danube Steamship Company, 150th anniv.

Fashion Design, by Theo Zasche, 1900 — A517

Photo. & Engr.
1979, Mar. 26   Perf. 13x13½
1117 A517 2.50s multicolored   .30 .15
50th Intl. Fashion Week, Vienna.

Wiener Neustadt Cathedral — A518

1979, Mar. 27 Engr.   Perf. 13½
1118 A518 4s violet blue   .50 .25
Cathedral of Wiener Neustadt, 700th anniv.

Teacher and Pupils, by Franz A. Zauner — A519
Population Chart and Barock Angel — A520

AUSTRIA

Photo. & Engr.
1979, Mar. 30   Perf. 14x13½
1119 A519 2.50s multicolored   .30 .15
Education of the deaf in Austria, 200th anniv.

1979, Apr. 6
1120 A520 2.50s multicolored   .30 .15
Austrian Central Statistical Bureau, 150th anniv.

Laurenz Koschier — A521

Diesel Motor — A522

Europa Issue, 1979

1979, May 4
1121 A521 6s ocher & purple   .80 .30

1979, May 4   Photo.
1122 A522 4s multicolored   .45 .20
13th CIMAC Congress (Intl. Org. for Internal Combustion Machines).

Arms of Ried, Schärding and Braunau — A523

Photo. & Engr.
1979, June 1   Perf. 14x13½
1123 A523 3s multicolored   .30 .15
200th anniversary of Innviertel District.

Flood and City — A524

1979, June 1   Perf. 13½x14
1124 A524 2.50s multicolored   .30 .15
Control and eliminate water pollution.

Arms of Rottenmann A525

Jodok Fink A526

Photo. & Engr.
1979, June 22   Perf. 14x13½
1125 A525 3s multicolored   .30 .15
700th anniversary of Rottenmann.

1979, June 29   Engr.   Perf. 14
1126 A526 3s brown carmine   .40 .15
Jodok Fink (1853-1929), governor of Vorarlberg.

Arms of Wels, Returnees' Emblem, "Europa Sail" — A527

1979, July 6   Photo.   Perf. 14x13½
1127 A527 4s yellow grn & blk   .45 .20
5th European Meeting of the Intl. Confederation of Former Prisoners of War, Wels, July 6-8.

Symbolic Flower, Conference Emblem — A528

1979, Aug. 20   Litho.   Perf. 14x13½
1128 A528 4s turq blue   .45 .20
UN Conf. for Science and Technology, Vienna, Aug. 20-31.

Donaupark, UNIDO and IAEA Emblems A529

1979, Aug. 24   Engr.   Perf. 13½x14
1129 A529 6s grayish blue   .75 .30
Opening of the Donaupark Intl. Center in Vienna, seat of the UN Industrial Development Org. (UNIDO) and the Intl. Atomic Energy Agency (IAEA).

Diseased Eye and Blood Vessels A530

1979, Sept. 10   Photo.   Perf. 14
1130 A530 2.50s multicolored   .35 .15
10th World Congress of Intl. Diabetes Federation, Vienna, Sept. 9-14.

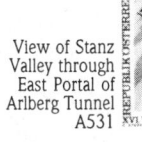

View of Stanz Valley through East Portal of Arlberg Tunnel A531

1979, Sept. 14   Photo. & Engr.
1131 A531 4s multicolored   .45 .20
16th World Road Cong., Vienna, Sept. 16-21.

Steam Printing Press A532

Photo. & Engr.
1979, Sept. 18   Perf. 13½x14
1132 A532 3s multicolored   .40 .15
Austrian Government Printing Office, 175th anniv.

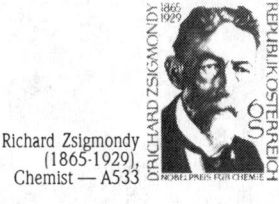

Richard Zsigmondy (1865-1929), Chemist — A533

1979, Sept. 21   Engr.   Perf. 14x13½
1133 A533 6s multicolored   .75 .30

"Save Energy" A534

1979, Oct. 1   Photo.   Perf. 14x13½
1134 A534 2.50s multicolored   .30 .15

Festival and Convention Center, Bregenz (Model) A535

1979, Oct. 1   Engr.   Perf. 14
1135 A535 2.50s purple   .30 .15

Lions International Emblem — A536

1979, Oct. 11   Photo. & Engr.
1136 A536 4s multicolored   .45 .25
25th Lions Europa Forum, Vienna, Oct. 11-13.

A537    A538

Photo. & Engr.
1979, Oct. 19   Perf. 13½x14
1137 A537 2.50s Wilhelm Exner   .30 .15
Centenary of Technological Handicraft Museum, founded by Wilhelm Exner.

1979, Oct. 23   Litho.   Perf. 13½x14
The Compassionate Christ, by Hans Fronius.
1138 A538 4s olive & ol blk   .50 .25
Modern Austrian art.

Locomotive and Arms A539

1979, Oct. 24   Photo.   Perf. 13½x14
1139 A539 2.50s multicolored   .30 .15
Raab-Odenburg-Ebenfurt railroad, cent.

August Musger — A540

Photo. & Engr.
1979, Oct. 30   Perf. 14x13½
1140 A540 2.50s bl gray & blk   .30 .15
August Musger (1868-1929), developer of slow-motion film technique.

Nativity, St. Barbara's Church A541

1979, Nov. 30   Perf. 13½x14
1141 A541 4s multicolored   .45 .25
Christmas.

Arms of Baden — A542

1980, Jan. 25   Perf. 14
1142 A542 4s multicolored   .45 .25
Baden, 500th anniversary.

A543    A544

1980, Feb. 21   Perf. 13½
1143 A543 2.50s red & aqua   .30 .15
Fight rheumatism.

1980, Feb. 21   Photo.   Perf. 14x13½
1144 A544 4s dark blue & red   .45 .25
Austrian exports.

Austrian Red Cross Centenary A545

1980, Mar. 14   Photo.   Perf. 13½x14
1145 A545 2.50s multicolored   .30 .15

Rudolph Kirchschlager — A546

Photo. & Engr.
1980, Mar. 20   Perf. 14x13½
1146 A546 4s sepia & red   .45 .25

AUSTRIA

Robert Hamerling (1830-1889), Poet — A547

1980, Mar. 24	Engr.	Perf. 13½x14
1147 A547 2.50s olive green		.35 .15

Seal of Hallein — A548

Maria Theresa, by Andreas Moller — A549

Photo. & Engr.
1980, Apr. 30		Perf. 14x13½
1148 A548 4s red & black		.45 .25

Hallein, 750th anniversary.

1980, May 13	Engr.	Perf. 13½

Empress Maria Theresa (1717-1780) Paintings by: 4s, Martin van Meytens. 6s, Josef Ducreux.
1149 A549 2.50s violet brown	.30 .25
1150 A549 4s dark blue	.45 .40
1151 A549 6s rose lake	.65 .75
Nos. 1149-1151 (3)	1.40 1.40

Flags of Austria and Four Powers — A550

1980, May 14	Photo.	Perf. 13½x14
1152 A550 4s multicolored		.45 .25

State Treaty, 25th anniversary.

St. Benedict, by Meinrad Guggenbichler A551

1980, May 16	Engr.	Perf. 14½
1153 A551 2.50s olive green		.30 .15

Congress of Benedictine Order of Austria.

Hygeia by Gustav Klimt — A552

1980, May 20	Photo.	Perf. 14
1154 A552 4s multicolored		.45 .25

Academic teaching of hygiene, 175th anniv.

Aflenz Ground Satellite Receiving Station Inauguration — A553

1980, May 30	Photo.	Perf. 14
1155 A553 6s multicolored		.85 .30

Steyr, Etching, 1693 A554

Photo. & Engr.
1980, June 4		Perf. 13½
1156 A554 4s multicolored		.45 .25

Millennium of Steyr.

Worker, Oil Drill Head — A555

1980, June 12		
1157 A555 2.50s multicolored		.30 .15

Austrian oil production, 25th anniversary.

Seal of Innsbruck, 1267 — A556

1980, June 23		Perf. 13½x14½
1158 A556 2.50s multicolored		.35 .15

Innsbruck, 800th anniversary.

Duke's Hat — A557

Bible Illustration, Book of Genesis — A559

	Perf. 14½x13½
1980, June 23	Photo.
1159 A557 4s multicolored	.45 .20

800th anniversary of Styria as a Duchy.

1980, Aug. 18	Engr.	Perf. 14
1160 A558 3s dark purple		.45 .20

1980, Aug. 25		Perf. 13½
1161 A559 4s multicolored		.45 .25

10th Intl. Cong. of the Org. for Old Testament Studies.

Europa Issue 1980

Robert Stolz (1880-1975), Composer — A560

1980, Aug. 25	Engr.	Perf. 14x13½
1162 A560 6s red brown		.85 .30

Old and Modern Bridges A561

1980, Sept. 1	Photo.	Perf. 13½
1163 A561 4s multicolored		.45 .25

11th Congress of the Intl. Assoc. for Bridge and Structural Engineering, Vienna.

Moon Figure, by Karl Brandstätter A562

Customs Service, Sesquicentennial A563

Photo. & Engr.
1980, Oct. 10		Perf. 14x13½
1164 A562 4s multicolored		.45 .25

1980, Oct. 13		Photo.
1165 A563 2.50s multicolored		.30 .15

Gazette Masthead, 1810 A564

1980, Oct. 23	Photo.	Perf. 13½
1166 A564 2.50s multicolored		.30 .15

Official Gazette of Linz, 350th anniversary.

Waidhofen Town Book Title Page, 14th Century — A565

Photo. & Engr.
1980, Oct. 24		Perf. 14
1167 A565 2.50s multicolored		.30 .15

Waidhofen on Thaya, 750th anniversary.

Federal Austrian Army, 25th Anniversary A566

1980, Oct. 24	Photo.	Perf. 13½x14
1168 A566 2.50s grnsh black & red		.30 .15

Alfred Wegener A567

1980, Oct. 31		Engr.
1169 A567 4s violet blue		.55 .25

Alfred Wegener (1880-1930), scientist, formulated theory of continental drift.

A568

A569

1980, Nov. 6		Perf. 14x13½
1170 A568 4s dark red brown		.55 .25

Robert Musil (1880-1942), poet.

Photo. & Engr.
1980, Nov. 28		Perf. 13½

Nativity, stained glass window, Klagenfurt.
| 1171 A569 4s multicolored | | .55 .25 |

Christmas.

25th Anniversary of Social Security A570

1981, Jan. 19	Litho.	Perf. 13½x14
1172 A570 2.50s multicolored		.30 .15

Niebelungen Saga, 1926, by Dachauer A571

Machinist in Wheelchair A572

1981, Apr. 6	Engr.	Perf. 14x13½
1173 A571 3s sepia		.40 .15

Wilhelm Dachauer (1881-1951), artist and engraver.

1981, Apr. 6		Photo. & Engr.
1174 A572 6s multicolored		.75 .35

Rehabilitation Intl., 3rd European Regional Conf.

Sigmund Freud — A573

Congress, Vienna — A574

1981, May 6		Engr.
1175 A573 3s rose violet		.40 .15

Sigmund Freud (1856-1939), psychoanalyst.

1981, May 11		Photo.
1176 A574 4s multicolored		.55 .15

AUSTRIA

A575
Azzo (founder of House of Kuenringer) and his followers, bear-skin manuscript.

1981, May 15	Photo. & Engr.
1177 A575 3s multicolored	.35 .15

Kuenringer Exhibition, Zwettl Monastery.

Europa — A576

1981, May 22	Photo.
1178 A576 6s Maypole	.80 .35

Telephone Service Centenary A577

1981 May 29	Photo. and Engr. Perf. 13½x14
1179 A577 4s multicolored	.45 .25

Seibersdorf Research Center, 25th Anniv. A578

1981, June 29	Photo. Perf. 13½
1180 A578 4s multicolored	.45 .25

The Frog King (Child's Drawing) A579

1981, June 29	Perf. 13½x14
1181 A579 3s multicolored	.35 .15

Town Hall and Town Seal of 1250 — A580

	Photo. & Engr.
1981, July 17	Perf. 13½x14
1182 A580 4s multicolored	.45 .25

St. Veit an der Glan, 800th anniv.

Johann Florian Heller (1813-1871), Pioneer of Urinalysis — A581

1981, Aug. 31	Perf. 14x13½
1183 A581 6s red brown	.75 .35

11th Intl. Clinical Chemistry Congress.

Ludwig Boltzmann (1844-1906), Physicist — A582

1981, Sept. 4	Engr. Perf. 14x13½
1184 A582 3s dark green	.45 .15

Scale — A583

1981, Sept. 7	Photo. & Engr. Perf. 14
1185 A583 6s multicolored	.75 .35

Intl. Pharmaceutical Federation World Congress, Vienna, Sept. 6-11.

Otto Bauer, Politician, Birth Centenary A584

Escher's Impossible Cube A585

1981, Sept. 7	Photo. Perf. 14x13½
1186 A584 4s multicolored	.45 .25

1981, Sept. 14	
1187 A585 4s dk blue & brt blue	.45 .25

10th Intl. Mathematicians' Cong., Innsbruck.

Kneeling Virgin, Detail of Coronation of Mary Altarpiece, St. Wolfgang, 500th Anniv. — A586

1981, Sept. 25	Engr. Perf. 14x13½
1188 A586 3s dark blue	.35 .15

South-East Fair, Graz, 75th Anniv. — A587

1981, Sept. 25	Photo. Perf. 13½x14
1189 A587 4s multicolored	.45 .25

Holy Trinity, 12th Cent. Byzantine Miniature A588

1981, Oct. 5	
1190 A588 6s multicolored	.75 .35

16th Intl. Byzantine Congress.

Hans Kelsen (1881-1973), Co-author of Federal Constitution A589

1981, Oct. 9	Engr.
1191 A589 3s dark carmine	.35 .15

Edict of Tolerance Bicen. — A590

1981, Oct. 9	Photo. & Engr. Perf. 14
1192 A590 4s Joseph II	.45 .25

World Food Day — A591

1981, Oct. 16	Photo. Perf. 13½
1193 A591 6s multicolored	.75 .35

Between the Times, by Oscar Asboth A592

1981, Oct. 22	Litho. Perf. 13½x14
1194 A592 4s multicolored	.55 .25

Intl. Catholic Workers' Day — A593

	Photo. & Engr.
1981, Oct. 23	Perf. 14x13½
1195 A593 4s multicolored	.35 .15

Baron Josef Hammer-Purgstall, Founder of Oriental Studies, 125th Death Anniv. — A594

	Photo. & Engr.
1981, Nov. 23	Perf. 14
1196 A594 3s multicolored	.35 .15

Julius Raab (1891-1964), Politician — A595

1981, Nov. 27	Engr. Perf. 13½
1197 A595 6s rose lake	.75 .35

Nativity, Corn Straw Figures A596

1981, Nov. 27	Photo. & Engr.
1198 A596 4s multicolored	.50 .20

Christmas.

Stefan Zweig (1881-1942), Poet — A597

1981, Nov. 27	Engr. Perf. 14x13½
1199 A597 4s dull violet	.50 .20

800th Anniv. of St. Nikola on the Danube — A598

1981, Dec. 4	Photo. & Engr.
1200 A598 4s multicolored	.55 .20

Vienna Emergency Medical Service Centenary A599

1981, Dec. 9	Photo. Perf. 13½x14
1201 A599 3s multicolored	.35 .15

Schladming-Haus Alpine World Skiing Championship A600

1982, Jan. 27	Perf. 14
1202 A600 4s multicolored	.45 .20

Dorotheum (State Auction Gallery), 275th Anniv. — A601

	Photo. & Engr.
1982, Mar. 12	Perf. 14
1203 A601 4s multicolored	.45 .20

Ordering on-line is
QUICK!
EASY!
CONVENIENT!
www.scottonline.com

AUSTRIA

A602 A603

1982, Mar. 19   Photo.   Perf. 14x13½
1204 A602 5s multicolored   .60 .30
Water Rescue Service, 25th anniv.

Photo. & Engr.
1982, Apr. 23   Perf. 14x13½
1205 A603 3s St. Severin   .35 .15
St. Severin and the End of the Roman Era exhibition.

A604 A605

1982, May 4   Perf. 14
1206 A604 4s multicolored   .55 .20
Intl. Kneipp Hydropathy Congress, Vienna.

1982, May 7
1207 A605 4s Printers' guild arms   .55 .20
Printing in Austria, 500th anniv.

A606 A607

Design: Urine analysis, Canone di Avicenna manuscript.

1982, May 12   Photo.
1208 A606 6s multicolored   .75 .35
5th European Urology Soc. Cong., Vienna.

1982, May 14   Photo. & Engr.
1209 A607 3s multicolored   .35 .15
800th birth anniv. of St. Francis of Assisi.

A608 A609

1982, May 19   Engr.   Perf. 13½
1210 A608 3s olive green   .35 .15
Haydn and His Time Exhibition, Rohrau.

1982, May 25   Photo.   Perf. 14x13½
1211 A609 7s multicolored   .90 .40
25th World Milk Day.

800th Anniv of Gfohl (Market Town) — A610

Photo. & Engr.
1982, May 28   Perf. 14
1212 A610 4s multicolored   .45 .20

Tennis Player and Austrian Tennis Federation Emblem — A611

1982, June 11
1213 A611 3s multicolored   .35 .15

900th Anniv. of City of Langenlois A612

Photo. & Engr.
1982, June 11   Perf. 13½x14
1214 A612 4s multicolored   .45 .20

800th Anniv. of City of Weiz — A613

Ignaz Seipel (1876-1932), Statesman — A614

1982, June 18   Photo.   Perf. 14x13½
1215 A613 4s Arms   .45 .20

1982, July 30   Engr.   Perf. 14x13½
1216 A614 3s brown violet   .35 .15

Europa Issue 1982

Sesquicentennial of Linz-Freistadt-Budweis Horse-drawn Railroad — A615

1982, July 30   Perf. 13½
1217 A615 6s brown   .90 .35

Mail Bus Service, 75th Anniv. — A616

Rocket Lift-off — A617

1982, Aug. 6   Photo.   Perf. 14x13½
1218 A616 4s multicolored   .50 .20

1982, Aug. 9   Perf. 14
1219 A617 4s multicolored   .50 .20
2nd UN Conference on Peaceful Uses of Outer Space, Vienna, Aug. 9-21.

Geodesists' Day — A618

Photo. & Engr.
1982, Sept. 1   Perf. 13½x14
1220 A618 3s Tower, Office of Standards   .35 .15

Protection of Endangered Species — A619

1982, Sept. 9   Perf. 14
1221 A619 3s Bustard   .45 .25
1222 A619 4s Beaver   .60 .30
1223 A619 6s Capercaillie   .90 .45
Nos. 1221-1223 (3)   1.95 1.00

10th Anniv. of Intl. Institute for Applied Systems Anaysis, Vienna A620

1982, Oct. 4   Photo.
1224 A620 3s Laxenburg Castle   .35 .15

St. Apollonia (Patron Saint of Dentists) A621

1982, Oct. 11   Photo. & Engr.
1225 A621 4s multicolored   .45 .20
70th Annual World Congress of Dentists.

Emmerich Kalman (1882-1953), Composer A622

1982, Oct. 22   Engr.   Perf. 13½
1226 A622 3s dark blue   .35 .15

Max Mell (1882-1971), Poet — A623

Christmas — A624

1982, Nov. 10   Photo.   Perf. 14x13½
1227 A623 3s multicolored   .35 .15

Photo. & Engr.
1982, Nov. 25   Perf. 13½
Design: Christmas crib, Damuls Church, Vorarlberg, 1630.
1228 A624 4s multicolored   .45 .20

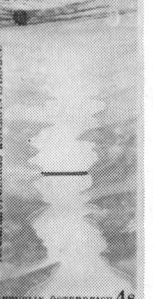

Centenary of St. George's College, Istanbul — A625

Portrait of a Girl, by Ernst Fuchs — A626

1982, Nov. 26   Litho.   Perf. 14
1229 A625 4s Bosporus   .45 .20

1982, Dec. 10   Photo. & Engr.
1230 A626 4s multicolored   .45 .20

Postal Savings Bank Centenary A627

Photo. & Engr.
1983, Jan. 12   Perf. 14
1231 A627 4s Bank   .55 .20

Hildegard Burjan (1883-1933), Founder of Caritas Socialis — A628

1983, Jan. 28   Engr.
1232 A628 4s rose lake   .55 .20

World Communications Year — A629

1983, Feb. 18   Photo.   Perf. 13½x14
1233 A629 7s multicolored   .95 .40

AUSTRIA

75th Anniv. Children's Friends Org. — A630

Photo. & Engr.
1983, Feb. 23   Perf. 14x13½
1234 A630 4s multicolored   .55 .20

Josef Matthias Hauer (1883-1959), Composer A631

1983, Mar. 18   Engr.   Perf. 14
1235 A631 3s deep lilac rose   .40 .15

25th Anniv. of Austrian Airlines A632

1983, Mar. 31   Photo.   Perf. 13½x14
1236 A632 6s multicolored   .85 .35

Work Inspection Centenary A633

1983, Apr. 8   Photo.   Perf. 13½
1237 A633 4s multicolored   .55 .20

Upper Austria Millennium Provincial Exhibition A634

1983, Apr. 28   Photo.   Perf. 13½
1238 A634 3s Wels Castle, by Matthaus Merian   .40 .15

Gottweig Monastery, 900th Anniv. A635

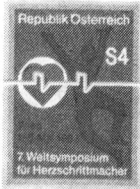

7th World Pacemakers Symposium A636

Photo. & Engr.
1983, Apr. 29   Perf. 13½
1239 A635 3s multicolored   .40 .15

1983, Apr. 29 Photo. Perf. 14x13½
1240 A636 4s multicolored   .55 .20

Catholic Students' Org. — A637

1983, May 20   Photo.   Perf. 14
1241 A637 4s multicolored   .55 .20

Weitra, 800th Anniv. A638

Photo. & Engr.
1983, May 20   Perf. 13½
1242 A638 4s multicolored   .55 .20

Granting of Town Rights to Hohenems, 650th Anniv. — A639

1983, May 27   Photo.   Perf. 14
1243 A639 4s multicolored   .55 .20

25th Anniv. of Stadthall, Vienna A640

1983, June 24   Photo.   Perf. 14
1244 A640 4s multicolored   .55 .20

Europa Issue 1983

A641   A642

1983, June 24   Engr.   Perf. 14x13½
1245 A641 6s dark green   .95 .35
Europa: Viktor Franz Hess (1883-1964), 1936 Nobel Prize winner in physics.

1983, July 1   Photo.   Perf. 13½
1246 A642 5s multicolored   .70 .30
Kiwanis Intl. Convention, Vienna, July 3-6.

7th World Congress of Psychiatry, Vienna — A643

1983, July 11   Photo.   Perf. 14
1247 A643 4s Emblem, St. Stephen's Cathedral   .55 .20

Baron Carl von Hasenauer (1833-1894), Architect A644

1983, July 20   Engr.   Perf. 13½x14
1248 A644 3s Natural History Museum, Vienna   .45 .15

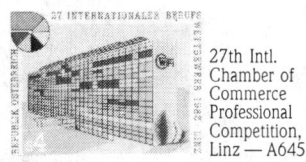

27th Intl. Chamber of Commerce Professional Competition, Linz — A645

1983, Aug. 16   Photo.
1249 A645 4s Chamber building   .55 .20

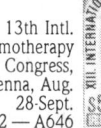

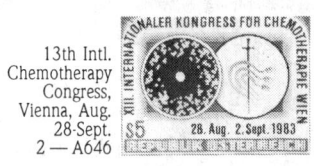

13th Intl. Chemotherapy Congress, Vienna, Aug. 28-Sept. 2 — A646

1983, Aug. 26
1250 A646 5s Penicillin test on cancer   .70 .30

Catholics' Day — A647   Visit of Pope John Paul II — A648

1983, Sept. 9 Photo. Perf. 14x13½
1251 A647 3s multicolored   .40 .15

Photo. & Engr.
1983, Sept. 9   Perf. 13½
1252 A648 6s multicolored   .90 .35

Souvenir Sheet

Battle of 1683 to Relieve Vienna, by Frans Geffel A649

1983, Sept. 9   Perf. 14
1253 A649 6s multicolored   .95 .50
300th anniv. of Vienna's rescue from Turkey.

Vienna Rathaus Centenary — A650

1983, Sept. 23   Perf. 13½x14
1254 A650 4s multicolored   .55 .20

Karl von Terzaghi (1883-1963), Founder of Scientific Subterranean Engineering A651

1983, Oct. 3   Engr.
1255 A651 3s dark blue   .40 .15

10th Trade Unions Federal Congress, Oct. 3-8 — A652

1983, Oct. 3   Photo.   Perf. 13½
1256 A652 3s black & red   .40 .15

Evening Sun in Burgenland, by Gottfried Kumpf — A653

Photo. & Engr.
1983, Oct. 7   Perf. 13½x14
1257 A653 4s multicolored   .55 .20

Modling-Hinterbruhl Electric Railroad Centenary — A654

1983, Oct. 21   Photo.
1258 A654 3s multicolored   .40 .15

Provincial Museum of Upper Austria Sesquicentennial — A655

1983, Nov. 4   Photo. & Engr.
1259 A655 4s Francisco-Carolinum Museum   .55 .20

Creche, St. Andreas Parish Church, Kitzbuhel A656

1983, Nov. 25   Perf. 14
1260 A656 4s multicolored   .55 .20
Christmas.

Parliament Bldg. Vienna, 100th Anniv. — A657

1983, Dec. 2   Engr.
1261 A657 4s slate blue   .55 .20

AUSTRIA

A658   A659

Altar picture, St. Nikola/Pram Church.

1983, Dec. 6   Photo.   Perf. 14x13½
1262 A658 3s multicolored   .40 .15

Perf. 14½x13½
1983, Dec. 15   Engr.
1263 A659 6s dark red brn   .90 .35
Wolfgang Pauli (1900-58), physicist, Nobel Prize winner.

Gregor Mendel (1822-1884), Genetics Founder — A660

Photo. & Engr.
1984, Jan. 5   Perf. 13½
1264 A660 4s multicolored   .55 .20

Anton Hanak (1875-1934), Sculptor — A661

1984, Jan. 5
1265 A661 3s red brown & blk   .40 .15

50th Anniv. of 1934 Uprising — A662

1984, Feb. 10   Photo.   Perf. 14
1266 A662 4.50s Memorial, Woellersdorf   .65 .30

Wernher von Reichersberg Family, Bas-relief, 15th Cent. — A663

Photo. & Engr.
1984, Apr. 25   Perf. 14x13½
1267 A663 3.50s brown & blue   .50 .25
900th anniv. of Reichersberg Monastery.

Tobacco Monopoly Bicentenary A665

1984, May 4   Perf. 13½
1269 A665 4.50s Cigar wrapper, tobacco plant   .65 .30

1200th Anniv. of Kostendorf Municipality — A666

1984, May 4
1270 A666 4.50s View, arms   .65 .30

Automobile Engineers World Congress A667

1984, May 4   Photo.   Perf. 13½x14
1271 A667 5s Wheel bearing cross-section   .70 .30

Europa (1959-1984) A668

1984, May 4   Perf. 13½
1272 A668 6s multicolored   .90 .35

A669   Aragonite — A670

Archduke Johann (1782-1859) by S. von Carolsfeld.

Photo. & Engr.
1984, May 11   Perf. 14
1273 A669 4.50s multicolored   .65 .30
1984, May 11   Perf. 13½
1274 A670 3.50s multicolored   .50 .20
Ore and Iron Provincial Exhibition.

Era of Emperor Francis Joseph Exhibition — A671

Design: Cover of Viribus Unitis, publ. by Max Herzig, 1898.

1984, May 18
1275 A671 3.50s red & gold   .50 .20

A672   A673

Photo. & Engr.
1984, May 30   Perf. 14x13½
1276 A672 4.50s Tower, arms   .65 .30
City of Vocklabruck, 850th anniv.

1984, June 1   Perf. 13½
Dionysius, Virinum mosaic.
1277 A673 3.50s multicolored   .50 .20
Museum of Carinthia, centenary.

Erosion Prevention Systems Centenary A674

1984, June 5   Engr.   Perf. 14
1278 A674 4.50s Stone reinforcement wall   .65 .30

Tyrol Provincial Celebration, 1809-1984 — A675

Art Exhibition: Meeting of Imperial Troops with South Tyrolean Reserves under Andreas Hofer near Sterzing in April 1809, by Ludwig Schnorr von Carolsfeld, 1830.

Photo. & Engr.
1984, June 5   Perf. 14x13½
1279 A675 3.50s multicolored   .50 .20

A676   A677

1984, June 5   Engr.
1280 A676 4s violet brown   .55 .25
Ralph Benatzky (1884-1957), composer.

1984, June 22   Photo.   Perf. 14
1281 A677 3.50s multicolored   .50 .20
Christian von Ehrenfels (1859-1932), philosopher.

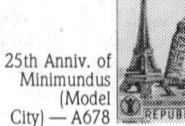

25th Anniv. of Minimundus (Model City) — A678

1984, June 22   Perf. 13½x14
1282 A678 4s Eiffel Tower, Tower of Pisa, ferris wheel   .55 .25

Blockheide Eibenstein Nature Park — A679

1984   Photo. & Engr.
1283 A679 4s shown   .55 .25
1284 A679 4s Lake Neusiedl   .55 .25
Issued: #1283, June 29; #1284, Aug. 13.

See Nos. 1349-1354, 1492-1496, 1744.

Monasteries and Abbeys — A679a

Designs: 3.50s, Geras Monastery, Lower Austria. 4s, Stams. 4.50s, Schlagl. 5s, Benedictine Abbey of St. Paul Levanttal. 6s, Rein-Hohenfurth.

1984-85   Perf. 14
1285   A679a   3.50s multicolored   .50 .20
1286   A679a   4s multicolored   .50 .20
1287   A679a   4.50s multicolored   .65 .30
1288   A679a   5s multicolored   .65 .30
1288A   A679a   6s multicolored   .90 .35
Nos. 1285-1288A (5)   3.20 1.45
Issued: 3.50s, 4/27/84; 4s, 9/28/84; 4.50s, 5/18/84; 5s, 9/27/85; 6s, 10/4/84.
See Nos. 1361-1365, 1464A-1468.

Schanatobel Railroad Bridge A680

Railroad Anniversaries: 3.50s, Arlberg centenary. 4.50s, Tauern, 75th.

1984, July 6   Perf. 14
1289 A680 3.50s shown   .50 .20
1290 A680 4.50s Falkenstein Bridge   .65 .20

A681   A682

1984, July 6   Photo.
1291 A681 6s Johan Stuwer's balloon   .90 .35
Balloon flight in Austria bicentenary.

1984, Aug. 31   Photo. & Engr.
1292 A682 7s Vienna Palace of Justice, emblem   .95 .45
Intl. Lawyers' Congress, Vienna.

A683   A684

1984, Sept. 3   Photo.
1293 A683 6s Josef Hyrtl, anatomist   .90 .35
7th European Anatomy Congress, Innsbruck, Sept. 3-7.

1984, Oct. 12
1294 A684 4s Window, by Karl Korab   .55 .20

AUSTRIA

A685 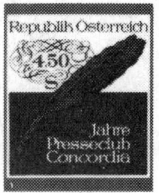 A686

1984, Oct. 18
1295 A685 3.50s Clock (Immset Uhr), 1555   .50 .20
Johannes of Gmunden, mathematician, 600th birth anniv.

1984, Nov. 9 Photo. *Perf. 13½*
1296 A686 4.50s Quill   .65 .30
Concordia Press Club, 125th anniv.

Fanny Eissler, Dancer, Birth Centenary — A687

1984, Nov. 23 Photo. & Engr.
1297 A687 4s multicolored   .55 .30

Christmas A688

Design: Christ is Born, Aggsbacher Altar, Herzogenburg Monastery.

1984, Nov. 30 *Perf. 14*
1298 A688 4.50s multicolored   .65 .20

A689  A690

1985, Jan. 4 *Perf. 14x13½*
1299 A689 3.50s Seal   .50 .15
Karl Franzens University, Graz, 400th anniv.

1985, Jan. 15 Engr.
1300 A690 4.50s dk rose lake   .60 .20
Dr. Lorenz Bohler, Surgeon, birth cent.

Nordic Events, Ski Championships, Seefeld — A691

1985, Jan. 17 Photo. *Perf. 13½*
1301 A691 4s Ski jumper, cross country racer   .55 .15

Linz Diocese Bicentenary A692

1985, Jan. 25
1302 A692 4.50s Linz Cathedral interior   .60 .20

Alban Berg (1885-1935), Composer — A693

1985, Feb. 8 Engr.
1303 A693 6s bluish black   .80 .25

Vocational Training Inst., 25th Anniv. — A694

1985, Feb. 15 Photo. *Perf. 13½x14*
1304 A694 4.50s multicolored   .60 .20

City of Bregenz, Bimillennium — A695

1985, Feb. 22 *Perf. 14x13½*
1305 A695 4s multicolored   .55 .15

Austrian Registration Labels Cent. — A696

1985, Mar. 15 *Perf. 13½x14*
1306 A696 4.50s Label, 1885   .60 .20

Josef Stefan (1835-1893), Physicist — A697

Photo. & Engr.
1985, Mar. 22 *Perf. 14x13½*
1307 A697 6s buff, dl red brn & dk brn .80 .25

A698  A699

1985, Mar. 29
1308 A698 3.50s multicolored   .50 .15
St. Leopold Exhibition, Klosterneuburg.

1985, Apr. 26 Photo.
1309 A699 4.50s multicolored   .60 .20
Liberation from German occupation forces, 40th anniv.

Painter Franz von Defregger (1835-1921) A700

1985, Apr. 26
1310 A700 3.50s Fairy tale teller   .50 .15

Europa Issue 1985

Johann Joseph Fux (1660-1741), Composer, Violin and Trombone A701

Photo. & Engr.
1985, May 3 *Perf. 13½*
1311 A701 6s lil gray & dk brn   .90 .25

Boheimkirchen (Market Town) Millennium — A702

1985, May 10 *Perf. 14*
1312 A702 4.50s View, coat of arms   .60 .20

A703  A704

Mercury staff, flags of member and affiliate nations.

1985, May 10 Photo. *Perf. 13½*
1313 A703 4s multicolored   .55 .15
European Free Trade Assoc., 25th anniv.

1985, May 15 Photo. & Engr.
Episcopal residence gate, St. Polten diocese arms.
1314 A704 4.50s multicolored   .60 .20
St. Polten Diocese, bicentenary.

The Gumpp Family of Builders, Innsbruck — A705

Perf. 14½x13½
1985, May 17 Photo.
1315 A705 3.50s multicolored   .50 .15

Garsten Market Town Millennium A706

Design: 17th century engraving by George Matthaus Fischer (1628-1696).

Photo. & Engr. *Perf. 13½x14*
1985, June 7
1316 A706 4.50s multicolored   .60 .20

UN, 40th Anniv. A707

Perf. 13½x14½
1985, June 26 Photo.
1317 A707 4s multicolored   .55 .20
Austrian membership, 30th anniv.

Intl. Assoc. for the Prevention of Suicide, 13th Congress — A708

Photo. & Engr. *Perf. 14*
1985, June 28
1318 A708 5s brn, lt ap grn & yel   .70 .30

Souvenir Sheet

Year of the Forest A709

1985, June 28 *Perf. 13½*
1319 A709 6s Healthy and damaged woodland   1.00 .35

Kurhaus, Bad Ischl Operetta Activities Emblem A710

1985, July 5 *Perf. 14*
1320 A710 3.50s multicolored   .50 .15
Bad Ischl Festival, 25th anniv.

AUSTRIA

Intl. Competition of Fire Brigades, Vocklabruck — A711

1985, July 18 Photo. *Perf. 14x13½*
1321 A711 4.50s Fireman, emblem .60 .20

Grossglockner Alpine Motorway, 50th Anniv. — A712

Photo. & Engr.
1985, Aug. 2 *Perf. 13½*
1322 A712 4s View of Fuschertorl .55 .20

World Chess Federation Congress, Graz — A713

1985, Aug. 28 Photo. *Perf. 13½*
1323 A713 4s Checkered globe, emblem .55 .20

The Legendary Foundation of Konigstetten by Charlemagne, by Auguste Stephan, c. 1870 — A714

Photo. & Engr.
1985, Aug. 30 *Perf. 14*
1324 A714 4.50s multicolored .60 .20
Konigstetten millennium.

Hofkirchen-Taufkirchen-Weibern Municipalities, 1200th Anniv. — A715

1985, Aug. 30 *Perf. 13½x14*
1325 A715 4.50s View of Weiburn, municipal arms .60 .20

Dr. Adam Politzer (1835-1920), Physician — A716

1985, Sept. 12 Engr. *Perf. 14*
1326 A716 3.50s blue violet .50 .15
Politzer pioneered aural therapy for auditory disorders.

Intl. Assoc. of Forwarding Agents, World Congress, Vienna — A717

1985, Oct. 7 Photo. *Perf. 13½*
1327 A717 6s multicolored .85 .35

Carnival Figures Riding High Bicycles, By Paul Flora A718

Photo. & Engr.
1985, Oct. 25 *Perf. 14*
1328 A718 4s multicolored .55 .20

St. Martin on Horseback A719

1985, Nov. 8 Photo.
1329 A719 4.50s multicolored .60 .30
Eisenstadt Diocese, 25th anniv.

Creche, Marble Bas-relief, Salzburg — A720

Photo. & Engr.
1985, Nov. 29 *Perf. 13½*
1330 A720 4.50s gold, dl vio & buff .60 .30
Christmas.

Hanns Horbiger (1860-1931), Inventor — A721

1985, Nov. 29 *Perf. 14*
1331 A721 3.50s gold & sepia .50 .20

Aqueduct, Hundsau Brook, Near Gostling A722

1985, Nov. 29 *Perf. 13½x14½*
1332 A722 3.50s red, bluish blk & brt ultra .50 .20
Vienna Aqueduct, 75th anniv.

Chateau de la Muette, Paris Headquarters A723

1985, Dec. 13
1333 A723 4s sep, rose lil & gold .55 .25
Org. for Economic Cooperation and Development, 25th anniv.

Johann Bohm (1886-1959), Pres. Austrian Trade Fed. — A724

1986, Jan. 24 Photo. *Perf. 14*
1334 A724 4.50s blk, ver & grayish black .65 .30

Intl. Peace Year — A725

Perf. 13½x14½
1986, Jan. 24 Photo.
1335 A725 6s multicolored .85 .35

Digital Telephone Service Introduction A726

1986, Jan. 29 Photo.
1336 A726 5s Push-button keyboard .75 .30

Johann Georg Albrechtsberger (b. 1736), Composer — A727

Perf. 13½x14½
1986, Jan. 31 Photo. & Engr.
1337 A727 3.50s Klosterneuburg organ .50 .20

Korneuburg, 850th Anniv. A728

1986, Feb. 7 Photo. *Perf. 14*
1338 A728 5s multicolored .75 .30

A729  A730

Self-portrait, by Oskar Kokoschka (b.1886).

Perf. 14½x13½
1986, Feb. 28 Photo.
1339 A729 4s multicolored .60 .30
1986, Feb. 28 Photo. *Perf. 13x13½*
1340 A730 6s multicolored .85 .35
Admission to Council of Europe, 30th anniv.

Clemens Holzmeister (b. 1886), Architect, Salzburg Festival Theater, 1926 — A731

Photo. & Engr.
1986, Mar. 27 *Perf. 13½*
1341 A731 4s sepia & redsh brn .60 .30

3rd Intl. Geotextile Congress, Vienna A732

Perf. 13½x14½
1986, Apr. 7 Photo.
1342 A732 5s multicolored .75 .30

Prince Eugen and Schlosshof Castle — A733

Photo. & Engr.
1986, Apr. 21 *Perf. 14*
1343 A733 4s multicolored .60 .30
Prince Eugen Exhibition, Schlosshof and Niederweiden.

St. Florian Monastery, Upper Austria A734

1986, Apr. 24
1344 A734 4s multicolored .60 .30
The World of Baroque provincial exhibition, St. Florian.

Herberstein Castle, Arms of Styria — A735

1986, May 2 *Perf. 13½x14½*
1345 A735 4s multicolored .60 .30

AUSTRIA

Europa
1986 — A736

1986, May 2   *Perf. 13½*
1346 A736 6s Pasque flower   .85 .45

Wagner, Scene from Opera Lohengrin
A737

1986, May 21
1347 A737 4s multicolored   .60 .30
Intl. Richard Wagner Congress, Vienna.

Antimonite
A738

1986, May 23   *Perf. 13½x14½*
1348 A738 4s multicolored   .60 .30
Burgenland Provincial Minerals Exhibition.

Scenery Type of 1984

1986-89   Photo. & Engr.   *Perf. 14*
1349 A679 5s Martinswall, Tyrol   .65 .35
1350 A679 5s Tschauko Falls, Carinthia   .65 .35
1351 A679 5s Dachstein Ice Caves   .80 .45
1352 A679 5s Gauertal, Montafon   .80 .45
1353 A679 5s Krimmler Waterfalls   .80 .60
1354 A679 5s Lusthauswasser   .80 .60
    Nos. 1349-1354 (6)   4.50 2.80
Issued: #1351, 6/11/87; #1352, 8/21/87; #1353, 8/19/88; #1354, 9/1/89.

Waidhofen on Ybbs Township, 800th Anniv.
A739

1986, June 20   Photo.   *Perf. 13½*
1355 A739 4s multicolored   .50 .30

Salzburg Local Railway, Cent.
A740

1986, Aug. 8   Photo.   *Perf. 14*
1356 A740 4s multicolored   .55 .30

Seals of Dukes Leopold Of Austria, Otakar of Styria, and Georgenberg Church
A741

1986, Aug. 14   Photo. & Engr.
1357 A741 5s multicolored   .70 .30
Georgenberg Treaty, 800th anniv.

Julius Tandler (1869-1936), Social Reformer — A742

1986, Aug. 22
1358 A742 4s multicolored   .60 .30

Sonnblick Observatory, Cent. — A743

   Perf. 13½x14½
1986, Aug. 27   Photo. & Engr.
1359 A743 4s Observatory, 1886   .60 .30

Discovery of Mandrake Root — A744

1986, Aug. 27   *Perf. 14½x13½*
1360 A744 5s multicolored   .75 .30
European Assoc. for Anesthesiology, 7th cong.

Monasteries and Abbeys Type of 1984

Designs: 5.50s, St. Gerold's Provostry, Vorarlberg. 7s, Loretto Monastery, Burgenland. 7.50s, Dominican Convent, Vienna. 8s, Zwettl Monastery. 10s, Wilten Monastery.

1986-88   Photo. & Engr.   *Perf. 14*
1361 A679a 5.50s multicolored   .80 .60
1362 A679a 7s multicolored   1.10 .90
1363 A679a 7.50s multicolored   1.10 .85
1364 A679a 8s multicolored   1.40 1.00
1365 A679a 10s multicolored   1.75 1.25
    Nos. 1361-1365 (5)   6.15 4.60
Issued: 5.50s, 9/12/86; 7.50s, 10/3; 7s, 8/14/87; 8s, 5/27/88; 10s, 3/18/88.

A745   A746

   Photo. & Engr.
1986, Sept. 3   *Perf. 14*
1366 A745 4s multicolored   .60 .30
Otto Stoessl (d. 1936), writer.

1986, Sept. 3   Photo.
1367 A746 4s Fireman, 1686   .60 .30
Vienna fire brigade, 300th anniv.

Silk Viennese Hunting Tapestry — A747

   Photo. & Engr.
1986, Sept. 3   *Perf. 14*
1368 A747 5s multicolored   .75 .40
Intl. conf. on Oriental Carpets, Vienna, Budapest.

A748   A749

   Photo. & Engr.
1986, Oct. 10   *Perf. 14*
1369 A748 5s Minister at pulpit   .70 .40
Protestant Act, 25th anniv., and Protestant Patent of Franz Josef I ensuring religious equality, 125th anniv.

1986, Oct. 17   *Perf. 13½x14*
Disintegration, by Walter Schmogner.
1370 A749 4s multicolored   .60 .30

Franz Liszt, Composer, and Birthplace, Burgenland
A750

1986, Oct. 17   *Perf. 13½*
1371 A750 5s green & sepia   .70 .40

Souvenir Sheet

European Security Conference, Vienna — A751

Illustration reduced.

1986, Nov. 4   *Perf. 13½x14*
1372 A751 6s Vienna   .95 .65

Strettweg Cart, 7th Cent. B.C. — A752

   Photo. & Engr.
1986, Nov. 26   *Perf. 14*
1373 A752 4s multicolored   .65 .30
Joanneum Styrian Land Museum, 175th anniv.

Christmas
A753

Design: The Little Crib, bas-relief by Schwanthaler (1740-1810), Schlierbach Monastery.

1986, Nov. 28
1374 A753 5s gold & rose lake   .80 .40

Federal Chamber of Commerce, 40th Anniv. — A754

1986, Dec. 2   Photo.
1375 A754 5s multicolored   .80 .40

Industry
A755

1986-91   *Perf. 14x13½*
1376 A755 4s Steel workers   .80 .30
1377 A755 4s Office worker, computer   .80 .35
1378 A755 4s Lab assistant   .80 .30
1378A A755 4.50s Textile worker   .75 .60
1379 A755 5s Bricklayer   .80 .60
    Nos. 1376-1379 (5)   3.95 2.15
Issued: #1376, 12/4/86; #1377, 10/5/87; #1378, 10/21/88; 5s, 10/10/89; 4.50s, 10/11/91.
This is an expanding set. Numbers will change if necessary.

The Educated Eye, by Arnulf Rainer — A756

1987, Jan. 13   Photo.   *Perf. 13½x14*
1386 A756 5s multicolored   .80 .40
Adult education in Vienna, cent.

The Large Blue Madonna, by Anton Faistauer (1887-1970)
A757

Paintings: 6s, Self-portrait, 1922, by A. Paris Gutersloh (1887-1973).

1987, Jan. 29   *Perf. 14*
1387 A757 4s multicolored   .55 .20
1388 A757 6s multicolored   .90 .40

Europa
1987 — A758

   Photo. & Engr.
1987, Apr. 6   *Perf. 13½x14*
1389 A758 6s Hundertwasser House   .95 .55

World Ice Hockey Championships, Vienna — A759

AUSTRIA

Perf. 13½x14½
1987, Apr. 17 Photo.
1390 A759 5s multicolored .80 .60

Opening of the Austria Center, Vienna A760

1987, Apr. 22
1391 A760 5s multicolored .80 .60

Salzburg City Charter, 700th Anniv. A761

1987, Apr. 24
1392 A761 5s multicolored .80 .60

A762  A763

Photo. & Engr.
1987, Apr. 29 Perf. 14
1393 A762 4s Factory, 1920 .65 .50
Work-Men-Machines, provincial exhibition, Upper Austria.

1987, Apr. 29 Photo. Perf. 13½
1394 A763 5s multicolored .80 .60
Equal rights for men and women.

A764  A765

Adele Block-Bauer I, abstract by Gustav Klimt.

Photo. & Engr.
1987, May 8 Perf. 13½
1395 A764 4s multicolored .65 .50
The Era of Emperor Franz Joseph, provincial exhibition, Lower Austria.

1987, May 15 Perf. 14½x13½
1396 A765 6s multicolored 1.00 .75
Arthur Schnitzler (1862-1931), poet.

Von Raitenau, View of Salzburg A766

1987, May 15 Perf. 14
1397 A766 4s multicolored .65 .50
Prince Archbishop Wolf Dietrich von Raitenau, patron of baroque architecture in Salzburg, provincial exhibition.

Lace, Lustenau Municipal Arms — A767

1987, May 22
1398 A767 5s multicolored .80 .60
Lustenau, 1100th anniv.

Souvenir Sheet

Austrian Railways Sesquicentenary — A768

1987, June 5 Photo. Perf. 13½
1399 A768 6s multicolored 1.00 .75

8th Intl. Congress of Engravers, Vienna A769

Photo. & Engr.
1987, June 17 Perf. 14
1400 A769 5s gray, gray brn & dull rose .80 .60

Dr. Karl Josef Bayer (1847-1904), Chemist — A770    Shipping on Achensee, Cent. — A771

1987, June 22 Perf. 14x13½
1401 A770 5s multicolored .80 .60
Eighth Intl. Light Metals Congress, June 22-26, Leoben and Vienna; Bayer Technique for producing aluminum oxide from bauxite, cent.

1987, June 26 Photo.
1402 A771 4s multicolored .65 .50

A772  A773

1987, July 1
1403 A772 5s Palais Rottal, Vienna .80 .60
Ombudsmen's office, 10th anniv.

1987, Aug. 11 Photo. & Engr.
1404 A773 5s dull olive bister, choc & buff .80 .60
Dr. Erwin Schrodinger (1887-1961), 1933 Nobel laureate in physics.

Freistadt Exhibitions, 125th Anniv. A774

1987, Aug. 11 Perf. 14x14½
1405 A774 5s multicolored .80 .60

Arbing, 850th Anniv. — A775

1987, Aug. 21 Perf. 13½
1406 A775 5s multicolored .80 .60

1987 World Cycling Championships, Villach to Vienna — A776

1987, Aug. 25 Perf. 14
1407 A776 5s multicolored .80 .60

World Congress of Savings Banks, Vienna A777

Perf. 13½x14½
1987, Sept. 9 Photo.
1408 A777 5s multicolored .80 .60

Johann Michael Haydn (1737-1806), Composer A778

Perf. 13½x14½
1987, Sept. 14 Engr.
1409 A778 4s dull violet .65 .50

Paul Hofhaymer (1459-1537), Composer A779

Photo. & Engr.
1987, Sept. 11 Perf. 14
1410 A779 4s gold, blk & ultra .65 .50

Bearded Vulture — A780

1987, Sept. 25
1411 A780 4s multicolored .65 .50
Innsbruck Zoo, 25th anniv.

Baumgottinnen, by Arnulf Neuwirth — A781

1987, Oct. 9 Perf. 14x13½
1412 A781 5s multicolored .80 .60
Modern Art.

Gambling Monopoly, 200th Anniv. — A782

Perf. 14½x13½
1987, Oct. 30 Photo.
1413 A782 5s Lottery drum .80 .60

Christoph Willibald Gluck (1714-1787), Composer A784

Photo. & Engr.
1987, Nov. 13 Perf. 14
1415 A784 5s cream & blk .88 .65

Oskar Helmer (b. 1887), Politician — A785

1987, Nov. 13
1416 A785 4s multicolored .70 .50

Joseph Mohr (1792-1848) and Franz Gruber (1787-1863), Opening Bars of "Silent Night, Holy Night" — A786

1987, Nov. 27
1417 A786 5s multicolored .90 .65
Christmas.

A787  A788

AUSTRIA

Photo. & Engr.
1988, Jan. 12   *Perf. 13½*
1418 A787 5s St. John Bosco, children .90 .65
Intl. Education Congress of Salesian Fathers.

Perf. 14½x13½
1988, Feb. 19   **Photo. & Engr.**
1419 A788 6s multicolored 1.05 .80
Ernst Mach (1838-1916), physicist.

Village with Bridge (1904), by Franz von Zulow (1883-1963), Painter — A789

1988, Feb. 25   **Photo.**   *Perf. 14½x14*
1420 A789 4s multicolored .70 .50

Biedermeier Provincial Exhibition, Vormarz in Vienna A790

Painting: Confiscation, by Ferdinand Georg Waldmuller (1793-1865).

Photo. & Engr.
1988, Mar. 11   *Perf. 14*
1421 A790 4s multicolored .70 .50

Anschluss of March 11, 1938 A791

1988, Mar. 11   **Photo.**   *Perf. 13½*
1422 A791 5s gray olive, brn blk & ver .85 .65

No. 2 Aigen Steam Locomotive, 1887 — A792

1988, Mar. 22   *Perf. 13½x14½*
1423 A792 4s shown .70 .50
1424 A792 5s Electric train, Josepsplatz .85 .65
Muhlkreis Railway, cent. (4s); Vienna Local Railway, cent. (5s).

World Wildlife Fund — A793

Photo. & Engr.
1988, Apr. 15   *Perf. 13½x14*
1425 A793 5s Bee eater .90 .65

Styrian Provincial Exhibition on Glass and Coal, Barnbach A794

1988, Apr. 29   *Perf. 13½*
1426 A794 4s Frosted glass .70 .50

Intl. Red Cross, 125th Anniv. — A795

1988, May 6   **Photo.**   *Perf. 14*
1427 A795 12s grn, brt red & blk 2.25 1.65

Gothic Silver Censer — A796

1988, May 6   **Photo. & Engr.**
1428 A796 4s multicolored .70 .50
Art and Monasticism at the Birth of Austria, lower Austrian provincial exhibition, Seitenstetten.

Europa 1988 A797

Communication and transportation.

1988, May 13   **Photo.**
1429 A797 6s multicolored 1.10 .80

Mattsee Monastery and Lion of Alz — A798

1988, May 18   **Photo. & Engr.**
1430 A798 4s multicolored .70 .50
Provincial exhibition at Mattsee Monastery: Bavarian Tribes in Salzburg.

Weinberg Castle — A799

Perf. 13½x14½
1988, May 20   **Photo.**
1431 A799 4s multicolored .70 .50
Upper Austrian provincial exhibition: Weinberg Castle.

Odon von Horwath (1901-1938), Dramatist — A800

Perf. 14½x13½
1988, June 1   **Photo. & Engr.**
1432 A800 6s olive bis & slate grn 1.10 .80

Stockerau Festival, 25th Anniv. — A801

1988, June 17   *Perf. 14*
1433 A801 5s Stockerau Town Hall .80 .60

Tauern Motorway Opening — A802

1988, June 24   **Photo.**   *Perf. 13½x14*
1434 A802 4s multicolored .65 .50

Brixlegg, 1200th Anniv. A803

Perf. 13½x14½
1988, July 1   **Photo. & Engr.**
1435 A803 5s multicolored .80 .60

View of Klagenfurt, Engraving by Matthaus Merian (1593-1650) A804

Photo. & Engr.
1988, Aug. 12   *Perf. 14*
1436 A804 5s multicolored .80 .60
Carinthian Postal Service, 400th Anniv.

Brixen-im-Thale, 1200th Anniv. — A805

1988, Aug. 12
1437 A805 5s multicolored .80 .60

Feldkirchen, 1100th Anniv. — A806

1988, Sept. 2   *Perf. 13½*
1438 A806 5s multicolored .80 .60

Feldbach, 800th Anniv. A807

1988, Sept. 15   **Photo. & Engr.**
1439 A807 5s multicolored .80 .60

Ansfelden, 1200th Anniv. — A808

1988, Sept. 23   *Perf. 14*
1440 A808 5s multicolored .80 .60

Exports — A809

1988, Oct. 18   **Photo.**   *Perf. 14x13½*
1441 A809 8s multicolored 1.50 1.25
No. 1441 has a holographic image. Soaking in water may affect the hologram.

Vienna Concert Hall, 75th Anniv. A810

Photo. & Engr.
1988, Oct. 19   *Perf. 13½*
1442 A810 5s multicolored .80 .60

The Watchmen, by Giselbert Hoke — A811

1988, Oct. 21   *Perf. 14*
1443 A811 5s multicolored .80 .60

AUSTRIA

Social Democrats Unification Party Congress, Cent. — A812

1988, Nov. 11 Photo. Perf. 14½x14
1444 A812 4s multicolored .65 .50

Leopold Schonbauer (1888-1963), Physician — A813

Perf. 14½x13½
1988, Nov. 11 Photo. & Engr.
1445 A813 4s multicolored .65 .50

Christmas A814

Nativity painting from St. Barbara's Church.

1988, Nov. 25 Perf. 14
1446 A814 5s multicolored .80 .60

Benedictine Monastery, Melk, 900th Anniv. A815

Design: Fresco by Paul Troger.

1989, Mar. 17 Photo. & Engr.
1447 A815 5s multicolored .80 .60

Madonna and Child, by Lucas Cranach (1472-1553) A816

Marianne Hainisch (1839-1936), Women's Rights Activist A817

1989, Mar. 17 Perf. 14½x13½
1448 A816 4s multicolored .60 .50

Diocese of Innsbruck, 25th anniv.

1989, Mar. 24 Perf. 14x13½
1449 A817 6s multicolored .95 .70

Glider Plane and Parachutist A818

1989, Mar. 31 Photo. Perf. 14
1450 A818 6s multicolored 1.00 .75

World Gliding Championships, Wiener Neustadt, and World Parachuting Championships, Damuls.

Bruck an der Leitha Commune, 750th Anniv. A819

Painting by Georg Matthaus Vischer (1628-1696).

1989, Apr. 21
1451 A819 5s multicolored .85 .60

A820    A821

Die Malerei, 1904, by Rudolf Jettmar (1869-1939).

Perf. 14½x13½
1989, Apr. 21 Photo.
1452 A820 5s multicolored .85 .60

1989, Apr. 26 Photo. & Engr.
1453 A821 5s multicolored .85 .60

Holy Trinity Church, Stadl-Paura.
Michael Prunner (1669-1739), baroque architect.

A822    A823

Eduard Suess (1831-1914, structural geologist) portrait by J. Krieher (1800-1876) and map.

1989, Apr. 26
1454 A822 6s multicolored 1.00 .75

1989, Apr. 26
1455 A823 5s multicolored .85 .60

Ludwig Wittgenstein (1889-1951), philosopher.

Styrian Provincial Exhibition, Judenburg A824

Design: Judenberg, 17th cent., an engraving by Georg Matthaus Vischer.

1989, Apr. 28 Perf. 14x13½
1456 A824 4s multicolored .70 .50

Industrial Technology Exhibition, Pottenstein — A825

1989, Apr. 28 Photo. Perf. 13½
1457 A825 4s Steam engine .70 .50

Radstadt Township, 700th Anniv. A826

1989, May 3 Photo. Perf. 13½x14½
1458 A826 5s multicolored .85 .60

Europa 1989 — A827

1989, May 5
1459 A827 6s Toy boat 1.00 .75

Monastery Church at Lambach, 900th Anniv. — A828

Photo. & Engr.
1989, May 19 Perf. 14
1460 A828 4s multicolored .70 .50

Paddle Steamer *Gisela* — A829

1989, May 19 Photo. Perf. 13½
1461 A829 5s multicolored .85 .60

Shipping on the Traunsee, 150th anniv.

St. Andra im Lavanttal, 650th Anniv. A830

Period cityscape by Matthaus Merian.

1989, May 26 Photo. & Engr.
1462 A830 5s multicolored .85 .60

Richard Strauss (1864-1949), Composer — A831

Perf. 14½x13½
1989, June 1 Photo. & Engr.
1463 A831 6s dark brn, gold & red brn 1.00 .75

Achensee Railway, Cent. — A832

1989, June 8 Photo. Perf. 13½
1464 A832 5s multicolored .85 .60

Monastery Type of 1984

Design: 50g, Vorau Abbey, Styria. 1s, Monastery of Mehrerau, Vorarlberg. 1.50s, Monastery of the German Order in Vienna. 2s, Bendictine Monastery, Michaelbeuern. 11s, Engelszell Abbey. 12s, Monastery of the Hospitalers, Eisenstadt. 17s, St. Peter, Salzburg. 20s, Wernberg Monastery.

1989-92 Photo. & Engr. Perf. 14
1464A A679a 50g multicolored .15 .15
1465 A679a 1s multicolored .15 .15
1465A A679a 1.50s multicolored .30 .25
1466 A679a 2s multicolored .35 .25
1467 A679a 11s multicolored 1.90 1.40
1467A A679a 12s multicolored 2.25 1.75
1468 A679a 17s multicolored 2.75 2.00
1469 A679a 20s multicolored 2.75 2.00
Nos. 1464A-1469 (8) 10.60 7.95

Issued: 1s, 9/1/89; 17s, 6/29/89; 11s, 3/9/90; 50g, 10/12/90; 20s, 5/3/91; 2s, 9/27/91; 1.50s, 10/23/92; 12s, 6/17/92.
This is an expanding set. Numbers will change if necessary.

Interparliamentary Union, Cent. — A833

Photo. & Engr.
1989, June 30 Perf. 14
1475 A833 6s Parliament, Vienna 1.00 .75

Social Security in Austria, Cent. — A834

1989, Aug. 1 Photo.
1476 A834 5s multicolored .70 .50

UN Offices in Vienna, 10th Anniv. A835

1989, Aug. 23
1477 A835 8s multicolored 1.10 .85

Wildalpen, 850th Anniv. A836

Photo. & Engr.
1989, Sept. 15 Perf. 13½x14
1478 A836 5s Foundry, coat of arms .80 .60

AUSTRIA

33rd Congress of the Association for Quality Assurance (EOQC) — A837

1989, Sept. 18 Photo. *Perf. 14x13½*
1479 A837 6s multicolored .90 .70

14th World Congress of the Soc. for Criminal Law (AIDP) A838

1989, Oct. 2 Photo. & Engr. *Perf. 13½*
1480 A838 6s Justice Palace, Vienna .90 .70

Lebensbaum, by Ernst Steiner — A839

1989, Oct. 10 *Perf. 13½x14*
1481 A839 5s multicolored .80 .60

1989, Nov. 6 *Perf. 14½x13½* Photo.
1482 A840 4s Trakl .60 .45
1483 A840 4s Anzengruber .60 .45

Georg Trakl (1887-1914), expressionist poet; Ludwig Anzengruber (1839-1889), playwright and novelist.

1989, Nov. 10 Photo. & Engr.
1484 A841 6s multicolored .90 .70

Alfred Fried (1864-1921), pacifist and publisher awarded the Nobel peace prize for 1911 with Tobias Asser.

Parish Church Christ Child, by Johann Carl Reslfeld A842

1989, Dec. 1 *Perf. 13½x14½*
1485 A842 5s multicolored .75 .60
Christmas.

The Young Post Rider, an Engraving by Albrecht Durer

1990, Jan. 12 Photo. & Engr. *Perf. 14*
1486 A843 5s multicolored .80 .60
Postal communications in Europe, 500th anniv. See Belgium No. 1332, Germany No. 1592, Berlin No. 9N584 and German Democratic Republic No. 2791.

Perf. 13½x14½
1990, Jan. 12 Photo.
1487 A844 5s multicolored .80 .60
Hahnenkamm alpine competition, Kitzbuhel, 50th anniv.

Perf. 14½x13½
1990, Jan. 17 Photo.
1488 A845 4.50s multicolored .70 .55
Salomon Sulzer (1804-90), cantor and composer.

1990, Jan. 22 Photo. & Engr.
1489 A846 6s claret & pale green .95 .70
Friedrich Emich (1860-1940), chemist.

Miniature from the *Market Book of Grein*, by Ulrich Schreier, c. 1490 A847

1990, Mar. 9 *Perf. 14*
1490 A847 5s sepia, buff & gray .80 .60
City of Linz, 500th anniv.

University Seals — A848

1990, Apr. 6
1491 A848 5s multicolored .85 .65
625th Anniv. of Vienna University and 175th anniv. of Vienna Technical University.

Scenery Type of 1984

1990-97 *Perf. 14*
1492 A679 5s Styrian Vineyards .85 .65
1493 A679 5s Obir Caverns .95 .70
1494 A679 5s Natural Bridge, Vorarlberg .90 .75
1495 A679 6s Wilder Kaiser Mountain, Tyrol 1.25 .95
1496 A679 6s Peggau Cave, Styria 1.00 .80
1497 A679 6s Moorland, swamp, Heidenreichstein 1.25 1.00
1498 A679 6s Hohe Tauern Natl. Park 1.25 1.00
1499 A679 6s Nussberg Vineyards 1.00 .80
Nos. 1492-1499 (8) 8.45 6.65
Issued: #1492, 4/27; #1493, 3/26/91; #1494, 2/5/92; #1495, 2/19/93; #1496, 4/29/94; #1497, 5/19/95; #1498, 3/29/96; #1499, 2/21/97.

A849  A850
Church and municipal arms.

1990, Apr. 27 Photo. *Perf. 14x13½*
1500 A849 7s multicolored 1.25 .25
1200th anniv. of Anthering.

1990, Apr. 30 Photo. *Perf. 13½*
1501 A850 4.50s multicolored .80 .60
Labor Day, cent.

Seckau Abbey, 850th Anniv. — A851    Ebene Reichenau Post Office — A852

1990, May 4 Engr. *Perf. 14x13½*
1502 A851 4.50s bluish black .80 .60

1990, May 4 Photo. *Perf. 13½x14*
1503 A852 7s multicolored 1.25 .25

A853  A854
Self Portraits: 4.50s, Hans Makart (1840-84). 5s, Egon Schiele (1890-1918).

1990, May 29 Photo. & Engr. *Perf. 14*
1504 A853 4.50s multicolored .80 .60
1505 A853 5s multicolored .85 .65

1990, June 1 Photo. *Perf. 14x13½*
1506 A854 4.50s multicolored .80 .60
Ferdinand Raimund (1790-1836), actor.

Christ Healing the Sick by Rembrandt A855

1990, June 5 Photo. & Engr. *Perf. 14*
1507 A855 7s multicolored 1.25 1.00
2nd Intl. Christus Medicus Cong., Bad Ischl.

Hardegg, 700th Anniv. — A856

1990, June 8 *Perf. 13½x14*
1508 A856 4.50s multicolored .80 .60

Oberdraburg, 750th Anniv. A857

1990, June 8 Photo.
1509 A857 5s multicolored .85 .65

Gumpoldskirchen, 850th Anniv. — A858

1990, June 15 Photo. & Engr. *Perf. 13½*
1510 A858 5s multicolored .85 .65

Mathias Zdarsky (1856-1940), Alpine Skier — A859

1990, June 20 *Perf. 14x13½*
1511 A859 5s multicolored .85 .65

Telegraph, 1880, Anton Tschechow, 1978 — A860

1990, June 28 Photo. *Perf. 14*
1512 A860 9s multicolored 1.50 1.10
Modern shipbuilding in Austria, 150th anniv.

A861  A862

1990, Aug. 3 Photo. & Engr. *Perf. 14x13½*
1513 A861 5s gold & brown .85 .65
Joseph Friedrich Perkonig (1890-1959), poet.

1990, Aug. 30 Photo. & Engr. *Perf. 13½x14*
Herr des Regenbogens, by Robert Zeppel-Sperl.
1514 A862 5s gold & brown .85 .65

European Dialysis and Transplantation
Society, 27th Congress — A863

1990, Sept. 4		Photo.	Perf. 14
1515	A863	7s multicolored	1.25 1.00

Franz Werfel (1890-1945), Writer — A864

Photo. & Engr.

1990, Sept. 11			Perf. 14x13½
1516	A864	5s multicolored	.95 .70

Austrian Forces in UN Peace Keeping Forces, 30th Anniv. A865

1990, Sept. 20		Photo.	Perf. 13½
1517	A865	7s multicolored	1.25 1.00

Federal and State Arms A866

1990, Sept. 24		Photo. & Engr.	
1518	A866	5s multicolored	.95 .70

Federalism in Austria.

A867    A868

1990, Oct. 22		Photo & Engr.	Perf. 14
1519	A867	4.50s blk, bl grn & red	.85 .65

Mining Univ., Leoben, 150th anniv.

Photo. & Engr.

1990, Nov. 8			Perf. 14x13½
1520	A868	4.50s multicolored	.85 .65

Karl Freiherr von Vogelsang (1818-90), politician.

Metalworkers and Miners Trade Union, Cent. — A869

1990, Nov. 16			Perf. 14
1521	A869	5s multicolored	.95 .70

3rd World Curling Championships A870

1990, Nov. 23		Photo.	Perf. 14x13½
1522	A870	7s multicolored	1.40 1.00

Palmhouse at Schonbrunn A871

1990, Nov. 30			Perf. 14
1523	A871	5s multicolored	.95 .70

A872    A873

Christmas: Altar in Klosterneuburg Abbey by the Master from Verdun.

Photo. & Engr.

1990, Nov. 23			Perf. 13½
1524	A872	5s multicolored	.95 .70

Photo. & Engr.

1991, Jan. 15			Perf. 14x13½
1525	A873	4.50s multicolored	.85 .65

Franz Grillparzer (1791-1872), dramatic poet.

A874    A875

1991, Jan. 21			Perf. 13½
1526	A874	5s multicolored	.95 .70

Alpine Skiing World Championship, Saalbach-Hinterglemm.

1991, Jan. 21		Photo.	Perf. 14x13½
1527	A875	5s multicolored	.95 .70

Bruno Kreisky (1911-90), chancellor.

Friedrich Freiherr von Schmidt (1825-1891), Architect A876

1991, Jan. 21			Perf. 14
1528	A876	7s multicolored	1.35 1.00

Visual Arts — A877

Designs: 4.50s, Donner Fountain, Vienna, by Raphael Donner (1693-1741), sculptor. 5s, Kitzbuhel in Winter, by Alfons Walde (1891-1958), painter. 7s, Vienna Stock Exchange, Theophil Hansen (1813-1891), architect.

1991, Feb. 8			
1529	A877	4.50s multicolored	.85 .65
1530	A877	5s multicolored	.95 .70
1531	A877	7s multicolored	1.40 1.00
Nos. 1529-1531 (3)			3.20 2.35

See No. 1543.

Marie von Ebner Eschenbach (1830-1916), Poet — A878

		Perf. 13½x14½	Engr.
1991, Mar. 12			
1532	A878	4.50s rose violet	.85 .65

Miniature Sheet

Wolfgang Amadeus Mozart (1756-1791), Composer — A879

Design: b, Magic Flute Fountain, Vienna.

1991, Mar. 22			Perf. 13½
1533		Sheet of 2 + label	1.65 1.25
a.-b.	A879	5s any single	.80 .60

Spittal an der Drau, 800th Anniv. A880

1991, Apr. 11			Perf. 14
1534	A880	4.50s multicolored	.75 .60

Europa A881

1991, May 3		Photo.	Perf. 14
1535	A881	7s ERS-1 satellite	1.10 .80

Garden Banquet by Anthony Bays A882

1991, May 10		Photo.	Perf. 13½
1536	A882	5s multicolored	.75 .60

Vorarlberg Provincial Exhibition, Hohenems.

Museum of Military History, Cent. A883

Design: 7s, Interior of Museum of Art History.

Photo. & Engr.

1991, May 24			Perf. 13½
1537	A883	5s multicolored	.95 .80
1538	A883	7s multicolored	1.25 1.00

Museum of Art History, Cent. (#1538).

Grein, 500th Anniv. A884

1991, May 24		Photo.	Perf. 14
1539	A884	4.50s multicolored	.90 .45

Tulln, 1200th Anniv. A885

1991, May 24			Perf. 13½x14
1540	A885	5s multicolored	.95 .80

Completion of Karawanken Tunnels — A886

1991, May 31			Perf. 14x13½
1541	A886	7s multicolored	1.25 1.00

5th Anniv. of St. Polten as Provincial Capital of Lower Austria A887

1991, July 5		Photo.	Perf. 14
1542	A887	5s multicolored	.80 .65

Visual Arts Type of 1991

Design: 4.50s, Karlsplatz Station of Vienna Subway by Otto Wagner (1841-1918), Architect.

1991, July 12		Photo. & Engr.	
1543	A877	4.50s multicolored	.75 .60

Rowing and Junior Canoeing World Championships, Vienna — A888

1991, Aug. 20		Photo.	Perf. 13½x14
1544	A888	5s multicolored	.85 .70

AUSTRIA

European Congress of Radiologists A889

1991, Sept. 13 *Perf. 14*
1545 A889 7s multicolored 1.10 .95

Paracelsus (1493-1541), Physician — A890

1991, Sept. 27 *Perf. 14x13½*
1546 A890 4.50s multicolored .75 .60

Joint Austrian-Soviet Space Mission — A891

1991, Oct. 2 *Perf. 14*
1547 A891 9s multicolored 1.50 1.25

Austrian Folk Festivals — A892

Designs: 4.50s, Almabtrieb, Tyrol. 5s, Winzerkrone, Vienna. 7s, Ernte-Monstranz, Styria.

1991, Oct. 4 *Photo. & Engr.*
1548 A892 4.50s multicolored .75 .60
1549 A892 5s multicolored .85 .70
1550 A892 7s multicolored 1.10 .95
Nos. 1548-1550 (3) 2.70 2.25

See Nos. 1577-1579, 1619-1621, 1633-1635, 1671-1673, 1694, 1705-1706, 1714, 1730, 1741, 1752-1753, 1762.

The General by Rudolph Pointner — A893

Photo. & Engr.
1991, Oct. 11 *Perf. 13½x14*
1551 A893 5s multicolored .85 .70

Birth of Christ, Baumgartenberg Church — A894

1991, Nov. 29
1552 A894 5s multicolored .85 .70
Christmas.

Julius Raab, Politician, Birth Cent. — A895

1991, Nov. 29 *Perf. 14x13½*
1553 A895 4.50s red brn & brn .75 .60

1992 Winter and Summer Olympic Games A897

1992, Jan. 14 *Photo. Perf. 14*
1555 A897 7s multicolored 1.25 1.00

Trade Union of Clerks in Private Enterprises, Cent. — A898

1992, Jan. 14
1556 A898 5.50s multicolored .95 .80

A899    A900

1992, Jan. 29 *Perf. 14x13½*
1557 A899 5s multicolored .90 .75
8th Natural Run Toboggan World Championships.

1992, Feb. 5 *Engr. Perf. 14x13½*
1558 A900 5.50s brown .95 .80
George Saiko, Poet, birth cent.

Worker's Sports, Cent. — A901

1992, Feb. 5 *Photo. Perf. 14*
1559 A901 5.50s multicolored .95 .80

Souvenir Sheet

Vienna Philharmonic Orchestra, 150th Anniv. — A902

Photo. & Engr.
1992, Mar. 27 *Perf. 14*
1560 A902 5.50s multicolored .95 .80

Scientists — A903

Designs: 5s, Franz Joseph Muller von Reichenstein (1742-1825), discoverer of tellurium. 5.50s, Dr. Paul Kitaibel (1757-1817), botanist. 6s, Christian Johann Doppler (1803-1853), physicist. 7s, Richard Kuhn (1900-1967), chemist.

1992, Mar. 27 *Photo.*
1561 A903 5s multicolored .85 .70
1562 A903 5.50s multicolored .95 .80
1563 A903 6s multicolored 1.00 .85
1564 A903 7s multicolored 1.25 .95
Nos. 1561-1564 (4) 4.05 3.30

Railway Workers Union, Cent. A904

1992, Apr. 2 *Perf. 14x13½*
1565 A904 5.50s black & red .95 .80

Norbert Hanrieder (1842-1913), Poet — A905

Photo. & Engr.
1992, Apr. 30 *Perf. 14x13½*
1566 A905 5.50s purple & buff .95 .80

Carl Zeller (1842-1898) and Karl Millocker (1842-1899), Operetta Composers A906

Photo. & Engr.
1992, Apr. 30 *Perf. 14*
1567 A906 6s multicolored 1.00 .85

LD Steel Mill, 40th Anniv. A907

1992, May 8 *Photo. Perf. 14x13½*
1568 A907 5s multicolored .85 .70

Discovery of America, 500th Anniv. A908

1992, May 8 *Photo. & Engr. Perf. 14*
1569 A908 7s multicolored 1.25 .95
Europa.

Austro-Swiss Treaty on Regulation of Rhine River, Cent. — A909

1992, May 8 *Photo. Perf. 13½x14*
1570 A909 7s multicolored 1.25 .95

Protection of the Alps — A910

1992, May 22 *Perf. 14x13½*
1571 A910 5.50s multicolored .95 .80

Dr. Anna Dengel (1892-1980), Physician — A911    Sebastian Rieger (1867-1953), Poet — A912

1992, May 22 *Photo. & Engr.*
1572 A911 5.50s multicolored .95 .80

1992, May 22 *Engr.*
1573 A912 5s red brown .85 .70

Lienz, 750th Anniv. A913

1992, June 17 *Photo. Perf. 14x13½*
1574 A913 5s Town Hall .90 .70

Intl. Congress of Austrian Society of Surgeons — A914

Photo. & Engr.
1992, June 17 *Perf. 14*
1575 A914 6s multicolored 1.10 .90

AUSTRIA

Dr. Kurt Waldheim, President of Austria, 1986-92 — A915

1992, June 22   Perf. 14x13½
1576 A915 5.50s multicolored   .95   .75

Folk Festivals Type of 1991
Designs: 5s, Marksman's target, Lower Austria. 5.50s, Peasant's chest, Carinthia. 7s, Votive icon, Vorarlberg.

Photo. & Engr.
1992, Sept. 18   Perf. 14
1577 A892 5s multicolored   .90   .70
1578 A892 5.50s multicolored   .95   .75
1579 A892 7s multicolored   1.25 1.00
   Nos. 1577-1579 (3)   3.10 2.45

Marchfeld Canal — A917

1992, Oct. 9   Photo.   Perf. 13½x14
1580 A917 5s multicolored   .90   .70

5th Intl. Ombudsman Conference, Vienna A918

1992, Oct. 9   Photo & Engr.   Perf. 14
1581 A918 5.50s multicolored   .95   .75

The Clearance of Seawater, by Peter Pongratz A919

1992, Oct. 9
1582 A919 5.50s multicolored   .95   .75

Academy of Fine Arts, 300th Anniv. — A920

Photo. & Engr.
1992, Oct. 23   Perf. 14
1583 A920 5s red & blue   1.00   .85

Birth of Christ, by Johann Georg Schmidt A921

1992, Nov. 27   Perf. 14x13½
1584 A921 5.50s multicolored   1.10   .90
Christmas.

Veit Koniger, Sculptor, Death Bicent. — A922

Photo. & Engr.
1992, Nov. 27   Perf. 14
1585 A922 5s multicolored   1.00   .80

Herman Potocnik, Theoretician of Geosynchronous Satellite Orbit, Birth Cent. — A923

1992, Nov. 27   Photo.
1586 A923 10s multicolored   2.00 1.65

Famous Buildings A924

Designs: 5s, Statues and dome of Imperial Palace, Vienna, designed by Joseph Emanuel Fischer von Erlach. 5.50s, Kinsky Palace, designed by Lukas von Hildebrandt. 7s, Vienna State Opera, designed by Eduard van der Null and August Siccard von Siccardsburg.

1993, Jan. 22   Photo. & Engr.
1587 A924 5s multicolored   1.00   .80
1588 A924 5.50s multicolored   1.10   .90
1589 A924 7s multicolored   1.40 1.10
   Nos. 1587-1589 (3)   3.50 2.80

Joseph Emanuel Fischer von Erlach, 300th birth anniv. (#1587). Johann Lukas von Hildebrandt, 325th birth anniv. (#1588). Eduard van der Null, August Siccard von Siccardsburg, 125th death anniv. (#1589).

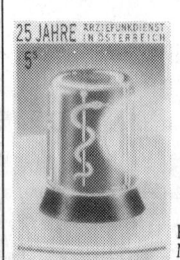

Radio Dispatched Medical Service, 25th Anniv. — A925

1993, Feb. 19   Photo.
1590 A925 5s multicolored   1.00   .80

Typewriter Made by Peter Mitterhofer (1822-1893) A926

1993, Feb. 19   Perf. 13½x14
1591 A926 17s multicolored   3.50 2.75

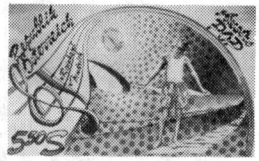

Popular Entertainers — A927

5.50s, Strada del Sole, by Rainhard Fendrich.

1993, Mar. 19   Photo.   Perf. 14
1592 A927 5.50s multicolored   1.00   .80
See Nos. 1626, 1639.

Charles Sealsfield (1793-1864), Writer A928

Photo. & Engr.
1993, Mar. 19   Perf. 13½x14
1593 A928 10s multicolored   1.75 1.40

Rights of the Child — A930

1993, Apr. 16   Photo.   Perf. 13½x14
1595 A930 7s multicolored   1.25 1.00

Flying Harlequin, by Paul Flora — A931

1993, Apr. 16   Photo. & Engr.
1596 A931 7s multicolored   1.25 1.00
Europa.

Monastery of Admont — A932

Designs: 1s, Detail of abbesse's crosier, St. Gabriel Abbey, Styria. 5.50s, Death, wooden statue by Josef Stammel (1695-1765). 6s, Stained glass, Mariastern-Gwiggen Monastery. 7s, Marble lion, Franciscan Monastery, Salzburg. 8s, Gothic entry, Wilhering Monastery, Upper Austria. 7.50s, Cupola fresco, by Paul Troger, Monastery of Altenburg. 10s, Altarpiece, St. Peregrinus praying, Maria Luggau Monastery. 20s, Crosier, Fiecht Monastery. 26s, Sculpture of Mater Dolorosa, Franciscan Monastery, Schwaz, Tirol. 30s, Madonna of Scottish Order, Schottenstift Monastery, Vienna.

Perf. 14x13½, 13½x14 (8s, 26s), 14 (1s, 30s)
1993-95   Photo. & Engr.
1599 A932 1s multicolored   .20   .15
1603 A932 5.50s green, black & yel   1.00   .80
    Perf. 14
1606 A932 6s multicolored   1.10   .90
1606A A932 7s gray, blk & yel   1.25 1.00
1607 A932 7.50s brown, blk & bl   1.25 1.00
1608 A932 8s multicolored   1.60 1.25
1609 A932 10s multicolored   1.75 1.40
1613 A932 20s multicolored   3.50 1.75
1613A A932 26s multicolored   5.25 4.25
1614 A932 30s multicolored   5.50 4.50
   Nos. 1599-1614 (10)   22.40 17.00

Issued: 5.50s, 4/16; 6s, 9/17; 20s, 10/8; 7.50s, 4/4/94; 10s, 8/26/94; 30s, 10/7/94; 7s, 11/18/94; 8s, 9/15/95; 26s, 10/6/95; 1s, 4/28/95.
This is an expanding set. Numbers may change.

Peter Rosegger (1843-1918), Writer — A933

1993, May 5   Photo.   Perf. 14x13½
1617 A933 5.50s green & black   1.00   .80

Lake Constance Steamer Hohentwiel A934

1993, May 5   Photo.   Perf. 14
1618 A934 6s multicolored   1.10   .85
See Germany No. 1786, Switzerland No. 931.

Folk Festivals Type of 1991
Designs: 5s, Corpus Christi Day Procession, Upper Austria. 5.50s, Blockdrawing, Burgenland. 7s, Cracking whip when snow is melting, Salzburg.

Photo. & Engr.
1993, June 11   Perf. 14
1619 A892 5s multicolored   .90   .70
1620 A892 5.50s multicolored   1.00   .80
1621 A892 7s multicolored   1.25 1.00
   Nos. 1619-1621 (3)   3.15 2.50

UN Conference on Human Rights, Vienna — A935

1993, June 11   Photo.
1622 A935 10s multicolored   1.75 1.40

Franz Jagerstatter (1907-1943), Resistance Fighter — A936

1993, Aug. 6   Photo.   Perf. 14x13½
1623 A936 5.50s multicolored   1.00   .80

Schafberg Railway, Cent. — A937

1993, Aug. 6   Perf. 13½x14
1624 A937 6s multicolored   1.10   .90

AUSTRIA

Self-portrait with Puppet, by Rudolf Wacker (1893-1939) A938

1993, Aug. 6   Photo. & Engr.   *Perf. 14*
1625   A938   6s multicolored   1.10   .90

Popular Entertainers Type of 1993
Design: 5.50s, Granny, by Ludwig Hirsch.

1993, Sept. 3   Photo.   *Perf. 14*
1626   A927   5.50s multicolored   1.00   .80

Vienna Mens' Choral Society, 150th Anniv. A940

1993, Sept. 17   Photo.   *Perf. 14*
1627   A940   5s multicolored   .90   .75

Easter, by Max Weiler A941   99 Heads, by Hundertwasser A942

Photo. & Engr.   *Perf. 13½x14*
1628   A941   5.50s multicolored   1.00   .80
1993, Oct. 8
1629   A942   7s multicolored   1.25   1.00

Council of Europe Conference, Vienna.

Austrian Republic, 75th Anniv. — A943

Design: 5.50s, Statue of Pallas Athena.

Photo. & Engr.
1993, Nov. 12   *Perf. 13½x14*
1630   A943   5.50s multicolored   1.00   .80

Trade Unions in Austria, Cent. A944

1993, Nov. 12   Photo.   *Perf. 14*
1631   A944   5.50s multicolored   1.00   .80

Birth of Christ, by Master of the Krainburger Altar — A945

Photo. & Engr.
1993, Nov. 26   *Perf. 13½x14*
1632   A945   5.50s multicolored   1.00   .80
Christmas.

Folklore and Customs Type of 1991
Antiques: 5.50s, Dolls, cradle, Vorarlberg. 6s, Sled, Steiermark. 7s, Godparent's bowl, Upper Austria.

1994, Jan. 28   Photo. & Engr.   *Perf. 14*
1633   A892   5.50s multicolored   1.00   .80
1634   A892   6s multicolored   1.10   .90
1635   A892   7s multicolored   1.25   1.00
Nos. 1633-1635 (3)   3.35   2.70

1994 Winter Olympics, Lillehammer, Norway — A946

1994, Feb. 9
1636   A946   7s multicolored   1.25   1.00

Vienna Mint, 800th Anniv. A947

1994, Feb. 18
1637   A947   6s multicolored   1.10   .90

Lying Lady, by Herbert Boeckl (1894-1966) A948

1994, Mar. 18   Photo.   *Perf. 14x13½*
1638   A948   5.50s multicolored   .95   .70

Popular Entertainers Type of 1993
Design: 6s, Rock Me Amadeus, by Falco.

1994, Mar. 18   *Perf. 14*
1639   A927   6s multicolored   1.00   .80

Wiener Neustadt, 800th Anniv. — A949

1994, Mar. 18
1640   A949   6s multicolored   1.00   .80

Lake Rudolph, Teleki-Hohnel Expedition — A950

Photo. & Engr.
1994, May 27   *Perf. 14x13½*
1641   A950   7s multicolored   1.25   1.00
Europa.

Daniel Gran, 300th Birth Anniv. A951

Fresco: 20s, Allegory of Theology, Jurisprudence and Medicine.

1994, May 27
1642   A951   20s multicolored   3.50   2.75

Carinthian Summer Festival, 25th Anniv. — A952

Design: 5.50s, Scene from The Prodigal Son.

Photo. & Engr.
1994, June 17   *Perf. 14*
1643   A952   5.50s lake & gold   .95   .75

Railway Centennials — A953

1994   Photo. & Engr.   *Perf. 14*
1647   A953   5.50s Gailtal   .95   .75
1648   A953   6s Murtal   1.00   .80
Issued: 5.50s, 6s, 6/17/94.

Hermann Gmeiner, 75th Birth Anniv. — A954

1994, June 17   *Perf. 14x13½*
1656   A954   7s multicolored   1.25   1.00

Karl Seitz (1869-1950) Politician — A955   Karl Bohm (1894-1981), Conductor — A956

1994, Aug. 12   Photo.   *Perf. 14*
1657   A955   5.50s multicolored   1.00   .80

Photo. & Engr.
1994, Aug. 26   *Perf. 14x13½*
1658   A956   7s gold & dk blue   1.25   1.00

Ethnic Minorities in Austria A957

1994, Sept. 9   Photo.   *Perf. 13½*
1659   A957   5.50s multicolored   1.00   .80

Franz Theodor Csokor (1885-1969), Writer — A958

Design: 7s, Joseph Roth (1894-1939), writer.

1994, Sept. 9   *Perf. 14x13½*
1660   A958   6s multicolored   1.00   .80
1661   A958   7s multicolored   1.25   1.00

Coin Bank — A959   Modern Art — A960

Photo. & Engr.
1994, Oct. 7   *Perf. 14x13½*
1662   A959   7s multicolored   1.25   1.00
Savings banks in Austria, 175th anniv.

1994, Oct. 7   *Perf. 13½x14*
Design: 6s, "Head," by Franz Ringel.
1663   A960   6s multicolored   1.10   .90

Austrian Working Environment — A961

1994, Nov. 18   Photo.   *Perf. 14*
1664   A961   6s Stewardess, child   1.10   .90
See Nos. 1690, 1703, 1736, 1773.

AUSTRIA

Richard Coudenhove Kalergi, Founder of PanEuropean Union, Birth Cent. — A962

Photo. & Engr.
1994, Nov. 18   Perf. 13½
1665 A962 10s multicolored   1.90   1.50

Birth of Christ, by Anton Wollenek A963

1994, Nov. 25   Perf. 14
1666 A963 6s multicolored   1.10   .90
Christmas.

Membership in European Union — A964

1995, Jan. 13   Photo.   Perf. 14
1667 A964 7s multicolored   1.25   1.00

Adolf Loos (1870-1933), Architect — A965

1995, Jan. 13
1668 A965 10s House, Vienna   1.90   1.50

Official Representation for Workers, 75th Anniv. — A966

1995, Feb. 24   Perf. 14x13½
1669 A966 6s multicolored   1.10   .90

Austrian Gymnastics and Sports Assoc., 50th Anniv. A967

1995, Feb. 24
1670 A967 6s multicolored   1.10   .90

Folklore and Customs Type of 1991

Designs: 5.50s, Belt, Gailtal, Carinthia. 6s, Vineyard watchman's costume, Vienna. 7s, Bonnet, Wachau, Lower Austria.

Photo. & Engr.
1995, Mar. 24   Perf. 14
1671 A892 5.50s multicolored   1.10   .90
1672 A892 6s multicolored   1.25   1.00
1673 A892 7s multicolored   1.40   1.10
   Nos. 1671-1673 (3)   3.75   3.00

Second Republic, 50th Anniv. — A968

1995, Apr. 27
1674 A968 6s State seal   1.25   1.00

History of Mining & Industry A969

Design: Blast furnaces, old Heft ironworks.

1995, Apr. 28   Perf. 13½x14
1675 A969 5.50s multicolored   1.10   .90
Carinthian Provincial Exhibition.

Nature Lovers Club, Cent. — A970

1995, Apr. 28   Perf. 14
1676 A970 5.50s multicolored   1.10   .90

Europa — A971

1995, May 19   Perf. 14
1677 A971 7s multicolored   1.50   1.25

1995 Conference of Ministers of Transportation, Vienna — A972

1995, May 26   Photo.   Perf. 14
1678 A972 7s multicolored   1.40   1.25

Bregenz Festival, 50th Anniv. A973

1995, June 9
1679 A973 6s multicolored   1.25   1.00

St. Gebhard (949-995) — A974

Design: Stained glass window, by Martin Hausle.

1995, June 9
1680 A974 7.50s multicolored   1.50   1.25

UN, 50th Anniv. — A975

1995, June 26   Photo.   Perf. 14
1681 A975 10s multicolored   2.00   2.00

Josef Loschmidt (1821-95), Chemist — A976

Photo. & Engr.
1995, June 26   Perf. 14x13½
1682 A976 20s multicolored   4.00   4.00

A977   A978

Photo. & Engr.
1995, Aug. 18   Perf. 13½x14
1683 A977 6s multicolored   1.25   1.00
Salzburg Festival, 75th anniv.

1995, Aug. 18   Perf. 14x13½
1684 A978 6s buff, black & red   1.25   1.00
Kathe Leichter, resistance member, birth cent.

Europaisches Landschaftsbild, by Adolf Frohner — A979

1995, Aug. 18
1685 A979 6s multicolored   1.25   1.00

Operetta Composers A980

Designs: 6s, Franz von Suppe (1819-95), scene from "The Beautiful Galathea." 7s, Nico Dostal (b. 1895), scene from "The Hungarian Wedding."

1995, Sept. 15   Perf. 14
1686 A980 6s multicolored   1.25   1.00
1687 A980 7s multicolored   1.40   1.10

University of Klagenfurt, 25th Anniv. — A981

1995, Oct. 6   Photo.   Perf. 14
1688 A981 5.50s multicolored   1.10   .90

Carinthian Referendum, 75th Anniv. A982

Photo. & Engr.
1995, Oct. 6
1689 A982 6s multicolored   1.25   1.00

Austria Working Environment Type of 1994

1995, Oct. 20
1690 A961 6s Post office official   1.25   1.00

Composers — A983

Designs: 6s, Anton von Webern (1883-1945). 7s, Ludwig van Beethoven (1770-1827).

1995, Oct. 20   Perf. 13½x14
1691 A983 6s orange & blue   1.25   1.00
1692 A983 7s orange & red   1.40   1.10

Christmas — A984

Photo. & Engr.
1995, Dec. 1   Perf. 13½
1693 A984 6s Christ Child   1.25   1.00

Folklore and Customs Type of 1991

Design: Roller and Scheller in "Procession of Masked Groups in Imst," Tyrol.

1996, Feb. 9   Photo. & Engr.   Perf. 14
1694 A892 6s multicolored   1.25   1.00

Maria Theresa Academy, 250th Anniv. — A985

1996, Feb. 9
1695 A985 6s multicolored   1.25   1.00

AUSTRIA

1996 World Ski Jumping Championships
A986

1996, Feb. 9 — Photo.
1696 A986 7s multicolored 1.40 1.10

New Western Pier, Vienna Intl. Airport — A987

1996, Mar. 28 Photo. *Perf. 14*
1697 A987 7s multicolored 1.40 1.10

A988   A989

6s, Mother with Child, by Peter Fendi (1796-1842). 7s, Self-portrait, by Leopold Kupelwieser (1795-1862).

1996, Mar. 29
1698 A988 6s multicolored 1.25 1.00
1699 A988 7s multicolored 1.40 1.10

Photo. & Engr.
1996, Apr. 26 *Perf. 14*
1700 A989 5.50s Organ, music 1.15 .90

Anton Bruckner (1824-96), composer, organist.

Georg Matthäus Vischer, 300th Death Anniv. A990

1996, Apr. 26
1701 A990 10s Kollmitz Castle 2.00 1.50

City of Klagenfurt, 800th Anniv. A991

1996, May 3
1702 A991 6s Ancient square 1.25 1.00

Austrian Working Environment Type of 1994
1996, May 17
1703 A961 6s Chef, waitress 1.25 1.00

Paula von Preradovic, Author A992

1996, May 17 *Perf. 13½x14*
1704 A992 7s black, gray & buff 1.40 1.10
Europa.

Folklore and Customs Type of 1991
Designs: 5.50s, Corpus Christi poles, Salzburg. 7s, Tyrolian riflemen.

Photo. & Engr.
1996, June 21 *Perf. 14*
1705 A892 5.50s multicolored 1.00 .80
1706 A892 7s multicolored 1.30 1.00

1996 Summer Olympic Games, Atlanta A993

1996, June 21
1707 A993 10s multicolored 1.90 1.50

Burgenland Province, 75th Anniv. A994

1996, Sept. 20
1708 A994 6s multicolored 1.10 .90

Austrian Mountain Rescue Service, Cent. — A995

1996, Sept. 27
1709 A995 6s multicolored 1.10 .90

Austria Millenium A996

Designs: a, Deed by Otto III. b, Empress Maria Theresa, Josef II. c, Duke Henry II. d, 1848 Revolution. e, Rudolf IV. f, Dr. Karl Renner, 1st Republic. g, Emperor Maximilian I. h, State Treaty of 1955, 2nd Republic. i, Imperial Crown of Rudolf II. j, Austria, Europe.

Photo. & Engr.
1996, Oct. 25 *Perf. 14*
1710   Sheet of 10 19.00 19.00
  a.-b. A996 6s any single 1.10 1.10
  c.-f. A996 7s any single 1.30 1.30
  g.-h. A996 10s any single 1.90 1.90
  i.-j. A996 20s any single 3.80 3.80

Power Station, by Reinhard Artberg A997

1996, Nov. 22
1711 A997 7s multicolored 1.30 1.30

UNICEF, 50th Anniv. — A998

1996, Nov. 22 Photo.
1712 A998 10s multicolored 1.90 1.90

Christmas — A999

1996, Nov. 29 Photo. & Engr.
1713 A999 6s multicolored 1.25 1.00

Folklore and Customs Type of 1991
Design: Epiphany Carol Singers, Burgenland.
1997, Jan. 17 Photo. & Engr. *Perf. 14*
1714 A892 7s multicolored 1.25 1.00

Theodor Kramer, Poet, Birth Cent. — A1000

1997, Jan. 17
1715 A1000 5.50s deep blue 1.00 .80

Austrian Academy of Sciences, 150th Anniv. — A1001

1997, Feb. 21 Photo. *Perf. 14*
1716 A1001 10s multicolored 1.65 1.35

Austrian Electricity Board, 50th Anniv. A1002

1997, Mar. 21
1717 A1002 6s multicolored 1.00 .80

The Cruel Lady of Forchtenstein Castle, Burgenland A1003

Erich Wolfgang Korngold (1897-1957), Composer A1004

Photo. & Engr.
1997, Mar. 21 *Perf. 14*
1718 A1003 7s multicolored 1.15 .95
See Nos. 1731, 1733, 1745-1746, 1763.

1997, Mar. 21
Design: Scene from opera, "The Dead City."
1719 A1004 20s blue, black & gold 3.30 1.65

Vienna Rapid, Austrian Soccer Champions A1005

1997, Apr. 25 Photo. *Perf. 14*
1720 A1005 7s multicolored 1.25 1.00
See No. 1754.

Deer Feeding in Wintertime A1006

1997, Apr. 25
1721 A1006 7s multicolored 1.25 1.00
See No. 1747.

St. Peter Canisius (1521-97) A1007

1997, Apr. 25 Photo. & Engr.
1722 A1007 7.50s Canisius Altar, Innsbruck 1.25 1.10

Composers A1008

Designs: 6s, Johannes Brahms (1833-1897). 10s, Franz Schubert (1797-1828).

1997, May 9
1723 A1008 6s gold & violet blue 1.00 .80
1724 A1008 10s purple & gold 1.75 1.40

471

AUSTRIA

Stamp Day — A1009

1997, May 9   *Perf. 13½*
1725 A1009 7s "A" and "E"   1.25   1.00
See Nos. B357-B362, 1765. The first letters will spell "Briefmarke," the second "Philatelie."

Child's View of "Town Band of Bremen" — A1010

1997, May 23   Photo.
1726 A1010 7s multicolored   1.25   1.00
Europa.

Technical Surveyance Assoc., 125th Anniv. — A1011

1997, June 13   Photo.   *Perf. 14*
1727 A1011 7s multicolored   1.40   1.15

Railways A1012

Designs: 6s, Hochschneeberg Cog Railway. 7.50s, Wiener Neustadt-Odenburg Railway.

1997, June 13   Photo. & Engr.
1728 A1012 6s multicolored   1.20   .95
1729 A1012 7.50s multicolored   1.50   1.20

Folklore and Customs Type of 1991
1997, July 11   Photo. & Engr.   *Perf. 14*
1730 A892 6.50s Marching band, Tyrol   1.30   1.00

Stories and Legends Type
Design: Dragon of Klagenfurt.
1997, July 11
1731 A1003 6.50s multicolored   1.30   1.00

Karl Heinrich Waggerl, Birth Cent. — A1013

1997, July 11
1732 A1013 7s multicolored   1.40   1.00

Stories and Legends Type of 1997
Design: Danube water nymph rescuing ferryman, Upper Austria.

Photo. & Engr.
1997, Sept. 19   *Perf. 14*
1733 A1003 14s multicolored   2.75   2.10

1997 Orthopedics Congress, Vienna A1014

1997, Sept. 19   Photo.   *Perf. 14*
1734 A1014 8s Adolph Lorenz   1.60   1.20

Vienna Agricultural University, 125th Anniv. — A1015

1997, Sept. 19
1735 A1015 9s multicolored   1.80   1.40

Austrian Working Environment Type of 1994
Photo. & Engr.
1997, Oct. 17   *Perf. 14*
1736 A961 6.50s Nurse, patient   1.30   1.00

"House in Wind," by Helmut Schickhofer A1016

1997, Oct. 17
1737 A1016 7s multicolored   1.40   1.00

Blind Persons Assocs. in Austria, Cent. — A1017

1997, Oct. 17   Photo. & Embossed
1738 A1017 7s multicolored   1.40   1.00
No. 1738 contains embossed Braille inscription.

A1018    A1019

Photo. & Engr.
1997, Oct. 31   *Perf. 14x13½*
1739 A1018 7s multicolored   1.40   1.00
Dr. Thomas Klestil, Pres. of Austria, 65th birthday.

1997, Oct. 31   *Perf. 14*
1740 A1019 7s multicolored   1.40   1.00
Oskar Werner (1922-84), actor.

Folklore and Customs Type of 1991
Upper Austria tower wind players, Steyr.
Photo. & Engr.
1997, Nov. 21   *Perf. 14*
1741 A892 6.50s multicolored   1.30   1.00

Light For All Relief Organization, 25th Anniv. — A1020

1997, Nov. 28   Photo.   *Perf. 14*
1742 A1020 7s multicolored   1.40   1.00

Christmas A1021

Photo. & Engr.
1997, Nov. 28   *Perf. 14*
1743 A1021 7s Mariazell Madonna   1.40   1.00

Scenery Type of 1984
Kalkalpen Natl. Park, Upper Austria.
1998, Jan. 23   Photo. & Engr.   *Perf. 14*
1744 A679 7s multicolored   1.10   .85

Stories and Legends Type of 1997
Designs: 9s, The Charming Augustin. 13s, Pied Piper from Korneuburg.

1998, Jan. 23
1745 A1003 9s multicolored   1.40   1.00
1746 A1003 13s multicolored   2.00   1.50

Hunting and Environment Type of 1997
1998, Feb. 6   Photo.
1747 A1006 9s Black cocks   1.40   1.00

1998 Winter Olympic Games, Nagano A1022

1998, Feb. 6   Photo. & Engr.
1748 A1022 14s multicolored   2.20   1.60

Lithographic Printing, Bicent. — A1023

Portrait of Aloys Senefelder (1771-1834), inventor of lithography, on printing stone.
1998, Mar. 13   Litho.   *Perf. 13½*
1749 A1023 7s multicolored   1.40   1.00

A1024    A1025

1998, Mar. 13   Photo.   *Perf. 14*
1750 A1024 7s Poster   1.40   1.00
Joseph Binder (1898-1972), graphic artist.

1998, Mar. 13   Photo. & Engr.
1751 A1025 8s multicolored   1.60   1.25
Wiener Secession, cent. (Assoc. of Artists in Austria-Viennese Secession).

Folklore and Customs Type of 1991
Designs: 6.50s, Fiacre, Vienna. 7s, Samson figure, Palm Sunday Donkey Procession, Tyrol.
1998, Apr. 3
1752 A892 6.50s multicolored   1.30   .95
1753 A892 7s multicolored   1.40   1.00

Soccer Champions Type of 1997
1998, Apr. 17   Photo.
1754 A1005 7s Austria-Memphis Club   1.40   1.00

Salzburg Archdiocese, 1200th Anniv. — A1026

1998, Apr. 17   Photo. & Engr.
1755 A1026 7s multicolored   1.40   1.00

St. Florian, Patron Saint of Fire Brigades A1027

1998, Apr. 17   Photo.
1756 A1027 7s multicolored   1.40   1.00

Railway Centennials A1028

No. 1757, Ybbs Railway. No. 1758, Pöstlingberg Railway. No. 1759, Pinzgau Railway.

1998   Photo. & Engr.   *Perf. 14*
1757 A1028 6.50s multicolored   1.25   1.00
1758 A1028 6.50s multicolored   1.25   1.00
1759 A1028 6.50s multicolored   1.25   1.00
Nos. 1757-1759 (5)   3.75   3.00

Issued: #1757, 5/15. #1758, 6/12. #1759, 7/17.

AUSTRIA

Ferdinandeum, Federal Museum of Tyrol, 175th Anniv. — A1029

1998, May 15
1760 A1029 7s multicolored 1.40 1.00

Vienna Festival Weeks — A1030

1998, May 15
1761 A1030 7s Townhall 1.40 1.00

Europa.

Folklore and Customs Type of 1991
Samson figure & the Zwergin, Lungau district, Salzburg.

1998, June 5
1762 A892 6.50s multicolored 1.30 1.00

Stories and Legends Type of 1997
Design: 25s, Saint Konrad collecting spring water in his handkerchief, Ems Castle.

1998, June 5
1763 A1003 25s multicolored 5.00 3.75

Christine Lavant, Poet, 25th Death Anniv. A1031

1998, June 5   Photo.
1764 A1031 7s multicolored 1.40 1.00

Stamp Day Type of 1997
Photo. & Engr.

1998, June 12   Perf. 13½
1765 A1009 7s "R" and "L" 1.40 1.00

See Nos. 1725, B357-B362. The first letters will spell "Briefmarke," the second "Philatelie."

Austrian Presidency of the European Union — A1032

1998, July 1   Photo.   Perf. 13½x14
1766 A1032 7s multicolored 1.40 1.00

The People's Opera, Vienna, 50th Anniv. & Franz Lehar (1870-1948), Composer — A1033

1998, Sept. 10   Photo.   Perf. 14
1767 A1033 6.50s multicolored 1.25 .85

Elizabeth, Empress of Austria (1837-98) A1034

1998, Sept. 10   Photo. & Engr.
1768 A1034 7s multicolored 1.40 .90

Vienna University for Commercial Sudies, Cent. A1035

1998, Sept. 10   Photo.
1769 A1035 7s multicolored 1.40 .90

Hans Kudlich, Emancipator of Peasants, 175th Birth Anniv. — A1036

Photo. & Engr.

1998, Oct. 23   Perf. 14
1770 A1036 6.50s multicolored 1.25 .90

"My Garden," by Hans Staudacher A1037

1998, Oct. 23
1771 A1037 7s multicolored 1.25 .90

City of Eisenstadt, 350th Anniv. A1038

1998, Oct. 23
1772 A1038 7s multicolored 1.25 .90

Austrian Working Environment Type of 1994

1998, Nov. 6   Photo. & Engr.   Perf. 14
1773 A961 6.50s Reporter, photographer 1.10 .85

Christmas A1039

: 1423 Fresco from Tainach/Tinje Church, Carinthia.

1998, Nov. 27
1774 A1039 7s multicolored 1.25 .85

SEMI-POSTAL STAMPS

Issues of the Monarchy

Emperor Franz Josef — SP1

The Firing Step — SP2

1914, Oct. 4   Typo.   Unwmk.   Perf. 12½
B1 SP1 5h green .15 .30
B2 SP1 10h rose .15 .35
Set, never hinged 1.10

Nos. B1-B2 were sold at an advance of 2h each over face value. Exist imperf.; value, set $50.

1915, May 1

Designs: 5h+2h, Cavalry. 10h+2h, Siege gun. 20h+3h, Battleship. 35h+3h, Airplane.

B3 SP2 3h + 1h violet brn .15 .40
B4 SP2 5h + 2h green .15 .15
B5 SP2 10h + 2h deep rose .15 .15
B6 SP2 20h + 3h Prus blue .45 2.00
B7 SP2 35h + 3h ultra 2.00 4.25
Nos. B3-B7 (5) 2.90 6.95
Set, never hinged 8.85

Exist imperf. Value, set $110.

Issues of the Republic

Kärnten

Types of Austria, 1919-20, Overprinted in Black

Abstimmung

1920, Sept. 16   Perf. 12½
B11 A44 5h gray, yellow .45 1.10
B12 A44 10h red, pink .35 1.00
B13 A43 15h bister, yel .25 .75
B14 A45 20h dark grn, bl .25 .60
B15 A43 25h violet, pink .25 .65
B16 A45 30h brown, buff 1.10 2.50
B17 A45 40h carmine, yel .25 .70
B18 A45 50h dark bl, blue .25 .55
B19 A43 60h ol grn, azure 1.10 2.50
B20 A47 80h red .30 .65
B21 A47 1k orange brown .35 .75
B22 A47 2k pale blue .35 .80

Granite Paper

Imperf

B23 A46 2½k brown red .35 .90
B24 A46 3k dk blue & green .45 1.10
B25 A46 4k carmine & violet .55 1.25
B26 A46 5k blue .55 1.10
B27 A46 7½k yellow green .60 1.10
B28 A46 10k gray grn & red .60 1.25
B29 A46 20k lilac & orange .65 1.75
Nos. B11-B29 (19) 9.00 21.00
Set, never hinged 15.00

Carinthia Plebiscite. Sold at three times face value for the benefit of the Plebiscite Propaganda Fund.
Nos. B11-B19 exist imperf. Value, set $125.

Hochwasser

Types of Regular Issues of 1919-21 Overprinted

1920

1921, Mar. 1   Perf. 12½
B30 A44 5h gray, yellow .25 .45
B31 A44 10h orange brown .25 .45
B32 A43 15h gray .25 .45
B33 A45 20h green, yellow .25 .45
B34 A43 25h blue, yellow .25 .45
B35 A45 30h violet, bl .45 .90
B36 A45 40h org brn, pink .50 1.10
B37 A45 50h green, blue 1.10 2.00
B38 A43 60h lilac, yellow .35 .90
B39 A47 80h pale blue .40 .80
B40 A47 1k red org, blue .35 .75
B41 A47 1½k green, yellow .20 .45
B42 A47 2k lilac brown .20 .40

Hochwasser

Overprinted

1920

B43 A46 2½k light blue .25 .45
B44 A46 3k ol grn & brn red .25 .45
B45 A46 4k lilac & orange .70 1.50
B46 A46 5k olive green .25 .55
B47 A46 7½k brown red .25 .65
B48 A46 10k blue & olive grn .25 .65
B49 A46 20k car rose & vio .45 1.00
Nos. B30-B49 (20) 7.20 14.75
Set, never hinged 12.75

Nos. B30-B49 were sold at three times face value, the excess going to help flood victims. Exists imperf. Value, set $175.

Franz Joseph Haydn — SP9

View of Bregenz — SP16

Musicians: 5k, Mozart. 7½k, Beethoven. 10k, Schubert. 25k, Anton Bruckner. 50k, Johann Strauss (son). 100k, Hugo Wolf.

1922, Apr. 24   Engr.   Perf. 12½
B50 SP9 2½k brown, perf. 11½ 6.00 10.50
  a. Perf. 12½ 7.25 12.00
B51 SP9 5k dark blue 1.10 1.50
B52 SP9 7½k black 1.40 2.50
  a. Perf. 11½ 90.00 140.00
B53 SP9 10k dark violet 1.90 3.00
  a. Perf. 11½ 2.50 5.25
B54 SP9 25k dark green 3.75 6.50
  a. Perf. 11½ 4.25 8.25
B55 SP9 50k claret 2.00 3.00
B56 SP9 100k brown olive 7.00 8.75
  a. Perf. 11½ 8.00 17.50
Nos. B50-B56 (7) 23.15 35.75
Set, never hinged 47.50

These stamps were sold at 10 times face value, the excess being given to needy musicians.
All values exist imperf. on both regular and handmade papers. Value, set $325.
A 1969 souvenir sheet without postal validity contains reprints of the 5k in black, 7½k in claret and 50k in dark blue, each overprinted "NEUDRUCK" in black at top. It was issued for the Vienna State Opera Centenary Exhibition.

1923, May 22   Perf. 12½

Designs: 120k, Mirabelle Gardens, Salzburg. 160k, Church at Eisenstadt. 180k, Assembly House, Klagenfurt. 200k, "Golden Roof," Innsbruck. 240k, Main Square, Linz. 400k, Castle Hill, Graz. 600k, Abbey at Melk. 1000k, Upper Belvedere, Vienna.

Various Frames

B57 SP16 100k dk green 2.75 5.00
B58 SP16 120k deep blue 2.50 5.00
B59 SP16 160k dk violet 2.50 5.00
B60 SP16 180k red violet 2.50 5.00
B61 SP16 200k lake 2.50 5.00
B62 SP16 240k red brown 2.50 5.00
B63 SP16 400k dark brown 2.50 5.00
B64 SP16 600k olive brn 2.75 5.00
B65 SP16 1000k black 4.00 5.00
Nos. B57-B65 (9) 24.50 45.00
Set, never hinged 55.50

Nos. B57-B65 were sold at five times face value, the excess going to needy artists.
All values exist imperf. on both regular and handmade papers. Value, set $325.

AUSTRIA

Feebleness
SP25

Siegfried Slays the Dragon
SP30

Designs: 300k+900k, Aid to industry. 500k+1500k, Orphans and widow. 600k+1800k, Indigent old man. 1000k+3000k, Alleviation of hunger.

1924, Sept. 6 — Photo.

B66	SP25	100k + 300k yel green	3.25 3.25
B67	SP25	300k + 900k red brn	4.50 9.00
B68	SP25	500k + 1500k brn vio	4.50 9.00
B69	SP25	600k + 1800k pck bl	4.50 9.00
B70	SP25	1000k + 3000k brn org	7.50 12.50
		Nos. B66-B70 (5)	24.25 42.75
		Set, never hinged	45.75

The surtax was for child welfare and anti-tuberculosis work. Set exists imperf. Value, $325.

1926, Mar. 8 — Engr.

Designs: 8g+2g, Gunther's voyage to Iceland. 15g+5g, Brunhild accusing Kriemhild. 20g+5g, Nymphs telling Hagen the future. 24g+6g, Rudiger von Bechelaren welcomes the Nibelungen. 40g+10g, Dietrich von Bern vanquishes Hagen.

B71	SP30	3g + 2g olive blk	1.10 .65
B72	SP30	8g + 2g indigo	.25 .35
B73	SP30	15g + 5g dk claret	.30 .35
B74	SP30	20g + 5g olive grn	.45 .75
B75	SP30	24g + 6g dk violet	.45 .75
B76	SP30	40g + 10g red brn	3.00 3.75
		Nos. B71-B76 (6)	5.55 6.60
		Set, never hinged	12.00

Nibelungen issue.

Nos. B71-B76 were printed in two sizes: 27½x28½mm and 28½x27½mm.

The surtax was for child welfare. Set exists imperf. Value, $250.

Pres. Michael Hainisch — SP36

Pres. Wilhelm Miklas — SP37

1928, Nov. 5

B77	SP36	10g dark brown	5.00 9.00
B78	SP36	15g red brown	5.00 9.00
B79	SP36	30g black	5.00 9.00
B80	SP36	40g indigo	5.00 9.00
		Nos. B77-B80 (4)	20.00 36.00
		Set, never hinged	31.00

Tenth anniversary of Austrian Republic. Sold at double face value, the premium aiding war orphans and children of war invalids.

Set exists imperf. Value $350.

1930, Oct. 4

B81	SP37	10g light brown	7.50 12.50
B82	SP37	20g red	7.50 12.50
B83	SP37	30g brown violet	7.50 12.50
B84	SP37	40g indigo	7.50 12.50
B85	SP37	50g dark green	7.50 12.50
B86	SP37	1s black brown	7.50 12.50
		Nos. B81-B86 (6)	45.00 75.00
		Set, never hinged	81.00

Nos. B81-B86 were sold at double face value. The excess aided the anti-tuberculosis campaign and the building of sanatoria in Carinthia.

Set exists imperf. Value, $425.

Regular Issue of 1929-30 Overprinted in Various Colors

CONVENTION WIEN 1931

1931, June 20

B87	A56	10g bister (Bl)	32.50 35.00
B88	A56	20g dk gray (R)	32.50 35.00
B89	A56	30g dk violet (Gl)	32.50 35.00
B90	A56	40g dk blue (Gl)	32.50 35.00
B91	A56	50g gray vio (O)	32.50 35.00
B92	A57	1s black brn (Bk)	32.50 35.00
		Nos. B87-B92 (6)	195.00 210.00
		Set, never hinged	465.00

Rotary convention, Vienna.

Nos. B87 to B92 were sold at double their face values. The excess was added to the beneficent funds of Rotary International.

Exists imperf.

Ferdinand Raimund — SP38

Poets: 20g, Franz Grillparzer. 30g, Johann Nestroy. 40g, Adalbert Stifter. 50g, Ludwig Anzengruber. 1s, Peter Rosegger.

1931, Sept. 12

B93	SP38	10g dark violet	12.00 17.50
B94	SP38	20g gray black	12.00 17.50
B95	SP38	30g orange red	12.00 17.50
B96	SP38	40g dull blue	12.00 17.50
B97	SP38	50g gray green	12.00 17.50
B98	SP38	1s yellow brown	12.00 17.50
		Nos. B93-B98 (6)	72.00 105.00
		Set, never hinged	114.00

Nos. B93-B98 were sold at double face value. The surtax aided unemployed young people.

Set exists imperf. Value, $425.

Chancellor Ignaz Seipel
SP44

Ferdinand Georg Waldmüller
SP45

1932, Oct. 12 — Perf. 13

B99	SP44	50g ultra	9.00 17.50
		Never hinged	16.00

Msgr. Ignaz Seipel, Chancellor of Austria, 1922-29. Sold at double face value, the excess aiding wounded veterans of World War I.

Exists imperf. Value, $150.

1932, Nov. 21

Artists: 24g, Moritz von Schwind. 30g, Rudolf von Alt. 40g, Hans Makart. 64g, Gustav Klimt. 1s, Albin Egger-Lienz.

B100	SP45	24g slate green	17.00 30.00
B101	SP45	24g dp violet	17.00 30.00
B102	SP45	30g dark red	17.00 30.00
B103	SP45	40g dark gray	17.00 30.00
B104	SP45	64g dark brown	17.00 30.00
B105	SP45	1s claret	17.00 30.00
		Nos. B100-B105 (6)	102.00 180.00
		Set, never hinged	156.00

Nos. B100 to B105 were sold at double their face values. The surtax was for the assistance of charitable institutions.

Set exists imperf. Value, $575.

Mountain Climbing
SP51

Designs: 24g, Ski gliding. 30g, Walking on skis. 50g, Ski jumping.

1933, Jan. 9 — Photo. — Perf. 12½

B106	SP51	12g dark green	7.00 11.50
B107	SP51	24g dark violet	67.50 95.00
B108	SP51	30g brown red	12.50 17.50
B109	SP51	50g dark blue	67.50 95.00
		Nos. B106-B109 (4)	154.50 219.00
		Set, never hinged	295.00

Meeting of the Intl. Ski Federation, Innsbruck, Feb. 8-13.

These stamps were sold at double their face value. The surtax was for the benefit of "Youth in Distress."

#B106-B109 exist imperf. Value $1,200.

Stagecoach, after Painting by Moritz von Schwind
SP55

1933, June 23 — Engr. — Perf. 12½

Ordinary Paper

B110	SP55	50g deep ultra	150.00 190.00
		Never hinged	225.00
a.		Granite paper	300.00 425.00
		Never hinged	450.00
		Sheets of 25.	

Nos. B110 and B110a exist imperf. Values $675 and $1,300.

Souvenir Sheet
Perf. 12
Granite Paper

B111		Sheet of 4	2,000. 2,750.
		Never hinged	2,500.
a.		SP55 50g deep ultra	375. 550.
		Never hinged	525.

Intl. Phil. Exhib., Vienna, 1933. In addition to the postal value of 50g the stamp was sold at a premium of 50g for charity and of 1.60s for the admission fee to the exhibition.

Size of No. B111: 126x103mm.

A 50g dark red in souvenir sheet, with dark blue overprint ("NEUDRUCK WIPA 1965"), had no postal validity.

Even though the margins No. B111 have no gum, the sheet sells for a premium when definitely never hinged.

St. Stephen's Cathedral in 1683 — SP56

Marco d'Aviano, Papal Legate — SP57

Designs: 30g, Count Ernst Rudiger von Starhemberg. 40g, John III Sobieski, King of Poland. 50g, Karl V, Duke of Lorraine. 64g, Burgomaster Johann Andreas von Liebenberg.

1933, Sept. 6 — Photo. — Perf. 12½

B112	SP56	12g dark green	21.00 25.00
B113	SP57	24g dark violet	19.00 22.50
B114	SP57	30g brown red	19.00 22.50
B115	SP57	40g blue black	27.50 37.50
B116	SP57	50g dark blue	19.00 22.50
B117	SP57	64g olive brown	24.00 35.00
		Nos. B112-B117 (6)	129.50 165.00
		Set, never hinged	242.50

Deliverance of Vienna from the Turks, 250th anniv., and Pan-German Catholic Congress, Sept. 6, 1933.

The stamps were sold at double their face value, the excess being for the aid of Catholic works of charity.

Set exists imperf. Value, $850.

Types of Regular Issue of 1925-30 Surcharged:

+2g WINTERHILFE
a

WINTERHILFE +6g
b

Winterhilfe +50g

WINTERHILFE
c

1933, Dec. 15

B118	A52(a)	5g + 2g olive grn	.25 .55
B119	A56(b)	12g + 3g lt blue	.25 .70
B120	A56(b)	24g + 6g brn orange	.25 .60
B121	A57(c)	1s + 50g orange red	25.00 40.00
		Nos. B118-B121 (4)	25.75 41.85
		Set, never hinged	41.75

Winterhelp. Exists imperf. Value, set $525.

Anton Pilgram — SP62

Architects: 24g, J. B. Fischer von Erlach. 30g, Jakob Prandtauer. 40g, A. von Siccardsburg & E. van der Null. 60g, Heinrich von Ferstel. 64g, Otto Wagner.

1934, Dec. 2 — Engr. — Perf. 12½
Thick Yellowish Paper

B122	SP62	12g black	9.00 15.00
B123	SP62	24g dull violet	9.00 15.00
B124	SP62	30g carmine	9.00 15.00
B125	SP62	40g brown	9.00 15.00
B126	SP62	60g blue	9.00 15.00
B127	SP62	64g dull green	9.00 15.00
		Nos. B122-B127 (6)	54.00 90.00
		Set, never hinged	81.00

Exist imperf. Value, set $425.

Nos. B124-B127 exist in horiz. pairs imperf. between. Value, each $160.

These stamps were sold at double their face value. The surtax on this and the following issues was devoted to general charity.

Types of Regular Issue of 1934 Surcharged in Black:

+50g

Winterhilfe +2g   WINTERHILFE
a   b

1935, Nov. 11 — Perf. 12, 12½

B128	A67(a)	5g + 2g emerald	.45 .90
B129	A67(a)	12g + 3g blue	.75 1.00
B130	A67(a)	24g + 6g lt brown	.45 .90
B131	A68(b)	1s + 50g ver	24.00 35.00
		Nos. B128-B131 (4)	25.65 37.80
		Set, never hinged	45.35

Winterhelp. Set exists imperf. Value, $125.

Prince Eugene of Savoy — SP68

Slalom Turn — SP74

Military Leaders: 24g, Field Marshal Laudon. 30g, Archduke Karl. 40g, Field Marshal Josef Radetzky. 60g, Admiral Wilhelm Tegetthoff. 64g, Field Marshal Franz Conrad Hotzendorff.

1935, Dec. 1 — Perf. 12½

B132	SP68	12g brown	9.00 14.00
B133	SP68	24g dark green	9.00 14.00
B134	SP68	30g claret	9.00 14.00
B135	SP68	40g slate	9.00 14.00
B136	SP68	60g deep ultra	9.00 14.00
B137	SP68	64g dark violet	9.00 14.00
		Nos. B132-B137 (6)	54.00 84.00
		Set, never hinged	81.00

These stamps were sold at double their face value. Set exists imperf. Value, $450.

1936, Feb. 20 — Photo.

Designs: 24g, Jumper taking off. 35g, Slalom turn. 60g, Innsbruck view.

B138	SP74	12g Prus green	2.50 3.00
B139	SP74	24g dp violet	4.50 4.50
B140	SP74	35g rose car	22.50 37.50
B141	SP74	60g sapphire	22.50 37.50
		Nos. B138-B141 (4)	52.00 82.50
		Set, never hinged	90.50

Ski concourse issue. These stamps were sold at twice face value. Set exists imperf. Value, $450.

AUSTRIA

St. Martin of Tours — SP78

Designs: 12g+3g, Medical clinic. 24g+6g, St. Elizabeth of Hungary. 1s+1s, "Flame of Charity."

1936, Nov. 2   Unwmk.
B142	SP78	5g + 2g dp green	.25	.40
B143	SP78	12g + 3g dp violet	.25	.40
B144	SP78	24g + 6g dp blue	.25	.40
B145	SP78	1s + 1s dk carmine	5.50	11.00
	Nos. B142-B145 (4)		6.25	12.20
	Set, never hinged		10.50	

Winterhelp. Set exists imperf. Value, $175.

Josef Ressel — SP82

Nurse and Infant — SP88

Inventors: 24g, Karl von Ghega. 30g, Josef Werndl. 40g, Carl Auer von Welsbach. 60g, Robert von Lieben. 64g, Viktor Kaplan.

1936, Dec. 6   Engr.
B146	SP82	12g dk brown	2.00	4.50
B147	SP82	24g dk violet	2.00	4.50
B148	SP82	30g dp claret	2.00	4.50
B149	SP82	40g gray violet	2.00	4.50
B150	SP82	60g vio blue	2.00	4.50
B151	SP82	64g dk slate green	2.00	4.50
	Nos. B146-B151 (6)		12.00	27.00
	Set, never hinged		24.00	

These stamps were sold at double their face value. Exists imperf. Value, set $350.

1937, Oct. 18   Photo.

12g+3g, Mother and child. 24g+6g, Nursing the aged. 1s+1s, Sister of Mercy with patient.

B152	SP88	5g + 2g dk green	.20	.35
B153	SP88	12g + 3g dk brown	.20	.35
B154	SP88	24g + 6g dk blue	.20	.35
B155	SP88	1s + 1s dk carmine	3.00	6.75
	Nos. B152-B155 (4)		3.60	7.80
	Set, never hinged		6.25	

Winterhelp. Set exists imperf. Value, $90.

Gerhard van Swieten — SP92

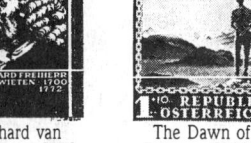

The Dawn of Peace — SP101

Physicians: 8g, Leopold Auenbrugger von Auenbrugg. 12g, Karl von Rokitansky. 20g, Joseph Skoda. 24g, Ferdinand von Hebra. 30g, Ferdinand von Arlt. 40g, Joseph Hyrtl. 60g, Theodor Billroth. 64g, Theodor Meynert.

1937, Dec. 5   Engr.   Perf. 12½
B156	SP92	5g choc	1.90	4.00
B157	SP92	8g dk red	1.90	4.00
B158	SP92	12g brown blk	1.90	4.00
B159	SP92	20g dk green	1.90	4.00
B160	SP92	24g dk violet	1.90	4.00
B161	SP92	30g brown car	1.90	4.00
B162	SP92	40g dp olive grn	1.90	4.00
B163	SP92	60g indigo	1.90	4.00
B164	SP92	64g brown vio	1.90	4.00
	Nos. B156-B164 (9)		17.10	36.00
	Set, never hinged		29.25	

These stamps were sold at double their face value. Set exists imperf. Value, $550.

> Catalogue values for unused stamps in this section, from this point to the end of the section, are for Never Hinged items.

1945, Sept. 10   Photo.   Perf. 14
B165	SP101	1s + 10s dk green	.85	1.40

No. 467 Surcharged in Black

+20 g

1946, June 25
B166	A110	30g + 20g dk red	3.00	5.00

First anniversary of United Nations.

Pres. Karl Renner SP102

1946   Engr.   Perf. 13½x14
B167	SP102	1s + 1s slate grn	2.00	4.00
B168	SP102	2s + 2s dk blue vio	2.00	4.00
B169	SP102	3s + 3s dk purple	2.00	4.00
B170	SP102	5s + 5s dk violet brn	2.00	4.00
	Nos. B167-B170 (4)		8.00	16.00

See Nos. B185-B188.

Nazi Sword Piercing Austria — SP103

Sweeping Away Fascist Symbols — SP104

Designs: 8g+6g, St. Stephen's Cathedral in Flames. 12g+12g, Pleading hand in concentration camp. 30g+30g, Hand choking Nazi serpent. 42g+42g, Hammer breaking Nazi pillar. 1s+1s, Oath of allegiance. 2s+2s, Austrian eagle and burning swastika.

Unwmk.
1946, Sept. 16   Photo.   Perf. 14
B171	SP103	5g + (3g) dk brown	.45	.65
B172	SP104	6g + (4g) dk slate grn	.30	.55
B173	SP104	8g + (6g) orange red	.30	.55
B174	SP104	12g + (12g) slate blk	.30	.55
B175	SP104	30g + (30g) violet	.30	.55
B176	SP104	42g + (42g) dull brn	.30	.55
B177	SP104	1s + 1s dk red	.45	.65
B178	SP104	2s + 2s dk car rose	.60	.65
	Nos. B171-B178 (8)		3.00	4.70

Anti-fascist propaganda.

Race Horse with Foal — SP111

Various Race Horses.

1946, Oct. 20   Engr.   Perf. 13½x14
B179	SP111	16g + 16g rose brown	2.00	3.00
B180	SP111	24g + 24g dk purple	2.00	3.00
B181	SP111	60g + 60g dk green	2.00	3.00
B182	SP111	1s + 1s dk blue gray	2.00	3.00
B183	SP111	2s + 2s yel brown	2.00	3.00
	Nos. B179-B183 (5)		10.00	15.00

Austria Prize race, Vienna.

St. Ruprecht's Church, Vienna — SP116

1946, Oct. 30   Perf. 14x13½
B184	SP116	30g + 70g dark red	.35	.70

Founding of Austria, 950th anniv. The surtax aided the Stamp Day celebration.

Renner Type of 1946
Souvenir Sheets
1946, Sept. 5   Imperf.
B185	Sheet of 8	500.00	900.00
a.	SP102 1s+1s dk slate grn	55.00	100.00
B186	Sheet of 8	500.00	900.00
a.	SP102 2s+2s dk blue vio	55.00	100.00
B187	Sheet of 8	500.00	900.00
a.	SP102 3s+3s dark purple	55.00	100.00
B188	Sheet of 8	500.00	900.00
a.	SP102 5s+5s dk vio brown	55.00	100.00

1st anniv. of Austria's liberation. Sheets of 8 plus center label showing arms.

Statue of Rudolf IV the Founder — SP118

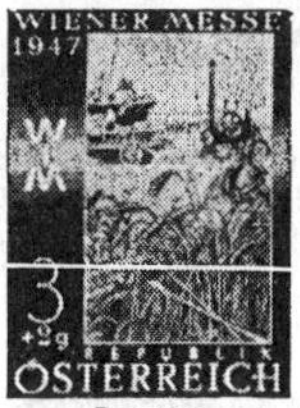

Reaping Wheat — SP128

Designs: 5g+20g, Tomb of Frederick III. 6g+24g, Main pulpit. 8g+32g, Statue of St. Stephen. 10g+40g, Madonna of the Domestics statue. 12g+48g, High altar. 30g+1.20s, Organ, destroyed in 1945. 50g+1.80s, Anton Pilgram statue. 1s+5s, Cathedral from northeast. 2s+10s, Southwest corner of cathedral.

1946, Dec. 12   Engr.   Perf. 14x13½
B189	SP118	3g + 12g brown	.25	.50
B190	SP118	5g + 20g dk vio brown	.25	.50
B191	SP118	6g + 24g dk blue	.25	.50
B192	SP118	8g + 32g dk green	.25	.50
B193	SP118	10g + 40g dp blue	.40	.75
B194	SP118	12g + 48g dk vio	.45	.80
B195	SP118	30g + 1.20s car	1.10	1.90
B196	SP118	50g + 1.80s dk bl	1.25	2.00
B197	SP118	1s + 5s brn vio	1.75	3.25
B198	SP118	2s + 10s vio brn	3.50	7.50
	Nos. B189-B198 (10)		9.45	18.20

The surtax aided reconstruction of St. Stephen's Cathedral, Vienna.

1947, Mar. 23   Perf. 14x13½

Designs: 8g+2g, Log raft. 10g+5g, Cement factory. 12g+8g, Coal mine. 18g+12g, Oil derricks. 30g+10g, Textile machinery. 35g+15g, Iron furnace. 60g+20g, Electric power lines.

B199	SP128	3g + 2g yel brown	.40	.50
B200	SP128	8g + 2g dk bl grn	.40	.50
B201	SP128	10g + 5g slate blk	.40	.50
B202	SP128	12g + 8g dark pur	.40	.50
B203	SP128	18g + 12g ol green	.40	.50
B204	SP128	30g + 10g deep cl	.40	.50
B205	SP128	35g + 15g crimson	.40	.50
B206	SP128	60g + 20g dk blue	.40	.50
	Nos. B199-B206 (8)		3.20	4.00

Vienna International Sample Fair, 1947.

Race Horse and Jockey SP136

1947, June 29   Perf. 13½x14
B207	SP136	60g + 20g deep blue, *pale pink*	.15	.20

Cup of Corvinus — SP137

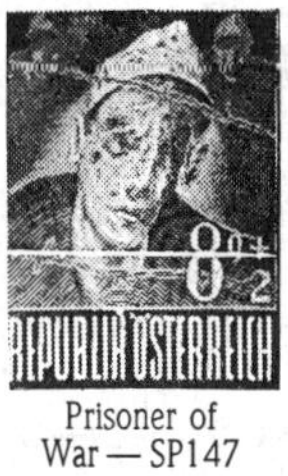

Prisoner of War — SP147

Designs: 8g+2g, Statue of Providence, Vienna. 10g+5g, Abbey at Melk. 12g+8g, Picture of a Woman, by Kriehuber. 18g+12g, Children at the Window, by Waldmuller. 20g+10g, Entrance, Upper Belvedere Palace. 30g+10g, Nymph Egeria, Schönbrunn Castle. 35g+15g, National Library, Vienna. 48g+12g, "Workshop of a Printer of Engravings," by Schmutzer. 60g+20g, Girl with Straw Hat, by Amerling.

1947, June 20   Perf. 14x13½
B208	SP137	3g + 2g brown	.30	.40
B209	SP137	8g + 2g dk blue grn	.30	.40
B210	SP137	10g + 5g dp claret	.30	.40
B211	SP137	12g + 8g dk purple	.30	.40
B212	SP137	18g + 12g golden brn	.30	.40
B213	SP137	20g + 10g sepia	.30	.40
B214	SP137	30g + 10g dk yel grn	.30	.40
B215	SP137	35g + 15g deep car	.30	.40
B216	SP137	48g + 12g dk brn vio	.30	.40
B217	SP137	60g + 20g dp blue	.30	.40
	Nos. B208-B217 (10)		3.00	4.00

1947, Aug. 30

Designs: 8g+2g dk green, Prisoners' Mail. 18g+12g, Prison camp visitor. 35g+15g, Family reunion. 60g+20g, "Industry" beckoning. 1s+40g, Sower.

B218	SP147	8g + 2g dk green	.20	.30
B219	SP147	12g + 8g dk vio brn	.20	.30
B220	SP147	18g + 12g black brn	.20	.30
B221	SP147	35g + 15g rose brn	.20	.30
B222	SP147	60g + 20g dp blue	.20	.30
B223	SP147	1s + 40g redsh brn	.20	.30
	Nos. B218-B223 (6)		1.20	1.80

Olympic Flame and Emblem SP153

Laabenbach Bridge Neulengbach SP154

1948, Jan. 16   Engr.
B224	SP153	1s + 50g dark blue	.35	.35

The surtax was used to help defray expenses of Austria's 1948 Olympics team.

1948, Feb. 18   Perf. 14x13½

Designs: 20g+10g, Dam, Vermunt Lake. 30g+10g, Danube Port, Vienna. 40g+20g, Mining, Erzberg. 45g+20g, Tracks, Southern Railway Station, Vienna. 60g+30g, Communal housing project, Vienna. 75g+35g, Gas Works, Vienna. 80g+40g, Oil refinery. 1s+50g, Gesäuse Highway, Styria. 1.40s+70g, Parliament Building, Vienna.

B225	SP154	10g + 5g slate blk	.20	.20
B226	SP154	20g + 10g lilac	.20	.20
B227	SP154	30g + 10g dull grn	.50	.50
B228	SP154	40g + 20g ol brn	.20	.20
B229	SP154	45g + 20g dk blue	.20	.20
B230	SP154	60g + 30g dk red	.20	.20
B231	SP154	75g + 35g dk vio brn	.15	.15
B232	SP154	80g + 40g vio brn	.20	.20
B233	SP154	1s + 50g dp blue	.20	.20
B234	SP154	1.40s + 70g dp car	.50	.50
	Set value		1.60	1.55

The surtax was for the Reconstruction Fund.

Violet — SP155

Hans Makart — SP156

Designs: 20g+10g, Anemone. 30g+10g, Crocus. 40g+20g, Yellow primrose. 45g+20g, Pasqueflower. 60g+30g, Rhododendron. 75g+35g, Dogrose. 80g+40g, Cyclamen. 1s+50g, Alpine Gentian. 1.40s+70g, Edelweiss.

1948, May 14   Engr. & Typo.
B235	SP155	10g + 5g multi	.35	.25
B236	SP155	20g + 10g multi	.15	.20
B237	SP155	30g + 10g multi	2.50	2.00
B238	SP155	40g + 20g multi	.50	.25
B239	SP155	45g + 20g multi	.15	.20
B240	SP155	60g + 30g multi	.15	.20
B241	SP155	75g + 35g multi	.15	.20
B242	SP155	80g + 40g multi	.30	.20
B243	SP155	1s + 50g multi	.40	.30
B244	SP155	1.40s + 70g multi	.65	.55
	Nos. B235-B244 (10)		5.30	4.35

AUSTRIA

1948, June 15   **Unwmk.**   **Engr.**

Designs: 20g+10g, Künstlerhaus, Vienna. 40g+20g, Carl Kundmann. 50g+25g, A. S. von Siccardsburg. 60g+30g, Hans Cannon. 1s+50g, William Unger. 1.40s+70g, Friedrich von Schmidt.

B245	SP156	20g + 10g dp yel green	6.25	5.00
B246	SP156	30g + 15g dark brown	3.00	1.90
B247	SP156	40g + 20g indigo	3.00	1.90
B248	SP156	50g + 25g dk vio	3.50	2.75
B249	SP156	60g + 30g dk red	3.50	2.75
B250	SP156	1s + 50g dk blue	6.25	5.00
B251	SP156	1.40s + 70g red brown	8.50	7.50
		Nos. B245-B251 (7)	34.00	26.80

Kunstlerhaus, home of the leading Austrian Artists Association, 80th anniv.

St. Rupert — SP157
Easter — SP158 

Designs: 30g+15g, Cathedral and Fountain. 40g+20g, Facade of Cathedral. 50g+25g, Cathedral from South. 60g+30g, Abbey of St. Peter. 80g+40g, Inside Cathedral. 1s+50g, Salzburg Cathedral and Castle. 1.40s+70g, Madonna by Michael Pacher.

1948, Aug. 6   **Perf. 14x13½**

B252	SP157	20g + 10g dp grn	6.00	5.50
B253	SP157	30g + 15g red brn	2.50	2.50
B254	SP157	40g + 20g sl blk	1.90	1.75
B255	SP157	50g + 25g choc	.40	.40
B256	SP157	60g + 30g dk red	.40	.40
B257	SP157	80g + 40g dk brn vio	.40	.40
B258	SP157	1s + 50g dp blue	.75	.50
B259	SP157	1.40s + 70g dk grn	1.50	1.25
		Nos. B252-B259 (8)	13.85	12.70

The surtax was to aid in the reconstruction of Salzburg Cathedral.

1949, Apr. 13   **Unwmk.**

Designs: 60g+20g, St. Nicholas Day. 1s+25g, Birthday. 1.40s+35g, Christmas.

Inscribed: "Gluckliche Kindheit"

B260	SP158	40g + 10g brn vio	17.00	12.50
B261	SP158	60g + 20g brn red	17.00	12.50
B262	SP158	1s + 25g op ultra	17.00	12.50
B263	SP158	1.40s + 35g dk grn	17.00	12.50
		Nos. B260-B263 (4)	68.00	50.00

The surtax was for Child Welfare.

Arms of Austria, 1230 — SP159
SP160 

1949, Aug. 17   **Engr. & Photo.**

B264 SP159   40g + 10g 1230   7.00   6.00

Engraved and Typographed

B265	SP159	60g + 15g 1450	7.00	6.00
B266	SP159	1s + 25g 1600	7.00	6.00
B267	SP159	1.60s + 40g 1945	7.00	6.00
		Nos. B264-B267 (4)	28.00	24.00

Surtax was for returned prisoners of war.

1949, Dec. 3   **Engr.**

Laurel Branch, Stamps and Magnifier

B268 SP160   60g + 15g dark red   2.25   1.50
Stamp Day, Dec. 3-4.

Arms of Austria and Carinthia — SP161
Carinthian with Austrian Flag — SP162 

Design: 1.70s+40g, Casting ballot.

1950, Oct. 10   **Photo.**   **Perf. 14x13½**

B269	SP161	60g + 15g	26.00	18.00
B270	SP162	1s + 25g	35.00	23.00
B271	SP162	1.70s + 40g	40.00	30.00
		Nos. B269-B271 (3)	101.00	68.00

Plebiscite in Carinthia, 30th anniv.

Collector Examining Cover — SP163
Miner and Mine — SP164 

1950, Dec. 2   **Engr.**

B272 SP163   60g + 15g blue grn   8.50   6.00
Stamp Day.

1951, Mar. 10   **Unwmk.**

Designs: 60g+15g, Mason holding brick and trowel. 1s+25g, Bridge builder with hook and chain. 1.70s+40g, Electrician, pole and insulators.

B273	SP164	40g + 10g dark brown	13.00	11.00
B274	SP164	60g + 15g dark brown	13.00	11.00
B275	SP164	1s + 25g red brown	13.00	11.00
B276	SP164	1.70s + 40g vio bl	13.00	11.00
		Nos. B273-B276 (4)	52.00	44.00

Issued to publicize Austrian reconstruction.

Laurel Branch and Olympic Circles SP165

1952, Jan. 26   **Perf. 13½x14**

B277 SP165   2.40s + 60g grnsh black   15.00   13.00

The surtax was used to help defray expenses of Austria's athletes in the 1952 Olympic Games.

Cupid as Postman — SP166

1952, Mar. 10   **Perf. 14x13½**

B278 SP166   1.50s + 35g dark brn car   17.50   16.00
Stamp Day.

Ordering on-line is
QUICK!
EASY!
CONVENIENT!
www.scottonline.com

Sculpture, "Christ, The Almighty" SP167

1952, Sept. 6   **Perf. 13½x14**

B279 SP167   1s + 25g grnsh gray   11.00   9.00
Austrian Catholic Conv., Vienna, Sept. 11-14.

Type of 1945-46 Overprinted in Gold

1953, Aug. 29   **Unwmk.**

B280 A124   1s + 25g on 5s dl bl   2.50   2.00
60th anniv. of labor unions in Austria.

Bummerlhaus Steyr SP168
Globe and Philatelic Accessories SP169 

Designs: 1s+25g, Johannes Kepler. 1.50s+40g, Lutheran Bible, 1st edition. 2.40s+60g, Theophil von Hansen. 3s+75g, Reconstructed Lutheran School, Vienna.

1953, Nov. 5   **Engr.**   **Perf. 14x13½**

B281	SP168	70g + 15g vio brn	.30	.30
B282	SP168	1s + 25g dk gray blue	.30	.30
B283	SP168	1.50s + 40g choc	.90	.90
B284	SP168	2.40s + 60g dk grn	2.50	2.25
B285	SP168	3s + 75g dk pur	6.00	5.75
		Nos. B281-B285 (5)	10.00	9.50

The surtax was used toward reconstruction of the Lutheran School, Vienna.

1953, Dec. 5

B286 SP169   1s + 25g chocolate   5.00   3.75
Stamp Day.

Type of 1945-46 with Denomination Replaced by Asterisks

Overprinted in Brown

1954, Feb. 19   **Perf. 13½x14**

B287 A124   1s + 20g blue gray   .15   .15
Surtax for aid to avalanche victims.

Patient Under Sun Lamp — SP170

Designs: 70g+15g, Physician using microscope. 1s+25g, Mother and children. 1.45s+35g, Operating room. 1.50s+35g, Baby on scale. 2.40s+60g, Nurse.

1954   **Engr.**   **Perf. 14x13½**

B288	SP170	30g + 10g purple	1.50	1.10
B289	SP170	70g + 15g dk brn	.25	.25
B290	SP170	1s + 25g dk bl	.30	.25
B291	SP170	1.45s + 35g dk bl green	.45	.40
B292	SP170	1.50s + 35g dk red	5.00	4.50
B293	SP170	2.40s + 60g dk red brown	6.00	5.50
		Nos. B288-B293 (6)	13.50	12.00

The surtax was for social welfare.

Early Vienna-Ulm Ferryboat SP171

1954, Dec. 4   **Perf. 13½x14**

B294 SP171   1s + 25g dk gray grn   4.50   4.00
Stamp Day.

"Industry" Welcoming Returned Prisoner of War — SP172

1955, June 29

B295 SP172   1s + 25g red brn   2.00   1.50
Surtax for returned prisoners of war and relatives of prisoners not yet released.

Collector Looking at Album — SP173
Ornamental Shield and Letter — SP174 

1955, Dec. 3   **Perf. 14x13½**

B296 SP173   1s + 25g vio brn   3.00   2.75
Stamp Day. The surtax was for the promotion of Austrian philately.

1956, Dec. 1   **Engr.**

B297 SP174   1s + 25g scarlet   2.75   2.50
Stamp Day. See note after No. B296.

Arms of Austria, 1945 — SP175

Perf. 14x13½

1956, Dec. 21   **Engr. & Typo.**

B298 SP175   1.50s + 50g on 1.60s + 40g gray & red   .25   .20
The surtax was for Hungarian refugees.

New Post Office, Linz 2 — SP176

Design: 2.40s+60g, Post office, Kitzbuhel.

1957-58   **Engr.**   **Perf. 13½x14**

B299	SP176	1s + 25g dk sl grn	2.75	2.50
B300	SP176	2.40s + 60g blue	.65	.60

Stamp Day. See note after B296. Issue dates: 1s, Nov. 30, 1957. 2.40s, Dec. 6, 1957. See No. B303.

AUSTRIA

Roman Carriage from Tomb at Maria Saal — SP177

Perf. 13½x14
1959, Dec. 5 Litho. & Engr.
B301 SP177 2.40s + 60g pale lil & blk .55 .50
Stamp Day.

Progressive Die Proof under Magnifying Glass — SP178

1960, Dec. 2 Engr. **Perf. 13½x14**
B302 SP178 3s + 70g vio brn .85 .70
Stamp Day.

Post Office Type of 1957
Design: 3s+70g, Post Office, Rust.

1961, Dec. 1 Unwmk. **Perf. 13½**
B303 SP176 3s + 70g dk bl grn .90 .70
Stamp Day. See note after No. B296.

Hands of Stamp Engraver at Work — SP179

1962, Nov. 30 **Perf. 13½x14**
B304 SP179 3s + 70g dull pur 1.25 .90
Stamp Day.

Railroad Exit, Post Office Vienna 101 — SP180

1963, Nov. 29 Litho. & Engr.
B305 SP180 3s + 70g tan & blk .80 .80
Stamp Day.

View of Vienna, North SP181

Designs: Various view of Vienna with compass indicating direction.

1964, July 20 Litho. **Perf. 13½x14**
B306 SP181 1.50s + 30g ("N") .20 .15
B307 SP181 1.50s + 30g ("NO") .20 .15
B308 SP181 1.50s + 30g ("O") .20 .15
B309 SP181 1.50s + 30g ("SO") .20 .15
B310 SP181 1.50s + 30g ("S") .20 .15
B311 SP181 1.50s + 30g ("SW") .20 .15
B312 SP181 1.50s + 30g ("W") .20 .15
B313 SP181 1.50s + 30g ("NW") .20 .15
Nos. B306-B313 (8) 1.60 1.20
Vienna Intl. Phil. Exhib. (WIPA 1965).

Post Bus Terminal, St. Gilgen, Wolfgangsee SP182

1964, Dec. 4 Unwmk. **Perf. 13½**
B314 SP182 3s + 70g multi .45 .45
Stamp Day.

Wall Painting, Tomb at Thebes — SP183

Development of Writing: 1.80s+50g, Cuneiform writing on stone tablet and man's head from Assyrian palace. 2.20s+60g, Wax tablet with Latin writing, Corinthian column. 3s+80g, Gothic writing on sealed letter, Gothic window from Munster Cathedral. 4s+1s, Letter with seal and postmark and upright desk. 5s+1.20s, Typewriter.

Perf. 14x13½
1965, June 4 Litho. & Engr.
B315 SP183 1.50s + 40g multi .15 .15
B316 SP183 1.80s + 50g multi .15 .15
B317 SP183 2.20s + 60g multi .35 .35
B318 SP183 3s + 80g multi .20 .20
B319 SP183 4s + 1s multi .45 .45
B320 SP183 5s + 1.20s multi .60 .60
Nos. B315-B320 (6) 1.90 1.90
Vienna Intl. Phil. Exhib., WIPA, June 4-13.

Mailman Distributing Mail — SP184

1965, Dec. 3 Engr. **Perf. 13½x14**
B321 SP184 3s + 70g blue grn .40 .35
Stamp Day.

Letter Carrier, 16th Century SP185

Letter Carrier, 16th Century Playing Card SP186

Litho. & Engr.
1966, Dec. 2 **Perf. 13½**
B322 SP185 3s + 70g multi .40 .35
Stamp Day. Design is from Ambras Heroes' Book, Austrian National Library.

Engr. & Photo.
1967, Dec. 1 **Perf. 13x13½**
B323 SP186 3.50s + 80g multi .40 .35
Stamp Day.

Mercury, Bas-relief from Purkersdorf SP187

Unken Post Station Sign, 1710 SP188

1968, Nov. 29 Engr. **Perf. 13½x14**
B324 SP187 3.50s + 80g slate green .40 .35
Stamp Day.

Engr. & Photo.
1969, Dec. 5 **Perf. 12**
B325 SP188 3.50s + 80g tan, red & blk .40 .35
Stamp Day. Design is from a watercolor by Friedrich Zeller.

Saddle, Bag, Harness and Post Horn — SP189

Perf. 13½x14
1970, Dec. 4 Engr. & Litho.
B326 SP189 3.50s + 80g gray blk & yel .40 .35
Stamp Day.

"50 Years" SP190

Engr. & Photo.
1971, Dec. 3 **Perf. 13½**
B327 SP190 4s + 1.50s gold & red brn .60 .45
50th anniversary of the Federation of Austrian Philatelic Societies.

Local Post Carrier — SP191

Gabriel, by Lorenz Luchsperger, 15th Century — SP192

1972, Dec. 1 Engr. **Perf. 14x13½**
B328 SP191 4s + 1s olive green .60 .45
Stamp Day.

1973, Nov. 30
B329 SP192 4s + 1s maroon .60 .45
Stamp Day.

Mail Coach Leaving Old PTT Building — SP193

1974, Nov. 29 Engr. **Perf. 14x13½**
B330 SP193 4s + 2s violet blue .70 .70
Stamp Day.

Alpine Skiing, Women's SP194

Designs: 1.50s+70g, Ice hockey. 2s+90g, Ski jump. 4s+1.90s, Bobsledding.

1975, Mar. 14 Photo. **Perf. 13½x14**
B331 SP194 1s + 50g multi .25 .25
B332 SP194 1.50s + 70g multi .30 .30
B333 SP194 2s + 90g multi .35 .35
B334 SP194 4s + 1.90s multi .70 .70
Nos. B331-B334 (4) 1.60 1.60

1975, Nov. 14
Designs: 70g+30g, Figure skating, pair. 2s+1s, Cross-country skiing. 2.50s+1s, Luge. 4s+2s, Biathlon.

B335 SP194 70g + 30g multi .15 .15
B336 SP194 2s + 1s multi .30 .30
B337 SP194 2.50s + 1s multi .40 .40
B338 SP194 4s + 2s multi .70 .70
Nos. B335-B338 (4) 1.55 1.55
12th Winter Olympic Games, Innsbruck, Feb. 4-15, 1976.

Austria Nos. 5, 250, 455 — SP195

Photo. & Engr.
1975, Nov. 28 **Perf. 14**
B339 SP195 4s + 2s multi .65 .65
Stamp Day; 125th anniv. of Austrian stamps.

Postilion's Gala Hat and Horn — SP196

1976, Dec. 3 **Perf. 13½x14**
B340 SP196 6s + 2s blk & lt vio .80 .80
Stamp Day.

Emanuel Herrmann — SP197

1977, Dec. 2 **Perf. 14x13½**
B341 SP197 6s + 2s multi .80 .80
Stamp Day. Emanuel Herrmann (1839-1902), economist, invented postal card. Austria issued first postal card in 1869.

Post Bus, 1913 — SP198

1978, Dec. 1 Photo. **Perf. 13½x14**
B342 SP198 10s + 5s multi 1.40 1.40
Stamp Day.

Heroes' Square, Vienna SP199

Photo. & Engr.
1979, Nov. 30 **Perf. 13½**
B343 SP199 16s + 8s multi 2.75 2.50

No. B343 Inscribed "2. Phase"
1980, Nov. 21
B344 SP199 16s + 8s multi 2.75 2.50

Souvenir Sheet
1981, Feb. 20
B345 SP199 16s + 8s multi 3.00 2.50
WIPA 1981 Phil. Exhib., Vienna, May 22-31. No. B345 contains one stamp without inscription.

AUSTRIA

Mainz-Weber Mailbox, 1870 — SP200

1982, Nov. 26   Photo. & Engr.
B346 SP200 6s + 3s multi   1.00 1.00
Stamp Day.

Boy Examining Cover — SP201

1983, Oct. 21   Perf. 14
B347 SP201 6s + 3s multi   1.10 1.10
Stamp Day. See Nos. B349-B352, B354-B355.

World Winter Games for the Handicapped SP202

1984, Jan. 5   Photo.   Perf. 13½x13
B348 SP202 4s + 2s Downhill skier   .75 .75

Stamp Day Type of 1983

Designs: No. B349, Seschemnofer III burial chamber detail, pyramid of Cheops, Gizeh. No. B350, Roman messenger on horseback. No. B351, Nuremberg messenger, 16th cent. No. B352, *The Postmaster* (detail), 1841, lithograph by Carl Schuster.

1984-87   Photo. & Engr.   Perf. 14
B349 SP201 6s + 3s multi   1.25 1.25
B350 SP201 6s + 3s multi   1.25 1.25
B351 SP201 6s + 3s multi   1.25 1.25
B352 SP201 6s + 3s multi   1.40 1.40
 Nos. B349-B352 (4)   5.15 5.15
Issue: #B349, 11/30/84; #B350, 11/28/85; #B351, 11/28/86; #B352, 11/19/87.

4th World Winter Sports Championships for the Disabled, Innsbruck — SP203

1988, Jan. 15   Photo.   Perf. 13½
B353 SP203 5s + 2.50s multi   1.10 1.10

Stamp Day Type of 1983

Designs: No. B354, Railway mail car. No. B355, Hansa-Brandenburg CI mail plane.

1988-89   Photo. & Engr.   Perf. 14
B354 SP201 6s +3s multi   1.40 1.40
B355 SP201 6s +3s multi   1.40 1.40
Issued: #B354, Nov. 17; #B355, May 24, 1989.

Stamp Day — SP204

1990, May 25   Photo.   Perf. 13½
B356 SP204 7s +3s multi   1.65 1.65

SP205    Stamp Day — SP205a

1991, May 29   Photo. & Engr.
B357 SP205 7s +3s "B" & "P"   1.75 1.75
1992, May 22
B358 SP205 7s +3s "R" & "H"   1.65 1.65
1993, May 5
B359 SP205 7s +3s "I" & "I"   1.75 1.75
1994, May 27
B360 SP205 7s +3s "E" & "L"   1.65 1.65
1995, May 26
B361 SP205a 10s +5s "F" & "A"   3.00 3.00
1996, May 17
B362 SP205a 10s +5s "M" & "T"   3.00 3.00
 Nos. B357-B362,1725,1765 (8)   15.45 14.80
The first letters will spell "Briefmarke," the second "Philatelie." For "A" & "E" see No. 1725; "R" & "L" No. 1765.

Special Olympics Winter Games SP206

1993, Mar. 19   Photo.   Perf. 13½x14
B367 SP206 6s +3s multi   1.65 1.65

WIPA 2000 SP207

Design: #5, postman on bicycle.

1997, May 23   Photo. & Engr.   Perf. 14
B368 SP207 27s +13s multi   6.75 6.75

Vienna Intl. Postage Stamp Exhibition (WIPA), 2000 — SP208

Design of #339, early mail truck.

1998, Nov. 6   Photo. & Engr.   Perf. 14
B369 SP208 32s +13s multi   7.50 7.50

AIR POST STAMPS

Issues of the Monarchy

FLUGPOST

Types of Regular Issue of 1916 Surcharged

2·50 K 2·50

1918, Mar. 30   Unwmk.   Perf. 12½
C1 A40 1.50k on 2k lilac   2.00 3.75
C2 A40 2.50k on 3k ocher   7.00 16.00
 a. Inverted surcharge   1,100.
 b. Perf. 11½   325.00 425.00
 c. Perf. 12½x11½   27.50 45.00

Overprinted **FLUGPOST**

C3 A40 4k gray   5.00 11.00
 Nos. C1-C3 (3)   14.00 30.75
 Set, never hinged   24.50

Set exists imperf. Value, $200.
Nos. C1-C3 also exist without surcharge or overprint. Value, set perf., $300; imperf., $275.
Nos. C1-C3 were printed on grayish and on white paper.
A 7k on 10k red brown was prepared but not regularly issued. Value, perf. or imperf., $300.

Issues of the Republic

Hawk — AP1    Wilhelm Kress — AP2

1922-24   Typo.   Perf. 12½
C4 AP1 300k claret   .30 1.25
C5 AP1 400k green ('24)   4.50 12.50
C6 AP1 600k bister   .15 .55
C7 AP1 900k brn orange   .15 .55

Engr.
C8 AP2 1200k brn violet   .15 .55
C9 AP2 2400k slate   .15 .55
C10 AP2 3000k dp brn ('23)   2.50 3.50
C11 AP2 4800k dark bl ('23)   2.50 3.75
 Nos. C4-C11 (8)   10.40 23.20
 Set, never hinged   22.35

Set exists imperf. Value, $250.

Plane and Pilot's Head — AP3    Airplane Passing Crane — AP4

1925-30   Typo.   Perf. 12½
C12 AP3 2g gray brown   .35 .90
C13 AP3 5g red   .20 .25
 a. Horiz. pair, imperf. btwn.   250.00
C14 AP3 6g dark blue   .80 1.40
C15 AP3 8g yel green   .90 1.60
C16 AP3 10g dp org ('26)   .90 1.60
 a. Horiz. pair, imperf. btwn.   250.00
C17 AP3 15g red vio ('26)   .35 .80
 a. Horiz. pair, imperf. btwn.   300.00
C18 AP3 20g org brn ('30)   10.00 6.25
C19 AP3 25g blk vio ('30)   3.75 7.50
C20 AP3 30g bister ('26)   7.00 8.25
C21 AP3 50g bl gray ('26)   12.50 12.50
C22 AP3 80g dk grn ('30)   1.90 3.25

Photo.
C23 AP4 10g orange red   .80 2.50
 a. Horiz. pair, imperf. btwn.   250.00
C24 AP4 15g claret   .55 1.40
C25 AP4 30g brn violet   .70 2.50
C26 AP4 50g gray black   .75 2.75
C27 AP4 1s deep blue   6.00 6.25
C28 AP4 2s dark green   1.50 3.50
 a. Vertical pair, imperf. btwn.   250.00
C29 AP4 3s red brn ('26)   42.50 52.50
C30 AP4 5s indigo ('26)   11.50 22.50

Size: 25½x32mm
C31 AP4 10s blk brown, *gray* ('26)   9.00 17.50
 Nos. C12-C31 (20)   111.95 155.95
 Set, never hinged   220.00

Exists imperf. Value, set $800.

Airplane over Güssing Castle — AP5    Airplane over the Danube — AP6

Designs (each includes plane): 10g, Maria-Worth. 15g, Durnstein. 20g, Hallstatt. 25g, Salzburg. 30g, Upper Dachstein and Schladminger Glacier. 40g, Lake Wetter. 50g, Arlberg. 60g, St. Stephen's Cathedral. 80g, Church of the Minorites. 2s, Railroad viaduct, Carinthia. 3s, Gross Glockner mountain. 5s, Aerial railway. 10s, Seaplane and yachts.

1935, Aug. 16   Engr.   Perf. 12½
C32 AP5 5g rose violet   .20 .40
C33 AP5 10g red orange   .15 .20
C34 AP5 15g yel green   .60 1.25
C35 AP5 20g gray blue   .15 .30
C36 AP5 25g violet brn   .15 .30
C37 AP5 30g brn orange   .15 .35
C38 AP5 40g gray green   .15 .35
C39 AP5 50g light sl bl   .15 .45
C40 AP5 60g black brn   .30 .65
C41 AP5 80g light brown   .35 .80
C42 AP6 1s rose red   .30 .70
C43 AP6 2s olive green   1.75 4.00
C44 AP6 3s yellow brn   7.00 15.00
C45 AP6 5s dark green   4.50 11.00
C46 AP6 10s slate blue   42.50 80.00
 Nos. C32-C46 (15)   58.40 115.75
 Set, never hinged   87.00

Set exists imperf. Value, $275.

Catalogue values for unused stamps in this section, from this point to the end of the section, are for Never Hinged items.

Windmill, Neusiedler Lake Shore — AP20

Designs: 1s, Roman arch, Carnuntum. 2s, Town Hall, Gmund. 3s, Schieder Lake, Hinterstoder. 4s, Praegraten, Eastern Tyrol. 5s, Torsäule, Salzburg. 10s, St. Charles Church, Vienna.

1947   Unwmk.   Perf. 14x13½
C47 AP20 50g black brown   .15 .20
C48 AP20 1s dark brn vio   .30 .25
C49 AP20 2s dark green   .35 .40
C50 AP20 3s chocolate   2.25 2.75
C51 AP20 4s dark green   1.40 2.00
C52 AP20 5s dark blue   1.40 2.00
C53 AP20 10s dark blue   .75 1.50
 Nos. C47-C53 (7)   6.60 9.10

Rooks — AP27

Birds: 1s, Barn swallows. 2s, Blackheaded gulls. 3s, Great cormorants. 5s, Buzzard. 10s, Gray heron. 20s, Golden eagle.

1950-53   Perf. 13½x14
C54 AP27 60g dark bl vio   2.50 1.10
C55 AP27 1s dark brn vio ('53)   17.50 15.00
C56 AP27 2s dark blue   15.00 6.00
C57 AP27 3s dk slate green ('53)   100.00 65.00
C58 AP27 5s red brn ('53)   100.00 65.00
C59 AP27 10s gray vio ('53)   45.00 30.00
C60 AP27 20s brn blk ('52)   10.00 4.00
 Nos. C54-C60 (7)   290.00 186.10
 Set, hinged   180.00

Value at lower left on Nos. C59 and C60.
No. C60 exists imperf.

Etrich "Dove" AP28

Designs: 3.50s, Twin-engine jet airliner. 5s, Four-engine jet airliner.

AUSTRIA 479

1968, May 31 Engr. *Perf. 13½x14*

C61 AP28 2s olive bister .30 .25
C62 AP28 3.50s slate green .50 .40
C63 AP28 5s dark blue .75 .60
Nos. C61-C63 (3) 1.55 1.25

IFA WIEN 1968 (International Air Post Exhibition), Vienna, May 30-June 4.

POSTAGE DUE STAMPS

Issues of the Monarchy

D1

D2

Perf. 10 to 13½

1894-95 Typo. Wmk. 91

J1 D1 1kr brown 1.60 1.40
a. Perf. 13½ 26.00 30.00
J2 D1 2kr brown ('95) 3.50 2.00
a. Pair, imperf. btwn. 175.00 200.00
J3 D1 3kr brown 2.75 1.00
J4 D1 5kr brown 2.50 1.40
a. Perf. 13½ 16.00 15.00
b. Pair, imperf. btwn. 160.00 175.00
J5 D1 6kr brown ('95) 2.50 5.00
J6 D1 7kr brown ('95) .80 4.50
a. Vert. pair, imperf. btwn. 250.00 300.00
b. Horiz. pair, imperf. btwn. 275.00 —
J7 D1 10kr brown 4.00 .50
J8 D1 20kr brown .80 4.50
J9 D1 50kr brown 35.00 55.00
Nos. J1-J9 (9) 53.45 75.30

Values for Nos. J1-J9 are for stamps that do not show the watermark. Stamps showing the watermark often sell for more.
See Nos. J204-J231.

1899-1900 *Imperf.*

J10 D2 1h brown .20 .40
J11 D2 2h brown .25 .50
J12 D2 3h brown ('00) .20 .40
J13 D2 4h brown 1.75 1.40
J14 D2 5h brown ('00) 2.25 1.10
J15 D2 6h brown .30 .85
J16 D2 10h brown .25 .40
J17 D2 12h brown .40 2.25
J18 D2 15h brown .40 1.40
J19 D2 20h brown 17.00 3.00
J20 D2 40h brown .80 2.50
J21 D2 100h brown 4.00 2.25
Nos. J10-J21 (12) 27.80 16.45

Perf. 10½, 12½, 13½ and Compound

J22 D2 1h brown .55 .20
J23 D2 2h brown .45 .20
J24 D2 3h brown ('00) .40 .15
J25 D2 4h brown .40 .15
J26 D2 5h brown ('00) .40 .15
J27 D2 6h brown .40 .15
J28 D2 10h brown .45 .15
J29 D2 12h brown .45 .65
J30 D2 15h brown .70 .80
J31 D2 20h brown .55 .30
J32 D2 40h brown 1.00 .75
J33 D2 100h brown 20.00 1.00
Nos. J22-J33 (12) 25.75 4.65

Nos. J10-J33 exist on unwmkd. paper.
For surcharges see Offices in the Turkish Empire Nos. J1-J5.

D3

1908-13 Unwmk. *Perf. 12½*

J34 D3 1h carmine 1.00 1.00
J35 D3 2h carmine .25 .25
J36 D3 4h carmine .15 .15
J37 D3 6h carmine .15 .15
J38 D3 10h carmine .25 .15
J39 D3 14h carmine ('13) 3.25 1.75
J40 D3 20h carmine 4.75 .15
J41 D3 25h carmine ('10) 4.50 3.50
J42 D3 30h carmine 5.00 .20
J43 D3 50h carmine 7.50 .25
J44 D3 100h carmine 13.50 .45
Nos. J34-J44 (11) 40.30 8.00

All values exist on ordinary paper, #J34-J38, J40, J42-J44 on chalky paper and #J34-J38, J40, J44 on thin ordinary paper. Values are for the least expensive stamp of the types. Some of the expensive types sell for considerably more.
All values exist imperf.
See Offices in the Turkish Empire type D3.

1911, July 16

J45 D3 5k violet 42.50 9.00
J46 D3 10k violet 175.00 2.75

Regular Issue of 1908 Overprinted or Surcharged in Carmine or Black:

PORTO
a

PORTO
15 15
b

1916, Oct. 21

J47 A22 1h gray (C) .15 .15
a. Pair, one without overprint 125.00
J48 A22 15h on 2h vio (Bk) .20 .35
Set, never hinged .40

D4

D5

1916, Oct. 1

J49 D4 5h rose red .15 .15
J50 D4 10h rose red .15 .15
J51 D4 15h rose red .15 .15
J52 D4 20h rose red .15 .15
J53 D4 25h rose red .30 .65
J54 D4 30h rose red .15 .25
J55 D4 40h rose red .15 .15
J56 D4 50h rose red .90 1.50
J57 D5 1k ultramarine .25 .15
a. Horiz. pair, imperf. btwn. 325.00 350.00
J58 D5 5k ultramarine 1.60 1.40
J59 D5 10k ultramarine 2.25 .90
Nos. J49-J59 (11) 6.20 5.60
Set, never hinged 17.00

Exists imperf. Value, set $80.
For overprints see J64-J74, Western Ukraine Nos. 54-55, NJ1-NJ6, Poland Nos. J1-J10.

Type of Regular Issue of 1916 Surcharged

PORTO
15 * 15

1917

J60 A38 10h on 24h blue 1.10 .40
J61 A38 15h on 36h violet .30 .15
J62 A38 20h on 54h orange .20 .30
J63 A38 50h on 42h chocolate .20 .20
Nos. J60-J63 (4) 1.80 1.05
Set, never hinged 5.00

All values of this issue are known imperforate, also without surcharge, perforated and imperforate.
For overprints see Western Ukraine Nos. 57-58.

Issues of the Republic

Postage Due Stamps of 1916 Overprinted

Deutschösterreich

1919

J64 D4 5h rose red .15 .15
a. Inverted overprint 225.00 225.00
J65 D4 10h rose red .15 .15
J66 D4 15h rose red .25 .35
J67 D4 20h rose red .25 .35
J68 D4 25h rose red 8.75 13.50
J69 D4 30h rose red .15 .25
J70 D4 40h rose red .25 .60
J71 D4 50h rose red .30 1.10
J72 D5 1k ultramarine 3.50 8.00
J73 D5 5k ultramarine 8.00 10.50
J74 D5 10k ultramarine 7.25 3.50
Nos. J64-J74 (11) 29.00 38.45
Set, never hinged 67.40

Nos. J64, J65, J67 and J70 exist imperforate.

D6

D7

1920-21 *Perf. 12½*

J75 D6 5h bright red .15 .30
J76 D6 10h bright red .15 .15
J77 D6 15h bright red .15 1.10
J78 D6 20h bright red .15 .15
J79 D6 25h bright red .15 .90
J80 D6 30h bright red .15 .25
J81 D6 40h bright red .15 .20
J82 D6 50h bright red .15 .20
J83 D6 80h bright red .15 .25
J84 D7 1k ultramarine .15 .15
J85 D7 1½k ultra ('21) .15 .15
J86 D7 2k ultra ('21) .15 .15
J87 D7 3k ultra ('21) .15 .50
J88 D7 4k ultra ('21) .15 .55
J89 D7 5k ultramarine .15 .15
J90 D7 8k ultra ('21) .15 .60
J91 D7 10k ultramarine .15 .25
J92 D7 20k ultra ('21) .15 1.10
Nos. J75-J92 (18) 2.70 7.10
Set, never hinged 3.40

Nos. J84 to J92 exist on white paper and on grayish white paper. They also exist imperf.; value, set $85.

Imperf

J93 D6 5h bright red .15 .35
J94 D6 10h bright red .15 .20
J95 D6 15h bright red .15 .90
J96 D6 20h bright red .15 .20
J97 D6 25h bright red .15 .90
J98 D6 30h bright red .15 .60
J99 D6 40h bright red .15 .35
J100 D6 50h bright red .15 .60
J101 D6 80h bright red .15 .35
Nos. J93-J101 (9) 1.35 4.45
Set, never hinged 1.60

No. 207a Surcharged in Dark Blue

Nachmarke
7½ K

1921, Dec. *Perf. 12½*

J102 A43 7½k on 15h bister .15 .15
Never hinged .15
a. Inverted surcharge 250.00 350.00

D8

D9

D10

1922

J103 D8 1k reddish buff .15 .25
J104 D8 2k reddish buff .15 .25
J105 D8 4k reddish buff .15 .50
J106 D8 5k reddish buff .15 .25
J107 D8 7½k reddish buff .15 .70
J108 D8 10k blue green .15 .25
J109 D8 15k blue green .15 .50
J110 D8 20k blue green .15 .35
J111 D8 25k blue green .15 .80
J112 D8 40k blue green .15 .30
J113 D8 50k blue green .15 .90
Nos. J103-J113 (11) 1.65 5.05
Set, never hinged 1.65

Issue date: Nos. J108-J113, June 2.

1922-24

J114 D9 10k cobalt blue .15 .30
J115 D9 15k cobalt blue .15 .35
J116 D9 20k cobalt blue .15 .45
J117 D9 50k cobalt blue .15 .35
J118 D10 100k plum .15 .15
J119 D10 150k plum .15 .15
J120 D10 200k plum .15 .15
J121 D10 400k plum .15 .15
J122 D10 600k plum ('23) .15 .35
J123 D10 800k plum .15 .15
J124 D10 1,000k plum ('23) .15 .15
J125 D10 1,200k plum ('23) .15 2.50
J126 D10 1,500k plum ('24) .15 .25
J127 D10 1,800k plum ('24) 1.50 5.25
J128 D10 2,000k plum ('23) .30 .85
J129 D10 3,000k plum ('24) 5.75 12.00
J130 D10 4,000k plum ('24) 3.75 9.75
J131 D10 6,000k plum ('24) 3.75 16.00
Nos. J114-J131 (18) 17.00 49.30
Set, never hinged 38.00

Value, Nos. J103-J131 imperf, $225.

D11

D12

1925-34 *Perf. 12½*

J132 D11 1g red .15 .15
J133 D11 2g red .15 .15
J134 D11 3g red .15 .15
J135 D11 4g red .15 .15
J136 D11 5g red ('27) .15 .15
J137 D11 6g red .20 .45
J138 D11 8g red .15 .20
J139 D11 10g dark blue .20 .15
J140 D11 12g dark blue .15 .15
J141 D11 14g dark blue ('27) .15 .15
J142 D11 15g dark blue .15 .15
J143 D11 16g dark blue ('29) .20 .20
J144 D11 18g dark blue ('34) 1.10 3.50
J145 D11 20g dark blue .15 .15
J146 D11 23g dark blue .25 .20
J147 D11 24g dark blue ('32) 1.10 .15
J148 D11 28g dark blue ('27) .90 .30
J149 D11 30g dark blue .20 .15
J150 D11 31g dark blue ('29) 1.10 .25
J151 D11 35g dark blue ('30) 1.10 .20
J152 D11 39g dark blue ('32) 1.40 .15
J153 D11 40g dark blue 1.25 1.75
J154 D11 60g dark blue .85 1.10
J155 D12 1s dark green 5.50 1.10
J156 D12 2s dark green 27.50 3.50
J157 D12 5s dark green 77.50 30.00
J158 D12 10s dark green 45.00 4.25
Nos. J132-J158 (27) 166.85 48.95
Set, never hinged 422.00

Issues of 1925-27 imperf, value, set $425.
Issued: 3g, 2s-10s, Dec; 5g, 28g, 1/1; 14g, June; 31g, 2/1; 35g, Jan; 24g, 39g, Sept; 16g, May; 18g, 6/25; others, 6/1.

Coat of Arms
D13 D14

1935, June 1

J159 D13 1g red .15 .15
J160 D13 2g red .15 .15
J161 D13 3g red .15 .15
J162 D13 5g red .15 .15
J163 D13 10g blue .15 .15
J164 D13 12g blue .15 .15
J165 D13 15g blue .15 .40
J166 D13 20g blue .15 .15
J167 D13 24g blue .15 .15
J168 D13 30g blue .20 .15
J169 D13 39g blue .20 .15
J170 D13 60g blue .75 .90
J171 D14 1s green .75 .30
J172 D14 2s green 1.10 .70
J173 D14 5s green 2.50 2.50
J174 D14 10s green 3.75 .60
Nos. J159-J174 (16) 10.60 6.90
Set, never hinged 41.40

On #J163-J170, background lines are horiz.
Nos. J159-J174 exist imperf. Value, set $125.

Catalogue values for unused stamps in this section, from this point to the end of the section, are for Never Hinged items.

D15

1945 Unwmk. Typo. *Perf. 10½*

J175 D15 1g vermilion .15 .15
J176 D15 2g vermilion .15 .15
J177 D15 3g vermilion .15 .15
J178 D15 5g vermilion .15 .15
J179 D15 10g vermilion .15 .15
J180 D15 12g vermilion .15 .15
J181 D15 20g vermilion .15 .15
J182 D15 24g vermilion .15 .15
J183 D15 30g vermilion .15 .15

J184 D15 60g vermilion	.15	*.20*
J185 D15 1s violet	.15	*.35*
J186 D15 2s violet	.15	*.45*
J187 D15 5s violet	.15	*.20*
J188 D15 10s violet	.15	*.20*
Nos. J175-J188 (14)	2.10	*2.75*

Issue dates: 1g-60g, Sept. 10, 1s-10s, Sept. 24.

Occupation Stamps of the Allied Military Government Overprinted in Black

PORTO

1946		*Perf. 11*
J189 OS1 3g deep orange	.15	.15
J190 OS1 5g bright green	.15	.15
J191 OS1 6g red violet	.15	.15
J192 OS1 8g rose pink	.15	.15
J193 OS1 10g light gray	.15	.20
J194 OS1 12g pale buff brown	.15	.15
J195 OS1 15g rose red	.15	.20
J196 OS1 20g copper brown	.15	.15
J197 OS1 25g deep blue	.15	.15
J198 OS1 30g bright violet	.15	.15
J199 OS1 40g light ultra	.15	.15
J200 OS1 60g light olive grn	.15	.15
J201 OS1 1s dark violet	.15	.20
J202 OS1 2s yellow	.25	.30
J203 OS1 5s deep ultra	.25	.30
Nos. J189-J203 (15)	2.45	2.70

Nos. J189-J203 were issued by the Renner Government. Inverted overprints exist on about half of the denominations.

Issue dates: 3g-60g, Apr. 23, 1s-5s, May 20.

Type of 1894-95
Inscribed "Republik Osterreich"

1947 Typo.		*Perf. 14*
J204 D1 1g chocolate	.15	.15
J205 D1 2g chocolate	.15	.15
J206 D1 3g chocolate	.15	.15
J207 D1 5g chocolate	.15	.15
J208 D1 8g chocolate	.15	.15
J209 D1 10g chocolate	.15	.15
J210 D1 12g chocolate	.15	.15
J211 D1 15g chocolate	.15	.15
J212 D1 16g chocolate	.20	.40
J213 D1 17g chocolate	.20	.40
J214 D1 18g chocolate	.20	.40
J215 D1 20g chocolate	.50	.15
J216 D1 24g chocolate	.30	.30
J217 D1 30g chocolate	.20	.20
J218 D1 36g chocolate	.50	.60
J219 D1 40g chocolate	.15	.15
J220 D1 42g chocolate	.50	.60
J221 D1 48g chocolate	.50	.60
J222 D1 50g chocolate	.55	.15
J223 D1 60g chocolate	.20	.15
J224 D1 70g chocolate	.15	.15
J225 D1 80g chocolate	3.75	1.65
J226 D1 1s blue	.20	.15
J227 D1 1.15s blue	2.50	.30
J228 D1 1.20s blue	3.00	1.00
J229 D1 2s blue	.40	.40
J230 D1 5s blue	.40	.40
J231 D1 10s blue	.40	.40
Nos. J204-J231 (28)	16.00	9.75

Issue dates: 1g, 20g, 50g, 80g, 1.15s, 1.20s, Sept. 25, others, Aug. 14.

D16

D17

1949-57		
J232 D16 1g carmine	.20	.15
J233 D16 2g carmine	.20	.15
J234 D16 4g carmine ('51)	1.00	.15
J235 D16 5g carmine	2.25	.25
J236 D16 8g carmine ('51)	2.75	1.50
J237 D16 10g carmine	.15	.15
J238 D16 20g carmine	.15	.15
J239 D16 30g carmine	.15	.15
J240 D16 40g carmine	.15	.15
J241 D16 50g carmine	.15	.15
J242 D16 60g carmine ('50)	7.50	.15
J243 D16 63g carmine ('57)	4.75	4.00
J244 D16 70g carmine	.15	.15
J245 D16 80g carmine	.15	.15
J246 D16 90g carmine ('50)	.20	.15
J247 D16 1s purple	.20	.15
J248 D16 1.20s purple	.35	.15
J249 D16 1.35s purple	.30	.15
J250 D16 1.40s purple ('51)	.45	.20
J251 D16 1.50s purple ('53)	.20	.15
J252 D16 1.65s purple ('50)	.40	.15
J253 D16 1.70s purple	.40	.15
J254 D16 2s purple	.35	.15
J255 D16 2.50s purple ('51)	.45	.15
J256 D16 3s purple ('51)	1.00	.15
J257 D16 4s purple ('51)	1.00	.40
J258 D16 5s purple	1.75	.20
J259 D16 10s purple	2.75	.20
Nos. J232-J259 (28)	29.50	9.90

Issued: 60g, 90g, 1.65s, 8/7; 4g, 8g, 1.40s, 2.50s-4s, 12/4; 1.50s, 2/18; 63g, 4/30; others, 11/17.

1985-89 Photo.		*Perf. 14*
Background Color		
J260 D17 10g brt yel ('86)	.15	.15
J261 D17 20g pink ('86)	.15	.15
J262 D17 50g orange ('86)	.15	.15
J263 D17 1s lt blue ('86)	.15	.15
J264 D17 2s pale brn ('86)	.30	.20
J265 D17 3s violet ('86)	.40	.30
J266 D17 5s ocher	.60	.40
J267 D17 10s pale grn ('89)	1.50	1.10
Nos. J260-J267 (8)	3.40	2.60

Issue dates: 5s, Dec. 12. 20g, 1s, 3s, Mar. 19. 10g, 50g, 2s, Oct. 3. 10s, June 30.

MILITARY STAMPS

Issues of the Austro-Hungarian Military Authorities for the Occupied Territories in World War I

See Bosnia and Herzegovina for similar designs inscribed "MILITARPOST" instead of "FELDPOST."

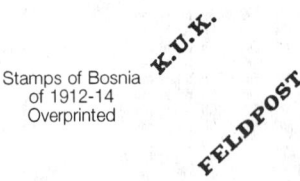

Stamps of Bosnia of 1912-14 Overprinted

K.U.K.
FELDPOST

1915 Unwmk.		*Perf. 12½*
M1 A23 1h olive green	.15	*.35*
M2 A23 2h bright blue	.15	*.35*
M3 A23 3h claret	.15	*.35*
M4 A23 5h green	.15	.15
M5 A23 6h dark gray	.15	*.35*
M6 A23 10h rose carmine	.15	.15
M7 A23 12h deep ol grn	.25	*.45*
M8 A23 20h orange brn	.30	*.55*
M9 A23 25h ultramarine	.25	*.45*
M10 A23 30h orange red	2.75	*5.25*
M11 A24 35h myrtle grn	2.25	*4.25*
M12 A24 40h dark violet	2.25	*4.25*
M13 A24 45h olive brown	2.50	*4.50*
M14 A24 50h slate blue	2.25	*4.25*
M15 A24 60h brn violet	.30	*3.25*
M16 A24 72h dark blue	2.25	*4.25*
M17 A25 1k brn vio, *straw*	2.50	*5.25*
M18 A25 2k dk gray, *blue*	2.25	*4.25*
M19 A26 3k car, *green*	20.00	*32.50*
M20 A26 5k dk vio, *gray*	18.00	*27.50*
M21 A25 10k dk ultra, *gray*	160.00	200.00
Nos. M1-M21 (21)	219.00	*302.65*
Set, never hinged	330.00	

Exists imperf. Value, set $275.

Nos. M1-M21 also exist with overprint double, inverted and in red. These varieties were made by order of an official but were not regularly issued.

M1

M2

Emperor Franz Josef

Perf. 11½, 12½ and Compound		
1915-17		**Engr.**
M22 M1 1h olive green	.15	.15
M23 M1 2h dull blue	.15	.15
M24 M1 3h claret	.15	.15
M25 M1 5h green	.15	.15
a. Perf. 11½	42.50	*60.00*
b. Perf. 11½x12½	55.00	*100.00*
c. Perf. 12½x11½	77.50	*110.00*
M26 M1 6h dark gray	.15	.15
M27 M1 10h rose carmine	.15	.15
M28 M1 10h gray bl ('17)	.15	.15
M29 M1 12h dp olive grn	.15	.15
M30 M1 15h car rose ('17)	.15	*.20*
a. Perf. 11½	7.00	*15.00*
M31 M1 20h orange brn	.30	*.35*
M32 M1 20h ol green ('17)	.30	*.35*
M33 M1 25h ultramarine	.15	*.20*
M34 M1 30h vermilion	.15	*.35*
M35 M1 35h dark green	.30	*.50*
M36 M1 40h dark violet	.30	*.50*
M37 M1 45h olive brown	.25	*.50*
M38 M1 50h myrtle green	.25	*.50*
M39 M1 60h brown violet	.25	*.50*
M40 M1 72h dark blue	.25	*.50*
M41 M1 80h org brn ('17)	.15	*.25*
M42 M1 90h magenta ('17)	.70	*1.10*
M43 M2 1k brn vio, *straw*	1.40	*2.10*
M44 M2 2k dk gray, *blue*	1.10	1.00
M45 M2 3k car, *green*	.80	*1.75*
M46 M2 4k dark violet, *gray* ('17)	.80	*2.75*
M47 M2 5k dk vio, *gray*	18.00	*27.50*
M48 M2 10k dk ultra, *gray*	2.75	*6.00*
Nos. M22-M48 (27)	29.55	*48.10*
Set, never hinged	63.40	

Nos. M22-M48 exist imperf. Value, set $125.

M3

M4

Emperor Karl I

1917-18		*Perf. 12½*
M49 M3 1h grnsh blue ('18)	.15	.15
a. Perf. 11½	3.25	*5.25*
M50 M3 2h red org ('18)	.15	.15
M51 M3 3h olive gray	.15	.15
a. Perf. 11½	12.00	*19.00*
b. Perf. 11½x12½	21.00	*35.00*
M52 M3 5h olive green	.15	.15
M53 M3 6h violet	.15	.15
M54 M3 10h orange brn	.15	.15
M55 M3 12h blue	.15	.15
a. Perf. 11½	2.00	*4.25*
M56 M3 15h bright rose	.15	.15
M57 M3 20h red brown	.15	.15
M58 M3 25h ultramarine	.30	.30
M59 M3 30h slate	.15	.15
M60 M3 40h olive bister	.15	.15
a. Perf. 11½	1.25	*2.10*
M61 M3 50h deep green	.15	.15
a. Perf. 11½	5.00	*9.00*
M62 M3 60h car rose	.15	.15
M63 M3 80h dull blue	.15	.15
M64 M3 90h dk violet	.40	*.50*
M65 M4 2k rose, *straw*	.15	.15
a. Perf. 11½	2.00	*3.50*
M66 M4 3k green, *blue*	.85	*1.75*
M67 M4 4k rose, *green*	13.50	*16.00*
a. Perf. 11½	25.00	*35.00*
M68 M4 10k dl vio, *gray*	2.00	*4.25*
a. Perf. 11½	10.00	*19.00*
Nos. M49-M68 (20)	19.30	*25.05*
Set, never hinged	35.00	

Nos. M49-M68 exist imperf. Value, set $45.

See No. M82. For surcharges and overprints see Italy Nos. N1-N19, Western Ukraine Nos. 34-53, 75-81.

Emperor Karl I — M5

1918 Typo.		*Perf. 12½*
M69 M5 1h grnsh blue	18.00	
M70 M5 2h orange	9.00	
M71 M5 3h olive gray	7.00	
M72 M5 5h yellow green	.25	
M73 M5 10h dark brown	.25	
M74 M5 20h red	.70	
M75 M5 25h blue	.70	
M76 M5 30h bister	67.50	
M77 M5 45h dark slate	67.50	
M78 M5 50h deep green	45.00	
M79 M5 60h violet	90.00	
M80 M5 80h rose	45.00	
M81 M5 90h brown violet	1.75	
Engr.		
M82 M4 1k ol bister, *blue*	.25	
Nos. M69-M82 (14)	352.90	
Set, never hinged	755.00	

Nos. M69-M82 were on sale at the Vienna post office for a few days before the Armistice signing. They were never issued at the Army Post Offices. They exist imperf.; value, set $450.

For surcharges see Italy Nos. N20-N33.

MILITARY SEMI-POSTAL STAMPS

Emperor Karl I — MSP7

Empress Zita — MSP8

Perf. 12½x13		
1918, July 20 Unwmk.		**Typo.**
MB1 MSP7 10h gray green	.25	.55
MB2 MSP8 20h magenta	.25	.55
MB3 MSP7 45h blue	.25	.55
Nos. MB1-MB3 (3)	.75	1.65
Set, never hinged	2.10	

Nos. M69-M82 were on sale at the Vienna post office for a few days before the Armistice signing. They were never issued at the Army Post Offices. They exist imperf.; value, set $450. These stamps were sold at a premium of 10h each over face value. The surtax was for "Karl's Fund."

For overprints see Western Ukraine Nos. 31-33. Exist imperf. Value, set $8.

MILITARY NEWSPAPER STAMPS

Mercury — MN1

1916 Unwmk. Typo.		*Perf. 12½*
MP1 MN1 2h blue	.15	*.20*
a. Perf. 11½	1.40	*1.60*
b. Perf. 12½x11½	150.00	*200.00*
MP2 MN1 6h orange	.50	*.80*
MP3 MN1 10h carmine	.60	*.80*
MP4 MN1 20h brown	.40	*.80*
a. Perf. 11½	1.90	*5.00*
Nos. MP1-MP4 (4)	1.65	*2.60*
Set, never hinged	3.20	

Exist imperf. Values, Nos. MP2-MP3, $1 each, Nos. MP1, MP4, $18 each.

For surcharges see Italy Nos. NP1-NP4.

NEWSPAPER STAMPS

From 1851 to 1866, the Austrian Newspaper Stamps were also used in Lombardy-Venetia.

Values for unused stamps 1851-67 are for fine copies with original gum. Specimens without gum sell for about a third or less of the figures quoted.

Issues of the Monarchy

Mercury — N1

Three Types
Type I - The "G" has no crossbar.
Type II - The "G" has a crossbar.
Type IIa - as type II but the rosette is deformed. Two spots of color in the "G."

1851-56 Unwmk. Typo.		*Imperf.*
Machine-made Paper		
P1 N1 (0.6kr) bl, type IIa	125.00	70.00
a. Blue, type I	160.00	85.00
b. Ribbed paper	375.00	140.00
c. Blue, type II	350.00	160.00
P2 N1 (6kr) yel, type I	*16,000.*	*7,000.*
P3 N1 (30kr) rose, type I	—	*9,000.*
P4 N1 (6kr) scar, type II ('56)	*37,500.*	*40,000.*

From 1852 No. P3 and from 1856 No. P2 were used as 0.6 kreuzer values.

Values for Nos. P2-P3 unused are for stamps without gum. Pale shades sell at considerably lower values.

Originals of Nos. P2-P3 are usually in pale colors and poorly printed. Values are for stamps clearly printed and in bright colors. Numerous reprints of Nos. P1-P4 were made between 1866 and 1904. Those of Nos. P2-P3 are always well printed and in

much deeper colors. All reprints are in type I, but occasionally show faint traces of a crossbar on "G" of "ZEITUNGS."

N2

N3

Two Types of the 1858-59 Issue
Type I - Loops of the bow at the back of the head broken.
Type II - Loops complete. Wreath projects further at top of head.

1858-59 **Embossed**

P5 N2 (1kr) blue, type I	450.00	550.00
P6 N2 (1kr) lilac, type II ('59)	650.00	275.00

1861

P7 N3 (1kr) gray	140.00	140.00
a. (1kr) gray lilac	350.00	200.00
b. (1kr) deep lilac	1,500.	575.00

The embossing on the reprints of the 1858-59 and 1861 issues is not as sharp as on the originals.

N4

Wmk. 91, or, before July 1864, Unwmkd.

1863

P8 N4 (1.05kr) gray	35.00	13.00
a. Tete beche pair	*18,000.*	
b. (1.05kr) gray lilac	60.00	17.50

Values are for stamps that do not show the watermark. Stamps showing the watermark often sell for more.

The embossing of the reprints is not as sharp as on the originals.

Mercury
N5 N6

Three Types
Type I - Helmet not defined at back, more or less blurred. Two thick short lines in front of wing of helmet. Shadow on front of face not separated from hair.
Type II - Helmet distinctly defined. Four thin short lines in front of wing. Shadow on front of face clearly defined from hair.
Type III - Outer white circle around head is open at top (closed on types I and II). Greek border at top and bottom is wider than on types I and II.

1867-73 **Typo.** **Wmk. 91**
Coarse Print

P9 N5 (1kr) vio, type I	37.50	4.00
a. (1kr) violet, type II ('73)	110.00	18.00

1874-76
Fine Print

P9B N5 (1kr) violet, type III ('76)	.55	.20
c. (1kr) gray lilac, type I ('76)	90.00	25.00
d. (1kr) violet, type II	27.50	5.00
e. Double impression, type III		175.00

Stamps of this issue, except No. P9c, exist in many shades, from gray to lilac brown and deep violet. Stamps in type III exist also privately perforated or rouletted.

1880

P10 N6 ½kr blue green	4.50	.85

Nos. P9B and P10 also exist on thicker paper without sheet watermark and No. P10 exists with unofficial perforation.

N7

1899 **Unwmk.** ***Imperf.***
Without Varnish Bars

P11 N7 2h dark blue	.20	.15
P12 N7 6h orange	2.00	1.75
P13 N7 10h brown	.80	.75
P14 N7 20h rose	1.75	1.75
Nos. P11-P14 (4)	4.75	4.40

1901
With Varnish Bars

P11a N7 2h dark blue	.60	.20
P12a N7 6h orange	8.50	*11.50*
P13a N7 10h brown	10.50	6.75
P14a N7 20h rose	19.00	*26.00*
Nos. P11a-P14a (4)	38.60	*44.45*

Nos. P11 to P14 were re-issued in 1905.

Mercury
N8 N9

1908 ***Imperf.***

P15 N8 2h dark blue	.50	.15
a. Tete beche pair	250.00	*300.00*
P16 N8 6h orange	2.50	.30
P17 N8 10h carmine	2.50	.30
P18 N8 20h brown	2.75	.25
Nos. P15-P18 (4)	8.25	1.00

All values are found on chalky, regular and thin ordinary paper. They exist privately perforated.

1916 ***Imperf.***

P19 N9 2h brown	.15	.15
P20 N9 4h green	.30	.30
P21 N9 6h dark blue	.25	*.60*
P22 N9 10h orange	.35	.35
P23 N9 30h claret	.30	.30
Nos. P19-P23 (5)	1.35	1.70
Set, never hinged	2.80	

Issues of the Republic

Newspaper Stamps of 1916 Overprinted

Deutschösterreich

1919

P24 N9 2h brown	.15	.15
P25 N9 4h green	.25	*.70*
P26 N9 6h dark blue	.15	*.70*
P27 N9 10h orange	.25	*.90*
P28 N9 30h claret	.15	*.45*
Nos. P24-P28 (5)	.95	*2.90*
Set, never hinged	1.70	

Mercury
N10 N11

1920-21 ***Imperf.***

P29 N10 2h violet	.15	.15
P30 N10 4h brown	.15	*.20*
P31 N10 5h slate	.15	.15
P32 N10 6h turq blue	.15	.15
P33 N10 8h green	.15	*.30*
P34 N10 9h yellow ('21)	.15	.15
P35 N10 10h red	.15	.15
P36 N10 12h blue	.15	*.30*
P37 N10 15h lilac ('21)	.15	.15
P38 N10 18h blue grn ('21)	.15	*.25*
P39 N10 20h orange	.15	*.25*
P40 N10 30h yellow brn ('21)	.15	.15
P41 N10 45h green ('21)	.15	*.35*
P42 N10 60h claret	.15	.15
P43 N10 72h chocolate ('21)	.15	*.45*
P44 N10 90h violet ('21)	.15	*.55*
P45 N10 1.20k red ('21)	.15	*.65*
P46 N10 2.40k yellow grn ('21)	.15	*.55*
P47 N10 3k gray ('21)	.15	*.40*
Nos. P29-P47 (19)	2.85	5.45
Set, never hinged	3.20	

Nos. P37-P40, P42, P44 and P47 exist also on thick gray paper.

1921-22

P48 N11 45h gray	.15	*.25*
P49 N11 75h brown org ('22)	.15	*.35*
P50 N11 1.50k ol bister ('22)	.15	*.50*
P51 N11 1.80k gray blue ('22)	.15	*.55*
P52 N11 2.25k light brown	.15	*.75*
P53 N11 3k dull green ('22)	.15	*.55*
P54 N11 6k claret ('22)	.15	*.65*
P55 N11 7.50k bister	.15	*.85*
Nos. P48-P55 (8)	1.20	*4.45*
Set, never hinged	1.40	

Nos. P24-P55 exist privately perforated.

NEWSPAPER TAX STAMPS

Values for unused stamps 1853-59 are for copies in fine condition with gum. Specimens without gum sell for about one-third or less of the figures quoted.

Issues of the Monarchy

NT1

NT2

Unwmk.
1853, Mar. 1 **Typo.** ***Imperf.***

PR1 NT1 2kr green	1,300.	50.00

The reprints are in finer print than the more coarsely printed originals, and on a smooth toned paper.

Wmk. 91, or, before July 1864, Unwmkd.

1858-59

Two Types.
Type I - The banderol on the Crown of the left eagle touches the beak of the eagle.
Type II - The banderol does not touch the beak.

PR2 NT2 1kr blue, type II ('59)	30.00	5.50
a. 1kr blue, type I	625.00	140.00
b. Printed on both sides, type II		—
PR3 NT2 2kr brown, type II ('59)	20.00	6.75
a. 2kr red brown, type II	350.00	140.00
PR4 NT2 4kr brn, type I	400.00	*1,000.*

Nos. PR2a, PR3a, and PR4 were printed only on unwatermarked paper. Nos. PR2 and PR3 exist on unwatermarked and watermarked paper.

Nos. PR2 and PR3 exist in coarse and (after 1874) in fine print, like the contemporary postage stamps.

The reprints of the 4kr brown are of type II and on a smooth toned paper.

Issue date: 4kr, Nov. 1.

See Lombardy-Venetia for the 1kr in black and the 2kr, 4fk in red.

NT3

NT4

1877 **Redrawn**

PR5 NT3 1kr blue	14.00	1.40
a. 1kr pale ultramarine		*1,600.*
PR6 NT3 2kr brown	12.50	1.50

In the redrawn stamps the shield is larger and the vertical bar has eight lines above the white square and nine below, instead of five.

Nos. PR5 and PR6 exist also watermarked "WECHSEL" instead of "ZEITUNGS-MARKEN."

1890, June 1

PR7 NT4 1kr brown	9.00	1.00
PR8 NT4 2kr green	10.00	1.50

#PR5-PR8 exist with private perforation.

NT5

Perf. 13, 12½
1890, June 1 **Wmk. 91**

PR9 NT5 25kr carmine	100.00	*425.00*

Nos. PR1-PR9 did not pay postage, but were a fiscal tax, collected by the postal authorities on newspapers.

Values for Nos. PR2-PR9 are for stamps that do not show the watermark. Stamps showing the watermark often sell for more.

SPECIAL HANDLING STAMPS

(For Printed Matter Only)
Issues of the Monarchy

Mercury — SH1

1916 **Unwmk.** ***Perf. 12½***

QE1 SH1 2h claret, *yel*	.60	*1.60*
QE2 SH1 5h dp green, *yel*	.60	*1.60*
Set, never hinged	3.50	

SH2

1917 ***Perf. 12¹***

QE3 SH2 2h claret, *yel*	.15	*.30*
a. Pair, imperf. between	175.00	*.ʖ0.00*
b. Perf. 11½x12½	55.00	*95.00*
c. Perf. 12½x11½	80.0'	*150.00*
d. Perf. 11½	' .0	*2.50*
QE4 SH2 5h dp green, *yel*	.15	*.30*
a. Pair, imperf. between	ɔ0.00	*250.00*
b. Perf. 11½x12½	45.00	*87.50*
c. Perf. 12½x11½	70.00	*125.00*
d. Perf. 11½	1.10	*2.50*
Set, never hinged	.60	

Nos. QE1-QE4 exist imperforate.

Issues of the Republic

Nos. QE3 and QE4 Overprinted

Deutschösterreich

1919

QE5 SH2 2h claret, *yel*	.15	.15
a. Inverted overprint	325.00	
b. Perf. 11½x12½	5.25	*8.00*
c. Perf. 12½x11½	65.00	*85.00*
d. Perf. 11½	.30	*.70*
QE6 SH2 5h deep green, *yel*	.15	.15
a. Perf. 11½x12½	2.25	*3.75*
b. Perf. 12½x11½	25.00	*35.00*
c. Perf. 11½	.20	*.45*
Set, never hinged	.30	

Nos. QE5 and QE6 exist imperforate.

SH3

Dark Blue Surcharge

1921

QE7 SH3 50h on 2h claret, *yel*	.15	*.20*
Never hinged	.15	

SH4

1922 ***Perf. 12½***

QE8 SH4 50h lilac, *yel*	.15	*.40*
Never hinged	.20	

#QE5-QE8 exist in vertical pairs, imperf between. No. QE8 exists imperf.

OCCUPATION STAMPS

Issued under Italian Occupation

Issued in Trieste

Austrian Stamps of 1916-18 Overprinted **Regno d'Italia Venezia Giulia 3. XI. 18.**

1918 Unwmk. *Perf. 12½*

N1	A37	3h bright vio	1.00	1.00
a.		Double overprint	30.00	30.00
b.		Inverted overprint	30.00	30.00
N2	A37	5h light grn	1.00	1.00
a.		Inverted overprint	30.00	30.00
c.		Double overprint	30.00	
N3	A37	6h dp orange	1.40	1.40
N4	A37	10h magenta	4.00	2.50
a.		Inverted overprint	30.00	30.00
N5	A37	12h light bl	2.00	2.00
a.		Double overprint	30.00	30.00
N6	A42	15h dull red	1.00	1.00
a.		Inverted overprint	30.00	30.00
b.		Double overprint	30.00	30.00
N7	A42	20h dark green	1.00	1.00
a.		Inverted overprint	30.00	30.00
c.		Double overprint	67.50	
N8	A42	25h deep blue	6.75	6.75
a.		Inverted overprint	110.00	110.00
N9	A42	30h dl violet	2.00	2.00
N10	A39	40h olive grn	85.00	85.00
N11	A39	50h dark green	7.00	6.75
N12	A39	60h deep blue	19.00	18.00
N13	A39	80h orange brn	11.00	12.00
a.		Inverted overprint	—	
N14	A39	1k car, *yel*	11.00	12.00
a.		Double overprint	67.50	
N15	A40	2k light bl	200.00	200.00
		Never hinged	400.00	
N16	A40	4k yellow grn	400.00	400.00
		Never hinged	800.00	

Handstamped

N17	A40	10k dp violet	*25,000.*	*25,000.*
		Never hinged	*27,500.*	

Granite Paper

N18	A40	2k light blue	300.00	
		Never hinged	600.00	
N19	A40	3k car rose	250.00	250.00
		Never hinged	500.00	
		Nos. N1-N14 (14)	153.15	152.40
		Set, never hinged, #N1-N14	295.00	

Some authorities question the authenticity of No. N18. Counterfeits of Nos. N10, N15-N19 are plentiful.

Italian Stamps of 1901-18 Overprinted **Venezia Giulia**

Wmk. 140 *Perf. 14*

N20	A42	1c brown	1.50	*2.00*
a.		Inverted overprint	20.00	20.00
N21	A43	2c orange brn	1.50	*2.00*
c.		Inverted overprint	17.00	*17.00*
N22	A48	5c green	.70	*1.00*
a.		Inverted overprint	35.00	*35.00*
b.		Double overprint	85.00	
N23	A48	10c claret	.70	*1.00*
a.		Inverted overprint	47.50	*47.50*
b.		Double overprint	85.00	
N24	A50	20c brn orange	.90	*1.10*
a.		Inverted overprint	67.50	*67.50*
b.		Double overprint	85.00	*85.00*
N25	A49	25c blue	1.00	*1.75*
a.		Double overprint	—	
b.		Inverted overprint	85.00	*85.00*
N26	A49	40c brown	8.00	*10.00*
a.		Inverted overprint	*35.00*	
N27	A45	45c olive grn	2.50	*3.50*
a.		Inverted overprint	95.00	*95.00*
N28	A49	50c violet	3.50	*4.75*
N29	A49	60c brown car	42.50	*55.00*
a.		Inverted overprint	—	
b.		Double overprint	190.00	
N30	A46	1 l brn & green	14.50	*21.00*
a.		Inverted overprint	—	
		Nos. N20-N30 (11)	77.30	*103.10*
		Set, never hinged	154.00	

Italian Stamps of 1901-18 Surcharged **Venezia Giulia 5 Heller**

N31	A48	5h on 5c green	1.00	*1.50*
		Never hinged	2.00	
a.		"5" omitted	85.00	*85.00*
b.		Inverted surcharge	85.00	*85.00*
N32	A50	20h on 20c brn org	1.00	1.50
		Never hinged	2.00	
a.		Double surcharge	85.00	*85.00*

Issued in the Trentino

Austrian Stamps of 1916-18 Overprinted **Regno d Italia Trentino 3 nov 1918**

1918 Unwmk. *Perf. 12½*

N33	A37	3h bright vio	4.00	3.00
a.		Double overprint	67.50	*67.50*
b.		Inverted overprint	55.00	*55.00*
N34	A37	5h light grn	3.50	1.75
a.		"8 nov. 1918"	*1,750.*	
b.		Inverted overprint	55.00	*55.00*
N35	A37	6h dp orange	50.00	40.00
N36	A37	10h magenta	3.50	2.00
a.		"8 nov. 1918"	95.00	95.00
N37	A37	12h light blue	125.00	110.00
N38	A42	15h dull red	4.00	3.00
N39	A42	20h dark green	2.00	2.00
a.		"8 nov. 1918"	110.00	*110.00*
b.		Double overprint	67.50	67.50
c.		Inverted overprint	22.50	22.50
N40	A42	25h deep blue	35.00	30.00
N41	A42	30h dl violet	12.00	10.00
N42	A39	40h olive grn	45.00	40.00
N43	A39	50h dark green	27.50	22.50
a.		Inverted overprint	110.00	110.00
N44	A39	60h deep blue	40.00	35.00
a.		Double overprint	110.00	*110.00*
N45	A39	80h orange brn	55.00	45.00
N46	A39	90h red violet	1,250.	1,000.
N47	A39	1k car, *yel*	55.00	45.00
N48	A40	2k light blue	375.00	275.00
N49	A40	4k yel green	*1,750.*	*1,500.*
N50	A40	10k dp violet	—	

Granite Paper

N51	A40	2k light blue	*450.00*	

Counterfeits of Nos. N33-N51 are plentiful.

Italian Stamps of 1901-18 Overprinted **Venezia Tridentina**

Wmk. 140 *Perf. 14*

N52	A42	1c brown	1.00	3.50
a.		Inverted overprint	55.00	55.00
b.		Double overprint	55.00	
N53	A43	2c orange brn	1.00	3.50
a.		Inverted overprint	55.00	55.00
N54	A48	5c green	1.00	3.50
a.		Inverted overprint	55.00	55.00
b.		Double overprint	55.00	55.00
N55	A48	10c claret	1.00	3.50
a.		Inverted overprint	75.00	75.00
b.		Double overprint	55.00	55.00
N56	A50	20c brn orange	1.00	3.50
a.		Inverted overprint	75.00	75.00
N57	A49	40c brown	55.00	35.00
N58	A45	45c olive grn	25.00	35.00
a.		Double overprint	140.00	*140.00*
N59	A49	50c violet	25.00	35.00
N60	A46	1 l brn & green	25.00	35.00
a.		Double overprint	140.00	*140.00*
		Nos. N52-N60 (9)	135.00	157.50

Italian Stamps of 1906-18 Surcharged **Venezia Tridentina 5 Heller**

N61	A48	5h on 5c green	1.00	*1.75*
N62	A48	10h on 10c claret	1.00	*1.75*
a.		Inverted surcharge	67.50	*67.50*
N63	A50	20h on 20c brn org	1.00	*1.75*
a.		Double surcharge	67.50	*67.50*
		Nos. N61-N63 (3)	3.00	*5.25*

General Issue

Italian Stamps of 1901-18 Surcharged **5 centesimi di corona**

1919

N64	A42	1c on 1c brown	.90	*1.25*
a.		Inverted surcharge	16.00	17.50
N65	A43	2c on 2c org brn	.90	*1.25*
a.		Double surcharge	175.00	
b.		Inverted surcharge	13.50	13.50
N66	A48	5c on 5c green	.85	.45
a.		Inverted surcharge	40.00	40.00
b.		Double surcharge	67.50	67.50
N67	A48	10c on 10c claret	.90	.45
a.		Inverted surcharge	40.00	40.00
b.		Double surcharge	67.50	*67.50*
N68	A50	20c on 20c brn org	.90	.45
a.		Double surcharge	87.50	*87.50*
N69	A49	25c on 25c blue	.85	*1.00*
a.		Double surcharge	87.50	
N70	A49	40c on 40c brown	.90	*2.00*
a.		"ccrona"	100.00	*100.00*
N71	A45	45c on 45c ol grn	.90	*2.00*
a.		Inverted surcharge	110.00	110.00
N72	A49	50c on 50c violet	.90	*2.00*
N73	A49	60c on 60c brn car	.90	*3.00*
a.		"00" for "60"	110.00	*110.00*

Surcharged **1 corona**

N74	A46	1cor on 1 l brn & grn	1.75	3.00
		Nos. N64-N74 (11)	10.65	16.85

Surcharges similar to these but differing in style or arrangement of type were used in Dalmatia.

OCCUPATION SPECIAL DELIVERY STAMPS

Issued in Trieste

Special Delivery Stamp of Italy of 1903 Overprinted

Venezia Giulia

1918 Wmk. 140 *Perf. 14*

NE1	SD1	25c rose red	30.00	37.50
		Never hinged	60.00	
a.		Inverted overprint	125.00	125.00

General Issue

Special Delivery Stamps of Italy of 1903-09 Surcharged **25 centesimi di corona**

1919

NE2	SD1	25c on 25c rose	1.10	*1.75*
a.		Double surcharge	67.50	*67.50*
NE3	SD2	30c on 30c bl & rose	1.50	*2.40*

OCCUPATION POSTAGE DUE STAMPS

Issued in Trieste

Postage Due Stamps of Italy, 1870-94, Overprinted **Venezia Giulia**

1918 Wmk. 140 *Perf. 14*

NJ1	D3	5c buff & mag	.25	.45
a.		Inverted overprint	13.50	13.50
b.		Double overprint	150.00	
NJ2	D3	10c buff & mag	.35	.50
a.		Inverted overprint	67.50	*67.50*
NJ3	D3	20c buff & mag	.75	1.10
a.		Double overprint	150.00	
b.		Inverted overprint	67.50	*67.50*
NJ4	D3	30c buff & mag	2.00	3.00
NJ5	D3	40c buff & mag	22.50	30.00
a.		Inverted overprint	200.00	*200.00*
NJ6	D3	50c buff & mag	50.00	67.50
a.		Inverted overprint	225.00	*250.00*
NJ7	D3	1 l bl & mag	150.00	200.00
		Nos. NJ1-NJ7 (7)	225.85	302.55

General Issue

Postage Due Stamps of Italy, 1870-1903 Surcharged **5 centesimi di corona**

1919

Buff & Magenta

NJ8	D3	5c on 5c	.50	.70
a.		Inverted overprint	19.00	19.00
NJ9	D3	10c on 10c	.50	.70
a.		Center and surcharge invtd.	125.00	*125.00*
NJ10	D3	20c on 20c	.70	1.00
a.		Double overprint	140.00	*140.00*
NJ11	D3	30c on 30c	.85	1.50
NJ12	D3	40c on 40c	.85	1.50
NJ13	D3	50c on 50c	.85	1.50

Surcharged **una corona**

NJ14	D3	1cor on 1 l bl & mag	.85	1.50
NJ15	D3	2cor on 2 l bl & mag	45.00	80.00
NJ16	D3	5cor on 5 l bl & mag	45.00	80.00
		Nos. NJ8-NJ16 (9)	95.10	168.40

A. M. G. ISSUE FOR AUSTRIA

Catalogue values for unused stamps in this section are for Never Hinged items.

Issued jointly by the Allied Military Government of the US and Great Britain, for civilian use in areas under American, British and French occupation. (Upper Austria, Salzburg, Tyrol, Vorarlberg, Styria and Carinthia).

OS1

1945 Unwmk. Litho. *Perf. 11*

4N1	OS1	1g aquamarine	.15	.15
4N2	OS1	3g deep orange	.15	.15
4N3	OS1	4g buff	.15	.15
4N4	OS1	5g bright green	.15	.15
4N5	OS1	6g red violet	.15	.15
4N6	OS1	8g rose pink	.15	.15
4N7	OS1	10g light gray	.15	.15
4N8	OS1	12g pale buff brown	.15	.15
4N9	OS1	15g rose red	.15	.15
4N10	OS1	20g copper brown	.15	.15
4N11	OS1	25g deep blue	.15	.15
4N12	OS1	30g bright violet	.15	.15
4N13	OS1	40g light ultra	.15	.15
4N14	OS1	60g light olive grn	.15	.18
4N15	OS1	1s dark violet	.15	.30
4N16	OS1	2s yellow	.20	.30
4N17	OS1	5s deep ultra	.40	.45

For Nos. 4N2, 4N4-4N17 overprinted "PORTO" see Nos. J189-J203.

AUSTRIAN OFFICES ABROAD

These stamps were on sale and usable at all Austrian post-offices in Crete and in the Turkish Empire.

100 Centimes = 1 Franc

OFFICES IN CRETE

Used values are italicized for stamps often found with false cancellations.

Stamps of Austria of 1899-1901 Issue, Surcharged in Black:

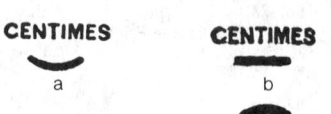

CENTIMES
a

CENTIMES
b

CENTIMES
c

FRANC
d

1903-04 Unwmk. *Perf. 12½, 13½*

On Nos. 73a, 75a, 77a, 81a

Granite Paper

With Varnish Bars

1	A15(a)	5c on 5h blue green	1.40	3.50
2	A16(b)	10c on 10h rose	.80	*3.75*
3	A16(b)	25c on 25h ultra	30.00	22.50
4	A17(c)	50c on 50h gray blue	7.50	*110.00*

On Nos. 83, 83a, 84, 85

Without Varnish Bars

5	A18(d)	1fr on 1k car rose	2.00	*100.00*
a.		1fr on 1k carmine	4.00	—
b.		Horiz. or vert. pair, imperf. between	175.00	
6	A18(d)	2fr on 2k ('04)	8.50	*225.00*
7	A18(d)	4fr on 4k ('04)	10.50	*450.00*
		Nos. 1-7 (7)	60.70	

AUSTRIA — AUSTRIAN OFFICES ABROAD — LOMBARDY-VENETIA

Surcharged on Austrian Stamps of 1904-05
1905
On Nos. 89, 97
Without Varnish Bars

8a	A19(a)	5c on 5h blue green	35.00	35.00
9	A20(b)	10c on 10h car	.70	9.00

On Nos. 89a, 97a, 99a, 103a
With Varnish Bars

8	A19(a)	5c on 5h bl grn	3.50	5.25
9a	A20(b)	10c on 10h carmine	18.00	22.50
10	A20(b)	25c on 25h ultra	.90	95.00
11	A21(b)	50c on 50h dl bl	.90	375.00

Surcharged on Austrian Stamps and Type of 1906-07
1907 Perf. 12½, 13½
Without Varnish Bars

12	A19(a)	5c on 5h yel green (#90)	.70	3.50
13	A20(b)	10c on 10h car (#92)	1.00	27.50
14	A20(b)	15c on 15h vio	1.10	26.00
		Nos. 12-14 (3)	2.80	57.00

A5    A6

1908 Typo. Perf. 12½

15	A5	5c green, *yellow*	.30	.60
16	A5	10c scarlet, *rose*	.35	.80
17	A5	15c brown, *buff*	.45	4.50
18	A5	25c dp blue, *blue*	10.50	5.00

Engr.

19	A6	50c lake, *yellow*	1.60	21.00
20	A6	1fr brown, *gray*	2.25	30.00
a.		Vert pair, imperf. btwn.	200.00	
		Nos. 15-20 (6)	15.45	61.90

Nos. 15-18 are on paper colored on the surface only. All values exist imperforate.
60th year of the reign of Emperor Franz Josef, for permanent use.

Paper Colored Through
1914 Typo.

21	A5	10c rose, *rose*	1.50	900.00
22	A5	25c ultra, *blue*	.60	110.00

Nos. 21 and 22 exist imperforate.

OFFICES IN THE TURKISH EMPIRE

From 1863 to 1867 the stamps of Lombardy-Venetia (Nos. 15 to 24) were used at the Austrian Offices in the Turkish Empire.

100 Soldi = 1 Florin
40 Paras = 1 Piaster

Values for unused stamps are for copies with gum. Specimens without gum sell for about one-third or less of the figures quoted.
Used values are italicized for stamps often found with false cancellations.

For similar designs in Kreuzers, see early Austria.

A1    A2

Two different printing methods were used, as in the 1867-74 issues of Austria. They may be distinguished by the coarse or fine lines of the hair and whiskers and by the paper, which is more transparent on the later issue.

1867 Typo. Wmk. 91 Perf. 9½
Coarse Print

1	A1	2sld orange	1.75	22.50
a.		2sld yellow	50.00	27.50
2	A1	3sld green	100.00	40.00
a.		3sld dark green	125.00	70.00
3	A1	5sld red	90.00	11.00
a.		5sld carmine	110.00	14.50
4	A1	10sld blue	95.00	1.75
a.		10sld light blue	110.00	2.50
b.		10sld dark blue	100.00	3.00
5	A1	15sld brown	16.00	6.50
a.		15sld dark brown	50.00	21.00
b.		15sld reddish brown	17.50	10.00
c.		15sld gray brown	45.00	9.00
6	A1	25sld violet	12.50	30.00
a.		25sld brown violet	16.00	35.00
b.		25sld gray violet	50.00	35.00
7	A2	50sld brn, perf. 10½	1.00	42.50
a.		Perf. 12	80.00	65.00
b.		Perf. 13	250.00	
e.		Perf. 9	25.00	50.00
i.		50sld pale red brn, perf. 12	55.00	600.00
m.		Vert. pair, imperf. btwn.	300.00	650.00
n.		Horiz. pair, imperf. btwn.	300.00	750.00
o.		Perf. 10½x9	60.00	100.00

Perf. 9, 9½, 10½ and Compound
1876-83 Fine Print

7C	A1	2sld yellow ('83)	.20	1,300.
7D	A1	3sld green ('78)	1.00	20.00
7E	A1	5sld red ('78)	.40	15.00
7F	A1	10sld blue	65.00	1.00
7I	A1	15sld org brn ('81)	9.00	125.00
7J	A1	25sld gray lilac ('83)	.50	275.00
		Nos. 7C-7J (6)	76.10	

The 10 soldi has been reprinted in deep dull blue, perforated 10½.

A3

1883 Perf. 9½, 10, 10½

8	A3	2sld brown	.20	110.00
9	A3	3sld green	1.00	25.00
10	A3	5sld rose	.20	16.00
11	A3	10sld blue	.75	.50
12	A3	20sld gray, perf. 10	1.00	60.00
a.		Perf. 9½	2.00	6.75
13	A3	50sld red lilac	1.40	16.00
		Nos. 8-13 (6)	4.55	

No. 9 Surcharged **10 PARA 10**

10 PARAS ON 3 SOLDI:
Type I - Surcharge 16½mm across. "PARA" about ½mm above bottom of "10." 2mm space between "10" and "P"; 1½mm between "A" and "10." Perf. 9½ only.
Type II - Surcharge 15¼ to 16mm across. "PARA" on same line with figures or slightly higher or lower. 1½mm space between "10" and "P"; 1mm between "A" and "10." Perf. 9½ and 10.

1886 Perf. 9½ and 10

14	A3	10pa on 3sld green, type II	.30	5.50
a.		Surcharge type I	170.00	325.00
b.		Inverted surcharge, type I		1,850.

Same Surcharge on Austria Nos. 42-46
1888

15	A11	10pa on 3kr grn	3.00	7.50
		"01 PARA 10"		400.00
16	A11	20pa on 5kr rose	.50	7.25
17	A11	1pi on 10kr blue	45.00	1.10
a.		Perf. 13½		225.00
b.		Double surcharge		275.00
18	A11	2pi on 20kr gray	1.50	4.00
19	A11	5pi on 50kr vio	2.00	15.00
		Nos. 15-19 (5)	52.00	

Austria Nos. 52-55, 58, 61 Surcharged **10 PARA 10**

1890-92 Unwmk. Perf. 9 to 13½
Granite Paper

20	A12	8pa on 2kr brn ('92)	.20	.50
a.		Perf. 9½	10.00	13.50
21	A12	10pa on 3kr green	.65	.50
22	A12	20pa on 5kr rose	.25	.50
23	A12	1pi on 10kr ultra	.35	.15
24	A12	2pi on 20kr ol grn	5.50	25.00
25	A12	5pi on 50kr violet	11.00	60.00
		Nos. 20-25 (6)	17.95	

See note after Austria No. 65 on missing numerals, etc.

Austria Nos. 66, 69 Surcharged **2 PIASTER 2**
1891 Perf. 10 to 13½

26	A14	2pi on 20kr green	4.25	1.25
a.		Perf. 9½	110.00	70.00
27	A14	5pi on 50kr violet	2.50	2.50

Two types of the surcharge on No. 26 exist.

Austria Nos. 62-65 Surcharged **10 PIAST.10**

1892 Perf. 10½, 11½

28	A13	10pi on 1gld blue	10.00	22.50
29	A13	20pi on 2gld car	12.00	35.00
a.		Double surcharge		

1896 Perf. 10½, 11½, 12½

30	A13	10pi on 1gld pale lilac	12.00	19.00
31	A13	20pi on 2gld gray grn	37.50	60.00

Austria Nos. 73, 75, 77, 81, 83-85 Surcharged

10 PARA 10 #32-35   **5 PIASTER 5** #36-38

Perf. 10½, 12½, 13½ and Compound
1900
Without Varnish Bars

32	A15	10pa on 5h bl grn	4.00	.80
33	A16	20pa on 10h rose	5.00	.75
b.		Perf. 12½x10½	250.00	85.00
34	A15	1pi on 25h ultra	3.00	.25
35	A17	2pi on 50h gray bl	7.25	3.25
36	A15	1pi on 1k car rose	1.00	.30
a.		5pi on 1k carmine	1.10	.90
b.		Horiz. or vert. pair, imperf. btwn.	110.00	
37	A18	10pi on 2k gray lil	2.50	2.25
38	A18	20pi on 4k gray grn	2.00	6.00
		Nos. 32-38 (7)	24.75	13.60

In the surcharge on Nos. 37 and 38 "piaster" is printed "PIAST."

1901
With Varnish Bars

32a	A15	10pa on 5h blue green	1.75	2.25
33a	A16	20pa on 10h rose	2.25	160.00
34a	A16	1pi on 25h ultra	1.50	.45
35a	A17	2pi on 50h gray blue	3.25	5.25
		Nos. 32a-35a (4)	8.75	

A4    A5

A6

1906 Perf. 12½ to 13½
Without Varnish Bars

39	A4	10pa dark green	11.00	2.50
40	A5	20pa rose	.80	.65
41	A5	1pi ultra	.35	.25
42	A6	2pi gray blue	.80	.65
		Nos. 39-42 (4)	12.95	4.05

1903
With Varnish Bars

39a	A4	10pa dark green	4.25	1.50
40a	A5	20pa rose	.80	.40
41a	A5	1pi ultra	1.60	1.25
42a	A6	2pi gray blue	125.00	2.25

1907
Without Varnish Bars

43	A4	10pa yellow green	.50	1.25
45	A5	30pa violet	.50	2.75

A7    A8

1908 Typo. Perf. 12½

46	A7	10pa green, *yellow*	.20	.25
47	A7	20pa scarlet, *rose*	.25	.25
48	A7	30pa brown, *buff*	.30	.50
49	A7	1pi deep bl, *blue*	11.00	
50	A7	60pa vio, *bluish*	.55	3.00

Engr.

51	A8	2pi lake, *yellow*	.35	.20
52	A8	5pi brown, *gray*	.60	.80
53	A8	10pi green, *yellow*	.80	1.50
54	A8	60pa vio, *bluish*	1.50	3.50
		Nos. 46-54 (9)	15.55	10.20

Nos. 46-50 are on paper colored on the surface only. 60th year of the reign of Emperor Franz Josef I, for permanent use. All values exist imperforate.

1913-14 Typo.
Paper Colored Through

57	A7	20pa rose, *rose* ('14)	.70	325.00
58	A7	1pi ultra, *blue*	.35	.45

Nos. 57 and 58 exist imperforate.

POSTAGE DUE STAMPS

Type of Austria D2 Surcharged **10 PARA**

Black Surcharge
1902 Unwmk. Perf. 12½, 13½

J1	D2	10pa on 5h green	1.10	2.75
J2	D2	20pa on 10h green	1.10	2.75
J3	D2	1pi on 20h green	1.75	3.25
J4	D2	2pi on 40h green	1.75	3.25
J5	D2	5pi on 100h green	2.75	2.75
		Nos. J1-J5 (5)	8.45	14.75

Shades of Nos. J1-J5 exist, varying from yellowish green to dark green.

D3

1908 Typo. Perf. 12½

J6	D3	¼pi green	2.50	5.50
J7	D3	½pi green	1.40	5.50
J8	D3	1pi green	1.50	5.50
J9	D3	1½pi green	.80	11.00
J10	D3	2pi green	1.75	13.50
J11	D3	5pi green	3.25	8.00
J12	D3	10pi green	16.00	100.00
J13	D3	20pi green	16.00	110.00
J14	D3	30pi green	13.00	11.50
		Nos. J6-J14 (9)	56.20	270.50

Nos. J6-J14 exist in distinct shades of green and on thick chalky, regular and thin ordinary paper. Values are for the least expensive variety. No. J6-J14 exist imperforate.
Forgeries exist.

LOMBARDY-VENETIA

Formerly a kingdom in the north of Italy forming part of the Austrian Empire. Milan and Venice were the two principal cities. Lombardy was annexed to Sardinia in 1859, and Venetia to the kingdom of Italy in 1866.

100 Centesimi = 1 Lira
100 Soldi = 1 Florin (1858)

Unused examples without gum of Nos. 1-24 are worth approximately 20% of the values given, which are for stamps with original gum as defined in the catalogue introduction.

For similar designs in Kreuzers, see early Austria.

Coat of Arms — A1

15 CENTESIMI:
Type I- "5" is on a level with the "1." One heavy line around coat of arms center.
Type II- As type I, but "5" is a trifle sideways and is higher than the "1."
Type III- As type II, but two, thinner, lines around center.

45 CENTESIMI:
Type I- Lower part of "45" is lower than "Centes." One heavy line around coat of arms center. "45" varies in height and distance from "Centes."
Type II- One heavy line around coat of arms center. Lower part of "45" is on a level with lower part of "Centes."
Type III- As type II, but two, thinner, lines around center.

AUSTRIA — LOMBARDY-VENETIA — AZERBAIJAN

Wmk. K.K.H.M. in Sheet or Unwmkd.
1850 Typo. Imperf.
Thick to Thin Paper

1	A1	5c buff	2,250.	125.00
a.		Printed on both sides	8,500.	225.00
b.		5c yellow	4,500.	325.00
c.		5c orange	2,500.	175.00
d.		5c lemon yellow		1,450.
3	A1	10c black	2,250.	110.00
a.		10c gray black	2,250.	100.00
4	A1	15c red, type III	1,000.	5.00
b.		15c red, type I	2,500.	20.00
c.		Ribbed paper, type III	—	750.00
d.		Ribbed paper, type I	11,000.	200.00
f.		Ribbed red, type II	1,200.	11.00
5	A1	30c brown	2,900.	8.00
a.		Ribbed paper	4,500.	125.00
6	A1	45c blue, type III	10,500.	30.00
a.		45c blue, type I	11,000.	—
b.		Ribbed paper, type I	—	375.00
c.		45c blue, type II	—	55.00

1854 Machine-made Paper, Type III

3c	A1	10c black	6,000.	225.00
4g	A1	15c pale red	650.00	3.50
5b	A1	30c brown	2,750.	7.50
6d	A1	45c blue	8,000.	35.00

See note about the paper of the 1850 issue of Austria. *The reprints are type III, in brighter colors.*

A2  A3
A4  A5 
A6 

Two Types of Each Value.
Type I- Loops of the bow at the back of the head broken.
Type II- Loops complete. Wreath projects further at top of head.

1858-62 Embossed Perf. 14½

7	A2	2s yel, type II	650.00	125.00
a.		2s yellow, type I	3,500.	600.00
8	A3	3s black, type II	6,500.	150.00
a.		3s black, type I	2,500.	300.00
b.		Perf. 16, type I		1,100.
c.		Perf. 15x16 or 16x15, type I	4,500.	400.00
9	A3	3s grn, type II ('62)	500.00	100.00
10	A4	5s red, type II	275.00	5.00
a.		5s red, type I	850.00	11.00
b.		Printed on both sides, type II		6,000.
11	A5	10s brown, type II	1,900.	11.00
a.		10s brown, type I	500.00	35.00
12	A6	15s blue, type II	2,250.	24.00
a.		15s blue, type I	3,500.	100.00
b.		Printed on both sides, type II		15,000.

The reprints are of type II and are perforated 10½, 11, 11½, 12, 12½ and 13. There are also imperforate reprints of Nos. 7-9.

A7  A8

1861-62 Perf. 14

13	A7	5s red	2,750.	3.00
14	A7	10s brown ('62)	4,000.	30.00

The reprints are perforated 9, 9½, 10½, 11, 12, 12½ and 13. There are also imperforate reprints of the 2 and 3s.

The 2, 3 and 15s of this type exist only as reprints.

1863 Imperf.

15	A8	2s yellow	150.00	150.00
16	A8	3s green	2,250.	100.00
17	A8	5s rose	2,750.	15.00
18	A8	10s blue	5,000.	85.00
19	A8	15s yellow brown	3,500.	140.00

1864-65 Wmk. 91 Perf. 9½

20	A8	2s yellow ('65)	200.00	500.00
21	A8	3s green	30.00	21.00
22	A8	5s rose	4.50	3.00
23	A8	10s blue	30.00	9.00
24	A8	15s yellow brown	275.00	170.00

Nos. 15-24 reprints are perforated 10½ and 13. There are also imperforate reprints of the 2s and 3s.

NEWSPAPER TAX STAMPS

From 1853 to 1858 the Austrian Newspaper Tax Stamp 2kr green (No. PR1) was also used in Lombardy-Venetia, at the value of 10 centesimi.

NT1

Type I - The banderol of the left eagle touches the beak of the eagle.
Type II - The banderol does not touch the beak.

1858-59 Unwmk. Typo. Imperf.

PR1	NT1	1kr black, type I ('59)	3,200.	3,200.
PR2	NT1	2kr red, type II ('59)	325.00	60.00
PR3	NT1	4kr red, type I	100,000.	3,500.

No. PR2 exists with watermark 91.
The reprints are on a smooth toned paper and are all of type II.

AZERBAIJAN

ˌa-zər-ˌbī-ˈjän

(Azerbaidjan)

LOCATION — Southernmost part of Russia in Eastern Europe, bounded by Georgia, Dagestan, Caspian Sea, Iran and Armenia
GOVT. — A Soviet Socialist Republic
AREA — 32,686 sq. mi.
POP. — 2,096,973 (1923)
CAPITAL — Baku

With Armenia and Georgia, Azerbaijan made up the Transcaucasian Federation of Soviet Republics.
Stamps of Azerbaijan were replaced in 1923 by those of Transcaucasian Federated Republics. descWith the breakup of the Soviet Union on Dec. 26, 1991, Azerbaijan and ten former Soviet republics established the Commonwealth of Independent States.

100 Kopecks = 1 Ruble
100 Giapiks = 1 Manat (1992)

Catalogue values for unused stamps in this country are for Never Hinged items, beginning with Scott 350 in the regular postage section.

National Republic

Standard Bearer — A1
Farmer at Sunset — A2 
Baku — A3 
Temple of Eternal Fires — A4 

1919 Unwmk. Litho. Imperf.

1	A1	10k multicolored	.15	.30
2	A1	20k multicolored	.15	.30
3	A2	40k green, yellow & blk	.15	.30
4	A2	60k red, yellow & blk	.25	.30
5	A1	1r blue, yellow & blk	.35	.50
6	A3	2r red, bister & blk	.35	.50
7	A3	5r blue, bister & blk	.45	.85
8	A3	10r olive grn, bis & blk	.65	.95
9	A4	25r blue, red & black	1.10	9.00
10	A4	50r ol grn, red & black	1.40	1.75
		Nos. 1-10 (10)	5.00	14.75

The two printings of Nos. 1-10 are distinguished by the grayish or thin white paper. Both have yellowish gum. White paper copies are worth five times the above values.
For surcharges see Nos. 57-64, 75-80.

Soviet Socialist Republic

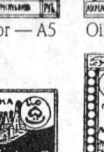

Symbols of Labor — A5 
Oil Well — A6 
Bibi Eibatt Oil Field — A7 
Khan's Palace, Baku — A8 
Globe and Workers — A9 
Maiden's Tower, Baku — A10

Goukasoff House A11
Blacksmiths A12 
Hall of Judgment, Baku — A13 

1922

15	A5	1r gray green	.20	.35
16	A6	2r olive black	.50	.50
17	A7	5r gray brown	.20	.35
18	A8	10r gray	.50	.65
19	A9	25r orange brown	.20	.40
20	A10	50r violet	.20	.40
21	A11	100r dull red	.35	.50
22	A12	150r blue	.35	.50
23	A9	250r violet & buff	.35	.50
24	A13	400r dark blue	.35	.50
25	A12	500r gray vio & blk	.35	.50
26	A13	1000r dk blue & rose	.35	.60
27	A8	2000r blue & black	.35	.50
28	A7	3000r brown & blue	.35	.50
a.		Tete beche pair	15.00	15.00
29	A11	5000r black, ol grn	.60	.75
		Nos. 15-29 (15)	5.20	7.50

Counterfeits exist of Nos. 1-29. They generally sell for more than genuine copies.
For overprints and surcharges see Nos. 32-41, 43, 45-55, 65-72, 300-304, 307-333.

Nos. 15, 17, 23, 28, 27 Handstamped from Metal Dies in a Numbering Machine

15000

1922

32	A5	10,000r on 1r	8.00	8.00
33	A7	15,000r on 5r	9.50	10.00
34	A9	33,000r on 250r	5.00	5.00
35	A7	50,000r on 3000r	5.00	5.00
36	A8	66,000r on 2000r	11.00	10.00
		Nos. 32-36 (5)	38.50	38.00

Same Surcharges on Regular Issue and Semi-Postal Stamps of 1922

1922-23

36A	A7	500r on 5r	60.00	67.50
37	A6	1000r on 2r	15.00	15.00
38	A8	2000r on 10r	5.00	4.00
39	A8	5000r on 2000r	5.00	3.00
40	A11	15,000r on 5000r	12.00	10.00
41	A5	20,000r on 1r	10.00	9.00
42	SP1	25,000r on 500r	35.00	
43	A7	50,000r on 5r	12.50	12.50
44	SP2	50,000r on 1000r	26.00	
45	A11	50,000r on 5000r	5.00	4.50
45A	A8	60,000r on 2000r	12.50	14.00
46	A11	70,000r on 5000r	20.00	20.00
47	A6	100,000r on 2r	15.00	15.00
48	A8	200,000r on 10r	10.00	10.00
49	A9	200,000r on 25r	15.00	15.00
50	A7	300,000r on 3000r	5.00	5.00
51	A8	500,000r on 2000r	15.00	10.00

Revalued

52	A7	500r on #33	200.00	200.00
53	A11	15,000r on #46	200.00	200.00
54	A7	300,000r on #35	200.00	200.00
55	A8	500,000r on #36	200.00	200.00

The surcharged semi-postal stamps were used for regular postage.

Same Surcharges on Stamps of 1919

57	A1	25,000r on 10k	.70	1.00
58	A1	50,000r on 20k	.70	1.00
59	A2	75,000r on 40k	1.75	2.50
60	A2	100,000r on 60k	.70	.95
61	A2	200,000r on 1r	.70	.95
62	A3	300,000r on 2r	.88	1.10

If you are a Collector of Lombardy-Venetia
Call the experts: *LIANE & SERGIO SISMONDO*
"THE CLASSIC COLLECTOR"
Visit our website: www.sismondostamps.com
BUYING, SELLING, APPRAISALS.
RARE AND CLASSIC STAMPS, POSTAL HISTORY, PROOFS.

10035 Carousel Center Drive
Syracuse, NY 13290-0001
Ph. 315-422-2331, Fax 315-422-2956
P.O. Box 6277, Station J,
Ottawa, Canada K2A 1T4.
Ph. 613-722-1621, Fax: 613-728-7305
e-mail: sismondo@dreamscape.com

AZERBAIJAN

63	A3	500,000r on 5r	1.00	1.10
64	A2	750,000r on 40k	3.50	2.75
		Nos. 57-64 (8)	9.93	11.35

Handstamped from Settings of Rubber Type in Black or Violet

100000 Nos. 65-66, 71-80 **200.000** Nos. 67-70

On Stamps of 1922

65	A6	100,000r on 2r	12.00	12.00
66	A8	200,000r on 10r	13.00	14.00
67	A8	200,000r on 10r (V)	17.50	15.00
68	A9	200,000r on 25r (V)	15.00	11.00
a.		Black surcharge	26.00	27.50
69	A7	300,000r on 3000r (V)	25.00	25.00
70	A8	500,000r on 2000r (V)	20.00	20.00
a.		Black surcharge	27.50	29.00
72	A11	1,500,000r on 5000r (V)	16.00	15.00
a.		Black surcharge	16.00	15.00

On Stamps of 1919

75	A1	50,000r on 20k	1.00	
76	A2	75,000r on 40k	.65	
77	A2	100,000r on 60k	1.25	
78	A2	200,000r on 1r	.15	.15
79	A3	300,000r on 2r	1.00	
80	A3	500,000r on 5r	1.25	

Inverted and double surcharges of Nos. 32-80 sell for twice the normal price.
Counterfeits exist of Nos. 32-80.

Baku Province
Regular and Semi-Postal Stamps of 1922 Handstamped in Violet or Black

БАКИНСКОЙ П. К.

The overprint reads "Bakinskoi P(ochtovoy) K(ontory)," meaning Baku Post Office.

1922   **Unwmk.**   **Imperf.**

300	A5	1r gray green	35.00
301	A7	5r gray brown	35.00
302	A12	150r blue	35.00
303	A9	250r violet & buff	35.00
304	A13	400r dark blue	35.00
305	SP1	500r blue & pale blue	35.00
306	SP2	1000r brown & bister	35.00
307	A8	2000r blue & black	35.00
308	A7	3000r brown & blue	35.00
309	A11	5000r black, ol grn	35.00
		Nos. 300-309 (10)	350.00

Stamps of 1922 Handstamped in Violet

Бакинскаго Г·П·Т·О.№1

Ovpt. reads: Baku Post, Telegraph Office No. 1.

1924

Overprint 24x2mm

312	A12	150r blue	30.00
313	A9	250r violet & buff	30.00
314	A13	400r dark blue	30.00
317	A8	2000r blue & black	30.00
318	A7	3000r brown & blue	30.00
319	A11	5000r black, ol grn	30.00

Overprint 30x3½mm

323	A12	150r blue	30.00
324	A9	250r violet & buff	30.00
325	A13	400r dark blue	30.00
328	A8	2000r blue & black	30.00
329	A7	3000r brown & blue	30.00
330	A11	5000r black, ol grn	30.00

Overprinted on Nos. 32-33, 35

331	A5	10,000r on 1r	30.00
332	A7	15,000r on 5r	30.00
333	A7	50,000r on 3000r	30.00
		Nos. 312-333 (15)	450.00

The overprinted semipostal stamps were used for regular postage.
A 24x2mm handstamp on #17, B1-B2, and 30x3½mm on #15, 17, B1-B2, was of private origin.

Catalogue values for unused stamps in this section, from this point to the end of the section, are for Never Hinged items.

Azerbaijan stamps can be mounted in the annual Scott Commonwealth of Independent States supplement.

Flag, Map — A20

Unwmk.

1992, Mar. 26   **Litho.**   **Perf. 14**
350 A20 35k multicolored 1.25 1.25

Park — A21

1992, May 7   **Perf. 12**
351	A21	25g on 15k multicolored	.25	.25
a.		Booklet pane of 12	3.00	
		Complete booklet, #351a	3.00	
352	A21	35g on 15k multicolored	.30	.30
353	A21	50g on 15k multicolored	.40	.40
354	A21	1.50m on 15k multicolored	1.25	1.25
355	A21	2.50m on 15k multicolored	2.25	2.25
		Nos. 351-355 (5)	4.45	4.45

Nos. 351-355 are overprinted or surcharged on a National Park series prepared for the Soviet Union with one stamp for each republic. Not issued without surcharge. Value, $4.
For additional surcharges see Nos. 435, 501-504.

Iran-Azerbaijan Telecommunications — A21a

1992   **Photo.**   **Perf. 13x13½**
355A A21a 15g multicolored 1.65 1.65

See Iran No. 2544.
For surcharges see Nos. 403-406.

Horses — A22

1993, Feb. 1   **Litho.**   **Perf. 13**
356	A22	20g shown	.15	.15
357	A22	30g Kabarda	.15	.15
358	A22	50g Qarabair	.15	.15
359	A22	1m Don	.20	.20
360	A22	2.50m Yakut	.45	.45
361	A22	5m Orlov	1.00	1.00
362	A22	10m Diliboz	2.00	2.00
		Nos. 356-362 (7)	4.10	4.10

Perf. 12½

Souvenir Sheet
362A A22 8m Qarabag .65 .65

For overprints see Nos. 629-636.

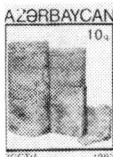

Ruins — A23    Government Building — A24

1992-93   **Litho.**   **Perf. 12½x12**
363	A23	10g blk & blue grn	.15	.15
365	A23	20g black & red	.15	.15
367	A23	50g black & blue grn	.15	.15
368	A23	50g black & yellow	.35	.35

370	A23	1m black & rose lilac	.20	.20
372	A23	1.50m black & blue	1.00	1.00
373	A23	2.50m black & yellow	.35	.35
374	A23	5m black & green	.65	.65
		Nos. 363-374 (8)	3.00	3.00

Issued: 10g, 20g, 1.50m, #367, Dec. 20; #368, 1m, 2.50m, 5m, June 20, 1993.
For surcharges see Nos. 550-557.
This is an expanding set. Numbers may change.

1993, Oct. 12   **Litho.**   **Perf. 12½**
375	A24	25g yellow & black	.15	.15
376	A24	30g green & black	.15	.15
377	A24	50g blue & black	.25	.25
378	A24	1m red & black	.50	.50
		Nos. 375-378 (4)	1.05	1.05

For surcharges see No. 407-414.

Flowers — A25

1993, Aug. 12   **Litho.**   **Perf. 12½**
379	A25	25g Tulipa eichleri	.15	.15
380	A25	50g Puschkinia scilloides	.15	.15
381	A25	1m Iris elegantissima	.15	.15
382	A25	1.50m Iris acutiloba	.25	.25
383	A25	5m Tulipa florenskyii	.80	.80
384	A25	10m Iris reticulata	1.50	1.50
		Nos. 379-384 (6)	3.00	3.00

Souvenir Sheet
Perf. 13
385 A25 10m Muscari elecostomum 1.50 1.50

No. 385 contains one 32x40mm stamp.

Fish — A26

1993, Aug. 27   **Perf. 12½**
386	A26	25g multicolored	.15	.15
387	A26	50g multicolored	.15	.15
388	A26	1m multicolored	.15	.15
389	A26	1.50m multicolored	.25	.25
390	A26	5m multicolored	.80	.80
391	A26	10m multicolored	1.50	1.50
		Nos. 386-391 (6)	3.00	3.00

Souvenir Sheet
Perf. 13
392 A26 10m multicolored 1.50 1.50

No. 392 contains one 40x32mm stamp.

25g, Acipenser guldenstadti. 50g, Acipenser stellatus. 1m, Rutilus frisii kutum. 1.50m, Rutilus lus caspicus. 5m, Salmo trutta caspius. No. 391, Alosa kessleri. #392, Huso huso.

Pres. Heydar A. Aliyev — A27

1993, Sept. 12   **Litho.**   **Perf. 12½x13**
393	A27	25m multicolored	1.00	1.00
394	A27	25m multicolored	1.00	1.00
a.		Pair, #393-394	2.00	2.00
b.		Souv. sheet #393-394, perf. 12	25.00	
c.		Souv. sheet #393-394, perf. 12	25.00	

Design: No. 394, Map of Nakhichevan.
Name on map spelled "Naxcivan" on #394c. It is spelled "Haxcivan" on #394-394b.
No. 394c issued Sept. 20, 1993.

Historic Buildings, Baku — A28

Style of tombs: 2m, Fortress, 13th-14th cent. 4m, Moorish gate, 15th cent. 8m, Oriental-style columns, 15th cent.

1994, Jan. 17   **Litho.**   **Perf. 11**
395	A28	2m red, silver & black	.20	.20
396	A28	4m green, silver & black	.35	.35
397	A28	8m blue, silver & black	.75	.75
		Nos. 395-397 (3)	1.30	1.30

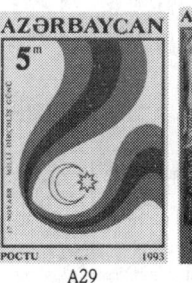

A29    A30

1994, Jan. 17   **Perf. 12½**
| 398 | A29 | 5m Natl. Colors, Star, Crescent | .45 | .45 |
| 399 | A29 | 8m Natl. coat of arms | .75 | .75 |

1994, Jan. 17   **Perf. 12½**
400 A30 10m multi + label .60 .60

Mohammed Fizuli (1494-1556), poet.

Mammed Amin Rasulzade (1884-1955), 1st President A31

Jalil Mamedkulizade, Writer, 125th Birth Anniv. — A32

1994, May 21   **Perf. 12½, 13 (#402)**
| 401 | A31 | 15m black, yellow & brown | 1.00 | 1.00 |
| 402 | A32 | 20m black, blue & gold | 1.00 | 1.00 |

No. 402 printed se-tenant with label.

No. 355A Surcharged

2 m.

1994, Jan. 18   **Photo.**   **Perf. 13x13½**
403	A21a	2m on 15g	.15	.15
404	A21a	20m on 15g	.35	.35
405	A21a	25m on 15g	.45	.45
406	A21a	50m on 15g	1.00	1.00
		Nos. 403-406 (4)	1.95	1.95

5 m.

Nos. 375-378 Surcharged

AZERBAIJAN

1994, Feb. 22	**Litho.**		*Perf. 12½*	
407 A24	5m on 1m #375		.15	.15
408 A24	10m on 30g #377		.15	.15
409 A24	15m on 30g #377		.15	.15
a.	Pair, #408-409		.30	.30
410 A24	20m on 50g #378		.25	.25
411 A24	25m on 1m #375		.30	.30
a.	Pair, #407, 411		.45	.45
412 A24	40m on 50g #378		.40	.40
a.	Pair, #410, 412		.65	.65
413 A24	50m on 25g #376		.50	.50
414 A24	100m on 25g #376		1.00	1.00
a.	Pair, #413-414		1.50	1.50
	Nos. 407-414 (8)		2.90	2.90

Baku Oil Fields — A33

Designs: 15m, Temple of Eternal Fires. 20m, Oil derricks. 25m, Early tanker. 50m, Ludwig Nobel, Robert Nobel, Petr Bilderling, Alfred Nobel.

1994, June 10	**Photo.**		*Perf. 13*	
415 A33	15m multicolored		.30	.30
416 A33	20m multicolored		.40	.40
417 A33	30m multicolored		.45	.45
418 A33	50m multicolored		1.00	1.00
a.	Souvenir sheet of 1		1.00	1.00
	Nos. 415-418 (4)		2.15	2.15

See Turkmenistan Nos. 39-43.

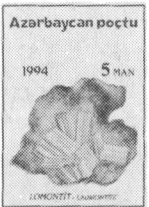

Minerals — A34

Posthorn — A35

1994, June 15	**Litho.**		*Perf. 13*	
419 A34	5m Laumontite		.30	.30
420 A34	10m Epidot calcite		.55	.55
421 A34	15m Andradite		.80	.80
422 A34	20m Amethyst		1.10	1.10
a.	Souvenir sheet, #420-423 + 2 labels, perf. 12		2.75	2.75
	Nos. 419-422 (4)		2.75	2.75

1994	**Litho.**		*Perf. 12½*	
426 A35	5m black & red		.15	.15
427 A35	10m black & green		.15	.15
428 A35	20m black & blue		.15	.15
429 A35	25m black & yellow		.25	.25
431 A35	40m black & brown		.40	.40
	Nos. 426-431 (5)		1.10	1.10

For surcharges see Nos. 487-489A.

400 M.

No. 351 Surcharged

25q

Unwmk.

1994, Oct. 17	**Litho.**		*Perf. 12*	
435 A21	400m on 25g multi		.85	.85

Souvenir Sheet

Pres. Heydar A. Aliyev — A36

Illustration reduced.

1994, Oct. 28	**Litho.**		*Perf. 14*	
436 A36	150m multicolored		2.25	2.25

Ships of the Caspian Sea A37

Designs: a, Tugboat, "Captain Racebov." b, "Azerbaijan." c, Balt Ro Ro line, "Merkuri I." d, Tanker, "Tovuz." e, Tanker.

1994, Oct. 28				
437 A37	50m Strip of 5, #a.-e.		1.75	1.75

Issued in sheets of 15 stamps. The background of the sheet shows a nautical chart, giving each stamp a different background.

1994 World Cup Soccer Championships, US — A38

Various soccer plays. Denominations: 5m, 10m, 20m, 25m, 30m, 50m, 80m.

1994, June 17	**Litho.**		*Perf. 13*	
438-444 A38	Set of 7		3.50	3.50
	Souvenir Sheet			
445 A38	100m multicolored		1.50	1.50

No. 445 contains one 32x40mm stamp and is a continuous design.

Dinosaurs A39

Designs: 5m, Coelophysis, segisaurus. 10m, Pentaceratops, tyrannosaurids. 20m, Segnosaurus, oviraptor. 25m, Albertosaurus, corythosaurus. 30m, Iguanodons. 50m, Stegosaurus, allosaurus. 80m, Tyrannosaurus, saurolophus. 100m, Phobetor.

1994, Sept. 15				
446-452 A39	Set of 7		3.50	3.50
	Souvenir Sheet			
	Perf. 12½			
453 A39	100m multicolored		1.50	1.50

No. 453 contains one 40x32mm stamp and is a continuous design.

Lyrurus Mlokosiewickzi — A40

a, 50m, Female on nest. b, 80m, Female on mountain cliff. c, 100m, 2 males. d, 120m, Male.

1994, Dec. 15	**Litho.**		*Perf. 12½*	
454 A40	Block of 4, #a.-d.		3.25	3.25

World Wildlife Fund.

Raptors A41

Designs: 10m, Haliaeetus albicilla. 15m, Aguila heliaca. 20m, Aguila rapax. 25m, Gypaetus barbatus, vert. 50m, Falco cherrug, vert.

100m, Aguila chrysaetos.

1994, Nov. 15	**Litho.**		*Perf. 13*	
458-462 A41	Set of 5		3.50	3.50
	Souvenir Sheet			
	Perf. 12½			
463 A41	100m multicolored		1.50	1.50

No. 463 contains one 40x32mm stamp and is a continuous design.

Cats A42

Designs: 10m, Felis libica, vert. 15m, Felis otocolobus, vert. 20m, Felis lyns, vert. 25m, Felis pardus. 50m, Panthera tigrus.
100m, Panthera tigrus adult and cub, vert.

1994, Dec. 14			*Perf. 13*	
464-468 A42	Set of 5		3.50	3.50
	Souvenir Sheet			
469 A42	100m multicolored		1.50	1.50

No. 469 contains one 32x40mm stamp and is a continuous design.
For overprints see Nos. 637-642.

Butterflies A43

Designs: 10m, Parnassius apollo. 25m, Zegris menestho. 50m, Manduca atropos. 60m, Pararge adrastoides.

1995, Jan. 23			*Perf. 14*	
470 A43	10m multicolored		.15	.15
471 A43	25m multicolored		.40	.40
472 A43	50m multicolored		.80	.80
473 A43	60m multicolored		1.00	1.00
a.	Souvenir sheet of 4, #470-473		2.50	2.50
	Nos. 470-473 (4)		2.35	2.35

Intl. Olympic Committee, Cent. — A44

Designs: No. 474, Pierre de Coubertin. No. 475, Discus. No. 476, Javelin.

1994, Dec. 15	**Litho.**		*Perf. 12*	
474-476 A44	100m Set of 3		2.00	2.00

A45 A46

1994 Winter Olympic medalists, Lillehammer: 10m, Aleksei Urnamov, Russia, figure skating. 25, Nancy Kerrigan, US, figure skating. 40m Bonnie Blair, US, speed skating, horiz. 50m, Takanori Kano, Japan, ski jumping, horiz. 80m, Philip Laros, Canada, freestyle skiing. 100m, Four-man bobsled, Germany.
200m, Katja Seizinger, skiing, Germany, vert.

1995, Feb. 10	**Litho.**		*Perf. 14*	
478-483 A45	Set of 6		2.00	2.00
	Souvenir Sheet			
484 A45	200m multicolored		1.75	1.75

1995, Feb. 21

Women in space: No. 485a, Mary Kliv, US. b, Valentina Tereshkova, Russia. c, Tamara Cernigan, US. d, Wendy Lourens, US.
No. 486a, Meg Jamison, US. b, Kitty Coleman, US. c, Ellen Sulman. US. d, M.I. Weber, US.

Miniature Sheets of 4

485-486 A46	100m each, #a.-d.			2.50

First manned moon landing, 25th anniv. (in 1994).

Nos. 426-428 Surcharged **100 M.**

1995	**Litho.**		*Perf. 12½*	
487 A35	100m on 5m #426		.15	.15
488 A35	250m on 10m #427		.40	.40
488A A35	400m on 25m No. 429		.50	.50
489 A35	500m on 20m #428		.65	.65
489A A35	900m on 40m No. 431		1.10	1.10
	Nos. 487-489A (5)		2.80	2.80

Issued: #488A, 7/7; #487-488, 489, 2/28.

Mushrooms — A47

Designs: 100m, Gymnopilus spectabilis. 250m, Fly agaris. 300m, Lepiota procera. 400m, Hygrophorus spectosus.
500m, Fly agaris, diff.

1995, Sept. 1	**Litho.**		*Perf. 14*	
490-493 A47	Set of 4		3.50	3.50
	Souvenir Sheet			
494 A47	500m multicolored		1.50	1.50

Singapore '95 A48

Orchids: 100m, Paphiopedilum argus, paphiopedilum barbatum. 250m, Maxillaria picta. 300m, Laeliocattleya. 400m, Dendrobium nobile.
500m, Cattleya gloriette.

1995, Sept. 1				
495-498 A48	Set of 4		3.50	3.50
	Souvenir Sheet			
499 A48	500m multicolored		1.50	1.50

UN, 50th Anniv. A49

Design: 250m, Azerbaijan Pres. Heydar A. Aliyev, UN Sec. Gen. Boutros Boutros-Ghali.

1995, Sept. 15				
500 A49	250m multicolored		2.00	2.00

200 M.

Nos. 352-355 Surcharged

1995	**Litho.**		*Perf. 12*	
501 A21	200m on 2.50m #355		.30	.30
502 A21	600m on 35g #352		.85	.85
503 A21	800m on 50g #353		1.10	1.10
504 A21	1000m on 1.50m #354		1.40	1.40
	Nos. 501-504 (4)		3.65	3.65

AZERBAIJAN

Uzeyir Hacibeyov
(1885-1948) — A50

Design: 400m, Oglu Iskenderov (1895-1965).

1995, June 30 Litho. Perf. 12x12½
| 505 | A50 | 250m silver gray & black | .60 | .60 |
| 506 | A50 | 400m gold bister & brown | .90 | .90 |

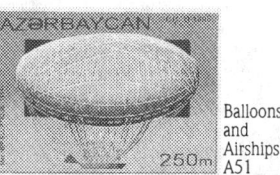

Balloons and Airships A51

Designs: 100m, First hydrogen balloon, 1784, vert. 150m, First motorized balloon, 1883, vert. 250m, First elliptical balloon, 1784. 300m, First Scott Baldwin dirigible, 1904. 400m, US Marine balloon, 1917. 500m, Pedal-powered dirigible, 1909.
800m, First rigid dirigible designed by Hugo Eckener, 1924.

1995, July 20 Litho. Perf. 13
507	A51	100m multicolored	.20	.20
508	A51	150m multicolored	.30	.30
509	A51	250m multicolored	.45	.45
510	A51	300m multicolored	.55	.55
511	A51	400m multicolored	.75	.75
512	A51	500m multicolored	.90	.90
		Nos. 507-512 (6)	3.15	3.15

Souvenir Sheet
| 513 | A51 | 800m multicolored | 1.50 | 1.50 |

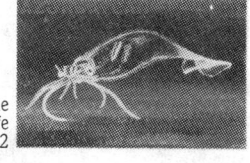

Marine Life A52

Designs: 50m, Loligo vulgaris. 100m, Orchistoma pileus. 150m, Pegea confoederata. 250m, Polyorchis karafutoensis, vert. 300m, Agalma okeni, vert.
500m, Corolla spectabilis.

1995, June 2 Litho. Perf. 13
514	A52	50m multicolored	.20	.20
515	A52	100m multicolored	.40	.40
516	A52	150m multicolored	.50	.50
517	A52	250m multicolored	.90	.90
518	A52	300m multicolored	1.10	1.10
		Nos. 514-518 (5)	3.10	3.10

Souvenir Sheet
| 519 | A52 | 500m multicolored | 1.50 | 1.50 |

Turtles A53

Designs: 50m, Chelus fimbriatus. 100m, Caretta caretta. 150m, Geochelone pardalis. 250m, Geochelone elegans. 300m, Testudo hermanni.
500m, Macroclemys temmincki.

1995, June 12 Litho. Perf. 13
520	A53	50m multicolored	.20	.20
521	A53	100m multicolored	.40	.40
522	A53	150m multicolored	.50	.50
523	A53	250m multicolored	.90	.90
524	A53	300m multicolored	1.10	1.10
		Nos. 520-524 (5)	3.10	3.10

Souvenir Sheet
| 525 | A53 | 500m multicolored | 1.50 | 1.50 |

1998 World Cup Soccer Championships, France — A54

Various soccer plays.

1995, Sept. 30 Litho. Perf. 12½
526	A54	100m orange & multi	.40	.40
527	A54	150m green & multi	.60	.60
528	A54	250m yellow orange & multi	.90	.90
529	A54	300m yellow & multi	1.10	1.10
530	A54	400m blue & multi	1.50	1.50
		Nos. 526-530 (5)	4.50	4.50

Souvenir Sheet Perf. 13
| 531 | A54 | 600m multicolored | 2.25 | 2.25 |

Domestic Cats — A55

1995, Oct. 30 Perf. 12½
532	A55	100m Persian	.20	.20
533	A55	150m Chartreux	.30	.30
534	A55	250m Somali	.45	.45
535	A55	300m Longhair Scottish fold	.55	.55
536	A55	400m Cumric	.75	.75
537	A55	500m Turkish angora	.90	.90
		Nos. 532-537 (6)	3.15	3.15

Souvenir Sheet
| 538 | A55 | 800m Birman | 1.50 | 1.50 |

No. 538 contains one 32x40mm stamp.

Fauna and Flora — A56

Designs: 100m, Horse. 200m, Muscari elecostomum, vert. 250m, Huso huso. 300m, Aquila chrysaetos. 400m, Panthera tigrus. 500m, Lyrurus miokosiewickzi, facing right. 1000m, Lyrurus miokosiewickzi, facing left.

1995, Nov. 30
539	A56	100m multicolored	.15	.15
540	A56	200m multicolored	.30	.30
541	A56	250m multicolored	.30	.30
542	A56	300m multicolored	.40	.40
543	A56	400m multicolored	.50	.50
544	A56	500m multicolored	.60	.60
545	A56	1000m multicolored	1.50	1.50
		Nos. 539-545 (7)	3.75	3.75

John Lennon (1940-80) A57

1995, Dec. 8 Perf. 14½
| 546 | A57 | 500m multicolored | .60 | .60 |

Issued in sheet of 16 plus label.

Miniature Sheet

Locomotives — A58

Designs: No. 547a, 4-4-0, America. b, J3 Hudson, US. c, 2-8-2. d, 2-6-2, Germany. e, 2-8-2, Germany. f, 2-6-2, Italy. g, G-C5, Japan. h, 2-10-2 QJ, China. i, 0-10-0, China.
500m, Electric passenger train, vert.

1996, Feb. 1 Perf. 14
| 547 | A58 | 100m Sheet of 9, #a.-i. | 6.00 | 6.00 |

Souvenir Sheet
| 548 | A58 | 500m multicolored | 3.00 | 3.00 |

Dr. M. Topcubasov, Surgeon — A59

1996, Feb. 1
| 549 | A59 | 300m multicolored | 1.50 | 1.50 |

Nos. 363, 365, 367-368, 370, 372-374 Surcharged 250 M.

1995, Jan. 4 Litho. Perf. 12½x12
550	A23	250m on 10g #363	.40	.40
551	A23	250m on 20g #365	.40	.40
552	A23	250m on 50g #368	.40	.40
553	A23	250m on 1.50m #372	.40	.40
554	A23	500m on 50g #367	.75	.75
555	A23	500m on 1m #370	.75	.75
556	A23	500m on 2.50m #373	.75	.75
557	A23	500m on 5m #374	.75	.75
		Nos. 550-557 (8)	4.60	4.60

1996 Olympic Games, Atlanta A60

1996, Apr. 9 Litho. Perf. 14
568	A60	50m Carl Lewis	.20	.20
569	A60	100m Muhammed Ali	.40	.40
570	A60	150m Li Ning	.60	.60
571	A60	200m Said Aouita	.80	.80
572	A60	250m Olga Korbut	1.00	1.00
573	A60	300m Nadia Comaneci	1.25	1.25
574	A60	400m Greg Louganis	1.50	1.50
		Nos. 568-574 (7)	5.75	5.75

Souvenir Sheet
| 575 | A60 | 500m Nazim Hüseynov, vert. | 2.00 | 2.00 |

Husein Aliyev (1911-91), Artist A61

Paintings: 100m, Water bird, swamp. 200m, Landscape.

1996, Apr. 16 Litho. Perf. 14
576	A61	100m multicolored	.75	.75
577	A61	200m multicolored	1.50	1.50
a.		Pair, #576-577 + label	2.25	2.25

No. 577a issued in sheets of 6 stamps.

Resid Behbudov (1915-89), Singer — A62

1996, Apr. 22 Perf. 12½
| 578 | A62 | 100m multicolored | 1.25 | 1.25 |

A63  A64

1996, Mar. 20
| 579 | A63 | 250m multicolored | 1.25 | 1.25 |

Novruz Bayrami, natl. holiday.

1996, May 28 Litho. Perf. 14
| 580 | A64 | 250m multicolored | 1.25 | 1.25 |

Independence, 5th anniv.

A65  A66

1996, Apr. 22 Litho. Perf. 12½
| 581 | A65 | 100m multicolored | 1.25 | 1.25 |

Yusif Memmedeliyev (1905-95), chemist.

1996, June 7 Perf. 14
Jerusalem, 3000th Anniv.: a, 100m, Wailing Wall. b, 250m, Inside cathedral. c, 300m, Dome of the Rock.
500m, Windmill.
| 582 | A66 | Sheet of 3, #a.-c. | 3.50 | 3.50 |

Souvenir Sheet
| 583 | A66 | 500m multicolored | 3.00 | 3.00 |

For overprints see Nos. 643-644.

Dogs A67

Designs: 50m, German shepherd. 100m, Basset hound. 150m, Collie. 200m, Bull terrier. 300m, Boxer. 400m, Cocker spaniel.
500m, Sharpei.

1996, June 18 Perf. 13
| 584-589 | A67 | Set of 6 | 5.00 | 5.00 |

Souvenir Sheet
| 590 | A67 | 500m multicolored | 2.50 | 2.50 |

Birds — A68

Designs: 50m, Tetraenura regia. 100m, Coliuspasser macrourus. 150m, Oriolus xanthornus. 200m, Oriolus oriolus. 300m, Sturnus vulgaris. 400m, Serinus mozambicus.
500m, Merops apiaster.

1996, June 19 Perf. 13
| 591-596 | A68 | Set of 6 | 5.00 | 5.00 |

Souvenir Sheet
| 597 | A68 | 500m multicolored | 2.50 | 2.50 |

AZERBAIJAN

Roses — A69

Designs: 50m, Burgundy. 100m, Virgo. 150m, Rose gaujard. 200m, Luna. 300m, Lady rose. 400m, Landora. 500m, Lougsor, horiz.

1996, June 19
598-603 A69 Set of 6   5.00 5.00
Souvenir Sheet
604 A69 500m multicolored   2.50 2.50

A70

A71

1996, July 8   Litho.   *Perf. 14*
605 A70 500m multicolored   1.25 1.25
UNICEF, 50th anniv.

1996, July 22
Competing teams: 100m, Spain, Bulgaria. 150m, Romania, France. 200m, Czech Republic, Germany. 250m, England, Israel. 300m, Croatia, Turkey. 400m, Italy, Russia. 500m, Trophy cup.
606-611 A71 Set of 6   3.25 3.25
Souvenir Sheet
612 A71 500m multicolored   1.50 1.50
Euro '96, European Soccer Championships, Great Britain.

Ships — A72

Ship, home country: 100m, Chinese junk. 150m, Danmark, Denmark. 200m, Nippon Maru, Japan. 250m, Mircea, Romania. 300m, Kruzenshtern, Russia. 400m, Ariadne, Germany. 500m, Tovarishch, Russia, vert.

1996, Aug. 26   Litho.   *Perf. 14*
613-618 A72 Set of 6   4.00 4.00
Souvenir Sheet
619 A72 500m multicolored   3.00 3.00
For overprints see Nos. 645-651.

Baxram Gur Kills a Dragon, Sculpture — A73

1997, Mar. 6   Litho.   *Perf. 13½x13*
620 A73 250m black & yellow   .45 .45
621 A73 400m black & vermilion   .60 .60
622 A73 500m black & green   .75 .75
623 A73 1000m black & purple   1.50 1.50
Nos. 620-623 (4)   3.30 3.30
See No. 671.

Famous Personalities — A74

Designs: No. 624, Mamed-Kerim Ogli Aliyev (1897-1962), politician. No. 625, Illyas Efendiyev (1914-96), writer. No. 626, Fatali Xan-Xoyskiy (1875-1920), politician. No. 627, Nariman Narimanov (1870-1925), politician, writer.

1997, Mar. 25   Litho.   *Perf. 14*
Background Color
624 A74 250m tan   1.10 1.10
625 A74 250m gray blue   1.10 1.10
626 A74 250m pale red   1.10 1.10
627 A74 250m pale olive   1.10 1.10
Nos. 624-627 (4)   4.40 4.40

Qobustan Prehistoric Art — A75

Rock carvings: a, Oxen. b, Large horned animals. c, Six figures.

1997, May 19   Litho.   *Perf. 14*
628 A75 500m Sheet of 3, #a.-c.   4.25 4.25
For overprint see No. 674.

#356-362A, 464-469 Ovptd. in Red

✚

Red Cross

1997, June 2   Litho.   *Perf. 13*
Denominations as Before
629-635 A22 Set of 7   8.00 8.00
Souvenir Sheet
636 A22 8m multicolored   5.00 5.00
Location of overprint varies. No. 636 is ovptd. both on stamp and in sheet margin.

1997, June 2
Denominations as Before
637-641 A42 Set of 5   6.00 6.00
Souvenir Sheet
642 A42 100m multicolored   5.00 5.00
Location of overprint varies. No. 642 is ovptd. both on stamp and in sheet margin.

Nos. 582-583, 613-619 Ovptd.

1997, June 2   *Perf. 14*
643 A66 Sheet of 3, #a.-c.   5.00 5.00
Souvenir Sheet
644 A66 500m multicolored   5.00 5.00
Size and location of overprint varies. Overprint appears both on stamp and in sheet margin.

1997, June 2   *Perf. 14*
Denominations as Before
645-650 A72 Set of 6   5.00 5.00
Souvenir Sheet
651 A72 500m multicolored   5.00 5.00
Location of overprint varies. No. 651 is ovptd. both on stamp and in sheet margin.

Grimm's Fairy Tales — A76

Bremen Musical: No. 652: a, Dog. b, Dancing horse, cat. c, Rooster.
500m, Animals looking through window at treaure chest, man.

1997, July 1   *Perf. 13½x14*
652 A76 250m Sheet of 3, #a.-c.   2.00 2.00
Souvenir Sheet
653 A76 500m multicolored   1.40 1.40

Caspian Seals A77

Designs: a, Seal looking right. b, Mountain top, seal looking forward. c, Seal, seagull. d, Seal looking left. e, Seal looking forward. f, Small seal.
500m, Mother nursing pup.

1997, July 1
654 A77 250m Sheet of 6, #a.-f.   4.25 4.25
Souvenir Sheet
655 A77 500m multicolored   1.40 1.40

Traditional Musical Instruments A77a

1997, Aug. 4   Litho.   *Perf. 14*
656 A77a 250m Qaval   .75 .75
657 A77a 250m Tanbur   .75 .75
658 A77a 500m Cenq   1.50 1.50
Nos. 656-658 (3)   3.00 3.00

A78   A79

Azerbaijan Oil Industry: a, Early oil derricks, building. b, Off-shore oil drilling platform.

1997, Aug. 18   *Perf. 14½*
Souvenir Sheet
659 A78 500m Sheet of 2, #a.-b.   3.00 3.00

1997, Sept. 12   *Perf. 14x13½*
660 A79 250m Hagani Shirvany, poet   1.00 1.00
No. 660 was issued in sheets of 4 + 5 labels.

Mosques A80

#661, Ashaqi mechet Qovqar-agi, Shusha, 1874-75. #662, Momuna-Zatun, Naxcivan, 1187. #663, Taza-pir, Baku (1905-14).

1997, Sept. 18   Litho.   *Perf. 14*
661 A80 250m multicolored   .85 .85
662 A80 250m multicolored   .85 .85
663 A80 250m multicolored   .85 .85
Nos. 661-663 (3)   2.55 2.55

H.C. Rasul Beyov (1917-1984), Communications Official — A81

1997, Oct. 6   Litho.   *Perf. 14*
664 A81 250m multicolored   2.00 2.00

1998 World Cup Soccer Championships, France — A82

Winning team photos: No. 665: a, Italy, 1938. b, Argentina, 1986. c, Uruguay, 1980. d, Brazil, 1994. e, England, 1966. f, Germany, 1990.
1500m, Tofiq Bahramov, "Golden Whistle" prize winner, 1966, vert.

1997, Oct. 15
665 A82 250m Sheet of 6, #a.-f.   5.00 5.00
Souvenir Sheet
666 A82 1500m multicolored   4.00 4.00

A83   A84

Figure skaters: No. 667: a, Katarina Witt, Germany. b, Elvis Stojko, Canada. c, Midori Ito, Japan. d, Silhouettes of various winter sports against natl. flag. e, Hand holding Olympic torch. f, Kristi Yamaguchi, US. g, John Curry, England. h, Lu Chen, China.
No. 668, Gordeyeva and Grinkov, Russia.

1997   Litho.   *Perf. 14*
667 A83 250m Sheet of 8, #a.-h.   2.50 2.50
Souvenir Sheet
668 A83 500m multicolored   .65 .65
1998 Winter Olympic Games, Nagano.

1998, Feb. 4   *Perf. 13½*
Diana, Princess of Wales (1961-97): No. 669, Wearing black turtleneck. No. 670, Wearing violet dress.
669 A84 400m multicolored   .50 .50
670 A84 400m multicolored   .50 .50
Nos. 669-670 were each issued in sheets of 6.

Sculpture Type of 1997
1998, Mar. 23   Litho.   *Perf. 13½x13*
671 A73 100m black & bright pink   1.00 1.00

Hasan Aliyev, Ecologist, 90th Birth Anniv. A85

1998, Apr. 3   *Perf. 14*
672 A85 500m multicolored   1.00 1.00

AZERBAIJAN — AZORES

Souvenir Sheet

Pres. Heydar Aliyev, 75th Birthday — A86

Illustration reduced.

1998, May 10			**Perf. 13½**
673	A86	500m multicolored	2.00 2.00

No. 628 Ovptd.

1998, May 13			**Perf. 14**
674	A75	500m Sheet of 3, #a.-c.	4.00 4.00

Additional inscription in sheet margin reads "ISRAEL 98 - WORLD STAMP EXHIBITION / TEL-AVIV 13-21 MAY 1998."

Musicians A87

Designs: No. 675, Gara Garayev. No. 676, Ashig Hasgar. No. 677, Sayid Mohammadhusein.

1998, June 7	**Litho.**		**Perf. 14**
675	A87	250m multicolored	.50 .50
676	A87	250m multicolored	.50 .50
677	A87	250m multicolored	.50 .50
		Nos. 675-677 (3)	1.50 1.50

Bul-Bul, Singer, Birth Cent. — A88

1998, July 7			
678	A88	500m multicolored	1.00 1.00

Disney Characters at World Rapid Chess Championship A89

No. 679: a, Minnie, Mickey. b, Goofy. c, Donald. d, Pluto. e, Minnie. f, Daisy. g, Goofy, Donald. h, Mickey.
#680, Donald, Mickey. #681, Minnie, Mickey.

1998, Nov. 13			**Perf. 13½x14**
679	A89	500m Sheet of 8, #a.-h.	8.00 8.00
Souvenir Sheets			
680-681	A89	4000m each	8.00 8.00

SEMI-POSTAL STAMPS

Carrying Food to Sufferers — SP1

1922	**Unwmk.**		**Imperf.**
B1	SP1	500r blue & pale blue	.40 .75

For overprint and surcharge see Nos. 42, 305.

Widow and Orphans — SP2

1922			
B2	SP2	1000r brown & bister	.50 1.25

Counterfeits exist.
For overprint and surcharge see Nos. 44, 306.

OCCUPATION AZIRBAYEDJAN

Russian stamps of 1909-18 were privately overprinted as above in red, blue or black by a group of Entente officers working with Russian soldiers returning from Persia. Azerbaijan was not occupied by the Allies. There is evidence that existing covers (some seemingly postmarked at Baku, dated Oct. 19, 1917, and at Tabriz, Russian Consulate, Apr. 25, 1917) are fakes.

AIR POST STAMP

Catalogue values for all stamps in this section are for never hinged items.

Eagle — AP1

1995, Oct. 16	**Litho.**		**Perf. 14**
C1	AP1	2200m multicolored	2.00 2.00

AZORES

'ā-ˌzōrz

LOCATION — Group of islands in the North Atlantic Ocean, due west of Portugal
GOVT. — Integral part of Portugal, former colony
AREA — 922 sq. mi.
POP. — 253,935 (1930)
CAPITAL — Ponta Delgada

Azores stamps were supplanted by those of Portugal in 1931.

1000 Reis = 1 Milreis
100 Centavos = 1 Escudo (1912)

See Portugal for other recent issues.

Stamps of Portugal Overprinted in Black or Carmine

AÇORES AÇORES
a

A second type of this overprint has a broad "O" and open "S."

		1868	**Unwmk.**	**Imperf.**
1	A14	5r black	3,250.	1,750.
2	A14	10r yellow	13,500.	7,500.
3	A14	20r bister	250.00	125.00
4	A14	50r green	250.00	125.00
5	A14	80r orange	250.00	125.00
6	A14	100r lilac	250.00	125.00

The reprints are on thick chalky white wove paper, ungummed, and on thin ivory paper with shiny white gum. Value $20 each.

		1868-70		**Perf. 12½**

5 REIS:
Type I - The "5" at the right is 1mm from end of label.
Type II - The "5" is 1½mm from end of label.

7	A14	5r black (C)	70.00	50.00
8	A14	10r yellow	90.00	50.00
a.		Inverted overprint	250.00	150.00
9	A14	20r bister	70.00	45.00
10	A14	25r rose	70.00	8.00
a.		Inverted overprint		—
11	A14	50r green	200.00	140.00
12	A14	80r orange	200.00	140.00
13	A14	100r lilac	200.00	140.00
14	A14	120r blue	170.00	90.00
15	A14	240r violet	600.00	300.00

The reprints are on thick chalky white paper ungummed, perf 13½, and on thin ivory paper with shiny white gum, perf 13½. Value $10 each.

		1871-75		**Perf. 12½, 13½**
21	A15	5r black (C)	12.50	6.00
a.		Inverted overprint	47.50	30.00
23	A15	10r yellow	27.50	20.00
a.		Inverted overprint		
24	A15	20r bister	25.00	19.00
25	A15	25r rose	16.00	3.00
b.		Double overprint	35.00	25.00
c.		Perf. 14	165.00	55.00
d.		Dbl. impression of stamp		
26	A15	50r green	80.00	30.00
27	A15	80r orange	110.00	50.00
28	A15	100r lilac	90.00	45.00
a.		Perf. 14	165.00	100.00
29	A15	120r blue	165.00	95.00
a.		Inverted overprint		
30	A15	240r violet	800.00	500.00

Nos. 21-29 exist with overprint "b."

The reprints are of type "b." They are on thick chalky white paper ungummed, perf 13½, and also on thin white paper with shiny white gum, perforated 13½.

Overprinted in Black

AÇORES
b

1875-80

15 REIS:
Type I - The figures of value, 1 and 5, at the right in upper label are close together.
Type II - The figures of value at the right in upper label are spaced.

31	A15	10r blue green	175.00	100.00
32	A15	10r blue green	100.00	60.00
33	A15	15r lilac brown	17.50	12.00
a.		Inverted overprint	125.00	
34	A15	50r blue	150.00	60.00
35	A15	150r blue	160.00	100.00
36	A15	150r yellow	200.00	175.00
37	A15	300r violet	80.00	50.00

The reprints have the same papers, gum and perforations as those of the preceding issue.

Black Overprint

		1880		**Perf. 12½, 13½**
38	A17	25r gray	125.00	30.00
39	A18	25r red lilac	50.00	6.00
b.		25r gray	50.00	6.00
		Double overprint		

Overprinted in Carmine or Black

		1881-82		
40	A16	5r black (C)	21.00	7.50
41	A23	25r brown ('82)	45.00	5.00
a.		Double overprint		
42	A19	50r blue	150.00	30.00
		Nos. 40-42 (3)	216.00	42.50

Reprints of Nos. 38, 39, 39a, 40 and 42 have the same papers, gum and perforations as those of preceding issues.

Overprinted in Red or Black

AÇORES
c

		1882-85	**Perf. 11½, 12½, 13½**

15, 20 REIS
Type I - The figures of value are some distance apart and close to the end of the label.
Type II - The figures are closer together and farther from the end of the label. On the 15 reis this is particularly apparent in the upper right figures.

43	A16	5r black (R)	25.00	10.00
44	A21	5r slate	15.00	3.00
a.		Double overprint		
c.		Inverted overprint		
45	A15	10r green	75.00	50.00
a.		Inverted overprint		
46	A22	10r green	25.00	10.00
47	A15	15r lilac brn	65.00	35.00
b.		Inverted overprint		
48	A15	20r bister	90.00	50.00
a.		Inverted overprint		
49	A15	20r carmine	125.00	80.00
a.		Double overprint	165.00	100.00
50	A23	25r brown	19.00	3.00
51	A15	50r blue	1,200.	1,000.
52	A24	50r blue	24.00	3.00
		Double overprint		
53	A15	80r yellow	70.00	40.00
		80r orange	110.00	70.00
b.		Double overprint		
54	A15	100r lilac	55.00	35.00
55	A15	150r blue	1,000.	750.00
56	A15	150r yellow	100.00	60.00
57	A15	300r violet	100.00	60.00

Reprints of the 1882-85 issues have the same papers, gum and perforations as those of preceding issues.

Red Overprint

58	A21	5r slate	20.00	4.00
59	A24a	500r black	160.00	110.00
60	A15	1000r black	125.00	85.00

Black Overprint

		1887		
61	A25	20r pink	25.00	10.00
a.		Inverted overprint		
b.		Double overprint		
62	A26	25r lilac rose	25.00	2.00
a.		Inverted overprint		
b.		Double ovpt., one invtd.		
63	A26	25r red violet	25.00	2.00
		Double overprint		
64	A24a	500r red violet	125.00	75.00
a.		Perf. 13½	400.00	200.00
		Nos. 61-64 (4)	200.00	89.00

Nos. 58-64 inclusive have been reprinted on thin white paper with shiny white gum and perforated 13½.

Prince Henry the Navigator Issue
Portugal Nos. 97-109 Overprinted AÇORES

		1894, Mar. 4		**Perf. 14**
65	A46	5r orange yel	3.00	2.00
a.		Inverted overprint	45.00	45.00
66	A46	10r violet rose	3.00	2.00
a.		Double overprint		
b.		Inverted overprint		
67	A46	15r brown	3.50	2.50
68	A46	20r violet	3.50	2.50
a.		Double overprint		
69	A47	25r green	4.00	3.00
a.		Double overprint	50.00	50.00
b.		Inverted overprint	50.00	50.00
70	A47	50r blue	10.00	4.25
71	A47	75r dp carmine	20.00	6.00
72	A47	80r yellow grn	21.00	6.00
73	A47	100r lt brn, pale buff	21.00	5.00
		Double overprint		
74	A48	150r lt car, pale rose	30.00	10.00
75	A48	300r dk bl, sal buff	40.00	17.50
76	A48	500r brn vio, pale lil	60.00	25.00
77	A48	1000r gray blk, yelsh	125.00	45.00
a.		Double overprint		
		Nos. 65-77 (13)	344.00	130.75

St. Anthony of Padua Issue
Portugal Nos. 132-146
Overprinted in Red or Black AÇORES

		1895, June 13		**Perf. 12**
78	A50	2½r black (R)	2.50	1.50
79	A51	5r brown yel	8.00	2.00
80	A51	10r red lilac	8.00	2.50
81	A51	15r red brown	12.50	4.00
82	A51	20r gray lilac	12.50	5.00
83	A51	25r green & vio	8.00	2.75
84	A52	50r blue & brn	25.00	14.00
85	A52	75r rose & brn	25.00	25.00
86	A52	80r lt green & brn	40.00	25.00
87	A52	100r choc & blk	50.00	25.00
88	A53	150r vio rose & bis	80.00	65.00
89	A53	200r blue & bis	100.00	60.00
90	A53	300r slate & bis	125.00	70.00
91	A53	500r vio brn & grn	200.00	100.00
92	A53	1000r violet & grn	400.00	200.00
		Nos. 78-92 (15)	1,096.	601.75

7th cent. of the birth of Saint Anthony of Padua.

490 AZORES

Common Design Types pictured following the introduction.

Vasco da Gama Issue
Common Design Types

1898, Apr. 1 *Perf. 14, 15*

93	CD20	2½r blue green	3.00	.80
94	CD21	5r red	3.00	1.00
95	CD22	10r gray lilac	5.00	2.00
96	CD23	25r yellow green	5.00	2.00
97	CD24	50r dark blue	8.00	6.00
98	CD25	75r violet brown	16.00	9.00
99	CD26	100r bister brown	20.00	9.00
100	CD27	150r bister	32.50	18.00
		Nos. 93-100 (8)	92.50	47.80

For overprints and surcharges see Nos. 141-148.

King Carlos — A28

King Manuel II — A29

1906 **Typo.** *Perf. 11½x12*

101	A28	2½r gray	.40	.15
a.		Inverted overprint	*25.00*	*25.00*
102	A28	5r orange yel	.40	.15
a.		Inverted overprint	*25.00*	*25.00*
103	A28	10r yellow grn	.40	.15
104	A28	20r gray vio	.50	.30
105	A28	25r carmine	.40	.15
106	A28	50r ultra	4.50	3.00
107	A28	75r brown, *straw*	1.50	*.80*
108	A28	100r dk blue, *bl*	1.50	*.90*
109	A28	200r red lilac, *pnksh*	1.50	*1.00*
110	A28	300r dk blue, *rose*	5.00	*3.25*
111	A28	500r black, *blue*	11.00	8.00
		Nos. 101-111 (11)	27.10	17.85

"Acores" and letters and figures in the corners are in red on the 2½, 10, 20, 75 and 500r and in black on the other values.

1910, Apr. 1 *Perf. 14x15*

112	A29	2½r violet	.25	.20
113	A29	5r black	.25	.20
114	A29	10r dk green	.30	.25
115	A29	15r lilac brn	.40	.50
116	A29	20r carmine	.45	.45
117	A29	25r violet brn	.25	.20
a.		Perf. 11½	1.25	.80
118	A29	50r blue	1.00	.70
119	A29	75r bister brn	1.75	1.25
120	A29	80r slate	1.75	1.25
121	A29	100r brown, *lt grn*	2.25	1.75
122	A29	200r green, *sal*	2.25	1.75
123	A29	300r black, *blue*	3.50	2.50
124	A29	500r olive & brown	7.00	7.00
125	A29	1000r blue & black	12.00	12.00
		Nos. 112-125 (14)	33.40	30.00

The errors of color 10r black, 15r dark green, 25r black and 50r carmine are considered to be proofs.

Stamps of 1910 Overprinted in Carmine or Green

REPUBLICA

1910

126	A29	2½r violet	.15	.15
a.		Inverted overprint	9.00	9.00
127	A29	5r black	.20	.15
a.		Inverted overprint	9.00	9.00
128	A29	10r dk green	.20	.20
a.		Inverted overprint	9.00	9.00
129	A29	15r lilac brn	.80	.65
a.		Inverted overprint	9.00	9.00
130	A29	20r carmine (G)	1.00	.80
a.		Inverted overprint	16.00	16.00
b.		Double overprint	16.00	16.00
131	A29	25r violet brn	.25	.15
a.		Perf. 11½	40.00	30.00
132	A29	50r blue	.60	.50
133	A29	75r bister brn	.35	.20
a.		Double overprint	9.00	9.00
134	A29	80r slate	.45	.35
135	A29	100r brown, *grn*	.40	.25
136	A29	200r green, *sal*	.60	*.60*
137	A29	300r black, *blue*	1.25	1.25
138	A29	500r olive & brn	1.25	*1.75*
139	A29	1000r blue & blk	3.50	*4.00*
		Nos. 126-139 (14)	11.00	*11.00*

Vasco da Gama Issue Overprinted or Surcharged in Black:

REPUBLICA
d

REPUBLICA REIS 15 REIS
e

REPUBLICA 1$000
f

1911 *Perf. 14, 15*

141	CD20(d)	2½r blue green	.35	.30
142	CD21(e)	15r on 5r red	.20	.20
143	CD23(d)	25r yellow grn	.40	.25
144	CD24(d)	50r dk blue	1.00	.70
145	CD25(d)	75r violet brn	.60	.60
146	CD27(e)	80r on 150r bister	.60	.60
147	CD26(d)	100r yellow brn	.60	.60
a.		Double surcharge	35.00	35.00
148	CD22(f)	1000r on 10r lilac	8.50	6.50
		Nos. 141-148 (8)	12.25	9.75

Postage Due Stamps of Portugal Overprinted or Surcharged in Black "ACORES" and

REPUBLICA

REPUBLICA Rs 300 Rs

1911 *Perf. 12*

149	D1	5r black	.75	.35
150	D1	10r magenta	1.75	1.25
a.		"Acores" double	20.00	20.00
151	D1	20r orange	2.00	2.00
152	D1	200r brn, *buff*	7.25	6.00
a.		"Acores" inverted		
153	D1	300r on 50r slate	7.25	6.00
154	D1	500r on 100r car, *pink*	7.25	6.00
		Nos. 149-154 (6)	26.25	21.60

AÇORES

Ceres Issue of Portugal Overprinted "ACORES" in Black or Carmine With Imprint

1912-31 *Perf. 12x11½, 15x14*

155	A30	¼c olive brown	.15	.15
a.		Inverted overprint	9.00	
156	A30	½c black (C)	.15	.15
157	A30	1c deep green	.55	.35
a.		Inverted overprint	9.00	
158	A30	1c deep brown ('18)	.15	.15
a.		Inverted overprint		
159	A30	1½c choc ('13)	.50	.40
a.		Inverted overprint	9.00	
160	A30	1½c deep green ('18)	.35	.15
a.		Inverted overprint		
161	A30	2c carmine	.30	.20
a.		Inverted overprint	14.00	
162	A30	2c orange ('18)	.20	.15
a.		Inverted overprint	18.00	
163	A30	2½c violet	.25	.15
164	A30	3c rose ('18)	.20	.15
165	A30	3c dull ultra ('25)	.20	.15
166	A30	3½c lt green ('18)	.30	.15
167	A30	4c lt green ('19)	.15	.15
168	A30	4c orange ('30)	.25	.20
169	A30	5c dp blue	.25	.15
170	A30	5c yellow brn ('18)	.25	.20
171	A30	5c olive brn ('23)	.15	.15
172	A30	5c black brn ('30)	2.75	2.50
173	A30	6c dull rose ('20)	.20	.15
174	A30	6c choc ('25)	.20	.15
175	A30	6c red brn ('31)	.35	*.80*
176	A30	7½c yel brn	4.75	1.25
177	A30	7½c deep blue ('18)	.60	.40
178	A30	8c slate ('13)	.55	.20
179	A30	8c blue grn ('22)	.25	.20
180	A30	8c orange ('25)	.50	.25
181	A30	10c orange brown	.30	.15
182	A30	12c blue gray ('20)	1.00	.70
183	A30	12c deep green ('22)	.45	.35
184	A30	13½c chlky bl ('20)	1.00	*3.25*
185	A30	14c dk bl, *yel* ('20)	3.25	*6.00*
186	A30	15c plum ('13)	.60	.60
187	A30	15c blk (R) ('23)	.40	.40
188	A30	16c brt ultra ('24)	.80	.40
189	A30	16c dp bl ('30)	1.25	*1.50*
190	A30	20c vio brn, *grn* ('13)	8.00	3.25
191	A30	20c choc ('20)	.60	.20
192	A30	20c deep green ('23)	.80	.80
a.		Double overprint		
193	A30	20c gray ('24)	.60	.20
194	A30	24c grnsh bl ('21)	.60	.40
195	A30	25c salmon ('23)	.30	.20
196	A30	30c brn, *pink* ('13)	40.00	22.50
197	A30	30c brn, *yel* ('19)	2.25	2.25
198	A30	30c gray brn ('21)	.80	.65
199	A30	32c dp green ('25)	4.00	1.00
200	A30	36c red ('21)	.40	.20
201	A30	40c dp blue ('23)	.40	.40
202	A30	40c black brn ('24)	.20	.15
203	A30	40c brt green ('30)	1.50	.40
204	A30	48c brt rose ('24)	1.50	1.00
205	A30	48c dull pink ('31)	6.25	6.00
206	A30	50c org, *sal* ('13)	5.25	1.00
207	A30	50c yellow ('23)	1.25	1.00
208	A30	50c bister ('30)	2.50	1.75
209	A30	50c red brn ('31)	2.00	1.50
210	A30	60c blue ('21)	1.00	.70
211	A30	64c pale ultra ('24)	1.50	1.00
212	A30	64c brown rose ('31)	45.00	45.00
213	A30	75c dull rose ('23)	4.25	4.00
214	A30	75c car rose ('30)	1.50	1.25
215	A30	80c dull rose ('21)	1.25	.65
216	A30	80c violet ('24)	1.25	.90
217	A30	80c dk green ('31)	1.50	1.25
218	A30	90c chlky bl ('21)	1.25	.75
219	A30	96c dp rose ('26)	8.25	4.50
220	A30	1e dp grn, *bl*	4.75	1.50
221	A30	1e violet ('21)	1.25	.75
222	A30	1e gray vio ('24)	1.50	1.00
223	A30	1e brn lake ('30)	12.50	10.00
224	A30	1.10e yel brn ('21)	1.25	1.25
225	A30	1.20e yel grn ('21)	1.50	1.00
226	A30	1.20e buff ('24)	3.75	1.75
227	A30	1.25e dk blue ('30)	1.50	.75
228	A30	1.50e blk vio ('23)	2.75	1.75
229	A30	1.50e lilac ('25)	2.75	1.75
230	A30	1.60e dp bl ('25)	2.75	1.75
231	A30	2e slate grn ('21)	4.25	2.00
232	A30	2.40e apple grn ('26)	60.00	50.00
233	A30	3e lilac pink ('26)	60.00	55.00
234	A30	3.20e gray grn ('25)	10.00	4.50
235	A30	5e emerald ('24)	20.00	12.00
236	A30	10e pink ('24)	40.00	20.00
237	A30	20e pale turq ('25)	125.00	75.00
		Nos. 155-237 (83)	525.00	369.00

For same overprint on surcharged stamps see Nos. 300-306. For same design without imprint see Nos. 307-313.

Castello-Branco Issue
Stamps of Portugal, 1925, Overprinted in Black or Red **AÇORES**

1925, Mar. 29 *Perf. 12½*

238	A73	2c orange	.20	*.50*
239	A73	3c green	.20	*.50*
240	A73	4c ultra (R)	.20	*.50*
241	A73	5c scarlet	.20	*.50*
242	A74	10c pale blue	.20	*.45*
243	A74	16c red orange	.25	*.75*
244	A75	25c car rose	.25	*.75*
245	A74	32c green	.55	*.80*
246	A75	40c grn & blk (R)	.25	*.75*
247	A74	48c red brn	1.25	*2.25*
248	A76	50c blue green	.80	*2.25*
249	A76	64c orange brn	1.40	*2.25*
250	A76	75c gray blk (R)	1.00	*3.00*
251	A75	80c brown	1.00	*3.00*
252	A76	96c car rose	1.25	*3.00*
253	A77	1.50e dk bl, *bl* (R)	1.25	*2.25*
254	A75	1.60e indigo (R)	1.25	*2.25*
255	A77	2e dk grn, *grn* (R)	1.50	*3.00*
256	A77	2.40e red, *org*	2.00	*3.25*
257	A77	3.20e blk, *grn* (R)	3.00	*5.00*
		Nos. 238-257 (20)	18.00	*37.00*

First Independence Issue
Stamps of Portugal, 1926, Overprinted in Red **AÇÔRES**

1926, Aug. 13 *Perf. 14, 14½*

Center in Black

258	A79	2c orange	.25	*.70*
259	A80	3c ultra	.25	*.70*
260	A79	4c yellow grn	.25	*.70*
261	A80	5c black brn	.25	*.70*
262	A79	6c ocher	.25	*.70*
263	A80	15c dk green	.50	*.90*
264	A81	20c dull violet	.50	*.90*
265	A82	25c scarlet	.50	*.90*
266	A81	32c deep green	.50	*.90*
267	A82	40c yellow brn	.50	*.90*
268	A82	50c olive bis	1.25	*2.00*
269	A82	75c red brown	1.25	*2.00*
270	A83	1e black violet	1.75	*3.25*
271	A84	4.50e olive green	2.00	*6.75*
		Nos. 258-271 (14)	10.00	*22.00*

The use of these stamps instead of those of the regular issue was obligatory on Aug. 13th and 14th, Nov. 30th and Dec. 1st, 1926.

Second Independence Issue
Same Overprint on Stamps of Portugal, 1927, in Red

1927, Nov. 29

Center in Black

272	A86	2c lt brown	.25	*.70*
273	A87	3c ultra	.25	*.70*
274	A86	4c orange	.25	*.70*
275	A88	5c dk brown	.25	*.70*
276	A89	6c orange brn	.25	*.70*
277	A87	15c black brn	.25	*.70*
278	A86	25c gray	1.00	*3.00*
279	A89	32c blue grn	1.00	*3.00*
280	A90	40c yellow grn	1.00	*3.00*
281	A90	96c red	2.50	*5.75*
282	A88	1.60e myrtle grn	2.50	*5.75*
283	A91	4.50e bister	4.50	*8.00*
		Nos. 272-283 (12)	14.00	*32.70*

Third Independence Issue
Same Overprint on Stamps of Portugal, 1928, in Red

1928, Nov. 27

Center in Black

284	A93	2c lt blue	.25	*.70*
285	A94	3c lt green	.25	*.70*
286	A95	4c lake	.25	*.70*
287	A96	5c olive grn	.25	*.70*
288	A97	6c orange brn	.25	*.70*
289	A94	15c slate	.40	*1.25*
290	A95	16c dk violet	.65	*2.25*
291	A93	25c ultra	.65	*2.00*
292	A97	32c dk green	.65	*2.00*
293	A96	40c olive brn	.65	*2.00*
294	A95	50c red orange	1.25	*3.00*
295	A94	80c lt gray	1.25	*3.00*
296	A97	96c carmine	1.75	*6.00*
297	A96	1e claret	1.75	*6.00*
298	A93	1.60e dk blue	1.75	*6.00*
299	A98	4.50e yellow	4.00	*8.50*
		Nos. 284-299 (16)	16.00	*45.50*

A31

A32

1929-30 *Perf. 12x11½, 15x14*

300	A31	4c on 25c pink ('30)	.35	.35
301	A31	4c on 60c dp blue	.35	.35
302	A31	10c on 25c pink	.80	.40
303	A31	12c on 25c pink	.80	.40
304	A31	15c on 25c pink	.65	.60
305	A31	20c on 25c pink	.80	.65
306	A31	40c on 1.10e yel brn	2.75	2.25
		Nos. 300-306 (7)	6.50	5.00

Black or Red Overprint

1930 *Perf. 14*

Without Imprint at Foot

307	A32	4c orange	.35	.40
308	A32	5c dp brown	1.50	1.00
309	A32	10c vermilion	.80	.55
310	A32	15c black (R)	.80	.55
311	A32	40c brt green	.80	.55
312	A32	80c violet	11.00	8.75
313	A32	1.60e dk blue	1.75	1.00
		Nos. 307-313 (7)	17.00	12.80

POSTAGE DUE STAMPS

D2

D3

Portugal Nos. J7-J13 Overprinted in Black

1904 **Unwmk.** *Perf. 12*

J1	D2	5r brown	.45	.65
J2	D2	10r orange	.45	.65
J3	D2	20r lilac	.85	1.10
J4	D2	30r gray green	1.00	1.10
a.		Double overprint		
J5	D2	40r gray violet	1.75	1.75
J6	D2	50r carmine	2.75	3.00
J7	D2	100r dull blue	4.25	4.50
		Nos. J1-J7 (7)	11.50	12.75

Same Overprinted in Carmine or Green (Portugal Nos. J14-J20) REPUBLICA

1911
J8 D2 5r brown .20 .20
J9 D2 10r orange .20 .20
J10 D2 20r lilac .20 .20
J11 D2 30r gray green .20 .20
J12 D2 40r gray violet .45 .45
J13 D2 50r carmine (G) 2.00 2.00
J14 D2 100r dull blue 1.25 1.25
Nos. J8-J14 (7) 4.50 4.50

Portugal Nos. J21-J27 Overprinted in Black

1918
J15 D3 ½c brown .15 .15
a. Inverted overprint 4.00 4.00
b. Double overprint 4.00 4.00
J16 D3 1c orange .15 .15
a. Inverted overprint 4.00 4.00
b. Double overprint 4.00 4.00
J17 D3 2c red lilac .15 .15
a. Inverted overprint 4.00 4.00
b. Double overprint 4.00 4.00
J18 D3 3c green .15 .15
a. Inverted overprint 4.00 4.00
b. Double overprint 4.00 4.00
J19 D3 4c gray .15 .15
a. Inverted overprint 4.00 4.00
b. Double overprint 4.00 4.00
J20 D3 5c rose .15 .15
b. Double overprint 4.00 4.00
J21 D3 10c dark blue .20 .20
Nos. J15-J21 (7) 1.10 1.10

Stamps and Type of Portugal Postage Dues, 1921-27, Overprinted in Black

1922-24 *Perf. 11½x12*
J30 D3 ½c gray green ('23) .15 .15
J31 D3 1c gray green ('23) .15 .15
J32 D3 2c gray green ('23) .15 .15
J33 D3 3c gray green ('24) .35 .35
J34 D3 8c gray green ('24) .20 .20
J35 D3 10c gray green ('24) .20 .20
J36 D3 12c gray green ('24) .20 .20
J37 D3 16c gray green ('24) .20 .20
J38 D3 20c gray green .60 .50
J39 D3 24c gray green .20 .20
J40 D3 32c gray green ('24) .20 .20
J41 D3 36c gray green .20 .20
J42 D3 40c gray green ('24) .50 .50
J43 D3 48c gray green ('24) .30 .30
J44 D3 50c gray green .60 .50
J45 D3 60c gray green .65 .35
J46 D3 72c gray green .65 .35
J47 D3 80c gray green ('24) 1.75 1.40
J48 D3 1.20e gray green 1.75 1.40
Nos. J30-J48 (19) 9.00 7.50

NEWSPAPER STAMPS

Newspaper Stamps of Portugal, Nos. P1, P1a, Overprinted Types b & c in Black or Red and:

N3

Perf. 11½, 12½ and 13½

1876-88 **Unwmk.**
P1 N1 2½r (a) olive 11.00 3.50
a. Inverted overprint
P2 N1 2½r (b) olive ('82) 5.00 1.00
a. Inverted overprint
b. Double overprint
P3 N3 2r black ('85) 5.00 2.00
a. Inverted overprint
b. Double overprint, one inverted
P4 N1 2½r (b) bister ('82) 5.00 1.00
a. Double overprint
P5 N3 2r black (R) ('88) 15.00 10.00
Nos. P1-P5 (5) 41.00 17.50

Reprints of the newspaper stamps have the same papers, gum and perforations as reprints of the regular issues. Value $2 each.

PARCEL POST STAMPS

Portugal Nos. Q1-Q17 Overprinted Like Nos. 155-237 in Black or Red

1921-22 **Unwmk.** *Perf. 12*
Q1 PP1 1c lilac brown .15 .15
a. Inverted overprint 4.00 4.00
Q2 PP1 2c orange .15 .15
a. Inverted overprint 4.00 4.00
Q3 PP1 5c light brown .15 .15
a. Inverted overprint 5.00 5.00
b. Double overprint 5.00 5.00
Q4 PP1 10c red brown .15 .25
a. Inverted overprint 5.00 5.00
b. Double overprint 5.00 5.00
Q5 PP1 20c gray blue .30 .25
a. Inverted overprint 5.00 5.00
b. Double overprint 5.00 5.00
Q6 PP1 40c carmine .30 .30
a. Double overprint 6.50 6.50
Q7 PP1 50c black (R) .55 .55
Q8 PP1 60c dark blue (R) .55 .55
Q9 PP1 70c gray brown 2.50 1.25
a. Double overprint
Q10 PP1 80c ultra 2.50 1.25
Q11 PP1 90c light violet 2.50 1.25
Q12 PP1 1e light green 3.00 1.25
Q13 PP1 2e pale lilac 4.00 2.50
Q14 PP1 3e olive 6.00 3.25
Q15 PP1 4e ultra 7.00 5.00
Q16 PP1 5e gray 7.00 5.00
Q17 PP1 10e chocolate 20.00 13.00
Nos. Q1-Q17 (17) 56.80 36.10

POSTAL TAX STAMPS

These stamps represent a special fee for the delivery of postal matter on certain days in the year. The money derived from their sale is applied to works of public charity.

Nos. 114 and 157 Overprinted in Carmine **ASSISTENCIA**

1911-13 **Unwmk.** *Perf. 14x15*
RA1 A29 10r dark green .55 .40

The 20r of this type was for use on telegrams.

Perf. 15x14
RA2 A30 1c deep green 1.25 1.25

The 2c of this type was for use on telegrams.

Postal Tax Stamp of Portugal, No. RA4, Overprinted Like Nos. 155-237 in Black

1915 *Perf. 12*
RA3 PT2 1c carmine .15 .15

The 2c of this type was for use on telegrams.

Postal Tax Stamp of 1915 Surcharged **15 ctvs.**

1924
RA4 PT1 15c on 1c rose .75 *1.25*

Comrades of the Great War Issue

Postal Tax Stamps of Portugal, 1925, Overprinted **AÇORES**

1925, Apr. 8 *Perf. 11*
RA5 PT3 10c brown .40 .30
RA6 PT3 10c green .40 .30
RA7 PT3 10c rose .40 .30
RA8 PT3 10c ultra .40 .30
Nos. RA5-RA8 (4) 1.60 1.20

The use of Nos. RA5-RA11 in addition to the regular postage was compulsory on certain days. If the tax represented by these stamps was not prepaid, it was collected by means of Postal Tax Due Stamps.

In 1934-45, #RA5-RA11, RAJ1-RAJ4 were used for regular postage in Portugal.

Pombal Issue
Common Design Types

1925 *Perf. 12½*
RA9 CD28 20c dp green & black .35 .30
RA10 CD29 20c dp green & black .35 .30
RA11 CD30 20c dp green & black .35 .30
Nos. RA9-RA11 (3) 1.05 .90

POSTAL TAX DUE STAMPS

Postal Tax Due Stamp of Portugal Overprinted like Nos. RA5-RA8

1925, Apr. 8 **Unwmk.** *Perf. 11x11½*
RAJ1 PTD1 20c brown orange .40 .40

See note after No. RA8.

Pombal Issue
Common Design Types

1925, May 8 *Perf. 12½*
RAJ2 CD28 40c dp green & black .60 *4.00*
RAJ3 CD29 40c dp green & black .60 *4.00*
RAJ4 CD30 40c dp green & black .60 *4.00*
Nos. RAJ2-RAJ4 (3) 1.80 *12.00*

See note after No. RA8.
See Portugal for later issues.

BAHAMAS

bə-'hä-məs

LOCATION — A group of about 700 islands and 2,000 rocks in the West Indies, off the coast of Florida. Only 30 islands are inhabited.
GOVT. — Independent state in British Commonwealth
AREA — 5,353 sq. mi.
POP. — 209,505 (1980)
CAPITAL — Nassau

The principal island, on which the capital is located, is New Providence. The Bahamas obtained internal self-government on January 7, 1964, and independence on July 10, 1973.

12 Pence = 1 Shilling
20 Shillings = 1 Pound
100 Cents = 1 Dollar (1966)

Catalogue values for unused stamps in this country are for Never Hinged items, beginning with Scott 130, and Scott C1 in the air post section.

Values for unused stamps are for examples with original gum as defined in the catalogue introduction. Very fine examples of Nos. 2-26 will have perforations touching the design or frameline on at least one side due to the narrow spacing of the stamps on the plates. Stamps with perfs clear of the design or framelines on all four sides are extremely scarce and will command higher prices.

Pen cancellations usually indicate revenue use. Such stamps sell for much less than postally canceled copies. Beware of stamps with revenue or pen cancellations removed and forged postal cancellations added.

Queen Victoria
A1 A2

1859-60 **Unwmk.** **Engr.** *Imperf.*
1 A1 1p dull lake ('60) 50. *1,500.*
a. 1p reddish lake *4,500.* *2,100.*
b. 1p brownish lake *4,500.* *2,250.*

Most unused copies of #1 are remainders, and false cancellations are plentiful. #1a and 1b are on thicker paper than #1.

1861 ***Rough Perf. 14 to 16***
2 A1 1p lake 925. 275.
a. Clean-cut perf. ('60) 2,100. 700.
3 A2 4p dull rose 1,600. 500.
a. Imperf. between, pair *20,000.*
4 A2 6p gray lilac 3,000. 575.
a. Pale lilac 3,250. 575.

1862 **Engr.** *Perf. 11½, 12*
5 A1 1p lake 800. 175.
a. Pair, imperf. between *5,000.*
6 A2 4p dull rose 3,000. 425.
7 A2 6p gray violet 4,750. 450.

No. 5a was not issued in the Bahamas. It is unique and faulty.

Nos. 5-7 exist with perf. 11½ or 12 compound with 11.

Perf. 13
8 A1 1p brown lake 600. 125.
a. 1p carmine lake 625. 150.
9 A2 4p rose 2,750. 400.
10 A2 6p gray violet 3,250. 400.
a. 6p dull violet 3,250. 500.

Queen Victoria — A3

1863-65 **Typo.** **Wmk. 1** *Perf. 12½*
11 A1 1p lake 85.00 70.00
a. 1p brown lake 85.00 70.00
b. 1p rose lake 95.00 70.00
12 A1 1p vermilion 65.00 50.00
a. 1p rose red 70.00 55.00
b. 1p red 70.00 55.00
13 A2 4p rose 375.00 70.00
a. 4p rose lake 400.00 90.00
b. 4p bright rose 250.00 70.00
14 A2 6p dk violet 160.00 80.00
a. 6p violet 250.00 100.00
b. 6p rose lilac 5,500. *3,500.*
c. 6p lilac 275.00 70.00
15 A3 1sh green ('65) 2,500. 325.00

For surcharge see No. 26.

1863-81 *Perf. 14*
16 A1 1p vermilion 45.00 20.00
17 A1 1p car lake (anil.) 1,500.
18 A2 4p rose 400.00 50.00
a. 4p deep rose ('76) 400.00 50.00
b. 4p dull rose 1,750. 50.00
19 A3 1sh green ('80) 7.50 7.50
a. 1shp dark green 120.00 45.00

Some copies of No. 16 show a light aniline appearance and care should be taken not to confuse these with No. 17. All known used copies of No. 17 bear fiscal cancels.

1882-98 **Wmk. 2**
20 A1 1p vermilion 350.00 65.00
21 A2 4p rose 800.00 65.00
22 A3 1sh green 30.00 17.50
23 A3 1sh blue grn ('98) 35.00 22.50

Perf. 12
24 A1 1p vermilion 40.00 22.50
25 A2 4p rose 500.00 60.00

No. 14a Surcharged in Black **FOURPENCE**

1883 **Wmk. 1** *Perf. 12½*
26 A2 4p on 6p violet 675. 500.
a. Inverted surcharge *7,250.* *4,500.*

The surcharge, being handstamped, is found in various positions. Counterfeit overprints exist.

Queen Victoria
A5

Queen's Staircase
A6

1884-90 **Typo.** **Wmk. 2** *Perf. 14*
27 A5 1p carmine rose 5.00 2.00
a. 1p pale rose 45.00 10.00
28 A5 2½p ultra 8.25 2.00
a. 2½p dull blue 47.50 15.00
29 A5 4p yellow 8.25 5.00
30 A5 6p violet 5.00 *25.00*
31 A5 5sh olive green 60.00 *70.00*
32 A5 £1 brown 325.00 275.00
Revenue cancellation *55.00*
Nos. 27-32 (6) 411.50 379.00

Cleaned fiscally used copies of No. 32 are often found with postmarks of small post offices added. Dangerous forged postmarks exist, especially dated "AU 29 94."

1901-03 **Engr.** **Wmk. 1**
33 A6 1p carmine & blk 5.50 *4.00*
34 A6 5p org & blk ('03) 10.00 *40.00*
35 A6 2sh ultra & blk ('03) 20.00 *45.00*
36 A6 3sh green & blk ('03) 22.50 *47.50*
Nos. 33-36 (4) 58.00 *136.50*

See Nos. 48, 58-62, 71, 78, 81-82.

Edward VII
A7

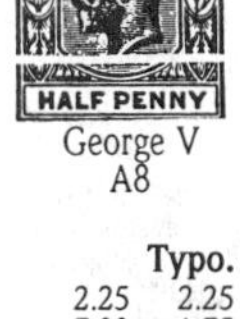

George V
A8

1902 **Wmk. 2** **Typo.**
37 A7 1p carmine rose 2.25 2.25
38 A7 2½p ultra 7.00 1.75
39 A7 4p orange 12.50 *42.50*
40 A7 6p bister brn 6.00 *14.00*
41 A7 1sh gray blk & car 16.00 *42.50*

42 A7 5sh violet & ultra 52.50 70.00
43 A7 £1 green & blk 325.00 350.00
Nos. 37-43 (7) 421.25 523.00

Beware of forged postmarks, especially dated "2 MAR 10."

1906-11 **Wmk. 3**
44 A7 ½p green 4.00 2.00
45 A7 1p car rose 19.00 2.00
46 A7 2½p ultra ('07) 19.00 21.00
47 A7 6p bister brn ('11) 35.00 50.00
Nos. 44-47 (4) 77.00 75.00

1910-16 **Engr.**
48 A6 1p red & gray blk ('16) 3.50 2.40
a. 1p carmine & black 5.50 5.50

For overprints see Nos. B1-B2.

1912-19 **Typo.**
49 A8 ½p green .85 6.00
50 A8 1p car rose (aniline) 2.10 .45
50A A8 2p gray ('19) 2.10 2.75
51 A8 2½p ultra 4.00 6.00
52 A8 4p orange 2.50 8.50
53 A8 6p bister brn 1.75 3.75

Chalky Paper
54 A8 1sh black & carmine 2.75 7.50
55 A8 5sh violet & ultra 32.50 57.50
56 A8 £1 dull grn & blk 225.00 275.00
Nos. 49-56 (9) 273.55 367.45

1917-19 **Engr.**
58 A6 3p reddish pur, *buff* 4.25 4.25
59 A6 3p brown & blk ('19) 2.75 5.50
60 A6 5p violet & blk 3.50 10.00
61 A6 2sh ultra & black 22.50 40.00
62 A6 3sh green & black 42.50 45.00
Nos. 58-62 (5) 75.50 104.75

Peace Commemorative Issue

King George V and Seal of Bahamas — A9

1920, Mar. 1 **Engr.** *Perf. 14*
65 A9 ½p gray green .85 3.75
66 A9 1p deep red 2.75 1.10
67 A9 2p gray 3.50 6.50
68 A9 3p brown 3.25 9.00
69 A9 1sh dark green 25.00 30.00
Nos. 65-69 (5) 35.35 50.35

Types of 1901-12

1921-34 **Typo., Engr. (A6)** **Wmk. 4**
70 A8 ½p green ('24) .45 .40
71 A6 1p car & black .90 1.00
72 A8 1p car rose 1.00 .20
73 A8 1½p fawn ('34) 1.50 1.40
74 A8 2p gray ('27) .90 2.75
75 A8 2½p ultra ('22) .80 2.75
76 A8 3p violet, *yel* ('31) 5.50 15.00
77 A8 4p yellow ('24) 1.60 5.25
78 A6 5p red vio & gray blk ('29) 6.50 32.50
79 A8 6p bister brn ('22) 1.25 3.25
80 A8 1sh blk & red ('26) 3.25 8.00
81 A6 2sh ultra & blk ('22) 32.50 55.00
82 A6 3sh grn & blk ('24) 55.00 65.00
83 A8 5sh vio & ultra ('24) 30.00 47.50
84 A8 £1 grn & blk ('26) 160.00 275.00
Nos. 70-84 (15) 301.15 515.00

The 3p, 1sh, 5sh and £1 are on chalky paper.

Seal of Bahamas — A10

1930, Jan. 2 **Engr.** *Perf. 12*
85 A10 1p red & black 1.50 2.50
86 A10 3p dp brown & blk 3.00 12.50
87 A10 5p dk vio & blk 3.50 12.50
88 A10 2sh ultra & black 20.00 37.50
89 A10 3sh dp green & blk 32.50 65.00
Nos. 85-89 (5) 60.50 130.00

The dates on the stamps commemorate important events in the history of the colony. The 1st British occupation was in 1629. The Bahamas were ceded to Great Britain in 1729 and a treaty of peace was signed by that country, France and Spain.

Type of 1930 Issue
Without Dates at Top

1931-46
90 A10 2sh ultra & black ('43) 4.75 2.50
a. 2sh ultra & slate purple 18.00 22.00
91 A10 3sh dp green & blk ('46) 3.75 1.90
a. 3sh deep grn & slate purple 27.50 22.50

Nos. 90a-91a are on thick paper with yellowish gum, Nos. 90-91 are on thin white paper with colorless gum.

For overprints see Nos. 126-127.

Common Design Types pictured following the introduction.

Silver Jubilee Issue
Common Design Type

1935, May 6 *Perf. 13½x14*
92 CD301 1½p car & blue .65 1.60
93 CD301 2½p blue & brn 2.50 5.00
94 CD301 6p ol grn & lt bl 5.00 7.50
95 CD301 1sh brt vio & ind 6.50 7.25
Nos. 92-95 (4) 14.65 21.35
Set, never hinged 30.00

Flamingos in Flight — A11

1935, May 22 *Perf. 12½*
96 A11 8p car & ultra 5.00 3.25
Never hinged 8.50

Coronation Issue
Common Design Type

1937, May 12 *Perf. 13½x14*
97 CD302 ½p dp green .15 .15
98 CD302 1½p brown .25 .25
99 CD302 2½p brt ultra .65 .65
Nos. 97-99 (3) 1.05 1.05
Set, never hinged 1.65

George VI — A12

Sea Gardens, Nassau — A13

Fort Charlotte A14

Flamingos in Flight — A15

1938-46 **Typo.** **Wmk. 4** *Perf. 14*
100 A12 ½p green .15 .65
101 A12 1p carmine 4.00 4.50
101A A12 1p gray ('41) .25 .50
102 A12 1½p red brown .60 1.00
103 A12 2p gray 12.00 5.75
103B A12 2p carmine ('41) .35 .55
c. "TWO PENCE" double 2,750.
104 A12 2½p ultra 1.90 2.00
104A A12 2½p lt violet ('43) .60 .65
b. "2½ PENNY" double 2,000. —
105 A12 3p lt violet 7.50 9.00
105A A12 3p ultra ('43) .40 .90

Engr.
Perf. 12½
106 A13 4p red org & blue .60 .65
107 A14 6p blue & ol grn .45 .65
108 A15 8p car & ultra 2.40 1.90

Typo.
Perf. 14
109 A12 10p yel org ('46) .95 .60
110 A12 1sh black & bright red 3.25 .50
112 A12 5sh pur & ultra 11.00 9.00
a. 5sh lilac & blue 12.50 10.50
113 A12 £1 bl grn & blk 37.50 42.50
Nos. 100-113 (17) 83.90 81.30
Set, never hinged 141.80

#110-113 printed on chalky & ordinary paper.
See Nos. 154-156. For overprints see Nos. 116-125, 128-129.

No. 104 Surcharged in Black **3d.**

1940, Nov. 28 *Perf. 14*
115 A12 3p on 2½p ultra .30 .30
Never hinged .55

Stamps of 1931-42 Overprinted in Black **1492 LANDFALL OF COLUMBUS 1942**

1942, Oct. 12 *Perf. 14, 12½, 12*
116 A12 ½p green .15 .15
117 A12 1p gray .15 .15
118 A12 1½p red brn .20 .15
119 A12 2p carmine .15 .15
120 A12 2½p ultra .15 .15
121 A12 3p ultra .15 .15
122 A13 4p red org & blue .25 .20
123 A14 6p blue & ol grn .35 .25
124 A15 8p car & ultra .50 .30
125 A12 1sh black & car 1.75 .40
126 A10 2sh dk ultra & blk 5.50 9.50
a. 2sh ultra & slate purple 7.50 15.00
127 A10 3sh dp grn & sl pur 3.00 9.00
a. 3sh deep green & black 19.00 17.00
128 A12 5sh lilac & ultra 8.50 9.00
129 A12 £1 green & black 20.00 30.00
Nos. 116-129 (14) 40.80 59.55
Set, never hinged 64.00

450th anniv. of the discovery of America by Columbus.

Nos. 125, 128-129 printed on chalky and ordinary paper.

Two printings of the basic stamps were overprinted, the first with dark gum, the second with white gum.

Catalogue values for unused stamps in this section, from this point to the end of the section, are for Never Hinged items.

Peace Issue
Common Design Type
Perf. 13½x14

1946, Nov. 11 **Engr.** **Wmk. 4**
130 CD303 1½p brown .15 .15
131 CD303 3p deep blue .20 .20

Infant Welfare Clinic — A16

Designs: 1p, Modern agriculture. 1½p, Sisal. 2p, Native straw work. 2½p, Modern dairying. 3p, Fishing fleet. 4p, Out island settlement. 6p, Tuna fishing. 8p, Paradise Beach. 10p, Modern hotel. 1sh, Yacht racing. 2sh, Water skiing. 3sh, Shipbuilding. 5sh, Modern transportation. 10sh, Modern salt production. £1, Parliament Building.

1948, Oct. 11 **Unwmk.** *Perf. 12*
132 A16 ½p orange .15 .15
133 A16 1p olive green .15 .15
134 A16 1½p olive bister .35 .35
135 A16 2p vermilion .25 .20
136 A16 2½p red brown .65 .60
137 A16 3p brt ultra .45 .45
138 A16 4p gray black .45 .75
139 A16 6p emerald .65 .75
140 A16 8p violet .65 .75
141 A16 10p rose car .70 .75
142 A16 1sh olive brn 1.25 1.10
143 A16 2sh claret 6.25 6.00
144 A16 3sh brt blue 6.25 6.00
145 A16 5sh purple 5.00 6.00
146 A16 10sh dk gray 5.00 7.00
147 A16 £1 red orange 10.00 12.00
Nos. 132-147 (16) 38.20 43.00

300th anniv., in 1947, of the settlement of the colony.

Silver Wedding Issue
Common Design Type
Perf. 14x14½

1948, Dec. 1 **Wmk. 4** **Photo.**
148 CD304 1½p red brown .20 .15

Engr.; Name Typo.
Perf. 11½x11
149 CD305 £1 gray green 30.00 35.00

UPU Issue
Common Design Types
Engr.; Name Typo. on #151 & 152

1949, Oct. 10 *Perf. 13½, 11x11½*
150 CD306 2½p violet .25 .25
151 CD307 3p indigo .50 .50
152 CD308 6p blue gray 1.00 1.00
153 CD309 1sh rose car 1.65 1.65
Nos. 150-153 (4) 3.40 3.40

George VI Type of 1938
Perf. 13½x14

1951-52 **Wmk. 4** **Typo.**
154 A12 ½p claret ('52) .50 .20
a. Wmk. 4a (error) 1,750.
155 A12 2p green .50 .40
156 A12 3p rose red ('52) .70 3.00
Nos. 154-156 (3) 1.70 3.60

Coronation Issue
Common Design Type

1953, June 3 **Engr.** *Perf. 13½x13*
157 CD312 6p blue & black .60 .60

Infant Welfare Clinic — A17

Designs: 1p, Modern Agriculture. 1½p, Out island settlement. 2p, Native strawwork. 3p, Fishing fleet. 4p, Water skiing. 5p, Modern dairying. 6p, Modern transportation. 8p, Paradise Beach. 10p, Modern hotels. 1sh, Yacht racing. 2sh, Sisal. 2sh6p, Shipbuilding. 5sh, Tuna fishing. 10sh, Modern salt production. £1, Parliament Building.

1954, Jan. 1 *Perf. 11x11½*
158 A17 ½p red org & blk .15 .15
159 A17 1p org brn & ol grn .15 .15
a. Booklet pane of 4 .55
160 A17 1½p black & blue .15 .15
a. Booklet pane of 4 .70
161 A17 2p dk grn & brn org .15 .15
a. Booklet pane of 4 .70
162 A17 3p dp car & blk .20 .15
163 A17 4p lil rose & bl green .30 .25
a. Booklet pane of 4 1.75
164 A17 5p dp ultra & brn .65 1.75
165 A17 6p blk & aqua .45 .25
a. Booklet pane of 4 2.25
166 A17 8p rose vio & blk .50 .25
a. Booklet pane of 4 2.50
167 A17 10p ultra & blk .55 .35
168 A17 1sh ol brn & ultra .65 .50
169 A17 2sh blk & brn org 1.10 .75
170 A17 2sh6p dp bl & blk 2.50 1.10
171 A17 5sh dp org & emer 5.00 2.50
172 A17 10sh grnsh blk & black 7.00 5.00
173 A17 £1 vio & grnsh black 15.00 11.00
Nos. 158-173 (16) 34.50 24.45

See No. 203. For types overprinted or surcharged see Nos. 181-182, 185-200, 202.

Queen Elizabeth II — A18

Wmk. 314

1959, June 10 **Engr.** *Perf. 13*
174 A18 1p dk red & black .15 .15
175 A18 2p green & black .15 .15
176 A18 6p blue & black .30 .30
177 A18 10p brown & black .55 .55
Nos. 174-177 (4) 1.15 1.15

Cent. of the 1st postage stamp of Bahamas.

Christ Church Cathedral, Nassau — A19

Perf. 14x13

1962, Jan. 30 **Photo.** **Unwmk.**
178 A19 8p shown .60 .60
179 A19 10p Public library .60 .60

Centenary of the city of Nassau.

Freedom from Hunger Issue
Common Design Type
Perf. 14x14½

1963, June 4		Wmk. 314
180 CD314 8p sepia	1.25	1.10
a. "8d" and "BAHAMAS" omitted	875.00	

Nos. 166-167 Overprinted: "BAHAMAS TALKS/ 1962"
Perf. 11x11½

1963, July 15	Engr.	Wmk. 4
181 A17 8p rose vio & black	1.00	.85
182 A17 10p ultra & black	1.75	1.65

Meeting of Pres. Kennedy and Prime Minister Harold Macmillan, Dec. 1962.

Red Cross Centenary Issue
Common Design Type
Wmk. 314

1963, Sept. 2	Litho.	Perf. 13
183 CD315 1p black & red	.20	.15
184 CD315 10p black & red	2.00	1.40

Type of 1954 Overprinted: "NEW CONSTITUTION/ 1964"
Designs as Before
Perf. 11x11½

1964, Jan. 7	Engr.	Wmk. 314
185 A17 ½p red org & blk	.15	.15
186 A17 1p org brn & ol green	.15	.15
187 A17 1½p black & blue	.15	.15
188 A17 2p dk grn & brn org	.15	.15
189 A17 3p dp car & blk	.15	.15
190 A17 4p lil rose & bl green	.20	.20
191 A17 5p dp ultra & brn	.20	.20
192 A17 6p blk & aqua	.25	.20
193 A17 8p rose vio & blk	.35	.30
194 A17 10p ultra & black	.45	.35
195 A17 1sh ol brn & ultra	.60	.45
196 A17 2sh blk & brn org	1.25	.95
197 A17 2sh6p dp bl & blk	1.50	1.25
198 A17 5sh dp org & emer	3.00	2.50
199 A17 10sh grnsh blk & black	5.50	4.75
200 A17 £1 vio & grnsh black	11.50	9.50
Nos. 185-200 (16)	25.55	21.35

Shakespeare Issue
Common Design Type
Perf. 14x14½

1964, Apr. 23	Photo.	Wmk. 314
201 CD316 6p greenish blue	.45	.35

Type of 1954 Surcharged with Olympic Rings, New Value and Bars
Perf. 11x11½

1964, Oct. 1	Engr.	Wmk. 314
202 A17 8p on 1sh ol brn & ultra	.45	.45

18th Olympic Games, Tokyo, Oct. 10-25.

Queen Type of 1954

1964, Oct. 6		Wmk. 314
203 A17 2p dk grn & brn org	.50	.50

Out Island Regatta — A21

Designs: ½p, Colony badge. 1½p, Princess Margaret Hospital. 2p, High School. 3p, Flamingo. 4p, Liner "Queen Elizabeth." 6p, Island development. 8p, Yachting. 10p, Public Square, Nassau. 1sh, Sea Garden, Nassau. 2sh, Cannons at Fort Charlotte. 2sh6p, Sea plane and jetliner. 5sh, 1914 Williamson film project and 1939 underwater post office. 10sh, Conch shell. £1, Columbus' flagship.

Engr. and Litho.

1965, Jan. 7		Perf. 13½x13
204 A21 ½p multi, bluish	.15	.15
205 A21 1p multi	.15	.15
a. Booklet pane of 4	.40	
206 A21 1½p multi	.15	.15
a. Booklet pane of 4	.45	
207 A21 2p multi	.15	.15
a. Booklet pane of 4	.55	
208 A21 3p multi	.20	.15
209 A21 4p multi	.25	.15
a. Booklet pane of 4	1.10	
210 A21 6p multi	.30	.15
a. Booklet pane of 4	1.25	
211 A21 8p multi	.40	.30
a. Booklet pane of 4	1.65	
212 A21 10p multi	.35	.15
213 A21 1sh multi, grnsh	.55	.25
214 A21 2sh multi, grnsh	1.10	.65
215 A21 2sh6p multi	1.50	.80
216 A21 5sh multi	3.00	1.60
217 A21 10sh multi	6.00	3.75
218 A21 £1 multi	12.00	7.25
Nos. 204-218 (15)	26.25	15.80

Booklet panes were issued Mar. 23, 1965.
See Nos. 252-266. For surcharges see Nos. 221, 230-244.

ITU Issue
Common Design Type
Perf. 11x11½

1965, May 17	Litho.	Wmk. 314
219 CD317 1p emerald & org	.20	.20
220 CD317 2sh lilac & olive	2.25	2.25

No. 211 Surcharged ≡ 9d

Perf. 13½x13

1965, July 12	Engr. & Litho.	
221 A21 9p on 8p multi	.60	.60

Intl. Cooperation Year Issue
Common Design Type
Perf. 14½

1965, Oct. 25	Wmk. 314	Litho.
222 CD318 ½p blue grn & claret	.15	.15
223 CD318 1sh lt violet & grn	.85	.70

Churchill Memorial Issue
Common Design Type

1966, Jan. 24	Photo.	Perf. 14
224 CD319 ½p multicolored	.15	.15
225 CD319 2p multicolored	.20	.20
226 CD319 10p multicolored	1.00	1.00
227 CD319 1sh multicolored	1.50	1.50
Nos. 224-227 (4)	2.85	2.85

Royal Visit Issue
Common Design Type Inscribed "Royal Visit / 1966"

1966, Feb. 4	Litho.	Perf. 11x12
228 CD320 6p violet blue	.65	.65
229 CD320 1sh dk car rose	1.65	1.65

Nos. 204-218 Surcharged ≡ 2c

Perf. 13½x13
Engr. & Litho.

1966, May 25		Wmk. 314
230 A21 1c on ½p multi	.15	.15
231 A21 2c on 1p multi	.15	.15
232 A21 3c on 2p multi	.15	.15
233 A21 4c on 3p multi	.15	.15
234 A21 5c on 4p multi	.15	.15
a. Surch. omitted, vert. strip of 7-10	3,000.	
235 A21 8c on 6p multi	.20	.20
236 A21 10c on 8p multi	.25	.25
237 A21 11c on 1½p multi	.35	.25
238 A21 12c on 10p multi	.40	.30
239 A21 15c on 1sh multi	.48	.35
240 A21 22c on 2sh multi	.65	.40
241 A21 50c on 2sh6p multi	1.40	1.25
242 A21 $1 on 5sh multi	2.50	2.50
243 A21 $2 on 10sh multi	5.50	5.00
244 A21 $3 on £1 multi	8.00	7.50
Nos. 230-244 (15)	20.48	18.75

The denominations are next to the bars instead of below on Nos. 232, 235-240; the length of the bars varies to cover old denomination.
No. 234a, if single, is identical with No. 209, but distinguishable if in vertical strip of 7 to 10. No. 234 was printed in sheets of 100 (10x10); No. 209 in sheets of 60 (10x6).

World Cup Soccer Issue
Common Design Type

1966, July 1		Perf. 14
245 CD321 8c multicolored	.30	.30
246 CD321 15c multicolored	.60	.60

WHO Headquarters Issue
Common Design Type

1966, Sept. 20	Litho.	Perf. 14
247 CD322 11c multicolored	.50	.50
248 CD322 15c multicolored	.70	.70

UNESCO Anniversary Issue
Common Design Type

1966, Dec. 1	Litho.	Perf. 14
249 CD323 3c "Education"	.15	.15
250 CD323 15c "Science"	.65	.65
251 CD323 $1 "Culture"	3.25	3.25
Nos. 249-251 (3)	4.05	4.05

Type of 1965 Values in Cents and Dollars
Perf. 13½x13

1967, May 25	Engr. & Litho.	

Designs: 1c, Colony badge. 2c, Out Island Regatta. 3c, High School. 4c, Flamingo. 5c, Liner "Oceanic." 8c, Island development. 10c, Yachting. 11c, Princess Margaret Hospital. 12c, Public Square, Nassau. 15c, Sea Garden, Nassau. 22c, Cannon at Fort Charlotte. 50c, Sea plane and jetliner. $1, 1914 Williamson film project and 1939 underwater post office. $2, Conch shell. $3, Columbus' flagship.

252 A21 1c brown & multi	.15	.15
253 A21 2c grn, slate & bl	.15	.15
254 A21 3c grn, indigo & vio	.15	.15
255 A21 4c ultra, blue & red	.15	.15
256 A21 5c pur, bl & indigo	.15	.15
257 A21 8c dk brn, bl & dl grn	.20	.20
258 A21 10c car rose, bl & pur	.25	.20
259 A21 11c bl, grn & rose red	.35	.25
260 A21 12c ol grn, bl & lt brn	.40	.20
261 A21 15c rose & multi	.50	.30
262 A21 22c rose red, brn & bl	.60	.40
263 A21 50c emer, ol & bl	1.40	.90
264 A21 $1 sep, brn org & dk blue	2.75	1.75
265 A21 $2 green & multi	5.50	4.25
266 A21 $3 pur, bl & brn org	8.50	6.75
Nos. 252-266 (15)	21.20	15.95

Nos. 252-266 are on toned paper. Printings on very white, untinted paper appeared between late 1969 and May, 1971. Value, set $500.

Seal of Bahamas, Queen Elizabeth II and Lord Baden-Powell — A22

60th anniv. of world Scouting: 15c, Scout emblem and portraits as on 3c.

Perf. 14x13½

1967, Sept. 1	Photo.	Wmk. 314
267 A22 3c multicolored	.25	.25
268 A22 15c multicolored	.85	.85

Human Rights Flame and Globe — A23

Intl. Human Rights Year: 12c, Human rights flame and scales of justice. $1, Human rights flame and Seal of Bahamas.

1968, May 13	Litho.	Perf. 14
269 A23 3c multicolored	.15	.15
270 A23 12c multicolored	.50	.50
271 A23 $1 multicolored	2.25	2.25
Nos. 269-271 (3)	2.90	2.90

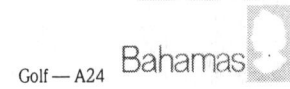

Golf — A24

Tourist Publicity: 11c, Yachting. 15c, Horse racing. 50c, Water skiing.

1968, Aug. 20	Unwmk.	Perf. 13½
272 A24 5c multicolored	.25	.25
273 A24 11c multicolored	.52	.52
274 A24 15c multicolored	.65	.65
275 A24 50c multicolored	2.25	2.25
Nos. 272-275 (4)	3.67	3.67

Olympic Monument and Sailboat — A25

Olympic Monument, San Salvador Island, Bahamas, and: 11c, Long jump. 50c, Running. $1, Sailing.

1968, Sept. 30	Photo.	Perf. 14½x14
276 A25 5c multicolored	.20	.20
277 A25 11c multicolored	.40	.40
278 A25 50c multicolored	1.65	1.65
279 A25 $1 multicolored	3.50	3.50
Nos. 276-279 (4)	5.75	5.75

19th Olympic Games, Mexico City, Oct. 12-27.

Legislative Building — A26

Designs: 10c, Bahamas mace and Big Ben, London, vert. 12c, Local straw market, vert. 15c, Horse-drawn surrey.

Perf. 14½

1968, Nov. 1	Unwmk.	Litho.
280 A26 3c brt blue & multi	.15	.15
281 A26 10c dark blue	.40	.40
282 A26 12c brt rose & multi	.45	.45
283 A26 15c multicolored	.50	.50
Nos. 280-283 (4)	1.50	1.50

14th Commonwealth Parliamentary Conf., Nassau, Nov. 1-8.

$100 Coin with Queen Elizabeth II and Landing of Columbus — A27

Gold Coins with Elizabeth II on Obverse: 12c, $50 coin and Santa Maria flagship. 15c, $20 coin and Nassau Harbor Lighthouse. $1, $10 coin and Fort.

Engr. on Gold Paper

1968, Dec. 2	Unwmk.	Perf. 13½
284 A27 3c dark red	.20	.20
285 A27 12c dark green	.65	.65
286 A27 15c lilac	.75	.75
287 A27 $1 black	4.50	2.50
Nos. 284-287 (4)	6.10	4.10

First gold coinage in the Bahamas.

Bahamas Postal Card and Airplane Wing — A28

Design: 15c, Seaplane, 1929.

Perf. 14½x14

1969, Jan. 30	Litho.	Unwmk.
288 A28 12c multicolored	.90	.90
289 A28 15c multicolored	1.10	1.10

50th anniv. of the 1st flight from Nassau, Bahamas, to Miami, Fla., Jan. 30, 1919.

Game Fishing Boats — A29

Designs: 11c, Paradise Beach. 12c, Sunfish sailboats. 15c, Parade on Rawson Square.

BAHAMAS

1969, Aug. 26   Litho.   Wmk. 314
290	A29	3c multicolored	.20	.20
291	A29	6c multicolored	.60	.60
292	A29	12c multicolored	.65	.65
293	A29	15c multicolored	.80	.80
a.	Souvenir sheet of 4, #290-293	4.25	4.25
	Nos. 290-293 (4)	2.25	2.25

Tourist publicity.

Holy Family, by Nicolas Poussin — A30

Paintings: 3c, Adoration of the Shepherds, by Louis Le Nain. 12c, Adoration of the Kings, by Gerard David. 15c, Adoration of the Kings, by Vincenzo Foppa.

1969, Oct. 15   Photo.   Perf. 12
294	A30	3c red & multi	.15	.15
295	A30	11c emerald & multi	.60	.60
296	A30	12c ultra & multi	.70	.70
297	A30	15c multicolored	.90	.90
	Nos. 294-297 (4)	2.35	2.35

Christmas.

Girl Guides, Globe and Flags — A31

Designs: 12c, Yellow elder and Brownie emblem. 15c, Ranger emblem.

1970, Feb. 23   Wmk. 314   Perf. 14½
298	A31	3c vio blue, yel & red	.20	.20
299	A31	12c dk brn, grn & yel	.60	.60
300	A31	15c vio bl, bluish grn & yel	.80	.80
	Nos. 298-300 (3)	1.60	1.60

60th anniversary of the Girl Guides.

Opening of UPU Headquarters, Bern — A32

1970, May 20   Litho.   Perf. 14½
301	A32	3c ver & multi	.15	.15
302	A32	15c orange & multi	.75	.75

Bus and Globe A33

Globe and: 11c, Train. 12c, Sailboat and ship. 15c, Plane.

1970, July 14   Perf. 13½x13
303	A33	3c orange & multi	.20	.20
304	A33	11c emerald & multi	.65	.65
305	A33	12c multicolored	.70	.70
306	A33	15c blue & multi	1.00	1.00
a.	Souvenir sheet of 4, #303-306	9.00	9.00
	Nos. 303-306 (4)	2.55	2.55

Issued to promote good will through world-wide travel and tourism.

People, Palms and Flamingo A34

15c, Red Cross Headquarters, Nassau & marlin.

1970, Aug. 18   Perf. 14x14½
307	A34	3c multicolored	.15	.15
308	A34	15c multicolored	.80	.80

Centenary of British Red Cross Society.

Nativity by G. B. Pittoni — A35

Christmas: 11c, Holy Family, by Anton Raphael Mengs. 12c, Adoration of the Kings, by Giorgione. 15c, Adoration of the Shepherds, School of Seville.

Perf. 12½x13

1970, Nov. 3   Litho.   Wmk. 314
309	A35	3c multicolored	.20	.20
310	A35	11c red org & multi	.55	.55
311	A35	12c emerald & multi	.65	.65
312	A35	15c blue & multi	.80	.80
a.	Souv. sheet of 4, #309-312 + 3 labels	2.25	2.25
	Nos. 309-312 (4)	2.20	2.20

International Airport — A36

Designs: 2c, Breadfruit. 3c, Straw market. 4c, 6c, Hawksbill turtle. 5c, Grouper. 8c, Yellow elder. 10c, Bahamian sponge boat. 11c, Flamingos. 7c, 12c, Hibiscus. 15c, Bonefish. 18c, 22c, Royal poinciana. 50c, Post office, Nassau. $1, Pineapple, vert. $2, Crayfish, vert. $3, "Junkanoo" (costumed drummer), vert.

Wmk. 314 Upright (Sideways on $1, $2, $3)

1971   Perf. 14½x14, 14x14½
313	A36	1c blue & multi	.15	.15
314	A36	2c red & multi	.15	.15
315	A36	3c lilac & multi	.15	.15
316	A36	4c brown & multi	.42	.42
317	A36	5c dp org & multi	.30	.28
318	A36	6c brown & multi	.15	.15
319	A36	7c green & multi	.30	.28
320	A36	8c yel & multi	.65	.40
321	A36	10c red & multi	.38	.38
322	A36	11c red & multi	.40	.40
323	A36	12c green & multi	1.10	1.10
324	A36	15c gray & multi	.32	.32
325	A36	18c multicolored	.40	.40
326	A36	22c green & multi	1.40	1.40
327	A36	50c multicolored	1.65	1.40
328	A36	$1 red & multi	3.50	2.75
329	A36	$2 blue & multi	6.75	5.50
330	A36	$3 vio bl & multi	10.00	8.75
	Nos. 313-330 (18)	28.17	24.38

See Nos. 398-401, 426-443.

Wmk. 314 Sideways (Upright on $1, $2, $3)

1973
317a	A36	5c	.16	.16
320a	A36	8c	.24	.24
327a	A36	50c	1.40	1.40
328a	A36	$1	3.00	3.00
329a	A36	$2	5.50	5.50
330a	A36	$3	8.50	8.50
	Nos. 317a-330a (6)	18.80	18.80

1976   Wmk. 373
313a	A36	1c	.15	.15
314a	A36	2c	.15	.15
315a	A36	3c	.15	.15
317b	A36	5c	.15	.15
320b	A36	8c	.15	.15
321a	A36	10c	.18	.18
327b	A36	50c	1.25	1.25
328b	A36	$1	2.50	2.50
329b	A36	$2	4.75	4.75
330b	A36	$3	7.50	7.50
	Nos. 313a-330b (10)	16.93	16.93

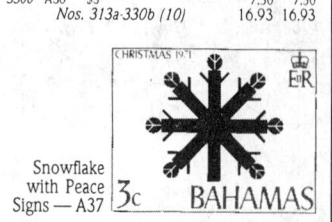

Snowflake with Peace Signs — A37

Christmas: 11c, "Peace on Earth" with doves. 15c, Christmas wreath around old Bahamas coat of arms. 18c, Star of Bethlehem over palms.

Perf. 14x14½

1971   Photo.   Wmk. 314
331	A37	3c dp lil rose, gold & org	.15	.15
332	A37	11c violet & gold	.45	.45
333	A37	15c gold embossed & multi	.65	.65
334	A37	18c brt bl, gold & vio bl	.90	.90
a.	Souv. sheet of 4, #331-334, perf. 15	2.50	2.50
	Nos. 331-334 (4)	2.15	2.15

High Jump, Arms of Bahamas A38

Olympic Rings, Compass, Arms of Bahamas and: 11c, Bicycling. 15c, Running. 18c, Sailing.

1972, June 27   Litho.   Perf. 13x13½
335	A38	10c lt violet & multi	.40	.40
336	A38	11c ocher & multi	.48	.48
337	A38	15c yel green & multi	.70	.70
338	A38	18c blue & multi	.95	.95
a.	Souvenir sheet of 4, #335-338	3.25	4.50
	Nos. 335-338 (4)	2.53	2.53

20th Olympic Games, Munich, Aug. 26-Sept. 10.

Shepherd and Star of Bethlehem — A39

Designs: 6c, Bells. 15c, Holly and monstrance. 20c, Poinsettia.

1972, Oct. 3   Wmk. 314   Perf. 14
339	A39	3c gold & multi	.15	.15
340	A39	6c black & multi	.28	.28
341	A39	15c black & multi	.70	.70
342	A39	20c gold & multi	.95	.95
a.	Souvenir sheet of 4, #339-342	2.75	3.25
	Nos. 339-342 (4)	2.08	2.08

Christmas. Gold on 15c is embossed.

Souvenir Sheet

Map of Bahama Islands — A40

1972, Nov. 1   Litho.   Perf. 15
343	A40	Sheet of 4	3.75	4.75
a.	11c blue & multi	.35	.35
b.	15c blue & multi	.45	.45
c.	18c blue & multi	.52	.52
d.	50c blue & multi	1.50	1.50

Tourism Year of the Americas.

Silver Wedding Issue, 1972
Common Design Type

Design: Queen Elizabeth II, Prince Philip, mace and galleon.

Perf. 14x14½

1972, Nov. 13   Photo.   Wmk. 314
344	CD324	11c car rose & multi	.35	.35
345	CD324	18c violet & multi	.55	.55

Weather Satellite, WMO Emblem A41

1973, Apr. 3   Litho.   Perf. 14
346	A41	15c shown	.65	.65
347	A41	18c Weather radar	.90	.90

Intl. meteorological cooperation, cent.

Clarence A. Bain — A42    Virgin in Prayer, by Sassoferrato — A43

Independence: 11c, New Bahamian coat of arms. 15c, New flag and Government House. $1, Milo B. Butler, Sr.

1973   Wmk. 314   Perf. 14½x14
348	A42	3c lilac & multi	.15	.15
349	A42	11c lt blue & multi	.30	.30
350	A42	15c lt green & multi	.45	.45
351	A42	$1 yel & multi	2.25	2.25
a.	Souvenir sheet of 4, #348-351	3.50	4.50
	Nos. 348-351 (4)	3.15	3.15

Issued: #348-350, July 10; #351, 351a, Aug. 1.

1973, Oct. 16   Litho.   Perf. 14

Christmas: 11c, Virgin and Child with St. John, by Filippino Lippi. 15c, Choir of Angels, by Marmion. 18c, The Two Trinities, by Murillo.

352	A43	3c blue & multi	.18	.18
353	A43	11c multicolored	.60	.60
354	A43	15c gray grn & multi	.80	.80
355	A43	18c lil rose & multi	1.10	1.10
a.	Souvenir sheet of 4, #352-355	2.75	3.75
	Nos. 352-355 (4)	2.68	2.68

Agriculture, Science and Medicine — A44

18c, Symbols of engineering, art, and law.

1974, Feb. 5   Litho.   Perf. 13½x14
356	A44	15c dull grn & multi	.48	.48
357	A44	18c multicolored	.65	.65

University of the West Indies, 25th anniv.

UPU Emblem A45

Designs: 13c, UPU emblem, vert. 14c, UPU emblem. 18c, UPU monument, Bern, vert.

1974, Apr. 23   Perf. 14
358	A45	3c multicolored	.15	.15
359	A45	13c multicolored	.45	.45
360	A45	14c olive bis & multi	.52	.52
361	A45	18c multicolored	.80	.80
a.	Souvenir sheet of 4, #358-361	1.90	2.25
	Nos. 358-361 (4)	1.92	1.92

Centenary of Universal Postal Union.

Roseate Spoonbills, Trust Emblem — A46

Protected Birds (National Trust Emblem and): 14c, White-crowned pigeons. 21c, White-tailed tropic birds. 36c, Bahamian parrot.

1974, Sept. 10   Litho.   Perf. 14
362	A46	13c multicolored	.95	.70
363	A46	14c multicolored	.95	.70
364	A46	21c multicolored	1.40	1.10

BAHAMAS

365 A46	36c multicolored	2.50	1.75
a.	Souvenir sheet of 4, #362-365	7.50	8.50
	Nos. 362-365 (4)	5.80	4.25

Bahamas National Trust, 15th anniv.

Holy Family, by Jacques de Stella — A47

Christmas: 10c, Virgin and Child, by Girolamo Romanino. 12c, Virgin and Child with St. John and St. Catherine, by Andrea Previtali. 21c, Virgin and Child with Angels, by Previtali.

1974, Oct. 29   Wmk. 314   Perf. 13

366 A47	8c black & multi	.40	.40
367 A47	10c green & multi	.48	.48
368 A47	12c red & multi	.60	.60
369 A47	21c ultra & multi	1.00	1.00
a.	Souvenir sheet of 4, #366-369	2.50	2.50
	Nos. 366-369 (4)	2.48	2.48

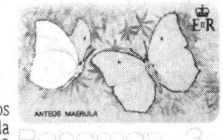

Anteos Maerula — A48

1975, Feb. 4   Litho.   Perf. 14x13½

370 A48	3c shown	.28	.24
371 A48	14c Eurema nicippe	1.00	.70
372 A48	18c Papilio andraemon	1.25	1.00
373 A48	21c Euptoieta hegesia	1.50	1.40
a.	Souvenir sheet of 4, #370-373	6.00	5.00
	Nos. 370-373 (4)	4.03	3.34

Sheep Raising — A49

Designs: 14c, Electric reel fishing, vert. 18c, Growing food. 21c, Crude oil refinery, vert.

Unwmk.

1975, May 27   Litho.   Perf. 14

374 A49	3c dull grn & multi	.15	.15
375 A49	14c green & multi	.50	.50
376 A49	18c brown & multi	.65	.65
377 A49	21c vio bl & multi	.75	.75
a.	Souvenir sheet of 4, #374-377	2.25	2.25
	Nos. 374-377 (4)	2.05	2.05

Economic diversification.

Rowena Rand, Staff and Chrismon — A50

Plant and IWY Emblem — A51

Wmk. 373

1975, July 22   Litho.   Perf. 14

378 A50	14c multicolored	.60	.60
379 A51	18c multicolored	.80	.80

International Women's Year.

Adoration of the Shepherds, by Perugino — A52

Christmas: 8c, 18c, Adoration of the Kings, by Ghirlandaio. 21c, like 3c.

1975, Dec. 2   Litho.   Perf. 13½

380 A52	3c dk green & multi	.15	.15
381 A52	8c dk violet & multi	.30	.30
382 A52	18c purple & multi	.70	.70
383 A52	21c maroon & multi	.85	.85
a.	Souvenir sheet of 4, #380-383	2.25	2.25
	Nos. 380-383 (4)	2.00	2.00

Telephones, 1876 and 1976 — A53

Designs: 16c, Radio-telephone link, Deleporte, Nassau (radar). 21c, Alexander Graham Bell. 25c, Communications satellite.

1976, Mar. 23   Litho.   Perf. 14

384 A53	3c multicolored	.15	.15
385 A53	16c multicolored	.40	.40
386 A53	21c multicolored	.52	.52
387 A53	25c multicolored	.65	.65
	Nos. 384-387 (4)	1.72	1.72

Centenary of first telephone call by Alexander Graham Bell, Mar. 10, 1876.

Bicycling and Olympic Rings — A54

Olympic Rings and: 16c, Long jump. 25c, Sailing. 40c, Boxing.

1976, July 13   Litho.   Perf. 14

388 A54	8c magenta & blue	.24	.24
389 A54	16c orange & brn	.42	.42
390 A54	25c magenta & blue	.60	.60
391 A54	40c orange & brn	1.10	1.10
a.	Souvenir sheet of 4, #388-391	2.75	2.75
	Nos. 388-391 (4)	2.36	2.36

21st Olympic Games, Montreal, Canada, July 17-Aug. 1.

John Murray, Earl of Dunmore — A55

Design: 16c, Map of US and Bahamas.

1976, June 1   Wmk. 373   Perf. 14

392 A55	16c multicolored	.52	.52
393 A55	$1 multicolored	2.50	2.50
a.	Souvenir sheet of 4, #393	10.00	10.00

American Bicentennial.

Virgin and Child, Filippo Lippi — A56

Christmas: 21c, Adoration of the Shepherds, School of Seville. 25c, Adoration of the Kings, by Vincenzo Foppa. 40c, Virgin and Child, by Vivarini.

1976, Oct. 19   Litho.   Perf. 14½x14

394 A56	3c brt blue & multi	.15	.15
395 A56	21c dp org & multi	.60	.60
396 A56	25c emerald & multi	.75	.75
397 A56	40c red lilac & multi	1.10	1.10
a.	Souvenir sheet of 4, #394-397	2.75	2.75
	Nos. 394-397 (4)	2.60	2.60

Type of 1971

Designs: 16c, Hibiscus. 21c, Breadfruit. 25c, Hawksbill turtle. 40c, Bahamian sponge boat.

1976, Nov. 2   Litho.   Wmk. 373

398 A36	16c emerald & multi	.35	.35
399 A36	21c vermilion & multi	.38	.38
400 A36	25c brown & multi	.52	.52
401 A36	40c vermilion & multi	.70	.70
	Nos. 398-401 (4)	1.95	1.95

Elizabeth II Seated under Gold Canopy — A57

Designs: 16c, Coronation. 21c, Taking and signing of oath. 40c, Queen holding orb and scepter.

1977, Feb. 7   Perf. 12

402 A57	8c silver & multi	.20	.20
403 A57	16c silver & multi	.35	.35
404 A57	21c silver & multi	.48	.48
405 A57	40c silver & multi	1.00	1.00
a.	Souvenir sheet of 4, #402-405	3.00	3.50
	Nos. 402-405 (4)	2.03	2.03

Reign of Queen Elizabeth II, 25th anniv. For surcharges see Nos. 412-415.

Featherduster — A58

Marine Life: 8c, Porkfish. 16c, Elkhorn coral. 21c, Soft coral and sponge.

1977, May 24   Litho.   Perf. 13½

406 A58	3c multicolored	.18	.18
407 A58	16c multicolored	.32	.32
408 A58	16c multicolored	.80	.80
409 A58	21c multicolored	.80	.80
a.	Souvenir sheet of 4, #406-409, perf. 14½	2.50	3.00
	Nos. 406-409 (4)	2.30	2.30

Campfire and Shower — A59

1977, Sept. 27   Litho.   Wmk. 373

410 A59	16c shown	.42	.42
411 A59	21c Boating	.52	.52

6th Caribbean Jamboree, Kingston, Jamaica, Aug. 5-14.

Nos. 402-405a Overprinted: "Royal Visit / October 1977"

1977, Oct. 19   Litho.   Perf. 12

412 A57	8c silver & multi	.16	.16
413 A57	16c silver & multi	.32	.32
414 A57	21c silver & multi	.38	.38
415 A57	40c silver & multi	.80	.80
a.	Souvenir sheet of 4	2.25	2.75
	Nos. 412-415 (4)	1.66	1.66

Caribbean visit of Queen Elizabeth II, Oct. 19-20.

Virgin and Child — A60

Nassau Public Library — A61

Crèche Figurines: 16c, Three Kings. 21c, Adoration of the Kings. 25c, Three Kings.

1977, Oct. 25   Litho.   Perf. 13½

416 A60	3c gold & multi	.15	.15
417 A60	16c gold & multi	.38	.38
418 A60	21c gold & multi	.48	.48
419 A60	25c gold & multi	.60	.60
a.	Souvenir sheet of 4, #416-419, perf. 14½	1.90	1.90
	Nos. 416-419 (4)	1.61	1.61

Christmas.

1978, Mar. 28   Litho.   Perf. 14½x14

Architectural Heritage: 8c, St. Matthew's Church. 16c, Government House. 18c, The Hermitage, Cat Island.

420 A61	3c black & yel green	.15	.15
421 A61	8c black & lt blue	.18	.18
422 A61	16c black & lilac rose	.32	.32
423 A61	18c black & salmon	.35	.35
a.	Souvenir sheet of 4, #420-423	1.10	1.10
	Nos. 420-423 (4)	1.00	1.00

Scepter, St. Edward's Crown, Orb — A62

Perf. 14x13½

1978, June 27   Litho.   Wmk. 373

424 A62	16c shown	.28	.28
425 A62	$1 Elizabeth II	1.65	1.65
a.	Souvenir sheet of 2, #424-425	2.25	2.25

Coronation of Queen Elizabeth II, 25th anniv.

Type of 1971

Designs as before and: 16c, Hibiscus. 25c, Hawksbill turtle.

Perf. 14½x14, 14x14½

1978, June   Unwmk.

426 A36	1c blue & multi	.15	.15
430 A36	5c dp org & multi	.15	.15
436 A36	16c brt grn & multi	.38	.38
439 A36	25c brown & multi	.60	.60
440 A36	50c lemon & multi	1.10	1.10
441 A36	$1 lemon & multi	2.50	2.50
442 A36	$2 blue & multi	4.75	4.75
443 A36	$3 vio bl & multi	7.25	7.25
	Nos. 426-443 (8)	16.88	16.88

Angels and Palms — A63

Christmas: 5c, Coat of arms within wreath, and sailing ships.

Perf. 14x14½

1978, Nov. 14   Litho.   Wmk. 373

444 A63	5c car, pink & gold	.15	.15
445 A63	21c ultra, dk bl & gold	.32	.32
a.	Souvenir sheet of 2, #444-445	2.50	2.50

Baby Walking, IYC Emblem — A64

IYC Emblem and: 16c, Children playing leapfrog. 21c, Girl skipping rope. 25c, Building blocks with "IYC" and emblem.

Perf. 13½x13

1979, May 15   Litho.   Wmk. 373

446 A64	5c multicolored	.15	.15
447 A64	16c multicolored	.25	.25
448 A64	21c multicolored	.35	.35
449 A64	25c multicolored	.40	.40
a.	Souv. sheet of 4, #446-449, perf. 14	1.10	1.10
	Nos. 446-449 (4)	1.15	1.15

International Year of the Child.

BAHAMAS

Rowland Hill and Penny Black — A65

Designs: 21c, Stamp printing press, 1840, and Bahamas No. 7. 25c, Great Britain No. 27 with 1850's Nassau cancellation, and Great Britain No. 29. 40c, Early mailboat and Bahamas No. 1.

1979, Aug. 14		**Perf. 13½x14**	
450 A65	10c multicolored	.16	.16
451 A65	21c multicolored	.35	.35
452 A65	25c multicolored	.40	.40
453 A65	40c multicolored	.65	.65
a.	Souvenir sheet of 4, #450-453	1.65	1.65
	Nos. 450-453 (4)	1.56	1.56

Sir Rowland Hill (1795-1879), originator of penny postage.

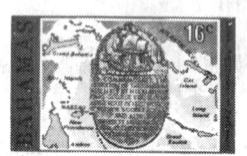

Commonwealth Plaque over Map of Bahamas — A66

Designs: 21c, Parliament buildings. 25c, Legislative chamber. $1, Senate chamber.

1979, Sept. 27	Litho.	**Perf. 13½**	
454 A66	16c multicolored	.25	.25
455 A66	21c multicolored	.35	.35
456 A66	25c multicolored	.40	.40
457 A66	$1 multicolored	1.65	1.65
a.	Souvenir sheet of 4, #454-457	2.75	2.75
	Nos. 454-457 (4)	2.65	2.65

Parliament of Bahamas, 250th anniv.

Headdress — A67

Christmas: Goombay Carnival costumes.

1979, Nov. 6	Litho.	**Perf. 13**	
458 A67	5c multicolored	.15	.15
459 A67	10c multicolored	.15	.15
460 A67	16c multicolored	.22	.22
461 A67	21c multicolored	.32	.32
462 A67	25c multicolored	.38	.38
463 A67	40c multicolored	.60	.60
a.	Souv. sheet of 6, 458-463, perf 13½	1.90	1.90
	Nos. 458-463 (6)	1.82	1.82

Columbus' Landing, 1492 — A68

1980, July 9	Litho.	**Perf. 15**	
464 A68	1c shown	.15	.15
465 A68	3c Blackbeard	.15	.15
466 A68	5c Articles, 1647, Eleuthera map	.15	.15
467 A68	10c Ceremonial mace	.20	.20
468 A68	12c Col. Andrew Deveaux	.24	.24
469 A68	15c Slave trading, Vendue House	.28	.28
470 A68	16c Shipwreck salvage, 19th cent.	.30	.30
471 A68	18c Blockade runner, 1860s	.32	.32
472 A68	21c Bootlegging, 1919-1929	.40	.40
473 A68	25c Pineapple cultivation	.24	.24
474 A68	40c Sponge clipping	.75	.75
475 A68	50c Victoria & Colonial Hotels		
476 A68	$1 Modern agriculture	2.00	2.00
477 A68	$2 Ship, jet	3.70	3.70
478 A68	$3 Central Bank, Arms	5.75	5.75
479 A68	$5 Prince Charles, Prime Minister Pindling	9.50	9.50
	Nos. 464-479 (16)	25.13	25.13

For overprints and surcharges see Nos. 496-499, 532-535.

1985, Nov. 6		**Wmk. 384**	
464a A68	1c	.15	.15
465a A68	3c	.15	.15
467a A68	10c	.20	.20
473a A68	25c	.48	.48
	Nos. 464a-473a (4)	.98	.98

Virgin and Child, Straw Figures — A69

1980, Oct. 28	Litho.	**Perf. 14½**	
480 A69	5c shown	.15	.15
481 A69	21c Three kings	.35	.35
482 A69	25c Angel	.40	.40
483 A69	$1 Christmas tree	1.65	1.65
a.	Souvenir sheet of 4, #480-483	2.50	2.50
	Nos. 480-483 (4)	2.55	2.55

Christmas.

Man with Crutch, Sun Rays A70

1981, Feb. 10	Litho.	**Perf. 14½**	
484 A70	5c shown	.15	.15
485 A70	$1 Man in wheelchair	1.65	1.65
a.	Souvenir sheet of 2, #484-485	1.75	1.75

International Year of the Disabled.

Grand Bahama Tracking Station A71

Satellite Views: 20c, Bahamas, vert. 25c, Eleuthera. 50c, Andros and New Providence, vert.

1981, Apr. 21	Litho.	**Perf. 13½**	
486 A71	10c multicolored	.18	.18
487 A71	20c multicolored	.35	.35
488 A71	25c multicolored	.45	.45
489 A71	50c multicolored	.90	.90
a.	Souvenir sheet of 4, #486-489	2.00	2.75
	Nos. 486-489 (4)	1.88	1.88

Prince Charles and Lady Diana — A72

1981, July 22	Litho.	**Wmk. 373**	
		Perf. 14½	
490 A72	30c shown	.52	.52
491 A72	$2 Charles, Prime Minister	3.50	3.50
a.	Souvenir sheet of 2, #490-491	5.00	5.75

Royal wedding.

Bahama Ducks — A73

1981, Aug. 25	Litho.	**Wmk. 373**	
		Perf. 14	
492 A73	5c shown	.25	.25
493 A73	20c Reddish egrets	1.00	1.00
494 A73	25c Brown boobies	1.00	1.00
495 A73	$1 West Indian tree ducks	2.50	2.50
a.	Souvenir sheet of 4, #492-495	5.25	5.25
	Nos. 492-495 (4)	4.75	4.75

See Nos. 514-517.

Nos. 466-467, 473, 475 Overprinted: "COMMONWEALTH FINANCE MINISTERS' MEETING 21-23 SEPTEMBER 1981"

1981, Sept.	Litho.	**Perf. 15**	
496 A68	5c multicolored	.15	.15
497 A68	10c multicolored	.16	.16
498 A68	25c multicolored	.42	.42
499 A68	50c multicolored	.85	.85
	Nos. 496-499 (4)	1.58	1.58

World Food Day — A74

1981, Oct. 16		**Wmk. 373**	
500 A74	5c Chickens	.18	.18
501 A74	20c Sheep	.40	.40
502 A74	30c Lobster	.60	.60
503 A74	50c Pigs	1.00	1.00
a.	Souvenir sheet of 4, #500-503	2.25	2.75
	Nos. 500-503 (4)	2.18	2.18

Christmas — A75

		Wmk. 373	
1981, Nov. 23	Litho.	**Perf. 14**	
504	Sheet of 9	5.00	5.00
a.	A75 5c Father Christmas	.20	.20
b.	A75 5c shown	.20	.20
c.	A75 5c St. Nicholas, Holland	.20	.20
d.	A75 25c Lussibruden, Sweden	.40	.40
e.	A75 25c Mother and child	.40	.40
f.	A75 25c King Wenceslas, Czechoslovakia	.40	.40
g.	A75 30c Mother and child	.45	.45
h.	A75 30c Mother and child standing	.45	.45
i.	A75 $1 Christkindl angel, Germany	1.75	1.75

TB Bacillus Centenary A76

1982, Feb. 3	Litho.	**Perf. 14**	
505 A76	5c Koch	.15	.15
506 A76	16c X-ray	.30	.30
507 A76	21c Microscopes	.42	.42
508 A76	$1 Mantoux test	1.90	1.90
a.	Souvenir sheet of 4, #505-508, perf. 14½	3.50	4.00
	Nos. 505-508 (4)	2.77	2.77

Flamingoes — A77

Designs: a, Females. b, Males. c, Nesting. d, Juvenile birds. e, Immature birds. No. 509 in continuous design.

		Wmk. 373	
1982, Apr. 28	Litho.	**Perf. 14**	
509	Strip of 5, multicolored	4.00	4.00
a.-e.	A77 25c any single	.80	.80

Princess Diana Issue Common Design Type

1982, July 1	Litho.	**Perf. 14**	
510 CD333	16c Arms	.25	.25
511 CD333	25c Diana	.38	.38
512 CD333	40c Wedding	.60	.60
513 CD333	$1 Portrait	1.50	1.50
	Nos. 510-513 (4)	2.73	2.73

Bird Type of 1981

		Wmk. 373	
1982, Aug. 18	Litho.	**Perf. 14**	
514 A73	10c Bat	.18	.18
515 A73	16c Hutia	.28	.28
516 A73	21c Racoon	.35	.35
517 A73	$1 Dolphins	1.75	1.75
a.	Souvenir sheet of 4, #514-517	3.25	3.25
	Nos. 514-517 (4)	2.56	2.56

28th Commonwealth Parliamentary Conference — A78

		Perf. 14x13½	
1982, Oct. 16	Litho.	**Wmk. 373**	
518 A78	5c Plaque	.15	.15
519 A78	25c Assoc. arms	.50	.50
520 A78	40c Natl. arms	.80	.80
521 A78	50c House of Assembly	1.00	1.00
	Nos. 518-521 (4)	2.45	2.45

Christmas A79

Designs: 5c, Wesley Methodist Church, Baillou Hill Road. 12c, Centerville Seventh Day Adventist Church. 15c, Church of God of Prophecy, East Street. 21c, Bethel Baptist Church, Meeting Street. 25c, St. Francis Xavier Catholic Church, West Hill Street. $1, Holy Cross Anglican Church, Highbury Park.

1982, Nov. 3		**Perf. 14**	
522 A79	5c multicolored	.15	.15
523 A79	12c multicolored	.24	.24
524 A79	15c multicolored	.28	.28
525 A79	21c multicolored	.40	.40
526 A79	25c multicolored	.48	.48
527 A79	$1 multicolored	1.90	1.90
	Nos. 522-527 (6)	3.45	3.45

A80

1983, Mar. 14			Litho.
528 A80	5c Lynden O. Pindling	.15	.15
529 A80	25c Flags	.40	.40
530 A80	35c Map	.55	.55
531 A80	$1 Ocean liner	1.65	1.65
	Nos. 528-531 (4)	2.75	2.75

Commonwealth Day.

Nos. 469-472 Surcharged

1983, Apr. 5	Litho.	**Perf. 15**	
532 A68	20c on 15c multi	.35	.35
533 A68	31c on 21c multi	.55	.55
534 A68	35c on 16c multi	.65	.65
535 A68	80c on 18c multi	1.50	1.50
	Nos. 532-535 (4)	3.05	3.05

For all your stamp supply needs

www.scottonline.com

BAHAMAS

30th Anniv. of Customs Cooperation Council — A81

10th Anniv. of Independence — A82

Perf. 14x13½
1983, May 31   Wmk. 373
| 536 | A81 | 31c Officers, ship | .52 | .52 |
| 537 | A81 | $1 Officers, jet | 1.65 | 1.65 |

1983, July 6   Litho.   Perf. 14
| 538 | A82 | $1 Flag raising | 1.50 | 1.50 |
| a. | Souvenir sheet, perf. 12 | | 1.50 | 1.50 |

Local Butterflies — A83

Perf. 14½x14
1983, Aug. 24
539	A83	5c Carters skipper	.18	.18
540	A83	25c Giant southern white	.90	.90
541	A83	31c Large orange sulphur	1.10	1.10
542	A83	50c Flambeau	1.75	1.75
a.	Souvenir sheet of 4		4.25	4.25
	Nos. 539-542 (4)		3.93	3.93

No. 542a contains Nos. 539-542, perf. 14 and perf. 14½x14.

American Loyalists Arrival Bicentenary — A84

Paintings by Alton Lowe.

1983, Sept. 28   Perf. 14
543	A84	5c Loyalist Dreams	.15	.15
544	A84	31c New Plymouth, Abaco	.55	.55
545	A84	35c New Plymouth Hotel	.60	.60
546	A84	50c Island Hope	.90	.90
a.	Souvenir sheet of 4, #543-546		2.25	2.25
	Nos. 543-546 (4)		2.20	2.20

Christmas — A85

125th Anniv. of Bahamas Stamps — A86

Children's designs: 5c, Christmas Bells, by Monica Pinder. 20c, The Flamingo by Cory Bullard. 25c, The Yellow Hibiscus with Christmas Candle by Monique A. Bailey. 31c, Santa goes a Sailing by Sabrina Seiler, horiz. 35c, Silhouette scene with palm trees by James Blake. 50c, Silhouette scene with Pelicans, by Erik Russell, horiz.

1983, Nov. 1   Perf. 14
547	A85	5c multicolored	.15	.15
548	A85	20c multicolored	.32	.32
549	A85	25c multicolored	.42	.42
550	A85	31c multicolored	.50	.50
551	A85	35c multicolored	.60	.60
552	A85	50c multicolored	.80	.80
	Nos. 547-552 (6)		2.79	2.79

1984, Feb. 22   Litho.   Perf. 14
| 553 | A86 | 5c No. 3 | .15 | .15 |
| 554 | A86 | $1 No. 1 | 1.65 | 1.65 |

Lloyd's List Issue
Common Design Type
Perf. 14½
1984, Apr. 25   Litho.   Wmk. 373
555	CD335	5c Trent	.52	.52
556	CD335	31c Orinoco	.55	.55
557	CD335	35c Nassau Harbor	.60	.60
558	CD335	50c Container ship Oropesa	.85	.85
	Nos. 555-558 (4)		2.15	2.15

1984 Summer Olympics — A87

1984, June 20   Litho.   Perf. 14x14½
559	A87	5c Running	.15	.15
560	A87	25c Discus	.42	.42
561	A87	31c Boxing	.52	.52
562	A87	$1 Basketball	1.65	1.65
a.	Souvenir sheet of 4, #559-562		2.75	2.75
	Nos. 559-562 (4)		2.74	2.74

Flags of Bahamas and Caribbean Community — A88

1984, July 4   Wmk. 373   Perf. 14
| 563 | A88 | 50c multicolored | .90 | .90 |

Conference of Heads of Government of Caribbean Community, 5th Meeting.

Allen's Cay Iguana — A89

1984, Aug. 15   Perf. 14
564	A89	5c shown	.15	.15
565	A89	25c Curly-tailed lizard	.60	.60
566	A89	35c Greenhouse frog	.80	.80
567	A89	50c Atlantic green turtle	1.00	1.00
a.	Souvenir sheet of 4, #564-567		3.00	3.00
	Nos. 564-567 (4)		2.55	2.55

25th Anniv. of Natl. Trust — A90

Christmas — A91

Wildlife: a, Calliphlox evelynae. b, Megaceryle alcyon, Eleutherodactylus planirostris. c, Phoebis sennae, Phoenicopterus ruber, Himantopus himantopus, Phoebus sennae. d, Urbanus proteus, Chelonia mydas. e, Pandion haliaetus. Continuous design.

1984, Aug. 15   Litho.   Perf. 14
| 568 | Strip of 5 | 5.25 | 5.25 |
| a.-e. | A90 31c any single | 1.10 | 1.10 |

1984, Nov. 7   Litho.   Perf. 13½x13

Madonna and Child Paintings.
569	A91	5c Titian	.15	.15
570	A91	31c Anais Colin	.55	.55
571	A91	35c Elena Caula	.60	.60
a.	Souvenir sheet of 3, #569-571		1.40	1.40
	Nos. 569-571 (3)		1.30	1.30

Girl Guides, 75th Anniv., Intl. Youth Year — A92

1985, Feb. 22   Litho.   Perf. 14
572	A92	5c Brownies	.15	.15
573	A92	25c Camping	.40	.40
574	A92	31c Girl Guides	.50	.50
575	A92	35c Rangers	.55	.55
a.	Souvenir sheet of 4, #572-575		1.65	1.65
	Nos. 572-575 (4)		1.60	1.60

Audubon Birth Bicentenary — A93

Wmk. 373
1985, Apr. 24   Litho.   Perf. 14
576	A93	5c Killdeer	.15	.15
577	A93	31c Mourning dove, vert.	.85	.85
578	A93	35c Mourning doves, diff., vert.	.90	.90
579	A93	$1 Killdeers, diff.	2.50	2.50
	Nos. 576-579 (4)		4.40	4.40

Queen Mother 85th Birthday
Common Design Type
Perf. 14½x14
1985, June 7   Litho.   Wmk. 384
580	CD336	5c Portrait, 1927	.15	.15
581	CD336	25c At christening of Peter Phillips	.42	.42
582	CD336	35c Portrait, 1985	.60	.60
583	CD336	50c Holding Prince Henry	.85	.85
	Nos. 580-583 (4)		2.02	2.02

Souvenir Sheet
| 584 | CD336 | $1.25 In a pony and trap | 2.00 | 2.00 |

UN and UN Food and Agriculture Org., 40th Anniv. — A94

1985, Aug. 26   Wmk. 373   Litho.   Perf. 14
| 585 | A94 | 25c Wheat, emblems | .42 | .42 |

Commonwealth Heads of Government Meeting, 1985 — A95

1985, Oct. 16   Wmk. 373   Perf. 14½
| 586 | A95 | 31c Queen Elizabeth II | .48 | .48 |
| 587 | A95 | 35c Flag, Commonwealth emblem | .55 | .55 |

Christmas — A96

Paintings by Alton Roland Lowe: 5c, Grandma's Christmas Bouquet. 25c, Junkanoo Romeo and Juliet, vert. 31c, Bunce Girl, vert. 35c, Home for Christmas.

1985, Nov. 5   Perf. 13
588	A96	5c multicolored	.15	.15
589	A96	25c multicolored	.48	.48
590	A96	31c multicolored	.62	.62
591	A96	35c multicolored	.65	.65
a.	Souv. sheet of 4, #588-591, perf. 14		1.90	1.90
	Nos. 588-591 (4)		1.90	1.90

Queen Elizabeth II 60th Birthday
Common Design Type

Designs: 10c, Age 1, 1927. 25c, Coronation, Westminster Abbey, 1953. 35c, Giving speech, royal visit, Bahamas. 40c, At Djakova, Yugoslavia, state visit, 1972. $1, Visiting Crown Agents, 1983.

1986, Apr. 21   Wmk. 384   Perf. 14½
592	CD337	10c scar, blk & sil	.16	.16
593	CD337	25c ultra & multi	.40	.40
594	CD337	35c green & multi	.55	.55
595	CD337	40c violet & multi	.65	.65
596	CD337	$1 rose vio & multi	1.65	1.65
	Nos. 592-596 (5)		3.41	3.41

AMERIPEX '86 — A97

1986, May 19   Perf. 14
597	A97	5c Nos. 464, 471	.15	.15
598	A97	25c Nos. 288-289	.45	.45
599	A97	31c No. 392	.55	.55
600	A97	50c No. 489a	.90	.90
601	A97	$1 Statue of Liberty, vert.	1.75	1.75
a.	Souvenir sheet of one		1.75	1.75
	Nos. 597-601 (5)		3.80	3.80

Statue of Liberty, cent.

Royal Wedding Issue, 1986
Common Design Type

Designs: 10c, Formal engagement. $1, Andrew in dress uniform.

1986, July 23   Perf. 14½x14
| 602 | CD338 | 10c multicolored | .16 | .16 |
| 603 | CD338 | $1 multicolored | 1.65 | 1.65 |

Fish — A98

1986-87   Wmk. 384   Perf. 14
604	A98	5c Rock beauty	.15	.15
605	A98	10c Stoplight parrotfish	.15	.15
606	A98	15c Jacknife fish	.22	.22
607	A98	20c Flamefish	.28	.28
608	A98	25c Swissguard basslet	.35	.35
609	A98	30c Spotfin butterflyfish	.42	.42
610	A98	35c Queen triggerfish	.52	.52
611	A98	40c Four-eyed butterflyfish	.55	.55
612	A98	45c Fairy basslet	.65	.65
613	A98	50c Queen angelfish	.70	.70
614	A98	60c Blue chromis	.85	.85
615	A98	$1 Spanish hogfish	1.40	1.40
616	A98	$2 Harlequin bass	2.75	2.75
617	A98	$3 Blackbar soldierfish	4.50	4.50
618	A98	$5 Pygmy angelfish	7.25	7.25
618A	A99	$10 Red hind ('87)	16.00	16.00
	Nos. 604-618A (16)		36.74	36.74

Nos. 605, 608, 611-613, 615, 617-618 exist inscribed "1990." Nos. 611, 615, 616 "1988."
Issue dates: $10, Jan. 2, others, Aug. 5.

1987, June 25   Wmk. 373
604a	5c	.15	.15
605a	10c	.15	.15
606a	15c	.22	.22
611a	40c	.55	.55
612a	45c	.65	.65
613a	50c	.70	.70
614a	60c	.85	.85
615a	$1	1.40	1.40
616a	$2	2.75	2.75
	Nos. 604a-616a (9)	7.42	7.42

Nos. 604a-616a dated 1987. No. 605a "1988."
No. 604a "1989."

Christ Church Cathedral — A99

BAHAMAS

1986, Sept. 16 Litho. Perf. 14½ Wmk. 373

619 A99	10c View, 19th cent.	.16	.16
620 A99	40c View, 1986	.65	.65
a.	Souvenir sheet of 2, #619-620	.85	.85

City of Nassau, Diocese of Nassau and the Bahamas and Christ Church, 125th anniv.

Christmas, Intl. Peace Year — A100

1986, Nov. 4 Litho. Wmk. 384 Perf. 14

621 A100	10c Nativity	.16	.16
622 A100	40c Flight to Egypt	.65	.65
623 A100	45c Children praying	.75	.75
624 A100	50c Exchanging gifts	.80	.80
a.	Souvenir sheet of 4, #621-624	2.50	2.50
	Nos. 621-624 (4)	2.36	2.36

Pirates of the Caribbean — A101

Map of the Bahamas — A102

1987, June 2 Litho. Perf. 14½ Wmk. 373

625 A101	10c Anne Bonney	.22	.22
626 A101	40c Blackbeard (d. 1718)	.90	.90
627 A101	45c Capt. Edward England	1.00	1.00
628 A101	50c Capt. Woodes Rogers (c. 1679-1732)	1.25	1.25
	Nos. 625-628 (4)	3.37	3.37

Souvenir Sheet

629 A102	$1.25 shown	2.75	2.75

Paintings of Lighthouses by Alton Roland Lowe — A103

1987, Mar. 31 Wmk. 384

630 A103	10c Great Isaac	.30	.30
631 A103	40c Bird Rock	1.25	1.25
632 A103	45c Castle Is.	1.50	1.50
633 A103	$1 Hole in the Wall	3.25	3.25
	Nos. 630-633 (4)	6.30	6.30

Tourist Transportation A104

1987, Aug. 26 Wmk. 373 Perf. 14

634	Strip of 5	3.75	3.75
a.-e.	A104 40c any single	.75	.75
635	Strip of 5	3.75	3.75
a.-e.	A104 40c any single	.75	.75

Ships: No. 634a, Cruise ship, sailboat. b, Cruise ships, tugboat, speedboat. c, Pleasure boat leaving harbor, sailboat. d, Pleasure boat docked, sailboats. e, Sailboats.
Aircraft: No. 635a, Bahamasair plane. b, Bahamasair and Pan Am aircraft. c, Aircraft, radar tower. d, Control tower, aircraft. e, Helicopter, planes.

Orchids Painted by Alton Roland Lowe — A105

1987, Oct. 20 Wmk. 384 Perf. 14½

636 A105	10c Cattleyopsis lindenii	.16	.16
637 A105	40c Encyclia lucayana	.65	.65
638 A105	45c Encyclia hodgeana	.75	.75
639 A105	50c Encyclia lleidae	.80	.80
a.	Souvenir sheet of 4, #636-639	2.50	2.50
	Nos. 636-639 (4)	2.36	2.36

Christmas.

Discovery of America, 500th Anniv. (in 1992) — A106

10c, Ferdinand & Isabella. 40c, Columbus before the Talavera Committee. 45c, Lucayan village. 50c, Lucayan potters. $1.50, Map, c. 1500.

1988, Feb. 23 Litho. Perf. 14x14½ Wmk. 373

640 A106	10c multicolored	.16	.16
641 A106	40c multicolored	.65	.65
642 A106	45c multicolored	.75	.75
643 A106	50c multicolored	.80	.80
	Nos. 640-643 (4)	2.36	2.36

Souvenir Sheet

644 A106	$1.50 multicolored	3.00	3.00

See Nos. 663-667, 688-692, 725-729, 749-753, 762.

World Wildlife Fund — A107

Whistling ducks, Dendrocygna arborea.

1988, Apr. 29 Perf. 14½

645 A107	5c Ducks in flight	.18	.15
646 A107	10c Among marine plants	.16	.16
647 A107	20c Adults, ducklings	.32	.32
648 A107	45c Wading	.75	.75
	Nos. 645-648 (4)	1.41	1.38

Abolition of Slavery, 150th Anniv. A108

1988, Aug. 9 Perf. 14

649 A108	10c African hut	.20	.20
650 A108	40c Basket weavers in hut, Grantstown	.80	.80

1988 Summer Olympics, Seoul A109

Games emblem and details of painting by James Martin: 10c, Olympic flame, high jump, hammer throw, basketball and gymnastics. 40c, Swimming, boxing, weight lifting, fencing and running. 45c, Gymnastics, shot put and javelin. $1, Running, cycling and gymnastics.

1988, Aug. 30 Litho. Wmk. 384 Perf. 14

651 A109	10c multicolored	.20	.20
652 A109	40c multicolored	.80	.80
653 A109	45c multicolored	.90	.90
654 A109	$1 multicolored	2.00	2.00
a.	Souvenir sheet of 4, #651-654	4.00	4.00
	Nos. 651-654 (4)	3.90	3.90

Lloyds of London, 300th Anniv.
Common Design Type

Designs: 10c, Lloyds List No. 560, 1740. 40c, Freeport Harbor, horiz. 45c, Space shuttle over the Bahamas, horiz. $1, Supply ship Yarmouth Castle on fire.

1988, Oct. 4 Wmk. 373

655 CD341	10c multicolored	.20	.20
656 CD341	40c multicolored	.80	.80
657 CD341	45c multicolored	.90	.90
658 CD341	$1 multicolored	2.00	2.00
	Nos. 655-658 (4)	3.90	3.90

Christmas Carols — A110

Designs: 10c, O' Little Town of Bethlehem. 40c, Little Donkey. 45c, Silent Night. 50c, Hark! The Herald Angels Sing.

1988, Nov. 21 Wmk. 384 Perf. 14½

659 A110	10c multicolored	.20	.20
660 A110	40c multicolored	.80	.80
661 A110	45c multicolored	.90	.90
662 A110	50c multicolored	1.00	1.00
a.	Souvenir sheet of 4, #659-662	2.90	2.90
	Nos. 659-662 (4)	2.90	2.90

Discovery of America Type of 1988

Design: 10c, Columbus as chartmaker. 40c, Development of the caravel. 45c, Navigational tools. 50c, Arawak artifacts. $1.50, Caravel under construction, an illumination from the Nuremburg Chronicles, 15th cent.

1989, Jan. 25 Litho. Perf. 14½x14 Wmk. 373

663 A106	10c multicolored	.20	.20
664 A106	40c multicolored	.80	.80
665 A106	45c multicolored	.90	.90
666 A106	50c multicolored	1.00	1.00
	Nos. 663-666 (4)	2.90	2.90

Souvenir Sheet

667 A106	$1.50 multicolored	3.00	3.00

Hummingbirds A111

1989, Mar. 29 Litho. Perf. 14½ Wmk. 384

668 A111	10c Cuban emerald	.20	.20
669 A111	40c Ruby-throated	.80	.80
670 A111	45c Bahama woodstar	.90	.90
671 A111	50c Rufous	1.00	1.00
	Nos. 668-671 (4)	2.90	2.90

Intl. Red Cross and Red Crescent Organizations, 125th Anniv. A112

1989, May 31 Perf. 14x14½

672 A112	10c Water safety	.20	.20
673 A112	$1 Dunant, Battle of Solferino	2.00	2.00

Moon Landing, 20th Anniv.
Common Design Type

Apollo 8: 10c, Apollo Communications System, Grand Bahama Is. 40c, James Lovell Jr., William Anders and Frank Borman. 45c, Mission emblem. $1, The Rising Earth (photograph). $2, Astronaut practicing lunar surface activities at Manned Spacecraft Center, Houston, in training for Apollo 11 mission.

1989, July 20 Perf. 14x13½
Size of Nos. 674-675: 29x29mm

674 CD342	10c multicolored	.20	.20
675 CD342	40c multicolored	.80	.80
676 CD342	45c multicolored	.90	.90
677 CD342	$1 multicolored	2.00	2.00
	Nos. 674-677 (4)	3.90	3.90

Souvenir Sheet

678 CD342	$2 multicolored	4.00	4.00

Christmas — A113

Designs: 10c, Church of the Nativity, Bethlehem. 40c, Basilica of the Annunciation, Nazareth. 45c, By the Sea of Galilee, Tabgha. $1, Church of the Holy Sepulcher, Jerusalem.

1989, Oct. 16 Perf. 14½x14 Wmk. 373

679 A113	10c multicolored	.20	.20
680 A113	40c multicolored	.80	.80
681 A113	45c multicolored	.90	.90
682 A113	$1 multicolored	2.00	2.00
a.	Souvenir sheet of 4, #679-682	4.00	4.00
	Nos. 679-682 (4)	3.90	3.90

World Stamp Expo '89 A114

Expo emblem and: 10c, Earth, #359. 40c, UPU Headquarters, #301. 45c, US Capitol, #601. $1, Passenger jet, #150. $2, Washington, DC, on map.

1989, Nov. 17 Wmk. 384 Perf. 14

683 A114	10c multicolored	.20	.20
684 A114	40c multicolored	.80	.80
685 A114	45c multicolored	.90	.90
686 A114	$1 multicolored	2.00	2.00
	Nos. 683-686 (4)	3.90	3.90

Souvenir Sheet
Perf. 14½x14

687 A114	$2 multicolored	4.00	4.00

No. 687 contains one 31x38mm stamp.

Discovery of America Type of 1988

10c, Caravel launch. 40c, Provisioning ships. 45c, Shortening sails. 50c, Lucayan fishermen. $1.50, Columbus's fleet departing from Cadiz.

1990, Jan. 24 Litho. Perf. 14½x14 Wmk. 373

688 A106	10c multicolored	.20	.20
689 A106	40c multicolored	.80	.80
690 A106	45c multicolored	.90	.90
691 A106	50c multicolored	1.00	1.00
	Nos. 688-691 (4)	2.90	2.90

Souvenir Sheet

692 A106	$1.50 multicolored	3.00	3.00

Organization of American States, Cent. — A115

1990, Mar. 14 Wmk. 384 Perf. 14

693 A115	40c multicolored	.80	.80

BAHAMAS

Souvenir Sheet

Stamp World London '90 — A116

Aircraft: a, Spitfire I. b, Hurricane IIc.

1990, May 3			Wmk. 384	
694	A116	Sheet of 2	4.00	4.00
a.-b.		$1 any single	2.00	2.00

For surcharge see No. B3.

Intl. Literacy Year A117

10c, Teacher helping student. 40c, Children reading to each other. 50c, Children reading aloud.

1990, June 27		Wmk. 384	Perf. 14	
695	A117	10c multicolored	.20	.20
696	A117	40c multicolored	.80	.80
697	A117	50c multicolored	1.00	1.00
		Nos. 695-697 (3)	2.00	2.00

Queen Mother, 90th Birthday
Common Design Types

1990, Aug. 4			Perf. 14x15	
698	CD343	40c Portrait, c. 1938	.80	.80
		Perf. 14½		
699	CD344	$1.50 At garden party, 1938	3.00	3.00

Bahamian Parrot — A118

1990, Sept. 26		Wmk. 373	Perf. 14	
700	A118	10c shown	.20	.20
701	A118	40c In flight	.80	.80
702	A118	45c Head	.90	.90
703	A118	50c On branch	1.00	1.00
		Nos. 700-703 (4)	2.90	2.90

Souvenir Sheet

| 704 | A118 | $1.50 On branch, diff. | 3.00 | 3.00 |

Christmas — A119    Birds — A120

1990, Nov. 5		Litho.	Wmk. 373	Perf. 13½
705	A119	10c Angel appears to Mary	.20	.20
706	A119	40c Nativity	.80	.80
707	A119	45c Angel appears to shepherds	.90	.90
708	A119	$1 Three kings	2.00	2.00
a.		Souvenir sheet of 4, #705-708	3.90	3.90
		Nos. 705-708 (4)	3.90	3.90

1991, Feb. 4		Litho.	Wmk. 384	Perf. 14
709	A120	5c Green heron	.15	.15
710	A120	10c Turkey vulture	.20	.20
711	A120	15c Osprey	.30	.30
712	A120	20c Clapper rail	.40	.40
713	A120	25c Royal tern	.50	.50
714	A120	30c Key West quail dove	.60	.60
715	A120	40c Smooth-billed ani	.80	.80
716	A120	45c Burrowing owl	.90	.90
717	A120	50c Hairy woodpecker	1.00	1.00
718	A120	55c Mangrove cuckoo	1.10	1.10
719	A120	60c Bahama mockingbird	1.20	1.20
720	A120	70c Red-winged blackbird	1.40	1.40
721	A120	$1 Thick-billed vireo	2.00	2.00
722	A120	$2 Bahama yellowthroat	4.00	4.00
723	A120	$5 Stripe-headed tanager	10.00	10.00
724	A120	$10 Greater Antillean bullfinch	20.00	20.00
		Nos. 709-724 (16)	44.55	44.55

Issued: $10, July 1; others, Feb. 4.

1993			Wmk. 373	
710a		10c	.20	.20
713a		25c	.50	.50
714a		30c	.60	.60
715a		40c	.80	.80
718a		55c	1.10	1.10
723a		$5	10.00	10.00
		Nos. 710a-723a (6)	13.20	13.20

Nos. 710a-723a dated 1993. 40c, 55c exist dated 1995.
Issued: 40c, 12/31/93; others, 9/23/93.

Discovery of America Type of 1988

Designs: 15c, Columbus practices celestial navigation. 40c, The fleet in rough seas. 55c, Natives on the beach. 60c, Map of voyage. $1.50, Pinta's crew sights land.

1991, Apr. 9		Litho.	Perf. 14½x14	Wmk. 384
725	A106	15c multicolored	.30	.30
726	A106	40c multicolored	.80	.80
727	A106	55c multicolored	1.10	1.10
728	A106	60c multicolored	1.20	1.20
		Nos. 725-728 (4)	3.40	3.40

Souvenir Sheet

| 729 | A106 | $1.50 multicolored | 3.00 | 3.00 |

Elizabeth & Philip, Birthdays
Common Design Types

1991, June 17		Litho.	Perf. 14½	Wmk. 384
730	CD346	15c multicolored	.30	.30
731	CD345	$1 multicolored	2.00	2.00
a.		Pair, #730-731 + label	2.30	2.30

Hurricane Awareness A121

Designs: 15c, Weather radar image of Hurricane Hugo. 40c, Anatomy of hurricane rotating around eye. 55c, Flooding caused by Hurricane David. 60c, Lockheed WP-3D Orion.

1991, Aug. 28				Perf. 14
732	A121	15c multicolored	.30	.30
733	A121	40c multicolored	.80	.80
734	A121	55c multicolored	1.10	1.10
735	A121	60c multicolored	1.20	1.20
		Nos. 732-735 (4)	3.40	3.40

Christmas A122

Designs: 15c, The Annunciation. 55c, Mary and Joseph traveling to Bethlehem. 60c, Angel appearing to shepherds. $1, Adoration of the Magi.

1991, Oct. 28		Wmk. 373	Perf. 14	
736	A122	15c multicolored	.30	.30
737	A122	55c multicolored	1.10	1.10
738	A122	60c multicolored	1.20	1.20
739	A122	$1 multicolored	2.00	2.00
a.		Souvenir sheet of 4, #736-739	4.60	4.60
		Nos. 736-739 (4)	4.60	4.60

Majority Rule, 25th Anniv. A123

Designs: 15c, First Progressive Liberal Party cabinet. 40c, Signing of Independence Constitution. 55c, Handing over constitutional instrument, vert. 60c, First Bahamian Governor-General, Sir Milo Butler, vert.

1992, Jan. 10		Wmk. 373	Litho.	Perf. 14
740	A123	15c multicolored	.28	.28
741	A123	40c multicolored	.75	.75
742	A123	55c multicolored	1.00	1.00
743	A123	60c multicolored	1.10	1.10
		Nos. 740-743 (4)	3.13	3.13

Queen Elizabeth II's Accession to the Throne, 40th Anniv.
Common Design Type

1992, Feb. 6		Litho.	Wmk. 373	Perf. 14
744	CD349	15c multicolored	.28	.28
745	CD349	40c multicolored	.75	.75
746	CD349	55c multicolored	1.00	1.00
747	CD349	60c multicolored	1.10	1.10
748	CD349	$1 multicolored	1.85	1.85
		Nos. 744-748 (5)	4.98	4.98

Discovery of America Type of 1988

Designs: 15c, Lucayans first sight of fleet. 40c, Approaching Bahamas coastline. 55c, Lucayans about to meet Columbus. 60c, Columbus gives thanks for safe arrival. $1.50, Monument to Columbus' landing.

1992, Mar. 17		Litho.	Perf. 14½x14	Wmk. 384
749	A106	15c multicolored	.28	.28
750	A106	40c multicolored	.75	.75
751	A106	55c multicolored	1.00	1.00
752	A106	60c multicolored	1.10	1.10
		Nos. 749-752 (4)	3.13	3.13

Souvenir Sheet

| 753 | A106 | $1.50 multicolored | 2.75 | 2.75 |

Templeton, Galbraith and Hansberger Ltd. Building — A124

1992, Apr. 22		Litho.	Perf. 14½	Wmk. 384
754	A124	55c multicolored	1.00	1.00

Templeton Prize for Progress in Religion, 20th Anniv.

1992 Summer Olympics, Barcelona — A125

1992, June 2			Perf. 14½x14	Wmk. 373
755	A125	15c Pole vault	.28	.28
756	A125	40c Javelin	.75	.75
757	A125	55c Hurdling	1.00	1.00
758	A125	60c Basketball	1.15	1.15
		Nos. 755-758 (4)	3.18	3.18

Souvenir Sheet

| 759 | A125 | $2 Sailing | 3.75 | 3.75 |

Intl. Conference on Nutrition A126

Designs: 15c, Drought-affected earth, starving child. 55c, Hand holding plant, stalks of grain.

		Perf. 14½x13		
1992, Aug. 11		Litho.	Wmk. 373	
760	A126	15c multicolored	.28	.28
761	A126	55c multicolored	1.00	1.00

Discovery of America Type of 1988
Souvenir Sheet

		Perf. 14x13½		
1992, Oct. 12		Litho.	Wmk. 384	
762	A106	$2 Coming ashore	3.75	3.75

Christmas — A127

1992, Nov. 2		Wmk. 373	Perf. 14	
763	A127	15c The Annunciation	.28	.28
764	A127	55c Nativity Scene	1.00	1.00
765	A127	60c Angel, shepherds	1.10	1.10
766	A127	70c The Magi	1.30	1.30
a.		Souvenir sheet of 4, #763-766	3.75	3.75
		Nos. 763-766 (4)	3.68	3.68

The Contract, Farm Labor Program, 50th Anniv. — A128

Bahamian, American flags and: 15c, Silhouette of worker's head. 55c, Onions. 60c, Citrus fruits. 70c, Apples.

1993, Mar. 16		Litho.	Perf. 14x14½	Wmk. 384
767	A128	15c multicolored	.28	.28
768	A128	55c multicolored	1.00	1.00
769	A128	60c multicolored	1.10	1.10
770	A128	70c multicolored	1.30	1.30
		Nos. 767-770 (4)	3.68	3.68

Royal Air Force, 75th Anniv.
Common Design Type

Designs: 15c, Westland Wapiti. 40c, Gloster Gladiator. 55c, DeHavilland Vampire. 70c, English Electric Lightning.

No. 775a, Avro Shackleton. b, Fairey Battle. c, Douglas Boston. d, DeHavilland DH9a.

1993, Apr. 1		Wmk. 373	Litho.	Perf. 14
771	CD350	15c multicolored	.26	.26
772	CD350	40c multicolored	.70	.70
773	CD350	55c multicolored	.95	.95
774	CD350	70c multicolored	1.25	1.25
		Nos. 771-774 (4)	3.16	3.16

Souvenir Sheet

| 775 | CD350 | 60c Sheet of 4, #a.-d. | 4.50 | 4.50 |

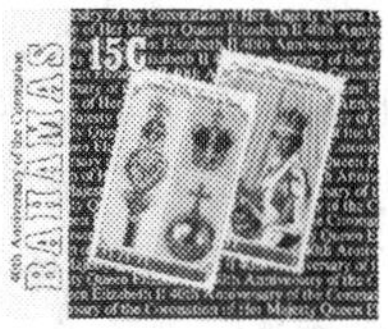

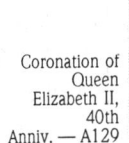

Coronation of Queen Elizabeth II, 40th Anniv. — A129

1993, June 2		Litho.	Perf. 13½	Wmk. 373
776	A129	15c Nos. 424-425	.28	.28
777	A129	55c No. 157	1.00	1.00
778	A129	60c Nos. 402-403	1.10	1.10
779	A129	70c Nos. 404-405	1.30	1.30
		Nos. 776-779 (4)	3.68	3.68

A130    A131

BAHAMAS

Natl. symbols: 15c, Lignum vitae. 55c, Yellow elder. 60c, Blue marlin. 70c, Flamingo.

1993, July 8   Litho.   *Perf. 14*

780 A130	15c multicolored	.28	.28
781 A130	55c multicolored	1.00	1.00
782 A130	60c multicolored	1.10	1.10
783 A130	70c multicolored	1.30	1.30
	Nos. 780-783 (4)	3.68	3.68

Independence, 20th anniv.

1993, Sept. 8   Litho.   *Perf. 14*

Wildflowers.

784 A131	15c Cordia	.30	.30
785 A131	55c Seaside morning glory	1.10	1.10
786 A131	60c Poinciana	1.25	1.25
787 A131	70c Spider lily	1.40	1.40
	Nos. 784-787 (4)	4.05	4.05

Christmas A132

1993, Nov. 1   Litho.   *Perf. 14*

788 A132	15c Angel, Mary	.28	.28
789 A132	55c Shepherds, angel	1.00	1.00
790 A132	60c Holy family	1.10	1.10
791 A132	70c Three wise men	1.25	1.25
	Nos. 788-791 (4)	3.63	3.63

Souvenir Sheet

792 A132	$1 Madonna and Child	1.90	1.90

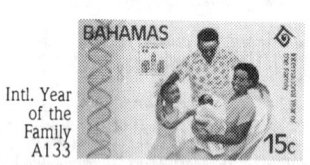

Intl. Year of the Family A133

1994, Feb. 18   *Perf. 13½*   Litho.   Wmk. 384

793 A133	15c shown	.28	.28
794 A133	55c Children studying	1.00	1.00
795 A133	60c Son, father fishing	1.10	1.10
796 A133	70c Children, grandmother	1.25	1.25
	Nos. 793-796 (4)	3.63	3.63

Hong Kong '94.

Royal Visit — A134

Designs: 15c, Bahamas, United Kingdom flags. 55c, Royal Yacht Britannia. 60c, Queen Elizabeth II. 70c, Prince Philip, Queen.

1994, Mar. 7   *Perf. 14x13½*   Wmk. 373

797 A134	15c multicolored	.28	.28
798 A134	55c multicolored	1.00	1.00
799 A134	60c multicolored	1.10	1.10
800 A134	70c multicolored	1.25	1.25
	Nos. 797-800 (4)	3.63	3.63

Natl. Family Island Regatta, 40th Anniv. A135

Designs: 15c, 55c, 60c, 70c, Various sailing boats at sea. $2, Beached yacht, vert.

1994, Apr. 27   Litho.   Wmk. 373   *Perf. 14*

801 A135	15c multicolored	.28	.28
802 A135	55c multicolored	1.00	1.00
803 A135	60c multicolored	1.10	1.10
804 A135	70c multicolored	1.25	1.25
	Nos. 801-804 (4)	3.63	3.63

Souvenir Sheet

805 A135	$2 multicolored	3.75	3.75

Intl. Olympic Committee, Cent. — A136

Flag, Olympic rings, and: 15c, Nos. 276-279, horiz. 55c, Nos. 388-391. 60c, Nos. 559-562, horiz. 70c, Nos. 755-758.

1994, May 31   Litho.   Wmk. 373   *Perf. 14*

806 A136	15c multicolored	.28	.28
807 A136	55c multicolored	1.00	1.00
808 A136	60c multicolored	1.10	1.10
809 A136	70c multicolored	1.25	1.25
	Nos. 806-809 (4)	3.63	3.63

Souvenir Sheet

First Recipients of the Order of the Caribbean Community — A137

Illustration reduced.

1994, July 5   Litho.   Wmk. 373   *Perf. 13x14*

810 A137	$2 multicolored	4.00	4.00

A138 / A139

Butterfly, flower: 15c, Canna skipper, canna. 55c, Cloudless sulphur, cassia. 60c, White peacock, passion flower. 70c, Devillier's swallowtail, calico flower.

1994, Aug. 16   Litho.   *Perf. 14*

811 A138	15c multicolored	.30	.30
812 A138	55c multicolored	1.10	1.10
813 A138	60c multicolored	1.25	1.25
814 A138	70c multicolored	1.40	1.40
	Nos. 811-814 (4)	4.05	4.05

1994, Sept. 13   *Perf. 13½x14*

Marine Life: a, Cuban hogfish, Spanish hogfish. b, Tomate, squirrelfish. c, French angelfish. d, Queen angelfish. e, Rock beauty.
$2, Rock beauty, queen angelfish.

815 A139	40c Strip of 5, #a.-e.	4.00	4.00

Souvenir Sheet

816 A139	$2 multicolored	4.00	4.00

Christmas A140

1994, Oct. 31   Litho.   Wmk. 384   *Perf. 14*

817 A140	15c Angel	.30	.30
818 A140	55c Holy family	1.10	1.10
819 A140	60c Shepherds	1.25	1.25
820 A140	70c Magi	1.40	1.40
	Nos. 817-820 (4)	4.05	4.05

Souvenir Sheet

821 A140	$2 Christ Child, vert.	3.75	3.75

College of the Bahamas, 20th Anniv. — A141

Designs: 15c, Lion. 70c, Queen Elizabeth II, college facade.

1995, Feb. 8   Litho.   Wmk. 373   *Perf. 14*

822 A141	15c multicolored	.30	.30
823 A141	70c multicolored	1.40	1.40

End of World War II, 50th Anniv.
Common Design Types

Designs: 15c, Bahamian soldiers on parade. 55c, Neutrality patrols flown by PBY-5A flying boats. 60c, Bahamian women in all three services. 70c, B-24 Liberator, Bahamians in RAF.
$2, Reverse of War Medal 1939-45.

1995, May 8   Litho.   Wmk. 373   *Perf. 13½*

824 CD351	15c multicolored	.30	.30
825 CD351	55c multicolored	1.10	1.10
826 CD351	60c multicolored	1.25	1.25
827 CD351	70c multicolored	1.40	1.40
	Nos. 824-827 (4)	4.05	4.05

Souvenir Sheet
Perf. 14

828 CD352	$2 multicolored	4.00	4.00

Kirtland's Warbler — A142

Designs: No. 829a, 25c, Female feeding young. b, 25c Immature bird feeding, prior to migration. c, 15c, Female at nest. d, 15c, Singing male.
$2, Female on branch overlooking lake.

1995, June 7   Litho.   Wmk. 373   *Perf. 13½*

829 A142	Strip of 4, #a.-d.	1.90	1.90

Souvenir Sheet
Perf. 13

830 A142	$2 multicolored	4.00	4.00

World Wildlife Fund (#829). No. 830 contains one 42x28mm stamp and has continuous design.

Tourism A143

Designs: 15c, Eleuthera Cliffs. 55c, Clarence Town, Long Island. 60c, Albert Lowe Museum. 70c, Yachting.

1995, July 18   Litho.   Wmk. 384   *Perf. 14½*

831 A143	15c multicolored	.30	.30
832 A143	55c multicolored	1.10	1.10
833 A143	60c multicolored	1.25	1.25
834 A143	70c multicolored	1.40	1.40
	Nos. 831-834 (4)	4.05	4.05

FAO, 50th Anniv. A144

Designs: 15c, Pig, poultry farming. 55c, Horticultural methods. 60c, Healthy eating. 70c, Sustainable fishing.

1995, Sept. 5   Litho.   Wmk. 373   *Perf. 13½x13*

835 A144	15c multicolored	.30	.30
836 A144	55c multicolored	1.10	1.10
837 A144	60c multicolored	1.25	1.25
838 A144	70c multicolored	1.40	1.40
	Nos. 835-838 (4)	4.05	4.05

UN, 50th Anniv.
Common Design Type

Designs: 15c, Sikorsky S-55, UNEF, Sinai, 1957. 55c, Ferret armored car, UNEF, Sinai, 1957. 60c, Fokker F-27, UNAMIC/UNTAC, Cambodia, 1991-93. 70c, Lockheed Hercules.

1995, Oct. 25   Litho.   Wmk. 373   *Perf. 14*

839 CD353	15c multicolored	.30	.30
840 CD353	55c multicolored	1.10	1.10
841 CD353	60c multicolored	1.25	1.25
842 CD353	70c multicolored	1.40	1.40
	Nos. 839-842 (4)	4.05	4.05

Christmas A145

Designs: 15c, St. Agnes Anglican Church. 55c, Church of God. 60c, Sacred Heart Roman Catholic Church. 70c, Salem Union Baptist Church.

1995, Nov. 17

843 A145	15c multicolored	.30	.30
844 A145	55c multicolored	1.10	1.10
845 A145	60c multicolored	1.25	1.25
846 A145	70c multicolored	1.40	1.40
	Nos. 843-846 (4)	4.05	4.05

World AIDS Day A146

1995, Dec. 1

847 A146	25c Virus in blood	.50	.50
848 A146	70c Scientific research	1.40	1.40

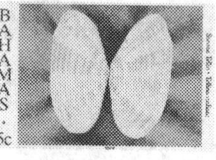

Shells A147

Designs: 5c, Sunrise tellin. 10c, Queen conch. 15c, Angular triton. 20c, True tulip. 25c, Reticulated cowrie-helmet. 30c, Sand dollar. 40c, Lace short-frond murex. 45c, Inflated sea biscuit. 50c, West Indian top shell (magpie). 55c, Spiny oyster. 60c, King helmet. 70c, Lion's paw. $1, Crown cone. $2, Atlantic partridge tun. $5, Wide-mouthed purpura. $10, Triton's trumpet.

1996   Litho.   Wmk. 373   *Perf. 14*

849 A147	5c multicolored	.15	.15
850 A147	10c multicolored	.20	.20
851 A147	15c multicolored	.30	.30
852 A147	20c multicolored	.40	.40
853 A147	25c multicolored	.50	.50
854 A147	30c multicolored	.60	.60
855 A147	40c multicolored	.80	.80
856 A147	45c multicolored	.90	.90
857 A147	50c multicolored	1.00	1.00
858 A147	55c multicolored	1.10	1.10
859 A147	60c multicolored	1.25	1.25
860 A147	70c multicolored	1.40	1.40
a.	Souvenir sheet of 1	1.40	1.40
861 A147	$1 multicolored	2.00	2.00
a.	A147 $1 Sheet of 1	2.00	2.00

BAHAMAS

862 A147 $2 multicolored 4.00 4.00
863 A147 $5 multicolored 10.00 10.00
864 A147 $10 multicolored 20.00 20.00
Nos. 849-864 (16) 44.60 44.60

No. 860a issued 6/20/97 for return of Hong Kong to China.
No. 861a issued 2/3/97 for Hong Kong '97.
Nos. 850, 861-864 exist dated "1997."
Issued: 5c, 10c, 15c, 20c, 25c, 30c, 40c, 45c, 50c, 55c, 60c, 70c, $1, $2, $5, 1/2/96.

Radio, Cent. — A148

Designs: 15c, East Goodwin Lightship, Marconi apparatus suspended from masthead. 55c, Arrest of Dr. Crippen, newspaper headline telling of wireless message from SS Montrose. 60c, SS Philadelphia, first readable transatlantic messages. 70c, Yacht Elettra, Guglielmo Marconi. $2, SS Titanic, SS Carpathia.

1996, Feb. 4   Litho.   Perf. 13½
865 A148 15c multicolored .30 .30
866 A148 55c multicolored 1.10 1.10
867 A148 60c multicolored 1.20 1.20
868 A148 70c multicolored 1.40 1.40
Nos. 865-868 (4) 4.00 4.00

Souvenir Sheet
869 A148 $2 multicolored 4.00 4.00

A149    A150

Perf. 13½
1996, June 25   Litho.   Wmk. 384
870 A149 15c Swimming .30 .30
871 A149 55c Track 1.10 1.10
872 A149 60c Basketball 1.20 1.20
873 A149 70c Long jump 1.40 1.40
Nos. 870-873 (4) 4.00 4.00

Souvenir Sheet
874 A149 $2 Javelin, 1896 4.00 4.00

Modern Olympic Games, cent.

Wmk. 384
1996, Sept. 3   Litho.   Perf. 14

Reptiles. 15c, Green anole. 55c, Fowl snake. 60c, Inagua freshwater turtle. 70c, Acklins rock iguana.

875 A150 15c multicolored .30 .30
876 A150 55c multicolored 1.10 1.10
877 A150 60c multicolored 1.20 1.20
878 A150 70c multicolored 1.40 1.40
a. Souvenir sheet, #875-878 4.00 4.00
Nos. 875-878 (4) 4.00 4.00

Environmental protection.

Christmas — A151

Designs: 15c, Angel Gabriel and Mary. 55c, Mary and Joseph. 60c, Shepherds. 70c, Magi. $2, Presentation at the Temple.

Wmk. 373
1996, Nov. 4   Litho.   Perf. 14
879 A151 15c multicolored .30 .30
880 A151 55c multicolored 1.10 1.10
881 A151 60c multicolored 1.20 1.20
882 A151 70c multicolored 1.40 1.40
Nos. 879-882 (4) 4.00 4.00

Souvenir Sheet
883 A151 $2 multicolored 4.00 4.00

Archives Dept., 25th Anniv. — A152

Perf. 14½x14
1996, Dec. 9   Litho.   Wmk. 384
884 A152 55c shown 1.10 1.10

Souvenir Sheet
Perf. 14x13½
885 A152 $2 Building, horiz. 4.00 4.00

Queen Elizabeth II and Prince Philip, 50th Wedding Anniv. — A153

Designs: No. 886, Queen. No. 887, Grenadier Guards. No. 888, Prince Philip. No. 889, Queen reviewing Grenadier Guards. No. 890, Prince holding trophy, Queen opening jewel box. No. 891, Prince on polo pony.
$2, Queen, Prince riding in open carriage, horiz.

Wmk. 373
1997, July 9   Litho.   Perf. 13
886 A153 50c multicolored 1.00 1.00
887 A153 50c multicolored 1.00 1.00
a. Pair, #886-887 2.00 2.00
888 A153 60c multicolored 1.20 1.20
889 A153 60c multicolored 1.20 1.20
a. Pair, #888-889 2.40 2.40
890 A153 70c multicolored 1.40 1.40
891 A153 70c multicolored 1.40 1.40
a. Pair, #890-891 2.80 2.80
Nos. 886-891 (6) 7.20 7.20

Souvenir Sheet
892 A153 $2 multicolored 4.00 4.00

Intl. Year of the Reefs A154

Various pictures of marine life and coral.

Perf. 14x14½
1997, Sept. 3   Litho.   Wmk. 384
893 A154 15c multicolored .30 .30
894 A154 55c multicolored 1.10 1.10
895 A154 60c multicolored 1.20 1.20
896 A154 70c multicolored 1.40 1.40
Nos. 893-896 (4) 4.00 4.00

Christmas — A155

Perf. 13x13½
1997, Oct. 6   Litho.   Wmk. 373
897 A155 15c Angel .30 .30
898 A155 55c Madonna & Child 1.10 1.10
899 A155 60c Shepherd 1.20 1.20
900 A155 70c Magi 1.40 1.40
Nos. 897-900 (4) 4.00 4.00

Souvenir Sheet
901 A155 $2 Christ Child 4.00 4.00

Diana, Princess of Wales (1961-97)
Common Design Type
Various portraits: 902: a, 55c. b, 60c. c, 70c.

Perf. 14½x14
1998, Mar. 31   Litho.   Wmk. 373
901A CD355 15c multicolored .30 .30
Sheet of 4
902 CD355 #a.-c., 901A 4.00 4.00

Organization of American States, 50th Anniv. — A156

Map of North and South America, national flags, and: 15c, "New Vision" paper. 55c, Building.

1998, Apr. 14   Perf. 13½x14
903 A156 15c multicolored .30 .30
904 A156 55c multicolored 1.10 1.10

University of the West Indies, 50th Anniv. — A157

1998, Apr. 14
905 A157 55c multicolored 1.10 1.10

Universal Declaration of Human Rights, 50th Anniv. — A158

1998, Apr. 14
906 A158 55c multicolored 1.10 1.10

Royal Air Force, 80th Anniv.
Common Design Type of 1993 Re-Inscribed

Designs: 15c, Handley Page Hyderabad. 55c, Hawker Demon. 60c, Gloster Meteor F.8. 70c, Lockheed Neptune MR.1.
No. 911: a, Sopwith Camel. b, Short 184. c, Supermarine Spitfire PR.19. d, North American Mitchell II.

1998, Apr. 1
907 CD350 15c multicolored .30 .30
908 CD350 55c multicolored 1.10 1.10
909 CD350 60c multicolored 1.20 1.20
910 CD350 70c multicolored 1.40 1.40
Nos. 907-910 (4) 4.00 4.00

Souvenir Sheet
911 CD350 50c Sheet of 4, #a.-d. 4.00 4.00

Independence, 25th Anniv. — A159

15c, Supreme Court Building. 55c, Nassau Library. 60c, Government House. 70c, Gregory Arch.
$2, Exuma-Family Island Regatta, George Town.

Perf. 13½
1998, July 10   Litho.   Wmk. 373
912 A159 15c multicolored .30 .30
913 A159 55c multicolored 1.10 1.10
914 A159 60c multicolored 1.25 1.25
915 A159 70c multicolored 1.40 1.40
Nos. 912-915 (4) 4.05 4.05

Souvenir Sheet
916 A159 $2 multicolored 4.00 4.00

Castaway Cay, Disney Cruise Lines A160

1998, Aug. 1   Perf. 14
917 A160 55c Daytime 1.10 1.10
918 A160 55c Nighttime 1.10 1.10
a. Pair, #917-918 2.20 2.20
b. Booklet pane, 5 each #917-918 11.00
Complete booklet, #918b 11.00

MS Ryndam, Half Moon Cay A161

1998, Aug. 19   Perf. 13½x13
919 A161 55c multicolored 1.10 1.10

Roses A162

Wmk. 373
1998, Sept. 8   Litho.   Perf. 14
920 A162 55c Yellow cream 1.10 1.10
921 A162 55c Big red 1.10 1.10
922 A162 55c Seven sisters 1.10 1.10
923 A162 55c Barrel pink 1.10 1.10
924 A162 55c Island beauty 1.10 1.10
a. Booklet pane, 2 each #920-924 11.00
Complete booklet, #924a 11.00
Nos. 920-924 (5) 5.50 5.50

Souvenir Sheet
925 A162 55c like #924 1.10 1.10

No. 925 has parts of other roses extending into center left and upper left area of stamp.

BAHAMIAN and WORLDWIDE STAMPS

1000's OF BAHAMIAN ITEMS IN STOCK AS WELL AS OTHER WORLDWIDE.
Write for FREE PRICE LISTS
...advising me of your collecting interests.

DON JOSS
BOX FH 14397
NASSAU, BAHAMAS
Ph:242-324-1146

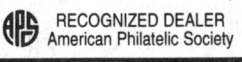

RECOGNIZED DEALER
American Philatelic Society

BAHAMAS — BAHRAIN

Intl. Year of the Ocean
A163

Wmk. 373
1998, Nov. 24 Litho. Perf. 14
926 A163 15c Killer whale .30 .30
927 A163 55c Tropical fish 1.10 1.10

Christmas
A164

1998, Dec. 11
928 A164 15c The Annunciation .30 .30
929 A164 55c Shepherds, star 1.10 1.10
930 A164 60c Magi 1.25 1.25
931 A164 70c Flight into Egypt 1.40 1.40
Nos. 928-931 (4) 4.05 4.05

Souvenir Sheet
932 A164 $2 Nativity scene 4.00 4.00

SEMI-POSTAL STAMPS

No. 48 Overprinted in Red

1.1.17.

1917, May 18 Wmk. 3 Perf. 14
B1 A6 1p car & black .40 1.25

Type of 1911 Overprinted in Red

WAR CHARITY
3.6.18.

1919, Jan. 1
B2 A6 1p red & black .40 2.25
a. Double overprint 3,500.
This stamp was originally scheduled for release in 1918.

Souvenir Sheet

No. 694 Surcharged **HURRICANE RELIEF + $1**

Wmk. 384
1992, Nov. 16 Litho. Perf. 14
B3 A116 Sheet of 2, #a.-b. 8.00 8.00

AIR POST STAMPS

Catalogue values for all unused stamps in this section are for Never Hinged items.

Manned Flight Bicentenary
AP1

Airplanes.

Wmk. 373
1983, Oct. 13 Litho. Perf. 14
C1 AP1 10c Consolidated Catalina .20 .20
a. Without emblem ('85) .20 .20
b. Without emblem, wmk. 384 ('86) .20 .20
C2 AP1 25c Avro Tudor IV .40 .40
a. Without emblem ('85) .45 .45
b. Without emblem, wmk. 384 ('86) .45 .45

C3 AP1 31c Avro Lancastrian .55 .55
a. Without emblem ('85) .55 .55
C4 AP1 35c Consolidated Commodore .60 .60
a. Without emblem ('85) .65 .65
Nos. C1-C4 (4) 1.75 1.75

Aircraft
AP2

1987, July 7
C5 AP2 15c Bahamasair Boeing 737 .25 .25
C6 AP2 40c Eastern Boeing 757 .65 .65
C7 AP2 45c Pan Am Airbus A300 B4 .75 .75
C8 AP2 50c British Airways Boeing 747 .85 .85
Nos. C5-C8 (4) 2.50 2.50

SPECIAL DELIVERY STAMPS

No. 34 Overprinted **SPECIAL DELIVERY**

1916 Wmk. 1 Perf. 14
E1 A6 5p orange & black 6.50 27.50
a. Double overprint 900.00 1,100.
b. Inverted overprint 1,400. 1,400.
c. Double ovpt., one invtd. 3,000. 3,000.
d. Pair, one without overprint 12,500. 16,000.
The No. E1 overprint exists in two types. Type I (illustrated) is much scarcer. Type II shows "SPECIAL" farther right, so that the letter "I" is slightly right of the vertical line of the "E" below it.

Type of Regular Issue of 1903 Overprinted **SPECIAL DELIVERY**

1917, July 2 Wmk. 3
E2 A6 5p orange & black .80 4.25

No. 60 Overprinted in Red **SPECIAL DELIVERY**

1918
E3 A6 5p violet & black .60 1.40

WAR TAX STAMPS

Stamps of 1912-18 Overprinted **WAR TAX**

1918, Feb. 21 Wmk. 3 Perf. 14
MR1 A8 ½p green 7.50 30.00
a. Double overprint 1,100. 1,100.
b. Inverted overprint 1,200. 1,300.
MR2 A8 1p car rose .80 1.00
a. Double overprint 1,250. 1,250.
b. Inverted overprint 1,250. 1,300.
MR3 A6 3p brown, yel 3.75 4.00
a. Inverted overprint 1,100. 1,100.
b. Double overprint 1,100. 1,100.
MR4 A8 1sh black & red 75.00 110.00
a. Double overprint 4,750. —
Nos. MR1-MR4 (4) 87.05 145.00

Same Overprint on No. 48a
1918, July 10
MR5 A6 1p car & black 3.50 5.50
a. Double overprint 1,500. 1,600.
b. Double ovpt... one invtd. 1,200.
c. Inverted overprint 1,250. 1,300.

Nos. 49-50, 54 Overprinted in Black or Red **WAR TAX**

MR6 A8 ½p green 1.00 1.25
MR7 A8 1p car rose .35 .30
a. Watermarked sideways 750.00
MR8 A8 1sh black & red (R) 6.00 2.50
Nos. MR6-MR8 (3) 7.35 4.05

Nos. 58-59 Overprinted **WAR TAX**

1918-19
MR9 A6 3p brown, yel .90 3.25
MR10 A6 3p brown & blk ('19) .90 3.75

Nos. 49-50, 54 Overprinted in Red or Black **WAR TAX**

1919, July 14
MR11 A8 ½p green (R) .30 1.10
MR12 A8 1p car rose 1.00 1.40
MR13 A8 1sh black & red (R) 8.50 24.00
Nos. MR11-MR13 (3) 9.80 26.50

No. 59 Overprinted **WAR TAX**

MR14 A6 3p brown & black .80 5.25

BAHRAIN

bä-'rān

LOCATION — An archipelago in the Persian Gulf, including the islands of Bahrain, Muharraq, Sitra, Nebi Saleh, Kasasifeh and Arad.
GOVT. — Independent sheikdom
AREA — 255 sq. mi.
POP. — 350,798 (1981)
CAPITAL — Manama

Bahrain was a British-protected territory until it became an independent state on August 15, 1971.

12 Pies = 1 Anna
16 Annas = 1 Rupee
100 Naye Paise = 1 Rupee (1957)
1000 Fils = 1 Dinar (1966)

Catalogue values for unused stamps in this country are for Never Hinged items, beginning with Scott 62 in the regular postage section and Scott MR2 in the postal tax section.

Indian Postal Administration

Stamps of India, 1926-32, Overprinted in Black

BAHRAIN
a

Wmk. Multiple Stars (196)
1933, Aug. 10 Perf. 14
1 A46 3p gray 2.25 .40
2 A47 ½a green 6.75 3.00
3 A68 9p dark green 3.25 .85
4 A48 1a dark brown 6.00 .85
5 A69 1a3p violet 3.25 .65
6 A60 2a vermilion 8.50 7.00
7 A51 3a blue 17.00 30.00
8 A70 3a6p deep blue 3.00 .50
9 A61 4a olive green 16.00 30.00
10 A54 8a red violet 5.00 .90
11 A55 12a claret 6.50 1.50

Overprinted in Black
b **BAHRAIN**

12 A56 1r green & brown 14.00 7.50
13 A56 2r brn org & car rose 30.00 30.00
14 A56 5r dk violet & ultra 80.00 110.00
Nos. 1-14 (14) 201.50 223.15

Stamps of India, 1926-32, Overprinted Type "a" in Black

1934
15 A72 1a dark brown 7.50 .35
16 A51 3a carmine rose 4.25 .35
17 A52 4a olive green 3.50 .35
Nos. 15-17 (3) 15.25 1.05

India Nos. 138, 111, 111a Overprinted Type "a" in Black

1935-37 Perf. 13½x14, 14
18 A71 ½a green 3.50 .50
19 A49 2a vermilion 30.00 7.00
a. Small die ('37) 42.50 .25

India Stamps of 1937 Overprinted Type "a" in Black

1938-41 Wmk. 196 Perf. 13½x14
20 A80 3p slate 4.00 2.50
21 A80 ½a brown 1.75 .15
22 A80 9p green 1.40 2.00
23 A80 1a carmine 1.25 .15
24 A81 2a scarlet 3.75 .90
26 A81 3a yel grn ('41) 7.75 4.25
27 A81 3a6p ultra 2.50 2.50
28 A81 4a dk brn ('41) 67.50 45.00
30 A81 8a bl vio ('40) 80.00 35.00
31 A81 12a car lake ('40) 60.00 42.50

Overprinted Type "b" in Black
32 A82 1r brn & slate 1.50 1.25
33 A82 2r dk brn & dk vio 7.50 2.50
34 A82 5r dp ultra & dk grn 20.00 13.00
35 A82 10r rose car & dk vio ('41) 37.50 22.50
36 A82 15r dk grn & dk brn ('41) 26.00 37.50
37 A82 25r dk vio & bl vio ('41) 55.00 65.00
Nos. 20-37 (16) 377.40 276.70
Set, never hinged 525.00

India Stamps of 1941-43 Overprinted Type "a" in Black

1942-44 Wmk. 196 Perf. 13½x14
38 A83 3p slate .55 .55
39 A83 1½a rose vio ('44) 2.00 .75
40 A83 9p lt green ('43) 6.25 8.75
41 A83 1a car rose ('44) 2.00 .40
42 A84 1a3p bister ('43) 4.50 10.00
43 A84 1½a dk pur ('43) 2.75 2.75
45 A84 2a scarlet ('43) 2.00 1.25
46 A84 3a violet ('43) 7.50 3.25
47 A84 3½a ultra 2.00 10.00
48 A85 4a chocolate 1.10 1.00
49 A85 6a peacock blue 5.50 6.25
50 A85 8a blue vio ('43) 1.90 1.60
51 A85 12a car lake 2.75 2.75
Nos. 38-51 (13) 40.80 49.20
Set, never hinged 62.50

British Postal Administration

See Oman (Muscat) for similar stamps with surcharge of new value only.

Great Britain Nos. 258 to 263, 243 and 248 Surcharged in Black

BAHRAIN
c
½
ANNA

1948-49 Wmk. 251 Perf. 14½x14
52 A101 ½a on ½p green .25 .40
53 A101 1a on 1p vermilion .25 .50
54 A101 1½a on 1½p lt red brn .25 .50
55 A101 2a on 2p lt orange .25 .15
56 A101 2½a on 2½p ultra .30 1.00
57 A101 3a on 3p violet .25 .15
58 A102 6a on 6p rose lilac .25 .15
59 A103 1r on 1sh brown 1.00 .45

Great Britain Nos. 249A, 250 and 251A Surcharged in Black

BAHRAIN
2 RUPEES

Wmk. 259 Perf. 14
60 A104 2r on 2sh6p yel grn 3.25 4.00
61 A104 5r on 5sh dull red 4.50 6.00
61A A105 10r on 10sh ultra 37.50 37.50
Nos. 52-61A (11) 48.05 50.80
Set, never hinged 70.00

Surcharge bars at bottom on No. 61A.
Issued: 10r, 7/4/49; others, 4/1/48.

Catalogue values for unused stamps in this section, from this point to the end of the section, are for Never Hinged items.

Silver Wedding Issue

Great Britain Nos. 267 and 268 Surcharged in Black

BAHRAIN
2½ ANNAS

BAHRAIN

Perf. 14½x14, 14x14½
1948, Apr. 26   Wmk. 251
62	A109	2½a on 2½p	.30	.20
63	A110	15r on £1	37.50	45.00

Three bars obliterate the original denomination on No. 63.

Olympic Issue
Great Britain Nos. 271 to 274 Surcharged "BAHRAIN" and New Value in Black
1948, July 29   Perf. 14½x14
64	A113	2½a on 2½p brt ultra	.50	.80
a.		Double surcharge	425.00	525.00
65	A114	3a on 3p dp vio	.50	1.50
66	A115	6a on 6p red vio	1.25	1.75
67	A116	1r on 1sh dk brn	1.40	1.75
		Nos. 64-67 (4)	3.65	5.80

A square of dots obliterates the original denomination on No. 67.

UPU Issue
Great Britain Nos. 276 to 279 Surcharged "BAHRAIN," New Value and Square of Dots in Black
1949, Oct. 10   Photo.   Perf. 14½x14
68	A117	2½a on 2½p brt ultra	.45	1.50
69	A118	3a on 3p brt vio	.75	2.00
70	A119	6a on 6p red vio	.70	2.25
71	A120	1r on 1sh brown	1.90	1.50
		Nos. 68-71 (4)	3.80	7.00

Great Britain Nos. 280, 281, 283-285 Surcharged Type "c" in Black
1950-51   Wmk. 251
72	A101	½a on ½p lt org	.55	.50
73	A101	1a on 1p ultra	1.40	.15
74	A101	1½a on 1½p green	1.40	6.75
75	A101	2a on 2p lt red brn	.55	.25
76	A101	2½a on 2½p ver	1.40	6.75
77	A102	4a on 4p ultra	1.40	1.25

Great Britain Nos. 286-288 Surcharged in Black

BAHRAIN
2 RUPEES
    Wmk. 259   Perf. 11x12
78	A121	2r on 2sh6p green	20.00	4.75
79	A121	5r on 5sh dl red	15.00	3.25
80	A122	10r on 10sh ultra	25.00	6.00
		Nos. 72-80 (9)	66.70	29.65

Longer bars, at lower right, on No. 80.
Issued: 4a, Nov. 2, 1950; others, May 3, 1951.

Stamps of Great Britain, 1952-54, Surcharged "BAHRAIN" and New Value in Black or Dark Blue
1952-54   Wmk. 298   Perf. 14½x14
81	A126	½a on ½p red org ('53)	.25	.25
a.		"½" omitted	200.00	225.00
82	A126	1a on 1p ultra	.25	.15
83	A126	1½a on 1½p grn	.25	.25
84	A126	2a on 2p red brn	.25	.25
85	A127	2½a on 2½p scar	.55	.25
86	A127	3a on 3p dk pur (Dk Bl)	.65	.25
87	A128	4a on 4p ultra	1.50	.75
88	A129	6a on 6p lil rose	1.25	.65
89	A132	12a on 1sh3p dk grn	4.00	1.50
90	A131	1r on 1sh6p dk bl	5.50	2.00
		Nos. 81-90 (10)	14.45	6.30

Issued: #83, 85, 12/5; #81-82, 84, 8/31/53; #87, 89-90, 11/2/53; #86, 88, 1/18/54.

Six stamps of this design picturing Sheik Sulman bin Hamad Al Kalifah were for local use in 1953-57.
Six stamps of similar design (same sheik, "Bahrain" vertical at left) were issued in 1961 for local use.

Coronation Issue
Great Britain Nos. 313-316 Surcharged "BAHRAIN" and New Value in Black
    Perf. 14½x14
1953, June 3   Wmk. 298
92	A134	2½a on 2½p scar	1.10	1.10
93	A135	4a on 4p brt ultra	1.75	1.75
94	A136	12a on 1sh3p dk grn	4.00	4.00
95	A137	1r on 1sh6p dk bl	5.25	5.25
		Nos. 92-95 (4)	12.10	12.10

Squares of dots obliterate the original denominations on Nos. 94-95.

Great Britain Nos. 309-311 Surcharged "BAHRAIN" and New Value in Black
1955   Wmk. 308   Engr.   Perf. 11x12
96	A133	2r on 2sh6p dk brn	3.00	1.25
97	A133	5r on 5sh crimson	9.50	4.00
98	A133	10r on 10sh brt ultra	20.00	6.50
		Nos. 96-98 (3)	32.50	11.75

Three slightly different types of surcharge are found on the 2r; two on 5r and 10r.

Great Britain Nos. 317, 323, 325, 332-333 Surcharged "BAHRAIN" and New Value
    Perf. 14½x14
1956-57   Wmk. 308   Photo.
99	A126	½a on 2½p red org	.25	.20
100	A128	4a on 4p ultra	5.00	6.25
101	A129	6a on 6p lil rose	.50	.40
102	A132	12a on 1sh3p dk green	6.25	12.00
103	A131	1r on 1sh6p dk bl ('57)	1.50	.75
		Nos. 99-103 (5)	13.50	19.60

Great Britain Nos. 317-325, 328, 332 Surcharged "BAHRAIN" and New Value
1957, Apr. 1
104	A129	1np on 5p lt brown	.15	.15
105	A126	3np on ½p red org	.25	.25
106	A126	6np on 1p ultra	.25	.25
107	A126	9np on 1½p green	.25	.25
108	A126	12np on 2p red brn	.30	.25
109	A127	15np on 2½p scar, Type I	.35	.15
a.		Type II	.40	.50
110	A127	20np on 3p dk pur	.25	.15
111	A128	25np on 4p ultra	.65	1.00
112	A129	40np on 6p lil rose	.65	.35
113	A130	50np on 9p dp ol grn	1.75	1.75
114	A132	75np on 1sh3p dk grn	1.50	.55
		Nos. 104-114 (11)	6.35	5.10

The arrangement of the surcharge varies on different values: there are three bars through value on No. 113.

Jubilee Jamboree Issue
Great Britain Nos. 334-336 Surcharged "BAHRAIN," New Value and Square of Dots in Black
    Perf. 14½x14
1957, Aug. 1   Photo.   Wmk. 308
115	A138	15np on 2½p scar	.35	.35
116	A138	25np on 4p ultra	.65	.40
117	A138	75np on 1sh3p dk grn	.80	.80
		Nos. 115-117 (3)	1.80	1.55

Great Britain No. 357 Surcharged "BAHRAIN/ NP 15 NP" in Black
1960   Wmk. 322   Perf. 14½x14
118	A127	15np on 2½p scar, type II	4.50	7.25

Sheik Sulman bin Hamad Al Khalifah — A1, A2

    Perf. 14½x14
1960, July 1   Photo.   Unwmk.
119	A1	5np lt ultra	.15	.15
120	A1	15np orange	.15	.15
121	A1	20np lt violet	.20	.15
122	A1	30np olive bister	.25	.15
123	A1	40np gray	.30	.15
124	A1	50np emerald	.30	.15
125	A1	75np red brown	.60	.15

    Engr.   Perf. 13x13½
126	A2	1r gray	.90	.20
127	A2	2r carmine	1.75	.50
128	A2	5r ultra	4.50	1.75
129	A2	10r olive green	12.00	2.25
		Nos. 119-129 (11)	21.10	5.75

Sheik Isa bin Sulman Al Khalifah — A3

Bahrain Airport — A4

Designs: 5r, 10r, Deep water jetty.

1964, Feb. 22   Photo.   Perf. 14½x14
130	A3	5np ultra	.15	.15
131	A3	15np orange	.15	.15
132	A3	20np brt purple	.15	.15
133	A3	30np brown olive	.20	.15
134	A3	40np slate	.20	.15
135	A3	50np emerald	.30	.15
136	A3	75np chestnut	.60	.25

    Engr.   Perf. 13½x13
137	A4	1r black	1.00	.35
138	A4	2r rose red	5.00	.85
139	A4	5r violet blue	8.50	5.00
140	A4	10r dull green	14.00	5.00
		Nos. 130-140 (11)	30.25	12.35

Bahrain Postal Administration

Sheik Isa bin Sulman Al Khalifah — A5

Sheik and Bahrain International Airport — A6

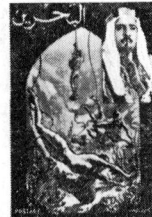

Pearl Divers — A7

Bab al Bahrain, Suq Al-Khamis Mosque, Sheik, Emblem, etc. — A8

Designs: 50f, 75f, Pier, Mina Sulman harbor. 200f, Falcon and horse race. 500f, "Hospitality," pouring coffee and Sheik's Palace.

    Perf. 14½x14
1966, Jan. 1   Photo.   Unwmk.
141	A5	5f green	.15	.15
142	A5	10f dark red	.15	.15
143	A5	15f ultra	.15	.15
144	A5	20f magenta	.20	.15

    Perf. 13½x14
145	A6	30f green & black	.28	.16
146	A6	40f blue & black	.32	.20
147	A6	50f dp car rose & blk	.42	.25
148	A6	75f violet & black	.60	.35

    Perf. 14½x14
149	A7	100f dk blue & yel	1.00	.50
150	A7	200f dk green & org	3.00	1.00
151	A7	500f red brown & yel	6.25	2.50
152	A8	1d multicolored	12.50	5.00
		Nos. 141-152 (12)	25.02	10.56

Produce, Date Palm, Ship, Truck and Plane — A9

Map of Bahrain and WHO Emblem — A10

1966, Mar. 28   Litho.   Perf. 13x13½
153	A9	10f red & blue green	.32	.32
154	A9	20f green & vio	.65	.65
155	A9	40f olive bis & lt bl	1.25	1.25
156	A9	200f vio blue & pink	6.25	6.25
		Nos. 153-156 (4)	8.47	8.47

6th Bahrain Trade Fair & Agricultural Show.

1968, June   Unwmk.   Perf. 13½x14
157	A10	20f gray & black	.55	.55
158	A10	40f blue grn & black	1.40	1.40
159	A10	150f dp rose & black	5.50	5.50
		Nos. 157-159 (3)	7.45	7.45

20th anniv. of the WHO.

Isa Town A11

1968, Nov. 18   Litho.   Perf. 14½
160	A11	50f shown	1.65	1.65
161	A11	80f Market	2.50	2.50
162	A11	120f Stadium	4.25	4.25
163	A11	150f Mosque	6.75	6.75
		Nos. 160-163 (4)	15.15	15.15

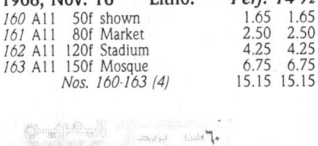

Education Symbol A12

1969, Apr.   Litho.   Perf. 13
164	A12	40f multicolored	1.25	1.25
165	A12	60f multicolored	2.00	2.00
166	A12	150f multicolored	4.25	4.25
		Nos. 164-166 (3)	7.50	7.50

50th anniversary of education in Bahrain.

Map of Arabian Gulf, Radar and Emblem A13

Designs: 40f, 150f, Radar installation and emblem of Cable & Wireless Ltd., vert.

    Perf. 14x13½, 13½x14
1969, July 14   Litho.
167	A13	20f lt green & multi	1.00	1.00
168	A13	40f vio blue & multi	2.25	2.25
169	A13	100f ocher & multi	5.25	5.25
170	A13	150f rose lilac & multi	9.00	9.00
		Nos. 167-170 (4)	17.50	17.50

Opening of the satellite earth station (connected through the Indian Ocean satellite Intelsat III) at Ras Abu Jarjur, July 14.

BAHRAIN

Municipal Building, Arms and Map of Bahrain — A14

1970, Feb. 23 Litho. Perf. 12x12½
171 A14 30f blue & multi 2.75 2.75
172 A14 150f multicolored 10.00 10.00
2nd Conf. of the Arab Cities' Org.

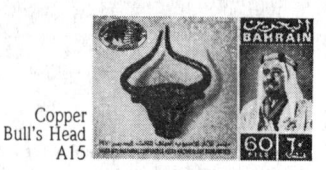

Copper Bull's Head — A15

Conf. Emblem and: 80f, Gateway to Qalat al Bahrain, 7th cent. B.C. 120f, Aerial view of grave mounds, Bahrain. 150f, Dilmun seal, 2000 B.C.

1970, Mar. 1 Photo. Perf. 14½
173 A15 60f multicolored 2.00 2.00
174 A15 80f multicolored 2.25 2.25
175 A15 120f multicolored 3.50 3.50
176 A15 150f multicolored 4.25 4.25
Nos. 173-176 (4) 12.00 12.00
3rd Intl. Asian Archaeological Conf., Bahrain.

Vickers VC 10, Big Ben and Minaret — A16

1970, Apr. 5 Litho. Perf. 14x14
177 A16 30f multicolored .90 .90
178 A16 60f multicolored 1.90 1.90
179 A16 120f multicolored 6.25 6.25
Nos. 177-179 (3) 9.05 9.05
1st flight to London from the Arabian Gulf Area by Gulf Aviation Company.

Intl. Education Year Emblem — A17

120f, Education Year emblem & students.

1970, Nov. 1 Litho. Perf. 14½x14
180 A17 60f blk, blue & org 3.25 3.25
181 A17 120f multicolored 8.00 8.00

Independent State

Government House, Manama — A18

UN Emblem and Sails — A19

Designs: 30f, "Freedom" with dove and torch, and globe. 120f, 150f, Bahrain coat of arms.

1971, Oct. 2 Photo. Perf. 14½x14
182 A18 30f gold & multi 1.65 1.65
183 A18 60f gold & multi 3.25 3.25
184 A18 120f gold & multi 6.50 6.50
185 A18 150f gold & multi 8.25 8.25
Nos. 182-185 (4) 19.65 19.65
Declaration of Bahrain independence, Aug. 15, 1971.

Perf. 14x14½, 14½x14
1972, Feb. 1 Litho.
Designs: 30f, 60f, Dhow with sails showing UN and Arab League emblems, horiz. 150f, as 120f.
186 A19 30f multicolored 2.50 2.50
187 A19 60f red, gray & multi 6.00 6.00
188 A19 120f dull blue & multi 12.50 12.50
189 A19 150f multicolored 14.00 14.00
Nos. 186-189 (4) 35.00 35.00
Bahrain's admission to the Arab League and the United Nations.

"Your Heart is your Health" — A20

1972, Apr. 7 Litho. Perf. 14½x14
190 A20 30f black & multi 3.75 3.75
191 A20 60f gray & multi 7.50 7.50
World Health Day.

UN and FAO Emblems — A21

1973, May 12 Litho. Perf. 12½x13
192 A21 30f org red, pur & grn 3.75 3.75
193 A21 60f ocher, brn & grn 6.50 6.50
World Food Programs, 10th anniversary.

People of Various Races, Human Rights Flame — A22

1973, Nov. Litho. Perf. 14x14½
194 A22 30f blue, blk & brn 4.00 4.00
195 A22 60f lake, blk & brn 7.75 7.75
25th anniversary of the Universal Declaration of Human Rights.

Flour Mill — A23

60f, Intl. Airport. 120f, Sulmaniya Medical Center. 150f, ALBA aluminum smelting plant.

1973, Dec. 16 Photo. Perf. 14½
196 A23 30f multicolored 1.00 1.00
197 A23 60f multicolored 1.75 1.75
198 A23 120f multicolored 3.50 3.50
199 A23 150f multicolored 4.25 4.25
Nos. 196-199 (4) 10.50 10.50
National Day.

Letters and UPU Emblem — A24

Carrier Pigeon and UPU Emblem — A25

60f, UPU emblem & letters. 150f, Like 120f.

1974, Feb. 4 Litho. Perf. 13½
200 A24 30f blue & multi 1.00 1.00
201 A24 60f emerald & multi 1.75 1.75
Perf. 12½x13½
202 A25 120f ultra & multi 3.00 3.00
203 A25 150f yellow & multi 4.25 4.25
Nos. 200-203 (4) 10.00 10.00
Bahrain's admission to UPU.

Traffic Signals — A26

1974, May 4 Litho. Perf. 14½
204 A26 30f org brown & multi 2.75 2.75
205 A26 60f brt blue & multi 6.25 6.25
International Traffic Day.

Jet, Globe, Mail Coach and UPU Emblem — A27

1974, Sept. 1 Photo. Perf. 14x14½
206 A27 30f multicolored .80 .80
207 A27 60f multicolored 1.65 1.65
208 A27 120f multicolored 3.25 3.25
209 A27 150f multicolored 4.00 4.00
Nos. 206-209 (4) 9.70 9.70
Centenary of Universal Postal Union.

National Day Emblem, Sitra Power Station — A28

Woman's Silk Gown — A29

National Day: 120f, 150f, Bahrain dry dock.

1974, Dec. 16 Litho. Perf. 14½
210 A28 30f blue & multi .90 .90
211 A28 60f green & multi 1.50 1.50
212 A28 120f lil rose & multi 3.50 3.50
213 A28 150f ver & multi 4.25 4.25
Nos. 210-213 (4) 10.15 10.15

Photo.; Gold Embossed
1975, Feb. 1 Perf. 14½x14
Design: Various women's costumes.
214 A29 30f blue grn & multi .70 .70
215 A29 60f vio blue & multi 1.10 1.10
216 A29 120f rose red & multi 2.75 2.75
217 A29 150f multicolored 3.50 3.50
Nos. 214-217 (4) 8.05 8.05

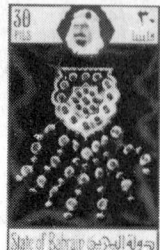

Pendant — A30

Woman Planting Flower, IWY Emblem — A31

Designs: Various jewelry.

1975, Apr. 1 Photo. Perf. 14½x14
218 A30 30f olive & multi .60 .60
219 A30 60f dp pur & multi 1.40 1.40
220 A30 120f dp car & multi 2.75 2.75
221 A30 150f dp blue & multi 3.50 3.50
Nos. 218-221 (4) 8.25 8.25

1975, July 28 Litho. Perf. 14½
60f, Educated woman holding IWY emblem.
222 A31 30f multicolored 1.50 1.50
223 A31 60f multicolored 3.50 3.50
International Women's Year.

Miniature Sheet

Arabian Stallion — A32

Arabian horses: a, Brown head. b, White mare. c, Mare and foal. d, White head. e, White mare. f, Mare and stallion. g, Bedouins on horseback. #224a, 224b, 224d are vert.

Perf. 14x14½, 14½x14
1975, Sept. 1 Photo.
224 Sheet of 8 52.50 32.50
a.-h. A32 60f any single 5.25 3.50

Flag of Bahrain — A33

Map of Bahrain — A34

Sheik Isa — A35

1976-80 Litho. Perf. 14½
225 A33 5f red & ultra .15 .15
226 A33 10f red & green .15 .15
227 A33 15f red & black .15 .15
228 A33 20f red & brown .15 .15
228A A34 25f gray & blk ('79) .15 .15
229 A34 40f blue & black .25 .25
229A A34 50f yel grn & blk ('79) .30 .30
230 A34 60f dl grn & blk ('77) .35 .35
231 A34 80f rose lil & blk .45 .45
232 A34 100f lt red brn & blk ('77) .55 .55
233 A34 150f org & black .85 .85
234 A34 200f yel & black 1.10 1.10
Engr.
Perf. 12x12½
235 A35 300f lt grn & grn 1.65 1.65
236 A35 400f pink & red brn 2.25 2.25
237 A35 500f lt bl & dk bl 2.75 2.75
238 A35 1d gray & sepia 5.50 5.00
239 A35 2d rose & vio ('80) 11.50 9.75
240 A35 3d buff & brn ('80) 17.00 14.00
Nos. 225-240 (18) 45.25 39.50
A later printing of the 100f-200f, and possibly others, has a larger printers imprint at bottom.

BAHRAIN

Concorde at London Airport — A36

Designs: No. 245, Concorde at Bahrain Airport. No. 246, Concorde over London to Bahrain map. No. 247, Concorde on runway at night.

1976, Jan. 22	Photo.	Perf. 13x14
244 A36 80f gold & multi	2.25	2.25
245 A36 80f gold & multi	2.25	2.25
246 A36 80f gold & multi	2.25	2.25
247 A36 80f gold & multi	2.25	2.25
a. Souvenir sheet of 4	8.00	8.00
b. Block of 4, #244-247	9.00	9.00

1st commercial flight of supersonic jet Concorde, London to Bahrain, Jan. 21. No. 247a contains 4 stamps with simulated perfs.

Soldier, Flag and Arms of Bahrain — A37

1976, Feb. 5	Litho.	Perf. 14½
248 A37 40f yellow & multi	2.00	2.00
249 A37 80f lt blue & multi	4.00	4.00

Defense Force Day.

Sheik Isa, King Khalid, Bahrain and Saudi Flags A38

1976, Mar. 23	Litho.	Perf. 14½
250 A38 40f gold & multi	1.75	1.75
251 A38 80f silver & multi	3.00	3.00

Visit of King Khalid of Saudi Arabia.

New Housing, Housing Ministry's Seal — A39

1976, Dec. 16	Litho.	Perf. 14½
252 A39 40f rose & multi	1.65	1.65
253 A39 80f blue & multi	3.25	3.25

National Day.

APU Emblem A40

1977, Apr. 12	Litho.	Perf. 14½
254 A40 40f silver & multi	1.50	1.50
255 A40 80f rose & multi	3.00	3.00

Arab Postal Union, 25th anniversary.

Miniature Sheet Dogs on Beach and Dhow A41

Saluki dogs: b, Dog and camels. c, Dog and gazelles. d, Dog and Ruler's Palace. e, Dog's head. f, Heads of two dogs. g, Dog in dunes. h, Playing dogs.

1977, July	Photo.	Perf. 14x14½
256 Sheet of 8	28.00	28.00
a.-h. A41 80f any single	2.75	2.75

Students and Candle A42

1977, Sept. 8	Litho.	Perf. 14½
257 A42 40f multicolored	1.50	1.50
258 A42 80f multicolored	3.00	3.00

International Literacy Day.

Shipyard and Flags A43

1977, Dec. 16	Litho.	Perf. 14½
259 A43 40f multicolored	1.50	1.50
260 A43 80f multicolored	3.00	3.00

Inauguration of Arab Shipbuilding and Repair Yard Co.

Antenna, ITU Emblem A44

1978, May 17	Litho.	Perf. 14½
261 A44 40f yellow & multi	1.50	1.50
262 A44 80f silver & multi	3.00	3.00

10th World Telecommunications Day.

Ganja Dhow A45

Dhows of the Arabian Gulf. #267-270 vertical.

	Perf. 14x14½, 14½x14	
1979, June 16		Photo.
263 A45 100f shown	3.25	3.25
264 A45 100f Zarook	3.25	3.25
265 A45 100f Shu'ai	3.25	3.25
266 A45 100f Jaliboot	3.25	3.25
267 A45 100f Baghla	3.25	3.25
268 A45 100f Sambuk	3.25	3.25
269 A45 100f Boom	3.25	3.25
270 A45 100f Kotia	3.25	3.25
a. Block of 8, #263-270	26.00	26.00

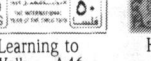

Learning to Walk — A46

IYC Emblem and: 100f, Hands surrounding girl, UN emblem.

1979	Litho.	Perf. 14½
271 A46 50f multicolored	1.50	1.50
272 A46 100f multicolored	3.00	3.00

International Year of the Child.

Hegira, 1,500th Anniv. — A47

1980	Photo.	Perf. 13x13½
273 A47 50f multicolored	.65	.65
274 A47 100f multicolored	1.25	1.25
a. Miniature sheet of 1	6.00	6.00
275 A47 150f multicolored	2.00	2.00
276 A47 200f multicolored	2.75	2.75
Nos. 273-276 (4)	6.65	6.65

Falcon A48

Designs: Falcons.

	Perf. 13½x14, 14x13½	
1980, Nov. 1		Photo.
277 Block of 8	15.00	15.00
a.-h. A48 100f any single	1.75	1.75

IYD Emblem, Sheik Isa — A49

1981, Mar. 21	Litho.	Perf. 14½
278 A49 50f multicolored	1.65	1.65
279 A49 100f multicolored	3.25	3.25

International Year of the Disabled.

50th Anniversary of Electricity in Bahrain A50

1981, Apr. 26	Litho.	Perf. 14½
280 A50 50f multicolored	1.65	1.65
281 A50 100f multicolored	3.25	3.25

Stone Cutting — A51

1981, July 1	Photo.	Perf. 14x13½
282 A51 50f shown	.75	.75
283 A51 100f Pottery	1.25	1.25
284 A51 150f Weaving	2.75	2.75
285 A51 200f Basket making	3.00	3.00
Nos. 282-285 (4)	7.75	7.75

Hegira (Pilgrimage Year) — A52

Designs: Various mosques.

1981, Oct. 1	Photo.	Perf. 14x13½
286 A52 50f multicolored	.80	.80
287 A52 100f multicolored	1.65	1.65
288 A52 150f multicolored	2.25	2.25
289 A52 200f multicolored	3.25	3.25
Nos. 286-289 (4)	7.95	7.95

Sheik Isa, 20th Anniv. of Coronation — A53

1981, Dec. 16	Photo.	Perf. 14x13½
290 A53 15f multicolored	.25	.25
291 A53 50f multicolored	.80	.80
292 A53 100f multicolored	1.75	1.75
293 A53 150f multicolored	2.50	2.50
294 A53 200f multicolored	3.50	3.50
Nos. 290-294 (5)	8.80	8.80

Wildlife in al Areen Park A54

Designs: a, Gazelle. b, Oryx. c, Dhub lizard. d, Arabian hares. e, Oryxes. f, Reems.

1982, Mar. 1	Photo.	Perf. 13½x14
295 Sheet of 6	14.00	14.00
a.-f. A54 100f any single	2.25	2.25

3rd Session of Gulf Supreme Council, Nov. — A55

1982, Nov. 9	Litho.	Perf. 14½
296 A55 50f blue & multi	.85	.85
297 A55 100f green & multi	2.25	2.25

Opening of Madinat Hamad Housing Development — A56

1983, Dec. 1	Litho.	Perf. 14½
298 A56 50f multicolored	.85	.85
299 A56 100f multicolored	2.25	2.25

BAHRAIN

Al Khalifa Dynasty Bicentenary — A57

Sheiks or Emblems: a, 500fr, Isa bin Sulman. b, Emblem (tan & multi). c, Isa bin Ali, 1869-1932. d, Hamad bin Isa, 1932-42. e, Sulman bin Hamad, 1942-61. f, Emblem (pale green & multi). g, Emblem (lemon & multi). h, Emblem (light blue & multi). i, Emblem (gray & multi).

1983, Dec. 16   Litho.   Perf. 14½
300		Sheet of 9	9.00	9.00
a.-i.	A57	100f any single	.80	.80

Souvenir Sheet
| 301 | A57 | 500f multicolored | 8.50 | 8.50 |

No. 301 contains one stamp 60x38mm.

Gulf Co-operation Council Traffic Week — A58

1984, Apr. 30   Litho.   Perf. 14½
302	A58	15f multicolored	.30	.30
303	A58	50f multicolored	1.00	1.00
304	A58	100f multicolored	2.00	2.00
		Nos. 302-304 (3)	3.30	3.30

1984 Summer Olympics A59

1984, Sept. 15   Perf. 14½
305	A59	15f Hurdles	.26	.26
306	A59	50f Equestrian	.80	.80
307	A59	100f Diving	1.65	1.65
308	A59	150f Fencing	2.00	2.00
309	A59	200f Shooting	3.50	3.50
		Nos. 305-309 (5)	8.21	8.21

Postal Service Cent. A60

1984, Dec. 8   Photo.   Perf. 12x11½
310	A60	15f multicolored	.40	.40
311	A60	50f multicolored	1.25	1.25
312	A60	100f multicolored	2.25	2.25
		Nos. 310-312 (3)	3.90	3.90

Miniature Sheet

Coastal Fish A61

1985, Feb. 10   Photo.   Perf. 13½x14
313		Sheet of 10	12.00	12.00
a.-j.	A61	100f any single	1.40	1.40

1st Arab Gulf States Week for Social Work A62

1985, Oct. 15   Litho.   Perf. 14½
314	A62	15f multicolored	.25	.25
315	A62	50f multicolored	.85	.85
316	A62	100f multicolored	1.90	1.90
		Nos. 314-316 (3)	3.00	3.00

Intl. Youth Year A63

1985, Nov. 16
317	A63	15f multicolored	.25	.25
318	A63	50f multicolored	.85	.85
319	A63	100f multicolored	1.90	1.90
		Nos. 317-319 (3)	3.00	3.00

Bahrain-Saudi Arabia Causeway Opening — A64

1986, Nov.   Litho.   Perf. 14½
320	A64	15f Causeway, aerial view	.25	.25
321	A64	50f Island	.85	.85
322	A64	100f Causeway	1.90	1.90
		Nos. 320-322 (3)	3.00	3.00

Sheik Isa, 25th Anniv. as the Emir — A65

1986, Dec. 16
323	A65	15f multicolored	.25	.25
324	A65	50f multicolored	.85	.85
325	A65	100f multicolored	1.90	1.90
a.		Souvenir sheet of 3, #323-325	5.50	5.50
		Nos. 323-325 (3)	3.00	3.00

WHO, 40th Anniv. A66

1988, Apr. 30   Litho.   Perf. 14½
326	A66	50f multicolored	.50	.50
327	A66	150f multicolored	1.40	1.40

Opening of Ahmed Al Fateh Islamic Center A67

1988, June 2   Litho.   Perf. 14½
328	A67	50f multicolored	.50	.50
329	A67	150f multicolored	1.40	1.40

1988 Summer Olympics, Seoul A68

1988, Sept. 17   Litho.   Perf. 14½
330	A68	50f Running	.28	.28
331	A68	80f Equestrian	.45	.45
332	A68	150f Fencing	.80	.80
333	A68	200f Soccer	1.10	1.10
		Nos. 330-333 (4)	2.63	2.63

Gulf Cooperation Council Supreme Council 9th Regular Session, Bahrain A69

1988, Dec. 19   Litho.   Perf. 14½
334	A69	50f multicolored	.50	.50
335	A69	150f multicolored	1.40	1.40

Miniature Sheets

Camels A70

No. 336: a, Close-up of head, rider in background. b, Camel kneeling at rest. c, Two adults, calf. d, Three adults. e, Camel facing right. f, Mount and rider (facing left).
No. 337: a, Man walking in front of camel, oil well. b, Man walking in front of camel. c, Oil well, camel's head. d, Mount and rider (facing forward). e, Mount and rider (facing right). f, Two dromedaries at a run. Nos. 337a-337f vert.

Perf. 13½x14, 14x13½
1989, June 15
336		Sheet of 6	6.00	6.00
a.-f.	A70	150f any single	1.00	1.00
337		Sheet of 6	6.00	6.00
a.-f.	A70	150f any single	1.00	1.00

Sheik Isa — A71

1989, Dec. 16   Litho.   Perf. 13½x14
338	A71	25f multicolored	.15	.15
339	A71	40f multicolored	.24	.24
340	A71	50f multicolored	.30	.30
341	A71	60f multicolored	.35	.35
342	A71	75f multicolored	.45	.45
343	A71	80f multicolored	.48	.48
344	A71	100f multicolored	.60	.60
345	A71	120f multicolored	.72	.72
346	A71	150f multicolored	.90	.90
347	A71	200f multicolored	1.20	1.20
a.		Souvenir sheet of 10, #338-347	6.00	6.00
		Nos. 338-347 (10)	5.39	5.39

Houbara (Bustard) — A72

Designs: a, Two birds facing right. b, Two birds facing each other. c, Chicks. d, Adult, chick. e, Adult, facing right, vert. f, In flight. g, Adult facing right. h, Chick, facing left, vert. i, Adult facing left. j, Adult male, close-up. k, Courtship display. l, Two birds facing left.

1990, Feb. 17   Photo.   Perf. 14
348		Sheet of 12	10.80	10.80
a.-l.	A72	150f any single	.90	.90

Gulf Air, 40th Anniv. A73

1990, Mar. 24   Litho.   Perf. 14½
360	A73	50f multicolored	.30	.30
361	A73	80f multicolored	.48	.48
362	A73	150f multicolored	.90	.90
363	A73	200f multicolored	1.20	1.20
		Nos. 360-363 (4)	2.88	2.88

Chamber of Commerce, 50th Anniv. A74

1990, May 26
364	A74	50f multicolored	.30	.30
365	A74	80f multicolored	.48	.48
366	A74	150f multicolored	.90	.90
367	A74	200f multicolored	1.20	1.20
		Nos. 364-367 (4)	2.88	2.88

Intl. Literacy Year A75

1990, Sept. 8   Litho.   Perf. 14½
368	A75	50f multicolored	.30	.30
369	A75	80f multicolored	.48	.48
370	A75	150f multicolored	.90	.90
371	A75	200f multicolored	1.20	1.20
		Nos. 368-371 (4)	2.88	2.88

Miniature Sheet

Indigenous Birds — A76

Designs: a, Galerida cristata. b, Upupa epops. c, Pycnonotus leucogenys. d, Streptopelia turtur. e, Streptopelia decaocto. f, Falco tinnunculus. g, Passer domesticus, horiz. h, Lanius excubitor, horiz. i, Psittacula krameri.

1991, Sept. 15   Litho.   Perf. 14½
372		Sheet of 9	9.00	9.00
a.-i.	A76	150f any single	1.10	1.10

See Nos. 382, 407.

Coronation of Sheik Isa, 30th Anniv. A77

Design: Nos. 374, 376, 378, 380, 381a, Portrait at left, leaves.

Litho. & Embossed
1991, Dec. 16   Perf. 14½
373	A77	50f multicolored	.35	.35
374	A77	50f multicolored	.35	.35
375	A77	80f multicolored	.55	.55
376	A77	80f multicolored	.55	.55
377	A77	150f multicolored	1.10	1.10
378	A77	150f multicolored	1.10	1.10
379	A77	200f multicolored	1.50	1.50
380	A77	200f multicolored	1.50	1.50
		Nos. 373-380 (8)	7.00	7.00

Souvenir Sheet
Perf. 14x14½
381		Sheet of 2	7.50	7.50
a.-b.	A77	500f any single	3.75	3.75

No. 381 contains 41x31mm stamps.

Miniature Sheet
Indigenous Birds Type of 1991

Designs: No. 382a, Ciconia ciconia. b, Merops apiaster. c, Sturnus vulgaris. d, Hypocolius ampelinus. e, Cuculus canorus. f, Turdus viscivorus. g, Coracias garrulus. h, Carduelis carduelis. i, Lanius collurio. j, Turdus iliacus, horiz. k, Motacilla alba,

BAHRAIN

horiz. l, Oriolus oriolus, horiz. m, Erithacus rubecula. n, Luscinia luscinia. o, Muscicapa striata. p, Hirundo rustica.

1992, Mar. 21	Litho.	Perf. 14½
382	Sheet of 16	13.50 13.50
a.-p.	A76 150f any single	.80 .80

Miniature Sheet

Horse Racing — A78

Designs: No. 383a, Horses leaving starting gate. b, Trainers leading horses. c, Horses racing around turn. d, Horses in stretch racing by flags. e, Two horses racing by grandstand. f, Five horses galloping. g, Two brown horses racing. h, Black horse, gray horse racing.

1992, May 22		
383	Sheet of 8	7.20 7.20
a.-h.	A78 150f any single	.90 .90

1992 Summer Olympics, Barcelona — A79

1992, July 25	Litho.	Perf. 14½
384 A79	50f Equestrian	.35 .35
385 A79	80f Running	.60 .60
386 A79	150f Judo	1.10 1.10
387 A79	200f Cycling	1.40 1.40
	Nos. 384-387 (4)	3.45 3.45

Bahrain Intl. Airport, 60th Anniv. — A80

1992, Oct. 27	Litho.	Perf. 14½
388 A80	50f multicolored	.35 .35
389 A80	80f multicolored	.55 .55
390 A80	150f multicolored	1.00 1.00
391 A80	200f multicolored	1.25 1.25
	Nos. 388-391 (4)	3.15 3.15

Children's Art — A81

Designs: 50f, Girl jumping rope, vert. 80f, Women in traditional dress, vert. 150f, Women stirring kettle. 200f, Fishermen.

1992, Nov. 28	Litho.	Perf. 14½
392 A81	50f multicolored	.30 .30
393 A81	80f multicolored	.50 .50
394 A81	150f multicolored	.95 .95
395 A81	200f multicolored	1.25 1.25
	Nos. 392-395 (4)	3.00 3.00

Inauguration of Expansion of Aluminum Bahrain — A82

Designs: 50f, Ore funicular. 80f, Smelting pot. 150f, Mill. 200f, Cylindrical aluminum ingots.

1992, Dec. 16		
396 A82	50f multicolored	.30 .30
397 A82	80f multicolored	.50 .50
398 A82	150f multicolored	.95 .95
399 A82	200f multicolored	1.25 1.25
	Nos. 396-399 (4)	3.00 3.00

Bahrain Defense Force, 25th Anniv. — A83

Designs: 50f, Artillery forces, vert. 80f, Fighters, tanks, and ship, vert. 150f, Frigate. 200f, Jet fighter.

Perf. 13½x13, 13x13½

1993, Feb. 5		Litho.
400 A83	50f multicolored	.30 .30
401 A83	80f multicolored	.50 .50
402 A83	150f multicolored	.95 .95
403 A83	200f multicolored	1.25 1.25
	Nos. 400-403 (4)	3.00 3.00

World Meteorology Day — A84

Designs: 50f, Satellite image of Bahrain, vert. 150f, Infrared satellite map of world. 200f, Earth, seen from space, vert.

1993, Mar. 23	Litho.	Perf. 14½
404 A84	50f multicolored	.45 .45
405 A84	150f multicolored	1.40 1.40
406 A84	200f multicolored	1.75 1.75
	Nos. 404-406 (3)	3.60 3.60

Bird Type of 1991
Miniature Sheet

Designs: a, Ardea purpurea. b, Gallinula chloropus. c, Phalacrocorax nigrogularis. d, Dromas ardeola. e, Alcedo atthis. f, Vanellus vanellus. g, Haematopus ostralegus, horiz. h, Nycticorax nycticorax. i, Sterna caspia, horiz. j, Arenaria interpres, horiz. k, Rallus aquaticus, horiz. l, Anas platyrhychos, horia. m, Larus fuscus, horiz.

1993, May 22	Litho.	Perf. 14½
407	Sheet of 13 + 2 labels	11.00 11.00
a.-m.	A76 150f any single	.85 .85

Gazella Subgutturosa Marica — A85

1993, July 24	Litho.	Perf. 14½
408 A85	25f Calf	.15 .15
409 A85	50f Female standing	.30 .30
410 A85	50f Female walking	.30 .30
411 A85	150f Male	.95 .95
	Nos. 408-411 (4)	1.70 1.70

World Wildlife Federation.

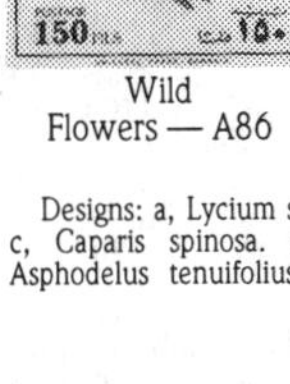

Wild Flowers — A86

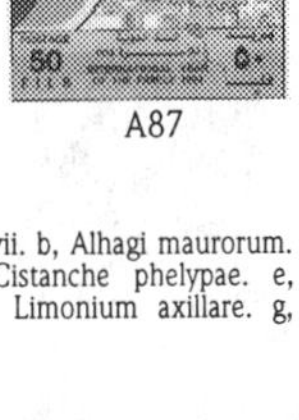

A87

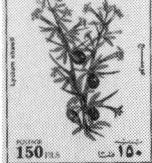

Designs: a, Lycium shawii. b, Alhagi maurorum. c, Caparis spinosa. d, Cistanche phelypae. e, Asphodelus tenuifolius. f, Limonium axillare. g, Cynomorium coccineum. h, Calligonum polygonoides.

1993, Oct. 16	Litho.	Perf. 13½x13
412 A86	150f Sheet of 8, #a.-h.	6.50 6.50

1994, Jan. 22	Litho.	Perf. 14½
Background Color		
413 A87	50f yellow	.30 .30
414 A87	80f blue green	.50 .50
415 A87	150f purple	.95 .95
416 A87	200f blue	1.25 1.25
	Nos. 413-416 (4)	3.00 3.00

Intl. Year of the Family.

A88 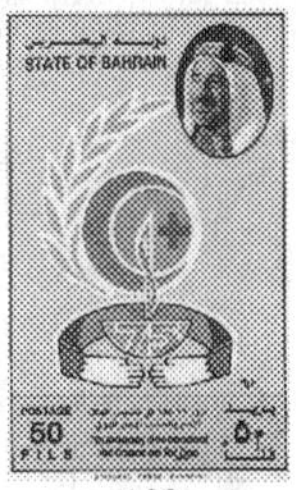   A89

Butterflies: No. 417a, Lepidochrysops arabicus. b, Ypthima bolanica. c, Eurema brigitta. d, Precis limnoria. e, Aglais urticae. f, Colotis protomedia. g, Salamis anacardii. h, Byblia ilithyia.

No. 418a, Papilio machaon. b, Agrodiaetus loewii. c, Vanessa cardui. d, Papilio demoleus. e, Hamanumida daedalus. f, Funonia orithya. g, Funonia chorimine. h, Colias croceus.

Perf. 13½x13, 13x13½

1994, Mar. 21		Litho.
417 A88	50f Sheet of 8, #a.-h.	2.50 2.50
418 A88	150f Sheet of 8, #a.-h.	7.50 7.50

No. 418 is horiz.

1994, May 8	Litho.	Perf. 14½
419 A89	50f lilac & multi	.30 .30
420 A89	80f yellow & multi	.50 .50
421 A89	150f salmon & multi	.95 .95
422 A89	200f green blue & multi	1.25 1.25
	Nos. 419-422 (4)	3.00 3.00

Intl. Red Cross & Red Crescent Societies, 75th anniv.

1994 World Cup Soccer Championships, US — A90

Designs: 50f, Goalkeeper. 80f, Heading ball. 150f, Dribbling ball. 200f, Slide tackle.

1994, June 17	Litho.	Perf. 14
423 A90	50f multicolored	.30 .30
424 A90	80f multicolored	.50 .50
425 A90	150f multicolored	.95 .95
426 A90	200f multicolored	1.25 1.25
	Nos. 423-426 (4)	3.00 3.00

Bahrain's First Satellite Earth Station, 25th Anniv. A91

1994, July 14		
427 A91	50f blue & multi	.30 .30
428 A91	80f yellow & multi	.50 .50
429 A91	150f violet & multi	.95 .95
430 A91	200f pink, yellow & multi	1.25 1.25
	Nos. 427-430 (4)	3.00 3.00

Education in Bahrain, 75th Anniv. — A92

1994, Nov. 19	Litho.	Perf. 14½
431 A92	50f yellow & multi	.30 .30
432 A92	80f buff & multi	.50 .50
433 A92	150f salmon & multi	.95 .95
434 A92	200f pink & multi	1.25 1.25
	Nos. 431-434 (4)	3.00 3.00

Gulf Cooperation Council Supreme Council, 15th Regular Session, Bahrain — A93

1994, Dec. 19		Perf. 14
435 A93	50f blue green & multi	.30 .30
436 A93	80f brown & multi	.50 .50
437 A93	150f lilac rose & multi	.95 .95
438 A93	200f blue & multi	1.25 1.25
	Nos. 435-438 (4)	3.00 3.00

Date Palm A94

Designs: 80f, Flowering stage. 100f, Dates beginning to ripen. 200f, Dates up close. 250f, Trees from distance.
500f, Pitcher, basket of dates.

1995, Mar. 21	Litho.	Perf. 14
439 A94	80f multicolored	.48 .48
440 A94	100f multicolored	.60 .60
441 A94	200f multicolored	1.25 1.25
442 A94	250f multicolored	1.50 1.50
	Nos. 439-442 (4)	3.83 3.83

Souvenir Sheet

| 443 A94 | 500f multicolored | 3.00 3.00 |

No. 443 contains one 65x48mm stamp.

Fight Against Polio — A95

1995, Apr. 22	Litho.	Perf. 13x13½
444 A95	80f pink & multi	.42 .42
445 A95	200f blue & multi	1.00 1.00
446 A95	250f lt brown & multi	1.40 1.40
	Nos. 444-446 (3)	2.82 2.82

World Health Day.

1st Natl. Industries Exhibition A96

1995, May 15		
447 A96	80f blue green & multi	.42 .42
448 A96	200f lilac & multi	1.00 1.00
449 A96	250f lt brown & multi	1.40 1.40
	Nos. 447-449 (3)	2.82 2.82

BAHRAIN

FAO, 50th Anniv. A97

Fields of various crops.

1995, June 17   Litho.   *Perf. 14*
450 A97 80f lilac & multi .42 .42
451 A97 200f blue & multi 1.00 1.00
452 A97 250f lt pink & multi 1.40 1.40
    Nos. 450-452 (3) 2.82 2.82

Arab League, 50th Anniv. — A98

1995, Sept. 14   Litho.   *Perf. 14½*
453 A98 80f pink & multi .40 .40
454 A98 200f blue & multi 1.10 1.10
455 A98 250f yellow & multi 1.40 1.40
    Nos. 453-455 (3) 2.90 2.90

UN, 50th Anniv. A99

1995, Oct. 24   Litho.   *Perf. 14½*
456 A99 80f yellow & multi .40 .40
457 A99 100f green & multi .55 .55
458 A99 200f pink & multi 1.10 1.10
459 A99 250f blue & multi 1.40 1.40
    Nos. 456-459 (4) 3.45 3.45

Miniature Sheet

Traditional Architecture — A100

Example of architecture, detail: a, Tower with balcony. b, Arched windows behind balcony. c, Double doors under arch. d, Four rows of square windows above row of arched windows. e, Door flanked by two windows. f, Three windows.

1995, Nov. 20   Litho.   *Perf. 14½*
460 A100 200f Sheet of 6, #a.-f. 6.50 6.50

National Day — A101

1995, Dec. 16   Litho.   *Perf. 14½*
461 A101 80f blue & multi .40 .40
462 A101 100f green & multi .55 .55
463 A101 200f violet & multi 1.10 1.10
464 A101 250f blue green & multi 1.40 1.40
    Nos. 461-464 (4) 3.45 3.45

Public Library, 50th Anniv. — A102

1996, Mar. 23   Litho.   *Perf. 14*
465 A102 80f pink & multi .40 .40
466 A102 200f green & multi 1.10 1.10
467 A102 250f blue & multi 1.40 1.40
    Nos. 465-467 (3) 2.90 2.90

Pearl Diving — A103

Designs: 80f, Group of divers on ship, three in water. 100f, Five divers in water, ship. 200f, Diver underneath water. 250f, Diver being pulled up, underwater scene.
500f, Lantern, weight, scales, pearls, knife. Illustration reduced.

1996, May 8   Litho.   *Perf. 14*
468 A103 80f multicolored .40 .40
469 A103 100f multicolored .55 .55
470 A103 200f multicolored 1.10 1.10
471 A103 250f multicolored 1.40 1.40
    Nos. 468-471 (4) 3.45 3.45

Souvenir Sheet
Perf. 14½
472 A103 500f multicolored 2.75 2.75

No. 472 contains one 70x70mm stamp.

1996 Summer Olympics, Atlanta A104

1996, July 19   Litho.   *Perf. 14*
473 A104 80f olive & multi .40 .40
474 A104 100f pink & multi .55 .55
475 A104 200f blue green & multi 1.10 1.10
476 A104 250f orange & multi 1.40 1.40
    Nos. 473-476 (4) 3.45 3.45

Interpol, Intl. Criminal Police Organization — A105

1996, Sept. 25   Litho.   *Perf. 14*
477 A105 80f blue & multi .40 .40
478 A105 100f yellow & multi .55 .55
479 A105 200f pink & multi 1.10 1.10
480 A105 250f green & multi 1.40 1.40
    Nos. 477-480 (4) 3.45 3.45

Aluminum Production in Bahrain, 25th Anniv. A106

1996, Nov. 20   Litho.   *Perf. 14*
481 A106 80f bister & multi .40 .40
482 A106 100f orange & multi .55 .55
483 A106 200f blue & multi 1.10 1.10
484 A106 250f green & multi 1.40 1.40
    Nos. 481-484 (4) 3.45 3.45

Accession to the Throne by Sheik Isa Bin Salman Al Khalifa, 35th Anniv. A107

1996, Dec. 16
485 A107 80f gray & multi .40 .40
486 A107 100f green & multi .55 .55
487 A107 200f pink & multi 1.10 1.10
488 A107 250f blue & multi 1.40 1.40
    Nos. 485-488 (4) 3.45 3.45

Bahrain Refinery, 60th Anniv. A108

1997, Jan. 15   Litho.   *Perf. 14*
489 A108 80f red & multi .45 .45
490 A108 200f blue & multi 1.10 1.10
491 A108 250f yellow & multi 1.30 1.30
    Nos. 489-491 (3) 2.85 2.85

Pure Breeds of Arabian Horses, Amiri Stud A109

Designs: a, Musannaan, Al-Jellabieh, Rabdaan. b, Kuheilaan weld umm zorayr. c, Al-Jellaby. d, Musannaan. e, Kuheilaan aladiyat. f, Kuheilaan aafas. g, Al-Dhahma. h, Mlolshaan. i, Al-Kray. j, Krush. k, Al Hamdaany. l, Hadhfaan. m, Rabda. n, Al-Suwaitieh. o, Al-Obeyah. p, Al-Shuwaimeh. q, Al-Ma'anaghieh. r, Al-Tuwaisah. s, Wadhna. t, Al-Saqlawieh. u, Al-Shawafah.

1997, Apr. 23   Litho.   *Perf. 14x14½*
492 A109 200f Sheet of 21, #a.-u. 22.50 22.50

9th Men's Junior World Volleyball Championship — A110

1997, Aug. 21   Litho.   *Perf. 14x14½*
493 A110 80f brown & multi .45 .45
494 A110 100f green & multi .55 .55
495 A110 200f gray brown & multi 1.10 1.10
496 A110 250f blue & multi 1.30 1.30
    Nos. 493-496 (4) 3.40 3.40

Montreal Protocol on Substances that Deplete Ozone Layer, 10th Anniv. — A111

1997, Sept. 16   Litho.   *Perf. 14½*
497 A111 80f yellow & multi .45 .45
498 A111 100f purple & multi .55 .55
499 A111 200f red & multi 1.10 1.10
500 A111 250f green & multi 1.30 1.30
    Nos. 497-500 (4) 3.40 3.40

Sheikh Isa Bin Salman Bridge A112

Designs: 80f, Pylon, supports. 200f, Center of bridge. 250f, 500f, Entire span.

1997, Dec. 28   Litho.   *Perf. 13x13½*
501 A112 80f multicolored .45 .45
502 A112 200f multicolored 1.10 1.10
    Size: 76x26mm
503 A112 250f multicolored 1.30 1.30
    Nos. 501-503 (3) 2.85 2.85

Souvenir Sheet
504 A112 500f multicolored 2.60 2.60

Inauguration of Urea Plant, GPIC (Refinery) Complex A113

Designs: 80f, View of plant from Persian Gulf. 200f, Plant facilities. 250f, Aerial view.

1998, Mar. 3   Litho.   *Perf. 13x13½*
505 A113 80f multicolored .45 .45
506 A113 200f multicolored 1.10 1.10
507 A113 250f multicolored 1.30 1.30
    Nos. 505-507 (3) 2.85 2.85

World Health Organization, 50th Anniv. — A114

1998, May 11   Litho.   *Perf. 14*
508 A114 80f orange & multi .45 .45
509 A114 200f green & multi 1.10 1.10
510 A114 250f gray & multi 1.30 1.30
    Nos. 508-510 (3) 2.85 2.85

1998 World Cup Soccer Championships, France — A115

Designs: 200f, Soccer balls, world maps, vert. 250f, Players, globe, vert.

1998, June 10
511 A115 80f multicolored .45 .45
512 A115 200f multicolored 1.10 1.10
513 A115 250f multicolored 1.30 1.30
    Nos. 511-513 (3) 2.85 2.85

14th Arabian Gulf Soccer Cup, Bahrain A116

Design: 200f, 250f, Soccer ball.

BAHRAIN — BANGKOK — BANGLADESH

1998, Oct. 30   Litho.   *Perf. 14*
514 A116   80f shown   .45   .45
515 A116   200f pale violet & multi   1.10   1.10
516 A116   250f bister & multi   1.25   1.25
     Nos. 514-516 (3)   2.80   2.80

WAR TAX STAMPS

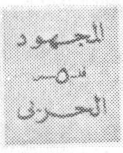

WT1    WT2

1973, Oct. 21   Litho.   *Perf. 14½*
MR1 WT1   5f sky blue

Catalogue values for all unused stamps in this section, from this point to the end of the section, are for Never Hinged items.

1974   Litho.   *Perf. 14½*
MR2 WT2   5f light blue   1.75   .25
   a.   Perf. 14½x13½   2.50

No. MR2a was issued around 1988.

BANGKOK
ˈbaŋ-ˌkäk

LOCATION — Capital of Siam (Thailand)

Stamps were issued by Great Britain under rights obtained in the treaty of 1855. These were in use until July 1, 1885, when the stamps of Siam were designated as the only official postage stamps to be used in the kingdom.

100 Cents = 1 Dollar

Excellent counterfeits of Nos. 1-22 are plentiful.

Stamps of Straits Settlements Overprinted in Black   B

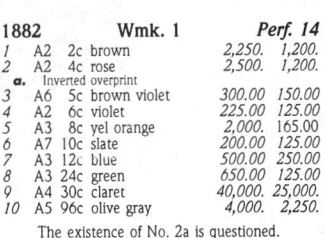

1882   Wmk. 1   *Perf. 14*
1   A2   2c brown   2,250.   1,200.
2   A2   4c rose   2,500.   1,200.
   a.   Inverted overprint
3   A6   5c brown violet   300.00   150.00
4   A3   6c violet   225.00   125.00
5   A3   8c yel orange   2,000.   165.00
6   A7   10c slate   200.00   125.00
7   A3   12c blue   500.00   250.00
8   A3   24c green   650.00   125.00
9   A4   30c claret   40,000.   25,000.
10   A5   96c olive gray   4,000.   2,250.

The existence of No. 2a is questioned.
See note after No. 20. No. 2 with two clear impressions: $6,000 used.

1882-83   Wmk. 2
11   A2   2c brown   325.00   250.00
12   A2   2c rose ('83)   40.00   40.00
   a.   Inverted overprint   20,000.   10,000.
   b.   Double overprint   1,750.
   c.   Triple overprint   10,000.
13   A2   4c rose   400.00   250.00
14   A2   4c brown ('83)   60.00   60.00
   a.   Double overprint
15   A6   5c ultra ('83)   165.00   165.00
16   A2   6c violet ('83)   100.00   100.00
   a.   Double overprint
17   A3   8c yel orange   125.00   80.00
   a.   Inverted overprint   17,500.   10,000.
18   A7   10c slate   125.00   80.00
19   A3   12c violet brn ('83)   175.00   140.00
20   A3   24c green   3,250.   2,250.

Partial double overprints exist on a number of values of these issues. They sell for a modest premium over catalogue value depending on how much of the impression is present.

1883   Wmk. 1
21   A5   2c on 32c pale red   2,250.   2,250.

On Straits Settlements No. 9
1885   Wmk. 38
22   A7   32c on 2a yel (B+B)   40,000.   50,000.

BANGLADESH
ˌbän-glə-ˈdesh

LOCATION — In southern, central Asia, touching India, Burma, and the Bay of Bengal
GOVT. — Republic in the British Commonwealth
AREA — 55,598 sq. mi.
POP. — 87,052,024 (1981)
CAPITAL — Dacca (Dhaka)

Bangladesh, formerly East Pakistan, broke away from Pakistan in April 1971, proclaiming its independence. It consists of 14 former eastern districts of Bengal and the former Sylhet district of Assam province of India.

100 Paisas = 1 Rupee
100 Paisas (Poishas) = 1 Taka (1972)

Catalogue values for all unused stamps in this country are for Never Hinged items.

Various stamps of Pakistan were handstamped locally for use in Bangladesh from March 26, 1971 until April 30, 1973.

Map of Bangladesh — A1   Sheik Mujibur Rahman — A2

Designs: 20p, "Dacca University Massacre." 50p, "A Nation of 75 Million People." 1r, Flag of Independence (showing map). 2r, Ballot box. 3r, Broken chain. 10r, "Support Bangladesh" and map.

Perf. 14x14½
1971, July 29   Litho.   Unwmk.
1   A1   10p red, dk pur & lt bl   .15   .15
2   A1   20p bl, grn, red & yel   .15   .15
3   A1   50p dp org, gray & brn   .15   .15
4   A1   1r red, emer & yel   .20   .20
5   A1   2r lil rose, lt & dk bl   .40   .40
6   A1   3r blue, emer & grn   .50   .50
7   A2   5r dp org, tan & blk   1.00   1.00
8   A1   10r gold, dk bl & lil rose   1.65   1.65
     Nos. 1-8 (8)   4.20   4.20

A set of 15 stamps of types A1 and A2 in new paisa-taka values and colors was rejected by Bangladesh officials and not issued. Bangladesh representatives in England released these stamps, which were not valid, on Feb. 1, 1972.
Imperfs of Nos. 1-8 were in the Format International liquidation. They are not errors.

Nos. 1-8 Overprinted in Black or Red   BANGLADESH LIBERATED

1971, Dec. 20
9   A1   10p multicolored   .15   .15
10   A1   20p multicolored   .15
11   A1   50p multicolored   .15
12   A1   1r multicolored   .30
13   A1   2r multicolored   .50
14   A1   3r multicolored   .90
15   A2   5r multicolored (R)   1.25   1.25
16   A1   10r multicolored   2.50   2.50
     Nos. 9-16 (8)   5.90

Liberation of Bangladesh.
The 10p, 5r and 10r were issued in Dacca, but Nos. 10-14 were not put on sale in Bangladesh.

Monument — A3   "Independence" — A4

1972, Feb. 21   Litho.   *Perf. 13*
32   A3   20p green & rose   .70   .30

Language Movement Martyrs.

1972, Mar. 26   Photo.   *Perf. 13*
33   A4   20p maroon & red   .15   .15
34   A4   60p dark blue & red   .30   .30
35   A4   75p purple & red   .30   .30
     Nos. 33-35 (3)   .75   .75

First anniversary of independence.

Doves of Peace — A5    Flower Growing from Ruin — A6

1972, Dec. 16   Litho.   *Perf. 13*
36   A5   20p ocher & multi   .15   .15
37   A5   60p lilac & multi   .30   .30
38   A5   75p yellow green & multi   .35   .35
     Nos. 36-38 (3)   .80   .80

Victory Day, Dec. 16.

1973, Mar. 25   Litho.   *Perf. 13*
39   A6   20p ocher & multi   .20   .20
40   A6   60p brown & multi   .40   .40
41   A6   1.35t violet blue & multi   1.00   1.00
     Nos. 39-41 (3)   1.60   1.60

Martyrs of the war of liberation.

Embroidered Quilt — A7 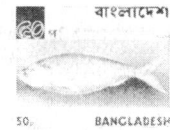   Hilsa — A8

Court of Justice — A9

Designs: 3p, Jute field. 5p, Jack fruit. 10p, Farmer plowing with ox team. 20p, Hibiscus rosenensis. 25p, Tiger. 60p, Bamboo and water lilies. 75p, Women picking tea. 90p, Handicraft. 2t, Collecting date palm juice, vert. 5t, Net fishing. 10t, Sixty-dome Mosque.

Perf. 14x14½, 14½x14
1973, Apr. 30   Litho.
Size: 21x28mm, 28x21mm
42   A7   2p black   .15   .15
43   A7   3p bright green   .15   .15
44   A7   5p light brown   .15   .15
45   A7   10p black   .15   .15
46   A7   20p olive   .70   .70
47   A7   25p red lilac   1.90   1.90
48   A8   50p rose lilac   1.50   1.50
49   A7   60p gray   .70   .70
50   A7   75p orange   1.25   1.25
51   A7   90p red brown   1.25   1.25

Taka Expressed as "TA"
Size: 35x22mm
52   A9   1t violet   3.50   3.50
53   A9   2t greenish gray   4.50   4.50
54   A9   5t grayish blue   6.00   6.00
55   A9   10t rose   6.50   6.50
     Nos. 42-55 (14)   28.40   28.40

See Nos. 82-85, 95-106, 165-176. For overprints see Nos. O1-O10, O13.

Human Rights Flame — A10   Family, Chart, Map of Bangladesh — A11

1973, Dec. 10   Litho.   *Perf. 13x13½*
56   A10   10p blue & multi   .15   .15
57   A10   1.25t violet & multi   .60   .60

25th anniversary of the Universal Declaration of Human Rights.

1974, Feb. 10   Litho.   *Perf. 13½*
58   A11   20p blue grn & multi   .15   .15
59   A11   25p brt blue & multi   .15   .15
60   A11   75p red & multi   .45   .45
     Nos. 58-60 (3)   .75   .75

First census in Bangladesh.
For overprints see Nos. 194-196.

Copernicus, Heliocentric System — A12   Flag and UN Headquarters — A13

1974, July 22   Litho.   *Perf. 13½*
61   A12   25p violet, blk & org   .20   .20
62   A12   75p emerald, blk & org   .60   .60

Nicolaus Copernicus (1473-1543), Polish astronomer.

1974, Sept. 25   Litho.   *Perf. 13½*
63   A13   25p lilac & multi   .15   .15
64   A13   1t blue & multi   .50   .50

Admission of Bangladesh to the UN.

A14    A15

Designs: 25p, 1.75t, UPU emblem. 1.25t, 5t, Mail runner. 25p, 1.25t, country and denomination appear on a yellow background, 1.75t, 5t, blue background.

1974, Oct. 9   *Perf. 13½*
65   A14   25p multicolored   .15   .15
66   A14   1.25t multicolored   .20   .20
67   A14   1.75t multicolored   .35   .35
68   A14   5t multicolored   .95   .95
   a.   Souv. sheet of 4, #65-68, imperf.   35.00
     Nos. 65-68 (4)   1.65   1.65

BANGLADESH

1974, Nov. 4			Litho.		
69	A15	25p Royal bengal tiger		.30	.30
70	A15	50p Tiger cub		1.25	1.25
71	A15	2t Swimming tiger		3.50	3.50
		Nos. 69-71 (3)		5.05	5.05

"Save the Tiger," World Wildlife Fund.

Type of 1973
Taka Expressed in Bengali

1974-75		Perf. 14½x14, 14x14½			
		Size: 35x22mm			
82	A9	1t violet		1.65	1.65
83	A9	2t grayish green		3.25	3.25
84	A9	5t grayish blue ('75)		4.50	4.50
85	A9	10t rose ('75)		8.00	8.00
		Nos. 82-85 (4)		17.40	17.40

For overprints see Nos. O11-O12, O14.

Family — A16
Children — A17  
Family — A18 

1974, Dec. 30			Litho.		Perf. 14
86	A16	25p ocher & multi		.15	.15
87	A17	70p claret & multi		.35	.35
88	A18	1.25t multicolored		.50	.50
		Nos. 86-88 (3)		1.00	1.00

Family planning. The numerals on No. 87 look like "90" but mean "70."

Betbunia Satellite Earth Station — A19

1975, June 14			Litho.		Perf. 14
89	A19	25p red, black & silver		.15	.15
90	A19	1t vio blue, blk & silver		.60	.60

Opening of Betbunia Satellite Earth Station.

Allegory, IWY Emblem A20

1975, Dec. 31			Litho.		Perf. 15
91	A20	50p rose & multi		.15	.15
92	A20	2t lt lilac & multi		.70	.70

International Women's Year.

Types of 1973 Redrawn

1976-77		Litho.			Perf. 15x14½
		Size: 18x23mm, 23x18mm			
95	A7	5p green		.15	.15
96	A7	10p black		.15	.15
97	A7	20p olive green		.20	.20
98	A7	25p rose lilac		.30	.30
99	A8	50p rose lilac		.45	.45
100	A7	60p gray		.60	.60
101	A7	75p olive		.70	.70
102	A7	90p red brown		.90	.90

Taka Expressed in Bengali
Size: 32x20mm, 20x32mm

103	A9	1t violet	.95	.95
104	A9	2t greenish gray	2.00	2.00
105	A9	5t grayish blue	5.25	5.25
106	A9	10t rose ('77)	10.00	10.00
		Nos. 95-106 (12)	21.65	21.65

For overprints see Nos. O16-O25.

Telephones, 1876 and 1976 — A21
Alexander Graham Bell — A22 

1976, Mar. 10		Litho.		Perf. 15
107	A21	2.25t multicolored	.40	.40
108	A22	5t multicolored	1.00	1.00

Centenary of first telephone call by Alexander Graham Bell, Mar. 10, 1876.

Eye and Healthful Food — A23

1976, Apr. 7		Litho.		Perf. 15
109	A23	30p yellow & multi	.35	.35
110	A23	2.25t orange & multi	1.65	1.65

World Health Day: Foresight prevents blindness.

Liberty Bell — A24

Designs: 2.25t, Statue of Liberty, New York Skyline. 5t, Mayflower. 10t, Mt. Rushmore, presidents' heads.

1976, May 29		Photo.		Perf. 13½x14
111	A24	30p multicolored	.15	.15
112	A24	2.25t multicolored	.30	.30
113	A24	5t multicolored	.70	.70
114	A24	10t multicolored	1.40	1.40
a.		Souv. sheet of 4, #111-114, perf. 13	3.50	3.50
		Nos. 111-114 (4)	2.55	2.55

American Bicentennial. Sheet exists imperf.

Weaver, Chemist, Farmer, Student and Emblem — A25

1976, July 29		Litho.		Perf. 15
115	A25	30p multicolored	.15	.15
116	A25	2.25t multicolored	.75	.75

25th anniversary of Colombo Plan.
For overprint see No. 252.

Hurdles — A26

Montreal Olympic Emblem and: 30p, Running, horiz. 1t, High jump. 2.25t, Swimming, horiz. 3.50t, Gymnastics. 5t, Soccer.

1976, Nov. 29		Litho.		Perf. 15
117	A26	25p multicolored	.15	.15
118	A26	30p multicolored	.15	.15
119	A26	1t multicolored	.20	.20
120	A26	2.25t multicolored	.50	.50
121	A26	3.50t multicolored	.70	.70
122	A26	5t multicolored	1.10	1.10
		Nos. 117-122 (6)	2.80	2.80

21st Olympic Games, Montreal, Canada, July 17-Aug. 1.

Coronation Ceremony — A27

Designs: 2.25t, Queen Elizabeth II. 10t, Queen and Prince Philip.

1977, Feb. 7				Perf. 14x15
123	A27	30p multicolored	.15	.15
124	A27	2.25t multicolored	.25	.25
125	A27	10t multicolored	1.00	1.00
a.		Souv. sheet of 3, #123-125, perf. 14½	1.50	1.50
		Nos. 123-125 (3)	1.40	1.40

25th anniv. of the reign of Elizabeth II.

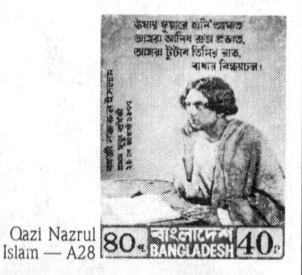

Qazi Nazrul Islam — A28
Nazrul A29 

1977, Aug. 29		Litho.		Perf. 14
126	A28	40p lt green & black	.15	.15
127	A29	2.25t multicolored	.65	.65

Qazi Nazrul Islam (1899-1976), natl. poet.

Pigeon Carrying Letter A30

1977, Sept. 29		Litho.		Perf. 14
128	A30	30p multicolored	.15	.15
129	A30	2.25t multicolored	.60	.60

Asian-Oceanic Postal Union (AOPU), 15th anniversary.

Leopard A31

40p and 1t are vert.

1977, Nov. 9		Litho.		Perf. 13
130	A31	40p Asiatic black bear	.15	.15
131	A31	1t Axis deer	.60	.60
132	A31	2.25t shown	.70	.70
133	A31	3.50t Gayal	.95	.95
134	A31	4t Elephant	1.50	1.50
135	A31	5t Bengal tiger	1.75	1.75
		Nos. 130-135 (6)	5.65	5.65

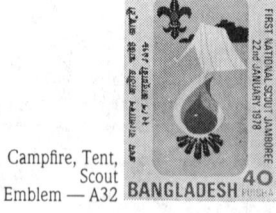

Campfire, Tent, Scout Emblem — A32

Designs: 3.50t, Emblem, first aid, signaling, horiz. 5t, Scout emblem and oath.

1978, Jan. 22		Litho.		Perf. 13
136	A32	40p multicolored	.15	.15
137	A32	3.50t multicolored	.90	.90
138	A32	5t multicolored	1.65	1.65
		Nos. 136-138 (3)	2.70	2.70

1st National Boy Scout Jamboree, Jan. 22.
For overprint see No. 269.

Champac A33

Flowers and Flowering Trees: 1t, Pudding pipe tree. 2.25t, Flamboyant tree. 3.50t, Water lilies. 4t, Butea. 5t, Anthocephalus indicus.

1978, Mar. 31		Litho.		Perf. 13
139	A33	40p multicolored	.20	.20
140	A33	1t multicolored	.50	.50
141	A33	2.25t multicolored	.85	.85
142	A33	3.50t multicolored	1.10	1.10
143	A33	4t multicolored	1.25	1.25
144	A33	5t multicolored	1.40	1.40
		Nos. 139-144 (6)	5.30	5.30

For overprints see Nos. 259A-259F.

Crown, Scepter and Staff of State — A34

Designs: 3.50t, Royal family on balcony. 5t, Queen Elizabeth II and Prince Philip. 10t, Queen in coronation regalia, Westminster Abbey.

1978, May 20				Perf. 14
145	A34	40p multicolored	.15	.15
146	A34	3.50t multicolored	.20	.20
147	A34	5t multicolored	.30	.30
148	A34	10t multicolored	.55	.55
a.		Souv. sheet of 4, #145-148, perf. 14½	1.40	1.40
		Nos. 145-148 (4)	1.20	1.20

Coronation of Queen Elizabeth II, 25th anniv.
For overprint see No. 228B.

Alan Cobham's DH50, 1926 A35

Planes: 2.25t, Capt. Hans Bertram's Junkers W33 Atlantis, 1932-33. 3.50t, Wright brothers' plane. 5t, Concorde.

BANGLADESH

1978, June 15   Litho.   Perf. 13
149	A35	40p multicolored	.20	.20
150	A35	2.25t multicolored	1.25	1.25
151	A35	3.50t multicolored	1.90	1.90
152	A35	5t multicolored	2.50	2.50
		Nos. 149-152 (4)	5.85	5.85

75th anniversary of powered flight.

Holy Kaaba, Mecca — A37

Design: 3.50t, Pilgrims at Mt. Arafat, horiz.

1978, Nov. 9   Litho.   Perf. 13
| 154 | A37 | 40p multicolored | .15 | .15 |
| 155 | A37 | 3.50t multicolored | .75 | .75 |

Pilgrimage to Mecca.

Jasim Uddin, Poet — A38

1979, Mar. 14   Litho.   Perf. 14
| 156 | A38 | 40p multicolored | .40 | .40 |

Rowland Hill — A39   Moulana Bhashani — A40

Hill and Stamps of Bangladesh: 3.50t, No. 1, horiz. 10t, No. 66, horiz.

1979, Aug. 27   Litho.   Perf. 14
157	A39	40p multicolored	.15	.15
158	A39	3.50t multicolored	.35	.35
159	A39	10t multicolored	1.10	1.10
a.		Souvenir sheet of 3, #157-159	2.75	2.75
		Nos. 157-159 (3)	1.60	1.60

Sir Rowland Hill (1795-1879), originator of penny postage.

1979, Nov. 17   Perf. 12½
| 160 | A40 | 40p multicolored | .55 | .55 |

Moulana Abdul Hamid Khan Bhashani (1880-1976), philosopher and statesman.

A41   A42

IYC Emblem and: 40p, Boys and Hoops. 3.50t, Boys flying kites. 5t, Children jumping.

1979, Dec. 17   Litho.   Perf. 14x14½
161	A41	40p multicolored	.15	.15
162	A41	3.50t multicolored	.45	.45
163	A41	5t multicolored	.65	.65
a.		Souv. sheet of 3, #161-163, perf. 14½	2.50	2.50
		Nos. 161-163 (3)	1.25	1.25

International Year of the Child.

Type of 1973

Designs: 5p, Lalbag Fort. 10p, Fenchungan Fertilizer Factory, vert. 15p, Pineapple. 20p, Gas well. 25p, Jute on boat. 30p, Banana tree. 40p, Baitul Mukarram Mosque. 50p, Baitul Mukarram Mosque. 80p, Garh excavations. 1ta, Dotara (musical instrument.) 2t, Karnaphuli Dam.

1979-82   Photo.   Perf. 14½
Size: 18x23mm, 23x18mm
165	A7	5p brown ('79)	.15	.15
166	A7	10p Prus blue	.15	.15
167	A7	15p yellow org ('81)	.20	.15
168	A7	20p dk carmine ('79)	.30	.15
169	A7	25p dk blue ('82)	.35	.15
170	A7	30p lt olive grn ('80)	.45	.15
171	A8	40p rose magenta ('79)	.55	.15
172	A9	50p black & gray ('81)	.75	.15
173	A7	80p dk brown ('80)	1.10	.15
174	A7	1t red lilac ('81)	1.50	.15
175	A7	2t brt ultra ('81)	2.75	1.00
		Nos. 165-175 (11)	8.25	2.50

For overprints see Nos. O27-O36.

1980, Feb. 23   Litho.   Perf. 14
Rotary Intl., 75th Anniv.: 40p, Rotary emblem, diff.
| 179 | A42 | 40p multicolored | .15 | .15 |
| 180 | A42 | 5t ultra & gold | .90 | .90 |

For overprints see Nos. 285-286.

Canal Digging A43

1980, Mar. 27   Litho.   Perf. 14
| 181 | A43 | 40p multicolored | .55 | .55 |

Sher-e-Bangla A.K. Fazlul Huq (1873-1962), Natl. Leader — A44

1980, Apr. 27   Litho.   Perf. 14
| 182 | A44 | 40p multicolored | .55 | .55 |

Early Mail Transport, London 1980 Emblem — A45

1980, May 5
183	A45	1t shown	.15	.15
184	A45	10t Modern mail transport	1.40	1.40
a.		Souvenir sheet of 2, #183-184	1.75	1.75

London 80 Intl. Stamp Exhib., May 6-14.

Dome of the Rock — A46   Adult Education — A47

1980, Aug. 21   Litho.   Perf. 14½
| 185 | A46 | 50p violet rose | .85 | .85 |

For the families of Palestinians.

1980, Aug. 23   Perf. 13½
| 186 | A47 | 50p multicolored | .55 | .55 |

Beach Scene A48

1980, Sept. 27   Litho.   Perf. 14
187	A48	50p shown	.15	.15
188	A48	5t Beach scene, diff.	1.40	1.40
a.		Souvenir sheet of 2, #187-188	1.50	1.50
b.		Pair, #187-188	1.50	1.50

World Tourism Conference, Manila, Sept. 27. No. 188b has continuous design.
For overprints see Nos. 243-244.

Hegira (Pilgrimage Year) — A49

1980, Nov. 11   Photo.   Perf. 14
| 189 | A49 | 50p multicolored | .40 | .40 |

A50   A51

Design: Deer and Boy Scout emblem.

1981, Jan. 1   Litho.   Perf. 14
| 190 | A50 | 50p multicolored | .15 | .15 |
| 191 | A50 | 5t multicolored | 1.40 | 1.40 |

5th Asia-Pacific and 2nd Bangladesh Scout Jamboree, 1980-1981.

1980, Dec. 9   Litho.   Perf. 14
| 192 | A51 | 50p multicolored | .15 | .15 |
| 193 | A51 | 2t multicolored | .55 | .55 |

Begum Roquiah (1880-1932), educator.

Nos. 58-60 Overprinted:
2nd / CENSUS / 1981

1981, Mar. 6   Perf. 13½
194	A11	20p multicolored	.15	.15
195	A11	50p multicolored	.15	.15
196	A11	75p multicolored	.35	.35
		Nos. 194-196 (3)	.65	.65

A52   A53

1981, Mar. 16   Litho.   Perf. 14
197	A52	1t multicolored	.15	.15
198	A52	15t multicolored	2.50	2.50
a.		Souvenir sheet of 2, #197-198	3.25	3.25

Queen Mother Elizabeth, 80th birthday (1980).

1981, Mar. 26
| 199 | A53 | 50p Citizen Holding Rifle & Flag | .15 | .15 |
| 200 | A53 | 2t People, map | .60 | .60 |

10th anniversary of independence.

UN Conference on Least-developed Countries, Paris — A54

1981, Sept. 1   Litho.   Perf. 14x13½
| 201 | A54 | 50p multicolored | .70 | .70 |

Birth Centenary of Kemal Ataturk (First President of Turkey) — A55

1981, Nov. 10   Litho.   Perf. 14
| 202 | A55 | 50p Portrait | .50 | .50 |
| 203 | A55 | 1t Portrait, diff. | .70 | .70 |

Intl. Year of the Disabled A56

1981, Dec. 26   Litho.   Perf. 14
| 204 | A56 | 50p Sign language, vert. | .35 | .35 |
| 205 | A56 | 2t Amputee | 1.10 | 1.10 |

World Food Day, Oct. 16 — A57

1981, Dec. 31   Litho.   Perf. 13½x14
| 206 | A57 | 50p multicolored | .80 | .80 |

A58   A59

1982, May 22   Litho.   Perf. 13½x14
| 207 | A58 | 50p Boat hauling rice straw | .70 | .70 |

10th Anniv. of UN Conf. on Human Environment.
For overprint see No. 281.

1982, Oct. 9
| 208 | A59 | 50p multicolored | .95 | .95 |

Dr. Kazi Motahar Hossain, educator and statistician.

Scouting Year — A60

1982, Oct. 21   Litho.   Perf. 14
| 209 | A60 | 50p Emblem, knots | .75 | .75 |
| 210 | A60 | 2t Baden-Powell, vert. | 3.25 | 3.25 |

BANGLADESH

Capt. Mohiuddin Jahangir — A61

Liberation Heroes (Tablet Color): b, Sepoy Hamidur Rahman (pale green). c, Sepoy Mohammed Mustafa Kamal (rose claret). d, Mohammad Ruhul Amin (yellow). e, M. Matiur Rahman (olive bister). f, Lance-Naik Munshi Abdur Rob (brown orange). g, Lance-Naik Nur Mouhammad (bright yellow green).

1982, Dec. 16		Litho.		Perf. 14	
211	Strip of 7			1.90	1.90
a.-g.	A61 50p multicolored			.25	.25

Metric System — A62

1983, Jan. 10		Litho.		Perf. 14	
212	A62	50p	Mail scale, vert.	.60	.60
213	A62	2t	Weights, measures	2.25	2.25

TB Bacillus Centenary — A63

1983, Feb. 20		Litho.		Perf. 14	
214	A63	50p	Koch	1.00	1.00
215	A63	1t	Slides, microscope	2.00	2.00

A64

1983, Mar. 14		Litho.		Perf. 14	
216	A64	1t	Open stage theater	.15	.15
217	A64	3t	Boat race	.20	.20
218	A64	5t	Snake dance	.65	.65
219	A64	15t	Tea garden	1.00	1.00
	Nos. 216-219 (4)			2.00	2.00

Commonwealth Day.

Jnantapash Shahidullah (1885-1969), Educator and Linguist — A65

1983, July 10		Litho.		Perf. 14	
220	A65 50p multicolored			.95	.95

Birds — A66

1983, Aug. 17		Litho.		Perf. 14	
221	A66	50p	Copsychus saulari	1.25	.65
222	A66	2t	Halcyon smyrnensis, vert.	2.00	2.00
223	A66	3.75t	Dinopium benghalense, vert.	2.25	2.25
224	A66	5t	Carina scutulota	3.00	3.00
a.	Souvenir sheet of 4, #221-224			11.00	11.00
	Nos. 221-224 (4)			8.50	7.90

No. 224a sold for 13t.

Local Fish — A67

1983, Oct. 31		Litho.		Perf. 14	
225	A67	50p	Macrobrachium rosenbergii	.60	.25
226	A67	2t	Stromateus cinereus	1.90	1.40
227	A67	3.75t	Labeo rohita	2.25	1.75
228	A67	5t	Anabas testudineus	2.75	2.25
a.	Souv. sheet of 4, #225-228, imperf.			7.50	7.50
	Nos. 225-228 (4)			7.50	5.65

No. 228a sold for 13t.

No. 148 Ovptd. "Nov. '83/Visit of Queen" in Red

1983, Nov. 14		Litho.		Perf. 14	
228B	A34 10t multicolored			5.25	5.25

World Communications Year — A68

1983, Dec. 21		Litho.		Perf. 14	
229	A68	50p	Messenger, vert.	.20	.20
230	A68	5t	Jet, train, ship, vert.	1.90	1.90
231	A68	10t	Dish antenna, messenger	3.50	3.50
	Nos. 229-231 (3)			5.60	5.60

Hall — A69   A70

1983, Dec. 5		Litho.		Perf. 14	
232	A69	50p	Sangsad Bhaban	.20	.20
233	A69	5t	Shait Gumbaz	2.25	2.25

14th Islamic Foreign Ministers Conference.

Perf. 11½x12½, 12½x11½
1983, Dec. 21

234	A70	5p	Mailboat	.15	.15
235	A70	10p	Dacca P.O. counter	.15	.15
236	A70	15p	IWTA Terminal	.15	.15
237	A70	20p	Sorting mail	.15	.15
238	A70	25p	Mail delivery	.15	.15
239	A70	30p	Postman at mailbox	.15	.15
240	A70	50p	Mobile post office	.20	.20

Size: 30½x18½mm
Perf. 12x11½

241	A70	1t	Kamalapur Railway Station	.25	.25
242	A70	2t	Zia Intl. Airport	.50	.50
242A	A70	5t	Khulna P.O.	1.25	1.25
	Nos. 234-242A (10)			3.10	3.10

Nos. 235-237, 239-242A horiz.
Nos. 234-240 reprinted on cream paper. See #270-271. For overprints see #O37-O46, O48, O51-O52.

No. 188b Overprinted in English
First Bangladesh National Philatelic Exhibition 1984
50p   50p
or Bengali in Red

1984, Feb. 1		Litho.		Perf. 14	
243	A48	50p	Beach Scene	.25	.25
244	A48	5t	Beach Scene, diff.	2.25	2.25
a.	Pair, #243-244			2.50	2.50

1st Bangladesh Natl. Philatelic Exhibition, 1984. No. 244a has continuous design.

A71

1984, May 17		Litho.		Perf. 14½	
245		50p	Girl examining stamp album	.25	.25
246		7.50t	Boy updating collection	2.00	2.00
a.	Souvenir sheet of 2, #245-246			4.00	4.00
b.	A71 Pair, #245-246			2.25	2.25
c.	As "a", overprinted			9.25	9.25

#246a sold for 10t.
Overprint in sheet margin of No. 246c reads: "SILVER JUBILEE / BANGLADESH POSTAGE STAMPS 1971-96."

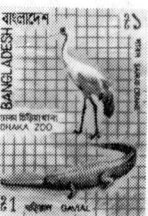

Dacca Zoo — A72   Postal Life Insurance, Cent. — A73

1984, July 17		Litho.		Perf. 14	
247	A72	1t	Sarus crane, gavial	1.40	1.40
248	A72	2t	Peafowl, royal Bengal tiger	2.75	2.75

1984, Dec. 3

249	A73	1t	Chicken hawk, hen	.40	.40
250	A73	5t	Beneficiaries	1.90	1.90

Abbasudin Ahmad, Bengali Singer — A74

1984, Dec. 24

| 251 | A74 | 3t | multicolored | 1.10 | 1.10 |

No. 116 Ovptd. for KHULNAPEX '84 Stamp Exhibition

1984, Dec. 29		Litho.		Perf. 15	
252	A25	2.25t	multicolored	1.10	1.10

1984 Summer Olympics, Los Angeles — A75

1984, Dec. 31				Perf. 14	
253	A75	1t	Bicycling	1.25	.25
254	A75	5t	Field hockey	2.50	2.50
255	A75	10t	Volleyball	3.50	3.50
	Nos. 253-255 (3)			7.25	6.25

Islamic Development Bank, 9th Annual Congress, Dacca — A76

1985, Feb. 2					
256	A76	1t	Farmer	.40	.40
257	A76	5t	Four Asian races	1.90	1.90

UN Child Survival Campaign — A77   UN Decade for Women — A78

1985, Mar. 14					
258	A77	1t	Breastfeeding	.30	.30
259	A77	10t	Growth monitoring	2.75	2.75

Nos. 139-144 Ovptd. in Bengali for Local Elections

উপজেলা নির্বাচন ১৯৮৫

1985, May 16		Litho.		Perf. 13	
259A	A33	40p	multicolored	.15	.15
259B	A33	1t	multicolored	.15	.15
259C	A33	2.25t	multicolored	.25	.25
259D	A33	3.50t	multicolored	.40	.40
259E	A33	4t	multicolored	.45	.45
259F	A33	5t	multicolored	.55	.55
	Nos. 259A-259F (6)			1.95	1.95

1985, July 18				Perf. 14	
260	A78	1t	shown	.15	.15
261	A78	10t	Technology	1.65	1.65

UN, 40th Anniv. A79

1985, Sept. 15					
262	A79	1t	UN building	.15	.15
263	A79	10t	World map, natl. flag	1.25	1.25

11th anniv. of UN admission.

Intl. Youth Year — A80

1985, Nov. 2		Litho.		Perf. 14	
264	A80	1t	Scissors, pencil	.15	.15
265	A80	5t	Hammer, wrenches	.70	.70

Seven Doves, Council Emblem — A81

BANGLADESH

1985, Dec. 8   Litho.   *Perf. 14*
266 A81 1t shown .15 .15
267 A81 5t Flags, lotus blossom .80 .80

1st South Asian Regional Council Summit, SARC, Dacca.

Shilpacharya Zainul Abedin (1914-1976), Founder, Dacca College of Art — A82

1985, Dec. 28
268 A82 3t multicolored 1.00 1.00

No. 138 Overprinted Reading Up

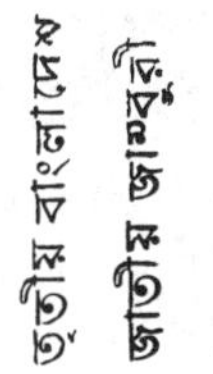

1985, Dec. 29   *Perf. 13*
269 A32 5t multicolored 2.75 2.75

3rd Natl. Scout Jamboree.
The overprint comes in two types.

Postal Services Type of 1983-84

1986, Jan. 11   Litho.   *Perf. 12x11½*
Size: 30½x19mm
270 A70 3t Sorting machine .30 .30

Perf. 12x12½
Size: 33½x22½mm
271 A70 4t Chittagong Port .55 .55

Issue dates: 3t, Jan. 11, 1986. 4t, Apr. 22, 1993.
For overprint see No. O46.
This is an expanding set. Numbers will change if necessary.

Fishing Net, by Safiuddin Ahmed A83

Paintings by Bengali artists: 5t, Happy Return, by Quamrul Hassan. 10t, Levelling the Plowed Field, by Zainul Abedin.

1986, Apr. 6   Litho.   *Perf. 14*
275 A83 1t multicolored .15 .15
276 A83 5t multicolored .55 .55
277 A83 10t multicolored 1.10 1.10
Nos. 275-277 (3) 1.80 1.80

1986 World Cup Soccer Championships, Mexico — A84

1986, June 29   *Perf. 15x14*
278 A84 1t Stealing the ball .30 .30
279 A84 10t Goal 3.00 3.00

Souvenir Sheet
Imperf
279A A84 20t multicolored 5.50 5.50

No. 279A contains one stamp 62x45mm with simulated perfs.

Gen. M.A.G. Osmani (1918-1984), Liberation Forces Commander-in-Chief — A85

1986, Sept. 10   Litho.   *Perf. 14*
280 A85 3t multicolored 1.50 1.50

No. 207 Ovptd. SAARC SEMINAR '86

1986, Dec. 3   Litho.   *Perf. 13½x14*
281 A58 50p on #207 1.75 1.75

Intl. Peace Year
A86   A87

1986, Dec. 25   Litho.   *Perf. 12x12½*
282 A86 1t shown .50 .25
283 A86 10t City ruins, flower 4.00 4.00

Souvenir Sheet
284 A87 20t shown 2.50 2.50

Nos. 179-180 Ovptd. or Surcharged
"CONFERENCE FOR DEVELOPMENT '87"

1987, Jan. 12   *Perf. 14*
285 A42 1t on 40p multicolored .15 .15
286 A42 5t multicolored .65 .65

Language Movement, 35th Anniv. — A88

Illustration reduced.

1987, Feb. 21   *Perf. 12½x12*
287 A88 3t Protestors 1.00 1.00
288 A88 3t Memorial 1.00 1.00
a. Pair, Nos. 287-288 2.00 2.00

World Health Day — A89
Bengali New Year — A90 

1987, Apr. 7   *Perf. 11½x12*
289 A89 1t Child immunization 2.50 2.50

See No. 318.

1987, Apr. 16   *Perf. 12x12½*
290 A90 1t Bengali script, embroidery .15 .15
291 A90 10t shown .75 .75

Jute Carpet A91

Exports: 1t, Jute shika (wall hanging, bowlholder and mats), vert. 10t, Table lamp and shade, vert.

Perf. 12x12½, 12½x12
1987, May 18   Litho.
292 A91 1t multicolored .15 .15
293 A91 5t shown .35 .35
294 A91 10t multicolored .75 .75
Nos. 292-294 (3) 1.25 1.25

Ustad Ayet Ali Khan (1884-1967), Composer, and Surbahar — A92

1987, Sept. 8   *Perf. 12x12½*
295 A92 5t multicolored .80 .80

Palanquin A93

Transportation.

1987, Oct. 24   Litho.   *Perf. 12½x12*
296 A93 2t shown .20 .20
297 A93 3t Bicycle rickshaw .30 .30
298 A93 5t Paddle steamer .55 .55
299 A93 7t Train .75 .75
300 A93 10t Ox cart 1.25 1.25
Nos. 296-300 (5) 3.05 3.05

For overprint see No. 424.

Hossain Shahid Suhrawardy (1893-1963), Politician — A94

1987, Dec. 5   Litho.   *Perf. 12x12½*
301 A94 3t multicolored .40 .40

Intl. Year of Shelter for the Homeless A95

1987, Dec. 15   *Perf. 12½x12*
302 A95 5t shown .50 .50
303 A95 5t Prosperous community .50 .50

Nos. 302-303 are printed se-tenant in a continuous design.

Natl. Democracy, 1st Anniv. — A96

Design: Pres. Hossain Mohammed Ershad addressing parliament.

1987, Dec. 31
304 A96 10t multicolored 1.90 1.90

Woman Tending Crop — A97

1988, Jan. 26
305 A97 3t shown .35 .35
306 A97 5t Milking cow, village .50 .50

Intl. Fund for Agricultural Development (IFAD) Seminar on Loans for Women in Rural Areas.

1988 Summer Olympics, Seoul — A98

1988 Summer Games emblem and Sports: a, Basketball. b, Weight lifting. c, Women's tennis. d, Shooting. e, Boxing.

1988, Sept. 29   Litho.   *Perf. 11½*
307   Strip of 5 3.00 3.00
a.-e. A98 5t any single .60 .60

Historical Sites — A99

Designs: 1t, Shait Gumbaz Mosque (interior), Bagerhat. 4t, Paharpur Monastery. 5t, Kantanagar Temple, Dinajpur. 10t, Lalbag Fort, Dacca.

1988, Oct. 9   *Perf. 12½x12*
308 A99 1t multicolored .15 .15
309 A99 4t multicolored .15 .15
310 A99 5t multicolored .25 .25
311 A99 10t multicolored .50 .50
Nos. 308-311 (4) 1.05 1.05

Qudrat-i-Khuda (1900-1977), Scientist — A100
Asia Cup Cricket — A101 

1988, Nov. 3   *Perf. 12x12½*
312 A100 5t multicolored .55 .55

BANGLADESH

1988, Nov. 27
313 Strip of 3 .... 3.25 3.25
 a. A101 1t Wicketkeeper .15 .15
 b. A101 5t Batsman .95 .95
 c. A101 10t Bowler 2.00 2.00

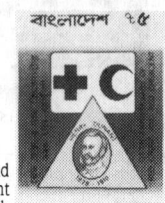

Intl. Red Cross and Red Crescent Organizations, 125th Anniv. — A102

1988, Oct. 26   Litho.   Perf. 12x12½
314 A102 5t Emblems, Dunant .50 .50
315 A102 10t Blood donation 1.00 1.00

Dacca G.P.O., 25th Anniv. — A103

1988, Dec. 6   Perf. 12
316 A103 1t Exterior .15 .15
317 A103 5t Sales counter .65 .65

World Health Day Type of 1987

1988, Jan. 16   Litho.   Perf. 11½x12
318 A89 25p Oral rehydration .70 .70

32nd Meeting of the Colombo Plan Consultative Committee, Dacca — A104

1988, Nov. 29   Perf. 12x12½
319 A104 3t multicolored .25 .25
320 A104 10t multicolored .75 .75

No. 191 Ovptd. ৫ম জাতীয় রোভার মুট ১৯৮৮-৮৯

1989, Dec. 29   Litho.   Perf. 14
321 A50 5t multicolored 1.25 1.25

5th Natl. Rover Moot (Scouting).

No. 277 Ovptd. চতুর্থ দ্বিবাষিক এশীয় চারুকলা প্রদর্শনী বাংলাদেশ ১৯৮৯

1989, Mar. 1
322 A83 10t multicolored 1.10 1.10

4th Asiatic Exposition.

A106    A107

1989, Mar. 13   Litho.   Perf. 12x12½
324 A106 10t multicolored .85 .85

Police academy, Sardah, 75th anniv.

1989, Mar. 7   Litho.   Perf. 12x12½
Modernizing water supply services.
325 A107 10t multicolored .85 .85

12th Natl. Science & Technology Week.

A108

French Revolution, Bicent. — A109

Scenes from the revolution: 5t, Close-up of revolutionaries destroying the Bastille, vert. No. 326b, Liberty guiding the people. No. 326c, Women's march on Versailles, vert. No. 327a, Celebration of the Federation on the Champ de Mars. No. 327b, Storming of the Bastille. 25t, Montage of scenes, #326a-326c.

1989, July 12   Perf. 14
326 Sheet of 3 + label 2.25 2.25
 a. A108 5t multicolored .45 .45
 b.-c. A108 10t any single .90 .90

Perf. 14x15
327 Strip of 2 + label 2.25 2.25
 a.-b. A109 17t any single 1.10 1.10

Size: 152x88mm
Imperf.
328 A108 25t multicolored 2.25 2.25
 Nos. 326-328 (3) 6.75 6.75

Labels picture the revolution anniv. emblem.

Rural Development in Asia and the Pacific (CIRDAP), 10th Anniv. — A110

1989, Aug. 10   Litho.   Perf. 12½x12
329 A110 5t shown .50 .50
330 A110 10t multi, diff. 1.00 1.00
 a. Pair, Nos. 329-330 1.50 1.50

No. 330a has a continuous design.

Child Survival A111

1989, Aug. 22
331 A111 1t shown .15 .15
332 A111 10t Women and children, diff. .90 .90

SOS Children's Village, 40th anniv.

Involvement of the Bangladesh Army in UN Peacekeeping Operations, 1st Anniv. — A112

1989, Sept. 12   Perf. 12x12½
333 A112 4t shown .65 .65
334 A112 10t Camp, two soldiers 1.65 1.65

2nd Asian Poetry Festival, Dacca — A113

1989, Nov. 17   Litho.   Perf. 12x12½
335 A113 2t multicolored .20 .20
336 A113 10t multicolored .90 .90

State Printing Office A114

1989, Dec. 7   Perf. 13½
337 A114 10t multicolored 1.25 1.25

Bangladesh Television, 25th Anniv. A115

1989, Dec. 25   Litho.   Perf. 12½x12
338 A115 5t shown .50 .50
339 A115 10t Emblem, flowers, diff. 1.00 1.00

World Wildlife Fund A116

Various gavials, (Gavialis gangeticus).

1990, Jan. 31   Litho.   Perf. 14
340 A116 50p shown .15 .15
341 A116 2t Reptile's jaws .55 .55
342 A116 4t 4 reptiles 1.00 1.00
343 A116 10t 2 reptiles resting 2.75 2.75
 a. Block of 4, #340-343 4.50 4.50

A117    A118

1990, Feb. 2   Perf. 14
344 A117 6t multicolored .85 .85

Natl. Population Day.

1990, May 6   Perf. 14
345 A118 7t shown 1.65 1.65
346 A118 10t Penny Black, No. 230 2.50 2.50

Penny Black, 150th anniv.

Justice Syed Mahbub Murshed, (1911-1979) — A119

1990, Apr. 3   Litho.   Perf. 12½x12
347 A119 5t multicolored 1.10 1.10

Intl. Literacy Year — A120

Design: 10t, Boy teaching girl to write.

1990, Apr. 10   Perf. 12x12½
348 A120 6t multicolored 1.40 1.40
349 A120 10t multicolored 2.00 2.00

Loading Cargo Plane — A121    Curzon Hall — A122

Fertilizer Plant — A123    Postal Academy, Rajshahi — A124

Salimullah Hall — A125

Bangla Academy — A126

1989-93   Perf. 12x11½, 12, 12x12½
350 A121 3t multicolored .15 .15
351 A122 5t gray blk & red brn .25 .25
352 A123 10t carmine .50 .50
353 A124 20t multicolored 1.10 1.10

Perf. 14½x14
354 A125 6t blue gray & yel .55 .55

Perf. 14x14½
355 A126 2t brown & green .15 .15
 Nos. 350-355 (6) 2.70 2.70

Issue dates: 5t, Mar. 31. 3t, Apr. 30. 10t, 20t, July 8. 6t, Jan. 30, 1991. 2t, Dec. 3, 1993. For overprints see Nos. O47A-O47B, O50. This is an expanding set. Numbers will change.

World Cup Soccer Championships, Italy — A133

BANGLADESH

1990, June 12   Litho.   *Perf. 14*
362 A133   8t shown   1.65   1.65
363 A133   10t Soccer player, diff.   2.25   2.25
     Size: 115x79mm
     Imperf
364 A133   25t Colosseum, soccer ball   6.00   6.00
     Nos. 362-364 (3)   9.90   9.90

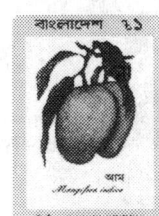

Fruits — A134

1990, July 16   *Perf. 12x12½*
365 A134   1t Mangifera indica   .15   .15
366 A134   2t Psidium guayava   .35   .35
367 A134   3t Citrullus vulgaris   .50   .50
368 A134   4t Carica papaya   .70   .70
369 A134   5t Artocarpus heterophyllus   .90   .90
370 A134   10t Averrhoa carambola   1.75   1.75
     Nos. 365-370 (6)   4.35   4.35

UN Conference on Least Developed Nations, Paris A135

1990, Sept. 3   Litho.   *Perf. 14*
371 A135   10t multicolored   1.90   1.90

Asia-Pacific Postal Training Center, 20th Anniv. — A136

Design: 6t, Map of Western Pacific, letters.

1990, Sept. 10   *Perf. 13½x14*
372 A136   2t shown   .50   .50
373 A136   6t multicolored   1.50   1.50
   a.   Pair, #372-373   2.00   2.00
     No. 373a has continuous design.

11th Asian Games, Beijing A137

1990, Sept. 22   *Perf. 14*
374 A137   2t Rowing   .40   .40
375 A137   4t Kabaddi   .85   .85
376 A137   8t Wrestling   1.75   1.75
377 A137   10t Badminton   2.00   2.00
     Nos. 374-377 (4)   5.00   5.00

Lalan Shah, Poet — A138

1990, Oct. 17   Litho.   *Perf. 14*
378 A138   6t multicolored   1.40   1.40

UN Development Program, 40th Anniv. — A139

1990, Oct. 24   Litho.   *Perf. 14*
379 A139   6t multicolored   1.25   1.25

Immunization Program — A139a

1990, Nov. 29   Litho.   *Perf. 14½x14*
379A   A139a 2t brown   .40   .40
     See No. 560.

Butterflies — A140

1990, Dec. 24   Litho.   *Perf. 13½x12*
380 A140   6t Danaus chrysippus   1.50   1.50
381 A140   6t Precis almana   1.50   1.50
382 A140   10t Ixias pyrene   2.50   2.50
383 A140   10t Danaus plexippus   2.50   2.50
   a.   Block of 4, #380-383   8.00   8.00

UN Decade Against Drugs A141

1991, Jan 1   Litho.   *Perf. 14x13½*
384 A141   2t Drugs, map   .75   .75
385 A141   4t shown   1.50   1.50

Third National Census — A142

1991, Mar. 12   Litho.   *Perf. 14*
386 A142   4t multicolored   .80   .80

Independence, 20th Anniv. A143

Designs: a, Invincible Bangla statue. b, Freedom Fighter statue. c, Mujibnagar Memorial. d, Eternal flame. e, National Martyrs' Memorial.

1991, Mar. 26   *Perf. 13½*
387 A143   4t Strip of 5, #a.-e.   2.75   2.75
     No. 387 printed in continuous design.

Pres. Ziaur Rahman, 10th Death Anniv. A144

1991, May 30   *Perf. 14*
388 A144   50p multicolored   .20   .20
389 A145   2t multicolored   .90   .90
   a.   Souvenir sheet of 2, #388-389   1.75   1.75
     No. 389a sold for 10t.

Endangered Animals — A146

1991, June 16   *Perf. 12*
390 A146   2t Petaurista petaurista   .40   .40
391 A146   4t Presbytis entellus, vert.   .75   .75
392 A146   6t Buceros bicornis, vert.   1.10   1.10
   a.   Pair, #391-392   1.85   1.85
393 A146   10t Manis crassicaudata   1.75   1.75
   a.   Pair, #390, 393   2.15   2.15
     Nos. 390-393 (4)   4.00   4.00

Kaikobad (1857-1951), Poet — A147

1991, July 21   Litho.   *Perf. 14*
394 A147   6t multicolored   .85   .85

Rabindranath Tagore, Poet, 50th Anniv. of Death — A148

1991, Aug. 7
395 A148   4t multicolored   .85   .85

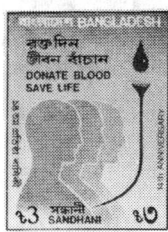

Blood and Eye Donations — A149

1991, Sept. 19
396 A149   3t shown   .60   .60
397 A149   5t Blind man and eye   .95   .95
     Sandhani, Medical Students Association, 14th anniversary.

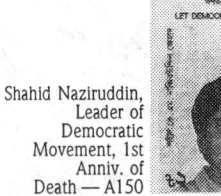

Shahid Naziruddin, Leader of Democratic Movement, 1st Anniv. of Death — A150

1991, Oct. 10
398 A150   2t multicolored   .80   .80

Shaheed Noor Hossain, 4th Death Anniv. — A151

1991, Nov. 10   Litho.   *Perf. 14*
399 A151   2t multicolored   .80   .80

Archaeological Treasures of Mainamati — A152

Designs: a, Bronze Stupa with images of Buddha. b, Bowl and pitcher. c, Ruins of Salban Vihara Monastery. d, Gold coins. e, Terra-cotta plaque.

1991, Nov. 26   Litho.   *Perf. 13½*
400 A152   4t Strip of 5, #a.-e.   4.00   4.00

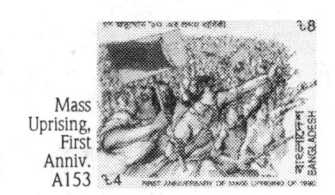

Mass Uprising, First Anniv. A153

1991, Dec. 6   *Perf. 14*
401 A153   4t multicolored   .80   .80

Miniature Sheets

Independence, 20th Anniv. — A154

Martyred intellectuals who died in 1971: No. 402a, A.N.M. Munier Chowdhury. b, Ghyasuddin Ahmad. c, S.M.A. Rashidul Hasan. d, Muhammad Anwar Pasha. e, Dr. Md. Mortaza. f, Shahid Saber. g, Fazlur Rahman Khan. h, Ranada Prasad Saha. i, Adhyaksha Joges Chandra Ghose. j, Santosh Chandra Bhattacharyya.

No. 403a, Dr. Gobinda Chandra Deb. b, A.N.M. Muniruzzaman. c, Mufazzal Haider Chaudhury. d, Dr. Abdul Alim Choudhury. e, Sirajuddin Hossain. f, Shahidulla Kaiser. g, Altaf Mahmud. h, Dr. Jyotirmay Guha Thakurta. i, Dr. Md. Abul Khair. j, Dr. Serajul Haque Khan.

No. 404a, Dr. Mohammad Fazle Rabbi. b, Mir Abdul Quyyum. c, A.N.M. Golam Mostafa. d, Dhirendranath Dutta. e, S.A. Mannan (Ladu Bhai). f, Nizamuddin Ahmad. g, Abul Bashar Chowdhury. h, Selina Parveen. i, Dr. Abul Kalam Azad. j, Saidul Hassan.

No. 404 l, LCDR. Moazzam Hussain. m, Muhammad Habibur Rahman. n, Khandoker Abu Taleb. o, Moshiur Rahman. p, Md. Abdul Muktadir. q, Nutan Chandra Sinha. r, Syed Nazmul Haque. s,

BANGLADESH

Dr. Mohammed Amin Uddin. t, Dr. N.A.M. Faizul Mohee. u, Sukha Ranjan Somaddar.

1991-93   Litho.   Perf. 13½
Sheets of 10
402 A154 2t #a.-j. + 5 labels   1.90 1.90
403 A154 2t #a.-j. + 5 labels   1.90 1.90
404 A154 2t #a.-j. + 5 labels   1.90 1.90

Perf. 14½
404K A154 2t #l.-u. + 5 labels   3.00 3.00

Issued: #402-404, 12/14/91; #404K, 12/14/93.
See Nos. 470-471, 499-500, 534-535, 558-559.

Shrimp A155

1991, Dec. 31   Perf. 14
405 A155 6t Penaeus monodon   1.25 1.25
406 A155 6t Metapenaeus monoceros 1.25 1.25
  a. Pair, #405-406   2.50 2.50

Shaheed Mirze Abu Raihan Jaglu, 5th Death Anniv. A156

1992, Feb. 8   Litho.   Perf. 14x13½
407 A156 2t multicolored   .95 .95

World Environment Day — A157

Design: 4t, Scenes of environmental protection and pollution control, vert.

1992, June 5   Litho.   Perf. 14
408 A157 4t multicolored   .45 .45
409 A157 10t multicolored   1.10 1.10

Nawab Sirajuddaulah of Bengal (1733-1757) A158

1992, July 2   Litho.   Perf. 14
410 A158 10t multicolored   1.00 1.00

Syed Ismail Hossain Sirajee (1880-1931), Social Reformer A159

1992, July 17
411 A159 4t multicolored   .80 .80

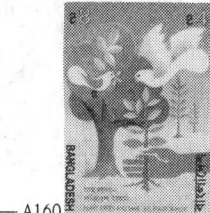

Tree Week — A160

1992, July 17   Litho.   Perf. 14
412 A160 2t Couple planting tree, horiz.   .50 .50
413 A160 4t Birds, trees   1.00 1.00

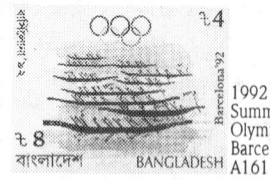

1992 Summer Olympics, Barcelona A161

Olympic rings and: a, 4t, Rowing. b, 6t, Hands holding Olympic torch. c, 10t, Peace doves. d, 10t, Clasped hands.

1992, July 25   Litho.   Perf. 14
414 A161 Block of 4, #a.-d.   2.75 2.75

The Star Mosque, 18th Cent. A162

1992, Oct. 29   Litho.   Perf. 14½x14
415 A162 10t multicolored   1.10 1.10

Masnad-E-Ala Isa Khan, 393rd Anniv. of Death — A163

1992, Sept. 15   Perf. 14x14½
416 A163 4t multicolored   .80 .80

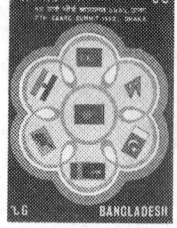

7th SAARC Summit, Dacca — A164

1992, Dec. 5
417 A164 6t Flags of members   .50 .50
418 A164 10t Emblem   .85 .85

1992 Bangladesh Natl. Philatelic Exhibition — A165

Designs: No. 419a, Elephant and mahout, ivory work, 19th cent. b, Post rider, mail box and postman delivering mail to villager.

1992, Sept. 26   Perf. 14½x14
419 A165 10t Pair, #a.-b. + label   2.50 2.50
  c. Souv. sheet, imperf.   2.75 2.75

No. 419c contains one strip of No. 419 with simulated perforations and sold for 25t.

1992 Intl. Conference on Nutrition, Rome — A166

1992, Dec. 5
420 A166 4t multicolored   .55 .55

Meer Nisar Ali Titumeer (1782-1831) — A167

1992, Nov. 19   Litho.   Perf. 14½x14
421 A167 10t multicolored   1.00 1.00

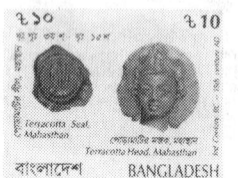

Archaeological Relics, Mahasthan — A168

Relics from 3rd century B.C.-15th century A.D.: No. 422a, Terracotta seal and head. b, Terracotta hamsa. c, Terracotta Surya image. d, Gupta stone columns.

1992, Nov. 30   Litho.   Perf. 14½x14
422 A168 10t Strip of 4, #a.-d.   4.00 4.00

Canal Digging A169

a, Workers digging canal. b, Completed project.

1993, Mar. 31   Litho.   Perf. 14½x14
423 A169 2t Pair, #a.-b.   1.40 1.40

No. 300 Ovptd.   **Banglapex '92**

1992, Aug. 18   Litho.   Perf. 12½x12
424 A93 10t multicolored   1.10 1.10

Syed Abdus Samad (1895-1964), Soccer Player — A170

1993, Feb. 2   Perf. 14x14½
425 A170 2t multicolored   .80 .80

A171

1993, Apr. 14
426 A171 2t multicolored   .70 .70

Completion of 14th cent. Bengali era.

Haji Shariat Ullah (1770-1839), Social Reformer, Religious and Political Leader — A172

1993, Mar. 10   Litho.   Perf. 14x14½
427 A172 2t multicolored   .70 .70

World Health Day A173

1993, Apr. 7   Perf. 14½x14, 14x14½
428 A173 6t Prevent accidents   .75 .75
429 A173 10t Prevent violence, vert. 1.25 1.25

Compulsory Primary Education — A174

1993, May 26
430 A174 2t Slate, chalk, books   .40 .40
431 A174 2t Hand writing, children, vert.   .40 .40

Nawab Sir Salimullah (1871-1915), Social Reformer — A175

1993, June 7   Litho.   Perf. 14½x14
432 A175 4t multicolored   .55 .55

Fishing Industry A176

1993, Aug. 15   Litho.   Perf. 14½x14
433 A176 2t multicolored   .55 .55

BANGLADESH

Tomb of Sultan Ghiyasuddin Azam Shah — A177

1993, Dec. 30   Litho.   *Perf. 14½x14*
434   A177   10t multicolored   1.10   1.10

Scenic Views A178

Designs: No. 435, Sunderban. No. 436, Madhabkunda Waterfall, vert. No. 437, River, mountains, vert. No. 438, Beach, Kuakata.

Perf. 14½x14, 14x14½
1993, Oct. 30
435   A178   10t multicolored   1.25   1.25
436   A178   10t multicolored   1.25   1.25
437   A178   10t multicolored   1.25   1.25
438   A178   10t multicolored   1.25   1.25
   a.   Souv. sheet of 4, #435-438, imperf.   5.50   5.50
     Nos. 435-438 (4)   5.00   5.00

#438a sold for 50t and has simulated perfs.

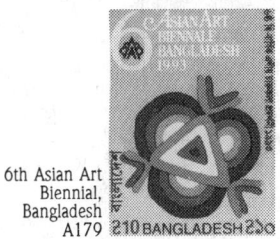

6th Asian Art Biennial, Bangladesh A179

1993, Nov. 7   Litho.   *Perf. 14x14½*
439   A179   10t multicolored   .85   .85

Foy's Lake A180

1993, Nov. 6   *Perf. 14½x14*
440   A180   10t multicolored   1.10   1.10
Tourism month.

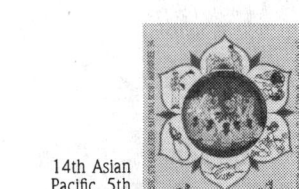

14th Asian Pacific, 5th Bangladesh Natl. Scout Jamboree A181

1994, Jan. 5   *Perf. 14x14½*
441   A181   2t multicolored   .55   .55

Oral Rehydration Solution, 25th Anniv. — A182

1994, Feb. 5   Litho.   *Perf. 13½x14*
442   A182   2t multicolored   .55   .55

6th SAF Games, Dhaka A183

1993, Dec. 6   *Perf. 14x13½, 13½x14*
443   A183   2t Shot put   .30   .30
444   A183   4t Runners, vert.   .65   .65

Mosques A184

Mosques: 4t, Interior, Chhota Sona, Nawabgonj. No. 446, Exterior, Chhota Sona. No. 447, Exterior, Baba Adam's, Munshigonj.

1994, Mar. 30   Litho.   *Perf. 14x13½*
445   A184   4t multicolored   .30   .30
446   A184   6t multicolored   .50   .50
447   A184   6t multicolored   .50   .50
     Nos. 445-447 (3)   1.30   1.30

For overprint see No. 509.

ILO, 75th Anniv. A185

Perf. 14x13½, 13½x14
1994, Apr. 11   Litho.
448   A185   4t multicolored   .40   .40
449   A185   10t multicolored   1.00   1.00

Designs: 4t, People, oxen working in fields. 10t, Man rotating gearwheel, vert.

Bangla Era, 15th Cent. — A186

1994, Apr. 14   *Perf. 13½x14*
450   A186   2t multicolored   .55   .55

Traditional Festivals A187

1994, May 12   *Perf. 14x13½*
451   A187   4t Folk Festival   .40   .40
452   A187   4t Baishakhi Festival   .40   .40

Intl. Year of the Family — A188

1994, May 15   *Perf. 13½x14*
453   A188   10t multicolored   1.50   1.50

Tree Planting Campaign A189

1994, June 15   Litho.   *Perf. 13½x14*
454   A189   4t Family planting trees   .55   .55
455   A189   6t Hands, seedlings   .80   .80

1994 World Cup Soccer Championships, US — A190

Soccer player's uniform colors: a, Red, yellow & blue. b, Yellow, green, & red.

1994, June 17   Litho.   *Perf. 14½*
456   A190   20t Pair, #a.-b. + label   4.25   4.25
     Complete booklet, #456   11.50

Jamuna Multi-Purpose Bridge — A191

1994, July 24   *Perf. 14½x14*
457   A191   4t multicolored   .40   .40

Birds — A192

Designs: 4t, Oriolus xanthornus. No. 459, Gallus gallus. No. 460, Dicrurus paradiseus. No. 461, Dendrocitta vagabunda.

1994, Aug. 31   *Perf. 14x14½*
458   A192   4t multicolored   .50   .50
459   A192   6t multicolored   .75   .75
460   A192   6t multicolored   .75   .75
461   A192   6t multicolored   .75   .75
   a.   Souvenir sheet, #458-461   2.75   2.75
     Nos. 458-461 (4)   2.75   2.75

No. 461a sold for 25t.

Dr. Mohammad Ibrahim (1911-89), Pioneer in Treatment of Diabetes A193

1994, Sept. 6   Litho.   *Perf. 14½x14*
462   A193   2t multicolored   .40   .40

Nawab Faizunnessa Chowdhurani (1834-1903), Social Reformer A194

1994, Sept. 23   *Perf. 14x14½*
463   A194   2t multicolored   .40   .40

12th Asian Games, Hiroshima, Japan — A195

1994, Oct. 2   *Perf. 14½x14*
464   A195   4t multicolored   .55   .55

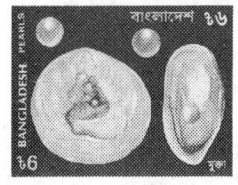

Shells A196

Designs: No. 465, White, pink pearls, oysters. No. 466, Snail, three other shells. No. 467, Scallop, other shells. No. 468, Spiral shaped shells, vert.

Perf. 14½x14, 14x14½
1994, Oct. 30   Litho.
465   A196   6t multicolored   .60   .60
466   A196   6t multicolored   .60   .60
467   A196   6t multicolored   .60   .60
468   A196   6t multicolored   .60   .60
     Nos. 465-468 (4)   2.40   2.40

Democracy Demonstration, Death of Dr. Shamsul Alam Khan Milon, 4th Anniv. — A197

1994, Nov. 27   *Perf. 14½x14*
469   A197   2t multicolored   .40   .40

Martyred Intellectual Type of 1991
Miniature Sheets of 8

Martyred intellectuals who died in 1971: No. 470: a, Dr. Harinath Dey. b, Dr. Lt. Col. A.F. Ziaur Rahman. c, Mamum Mahmud. d, Mohsin Ali Dewan. e, Dr. Lt. Col. N.A.M. Jahangir. f, Shah Abdul Majid. g, Muhammad Akhter. h, Meherunnesa.
No. 471: a, Dr. Kasiruddin Talukder. b, Fazlul Haque Choudhury. c, Md. Shamsuzzaman. d, A.K.M. Shamsuddin. e, Lt. Mohammad Anwarul Azim. f, Nurul Amin Khan. g, Mohammad Sadeque. h, Md. Araz Ali.

BANGLADESH

1994, Dec. 14 — Perf. 14½
470 A154 2t #a.-h. + 4 labels	1.25	1.25
471 A154 2t #a.-h. + 4 lables	1.25	1.25

Vegetables — A199

Perf. 14x14½, 14½x14
1994, Dec. 24
472 A199 4t Diplazium esculentum	.25	.25
473 A199 4t Momordica charantia	.25	.25
474 A199 6t Lagenaria siceraria	.50	.50
475 A199 6t Trichosanthes dioica	.50	.50
476 A199 10t Solanum melongena	.85	.85
477 A199 10t Cucurbita maxima	.85	.85
Nos. 472-477 (6)	3.20	3.20

Nos. 472-476 are vert.

World Tourism Organization, 20th Anniv. — A200

1995, Jan. 2 — Perf. 14½x14
478 A200 10t multicolored   .95 .95

Intl. Trade Fair, Dhaka — A201

Designs: 4t, Trade products. 6t, Factories, emblems of industry.

1995, Jan. 7 Litho. **Perf. 14x14½**
479 A201 4t multicolored	.30	.30
480 A201 6t multicolored	.60	.60

Bangladesh Rifles, Bicent. — A202

1995, Jan. 10 Litho. **Perf. 14½x14**
481 A202 2t shown	.30	.30
482 A202 4t Building, battalion	.60	.60

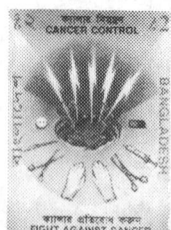

Fight Against Cancer — A203

1995, Apr. 7 Litho. **Perf. 14x14½**
483 A203 2t multicolored   .40 .40

Natl. Diabetes Awareness Day — A204

1995, Feb. 28 Perf. 14
484 A204 2t multicolored   .55 .55

For overprint see No. O49.

Munshi Mohammad Meherullah (1861-1907), Educator — A205

1995, June 7 Litho. **Perf. 14x14½**
485 A205 2t multicolored   .55 .55

FAO, 50th Anniv. — A206

1995, Oct. 16 Litho. **Perf. 14**
486 A206 10t multicolored   .90 .90

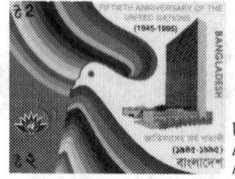

UN, 50th Anniv. A207

UN emblem, "50," and: 2t, Dove of peace, UN headquarters. No. 488, "1945," earth from space, "1995." No. 489, Hands of different nationalities clasping, UN headquarters.

1995, Oct. 24 **Perf. 14½x14**
487 A207 2t multicolored	.20	.20
488 A207 10t multicolored	1.00	1.00
489 A207 10t multicolored	1.00	1.00
Nos. 487-489 (3)	2.20	2.20

Flowers — A208

Designs: No. 490, Bombax ceiba. No. 491, Lagerstroemia speciosa. No. 492, Gloriosa superba. No. 493, Canna indica. No. 494, Bauhinia purpurea. No. 495, Passiflora incarnata.

1995, Oct. 9 Perf. 14½x14, 14x14½
490 A208 6t multicolored	.65	.65
491 A208 6t multi, vert.	.65	.65
492 A208 10t multi, vert.	1.00	1.00
493 A208 10t multi, vert.	1.00	1.00
494 A208 10t multi, vert.	1.00	1.00
495 A208 10t multi, vert.	1.00	1.00
Nos. 490-495 (6)	5.30	5.30

18th Eastern Regional Conference on Tuberculosis and Respiratory Diseases, Dhaka — A209

1995, Oct. 29 Litho. **Perf. 14½x14**
497 A209 6t multicolored   .55 .55

South Asian Assoc. for Regional Cooperation (SAARC), 10th Anniv. — A210

1995, Dec. 8 Litho. **Perf. 14x14½**
498 A210 2t multicolored   .70 .70

Martyred Intellectual Type of 1991 Sheets of 8

Martyred intellectuals who died in 1971: No. 499a, Shaikh Habibur Rahman. b, Dr. Major Naimul Islam. c, Md. Shahidullah. d, Ataur Rahman Khan Khadim. e, A.B.M. Ashraful Islam Bhuiyan. f, Dr. Md. Sadat Ali. g, Sarafat Ali. h, M.A. Sayeed.
No. 500: a, Abdul Ahad. b, Lt. Col. Mohammad Abdul Qadir. c, Mozammel Hoque Chowdhury. d, Rafiqul Haider Chowdhury. e, Dr. Azharul Haque. f, A.K. Shamsuddin. g, Anudwaipayan Bhattacharjee. h, Lutfunnahar Helena.

1995, Dec. 14 Litho. **Perf. 14½x14**
499 A154 2t #a.-h. + 4 labels	1.50	1.50
500 A154 2t #a.-h. + 4 labels	1.50	1.50

Second Asian Pacific Community Development Scout Camp — A211

1995, Dec. 18 Litho. **Perf. 14x14½**
501 A211 2t multicolored   .55 .55

Volleyball, Cent. — A212

1995, Dec. 25
502 A212 6t multicolored   .55 .55

Traditional Costumes — A213

Designs: No. 503, Man in punjabi and lungi, vert. No. 504, Woman in sari, vert. No. 505, Christian bride and groom, vert. No. 506, Muslim bridal couple, vert. No. 507, Hindu bridal couple. No. 508, Buddhist bridal couple.

Perf. 14x14½, 14½x14
1995, Dec. 25
503 A213 6t multicolored	.60	.60
504 A213 6t multicolored	.60	.60
505 A213 10t multicolored	1.00	1.00
506 A213 10t multicolored	1.00	1.00
507 A213 10t multicolored	1.00	1.00
508 A213 10t multicolored	1.00	1.00
Nos. 503-508 (6)	5.20	5.20

No. 446 Ovptd. in Red

রাজশাহীপেক্স-৯৫

1995 Litho. **Perf. 14x13½**
509 A184 6t multicolored   1.50 1.50

This stamp was released for a brief period in 1995. Scott has recently received several copies of the stamp from various sources. Anyone with information about this stamp is asked to contact the New Issues Editor.

Shaheed Amanullah Mohammad Asaduzzaman (1942-69) A214

1996, Jan. 20 **Perf. 14x14½**
510 A214 2t multicolored   .50 .50

1996 World Cup Cricket Championships — A215

Perf. 14x14½, 14½x14
1996, Feb. 14
511 A215 4t Pitching, vert.	.60	.60
512 A215 6t At bat, vert.	.85	.85
513 A215 10t shown	1.40	1.40
Nos. 511-513 (3)	2.85	2.85

Independence, 25th Anniv. — A216

Designs: No. 514, Natl. Martyrs' Memorial. No. 515, Industrial development. No. 516, 1971 Destruction of war. No. 517, Educational development. No. 518, Development in communication. No. 519, Development in health.

1996, Mar. 26 Litho. **Perf. 14x14½**
514 A216 4t multicolored	.35	.35
515 A216 4t multicolored	.35	.35
516 A216 4t multicolored	.35	.35
517 A216 4t multicolored	.35	.35
518 A216 4t multicolored	.35	.35
519 A216 4t multicolored	.35	.35
Nos. 514-519 (6)	2.10	2.10

BANGLADESH

Michael Madhusudan Dutt (1824-73), Writer — A217

1996, June 29 Litho. Perf. 14x14½
520 A217 4t multicolored .60 .60

1996 Summer Olympic Games, Atlanta A218

1996, July 19 Litho. Perf. 14
521 A218 4t Gymnast, vert. .60 .60
522 A218 6t Judo, vert. .90 .90
523 A218 10t High jumper 1.40 1.40
524 A218 10t Runners 1.40 1.40
  a. Souvenir sheet, #521-524 7.00 7.00
    Nos. 521-524 (4) 4.30 4.30

No. 524a sold for 50t.

Sheikh Mujibur Rahman (1920-75), Prime Minister — A219

Design: No. 527, Maulana Mohammad Akrum Khan (1868-1968).

1996 Litho. Perf. 14x14½
526 A219 4t multicolored .60 .60
527 A219 4t multicolored .60 .60

Issued: No. 526, 8/15/96, No. 527, 8/18/96.

Ustad Alauddin Khan (1862-1972), Musician A220

1996, Sept. 6 Litho. Perf. 14x14½
528 A220 4t multicolored .20 .20

Children's Paintings A221

Perf. 14x14½, 14½x14
1996, Oct. 9 Litho.
529 A221 2t Kingfisher, vert. .45 .45
530 A221 4t River Crossing .95 .95

Jailed, 21st Death Anniv. — A222

a, Syed Nazrul Islam. b, Tajuddin Ahmad. c, M. Monsoor Ali. d, A.H.M. Quamaruzzaman.

1996, Nov. 3 Litho. Perf. 14x14½
531 A222 4t Block of 4, #a.-d. 2.00 2.00

UNICEF, 50th Anniv. — A223

Designs: 4t, Children receiving food, medicine, aid. 10t, Mother holding infant.

1996, Dec. 11
532 A223 4t multicolored .65 .65
533 A223 10t multicolored 1.65 1.65

Martyred Intellectual Type of 1991

Martyred intellectuals who died in 1971: No. 534: a, Dr. Jekrul Haque. b, Munshi Kabiruddin Ahmed. c, Md. Abdul Jabbar. d, Mohammad Amir. e, A.K.M. Shamsul Huq Khan. f, Dr. Siddique Ahmed. g, Dr. Soleman Khan. h, S.B.M. Mizanur Rahman.
No. 535: a, Aminuddin. b, Md. Nazrul Islam. c, Zahirul Islam. d, A.K. Lutfor Rahman. e, Afsar Hossain. f, Abul Hashem Mian. g, A.T.M. Alamgir. h, Baser Ali.

1996, Dec. 14 Litho. Perf. 14½x14
Sheets of 8
534 A154 2t #a.-h. + 4 labels 2.25 2.25
535 A154 2t #a.-h. + 4 labels 2.25 2.25

Victory Day, 25th Anniv. A224

Designs: 4t, People celebrating, natl. flag. 6t, Soldiers, monument, vert.

Perf. 14½x14, 14x14½
1996, Dec. 16
536 A224 4t multicolored .65 .65
537 A224 6t multicolored 1.00 1.00

Paul Harris (1868-1947), Founder of Rotary Intl. — A225

1997, Feb. 18 Litho. Perf. 14x14½
538 A225 4t multicolored .40 .40

Sheikh Mujibur Rahman's Mar. 7 Speech, 26th Anniv. — A226

1997, Mar. 7 Perf. 12½
539 A226 4t multicolored .40 .40

Sheikh Mujibur Rahman (1920-75) A227

1997, Mar. 17 Perf. 14x14½
540 A227 4t multicolored .40 .40

Heinrich von Stephan (1831-97) A229

1997, Apr. 8 Litho. Perf. 14x14½
542 A229 4t multicolored .40 .40

Livestock A230

1997, Apr. 10 Litho. Perf. 14½x14
543 A230 4t Goat .35 .35
544 A230 4t Sheep .35 .35
545 A230 6t Cow .50 .50
546 A230 6t Buffalo .50 .50
    Nos. 543-546 (4) 1.70 1.70

Paintings — A231

Designs: 6t, "Tilling the Field-2," by S.M. Sultan (1923-94). 10t, "Three Women," by Quamrul Hassan (1921-88).

1997, June 26 Litho. Perf. 12½
547 A231 6t multicolored .60 .60
548 A231 10t multicolored .95 .95

6th Intl. Cricket Council Trophy Championship, Malaysia — A232

1997, Sept. 4
549 A232 10t multicolored 1.00 1.00

Ancient Mosques A233

Designs: 4t, Kusumba Mosque, Naogaon, 1558. 6t, Atiya Mosque, Tangail, 1609. 10t, Bagha Mosque, Rajshahi, 1523.

1997, Sept. 4 Litho. Perf. 14½x14
550 A233 4t multicolored .25 .25
551 A233 6t multicolored .35 .35
552 A233 10t multicolored .60 .60
    Nos. 550-552 (3) 1.20 1.20

Abdul Karim Sahitya Visharad (1871-1953), Scholar — A234

1997, Oct. 11 Perf. 14x14½
553 A234 4t multicolored .25 .25

9th Asia-Pacific, 7th Bangladesh Rover Moot '97 — A235

1997, Oct. 25 Perf. 14x14½
554 A235 2t multicolored .35 .35

Armed Forces, 25th Anniv. A236

1997, Nov. 11 Perf. 14½x14
555 A236 2t multicolored .15 .15

East Bengal Regiment, 50th Anniv. A237

1997
556 A237 2t multicolored .15 .15

Mohammad Mansooruddin (1904-87) — A238

1997 Perf. 14x14½
557 A238 4t multicolored .25 .25

BANGLADESH

Martyred Intellectual Type of 1991
Sheets of 8 + 4 Labels

Martyred intellectuals who died in 1971: No. 558: a, Dr. Shamsuddin Ahmed. b, Mohammad Salimullah. c, Mohiuddin Haider. d, Abdur Rahim. e, Nitya Nanda Paul. f, Abdul Jabber. g, Dr. Humayun Kabir. h, Khaja Nizamuddin Bhuiyan.

No. 559: a, Gulam Hossain. b, Ali Karim. c, Md. Moazzem Hossain. d, Rafiqul Islam. e, M. Nur Hussain. f, Captain Mahmood Hossain Akonda. g, Abdul Wahab Talukder. h, Dr. Hasimoy Hazra.

1997, Dec. 14
558-559 A154 2t #a.-h., each   1.00 1.00

Immunization Type of 1990
1998, Jan. 22   Perf. 14½x14
560 A139a 1t green   .15 .15

For overprint see No. O53.

Bulbul Chowdhury (1919-54), Dancer — A239

1998   Perf. 14x14½
561 A239 4t multicolored   .25 .25

Opening of the Bangabandhu Bridge — A240

Designs: 4t, East approach road. 6t, West approach road. 8t, River training works. 10t, Bangabandhu Bridge.

1998   Perf. 14
562 A240 4t multicolored   .25 .25
563 A240 6t multicolored   .35 .35
564 A240 8t multicolored   .45 .45
565 A240 10t multicolored   .55 .55
     Nos. 562-565 (4)   1.60 1.60

1998 World Cup Soccer Championships, France — A241

1998
566 A241 6t Trophy   .35 .35
567 A241 18t Player, trophy 1.00 1.00

OFFICIAL STAMPS

Nos. 42-47, 49-50, 52, 82-84 and 54 Overprinted **SERVICE** in Black or Red

Perf. 14x14½, 14½x14
1973-75   Litho.
O1   A7   2p black (R)   .15 .15
O2   A7   3p brt green   .15 .15
O3   A7   5p lt brown   .15 .15
O4   A7   10p black (R)   .15 .15
O5   A7   20p olive   1.10 .15
O6   A7   25p red lilac   3.00 .15
O7   A7   60p gray (R)   3.00 .20
O8   A7   75p orange ('74)   1.10 .25
O9   A9   1t violet (#52)   12.00 3.25
O10 A9   1t violet (#82)   2.25 .35
O11 A9   2t grayish grn ('74) 3.75 1.25
O12 A9   5t gray blue (#54) 5.25 4.50
O13 A9   5t grysh bl (#84) ('75) 6.00 5.00
O14 A9   Nos. O1-O14 (13)   38.55 15.70

Issue date: Apr. 30, 1973.

Nos. 95-101, 103-105 Overprinted "SERVICE" in Black or Red

1976   Litho.   Perf. 15x14½, 14½x15
O16 A7   5p green   .30 .30
O17 A7   10p black (R)   .30 .30
O18 A7   20p olive   .30 .30
O19 A7   25p rose   .30 .30
O20 A8   50p rose lilac   .40 .40
O21 A7   60p gray (R)   .50 .50
O22 A7   75p olive   .55 .55

Perf. 15
O23 A9   1t violet   .85 .85
O24 A9   2t greenish gray   1.65 1.65
O25 A9   5t grayish blue   4.25 4.25
     Nos. O16-O25 (10)   9.40 9.40

Nos. 165-169, 171-175 Ovptd. "SERVICE"
1979-82   Photo.   Perf. 14½
O27 A7   5p brown   .15 .15
O28 A7   10p Prussian blue .15 .15
O29 A7   15p yellow orange .15 .15
O30 A7   20p dk carmine   .20 .20
O31 A7   25p dk blue ('82) .25 .25
O32 A9   40p rose magenta   .45 .45
O33 A9   50p gray ('81)   .55 .55
O34 A7   80p dark brown   .80 .80
O35 A7   1t red lilac ('81) 1.10 1.10
O36 A7   2t brt ultra ('81) 1.90 1.90
     Nos. O27-O36 (10)   5.70 5.70

#234-242, 271 Ovptd. "Service" in Red, Diagonally Up on #O43A, 1t, 2t, 4t

Perf. 11½x12½, 12½x11½
1983-93
O37 A70 5p bluish green   .15 .15
O38 A70 10p deep magenta   .15 .15
O39 A70 15p blue   .15 .15
O40 A70 20p dark gray   .15 .15
O41 A70 25p slate   .15 .15
O42 A70 30p gray brown   .15 .15
O43 A70 50p yellow brown   .15 .15
O43A A70 50p yellow brown   .15 .15

Size: 30½x28½mm
Perf. 12x11½
O44 A70 1t ultramarine   .30 .30
O45 A70 2t Prussian blue   .60 .60

Perf. 12
O46 A70 4t blue   1.40 1.40
     Nos. O37-O46 (11)   3.50 3.50

Issued: 4t, 7/27/92; #O43A, 1993(?); others, 12/21/83.

No. 350 Ovptd. "Service" Diagonally in Red
1994, July 16 Litho. Perf. 12x11½
O47A A122 3t multicolored   11.50 11.50

No. 354 Ovptd. in Red সার্ভিস

1992, Nov. 22 Litho. Perf. 14½x14
O47B A125 6t blue gray & yel 6.75 6.75

No. 241 Ovptd. in Red সার্ভিস

1992, Sept. 16 Litho. Perf. 12x11½
O48 A70 1t ultramarine   .15 .15

No. 484 Ovptd. in Red সার্ভিস

1996   Litho.   Perf. 14
O49 A204 2t multicolored   2.75 2.75

No. 351 Ovptd. in Blue

1997? Litho.   Perf. 12
O50 A122 5t multicolored   .30 .30

Bengali overprint reads from top to bottom.

Nos. 235, 237 Ovptd. in Black or Red সার্ভিস

1997?   Perf. 12½x11½
O51 A70 10p on #235   .65 .65
O52 A70 20p on #237 (R)   1.25 1.25

No. 560 Ovptd. in Red

1998   Litho.   Perf. 14½x14
O53 A139a 1t green   .15 .15

BARBADOS

bär-'bā-(,)dōs

LOCATION — A West Indies island east of the Windwards
GOVT. — Independent state in the British Commonwealth
AREA — 166 sq. mi.
POP. — 270,500 (1981)
CAPITAL — Bridgetown

The British colony of Barbados became an independent state on November 30, 1966.

4 Farthings = 1 Penny
12 Pence = 1 Shilling
20 Shillings = 1 Pound
100 Cents = 1 Dollar (1950)

Catalogue values for unused stamps in this country are for Never Hinged items, beginning with Scott 207 in the regular postage section, Scott B2 in the semi-postal section and Scott J1 in the postage due section.

Watermarks

Wmk. 5- Small Star   Wmk. 6- Large Star

Values for unused stamps are for examples with original gum as defined in the catalogue introduction. Very fine examples of Nos. 10-42a, 44-59a will have perforations touching the design on at least one side due to the narrow spacing of the stamps on the plates and imperfect perforation methods. Stamps with perfs clear of the design on all four sides are extremely scarce and will command higher prices.

Britannia
A1   A2
1852-55 Unwmk. Engr. Imperf.
Blued Paper
1   A1 (½p) deep green   100.00 300.00
a.   (½p) yellow green   9,000. 800.00
2   A1 (1p) dark blue   18.00 70.00
a.   (1p) blue   22.00 200.00
3   A1 (2p) slate blue   15.00
a.   (2p) grayish slate   225.00 1,100.
b.   As "a", vert. half used as 1p on cover   6,750.
4   A1 (4p) brown red ('55) 55.00 300.00
        Nos. 1-4 (4)   188.00

No. 3 was not placed in use. Beware of color changelings of Nos. 2-3 that may resemble No. 3a. Certificates of authenticity are required for Nos. 3a and 3b.

1855-58
White Paper
5   A1 (½p) deep green ('58) 85.00 200.00
a.   (½p) yellow green ('57) 450.00 110.00
6   A1 (1p) blue   21.00 50.00
a.   (1p) pale blue   55.00 60.00

It is believed that the (4p) brownish red on white paper exists only as No. 17b.

1859
8   A2   6p rose red   600.00 110.00
9   A2   1sh black   140.00 70.00

Pin-perf. 14
10 A1   (½p) pale yel grn   2,500. 375.00
11 A1   (1p) blue   2,500. 150.00

Pin-perf. 12½
12 A1   (½p) pale yel grn   6,000. 550.
12A A1   (1p) blue   16,000. 1,400.

1861   Clean-Cut Perf. 14 to 16
13 A1   (½p) dark blue grn 60.00 10.00
14 A1   (1p) pale blue   625.00 35.00
b.   (1p) blue   725.00
b.   Half used as ½p on cover   3,500.

Rough Perf. 14 to 16
15 A1   (½p) green   9.00   9.00
a.   (½p) blue green   65.00 75.00
b.   Imperf., pair   500.00
16 A1   (1p) blue   24.00 1.50
a.   Diagonal half used as ½p on cover   1,750.
b.   Imperf., pair   550.00
17 A1   (4p) rose red   60.00 25.00
a.   (4p) brown red   100.00 32.50
b.   As "a", imperf., pair 850.00
c.   (4p) rose red, imperf., pair   750.00
18 A1   (4p) vermilion   175.00 60.00
         Imperf., pair   850.00
19 A2   6p rose red   175.00 12.00
20 A2   6p orange ver   55.00 13.00
         6p vermilion   55.00 13.00
         Imperf., pair   450.00 800.00
21 A2   1sh brownish black 35.00 3.50
a.   Horiz. pair, imperf. btwn.   5,750.
c.   1sh blue (error)   15,000.

No. 21c was never placed in use. All copies are pen-marked (some have been removed) and have clipped perfs on one or more sides.

Perf. 11 to 13
22 A1   (½p) deep green   6,500.
23 A1   (1p) blue   2,250.

Nos. 22 and 23 were never placed in use.

1870 Wmk. 6 Rough Perf. 14 to 16
24 A1   (½p) green   75.00 10.00
a.   Imperf., pair (#24) 675.00
b.   (½p) yellow green   90.00 40.00
25 A1   (1p) blue   1,200. 30.00
a.   Imperf., pair   1,500.
26 A1   (4p) dull red   650.00 75.00
27 A2   6p vermilion   625.00 50.00
28 A2   1sh black   225.00 17.50

1871   Wmk. 5
29 A1   (1p) blue   75.00 10.00
30 A1   (4p) rose red   575.00 25.00
31 A2   6p vermilion   350.00 20.00
32 A2   1sh black   125.00 10.00

Clean-Cut Perf. 14½ to 16
33 A1   (1p) blue   200.00 10.00
a.   Diagonal half used as ½p on cover   1,500.
34 A2   6p vermilion   550.00 45.00
35 A2   1sh black   125.00 10.00

Perf. 11 to 13x14½ to 16
36 A1   (½p) blue green   225.00 25.00
37 A1   (4p) vermilion   450.00 75.00

1873   Perf. 14
38 A2   3p claret   475.00 110.00

Wmk. 6
Clean-Cut Perf. 14½ to 16
39 A1   (½p) blue green   175.00 17.50
40 A1   (4p) rose red   725.00 125.00
41 A2   6p vermilion   575.00 60.00
a.   Imperf., pair   90.00 1,500.
b.   Horiz. pair, imperf. btwn.   4,500.
42 A2   1sh black   90.00 12.00
a.   Horiz. pair, imperf. btwn.   4,500.

Britannia — A3
1873   Wmk. 5   Perf. 15½x15
43 A3   5sh dull rose   1,100. 325.00

For surcharged bisects see Nos. 57-59.

1874   Wmk. 6   Perf. 14
44 A2   ½p blue green   17.50 7.50
45 A2   1p blue   67.50 9.00

Clean-Cut Perf. 14½ to 16
45A A2   1p blue   14,000.

1875   Wmk. 1   Perf. 12½
46 A2   ½p yellow green   21.00 3.00
47 A2   4p scarlet   165.00 10.00
48 A2   6p orange   600.00 65.00
49 A2   1sh purple   450.00 17.50
         Nos. 46-49 (4)   1,236. 95.50

1875-78 *Perf. 14*

50	A2	½p yel green ('76)	6.00	1.75
51	A2	1p ultramarine	30.00	1.00
a.		1p gray blue	30.00	.75
b.		Half used as ½p on cover		1,200.
c.		Watermarked sideways		1,750.
52	A2	3p violet ('78)	80.00	10.00
53	A2	4p rose red	80.00	8.00
a.		4p scarlet	125.00	5.00
b.		As "a," perf. 14x12½	4,500.	
54	A2	4p lake	375.00	5.00
55	A2	6p chrome yel	100.00	3.25
a.		6p yellow	300.00	12.50
56	A2	1sh purple ('76)	125.00	5.00
a.		1sh violet	2,100.	45.00
b.		1sh dull mauve	275.00	4.00
c.		Half used as 6p on cover		5,000.

#48, 49, 55, 56 have the watermark sideways.
No. 53b was never placed in use.

A4

A5

Large Surcharge, ("1" 7mm High, "D" 2¾mm High)

1878 **Wmk. 5** *Perf. 15½x15*

Slanting Serif

57	A4	1p on half of 5sh	4,000.	650.
a.		Unsevered pair	16,000.	2,500.
b.		Unsevered horiz. pair, #57 + 58		4,000.
d.		Unsevered horiz. pair, #57 + 58, imperf. between		—
e.		Unsevered horiz. pair, #57 + 59, imperf. between	25,000.	8,500.

Straight Serif

58	A4	1p on half of 5sh	4,750.	950.
a.		Unsevered pair		4,250.

Small Surcharge, ("1" 6mm, "D" 2½mm High)

59	A5	1p on half of 5sh	5,250.	1,100.
a.		Unsevered pair	15,000.	4,250.

On Nos. 57, 58 and 59 the surcharge is found reading upwards or downwards.

The perforation, which divides the stamp into halves, measures 11½ to 13.

The old denomination has been cut off the bottom of the stamps.

Queen Victoria — A6

1882-85 **Typo.** **Wmk. 2** *Perf. 14*

60	A6	½p green	5.25	.80
61	A6	1p carmine rose	4.75	.50
a.		1p rose	30.00	1.50
b.		Half used as ½p on cover		750.00
62	A6	2½p dull blue	52.50	.75
a.		2½p ultramarine	47.50	1.00
63	A6	3p magenta	3.00	8.75
a.		3p lilac	70.00	30.00
64	A6	4p slate	175.00	2.00
65	A6	4p brown ('85)	2.75	1.00
66	A6	6p olive gray	52.50	25.00
67	A6	1sh orange brown	17.00	18.00
68	A6	5sh bister	125.00	175.00
		Nos. 60-68 (9)	437.75	231.80

No. 65 Surcharged in Black HALF-PENNY

1892

69	A6	½p on 4p brown	1.00	2.00
a.		Without hyphen	6.00	11.00
b.		Double surcharge		
c.		Double surch., red & black	500.00	1,200.
d.		As "c," without hyphen	1,500.	1,500.

Badge of Colony
A8 A9

1892-1903 **Wmk. 2**

70	A8	1f sl & car ('96)	.85	.20
71	A8	½p green	.55	.20
72	A8	1p carmine rose	1.75	.20
73	A8	2p sl & org ('99)	5.25	1.50
74	A8	2½p ultramarine	8.75	.30
75	A8	5p olive brn	4.25	4.25
76	A8	6p vio & car	6.00	3.50
77	A8	8p org & ultra	2.25	15.00
78	A8	10p bl grn & car	4.50	6.00
79	A8	2sh6p slate & org	35.00	35.00
80	A8	2sh6p pur & grn ('03)	47.50	75.00
		Nos. 70-80 (11)	116.65	141.15

See Nos. 90-101. For surcharge see No B1.

Victoria Jubilee Issue

1897 **Wmk. 1**

81	A9	1f gray & car	1.25	.30
82	A9	½p gray green	1.75	.30
83	A9	1p carmine rose	2.00	.35
84	A9	2½p ultra	4.25	.70
85	A9	5p dk olive brn	8.50	9.25
86	A9	6p vio & car	12.00	14.00
87	A9	8p org & ultra	7.00	15.00
88	A9	10p bl grn & car	30.00	35.00
89	A9	2sh6p slate & org	35.00	42.50
		Nos. 81-89 (9)	101.75	117.40

Bluish Paper

81a	A9	1f gray & car	25.00	30.00
82a	A9	½p gray green	25.00	30.00
83a	A9	1p carmine rose	35.00	40.00
84a	A9	2½p ultra	37.50	45.00
85a	A9	5p dk olive brn	225.00	250.00
86a	A9	6p vio & car	100.00	110.00
87a	A9	8p org & ultra	85.00	100.00
88a	A9	10p bl grn & car	140.00	150.00
89a	A9	2sh6p slate & org	90.00	95.00
		Nos. 81a-89a (9)	762.50	850.00

Badge Type of 1892-1903

1904-10 **Wmk. 3**

90	A8	1f gray & car	3.50	1.25
91	A8	1f brown ('09)	.90	.25
92	A8	½p green	7.00	.15
93	A8	1p carmine rose	5.75	.20
94	A8	1p carmine ('09)	4.00	.15
95	A8	2p gray ('09)	4.00	7.75
96	A8	2½p ultramarine	4.00	.40
97	A8	6p vio & car	15.00	12.50
98	A8	6p dl vio & vio ('10)	5.00	12.00
99	A8	8p org & ultra	22.50	52.50
100	A8	1sh blk, grn ('10)	7.50	12.00
101	A8	2sh6p pur & green	27.50	55.00
		Nos. 90-101 (12)	106.65	154.15

Nelson Centenary Issue

Lord Nelson Monument — A10

1906 **Engr.** **Wmk. 1**

102	A10	1f gray & black	2.00	.60
103	A10	½p green & black	3.00	.40
104	A10	1p car & black	3.50	.30
105	A10	2p org & black	4.00	4.25
106	A10	2½p ultra & black	5.00	4.00
107	A10	6p lilac & black	15.00	19.00
108	A10	1sh rose & black	17.50	32.50
		Nos. 102-108 (7)	50.00	61.05

See Nos. 110-112.

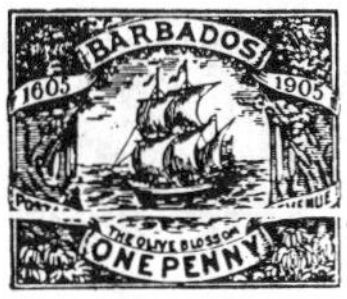
The "Olive Blossom" — A11

1906, Aug. 15 **Wmk. 3**

109	A11	1p blk, green & blue	8.00	1.25

Tercentenary of the 1st British landing.

Nelson Type of 1906

1907, July 6 **Wmk. 3**

110	A10	1f gray & black	2.50	2.00
111	A10	2p org & black	12.50	15.00
112	A10	2½p ultra & black	10.00	12.50
a.		2½p indigo & black	850.00	1,200.
		Nos. 110-112 (3)	25.00	29.50

A12

A13

King George V — A14

1912 **Typo.**

116	A12	¼p brown	.40	.30
117	A12	½p green	1.50	.20
a.		Booklet pane of 6		
118	A12	1p carmine	3.00	.15
a.		1p scarlet	10.00	1.00
b.		Booklet pane of 6		
119	A12	2p gray	1.65	6.50
120	A12	2½p ultramarine	1.00	.50
121	A13	3p violet, yel	1.00	4.00
122	A13	4p blk & scar, yel	1.00	7.50
123	A13	6p vio & red vio	6.00	5.00
124	A14	1sh black, green	4.00	7.00
125	A14	2sh vio & ultra, bl	24.00	32.50
126	A14	3sh grn & violet	47.50	37.50
		Nos. 116-126 (11)	91.05	101.15

Seal of the Colony — A15

1916-18 **Engr.**

127	A15	¼p brown	.30	.25
128	A15	½p green	.75	.20
129	A15	1p red	1.00	.20
130	A15	2p gray	3.50	10.00
131	A15	2½p ultramarine	.85	.75
132	A15	3p violet, yel	2.25	2.50
133	A15	4p red, yel	.60	5.00
134	A15	4p red & black ('18)	.85	2.50
135	A15	6p claret	1.50	2.25
136	A15	1sh black, green	3.50	5.00
137	A15	2sh violet, blue	15.00	8.50
138	A15	3sh dark violet	32.50	70.00
139	A15	3sh dk vio & grn ('18)	15.00	30.00
a.		3sh bright violet & green ('18)	140.00	150.00
		Nos. 127-139 (13)	77.60	137.15

Nos. 134 and 139 are from a re-engraved die. The central medallion is not surrounded by a line and there are various other small alterations.

Victory Issue

Victory
A16 A17

1920, Sept. 9 **Wmk. 3**

140	A16	¼p bister & black	.25	.35
141	A16	½p yel green & blk	.80	.30
a.		Booklet pane of 2		
142	A16	1p org red & blk	1.25	.20
a.		Booklet pane of 2		
143	A16	2p gray & black	1.50	4.50
144	A16	2½p ultra & dk bl	2.00	4.75
145	A16	3p red lilac & blk	.85	2.00
146	A16	4p gray grn & blk	1.40	3.50
147	A16	6p orange & blk	1.75	4.50
148	A17	1sh yel green & blk	5.00	10.00
149	A17	2sh brown & blk	10.00	15.00
150	A17	3sh orange & blk	15.00	20.00
		Nos. 140-150 (11)	39.80	65.10

1921, Aug. 22 **Wmk. 4**

151	A16	1p orange red & blk	8.00	.30
		Nos. 140-151 (12)	47.80	65.40

A18

A19

1921-24 **Wmk. 4**

152	A18	¼p brown	.15	.15
153	A18	½p green	.35	.15
154	A18	1p carmine	.30	.15
155	A18	2p gray	1.00	.30
156	A18	2½p ultramarine	.90	1.50
158	A18	6p claret	1.50	1.50
159	A18	1sh blk, emer ('24)	30.00	32.50
160	A18	2sh dk vio, blue	13.00	17.50
161	A18	3sh dark violet	13.00	22.50

Wmk. 3

162	A18	3p violet, yel	.75	1.50
163	A18	4p red, yel	.70	3.00
164	A18	1sh black, green	4.00	10.00
		Nos. 152-164 (12)	65.65	90.75

1925-35 **Wmk. 4** *Perf. 14*

165	A19	¼p brown	.15	.15
166	A19	½p green	.15	.15
a.		Perf. 13½x12½ ('32)	1.25	.15
b.		Booklet pane of 10		
167	A19	1p carmine	.15	.15
a.		Perf. 13½x12½ ('32)	.90	.30
b.		Booklet pane of 10		
168	A19	1½p org, perf. 13½x12½ ('32)	.75	.60
a.		Booklet pane of 6		
b.		Perf. 14	3.50	.80
169	A19	2p gray	.50	1.25
170	A19	2½p ultramarine	.50	.50
a.		Perf. 13½x12½ ('32)	3.00	1.00
171	A19	3p vio brn, yel	.60	.40
172	A19	3p red brn, yel ('35)	6.00	6.00
173	A19	4p red, yel	.80	.80
174	A19	6p claret	.80	.80
175	A19	1sh blk, emerald	1.50	2.50
a.		Perf. 13½x12½ ('32)	15.00	10.00
176	A19	1sh brn blk, yel grn ('32)	4.25	7.50
177	A19	2sh violet, bl	5.00	4.00
178	A19	2sh6p car, blue ('32)	15.00	17.50
179	A19	3sh dark violet	8.00	12.50
		Nos. 165-179 (15)	44.15	54.80

Charles I and George V — A20

1927, Feb. 17 *Perf. 12½*

180	A20	1p carmine lake	.75	.60

Tercentenary of the settlement of Barbados.

Common Design Types pictured following the introduction.

Silver Jubilee Issue

Common Design Type

1935, May 6 *Perf. 11x12*

186	CD301	1p car & dk bl	.20	.20
187	CD301	1½p blk & ultra	.40	.30
188	CD301	2½p ultra & brn	.85	.85
189	CD301	1sh brn vio & ind	5.00	5.00
		Nos. 186-189 (4)	6.45	6.35
		Set, never hinged	15.00	

Coronation Issue

Common Design Type

1937, May 14 *Perf. 13½x14*

190	CD302	1p carmine	.15	.15
191	CD302	1½p brown	.20	.20
192	CD302	2½p bright ultra	.40	.40
		Nos. 190-192 (3)	.75	.75
		Set, never hinged	1.00	

A21

1938-47 *Perf. 13-14 & Compound*

193	A21	½p green	.40	.15
b.		Perf. 14	22.50	1.40
c.		Booklet pane of 10		
193A	A21	½p bister ('42)	.15	.15
194	A21	1p carmine	1.75	.15
b.		Perf. 13½x13	50.00	1.40
c.		Booklet pane of 10		
194A	A21	1p green ('42)	.15	.15
d.		Perf. 13½x13	.30	.15
195	A21	1½p red orange	.15	.15
c.		Perf. 14	.60	.15
d.		Booklet pane of 6		
195A	A21	2p rose lake ('41)	1.10	.50
195B	A21	2p bright rose red ('43)	.20	.15
e.		Perf. 14	.15	.15
196	A21	2½p ultramarine	.20	.15
197	A21	3p brown	.20	.50
b.		Perf. 14	.25	.20
197A	A21	3p deep bl ('47)	.20	.15
198	A21	4p black	.20	.15
a.		Perf. 14	.30	.30
199	A21	6p violet	.20	.15
199A	A21	8p red vio ('46)	.65	.65
200	A21	1sh brn olive	.50	.20
a.		1sh olive green	5.00	1.40

BARBADOS

201 A21	2sh6p brown vio	2.75	.65
201A A21	5sh indigo ('41)	2.75	1.40
	Nos. 193-201A (16)	11.55	5.40
	Set, never hinged	25.00	

For surcharge see No. 209.

Kings Charles I, George VI Assembly Chamber and Mace — A22

Perf. 13½x14
1939, June 27 Engr. Wmk. 4

202 A22	½p deep green	.25	.15
203 A22	1p scarlet	.25	.15
204 A22	1½p deep orange	.35	.25
205 A22	2½p ultramarine	.60	.80
206 A22	3p yellow brown	.65	.80
	Nos. 202-206 (5)	2.10	2.15
	Set, never hinged	5.00	

Tercentenary of the General Assembly.

Catalogue values for unused stamps in this section, from this point to the end of the section, are for Never Hinged items.

Peace Issue
Common Design Type
1946, Sept. 18

207 CD303	1½p deep orange	.15	.15
208 CD303	3p brown	.15	.15

Nos. 195e, 195B, Surcharged in Black **ONE PENNY**

1947, Apr. 21 Perf. 14
209 A21	1p on 2p brt rose red	.55	.55
a.	Double surcharge		
b.	Perf. 13½x13	.65	.65

Silver Wedding Issue
Common Design Types
Perf. 14x14½
1948, Nov. 24 Photo. Wmk. 4
| 210 CD304 | 1½p orange | .15 | .15 |

Engraved; Name Typographed
Perf. 11½x11
| 211 CD305 | 5sh dark blue | 10.00 | 10.00 |

UPU Issue
Common Design Types
1949, Oct. 10 Perf. 13½, 11x11½

212 CD306	1½p red orange	.32	.35
213 CD307	3p indigo	.55	.55
214 CD308	4p gray	1.00	1.00
215 CD309	1sh olive	1.40	1.40
	Nos. 212-215 (4)	3.27	3.30

Dover Fort — A23

Admiral Nelson Statue — A24

Designs: 2c, Sugar cane breeding. 3c, Public buildings. 6c, Casting net. 8c, Intercolonial schooner. 12c, Flying Fish. 24c, Old Main Guard Garrison. 48c, Cathedral. 60c, Careenage. $1.20, Map. $2.40, Great Seal, 1660.

Perf. 11x11½ (A23), 13x13½ (A24)
1950, May 1 Engr. Wmk. 4

216 A23	1c slate	.15	.15
217 A23	2c emerald	.15	.15
218 A23	3c slate & brown	.15	.15
219 A24	4c carmine	.30	.30
220 A23	6c blue	.35	.30
221 A23	8c choc & blue	.60	.15
222 A23	12c olive & aqua	1.25	.75
223 A23	24c gray & red	1.50	1.00
224 A24	48c violet	4.00	2.75
225 A23	60c brn car & bl grn	2.50	3.00
226 A24	$1.20 olive & car	9.00	5.25
227 A23	$2.40 gray	21.00	13.00
	Nos. 216-227 (12)	40.95	27.20

University Issue
Common Design Types
1951, Feb. 16 Perf. 14x14½
228 CD310	3c turq bl & choc	.15	.15
229 CD311	12c ol brn & turq bl	.75	.75

Stamp of 1852 — A25

Perf. 13½
1952, Apr. 15 Wmk. 4 Engr.
230 A25	3c slate bl & dp grn	.15	.15
231 A25	4c rose pink & bl	.25	.25
232 A25	12c emer & slate bl	.40	.40
233 A25	24c gray blk & red brn	.65	.65
	Nos. 230-233 (4)	1.45	1.45

Centenary of Barbados postage stamps.

Coronation Issue
Common Design Type
1953, June 4 Perf. 13½x13
| 234 CD312 | 4c red orange & black | .15 | .15 |

Harbor Police — A26

Designs as in 1950 with portrait of Queen Elizabeth II. $2.40, Great Seal, 1660 ("E II R").

Perf. 11x11½ (horiz.), 13x13½ (vert.)
1953-57 Engr.

235 A23	1c slate ('53)	.15	.15
236 A23	2c grnsh blue & deep org	.15	.15
237 A23	3c emerald & blk	.15	.15
238 A24	4c orange & gray	.15	.15
239 A26	5c dp car & dp bl	.20	.15
240 A23	6c red brown	.20	.15
241 A23	8c brt blue & blk	.30	.15
242 A23	12c brn ol & aqua	.40	.15
243 A23	24c gray & red ('56)	.55	.20
244 A24	48c violet ('56)	1.75	1.10
245 A23	60c brown car & blue grn ('56)	3.00	1.75
246 A24	$1.20 ol & car ('56)	5.25	3.25
247 A23	$2.40 gray ('57)	11.00	6.25
	Nos. 235-247 (13)	23.25	13.75

See Nos. 257-264.

West Indies Federation
Common Design Type
Perf. 11½x11
1958, Apr. 23 Wmk. 314
248 CD313	3c green	.15	.15
249 CD313	6c blue	.40	.40
250 CD313	12c carmine rose	.50	.50
	Nos. 248-250 (3)	1.05	1.05

Deep Water Harbor, Bridgetown — A27

1961, May 6 Engr. Perf. 11x11½
251 A27	4c orange & black	.15	.15
252 A27	8c ultra & black	.30	.30
253 A27	24c black & pink	.65	.65
	Nos. 251-253 (3)	1.10	1.10

Deep Water Harbor at Bridgetown opening.

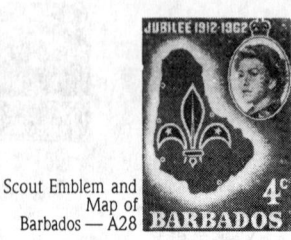

Scout Emblem and Map of Barbados — A28

Perf. 11½x11
1962, Mar. 9 Wmk. 314
254 A28	4c orange & black	.15	.15
255 A28	12c gray & blue	.30	.30
256 A28	$1.20 greenish gray & carmine rose	2.00	2.00
	Nos. 254-256 (3)	2.45	2.45

50th anniv. of the founding of the Boy Scouts of Barbados.

Queen Types of 1953-57
Perf. 11x11½, 13x13½
1964-65 Engr. Wmk. 314

257 A23	1c slate	.25	.25
258 A24	4c orange & gray	.35	.35
259 A23	8c brt bl & blk ('65)	.50	.45
260 A23	12c brn ol & aqua ('65)	.60	
261 A23	24c gray & red	.60	.50
262 A24	48c violet	2.50	2.50
263 A23	60c brn car & bl grn	3.50	3.50
264 A23	$2.40 gray ('65)	5.50	5.50
	Nos. 257-264 (8)	13.80	
	Nos. 257-259,261-264 (7)		13.05

The 12c was never put on sale in Barbados.

ITU Issue
Common Design Type
Perf. 11x11½
1965, May 17 Litho. Wmk. 314
265 CD317	2c lilac & ver	.15	.15
266 CD317	48c yellow & gray	1.50	1.50

Sea Horse — A29

Designs: 1c, Deep sea coral. 2c, Lobster. 4c, Sea urchin. 5c, Staghorn coral. 6c, Butterflyfish. 8c, File shell. 12c, Balloonfish. 15c, Angelfish. 25c, Brain coral. 35c, Brittle star. 50c, Flyingfish. $1, Queen conch shell. $2.50, Fiddler crab.

Wmk. 314 Upright
1965, July 15 Photo. Perf. 14x13½

267 A29	1c dk blue, pink & black	.15	.15
268 A29	2c car rose, sepia & orange	.15	.15
269 A29	3c org, brn & sep ("Hippocanpus")	.15	.15
270 A29	4c ol grn & dk bl	.15	.15
a.	Imperf., pair	450.00	
271 A29	5c lil, brn & pink	.15	.15
272 A29	6c greenish bl, yel & blk	.15	.15
273 A29	8c ultra, orange, red & black	.25	.20
274 A29	12c rose lil, yel & blk	.40	.25
275 A29	15c red, yel & blk	.75	.50
276 A29	25c yel brn & ultra	1.10	.80
277 A29	35c grn, rose brn & blk	1.75	1.00
278 A29	50c yel grn & ultra	2.75	1.65
279 A29	$1 gray & multi	5.50	4.00
280 A29	$2.50 lt bl & multi	12.00	10.00
	Nos. 267-280 (14)	25.40	19.30

1966-69 Wmk. 314 Sideways

Design: $5, "Dolphin" (coryphaena hippurus).

267a A29	1c	.15	.15
268a A29	2c ('67)	.15	.15
269A A29	3c ("Hippocampus") ('67)	.18	.15
270b A29	4c	.15	.15
271a A29	5c	.15	.15
272a A29	6c ('67)	.20	.15
273a A29	8c	.25	.20
274a A29	12c ('67)	.35	.20
275a A29	15c	.50	.35
276a A29	25c	.60	.55
277a A29	35c	.85	.60
278a A29	50c	1.25	1.10
279a A29	$1	2.50	1.90
280a A29	$2.50	6.25	6.00
280B A29	$5 dk ol & multi ('69)	12.50	12.50
	Nos. 267a-280B (15)	26.03	24.30

For surcharge see No. 327.

Churchill Memorial Issue
Common Design Type
1966, Jan. 24 Wmk. 314 Perf. 14
281 CD319	1c multicolored	.15	.15
282 CD319	4c multicolored	.20	.20
283 CD319	25c multicolored	1.00	1.00
284 CD319	35c multicolored	1.40	1.40
	Nos. 281-284 (4)	2.75	2.75

Royal Visit Issue
Common Design Type
1966, Feb. 4 Litho. Perf. 11x12
285 CD320	3c violet blue	.20	.20
286 CD320	35c dark car rose	1.75	1.75

UNESCO Anniversary Issue
Common Design Type
1967, Jan. 6 Litho. Perf. 14
287 CD323	4c "Education"	.15	.15
288 CD323	12c "Science"	.55	.55
289 CD323	25c "Culture"	1.40	1.40
	Nos. 287-289 (3)	2.10	2.10

Arms of Barbados — A30

Policeman and Anchor Monument — A31

Designs: 25c, Hilton Hotel, horiz. 35c, Garfield Sobers, captain of Barbados and West Indies Cricket Team. 50c, Pine Hill Dairy, horiz.

1966, Dec. 2 Unwmk. Photo.
290 A30	4c multicolored	.15	.15
291 A30	25c multicolored	.35	.35
292 A30	35c multicolored	.50	.50
293 A30	50c multicolored	.75	.75
	Nos. 290-293 (4)	1.75	1.75

Barbados' independence, Nov. 30, 1966.

1967, Oct. 16 Litho. Perf. 13½x14

Designs: 25c, Policeman with telescope. 35c, Police motor launch, horiz. 50c, Policemen at Harbor Gate.

294 A31	4c multicolored	.15	.15
295 A31	25c multicolored	.30	.30
296 A31	35c multicolored	.50	.50
297 A31	50c multicolored	.80	.80
	Nos. 294-297 (4)	1.75	1.75

Centenary of Bridgetown Harbor Police.
For surcharge see No. 322.

Independence Arch — A32

1st Anniv. of Independence: 4c, Sir Winston Scott, Governor-General, vert. 35c, Treasury Building. 50c, Parliament Building.

Perf. 14½x14, 14x14½
1967, Dec. 4 Photo. Unwmk.
298 A32	4c multicolored	.15	.15
299 A32	25c multicolored	.25	.25
300 A32	35c multicolored	.40	.40
301 A32	50c multicolored	.60	.60
	Nos. 298-301 (4)	1.40	1.40

UN Building, Santiago, Chile — A33

1968, Feb. 27 Perf. 14½x14
| 302 A33 | 15c multicolored | .20 | .20 |

20th anniv. of the UN Economic Commission for Latin America.

Radar Antenna on Top of Old Sugar Mill, Sugar Cane — A34

Designs: 25c, Caribbean Meteorological Institute, Barbados, horiz. 50c, HARP gun used in High Altitude Research Program, at Paragon in Christ Church, Barbados.

Perf. 14x14½, 14½x14

1968, June 4	Photo.	Unwmk.	
303 A34	3c violet & multi	.15	.15
304 A34	25c vermilion & multi	.30	.30
305 A34	50c orange & multi	.70	.70
Nos. 303-305 (3)		1.15	1.15

World Meteorological Day.

Girl Scout at Campfire, Lady Baden-Powell and Queen Elizabeth II — A35

Lady Baden-Powell, Queen Elizabeth II and: 25c, Pax Hill Headquarters. 35c, Girl Scout badge.

Perf. 14x14½

1968, Aug. 29	Photo.	Unwmk.	
306 A35	3c dp ultra, blk & gold	.15	.15
307 A35	25c bluish green, black & gold	.35	.35
308 A35	35c org yel, blk & gold	.70	.70
Nos. 306-308 (3)		1.20	1.20

Barbados Girl Scouts' 50th anniv.

Human Rights Flame and Escape to Freedom A36

Designs: 4c, Human Rights flame, hands, and broken chain. 25c, Human Rights flame, family and broken chain.

Perf. 11x11½

1968, Dec. 10	Litho.	Unwmk.	
309 A36	4c violet, gray grn & red brown	.15	.15
310 A36	25c org, blk & blue	.40	.40
311 A36	35c greenish blue, blue, blk & org	.55	.55
Nos. 309-311 (3)		1.10	1.10

International Human Rights Year.

In the Paddock A37

Horse Racing: 25c, "They're off!" 35c, On the flat. 50c, The Finish.

1969, Mar. 15	Litho.	Perf. 14½
312 A37	4c multicolored	.15 .15
313 A37	25c multicolored	.25 .25
314 A37	35c multicolored	.35 .35
315 A37	50c multicolored	.55 .55
a. Souvenir sheet of 4, #312-315		2.50 3.00
Nos. 312-315 (4)		1.30 1.30

Map of Caribbean — A38

Design: 12c, 50c, "Strength in Unity," horiz.

Perf. 14x14½, 14½x14

1969, May 6	Photo.	Wmk. 314
316 A38	5c brown & multi	.15 .15
317 A38	12c ultra & multi	.20 .20
318 A38	25c green & multi	.30 .30
319 A38	50c magenta & multi	.65 .65
Nos. 316-319 (4)		1.30 1.30

1st anniv. of CARIFTA (Caribbean Free Trade Area).

ILO Emblem A39

Perf. 14x13

1969, Aug. 5	Litho.	Unwmk.
320 A39	4c bl grn, brt grn & blk	.15 .15
321 A39	25c red brn, brt mag & red	.40 .40

50th anniv. of the ILO.

No. 294 Surcharged **ONE CENT**

Perf. 13½x14

1969, Aug. 30		
322 A31	1c on 4c multicolored	.35 .35

Barbados Boy Scout Emblem A40

Designs: 25c, Sea Scouts rowing in Bridgetown harbor. 35c, Campfire. 50c, Various Scouts in front of National Headquarters and Training Center, Hazelwood.

Perf. 13½x13

1969, Dec. 16	Litho.	Unwmk.
323 A40	5c multicolored	.15 .15
324 A40	25c multicolored	.50 .50
325 A40	50c multicolored	.65 .65
326 A40	50c multicolored	1.00 1.00
a. Souvenir sheet of 4, #323-326		10.00 12.00
Nos. 323-326 (4)		2.30 2.30

Attainment of independence by the Barbados Boy Scout Assoc.

No. 271a Surcharged **4 x**

Wmk. 314 Sideways

1970, Mar. 11	Photo.	Perf. 14x13½
327 A29	4c on 5c multicolored	.20 .20

This locally applied surcharge exists in several variations: double, triple, on back, in pair with one missing, etc.

Lion at Gun Hill — A41

Barbados Museum A42

2c, Trafalgar Fountain. 3c, Montefiore Drinking Fountain. 4c, St. James' Monument. 5c, St. Ann's Fort. 6c, Old Sugar Mill, Morgan Lewis. 8c, Cenotaph. 10c, South Point Lighthouse. 15c, Sharon Moravian Church. 25c, George Washington House. 35c, St. Nicholas Abbey. 50c, Bowmanston Pumping Station. $1, Queen Elizabeth Hospital. $2.50, Modern sugar factory. $5, Seawell Intl. Airport.

Wmk. 314 Upright (A41), Sideways (A42)

Perf. 12½x13, 13x12½

1970, May 4		Photo.
328 A41	1c blue grn & multi	.15 .15
329 A41	2c crimson & multi	.15 .15
330 A41	3c blue & multi	.15 .15
331 A41	4c yellow & multi	.15 .15
332 A41	5c dp org & multi	.15 .15
333 A41	6c dull yel & multi	.15 .15
334 A41	8c dp blue & multi	.15 .15
335 A41	10c red & multi	.15 .15
336 A42	12c ultra & multi	.20 .20
337 A42	15c yellow & multi	.22 .20
338 A42	25c orange & multi	.40 .40
339 A42	35c pink & multi	.60 .60
340 A42	50c bl grn & multi	.65 .65
341 A42	$1 emerald & multi	1.40 1.40
342 A42	$2.50 ver & multi	3.50 3.50
343 A42	$5 yellow & multi	6.50 6.50
Nos. 328-343 (16)		14.67 14.65

Nos. 328-332, 334-343 were reissued in 1971 on glazed paper.

Wmk. 314 Sideways (A41), Upright (A42)

1972-74

331a A41	4c	.15 .15
332a A41	5c	.15 .15
333a A41	6c	.15 .15
334a A41	8c	.15 .15
335a A41	10c ('74)	.25 .25
336a A42	12c	.25 .25
337a A42	25c	.30 .30
338a A42	25c	.55 .55
339a A42	35c	.85 .85
340a A42	50c	1.25 1.25
341a A42	$1	2.50 2.50
342a A42	$2.50 ('73)	6.50 6.50
343a A42	$5 ('73)	13.00 13.00
Nos. 331a-343a (13)		26.05 26.05

For surcharge, see No. 391.

Primary Education, UN and Education Year Emblems A43

Designs (UN and Education Year Emblems and): 5c, Secondary education (student with microscope). 25c, Technical education (men working with power drill). 50c, University building.

1970, June 26	Litho.	Perf. 14
344 A43	4c multicolored	.15 .15
345 A43	5c multicolored	.15 .15
346 A43	25c multicolored	.35 .35
347 A43	50c multicolored	.75 .75
Nos. 344-347 (4)		1.40 1.40

UN, 25th anniv., and Intl. Education Year.

Minnie Root A44

Flowers: 1c, Barbados Easter lily, vert. 10c, Eyelash orchid. 25c, Pride of Barbados, vert. 35c, Christmas hope.

1970, Aug. 24 Litho. Wmk. 314
Flowers in Natural Colors

348 A44	1c green	.20 .15
349 A44	5c deep magenta	.20 .15
350 A44	10c dark blue	.45 .25
351 A44	25c brt orange brown	1.25 .55
352 A44	35c blue	1.75 .90
a. Souvenir sheet of 5		3.00 2.25
Nos. 348-352 (5)		3.85 2.00

No. 352a contains 5 imperf. stamps similar to Nos. 348-352 with simulated perforations.

Christ Carrying Cross — A45

Easter: 10c, 50c, Resurrection, by Benjamin West, St. George's Anglican Church. 35c like 4c, Window from St. Margaret's Anglican Church, St. John.

1971, Apr. 7	Wmk. 314	Perf. 14
353 A45	4c purple & multi	.15 .15
354 A45	10c silver & multi	.15 .15
355 A45	35c brt blue & multi	.50 .50
356 A45	50c gold & multi	.80 .80
Nos. 353-356 (4)		1.60 1.60

Sailfish Craft — A46

Tourism: 5c, Tennis. 12c, Horseback riding. 25c, Water-skiing. 50c, Scuba diving.

1971, Aug. 17		Perf. 14x14½
357 A46	1c multicolored	.15 .15
358 A46	5c multicolored	.15 .15
359 A46	12c multicolored	.20 .20
360 A46	25c multicolored	.50 .50
361 A46	50c multicolored	1.00 1.00
Nos. 357-361 (5)		2.00 2.00

Samuel Jackman Prescod — A47

1971, Sept. 26		Perf. 14
362 A47	3c orange & multi	.15 .15
363 A47	35c ultra & multi	.65 .65

Samuel Jackman Prescod (1806-1871), 1st black member of Barbados Assembly.

Coat of Arms — A48

Designs: 15c, 50c, Flag and map of Barbados.

1971, Nov. 23		
364 A48	4c light blue & multi	.15 .15
365 A48	15c multicolored	.30 .30
366 A48	25c yel green & multi	.45 .45
367 A48	50c blue & multi	.90 .90
Nos. 364-367 (4)		1.80 1.80

5th anniv. of independence.

Telegraphy, 1872 and 1972 A49

Designs: 10c, "Stanley Angwin" off St. Lawrence Coast. 35c, Earth station and Intelsat 4. 50c, Mt. Misery tropospheric scatter station.

1972, Mar. 28	Litho.	Perf. 14
368 A49	4c purple & multi	.15 .15
369 A49	10c emerald & multi	.25 .25
370 A49	35c red & multi	.55 .55
371 A49	50c orange & multi	.85 .85
Nos. 368-371 (4)		1.80 1.80

Centenary of telecommunications to and from Barbados.

Lord Baden-Powell, Charles W. Springer, George B. Burton — A50

Designs: 5c, Map of Barbados and Combermere School, vert. 25c, Photograph of 1922 troop. 50c, Flags of various Boy Scout troops.

BARBADOS

1972, Aug. 1

372 A50	5c ultra & multi	.15	.15
373 A50	15c ultra & multi	.40	.40
374 A50	25c ultra & multi	.60	.60
375 A50	50c ultra & multi	1.10	1.10
	Nos. 372-375 (4)	2.25	2.25

60th anniv. of Barbados Boy Scouts and 4th Caribbean Jamboree.

Bookmobile, Open Book — A51

Intl. Book Year: 15c, Visual aids truck. 25c, Central Library, Bridgetown. $1, Codrington College.

1972, Oct. 31   Litho.   Wmk. 314

376 A51	4c brt pink & multi	.15	.15
377 A51	15c dull org & multi	.25	.25
378 A51	25c buff & multi	.40	.40
379 A51	$1 lt violet & multi	1.90	1.90
	Nos. 376-379 (4)	2.70	2.70

Pottery Wheels A52

Barbados pottery industry: 15c, Kiln. 25c, Finished pottery, Chalky Mount. $1, Pottery on sale at market.

1973, Mar. 1   Wmk. 314   Perf. 14

380 A52	5c dull red & multi	.15	.15
381 A52	15c olive grn & multi	.20	.20
382 A52	25c gray & multi	.35	.35
383 A52	$1 yellow & multi	1.40	1.40
	Nos. 380-383 (4)	2.10	2.10

First Flight in Barbados, Wright Box Kite, 1911 — A53

Aircraft: 15c, First flight to Barbados, De Havilland biplane, 1928. 25c, Passenger plane, 1939. 50c, Vickers VC-10 over control tower, 1973.

1973, July 25   Perf. 12½x12

384 A53	5c blue & multi	.15	.15
385 A53	15c vio blue & multi	.40	.40
386 A53	25c multicolored	.65	.65
387 A53	50c blue & multi	1.40	1.40
	Nos. 384-387 (4)	2.60	2.60

Chancellor Sir Hugh Wooding A54

Designs: 25c, Sherlock Hall, Cave Hill Campus. 35c, Cave Hill Campus.

1973, Dec. 11   Perf. 13x14

388 A54	5c dp orange & multi	.15	.15
389 A54	25c red brown & multi	.40	.40
390 A54	35c multicolored	.60	.60
	Nos. 388-390 (3)	1.15	1.15

25th anniv. of the Univ. of the West Indies.

No. 338a Surcharged **4c.**

1974, Apr. 30   Photo.   Perf. 13x12½

391 A42	4c on 25c multi	.15	.15
a.	"4c." omitted	20.00	

Barbados stamps can be mounted in the annual Scott Barbados supplement.

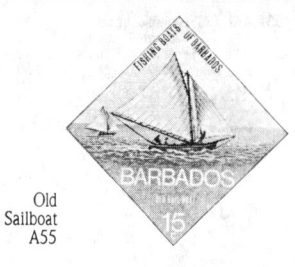

Old Sailboat A55

Designs: 25c, Rowboat. 50c, Motor-powered fishing boat. $1, Trawler "Calamar."

1974, June 11   Wmk. 314   Perf. 14

392 A55	15c blue & multi	.25	.25
393 A55	35c multicolored	.50	.50
394 A55	50c vio blue & multi	.70	.70
395 A55	$1 blue & multi	1.40	1.40
a.	Souvenir sheet of 4, #392-395	3.00	3.75
	Nos. 392-395 (4)	2.85	2.85

Fishing boats of Barbados.

Fire Orchid — A56

Orchids. 1c, 20c, 25c, $2.50, $5 horizontal.

Wmk. 314 Sideways; Upright (1c, 20c, 25c, $1, $10)

1974-77   Photo.   Perf. 14

396 A56	1c Cattleya gaskelliana alba	.15	.15
397 A56	2c shown	.15	.15
398 A56	3c Rose Marie	.15	.15
399 A56	4c Fiery red orchid	.15	.15
400 A56	5c Schomburgkia humboltii	.15	.15
401 A56	8c Dancing dolls	.15	.15
402 A56	10c Spider orchids	.20	.15
403 A56	12c Dendrobium aggregatum	.25	.20
404 A56	15c Lady slippers	.40	.35
404C A56	20c Spathoglottis	.45	.40
405 A56	25c Eyelash	.75	.55
406 A56	35c Bletia patula	.80	.65
406B A56	45c Sunset Glow	1.10	.85
407 A56	50c Sunset Glow	1.10	.85

Perf. 14½x14, 14x14½

408 A56	$1 Ascocenda red gem	2.00	1.50
409 A56	$2.50 Brassolaeliocattleya nugget	4.75	3.75
410 A56	$5 Caularthron bicornutum	9.50	8.00
411 A56	$10 Moon orchid	17.50	15.00
	Nos. 396-411 (18)	39.70	33.15

Issued: 20c, 45c, 5/3/77; others, 9/16/74. For surcharge see No. B2.

Wmk. 314 Upright; Sideways (1c, 25c, $1)

1976   Perf. 14

396a A56	1c multicolored	.15	.15
397a A56	2c multicolored	.15	.15
398a A56	3c multicolored	.20	.15
399a A56	4c multicolored	.25	.20
402a A56	10c multicolored	.45	.40
404a A56	15c multicolored	.80	.70
405a A56	25c multicolored	1.00	.90
406a A56	35c multicolored	1.50	1.25

Perf. 14½x14

408a A56		4.00	3.50
	Nos. 396a-408a (9)	8.50	7.40

1975   Wmk. 373   Perf. 14

396b A56	1c multicolored	.15	.15
397b A56	2c multicolored	.15	.15
398b A56	3c multicolored	.15	.15
399b A56	4c multicolored	.25	.22
400b A56	5c multicolored	.15	.15
402b A56	10c multicolored	.20	.20
403b A56	12c multicolored	.25	.25
404b A56	15c multicolored	.50	.45
406c A56	45c multicolored	1.10	.90

Perf. 14½x14, 14x14½

408b A56	$1 multicolored	2.00	1.90
409b A56	$2.50 multicolored	5.00	4.50
410b A56	$5 multicolored	10.00	9.90
411b A56	$10 multicolored	18.00	18.00
	Nos. 396b-411b (13)	37.90	36.52

UPU Emblem, Barbados No. 64 A57

Cent. of the UPU: 35c, Letters encircling globe. 50c, Barbados coat of arms. $1, Map of Barbados, sailing ship and jet.

1974, Oct. 9   Litho.   Perf. 14½

412 A57	8c brt rose, org & gray	.15	.15
413 A57	35c red, blk, & ocher	.45	.45
414 A57	50c vio blue, bl & sil	.65	.65
415 A57	$1 ultra, blk & brn	1.25	1.25
a.	Souvenir sheet of 4, #412-415	3.00	3.00
	Nos. 412-415 (4)	2.50	2.50

Yacht Britannia off Barbados A58

Royal Visit, Feb. 1975: 35c, $1, Palms and sunset.

1975, Feb. 18

416 A58	8c brown & multi	.15	.15
417 A58	25c blue & multi	.40	.40
418 A58	35c purple & multi	.60	.60
419 A58	$1 violet & multi	1.65	1.65
	Nos. 416-419 (4)	2.80	2.80

St. Michael's Cathedral — A59

Designs: 15c, Bishop Coleridge. 50c, All Saint's Church. $1, St. Michael, stained glass window, St. Michael's Cathedral.

1975, July 29   Wmk. 314   Litho.   Perf. 14

420 A59	5c blue & multi	.15	.15
421 A59	15c lilac & multi	.20	.20
422 A59	50c green & multi	.55	.55
423 A59	$1 multicolored	1.00	1.00
a.	Souvenir sheet of 4, #420-423	2.25	2.75
	Nos. 420-423 (4)	1.90	1.90

Anglican Diocese in Barbados, sesquicentennial.

Pony Float A60

Designs: 25c, Stiltsman (band and masqueraders). 35c, Maypole dancing. 50c, Cuban dancers.

1975, Nov. 18   Wmk. 373

424 A60	8c yellow & multi	.15	.15
425 A60	25c buff & multi	.30	.30
426 A60	35c ultra & multi	.40	.40
427 A60	50c orange & multi	.65	.65
a.	Souvenir sheet of 4, #424-427	1.75	1.75
	Nos. 424-427 (4)	1.50	1.50

Crop-over (harvest) festival.

Sailing Ship, 17th Cent. — A61

Coat of Arms — A62

350th Anniv. of 1st Settlement: 10c, Bearded fig tree and fruit. 25c, Ogilvy's 17th cent. map. $1, Capt. John Powell.

1975, Dec. 17   Wmk. 373   Perf. 13½

428 A61	4c lt blue & multi	.15	.15
429 A61	10c lt blue & multi	.20	.15
430 A61	25c yellow & multi	.55	.50
431 A61	$1 lt red & multi	1.90	1.65
a.	Souvenir sheet of 4, #428-431	3.00	2.75
	Nos. 428-431 (4)	2.80	2.45

Coil Stamps

1975, Dec.   Unwmk.   Perf. 15x14

432 A62	5c light blue	.15	.15
433 A62	25c violet	.25	.25

Map of West Indies, Bats, Wicket and Ball — A63

BARBADOS Prudential Cup — A64

1976, July 7   Litho.   Perf. 14

438 A63	25c lt blue & multi	.85	.50
439 A64	45c lilac rose & black	1.10	1.00

World Cricket Cup, won by West Indies Team, 1975.

Map of South Carolina settled by Barbadians — A65

American Bicentennial: 25c, George Washington and map of Bridge Town area. 50c, Declaration of Independence. $1, Masonic emblem and Prince Hall, founder and Grand Master of African Grand Lodge, Boston, 1790-1807.

1976, Aug. 17   Wmk. 373   Perf. 13½

440 A65	15c multicolored	.20	.20
441 A65	25c multicolored	.35	.35
442 A65	50c multicolored	.65	.65
443 A65	$1 multicolored	1.40	1.40
	Nos. 440-443 (4)	2.60	2.60

Mailman with Bicycle A66

PO Act, 125th anniv.: 35c, Mailman on motor scooter. 50c, Cover with Barbados No. 2. $1, Mail truck.

1976, Oct. 19   Litho.   Perf. 14

444 A66	8c rose red, blk & bis	.15	.15
445 A66	35c multicolored	.40	.40
446 A66	50c vio blue & multi	.60	.60
447 A66	$1 red & multi	1.10	1.10
	Nos. 444-447 (4)	2.25	2.25

Coast Guard Vessels A67

Designs: 15c, Bank note, reverse, showing Barbados Parliament. 25c, National anthem by Van Roland Edwards (music) and Irvine Burgie (lyrics). $1, Independence Day parade.

1976, Nov. 30   Perf. 13x13½

448 A67	5c multicolored	.15	.15
449 A67	15c multicolored	.15	.15
450 A67	25c yel, brown & blk	.25	.25

BARBADOS

451 A67 $1 multicolored 1.00 1.00
    a. Souvenir sheet of 4, #448-451 2.00 2.00
    Nos. 448-451 (4) 1.55 1.55

10th anniv. of independence.

Queen Knighting Garfield Sobers, 1957 Visit — A68

Designs: 50c, Queen arriving at Westminster Abbey. $1, Queen leaving coach.

1977, Feb. 7   **Perf. 14x13½**
452 A68 15c silver & multi .20 .20
453 A68 50c silver & multi .60 .60
454 A68 $1 silver & multi 1.25 1.25
    Nos. 452-454 (3) 2.05 2.05

25th anniv. of the reign of Queen Elizabeth II. See Nos. 467-469.

Underwater Park — A69

Beauty of Barbados: 35c, Royal palms, vert. 50c, Underwater caves. $1, Stalagmite in Harrison's Cave, vert.

1977, May 3   **Wmk. 373**   **Perf. 14**
455 A69 5c multicolored .15 .15
456 A69 35c multicolored .50 .50
457 A69 50c multicolored .65 .65
458 A69 $1 multicolored 1.40 1.40
    a. Souvenir sheet of 4, #455-458 2.75 2.75
    Nos. 455-458 (4) 2.70 2.70

House of Commons Maces — A70

Charles I Handing Charter to Carlisle — A71

Designs: 25c, Speaker's chair. 50c, Senate Chamber. $1, Sam Lord's Castle, horiz.

1977, Aug. 2   **Litho.**   **Perf. 13½**
459 A70 10c red brown & yel .15 .15
460 A70 25c slate grn & org .30 .30
461 A70 50c dk green, grn & yel .60 .60
462 A70 $1 dk & lt blue & org 1.10 1.10
    Nos. 459-462 (4) 2.15 2.15

13th Regional Conference of Commonwealth Parliamentary Association.

Perf. 13½x13, 13x13½
1977, Oct. 11   **Litho.**   **Wmk. 373**

Designs: 12c, Charter scroll. 45c, Charles I and Earl of Carlisle, horiz. $1, Map of Barbados, by Richard Ligon, 1657, horiz.

463 A71 12c buff & multi .15 .15
464 A71 25c buff & multi .30 .30
465 A71 45c buff & multi .55 .55
466 A71 $1 buff & multi 1.10 1.10
    Nos. 463-466 (4) 2.10 2.10

350th anniv. of charter granting Barbados to the Earl of Carlisle.

Silver Jubilee Type, 1977, Inscribed: "ROYAL VISIT"

1977, Oct. 31   **Unwmk.**   **Roulette 5**
Self-adhesive
467 A68 15c silver & multi .20 .20
468 A68 50c silver & multi .60 .60
469 A68 $1 silver & multi 1.10 1.10
    Nos. 467-469 (3) 1.90 1.90

Caribbean visit of Queen Elizabeth II. Printed on peelable paper backing inscribed in ultramarine multiple rows: "SILVER JUBILEE ROYAL VISIT BARBADOS." Printed with die-cut label inscribed in black "BEND & PEEL" attached at left of stamp. Sheets of 50 stamps and 50 labels.

Gibson's Map of Bridgetown, 1766 — A72

25c, Bridgetown, engraving by S. Copens, 1695. 45c, Trafalgar Square, Bridgetown, drawing by J. M. Carter, 1835. $1, The Bridges, 1978.

Perf. 14½
1978, Mar. 1   **Wmk. 373**
470 A72 12c gold & multi .15 .15
471 A72 25c gold & multi .25 .25
472 A72 45c gold & multi .45 .45
473 A72 $1 gold & multi .85 .85
    Nos. 470-473 (4) 1.70 1.70

350th anniv. of founding of Bridgetown.

Elizabeth II Coronation Anniv. Issue
Souvenir Sheet
Common Design Types

1978, Apr. 21   **Unwmk.**   **Perf. 15**
474   Sheet of 6 3.00 3.00
    a. CD326 50c Griffin of Edward III .50 .50
    b. CD327 50c Elizabeth II .50 .50
    c. CD328 50c Pelican .50 .50

No. 474 contains 2 se-tenant strips of Nos. 474a-474c, separated by horizontal gutter with commemorative and descriptive inscriptions and showing central part of coronation with coach.

Freak Bridge Hand A73

Designs: 10c, World Bridge Fed. emblem. 45c, Central American and Caribbean Bridge Fed. emblem. $1, Map of Caribbean and cards.

Perf. 14½
1978, June 6   **Litho.**   **Wmk. 373**
475 A73 5c multicolored .15 .15
476 A73 10c multicolored .15 .15
477 A73 45c multicolored .50 .50
478 A73 $1 multicolored 1.00 1.00
    a. Souvenir sheet of 4, #475-478 1.50 1.50
    Nos. 475-478 (4) 1.80 1.80

7th Regional Bridge Tournament, Dover Centre, Barbados, June 5-14.

Girl Guides' Camp — A74

Designs: 28c, Girl Guides helping children and handicapped. 50c, Badge with "60", vert. $1, Badge with initials, vert.

1978, Aug. 1   **Litho.**   **Perf. 13½**
479 A74 12c multicolored .15 .15
480 A74 28c multicolored .30 .30
481 A74 50c multicolored .50 .50
482 A74 $1 multicolored 1.00 1.00
    Nos. 479-482 (4) 1.95 1.95

Girl Guides of Barbados, 60th anniv.

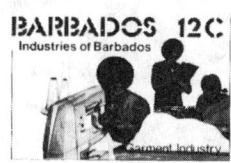

Garment Industry A75

Industries of Barbados: 28c, Cooper, vert. 45c, Blacksmith, vert. 50c, Wrought iron industry.

1978, Nov. 14   **Litho.**   **Perf. 14**
483 A75 12c multicolored .15 .15
484 A75 28c multicolored .30 .30
485 A75 45c multicolored .40 .40
486 A75 50c multicolored .50 .50
    Nos. 483-486 (4) 1.35 1.35

Early Mail Steamer A76

Ships: 25c, Q.E.II in Deep Water Harbour. 50c, Ra II (raft) nearing Barbados. $1, Early mail steamer.

1979, Feb. 8   **Litho.**   **Perf. 13x13½**
487 A76 12c multicolored .15 .15
488 A76 25c multicolored .30 .30
489 A76 50c multicolored .50 .50
490 A76 $1 multicolored 1.00 1.00
    Nos. 487-490 (4) 1.95 1.95

Barbados No. 235 A77

28c, Barbados #430, vert. 45c, Penny Black and Maltese postmark, vert. 50c, Barbados #21b.

Wmk. 373
1979, May 8   **Litho.**   **Perf. 14**
491 A77 12c multicolored .15 .15
492 A77 28c multicolored .20 .20
493 A77 45c multicolored .30 .30
    Nos. 491-493 (3) .65 .65

Souvenir Sheet
494 A77 50c multicolored .40 .40

Sir Rowland Hill (1795-1879), originator of penny postage.

Birds — A78

Launcher Transported through Barbados — A79

1979-81   **Photo.**   **Wmk. 373**   **Perf. 14**
495 A78 1c Grass canaries .15 .15
496 A78 2c Rain birds .15 .15
497 A78 5c Sparrows .15 .15
498 A78 8c Frigate birds .15 .15
499 A78 10c Cattle egrets .15 .15
500 A78 12c Green gaulins .15 .15
501 A78 20c Hummingbirds .25 .15
502 A78 25c Ground doves .25 .25
503 A78 28c Blackbirds .30 .30
504 A78 35c Green-throated
             caribs .40 .40
505 A78 45c Wood doves .55 .55
506 A78 50c Ramiers .65 .65
506A A78 55c Black-breasted
             plover ('81) .80 .80
507 A78 70c Yellow breasts .80 .80
508 A78 $1 Pee whistlers 1.25 1.25
509 A78 $2.50 Christmas birds 3.25 3.25
510 A78 $5 Kingfishers 7.00 2.00
511 A78 $10 Red-seal coot 14.00 14.00
    Nos. 495-511 (18) 30.40 25.30

Issue dates: 55c, Sept. 1; others, Aug. 7.
See #570-572. For surcharges see #563-565.

1979, Oct. 9   **Photo.**
Designs: 10c, Gun on landing craft, Foul Bay, horiz. 20c, Firing of 16-inch launcher by day. 28c, Bath Earth Station and Intelsat IV-A, horiz. 45c, Intelsat over Caribbean, horiz. 50c, Intelsat IV-A over Atlantic, and globe. $1, Lunar landing module, horiz.

512 A79 10c multicolored .15 .15
513 A79 12c multicolored .15 .15
514 A79 20c multicolored .15 .15
515 A79 28c multicolored .20 .20
516 A79 45c multicolored .30 .30
517 A79 $1 multicolored .35 .35
    Nos. 512-517 (6) 1.30 1.30

Souvenir Sheet
518 A79 $1 multicolored .85 .85

Space exploration. No. 518 commemorates 10th anniversary of first moon landing.

Family, IYC Emblem — A80

IYC Emblem and: 28c, Children holding hands and map of Barbados. 45c, Boy and teacher. 50c, Children playing. $1, Boy and girl flying kite.

1979, Nov. 27   **Litho.**   **Perf. 14**
519 A80 12c multicolored .15 .15
520 A80 28c multicolored .20 .20
521 A80 45c multicolored .30 .30
522 A80 50c multicolored .35 .35
523 A80 $1 multicolored .65 .65
    Nos. 519-523 (5) 1.65 1.65

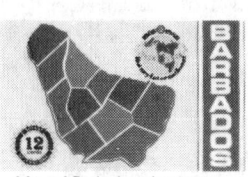

Map of Barbados, Anniversary Emblem — A81

Rotary Intl., 75th Anniv.: 28c, Map of district 404. 50c, 75th anniv. emblem. $1, Paul P. Harris, founder.

1980, Feb. 19   **Litho.**   **Perf. 13½**
524 A81 12c multicolored .15 .15
525 A81 28c multicolored .20 .20
526 A81 50c multicolored .35 .35
527 A81 $1 multicolored .65 .65
    Nos. 524-527 (4) 1.35 1.35

A82   A83

12c, Regiment volunteer, artillery company, 1909. 35c, Drum major. 50c, Sovereign's, regimental flags. $1, e, Women's corps.

Perf. 14½
1980, Apr. 8   **Litho.**   **Wmk. 373**
528 A82 12c multicolored .15 .15
529 A82 35c multicolored .20 .20
530 A82 50c multicolored .35 .35
531 A82 $1 multicolored .65 .65
    Nos. 528-531 (4) 1.35 1.35

Barbados Regiment, 75th anniv.

BARBADOS

Souvenir Sheets
Wmk. 373

1980, May 6   Litho.   *Perf. 14*

Early mailman, London 1980 emblem. The vignette is a different color for each stamp.

532	Sheet of 6	1.10	1.10
a.-f.	A83 28c any single	.15	.15
533	Sheet of 6	2.25	2.25
a.-f.	A83 50c any single	.35	.35

London 80 Intl. Stamp Exhib., May 6-14.

Underwater Scenes — A84

1980, Sept. 30   Litho.   *Perf. 13½*

534	A84 12c multicolored	.15	.15
535	A84 28c multicolored	.25	.25
536	A84 50c multicolored	.40	.40
537	A84 $1 multicolored	.75	.75
a.	Souvenir sheet of 4, #534-537	1.50	1.50
	Nos. 534-537 (4)	1.55	1.55

Bathsheba Railroad Station A85

1981, Jan. 13   Litho.   *Perf. 14½*

538	A85 12c shown	.15	.15
539	A85 28c Cab stand, The Green	.20	.20
540	A85 45c Mule-drawn tram	.30	.30
541	A85 70c Horse-drawn bus	.50	.50
542	A85 $1 Fairchild St. railroad station	.65	.65
	Nos. 538-542 (5)	1.80	1.80

Visually Handicapped Girl at Typewriter — A86

1981, May 19   Litho.   *Perf. 14*

543	A86 10c shown	.15	.15
544	A86 25c Sign language alphabet, vert.	.15	.15
545	A86 45c Blind people crossing street, vert.	.30	.30
546	A86 $2.50 Baseball game	1.65	1.65
	Nos. 543-546 (4)	2.25	2.25

International Year of the Disabled.

Royal Wedding Issue
Common Design Type
Perf. 13½

1981, July 22   Litho.   Wmk. 373

547	CD331 28c Bouquet	.20	.20
548	CD331 50c Charles	.35	.35
549	CD331 $2.50 Couple	1.65	1.65
	Nos. 547-549 (3)	2.20	2.20

4th Caribbean Arts Festival (CARIFESTA), July 19-Aug. 3 — A87

1981, Aug. 11   Litho.   *Perf. 14½*

550	A87 15c Landship maneuver	.15	.15
551	A87 20c Yoruba dancer	.15	.15
552	A87 40c Tuk band	.30	.30
553	A87 55c Frank Collymore (sculpture)	.40	.40
554	A87 $1 Barbados Harbor (painting)	.75	.75
	Nos. 550-554 (5)	1.75	1.75

Hurricane Gladys, View from Apollo A88

1981, Sept. 29   Litho.   *Perf. 14*

555	A88 35c Satellite view over Barbados	.30	.30
556	A88 50c shown	.40	.40
557	A88 60c Police watch	.50	.50
558	A88 $1 Spotter plane	.85	.85
	Nos. 555-558 (4)	2.05	2.05

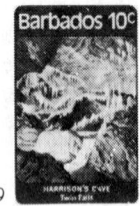

Harrison's Cave — A89

Perf. 14x14½

1981, Dec. 1   Litho.   Wmk. 373

559	A89 10c Twin Falls	.15	.15
560	A89 20c Rotunda Room Stream	.15	.15
561	A89 55c Rotunda Room formation	.35	.35
562	A89 $2.50 Cascade Pool	1.65	1.65
	Nos. 559-562 (4)	2.30	2.30

Nos. 503, 505, 507 Surcharged

1982, Feb. 1   Photo.   *Perf. 14*

563	A78 15c on 28c multi	.15	.15
564	A78 40c on 45c multi	.40	.40
565	A78 60c on 70c multi	.60	.60
	Nos. 563-565 (3)	1.15	1.15

Black Belly Sheep A90

1982, Feb. 9   Litho.

566	A90 40c Ram	.40	.40
567	A90 50c Ewe	.50	.50
568	A90 60c Ewe, lambs	.60	.60
569	A90 $1 Pair, map	1.00	1.00
	Nos. 566-569 (4)	2.50	2.50

Bird Type of 1979
Wmk. 373

1982, Mar. 1   Photo.   *Perf. 14*

570	A78 15c like #503	.15	.15
571	A78 40c like #506	.40	.40
572	A78 60c like #507	.60	.60
	Nos. 570-572 (3)	1.15	1.15

Early Marine Transport A91

1982, Apr. 6   Litho.   *Perf. 14½*

577	A91 20c Lighter	.20	.20
578	A91 35c Rowboat	.35	.35
579	A91 55c Speightstown schooner	.55	.55
580	A91 $2.50 Inter-colonial schooner	2.50	2.50
	Nos. 577-580 (4)	3.60	3.60

Visit of Pres. Ronald Reagan A92

1982, Apr. 8   Litho.   *Perf. 14*

581	A92 20c Barbados Flag, arms	.20	.20
582	A92 20c US Flag, arms	.20	.20
a.	Pair, Nos. 581-582	.40	.40
583	A92 55c like #581	.55	.50
584	A92 55c like #582	.55	.50
a.	Pair, Nos. 583-584	1.10	1.10
	Nos. 581-584 (4)	1.50	1.40

Printed in sheets of 8 with gutter showing Pres. Reagan and Prime Minister Tom Adams.

Princess Diana Issue
Common Design Type

1982, July 1   Litho.   *Perf. 14½*

585	CD333 20c Arms	.15	.15
586	CD333 60c Diana	.45	.45
587	CD333 $1.20 Wedding	.90	.90
588	CD333 $2.50 Portrait	1.75	1.75
	Nos. 585-588 (4)	3.25	3.25

Scouting Year — A93   Washington's 250th Birth Anniv. — A94

1982, Sept. 7   Wmk. 373   *Perf. 14*

589	A93 15c Helping woman	.15	.15
590	A93 40c Sign, emblem, flag, horiz.	.45	.45
591	A93 55c Religious service, horiz.	.55	.55
592	A93 $1 Flags	1.00	1.00
	Nos. 589-592 (4)	2.15	2.15

Souvenir Sheet

593	A93 $1.50 Laws	1.65	1.65

1982, Nov. 2   *Perf. 13½x13*

594	A94 10c Arms	.15	.15
595	A94 55c Washington's house, Barbados	.55	.55
596	A94 60c Taking command	.60	.60
597	A94 $2.50 Taking oath	2.50	2.50
	Nos. 594-597 (4)	3.80	3.80

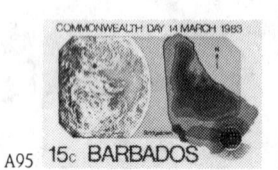

A95   15c BARBADOS

1983, Mar. 14   Litho.   *Perf. 14*

598	A95 15c Map, globe	.15	.15
599	A95 40c Beach	.40	.40
600	A95 60c Sugar cane harvest	.60	.60
601	A95 $1 Cricket game	1.00	1.00
	Nos. 598-601 (4)	2.15	2.15

Commonwealth day.

Gulf Fritillary A96

1983, Feb. 8   Litho.   *Perf. 13½x13*

602	A96 20c shown	.25	.25
603	A96 40c Monarch	.45	.45
604	A96 55c Mimic	.60	.60
605	A96 $2.50 Hanno Blue	3.00	3.00
	Nos. 602-605 (4)	4.30	4.30

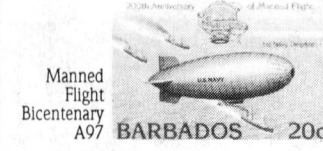

Manned Flight Bicentenary A97

1983, June 14   Litho.   *Perf. 14*

606	A97 20c US Navy dirigible	.30	.30
607	A97 40c Douglas DC-3	.85	.85
608	A97 55c Vickers Viscount	1.25	1.25
609	A97 $1 Lockheed TriStar	2.50	2.50
	Nos. 606-609 (4)	4.90	4.90

Nash 600, 1941 A98

1983, Aug. 9   Litho.   *Perf. 14*

610	A98 25c shown	.25	.25
611	A98 45c Dodge, 1938	.45	.45
612	A98 75c Ford Model AA, 1930	.75	.75
613	A98 $2.50 Dodge Four, 1918	2.50	2.50
	Nos. 610-613 (4)	3.95	3.95

A99   A100

1983, Aug. 30   Litho.   *Perf. 14*

614	A99 20c Players	.20	.20
615	A99 65c Emblem, map	.65	.65
616	A99 $1 Cup	1.00	1.00
	Nos. 614-616 (3)	1.85	1.85

World Cup Table Tennis Championship.

1983, Nov. 1   *Perf. 14*

Christmas: 10c, 25c, Angel with lute, painting details. $2, The Virgin and Child, by Masaccio.

617	A100 10c multicolored	.15	.15
618	A100 25c multicolored	.25	.25

Souvenir Sheet

619	A100 $2 multicolored	2.00	2.00

Barbados Museum, Golden Jubilee A101

Museum Paintings: 45c, by Richard Day. 75c, St. Ann's Garrison in Barbados by W.S. Hedges. $2.50, Needham's Point, Carlisle Bay.

1983, Nov. 1   *Perf. 14*

620	A101 45c multicolored	.45	.45
621	A101 75c multicolored	.75	.75
622	A101 $2.50 multicolored	2.50	2.50
	Nos. 620-622 (3)	3.70	3.70

1984 Olympics, Los Angeles A102

1984, Apr. 3   Litho.   *Perf. 14*

623	A102 50c Track & field	.50	.50
624	A102 65c Shooting	.65	.65
625	A102 75c Sailing	.75	.75
626	A102 $1 Bicycling	1.00	1.00
a.	Souvenir sheet of 4, #623-626	3.00	3.00
	Nos. 623-626 (4)	2.90	2.90

Lloyd's List Issue
Common Design Type

1984, Apr. 25   Litho.   *Perf. 14½*

627	CD335 45c World map	.45	.45
628	CD335 50c Bridgetown Harbor	.50	.50
629	CD335 75c Philosopher	.75	.75
630	CD335 $1 Sea Princess	1.00	1.00
	Nos. 627-630 (4)	2.70	2.70

BARBADOS

1984 UPU Congress A103

1984, June 6   Litho.   Perf. 13½
631 A103 $2 #213, UPU emblem   2.00 2.00

World Chess Fed., 60th Anniv. — A104

1984, Aug. 8   Perf. 14x14½
632 A104 25c Junior match   .30 .30
633 A104 45c Knights   .50 .50
634 A104 65c Queens   .75 .75
635 A104 $2 Rooks   2.25 2.25
  Nos. 632-635 (4)   3.80 3.80

Christmas — A105

1984, Oct. 24   Litho.   Perf. 14
636 A105 50c Poinsettia   .50 .50
637 A105 65c Snow-on-the-mountain   .65 .65
638 A105 75c Christmas candle   .75 .75
639 A105 $1 Christmas hope   1.00 1.00
  Nos. 636-639 (4)   2.90 2.90

Marine Life A106

1985   Litho.   Wmk. 373   Perf. 14
640 A106   1c Bristle worm   .15 .15
641 A106   2c Spotted trunk fish   .15 .15
642 A106   5c Coney fish   .15 .15
643 A106 10c Pink-tipped anemone   .15 .15
645 A106 20c Christmas tree worm   .30 .30
646 A106 25c Hermit crab   .35 .35
648 A106 35c Animal flower   .50 .50
649 A106 40c Vase sponge   .60 .60
650 A106 45c Spotted moray   .65 .65
651 A106 50c Ghost crab   .75 .75
653 A106 65c Flaming tongue snail   .95 .95
654 A106 75c Sergeant major fish   1.10 1.10
656 A106 $1 Caribbean warty anemone   1.50 1.50
657 A106 $2.50 Green turtle   3.75 3.75
658 A106 $5 Rock beauty   7.25 7.25
659 A106 $10 Elkhorn coral   15.00 15.00
  Nos. 640-659 (16)   33.30 33.30

Issue dates: 10c, 20c, 25c, 50c, $2.50 and $5, Feb. 26; 5c, 35c, 40c, 65c and $10, Apr. 9; 1c, 2c, 45c, 75c and $1, May 7.
Exist inscribed "1987," etc.

1986 (?)   Wmk. 384
640a A106   1c   .15 .15
641a A106   2c   .15 .15
642a A106   5c   .15 .15
643a A106 10c   .15 .15
645a A106 20c   .30 .30
646a A106 25c   .35 .35
648a A106 35c   .45 .45
649a A106 40c   .60 .60
650a A106 45c   .65 .65
651a A106 50c   .75 .75
653a A106 65c   .95 .95
654a A106 75c   1.10 1.10
656a A106 $1   1.50 1.50
657a A106 $2.50   3.75 3.75
658a A106 $5   7.25 7.25
659a A106 $10   15.00 15.00
  Nos. 640a-659a (16)   33.25 33.25

Some inscribed "1986." Also exist with "1987," "1988," and with no date.

Queen Mother 85th Birthday
Common Design Type
Perf. 14½x14

1985, June 7   Litho.   Wmk. 384
660 CD336 25c At Buckingham Palace, 1930   .25 .25
661 CD336 65c With Lady Diana, 1981   .65 .65
662 CD336 75c At the docks   .75 .75
663 CD336 $1 Holding Prince Henry   1.00 1.00
  Nos. 660-663 (4)   2.65 2.65

Souvenir Sheet
664 CD336 $2 Opening the Garden Center, Syon House   2.00 2.00

Audubon Birth Bicentenary A107

Illustrations of North American bird species. Nos. 666-668 vert.

Wmk. 373
1985, Aug. 6   Litho.   Perf. 14
665 A107 45c Falco peregrinus   .60 .60
666 A107 65c Dendroica discolor   .90 .90
667 A107 $1 Ardea herodias   1.10 1.10
668 A107 $1 Dendroica petechia   1.40 1.40
  Nos. 665-668 (4)   4.00 4.00

Satellite Orbiting Earth A108

1985, Sept. 10
669 A108 75c multicolored   .75 .75

INTELSAT, Intl. Telecommunications Satellite Consortium, 20th anniv.

Royal Barbados Police, 150th Anniv. — A109

1985, Nov. 19
670 A109 25c Traffic Dept.   .25 .25
671 A109 50c Police Band   .50 .50
672 A109 65c Dog Force   .65 .65
673 A109 $1 Mounted Police   1.00 1.00
  Nos. 670-673 (4)   2.40 2.40

Souvenir Sheet
674 A109 $2 Band on parade, horiz.   2.00 2.00

Queen Elizabeth II 60th Birthday
Common Design Type

Designs: 25c, Age 2. 50c, Senate House opening, University College of the West Indies, Jamaica, 1953. 65c, With Prince Philip, Caribbean Tour, 1985. 75c, Banquet, state visit to Sao Paulo, Brazil, 1968. $2, Visiting Crown Agents, 1983.

Perf. 14x14½
1986, Apr. 21   Litho.   Wmk. 384
675 CD337 25c scar, blk & sil   .20 .20
676 CD337 50c ultra & multi   .45 .45
677 CD337 65c green & multi   .60 .60
678 CD337 75c violet & multi   .70 .70
679 CD337 $2 rose vio & multi   1.90 1.90
  Nos. 675-679 (5)   3.85 3.85

EXPO '86, Vancouver A110

1986, May 2   Perf. 14
680 A110 50c Trans-Canada North Star   .50 .50
681 A110 $2.50 Lady Nelson   2.50 2.50

AMERIPEX '86 A111

1986, May 22   Wmk. 373
682 A111 45c No. 441   .45 .45
683 A111 50c No. 442   .50 .50
684 A111 65c No. 558   .65 .65
685 A111 $1 Nos. 583-584   1.00 1.00
  Nos. 682-685 (4)   2.60 2.60

Souvenir Sheet
686 A111 $2 Statue of Liberty, NY Harbor   2.00 2.00

Statue of Liberty, cent.

Royal Wedding Issue, 1986
Common Design Type

Designs: 45c, Informal portrait. $1, Andrew in navy uniform.

Perf. 14½x14
1986, July 23   Litho.   Wmk. 384
687 CD338 45c multicolored   .45 .45
688 CD338 $1 multicolored   1.00 1.00

Electrification of Barbados, 75th Anniv. — A112

Designs: 10c, Transporting utility poles, 1923. 25c, Heathfield ladder, 1935, vert. 65c, Transport fleet, 1941. $2, Bucket truck, 1986, vert.

Wmk. 384
1986, Sept. 16   Litho.   Perf. 14
689 A112 10c multicolored   .15 .15
690 A112 25c multicolored   .25 .25
691 A112 65c multicolored   .65 .65
692 A112 $2 multicolored   2.00 2.00
  Nos. 689-692 (4)   3.05 3.05

Christmas — A113

Church windows and flowers.

1986, Oct. 28   Wmk. 373
693 A113 25c Alpinia purpurata   .25 .25
694 A113 50c Anthurium andreanum   .50 .50
695 A113 75c Heliconia rostrata   .75 .75
696 A113 $2 Heliconia psittacorum   2.00 2.00
  Nos. 693-696 (4)   3.50 3.50

Natl. Special Olympics, 10th Anniv. A114

1987, Mar. 27   Wmk. 373   Perf. 14
697 A114 15c Shot put   .15 .15
698 A114 45c Wheelchair race   .45 .45
699 A114 65c Girl's long jump   .65 .65
700 A114 $2 Emblem, creed   2.00 2.00
  Nos. 697-700 (4)   3.25 3.25

CAPEX '87 — A115

1987, June 12
701 A115 25c Barn swallow   .35 .35
702 A115 50c Yellow warbler   .75 .75
703 A115 65c Audubon's shearwater   .90 .90
704 A115 75c Black-whiskered vireo   1.10 1.10
705 A115 $1 Scarlet tanager   1.50 1.50
  Nos. 701-705 (5)   4.60 4.60

Natl. Scouting Movement, 75th Anniv. — A116

1987, July 24   Perf. 14x14½
706 A116 10c Scout sign   .15 .15
707 A116 25c Campfire   .25 .25
708 A116 65c Merit badges, etc.   .65 .65
709 A116 $2 Marching band   2.00 2.00
  Nos. 706-709 (4)   3.05 3.05

Bridgetown Synagogue Restoration A117

1987, Oct. 6   Wmk. 384   Perf. 14½
710 A117 50c Exterior   .65 .65
711 A117 65c Interior   .85 .85
712 A117 75c Ten Commandments, vert.   1.00 1.00
713 A117 $1 Marble laver, vert.   1.40 1.40
  Nos. 710-713 (4)   3.90 3.90

Natl. Independence, 21st Anniv. — A118

E.W. Barrow (1920-87), Father of Independence A119

Designs: 25c, Coat of arms and seal of the colony. 45c, Natl. flag and the Union Jack. 65c, Silver dollar and penny. $2, Old and new regimental flags and Queen Elizabeth's colors.

1987, Nov. 24   Litho.   Perf. 14½
714 A118 25c multicolored   .25 .25
715 A118 45c multicolored   .45 .45
716 A118 65c multicolored   .65 .65
717 A118 $2 multicolored   2.00 2.00
  Nos. 714-717 (4)   3.35 3.35

Souvenir Sheet
718 A119 $1.50 multicolored   1.50 1.50

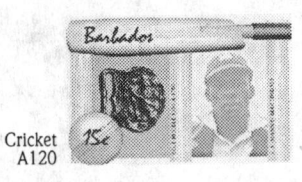

BARBADOS

Cricket — A120

Bat, wicket posts, ball, 18th cent. belt buckle and batters: 15c, E.A. "Manny" Martindale. 45c, George Challenor. 50c, Herman C. Griffith. 75c, Harold Austin. $2, Frank Worrell.

1988		Litho.	Wmk. 373	Perf. 14
719	A120	15c multicolored	.15	.15
720	A120	45c multicolored	.45	.45
720A	A120	50c multicolored	.50	.50
721	A120	75c multicolored	.75	.75
722	A120	$2 multicolored	2.00	2.00
		Nos. 719-722 (5)	3.85	3.85

The 50c was originally printed with the wrong photograph but was not issued. Copies of the error have appeared on the market.

Issued: No. 720A, July 11; others, June 6.

Lizards — A121

1988 Summer Olympics, Seoul — A122

1988, June 13

723	A121	10c Kentropyx borckianus	.15	.15
724	A121	50c Hemidactylus mabouia	.60	.60
725	A121	65c Anolis extremus	.75	.75
726	A121	$2 Gymnophthalmus underwoodii	2.25	2.25
		Nos. 723-726 (4)	3.75	3.75

				Perf. 14½
1988, Aug. 2		**Litho.**	**Wmk. 373**	
727	A122	25c Cycling	.25	.25
728	A122	45c Running	.45	.45
729	A122	75c Swimming	.75	.75
730	A122	$2 Yachting	2.00	2.00
a.		Souvenir sheet of 4, #727-730	3.50	3.50
		Nos. 727-730 (4)	3.45	3.45

Lloyds of London, 300th Anniv.
Common Design Type

Designs: 40c, Royal Exchange, 1774. 50c, Sugar mill (windmill), horiz. 65c, Container ship Author, horiz. $2, Sinking of the Titanic, 1912.

1988, Oct. 18		Litho.		Perf. 14
731	CD341	40c multicolored	.40	.40
732	CD341	50c multicolored	.50	.50
733	CD341	65c multicolored	.65	.65
734	CD341	$2 multicolored	2.00	2.00
		Nos. 731-734 (4)	3.55	3.55

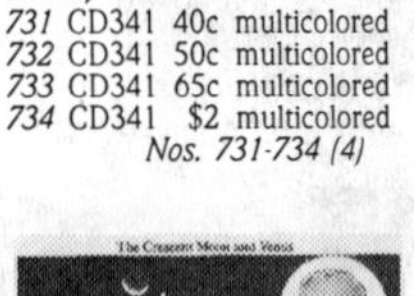

Harry Bayley Observatory, 25th Anniv. — A123

Designs: 25c, Observatory, crescent Moon, Venus and Harry Bayley. 65c, Observatory and constellations. 75c, Andromeda Galaxy and telescope. $2, Orion Constellation.

1988, Nov. 28		Wmk. 384		Perf. 14½
735	A123	25c multicolored	.25	.25
736	A123	65c multicolored	.65	.65
737	A123	75c multicolored	.75	.75
738	A123	$2 multicolored	2.00	2.00
		Nos. 735-738 (4)	3.65	3.65

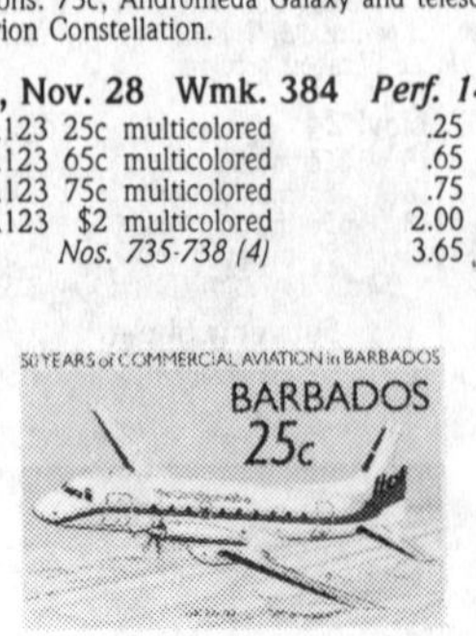

Commercial Aviation, 50th Anniv. — A124

Designs: 25c, Caribbean Airline Liat BAe748. 65c, Pan American DC-8. 75c, Two British Airways Concordes, Grantley Adams Intl. Airport. $2, Two Caribbean Air Cargo Boeing 707-351c.

1989, Mar. 20		Litho.		Perf. 14
739	A124	25c multicolored	.25	.25
740	A124	65c multicolored	.65	.65
741	A124	75c multicolored	.75	.75
742	A124	$2 multicolored	2.00	2.00
		Nos. 739-742 (4)	3.65	3.65

Parliament, 350th Anniv. — A125

1989, July 19		Litho.		Perf. 13½
743	A125	25c Assembly chamber	.25	.25
744	A125	50c The Speaker	.50	.50
745	A125	75c Parliament, c. 1882	.75	.75
746	A125	$2.50 Queen in Parliament	2.50	2.50
		Nos. 743-746 (4)	4.00	4.00

Parliament, 350th anniv. See No. 752.

Wildlife Preservation — A126

1989, Aug. 1				Perf. 14x13½
747	A126	10c Wild hare, vert.	.20	.20
748	A126	50c Red-footed tortoise	.75	.75
749	A126	65c Green monkey, vert.	1.00	1.00
750	A126	$2 Toad	3.00	3.00
		Nos. 747-750 (4)	4.95	4.95

Souvenir Sheet

751	A126	$1 Mongoose, vert.	2.00	2.00

Parliament Anniv. Type of 1989
Souvenir Sheet

1989, Oct. 9		Wmk. 373		Perf. 13½
752	A125	$1 The Mace	1.00	1.00

35th Commonwealth Parliamentary Conf.

Wild Plants — A127

World Stamp Expo '89, Washington, DC — A128

1989-92		Wmk. 373		Perf. 14½
753	A127	2c Bread'n cheese	.15	.15
754	A127	5c Scarlet cordia	.15	.15
755	A127	10c Columnar cactus	.15	.15
756	A127	20c Spiderlily	.20	.20
757	A127	25c Rock balsam	.25	.25
758	A127	30c Hollyhock	.30	.30
758A	A127	35c Red sage	.35	.35
759	A127	45c Yellow shakshak	.45	.45
760	A127	50c Whitewood	.50	.50
761	A127	55c Bluebell	.55	.55
762	A127	65c Prickly sage	.65	.65
763	A127	70c Seaside samphire	.70	.70
764	A127	80c Flat-hand dildo	.80	.80
764A	A127	90c Herringbone	.90	.90
765	A127	$1.10 Lent tree	1.10	1.10
766	A127	$2.50 Rodwood	2.50	2.50
767	A127	$5 Cowitch	5.00	5.00
768	A127	$10 Maypole	10.00	10.00
		Nos. 753-768 (18)	24.70	24.70

Issue dates: 35c, 90c, June 9, 1992 (inscribed 1991). Others, Nov. 1.
Nos. 754-756, 763, 765 exist inscribed "1991."
For overprints see Nos. 788-790.

1990		Litho.		Wmk. 384
753a	A127	2c	.15	.15
754a	A127	5c	.15	.15
755a	A127	10c	.15	.15
756a	A127	20c	.20	.20
757a	A127	25c	.25	.25
759a	A127	45c	.40	.40
760a	A127	50c	.45	.45
762a	A127	65c	.60	.60
766a	A127	$2.50	2.25	2.25
767a	A127	$5	4.50	4.50
768a	A127	$10	9.00	9.00
		Nos. 753a-768a (11)	18.10	18.10

Inscribed 1990.

1989, Nov. 17		Wmk. 384		Perf. 14

Water sports.

769	A128	25c Water skiing	.25	.25
770	A128	50c Yachting	.50	.50
771	A128	65c Scuba diving	.65	.65
772	A128	$2.50 Surfing	2.50	2.50
		Nos. 769-772 (4)	3.90	3.90

Horse Racing — A129

Wmk. 373

1990, May 3		Litho.		Perf. 14
773	A129	25c Bugler, jockeys	.25	.25
774	A129	45c Parade ring	.45	.45
775	A129	75c In the straight	.75	.75
776	A129	$2 Winner, vert.	2.00	2.00
		Nos. 773-776 (4)	3.45	3.45

Barbados No. 2 — A130

Stamps on stamps: No. 778, Barbados #61. 65c, Barbados #73. $2.50, Barbados #121. No. 781a, Great Britain #1. No. 781b, Barbados #108.

1990, May 3

777	A130	25c shown	.25	.25
778	A130	50c multicolored	.50	.50
779	A130	65c multicolored	.65	.65
780	A130	$2.50 multicolored	2.50	2.50
		Nos. 777-780 (4)	3.90	3.90

Souvenir Sheet

| 781 | | Sheet of 2 | 1.00 | 1.00 |
| a.-b. | | A130 50c any single | .50 | .50 |

Stamp World London '90.

Queen Mother, 90th Birthday
Common Design Types

1990, Aug. 8		Wmk. 384		Perf. 14x15
782	CD343	75c At age 23	.75	.75

				Perf. 14½
783	CD344	$2.50 Engagement portrait, 1923	2.50	2.50

Insects — A131

Wmk. 373

1990, Oct. 16		Litho.		Perf. 14
784	A131	50c Dragonfly	.50	.50
785	A131	65c Black hardback beetle	.65	.65
786	A131	75c Green grasshopper	.75	.75
787	A131	$2 God-horse	2.00	2.00
		Nos. 784-787 (4)	3.90	3.90

Nos. 757, 764 and 766 Overprinted

VISIT OF HRH THE PRINCESS ROYAL OCTOBER 1990

1990, Nov. 21				Perf. 14½
788	A127	25c on No. 757	.25	.25
789	A127	80c on No. 764	.80	.80
790	A127	$2.50 on No. 766	2.50	2.50
		Nos. 788-790 (3)	3.55	3.55

Christmas — A132

1990, Dec. 4				Perf. 14
791	A132	20c Christmas star	.20	.20
792	A132	50c Nativity scene	.50	.50
793	A132	$1 Stained glass window	1.00	1.00
794	A132	$2 Angel	2.00	2.00
		Nos. 791-794 (4)	3.70	3.70

Yellow Warbler — A133

1991, Mar. 4				
795	A133	10c shown	.25	.25
796	A133	20c Male, female, nest	.55	.55
797	A133	45c Female, chicks	1.25	1.25
798	A133	$1 Male, fledgling	2.75	2.75
		Nos. 795-798 (4)	4.80	4.80

World Wildlife Fund.

Fishing — A134

				Perf. 13½x14, 14x13½
1991, June 18		**Litho.**		**Wmk. 373**
799	A134	5c Daily catch, vert.	.15	.15
800	A134	50c Line fishing	.50	.50
801	A134	75c Cleaning fish	.75	.75
802	A134	$2.50 Game fishing, vert.	2.50	2.50
		Nos. 799-802 (4)	3.90	3.90

Freemasonry in Barbados, 250th Anniv. — A135

Designs: 25c, Masonic Building, Bridgetown. 65c, Compass and square. 75c, Royal arch jewel. $2.50, Columns, apron and centenary badge.

1991, Sept. 17				Perf. 14
803	A135	25c multicolored	.25	.25
804	A135	65c multicolored	.65	.65
805	A135	75c multicolored	.75	.75
806	A135	$2.50 multicolored	2.50	2.50
		Nos. 803-806 (4)	4.15	4.15

Butterflies — A136

1991, Nov. 15				Wmk. 384
807	A136	20c Polydamus swallowtail	.25	.25
808	A136	50c Long-tailed skipper, vert.	.65	.65
809	A136	65c Cloudless sulphur	.85	.85

BARBADOS

810	A136	$2.50 Caribbean buckeye, vert.	3.25	3.25
		Nos. 807-810 (4)	5.00	5.00

Souvenir Sheet

811	A136	$4 Painted lady	6.00	6.00

Phila Nippon '91.

Independence, 25th Anniv. — A137

Governor-General Dame Nita Barrow and: 10c, Students in classroom. 25c, Barbados Workers Union headquarters. 65c, Building industry. 75c, Agriculture. $1, Inoculations given at health clinic. $2.50, Gordon Greenidge, Desmond Haynes, cricket players (no portrait).

1991, Nov. 20   Wmk. 373

812	A137	10c multicolored	.15	.15
813	A137	25c multicolored	.25	.25
814	A137	65c multicolored	.65	.65
815	A137	75c multicolored	.75	.75
816	A137	$1 multicolored	1.00	1.00
		Nos. 812-816 (5)	2.80	2.80

Souvenir Sheet

817	A137	$2.50 multi, vert.	2.40	2.50

Easter — A138

1992, Apr. 7   Litho.   Wmk. 384   Perf. 14

818	A138	35c Christ carrying cross	.35	.35
819	A138	70c Christ on cross	.70	.70
820	A138	90c Christ taken down from cross	.90	.90
821	A138	$3 Christ risen	3.00	3.00
		Nos. 818-821 (4)	4.95	4.95

Flowering Trees A139

1992, June 9   Litho.   Wmk. 373   Perf. 14x13½

822	A139	10c Cannon ball	.15	.15
823	A139	30c Golden shower	.30	.30
824	A139	80c Frangipani	.80	.80
825	A139	$1.10 Flamboyant	1.10	1.10
		Nos. 822-825 (4)	2.35	2.35

Orchids A140

Designs: 55c, Epidendrum "Costa Rica." 65c, Cattleya guttaca. 70c, Laeliacattleya "Splashing Around." $1.40, Phalaenopsis "Kathy Saegert."

1992, Sept. 8   Perf. 13½x14

826	A140	55c multicolored	.55	.55
827	A140	65c multicolored	.65	.65
828	A140	70c multicolored	.70	.70
829	A140	$1.40 multicolored	1.40	1.40
		Nos. 826-829 (4)	3.30	3.30

For overprints see Nos. 838-841.

Transport and Tourism A141

Designs: 5c, Mini Moke, Gun Hill Signal Station, St. George. 35c, Tour bus, Bathsheba Beach, St. Joseph. 90c, BWIA McDonnell Douglas MD 83, Grantley Adams Airport. $2, Cruise ship Festivale, deep water harbor, Bridgetown.

1992, Dec. 15   Litho.   Wmk. 373   Perf. 14½

830	A141	5c multicolored	.15	.15
831	A141	35c multicolored	.35	.35
832	A141	90c multicolored	.90	.90
833	A141	$2 multicolored	2.00	2.00
		Nos. 830-833 (4)	3.40	3.40

Cacti and Succulents — A142

1993, Feb. 9   Litho.   Wmk. 373   Perf. 14

834	A142	10c Barbados gooseberry	.15	.15
835	A142	35c Night-blooming cereus	.35	.35
836	A142	$1.40 Aloe	1.40	1.40
837	A142	$2 Scruncineel	2.00	2.00
		Nos. 834-837 (4)	3.90	3.90

Nos. 826-829 Ovptd. "WORLD ORCHID CONFERENCE 1993" on 2 or 4 lines

1993, Apr. 1   Litho.   Wmk. 373   Perf. 13½x14

838	A140	55c on #826 multi	.55	.55
839	A140	65c on #827 multi	.65	.65
840	A140	70c on #828 multi	.70	.70
841	A140	$1.40 on #829 multi	1.40	1.40
		Nos. 838-841 (4)	3.30	3.30

Royal Air Force, 75th Anniv.
Common Design Type

Designs: 10c, Hawker Hunter. 30c, Handley Page Victor. 70c, Hawker Typhoon. $3, Hawker Hurricane.

No. 846a, Armstrong Whitworth Siskin 3a. b, Supermarine S.6B. c, Supermarine Walrus. d, Hawker Hart.

1993, Apr. 1   Perf. 14

842	CD350	10c multicolored	.15	.15
843	CD350	30c multicolored	.30	.30
844	CD350	70c multicolored	.70	.70
845	CD350	$3 multicolored	3.00	3.00
		Nos. 842-845 (4)	4.15	4.15

Souvenir Sheet

846	CD350	50c Sheet of 4, #a.-d.	2.00	2.00

Cannon A143

Designs: 5c, 18-pounder Culverin, 1625, Denmark Fort. 45c, 6-pounder Commonwealth gun, 1649-1660, St. Ann's Fort. $1, 9-pounder Demi-culverin, 1691, The Main Guard. $2.50, 32-pounder Demi-cannon, 1693-94, Charles Fort.

1993, June 8   Wmk. 373   Perf. 13

847	A143	5c multicolored	.15	.15
848	A143	45c multicolored	.45	.45
849	A143	$1 multicolored	1.00	1.00
850	A143	$2.50 multicolored	2.50	2.50
		Nos. 847-850 (4)	4.10	4.10

Barbados Museum, 60th Anniv. — A144

Designs: 10c, Shell box, carved figure. 75c, Map, print of three people. 90c, Silver cup, print of soldier. $1.10, Map.

1993, Sept. 14   Wmk. 373   Litho.   Perf. 14

851	A144	10c multicolored	.15	.15
852	A144	75c multicolored	.75	.75
853	A144	90c multicolored	.90	.90
854	A144	$1.10 multicolored	1.10	1.10
		Nos. 851-854 (4)	2.90	2.90

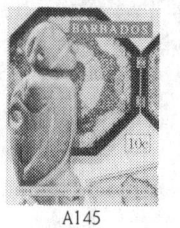

A145    A146

Prehistoric Aquatic Reptiles: a, Plesiosaurus. b, Ichthyosaurus. c, Elasmosaurus. d, Mosasaurus. e, Archelon. Continuous design.

Wmk. 373

1993, Oct. 28   Litho.   Perf. 13

855	A145	90c Strip of 5, #a.-e.	5.00	5.00

Wmk. 384

1994, Jan. 11   Litho.   Perf. 14

856	A146	10c Cricket	.15	.15
857	A146	35c Motor racing	.35	.35
858	A146	50c Golf	.50	.50
859	A146	70c Run Barbados 10k	.70	.70
860	A146	$1.40 Swimming	1.40	1.40
		Nos. 856-860 (5)	3.10	3.10

Sports & tourism.

Migratory Birds A147

1994, Feb. 18   Wmk. 373   Litho.   Perf. 14

861	A147	10c Whimbrel	.15	.15
862	A147	35c American golden plover	.35	.35
863	A147	70c Ruddy turnstone	.70	.70
864	A147	$3 Tricolored heron	3.00	3.00
		Nos. 861-864 (4)	4.20	4.20

Hong Kong '94.

1st UN Conference of Small Island Developing States — A148

1994, Apr. 25   Perf. 14x14½

865	A148	10c Bathsheba	.15	.15
866	A148	65c Pico Tenneriffe	.65	.65
867	A148	90c Ragged Point Lighthouse	.90	.90
868	A148	$2.50 Consett Bay	2.50	2.50
		Nos. 865-868 (4)	4.20	4.20

Order of the Caribbean Community — A149

First award recipients: No. 869, Sir Shridath Ramphal, statesman, Guyana. No. 870, Derek Walcott, writer, Nobel Laureate, St. Lucia. No. 871, William Demas, economist, Trinidad and Tobago.

1994, July 4   Wmk. 373   Litho.   Perf. 14

869	A149	70c multicolored	.70	.70
870	A149	70c multicolored	.70	.70
871	A149	70c multicolored	.70	.70
		Nos. 869-871 (3)	2.10	2.10

Ships A150

Designs: 5c, Dutch Flyut, 1695. 10c, Geestport, 1994. 25c, HMS Victory, 1805. 30c, Royal Viking Queen, 1994. 35c, HMS Barbados, 1945. 45c, Faraday, 1924. 50c, USCG Hamilton, 1974. 65c, HMCS Saguenay, 1939. 70c, Inanda, 1928. 80c, HMS Rodney, 1944. 90c, USS John F. Kennedy, 1982. $1.10, William & John, 1627. $5, USCG Champlain, 1931. $10, Artist, 1877.

1994, Aug. 16   Wmk. 373   Litho.   Perf. 14

872	A150	5c multicolored	.15	.15
873	A150	10c multicolored	.15	.15
874	A150	25c multicolored	.25	.25
875	A150	30c multicolored	.30	.30
876	A150	35c multicolored	.35	.35
877	A150	45c multicolored	.45	.45
878	A150	50c multicolored	.50	.50
879	A150	65c multicolored	.65	.65
880	A150	70c multicolored	.70	.70
881	A150	80c multicolored	.80	.80
882	A150	90c multicolored	.90	.90
883	A150	$1.10 multicolored	1.10	1.10
884	A150	$5 multicolored	5.00	5.00
885	A150	$10 multicolored	10.00	10.00
		Nos. 872-885 (14)	21.30	21.30

1996   Litho.   Wmk. 384

872a	A150	5c	.15	.15
873a	A150	10c	.15	.15
878a	A150	50c	.50	.50
883a	A150	$1.10	1.10	1.10
884a	A150	$5	5.00	5.00
		Nos. 872a-884a (5)	6.90	6.90

Nos. 872-873, 877, 880 exist inscribed "1998."

No. 822 exists inscribed "1996"; Nos. 872-877, 880, 885 "1997."

West India Regiment, Bicent. — A151

Designs: 30c, 2nd Regiment, 1860. 50c, 4th Regiment, Light Company, 1795. 70c, 3rd Regiment, drum major, 1860. $1, 5th Regiment, undress, working dress, 1815. $1.10, 1st, 2nd Regiments, Review Order, 1874.

1995, Feb. 21   Perf. 15x14

886	A151	30c multicolored	.30	.30
887	A151	50c multicolored	.50	.50
888	A151	70c multicolored	.70	.70
889	A151	$1 multicolored	1.00	1.00
890	A151	$1.10 multicolored	1.10	1.10
		Nos. 886-890 (5)	3.60	3.60

End of World War II
Common Design Type

10c, Barbadians serving in the Middle East. 35c, Lancaster bomber. 55c, Spitfire fighter. $2.50, SS Davisian sunk off Barbados, July 10, 1940. $2, Reverse of War Medal 1939-45.

1995, May 8   Wmk. 373   Litho.   Perf. 14

891	CD351	10c multicolored	.15	.15
892	CD351	35c multicolored	.30	.30
893	CD351	55c multicolored	.55	.55
894	CD351	$2.50 multicolored	2.50	2.50
		Nos. 891-894 (4)	3.50	3.50

Souvenir Sheet

895	CD352	$2 multicolored	2.50	2.50

BARBADOS

Combermere School, 300th Anniv. — A152

Designs: 5c, Scouting, Combermere 1st Barbados, 1912. 20c, Violin, sheet music. 35c, Cricket, Sir Frank Worrell, vert. 90c, Frank Collymore, #553. $3, Landscape.

		Wmk. 373		
1995, July 25		Litho.		Perf. 14
896 A152	5c multicolored		.15	.15
897 A152	20c multicolored		.20	.20
898 A152	35c multicolored		.35	.35
899 A152	$3 multicolored		3.00	3.00
	Nos. 896-899 (4)		3.70	3.70
	Souvenir Sheet			
900	Sheet of 5, #896-899, 900a		4.50	4.50
a.	A152 90c multicolored		.90	.90

UN, 50th Anniv.
Common Design Type

Designs: 30c, Douglas C-124 Globemaster, Korea 1950-53. 45c, Royal Navy Sea King helicopter. $1.40, Wessex helicopter, UNFICYP, Cyprus 1964. $2, Gazelle helicopter, UNFICYP, Cyprus 1964.

		Wmk. 373		
1995, Oct. 24		Litho.		Perf. 14
901 CD353	30c multicolored		.30	.30
902 CD353	45c multicolored		.45	.45
903 CD353	$1.40 multicolored		1.40	1.40
904 CD353	$2 multicolored		2.00	2.00
	Nos. 901-904 (4)		4.15	4.15

Water Lilies — A153

		Wmk. 373		
1995, Dec. 19		Litho.		Perf. 14
905 A153	10c Blue beauty		.15	.15
906 A153	65c White water lily		.65	.65
907 A153	70c Sacred lotus		.70	.70
908 A153	$3 Water hyacinth		3.00	3.00
	Nos. 905-908 (4)		4.50	4.50

Barbados Philatelic Society, Cent. A154

Magnifying glass, tongs, and: 10c, #70. 55c, #109. $1.10, #148. $1.40, #192.

		Wmk. 373		
1996, Jan. 30		Litho.		Perf. 14
909 A154	10c multicolored		.15	.15
910 A154	55c multicolored		.55	.55
911 A154	$1.10 multicolored		1.10	1.10
912 A154	$1.40 multicolored		1.40	1.40
	Nos. 909-912 (4)		3.20	3.20

A155

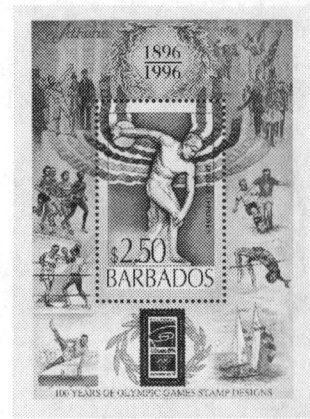

Modern Olympic Games, Cent. — A156

1996, Apr. 2		Litho.		Perf. 14
913 A155	20c Soccer		.20	.20
914 A155	30c Relay race		.30	.30
915 A155	55c Basketball		.55	.55
916 A155	$3 Rhythmic gymnastics		3.00	3.00
	Nos. 913-916 (4)		4.05	4.05
	Souvenir Sheet			
917 A156	$2.50 Discus thrower		2.50	2.50

Olymphilex '96 (No. 917).

CAPEX '96 — A157

Transportation links with Canada: 10c, Canadian Airlines DC10. 90c, Air Canada Boeing 767. $1, Air Canada 320 Airbus. $1.40, Canadian Airlines Boeing 767.

		Wmk. 373		
1996, June 7		Litho.		Perf. 14
918 A157	10c multicolored		.15	.15
919 A157	90c multicolored		.90	.90
920 A157	$1 multicolored		1.00	1.00
921 A157	$1.40 multicolored		1.40	1.40
	Nos. 918-921 (4)		3.45	3.45

Chattel Houses A158

House features: 35c, Shed roof, lattice work. 70c, Pedimented porch, carved wooden trim. $1.10, Decorative, elegant porch. $2, Hip roof, bell pelmet window hoods.

1996, June 7				
922 A158	35c multicolored		.35	.35
923 A158	70c multicolored		.70	.70
924 A158	$1.10 multicolored		1.10	1.10
925 A158	$2 multicolored		2.00	2.00
	Nos. 922-925 (4)		4.15	4.15

Christmas A159

Children's paintings: 10c, Going to Church on Christmas morning. 30c, The Tuk Band. 55c, Caroling on Christmas. $2.50, Decorated houses.

			Perf. 14½	
1996, Nov. 12		Litho.		Wmk. 373
926 A159	10c multicolored		.15	.15
927 A159	30c multicolored		.30	.30
928 A159	55c multicolored		.55	.55
929 A159	$2.50 multicolored		2.50	2.50
	Nos. 926-929 (4)		3.50	3.50

UNICEF, 50th anniv.

Hong Kong '97 — A160

Dogs: 10c, Doberman pinscher. 30c, German shepherd. 90c, Japanese akita. $3, Irish red setter.

			Perf. 14x14½	
1997, Feb. 12		Litho.		Wmk. 373
930 A160	10c multicolored		.15	.15
931 A160	30c multicolored		.30	.30
932 A160	90c multicolored		.90	.90
933 A160	$3 multicolored		3.00	3.00
	Nos. 930-933 (4)		4.35	4.35

Visit of US Pres. Clinton to Barbados, May 1997 A161

35c, Barbados flag, arms. 90c, US flag, arms.

		Wmk. 373		
1997, May 9		Litho.		Perf. 14
934 A161	35c multicolored		.35	.35
935 A161	90c multicolored		.90	.90
a.	Pair, #934-935		1.25	1.25

Issued in sheets of 8 stamps + 2 labels.

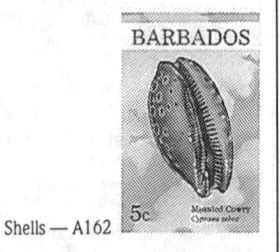

Shells — A162

Designs: 5c, Measled cowry. 35c, Trumpet triton. 90c, Scotch bonnet. $2, West Indian murex. $2.50, Sea bottom with miscellaneous shells.

1997, July 29		Litho.		Perf. 14
936 A162	5c multicolored		.15	.15
937 A162	35c multicolored		.35	.35
938 A162	90c multicolored		.90	.90
939 A162	$2 multicolored		1.90	1.90
	Nos. 936-939 (4)		3.30	3.30
	Souvenir Sheet			
940 A162	$2.50 multicolored		2.40	2.40

Public Library, 150th Anniv. A163

Designs: 10c, Lucas manuscripts. 30c, Storytelling to children. 70c, Bookmobile. $3, Information technology.

		Wmk. 373		
1997, Oct. 1		Litho.		Perf. 14
941 A163	10c multicolored		.15	.15
942 A163	30c multicolored		.30	.30
943 A163	70c multicolored		.70	.70
944 A163	$3 multicolored		3.10	3.10
	Nos. 941-944 (4)		4.25	4.25

Fruit — A164

			Perf. 14½	
1997, Dec. 16		Litho.		Wmk. 373
945 A164	35c Barbados cherry		.35	.35
946 A164	40c Sugar apple		.40	.40
947 A164	$1.15 Soursop		1.10	1.10
948 A164	$1.70 Papaya		1.60	1.60
	Nos. 945-948 (4)		3.45	3.45
	Souvenir Sheet			

Sir Grantley Adams, Birth Cent. — A165

a, Natl. Arms. b, Grantley Adams. c, Natl. flag.

		Wmk. 373		
1998, Apr. 27		Litho.		Perf. 13
949 A165	$1 Sheet of 3, #a.-c.		3.00	3.00

Diana, Princess of Wales (1961-97)
Common Design Type of 1998

Portraits wearing: a, Blue hat. b, Red suit jacket. c, Tiara. d, Black and white.

1998, May		Wmk. 373		Perf. 14½x14
950 CD355	$1.15 Sheet of 4, #a.-d.		6.50	6.50

Organization of American States, 50th Anniv. A166

Designs: 15c, Beach during storm, beach during sunny day. $1, Dancers in native costumes. $2.50, Judge reading at podium, statue of justice.

		Wmk. 373		
1998, June 30		Litho.		Perf. 14
951 A166	15c multicolored		.15	.15
952 A166	$1 multicolored		.95	.95
953 A166	$2.50 multicolored		2.50	2.50
	Nos. 951-953 (3)		3.60	3.60

University of West Indies, 50th Anniv. — A167

			Perf. 14½	
1998, July 20		Litho.		Wmk. 373
954 A167	40c Frank Worrell Hall		.40	.40
955 A167	$1.15 Graduation		1.10	1.10
956 A167	$1.40 Plaque, hummingbird		1.40	1.40
957 A167	$1.75 Quadrangle		1.75	1.75
	Nos. 954-957 (4)		4.65	4.65

Tourism A168

		Wmk. 373		
1998, Dec. 1		Litho.		Perf. 14
958 A168	10c Catamaran, vert.		.15	.15
959 A168	45c Jolly Roger		.45	.45
960 A168	70c Atlantis submarine		.70	.70
961 A168	$2 MV Harbor Master, vert.		2.00	2.00
	Nos. 958-961 (4)		3.30	3.30

SEMI-POSTAL STAMPS

Kingston Relief Fund. 1d.

No. 73 Surcharged in Red

BARBADOS — BARBUDA

Wmk. 2
1907, Jan. 25   Typo.   Perf. 14

B1	A8	1p on 2p sl & org	1.75	2.50
a.		No period after 1d	15.00	17.50
b.		Inverted surcharge	1.75	2.50
c.		Inverted surcharge, no period after 1d	15.00	17.50
d.		Double surcharge	750.00	
e.		Dbl. surch., both invtd.	750.00	

Catalogue values for unused stamps in this section, from this point to the end of the section, are for Never Hinged items.

28c + 4c

No. 406 Surcharged

ST. VINCENT RELIEF FUND

1979, May 29   Photo.   Wmk. 314

B2	A56	28c + 4c on 35c multi	.30	.30

The surtax was for victims of the eruption of Mt. Soufrière.

POSTAGE DUE STAMPS

Catalogue values for unused stamps in this section are for Never Hinged items.

D1

1934-47   Typo.   Wmk. 4   Perf. 14

J1	D1	½p green ('35)	.75	.75
J2	D1	1p black	1.40	1.40
J3	D1	3p dk car rose ('47)	22.50	22.50
		Nos. J1-J3 (3)	24.65	24.65

A 2nd die of the 1p was introduced in 1947.

1950

J4	D1	1c green	.20	.20
J5	D1	2c black	.40	.40
J6	D1	6c carmine rose	1.50	1.75
		Nos. J4-J6 (3)	2.10	2.35

Values are for 1953 chalky paper printing.

Wmk. 4a (error)

J4a	D1	1c green	140.00
J5a	D1	2c black	190.00
J6a	D1	6c carmine rose	110.00
		Nos. J4a-J6a (3)	440.00

1965, Aug. 3   Wmk. 314   Perf. 14

J7	D1	1c green	.30	.30
J8	D1	2c black	.35	.35
J9	D1	6c carmine rose	.65	.65
a.		Wmk. sideways, perf. 14x13½ ('74)	2.25	2.25
		Nos. J7-J9 (3)	1.30	1.30

Issued: No. J9a, 2/4/74.

Wmk. 314 Sideways

1974, Dec. 4   Perf. 13x13½

J8b	D1	2c	1.50	1.50
J9b	D1	6c	1.50	1.50

D2

Designs: Each stamp shows different stylized flower in background.

Perf. 13½x14

1976, May 12   Litho.   Wmk. 373

J10	D2	1c brt pink & mag	.15	.15
J11	D2	2c lt & dk vio blue	.15	.15
J12	D2	5c yellow & brown	.15	.15
J13	D2	10c lilac & purple	.15	.15
J14	D2	25c yel green & dk grn	.25	.25
J15	D2	$1 rose & red	.90	.90
		Nos. J10-J15 (6)	1.75	1.75

1985, July   Perf. 15x14

J10a	D2	1c	.15	.15
J11a	D2	2c	.15	.15
J12a	D2	5c	.15	.15
J13a	D2	10c	.15	.15
J14a	D2	25c	.25	.25
		Nos. J10a-J14a (5)	.85	.85

WAR TAX STAMP

No. 118 Overprinted **WAR TAX**

1917   Wmk. 3   Perf. 14

MR1	A12	1p carmine	.15	.15
a.		Imperf., pair	4,000.	

BARBUDA
bär-'büd-ə

LOCATION — Northernmost of the Leeward Islands, West Indies
GOVT. — Dependency of Antigua
AREA — 63 sq. mi.
POP. — 1,000 (estimated)
See Antigua.

12 Pence = 1 Shilling

Catalogue values for unused stamps in this country are for Never Hinged items, beginning with Scott 12 in the regular postage section, and Scott B1 in the semi-postal section.

Watermark

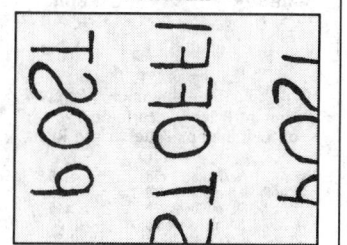

Wmk. 380- "POST OFFICE"

Leeward Islands Stamps and Types of 1912-22 Overprinted in Black or Red

BARBUDA

Die II

For description of dies I and II, see back of this section of the Catalogue.

1922, July 13   Wmk. 4   Perf. 14

1	A5	½p green	1.50	4.50
2	A5	1p rose red	1.50	4.50
3	A5	2p gray	1.60	4.00
4	A5	2½p ultramarine	1.60	4.50
5	A5	6p vio & red vio	4.00	10.00
6	A5	2sh vio & ultra, bl	15.00	30.00
7	A5	3sh green & violet	32.50	50.00
8	A5	4sh blk & scar (R)	35.00	50.00

Wmk. 3

9	A5	3p violet, yel	1.50	4.75
10	A5	1sh blk, emer (R)	3.25	4.75
11	A5	5sh grn & red, yel	95.00	125.00
		Nos. 1-11 (11)	192.45	292.00

Catalogue values for unused stamps in this section, from this point to the end of the section, are for Never Hinged items.

Map — B1

Fish — B2

1968-70   Litho.   Unwmk.   Perf. 14

12	B1	½c blk, salmon pink & red brn	.15	.15
13	B1	1c blk, org & brt org	.15	.15
14	B1	2c blk, brt pink & brt rose	.15	.15
15	B1	3c blk, yel & org yel	.15	.15
16	B1	4c blk, lt grn & brt grn	.15	.15
17	B1	5c blk, bl grn & brt bl grn	.15	.15
18	B1	6c blk, lt lil & red lil	.15	.15
19	B1	10c blk, lt bl & dk bl	.15	.15
20	B1	15c blk, dl grn & grn	.20	.20
21	B2	20c Great barracuda	.75	1.25
22	B2	25c Great amberjack	.30	.25
23	B2	35c French angelfish	.40	.40
24	B2	50c Porkfish	.55	.55
25	B2	75c Striped parrotfish	.80	.80
26	B2	$1 Longspine squirrelfish	1.10	1.10
27	B2	$2.50 Catalufa	2.75	2.75
28	B2	$5 Blue chromis	5.00	6.00
		Nos. 12-28 (17)	13.05	14.50

Issued: ½c-15c, 11/19/68; 20c, 7/22/70; 25c-75c, 2/5/69; others, 3/6/69.
For surcharge see No. 80.

1968 Summer Olympics, Mexico City — B3

Designs: 25c, Running, Aztec calendar stone. 35c, High jumping, Aztec statue. 75c, Yachting, Aztec lion mask. $1, Soccer, Aztec carved stone.

1968, Dec. 20

29	B3	25c multicolored	.25	.25
30	B3	35c multicolored	.35	.35
31	B3	75c multicolored	.75	.75
		Nos. 29-31 (3)	1.35	1.35

Souvenir Sheet

32	B3	$1 multicolored	2.75	2.75

The Ascension, by Orcagna — B4

1969, Mar. 24

33	B4	25c blue & black	.15	.15
34	B4	35c dp carmine & blk	.15	.20
35	B4	75c violet & black	.30	.30
		Nos. 33-35 (3)	.60	.70

Easter.

3rd Caribbean Boy Scout Jamboree — B5

1969, Aug. 7

36	B5	25c Flag ceremony	.45	.45
37	B5	35c Campfire	.65	.65
38	B5	75c Rowing	1.40	1.40
		Nos. 36-38 (3)	2.50	2.50

The Sistine Madonna, by Raphael — B6

1969, Oct. 20

39	B6	½c multicolored	.15	.15
40	B6	25c multicolored	.15	.15
41	B6	35c multicolored	.25	.25
42	B6	75c multicolored	.55	.55
		Nos. 39-42 (4)	1.10	1.10

Christmas.

English Monarchs — B7

1970-71   Perf. 14½x14

43	B7	35c William I	.15	.15
44	B7	35c William II	.15	.15
45	B7	35c Henry I	.15	.15
46	B7	35c Stephen	.15	.15
47	B7	35c Henry II	.15	.15
48	B7	35c Richard I	.15	.15
49	B7	35c John	.15	.15
50	B7	35c Henry III	.15	.15
51	B7	35c Edward I	.15	.15
52	B7	35c Edward II	.15	.15
53	B7	35c Edward III	.15	.15
54	B7	35c Richard II	.15	.15
55	B7	35c Henry IV	.15	.15
56	B7	35c Henry V	.15	.15
57	B7	35c Henry VI	.15	.15
58	B7	35c Edward IV	.15	.15
59	B7	35c Edward V	.15	.15
60	B7	35c Richard III	.15	.15
61	B7	35c Henry VII	.15	.15
62	B7	35c Henry VIII	.15	.15
63	B7	35c Edward VI	.15	.15
64	B7	35c Lady Jane Grey	.15	.15
65	B7	35c Mary I	.15	.15
66	B7	35c Elizabeth I	.15	.15
67	B7	35c James I	.15	.15
68	B7	35c Charles I	.15	.15
69	B7	35c Charles II	.15	.15
70	B7	35c James II	.15	.15
71	B7	35c William III	.15	.15
72	B7	35c Mary II	.15	.15
73	B7	35c Anne	.15	.15
74	B7	35c George I	.15	.15
75	B7	35c George II	.15	.15
76	B7	35c George III	.15	.15
77	B7	35c George IV	.15	.15
78	B7	35c William IV	.15	.15
79	B7	35c Victoria	.15	.15
		Nos. 43-79 (37)	5.55	5.55

Issued: 1970, #43, 2/16; #44, 3/2; #45, 3/16; #46, 4/4; #47, 4/15; #48, 5/1; #49, 5/15; #50, 6/1; #51, 6/15; #52, 7/1; #53, 7/15; #54, 8/1; #55, 8/15; #56, 9/1; #57, 9/15; #58, 10/1; #59, 10/15; #60, 11/2; #61, 11/16; #62, 12/1; #63, 12/15.
1971: #64, 1/2; #65, 1/15; #66, 2/1; #67, 2/15; #68, 3/1; #69, 3/15; #70, 4/1; #71, 4/15; #72, 5/1; #73, 5/15; #74, 6/1; #75, 6/15; #76, 7/1; #77, 7/15; #78, 8/2; #79, 8/16.
See Nos. 622-627 for other Monarchs.

20c

No. 12 Surcharged

1970, Feb. 26   Perf. 14

80	B1	20c on ½c multicolored	.15	.15

Ordering on-line is QUICK! EASY! CONVENIENT!
www.scottonline.com

BARBUDA

Easter — B8

1970, Mar. 16
81	B8	25c Carrying Cross		.15	.15
82	B8	35c Descent from cross		.15	.20
83	B8	75c Crucifixion		.35	.35
a.		Strip of 3, #81-83		.70	.70

Charles Dickens B9

1970, July 10
84	B9	20c Oliver Twist	.15	.15
85	B9	75c Old Curiosity Shop	.40	.50

Christmas B10

Designs: 20c, Madonna of the Meadow, by Giovanni Bellini. 50c, Madonna, Child and Angels from Wilton Diptych. 75c, Nativity, by Piero della Francesca.

1970, Oct. 15
86	B10	20c multicolored	.15	.15
87	B10	50c multicolored	.20	.25
88	B10	75c multicolored	.35	.40
		Nos. 86-88 (3)	.70	.80

British Red Cross, Cent. B11

1970, Dec. 21
89	B11	20c Patient in wheelchair, vert.	.20	.25
90	B11	35c shown	.35	.40
91	B11	75c Child care	.60	.80
		Nos. 89-91 (3)	1.15	1.45

Easter — B12

Details from the Mond Crucifixion, by Raphael.

1971, Apr. 7
92	B12	35c Angel	.20	.30
93	B12	50c Crucifixion	.30	.35
94	B12	75c Angel, diff.	.45	.75
a.		Strip of 3, #92-94	1.00	1.00

Martello Tower B13

1971, May 10
95	B13	20c shown	.15	.15
96	B13	25c Sailboats	.15	.15
97	B13	50c Hotel bungalows	.30	.30
98	B13	75c Government House, mystery stone	.45	.45
		Nos. 95-98 (4)	1.05	1.05

Christmas — B14

Paintings: ½c, The Granduca Madonna, by Raphael. 35c, The Ansidei Madonna, by Raphael. 50c, The Virgin and Child, by Botticelli. 75c, The Madonna of the Trees, by Bellini.

1971, Oct. 4
99	B14	½c multicolored	.15	.15
100	B14	35c multicolored	.25	.25
101	B14	50c multicolored	.38	.38
102	B14	75c multicolored	.60	.60
		Nos. 99-102 (4)	1.38	1.38

A set of four stamps for Durer (20c, 35c, 50c, 75c) was not authorized.

All stamps are types of Antigua or overprinted on stamps of Antigua unless otherwise specified. Many of the "BARBUDA" overprints are vertical.

Nos. 321-322 Ovptd. "BARBUDA"
1973, Nov. 14   Perf. 13½
103	A65	35c multicolored	1.50	1.50
104	A65	$2 multicolored	8.00	8.00

Nos. 313-315a Ovptd. in Red "BARBUDA"
1973, Nov. 26   Perf. 13½x14
105	A63	20c multicolored	.24	.24
106	A63	35c multicolored	.40	.40
107	A63	75c multicolored	.85	.85
		Nos. 105-107 (3)	1.49	1.49

Souvenir Sheet
108		Sheet of 4, #105-107, 108a	4.00	4.00
a.		A63 5c multicolored		

Carnival, 1973.

Nos. 307, 309, 311, 311a Ovptd. "BARBUDA"
Perf. 14x13½
1973, Nov. 26   Wmk. 314
109	A53	½c multicolored	.15	.15
110	A53	20c multicolored	.20	.20
111	A53	75c multicolored	.80	.80
		Nos. 109-111 (3)	1.15	1.15

Souvenir Sheet
112		Sheet of 5, #109-111, 112a-112b + label	3.50	3.50
a.		A53 10c multicolored		
b.		A53 35c multicolored		

Nos. 241a, 242-243, 244a, 245-248, 249a, 250-254, 255a, 256, 256a, 257 Ovptd. "BARBUDA"
1973-74   Wmk. 314 Sideways, Upright   Perf. 14
113	A51	½c multicolored	.15	.15
114	A51	1c multicolored	.15	.15
115	A51	2c multicolored	.15	.15
116	A51	3c multicolored	.15	.15
117	A51	4c multicolored	.15	.15
118	A51	5c multicolored	.15	.15
119	A51	6c multicolored	.15	.15
120	A51	10c multicolored	.18	.18
121	A51	15c multicolored	.28	.28
122	A51	20c multicolored	.38	.38
123	A51	25c multicolored	.45	.45
124	A51	35c multicolored	.65	.65
125	A51	50c multicolored	.95	.95
126	A51	75c multicolored	1.40	1.40
127	A51	$1 multicolored	1.90	1.90
128	A51	$2.50 multicolored	4.75	4.75
a.		Wmk. upright	9.25	9.25
129	A51	$5 multicolored	9.25	9.25
		Nos. 113-129 (17)	21.24	21.24

Issue dates: ½c, 3c, 15c, $1, $2.50, Feb. 18, 1974. Others, Nov. 26.

Nos. 316-320a Ovptd. in Silver or Red "BARBUDA"
Perf. 14½
1973, Dec. 11   Photo.   Unwmk.
130	A64	3c multicolored	.15	.15
131	A64	5c multicolored	.15	.15
132	A64	20c multicolored	.30	.30
133	A64	35c multicolored (R)	.55	.55
134	A64	$1 multicolored (R)	1.50	1.50
		Nos. 130-134 (5)	2.65	2.65

Souvenir Sheet
135		Sheet of 5 + label	9.00	9.00
a.		A64 35c multicolored (S)		
b.		A64 $1 multicolored (S)		

No. 135 contains Nos. 130-132, 135a-135b.

Nos. 323-324a Ovptd. "BARBUDA"
1973, Dec. 16   Litho.   Perf. 13½
136	A65	35c multicolored	.32	.32
137	A65	$2 multicolored	1.75	1.75
a.		Souvenir sheet of 2, #136-137	2.50	2.50

Nos. 325-328 Ovptd. "BARBUDA"
1974, Feb. 18   Wmk. 314
138	A66	5c multicolored	.15	.15
139	A66	20c multicolored	.18	.18
140	A66	35c multicolored	.32	.32
141	A66	75c multicolored	.70	.70
		Nos. 138-141 (4)	1.35	1.35

Nos. 329-333 Ovptd. "BARBUDA"
1974, May 1   Perf. 14x13½
142	A53	½c multicolored	.15	.15
143	A53	10c multicolored	.15	.15
144	A53	20c multicolored	.30	.30
145	A53	52c multicolored	.52	.52
146	A53	75c multicolored	1.10	1.10
		Nos. 142-146 (5)	2.22	2.22

No. 333a exists with overprint.

Nos. 334-340 Ovptd. Type "a" or "b" and No. 340 "BARBUDA" in Red

BARBUDA	BARBUDA
15 SEPT.	13 JULY 1922
1874 G.P.U.	
a	b

1974, July 15   Unwmk.   Perf. 14½
Se-tenant Pairs Overprinted Type "a" on Left Stamp, Type "b" on Right Stamp
148	A67	½c multicolored	.15	.15
149	A67	1c multicolored	.15	.15
150	A67	2c multicolored	.15	.15
151	A67	5c multicolored	.40	.40
152	A67	20c multicolored	1.50	1.50
153	A67	35c multicolored	2.75	2.75
154	A67	$1 multicolored	7.50	7.50
		Nos. 148-154 (7)	12.60	12.60

Souvenir Sheet   Perf. 13
155		Sheet of 7 + label	10.00	10.00
a.		A67 ½c multicolored	.15	.15
b.		A67 1c multicolored	.15	.15
c.		A67 2c multicolored	.15	.15
d.		A67 5c multicolored	.30	.30
e.		A67 20c multicolored	1.25	1.25
f.		A67 35c multicolored	2.00	2.00
g.		A67 $1 multicolored	6.00	6.00

UPU, cent.

Nos. 341-344a Ovptd. "BARBUDA"
1974, Aug. 14   Wmk. 314   Perf. 14
156	A68	5c multicolored	.15	.15
157	A68	20c multicolored	.18	.18
158	A68	35c multicolored	.32	.32
159	A68	75c multicolored	.65	.65
a.		Souvenir sheet of 4, #156-159	1.25	1.25
		Nos. 156-159 (4)	1.30	1.30

Nos. 345-348a Ovptd. "BARBUDA" and

World Cup Soccer Championships — B16

Various soccer plays.

1974, Sept. 2   Unwmk.   Perf. 15, 14
160	A69	5c multicolored	.15	.15
161	A69	20c multicolored	.30	.30
162	B16	35c multicolored	.16	.16
163	A69	75c multicolored	.65	.65
164	A69	$1 multicolored	.85	.85
a.		Souv. sheet of 4, #160-161, 163-164 + 2 labels, perf. 13½	2.25	2.25
165	B16	$1.20 multicolored	.55	.55
166	B16	$2.50 multicolored	1.25	1.25
a.		Souv. sheet of 3, #162, 165-166	3.00	3.00
		Nos. 160-166 (7)	3.91	3.91

UPU, Cent. — B17

1974, Sept. 30   Perf. 14x13½
167	B17	35c Ship letter, 1833	.15	.15
168	B17	$1.20 #1, 2 on FDC	.48	.48
169	B17	$2.50 Airplane, map	1.00	1.00
a.		Souvenir sheet of 3, #167-169	4.00	4.00
		Nos. 167-169 (3)	1.63	1.63

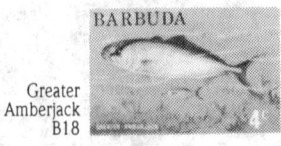

Greater Amberjack B18

1974-75   Perf. 14x14½, 14½x14
170	B18	½c Oleander, rose bay	.15	.15
171	B18	1c Blue petrea	.15	.15
172	B18	2c Poinsettia	.15	.15
173	B18	3c Cassia tree	.15	.15
174	B18	4c shown	.15	.15
175	B18	5c Holy Trinity School	.15	.15
176	B18	6c Snorkeling	.15	.15
177	B18	10c Pilgrim Holiness Church	.15	.15
178	B18	15c New Cottage Hospital	.15	.15
179	B18	20c Post Office & Treasury	.16	.16
180	B18	25c Island jetty & boats	.20	.20
181	B18	35c Martello Tower	.28	.28

Size: 39x25mm   Perf. 14
182	B18	50c Warden's House	.40	.40
183	B18	75c Inter-island air service	.60	.60
184	B18	$1 Tortoise	.80	.80

Size: 45x29mm   Perf. 13½x14
185	B18	$2.50 Spiny lobster	2.00	2.00
186	B18	$5 Frigate birds	4.00	4.00
a.		Perf. 14x15		

Size: 34x47mm
187	B18	$10 Hibiscus	8.00	8.00
		Nos. 170-187 (18)	17.79	17.79

Nos. 170-173, 180, 187 vert.

Issued: 4c, 5c, 6c, 10c, 15c, 20c, 25c, 35c, 75c, 10/15/74; ½c, 1c, 2c, 3c, 50c, $1, $2.50, #186a, 1/6/75; #186a, 7/24/75; $10, 9/19/75.
For overprints see Nos. 213-214.

Nos. 349-352a Ovptd. "BARBUDA" in Red and

Winston Churchill, Birth Cent. — B19

1974   Perf. 14½, 13½x14
188	A70	5c multicolored	.15	.15
189	B19	5c Making broadcast	.15	.15
190	A70	35c multicolored	.70	.70
191	B19	35c Portrait	.28	.28
192	A70	75c multicolored	1.50	1.50
193	B19	75c Painting	.60	.60
194	A70	$1 multicolored	2.00	2.00
a.		Souv. sheet of 4, #188, 190, 192, 194	8.50	8.50
195	B19	$1 Victory sign	.80	.80
a.		Souv. sheet of 4, #189, 191, 193, 195	3.50	3.50
		Nos. 188-195 (8)	6.18	6.18

Issue dates: Nos. 188, 190, 192, 194, Oct. 15, others, Nov. 20. For overprints see Nos. 213-214.

Nos. 353-360a Ovptd. "BARBUDA"
1974, Nov. 25   Perf. 14½
196	A71	½c multicolored	.15	.15
197	A71	1c multicolored	.15	.15
198	A71	2c multicolored	.15	.15
199	A71	3c multicolored	.15	.15
200	A71	5c multicolored	.15	.15
201	A71	20c multicolored	.20	.20
202	A71	35c multicolored	.38	.38

203 A71 75c multicolored .80 .80
a. Souv. sheet of 4, #200-203, perf. 13½ 1.40 1.40
Nos. 196-203 (8) 2.13 2.13

Nos. 369-373a Ovptd. "BARBUDA"

1975, Mar. 17
204 A72 5c multicolored .15 .15
205 A72 15c multicolored .28 .28
206 A72 35c multicolored .65 .65
207 A72 50c multicolored .90 .90
208 A72 $1 multicolored 1.75 1.75
a. Souv. sheet of 5, #204-208 + label, perf. 13½x14 4.50 4.50
Nos. 204-208 (5) 3.73 3.73

Stamps from No. 208a are 43x28mm.

Battle of the Saints B20

1975, May 30 *Perf. 13½x14*
209 B20 35c shown 1.00 1.00
210 B20 50c Two ships 1.40 1.40
211 B20 75c Ships firing 2.00 2.00
212 B20 95c Sailors abandoning ship 2.50 2.50
Nos. 209-212 (4) 6.90 6.90

Barbuda No. 186a Ovptd.

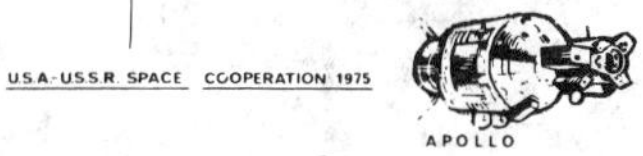

a

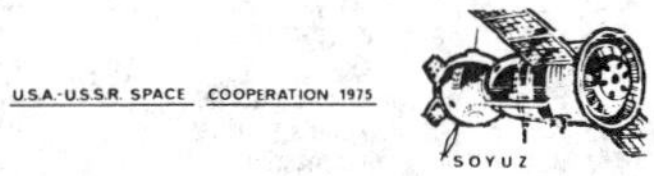

b

1975, July 2 *Perf. 14x15*
213 B18 (a) $5 multicolored
214 B18 (b) $5 multicolored

Overprint "a" is in 1st and 3rd vertical rows, "b" 2nd and 4th. The 5th row has no overprint. This can be collected se-tenant either as Nos. 213, 214 or 213, 214 and 186a.

Military Uniforms — B21

Designs: 35c, Officer of 65th Foot, 1763. 50c, Grenadier, 27th Foot, 1701-1710. 75c, Officer of 21st Foot, 1793-1796. 95c, Officer, Royal Regiment of Artillery, 1800.

1975, Sept. 17 *Perf. 14*
215 B21 35c multicolored .70 .70
216 B21 50c multicolored 1.00 1.00
217 B21 75c multicolored 1.50 1.50
218 B21 95c multicolored 1.90 1.90
Nos. 215-218 (4) 5.10 5.10

Barbuda Nos. 189, 191, 193, 195 Ovptd. "30th ANNIVERSARY / UNITED NATIONS / 1945 - 1975"

1975, Oct. 24 *Perf. 13½x14*
219 B19 5c multicolored .15 .15
220 B19 35c multicolored .15 .15
221 B19 75c multicolored .25 .25
222 B19 $1 multicolored .60 .60
Nos. 219-222 (4) 1.15 1.15

Nos. 394-401a Ovptd. "BARBUDA"

1975, Nov. 17 *Perf. 14*
223 A77 ½c multicolored .15 .15
224 A77 1c multicolored .15 .15
225 A77 2c multicolored .15 .15
226 A77 3c multicolored .15 .15
227 A77 5c multicolored .15 .15
228 A77 10c multicolored .15 .15
229 A77 35c multicolored .20 .20
230 A77 $2 multicolored 1.25 1.25
a. Souvenir sheet of 4, #227-230 2.50 2.50
Nos. 223-230 (8) 2.35 2.35

Nos. 402-404 Ovptd. "BARBUDA"

1975, Dec. 15 *Perf. 14*
231 A78 5c multicolored .15 .15
232 A78 35c multicolored .85 .85
233 A78 $2 multicolored 5.00 5.00
Nos. 231-233 (3) 6.00 6.00

American Revolution, Bicent. — B22

Details from Surrender of Cornwallis at Yorktown, by Trumbull: No. 234a, British officers. b, Gen. Benjamin Lincoln. c, Washington, Allied officers.

The Battle of Princeton: No. 235a, Infantry. b, Battle. c, Cannon fire.

Surrender of Burgoyne at Saratoga by Trumbull: No. 236a, Mounted officer. b, Washington, Burgoyne. c, American officers.

Signing the Declaration of Independence, by Trumbull: No. 237a, Delegates to Continental Congress. b, Adams, Sherman, Livingston, Jefferson and Franklin. c, Hancock, Thomson, Read, Dickinson, and Rutledge. Strips of 3 have continuous designs.

1976, Mar. 8 *Perf. 13½x13*
234 B22 15c Strip of 3, #a.-c. .32 .32
235 B22 35c Strip of 3, #a.-c. .75 .75
d. Souvenir sheet, #234-235 1.65 1.65
236 B22 $1 Strip of 3, #a.-c. 2.25 2.25
237 B22 $2 Strip of 3, #a.-c. 4.25 4.25
d. Souvenir sheet, #236-237 10.00 10.00

See Nos. 244-247.

Birds B23

1976, June 30 *Perf. 13½x14*
238 B23 35c Bananaquits 1.40 1.40
239 B23 50c Blue-hooded euphonia 2.00 2.00
240 B23 75c Royal tern 3.00 3.00
241 B23 95c Killdeer 3.75 3.75
242 B23 $1.25 Glossy cowbird 5.00 5.00
243 B23 $2 Purple gallinule 8.25 8.25
Nos. 238-243 (6) 23.40 23.40

Barbuda #234-237 With Inscription Added at Top Across the Three Stamps in Blue
"H.M. Queen Elizabeth" "Royal Visit 6th July 1976" "H.R.H. Duke of Edinburgh"

1976, Aug. 12 *Perf. 13½x14*
Size: 38x31mm
244 B22 15c Strip of 3, #a.-c. .30 .30
245 B22 35c Strip of 3, #a.-c. .70 .70
d. Souvenir sheet of 2, #244-245 1.10 1.10
246 B22 $1 Strip of 3, #a.-c. 2.00 2.00
247 B22 $2 Strip of 3, #a.-c. 4.00 4.00
d. Souvenir sheet, #246-247 7.00 7.00

Nos. 244-247 are perforated on outside edges; imperf. vertically within.

Nos. 448-452 Ovptd. "BARBUDA"

1976, Dec. 2 *Perf. 14*
248 A85 8c multicolored .15 .15
249 A85 10c multicolored .15 .15
250 A85 15c multicolored .15 .15
251 A85 50c multicolored .32 .32
252 A85 $1 multicolored .65 .65
Nos. 248-252 (5) 1.42 1.42

Nos. 431-437 Ovptd. "BARBUDA"

1976, Dec. 28 *Perf. 15*
253 A82 ½c yellow & multi .15 .15
254 A82 1c purple & multi .15 .15
255 A82 2c emerald & multi .15 .15
256 A82 15c brt blue & multi .15 .15
257 A82 30c olive & multi .20 .20
258 A82 $1 orange & multi .65 .65
259 A82 $2 red & multi 1.25 1.25
a. Souv. sheet of 4, #256-259, perf. 13½ 3.50 3.50
Nos. 253-259 (7) 2.70 2.70

Telephone, Cent. — B24

1977, Jan. 31 *Perf. 14*
260 B24 75c shown .30 .30
261 B24 $1.25 Satellite dish, television .45 .45
262 B24 $2 Satellites in earth orbit .75 .75
a. Souv. sheet of 3, #260-262, perf. 15 3.50 3.50
Nos. 260-262 (3) 1.50 1.50

Coronation of Queen Elizabeth II, 25th Anniv. — B25

Designs: Nos. 263a, St. Margaret's Church, Westminster. b, Westminster Abbey entrance. c, Westminster Abbey.

Nos. 264a, Riders on horseback. b, Coronation coach. c, Team of horses. Strips of 3 have continuous designs.

1977, Feb. 7 *Perf. 13½x13*
263 B25 75c Strip of 3, #a.-c. .85 .85
264 B25 $1.25 Strip of 3, #a.-c. 1.35 1.35

Souvenir Sheet
265 B25 Sheet of 6 2.25 2.25

Nos. 263a-264c se-tenant with labels. No. 265 contains Nos. 263a-264c with silver borders.

Nos. 405-422 Ovptd. "BARBUDA"

1977, Apr. 4 *Perf. 15*
266 A79 ½c multicolored .15 .15
267 A79 1c multicolored .15 .15
268 A79 2c multicolored .15 .15
269 A79 3c multicolored .15 .15
270 A79 4c multicolored .15 .15
271 A79 5c multicolored .15 .15
272 A79 6c multicolored .15 .15
273 A79 10c multicolored .15 .15
274 A79 15c multicolored .15 .15
275 A79 20c multicolored .15 .15
276 A79 25c multicolored .18 .18
277 A79 35c multicolored .28 .28
278 A79 50c multicolored .38 .38
279 A79 75c multicolored .52 .52
280 A79 $1 multicolored .70 .70

Perf. 13½x14
281 A80 $2.50 multicolored 1.75 1.75
282 A80 $5 multicolored 3.50 3.50
283 A80 $10 multicolored 7.25 7.25
Nos. 266-283 (18) 16.06 16.06

For overprints see Nos. 506-516.

Nos. 459-464 Ovptd. "BARBUDA"

1977, Apr. 4 *Perf. 13½x14, 12*
284 A87 10c multicolored .15 .15
285 A87 30c multicolored .28 .28
286 A87 50c multicolored .45 .45
287 A87 90c multicolored .85 .85
288 A87 $2.50 multicolored 2.25 2.25
Nos. 284-288 (5) 3.98 3.98

Souvenir Sheet
289 A87 $5 multicolored 4.50 4.50

A booklet of self-adhesive stamps contains one pane of six rouletted and die cut 50c stamps in design of 90c (silver overprint), and one pane of one die cut $5 (gold overprint) in changed colors. Panes have marginal inscriptions.

For overprints see Nos. 312-317.

Nos. 465-471a Ovptd. "BARBUDA"

1977, June 13 *Perf. 14*
290 A88 ½c multicolored .15 .15
291 A88 1c multicolored .15 .15
292 A88 2c multicolored .15 .15
293 A88 10c multicolored .15 .15
294 A88 30c multicolroed .45 .45
295 A88 50c multicolored .75 .75
296 A88 $2 multicolored 3.00 3.00
a. Souvenir sheet of 3, #294-296 5.00 5.00
Nos. 290-296 (7) 4.80 4.80

Overprint is slightly smaller on No. 296a.

Nos. 472-476a Ovptd. "BARBUDA"

1977, Aug. 12
297 A89 10c multicolored .15 .15
298 A89 30c multicolored .22 .22
299 A89 50c multicolored .38 .38
300 A89 90c multicolored .65 .65
301 A89 $1 multicolored .75 .75
a. Souvenir sheet of 4, #298-301 2.50 2.50
Nos. 297-301 (5) 2.15 2.15

Royal Visit B26

1977, Oct. 27 *Perf. 14½*
302 B26 50c Royal yacht Britannia .24 .24
303 B26 $1.50 Jubliee emblem .65 .65
304 B26 $2.50 Flags 1.10 1.10
a. Souvenir sheet of 3, #302-304 3.00 3.00
Nos. 302-304 (3) 1.99 1.99

Nos. 483-489 Ovptd. "BARBUDA"

1977, Nov. 15 *Perf. 14*
305 A90 ½c multicolored .15 .15
306 A90 1c multicolored .15 .15
307 A90 2c multicolored .15 .15
308 A90 8c multicolored .15 .15
309 A90 10c multicolored .15 .15
310 A90 25c multicolored .20 .20
311 A90 $2 multicolored 1.65 1.65
a. Souvenir sheet of 4, #308-311 2.50 2.50
Nos. 305-311 (7) 2.60 2.60

Nos. 477-482 Ovptd. "BARBUDA" in Black

1977, Dec. 20 *Perf. 12*
312 A87 10c multicolored .15 .15
313 A87 30c multicolored .18 .18
314 A87 50c multicolored .28 .28
315 A87 90c multicolored .52 .52
316 A87 $2.50 multicolored 1.50 1.50
Nos. 312-316 (5) 2.63 2.63

Nos. 312-316 exist with blue overprint.

1977, Nov. 28 *Perf. 13½x14*
312a A87 10c multicolored .15 .15
313a A87 30c multicolored .28 .28
314a A87 50c multicolored .38 .38
315a A87 90c multicolored .70 .70
316a A87 $2.50 multicolored 2.00 2.00
Nos. 312a-316a (5) 3.51 3.51

Souvenir Sheet
317 A87 $5 multicolored 3.75 3.75

Overprint of Nos. 312a-316a differs from that on Nos. 312-316.

Anniversaries — B27

First navigable airships, 75th anniv: No. 318a, Zeppelin LZ1. b, German Naval airship L31. c, Graf Zeppelin. d, Gondola on military airship.

Soviet space program, 20th anniv: No. 319a, Sputnik, 1957. b, Vostok rocket, 1961. c, Voskhod rocket, 1964. d, Space walk, 1965.

Lindbergh's Atlantic crossing, 50th anniv: No. 320a, Fueling for flight. b, New York take-off. c, Spirit of St. Louis. d, Welcome in England.

Coronation of Queen Elizabeth II, 25th anniv: No. 321a, Lion of England. b, Unicorn of Scotland. c, Yale of Beaufort. d, Falcon of Plantagenets.

Rubens, 400th birth anniv: No. 322a, Two lions. b, Daniel in the Lion's Den. c, Two lions lying down. d, Lion at Daniel's feet. Block of 4 has continuous design.

1977, Dec. 29 *Perf. 14½x14*
318 B27 75c Block of 4, #a.-d. 1.25 1.25
319 B27 95c Block of 4, #a.-d. 1.65 1.65
320 B27 $1.25 Block of 4, #a.-d. 2.00 2.00
321 B27 $2 Block of 4, #a.-d. 3.25 3.25
322 B27 $5 Block of 4, #a.-d. 8.50 8.50
e. Min. sheet, #318-322 + 4 labels 17.00 17.00
Nos. 318-322 (5) 16.65 16.65

Nos. 490-494a Ovptd. "BARBUDA"

1978, Feb. 15 *Perf. 13x13½*
323 A91 10c multicolored .15 .15
324 A91 15c multicolored .15 .15
325 A91 50c multicolored .28 .28
326 A91 90c multicolored .52 .52
327 A91 $2 multicolored 1.10 1.10
a. Souv. sheet of 4, #324-327, perf. 14 2.25 2.25
Nos. 323-327 (5) 2.20 2.20

Pieta, by Michelangelo — B28

Works by Michelangelo: 95c, Holy Family. $1.25, Libyan Sibyl. $2, The Flood.

1978, Mar. 23 *Perf. 13½x14*

328 B28 75c multicolored .38 .38
329 B28 95c multicolored .50 .50
330 B28 $1.25 multicolored .65 .65
331 B28 $2 multicolored 1.00 1.00
a. Souvenir sheet of 4, #328-331 3.00 3.00
Nos. 328-331 (4) 2.53 2.53

Nos. 495-502 Ovptd. "BARBUDA"

1978, Mar. 23 *Perf. 14*

332 A92 ½c multicolored .15 .15
333 A92 1c multicolored .15 .15
334 A92 2c multicolored .15 .15
335 A92 10c multicolored .15 .15
336 A92 50c multicolored .35 .35
337 A92 90c multicolored .60 .60
338 A92 $2 multicolored 1.40 1.40
Nos. 332-338 (7) 2.95 2.95

Souvenir Sheet

339 A92 $2.50 multicolored 1.75 1.75

Nos. 503-507 Ovptd. "BARBUDA"

1978, May 22 *Perf. 14½*

340 A93 10c multicolored .15 .15
341 A93 50c multicolored .40 .40
342 A93 90c multicolored .75 .75
343 A93 $2 multicolored 1.65 1.65
Nos. 340-343 (4) 2.95 2.95

Souvenir Sheet

344 A93 $2.50 multicolored 2.00 2.00

Coronation of Queen Elizabeth II, 25th Anniv. — B29

Crowns: No. 345a, St. Edward's. b, Imperial State. No. 346a, Queen Mary's. b, Queen Mother's. No. 347a, Queen Consort's. b, Queen Victoria's.

1978, June 2 *Perf. 15*

Miniature Sheets of Two Each Plus Two Labels

345 B29 75c Sheet of 4 1.30 1.30
346 B29 $1.50 Sheet of 4 2.50 2.50
347 B29 $2.50 Sheet of 4 4.50 4.50

Souvenir Sheet

Perf. 14½

348 B29 Sheet of 6, #345a-347b 4.00 4.00

Nos. 508-514 Ovptd. in Black or Deep Rose Lilac "BARBUDA"

1978 *Perf. 14*

349 A94 10c multicolored .15 .15
350 A94 30c multicolored .18 .18
351 A94 50c multicolored .28 .28
352 A94 90c multicolored .52 .52
353 A94 $2.50 multicolored 1.50 1.50
Nos. 349-353 (5) 2.63 2.63

Souvenir Sheet

354 A94 $5 multicolored 3.00 3.00

Self-adhesive

355 Souvenir booklet
a. A95 Bklt. pane, 3 each 25c and 50c, die cut, rouletted (DRL)
b. A95 $5 Bklt. pane of 1, die cut

Issue dates: #349-354, June 2, #355, Oct. 12.

Nos. 515-518 Ovptd. "BARBUDA"

1978, Sept. 12 *Perf. 15*

356 A96 10c multicolored .15 .15
357 A96 15c multicolored .15 .15
358 A96 $3 multicolored 2.25 2.25
Nos. 356-358 (3) 2.55 2.55

Souvenir Sheet

359 Sheet of 4 2.50 2.50
a. A96 25c multicolored .18 .18
b. A96 30c multicolored .22 .22
c. A96 50c multicolored .38 .38
d. A96 $2 multicolored 1.50 1.50

Nos. 519-523 Ovptd. "BARBUDA"

1978, Nov. 20 *Perf. 14*

360 A97 25c multicolored .26 .26
361 A97 50c multicolored .52 .52
362 A97 90c multicolored .95 .95
363 A97 $2 multicolored 2.25 2.25
Nos. 360-363 (4) 3.98 3.98

Souvenir Sheet

364 A97 $2.50 multicolored 3.00 3.00

Flora and Fauna B30

1978, Nov. 20 *Perf. 15*

365 B30 25c Blackbar soldierfish .50 .50
366 B30 50c Painted lady 1.00 1.00
367 B30 75c Dwarf poinciana 1.50 1.50
368 B30 95c Zebra butterfly 1.90 1.90
369 B30 $1.25 Bougainvillea 2.50 2.50
Nos. 365-369 (5) 7.40 7.40

Nos. 524-527 Ovptd. in Silver "BARBUDA"

1978, Nov. 20 *Perf. 14*

370 A98 8c multicolored .15 .15
371 A98 25c multicolored .18 .18
372 A98 $2 multicolored 1.50 1.50
Nos. 370-372 (3) 1.83 1.83

Souvenir Sheet

373 A98 $4 multicolored 3.25 3.25

Events and Annivs. B31

Designs: 75c, 1978 World Cup Soccer Championships, vert. 95c, Wright Brothers 1st powered flight, 75th anniv. $1.25, First Trans-Atlantic balloon flight, Aug. 1978. $2, Coronation of Elizabeth II, 25th anniv., vert.

1978, Dec. 20 *Perf. 14*

374 B31 75c multicolored .40 .40
375 B31 95c multicolored .50 .50
376 B31 $1.25 multicolored .60 .60
377 B31 $2 multicolored 1.00 1.00
a. Souv. sheet of 4, #374-377, imperf. 4.00 4.00
Nos. 374-377 (4) 2.50 2.50

No. 377a has simulated perfs.

Nos. 528-532 Ovptd. in Bright Blue "BARBUDA" and

Sir Rowland Hill, Death Cent. B32

1979, Apr. 4

378 A99 25c multicolored .16 .16
379 A99 50c multicolored .35 .35
380 B32 75c Sir Rowland Hill, vert. .42 .42
381 B32 95c Mail coach, 1840 .52 .52
382 A99 $1 multicolored .65 .65
383 B32 $1.25 London's first pillar box, 1855 .70 .70
384 B32 $2 St. Martin's Post Office, London, vert. 1.10 1.10
a. Souvenir sheet of 4, #380-381, 383-384, imperf. 2.75 2.75
385 A99 $2 multicolored 1.40 1.40
Nos. 378-385 (8) 5.30 5.30

Souvenir Sheet

386 A99 $2.50 multicolored 2.00 2.00

No. 384a has simulated perfs.
For overprints see Nos. 423-426.

Nos. 533-536 Ovptd. "BARBUDA"

1979, Apr. 16

387 A100 10c multicolored .15 .15
388 A100 50c multicolored .35 .35
389 A100 $4 multicolored 2.50 2.50
Nos. 387-389 (3) 3.00 3.00

Souvenir Sheet

390 A100 $2.50 multicolored 1.90 1.90

Intl. Civil Aviation Organization, 30th Anniv. — B33

1979, May 24 *Perf. 13½x14*

391 B33 75c Passengers leaving 747 .50 .50
392 B33 95c Air traffic controllers .65 .65
393 B33 $1.25 Plane on runway .85 .85
a. Block of 3, #391-393 + label 2.00 2.00

Nos. 537-541 Ovptd. "BARBUDA"

1979, May 24 *Perf. 14*

394 A101 25c multicolored .18 .18
395 A101 50c multicolored .38 .38
396 A101 90c multicolored .65 .65
397 A101 $2 multicolored 1.40 1.40
Nos. 394-397 (4) 2.61 2.61

Souvenir Sheet

398 A101 $5 multicolored 3.50 3.50

Nos. 542-546 Ovptd. "BARBUDA"

1979, Aug. 1 *Perf. 14½*

399 A102 30c multicolored .24 .24
400 A102 50c multicolored .42 .42
401 A102 90c multicolored .70 .70
402 A102 $3 multicolored 2.50 2.50
Nos. 399-402 (4) 3.86 3.86

Souvenir Sheet

403 A102 $2.50 multicolored 2.50 2.50

Nos. 547-551 Ovptd. "BARBUDA"

1979, Aug. 1 *Perf. 14*

404 A103 25c multicolored .16 .16
405 A103 50c multicolored .38 .38
406 A103 90c multicolored .65 .65
407 A103 $3 multicolored 2.25 2.25
Nos. 404-407 (4) 3.44 3.44

Souvenir Sheet

408 A103 $2.50 multicolored 2.00 2.00

Intl. Year of the Child — B34

Details of the Christ Child from various paintings by Durer: 25c, 1512. 50c, 1516. 75c, 1526. $1.25, 1502.

1979, Sept. 24 *Perf. 14x13½*

409 B34 25c multicolored .18 .18
410 B34 50c multicolored .38 .38
411 B34 75c multicolored .58 .58
412 B34 $1.25 multicolored .90 .90
a. Souvenir sheet of 4, #409-412 2.25 2.25
Nos. 409-412 (4) 2.04 2.04

Nos. 552-556 Ovptd. "BARBUDA"

1979, Nov. 21 *Perf. 14*

413 A104 8c multicolored .15 .15
414 A104 25c multicolored .15 .15
415 A104 50c multicolored .30 .30
416 A104 $4 multicolored 2.50 2.50
Nos. 413-416 (4) 3.10 3.10

Souvenir Sheet

Perf. 12x12½

417 A104 $3 multicolored 2.25 2.25

Nos. 557-561 Ovptd. "BARBUDA"

1980, Mar. 18

418 A105 10c multicolored .15 .15
419 A105 25c multicolroed .15 .15
420 A105 $1 multicolored .52 .52
421 A105 $2 multicolored 1.00 1.00
Nos. 418-421 (4) 1.82 1.82

Souvenir Sheet

422 A105 $3 multicolored 2.00 2.00

Nos. 571A-571D Overprinted "BARBUDA" in Dark Blue

1980, May 6 *Perf. 12*

423 A99 25c multicolored .18 .18
424 A99 50c multicolored .42 .42
425 A99 $1 multicolored .75 .75
426 A99 $2 multicolored 1.65 1.65
Nos. 423-426 (4) 3.00 3.00

First Moon Landing, 10th Anniv. — B35

1980, May 21 *Perf. 13½x14*

427 B35 75c Crew badge .45 .45
428 B35 95c Plaque left on moon .60 .60
429 B35 $1.25 Lunar, command modules .75 .75
430 B35 $2 Lunar module 1.25 1.25
a. Souvenir sheet of 4, #427-430 3.25 3.25
Nos. 427-430 (4) 3.05 3.05

American Widgeon B36

1980, June 16 *Perf. 14½x14*

431 B36 1c shown .55 .40
432 B36 2c Snowy plover .55 .40
433 B36 4c Rose-breasted grosbeak .65 .40
434 B36 6c Mangrove cuckoo .65 .40
435 B36 10c Adelaide's warbler .65 .40
436 B36 15c Scaly-breasted thrasher .65 .40
437 B36 20c Yellow-crowned night heron .75 .40
438 B36 25c Bridled quail dove .75 .40
439 B36 35c Carib grackle .75 .40
440 B36 50c Northern pintail .75 .40
441 B36 75c Black-whiskered vireo .75 .45
442 B36 $1 Blue-winged teal 1.10 .75

Perf. 14x14½

443 B36 $1.50 Green-throated carib 1.40 1.00
444 B36 $2 Red-necked pigeon 2.00 1.40
445 B36 $2.50 Stolid flycatcher 2.75 1.65
446 B36 $5 Yellow-bellied sapsucker 3.25 3.25
447 B36 $7.50 Caribbean elaenia 4.75 4.75
448 B36 $10 Great egret 6.50 6.50
Nos. 431-448 (18) 29.20 23.75

Nos. 443-448 vert.

Nos. 572-578 Ovptd. "BARBUDA"

Perf. 13½x14, 14x13½

1980, July 29

449 A106a 10c multicolored .15 .15
450 A106a 30c multicolored .20 .20
451 A106a 50c multicolored .35 .35
452 A106a 90c multicolored .60 .60
453 A106a $1 multicolored .60 .60
454 A106a $4 multicolored 2.50 2.50
Nos. 449-454 (6) 4.40 4.40

Souvenir Sheet

Perf. 14

455 A106a $5 multicolored 3.00 3.00

Nos. 579-583 Ovptd. "BARBUDA"

1980, Sept. 8 *Perf. 14*

456 A107 30c multicolored .20 .20
457 A107 50c multicolored .35 .35
458 A107 90c multicolored .60 .60
459 A107 $3 multicolored 2.00 2.00
Nos. 456-459 (4) 3.15 3.15

Souvenir Sheet

460 A107 $5 multicolored 3.50 3.50

Nos. 584-586 Optd. "BARBUDA"

1980, Oct. 6

461 A108 10c multicolored .15 .15
462 A108 $2.50 multicolored 2.50 2.50

Souvenir Sheet

Perf. 12

463 A108 $3 multicolored 2.75 2.75

Nos. 587-591 Ovptd. "BARBUDA"

1980, Dec. 8 *Perf. 14*
464 A109 10c multicolored .20 .20
465 A109 30c multicolored .55 .55
466 A109 $1 multicolored 1.75 1.75
467 A109 $2 multicolored 3.50 3.50
Nos. 464-467 (4) 6.00 6.00

Souvenir Sheet

468 A109 $2.50 multicolored 3.25 3.25

Nos. 602-606 Ovptd. "BARBUDA"

1981, Jan. 26
469 A111 25c multicolored .20 .20
470 A111 50c multicolored .45 .45
471 A111 90c multicolored .80 .80
472 A111 $3 multicolored 2.75 2.75
Nos. 469-472 (4) 4.20 4.20

Souvenir Sheet

473 A111 $2.50 multicolored 2.50 2.50

Famous Women — B37

1981, Mar. 9 *Perf. 14x13½*
474 B37 50c Florence Nightingale .25 .25
475 B37 90c Marie Curie .50 .50
476 B37 $1 Amy Johnson .55 .55
477 B37 $4 Eleanor Roosevelt 2.25 2.25
Nos. 474-477 (4) 3.55 3.55

Walt Disney Characters at Sea — B38

1981, May 15 *Perf. 13½x14*
478 B38 10c Goofy .15 .15
479 B38 20c Donald Duck .30 .30
480 B38 25c Mickey Mouse .45 .45
481 B38 30c Goofy fishing .50 .50
482 B38 35c Goofy sailing .60 .60
483 B38 40c Mickey fishing .65 .65
484 B38 75c Donald Duck boating 1.25 1.25
485 B38 $1 Minnie Mouse 1.75 1.75
486 B38 $2 Chip 'n Dale 3.50 3.50
Nos. 478-486 (9) 9.15 9.15

Souvenir Sheet

487 B38 $2.50 Donald Duck, diff. 8.00 8.00

Nos. 618-622 Ovptd. "BARBUDA"

1981, June 9 *Perf. 14*
488 A112 10c multicolored .15 .15
489 A112 50c multicolored .35 .35
490 A112 90c multicolored .60 .60
491 A112 $4 multicolored 2.75 2.75
Nos. 488-491 (4) 3.85 3.85

Souvenir Sheet

Perf. 14x14½

492 A112 $5 multicolored 4.50 4.50

Miniature Sheets

Royal Wedding — B39

Designs: $1, Buckingham Palace. $1.50, Caernarvon Castle. $4, Highgrove House.

1981, July 27 *Perf. 11x11½*
493 B39 Sheet of 6 8.00 8.00
494 B39 Sheet of 6 8.00 8.00
495 B39 Sheet of 6 8.00 8.00

Souvenir Sheet

Perf. 11½x11

496 B39 $5 St. Paul's Cathedral, vert. 2.25 2.25

Sheets of 6 contain two of each denomination. Stamps of same denomination have continuous design. For surcharges see Nos. 592-594.

Common Design Types pictured following the introduction.

Nos. 623-627 Ovptd. in Black or Silver "BARBUDA"

1981, Aug. 14 *Perf. 14*
497 CD331 25c multicolored .15 .15
498 CD331 50c multicolored .30 .30
499 CD331 $4 multicolored 2.00 2.00
Nos. 497-499 (3) 2.45 2.45

Souvenir Sheet

500 CD331 $5 multicolored 3.50 3.50

Self-adhesive

501 CD331 Booklet 15.00 15.00
a. Pane of 6 (2x25c, 2x$1, 2x$2), Charles, die cut, rouletted (S) 8.00 8.00
b. Pane of 1, $5 Couple, die cut (S) 6.50 6.50

Issued: #497-500, Aug. 24; #501, Oct. 12.
For surcharge see No. B1.

Intl. Year of the Disabled B40

1981, Sept. 14 *Perf. 14*
502 B40 50c Travel .35 .35
503 B40 90c Braille, sign language .65 .65
504 B40 $1 Helping hands .70 .70
505 B40 $4 Mobility aids 2.75 2.75
Nos. 502-505 (4) 4.45 4.45

Nos. 607-617 Ovptd. "BARBUDA"

1981, Nov. 1 *Perf. 15*
506 A79 6c multicolored .15 .15
507 A79 10c multicolored .15 .15
508 A79 20c multicolored .15 .15
509 A79 25c multicolored .20 .20
510 A79 35c multicolored .30 .30
511 A79 50c multicolored .40 .40
512 A79 75c multicolored .60 .60
513 A79 $1 multicolored .75 .75

Perf. 13½x14

514 A80 $2.50 multicolored 1.90 1.90
515 A80 $5 multicolored 3.75 3.75
516 A80 $10 multicolored 7.50 7.50
Nos. 506-516 (11) 15.85 15.85

Nos. 628-632 Ovptd. "BARBUDA"

1981, Dec. 14 *Perf. 15*
517 A113 10c multicolored .15 .15
518 A113 50c multicolored .50 .50
519 A113 90c multicolored .90 .90
520 A113 $2.50 multicolored 2.50 2.50
Nos. 517-520 (4) 4.05 4.05

Souvenir Sheet

521 A113 $5 multicolored 4.00 4.00

Nos. 643-647 Ovptd. "BARBUDA"

1981, Dec. 14
522 A116 10c multicolored .15 .15
523 A116 50c multicolored .55 .55
524 A116 90c multicolored 1.00 1.00
525 A116 $2 multicolored 2.25 2.25
Nos. 522-525 (4) 3.95 3.95

Souvenir Sheet

526 A116 $4 multicolored 3.00 3.00

Nos. 638-642 Ovptd. in Black or Silver "BARBUDA"

1981, Dec. 22
527 A115 8c multi .15 .15
528 A115 30c multi .20 .20
529 A115 $1 multi (S) .65 .65
530 A115 $3 multi 2.00 2.00
Nos. 527-530 (4) 3.00 3.00

Souvenir Sheet

531 A115 $5 multi 3.50 3.50

Birth of Prince William — B41

Various portraits.

1982, June 21 Wmk. 380 *Perf. 14*
532 B41 $1 buff & multi .60 .60
533 B41 $2.50 lt pink & multi 1.50 1.50
534 B41 $5 lt lilac & multi 3.00 3.00
Nos. 532-534 (3) 5.10 5.10

Souvenir Sheet

535 B41 $5 Couple 4.00 4.00

See Nos. 540-543.

The overprint on stamps of Antigua, from here on, read "BARBUDA MAIL" in one or two lines.

#672-675 Ovptd. in Black or Silver

Perf. 14½x14

1982, Oct. 12 **Unwmk.**
536 CD332 90c multi .65 .65
537 CD332 $1 multi (S) .75 .75
538 CD332 $4 multi (S) 3.00 3.00
Nos. 536-538 (3) 4.40 4.40

Souvenir Sheet

539 CD332 $5 multi 3.50 3.50

Barbuda Nos. 532-535 Inscribed "Twenty First Birthday Greetings to H.R.H. The Princess of Wales"

Various portraits.

Perf. 14x14½

1982, July 1 **Wmk. 380**
540 B41 $1 lt grn & multi .60 .60
541 B41 $2.50 pale salmon & multi 1.50 1.50
542 B41 $5 lt bl & multi 3.00 3.00
Nos. 540-542 (3) 5.10 5.10

Souvenir Sheet

543 B41 $4 Couple 3.50 3.50

#663-666 Ovptd. in Black or Silver

Perf. 14½x14

1982, Aug. 30 **Unwmk.**
544 CD332 90c multi .75 .75
545 CD332 $1 multi (S) .85 .85
546 CD332 $4 multi 3.25 3.25
Nos. 544-546 (3) 4.85 4.85

Souvenir Sheet

547 CD332 $5 multi 4.50 4.50

Nos. 676-683 Overprinted

1982, Dec. 6 *Perf. 15*
551 A121 10c multicolored .15 .15
552 A121 25c multicolored .22 .22
553 A121 45c multicolored .40 .40
554 A121 60c multicolored .55 .55
555 A121 $1 multicolored .90 .90
556 A121 $3 multicolored 2.75 2.75
Nos. 551-556 (6) 4.97 4.97

Souvenir Sheets

557 A121 $4 on #682 3.25 3.25
558 A121 $4 on #683 3.25 3.25

Nos. 684-688 Overprinted

1982, Dec. 6 *Perf. 14*
559 A122 10c multicolored .15 .15
560 A122 30c multicolored .22 .22
561 A122 $1 multicolored .75 .75
562 A122 $4 multicolored 3.00 3.00
Nos. 559-562 (4) 4.12 4.12

Souvenir Sheet

563 A122 $5 multicolored 3.75 3.75

Nos. 689-693 Overprinted

1983, Mar. 14 *Perf. 14½*
564 A123 45c multicolored .32 .32
565 A123 50c multicolored .38 .38
566 A123 60c multicolored .45 .45
567 A123 $4 multicolored 3.00 3.00
Nos. 564-567 (4) 4.15 4.15

Souvenir Sheet

568 A123 $5 multicolored 3.75 3.75

Nos. 694-697 Overprinted

1983, Mar. 14 *Perf. 14*
569 A124 25c multicolored .22 .22
570 A124 45c multicolored .42 .42
571 A124 60c multicolored .55 .55
572 A124 $3 multicolored 2.75 2.75
Nos. 569-572 (4) 3.94 3.94

Nos. 698-702 Overprinted

1983, Apr. 12
573 A125 15c multicolored .15 .15
574 A125 50c multicolored .48 .48
575 A125 60c multicolored .55 .55
576 A125 $3 multicolored 3.00 3.00
Nos. 573-576 (4) 4.18 4.18

Souvenir Sheet

577 A125 $5 multicolored 4.00 4.00

First Manned Balloon Flight, Bicent. — B43

1983, June 13
578 B43 $1 Vincenzo Lunardi, 1785 1.00 1.00
579 B43 $1.50 Montgolfier brothers, 1783 1.50 1.50
580 B43 $2.50 Blanchard & Jeffries, 1785 2.50 2.50
Nos. 578-580 (3) 5.00 5.00

Souvenir Sheet

581 B43 $5 Graf Zeppelin, 1928 3.75 3.75

Nos. 703-707 Overprinted

1983, July 4 *Perf. 15*
582 A126 15c multicolored .15 .15
583 A126 50c multicolored .45 .45
584 A126 60c multicolored .55 .55
585 A126 $3 multicolored 2.75 2.75
Nos. 582-585 (4) 3.90 3.90

Souvenir Sheet

586 A126 $5 multicolored 4.50 4.50

Nos. 726-730 Overprinted

1983, Sept. 12
587 A128 30c multicolored .26 .26
588 A128 50c multicolored .45 .45
589 A128 60c multicolored .52 .52
590 A128 $4 multicolored 3.50 3.50
Nos. 587-590 (4) 4.73 4.73

Souvenir Sheet

591 A128 $5 multicolored 4.50 4.50

Barbuda Nos. 493-495 Surcharged 45c on $1, 50c on $1.50, or 60c on $4

1983, Oct. 21 *Perf. 11½x11*
592 Sheet of 6 11.00 11.00
593 Sheet of 6 11.00 11.00
594 Sheet of 6 11.00 11.00

Nos. 708-725 Overprinted

1983, Oct. 28 *Perf. 14*
595 A127 1c multicolored .15 .15
596 A127 2c multicolored .15 .15
597 A127 3c multicolored .15 .15
598 A127 5c multicolored .15 .15
599 A127 10c multicolored .15 .15
600 A127 15c multicolored .15 .15
601 A127 20c multicolored .15 .15
602 A127 25c multicolored .20 .20
603 A127 30c multicolored .25 .25
604 A127 40c multicolored .35 .35
605 A127 45c multicolored .35 .35
606 A127 50c multicolored .45 .45
607 A127 60c multicolored .50 .50
608 A127 $1 multicolored .85 .85
609 A127 $2 multicolored 1.75 1.75
610 A127 $2.50 multicolored 2.25 2.25
611 A127 $5 multicolored 4.25 4.25
612 A127 $10 multicolored 8.00 8.00
Nos. 595-612 (18) 20.25 20.25

Nos. 731-735 Overprinted

1983, Oct. 28 *Perf. 14*
613 A129 10c multicolored .15 .15
614 A129 30c multicolored .20 .20
615 A129 $1 multicolored .75 .75
616 A129 $4 multicolored 3.00 3.00
Nos. 613-616 (4) 4.10 4.10

Souvenir Sheet

617 A129 $5 multicolored 3.75 3.75

BARBUDA

#736-739 Ovptd. in Black or Silver
1983, Dec. 14   *Perf. 14*
618 A130   15c multicolored (S)   .15 .15
619 A130   50c multicolored (S)   .45 .45
620 A130   60c multicolored   .50 .50
621 A130 $3 multicolored   2.75 2.75
  Nos. 618-621 (4)   3.85 3.85

Members of Royal Family — B44

1984, Feb. 14   *Perf. 14½x14*
622 B44 $1 Edward VII   1.00 1.00
623 B44 $1 George V   1.00 1.00
624 B44 $1 George VI   1.00 1.00
625 B44 $1 Elizabeth II   1.00 1.00
626 B44 $1 Prince Charles   1.00 1.00
627 B44 $1 Prince William   1.00 1.00
  Nos. 622-627 (6)   6.00 6.00

Nos. 740-744 Overprinted and

1984 Summer Olympics, Los Angeles B45

1984   *Perf. 15, 13½ (B45)*
628 A131   25c multicolored   .20 .20
629 A131   50c multicolored   .40 .40
630 A131   90c multicolored   .45 .45
631 B45 $1.50 Olympic Stadium, Athens   1.10 1.10
632 B45 $2.50 Olympic Stadium, Los Angeles   1.90 1.90
633 A131 $3 multicolored   2.50 2.50
634 B45 $5 Torch bearer   4.00 4.00
  a. Souv. sheet of 1, perf. 15   4.00 4.00
  Nos. 628-634 (7)   10.55 10.55

Souvenir Sheet
635 A131 $5 multicolored   4.00 4.00
  Issue dates: A131, Apr. 26; B45, July 27.

Nos. 755-759 Overprinted
1984, July 12   *Perf. 15*
636 A133   15c multicolored   .15 .15
637 A133   50c multicolored   .45 .45
638 A133   60c multicolored   .55 .55
639 A133 $3 multicolored   2.75 2.75
  Nos. 636-639 (4)   3.90 3.90

Souvenir Sheet
640 A133 $5 multicolored   4.25 4.25

Nos. 745-749 Overprinted
1984, July 12
641 A132   45c multicolored   .40 .40
642 A132   50c multicolored   .45 .45
643 A132   60c multicolored   .50 .50
644 A132 $4 multicolored   3.50 3.50
  Nos. 641-644 (4)   4.85 4.85

Souvenir Sheet
645 A132 $5 multicolored   4.50 4.50

#760-767 Ovptd. in Black or Silver
1984, Oct. 1   *Perf. 14*
646 A134   10c multicolored (S)   .15 .15
647 A134   20c multicolored   .15 .15
648 A134   30c multicolored   .25 .25
649 A134   40c multicolored   .30 .30
650 A134   90c multicolored (S)   .70 .70
651 A134 $1.10 multicolored   .90 .90
652 A134 $1.50 multicolored (S)   1.25 1.25
653 A134 $2 multicolored   1.65 1.65
  Nos. 646-653 (8)   5.35 5.35

Nos. 768-772 Overprinted
1984, Oct. 1
654 A135   40c multicolored   .35 .35
655 A135   50c multicolored   .45 .45
656 A135   60c multicolored   .50 .50
657 A135 $3 multicolored   2.75 2.75
  Nos. 654-657 (4)   4.05 4.05

Souvenir Sheet
658 A135 $5 multicolored   4.25 4.25

Nos. 773-778 Overprinted
1984, Nov. 21   *Perf. 15*
659 A136   40c multicolored   .40 .40
660 A136   50c multicolored   .50 .50
661 A136   60c multicolored   .60 .60
662 A136 $2 multicolored   2.00 2.00
663 A136 $3 multicolored   3.00 3.00
  Nos. 659-663 (5)   6.50 6.50

Souvenir Sheet
664 A136 $5 multicolored   5.00 5.00

Nos. 782-791 Overprinted in Silver
1984   *Perf. 15*
665 A137a   15c multicolored   .15 .15
666 A137a   25c multicolored   .20 .20
667 A137a   50c multicolored   .40 .40
668 A137a   60c multicolored   .50 .50
669 A137a   70c multicolored   .55 .55
670 A137a   90c multicoloed   .75 .75
671 A137a $3 multicolored   2.50 2.50
672 A137a $4 multicolored   3.25 3.25
  Nos. 665-672 (8)   8.30 8.30

Souvenir Sheets
673 A137a $5 #790   4.50 4.50
674 A137a $5 #791, horiz.   4.50 4.50
  Issue dates: Correggio, Nov. 21; Degas, Nov. 30.

Nos. 779-781 Overprinted
1984, Nov. 30
675 A137 $1 multicolored   .80 .80
676 A137 $5 multicolored   4.00 4.00

Souvenir Sheet
677 A137 $5 multicolored   4.50 4.50

Nos. 819-827 Overprinted
1985, Feb. 18
678 A139   60c multicolored   .45 .45
679 A139   60c multicolored   .45 .45
680 A139   60c multicolored   .45 .45
681 A139   60c multicolored   .45 .45
682 A139 $1 multicolored   .75 .75
683 A139 $1 multicolored   .75 .75
684 A139 $1 multicolored   .75 .75
685 A139 $1 multicolored   .75 .75
  Nos. 678-685 (8)   4.80 4.80

Souvenir Sheet
686 A139 $5 multicolored   4.50 4.50

Queen Mother (Lady Elizabeth Bowes-Lyon), 1907 — B46

1985, Feb. 26   *Perf. 14x14½*
687 B46   15c shown   .15 .15
688 B46   45c Duchess of York, 1926   .35 .35
689 B46   50c Coronation, 1937   .40 .40
690 B46   60c Queen Mother   .50 .50
691 B46   90c Wearing tiara   .70 .70
692 B46 $2 Wearing blue hat   1.65 1.65
693 B46 $3 With children   2.50 2.50
  Nos. 687-693 (7)   6.25 6.25

For overprints see Nos. 724-728, 733, 735.

Nos. 828-834 Overprinted
1985, May 10   *Perf. 15*
694 A140   25c multicolored   .20 .20
695 A140   30c multicolored   .25 .25
696 A140   50c multicolored   .40 .40
697 A140   90c multicolored   .70 .70
698 A140 $1 multicolored   .80 .80
699 A140 $3 multicolored   2.50 2.50
  Nos. 694-699 (6)   4.85 4.85

Souvenir Sheet
700 A140 $5 multicolored   4.00 4.00

Audubon, Birth Bicentenary — B47

1985, Apr. 4   *Perf. 14*
701 B47   45c Roseate tern   .40 .40
702 B47   50c Mangrove cuckoo   .45 .45
703 B47   60c Yellow-crowned night heron   .55 .55
704 B47 $5 Brown pelican   4.50 4.50
  Nos. 701-704 (4)   5.90 5.90

Nos. 845-849, 910-913 Ovptd. in Black or Silver
1985-86   *Perf. 15, 12½x12*
705 A143   60c on #910 (S)   .48 .48
706 A143   90c on #845   .70 .70
707 A143   90c on #911 (S)   .70 .70
708 A143 $1 on #846   .80 .80
709 A143 $1.50 on #847   1.25 1.25
710 A143 $1.50 on #912   1.25 1.25
711 A143 $3 on #848   2.50 2.50
712 A143 $3 on #913   2.50 2.50
  Nos. 705-712 (8)   10.18 10.18

Souvenir Sheet
713 A143 $5 on #849   4.50 4.50
  Issue dates: Nos. 706, 708-709, 711, 713, July 18, 1985. Others, Dec. 1986.

Nos. 850-854 Overprinted
1985, July 18   *Perf. 14*
714 A144   25c multicolored   .22 .22
715 A144   60c multicolored   .52 .52
716 A144   95c multicolored   .80 .80
717 A144 $4 multicolored   3.50 3.50
  Nos. 714-717 (4)   5.04 5.04

Souvenir Sheet
718 A144 $5 multicolored   4.50 4.50

Nos. 840-844 Overprinted
1985, Aug. 2
719 A142   10c multicolored   .15 .15
720 A142   30c multicolored   .28 .28
721 A142   60c multicolored   .52 .52
722 A142 $4 multicolored   3.75 3.75
  Nos. 719-722 (4)   4.70 4.70

Souvenir Sheet
723 A142 $5 multicolored   4.50 4.50

Barbuda Nos. 687-693 Ovptd. "4TH AUG 1900-1985" and Antigua Nos. 866A-870 Ovptd. "BARBUDA / MAIL" in Silver or Black

Perf. 14, 12x12½ (#729, 731, 736)
1985-86
724 B46   15c multi   .15 .15
725 B46   45c multi   .35 .35
726 B46   50c multi   .40 .40
727 B46   60c multi   .48 .48
728 B46   90c multi   .70 .70
729 A148   90c multi   .70 .70
730 A148 $1 multi (S)   .80 .80
731 A148 $1 like #730   .80 .80
732 A148 $1.50 multi (S)   1.20 1.20
733 B46 $2 multi   1.65 1.65
734 A148 $2.50 multi   2.00 2.00
735 B46 $3 multi   2.50 2.50
736 A148 $3 multi   2.50 2.50
  Nos. 724-736 (13)   14.23 14.23

Souvenir Sheet
737 A148 $5 multi   4.50 4.50
  Queen Mother's 85th birthday.
  Issue dates: 15c, 45c, 50c, 60c, No. 728, $2, No. 735, Aug. 2. No. 730, $1.50, $2.50, Nov. 8. Others, Dec. 1986. Nos. 729, 731, 736 issued in sheets of 5 plus label.

Nos. 835-839 Overprinted
1985, Aug. 30   *Perf. 15*
738 A141   15c multicolored   .15 .15
739 A141   50c multicolored   .40 .40
740 A141   60c multicolored   .45 .45
741 A141 $3 multicolored   2.50 2.50
  Nos. 738-741 (4)   3.50 3.50

Souvenir Sheet
742 A141 $5 multicolored   4.00 4.00

Nos. 855-859 Overprinted
1985, Aug. 30   *Perf. 14*
743 A145   30c multicolored   .24 .24
744 A145   90c multicolored   .70 .70
745 A145 $1.50 multicolored   1.25 1.25
746 A145 $3 multicolored   2.50 2.50
  Nos. 743-746 (4)   4.69 4.69

Souvenir Sheet
747 A145 $5 multicolored   4.25 4.25

Nos. 860-861 Overprinted
1985, Nov. 25   *Perf. 14*
748 A146 $2 yellow green   1.65 1.65

Souvenir Sheet
749 A146 $5 deep brown   4.00 4.00

#871-875 Ovptd. in Black or Silver
1985, Nov. 25
750 A149   15c multi (S)   .15 .15
751 A149   45c multi   .40 .40
752 A149   60c multi   .55 .55
753 A149 $3 multi (S)   3.00 3.00
  Nos. 750-753 (4)   4.10 4.10

Souvenir Sheet
754 A149 $5 multi   4.50 4.50

Nos. 862-866 Overprinted
1986, Feb. 17
755 A147   25c multicolored   .20 .20
756 A147   50c multicolored   .40 .40
757 A147   60c multicolored   .48 .48
758 A147 $3 multicolored   2.50 2.50
  Nos. 755-758 (4)   3.58 3.58

Souvenir Sheet
759 A147 $5 multicolored   4.00 4.00

Nos. 886-889 Overprinted
1986, Feb. 17   *Perf. 14½*
760 A152   60c multicolored   .48 .48
761 A152 $1 multicolored   .80 .80
762 A152 $4 multicolored   3.25 3.25
  Nos. 760-762 (3)   4.53 4.53

Souvenir Sheet
763 A152 $5 multicolored   4.00 4.00

Nos. 876-880 Overprinted
1986, Mar. 10   *Perf. 14*
764 A150   25c multicolored   .20 .20
765 A150   50c multicolored   .40 .40
766 A150 $1 multicolored   .80 .80
767 A140 $3 multicolored   2.50 2.50
  Nos. 764-767 (4)   3.90 3.90

Souvenir Sheet
768 A150 $5 multicolored   4.00 4.00

Nos. 881-885 Overprinted
1986, Mar. 10   *Perf. 14*
769 A151   15c multicolored   .15 .15
770 A151   45c multicolored   .35 .35
771 A151   60c multicolored   .48 .48
772 A151 $3 multicolored   2.50 2.50
  Nos. 769-772 (4)   3.48 3.48

Souvenir Sheet
773 A151 $5 multicolored   4.00 4.00

Nos. 905-909 Overprinted
1986, Apr. 4   *Perf. 15*
774 A156   10c multicolored   .15 .15
775 A156   25c multicolored   .20 .20
776 A156   60c multicolored   .48 .48
777 A156 $4 multicolored   3.25 3.25
  Nos. 774-777 (4)   4.08 4.08

Souvenir Sheet
778 A156 $5 multicolored   4.00 4.00

1986, Apr. 21
779 B48 $1 Shaking hands   .80 .80
780 B48 $2 Talking with woman   1.65 1.65
781 B48 $2.50 With officer   2.00 2.00
  Nos. 779-781 (3)   4.45 4.45

Souvenir Sheet
  Perf. 13½x14
782 B48 $5 Portraits   4.00 4.00
  No. 782 contains one 34x27mm stamp.

Nos. 925-928 Overprinted in Silver or Black
1986, Aug. 12
783 CD339   60c multi   .48 .48
784 CD339 $1 multi   .80 .80
785 CD339 $4 multi   3.25 3.25
  Nos. 783-785 (3)   4.53 4.53

Souvenir Sheet
786 CD339 $5 multi (Bk)   4.00 4.00

Nos. 920-924 Overprinted and

Halley's Comet B49

1986   *Perf. 14, 15 (B49)*
787 A158   5c multicolored   .15 .15
788 A158   10c multicolored   .15 .15
789 A158   60c multicolored   .48 .48
790 B49 $1 shown   .80 .80
791 B49 $2.50 Early telescope, dish antenna, vert.   2.00 2.00
792 A158 $4 multicolored   3.25 3.25

BARBUDA 537

793 B49 $5 World map, comet 4.00 4.00
Nos. 787-793 (7) 10.83 10.83

Souvenir Sheet

794 A159 $5 multicolored 4.00 4.00

Issued: #790-791, 793, 7/10; others, 9/22.

Nos. 901-904 Overprinted

1986, Aug. 12 *Perf. 13½x14*

795 A155 40c multicolored .32 .32
796 A155 $1 multicolored .80 .80
797 A155 $3 multicolored 2.50 2.50
Nos. 795-797 (3) 3.62 3.62

Souvenir Sheet

Perf. 14x13½

798 A155 $5 multicolored 4.00 4.00

Nos. 915-919 Overprinted

1986, Aug. 28 *Perf. 14*

799 A157 30c multicolored .24 .24
800 A157 60c multicolored .48 .48
801 A157 $1 multicolored .80 .80
802 A157 $4 multicolored 3.25 3.25
Nos. 799-802 (4) 4.77 4.77

Souvenir Sheet

803 A157 $5 multicolored 4.00 4.00

See Nos. 848-851.

Nos. 934-938 Overprinted

1986, Aug. 28 Litho. *Perf. 15*

804 A161 25c multicolored .20 .20
805 A161 50c multicolored .40 .40
806 A161 $1 multicolored .80 .80
807 A161 $3 multicolored 2.50 2.50
Nos. 804-807 (4) 3.90 3.90

Souvenir Sheet

808 A161 $5 multicolored 4.00 4.00

Nos. 939-942 Ovptd. in Silver

1986, Sept. 22 *Perf. 14*

809 CD340 45c multicolored .42 .42
810 CD340 60c multicolored .60 .60
811 CD340 $4 multicolored 4.00 4.00
Nos. 809-811 (3) 5.02 5.02

Souvenir Sheet

812 CD340 $5 multicolored 5.00 5.00

Nos. 943-947 Overprinted in Silver or Black

1986, Nov. 10 *Perf. 15*

813 A162 15c multicolored .15 .15
814 A162 45c multicolored .32 .32
815 A162 60c multicolored .45 .45
816 A162 $3 multicolored 2.25 2.25
Nos. 813-816 (4) 3.17 3.17

Souvenir Sheet

817 A162 $5 multi (Bk) 4.00 4.00

Nos. 948-957 Overprinted

1986, Nov. 10

818 A163 10c multicolored .15 .15
819 A163 15c multicolored .15 .15
820 A163 50c multicolored .38 .38
821 A163 60c multicolored .45 .45
822 A163 70c multicolored .52 .52
823 A163 $1 multicolored .75 .75
824 A163 $3 multicolored 2.25 2.25
825 A163 $4 multicolored 3.00 3.00
Nos. 818-825 (8) 7.65 7.65

Souvenir Sheets

826 A163 $4 multicolored 3.25 3.25
827 A163 $5 multicolored 4.00 4.00

Nos. 958-962 Overprinted

1986, Nov. 28

828 A164 10c multicolored .15 .15
829 A164 50c multicolored .38 .38
830 A164 $1 multicolored .75 .75
831 A164 $4 multicolored 3.00 3.00
Nos. 828-831 (4) 4.28 4.28

Souvenir Sheet

832 A164 $5 multicolored 4.00 4.00

Nos. 929-933 Overprinted

1987, Jan. 12 *Perf. 14*

833 A160 30c multicolored .28 .28
834 A160 60c multicolored .55 .55
835 A160 $1 multicolored .90 .90
836 A160 $3 multicolored 2.75 2.75
Nos. 833-836 (4) 4.48 4.48

Souvenir Sheet

837 A160 $5 multicolored 4.00 4.00

Nos. 968-972A Overprinted

1987, Jan. 12

838 A165 10c multicolored .15 .15
839 A165 15c multicolored .15 .15
840 A165 50c multicolored .40 .40
841 A165 60c multicolored .48 .48
842 A165 70c multicolored .55 .55
843 A165 $1 multicolored .80 .80
844 A165 $3 multicolored 2.50 2.50
845 A165 $4 multicolored 3.25 3.25
Nos. 838-845 (8) 8.28 8.28

Souvenir Sheets

846 A165 $5 multi (#972) 4.00 4.00
847 A165 $5 multi (#972A) 4.00 4.00

Automobile, cent.

Nos. 963-966 Overprinted

1987, Mar. 10

848 A157 30c multicolored .22 .22
849 A157 60c multicolored .45 .45
850 A157 $1 multicolored .75 .75
851 A157 $4 multicolored 3.00 3.00
Nos. 848-851 (4) 4.42 4.42

See Nos. 799-802.

Nos. 1000-1004 Overprinted

1987, Apr. 23 *Perf. 15*

852 A170 30c multicolored .22 .22
853 A170 60c multicolored .45 .45
854 A170 $1 multicolored 2.25 2.25
855 A170 $3 multicolored .75 .75
Nos. 852-855 (4) 3.67 3.67

Souvenir Sheet

856 A171 $5 multicolored 5.00 5.00

Nos. 1005-1014 Overprinted

1987, July 1 *Perf. 14*

857 A172 15c multicolored .15 .15
858 A173 30c multicolored .22 .22
859 A172 40c multicolored .30 .30
860 A173 50c multicolored .38 .38
861 A172 60c multicolored .45 .45
862 A172 $1 multicolored .75 .75
863 A173 $2 multicolored 1.50 1.50
864 A173 $3 multicolored 2.25 2.25
Nos. 857-864 (8) 6.00 6.00

Souvenir Sheets

865 A172 $5 multicolored 4.00 4.00
866 A173 $5 multicolored 4.00 4.00

Nos. 1025-1034 Overprinted

1987, July 28 *Perf. 15*

867 A175 10c multicolored .15 .15
868 A175 15c multicolored .15 .15
869 A175 30c multicolored .24 .24
870 A175 50c multicolored .40 .40
871 A175 60c multicolored .48 .48
872 A175 70c multicolored .55 .55
873 A175 90c multicolored .70 .70
874 A175 $1.50 multicolored 1.20 1.20
875 A175 $2 multicolored 1.65 1.65
876 A175 $3 multicolored 2.25 2.25
Nos. 867-876 (10) 7.77 7.77

Marine Life
B50

1987, July 28

877 B50 5c Shore crab .15 .15
878 B50 10c Sea cucumber .15 .15
879 B50 15c Stop light parrotfish .15 .15
880 B50 25c Banded coral shrimp .18 .18
881 B50 35c Spotted drum .26 .26
882 B50 60c Thorny star-fish .45 .45
883 B50 75c Atlantic trumpet triton .55 .55
884 B50 90c Feather-star, yellow beaker sponge .65 .65
885 B50 $1 Blue gorgonian, vert. .75 .75
886 B50 $1.25 Slender filefish, vert. .90 .90
887 B50 $5 Barred hamlet, vert. 3.75 3.75
888 B50 $7.50 Fairy basslet, vert. 5.50 5.50
889 B50 $10 Fire coral, butterfly fish, vert. 7.50 7.50
Nos. 877-889 (13) 20.94 20.94

For surcharges see Nos. 1133-1134.

#1048-1052 Ovptd. in Silver or Black

1987, Oct. 12 *Perf. 14*

890 A178 10c multicolored .15 .15
891 A178 60c multicolored .48 .48
892 A178 $1 multicolored .80 .80
893 A178 $3 multicolored 2.25 2.25
Nos. 890-893 (4) 3.68 3.68

Souvenir Sheet

894 A178 $5 multi (Bk) 4.00 4.00

1988 Summer Olympics, Seoul.

#990-999 Ovptd. in Black or Silver

1987, Oct. 12 *Perf. 13½x14*

895 A169 10c multicolored .15 .15
896 A169 30c multicolored .24 .24
897 A169 40c multicolored .32 .32
898 A169 60c multicolored .48 .48
899 A169 90c multicolored .70 .70
900 A169 $1 multicolored (S) .80 .80
901 A169 $3 multicolored 2.25 2.25
902 A169 $4 multicolored 3.00 3.00
Nos. 895-902 (8) 7.94 7.94

Size: 110x95mm

Imperf

903 A169 $5 multicolored 4.00 4.00
904 A169 $5 multicolored (S) 4.00 4.00

#1015-1024 Ovptd. in Silver or Black

1987, Nov. 5 *Perf. 14*

905 A174 15c multicolored .15 .15
906 A174 30c multicolored .24 .24
907 A174 45c multicolored .35 .35
908 A174 50c multicolored (Bk) .40 .40
909 A174 60c multicolored .48 .48
910 A174 90c multicolored .70 .70
911 A174 $1 multicolored .80 .80
912 A174 $2 multicolored 1.65 1.65
913 A174 $3 multicolored (Bk) 2.25 2.25
914 A174 $5 multicolored 4.00 4.00
Nos. 905-914 (10) 11.02 11.02

#1040-1047 Ovptd. in Black or Silver

1987, Nov. 5

915 A177 15c multicolored .15 .15
916 A177 30c multicolored .28 .28
917 A177 45c multicolored .42 .42
918 A177 50c multicolored .48 .48
919 A177 60c multicolored .55 .55
920 A177 $1 multicolored .95 .95
921 A177 $2 multicolored 2.00 2.00
922 A177 $3 multicolored (S) 2.75 2.75
Nos. 915-922 (8) 7.58 7.58

Nos. 1035-1039 Overprinted

1987, Dec. 8

923 A176 30c multicolored .24 .24
924 A176 60c multicolored .48 .48
925 A176 $1 multicolored .80 .80
926 A176 $3 multicolored 2.25 2.25
Nos. 923-926 (4) 3.77 3.77

Souvenir Sheet

927 A176 $5 multicolored 4.00 4.00

Nos. 1063-1067 Overprinted

1988, Jan. 12

928 A181 45c multicolored .32 .32
929 A181 60c multicolored .45 .45
930 A181 $1 multicolored .75 .75
931 A181 $4 multicolored 3.00 3.00
Nos. 928-931 (4) 4.52 4.52

Souvenir Sheet

932 A181 $5 multicolored 4.00 4.00

Nos. 1083-1091 Overprinted

1988, Mar. 25

933 A184 25c multicolored .20 .20
934 A184 30c multicolored .24 .24
935 A184 40c multicolored .32 .32
936 A184 45c multicolored .35 .35
937 A184 50c multicolored .40 .40
938 A184 60c multicolored .48 .48
939 A184 $1 multicolored .80 .80
940 A184 $2 multicolored 1.65 1.65
Nos. 933-940 (8) 4.44 4.44

Souvenir Sheet

941 A184 $5 multicolored 4.00 4.00

Nos. 1058-1062 Ovptd. in Silver

1988, May 6

942 A180 15c multicolored .15 .15
943 A180 45c multicolored .35 .35
944 A180 60c multicolored .48 .48
945 A180 $4 multicolored 3.25 3.25
Nos. 942-945 (4) 4.23 4.23

Souvenir Sheet

946 A180 $5 multicolored 4.00 4.00

Nos. 1068-1072 Overprinted

1988, July 4

947 A182 25c multicolored .20 .20
948 A182 60c multicolored .48 .48
949 A182 $2 multicolored 1.65 1.65
950 A182 $3 multicolored 2.25 2.25
Nos. 947-950 (4) 4.58 4.58

Souvenir Sheet

951 A182 $5 multicolored 4.00 4.00

Nos. 1073-1082 Overprinted

1988, July 4

952 A183 10c multicolored .15 .15
953 A183 15c multicolored .15 .15
954 A183 50c multicolored .40 .40
955 A183 60c multicolored .48 .48
956 A183 70c multicolored .55 .55
957 A183 $1 multicolored .80 .80
958 A183 $3 multicolored 2.25 2.25
959 A183 $4 multicolored 3.25 3.25
Nos. 952-959 (8) 8.03 8.03

Souvenir Sheets

960 A183 $5 multi (#1081) 4.00 4.00
961 A183 $5 multi (#1082) 4.00 4.00

Nos. 1092-1101 Overprinted

1988, July 25

962 A185 10c multicolored .15 .15
963 A185 30c multicolored .25 .25
964 A185 45c multicolored .38 .38
965 A185 60c multicolored .50 .50
966 A185 90c multicolored .75 .75
967 A185 $1 multicolored .85 .85
968 A185 $3 multicolored 2.50 2.50
969 A185 $4 multicolored 3.50 3.50
Nos. 962-969 (8) 8.88 8.88

Souvenir Sheets

970 A185 $5 multi (#1100) 4.00 4.00
971 A185 $5 multi (#1101) 4.00 4.00

Nos. 1102-1111 Overprinted

1988, July 25 *Perf. 13½x14*

972 A187 30c multicolored .24 .24
973 A187 40c multicolored .32 .32
974 A187 45c multicolored .35 .35
975 A187 50c multicolored .40 .40
976 A187 $1 multicolored .80 .80
977 A187 $2 multicolored 1.65 1.65
978 A187 $3 multicolored 2.25 2.25
979 A187 $4 multicolored 3.25 3.25
Nos. 972-979 (8) 9.26 9.26

Souvenir Sheets

980 A187 $5 multi (#1110) 4.00 4.00
981 A187 $5 multi (#1111) 4.00 4.00

Nos. 1053-1057 Overprinted

1988, Aug. 25 *Perf. 15*

982 A179 10c multicolored .15 .15
983 A179 60c multicolored .45 .45
984 A179 $1 multicolored .75 .75
985 A179 $3 multicolored 2.25 2.25
Nos. 982-985 (4) 3.60 3.60

Souvenir Sheet

986 A179 $5 multicolored 4.00 4.00

Nos. 1112-1116 Overprinted

1988, Aug. 25

987 A188 30c multicolored .24 .24
988 A188 60c multicolored .48 .48
989 A188 $1 multicolored .80 .80
990 A188 $3 multicolored 2.25 2.25
Nos. 987-990 (4) 3.77 3.77

Souvenir Sheet

991 A188 $5 multicolored 4.00 4.00

Nos. 1127-1136 Overprinted

1988, Sept. 16 *Perf. 14*

992 A190 10c multicolored .15 .15
993 A190 30c multicolored .22 .22
994 A190 50c multicolored .38 .38
995 A190 90c multicolored .65 .65
996 A190 $1 multicolored .75 .75
997 A190 $2 multicolored 1.65 1.65
998 A190 $3 multicolored 2.25 2.25
999 A190 $4 multicolored 3.00 3.00
Nos. 992-999 (8) 9.05 9.05

Souvenir Sheets

1000 A191 $5 multi (#1135) 4.00 4.00
1001 A191 $5 multi (#1136) 4.00 4.00

Nos. 1140-1144 Overprinted

1988, Sept. 16

1002 A192 40c multicolored .32 .32
1003 A192 60c multicolored .48 .48
1004 A192 $1 multicolored .80 .80
1005 A192 $3 multicolored 2.25 2.25
Nos. 1002-1005 (4) 3.85 3.85

Souvenir Sheet

1006 A192 $5 multicolored 4.00 4.00

Nos. 1145-1162 Overprinted

1988-90

1007 A193 1c multicolored .15 .15
1008 A193 2c multicolored .15 .15
1009 A193 3c multicolored .15 .15
1010 A193 5c multicolored .15 .15
1011 A193 10c multicolored .15 .15
1012 A193 15c multicolored .15 .15
1013 A193 20c multicolored .16 .16
1014 A193 25c multicolored .20 .20
1015 A193 30c multicolored .24 .24
1016 A193 40c multicolored .32 .32
1017 A193 45c multicolored .35 .35
1018 A193 50c multicolored .40 .40
1019 A193 60c multicolored .48 .48
1020 A193 $1 multicolored .80 .80
1021 A193 $2 multicolored 1.65 1.65
1022 A193 $2.50 multicolored 2.00 2.00
1023 A193 $5 multicolored 4.00 4.00
1024 A193 $10 multicolored 8.00 8.00
1025 A193 $20 multi ('90) 16.00 16.00
Nos. 1007-1025 (19) 35.50 35.50

Issue dates: $20, May 4, others Dec. 8.

Nos. 1162A-1167 Overprinted

1989, Apr. 28

1026 A194 1c multicolored .15 .15
1027 A194 2c multicolored .15 .15
1028 A194 3c multicolored .15 .15
1029 A194 4c multicolored .15 .15
1030 A194 30c multicolored .24 .24
1031 A194 60c multicolored .48 .48
1032 A194 $1 multicolored .80 .80
1033 A194 $4 multicolored 3.25 3.25
Nos. 1026-1033 (8) 5.37 5.37

Souvenir Sheet

1034 A194 $5 multicolored 4.00 4.00

Nos. 1175-1176 Overprinted

1989, May 24

1035 A196 $1.50 Strip of 4, #a.-d. 4.75 4.75

Souvenir Sheet

1036 A196 $6 multicolored 4.75 4.75

Nos. 1177-1186 Overprinted

1989, May 29

1037 A197 10c multicolored .15 .15
1038 A197 30c multicolored .35 .35
1039 A197 40c multicolored .48 .48
1040 A197 60c multicolored .70 .70
1041 A197 $1 multicolored 1.20 1.20
1042 A197 $2 multicolored 2.25 2.25
1043 A197 $3 multicolored 3.50 3.50
1044 A197 $4 multicolored 4.75 4.75
Nos. 1037-1044 (8) 13.38 13.38

Souvenir Sheets

1045 A197 $7 multi (#1185) 5.50 5.50
1046 A197 $7 multi (#1186) 5.50 5.50

Nos. 1187-1196 Overprinted

1989, Sept. 18

1047 A198 25c multicolored .18 .18
1048 A198 45c multicolored .32 .32
1049 A198 50c multicolored .38 .38
1050 A198 60c multicolored .45 .45
1051 A198 75c multicolored .55 .55
1052 A198 90c multicolored .65 .65
1053 A198 $3 multicolored 2.25 2.25
1054 A198 $4 multicolored 3.00 3.00
Nos. 1047-1054 (8) 7.78 7.78

Souvenir Sheets

1055 A198 $6 multi (#1195) 4.50 4.50
1056 A198 $6 multi (#1196) 4.50 4.50

Nos. 1197-1206 Overprinted

1989, Dec. 14 *Perf. 14x13½*

1057 A199 25c multicolored .18 .18
1058 A199 45c multicolored .32 .32
1059 A199 50c multicolored .38 .38
1060 A199 60c multicolored .45 .45
1061 A199 $1 multicolored .75 .75
1062 A199 $2 multicolored 1.50 1.50
1063 A199 $3 multicolored 2.25 2.25
1064 A199 $4 multicolored 3.00 3.00
Nos. 1057-1064 (8) 8.83 8.83

Souvenir Sheets

1065 A199 $5 multi (#1205) 3.75 3.75
1066 A199 $5 multi (#1206) 3.75 3.75

Nos. 1217-1222 Overprinted

1989, Dec. 20 *Perf. 14*

1067 A201 15c multicolored .15 .15
1068 A201 25c multicolored .18 .18
1069 A201 $1 multicolored .75 .75
1070 A201 $4 multicolored 3.00 3.00
Nos. 1067-1070 (4) 4.08 4.08

Souvenir Sheets

1071 A201 $5 multi (#1221) 3.75 3.75
1072 A201 $5 multi (#1222) 3.75 3.75

Nos. 1264-1273 Overprinted

1989, Dec. 20

1073 A208 10c multicolored .15 .15
1074 A208 25c multicolored .18 .18
1075 A208 30c multicolored .22 .22
1076 A208 50c multicolored .38 .38
1077 A208 60c multicolored .45 .45
1078 A208 70c multicolored .52 .52
1079 A208 $4 multicolored 3.00 3.00
1080 A208 $5 multicolored 3.75 3.75
Nos. 1073-1080 (8) 8.65 8.65

Souvenir Sheets

1081 A208 $5 multi (#1272) 3.75 3.75
1082 A208 $5 multi (#1273) 3.75 3.75

Nos. 1223-1232 Overprinted

1990, Feb. 21

1083 A202 10c multicolored .15 .15
1084 A202 25c multicolored .18 .18
1085 A202 50c multicolored .38 .38
1086 A202 60c multicolored .45 .45
1087 A202 75c multicolored .55 .55
1088 A202 $1 multicolored .75 .75
1089 A202 $3 multicolored 2.25 2.25
1090 A202 $4 multicolored 3.00 3.00
Nos. 1083-1090 (8) 7.71 7.71

Souvenir Sheets

1091 A202 $6 multi (#1231) 4.50 4.50
1092 A202 $6 multi (#1232) 4.50 4.50

Nos. 1233-1237 Overprinted

1990, Mar. 30

1093 A203 25c multicolored .18 .18
1094 A203 45c multicolored .32 .32
1095 A203 60c multicolored .45 .45
1096 A203 $4 multicolored 3.00 3.00
Nos. 1093-1096 (4) 3.95 3.95

Souvenir Sheet

1097 A203 $5 multicolored 3.75 3.75

Nos. 1258-1262 Overprinted

1990, Mar. 30

1098 A206 10c multicolored .15 .15
1099 A206 45c multicolored .32 .32
1100 A206 $1 multicolored .75 .75
1101 A206 $4 multicolored 3.00 3.00
Nos. 1098-1101 (4) 4.22 4.22

Souvenir Sheet

1102 A206 $5 multicolored 3.75 3.75

Nos. 1275-1284 Overprinted

1990, June 6

1103 A210 10c multicolored .15 .15
1104 A210 20c multicolored .15 .15
1105 A210 25c multicolored .18 .18
1106 A210 45c multicolored .32 .32
1107 A210 60c multicolored .45 .45
1108 A210 $2 multicolored 1.50 1.50
1109 A210 $3 multicolored 2.25 2.25
1110 A210 $4 multicolored 3.00 3.00
Nos. 1103-1110 (8) 8.00 8.00

Souvenir Sheets

1111 A210 $5 multi (#1283) 3.75 3.75
1112 A210 $5 multi (#1284) 3.75 3.75

Nos. 1285-1294 Overprinted

1990, July 12

1113 A211 15c multicolored .15 .15
1114 A211 45c multicolored .32 .32
1115 A211 50c multicolored .38 .38
1116 A211 60c multicolored .45 .45
1117 A211 $1 multicolored .75 .75
1118 A211 $2 multicolored 1.50 1.50
1119 A211 $3 multicolored 2.25 2.25
1120 A211 $5 multicolored 3.75 3.75
Nos. 1113-1120 (8) 9.55 9.55

Souvenir Sheets

1121 A211 $6 multi (#1293) 4.50 4.50
1122 A211 $6 multi (#1294) 4.50 4.50

Nos. 1295-1304 Overprinted

1990, Aug. 14

1123 A212 10c multicolored .15 .15
1124 A212 15c multicolored .15 .15
1125 A212 50c multicolored .38 .38
1126 A212 60c multicolored .45 .45
1127 A212 $1 multicolored .75 .75
1128 A212 $2 multicolored 1.50 1.50
1129 A212 $3 multicolored 2.25 2.25
1130 A212 $4 multicolored 3.00 3.00
Nos. 1123-1130 (8) 8.63 8.63

Souvenir Sheets

1131 A212 $5 multi (#1303) 3.75 3.75
1132 A212 $5 multi (#1304) 3.75 3.75

Barbuda Nos. 888-889 Surcharged "1st Anniversary / Hurricane Hugo / 16th September, 1989-1990"

1990, Sept. 17 *Perf. 15*

1133 A50 $5 on $7.50 3.75 3.75
1134 A50 $7.50 on $10 5.50 5.50

Nos. 1324-1328 Overprinted

1990, Oct. 12 *Perf. 14*

1135 A217 15c multicolored .15 .15
1136 A217 35c multicolored .28 .28
1137 A217 75c multicolored .55 .55
1138 A217 $3 multicolored 2.25 2.25
Nos. 1135-1138 (4) 3.23 3.23

Souvenir Sheet

1139 A217 $6 multicolored 4.50 4.50

No. 1313 Ovptd. in Silver
Miniature Sheet

1990, Dec. 14

1140 A215 45c Sheet of 20, #a.-t. 6.75 6.75

Nos. 1360-1369 Overprinted

Perf. 14x13½, 13½x14

1990, Dec. 14

1141 A221 25c multicolored .18 .18
1142 A221 30c multicolored .22 .22
1143 A221 40c multicolored .30 .30
1144 A221 60c multicolored .45 .45
1145 A221 $1 multicolored .75 .75
1146 A221 $2 multicolored 1.50 1.50
1147 A221 $4 multicolored 3.00 3.00
1148 A221 $5 multicolored 3.75 3.75
Nos. 1141-1148 (8) 10.15 10.15

Souvenir Sheets

1149 A221 $6 multi (#1368) 4.50 4.50
1150 A221 $6 multi (#1369) 4.50 4.50

Nos. 1305-1308 Overprinted

1991, Feb. 4 *Perf. 15x14*

1151 A213 45c green .35 .35
1152 A213 60c bright rose .45 .45
1153 A213 $5 bright ultra 3.75 3.75
Nos. 1151-1153 (3) 4.55 4.55

Souvenir Sheet

1154 A213 $6 black 4.50 4.50

Nos. 1309-1312 Overprinted

1991, Feb. 4 *Perf. 13½*

1155 A214 50c red & deep grn .38 .38
1156 A214 75c red & vio brn .55 .55
1157 A214 $4 red & brt ultra 3.00 3.00
Nos. 1155-1157 (3) 3.93 3.93

Souvenir Sheet

1158 A214 $6 red & black 4.50 4.50

Birds — B52

1991, Mar. 25 **Litho.** *Perf. 14*

1164 B52 60c Troupial .45 .45
1168 B52 $2 Christmas bird 1.50 1.50
1169 B52 $4 Rose-breasted grosbeak 3.00 3.00
1171 B52 $7 Stolid flycatcher 5.25 5.25
Nos. 1164-1171 (4) 10.20 10.20

This is an expanding set. Numbers will change.

Nos. 1329-1333 Overprinted

1991, Apr. 23 **Litho.** *Perf. 14*

1173 A218 50c multicolored .38 .38
1174 A218 75c multicolored .55 .55
1175 A218 $1 multicolored .75 .75
1176 A218 $5 multicolored 3.75 3.75
Nos. 1173-1176 (4) 5.43 5.43

Souvenir Sheet

1177 A218 $6 multicolored 4.50 4.50

Nos. 1350-1359 Overprinted

1991, Apr. 23

1178 A220 10c multicolored .15 .15
1179 A220 25c multicolored .18 .18
1180 A220 50c multicolored .38 .38
1181 A220 60c multicolored .45 .45
1182 A220 $1 multicolored .75 .75
1183 A220 $2 multicolored 1.50 1.50
1184 A220 $3 multicolored 2.25 2.25
1185 A220 $4 multicolored 3.00 3.00
Nos. 1178-1185 (8) 8.66 8.66

Souvenir Sheets

1186 A220 $6 multi (#1358) 4.50 4.50
1187 A220 $6 multi (#1359) 4.50 4.50

Nos. 1370-1379 Overprinted

1991, June 21 *Perf. 14x13½*

1188 A222 25c multicolored .18 .18
1189 A222 45c multicolored .35 .35
1190 A222 50c multicolored .38 .38
1191 A222 60c multicolored .45 .45
1192 A222 $1 multicolored .75 .75
1193 A222 $2 multicolored 1.50 1.50
1194 A222 $3 multicolored 2.25 2.25
1195 A222 $4 multicolored 3.00 3.00
Nos. 1188-1195 (8) 8.86 8.86

Souvenir Sheets

1196 A222 $6 multi (#1378) 4.50 4.50
1197 A222 $6 multi (#1379) 4.50 4.50

Nos. 1380-1390 Overprinted

1991, July 25 **Litho.** *Perf. 14*

1198 A223 10c multicolored .15 .15
1199 A223 15c multicolored .15 .15
1200 A223 25c multicolored .18 .18
1201 A223 45c multicolored .35 .35
1202 A223 50c multicolored .38 .38
1203 A223 $1 multicolored .75 .75
1204 A223 $2 multicolored 1.50 1.50
1205 A223 $4 multicolored 3.00 3.00
1206 A223 $5 multicolored 3.75 3.75
Nos. 1198-1206 (9) 10.21 10.21

Souvenir Sheets

1207 A223 $6 multi (#1389) 4.50 4.50
1208 A223 $6 multi (#1390) 4.50 4.50

Nos. 1411-1420 Overprinted

1991, Aug. 26 **Litho.** *Perf. 14*

1209 A226 10c multicolored .15 .15
1210 A226 15c multicolored .15 .15
1211 A226 45c multicolored .35 .35
1212 A226 60c multicolored .45 .45
1213 A226 $1 multicolored .75 .75
1214 A226 $2 multicolored 1.50 1.50
1215 A226 $4 multicolored 3.00 3.00
1216 A226 $5 multicolored 3.75 3.75
Nos. 1209-1216 (8) 10.10 10.10

Souvenir Sheets

1217 A226 $6 multi (#1419) 4.50 4.50
1218 A226 $6 multi (#1420) 4.50 4.50

Nos. 1401-1410 Overprinted

1991, Oct. 18

1219 A225 10c multicolored .15 .15
1220 A225 35c multicolored .26 .26
1221 A225 50c multicolored .38 .38
1222 A225 75c multicolored .55 .55
1223 A225 $1 multicolored .75 .75
1224 A225 $2 multicolored 1.50 1.50
1225 A225 $4 multicolored 3.00 3.00
1226 A225 $5 multicolored 3.75 3.75
Nos. 1219-1226 (8) 10.34 10.34

Souvenir Sheets

1227 A225 $6 multi (#1409) 4.50 4.50
1228 A225 $6 multi (#1410) 4.50 4.50

Nos. 1446-1455 Overprinted

1991, Nov. 18

1229 CD347 10c multicolored .15 .15
1230 CD347 15c multicolored .15 .15
1231 CD347 20c multicolored .15 .15
1232 CD347 40c multicolored .30 .30
1233 CD347 $1 multicolored .75 .75
1234 CD347 $2 multicolored 1.50 1.50
1235 CD347 $4 multicolored 3.00 3.00
1236 CD347 $5 multicolored 3.75 3.75
Nos. 1229-1236 (8) 9.75 9.75

Souvenir Sheets

1237 CD347 $4 multi (#1454) 3.00 3.00
1238 CD347 $4 multi (#1455) 3.00 3.00

Nos. 1503-1510 Overprinted

1991, Dec. 24 *Perf. 12*

1239 A238 10c multicolored .15 .15
1240 A238 30c multicolored .22 .22
1241 A238 40c multicolored .30 .30
1242 A238 60c multicolored .45 .45
1243 A238 $1 multicolored .75 .75
1244 A238 $3 multicolored 2.25 2.25
1245 A238 $4 multicolored 3.00 3.00
1246 A238 $5 multicolored 3.75 3.75
Nos. 1239-1246 (8) 10.87 10.87

Nos. 1421-1435 Overprinted

1992, Feb. 20 *Perf. 13½*

1249 A227 5c multicolored .15 .15
1250 A227 10c multicolored .15 .15
1251 A227 15c multicolored .15 .15
1252 A227 25c multicolored .18 .18
1253 A227 30c multicolored .22 .22
1254 A227 40c multicolored .30 .30
1255 A227 50c multicolored .38 .38
1256 A227 75c multicolored .55 .55
1257 A227 $2 multicolored 1.50 1.50
1258 A227 $3 multicolored 2.25 2.25
1259 A227 $4 multicolored 3.00 3.00
1260 A227 $5 multicolored 3.75 3.75
Nos. 1249-1260 (12) 12.58 12.58

Size: 102x76mm

Imperf

1261 A227 $5 multi (#1433) 3.75 3.75
1262 A227 $5 multi (#1434) 3.75 3.75
1263 A227 $6 multi 4.50 4.50

Nos. 1476-1483 Overprinted

1992, Apr. 7 **Litho.** *Perf. 14*

1264 A231 10c multi .15 .15
1265 A231 15c multi, vert. .15 .15
1266 A231 45c multi, vert. .35 .35
1267 A231 60c multi, vert. .45 .45
1268 A231 $1 multi .75 .75
1269 A231 $2 multi 1.50 1.50
1270 A231 $4 multi 3.00 3.00
1271 A231 $5 multi, vert. 3.75 3.75
Nos. 1264-1271 (8) 10.10 10.10

Nos. 1484-1485 Overprinted

1992, Apr. 7 **Litho.** *Perf. 14*

Souvenir Sheets

1272 A231 $6 multi (#1484) 5.00 5.00
1273 A231 $6 multi (#1485) 5.00 5.00

Nos. 1551-1560 Overprinted

1992, Apr. 16 **Litho.** *Perf. 14x13½*

1274 A242 10c multicolored .15 .15
1275 A242 15c multicolored .15 .15
1276 A242 30c multicolored .25 .25
1277 A242 40c multicolored .35 .35
1278 A242 $1 multicolored .85 .85
1279 A242 $2 multicolored 1.65 1.65

1280 A242 $4 multicolored 3.30 3.30
1281 A242 $5 multicolored 4.15 4.15
Nos. 1274-1281 (8) 10.85 10.85

Souvenir Sheets

1282 A242 $6 multi (#1559) 5.00 5.00
1283 A242 $6 multi (#1560) 5.00 5.00

Nos. 1489-1492 Overprinted

1992, June 19 Litho. ***Perf. 14***

1284 A234 75c multi .55 .55
1285 A234 $2 multi, vert. 1.50 1.50
1286 A234 $3.50 multi 2.65 2.65
Nos. 1284-1286 (3) 4.70 4.70

Souvenir Sheet

1287 A234 $5 multi, vert. 4.25 4.25

Nos. 1493-1494 Overprinted

1992, June 19

1288 A235 $1.50 multi 1.10 1.10
1289 A235 $4 multi 3.00 3.00

Nos. 1495-1496 Overprinted

1992, June 19

1290 A236 $2 multi 1.50 1.50
1291 A236 $2.50 multi, vert. 1.90 1.90

Nos. 1499-1502 Overprinted

1992, June 19

1292 A237 25c multicolored .18 .18
1293 A237 $2 multicolored 1.50 1.50
1294 A237 $3 multicolored 2.25 2.25
1295 A237 $4 multicolored 3.50 3.50
Nos. 1292-1295 (4) 7.43 7.43

Nos. 1571-1578 Overprinted

1992, Oct. 12 Litho. ***Perf. 14***

1296 A244 15c multicolored .15 .15
1297 A244 30c multicolored .22 .22
1298 A244 40c multicolored .30 .30
1299 A244 $1 multicolored .75 .75
1300 A244 $2 multicolored 1.50 1.50
1301 A244 $4 multicolored 3.00 3.00
Nos. 1296-1301 (6) 5.92 5.92

Souvenir Sheets

1302 A244 $6 multicolored 4.50 4.50
1303 A244 $6 multicolored 4.50 4.50

Nos. 1599-1600 Overprinted

1992, Oct. 12 ***Perf. 14½***

1304 A247 $1 multicolored .75 .75
1305 A247 $2 multicolored 1.50 1.50

Nos. 1513-1518 Overprinted

1992, Nov. 3 ***Perf. 14***

1306 CD348 10c multicolored .15 .15
1307 CD348 30c multicolored .22 .22
1308 CD348 $1 multicolored .75 .75
1309 CD348 $5 multicolored 3.75 3.75
Nos. 1306-1309 (4) 4.87 4.87

Souvenir Sheets

1310 CD348 $6 multi (#1517) 4.50 4.50
1311 CD348 $6 multi (#1518) 4.50 4.50

Nos. 1541-1550 Ovptd. "BARBUDA / MAIL"

1992, Dec. 8

1312 A241 10c multicolored .15 .15
1313 A241 15c multicolored .15 .15
1314 A241 30c multicolored .22 .22
1315 A241 50c multicolored .38 .38
1316 A241 $1 multicolored .75 .75
1317 A241 $2 multicolored 1.50 1.50
1318 A241 $4 multicolored 3.00 3.00
1319 A241 $5 multicolored 3.75 3.75
Nos. 1312-1319 (8) 9.90 9.90

Souvenir Sheets

1320 A241 $6 multi (#1549) 5.50 5.50
1321 A241 $6 multi (#1550) 5.50 5.50

Nos. 1608-1617 Ovptd. "BARBUDA MAIL"

1992, Dec. 8 Litho. ***Perf. 13½x14***

1322 A251 10c multicolored .15 .15
1323 A251 25c multicolored .18 .18
1324 A251 30c multicolored .22 .22
1325 A251 40c multicolored .30 .30
1326 A251 60c multicolored .45 .45
1327 A251 $1 multicolored .75 .75
1328 A251 $4 multicolored 3.00 3.00
1329 A251 $5 multicolored 3.75 3.75
Nos. 1322-1329 (8) 8.80 8.80

Souvenir Sheets

1330 A251 $6 multi (#1616) 5.50 5.50
1331 A251 $6 multi (#1617) 5.50 5.50

No. 1601 Ovptd. "BARBUDA MAIL"

1992 Litho. ***Perf. 14***

Souvenir Sheet

1332 A248 $6 multicolored 4.50 4.50

Nos. 1519-1528 Ovptd.

1993, Jan. 25 Litho. ***Perf. 14***

1333 A239 10c multicolored .15 .15
1334 A239 15c multicolored .15 .15
1335 A239 30c multicolored .28 .28
1336 A239 40c multicolored .35 .35
1337 A239 $1 multicolored .90 .90
1338 A239 $2 multicolored 1.80 1.80
1339 A239 $4 multicolored 3.50 3.50
1340 A239 $5 multicolored 4.50 4.50
Nos. 1332-1339 (8) 11.63 11.63

Souvenir Sheets

1341 A239 $6 multi (#1527) 5.50 5.50
1342 A239 $6 multi (#1528) 5.50 5.50

Nos. 1561-1570 Ovptd.

1993, Mar. 22 Litho. ***Perf. 13***

1343 A243 10c multicolored .15 .15
1344 A243 15c multicolored .15 .15
1345 A243 30c multicolored .22 .22
1346 A243 40c multicolored .30 .30
1347 A243 $1 multicolored .75 .75
1348 A243 $2 multicolored 1.50 1.50
1349 A243 $4 multicolored 3.00 3.00
1350 A243 $5 multicolored 3.75 3.75
Nos. 1343-1350 (8) 9.82 9.82

Imperf

Size: 120x95mm

1351 A243 $6 multi (#1569) 5.50 5.50
1352 A243 $6 multi (#1570) 5.50 5.50

Nos. 1589-1598 Ovptd.

1993, May 10 Litho. ***Perf. 14***

1353 A246 10c multicolored .15 .15
1354 A246 25c multicolored .18 .18
1355 A246 45c multicolored .35 .35
1356 A246 60c multicolored .45 .45
1357 A246 $1 multicolored .75 .75
1358 A246 $2 multicolored 1.50 1.50
1359 A246 $4 multicolored 3.00 3.00
1360 A246 $5 multicolored 3.75 3.75
Nos. 1353-1360 (8) 10.13 10.13

Souvenir Sheets

1361 A246 $6 multi (#1597) 5.50 5.50
1362 A246 $6 multi (#1598) 5.50 5.50

Nos. 1603-1608 Ovptd.

1993, June 29 Litho. ***Perf. 14***

1363 A250 10c multicolored .15 .15
1364 A250 25c multicolored .22 .22
1365 A250 30c multicolored .28 .28
1366 A250 40c multicolored .35 .35
1367 A250 60c multicolored .55 .55
1368 A250 $1 multicolored .90 .90
1369 A250 $4 multicolored 3.60 3.60
1370 A250 $5 multicolored 4.50 4.50
Nos. 1363-1370 (8) 10.55 10.55

Souvenir Sheets

1371 A250 $6 multi (#1607) 5.50 5.50
1372 A250 $6 multi (#1608) 5.50 5.50

Nos. 1619-1632 Ovptd.

1993, Aug. 16 Litho. ***Perf. 14***

1373 A252 10c multicolored .15 .15
1374 A252 40c multicolored .30 .30
1375 A253 45c multicolored .35 .35
1376 A252 75c multicolored .58 .58
1377 A252 $1 multicolored .75 .75
1378 A252 $1.50 multicolored 1.15 1.15
1379 A252 $2 multicolored 1.50 1.50
1380 A253 $2 multi (#1626) 1.50 1.50
1381 A253 $2 multi (#1627) 1.50 1.50
1382 A252 $2.25 multicolored 1.70 1.70
1383 A252 $3 multicolored 2.25 2.25
1384 A252 $4 multi (#1630) 3.00 3.00
1385 A252 $4 multi (#1631) 3.00 3.00
1386 A252 $6 multicolored 4.50 4.50
Nos. 1373-1386 (14) 22.23 22.23

Numbers have been reserved for four souvenir sheets in this set.

Nos. 1650-1657 Ovptd.

1993, Sept. 21 Litho. ***Perf. 14***

1391 A256 15c multicolored .15 .15
1392 A256 25c multicolored .18 .18
1393 A256 30c multicolored .22 .22
1394 A256 40c multicolored .30 .30
1395 A256 $1 multicolored .75 .75
1396 A256 $2 multicolored 1.50 1.50
1397 A256 $4 multicolored 3.00 3.00
1398 A256 $5 multicolored 3.75 3.75
Nos. 1391-1398 (8) 9.85 9.85

Numbers have been reserved for two souvenir sheets with this set.

No. 1660 Ovptd.

1993, Nov. 11 Litho. ***Perf. 14***

1401 A257 $1 Sheet of 12, #a.-l. 9.00 9.00

Numbers have been reserved for two souvenir sheets in this set.

Nos. 1697-1710 Ovptd.

1994, Mar. 3 Litho. ***Perf. 14***

1404-1415 A267 $2 Set of 12 18.00 18.00

Souvenir Sheets

1416-1417 A267 $6 each 4.50 4.50

Nos. 1676-1678 Ovptd.

1994, Apr. 21 Litho. ***Perf. 14***

1418 A260 40c multicolored .30 .30
1419 A260 $3 multicolored 2.25 2.25

Souvenir Sheet

1420 A260 $6 multicolored 4.50 4.50

Nos. 1679-1682 Ovptd.

1994, Apr. 21

1421-1423 A261 Set of 3 4.50 4.50

Souvenir Sheet

1424 A261 $6 multicolored 4.50 4.50

Nos. 1683-1685 Ovptd.

1994, Apr. 21

1425 A262 40c multicolored .32 .32
1426 A262 $4 multicolored 3.25 3.25

Souvenir Sheet

1427 A262 $5 multicolored 3.75 3.75

Nos. 1686-1688 Ovptd.

1994, Apr. 21

1428 A263 30c multicolored .25 .25
1429 A263 $4 multicolored 3.25 3.25

Souvenir Sheet

1430 A263 $6 multicolored 4.50 4.50

Nos. 1692-1693 Ovptd.

1994, Apr. 21

1431 A265 $5 multicolored 4.00 4.00

Souvenir Sheet

1432 A265 $6 multicolored 4.50 4.50

Nos. 1694-1696 Ovptd.

1994, Apr. 21

1433 A266 15c multicolored .15 .15
1434 A266 $5 multicolored 4.00 4.00

Souvenir Sheet

1435 A266 $6 multicolored 4.50 4.50

Nos. 1732-1735 Ovptd.

1994, Apr. 21

1436-1439 A270 Set of 4 1.10 1.10

Nos. 1711-1720 Ovptd.

1994, June 15

1440-1446 A268 Set of 7 12.00 12.00

Souvenir Sheets

1447-1449 A268 $6 each 4.50 4.50

Nos. 1736-1741 Ovptd.

1994, June 15

1450-1453 A271 30c Set of 4 7.25 7.25

Souvenir Sheets

1454-1455 A271 $6 each 4.50 4.50

Nos. 1689-1691 Ovptd.

1994, Sept. 21 Litho. ***Perf. 14***

1456 A264 $1 multicolored .75 .75
1457 A264 $3 multicolored 2.25 2.25

Souvenir Sheet

1458 A264 $6 multicolored 4.50 4.50

Nos. 1786-1795 Ovptd.

1994, Sept. 21 Litho. ***Perf. 14***

1459-1466 A279 Set of 8 10.00 10.00

Souvenir Sheets

1467-1468 A279 $6 each 4.50 4.50

Nos. 1776-1779 Ovptd.

1994, Nov. 3 Litho. ***Perf. 14***

1469 A277 $1.50 multi (#1776) 9.00 9.00
1470 A277 $1.50 multi (#1777) 9.00 9.00

Souvenir Sheets

1471 A277 $1.50 multi (#1778) 1.10 1.10
1472 A277 $1.50 multi (#1779) 1.10 1.10

Nos. 1835-1842 Ovptd.

1995, Jan. 12 Litho. ***Perf. 14***

1473-1478 A291 Set of 6 8.50 8.50

Souvenir Sheets

1479 A291 $6 multi (#1841) 4.50 4.50
1480 A291 $6 multi (#1842) 4.50 4.50

Nos. 1857-1866 Ovptd.

1995, Jan. 12 Litho. ***Perf. 14***

1481-1488 A295 Set of 8 6.75 6.75

Souvenir Sheets

Perf. 13½x14

1489 A295 $6 multi (#1865) 4.50 4.50
1490 A295 $6 multi (#1866) 4.50 4.50

Nos. 1829-1834 Ovptd.

1996, Feb. 14 Litho. ***Perf. 14***

1491 A290 75c multi (#1829) 5.50 5.50
1492 A290 75c multi (#1830) 5.50 5.50
1493 A290 75c multi (#1831) 5.50 5.50

Souvenir Sheets

1494 A290 $6 multi (#1832) 5.50 5.50
1495 A290 $6 multi (#1833) 5.50 5.50
1496 A290 $6 multi (#1834) 5.50 5.50

Nos. 1867-1881 Ovptd.

1995 Litho. ***Perf. 14½x14***

1497 A296 15c multi (#1867) .15 .15
1498 A296 25c multi (#1868) .20 .20
1499 A296 35c multi (#1869) .30 .30
1500 A296 40c multi (#1870) .35 .35
1501 A296 45c multi (#1871) .40 .40
1502 A296 60c multi (#1872) .55 .55
1503 A296 65c multi (#1873) .60 .60
1504 A296 70c multi (#1873) .65 .65
1505 A296 75c multi (#1874) .70 .70
1506 A296 90c multi (#1875) .80 .80
1507 A296 $1.20 multi (#1876) 1.10 1.10
1508 A296 $2 multi (#1877) 1.80 1.80
1509 A296 $5 multi (#1878) 4.50 4.50
1510 A296 $10 multi (#1879) 9.00 9.00
1511 A296 $20 multi (#1880) 18.00 18.00
Nos. 1497-1511 (15) 39.10 39.10

Nos. 1806-1808 Ovptd.

1996, Jan. 22 Litho. ***Perf. 14***

1512 A281 50c Sheet of 9, #a.-i. 3.50 3.50

Souvenir Sheets

1513 A281 $6 multi (#1807) 4.50 4.50
1514 A281 $6 multi (#1808) 4.50 4.50

Nos. 1949-1956 Ovptd.

1996, Jan. 22 ***Perf. 13½x14***

1515-1520 A314 Set of 6 6.75 6.75

Souvenir Sheets

1521 A314 $5 multi (#1955) 3.75 3.75
1522 A314 $6 multi (#1956) 4.50 4.50

Nos. 1810-1813 Ovptd.

1995, Sept. 29 Litho. ***Perf. 14***

1546-1548 A283 Set of 3 4.00 4.00

Souvenir Sheet

1549 A283 $6 multi (on #1813) 5.50 5.50

Nos. 1848, 1851, 1854-1856 Ovptd.

1996, Feb. 14 Litho. ***Perf. 14***

1553 A294 15c multi (#1848) .15 .15
1554 A294 $1 multi (#1851) .75 .75
1555 A294 $4 multi (#1854) 3.00 3.00
Nos. 1553-1555 (3) 3.90 3.90

Souvenir Sheets

1556 A294 $6 multi (#1855) 4.50 4.50
1557 A294 $6 multi (#1856) 4.50 4.50

Nos. 1882-1890 Ovptd.

1996, June 13 Litho. ***Perf. 14***

1558-1563 A297 Set of 6 7.50 7.50
1564 A297 75c Sheet of 12, #a.-l. 8.25 8.25

Souvenir Sheets

1565 A297 $6 multi (#1889) 5.50 5.50
1566 A297 $6 multi (#1890) 5.50 5.50

Nos. 1891-1898 Ovptd.

1996, July 16 Litho. ***Perf. 14***

1567-1572 A298 Set of 6 7.00 7.00

Souvenir Sheets

1573 A298 $6 multi (#1897) 5.10 5.10
1574 A298 $6 multi (#1898) 5.10 5.10

Nos. 1930-1933 Ovptd.

1996, Sept. 10

1575-1576 A310 Strip of 3, #a.-c., each 3.10 3.10

Souvenir Sheets

1577 A310 $6 multi (#1932) 5.10 5.10
1578 A310 $6 multi (#1933) 5.10 5.10

Nos. 1945-1948 Ovptd.

1996, Oct. 25 Litho. ***Perf. 14***

1579 A313 $1 Sheet of 9, #a.-i. (#1945) 8.00 8.00
1580 A313 $1 Sheet of 9, #a.-i. (#1946) 8.00 8.00

Souvenir Sheets

1581 A313 $6 multi (#1947) 5.25 5.25
1582 A313 $6 multi (#1948) 5.25 5.25

Nos. 2001-2002 Ovptd.
1996, Nov. 14   Perf. 13½x14
1583 A323 $2 Strip of 3, #a.-c.   5.25 5.25
Souvenir Sheet
1584 A323 $6 multicolored   5.25 5.25

Nos. 2018-2025 Ovptd.
1997, Jan. 28   Litho.   Perf. 13½x14
1585-1590 A328 Set of 6   6.50 6.50
Souvenir Sheets
1591 A328 $6 multi (#2024)   5.50 5.50
1592 A328 $6 multi (#2025)   5.50 5.50

Nos. 1905-1906 Ovptd.
1997, Feb. 24   Perf. 14
1593 A301 Strip of 3, #a.-c.   2.60 2.60
Souvenir Sheet
1594 A301 $6 multicolored   5.50 5.50

Nos. 1907-1908 Ovptd.
1997, Feb. 24
1595 A302 $5 multicolored   4.50 4.50
Souvenir Sheet
1596 A302 $6 multicolored   5.50 5.50

Nos. 1899-1902 Ovptd.
Sheets of 6 or 8 + Label
1997, Apr. 4   Litho.   Perf. 14
1597 A299 $1.20 #a.-f.   6.50 6.50
1598 A299 $1.20 #a.-h.   8.50 8.50
Souvenir Sheets
1599 A299 $3 multicolored   2.75 2.75
1600 A299 $6 multicolored   5.50 5.50

Nos. 1903-1904 Ovptd.
1997   Litho.   Perf. 14
1601 A300 Strip of 3, #a.-c.   2.50 2.50
Souvenir Sheet
1602 A300 $6 multicolored   5.50 5.50

Nos. 1909-1910 Ovptd.
1997   Perf. 13½x14
1603 A303 $1.50 Strip or block of 4, #a.-d.   5.50 5.50
Souvenir Sheet
1604 A303 $6 multicolored   5.50 5.50

Nos. 1913-1917 Ovptd.
1997   Litho.   Perf. 14
1605-1608 A305 Set of 4   5.00 5.00
Souvenir Sheet
1609 A305 $6 multicolored   5.50 5.50

Nos. 1918-1919 Ovptd.
1997
1610 A306 45c Sheet of 12, #a.-l.   4.75 4.75
Souvenir Sheet
1611 A306 $6 multicolored   5.50 5.50

Nos. 1928-1929 Ovptd.
1997
1612 A309 75c Sheet of 12, #a.-l.   8.00 8.00
Souvenir Sheet
1613 A309 $6 multicolored   5.50 5.50

Nos. 1934-1942 Ovptd.
1997, May 30   Litho.   Perf. 14
1614-1619 A311 Set of 6   7.50 7.50
Sheet of 9
1620 A311 $1.20 #a.-i.   8.25 8.25
Souvenir Sheets
1621 A311 $6 multi (#1941)   4.50 4.50
1621A A311 $6 multi (#1942)   4.50 4.50

Nos. 1911-1912 Ovptd.
1997   Litho.   Perf. 14
1622 A304 75c Sheet of 12, #a.-l.   8.00 8.00
Souvenir Sheet
1623 A304 $6 multicolored   5.50 5.50

Nos. 1943-1944 Ovptd.
1997
1624 A312 75c Sheet of 12, #a.-l.   8.00 8.00
Souvenir Sheet
1625 A312 $6 multicolored   5.50 5.50

Nos. 1967-1970 Ovptd.
1997
1626-1627 A317 75c Strips of 4, #a.-d., each   2.75 2.75

Souvenir Sheets
1628 A317 $6 multi (#1969)   5.50 5.50
1629 A317 $6 multi (#1970)   5.50 5.50

Nos. 1970A-1974 Ovptd.
1997, Nov. 3   Litho.   Perf. 14
1629A-1629F A318 Set of 6   2.50 2.50
Sheets of 6
1629G A318 $1.20 #k.-p. (#1971)   5.50 5.50
1629H A318 $1.50 #q.-v. (#1972)   6.75 6.75
Souvenir Sheets
1629I A318 $6 multi (#1973)   4.50 4.50
1629J A318 $6 multi (#1974)   4.50 4.50

Nos. 2111-2118 Ovptd.
1997   Litho.   Perf. 14
1630-1635 A345 Set of 6   5.25 5.25
Souvenir Sheets
1636 A345 $6 multi (#2117)   4.50 4.50
1637 A345 $6 multi (#2118)   4.50 4.50

Nos. 2069-2070
1997, Nov. 3   Litho.   Perf. 14
Sheet of 6
1637A A337 $1 #c.-h. (#2069)   4.50 4.50
Souvenir Sheet
1637B A337 $6 multi (#2070)   4.50 4.50

Nos. 1983-1986 Ovptd.
1998   Litho.   Perf. 14
1640 A320 75c Vert. strip, #a.-d. (#1983)   2.75 2.75
1641 A320 75c Vert. strip, #a.-d. (#1984)   2.75 2.75
Souvenir Sheets
1643 A320 $5 multicolored   4.50 4.50
1644 A320 $6 multicolored   5.50 5.50

Nos. 2003-2004 Ovptd.
1998   Litho.   Perf. 14
1645 A324 60c Block of 4, #a.-d.   2.00 2.00
Souvenir Sheet
1646 A324 $6 multi   5.25 5.25

Nos. 2094-2102 Ovptd.
1998
1647-1652 A342 Set of 6   5.75 5.75
1653 A342 $1 Sheet of 8 + label   6.75 6.75
Souvenir Sheets
1654 A342 $6 multi (#2101)   5.25 5.25
1655 A342 $6 multi (#2102)   5.25 5.25

Nos. 2005-2008 Ovptd.
1998   Litho.   Perf. 14
1656-1658 A325 Set of 3   2.50 2.50
Souvenir Sheet
1659 A325 $6 multicolored   5.25 5.25

Nos. 2009-2012 Ovptd.
1998
1660-1662 A326 Set of 3   2.50 2.50
Souvenir Sheet
1663 A326 $6 multicolored   5.25 5.25

Nos. 2119-2122 Ovptd.
1998   Litho.   Perf. 14
Sheets of 6
1664 A346 $1.65 #a.-f. (#2119)   8.50 8.50
1665 A346 $1.65 #a.-f. (#2120)   8.50 8.50
Souvenir Sheets
1666 A346 $6 multi (#2121)   5.25 5.25
1667 A346 $6 multi (#2122)   5.25 5.25

SEMI-POSTAL STAMP

Catalogue values for unused stamps in this section are for Never Hinged items.

Barbuda No. 501 Crudely Surcharged

S. Atlantic Fund + 50c

1982, June 28
Self-Adhesive
B1 CD331 Booklet   16.00

BASUTOLAND
bə-ˈsü-tə-ˌland

LOCATION — An enclave in the state of South Africa
GOVT. — Former British Crown Colony
AREA — 11,716 sq. mi.
POP. — 733,000 (est. 1964)
CAPITAL — Maseru

The Colony, a former independent native state, was annexed to the Cape Colony in 1871. In 1883 control was transferred directly to the British Crown. Stamps of the Cape of Good Hope were used from 1871 to 1910 and those of the Union of South Africa from 1910 to 1933. Basutoland became the independent state of Lesotho on Oct. 4, 1966.

12 Pence = 1 Shilling
100 Cents = 1 Rand (1961)

Catalogue values for unused stamps in this country are for Never Hinged items, beginning with Scott 29 in the regular postage section and Scott J1 in the postage due section.

George V — A1
George VI — A2 

Crocodile and River Scene

Perf. 12½
1933, Dec. 1   Engr.   Wmk. 4
1 A1 ½p emerald   .20 .60
2 A1 1p carmine   .30 .20
3 A1 2p red violet   .50 1.10
4 A1 3p ultra   .50 1.75
5 A1 4p slate   1.75 2.50
6 A1 6p yellow   2.25 2.50
7 A1 1sh red orange   3.50 5.25
8 A1 2sh6p dk brown   17.50 22.50
9 A1 5sh violet   35.00 50.00
10 A1 10sh olive green   100.00 125.00
Nos. 1-10 (10)   161.50 211.40

Common Design Types pictured following the introduction.

Silver Jubilee Issue
Common Design Type
1935, May 4   Perf. 13½x14
11 CD301 1p car & blue   .25 .25
12 CD301 2p gray blk & ultra   .60 2.00
13 CD301 3p blue & brown   2.50 3.25
14 CD301 6p brt vio & indigo   3.50 6.50
Nos. 11-14 (4)   6.85 12.00
Set, never hinged   14.50

Coronation Issue
Common Design Type
1937, May 12   Perf. 13½x14
15 CD302 1p carmine   .15 .15
16 CD302 2p rose violet   .30 .30
17 CD302 3p bright ultra   .40 .40
Nos. 15-17 (3)   .85 .85
Set, never hinged   1.40

1938, Apr. 1   Perf. 12½
18 A2 ½p emerald   .30 .30
19 A2 1p rose car   .30 .15
20 A2 1½p light blue   .30 .20
21 A2 2p rose lilac   .30 .30
22 A2 3p ultra   .35 .35
23 A2 4p gray   .45 1.25
24 A2 6p yel ocher   .55 .60
25 A2 1sh red orange   .75 .85
26 A2 2sh6p black brown   2.75 2.75
27 A2 5sh violet   11.00 11.00
28 A2 10sh olive green   15.00 17.00
Nos. 18-28 (11)   32.05 34.75
Set, never hinged   60.00

Catalogue values for unused stamps in this section, from this point to the end of the section, are for Never Hinged items.

Peace Issue
South Africa Nos. 100-102 Overprinted **Basutoland**

Basic stamps inscribed alternately in English and Afrikaans.

1945, Dec. 3   Wmk. 201   Perf. 14
29 A42 1p rose pink & choc, pair   .25 .25
   a. Single, English   .15 .15
   b. Single, Afrikaans   .15 .15
30 A43 2p vio & slate blue, pair   .30 .30
   a. Single, English   .15 .15
   b. Single, Afrikaans   .15 .15
31 A43 3p ultra & dp ultra, pair   .45 .45
   a. Single, English   .15 .15
   b. Single, Afrikaans   .15 .15
Nos. 29-31 (3)   1.00 1.00

King George VI — A3
King George VI and Queen Elizabeth — A4 
Princess Margaret Rose and Princess Elizabeth — A5 
Royal British Family — A6 

Perf. 12½
1947, Feb. 17   Wmk. 4   Engr.
35 A3 1p red   .15 .15
36 A4 2p green   .15 .15
37 A5 3p ultra   .15 .15
38 A6 1sh dark violet   .25 .25
Nos. 35-38 (4)   .70 .70

Visit of the British Royal Family, Mar. 11-12, 1947.

Silver Wedding Issue
Common Design Types
1948, Dec. 1   Photo.   Perf. 14x14½
39 CD304 1½p brt ultra   .15 .15
Engr.; Name Typo.
Perf. 11½
40 CD305 10sh dk brown olive   40.00 32.00

UPU Issue
Common Design Types
Engr.; Name Typo. on 3p, 6p
Perf. 13½, 11x11½
1949, Oct. 10   Wmk. 4
41 CD306 1½p blue   .30 .30
42 CD307 3p indigo   .75 .65
43 CD308 6p orange yel   1.00 .90
44 CD309 1sh red brown   1.10 1.10
Nos. 41-44 (4)   3.15 2.95

Coronation Issue
Common Design Type
1953, June 3   Engr.   Perf. 13½x13
45 CD312 2p red violet & black   .25 .25

Qiloane Hill — A7
Shearing Angora Goats — A8 

Designs: 1p, Orange River. 2p, Mosotho horseman. 3p, Basuto household. 4½p, Maletsunyane falls. 6p, Herdboy with lesiba. 1sh, Pastoral scene. 1sh3p, Plane at Lancers Gap. 2sh6p, Old Fort Leribe. 5sh, Mission cave house.

1954, Oct. 18 Wmk. 4 *Perf. 13½*

46	A7	½p dk brown & gray	.15	.15
47	A7	1p dp grn & gray blk	.15	.15
48	A7	2p org & dp blue	.30	.25
49	A7	3p car & ol green	.35	.30
50	A7	4½p dp blue & ind	.80	.65
51	A7	6p dk grn & org brn	.75	.60
52	A7	1sh rose vio & dk ol green	1.40	1.10
53	A7	1sh3p aqua & brown	1.75	1.40
54	A7	2sh6p lilac rose & dp ultra	6.25	5.00
55	A7	5sh dp car & black	9.00	7.50
56	A8	10sh dp cl & black	19.00	15.00
		Nos. 46-56 (11)	39.90	32.10

See Nos. 72-82, 87-91. For surcharges see Nos. 57, 61-71.

No. 48 Surcharged ½d. ■

1959, Aug. 1

57	A7	½p on 2p org & dp blue	.20	.20

Chief Moshoeshoe (Moshesh) — A9

Designs: 1sh, Council chamber. 1sh3p, Mosotho on horseback.

Perf. 13x13½

1959, Dec. 15 Wmk. 314

58	A9	3p lt yel, grn & blk	.15	.15
59	A9	1sh green & pink	.35	.35
60	A9	1sh3p orange & ultra	.60	.60
		Nos. 58-60 (3)	1.10	1.10

Institution of the Basutoland National Council.

Nos. 46-56 Surcharged with New Value

2½c I 2½c II 3½c I 3½c II

5c I 5c II 10c I 10c II

12½c I 12½c II

25c I 25c II 25c III

50c I 50c II R1 I R1 II R1 III

1961, Feb. 14 Wmk. 4 *Perf. 13½*

61	A7	½c on ½p dk brn & gray	.15	.15
a.		Double surcharge	250.00	
62	A7	1c on 1p dp grn & gray blk	.15	.15
63	A7	2c on 2p org & dp bl	.15	.15
a.		Inverted surcharge	125.00	
64	A7	2½c on 3p (II)	.15	.15
a.		Type I	.15	.15
b.		Inverted surcharge (II)	1,750.	1,000.
65	A7	3½c on 4½p (I)	.15	.15
a.		Type II	4.50	4.50
66	A7	5c on 6p (II)	.15	.15
a.		Type I	.15	.15
67	A7	10c on 1sh (I)	.20	.20
a.		Type II	40.00	40.00
68	A7	12½c on 1sh3p (II)	.35	.35
a.		Type I	.65	.65
69	A7	25c on 2sh6p (I)	.65	.65
a.		Type II	12.00	12.00
b.		Type III	.65	.65
70	A7	50c on 5sh (II)	1.40	1.40
a.		Type I	2.25	2.25
71	A8	1r on 10sh (III)	2.75	2.75
a.		Type I	12.00	12.00
b.		Type II	12.00	12.00
		Nos. 61-71 (11)	6.25	6.25

Surcharge types on Nos. 64-71 are numbered chronologically.

Types of 1954
Value in Cents and Rands

Designs: ½c, Qiloane Hill. 1c, Orange River. 2c, Mosotho horseman. 2½c, Basuto household. 3½c, Maletsunyane Falls. 5c, Herdboy with lesiba. 10c, Pastoral scene. 12½c, Plane at Lancers Gap. 25c, Old Fort Leribe. 50c, Mission cave house. 1r, Shearing Angora goats.

1961-63 Wmk. 4 Engr. *Perf. 13½*

72	A7	½c dk brn & gray ('62)	.15	.15
73	A7	1c dp grn & gray blk ('62)	.15	.15
74	A7	2c org & dp bl ('62)	.15	.15
75	A7	2½c car & ol grn	.45	.15
76	A7	3½c dp bl & ind ('62)	.40	.15
77	A7	5c dk grn & org brn ('62)	.60	.30
78	A7	10c rose vio & dk ol ('62)	.95	.40
79	A7	12½c aqua & brn ('62)	1.25	.55
80	A7	25c lilac rose & dp ultra ('62)	2.25	1.00
81	A7	50c dp car & blk ('62)	9.00	4.00
		Perf. 11½		
82	A8	1r dp cl & blk ('63)	15.00	6.50
		Nos. 72-82 (11)	30.35	13.50

See Nos. 87-91. For overprints on stamps and types see Lesotho Nos. 5-14, 20a.

Freedom from Hunger Issue
Common Design Type
Perf. 14x14½

1963, June 4 Photo. Wmk. 314

83	CD314	12½c lilac	.50	.40

Red Cross Centenary Issue
Common Design Type

1963, Sept. 2 Litho. *Perf. 13*

84	CD315	2½c black & red	.20	.15
85	CD315	12½c ultra & red	.70	.70

Queen Type of 1961-63

1964 Engr. *Perf. 13½*

87	A7	1c grn & gray blk	.15	.15
88	A7	2½c car & ol green	.30	.15
89	A7	5c dk green & org brn	.70	.60
90	A7	12½c aqua & brown	1.50	1.40
91	A7	50c dp car & black	6.00	4.75
		Nos. 87-91 (5)	8.65	7.05

Mosotho Woman and Child — A10

Designs: 3½c, Maseru border post. 5c, Mountains. 12½c, Legislative Building.

Perf. 14x13½

1965, May 10 Photo. Wmk. 314

97	A10	2½c ultra & multi	.15	.15
98	A10	3½c blue & bister	.20	.15
99	A10	5c blue & ocher	.20	.20
100	A10	12½c lt blue, blk & buff	.40	.40
		Nos. 97-100 (4)	.95	.90

Attainment of self-government.

ITU Issue
Common Design Type

1965, May 17 Litho. *Perf. 11x11½*

101	CD317	1c ver & red lilac	.15	.15
102	CD317	20c grnsh bl & org brn	.85	.65

Intl. Cooperation Year Issue
Common Design Type

1965, Oct. 25 Wmk. 314 *Perf. 14½*

103	CD318	½c blue grn & cl	.15	.15
104	CD318	12½c lt vio & green	.90	.70

Churchill Memorial Issue
Common Design Type

1966, Jan. 24 Photo. *Perf. 14*
Design in Black, Gold and Carmine Rose

105	CD319	1c bright blue	.15	.15
106	CD319	2½c green	.15	.15
107	CD319	10c brown	.50	.50
108	CD319	22½c violet	1.25	1.25
		Nos. 105-108 (4)	2.05	2.05

POSTAGE DUE STAMPS

Catalogue values for all unused stamps in this section are for Never Hinged items.

D1

1933-38 Wmk. 4 Typo. *Perf. 14*

J1	D1	1p dark red ('38)	.40	.20
a.		1p dark carmine	1.00	1.10
b.		Wmk. 4a (error)	67.50	
J2	D1	2p lt violet	.30	.20
a.		Wmk. 4a (error)	67.50	

Nos. J1-J2 valued on chalky paper.
For surcharge see No. J7.

Coat of Arms — D2

1956, Dec. 1

J3	D2	1p carmine	.35	.25
J4	D2	2p dark purple	.35	.25

Nos. J2-J4 Surcharged with New Value

1961

J5	D2	1c on 1p carmine	.15	.15
J6	D2	1c on 2p dk purple	.15	.15
J7	D1	5c on 2p lt violet	3.00	3.00
a.		Wmk. 4a (error)	275.00	
J8	D2	5c on 2p dark pur ("5" 7½mm high)	.15	.15
a.		"5" 3½mm high	17.50	25.00
		Nos. J5-J8 (4)	3.45	3.45

Value in Cents

1964 Wmk. 314 *Perf. 14*

J9	D2	1c carmine	2.25	2.25
J10	D2	5c dark purple	2.25	2.25

For overprints see Lesotho Nos. J1-J2.

OFFICIAL STAMPS

Nos. 1-3 and 6 Overprinted "OFFICIAL"

1934 Wmk. 4 Engr. *Perf. 12½*

O1	A1	½p emerald	*4,000.*	*4,000.*
O2	A1	1p carmine	*1,100.*	*1,750.*
O3	A1	2p red violet	*1,750.*	*1,000.*
O4	A1	6p yellow	*4,000.*	*2,250.*

Counterfeits exist.

BATUM

LOCATION — A seaport on the Black Sea

Batum is the capital of Adzhar, a territory which, in 1921, became an autonomous republic of the Georgian Soviet Socialist Republic.

Stamps of Batum were issued under the administration of British forces which occupied Batum and environs between December, 1918, and July, 1920, following the Treaty of Versailles.

100 Kopecks = 1 Ruble

Counterfeits exist of Nos. 1-65.

Basic Russian Designs

A8

A11

A14

A15

A19

A1

1919 Unwmk. Litho. *Imperf.*

1	A1	5k green	.55	.55
2	A1	10k ultramarine	.55	.55
3	A1	50k yellow	.35	*.45*
4	A1	1r red brown	.50	*.60*
5	A1	3r violet	1.90	*3.25*
6	A1	5r brown	3.00	*5.25*
		Nos. 1-6 (6)	6.85	*10.65*

For overprints and surcharges see #13-20, 51-65.

Russian Stamps of 1909-17 Surcharged

БАТУМ. ОБ.
Руб 10 Руб.

1919 On Stamps of 1917

7	A14	10r on 1k orange	25.00	*27.50*
8	A14	10r on 3k red	12.00	*16.00*
		On Stamp of 1909-12 ***Perf. 14x14½***		
9	A14	10r on 5k claret	250.00	250.00
		On Stamp of 1917		
10	A14	10r on 10k on 7k light blue	200.00	200.00
		Nos. 7-10 (4)	487.00	493.50

Russian Stamps of 1909-13 Surcharged

БАТУМ. ОБ.
Коп 35 Коп.

1919

11	A15	35k on 4k carmine	*1,650.*	
12	A19	35k on 4k dull red	*6,500.*	

This surcharge was intended for postal cards. A few cards which bore adhesive stamps were also surcharged.

Values are for stamps off card and without gum.

Type of 1919 Issue Overprinted

BRITISH
OCCUPATION

1919 Unwmk. *Imperf.*

13	A1	5k green	1.25	*1.75*
14	A1	10k dark blue	1.25	*1.75*
15	A1	25k orange	1.25	*1.75*
16	A1	1r pale blue	.90	*1.25*
17	A1	2r salmon pink	.40	*.55*
18	A1	3r violet	.40	*.55*
19	A1	5r brown	.40	*.55*
a.		"CCUPATION"	*190.00*	*190.00*
20	A1	7r dull red	1.25	*1.75*
		Nos. 13-20 (8)	7.10	*9.90*

Russian Stamps of 1909-17 Surcharged in Various Colors:

БАТУМ ОБЛАС.
P 10 P.
BRITISH
OCCUPATION
10r & 50r

БАТУМЪ
BRITISH
P. 15 P.
OCCUPATION
ОБЛ.
15r

On Stamps of 1917

1919-20 *Imperf.*

21	A14	10r on 3k red	25.00	22.50
22	A14	15r on 1k org (R)	50.00	45.00
23	A14	15r on 1k org (Bk)	75.00	65.00
24	A14	15r on 1k org (V)	50.00	45.00
25	A14	50r on 1k org	300.00	275.00
26	A14	50r on 2k green	350.00	350.00

On Stamps of 1909-17
Perf. 14x14½

27	A14	50r on 2k green	350.00	350.00
28	A14	50r on 3k red	500.00	500.00
29	A15	50r on 4k car	350.00	350.00
30	A14	50r on 5k claret	350.00	350.00
31	A15	50r on 10k dk blue (R)	850.00	850.00
32	A11	50r on 15k red brn & blue	325.00	325.00

BATUM — BECHUANALAND — BECHUANALAND PROTECTORATE

BATUM

Surcharged БАТУМ.ОБЛ. P.25P. BRITISH OCCUPATION

On Stamps of 1909-17

33	A14	25r on 5k cl (Bk)	50.00	50.00
34	A14	25r on 5k cl (Bl)	50.00	50.00
35	A14	25r on 10k on 7k lt blue (Bk)	75.00	75.00
36	A14	25r on 10k on 7k lt blue (Bl)	45.00	45.00
37	A11	25r on 20k on 14k bl & rose (Bk)	75.00	75.00
38	A11	25r on 20k on 14k bl & rose (Bl)	40.00	40.00
39	A11	25r on 25k grn & gray vio (Bk)	100.00	100.00
40	A11	25r on 25k grn & gray vio (Bl)	100.00	100.00
41	A8	25r on 50k vio & green (Bk)	45.00	45.00
42	A8	25r on 50k vio & green (Bl)	47.50	47.50
43	A14	50r on 2k green	65.00	65.00
44	A14	50r on 3k red	65.00	65.00
45	A15	50r on 4k car	100.00	100.00
46	A14	50r on 5k claret	100.00	100.00

On Stamps of 1917 — Imperf

47	A14	50r on 2k green	150.00	150.00
48	A14	50r on 3k red	250.00	250.00
49	A14	50r on 5k claret	600.00	600.00

On Stamp of 1913 — Perf. 13½

50	A19	50r on 4k dull red (Bl)	75.00	75.00

Nos. 3, 13 and 15 Surcharged in Black or Blue:

РУБ 25 ПЕН   R.50R. BRITISH OCCUPATION   25 РУБ. 25 РУБ.

1920 — Imperf.

51	A1	25r on 5k green	24.00	24.00
52	A1	25r on 5k grn (Bl)	30.00	30.00
53	A1	25r on 25k orange	17.00	17.00
54	A1	25r on 25k org (Bl)	65.00	65.00
55	A1	50r on 50k yellow	15.00	15.00
56	A1	50r on 50k yel (Bl)	60.00	60.00
		Nos. 51-56 (6)	211.00	211.00

The surcharges on Nos. 21-56 inclusive are handstamped and are known double, inverted, etc.

Tree Type of 1919 Overprinted Like Nos. 13-20

1920

57	A1	1r orange brown	.60	.90
58	A1	2r gray blue	.60	.90
59	A1	3r rose	.60	.90
60	A1	5r black brown	.60	.90
61	A1	7r yellow	.60	.90
62	A1	10r dark green	.60	.90
63	A1	15r violet	.75	1.25
64	A1	25r vermilion	.75	1.25
65	A1	50r dark blue	.90	1.90
		Nos. 57-65 (9)	6.00	9.80

The variety "BPITISH" occurs on #57-65.

BECHUANALAND

,bech-'wä-nə-,land

(British Bechuanaland)

LOCATION — Southern Africa
GOVT. — A British Crown Colony, annexed in 1895 to the Cape of Good Hope Colony which became a province in the Union of South Africa.
AREA — 51,424 sq. mi.
POP. — 84,210 (1904)
CAPITAL — Mafeking

12 Pence = 1 Shilling
20 Shillings = 1 Pound

Watermarks

Wmk. 29 - Orb
Wmk. 14 - VR in Italics

Cape of Good Hope Stamps of 1871-85 Overprinted British Bechuanaland

1886 — Wmk. 1 — Perf. 14 — Black Overprint

1	A6	4p blue	50.00	55.00

Wmk. 2 — Black Overprint

3	A6	3p claret	30.00	30.00

Wmk. Anchor (16) — Red Overprint

4	A6	½p black	10.00	10.00
a.		Double overprint in red & blk	850.00	

Wmk. Anchor (16) — Black Overprint

5	A6	½p black	6.00	10.00
a.		"ritish"	1,800.	1,800.
6	A6	1p rose	8.00	6.50
b.		"ritish"	1,800.	1,600.
7	A6	2p bister	22.50	10.00
a.		"ritish"	4,500.	4,500.
8	A3	6p violet	60.00	32.50
9	A3	1sh green	215.00	125.00
		"ritish"	10,000.	8,000.

There is no period after Bechuanaland in the genuine stamps.

Black Ovpt. on Great Britain #111

1887 — Wmk. 30

10	A54	½p vermilion	.60	1.00
a.		Double overprint	2,250.	

For overprints see Bechuanaland Protectorate Nos. 51-53.

1887 — Typo. — Wmk. 29 — Country Name in Black

11	A1	1p lilac	12.00	4.75
12	A1	2p lilac	30.00	20.00
13	A1	3p lilac	3.25	4.75
14	A1	4p lilac	35.00	5.50
15	A1	6p lilac	40.00	18.00

Wmk. 14

16	A2	1sh green	30.00	5.00
17	A2	2sh green	45.00	30.00
18	A2	2sh6p green	55.00	40.00
19	A2	5sh green	90.00	90.00
20	A2	10sh green	190.00	225.00

Wmk. 29

21	A3	£1 lilac	900.	800.
22	A3	£5 lilac	2,750.	1,400.
		Pen cancellation		165.

The corner designs and central oval differs on No. 22.

For overprints see Bechuanaland Protectorate Nos. 54-58, 60-66. For surcharges see Nos. 23-28, 30, Cape of Good Hope No. 171.

Nos. 11-12, 14-16 Surcharged **1d.**

1888 — Country Name in Black — Black Surcharge

23	A1	1p on 1p lilac	7.00	5.00
a.		Double surcharge		
24	A1	6p on 6p lilac	90.00	22.50

Red Surcharge

25	A1	2p on 2p lilac	12.50	3.00
a.		"2" with curved tail	190.00	150.00
26	A1	4p on 4p lilac	150.00	200.00

Green Surcharge

27	A1	2p on 2p lilac		2,750.

Blue Surcharge

27A	A1	6p on 6p lilac		4,500.

Wmk. 14 — Black Surcharge

28	A2	1sh on 1sh green	85.00	47.50

British Bechuanaland — One Half-Penny
No. 29 — No. 30

Green Ovpt. on Cape of Good Hope #41

1889 — Wmk. 16

29	A4	½p black	4.75	13.00

Vertical overprint, double overprints one inverted or double, and varieties such as "British" omitted probably are from printers waste.

Wmk. 29 — Black Surcharge on No. 13

30	A1	½p on 3p lilac & blk	125.00	135.00

Cape of Good Hope Nos. 43-44 Overprinted in Black — British Bechuanaland

1891 — Wmk. 16

31	A4	1p rose	10.00	9.50
a.		Horiz. pair, one without overprint	1,500.	
b.		"British" omitted		575.00
c.		"Bechuanaland" omitted	850.00	
32	A4	2p bister	3.00	3.00
a.		Without period	200.00	

See Nos. 38-39.

Stamps of Great Britain Overprinted in Black — BRITISH BECHUANALAND

1891-94 — Wmk. 30

33	A40	1p lilac	5.00	1.00
34	A56	2p green & car	3.00	2.50
35	A59	4p brown & green	2.50	.75
36	A62	6p violet, rose	2.50	1.75
37	A65	1sh green ('94)	11.00	13.00
		Nos. 33-37 (5)	24.00	19.00

For surcharges see Cape of Good Hope Nos. 172, 176-177.

Cape of Good Hope Nos. 43-44 Overprinted Like Nos. 31-32 but Reading Down

1893-95 — Wmk. 16

38	A6	1p rose	2.50	2.75
a.		No dots over the "i"s of "British"	80.00	80.00
b.		"British" omitted	650.00	
c.		As "a," reading up		750.00
d.		Pair, one without overprint		
39	A6	2p bister ('95)	4.75	2.75
a.		Double overprint	900.00	900.00
b.		No dots over the "i"s of "British"	125.00	125.00
c.		"British" omitted	350.00	325.00
d.		As "b," reading up		

Cape of Good Hope No. 42 Overprinted BRITISH BECHUANALAND

"BECHUANALAND" 16mm Long Overprint Lines 13mm Apart

1897

40	A6	½p light green	2.50	5.00

"BECHUANALAND" 15mm Long Overprint Lines 10½mm Apart

41	A6	½p light green	10.00	27.50

"BECHUANALAND" 15mm Long Overprint Lines 13½mm Apart

42	A6	½p light green	17.50	45.00
		Nos. 40-42 (3)	30.00	77.50

BECHUANALAND PROTECTORATE

,bech-'wä-nə-,land prə-'tek-t(ə-)rət

LOCATION — In central South Africa, north of the Republic of South Africa, east of South-West Africa and bounded on the north and east by Angola and Southern Rhodesia
GOVT. — British Protectorate
AREA — 222,000 sq. mi.
POP. — 540,400 (1964)

Bechuanaland Protectorate became the independent republic of Botswana, Sept. 30, 1966.

12 Pence = 1 Shilling
20 Shillings = 1 Pound
100 Cents = 1 Rand (1961)

Catalogue values for unused stamps in this country are for Never Hinged items, beginning with Scott 137 in the regular postage section and Scott J7 in the postage due section.

Additional Overprint in Black on Bechuanaland No. 10

Protectorate (a)   Protectorate (b)
Protectorate (c)

1888-90 — Wmk. 30 — Perf. 14

51	A54(a)	½p vermilion	110.00	150.00
a.		Double overprint	575.00	
52	A54(b)	½p vermilion ('89)	2.50	16.00
a.		Double overprint	300.00	
53	A54(c)	½p vermilion	90.00	100.00
a.		Inverted overprint	65.00	80.00
b.		Double overprint	85.00	95.00
c.		As "a," double	600.00	600.00

For surcharge see No. 68.

Bechuanaland Nos. 16-20 Overprinted Type "b" in Black — Wmk. 14 — Country Name in Black

54	A2	1sh green	55.00	50.00
a.		First "o" omitted	3,250.	3,000.
55	A2	2sh green	475.00	625.00
a.		First "o" omitted	5,750.	4,250.
56	A2	2sh6p green	500.00	625.00
a.		First "o" omitted	6,000.	4,500.
57	A2	5sh green	1,100.	1,500.
a.		First "o" omitted	6,750.	6,000.
58	A2	10sh green	3,250.	4,000.
a.		First "o" omitted	12,000.	

Bechuanaland Nos. 11-15 Overprinted Type "b" and Surcharged in Black

1888 — Wmk. 29 — Country Name in Black

60	A1	1p on 1p lilac	5.50	10.00
a.		Short "1"	275.00	300.00
61	A1	2p on 2p lilac	17.50	15.00
a.		"2" with curved tail	300.00	300.00

63 A1 3p on 3p lilac 80.00 *110.00*
64 A1 4p on 4p lilac 175.00 175.00
65 A1 6p on 6p lilac 50.00 40.00

In #60 the "1" is 2½mm high; in #60a, 2mm.

Value Surcharged in Red

66 A1 4p on 4p lilac 50.00 42.50

Cape of Good Hope Type of 1886 Overprinted in Green

Bechuanaland

Protectorate.

1889 Wmk. 16

67 A6 ½p black 3.75 *20.00*
a. Double overprint 400.00 475.00
b. "Bechuanaland" omitted 600.00 600.00

Black Surcharge on Bechuanaland Protectorate No. 52

Wmk. 30

68 A54 4p on ½p ver 15.00 3.00
a. Inverted surcharge *4,500.*

Stamps of Great Britain 1881-87, Overprinted in Black

BECHUANALAND PROTECTORATE

1897, Oct.

69 A54 ½p vermilion 1.00 1.00
70 A40 1p lilac 3.50 .50
71 A56 2p green & car 2.00 4.00
72 A58 3p violet, *yel* 5.00 *7.50*
73 A59 4p brown & green 10.00 10.00
74 A62 6p violet, *rose* 17.50 10.50
Nos. 69-74 (6) 39.00 33.50

For surcharges see Cape of Good Hope Nos. 167-170, 173-175.

Same on Great Britain No. 125

1902, Feb. 25

75 A54 ½p blue green 1.50 1.25

Stamps of Great Britain, 1902, Overprinted in Black

BECHUANALAND PROTECTORATE

1904-12

76 A66 ½p gray green ('06) 3.50 3.50
77 A66 1p car ('05) 4.75 1.25
78 A66 2½p ultra 6.25 5.75
79 A74 1sh scar & grn ('12) 12.00 15.00
Nos. 76-79 (4) 26.50 25.50

Same on Great Britain No. 143

1908

80 A66 ½p pale yel green 2.00 *3.00*

Bechuanaland

Transvaal No. 274 Overprinted

Protectorate

1910 Wmk. 3

81 A27 6p brn org & blk 180.00 *210.00*

This stamp was issued for fiscal use, although it is known postally used.

Great Britain No. 154 Overprinted Like Nos. 76-79

1912, Sept. Wmk. 30 *Perf. 15x14*

82 A81 1p scarlet 1.10 1.00

Great Britain Stamps of 1912-13 Overprinted Like Nos. 76-79

1914-24 Wmk. Crown and GvR (33)

83 A82 ½p green .95 1.25
84 A83 1p scarlet 2.50 .30
85 A84 1½p red brn ('20) 1.50 2.00
86 A85 2p orange (I) 2.25 2.25
a. 2p orange (II) ('24) 30.00 3.50
87 A86 2½p ultra 2.50 *10.00*
88 A87 3p bluish violet 4.75 *11.00*
89 A88 4p slate green 5.25 *9.50*
90 A89 6p dull violet 5.75 *11.00*
91 A90 1sh bister 6.50 *12.00*
Nos. 83-91 (9) 31.95 59.30

The dies of No. 86 are the same as in Great Britain 1912-13 issue.

Overprinted **BECHUANALAND PROTECTORATE**

Wmk. 34 *Perf. 11x12*

92 A91 2sh6p dk brown 100.00 140.00
a. 2sh6p light brown ('16) 125.00 140.00
93 A91 5sh rose car 150.00 200.00
a. 5sh carmine ('20) 200.00 250.00

Nos. 92, 93 were printed by Waterlow Bros. & Layton; Nos. 92a, 93a were printed by Thomas De La Rue & Co.

Same Overprint On Retouched Stamps of 1919

1920-23

94 A91 2sh6p gray brown 100.00 125.00
95 A91 5sh car rose 140.00 165.00

Great Britain Stamps of 1924 Overprinted like Nos. 76-79

Wmk. Crown and Block GvR Multiple (35)

1925-26 *Perf. 15x14*

96 A82 ½p green 1.00 1.65
97 A83 1p scarlet 1.25 1.65
99 A85 2p deep org (II) 2.50 2.25
101 A87 3p violet 3.25 *6.50*
102 A88 4p slate green 4.00 *12.00*
103 A89 6p dull violet 5.25 *16.00*
104 A90 1sh bister 14.00 *21.00*
Nos. 96-104 (7) 31.25 *61.05*

George V
A11

George VI, Cattle and Baobab Tree
A12

Perf. 12½

1932, Dec. 12 Engr. Wmk. 4

105 A11 ½p green .50 .35
106 A11 1p carmine .50 .35
107 A11 2p red brown .50 .45
108 A11 3p ultra 1.00 1.00
109 A11 4p orange 1.00 2.00
110 A11 6p red violet 2.50 1.25
111 A11 1sh blk & ol grn 5.00 5.00
112 A11 2sh black & org 22.50 25.00
113 A11 2sh6p black & car 17.50 20.00
114 A11 3sh black & red vio 25.00 *27.50*
115 A11 5sh black & ultra 35.00 *40.00*
116 A11 10sh blk & red brown 85.00 95.00
Nos. 105-116 (12) 196.00 217.90

Common Design Types pictured following the introduction.

Silver Jubilee Issue

Common Design Type

1935, May 4 *Perf. 11x12*

117 CD301 1p car & blue .25 .35
118 CD301 2p black & ultra .90 .90
119 CD301 3p ultra & brown 1.10 1.10
120 CD301 6p brown vio & ind 2.50 1.75
Nos. 117-120 (4) 4.75 4.10

Coronation Issue

Common Design Type

1937, May 12 *Perf. 13½x14*

121 CD302 1p carmine .15 .15
122 CD302 2p brown .15 .15
123 CD302 3p bright ultra .25 .25
Nos. 121-123 (3) .55 .55
Set, never hinged 1.50

1938, Apr. 1 *Perf. 12½*

124 A12 ½p green 1.25 *2.00*
125 A12 1p rose car .25 *.35*
126 A12 1½p light blue .25 *.60*
127 A12 2p brown .25 *.35*
128 A12 3p ultra .25 *1.25*
129 A12 4p orange .90 *2.00*
130 A12 6p rose violet 1.90 *2.25*
131 A12 1sh blk & ol grn 1.90 *2.50*
133 A12 2sh6p black & car 8.75 *7.50*
135 A12 5sh black & ultra 19.00 7.50
136 A12 10sh black & brn 8.75 *14.50*
Nos. 124-136 (11) 43.45 *40.80*
Set, never hinged 67.50

Catalogue values for unused stamps in this section, from this point to the end of the section, are for Never Hinged items.

Peace Issue

South Africa Nos. 100-102 Overprinted **Bechuanaland**

Basic stamps inscribed alternately in English and Afrikaans.

1945, Dec. 3 Wmk. 201 *Perf. 14*

137 A42 1p rose pink & choc, pair .30 .30
a. Single, English .15 .15
b. Single, Afrikaans .15 .15
138 A43 2p vio & slate blue, pair .40 .40
a. Single, English .20 .20
b. Single, Afrikaans .20 .20
139 A43 3p ultra & dp ultra, pair .50 .50
a. Single, English .25 .25
b. Single, Afrikaans .25 .25
Nos. 137-139 (3) 1.20 1.20

World War II victory of the Allies.

Royal Visit Issue

Types of Basutoland, 1947

Perf. 12½

1947, Feb. 17 Wmk. 4 Engr.

143 A3 1p red .15 .15
144 A4 2p green .15 .15
145 A5 3p ultra .15 .15
146 A6 1sh dark violet .30 .30
Nos. 143-146 (4) .75 .75

Visit of the British Royal Family, Apr. 17, 1947.

Silver Wedding Issue

Common Design Types

1948, Dec. 1 Photo. *Perf. 14x14½*

147 CD304 1½p brt ultra .15 .15

Engr.; Name Typo.

Perf. 11½x11

148 CD305 10sh gray black 24.00 *30.00*

UPU Issue

Common Design Types

Engr.; Name Typo. on 3p and 6p

1949, Oct. 10 *Perf. 13½, 11x11½*

149 CD306 1½p blue .25 .25
150 CD307 3p indigo .35 .35
151 CD308 6p red lilac .80 .80
152 CD309 1sh olive 1.50 1.50
Nos. 149-152 (4) 2.90 2.90

Coronation Issue

Common Design Type

1953, June 3 Engr. *Perf. 13½x13*

153 CD312 2p brown & black .30 .30

Elizabeth II
A13

Victoria, Elizabeth II and Water Hole
A14

1955-58 *Perf. 13x13½*

154 A13 ½p green .25 .25
155 A13 1p rose car .25 .25
156 A13 2p brown .25 .25
157 A13 3p ultra .35 .35
158 A13 4p orange ('58) *4.25* *4.25*
159 A13 4½p indigo 1.25 1.25
160 A13 6p rose violet .80 .80
161 A13 1sh blk & ol grn 1.50 1.50
162 A13 1sh3p blk & rose vio 2.00 *6.50*
163 A13 2sh6p black & car 5.50 10.50
164 A13 5sh black & ultra 10.50 16.00
165 A13 10sh black & brn 24.00 30.00
Nos. 154-165 (12) 50.90 71.90

For surcharges see Nos. 169-179.

Perf. 14½x14

1960, Jan. 21 Photo. Wmk. 314

166 A14 1p brown & black .15 .15
167 A14 3p car rose & black .16 .16
168 A14 6p ultra & black .32 .32
Nos. 166-168 (3) .63 .63

Proclamation of the Protectorate, 75th anniv.

Bechuanaland Protectorate stamps can be mounted in the Scott British Africa album.

Nos. 155-165 Surcharged

1c 1c 3½c 3½c 3½c
I II I II III

5c 5c R1 R1
I II I II

Perf. 13x13½

1961, Feb. 14 Wmk. 4 Engr.

169 1c on 1p (I) .15 .15
a. Type II .15 .15
170 2c on 2p .15 .15
171 2½c on 2p .15 .15
a. Pair, one without surcharge *700.00*
172 2½c on 3p .90 .90
173 3½c on 4p (III) .18 .18
a. Type I .52 .52
b. Type II 1.65 1.65
174 5c on 6p (II) .22 .22
a. Type I .75 .75
175 10c on 1sh .32 .32
a. Pair, one without surcharge *700.00*
176 12½c on 1sh3p ("12½c" 11¼mm wide) .55 .55
a. "12½c" 12½mm wide .75 .75
177 25c on 2sh6p .90 .90
178 50c on 5sh 1.90 1.90
179 1r on 10sh (II, "R1" at lower center) 4.50 4.50
a. Type II, "R1" at lower left 6.50 6.50
b. Type I 300.00 110.00
Nos. 169-179 (11) 9.92 9.92

Nos. 173a and 173b are found in the same sheet; each comes with "3½c" in both wide and narrow settings.

Surcharge types are numbered chronologically.

African Golden Oriole — A15

Baobab Tree — A16

Designs: 2c, African hoopoe. 2½c, Scarlet-chested sunbird. 3½c, Cape widow bird (Yellow bishop). 5c, Swallow-tailed bee-eater. 7½c, Gray hornbill. 10c, Red-headed weaver. 12½c, Brown-hooded kingfisher. 20c, Woman musician. 35c, Woman grinding corn. 50c, Bechuana ox. 1r, Lion. 2r, Police camel patrol.

Perf. 14x14½, 14½x14

1961, Oct. 2 Photo. Wmk. 314

180 A15 1c lilac, blk & yel .20 .20
181 A15 2c pale ol, blk & org .20 .20
182 A15 2½c bis, blk, grn & dp car .25 .20
183 A15 3½c pink, blk & yel .35 .25
184 A15 5c dl org, blk, grn & bl .45 .30
185 A15 7½c yel grn, blk, red & brn .65 .40
186 A15 10c aqua & multi .80 .50
187 A15 12½c gray, yel, red & blue 1.10 .55
188 A15 20c gray & brn 1.40 1.10
189 A16 25c yel & dk brn 2.50 1.40
190 A15 35c dp org & ultra 2.75 1.75
191 A16 50c lt ol grn & sep 4.00 2.75
192 A15 1r ocher & black 8.25 5.25
193 A15 2r blue & brn 16.00 10.50
Nos. 180-193 (14) 38.90 25.35

Freedom from Hunger Issue

Common Design Type

1963, June 4 *Perf. 14x14½*

194 CD314 12½c green .48 .48

Red Cross Centenary Issue

Common Design Type

1963, Sept. 2 Litho. *Perf. 13*

195 CD315 2½c black & red .20 .20
196 CD315 12½c ultra & red .80 .80

Shakespeare Issue

Common Design Type

1964, Apr. 23 Photo. *Perf. 14x14½*

197 CD316 12½c red brown .28 .28

Notwani River Dam, Gaberones Water Supply
A17

BECHUANALAND PROTECTORATE

Perf. 14½
1965, Mar. 1   Photo.   Wmk. 314
198	A17	2½c dark red & gold	.15	.15
199	A17	5c deep ultra & gold	.15	.15
200	A17	12½c brown & gold	.30	.30
201	A17	25c emerald & gold	.55	.55
		Nos. 198-201 (4)	1.15	1.15

Internal self-government, Mar. 1, 1965.

ITU Issue
Common Design Type
Perf. 11x11½
1965, May 17   Litho.   Wmk. 314
202	CD317	2½c ver & dl yel	.15	.15
203	CD317	12½c red lil & pale brn	.70	.70

Intl. Cooperation Year Issue
Common Design Type
1965, Oct. 25   Perf. 14½
204	CD318	1c bl grn & claret	.16	.16
205	CD318	12½c lt vio & grn	.85	.85

Churchill Memorial Issue
Common Design Type
1966, Jan. 24   Photo.   Perf. 14
Design in Black, Gold and Carmine Rose
206	CD319	1c bright blue	.15	.15
207	CD319	2½c green	.16	.16
208	CD319	12½c brown	.65	.65
209	CD319	20c violet	1.10	1.10
		Nos. 206-209 (4)	2.06	2.06

Haslar Smoke Generator — A18

Perf. 14½
1966, June 1   Photo.   Wmk. 314
210	A18	2½c shown	.15	.15
211	A18	5c Bugler	.15	.15
212	A18	15c Gun site	.38	.38
213	A18	35c Regimental cap badge	.85	.85
		Nos. 210-213 (4)	1.53	1.53

25th anniv. of the Bechuanaland Pioneers and Gunners.

POSTAGE DUE STAMPS

Postage Due Stamps of Great Britain Overprinted **BECHUANALAND PROTECTORATE**

On Stamp of 1914-22
1926   Wmk. 33   Perf. 14x14½
J1	D1	1p carmine	3.75	40.00

On Stamps of 1924-30
Wmk. 35
J2	D1	½p emerald	3.75	40.00

Overprinted **BECHUANALAND PROTECTORATE**
J3	D1	2p black brown	7.25	80.00
		Nos. J1-J3 (3)		14.75

D2

1932   Wmk. 4   Typo.   Perf. 14½
J4	D2	½p olive green	6.00	21.00
J5	D2	1p carmine rose	6.00	7.00
J6	D2	2p dull violet	8.00	24.00
		Nos. J4-J6 (3)	20.00	52.00

Catalogue values for unused stamps in this section, from this point to the end of the section, are for Never Hinged items.

Nos. J4-J6 Surcharged

2c I   **2c** II

1961, Feb. 14
J7	D2	1c on 1p car rose (II)	.15	.15
a.		Type I	.28	.28
b.		Double surcharge (II)	140.00	
J8	D2	2c on 2p dull vio (II)	.25	.25
a.		Type I	.35	.35
J9	D2	5c on ½p ol green (I)	.52	.52
		Nos. J7-J9 (3)	.92	.92

Nos. J6, J7a, J8 and J8a are on chalky paper. Nos. J7 and J8 printed on ordinary paper sell for much more.

Denominations in Cents
1961   Wmk. 4   Perf. 14
J10	D2	1c carmine rose	.15	.15
J11	D2	2c dull violet	.16	.16
J12	D2	5c olive green	.40	1.25
		Nos. J10-J12 (3)	.71	1.56

BELARUS
ˌbē-lə-ˈrüs

(Byelorussia)

(White Russia)

LOCATION — Eastern Europe, bounded by Russia, Latvia, Lithuania and Poland
GOVT. — Independent republic, member of the Commonwealth of Independent States
AREA — 80,200 sq. mi.
POP. — 10,200,000 (1989)
CAPITAL — Minsk

With the breakup of the Soviet Union on Dec. 26, 1991, Belarus and ten former Soviet republics established the Commonwealth of Independent States.

100 Kopecks = 1 Ruble

Catalogue values for all unused stamps in this country are for Never Hinged items.

Cross of Ephrosinia of Polotsk — A1

Five denominations, perf and imperf, of this design produced in 1920 were not put in use and were probably propaganda labels. They are common.

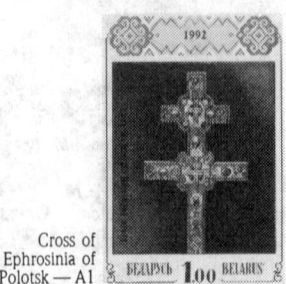

1992, Mar. 20   Litho.   Perf. 12x12½
1	A1	1r multicolored	.15	.15

R.R. Schurma (1892-1978), Composer — A2

1992, Apr. 10   Photo.   Perf. 12x11½
2	A2	20k blue & black	.15	.15

For surcharge see No. 203.

Arms of Polotsk — A3

Designs: No. 13, Stag jumping fence. No. 14, Man's head, sword.

1992-94   Photo.   Perf. 12x11½
11	A3	2r shown	.15	.15

Perf. 12x12½
12	A3	25r Minsk	.15	.15
13	A3	700r Grodno	.15	.15
14	A3	700r Vitebsk	.15	.15
		Nos. 11-14 (4)	.60	.60

Issued: 2r, 6/9/92; 25r, 11/11/93; #13, 14, 10/17/94.
This is an expanding set. Numbers will change if necessary.

National Symbols — A4

Designs: No. 15, Natl. arms. No. 16, Map, flag.

1992, Aug. 31   Litho.   Perf. 12x12½
15	A4	5r black, red & yellow	.15	.15
16	A4	5r multicolored	.15	.15

For surcharges see Nos. 55-58, 61-64.

No. 1 Overprinted

1992, Sept. 25   Litho.   Perf. 12x12½
17	A1	1r on #1 multi	.15	.15

Cross of Ephrosinia of Polotsk — A5

A5 illustration reduced.

Souvenir Sheet
Perf. 12
18	A5	5r multicolored	.30	.30

Orthodox Church in Belarus, 1000th anniv. No. 18, imperf, was issued Feb. 15, 1993. For surcharges see Nos. 59-60, 65-66.

Buildings A6

Designs: No. 19, Church of Boris Gleb, Grodno, 12th cent. No. 20, World Castle, 16th cent. No. 21, Nyasvizh Castle, 16th-19th cent. No. 22, Kamyanets Tower, 12th-13th cent, vert. No. 23, Church of Ephrosinia of Polotsk, 12th cent., vert. No. 24, Calvinist Church, Zaslaw, 16th cent., vert.

1992, Oct. 15   Litho.   Perf. 12
19	A6	2r multicolored	.15	.15
20	A6	2r multicolored	.15	.15
21	A6	2r multicolored	.15	.15
22	A6	2r multicolored	.15	.15
23	A6	2r multicolored	.15	.15
24	A6	2r multicolored	.15	.15
		Nos. 19-24 (6)	.90	.90

Centuries of construction are in Roman numerals.

Natl. Arms — A7

1992-94   Litho.   Perf. 12x12½
25	A7	30k light blue	.15	.15
26	A7	45k olive green	.15	.15
27	A7	50k green	.15	.15
28	A7	1r brown	.15	.15
29	A7	2r red brown	.15	.15
30	A7	3r org yellow	.15	.15
31	A7	5r blue	.15	.15
32	A7	10r red	.20	.20
33	A7	15r violet	.25	.25
34	A7	25r yellow green	.40	
35	A7	50r bright pink	.15	.15
36	A7	100r henna brown	.25	
37	A7	150r plum	.40	.40
38	A7	200r blue green	.15	.15
39	A7	300r salmon pink	.15	.15
40	A7	600r light lilac	.15	.15
40A	A7	1000r rose carmine	.25	.25
40B	A7	3000r gray blue	.50	.50
		Nos. 25-40B (18)	3.90	3.50

Issued: 30k, 45k, 50k, 11/10; 1r-3r, 10r, 1/4/93; 5r, 15r, 25r, 2/9/93; 50r, 100r, 150r, 6/16/93; 200r-3,000r, 12/28/94; others, 1992.
For surcharges see Nos. 141-142, 211A-212.

Ceramics — A8

Designs: No. 41, Pitcher and bowl. No. 42, Four pieces on tree branches. No. 43, Two large pitchers. No. 44, One large pitcher.

1992, Dec. 24   Litho.   Perf. 11½
41	A8	1r multicolored	.15	.15
42	A8	1r multicolored	.15	.15
43	A8	1r multicolored	.15	.15
44	A8	1r multicolored	.15	.15
		Nos. 41-44 (4)	.60	.60

M. I. Garetzky (1893-1938), Writer — A9

1993, June 22   Photo.   Perf. 12x11½
45	A9	50r magenta	.30	.30

Straw Figures — A10

Designs: 5r, Chickens. 10r, Child, mother, vert. 15r, Woman, vert. 25r, Man with scythe, woman with rake, vert.

BELARUS

Perf. 12x11½, 11½x12
1993, Apr. 22 Litho.
47 A10 5r multicolored .15 .15
48 A10 10r multicolored .15 .15
49 A10 15r multicolored .15 .15
50 A10 25r multicolored .15 .15
Nos. 47-50 (4) .60 .60

First World Congress of White Russians — A11

1993, July 8 Litho. Perf. 12
51 A11 50r multicolored 1.25 1.25

Europa — A12

Paintings by Chagall: No. 52, Promenade, vert. No. 53, Man Over Vitebsk. 2500r, Allegory.

1993, Oct. 12 Litho. Perf. 14
52 A12 1500r multicolored 3.00 3.00
53 A12 1500r multicolored 3.00 3.00
a. Pair, #52-53 6.00 6.00

Souvenir Sheet
54 A12 2500r multicolored 45.00 45.00

Nos. 15-16, 18 Surcharged

1500 a

WINTER PRE-OLYMPICS GAMES LILLEHAMMER, NORWAY

1500 b

Size and location of surcharge varies.

1993, Oct. 15 Litho. Perf. 12x12½
55 A4(a) 1500r on 5r #15 3.50 3.50
56 A4(b) 1500r on 5r #15 3.50 3.50
a. Pair, #55-56 7.00 7.00
57 A4(a) 1500r on 5r #16 3.50 3.50
58 A4(b) 1500r on 5r #16 3.50 3.50
a. Pair, #57-58 7.00 7.00
Nos. 55-58 (4) 14.00 14.00

Souvenir Sheets
Perf. 12
59 A5(a) 1500r on 5r #18 3.50 3.50
60 A5(b) 1500r on 5r #18 3.50 3.50
No. 59 exists imperf.

Nos. 15-16, 18 Surcharged

ЧЭМПІЯНАТ СВЕТУ ПА ФУТБОЛУ, ЗША. 1994

1500 c

WORLD CUP USA 94

1500 d

Size and location of surcharge varies.

1993, Oct. 15 Litho. Perf. 12x12½
61 A4(c) 1500r on 5r #15 3.50 3.50
62 A4(d) 1500r on 5r #15 3.50 3.50
a. Pair, #61-62 7.00 7.00
63 A4(c) 1500r on 5r #16 3.50 3.50
64 A4(d) 1500r on 5r #16 3.50 3.50
a. Pair, #63-64 7.00 7.00
Nos. 61-64 (4) 14.00 14.00

Souvenir Sheets
Perf. 12
65 A5(c) 1500r on 5r #18 3.50 3.50
66 A5(d) 1500r on 5r #18 3.50 3.50

Stansilavski Church — A13

1993, Nov. 24 Litho. Perf. 12
67 A13 150r multicolored .35 .35
For surcharge see No. 242.

Famous People — A14

Designs: 50r, Kastus Kalinovsky, led 1863 independence movement. No. 69, Prince Rogvold of Polotsk, map of Polotsk. No. 70, Princess Rogneda, daughter of Rogvold, fortress. 100r, Statue of Simon Budny (1530-93), writer and printer, vert.

1993 Perf. 12x12½, 12½x12
68 A14 50r multicolored .15 .15
69 A14 75r multicolored .20 .20
70 A14 75r multicolored .20 .20
71 A14 100r multicolored .35 .35
Nos. 68-71 (4) .90 .90

Issued: 50r, 12/29; 75r, 12/30; 100r, 12/31.

Nos. 27, 29, 30 Surcharged
15.00

1994, Feb. 1 Photo. Perf. 12x12½
72 A7 15r on 30k light green .15 .15
73 A7 25r on 45k olive green .15 .15
74 A7 50r on 50k green .15 .15
Nos. 72-74 (3) .45 .45

Birds A15

1994, Jan. 19 Litho. Perf. 11½
75 A15 20r Aguila chrysaetos .15 .15
76 A15 40r Cygnus olor .15 .15
77 A15 40r Alcedo atthis .15 .15
a. Block of 3, #75-77 + label .40 .40
See Nos. 87-89.

Six World Wildlife Fund labels with 1000r denominations depicting 3 different animals and 3 different birds exist. They were not valid for postage.

Liberation of Soviet Areas, 50th Anniv. A16

Battle maps and: a, Katyusha rockets, liberation of Russia. b, Fighter planes, liberation of Ukraine. c, Combined offensive, liberation of Belarus.

1994, July 3 Litho. Perf. 12
78 A16 500r Block of 3 + label .45 .45
See Russia No. 6213, Ukraine No. 195.

1994 Winter Olympics, Lillehammer — A17

1994, Aug. 30 Litho. Perf. 12x12½
79 A17 1000r Speed skating .15 .15
80 A17 1000r Women's figure skating .15 .15
81 A17 1000r Hockey .15 .15
82 A17 1000r Cross-country skiing .15 .15
83 A17 1000r Biathlon .15 .15
Nos. 79-83 (5) .75 .75

Painters — A18

Designs: No. 84, Farmer, oxen in field, by Ferdinand Rushchyts. No. 85, Knight on horseback, by Jasev Drazdovich. No. 86, Couple walking up path, by Petra Sergievich. Illustration reduced

1994, July 18 Litho. Perf. 12
84 A18 300r multicolored .15 .15
85 A18 300r multicolored .15 .15
86 A18 300r multicolored .15 .15
Nos. 84-86 (3) .45 .45
For overprint see No. 127.

Bird Type of 1994
1994, Sept. 30 Perf. 11½
87 A15 300r like #75 .15 .15
88 A15 400r like #76 .15 .15
89 A15 400r like #77 .15 .15
Nos. 87-89 (3) .45 .45

Ilya Yefimovich Repin (1844-1930), Ukrainian Painter — A19

Designs: #90, Self-portrait. #91, Repin Museum.

1994, Oct. 31 Litho. Perf. 12x12½
90 A19 1000r multicolored .30 .30
91 A19 1000r multicolored .30 .30
a. Pair, #90-91 .60 .60

Churches A20

Designs: No. 92, Sacred Consolidated Church, Sinkavitsch, 16th cent. No. 93, Sts. Peter and Paul Cathedral, Gomel, 19th cent.

1994, Oct. 20 Litho. Perf. 12
92 A20 700r multicolored .20 .20
93 A20 700r multicolored .20 .20

Kosciuszko Uprising, Bicent. (in 1994) A21

Battle scene and: No. 94, Tomasz Vaishetcki (1754-1816). No. 95, Jakov Jasinski (1761-94). No. 96, Tadeusz Kosziuszko (1746-1817). No. 97, Mikhail K. Aginski (1765-1833).

1995, Jan. 11 Perf. 12½x12
94 A21 600r multicolored .15 .15
95 A21 600r multicolored .15 .15
96 A21 1000r multicolored .30 .30
97 A21 1000r multicolored .30 .30
Nos. 94-97 (4) .90 .90

End of World War II, 50th Anniv. — A22

1995, May 4 Litho. Perf. 13½
98 A22 180r multicolored .15 .15
99 A22 600r multicolored .20 .20

Radio, Cent. — A23

1995, May 7 Perf. 14
100 A23 600r A Popov .20 .20
Exists imperf.

Monument — A24

BELARUS

1995-96 Litho. Perf. 13x14
102 A24 180r olive brown & red .15 .15
103 A24 200r gray green & bister .15 .15
105 A24 280r green & blue .20 .20
109 A24 600r plum & bister .20 .20
Nos. 102-109 (4) .70 .70
No. 102 exists imperf.
Issued: 180r, 5/10/95; 280r, 5/18/95; 600r, 8/29/95; 200r, 1/30/96.
This is an expanding set. Numbers may change.

Ivan Chersky (1845-92), Geographer — A25

1995, May 15 Litho. Perf. 13½x14
113 A25 600r multicolored .20 .20
Exists imperf.

A26  A27

Traditional Costumes: 600r, Woman wearing shawl, coat, ankle length skirt, man with long coat. 1200r, Woman wearing shawl & apron holding child, man wearing vest, knickers.

1995, July 13 Litho. Perf. 14½x14
114 A26 180r multicolored .15 .15
115 A26 600r multicolored .15 .15
116 A26 1200r multicolored .35 .35
Nos. 114-116 (3) .65 .65
See Nos. 164-167, 214-216.

1995, July 20 Perf. 12
World Wildlife Fund: Various pictures of a beaver.
117 A27 300r multi .15 .15
118 A27 450r multi .15 .15
119 A27 450r multi, horiz. .15 .15
120 A27 800r multi, horiz. .20 .20
Nos. 117-120 (4) .65 .65

A28  A29

1995, Aug. 29 Litho. Perf. 14
121 A28 600r Book Fair .20 .20
Exists imperf.

1995, Oct. 3 Litho. Perf. 14
122 A29 600r Natl. arms .20 .20
123 A29 600r Flag .20 .20
New national symbols. Exist imperf.

UN, 50th Anniv. — A30

1995, Oct. 24 Litho. Perf. 13½x14
124 A30 600r bister, black & blue .20 .20
Exists imperf.

Churches — A31

Designs: No. 125, Mstislav, 17th-19th cent. No. 126, Kamai, 17th cent.

1995, Nov. 21 Perf. 14
125 A31 600r multicolored .20 .20
126 A31 600r multicolored .20 .20

No. 84 Ovptd. **1995 125 год з дня нараджэння**

1995, Dec. 27 Litho. Perf. 12
127 A18 300r multicolored .20 .20

P. V. Sukhi (1895-1975), Airplane Designer — A32

1995, Dec. 27 Litho. Perf. 13½
128 A32 600r multicolored .20 .20

Wildlife — A33

Designs: 1000r, Lynx lynx. No. 130, Capreolus capreolus, vert. No. 131, Ursus arctos. 3000r, Alces alces, vert. 5000r, Bison bonasus. 10,000r, Cervus elaphus, vert.

1995-96 Litho. Perf. 14
129 A33 1000r multicolored .25 .25
130 A33 2000r multicolored .40 .40
131 A33 2000r multicolored .40 .40
132 A33 3000r multicolored .65 .65
133 A33 5000r multicolored 1.10 1.10
Nos. 129-133 (5) 2.80 2.80
Souvenir Sheet
Imperf
134 A33 10,000r multicolored 1.75 1.75
Issued: #129-133, 2/6/96; #134, 12/29/95.

Famous People — A34

Designs: 600r, L. Sapega (1557-1633), statesman. 1200r, K. Semyanovitch (1600-51), military scholar. 1800r, S. Polotzki (1629-80), writer. Illustration reduced.

1995, Dec. 30 Litho. Perf. 12
135 A34 600r multicolored .15 .15
136 A34 1200r multicolored .30 .30
137 A34 1800r multicolored .45 .45
Nos. 135-137 (3) .90 .90

Miniature Sheet

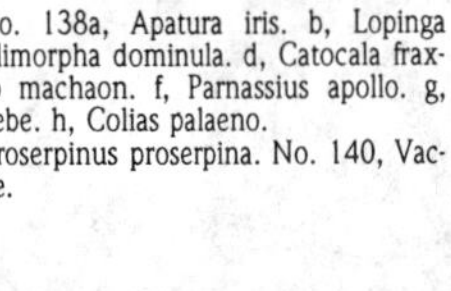

Butterflies — A35

Designs: No. 138a, Apatura iris. b, Lopinga achine. c, Callimorpha dominula. d, Catocala fraxini. e, Papilio machaon. f, Parnassius apollo. g, Ammobiota hebe. h, Colias palaeno.
No. 139, Proserpinus proserpina. No. 140, Vacciniina optilete.

1996, Mar. 29 Litho. Perf. 14
138 A35 300r Sheet of 8, #a.-h. 10.00 10.00
Souvenir Sheets
139-140 A35 1000r each 4.00 4.00
Inscribed 1995.

Nos. 28, 34 Surcharged in Green or Red

1996 Litho. Perf. 12x12½
141 A7 (B) on 1r #28 (G) .15 .15
142 A7 (A) on 25r #34 (R) .15 .15
Nos. 141-142 were valued at 200r and 400r, respectively, on day of issue. Issued: No. 141, 2/28/96. No. 142, 3/13/96.

Souvenir Sheet

Beaver — A36

Illustration reduced.

1996, Mar. 26 Litho. Perf. 12½x12
143 A36 1200r multicolored .35 .35

Kondrat Krapiva (1896-1991), Writer — A37

1996, Mar. 5 Litho. Perf. 14x14½
144 A37 1000r multicolored .35 .35

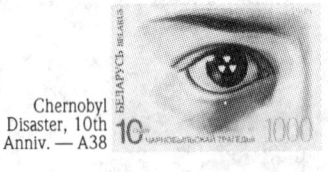

Chernobyl Disaster, 10th Anniv. — A38

Radiation symbol and: a, Eye. b, Leaf showing contamination. c, Boarded-up window.

1996, Apr. 10 Perf. 14
145 A38 1000r Block of 3, #a.-c. + label .50 .50

Coat of Arms — A39

1996, May 6 Litho. Perf. 13½
146 A39 100r blue & black .15 .15
147 A39 500r green & black .15 .15
148 A39 600r vermilion & black .15 .15
149 A39 1000r orange & black .15 .15
150 A39 1500r dp lilac rose & blk .25 .25
151 A39 1800r violet & black .30 .30
152 A39 2200r rose violet & black .40 .40
153 A39 3300r yellow & black .50 .50
154 A39 5000r green blue & blk .75 .75
155 A39 10,000r apple green & blk 1.50 1.50
156 A39 30,000r brown & black 4.50 4.50
157 A39 50,000r red brown & blk 7.50 7.50
Nos. 146-157 (12) 16.30 16.30
See Nos. 182, 192-200.

Agreement with Russia — A40

1996, June 14 Perf. 13½x14
158 A40 1500r multicolored .30 .30

1996 Summer Olympic Games, Atlanta — A41

1996, July 15 Litho. Perf. 14
159 A41 3000r Rhythmic gymnastics .25 .25
160 A41 3000r Discus .25 .25
161 A41 3000r Wrestling .25 .25
162 A41 3000r Weight lifting .25 .25
Nos. 159-162 (4) 1.00 1.00
Souvenir Sheet
Imperf
163 A41 5000r Shooting, vert. 1.00 1.00
No. 163 has simulated perforations.

Regional Costume Type of 1995
Couples in traditional 19th cent. costumes: 1800r, Kapilska-Kletzky region. 2200r, David-Gorodok-Turai region. 3300r, Kobrin region. 5000r, Naralyan region.

1996, Aug. 13 Litho. Perf. 14
164 A26 1800r multicolored .20 .20
165 A26 2200r multicolored .25 .25
166 A26 3300r multicolored .40 .40
Nos. 164-166 (3) .85 .85
Souvenir Sheet
Imperf
167 A26 5000r multicolored 1.00 1.00

Medicinal Plants — A42

No. 168, Sanguisorba officinaus. No. 169, Acorus calamus. 2200r, Potentilla erecta. 3300r, Frangula alnus. 5000r, Menyanthes trifoliata.

1996, Aug. 15 Perf. 14x13½
168 A42 1500r multicolored .25 .25
169 A42 1500r multicolored .25 .25
170 A42 2200r multicolored .40 .40
171 A42 3300r multicolored .60 .60
Nos. 168-171 (4) 1.50 1.50
Souvenir Sheet
Imperf
172 A42 5000r multicolored 1.00 1.00

Birds — A44

No. 173: a, Ardea cinerea. b, Ciconia nigra. c, Phalacrocorax caroo. d, Ciconia ciconia. e, Larus ridibundus. f, Gallinago gallinago. g, Chlidonias leucopterus. h, Remiz pendulinus. i, Botaurus stellaris. j, Fulica atra. k, Ixobrychus minutus. l, Alcedo atthts.
No. 174: a, Anas crecca. b, Anas strepera. c, Anas acuta. d, Anas platyrhynchos. e, Aythya marila. f, Clangula hyemalis. g, Anas clypeata. h, Anas querquedula. i, Anas penelope. j, Arthya nyroca. k, Bucephala clangula. l, Mergus merganser. m, Mergus albellus. n, Aythya fuligula. o, Mergus serrator. p, Aythya ferina.
No. 175, Aythya ferina, diff. No. 176, Gallinago gallinago, diff.

1996, Sept. 10 Litho. Perf. 14
173 A44 400r Sheet of 12, #a.-l. 6.00 6.00

BELARUS

174	A44 400r Sheet of 16, #a.-p.	8.00	8.00

Souvenir Sheets

175-176	A44 1000r each	4.00	4.00

Grammar Book, 1596 — A45

1996, Sept. 19   Litho.   Perf. 14x13½

177	A45 1500r multicolored	.30	.30

Churches A46

1996, Sept. 24   Perf. 14x14½

178	A46 3300r Pinsk	.50	.50
179	A46 3300r Mogilev, 17th cent.	.50	.50

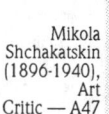

Mikola Shchakatskin (1896-1940), Art Critic — A47

1996, Oct. 16

180	A47 2000r multicolored	.35	.35

Minsk Telephone Station, Cent. — A48

1996, Nov. 14

181	A48 2000r multicolored	.35	.35

Natl. Arms Type of 1996

1996, Nov. 21   Litho.   Perf. 13½x14

182	A39 200r gray green & black	.15	.15

Pres. Aleksandr G. Lukashenka, Natl. Flag — A49

1996, Dec. 6   Litho.   Perf. 13½

183	A49 2500r multicolored	.50	.50

Famous Men — A50

1996, Dec. 17   Perf. 13½

184	A50 3000r multicolored	.40	.40
185	A50 3000r multicolored	.40	.40
186	A50 3000r multicolored	.40	.40
	Nos. 184-186 (3)	1.20	1.20

New Year — A51

1500r, Christmas tree, buildings in Minsk.

1996, Dec. 21   Perf. 14

187	A51 1500r multicolored	.30	.30
188	A51 2000r multicolored, vert.	.40	.40

Natl. Museum of Art, Minsk — A52

Icons: No. 189, Madonna and Child, Smolensk, 16th cent. No. 190, Paraskeva, 16th cent. No. 191, Ilya, 17th cent. No. 192, Three saints, 18th cent. 5000r, Birth of Christ, by Peter Yacijevitsch, 1649.

1996, Dec. 26   Perf. 13½

189	A52 3500r multicolored	.50	.50
190	A52 3500r multicolored	.50	.50
191	A52 3500r multicolored	.50	.50
192	A52 3500r multicolored	.50	.50
	Nos. 189-192 (4)	2.00	2.00

Souvenir Sheet
Imperf

193	A46 5000r multicolored	.75	.75

Georgi K. Zhukov (1896-1974), Soviet Marshal — A53

1997, Jan. 3   Perf. 13½

194	A53 2000r multicolored	.35	.35

Kupala Natl. Theater, Minsk — A54

1997, Jan. 3   Perf. 13½x14

195	A54 3500r multicolored	.55	.55

Coat of Arms Type of 1996

1997   Litho.   Perf. 13½x14

196	A39 400r lt brown & black	.15	.15
198	A39 1500r brt pink & black	.45	.45
199	A39 2000r apple green & black	.60	.60
200	A39 2500r dk blue & black		
	Nos. 196-199 (3)	1.20	1.20

Issued: 400r, 2000r, 1/9; 1500r, 1/16; 2500r, 9/22.

Numbers have been reserved for two other stamps released 9/22. The editors would like to examine them.

V.K. Byalynitsky-Birulya (1872-1957), Painter — A55

1997, Feb. 26   Perf. 14

202	A55 2000r multicolored	.60	.60

No. 2 Surcharged in Gray

1997, Mar. 10   Photo.   Perf. 12x11½

203	A2 3500r on 20k blue & black	1.00	1.00

Fish — A56

2000r, Salmo trutta. 3000r, Vimba vimba. #206, Thymallus thymallus. #207, Barbus barbus. 5000r, Acipenser ruthenus.

1997, Apr. 10   Litho.   Perf. 13½x14

204	A56 2000r multicolored	.60	.60
205	A56 3000r multicolored	.90	.90
206	A56 4500r multicolored	1.30	1.30
207	A56 4500r multicolored	1.30	1.30
	Nos. 204-207 (4)	4.10	4.10

Souvenir Sheet

208	A56 5000r multicolored	1.40	1.40

Intl. Conference on Sustainable Development of Countries with Economies in Transition — A57

Designs: 3000r, Earth with "SOS" formed in atmosphere. 4500r, Hand above flora and fauna.

1997, Apr. 16   Perf. 14x14½

209	A57 3000r multicolored	.85	.85
210	A57 4500r multicolored	1.30	1.30
a.	Pair, #209-210 + label	2.20	2.20

Entry into UPU, 50th Anniv. — A58

1997, May 13   Perf. 14½x14

211	A58 3000r multicolored	.90	.90

Nos. 28-29 Surcharged in Violet Blue

1997   Litho.   Perf. 12x12½

211A	A7 100r on 1r brown	5.00	5.00
212	A7 100r on 2r red brown	.15	.15

Issued: 2r, 5/22.

World War II Liberation Day, July 3 — A59

1997, June 26   Perf. 14½x14

213	A59 3000r multicolored	.90	.90

Traditional Costume Type of 1995

Men and women in 19th cent. costumes, regions: 2000r, Dzisna. 3000r, Navagrudak. 4500r, Byhau.

1997, July 10

214	A26 2000r multicolored	.55	.55
215	A26 3000r multicolored	.85	.85
216	A26 4500r multicolored	1.30	1.30
	Nos. 214-216 (3)	2.70	2.70

Book Printing in Belarus, 480th Anniv. — A60

#217, Text, Vilnius period. #218, Text, Prague period. 4000r, F. Skorina (1488-1535), Polatsk period. 7500r, F. Skorina, Krakow period.

1997, Sept. 7   Perf. 13½

217	A60 3000r shown	.85	.85
218	A60 3000r gray, black & red	.85	.85
219	A60 4000r gray, black & red	1.10	1.10
220	A60 7500r gray, black & red	2.00	2.00
	Nos. 217-220 (4)	4.80	4.80

Pinsk Jesuit College, 900th Anniv. — A61

1997, Sept. 13   Perf. 14x14½

221	A61 3000r multicolored	.85	.85

National Library, 75th Anniv. — A62

1997, Sept. 15

222	A62 3000r multicolored	.90	.90

Intl. Children's Day — A64

1997, Sept. 28   Litho.   Perf. 14x14½

224	A64 3000r multicolored	.85	.85

Fight Against AIDS — A65

1997, Oct. 14   Perf. 14½x14

225	A65 4000r multicolored	1.10	1.10

Designs: No. 184, Kyril Turovski (1130-81), Bishop of Turov. No. 185, Mikola Gusovski (1470-1533), writer. No. 186, Mikolaj Radziwil (1515-65), chancellor of Lithuania.

BELARUS — BELGIAN CONGO

Farm Tractors — A66

3300r, Belarus "1221." 4400r, First wheel tractor, 1953. #228, Belarus "952." #229, Belarus "680."

		1997, Oct. 16		Perf. 14x14½
226	A66	3300r multicolored	1.00	1.00
227	A66	4400r multicolored	1.25	1.25
228	A66	7500r multicolored	2.00	2.00
229	A66	7500r multicolored	2.00	2.00
a.		Sheet, 2 each, #226-229 + label	13.00	13.00
		Nos. 226-229 (4)	6.25	6.25

1998 Winter Olympic Games, Nagano — A69

Designs: a, 2000r, Cross country skiing. b, 3300r, Ice hockey. c, 4400r, Biathlon. d, 7500r, Freestyle skiing.

		1998, Feb. 3	Litho.	Perf. 13½
233	A69	Block of 4, #a.-d.		2.50

P.M. Mascherov (1918-80), Author A70

		1998, Feb. 12	Litho.	Perf. 13½
234	A70	2500r multicolored	.30	.30

Minsk Automobile Plant — A71

Dump trucks: 1400r, 1947 MAZ-205. 2000r, 1968 MAZ-503B. 3000r, 1977 MAZ-5549. 4400r, 1985 MAZ-5551. 7500r, 1994 MAZ-5516.

		1998, Apr. 23	Litho.	Perf. 13½
235	A71	1400r multicolored	.20	.20
236	A71	2000r multicolored	.25	.25
237	A71	3000r multicolored	.40	.40
238	A71	4400r multicolored	.55	.55
239	A71	7500r multicolored	.95	.95
a.		Souvenir sheet, #235-239 + label	2.50	2.50
		Nos. 235-239 (5)	2.35	2.35

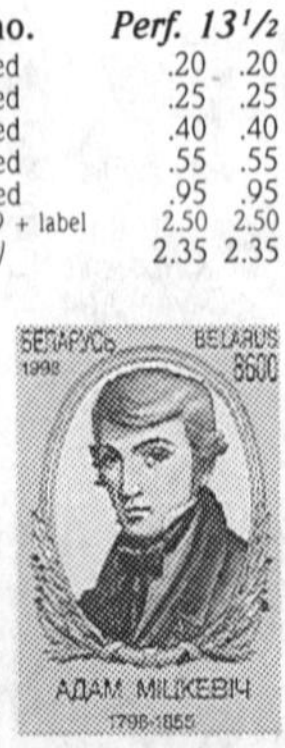

Adam Mickiewicz (1798-1855), Poet — A73

		1998, May 20	Litho.	Perf. 14
241	A73	8600r multicolored	1.10	1.10

No. 67 Surcharged in Silver with Post Horn, New Value and Cyrillic Text

		1998, May 22		Perf. 12
242	A13	8600r on 150r multi	1.10	1.10

St. Petersburt-Mahilyou Post Route, 225th anniv.

Songbirds from Red Book of Belarus — A74

Designs: 1500r, Luscinia svecica. 3200r, Remiz pendulinus. 3800r, Acrocephalus paludicola. 5300r, Locustella luscinioides. 8600r, Parus cyanus.

		1998, May 29		Perf. 14
243	A74	1500r multicolored	.20	.20
244	A74	3200r multicolored	.40	.40
245	A74	3800r multicolored	.50	.50
246	A74	5300r multicolored	.65	.65
247	A74	8600r multicolored	1.10	1.10
a.		Sheet of 2 each #243-247	5.75	5.75
		Nos. 243-247 (5)	2.85	2.85

Mills, Musical Instruments — A75

Designs: 100r, Water-powered mill. 200r, Windmill. 3200r, Dulcimer. 5300r, Hurdy-gurdy.

		1998		Perf. 13½x14
248	A75	100r green & black	.15	.15
249	A75	200r brown & black	.15	.15
251	A75	3200r apple green & black	1.00	1.00
252	A75	5300r bister, black & buff	1.75	1.75
		Nos. 248-252 (4)	3.05	3.05

Issued: 100r, 200r, 7/1/98. 3200r, 5300r, 6/23/98. Numbers have been reserved for additional values in this set.

BELGIAN CONGO

ˈbel-jən ˈkäŋ-(ˌ)gō

LOCATION — Central Africa
GOVT. — Belgian colony
AREA — 902,082 sq. mi. (estimated)
POP. — 12,660,000 (1956)
CAPITAL — Léopoldville

Congo was an independent state, founded by Leopold II of Belgium, until 1908 when it was annexed to Belgium as a colony. In 1960 it became the independent Republic of the Congo. See Congo Democratic Republic and Zaire.

100 Centimes = 1 Franc

Catalogue values for unused stamps in this country are for Never Hinged items, beginning with Scott 187 in the regular postage section, Scott B32 in the semi-postal section, Scott C17 in the airpost section, and Scott J8 in the postage due section.

Independent State

King Leopold II
A1 A2 A3

		1886	Unwmk.	Typo.	Perf. 15
1	A1	5c green		8.00	20.00
2	A1	10c rose			
3	A2	25c blue		40.00	32.50
4	A3	50c olive green		6.00	6.00

5	A1	5fr lilac	325.00	250.00
a.		Perf. 14	800.00	
b.		5fr deep lilac	700.00	475.00

Counterfeits exist.
For surcharge see No. Q1.

King Leopold II — A4

		1887-94		
6	A4	5c grn ('89)	.75	.75
7	A4	10c rose ('89)	1.25	1.25
8	A4	25c blue ('89)	1.25	1.25
9	A4	50c reddish brown	45.00	20.00
10	A4	50c gray ('94)	2.50	15.00
11	A4	5fr violet	900.00	375.00
12	A4	5fr gray ('92)	110.00	95.00
13	A4	10fr buff ('91)	400.00	275.00

The 25fr and 50fr in gray were not issued. Values, each $20.

Counterfeits exist of Nos. 10-13, 25fr and 50fr, unused, used, genuine stamps with faked cancels and counterfeit stamps with genuine cancels.
For surcharges see Nos. Q3-Q6.

Port Matadi — A5

River Scene on the Congo, Stanley Falls — A6

Inkissi Falls — A7

Railroad Bridge on M'pozo River — A8

Hunting Elephants A9

Bangala Chief and Wife — A10

		1894-1901	Engr.	Perf. 12½ to 15
14	A5	5c pale bl & blk	12.50	12.50
15	A5	5c red brn & blk ('95)	3.25	1.35
16	A5	5c grn & blk ('00)	1.75	.50
17	A6	10c red brn & blk	12.50	12.50
18	A6	10c grnsh bl & blk ('95)	1.50	1.25
a.		Center inverted	1,850.	2,250.
19	A6	10c car & blk ('00)	3.00	.75
20	A7	25c yel org & blk	3.25	2.25
21	A7	25c lt bl & blk ('00)	3.00	1.25
22	A8	50c grn & blk	1.25	1.25
23	A8	50c ol & blk ('00)	3.00	.75
24	A9	1fr lilac & blk	20.00	11.00
a.		1fr rose lilac & black	225.00	22.50
25	A9	1fr car & blk ('01)	200.00	5.00
26	A10	5fr lake & blk	40.00	25.00
a.		5fr carmine rose & black	85.00	35.00
		Nos. 14-26 (13)	305.00	75.35

For overprints see Nos. 31-32, 34, 36-37, 39.

Climbing Oil Palms — A11

Congo Canoe — A12

		1896		
27	A11	15c ocher & blk	3.25	.95
28	A12	40c bluish grn & blk	3.25	2.50

For overprints see Nos. 33, 35.

Congo Village — A13

River Steamer on the Congo — A14

		1898		
29	A13	3.50fr red & blk	140.00	80.00
a.		Perf. 14x12	350.00	225.00
30	A14	10fr yel grn & blk	90.00	24.00
a.		Center inverted	25,000.	
b.		Perf. 12	525.00	22.50
c.		Perf. 12x14	325.00	
		As "c," pen canceled		14.00

For overprints see Nos. 38, 40.

Belgian Congo

Overprinted **CONGO BELGE**

		1908		
31	A5	5c green & blk	7.00	7.00
a.		Handstamped	2.50	1.75
32	A6	10c carmine & blk	12.00	12.00
a.		Handstamped	2.50	1.75
33	A11	15c ocher & blk	7.00	7.00
a.		Handstamped	5.50	
34	A7	25c lt blue & blk	3.75	2.50
a.		Handstamped	7.00	3.50
c.		Double overprint (#34)	185.00	
35	A12	40c bluish grn & blk	2.25	2.25
a.		Handstamped	7.00	5.50
36	A8	50c olive & blk	4.00	2.25
a.		Handstamped	3.75	
b.		Inverted overprint (#36)	500.00	
37	A9	1fr carmine & blk	19.00	2.25
a.		Handstamped	25.00	7.00
38	A13	3.50fr red & blk	25.00	20.00
a.		Handstamped	160.00	110.00
39	A10	5fr carmine & blk	40.00	24.00
a.		Handstamped	60.00	40.00
40	A14	10fr yel grn & blk	85.00	20.00
a.		Perf. 14	225.00	
b.		Handstamped	125.00	45.00
c.		Handstamped, perf. 14	275.00	225.00
		Nos. 31-40 (10)	205.00	99.25

Most of the above handstamps are also found inverted and double.
Values for handstamped overprints are for those applied locally.
Counterfeits of the handstamped overprints exist.

Port Matadi — A15

River Scene on the Congo, Stanley Falls — A16

Climbing Oil Palms — A17

BELGIAN CONGO

Railroad Bridge on M'pozo River — A18

1909 *Perf. 14*
41	A15	5c green & blk	.75	.75
42	A16	10c carmine & blk	.75	.50
43	A17	15c ocher & blk	25.00	15.00
44	A18	50c olive & blk	3.00	2.50
		Nos. 41-44 (4)	29.50	18.75

Port Matadi — A19

River Scene on the Congo, Stanley Falls — A20

Climbing Oil Palms — A21

Inkissi Falls — A22

Congo Canoe — A23

Railroad Bridge on M'pozo River — A24

Hunting Elephants A25

Congo Village — A26

Bangala Chief and Wife — A27

River Steamer on the Congo — A28

1910-15 *Engr.* *Perf. 14, 15*
45	A19	5c green & blk	.75	.15
46	A20	10c carmine & blk	.40	.15
47	A21	15c ocher & blk	.40	.15
48	A21	15c grn & blk ('15)	.20	.15
	a.	Booklet pane of 10	14.00	
49	A22	25c blue & blk	1.50	.30
50	A23	40c bluish grn & blk	2.00	1.75
51	A23	40c brn red & blk ('15)	3.75	1.75
52	A24	50c olive & blk	3.00	1.50
53	A24	50c brn lake & blk ('15)	6.00	1.75
54	A25	1fr carmine & blk	2.75	2.10
55	A25	1fr ol bis & blk ('15)	2.00	.65
56	A26	3fr red & blk	15.00	10.00
57	A27	5fr carmine & blk	17.00	14.00
58	A27	5fr ocher & blk ('15)	1.50	.65
59	A28	10fr green & blk	16.00	12.50
		Nos. 45-59 (15)	72.25	47.55

Nos. 48, 51, 53, 55 and 58 exist imperforate.
For overprints and surcharges see Nos. 64-76, 81-86, B5-B9.

Port Matadi — A29

Stanley Falls, Congo River — A30

Inkissi Falls — A31

TEN CENTIMES.
Type I - Large white space at top of picture and two small white spots at lower edge. Vignette does not fill frame.
Type II - Vignette completely fills frame.

1915
60	A29	5c green & blk	.15	.15
	a.	Booklet pane of 10	7.50	
61	A30	10c car & blk (II)	.20	.15
		10c carmine & black (I)	.20	.15
	d.	Booklet pane of 10 (II)	14.00	
62	A31	25c blue & blk	.85	.25
	a.	Booklet pane of 10	65.00	
		Nos. 60-62 (3)	1.20	.55

Nos. 60 to 62 exist imperforate.
For surcharges see Nos. 77-80, 87, B1-B4.

Stamps of 1910 Issue Surcharged in Red or Black

10ᶜ   **10ᶜ**

1921
64	A23	5c on 40c bluish grn & blk (R)	.25	.25
65	A19	10c on 5c grn & blk (R)	.25	.25
66	A24	10c on 50c ol & blk (R)	.25	.25
67	A21	25c on 15c ocher & blk (R)	1.50	1.00
68	A20	30c on 10c car & blk	.35	.35
69	A22	50c on 25c bl & blk (R)	1.40	.90
		Nos. 64-69 (6)	4.00	3.00

The position of the new value and the bars varies on Nos. 64 to 69.

Overprinted **1921**

1921
70	A25	1fr carmine & blk	.75	.75
	a.	Double overprint	20.00	
71	A26	3fr red & blk	2.50	2.50
72	A27	5fr carmine & blk	4.75	4.75
73	A28	10fr green & blk (R)	4.25	2.50
		Nos. 70-73 (4)	12.25	10.50

Belgian Surcharges
Nos. 51, 53, 60-62 Surcharged in Black or Red **•10ᶜ**

1922
74	A24	5c on 50c	.35	.30
75	A29	10c on 5c (R)	.35	.25
76	A23	25c on 40c (R)	2.00	.30
77	A30	30c on 10c (II)	.15	.15
	a.	30c on 10c (I)	.15	.15
	b.	Double surcharge	4.75	4.75
78	A31	50c on 25c (R)	.40	.25
		Nos. 74-78 (5)	3.25	1.25

No. 74 has the surcharge at each side.

Congo Surcharges
Nos. 60, 51 Surcharged in Red or Black:

10 c.
≡ a ≡

25 c.
b

1922
80	A29	10c on 5c (R)	.55	.55
	a.	Inverted surcharge	17.50	17.50
	b.	Double surcharge	4.75	
	c.	Double surch., one invtd.	40.00	
	d.	Pair, one without surcharge	42.50	
	e.	On No. 45	125.00	125.00
81	A23	25c on 40c	.70	.35
	a.	Inverted surcharge	17.50	17.50
	b.	Double surcharge	5.50	
	c.	"25c" double		
	d.	25c on 5c, No. 60	100.00	100.00

Nos. 55, 58 Surcharged with vertical bars over original values **10 c.**

1922
84	A25	10c on 1fr (R)	.55	.55
	a.	Double surcharge	14.00	
	b.	Inverted surcharge	17.50	17.50
85	A27	25c on 5fr	1.50	1.50

Nos. 68, 77 Handstamped **0,25**

86	A20	25c on 30c on 10c	7.00	8.50
87	A30	25c on 30c on 10c (II)	7.00	8.50

Nos. 86-87 exist with handstamp surcharge inverted.
Counterfeit handstamped surcharges exist.

Ubangi Woman — A32

Watusi Cattle — A44

Designs: 10c, Baluba woman. 15c, Babuende woman. No. 90, 40c, 1.25fr, 1.50fr, 1.75fr, Ubangi man. 25c, Basketmaking. 30c, 35c, Nos. 101, 102, Carving wood. 50c, Archer. Nos. 92, 100, Weaving. 1fr, Making pottery. 3fr, Working rubber. 5fr, Making palm oil. 10fr, African elephant.

1923-27 *Engr.* *Perf. 12*
88	A32	5c yellow	.15	.15
89	A32	10c green	.15	.15
90	A32	15c olive brn	.15	.15
91	A32	20c olive grn ('24)	.15	.15
92	A44	20c green ('26)	.15	.15
93	A44	25c red brown	.25	.15
94	A44	30c rose red ('26)	.45	.45
95	A44	30c olive grn ('25)	.15	.15
96	A44	35c green ('27)	.45	.35
97	A32	40c violet ('25)	.25	.15
98	A44	50c gray blue	.25	.15
99	A44	50c buff ('25)	.30	.15
100	A44	75c red orange	.25	.20
101	A44	75c gray bl ('25)	.40	.25
102	A44	75c salmon red ('26)	.20	.15
103	A44	1fr bister brn	.55	.15
104	A44	1fr dl blue ('25)	.35	.15
105	A44	1fr rose red ('27)	.85	.15
106	A32	1.25fr dl blue ('26)	.30	.20
107	A32	1.50fr dl blue ('26)	.30	.15
108	A32	1.75fr dl blue ('27)	3.75	3.25
109	A44	3fr gray brn ('24)	4.00	2.25
110	A44	5fr gray ('24)	10.00	4.75
111	A44	10fr gray blk ('24)	17.50	8.50

1925-26
112	A44	45c dk vio ('26)	.40	.25
113	A44	60c carmine rose	.40	.15
		Nos. 88-113 (26)	42.00	22.85

For surcharges see Nos. 114, 136-138, 157.

No. 107 Surcharged **1.75**

1927, June 14
114	A32	1.75fr on 1.50fr dl bl	.30	.20

Sir Henry Morton Stanley — A45

1928, June 30 *Perf. 14*
115	A45	5c gray blk	.15	.15
116	A45	10c dp violet	.15	.15
117	A45	20c orange red	.35	.25
118	A45	35c green	1.00	.75
119	A45	40c red brown	.40	.15
120	A45	60c black brn	.40	.15
121	A45	1fr carmine	.40	.15
122	A45	1.60fr dk gray	4.00	3.25
123	A45	1.75fr dp blue	1.65	.80
124	A45	2fr dk brown	1.10	.30
125	A45	2.75fr red violet	4.50	.45
126	A45	3.50fr rose lake	1.40	.75
127	A45	5fr slate grn	1.10	.30
128	A45	10fr violet blue	1.65	.75
129	A45	20fr claret	6.75	2.25
		Nos. 115-129 (15)	25.00	10.60

Sir Henry M. Stanley (1841-1904), explorer.

Nos. 118, 121-123, 125-126 Surcharged in Red, Blue or Black

1ᶠ25

1931, Jan. 15
130	A45	40c on 35c	.50	.40
131	A45	1.25fr on 1fr (Bl)	.40	.15
132	A45	2fr on 1.60fr	.80	.30
133	A45	2fr on 1.75fr	.75	.30
134	A45	3.25fr on 2.75fr (Bk)	2.25	2.00
135	A45	3.25fr on 3.25fr (Bk)	3.00	2.10

BELGIAN PHILATELIC SPECIALISTS, INC.

We maintain the largest stock of Belgian Colonies philatelic material in the U.S. today. Draw from the finest stock to fill out your collection. We have all Scott listed material as well as all material found in the specialized European Catalogs.

BELGIAN CONGO

88/111 NH	110.00	231/56 NH	55.00
88/111 LH	55.00	231/56 LH	35.00
115/29 NH	65.00	B12/20 NH	90.00
115/29 LH	25.00	B12/20 LH	40.00
139/56 NH	14.00	B27/31 NH	60.00
173/83 NH	30.00	B27/31 LH	34.00
187/227 NH	50.00	C7/15 NH	17.00
187/227 LH	37.50		

RUANDA-URUNDI
6-23 NH 70.00
56-59 NH 42.00
J1-7 NH 3.50

KATANGA
Complete NH 88 values $225.00

SUD KASAII
Complete NH 29 values $140.00

CONGO Specialty Items
Booklet Panes, Covers
Message Sheets, etc., all in stock.

COMPLETE PRICE LIST AVAILABLE

All are in stock. Order with confidence. Satisfaction guaranteed. Prices in U.S. Dollars.
N.Y. residents please add sales tax.

**P.O. BOX 599
LARCHMONT, NY 10538**

BELGIAN CONGO

Nos. 96, 108, 112 Surcharged in Red

= **50ᶜ** =

		Perf. 12½, 12		
136	A44	40c on 35c grn	3.25	3.00
137	A44	50c on 45c dk vio	2.00	1.10

Surcharged **2**

138	A32	2(fr) on 1.75fr dl bl	8.50	7.50
		Nos. 130-138 (9)	21.45	16.85

View of Sankuru River — A46

Flute Players — A50

Designs: 15c, Kivu Kraal. 20c, Sankuru River rapids. 25c, Uele hut. 50c, Musicians of Lake Leopold II. 60c, Batetelas drummers. 75c, Mangbetu woman. 1fr, Domesticated elephant of Api. 1.25fr, Mangbetu chief. 1.50fr, 2fr, Village of Mondimbi. 2.50fr, 3.25fr, Okapi. 4fr, Canoes at Stanleyville. 5fr, Woman preparing cassava. 10fr, Baluba chief. 20fr, Young woman of Irumu.

1931-37		Engr.	Perf. 11½	
139	A46	10c gray brn ('32)	.15	.15
140	A46	15c gray ('32)	.15	.15
141	A46	20c brn lil ('32)	.15	.15
142	A46	25c dp blue ('32)	.15	.15
143	A46	40c dp grn ('32)	.20	.20
144	A46	50c violet ('32)	.15	.15
b.		Booklet pane of 8	6.25	
145	A46	60c vio brn ('32)	.15	.15
146	A46	75c rose ('32)	.15	.15
b.		Booklet pane of 8	1.25	
147	A50	1fr rose red ('32)	.15	.15
148	A50	1.25fr red brown	.15	.15
b.		Booklet pane of 8	1.25	
149	A46	1.50fr dk ol gray ('37)	.15	.15
b.		Booklet pane of 8	6.00	
150	A46	2fr ultra ('32)	.20	.15
151	A46	2.50fr dp blue ('37)	.30	.15
b.		Booklet pane of 8	8.50	
152	A46	3.25fr gray blk ('32)	.45	.30
153	A46	4fr dl vio ('32)	.20	.15
154	A50	5fr dp vio ('32)	.50	.25
155	A50	10fr red ('32)	.50	.40
156	A50	20fr blk blk ('32)	1.50	1.25
		Nos. 139-156 (18)	5.35	4.35

No. 109 Surcharged in Red

= **3ᶠ25** =

1932, Mar. 15			Perf. 12	
157	A44	3.25fr on 3fr gray brn	2.75	2.25

King Albert Memorial Issue

King Albert — A62

1934, May 7		Photo.	Perf. 11½	
158	A62	1.50fr black	.65	.35

Leopold I, Leopold II, Albert I, Leopold III — A63

1935, Aug. 15		Engr.	Perf. 12½x12	
159	A63	50c green	.65	.50
160	A63	1.25fr dk carmine	.65	.15
161	A63	1.50fr brown vio	.65	.15
162	A63	2.40fr brown org	2.00	2.00
163	A63	3fr lt blue	2.00	.90
164	A63	4fr brt violet	2.00	1.25
165	A63	5fr black brn	2.00	1.50
		Nos. 159-165 (7)	9.95	6.45

Founding of Congo Free State, 50th anniv. For surcharges see Nos. B21-B22.

Molindi River — A64

Bamboos — A65

Suza River — A66

Rutshuru River — A67

Karisimbi — A68

Mitumba Forest — A69

1937-38		Photo.	Perf. 11½	
166	A64	5c purple & blk	.15	.15
167	A65	90c car & brn	.40	.30
168	A66	1.50fr dp red brn & blk	.15	.15
169	A67	2.40fr ol blk & brn	.15	.15
170	A68	2.50fr dp ultra & blk	.30	.15
171	A69	4.50fr dk grn & brn	.30	.15
172	A69	4.50fr car & sep	.20	.20
		Nos. 166-171 (7)	1.65	1.25

National Parks.

No. 172 was issued in sheets of four measuring 140x111mm. It was sold by subscription, the subscription closing Oct. 20, 1937. Value, $1.60.
Nos. 166-171 were issued Mar. 1, 1938.
See No. B26. For surcharges see Nos. 184, 186.

King Albert Memorial, Leopoldville — A70

1941, Feb. 7		Litho.	Perf. 11	
173	A70	10c lt gray	.20	.15
174	A70	15c brown vio	.25	.15
175	A70	25c lt blue	.30	.15
176	A70	50c lt violet	.25	.15
177	A70	75c rose pink	.95	.30
178	A70	1.25fr gray	.30	.15
179	A70	1.75fr orange	.95	.45
180	A70	2.50fr carmine	.65	.15
181	A70	2.75fr vio blue	.95	.60
182	A70	5fr lt olive grn	4.00	1.50
183	A70	10fr rose red	2.75	1.75
		Nos. 173-183 (11)	11.55	5.50

Exist imperforate.
For surcharge see No. 185.

Nos. 168, 179, 169 Surcharged in Blue or Black

5 c.

75 c.

Nos. 184, 186   No. 185

1941-42			Perf. 11½, 11	
184	A66	5c on 1.50fr (Bl)	.15	.15
a.		Inverted surcharge	14.00	14.00
185	A70	75c on 1.75fr ('42)	.35	.35
a.		Inverted surcharge	14.00	14.00
186	A67	2.50fr on 2.40fr ('42)	.85	.70
a.		Double surcharge	27.50	27.50
b.		Inverted surcharge	14.00	14.00
		Nos. 184-186 (3)	1.35	1.20

Catalogue values for unused stamps in this section, from this point to the end of the section, are for Never Hinged items.

Oil Palms

A71   A72

Congo Woman — A73

Askari — A75

Leopard A74

Okapi — A76

Inscribed "Congo Belge Belgisch Congo"

1942, May 23		Engr.	Perf. 12½	
187	A71	5c red	.15	.15
188	A72	10c olive grn	.15	.15
189	A72	15c brown car	.15	.15
190	A72	20c dp ultra	.15	.15
191	A72	25c brown vio	.15	.15
192	A72	30c blue	.15	.15
193	A72	50c dp green	.15	.15
194	A72	60c chestnut	.15	.15
195	A73	75c dl lil & blk	.15	.15
196	A73	1fr dk brn & blk	.20	.15
197	A73	1.25fr rose red & blk	.20	.15
198	A74	1.75fr dk gray brn	.75	.35
199	A74	2fr ocher	.75	.15
200	A74	2.50fr carmine	.75	.15
201	A75	3.50fr dk ol grn	.35	.15
202	A75	5fr orange	.70	.15
203	A75	6fr brt ultra	.50	.15
204	A75	7fr black	.60	.15
205	A75	10fr dp brown	.75	.15
206	A76	20fr plum & blk	8.00	.65
		Nos. 187-206 (20)	14.90	3.70

Same Inscribed "Belgisch Congo Congo Belge"

207	A72	10c olive grn	.15	.15
208	A72	15c brown car	.15	.15
209	A72	20c dp ultra	.15	.15
210	A72	25c brown vio	.15	.15
211	A72	30c blue	.15	.15
212	A72	50c dp green	.15	.15
213	A72	60c chestnut	.15	.15
214	A73	75c dl lil & blk	.15	.15
215	A73	1fr dk brn & blk	.20	.15
216	A73	1.25fr rose red & blk	.20	.15
217	A74	1.75fr dk gray brn	.75	.35
218	A74	2fr ocher	.75	.15
219	A74	2.50fr carmine	.75	.15
220	A75	3.50fr dk ol grn	.30	.15
221	A75	5fr orange	.55	.15
222	A75	6fr brt ultra	.55	.15
223	A75	7fr black	.55	.15
224	A75	10fr dp brown	.65	.15
225	A76	20fr plum & blk	7.00	.65
		Nos. 207-225 (19)	13.45	3.55

Miniature sheets of Nos. 193, 194, 197, 200, 211, 214, 217 and 219 were printed in 1944 by the Belgian Government in London and given to the Belgian political review, Message, which distributed them to its subscribers, one a month. Value per sheet, about $12.50.

Remainders of these eight miniature sheets received marginal overprints in various colors in 1950, specifying a surtax of 100fr per sheet and paying tribute to the UPU. These sheets, together with four of Ruanda-Urundi, were sold by the Committee of Cultural Works (and not at post offices) in sets of 12 for 1,217.15 francs. Set value, about $150.

Nos. 187-227 imperforate had no franking value.
For surcharges see Nos. B34-B37.

Congo Woman — A77

Askari — A78

1943, Jan. 1				
226	A77	50fr ultra & blk	6.50	.40
227	A78	100fr car & blk	7.50	.60

Slaves and Arab Guards A79

Auguste Lambermont A80

Design: 10fr, Leopold II.

		Perf. 13x11½, 12½x12		
1947		Engr.	Unwmk.	
228	A79	1.25fr black brown	.25	.15
229	A80	3.50fr dark blue	.40	.15
230	A80	10fr red orange	.75	.15
		Nos. 228-230 (3)	1.40	.45

50th anniv. of the abolition of slavery in Belgian Congo. See Nos. 261-262.

Baluba Carving of Former King — A82

Carved Figures and Masks of Baluba Tribe: 10c, 50c, 2fr, "Ndoha," figure of tribal king. 15c, 70c, 1.20fr, 2.50fr, "Tshimanyi," an idol. 20c, 75c, 1.60fr, 3.50fr, "Buangakokoma," statue of kneeling beggar. 25c, 1fr, 2.40fr, 5fr, "Mbuta," sacred double cup, carved with two faces, Man and Woman. 40c, 1.25fr, 6fr, 8fr, "Ngadimuashi," female mask. 1.50fr, 3fr, 10fr, 50fr, "Buadi-Muadi," mask with squared features. 6.50fr, 20fr, 100fr, "Mbowa," executioner's mask with buffalo horns.

1947-50			Perf. 12½	
231	A82	10c dp org ('48)	.15	.15
232	A82	15c ultra ('48)	.15	.15
233	A82	20c brt bl ('48)	.15	.15
234	A82	25c rose car ('48)	.20	.15
235	A82	40c violet ('48)	.15	.15

BELGIAN CONGO

236	A82	50c olive brn	.15	.15
237	A82	70c yel grn ('48)	.15	.15
238	A82	75c magenta ('48)	.15	.15
239	A82	1fr yel org & dk vio	1.50	.15
240	A82	1.20fr gray & brn ('50)	.20	.15
241	A82	1.25fr lt brn & mag ('48)	.30	.15
242	A82	1.50fr ol & mag ('50)	14.00	1.10
243	A82	1.60fr bl gray & brt bl ('50)	.40	.15
244	A82	2fr org & mag ('48)	.20	.15
245	A82	2.40fr bl grn & dk grn ('50)	.30	.15
246	A82	2.50fr brn red & bl grn	.30	.15
247	A82	3fr lt ultra & ind ('49)	4.25	.15
248	A82	3.50fr lt bl & blk ('48)	3.50	.15
249	A82	5fr bis & mag ('48)	1.25	.15
250	A82	6fr brn org & ind ('48)	1.40	.15
251	A82	6.50fr red org & red brn ('49)	1.90	.15
252	A82	8fr gray bl & dk grn ('50)	1.25	.15
253	A82	10fr pale vio & red brn ('48)	4.00	.15
254	A82	20fr red org & vio brn ('48)	1.90	.15
255	A82	50fr dp org & blk ('48)	3.75	.15
256	A82	100fr crim & blk brn ('48)	4.00	.30
		Nos. 231-256 (26)	45.65	5.00

Railroad Train and Map — A83

1948, July 1   Unwmk.   Perf. 13½

257	A83	2.50fr dp bl & grn	1.00	.15

50th anniv. of railway service in the Congo.

Globe and Ship — A84

1949, Nov. 21   Perf. 11½
Granite Paper

258	A84	4fr violet blue	.85	.15

75th anniv. of the UPU.

Allegorical Figure and Map — A85

1950, Aug. 12   Perf. 12x12½

259	A85	3fr blue & indigo	1.75	.15
260	A85	6.50fr car rose & blk brn	2.00	.25

Establishment of Katanga Province, 50th anniv.

Portrait Type of 1947
1.50fr, Cardinal Lavigerie. 3fr, Baron Dhanis.

Perf. 12½x12
1951, June 25   Unwmk.

261	A80	1.50fr purple	2.00	.25
262	A80	3fr black brown	2.00	.15

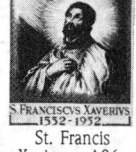

Littonia — A86    St. Francis Xavier — A86a

1952-53   Photo.   Perf. 11½
Granite Paper
Flowers in Natural Colors
Size: 21x25½mm

263	A86	10c Dissotis	.15	.15
264	A86	15c Protea	.15	.15
265	A86	20c Vellozia	.15	.15
266	A86	25c shown	.15	.15
267	A86	40c Ipomoea	.20	.15
268	A86	50c Angraecum	.15	.15
269	A86	60c Euphorbia	.15	.15
270	A86	75c Ochna	.15	.15
271	A86	1fr Hibiscus	.15	.15
272	A86	1.25fr Protea ('53)	.65	.45
273	A86	1.50fr Schrizoglossum	.15	.15
274	A86	2fr Ansellia	.25	.15
275	A86	3fr Costus	.25	.15
276	A86	4fr Nymphaea	.30	.15
277	A86	5fr Thunbergia	.45	.15
278	A86	6.50fr Thonningia	.55	.15
279	A86	7fr Gerbera	.55	.15
280	A86	8fr Gloriosa ('53)	.90	.15
281	A86	10fr Silene ('53)	1.65	.15
282	A86	20fr Aristolochia	1.40	.15

Size: 22x32mm

283	A86	50fr Eulophia ('53)	7.00	.45
284	A86	100fr Crytosepalum ('53)	11.00	1.00
		Nos. 263-284 (22)	26.50	4.75

Nos. 264, 269 and 270 with additional surcharges are varieties of Congo Democratic Republic Nos. 324, 327 and 328.

1953, Jan. 5   Engr.   Perf. 12½x13

285	A86a	1.50fr ultra & gray blk	.75	.30

400th death anniv. of St. Francis Xavier.

Canoe on Lake Kivu — A87

1953, Jan. 5   Perf. 14

286	A87	3fr car & blk	1.25	.20
287	A87	7fr dp bl & brn org	1.25	.25

Issued to publicize the Kivu Festival, 1953.

Royal Colonial Institute Jubilee Medal — A88

Design: 6.50fr, Same with altered background and transposed inscriptions.

1954, Dec. 27   Photo.   Perf. 13½

288	A88	4.50fr indigo & gray	1.10	.28
289	A88	6.50fr dk grn & brn	.90	.15

25th anniv. of the founding of the Belgian Royal Colonial Institute.

King Baudouin and Tropical Scene — A89

Designs: King and various views.

Inscribed "Congo Belge-Belgisch Congo"
Engr.; Portrait Photo.
1955, Feb. 15   Unwmk.   Perf. 11½
Portrait in Black

290	A89	1.50fr rose car	.70	.25
291	A89	3fr green	.25	.15
292	A89	4.50fr ultra	.30	.15
293	A89	6.50fr dp claret	.55	.15

Inscribed "Belgisch Congo-Congo Belge"

294	A89	1.50fr rose car	.30	.16
295	A89	3fr green	.25	.15
296	A89	4.50fr ultra	.30	.15
297	A89	6.50fr deep claret	.55	.15
		Nos. 290-297 (8)	3.20	1.31

Map of Africa and Emblem of Royal Touring Club — A90

1955, July 26   Engr.   Perf. 11½
Inscription in French

298	A90	6.50fr vio blue	3.25	.25

Inscription in Flemish

299	A90	6.50fr vio blue	3.25	.25

5th International Congress of African Tourism, Elisabethville, July 26-Aug. 4. Nos. 298-299 printed in alternate rows.

Kings of Belgium — A91

1958, July 1   Unwmk.   Perf. 12½

300	A91	1fr rose vio	.22	.15
301	A91	1.50fr ultra	.22	.15
302	A91	3fr rose car	.22	.15
303	A91	5fr green	.70	.32
304	A91	6.50fr brn red	.45	.15
305	A91	10fr dl vio	.65	.15
		Nos. 300-305 (6)	2.46	1.07

Belgium's annexation of Congo, 50th anniv.

Roan Antelope — A92   Black Buffaloes — A93

Animals: 20c, White rhinoceros. 40c, Giraffe. 50c, Thick-tailed bushbaby. 1fr, Gorilla. 2fr, Black-and-white colobus (monkey). 3fr, Elephants. 5fr, Okapis. 6.50fr, Impala. 8fr, Giant pangolin. 10fr, Eland and zebras.

1959, Oct. 15   Photo.   Perf. 11½
Granite Paper

306	A92	10c bl & brn	.15	.15
307	A93	20c red org & slate	.15	.15
308	A92	40c brn & bl	.15	.15
309	A93	50c brt ultra, red & sep	.15	.15
310	A92	1fr brn, grn & blk	.15	.15
311	A93	1.50fr blk & org yel	.15	.15
312	A92	2fr crim, blk & brn	.15	.15
313	A93	3fr blk, gray & lil rose	.25	.15
314	A92	5fr brn, dk brn & brt grn	.40	.20
315	A93	6.50fr bl, brn & org yel	.45	.15
316	A92	8fr org brn, ol bis & lil	.50	.30
317	A93	10fr multi	.60	.15
		Nos. 306-317 (12)	3.25	2.00

Madonna and Child — A94

1959, Dec. 1   Unwmk.   Perf. 11½

318	A94	50c golden brn, ocher & red brn	.15	.15
319	A94	1fr dk bl, pur & red brn	.15	.15
320	A94	2fr gray, brt bl & red brn	.20	.15
		Nos. 318-320 (3)	.50	.45

Map of Africa and Symbolic Honeycomb — A95

1960, Feb. 19   Unwmk.   Perf. 11½
Inscription in French

321	A95	3fr gray & red	.25	.15

Inscription in Flemish

322	A95	3fr gray & red	.25	.15

Commission for Technical Co-operation in Africa South of the Sahara (C. C. T. A.), 10th anniv.

SEMI-POSTAL STAMPS

Types of 1910-15 Issues Surcharged in Red   **+ 10c**

1918, May 15   Unwmk.   Perf. 14, 15

B1	A29	5c + 10c grn & bl	.15	.20
B2	A30	10c + 15c car & bl (I)	.15	.20
B3	A21	15c + 20c bl grn & bl	.15	.20
B4	A31	25c + 25c dp bl & pale bl	.20	.25
B5	A23	40c + 40c brn red & bl	.40	.45
B6	A24	50c + 50c brn lake & bl	.40	.45
B7	A25	1fr + 1fr ol bis & bl	2.00	2.25
B8	A27	5fr + 5fr ocher & bl	11.00	17.50
B9	A28	10fr + 10fr grn & bl	85.00	150.00
		Nos. B1-B9 (9)	99.45	171.50

The position of the cross and the added value varies on the different stamps.
Nos. B1-B9 exist imperforate.

SP1

Design: #B11 inscribed "Belgisch Congo."

1925, July 8   Perf. 12½

B10	SP1	25c + 25c carmine & blk	.20	.25
B11	SP1	25c + 25c carmine & blk	.20	.25
a.		Pair, Nos. B10-B11	.40	.50

Colonial campaigns in 1914-1918.
The surtax helped erect at Kinshasa a monument to those who died in World War I.

Nurse Weighing Child — SP3

First Aid Station — SP5

20c+10c, Missionary & Child. 60c+30c, Congo hospital. 1fr+50c, Dispensary service. 1.75fr+75c, Convalescent area. 3.50fr+1.50fr, Instruction on bathing infant. 5fr+2.50fr, Operating room. 10fr+5fr, Students.

1930, Jan. 16   Engr.   Perf. 11½

B12	SP3	10c + 5c ver	.55	.55
B13	SP3	20c + 10c dp brn	.70	.70
B14	SP5	35c + 15c dp grn	1.25	1.25
B15	SP5	60c + 30c dl vio	1.50	1.50
B16	SP3	1fr + 50c dk car	2.25	2.25
B17	SP5	1.75fr + 75c dp bl	4.25	4.50
B18	SP5	3.50fr + 1.50fr rose lake	8.50	8.50
B19	SP5	5fr + 2.50fr red brn	7.50	7.50
B20	SP5	10fr + 5fr gray blk	8.50	8.50
		Nos. B12-B20 (9)	35.00	35.25

The surtax was intended to aid welfare work among the natives, especially the children.

Nos. 161, 163 Surcharged "+50c" in Blue or Red

1936, May 15   Perf. 12½x12

B21	A63	1.50fr + 50c (Bl)	2.50	3.00
B22	A63	2.50fr + 50c (R)	2.00	2.00

Surtax was for the King Albert Memorial Fund.

Queen Astrid with Congolese Children — SP12

BELGIAN CONGO — BELGIUM

1936, Aug. 29   Photo.   *Perf. 12½*
B23	SP12	1.25fr + 5c dark brown	.40 .35
B24	SP12	1.50fr + 10c dull rose	.40 .35
B25	SP12	2.50fr + 25c dark blue	.60 .60
		Nos. B23-B25 (3)	1.40 1.30

Issued in memory of Queen Astrid. The surtax was for the aid of the National League for Protection of Native Children.

National Park Type of 1937-38
Souvenir Sheet

1938, Oct. 3   *Perf. 11½*
Star in Yellow
B26		Sheet of 6	18.00 18.00
a.	A64	5c ultra & light brown	3.00 3.00
b.	A65	90c ultra & light brown	3.00 3.00
c.	A66	1.50fr ultra & light brown	3.00 3.00
d.	A67	2.40fr ultra & light brown	3.00 3.00
e.	A68	2.50fr ultra & light brown	3.00 3.00
f.	A69	4.50fr ultra & light brown	3.00 3.00

Intl. Tourist Cong. A surtax of 3.15fr was for the benefit of the Congo Tourist Service.

Marabou Storks and Vultures — SP14

Buffon's Kob — SP15

Designs: 1.50fr+1.50fr, Pygmy chimpanzees. 4.50fr+4.50fr, Dwarf crocodiles. 5fr+5fr, Lioness.

1939   Photo.   *Perf. 14*
B27	SP14	1fr + 1fr dp claret	5.50 5.50
B28	SP15	1.25fr + 1.25fr car	5.50 5.50
B29	SP15	1.50fr + 1.50fr brt pur	7.50 7.50
B30	SP14	4.50fr + 4.50fr sl grn	5.50 5.50
B31	SP15	5fr + 5fr brown	6.00 6.00
		Nos. B27-B31 (5)	30.00 30.00

Surtax for the Leopoldville Zoological Gardens. Sold in full sets by subscription.

> Catalogue values for unused stamps in this section, from this point to the end of the section, are for Never Hinged items.

Lion of Belgium and Inscription "Belgium Shall Rise Again" — SP19

1942, Feb. 17   Engr.   *Perf. 12½*
B32	SP19	10fr + 40fr brt grn	1.50 1.75
B33	SP19	10fr + 40fr vio bl	1.50 1.75

Nos. 193, 216, 198 and 220 Surcharged in Red

Au profit de la Croix Rouge + 50 Fr. Ten voordeele van het Roode Kruis
a

Ten voordeele van het Roode Kruis + 100 Fr. Au profit de la Croix Rouge
b

Au profit de la Croix Rouge + 100 Fr. Ten voordeele van het Roode Kruis
c

1945
B34	A72 (a)	50c + 50fr	2.00 3.25
B35	A73 (b)	1.25fr + 100fr	2.00 3.25
B36	A74 (c)	1.75fr + 100fr	2.00 3.50
B37	A75 (b)	3.50fr + 100fr	2.00 3.50
		Nos. B34-B37 (4)	8.00 13.50

The surtax was for the Red Cross. Sold in full sets by subscription.

Mozart at Age 7 — SP20

Queen Elisabeth and Sonata by Mozart — SP21

Perf. 11½
1956, Oct. 10   Unwmk.   Engr.
B38	SP20	4.50fr + 1.50fr brt lil	2.00 2.00
B39	SP21	6.50fr + 2.50fr ultra	3.00 3.00

200th anniv. of the birth of Wolfgang Amadeus Mozart.
The surtax was for the Pro-Mozart Committee.

Nurse and Children — SP22

Designs: 4.50fr+50c, Patient receiving injection. 6.50fr+40c, Patient being bandaged.

1957, Dec. 10   Photo.   *Perf. 13x10½*
Cross in Carmine
B40	SP22	3fr + 50c dk bl	.90 .85
B41	SP22	4.50fr + 50c dk grn	.80 .75
B42	SP22	6.50fr + 50c red brn	1.00 .95
		Nos. B40-B42 (3)	2.70 2.55

The surtax was for the Red Cross.

High Jump — SP23

1960, May 2   Unwmk.   *Perf. 13½*
B43	SP23	50c + 25c shown	.15 .20
B44	SP23	1.50fr + 50c Hurdles	.20 .20
B45	SP23	2fr + 1fr Soccer	.20 .25
B46	SP23	3fr + 1.25fr Javelin	.75 .80
B47	SP23	6.50fr + 3.50fr Discus	1.00 1.10
		Nos. B43-B47 (5)	2.30 2.55

17th Olympic Games, Rome, Aug. 25-Sept. 11. The surtax was for the youth of Congo.

AIR POST STAMPS

Wharf on Congo River AP1

Congo "Country Store" AP2

View of Congo River AP3

Stronghold in the Interior — AP4

1920, July 1   Unwmk.   Engr.   *Perf. 12*
C1	AP1	50c orange & blk	.15 .15
C2	AP2	1fr dull vio & blk	.15 .15
C3	AP3	2fr blue & blk	.50 .20
C4	AP4	5fr green & blk	.90 .40
		Nos. C1-C4 (4)	1.70 .90

Kraal — AP5

Porters on Safari AP6

1930, Apr. 2
C5	AP5	15fr dk brn & blk	1.90 .75
C6	AP6	30fr brn vio & blk	2.25 .75

Fokker F VII over Congo — AP7

1934, Jan. 22   *Perf. 13½x14*
C7	AP7	50c gray black	.15 .15
C8	AP7	1fr dk carmine	.20 .15
a.		Booklet pane of 8	5.25
C9	AP7	1.50fr green	.15 .15
C10	AP7	3fr brown	.20 .15
C11	AP7	4.50fr brt ultra	.25 .15
a.		Booklet pane of 8	10.00
C12	AP7	5fr red brown	.20 .15
C13	AP7	15fr brown vio	.40 .25
C14	AP7	30fr red-orange	.70 .60
C15	AP7	5fr violet	2.00 .95
		Nos. C7-C15 (9)	4.25 2.70

The 1fr, 3fr, 4.50fr, 5fr, 15fr exist imperf.

No. C10 Surcharged in Blue with New Value and Bars

1936, Mar. 25
C16	AP7	3.50fr on 3fr brown	.20 .15

> Catalogue values for unused stamps in this section, from this point to the end of the section, are for Never Hinged items.

No. C9 Surcharged in Black

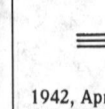

50 c.

1942, Apr. 27
C17	AP7	50c on 1.50fr green	.35 .15
a.		Inverted surcharge	6.50 6.50

POSTAGE DUE STAMPS

In 1908-23 regular postage stamps handstamped "TAXES" or "TAXE," usually boxed, were used in lieu of postage due stamps.

D1

1923-29(?)   Typo.   Unwmk.   *Perf. 14*
J1	D1	5c black brown	.15 .15
J2	D1	10c rose red	.15 .15
J3	D1	15c violet	.15 .15
J4	D1	30c green	.25 .25
J5	D1	50c ultramarine	.30 .30
J6	D1	50c blue ('29)	.30 .30
J7	D1	1fr gray	.45 .45
		Nos. J1-J7 (7)	1.75 1.50

> Catalogue values for unused stamps in this section, from this point to the end of the section, are for Never Hinged items.

D2   D3

1943   *Perf. 14x14½*
J8	D2	10c olive green	.15 .15
J9	D2	20c dark ultra	.15 .15
J10	D2	50c green	.15 .15
J11	D2	1fr dark brown	.20 .15
J12	D2	2fr yellow orange	.25 .25
		Nos. J8-J12 (5)	.90 .90

1943   *Perf. 12½*
J8a	D2	10c olive green	.30 .30
J9a	D2	20c dark ultramarine	.30 .30
J10a	D2	50c green	.30 .30
J11a	D2	1fr dark brown	.45 .45
J12a	D2	2fr yellow orange	.45 .45
		Nos. J8a-J12a (5)	1.80 1.80

1957   Engr.   *Perf. 11½*
J13	D3	10c olive brown	.15 .15
J14	D3	15c claret	.15 .15
J15	D3	50c green	.15 .15
J16	D3	1fr light blue	.25 .25
J17	D3	2fr vermilion	.40 .25
J18	D3	4fr purple	.60 .35
J19	D3	6fr violet blue	.75 .45
		Nos. J13-J19 (7)	2.50 1.75

PARCEL POST STAMPS

PP1   PP2

PP3

Handstamped Surcharges on Nos. 5, 11-12

1887-93   Unwmk.   *Perf. 15*
Blue-Black Surcharge
Q1	PP1	3.50fr on 5fr lilac	950.00 725.00

Black Surcharge
Q3	PP2	3.50fr on 5fr vio	850.00 500.00
Q4	PP3	3.50fr on 5fr vio ('88)	575.00 325.00
a.		Blue surcharge	625.00 375.00
Q6	PP3	3.50fr on 5fr gray ('93)	95.00 70.00

Nos. Q1, Q3-Q4, Q4a and Q6 are known with inverted surcharge, No. Q1 with double surcharge and No. Q6 in pair with unsurcharged stamp. These varieties sell for somewhat more than the normal surcharges.

Genuine stamps with counterfeit surcharges, counterfeit stamps with counterfeit surcharges, and both with counterfeit cancels exist.

BELGIUM

ˈbel-jəm

LOCATION — Western Europe, bordering the North Sea
GOVT. — Constitutional Monarchy
AREA — 11,778 sq. mi.
POP. — 9,853,000 (est. 1983)

BELGIUM

CAPITAL — Brussels

100 Centimes = 1 Franc

Catalogue values for unused stamps in this country are for Never Hinged items, beginning with Scott 322 in the regular postage section, Scott B370 in the semi-postal section, Scott C8 in the airpost section, Scott CB1 in the airpost semi-postal section, Scott J40 in the postage due section, Scott M1 in the military stamp section, Scott O36 in the officials section, and Scott Q267 in the parcel post section.

Watermark

Wmk. 96 (No Frame)

King Leopold I
A1   A2

Wmk. Two "L's" Framed (96)

1849	Engr.		Imperf.
1	A1	10c brown	2,300. 75.00
a.		10c red brown	3,500. 475.00
b.		10c bister brown	2,500. 120.00
2	A1	20c blue	2,850. 57.50
a.		20c milky blue	3,250. 160.00
b.		20c greenish blue	3,500. 290.00

The reprints are on thick and thin wove and thick laid paper unwatermarked.

A pale blue shade exists that is often confused with the milky blue.

A souvenir sheet containing reproductions of the 10c, 20c and 40c of 1849-51 with black burelage on back was issued Oct. 17, 1949, for the cent. of the 1st Belgian stamps. It was sold at BEPITEC 1949, an intl. stamp exhib. at Brussels, and was not valid.

1849-50

3	A2	10c brown ('50)	2,000. 90.00
4	A2	20c blue ('50)	1,750. 52.50
5	A2	40c carmine rose	1,625. 425.00

Nos. 3-5 were printed on both thick and thin paper and sell for about the same prices.

Wmk. Two "L's" Without Frame (96)

1851-54

6	A2	10c brown	525.00 8.50
a.		Ribbed paper ('54)	900.00 50.00
7	A2	20c blue	550.00 8.00
a.		Ribbed paper ('54)	900.00 47.50
8	A2	40c car rose	2,750. 95.00
a.		Ribbed paper ('54)	3,500. 260.00

Nos. 6-8 were printed on both thin and thick paper and sell for about the same prices.

Nos. 6a, 7a, 8a must have regular and parallel ribs covering the whole stamp.

1858-61 Unwmk.

9	A2	1c green ('61)	225.00 125.00
10	A2	10c brown	375.00 7.50
11	A2	20c blue	400.00 9.00
12	A2	40c carmine rose	2,400. 70.00

Nos. 9 and 13 were valid for postage on newspapers and printed matter only.

Nos. 10-12 were printed in two sizes: 21mm high (with a 16½mm high oval) and 22mm high (with a 17¼mm high oval). The 22mm high stamps were issued in 1861. The 21mm high stamps sell for more.

Reprints of Nos. 9 to 12 are on thin wove paper. The colors are brighter than those of the originals. They were made from the dies and show lines outside the stamps.

1863-65 Perf. 14½

13	A2	1c green ('65)	35.00 25.00
14	A2	10c brown ('65)	47.50 3.25
15	A2	20c blue ('65)	50.00 9.00
16	A2	40c carmine rose ('65)	325.00 25.00
		Nos. 13-16 (4)	457.50 56.50

Values for Nos. 13-16 are for copies with perfs cutting into design.

Nos. 13-16 also come perf 12½ and 12½x13, which were issued in 1863. Values differ. See the Scott Classic Specialized Catalogue.

King Leopold I
A3   A3a

A4   A4a

A5

London Print

1865 Typo. Perf. 14
17 A5 1fr pale violet   1,300. 110.00

Brussels Print
Thick or Thin Paper

1865-67 Perf. 15

18	A3	10c slate ('67)	125.00 1.50
b.		Pair, imperf. between	
19	A3a	20c blue ('67)	175.00 1.50
a.		20c lilac blue	190.00 2.00
20	A4	30c brown ('67)	425.00 11.00
b.		Pair, imperf. between	1,100.
21	A4a	40c rose ('67)	450.00 20.00
22	A5	1fr violet	1,200. 90.00

Nos. 18-22 also come perf. 14½x14, issued in 1865-66. Values differ. See the Scott Classic Specialized Catalogue. Nos. 18b and 20b are from the earlier printings.

The reprints are on thin paper, imperforate and ungummed.

Coat of Arms — A6

1866-67 Imperf.
23 A6 1c gray   250.00 150.00

Perf. 15, 14½x14

24	A6	1c gray	45.00 16.00
25	A6	2c blue ('67)	135.00 90.00
26	A6	5c brown	150.00 90.00
		Nos. 23-26 (4)	580.00 346.00

Nos. 23-26 were valid for postage on newspapers and printed matter only.

Values are for perf. 15 stamps. Values for 14½x14 differ. See the Scott Classic Specialized Catalogue.

Counterfeits exist.

Reprints of Nos. 24-26 are on thin paper, imperforate and ungummed.

Imperf. varieties of 1869-1912 (between Nos. 28-105) are without gum.

A7   A8   A9

A10   A11   A12

King Leopold II
A13   A14   A15

1869-70 Perf. 15

28	A7	1c green	6.50 .30
29	A7	2c ultra ('70)	20.00 1.50
30	A7	5c buff ('70)	45.00 .75
31	A7	8c lilac ('70)	80.00 50.00
32	A8	10c green	20.00 .40
33	A9	20c lt ultra ('70)	140.00 .90
34	A10	30c buff ('70)	75.00 4.00
35	A11	40c brt rose ('70)	110.00 6.00
36	A12	1fr dull lilac ('70)	350.00 17.00
a.		1fr rose lilac	350.00 20.00
		Nos. 28-36 (9)	846.50 80.85

The frames and inscriptions of Nos. 30, 31 and 42 differ slightly from the illustration.

Minor "broken letter" varieties exist on several values.

Nos. 28-30, 32-33, 35-38 also were printed in aniline colors. These are not valued separately.

See Nos. 40-43, 49-51, 55.

1875-78

37	A13	25c olive bister	135.00 1.25
a.		25c ocher	135.00 1.50
38	A14	50c gray	200.00 8.50
		Roller cancel	12.50
a.		50c gray black	325.00 55.00
b.		50c deep black	1,750. 225.00
39	A15	5fr dp red brown	1,500. 1,250.
		Roller cancel	575.00
a.		5fr pale brown ('78)	3,750. 1,250.
		Roller cancel	575.00

Dangerous counterfeits of No. 39 exist.

Printed in Aniline Colors

1881 Perf. 14

40	A7	1c gray green	20.00 .60
41	A7	2c lt ultra	17.50 2.50
42	A7	5c orange buff	57.50 1.10
a.		5c red orange	57.50 1.10
43	A8	10c gray green	30.00 .80
44	A13	25c olive bister	75.00 2.50
		Nos. 40-44 (5)	200.00 7.50

See note following No. 36.

A16   A17

A18   A19

1883

45	A16	10c carmine	27.50 2.50
46	A17	20c gray	150.00 7.75
47	A18	25c blue	260.00 35.00
		Roller cancel	15.00
48	A19	50c violet	260.00 35.00
		Roller cancel	15.00
		Nos. 45-48 (4)	697.50 80.25

A20   A21

A22

1884-85 Perf. 14

49	A7	1c olive green	13.50 .85
50	A7	1c gray	4.00 .30
51	A7	5c green	32.50 .40

BELGIAN PHILATELIC SPECIALISTS, INC.

BELGIUM & COLONIES

We maintain the most comprehensive, specialized stock of philatelic material of Belgium and her former African Colonies through the independence struggle of the 1960's. Why look anywhere else? We have it all!! All conditions in stock:
NH, LH, ☉, FDC, New Issues, Folders, Philatelic Literature, etc.!
Some samples from our extensive holdings:

REGULAR ISSUES

Sc.#	Price	Sc.#	Price
108-122 LH	$350.00	172-184 NH	$175.00
(Type I, II, III, and Ia in stock!)		172-184 LH	70.00
144-161 LH	$12.00	185-190 LH	90.00
162-169 NH	75.00	212-215 LH	160.00
162-169 LH	33.00	(All Varieties in Stock)	

BACK-OF-THE-BOOK-ISSUES

Sc.#	Price	Sc.#	Price
C1-4 LH	$7.00	Q328-35 LH	$27.00
C5 LH	27.00	Q343-61B LH	165.00
C6-7 LH	11.00	Same, Used	6.00
C8-11 LH	9.00	Q388-406 LH	110.00
C10a/11a LH	175.00	Same, Used	8.50
J3-11 LH	67.50	Q410-12 NH	75.00
J12-16 LH	225.00	Same, Used	16.00
042-46 LH	30.00	Q437 NH	49.00
047-55 LH	30.00	Q438-59 NH	100.00
P1-19 LH	110.00	Same, Used	25.00
P20-40 LH	135.00	Q466-70 NH	21.00
Q267-90 LH	15.00		

All other BACK-OF-THE-BOOK Material in Stock
ORDER WITH CONFIDENCE.
Prices in U.S. Dollars.
N.Y. residents please add sales tax.
P.O. BOX 599
LARCHMONT, NY 10538

Belgium

FREE PRICE LISTS
Sets & Singles • Year Sets • Parcel Post • Covers & Specialized • Colonies • Complete stock of Imperfs & Proofs

WE BUY! - TOP PRICES PAID!

Save 10%!
Complete Run Mint NH 1958-1998
Purchase the complete run of Belgium Year Sets 1958-1998 and save 10%!
Regularly — $1483.25
10%Off! — $1334.90

For buying or selling Belgium and all other U.S., Asia & Worldwide call

1-800-9-4-STAMP
(1-800-947-8267)

Henry Gitner Philatelists, Inc.
P.O. Box 3077-S
Middletown, NY 10940
Toll Free: 1-800-947-8267
Fax: 914-343-0068
E-mail: hgitner@hgitner.com
http://www.hgitner.com

Philately-The Quiet Excitement!

BELGIUM

52	A20	10c rose, *bluish*	10.00	.40
a.		Grayish paper	11.00	.50
c.		Yellowish paper	200.00	35.00
53	A21	25c blue, *pink* ('85)	11.00	.75
54	A22	1fr brown, *grnsh*	600.00	17.50

The frame and inscription of No. 51 differ slightly from the illustration.
See note after No. 36.

A23  A24
A25  A26 

1886-91

55	A7	2c purple brn ('88)	12.50	1.50
56	A23	20c olive, *grnsh*	140.00	1.25
57	A24	35c vio brn, *brnsh* ('91)	18.00	3.00
58	A25	50c bister, *yelsh*	9.50	2.25
59	A26	2fr violet, *pale lil*	100.00	45.00
		Roller cancel		6.00
		Nos. 55-59 (5)	280.00	53.00

Coat of Arms A27   King Leopold A28

1893-1900

60	A27	1c gray	1.10	.20
61	A27	2c yellow	1.25	1.10
a.		Wmkd. coat of arms in sheet ('95)	—	—
62	A27	2c violet brn ('94)	1.65	.30
63	A27	2c red brown ('98)	3.25	.50
64	A27	5c yellow grn	7.75	.30
65	A28	10c orange brn	5.00	.30
66	A28	10c brt rose ('96)	3.50	.40
67	A28	20c olive green	22.50	.60
68	A28	25c ultra	20.00	.50
a.		No ball to "5" in upper left corner	32.50	12.50
69	A28	35c violet brn	25.00	1.50
a.		35c red brown	42.50	2.40
70	A28	50c bister	62.50	20.00
71	A28	50c gray ('97)	57.50	2.50
72	A28	1fr car, *lt grn*	75.00	20.00
73	A28	1fr orange ('00)	90.00	5.00
74	A28	2fr lilac, *rose*	90.00	70.00
75	A28	2fr lilac ('00)	150.00	13.50
		Nos. 60-75 (16)	616.00	136.70

Values quoted for Nos. 60-107 are for stamps with label attached. Stamps without label sell for much less.

Antwerp Exhibition Issue

Arms of Antwerp — A29

1894

76	A29	5c green, *rose*	4.75	3.25
77	A29	10c carmine, *bluish*	3.75	2.50
78	A29	25c blue, *rose*	1.00	1.00
		Nos. 76-78 (3)	9.50	6.75

Belgium stamps can be mounted in the annually supplemented Scott Belgium album.

Brussels Exhibition Issue

St. Michael and Satan
A30   A31

1896-97   Perf. 14x14½

79	A30	5c deep violet	1.00	.60
80	A31	10c orange brown	8.50	3.50
81	A31	10c lilac brown	.50	.35
		Nos. 79-81 (3)	10.00	4.45

A32  A33
A34  A35 
A36  A37  
A38  A39  

Two types of 1c:
I - Periods after "Dimanche" and "Zondag" in label.
II - No period after "Dimanche." Period often missing after "Zondag."

1905-11   Perf. 14

82	A32	1c gray (I) ('07)	1.50	.20
a.		Type II ('08)	2.00	.60
83	A32	2c red brown ('07)	14.50	5.75
84	A32	5c green ('07)	11.50	.60
85	A33	10c dull rose	1.75	.60
86	A34	20c olive grn	26.00	1.00
87	A35	25c ultra	12.00	.85
a.		25c deep blue '11	13.50	2.00
88	A36	35c red brn	25.00	1.75
89	A37	50c bluish gray	95.00	4.00
90	A38	1fr yellow orange	110.00	8.00
91	A39	2fr violet	75.00	22.50
		Bar cancellation		5.00
		Nos. 82-91 (10)	372.25	45.25

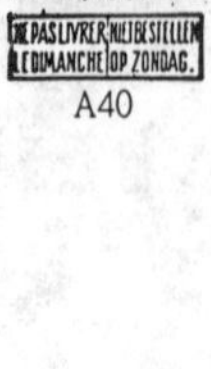

A40 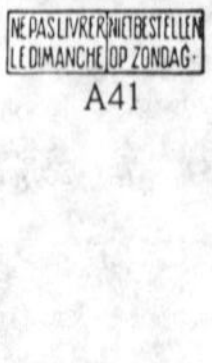 A41

Lion of Belgium — A42   A43

King Albert I — A44

1912

92	A40	1c orange	.15	.15
93	A41	2c orange brn	.25	.45
94	A42	5c green	.15	.15
95	A43	10c red	.75	.40
96	A43	20c olive grn	16.00	4.00
97	A43	35c bister brn	1.00	.70
98	A43	40c green	16.00	14.50
99	A43	50c gray	1.00	.80
100	A43	1fr orange	4.00	3.00
101	A43	2fr violet	17.50	17.50
102	A43	5fr plum	80.00	25.00
		Nos. 92-102 (11)	136.80	66.65

Counterfeits exist of Nos. 97-102. Those of No. 102 are common.
For overprints see Nos. Q49-Q50, Q52, Q55-Q55A, Q57-Q60.

A45

1912-13   Larger Head

103	A45	10c red	.40	.20
a.		Without engraver's name	.15	.25
104	A45	20c olive grn ('13)	.40	.40
a.		Without engraver's name	2.00	2.00
105	A45	25c ultra	.25	.40
a.		With engraver's name	4.25	3.00
107	A45	40c green ('13)	.50	.60
		Nos. 103-107 (4)	1.55	1.60

For overprints see #Q51, Q53-Q54, Q56.

Albert I A46   Cloth Hall of Ypres A47

Bridge of Dinant — A48

Library of Louvain — A49

Scheldt River at Antwerp A50

Anti-slavery Campaign in the Congo — A51

King Albert I at Furnes — A52

Kings of Belgium Leopold I, Albert I, Leopold II A53

1915-20   Typo.   Perf. 14, 14½

108	A46	1c orange	.15	.15
109	A46	2c chocolate	.15	.15
110	A46	3c gray blk ('20)	.30	.15
111	A46	5c green	1.00	.15
112	A46	10c carmine	.90	.15
113	A46	15c purple	1.50	.15
114	A46	20c red violet	3.00	.20
115	A46	25c blue	.50	.40

Engr.

116	A47	35c brown org & blk	.50	.30
117	A48	40c green & black	1.00	.30
a.		Vert. pair, imperf. btwn.	4.50	.30
118	A49	50c car rose & blk	4.50	.30
119	A50	1fr violet	32.50	1.00
120	A51	2fr slate	21.00	2.00
121	A52	5fr dp blue	275.00	125.00
		Telegraph or railroad cancel		55.00
122	A53	10fr brown	20.00	20.00
		Nos. 108-122 (15)	362.00	150.40

Two types each of the 1c, 10c and 20c; three of the 2c and 15c; four of the 5c, differing in the top left corner.
See No. 138. For surcharges see Nos. B34-B47.

Perron of Liege (Fountain) A54   King Albert in Trench Helmet A55

1919   Perf. 11½

123	A54	25c deep blue	2.40	.35
a.		Sheet of 10	5,500.	5,750.

Perf. 11, 11½, 11½x11, 11x11½
1919

Size: 18½x22mm

124	A55	1c lilac brn	.15	.15
125	A55	2c olive	.15	.15

Size: 22x26

126	A55	5c green	.20	.20
127	A55	10c carmine, 22x26¾mm	.25	.25
a.		Size: 22½x26mm	1.00	.60
128	A55	15c gray vio, 22x26¾mm	.30	.30
a.		Size: 22½x26mm	2.40	
129	A55	20c olive blk	1.10	1.10
130	A55	25c deep blue	1.60	1.60
131	A55	35c bister brn	3.00	3.00
132	A55	40c red	5.00	5.00
133	A55	50c red brn	9.50	10.00
134	A55	1fr lt orange	40.00	40.00
135	A55	2fr violet	375.00	375.00

Size: 28x33½mm

136	A55	5fr car lake	100.00	100.00
137	A55	10fr claret	110.00	110.00
		Nos. 124-137 (14)	646.25	646.75
		Set, never hinged		1,143.

Type of 1915 Inscribed: "FRANK" instead of "FRANKEN"

1919, Dec.   Perf. 14, 15

138	A52	5fr deep blue	1.75	1.25

BELGIUM

Town Hall at Termonde — A56

1920   *Perf. 11½*
139	A56	65c claret & black, 27x22mm	.75	.20
		Never hinged	1.50	
a.		Center inverted	57,500.	
b.		Size: 26¼x22½mm	5.75	2.40

For surcharge see No. 143.

Nos. B48-B50 Surcharged in Red or Black

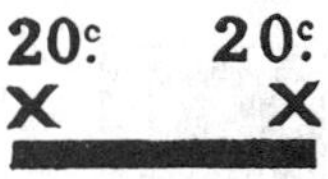

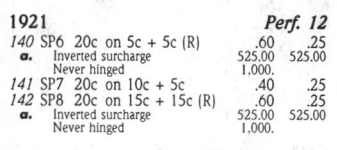

1921   *Perf. 12*
140	SP6	20c on 5c + 5c (R)	.60	.25
a.		Inverted surcharge	525.00	525.00
		Never hinged	1,000.	
141	SP7	20c on 10c + 5c	.40	.25
142	SP8	20c on 15c + 15c (R)	.60	.25
a.		Inverted surcharge	525.00	525.00
		Never hinged	1,000.	

No. 139 Surcharged in Red

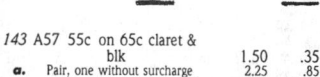

143	A57	55c on 65c claret & blk	1.50	.35
a.		Pair, one without surcharge	2.25	.85
		Nos. 140-143 (4)	3.10	1.10
		Set, never hinged	7.30	

A58    A59

1922-27   Typo.   *Perf. 14*
144	A58	1c orange	.15	.15
145	A58	2c olive ('26)	.20	.20
146	A58	3c fawn	.15	.15
147	A58	5c gray	.15	.15
148	A58	10c blue grn	.15	.15
149	A58	15c plum ('23)	.15	.15
150	A58	20c black brn	.20	.15
151	A58	25c magenta	.20	.20
a.		25c dull violet ('23)	.50	.15
152	A58	30c vermilion	.50	.15
153	A58	30c rose ('25)	.35	.15
154	A58	35c red brown	.35	.30
155	A58	35c blue grn ('27)	.80	.35
156	A58	40c rose	.50	.15
157	A58	50c bister ('25)	.50	.20
158	A58	60c olive brn ('27)	3.00	.15
159	A58	1.25fr dp blue ('26)	1.10	1.10
160	A58	1.50fr brt blue ('26)	1.60	.40
161	A58	1.75fr ultra ('27)	1.25	.15
a.		Tete beche pair	5.00	5.00
c.		Bklt. pane of 4 + 2 labels	40.00	
		Nos. 144-161 (18)	11.30	4.40
		Set, never hinged	27.00	

See Nos. 185-190. For overprints and surcharges see Nos. 191-195, 197, B56, O1-O6.

Perf. 11, 11x11½, 11½, 11½x11, 11½x12, 11½x12½, 12½
1921-25   Engr.
162	A59	50c dull blue	.30	.15
163	A59	75c scarlet ('22)	.25	.25
164	A59	75c ultra ('24)	.45	.15
165	A59	1fr black brn ('22)	.80	.15
166	A59	1fr blue ('25)	.60	.20
167	A59	2fr dk green ('22)	.90	.25
168	A59	5fr brown vio ('23)	13.50	15.00
169	A59	10fr magenta ('22)	9.00	6.50
		Nos. 162-169 (8)	25.80	22.65
		Set, never hinged	50.00	

No. 162 measures 18x20¾mm and was printed in sheets of 100.

Philatelic Exhibition Issues

1921, May 26   *Perf. 11½*
170	A59	50c dark blue	3.50	3.50
		Never hinged	4.75	
a.		Sheet of 25	200.00	175.00
		Never hinged	225.00	

No. 170 measures 17½x21¼mm, was printed in sheets of 25 and sold at the Philatelic Exhibition at Brussels.

The sheet normally has pin holes and a cancellation-like marking in the margin. These are considered unused and the condition valued here.

Souvenir Sheet

1924, May 24   *Perf. 11½*
171		Sheet of 4	140.00	140.00
		Never hinged	250.00	
a.		A59 5fr red brown	10.00	10.00
		Never hinged	12.00	

Sold only at the Intl. Phil. Exhib., Brussels. Sheet size: 130x145mm.

The sheet normally has pin holes and a cancellation-like marking in the margin. These are considered unused and the condition valued here.

Kings Leopold I and Albert I — A60

1925   *Perf. 14*
172	A60	10c dp green	7.25	7.25
173	A60	15c dull vio	3.75	4.50
174	A60	20c red brown	3.75	4.50
175	A60	25c grnsh black	3.75	4.50
176	A60	30c vermilion	3.75	4.50
177	A60	35c lt blue	3.75	4.50
178	A60	40c brnsh blk	3.75	4.50
179	A60	50c yellow brn	3.75	4.50
180	A60	75c dk blue	3.75	4.50
181	A60	1fr dk violet	6.50	6.50
182	A60	2fr ultra	4.00	4.00
183	A60	5fr blue blk	3.75	4.50
184	A60	10fr dp rose	6.50	8.00
		Nos. 172-184 (13)	58.00	66.25
		Set, never hinged	125.00	

75th anniv. of Belgian postage stamps.
Nos. 172-184 were sold only in sets and only by The Administration of Posts, not at post offices.

A61

1926-27   Typo.
185	A61	75c dk violet	.75	.70
186	A61	1fr pale yellow	.60	.35
187	A61	1fr rose red ('27)	1.00	.35
a.		Tete beche pair	7.50	4.50
c.		Bklt. pane 4 + 2 labels	25.00	
188	A61	2fr Prus blue	2.50	.45
189	A61	5fr emerald ('27)	27.50	1.65
190	A61	10fr dk brown ('27)	60.00	7.75
		Nos. 185-190 (6)	92.35	11.10
		Set, never hinged	250.00	

For overprints and surcharge see Nos. 196, Q174-Q175.

Stamps of 1921-27 Surcharged in Carmine, Red or Blue — 1F75

1927
191	A58	3c on 2c olive (C)	.15	.15
192	A58	10c on 15c plum (R)	.15	.15
193	A58	35c on 40c rose (Bl)	.45	.15
194	A58	1.75fr on 1.50fr brt bl (C)	2.25	.80
		Nos. 191-194 (4)	3.00	1.25
		Set, never hinged	3.70	

Nos. 153, 185 and 159 Surcharged in Black — BRUXELLES 1929 BRUSSEL =5c=

1929, Jan. 1
195	A58	5c on 30c rose	.15	.15
196	A61	5c on 75c dk violet	.15	.15
197	A58	5c on 1.25fr dp blue	.15	.15
		Nos. 195-197 (3)	.45	.45
		Set, never hinged	.60	

The surcharge on Nos. 195-197 is a precancelation which alters the value of the stamp to which it is applied.
Values for precanceled stamps in unused column are for those which have not been through the post and have original gum. Values in second column are for postally used, gumless stamps.

A63    A64

1929-32   Typo.   *Perf. 14*
198	A63	1c orange	.15	.15
199	A63	2c emerald ('31)	.45	.45
200	A63	3c red brown	.15	.15
201	A63	5c slate	.15	.15
c.		Bklt. pane of 4 + 2 labels	8.25	
202	A63	10c olive grn	.15	.15
c.		Bklt. pane of 4 + 2 labels	4.50	
203	A63	20c brt violet	1.00	.25
204	A63	25c rose red	.45	.15
c.		Bklt. pane of 4 + 2 labels	8.25	
205	A63	35c green	.60	.15
c.		Bklt. pane of 4 + 2 labels	9.75	
206	A63	40c red vio ('30)	.30	.15
c.		Bklt. pane of 4 + 2 labels	9.75	
207	A63	50c dp blue	.45	.15
c.		Bklt. pane of 4 + 2 labels	8.25	
208	A63	60c rose ('30)	1.90	.20
c.		Bklt. pane of 4 + 2 labels	30.00	
209	A63	70c org brn ('30)	1.10	.15
c.		Bklt. pane of 4 + 2 labels	22.50	
210	A63	75c dk blue ('30)	2.00	.15
211	A63	75c dp brown ('32)	6.00	.15
b.		Bklt. pane of 4 + 2 labels	100.00	
		Nos. 198-211 (14)	14.85	2.55
		Set, never hinged	53.00	

For overprints and surcharges see Nos. 225-226, 240-241, 254-256, 309, O7-O15.

Tete Beche Pairs

201a	A63	5c	.60	.60
202a	A63	10c	.30	.30
204a	A63	25c	1.75	1.75
205a	A63	35c	2.75	2.75
206a	A63	40c	2.75	2.75
207a	A63	50c	2.25	2.25
208a	A63	60c	8.00	7.50
209a	A63	70c	6.00	5.00
210a	A63	75c	9.00	8.50
211a	A63	75c	27.50	25.00
		Nos. 201a-211a (10)	60.90	56.40
		Set, never hinged	116.00	

1929, Jan. 25   Engr.   *Perf. 14½, 14*
212	A64	10fr dk brown	15.00	4.50
213	A64	20fr dk green	85.00	20.00
214	A64	50fr red violet	13.50	13.50
a.		Perf. 14½	37.50	40.00
215	A64	100fr brownish lake	13.50	13.50
a.		Perf. 14½	37.50	40.00
		Nos. 212-215 (4)	127.00	51.50
		Set, never hinged	275.00	

Peter Paul Rubens — A65    Zenobe Gramme — A66

1930, Apr. 26   Photo.   *Perf. 12½x12*
216	A65	35c blue green	.40	.20
217	A66	35c blue green	.40	.20
		Set, never hinged	2.10	

No. 216 issued for the Antwerp Exhibition, No. 217 the Liege Exhibition.

Leopold I, by Jacques de Winne — A67    Leopold II, by Joseph Lempoels — A68

Design: 1.75fr, Albert I.

1930, July 1   Engr.   *Perf. 11½*
218	A67	60c brown violet	.20	.20
219	A68	1fr carmine	1.10	1.10
220	A68	1.75fr dk blue	2.75	1.25
		Nos. 218-220 (3)	4.05	2.55
		Set, never hinged	10.00	

Centenary of Belgian independence.
For overprints see Nos. 222-224.

Antwerp Exhibition Issue
Souvenir Sheet

Arms of Antwerp — A70

1930, Aug. 9   *Perf. 11½*
221	A70	4fr Sheet of 1	87.50	87.50
		Never hinged	125.00	

Size: 142x141mm. Inscription in lower margin "ATELIER DU TIMBRE-1930-ZEGELFABRIEK." Each purchaser of a ticket to the Antwerp Phil. Exhib., Aug. 9-15, was allowed to purchase one stamps. The ticket cost 6 francs.

The sheet normally has pin holes and a cancellation-like marking in the margin. These are considered unused and the condition valued here.

Nos. 218-220 Overprinted in Blue or Red — B.I.T. OCT. 1930

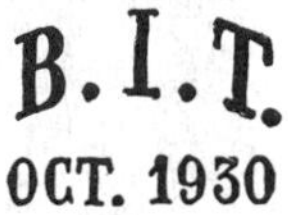

1930, Oct.
222	A67	60c brown vio (Bl)	2.00	2.00
223	A68	1fr carmine (Bl)	8.25	7.75
224	A68	1.75fr dk blue (R)	14.50	14.50
		Nos. 222-224 (3)	24.75	24.25
		Set, never hinged	54.00	

50th meeting of the administrative council of the Intl. Labor Bureau at Brussels.
The names of the painters and the initials of the engraver have been added at the foot of these stamps.

Stamps of 1929-30 Surcharged in Blue or Black: BELGIQUE 1931 BELGIË =2c= 10c

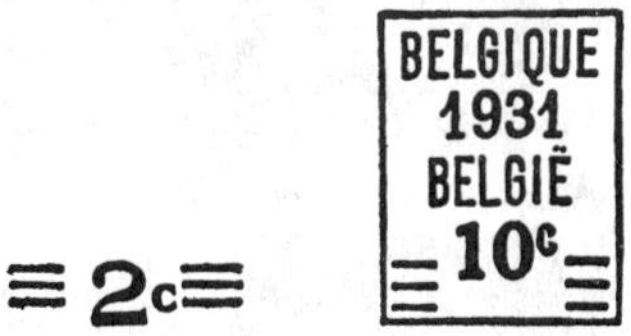

1931, Feb. 20   *Perf. 14*
225	A63	2c on 3c red brown (Bl)	.15	.15
226	A63	10c on 60c rose (Bk)	.50	.20
		Set, never hinged	3.75	

The surcharge on No. 226 is a precancelation which alters the denomination. See note after No. 197.

King Albert   A71   A71a

1931, June 15   Photo.
227	A71	1fr brown carmine	.50	.20
		Never hinged	1.00	

1932, June 1
228	A71a	75c bister brown	1.25	.15
		Never hinged	5.00	
a.		Tete beche pair	6.75	6.75
		Never hinged	17.50	
c.		Bklt. pane 4 + 2 labels	27.50	

See No. 257. For overprint see No. O18.

A72

1931-32   Engr.
229	A72	1.25fr gray black	.75	.50
230	A72	1.50fr brown vio	1.25	.50
231	A72	1.75fr dp blue	.80	.15
232	A72	2fr red brown	1.10	.20
233	A72	2.45fr dp violet	1.90	.40
234	A72	2.50fr black brn ('32)	10.00	.50

BELGIUM

235	A72	5fr dp green	18.00 1.10
236	A72	10fr claret	42.50 12.50
		Nos. 229-236 (8)	76.30 15.85
		Set, never hinged	250.00

Nos. 206 and 209 Surcharged as No. 226, but dated "1932"

1932, Jan. 1

240	A63	10c on 40c red vio	2.50 .30
241	A63	10c on 70c org brn	2.00 .20
		Set, never hinged	13.50

See note after No. 197.

Gleaner A73

Mercury A74

1932, June 1   Typo.   Perf. 13½x14

245	A73	2c pale green	.35 .35
246	A74	5c dp orange	.15 .15
247	A73	10c olive grn	.25 .15
a.		Tete beche pair	4.00 4.00
b.		Bklt. pane 4 + 2 labels	15.00
248	A74	20c brt violet	1.00 .20
249	A73	25c deep red	.60 .15
a.		Tete beche pair	3.50 3.50
b.		Bklt. pane 4 + 2 labels	15.00
250	A74	35c dp green	2.40 .15
		Nos. 245-250 (6)	4.75 1.15
		Set, never hinged	15.30

For overprints see Nos. O16-O17.

Auguste Piccard's Balloon — A75

1932, Nov. 26   Engr.   Perf. 11½

251	A75	75c red brown	3.50 .30
252	A75	1.75fr dk blue	13.50 2.10
253	A75	2.50fr dk violet	17.00 11.50
		Nos. 251-253 (3)	34.00 13.90
		Set, never hinged	94.50

Issued in commemoration of Prof. Auguste Piccard's two ascents to the stratosphere.

Nos. 206 and 209 Surcharged as No. 226, but dated "1933"

1933, Nov.   Perf. 14

254	A63	10c on 40c red vio	14.00 4.00
255	A63	10c on 70c org brn	12.50 1.50
		Set, never hinged	65.00

No. 206 Surcharged as No. 226, but dated "1934"

1934, Feb.

256	A63	10c on 40c red vio	12.50 1.50
		Never hinged	3.00

For Nos. 254 to 256 see note after No. 197. Regummed copies of Nos. 254-256 abound.

King Albert Memorial Issue
Type of 1932 with Black Margins

1934, Mar. 10   Photo.

257	A71a	75c black	.30 .15
		Never hinged	.60

Congo Pavilion — A76

Designs: 1fr, Brussels pavilion. 1.50fr, "Old Brussels." 1.75fr, Belgian pavilion.

1934, July 1   Perf. 14x13½

258	A76	35c green	.70 .30
259	A76	1fr dk carmine	1.25 .40
260	A76	1.50fr brown	5.00 .80
261	A76	1.75fr blue	5.00 .30
		Nos. 258-261 (4)	11.95 1.80
		Set, never hinged	43.75

Brussels Intl. Exhib. of 1935.

King Leopold III
A80   A81

1934-35   Perf. 13½x14

262	A80	70c olive blk ('35)	.35 .15
a.		Tete beche pair	1.50 1.00
c.		Bklt. pane 4 + 2 labels	6.25
263	A80	75c brown	.65 .25

Perf. 14x13½

264	A81	1fr rose car ('35)	3.00 .35
		Nos. 262-264 (3)	4.00 .75
		Set, never hinged	10.25

For overprint see No. O19.

Coat of Arms — A82

1935-48   Typo.   Perf. 14

265	A82	2c green ('37)	.15 .15
266	A82	5c orange	.15 .15
267	A82	10c olive bister	.15 .15
a.		Tete beche pair	.25 .25
b.		Bklt. pane 4 + 2 labels	4.50
268	A82	15c dk violet	.15 .15
269	A82	20c lilac	.15 .15
270	A82	25c carmine rose	.15 .15
a.		Tete beche pair	.30 .25
c.		Bklt. pane 4 + 2 labels	4.50
271	A82	25c yel grn ('46)	.15 .15
272	A82	30c brown	.15 .15
273	A82	35c green	.15 .15
a.		Tete beche pair	.30 .15
b.		Bklt. pane 4 + 2 labels	3.00
274	A82	40c red vio ('38)	.20 .15
275	A82	50c blue	.40 .15
276	A82	60c slate ('41)	.15 .15
277	A82	65c red lilac ('46)	.25 .15
278	A82	70c lt blue grn ('45)	.25 .25
279	A82	75c lilac rose ('45)	.25 .15
280	A82	80c green ('48)	3.50 .40
281	A82	90c dull vio ('46)	.15 .15
282	A82	1fr red brown ('45)	.15 .15
		Nos. 265-282 (18)	6.65 3.05
		Set, never hinged	15.00

Several stamps of type A82 exist in various shades.
Nos. 265, 361 were privately overprinted and surcharged "+10FR." by the Association Belgo-Americaine for the dedication of the Bastogne Memorial, July 16, 1950. The overprint is in six types.
See design O1. For overprints and surcharges see Nos. 312-313, 361-364, 390-394, O20-O22, O24, O26-O28, O33.

A83    A83a

Perf. 14, 14x13½, 11½

1936-51   Photo.

Size: 17½x21¾mm

283	A83	70c brown	.30 .15
a.		Tete beche pair	.80 .80
c.		Bklt. pane 4 + 2 labels	7.50

Size: 20¾x24mm

284	A83a	1fr rose car	.30 .15
285	A83a	1.20fr dk brown ('51)	.80 .15
286	A83a	1.50fr brt red vio ('43)	.40 .30
287	A83a	1.75fr dp ultra ('43)	.20 .20
288	A83a	1.75fr dk car ('50)	.15 .15
289	A83a	2fr dk pur ('43)	1.00 1.00
290	A83a	2.25fr grnsh blk ('43)	.25 .20
291	A83a	2.50fr org red ('51)	1.75 .30
292	A83a	3.25fr chestnut ('43)	.20 .20
293	A83a	5fr dp green ('43)	1.00 .40
		Nos. 283-293 (11)	6.35 3.20
		Set, never hinged	16.65

Nos. 287-288, 290-291, 293 inscribed "Belgie-Belgique."
See designs A85, A91. For overprints and surcharges see #314, O23, O25, O29, O31, O34.

A84   A85

1936-51   Engr.   Perf. 14x13½

294	A84	1.50fr rose lilac	.60 .35
295	A84	1.75fr dull blue	.20 .15
296	A84	2fr dull vio	.40 .30
297	A84	2.25fr gray vio ('41)	.25 .25
298	A84	2.45fr black	32.50 .70
299	A84	2.50fr ol blk ('40)	2.00 .25
300	A84	3.25fr org brn ('41)	.30 .20
301	A84	5fr dull green	2.40 .50
302	A84	10fr vio brn	.60 .15
a.		10fr light brown	1.00 .20
303	A84	20fr vermilion	1.00 .30

Perf. 11½

304	A84	3fr yel brn ('51)	.55 .15
305	A84	4fr bl, *bluish* ('50)	1.50 .15
a.		White paper	5.50 .15
306	A84	6fr brt rose car ('51)	2.75 .20
307	A84	10fr brn vio ('51)	.55 .15
308	A84	20fr red ('51)	1.10 .20
		Nos. 294-308 (15)	46.70 4.65
		Set, never hinged	144.00

See No. 1159. For overprint and surcharges see Nos. 316-317, O32.

No. 206 Surcharged as No. 226, but dated "1937"

1937   Unwmk.   Perf. 14

309	A63	10c on 40c red vio	.20 .20
		Never hinged	.30

See note after No. 197.

1938-41   Photo.   Perf. 13½x14

310	A85	75c olive gray	.25 .15
a.		Tete beche pair	.75 .75
c.		Bklt. pane 4 + 2 labels	6.75
311	A85	1fr rose pink ('41)	.15 .15
a.		Tete beche pair	.25 .25
b.		Booklet pane of 6	2.25
c.		Bklt. pane 4 + 2 labels	2.25
		Set, never hinged	.75

For overprints and surcharges see Nos. 315, O25, O30, O35.

Nos. 272, 274, 283, 310, 299, 298 Surcharged in Blue, Black, Carmine or Red

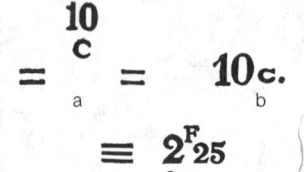

= 10c = 10c.
  a   b

= 2F25
   c

1938-42

312	A82 (a)	10c on 30c (Bl)	.15 .15
313	A82 (a)	10c on 40c (Bl)	.15 .15
314	A83 (b)	10c on 70c (Bk)	.15 .15
315	A85 (b)	50c on 75c (C)	.20 .15
316	A84 (c)	2.25fr on 2.50fr (C)	.45 .45
317	A84 (c)	2.50fr on 2.45fr (R)	11.00 .20
		Nos. 312-317 (6)	12.10 1.25
		Set, never hinged	26.55

Issue date: No. 317, Oct. 31, 1938.

Basilica and Bell Tower — A86

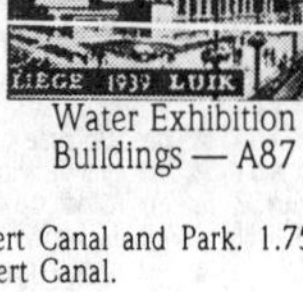

Water Exhibition Buildings — A87

Designs: 1.50fr, Albert Canal and Park. 1.75fr, Eygenbilsen Cut in Albert Canal.

Perf. 14x13½, 13½x14

1938, Oct. 31

318	A86	35c dk blue grn	.20 .20
319	A87	1fr rose red	.45 .30
320	A87	1.50fr vio brn	1.10 .60
321	A87	1.75fr ultra	1.25 .20
		Nos. 318-321 (4)	3.00 1.30
		Set, never hinged	10.80

Intl. Water Exhibition, Liège, 1939.

Catalogue values for unused stamps in this section, from this point to the end of the section, are for Never Hinged items.

Lion Rampant A90

Leopold III, Crown and V A91

1944   Unwmk.   Photo.   Perf. 12½
Inscribed: "Belgique-Belgie"

322	A90	5c chocolate	.15 .15
323	A90	10c green	.15 .15
324	A90	25c lt blue	.15 .15
325	A90	35c brown	.15 .15
326	A90	50c lt bl grn	.15 .15
327	A90	75c purple	.15 .15
328	A90	1fr vermilion	.15 .15
329	A90	1.25fr chestnut	.20 .15
330	A90	1.50fr orange	.45 .40
331	A90	1.75fr brt ultra	.15 .15
332	A90	2fr aqua	3.75 1.90
333	A90	2.75fr dp mag	.20 .15
334	A90	3fr claret	.75 .60
335	A90	3.50fr sl blk	.75 .60
336	A90	5fr dk olive	6.75 4.75
337	A90	10fr black	1.25 1.10
		Nos. 322-337 (16)	15.30 10.85

Inscribed: "Belgie-Belgique"

338	A90	5c chocolate	.15 .15
339	A90	10c green	.15 .15
340	A90	25c lt bl	.15 .15
341	A90	35c brown	.15 .15
342	A90	50c lt bl grn	.15 .15
343	A90	75c purple	.15 .15
344	A90	1fr vermilion	.15 .15
345	A90	1.25fr chestnut	.15 .20
346	A90	1.50fr orange	.30 .45
347	A90	1.75fr brt ultra	.15 .15
348	A90	2fr aqua	2.00 2.00
349	A90	2.75fr dp magenta	.20 .15
350	A90	3fr claret	.65 .75
351	A90	3.50fr slate blk	.65 .75
352	A90	5fr dark olive	5.75 5.00
353	A90	10fr black	1.00 1.25
		Nos. 338-353 (16)	11.90 11.75

1944-57   Perf. 14x13½

354	A91	1fr brt rose red	.35 .15
355	A91	1.50fr magenta	.50 .15
356	A91	1.75fr dp ultra	.50 .55
357	A91	2fr dp vio	1.50 .15
358	A91	2.25fr grnsh blk	.55 .65
359	A91	3.25fr chnt brn	.75 .15
360	A91	5fr dk bl grn	3.00 .15
a.		Perf. 11½ ('57)	75.00 .15
		Nos. 354-360 (7)	7.15 1.95

Nos. 355, 357, 359 inscribed "Belgique-Belgie." For surcharges see Nos. 365-367 and footnote following No. 367.

Stamps of 1935-41 Overprinted in Red V

1944   Perf. 14

361	A82	2c pale green	.15 .15
362	A82	15c indigo	.15 .15
363	A82	20c brt violet	.15 .15
364	A82	60c slate	.25 .15
		Nos. 361-364 (4)	.70 .60

See note following No. 282.

Nos. 355, 357, and 360 Surcharged Typographically in —10% Black or Carmine

1946   Perf. 14x13½

365	A91	On 1.50fr magenta	.40 .15
366	A91	On 2fr dp vio (C)	1.50 .15
367	A91	On 5fr dk bl grn (C)	2.00 .30
		Nos. 365-367 (3)	3.90 .90

To provide denominations created by a reduction in postal rates, the Government produced #365-367 by typographed surcharge. Also, each post

BELGIUM

office was authorized on May 20, 1946, to surcharge its stock of 1.50fr, 2fr and 5fr stamps "-10 percent." Hundreds of types and sizes of this surcharge exist, both hand-stamped and typographed. These include the "1,35," "1,80" and "4,50" applied at Ghislenghien.

M. S. Prince Baudouin — A92

2.25fr, S.S. Marie Henriette. 3.15fr, S.S. Diamant.

Perf. 14x13½, 13½x14
1946, June 15   Photo.   Unwmk.
368	A92	1.35fr brt bluish grn	.15	.15
369	A92	2.25fr slate green	.30	.15
370	A92	3.15fr slate black	.30	.15
		Nos. 368-370 (3)	.75	.45

Centenary of the steamship line between Ostend and Dover.
#368 exists in two sizes: 21¼x18¼mm and 21x17mm. #369-370 are 24½x20mm.

Capt. Adrien de Gerlache A95

Belgica and Explorers A96

1947, June   Perf. 14x13½, 11½
371	A95	1.35fr crimson rose	.45	.15
372	A96	2.25fr gray black	2.75	2.00

50th anniv. of Capt. Adrien de Gerlache's Antarctic Expedition.

Joseph A. F. Plateau — A97

1947, June   Perf. 14x13½
| 373 | A97 | 3.15fr deep blue | .80 | .15 |

Issued to mark the World Film and Fine Arts Festival, Brussels, June, 1947.

Chemical Industry — A98

Industrial Arts — A99

Agriculture — A100

Textile Industry — A102

Communications Center — A101

Iron Manufacture A103

Photogravure (#374-376, 378),
Typographed (#377, 380), Engraved
1948   Unwmk.   Perf. 11½
374	A98	60c blue grn	.85	.20
375	A98	1.20fr brown	2.25	.15
376	A99	1.35fr red brown	.85	.15
377	A99	1.75fr brt red	1.65	.15
378	A99	1.75fr dk gray grn	1.10	.15
379	A101	2.25fr gray blue	2.00	1.75
380	A100	2.50fr dk car rose	6.75	.20
381	A101	3fr brt red vio	9.00	.30
382	A101	3.15fr deep blue	2.00	.20
383	A102	4fr brt ultra	8.25	.20
384	A103	6fr blue green	13.00	.20
385	A103	6.30fr brt red vio	4.00	3.75
		Nos. 374-385 (12)	51.70	7.40

See Nos. O42-O46.

Leopold I — A104

1949, July 1   Engr.   Perf. 14x13½
386	A104	90c dk green	1.10	.60
387	A104	1.75fr brown	.90	.15
388	A104	3fr red	3.50	3.00
389	A104	4fr deep blue	5.00	1.25
		Nos. 386-389 (4)	10.50	5.00

Cent. of Belgium's 1st postage stamps.
See note on souvenir sheet below No. 2.

Stamps of 1935-45 Precanceled and Surcharged in Black

1949   Perf. 14
390	A82	5c on 15c dk vio	.15	.15
391	A82	5c on 30c brown	.15	.15
392	A82	5c on 40c red vio	.15	.15
393	A82	20c on 70c lt bl grn	.30	.35
394	A82	20c on 75c lil rose	.20	.15

Similar Surcharge and Precancellation in Black on Nos. B455-B458
Perf. 14x13½
395	SP251	10c on #B455	3.50	3.00
396	SP251	40c on #B456	1.10	.85
397	SP251	80c on #B457	.65	.50
398	SP251	1.20fr on #B458	2.25	1.50
		Nos. 390-398 (9)	8.45	6.80

See note after No. 197.

St. Mary Magdalene, from Painting by Gerard David — A105

1949, July 15   Photo.   Perf. 11
| 399 | A105 | 1.75fr dark brown | .70 | .35 |

Gerard David Exhibition at Bruges, 1949.

Allegory of UPU — A106

1949, Oct. 1   Engr.   Perf. 11½
| 400 | A106 | 4fr deep blue | 4.50 | 2.50 |

75th anniv. of the UPU.

Symbolical of Pension Fund A107

Lion Rampant A108

Perf. 11½
1950, May 1   Unwmk.   Photo.
| 401 | A107 | 1.75fr dark brown | .50 | .25 |

General Pension Fund founding, cent.

1951, Feb. 15   Engr.   Perf. 11½
| 402 | A108 | 20c blue | .25 | .15 |

1951-75   Typo.   Perf. 13½x14
Size: 17½x21mm
403	A108	2c org brn ('60)	.15	.15
404	A108	3c brt lil ('60)	.15	.15
405	A108	5c pale violet	.15	.15
406	A108	5c brt pink ('74)	.15	.15
407	A108	10c red orange	.15	.15
408	A108	15c brt pink ('59)	.15	.15
409	A108	20c claret	.15	.15
410	A108	25c green	1.75	.25
411	A108	25c lt bl grn ('66)	.15	.15
412	A108	30c gray grn ('57)	.15	.15
413	A108	40c brown olive	.15	.15
414	A108	50c ultra	.15	.15
a.		50c light blue	.15	.15
415	A108	60c lilac rose	.20	.15
416	A108	65c violet brn	12.50	.55
417	A108	75c bluish lilac	.15	.15
418	A108	80c emerald	.75	.15
419	A108	90c deep blue	.75	.15
420	A108	1fr rose	.20	.15
421	A108	2fr emerald ('73)	.15	.15
422	A108	2.50fr brown ('70)	.20	.15
423	A108	3fr brt pink ('70)	.15	.15
424	A108	4fr brt rose lil ('74)	.25	.15
425	A108	4.50fr blue ('74)	.30	.15
426	A108	5fr brt lilac ('75)	.30	.15

Size: 17x20½mm
| 427 | A108 | 1.50fr dk sl grn ('69) | .15 | .15 |

Perf. 13½x13
| 428 | A108 | 2fr emerald ('68) | .15 | .15 |

Photo.   Perf. 11½
Size: 20½x24mm
429	A108	50c light blue ('61)	.45	.15
430	A108	60c lilac rose ('66)	1.10	.70
431	A108	1fr carmine rose ('59)	.15	.15

Perf. 13½x12½
Size: 17½x22mm
432	A108	50c lt blue ('75)	.15	.15
a.	Booklet pane of 4 (#432, 784 and 2 #785) + labels		1.00	
b.	Booklet pane of 4 (#432 and 3 #787) + labels		1.35	
433	A108	1fr rose ('69)	2.00	.90
434	A108	2fr emerald ('72)	.50	.20
e.	Booklet pane of 6 (4 #434 + 2 #475)		5.50	
f.	Booklet pane of 5 (#434, 4 #476 + label)		8.00	
		Nos. 403-434 (32)	23.95	6.75

Counterfeits exist of No. 416. Nos. 429, 431 also issued in coils with black control number on back of every fifth stamp. Nos. 432-434 issued in booklet panes only. No. 432 has one straightedge, and stamps in the pane are tete-beche. Each pane has 2 labels showing Belgian postal emblem and a large selvage with postal code instructions.
Nos. 433-434 have 1 or 2 straight-edges. Panes have a large selvage with inscription or map of Belgium showing postal zones.
See designs A386, O5. For surcharges see Nos. 477-478, 563-567.

Francois de Tassis (Franz von Taxis) — A109

Portraits: 1.75fr, Jean-Baptiste of Thurn & Taxis. 2fr, Baron Leonard I. 2.50fr, Count Lamoral I. 3fr, Count Leonard II. 4fr, Count Lamoral II. 5fr, Prince Eugene Alexander. 5.75fr, Prince Anselme Francois. 8fr, Prince Alexander Ferdinand. 10fr, Prince Charles Anselme. 20fr, Prince Charles Alexander.

1952, May 14   Engr.   Perf. 11½
Laid Paper
435	A109	80c olive grn	.75	.30
436	A109	1.75fr red org	.75	.30
437	A109	2fr violet brn	1.50	.40
438	A109	2.50fr carmine	2.25	1.65
439	A109	3fr olive vio	2.00	1.00
440	A109	4fr ultra	3.00	.85
441	A109	5fr red brn	4.00	1.75
442	A109	5.75fr blue vio	6.75	2.25
443	A109	8fr gray	12.50	2.75
444	A109	10fr rose vio	12.50	4.50
445	A109	20fr brown	60.00	22.50
		Nos. 435-445,B514 (12)	291.00	213.25

13th UPU Cong., Brussels, 1952.

King Baudouin
A110   A111

1952-58   Engr.   Perf. 11½
Size: 21x24mm
446	A110	1.50fr gray green	.55	.15
447	A110	2fr crimson	.40	.15
448	A110	4fr ultra	3.50	.20

Size: 24½x35mm
449	A110	50fr gray brn	1.75	.20
a.		50fr violet brown	35.00	.60
450	A110	100fr rose red ('58)	5.00	.25

1953-72   Photo.   Perf. 11½
451	A111	1.50fr gray	.25	.15
452	A111	2fr rose carmine	6.75	.15
453	A111	2fr green	.25	.15
454	A111	2.50fr red brn ('57)	.60	.15
a.		2.50fr orange brown ('70)	.25	.15
455	A111	3fr rose lilac ('57)	.40	.15
456	A111	3.50fr brt yel grn ('58)	.75	.15
457	A111	4fr brt ultra	.50	.15
458	A111	4.50fr dk red brn ('62)	3.00	.15
459	A111	5fr violet ('57)	1.25	.15
460	A111	6fr dp pink ('58)	.75	.15
461	A111	6.50fr gray ('60)	62.50	15.00
462	A111	7fr blue ('60)	.90	.15
463	A111	7.50fr grysh brn ('58)	47.50	14.00
464	A111	8fr bluish gray ('58)	1.25	.15
465	A111	8.50fr claret ('58)	15.00	.30
466	A111	9fr gray ('58)	47.50	.75
467	A111	12fr lt bl grn ('66)	.90	.15
468	A111	30fr red org ('58)	5.50	.15

Redrawn
469	A111	2.50fr orange brn ('71)	.35	.15
470	A111	4.50fr brown ('72)	2.25	.60
471	A111	7fr blue ('71)	.60	.15

Perf. 13½x12½
Size: 17½x22mm
472	A111	1.50fr gray ('70)	.60	.30
b.	Bklt. pane of 10		6.50	
c.	Bklt. pane, 3 #472, 3 #475		15.00	
473	A111	2.50fr org brn ('71)	9.00	6.25
h.	Bklt. pane, 1 #473, 5 #475		16.00	
474	A111	3fr lilac rose ('69)	.60	.15
a.	Bklt. pane of 5 + label		25.00	
b.	Bklt. pane, 2 #433, 6 #474		18.00	
475	A111	3.50fr brt yel grn ('70)	.60	.25
476	A111	4.50fr dull red brn ('72)	.75	.45
		Nos. 446-476 (31)	221.50	41.40

Nos. 451, 453, 454a, 455, 456, 458 also issued in coils with black control number on back of every fifth stamp. These coils, except for No. 451, are on luminescent paper.
On Nos. 469-471, the 2, 4 and 7 are 3mm high. The background around the head is white. On Nos. 454, 458, 462 the 2, 4 and 7 are 2½mm high and the background is tinted.
Nos. 472-476 issued in booklets only and have 1 or 2 straight-edges. All panes have a large selvage with inscription or map.
See designs M1, O3.

Luminescent Paper
Stamps issued on both ordinary and luminescent paper include: Nos. 307-308, 430-431, 449-451, 453-460, 462, 464, 467-468, 472, 643-644, 650-651, 837, Q385, Q410.
Stamps issued only on luminescent paper include: Nos. 433, 454a, 472b, 473-474, 649, 652-658, 664-670, 679-682, 688-690, 694-696, 698-703, 705-711, 713-726, 729-747, 751-754, 756-757, 759, 761-762, 764, 766, 769, 772, 774, 778, 789, 791-793, 795, 797-799, 801-807, 809-811, 814-818, 820-834, 836, 838-848.
See note after No. 857.

BELGIUM

Nos. 416 and 419 Surcharged and Precanceled in Black

20c
I-I-54
31-XII-54

1954, Jan. 1   Unwmk.   Perf. 13½x14
477 A108 20c on 65c vio brn   1.75   .30
478 A108 20c on 90c dp blue   1.75   .20
See note after No. 197.

Map and Rotary Emblem — A112

Designs: 80c, Mermaid and Mercury holding emblem. 4fr, Rotary emblem and two globes.

1954, Sept. 10   Engr.   Perf. 11½
479 A112 20c red   .25   .15
480 A112 80c dark green   .65   .35
481 A112 4fr ultra   1.40   .50
     Nos. 479-481 (3)   2.30 1.00

5th regional conf. of Rotary Intl. at Ostend. No. 481 for Rotary 50th Anniv. (in 1955).
A souv. sheet containing one each, imperf., was sold for 500 francs. It was not valid for postage.

The Rabot and Begonia — A113

Designs: 2.50fr, The Oudeburg and azalea. 4fr, "Three Towers" and orchid.

1955, Feb. 15   Photo.
482 A113 80c brt carmine   .85   .35
483 A113 2.50fr black brn   5.25 2.75
484 A113 4fr dk rose brn   5.00   .90
     Nos. 482-484 (3)   11.10 4.00

Ghent Intl. Flower Exhibition, 1955.

Homage to Charles V as a Child, by Albrecht de Vriendt — A114

Charles V, by Titian — A115

4fr, Abdication of Charles V, by Louis Gallait.

1955, Mar. 25   Unwmk.   Perf. 11½
485 A114 20c rose red   .25   .20
486 A115 2fr dk gray green   1.90   .15
487 A114 4fr blue   5.00 1.25
     Nos. 485-487 (3)   7.15 1.60

Charles V Exhibition, Ghent, 1955.

Emile Verhaeren, by Montald Constant — A116

1955, May 11   Engr.
488 A116 20c dark gray   .15   .15
Birth cent. of Verhaeren, poet.

Allegory of Textile Manufacture A117

1955, May 11
489 A117 2fr violet brown   1.00   .15
2nd Intl. Textile Exhibition, Brussels, June 1955.

"The Foolish Virgin" by Rik Wouters — A118

"Departure of Volunteers from Liege, 1830" by Charles Soubre — A119

1955, June 10
490 A118 1.20fr olive green   1.10 1.10
491 A118 2fr violet   1.65   .15
3rd biennial exhibition of sculpture, Antwerp, June 11-Sept. 10, 1955.

1955, Sept. 10   Photo.
492 A119 20c grnsh slate   .20   .15
493 A119 2fr chocolate   .90   .20

Exhibition "The Romantic Movement in Liege Province," Sept. 10-Oct. 31, 1955; and 125th anniv. of Belgium's independence from the Netherlands.

Pelican Giving Blood to Young — A120

Buildings of Tournai, Ghent and Antwerp — A121

1956, Jan. 14   Engr.
494 A120 2fr brt carmine   .35   .18
Blood donor service of the Belgian Red Cross.

1956, July 14   Photo.
495 A121 2fr brt ultra   .30   .18
The Scheldt exhibition (Scaldis) at Tournai, Ghent and Antwerp, July-Sept. 1956.

Europa Issue

"Rebuilding Europe" — A122

1956, Sept. 15   Engr.
496 A122 2fr lt green   1.75   .15
497 A122 4fr purple   8.75   .70

Issued to symbolize the cooperation among the six countries comprising the Coal and Steel Community.

Train on Map of Belgium and Luxembourg A123

1956, Sept. 29
498 A123 2fr dark blue   .45   .20
Issued to mark the electrification of the Brussels-Luxembourg railroad.

Edouard Anseele — A124

"The Atom" and Exposition Emblem — A125

1956, Oct. 27
499 A124 20c violet brown   .15   .15
Cent. of the birth of Edouard Anseele, statesman, and in connection with an exhibition held in his honor at Ghent.

1957-58   Unwmk.
500 A125 2fr carmine rose   .25   .15
501 A125 2.50fr green ('58)   .40   .15
502 A125 4fr brt violet blue   .95   .20
503 A125 5fr claret ('58)   .85   .50
     Nos. 500-503 (4)   2.45 1.00

1958 World's Fair at Brussels.

Emperor Maximilian I Receiving Letter — A126

1957, May 19
504 A126 2fr claret   .40   .15
Day of the Stamp, May 19, 1957.

Sikorsky S-58 Helicopter A127

1957, June 15
505 A127 4fr gray grn & brt bl   .80   .45
100,000th passenger carried by Sabena helicopter service, June 15, 1957.

Zeebrugge Harbor A128

1957, July 6
506 A128 2fr dark blue   .40   .15
50th anniv. of the completion of the port of Zeebrugge-Bruges.

Leopold I Entering Brussels, 1831 — A129

Leopold I Arriving at Belgian Border — A130

1957, July 17   Photo.
507 A129 20c dk gray grn   .15   .15
508 A130 2fr lilac   .50   .20
126th anniv. of the arrival in Belgium of King Leopold I.

Boy Scout and Girl Scout Emblems A131

Design: 4fr, Robert Lord Baden-Powell, painted by David Jaggers, vert.

Perf. 11½
1957, July 29   Unwmk.   Engr.
509 A131 80c gray   .25   .15
510 A131 4fr light green   1.00   .15
Cent. of the birth of Lord Baden-Powell, founder of the Boy Scout movement.

"Kneeling Woman" by Lehmbruck A132

"United Europe" A133

1957, Aug. 20   Photo.
511 A132 2.50fr dk blue grn   1.10   .85
4th Biennial Exposition of Sculpture, Antwerp, May 25-Sept. 15.

1957, Sept. 16   Engr.   Perf. 11½
512 A133 2fr dk violet brn   1.00   .15
513 A133 4fr dark blue   1.90   .45
Europa: United Europe for peace and prosperity.

Queen Elisabeth Assisting at Operation, by Allard L'Olivier A134

Perf. 11½
1957, Nov. 23   Unwmk.   Engr.
514 A134 30c rose lilac   .15   .15
50th anniv. of the founding of the Edith Cavell-Marie Depage and St. Camille schools of nursing.

Post Horn and Historic Postal Insignia A135

1958, Mar. 16   Photo.   Perf. 11½
515 A135 2.50fr gray   .25   .15
Postal Museum Day.

United Nations Issue

International Labor Organization A136

BELGIUM

Allegory of UN — A137

Designs: 1fr, FAO. 2fr, World Bank. 2.50fr, UNESCO. 3fr, UN Pavilion. 5fr, ITU. 8fr, Intl. Monetary Fund. 11fr, WHO. 20fr, UPU.

1958, Apr. 17   Unwmk.   Perf. 11½   Engr.

516	A136	50c gray	.90	1.40
517	A136	1fr claret	.30	.45
518	A137	1.50fr dp ultra	.30	.45
519	A137	2fr gray brown	.85	1.25
520	A136	2.50fr olive grn	.30	.45
521	A136	3fr grnsh blue	.85	1.25
522	A137	5fr rose lilac	.55	.90
523	A136	8fr red brown	1.00	1.65
524	A136	11fr dull lilac	1.25	2.00
525	A136	20fr car rose	1.65	2.50
	Nos. 516-525,C15-C20 (16)		10.25	14.75

World's Fair, Brussels, Apr. 17-Oct. 19.
Postally valid only from the UN pavilion at the Brussels Fair. Proceeds went toward financing the UN exhibits.

Eugène Ysaÿe — A138

1958, Sept. 1

526   A138   30c dk blue & plum   .15   .15

Ysaÿe (1858-1931), violinist, composer.

Common Design Types pictured in section at front of book.

Europa Issue, 1958
Common Design Type

1958, Sept. 13   Photo.
Size: 24½x35mm

| 527 | CD1 | 2.50fr brt red & blue | .20 | .15 |
| 528 | CD1 | 5fr brt blue & red | .35 | .35 |

Issued to show the European Postal Union at the service of European integration.

Infant and UN Emblem — A140

Charles V and Jean-Baptiste of Thurn and Taxis — A141

1958, Dec. 10   Engr.
529   A140   2.50fr blue gray   .30   .15

10th anniv. of the signing of the Universal Declaration of Human Rights.

1959, Mar. 15   Unwmk.
530   A141   2.50fr green   .35   .15

Issued for the Day of the Stamp. Design from painting by J.-E. van den Bussche.

NATO Emblem A142

City Hall, Audenarde A143

1959, Apr. 3   Photo.   Perf. 11½

| 531 | A142 | 2.50fr dp red & dk bl | .45 | .15 |
| 532 | A142 | 5fr emerald & dk bl | 1.25 | 1.40 |

10th anniv. of NATO. See No. 720.

1959, Aug. 17   Engr.
533   A143   2.50fr deep claret   .30   .15

Pope Adrian VI, by Jan van Scorel — A144

1959, Aug. 31   Perf. 11½

| 534 | A144 | 2.50fr dark red | .20 | .15 |
| 535 | A144 | 5fr Prus blue | .55 | .55 |

500th anniv. of the birth of Pope Adrian VI.

Europa Issue, 1959
Common Design Type

1959, Sept. 19   Photo.
Size: 24x35½mm

| 536 | CD2 | 2.50fr dark red | .20 | .15 |
| 537 | CD2 | 5fr brt grnsh blue | .45 | .45 |

Boeing 707 A146

Engraved and Photogravure

1959, Dec. 1   Perf. 11½
538   A146   6fr dk bl gray & car   1.75   .80

Inauguration of jet flights by Sabena Airlines.

Countess of Taxis — A147

Indian Azalea — A148

1960, Mar. 21   Engr.   Perf. 11½
539   A147   3fr dark blue   .85   .15

Alexandrine de Rye, Countess of Taxis, Grand Mistress of the Netherlands Posts, 1628-1645, and day of the stamp, Mar. 21, 1960. The painting of the Countess is by Nicholas van der Eggermans.

1960, Mar. 28   Unwmk.

540	A148	40c shown	.20	.15
541	A148	3fr Begonia	.90	.15
542	A148	6fr Anthurium, bromelia	1.00	.90
	Nos. 540-542 (3)		2.10	1.20

24th Ghent Intl. Flower Exhibition, Apr. 23-May 2, 1960.

Steel Workers, by Constantin Meunier — A149

Design: 3fr, The sower, field and dock workers, from "Monument to Labor," Brussels, by Constantin Meunier, horiz.

Engraved and Photogravure

1960, Apr. 30   Perf. 11½

| 543 | A149 | 40c claret & brt red | .15 | .15 |
| 544 | A149 | 3fr brown & brt red | .85 | .25 |

Socialist Party of Belgium, 75th anniv.

Congo River Boat Pilot — A150

Designs: 40c, Medical team. 1fr, Planting tree. 2fr, Sculptors. 2.50fr, Shot put. 3fr, Congolese officials. 6fr, Congolese and Belgian girls playing with doll. 8fr, Boy pointing on globe to independent Congo.

1960, June 30   Photo.   Perf. 11½
Size: 35x24mm

545	A150	10c bright red	.30	.15
546	A150	40c rose claret	.45	.15
547	A150	1fr brt lilac	.85	.75
548	A150	2fr gray green	.95	.85
549	A150	2.50fr blue	.85	.75
550	A150	3fr dk bl gray	1.00	.45

Size: 51x35mm

551	A150	6fr violet bl	3.00	1.90
552	A150	8fr dk brown	5.00	4.00
	Nos. 545-552 (8)		12.40	9.00

Independence of Congo.

Europa Issue, 1960
Common Design Type

1960, Sept. 17   Photo.
Size: 35x24½mm

| 553 | CD3 | 3fr claret | .60 | .15 |
| 554 | CD3 | 6fr gray | 1.25 | .40 |

Children Examining Stamp and Globe A152

H. J. W. Frère-Orban A153

1960, Oct. 1   Photo.   Perf. 11½
555   A152   40c bister & blk + label   .15   .15

Promoting stamp collecting among children.

Engraved and Photogravure

1960, Oct. 17   Unwmk.
Portrait in Brown

556	A153	10c orange yel	.15	.15
557	A153	40c blue grn	.15	.15
558	A153	1.50fr brt violet	.70	.70
559	A153	3fr red	1.10	.15
	Nos. 556-559 (4)		2.10	1.15

Centenary of Communal Credit Society.

King Baudouin and Queen Fabiola A154

1960, Dec. 13   Photo.   Perf. 11½
Portraits in Dark Brown

560	A154	40c green	.15	.15
561	A154	3fr red lilac	.30	.15
562	A154	6fr dull blue	1.25	.60
	Nos. 560-562 (3)		1.70	.90

Wedding of King Baudouin and Dona Fabiola de Mora y Aragon, Dec. 15, 1960.

Nos. 412, 414 Surcharged

1961-68   Typo.   Perf. 13½x14

563	A108	15c on 30c gray grn	.15	.15
564	A108	15c on 50c blue ('68)	.15	.15
565	A108	20c on 30c gray grn	.15	.15
	Nos. 563-565 (3)		.45	.45

No. 412 Surcharged and Precanceled

1961

| 566 | A108 | 15c on 30c gray grn | .90 | .15 |
| 567 | A108 | 20c on 30c gray grn | 1.90 | 1.40 |

See note after No. 197.

Nicolaus Rockox, by Anthony Van Dyck — A155

Seal of Jan Bode, Alderman of Antwerp, 1264 — A156

Engraved and Photogravure

1961, Mar. 18   Perf. 11½
568   A155   3fr bister, blk & brn   .35   .15

400th anniv. of the birth of Nicolaus Rockox, mayor of Antwerp.

1961, Apr. 16   Photo.
569   A156   3fr buff & brown   .35   .15

Issued for Stamp Day, April 16.

Senate Building, Brussels, Laurel and Sword — A157

Engraved and Photogravure

1961, Sept. 14   Unwmk.   Perf. 11½

| 570 | A157 | 3fr brn & Prus grn | .30 | .15 |
| 571 | A157 | 6fr dk brn & dk car | 2.75 | 1.00 |

50th Conference of the Interparliamentary Union, Brussels, Sept. 14-22.

Europa Issue, 1961
Common Design Type

1961, Sept. 16   Photo.

| 572 | CD4 | 3fr yel grn & dk grn | .25 | .20 |
| 573 | CD4 | 6fr org brn & blk | .35 | .25 |

Atomic Reactor Plant, BR2, Mol — A159

Designs: 3fr, Atomic Reactor BR3, vert. 6fr, Atomic Reactor plant BR3.

BELGIUM

1961, Nov. 8   Unwmk.   Perf. 11½
574 A159 40c dk blue grn   .15 .15
575 A159 3fr red lilac   .15 .15
576 A159 6fr bright blue   .35 .25
Nos. 574-576 (3)   .65 .55
Aatomic nuclear research center at Mol.

Horta Museum — A160

1962, Feb. 15   Engr.
577 A160 3fr red brown   .25 .15
Baron Victor Horta (1861-1947), architect.

Postrider, 16th Century A161

Engraved and Photogravure
1962, Mar. 25   Perf. 11½
Chalky Paper
578 A161 3fr brn & slate grn   .30 .15
Stamp Day. See No. 677.

Gerard Mercator — A162

Bro. Alexis-Marie Gochet — A163

Engraved and Photogravure
1962, Apr. 14   Unwmk.
579 A162 3fr sepia & gray   .30 .15
Mercator (Gerhard Kremer, 1512-1594), geographer and map maker.

1962, May 19   Engr.   Perf. 11½
Portrait: 3fr, Canon Pierre-Joseph Triest.
580 A163 2fr dark blue   .30 .15
581 A163 3fr golden brown   .30 .15
Brother Alexis-Marie Gochet (1835-1910), geographer and educator, and Canon Pierre-Joseph Triest (1760-1836), educator and founder of hospitals and orphanages.

Europa Issue, 1962
Common Design Type
1962, Sept. 15   Photo.
582 CD5 3fr dp car, citron & blk   .25 .15
583 CD5 6fr olive, citron & blk   .35 .35

Hand with Barbed Wire and Freed Hand — A165

1962, Sept. 16   Engr. & Photo.
584 A165 40c lt blue & blk   .15 .15
Issued in memory of concentration camp victims.

Adam, by Michelangelo, Broken Chain and UN Emblem A166

1962, Nov. 24   Perf. 11½
585 A166 3fr gray & blk   .25 .15
586 A166 6fr lt redsh brn & dk brn   .40 .30
UN Declaration of Human Rights.

Henri Pirenne (1862-1935), Historian — A167

1963, Jan. 15   Engr.
587 A167 3fr ultramarine   .35 .15

Swordsmen and Ghent Belfry — A168

Designs: 3fr, Modern fencers. 6fr, Arms of the Royal and Knightly Guild of St. Michael, vert.

Engraved and Photogravure
1963, Mar. 23   Unwmk.   Perf. 11½
588 A168 1fr brn red & pale bl   .15 .15
589 A168 3fr dk vio & yel grn   .15 .15
590 A168 6fr gray, blk, red, bl & gold   .30 .25
Nos. 588-590 (3)   .60 .55
350th anniv. of the granting of a charter to the Ghent guild of fencers.

Stagecoach A169

1963, Apr. 7
591 A169 3fr gray & ocher   .25 .15
Stamp Day. See No. 678.

Hotel des Postes, Paris, Stagecoach and Stamp, 1863 A170

Perf. 11½
1963, May 7   Unwmk.   Engr.
592 A170 6fr dk brn, gray & yel grn   .40 .35
Cent. of the 1st Intl. Postal Conf., Paris, 1863.

"Peace," Child in Rye Field — A171

1963, May 8   Engr. & Photo.
593 A171 3fr grn, blk, yel & brn   .15 .15
594 A171 6fr buff, blk, brn & org   .35 .25
May 8th Movement for Peace. (On May 8, 1945, World War II ended in Europe).

Allegory and Shields of 17 Member Nations A172

1963, June 13   Unwmk.   Perf. 11½
595 A172 6fr blue & black   .40 .30
10th anniversary of the Conference of European Transport Ministers.

Seal of Union of Belgian Towns — A173

1963, June 17
596 A173 6fr grn, red, blk & gold   .40 .35
Intl. Union of Municipalities, 50th anniv.

Caravelle over Brussels National Airport A174

Photogravure and Engraved
1963, Sept. 1   Unwmk.   Perf. 11½
597 A174 3fr green & gray   .25 .15
40th anniversary of SABENA airline.

Europa Issue, 1963
Common Design Type
1963, Sept. 14   Photo.
Size: 35x24mm
598 CD6 3fr blk, dl red & lt brn   .60 .15
599 CD6 6fr blk, lt bl & lt brn   1.65 .35

Jules Destrée A176

Design: No. 601, Henry Van de Velde.

Perf. 11½
1963, Nov. 16   Unwmk.   Engr.
600 A176 1fr rose lilac   .15 .15
601 A176 1fr green   .15 .15
Jules Destrée (1863-1936), statesman and founder of the Royal Academy of French Language and Literature, and of Henry Van de Velde (1863-1957), architect.
No. 600 incorrectly inscribed "1864."

Development of the Mail, Bas-relief A177

1963, Nov. 23   Engr. & Photo.
602 A177 50c dl red, slate & blk   .15 .15
50th anniversary of the establishment of postal checking service.

Dr. Armauer G. Hansen A178

Fight Against Leprosy: 2fr, Leprosarium. 5fr, Father Joseph Damien.

1964, Jan. 25   Unwmk.   Perf. 11½
603 A178 1fr brown org & blk   .15 .15
604 A178 2fr brown org & blk   .20 .20
605 A178 5fr brown org & blk   .25 .25
 a. Souvenir sheet of 3, #603-605   1.90 1.90
Nos. 603-605 (3)   .60 .50
No. 605a sold for 12fr.

Andreas Vesalius (1514-64), Anatomist — A179

Jules Boulvin (1855-1920), Mechanical Engineer A180

Design: 2fr, Henri Jaspar (1870-1939), statesman and lawyer.

Engraved and Photogravure
1964, Mar. 2   Unwmk.   Perf. 11½
606 A179 50c pale grn & blk   .15 .15
607 A180 1fr pale grn & blk   .15 .15
608 A180 2fr pale grn & blk   .15 .15
Nos. 606-608 (3)   .45 .45

Postilion of Liege, 1830-40 — A181

1964, Apr. 5   Engr.   Perf. 11½
609 A181 3fr black   .20 .15
Issued for Stamp Day 1964.

Arms of Ostend A182

1964, May 16   Photo.
610 A182 3fr ultra, ver, gold & blk   .20 .15
Millennium of Ostend.

Flame, Hammer and Globe — A183

1fr, "SI" and globe. 2fr, Flame over wavy lines.

1964, July 18   Unwmk.   Perf. 11½
611 A183 50c dark blue & red   .15 .15
612 A183 1fr dark blue & red   .15 .15
613 A183 2fr dark blue & red   .15 .15
Nos. 611-613 (3)   .45 .45
Centenary of the First Socialist International, founded in London, Sept. 28, 1864.

Europa Issue, 1964
Common Design Type
1964, Sept. 12   Photo.   Perf. 11½
Size: 24x35½mm
614 CD7 3fr yel grn, dk car & gray   .25 .15
615 CD7 6fr car rose, yel grn & bl   .40 .40

BELGIUM

Benelux Issue

King Baudouin, Queen Juliana and Grand Duchess Charlotte — A185

1964, Oct. 12
616 A185 3fr olive, lt grn & mar .15 .15

20th anniv. of the customs union of Belgium, Netherlands and Luxembourg.

Hand, Round & Pear-shaped Diamonds A186

Symbols of Textile Industry A187

1965, Jan. 23 Unwmk. Perf. 11½
617 A186 2fr ultra, dp car & blk .15 .15

Diamond Exhibition "Diamantexpo," Antwerp, July 10-28, 1965.

1965, Jan. 25 Photo.
618 A187 1fr blue, red & blk .15 .15

Eighth textile industry exhibition "Textirama," Ghent, Jan. 29-Feb. 2, 1965.

Vriesia — A188

Paul Hymans — A189

Designs: 2fr, Echinocactus. 3fr, Stapelia.

1965, Feb. 13 Engr. & Photo.
619 A188 1fr multicolored .15 .15
620 A188 1fr multicolored .15 .15
621 A188 3fr multicolored .15 .15
  a. Souvenir sheet of 3, #619-621 1.75 1.75
    Nos. 619-621 (3) .45 .45

25th Ghent International Flower Exhibition, Apr. 24-May 3, 1965.
No. 621a was issued Apr. 26 and sold for 20fr.

1965, Feb. 24 Engr. Perf. 11½
622 A189 1fr dull purple .15 .15

Paul Hymans (1865-1941), Belgian Foreign Minister and first president of the League of Nations.

Peter Paul Rubens A190

Sir Rowland Hill as Philatelist A191

Portraits: 2fr, Frans Snyders. 3fr, Adam van Noort. 6fr, Anthony Van Dyck. 8fr, Jacob Jordaens.

1965, Mar. 15 Photo. & Engr.
Portraits in Sepia
623 A190 1fr carmine rose .15 .15
624 A190 2fr blue green .15 .15
625 A190 3fr plum .15 .15
626 A190 6fr deep carmine .25 .15
627 A190 8fr dark blue .35 .35
    Nos. 623-627 (5) 1.05 .95

Issued to commemorate the founding of the General Savings and Pensions Bank.

1965, Mar. 27 Engr. Perf. 11½
628 A191 50c blue green .15 .15

Issued to publicize youth philately. The design is from a mural by J. E. Van den Bussche in the General Post Office, Brussels.

Postmaster, c. 1833 — A192

Staircase, Affligem Abbey — A194

Telephone, Globe and Teletype Paper — A193

1965, Apr. 26 Unwmk. Perf. 11½
629 A192 3fr emerald .15 .15

Issued for Stamp Day.

1965, May 8 Photo.
630 A193 2fr dull purple & blk .15 .15

Cent. of the ITU.

1965, May 27 Engr.
631 A194 1fr gray blue .15 .15

St. Jean Berchmans and his Birthplace A195

1965, May 27 Engr. & Photo.
632 A195 2fr dk brn & red brn .15 .15

Issued to honor St. Jean Berchmans (1599-1621), Jesuit "Saint of the Daily Life."

TOC H Lamp and Arms of Poperinge A196

Farmer with Tractor A197

1965, June 19 Photo. Perf. 11½
633 A196 3fr ol bis, blk & car .15 .15

50th anniv. of the founding of Talbot House in Poperinge, where British soldiers in World War I, and where the TOC H Movement began (Christian Social Service; TOC H is army code for Poperinge Center).

Engraved and Photogravure
1965, July 17 Unwmk. Perf. 11½

Design: 3fr, Farmer with horse-drawn roller.

634 A197 50c bl, ol, bis brn & blk .15 .15
635 A197 3fr bl, ol grn, ol & blk .15 .15

75th anniv. of the Belgian Farmers' Association (Boerenbond).

Europa Issue, 1965
Common Design Type

1965, Sept. 25 Perf. 11½
Size: 35½x24mm
636 CD8 1fr dl rose & blk .15 .15
637 CD8 3fr grnsh gray & blk .15 .15

Leopold I A199

Joseph Lebeau A200

1965, Nov. 13 Engr.
638 A199 3fr sepia .20 .15
639 A199 6fr bright violet .25 .25

King Leopold I (1790-1865). The designs of the vignettes are similar to A4 and A5.

1965, Nov. 13 Photo.
640 A200 1fr multicolored .15 .15

Joseph Lebeau (1794-1865), Foreign Minister.

Tourist Issue

Grapes and Houses, Hoeilaart A201

Bridge and Castle, Huy A202

Designs: No. 643, British War Memorial, Ypres. No. 644, Castle Spontin. No. 645, City Hall, Louvain. No. 646, Ourthe Valley. No. 647, Romanesque Cathedral, gothic fountain, Nivalles. No. 648, Water mill, Kasterlee. No. 649, City Hall, Cloth Guild and Statue of Margarethe of Austria, Malines. No. 650, Town Hall, Lier. No. 651, Castle Bouillon. No. 652, Fountain and Kursaal Spa. No. 653, Windmill, Bokrijk. No. 654, Mountain road, Vielsalm. No. 655, View of Furnes. No. 656, City Hall and Belfry, Mons. No. 657, St. Martin's Church, Aalst. No. 658, Abbey and fountain, St. Hubert.

1965-71 Engr. Perf. 11½
641 A201 50c vio bl, lt bl & yel grn .15 .15
642 A202 50c sl grn, lt bl & red brn .15 .15
643 A202 1fr grn, lt bl, sal & brn .15 .15
644 A202 1fr ind, lt bl & ol .15 .15
645 A201 1fr brt rose lil, lt bl & blk .15 .15
646 A202 1fr blk, grnsh bl & ol .15 .15
647 A201 1.50fr sl, sky bl & bis .15 .15
648 A201 1.50fr blk, bl & ol .15 .15
649 A202 1.50fr dk bl & buff .18 .15
650 A201 2fr brn, lt bl & ind .18 .15
651 A201 2fr dk brn, grn & ocher .18 .15
652 A202 2fr bl, brt grn & blk .15 .15
653 A202 2fr blk, lt bl & yel .15 .15
654 A202 2fr blk, lt bl & yel grn .15 .15
655 A202 2fr car, lt bl & dk brn .15 .15
656 A201 2.50fr vio, buff & blk .18 .15
657 A201 2.50fr vio, lt bl, blk & ol .25 .15
658 A201 2.50fr vio bl & yel .25 .15
    Nos. 641-658 (18) 3.02 2.70

Issued: #641-642, 11/13/65; #643-644, 7/15/67; #645-646, 12/16/68; #647-648, 7/6/70; #649, 656, 12/11/71; #650-651, 11/11/66; #652-653, 6/24/68; #654-655, 9/6/69; #657-658, 9/11/71.

Queen Elisabeth Type of Semi-Postal Issue, 1956

1965, Dec. 23 Photo. Perf. 11½
659 SP305 3fr dark gray .22 .15

Queen Elisabeth (1876-1965).
A dark frame has been added in design of No. 659; 1956 date has been changed to 1965; inscription in bottom panel is Koningin Elisabeth Reine Elisabeth 3F.

"Peace on Earth" — A203

Arms of Pope Paul VI — A204

Rural Mailman, 19th Century — A205

Design: 1fr, "Looking toward a Better Future" (family, new buildings, sun and landscape).

1966, Feb. 12 Photo. Perf. 11½
660 A203 50c multicolored .15 .15
661 A203 1fr ocher, blk & bl .15 .15
662 A204 3fr gray, gold, car & blk .15 .15
    Nos. 660-662 (3) .45 .45

75th anniv. of the encyclical by Pope Leo XIII "Rerum Novarum," which proclaimed the general principles for the organization of modern industrial society.

1966, Apr. 17 Photo. Unwmk.
663 A205 3fr blk, dl yel & pale lil .18 .15

Stamp Day. For overprint see No. 673.

Iguanodon, Natural Science Institute A206

Arend-Roland Comet, Observatory — A207

Designs: No. 665, Ancestral head and spiral pattern, Kasai; Central Africa Museum. No. 666, Snowflakes, Meteorological Institute. No. 667, Seal of Charles V, Royal Archives. No. 668, Medieval scholar, Royal Library. 8fr, Satellite and rocket, Space Aeronautics Institute.

1966, May 28 Engr. & Photo.
664 A206 1fr green & blk .15 .15
665 A206 2fr gray, blk & brn org .15 .15
666 A206 2fr blue, blk & yel .15 .15
667 A207 3fr dp rose, blk & gold .15 .15
668 A207 3fr multicolored .22 .15
669 A207 6fr ultra, yel & blk .22 .15
670 A207 8fr multicolored .30 .30
    Nos. 664-670 (7) 1.27 1.20

National scientific heritage.

Atom Symbol and Retort — A208

August Kekulé, Benzene Ring — A209

BELGIUM

Engraved and Photogravure
1966, July 9   **Unwmk.**   *Perf. 11½*
671 A208 6fr gray, blk & red   .30 .18
Issued to publicize the European chemical plant, EUROCHEMIC, at Mol.

1966, July 9
672 A209 3fr brt blue & blk   .18 .15
August Friedrich Kekule (1829-96), chemistry professor at University of Ghent (1858-67).

No. 663 Overprinted with Red and Blue Emblem

1966, July 11   Photo.
673 A205 3fr multicolored   .18 .15
19th Intl. P.T.T. Cong., Brussels, July 11-15.

Rik Wouters (1882-1916), Self-portrait — A210

1966, Sept. 6   Photo.   *Perf. 11½*
674 A210 60c multicolored   .15 .15

Europa Issue, 1966
Common Design Type
1966, Sept. 24   Engr.   *Perf. 11½*
Size: 24x34mm
675 CD9 3fr brt green   .15 .15
676 CD9 6fr brt rose lilac   .32 .28

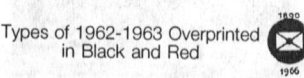

Types of 1962-1963 Overprinted in Black and Red

1966, Nov. 11   Engr. & Photo.
677 A161 60c sepia & grnsh gray   .15 .15
678 A169 3fr sepia & pale bister   .15 .15
75th anniv., Royal Fed. of Phil. Circles of Belgium. Overprint shows emblem of F.I.P.

Lions Emblem — A214

1967, Jan. 14   *Perf. 11½*
679 A214 3fr gray, blk & bl   .15 .15
680 A214 6fr lt green, blk & vio   .28 .15
Lions Club Intl., 50th anniv.

Pistol by Leonhard Cleuter A215

1967, Feb. 11   Photo.
681 A215 2fr dp car, blk & cream   .15 .15
Fire Arms Museum in Liege.

International Tourist Year Emblem A216

1967, Feb. 11
682 A216 6fr ver, ultra & blk   .28 .15
International Tourist Year, 1967.

Birches and Trientalis A217

Design: No. 684, Dunes, beach grass, privet and blue thistles.

1967, Mar. 11   Photo.   *Perf. 11½*
683 A217 1fr multicolored   .15 .15
684 A217 1fr multicolored   .15 .15
Issued to publicize the nature preserves at Hautes Fagnes and Westhoek.

Paul E. Janson — A218

1967, Apr. 15   Engr.   *Perf. 11½*
685 A218 10fr blue   .35 .18
Issued in memory of Paul Emile Janson (1872-1944), lawyer and statesman.

Postilion A219

1967, Apr. 16   Photo. & Engr.
686 A219 3fr rose red & claret   .18 .15
Issued for Stamp Day, 1967.

Inscribed: "FITCE"
1967, June 24   *Perf. 11½*
687 A219 10fr ultra, sep & emer   .42 .30
Issued to commemorate the meeting of the Federation of Common Market Telecommunications Engineers, Brussels, July 3-8.

Europa Issue, 1967
Common Design Type
1967, May 2   Photo.
Size: 24x35mm
688 CD10 3fr blk, lt bl & red   .18 .15
689 CD10 6fr blk, grnsh gray & yel   .30 .28

Flax, Shuttle and Mills — A221

1967, June 3   Photo.   *Perf. 11½*
690 A221 6fr tan & multi   .28 .20
Belgian linen industry.

Old Kursaal, Ostend — A222

1967, June 3   Engr. & Photo.
691 A222 2fr dk brn, lt bl & yel   .15 .15
700th anniversary of Ostend as a city.

A223    A224

Designs: #692, Caesar Crossing Rubicon, 15th Century Tapestry. #693, Emperor Maximilian Killing a Boar, 16th cent. tapestry.

1967, Sept. 2   Photo.   *Perf. 11½*
692 A223 1fr multicolored   .15 .15
693 A223 1fr multicolored   .15 .15
Issued for the Charles Plisnier and Lodewijk de Raet Foundations.

Engraved and Photogravure
1967, Sept. 30   *Perf. 11½*
Arms of Universities: #694, Ghent. #695, Liege.
694 A224 3fr gray & multi   .15 .15
695 A224 3fr gray & multi   .15 .15
Universities of Ghent and Liège, 150th anniv.

Princess Margaret of York — A225
"Virga Jesse," Hasselt — A226 

1967, Sept. 30   Photo.
696 A225 6fr multicolored   .28 .24
British Week, Sept. 28-Oct. 2.

1967, Nov. 11   Engr.   *Perf. 11½*
697 A226 1fr slate blue   .15 .15
Christmas, 1967.

Hand Guarding Worker — A227
Military Mailman, 1916, by James Thiriar — A228 

1968, Feb. 3   Photo.   *Perf. 11½*
698 A227 3fr multicolored   .18 .15
Issued to publicize industrial safety.

Engraved and Photogravure
1968, Mar. 17   *Perf. 11½*
699 A228 3fr sepia, lt bl & brn   .18 .15
Issued for Stamp Day, 1968.

View of Grammont and Seal of Baudouin VI — A229
Stamp of 1866, No. 23 — A230 

Historic Sites: 3fr, Theux-Franchimont fortress, sword and seal. 6fr, Neolithic cave and artifacts, Spiennes. 10fr, Roman oil lamp and St. Medard's Church, Wervik.

1968, Apr. 13   Photo.   *Perf. 11½*
700 A229 2fr bl, blk, lil & rose   .15 .15
701 A229 3fr orange, blk & car   .15 .15
702 A229 6fr ultra, ind & bis   .25 .15
703 A229 10fr tan, blk, yel & gray   .40 .28
Nos. 700-703 (4)   .95 .73

1968, Apr. 13   Engr.   *Perf. 13*
704 A230 1fr black   .15 .15
Centenary of the Malines Stamp Printery.

Europa Issue, 1968
Common Design Type
1968, Apr. 27   Photo.   *Perf. 11½*
Size: 35x24mm
705 CD11 3fr dl grn, gold & blk   .15 .15
706 CD11 6fr carmine, sil & blk   .35 .25

St. Laurent Abbey, Liège A232

Designs: 3fr, Gothic Church, Lisseweghe. No. 709, Barges in Zandvliet locks. No. 710, Ship in Neuzen lock, Ghent Canal. 10fr, Ronquieres canal ship lift.

Engraved and Photogravure
1968, Sept. 7   *Perf. 11½*
707 A232 2fr ultra, gray ol & sep   .15 .15
708 A232 3fr ol bis, gray & sep   .15 .15
709 A232 6fr ind, brt bl & sep   .30 .15
710 A232 6fr black, grnsh bl & ol   .22 .15
711 A232 10fr bister, brt bl & sep   .50 .32
Nos. 707-711 (5)   1.32 .92

No. 710 issued Dec. 14 for opening of lock at Neuzen, Netherlands.

Christmas Candle — A233

1968, Dec. 7   *Perf. 11½*
712 A233 1fr multicolored   .15 .15
Christmas, 1968.

St. Albertus Magnus — A234

1969, Feb. 15   Engr.   *Perf. 11½*
713 A234 2fr sepia   .15 .15
The Church of St. Paul in Antwerp (16th century) was destroyed by fire in Apr. 1968.

BELGIUM

Ruins of Aulne Abbey, Gozee — A235

1969, Feb. 15   Engr. & Photo.
714 A235 3fr brt pink & blk   .15 .15
Aulne Abbey was destroyed in 1794 during the French Revolution.

The Travelers, Roman Sculpture — A236

Broodjes Chapel, Antwerp — A237

1969, Mar. 15   Engr.   Perf. 11½
715 A236 2fr violet brown   .15 .15
2,000th anniversary of city of Arlon.

1969, Mar. 15   Engr. & Photo.
716 A237 3fr gray & blk   .15 .15
150th anniv. of public education in Antwerp.

Post Office Train — A238

1969, Apr. 13   Photo.   Perf. 11½
717 A238 3fr multicolored   .15 .15
Issued for Stamp Day.

Europa Issue, 1969
Common Design Type
1969, Apr. 26
Size: 35x24mm
718 CD12 3fr lt grn, brn & blk   .20 .15
719 CD12 6fr salmon, rose car & blk   .30 .30

NATO Type of 1959 Redrawn and Dated "1949-1969"
1969, May 31   Photo.   Perf. 11½
720 A142 6fr org brn & ultra   .28 .28
20th anniv. of NATO. No. 720 inscribed Belgique-Belgie and OTAN-NAVO.

Construction Workers, by F. Leger — A240

Bicyclist A241

1969, May 31
721 A240 3fr multicolored   .15 .15
50th anniversary of the ILO.

1969, July 5   Photo.   Perf. 11½
722 A241 6fr rose & multi   .28 .24
World Bicycling Road Championships, Terlaemen to Zolder, Aug. 10.

Ribbon in Benelux Colors — A242

1969, Sept. 6   Photo.   Perf. 11½
723 A242 3fr blk, red, ultra & yel   .20 .15
25th anniv. of the signing of the customs union of Belgium, Netherlands and Luxembourg.

Annevoie Garden and Pascali Rose — A243

Design: No. 725, Lochristi Garden and begonia.

1969, Sept. 6
724 A243 2fr multicolored   .15 .15
725 A243 2fr multicolored   .15 .15

Armstrong, Collins, Aldrin and Map Showing Tranquillity Base — A245

1969, Sept. 20   Photo.
726 A245 6fr black   .28 .24
See note after Algeria #427. See #B846.

Wounded Veteran — A246

Mailman — A247

1969, Oct. 11   Engr.   Perf. 11½
727 A246 1fr blue gray   .15 .15
Natl. war veterans' aid organization (O.N.I.G.). The design is similar to type SP10.

1969, Oct. 18   Photo.
728 A247 1fr deep rose & multi   .15 .15
Issued to publicize youth philately. Design by Danielle Saintenoy, 14.

Kennedy Tunnel Under the Schelde, Antwerp A248

6fr, Three highways crossing near Loncin.

1969, Nov. 8   Engr.   Perf. 11½
729 A248 3fr multicolored   .22 .15
730 A248 6fr multicolored   .28 .28
Issued to publicize the John F. Kennedy Tunnel under the Schelde and the Walloon auto route and interchange near Loncin.

Henry Carton de Wiart, by Gaston Geleyn — A249

1969, Nov. 8
731 A249 6fr sepia   .28 .20
Count de Wiart (1869-1951), statesman.

The Census at Bethlehem (detail), by Peter Brueghel A250

1969, Dec. 13   Photo.
732 A250 1.50fr multicolored   .15 .15
Christmas, 1969.

Symbols of Bank's Activity, 100fr Coin — A251

1969, Dec. 13   Engr. & Photo.
733 A251 3.50fr lt ultra, blk & sil   .15 .15
50th anniv. of the Industrial Credit Bank (Societe nationale de credit a l'industrie).

Camellia — A252

Beeches in Botanical Garden — A253

1970, Jan. 31   Photo.   Perf. 11½
734 A252 1.50fr shown   .15 .15
735 A252 2.50fr Water lily   .15 .15
736 A252 3.50fr Azalea   .15 .15
   a. Souvenir sheet of 3, #734-736   2.00 2.00
     Nos. 734-736 (3)   .45 .45
Ghent Int'l Flower Exhibition. No. 736a was issued Apr. 25 and sold for 25fr.

1970, Mar. 7   Engr. & Photo.
737 A253 3.50fr shown   .20 .15
738 A253 7fr Birches   .30 .30
European Nature Conservation Year.

Mailman A254

1970, Apr. 4   Photo.
739 A254 1.50fr multicolored   .15 .15
Issued for Youth Stamp Day.

New UPU Headquarters and Monument, Bern — A255

1970, Apr. 12   Engr. & Photo.
740 A255 3.50fr grn & lt grn   .30 .15
Opening of the new UPU Headquarters, Bern.

Europa Issue, 1970
Common Design Type
1970, May 1   Photo.   Perf. 11½
Size: 35x24mm
741 CD13 3.50fr rose cl, yel & blk   .20 .15
742 CD13 7fr ultra, pink & blk   .40 .30

Cooperative Alliance Emblem — A257

1970, June 27   Photo.   Perf. 11½
743 A257 7fr black & org   .30 .15
Intl. Cooperative Alliance, 75th anniv.

Ship in Ghent Terneuzen Lock, Zelzate A258

Design: No. 745, Clock Tower, Virton, vert.

1970, June 27   Engr. & Photo.
744 A258 2.50fr indigo & lt bl   .15 .15
745 A258 2.50fr dk pur & ocher   .15 .15

King Baudouin — A259

1970-80   Engr.   Perf. 11½
746 A259 1.75fr green ('71)   .24 .15
747 A259 2.25fr gray grn ('72)   .35 .15
748 A259 2.50fr gray grn ('74)   .16 .15
749 A259 3fr emerald ('73)   3.00 2.00
750 A259 3.25fr violet brn ('75)   .20 .15
751 A259 3.50fr orange brn   .24 .15
752 A259 3.50fr brown ('71)   .24 .15
753 A259 4fr blue ('72)   .35 .15
754 A259 4.50fr brown ('72)   .24 .15
755 A259 4.50fr grnsh bl ('74)   .24 .15
756 A259 5fr lilac ('72)   .24 .15
757 A259 6fr rose car ('72)   .28 .15
758 A259 6.50fr vio blk ('74)   .35 .15
759 A259 7fr ver ('71)   .35 .15
760 A259 7.50fr brt pink ('75)   .35 .15
761 A259 8fr black ('72)   .35 .15
762 A259 9fr ol bis ('71)   .60 .15
763 A259 9fr red brn ('79)   .45 .15
764 A259 10fr rose car ('71)   .48 .15
765 A259 11fr gray ('76)   .52 .15
766 A259 12fr Prus bl ('72)   .60 .15
767 A259 13fr slate ('75)   .70 .15
768 A259 14fr gray grn ('76)   .65 .15
769 A259 15fr lt vio ('71)   .70 .15
770 A259 16fr green ('77)   .70 .15
771 A259 17fr dull mag ('75)   .80 .15
772 A259 18fr bist bl ('71)   1.00 .20
773 A259 18fr grnsh bl ('80)   .90 .15
774 A259 20fr vio bl ('71)   1.00 .15
775 A259 22fr black ('74)   1.40 1.25
776 A259 22fr lt grn ('79)   1.10 .15
777 A259 25fr lilac ('72)   1.25 .15
778 A259 30fr ocher ('72)   1.50 .15
779 A259 35fr emer ('70)   1.50 .20
780 A259 40fr dk blue ('77)   2.00 .15
781 A259 45fr brown ('80)   2.25 .20

Perf. 12½x13½
Photo.
Size: 22x17mm
782 A259 3fr emerald ('73)   3.00 2.50
   a. Booklet pane of 4 (#782 and 3 #783) + labels   10.00
783 A259 4fr blue ('73)   .70 .60
784 A259 4.50fr grnsh bl ('75)   .40 .30
785 A259 5fr lilac ('73)   .24 .15
   a. Booklet pane of 4 + labels   2.75

786	A259	6fr carmine ('78)	.28	.16
787	A259	6.50fr dull pur ('75)	.45	.20
788	A259	8fr gray ('78)	.35	.15
	Nos. 746-788 (43)		32.70	12.56

No. 751 issued Sept. 7, 1970, King Baudouin's 40th birthday, and is inscribed "1930-1970." Dates are omitted on other stamps of type A259.

Nos. 754, 756 also issued in coils in 1973 and Nos. 757, 761 in 1978, with black control number on back of every fifth stamp.

Nos. 782-788 issued in booklets only. Nos. 782, 784 have one straight-edge, Nos. 786, 788 have two. The rest have one or two. Stamps in the panes are tete-beche. Each pane has two labels showing Belgian Postal emblem with a large selvage with postal code instructions. Nos. 786, 788 not luminescent.

See designs M2, O4. See Nos. 432a, 432b, 977a, 977b.

UN Headquarters, NY — A260

Fair Emblem — A261

1970, Sept. 12 Engr. & Photo.
789 A260 7fr dk brn & Prus bl .30 .15
25th anniversary of the United Nations.

1970, Sept. 19
790 A261 1.50fr bister, org & brn .15 .15
Issued to publicize the 25th International Fair at Ghent, Sept. 12-27.

Queen Fabiola — A262

The Mason, by Georges Minne — A263

1970, Sept. 19
791 A262 3.50fr lt blue & blk .15 .15
Issued to publicize the Queen Fabiola Foundation for Mental Health.

1970, Oct. 17 Perf. 11½
792 A263 3.50fr dull yel & sep .15 .15
50th anniv. of the National Housing Society.

Man, Woman and City — A264

1970, Oct. 17 Photo.
793 A264 2.50fr black & multi .15 .15
Social Security System, 25th anniv.

Have you found a typo or other error in this catalogue? Inform the editors via our web site or e-mail

sctcat@
scottonline.com

Madonna with the Grapes, by Jean Gossaert — A265

1970, Nov. 14 Engr. Perf. 11½
794 A265 1.50fr dark brown .15 .15
Christmas 1970.

Arms of Eupen, Malmédy and Saint-Vith — A266

Engraved and Photogravure
1970, Dec. 12 Perf. 11½
795 A266 7fr sepia & dk brn .30 .15
The 50th anniversary of the return of the districts of Eupen, Malmédy and Saint-Vith.

Automatic Telephone — A267

Touring Club Emblem — A269

"Auto" A268

1971, Jan. 16 Photo. Perf. 11½
796 A267 1.50fr multicolored .15 .15
Automatization of Belgian telephone system.

1971, Jan. 16
797 A268 2.50fr carmine & blk .15 .15
50th Automobile Show, Brussels, Jan. 19-31.

1971, Feb. 13
798 A269 3.50fr ultra & multi .18 .15
Belgian Touring Club, 75th anniversary.

Tournai Cathedral — A270

1971, Feb. 13 Engr.
799 A270 7fr bright blue .30 .20
Cathedral of Tournai, 8th centenary.

"The Letter Box," by T. Lobrichon — A271

1971, Mar. 13 Engr. Perf. 11½
800 A271 1.50fr dark brown .15 .15
Youth philately.

Albert I, Jules Destrée and Academy — A272

Engraved and Photogravure
1971, Apr. 17 Perf. 11½
801 A272 7fr gray & blk .30 .20
50th anniversary of the founding of the Royal Academy of Language and French Literature.

Stamp Day — A273

1971, Apr. 25
802 A273 3.50fr Mailman .15 .15

Europa Issue, 1971
Common Design Type
1971, May 1 Photo.
Size: 35x24mm
803 CD14 3.50fr olive & blk .24 .15
804 CD14 7fr dk ol grn & blk .35 .15

Radar Ground Station — A275

1971, May 15 Photo. Perf. 11½
805 A275 7fr multicolored .30 .15
3rd World Telecommunications Day.

Antarctic Explorer, Ship and Penguins — A276

1971, June 19 Photo. Perf. 11½
806 A276 10fr multicolored .50 .50
Tenth anniversary of the Antarctic Treaty pledging peaceful uses of and scientific cooperation in Antarctica.

Orval A277

G. Hubin A278

1971, June 26 Engr. Perf. 11½
807 A277 2.50fr Orval Abbey .15 .15
9th cent. of the Abbey of Notre Dame, Orval.

1971, June 26 Engr. & Photo.
808 A278 1.50fr vio bl & blk .15 .15
Georges Hubin (1863-1947), socialist leader and Minister of State.

Mr. and Mrs. Goliath, the Giants of Ath — A279

View of Ghent A280

1971, Aug. 7 Photo.
809 A279 2.50fr multicolored .15 .15

Engr.
810 A280 2.50fr gray brown .15 .15

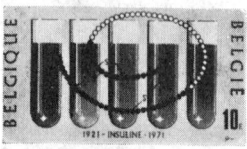

Test Tubes and Insulin Molecular Diagram — A281

1971, Aug. 7 Photo.
811 A281 10fr lt gray & multi .40 .30
50th anniversary of the discovery of insulin.

Family and "50" — A283

1971, Sept. 11 Photo.
812 A283 1.50fr green & multi .15 .15
Belgian Large Families League, 50th anniv.

Achaemenidaen Tomb, Buzpar, and Persian Coat of Arms — A284

BELGIUM

Engraved and Photogravure

1971, Oct. 2   Perf. 11½
813 A284 7fr multicolored   .30 .15

2500th anniversary of the founding of the Persian empire by Cyrus the Great.

Dr. Jules Bordet — A285
Flight into Egypt, Anonymous — A286 

Portrait: No. 815, Stijn Streuvels.

1971, Oct. 2   Engr.
814 A285 3.50fr slate green   .15 .15
815 A285 3.50fr dark brown   .15 .15

No. 814 honors Dr. Jules Bordet (1870-1945), serologist and immunologist; No. 815, Stijn Streuvels (1871-1945), novelist whose pen name was Frank Lateur.

1971, Nov. 13   Photo.
816 A286 1.50fr multicolored   .15 .15

Christmas 1971.

Federation Emblem — A287
Book Year Emblem — A288 

1971, Nov. 13
817 A287 3.50fr black, ultra & gold   .18 .15

25th anniversary of the Federation of Belgian Industries (FIB).

1972, Feb. 19
818 A288 7fr bister, blk & bl   .30 .20

International Book Year 1972.

Coins of Belgium and Luxembourg — A289
Traffic Signal and Road Signs — A290 

1972, Feb. 19   Engr. & Photo.
819 A289 1.50fr orange, blk & sil   .15 .15

Economic Union of Belgium and Luxembourg, 50th anniversary.

1972, Feb. 19   Photo.
820 A290 3.50fr blue & multi   .15 .15

Via Secura (road safety), 25th anniversary.

Belgica '72 Emblem — A291

1972, Mar. 27
821 A291 3.50fr choc, bl & lil   .15 .15

International Philatelic Exhibition, Brussels, June 24-July 9.

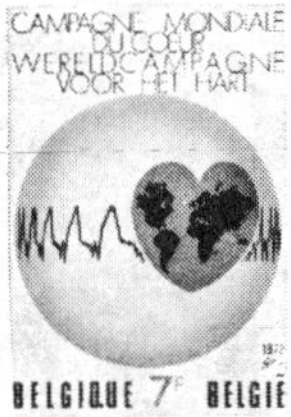

"Your Heart is your Health" — A292
Auguste Vermeylen — A293 

1972, Mar. 27
822 A292 7fr blk, gray, red & bl   .25 .18

World Health Day.

1972, Mar. 27
823 A293 2.50fr multicolored   .15 .15

Centenary of the birth of Auguste Vermeylen (1872-1945), Flemish writer and educator. Portrait by Isidore Opsomer.

A294
A296 

1972, Apr. 23
824 A294 3.50fr Astronaut on Moon   .15 .15

Stamp Day 1972.

Europa Issue 1972
Common Design Type

1972, Apr. 29   Size: 24x35mm
825 CD15 3.50fr light blue & multi   .20 .15
826 CD15 7fr rose & multi   .40 .30

1972, May 13   Photo.   Perf. 11½
827 A296 2.50fr "Freedom of the Press"   .15 .15

50th anniv. of the BELGA news information agency and 25th Congress of the Intl. Federation of Newspaper Editors (F.I.E.J.), Brussels, May 15-19.

Freight Cars with Automatic Coupling — A297

1972, June 3
828 A297 7fr blue & multi   .30 .20

Intl. Railroad Union, 50th anniv.

View of Couvin — A298

No. 830, Aldeneik Church, Maaseik, vert.

1972, June 24   Engr.   Perf. 13½x14
829 A298 2.50fr bl, vio brn & sl grn   .20 .20
830 A298 2.50fr dk brown & bl   .20 .20

Beatrice, by Gustave de Smet — A299
Radar Station, Intelsat 4 — A300 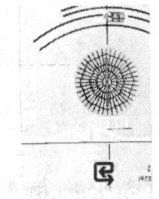

1972, Sept. 9   Photo.   Perf. 11½
831 A299 3fr multicolored   .18 .15

Youth philately.

1972, Sept. 16
832 A300 3.50fr lt bl, sil & blk   .18 .15

Opening of the Lessive satellite earth station.

Frans Masereel, Self-portrait — A301
Adoration of the Kings, by Felix Timmermans — A302 

1972, Oct. 21
833 A301 4.50fr lt olive & blk   .18 .15

Frans Masereel (1889-1972), wood engraver.

1972, Nov. 11   Photo.   Perf. 11½
834 A302 3.50fr black & multi   .18 .15

Christmas 1972.

Maria Theresa, Anonymous — A303

1972, Dec. 16   Photo.
835 A303 2fr multicolored   .15 .15

200th anniversary of the Belgian Academy of Science, Literature and Art, founded by Empress Maria Theresa.

WMO Emblem, Meteorological Institute, Ukkel — A304

1973, Mar. 24   Photo.   Perf. 11½
836 A304 9fr blue & multi   .38 .18

Cent. of intl. meteorological cooperation.

"Fire" — A305
Man and WHO Emblem — A306 

1973, Mar. 24
837 A305 2fr multicolored   .15 .15

Natl. industrial fire prevention campaign.

1973, Apr. 7
838 A306 8fr dk red, ocher & blk   .32 .24

25th anniv. of WHO.

Europa Issue 1973
Common Design Type

1973, Apr. 28   Size: 35x24mm
839 CD16 4.50fr org brn, vio bl & yel   .22 .15
840 CD16 8fr olive, dk bl & yel   .55 .45

Thurn and Taxis Courier — A308
Arrows Circling Globe — A309 

Engraved and Photogravure

1973, Apr. 28   Perf. 11½
841 A308 4.50fr black & red brn   .20 .15

Stamp Day.

1973, May 12   Photo.
842 A309 3.50fr dp ocher & multi   .16 .15

5th International Telecommunications Day.

Workers' Sports Exhibition Poster, Ghent, 1913 — A310

1973, May 12
843 A310 4.50fr multicolored   .20 .15

60th anniversary of the International Workers' Sports Movement.

Fair Emblem — A311

1973, May 12   Photo.   Perf. 11½
844 A311 4.50fr multicolored   .18 .15

25th International Fair, Liege, May 12-27.

BELGIUM

DC-10 and 1923 Biplane over Brussels Airport — A312

Design: 10fr, Tips biplane, 1908.

1973, May 19		Engr. & Photo.	
845 A312	8fr gray bl, blk & ultra	.28	.20
846 A312	10fr grn, lt bl & blk	.45	.35

50th anniv. of SABENA, Belgian airline (8fr) and 25th anniv. of the "Vieilles Tiges" Belgian flying pioneers' society (10fr).

Adolphe Sax and Tenor Saxophone — A313

Fresco from Bathhouse, Ostend — A314

1973, Sept. 15		Photo.	
847 A313	9fr green, blk & bl	.40	.20

Adolphe Sax (1814-1894), inventor of saxophone.

1973, Sept. 15			
848 A314	4.50fr multicolored	.22	.15

Year of the Spa.

St. Nicholas Church, Eupen — A315

Charley, by Henri Evenepoel — A316

Designs: No. 850, Town Hall, Leau. No. 851, Aarshot Church. No. 852, Chiman Castle. No. 853, Gemmenich Border: Belgium, Germany, Netherlands. No. 854, St. Monan and church, Nassogne. No. 855, Church tower, Dottignes. No. 856, Grand-Place, Sint-Truiden.

1973-75		Engr.	Perf. 13
849 A315	2fr plum, sep & lt vio	.20	.15
850 A315	3fr black, lt bl & mar	.50	.15
851 A315	3fr brn blk & yel	.32	.15
852 A315	4fr grnsh blk & grnsh bl	.35	.15
853 A315	4fr grnsh blk & bl	.40	.18
854 A315	4fr grnsh blk & bl	.40	.18
855 A315	4.50fr multicolored	.50	.20
856 A315	5fr multicolored	.50	.18
Nos. 849-856 (8)		3.17	1.34

Nos. 851, 855 not luminescent. Nos. 850, 852-854, 856 horiz.

1973, Oct. 13		Photo.	Perf. 11½
857 A316	3fr multicolored	.18	.15

Youth philately.

Luminescent Paper
Starting with No. 858, all stamps are on luminescent paper unless otherwise noted.

Jean-Baptiste Moens — A317

1973, Oct. 13		Engr. & Photo.	
858 A317	10fr gray & multi	.42	.20

50th anniversary of the Belgian Stamp Dealers' Association. Printed in sheets of 12 stamps and 12 labels showing association emblem.

Adoration of the Shepherds, by Hugo van der Goes — A318

Louis Pierard, by M. I. Ianchelevici — A319

1973, Nov. 17		Engr.	Perf. 11½
859 A318	4fr blue	.18	.15

Christmas 1973.

1973, Nov. 17		Engr. & Photo.	
860 A319	4fr vermilion & buff	.25	.15

Louis Pierard (1886-1952), journalist, member of Parliament.

Highway, Automobile Club Emblem — A320

1973, Nov. 17		Photo.	
861 A320	5fr yellow & multi	.25	.15

Flemish Automobile Club, 50th anniv.

Early Microphone, Emblem of Radio Belgium — A321

1973, Nov. 24		Engr. & Photo.	
862 A321	4fr blue & black	.18	.15

50th anniversary of Radio Belgium.

Felicien Rops, Self-portrait — A323

Engraved and Photogravure

1973, Dec. 8			Perf. 11½
863 A323	7fr tan & black	.32	.15

Felicien Rops (1833-1898), painter and engraver.

King Albert, (1875-1934) — A324

Sun, Bird, Flowers and Girl — A325

1974, Feb. 16		Photo.	Perf. 11½
864 A324	4fr Prus green & blk	.22	.15

1974, Mar. 25		Photo.	Perf. 11½
865 A325	3fr violet & multi	.15	.15

Protection of the environment.

NATO Emblem — A326

1974, Apr. 20		Photo.	Perf. 11½
866 A326	10fr dp to lt blue	.45	.25

25th anniversary of the signing of the North Atlantic Treaty.

Hubert Krains — A327

"Destroyed City," by Ossip Zadkine — A328

1974, Apr. 27		Engr. & Photo.	
867 A327	5fr black & gray	.20	.15

Stamp Day.

Europa Issue 1974
1974, May 4
Design: 10fr, Solidarity, by Georges Minne.

| 868 A328 | 5fr black & red | .24 | .15 |
| 869 A328 | 10fr black & ultra | .60 | .30 |

Children — A329

1974, May 18		Photo.	Perf. 11½
870 A329	4fr lt blue & multi	.20	.15

10th Lay Youth Festival.

Planetarium, Brussels — A330

Soleilmont Abbey Ruins — A331

Designs: 4fr, Pillory, Braine-le-Chateau. 7fr, Fountain, Ghent (procession symbolic of Chamber of Rhetoric). 10fr, Belfry, Bruges, vert.

1974, June 22		Engr. and Photo.	Perf. 11½
871 A330	3fr sky blue & blk	.15	.15
872 A330	4fr lilac rose & blk	.18	.15
873 A331	5fr lt green & blk	.28	.15
874 A331	7fr dull yellow & blk	.35	.20
875 A330	10fr black, blue & brn	.45	.15
Nos. 871-875 (5)		1.41	.80

Historic buildings and monuments.

"BENELUX" — A332

1974, Sept. 7		Photo.	Perf. 11½
876 A332	5fr bl grn, dk grn & lt bl	.25	.15

30th anniversary of the signing of the customs union of Belgium, Netherlands and Luxembourg.

Jan Vekemans, by Cornelis de Vos — A333

1974, Sept. 14			
877 A333	3fr multicolored	.18	.15

Youth philately.

Leon Tresignies, Willebroek Canal Bridge — A334

1974, Sept. 28		Engr. & Photo.	
878 A334	4fr brn & ol grn	.18	.15

60th death anniversary of Corporal Leon Tresignies (1886-1914), hero of World War I.

Montgomery Blair, UPU Emblem — A335

10fr, Heinrich von Stephan and UPU emblem.

1974, Oct. 5			Perf. 11½
879 A335	5fr green & blk	.20	.15
880 A335	10fr brick red & blk	.40	.28

Centenary of Universal Postal Union.

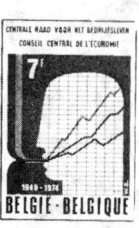

Symbolic Chart — A336

1974, Oct. 12		Photo.	Perf. 11½
881 A336	7fr multicolored	.30	.20

Central Economic Council, 25th anniv.

BELGIUM

Rotary Emblem A337

1974, Oct. 19
882 A337 10fr multicolored .42 .20
Rotary International of Belgium.

A338    A341

1974, Oct. 26
883 A338 3fr multicolored .18 .15
Granting of the colors to the Ardennes Chasseurs Regiment, 40th anniversary.

1974, Nov. 16 Perf. 11½
884 A341 4fr rose lilac .20 .15
Christmas 1974. The Angel shown is from the triptyque "The Mystical Lamb" in the Saint-Bavon Cathedral, Ghent.

A342   A343

Adolphe Quetelet, by J. Odevaere.

1974, Dec. 14 Engr. & Photo.
885 A342 10fr black & buff .42 .20
Death centenary of Adolphe Quetelet (1796-1874), statistician, astronomer and Secretary of Royal Academy of Brussels.

1975, Feb. 15 Photo. Perf. 11½
912 A343 6.50fr Themabelga emblem .30 .15
Themabelga, International Thematic Stamp Exhibition, Brussels, Dec. 13-21, 1975.

A344    A345

1975, Feb. 22
913 A344 4.50fr Neoregelia carolinae .22 .15
Photogravure and Engraved
914 A344 5fr Coltsfoot .25 .16
915 A344 6.50fr Azalea .30 .15
  Nos. 913-915 (3) .77 .46
Ghent Intl. Flower Exhib., Apr. 26-May 5.

1975, Mar. 15 Perf. 11½
School emblem, man Leading boy.
916 A345 4.50fr black & multi .20 .15
Centenary of the founding of the Charles Buls Normal School for Boys, Brussels.

Davids Foundation Emblem A346

1975, Mar. 22 Photo.
917 A346 5fr yellow & multi .25 .15
Centenary of the Davids Foundation, a Catholic organization for the promotion of Flemish through education and books.

King Albert (1875-1934) A347

Mailman, 1840, by James Thiriar A348

1975, Apr. 5 Engr. & Photo.
918 A347 10fr black & maroon .45 .25

1975, Apr. 19 Engr. Perf. 11½
919 A348 6.50fr dull magenta .30 .15
Stamp Day 1975.

St. John, from Last Supper, by Bouts — A349

Concentration Camp Symbols — A350

1975, Apr. 26 Engr. & Photo.
920 A349 6.50fr black, grn & blue .35 .15
921 A349 10fr black, ocher & red .60 .32
Europa: 10fr, Woman's Head, detail from "Trial by Fire," by Dirk Bouts.

1975, May 3 Photo.
Design: "B" denoted political prisoners, "KG" prisoners of war.
922 A350 4.50fr multicolored .20 .15
Liberation of concentration camps, 30th anniv.

Hospice of St. John, Bruges A351

Church of St. Loup, Namur — A352

Design: 10fr, Martyrs' Square, Brussels.

1975, May 12 Engr. Perf. 11½
926 A351 4.50fr deep rose lilac .22 .20
927 A352 5fr slate green .22 .15
928 A351 10fr bright blue .45 .32
  Nos. 926-928 (3) .89 .67
European Architectural Heritage Year.

Library, Louvain University, Ryckmans and Cerfaux A355

1975, June 7 Photo.
931 A355 10fr dull blue & sepia .40 .20
25th anniversary of Louvain Bible Colloquium, founded by Professors Gonzague Ryckmans (1887-1969) and Lucien Cerfaux (1883-1968).

"Metamorphose" by Pol Mara — A356

Marie Popelin, Palace of Justice, Brussels — A357

1975, June 14
932 A356 7fr multicolored .30 .20
Queen Fabiola Mental Health Foundation.

1975, June 21 Engr. & Photo.
933 A357 6.50fr green & claret .30 .15
International Women's Year 1975. Marie Popelin (1846-1913), first Belgian woman doctor of law.

Assia, by Charles Despiau — A358

Cornelia Vekemans, by Cornelis de Vos — A359

1975, Sept. 6 Perf. 11½
934 A358 5fr yellow grn & blk .24 .15
Middelheim Outdoor Museum, 25th anniv.

1975, Sept. 20 Photo.
935 A359 4.50fr multicolored .20 .15
Youth philately.

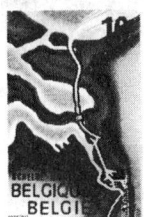

Map of Schelde-Rhine Canal — A360

1975, Sept. 20
936 A360 10fr multicolored .45 .22
Opening of connection between the Schelde and Rhine, Sept. 23, 1975.

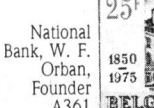

National Bank, W. F. Orban, Founder A361

Photogravure and Engraved
1975, Oct. 11 Perf. 12½x13
937 A361 25fr multicolored 1.00 .30
Natl. Bank of Belgium, 125th anniv.

Edmond Thieffry and Plane, 1925 — A362

1975, Oct. 18 Perf. 11½
938 A362 7fr black & lilac .30 .20
First flight Brussels to Kinshasa, Congo, 50th anniversary.

"Seat of Wisdom" St. Peter's, Louvain — A363

1975, Nov. 8 Perf. 11½
939 A363 6.50fr blue, blk & grn .28 .15
University of Louvain, 550th anniversary.

Angels, by Rogier van der Weyden A364

1975, Nov. 15
940 A364 5fr multicolored .24 .15
Christmas 1975.

Willemsfonds Emblem — A365

American Bicentennial Emblem — A366

1976, Feb. 21 Photo. Perf. 11½
941 A365 5fr multicolored .24 .15
125th anniversary of the Willems Foundation, which supports Flemish language and literature.

1976, Mar. 13 Photo. Perf. 11½
942 A366 14fr gold, red, bl & blk .60 .30
American Bicentennial. No. 942 printed checkerwise in sheets of 30 stamps and 30 gold and black labels which show medal with 1626 seal of New York. Black engraved inscription on labels commemorates arrival of first Walloon settlers in Nieu Nederland.

Cardinal Mercier — A367

Symbolic of V.E.V. — A368

1976, Mar. 20 Engr.
943 A367 4.50fr brt rose lilac .20 .15
Desire Joseph Cardinal Mercier (1851-1926), professor at Louvain University, spiritual and patriotic leader during World War I, 50th death anniversary.

1976, Apr. 3 Photo. Perf. 11½
944 A368 6.50fr multicolored .28 .15
Flemish Economic Organization (Vlaams Ekonomisch Verbond), 50th anniversary.

BELGIUM

General Post Office, Brussels — A369

1976, Apr. 24   Engr.   *Perf. 11½*
945 A369 6.50fr sepia   .28 .15
Stamp Day.

Potter's Hands — A370

Europa: 6.50fr, Basket maker, vert.

1976, May 8   Photo.
946 A370 6.50fr multicolored   .45 .15
947 A370 14fr multicolored   .65 .38

Truck on Road — A371

1976, May 8
948 A371 14fr black, yel & red   .65 .35
15th Intl. Road Union Cong., Brussels, May 9-13.

Queen Elisabeth (1876-1965) — A372

1976, May 24   *Perf. 11½*
949 A372 14fr green   .60 .30

Ardennes Draft Horses — A373

1976, June 19
950 A373 5fr multicolored   .22 .15
Ardennes Draft Horses Association, 50th anniversary.

Souvenir Sheets

King Baudouin — A374

1976, June 26
951 A374 Sheet of 3   2.50 .50
a. 4.50fr gray   .70 .70
b. 6.50fr ocher   .70 .70
c. 10fr brick red   .70 .70
952 A374 Sheet of 2   3.50 3.50
a. 20fr yellow green   .85 .85
b. 30fr Prussian blue   .85 .85

25th anniv. of the reign of King Baudouin. No. 951 sold for 30fr, No. 952 for 70fr. The surtax went to a new foundation for the improvement of living conditions in honor of the King.

Electric Train and Society Emblem — A375

1976, Sept. 11   Photo.   *Perf. 11½*
953 A375 6.50fr multi   .30 .15
Natl. Belgian Railroad Soc., 50th anniv.

William of Nassau, Prince of Orange — A376

1976, Sept. 11   Engr.
954 A376 10fr slate green   .42 .20
400th anniv. of the pacification of Ghent.

New Subway Train — A377

1976, Sept. 18   Photo.
955 A377 6.50fr multi   .30 .15
Opening of first line of Brussels subway.

Young Musician, by W. C. Duyster — A378

1976, Oct. 2   Photo.   *Perf. 11½*
956 A378 4.50fr multi   .20 .15
Young musicians and youth philately.

Charles Bernard — A379

St. Jerome in the Mountains, by Le Patinier — A380

Blind Leading the Blind, by Breughel the Elder — A381

#958, Fernand Victor Toussaint van Boelaere.

1976, Oct. 16   Engr.
957 A379 5fr violet   .15 .15
958 A379 5fr red brn & sepia   .15 .15
959 A380 6.50fr dark brown   .30 .15
960 A381 6.50fr slate green   .30 .15
Nos. 957-960 (4)   .90 .60

Charles Bernard (1875-1961), French-speaking journalist; Toussaint van Boelaere (1875-1947), Flemish journalist; No. 959, Charles Plisnier Belgian-French Cultural Society. No. 960, Assoc. for Language Promotion.

Remouchamps Caves — A382

Hunnegem Priory, Gramont, and Madonna — A383

Designs: No. 963, River Lys and St. Martin's Church. No. 964, Ham-sur-Heure Castle.

1976, Oct. 23   Engr.   *Perf. 13*
961 A382 4.50fr multi   .15 .15
962 A383 4.50fr multi   .15 .15
963 A383 5fr multi   .22 .15
964 A383 5fr multi   .22 .15
Nos. 961-964 (4)   .74 .60

Tourism. #961-962 are not luminescent.

Nativity, by Master of Flemalle — A384

1976, Nov. 20   *Perf. 11½*
965 A384 5fr violet   .22 .18
Christmas 1976.

Rubens' Monogram — A385

1977, Feb. 12   Photo. & Engr.
966 A385 6.50fr lilac & blk   .30 .15
Peter Paul Rubens (1577-1640), painter.

Heraldic Lion — A386

1977-85   Typo.   *Perf. 13½x14*
Size: 17x20mm
967 A386 50c brn ('80)   .15 .15
a. 50c orange brown ('85)   .15 .15
968 A386 1fr brt lil   .15 .15
a. 1fr bright rose lilac ('84)   .15 .15
969 A386 1.50fr gray ('78)   .15 .15
970 A386 2fr yel ('78)   .15 .15
970A A386 2.50fr yel grn ('81)   .15 .15
971 A386 2.75fr Prus bl ('80)   .30 .15
972 A386 3fr vio ('78)   .30 .15
a. 3fr dull violet ('84)   .18 .15
973 A386 4fr red brn ('80)   .25 .15
a. 4fr rose brown ('85)   .25 .15
974 A386 4.50fr lt ultra   .30 .15
975 A386 5fr grn ('80)   .30 .15
a. 5fr emerald green ('84)   .20 .15
976 A386 6fr dl red brn   .35 .15
a. 6fr light red brown ('85)   .35 .15
Nos. 967-976 (11)   2.55 1.65

1978, Aug.   Photo.   *Perf. 13½x12½*
Size: 17x22mm
Booklet Stamps
977 A386 1fr brt lilac   .15 .15
a. Bklt. pane, #977-978, 2 #786   1.50
b. Bklt. pane, #977, 979, 2 #788   2.00
978 A386 2fr yellow   .30 .30
979 A386 3fr violet   .45 .45
Nos. 977-979 (3)   .90 .90

Each pane has 2 labels showing Belgian Postal emblem, also a large selvage with zip code instructions. No. 977-979 not luminescent.

See Nos. 1084-1088, design O5.

Anniversary Emblem — A387

1977, Mar. 14   Photo.   *Perf. 11½*
982 A387 6.50fr sil & multi   .30 .15
Royal Belgian Association of Civil and Agricultural Engineers, 50th anniversary.

Birds and Lions Emblem — A388

1977, Mar. 28
983 A388 14fr multi   .60 .30
Belgian District #112 of Lions Intl., 25th anniv.

Pillar Box, 1852 — A389

1977, Apr. 23   Engr.
984 A389 6.50fr slate green   .45 .15
Stamp Day 1977.

Gileppe Dam, Jalhay — A390

Europa: 14fr, War Memorial, Yser at Nieuport.

1977, May 7   Photo.   *Perf. 11½*
985 A390 6.50fr multi   .40 .15
986 A390 14fr multi   .90 .45

Mars and Mercury Association Emblem — A391

1977, May 14
987 A391 5fr multi   .25 .15
Mars and Mercury Association of Reserve and Retired Officers, 50th anniversary.

Prince de Hornes Coat of Arms — A392

Conversion of St. Hubertus — A394

BELGIUM

Battle of the Golden Spur, from Oxford Chest — A393

Design: 6.50fr, Froissart writing book.

1977, June 11 Engr. Perf. 11½
988 A392 4.50fr violet .30 .15
989 A393 5fr red .35 .15
990 A394 6.50fr dark brown .40 .15
991 A394 14fr slate green .75 .15
  Nos. 988-991 (4) 1.80 .80

300th anniv. of the Principality of Overijse (4.50fr); 675th anniv. of the Battle of the Golden Spur (5f); 600th anniv. of publication of 1st volume of the Chronicles of Jehan Froissart (6.50fr); 1250th anniv. of the death of St. Hubertus (14fr).

Rubens, Self-portrait — A395

1977, June 25 Photo.
992 A395 5fr multi .25 .15
  a. Souvenir sheet of 3 1.25 .90

Peter Paul Rubens (1577-1640), painter. No. 992a sold for 20fr.

Open Book, from The Lamb of God, by Van Eyck Brothers — A396

1977, Sept. 3 Photo. Perf. 11½
993 A396 10fr multi .45 .25

Intl. Federation of Library Associations (IFLA), 50th Anniv. Congress, Brussels, Sept. 5-10.

Gymnast and Soccer Player — A397

Designs: 6.50fr, Fencers in wheelchairs, horiz. 10fr, Basketball players. 14fr, Hockey players.

1977, Sept. 10
994 A397 4.50fr multi .25 .15
995 A397 6.50fr multi .40 .15
996 A397 10fr multi .60 .20
997 A397 14fr multi .80 .30
  Nos. 994-997 (4) 2.05 .80

Workers' Gymnastics and Sports Center, 50th anniversary (4.50fr); sport for the Handicapped (6.50fr); 20th European Basketball Championships (10fr); First World Hockey Cup (14fr).

Europalia 77 Emblem — A398

1977, Sept. 17
998 A398 5fr gray & multi .22 .15

5th Europalia Arts Festival, featuring German Federal Republic, Belgium, Oct.-Nov. 1977.

The Egg Farmer, by Gustave De Smet — A399

1977, Oct. 8 Engr. & Photo.
999 A399 4.50fr bister & blk .22 .15

Publicity for Belgian eggs.

Mother and Daughter with Album, by Constant Cap — A400

1977, Oct. 15 Engr.
1000 A400 4.50fr dark brown .22 .15

Youth Philately.

Bailiff's House, Gembloux — A401

Market Square, St. Nicholas — A402

No. 1002, St. Aldegonde Church and Cultural Center. No. 1004, Statue and bridge, Liège.

1977, Oct. 22
1001 A401 4.50fr multi .22 .15
1002 A401 4.50fr multi .22 .15
1003 A402 5fr multi .22 .18
1004 A402 5fr multi .22 .18
  Nos. 1001-1004 (4) .88 .66

Tourism. Nos. 1001-1004 not luminescent. See Nos. 1017-1018, 1037-1040.

Nativity, by Rogier van der Weyden — A403

1977, Nov. 11 Engr.
1005 A403 5fr rose red .30 .15

Christmas 1977.

Symbols of Transportation and Map — A404

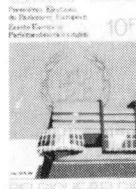

Parliament of Europe, Strasbourg, and Emblem — A405

Campidoglio Palace, Rome, and Map — A406

Design: No. 1009, Paul-Henri Spaak and map of 19 European member countries.

1978, Mar. 18 Photo. Perf. 11½
1006 A404 10fr blue & multi .55 .20
1007 A405 10fr blue & multi 1.10 .20
1008 A406 14fr blue & multi .65 .55
1009 A406 14fr blue & multi .65 .55
  Nos. 1006-1009 (4) 2.95 1.50

European Action: 25th anniversary of the European Transport Ministers' Conference; 1st general elections for European Parliament; 20th anniversary of the signing of the Treaty of Rome; Paul Henri Spaak (1899-1972), Belgian statesman who worked for the establishment of European Community.

Grimbergen Abbey — A407

1978, Apr. 1 Engr.
1010 A407 4.50fr red brown .22 .15

850th anniversary of the Premonstratensian Abbey at Grimbergen.

Emblem — A408

No. 39 with First Day Cancel — A409

1978, Apr. 8 Photo.
1011 A408 8fr multicolored .50 .15

Ostend Chamber of Commerce and Industry, 175th anniversary.

1978, Apr. 15
1012 A409 8fr multicolored .35 .15

Stamp Day.

Europa Issue

Pont des Trous, Tournai — A410

8fr, Antwerp Cathedral, by Vaclav Hollar.

Photogravure and Engraved
1978, May 6 Perf. 11½
1013 A410 8fr multi, vert. .50 .15
1014 A410 14fr multi .75 .30

Virgin of Ghent, Porcelain Plaque — A411

Paul Pastur Workers' University, Charleroi — A412

1978, Sept. 16 Photo. Perf. 11½
1015 A411 6fr multicolored .42 .15
1016 A412 8fr multicolored .55 .15

Municipal education in Ghent, 150th anniversary; Paul Pastur Workers' University, Charleroi, 75th anniv. #1015-1016 are not luminescent.

Types of 1977 and Tourist Guide, Brussels — A413

#1017, Jonathas House, Enghien. #1018, View of Wetteren and couple in local costume. #1020, Prince Carnival, Eupen-St. Vith.

1978, Sept. 25 Photo. & Engr.
1017 A401 4.50fr multi .16 .15
1018 A402 4.50fr multi .16 .15
1019 A413 6fr multi .25 .15
1020 A413 6fr multi .25 .15
  Nos. 1017-1020 (4) .82 .60

Tourism. #1017-1020 are not luminescent.

Emblem — A414

1978, Oct. 7 Photo.
1021 A414 8fr red & blk .35 .15

Royal Flemish Engineer's Organization, 50th anniversary.

Young Philatelist — A415

1978, Oct. 14 Engr. Perf. 11½
1022 A415 4.50fr dk violet .22 .15

Youth philately.

Nativity, Notre Dame, Huy — A416

1978, Nov. 18 Engr. Perf. 11½
1023 A416 6fr black .28 .15

Christmas 1978.

Tyll Eulenspiegel, Lay Action Emblem — A417

European Parliament Emblem — A418

1979, Mar. 3 Photo. Perf. 11½
1024 A417 4.50fr multi .28 .15

10th anniversary of Lay Action Centers.

1979, Mar. 3
1025 A418 8fr multicolored .50 .15

European Parliament, first direct elections, June 7-10.

569

BELGIUM

St. Michael Banishing
Lucifer — A419

1979, Mar. 17   Photo. & Engr.
1026 A419 4.50fr rose red & blk   .20 .15
1027 A419 8fr brt green & blk   .30 .15
Millennium of Brussels.

NATO Emblem
and Monument
A420

1979, Mar. 31   Photo.
1028 A420 3fr multicolored   1.75 .45
NATO, 30th anniv.

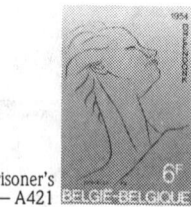

Prisoner's
Head — A421

1979, Apr. 7   Photo. & Engr.
1029 A421 6fr orange & blk   .25 .15
25th anniversary of the National Political Prisoners' Monument at Breendonk.

Belgium No.
O2 — A422

1979, Apr. 21   Photo.   Perf. 11½
1030 A422 8fr multicolored   .50 .15
Stamp Day 1979.

Mail
Coach
and
Truck
A423

Europa: 14fr, Chappe's heliograph, Intelsat satellite and dish antenna.

1979, Apr. 28   Photo. & Engr.
1031 A423 8fr multicolored   .45 .15
1032 A423 14fr multicolored   .90 .40

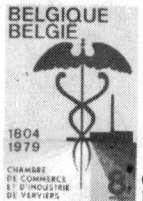

Chamber of Commerce
Emblem — A424

1979, May 19   Photo.   Perf. 11½
1033 A424 8fr multicolored   .35 .15
Verviers Chamber of Commerce and Industry, 175th anniversary.

"50" Emblem
A425

1979, June 9   Photo.   Perf. 11½
1034 A425 4.50fr gold & ultra   .30 .15
Natl. Fund for Professional Credit, 50th anniv.

Merchants,
Roman Bas-
relief A426

1979, June 9
1035 A426 10fr multicolored   .60 .16
Belgian Chamber of Trade and Commerce, 50th anniversary.

"Tintin" as
Philatelist
A427

1979, Sept. 29   Photo.   Perf. 11½
1036 A427 8fr multicolored   1.10 .15
Youth philately.

Tourism Types of 1977
Designs: No. 1037, Belfry, Thuin. No. 1038, Royal Museum of Central Africa, Tervuren. No. 1039, St. Nicholas Church and cattle, Ciney. No. 1040, St. John's Church and statue of Our Lady, Poperinge.

Perf. 11½ (A401), 13 (A402)
1979, Oct. 22   Photo. & Engr.
1037 A401 5fr multicolored   .20 .15
1038 A402 5fr multicolored   .20 .15
1039 A401 6fr multicolored   .35 .15
1040 A402 6fr multicolored   .35 .15
   Nos. 1037-1040 (4)   1.10 .60

Francois Auguste
Gevaert
A429

Piano, String
Instruments
A430

Design: 6fr, Emmanuel Durlet.

1979, Nov. 3   Perf. 11½
1041 A429 5fr brown   .35 .15
1042 A429 6fr brown   .42 .15
1043 A430 14fr brown   .90 .35
   Nos. 1041-1043 (3)   1.67 .65

Francois Auguste Gevaert (1828-1908), musicologist and composer; Emmanuel Durlet (1893-1977), pianist; Queen Elisabeth Musical Chapel Foundation, 40th anniv.

Virgin and Child, Notre
Dame, Foy — A431

1979, Nov. 24   Photo. & Engr.
1044 A431 6fr lt grnsh blue   .30 .15
Christmas 1979.

Independence,
150th
Anniversary
A432

1980, Jan. 26   Photo.   Perf. 11½
1045 A432 9fr purple   .40 .15

Frans van
Cauwelaert
A433

Spring Flowers
A434

1980, Feb. 25   Engr.
1046 A433 5fr gray   .22 .15
Frans van Cauwelaert (1880-1961), Minister of State.

1980, Mar. 10   Photo.
1047 A434 5fr shown   .24 .15
1048 A434 6.50fr Summer flowers   .32 .15
1049 A434 9fr Autumn flowers   .45 .15
   Nos. 1047-1049 (3)   1.01 .45
Ghent Flower Show, Apr. 19-27.

P.T.T., 50th
Anniv.
A435

1980, Apr. 14   Photo.   Perf. 11½
1050 A435 10fr multicolored   .45 .22

Belgium No.
C4 — A436

1980, Apr. 21
1051 A436 9fr multicolored   .50 .15
Stamp Day.

A437    A438

Europa: 9fr, St. Benedict, by Hans Memling. 14fr, Margaret of Austria (1480-1530).

1980, Apr. 28
1052 A437 9fr multicolored   .45 .15
1053 A437 14fr multicolored   .70 .24

1980, May 10   Photo.   Perf. 11½
1054 A438 5fr Palais des Nations, Brussels   .25 .15
4th Interparliamentary Conference for European Cooperation and Security, Brussels, May 12-18.

Golden
Carriage, 1780,
Mons — A439

Tourism: #1056, Canal landscape, Damme.

1980, May 17
1055 A439 6.50fr multi   .32 .20
1056 A439 6.50fr multi   .32 .20

Souvenir Sheet

Royal Mint Theater, Brussels — A440

Photo. & Engr.
1980, May 31   Perf. 11½
1057 A440 50fr black   3.25 3.25
150th anniv. of independence. Sold for 75fr.

King Baudouin, 50th
Birthday — A441

1980, Sept. 6   Photo.   Perf. 11½
1058 A441 9fr rose claret   .42 .15

View of
Chiny
A442

Portal and Court,
Diest — A443

1980   Engr.   Perf. 13
1059 A442 5fr multicolored   .25 .15
1060 A443 5fr multicolored   .25 .15
Tourism. Nos. 1059-1060 are not luminescent. Issue dates: No. 1059, Sept. 27; No. 1060, Dec. 13. See Nos. 1072-1075, 1120-1125.

Emblem of
Belgian Heart
League
A444

1980, Oct. 4   Photo.   Perf. 11½
1061 A444 14fr blue & magenta   .55 .25
Heart Week, Oct. 20-25.

BELGIUM

Rodenbach Statue, Roulers — A445

1980, Oct. 11
1062 A445 9fr multicolored .40 .15
Albrecht Rodenbach (1856-1880), poet.

Youth Philately — A446

1980, Oct. 27   Photo.   Perf. 11½
1063 A446 5fr multicolored .22 .15

National Broadcasting Service, 50th Anniversary — A447

1980, Nov. 10
1064 A447 10fr gray & blk .45 .22

Garland and Nativity, by Daniel Seghers, 17th Century A448

1980, Nov. 17
1065 A448 6.50fr multicolored .40 .15
Christmas 1980.

Baron de Gerlache, by F.J. Navez — A449

Leopold I, By Geefs — A450

Design: 9fr, Baron de Stassart, by F.J. Navez.

1981, Mar. 16   Photo.   Perf. 11½
1066 A449 6fr multicolored .35 .15
1067 A449 9fr multicolored .55 .15

Photogravure and Engraved
1068 A450 50fr multicolored 3.00 .55
Sesquicentennial of Chamber of Deputies, Senate and Dynasty.

Europa Issue 1981

Tchantchès and Op-Signoorke, Puppets — A451

Photogravure and Engraved
1981, May 4   Perf. 11½
1069 A451 9fr shown .40 .15
1070 A451 14fr d'Artagnan and Woltje .65 .35

Impression of M.A. de Cock (Founder of Post Museum) — A452

1981, May 18   Photo.
1071 A452 9fr multicolored .40 .15
Stamp Day.

Tourism Types of 1980

Designs: No. 1072, Virgin and Child statue, Our Lady's Church, Tongre-Notre Dame. No. 1073, Egmont Castle, Zottegem. No. 1074, Eau d'Heure River. No. 1075, Tongerlo Abbey, Antwerp.

1981, June 15   Engr.   Perf. 11½
1072 A442 6fr multi .35 .15
1073 A442 6fr multi .35 .20
1074 A443 6.50fr multi .35 .20
1075 A443 6.50fr multi .35 .20
Nos. 1072-1075 (4) 1.40 .75

Soccer Player — A453

E. Remouchamps, Founder — A454

1981, Sept. 5   Photo.   Perf. 11½
1076 A453 6fr multicolored .35 .15
Soccer in Belgium centenary; Royal Antwerp Soccer Club.

1981, Sept. 5   Photo. & Engr.
1077 A454 6.50fr multi .40 .15
Walloon Language and Literature Club 125th anniv.

Audit Office Sesquicentennial — A455

1981, Sept. 12   Engr.
1078 A455 10fr tan & dk brn .60 .24

French Horn — A456

1981, Sept. 12   Photo.
1079 A456 6.50fr multi .40 .15
Vredekring (Peace Circle) Band of Antwerp centenary.

Souvenir Sheet

Pieta, by Ben Genaux — A457

1981, Sept. 19   Photo.   Perf. 11½
1080 A457 20fr multicolored 1.75 1.40
Mining disaster at Marcinelle, 25th anniv. Sold for 30fr.

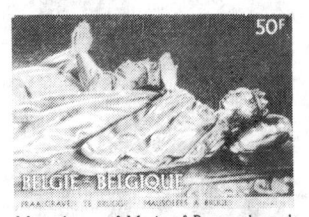

Mausoleum of Marie of Burgundy and Charles the Bold, Bruges — A458

1981, Oct. 10   Photo. & Engr.
1081 A458 50fr multi 2.75 .60

Youth Philately — A459

1981, Oct. 24   Photo.
1082 A459 6fr multi .28 .15

Type of 1977 and

A459a   A460

King Baudouin A460a

Photo. and Engr.; Photo.
1980-86   Perf. 13½x14, 11½
1084 A386 65c brt rose .20 .15
1085 A386 1fr on 5fr grn .20 .15
1086 A386 7fr brt rose .55 .15
1087 A386 8fr grnsh bl .60 .15
1088 A386 9fr dl org .55 .15
1089 A459a 10fr blue .85 .15
1090 A459a 11fr dl red .90 .15
1091 A459a 12fr grn .90 .15
1092 A459a 13fr scar .85 .15
1093 A459a 15fr red org 1.25 .20
1094 A459a 20fr dk bl 1.50 .28
1095 A459a 22fr lilac 1.65 .30
1096 A459a 23fr gray grn 1.00 .55
1097 A459a 30fr brown 2.25 .40
1098 A459a 40fr red org 2.50 .55
1099 A460 50fr lt grnsh bl & bl 3.25 .30
1100 A460a 50fr tan & dk brn 3.25 .60
1101 A460 65fr pale lil & blk 4.50 .90
1102 A460a 100fr lt bis brn & dk bl 6.75 1.25
1103 A460a 100fr lt bl & dk bl 6.75 1.25
Nos. 1084-1103 (20) 40.25 7.93

Issued: 65c, 4/14/80; 1fr, 5/3/82; 7fr, 5/17/82; 8fr, 5/9/83; 9fr, 2/11/85; 65fr, No. 1099, 1102, 11/5/81; 10fr, 11/15/82; 11fr, 4/5/83; 12fr, 1/23/84; 15fr, 22fr, 30fr, No. 1100, 3/26/84; 20fr, 40fr, No. 1103, 6/12/84; 23fr, 2/25/85; 13fr, 3/10/86. See Nos. 1231-1234.

Max Waller, Movement Founder A461

The Spirit Drinkers, by Gustave van de Woestyne A462

Fernand Severin, Poet, 50th Death Anniv. — A463

Jan van Ruusbroec, Flemish Mystic, 500th Birth Anniv. — A464

Thought and Man TV Series, 25th Anniv. A465

Nativity, 16th Cent. Engraving A466

1981, Nov. 7
1104 A461 6fr multi .30 .15
1105 A462 6.50fr multi .35 .18
1106 A463 9fr multi .50 .15
1107 A464 10fr multi .80 .22
1108 A465 14fr multi .75 .35
Nos. 1104-1108 (5) 2.70 1.05
La Jeune Belgique cultural movement cent. (6fr).

1981, Nov. 21
1109 A466 6.50fr multi .30 .15
Christmas 1981.

Royal Conservatory of Music Sesquicentennial — A467

Design: 9fr, Judiciary sesquicentennial.

1982, Jan. 25   Photo.   Perf. 11½
1110 A467 6.50fr multi .30 .15
1111 A467 9fr multi .40 .15

A468   A469

1982, Mar. 1

1112	A468	6fr Cyclotron	.35	.15
1113	A468	14fr Galaxy, telescope	.85	.35
1114	A468	50fr Koch	3.00	.65
		Nos. 1112-1114 (3)	4.20	1.15

Radio-isotope production, Natl. Radio-elements Institute, Fleurus (6fr); Royal Belgian Observatory (14fr); centenary of TB bacillus discovery (50fr).

1982, Apr. 17 Photo. *Perf. 11½*

1115	A469	6.50fr multi	.32	.15

Joseph Lemaire (1882-1966), Minister of State.

Europa 1982 — A470

1982, May 1

1116	A470	10fr Universal suffrage	.48	.15
1117	A470	17fr Edict of Tolerance, 1781	.80	.40

Stamp Day — A471

1982, May 22 Photo. & Engr.

1118	A471	10fr multi	.50	.15

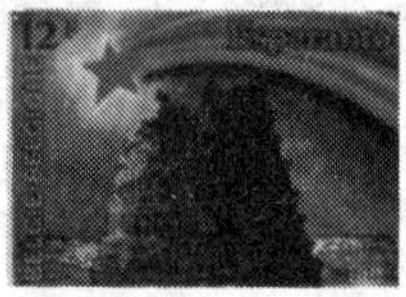

67th World Esperanto Congress, Anvers A472

1982, June 7 Photo. *Perf. 11½*

1119	A472	12fr Tower of Babel	.60	.30

Tourism Type of 1980

Designs: No. 1120, Tower of Gosselies. No. 1121, Zwijveke Abbey, Dendermonde. No. 1122, Stavelot Abbey. No. 1123, Villers-la-Ville Abbey ruins. No. 1124, Geraardsbergen Abbey entrance. No. 1125, Beveren Pillory.

1982, June 21 Photo. & Engr.

1120	A443	7fr lt bl & blk	.50	.15
1121	A443	7fr lt grn & blk	.50	.15
1122	A442	7.50fr tan & dk brn	.55	.25
1123	A442	7.50fr lt vio & pur	.55	.25
1124	A443	7.50fr slate & blk	.55	.25
1125	A443	7.50fr beige & blk	.55	.25
		Nos. 1120-1125 (6)	3.20	1.30

Self Portrait, by L.P. Boon (b. 1912) A473

Abraham Hans, Writer (1882-1932) A474

Designs: 10fr, Adoration of the Shepherds, by Hugo van der Goes (1440-1482). 12fr, The King on His Throne, carving by M. de Ghelderode (1898-1962). 17fr, Madonna and Child, by Pieter Paulus (1881-1959).

1982, Sept. 13 Photo. *Perf. 11½*

1126	A473	7fr multicolored	.50	.15
1127	A473	10fr multicolored	.60	.15
1128	A473	12fr multicolored	.70	.35
1129	A473	17fr multicolored	1.00	.35
		Nos. 1126-1129 (4)	2.80	1.00

1982, Sept. 27

1130	A474	17fr multicolored	1.10	.35

Youth Philately and Scouting A475

1982, Oct. 2 Photo. *Perf. 11½*

1131	A475	7fr multicolored	.50	.15

Grand Orient Lodge of Belgium Sesquicentennial A476

1982, Oct. 16 Photo. & Engr.

1132	A476	10fr Man taking oath	.60	.15

Cardinal Joseph Cardijn (1882-1967) A477

1982, Nov. 13 Photo.

1133	A477	10fr multicolored	.48	.15

St. Francis of Assisi (1182-1226) — A478

1982, Nov. 27

1134	A478	20fr multicolored	.90	.30

Horse-drawn Trolley A479

1983, Feb. 12 Photo. *Perf. 11½*

1135	A479	7.50fr shown	.38	.22
1136	A479	10fr Electric trolley	.50	.15
1137	A479	50fr Trolley, diff.	2.50	.50
		Nos. 1135-1137 (3)	3.38	.87

Intl. Fed. for Periodical Press, 24th World Congress, Brussels, May 11-13 — A480

1983, Mar. 19 Photo. *Perf. 11½*

1138	A480	20fr multicolored	1.00	.25

Homage to Women A481

1983, Apr. 16

1139	A481	8fr Operator	.45	.15
1140	A481	11fr Homemaker	.55	.15
1141	A481	20fr Executive	.95	.25
		Nos. 1139-1141 (3)	1.95	.55

Stamp Day — A482

1983, Apr. 23

1142	A482	11fr multicolored	.60	.15

Procession of the Precious Blood, Bruges A483

1983, Apr. 30 Photo. *Perf. 11½*

1143	A483	8fr multi	.60	.15

Europa 1983 A484

Paintings by P. Delvaux. 11fr vert.

1983, May 14

1144	A484	11fr Common Man	.65	.15
1145	A484	20fr Night Train	1.25	.45

Manned Flight Bicentenary A485

1983, June 11 Photo. *Perf. 11½*

1146	A485	11fr Balloon over city	.65	.15
1147	A485	22fr Country	1.40	.45

Our Lady's Church, Hastiere A486

1983, June 25

1148	A486	8fr shown	.40	.18
1149	A486	8fr Landen	.40	.18
1150	A486	8fr Park, Mouscron	.40	.18
1151	A486	8fr Wijnendale Castle, Torhout	.40	.18
		Nos. 1148-1151 (4)	1.60	.72

Tineke Festival, Heule — A487

1983, Sept. 10 Photo.

1152	A487	8fr multi	.40	.15

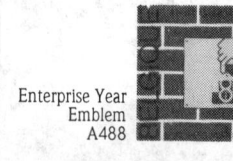

Enterprise Year Emblem A488

1983, Sept. 24

1153	A488	11fr multicolored	.55	.15

European year for small and medium-sized enterprises and craft industry.

Youth Philately — A489

1983, Oct. 10 Photo. *Perf. 11½*

1154	A489	8fr multicolored	.40	.15

Belgian Exports — A490

1983, Oct. 24 *Perf. 11½*

1155	A490	10fr Diamond industry	.55	.15
1156	A490	10fr Metallurgy	.55	.15
1157	A490	10fr Textile industry	.55	.15
		Nos. 1155-1157 (3)	1.65	.45

See Nos. 1161-1164.

A491

A492

1983, Nov. 7

1158	A491	20fr multicolored	1.00	.25

Hendrik Conscience, novelist (1812-1883).

Leopold III Type of 1936

1983, Dec. 12 Engr. *Perf. 12x11½*

1159	A84	11fr black	.55	.15

Leopold III memorial (1901-1983), King 1934-1951.

Photogravure and Engraved

1984, Jan. 14 *Perf. 11½*

1160	A492	11fr multicolored	.55	.15

Free University of Brussels, sesquicentennial.

Exports Type of 1983

1984, Jan. 28 Photo.

1161	A490	11fr Chemicals	.55	.15
1162	A490	11fr Food	.55	.15
1163	A490	11fr Transportation equipment	.55	.15
1164	A490	11fr Technology	.55	.15
		Nos. 1161-1164 (4)	2.20	.60

A494

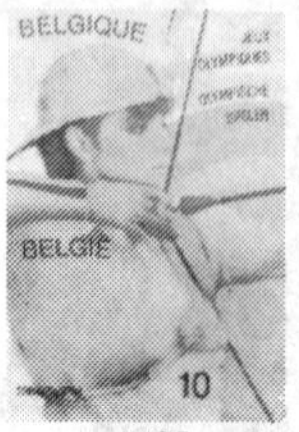

A495

1984, Feb. 11 Photo. & Engr.

1165	A494	8fr tan & dk brn	.40	.15

50th death anniv. of King Albert I.

1984, Mar. 3 Photo.

Souvenir Sheet

1166	Sheet of 2	2.00	2.00
a.	A495 10fr Archery	.55	.55
b.	A495 24fr Dressage	1.40	1.40

1984 Olympics. See Nos. B1029-B1030.

BELGIUM

Family, Globe, Birds A496

St. John Bosco Canonization A497

1984, Mar. 24 Photo. Perf. 11½
1167 A496 12fr multicolored .60 .15
"Movement without a Name" peace org.

1984, Apr. 7
1168 A497 8fr multicolored .40 .15

Europa (1959-84) A498

1984, May 5 Photo. Perf. 11½
1169 A498 12fr black & red .75 .15
1170 A498 22fr black & ultra 1.40 .30

Stamp Day — A499

1984, May 19
1171 A499 12fr No. 52 .60 .15

2nd European Parliament Elections A500

1984, May 26
1172 A500 12fr multicolored .60 .15

Royal Military School, 150th Anniv. — A501

1984, June 9 Photo. Perf. 11½
1173 A501 22fr Hat 1.10 .25

Notre-Dame de la Chappelle, Brussels A502

Churches: No. 1175, St. Martin's, Montignyle-Tilleul. No. 1176, Tielt, vert.

Perf. 11½x12, 12x11½
1984, June 23 Photo. & Engr.
1174 A502 10fr multicolored .55 .15
1175 A502 10fr multicolored .55 .15
1176 A502 10fr multicolored .55 .15
Nos. 1174-1176 (3) 1.65 .45

50th Anniv. of Chirojeugd (Christian Youth Movement) A503

1984, Sept. 15 Photo. Perf. 11½
1177 A503 10fr Emblem .50 .15

Affligem Abbey A504

1984, Oct. 6 Photo. & Engr.
1178 A504 8fr Averbode, vert. .40 .25
1179 A504 22fr Chimay, vert. 1.25 .25
1180 A504 24fr Rochefort, vert. 1.25 .38
1181 A504 50fr shown 2.50 .50
Nos. 1178-1181 (4) 5.40 1.38

Youth Philately A505

1984, Oct. 20 Photo.
1182 A505 8fr Postman smurf .45 .15

Arthur Meulemans (1884-1966), Composer — A506

1984, Nov. 17 Photo. & Engr.
1183 A506 12fr multi .60 .15

St. Norbert, 850th Death Anniv. — A507

Europalia '85 — A508

1985, Jan. 14 Photo. & Engr.
1184 A507 22fr sepia & beige 1.10 .30

1985, Jan. 21 Photo.
1185 A508 12fr Virgin of Louvain .65 .15

Belgian Assoc. of Professional Journalists, Cent. — A509

1985, Feb. 11 Photo.
1186 A509 9fr multicolored .42 .15

Ghent Flower Festival, Orchids A510

Visit of Pope John Paul II A511

Photogravure and Engraved
1985, Mar. 18 Perf. 11½
1187 A510 12fr Vanda coerules .70 .15
1188 A510 12fr Phalaenopsis .70 .15
1189 A510 12fr Suphrolaelio cattlea riffe .70 .15
Nos. 1187-1189 (3) 2.10 .45

1985, Apr. 1 Photo.
1190 A511 12fr multicolored .60 .15

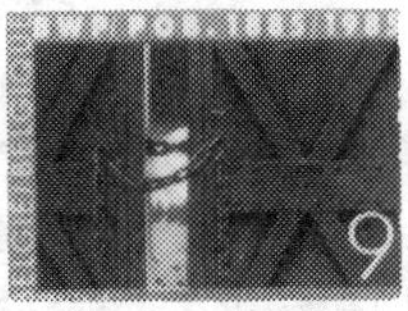

Belgian Worker's Party Cent. — A512

1985, Apr. 15 Photo.
1191 A512 9fr Chained factory gate .42 .15
1192 A512 12fr Broken wall, red flag .60 .15
Set value .24

Jean de Bast (1883-1975), Engraver A513

1985, Apr. 22 Engr.
1193 A513 12fr blue black .60 .15
Stamp Day.

Public Transportation Year — A514

Design: 9fr, Steam tram locomotive Type 18, 1896. 12fr, Locomotive Elephant and tender, 1835. 23fr, Type 23 tank engine, 1904. 24fr, Type I Pacific locomotive, 1935. 50fr, Type 27 electric locomotive, 1975.

1985, May 6 Photo.
1194 A514 9fr multicolored .65 .20
1195 A514 12fr multicolored .85 .20
1196 A514 23fr multicolored 1.50 .35
1197 A514 24fr multicolored 1.90 .40
Nos. 1194-1197 (4) 4.90 1.15

Souvenir Sheet
1198 A514 50fr multicolored 4.50 3.75

Europa 1985 — A515

1985, May 13 Photo.
1199 A515 12fr Cesar Franck at organ, 1887 .80 .15
1200 A515 23fr Folk figures 1.50 .25

26th Navigation Congress, Brussels A516

1985, June 10 Photo. Perf. 11½
1201 A516 23fr Zeebruge Harbor 1.25 .25
1202 A516 23fr Projected lock at Strepy-Thieu 1.25 .25

St. Martin's Church, Marcinelle A517

Tourism: No. 1203, Church of the Assumption of Our Lady, Avernas-le-Baudouin, vert. No. 1204, Church of the Old Beguinage, Tongres, vert. No. 1206, Private residence, Puyenbroeck.

1985, June 24 Perf. 11½
1203 A517 12fr multicolored .60 .15
1204 A517 12fr multicolored .60 .15
1205 A517 12fr multicolored .60 .15
1206 A517 12fr multicolored .60 .15
Nos. 1203-1206 (4) 2.40 .60

Queen Astrid (1905-1935) A518

Baking Pies for the Mattetart of Geraardsbergen A519

1985, Sept. 2 Perf. 11½
1207 A518 12fr brown .60 .15

1985, Sept. 16
Folk events: 24fr, Children dancing, centenary of the St. Lambert de Hermalle-Argenteau Le Rouges youth organization.
1208 A519 12fr multicolored .60 .15
1209 A519 24fr multicolored .95 .28

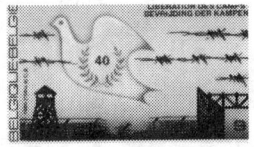

Liberation from German Occupation, 40th Anniv. — A520

Allegories: 9fr, Dove, liberation of concentration camps. 23fr, Battle of Ardennes. 24fr, Destroyer, liberation of the River Scheldt estuary.

1985, Sept. 30 Photo. Perf. 11½
1210 A520 9fr multicolored .50 .25
1211 A520 23fr multicolored 1.25 .65
1212 A520 24fr multicolored 1.25 .68
Nos. 1210-1212 (3) 3.00 1.58

Ernest Claes (1885-1968), Author A521

1985, Oct. 7
1213 A521 9fr Portrait, book character .48 .25

Intl. Youth Year — A522

1985, Oct. 21
1214 A522 9fr Nude in repose, angel .50 .25

King Baudouin & Queen Fabiola, 25th Wedding Anniv. — A523

1985, Dec. 9
1215 A523 12fr multicolored .52 .38

BELGIUM

Birds — A524

Photo. (50c-2fr, No. 1220, 4.50fr-6fr, No. 1229, 10fr), Typo. (Others)
1985-91 Perf. 11½
1216 A524 50c Roitelet huppe .15 .15
1217 A524 1fr Pic Epechette .15 .15
1218 A524 2fr Moineau friquet .15 .15
1219 A524 3fr Gros bec .15 .15
1220 A524 3fr Bruant des roseax .25 .15
1221 A524 3.50fr Rouge gorge .20 .15
1222 A524 4fr Gorge bleue .25 .15
1223 A524 4.50fr Traquet Patre .35 .15
1224 A524 5fr Sittele tporchepot .35 .15
1225 A524 6fr Bouvreuil .40 .15
1226 A524 7fr Mesange bleue .45 .15
1227 A524 8fr Martin-pechuer .45 .15
1228 A524 9fr Chardonneret .35 .15
1229 A524 9fr Grive musicienne .65 .15
1230 A524 10fr Pinson .65 .15
  Nos. 1216-1230 (15) 4.95 2.25
  Issued: 7fr, 9/7/87; 5fr, 6fr, 9/12/88; 4fr, 4/17/89; 2fr, 12/4/89; 1fr, 1/8/90; 10fr, 1/15/90; 50c, #1220, 1229, 9/30/91; others, 9/30/85.
  See #1432-1447, 1627, 1641, 1645, 1651, 1660, 1676, 1696, 1700, 1702-1703.

King Type of 1981
1986-90 Photo. Perf. 11½
1231 A459a 14fr black .80 .20
1232 A459a 24fr dk grysh green 1.10 .85
1233 A459a 25fr blue black 1.45 .38
1234 A460a 200fr sage grn & dl gray grn 11.00 2.00
  Nos. 1231-1234 (4) 14.35 3.43
  Issued: 24fr, 4/7/86; 200fr, 11/3/86; 14fr, 1/15/90; 25fr, 2/19/90.

Congo Stamp Cent. — A525

1986, Jan. 27 Photo. Perf. 11½
1236 A525 10fr Belgian Congo #3 .42 .15
  See Zaire No. 1230.

Carnival Cities of Aalst and Binche A526

Folklore: masks, giants.
1986, Feb. 3
1237 A526 9fr Aalst Belfry .48 .15
1238 A526 12fr Binche Gilles .60 .18

Intl. Peace Year — A527

1986, Mar. 10
1239 A527 23fr Emblem, dove 1.25 .35

Stamp Day — A528

1986, Apr. 21 Photo. Perf. 11½
1240 A528 13fr Artifacts .65 .42

Europa 1986 — A529

1986, May 5
1241 A529 13fr Fish .65 .42
1242 A529 24fr Flora 1.40 .85

Dogs — A530

St. Ludger's Church, Zele — A531

1986, May 26 Photo. Perf. 11½
1243 A530 9fr Malines sheepdog .65 .30
1244 A530 13fr Tervueren sheepdog .85 .45
1245 A530 24fr Groenendael sheepdog 1.65 .82
1246 A530 26fr Flemish cattle dog 1.65 .85
  Nos. 1243-1246 (4) 4.80 2.42

1986, June 30 Photo. & Engr.
  Designs: No. 1248, Waver Town Hall. No. 1249, Nederzwalm Canal, horiz. No. 1250, Chapel of Our Lady of the Dunes, Bredene. No. 1251, Licot Castle, Viroinval, horiz. No. 1252, Eynenbourg Castle, La Calamine, horiz.
1247 A531 9fr multicolored .60 .30
1248 A531 9fr multicolored .60 .30
1249 A531 13fr multicolored .80 .45
1250 A531 13fr multicolored .80 .45
1251 A531 13fr multicolored .80 .45
1252 A531 13fr multicolored .80 .45
  Nos. 1247-1252 (6) 4.40 2.40

Youth Philately A532

1986, Sept. 1 Photo. Perf. 11½
1253 A532 9fr dl ol grn, blk & dk red .50 .32
  Cartoon Exhibition, Knokke.

Famous Men — A533

  Designs: 9fr, Constant Permeke, painter, sculptor. 13fr, Baron Michel-Edmond de Selys Longchamps, scientist. 24fr, Felix Timmermans, writer. 26fr, Maurice Careme, poet.
1986, Sept. 29
1254 A533 9fr multicolored .52 .32
1255 A533 13fr multicolored .75 .45
1256 A533 24fr multicolored 1.40 .82
1257 A533 26fr multicolored 1.50 .90
  Nos. 1254-1257 (4) 4.17 2.49

Royal Academy for Dutch Language and Literature, Cent. — A534

1986, Oct. 6 Engr.
1258 A534 9fr dark blue .52 .32

Natl. Beer Industry A535

Perf. 12½x11½
1986, Oct. 13 Photo.
1259 A535 13fr Glass, barley, hops .70 .50

Provincial Law and Councils, 150th Anniv. A536

1986, Oct. 27 Perf. 11½
1260 A536 13fr Stylized map .70 .50

Christian Trade Union, Cent. — A537

1986, Dec. 13 Photo. Perf. 11½
1261 A537 9fr shown .45 .35
1262 A537 13fr design reversed .65 .50

Flanders Technology Intl. — A538

1987, Mar. 2 Photo.
1263 A538 13fr multi .70 .50

EUROPALIA '87, Austrian Cultural Events — A539

  Design: Woman, detail of a fresco by Gustav Klimt, Palais Stoclet, Brussels.
1987, Apr. 4 Photo. Perf. 11½
1264 A539 13fr multicolored .70 .50

Stamp Day 1987 — A540

  Portrait: Jakob Wiener (1815-1899), 1st engraver of Belgian stamps.
1987, Apr. 11 Photo. & Engr.
1265 A540 13fr lt greenish blue & sage grn .70 .50

Folklore A541

1987, Apr. 25 Photo.
1266 A541 9fr Penitents procession, Veurne .45 .35
1267 A541 13fr Play of John and Alice, Wavre .65 .50

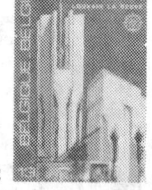

Europa 1987 — A542

  Modern architecture: 13fr, Louvain-la-Neuve Church. 24fr, Regional Housing Assoc. Tower, St. Maartensdal at Louvain.
1987, May 9 Photo.
1268 A542 13fr multicolored .85 .55
1269 A542 24fr multicolored 1.50 1.00

Statue of Andre-Ernest Gretry (1741-1813), French Composer A543

1987, May 23
1270 A543 24fr multicolored 1.50 1.00
  Wallonie Royal Opera, Liege, 20th anniv.

Tourism — A544

  Designs: No. 1271, Statues of Jan Breydel and Pieter de Conin, Bruges. No. 1272, Boondael Chapel, Brussels. No. 1273, Windmill, Keerbergen. No. 1274, St. Christopher's Church, Racour. No. 1275, Virelles Lake, Chimay.
1987, June 13
1271 A544 13fr multicolored 1.00 .55
1272 A544 13fr multicolored 1.00 .55
1273 A544 13fr multicolored 1.00 .55
1274 A544 13fr multicolored 1.00 .55
1275 A544 13fr multicolored 1.00 .55
  Nos. 1271-1275 (5) 5.00 2.75

BELGIUM

Royal Belgian Rowing Assoc., Cent. — A545

European Volleyball Championships A546

1987, Sept. 5
1276 A545 9fr multicolored .50 .38
1277 A546 13fr multicolored .75 .55

Foreign Trade Year — A547

1987, Sept. 12
1278 A547 13fr multi .75 .55

Belgian Social Reform, Cent. — A548

1987, Sept. 19
1279 A548 26fr Leisure, by P. Paulus 1.45 1.10

Youth Philately A549

1987, Oct. 3
1280 A549 9fr multi .50 .38

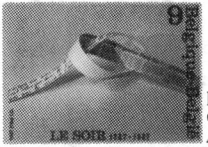

Newspaper Centennials A550

1987, Dec. 12
1281 A550 9fr Le Soir .55 .42
1282 A550 9fr Het Laatste Nieuws, vert. .55 .42

The Sea — A551

Designs: a, Lighthouse, trawler, rider and mount. b, Trawler, youths playing volleyball on beach. c, Cruise ship, sailboat, beach and cabana. d, Shore, birds.

1988, Feb. 6 Photo. Perf. 11½
1283 Strip of 4 + label 2.50 1.80
a.-d. A551 10fr any single .62 .45
No. 1283 has a continuous design.

Dynamism of the Regions A552

1988, Mar. 5 Photo. Perf. 11½
1284 A552 13fr Operation Athena .80 .58
1285 A552 13fr Flanders Alive Campaign .80 .58

Stamp Day — A553

Europa 1988 — A554

1988, Apr. 16 Photo. & Engr.
1286 A553 13fr buff & sepia .80 .58

1988, May 9 Photo. Perf. 11½
Transport and communication.
1287 A554 13fr Satellite dish 1.10 .58
1288 A554 24fr Non-polluting combustion engine 1.90 1.10

Tourism A555

Designs: No. 1289, Romanesque watchtower, ca. 12th-13th cent., Amay, vert. No. 1290, Our Lady of Hanswijk Basilica, 988, Mechelen, vert. No. 1291, St. Sernin's Church, 16th cent., Waimes. No. 1292, Old Town Hall, 1637, and village water pump, 1761, Peer, vert. No. 1293, Our Lady of Bon-Secours Basilica, 1892, Peruwelz.

1988, June 20 Photo. & Engr. Perf. 11½
1289 A555 9fr beige & blk .50 .38
1290 A555 9fr lt blue & blk .50 .38
1291 A555 9fr pale blue grn & blk .50 .38
1292 A555 13fr pale pink & blk .75 .55
1293 A555 13fr pale gray & blk .75 .55
Nos. 1289-1293 (5) 3.00 2.24
Our Lady of Hanswijk Basilica millennium (No. 1290); Waimes village, 1100th anniv. (No. 1291).

Jean Monnet (1888-1979), French Economist — A556

Tapestry in the Hall of the Royal Academy of Medicine — A557

1988, Sept. 12 Perf. 11½
1294 A556 13fr black .70 .52

1988, Sept. 17 Photo.
Academies building and: No. 1296, Lyre, quill pen, open book and atomic symbols.
1295 A557 9fr shown .50 .38
1296 A557 9fr multi .50 .38
Royal Academy of Medicine (#1295); Royal Academy of Science, Literature and Fine Arts (#1296).

Cultural Heritage A558

Artifacts: 9fr, Statue and mask in the Antwerp Ethnographical Museum. 13fr, Sarcophagus, St. Martin's Church, Trazegnies. 24fr, Church organ, Geraardsbergen. 26fr, Shrine, St. Hadelin's Church, Vise.

1988, Sept. 24
1297 A558 9fr multi .50 .38
1298 A558 13fr multi .70 .52
1299 A558 24fr multi 1.30 1.00
1300 A558 26fr multi 1.40 1.05
Nos. 1297-1300 (4) 3.90 2.95

Youth Philately A559

1988, Oct. 10
1301 A559 9fr multi .50 .38

Natl. Postal Savings Bank, 75th Anniv. A560

1988, Nov. 7
1302 A560 13fr multi .70 .52

Christmas 1988 and New Year 1989 — A561

1988, Nov. 21
1303 A561 9fr Winter landscape .50 .38

Royal Mounted Guard, 50th Anniv. A562

1988, Dec. 12
1304 A562 13fr multi .75 .55

Printing Presses A563

9fr, J. Moretus I, Antwerp Museum, vert. 24fr, Stanhope, Printing Museum, Brussels, vert. 26fr, Litho Krause, Royal Museum, Mariemont.

1988, Dec. 19 Engr.
1305 A563 9fr bl blk & blk .52 .40
1306 A563 24fr dark red brn 1.40 1.05
1307 A563 26fr grn & slate grn 1.50 1.15
Nos. 1305-1307 (3) 3.42 2.60

Lace — A564

1989, Mar. 20 Photo.
1308 A564 9fr Marche-en-Famenne .50 .38
1309 A564 13fr Brussels .70 .52
1310 A564 13fr Brugge .70 .52
Nos. 1308-1310 (3) 1.90 1.42

Stamp Day — A565

1989, Apr. 24 Photo. & Engr.
1311 A565 13fr Mail coach, post chaise .75 .55

Europa 1989 — A566

Royal Academy of Fine Arts, Antwerp, 325th Anniv. — A567

Children's toys.

1989, May 8 Photo.
1312 A566 13fr Marbles, horiz. .75 .52
1313 A566 24fr Jumping-jack 1.35 1.00

1989, May 22 Perf. 11½
1314 A567 13fr multi .75 .52

European Parliament 3rd Elections — A568

Illustration reduced.

1989, June 5 Photo.
1315 A568 13fr Brussels .75 .52

Declaration of Rights of Man and the Citizen, Bicent. — A569

1989, June 12 Perf. 11½
1316 A569 13fr multi + label .75 .52

Tourism A570

BELGIUM

Designs: No. 1317, St. Tillo's Church, Izegem. No. 1318, Logne Castle, Ferrieres. No. 1319, St. Laurentius's Church, Lokeren. No. 1320, Antoing Castle, Antoing. Nos. 1318-1320 vert.

1989, June 26			Photo. & Engr.
1317 A570	9fr shown	.50	.38
1318 A570	9fr multi	.50	.38
1319 A570	13fr multi	.75	.52
1320 A570	13fr multi	.75	.52
	Nos. 1317-1320 (4)	2.50	1.80

Ducks — A571

1989, Sept. 4	Photo.	Perf. 12
Booklet Stamps		
1321 A571	13fr Mallard (8a)	1.25 .50
1322 A571	13fr Winter teal (8b)	1.25 .50
1323 A571	13fr Shoveller (8c)	1.25 .50
1324 A571	13fr Pintail (8d)	1.25 .50
a.	Bklt. pane of 4, #1321-1324	5.00

Shigefusa Uesugi, a Seated Japanese Warrior, 13th Cent. A572

1989, Sept. 18		Perf. 11½
1325 A572	24fr multicolored	1.50 .50

Europalia.

Education League, 125th Anniv. — A573

1989, Sept. 25		
1326 A573	13fr multicolored	.80 .20

Treaty of London, 150th Anniv. — A574

Mr. Nibbs — A575

1989, Oct. 2		Photo.
1327 A574	13fr Map of Limburg Provinces	.80 .20

See Netherlands No. 750.

1989, Oct. 9		Perf. 11½
1328 A575	9fr multicolored	.60 .20

Youth philately promotion.

Christmas, New Year 1990 A576

1989, Nov. 20		Photo.
1329 A576	9fr Salvation Army band	.60 .15

Fr. Damien (1840-89), Missionary, Molokai Is. Leper Colony, Hawaii A577

1989, Nov. 27		Photo.
1330 A577	24fr multicolored	1.50 .50

Father Adolf Daens — A578

1989, Dec. 11		Photo. & Engr.
1331 A578	9fr pale & dk grn	.55 .15

The Young Post Rider, an Engraving by Albrecht Durer A579

Ghent Flower Festival A580

1990, Jan. 12		Photo. & Engr.
1332 A579	14fr buff & red blk	.75 .55

Postal communications in Europe, 500th anniv. See Austria No. 1486, Germany No. 1592, Berlin No. 9N584 and German Democratic Republic No. 2791.

1990, Mar. 3		Photo.
1333 A580	10fr Iris florentina	.55 .40
1334 A580	14fr Cattleya harrisoniana	.75 .55
1335 A580	14fr Lilium bulbiferum	.75 .55
	Nos. 1333-1335 (3)	2.05 1.50

Intl. Women's Day — A581

1990, Mar. 12	Photo.	Perf. 11½
1336 A581	25fr Emilienne Brunfaut	1.45 1.05

Wheelchair Basketball — A582

Sports.

1990, Mar. 19		
1337 A582	10fr multicolored	.58 .42
1338 A582	14fr multicolored	.80 .60
1339 A582	25fr shown	1.45 1.05
	Nos. 1337-1339 (3)	2.83 2.07

Special Olympics (10fr); and 1990 World Cup Soccer Championships, Italy (14fr).

Natl. Water Supply Soc., 75th Anniv. A583

1990, Apr. 2		
1340 A583	14fr Water means life	.80 .60

Postman Roulin, by Van Gogh — A584

1990, Apr. 9		
1341 A584	14fr multicolored	.80 .60

Stamp Day.

Labor Day, Cent. A585

1990, Apr. 30		
1342 A585	25fr multicolored	1.45 1.05

Europa 1990 A586

Post offices.

1990, May 7		Photo. & Engr.
1343 A586	14fr Ostend 1	.80 .60
1344 A586	25fr Liege 1, vert.	1.45 1.05

18-Day Campaign, 1940 — A587

1990, May 14	Photo.	Perf. 11½
1345 A587	14fr Lys Monument, Courtrai	.80 .60

Resistance of German occupation.

Stamp Collecting Promotion Type of 1988 Souvenir Sheet

Various flowers from Sixty Roses for a Queen, by P.J. Redoute (1759-1840): a, Rose tricolore. b, Belle Rubaree. c, Mycrophylla. d, Amelie rose. e, Adelaide rose. f, Helene rose.

1990, June 2		Photo. & Engr.
1346	Sheet of 6	40.00 40.00
a.-c.	SP487 14fr any single	1.40 1.40
d.-f.	SP487 25fr any single	2.50 2.50

BELGICA '90, Brussels, June 2-10. sold for 220fr.

Battle of Waterloo, 1815 — A588

Design: Marshal Ney leading the French cavalry. (Illustration reduced).

1990, June 18		Photo.
1352 A588	25fr multi + label	1.60 1.15

Tourism A589

1990, July 9		
1353 A589	10fr Antwerp	.58 .45
1354 A589	10fr Dendermonde	.58 .45
1355 A589	14fr Gerpinnes, vert.	.80 .60
1356 A589	14fr Lommel	.80 .60
1357 A589	14fr Watermael	.80 .60
	Nos. 1353-1357 (5)	3.56 2.70

A590 A590a

King Baudouin A590b

1990-92	Photo.	Perf. 11½
1364 A590	14fr multicolored	.80 .60
1365 A590a	15fr rose car	.85 .65
1366 A590a	28fr blue green	1.75 1.30
1367 A590b	100fr slate green	6.00 1.50
	Nos. 1364-1367 (4)	9.40 4.05

Issue dates: 14fr, Sept. 7; 15fr, Apr. 1; 28fr, Aug. 3, 1992; 100fr, Sept. 14, 1992.

Fish — A591

Designs: No. 1383, Perch (Perche). No. 1384, Minnow (Vairon). No. 1385, Bitterling (Bouviere). No. 1386, Stickleback (Epinoche).

1990, Sept. 8		Perf. 12
1383 A591	14fr multicolored	1.25 .60
1384 A591	14fr multicolored	1.25 .60
1385 A591	14fr multicolored	1.25 .60
1386 A591	14fr multicolored	1.25 .60
a.	Bklt. pane of 4, #1383-1386	5.00

Youth Philately A592

1990, Oct. 13		Perf. 11½
1387 A592	10fr multicolored	.58 .45

BELGIUM

St. Bernard, 900th Birth Anniv. — A593

1990, Nov. 5   Photo. & Engr.
1388 A593 25fr black & buff   1.45   1.10

Winter Scene by Jozef Lucas A594

1990, Nov. 12   Photo.
1389 A594 10fr   .58   .42
Christmas.

Self-Portrait A595

Paintings by David Teniers (1610-1690).

1990, Dec. 3
1390 A595 10fr shown   .58   .42
1391 A595 14fr Dancers   .82   .62
1392 A595 25fr Bowlers   1.45   1.10
Nos. 1390-1392 (3)   2.85   2.14

A596   A597

Designs: 14fr, The Sower by Constantin Meunier (1831-1905). 25fr, Brabo Fountain by Jef Lambeaux (1852-1908).

Photo. & Engr.

1991, Mar. 18   Perf. 11½
1393 A596 14fr buff & blk   .82   .62
1394 A596 25fr lt bl & dk bl   1.45   1.10

1991, Apr. 8   Photo.   Perf. 11½
1395 A597 10fr Rhythmic gymnastics   .65   .50
1396 A597 10fr Korfball   .65   .50
No. 1395, European Youth Olympics. No. 1396, Korfball World Championships.

Stamp Printing Office, Mechlin — A598

1991, Apr. 22
1397 A598 14fr multicolored   .90   .65
Stamp Day.

Liberal Trade Union, Cent. A599

1991, Apr. 29
1398 A599 25fr blue & lt blue   1.50   1.15

Europa A600

1991, May 6
1399 A600 14fr Olympus-1 satellite   .90   .65
1400 A600 25fr Hermes space shuttle   1.50   1.15

Rerum Novarum Encyclical, Cent. A601

1991, May 13   Photo.   Perf. 11½
1401 A601 14fr multicolored   .85   .65

Princess Isabel & Philip le Bon — A602

1991, May 27   Photo.   Perf. 11½
1402 A602 14fr multicolored   .85   .65
Europalia '91. See Portugal No. 1861.

Tourism A603

Designs: No. 1403, Neptune's Grotto, Couvin. No. 1404, Dieleghem Abbey, Jette. No. 1405, Town Hall, Niel, vert. No. 1406, Nature Reserve, Hautes Fagnes. No. 1407, Legend of giant Rolarius, Roeselare, vert.

1991, June 17   Photo. & Engr.
1403 A603 14fr multicolored   .85   .65
1404 A603 14fr multicolored   .85   .65
1405 A603 14fr multicolored   .85   .65
1406 A603 14fr multicolored   .85   .65
1407 A603 14fr multicolored   .85   .65
Nos. 1403-1407 (5)   4.25   3.25

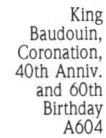

King Baudouin, Coronation, 40th Anniv. and 60th Birthday A604

1991, June 24   Photo.
1408 A604 14fr multicolored   .85   .65

Royal Academy of Medicine, 150th Anniv. — A605

Photo. & Engr.

1991, Sept. 2   Perf. 11½
1409 A605 10fr multicolored   .65   .50

The English Coast at Dover by Alfred W. Finch (1854-1930) — A606

1991, Sept. 9   Photo.
1410 A606 25fr multicolored   1.50   1.15
See Finland Nos. 868-869.

Mushrooms — A607

1991, Sept. 16   Photo.   Perf. 12
Booklet Stamps
1411   14fr Amanita phalloides (13A)   1.25   .65
1412   14fr Amanita rubescens (13B)   1.25   .65
1413   14fr Boletus erythropus (13C)   1.25   .65
1414   14fr Hygrocybe persistens (13D)   1.25   .65
   a. Bklt. pane of 4, #1411-1414   5.00

Doctors Without Borders A608

Design: No. 1415, Amnesty Intl.

1991, Sept. 23   Perf. 11½
1415 A608 25fr multicolored   1.50   1.15
1416 A608 25fr multicolored   1.50   1.15

Telecom '91 — A609

1991, Oct. 7   Photo.   Perf. 11½
1417 A609 14fr multicolored   .90   .70
6th World Forum and Exposition on Telecommunications, Geneva, Switzerland.

Youth Philately — A610

Cartoon characters: No. 1418, Blake and Mortimer, by Edgar P. Jacobs (16a). No. 1419, Cori the ship boy, by Bob De Moor (16b). No. 1420, Cities of the Fantastic, by Francois Schuiten (16c). No. 1421, Boule and Bill, by Jean Roba (16d).

1991, Oct. 14   Perf. 12
Booklet Stamps
1418 A610 14fr multicolored   .90   .70
1419 A610 14fr multicolored   .90   .70
1420 A610 14fr multicolored   .90   .70
1421 A610 14fr multicolored   .90   .70
   a. Bklt. pane of 4, #1418-1421   3.60

Belgian Newspapers, Cent. A611

1991, Nov. 4   Photo.   Perf. 11½
1422 A611 10fr Gazet Van Antwerpen   .65   .50
1423 A611 10fr Het Volk   .65   .50

Icon of Madonna and Child, Chevetogne Abbey — A612

1991, Nov. 25   Photo.   Perf. 11½
1424 A612 10fr multicolored   .65   .50
Christmas.

Wolfgang Amadeus Mozart, Death Bicent. — A613

1991, Dec. 2   Photo.   Perf. 11½
1425 A613 25fr multicolored   1.70   1.30

A614   A615

1992, Feb. 10   Photo.   Perf. 11½
1426 A614 14fr Fire fighting   .80   .60

1992, Feb. 24
1427 A615 14fr multicolored   .80   .60
Belgian resistance in WWII.

BELGIUM

Belgian Carpet Industry — A616

Antwerp Diamond Club, Cent. — A617

Design: 14fr, Chef's hat, cutlery.

1992, Mar. 9
1428	A616	10fr multicolored	.55	.42
1429	A616	14fr multicolored	.80	.60
1430	A617	27fr multicolored	1.50	1.15
		Nos. 1428-1430 (3)	2.85	2.17

Belgian Association of Master Chefs.

Expo '92, Seville — A618

1992, Mar. 23
1431	A618	14fr multicolored	.80	.60

Bird Type of 1985

1992-96 Photo. Perf. 11½
1432	A524	1fr Sizerin flamme	.15	.15
1433	A524	2fr Merle noir	.15	.15
1434	A524	2fr Grive mauvis	.15	.15
1435	A524	4fr Gobe mouche noir	.30	.22
1436	A524	4fr Bergeronette grise	.25	.15
1437	A524	5fr Etourneau sansonnet	.35	.15
1438	A524	5fr Hirondelle de cheminee	.32	.15
1439	A524	5.50fr Geai des chenes	.30	.22
1440	A524	6fr Cincle plongeur	.35	.15
1441	A524	6.50fr Phragmite des jongs	.45	.30
1442	A524	7fr Loriot	.45	.15
1443	A524	8fr Mesange charbonniere	.45	.15
1444	A524	10fr Verdier	.58	.15
1445	A524	11fr Troglodyte mignon	.65	.15
1446	A524	13fr Moineau domestique	.70	.18
1446A	A524	14fr Pouillot fitis	.95	.20
1447	A524	16fr Jaseur boreal	.90	.22
		Nos. 1432-1447 (17)	7.45	2.99

Issued: 11fr, 4/1/92; 1fr, 2fr, 6fr, 8fr, 10fr, 6/92; 4fr, 5fr, 7fr, 9/7/92; 5.50fr, 9/27/93; 13fr, 16fr, 1/3/94; 6.50fr, 10/3/94; 14fr, 12/18/95; 30fr, 5/6/96; #1435A, 5/6/96; #1433A, 1434, 7/1/96.

Jean Van Noten (1903-1982), Stamp Designer — A619

1992, Apr. 13   Photo. & Engr.   Perf. 11½
1448	A619	15fr ver & black	.90	.70

Stamp Day.

For all your stamp supply needs
www.scottonline.com

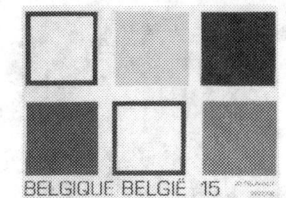

Abstract Painting by Jo Delahaut — A620

#1449, Witte Magie No. 6, by Roger Raveel.

1992, Apr. 27   Photo.   Perf. 11½
1449	A620	15fr multi, vert.	.85	.65
1450	A620	15fr multi	.85	.65

Discovery of America, 500th Anniv. — A621

1992, May 4
1451	A621	15fr shown	.85	.65
1452	A621	28fr 500, globe, astrolabe	1.60	1.20

Europa.

Fight Racism — A622

1992, May 18   Photo.   Perf. 11½
1453	A622	15fr black, gray & pink	.90	.70

Paintings from Orsay Museum, Paris — A623

Paintings by Belgian artists: 11fr, The Hamlet, by Jacob Smits. 15fr, The Bath, by Alfred Stevens. 30fr, The Man at the Helm, by Theo Van Rysselberghe.

1992, June 15   Photo.   Perf. 11½
1454	A623	11fr multicolored	.65	.48
1455	A623	15fr multicolored	.90	.70
1456	A623	30fr multicolored	1.75	1.35
		Nos. 1454-1456 (3)	3.30	2.53

Tourism — A624

Designs: No. 1457, Manneken Pis Fountain, Brussels. No. 1458, Landcommander Castle Alden Biesen, Bilzen, horiz. No. 1459, Building facade, Andenne. No. 1460, Fools' Monday Carnival, Renaix, horiz. No. 1461, Great Procession, Tournai, horiz.

1992, July 6   Photo. & Engr.   Perf. 11½
1457	A624	15fr multicolored	.90	.70
1458	A624	15fr multicolored	.90	.70
1459	A624	15fr multicolored	.90	.70
1460	A624	15fr multicolored	.90	.70
1461	A624	15fr multicolored	.90	.70
		Nos. 1457-1461 (5)	4.50	3.50

Village of Andenne, 1300th anniv. (#1459). Grand Procession of Tournai, 900th anniv. (#1461).

Animals — A625

1992, Sept. 7   Photo.   Perf. 12
Booklet Stamps
1462	A625	15fr Polecat (13a)	1.05	.80
1463	A625	15fr Squirrel (13b)	1.05	.80
1464	A625	15fr Hedgehog (13c)	1.05	.80
1465	A625	15fr Dormouse (13d)	1.05	.80
a.		Bklt. pane of 4, #1462-1465	4.25	

Brabant Revolution — A626

Design: 15fr, Troops fighting and Henri Van der Noot, Jean Andre Van der Meersch, and Jean Francois Vonck, rebel leaders.

1992, Sept. 21   Photo. & Engr.   Perf. 11½
1466	A626	15fr multicolored	.90	.70

Arms of Thurn and Taxis — A627

1992, Oct. 5   Photo.   Perf. 11½
1467	A627	15fr multicolored	.90	.70

Gaston Lagaffe, by Andre Franquin — A628

1992, Oct. 12
1468	A628	15fr multicolored	.90	.70

Youth philately.

Single European Market — A629

1992, Oct. 26
1469	A629	15fr multicolored	.90	.70

Antwerp Zoo, 150th Anniv. — A630

1992, Nov. 16
1470	A630	15fr Okapi	.90	.70
1471	A630	30fr Tamarin	1.80	1.40

The Brussels Place Royale in Winter, by Luc De Decker — A631

1992, Nov. 23
1472	A631	11fr multicolored	.70	.52

Christmas.

History — A632

Designs: 11fr, Council of Leptines, 1250th anniv. 15fr, 28fr, Missale Romanum of Matthias Corvinus (Matyas Hunyadi, King of Hungary) (diff. details). 30fr, Battles of Neerwinden (1693, 1793).

1993, Mar. 15   Photo.   Perf. 11½
1473	A632	11fr multicolored	.65	.48
1474	A632	15fr multicolored	.90	.70
1475	A632	30fr multicolored	1.80	1.35
		Nos. 1473-1475 (3)	3.35	2.53

Souvenir Sheet
1476	A632	28fr multicolored	1.75	1.30

Size of No. 1474, 80x28mm. No. 1476 contains one 55x40mm stamp.
See Hungary No. 3385-3386.

A633

A634

Antwerp, Cultural City of Europe — A635

Designs: No. 1477, Panoramic view of Antwerp (illustration reduced). No. 1478, Antwerp Town Hall, designed by Cornelis Floris. No. 1479, Woman's Head and Warrior's Torso, by Jacob

BELGIUM

Jordaens. No. 1480, St. Job's Altar (detail), Schoonbroek. No. 1481, Angels on stained glass window, Mater Dei Chapel of Institut Marie-Josee, by Eugeen Yoors, vert.

1993, Mar. 22
1477	A633	15fr multicolored	.90	.70
1478	A634	15fr multicolored	.90	.70
1479	A635	15fr gray & multi	.90	.70
1480	A635	15fr green & multi	.90	.70
1481	A635	15fr blue & multi	.90	.70
		Nos. 1477-1481 (5)	4.50	3.50

Antwerp '93.

Stamp Day — A636

1993, Apr. 5
| 1482 | A636 | 15fr No. 74 | .90 | .70 |

Contemporary Paintings — A637

Europa: 15fr, Florence 1960, by Gaston Bertrand. 28fr, De Sjees, by Constant Permeke.

1993, Apr. 26   Photo.   Perf. 11½
| 1483 | A637 | 15fr multicolored | .90 | .70 |
| 1484 | A637 | 28fr multicolored | 1.70 | 1.35 |

Butterflies — A638

1993, May 10
1485	A638	15fr Vanessa atalanta	.90	.70
1486	A638	15fr Apatura iris	.90	.70
1487	A638	15fr Inachis io	.90	.70
1488	A638	15fr Aglais urticae	.90	.70
		Nos. 1485-1488 (4)	3.60	2.80

Alumni Assoc. (UAE), Free University of Brussels, 150th Anniv. A639

1993, May 17
| 1489 | A639 | 15fr blue & black | .90 | .70 |

Europalia '93 — A640

1993, May 24
| 1490 | A640 | 15fr Mayan statuette | .90 | .70 |

Folklore A641

Designs: 11fr, Ommegang Procession, Brussels. 15fr, Royal Moncrabeau Folk Group, Namur. 28fr, Stilt walkers of Merchtem, vert.

1993, June 7   Photo.   Perf. 11½
1491	A641	11fr multicolored	.65	.48
1492	A641	15fr multicolored	.90	.70
1493	A641	28fr multicolored	1.65	1.30
		Nos. 1491-1493 (3)	3.20	2.48

Tourism A642

Castles: No. 1494, La Hulpe. No. 1495, Cortewalle (Beveren). No. 1496, Jehay. No. 1497, Arenberg (Heverlee), vert. No. 1498, Raeren.

1993, June 21   Photo. & Engr.   Perf. 11½
1494	A642	15fr pale green & black	.90	.70
1495	A642	15fr pale lilac & black	.90	.70
1496	A642	15fr pale blue & black	.90	.70
1497	A642	15fr pale brown & black	.90	.70
1498	A642	15fr pale olive & black	.90	.70
		Nos. 1494-1498 (5)	4.50	3.50

Intl. Triennial Exhibition of Tournai A643

1993, July 5   Photo.   Perf. 11½
| 1499 | A643 | 15fr black, blue & red | .90 | .70 |

Belgian Presidency of European Community Council A644

1993, Aug. 9   Photo.   Perf. 11½
| 1500 | A644 | 15fr multicolored | .90 | .70 |

Rene Magritte (1898-1967), Artist A645

1993, Aug. 9
| 1501 | A645 | 30fr multicolored | 1.75 | 1.40 |

King Baudouin (1930-1993) — A646

1993, Aug. 17   Photo.   Perf. 11½
| 1502 | A646 | 15fr black & gray | .90 | .70 |

European House Cats — A647

1993, Sept. 6   Photo.   Perf. 12
Booklet Stamps
1503	A647	15fr Brown & white (10a)	.90	.70
1504	A647	15fr Black & white (10b)	.90	.70
1505	A647	15fr Gray tabby (10c)	.90	.70
1506	A647	15fr Calico (10d)	.90	.70
a.		Booklet pane of 4, #1503-1506	3.75	

Publication of De Humani Corporis Fabrica, by Andreas Vesalius, 1543 — A648

1993, Oct. 4   Photo.   Perf. 11½
| 1507 | A648 | 15fr multicolored | .90 | .70 |

Air Hostess Natacha, by Francois Walthery — A649

1993, Oct. 18
| 1508 | A649 | 15fr multicolored | .85 | .65 |

Youth philately.

Publication of "Faux Soir," 50th Anniv. — A650

1993, Nov. 8   Photo.   Perf. 11½
| 1509 | A650 | 11fr multicolored | .60 | .45 |

Notre-Dame de la Chapelle, Brussels A651

1993, Nov. 22   Photo.   Perf. 11½
| 1510 | A651 | 11fr multicolored | .65 | .48 |

Christmas, New Year.

Children, Future Decisionmakers — A652

1993, Dec. 13   Photo.   Perf. 11½
| 1511 | A652 | 15fr multicolored | .90 | .70 |

King Albert II

A653    A654

A655    A655a

1993-98   Photo.   Perf. 11½
1519	A653	16fr lt gray & multi	.95	.25
1520	A653	16fr lt & dk bl grn	1.00	.75
1521	A653	16fr multicolored	1.10	.80
1521A	A655	16fr blue	1.10	.80
1521B	A655	17fr blue	1.10	.80
1521C	A655	18fr olive black	1.00	.75
1521D	A655	19fr dp gray violet	1.35	1.00
1522	A653	20fr cream & brown	1.25	.32
1522A	A655	20fr brown	1.10	.85
1523	A655	25fr sepia	1.40	1.00
1524	A655	28fr claret	1.90	1.40
1526	A653	30fr red lilac	1.65	.40
1526A	A655	32fr violet blue	1.90	1.40
1527	A653	32fr cream & org brn	1.90	.48
1527A	A655	34fr dark blue gray	2.00	1.50
1527B	A655	36fr dark slate blue	2.20	1.65
1528	A653	40fr pink & carmine	2.50	.60
1529	A653	50fr green	3.00	.75
1530	A653	50fr green	3.30	2.50
1533	A654	100fr multicolored	6.25	4.75
1535	A654	200fr multicolored	14.00	3.50
		Nos. 1519-1535 (18)	47.55	23.00

Coil Stamp
| 1536 | A655a | 19fr deep gray violet | 1.25 | .90 |

Issued: #1519, 12/15/93; #1520, 1/17/94; 30fr, 2/4/94; #1527, 3/7/94; 50fr, 4/18/94; #1522, 6/6/94; 40fr, 6/20/94; 100fr, 10/3/94; 200fr, 5/2/95; #1521, 6/6/96; #1521A, 1530, 28fr, 9/2/96; 17fr, 12/16/96; 34fr, 36fr, 2/10/97; 18fr, 4/7/97; #1521D, 7/7/97; 25fr, 4/20/98; #1536, 8/10/98; #1522A, 10/19/98; #1526a, 11/9/98.

This is an expanding set. Numbers will change.

Paintings A656

Designs: No. 1537, The Malleable Darkness, by Octave Landuyt. No. 1538, Ma Toute Belle, by Serge Vandercam, vert.

1994, Jan. 31   Photo.   Perf. 11½
| 1537 | A656 | 16fr multicolored | .90 | .70 |
| 1538 | A656 | 16fr multicolored | .90 | .70 |

Airplanes A657

13fr, Hanriot-Dupont HD-1. 15fr, Spad XIII. 30fr, Schreck FBA-H. 32fr, Stampe-Vertongen SV-4B.

1994, Feb. 28
1539	A657	13fr multicolored	.70	.52
1540	A657	15fr multicolored	.85	.65
1541	A657	30fr multicolored	1.65	1.25
1542	A657	32fr multicolored	1.75	1.40
		Nos. 1539-1542 (4)	4.95	3.82

Daily Newspapers A658

BELGIUM

Designs: No. 1543, "Le Jour-Le Courier," cent., vert. No. 1544, "La Wallonie," 75th anniv.

1994, Mar. 21   Photo.   Perf. 11½
1543 A658 16fr multicolored   .95   .70
1544 A658 16fr multicolored   .95   .70

Fall of the Golden Calf (Detail), by Fernand Allard l'Olivier — A659

1994, Mar. 28
1545 A659 16fr multicolored   .95   .70
Charter of Quaregnon, cent.

Stamp Day — A660

1994, Apr. 11   Photo.   Perf. 11½
1546 A660 16fr No. 102   .95   .70

History A661

Scenes from Brabantse Yeesten, 15th cent. illuminated manuscript: 13fr, Reconciliation between John I and Arnold, squire of Wezemaal. 16fr, Tournament at wedding of John II and Margaret of York. 30fr, Battle of Woeringen.

1994, Apr. 25
1547 A661 13fr multicolored   .75   .55
1548 A661 16fr multicolored   .95   .70
1549 A661 30fr multicolored   1.75   1.25
    Nos. 1547-1549 (3)   3.45   2.50
No. 1549 is 81x28mm.

Europa — A662

Designs: 16fr, Abbe Georges Lemaitre (1894-1966), proposed "big-bang" theory of origins of universe. 30fr, Gerardus Mercator (1512-94), cartographer, astronomer.

1994, May 9   Photo.   Perf. 11½
1550 A662 16fr multicolored   .95   .70
1551 A662 30fr multicolored   1.75   1.25

Papal Visit A663

#1552, Father Damien (1840-89). #1553, St. Mutien-Marie (1841-1917), Christian educator.

1994, May 16   Perf. 11½x12
1552 A663 16fr multicolored   .95   .70
1553 A663 16fr multicolored   .95   .70

Tourism A664

Churches: No. 1554, St. Peter's, Bertem. No. 1555, St. Bavo's, Kanegem, vert. No. 1556, Royal St. Mary's, Schaarbeek. No. 1557, St. Gery's, Aubechies. No. 1558, Sts. Peter and Paul, Saint-Severin, Condroz, vert.

1994, June 13   Photo.   Perf. 11½
1554 A664 16fr multicolored   .95   .70
1555 A664 16fr multicolored   .95   .70
1556 A664 16fr multicolored   .95   .70
1557 A664 16fr multicolored   .95   .70
1558 A664 16fr multicolored   .95   .70
    Nos. 1554-1558 (5)   4.75   3.50

Guillaume Lekeu (1870-94), Composer A665

Design: No. 1560, Detail of painting by Hans Memling (c.1430-94).

1994, Aug. 16   Photo.   Perf. 11½
1559 A665 16fr multicolored   1.10   .75
1560 A665 16fr multicolored   1.10   .75

Liberation of Belgium, 50th Anniv. — A666

Design: 16fr, General Crerar, Field Marshal Montgomery, Gen. Bradley, Belgium landscape. Illustration reduced.

1994, Sept. 5   Photo.   Perf. 11x11½
1561 A666 16fr multicolored   .95   .70

Wildflowers — A667

Designs: No. 1562, Caltha palustris. No. 1563, Cephalanthera damasonium. No. 1564, Calystegia soldanella. No. 1565, Epipactis helleborine.

1994, Sept. 26   Photo.   Perf. 12
Booklet Stamps
1562 A667 16fr multi (14a)   1.10   .75
1563 A667 16fr multi (14b)   1.10   .75
1564 A667 16fr multi (14c)   1.10   .75
1565 A667 16fr multi (14d)   1.10   .75
  a. Booklet pane of 4, #1562-1565   4.50

Cubitus the Dog, by Luc Dupanloup — A668

1994, Oct. 10   Perf. 11½
1566 A668 16fr multicolored   1.10   .75
Youth philately.

Georges Simenon (1903-89), Writer A669

Photo. & Engr.
1994, Oct. 17   Perf. 11½
1567 A669 16fr multicolored   1.10   .75
See France No. 2443, Switzerland No. 948.

Christmas A670

1994, Dec. 5   Photo.   Perf. 11½
1568 A670 13fr multicolored   .85   .65

Anniversaries and Events A671

Designs: No. 1569, August Vermeylen Fund, 50th anniv. No. 1570, Belgian Touring Club, cent. No. 1571, Assoc. of Belgian Enterprises, cent. No. 1572, Dept. of Social Security, 50th anniv.

1995, Feb. 13   Photo.   Perf. 11½
1569 A671 16fr multicolored   1.10   .75
1570 A671 16fr multicolored   1.10   .75
1571 A671 16fr multicolored   1.10   .75
1572 A671 16fr multicolored   1.10   .75
    Nos. 1569-1572 (4)   4.40   3.00

Flowers of Ghent A672

1995, Mar. 6
1573 A672 13fr Hibiscus rosa-sinensis   .95   .70
1574 A672 16fr Rhododendron simsii   1.10   .75
1575 A672 30fr Fuchsia hybrida   2.25   1.65
    Nos. 1573-1575 (3)   4.30   3.10

Games — A673    Stamp Day — A674

1995, Mar. 20
1576 A673 13fr Crossword puzzles   .95   .70
1577 A673 16fr Chess   1.10   .75
1578 A673 30fr Scrabble   2.25   1.65
1579 A673 34fr Cards   2.50   1.75
    Nos. 1576-1579 (4)   6.80   4.85

1995, Apr. 10   Photo. & Engr.
1580 A674 16fr Frans de Troyer   1.10   .75

Peace & Freedom A675

Europa: 16fr, Broken barbed wire, prison guard tower. 30fr, Mushroom cloud, "Never again."

1995, Apr. 24   Photo.   Perf. 11½
1581 A675 16fr multicolored   1.10   .75
1582 A675 30fr multicolored   2.25   1.75
Liberation of concentration camps, 50th anniv. (#1581). Nuclear Non-Proliferation Treaty, 25th anniv. (#1582).

Battle of Fontenoy, 250th Anniv. — A676

Design: 16fr, Irish soldiers, Cross of Fontenoy.

1995, May 15   Photo.   Perf. 11½
1583 A676 16fr multicolored   1.10   .75
See Ireland No. 967.

UN, 50th Anniv. A677

1995, May 22   Photo.   Perf. 11½
1584 A677 16fr multicolored   1.10   .75

"Sauvagemont, Maransart," by Pierre Alechinsky — A678

No. 1586: "Telegram-style," by Pol Mara.

1995, June 6
1585 A678 16fr multicolored   1.10   .75
1586 A678 16fr multicolored   1.10   .75

Tourism A679

Architectural designs: No. 1587, Cauchie house, Brussels, by Paul Cauchie (1875-1952). No. 1588, De Viif Werelddelen, corner building. Antwerp, by Frans Smet-Verhas (1851-1925). No. 1589, House, Liege, by Paul Jaspar (1859-1945).

1995, June 26
1587 A679 16fr multicolored   1.10   .75
1588 A679 16fr multicolored   1.10   .75
1589 A679 16fr multicolored   1.10   .75
    Nos. 1587-1589 (3)   3.30   2.25

Sailing Ships — A680

BELGIUM

1995, Aug. 21   Photo.   *Perf. 12*
Booklet Stamps

1590	A680	16fr Mercator	1.10	.80
1591	A680	16fr Kruzenstern	1.10	.80
1592	A680	16fr Sagres II	1.10	.80
1593	A680	16fr Amerigo Vespucci	1.10	.80
a.		Booklet pane of 4, #1590-1593	4.50	
		Complete booklet, #1593a	4.50	

Classic Motorcycles — A681

1995, Sept. 25   Photo.   *Perf. 11½*

1594	A681	13fr 1908 Minerva	.90	.65
1595	A681	16fr 1913 FN, vert.	1.10	.80
1596	A681	30fr 1929 La Mondiale	2.00	1.50
1597	A681	32fr 1937 Gillet, vert.	2.25	1.65
		Nos. 1594-1597 (4)	6.25	4.60

Comic Character, Sammy, by Arthur Berckmans — A682

1995, Oct. 9   Photo.   *Perf. 11½*

| 1598 | A682 | 16fr multicolored | 1.10 | .80 |

Youth philately.

King's Day — A683

Design: 16fr, King Albert II and Queen Paola.

1995, Nov. 15   Photo.   *Perf. 11½*

| 1599 | A683 | 16fr multicolored | 1.10 | .80 |

A684   A685

Christmas: 13fr, Nativity scene from "Breviary," book of devotions, c. 1500.

1995, Nov. 20

| 1600 | A684 | 13fr multicolored | .90 | .70 |

1996, Mar. 4   Photo.   *Perf. 11½*

| 1601 | A685 | 16fr multicolored | 1.10 | .80 |

Liberal Party, 150th anniv.

Portrait of Emile Mayrisch (1862-1928), by Théo Van Rysselberghe (1862-1926) — A686

1996, Mar. 4

| 1602 | A686 | (A) multicolored | 1.10 | .80 |

No. 1602 was valued at 16fr on day of issue. See Luxemburg No. 939.

Oscar Bonnevalle, Stamp Designer — A687

1996, Apr. 1

| 1603 | A687 | 16fr multicolored | 1.10 | .80 |

Stamp Day.

Insects — A688

Designs: No. 1604, Sympetrum sanguineum. No. 1605, Bombus terrestris. No. 1606, Lucanus cervus. No. 1607, Melolontha melolontha. No. 1608, Gryllus campestris. No. 1609, Coccinella septempunctata.

1996, Apr. 1   Photo.   *Perf. 12*
Booklet Stamps

1604	A688	16fr multicolored	1.10	.80
1605	A688	16fr multicolored	1.10	.80
1606	A688	16fr multicolored	1.10	.80
1607	A688	16fr multicolored	1.10	.80
1608	A688	16fr multicolored	1.10	.80
1609	A688	16fr multicolored	1.10	.80
a.		Booklet pane, #1604-1609	6.60	
		Complete booklet, #1609a	6.60	

Famous Women — A689

Europa: 16fr, Yvonne Nevejean (1900-87), saved Jewish children during World War II. 30fr, Marie Gevers (1883-1975), poet.

1996, May 6   *Perf. 11½*

1610	A689	16fr multicolored	1.10	.80
1611	A689	30fr multicolored	2.00	1.50

Tourism — A690

Architecture in Brussels — A691

Designs: No. 1612, Grotto of Han-Sur-Lesse, horiz. No. 1613, Village of Begijnendijk as separate community, bicent.

1996, June 10   Photo.   *Perf. 11½*

1612	A690	16fr multicolored	1.10	.80
1613	A690	16fr multicolored	1.10	.80

Designs: No. 1614, La Maison du Roi (Grand Place). No. 1615, Galeries Royales Saint-Hubert. No. 1616, Le Palais d'Egmont, Le Petit Sablon, horiz. No. 1617, Le Cinquantenaire, horiz.

1996, June 10

1614	A691	16fr multi (7a)	1.10	.80
1615	A691	16fr multi (7b)	1.10	.80
1616	A691	16fr multi (7c)	1.10	.80
1617	A691	16fr multi (7d)	1.10	.80
		Nos. 1614-1617 (4)	4.40	3.20

Auto Races at Spa, Cent. — A692

1996, July 1

1618	A692	16fr 1900 German 6CV	1.10	.80
1619	A692	16fr 1925 Alfa Romeo P2	1.10	.80
1620	A692	16fr 1939 Mercedes Benz W154	1.10	.80
1621	A692	16fr 1967 Ferrari 330P	1.10	.80
		Nos. 1618-1621 (4)	4.40	3.20

Paintings of Historical Figures — A693

Portraits from town hall triptych, Zierikzee, Netherlands: No. 1622, Philip I, the Handsome (1478-1506). No. 1623, Juana of Castile, the Mad (1479-1555).

1996, Sept. 2   Photo.   *Perf. 11½*

1622	A693	16fr multicolored	1.10	.80
1623	A693	16fr multicolored	1.10	.80

A694   A695

Paintings from National Gallery, London: 14fr, Reading Man, by Rogier Van Der Weyden (1399-1464). 16fr, Susanna Fourment, by Peter Paul Rubens (1577-1640). 30fr, A Man in a Turban, by Jan Van Eyck (1390-1441).

1996, Sept. 2

1624	A694	14fr multicolored	.95	.70
1625	A694	16fr multicolored	1.10	.80
1626	A694	30fr multicolored	2.00	1.50
		Nos. 1624-1626 (3)	4.05	3.00

Bird Type of 1985

1996, Oct. 7   Photo.   *Perf. 11½*

| 1627 | A524 | 6fr Tarin des aulnes | .40 | .30 |

1996, Oct. 7

Comic Character, Cloro, by Raymond Macherot.

| 1628 | A695 | 16fr multicolored | 1.10 | .80 |

Youth Philately.

Almanac of Mons, by Fr. Charles Letellier, 150th Anniv. — A696

1996, Oct. 7

| 1629 | A696 | 16fr multicolored | 1.10 | .80 |

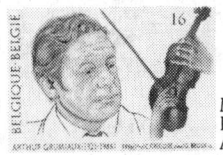

Music and Literature — A697

Designs: No. 1630, Arthur Grumiaux (1921-86), violinist. No. 1631, Flor Peeters (1903-86), organist. No. 1632, Christian Dotremont (1922-79), poet, artist. No. 1633, Paul Van Ostaijen (1896-1928), writer.

BELGIAN PHILATELIC SPECIALISTS, INC.

Choose from the widest selection of material available for the Belgophile.

Year Units

Includes regular and semi postal issues only. No long definitive series. All NH!

1970	21.00	1985	42.50
1971	16.00	1986	49.00
1972	17.00	1987	37.00
1973	17.00	1988	54.00
1974	17.00	1989	48.50
1975	26.00	1990	125.00
1976	27.00	1991	55.00
1977	19.00	1992	50.00
1978	21.00	1993	50.00
1979	25.00	1994	43.00
1980	26.00	1995	40.00
1981	33.00	1996	40.00
1982	43.50	1997	40.00
1983	29.00	1998	47.50
1984	36.00		

All Others Available.
SPECIAL! 5 UNITS - TAKE 5% OFF
10 UNITS TAKE 7 1/2% OFF

Also available are official catalog listed items such as Bagages ($1300. LH), Telephone ($27.00 LH), Telegraph, Precancels, Pubs, Occupations, Booklet Coils, Errors, Varieties, etc.

Highly recommended!
1999 OFFICIEL CATALOGUE
$38.00 ppd.

Precancel catalog $50.00
Order with confidence. All items are in stock. Prices in U.S. Dollars. N.Y. residents please add sales tax.
**P.O. BOX 599
LARCHMONT, NY 10538**

CAMPO RODAN
RUE DU LOMBARD 9
1000 BRUSSELS, BELGIUM
PHONE: 011-32-2-514-5292
FAX: 011-32-2-514-5415

Specialists in...
BELGIUM
and former territories:
**CONGO - ZAIRE
KATANGA
SOUTH KASAI
RUANDA
URUNDI
RWANDA
BURUNDI
LUXEMBOURG
EUROPE**

Charge it! We accept:
VISA   DINERS CLUB   MasterCard

BELGIUM

Photo. & Engr.
1996, Oct. 28   *Perf. 11½*
1630	A697	16fr multicolored	1.10	.80
1631	A697	16fr multicolored	1.10	.80
1632	A697	16fr multicolored	1.10	.80
1633	A697	16fr multicolored	1.10	.80
		Nos. 1630-1633 (4)	4.40	3.20

Christmas and New Year — A698

Scenes from Christmas Market: a, Decorated trees, rooftops. b, Lighted greeting signs. c, Church. d, Selling desert items. e, Selling Nativity scenes. f, Selling meat. g, Santa ringing bell. h, Man smoking pipe, people with presents. i, People shopping.

1996, Nov. 18   Photo.   *Perf. 11½*
| 1634 | A698 | 14fr Sheet of 9, #a.-i. | 8.25 | 6.25 |

Catholic Faculty University, Mons, Cent. — A699

1997, Jan. 20   Photo.   *Perf. 11½*
| 1635 | A699 | 17fr multicolored | 1.10 | .80 |

Opera at Theatre Royal de la Monnaie, Brussels — A700

#1636, Marie Sasse (1834-1907), soprano.
#1637, Ernest Van Dijck (1861-1923), tenor.
#1638, Hector Dufranne (1870-1951), baritone.
#1639, Clara Clairbert (1899-1970), soprano.

1997, Feb. 10
1636	A700	17fr multicolored	1.00	.75
1637	A700	17fr multicolored	1.00	.75
1638	A700	17fr multicolored	1.00	.75
1639	A700	17fr multicolored	1.00	.75
		Nos. 1636-1639 (4)	4.00	3.00

Eastern Cantons — A701

Illustration reduced.

1997, Feb. 10   Photo.   *Perf. 11½*
| 1640 | A701 | 17fr multicolored | 1.00 | .75 |

Bird Type of 1985
1997, Mar. 10
| 1641 | A524 | 15fr Mesange boreale | .90 | .70 |

UN Peace-Keeping Forces — A702

1997, Mar. 10
| 1642 | A702 | 17fr multicolored | 1.00 | .75 |

Stories and Legends
A703

Europa: 17fr, "De Bokkenrijders" (The Goat Riders). 30fr, Jean de Berneau.

1997, Mar. 10   Photo.   *Perf. 11½*
| 1643 | A703 | 17fr multicolored | 1.00 | .75 |
| 1644 | A703 | 30fr multicolored | 1.75 | 1.30 |

Bird Type of 1985
1997, Apr. 7   Size: 35x25mm
| 1645 | A524 | 150fr Ekster | 8.50 | 6.25 |

Constant Spinoy (1924-93), Stamp Engraver — A704

1997, Apr. 7   Photo. & Engr.
| 1646 | A704 | 17fr multicolored | 1.00 | .75 |
Stamp Day.

Intl. Flower Show, Liege
A705

Paintings by Paul Delvaux (1897-1994)
A706

1997, Apr. 21   Photo.
| 1647 | A705 | 17fr multicolored | 1.00 | .75 |

1997, Apr. 21
Details or entire paintings: 15fr, Woman with garland of leaves in hair. 17fr, Nude, horiz. 32fr, Woman wearing hat, trolley.

1648	A706	15fr multicolored	.85	.65
1649	A706	17fr multicolored	1.00	.75
1650	A706	32fr multicolored	1.75	1.35
		Nos. 1648-1650 (3)	3.60	2.75

Bird Type of 1985
1997, May 7   Photo.   *Perf. 11½*
| 1651 | A524 | 3fr Alouette des champs | .25 | .20 |

Queen Paola, 60th Birthday
A707

1997, May 26
| 1652 | A707 | 17fr Belvedere Castle | 1.00 | .75 |
See Italy No. 2147.

Cartoon Character, "Jommeke," by Jef Nys — A708

1997, May 26
| 1653 | A708 | 17fr multicolored | 1.00 | .75 |

A709    A710

Roses: No. 1654, Rosa damascena coccinea. No. 1655, Rosa sulfurea. No. 1656, Rosa centifolia.

1997, July 7   Photo.   *Perf. 11½*
1654	A709	17fr multicolored	1.20	.90
1655	A709	17fr multicolored	1.20	.90
1656	A709	17fr multicolored	1.20	.90
		Nos. 1654-1656 (3)	3.60	2.70

World Congress of Rose Societies.

1997, July 7   Photo. & Engr.
Churches: No. 1657, Basilica of St. Martin, Halle. No. 1658, Notre Dame Church, Laeken, horiz. No. 1659, Basilica of St. Martin, Liège.

1657	A710	17fr multicolored	1.20	.90
1658	A710	17fr multicolored	1.20	.90
1659	A710	17fr multicolored	1.20	.90
		Nos. 1657-1659 (3)	3.60	2.70

Bird Type of 1985
1997, Sept. 1   Photo.   *Perf. 11½*
| 1660 | A525 | 7fr Bergeronnette printaniere | .40 | .30 |

Bees and Apiculture — A711

Designs: No. 1661, Queen, workers. No. 1662, Development of the larvae. No. 1663, Bee exiting cell. No. 1664, Bee collecting nectar. No. 1665, Two bees. No. 1666, Two bees on honeycomb.

1997, Sept. 1   Photo.   *Perf. 12*
Booklet Stamps
1661	A711	17fr multicolored (15a)	1.00	.75
1662	A711	17fr multicolored (15b)	1.00	.75
1663	A711	17fr multicolored (15c)	1.00	.75
1664	A711	17fr multicolored (15d)	1.00	.75
1665	A711	17fr multicolored (15e)	1.00	.75
1666	A711	17fr multicolored (15f)	1.00	.75
a.		Booklet pane of 6, #1661-1666	6.00	
		Complete booklet, #1666a	6.00	

Craftsmen
A712

1997, Sept. 1   *Perf. 11½*
1667	A712	17fr Stone cutter	.75	.60
1668	A712	17fr Mason	.75	.60
1669	A712	17fr Carpenter	.75	.60
1670	A712	17fr Blacksmith	.75	.60
		Nos. 1667-1670 (4)	3.00	2.40

Antarctic Expedition by the Belgica, Cent. — A713

1997, Sept. 22   Photo.   *Perf. 11½*
| 1671 | A713 | 17fr multicolored | 1.00 | .75 |

A714    A715

Royal Museum of Central Africa, Cent.: No. 1672, Mask, Shaba, Congo. No. 1673, Outside view of museum, horiz. 34fr, Dish Bearer sculpture, Buli area, Congo.

1997, Sept. 22   Photo.   *Perf. 11½*
1672	A714	17fr multicolored	1.00	.75
1673	A714	17fr multicolored	1.00	.75
1674	A714	34fr multicolored	1.00	.75
		Nos. 1672-1674 (3)	3.00	2.25

No. 1673 is 25x73mm.

1997, Oct. 25   Photo.   *Perf. 11½*
Christmas: "Fairon," by Pierre Grahame.
| 1675 | A715 | 15fr multicolored | .90 | .70 |

Bird Type of 1985
1997, Dec. 1   Photo.   *Perf. 11½*
| 1676 | A524 | 15fr Mesange boreale, horiz. | .90 | .70 |

No. 1676 issued in coil rolls with every fifth stamp numbered on reverse.

Rhododendron
A716

Serpentine Die Cut 13½ on 2 or 3 Sides
1997, Dec. 1
Booklet Stamp
Self-Adhesive
| 1677 | A716 | (17fr) multicolored | 1.00 | .75 |
| a. | | Booklet pane of 10 | 10.00 | |

By its nature, No. 1677a is a complete booklet. The peelable backing serves as a booklet cover.

"Thalys" High Speed Train — A717

1998, Jan. 19   Photo.   *Perf. 11½*
| 1678 | A717 | 17fr multicolored | 1.00 | .75 |

Shop with Scott Publishing Co. 24 hours a day 7 days a week at www.scottonline.com

BELGIUM

Woman Suffrage in Belgium, 50th Anniv. — A718

1998, Jan. 19
1679 A718 17fr multicolored   1.00   .75

Paintings, by René Magritte (1898-1967) A720

#1682, "La Magie Noire (Black Magic)," nude woman. #1683, "La Corde Sensible (Heartstring)," cloud over champagne glass. #1684, "Le Chateau des Pyrenees (Castle of the Pyrenees)," castle atop floating rock.

1998, Mar. 9   Photo.   Perf. 11½
1682 A720 17fr multi, vert.   .95   .70
1683 A720 17fr multi   .95   .70
1684 A720 17fr multi, vert.   .95   .70
     Nos. 1682-1684 (3)   2.85 2.10

Belgian Artists — A721

Details or entire paintings: No. 1685, "La Foire aux Amours," by Félicien Rops (1833-98). No. 1686, "Hospitality for the Strangers," by Gustave van de Woestijne (1881-1947). No. 1687, Self-portrait, "The Man with the Beard," by Felix de Boeck (1898-1995). No. 1688, "Black Writing Mixed with Colors," by Karel Appel & Christian Cotremont of COBRA.

1998, Mar. 9   Perf. 12
Booklet Stamps
1685 A721 17fr multicolored   .95   .70
1686 A721 17fr multicolored   .95   .70
1687 A721 17fr multicolored   .95   .70
1688 A721 17fr multicolored   .95   .70
   a. Booklet pane, #1685-1688   3.80
     Complete booklet, #1688a   3.80

Museum of Fine Arts, Ghent, bicent. (#1686). COBRA art movement of painters and poets, 50th anniv. (#1688).

Sabena Airlines, 75th Anniv. — A722

1998, Apr. 20   Photo.   Perf. 11½
1689 A722 17fr multicolored   .95   .70

Belgian Stamp Dealers' Assoc., 75th Anniv. A723

1998, Apr. 20
1690 A723 17fr multicolored   .95   .70

"The Return," by René Magritte (1898-1967) — A724

1998, Apr. 20
1691 A724 17fr multicolored   .95   .70
See France No. 2637.

Wildlife A725

1998, Apr. 20
1692 A725 17fr Vulpes vulpes   .95   .70
1693 A725 17fr Cervus elaphus   .95   .70
1694 A725 17fr Sus scrofa   .95   .70
1695 A725 17fr Capreolus capreolus   .95   .70
     Nos. 1692-1695 (4)   3.80 2.80

Bird Type of 1985

1998, May 4   Photo.   Perf. 11½
1696 A524 1fr Mesange huppee   .15   .15

Edmund Struyf (1911-96), Founder of Pro-Post, Assoc. for Promotion of Philately — A726

1998, May 4   Photo. & Engr.
1697 A726 17fr multicolored   .95   .70
Stamp Day.

Natl. Festivals A727

1998, May 4   Photo.   Perf. 11½
1698 A727 17fr Torhout & Werchter Rock Festival   .95   .70
1699 A727 17fr Wallonia Festival   .95   .70
Europa.

Bird Type of 1985

1998, July 6   Photo.   Perf. 11½
1700 A524 7.50fr Pie-grieche grise   .45   .35

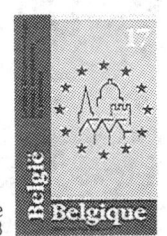

European Heritage Days — A728

Designs: a, Logo. b, Bourla Theatre, Antwerp. c, La Halle, Durbuy. d, Halletoren, Kortrijk. e, Louvain Town Hall. f, Perron, Liège. g, Royal Theatre, Namur. h, Aspremont-Lynden Castle, Rekem. i, Neo-Gothic kiosk, Sint-Niklaas. j, Chapelle Saint Vincent, Tournai. k, Villers-la-Ville Abbey. l, Saint Gilles Town Hall, Brussels.

1998, July 6
1701 A728 17fr Sheet of 12, #a.-l.   11.00 8.50

Bird Type of 1985

1998   Photo.   Perf. 11½
1702 A524 9fr Pic vert   .50   .40
1703 A524 10fr Turtle dove   .60   .45
Issued: 9fr, 8/10; 10fr, 9/28/98.

Free Thinking A729

1998, Aug. 10   Photo.   Perf. 11½
1704 A729 17fr multicolored   1.00   .75

Philips van Marnix van Sint-Aldegonde (1540-98), Author — A730

1998, Aug. 10
1705 A730 17fr multicolored   1.00   .75

Mniszech Palace (Belgian Embassy), Warsaw, Bicent. A731

1998, Sept. 28   Photo. & Engr.   Perf. 11½
1706 A731 17fr multicolored   1.00   .75
See Poland No. .

Contemporary Belgium Films — A732

1998, Sept. 28   Photo.
1707 A732 17fr "Le Huitieme Jour"   1.00   .75
1708 A732 17fr "Daens"   1.00   .75

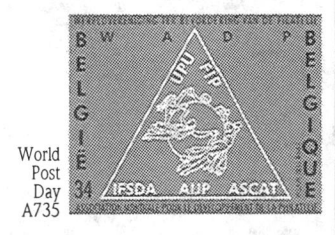

World Post Day A735

1998, Oct. 19   Photo.   Perf. 11½
1711 A735 34fr blue & dark blue   2.00 1.50
World Assoc. for the Development of Philately.

SEMI-POSTAL STAMPS

Values quoted for Nos. B1-B24 are for stamps with label attached. Copies without label sell for one-tenth or less.

Belgium **
COMPLETE YEAR SETS MINT NH
including «B» and Blocks as in our country
When US.$ = 1.15 EUR net price =$.

Year	Contents	Price
1944/45	72 val	42,70
1946	23 val	40,00
1947	13 val	60,50
1948	31 val +Bk	267,00
1949	31 val	280,00
1950	18 val + Bk	140,50
1951	38 val	183,50
1952	32 val + Bk	672,00
1953	30 val	167,00
1954	23 val	213,50
1955	25 val	75,00
1956	19 val	43,00
1957	43 val + Bk	151,50
1958	53 val (with air)	229,50
1959	31 val	31,80
1960	55 val +Bk	113,00
1961	30 val	21,00

If hinged before '61 deduct 40%

Year	Contents	Price
1962	36 val + Bk	16,50
1963	38 val + Bk	14,40
1964	38 val + 3Bk	12,00
1965	47 val + 2Bk	11,00
1966	44 val + 3Bk	15,50
1967	39 val + 2Bk	9,50
1968	39 val	9,00
1969	41 val + Bk	18,00
1970	44 val + 2Bk	23,00
1971	49 val	10,20
1972	41 val	15,00
1973	40 val + 2Bkt	12,40
1974	43 val	12,40
1975	46 val + 2 Bkt	17,50
1976	43 val + 3Bk	23,00
1977	43 val + Bk	13,50
1978	35 v+Bk+2Bkt	13,00
1979	40 val + Bk	16,50
1980	37 val + 2Bk	21,60
1981	36 val + Bk	27,00
1982	44 val + 2Bk	37,00
1983	34 val	19,00
1984	44 val + Bk	33,00
1985	43 val + Bk	35,00
1986	42 val + Bk	44,80
1987	32 val	23,25
1988	37 val + Bk	46,00
1989	37 val + Bk	33,50
1990	49 val + 2 Bk	104,00

1991,1992,1993 = @ 33,90
1994,1995,1996 = @ 49,00

Minimum order 50$+ postage
(air reg.letter 7-$ free for order >200$)
COMPLETE PRICE LIST of sets, NH, LH or used on request.

Prices mint NH. are based on the real market price, not according Scott valuations for mint LH. !
Belgium National catalogue in full color (30,00 $) offered for order >500 $

IMPERF, DELUXE, FDC,
Single stamps, parts of collections, available.

BELGIAN CONGO
ZAÏRE • BURUNDI
RUANDA-URUNDI.
Large choice for topical & advanced collector

VISA   AMERICAN EXPRESS

CENTRALE PHILATÉLIQUE
rue du Midi 163
1000 Brussels. Belgium
(est.1942 - Member ASDA)
Fax ++32.2. 512 74 15

BELGIUM

St. Martin of Tours Dividing His
Cloak with a Beggar
SP1   SP2

Unwmk.

1910, June 1		Typo.		Perf. 14
B1	SP1	1c gray	1.65	1.25
B2	SP1	2c purple brn	13.00	9.25
B3	SP1	5c peacock blue	3.50	2.50
B4	SP1	10c brown red	3.50	2.50
B5	SP2	1c gray green	3.50	2.50
B6	SP2	2c violet brn	10.00	7.25
B7	SP2	5c peacock blue	3.50	2.50
B8	SP2	10c carmine	3.50	2.50
		Nos. B1-B8 (8)	42.15	30.25

Overprinted "1911" in Black

1911, Apr. 1				
B9	SP1	1c gray	20.00	14.00
a.		Inverted overprint		
B10	SP1	2c purple brn	50.00	45.00
B11	SP1	5c peacock blue	5.75	4.00
B12	SP1	10c brown red	5.75	4.00
B13	SP2	1c gray green	40.00	35.00
B14	SP2	2c violet brn	36.00	27.50
B15	SP2	5c peacock blue	5.75	4.00
B16	SP2	10c carmine	5.75	4.00
		Nos. B9-B16 (8)	169.00	137.50

Overprinted "CHARLEROI·1911"

1911, June				
B17	SP1	1c gray	5.00	5.00
B18	SP1	2c purple brn	17.00	17.00
B19	SP1	5c peacock blue	8.00	8.00
B20	SP1	10c brown red	7.50	7.50
B21	SP2	1c gray green	5.00	5.00
B22	SP2	2c violet brn	16.00	16.00
B23	SP2	5c peacock blue	6.75	6.75
B24	SP2	10c carmine	5.00	5.00
		Nos. B17-B24 (8)	70.25	70.25

Nos. B1-B24 were sold at double face value, except the 10c denominations which were sold for 15c. The surtax benefited the national anti-tuberculosis organization.

SP3

Merode Monument — SP4    King Albert I — SP5

1914, Oct. 3				Litho.
B25	SP3	5c green & red	1.65	2.00
B26	SP3	10c red	.45	.50
B27	SP3	20c violet & red	10.50	13.00
		Nos. B25-B27 (3)	12.60	15.50

Counterfeits of Nos. B25-B27 abound. Probably as many as 90% of the stamps on the market are counterfeits. Competently certified copies sell for much more.

1914, Oct. 3				
B28	SP4	5c green & red	4.50	5.00
B29	SP4	10c red	4.50	5.00
B30	SP4	20c violet & red	42.50	47.50
		Nos. B28-B30 (3)	51.50	57.50

Counterfeits of Nos. B28-B30 abound. Probably as many as 90% of the stamps on the market are counterfeits. Competently certified copies sell for much more.

1915, Jan. 1				Perf. 12, 14
B31	SP5	5c green & red	5.00	3.00
a.		Perf. 12x14	16.00	12.00
B32	SP5	10c rose & red	20.00	6.00
B33	SP5	20c violet & red	25.00	14.00
a.		Perf. 14x12	500.00	240.00
b.		Perf. 12	50.00	32.50
		Nos. B31-B33 (3)	50.00	23.00

Nos. B25-B33 were sold at double face value. The surtax benefited the Red Cross.

Types of Regular Issue of 1915 Surcharged in Red:

+ 1c   Nos. B34-B40
+ 35c   Nos. B41-B43
+ 1F   Nos. B44-B47

1918, Jan. 15		Typo.		Perf. 14
B34	A46	1c + 1c dp orange	.50	.50
B35	A46	2c + 2c brown	.60	.60
B36	A46	5c + 5c blue grn	1.25	1.25
B37	A46	10c + 10c red	2.25	2.25
B38	A46	15c + 15c brt violet	3.25	3.25
B39	A46	20c + 20c plum	7.50	7.50
B40	A46	25c + 25c ultra	7.50	7.50
		Engr.		
B41	A47	35c + 35c lt vio & blk	10.00	10.00
B42	A48	40c + 40c dull red & blk	10.00	10.00
B43	A49	50c + 50c turq blue & blk	12.00	12.00
B44	A50	1fr + 1fr bluish slate	35.00	35.00
B45	A51	2fr + 2fr dp gray grn	100.00	100.00
B46	A52	5fr + 5fr brown	250.00	250.00
B47	A53	10fr + 10fr dp blue	500.00	500.00
		Nos. B34-B47 (14)	939.85	939.85

Discus Thrower — SP6    Racing Chariot — SP7

Runner — SP8

1920, May 20		Engr.		Perf. 12
B48	SP6	5c + 5c dp green	1.40	1.40
B49	SP7	10c + 5c carmine	1.40	1.40
B50	SP8	15c + 15c dk brown	3.00	3.00
		Nos. B48-B50 (3)	5.80	5.80

7th Olympic Games, 1920. Surtax benefited wounded soldiers. Exists imperf.
For surcharges see Nos. 140-142.

Allegory: Asking Alms from the Crown — SP9     Wounded Veteran — SP10

1922, May 20				
B51	SP9	20c + 20c brown	1.40	1.40

1923, July 5				
B52	SP10	20c + 20c slate gray	1.75	1.75

Surtax on #B51-B52 was to aid wounded veterans.

SP11    SP12

St. Martin, by Van Dyck
SP13   SP14

1925, Dec. 15		Typo.		Perf. 14
B53	SP11	15c + 15c dull vio & red	.25	.20
B54	SP11	30c + 5c gray & red	.25	.20
B55	SP11	1fr + 10c chalky blue & red	1.25	1.40
		Nos. B53-B55 (3)	2.00	1.80

Surtax for the Natl. Anti-Tuberculosis League.

1926, Feb. 10				
B56	SP12	30c + 30c bluish grn (red surch.)	.50	.55
B57	SP13	1fr + 1fr lt blue	7.25	7.25
B58	SP14	1fr + 1fr lt blue	1.10	1.25
		Nos. B56-B58 (3)	8.85	9.05

The surtax aided victims of the Meuse flood.

Lion and Cross of Lorraine SP15    Queen Elisabeth and King Albert SP16

1926, Dec. 6		Typo.		Perf. 14
B59	SP15	5c + 5c dk brown	.25	.20
B60	SP15	20c + 5c red brown	.45	.40
B61	SP15	50c + 5c dull violet	.30	.20
		Engr.		Perf. 11½
B62	SP16	1.50fr + 25c dk blue	.75	.70
B63	SP16	5fr + 1fr rose red	6.50	6.00
		Nos. B59-B63 (5)	8.25	7.50

Surtax was used to benefit tubercular war veterans.

Boat Adrift — SP17

1927, Dec. 15		Engr.		Perf. 11½, 14
B64	SP17	25c + 10c dk brown	.70	.70
B65	SP17	35c + 10c yel grn	.70	.70
B66	SP17	60c + 10c dp violet	.60	.40
B67	SP17	1.75fr + 25c dk blue	1.50	2.00
B68	SP17	5fr + 1fr plum	4.50	4.75
		Nos. B64-B68 (5)	8.00	8.55

The surtax on these stamps was divided among several charitable associations.

Ogives of Orval Abbey — SP18    Monk Carving Capital of Column — SP19

Ruins of Orval Abbey — SP20

Design: 60c+15c, 1.75fr+25c, 3fr+1fr, Countess Matilda recovering her ring.

1928, Sept. 15		Photo.		Perf. 11½
B69	SP18	5c + 5c red & gold	.25	.30
B70	SP18	25c + 5c dk vio & gold	.45	.50
		Engr.		
B71	SP19	35c + 10c dp green	1.10	1.10
B72	SP19	60c + 15c red brown	1.65	1.65
B73	SP19	1.75fr + 25c dk blue	3.50	3.50
B74	SP19	2fr + 40c dp violet	13.00	13.00
B75	SP19	3fr + 1fr red	15.00	15.00
		Perf. 14		
B76	SP20	5fr + 5fr rose lake	15.00	15.00
B77	SP20	10fr + 10fr ol green	15.00	15.00
		Nos. B69-B77 (9)	64.95	65.05

Surtax for the restoration of the ruined Orval Abbey.
For overprints see Nos. B84-B92.

St. Waudru, Mons — SP22    St. Rombaut, Malines — SP23

Designs: 25c + 15c, Cathedral of Tournai. 60c + 15c, St. Bavon, Ghent. 1.75fr + 25c, St. Gudule, Brussels. 5fr + 5fr, Louvain Library.

1928, Dec. 1		Photo.		Perf. 14, 11½
B78	SP22	5c + 5c carmine	.20	.20
B79	SP22	25c + 15c ol brn	.35	.38
		Engr.		
B80	SP23	35c + 10c dp green	1.25	1.25
B81	SP23	60c + 15c red brn	.50	.25
B82	SP23	1.75fr + 25c vio blue	8.50	7.00
B83	SP23	5fr + 5fr red vio	16.00	15.00
		Nos. B78-B83 (6)	26.80	24.08

The surtax was for anti-tuberculosis work.

Nos. B69-B77 with this overprint in blue or red was privately produced. They are for the laying of the 1st stone toward the restoration of the ruined Abbey of Orval. Forgeries of the overprint exist. Value, set, $650.

Waterfall at Coo — SP28

Bayard Rock, Dinant — SP29

Designs: 35c+10c, Menin Gate, Ypres. 60c+15c, Promenade d'Orleans, Spa. 1.75fr+25c, Antwerp Harbor. 5fr+5fr, Quai Vert, Bruges.

1929, Dec. 2		Engr.		Perf. 11½
B93	SP28	5c + 5c red brown	.20	.25
B94	SP28	25c + 15c gray blk	.65	.60
B95	SP28	35c + 10c green	.80	.95
B96	SP28	60c + 15c rose lake	.55	.50
B97	SP28	1.75fr + 25c dp blue	4.50	4.50
		Perf. 14		
B98	SP29	5fr + 5fr dl vio	27.50	27.50
		Nos. B93-B98 (6)	34.20	34.30

BELGIUM

Bornhem — SP34
Beloeil — SP35 
Gaesbeek SP36 

Designs: 25c + 15c, Wynendaele. 70c + 15c, Oydonck. 1fr + 25c, Ghent. 1.75fr + 25c, Bouillon.

1930, Dec. 1   Photo.   Perf. 14
B99	SP34	10c + 5c violet	.25	.30
B100	SP34	25c + 15c olive brn	.60	.60

Engr.
B101	SP35	40c + 10c brown vio	.80	1.00
B102	SP35	70c + 15c gray blk	.55	.55
B103	SP35	1fr + 25c rose lake	3.50	3.50
B104	SP35	1.75fr + 25c dp blue	4.50	2.75
B105	SP36	5fr + 5fr gray grn	27.50	32.50
		Nos. B99-B105 (7)	37.70	41.20

Prince Leopold SP41
Queen Elisabeth SP42 

Philatelic Exhibition Issue
Souvenir Sheet

1931, July 18   Photo.   Perf. 14
B106	SP41	2.45fr + 55c car brn	140.00	140.00

Sold exclusively at the Brussels Phil. Exhib., July 18-21, 1931. Size: 122x159mm. Surtax for the Veterans' Relief Fund.

The sheet normally has pin holes and a cancellation-like marking in the margin. These are considered unused and the condition valued here.

1931, Dec. 1   Engr.
B107	SP42	10c + 5c red brown	.30	.52
B108	SP42	25c + 15c dk violet	1.10	1.25
B109	SP42	50c + 10c dk green	.95	1.00
B110	SP42	75c + 15c black brn	.90	.65
B111	SP42	1fr + 25c rose lake	6.75	6.00
B112	SP42	1.75fr + 25c ultra	4.75	4.00
B113	SP42	5fr + 5fr brown vio	55.00	55.00
		Nos. B107-B113 (7)	69.75	68.42

The surtax was for the National Anti-Tuberculosis League.

Désiré Cardinal Mercier SP43
Mercier Protecting Children and Aged at Malines SP44 
Mercier as Professor at Louvain University — SP45 
Mercier in Full Canonicals, Giving His Blessing SP46 

1932, June 10   Photo.   Perf. 14½x14
B114	SP43	10c + 10c dk violet	.40	.60
B115	SP43	50c + 30c brt violet	2.25	2.50
B116	SP43	75c + 25c olive brn	2.25	2.25
B117	SP43	1fr + 2fr brown red	6.00	6.00

Engr.   Perf. 11½
B118	SP44	1.75fr + 75c dp blue	70.00	82.50
B119	SP45	2.50fr + 2.50fr dk brn	70.00	70.00
B120	SP44	3fr + 4.50fr dull grn	70.00	70.00
B121	SP45	5fr + 20fr vio brn	80.00	82.50
B122	SP46	10fr + 40fr brn lake	175.00	210.00
		Nos. B114-B122 (9)	475.90	526.35

Issued in commemoration of Cardinal Mercier and to obtain funds to erect a monument to his memory.

Belgian Infantryman SP47
Sanatorium at Waterloo SP48 

1932, Aug. 4   Perf. 14½x14
B123	SP47	75c + 3.25fr red brn	55.00	55.00
B124	SP47	1.75fr + 4.25fr dk blue	55.00	55.00

Honoring Belgian soldiers who fought in WWI and to obtain funds to erect a natl. monument to their glory.

1932, Dec. 1   Photo.   Perf. 13½x14
B125	SP48	10c + 5c dk vio	.30	.90
B126	SP48	25c + 15c red vio	1.00	1.25
B127	SP48	50c + 10c red brn	1.00	1.25
B128	SP48	75c + 15c ol brn	1.00	.80
B129	SP48	1fr + 25c dp red	13.00	10.50
B130	SP48	1.75fr + 25c dp blue	10.50	9.25
B131	SP48	5fr + 5fr gray grn	85.00	99.00
		Nos. B125-B131 (7)	111.80	113.95

Surtax for the assistance of the Natl. Anti-Tuberculosis Society at Waterloo.

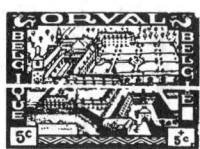

View of Old Abbey — SP49
Ruins of Old Abbey — SP50 
Count de Chiny Presenting First Abbey to Countess Matilda SP56 
Restoration of Abbey in XVI and XVII Centuries SP57 
Abbey in XVIII Century, Maria Theresa and Charles V — SP58 
Madonna and Arms of Seven Abbeys — SP60 

Designs: 25c+15c, Guests, courtyard, 50c+25c, Transept. 75c+50c, Bell Tower. 1fr+1.25fr, Fountain. 1.25fr+1.75fr, Cloisters. 5fr+20fr, Duke of Brabant placing 1st stone of new abbey.

1933, Oct. 15   Perf. 14
B132	SP49	5c + 5c dull grn	35.00	40.00
B133	SP50	10c + 15c ol grn	32.50	35.00
B134	SP49	25c + 15c dk brn	32.50	35.00
B135	SP50	50c + 25c red brn	32.50	35.00
B136	SP50	75c + 50c dp grn	32.50	35.00
B137	SP50	1fr + 1.25fr cop red	32.50	35.00
B138	SP49	1.25fr + 1.75fr gray blk	32.50	35.00
B139	SP56	1.75fr + 2.75fr blue	37.50	40.00
B140	SP57	2fr + 3fr mag	37.50	40.00
B141	SP58	2.50fr + 5fr dull grn	37.50	40.00
B142	SP56	5fr + 20fr vio	40.00	40.00

Perf. 11½
B143	SP60	10fr + 40fr blue	225.00	225.00
		Nos. B132-B143 (12)	607.50	635.00

The surtax was for a fund to aid in the restoration of Orval Abbey. Counterfeits exist.

"Tuberculosis Society" SP61
Peter Benoit SP62 

1933, Dec. 1   Engr.   Perf. 14x13½
B144	SP61	10c + 5c black	.85	.85
B145	SP61	25c + 15c violet	3.00	3.00
B146	SP61	50c + 10c red brn	2.25	2.25
B147	SP61	75c + 15c blk brn	9.25	9.00
B148	SP61	1fr + 25c claret	10.50	10.50
B149	SP61	1.75fr + 25c vio bl	12.50	12.50
B150	SP61	5fr + 5fr lilac	115.00	115.00
		Nos. B144-B150 (7)	153.35	153.10

The surtax was for anti-tuberculosis work.

1934, June 1   Photo.
B151	SP62	75c + 25c olive brn	5.50	5.50

The surtax was to raise funds for the Peter Benoit Memorial.

King Leopold III
SP63   SP64

1934, Sept. 15
B152	SP63	75c + 25c ol blk	18.00	17.00
a.		Sheet of 20	750.00	750.00
B153	SP64	1fr + 25c red vio	17.00	16.00
a.		Sheet of 20	750.00	750.00

The surtax aided the National War Veterans' Fund. Sold for 4.50fr a set at the Exhibition of War Postmarks 1914-18, held at Brussels by the Royal Philatelic Club of Veterans. The price included an exhibition ticket. Sold at Brussels post office Sept. 18-22. No. B152 printed in sheets of 20 (4x5) and 100 (10x10). No. B153 printed in sheets of 20 (4x5) and 150 (10x15).

1934, Sept. 24
B154	SP63	75c + 25c violet	1.25	1.25
B155	SP64	1fr + 25c red brn	7.00	7.00

The surtax aided the National War Veterans' Fund. No. B154 printed in sheets of 100 (10x10); No. B155 in sheets of 150 (10x15). These stamps remained in use one year.

Crusader — SP65

1934, Nov. 17   Engr.   Perf. 13½x14
Cross in Red
B156	SP65	10c + 5c black	1.25	1.25
B157	SP65	25c + 5c brown	1.75	1.75
B158	SP65	50c + 10c dull grn	1.75	1.75
B159	SP65	75c + 15c vio brn	.85	.85
B160	SP65	1fr + 25c rose	8.50	8.50
B161	SP65	1.75fr + 25c ultra	7.50	7.50
B162	SP65	5fr + 5fr brn vio	105.00	105.00
		Nos. B156-B162 (7)	126.60	126.60

The surtax was for anti-tuberculosis work.

Prince Baudouin, Princess Josephine and Prince Albert SP66

1935, Apr. 10   Photo.
B163	SP66	35c + 15c dk green	.85	.75
B164	SP66	70c + 30c red brn	.85	.60
B165	SP66	1.75fr + 50c dk blue	3.00	3.50
		Nos. B163-B165 (3)	4.70	4.85

Surtax was for Child Welfare Society.

Stagecoach SP67
Franz von Taxis — SP68 
Queen Astrid — SP69 

1935, Apr. 27
B166	SP67	10c + 10c ol blk	.55	.65
B167	SP67	25c + 25c bis brn	1.90	1.75
B168	SP67	35c + 25c dk green	2.50	2.25
		Nos. B166-B168 (3)	4.95	4.65

Printed in sheets of 10. Value, set of 3, $175.

Souvenir Sheet

1935, May 25   Engr.   Perf. 14
B169	SP68	5fr + 5fr grnsh blk	125.00	125.00

Sheets measure 91½x117mm.

Nos. B166-B169 were issued for the Brussels Philatelic Exhibition (SITEB).

The sheet normally has pin holes and a cancellation-like marking in the margin. These are considered unused and the condition valued here.

BELGIUM

1935	**Photo.**		***Perf. 11½***
	Borders in Black		
B170 SP69	10c + 5c ol blk	.15	.15
B171 SP69	25c + 15c brown	.15	.30
B172 SP69	35c + 5c dk green	.20	.25
B173 SP69	50c + 10c rose lil	.65	.55
B174 SP69	70c + 5c gray blk	.15	.15
B175 SP69	1fr + 25c red	.90	.70
B176 SP69	1.75fr + 25c blue	2.00	1.50
B177 SP69	2.45fr + 55c dk vio	2.50	2.75
	Nos. B170-B177 (8)	6.70	6.35

Queen Astrid Memorial issue. The surtax was divided among several charitable organizations. Issued: #B174, 10/31; others, 12/1.

Borgerhout Philatelic Exhibition Issue
Souvenir Sheet

Town Hall, Borgerhout — SP70

1936, Oct. 3
B178 SP70 70c + 30c pur brn 50.00 35.00

Sheet measures 115x126mm.
The sheet normally has pin holes and a cancellation-like marking in the margin. These are considered unused and the condition valued here.

Town Hall and Belfry of Charleroi SP71

Prince Baudouin SP72

Charleroi Youth Exhibition
Souvenir Sheet

1936, Oct. 18 **Engr.**
B179 SP71 2.45fr + 55c gray blue 42.50 40.00

Sheet measures 95x120mm.
The sheet normally has pin holes and a cancellation-like marking in the margin. These are considered unused and the condition valued here.

1936, Dec. 1	**Photo.**		***Perf. 14x13½***
B180 SP72	10c + 5c dk brown	.15	.20
B181 SP72	25c + 5c violet	.20	.25
B182 SP72	35c + 5c dk green	.20	.25
B183 SP72	50c + 5c vio brn	.30	.35
B184 SP72	70c + 5c ol grn	.20	.20
B185 SP72	1fr + 25c cerise	.65	.45
B186 SP72	1.75fr + 25c ultra	1.10	.65
B187 SP72	2.45fr + 2.55fr vio rose	3.00	4.00
	Nos. B180-B187 (8)	5.80	6.35

The surtax was for the assistance of the National Anti-Tuberculosis Society.

1937, Jan. 10
B188 SP72 2.45fr + 2.55fr slate 1.50 1.50

Intl. Stamp Day. Surtax for the benefit of the Brussels Postal Museum, the Royal Belgian Phil. Fed. and the Anti-Tuberculosis Soc.

Queen Astrid and Prince Baudouin SP73

Queen Mother Elisabeth SP74

1937, Apr. 15			***Perf. 11½***
B189 SP73	10c + 5c magenta	.15	.15
B190 SP73	25c + 5c ol blk	.20	.25
B191 SP73	35c + 5c dk grn	.20	.25
B192 SP73	50c + 5c violet	.50	.55
B193 SP73	70c + 5c slate	.20	.30
B194 SP73	1fr + 25c dk car	.65	.65
B195 SP73	1.75fr + 25c dp ultra	1.10	1.10
B196 SP73	2.45fr + 1.55fr dk brn	2.75	2.75
	Nos. B189-B196 (8)	5.75	6.00

The surtax was to raise funds for Public Utility Works.

1937, Sept. 15			***Perf. 14x13½***
B197 SP74	70c + 5c int black	.30	.30
B198 SP74	1.75fr + 25c brt ultra	.70	.70

Souvenir Sheet
Perf. 11½

B199	Sheet of 4	26.00	15.00
a.	SP74 1.50fr+2.50fr red brown	3.75	3.25
b.	SP74 2.45fr+3.55fr red violet	3.25	2.00

Issued for the benefit of the Queen Elisabeth Music Foundation in connection with the Eugene Ysaye intl. competition.
No. B199 contains two se-tenant pairs of Nos. B199a and B199b. Size: 111x145mm. On sale one day, Sept. 15, at Brussels.
The sheet normally has pin holes and a cancellation-like marking in the margin. These are considered unused and the condition valued here.

Princess Josephine-Charlotte SP75

1937, Dec. 1			***Perf. 14x13½***
B200 SP75	10c + 5c sl grn	.15	.20
B201 SP75	25c + 5c lt brn	.20	.20
B202 SP75	35c + 5c yel grn	.20	.20
B203 SP75	50c + 5c ol gray	.40	.35
B204 SP75	70c + 5c brn red	.15	.20
B205 SP75	1fr + 25c red	.70	.55
B206 SP75	1.75fr + 25c vio bl	.80	.70
B207 SP75	2.45fr + 2.55fr mag	3.25	3.50
	Nos. B200-B207 (8)	5.85	5.90

King Albert Memorial Issue
Souvenir Sheet

King Albert Memorial — SP76

1938, Feb. 17 ***Perf. 11½***
B208 SP76 2.45fr + 7.55fr brn vio 13.00 11.00

Dedication of the monument to King Albert.
The sheet normally has pin holes and a cancellation-like marking in the margin. These are considered unused and the condition valued here.

King Leopold III in Military Plane — SP77

1938, Mar. 15			
B209 SP77	10c + 5c car brn	.20	.30
B210 SP77	35c + 5c dp grn	.35	.90
B211 SP77	70c + 5c gray blk	.65	.50
B212 SP77	1.75fr + 25c ultra	1.50	1.40
B213 SP77	2.45fr + 2.55fr pur	3.50	3.00
	Nos. B209-B213 (5)	6.20	6.10

The surtax was for the benefit of the National Fund for Aeronautical Propaganda.

Basilica of Koekelberg SP78

Interior View of the Basilica of Koekelberg — SP79

1938, June 1	**Photo.**		
B214 SP78	10c + 5c lt brn	.15	.20
B215 SP78	35c + 5c grn	.20	.20
B216 SP78	70c + 5c gray grn	.20	.20
B217 SP78	1fr + 25c car	.65	.55
B218 SP78	1.75fr + 25c ultra	.65	.65
B219 SP78	2.45fr + 2.55fr brn vio	2.75	3.50

Engr.
B220 SP79 5fr + 5fr dl grn 11.00 10.50
Nos. B214-B220 (7) 15.60 15.80

Souvenir Sheet
1938, July 21 **Engr.** ***Perf. 14***
B221 SP79 5fr + 5fr lt vio 14.00 14.00

The surtax was for a fund to aid in completing the National Basilica of the Sacred Heart at Koekelberg.
Nos. B214, B216 and B218 are different views of the exterior of the Basilica.
The sheet normally has pin holes and a cancellation-like marking in the margin. These are considered unused and the condition valued here.

Stamps of 1938 Surcharged in Black:

Nos. B222-B223

No. B224

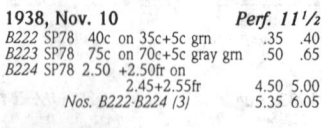

1938, Nov. 10			***Perf. 11½***
B222 SP78	40c on 35c+5c grn	.35	.40
B223 SP78	75c on 70c+5c gray grn	.50	.65
B224 SP78	2.50 +2.50fr on 2.45+2.55fr	4.50	5.00
	Nos. B222-B224 (3)	5.35	6.05

Prince Albert of Liege — SP81

1938, Dec. 10	**Photo.**		***Perf. 14x13½***
B225 SP81	10c + 5c brown	.15	.20
B226 SP81	30c + 5c magenta	.20	.30
B227 SP81	40c + 5c olive gray	.20	.30
B228 SP81	75c + 5c slate grn	.15	.20
B229 SP81	1fr + 25c dk car	.55	.75
B230 SP81	1.75fr + 25c ultra	.55	.75
B231 SP81	2.50fr + 2.50fr dp grn	3.50	5.50
B232 SP81	5fr + 5fr brn lake	11.00	8.50
	Nos. B225-B232 (8)	16.30	16.50

Henri Dunant SP82

Florence Nightingale SP83

Queen Mother Elisabeth and Royal Children — SP84

Queen Astrid — SP86

King Leopold and Royal Children SP85

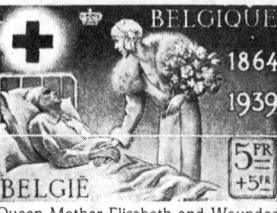

Queen Mother Elisabeth and Wounded Soldier — SP87

1939, Apr. 1	**Photo.**		***Perf. 11½***
	Cross in Carmine		
B233 SP82	10c + 5c brn	.15	.20
B234 SP83	30c + 5c brn car	.30	.30
B235 SP84	40c + 5c ol gray	.20	.30
B236 SP85	75c + 5c slate blk	.40	.20
B237 SP84	1fr + 25c brt rose	1.90	1.10
B238 SP85	1.75fr + 25c brt ultra	.60	.85
B239 SP86	2.50fr + 2.50fr dl vio	1.25	1.65
B240 SP87	5fr + 5fr gray grn	4.25	5.50
	Nos. B233-B240 (8)	9.05	10.10

75th anniversary of the founding of the International Red Cross Society.

Rubens' House, Antwerp SP88

"Albert and Nicolas Rubens" — SP89

Arcade, Rubens' House SP90

"Helena Fourment and Her Children" — SP91

Rubens and Isabelle Brandt — SP92

BELGIUM

Peter Paul Rubens — SP93

"The Velvet Hat" — SP94

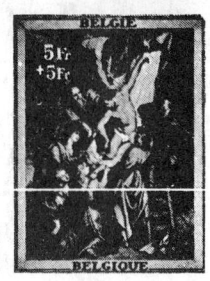

Bishop Heylen of Namur, Madonna and Abbot General Smets of the Trappists — SP101

Queen Elisabeth Music Chapel SP120

Maria Theresa — SP129

Charles the Bold — SP130

"Descent from the Cross" SP95

King Albert I and King Leopold III and Shrine — SP102

Bust of Prince Albert of Liege — SP121

Portraits (in various frames): 35c+5c, Charles of Lorraine. 50c+10c, Margaret of Parma. 60c+10c, Charles V. 1fr+15c, Johanna of Castile. 1.50fr+1fr, Philip the Good. 1.75fr+1.75fr, Margaret of Austria. 3.25fr+3.25fr, Archduke Albert. 5fr+5fr, Archduchess Isabella.

1940, Nov.   Photo.   Perf. 11½

B273	SP120	75c + 75c slate	1.25	1.25
B274	SP120	1fr + 1fr rose red	1.25	1.25
B275	SP121	1.50fr + 1.50fr Prus grn	1.25	1.25
B276	SP121	1.75fr + 1.75fr ultra	1.25	1.25
B277	SP120	2.50fr + 2.50fr brn org	2.50	2.50
B278	SP121	5fr + 5fr red vio	3.00	3.00
		Nos. B273-B278 (6)	10.50	10.50

1941-42   Photo.

B293	SP129	10c + 5c ol blk	.15	.15
B294	SP129	35c + 5c dl grn	.15	.15
B295	SP129	50c + 10c brn	.15	.15
B296	SP129	60c + 10c pur	.15	.15
B297	SP129	1fr + 15c brt car rose	.15	.15
B298	SP129	1.50fr + 1fr red vio	.20	.20
B299	SP129	1.75fr + 1.75fr ryl bl	.20	.20
B300	SP130	2.25fr + 2.25fr dl red brn	.30	.30
B301	SP129	3.25fr + 3.25fr lt brn	.35	.45
B302	SP129	5fr + 5fr sl grn	.40	.45
		Nos. B293-B302 (10)	2.20	2.35

1939, July 1

B241	SP88	10c + 5c brn	.15	.20
B242	SP89	40c + 5c brn car	.30	.30
B243	SP90	75c + 5c ol blk	.60	.50
B244	SP91	1fr + 25c rose	1.65	1.50
B245	SP92	1.50fr + 25c sep	1.65	1.50
B246	SP93	1.75fr + 25c dp ultra	2.25	1.65
B247	SP94	2.50fr + 2.50fr brt red vio	9.25	10.50
B248	SP95	5fr + 5fr slate gray	14.00	14.00
		Nos. B241-B248 (8)	29.85	30.15

Issued to honor Peter Paul Rubens. The surtax was used to restore Rubens' home in Antwerp.

1939, July 20

B250	SP97	75c + 75c ol blk	2.50	2.75
B251	SP98	1fr + 1fr rose red	1.65	1.65
B252	SP99	1fr + 1.50fr dl brn	1.65	1.50
B253	SP100	1.75fr + 1.75fr saph	1.65	1.65
B254	SP101	2.50fr + 2.50fr brt red vio	7.25	6.50
B255	SP102	5fr + 5fr brn car	7.25	7.25
		Nos. B250-B255 (6)	21.95	21.45

The surtax was used for the restoration of the Abbey of Orval.

"Martin van Nieuwenhove" by Hans Memling (1430?-1495), Flemish Painter — SP96

1939, July 1

| B249 | SP96 | 75c + 75c olive blk | 2.75 | 2.75 |

Bruges SP103

Furnes SP104

Belfries: 30c+5c, Thuin. 40c+5c, Lierre. 75c+5c, Mons. 1.75fr+25c, Namur. 2.50fr+2.50fr, Alost. 5fr+5fr, Tournai.

1939, Dec. 1   Photo.   Perf. 14x13½

B256	SP103	10c + 5c ol gray	.15	.25
B257	SP103	30c + 5c brn org	.25	.35
B258	SP103	40c + 5c brt red vio	.40	.45
B259	SP103	75c + 5c olive blk	.15	.25

Engr.

B260	SP104	1fr + 25c rose car	1.00	1.25
B261	SP104	1.75fr + 25c dk blue	1.00	1.25
B262	SP104	2.50fr + 2.50fr dp red brn	7.25	8.00
B263	SP104	5fr + 5fr purple	10.00	11.00
		Nos. B256-B263 (8)	20.20	22.80

The surtax was for the Queen Elisabeth Music Foundation. Nos. B273-B278 were not authorized for postal use, but were sold to advance subscribers either mint or canceled to order. See Nos. B317-B318.

Arms Types of 1940-41
Souvenir Sheets
Perf. 14x13½, Imperf.

1941, May   Typo.
Cross and City Name in Carmine
Arms in Color of Stamp

B279		Sheet of 9	13.00	13.00
a.	SP111	10c + 5c slate	1.10	1.25
b.	SP112	30c + 5c emerald	1.10	1.25
c.	SP111	40c + 10c chocolate	1.10	1.25
d.	SP112	50c + 10c light violet	1.10	1.25
e.	SP111	75c + 15c dull purple	1.10	1.25
f.	SP112	1fr + 25c carmine	1.10	1.25
g.	SP111	1.75fr + 50c dull blue	1.10	1.25
h.	SP112	2.50fr + 2.50fr olive gray	1.10	1.25
i.	SP111	5fr + 5fr dull violet	4.00	4.25

The sheets measure 106x148mm. The surtax was used for relief work.

Archduke Albert and Archduchess Isabella — SP139

B302A	SP139	Sheet of 2 ('42)	6.00	6.00
b.		3.25fr+6.75fr turquoise blue	2.25	2.25
c.		5fr+10fr dark carmine	2.25	2.25

The surtax was for the benefit of National Social Service Work among soldiers' families.

Twelfth Century Monks at Work — SP97

Reconstructed Tower Seen through Cloister — SP98

Monks Laboring in the Fields — SP99

Mons SP111

Ghent SP112

Coats of Arms: 40c+10c, Arel. 50c+10c, Bruges. 75c+15c, Namur. 1fr+25c, Hasselt. 1.75fr+50c, Brussels. 2.50fr+2.50fr, Antwerp. 5fr+5fr, Liege.

1940-41   Typo.   Perf. 14x13½

B264	SP111	10c + 5c multi	.15	.15
B265	SP112	30c + 5c multi	.20	.15
B266	SP111	40c + 10c multi	.20	.15
B267	SP112	50c + 10c multi	.20	.15
B268	SP111	75c + 15c multi	.15	.15
B269	SP112	1fr + 25c multi	.30	.30
B270	SP111	1.75fr + 50c multi	.45	.40
B271	SP112	2.50fr + 2.50fr multi	1.25	1.25
B272	SP111	5fr + 5fr multi	1.50	1.50
		Nos. B264-B272 (9)	4.40	4.20

Nos. B264, B269-B272 issued in 1941. Surtax for winter relief. See No. B279.

Orval Abbey, Aerial View — SP100

Painting SP123

Sculpture SP124

Monks Studying Plans of Orval Abbey — SP128

Designs: 40c+60c, 2fr+3.50fr, Monk carrying candle. 50c+65c, 1.75fr+2.50fr, Monk praying. 75c+1fr, 3fr+5fr, Two monks singing.

1941, June   Photo.   Perf. 11½

B281	SP123	10c + 15c brn org	.35	.40
B282	SP124	30c + 30c ol gray	.35	.40
B283	SP124	40c + 60c dp brn	.35	.40
B284	SP124	50c + 65c vio	.35	.40
B285	SP124	75c + 1fr brt red vio	.35	.40
B286	SP124	1fr + 1.50fr rose red	.35	.40
B287	SP123	1.25fr + 1.75fr dp yel grn	.35	.40
B288	SP123	1.75fr + 2.50fr dp ultra	.35	.40
B289	SP123	2fr + 3.50fr red vio	.35	.40
B290	SP124	2.50fr + 4.50fr dl red brn	.35	.40
B291	SP124	3fr + 5fr dk ol grn	.35	.40
B292	SP128	5fr + 10fr grnsh blk	1.25	1.25
		Nos. B281-B292 (12)	5.10	5.65

The surtax was used for the restoration of the Abbey of Orval.

Souvenir Sheets

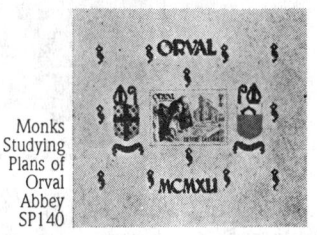

Monks Studying Plans of Orval Abbey SP140

1941, Oct.   Photo.   Perf. 11½
Inscribed "Belgie-Belgique"

| B303 | SP140 | 5fr + 15fr ultra | 7.00 | 7.00 |

Inscribed "Belgique-Belgie"

| B304 | SP140 | 5fr + 15fr ultra | 7.00 | 7.00 |

Surtax for the restoration of Orval Abbey. No. B304 exists perforated.
In 1942 these sheets were privately trimmed and overprinted "1142 1942" and ornament.

St. Martin Statue, Church of Dinant SP141

Lennik, Saint-Quentin SP142

BELGIUM

St. Martin's Church, Saint-Trond — SP146

Statues of St. Martin: 50c+10c, 3.25fr+3.25fr, Beck, Limburg. 60c+10c, 2.25fr+2.25fr, Dave on the Meuse. 1.75fr+50c, Hal, Brabant.

1941-42   Photo.   Perf. 11½
B305	SP141	10c + 5c chestnut	.15	.15
B306	SP142	35c + 5c dk bl grn	.15	.15
B307	SP142	50c + 10c violet	.15	.15
B308	SP142	60c + 10c dp brn	.15	.15
B309	SP142	1fr + 15c carmine	.15	.15
B310	SP141	1.50fr + 25c sl grn	.20	.20
B311	SP142	1.75fr + 50c dk ultra	.30	.30
B312	SP142	2.25fr + 2.25fr red vio	.30	.30
B313	SP142	3.25fr + 3.25fr brn vio	.30	.30
B314	SP146	5fr + 5fr dk ol grn	.45	.45
		Nos. B305-B314 (10)	2.30	2.30

Souvenir Sheets
Inscribed "Belgie-Belgique"

B315	SP146	5fr + 20fr vio brn ('42)	12.50	12.50

Inscribed "Belgique-Belgie"

B316	SP146	5fr + 20fr vio brn ('42)	12.50	12.50

In 1956, the Bureau Europeen de la Jeunesse et de l'Enfance privately overprinted Nos. B315-B316: "Congres Europeen de l'education 7-12 Mai 1956," in dark red and dark green respectively. A black bar obliterates "Winterhulp-Secours d'Hiver."

Souvenir Sheets

Queen Elisabeth Music Chapel — SP147

1941, Dec. 1   Photo.   Perf. 11½
Inscribed "Belgique-Belgie"

B317	SP147	10fr + 15fr ol blk	4.50	4.00

Inscribed "Belgie-Belique"

B318	SP147	10fr + 15fr ol blk	4.50	4.00

The surtax was for the Queen Elisabeth Music Foundation. These sheets were perforated with the monogram of Queen Elisabeth in 1942.

In 1954 Nos. B317-B318 were overprinted to for the birth cent. of Edgar Tinel, composer. These overprinted sheets were not postally valid.

Jean Bollandus SP148

Christophe Plantin SP156

Designs: 35c+5c, Andreas Vesalius. 50c+10c, Simon Stevinus. 60c+10c, Jean Van Helmont. 1fr+15c, Rembert Dodoens. 1.75fr+50c, Gerardus Mercator. 3.25fr+3.25fr, Abraham Ortelius. 5fr+5fr, Justus Lipsius.

1942, May 15   Photo.   Perf. 14x13½
B319	SP148	10c + 5c dl brn	.15	.15
B320	SP148	35c + 5c gray grn	.15	.15
B321	SP148	50c + 10c fawn	.15	.15
B322	SP148	60c + 10c grnsh blk	.15	.15

Engr.
B323	SP148	1fr + 15c brt rose	.15	.15
B324	SP148	1.75fr + 50c dl bl	.20	.20
B325	SP148	3.25fr + 3.25fr lil rose	.20	.20
B326	SP148	5fr + 5fr vio	.25	.25

Perf. 13½x14
B327	SP156	10fr + 30fr red org	.95	1.00
		Nos. B319-B327 (9)	2.35	2.40

The surtax was used to help fight tuberculosis. No. B327 was sold by subscription at the Brussels Post Office, July 1-10, 1942.

Belgian Prisoner — SP158

1942, Oct. 1   Perf. 11½
B331	SP158	5fr + 45fr olive gray	5.50	5.50

The surtax was for prisoners of war. Value includes a brown inscribed label which alternates with the stamps in the sheet.

SP159

SP164

SP162

SP168

Various Statues of St. Martin.

1942-43
B332	SP159	10c + 5c org	.15	.15
B333	SP159	35c + 5c dk bl grn	.15	.15
B334	SP159	50c + 10c dp brn	.15	.15
B335	SP162	60c + 10c blk	.15	.15
B336	SP159	1fr + 15c brt rose	.15	.15
B337	SP164	1.50fr + 25c grnsh blk	.20	.20
B338	SP164	1.75fr + 50c dk bl	.20	.20
B339	SP162	2.25fr + 2.25fr brn	.20	.25
B340	SP162	3.25fr + 3.25fr brt red vio	.35	.40
B341	SP168	5fr + 10fr hn brn	.50	.45
B342	SP168	10fr + 20fr rose brn & vio brn ('43)	.65	.65

Inscribed "Belgique-Belgie"

B343	SP168	10fr + 20fr gldn brn & vio brn ('43)	.65	.65
		Nos. B332-B343 (12)	3.60	3.45

The surtax was for winter relief.
Issue dates: Nos. B332-B341, Nov. 12, 1942. Nos. B342-B343, Apr. 3, 1943.

Prisoners of War — SP170

#B345, 2 prisoners with package from home.

1943, May   Photo.   Perf. 11½
B344	SP170	1fr + 30fr ver	2.50	2.50
B345	SP170	1fr + 30fr brn rose	2.50	2.50

The surtax was used for prisoners of war.

Roof Tiler SP172

Coppersmith SP173

Statues in Petit Sablon Park, Brussels: 35c+5c, Blacksmith. 60c+10c, Gunsmith. 1fr+15c, Armsmith. 1.75fr+75c, Goldsmith. 3.25fr+3.25fr, Fishdealer. 5fr+25fr, Watchmaker.

1943, June 1
B346	SP172	10c + 5c chnt brn	.15	.15
B347	SP172	35c + 5c grn	.15	.15
B348	SP173	50c + 10c dk brn	.15	.15
B349	SP173	60c + 10c slate	.15	.15
B350	SP173	1fr + 15c dl rose brn	.15	.15
B351	SP173	1.75fr + 75c ultra	.20	.20
B352	SP173	3.25fr + 3.25fr brt red vio	.30	.40
B353	SP173	5fr + 25fr dk pur	.50	.55
		Nos. B346-B353 (8)	1.75	1.90

Surtax for the control of tuberculosis.

"O" — SP180

"ORVAL" — SP185

1943, Oct. 9
B354	SP180	50c + 1fr "O"	.50	.50
B355	SP180	60c + 1.90fr "R"	.30	.25
B356	SP180	1fr + 3fr "V"	.30	.25
B357	SP180	1.75fr + 5.25fr "A"	.30	.25
B358	SP180	3.25fr + 16.75fr "L"	.40	.40
B359	SP185	5fr + 30fr dp brn	.75	.75
		Nos. B354-B359 (6)	2.55	2.40

Surtax aided restoration of Orval Abbey.

St. Leonard Church, Leau — SP186

St. Martin Church, Courtrai SP190

Basilica of St. Martin, Angre SP191

Notre Dame, Hal — SP193

St. Martin SP194

Designs: 35c+5c, St. Martin Church, Dion-le-Val. 50c+15c, St. Martin Church, Alost. 60c+20c, St. Martin Church, Liege. 3.25fr+11.75fr, St. Martin Church, Loppem. No. B369, St. Martin, beggar and Meuse landscape.

1943-44
B360	SP186	10c + 5c dp brn	.15	.15
B361	SP186	35c + 5c dk bl grn	.20	.20
B362	SP186	50c + 15c ol blk	.30	.30
B363	SP186	60c + 20c brt red vio	.30	.40
B364	SP190	1fr + 1fr rose brn	.40	.40
B365	SP191	1.75fr + 4.25fr dp ultra	.90	.65
B366	SP186	3.25fr + 11.75fr red lil	.90	.65
B367	SP193	5fr + 25fr dk bl	1.25	1.25
B368	SP194	10fr + 30fr gray grn ('44)	.90	.90
B369	SP194	10fr + 30fr blk brn ('44)	.90	.90
		Nos. B360-B369 (10)	6.20	5.75

Surtax for winter relief.

> Catalogue values for unused stamps in this section, from this point to the end of the section, are for Never Hinged items.

"Daedalus and Icarus" SP196

Sir Anthony Van Dyck, Self-portrait SP200

Paintings by Van Dyck: 50c+2.50fr, "The Good Samaritan." 60c+3.40fr, Detail of "Christ Healing the Paralytic." 1fr+5fr, "Madonna and Child." 5fr+30fr, "St. Sebastian."

1944, Apr. 16   Photo.   Perf. 11½
Crosses in Carmine
B370	SP196	35c + 1.65fr dk sl grn	.40	.30
B371	SP196	50c + 2.50fr grnsh blk	.40	.30
B372	SP196	60c + 3.40fr blk brn	.40	.30
B373	SP196	1fr + 5fr dk car	.60	.45
B374	SP200	1.75fr + 8.25fr int bl	.75	.60
B375	SP196	5fr + 30fr cop brn	.75	.60
		Nos. B370-B375 (6)	3.30	2.55

The surtax was for the Belgian Red Cross.

BELGIUM

Jan van Eyck — SP202
Godfrey of Bouillon — SP203 

Designs: 50c+25c, Jacob van Maerlant. 60c+40c, Jean Joses de Dinant. 1fr+50c, Jacob van Artevelde. 1.75fr+4.25fr, Charles Joseph de Ligne. 2.25fr+8.25fr, Andre Gretry. 3.25fr+11.25fr, Jan Moretus-Plantin. 5fr+35fr, Jan van Ruysbroeck.

1944, May 31

B376	SP202	10c + 15c dk pur	.40	.25
B377	SP203	35c + 15c green	.40	.25
B378	SP203	50c + 25c chnt brn	.40	.25
B379	SP203	60c + 40c ol blk	.40	.25
B380	SP203	1fr + 50c rose brn	.40	.25
B381	SP203	1.75fr + 4.25fr ultra	.40	.25
B382	SP203	2.25fr + 8.25fr grnsh blk	1.00	.55
B383	SP203	3.25fr + 11.25fr dk brn	.40	.25
B384	SP203	5fr + 35fr sl bl	.70	.70
		Nos. B376-B384 (9)	4.50	3.00

The surtax was for prisoners of war.

Sons of Aymon Astride Bayard — SP211
Brabo Slaying the Giant Antigoon — SP212 
Till Eulenspiegel Singing to Nele — SP214 

Designs: 50c+10c, St. Hubert converted by stag with crucifix. 1fr+15fr, St. George slaying the dragon. 1.75fr+5.25fr, Genevieve of Brabant with son and roe-deer. 3.25fr+11.75fr, Tchantches wrestling with the Saracen. 5fr+25fr, St. Gertrude rescuing the knight with the cards.

1944, June 25

B385	SP211	10c + 5c choc	.15	.20
B386	SP212	35c + 5c dk bl grn	.15	.20
B387	SP211	50c + 10c dl vio	.15	.20
B388	SP214	60c + 10c blk brn	.15	.20
B389	SP211	1fr + 15c rose brn	.15	.20
B390	SP214	1.75fr + 5.25fr ultra	.20	.30
B391	SP214	3.25fr + 11.75fr grnsh blk	.35	.50
B392	SP211	5fr + 25fr dk bl	.45	.70
		Nos. B385-B392 (8)	1.75	2.50

The surtax was for the control of tuberculosis. Nos. B385-B389 were overprinted "Breendonk+10fr." in 1946 by the Union Royale Philatelique for an exhibition at Brussels. They had no postal validity.

Union of the Flemish and Walloon Peoples in their Sorrow — SP219

Union in Reconstruction — SP220

1945, May 1 Perf. 11½ Unwmk. Photo.

B395	SP219	1fr + 30fr carmine	1.25	.90
B396	SP220	1¾fr + 30fr brt ultra	1.25	.90

1945, July 21 Size: 34½x23½mm

B397	SP219	1fr + 9fr scarlet	.25	.20
B398	SP220	1fr + 9fr car rose	.25	.20
		Nos. B395-B398 (4)	3.00	2.20

Surtax for the postal employees' relief fund.

Prisoner of War — SP221
Reunion — SP222 
Awaiting Execution — SP223 
Symbolical Figures "Recovery of Freedom" — SP225 

Design: 70c+30c, 3.50fr+3.50fr, Member of Resistance Movement.

1945, Sept. 10

B399	SP221	10c + 15c orange	.15	.15
B400	SP222	20c + 20c dp purple	.15	.15
B401	SP223	60c + 25c sepia	.15	.15
B402	SP221	70c + 30c dp yel grn	.15	.15
B403	SP221	75c + 50c org brn	.15	.15
B404	SP222	1fr + 75c brt bl grn	.25	.20
B405	SP223	1.50fr + 1fr brt red	.25	.20
B406	SP221	3.50fr + 3.50fr brt bl	1.10	1.00
B407	SP225	5fr + 40fr brown	.90	.90
		Nos. B399-B407 (9)	3.25	3.05

The surtax was for the benefit of prisoners of war, displaced persons, families of executed victims and members of the Resistance Movement.

Arms of West Flanders — SP226

Arms of Provinces: 20c+20c, Luxembourg. 60c+25c, East Flanders. 70c+30c, Namur. 75c+50c, Limburg. 1fr+75c, Hainaut. 1.50fr+1fr, Antwerp. 3.50fr+1.50fr, Liege. 5fr+45fr, Brabant.

1945, Dec. 1

B408	SP226	10c + 15c sl blk & sl gray	.15	.15
B409	SP226	20c + 20c rose car & rose	.15	.15
B410	SP226	60c + 25c dk brn & pale brn	.15	.15
B411	SP226	70c + 30c dk grn & lt grn	.15	.15
B412	SP226	75c + 50c org brn & pale org brn	.25	.20
B413	SP226	1fr + 75c pur & lt pur	.15	.15
B414	SP226	1.50fr + 1fr car & rose	.15	.15
B415	SP226	3.50fr + 1.50fr dp bl & gray bl	.30	.20
B416	SP226	5fr + 45fr dp mag & cerise	2.25	1.90
		Nos. B408-B416 (9)	3.70	3.20

The surtax was for tuberculosis prevention.

Father Joseph Damien — SP227
Father Damien Comforting Leper — SP229 
Leper Colony, Molokai Island, Hawaii — SP228 
Symbols of Wisdom and Patriotism — SP230 
"In Memoriam" — SP232 
François Bovesse — SP231 
Emile Vandervelde — SP233 
Sower — SP235 
Vandervelde, Laborer and Family — SP234 

1946, July 15 Perf. 11½ Unwmk. Photo.

B417	SP227	65c + 75c dk blue	1.00	.65
B418	SP228	1.35fr + 2fr brown	1.00	.65
B419	SP229	1.75fr + 18fr rose brn	1.65	1.10

The surtax was for the erection of a museum in Louvain.

1946, July 15

B420	SP230	65c + 75c violet	1.00	.65
B421	SP231	1.35fr + 2fr dk org brn	1.40	.80
B422	SP232	1.75fr + 18fr car rose	1.90	1.10

The surtax was for the erection of a "House of the Fine Arts" at Namur.

1946, July 15

B423	SP233	65c + 75c dk sl grn	1.25	.65
B424	SP234	1.35fr + 2fr dk vio bl	1.40	.80
B425	SP235	1.75fr + 18fr dp car	1.90	1.10
		Nos. B417-B425 (9)	12.50	7.50

The surtax was for the Emile Vandervelde Institute, to promote social, economic and cultural activities.
For surcharges see Nos. CB4-CB12.

Pepin of Herstal — SP236
Malines — SP241 

1fr+50c, Charlemagne. 1.50fr+1fr, Godfrey of Bouillon. 3.50fr+1.50fr, Robert of Jerusalem. #B430-B431, Baldwin of Constantinople.

1946, Sept. 15 Engr. Perf. 11½x11

B426	SP236	75c + 25c green	.60	.35
B427	SP236	1fr + 50c violet	.90	.50
B428	SP236	1.50fr + 1fr plum	1.25	.65
B429	SP236	3.50fr + 1.50fr brt bl	1.50	.75
B430	SP236	5fr + 45fr red vio	12.00	7.00
B431	SP236	5fr + 45fr red org	15.00	7.75
		Nos. B426-B431 (6)	31.25	17.00

The surtax on Nos. B426-B429 was for the benefit of former prisoners of war, displaced persons, the families of executed patriots, and former members of the Resistance Movement.
The surtax on Nos. B430-B431 was divided among several welfare, national celebration and educational organizations.
Issue dates: Nos. B426-B429, Apr. 15; No. B430, Sept. 15; No. B431, Nov. 15.
See Nos. B437-B441, B465-B466, B472-B476.

1946, Dec. 2 Perf. 11½

Coats of Arms: 90c+60c, Dinant. 1.35fr+1.15fr, Ostend. 3.15fr+1.85fr, Verviers. 4.50fr+45.50fr, Louvain.

B432	SP241	65c + 35c rose car	.50	.50
B433	SP241	90c + 60c lemon	.50	.50
B434	SP241	1.35fr + 1.15fr dp grn	.50	.50
B435	SP241	3.15fr + 1.85fr blue	1.50	1.25
B436	SP241	4.50fr + 45.50fr dk vio brn	13.00	12.00
		Nos. B432-B436 (5)	16.00	14.75

The surtax was for anti-tuberculosis work. See Nos. B442-B446.

Type of 1946

Designs: 65c+35c, John II, Duke of Brabant. 90c+60c, Count Philip of Alsace. 1.35fr+1.15fr, William the Good. 3.15fr+1.85fr, Bishop Notger of Liege. 20fr+20fr, Philip the Noble.

1947, Sept. 25 Engr. Perf. 11½x11

B437	SP236	65c + 35c Prus grn	.60	.50
B438	SP236	90c + 60c yel grn	1.00	.75
B439	SP236	1.35fr + 1.15fr car	1.40	1.10
B440	SP236	3.15fr + 1.85fr ultra	2.00	1.65
B441	SP236	20fr + 20fr red vio	52.50	42.50
		Nos. B437-B441 (5)	57.50	46.50

The surtax was for victims of World War II.

Arms Type of 1946 Dated "1947"

Coats of Arms: 65c+35c, Nivelles. 90c+60c, St. Trond. 1.35fr+1.15fr, Charleroi. 3.15fr+1.85fr, St. Nicolas. 20fr+20fr, Bouillon.

1947, Dec. 15 Perf. 11½

B442	SP241	65c + 35c orange	.80	.65
B443	SP241	90c + 60c dp cl	.70	.65
B444	SP241	1.35fr + 1.15fr dk brn	1.00	.70
B445	SP241	3.15fr + 1.85fr dp bl	2.50	1.75
B446	SP241	20fr + 20fr dk grn	20.00	12.50
		Nos. B442-B446 (5)	25.00	16.25

The surtax was for anti-tuberculosis work.

BELGIUM

St. Benedict and King Totila — SP247

Achel Abbey SP248

Designs: 3.15fr+2.85fr, St. Benedict, legislator and builder. 10fr+10fr, Death of St. Benedict.

1948, Apr. 5   Photo.
B447 SP247   65c + 65c red brn   1.25   .55
B448 SP248   1.35fr + 1.35fr gray   1.75   .55
B449 SP247   3.15fr + 2.85fr dp ultra   2.50   1.90
B450 SP247   10fr + 10fr brt red vio   12.50   10.00
Nos. B447-B450 (4)   18.00   13.00

The surtax was to aid the Abbey of the Trappist Fathers at Achel.

St. Begga and Chevremont Castle — SP249

Chevremont Basilica and Convent SP250

Designs: 3.15fr+2.85fr, Madonna of Chevremont and Chapel. 10fr+10fr, Madonna of Mt. Carmel.

1948, Apr. 5   Unwmk.
B451 SP249   65c + 65c bl grn   1.00   .55
B452 SP250   1.35fr + 1.35fr dk car rose   1.65   1.05
B453 SP249   3.15fr + 2.85fr dp bl   2.25   1.90
B454 SP249   10fr + 10fr dp brn   12.00   10.00
Nos. B451-B454 (4)   16.90   13.00

The surtax was to aid the Basilica of the Carmelite Fathers of Chèvremont.

Anseele Monument Showing French Inscription — SP251

90c+60c, View of Ghent. 1.35fr+1.15fr, Van Artevelde monument, Ghent. 3.15fr+1.85fr, Anseele Monument, Flemish inscription.

1948, June 21   Perf. 14x13½
B455 SP251   65c + 35c rose red   2.75   1.10
B456 SP251   90c + 60c gray   3.50   1.90
B457 SP251   1.35fr + 1.15fr hn brn   2.25   1.50
B458 SP251   3.15fr + 1.85fr brt bl   8.50   5.00
a.   Souv. sheet of 4, #B455-B458   140.00   55.00
Nos. B455-B458 (4)   17.00   9.50

Issued to honor Edouard Anseele, statesman, founder of the Belgian Socialist Party.
No. B458a sold for 50fr.
For surcharges see Nos. 395-398.

Statue "The Unloader" SP252

Underground Fighter SP253

1948, Sept. 4   Perf. 11½x11
B460 SP252   10fr + 10fr gray grn   35.00   19.00
B461 SP253   10fr + 10fr red brn   20.00   11.00

The surtax was used toward erection of monuments at Antwerp and Liege.

Portrait Type of 1946 and

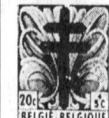

Double Barred Cross — SP254

Designs: 4fr+3.25fr, Isabella of Austria. 20fr+20fr, Archduke Albert of Austria.

1948, Dec. 15   Photo.   Perf. 13½x14
B462 SP254   20c + 5c dk sl grn   .50   .15
B463 SP254   1.20fr + 30c magenta   1.25   .70
B464 SP254   1.75fr + 25c red   1.75   .60

     Engr.   Perf. 11½x11
B465 SP236   4fr + 3.25fr ultra   9.50   6.50
B466 SP236   20fr + 20fr Prus grn   42.50   30.00
Nos. B462-B466 (5)   55.50   37.95

The surtax was divided among several charities.

Souvenir Sheets

Rogier van der Weyden Paintings — SP255

Paintings by van der Weyden (No. B466A): 90c, Virgin and Child. 1.75fr, Christ on the Cross. 4fr, Mary Magdalene.
Paintings by Jordaens (No. B466B): 90c, Woman Reading. 1.75fr, The Flutist. 4fr, Old Woman Reading Letter.

1949, Apr. 1   Photo.   Perf. 11½
B466A SP255   Sheet of 3   125.00   110.00
c.   90c deep brown   37.50   32.50
d.   1.75fr deep rose lilac   37.50   32.50
e.   4fr dark violet blue   37.50   32.50
B466B SP255   Sheet of 3   125.00   110.00
f.   90c dark violet   37.50   32.50
g.   1.75fr red   37.50   32.50
h.   4fr blue   37.50   32.50

The surtax went to various cultural and philanthropic organizations. Sheets sold for 50fr each.
Gum on Nos. B466A-B466B is irregularly applied.

Guido Gezelle — SP256

1949, Nov. 15   Photo.   Perf. 14x13½
B467 SP256   1.75fr + 75c dk Prus grn   2.50   1.75

50th anniversary of the death of Guido Gezelle, poet. The surtax was for the Guido Gezelle Museum, Bruges.

Arnica — SP257

Designs: 65c+10c, Sand grass. 90c+10c, Wood myrtle. 1.20fr+30c, Field poppy. 1.75fr+25c, Philip the Good. 3fr+1.50fr, Charles V. 4fr+2fr, Maria-Christina. 6fr+3fr, Charles of Lorraine. 8fr+4fr, Maria-Theresa.

1949, Dec. 20   Typo.   Perf. 13½x14
B468 SP257   20c + 5c multi   .50   .50
B469 SP257   65c + 10c multi   1.25   1.10
B470 SP257   90c + 10c multi   2.00   1.50
B471 SP257   1.20fr + 30c multi   2.50   1.75

     Engr.   Perf. 11½x11
B472 SP236   1.75fr + 25c red org   1.40   .80
B473 SP236   3fr + 1.50fr dp claret   10.00   6.75
B474 SP236   4fr + 2fr ultra   10.00   8.00
B475 SP236   6fr + 3fr choc   16.00   11.00
B476 SP236   8fr + 4fr dl grn   16.00   8.75
Nos. B468-B476 (9)   59.65   40.15

The surtax was apportioned among several welfare organizations.

Arms of Belgium and Great Britain SP258

British Memorial SP260

Design: 2.50fr+50c, British tanks at Hertain.

     Perf. 13½x14, 11½
1950, Mar. 15
B477 SP258   80c + 20c green   1.50   1.00
B478 SP258   2.50fr + 50c red   5.00   3.75
B479 SP260   4fr + 2fr dp bl   9.25   6.25
Nos. B477-B479 (3)   15.75   11.00

6th anniv. of the liberation of Belgian territory by the British army.

Hurdling SP261

Relay Race SP262

Designs: 90c+10c, Javelin throwing. 4fr+2fr, Pole vault. 8fr+4fr, Foot race.

1950, July 1   Engr.   Perf. 14x13½, 13½x14
B480 SP261   20c + 5c brt grn   .90   .75   Unwmk.
B481 SP261   90c + 10c vio brn   3.75   1.90
B482 SP262   1.75fr + 25c car   4.50   1.90
a.   Souvenir sheet of 2   55.00   42.50
B483 SP261   4fr + 2fr lt bl   35.00   19.00
B484 SP261   8fr + 4fr dp grn   40.00   24.00
Nos. B480-B484 (5)   84.15   47.55

Issued to publicize the European Athletic Games, Brussels, August 1950.
The margins of No. B482a were trimmed in April, 1951, and an overprint ("25 Francs pour le Fonds Sportif-25e Fofre Internationale Bruxelles") was added in red in French and in black in Flemish by a private committee. These pairs of altered sheets were sold at the Brussels Fair.

Gentian SP263

Sijsele Sanatorium SP264

Tombeek Sanatorium — SP265

Designs: 65c+10c, Cotton Grass. 90c+10c, Foxglove. 1.20fr+30c, Limonia. 4fr+2fr, Jauche Sanatorium.

1950, Dec. 20   Typo.   Perf. 14x13½
B485 SP263   20c + 5c multi   .80   .40
B486 SP263   65c + 10c multi   1.50   .80
B487 SP263   90c + 10c multi   1.65   1.10
B488 SP263   1.20fr + 30c multi   2.75   2.25

     Perf. 11½
     Engr.
     Cross in Red
B489 SP264   1.75fr + 25c car   2.50   1.40
B490 SP264   4fr + 2fr blue   13.00   7.00
B491 SP265   8fr + 4fr bl grn   21.00   15.00
Nos. B485-B491 (7)   43.20   27.95

The surtax was for tuberculosis prevention and other charitable purposes.

Chemist — SP266

Allegory of Peace — SP268

Colonial Instructor and Class — SP267

1951, Mar. 27   Unwmk.
B492 SP266   80c + 20c grn   1.40   1.00
B493 SP267   2.50fr + 50c vio brn   9.50   5.00
B494 SP268   4fr + 2fr dp bl   10.25   6.00
Nos. B492-B494 (3)   21.15   12.00

Surtax for the reconstruction fund of the UNESCO.

Monument to Political Prisoners SP269

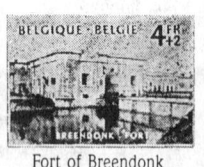

Fort of Breendonk SP270

8fr+4fr, Monument: profile of figure on pedestal.

1951, Aug. 20   Photo.   Perf. 11½
B495 SP269   1.75fr + 25c blk brn   2.50   1.75
B496 SP270   4fr + 2fr bl & sl gray   17.00   14.00
B497 SP269   8fr + 4fr dk bl grn   22.50   17.00
Nos. B495-B497 (3)   42.00   32.75

The surtax was for the erection of a national monument.

Queen Elisabeth — SP271

BELGIUM

1951, Sept. 22

B498 SP271	90c + 10c grnsh gray	1.75	.75
B499 SP271	1.75fr + 25c plum	2.25	1.50
B500 SP271	3fr + 1fr green	21.00	9.25
B501 SP271	4fr + 2fr gray bl	24.00	12.00
B502 SP271	8fr + 4fr sepia	30.00	14.00
Nos. B498-B502 (5)		79.00	37.50

The surtax was for the Queen Elisabeth Medical Foundation.

Cross, Sun Rays and Dragon SP272

Beersel Castle SP273

Horst Castle — SP274

Castles: 4fr+2fr, Lavaux St. Anne. 8fr+4fr, Veves.

1951, Dec. 17   Engr.   Unwmk.

B503 SP272	20c + 5c red	.25	.20
B504 SP272	65c + 10c dp ultra	.85	.60
B505 SP272	90c + 10c sepia	.90	.80
B506 SP272	1.20fr + 30c rose vio	1.25	.90
B507 SP273	1.75fr + 75c red brn	1.75	1.50
B508 SP274	3fr + 1fr yel grn	12.00	7.50
B509 SP273	4fr + 2fr blue	14.00	8.50
B510 SP274	8fr + 4fr gray	19.00	11.00
Nos. B503-B510 (8)		50.00	31.00

The surtax was for anti-tuberculosis work. See Nos. B523-B526, B547-B550.

Main Altar SP275

Basilica of the Sacred Heart Koekelberg SP276

Procession Bearing Relics of St. Albert of Louvain — SP277

1952, Mar. 1   Photo.   Perf. 11½

B511 SP275	1.75fr + 25c blk brn	1.50	1.25
B512 SP276	4fr + 2fr indigo	11.00	7.50

Engr.

B513 SP277	8fr + 4fr vio brn	15.00	9.25
a.	Souvenir sheet, #B511-B513	250.00	125.00
Nos. B511-B513 (3)		27.50	18.00

25th anniv. of the Cardinalate of J. E. Van Roey, Primate of Belgium. The surtax was for the Basilica. No. B513a sold for 30fr.

Beaulieu Castle, Malines SP278

August Vermeylen SP279

1952, May 14   Engr.   Laid Paper

B514 SP278	40fr + 10fr lt grnsh bl	175.00	175.00

Issued on the occasion of the 13th Universal Postal Union Congress, Brussels, 1952.

Perf. 11½

1952, Oct. 24   Unwmk.   Photo.

Portraits: 80c+40c, Karel Van de Woestijne. 90c+45c, Charles de Coster. 1.75fr+75c, M. Maeterlinck. 4fr+2fr, Emile Verhaeren. 8fr+4fr, Hendrik Conscience.

B515 SP279	65c + 30c purple	1.75	.90
B516 SP279	80c + 40c dk grn	3.75	1.10
B517 SP279	90c + 45c sepia	2.75	1.25
B518 SP279	1.75fr + 75c cer	3.75	1.75
B519 SP279	4fr + 2fr bl vio	30.00	19.00
B520 SP279	8fr + 4fr dk brn	30.00	21.00
Nos. B515-B520 (6)		72.00	45.00

1952, Nov. 15

4fr, Emile Verhaeren. 8fr, Hendrik Conscience.

B521 SP279	4fr (+ 9fr) blue	100.00	67.50
B522 SP279	8fr (+ 9fr) dk car rose	100.00	67.50

On Nos. B521-B522, the denomination is repeated at either side of the stamp. The surtax is expressed on se-tenant labels bearing quotations of Verhaeren (in French) and Conscience (in Flemish). Value is for stamp with label.

A 9-line black overprint was privately applied to these labels: "Conference Internationale de la Musique Bruxelles UNESCO International Music Conference Brussels 1953*".

Type of 1951 Dated "1952," and

Arms of Malmédy — SP281

Castle Ruins, Burgreuland SP282

Designs: 4fr+2fr, Vesdre Dam, Eupen. 8fr+4fr, St. Vitus, patron saint of Saint-Vith.

1952, Dec. 15   Engr.

B523 SP272	20c + 5c red brn	.40	.40
B524 SP272	80c + 20c green	.85	.60
B525 SP272	1.20fr + 30c lil rose	1.75	1.00
B526 SP272	1.75fr + 50c ol brn	1.75	1.00
B527 SP281	2fr + 75c carmine	3.25	2.25
B528 SP282	3fr + 1.50fr choc	14.00	8.75
B529 SP281	4fr + 2fr blue	12.00	8.00
B530 SP281	8fr + 4fr vio brn	21.00	11.00
Nos. B523-B530 (8)		55.00	33.00

The surtax on Nos. B523-B530 was for anti-tuberculosis and other charitable works.

Walthère Dewé SP283

Princess Josephine-Charlotte SP284

1953, Feb. 16   Photo.

B531 SP283	2fr + 1fr brn car	3.25	1.75

The surtax was for the construction of a memorial to Walthère Dewé, Underground leader in World War II.

1953, Mar. 14   Cross in Red

B532 SP284	80c + 20c ol grn	1.25	.70
B533 SP284	1.20fr + 30c brown	1.75	.80
B534 SP284	2fr + 50c rose lake	1.25	1.25
a.	Booklet pane of 8	80.00	65.00
B535 SP284	2.50fr + 50c crimson	14.00	6.75
B536 SP284	4fr + 1fr brt blue	9.25	5.25
B537 SP284	5fr + 2fr sl grn	11.00	6.75
Nos. B532-B537 (6)		38.50	21.50

The surtax was for the Belgian Red Cross. The selvage of No. B534a is inscribed in French or Dutch. The value is for the French.

Boats at Dock — SP285

Bridge and Citadel, Namur — SP286

Allegory — SP287

Designs: 1.20fr+30c, Bridge at Bouillon. 2fr+50c, Antwerp waterfront. 4fr+2fr, Wharf at Ghent. 8fr+4fr, Meuse River at Freyr.

1953, June 22   Unwmk.   Perf. 11½

B538 SP285	80c + 20c green	1.00	.85
B539 SP285	1.20fr + 30c redsh brn	1.75	1.65
B540 SP285	2fr + 50c sepia	2.25	2.00
B541 SP286	2.50fr + 50c dp mag	11.00	8.50
B542 SP286	4fr + 2fr vio bl	16.00	8.50
B543 SP286	8fr + 4fr gray blk	20.00	8.50
Nos. B538-B543 (6)		52.00	30.00

The surtax was used to promote tourism in the Ardenne-Meuse region and for various cultural works.

1953, Oct. 26   Engr.

B544 SP287	80c + 20c green	3.50	2.50
B545 SP287	2.50fr + 1fr rose car	32.50	24.00
B546 SP287	4fr + 1.50fr blue	37.50	30.00
Nos. B544-B546 (3)		73.50	56.50

The surtax was for the European Bureau of Childhood and Youth.

Type of 1951 Dated "1953," and

Ernest Malvoz — SP288

Robert Koch — SP289

Portraits: 3fr+1.50fr, Carlo Forlanini. 4fr+2fr, Leon Charles Albert Calmette.

1953, Dec. 15

B547 SP272	20c + 5c blue	.50	.45
B548 SP272	80c + 20c rose vio	1.00	.60
B549 SP272	1.20fr + 30c choc	1.25	.80
B550 SP272	1.50fr + 50c dk gray	1.75	1.00
B551 SP288	2fr + 75c dk grn	3.00	1.65
B552 SP288	3fr + 1.50fr dk red	13.00	8.50
B553 SP288	4fr + 2fr ultra	11.00	7.00
B554 SP289	8fr + 4fr choc	17.50	11.00
Nos. B547-B554 (8)		49.00	30.00

The surtax was for anti-tuberculosis and other charitable works.

King Albert I Statue — SP290

Albert I Monument, Namur SP291

Design: 9fr+4.50fr, Cliffs of Marche-les-Dames.

1954, Feb. 17   Photo.

B555 SP290	2fr + 50c chnt brn	2.50	1.75
B556 SP291	4fr + 2fr blue	15.00	11.00
B557 SP290	9fr + 4.50fr ol blk	22.50	12.00
Nos. B555-B557 (3)		40.00	24.75

20th anniv. of the death of King Albert I. The surtax aided in the erection of the monument pictured on #B556.

Political Prisoners' Monument — SP292

Camp and Fort, Breendonk SP293

Design: 9fr+4.50fr, Political prisoners' monument (profile).

1954, Apr. 1   Unwmk.   Perf. 11½

B558 SP292	2fr + 1fr red	12.50	7.00
B559 SP293	4fr + 2fr dk brn	30.00	17.50
B560 SP292	9fr + 4.50fr ol grn	32.50	17.50
Nos. B558-B560 (3)		75.00	42.00

The surtax was used toward the creation of a monument to political prisoners.

Gatehouse and Gateway SP294

Nuns in Courtyard — SP295

BELGIUM

Our Lady of the Vine — SP296

Designs: 2fr+1fr, Swans in stream. 7fr+3.50fr Nuns at well. 8fr+4fr, Statue above door.

1954, May 15
B561	SP294	80c + 20c dk bl grn	1.00	.75
B562	SP294	2fr + 1fr crimson	11.00	1.50
B563	SP295	4fr + 2fr violet	16.00	9.25
B564	SP295	7fr + 3.50fr lil rose	35.00	22.50
B565	SP295	8fr + 4fr brown	32.50	19.00
B566	SP296	9fr + 4.50fr gray bl	55.00	30.00
		Nos. B561-B566 (6)	150.50	83.00

The surtax was for the Friends of the Beguinage of Bruges.

Child's Head SP297

"The Blind Man and the Paralytic," by Antoine Carte SP298

1954, Dec. 1   Engr.
B567	SP297	20c + 5c dk grn	.50	.50
B568	SP297	80c + 20c dk gray	1.00	.85
B569	SP297	1.20fr + 30c org brn	1.50	1.00
B570	SP297	1.50fr + 50c purple	1.75	1.65
B571	SP298	2fr + 75c rose car	7.25	3.50
B572	SP298	4fr + 1fr brt blue	16.00	9.50
		Nos. B567-B572 (6)	28.00	17.00

The surtax was for anti-tuberculosis work.

Ernest Solvay SP299

Jean-Jacques Dony — SP300

Portraits: 1.20fr+30c, Egide Walschaerts. 25fr+50c, Leo H. Baekeland. 3fr+1fr, Jean-Etienne Lenoir. 4fr+2fr, Emile Fourcault and Emile Gobbe.

Perf. 11½
1955, Oct. 22   Unwmk.   Photo.
B573	SP299	20c + 5c brn & dk brn	.40	.35
B574	SP300	80c + 20c violet	1.00	.50
B575	SP300	1.20fr + 30c indigo	1.10	.65
B576	SP300	2fr + 50c dp car	4.00	2.50
B577	SP300	3fr + 1fr dk grn	12.50	6.25
B578	SP299	4fr + 2fr brown	12.50	6.25
		Nos. B573-B578 (6)	31.50	16.50

Issued in honor of Belgian scientists.
The surtax was for the benefit of various cultural organizations.

"The Joys of Spring" by E. Canneel — SP301

Einar Holböll — SP302

Portraits: 4fr+2fr, John D. Rockefeller. 8fr+4fr, Sir Robert W. Philip.

1955, Dec. 5   Unwmk.   Perf. 11½
B579	SP301	20c + 5c red lilac	.70	.30
B580	SP301	80c + 20c green	1.00	.65
B581	SP301	1.20fr + 30c redsh brn	1.40	.80
B582	SP301	1.50fr + 50c vio bl	1.40	1.00
B583	SP302	2fr + 50c carmine	8.50	4.75
B584	SP302	4fr + 2fr ultra	17.50	10.00
B585	SP302	8fr + 4fr ol gray	21.00	12.50
		Nos. B579-B585 (7)	51.50	30.00

The surtax was for anti-tuberculosis work.

Palace of Charles of Lorraine — SP303

Queen Elisabeth and Sonata by Mozart — SP304

Design: 2fr+1fr, Mozart at age 7.

1956, Mar. 5   Engr.
B586	SP303	80c + 20c steel bl	1.00	1.00
B587	SP303	2fr + 1fr rose lake	4.25	3.00
B588	SP304	4fr + 2fr dull pur	6.75	3.75
		Nos. B586-B588 (3)	12.00	7.75

200th anniversary of the birth of Wolfgang Amadeus Mozart, composer.
The surtax was for the benefit of the Pro-Mozart Committee in Belgium.

Queen Elisabeth — SP305

1956, Aug. 16   Photo.
B589	SP305	80c + 20c slate grn	1.00	1.00
B590	SP305	2fr + 1fr deep plum	2.75	1.50
B591	SP305	4fr + 2fr brown	4.25	2.50
		Nos. B589-B591 (3)	8.00	5.00

Issued in honor of the 80th birthday of Queen Elisabeth. The surtax went to the Queen Elisabeth Foundation. See No. 659.

Ship with Cross SP306

Infant on Scales SP307

Rehabilitation — SP308

Design: 4fr+2fr, X-Ray examination.

1956, Dec. 17   Engr.
B592	SP306	20c + 5c redsh brn	.35	.30
B593	SP306	80c + 20c green	.75	.60
B594	SP306	1.20fr + 30c dl lil	.90	.60
B595	SP306	1.5fr + 50c lt sl bl	.95	.90
B596	SP307	2fr + 50c ol grn	2.25	1.65
B597	SP307	4fr + 2fr dl pur	11.00	6.25
B598	SP308	8fr + 4fr dp car	11.00	7.25
		Nos. B592-B598 (7)	27.20	17.55

The surtax was for anti-tuberculosis work.

Charles Plisnier and Albrecht Rodenbach SP309

80c+20c, Emiel Vliebergh & Maurice Wilmotte. 1.20fr+30c, Paul Pastur & Julius Hoste. 2fr+50c, Lodewijk de Raet & Jules Destree. 3fr+1fr, Constantin Meunier & Constant Permeke. 4fr+2fr, Lieven Gevaert & Edouard Empain.

Perf. 11½
1957, June 8   Unwmk.   Photo.
B599	SP309	20c + 5c brt vio	.40	.35
B600	SP309	80c + 20c lt red brn	.55	.35
B601	SP309	1.20f + 30c blk brn	.65	.60
B602	SP309	2fr + 50c claret	1.65	.95
B603	SP309	3fr + 1fr dk ol grn	2.25	1.75
B604	SP309	4fr + 2fr vio bl	3.25	2.50
		Nos. B599-B604 (6)	8.75	6.50

The surtax was for the benefit of various cultural organizations.

Dogs and Antarctic Camp SP310

1957, Oct. 18   Engr.   Perf. 11½
B605	SP310	5fr + 2.50fr gray, org & vio brn	3.00	2.25
a.		Sheet of 4, #B605b	140.00	125.00
b.		Blue, slate & red brown	30.00	25.00

Surtax for Belgian Antarctic Expedition, 1957-58.

Gen. Patton's Grave and Flag — SP311

Gen. George S. Patton, Jr. — SP312

Designs: 2.50fr+50c, Memorial, Bastogne. 3fr+1fr, Gen. Patton decorating Brig. Gen. Anthony C. McAuliffe. 6fr+3fr, Tanks of 1918 and 1944.

1957, Oct. 28   Photo.
Size: 36x25mm, 25x36mm
B606	SP311	1fr + 50c dk gray	1.25	.85
B607	SP311	2.50fr + 50c ol grn	1.75	1.50
B608	SP311	3fr + 1fr red brn	2.75	1.65
B609	SP312	5fr + 2.50fr grysh bl	6.25	5.00

Size: 53x35mm
B610	SP311	6fr + 3fr pale brn car	10.00	6.00
		Nos. B606-B610 (5)	22.00	15.00

The surtax was for the General Patton Memorial Committee and Patriotic Societies.

Adolphe Max — SP313

1957, Nov. 10   Engr.
B611	SP313	2.50fr + 1fr ultra	1.25	.75

18th anniversary of the death of Adolphe Max, mayor of Brussels. The surtax was for the national "Adolphe Max" fund.

"Chinels," Fosses SP314

"Op Signoorken," Malines SP315

Infanta Isabella Shooting Crossbow SP316

Legends: 1.50fr+50c, St. Remacle and the wolf. 2fr+1fr, Longman and the pea soup. 5fr+2fr, The Virgin with Inkwell, vert. 6fr+2.50fr, "Gilles" (clowns), Binche.

1957, Dec. 14   Engr. & Photo.
B612	SP314	30c + 20c	.20	.30
B613	SP315	1fr + 50c	.40	.30
B614	SP314	1.50fr + 50c	.80	.50
B615	SP315	2fr + 1fr	1.10	1.00
B616	SP316	2.50fr + 1fr	1.25	.90
B617	SP316	5fr + 2fr	3.25	2.25
B618	SP316	6fr + 2.50fr	4.50	3.25
		Nos. B612-B618 (7)	11.50	8.50

The surtax was for anti-tuberculosis work. See Nos. B631-B637.

Benelux Gate — SP317

Designs: 1fr+50c, Civil Engineering Pavilion. 1.50fr+50c, Ruanda-Urundi Pavilion. 2.50fr+1fr, Belgium 1900. 3fr+1.50fr, Atomium. 5fr+3fr, Telexpo Pavilion.

Perf. 11½
1958, Apr. 15   Unwmk.   Engr.
Size: 35½x24½mm
B619	SP317	30c + 20c multi	.15	.15
B620	SP317	1fr + 50c multi	.15	.15
B621	SP317	1.50fr + 50c multi	.25	.25
B622	SP317	2.50fr + 1fr multi	.45	.45
B623	SP317	3fr + 1.50fr multi	.90	.50

Size: 49x33mm
B624	SP317	5fr + 3fr multi	1.10	.50
		Nos. B619-B624 (6)	3.00	2.00

World's Fair, Brussels, Apr. 17-Oct. 19.

BELGIUM

Marguerite van Eyck
by Jan van
Eyck — SP318

Christ Carrying
Cross, by
Hieronymus
Bosch — SP319

Paintings: 1.50fr+50c, St. Donatien, Jan Gossart. 2.50fr+1fr, Self-portrait, Lambert Lombard. 3fr+1.50fr, The Rower, James Ensor. 5fr+3fr, Henriette, Henri Evenepoel.

1958, Oct. 30   Photo.   Perf. 11½
Various Frames in Ocher and Brown
B625	SP318	30c + 20c dk ol grn	.25	.30
B626	SP319	1fr + 50c mar	.75	.70
B627	SP318	1.50fr + 50c vio bl	1.00	.75
B628	SP318	2.50fr + 1fr dk brn	2.00	1.25
B629	SP319	3fr + 1.50fr dl red	2.75	2.00
B630	SP318	5fr + 3fr brt bl	5.25	5.00
		Nos. B625-B630 (6)	12.00	10.00

The surtax was for the benefit of various cultural organizations.

Type of 1957

Legends: 40c+10c, Elizabeth, Countess of Hoogstraten. 1fr+50c, Jean de Nivelles. 1.50fr+50c, St. Evermare play, Russon. 2fr+1fr, The Penitents of Furnes. 2.50fr+1fr, Manger and "Pax." 5fr+2fr, Sambre-Meuse procession. 6fr+2.50fr, Our Lady of Peace and "Pax," vert.

Engraved and Photogravure
1958, Dec. 6   Unwmk.   Perf. 11½
B631	SP314	40c + 10c ultra & brt grn	.30	.20
B632	SP315	1fr + 50c gray brn & org	.40	.30
B633	SP315	1.50fr + 50c cl & brt grn	.60	.35
B634	SP314	2fr + 1fr brn & red	.70	.50
B635	SP316	2.50fr + 1fr vio brn & bl grn	2.50	1.90
B636	SP316	5fr + 2fr cl & bl	3.75	3.00
B637	SP316	6fr + 2.50fr bl & rose red	4.75	4.50
		Nos. B631-B637 (7)	13.00	10.75

The surtax was for anti-tuberculosis work.

"Europe of the Heart" SP320

1959, Feb. 25   Photo.   Unwmk.
B638	SP320	1fr + 50c red lilac	.55	.30
B639	SP320	2.50fr + 1fr dk green	.95	.90
B640	SP320	5fr + 2.50fr dp brn	1.25	1.10
		Nos. B638-B640 (3)	2.75	2.30

The surtax was for aid for displaced persons.

Allegory of Blood Transfusion — SP321

Henri Dunant and Battlefield at Solferino — SP322

Design: 2.50fr+1fr, 3fr+1.50fr, Red Cross, broken sword and drop of blood, horiz.

1959, June 10   Photo.   Perf. 11½
B641	SP321	40c + 10c	.60	.30
B642	SP321	1fr + 50c	1.10	.45
B643	SP321	1.50fr + 50c	1.40	.60
B644	SP321	2.50fr + 1fr	1.90	1.10
B645	SP321	3fr + 1.50fr	4.75	2.50
B646	SP322	5fr + 3fr	7.25	3.25
		Nos. B641-B646 (6)	17.00	8.20

Cent. of the Intl. Red Cross idea. Surtax for the Red Cross and patriotic organizations.

Philip the Good — SP323

Arms of Philip the Good SP324

Designs: 1fr+50c, Charles the Bold. 1.50fr+50c, Emperor Maximilian of Austria. 2.50fr+1fr, Philip the Fair. 3fr+1.50fr, Charles V. Portraits from miniatures by Simon Bening (c. 1483-1561).

1959, July 4   Engr.
B647	SP323	40c + 10c multi	.50	.35
B648	SP323	1fr + 50c multi	.80	.50
B649	SP323	1.50fr + 50c multi	.95	.75
B650	SP323	2.50fr + 1fr multi	1.25	1.40
B651	SP323	3fr + 1.50fr multi	3.25	3.00
B652	SP324	5fr + 3fr multi	5.25	4.00
		Nos. B647-B652 (6)	12.00	10.00

The surtax was for the Royal Library, Brussels. Portraits show Grand Masters of the Order of the Golden Fleece.

Whale, Antwerp SP325

Carnival, Stavelot SP326

Designs: 1fr+50c, Dragon, Mons. 2fr+50c, Prince Carnival, Eupen. 3fr+1fr, Jester and cats, Ypres. 6fr+2fr, Holy Family, horiz. 7fr+3fr, Madonna, Liége, horiz.

Engraved and Photogravure
1959, Dec. 5   Perf. 11½
B653	SP325	40c + 10c cit, Prus bl & red	.45	.40
B654	SP325	1fr + 50c ol & grn	.75	.60
B655	SP325	2fr + 50c lt brn, org & cl	.50	.40
B656	SP326	2.50fr + 1fr gray, pur & ultra	.80	.60
B657	SP326	3fr + 1fr gray, mar & yel	1.75	1.25
B658	SP326	6fr + 2fr ol, brt bl & hn brn	3.25	2.50
B659	SP326	7fr + 3fr chlky bl & org yel	5.00	4.25
		Nos. B653-B659 (7)	12.50	10.00

The surtax was for anti-tuberculosis work.

Child Refugee — SP327

Designs: 3fr+1.50fr, Man. 6fr+3fr, Woman.

1960, Apr. 7   Engr.
B660	SP327	40c + 10c rose claret	.20	.15
B661	SP327	3fr + 1.50fr gray brn	.65	.50
B662	SP327	6fr + 3fr dk bl	1.65	1.10
a.		Souvenir sheet of 3	50.00	45.00
		Nos. B660-B662 (3)	2.50	1.75

World Refugee Year, July 1, 1959-June 30, 1960. No. B662a contains Nos. B660-B662 with colors changed: 40c+10c, dull purple; 3fr+1.50fr, red brown; 6fr+3fr, henna brown.

Parachutists and Plane SP328

Designs: 2fr+50c, 2.50fr+1fr, Parachutists coming in for landing, vert 3fr+1fr, 6fr+2fr, Parachutist walking with parachute.

Photogravure and Engraved
1960, June 13   Perf. 11½
B663	SP328	40c + 10c lt ultra & blk	.15	.15
B664	SP328	1fr + 50c bl & blk	.85	.60
B665	SP328	2fr + 50c bl, blk & ol	2.75	1.25
B666	SP328	2.50fr + 1fr grnsh bl, blk & gray ol	3.00	2.00
B667	SP328	3fr + 1fr bl, blk & sl grn	3.00	2.00
B668	SP328	6fr + 2fr lt vio bl, blk & ol	6.25	4.00
		Nos. B663-B668 (6)	16.00	10.00

The surtax was for various patriotic and cultural organizations.

Mother and Child, Planes and Rainbow SP329

Designs: 40c+10c, Brussels Airport, planes and rainbow. 6fr+3fr, Rainbow connecting Congo and Belgium, and planes, vert

Perf. 11½
1960, Aug. 3   Unwmk.   Photo.
Size: 35x24mm
B669	SP329	40c + 10c grnsh blue	.15	.15
B670	SP329	3fr + 1.50fr brt red	2.50	2.25

Size: 35x52mm
B671	SP329	6fr + 3fr violet	3.75	3.00
		Nos. B669-B671 (3)	6.40	5.40

The surtax was for refugees from Congo.

Infant, Milk Bottle and Mug — SP330

UNICEF: 1fr+50c, Nurse and children of 3 races. 2fr+50c, Refugee woman carrying gift clothes. 2.50fr+1fr, Negro nurse weighing infant. 3fr+1fr, Children of various races dancing. 6fr+2fr, Refugee boys.

Photogravure and Engraved
1960, Oct. 8   Perf. 11½
B672	SP330	40c + 10c gldn brn, yel & bl grn	.15	.15
B673	SP330	1fr + 50c ol gray, mar & slate	1.40	.75
B674	SP330	2fr + 50c vio, pale brn & brt grn	1.50	1.10
B675	SP330	2.50fr + 1fr dk red, sep & lt bl	1.75	1.40
B676	SP330	3fr + 1fr bl grn, red org & dl vio	.95	.85
B677	SP330	6fr + 2fr ultra, emer & brn	3.75	3.25
		Nos. B672-B677 (6)	9.50	7.50

Tapestry SP331

Belgian handicrafts: 1fr+50c, Cut crystal vases, vert. 2fr+50c, Lace, vert. 2.50fr+1fr, Metal plate & jug. 3fr+1fr, Diamonds. 6fr+2fr, Ceramics.

1960, Dec. 5   Perf. 11½
B678		40c + 10c bl, bis & brn	.15	.15
B679		1fr + 50c ind & org brn	1.10	1.00
B680		2fr + 50c dk red brn, blk & cit	2.00	1.50
B681		2.50fr + 1fr choc & yel	2.50	2.25
B682		3fr + 1fr org brn, blk & ultra	1.25	1.10
B683		6fr + 2fr dp blk & yel	5.00	4.00
		Nos. B678-B683 (6)	12.00	10.00

The surtax was for anti-tuberculosis work.

Jacob Kats and Abbe Nicolas Pietkin SP332

Portraits: 1fr+50c, Albert Mockel and J. F. Willems. 2fr+50c, Jan van Rijswijck and Xavier M. Neujean. 2.50fr+1fr, Joseph Demarteau and A. Van de Perre. 3fr+1fr, Canon Jan-Baptist David and Albert du Bois. 6fr+2fr, Henri Vieuxtemps and Willem de Mol.

1961, Apr. 22   Unwmk.   Perf. 11½
Portraits in Gray Brown
B684		40c + 10c ver & mar	.15	.15
B685		1fr + 50c bis brn & mar	1.50	1.10
B686		2fr + 50c yel & crim	1.75	1.50
B687		2.50fr + 1fr pale cit & dk grn	2.75	1.50
B688		3fr + 1fr lt & dk bl	2.75	2.50
B689		6fr + 2fr lil & ultra	5.00	4.25
		Nos. B684-B689 (6)	13.90	11.00

The surtax was for the benefit of various cultural organizations.

White Rhinoceros SP333

Antonius Cardinal Perrenot de Granvelle SP334

Animals: 1fr+50c, Przewalski horses. 2fr+50c, Okapi. 2.50fr+1fr, Giraffe, horiz. 3fr+1fr, Lesser panda, horiz. 6fr+2fr, European elk, horiz.

Perf. 11½
1961, June 5   Unwmk.   Photo.
B690		40c + 10c bis brn & dk brn	.15	.15
B691		1fr + 50c gray & brn	.90	.90
B692		2fr + 50c dp rose & blk	1.40	1.25
B693		2.50fr + 1fr red org & brn	1.10	1.10
B694		3fr + 1fr org & brn	1.00	1.00
B695		6fr + 2fr bl & bis brn	2.25	1.50
		Nos. B690-B695 (6)	6.80	5.90

The surtax was for various philanthropic organizations.

1961, July 29   Engr.

Designs: 3fr+1.50fr, Arms of Cardinal de Granvelle. 6fr+3fr, Tower and crosier, symbolic of collaboration between Malines and the Archbishopric.

B696	SP334	40c + 10c magenta, car & brn	.15	.15
B697	SP334	3fr + 1.50fr multi	.65	.50
B698	SP334	6fr + 3fr mag pur & bis	1.25	1.10
		Nos. B696-B698 (3)	2.05	1.75

400th anniv. of Malines as an Archbishopric.

BELGIUM

Mother and Child by Pierre Paulus — SP335

Castle of the Counts of Male — SP336

Plaintings: 1fr+50c, Mother Love, Francois-Joseph Navez. 2fr+50c, Motherhood, Constant Permeke. 2.50fr+1fr, Madonna and Child, Rogier van der Weyden. 3fr+1fr, Madonna with Apple, Hans Memling. 6fr+2fr, Madonna of the Forget-me-not, Peter Paul Rubens.

1961, Dec. 2 Photo. Perf. 11½
Gold Frame

B699	SP335	40c + 10c dp brn	.15	.15
B700	SP335	1fr + 50c brt bl	.40	.30
B701	SP335	2fr + 50c rose red	.60	.45
B702	SP335	2.50fr + 1fr magenta	.85	.75
B703	SP335	3fr + 1fr vio bl	1.00	.85
B704	SP335	6fr + 2fr dk sl grn	1.75	1.50
		Nos. B699-B704 (6)	4.75	4.00

The surtax was for anti-tuberculosis work.

1962, Mar. 12 Engr. Perf. 11½

Designs: 90c+10c, Royal library, horiz. 1fr+50c, Church of Our Lady, Tongres. 2fr+50c, Collegiate Church, Soignies, horiz. 2.50fr+1fr, Church of Our Lady, Malines. 3fr+1fr, St. Denis Abbey, Broqueroi. 6fr+2fr, Cloth Hall, Ypres, horiz.

B705	SP336	40c + 10c brt grn	.15	.15
B706	SP336	90c + 10c lil rose	.20	.20
B707	SP336	1fr + 50c dl vio	.45	.45
B708	SP336	2fr + 50c violet	.70	.60
B709	SP336	2.50fr + 1fr red brn	1.00	.85
B710	SP336	3fr + 1fr bl grn	1.00	.85
B711	SP336	6fr + 2fr car rose	1.50	1.40
		Nos. B705-B711 (7)	5.00	4.50

The surtax was for various cultural and philanthropic organizations.

Andean Cock of the Rock — SP337

Handicapped Child — SP338

Birds: 1fr+50c, Red lory. 2fr+50c, Guinea touraco. 2.50fr+1fr, Keel-billed toucan. 3fr+1fr, Great bird of paradise. 6fr+2fr, Congolese peacock.

Engraved and Photogravure
1962, June 23 Unwmk. Perf. 11½

B712	SP337	40c + 10c multi	.15	.15
B713	SP337	1fr + 50c multi	.45	.30
B714	SP337	2fr + 50c multi	.50	.40
B715	SP337	2.50fr + 1fr multi	.55	.45
B716	SP337	3fr + 1fr multi	1.10	.95
B717	SP337	6fr + 2fr multi	2.00	1.75
		Nos. B712-B717 (6)	4.75	4.00

The surtax was for various philanthropic organizations.

1962, Sept. 22 Photo.

Handicapped Children: 40c+10c, Reading Braille. 2fr+50c, Deaf-mute girl with earphones and electronic equipment, horiz. 2.50fr+1fr, Child with ball (cerebral palsy). 3fr+1fr, Girl with crutches (polio). 6fr+2fr, Sitting boys playing ball, horiz.

B718	SP338	40c + 10c choc	.15	.15
B719	SP338	1fr + 50c rose red	.30	.30
B720	SP338	2fr + 50c brt lil	.60	.60
B721	SP338	2.50fr + 1fr dl grn	.65	.65
B722	SP338	3fr + 1fr dk blue	.80	.80
B723	SP338	6fr + 2fr dk brn	1.50	1.25
		Nos. B718-B723 (6)	4.00	3.75

The surtax was for various institutions for handicapped children.

Queen Louise-Marie — SP339

Belgian Queens: No. B725, like No. B724 with "ML" initials. 1fr+50c, Marie-Henriette. 2fr+1fr, Elisabeth. 3fr+1.50fr, Astrid. 8fr+2.50fr, Fabiola.

1962, Dec. 8 Photo. & Engr.
Gray, Black & Gold

B724	SP339	40c + 10c ("L")	.15	.15
B725	SP339	40c + 10c ("ML")	.15	.15
B726	SP339	1fr + 50c	.50	.50
B727	SP339	2fr + 1fr	.85	.85
B728	SP339	3fr + 1.50fr	.95	.85
B729	SP339	8fr + 2.50fr	1.40	1.00
		Nos. B724-B729 (6)	4.00	3.50

The surtax was for anti-tuberculosis work.

British War Memorial (Porte de Menin), Ypres — SP340

1962, Dec. 26 Engr. Perf. 11½

| B730 | SP340 | 1fr + 50c multi | .50 | .50 |

Millennium of the city of Ypres. Issued in sheets of eight.

Peace Bell Ringing over Globe SP341

The Sower by Brueghel SP342

Engraved and Photogravure
1963, Feb. 18 Unwmk. Perf. 11½

B731		3fr + 1.50fr blk, bl, org & grn	1.50	1.50
a.		Sheet of 4	7.25	7.25
B732		6fr + 3fr blk, brn & org	.75	.75

The surtax was for the installation of the Peace Bell (Bourdon de la Paix) at Koekelberg Basilica and for the benefit of various cultural organizations.

No. B731 was issued in sheets of 4. No. B732 was issued in sheets of 30.

1963, Mar. 21 Perf. 11½

Designs: 3fr+1fr, The Harvest, by Brueghel, horiz. 6fr+2fr, "Bread," by Anton Carte, horiz.

B733		2fr + 1fr grn, ocher & blk	.15	.15
B734		3fr + 1fr red lil, ocher & blk	.40	.35
B735		6fr + 2fr red brn, cit & blk	.55	.50
		Nos. B733-B735 (3)	1.10	1.00

FAO "Freedom from Hunger" campaign.

Speed Racing — SP343

2fr+1fr, Bicyclists at check point, horiz. 3fr+1.50fr, Team racing, horiz. 6fr+3fr, Pace setters.

Perf. 11½
1963, July 13 Unwmk. Engr.

B736	SP343	1fr + 50c multi	.15	.15
B737	SP343	2fr + 1fr bl, car, blk & ol gray	.20	.20
B738	SP343	3fr + 1.50fr multi	.35	.35
B739	SP343	6fr + 3fr multi	.50	.50
		Nos. B736-B739 (4)	1.20	1.20

80th anniversary of the founding of the Belgian Bicycle League. The surtax was for athletes at the 1964 Olympic Games.

Princess Paola with Princess Astrid — SP344

Prince Albert and Family SP345

Designs: 40c+10c, Prince Philippe. 2fr+50c, Princess Astrid. 2.50fr+1fr, Princess Paola. 6fr+2fr, Prince Albert.

1963, Sept. 28 Photo.

B740	SP344	40c + 10c	.15	.15
B741	SP344	1fr + 50c	.35	.30
B742	SP344	2fr + 50c	.45	.40
B743	SP344	2.50fr + 1fr	.45	.45
B744	SP345	3fr + 1fr	.45	.45
B745	SP345	3fr + 1fr	1.50	1.40
a.		Booklet pane of 8	17.00	17.00
B746	SP345	6fr + 2fr	.90	.85
		Nos. B740-B746 (7)	4.25	4.00

Cent. of the Intl. Red Cross. No. B745 issued in booklet panes of 8, which are in two forms: French and Flemish inscriptions in top and bottom margins transposed.

Daughter of Balthazar Gerbier, Painted by Rubens — SP346

Jesus, St. John and Cherubs by Rubens — SP347

Portraits (Rubens' sons): 1fr+40c, Nicolas, 2 yrs. old. 2fr+50c, Franz. 2.50fr+1fr, Nicolas, 6 yrs. old. 3fr+1fr, Albert.

Photogravure and Engraved
1963, Dec. 7 Unwmk. Perf. 11½

B747	SP346	50c + 10c	.15	.15
B748	SP346	1fr + 40c	.15	.15
B749	SP346	2fr + 50c	.20	.20
B750	SP346	2.50fr + 1fr	.45	.45
B751	SP346	3fr + 1fr	.35	.35
B752	SP347	6fr + 2fr	.45	.45
		Nos. B747-B752 (6)	1.75	1.75

The surtax was for anti-tuberculosis work. See No. B771.

John Quincy Adams and Lord Gambier Signing Treaty of Ghent, by Amédée Forestier — SP348

1964, May 16 Photo. Perf. 11½

| B753 | SP348 | 6fr + 3fr dk blue | .75 | .75 |

Signing of the Treaty of Ghent between the US and Great Britain, Dec. 24, 1814.

Philip van Marnix — SP349

Portraits: 3fr+1.50fr, Ida de Bure Calvin. 6fr+3fr, Jacob Jordaens.

1964, May 30 Engr.

B754	SP349	1fr + 50c blue gray	.15	.15
B755	SP349	3fr + 1.50fr rose pink	.25	.25
B756	SP349	6fr + 3fr redsh brn	.45	.45
		Nos. B754-B756 (3)	.85	.85

Issued to honor Protestantism in Belgium. The surtax was for the erection of a Protestant church.

Foot Soldier, 1918 — SP350

Battle of Bastogne — SP351

Designs: 2fr+1fr, Flag bearer, Guides Regiment, 1914. 3fr+1.50fr, Trumpeter of the Grenadiers and drummers, 1914.

1964, Aug. 1 Photo. Perf. 11½

B757	SP350	1fr + 50c multi	.15	.15
B758	SP350	2fr + 1fr multi	.24	.24
B759	SP350	3fr + 1.50fr multi	.24	.24
		Nos. B757-B759 (3)	.63	.63

50th anniversary of the German aggression against Belgium in 1914. The surtax aided patriotic undertakings.

1964, Aug. 1 Unwmk.

6fr+3fr, Liberation of the estuary of the Escaut.

B760	SP351	3fr + 1fr multi	.18	.18
B761	SP351	6fr + 3fr multi	.28	.28

Belgium's Resistance and liberation of World War II. The surtax was to help found an International Student Center at Antwerp and to aid cultural undertakings.

Souvenir Sheets

Rogier van der Weyden Paintings — SP352

BELGIUM

Descent From the Cross — SP353

1964, Sept. 19   Photo.   Perf. 11½
B762 SP352   Sheet of 3   2.25   2.25
   a.   1fr Philip the Good   .52   .52
   b.   2fr Portrait of a Lady   .52   .52
   c.   3fr Man with Arrow   .52   .52

Engr.
B763 SP353   8fr red brown   2.25   2.25

Rogier van der Weyden (Roger de La Pasture, 1400-64). The surtax went to various cultural organizations. #B762 sold for 14fr; #B763 for 16fr.

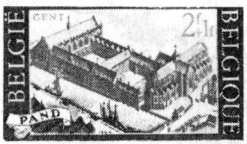

Ancient View of the Pand SP354

3fr+1fr, Present view of the Pand from Lys River.

1964, Oct. 10   Photo.
B764 SP354   2fr + 1fr blk, grnsh bl & ultra   .40   .40
B765 SP354   3fr + 1fr lil rose, bl & dk brn   .40   .40

The surtax was for the restoration of the Pand Dominican Abbey in Ghent.

Type of 1963 and

Child of Charles I, Painted by Van Dyck — SP355

Designs: 1fr+40c, William of Orange with his bride, by Van Dyck. 2fr+1fr, Portrait of a small boy with dogs by Erasmus Quellin and Jan Fyt. 3fr+1fr, Alexander Farnese by Antonio Moro. 4fr+2fr, William II, Prince of Orange by Van Dyck. 6fr+3fr, Artist's children by Cornelis De Vos.

1964, Dec. 5   Engr.   Perf. 11½
B766 SP355   50c + 10c rose claret   .15   .15
B767 SP355   1fr + 40c car rose   .15   .15
B768 SP355   2fr + 1fr vio brn   .15   .15
B769 SP355   3fr + 1fr gray   .15   .15
B770 SP355   4fr + 2fr vio bl   .24   .24
B771 SP347   6fr + 3fr brt pur   .24   .24
   Nos. B766-B771 (6)   1.08   1.08

The surtax was for anti-tuberculosis work.

Liberator, Shaking Prisoner's Hand, Concentration Camp — SP356

Designs: 1fr+50c, Prisoner's hand reaching for the sun. 3fr+1.50fr, Searchlights and tank breaking down barbed wire, horiz. 8fr+5fr, Rose growing amid the ruins, horiz.

Engraved and Photogravure
1965, May 8   Unwmk.   Perf. 11½
B772 SP356   50c + 50c tan, blk & buff   .15   .15
B773 SP356   1fr + 50c multi   .15   .15
B774 SP356   3fr + 1.50fr dl lil & blk   .18   .18
B775 SP356   8fr + 5fr multi   .35   .35
   Nos. B772-B775 (4)   .83   .83

20th anniv. of the liberation of the concentration camps for political prisoners and prisoners of war.

Stoclet House, Brussels SP357

Stoclet House: 6fr+3fr, Hall with marble foundation, vert. 8fr+4fr, View of house from garden.

1965, June 21
B776 SP357   3fr + 1fr slate & tan   .22   .22
B777 SP357   6fr + 3fr sepia   .32   .32
B778 SP357   8fr + 4fr vio brn & tan   .42   .42
   Nos. B776-B778 (3)   .96   .96

Austrian architect Josef Hoffmann (1870-1956), builder of the art nouveau residence of Adolphe Stoclet, engineer and financier.

Jackson's Chameleon SP358

Animals from Antwerp Zoo: 2fr+1fr, Common iguanas. 3fr+1.50fr, African monitor. 6fr+3fr, Komodo monitor. 8fr+4fr, Nile softshell turtle.

1965, Oct. 16   Photo.   Perf. 11½
B779 SP358   1fr + 50c multi   .15   .15
B780 SP358   2fr + 1fr multi   .16   .16
B781 SP358   3fr + 1.50fr multi   .22   .22
B782 SP358   6fr + 3fr multi   .45   .45
   Nos. B779-B782 (4)   .98   .98

Miniature Sheet
B783 SP358   8fr + 4fr multi   1.75   1.75

The surtax was for various cultural and philanthropic organizations. No. B783 contains one stamp, size: 52x35mm.

Boatmen's and Archers' Guild Halls — SP359

Buildings on Grand-Place, Brussels: 1fr+40c, Brewers' Hall. 2fr+1fr, "King of Spain." 3fr+1.50fr, "Dukes of Brabant." 10fr+4.50fr, Tower of City Hall and St. Michael.

1965, Dec. 4   Engr.   Perf. 11½
Size: 35x24mm
B784 SP359   50c + 10c ultra   .15   .15
B785 SP359   1fr + 40c bl grn   .15   .15
B786 SP359   2fr + 1fr rose claret   .18   .18
B787 SP359   3fr + 1.50fr violet   .20   .20
Size: 24x44mm
B788 SP359   10fr + 4.50fr sep & gray   .32   .32
   Nos. B784-B788 (5)   1.00   1.00

The surtax was for anti-tuberculosis work.

Souvenir Sheets

Queen Elisabeth — SP360

Design: No. B790, Types of 1931 and 1956.

1966, Apr. 16   Photo.
B789 SP360   Sheet of 2 + label   1.50   1.50
   a.   SP74 3fr dk brn & gray grn   .60   .60
   b.   SP87 3fr dk brn, yel grn & gold   .60   .60
B790 SP360   Sheet of 2 + label   1.50   1.50
   a.   SP42 3fr dk brn & dl bl   .60   .60
   b.   SP304 3fr dk brn & gray   .60   .60

The surtax went to various cultural organizations. Each sheet sold for 20fr.

Luminescent Paper was used in printing Nos. B789-B790, B801-B806, B808-B809, B811-B823, B825-B831, B833-B835, B837-B840, B842-B846, B848-B850, B852-B854, B856-B863, and from B865 onward unless otherwise noted.

Diver — SP361

Design: 10fr+4fr, Swimmer at start.

1966, May 9   Engr.
B791 SP361   60c + 40c Prus grn, ol & org brn   .15   .15
B792 SP361   10fr + 4fr ol grn, org brn & mag   .38   .38

Issued to publicize the importance of swimming instruction.

Minorites' Convent, Liège — SP362

Designs: 1fr+50c, Val-Dieu Abbey, Aubel. 2fr+1fr, View and seal of Huy. 10fr+4.50fr, Statue of Ambiorix by Jules Bertin, and tower, Tongeren.

1966, Aug. 27   Engr.   Perf. 11½
B793 SP362   60c + 40c multi   .15   .15
B794 SP362   1fr + 50c multi   .15   .15
B795 SP362   2fr + 1fr multi   .15   .15
B796 SP362   10fr + 4.50fr multi   .42   .42
   Nos. B793-B796 (4)   .87   .87

The surtax was for various patriotic and cultural organizations.

Surveyor and Dog Team — SP363

Designs: 3fr+1.50fr, Adrien de Gerlache and "Belgica." 6fr+3fr, Surveyor, weather balloon and ship. 10fr+5fr, Penguins and "Magga Dan" (ship used for 1964, 1965 and 1966 expeditions).

1966, Oct. 8   Engr.   Perf. 11½
B797 SP363   1fr + 50c bl grn   .15   .15
B798 SP363   3fr + 1.50fr pale vio   .20   .20
B799 SP363   6fr + 3fr dk car   .35   .35
   Nos. B797-B799 (3)   .70   .70

Souvenir Sheet
Engraved and Photogravure
B800 SP363   10fr + 5fr dk gray, sky bl & dk red   .70   .70

Belgian Antarctic expeditions. #B800 contains one 52x35mm stamp.

Boy with Ball and Dog — SP364

Designs: 2fr+1fr, Girl skipping rope. 3fr+1.50fr, Girl and boy blowing soap bubbles. 6fr+3fr, Girl and boy rolling hoops, horiz. 8fr+3.50fr, Four children at play and cat, horiz.

1966, Dec. 3   Perf. 11½
B801 SP364   1fr + 1fr pink & blk   .15   .15
B802 SP364   2fr + 1fr lt bluish grn & blk   .15   .15
B803 SP364   3fr + 1.50fr lt vio & blk   .15   .15
B804 SP364   6fr + 3fr pale sal & dk brn   .24   .24
B805 SP364   8fr + 3.50fr lt yel grn & dk brn   .28   .28
   Nos. B801-B805 (5)   .97   .97

The surtax was for anti-tuberculosis work.

Souvenir Sheet

Refugees — SP365

Designs: 1fr, Boy receiving clothes. 2fr, Tibetan children. 3fr, African mother and children.

1967, Mar. 11   Photo.   Perf. 11½
B806 SP365   Sheet of 3   1.25   1.25
   a.   1fr black & yellow   .28   .28
   b.   2fr black & blue   .28   .28
   c.   3fr black & orange   .40   .40

Issued to help refugees around the world. Sheet has black border with Belgian P.T.T. and UN Refugee emblems. Sold for 20fr.

Robert Schuman — SP366

Colonial Brotherhood Emblem — SP368

Kongolo Memorial, Gentinnes SP367

1967, June 24   Engr.   Perf. 11½
B807 SP366   2fr + 1fr gray blue   .24   .24

Engraved and Photogravure
B808 SP367   5fr + 2fr brn & olive   .28   .28
B809 SP368   10fr + 5fr multi   .45   .35

Robert Schuman (1886-1963), French statesman, one of the founders of European Steel and Coal Community, 1st pres. of European Parliament (2fr+1fr); Kongolo Memorial, erected in memory of missionary and civilian victims in the Congo (5fr+2fr); a memorial for African Troops, Brussels (10fr+5fr).

Preaching Fool from "Praise of Folly" by Erasmus — SP369

Erasmus, by Quentin Massys — SP370

Designs: 2fr+1fr, Exhorting Fool from Praise of Folly. 5fr+2fr, Thomas More's Family, by Hans Holbein, horiz. 6fr+3fr, Pierre Gilles (Aegidius), by Quentin Massys.

BELGIUM

Photogravure and Engraved (SP369); Photogravure (SP370)

1967, Sept. 2   Unwmk.   Perf. 11
B810	SP369	1fr + 50c tan, blk, bl & car	.15	.15
B811	SP369	2fr + 1fr tan, blk & car	.15	.15
B812	SP369	3fr + 1.50fr multi	.15	.15
B813	SP369	5fr + 2fr tan, blk & car	.18	.18
B814	SP370	6fr + 3fr multi	.24	.24
		Nos. B810-B814 (5)	.87	.87

Issued to commemorate Erasmus (1466(?)-1536), Dutch scholar and his era.

Souvenir Sheet

Pro-Post Association Emblem — SP371

Engraved and Photogravure
1967, Oct. 21   Perf. 11½
B815	SP371	10fr + 5fr multi	.75	.75

Issued to publicize the POSTPHILA Philatelic Exhibition, Brussels, Oct. 21-29.

Detail from Brueghel's "Children's Games" — SP372

Designs: Various Children's Games. Singles of Nos. B816-B821 arranged in 2 rows of 3 show complete painting by Pieter Brueghel.

1967, Dec. 9   Photo.   Perf. 11½
B816	SP372	1fr + 50c multi	.15	.15
B817	SP372	2fr + 1fr multi	.18	.18
B818	SP372	3fr + 1fr multi	.18	.18
B819	SP372	6fr + 3fr multi	.30	.30
B820	SP372	10fr + 4fr multi	.40	.40
B821	SP372	13fr + 6fr multi	.60	.60
		Nos. B816-B821 (6)	1.81	1.81

Queen Fabiola Holding Refugee Child from Congo — SP373

6fr+3fr, Queen Elisabeth & Dr. Depage.

1968, Apr. 27   Photo.   Perf. 11½
Cross in Red
B822	SP373	6fr + 3fr sepia & gray	.25	.25
B823	SP373	10fr + 5fr sepia & gray	.45	.45

The surtax was for the Red Cross.

Woman Gymnast and Calendar Stone SP374

Yachting and "The Swimmer" by Andrien SP375

"Explosion" SP376

Designs: 2fr+1fr, Weight lifter and Mayan motif. 3fr+1.50fr, Hurdler, colossus of Tula and animal head from Kukulkan. 6fr+2fr, Bicyclists and Chichen Itza Temple.

Engraved and Photogravure
1968, May 27   Perf. 11½
B824	SP374	1fr + 50c multi	.15	.15
B825	SP374	2fr + 1fr multi	.15	.15
B826	SP374	3fr + 1.50fr multi	.15	.15
B827	SP374	6fr + 3fr multi	.24	.24

Photo.
B828	SP375	13fr + 5fr multi	.52	.52
		Nos. B824-B828 (5)	1.21	1.21

Issued to publicize the 19th Olympic Games, Mexico City, Oct. 12-27.

1968, June 22   Photo.

Designs (Paintings by Pol Mara): 12fr+5fr, "Fire." 13fr+5fr, "Tornado."

B829	SP376	10fr + 5fr multi	.40	.40
B830	SP376	12fr + 5fr multi	.65	.65
B831	SP376	13fr + 5fr multi	.70	.70
		Nos. B829-B831 (3)	1.75	1.75

The surtax was for disaster victims.

Undulate Triggerfish SP377

Tropical Fish: 3fr+1.50fr, Angelfish. 6fr+3fr, Turkeyfish (Pterois volitans). 10fr+5fr, Orange butterflyfish.

1968, Oct. 19   Engr. & Photo.
B832	SP377	1fr + 50c multi	.15	.15
B833	SP377	3fr + 1.50fr multi	.15	.15
B834	SP377	6fr + 3fr multi	.30	.30
B835	SP377	10fr + 5fr multi	.42	.42
		Nos. B832-B835 (4)	1.02	1.02

King Albert and Queen Elisabeth Entering Brussels SP378

Tomb of the Unknown Soldier and Eternal Flame, Brussels — SP379

Designs: 1fr+50c, King Albert, Queen Elisabeth and Crown Prince Leopold on balcony, Bruges, vert. 6fr+3fr, King and Queen entering Liège.

1968, Nov. 9   Photo.   Perf. 11½
B836	SP378	1fr + 50c multi	.15	.15
B837	SP378	3fr + 1.50fr multi	.15	.15
B838	SP378	6fr + 3fr multi	.30	.30

Engraved and Photogravure
B839	SP379	10fr + 5fr multi	.40	.40
		Nos. B836-B839 (4)	1.00	1.00

50th anniv. of the victory in World War I.

Souvenir Sheet

The Painter and the Amateur, by Peter Brueghel — SP380

1969, May 10   Engr.   Perf. 11½
B840	SP380	10fr + 5fr sepia	1.10	1.10

Issued to publicize the POSTPHILA 1969 Philatelic Exhibition, Brussels, May 10-18.

Huts, by Ivanka D. Pancheva, Bulgaria SP381

Msgr. Victor Scheppers SP382

Children's Drawings and UNICEF Emblem: 3fr+1.50fr, "My Art" (Santa Claus), by Claes Patric, Belgium. 6fr+3fr, "In the Sun" (young boy), by Helena Rejchlova, Czechoslovakia. 10fr+5fr, "Out for a Walk" by Phillis Sporn, US, horiz.

1969, May 31   Photo.   Perf. 11½
B841	SP381	1fr + 50c multi	.15	.15
B842	SP381	3fr + 1.50fr multi	.16	.16
B843	SP381	6fr + 3fr multi	.35	.35
B844	SP381	10fr + 5fr multi	.52	.52
		Nos. B841-B844 (4)	1.18	1.18

The surtax was for philanthropic purposes.

1969, July 5   Engr.
B845	SP382	6fr + 3fr rose claret	.45	.45

Msgr. Victor Scheppers (1802-77), prison reformer and founder of the Brothers of Mechlin (Scheppers).

Moon Landing Type of 1969
Souvenir Sheet

Design: 20fr+10fr, Armstrong, Collins and Aldrin and moon with Tranquillity Base, vert.

1969, Sept. 20   Photo.   Perf. 11½
B846	A245	20fr + 10fr indigo	3.00	3.00

See note after No. 726.

Heads from Alexander the Great Tapestry, 15th Century — SP383

Designs from Tapestries: 3fr+1.50fr, Fiddler from "The Feast," c. 1700. 10fr+4fr, Head of beggar from "The Healing of the Paralytic," 16th century.

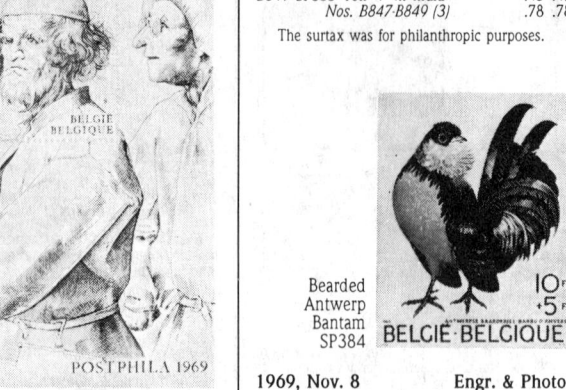

1969, Sept. 20
B847	SP383	1fr + 50c multi	.15	.15
B848	SP383	3fr + 1.50fr multi	.18	.18
B849	SP383	10fr + 4fr multi	.45	.45
		Nos. B847-B849 (3)	.78	.78

The surtax was for philanthropic purposes.

Bearded Antwerp Bantam SP384

1969, Nov. 8   Engr. & Photo.
B850	SP384	10fr + 5fr multi	.70	.70

Angel Playing Lute — SP385

Designs from Stained Glass Windows: 1.50fr+50c, Angel with trumpet, St. Waudru's, Mons. 7fr+3fr, Angel with viol, St. Jacques', Liege. 9fr+4fr, King with bagpipes, Royal Art Museum, Brussels.

1969, Dec. 13   Photo.
Size: 24x35mm
B851	SP385	1.50fr + 50c multi	.15	.15
B852	SP385	3.50fr + 1.50fr multi	.18	.18
B853	SP385	7fr + 3fr multi	.35	.35

Size: 35x52mm
B854	SP386	9fr + 4fr multi	.52	.52
		Nos. B851-B854 (4)	1.20	1.20

The surtax was for philanthropic purposes.

Farm and Windmill, Open-air Museum, Bokrijk SP386

Belgian Museums: 3.50fr+1.50fr, Stage Coach Inn, Courcelles. 7fr+3fr, "The Thresher of Trevires," Gallo-Roman sculpture, Gaumais Museum, Virton. 9fr+4fr, "The Sovereigns," by Henry Moore, Middelheim Museum, Antwerp.

Engraved and Photogravure
1970, May 30   Perf. 11½
B855	SP386	1.50fr + 50c multi	.15	.15
B856	SP386	3.50fr + 1.50fr multi	.25	.25
B857	SP386	7fr + 3fr multi	.35	.35
B858	SP386	9fr + 4fr multi	.40	.40
		Nos. B855-B858 (4)	1.15	1.15

The surtax went to various culture organizations.

"Resistance" — SP387

Design: 7fr+3fr, "Liberation of Camps." The designs were originally used as book covers.

1970, July 4   Photo.   Perf. 11½
B859	SP387	3.50fr + 1.50fr blk, gray grn & dp car	.20	.20
B860	SP387	7fr + 3fr blk, lil & dp car	.40	.40

Honoring the Resistance Movement and 25th anniv. of the liberation of concentration camps.

BELGIUM

Fishing Rod and Reel — SP388

Design: 9fr+4fr, Hockey stick and puck, vert.

1970, Sept. 19   Engr. & Photo.
B861 SP388   3.50fr + 1.50fr multi   .28 .28
B862 SP388   9fr + 4fr multi   .48 .48

Souvenir Sheet

Belgium Nos. 31, 36, 39 — SP389

1970, Oct. 10   Perf. 11½
B863 SP389   Sheet of 3   4.75 4.75
   a.   1.50fr + 50c black & dull lilac   1.40 1.40
   b.   3.50fr + 1.50fr black & lilac   1.40 1.40
   c.   9fr + 4fr black & red brown   1.40 1.40

BELGICA 72 International Philatelic Exhibition, Brussels, June 24-July 9.

Camille Huysmans (1871-1968) SP390

"Anxious City" (Detail) by Paul Delvaux SP391

Portraits: 3.50fr+1.50fr, Joseph Cardinal Cardijn (1882-1967). 7fr+3fr, Maria Baers (1883-1959). 9fr+4fr, Paul Pastur (1866-1938).

1970, Nov. 14   Perf. 11½
Portraits in Sepia
B864 SP390   1.50fr + 50c car rose   .15 .15
B865 SP390   3.50fr + 1.50fr lilac   .20 .20
B866 SP390   7fr + 3fr green   .40 .40
B867 SP390   9fr + 4fr blue   .48 .48
   Nos. B864-B867 (4)   1.23 1.23

1970, Dec. 12   Photo.
7fr+3fr, "The Memory," by Rene Magritte.
B868 SP391   3.50fr + 1.50fr multi   .18 .18
B869 SP391   7fr + 3fr multi   .38 .38

Notre Dame du Vivier, Marche-les-Dames — SP392

7fr+3fr, Turnhout Beguinage and Beguine.

1971, Mar. 13   Perf. 11½
B870 SP392   3.50fr + 1.50fr multi   .20 .20
B871 SP392   7fr + 3fr multi   .40 .40

The surtax was for philanthropic purposes.

Red Cross — SP393

1971, May 22   Photo.   Perf. 11½
B872 SP393   10fr + 5fr crim & blk   .75 .75

Belgian Red Cross.

Discobolus and Munich Cathedral SP394

Festival of Flanders SP395

1971, June 19   Engr. & Photo.
B873 SP394   7fr + 3fr bl & blk   .42 .42

Publicity for the 20th Summer Olympic Games, Munich 1972.

1971, Sept. 11   Photo.   Perf. 11½
Design: 7fr+3fr, Wallonia Festival.
B874 SP395   3.50fr + 1.50fr multi   .18 .18
B875 SP395   7fr + 3fr multi   .38 .38

Attre Palace — SP396

Steen Palace, Elewijt — SP397

Design: 10fr+5fr, Royal Palace, Brussels.

1971, Oct. 23   Engr.
B876 SP396   3.50fr + 1.50fr sl grn   .30 .30
B877 SP397   7fr + 3fr red brn   .50 .50
B878 SP396   10fr + 5fr vio bl   .70 .70
   Nos. B876-B878 (3)   1.50 1.50

Surtax was for BELGICA 72, International Philatelic Exposition.

Ox Fly — SP398

Insects: 1.50fr+50c, Luna moth, vert. 7fr+3fr, Wasp, polistes gallicus. 9fr+4fr, Tiger beetle, vert.

1971, Dec. 11   Photo.   Perf. 11½
B879 SP398   1.50fr + 50c multi   .20 .20
B880 SP398   3.50fr + 1.50fr multi   .20 .20
B881 SP398   7fr + 3fr multi   .40 .40
B882 SP398   9fr + 4fr multi   .60 .60
   Nos. B879-B882 (4)   1.40 1.40

Surtax was for philanthropic purposes.

Leopold I on #1 — SP399

Epilepsy Emblem — SP400

Designs: 2fr+1fr, Leopold I on No. 5. 2.50fr+1fr, Leopold II on No. 45. 3.50fr+1.50fr, Leopold II on No. 48. 6fr+3fr, Albert I on No. 135. 7fr+3fr, Albert I on No. 214. 10fr+5fr, Albert I on No. 231. 15fr+7.50fr, Leopold III on No. 290. 20fr+10fr, King Baudouin on No. 718.

Engraved and Photogravure

1972, June 24   Perf. 11½
B883 SP399   1.50fr + 50c   .16 .16
B884 SP399   2fr + 1fr   .16 .16
B885 SP399   2.50 + 1fr   .20 .20
B886 SP399   3.50fr + 1.50fr   .32 .32
B887 SP399   6fr + 3fr   .52 .52
B888 SP399   7fr + 3fr   .70 .70
B889 SP399   10fr + 5fr   .90 .90
B890 SP399   15fr + 7fr   1.10 1.10
B891 SP399   20fr + 10fr   2.00 2.00
   Nos. B883-B891 (9)   6.06 6.06

Belgica 72, Intl. Philatelic Exhibition, Brussels, June 24-July 9. Nos. B883-B891 issued in sheets of 10 and of 20 (2 tete beche sheets with gutter between). Sold in complete sets.

1972, Sept. 9   Photo.   Perf. 11½
B892 SP400   10fr + 5fr multi   .55 .55

The surtax was for the William Lennox Center for epilepsy research and treatment.

Gray Lag Goose — SP401

Designs: 4.50fr+2fr, Lapwing. 8fr+4fr, Stork. 9fr+4.50fr, Kestrel, horiz.

1972, Dec. 16   Photo.   Perf. 11½
B893 SP401   2fr + 1fr multi   .22 .22
B894 SP401   4.50fr + 2fr multi   .32 .32
B895 SP401   8fr + 4fr multi   .60 .60
B896 SP401   9fr + 4.50fr multi   .60 .60
   Nos. B893-B896 (4)   1.74 1.74

Bijloke Abbey, Ghent — SP402

Designs: 4.50fr+2fr, St. Ursmer Collegiate Church, Lobbes. 8fr+4fr, Park Abbey, Heverle. 9fr+4.50fr, Abbey, Floreffe.

1973, Mar. 24   Engr.   Perf. 11½
B897 SP402   2fr + 1fr slate grn   .16 .16
B898 SP402   4.50fr + 2fr brown   .24 .24
B899 SP402   8fr + 4fr rose lil   .48 .48
B900 SP402   9fr + 4.50fr brt bl   .60 .60
   Nos. B897-B900 (4)   1.48 1.48

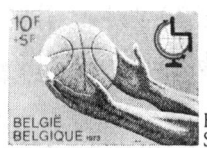

Basketball SP403

1973, Apr. 7   Photo. & Engr.
B901 SP403   10fr + 5fr multi   .60 .60

First World Basketball Championships of the Handicapped, Bruges, Apr. 16-21.

Dirk Martens' Printing Press — SP404

Lady Talbot, by Petrus Christus — SP405

Hadrian and Marcus Aurelius Coins — SP406

Council of Malines, by Coussaert — SP407

Designs: 3.50fr+1.50fr, Head of Amon and Tutankhamen's cartouche. 10fr+5fr, Three-master of Ostend Merchant Company.

Photogravure and Engraved; Photogravure (#B906)

1973, June 23   Perf. 11½
B902 SP404   2fr + 1fr multi   .15 .15
B903 SP404   3.50fr + 1.50fr multi   .15 .15
B904 SP405   4.50fr + 2fr multi   .20 .20
B905 SP406   8fr + 4fr multi   .60 .60
B906 SP407   9fr + 4.50fr multi   .85 .85
B907 SP407   10fr + 5fr multi   1.50 1.50
   Nos. B902-B907 (6)   3.45 3.45

500th anniv. of 1st book printed in Belgium (#B902); 50th anniv. of Queen Elisabeth Egyptological Foundation (#B903); 500th anniv. of death of painter Petrus Christus (#B904); Discovery of Roman treasure at Luttre-Liberchies (#B905); 500th anniv. of Great Council of Malines (#B906); 250th anniv. of the Ostend Merchant Company (#B907). No. B902 is not luminescent.

Queen of Hearts SP408

Symbol of Blood Donations SP409

Old Playing Cards: #B909, King of Clubs. #B910, Jack of Diamonds. #B911, King of Spades.

1973, Dec. 8   Photo.   Perf. 11½
B908 SP408   5fr + 2.50fr multi   .38 .38
B909 SP408   5fr + 2.50fr multi   .38 .38
B910 SP408   5fr + 2.50fr multi   .38 .38
B911 SP408   5fr + 2.50fr multi   .38 .38
   a.   Block of 4, #B908-B911   1.60 1.60

Surtax was for philanthropic purposes.

1974, Feb. 23   Photo.   Perf. 11½
Design: 10fr+5fr, Traffic lights, Red Cross (symbolic of road accidents).
B912 SP409   4fr + 2fr multi   .24 .24
B913 SP409   10fr + 5fr multi   .55 .55

The Red Cross as blood collector and aid to accident victims.

BELGIUM

Armand Jamar, Self-portrait SP410

Van Gogh, Self-portrait and House at Cuesmes SP411

Designs: 5fr+2.50fr, Anton Bergmann and view of Lierre. 7fr+3.50fr, Henri Vieuxtemps and view of Verviers. 10fr+5fr, James Ensor, self-portrait, and masks.

1974, Apr. 6	Photo.	Perf. 11½
Size: 24x35mm		
B914 SP410 4fr + 2fr multi	.24	.24
B915 SP410 5fr + 2.50fr multi	.32	.32
B916 SP410 7fr + 3.50fr multi	.40	.40
Size: 35x52mm		
B917 SP410 10fr + 5fr multi	.65	.65
Nos. B914-B917 (4)	1.61	1.61

1974, Sept. 21	Photo.	Perf. 11½
B918 SP411 10fr + 5fr multi	.55	.55

Opening of Vincent van Gogh House at Cuesmes, where he worked as teacher.

Gentian — SP412

Spotted Cat's Ear — SP414

Badger SP413

Design: 7fr+3.50fr, Beetle.

1974, Dec. 8	Photo.	Perf. 11½
B919 SP412 4fr + 2fr multi	.25	.25
B920 SP413 5fr + 2.50fr multi	.30	.30
B921 SP413 7fr + 3.50fr multi	.40	.40
B922 SP414 10fr + 5fr multi	.60	.60
Nos. B919-B922 (4)	1.55	1.55

Pesaro Palace, Venice SP415

St. Bavon Abbey, Ghent SP416

Virgin and Child, by Michelangelo — SP417

1975, Apr. 12	Engr.	Perf. 11½
B923 SP415 6.50fr + 2.50fr brn	.35	.35
B924 SP416 10fr + 4.50 vio brn	.60	.60
B925 SP417 15fr + 6.50fr brt bl	.80	.80
Nos. B923-B925 (3)	1.75	1.75

Surtax was for various cultural organizations.

Frans Hemerijckx and Leprosarium, Kasai — SP418

1975, Sept. 13	Photo.	Perf. 11½
B926 SP418 20fr + 10fr multi	1.40	1.40

Dr. Frans Hemerijckx (1902-1969), tropical medicine and leprosy expert.

Emile Moyson — SP419

Beheading of St. Dympna — SP420a

Hand Reading Braille SP420

6.50fr+3fr, Dr. Ferdinand Augustin Snellaert.

1975, Nov. 22	Engr.	Perf. 11½
B927 SP419 4.50fr + 2fr lilac	.24	.24
B928 SP419 6.50fr + 3fr green	.35	.35

Engraved and Photogravure

B929 SP420 10fr + 5fr multi	.50	.50

Photo.

B930 SP420a 13fr + 6fr multi	.70	.70
Nos. B927-B930 (4)	1.79	1.79

Emile Moyson (1838-1868), freedom fighter for the rights of Flemings and Walloons; Dr. Snellaert (1809-1872), physician and Flemish patriot; Louis Braille (1809-1852), sesquicentennial of invention of Braille system of writing for the blind; St. Dympna, patron saint of Geel, famous for treatment of mentally ill.

The Cheese Vendor — SP421

Designs (THEMABELGA Emblem and): No. B932, Potato vendor. No. B933, Basket carrier. No. B934, Shrimp fisherman with horse, horiz. No. B935, Knife grinder, horiz. No. B936, Milk vendor with dog cart, horiz.

1975, Dec. 13	Engr. & Photo.	
B931 SP421 4.50fr + 1.50fr multi	.15	.15
B932 SP421 6.50fr + 3fr multi	.32	.32
B933 SP421 6.50fr + 3fr multi	.32	.32
B934 SP421 10fr + 5fr multi	.45	.45
B935 SP421 10fr + 5fr multi	.45	.45
B936 SP421 30fr + 15fr multi	1.50	1.50
Nos. B931-B936 (6)	3.19	3.19

THEMABELGA Intl. Topical Philatelic Exhib., Brussels, Dec. 13-21. Issued in sheets of 10 (5x2).

Blackface Fund Collector — SP422

1976, Feb. 14	Photo.	Perf. 11½
B937 SP422 10fr + 5fr multi	.55	.55

"Conservatoire Africain" philanthropic soc., cent., and to publicize the Princess Paola creches.

Swimming and Olympic Emblem SP423

Montreal Olympic Games Emblem and: 5fr+2fr, Running, vert. 6.50fr+2.50fr, Equestrian.

1976, Apr. 10	Photo.	Perf. 11½
B938 SP423 4.50fr + 1.50fr multi	.18	.18
B939 SP423 5fr + 2fr multi	.25	.25
B940 SP423 6.50fr + 2.50fr multi	.45	.45
Nos. B938-B940 (3)	.88	.88

21st Olympic Games, Montreal, Canada, July 17-Aug. 1.

Queen Elisabeth Playing Violin SP424

	Perf. 11½	
B941 SP424 14fr + 6fr blk & claret	.95	.95

Queen Elisabeth International Music Competition, 25th anniversary.

Souvenir Sheet

Jan Olieslagers, Bleriot Monoplane, Aero Club Emblem SP425

Engraved and Photogravure

1976, June 12		Perf. 11½
B942 SP425 25fr + 10fr multi	2.25	2.25

Royal Belgian Aero Club, 75th anniversary, and Jan Olieslagers (1883-1942), aviation pioneer.

Adoration of the Shepherds (detail), by Rubens SP426

Dwarf, by Velazquez SP427

Rubens Paintings (Details): 4.50fr, Descent from the Cross. No. B945, The Virgin with the Parrot. No. B946, Adoration of the Kings. No. B947, Last Communion of St. Francis. 30fr+15fr, Virgin and Child.

1976, Sept. 4	Photo.	Perf. 11½
Size: 35x52mm		
B943 SP426 4.50fr + 1.50fr multi	.35	.35
Size: 24x35mm		
B944 SP426 6.50fr + 3fr multi	.55	.55
B945 SP426 6.50fr + 3fr multi	.55	.55
B946 SP426 10fr + 5fr multi	.85	.85
B947 SP426 10fr + 5fr multi	.85	.85
Size: 35x52mm		
B948 SP426 30fr + 15fr multi	1.75	1.75
Nos. B943-B948 (6)	4.90	4.90

Peter Paul Rubens (1577-1640), Flemish painter, 400th birth anniversary.

1976, Nov. 6	Photo.	Perf. 11½
B949 SP427 14fr + 6fr multi	.80	.80

Surtax was for the National Association for the Mentally Handicapped.

Dr. Albert Hustin — SP428

Red Cross and Rheumatism Year Emblem — SP429

1977, Feb. 19	Photo.	Perf. 11½
B950 SP428 6.50fr + 2.50 multi	.38	.38
B951 SP429 14fr + 7fr multi	.75	.75

Belgian Red Cross.

Bordet Atheneum, Empress Maria Theresa — SP430

Conductor and Orchestra, by E. Tytgat — SP431

Lucien Van Obbergh, Stage — SP432

Humanistic Society Emblem SP433

Camille Lemonnier SP434

Design: No. B953, Marie-Therese College, Herve, and coat of arms.

1977, Mar. 21	Photo.	Perf. 11½
B952 SP430 4.50fr + 1fr multi	.20	.20
B953 SP430 4.50fr + 1fr multi	.20	.20
B954 SP431 5fr + 2fr multi	.24	.24
B955 SP432 6.50fr + 2fr multi	.32	.32
B956 SP433 6.50fr + 2fr blk & red	.32	.32

BELGIUM

		Engr.		
B957	SP434	10fr + 5fr slate bl	.48	.48
	Nos. B952-B957 (6)		1.76	1.76

Bicentenaries of the Jules Bordet Atheneum, Brussels, and the Marie-Therese College, Herve (#B952-B953); 50th anniv. of the Brussels Philharmonic Soc., and Artists' Union (#B954-B955): 25th anniv. of the Flemish Humanistic Organization (#B956); 75th anniv. of the French-speaking Belgian writers' organization (#957).

Young Soccer Players — SP435

Albert-Edouard Janssen, Financier — SP436

1977, Apr. 18   Photo.
B958 SP435 10fr + 5fr multi   .55 .55

30th Intl. Junior Soccer Tournament.

1977, Dec. 3   Engr.   Perf. 11½

Famous Men: No. B960, Joseph Wauters (1875-1929), editor of Le Peuple, and newspaper. No. B961, Jean Capart (1877-1947), Egyptologist, and hieroglyph. No. B962, August de Boeck (1865-1937), composer, and score.

B959	SP436	5fr + 2.50fr brown	.28	.28
B960	SP436	5fr + 2.50fr red	.28	.28
B961	SP436	10fr + 5fr magenta	.55	.55
B962	SP436	10fr + 5fr blue gray	.55	.55
	Nos. B959-B962 (4)		1.66	1.66

Abandoned Child — SP437

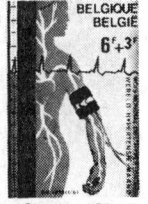

Checking Blood Pressure — SP438

De Mick Sanatorium, Brasschaat — SP439

1978, Feb. 18   Photo.   Perf. 11½
B963	SP437	4.50fr + 1.50fr multi	.15	.15
B964	SP438	6fr + 3fr multi	.38	.38
B965	SP439	10fr + 5fr multi	.60	.60
	Nos. B963-B965 (3)		1.13	1.13

Help for abandoned children (No. B963); fight against hypertension (No. B964); fight against tuberculosis (No. B965).

Actors and Theater SP440

Karel van de Woestijne SP441

Designs: No. B967, Harquebusier, Harquebusier Palace and coat of arms. 10fr+5fr, John of Austria and his signature.

Engraved and Photogravure
1978, June 17   Perf. 11½
| B966 | SP440 | 6fr + 3fr multi | .38 | .38 |
| B967 | SP440 | 6fr + 3fr multi | .38 | .38 |

		Engr.		
B968	SP441	8fr + 4fr black	.45	.45
B969	SP441	10fr + 5fr black	.55	.55
	Nos. B966-B969 (4)		1.76	1.76

Cent. of Royal Flemish Theater, Brussels (#B966); 400th anniv. of Harquebusiers' Guild of Vise, Liege (#967); Karel van de Woestijne (1878-1929), poet (#B968); 400th anniv. of signing of Perpetual Edict by John of Austria (#969).

Lake Placid '80 and Belgian Olympic Emblems — SP442

Designs (Moscow '80 Emblem and): 8fr+3.50fr, Kremlin Towers and Belgian Olympic Committee emblem. 7fr+3fr, Runners from Greek vase, Lake Placid '80 emblem and Olympic rings. 14fr+6fr, Olympic flame, Lake Placid '80 and Belgian emblems, Olympic rings.

1978, Nov. 4   Photo.   Perf. 11½
| B970 | SP442 | 6fr + 2.50fr multi | .30 | .30 |
| B971 | SP442 | 8fr + 3.50fr multi | .45 | .45 |

Souvenir Sheet
B972		Sheet of 2	1.50	1.50
a.		SP442 7fr + 3fr multi	.55	.55
b.		SP442 14fr + 6fr multi	.90	.90

Surtax was for 1980 Olympic Games.

Great Synagogue, Brussels — SP443

Dancers SP444

Father Pire, African Village SP445

1978, Dec. 2   Engr.   Perf. 11½
| B973 | SP443 | 6fr + 2fr sepia | .45 | .45 |

Photo.
B974	SP444	8fr + 3fr multi	.35	.35
B975	SP445	14fr + 7fr multi	.65	.65
	Nos. B973-B975 (3)		1.45	1.45

Centenary of Great Synagogue of Brussels; Flemish Catholic Youth Action Organization, 50th anniversary; Nobel Peace Prize awarded to Father Dominique Pire for his "Heart Open to the World" movement, 20th anniversary.

Young People Giving First Aid — SP446

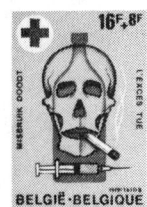

Skull with Bottle, Cigarette, Syringe — SP447

1979, Feb. 10   Photo.   Perf. 11½
| B976 | SP446 | 8fr + 3fr multi | .35 | .35 |
| B977 | SP447 | 16fr + 8fr multi | .85 | .85 |

Belgian Red Cross.

Beatrice Soetkens with Statue of Virgin Mary — SP448

Details from Tapestries, 1516-1518, Showing Legend of Our Lady of Sand: 8fr+3fr, Francois de Tassis accepting letter from Emperor Frederick III (beginning of postal service). 14fr+7fr, Arrival of statue, Francois de Tassis and Philip the Fair. No. B981, Statue carried in procession by future Emperor Charles V and his brother Ferdinand. No. B982, Ship carrying Beatrice Soetkens with statue to Brussels, horiz.

1979, May 5   Photo.   Perf. 11½
B978	SP448	6fr + 2fr multi	.25	.25
B979	SP448	8fr + 3fr multi	.40	.40
B980	SP448	14fr + 7fr multi	.65	.65
B981	SP448	20fr + 10fr multi	1.10	1.10
	Nos. B978-B981 (4)		2.40	2.40

Souvenir Sheet
| B982 | SP448 | 20fr + 10fr multi | .90 | .90 |

The surtax was for festivities in connection with the millennium of Brussels.

Notre Dame Abbey, Brussels SP449

Designs: 8fr+3fr, Beauvoorde Castle. 14fr+7fr, 1st issue of "Courrier de L'Escaut" and Barthelemy Dumortier, founder. 20fr+10fr, Shrine of St. Hermes, Renaix.

Engraved and Photogravure
1979, Sept. 15   Perf. 11½
B983	SP449	6fr + 2fr multi	.35	.35
B984	SP449	8fr + 3fr multi	.50	.50
B985	SP449	14fr + 7fr multi	.60	.60
B986	SP449	20fr + 10fr multi	1.10	1.10
	Nos. B983-B986 (4)		2.55	2.55

50th anniv. of restoration of Notre Dame de la Cambre Abbey; historic Beauvoorde Castle, 15th cent. sesquicentennial of the regional newspaper "Le Courrier de L'Escaut"; 850th anniv. of the consecration of the Collegiate Church of St. Hermes, Renaix.

Grand-Hornu Coal Mine — SP450

1979, Oct. 22   Engr.   Perf. 11½
| B987 | SP450 | 10fr + 5fr blk | .55 | .55 |

Henry Heyman — SP451

Veterans Organization Medal — SP452

Boy and IYC Emblem SP453

1979, Dec. 8   Photo.   Perf. 11½
B988	SP451	8fr + 3fr multi	.45	.45
B989	SP452	10fr + 5fr multi	.55	.55
B990	SP453	16fr + 8fr multi	.75	.75
	Nos. B988-B990 (3)		1.75	1.75

Henri Heyman (1879-1958), Minister of State; Disabled Veterans' Organization, 50th anniv.; Intl. Year of the Child.

Ivo Van Damme, Olympic Rings — SP454

1980, May 3   Photo.   Perf. 11½
| B991 | SP454 | 20fr + 10fr multi | 1.10 | 1.10 |

Ivo Van Damme (1954-1976), silver medalist, 800-meter race, Montreal Olympics, 1976. Surtax was for Van Damme Memorial Foundation.

Queen Louis, King Leopold I SP455

150th Anniversary of Independence (Queens and Kings): 9fr+3fr, Marie Henriette. Leopold II. 14fr+6fr, Elisabeth, Albert I. 17fr+8fr, Astrid, Leopold III. 25fr+10fr, Fabiola, Baudouin.

Photogravure and Engraved
1980, May 31   Perf. 11½
B992	SP455	6.50 + 1.50fr multi	.28	.28
B993	SP455	9 + 3fr multi	.50	.50
B994	SP455	14 + 6fr multi	.70	.70
B995	SP455	17 + 8fr multi	1.00	1.00
B996	SP455	25 + 10fr multi	1.25	1.25
	Nos. B992-B996 (5)		3.73	3.73

Miner, by Constantine Meunier SP456

Seal of Bishop Notger, First Prince-Bishop — SP457

9fr+3fr, Brewer, 16th century, from St. Lambert's reliquary, vert. 25fr+10fr, Virgin and Child, 13th century, St. John's Collegiate Church, Liege.

1980, Sept. 13   Photo.   Perf. 11½
B997	SP456	9 + 3fr multi	.35	.35
B998	SP456	17 + 6fr multi	.70	.70
B999	SP456	25 + 10fr multi	1.10	1.10
	Nos. B997-B999 (3)		2.15	2.15

Souvenir Sheet
| B1000 | SP457 | 20 + 10fr multi | 1.25 | 1.25 |

Millennium of the Principality of Liege.

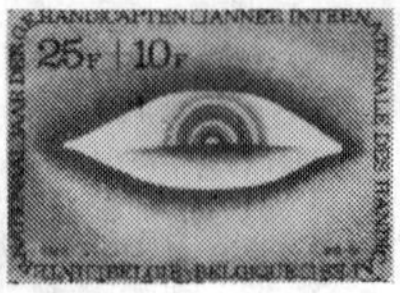

BELGIUM

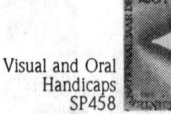

Visual and Oral Handicaps SP458

Intl. Year of the Disabled: 10fr+5fr, Cerebral handicap, vert.

1981, Feb. 9		Photo.	Perf. 11½
B1001	SP458 10 + 5fr multi	.70	.70
B1002	SP458 25 + 10fr multi	1.65	1.65

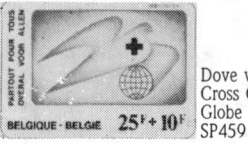

Dove with Red Cross Carrying Globe SP459

Design: 10fr+5fr, Atomic model, vert.

1981, Apr. 6		Photo.	Perf. 11½
B1003	SP459 10 + 5fr multi	.70	.70
B1004	SP459 25 + 10fr multi	1.65	1.65

Red Cross and: 15th Intl. Radiology Congress, Brussels, June 24-July 1 (#B1003); intl. disaster relief (#B1004).

Ovide Decroly SP460

1981, June 1		Photo.	Perf. 11½
B1005	SP460 35 + 15fr multi	2.00	2.00

Ovide Decroly (1871-1932), developer of educational psychology.

Mounted Police Officer — SP461

Billiards — SP462

Anniversaries: 9fr+4fr, Gendarmerie (State Police Force), 150th. 20fr+7fr, Carabineers Regiment, 150th. 40fr+20fr, Guides Regiment.

1981, Dec. 7		Photo.	Perf. 11½
B1006	SP461 9 + 4fr multi	.60	.60
B1007	SP461 20 + 7fr multi	1.25	1.25
B1008	SP461 40 + 20fr multi	2.75	2.75
	Nos. B1006-B1008 (3)	4.60	4.60

1982, Mar. 29		Photo.	Perf. 11½
B1009	SP462 6 + 2fr shown	.38	.38
B1010	SP462 9 + 4fr Cycling	.60	.60
B1011	SP462 10 + 5fr Soccer	.70	.70
B1012	SP462 50 + 14fr Yachting	3.00	3.00
	Nos. B1009-B1012 (4)	4.68	4.68

Souvenir Sheet

B1013	Sheet of 4	5.00	5.00
a.	SP462 25fr like #B1009	1.40	1.40
b.	SP462 25fr like #B1010	1.40	1.40
c.	SP462 25fr like #B1011	1.40	1.40
d.	SP462 25fr like #B1012	1.40	1.40

#B1013 shows designs in changed colors.

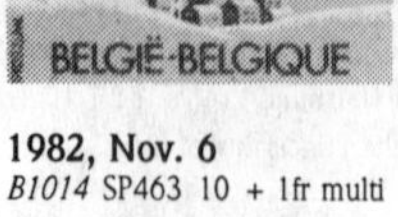

Christmas SP463

1982, Nov. 6			
B1014	SP463 10 + 1fr multi	.60	.45

Surtax was for tuberculosis research.

Belgica '82 Intl. Stamp Exhibition, Brussels, Dec. 11-19 SP464

Messengers (Prints). Nos. B1016-B1018 vert.

Photogravure and Engraved

1982, Dec. 11		Perf. 11½
B1015	SP464 7 + 2fr multi	.38 .38
B1016	SP464 7.50 + 2.50fr multi	.45 .45
B1017	SP464 10 + 3fr multi	.55 .55
B1018	SP464 17 + 7fr multi	1.10 1.10
B1019	SP464 20 + 9fr multi	1.25 1.25
B1020	SP464 25 + 10fr multi	1.50 1.50
	Nos. B1015-B1020 (6)	5.23 5.23

Souvenir Sheet

| B1021 | SP464 50 + 25fr multi | 6.00 6.00 |

No. B1021 contains one 48x37mm stamp.

50th Anniv. of Catholic Charities SP465

Mountain Climbing SP466

1983, Jan. 22		Photo.	Perf. 11½
B1022	SP465 10 + 2fr multi	.65	.65

1983, Mar. 7		Photo.	
B1023	SP466 12 + 3fr shown	.80	.80
B1024	SP466 20 + 5fr Hiking	1.25	1.25

Surtax was for Red Cross.

Madonna by Jef Wauters — SP467

Rifles Uniform — SP468

1983, Nov. 21		Photo.	Perf. 11½
B1025	SP467 11 + 1fr multi	.60	.60

1983, Dec. 5		Photo.	Perf. 11½
B1026	SP468 8 + 2fr shown	.50	.50
B1027	SP468 11 + 2fr Lancers uniform	.75	.75
B1028	SP468 50 + 12fr Grenadiers uniform	3.50	3.50
	Nos. B1026-B1028 (3)	4.75	4.75

Type of 1984

1984, Mar. 3		Photo.	Perf. 11½
B1029	A495 8 + 2fr Judo, horiz.	.55	.55
B1030	A495 12 + 3fr Wind surfing	.85	.85

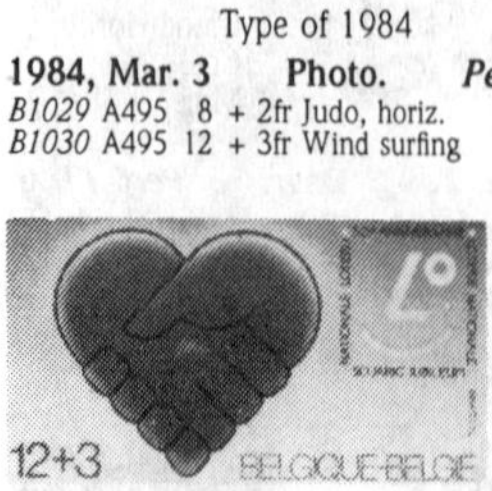

50th Anniv. of Natl. Lottery SP469

1984, Mar. 31		Photo.	Perf. 11½
B1031	SP469 12 + 3fr multi	.75	.75

Brussels Modern Art Museum Opening SP470

Paintings: 8fr+2fr, Les Masques Singuliers, by James Ensor. 12fr+3fr, Empire des Lumieres, by Rene Magritte. 22fr+5fr, The End, by Jan Cox. 50fr+13fr, Rhythm No. 6, by Jo Delahaut.

1984, Sept. 1		Photo.	
B1032	SP470 8 + 2fr multi	.60	.60
B1033	SP470 12 + 3fr multi	.90	.90
B1034	SP470 22 + 5fr multi	1.65	1.65
B1035	SP470 50 + 13fr multi	3.75	3.75
	Nos. B1032-B1035 (4)	6.90	6.90

Child with Parents — SP471

1984, Nov. 3		Photo.	
B1036	SP471 10 + 2fr shown	.60	.60
B1037	SP471 12 + 3fr Siblings	.75	.75
B1038	SP471 15 + 3fr Merry-go-round	.85	.85
	Nos. B1036-B1038 (3)	2.20	2.20

Surtax was for children's programs.

Christmas 1984 SP472

1984, Dec. 1			
B1039	SP472 12 + 1fr Three Kings	.75	.75

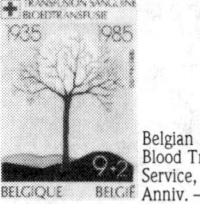

Belgian Red Cross Blood Transfusion Service, 50th Anniv. — SP473

1985, Mar. 4		Photo.	Perf. 11½
B1040	SP473 9 + 2fr Tree	.60	.60
B1041	SP473 23 + 5fr Hearts	1.40	1.40

Surtax was for the Belgian Red Cross.

Solidarity SP474

Castles.

1985, Nov. 4		Photo. & Engr.	
B1042	SP474 9 + 2fr Trazegnies	.60	.60
B1043	SP474 12 + 3fr Laarne	.80	.80
B1044	SP474 23 + 5fr Turnhout	1.40	1.40
B1045	SP474 50 + 12fr Colonster	3.50	3.50
	Nos. B1042-B1045 (4)	6.30	6.30

Christmas 1985, New Year 1986 — SP475

Painting: Miniature from the Book of Hours, by Jean duc de Berry.

1985, Nov. 25		Photo.	
B1046	SP475 12 + 1fr multi	.70	.70

King Baudouin Foundation SP476

1986, Mar. 24		Photo.	
B1047	SP476 12 + 3fr Emblem	.80	.80

Surtax for the foundation.

Madonna SP477

Adoration of the Mystic Lamb, St. Bavon Cathedral Altarpiece, Ghent — SP478

Paintings by Hubert van Eyck (c. 1370-1426).

1986, Apr. 5		Photo.	Perf. 11½
B1048	SP477 9 + 2fr shown	.65	.65
B1049	SP477 13 + 3fr Christ in Majesty	.95	.95
B1050	SP477 24 + 6fr St. John the Baptist	1.75	1.75
	Nos. B1048-B1050 (3)	3.35	3.35

Souvenir Sheet

| B1051 | SP478 50 + 12fr multi | 5.25 | 5.25 |

Surtax for cultural organizations.

Antique Automobiles SP479

1986, Nov. 3		Photo.	
B1052	SP479 9 + 2fr Lenoir, 1863	.65	.65
B1053	SP479 13 + 3fr Pipe de Tourisme, 1911	.90	.90
B1054	SP479 24 + 6fr Minerva 22 HP, 1930	1.75	1.75
B1055	SP479 26 + 6fr FN 8 Cylinder, 1931	1.90	1.90
	Nos. B1052-B1055 (4)	5.20	5.20

BELGIUM

Christmas 1986, New Year 1987 — SP480

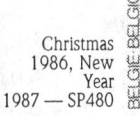

1986, Nov. 24   *Photo.*
B1056 SP480 13 + 1fr Village in winter   .75   .75

Natl. Red Cross — SP482

European Conservation Year — SP483

Nobel Prize winners for physiology (1938) and medicine (1974): No. B1058, Corneille Heymans (1892-1968). No. B1059, A. Claude (1899-1983).

Photogravure and Engraved
1987, Feb. 16   *Perf. 11½*
B1058 SP482 13 + 3fr dk brn & red   .90   .90
B1059 SP482 24 + 6fr dk brn & red   1.65   1.65

1987, Mar. 16   *Photo.*
B1060 SP483 9 + 2fr Bee orchid   .60   .60
B1061 SP483 24 + 6fr Horseshoe bat   1.65   1.65
B1062 SP483 26 + 6fr Peregrine falcon   1.75   1.75
     Nos. B1060-B1062 (3)   4.00   4.00

Castles — SP484

1987, Oct. 17   *Photo. & Engr.*
B1063 SP484 9 + 2fr Rixensart   .60   .60
B1064 SP484 13 + 3fr Westerlo   .90   .90
B1065 SP484 26 + 5fr Fallais   1.75   1.75
B1066 SP484 50 + 12fr Gaasbeek   3.50   3.50
     Nos. B1063-B1066 (4)   6.75   6.75

Christmas 1987 — SP485

White and Yellow Cross of Belgium, 50th Anniv. — SP486

Painting: Holy Family, by Rev. Father Lens.

1987, Nov. 14   *Photo.*
B1067 SP485 13 + 1fr multi   .85   .85

1987, Dec. 5
B1068 SP486 9 + 2fr multi   .70   .70

Promote Philately — SP487

Various flowers from *Sixty Roses for a Queen*, by P. J. Redoute (1759-1840).

1988, Apr. 25   *Photo.*   *Perf. 11½*
B1069 SP487 13 + 3fr shown   1.00   1.00
B1070 SP487 24 + 6fr multi, diff.   1.75   1.75
     Souvenir Sheet
B1071 SP487 50 + 12fr multi, diff.   3.75   3.75
     See Nos. B1081-B1083, B1089-B1091, 1346.

1988 Summer Olympics, Seoul — SP488

1988, June 6   *Photo.*   *Perf. 11½*
B1072 SP488 9fr + 2fr Table tennis   .65   .65
B1073 SP488 13fr + 3fr Cycling   .95   .95
     Souvenir Sheet
B1074 SP488 50fr + 12fr Marathon runners   3.70   3.70

Solidarity — SP489

1988, Oct. 24   *Photo.*   *Perf. 12x11½*
B1075 SP489 9fr + 2fr Jacques Brel   .60   .60
B1076 SP489 13fr + 3fr Jef Denyn   .90   .90
B1077 SP489 26fr + 6fr Fr. Ferdinand Verbiest   1.75   1.75
     Nos. B1075-B1077 (3)   3.25   3.25

Belgian Red Cross SP490

Paintings: No. B1078, *Crucifixion of Christ*, by Rogier van der Weyden (c. 1399-1464). No. B1079, *Virgin and Child*, by David (c. 1460-1523). B1089, *The Good Samaritan*, by Denis van Alsloot.

1989, Feb. 20   *Photo.*   *Perf. 11½*
B1078 SP490 9fr + 2fr multi   .60   .60
B1079 SP490 13fr + 3fr multi   .90   .90
B1080 SP490 24fr + 6fr multi   1.65   1.65
     Nos. B1078-B1080 (3)   3.15   3.15

Stamp Collecting Promotion Type of 1988

Various flowers from *Sixty Roses for a Queen*, by P.J. Redoute (1759-1840) and inscriptions: No. B1081, "Centfeuille unique melee de rouge." No. B1082, "Bengale a grandes feuilles." No. B1083, Aeme vibere (tea roses).

1989, Apr. 17
B1081 SP487 13fr + 5fr multi   1.00   1.00
B1082 SP487 24fr + 6fr multi   1.65   1.65
     Souvenir Sheet
B1083 SP487 50fr + 17fr multi   3.75   3.75

Solidarity SP491

Royal Greenhouses of Laeken.

1989, Oct. 23
B1084 SP491 9fr + 3fr Exterior   .60   .60
B1085 SP491 13fr + 4fr Interior, vert.   .85   .85
B1086 SP491 24fr + 5fr Dome exterior, vert.   1.40   1.40
B1087 SP491 26fr + 6fr Dome interior, vert.   1.50   1.50
     Nos. B1084-B1087 (4)   4.35   4.35

Queen Elisabeth Chapelle Musicale, 50th Anniv. — SP492

1989, Nov. 6
B1088 SP492 24fr + 6fr G clef   1.45   1.45

Stamp Collecting Promotion Type of 1988

Various flowers from *Sixty Roses for a Queen*, by P.J. Redoute (1759-1840): No. B1089, *Bengale desprez*. No. B1090, *Bengale philippe*. No. B1091, *Maria leonida*.

1990, Feb. 5
B1089 SP487 14fr + 7fr multi   1.15   1.15
B1090 SP487 25fr + 12fr multi   2.00   2.00
     Souvenir Sheet
B1091 SP487 50fr + 20fr multi   3.75   3.75

Youth and Music — SP493

Designs: 14fr+3fr, Beethoven and Lamoraal, Count of Egmont (1522-1568). 25fr+6fr, Joseph Cantre (1890-1957), drawing and sculpture.

1990, Oct. 6
B1092 SP493 10fr + 2fr multi   .70   .70
B1093 SP493 14fr + 3fr multi   1.00   1.00
B1094 SP493 25fr + 6fr multi   1.80   1.80
     Nos. B1092-B1094 (3)   3.50   3.50

King Baudouin & Queen Fabiola, 30th Wedding Anniv. — SP494

1990, Dec. 10
B1095 SP494 50fr +15fr multi   4.25   4.25

Belgian Red Cross SP495

Details from paintings: No. B1096, The Temptation of St. Anthony by Hieronymus Bosch. No. B1097, The Annunciation by Dirk Bouts.

1991, Feb. 25,   *Photo.*   *Perf. 11½*
B1096 SP495 14fr +3fr multi   1.10   1.10
B1097 SP495 25fr +6fr multi   2.00   2.00

Belgian Film Personalities — SP496

Designs: 10fr+2fr, Charles Dekeukeleire (1905-1971), producer. 14fr+3fr, Jacques Ledoux (1921-1988), film conservationist. 25fr+6fr, Jacques Feyder (1899-1948), director.

1991, Oct. 28   *Photo.*   *Perf. 11½*
B1098 SP496 10fr +2fr multi   .75   .75
B1099 SP496 14fr +3fr multi   1.05   1.05
B1100 SP496 25fr +6fr multi   1.90   1.90
     Nos. B1098-B1100 (3)   3.70   3.70

1992 Winter and Summer Olympics, Albertville and Barcelona — SP497

1992, Jan. 20   *Photo.*   *Perf. 11½*
B1101 SP497 10fr +2fr Speed skating   .75   .75
B1102 SP497 10fr +2fr Baseball   .75   .75
B1103 SP497 14fr +3fr Women's tennis, horiz.   1.05   1.05
B1104 SP497 25fr +6fr Skeet shooting   1.90   1.90
     Nos. B1101-B1104 (4)   4.45   4.45

Folk Legends SP498

11fr + 2fr, Proud Margaret. 15fr + 3fr, Gustine Maca & the Witches. 28fr + 6fr, Reynard the Fox.

1992, June 22   *Photo.*   *Perf. 11½*
B1105 SP498 11fr +2fr multi   .78   .78
B1106 SP498 15fr +3fr multi   1.10   1.10
B1107 SP498 28fr +6fr multi   2.00   2.00
     Nos. B1105-B1107 (3)   3.88   3.88

Belgian Red Cross SP499

Paintings: 15fr + 3fr, Man with the Pointed Hat, by Adriaen Brouwer (1605-1638). 28fr + 7fr, Nereid and Triton, by Peter Paul Rubens, horiz.

1993, Feb. 15   *Photo.*   *Perf. 11½*
B1108 SP499 15fr +3fr multi   1.10   1.10
B1109 SP499 28fr +7fr multi   2.10   2.10

Fight Against Cancer SP500

1993, Sept. 20   *Photo.*   *Perf. 11½*
B1110 SP500 15fr +3fr multicolored   1.10   1.10

Intl. Olympic Committee, Cent. — SP501

#B1112, Soccer players. #B1113, Figure skater.

1994, Feb. 14   *Photo.*   *Perf. 11½*
B1111 SP501 16fr +3fr multi   1.00   1.00
B1112 SP501 16fr +3fr multi   1.00   1.00
B1113 SP501 16fr +3fr multi   1.00   1.00
     Nos. B1111-B1113 (3)   3.00   3.00
1994 World Cup Soccer Championships, Los Angeles (#B1112). 1994 Winter Olympics, Lillehammer, Norway (#B1113).

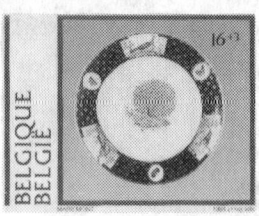

BELGIUM

Porcelain — SP502

Designs: No. B1114, Tournai plate, Museum of Mariemont-Morlanweiz. No. B1115, Etterbeek cup, saucer, Municipal Museum, Louvain. 50fr+11fr, Delft earthenware jars, Pharmacy Museum of Maaseik.

1994, June 27 Photo. Perf. 11½
B1114	SP502	16fr +3fr multi	1.10	1.10
B1115	SP502	16fr +3fr multi	1.10	1.10

Souvenir Sheet
B1116	SP502	50fr +11fr multi	3.50	3.50

No. B1116 contains one 49x38mm stamp.

Solidarity — SP503

Design: 16fr+3fr, Hearing-impaired person.

1994, Nov. 14 Photo. Perf. 11½
B1117	SP503	16fr +3fr multi	1.25	1.25

Museums — SP504

#B1118, Natl. Flax Museum, Kortrijk. #B1119, Natl. Water & Fountain Museum, Genval. 34fr+6fr, Intl. Carnival and Mask Museum, Binche.

1995, Jan. 30 Photo. Perf. 11½
B1118	SP504	16fr +3fr multi	1.25	1.25
B1119	SP504	16fr +3fr multi	1.25	1.25

Souvenir Sheet
B1120	SP504	34fr +6fr multi	2.75	2.75

Surtax for promotion of philately.

"Souvenir Sheets"
Beginning in 1995 items looking like souvenir sheets have appeared in the market. The 1995 one has the design used for No. B1120. The 1996 one has the design similar to the one used for No. B1128. The 1997 one has the design used for No. B1131. These have no postal value.

Royal Belgian Soccer Assoc., Cent. SP505

1995, Aug. 21 Photo. Perf. 11½
B1121	SP505	16fr +4fr multi	1.40	1.40

Belgian Red Cross SP506

Designs: No. B1122, Princess Astrid, chairwoman of Belgian Red Cross. No. B1123, Wilhelm C. Röntgen (1845-1923), discoverer of the X-ray. No. B1124, Louis Pasteur (1822-95), scientist.

1995, Sept. 11
B1122	SP506	16fr +3fr multi	1.25	1.25
B1123	SP506	16fr +3fr multi	1.25	1.25
B1124	SP506	16fr +3fr multi	1.25	1.25
		Nos. B1122-B1124 (3)	3.75	3.75

Solidarity — SP507

1995, Nov. 6 Photo. Perf. 11½
B1125	SP507	16fr +4fr multi	1.30	1.30

Surtax for fight against AIDS.

Museums — SP508

Designs: No. B1126, Museum of Walloon Life, Liège. No. B1127, Natl. Gin Museum, Hasselt. 34fr+6fr, Butchers' Guild Hall Museum, Antwerp.

1996, Feb. 19 Photo. Perf. 11½
B1126	SP508	16fr +4fr multi	1.30	1.30
B1127	SP508	16fr +4fr multi	1.30	1.30

Souvenir Sheet
B1128	SP508	34fr +6fr multi	2.60	2.60

Modern Olympic Games, Cent. SP509

1996, July 1 Photo. Perf. 11½
B1129	SP509	16fr +4fr Table tennis	1.30	1.30
B1130	SP509	16fr +4fr Swimming	1.30	1.30

Souvenir Sheet
B1131	SP509	34fr +6fr High jump	2.60	2.60

No. B1131 contains one 49x38mm stamp.

UNICEF, 50th Anniv. — SP510

1996, Nov. 18 Photo. Perf. 11½
B1132	SP510	16fr +4fr multi	1.40	1.40

Museums SP511

#B1133, Deportation and Resistance Museum, Mechlin. #B1134, Iron Museum, Saint Hubert. 41fr+9fr, Horta Museum, Saint Gilles.

1997, Jan. 20 Photo. Perf. 11½
B1133	SP511	17fr +4fr multi	1.30	1.30
B1134	SP511	17fr +4fr multi	1.30	1.30

Souvenir Sheet
B1135	SP511	41fr +9fr multi	3.10	3.10

Surtax for "Pro-Post" association.

Judo — SP512   Solidarity — SP513

1997, May 5 Photo. Perf. 11½
B1136	SP512	17fr +4fr Men's (10a)	1.25	1.25
B1137	SP512	17fr +4fr Women's (10b)	1.25	1.25

Surtax for Belgian Olympic Committee.

1997, Oct. 25
B1138	SP513	17fr +4fr multi	1.25	1.25

Surtax for Multiple Sclerosis research.

King Leopold III — SP514

32fr+15fr, King Baudouin I. 50fr+25fr, King Albert II.

1998, Feb. 16 Engr. Perf. 11½
B1139	SP514	17fr +8fr dk grn	1.50	1.50
B1140	SP514	32fr +15fr dk brn blk	2.75	2.75

Souvenir Sheet
B1141	SP514	50fr +25fr dk vio brn	4.50	4.50

Sports SP515

1998, June 8 Photo. Perf. 11½
B1142	SP515	17fr +4fr Pelota	1.25	1.25
B1143	SP515	17fr +4fr Handball	1.25	1.25

Souvenir Sheet
B1144	SP515	30fr +7fr Soccer	2.00	2.00

1998 World Cup Soccer Championships, France (#B1144).

AIR POST STAMPS

Fokker FVII/3m over Ostend — AP1

Designs: 1.50fr, Plane over St. Hubert. 2fr, over Namur. 5fr, over Brussels.

Perf. 11½
1930, Apr. 30 Unwmk. Photo.
C1	AP1	50c blue	.40	.40
C2	AP1	1.50fr black brn	2.25	2.50
C3	AP1	2fr deep green	2.00	.55
C4	AP1	5fr brown lake	1.75	.95
		Nos. C1-C4 (4)	6.40	4.40

Exist imperf.

1930, Dec. 5
C5	AP1	5fr dark violet	30.00	30.00

Issued for use on a mail carrying flight from Brussels to Leopoldville, Belgian Congo, starting Dec. 7. Exists imperf.

Nos. C2 and C4 Surcharged in Carmine or Blue

1fr   1fr
×   ×

1935, May 23
C6	AP1	1fr on 1.50fr (C)	.55	.40
C7	AP1	4fr on 5fr (Bl)	7.50	7.00

Catalogue values for unused stamps in this section, from this point to the end of the section, are for Never Hinged items.

DC-4 Skymaster, Sabena Airline AP5

1946, Apr. 20 Engr. Perf. 11½
C8	AP5	6fr blue	.75	.25
C9	AP5	8.50fr violet brn	1.00	.35
C10	AP5	50fr yellow grn	5.00	.60
a.		Perf. 12x11½ ('54)	325.00	
C11	AP5	100fr gray	8.25	1.10
a.		Perf. 12x11½ ('54)	65.00	1.10
		Nos. C8-C11 (4)	15.00	

Evolution of Postal Transportation — AP6

1949, July 1
C12	AP6	50fr dark brown	42.50	15.00

Centenary of Belgian postage stamps.

Glider — AP7

Design: 7fr, "Tipsy" plane.

1951, June 18 Photo. Perf. 13½
C12A		Strip of 2 + label	70.00	60.00
b.	AP7	6fr dark blue	25.00	17.50
c.	AP7	7fr carmine rose	25.00	17.50

For the 50th anniv. of the Aero Club of Belgium. The strip sold for 50fr.

1951, July 25 Perf. 13½
C13	AP7	6fr sepia	4.50	.15
C14	AP7	7fr Prus green	3.50	.95

UN Types of Regular Issue, 1958

Designs: 5fr, ICAO. 6fr, World Meteorological Organization. 7.50fr, Protection of Refugees. 8fr, General Agreement on Tariffs and Trade. 9fr, UNICEF. 10fr, Atomic Energy Agency.

Perf. 11½
1958, Apr. 17 Unwmk. Engr.
C15	A137	5fr dull blue	.30	.30
C16	A136	6fr yellow grn	.30	.45
C17	A137	7.50fr lilac	.30	.30
C18	A136	8fr sepia	.30	.30

BELGIUM

C19	A137	9fr carmine	.40	.50
C20	A136	10fr redsh brown	.75	.60
		Nos. C15-C20 (6)	2.30	2.45

World's Fair, Brussels, Apr. 17-Oct. 19. See note after No. 476.

AIR POST SEMI-POSTAL STAMPS

Catalogue values for unused stamps in this section are for Never Hinged items.

American Soldier in Combat — SPAP1

1946, June 15   Unwmk.   *Perf. 11x11½*   Engr.

CB1	SPAP1	17.50fr + 62.50fr dl brn	1.25	.90
CB2	SPAP1	17.50fr + 62.50fr dl gray grn	1.25	.90

Surtax for an American memorial at Bastogne.

An overprint, "Hommage a Roosevelt," was privately applied to Nos. CB1-CB2 in 1947 by the Association Belgo-Americaine.

In 1950 another private overprint was applied, in red, to Nos. CB1-CB2. It consists of "16-12-1944, 25-1-1945, Dedication July 16, 1950" and outlines of the American eagle emblem and the Bastogne Memorial. Similar overprints were applied to Nos. 265 and 345.

Flight Allegory — SPAP2

1946, Sept. 7   *Perf. 11½*

CB3	SPAP2	2fr + 8fr brt vio	.60	1.00

The surtax was for the benefit of aviation.

Nos. B417-B425 Surcharged in Various Arrangements in Red or Dark Blue

POSTE AERIENNE   LUCHTPOST
1F   2F 1F   +2F
LUCHTPOST   POSTE AERIENNE

Type I- Top line "POSTE AERIENNE"
Type II- Top line "LUCHTPOST"

1947, May 18   Photo.   *Perf. 11½*

Type I

CB4	1fr + 2fr on #B417 (R)	.60	.90
CB5	1.50fr + 2.50fr on #B418	.60	.90
CB6	2fr + 45fr on #B419	.60	.90
CB7	1fr + 2fr on #B420 (R)	.60	.90
CB8	1.50fr + 2.50fr on #B421	.60	.90
CB9	2fr + 45fr on #B422	.60	.90
CB10	1fr + 2fr on #B423 (R)	.60	.90
CB11	1.50fr + 2.50fr on #B424 (R)	.60	.90
CB12	2fr + 45fr on #B425	.60	.90

Type II

CB4A	1fr + 2fr on #B417 (R)	.60	.90
CB5A	1.50fr + 2.50fr on #B418	.60	.90
CB6A	2fr + 45fr on #B419	.60	.90
CB7A	1fr + 2fr on #B420 (R)	.60	.90
CB8A	1.50fr + 2.50fr on #B421	.60	.90
CB9A	2fr + 45fr on #B422	.60	.90
CB10A	1fr + 2fr on #B423 (R)	.60	.90
CB11A	1.50fr + 2.50fr on #B424 (R)	.60	.90
CB12A	2fr + 45fr on #B425	.60	.90
	Nos. CB4-CB12A (18)	10.80	16.20

Issued for CIPEX, NYC. In 1948 Nos. CB4-CB12 and CB4A-CB12A were punched with the letters "IMABA", and the inscription "Imaba du 21 au 29 aout 1948" was applied to the backs. Value $20.

Helicopter Leaving Airport — SPAP3

1950, Aug. 7

CB13	SPAP3	7fr + 3fr blue	9.00	5.25

Surtax for the Natl. Aeronautical Committee.

SPECIAL DELIVERY STAMPS

From 1874 to 1903 certain hexagonal telegraph stamps were used as special delivery stamps.

Town Hall, Brussels — SD1   Eupen — SD2

Designs: 2.35fr, Street in Ghent. 3.50fr, Bishop's Palace, Liege. 5.25fr, Notre Dame Cathedral, Antwerp.

1929   Unwmk.   Photo.   *Perf. 11½*

E1	SD1	1.75fr dark blue	.80	.32
E2	SD1	2.35fr carmine	1.50	.45
E3	SD1	3.50fr dark violet	10.00	9.00
E4	SD1	5.25fr olive green	5.50	5.25

1931

E5	SD2	2.45fr dark green	11.00	2.50
		Nos. E1-E5 (5)	28.80	17.52

No. E5 Surcharged in Red   **2Fr 50**

1932

E6	SD2	2.50fr on 2.45fr dk grn	9.00	1.25

POSTAGE DUE STAMPS

D1   D2

1870   Unwmk.   Typo.   *Perf. 15*

J1	D1	10c green	3.75	2.00
J2	D1	20c ultra, thin paper	30.00	3.75

In 1909 many bisects of Nos. J1-J2 were created. The 10c bisect used as 5c on piece sells for $3.50. No. J2 was also printed on thicker paper and in aniline ink on thin paper.

1895-09   *Perf. 14*

J3	D2	5c yellow grn	.15	.15
J4	D2	10c orange brn	17.50	1.75
J5	D2	10c carmine ('00)	.15	.15
J6	D2	20c olive green	.15	.15
J7	D2	30c pale blue ('09)	.30	.25
J8	D2	50c yellow brn	17.50	5.00
J9	D2	50c gray ('00)	.75	.45
J10	D2	1fr carmine	20.00	11.50
J11	D2	1fr ocher ('00)	6.50	5.00
		Nos. J3-J11 (9)	63.00	24.40

1916   Redrawn

J12	D2	5c blue grn	25.00	7.00
J13	D2	10c carmine	42.50	11.00
J14	D2	20c dp gray grn	42.50	15.00
J15	D2	30c brt blue	6.00	5.00
J16	D2	50c gray	110.00	60.00
		Nos. J12-J16 (5)	226.00	98.00

In the redrawn stamps the lions have a heavy, colored outline. There is a thick vertical line at the outer edge of the design on each side.

D3   D4

1919   *Perf. 14*

J17	D3	5c green	.40	.50
J18	D3	10c carmine	.95	.40
J19	D3	20c gray green	7.25	1.25
J20	D3	30c bright blue	1.40	.40
J21	D3	50c gray	2.75	.50
		Nos. J17-J21 (5)	12.75	3.05

1922-32

J22	D4	5c dk gray	.15	.15
J23	D4	10c green	.15	.15
J24	D4	20c deep brown	.15	.15
J25	D4	30c ver ('24)	.65	.15
a.		30c rose red	1.00	.45
J26	D4	40c red brn ('25)	.25	.15
J27	D4	50c ultra	1.90	.15
J28	D4	70c red brn ('29)	.30	.15
J29	D4	1fr violet ('25)	.45	.15
J30	D4	1fr rose lilac ('32)	.55	.60
J31	D4	1.20fr ol grn ('29)	.65	.45
J32	D4	1.50fr ol grn ('32)	.65	.45
J33	D4	2fr violet ('29)	.75	.20
J34	D4	3.50fr dp blue ('29)	1.00	.25
		Nos. J22-J34 (13)	7.60	2.70

1934-46   *Perf. 14x13½*

J35	D4	35c green ('35)	.40	.45
J36	D4	50c slate	.20	.15
J37	D4	60c carmine ('38)	.40	.30
J38	D4	80c slate ('38)	.30	.15
J39	D4	1.40fr gray ('35)	.65	.45
J39A	D4	3fr org brn ('46)	1.50	.60
J39B	D4	7fr brt red vio ('46)	2.25	3.25
		Nos. J35-J39B (7)	5.70	5.35

See Nos. J54-J61.

Catalogue values for unused stamps in this section, from this point to the end of the section, are for Never Hinged items.

D5   D6

1945   Typo.   *Perf. 12½*
Inscribed "TE BETALEN" at Top

J40	D5	10c gray olive	.15	.15
J41	D5	20c ultramarine	.15	.15
J42	D5	30c carmine	.15	.15
J43	D5	40c black violet	.15	.15
J44	D5	50c dl bl grn	.15	.15
J45	D5	1fr sepia	.15	.15
J46	D5	2fr red orange	.15	.15

Inscribed "A PAYER" at Top

J47	D5	10c gray olive	.15	.15
J48	D5	20c ultramarine	.15	.15
J49	D5	30c carmine	.15	.15
J50	D5	40c black vio	.15	.15
J51	D5	50c dl bl grn	.15	.15
J52	D5	1fr sepia	.15	.15
J53	D5	2fr red orange	.15	.15
		Nos. J40-J53 (14)	2.10	2.10

Type of 1922-32

1949-53   Typo.   *Perf. 14x13½*

J54	D4	65c emerald	7.00	3.75
J55	D4	1.60fr lilac rose ('53)	14.00	6.50
J56	D4	1.80fr red	15.00	6.50
J57	D4	2.40fr gray lilac ('53)	9.00	4.00
J58	D4	4fr deep blue ('53)	11.00	.50
J59	D4	5fr red brown	3.50	.40
J60	D4	8fr lilac rose	7.25	3.75
J61	D4	10fr dark violet	7.25	3.75
		Nos. J54-J61 (8)	74.00	29.15

Numerals 6½mm or More High

1966-70   Photo.

J62	D6	1fr brt pink	.15	.15
J63	D6	2fr blue green	.15	.15
J64	D6	3fr blue	.15	.15
J65	D6	5fr purple	.25	.15
J66	D6	6fr bister brn	.40	.15
J67	D6	7fr red org ('70)	.45	.30
J68	D6	20fr slate grn	1.50	1.00
		Nos. J62-J68 (7)	3.05	2.15

Printed on various papers.

Numerals 4½-5½mm High

1985-87   Photo.   *Perf. 14x13½*

J69	D6	1fr lilac rose	.15	.15
J70	D6	2fr dull blue grn	.15	.15
J71	D6	3fr greenish blue	.15	.15
J72	D6	4fr green	.20	.15
J73	D6	5fr lt violet	.25	.20
J74	D6	7fr brt orange	.35	.30
J75	D6	8fr pale gray	.40	.30
J76	D6	9fr rose lake	.45	.35
J77	D6	10fr lt red brown	.50	.40
J78	D6	20fr lt olive grn	1.10	1.10
		Nos. J69-J78 (10)	3.70	3.25

Printed on various papers.

Issue dates: 3fr, 4fr, 8fr-10fr, Mar. 25, 1985. 2fr, 20fr, 1986. 1fr, 5fr, 7fr, 1987.

This is an expanding set. Numbers will change again if necessary.

MILITARY STAMPS

Catalogue values for unused stamps in this section are for Never Hinged items.

King Baudouin
M1   M2

1967, July 17   Unwmk.   Photo.   *Perf. 11*

M1	M1	1.50fr greenish gray	.25	.25

1971-75   Engr.   *Perf. 11½*

M2	M2	1.75fr green	.50	.45
M3	M2	2.25fr gray green ('72)	.30	.30
M4	M2	2.50fr gray green ('74)	.20	.20
M5	M2	3fr gray brown ('75)	.25	.20
		Nos. M2-M5 (4)	1.25	1.15

#M1-M3 are luminescent, #M4-M5 are not.

MILITARY PARCEL POST STAMP

Type of Parcel Post Stamp of 1938 Surcharged with New Value and "M" in Blue.

1939   Unwmk.   *Perf. 13½*

MQ1	PP19	3fr on 5.50fr copper red	.30	.20

OFFICIAL STAMPS

For franking the official correspondence of the Administration of the Belgian National Railways.

Counterfeits exist of Nos. O1-O25.

Regular Issue of 1921-27 Overprinted in Black

1929-30   Unwmk.   *Perf. 14*

O1	A58	5c gray	.20	.20
O2	A58	10c blue green	.30	.40
O3	A58	35c blue green	.40	.30
O4	A58	60c olive green	.45	.30
O5	A58	1.50fr brt blue	8.00	6.25
O6	A58	1.75fr ultra ('30)	1.75	.60
		Nos. O1-O6 (6)	11.10	9.45

Same Overprint, in Red or Black, on Regular Issues of 1929-30

1929-31

O7	A63	5c slate (R)	.25	.35
O8	A63	10c olive grn (R)	.50	.40
O9	A63	25c rose red (Bk)	1.50	.85
O10	A63	35c dp green (R)	1.75	.50
O11	A63	40c red vio (Bk)	1.25	.45
O12	A63	50c dp blue (R) ('31)	.80	.35
O13	A63	60c rose (Bk)	6.00	6.00
O14	A63	70c orange brn (Bk)	4.25	.30
O15	A63	75c black vio (R) ('31)	4.00	.85
		Nos. O7-O15 (9)	20.30	11.00

Overprinted on Regular Issue of 1932

1932

O16	A73	10c olive grn (R)	.55	.60
O17	A74	35c dp green	9.00	.75
O18	A71a	75c bister brn (R)	1.50	.30
		Nos. O16-O18 (3)	11.05	1.65

BELGIUM

Overprinted on No. 262 in Red
1935 — Perf. 13½x14
O19 A80 70c olive black 2.75 .25

Regular Stamps of 1935-36 Overprinted in Red
1936-38 — Perf. 13½, 13½x14, 14
O20 A82 10c olive bister .15 .35
O21 A82 35c green .25 .40
O22 A82 50c dark blue .45 .35
O23 A83 70c brown 1.50 .65

Overprinted in Black or Red on Regular Issue of 1938
Perf. 13½x14
O24 A82 40c red violet (Bk) .30 .35
O25 A85 75c olive gray (R) .65 .30
Nos. O20-O25 (6) 3.30 2.40

Regular Issues of 1935-41 Overprinted in Red or Dark Blue
1941-44 — Perf. 14, 14x13½, 13½x14
O26 A82 10c olive bister .15 .15
 a. Inverted overprint 40.00
O27 A82 40c red violet .55 .75
O28 A82 50c dark blue .15 .15
 a. Inverted overprint
O29 A83a 1fr rose car (Bl) .45 .35
O30 A83 1fr rose pink (Bl) .15 .15
O31 A83a 2.25fr grnsh blk ('44) .30 .50
O32 A84 2.25fr gray violet .45 .70
Nos. O26-O32 (7) 2.20 2.75

Nos. O21, O23 and O25 Surcharged with New Values in Black or Red
1942
O33 A82 10c on 35c green .20 .35
O34 A83 50c on 70c brown .15 .20
O35 A85 50c on 75c ol gray (R) .15 .20
Nos. O33-O35 (3) .50 .75

Catalogue values for unused stamps in this section, from this point to the end of the section, are for Never Hinged items.

O1    O2

1946-48 — Unwmk. — Perf. 14
O36 O1 10c olive bister .25 .15
O37 O1 20c brt violet 2.00 .50
O38 O1 50c dk blue .25 .15
O39 O1 65c red lilac ('48) 3.25 .75
O40 O1 75c lilac rose .25 .20
O41 O1 90c brown violet 4.25 .35
Nos. O36-O41 (6) 10.25 2.10

Types A99, A101 and A102 with "B" Emblem Added to Design
1948 — Perf. 11½
O42 A99 1.35fr red brown 4.25 .75
O43 A99 1.75fr dk gray green 4.75 .25
O44 A101 3fr brt red violet 25.00 3.50
O45 A102 3.15fr deep blue 11.00 7.00
O46 A102 4fr brt ultra 20.00 13.00
Nos. O42-O46 (5) 65.00 24.50

1953-66 Typo. — Perf. 13½x14
O47 O2 10c orange .65 .15
O48 O2 20c red lilac .80 .25
O49 O2 30c gray green ('58) .80 .55
O50 O2 40c olive gray .50 .15
O51 O2 50c light blue .75 .15
O51A O2 60c lilac rose ('66) 1.10 .55
O52 O2 65c red lilac 27.50 21.00
O53 O2 80c emerald 4.50 .70
O54 O2 90c deep blue 6.00 .85
O55 O2 1fr rose .40 .15
Nos. O47-O55 (10) 43.00 24.50
See Nos. O66, O68.

King Baudouin
O3   O4

1954-70 Photo. — Perf. 11½
O56 O3 1.50fr gray .30 .15
O57 O3 2fr rose red 37.50 .15
O58 O3 2fr blue grn ('59) .25 .15
O59 O3 2.50fr red brown ('58) 27.50 .75
O60 O3 3fr red lilac ('58) 1.25 .15
O61 O3 3.50fr yel green ('70) .75 .15
O62 O3 4fr brt blue .90 .25
O63 O3 6fr car rose ('58) 1.50 .60
Nos. O56-O63 (8) 70.00 2.45

Type of 1953-66 Redrawn
1970-75 Typo. — Perf. 13½x14
O66 O2 1.50fr grnsh gray ('75) .20 .15
O68 O2 2.50fr brown .20 .15

1971-73 Engr. — Perf. 11½
O71 O4 3.50fr org brn ('73) .25 .25
O72 O4 4.50fr brown ('73) .25 .25
O73 O4 7fr red .40 .50
O74 O4 7fr violet .75 .30
Nos. O71-O74 (4) 1.65 1.30
Nos. O71-O74 are on luminescent paper.

1974-80
O75 O4 3fr yellow grn 1.50 1.00
O76 O4 4fr blue 1.50 .50
O77 O4 4.50fr grnsh bl ('75) .30 .15
O78 O4 5fr lilac .30 .15
O79 O4 6fr carmine ('78) .35 .20
O80 O4 6.50fr black ('76) .40 .35
O81 O4 8fr bluish blk ('78) .50 .25
O82 O4 8fr lt red brn ('80) .55 .25
O83 O4 10fr rose carmine .60 .15
O84 O4 25fr lilac ('76) 1.50 .50
O85 O4 30fr org brn ('78) 1.75 .50
Nos. O75-O85 (11) 9.25 4.10

Heraldic Lion — O5

1977-82 Typo. — Perf. 13½x14
O87 O5 50c brown ('82) .15 .15
O92 O5 1fr lilac ('82) .15 .15
O94 O5 2fr orange ('82) .20 .15
O95 O5 4fr red brown .25 .20
O96 O5 5fr green ('80) .25 .25
Nos. O87-O96 (5) 1.00 .90

NEWSPAPER STAMPS

Counterfeits exist of Nos. P1-P40.

Parcel Post Stamps of 1923-27 Overprinted JOURNAUX DAGBLADEN 1928
Perf. 14½x14, 14x14½
1928 Unwmk.
P1 PP12 10c vermilion .25 .40
P2 PP12 20c turq blue .25 .40
P3 PP12 40c olive grn .25 .40
P4 PP12 60c orange .70 .90
P5 PP12 70c dk brown .45 .40
P6 PP12 80c violet .60 .70
P7 PP12 90c slate 2.25 2.00
P8 PP13 1fr brt blue .90 .60
 a. 1fr ultramarine 12.00 5.00
P10 PP13 2fr olive grn 1.50 .60
P11 PP13 3fr orange red 1.65 .90
P12 PP13 4fr rose 2.25 1.10
P13 PP13 5fr violet 2.25 1.00
P14 PP13 6fr bister brn 4.50 1.75
P15 PP13 7fr orange 5.00 2.25
P16 PP13 8fr dk brown 6.00 2.75
P17 PP13 9fr red violet 10.00 3.00
P18 PP13 10fr blue green 9.00 2.75
P19 PP13 20fr magenta 15.00 7.00
Nos. P1-P8, P10-P19 (18) 62.80 28.90

Parcel Post Stamps of 1923-28 Overprinted JOURNAUX DAGBLADEN
1929-31
P20 PP12 10c vermilion .25 .20
P21 PP12 20c turq blue .25 .20
P22 PP12 40c olive green .30 .20
 a. Inverted overprint
P23 PP12 60c orange .55 .35
P24 PP12 70c dk brown .55 .20
P25 PP12 80c violet .60 .25
P26 PP12 90c gray 2.00 1.00
P27 PP13 1fr ultra .65 .30
 a. 1fr bright blue 4.00 2.50
P28 PP13 1.10fr org brn ('31) 6.25 1.40
P29 PP13 1.50fr gray vio ('31) 6.25 1.90
P30 PP13 2fr olive green 2.00 .25
P31 PP13 2.10fr sl gray ('31) 17.00 12.00

P32 PP13 3fr orange red 2.25 .45
P33 PP13 4fr rose 2.25 .70
P34 PP13 5fr violet 3.00 .55
P35 PP13 6fr bister brn 3.75 1.00
P36 PP13 7fr orange 3.75 1.00
P37 PP13 8fr dk brown 3.75 1.10
P38 PP13 9fr red violet 5.25 1.50
P39 PP13 10fr blue green 3.75 1.10
P40 PP13 20fr magenta 13.00 4.50
Nos. P20-P40 (21) 77.35 30.10

PARCEL POST AND RAILWAY STAMPS

Values for used Railway Stamps (Chemins de Fer) stamps are for copies with railway cancellations. Railway Stamps with postal cancellations sell for twice as much.

Coat of Arms — PP1

1879-82 Unwmk. Typo. — Perf. 14
Q1 PP1 10c violet brown 57.50 5.75
Q2 PP1 20c blue 175.00 17.50
Q3 PP1 25c green ('81) 225.00 10.00
Q4 PP1 50c carmine 1,250. 10.00
Q5 PP1 80c yellow 1,300. 57.50
Q6 PP1 1fr gray ('82) 175.00 16.00

Used copies of Nos. Q1-Q6 with pinholes, a normal state, sell for approximately one third the values given.

Most of the stamps of 1882-1902 (Nos. Q7 to Q28) are without watermark. Twice in each sheet of 100 stamps they have one of three watermarks: (1) A winged wheel and "Chemins de Fer de l'Etat Belge," (2) Coat of Arms of Belgium and "Royaume de Belgique," (3) Larger Coat of Arms, without inscription.

PP2

1882-94 — Perf. 15½x14½
Q7 PP2 10c brown ('86) 20.00 1.50
Q8 PP2 15c gray ('94) 8.75 7.25
Q9 PP2 20c blue ('86) 65.00 7.00
 a. 20c ultra ('90) 75.00 4.00
Q10 PP2 25c yel grn ('91) 72.50 4.25
 a. 25c blue green ('87) 67.50 4.00
Q11 PP2 50c carmine 67.50 .75
Q12 PP2 80c brnsh buff 67.50 .80
Q13 PP2 80c lemon 75.00 1.60
Q14 PP2 1fr lavender 350.00 3.00
Q15 PP2 2fr yel buff ('94) 210.00 67.50
Counterfeits exist.

PP3

Name of engraver below frame
1895-97
Numerals in Black, except 1fr, 2fr
Q16 PP3 10c red brown ('96) 11.00 .60
Q17 PP3 15c gray 11.00 7.00
Q18 PP3 20c blue 17.50 1.00
Q19 PP3 25c green 17.50 1.25
Q20 PP3 50c carmine 25.00 .80
Q21 PP3 60c violet ('96) 50.00 1.40
Q22 PP3 80c ol yel ('96) 50.00 1.40
Q23 PP3 1fr lilac brown 175.00 3.00
Q24 PP3 2fr yel buff ('97) 200.00 15.00
Counterfeits exist.

1902
Numerals in Black
Q25 PP3 30c orange 21.00 2.00
Q26 PP3 40c green 26.00 1.75
Q27 PP3 70c blue 50.00 1.40
 a. Numerals omitted 750.00
 b. Numerals printed on reverse 750.00
Q28 PP3 90c red 65.00 1.65
Nos. Q25-Q28 (4) 162.00 6.80

Winged Wheel — PP4
Without engraver's name

1902-14 Perf. 15
Q29 PP3 10c yel brn & slate .15 .15
Q30 PP3 15c slate & vio .20 .15
Q31 PP3 20c ultra & yel brn .15 .15
Q32 PP3 25c yel grn & red .20 .15
Q33 PP3 30c orange & bl grn .15 .15
Q34 PP3 35c bister & bl grn ('12) .35 .15
Q35 PP3 40c blue grn & vio .15 .15
Q36 PP3 50c pale rose & vio .15 .15
Q37 PP3 55c lilac brn & ultra ('14) .35 .20
Q38 PP3 60c violet & red .15 .15
Q39 PP3 70c blue & red .15 .15
Q40 PP3 80c lemon & vio brn .15 .15
Q41 PP3 90c red & yel grn .20 .15
Q42 PP4 1fr vio brn & org .20 .15
Q43 PP4 1.10fr rose & blk ('06) .20 .15
Q44 PP4 2fr ocher & red .20 .15
Q45 PP4 3fr black & ultra .35 .20
Q46 PP4 4fr yel grn & red ('13) 1.25 .70
Q47 PP4 5fr org & bl grn ('13) .55 .55
Q48 PP4 10fr ol yel & brn vio ('13) .90 .55
Nos. Q29-Q48 (20) 6.30 4.50

Regular Issues of 1912-13 Handstamped in Violet

1915 Perf. 14
Q49 A42 5c green 165.00 165.00
Q50 A43 10c red 800.00 800.00
Q51 A45 10c red 175.00 175.00
 a. With engraver's name 750.00 750.00
Q52 A43 20c olive grn 1,200. 1,200.
Q53 A45 20c olive grn 200.00 200.00
 a. With engraver's name 750.00 750.00
Q54 A45 25c ultra 200.00 200.00
 a. With engraver's name 750.00 750.00
Q55 A43 35c bister brn 250.00 250.00
Q55A A43 40c green 1,750. 1,750.
Q56 A45 40c green 250.00 250.00
Q57 A43 50c gray 250.00 250.00
Q58 A43 1fr orange 200.00 200.00
Q59 A43 2fr violet 1,650. 1,650.
Q60 A44 5fr plum 3,500. 3,500.
Excellent forgeries of this overprint exist.

PP5   PP6

1916 Litho. — Perf. 13½
Q61 PP5 10c pale blue 1.10 .20
Q62 PP5 15c olive grn 1.40 .50
Q63 PP5 20c red 2.25 .50
Q64 PP5 25c lt brown 2.25 .50
Q65 PP5 30c lilac 1.40 .45
Q66 PP5 35c gray 1.40 .45
Q67 PP5 40c orange yel 3.00 1.50
Q68 PP5 50c bister 2.25 .45
Q69 PP5 55c brown 3.00 2.25
Q70 PP5 60c gray vio 2.25 .45
Q71 PP5 70c green 2.25 .45
Q72 PP5 80c red brown 2.25 .45
Q73 PP5 90c blue 2.25 .45
Q74 PP6 1fr gray 2.25 .45
Q75 PP6 1.10fr ultra (Franken) 27.50 21.00
Q76 PP6 2fr red 25.00 .45
Q77 PP6 3fr violet 25.00 .45
Q78 PP6 4fr emerald 45.00 1.50
Q79 PP6 5fr brown 45.00 3.00
Q80 PP6 10fr orange 45.00 1.50
Nos. Q61-Q80 (20) 241.80 36.95

Type of 1916 Inscribed "FRANK" instead of "FRANKEN"

1920
Q81 PP6 1.10fr ultra 2.00 .45

BELGIUM

PP7  PP8

1920   *Perf. 14*

Q82	PP7	10c blue grn	1.75	.75
Q83	PP7	15c olive grn	1.75	.75
Q84	PP7	20c red	1.75	.75
Q85	PP7	25c gray brn	2.50	.75
Q86	PP7	30c red vio	27.00	22.50
Q87	PP7	40c pale org	11.00	.75
Q88	PP7	50c bister	9.00	.75
Q89	PP7	55c pale brown	5.50	4.50
Q90	PP7	60c dk violet	10.00	.75
Q91	PP7	70c green	18.00	1.10
Q92	PP7	80c red brown	40.00	1.50
Q93	PP7	90c dull blue	10.00	.75
Q94	PP8	1fr gray	85.00	1.50
Q95	PP8	1.10fr ultra	26.00	2.00
Q96	PP8	1.20fr dk green	11.00	.75
Q97	PP8	1.40fr black brn	11.00	.75
Q98	PP8	2fr vermilion	110.00	1.25
Q99	PP8	3fr red vio	120.00	.85
Q100	PP8	4fr yel grn	120.00	.75
Q101	PP8	5fr bister brn	120.00	.75
Q102	PP8	10fr brown org	120.00	.75
	Nos. Q82-Q102 (21)		861.25	45.30

PP9  PP10

Types PP7 and PP9 differ in the position of the wheel and the tablet above it.
Types PP8 and PP10 differ in the bars below "FR".
There are many other variations in the designs.

1920-21   *Typo.*

Q103	PP9	10c carmine	.30	.15
Q104	PP9	15c yel grn	.30	.15
Q105	PP9	20c blue grn	.70	.20
Q106	PP9	25c ultra	.65	.20
Q107	PP9	30c chocolate	.85	.20
Q108	PP9	35c orange brn	.90	.30
Q109	PP9	40c orange	1.10	.15
Q110	PP9	50c rose	1.10	.15
Q111	PP9	55c yel ('21)	4.50	3.25
Q112	PP9	60c dull rose	1.10	.20
Q113	PP9	70c emerald	3.00	.40
Q114	PP9	80c violet	2.25	.15
Q115	PP9	90c lemon	37.50	21.00
Q116	PP9	90c claret	4.50	.40
Q117	PP10	1fr buff	4.50	.35
Q118	PP10	1fr red brown	4.00	.30
Q119	PP10	1.10fr ultra	1.65	.45
Q120	PP10	1.20fr orange	6.25	.30
Q121	PP10	1.40fr yellow	10.00	1.75
Q122	PP10	1.60fr turq blue	18.00	.70
Q123	PP10	1.60fr emerald	40.00	.70
Q124	PP10	2fr pale rose	26.00	.30
Q125	PP10	3fr dp rose	24.00	.30
Q126	PP10	4fr emerald	24.00	.30
Q127	PP10	5fr lt violet	17.50	.30
Q128	PP10	10fr lemon	110.00	9.00
Q129	PP10	10fr dk brown	22.50	.30
Q130	PP10	15fr dp rose ('21)	22.50	.30
Q131	PP10	20fr dk blue ('21)	325.00	3.00
	Nos. Q103-Q131 (29)		714.65	45.25

PP11

1922   *Engr.*   *Perf. 11½*

Q132	PP11	2fr black	4.00	.15
Q133	PP11	3fr brown	37.50	.20
Q134	PP11	4fr green	9.00	.15
Q135	PP11	5r caret	9.00	.15
Q136	PP11	10fr yel brown	10.00	.15
Q137	PP11	15fr rose red	10.00	.25
Q138	PP11	20fr blue	67.50	.25
	Nos. Q132-Q138 (7)		147.00	1.30

PP12  PP13

Perf. 14x13½, 13½x14

1923-40   *Typo.*

Q139	PP12	5c red brown	.20	.25
Q140	PP12	10c vermilion	.15	.15
Q141	PP12	15c ultra	.20	.30
Q142	PP12	20c turq blue	.15	.15
Q143	PP12	30c brn vio ('27)	.20	.15
Q144	PP12	40c olive grn	.20	.15
Q145	PP12	50c magenta ('27)	.20	.15
Q146	PP12	60c orange	.25	.15
Q147	PP12	70c dk brown ('24)	.15	.15
Q148	PP12	80c violet	.20	.15
Q149	PP12	90c slate ('27)	1.25	.15
Q150	PP13	1fr ultra	.35	.15
Q151	PP13	1fr brt blue ('28)	.55	.15
Q152	PP13	1.10fr orange	3.00	.30
Q153	PP13	1.50fr turq blue	3.25	.30
Q154	PP13	1.70fr dp brown ('31)	.75	.60
Q155	PP13	1.80fr claret	4.25	.60
Q156	PP13	2fr olive grn ('24)	.35	.20
Q157	PP13	2.10fr gray grn	7.50	.85
Q158	PP13	2.40fr dp violet	4.00	.85
Q159	PP13	2.70fr gray ('24)	12.00	.75
Q160	PP13	3fr orange red	.45	.15
Q161	PP13	3.30fr brown ('24)	12.50	.75
Q162	PP13	4fr rose ('24)	.55	.15
Q163	PP13	5fr violet ('24)	.90	.15
Q163A	PP13	5fr brn vio ('40)	.45	.30
Q164	PP13	6fr bis brn ('27)	.50	.15
Q165	PP13	7fr orange ('27)	.90	.15
Q166	PP13	8fr dp brown ('27)	.75	.15
Q167	PP13	9fr red vio ('27)	2.50	.15
Q168	PP13	10fr blue grn ('27)	1.10	.20
Q168A	PP13	10fr black ('40)	4.00	3.75
Q169	PP13	20fr magenta ('27)	1.90	.15
Q170	PP13	30fr turq green ('31)	6.00	.40
Q171	PP13	40fr gray ('31)	55.00	.75
Q172	PP13	50fr bister ('27)	9.00	.30
	Nos. Q139-Q172 (36)		135.65	14.25

See Nos. Q239-Q262. For overprints see Nos. Q216-Q238. Stamps overprinted "Bagages Reisgoed" are revenues.

No. Q158 Surcharged

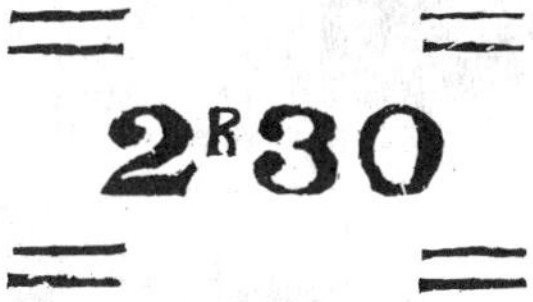

2R30

1924   *Green Surcharge*

Q173	PP13	2.30fr on 2.40fr violet	3.00	.50
	a. Inverted surcharge		57.50	

Type of Regular Issue of 1926-27 Overprinted

Colis Postal Postcollo

1928   *Perf. 14*

Q174	A61	4fr buff	6.50	.90
Q175	A61	5fr bister	6.50	1.10

Central P.O., Brussels — PP15

1929-30   *Engr.*   *Perf. 11½*

Q176	PP15	3fr black brn	1.40	.20
Q177	PP15	4fr gray	1.40	.20
Q178	PP15	5fr carmine	1.40	.20
Q179	PP15	6fr vio brn ('30)	22.50	25.00
	Nos. Q176-Q179 (4)		26.70	25.60

No. Q179 Surcharged in Blue

×4 4×

1933

Q180	PP15	4(fr) on 6fr vio brn	25.00	.25

Modern Locomotive — PP16

1934   *Photo.*   *Perf. 13½x14*

Q181	PP16	3fr dk green	15.00	2.25
Q182	PP16	4fr red violet	4.00	.20
Q183	PP16	5fr dp rose	14.00	.20
	Nos. Q181-Q183 (3)		33.00	2.65
	Set, never hinged		150.00	

Modern Railroad Train — PP17  Old Railroad Train — PP18

1935   *Engr.*   *Perf. 14x13½, 13½x14*

Q184	PP17	10c rose car	.30	.15
Q185	PP17	20c violet	.35	.15
Q186	PP17	30c black brn	.45	.30
Q187	PP17	40c dk blue	.55	.15
Q188	PP17	50c orange red	.55	.15
Q189	PP17	60c green	.65	.15
Q190	PP17	70c ultra	.70	.15
Q191	PP17	80c olive blk	.65	.15
Q192	PP17	90c rose lake	.85	.45
Q193	PP18	1fr brown vio	.85	.15
Q194	PP18	2fr gray blk	2.00	.15
Q195	PP18	3fr red org	2.50	.15
Q196	PP18	4fr violet brn	3.00	.15
Q197	PP18	5fr plum	3.25	.15
Q198	PP18	6fr dp green	3.50	.15
Q199	PP18	7fr dp violet	17.00	.15
Q200	PP18	8fr olive blk	17.00	.20
Q201	PP18	9fr dk blue	17.00	.15
Q202	PP18	10fr car lake	17.00	.15
Q203	PP18	20fr green	90.00	.20
Q204	PP18	30fr violet	90.00	2.00
Q205	PP18	40fr black brn	90.00	2.50
Q206	PP18	50fr rose car	100.00	2.00
Q207	PP18	100fr ultra	250.00	45.00
	Nos. Q184-Q207 (24)		708.15	55.05
	Set, never hinged		1,750.	

Centenary of Belgian State Railway.

Winged Wheel — PP19

Surcharge in Red or Blue

1938   *Photo.*   *Perf. 13½*

Q208	PP19	5fr on 3.50fr dk grn	6.50	.45
Q209	PP19	5fr on 4.50fr rose vio (Bl)	.15	.15
Q210	PP19	6fr on 5.50fr cop red (Bl)	.35	.15
	a. Half used as 3fr on piece			1.50
	Nos. Q208-Q210 (3)		7.00	.75
	Set, never hinged		50.00	

See Nos. MQ1, Q297-Q299.

Symbolizing Unity Achieved Through Railroads — PP20

1939   *Engr.*   *Perf. 13½x14*

Q211	PP20	20c redsh brn	3.50	3.75
Q212	PP20	50c vio bl	3.50	3.75
Q213	PP20	2fr rose red	3.50	3.75
Q214	PP20	5fr dp violet	3.50	3.75
Q215	PP20	10fr dk vio	3.50	3.75
	Nos. Q211-Q215 (5)		17.50	18.75
	Set, never hinged		22.50	

Issued in commemoration of the Railroad Exposition and Congress held at Brussels.

Parcel Post Stamps of 1925-27 Overprinted in Blue or Carmine **B**

Perf. 14½x14, 14x14½

1940   *Unwmk.*

Q216	PP12	10c vermilion	.15	.15
Q217	PP12	20c turq bl (C)	.15	.15
Q218	PP12	30c brn vio	.15	.15
Q219	PP12	40c ol grn (C)	.15	.15
Q220	PP12	50c magenta	.15	.15
Q221	PP12	60c orange	.15	.25
Q222	PP12	70c dk brn	.15	.15
Q223	PP12	80c vio (C)	.15	.15
Q224	PP12	90c slate	.25	.25
Q225	PP13	1fr ultra	.25	.15
Q226	PP13	2fr ol grn (C)	.25	.15
Q227	PP13	3fr org red	.25	.15
Q228	PP13	4fr rose	.25	.15
Q229	PP13	5fr vio (C)	.25	.15
Q230	PP13	6fr bis brn	.35	.25
Q231	PP13	7fr orange	.35	.15
Q232	PP13	8fr dp brn	.35	.15
Q233	PP13	9fr red vio	.35	.15
Q234	PP13	10fr bl grn (C)	.35	.25
Q235	PP13	20fr magenta	.60	.15
Q236	PP13	30fr turq grn (C)	1.10	.75
Q237	PP13	40fr gray (C)	1.40	2.00
Q238	PP13	50fr bister	1.65	1.15
	Nos. Q216-Q238 (23)		9.20	7.35
	Set, never hinged		16.00	

Types of 1923-40

1941

Q239	PP12	10c dl olive	.15	.15
Q240	PP12	20c lt vio	.15	.15
Q241	PP12	30c fawn	.15	.15
Q242	PP12	40c dull blue	.15	.15
Q243	PP12	50c lt grn	.15	.15
Q244	PP12	60c gray	.15	.15
Q245	PP12	70c chalky grn	.15	.15
Q246	PP12	80c orange	.15	.15
Q247	PP12	90c rose lilac	.15	.15
Q248	PP13	1fr lt yel grn	.15	.15
Q249	PP13	2fr vio brn	.40	.15
Q250	PP13	3fr slate	.45	.15
Q251	PP13	4fr dl olive	.50	.15
Q252	PP13	5fr rose lilac	.50	.15
Q253	PP13	5fr black	.80	.15
Q254	PP13	6fr org ver	.75	.30
Q255	PP13	7fr lilac	.75	.15
Q256	PP13	8fr chalky grn	.75	.15
Q257	PP13	9fr blue	.90	.15
Q258	PP13	10fr rose lilac	.90	.15
Q259	PP13	20fr milky blue	2.00	.15
Q260	PP13	30fr orange	4.50	.35
Q261	PP13	40fr rose	5.00	.35
Q262	PP13	50fr brt red vio	6.75	.15
	Nos. Q239-Q262 (24)		26.45	4.30
	Set, never hinged		90.00	

Adjusting Tie Plates — PP21  Engineer at Throttle — PP22

Freight Station Interior — PP23  Signal and Electric Train — PP24

BELGIUM

1942   Engr.   Perf. 14x13½

Q263	PP21	9.20fr red org	.60	.80
Q264	PP22	12.30fr dp grn	.60	.85
Q265	PP23	14.30fr dk car	.85	1.25

Perf. 11½

Q266	PP24	100fr ultra	20.00	17.00
	Nos. Q263-Q266 (4)		22.05	19.90
	Set, never hinged		25.00	

Catalogue values for unused stamps in this section, from this point to the end of the section, are for Never Hinged items.

PP25    PP26

PP27

1945-46   Photo.   Unwmk.

Q267	PP25	10c ol blk ('46)	.30	.15
Q268	PP25	20c dp vio	.30	.15
Q269	PP25	30c chnt brn ('46)	.30	.15
Q270	PP25	40c dp bl ('46)	.30	.15
Q271	PP25	50c peacock grn	.30	.15
Q272	PP25	60c blk ('46)	.30	.15
Q273	PP25	70c emer ('46)	.45	.15
Q274	PP25	80c orange	.75	.20
Q275	PP25	90c brn vio ('46)	.30	.15
Q276	PP26	1fr bl grn ('46)	.30	.15
Q277	PP26	2fr blk brn	.30	.15
Q278	PP26	3fr grnsh blk ('46)	2.00	.20
Q279	PP26	4fr dark blue	.45	.20
Q280	PP26	5fr sepia	.45	.15
Q281	PP26	6fr dk ol grn ('46)	2.25	.15
Q282	PP26	7fr dk vio ('46)	.75	.15
Q283	PP26	8fr red org	.75	.15
Q284	PP26	9fr dp bl ('46)	.90	.15
Q285	PP27	10fr dk red ('46)	3.25	.15
Q286	PP27	10fr sepia ('46)	1.65	.25
Q287	PP27	17fr dk yel grn ('46)	.75	.15
Q288	PP27	30fr dp vio	1.00	.15
Q289	PP27	40fr rose pink	.90	.15
Q290	PP27	50fr brt bl ('46)	12.00	.15
	Nos. Q267-Q290 (24)		31.00	4.15

Mercury — PP28

1945-46   Perf. 13½x13

Q291	PP28	3fr emer ('46)	.25	.25
Q292	PP28	5fr ultra	.15	.15
Q293	PP28	6fr red	.15	.15

Inscribed "Belgique-Belgie"

Q294	PP28	3fr emer ('46)	.25	.25
Q295	PP28	5fr ultra	.15	.15
Q296	PP28	6fr red	.15	.15
	Nos. Q291-Q296 (6)		1.10	1.10

Winged Wheel Type of 1938
Carmine Surcharge

1946   Perf. 13½x14

Q297	PP19	8fr on 5.50fr brn	.65	.15
Q298	PP19	10fr on 5.50fr dk bl	.75	.20
Q299	PP19	12fr on 5.50fr vio	1.10	.20
	Nos. Q297-Q299 (3)		2.50	.55

Railway Crossing PP29

1947   Engr.   Perf. 12½

Q300	PP29	100fr dark green	7.00	.25

Crossbowman with Train — PP30

1947   Photo.   Perf. 11½

Q301	PP30	8fr dark olive brn	1.00	.20
Q302	PP30	10fr gray & blue	1.10	.25
Q303	PP30	12fr dark violet	1.65	.45
	Nos. Q301-Q303 (3)		3.75	.90

Surcharged with New Value and Bars in Carmine

1948

Q304	PP30	9fr on 8fr	1.25	.15
Q305	PP30	11fr on 10fr	1.25	.25
Q306	PP30	13.50fr on 12fr	2.00	.25
	Nos. Q304-Q306 (3)		4.50	.65

Delivery of Parcel — PP31

1948

Q307	PP31	9fr chocolate	6.50	.15
Q308	PP31	11fr brown car	7.00	.15
Q309	PP31	13.50fr gray	10.50	.15
	Nos. Q307-Q309 (3)		24.00	.55

Locomotive of 1835 — PP32

Various Locomotives.
Lathe Work in Frame Differs

1949   Engr.   Perf. 12½

Q310	PP32	½fr dark brown	.60	.15
Q311	PP32	1fr carmine rose	.70	.15
Q312	PP32	2fr deep ultra	.95	.15
Q313	PP32	3fr dp magenta	2.00	.15
Q314	PP32	4fr blue green	2.75	.15
Q315	PP32	5fr orange red	2.75	.15
Q316	PP32	6fr brown vio	3.00	.25
Q317	PP32	7fr yellow grn	4.00	.15
Q318	PP32	8fr grnsh blue	5.00	.15
Q319	PP32	9fr yellow brn	6.00	.25
Q320	PP32	10fr citron	7.25	.15
Q321	PP32	20fr orange	11.00	.15
Q322	PP32	30fr blue	15.00	.15
Q323	PP32	40fr lilac rose	21.00	.15
Q324	PP32	50fr violet	21.00	.30
Q325	PP32	100fr red	65.00	.25

Engraved; Center Typographed

Q326	PP32	10fr car rose & blk	9.00	.80
	Nos. Q310-Q326 (17)		177.00	3.75

See No. Q337.

1949   Engr.

Design: Electric locomotive.

Q327	PP32	60fr black brown	20.00	.20

Opening of Charleroi-Brussels electric railway line, Oct. 15, 1949.

Mailing Parcel Post — PP33

Sorting PP34

Loading PP35

1950-52   Perf. 12, 12½

Q328	PP33	11fr red orange	6.00	.20
Q329	PP33	12fr red vio ('51)	20.00	1.50
Q330	PP34	13fr dk blue grn	6.00	.20
Q331	PP34	15fr ultra ('51)	15.00	.30
Q332	PP35	16fr gray	6.00	.20
Q333	PP35	17fr brown ('52)	8.00	.20
Q334	PP35	18fr brt car ('51)	16.00	.45
Q335	PP35	20fr brn org ('52)	8.00	.20
	Nos. Q328-Q335 (8)		85.00	3.25

For surcharges see Nos. Q338-Q340.

Mercury and Winged Wheel — PP36

1951

Q336	PP36	25fr dark blue	10.00	8.50

25th anniv. of the founding of the Natl. Soc. of Belgian Railroads.

Type of 1949

Design: Electric locomotive.

1952   Unwmk.   Perf. 11½

Q337	PP32	300fr red violet	150.00	.50

Nos. Q331, Q328 and Q334 Surcharged with New Value and "X" in Red, Blue or Green

1953   Perf. 12

Q338	PP34	13fr on 15fr (R)	60.00	3.00
Q339	PP33	17fr on 11fr (Bl)	35.00	2.25
Q340	PP35	20fr on 18fr (G)	30.00	2.50
	Nos. Q338-Q340 (3)		125.00	7.75

Electric Train, 1952 — PP37

1953   Engr.

Q341	PP37	200fr dk yel grn & vio brn	250.00	4.00
Q342	PP37	200fr dk green	225.00	1.00

No. Q341 was issued to commemorate the opening of the railway link connecting Brussels North and South Stations, Oct. 4, 1952.

New North Station, Brussels — PP38

Chapelle Station, Brussels PP39

Designs: No. Q348, 15fr, Congress Station. 10fr, 20fr, 30fr, 40fr, 50fr, South Station. 100fr, 200fr, 300fr, Central Station.

1953-57   Unwmk.   Perf. 11½

Q343	PP38	1fr bister	.30	.15
Q344	PP38	2fr slate	.40	.15
Q345	PP38	3fr blue grn	.60	.15
Q346	PP38	4fr orange	.80	.15
Q347	PP38	5fr red brn	.80	.15
Q348	PP38	5fr dk red brn	10.00	.15
Q349	PP38	6fr rose vio	1.10	.15
Q350	PP38	7fr brt green	1.10	.15
Q351	PP38	8fr rose red	1.40	.15
Q352	PP38	9fr brt grnsh bl	2.00	.15
Q353	PP38	10fr lt grn	2.25	.15
Q354	PP38	15fr dl red	13.00	.15
Q355	PP38	20fr blue	4.00	.15
Q356	PP38	30fr purple	6.25	.15
Q357	PP38	40fr brt purple	8.00	.15
Q358	PP38	50fr lilac rose	10.00	.15
Q359	PP39	60fr brt purple	20.00	.15
Q360	PP39	80fr brown vio	30.00	.15
Q361	PP39	100fr emerald	18.00	.15
Q361A	PP39	200fr brt vio bl	95.00	1.65
Q361B	PP39	300fr lilac rose	175.00	2.25
	Nos. Q343-Q361B (21)		400.00	6.85

Issued: #Q347, 20fr, 30fr, 1953; 80fr, 1955; 200fr, 1956; 300fr, 1957; others, 1954.

See Nos. Q407, Q431-Q432.

Electric Train — PP40    Mercury and Winged Wheel — PP41

1954

Q362	PP40	13fr chocolate	14.00	.15
Q363	PP40	19fr olive	17.00	.15
Q364	PP40	21fr lilac rose	18.00	.45
	Nos. Q362-Q364 (3)		49.00	.75

Nos. Q362-Q364 Surcharged with New Value and "X" in Blue, Red or Green

1956

Q365	PP40	14fr on 13fr (B)	8.00	.15
Q366	PP40	19fr on 18fr (R)	8.25	.15
Q367	PP40	22fr on 21fr (G)	8.75	.45
	Nos. Q365-Q367 (3)		25.00	.85

1957   Engr.   Perf. 11½

Q368	PP41	14fr brt green	7.75	.15
Q369	PP41	19fr olive gray	8.00	.20
Q370	PP41	22fr carmine rose	8.75	.30
	Nos. Q368-Q370 (3)		24.50	.65

Nos. Q369-Q370 Surcharged with New Value and "X" in Pink or Green

1959

Q371	PP41	20fr on 19fr (P)	22.50	.35
Q372	PP41	20fr on 22fr (G)	27.50	.55

Old North Station, Brussels PP42

1959   Engr.   Perf. 11½

Q373	PP42	20fr olive green	14.00	.20

See Nos. Q381, Q383. For surcharges see Nos. Q378, Q382, Q384.

Diesel and Electric Locomotives and Association Emblem PP43

1960   Unwmk.   Perf. 11½

Q374	PP43	20fr red	42.50	30.00
Q375	PP43	50fr dark blue	42.50	30.00
Q376	PP43	60fr red lilac	42.50	30.00
Q377	PP43	70fr emerald	42.50	30.00
	Nos. Q374-Q377 (4)		170.00	120.00

Intl. Assoc. of Railway Congresses, 75th anniv.

No. Q373 Surcharged with New Value and "X" in Red

1961

Q378	PP42	24fr on 20fr ol grn	65.00	.25

South Station, Brussels — PP44

1962   Unwmk.   Perf. 11½

Q379	PP44	24fr dull red	6.25	.25

BELGIUM

No. Q379 Surcharged with New Value and "X" in Light Green

1963
Q380 PP44 26fr on 24fr dl red   6.50 .25

Type of 1959
Design: 26fr, Central Station, Antwerp.

1963 Engr. Perf. 11½
Q381 PP42 26fr blue   6.25 1.75

No. Q381 Surcharged in Red

1964, Apr. 20
Q382 PP42 28fr on 26fr blue   6.25 .25

Type of 1959
Design: 28fr, St. Peter's Station, Ghent.

1965 Perf. 11½
Q383 PP42 28fr red lilac   6.25 1.40

Nos. Q383 Surcharged with New Value and "X" in Green

1966
Q384 PP42 35fr on 28fr red lil   6.25 .20

Arlon Railroad Station — PP45

Perf. 11½
1967, Aug. Unwmk. Engr.
Q385 PP45 25fr bister   10.00 .15
Q386 PP45 30fr blue green   5.00 .20
Q387 PP45 35fr deep blue   7.00 .35
Nos. Q385-Q387 (3)   22.00 .70

See #Q408. For surcharges see #Q410-Q412.

Electric Train — PP46

Designs: 2fr, 3fr, 4fr, 5fr, 6fr, 7fr, 8fr, 9fr, like 1fr. 10fr, 20fr, 30fr, 40fr, Train going right. 50fr, 60fr, 70fr, 80fr, 90fr, Train going left. 100fr, 200fr, 300fr, Diesel train.

1968-73 Engr. Perf. 11½
Q388 PP46 1fr olive bis   .20 .20
Q389 PP46 2fr slate   .25 .20
Q390 PP46 3fr blue green   .55 .20
Q391 PP46 4fr orange   .55 .20
Q392 PP46 5fr brown   .65 .20
Q393 PP46 6fr plum   .55 .20
Q394 PP46 7fr brt green   .65 .20
Q395 PP46 8fr carmine   .80 .20
Q396 PP46 9fr blue   1.40 .20
Q397 PP46 10fr green   2.75 .20
Q398 PP46 20fr dk blue   1.65 .20
Q399 PP46 30fr dk purple   4.00 .20
Q400 PP46 40fr brt lilac   5.50 .20
Q401 PP46 50fr brt pink   6.75 .20
Q402 PP46 60fr brt violet   8.25 .30
Q402A PP46 70fr dp bister ('73)   6.75 .30
Q403 PP46 80fr dk brown   6.75 .30
Q403A PP46 90fr yel grn ('73)   5.50 .30
Q404 PP46 100fr emerald   11.00 .25
Q405 PP46 200fr violet blue   13.00 .50
Q406 PP46 300fr lilac rose   22.50 1.25
Nos. Q388-Q406 (21)   100.00 5.90

See No. Q409.

Types of 1953-68
Designs: 10fr, Congress Station, Brussels. 40fr, Arlon Station. 500fr, Electric train going left.

1968, June Engr. Perf. 11½
Q407 PP38 10fr gray   1.50 .20
Q408 PP45 40fr vermilion   22.50 1.10
Q409 PP46 500fr yellow   30.00 1.90
Nos. Q407-Q409 (3)   54.00 2.25

Nos. Q385, Q387 and Q408 Surcharged with New Value and "X"

1970, Dec.
Q410 PP45 37fr on 25fr bister   45.00 3.00
Q411 PP45 48fr on 35fr dp bl   13.00 5.00
Q412 PP45 53fr on 40fr ver   15.00 6.00
Nos. Q410-Q412 (3)   73.00 14.00

Ostend Station PP47

1971, Mar. Engr. Perf. 11½
Q413 PP47 32fr bis & blk   2.50 2.25
Q414 PP47 37fr gray & blk   2.50 2.50
Q415 PP47 42fr bl & blk   4.00 3.00
Q416 PP47 44fr brt rose & blk   4.50 3.00
Q417 PP47 46fr vio & blk   4.50 3.00
Q418 PP47 50fr brick red & blk   5.25 3.25
Q419 PP47 52fr sep & blk   5.25 3.25
Q420 PP47 54fr yel grn & blk   5.75 3.25
Q421 PP47 61fr grnsh bl & blk   5.75 4.00
Nos. Q413-Q421 (9)   40.00 27.50

Nos. Q413-Q416, Q419-Q421 Surcharged with New Value and "X"

1971, Dec. 15
Denomination in Black
Q422 PP47 34fr on 32fr bister   2.00 .55
Q423 PP47 40fr on 37fr gray   2.50 .70
Q424 PP47 47fr on 44fr brt rose   2.75 .80
Q425 PP47 53fr on 42fr blue   3.25 .85
Q426 PP47 56fr on 52fr sepia   3.25 1.00
Q427 PP47 59fr on 54fr yel grn   3.25 1.00
Q428 PP47 66fr on 61fr grnsh blue   4.00 1.10
Nos. Q422-Q428 (7)   21.00 6.00

Track, Underpinning of Railroad Car and Emblems PP48

1972, Mar. Photo.
Q429 PP48 100fr emer, red & blk   10.00 1.10
Centenary of International Railroad Union.

Congress Emblem — PP49

1974, Apr. Photo. Perf. 11½
Q430 PP49 100fr yel, blk & red   8.00 1.25
4th International Symposium on Railroad Cybernetics, Washington, DC, Apr. 1974.

Type of 1953-1957

1975, June 1 Engr. Perf. 11½
Q431 PP38 20fr emerald   1.75 .20
Q432 PP38 50fr blue   3.75 .55

Railroad Tracks — PP50

1976, June 10 Photo. Perf. 11½
Q433 PP50 20fr ultra & multi   3.00 .20
Q434 PP50 50fr brt grn & multi   1.75 .50
Q435 PP50 100fr dp org & multi   4.00 1.00
Q436 PP50 150fr brt lil & multi   6.25 1.75
Nos. Q433-Q436 (4)   15.00 3.45

Railroad Station — PP51

1977 Photo. Perf. 11½
Q437 PP51 1000fr multi   45.00 8.00

Freight Car — PP52

Designs: 1fr-9fr, Freight car. 10fr-40fr, Hopper car. 50fr-90fr, Maintenance car. 100fr-500fr, Liquid fuel car.

1980, Dec. 16 Engr. Perf. 11½
Q438 PP52 1fr bis brn & blk   .15 .15
Q439 PP52 2fr claret & blk   .15 .15
Q440 PP52 3fr brt bl & blk   .15 .15
Q441 PP52 4fr grnsh blk & blk   .15 .15
Q442 PP52 5fr sepia & blk   .20 .15
Q443 PP52 6fr dp org & blk   .35 .15
Q444 PP52 7fr purple & blk   .40 .15
Q445 PP52 8fr black   .40 .15
Q446 PP52 9fr green & blk   .45 .15
Q447 PP52 10fr yel bis & blk   .50 .15
Q448 PP52 20fr grnsh bl & blk   1.10 .20
Q449 PP52 30fr bister & blk   2.25 .35
Q450 PP52 40fr lt lil & blk   2.50 .40
Q451 PP52 50fr dk brn & blk   2.75 .55
Q452 PP52 60fr olive & blk   2.75 .70
Q453 PP52 70fr vio bl & blk   3.50 .75
Q454 PP52 80fr vio brn & blk   4.00 .85
Q455 PP52 90fr lil rose & blk   5.00 .95
Q456 PP52 100fr crim rose & blk   5.25 1.00
Q457 PP52 200fr brn & blk   10.00 2.00
Q458 PP52 300fr ol gray & blk   14.00 3.00
Q459 PP52 500fr dl pur & blk   25.00 5.25
Nos. Q438-Q459 (22)   81.00 17.50

Train in Station PP53    Electric Locomotives PP54

1982 Engr. Perf. 11½
Q460 PP53 10fr red & blk   1.75 .25
Q461 PP53 20fr green & blk   1.25 .50
Q462 PP53 50fr sepia & blk   4.25 .75
Q463 PP53 100fr blue & blk   7.25 2.75
Nos. Q460-Q463 (4)   14.50 4.25

1985, May 3 Photo. Perf. 11½
Q464 PP54 250fr BB-150   11.00 2.00
Q465 PP54 500fr BB-120   24.00 10.00

Stylized Castle, Gabled Station and Electric Rail Car — PP55

1987, Oct. 12 Engr. Perf. 11½
Q466 PP55 10fr dk red & blk   .50 .40
Q467 PP55 20fr dk grn & blk   1.00 .75
Q468 PP55 50fr dk brn & blk   2.50 1.90
Q469 PP55 100fr dk lil & blk   5.25 3.75
Q470 PP55 150fr dark olive bister & blk   7.75 5.65
Nos. Q466-Q470 (5)   17.00 12.45

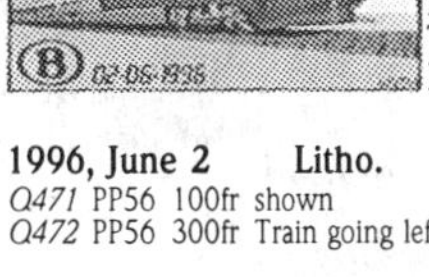

High Speed Trains PP56

1996, June 2 Litho. Perf. 11½
Q471 PP56 100fr shown   6.00 4.50
Q472 PP56 300fr Train going left   18.50 13.50

Electric Trains PP57

Designs: 50fr, Passenger railcars. 100fr, End car. 200fr, Front car.

1997, Oct. 14 Photo. Perf. 11½
Q473 PP57 50fr multicolored   2.75 2.10
Q474 PP57 100fr multicolored   5.50 4.25
Q475 PP57 200fr multicolored   11.00 8.50
Nos. Q473-Q475 (3)   19.25 14.85

Electric Trains PP58

Designs: No. Q476, Eurostar (yellow & white train). No. Q477, Thalys (red & white train). 160fr, Eurostar, Thalys side by side.

1998 Photo. Perf. 11½
Q476 PP58 80fr multicolored   4.75 3.50
Q477 PP58 80fr multicolored   4.75 3.50
Q478 PP58 160fr multicolored   9.50 7.25
Nos. Q476-Q478 (3)   19.00 14.25

ISSUED UNDER GERMAN OCCUPATION

German Stamps of 1906-11 Surcharged

Belgien 3 Centimes
Nos. N1-N6

1 Fr. 25 C.

Belgien
Nos. N7-N9

Wmk. Lozenges (125)
1914-15 Perf. 14, 14½
N1 A16 3c on 3pf brown   .45 .25
N2 A16 5c on 5pf green   .40 .25
N3 A16 10c on 10pf car   .50 .25
N4 A16 25c on 20pf ultra   .55 .35
N5 A16 50c on 40pf lake & blk   2.25 1.65
N6 A16 75c on 60pf mag   .90 1.25
N7 A16 1fr on 80pf lake & blk, rose   2.50 2.00
N8 A17 1fr25c on 1m car   22.50 18.00
N9 A21 2fr50c on 2m gray bl   20.00 22.50
Nos. N1-N9 (9)   50.05 46.50

German Stamps of 1906-18 Surcharged

Belgien 3 Cent.   **Belgien 1 F.**
Nos. N10-N21   No. N22

1 F. 25 Cent.

Belgien
Nos. N23-N25

1916-18
N10 A22 2c on 2pf drab   .25 .25
N11 A16 3c on 3pf brn   .35 .25
N12 A16 5c on 5pf grn   .35 .25
N13 A22 8c on 7½pf org   .65 .35
N14 A16 10c on 10pf car   .25 .25
N15 A22 15c on 15pf yel brn   .65 .25
N16 A22 15c on 15pf dk vio   .65 .45
N17 A16 20c on 25pf org & blk, yel   .35 .35
N18 A16 25c on 20pf ultra   .35 .25
a. 25c on 20pf blue   .40 .25
N19 A16 40c on 80pf org & blk, buff   .40 .35
N20 A16 50c on 40pf lake & blk   .35 .35
N21 A16 75c on 60pf mag   .65 8.50
N22 A16 1fr on 80pf lake & blk, rose   2.00 2.50
N23 A17 1fr25c on 1m car   3.25 3.25

BELGIUM — BELIZE

N24 A21 2fr50c on 2m gray bl	30.00	30.00
a. 2fr50c on 1m carmine (error)		3,500.
N25 A20 6fr25c on 5m sl & car	40.00	37.50
Nos. N10-N25 (16)	80.50	85.10

A similar series of stamps without "Belgien" was used in parts of Belgium and France while occupied by German forces. See France Nos. N15-N26.

BELIZE
bə-'lēz

LOCATION — Central America bordering on Caribbean Sea to east, Mexico to north, Guatemala to west
GOVT. — Independent state
AREA — 8,867 sq. mi.
POP. — 152,000 (1982 est.)
CAPITAL — Belmopan

Belize was known as British Honduras until 1973. The former British colony achieved independence in September 1981.

100 Cents = 1 Dollar

Catalogue values for all unused stamps in this country are for Never Hinged items.

Fish-Animal Type of British Honduras Regular Issue 1968-72 Overprinted in Black on Silver Panel

※ BELIZE ※

Wmk. 314 (½c, 5c, $5), Unwmkd.
1973, June 1   Litho.   Perf. 13x12½

312 A37 ½c multi (#235)	.15	.15
313 A37 1c multi (#214)	.15	.15
314 A37 2c multi (#215)	.15	.15
315 A37 3c multi (#216)	.15	.15
316 A37 4c multi (#217)	.15	.15
317 A37 5c multi (#238)	.15	.15
318 A37 10c multi (#219)	.15	.15
319 A37 15c multi (#220)	.15	.15
320 A37 25c multi (#221)	.30	.30
321 A37 50c multi (#222)	.50	.50
322 A37 $1 multi (#223)	.90	1.25
323 A37 $2 multi (#224)	2.00	2.50
324 A37 $5 multi (#240)	5.50	7.00
Nos. 312-324 (13)	10.40	12.75

No. 315 with silver panel omitted exists canceled. Nos. 313 and 319 exist with silver panel double.

Common Design Types pictured following the introduction.

Princess Anne's Wedding Issue
Common Design Type
1973, Nov. 14   Wmk. 314   Perf. 14

325 CD325 26c blue grn & multi	.15	.25
326 CD325 50c ocher & multi	.35	.50

Crana — A50

1974, Jan. 1   Litho.   Perf. 13½

327 A50 ½c shown	.15	.15
328 A50 1c Jewfish	.15	.15
329 A50 2c White-lipped peccary	.15	.15
330 A50 3c Grouper	.15	.15
331 A50 4c Collared anteater	.15	.15
332 A50 5c Bonefish	.15	.15
333 A50 10c Paca	.15	.15
334 A50 15c Dolphinfish	.15	.15
335 A50 25c Kinkajou	.25	.25
336 A50 50c Muttonfish	.55	.55
337 A50 $1 Tayra	1.00	1.00
338 A50 $2 Great barracudas	2.00	2.00
339 A50 $5 Mountain lion	5.25	5.25
Nos. 327-339 (13)	10.25	10.25

Stag, Mayan Pottery A51

Designs: Mayan pottery decorations.
1974, May 1   Perf. 14½

340 A51 3c shown	.15	.15
341 A51 6c Fire snake	.15	.15
342 A51 16c Mouse	.20	.20
343 A51 26c Eagle	.30	.30
344 A51 50c Parrot	.65	.65
Nos. 340-344 (5)	1.45	1.45

Parides Arcas A52

Designs: Butterflies of Belize.
1974-77   Perf. 14

345 A52 ½c shown	.15	.15
346 A52 1c Thecla regalis	.15	.15
347 A52 2c Colobura dirce	.15	.15
348 A52 3c Catonephele numilia	.15	.15
349 A52 4c Battus belus	.15	.15
350 A52 5c Callicore patelina	.35	.20
351 A52 10c Callicore astala	.70	.35

Perf. 14x15; 14 (26, 35c)

352 A52 15c Nessaea aglaura	.80	.50
a. Watermark upright ('75)	.70	.40
353 A52 16c Prepona pseudojoiceyi	.45	.25
354 A52 25c Papilio thoas	1.10	.65
a. Watermark upright ('77)	.80	.45
355 A52 26c Hamadryas arethusa	7.00	7.50
356 A52 50c Thecla bathildis	2.25	1.25
a. Watermark upright ('77)	1.00	.60
357 A52 $1 Caligo uranus	2.25	1.20
358 A52 $2 Heliconius sapho	4.25	2.40
359 A52 $5 Eurytides philolaus	13.00	7.50
a. Watermark upright ('75)	11.00	6.00
360 A52 $10 Philaethria dido	21.00	12.00
Nos. 345-360 (16)	53.90	34.55

Issue dates: No. 355A, July 25, 1977; No. 360, Jan. 2, 1975; others Sept. 2, 1974.
For surcharges, see Nos. 380, 386. For overprint, see No. 395.

1975-78   Wmk. 373

345a A52 ½c multicolored	.15	.15
347a A52 2c multi ('77)	.15	.15
348a A52 3c multi ('77)	.20	.20
349a A52 4c multi ('77)	.25	.25
350a A52 5c multi ('77)	.30	.30
351a A52 10c multicolored	.65	.65
352b A52 15c multi ('77)	.90	.90
354b A52 25c multi ('78)	1.25	1.25
355A A52 35c Parides arcas ('77)	2.00	2.00
Nos. 345a-355A (9)	5.85	5.85

For overprints and surcharges see Nos. 395-396, 424, 426-427.

Churchill and Coronation Coach of Queen Elizabeth II — A53

$1, Churchill & Williamsburg, VA Liberty Bell.

Wmk. 373
1974, Nov. 30   Litho.   Perf. 14

363 A53 50c multicolored	.15	.15
364 A53 $1 multicolored	.35	.35

Sir Winston Churchill (1874-1965).

Mayan Urn — A54 Maya art

Designs: Various Mayan vessels.
1975, June 2   Wmk. 314   Perf. 14

365 A54 3c lt green & multi	.15	.15
366 A54 6c lt blue & multi	.15	.15
367 A54 16c dull yel & multi	.20	.20
368 A54 26c lilac & multi	.30	.30
369 A54 50c lt brown & multi	.65	.65
Nos. 365-369 (5)	1.45	1.45

Musicians A55

Christmas: 26c, Nativity (Thatched hut and children). 50c, Drummers, vert. $1, Map of Belize, star, fleeing family, vert.

Perf. 14x14½, 14½x14
1975, Nov. 17   Litho.   Wmk. 314

370 A55 6c multicolored	.15	.15
371 A55 26c multicolored	.15	.15
372 A55 50c multicolored	.25	.25
373 A55 $1 multicolored	.55	.55
Nos. 370-373 (4)	1.10	1.10

William Wrigley, Jr., Sapodilla Tree A56

Bicentennial Emblem and: 35c, Charles Lindbergh and "Spirit of St. Louis." $1, John Lloyd Stephens and Mayan temple.

1976, Mar. 29   Wmk. 373   Perf. 14½

374 A56 10c multicolored	.15	.15
375 A56 35c multicolored	.25	.25
376 A56 $1 multicolored	.65	.65
Nos. 374-376 (3)	1.05	1.05

American Bicentennial.

Bicycling A57

Perf. 14½
1976, July 17   Litho.   Wmk. 373

377 A57 35c shown	.20	.20
378 A57 45c Running	.20	.20
379 A57 $1 Shooting	.45	.45
Nos. 377-379 (3)	.85	.85

21st Olympic Games, Montreal, Canada, July 17-Aug. 1.

No. 355 Surcharged with New Value and Bar
Wmk. 314
1976, Aug. 30   Litho.   Perf. 14

380 A52 20c on 26c multi	1.40	1.40

Map of West Indies, Bats, Wicket and Ball — A57a

Prudential Cup — A57b

Unwmk.
1976, Oct. 18   Litho.   Perf. 14

381 A57a 35c lt blue & multi	.45	.45
382 A57b $1 lilac rose & blk	1.25	1.25

World Cricket Cup, won by West Indies Team, 1975.

Royal Visit, 1975 A58

Designs: 35c, Rose window and Queen's head. $2, Queen surrounded by bishops.

1977, Feb. 7   Litho.   Perf. 13½x14

383 A58 10c multicolored	.15	.15
384 A58 35c multicolored	.25	.25
385 A58 $2 multicolored	1.10	1.10
Nos. 383-385 (3)	1.50	1.50

25th anniv. of the reign of Elizabeth II.

No. 352 Surcharged with New Value and Bar
1977   Wmk. 314   Perf. 14x15

386 A52 5c on 15c multi	.30	.30

The first setting has the "5c" close to the right edge of the block (varies). The second, and more common, setting has about 7mm from the right edge to the "5c."

Red-capped Manakin — A59

Designs: Birds of Belize.

Perf. 14½
1977, Sept. 3   Litho.   Wmk. 373

387 A59 8c shown	.30	.30
388 A59 10c Hooded oriole	.30	.20
389 A59 25c Blue-crowned motmot	.90	.45
390 A59 35c Slaty-breasted tinamou	1.00	.60
391 A59 45c Ocellated turkey	1.50	.75
392 A59 $1 White hawk	3.00	1.75
a. Souvenir sheet of 6, #387-392	8.50	4.25
Nos. 387-392 (6)	7.00	3.90

See Nos. 398-403, 416-421, 500-501. For overprints and surcharges see No. 502.

Medical Laboratory A60

Design: $1, Mobile medical unit and children receiving treatment.

1977, Dec. 2   Perf. 13½

393 A60 35c multicolored	.30	.30
394 A60 $1 multicolored	.75	.75
a. Souvenir sheet of 2, #393-394	1.10	1.10

Pan American Health Org., 75th anniv.

Nos. 351 and 355A Overprinted in Gold: "BELIZE DEFENCE FORCE / 1ST JANUARY 1978"
Wmk. 314, 373
1978, Feb. 15   Litho.   Perf. 14

395 A52 10c multicolored	.30	.30
396 A52 35c multicolored	.35	.35

Elizabeth II Coronation Anniversary Issue
Common Design Types
Souvenir Sheet
1978, Apr. 21   Unwmk.   Perf. 15

397 Sheet of 6	1.25	1.25
a. CD326 75c White lion of Mortimer	.20	.20
b. CD327 75c Elizabeth II	.20	.20
c. CD328 75c Jaguar (Maya god)	.20	.20

No. 397 contains 2 se-tenant strips of Nos. 397a-397c, separated by horizontal gutter with commemorative and descriptive inscriptions and showing central part of coronation procession with coach.

BELIZE

Bird Type of 1977
1978, July 31   Litho.   Wmk. 373   Perf. 14½

398	A59	10c White-crowned parrot	.40	.20
399	A59	25c Crimson-collared tanager	.90	.45
400	A59	35c Citreoline trogon	1.00	.50
401	A59	45c Sungrebe	1.10	.60
402	A59	50c Muscovy duck	1.25	.65
403	A59	$1 King vulture	2.25	1.25
a.		Souvenir sheet of 6, #398-403	9.50	4.00
		Nos. 398-403 (6)	6.90	3.65

Russelia Sarmentosa — A61

Wild Flowers and Ferns: 15c, Lygodium polymorphum. 35c, Heliconia aurantiaca. 45c, Adiantum tetraphyllum. 50c, Angelonia ciliaris. $1, Thelypteris obliterata.

1978, Oct. 16   Litho.   Perf. 14x13½

404	A61	10c multicolored	.15	.15
405	A61	15c multicolored	.20	.20
406	A61	35c multicolored	.40	.40
407	A61	45c multicolored	.50	.50
408	A61	50c multicolored	.55	.55
409	A61	$1 multicolored	1.10	1.10
		Nos. 404-409 (6)	2.90	2.90

Christmas.

Internal Airmail Service, 1937 — A62

Mail Service: 10c, MV Heron, 1949. 35c, Dugout canoe on river, 1920. 45c, Stann Creek railroad, 1910. 50c, Mounted courier, 1882. $2, RMS Eagle, 1856, and "paid" cancel.

1979, Jan. 15   Litho.   Wmk. 373   Perf. 13½x14

410	A62	5c multicolored	.15	.15
411	A62	10c multicolored	.15	.15
412	A62	35c multicolored	.30	.30
413	A62	45c multicolored	.40	.40
414	A62	50c multicolored	.45	.45
415	A62	$2 multicolored	1.75	1.75
		Nos. 410-415 (6)	3.20	3.20

Centenary of membership in UPU.

Bird Type of 1977
1979, Apr. 16   Unwmk.   Perf. 14½

416	A59	10c Boat-billed heron	.25	.25
417	A59	25c Gray-necked wood rail	.70	.60
418	A59	35c Lineated woodpecker	.85	.85
419	A59	50c Blue gray tanager	1.10	1.10
420	A59	50c Laughing falcon	1.25	1.20
421	A59	$1 Long-tailed hermit	2.50	2.50
a.		Souvenir sheet of 6, #416-421	7.25	7.00
		Nos. 416-421 (6)	6.65	6.50

Nos. 477, 354b, 595, 355A, 599, 651 Surcharged with New Value and Bar

10c $1.25

1979-83   Litho.   Perf. 14

422	A67	10c on 15c multi	.65	.65
423	A67	10c on 15c multi	.65	.65
424	A52	10c on 25c multi	.65	.65
424A	A67	10c on 35c multi		
b.		Round obliterator		
425	A76	10c on 35c multi		
426	A52	15c on 35c multi		
427	A52	15c on 35c multi	.30	.30
428	A76	$1.25 on $2 multi	2.00	2.00
429	A81	$1.25 on $2 multi	2.00	2.00

No. 422 has a square the width of the "10c" obliterating the old value. No. 423 has a rectangle that is wider than the "10c".
No. 424A has a square obliterator.
No. 426 has "15c" at top of stamp, No. 427 has "15c" at right of rectangle. Type differs.

No. 429 has rectangular obliterator with new value at top of stamp.
Many errors exist from printer's waste.
Issue dates: #426, Mar. 1979. #427, June, 1979. #424, Mar. 31, 1980. #422, Aug. 22, 1981. #423, Jan. 28, 1983. #425, Apr. 15, 1983. #428-429, June 9, 1983.

Used Stamps
Postally used copies are valued the same as unused. CTO's are of minimal value. Most used stamps from No. 430-679 exist CTO. Most of these appeared on the market after the contract was canceled and were not authorized. The cancellations are printed and the paper differs from the issued stamps.

Imperforate Stamps
Stamps from No. 430-679 exist imperforate in small quantities.

Queen Elizabeth II, 25th Anniv. of Coronation — A63

Designs: 25c, No. 439, Paslow Bldg., #397c. 50c, Parliament, London, #397a. 75c, Coronation coach. $1, Queen on horseback, vert. $2, Prince of Wales, vert. $3, Queen and Prince Philip, vert. $4, Queen Elizabeth II, portrait, vert. No. 437, St. Edward's Crown, vert. No. 438a, $5, Princess Anne on horseback, Montreal Olympics, vert. No. 438b, $10, Queen, Montreal Olympics, vert.

Unwmk.
1979, May 31   Litho.   Perf. 14

430	A63	25c multicolored	.20	
431	A63	50c multicolored	.45	
432	A63	75c multicolored	.70	
433	A63	$1 multicolored	.90	
434	A63	$2 multicolored	1.75	
435	A63	$3 multicolored	2.75	
436	A63	$4 multicolored	3.75	
437	A63	$5 multicolored	4.50	
		Nos. 430-437 (8)	15.00	

Souvenir Sheets

438	A63	Sheet of 2, #a.-b.	10.00	
439	A63	$15 multicolored	10.00	

Powered Flight, 75th Anniv. — A64

1979, July 30

440	A64	4c Safety, 1909	
441	A64	25c Boeing 707	
442	A64	50c Concorde	
443	A64	75c Handley Page W8b, 1922	
444	A64	$1 AVRO F, 1912	
445	A64	$1.50 Cody, 1910	
446	A64	$2 Triplane Roe II, 1909	
447	A64	$3 Santos-Dumont, 1906	
448	A64	$4 Wright Brothers Flyer, 1903	

Souvenir Sheets   Perf. 14½

449		Sheet of 2
a.		A64 $5 Dunne D.5, 1910
b.		A64 $5 Great Britain #581
450	A64	$10 Belize Airways Jet

Sir Rowland Hill, death cent., "75th anniv." of ICAO.

1980 Summer Olympics, Moscow — A65

1979, Oct. 10   Perf. 14

451	A65	25c Handball	.20
452	A65	50c Weight lifting	.45
453	A65	75c Track	.70
454	A65	$1 Soccer	.90
455	A65	$2 Sailing	1.75
456	A65	$3 Swimming	2.75
457	A65	$4 Boxing	3.75
458	A65	$5 Cycling	4.50
		Nos. 451-458 (8)	15.00

Souvenir Sheets   Perf. 14½

459		Sheet of 2	12.00
a.		A65 $5 Track, diff.	4.00
b.		A65 $10 Boxing, diff.	8.00
460	A65	$15 Cycling, diff.	12.00

1980 Winter Olympics, Lake Placid — A66

1979, Dec. 4   Perf. 14

461	A66	25c Torch	.20
462	A66	50c Slalom skiing	.40
463	A66	75c Figure skating	.65
464	A66	$1 Downhill skiing	.85
465	A66	$2 Speed skating	1.75
466	A66	$3 Cross country skiing	2.50
467	A66	$4 Biathlon	3.50
468	A66	$5 Olympic medals	4.25
		Nos. 461-468 (8)	14.10

Souvenir Sheets   Perf. 14½

469		Sheet of 2	12.00
a.		A66 $5 Torch bearers	4.00
b.		A66 $10 Medals, diff.	8.00
470	A66	$15 Torch, diff.	12.00

See Nos. 503-512.

Cypraea Zebra — A67

1980, Jan. 7   Litho.   Perf. 14

471	A67	1c shown	.15	.15
472	A67	2c Macrocallista maculata	.15	.15
473	A67	3c Arca zebra, vert.	.15	.15
474	A67	4c Chama macerophylla, vert.	.15	.15
475	A67	5c Latirus cariniferus	.15	.15
476	A67	10c Conus spurius, vert.	.15	.15
477	A67	15c Murex cabritii, vert.	.20	.15
478	A67	20c Atrina rigida	.25	.15
479	A67	25c Chlamys imbricata, vert.	.30	.15
480	A67	35c Conus granulatus	.40	.15
481	A67	45c Tellina radiata, vert.	.55	.15
482	A67	50c Leucozonia nassa	.60	.20
483	A67	85c Tripterotyphis triangularis	1.05	.35
484	A67	$1 Strombus gigas, vert.	1.25	.35
485	A67	$2 Strombus gallus, vert.	2.50	.75
486	A67	$5 Fasciolaria tulipa	6.25	1.75
487	A67	$10 Arene cruentata	12.50	3.50
		Nos. 471-487 (17)	26.75	8.50

Souvenir Sheets

488	A67	Sheet of 2, 85c, $5	7.50	7.50
489	A67	Sheet of 2, $2, $10	15.00	17.50

Stamps in Nos. 488-489 have colored border and are of a slightly different size than the sheet stamps.
The 10c, 50c, 85c, $1 exist dated 1981.
For overprints and surcharges see Nos. 422-423, 424A, 572-589, 592-593.

Intl. Year of the Child — A68

Various children. No. 498a, Three children. No. 498b, Madonna and Child by Durer. No. 499, Children before Christmas tree.

1980, Mar. 15   Litho.   Perf. 14

490	A68	25c multicolored	.15
491	A68	50c multicolored	.35
492	A68	75c multicolored	.50
493	A68	$1 multicolored	.65
494	A68	$1.50 multicolored	1.00
495	A68	$2 multicolored	1.40
496	A68	$3 multicolored	2.00
497	A68	$4 multicolored	2.75
		Nos. 490-497 (8)	8.80

Souvenir Sheets   Perf. 13½

498	A68	$5 Sheet of 2, #a.-b.	6.00
499	A68	$10 multicolored	6.00

No. 498 contains two 35x54mm stamps. No. 499 contains one 73x110mm stamp.

Bird Type of 1977
Souvenir Sheets
1980, June 16   Unwmk.   Perf. 13½

500		Sheet of 6	5.50	4.50
a.	A59	10c Jabiru	.20	.15
b.	A59	25c Barred antshrike	.50	.35
c.	A59	35c Royal flycatcher	.65	.50
d.	A59	45c White-necked puffbird	.75	.65
e.	A59	50c Ornate hawk-eagle	.85	.75
f.	A59	$1 Golden-masked tanager	1.90	1.50
g.		Sheet of 12	11.00	9.00
501		Sheet of 2	8.00	8.00
a.	A59	$2 Jabiru	3.00	3.00
b.	A59	$3 Golden-masked tanager	4.50	4.50

No. 500g contains 2 each Nos. 500a-500f with gutter between; inscribed "Protection of Environment" and "Wildlife Protection."

No. 500 Overprinted or Surcharged with Exhibition Emblem
1980, Oct. 3   Litho.   Perf. 13½

502		Sheet of 6	4.00	4.00
a.	A59	10c multicolored	.20	.20
b.	A59	25c multicolored	.50	.50
c.	A59	35c multicolored	.65	.65
d.	A59	40c on 45c multi	.85	.85
e.	A59	40c on 50c multi	.85	.85
f.	A59	40c on $1 multi	.85	.85

ESPAMER '80 Stamp Exhibition, Madrid, Spain, Oct. 3-12.

1980 Winter Olympics, Lake Placid — A69

Events and winning country: 25c, Men's speed skating, US. 50c, Ice hockey, US. 75c, No. 512, Men's figure skating, Great Britain. $1, Alpine skiing, Austria. $1.50, Women's giant slalom, Germany. $2, Women's speed skating, Netherlands. $3, Cross country skiing, Sweden. $5, Men's giant slalom, Sweden. Nos. 511a ($5), 511b ($10), Speed skating, US.

BELIZE

1980, Aug. 20   Litho.   Perf. 14
503	A69	25c multicolored	.25
504	A69	50c multicolored	.50
505	A69	75c multicolored	.75
506	A69	$1 multicolored	.95
507	A69	$1.50 multicolored	1.50
508	A69	$2 multicolored	1.90
509	A69	$3 multicolored	3.00
510	A69	$5 multicolored	4.75
		Nos. 503-510 (8)	13.60

Souvenir Sheets
Perf. 14½
511	A69	Sheet of 2, #a.-b.	9.50
512	A69	$10 multicolored	9.50

Nos. 503-510 issued with se-tenant label.

Intl. Year of the Child — A70

Nos. 513-521: Scenes from Sleeping Beauty. $8, Detail from Paumgartner Family Altarpiece by Albrecht Durer.

1980, Nov. 24   Perf. 14
513	A70	35c multicolored	.30
514	A70	40c multicolored	.35
515	A70	50c multicolored	.40
516	A70	75c multicolored	.65
517	A70	$1 multicolored	.85
518	A70	$1.50 multicolored	1.25
519	A70	$3 multicolored	2.50
520	A70	$4 multicolored	3.50
		Nos. 513-520 (8)	9.80

Souvenir Sheets
Perf. 14½
521		Sheet of 2	9.50
a.		A70 $5 Marriage	4.25
b.		A70 $5 Couple on horseback	4.25
522	A70	$8 multicolored	7.50

Nos. 513-520 issued with se-tenant label.

Queen Mother Elizabeth, 80th Birthday A71

1980, Dec. 12
523	A71	$1 multicolored	1.00	1.00

Souvenir Sheet
Perf. 14½
524	A71	$5 multicolored	

No. 524 contains one 46x31mm stamp.
No. 523 issued in sheet of 6.

Christmas — A72

1980, Dec. 30   Litho.   Perf. 14
525	A72	25c Annunciation	.20
526	A72	50c Bethlehem	.40
527	A72	75c Holy Family	.65
528	A72	$1 Nativity	.85
529	A72	$1.50 Flight into Egypt	1.25
530	A72	$2 Shepards	1.65
531	A72	$3 With angel	2.50
532	A72	$4 Adoration	3.25
		Nos. 525-532 (8)	10.75

Souvenir Sheets
Perf. 14½
533	A72	$5 Nativity	5.00
534	A72	$10 Madonna & Child	10.00

Nos. 525-532 each issued in sheets of 20 + 10 labels. The 2nd and 5th vertical rows consist of labels.

Nos. 529, 532, 534 Surcharged $2
WIPA 1981

1981, May 22
535	A72	$1 on $1.50 multi	
536	A72	$2 on $4 multi	

Souvenir Sheet
Perf. 14½
537	A72	$2 on $10 multi	

Location of overprint and surcharge varies.

Intl. Rotary Club — A73

Designs: 25c, Paul P. Harris, founder. 50c, No. 546, Rotary, project emblem. $1, No. 545b, 75th anniv. emblem. $1.50 Diploma, horiz. $2, No. 545a, Project Hippocrates. $3, 75th anniv. project emblems, horiz. No. 544, Hands reach out, horiz.

1981, May 26   Perf. 14
538	A73	25c multicolored	.25
539	A73	50c multicolored	.50
540	A73	$1 multicolored	.95
541	A73	$1.50 multicolored	1.40
542	A73	$2 multicolored	1.90
543	A73	$3 multicolored	2.75
544	A73	$5 multicolored	4.75
		Nos. 538-544 (7)	12.50

Souvenir Sheets
Perf. 14½
545		Sheet of 2	18.00
a.		A73 $5 multicolored	5.75
b.		A73 $10 multicolored	12.00
546	A73	$10 multicolored	12.00

Originally scheduled to be issued Mar. 30, the set was postponed and issued without a 75c stamp. Supposedly some of the 75c were sold to the public.
For overprints and surcharges see Nos. 563-571, 590-591.

Royal Wedding of Prince Charles and Lady Diana — A74

1981, July 16   Perf. 13½x14
548	A74	50c Coat of Arms	.20
549	A74	$1 Prince Charles	.40
550	A74	$1.50 Couple	.65

Size: 25x43mm
Perf. 13½
551	A74	50c like No. 548	.20
552	A74	$1 like No. 549	.40
553	A74	$1.50 like No. 550	.65
		Nos. 548-553 (6)	2.50

Miniature Sheet
Perf. 14½
554		Sheet of 3, #554a-554c	5.00
a.		A74 $3 like No. 550	1.65
b.		A74 $3 like No. 548	1.65
c.		A74 $3 like No. 549	1.65

Nos. 551-553 issued in sheets of 6 + 3 labels.
No. 554 contains three 35x50mm stamps.
For overprints see Nos. 659-665.

1984 Olympics — A75

1981, Sept. 14   Perf. 14
555	A75	85c Track	.75
556	A75	$1 Cycling	.90
557	A75	$1.50 Boxing	1.40
558	A75	$2 Emblems	1.90
559	A75	$3 Baron Coubertin	2.75
560	A75	$5 Torch, emblems	4.50
		Nos. 555-560 (6)	12.20

Souvenir Sheets
Perf. 13½
561		Sheet of 2	10.00
a.		A75 $5 like No. 559	3.25
b.		A75 $10 like No. 560	6.75

Perf. 14½
562	A75	$15 like No. 558	10.00

No. 561 contains two 35x54mm stamps. No. 562 contains one 46x68mm stamp.
Nos. 561-562 exist with gold background.

Nos. 538-546 Overprinted in Black or Gold INDEPENDENCE 21 SEPT.,1981

1981, Sept. 21   Perf. 14
563	A73	25c multicolored (G)	
564	A73	50c multicolored	
565	A73	$1 multicolored	
566	A73	$1.50 multicolored	
567	A73	$2 multicolored (G)	
568	A73	$3 multicolored	
569	A73	$5 multicolored	

Souvenir Sheets
Perf. 14½
570	A73	Sheet of 2, #a.-b. (G)	
571	A73	$10 multicolored	

Size of overprint varies.

Nos. 471-483, 485-489 Overprinted Independence 21 Sept.,1981

1981, Sept. 21
572	A67	1c multicolored	
573	A67	2c multicolored	
574	A67	3c multicolored	
575	A67	4c multicolored	
576	A67	5c multicolored	
577	A67	10c multicolored	
578	A67	15c multicolored	
579	A67	20c multicolored	
580	A67	25c multicolored	
581	A67	35c multicolored	
582	A67	45c multicolored	
583	A67	50c multicolored	
584	A67	75c multicolored	
585	A67	$2 multicolored	
586	A67	$5 multicolored	
587	A67	$10 multicolored	

Souvenir Sheets
588	A67	Sheet of 2, #488	
589	A67	Sheet of 2, #489	

Size and style of overprint varies, italic on horiz. stamps, upright on vert. stamps and upright capitals on souvenir sheets.
The 10c is dated 1981. Less than 16 sheets dated 1980 were also overprinted.

Nos. 541, 545 Surcharged $1

1981, Nov. 13   Perf. 14
590	A73	$1 on $1.50 multi	

Souvenir Sheet
Perf. 14½
591		Sheet of 2	
a.		A73 $1 on $5 multicolored	
b.		A73 $1 on $10 multicolored	

Espamer '81.

Nos. 488, 489 Surcharged in Red $1
PHILATELIA'81
14-18.XI.1981

1981, Nov. 14   Perf. 14½
Souvenir Sheets
592		Sheet of 2	2.50
a.		A67 $1 on 85c	
b.		A67 $1 on $5	
593		Sheet of 2	2.50
a.		A67 $1 on $2	
b.		A67 $1 on $10	

Independence — A76

1981-82   Perf. 14
594	A76	10c Flag	
595	A76	35c Map, vert.	
596	A76	50c Black orchid, vert.	
597	A76	85c Tapir	
598	A76	$1 Mahogany tree, vert.	
599	A76	$2 Keel-billed toucan	

Souvenir Sheet
Perf. 14½
600	A76	$5 like 10c	

Issued: 50c-$2, 12/18; 10c, 35c, $5, 2/10/82.
For surcharges see Nos. 425, 428, 616.

1982 World Cup Soccer Championships, Spain — A77

1981, Dec. 28   Perf. 14
601	A77	10c Uruguay '30, '50	.15
602	A77	25c Italy '34, '38	.15
603	A77	50c Germany '54, '74	.40
604	A77	$1 Brazil '58, '62, '70	.75
605	A77	$1.50 Argentina '78	1.25
606	A77	$2 England '66	1.75
		Nos. 601-606 (6)	4.45

Souvenir Sheets
Perf. 14½
607	A77	$2 Emblem	1.75
608	A77	$3 Player	2.50

No. 608 contains one 46x78mm stamp.
For surcharge see No. 617.

Sailing Ships A78

1982, Mar. 15   Perf. 14
609	A78	10c Man of war, 19th cent.	
610	A78	25c Madagascar, 1837	
611	A78	35c Whitby, 1838	
612	A78	50c China, 1838	
613	A78	85c Swiftsure, 1850	
614	A78	$2 Windsor Castle, 1857	

BELIZE

Souvenir Sheet
Perf. 14½
615 A78 $5 19th cent. ships

Nos. 599 and 606 Surcharged

1982, Apr. 28
616 A76 $1 on $2 multi 2.25
617 A77 $1 on $2 multi 2.25
Essen '82 Philatelic Exhibition.

Princess of Wales, 21st Birthday — A79

Various portraits.

1982, May 20 *Perf. 13½x14*
618 A79 50c multicolored .25
619 A79 $1 multicolored .50
620 A79 $1.50 multicolored .75
Size: 25x42mm
Perf. 13½
621 A79 50c like No. 618 .25
622 A79 $1 like No. 619 .50
623 A79 $1.50 like No. 620 .75
Nos. 618-623 (6) 3.00

Souvenir Sheet
Stamp Size: 31x47mm
Perf. 14½
624 A79 $3 Sheet of 3, #a.-c. like #618-620 4.00

Nos. 618-620 also exist with gold borders, size: 30x45mm.

BIRTH OF H.R.H.

Overprinted in Silver
PRINCE
WILLIAM ARTHUR
PHILIP LOUIS
21ST JUNE 1982

1982, Oct. 21 *Perf. 13½x14*
628 A79 50c multicolored .40
629 A79 $1 multicolored .80
630 A79 $1.50 multicolored 1.25
Size: 25x42mm
Perf. 13½
631 A79 50c multicolored .40
632 A79 $1 multicolored .80
633 A79 $1.50 multicolored 1.25
Nos. 628-633 (6) 4.90

Souvenir Sheet
Perf. 14½
634 A79 $3 Sheet of 3, #a.-c. 8.50

Size of overprint varies. The overprint exists on the gold bordered stamps. No. 634 exists with a second type of overprint.

Boy Scouts A80

1982, Aug. 31 *Perf. 14*
638 A80 10c Building camp fire .15
639 A80 25c Bird watching .35
640 A80 35c Playing guitar .50
641 A80 50c Hiking .75
642 A80 85c Flag, scouts 1.25
643 A80 $2 Salute 2.75
Nos. 638-643 (6) 5.75

Souvenir Sheets
Perf. 14½
644 A80 $2 Scout holding flag, vert. 4.00
645 A80 $3 Lord Baden Powell, vert. 6.00

Scouting, 75th anniv. and Lord Baden Powell, 125th birth anniv.
For overprints see Nos. 653-658.

Marine Life — A81

1982, Sept. 20 *Perf. 14*
646 A81 10c Gorgonia ventalina
647 A81 35c Carpilius corallinus
648 A81 50c Plexaura flexuosa
649 A81 85c Condylactis gigantea
650 A81 $1 Stenopus hispidus
651 A81 $2 Abudefduf saxatilis

Souvenir Sheet
Perf. 14½
652 A81 $5 Scyllarides aequinoctialis

For surcharge see No. 429.

Nos. 638-643 Ovptd. in Gold:
BELGICA 82
INT. YEAR OF THE CHILD
SIR ROWLAND HILL 1795 1879
Picasso CENTENARY OF BIRTH
and Emblems

1982, Oct. 1 *Perf. 14*
653 A80 10c Building camp fire
654 A80 25c Bird watching
655 A80 35c Playing guitar
656 A80 50c Hiking
657 A80 85c Flag, scouts
658 A80 $2 Salute

Overprint is different on Nos. 654-655.
Sheets include labels with native Christmas themes.

Nos. 548-554 Overprinted in Gold Similar to Nos. 628-634

1982, Oct. 25 *Perf. 13½x14*
659 A74 50c Coat of Arms 1.40
660 A74 $1 Prince Charles 2.75
661 A74 $1.50 Couple 4.25
Size: 25x43mm
Perf. 13½
662 A74 50c like No. 659 1.40
663 A74 $1 like No. 660 2.75
664 A74 $1.50 like No. 661 4.25
Nos. 659-664 (6) 16.80

Miniature Sheet
Perf. 14½
665 Sheet of 3, #665a-665c 14.00
  a. A74 $3 like No. 661 3.50
  b. A74 $3 like No. 659 3.50
  c. A74 $3 like No. 660 3.50

Nos. 662-664 issued in sheets of 6 plus 3 labels.
No. 665 contains three 35x50mm stamps. Size and style of overprint varies.

Visit by Pope John Paul II A82

1983, Mar. 7 *Perf. 13½*
666 A82 50c Belize Cathedral 1.90

Souvenir Sheet
Perf. 14½
667 A82 $2.50 Pope John Paul II 4.75
No. 667 contains one 30x47mm stamp.
No. 666 issued in sheet of 6.

Commonwealth Day — A83

1983, Mar. 14 *Perf. 13½*
668 A83 35c Map, vert. .30
669 A83 50c Maya Stella .40
670 A83 85c Supreme Court Bldg. .80
671 A83 $2 University Center 2.00
Nos. 668-671 (4) 3.50

Issued in miniature sheets of 4. Other formats are suspect.

First Manned Flight, Bicent. — A84

1983, May 16 *Perf. 14*
672 A84 10c Flying boat, 1670 .15
673 A84 25c Flying machine, 1709 .16
674 A84 50c Airship Guyton de Morveau .30
675 A84 85c Dirigible .52
676 A84 $1 Clement Bayard .60
677 A84 $1.50 Great Britain R-34 .95
Nos. 672-677 (6) 2.68

Souvenir Sheets
Perf. 14½
678 A84 $3 Nassau Balloon 1.65
679 A84 $3 Montgolfier Brothers balloon, vert. 1.65

"Errors"

Many "errors," including imperforates, exist of Nos. 680-898. These unauthorized varieties were printed without the knowledge of the Belize postal service. There may be large quantities of them.

Mayan Monuments — A85

1983, Nov. 14 Litho. *Perf. 13½x14*
680 A85 10c Altun Ha .15 .15
681 A85 15c Xunantunich .15 .15
682 A85 75c Cerros .60 .60
683 A85 $2 Lamanai 1.40 1.40
Nos. 680-683 (4) 2.30 2.30

Souvenir Sheet
684 A85 $3 Xunantunich, diff. 2.75 2.75

World Communications Year — A86

1983, Nov. 28 *Perf. 14*
685 A86 10c Belmopan Earth Station .15 .15
686 A86 15c Telstar 2 .15 .15
687 A86 75c UPU monument .75 .75
688 A86 $2 Mail boat 2.00 2.00
Nos. 685-688 (4) 3.05 3.05

Jaguar, World Wildlife Fund Emblem A87

1983, Dec. 9
689 A87 5c Sitting .15 .15
690 A87 10c Standing .15 .15
691 A87 85c Swimming 1.10 1.10
692 A87 $1 Walking 1.40 1.40
Nos. 689-692 (4) 2.80 2.80

Souvenir Sheet
693 A87 $3 Sitting in tree 3.25 3.25

No. 693 contains one stamp 45x28mm.

Christmas — A88

Scenes from mass celebrated by Pope John Paul II during visit, Mar.

1983, Dec. 22
694 A88 10c multicolored .15 .15
695 A88 15c multicolored .15 .15
696 A88 75c multicolored .75 .75
697 A88 $2 multicolored 2.00 2.00
Nos. 694-697 (4) 3.05 3.05

Souvenir Sheet
698 A88 $3 multicolored 3.25 3.25

Foureye Butterflyfish A89

1984, Feb. 27 *Perf. 15*
699 A89 1c shown .15 .15
700 A89 2c Cushion star .15 .15
701 A89 3c Flower coral .15 .15
702 A89 4c Fairy bassletts .15 .15
703 A89 5c Spanish hogfish .15 .15
704 A89 6c Star-eyed hermit crab .15 .15
705 A89 10c Sea fans, fire sponge .15 .15
706 A89 15c Blueheads .15 .15
707 A89 25c Blue-striped grunt .25 .25
708 A89 50c Coral crab .50 .50
709 A89 60c Tube sponge .60 .60
710 A89 75c Brain coral .75 .75
711 A89 $1 Yellow-tail snapper 1.00 1.00
712 A89 $2 Common lettuce slug 2.00 2.00
713 A89 $5 Yellow damselfish 5.00 5.00
714 A89 $10 Rock beauty 10.00 10.00
Nos. 699-714 (16) 21.30 21.30

For overprints and surcharge see Nos. 715-716, 762A-762C, 922.
The 50c, 60c, 75c, $1 exist inscribed "1986."

1988, July *Perf. 13½*
705a A89 10c .15 .15
706a A89 15c .15 .15
707a A89 25c .25 .25
708a A89 50c .48 .48
709a A89 60c .58 .58
711a A89 $1 .95 .95
Nos. 705a-711a (6) 2.56 2.56

Nos. 705, 708 Overprinted: "VISIT OF THE LORD / ARCHBISHOP OF CANTERBURY / 8th-11th MARCH 1984"

1984, Mar. 8
715 A89 10c multicolored .15 .15
716 A89 50c multicolored .60 .60

1984 Summer Olympics — A90

1984, Apr. 30 *Perf. 13½x14*
717 A90 25c Shooting .25 .25
718 A90 75c Boxing .75 .75
719 A90 $1 Running 1.10 1.10
720 A90 $2 Bicycling 1.90 1.90
Nos. 717-720 (4) 4.00 4.00

Souvenir Sheet
721 A90 $3 Discus 2.25 2.25

BELIZE

1984 Summer Olympics — A91

1984, Apr. 30   Litho.   Perf. 14½
Booklet Stamps
722	A91	5c Running	.15	.15
a.		Booklet pane of 4	.30	
723	A91	20c Javelin	.25	.25
a.		Booklet pane of 4	1.10	
724	A91	25c Shot put	.35	.35
a.		Booklet pane of 4	1.50	
725	A91	$2 Torch	2.50	2.50
a.		Booklet pane of 4	10.50	
		Nos. 722-725 (4)	3.25	3.25

Ausipex '84 — A92

1984, Sept. 26   Litho.   Perf. 15
726	A92	15c Br. Honduras #3	.15	.15
727	A92	30c Bath-Bristol mail coach, 1784	.30	.30
728	A92	65c Penny Black, Rowland Hill	.65	.65
729	A92	75c Railroad Pier, Commerce Bight	.75	.75

Perf. 14
730	A92	$2 Royal Exhibition Bldgs.	2.00	2.00
		Nos. 726-730 (5)	3.85	3.85

Souvenir Sheet
731	A92	$3 Australia #132, Br. Hond. #3	3.00	3.00

House of Tudor, 500th Anniv. — A93
White-fronted Parrot — A94 

1984, Oct. 15   Perf. 14
732	A93	50c Queen Victoria	.35	.35
733	A93	50c Prince Albert	.35	.35
a.		Sheet of 4, 2 each, #732-733	1.50	
734	A93	75c King George VI	.55	.55
735	A93	75c Queen Elizabeth	.55	.55
a.		Sheet of 4, 2 each, #734-735	2.25	
736	A93	$1 Prince Charles	.75	.75
737	A93	$1 Princess Diana	.75	.75
a.		Sheet of 4, 2 each, #736-737	3.00	
		Nos. 732-737 (6)	3.30	3.30

Souvenir Sheet
738		Sheet of 2	2.00	2.00
a.	A93	$1.50 Prince Philip	1.00	1.00
b.	A93	$1.50 Queen Elizabeth II	1.00	1.00

1984, Nov. 1   Perf. 11
Parrots: b, White-capped. c, Red-lored. d, Mealy. b, d, horiz.

739		Block of 4	4.00	4.00
a.-d.	A94	$1 any single	1.00	1.00

Miniature Sheet   Perf. 14
740	A94	$3 Scarlet macaw	3.00	3.00

No. 740 contains one 48x32mm stamp.

Ordering on-line is QUICK! EASY! CONVENIENT!
www.scottonline.com

Mayan Artifacts — A95

1984, Nov. 30   Perf. 15
741	A95	25c Incense holder, 1450	.25	.25
742	A95	75c Cylindrical vase, 675	.75	.75
743	A95	$1 Tripod vase, 500	1.00	1.00
744	A95	$2 Kinich Ahau (sun god)	2.00	2.00
		Nos. 741-744 (4)	4.00	4.00

Girl Guides 75th Anniv., Intl. Youth Year — A96

1985, Mar. 15   Litho.   Perf. 15
745	A96	25c Gov.-Gen. Gordon	.25	.25
746	A96	50c Camping	.50	.50
747	A96	90c Map reading	.90	.90
748	A96	$1.25 Students in laboratory	1.25	1.25
749	A96	$2 Lady Baden-Powell	2.00	2.00
		Nos. 745-749 (5)	4.90	4.90

Each stamp shows the scouting and IYY emblems.
For overprints see Nos. 777-781.

Audubon Birth Bicentenary — A97

Illustrations by Audubon. 10c, 25c, 75c, $1, $5 vert.

Perf. 14, 15 ($1)
1985, May 30-1988   Litho.
750	A97	10c White-tailed kite	.15	.15
751	A97	15c Cuvier's kinglet	.15	.15
752	A97	25c Painted bunting	.35	.35
752A	A97	60c like #752 ('88)		
753	A97	75c Belted kingfisher	1.00	1.00
754	A97	$1 Northern cardinal	1.40	1.40
755	A97	$3 Long-billed curlew	4.00	4.00
		Nos. 750-752, 753-755 (6)	7.05	7.05

Souvenir Sheet   Perf. 13½x14
756	A97	$5 Portrait of Audubon, 1826, by John Syme	5.00	5.00

No. 756 contains one 38x51mm stamp.

Queen Mother, 85th Birthday — A98

Designs: 10c, The Queen Consort and Princess Elizabeth, 1928. 15c, Queen Mother, Elizabeth. 75c, Queen Mother waving a greeting. No. 760, Royal family photograph, christening of Prince Henry. $2, Holding the infant Prince Henry. No. 762, Queen Mother, diff.

1985, June 20
757	A98	10c shown	.15	.15
758	A98	15c multicolored	.15	.15
759	A98	75c multicolored	.75	.75
760	A98	$5 multicolored	5.00	5.00
		Nos. 757-760 (4)	6.05	6.05

Souvenir Sheets
761	A98	$2 multicolored	1.75	1.75
762	A98	$5 multicolored	4.25	4.25

Nos. 761-762 contain one 38x51mm stamp.
For overprints see Nos. 771-776.

Nos. 705-706, 708 Ovptd.:   INAUGURATION OF NEW GOVERNMENT 21st. DECEMBER 1984

1985, June 24   Perf. 15
762A	A89	10c multicolored	.30	.30
762B	A89	15c multicolored	.45	.45
762C	A89	50c multicolored	1.25	1.25
		Nos. 762A-762C (3)	2.00	2.00

Miniature Sheet

Commonwealth Stamp Omnibus, 50th Anniv. — A99

British Honduras Nos. 111-112, 127, 129, 143, 194, 307 and Belize Nos. 326, 385 and 397b on: a, George V and Queen Mary in an open carriage. b, George VI and Queen Consort Elizabeth crowned. c, Civilians celebrating the end of WWII. d, George VI and Queen Consort at mass service. e, Elizabeth II wearing robes of state and the imperial crown. f, Winston Churchill, WWII fighter planes. g, Bridal photograph of Elizabeth II and Prince Philip. h, Bridal photograph of Princess Anne and Capt. Mark Phillips. i, Elizabeth II. j, Imperial crown.

1985, July 25   Perf. 14½x14
763		Sheet of 10	5.00	5.00
a.-j.	A99	50c any single	.50	.50

Souvenir Sheet   Perf. 14
764	A99	$5 Elizabeth II coronation photograph	5.00	5.00

No. 764 contains one 38x51mm stamp.
For overprints see Nos. 796-797.

British Post Office, 350th Anniv. — A100

1985, Aug. 1   Perf. 15
765	A100	10c Postboy, letters	.15	.15
766	A100	15c Packet, privateer	.15	.15
767	A100	25c Duke of Marlborough	.25	.25
768	A100	75c Diana	.75	.75
769	A100	$1 Falmouth P.O. packet	1.00	1.00
770	A100	$3 S. S. Conway	3.00	3.00
		Nos. 765-770 (6)	5.30	5.30

Nos. 757-762 Ovptd. in Silver   "COMMONWEALTH SUMMIT / CONFERENCE, BAHAMAS / 16th-22nd OCTOBER 1985"

1985, Sept. 5   Litho.   Perf. 15
771	A98	10c multicolored	.15	.15
772	A98	15c multicolored	.15	.15
773	A98	75c multicolored	.75	.75
774	A98	$5 multicolored	5.00	5.00
		Nos. 771-774 (4)	6.05	6.05

Souvenir Sheets
775	A98	$2 multicolored	1.90	1.90
776	A98	$5 multicolored	4.75	4.75

Nos. 745-749 Ovptd. "80th ANNIVERSARY OF / ROTARY INTERNATIONAL"

1985, Sept. 25   Perf. 15
777	A96	25c multicolored	.25	.25
778	A96	50c multicolored	.50	.50
779	A96	90c multicolored	.90	.90
780	A96	$1.25 multicolored	1.25	1.25
781	A96	$2 multicolored	2.00	2.00
		Nos. 777-781 (5)	4.90	4.90

Royal Visit — A101

1985, Oct. 9   Perf. 15x14½
782	A101	25c Royal and natl. flags	.25	.25
783	A101	75c Elizabeth II	.75	.75

Size: 81x38mm
784	A101	$4 Britannia	4.00	4.00
a.		Strip of 3, #782-784	5.00	
		Nos. 782-784 (3)	5.00	5.00

Souvenir Sheet   Perf. 13½x14
785	A101	$5 Elizabeth II, diff.	5.00	5.00

No. 785 contains one 38x51mm stamp.

Disneyland, 30th Anniv. — A102

Characters from "It's a Small World."

1985, Nov. 1   Perf. 11
786	A102	1c Royal Canadian Mounted Police	.15	.15
787	A102	2c American Indian	.15	.15
788	A102	3c Inca of the Andes	.15	.15
789	A102	4c Africa	.15	.15
790	A102	5c Far East	.15	.15
791	A102	6c Belize	.15	.15
792	A102	50c Balkans	.50	.50
793	A102	$1.50 Saudi Arabia	1.50	1.50
794	A102	$3 Japan	3.00	3.00
		Nos. 786-794 (9)	5.90	5.90

Souvenir Sheet   Perf. 14
795	A102	$4 Montage	4.00	4.00

Christmas.

Nos. 763-764 Ovptd. "PRE 'WORLD CUP FOOTBALL' / MEXICO 1986"

1985, Dec. 20   Perf. 14½x14
796		Sheet of 10	5.00	5.00
a.-j.	A99	50c, any single	.50	.50

Souvenir Sheet
797	A99	$5 multicolored	5.00	5.00

Women in Folk Costumes — A103

1986, Jan. 15   Perf. 15
798	A103	5c India	.15	.15
799	A103	10c Maya	.15	.15
800	A103	15c Garifuna	.15	.15
801	A103	25c Creole	.30	.30
802	A103	50c China	.65	.65
803	A103	75c Lebanon	1.00	1.00
804	A103	$1 Europe	1.25	1.25
805	A103	$2 South America	2.50	2.50
		Nos. 798-805 (8)	6.15	6.15

Souvenir Sheet   Perf. 14
806	A103	$5 Maya, So. America	6.25	6.25

No. 806 contains one 38x51mm stamp.

Miniature Sheet

A104

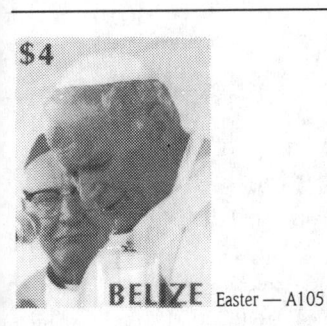

BELIZE

Easter — A105

Papal arms, crucifix and: a, Pius X. b, Benedict XV. c, Pius XI. d, Pius XII. e, John XXIII. f, Paul VI. g, John Paul I. h, John Paul II. No. 573, John Paul II saying mass in Belize.

1986, Apr. 15	Litho.	Perf. 11		
807	Sheet of 8 + label		6.25	6.25
a.-h.	A104 50c, any single		.80	.80

Souvenir Sheet
Perf. 14

808	A105	$4 multi	6.50	6.50

No. 807 contains center label picturing the Vatican, and papal crest.

Queen Elizabeth II, 60th Birthday — A107

A106

1986, Apr. 21		Perf. 14		
809	Strip of 3		1.50	1.50
a.	A106 25c Age 2		.25	.25
b.	A106 50c Coronation		.50	.50
c.	A106 75c Riding horse		.75	.75
810	A106 $3 Wearing crown jewels		3.00	3.00

Souvenir Sheet

811	A107	$4 Portrait	3.25	3.25

A108

Halley's Comet — A109

1986, Apr. 30				
812	Strip of 3		.75	.75
a.	A108 10c Planet-A probe		.15	.15
b.	A108 15c Sighting, 1910		.15	.15
c.	A108 50c Giotto probe		.50	.50
813	Strip of 3		3.75	3.75
a.	A108 75c Weather bureau		.75	.75
b.	A108 $1 US space telescope, shuttle		1.00	1.00
c.	A108 $2 Edmond Halley		2.00	2.00

Souvenir Sheet

814	A109	$4 Computer graphics	4.00	4.00

Miniature Sheet

A110

US Presidents A111

1986, May		Perf. 11		
815	Sheet of 6 + 3 labels		3.75	3.75
a.	A110 10c George Washington		.15	.15
b.	A110 20c John Adams		.15	.15
c.	A110 30c Thomas Jefferson		.25	.25
d.	A110 50c James Madison		.40	.40
e.	A110 $1.50 James Monroe		1.10	1.10
f.	A110 $2 John Quincy Adams		1.65	1.65

Souvenir Sheet
Perf. 14

816	A111	$4 Washington	4.00	4.00

No. 815 contains 3 center labels picturing the great seal of the US. Issue dates: #815, May 5. #816, May 7.

A112

A114

Statue of Liberty, Cent. — A113

Designs: 25c, Bartholdi, statue. 50c, Statue, US centennial celebration, Philadelphia, 1876. 75c, Statue close-up, flags, 1886 unveiling. $3, Flags, statue close-up. $4, Statue, New York City skyline.

1986, May 15		Perf. 14		
817	Strip of 3		4.00	4.00
a.	A112 25c multicolored		.25	.25
b.	A112 75c multicolored		.75	.75
c.	A112 $3 multicolored		3.00	3.00
818	A112 50c multicolored		.50	.50

Souvenir Sheet

819	A113	$4 multicolored	4.00	4.00

AMERIPEX '86, Chicago, May 22-June 1 — A115

1986, May 22				
820	Strip of 3		.75	.75
a.	A114 10c British Honduras No. 3		.15	.15
b.	A114 15c Stamp of 1981		.15	.15
c.	A114 50c US No. C3a		.50	.50
821	Strip of 3		3.75	3.75
a.	A114 75c USS Constitution		.75	.75
b.	A114 $1 Liberty Bell		1.00	1.00
c.	A114 $2 White House		2.00	2.00

Souvenir Sheet

822	A115	$4 Capitol Building	3.50	3.50

For overprints Nos. 835-837.

1986 World Cup Soccer Championships, Mexico — A116

Designs: 25c, England vs. Brazil. 50c, Mexican player, Mayan statues. 75c, Belize players. $3, Aztec calendar stone, Mexico. $4, Flags composing soccer balls.

1986, June 16		Litho.	Perf. 11	
823	A116 25c multicolored		.25	.25
824	A116 50c multicolored		.50	.50
825	A116 75c multicolored		.75	.75
826	A116 $3 multicolored		3.00	3.00
	Nos. 823-826 (4)		4.50	4.50

Souvenir Sheet
Perf. 14

827	A116	$4 multicolored	4.00	4.00

Nos. 823-826 printed in sheets of 8 plus label picturing Azteca Stadium, 2 each value per sheet.

Nos. 823-827 Overprinted "ARGENTINA -/WINNERS 1986"

1986, Aug. 15				
828	A116 25c multicolored		.25	.25
829	A116 50c multicolored		.50	.50
830	A116 75c multicolored		.75	.75
831	A116 $3 multicolored		3.00	3.00
	Nos. 828-831 (4)		4.50	4.50

Souvenir Sheet

832	A116	$4 multicolored	4.00	4.00

Wedding of Prince Andrew and Sarah Ferguson
A117   A118

1986, July 23		Perf. 14x14½		
833	Strip of 3		3.25	3.25
a.	A117 25c Sarah		.20	.20
b.	A117 75c Andrew		.60	.60
c.	A117 $3 Couple		2.25	2.25

Souvenir Sheet
Perf. 14½

834	Sheet of 2		4.00	4.00
a.	A118 $1 Sarah, diff.		1.00	1.00
b.	A118 $3 Andrew, diff.		3.00	3.00

Size of No. 833c: 92x41mm.

Nos. 820-822 Ovptd. with STOCKHOLMIA '86 Emblems

1986, Aug. 28		Litho.	Perf. 14	
835	Strip of 3		.75	.75
a.	A114 10c multicolored		.15	.15
b.	A114 15c multicolored		.15	.15
c.	A114 50c multicolored		.50	.50
836	Strip of 3		3.75	3.75
a.	A114 75c multicolored		.75	.75
b.	A114 $1 multicolored		1.00	1.00
c.	A114 $2 multicolored		2.00	2.00

Souvenir Sheet

837	A115	$4 multicolored	4.00	4.00

Intl. Peace Year — A120

Children.

1986, Oct. 3		Litho.	Perf. 14	
838	A119 25c Infant		.25	.25
839	A119 50c Caucasians		.50	.50
840	A119 75c Oriental		.75	.75
841	A119 $3 Indian, caucasian		3.00	3.00
	Nos. 838-841 (4)		4.50	4.50

Souvenir Sheet

842	A120	$4 shown	4.00	4.00

Nos. 838-841 printed se-tenant in sheets of 8 (2 each) plus center label.

Fungi — A121    Toucans — A122

1986, Oct. 30			Perf. 14	
843	A121	5c Amanita lilloi	.15	.15
844	A122	10c Keel-billed toucan	.15	.15
845	A121	20c Boletellus cubensis	.30	.30
846	A122	25c Collared aracari	.40	.40
847	A121	75c Psilocybe caerules-cens	1.25	1.25
848	A122	$1 Emerald toucanet	1.50	1.50
849	A122	$1.25 Crimson-rumped toucan	1.75	1.75
850	A121	$2 Russula puiggarii	3.00	3.00
	Nos. 843-850 (8)		8.50	8.50

Stamps of the same design printed in sheets of 8 plus center label picturing Audubon Society emblem.

Christmas A123

Disney characters.

BELIZE

1986, Nov. 14			Perf. 11	
851		Sheet of 9	6.50	6.50
a.	A123	2c Jose Carioca	.15	.15
b.	A123	3c Carioca, Panchito, Donald	.15	.15
c.	A123	4c Daisy	.15	.15
d.	A123	5c Mickey, Minnie	.15	.15
e.	A123	6c Carioca playing music	.15	.15
f.	A123	50c Panchito, Donald	.65	.65
g.	A123	65c Donald, Carioca	.90	.90
h.	A123	$1.35 Donald	1.75	1.75
i.	A123	$2 Goofy	2.75	2.75

Souvenir Sheet
Perf. 14

| 852 | A123 | $4 Donald | 6.00 | 6.00 |

A124

Marriage of Queen Elizabeth II and the Duke of Edinburgh, 40th Anniv. — A125

1987, Oct. 7	Litho.		Perf. 15	
853	A124	25c Elizabeth, 1947	.20	.20
854	A124	75c Couple, c. 1980	.55	.55
855	A124	$1 Elizabeth, 1986	.75	.75
856	A124	$4 Wearing robes of Order of the Garter	3.00	3.00
	Nos. 853-856 (4)		4.50	4.50

Souvenir Sheet
Perf. 14

| 857 | A125 | $6 shown | 6.00 | 6.00 |

A126

America's Cup 1986-87 — A127

Yachts that competed in the 1987 finals.

1987, Oct. 21			Perf. 15	
858	A126	25c America II	.25	.25
859	A126	75c Stars and Stripes	.75	.75
860	A126	$1 Australia II	1.00	1.00
861	A126	$4 White Crusader	4.00	4.00
	Nos. 858-861 (4)		6.00	6.00

Souvenir Sheet
Perf. 14

| 862 | A127 | $6 Australia II sails | 6.00 | 6.00 |

A128

Woodcarvings by Sir George Gabb (b. 1928) — A129

1987, Nov. 4			Perf. 15	
863	A128	25c Mother and Child	.20	.20
864	A128	75c Standing Form	.60	.60
865	A128	$1 Love-Doves	.80	.80
866	A128	$4 Depiction of Music	3.25	3.25
	Nos. 863-866 (4)		4.85	4.85

Souvenir Sheet
Perf. 14

| 867 | A129 | $6 African Heritage | 4.50 | 4.50 |

A130

Indigenous Primates — A131

1987, Nov. 11			Perf. 15	
868	A130	25c Black spider monkey	.25	.25
869	A130	75c Male black howler	.75	.75
870	A130	$1 Spider monkeys	1.00	1.00
871	A130	$4 Howler monkeys	4.00	4.00
	Nos. 868-871 (4)		6.00	6.00

Souvenir Sheet
Perf. 14

| 872 | A131 | $6 Black spider, diff. | 6.00 | 6.00 |

Natl. Girl Guides Movement, 50th Anniv. A132

Lady Olave Baden-Powell, Founder — A133

1987, Nov. 25			Perf. 15	
873	A132	25c Flag-bearers	.25	.25
874	A132	75c Camping	.75	.75
875	A132	$1 On parade, camp	1.00	1.00
876	A132	$4 Olave Baden-Powell	4.00	4.00
	Nos. 873-876 (4)		6.00	6.00

Souvenir Sheet
Perf. 14

| 877 | A133 | $6 Lady Olave, diff. | 6.00 | 6.00 |

Intl. Year of Shelter for the Homeless A134

1987, Dec. 3			Perf. 15	
878	A134	25c Tent dwellings	.25	.25
879	A134	75c Urban slum	.75	.75
880	A134	$1 Tents, diff.	1.00	1.00
881	A134	$4 Construction	4.00	4.00
	Nos. 878-881 (4)		6.00	6.00

Orchids A135

Designs: Illustrations from Reichenbachia, published by Henry F. Sander in 1886.

1987, Dec. 16	Litho.		Perf. 14	
882	A135	1c Laelia euspatha	.15	.15
883	A135	2c Cattleya citrina	.15	.15
884	A135	3c Masdevallia bachousiana	.15	.15
885	A135	4c Cypripedium tautzianum	.15	.15
886	A135	5c Trichopilia suavis alba	.15	.15
887	A135	6c Odontoglossum hebraicum	.15	.15
888	A135	7c Cattleya trianaei schroederiana	.15	.15
889	A135	10c Saccolabium giganteum	.15	.15
890	A135	30c Cattleya warscewiczii	.40	.40
891	A135	50c Chysis bractescens	.65	.65
892	A135	70c Cattleya rochellensis	.95	.95
893	A135	$1 Laelia elegans schilleriana	1.40	1.40
894	A135	$1.50 Laelia anceps percivaliana	2.00	2.00
895	A135	$3 Laelia gouldiana	4.00	4.00
	Nos. 882-895 (14)		10.60	10.60

Miniature Sheets

| 896 | A135 | $3 Odontoglossum roezlii | 3.00 | 3.00 |
| 897 | A135 | $5 Cattleya dowiana aurea | 5.00 | 5.00 |

Nos. 882-887 and 889-894 printed in blocks of six. Sheets of 14 contain 2 blocks of Nos. 882-887 plus 2 No. 888 and center label or 2 blocks of Nos. 889-894 plus center strip containing 2 No. 895 and center label. Center labels picture various illustrations from Reichenbachia.

Nos. 896, 897 contain one 44x51mm stamp.

Easter — A136

Stations of the Cross (in sequential order): a, Jesus condemned to death. b, Carries the cross. c, Falls the first time. d, Meets his mother, Mary. e, Cyrenean takes up the cross. f, Veronica wipes Jesus's face. g, Falls the second time. h, Consoles the women of Jerusalem. i, Falls the third time. j, Stripped of his robes. k, Nailed to the cross. l, Dies. m, Taken down from the cross. n, Laid in the sepulcher.

1988, Mar. 21			Perf. 14	
898		Sheet of 14 + label	5.60	5.60
a.-n.	A136	40c, any single	.40	.40

A $6 souvenir sheet was prepared but not issued.

1988 Summer Olympics, Seoul — A137

1988, Aug. 15	Litho.		Perf. 14	
899	A137	10c Basketball	.15	.15
900	A137	25c Volleyball	.25	.25
901	A137	60c Table tennis	.60	.60
902	A137	75c Diving	.75	.75
903	A137	$1 Judo	1.00	1.00
904	A137	$2 Field hockey	2.00	2.00
	Nos. 899-904 (6)		4.75	4.75

Souvenir Sheet

| 905 | A137 | $3 Women's gymnastics | 3.00 | 3.00 |

Intl. Red Cross, 125th Anniv. A138

1988, Nov. 18	Litho.		Perf. 14	
906	A138	60c Travelling nurse, 1912	.60	.60
907	A138	75c Hospital ship, ambulance boat, 1937	.75	.75
908	A138	$1 Ambulance, 1956	1.00	1.00
909	A138	$2 Ambulance plane, 1940	2.00	2.00
	Nos. 906-909 (4)		4.35	4.35

Indigenous Small Animals A139

1989	Litho.	Wmk. 384	Perf. 14	
910	A139	10c Gibnut (agouti)	.25	.25

Unwmk.

911	A139	25c Four-eyed opossum, vert.	.65	.65
a.		Wmk. 384	.65	.65
912	A139	50c Ant bear	1.40	1.40
913	A139	60c like 10c	1.65	1.65
914	A139	75c Antelope	2.00	2.00
915	A139	$2 Peccary	5.50	5.50
	Nos. 910-915 (6)		11.45	11.45

Issued: 10c, 7/23; #911a, 12/6; others, 2/24.

Moon Landing, 20th Anniv.
Common Design Type

Apollo 9: 25c, Command service and lunar modules docked in space. 50c, Command service module. 75c, Mission emblem. $1, First manned lunar module in space. $5, Apollo 11 command service module.

BELIZE

	Perf. 14x13½	
1989, July 20		Wmk. 384

Size of Nos. 680-681: 29x29mm

916	CD342	25c multicolored	.20	.20
917	CD342	50c multicolored	.45	.45
918	CD342	75c multicolored	.65	.65
919	CD342	$1 multicolored	.90	.90
	Nos. 916-919 (4)		2.20	2.20

Souvenir Sheet

| 920 | CD342 | $5 multi | 5.00 | 5.00 |

No. 920 Overprinted

WORLD STAMP EXPO '89™
United States Postal Service
Nov. 17 — 20 and
Nov. 24 — Dec. 3, 1989
Washington Convention Center
Washington, DC

		Perf. 14x13½
1989, Nov. 17		
921	CD342 $5 multicolored	5.00 5.00

World Stamp Expo '89.

No. 704 Surcharged

5c

1989, Nov. 15		Perf. 15
922	A89 5c on 6c multi	2.00

Christmas — A140

A141

Wmk. 384

1989, Dec. 13	Litho.	Perf. 14
927 A140	10c Wesley	.15 .15
928 A140	25c Baptist	.25 .25
929 A140	60c St. John's Cathedral	.60 .60
930 A140	75c St. Andrew's Presbyterian	.75 .75
931 A140	$1 Holy Redeemer Cathedral	1.00 1.00
	Nos. 927-931 (5)	2.75 2.75

Wmk. 373

1990, Mar. 1	Litho.	Perf. 14

Birds and Butterflies: 5c, *Piranga leucoptera*, *Catonephele numilia* female. 10c, *Ramphastos sulfuratus*, *Nessaea aglaura*. 15c, *Fregata magnificens*, *Eurytides philolaus*. 25c, *Jabiru mycteria*, *Heliconius sapho*. 30c, *Ardea herodias*, *Colobura dirce*. 50c, *Icterus galbula*, *Hamadryas arethusia*. 60c, *Ara macao*, *Thecla regalis*. 75c, *Cyanerpes cyaneus*, *Callicore patelina*. $1, *Pulsatrix perspicillata*, *Caligo uranus*. $2, *Cyanocorax yncas*, *Philaethria dido*. $5, *Cathartes aura*, *Battus belus*. $10, *Pandion haliaetus*, *Papilio thoas*.

932 A141	5c multicolored	.15 .15
933 A141	10c multicolored	.15 .15
934 A141	15c multicolored	.15 .15
935 A141	25c multicolored	.25 .25
936 A141	30c multicolored	.30 .30
937 A141	50c multicolored	.50 .50
938 A141	60c multicolored	.60 .60
939 A141	75c multicolored	.75 .75
940 A141	$1 multicolored	1.00 1.00
941 A141	$2 multicolored	2.00 2.00
942 A141	$5 multicolored	5.00 5.00
943 A141	$10 multicolored	10.00 10.00
	Nos. 932-943 (12)	20.85 20.85

The 10c exists inscribed "1993."
For overprints and surcharge see Nos. 944, 1021, 1030.

No. 940 Overprinted in Gold:
"FIRST DOLLAR / COIN / 1990"

1990, Mar. 1		
944 A141	$1 multicolored	1.00 1.00

Turtles A142

Wmk. 373

1990, Aug. 8	Litho.	Perf. 14
945 A142	10c Green	.15 .15
946 A142	25c Hawksbill	.25 .25
947 A142	60c Loggerhead	.60 .60
948 A142	75c Loggerhead, diff.	.75 .75
949 A142	$1 Bocatora	1.00 1.00
950 A142	$2 Hicatee	2.00 2.00
	Nos. 945-950 (6)	4.75 4.75

Battle of Britain, 50th Anniv. A143

Aircraft.

1990, Sept. 15	Wmk. 384	Perf. 13½
951 A143	10c Fairey Battle	.15 .15
952 A143	25c Bristol Beaufort	.25 .25
953 A143	60c Bristol Blenheim	.60 .60
954 A143	75c Armstrong-Whitworth Whitley	.75 .75
955 A143	$1 Vickers-Armstrong Wellington	1.00 1.00
956 A143	$2 Handley-Page Hampden	2.00 2.00
	Nos. 951-956 (6)	4.75 4.75

Orchids — A144

1990, Nov. 1	Wmk. 384	Perf. 14
957 A144	25c Cattleya bowringiana	.25 .25
958 A144	50c Rhyncholaelia digbyana	.50 .50
959 A144	60c Sobralia macrantha	.60 .60
960 A144	75c Chysis bractescens	.75 .75
961 A144	$1 Vanilla planifolia	1.00 1.00
962 A144	$2 Epidendrum polyanthum	2.00 2.00
	Nos. 957-962 (6)	5.10 5.10

Christmas.

Indigenous Fauna A145

1991, Apr. 10		
963 A145	25c Iguana	.25 .25
964 A145	50c Crocodile	.50 .50
965 A145	60c Manatee	.60 .60
966 A145	75c Boa constrictor	.75 .75
967 A145	$1 Tapir	1.00 1.00
968 A145	$2 Jaguar	2.00 2.00
	Nos. 963-968 (6)	5.10 5.10

Elizabeth & Philip, Birthdays
Common Design Types

1991, June 17		Perf. 14½
969 CD345	$1 multicolored	1.00 1.00
970 CD346	$1 multicolored	1.00 1.00
a.	Pair, #969-970 + label	2.00 2.00

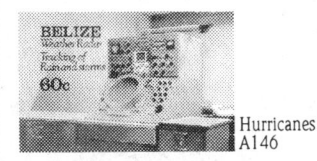

Hurricanes A146

1991, July 31	Wmk. 373	Perf. 14
971 A146	60c Weather radar	.60 .60
972 A146	75c Weather observation station	.75 .75
973 A146	$1 Scene after hurricane	1.00 1.00
974 A146	$2 Hurricane Gilbert	2.00 2.00
	Nos. 971-974 (4)	4.35 4.35

Independence, 10th Anniv. — A147

Famous Men: 25c, Thomas V. Ramos (1887-1955). 60c, Sir Isaiah Morter (1860-1924). 75c, Antonio Soberanis (1897-1975). $1, Santiago Ricalde (1920-1975).

1991, Sept. 4		Wmk. 384
975 A147	25c multicolored	.28 .28
976 A147	60c multicolored	.65 .65
977 A147	75c multicolored	.80 .80
978 A147	$1 multicolored	1.10 1.10
	Nos. 975-978 (4)	2.83 2.83

Folktales A148

Christmas.

Wmk. 373

1991, Nov. 6	Litho.	Perf. 14
979 A148	25c Anansi	.28 .28
980 A148	50c Jack-O-Lantern	.55 .55
981 A148	60c Tata Duende, vert.	.65 .65
982 A148	75c Xtabai	.80 .80
983 A148	$1 Warrie Massa, vert.	1.10 1.10
984 A148	$2 Old Heg	2.20 2.20
	Nos. 979-984 (6)	5.58 5.58

Orchids — A149

Easter: 25c, Gongora quinquenervis. 50c, Oncidium sphacelatum. 60c, Encyclia bractescens. 75c, Epidendrum ciliare. $1, Psygmorchis pusilla. $2, Galeandra batemanii.

1992, Apr. 1		
985 A149	25c multicolored	.28 .28
986 A149	50c multicolored	.55 .55
987 A149	60c multicolored	.65 .65
988 A149	75c multicolored	.80 .80
989 A149	$1 multicolored	1.10 1.10
990 A149	$2 multicolored	2.20 2.20
	Nos. 985-990 (6)	5.58 5.58

Famous Belizeans A150

Designs: 25c, Gwendolyn Lizarraga, MBE (1901-75). 60c, Rafael Fonseca, CMG, OBE (1921-78). 75c, Vivian Seay, MBE (1881-1971). $1, Samuel A. Haynes (1898-1971).

1992, Aug. 26		Perf. 13x12½
991 A150	25c multicolored	.28 .28
992 A150	60c multicolored	.65 .65
993 A150	75c multicolored	.80 .80
994 A150	$1 multicolored	1.10 1.10
	Nos. 991-994 (4)	2.83 2.83

See Nos. 1013-1016.

Discovery of America, 500th Anniv. — A151

Mayan ruins, modern buildings: 25c, Xunantunich, National Assembly. 60c, Altun Ha, Supreme Court Building. 75c, Santa Rita, Tower Hill Sugar Factory. $5, Lamanai, The Citrus Company.

	Perf. 13½x14	
1992, Oct. 1	Litho.	Wmk. 384
995 A151	25c multicolored	.28 .28
996 A151	60c multicolored	.65 .65
997 A151	75c multicolored	.80 .80
998 A151	$5 multicolored	5.50 5.50
	Nos. 995-998 (4)	7.23 7.23

Folklore Type of 1991

Christmas.

	Perf. 13x12½	
1992, Nov. 16	Litho.	Wmk. 373
999 A148	25c Hashishi Pampi	.25 .25
1000 A148	60c Cadejo	.62 .62
1001 A148	$1 La Sucia, vert.	1.05 1.05
1002 A148	$5 Sisimito	5.00 5.00
	Nos. 999-1002 (4)	6.92 6.92

Royal Air Force, 75th Anniv.
Common Design Type

Designs: 25c, Aerospatiale Puma. 50c, British Aerospace Harrier. 60c, DeHavilland Mosquito. 75c, Avro Lancaster. $1, Consolidated Liberator. $3, Short Stirling.

	Wmk. 373	
1993, Apr. 1	Litho.	Perf. 14
1003 CD350	25c multicolored	.25 .25
1004 CD350	50c multicolored	.52 .52
1005 CD350	60c multicolored	.65 .65
1006 CD350	75c multicolored	.80 .80
1007 CD350	$1 multicolored	1.05 1.05
1008 CD350	$3 multicolored	3.15 3.15
	Nos. 1003-1008 (6)	6.42 6.42

1993 World Orchid Conference, Glasgow — A152

	Perf. 14½x14	
1993, Apr. 24	Litho.	Wmk. 384
1009 A152	25c Lycaste aromatica	.28 .28
1010 A152	60c Sobralia decora	.65 .65
1011 A152	$1 Maxillaria alba	1.10 1.10
1012 A152	$2 Brassavola nodosa	2.20 2.20
	Nos. 1009-1012 (4)	4.23 4.23

Famous Belizeans Type of 1992

Designs: 25c, Herbert Watkin Beaumont (1880-1978). 60c, Dr. Selvyn Walford Young (1899-1977). 75c, Cleopatra White (1898-1987). $1, Dr. Karl Heusner (1872-1960).

Wmk. 384

1993, Aug. 11	Litho.	Perf. 14
1013 A150	25c multicolored	.28 .28
1014 A150	60c multicolored	.65 .65
1015 A150	75c multicolored	.85 .65
1016 A150	$1 multicolored	1.10 1.10
	Nos. 1013-1016 (4)	2.88 2.68

Christmas A153

Wmk. 373

1993, Nov. 3	Litho.	Perf. 14
1017 A153	25c Boom and chime band	.28 .28
1018 A153	60c John Canoe dance	.65 .65
1019 A153	75c Cortez dance	.80 .80
1020 A153	$2 Maya Musical Group	2.25 2.25
	Nos. 1017-1020 (4)	3.98 3.98

BELIZE

No. 940 Ovptd. with Hong Kong '94 Emblem
Wmk. 373

1994, Feb. 18	Litho.		*Perf. 14*	
1021	A141	$1 multicolored	1.10	1.10

Royal Visit — A154

Designs: 25c, Belize, United Kingdom Flags. 60c, Queen Elizabeth II wearing hat. 75c, Queen. $1, Queen, Prince Philip.

1994, Feb. 24	Litho.		*Perf. 14½x14*	Wmk. 373
1022	A154	25c multicolored	.28	.28
1023	A154	60c multicolored	.65	.65
1024	A154	75c multicolored	.80	.80
1025	A154	$1 multicolored	1.10	1.10
		Nos. 1022-1025 (4)	2.83	2.83

Bats A155

1994, May 30	Litho.		**Wmk. 384**	*Perf. 14*
1026	A155	25c Insect feeder	.25	.25
1027	A155	60c Fruit feeder	.60	.60
1028	A155	75c Fish feeder	.75	.75
1029	A155	$2 Common vampire	2.00	2.00
		Nos. 1026-1029 (4)	3.60	3.60

No. 939 Surcharged

10c

1994, Aug. 18	Litho.		**Wmk. 373**	*Perf. 14*
1030	A141	10c on 75c multi	.15	.15

Christmas — A156

Orchids: 25c, Cycnoches chlorochilon. 60c, Brassavolas cucullata. 75c, Sobralia mucronata. $1, Nidema Boothii.

1994, Nov. 7			Wmk. 384	
1031	A156	25c multicolored	.25	.25
1032	A156	60c multicolored	.60	.60
1033	A156	75c multicolored	.75	.75
1034	A156	$1 multicolored	1.00	1.00
		Nos. 1031-1034 (4)	2.60	2.60

For overprints see Nos. 1051-1054.

Insects A157

1995, Jan. 11	**Wmk. 373** Litho.		*Perf. 14*	
1035	A157	5c Ground beetle	.15	.15
1036	A157	10c Harlequin beetle	.15	.15
1037	A157	15c Giant water bug	.15	.15
1038	A157	25c Peanut-head bug	.25	.25
1039	A157	30c Coconut weevil	.30	.30
1040	A157	50c Mantis	.50	.50
1041	A157	60c Tarantula wasp	.60	.60
1042	A157	75c Rhinoceros beetle	.75	.75
1043	A157	$1 Metallic wood borer	1.00	1.00
1044	A157	$2 Dobson fly	2.00	2.00
1045	A157	$5 Click beetle	5.00	5.00
1046	A157	$10 Long-horned beetle	10.00	10.00
		Nos. 1035-1046 (12)	20.85	20.85

Nos. 1035-1046 exist inscribed "1996."
For overprints see Nos. 1063-1066.

End of World War II, 50th Anniv.
Common Design Type

Designs: 25c, War Memorial Cenotaph. 60c, Remembrance Sunday. 75c, British Honduras Forestry Unit. $1, Wellington Bomber.

1995, May 8	Litho.		*Perf. 13½*	Wmk. 373
1047	CD351	25c multicolored	.28	.28
1048	CD351	60c multicolored	.65	.65
1049	CD351	75c multicolored	.80	.80
1050	CD351	$1 multicolored	1.10	1.10
		Nos. 1047-1050 (4)	2.83	2.83

Nos. 1031-1034 Ovptd. in Blue

1995, Sept. 1		Wmk. 384	*Perf. 14*	
1051	A156	25c on No. 1031	.25	.25
1052	A156	60c on No. 1032	.60	.60
1053	A156	75c on No. 1033	.75	.75
1054	A156	$1 on No. 1034	1.00	1.00
		Nos. 1051-1054 (4)	2.60	2.60

UN, 50th Anniv.
Common Design Type

Designs: 25c, M113 Light reconnaissance vehicle. 60c, Sultan, armored command vehicle. 75c, Leyland/DAF 8x4 "Drops" vehicle. $2, Warrior infantry combat vehicle.

1995, Oct. 24		Wmk. 384 Litho.	*Perf. 14*	
1055	CD353	25c multicolored	.25	.25
1056	CD353	60c multicolored	.60	.60
1057	CD353	75c multicolored	.75	.75
1058	CD353	$2 multicolored	2.00	2.00
		Nos. 1055-1058 (4)	3.60	3.60

Christmas — A158

Doves: 25c, Blue ground. 60c, White-fronted. 75c, Ruddy ground. $1, White-winged.

1995, Nov. 6			Wmk. 373	
1059	A158	25c multicolored	.25	.25
1060	A158	60c multicolored	.60	.60
1061	A158	75c multicolored	.75	.75
1062	A158	$1 multicolored	1.00	1.00
		Nos. 1059-1062 (4)	2.60	2.60

Nos. 1037, 1039-1040, 1044 Ovptd.

1996, May 17		Wmk. 373 Litho.	*Perf. 14*	
1063	A157	15c on #1037	.15	.15
1064	A157	30c on #1039	.30	.30
1065	A157	50c on #1040	.50	.50
1066	A157	$2 on #1044	2.00	2.00
		Nos. 1063-1066 (4)	2.95	2.95

CAPEX '96 A159

Trains: 25c, Unloading banana train onto freighter, Commerce Bight Pier. 60c, Engine No. 1, Stann Creek Station. 75c, Mahogany log train, Hunslet 0-6-0 Side Tank Engine No. 4. $3, LMS Jubilee Class 4-6-0 Locomotive No. 5602 "British Honduras."

1996, June 6	Litho.		*Perf. 13½x13*	Wmk. 373
1067	A159	25c multicolored	.25	.25
1068	A159	60c multicolored	.60	.60
1069	A159	75c multicolored	.75	.75
1070	A159	$3 multicolored	3.00	3.00
		Nos. 1067-1070 (4)	4.60	4.60

Christmas — A160

Orchids: 25c, Epidendrum stamfordianum. 60c, Oncidium carthagenense. 75c, Oerstedella verrucosa. $1, Coryanthes speciosa.

1996, Nov. 6	Litho.		**Wmk. 373**	*Perf. 14*
1071	A160	25c multicolored	.25	.25
1072	A160	60c multicolored	.60	.60
1073	A160	75c multicolored	.75	.75
1074	A160	$1 multicolored	1.00	1.00
		Nos. 1071-1074 (4)	2.60	2.60

Hong Kong '97 — A161

Cattle: 25c, Red poll. 60c, Brahman. 75c, Longhorn. $1, Charbray.

1997, Feb. 12		**Wmk. 373**	*Perf. 14*	
1075	A161	25c multicolored	.30	.30
1076	A161	60c multicolored	.70	.70
1077	A161	75c multicolored	.85	.85
1078	A161	$1 multicolored	1.10	1.10
		Nos. 1075-1078 (4)	2.95	2.95

Snakes — A162    Howler Monkeys — A163

25c, Coral snake. 60c, Green vine snake. 75c, Yellow-jawed tommygoff. $1, Speckled racer.

1997, May 28		**Wmk. 373**	*Perf. 14*	
1079	A162	25c multicolored	.30	.30
1080	A162	60c multicolored	.65	.65
1081	A162	75c multicolored	.80	.80
1082	A162	$1 multicolored	1.10	1.10
		Nos. 1079-1082 (4)	2.85	2.85

1997, Aug. 13	Litho.		**Wmk. 373**	*Perf. 14*

World Wildlife Fund: 10c, Adult male. 25c, Female feeding. 60c, Female with infant. 75c, Juvenile feeding.

1083	A163	10c multicolored	.15	.15
1084	A163	25c multicolored	.25	.25
1085	A163	60c multicolored	.60	.60
1086	A163	75c multicolored	.75	.75
		Nos. 1083-1086 (4)	1.75	1.75

Christmas — A164

Orchids: 25c, Maxillaria elatior. 60c, Dimerandra emarginata. 75c, Macradenia brassavolae. $1, Ornithocephalus gladiatus.

1997, Nov. 21	Litho.		**Wmk. 373**	*Perf. 14*
1087	A164	25c multicolored	.25	.25
1088	A164	60c multicolored	.65	.65
1089	A164	75c multicolored	.80	.80
1090	A164	$1 multicolored	1.10	1.10
		Nos. 1087-1090 (4)	2.80	2.80

Diana, Princess of Wales (1961-97)
Common Design Type

Designs: a, Up close portrait, smiling. b, Wearing evening dress. c, Up close portrait, serious. d, Holding bouquet of flowers.

1998, Mar. 31	Litho.		*Perf. 14½x14*	Wmk. 373
1091	CD355	$1 Sheet of 4, #a.-d.	4.50	4.50

University of West Indies, 50th Anniv. — A165

1998, July 22	Litho.		**Wmk. 373**	*Perf. 13*
1092	A165	$1 multicolored	1.00	1.00

Organization of American States, 50th Anniv. A166

Designs: 25c, Children working computers, connecting high schools to the internet. $1, Map of Central America, Inter American Drug Abuse Control Commission.

1998, July 22				
1093	A166	25c multicolored	.25	.25
1094	A166	$1 multicolored	1.00	1.00

Battle of St. George's Cay, Bicent. A167

Views of Old Belize from St. George, vert: No. 1095, Woman, child beside small boat. No. 1096, Soldiers at dock, cannon. No. 1097, Cannon balls, cannon, boats in water.
25c, Bayman gun flats. 60c, Bayman sloops. 75c, Schooners. $1, HMS Merlin. $2, Spanish flagship.

1998, Aug. 5			*Perf. 13½*	
1095	A167	10c multicolored	.15	.15
1096	A167	10c multicolored	.15	.15
1097	A167	10c multicolored	.15	.15
	a.	Strip of 3, #1095-1097	.30	.30
1098	A167	25c multicolored	.25	.25
1099	A167	60c multicolored	.60	.60
1100	A167	75c multicolored	.75	.75
1101	A167	$1 multicolored	1.00	1.00
1102	A167	$2 multicolored	2.00	2.00
		Nos. 1095-1102 (8)	5.05	5.05

BELIZE — Cayes of Belize — BENIN — BENIN — People's Republic of Benin

Christmas — A168

Flowers: 25c, Brassia maculata. 60c, Encyclia radiata. 75c, Stanhopea ecornuta. $1, Isochilius carnosiflorus.

1998	Litho.	Wmk. 373	Perf. 14
1103	A168	25c multicolored	.25 .25
1104	A168	60c multicolored	.60 .60
1105	A168	75c multicolored	.75 .75
1106	A168	$1 multicolored	1.00 1.00
		Nos. 1103-1106 (4)	2.60 2.60

SEMI-POSTAL STAMPS

World Cup Soccer Championship — SP1

Designs: 20c+10c, Scotland vs. New Zealand (diff.). 40c+20c, Kuwait vs. France. 60c+30c, Italy vs. Brazil. No. B5, France vs. Northern Ireland. $1.50+75c, Austria vs. Chile. No. B7, Italy vs. Germany, vert. $2+$1, England vs. France, vert.

1982, Dec. 10	Litho.		Perf. 14
B1	SP1	20c +10c multi	.25 .25
B2	SP1	30c +15c multi	.35 .35
B3	SP1	40c +20c multi	.45 .45
B4	SP1	60c +30c multi	.75 .75
B5	SP1	$1 +50c multi	3.00 3.00
B6	SP1	$1.50 +75c multi	5.00 5.00
		Nos. B1-B6 (6)	9.80 9.80

Souvenir Sheets
Perf. 14½

| B7 | SP1 | $1 +50c multi | 3.50 3.50 |
| B8 | SP1 | $2 +$1 multi | 6.00 6.00 |

Nos. B7-B8 each contain one 50x70mm stamp.

POSTAGE DUE STAMPS

Numeral — D1

Each denomination has different border.

1976, July 1	Litho.	Wmk. 373
J6	D2	1c green & red	.15 .15
J7	D2	2c violet & rose lil	.15 .15
J8	D2	5c ocher & brt grn	.15 .15
J9	D2	15c brown org & yel grn	.30 .30
J10	D2	25c slate grn & org	.50 .50
		Nos. J6-J10 (5)	1.25 1.25

CAYES OF BELIZE

Catalogue values for all unused stamps in this country are for Never Hinged items.

Spiny Lobster — A1

Perf. 14½x14, 14x14½

1984, May 30	Litho.	Unwmk.
1	A1	1c shown	.15 .15
2	A1	2c Blue crab	.15 .15
3	A1	5c Red-footed booby	.15 .15
4	A1	10c Brown pelican	.15 .15
5	A1	15c White-tailed deer	.15 .15
6	A1	25c Lighthouse, English Caye	.20 .20
7	A1	75c Spanish galleon, Santa Yaga, c. 1750	.55 .55
8	A1	$3 Map of Ambergris Caye, vert.	2.25 2.25
9	A1	$5 Jetty, windsurfers	3.75 3.75
		Nos. 1-9 (9)	7.50 7.50

The $1 stamp was not issued. Eighteen sheets of 40 were sold for postage by accident.

Lloyd's List Issue
Common Design Type

1984, June 6		Perf. 14½x14
10	CD335	25c Queen Elizabeth 2	.20 .20
11	CD335	75c Lutine Bell	.55 .55
12	CD335	$1 Loss of the Fishburn	.75 .75
13	CD335	$2 Trafalgar Sword	1.50 1.50
		Nos. 10-13 (4)	3.00 3.00

1984 Summer Olympics, Los Angeles — A2

1984, Oct. 5		Perf. 15
14	A2	10c Yachting	.15 .15
15	A2	15c Windsurfing	.15 .15
16	A2	75c Swimming	.75 .75
17	A2	$2 Kayaking	2.00 2.00
		Nos. 14-17 (4)	3.05 3.05

No. 17 inscribed Canoeing.

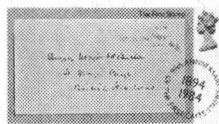

First Cayes Stamps, 90th Anniv. A3

1984, Nov. 5		
18	A3	10c 1895 cover	.15 .15
19	A3	15c Sydney Cuthbert	.15 .15
20	A3	75c Cuthbert's steam yacht	.55 .55
21	A3	$2 British Honduras #133	1.50 1.50
		Nos. 18-21 (4)	2.35 2.35

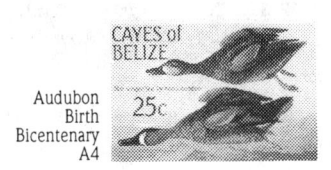

Audubon Birth Bicentenary A4

Illustrations by Audubon.

1985, May 20		Perf. 14
22	A4	25c Blue-winged teal	.20 .20
23	A4	75c Semipalmated sandpiper	.55 .55
24	A4	$1 Yellow-crowned night heron, vert.	.75 .75
25	A4	$3 Common gallinule	2.25 2.25
		Nos. 22-25 (4)	3.75 3.75

Shipwrecks — A5

Designs: a, Oxford, c. 1675. b, Santa Yaga, 1780. c, No. 27, Comet, 1822. d, Yeldham, 1800.

1985, June 5		Perf. 15
26	A5	$1 Strip of 4+label, #a.-d.	4.00 4.00

Souvenir Sheet
Perf. 13½x14

| 27 | A5 | $5 multicolored | 5.00 5.00 |

No. 27 contains one 38x51mm stamp. No. 26 has continuous design.

BENIN
bə-'nin

French Colony

LOCATION — West Coast of Africa
GOVT. — French Possession
AREA — 8,627 sq. mi.
POP. — 493,000 (approx.)
CAPITAL — Benin

In 1895 the French possessions known as Benin were incorporated into the colony of Dahomey and postage stamps of Dahomey superseded those of Benin. Dahomey took the name Benin when it became a republic in 1975.

100 Centimes = 1 Franc

Catalogue values for unused stamps in this country are for Never Hinged items, beginning with Scott 342 in the regular postage section, Scott C240 in the airpost section, Scott J44 in the postage due section, and Scott Q8 in the parcel post section.

Handstamped on Stamps of French Colonies
BÉNIN

1892	Unwmk.		Perf. 14x13½
		Black Overprint	
1	A9	1c blk, bluish	115.00 95.00
2	A9	2c brn, buff	85.00 72.50
3	A9	4c claret, lav	35.00 30.00
4	A9	5c grn, grnsh	13.00 12.00
5	A9	10c blk, lavender	57.50 45.00
6	A9	15c blue	20.00 8.00
7	A9	20c red, grn	165.00 150.00
8	A9	25c blk, rose	67.50 37.50
9	A9	30c brn, yelsh	135.00 100.00
10	A9	35c blk, orange	135.00 100.00
11	A9	40c red, straw	110.00 90.00
12	A9	75c car, rose	275.00 225.00
13	A9	1fr brnz grn, straw	300.00 275.00
		Red Overprint	
14	A9	15c blue	70.00 45.00
		Blue Overprint	
15	A9	5c grn, grnsh	1,750. 700.00
15A	A9	15c blue	1,750. 700.00

Nos. 1-13 all exist with overprint inverted, and several with it double. These sell for more (see the Scott Classic Specialized Catalogue). The overprints of Nos. 1-15A are of four types, three without accent mark on "E." They exist diagonal. Counterfeits exist of Nos. 1-19.

Additional Surcharge in Red or Black 40

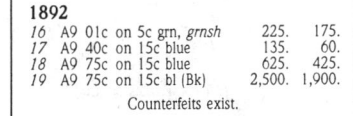

1892			
16	A9	01c on 5c grn, grnsh	225. 175.
17	A9	40c on 15c blue	135. 60.
18	A9	75c on 15c blue	625. 425.
19	A9	75c on 15c bl (Bk)	2,500. 1,900.

Counterfeits exist.

Navigation and Commerce
A3 A4

1893	Typo.		Perf. 14x13½
		Name of Colony in Blue or Carmine	
20	A3	1c blk, bluish	1.90 1.40
21	A3	2c brn, buff	2.25 1.75
22	A3	4c claret, lav	2.50 1.75
23	A3	5c grn, grnsh	3.25 2.00
24	A3	10c blk, lavender	3.25 2.40
25	A3	15c blue, quadrille paper	20.00 14.00

26	A3	20c red, grn	10.00 6.50
27	A3	25c blk, rose	27.50 16.00
28	A3	30c brn, bis	12.50 9.50
29	A3	40c red, straw	3.75 2.25
30	A3	50c car, rose	3.00 2.00
31	A3	75c vio, org	6.25 4.25
32	A3	1fr brnz grn, straw	42.50 35.00
		Nos. 20-32 (13)	138.65 98.80

Perf. 13½x14 stamps are counterfeits.

1894			Perf. 14x13½
33	A4	1c blk, bluish	2.00 1.40
34	A4	2c brn, buff	2.00 1.40
35	A4	4c claret, lav	2.00 1.40
36	A4	5c grn, grnsh	2.50 1.40
37	A4	10c blk, lavender	3.50 2.25
38	A4	15c bl, quadrille paper	4.50 2.25
39	A4	20c red, grn	4.50 3.50
40	A4	25c blk, rose	6.50 2.50
41	A4	30c brn, bis	4.00 2.50
42	A4	40c red, straw	11.00 7.00
43	A4	50c car, rose	15.00 7.50
44	A4	75c vio, org	9.50 8.00
45	A4	1fr brnz grn, straw	2.50 2.00
		Nos. 33-45 (13)	69.50 43.10

Perf. 13½x14 stamps are counterfeits.

PEOPLE'S REPUBLIC OF BENIN

LOCATION — West Coast of Africa
GOVT. — Republic.
AREA — 43,483 sq. mi.
POP. — 3,832,000 (est. 1984)
CAPITAL — Porto Novo

The Republic of Dahomey proclaimed itself the People's Republic of Benin on Nov. 30, 1975. See Dahomey for stamps issued before then.

Catalogue values for unused stamps in this section are for Never Hinged items.

Allamanda Cathartica — A83

Flag Bearers, Arms of Benin — A84

Flowers: 35fr, Ixora coccinea. 45fr, Hibiscus, 60fr, Phaemeria magnifica.

		Unwmk.	
1975, Dec. 8	Photo.		Perf. 13
342	A83	10fr lilac & multi	.15 .15
343	A83	35fr gray & multi	.22 .15
344	A83	45fr multi	.35 .22
345	A83	60fr blue & multi	.40 .30
		Nos. 342-345 (4)	1.12 .82

For surcharges see Nos. 618, 719, 723, 788.

1976, Apr. 30	Litho.		Perf. 12

Design: 60fr, Speaker, wall with "PRPB," flag and arms of Benin. 100fr, Flag and arms of Benin.

346	A84	40fr ocher & multi	.28 .20
347	A84	60fr ocher & multi	.30 .20
348	A84	100fr multi	.55 .40
		Nos. 346-348 (3)	1.13 .80

Proclamation of the People's Republic of Benin. Nov. 30, 1975.

The Scott editorial staff regrettably cannot accept requests to identify, authenticate or appraise stamps and postal markings.

617

BENIN — People's Republic of Benin

A.G. Bell, Satellite and 1876 Telephone — A85

1976, July 9 Litho. *Perf. 13*
349 A985 200fr lilac, red & brn 1.10 .45
Centenary of first telephone call by Alexander Graham Bell, Mar. 10, 1876.

Dahomey Nos. 277-278 Surcharged
1976, July 19 Photo. *Perf. 12½x13*
350 A57 50fr on 1fr multi .32 .15
351 A57 60fr on 2fr multi .42 .15
For overprint and surcharge see Nos. 654A, 711.

African Jamboree, Nigeria 1976 — A86

1976, Aug. 16 Litho. *Perf. 12½x13*
352 A86 50fr Scouts Cooking .28 .20
353 A86 70fr Three scouts .38 .28

Blood Bank, Cotonou — A87

Designs: 50fr, Accident and first aid station. 60fr, Blood donation.

1976, Sept. 24 Litho. *Perf. 13*
354 A87 5fr multicolored .15 .15
355 A87 50fr multicolored .28 .20
356 A87 60fr multicolored .35 .22
  Nos. 354-356 (3) .78 .57
National Blood Donors Day.

A88  A89

1976, Oct. 4 Litho. *Perf. 13x12½*
357 A88 20fr Manioc .15 .15
358 A88 50fr Corn .28 .20
359 A88 60fr Cacao .30 .20
360 A88 150fr Cotton .80 .60
  Nos. 357-360 (4) 1.53 1.15
Natl. agricultural production campaign. For surcharge see No. 565.

1976, Oct. 25
361 A89 50fr Classroom .28 .20
Third anniversary of KPARO newspaper, used in local language studies.

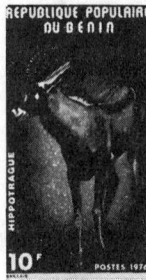

Roan Antelope — A90    Flags, Wall, Broken Chains — A91

Penhari National Park: 30fr, Buffalo. 50fr, Hippopotamus, horiz. 70fr, Lion.

1976, Nov. 8 Photo.
362 A90 10fr multicolored .15 .15
363 A90 30fr multicolored .16 .15
364 A90 50fr multicolored .28 .20
365 A90 70fr multicolored .38 .22
  Nos. 362-365 (4) .97 .72

1976, Nov. 30 Litho. *Perf. 12½*
Design: 150fr, Corn, raised hands with weapons.
366 A91 40fr multicolored .20 .15
367 A91 150fr multicolored .80 .60
First anniversary of proclamation of the People's Republic of Benin.

Table Tennis, Map of Africa (Games' Emblem) — A92

Design: 50fr, Stadium, Cotonou.

1976, Dec. 26 Litho. *Perf. 13*
368 A92 10fr multi .15 .15
369 A92 50fr multi .28 .20
West African University Games, Cotonou, Dec. 26-31.

Europafrica Issue

Planes over Africa and Europe — A93

1977, May 13 Litho. *Perf. 13*
370 A93 200fr multi .70 .55
For surcharge see No. 590.

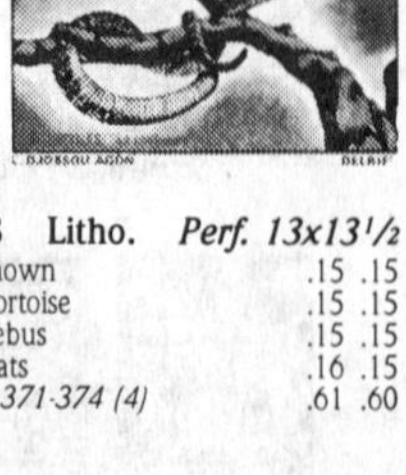

Snake — A94

1977, June 13 Litho. *Perf. 13x13½*
371 A94 2fr shown .15 .15
372 A94 3fr Tortoise .15 .15
373 A94 5fr Zebus .15 .15
374 A94 10fr Cats .16 .15
  Nos. 371-374 (4) .61 .60

Patients at Clinic — A95

1977, Aug. 2 Litho. *Perf. 12½*
375 A95 100fr multi .60 .40
World Rheumatism Year.

Karate, Map of Africa — A96

Designs: 100fr, Javelin, map of Africa, Benin Flag, horiz. 150fr, Hurdles.

1977, Aug. 30 Litho. *Perf. 12½*
376 A96 90fr multi .35 .25
377 A96 100fr multi .45 .35
378 A96 150fr multi .60 .45
  a. Souvenir sheet of 3, #376-378 2.00 2.00
  Nos. 376-378 (3) 1.40 1.05
2nd West African Games, Lagos, Nigeria. For surcharge see No. 925.

Chairman Mao — A97    Lister and Vaporizer — A98

1977, Sept. 9 Litho. *Perf. 13x12½*
379 A97 100fr multicolored .50 .40
Mao Tse-tung (1893-1976), Chinese communist leader.

1977, Sept. 20 Engr. *Perf. 13*
Designs: 150fr, Scalpels and flames, symbols of antisepsis, and Red Cross.
380 A98 150fr multi .80 .60
381 A98 210fr multi 1.20 .80
Joseph Lister (1827-1912), surgeon, founder of antiseptic surgery.
For surcharges see Nos. 560, 566, 919.

Guelege Mask, Ethnographic Museum, Porto Novo — A99

Designs: 50fr, Jar, symbol of unity, emblem of King Ghezo, Historical Museum, Abomey, vert. 210fr, Abomey Museum.

1977, Oct. 17 *Perf. 13*
382 A99 50fr red & multi .28 .20
383 A99 60fr blk, bl & bister .35 .22
384 A99 210fr multi 1.20 .80
  Nos. 382-384 (3) 1.83 1.22
For surcharge see Nos. 562, 920.

Atacora Falls — A100    Mother and Child, Owl of Wisdom — A101

Tourist Publicity: 60fr, Pile houses, Ganvie, horiz. 150fr, Round huts, Savalou.

1977, Oct. 24 Litho. *Perf. 12½*
385 A100 50fr multi .32 .24
386 A100 60fr multi .42 .25
387 A100 150fr multi 1.00 .70
  a. Souvenir sheet of 3, #385-387 2.00 2.00
  Nos. 385-387 (3) 1.74 1.19

Perf. 12½x13, 13x12½
1977, Dec. 3 Photo.
150fr, Chopping down magical tree, horiz.
388 A101 60fr multi .35 .35
389 A101 150fr multi .80 .60
Campaign against witchcraft. For surcharge see No. 576.

Battle Scene A102

1978, Jan. 16 Litho. *Perf. 12½*
390 A102 50fr multi .35 .20
Victory of people of Benin over imperialist forces.

Map, People and Houses of Benin — A103

1978, Feb. 1
391 A103 50fr multi .35 .20
General population and dwelling census.

Alexander Fleming, Microscope and Penicillin — A104

1978, Mar. 12 Litho. *Perf. 13*
392 A104 300fr multi 2.00 1.10
Alexnader Fleming (1881-1955), 50th anniversary of discovery of penicillin.

BENIN — People's Republic of Benin

Abdoulaye Issa, Weapons and Fighters — A105

1978, Apr. 1 Perf. 12½x13
393 A105 100fr red, blk & gold .65 .38
First anniversary of death of Abdoulaye Issa and National Day of Benin's Youth.

Ed Hadj Omar and Horseback Rider — A106

Design: 90fr, L'Almamy Samory Toure (1830-1900) and horseback riders.

1976, Apr. 10 Perf. 13x12½
394 A106 90fr red & multi .60 .35
395 A106 100fr multi .65 .38
African heroes of resistance against colonialism.

ITU Emblem, Satellite, Landscape — A107

1978, May 17 Litho. Perf. 13
396 A107 100fr multi .65 .38
10th World Telecommunications Day.

Soccer Player, Stadium, Argentina '78 Emblem — A108

Designs (Argentina '78 Emblem and): 300fr, Soccer players and ball, vert. 500fr, Soccer player, globe with ball on map.

1978, June 1 Litho. Perf. 12½
397 A108 200fr multi 1.40 .70
398 A108 300fr multi 2.00 1.10
399 A108 500fr multi 3.50 1.75
 a. Souvenir sheet of 3 7.00 7.00
 Nos. 397-399 (3) 6.90 3.55
11th World Cup Soccer Championship, Argentina, June 1-25. No. 399a contains 3 stamps similar to Nos. 397-399 in changed colors.
For surcharges see Nos. 591, 593, 595-596.

Nos. 397-399a Overprinted in Red Brown:
 a. FINALE / ARGENTINE: 3 / HOLLANDE: 1
 b. CHAMPION / 1978 / ARGENTINE
 c. 3e BRESIL / 4e ITALIE

1978, June 25 Litho. Perf. 12½
400 A108 (a) 200fr multi 1.40 .75
401 A108 (b) 300fr multi 2.00 1.10
402 A108 (c) 500fr multi 3.50 1.75
 a. Souvenir sheet of 3 7.00 7.00
 Nos. 400-402 (3) 6.90 3.60
Argentina's victory in 1978 Soccer Championship.

Games' Flag over Africa, Basketball Players — A109

Designs: 60fr, Map of Africa, volleyball players. 80fr, Map of Benin, bicyclists.

1978, July 13 Perf. 13x12½
403 A109 50fr lt bl & multi .35 .20
404 A109 60fr ultra & multi .40 .22
405 A109 80fr multi .55 .35
 a. Souvenir sheet of 3 1.40 1.40
 Nos. 403-405 (3) 1.30 .77
3rd African Games, Algiers, July 13-28. No. 405a contains 3 stamps in changed colors similar to Nos. 403-405.

Martin Luther King, Jr. — A110

1978, July 30 Perf. 12½
406 A110 300fr multi 2.00 1.10
Martin Luther King, Jr. (1929-1968), American civil rights leader.
For surcharge see No. 592.

Kanna Taxi, Oueme — A111

60fr Leatherworker & goods. 70fr, Drummer & tom-toms. 100fr, Metalworker & calabashes.

1978, Aug. 26
407 A111 50fr multi .35 .20
408 A111 60fr multi .40 .22
409 A111 70fr multi .45 .28
410 A111 100fr multi 1.65 1.10
 Nos. 407-410 (4) 1.85 1.10
Getting to know Benin through its provinces.

Map of Italy and Exhibition Poster — A112

1978, Aug. 26 Litho. Perf. 13
411 A112 200fr multi 1.40 .70
Riccione 1978 Philatelic Exhibition.
For overprint see No. 537.

Poultry Breeding — A113

1978 Oct. 5 Photo. Perf. 12½x13
412 A113 10fr Turkeys .15 .15
413 A113 20fr Ducks .15 .15
414 A113 50fr Chicken .35 .35
415 A113 60fr Guinea fowl .40 .40
 Nos. 412-415 (4) 1.05 1.05

Royal Messenger, UPU Emblem — A114

UPU Emblem and: 60fr, Boatsman, ship & car, vert. 90fr, Special messenger & plane, vert.

Perf. 13x12½, 12½x13
1978, Oct. 16
416 A114 50fr multi .35 .35
417 A114 60fr multi .40 .40
418 A114 90fr multi .60 .60
 Nos. 416-418 (3) 1.35 1.35
Centenary of change of "General Postal Union" to "Universal Postal Union."
For surcharge see No. 1009.

Raoul Follereau — A115

1978, Dec. 17 Litho. Perf. 12½
419 A115 200fr multi 1.75 1.75
Raoul Follereau (1903-1977), apostle to the lepers and educator of the blind.

IYC Emblem — A116

Intl. Year of the Child: 20fr, Glove as balloon carrying children. 50fr, Children of various races surrounding globe.

1979, Feb. 20 Litho. Perf. 12x13
420 A116 10fr multi .15 .15
421 A116 20fr multi .15 .15
422 A116 50fr multi .35 .35
 Nos. 420-422 (3) .65 .65

Hydrangea — A117

Flowers: 25fr, Assangokan. 30fr, Geranium. 40fr, Water lilies, horiz.

Perf. 13x12½, 12½x13
1979, Feb. 28
423 A117 20fr multi .15 .15
424 A117 25fr multi .16 .16
425 A117 30fr multi .20 .20
426 A117 40fr mutli .25 .25
 Nos. 423-426 (4) .76 .76

Emblem: Map of Africa and Members' Flags — A118

60fr, Map of Benin & flags. 80fr, OCAM flag & map of Africa showing member states.

1979, Mar. 20 Litho. Perf. 12x13
427 A118 50fr multi .40 .40
428 A118 60fr multi .45 .45
429 A118 80fr multi .65 .65
 Nos. 427-429 (3) 1.50 1.50
OCAM Summit Conf., Cotonou, Mar. 20-28.
For overprints see Nos. 434-436.

Tower, Waves, Satellite, ITU Emblem — A119

1979, May 17 Litho. Perf. 12½
430 A119 50fr multi .40 .40
World Telecommunications Day.

Bank Building and Sculpture — A120

1979, May 26 Litho.
431 A120 50fr multi .35 .35
Opening of Headquarters of West African Savings Bank in Dakar.

Guelede Mask, Abomey Tapestry, Malaconotus Bird — A121

Design: 50fr, Jet, canoe, satellite, UPU and exhibition emblems.

1979, June 8 Litho. Perf. 13
432 A121 15fr multi .15 .15
 Engr.
433 A121 50fr multi .35 .35
Philexafrique II, Libreville, Gabon, June 8-17. Nos. 432, 433 each printed in sheets of 10 with 5 labels showing exhibition emblem.

619

BENIN — People's Republic of Benin

Nos. 427-429 Overprinted: "26 au 28 juin 1979" and Dots

1979, June 26
434	A118	50fr multi	.35	.35
435	A118	60fr multi	.40	.40
436	A118	80fr multi	.55	.55
		Nos. 434-436 (3)	1.30	1.30

2nd OCAM Summit Conf., June 26-28.

Olympic Flame, and Emblems — A122

Pre-Olympic Year: 50fr, High jump.

1979, July 1   Litho.
| 437 | A122 | 10fr multi | .15 | .15 |
| 438 | A122 | 50fr multi | .35 | .35 |

Antelope — A123

Animals: 10fr, Giraffes, map of Benin, vert 20fr, Chimpanzee. 50fr, Elephants, map of Benin, vert.

1979, Oct. 1   Litho.   Perf. 13
439	A123	5fr multi	.15	.15
440	A123	10fr multi	.15	.15
441	A123	20fr multi	.15	.15
442	A123	50fr multi	.35	.35
		Nos. 439-442 (4)	.80	.80

Map of Africa, Emblem and Jet — A124

1979, Dec. 12   Litho.   Perf. 12½
| 443 | A124 | 50fr multi | .35 | .35 |
| 444 | A124 | 60fr multi | .40 | .40 |

ASECNA (Air Safety Board), 20th anniv.

Mail Services — A125

Design: 50fr, Post Office and headquarters, vert.

1979, Dec. 19   Litho.   Perf. 13
| 445 | A125 | 50fr multi | .35 | .35 |
| 446 | A125 | 60fr multi | .40 | .40 |

Office of Posts and Telecommunications, 20th anniversary.

Lenin and Globe — A126

1980, Apr. 22   Litho.   Perf. 12½
| 447 | A126 | 50fr shown | .25 | .25 |
| 448 | A126 | 150fr Lenin in library | .80 | .80 |

Lenin, 110th birth anniversary.

Monument to King Behanzin — A126a

Litho. & Embossed

1980, May 31   Perf. 12½
| 448A | A126a | 1000fr gold & multi | 5.50 | 5.50 |

For overprint see No. Q10A.

Cotonou Club Emlem — A127    Galileo, Astrolabe — A128

1980, Feb. 23   Litho.   Perf. 12½
| 449 | A127 | 90fr shown | .60 | .60 |
| 450 | A127 | 200fr Rotary emblem on globe, horiz. | 1.40 | 1.40 |

Rotary International, 75th anniversary. For surcharge see No. 915.

1980, Apr. 2
| 451 | A128 | 100fr shown | .45 | .45 |
| 452 | A128 | 100fr Copernicus, solar system | .65 | .65 |

Discovery of Pluto, 50th anniversary.

Abu Simbel, UNESCO Emblem — A129

1980, Apr. 15   Perf. 13
453	A129	50fr Column, vert.	.35	.35
454	A129	60fr Ramses II, vert.	.40	.40
455	A129	150fr shown	1.00	1.00
		Nos. 453-455 (3)	1.75	1.75

UNESCO campaign to save Nubian monuments, 20h anniversary.

Monument, Martyrs' Square, Cotonou — A130

Designs: Various monuments in Martyrs' Square. Cotonou. 60fr, 70fr, 100fr, horiz.

1980, May 2   Perf. 12½x13, 13x12½
456	A130	50fr multi	.35	.35
457	A130	60fr multi	.40	.40
458	A130	70fr multi	.45	.45
459	A130	100fr multi	.65	.65
		Nos. 456-459 (4)	1.85	1.85

For surcharge see No. 539.

Musical Instruments — A131

1980, May 20   Perf. 12½
460	A131	5fr Assan, vert.	.15	.15
461	A131	10fr Tinbo	.15	.15
462	A131	15fr Tam-tam sato, vert.	.15	.15
463	A131	20fr Kora	.15	.15
464	A131	30fr Gangan	.20	.20
465	A131	50fr Sinhoun	.35	.35
		Nos. 460-465 (6)	1.15	1.15

First Non-stop Flight, Paris-New York — A132

1980, June 2   Litho.   Perf. 12½
| 466 | A132 | 90fr shown | .60 | .60 |
| 467 | A132 | 100fr Dieudonne Coste, Maurice Bellonte | .65 | .65 |

For surcharge see No. 564.

Lunokhod I on the Moon — A133

1980, June 15   Engr.   Perf. 13
| 468 | A133 | 90fr multi | .60 | .60 |

Lunokhod I Soviet unmanned moon mission, 10th anniv. See #C290. For surcharge see #C305.

Olympic Flame and Mischa, Moscow '80 Emblem — A134

1980, July 16   Litho.   Perf. 12½
469	A134	50fr shown	.35	.35
470	A134	60fr Equestrian, vert.	.40	.40
471	A134	70fr Judo	.50	.50
472	A134	200fr Flag, sports, globe, vert.	1.40	1.40
473	A134	300fr Weight lifting, vert.	2.25	2.25
		Nos. 469-473 (5)	4.90	4.90

22nd Summer Olympic Games, Moscow, July 19-Aug. 3. For surcharges see Nos. 559, 561.

Telephone and Rising Sun — A135

World Telecommunications Day: 50fr, Farmer on telephone, vert.

1980, May 17   Litho.   Perf. 12½
| 474 | A135 | 50fr multi | .35 | .35 |
| 475 | A135 | 60fr multi | .40 | .40 |

Cotonou West African Community Village — A136

Designs: View of Cotonou.

1980, July 26   Perf. 13x13½
476	A136	50fr multi	.35	.35
477	A136	60fr multi	.40	.40
478	A136	70fr multi	.45	.45
		Nos. 476-478 (3)	1.20	1.20

For surcharge see No. 540.

Agbadja Dancers — A137

Designs: Dancers and muscians.

1980, Aug. 1   Perf. 12½
479	A137	30fr multi	.20	.20
480	A137	50fr multi	.35	.35
481	A137	66fr multi	.40	.40
		Nos. 479-481 (3)	.95	.95

Fisherman — A138    Philippines under Magnifier — A139

Designs: 5fr, Throwing net. 15fr, Canoe and shore fishing. 20fr, Basket traps. 50fr, Hauling net. 60fr, River fishing. All horiz.

1980, Sept. 1
482	A138	5fr multi	.15	.15
483	A138	10fr multi	.15	.15
484	A138	15fr multi	.15	.15
485	A138	20fr multi	.15	.15
486	A138	50fr multi	.35	.35
487	A138	60fr multi	.40	.40
		Nos. 482-487 (6)	1.35	1.35

For surcharge see No. 535.

Perf. 13x13½, 13x½x13

1980, Sept. 27

World Tourism Conference, Manila, Sept. 27: 60fr, Emblem on flag, hand pointing to Manila on globe, horiz.

| 488 | A139 | 50fr multi | .35 | .35 |
| 489 | A139 | 60fr multi | .40 | .40 |

For surcharge see No. 557.

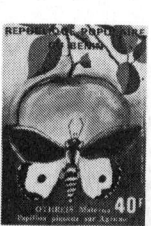

A140    A141

1980, Oct. 1   Perf. 12½
490	A140	40fr Othreis materna	.25	.25
491	A140	50fr Othreis fullonia	.35	.35
492	A140	200fr Oryctes sp.	1.40	1.40
		Nos. 490-492 (3)	2.00	2.00

1980, Oct. 24   Photo.   Perf. 13½
| 493 | A141 | 75fr multi | .50 | .50 |

African Postal Union, 5th Anniv.

BENIN — People's Republic of Benin

A142

A143

1980, Nov. 4   *Perf. 12½x13*
- 494 A142 30fr shown .20 .20
- 495 A142 50fr Freed prisoner .35 .35
- 496 A142 60fr Man holding torch .40 .40
- Nos. 494-496 (3) .95 .95

Declaration of human rights, 30th anniv.

1980, Dec. 1   *Litho.*   *Perf. 13*
- 497 A143 100fr shown .75 .75
- 498 A143 300fr Facteur Roulin 2.25 2.25

Vincent van Gogh (1853-1890), artist.
For surcharge see No. 579.

Offenbach and Scene from Orpheus in the Underworld — A144

1980, Dec. 15   *Engr.*
- 499 A144 50fr shown .40 .40
- 500 A144 60fr Paris Life .45 .45

Jacques Offenbach (1819-1880), composer.

Kepler and Satellites — A145

1980, Dec. 20
- 501 A145 50fr Kepler, diagram, vert. .35 .35
- 502 A145 60fr shown .40 .40

Johannes Kepler (1571-1630), astronomer.

Intl. Year of the Disabled — A146

1981, Apr. 10   *Litho.*   *Perf. 12½*
- 503 A146 115fr multi .75 .75

For surcharge see No. 582.

20th Anniv. of Manned Space Flight — A147

1981, May 30   *Perf. 13*
- 504 A147 500fr multi 3.50 3.50

For surcharges see Nos. 580, 790.

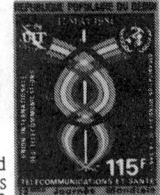

13th World Telecommunications Day — A148

1981, May 30   *Litho.*   *Perf. 12½*
- 505 A148 115fr multi .75 .75

For surcharge see No. 583.

Amaryllis A149

1981, June 20   *Perf. 12½*
- 506 A149 10fr shown .15 .15
- 507 A149 20fr Eischornia crassipes, .15 .15
- 508 A149 80fr Parkia biglobosa, vert. .55 .55
- Nos. 506-508 (3) .85 .85

For surcharge see No. 542.

Benin Sheraton Hotel — A150

1981, July
- 509 A150 100fr multi .65 .65

For surcharge see No. 541.

Guinea Pig — A151

1981, July 31   *Perf. 13x13½*
- 510 A151 5fr shown .15 .15
- 511 A151 60fr Cat .40 .40
- 512 A151 80fr Dogs .55 .55
- Nos. 510-512 (3) 1.10 1.10

For surcharges see Nos. 536, 543, 563.

World UPU Day — A152

1981, Oct. 9   *Engr.*   *Perf. 13*
- 513 A152 100fr red brn & blk .65 .65

25th Intl. Letter Writing Week, Oct. 6-12 — A153

1981, Oct. 15
- 514 A153 100fr dk bl & pur .65 .65

For surcharge see No. 558.

West African Economic Community A154

1981, Nov. 20   *Litho.*   *Perf. 12½*
- 515 A154 60fr multi .40 .40

West African Rice Development Assoc. 10th Anniv. A155

1981, Dec. 10   *Perf. 13x13½*
- 516 A155 60fr multi .40 .40

TB Bacillus Centenary A156

1982, Mar. 1   *Litho.*   *Perf. 13*
- 517 A156 115fr multi 1.20 1.20

For surcharge see No. 584.

West African Economic Community, 5th Summit Conference — A157

1982, May 27   *Perf. 12½*
- 518 A157 60fr multi .40 .40

1982 World Cup A158

1982, June 1   *Perf. 13*
- 519 A158 90fr Players .65 .65
- 520 A158 300fr Flags on leg 2.25 2.25

For overprints and surcharges see #523-524, 594, 789.

France No. B349 Magnified, Map of France — A159

1982, June 11
- 521 A159 90fr multi .60 .60

For surcharge see No. 916.

PHILEXFRANCE '82 Stamp Exhibition, Paris, June 11-21.

George Washington A160

1982, Mar. 10   *Litho.*   *Perf. 14*
- 522 A160 200fr Washington, flag, map 1.00 1.00

For surcharge see No. 577.

Nos. 519-520 Overprinted with Finalists Names

1982, Aug. 16   *Perf. 12½*
- 523 A158 90fr multi .60 .60
- 524 A158 300fr multi 2.00 2.00

Italy's victory in 1982 World Cup.
For surcharge see No. 811.

Bluethroat A161

Perf. 14x14½, 14½x14

1982, Sept. 1
- 525 A161 5fr Daoelo gigas, vert. .15 .15
- 526 A161 10fr shown .15 .15
- 527 A161 15fr Swallow, vert. .15 .15
- 528 A161 20fr Kingfisher, weaver bird, vert. .16 .16
- 529 A161 30fr Great sedge warbler .25 .25
- 530 A161 60fr Common warbler .50 .50
- 531 A161 80fr Owl, vert. .65 .65
- 532 A161 100fr Cockatoo, vert. .80 .80
- Nos. 525-532 (8) 2.81 2.81

ITU Plenipotentiaries Conference, Nairobi, Sept. — A162

1982, Sept. 26   *Perf. 13*
- 533 A162 200fr Map 1.00 1.00

For surcharge see No. 585.

13th World UPU Day A163

1982, Oct. 9   *Engr.*   *Perf. 13*
- 534 A163 100fr Monument .65 .65

Nos. 482, 510, 411 Overprinted in Red or Blue:
- #535 "Croix Rouge / 8 Mai 1982"
- #536 "UAPT 1982"
- #537 "RICCONE 1982"

Perf. 13, 12½, 13x13½

1982, Nov.   *Litho.*
- 535 A138 60fr on 5fr multi .40 .40
- 536 A151 60fr on 5fr multi .40 .40
- 537 A112 200fr multi (Bl) 1.40 1.40
- Nos. 535-537 (3) 2.20 2.20

15-Cent Minimum Value
The minimum catalogue value is 15 cents. Separating se-tenant pieces into individual stamps does not increase the value of the stamps since demand for the separated stamps may be small.

BENIN — People's Republic of Benin

Visit of French Pres. Francois Mitterand A164

1983, Jan. 15   Litho.   Perf. 12½x13
538 A164 90fr multi .60 .60
For surcharge see No. 917.

Nos. 458, 476, 508-509, 512 Surcharged
Perf. 13x12½, 13x13½, 12½
1983   Litho.
539 A130 60fr on 70fr multi   .40 .40
540 A136 60fr on 80fr multi   .40 .40
541 A150 60fr on 100fr multi   .40 .40
542 A149 75fr on 80fr multi   .50 .50
543 A151 75fr on 80fr multi   .50 .50
Nos. 539-543 (5)   2.20 2.20

Seme Oil Rig — A165

1983, Apr. 28   Litho.   Perf. 13x12½
544 A165 125fr multi   .80 .80

World Communications Year — A166

1983, May 17   Litho.   Perf. 13
545 A166 185fr multi   1.00 1.00
For surcharge see No. 898.

Riccione '83, Stamp Show — A167

1983, Aug. 27   Litho.   Perf. 13
546 A167 500fr multi   3.25 3.25
For surcharge see No. 922.

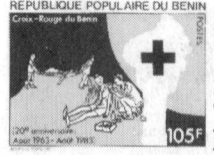

Benin Red Cross, 20th Anniv. A168

1983, Sept. 5   Photo.   Perf. 13
547 A168 105fr multi   .70 .70
For surcharge see No. 581.

Handicrafts A169

Designs: 75fr, Handcarved lion chairs and table. 90fr, Natural tree table and stools. 200fr, Monkeys holding jar.

1983, Sept. 18   Litho.   Perf. 13
548 A169 75fr multi   .40 .40
549 A169 90fr multi   .50 .50
550 A169 200fr multi   1.10 1.10
Nos. 548-550 (3)   2.00 2.00
For surcharge see No. 578.

14th UPU Day — A170

1983, Oct. 9   Engr.   Perf. 13
551 A170 125fr multi   .80 .80
For surcharge see No. 575.

Religious Movements A171

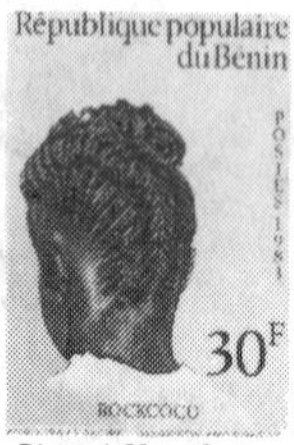

Plaited Hair Styles A172

1983, Oct. 31   Litho.   Perf. 14x15
552 A171 75fr Zangbeto   .35 .35
553 A171 75fr Egoun   .35 .35

1983, Nov. 14
554 A172 30fr Rockcoco   .15 .15
555 A172 75fr Serpent   .35 .35
556 A172 90fr Songas   .40 .40
Nos. 554-556 (3)   .90 .90

Stamps of 1976-81 Surcharged
1983, Nov.
557 A139 5fr on 50fr #488   .15 .15
558 A153 10fr on 100fr #514   .15 .15
559 A134 15fr on 200fr #472   .15 .15
560 A98   15fr on 210fr #381   .15 .15
561 A134 25fr on 70fr #471   .15 .15
562 A99   25fr on 210fr #384   .15 .15
563 A151 75fr on 5fr #510   .35 .35
564 A132 75fr on 100fr #467   .35 .35
565 A88   75fr on 150fr #360   .35 .35
566 A98   75fr on 150fr #380   .35 .35
Nos. 557-566 (10)   2.30 2.30

Alfred Nobel (1833-96) A173

1983, Dec. 19   Litho.   Perf. 15x14
567 A173 300fr multi   1.40 1.40
For surcharge see No. 923.

Council of Unity — A174

1984, May 29   Litho.   Perf. 12
568 A174 75fr multi   .35 .35
569 A174 90fr multi   .40 .40
For surcharge see No. 918.

1984 UPU Congress A175

1984, June 18   Litho.   Perf. 13
570 A175 90fr multi   .40 .40

Abomey Calavi Earth Station A176

1984, June 29   Litho.   Perf. 12½x13
571 A176 75fr Satellite dish   .35 .35

Traditional Costumes — A177

1984, July 2   Litho.   Perf. 13½x13
572 A177 5fr Koumboro   .15 .15
573 A177 10fr Taka   .15 .15
574 A177 20fr Toko   .15 .15
Set value   .17 .17

Nos. 389, 498, 503-505, 517, 522, 533, 547, 550 and 551 Surcharged
1984, Sept.
575 A170 5fr on 125fr #551   .15 .15
576 A101 5fr on 150fr #389   .15 .15
577 A160 10fr on 200fr #522   .15 .15
578 A169 10fr on 200fr #550   .15 .15
579 A143 15fr on 300fr #498   .15 .15
580 A147 40fr on 500fr #504   .15 .15
581 A168 75fr on 105fr #547   .35 .35
582 A146 75fr on 115fr #503   .35 .35
583 A148 75fr on 115fr #505   .35 .35
584 A156 75fr on 115fr #517   .35 .35
585 A162 75fr on 200fr #533   .35 .35
Nos. 575-585 (11)   2.65 2.65

World Food Day — A178

Dinosaurs — A179

1984, Oct. 16   Litho.   Perf. 12½
586 A178 100fr Malnourished child   .30 .30

1984, Dec. 14   Litho.   Perf. 13½
587 A179 75fr Anatosaurus   .22 .22
588 A179 90fr Brontosaurus   .25 .25

Cultural & Technical Cooperation Agency, 15th Anniv. A180

1985, Mar 20   Litho.   Perf. 13
589 A180 300fr Emblem, globe, hands, book   .90 .90

Stamps of 1977-82 Surcharged
1985, Mar.
590 A93   75fr on 200fr No. 370   .20 .20
591 A108 75fr on 200fr No. 397   .20 .20
592 A110 75fr on 300fr No. 406   .20 .20
593 A108 75fr on 300fr No. 398   .20 .20
594 A158 90fr on 300fr No. 520   .25 .25
595 A108 90fr on 500fr No. 399   .25 .25
596 A108 90fr on 500fr No. 402   .25 .25
Nos. 590-596 (7)   1.55 1.55

End of World War II, 40th Anniv. — A180a

1985, May   Litho.   Perf. 12
596A A180a 100fr multicolored

Traditional Dances A181

1985, June 1   Litho.   Perf. 15x14½
597 A181 75fr Teke, Borgou Tribe   .20 .20
598 A181 100fr Tipen'ti, L'Atacora Tribe   .28 .28

Intl. Youth Year — A182

1985, July 16   Perf. 13½
599 A182 150fr multi   .45 .45

1986 World Cup Soccer Championships, Mexico — A183

1985, July 22   Perf. 13x12½
600 A183 200fr multi   .60 .60

Beginning with Scott 601, Benin again surcharged stamps of Dahomey with a variety of surcharges. While the listings that follow contain more than 80 surcharged stamps, the Scott editors still need to examine more than 60 other stamps, in order to list all of those that are currently known to exist.

The size and location of the surcharge varies from stamp to stamp. The type face used in the surcharge may also vary from issue to issue.

REPUBLIQUE POPULAIRE
DU BÉNIN
15 f

a

BENIN — People's Republic of Benin

Dahomey No. 336 Surcharged with Black Bars and New Value

1985, Aug.   *Perf. 12½*
601 A78(a) 15fr on 40fr multi   .18 .18

ASECNA Airlines, 25th Anniv. — A184

1985, Sept. 16   *Perf. 13*
602 A184 150fr multi   .45 .45

UN 40th Anniv. A185

1985, Oct. 24   *Perf. 12½*
603 A185 250fr multi   .90 .90
Benin UN membership, 25th anniv.

ITALIA '85, Rome — A186

1985, Oct. 25   *Perf. 13½*
604 A186 200fr multi   .75 .75

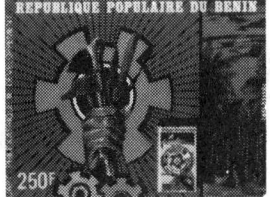

PHILEXAFRICA '85, Lome — A187

1985, Nov. 16   *Perf. 13*
605 A187 250fr #569, labor emblem   .90 .90
606 A187 250fr #C252, Gabon #366, magnified stamp   .90 .90
   a. Pair, Nos. 605-606 + label   1.80 1.80

Audubon Birth Bicent. — A188 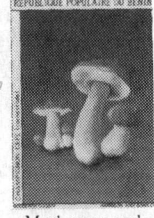   Mushrooms and Toadstools — A189

1985, Oct. 17   *Litho.*   *Perf. 14x15*
607 A188 150fr Skua gull   .55 .55
608 A188 300fr Oyster catcher   1.10 1.10

1985, Oct. 17
609 A189 35fr Boletus edible   .15 .15
610 A189 40fr Amanite phalloide   .15 .15
611 A189 100fr Brown chanterelle   .38 .38
   Nos. 609-611 (3)   .68 .68

Dahomey Nos. 282, 292, Benin No. 343 Surcharged

1986, Mar.   *Photo.*
612 A83(b) 75fr on 35fr #343   .25 .25
613 A57(c) 90fr on 70fr #282   .35 .35
614 A60(b) 90fr on 140fr #292   .35 .35
   Nos. 612-614 (3)   .95 .95

African Parliamentary Union, 10th Anniv. — A190

1986, May 8   *Litho.*   *Perf. 13x12½*
615 A190 100fr multi   .38 .38
9th Conference, Cotonou, May 8-10.

Halley's Comet — A191

1986, May 30   *Perf. 12½x12*
616 A191 250fr multi   .75 .75
For surcharge see No. 809.

Dahomey No. 283, Benin No. 344 Surcharged
Engraved, Photogravure
1986, June   *Perf. 13*
617 A58(b) 100fr on 40fr #283   .38 .38
618 A83(b) 150fr on 45fr #344   .55 .55

1986 World Cup Soccer Championships, Mexico — A192

1986, June 29   *Litho.*
619 A192 500fr multi   1.75 1.75
For surcharge see No. 792.

Fight against Desert Encroachment A193

1986, July 16   *Perf. 13½*
620 A193 150fr multi   .55 .55

King Behanzin A194    Amazon A194a

1986-88   *Engr.*   *Perf. 13*
621 A194 40fr black   .20 .20
622 A194a 100fr brt blue   .40 .40
623 A194 125fr maroon   .60 .60
624 A194a 150fr violet   .60 .60
625 A194 190fr dark ultra   .90 .90
627 A194 220fr dark grn   1.00 1.00
   Nos. 621-627 (6)   3.70 3.70
Issued: 100fr, 150fr, 8/1; others, 10/1/88.
See No. 636. For surcharge see No. 787.

Flowers — A195    Butterflies — A196

Perf. 13x12½, 12½x13
1986, Sept. 1   *Litho.*
631 A195 100fr Haemanthus   .42 .42
632 A195 205fr Hemerocalle, horiz.   .90 .90

1986, Sept. 15
#633, Day peacock, little tortoiseshell, morio.
#634, Aurora, machaon and fair lady.
633 A196 150fr multi   .60 .60
634 A196 150fr multi   .60 .60

Dahomey Nos. 290, 307 Overprinted
1985, Oct. 15
Perfs. & Printing Methods as Before
634A A67(b) 50fr on #307
634B A60(d) 150fr on 100fr #290

Statue of Liberty, Cent. — A197    King Behanzin — A198

1986, Oct. 28   *Litho.*   *Perf. 12½*
635 A197 250fr multi   .90 .90

1986, Oct. 30   *Perf. 13½*
636 A198 440fr multi   1.60 1.60
Behanzin, leader of resistance movement against French occupation (1886-1894).
For surcharge see No. 921.

Brazilian Cultural Week, Cotonou — A200

1987, Jan. 17   *Perf. 12½*
638 A200 150fr multi   .88 .88

BENIN — People's Republic of Benin

Rotary Intl. District 910 Conference, Cotonou, Apr. 23-25 — A201

1987, Apr. 23   Litho.   Perf. 13½
639 A201 300fr Center for the Blind, Cotonou   1.75 1.75

Automobile Cent. — A202

Modern car and: 150fr, Steam tricycle, by De Dion-Bouton and Trepardoux, 1887. 300fr, Gas-driven Victoria, by Daimler, 1886.

1987, July 1   Perf. 12½
640 A202 150fr multi   .88 .88
641 A202 300fr multi   1.75 1.75

For surcharge see No. 679B.

Snake Temple Baptism — A203

1987, July 20   Perf. 13½
642 A203 100fr multi   .55 .55

Shellfish A204

1987, July 24   Perf. 12½
643 A204 100fr crayfish   .55 .55
644 A204 150fr crab   .90 .90

G. Hansen, R. Follerau — A205

1987, Sept. 4   Perf. 13
645 A205 200fr Cure Leprosy   1.10 1.10

Beginning of Benin Revolution, 15th Anniv. — A205a

1987, Oct. 28   Litho.   Perf. 12x12½
645A A205a 100fr multicolored

Locust Control A206

1987, Dec. 7   Litho.   Perf. 12½x13
646 A206 100fr multi   .72 .72

Christmas 1987 — A207

1987, Dec. 21   Perf. 13
647 A207 150fr multi   1.10 1.10

Dahomey Nos. 268, 284 Ovptd. or Surchd.

1987   Engr.   Perf. 13
647A A58(b) 15fr on 100fr #284
647B A53(b) 40fr on #268

See Nos. C362, C369.

Intl. Red Cross and Red Crescent Organizations, 125th Anniv. — A208

1988, May 25   Litho.   Perf. 13½
648 A208 200fr multi   1.30 1.30

A209   A210

1988, July 11   Perf. 12½
649 A209 200fr multi   1.30 1.30

Martin Luther King, Jr. (1929-68), American civil rights leader.

1988, May 25   Litho.   Perf. 13½
650 A210 125fr multi   .88 .88

Organization of African Unity, 25th anniv.

WHO, 40th Anniv. — A211

1988, Sept. 1   Litho.   Perf. 13x12½
651 A211 175fr multi   1.15 1.15

Alma Ata Declaration, 10th anniv.; Health Care for All on Earth by the Year 2000.
For surcharge see No. 786.

Ganvie Lake Village A212

1988, Sept. 4   Perf. 13½
652 A212 125fr shown   .85 .85
653 A212 190fr Boatman, village, diff.   1.25 1.25

A213   A214

1988, Aug. 14   Perf. 12½
654 A213 125fr multi   .88 .88

1st Benin Scout Jamboree, Aug. 12-19.

Benin No. 351, Dahomey Nos. 296, 328 Surcharged

1988   Printing Method & Perfs as Before
654A A57(d) 10fr on 60fr on 2fr #351
654B A62(d) 10fr on 65fr #296
654E A74(d) 150fr on 200fr #328

1988, Dec. 30   Litho.   Perf. 13
Ritual Offering to Hebiesso, God of Thunder and Lightning.
655 A214 125fr multicolored   .82 .82

Dahomey Nos. 161, 247, 302, 333, 339, 341 Surcharged

1988   Photo.   Perf. 12½x13
655A A19(d) 5fr on 3fr #161
655C A82(d) 30fr on 150fr #341
655D A76(d) 25fr on 100fr #333
655E A45(b) 50fr on 45fr #247
655F A81(d) 55fr on 200fr #339
655G A65(b) 65fr on 85fr #302

These are part of a set of 10. Another set of 19 surcharges also is known to exist. The editors need to see the rest of these stamps before listings can be created.

Rural Development Council, 30th Anniv. A214a

1989, May 29   Litho.   Perf. 15x14
655K A214a 75fr multicolored

World Wildlife Fund — A216

Roseate terns, Sterna dougalli.

1989, Jan. 30   Litho.   Perf. 13
657 A216 10fr Three terns   .15 .15
658 A216 15fr Feeding on fish   .15 .15
659 A216 50fr Perched   .32 .32
660 A216 125fr In flight   .82 .82
    Nos. 657-660 (4)   1.44 1.44

Eiffel Tower Cent. — A217

1989, Apr. 24   Litho.   Perf. 13x12½
661 A217 190fr multi   1.10 1.10

PHILEXFRANCE '89, French Revolution Bicent. — A218

Design: Bastille, emblems, Declaration of Human Rights and Citizenship, France No. B252-B253.

1989, July 7   Perf. 13
662 A218 190fr multicolored   1.10 1.10

Electric Corp. of Benin, 20th Anniv. A219

1989, Oct.   Litho.   Perf. 12½x13
663 A219 125fr multicolored   .80 .80

Fish — A220

1989, Sept. 22   Perf. 13½
664 A220 125fr Lote   .80 .80
665 A220 190fr Pike, salmon   1.20 1.20

Death of King Glele, Cent. — A221

1989, Dec. 16   Litho.   Perf. 13½
666 A221 190fr multicolored   1.25 1.25

BENIN — People's Republic of Benin

Christmas
A222

1989, Dec. 25   *Perf. 13*
667 A222 200fr Holy family   1.30   1.30

Benin Posts & Telecommunications, Cent. — A223

1990, Jan. 1   *Perf. 13½*
668 A223 125fr multicolored   .82   .82

Fruits and Flora
A224

1990, Jan. 23   *Litho.*   *Perf. 11½*
669 A224 60fr Oranges   .42   .42
670 A224 190fr Kaufmann Tulips, vert.   1.40   1.40
671 A224 250fr Cashews, vert.   1.75   1.75
Nos. 669-671 (3)   3.57   3.57
Dated 1989.

Moon Landing, 20th Anniv.
A225

1990, Jan. 23
672 A225 190fr multicolored   1.40   1.40
Dated 1989.

World Cup Soccer Championships, Italy — A226

1990, June 8   *Litho.*   *Perf. 12½*
673 A226 125fr shown   1.00   1.00
674 A226 190fr Character trademark, vert.   1.50   1.50
For overprint see No. 676.

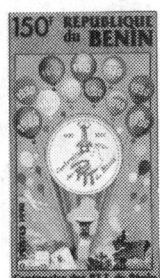

Post, Telephone & Telegraph Administration in Benin, Cent. — A227

1990, July 1   *Perf. 13*
675 A227 150fr multicolored   1.25   1.25

FINALE
No. 673   R.F.A. - ARGENTINE
Ovptd.   1 - 0

1990   *Litho.*   *Perf. 12½*
676 A226 125fr multicolored   1.00   1.00

Charles de Gaulle (1890-1970)
A228

1990, Nov. 22   *Litho.*   *Perf. 13*
677 A228 190fr multicolored   1.50   1.50
See No. 689.

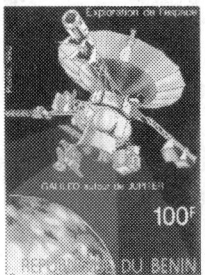

Galileo Probe and Jupiter
A229

1990, Dec. 1
678 A229 100fr multicolored   .75   .75
For overprint see No. 681.

A230

1990, Dec. 25   *Litho.*   *Perf. 12½x13*
679 A230 200fr multicolored   1.75   1.75
Christmas.

Benin No. 641 Surcharged

1990
Perf. & Printing Method as Before
679B A202(e) 190fr on 300fr #641

A230a    A231

1990   *Litho.*   *Perf. 11½x12*
679C A230a 125fr multicolored
National People's Congress.

1991, Sept. 3   *Litho.*   *Perf. 13½*
680 A231 125fr multicolored   1.05   1.05
Independence, 31st anniv.

No. 678 Ovptd. in "Riccione 91" Red

1991   *Perf. 13*
681 A229 100fr multicolored   .85   .85

French Open Tennis Championships, Cent. — A232

1991   *Perf. 13½*
682 A232 125fr multicolored   1.05   1.05

African Tourism Year — A233

1991
683 A233 190fr multicolored   1.65   1.65

Christmas
A234

1991, Dec. 2   *Litho.*   *Perf. 13½*
684 A234 125fr multicolored   1.05   1.05

Dancer of Guelede — A235    Wolfgang Amadeus Mozart, Death Bicent. — A236

1991, Dec. 2
685 A235 190fr multicolored   1.65   1.65

1991, Dec. 2
686 A236 1000fr multicolored   8.50   8.50
For surcharge see No. 793.

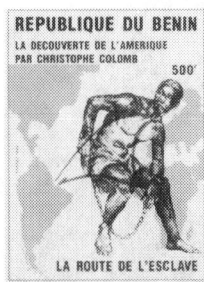

Discovery of America, 500th Anniv.
A237

Design: 1000fr, Columbus coming ashore, horiz.

1992, Apr. 24   *Litho.*   *Perf. 13*
687 A237 500fr blk, blue & brn   3.75   3.75
688 A237 1000fr multicolored   7.50   7.50
a. Souvenir sheet of 2, #687-688   11.25   11.25

De Gaulle Type of 1990

1992   *Litho.*   *Perf. 13*
689 A228 300fr like #677   2.25   2.25

Intl. Conference on Nutrition, Rome — A238

1992, Dec. 5   *Litho.*   *Perf. 13*
690 A238 190fr multicolored   1.60   1.60

Dahomey Nos. 160, 266, 303, 311, 327, 334, 338, C161 Surcharged or Overprinted (#690A)

1992
Perfs. & Printing Methods as Before
690A A66(e)   5fr on #303
690E A80(f)   35fr on #338
690F A19(e)   125fr on 2fr #160
690G AP54(f)   125fr on 65fr #C161
690H A77(f)   125fr on 65fr #334
     (G)
690I CD137(e)   125fr on 100fr #311
690J A52(f)   190fr on 45fr #266
690K A74(f)   125fr on 100fr #327

Have you found a typo or other error in this catalogue?

Inform the editors via our web site or e-mail

sctcat@ scottonline.com

BENIN — People's Republic of Benin

Visit of Pope John Paul II, Feb. 3-5 — A239

Ouidah 92, First Festival of Voodoo Culture — A240

1993, Feb. 3   Litho.   Perf. 13x12½
691 A239 190fr multicolored   1.50 1.50

1993, Feb. 8   Perf. 13½
692 A240 125fr multicolored   1.00 1.00

Well of Possotome, Eurystome — A241

1993, May 25   Litho.   Perf. 12½
693 A241 125fr multicolored   1.00 1.00

OAU, 30th Anniv. — A242

1993, June 7   Litho.   Perf. 13½
694 A242 125fr multicolored   1.00 1.00

John F. Kennedy — A243

1993, June 24   Perf. 13
695 A243 190fr shown   1.50 1.50
696 A243 190fr Martin Luther King, vert.   1.50 1.50

Assassinations of Kennedy, 30th anniv. (#695), and King, 25th anniv. (#696).

Dahomey Nos. 161, 173, 175, 277, 335 Overprinted or Surcharged

1993
Perfs. & Printing Methods as Before
697 A21(e) 5fr on #175
700 A19(f) 10fr on 3fr #161
701 A77(f) 10fr on 100fr #335
703 A57(f) 20fr on 1fr #277
704 A21(f) 25fr on 1fr #173

Benin Nos. 343, 345, 350, Dahomey Nos. 169, 226-227, 249, 276, 295, 283, 319, 333
Surcharged or Overprinted (#711, 713)

1994-95
707 A38(f) 5fr on 1fr #226
709 A71(f) 25fr on #319
711 A57(e) 50fr on 1fr #350
712 A58(e) 80fr on 40fr #283
713 A76(g) 100fr on #333
715 A38(f) 135fr on 3fr #227
718 A62(e) 135fr on 30fr #295
719 A83(g) 135fr on 35fr #343
720 A56(h) 135fr on 40fr multi
722 A20(f) 135fr on 60fr #169
723 A83(g) 135fr on 60fr #345
725 A45(e) 200fr on 100fr #249

UNESCO Conference on The Slave Route — A244

1994   Litho.   Perf. 13x13½
729 A244 200fr multicolored
730 A244 300fr multicolored

The editors would like to see the 135fr value in this set, for which a number has been reserved.

Intl. Year of the Family — A246

1994   Litho.   Perf. 12½
732 A246 200fr multicolored

1994 World Cup Soccer Championships, US — A247

1994   Litho.   Perf. 13x13½
733 A247 300fr multicolored

1996 Summer Olympics, Atlanta — A248

Perf. 12½x13, 13x12½
1995, Apr. 30   Litho.
734 A248 45fr Water polo   .45 .45
735 A248 50fr Javelin   .50 .50
736 A248 75fr Weight lifting   .75 .75
737 A248 100fr Tennis   1.00 1.00
738 A248 135fr Baseball   1.40 1.40
739 A248 200fr Synchronized swimming   2.00 2.00
Nos. 734-739 (6)   6.10 6.10

Souvenir Sheet
740 A248 300fr Diving   4.50 4.50

Nos. 735-740 are vert. No. 740 contains one 32x40mm stamp.

Dogs — A249

1995, Aug. 23   Litho.   Perf. 12½
741 A249 40fr German shepherd   .40 .40
742 A249 50fr Beagle   .50 .50
743 A249 75fr Great dane   .75 .75
744 A249 100fr Boxer   1.00 1.00
745 A249 135fr Pointer   1.40 1.40
746 A249 200fr Fox terrier   2.00 2.00
Nos. 741-746 (6)   6.05 6.05

Souvenir Sheet
747 A249 300fr Schnauzer   6.50 6.50

Ships — A250

Designs: 40fr, Steam driven paddle boat, 1788. 50fr, Paddle steamer Charlotte, 1802. 75fr, Transatlantic steamship, Citta de Catania. 100fr, Hovercraft Mountbatten SR-N4. 135fr, QE II. 200fr, Japanese experimental atomic energy ship, Mutsu-NEF. 300fr, Paddle-steamer Savannah, 1819.

1995, May 20
748 A250 40fr multicolored   .40 .40
749 A250 50fr multicolored   .50 .50
750 A250 75fr multicolored   .75 .75
751 A250 100fr multicolored   1.00 1.00
752 A250 135fr multicolored   1.40 1.40
753 A250 200fr multicolored   2.00 2.00
Nos. 748-753 (6)   6.05 6.05

Souvenir Sheet
754 A250 300fr multicolored   4.50 4.50

No. 754 contains one 40x32mm stamp.

Primates — A251

1995, June 30
755 A251 50fr Pan troglodytes   .50 .50
756 A251 75fr Mandrillus sphinx   .75 .75
757 A251 100fr Colobus   1.00 1.00
758 A251 135fr Macaca sylvanus   1.40 1.40
759 A251 200fr Comopithecus hamadryas   2.00 2.00
Nos. 755-759 (5)   5.65 5.65

Souvenir Sheet
760 A251 300fr Papio cynocephalus   4.50 4.50

No. 760 contains one 32x40mm stamp.

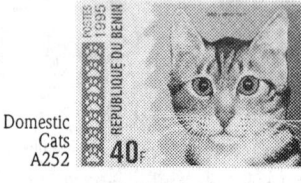

Domestic Cats — A252

1995, July 30   Litho.   Perf. 12½x13
761 A252 40fr Shorthair tabby   .40 .40
762 A252 50fr Ruddy red   .50 .50
763 A252 75fr White longhair   .75 .75
764 A252 100fr Seal color point   1.00 1.00
765 A252 135fr Tabby point   1.40 1.40
766 A252 200fr Black shorthair   2.00 2.00
Nos. 761-766 (6)   6.05 6.05

Souvenir Sheet
767 A252 300fr Cat in basket   4.50 4.50

No. 767 contains one 40x32mm stamp.

Flowers — A253

Designs: 40fr, Dracunculus vulgaris. 50fr, Narcissus watieri. 75fr, Amaryllis belladonna. 100fr, Nymphaea capensis. 135fr, Chrysanthemum carinatum. 200fr, Iris tingitana.

1995, Oct. 15   Litho.   Perf. 12½
768 A253 40fr multicolored   .40 .40
769 A253 50fr multicolored   .55 .55
770 A253 75fr multicolored   .80 .80
771 A253 100fr multicolored   1.10 1.10
772 A253 135fr multicolored   1.40 1.40
773 A253 200fr multicolored   2.25 2.25
Nos. 768-773 (6)   6.50 6.50

Wild Animals — A254

Designs: 50fr, Panthera leo. 75fr, Syncerus caffer. 100fr, Pan troglodytes. 135fr, Aepyceros melampus. 200fr, Geosciurus inaurus. 300fr, Loxodonta, vert.

Perf. 13x12½, 12½x13
1995, Sept. 20
774 A254 50fr multicolored   .55 .55
775 A254 75fr multicolored   .80 .80
776 A254 100fr multicolored   1.10 1.10
777 A254 135fr multicolored   1.50 1.50
778 A254 200fr multicolored   2.25 2.25
Nos. 774-778 (5)   6.20 6.20

Souvenir Sheet
779 A254 300fr multicolored   4.75 4.75

Nos. 774-777 are vert. No. 779 contains one 32x40mm stamp.

Birds Feeding Their Chicks — A255

Designs: 40fr, Cocothraustes cocothraustes. 50fr, Streptopelia chinensis. 75fr, Falco peregrinus. 100fr, Dendroica fusca. 135fr, Larus ridibundus. 200fr, Pelecanus onocrotalus.

1995, Aug. 28   Perf. 12½x13
780 A255 40fr multicolored   .40 .40
781 A255 50fr multicolored   .55 .55
782 A255 75fr multicolored   .80 .80
783 A255 100fr multicolored   1.10 1.10
784 A255 135fr multicolored   1.40 1.40
785 A255 200fr multicolored   2.25 2.25
Nos. 780-785 (6)   6.50 6.50

Benin Nos. 344, 504, 520, 619, 627, 651, 686 and Dahomey No. 291 Surcharged

1994-95
Printing Method and Perfs as Before
786 A211 25fr on 175fr #651
787 A194 50fr on 220fr #627
788 A83(h) 150fr on 45fr #344
789 A158 150fr on 90fr #520
790 A147 150fr on 500fr #504
791 A60(f) 200fr on 135fr #291
792 A192 200fr on 500fr #619
793 A236 250fr on 1000fr #686

Natl. Arms — A256

1995   Litho.   Perf. 12½
793A A256 135fr yellow & multi   1.30 1.30
793B A256 150fr yel grn & multi   1.45 1.45
794   A256 200fr multicolored

See Nos. 948-951.

Orchids — A257

Designs: 40fr, Angraecum sesquipedale. 50fr, Polystachya virginea. 75fr, Disa uniflora. 100fr,

BENIN — People's Republic of Benin

Ansellia africana. 135fr, Angraecum eichlerianum. 200fr, Jumellea confusa.

1995, Nov. 10   Litho.   Perf. 12½

795	A257	40fr multicolored	.40	.40
796	A257	50fr multicolored	.50	.50
797	A257	75fr multicolored	.75	.75
798	A257	100fr multicolored	1.00	1.00
799	A257	135fr multicolored	1.35	1.35
800	A257	200fr multicolored	2.00	2.00
		Nos. 795-800 (6)	6.00	6.00

Butterflies — A258

Designs: 40fr, Graphium policenes. 50fr, Vanessa atalanta. 75fr, Polymmatus icarus. 100fr, Danaus chrysipus. 135fr, Cynthia cardui. 200fr, Argus celbulina.
1000fr, Charaxes jasius.

1996, Mar. 10

801	A258	40fr multicolored	.40	.40
802	A258	50fr multicolored	.50	.50
803	A258	75fr multicolored	.75	.75
804	A258	100fr multicolored	1.00	1.00
805	A258	135fr multicolored	1.35	1.35
806	A258	200fr multicolored	2.00	2.00
		Nos. 801-806 (6)	6.00	6.00

Souvenir Sheet

807	A258	1000fr multicolored	6.00	6.00

CHINA '96, Beijing A259

Designs: a, 40fr, Dancer in traditional Chinese costume. b, 50fr, Exhibition emblem. c, 75fr, Water lily. d, 100fr, Temple of Heaven.

1996, Apr. 8

808	A259	Block of 4, #a.-d.	5.10	5.10

Benin Nos. 523, 616 and Dahomey No. 306 Surcharged or Overprinted (#810)

1996?
Perfs. & Printing Methods as Before

809	A191	5fr on 250fr #616	
810	A67(g)	35fr on #306	
811	A158	150fr on 90fr #523	

15th Lions Intl. District Convention — A260

1996   Litho.   Perf. 12½

811A	A260	100fr multicolored	.45	.45
811B	A260	135fr green & multi	1.40	1.40
812	A260	150fr yellow & multi	1.50	1.50
813	A260	200fr red & multi	2.00	2.00
		Nos. 811A-813 (4)	3.96	5.35

Issued: #811A, 12/27; others, 5/2.

La Francoponie Conference A261

1995, Dec. 2   Litho.   Perf. 12½

814	A261	150fr pink & multi	1.30	1.30
815	A261	200fr blue & multi	1.75	1.75

Cats — A262

1995, Nov. 2   Litho.   Perf. 13

816	A262	40fr Lynx lynx	.40	.40
817	A262	50fr Felis concolor	.50	.50
818	A262	75fr Acinonyx jubatus	.70	.70
819	A262	100fr Panthera pardus	.95	.95
820	A262	135fr Panthera tigris	1.30	1.30
821	A262	200fr Panthera leo	1.90	1.90
		Nos. 816-821 (6)	5.75	5.75

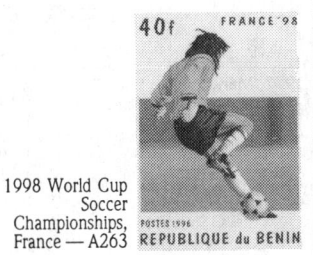

1998 World Cup Soccer Championships, France — A263

1996, Feb. 10   Litho.   Perf. 13

822	A263	40fr multicolored	.40	.40
823	A263	50fr multicolored	.50	.50
824	A263	75fr multicolored	.75	.75
825	A263	100fr multicolored	1.00	1.00
826	A263	135fr multicolored	1.35	1.35
827	A263	200fr multicolored	2.00	2.00
		Nos. 822-827 (6)	6.00	6.00

Souvenir Sheet
Perf. 12½

828	A263	1000fr multicolored	6.00	6.00

No. 828 contains one 32x40mm stamp.

1996 Summer Olympic Games, Atlanta — A264

1996, Jan. 28   Litho.   Perf. 13

829	A264	40fr Diving	.40	.40
830	A264	50fr Tennis	.50	.50
831	A264	75fr Running	.75	.75
832	A264	100fr Gymnastics	1.00	1.00
833	A264	135fr Weight lifting	1.35	1.35
834	A264	200fr Shooting	2.00	2.00
		Nos. 829-834 (6)	6.00	6.00

Souvenir Sheet

835	A264	1000fr Water polo	6.00	6.00

No. 835 contains one 32x40mm stamp.

Christmas Paintings — A265

Entire paintings or details: 40fr, Holy Family Under the Oak Tree, by Raphael. 50fr, The Holy Family, by Raphael. 75fr, St. John the Baptist as a Child, by Murillo. 100fr, The Virgin of Balances, by Leonardo da Vinci. 135fr, The Virgin and the Infant, by Gerard David. 200fr, Adoration of the Magi, by Juan Batista Mayno.
1000fr, Rest on the Flight into Egypt, by Murillo.

1996, May 5   Litho.   Perf. 13

836	A265	40fr multicolored	.40	.40
837	A265	50fr multicolored	.55	.55
838	A265	75fr multicolored	.80	.80
839	A265	100fr multicolored	1.00	1.00
840	A265	135fr multicolored	1.40	1.40
841	A265	200fr multicolored	2.10	2.10
		Nos. 836-841 (6)	6.25	6.25

Souvenir Sheet

842	A265	1000fr multicolored	6.25	6.25

No. 842 contains one 40x32mm stamp.

Wild Cats — A266

Designs: 40fr, Leptailurus serval. 50fr, Profelis temmincki. 75fr, Leopardus pardalis. 100fr, Lynx rufus. 135fr, Prionailurus bengalensis. 200fr, Felis euphtilura.
1000fr, Neofelis nebulosa.

1996, June 10   Litho.   Perf. 12x12½

843	A266	40fr multicolored	.40	.40
844	A266	50fr multicolored	.55	.55
845	A266	75fr multicolored	.80	.80
846	A266	100fr multicolored	1.00	1.00
847	A266	135fr multicolored	1.40	1.40
848	A266	200fr multicolored	2.10	2.10
		Nos. 843-848 (6)	6.25	6.25

Souvenir Sheet
Perf. 12½

849	A266	1000fr multicolored	6.25	6.25

No. 849 contains one 32x40mm stamp.

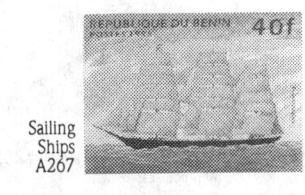

Sailing Ships A267

1996, May 27   Perf. 13x12½

850	A267	40fr Thermopylae	.40	.40
851	A267	50fr 5-masted bark	.55	.55
852	A267	75fr Nightingale	.80	.80
853	A267	100fr Opium clipper	1.00	1.00
854	A267	135fr The Torrens	1.40	1.40
855	A267	200fr English clipper	2.10	2.10
		Nos. 850-855 (6)	6.25	6.25

Souvenir Sheet
Perf. 13

856	A267	1000fr Opium clipper, diff.	6.25	6.25

No. 856 contains one 32x40mm stamp.

Olymphilex '96 — A268

1996, July 2   Perf. 13

857	A268	40fr Running	.40	.40
858	A268	50fr Kayaking	.55	.55
859	A268	75fr Gymnastics	.80	.80
860	A268	100fr Soccer	1.00	1.00
861	A268	135fr Tennis	1.40	1.40
862	A268	200fr Baseball	2.00	2.00
		Nos. 857-862 (6)	6.15	6.15

Souvenir Sheet

863	A268	1000fr Basketball	6.25	6.25

No. 863 contains one 32x40mm stamp.

Modern Olympic Games, Cent. — A269

a, 40fr, Gold medal, woman hurdler. b, 50fr, Runner, Olympic flame. c, 75fr, Pierre de Coubertin, map of US. d, 100fr, Map of US, "1996."

1996, June 20

864	A269	Block of 4, #a.-d.	5.30	5.30

No. 864 is a continuous design.

Horses A270

Various horses.

1996, Aug. 10   Litho.   Perf. 13

865	A270	40fr multi, vert.	.40	.40
866	A270	50fr multi, vert.	.50	.50
867	A270	75fr multi, vert.	.75	.75
868	A270	100fr multi, vert.	1.00	1.00
869	A270	135fr multi, vert.	1.35	1.35
870	A270	200fr multicolored	2.00	2.00
		Nos. 865-870 (6)	6.00	6.00

Flowering Cacti — A271

40fr, Parodia subterranea. 50fr, Astrophytum senile. 75fr, Echinocereus melanocentrus. 100fr, Turbinicarpus kinkerianus. 135fr, Astrophytum capricorne. 200fr, Nelloydia grandiflora.

1996, July 25

871	A271	40fr multicolored	.40	.40
872	A271	50fr multicolored	.50	.50
873	A271	75fr multicolored	.75	.75
874	A271	100fr multicolored	1.00	1.00
875	A271	135fr multicolored	1.35	1.35
876	A271	200fr multicolored	2.00	2.00
		Nos. 871-876 (6)	6.00	6.00

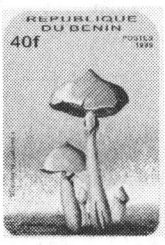

Mushrooms A272

Designs: 40fr, Stropharia cubensis. 50fr, Psilocybe zapotecorum. 75fr, Psilocybe mexicana. 100fr, Conocybe siliginoides. 135fr, Psilocybe caerulescens mazatecorum. 200fr, Psilocybe caerulescens nigripes.
1000fr, Psilocybe aztecorum, horiz.

1996, Sept. 30

877	A272	40fr multicolored	.40	.40
878	A272	50fr multicolored	.50	.50
879	A272	75fr multicolored	.75	.75
880	A272	100fr multicolored	1.00	1.00
881	A272	135fr multicolored	1.35	1.35
882	A272	200fr multicolored	2.00	2.00
		Nos. 877-882 (6)	6.00	6.00

Souvenir Sheet
Perf. 12½

883	A272	1000fr multicolored	6.00	6.00

No. 883 contains one 40x32mm stamp.

BENIN — People's Republic of Benin

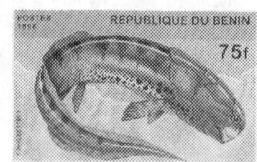

Prehistoric Animals — A273

1996, Aug. 30   *Perf. 12½*
884	A273	40fr Longisquama, vert.	.40	.40
885	A273	50fr Dimophodon, vert.	.50	.50
886	A273	75fr Dunkleosteus	.75	.75
887	A273	100fr Eryops	1.00	1.00
888	A273	135fr Peloneustes	1.35	1.35
889	A273	200fr Deinonychus	2.00	2.00
		Nos. 884-889 (6)	6.00	6.00

Birds — A274

Designs: 40fr, Campephilus principalis. 50fr, Picathartes oreas. 75fr, Strigops habroptilus. 100fr, Amazona vittata. 135fr, Nipponia nippon. 200fr, Gymnogyps californianus. 1000fr, Paradisea rudolphi.

1996, Sept. 10
890	A274	40fr multicolored	.40	.40
891	A274	50fr multicolored	.50	.50
892	A274	75fr multicolored	.75	.75
893	A274	100fr multicolored	1.00	1.00
894	A274	135fr multicolored	1.35	1.35
895	A274	200fr multicolored	2.00	2.00
		Nos. 890-895 (6)	6.00	6.00

Souvenir Sheet
896	A274	1000fr multicolored	6.00	6.00

No. 896 contains one 32x40mm stamp.

Dahomey No. 235 Overprinted Benin No. 545 Surcharged

199?
Perfs. & Printing Methods as Before
897	A40(e)	30fr on #235		
898	A166	75fr on 185fr #545		

Dahomey Nos. 208, 239-241, 257-258, 261, 269, 274, 283, 320, 326, 334-336, 337 Surcharged or Overprinted (#899)

1996?
Perfs. & Printing Methods as Before
899	A77(f)	100fr on #335	
900	A79(e)	125fr on 150fr #337	
901	A77(h)	135fr on 65fr #334	
902	A42(e)	150fr on 30fr #239	
903	A43(h)	150fr on 30fr #241	
904	A48(h)	150fr on 30fr #257	
905	A50(h)	150fr on 30fr #261	
906	CD132(h)	150fr on 40fr #269	
907	A58(h)	150fr on 40fr #283	
908	A71(e)	150fr on 40fr #320	
909	A74(e)	150fr on 40fr #326	
910	A78(e)	150fr on 40fr #336	
911	A32(e)	150fr on 50fr #208	
912	A42(e)	150fr on 70fr #240	
913	A48(h)	150fr on 70fr #258	
914	A55(h)	150fr on 200fr #274	

Benin Nos. 381, 384, 449, 521, 538, 546, 567, 569, 636, Surcharged

1996?
Perfs. & Printing Methods as Before
915	A127	10fr on 90fr #449	
916	A159	10fr on 90fr #521	
917	A164	10fr on 90fr #538	
918	A174	10fr on 90fr #569	
919	A98	40fr on 210fr #381	
920	A99	40fr on 210fr #384	
921	A198	75fr on 440fr #636	
922	A167	10fr on 500fr #546	
923	A173	125fr on 300fr #567	

Obliterator on No. 922 has either one or two bars. Pairs of No. 922 exist with each stamp having a different obliterator.

Benin No. 376 Surcharged

1995
Perfs. & Printing Methods as Before
925	A96	10fr on 90fr #376	

Ungulates — A275

Designs: 40fr, Aepyceros melampus. 50fr, Kobus ellipsiprymnus. 75fr, Caffer caffer. 100fr, Connochaetes taurinus. 135fr, Okapia johnstoni. 200fr, Tragelaphus strepsiceros.

1996, Oct. 15   *Litho.*   *Perf. 12½x12*
930	A275	40fr multicolored	.40	.40
931	A275	50fr multicolored	.50	.50
932	A275	75fr multicolored	.75	.75
933	A275	100fr multicolored	1.00	1.00
934	A275	135fr multicolored	1.35	1.35
935	A275	200fr multicolored	2.00	2.00
		Nos. 930-935 (6)	6.00	6.00

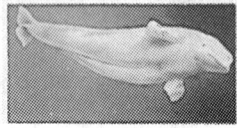

Marine Mammals A276

Designs: 40fr, Delphinapterus leucas. 50fr, Tursiops truncatus. 75fr, Belaenoptera musculus. 100fr, Eubalaena australis. 135fr, Gramphidelphis griseus. 200fr, Orcinus orca.

1996, Nov. 5   *Perf. 13*
936	A276	40fr multicolored	.40	.40
937	A276	50fr multicolored	.50	.50
938	A276	75fr multicolored	.75	.75
939	A276	100fr multicolored	1.00	1.00
940	A276	135fr multicolored	1.35	1.35
941	A276	200fr multicolored	2.00	2.00
		Nos. 936-941 (6)	6.00	6.00

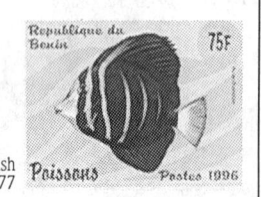

Fish A277

1996, Dec. 4   *Litho.*   *Perf. 12½*
942	A277	50fr Pomacanthidae, vert.	.50	.50
943	A277	75fr Acanthuridae	.75	.75
944	A277	100fr Carangidae	1.00	1.00
945	A277	135fr Chaetodontidae	1.35	1.35
946	A277	200fr Chaetodontidae, diff.	2.00	2.00
		Nos. 942-946 (5)	5.60	5.60

Souvenir Sheet
947	A277	1000fr Scaridae	6.00	6.00

No. 947 contains one 40x32mm stamp.

Coat of Arms Type of 1995

1996-97   *Perf. 12½*
948	A256	100fr multicolored	.45	.45
949	A256	135fr lt yellow & multi	.55	.55
950	A256	150fr lt blue green & multi	.60	.60
951	A256	200fr lt orange & multi	.80	.80
		Nos. 949-951 (3)	1.95	1.95

Issued: 100fr, 12/27/96; 135fr, 150fr, 200fr, 5/15/97.

Military Uniforms — A278

Regiments of European infantry: 135fr, Grenadier, Glassenapp. 150fr, Officer, Von Groben. 200fr, Musketeer, Comte Dohna. 270fr, Bombardier. 300fr, Gendarme. 400fr, Dragoon, Mollendorf. 1000fr, Soldiers, flag, horses, vert.

1997, Feb. 20
952	A278	135fr multicolored	.55	.55
953	A278	150fr multicolored	.60	.60
954	A278	200fr multicolored	.80	.80
955	A278	270fr multicolored	1.10	1.10
956	A278	300fr multicolored	1.25	1.25
957	A278	400fr multicolored	1.60	1.60
		Nos. 952-957 (6)	5.90	5.90

Souvenir Sheet   *Perf. 13*
958	A278	1000fr multicolored	4.00	4.00

No. 958 contains one 32x40mm stamp.

Trains A279

135fr, Steam turbine, Reid Maclead, 1920. 150fr, Experimental high speed, 1935. 200fr, Renard Argent, 1935. 270fr, Class No. 21-C-6, 1941. 300fr, Diesel, 1960. 400fr, Diesel, 1960, diff. 1000fr, Coronation Scot, 1937.

1997, Mar. 26   *Litho.*   *Perf. 13*
959	A279	135fr multicolored	.50	.50
960	A279	150fr multicolored	.55	.55
961	A279	200fr multicolored	.75	.75
962	A279	270fr multicolored	1.00	1.00
963	A279	300fr multicolored	1.10	1.10
964	A279	400fr multicolored	1.50	1.50
		Nos. 959-964 (6)	5.40	5.40

Souvenir Sheet
965	A279	1000fr multicolored	3.75	3.75

No. 965 contains one 40x32mm stamp.

1998 World Cup Soccer Championship, France — A280

Various soccer plays.

1997, Apr. 9   *Perf. 12½x13*
966	A280	135fr multicolored	.50	.50
967	A280	150fr multicolored	.55	.55
968	A280	200fr multicolored	.75	.75
969	A280	270fr multicolored	1.00	1.00
970	A280	300fr multi, horiz.	1.10	1.10
971	A280	400fr multi, horiz.	1.50	1.50
		Nos. 966-971 (6)	5.40	5.40

Souvenir Sheet
972	A280	1000fr multicolored	3.75	3.75

No. 972 contains one 40x32mm stamp.

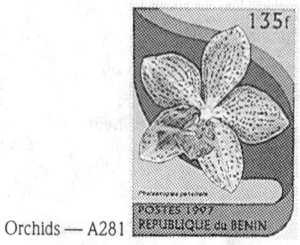

Orchids — A281

Phalaenopsis: 135fr, Penetrate. 150fr, Golden sands. 200fr, Sun spots. 270fr, Fuscata. 300fr, Christi floyd. 400fr, Cayanne. 1000fr, Janet kuhn.

1997, June 9   *Litho.*   *Perf. 12½x13*
973	A281	135fr multicolored	.50	.50
974	A281	150fr multicolored	.55	.55
975	A281	200fr multicolored	.70	.70
976	A281	270fr multicolored	1.00	1.00
977	A281	300fr multicolored	1.10	1.10
978	A281	400fr multicolored	1.40	1.40
		Nos. 973-978 (6)	5.25	5.25

Souvenir Sheet   *Perf. 12½*
979	A281	1000fr multicolored	3.60	3.60

No. 979 contains one 32x40mm stamp.

Dogs — A282

Designs: 135fr, Irish setter. 150fr, Saluki. 200fr, Doberman pinscher. 270fr, Siberian husky. 300fr, Basenji. 400fr, Boxer. 1000fr, Rhodesian ridgeback.

1997, May 30   *Perf. 13*
980	A282	135fr multicolored	.50	.50
981	A282	150fr multicolored	.55	.55
982	A282	200fr multicolored	.70	.70
983	A282	270fr multicolored	1.00	1.00
984	A282	300fr multicolored	1.10	1.10
985	A282	400fr multicolored	1.40	1.40
		Nos. 980-985 (6)	5.25	5.25

Souvenir Sheet   *Perf. 12½*
986	A282	1000fr multicolored	3.60	3.60

No. 986 contains one 32x40mm stamp.

Antique Automobiles — A283

1997, July 5   *Litho.*   *Perf. 13x12½*
987	A283	135fr 1905 Buick	.45	.45
988	A283	150fr 1903 Ford	.50	.50
989	A283	200fr 1913 Stanley	.70	.70
990	A283	270fr 1911 Stoddar-Dayton	.90	.90
991	A283	300fr 1934 Cadillac	1.00	1.00
992	A283	400fr 1931 Cadillac	1.40	1.40
		Nos. 987-992 (6)	4.95	4.95

Souvenir Sheet   *Perf. 13*
993	A283	1000fr 1928 Ford	3.40	3.40

No. 993 contains one 40x32mm stamp.

Songbirds A284

Designs: 135fr, Pyrrhula pyrrhula. 150fr, Carduelis spinus. 200fr, Turdus torquatus. 270fr, Parus cristatus. 300fr, Nucifraga caryocatactes. 400fr, Luscinia megarhynchos. 1000fr, Motacilla flava.

1997, July 30   *Perf. 13x12½*
994	A284	135fr multicolored	.45	.45
995	A284	150fr multicolored	.50	.50
996	A284	200fr multicolored	.70	.70
997	A284	270fr multicolored	.90	.90
998	A284	300fr multicolored	1.00	1.00
999	A284	400fr multicolored	1.40	1.40
		Nos. 994-999 (6)	4.95	4.95

Souvenir Sheet   *Perf. 12½*
1000	A284	1000fr multicolored	3.40	3.40

No. 1000 contains one 32x40mm stamp.

Flowering Cactus — A285

BENIN — People's Republic of Benin

Designs: 135fr, Faucaria lupina. 150fr, Conophytum bilobun. 200fr, Lithops aucampiae. 270fr, Lithops helmutii. 300fr, Stapelia grandiflora. 400fr, Lithops fulviceps. 1000fr, Pleiospilos willowmorensis.

1997, Aug. 30   Litho.   Perf. 13x12½
1001	A285	135fr multicolored	.45	.45
1002	A285	150fr multicolored	.50	.50
1003	A285	200fr multicolored	.70	.70
1004	A285	270fr multicolored	.90	.90
1005	A285	300fr multicolored	1.00	1.00
1006	A285	400fr multicolored	1.30	1.30
		Nos. 1001-1006 (6)	4.85	4.85

Souvenir Sheet   Perf. 12½
| 1007 | A285 | 1000fr multicolored | 3.40 | 3.40 |

No. 1007 contains one 32x40mm stamp.

Benin No. 418 Surcharged

1995
Perfs. & Printing Methods as Before
| 1009 | A114 | 10fr on 90fr #418 | | |

Early Locomotives — A265

Designs: 135fr, Puffing Billy, 1813. 150fr, La Fusée, 1829. 200fr, Royal George, 1827. 270fr, Nouveauté, 1829. 300fr, Locomotion, 1825, vert. 400fr, Sans Pareil, 1829, vert. 1000fr, Trevithick locomotive.

1997, Dec. 3   Litho.   Perf. 13
1022	A265	135fr multicolored	.45	.45
1023	A265	150fr multicolored	.50	.50
1024	A265	200fr multicolored	.70	.70
1025	A265	270fr multicolored	.95	.95
1026	A265	300fr multicolored	1.00	1.00
1027	A265	400fr multicolored	1.40	1.40
		Nos. 1022-1027 (6)	5.00	5.00

Souvenir Sheet
| 1028 | A265 | 1000fr multicolored | 3.50 | 3.50 |

No. 1028 contains one 40x32mm stamp.

Mushrooms A266

Designs: 135fr, Amanita caesarea. 150fr, Cortinarius collinitus. 200fr, Amanita bisporigera. 270fr, Amanita rubescens. 300fr, Russula virescens. 400fr, Amanita inaurata. 1000fr, Amanita muscaria.

1997, Nov. 5   Litho.   Perf. 13
1029	A266	135fr multicolored	.45	.45
1030	A266	150fr multicolored	.55	.55
1031	A266	200fr multicolored	.70	.70
1032	A266	270fr multicolored	.95	.95
1033	A266	300fr multicolored	1.00	1.00
1034	A266	400fr multicolored	1.40	1.40
		Nos. 1029-1034 (6)	5.05	5.05

Souvenir Sheet
| 1035 | A266 | 1000fr multicolored | 3.50 | 3.50 |

No. 1035 contains one 32x40mm stamp.

Assoc. of African Petroleum Producers, 10th Anniv. — A267

1997, Oct. 20   Litho.   Perf. 13
1036	A267	135fr green & multi		
1037	A267	200fr orange & multi		
1038	A267	300fr blue & multi		
1039	A267	500fr yellow & multi	1.75	1.75

Souvenir Sheet

Arabian Horse — A270

1997   Litho.   Perf. 12½
| 1054 | A270 | 1000fr multicolored | 3.50 | 3.50 |

Diana, Princess of Wales (1961-97) — A274

Various portraits: a, 135fr. b, 150fr. c, 200fr. d, 270fr. e, 300fr. f, 400fr. g, 500fr. h, 600fr. i, 700fr.

1998, July 10   Litho.   Perf. 12½
| 1083 | A274 | Sheet of 9, #a.-i. | 11.50 | 11.50 |

Dahomey No. 302 Surcharged

1997?
Perfs. & Printing Method as Before
| 1084 | A65(h) | 35fr on 85fr #302 | | |

AIR POST STAMPS
PEOPLE'S REPUBLIC

Catalogue values for unused stamps in this section are for Never Hinged items.

Nativity, by Aert van Leyden — AP84

Christmas: 85fr, Adoration of the Kings, by Rubens, vert. 140fr, Adoration of the Shepherds, by Charles Lebrun. 300fr, The Virgin with the Blue Diadem, by Raphael, vert.

1975, Dec. 19   Litho.   Perf. 13
C240	AP84	40fr gold & multi	.20	.15
C241	AP84	85fr gold & multi	.42	.15
C242	AP84	140fr gold & multi	.60	.25
C243	AP84	300fr gold & multi	1.40	.65
		Nos. C240-C243 (4)	2.62	1.20

For surcharges see Nos. C362, C367, C407.

Slalom, Innsbruck Olympic Emblem — AP85

Innsbruck Olympic Games Emblem and: 150fr, Bobsledding, vert. 300fr, Figure skating, pairs.

1976, June 28   Litho.   Perf. 12½
C244	AP85	60fr multi	.25	.15
C245	AP85	150fr multi	.65	.25
C246	AP85	300fr multi	1.25	.55
		Nos. C244-C246 (3)	2.15	.95

12th Winter Olympic Games, Innsbruck, Austria, Feb. 4-15.

Dahomey Nos. C263-C265 Overprinted or Surcharged: "POPULAIRE / DU BENIN" and Bars

1976, July 4   Engr.   Perf. 13
C247	AP86	135fr multi	.55	.25
C248	AP86	210fr on 300fr multi	.90	.35
C249	AP86	380fr on 500fr multi	1.50	.65
		Nos. C247-C249 (3)	2.95	1.25

The overprint includes a bar covering "DU DAHOMEY" in shades of brown; "POPULAIRE DU BENIN" is blue on Nos. C247-C248, red on No. C249. The surcharge and bars over old value are blue on No. C248, red, brown on No. C249.

Long Jump AP86

Designs (Olympic Rings and): 150fr, Basketball, vert. 200fr, Hurdles.

1976, July 16   Photo.   Perf. 13
C250	AP86	60fr multi	.32	.15
C251	AP86	150fr multi	.85	.30
C252	AP86	200fr multi	1.25	.45
a.		Souv. sheet of 3, #C250-C252	3.00	3.00
		Nos. C250-C252 (3)	2.42	.90

21st Olympic Games, Montreal, Canada, July 17-Aug 1.

Konrad Adenauer and Cologne Cathedral — AP87

Design: 90fr, Konrad Adenauer, vert.

1976, Aug. 27   Engr.   Perf. 13
| C253 | AP87 | 90fr multi | .60 | .25 |
| C254 | AP87 | 250fr multi | 1.75 | .70 |

Konrad Adenauer (1876-1967), German Chancellor, birth centenary.
For surcharge see No. C289B.

Children's Heads and Flying Fish (Dahomey Type A32) — AP88

210fr, Lion cub's head and Benin type A3, vert.

1976, Sept. 13
| C255 | AP88 | 60fr Prus bl & vio bl | .35 | .15 |
| C256 | AP88 | 210fr multi | 1.10 | .45 |

JUVAROUEN 76, Intl. Youth Phil. Exhib., Rouen, France, Apr. 25-May 2.
For surcharge see No. C300.

Apollo 14 Emblem and Blast-off — AP89

Design: 270fr, Landing craft and man on moon.

1976, Oct. 18   Engr.   Perf. 13
| C257 | AP89 | 130fr multi | .45 | .30 |
| C258 | AP89 | 270fr multi | 1.00 | .65 |

Apollo 14 Moon Mission, 5th anniversary.
For surcharges see Nos. C312, C454.

Annunciation, by Master of Jativa — AP90

Christmas: 60fr, Nativity, by Gerard David. 270fr, Adoration of the Kings, Dutch School. 300fr, Flight into Egypt, by Gentile Fabriano, horiz.

1976, Dec. 20   Litho.   Perf. 12½
C259	AP90	50fr gold & multi	.25	.16
C260	AP90	60fr gold & multi	.35	.22
C261	AP90	270fr gold & multi	1.50	.60
C262	AP90	300fr gold & multi	1.60	1.00
		Nos. C259-C262 (4)	3.70	1.98

For surcharges see Nos. C310, C321, C484.

Gamblers and Lottery Emblem — AP91

1977, Mar. 13   Litho.   Perf. 13
| C263 | AP91 | 50fr multi | .25 | .20 |

National lottery, 10th anniversary.

Sassenage Castle, Grenoble — AP92

1977, May 16   Perf. 12½
| C264 | AP92 | 200fr multi | .80 | .60 |

10th anniv. of Intl. French Language Council.
For surcharge see No. C334.

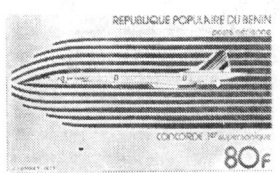

Concorde, Supersonic Plane — AP93

BENIN — People's Republic of Benin

Designs: 150fr, Zeppelin. 300fr, Charles A. Lindbergh and Spirit of St. Louis. 500fr, Charles Nungesser and François Coli, French aviators lost over Atlantic, 1927.

1977, July 25	Engr.		Perf. 13	
C265	AP93	80fr ultra & red	.40	.35
C266	AP93	150fr multi	.80	.60
C267	AP93	300fr multi	1.60	1.20
C268	AP93	500fr multi	2.50	2.00
	Nos. C265-C268 (4)		5.30	4.15

Aviation history.
For overprint and surcharges see Nos. C274, C316, C336.

Soccer Player — AP94

200fr, Soccer players and Games' emblem.

1977, July 28	Litho.		Perf. 12½x12	
C269	AP94	60fr multi	.35	.20
C270	AP94	200fr multi	1.10	.80

World Soccer Cup elimination games.
For surcharges see Nos. C289A, C308.

Miss Haverfield, by Gainsborough — AP95

Designs: 150fr, Self-portrait, by Rubens. 200fr, Anguish, man's head by Da Vinci.

1977, Oct. 3	Engr.		Perf. 13	
C271	AP95	100fr sl grn & mar	.55	.40
C272	AP95	150fr red brn & dk brn	.80	.60
C273	AP95	200fr brn & red	1.10	.80
	Nos. C271-C273 (3)		2.45	1.80

For surcharges see Nos. C309, C317.

No. C265 Overprinted: "1er VOL COMMERCIAL / 22.11.77 PARIS NEW-YORK"

1977, Nov. 22	Engr.		Perf. 13	
C274	AP93	80fr ultra & red	.42	.35

Concorde, 1st commercial flight, Paris to NY.

Viking on Mars — AP96

Designs: 150fr, Isaac Newton, apple globe, stars. 200fr, Vladimir M. Komarov, spacecraft and earth. 500fr, Dog Laika, rocket and space.

1977, Nov. 28	Engr.		Perf. 13	
C275	AP96	100fr multi	.55	.40
C276	AP96	150fr multi	.80	.60
C277	AP96	200fr multi	1.10	.80
C278	AP96	500fr multi	2.75	2.00
	Nos. C275-C278 (4)		5.20	3.80

Operation Viking on Mars; Isaac Newton (1642-1727); 10th death anniv. of Russian cosmonaut Vladimir M. Komarov; 20th anniv. of 1st living creature in space.
For surcharges see Nos. C301, C314.

Monument, Red Star Place, Cotonou AP97

Lithographed; Gold Embossed				
1977, Nov. 30			Perf. 12½	
C279	AP97	500fr multi	1.75	1.10

Suzanne Fourment, by Rubens — AP98

Design: 380fr, Nicholas Rubens, By Rubens.

1977, Dec. 12	Engr.		Perf. 13	
C280	AP98	200fr multi	1.10	.80
C281	AP98	380fr claret & ocher	2.00	1.40

For surcharges see Nos. C311, C313, C483.

Parthenon and UNESCO Emblem — AP99

Designs: 70fr, Acropolis and frieze showing Pan-Athenaic procession, vert. 250fr, Parthenon and frieze showing horsemen, vert.

1978, Sept. 22	Litho.		Perf. 12½x12	
C282	AP99	70fr multi	.35	.20
C283	AP99	250fr multi	1.25	.80
C284	AP99	500fr multi	2.75	1.50
	Nos. C282-C284 (3)		4.35	2.50

Save the Parthenon in Athens campaign.
For surcharge see No. C338.

Philexafrique II—Essen Issue
Common Design Types

Designs: No. C285, Buffalo and Dahomey #C33. No. C286, Wild ducks and Baden #1.

1978, Nov. 1	Litho.		Perf. 12½	
C285	CD138	100fr multi	.65	.40
C286	CD139	100fr multi	.65	.40
a.	Pair, #C285-C286		1.30	1.00

Wilbur and Orville Wright and Flyer — AP100

1978, Dec. 28	Engr.		Perf. 13	
C287	AP100	500fr multi	3.50	2.00

75th anniversary of 1st powered flight.
For surcharge see No. C339.

Cook's Ships, Hawaii, World Map — AP101

Design: 50fr, Battle at Kowrowa.

1979, June 1	Engr.		Perf. 13	
C288	AP101	20fr multi	.20	.20
C289	AP101	50fr multi	.45	.45

Capt. James Cook (1728-1779), explorer.

No. C253, C269 Surcharged
1979
Perfs. & Printing Method as Before
| C289A | AP94 | 50fr on 60fr #C269 | | |
| C289B | AP87 | 50fr on 90fr multi | | |

Lunokhod Type of 1980
1980, June 15		Perf. 13	
Size: 27x48mm			
C290	A133	210fr multi	1.40	1.40

For surcharges see Nos. C305, C450.

Soccer Players — AP102

1981, Mar. 31	Litho.		Perf. 13	
C291	AP102	200fr Ball, globe	.90	.90
C292	AP102	500fr shown	2.50	2.50

ESPANA '82 World Soccer Cup eliminations.
For surcharges see Nos. C335, Q10B.

Prince Charles and Lady Diana, London Bridge — AP103

1981, July 29	Litho.		Perf. 12½	
C293	AP103	500fr multi	3.00	3.00

Royal wedding.
For surcharges see Nos. C323, C500.

Three Musicians, by Pablo Picasso (1881-1973) — AP104

Perf. 12½x13, 13x12½
1981, Nov. 2		Litho.	
C294	AP104	300fr Dance, vert.	2.00	2.00
C295	AP104	500fr shown	3.50	3.50

For surcharges see Nos. C320, C340.

1300th Anniv. of Bulgaria — AP105

1981, Dec. 2	Litho.		Perf. 13	
C296	AP105	100fr multi	.60	.60

Visit of Pope John Paul II — AP106

1982, Feb. 17	Litho.		Perf. 13	
C297	AP106	80fr multi	.55	.55

20th Anniv. of John Glenn's Flight — AP107

1982, Feb. 21	Litho.		Perf. 13	
C298	AP107	500fr multi	3.00	3.00

For surcharge see No. C315.

Scouting Year AP108

1982, June 1			Perf. 12½	
C299	AP108	105fr multi	.70	.70

For surcharge see No. C324.

Nos. C256, C275 Surcharged
1982, Nov.	Engr.		Perf. 13	
C300	AP88	50fr on 210fr multi	.35	.35
C301	AP96	50fr on 100fr multi	.35	.35

Monet in Boat, by Claude Monet (1832-1883) — AP109

1982, Dec. 6	Litho.		Perf. 13x12½	
C302	AP109	300fr multi	2.00	2.00

For surcharge see No. C326.

BENIN — People's Republic of Benin

Christmas 1982 AP110

Virgin and Child Paintings.
1982, Dec. 20   *Perf. 12½x13*
C303 AP110 200fr Matthias Grune-
    wald   1.25 1.25
C304 AP110 300fr Correggio   1.75 1.75
For surcharges see Nos. C325, C337.

No. C290 Surcharged
1983   **Engr.**   *Perf. 13*
C305 A133 75fr on 210fr multi   .50 .50

Bangkok '83 Stamp Exhibition AP111

1983, Aug. 4   Photo.   *Perf. 13*
C306 AP111 300fr multi   1.50 1.50
For surcharge see No. C322.

Christmas 1983 AP112

1983, Dec. 26   Litho.   *Perf. 12½x13*
C307 AP112 200fr Loretto Madonna,
    by Raphael   .65 .65
For surcharge see No. C319.

Types of 1976-82 Surcharged
1983, Nov.
C308 AP94 10fr on 200fr C270   .15 .15
C309 AP95 15fr on 200fr C273   .15 .15
C310 AP90 15fr on 270fr C261   .15 .15
C311 AP98 20fr on 200fr C280   .15 .15
C312 AP89 25fr on 270fr C258   .15 .15
C313 AP98 25fr on 380fr C281   .15 .15
C314 AP96 30fr on 200fr C277   .15 .15
C315 AP107 40fr on 500fr C298   .20 .20
C316 AP93 75fr on 150fr C266   .38 .38
C317 AP95 75fr on 150fr C272   .38 .38
    Nos. C308-C317 (10)   2.01 2.01

Summer Olympics — AP113

1984, July 16   Litho.   *Perf. 13x13½*
C318 AP113 300fr Sam the Eagle,
    mascot   1.00 1.00

Nos. C262, C293-C294, C299, C302-
C303, C306-C307 Surcharged
1984, Sept.
C319 AP94 15fr on 200fr multi   .15 .15
C320 AP104 15fr on 300fr multi   .15 .15
C321 AP90 25fr on 300fr multi   .15 .15
C322 AP111 25fr on 300fr multi   .15 .15
C323 AP103 40fr on 500fr multi   .15 .15
C324 AP108 75fr on 105fr multi   .25 .25

C325 AP110 90fr on 200fr multi   .30 .30
C326 AP109 90fr on 300fr multi   .30 .30
    Nos. C319-C326 (8)   1.60 1.60

Christmas 1984 AP114

1984, Dec. 17   Litho.   *Perf. 12½x13*
C327 AP114 500fr Virgin and Child,
    by Murillo   1.50 1.50
For surcharge see No. C486.

Ships — AP115

1984, Dec. 28   Litho.   *Perf. 13*
C328 AP115 90fr Sidon merchant ship   .30 .30
C329 AP115 125fr Wavertree, vert.   .38 .38

Benin-S.O.M. Postal Convention AP116

1985, Apr. 15   Litho.   *Perf. 13½*
C330 AP116 75fr Benin arms   .22 .22
C331 AP116 75fr Sovereign Order of
    Malta   .22 .22
  a. Pair, #C330-C331   .45 .45

PHILEXAFRICA III, Lome — AP117

1985, June 24   *Perf. 13*
C332 AP117 200fr Oil platform   .60 .60
C333 AP117 200fr Soccer players   .60 .60
  a. Pair, #C332-C333 + label   1.25 1.25
For surcharges see Nos. C485-C485A.

Stamps of 1977-82 Surcharged
1985, Mar.
C334 AP92 75fr on 200fr #C264   .20 .20
C335 AP102 75fr on 200fr #C291   .20 .20
C336 AP93 75fr on 300fr #C267   .20 .20
C337 AP110 75fr on 300fr #C304   .20 .20
C338 AP99 90fr on 500fr #C284   .25 .25
C339 AP100 90fr on 500fr #C287   .25 .25
C340 AP104 90fr on 500fr #C295   .25 .25
    Nos. C334-C340 (7)   1.55 1.55

Dahomey Stamps of 1971-75 Surcharged
1985, Aug.
C341 AP87(i) 25fr on 40fr #C266   .15 .15
C342 AP49(a) 40fr on #C142   .15 .15
C343 AP56(i) 75fr on 85fr #C164   .20 .20
C344 AP60(a) 75fr on 100fr
    #C173   .20 .20
C345 AP64(i) 75fr on 125fr
    #C186   .20 .20
C346 AP56(i) 90fr on 20fr #C163   .25 .25
C347 A61(i) 90fr on 150fr
    #C153   .25 .25
C348 AP49(a) 90fr on 200fr
    #C143   .25 .25

C349 AP78(j) 90fr on 200fr
    #C237   .25 .25
C350 AP78(j) 150fr on #C236   .45 .45
    Nos. C341-C350 (10)   2.35 2.35

Christmas — AP118

1985, Dec. 20   Litho.   *Perf. 13x12½*
C351 AP118 500fr multi   1.75 1.75
For surcharge see No. C449.

Dahomey Nos. C34-C37, C84, C131
Surcharged or Overprinted
1986   Photo.   Perfs. as before
C352 AP33(b) 75fr on 70fr #C84   .25 .25
C353 AP14(b) 75fr on 100fr #C34   .25 .25
C354 AP15(b) 75fr on 200fr #C35   .25 .25
C355 AP15(b) 90fr on 250fr #C36   .35 .35
C356 AP45(b) 100fr on #C131   .38 .38
C357 AP14(b) 150fr on 500fr #C37   .55 .55
    Nos. C352-C357 (6)   2.03 2.03
Issued: 75fr, 90fr, Mar; 100fr, 150fr, June.

Dahomey Nos. C82, C139, C141, C146
Surcharged
1986
Perfs. & Printing Methods as Before
C357A AP33(d) 15fr on 45fr
    #C82
C357B AP48(d) 25fr on 200fr
    #C141 (S)
C357D AP48(d) 100fr on #C139
C357E CD135(d) 100fr on #C146

Christmas — AP119

1986, Dec. 24   Litho.   *Perf. 13x12½*
C358 AP119 300fr multi   1.20 1.20

Air Africa, 25th Anniv. AP120

1986, Dec. 30   *Perf. 12½*
C359 AP120 100fr multi   .40 .40

Intl. Agricultural Development Fund (FIDA), 10th Anniv. AP121

1987, Dec. 14   Litho.   *Perf. 13½*
C360 AP121 500fr multi   3.50 3.50

Christmas — AP122

1988, Dec. 23   Litho.   *Perf. 13x12½*
C361 AP122 500fr Adoration of the
    Magi, storyteller   3.25 3.25

No. C241 Surcharged

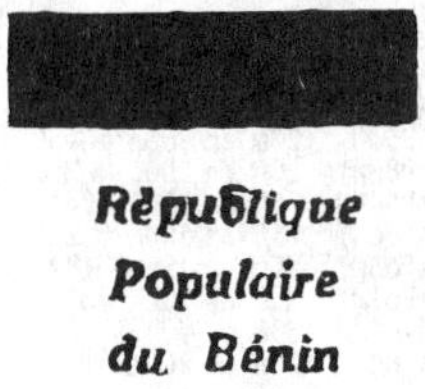

République Populaire du Bénin

15 f ═

1989, Apr. 24   Litho.   *Perf. 13*
C362 AP84(b) 15fr on 85fr multi   .15 .15

Dahomey Nos. C37, C53, C152, C156,
C165, C175, C182, C234
Benin No. C242 Surcharged or
Overprinted

République Populaire du Bénin

1987
Perfs. & Printing Methods as Before
C363 AP77 20fr on 250fr #C234
C364 AP48(b) 25fr on 150fr #C175
    (S&B)
C365 AP63(b) 40fr on 15fr #C182
C366 AP48(b) 40fr on 100fr #C152
C367 AP84(b) 50fr on 140fr #C242
C368 AP14(b) 50fr on 500fr #C37
C369 AP22(b) 80fr on #C53
C370 AP56(b) 80fr on 150fr #C165
C373 AP52(b) 100fr on #C156

Dahomey Nos. C140, C144, C158, C166,
C177, C185, C188 C191, C195, C207,
C262 Surcharged
1988
Perfs. & Printing Methods as Before
C374 AP50(d) 10fr on 50fr #C144
C375 AP64(d) 10fr on 65fr #C185
C376 AP72(d) 15fr on 150fr #C207
C377 AP67(d) 25fr on 200fr #C191
C378 AP61(d) 40fr on 35fr #C195
C380 AP53(d) 70fr on 250fr #C158
C381 AP48(d) 100fr on #C140
C382 AP65(d) 100fr on #C188
C384 AP61(f) 125fr on #C177
C385 AP86(d) 125fr on 75fr #C262
C386 AP57(d) 150fr on 100fr #C166

Dahomey Nos. C181, C196, C208
Surcharged
1988
Perfs. & Printing Methods as Before
C388 AP61(d) 25fr on 100fr #C196
C390 AP62 40fr on 100fr #C181
C391 AP73(d) 40fr on 150fr #C208

Dahomey Nos. C108, C147-C148, C162,
C167, C178, C187, C194
1992
Perfs. & Printing Methods as Before
C394 AP51(f) 70fr on #C148
C395 AP55(e) 100fr on #C162
C396 AP68(g) 100fr on #C194
C397 AP51(e) 125fr on 40fr #C147
C398 A52(f) 125fr on 70fr #C108
C400 AP64a(e) 125fr on 100fr #C187
C401 AP61(f) 190fr on 140fr #C178
C402 AP58(f) 190fr on 150fr #C167

Dahomey Nos. C145, C149-C150, C182,
C189, C198,
C257, C264-C265 Surcharged
Benin No. C241 Surcharged

1993
Perfs. & Printing Methods as Before

C403	AP51(e)	5fr on 100fr #C149
C404	AP50(f)	10fr on 100fr #C145
C405	AP51(f)	20fr on 200fr #C150
C406	AP83(f)	20fr on 500fr #C257
C407	AP84	25fr on 85fr #C241
C408	AP86(f)	25fr on 500fr #C265
C409	AP63(f)	30fr on 15fr #C182
C410	AP61(f)	30fr on 200fr #C198
C411	AP66(b)	35fr on #C189
C412	AP86(g)	300fr on #C264

Dahomey Nos. C14, C31, C34, C101,
C110, C144, C151, C153, C155, C197,
C222, C234, C250, C254, C256, C261,
Benin C242 Surcharged or Overprinted

1994-95?
Perfs. & Printing Methods as Before

C414	AP52(e)	15fr on 40fr #C155
C415	AP83(f)	20fr on 200fr #C256
C417	AP49(g)	50fr on #C101
C418	AP48(g)	75fr on 40fr #C151
C419	AP4(g)	100fr on #C14
C421	AP50(g)	125fr on 50fr #C144
C422	AP75(e)	125fr on 65fr #C222
C425	AP21(f)	135fr on 45fr #C110
C430	AP81(f)	135fr on 250fr #C222
C432	AP84(f)	150fr on 140fr #C242
C433	A61(b)	150fr on #C153
C434	AP61(f)	150fr on #C197
C435	AP13(e)	200fr on 100fr #C31
C436	AP14(e)	200fr on 100fr #C34
C445	AP61(e)	200fr on 250fr #C234
C446	AP61(e)	200fr on 250fr #C254
C447	AP85(f)	300fr on #C261

Dahomey No. C37, Benin No. C351
Surcharged

1994-95
Printing Method and Perfs as Before

C448	AP14	150fr on 500fr #C37
C449	AP118	200fr on 500fr #C351

Benin No. C290 Surcharged
Dahomey Nos. C206, C257 Surcharged

1996?
Perfs. & Printing Methods as Before

C450	A133	40fr on 210fr #C290
C451	AP83(f)	200fr on 500fr #C257
C452	AP72(f)	1000fr on 150fr #C206

Dahomey No. C265 Surcharged
Benin Nos. C258, C292 Surcharged

1996?
Perfs. & Printing Methods as Before

C453	AP86(g)	25fr on 500fr #C265
C454	AP89	35fr on 270fr #C258
C455	AP102	100fr on 500fr #C292

Dahomey Nos. C61, C74, C85, C88, C94,
C106, C109, C111, C113, C115, C120,
C124-C125, C130, C135-C136, C138,
C142-C143, C150, C157, C204-C205,
C207-C208, C260, C263 Surcharged

1996?
Perfs. & Printing Methods as Before

C456	AP48(e)	70fr on #C138
C457	AP34(h)	150fr on #C88
C458	AP21(e)	150fr on #C115
C459	AP72(e)	150fr on #C207
C460	AP73(h)	150fr on #C208
C461	AP34(e)	150fr on #C85
C462	AP31(h)	150fr on 30fr #C74
C463	AP21(e)	150fr on #C109
C464	AP40(e)	150fr on 40fr on 30fr #C120
C465	AP47(s)	150fr on 40fr #C136
C466	AP49(e)	150fr on 40fr #C142
C467	CD128(h)	150fr on 50fr #C94
C468	AP38(h)	150fr on 50fr #C106
C469	AP71(e)	150fr on 50fr #C204
C470	AP54(e)	150fr on 70fr #C124
C471	CD124(h)	150fr on 100fr #C61
C472	AP21(e)	150fr on 100fr #C113
C473	AP31(h)	150fr on 100fr #C157
C474	AP84(h)	150fr on 100fr #C260
C475	AP21(h)	150fr on 110fr #C111
C476	AP44(h)	150fr on 110fr #C130
C477	AP54(e)	150fr on 120fr #C125
C478	AP86(g)	150fr on 135fr #C263
C479	AP46(h)	150fr on 200fr #C135
C480	AP49(e)	150fr on 200fr #C143
C481	AP51(h)	150fr on 200fr #C150
C482	AP71(e)	150fr on 200fr #C205

Benin Nos. C261, C281, C327, C332-C333 Surcharged
Dahomey No. C201 Surcharged

1996-97?
Perfs. & Printing Methods as Before

C483	AP98	30fr on 380fr #C261
C484	AP90	35fr on 270fr #C281
C485	AP117	125fr on 200fr #C332
C485A	AP117	125fr on 200fr #C333
C486	AP114	200fr on 500fr #C327
C489	AP70(f)	150fr on #C201

Dahomey No. C250 Surcharged Type f

1997?
Perf. & Printing Method as Before

C509	AP81(f)	150fr on 250fr #C250

Benin No. C293 Surcharged
Dahomey No. C126 Surcharged

1995-97?
Perfs. & Printing Methods as Before

C500	AP103	150fr on 500fr #C293
C515	AP42(h)	35fr on 100fr on 200fr #C126

POSTAGE DUE STAMPS

French Colony
Handstamped in Black on Postage Due
Stamps of French Colonies

BENIN

1894 Unwmk. Imperf.

J1	D1	5c black	120.00 45.00
J2	D1	10c black	120.00 45.00
J3	D1	20c black	120.00 45.00
J4	D1	30c black	120.00 45.00
		Nos. J1-J4 (4)	480.00 180.00

Nos. J1-J4 exist with overprint in various positions.

Catalogue values for unused stamps in this section are for Never Hinged items.

People's Republic

Pineapples
D6

Mail Delivery — D7

Designs: 20fr, Cashew, vert. 40fr, Oranges. 50fr, Akee. 80fr, Mail delivery by boat.

1978, Sept. 5 Photo. Perf. 13

J44	D6	10fr multi	.15	.15
J45	D6	20fr multi	.15	.15
J46	D6	40fr multi	.28	.16
J47	D6	50fr multi	.45	.25

Engr.

J48	D7	60fr multi	.32	.22
J49	D7	80fr multi	.45	.28
		Nos. J44-J49 (6)	1.80	1.21

PARCEL POST STAMPS

Catalogue values for unused stamps in this section are for Never Hinged items.

Nos. 448-448A, 459, 473, C292
Overprinted or Surcharged "Colis Postaux"
Perfs. and Printing Methods as Before

1982, Nov.

Q8	A126	100fr on 150fr	.40	.20
Q9	A130	100fr multi	.40	.20
Q10	A134	300fr multi	1.20	.60
Q10A	A126	1000fr multi	5.50	5.50
Q10B	AP102	5000fr on 500fr	27.50	27.50
		Nos. Q8-Q10B (5)	35.00	34.00

Dahomey No. C205 Surcharged

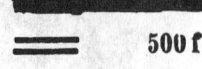

═══
500 f
═══
République
Populaire
du Bénin

colis postaux

1989 Photo. Perf. 12½x13

Q11	AP71	500fr on 200fr multi	3.25 3.25

BERMUDA

(,)bər-'myü-də

LOCATION — A group of about 150 small islands of which only 20 are inhabited, lying in the Atlantic Ocean about 580 miles southeast of Cape Hatteras.
GOVT. — British Crown Colony
AREA — 20.5 sq. mi.
POP. — 54,893 (1980)
CAPITAL — Hamilton

Bermuda achieved internal self-government in 1968.

4 Farthings = 1 Penny
12 Pence = 1 Shilling
20 Shillings = 1 Pound
100 Cents = 1 Dollar (1970)

Catalogue values for unused stamps in this country are for Never Hinged items, beginning with Scott 131.

POSTMASTER STAMPS

PM1

1848-54 Unwmk. Imperf.

X1	PM1	1p blk, bluish (1848, 1849)	125,000.
X2	PM1	1p red, bluish (1854, 1856)	175,000.
X3	PM1	1p red (1853)	160,000.

PM2

1860

X4	PM2	(1p) red, yellowish	100,000.

Same inscribed "HAMILTON"

1861

X5	PM2	(1p) red, bluish	125,000.

Nos. X1-X3 were produced and used by Postmaster William B. Perot of Hamilton. No. X4 is attributed to Postmaster James H. Thies of St. George's.

Only a few of each stamp exist. Values reflect actual sales figures for stamps in the condition in which they are found.

GENERAL ISSUES

Values for unused stamps are for examples with original gum as defined in the catalogue introduction. Very fine examples of Nos. 1-1a, 2-15b will have perforations touching the design (or framelines where applicable) on at least one side due to the narrow spacing of the stamps on the plates. Stamps with perfs clear of the design on all four sides are scarce and will command higher prices.

Queen Victoria
A1 A2
A3 A4
A5

1865-74 Typo. Wmk. 1 Perf. 14

1	A1	1p rose red	80.00	3.00
a.		1p dull rose	100.00	3.00
b.		Imperf.	20,000.	11,000.
2	A2	2p blue ('66)	140.00	11.00
3	A3	3p buff ('73)	425.00	60.00
4	A4	6p brown lilac	900.00	110.00
5	A4	6p lilac ('74)	22.50	17.50
6	A5	1sh green	175.00	35.00
		Nos. 1-6 (6)	1,742.	236.50

See Nos. 7-9, 19-21, 23, 25. For surcharges see Nos. 10-15.

1882-1903 Perf. 14x12½

7	A3	3p buff	165.00	50.00
8	A4	6p violet ('03)	15.00	17.50
9	A5	1sh green ('94)	22.50	80.00
a.		Vert. strip of 3, perf. all around & imperf. btwn.	13,000.	
		Nos. 7-9 (3)	202.50	147.50

Handstamped Diagonally **THREE PENCE**

1874 Perf. 14

10	A5	3p on 1sh green	1,400.	950.

Handstamped Diagonally *THREE PENCE*

11	A1	3p on 1p rose	12,000.	
12	A5	3p on 1sh green	2,100.	900.
a.		"P" with top like "R"	2,250.	1,200.

No. 11 is stated to be an essay, but a few copies are known used. Nos. 10-12 are found with double or partly double surcharges.

Surcharged in Black **One Penny.**

1875

13	A2	1p on 2p blue	700.00	375.00
a.		Without period	11,000.	7,250.
14	A3	1p on 3p buff	450.00	350.00
15	A5	1p on 1sh green	500.00	300.00
a.		Inverted surcharge	—	—
b.		Without period	—	—

BERMUDA

A6  / **A7**

1880 — Wmk. 1
16	A6	½p brown	1.75	2.75
17	A7	4p orange	15.00	2.50

See Nos. 18, 24.

A8  / **A9**

1883-1904 — Wmk. 2
18	A6	½p green ('92)	1.50	1.00
19	A1	1p aniline car ('89)	6.00	.30
a.		1p dull rose	110.00	4.00
b.		1p rose red	60.00	2.25
c.		1p carmine rose ('86)	25.00	1.00
20	A2	2p blue ('86)	35.00	3.00
21	A2	2p brown purple ('98)	3.00	2.50
a.		2p aniline pur ('93)	8.50	4.00
22	A8	2½p ultra ('84)	6.00	.40
23	A3	3p gray ('86)	14.00	5.50
24	A7	4p brown org ('04)	24.00	60.00
25	A5	1sh ol bis ('93)	13.00	12.00
a.		1sh yellow brown	15.00	13.00
		Nos. 18-25 (8)	102.50	84.70

Black Surcharge
1901
26	A9	1f on 1sh gray	.40	.25

Dry Dock — **A10**

1902-03
28	A10	½p gray grn & blk ('03)	8.25	2.50
29	A10	1p car rose & brown	7.50	.40
30	A10	3p ol grn & violet	1.75	3.75
		Nos. 28-30 (3)	17.50	6.65

1906-10 — Wmk. 3
31	A10	¼p pur & brn ('08)	1.10	1.25
32	A10	½p gray grn & blk	11.50	1.65
33	A10	½p green ('09)	7.00	2.25
34	A10	1p car rose & brn	14.00	.30
35	A10	1p carmine ('08)	13.00	.40
36	A10	2p orange & gray	5.75	5.75
37	A10	2½p blue & brown	10.00	13.00
38	A10	2½p ultra ('10)	9.50	9.50
39	A10	4p vio brn & blue ('09)	2.25	9.50
		Nos. 31-39 (9)	74.10	43.60

Caravel **A11** / King George V **A12**

1910-20 — Engr. — Perf. 14
40	A11	¼p brown	.45	1.25
41	A11	½p yel green	.90	.30
a.		½p dark green	3.00	1.40
42	A11	1p rose red (I)	7.00	.35
a.		1p carmine (I)	25.00	3.50
43	A11	2p gray	2.00	4.00
44	A11	2½p ultra (I)	2.25	.50
45	A11	3p violet, yel	1.40	6.00
46	A11	4p red, yellow	2.75	6.00
47	A11	6p claret	8.00	8.00
48	A11	1sh blk, green	4.00	5.00
a.		1sh black, olive	3.75	8.00

Typographed — Chalky Paper
49	A12	2sh ultra & dl vio, bl ('20)	14.00	32.50
50	A12	2sh6p red & blk, bl	18.00	42.50
51	A12	4sh car & black ('20)	40.00	70.00
52	A12	5sh red & grn, yellow	50.00	70.00
53	A12	10sh red & grn, green	140.00	125.00
54	A12	£1 black & vio, red	350.00	450.00
		Nos. 40-54 (15)	640.75	820.40

Types I of 1p and 2½p are illustrated above Nos. 81-97.

The 1p was printed from two plates, the 2nd of which, #42a, exists only in carmine on opaque paper with a bluish tinge. Compare #MR1 (as #42) and MR2 (as #42a).

Revenue cancellations are found on Nos. 52-54. See Nos. 81-97.

Seal of the Colony and King George V — **A13**

1920-21 — Wmk. 3 — Ordinary Paper
55	A13	¼p brown	.80	5.00
56	A13	½p green	1.00	6.00
57	A13	2p gray	6.50	17.50

Chalky Paper
58	A13	3p vio & dl vio, yel	6.00	15.00
59	A13	4p red & blk, yellow	6.50	15.00
60	A13	1sh blk, gray grn	14.00	35.00

Ordinary Paper — Wmk. 4
67	A13	1p rose red	1.00	.60
68	A13	2½p ultra	5.50	8.00

Chalky Paper
69	A13	6p red vio & dl vio	12.50	35.00
		Nos. 55-60,67-69 (9)	53.80	137.10

Issued: 6p, Jan. 19, 1921; others, Nov. 11, 1920.

King George V — **A14**

1921, May 12 — Engr.
71	A14	¼p brown	.45	1.50
72	A14	½p green	3.50	4.00
73	A14	1p carmine	2.50	1.00

Wmk. 3
74	A14	2p gray	6.00	10.00
75	A14	2½p ultra	6.00	4.00
76	A14	3p vio, orange	4.25	10.00
77	A14	4p scarlet, org	8.00	12.00
78	A14	6p claret	8.50	25.00
79	A14	1sh blk, green	16.00	30.00
		Nos. 71-79 (9)	55.20	97.50

Tercentenary of "Local Representative Institutions" (Nos. 55-79).

Types of 1910-20 Issue

Types of 1p: **1d** I **1d** II **1d** III

Types of 2½p: **2½d** I **2½d** II

1922-34 — Wmk. 4
81	A11	¼p brown ('28)	.30	.75
82	A11	½p green	.20	.15
83	A11	1p car, III ('28)	7.50	.30
a.		1p carmine, II ('26)	8.00	.60
b.		1p carmine, I	8.00	.40
84	A11	1½p red brown ('34)	3.00	.30
85	A11	2p gray ('23)	1.00	1.00
86	A11	2½p ap grn ('23)	1.00	1.00
87	A11	2½p ultra, II ('32)	2.00	.35
a.		2½p ultra, I ('26)	1.75	.35
88	A11	3p ultra ('24)	14.00	20.00
89	A11	3p vio, yellow ('26)	.80	.60
90	A11	4p red, yellow ('24)	1.00	1.00
91	A11	6p claret ('24)	.80	.80
92	A11	1sh blk, emer ('27)	5.00	5.00
93	A11	1sh brn blk, yel grn ('34)	30.00	40.00

Chalky Paper
94	A12	2sh ultra & vio, bl ('27)	30.00	40.00
a.		2sh bl & dp vio, dp bl ('31)	35.00	40.00
95	A12	2sh 6p red & blk, bl ('27)	40.00	37.50
a.		2sh6p pale org ver & blk, gray bl ('30)	2,750.	2,250.
b.		2sh6p dp ver & blk, deep blue ('31)	55.00	60.00
96	A12	10sh red & grn, emer ('24)	150.00	175.00
a.		10sh dp red & pale grn, dp emer ('31)	150.00	175.00
97	A12	12sh 6p ocher & gray blk ('32)	300.00	350.00
		Nos. 81-97 (17)	586.60	673.75

Revenue cancellations are found on Nos. 94-97. The 12sh6p with "Revenue" on both sides, was used postally from Feb. 1 to Apr., 1937. Copies with postal cancels in that time period are valued at three times No. 97.

Common Design Types
pictured following the introduction.

Silver Jubilee Issue
Common Design Type

1935, May 6 — Perf. 11x12
100	CD301	1p car & dk bl	.15	.15
101	CD301	1½p blk & ultra	.45	.45
102	CD301	2½p ultra & brn	1.50	1.50
103	CD301	1sh brn vio & ind	6.00	10.00
		Nos. 100-103 (4)	8.10	12.10
		Set, never hinged	14.00	

Hamilton Harbor — **A15**  / Yacht "Lucie" — **A17**

South Shore — **A16**  / Grape Bay — **A18**

For Bermuda & the Entire British Commonwealth Pre-1960

Aron R. Halberstam Philatelists, Ltd.

POB 150168, Van Brunt Station
Brooklyn, NY 11215-0168
Tel: 718-788-3978
Fax: 718-965-3099
Toll Free: 800-343-1303

Call or write for our Free Price List, or send us your Want Lists.

VISA MasterCard AMERICAN EXPRESS

Accepted on all orders.

We are also eager buyers of better Commonwealth collections and singles or sets. Let us know what you have to offer.

PTS APS ASDA

BRITISH EMPIRE EXCLUSIVELY

REQUEST A CATALOGUE FOR OUR NEXT **PUBLIC AUCTION**.

PLEASE SPECIFY YOUR INTERESTS.

WANT LISTS INVITED FROM SERIOUS COLLECTORS OF **BERMUDA**.

EMPHASIS ON PRE-1935. REFERENCES PLEASE.

SELLING? ASK US ABOUT CONSIGNING YOUR COLLECTION TO A FUTURE SALE.

Victoria Stamp Company

Established 1962

PHOEBE A. MacGILLIVARY
P.O. BOX 745, RIDGEWOOD, NJ 07451
PHONE 201-652-7283 • FAX 201-612-0024

ASDA PTS

BERMUDA

Typical Cottage
A19

Scene at Par-la-Ville
A20

1936-40   Perf. 12
105	A15	½p blue green	.15	.15
106	A16	1p car & black	.30	.15
107	A16	1½p choc & black	.30	.15
108	A17	2p lt bl & blk	2.50	2.00
109	A17	2p brn blk & turq bl ('38)	22.50	8.00
109A	A17	2p red & ultra ('40)	.25	.15
110	A18	2½p dk bl & lt bl	.55	.15
111	A19	3p car & black	2.50	1.50
112	A20	6p vio & rose lake	.30	.20
113	A18	1sh deep green	5.50	6.00
114	A15	1sh6p brown	.50	.40
		Nos. 105-114 (11)	35.35	18.05
		Set, never hinged	50.00	

No. 108, blue border and black center.
No. 109, black border, blue center.

Coronation Issue
Common Design Type
1937, May 14   Perf. 13½x14
115	CD302	1p carmine	.15	.15
116	CD302	1½p brown	.20	.15
117	CD302	2½p bright ultra	.50	.25
		Nos. 115-117 (3)	.85	.55
		Set, never hinged	1.50	

Hamilton Harbor — A21

Grape Bay — A22

St. David's Lighthouse
A23

King George VI
A25

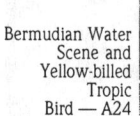

Bermudian Water Scene and Yellow-billed Tropic Bird — A24

1938-51   Wmk. 4   Perf. 12
118	A21	1p red & black ('40)	.15	.15
a.		1p rose red & black	12.00	1.00
119	A21	1½p vio brn & blue	.50	.25
a.		1½p dl vio brn & bl ('43)	.20	.15
120	A22	2½p blue & lt bl	2.50	.75
120A	A22	2½p brn & lt bl ('41)	.30	.15
b.		2½p dk ol blk & pale blue ('43)	.30	.15
121	A23	3p car & blk	4.50	1.75
121A	A23	3p dp ultra & blk ('42)	.25	.15
c.		3p brt ultra & blk ('41)	.25	.15
121D	A24	7½p yel grn, bl & blk ('41)	1.25	1.00
122	A22	1sh green	1.00	.35

Typo.   Perf. 13
123		2sh ultra & red vio, bl ('50)	6.00	4.00
a.		2sh ultra & vio, bl	5.00	3.50
b.		2sh ultra & dl vio, bl (mottled paper), perf. 14 ('42)	5.00	3.50
124	A25	2sh 6p red & blk, bl	8.00	6.00
a.		Perf. 14	8.00	3.50
125	A25	5sh red & grn, yel	10.00	7.50
a.		Perf. 14	13.00	7.50
126	A25	10sh red & grn, grn ('51)	20.00	14.00
a.		brn lake & grn, perf. 14	175.00	200.00
b.		red & grn, grn, perf. 14 ('39)	40.00	40.00
127	A25	12sh 6p org & gray blk	55.00	50.00
a.		orange & gray, perf. 14	45.00	35.00
b.		yel & gray, perf. 14 ('47)	600.00	525.00
c.		brn orange & gray, perf. 14	300.00	300.00

Wmk. 3
128	A25	£1 blk & vio, red ('51)	35.00	30.00
a.		£1 blk & pur, red, perf. 14	190.00	100.00
b.		£1 blk & dk vio, salmon, perf. 14 ('42)	40.00	25.00
		Nos. 118-128 (14)	144.45	116.05
		Set, never hinged	220.00	

No. 127b is the so-called "lemon yellow" shade. Revenue cancellations are found on Nos. 123-128. Copies with removed revenue cancellations and forged postmarks are abundant.

HALF PENNY

No. 118a Surcharged in Black

X   X

1940, Dec. 20   Wmk. 4   Perf. 12
129	A21	½p on 1p rose red & blk	.30	.30
		Never hinged	.50	

Catalogue values for unused stamps in this section, from this point to the end of the section, are for Never Hinged items.

Peace Issue
Common Design Type
Perf. 13½x14
1946, Nov. 6   Engr.   Wmk. 4
131	CD303	1½p brown	.20	.20
132	CD303	3p deep blue	.30	.30

Silver Wedding Issue
Common Design Types
1948, Dec. 1   Photo.   Perf. 14x14½
133	CD304	1½p red brown	.15	.15

Engr.; Name Typo.
Perf. 11½x11
134	CD305	£1 rose carmine	47.50	35.00

Postmaster Stamp of 1848 — A26

1949, Apr. 11   Engr.   Perf. 13x13½
135	A26	2½p dk brown & dp bl	.20	.20
136	A26	3p dp blue & black	.20	.20
137	A26	6p green & rose vio	.45	.45
		Nos. 135-137 (3)	.85	.85

No. 137 shows a different floral arrangement. Bermuda's first postage stamp, cent.

UPU Issue
Common Design Types
Perf. 13½, 11x11½
1949, Oct. 10   Engr.; Name Typo.
138	CD306	2½p slate	.55	.55
139	CD307	3p indigo	.70	.70
140	CD308	6p rose violet	1.10	1.10
141	CD309	1sh blue green	2.25	2.25
		Nos. 138-141 (4)	4.60	4.60

Coronation Issue
Common Design Type
1953, June 4   Engr.   Perf. 13½x13
142	CD312	1½p dk blue & blk	.40	.20

A27

Easter Lilies — A28

Designs: 1p, 4p, Perot stamp. 2p, Racing dinghy. 2½p, Sir George Somers and "Sea Venture." 3p, 1sh3p, Map. 4½p, 9p, "Sea Venture," boat, hog coin and Perot stamp. 6p, 8p, Yellow-billed tropic bird. 1sh, Hog coins. 2sh, Arms of St. George. 2sh6p, Warwick Fort. 5sh, Hog coin. 10sh, Earliest hog coin. £1, Arms of Bermuda.

1953-58   Perf. 13½x13, 13x13½
143	A27	½p olive green	.15	.15
144	A27	1p rose red & blk	.15	.15
145	A28	1½p dull green	.15	.15
146	A27	2p red & ultra	.15	.15
147	A27	2½p carmine rose	.50	.15
148	A27	3p vio (Sandy's)	.45	.25
149	A27	3p violet (Sandys) ('57)	.55	.20
150	A27	4p dp ultra & blk	.25	.25
151	A27	4½p green	.60	.60
152	A27	6p dk bluish grn & blk	2.50	.30
153	A27	8p red & blk ('55)	.95	.35
154	A27	9p violet ('58)	2.00	.95
155	A27	1sh orange	.40	.20
156	A27	1sh3p blue (Sandy's)	2.00	.35
157	A27	1sh3p blue (Sandys) ('57)	4.00	.50
158	A27	2sh yellow brown	2.00	.65
159	A28	2sh6p scarlet	2.00	1.25
160	A27	5sh dp car rose	7.50	2.00
161	A27	10sh deep ultra	11.00	4.50

Engr. and Typo.
162	A27	£1 dp ol grn & multi	20.00	17.50
		Nos. 143-162 (20)	57.30	30.60

For overprints, see Nos. 164-167.

Type of 1953 Inscribed "ROYAL VISIT 1953"

Design: 6p, Yellow-billed tropic bird.

1953, Nov. 26   Engr.
163	A27	6p dk bluish grn & blk	.40	.35

Visit of Queen Elizabeth II and the Duke of Edinburgh, 1953.

Nos. 148 and 156 Overprinted in Violet Blue or Red

Three Power Talks December, 1953

1953, Dec. 8   Perf. 13½x13
164	A27	3p violet	.20	.20
165	A27	1sh3p blue (R)	.45	.40

Three Power Conference, Tucker's Town, December 1953.

Nos. 153 and 156 Overprinted in Black or Red

50TH ANNIVERSARY
U S — BERMUDA
OCEAN RACE 1956

1956, June 22
166	A27	8p red & black	.25	.30
167	A27	1sh3p blue (R)	.35	.50

Newport-Bermuda Yacht Race, 50th anniv.

Perot Post Office, Hamilton
A29

Perf. 13½x13
1959, Jan. 1   Engr.   Wmk. 4
168	A29	6p lilac & black	.20	.20

Restoration and reopening of the post office operated at Hamilton by W. B. Perot in the mid-nineteenth century.

Arms of James I and Elizabeth II — A30

Engr. and Litho.
1959, July 29   Wmk. 314   Perf. 13
Coats of Arms in Blue, Yellow & Red
169	A30	1½p dark blue	.15	.15
170	A30	3p gray	.30	.30
171	A30	4p rose violet	.35	.35
172	A30	8p violet gray	.75	.75
173	A30	9p olive green	.95	.95
174	A30	1sh3p orange brown	1.50	1.50
		Nos. 169-174 (6)	4.00	4.05

350th anniv. of the shipwreck of the "Sea Venture" which resulted in the first permanent settlement of Bermuda.

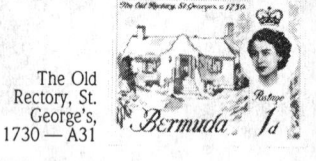

The Old Rectory, St. George's, 1730 — A31

Designs: 2p, Church of St. Peter. 3p, Government House. 4p, Cathedral, Hamilton. 5p, No. 185A, H.M. Dockyard. 6p, Perot's Post Office, 1848. 8p, General Post Office, 1869. 9p, Library and Historical Society. 1sh, Christ Church, Warwick, 1719. 1sh3p, City Hall, Hamilton. 10p, No. 185, Bermuda Cottage, 1705. 2sh, Town of St. George. 2sh3p, Bermuda House, 1710. 2sh6p, Bermuda House, 18th century. 5sh, Colonial Secretariat, 1833. 10sh, Old Post Office, Somerset, 1890. £1, House of Assembly, 1815.

Wmk. 314 Upright
1962-65   Photo.   Perf. 12½
175	A31	1p org, lil & blk	.15	.15
176	A31	2p sl, lt vio, grn & yel	.15	.15
a.		Light vio omitted	650.00	
b.		Green omitted		
d.		Imperf., pair	650.00	
177	A31	3p lt bl & yel brn	.15	.15
a.		Yellow brown omitted	1,250.	
178	A31	4p car rose & red brn	.15	.15
179	A31	5p dk blue & pink	.32	.32
180	A31	6p emer, lt & dk blue	.18	.15
181	A31	8p grn, dp org & ultra	.35	.30
182	A31	9p org brn & grnsh bl	.32	.28
182A	A31	10p brt vio & bister ('65)	.65	.55
183	A31	1sh multicolored	.42	.26
184	A31	1sh3p sl, lem & rose car	.48	.26
185	A31	1sh6p brt vio & bis	2.75	2.25
186	A31	2sh brown & org	1.25	.85
187	A31	2sh3p brn & brt yel green	2.50	2.00
188	A31	2sh6p grn, yel & sep	1.50	1.10
189	A31	5sh choc & brt green	2.50	1.65
190	A31	10p dl grn, buff & rose car	4.00	3.50
191	A31	£1 cit, bis, blk & orange	9.50	7.75
		Nos. 175-191 (18)	27.32	21.82

See No. 252a. For surcharges see Nos. 238, 240-244, 247, 250-254.

1966-69   Wmk. 314 Sideways
Unnamed Colors as in 1962-65 Issue
176c	A31	2p ('69)	2.50	1.65
181a	A31	8p ('67)	1.10	1.10
182b	A31	10p	1.40	1.10
183a	A31	1sh ('67)	1.40	1.25
185A	A31	1sh6p indigo & rose	2.50	3.00
186a	A31	2sh ('67)	4.50	4.50
		Nos. 176c-186a (6)	13.40	12.40

For surcharges see #239, 245-246, 248-249.

Freedom from Hunger Issue
Common Design Type
1963, June 4   Perf. 14x14½
192	CD314	1sh3p sepia	2.75	2.25

Red Cross Centenary Issue
Common Design Type
Wmk. 314
1963, Sept. 2   Litho.   Perf. 13
193	CD315	3p black & red	.50	.30
194	CD315	1sh3p ultra & red	5.50	6.00

BERMUDA

Finn Boat — A32

Perf. 13½
1964, Sept. 28 Photo. Wmk. 314
195 A32 3p blue, vio & red   .28 .28
18th Olympic Games, Tokyo, Oct. 10-25.

ITU Issue
Common Design Type
Perf. 11x11½
1965, May 17 Photo. Wmk. 314
196 CD317 3p blue & emerald   .42 .30
197 CD317 2sh yel & vio blue   3.50 3.50

Scout Badge and Royal Cipher A33

1965, July 24 Photo. Perf. 12½
198 A33 2sh multicolored   .85 .85
50th anniversary of Scouting in Bermuda.

Intl. Cooperation Year Issue
Common Design Type
1965, Oct. 25 Litho. Perf. 14½
199 CD318 4p blue grn & cl   .30 .30
200 CD318 2sh6p lt violet & grn   2.25 2.25

Churchill Memorial Issue
Common Design Type
1966, Jan. 24 Photo. Perf. 14
Design in Black, Gold and Carmine Rose
201 CD319 3p bright blue   .30 .20
202 CD319 6p green   .65 .45
203 CD319 10p brown   1.25 1.00
204 CD319 1sh3p violet   2.50 2.00
  Nos. 201-204 (4)   4.70 3.65

World Cup Soccer Issue
Common Design Type
1966, July 1 Litho. Perf. 14
205 CD321 10p multicolored   .65 .65
206 CD321 2sh6p multicolored   1.75 1.75

UNESCO Anniversary Issue
Common Design Type
1966, Dec. 1 Litho. Perf. 14
207 CD323 4p "Education"   .40 .40
208 CD323 1sh3p "Science"   1.50 1.50
209 CD323 2sh "Culture"   2.50 2.50
  Nos. 207-209 (3)   4.40 4.40

Post Office, Hamilton A34

Perf. 14½
1967, June 23 Photo. Wmk. 314
210 A34 3p vio blue & multi   .15 .15
211 A34 1sh orange & multi   .40 .40
212 A34 1sh6p green & multi   .70 .70
213 A34 2sh6p red & multi   1.10 1.10
  Nos. 210-213 (4)   2.35 2.35
Opening of the new GPO, Hamilton.

Cable Ship Mercury A35

Designs: 1sh, Map of Bermuda and Virgin Islands, telephone and microphone. 1sh6p, Radio tower, television set, telephone and cable. 2sh6p, Cable at sea bottom and ship.

1967, Sept. 14 Photo. Wmk. 314
214 A35 3p multicolored   .15 .15
215 A35 1sh multicolored   .40 .40
216 A35 1sh6p multicolored   .70 .70
217 A35 2sh6p multicolored   1.10 1.10
  Nos. 214-217 (4)   2.35 2.35
Completion of the Bermuda-Tortola, Virgin Islands, telephone link.

Human Rights Flame, Globe and Doves A36

1968, Feb. 1 Litho. Perf. 14x14½
218 A36 3p indigo, lt grn & bl   .15 .15
219 A36 1sh brown, lt bl & bl   .45 .45
220 A36 1sh6p black, pink & blue   .75 .75
221 A36 2sh6p green, yellow & bl   .95 .95
  Nos. 218-221 (4)   2.30 2.30
International Human Rights Year.

Mace A37

Design: 1sh6p, 2sh6p, House of Assembly, Bermuda; Parliament, London, and royal cipher.

1968, July 1 Photo. Perf. 14½
222 A37 3p rose red & multi   .15 .15
223 A37 1sh ultra & multi   .45 .45
224 A37 1sh6p yellow & multi   .75 .75
225 A37 2sh6p multicolored   .95 .95
  Nos. 222-225 (4)   2.30 2.30
New constitution.

Olympic Sports and Rings — A38

1968, Sept. 24 Wmk. 314 Perf. 12½
226 A38 3p lilac & multi   .15 .15
  a. Rose brown omitted ("3d BERMUDA")   2,000.
227 A38 1sh multicolored   .42 .35
228 A38 1sh6p multicolored   .60 .60
229 A38 2sh6p multicolored   1.00 1.00
  Nos. 226-229 (4)   2.17 2.10
19th Olympic Games, Mexico City, Oct. 12-27.

Girl Guides A39

Designs: 1sh, Like 3p. 1sh6p, 2sh6p, Girl Guides and arms of Bermuda.

1969, Feb. 17 Litho. Perf. 14
230 A39 3p lilac & multi   .15 .15
231 A39 1sh green & multi   .35 .35
232 A39 1sh6p gray & multi   .55 .55
233 A39 2sh6p red & multi   1.00 1.00
  Nos. 230-233 (4)   2.05 2.05
Bermuda Girl Guides, 50th anniv.

Gold and Emerald Cross — A40

Design: 4p, 2sh, Different background.

1969, Sept. 29 Photo. Perf. 14½x14
Cross in Yellow, Brown and Emerald
234 A40 4p violet   .24 .24
235 A40 1sh3p green   .75 .75
236 A40 2sh black   1.10 1.10
237 A40 2sh6p carmine rose   1.40 1.25
  Nos. 234-237 (4)   3.49 3.34
Treasures salvaged off the coast of Bermuda. The cross shown is from the Tucker treasure from the 16th century Spanish galleon San Pedro.

Buildings Issue and Type of 1962-69 Surcharged with New Value and Bar in Black or Brown

1970, Feb. 6 Wmk. 314 Perf. 12½
238 A31 1c on 1p multi   .15 .15
239 A31 2c on 2p multi   .15 .15
  a. Watermark upright   1.25 1.25
  b. Light violet omitted   650.00
  c. Pair, one without surch.   2,000.
240 A31 3c on 3p multi   .15 .15
241 A31 4c on 4p multi (Br)   .15 .15
242 A31 5c on 6p multi   .15 .15
243 A31 6c on 8p multi   .15 .15
244 A31 9c on 9p multi (Br)   .22 .40
245 A31 10c on 10p multi   .28 .50
246 A31 12c on 1sh multi   .32 .60
247 A31 15c on 1sh3p multi   .70 1.10
248 A31 18c on 1sh6p multi   .70 1.25
249 A31 24c on 2sh multi   .85 1.50
250 A31 30c on 2sh6p multi   1.00 1.90
251 A31 36c on 2sh6p multi   1.25 2.50
252 A31 60c on 5sh multi   2.00 3.75
  a. Surcharge omitted   450.00
253 A31 $1.20 on 10sh multi   4.00 7.50
254 A31 $2.40 on £1 multi   8.00 15.00
  Nos. 238-254 (17)   20.22 36.90
Watermark upright on 1c, 3c to 9c and 36c; sideways on others. Watermark is sideways on No. 252a, upright on No. 189.

Spathiphyllum — A41

Flowers: 2c, Bottlebrush. 3c, Oleander, vert. 4c, Bermudiana. 5c, Poinsettia. 6c, Hibiscus. 9c, Cereus. 10c, Bougainvillea, vert. 12c, Jacaranda. 15c, Passion flower. 18c, Coralita. 24c, Morning glory. 30c, Tecoma. 36c, Angel's trumpet. 60c, Plumbago. $1.20, Bird of paradise. $2.40, Chalice cup.

Wmk. 314, Sideways on Horiz. Stamps
1970, July 6 Perf. 14
255 A41 1c lt green & multi   .15 .15
256 A41 2c pale bl & multi   .26 .15
257 A41 3c yellow & multi   .16 .15
258 A41 4c buff & multi   .18 .15
259 A41 5c pink & multi   .60 .26
  a. Imperf., pair   800.00
260 A41 6c orange & multi   .60 .30
261 A41 9c lt green & multi   .35 .16
262 A41 10c pale salmon & multi   .35 .16
263 A41 12c pale yellow & multi   1.65 .85
264 A41 15c buff & multi   1.40 .70
265 A41 18c pale salmon & multi   2.50 1.10
266 A41 24c pink & multi   1.65 .75
267 A41 30c plum & multi   1.65 .75
268 A41 36c dark gray & multi   2.50 1.10
269 A41 60c gray & multi   3.25 1.75
270 A41 $1.20 blue & multi   7.50 3.50
271 A41 $2.40 multicolored   15.00 8.25
  Nos. 255-271 (17)   39.75 20.23
See #322-328. For overprints see #288-291.

1974-76 Wmk. 314 Upright
259b A41 5c multicolored   1.00 1.00
260a A41 6c multicolored   2.25 2.25
263a A41 12c multicolored   1.65 1.65
267a A41 30c multicolored ('76)   3.00 3.00
  Nos. 259b-267a (4)   7.90 7.90
Issued: 30c, June 11; others, June 13.

1975-76 Wmk. 373
256a A41 2c multicolored   1.00 1.00
260b A41 6c multicolored   2.00 2.00
Issued: 2c, Dec. 8; 6c, June 11, 1976.

State House, St. George's, 1622-1815 A42

Designs: 15c, The Sessions House, Hamilton, 1893. 18c, First Assembly House, St. Peter's Church, St. George's. 24c, Temporary Assembly House, Hamilton, 1815-26.

1970, Oct. 12 Litho. Perf. 14
272 A42 4c multicolored   .15 .15
273 A42 15c multicolored   .45 .45
274 A42 18c multicolored   .65 .65
275 A42 24c multicolored   1.10 1.10
  a. Souvenir sheet of 4, #272-275   3.75 4.25
  Nos. 272-275 (4)   2.35 2.35
350th anniv. of Bermuda's Parliament.

Street in St. George's A43

"Keep Bermuda Beautiful": 15c, Horseshoe Bay. 18c, Gibb's Hill Lighthouse. 24c, View of Hamilton Harbor.

1971, Feb. 8 Wmk. 314 Perf. 14
276 A43 4c multicolored   .24 .24
277 A43 15c multicolored   .70 .70
278 A43 18c multicolored   .90 .90
279 A43 24c multicolored   1.50 1.50
  Nos. 276-279 (4)   3.34 3.34

Building of "Deliverance" — A44

Designs: 15c, "Deliverance" and "Patience" arriving in Jamestown, Va., 1610, vert. 18c, Wreck of "Sea Venture," vert. 24c, "Deliverance" and "Patience" under sail, 1610.

1971, May 10 Litho. Wmk. 314
280 A44 4c multicolored   .40 .40
281 A44 15c brown & multi   1.40 1.40
282 A44 18c purple & multi   1.75 1.75
283 A44 24c blue & multi   2.50 2.50
  Nos. 280-283 (4)   6.05 6.05
Voyage of Sir George Somers to Jamestown, Va., from Bermuda, 1610.

Ocean View Golf Course A45

Golf Courses: 15c, Port Royal. 18c, Castle Harbour. 24c, Belmont.

1971, Nov. 1 Perf. 13
284 A45 4c multicolored   .18 .18
285 A45 15c multicolored   .65 .65
286 A45 18c multicolored   .75 .75
287 A45 24c multicolored   1.10 1.10
  Nos. 284-287 (4)   2.68 2.68
Golfing in Bermuda.

BERMUDA

Nos. 258, 264-266 Overprinted: "HEATH-NIXON / DECEMBER 1971"

1971, Dec. 20 Photo. Perf. 14
288	A41	4c buff & multi	.15	.15
289	A41	15c buff & multi	.42	.42
290	A41	18c pale sal & multi	.52	.52
291	A41	24c pink & multi	.70	.70
		Nos. 288-291 (4)	1.79	1.79

Meeting of President Richard M. Nixon and Prime Minister Edward Heath of Great Britain, at Hamilton, Dec. 20-21, 1971.

Bonefish A46

1972, Aug. 7 Litho. Perf. 13½x14
292	A46	4c shown	.26	.26
293	A46	15c Wahoo	.75	.75
294	A46	18c Yellowfin tuna	.90	.90
295	A46	24c Greater amberjack	1.40	1.40
		Nos. 292-295 (4)	3.31	3.31

World fishing records.

Silver Wedding Issue, 1972
Common Design Type

Design: Queen Elizabeth II, Prince Philip, Admiralty oar and mace.

1972, Nov. 20 Photo. Perf. 14x14½
| 296 | CD324 | 4c violet & multi | .15 | .15 |
| 297 | CD324 | 15c car rose & multi | .52 | .52 |

Palmettos — A47

1973, Sept. 3 Wmk. 314 Perf. 14
298	A47	4c shown	.25	.25
299	A47	15c Olivewood	.75	.75
300	A47	18c Bermuda cedar	1.00	1.20
301	A47	24c Mahogany	1.25	1.25
		Nos. 298-301 (4)	3.25	3.45

Bermuda National Trust, and "Plant a Tree" campaign.

Princess Anne's Wedding Issue
Common Design Type

1973, Nov. 21 Litho.
| 302 | CD325 | 15c lilac & multi | .35 | .35 |
| 303 | CD325 | 18c slate & multi | .45 | .45 |

National Tennis Stadium, Pembroke, 1973 A48

15c, Bermuda's 1st tennis court, Pembroke, 1873. 18c, Britain's 1st tennis court, Leamington Spa, 1872. 24c, 1t US tennis club, Staten Island, 1874.

1973, Dec. 17 Wmk. 314
304	A48	4c black & multi	.20	.20
305	A48	15c black & multi	.65	.65
306	A48	18c black & multi	.90	.90
307	A48	24c black & multi	1.25	1.25
		Nos. 304-307 (4)	3.00	3.00

Centenary of tennis in Bermuda.

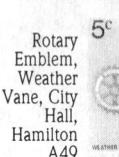

Rotary Emblem, Weather Vane, City Hall, Hamilton A49

Rotary Emblem and: 17c, St. Peter's Church, St. George's. 20c, Somerset Drawbridge, Somerset. 25c, Map of Bermuda on globe, 1626.

1974, June 24
308	A49	5c emerald & multi	.22	.22
309	A49	17c blue & multi	.75	.75
310	A49	20c yel org & multi	.85	.85
311	A49	25c lt violet & multi	1.10	1.10
		Nos. 308-311 (4)	2.92	2.92

50th anniv. of Rotary Intl. in Bermuda.

Jack of Clubs and a Good Bridge Hand — A50

Bermuda Bowl and: 17c, Queen of diamonds. 20c, King of hearts. 25c, Ace of spades.

1975, Jan. 27 Litho. Wmk. 314
312	A50	5c blue & multi	.24	.24
313	A50	17c dull yel & multi	.75	.75
314	A50	20c ver & multi	.80	.80
315	A50	25c lilac & multi	1.10	1.10
		Nos. 312-315 (4)	2.89	2.89

World Bridge Championship, Bermuda, Jan. 1975.

Queen Elizabeth II and Prince Philip — A51

1975, Feb. 17 Photo. Perf. 14x14½ Wmk. 373
| 316 | A51 | 17c multicolored | .60 | .60 |
| 317 | A51 | 20c dk blue & multi | .80 | .80 |

Royal Visit, Feb. 16-18, 1975.

British Cavalier Flying Boat, 1937 A52

Designs: 17c, U.S. Navy airship "Los Angeles," 1925, flying from Lakehurst, N.J. to Hamilton, Bermuda. 20c, Constellation over Kindley Field, 1946. 25c, Boeing 747 on tarmac, 1970.

1975, Apr. 28 Perf. 14
318	A52	5c lt green & multi	.42	.42
319	A52	17c lt ultra & multi	1.25	1.25
320	A52	20c multicolored	1.75	1.75
321	A52	25c rose lil & multi	2.00	2.00
a.		Souvenir sheet of 4, #318-321	6.00	7.50
		Nos. 318-321 (4)	5.42	5.42

Airmail service to Bermuda, 50th anniv.

Flower Type of 1970

1975, June 2 Photo. Wmk. 314
322	A41	17c Passion flower	1.25	1.25
323	A41	20c Coralita	1.25	1.25
324	A41	25c Morning glory	1.25	1.25
325	A41	40c Angel's trumpet	1.25	1.25
326	A41	$1 Plumbago	2.00	2.00
327	A41	$2 Bird-of-paradise flower	3.50	3.50
328	A41	$3 Chalice cup	6.00	6.00
		Nos. 322-328 (7)	16.50	16.50

Royal Magazine Break-in A54

Designs: 17c, Sympathizers rowing towards magazine. 20c, Loading gun powder barrels onto ships. 25c, Gun powder barrels on beach.

Perf. 13x13½
1975, Oct. 27 Litho. Wmk. 373
329	A54	5c multicolored	.24	.24
330	A54	17c multicolored	.75	.75
331	A54	20c multicolored	.85	.85
332	A54	25c multicolored	1.25	1.25
a.		Souv. sheet of 4, #329-332, perf. 14	4.00	5.00
		Nos. 329-332 (4)	3.09	3.09

Gunpowder Plot, 1775, American War of Independence.

Bermuda Biological Station A55

Designs: 5c, Launching of bathysphere from "Ready," vert. 20c, Sailing ship Challenger, 1873. 25c, Descent of Beebe's bathysphere, 1934, and marine life, vert.

1976, Mar. 29 Litho. Perf. 14
333	A55	5c multicolored	.28	.28
334	A55	17c multicolored	.70	.70
335	A55	20c multicolored	.85	.85
336	A55	25c multicolored	1.00	1.00
		Nos. 333-336 (4)	2.83	2.83

Bermuda Biological Station, 50th anniv.

Christian Radich, Norway A56

Tall Ships: 12c, Juan Sebastian de Elcano, Spain. 17c, Eagle, US. 20c, Sir Winston Churchill, Great Britain. 40c, Krunzenshtern, USSR. $1, Cutty Sark (silver trophy).

1976, June 15 Litho. Perf. 13
337	A56	5c lt green & multi	.30	.30
338	A56	12c violet & multi	.55	.55
339	A56	17c ultra & multi	.75	.75
340	A56	20c blue & multi	1.00	1.00
341	A56	40c yellow & multi	1.50	1.50
342	A56	$1 sl grn & multi	4.50	4.50
		Nos. 337-342 (6)	8.60	8.60

Trans-Atlantic Cutty Sark International Tall Ships Race, Plymouth, England-New York City (Operation Sail '76).

Silver Cup Trophy and Crossed Club Flags A57

Designs: 17c, St. George's Cricket Club and emblem. 20c, Somerset Cricket Club and emblem. 25c, Cricket match.

1976, Aug. 16 Wmk. 373 Perf. 14½
343	A57	5c multicolored	.26	.26
344	A57	17c multicolored	.85	.85
345	A57	20c multicolored	.95	.95
346	A57	25c multicolored	1.40	1.40
		Nos. 343-346 (4)	3.46	3.46

St. George's and Somerset Cricket Club matches, 75th anniversary.

Queen's Visit to Bermuda, 1975 — A58

Designs: 20c, St. Edward's Crown. $1, Queen seated in Chair of Estate.

1977, Feb. 7 Litho. Perf. 14x13½
347	A58	5c silver & multi	.18	.18
348	A58	20c silver & multi	.50	.50
349	A58	$1 silver & multi	2.25	2.25
		Nos. 347-349 (3)	2.93	2.93

Reign of Queen Elizabeth II, 25th anniv.

Stockdale House, St. George's A59

UPU Emblem and: 15c, Perot Post Office and Perot Stamp. 17c, St. George's Post Office, c. 1860. 20c, Old GPO, Hamilton, c. 1935. 40c, New GPO, Hamilton, 1967.

1977, June 20 Litho. Perf. 13x13½
350	A59	5c multicolored	.15	.15
351	A59	15c multicolored	.35	.35
352	A59	17c multicolored	.40	.40
353	A59	20c multicolored	.50	.50
354	A59	40c multicolored	1.00	1.00
		Nos. 350-354 (5)	2.40	2.40

Bermuda's UPU membership, cent.

Sailing Ship, 17th Century, Approaching Castle Island — A60

Designs: 15c, King's pilot leaving 18th century naval ship at Murray's Anchorage. 17c, Pilot gigs racing to meet steamship, early 19th century. 20c, Harvest Queen, late 19th century. 40c, Pilot cutter and Queen Elizabeth II off St. David's Lighthouse.

Perf. 13½x14
1977, Sept. 26 Wmk. 373
355	A60	5c multicolored	.15	.15
356	A60	15c multicolored	.42	.42
357	A60	17c multicolored	.48	.48
358	A60	20c multicolored	.60	.60
359	A60	40c multicolored	1.25	1.25
		Nos. 355-359 (5)	2.90	2.90

Piloting in Bermuda waters.

Elizabeth II — A61

Designs: 8c, Great Seal of Elizabeth I. 50c, Great Seal of Elizabeth II.

1978, Aug. 28 Litho. Perf. 14x13½
360	A61	8c gold & multi	.15	.15
361	A61	50c gold & multi	.85	.85
362	A61	$1 gold & multi	1.65	1.65
		Nos. 360-362 (3)	2.65	2.65

25th anniv. of coronation of Elizabeth II.

White-tailed Tropicbird — A62

Perf. 14; 14x14½ (4c, 5c, $2, $3, $5)
1978-79 Photo. Wmk. 373
363	A62	3c shown	.15	.15
364	A62	4c White-eyed vireo	.15	.15
365	A62	5c Eastern bluebird	.15	.15
366	A62	7c Whistling tree frog	.15	.15
367	A62	8c Cardinal	.15	.15
368	A62	10c Spiny lobster	.15	.15

BERMUDA

369	A62	12c Land crab	.20	.20
370	A62	15c Skink	.25	.25
371	A62	20c Four-eyed butterflyfish	.35	.35
372	A62	25c Red hind	.45	.45
373	A62	30c Monarch butterfly	.50	.50
374	A62	40c Rock beauty	.70	.70
375	A62	50c Banded butterflyfish	1.00	1.00
376	A62	$1 Blue angelfish	2.00	2.00
377	A62	$2 Humpback whale	4.25	4.25
378	A62	$3 Green turtle	6.25	6.25
379	A62	$5 Bermuda Petrel	10.50	10.50
		Nos. 363-379 (17)	27.35	27.35

Issued: 3c, 4c, 5c, 8c, $5, 1978; others, 1979.
For surcharge see No. 509.

Map of Bermuda, by George Somers, 1609 — A63

Old Maps of Bermuda: 15c, by John Seller, 1685. 20c, by Herman Moll, 1729, vert. 25c, by Desbruslins, 1740. 50c, by John Speed, 1626.

1979, May 14 Litho. *Perf. 13½*

380	A63	8c multicolored	.16	.16
381	A63	15c multicolored	.30	.30
382	A63	20c multicolored	.40	.40
383	A63	25c multicolored	.45	.45
384	A63	50c multicolored	.95	.95
		Nos. 380-384 (5)	2.26	2.26

Bermuda Police Centenary — A64

Designs: 20c, Traffic direction, horiz. 25c, Water patrol, horiz. 50c, Motorbike and patrol car.

1979, Nov. 26 Wmk. 373 *Perf. 14*

385	A64	8c multicolored	.16	.16
386	A64	20c multicolored	.40	.40
387	A64	25c multicolored	.50	.50
388	A64	50c multicolored	1.00	1.00
		Nos. 385-388 (4)	2.06	2.06

Bermuda No. X1, Penny Black — A65

Bermuda #X1 and: 20c, Hill. 25c, "Paid 1" marking on cover. 50c, "Paid 1" marking.

1980, Feb. 25 Litho. *Perf. 13½x14*

389	A65	8c multicolored	.16	.16
390	A65	20c multicolored	.40	.40
391	A65	25c multicolored	.50	.50
392	A65	50c multicolored	1.00	1.00
		Nos. 389-392 (4)	2.06	2.06

Sir Rowland Hill (1795-1879), originator of penny postage.

Tristar-500, London 1980 Emblem — A66

1980, May 6 Litho. *Perf. 13x14*

393	A66	25c shown	.35	.35
394	A66	50c "Orduna," 1926	.70	.70
395	A66	$1 "Delta," 1856	1.50	1.50
396	A66	$2 "Lord Sidmouth," 1818	3.00	3.00
		Nos. 393-396 (4)	5.55	5.55

London 1980 Intl. Stamp Exhib., May 6-14.

Gina Swainson, Miss World, 1979-80, Arms of Bermuda — A67

1980, May 8 *Perf. 14*

397	A67	8c shown	.15	.15
398	A67	20c After crowning ceremony	.35	.35
399	A67	50c Welcome home party	.90	.90
400	A67	$1 In carriage	1.75	1.75
		Nos. 397-400 (4)	3.15	3.15

Queen Mother Elizabeth Birthday Issue
Common Design Type

1980, Aug. 4 Wmk. 373 *Perf. 14*

401	CD330	25c multicolored	.46	.46

Camden, Prime Minister's House A68

1980, Sept. 24 Litho. *Perf. 14*

402	A68	8c View from satellite	.16	.16
403	A68	20c shown	.40	.40
404	A68	25c Princess Hotel, Hamilton	.50	.50
405	A68	50c Government House	1.00	1.00
		Nos. 402-405 (4)	2.06	2.06

Commonwealth Finance Ministers Meeting, Bermuda, Sept.

18th Century Kitchen A69

1981, May 21 Wmk. 373 *Perf. 14*

406	A69	8c shown	.15	.15
407	A69	25c Gathering Easter lilies	.42	.42
408	A69	30c Fisherman	.52	.52
409	A69	40c Stone cutting, 19th cent.	.70	.70
410	A69	50c Onion shipping, 19th cent.	.85	.85
411	A69	$1 Ships, 17th cent.	1.75	1.75
		Nos. 406-411 (6)	4.39	4.39

Royal Wedding Issue
Common Design Type

1981, July 22 Wmk. 373 *Perf. 14*

412	CD331	30c Bouquet	.52	.52
413	CD331	50c Charles	.90	.90
414	CD331	$1 Couple	1.75	1.75
		Nos. 412-414 (3)	3.17	3.17

Girl Helping Blind Man Cross Street — A70

1981, Sept. 28 Litho. *Perf. 14*

415	A70	10c shown	.18	.18
416	A70	25c Kayaking, Paget Island	.48	.48
417	A70	30c Mountain climbing, St. David's Island	.55	.55
418	A70	$1 Duke of Edinburgh	1.90	1.90
		Nos. 415-418 (4)	3.11	3.11

Duke of Edinburgh's Awards, 25th anniv.

Conus Species A71

1982, May 13 Wmk. 373 *Perf. 14*

419	A71	10c shown	.20	.20
420	A71	25c Bursa finlayi	.50	.50
421	A71	30c Sconsia striata	.60	.60
422	A71	$1 Murex pterynotus lightbourni	1.90	1.90
		Nos. 419-422 (4)	3.20	3.20

Bermuda Regiment A72

1982, June 17 Litho. Wmk. 373

423	A72	10c Color guard	.16	.16
424	A72	25c Queen's birthday parade	.40	.40
425	A72	30c Governor inspecting honor guard	.60	.60
426	A72	40c Beating the retreat	.75	.75
427	A72	50c Ceremonial gunners	1.00	1.00
428	A72	$1 Royal visit, 1975	2.00	2.00
		Nos. 423-428 (6)	4.91	4.91

Southampton Fort — A73

1982, Nov. 18 Litho. Wmk. 373

429	A73	10c Charles Fort, vert.	.20	.20
430	A73	25c Pembroks Fort, vert.	.50	.50
431	A73	30c shown	.60	.60
432	A73	$1 Smiths and Pagets Forts	1.90	1.90
		Nos. 429-432 (4)	3.20	3.20

Arms of Sir Edwin Sandys (1561-1629) — A74

Fitted Dinghies — A75

Coats of Arms: 25c, Bermuda Company. 50c, William Herbert, 3rd Earl of Pembroke (1584-1630). $1, Sir George Somers (1554-1610).

1983, Apr. 14 Litho. *Perf. 13½*

433	A74	10c multicolored	.18	.18
434	A74	25c multicolored	.45	.45
435	A74	50c multicolored	.90	.90
436	A74	$1 multicolored	1.75	1.75
		Nos. 433-436 (4)	3.28	3.28

See Nos. 457-460, 474-477.

1983, July 21 Wmk. 373 *Perf. 14*

Old and modern boats.

437	A75	12c multicolored	.22	.22
438	A75	30c multicolored	.55	.55
439	A75	40c multicolored	.70	.70
440	A75	$1 multicolored	1.75	1.75
		Nos. 437-440 (4)	3.22	3.22

Manned Flight Bicentenary A76

Designs: 12c, Curtiss Jenny, 1919 (first flight over Bermuda). 30c, Stinson Pilot Radio, 1930 (first completed US-Bermuda flight). 40c, Cavalier, 1937 (first scheduled passenger flight). $1, USS Los Angeles airship moored to USS Patoka, 1925.

1983, Oct. 13 Litho. *Perf. 14*

441	A76	12c multicolored	.28	.28
442	A76	30c multicolored	.65	.65
443	A76	40c multicolored	.90	.90
444	A76	$1 multicolored	1.75	1.75
		Nos. 441-444 (4)	3.58	3.58

Newspaper and Postal Services, 200th Anniv. — A77

1984, Jan. 26 Litho. *Perf. 14*

445	A77	12c Joseph Stockdale	.22	.22
446	A77	30c First Newspaper	.55	.55
447	A77	40c Stockdale's Postal Service, horiz.	.70	.70
448	A77	$1 "Lady Hammond," horiz.	1.75	1.75
		Nos. 445-448 (4)	3.22	3.22

375th Anniv. of Bermuda Settlement A78

Designs: 12c, Thomas Gates, George Somers. 30c, Jamestown, Virginia, US. 40c, Sea Venture shipwreck. $1, Fleet leaving Plymouth, England.

1984, May 3 Litho. Wmk. 373

449	A78	12c multicolored	.22	.22
450	A78	30c multicolored	.55	.55
451	A78	40c multicolored	.70	.70
452	A78	$1 multicolored	1.75	1.75
	a.	Souv. sheet of 2, #450, 452	5.00	5.00
		Nos. 449-452 (4)	3.22	3.22

1984 Summer Olympics A79

1984, July 19 Litho. *Perf. 14*

453	A79	12c Swimming, vert.	.20	.20
454	A79	30c Track & field	.48	.48
455	A79	40c Equestrian, vert.	.65	.65
456	A79	$1 Sailing	1.65	1.65
		Nos. 453-456 (4)	2.98	2.98

Arms Type of 1983

1984, Sept. 27 Litho. *Perf. 13½*

457	A74	12c Southampton	.20	.20
458	A74	30c Smith	.60	.60
459	A74	40c Devonshire	.75	.75
460	A74	$1 St. George	1.65	1.65
		Nos. 457-460 (4)	3.20	3.20

Architecture, Buttery — A80

1985, Jan. 24 Litho. *Perf. 13½x13*

461	A80	12c Buttery	.35	.35
462	A80	30c Rooftops	.75	.75
463	A80	40c Chimneys	1.00	1.00
464	A80	$1.50 Archway	3.50	3.50
		Nos. 461-464 (4)	5.60	5.60

Audubon Birth Bicentenary A81

BERMUDA

1985, Mar. 21   Wmk. 373   Perf. 14
465	A81	12c Osprey, vert.	.30	.30
466	A81	30c Yellow-crowned night heron, vert.	.75	.75
467	A81	40c Great egret	1.00	1.00
468	A81	$1.50 Bluebird, vert.	3.50	3.50
		Nos. 465-468 (4)	5.55	5.55

Queen Mother 85th Birthday Issue
Common Design Type

Designs: 12c, Queen Consort, 1937. 30c, With grandchildren, 80th birthday. 40c, At Clarence House, 83rd birthday. $1.50, Holding Prince Henry. No. 473, In coach with Prince Charles.

Perf. 14½x14
1985, June 7   Wmk. 384
469	CD336	12c gray, bl & blk	.35	.35
470	CD336	30c multicolored	.75	.75
471	CD336	40c multicolored	1.00	1.00
472	CD336	$1.50 multicolored	3.50	3.50
		Nos. 469-472 (4)	5.60	5.60

Souvenir Sheet
473	CD336	$1 multicolored	4.50	4.50

Arms Type of 1983

Coats of Arms: 12c, James Hamilton, 2nd Marquess of Hamilton (1589-1625). 30c, William Paget, 4th Lord Paget (1572-1629). 40c, Robert Rich, 2nd Earl of Warwick (1587-1658). $1.50, Hamilton, 1957.

1985, Sept. 19   Litho.   Perf. 13½
474	A74	12c multicolored	.30	.30
475	A74	30c multicolored	.75	.75
476	A74	40c multicolored	1.00	1.00
477	A74	$1.50 multicolored	3.75	3.75
		Nos. 474-477 (4)	5.80	5.80

Halley's Comet — A82

1985, Nov. 21   Wmk. 384   Perf. 14½
478	A82	15c Bermuda Archipelago	.38	.38
479	A82	40c Nuremberg Chronicles, 1493	1.00	1.00
480	A82	50c Peter Apian woodcut, 1532	1.25	1.25
481	A82	$1.50 Painting by Samuel Scott (c.1702-72)	3.75	3.75
		Nos. 478-481 (4)	6.38	6.38

Shipwrecks A83

1986   Wmk. 384   Perf. 14
482	A83	3c Constellation, 1943	.15	.15
483	A83	5c Early Riser, 1876	.15	.15
484	A83	7c Madiana, 1903	.15	.15
485	A83	10c Curlew, 1856	.20	.20
486	A83	12c Warwick, 1619	.20	.20
487	A83	15c HMS Vixen, 1890	.30	.30
488	A83	20c San Pedro, 1594	.35	.35
489	A83	25c Alert, 1877	.50	.50
490	A83	40c North Carolina, 1880	.75	.75
491	A83	50c Mark Antonie, 1777	1.00	1.10
492	A83	60c Mary Celestia, 1864	1.10	1.10
493	A83	$1 L'Herminie, 1839	1.75	1.75
494	A83	$1.50 Caesar, 1818	2.75	2.75
495	A83	$2 Lord Amherst, 1778	3.50	3.50
496	A83	$3 Minerva, 1849	5.50	5.50
497	A83	$5 Caraquet, 1923	9.00	9.00
498	A83	$8 HMS Pallas, 1783	14.50	14.50
		Nos. 482-498 (17)	41.85	41.95

Nos. 493, 495-496 exist inscribed "1989." Nos. 482, 488, "1990."
See #545-546. For surcharges see #598-600.

Inscribed "1992"
1992   Litho.   Wmk. 373   Perf. 14
485a	A83	10c	.18	.18
487a	A83	15c	.28	.28
488a	A83	20c	.36	.36
489a	A83	25c	.45	.45
492a	A83	60c	1.10	1.10
497a	A83	$5	9.25	9.25
498a	A83	$8	14.75	14.75
		Nos. 485a-498a (7)	26.37	26.37

Queen Elizabeth II 60th Birthday
Common Design Type

Designs: 15c, Age 3. 40c, With the Earl of Rosebury, Oaks May Meeting, Epsom, 1954. 50c, With Prince Philip, state visit, 1979. 60c, At the British embassy in Paris, state visit, 1972. $1.50, Visiting Crown Agents' offices, 1983.

1986, Apr. 21   Wmk. 384   Perf. 14½
499	CD337	15c scar, blk & sil	.24	.24
500	CD337	40c ultra & multi	.65	.65
501	CD337	50c green & multi	.80	.80
502	CD337	60c violet & multi	.95	.95
503	CD337	$1.50 rose vio & multi	2.50	2.50
		Nos. 499-503 (5)	5.14	5.14

AMERIPEX '86 — A84

1986, May 22   Perf. 14
504	A84	15c No. 452a	.24	.24
505	A84	40c No. 307	.65	.65
506	A84	50c No. 441	.80	.80
507	A84	$1 No. 339	1.65	1.65
		Nos. 504-507 (4)	3.34	3.34

Souvenir Sheet
508	A84	1.50 Statue of Liberty, S.S. Queen of Bermuda	4.50	4.50

Statue of Liberty, cent.

No. 378 Surcharged
Perf. 14x14½
1986, Dec. 4   Photo.   Wmk. 373
509	A62	90c on $3 multi	3.00	3.00

Exists with double surcharge.

Transport Railway, c. 1931-1947 — A85

Wmk. 373
1987, Jan. 22   Litho.   Perf. 14
510	A85	15c Front Street, c. 1940	.24	.24
511	A85	40c Springfield Trestle	.65	.65
512	A85	50c No. 101, Bailey's Bay Sta.	.80	.80
513	A85	$1.50 No. 31, ship Prince David	2.50	2.50
		Nos. 510-513 (4)	4.19	4.19

Paintings by Winslow Homer (1836-1910) A86

1987, Apr. 30   Perf. 14½
514	A86	15c Bermuda Settlers, 1901	.28	.28
515	A86	30c Bermuda, 1900	.55	.55
516	A86	40c Bermuda Landscape, 1901	.75	.75
517	A86	50c Inland Water, 1901	.95	.95
518	A86	$1.50 Salt Kettle, 1899	3.00	3.00
		Nos. 514-518 (5)	5.53	5.53

Booklet Stamps
519	A86	40c like 15c	.65	.65
520	A86	40c like 30c	.65	.65
521	A86	40c like No. 516	.65	.65
522	A86	40c like 50c	.65	.65
523	A86	40c like $1.50	.65	.65
a.		Bklt. pane, 2 each #519-523	6.50	

Nos. 519-523 printed in strips of 5 within pane. "ER" at lower left.

Intl. Flights Inauguration — A87

1987, June 18   Perf. 14
524	A87	15c Sikorsky S-42B, 1937	.50	.50
525	A87	40c Shorts S-23 Cavalier	1.40	1.40
526	A87	50c S-42B Bermuda Clipper	1.65	1.65
527	A87	$1.50 Cavalier, Bermuda Clipper	5.00	5.00
		Nos. 524-527 (4)	8.55	8.55

Bermuda Telephone Company, Cent. — A88

1987, Oct. 1   Litho.   Wmk. 384
528	A88	15c Telephone poles on wagon	.25	.25
529	A88	40c Operators	.70	.70
530	A88	50c Telephones	.85	.85
531	A88	$1.50 Satellite, fiber optics, world	2.50	2.50
		Nos. 528-531 (4)	4.30	4.30

Horse-drawn Commercial Vehicles — A89

1988, Mar. 3   Litho.   Perf. 14
532	A89	15c Mail wagon, c. 1869	.28	.28
533	A89	40c Open cart, c. 1823	.75	.75
534	A89	50c Closed cart, c. 1823	.95	.95
535	A89	$1.50 Two-wheel wagon, c. 1930	2.75	2.75
		Nos. 532-535 (4)	4.73	4.73

Old Garden Roses — A90

1988, Apr. 21   Wmk. 373
536	A90	15c Old blush	.26	.26
537	A90	30c Anna Olivier	.52	.52
538	A90	40c Rosa chinensis semperflorens, vert.	.70	.70
539	A90	50c Archduke Charles	.90	.90
540	A90	$1.50 Rosa chinensis viridiflora, vert.	2.75	2.75
		Nos. 536-540 (5)	5.13	5.13

See Nos. 561-575.

Lloyds of London, 300th Anniv.
Common Design Type

Designs: 18c, Loss of the H.M.S. Lutine, 1799. 50c, Cable ship Sentinel, horiz. 60c, The Bermuda, Hamilton, 1931, horiz. $2, Valerian, lost during a hurricane, 1926.

1988, Oct. 13   Litho.   Wmk. 384
541	CD341	18c multi	.32	.32
542	CD341	50c multi	.90	.90
543	CD341	60c multi	1.10	1.10
544	CD341	$2 multi	3.50	3.50
		Nos. 541-544 (4)	5.82	5.82

Shipwreck Type of 1986
1988   Litho.   Wmk. 384   Perf. 14
545	A83	18c like 7c	.35	.35
546	A83	70c like $1.50	1.40	1.40

Issue dates: 18c, Sept. 22; 70c, Oct. 27.

Military Uniforms — A91

Designs: 18c, Devonshire Parish Militia, 1812. 50c, 71st Regiment Highlander, 1831-34. 60c, Cameron Highlander, 1942. $2, Troop of Horse, 1774.

1988, Nov. 10   Wmk. 373   Perf. 14½
547	A91	18c multicolored	.30	.30
548	A91	50c multicolored	.85	.85
549	A91	60c multicolored	1.00	1.00
550	A91	$2 multicolored	3.50	3.50
		Nos. 547-550 (4)	5.65	5.65

Ferry Service A92

1989   Litho.   Wmk. 384   Perf. 14
551	A92	18c Corona	.30	.30
552	A92	50c Rowboat ferry	.85	.85
553	A92	60c St. George's Ferry	1.00	1.00
554	A92	$2 Laconia	3.50	3.50
		Nos. 551-554 (4)	5.65	5.65

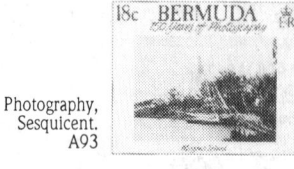

Photography, Sesquicent. A93

Perf. 14x14½
1989, May 11   Litho.   Wmk. 373
555	A93	18c Morgan's Is.	.35	.35
556	A93	30c Front Street, Hamilton (cannon in square)	.60	.60
557	A93	50c Front Street (seascape)	1.00	1.00
558	A93	60c Crow Lane, Hamilton Harbor	1.20	1.20
559	A93	70c Hamilton Harbor (shipbuilding)	1.40	1.40
560	A93	$1 Dockyard	2.00	2.00
		Nos. 555-560 (6)	6.55	6.55

Old Garden Roses Type of 1988
1989, July 13   Perf. 14
561	A90	18c Agrippina	.35	.35
562	A90	30c Smith's Parish	.60	.60
563	A90	50c Champney's pink cluster	1.00	1.00
564	A90	60c Rosette delizy	1.20	1.20
565	A90	$1.50 Rosa bracteata	3.00	3.00
		Nos. 561-565 (5)	6.15	6.15

Nos. 561-562 vert.

Old Garden Roses Type of 1988 with Royal Cipher Instead of Queen's Silhouette
1989, July 13   Booklet Stamps
566	A90	50c like No. 562	1.00	1.00
567	A90	50c like No. 540	1.00	1.00
568	A90	50c like No. 561	1.00	1.00
569	A90	50c like No. 538	1.00	1.00
570	A90	50c like No. 563	1.00	1.00
571	A90	50c like No. 536	1.00	.85
572	A90	50c like No. 564	1.00	1.00
573	A90	50c like No. 537	1.00	1.00
574	A90	50c like No. 565	1.00	1.00
575	A90	50c like No. 539	1.00	1.00
a.		Bkt. pane of 10, #566-575	10.00	
		Nos. 566-575 (10)	10.00	10.00

Bermuda Library, 150th Anniv. — A94

1989, Sept. 14   Perf. 13½x14
576	A94	18c Hamilton Main Library	.30	.30
577	A94	50c St. George's, The Old Rectory	.85	.85
578	A94	60c Springfield, Sommerset Library	1.00	1.00
579	A94	$2 Cabinet Building	3.50	3.50
		Nos. 576-579 (4)	5.65	5.65

BERMUDA

Commonwealth Postal Conference — A95

1989, Nov. 3   Wmk. 384   Perf. 14

580	A95	18c No. 1	.30	.30
581	A95	50c No. 2	.85	.85
582	A95	60c Type A4	1.00	1.00
583	A95	$2 No. 6	3.50	3.50
		Nos. 580-583 (4)	5.65	5.65

For overprints see Nos. 594-597.

Fairylands, Bermuda, c. 1890, by Ross Sterling Turner — A96

Paintings: 50c, *Shinebone Alley, c. 1953,* by Ogden M. Pleissner. 60c, *Salt Kettle, 1916,* by Prosper Senate. $2, *St. George's, 1934,* by Jack Bush.

1990, Apr. 19

590	A96	18c multicolored	.30	.30
591	A96	50c multicolored	.85	.85
592	A96	60c multicolored	1.00	1.00
593	A96	$2 multicolored	3.50	3.50
		Nos. 590-593 (4)	5.65	5.65

Nos. 580-583 Overprinted *Stamp World London 90*

1990, May 3

594	A95	18c multicolored	.35	.35
595	A95	50c multicolored	1.00	1.00
596	A95	60c multicolored	1.20	1.20
597	A95	$2 multicolored	4.00	4.00
		Nos. 594-597 (4)	6.55	6.55

Stamp World London '90.

Nos. 486, 491, 494 Surcharged 80c

1990, Aug. 13

598	A83	30c on 12c No. 486	.55	.55
599	A83	55c on 50c No. 491	1.00	1.00
600	A83	80c on $1.50 No. 494	1.50	1.50
		Nos. 598-600 (3)	3.05	3.05

Nova Scotia-Bermuda Cable, Cent. — A97

1990, Oct. 18   Litho.   Unwmk.

601	A97	20c Office	.35	.35
602	A97	55c Cableship SS Westmeath	1.00	1.00
603	A97	70c Radio station, 1928	1.25	1.25
604	A97	$2 Cableship Sir Eric Sharp	3.50	3.50
		Nos. 601-604 (4)	6.10	6.10

Nos. 601-602 with Added Inscription: "BUSH-MAJOR / 16 MARCH 1991"

1991, Mar.   Unwmk.   Perf. 14

605	A97	20c like #601	.40	.40
606	A97	55c like #602	1.10	1.10

Carriages A98

Designs: 20c, Two-seat pony cart, c. 1805. 30c, Varnished rockaway, c. 1830. 55c, Vis-a-Vis Victoria, c. 1895. 70c, Semi-formal phaeton, c. 1900. 80c, Pony runabout, c. 1905. $1, Ladies' phaeton, c. 1910.

Perf. 14x14½

1991, Mar. 21   Litho.   Wmk. 373

607	A98	20c green & multi	.40	.40
608	A98	30c bl gray & multi	.60	.60
609	A98	55c dk car & multi	1.10	1.10
610	A98	70c blue & multi	1.40	1.40
611	A98	80c yel org & multi	1.60	1.60
612	A98	$1 dk gray & multi	2.00	2.00
		Nos. 607-612 (6)	7.10	7.10

Paintings A99

Designs: 20c, Bermuda by Prosper Senat, vert. 55c, Bermuda Cottage by Frank Allison. 70c, Old Maid's Lane by Jack Bush, vert. $2, St. George's by Ogden M. Pleissner.

Perf. 14x13½

1991, May 16   Litho.   Wmk. 373

613	A99	20c multicolored	.40	.40
614	A99	55c multicolored	1.10	1.10
615	A99	70c multicolored	1.40	1.40
616	A99	$2 multicolored	4.00	4.00
		Nos. 613-616 (4)	6.90	6.90

Elizabeth & Philip, Birthdays
Common Design Types

1991, June 20   Wmk. 384   Perf. 14½

617	CD346	55c multicolored	1.10	1.10
618	CD345	70c multicolored	1.40	1.40
a.		Pair, #617-618 + label	2.50	2.50

Bermuda in World War II A100

Designs: 20c, Floating drydock. 55c, Kindley Air Field. 70c, Trans-atlantic air route, Boeing 314. $2, Censored trans-atlantic mail.

1991, Sept. 19   Wmk. 373   Perf. 14

619	A100	20c multicolored	.40	.40
620	A100	55c multicolored	1.10	1.10
621	A100	70c multicolored	1.40	1.40
622	A100	$2 multicolored	4.00	4.00
		Nos. 619-622 (4)	6.90	6.90

Queen Elizabeth II's Accession to the Throne, 40th Anniv.
Common Design Type

1992, Feb. 6

623	CD349	20c multicolored	.40	.40
624	CD349	30c multicolored	.60	.60
625	CD349	55c multicolored	1.10	1.10
626	CD349	70c multicolored	1.40	1.40
627	CD349	$1 multicolored	2.00	2.00
		Nos. 623-627 (5)	5.50	5.50

Age of Exploration — A101

Artifacts: 25c, Rings, medallion. 35c, Ink wells. 60c, Gold pieces. 75c, Bishop button, crucifix. 85c, Pearl earrings and buttons. $1, 8-real coin, jug and measuring cups.

1992, July 23   Perf. 13½

628	A101	25c multicolored	.50	.50
629	A101	35c multicolored	.70	.70
630	A101	60c multicolored	1.20	1.20
631	A101	75c multicolored	1.50	1.50
632	A101	85c multicolored	1.70	1.70
633	A101	$1 multicolored	2.00	2.00
		Nos. 628-633 (6)	7.60	7.60

Stained Glass Windows — A102

Designs: 25c, Ship wreck. 60c, Birds in tree. 75c, St. Francis feeding bird. $2, Seashells.

1992, Sept. 24   Perf. 14

634	A102	25c multicolored	.50	.50
635	A102	60c multicolored	1.20	1.20
636	A102	75c multicolored	1.50	1.50
637	A102	$2 multicolored	4.00	4.00
		Nos. 634-637 (4)	7.20	7.20

7th World Congress of Kennel Clubs — A103

Perf. 13½x14, 14x13½

1992, Nov. 12   Litho.   Wmk. 373

638	A103	25c German shepherd	.48	.48
639	A103	35c Irish setter	.65	.65
640	A103	60c Whippet, vert.	1.15	1.15
641	A103	75c Border terrier, vert.	1.40	1.40
642	A103	85c Pomeranian, vert.	1.60	1.60
643	A103	$1 Schipperke, vert.	1.85	1.85
		Nos. 638-643 (6)	7.13	7.13

Tourist Posters
A104   A105

1993, Feb. 25   Wmk. 373   Perf. 14

644	A104	25c Cyclist, carriage, ship	.48	.48
645	A105	60c Golf course	1.15	1.15
646	A105	75c Coastline	1.40	1.40
647	A104	$2 Dancers	3.70	3.70
		Nos. 644-647 (4)	6.73	6.73

Royal Air Force, 75th Anniv.
Common Design Type

Designs: 25c, Consolidated Catalina. 60c, Supermarine Spitfire. 75c, Bristol Beaufighter. $2, Handley Page Halifax.

1993, Apr. 1

648	CD350	25c multicolored	.48	.48
649	CD350	60c multicolored	1.15	1.15
650	CD350	75c multicolored	1.40	1.40
651	CD350	$2 multicolored	3.70	3.70
		Nos. 648-651 (4)	6.73	6.73

Duchesse de Brabant Rose, Bee — A106

1993, Apr. 1   Wmk. 384
Booklet Stamps

652	A106	10c green & multi	.20	.20
653	A106	25c violet & multi	.48	.48
a.		Booklet pane of 5	2.40	
654	A106	50c sepia & multi	1.00	1.00
a.		Booklet pane, 2 #652, 3 #654	3.50	
655	A106	60c vermilion & multi	1.10	1.10
a.		Booklet pane of 5	5.50	
		Nos. 652-655 (4)	2.78	2.78

Hamilton, Bicent. — A107

Designs: 25c, Modern skyline. 60c, Front Street, ships at left. 75c, Front Street, horse carts. $2, Hamilton Harbor, 1823.

Perf. 14½

1993, Sept. 16   Litho.   Wmk. 373

656	A107	25c multicolored	.48	.48
657	A107	60c multicolored	1.10	1.10
658	A107	75c multicolored	1.40	1.40
659	A107	$2 multicolored	3.75	3.75
		Nos. 656-659 (4)	6.73	6.73

Furness Lines — A108

Designs: 25c, Furness Liv-Aboard Bermuda cruises, vert. 60c, SS Queen of Bermuda entering port. 75c, SS Queen of Bermuda, SS Ocean Monarch. $2, Starlit night aboard ship, vert.

Perf. 15x14, 14x15

1994, Jan. 20   Litho.   Wmk. 373

660	A108	25c multicolored	.48	.48
661	A108	60c multicolored	1.10	1.10
662	A108	75c multicolored	1.40	1.40
663	A108	$2 multicolored	3.75	3.75
		Nos. 660-663 (4)	6.73	6.73

Royal Visit — A109

Designs: 25c, Queen Elizabeth II. 60c, Queen Elizabeth II, Duke of Edinburgh. 75c, Royal yacht Britannia.

1994, Mar. 9   Perf. 13½   Litho.   Wmk. 373

664	A109	25c multicolored	.48	.48
665	A109	60c multicolored	1.10	1.10
666	A109	75c multicolored	1.50	1.50
		Nos. 664-666 (3)	3.08	3.08

Flowering Fruits A110

1994-95   Litho.   Wmk. 373   Perf. 14

668	A110	5c Peach	.15	.15
669	A110	7c Fig	.15	.15
670	A110	10c Calabash, vert.	.20	.20
671	A110	15c Natal plum	.30	.30
672	A110	18c Locust & wild honey	.35	.35
673	A110	20c Pomegranate	.38	.38
674	A110	25c Mulberry, vert.	.48	.48
675	A110	35c Grape, vert.	.70	.70
676	A110	55c Orange, vert.	1.10	1.10
677	A110	60c Surinam cherry	1.25	1.25
678	A110	75c Loquat	1.50	1.50
679	A110	90c Sugar apple	1.75	1.75
680	A110	$1 Prickly pear, vert.	2.00	2.00
681	A110	$2 Paw paw	4.00	4.00
682	A110	$3 Bay grape	6.00	6.00
683	A110	$5 Banana, vert.	10.00	10.00
684	A110	$8 Lemon	16.00	16.00
		Nos. 668-684 (17)	46.31	46.31

No. 672 exists dated "1996." Nos. 668, 671-674, 678-680 dated "1998."

Issued: 5c, 7c, 15c, 20c, $8, 7/14/94; 10c, 25c, 35c, 55c, $1, $5, 10/6/94; 18c, 60c, 75c, 90c, $2, $3, 3/23/95.

BERMUDA

Hospital Care, Cent. — A111

1994, Sept. 15   *Perf. 15x14*
685	A111	25c Child birth	.48	.48
686	A111	60c Dialysis	1.10	1.10
687	A111	75c Emergency	1.50	1.50
688	A111	$2 Therapy	4.00	4.00
		Nos. 685-688 (4)	7.08	7.08

Christmas — A112

1994, Nov. 10   *Perf. 14x15*
689	A112	25c Gombey dancers	.48	.48
690	A112	60c Carollers	1.10	1.10
691	A112	75c Marching band	1.50	1.50
692	A112	$2 Nat'l. dance group	4.00	4.00
		Nos. 689-692 (4)	7.08	7.08

Decimalization, 25th Anniv. — A113

Stamps, 1970 coins: 25c, #255, one cent. 60c, #259, five cents. 75c, #262, ten cents. $2, #324, twenty-five cents.

Wmk. 373
1995, Feb. 6   Litho.   *Perf. 14*
693	A113	25c multicolored	.48	.48
694	A113	60c multicolored	1.10	1.10
695	A113	75c multicolored	1.50	1.50
696	A113	$2 multicolored	4.00	4.00
		Nos. 693-696 (4)	7.08	7.08

Outdoor Celebrations — A114

1995, May 30   Litho.   Wmk. 373   *Perf. 14x15*
697	A114	25c Kite flying	.50	.50
698	A114	60c Majorettes	1.10	1.10
699	A114	75c Portuguese dancers	1.50	1.50
700	A114	$2 Floral float	4.00	4.00
		Nos. 697-700 (4)	7.10	7.10

Parliament, 375th Anniv. — A115

1995, Nov. 3   Litho.   Wmk. 373   *Perf. 14x13½*
701	A115	25c blue & multi	.50	.50
702	A115	$1 green & multi	2.00	2.00
		See No. 731.		

Designs: 25c, $1, Bermuda coat of arms.

Military Bases A116

Force insignia and: 20c, Ordnance Island Submarine Base. 25c, Royal Naval Dockyard. 60c, Fort Bell and Kindley Field. 75c, Darrell's Island. 90c, US Navy Operating Base. $1, Canadian Forces Station, Daniel's Head.

1995, Dec. 4   *Perf. 14*
703	A116	20c multicolored	.40	.40
704	A116	25c multicolored	.50	.50
705	A116	60c multicolored	1.25	1.25
706	A116	75c multicolored	1.50	1.50
707	A116	90c multicolored	1.75	1.75
708	A116	$1 multicolored	2.00	2.00
		Nos. 703-708 (6)	7.40	7.40

Modern Olympic Games, Cent. — A117

Wmk. 384
1996, May 21   Litho.   *Perf. 14*
709	A117	25c Track & field	.50	.50
710	A117	30c Cycling	.60	.60
711	A117	65c Sailing	1.30	1.30
712	A117	80c Equestrian	1.60	1.60
		Nos. 709-712 (4)	4.00	4.00

CAPEX '96 — A118

Methods of transportation: 25c, Sommerset Express, c. 1900. 60c, Bermuda Railway, 1930's. 75c, First bus, 1946. $2, Early sightseeing bus, c.1947.

1996, June 7   *Perf. 13½x14*   Wmk. 373
713	A118	25c multicolored	.50	.50
714	A118	60c multicolored	1.20	1.20
715	A118	75c multicolored	1.50	1.50
716	A118	$2 multicolored	4.00	4.00
		Nos. 713-716 (4)	7.20	7.20

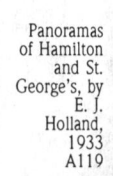

Panoramas of Hamilton and St. George's, by E. J. Holland, 1933 A119

Hamilton, looking across water from Bostock Hill: No. 717, Palm trees, Furness Line ship coming through Two Rock Passage. No. 718, House, buildings on other side. No. 719, Sailboats on water, Princess Hotel. No. 720, Island, Bermudiana Hotel, Cathedral. No. 721, Coral roads on hillside, city of Hamilton.

St. George's, looking across water from St. David's: No. 722, Island, harbor. No. 723, Sailboat, buildings along shore. No. 724, Sailboat, St. George's Hotel, buildings. No. 725, Hillside, ship. No. 726, Homes on hill top, passage out of harbor.

1996, May 21   *Perf. 14x14½*   Wmk. 373
Booklet Stamps
717	A119	60c multicolored	1.20	1.20
718	A119	60c multicolored	1.20	1.20
719	A119	60c multicolored	1.20	1.20
720	A119	60c multicolored	1.20	1.20
721	A119	60c multicolored	1.20	1.20
a.		Strip of 5, #717-721	6.00	6.00
722	A119	60c multicolored	1.20	1.20
723	A119	60c multicolored	1.20	1.20
724	A119	60c multicolored	1.20	1.20
725	A119	60c multicolored	1.20	1.20
726	A119	60c multicolored	1.20	1.20
a.		Strip of 5, #722-726	6.00	6.00
b.		Booklet pane, #721a, 726a	12.00	
		Complete booklet, #726b	12.00	

Lighthouses — A120

Designs: 30c, Hog Fish Beacon. 65c, Gibbs Hill Lighthouse. 80c, St. David's Lighthouse. $2, North Rock Beacon.

1996, Aug. 15   *Perf. 14x13½*   Litho.   Wmk. 373
727	A120	30c multicolored	.60	.60
728	A120	65c multicolored	1.30	1.30
729	A120	80c multicolored	1.60	1.60
730	A120	$2 multicolored	4.00	4.00
		Nos. 727-730 (4)	7.50	7.50
		See Nos. 737-740.		

Bermuda Coat of Arms Type of 1995
Inscribed "Commonwealth Finance Ministers Meeting"
Perf. 14x13½
1996, Sept. 24   Litho.   Wmk. 373
731	A115	$1 red & multi	2.00	2.00

Queen Elizabeth II — A121

1996, Nov. 7
732	A121	$22 blue & org brn	44.00	44.00

Architectural Heritage — A122

Wmk. 384
1996, Nov. 28   Litho.   *Perf. 14*
733	A122	30c Waterville	.60	.60
734	A122	65c Bridge House	1.30	1.30
735	A122	80c Fannie Fox's Cottage	1.60	1.60
736	A122	$2.50 Palmetto House	5.00	5.00
		Nos. 733-736 (4)	8.50	8.50

Lighthouse Type of 1996 Redrawn
Wmk. 373
1997, Feb. 12   Litho.   *Perf. 14*
737	A120	30c Like #727	.60	.60
738	A120	65c Like #728	1.30	1.30
739	A120	80c Like #729	1.60	1.60
740	A120	$2.50 Like #730	5.00	5.00
		Nos. 737-740 (4)	8.50	8.50

Nos. 737-740 each have Hong Kong '97 emblem. No. 738 inscribed "Gibbs Hill Lighthouse c. 1900." No. 739 inscribed "St. David's Lighthouse c. 1900."

Birds A123

Designs: 30c, White-tailed tropicbird. 60c, White-tailed tropicbird, adult, chick, vert. 80c, Cahow, adult, chick, vert. $2.50, Cahow.

Wmk. 384
1997, Apr. 17   Litho.   *Perf. 14*
741	A123	30c multicolored	.60	.60
742	A123	60c multicolored	1.20	1.20
743	A123	80c multicolored	1.60	1.60
744	A123	$2.50 multicolored	5.00	5.00
		Nos. 741-744 (4)	8.40	8.40

Queen Elizabeth II and Prince Philip, 50th Wedding Anniv. A124

Perf. 14x14½
1997, Oct. 9   Litho.   Wmk. 373
745	A124	30c Queen, crowd	.60	.60
746	A124	$2 Queen, Prince	4.00	4.00
a.		Souvenir sheet of 2, #745-746	4.60	4.60

Education in Bermuda A125

Designs: 30c, Man, children using blocks. 40c, Teacher, students with map. 60c, Boys holding sports trophy. 65c, Students in front of Berkeley Institute. 80c, Students working in lab. 90c, Students in graduation gowns.

Wmk. 384
1997, Dec. 18   Litho.   *Perf. 14*
747	A125	30c multicolored	.60	.60
748	A125	40c multicolored	.80	.80
749	A125	60c multicolored	1.20	1.20
750	A125	65c multicolored	1.30	1.30
751	A125	80c multicolored	1.60	1.60
752	A125	90c multicolored	1.80	1.80
		Nos. 747-752 (6)	7.30	7.30

Diana, Princess of Wales (1961-97)
Common Design Type
Various portraits: a. 30c. b, 40c. c, 65c. d, 80c.

Perf. 14x14½
1998, Mar. 31   Litho.   Wmk. 373
753	CD355	Sheet of 4, #a.-d.	4.75	4.75

No. 753 sold for $2.15 + 25c, with surtax from international sales being donated to the Princess Diana Memorial Fund and surtax from national sales being donated to designated local charity.

Paintings of the Islands A126

Designs: 30c, Fox's Cottage, St. David's. 40c, East Side, Somerset. 65c, Long Bay Road, Somerset. $2, Flatts Village.

1998, June 4   *Perf. 13½x14*
754	A126	30c multicolored	.60	.60
755	A126	40c multicolored	.80	.80
756	A126	65c multicolored	1.25	1.25
757	A126	$2 multicolored	3.90	3.90
		Nos. 754-757 (4)	6.55	6.55

Hospitality for Tourists in Bermuda — A127

Designs: 25c, Carriage ride. 30c, Golfer at registration desk. 65c, Maid leaving flowers on hotel bed. 75c, Chefs preparing food. 80c, Waiter serving couple. 90c, Singer, bartender, guests.

1998   Litho.   Wmk. 384   *Perf. 14½*
758	A127	25c multicolored	.50	.50
759	A127	30c multicolored	.60	.60
760	A127	65c multicolored	1.25	1.25
761	A127	75c multicolored	1.50	1.50

BERMUDA — BHUTAN

762	A127 80c multicolored	1.60	1.60
763	A127 90c multicolored	1.75	1.75
	Nos. 758-763 (6)	7.20	7.20

Bermuda's Botanical Gardens, Cent. — A128

1998	Litho.	Wmk. 373	Perf. 14
764	A128 30c Agave attenuata	.60	.60
765	A128 65c Bermuda palmetto tree	1.25	1.25
766	A128 $1 Banyan tree	2.00	2.00
767	A128 $2 Cedar tree	4.00	4.00
	Nos. 764-767 (4)	7.85	7.85

WAR TAX STAMPS

No. 42 Overprinted **WAR TAX**

1918	Wmk. 3		Perf. 14
MR1	A11 1p rose red	.50	.40

No. 42a Overprinted **WAR TAX**

1920			
MR2	A11 1p carmine	.45	.80

BHUTAN
bü-'tän

LOCATION — Eastern Himalayas
GOVT. — Kingdom
AREA — 18,000 sq. mi.
POP. — 1,250,000 (est. 1983)
CAPITAL — Thimphu

100 Chetrum = 1 Ngultrum or Rupee

Catalogue values for all unused stamps in this country are for Never Hinged items.

Postal Runner — A1

Designs: 3ch, 70ch, Archer. 5ch, 1.30nu, Yak. 15ch, Map of Bhutan, portrait of Druk Gyalpo (Dragon King) Ugyen Wangchuk (1867-1902) and Paro Dzong (fortress-monastery). 33ch, Postal runner. All horiz. except 2ch and 33ch.

	Perf. 14x14½, 14½x14		
1962	Litho.		Unwmk.
1	A1 2ch red & gray	.15	.15
2	A1 3ch red & ultra	.20	.20
3	A1 5ch green & brown	.80	.80
4	A1 15ch red, blk & org yel	.15	.15
5	A1 33ch blue grn & lil	.20	.20
6	A1 70ch dp ultra & lt blue	.60	.60
7	A1 1.30nu blue & black	1.65	1.65
	Nos. 1-7 (7)	3.75	3.75

Nos. 1-7 were issued for inland use in April, 1962, and became valid for international mail on Oct. 10, 1962.
For overprint and surcharges see #42, 72-73.

Refugee Year Emblem and Arms of Bhutan — A2

1962, Oct. 10		Perf. 14½x14
8	A2 1nu dk blue & dk car rose	.65 .65
9	A2 2nu yel grn & red lilac	1.25 1.25

World Refugee Year. For surcharges see #68-69.

Equipment of Ancient Warrior — A3

Boy Filling Grain Box and Wheat Emblem — A4

1963	Unwmk.	Perf. 14x14½
10	A3 33ch multicolored	.20 .20
11	A3 70ch multicolored	.40 .40
12	A3 1.30nu multicolored	.75 .75
	Nos. 10-12 (3)	1.35 1.35

Bhutan's membership in Colombo Plan.

1963, July 15		Perf. 13½x14
13	A4 20ch lt blue, yel & red brn	.15 .15
14	A4 1.50nu rose lil, bl & red brn	.65 .65

FAO "Freedom from Hunger" campaign. For surcharge see No. 117M.

Masked Dancer A5

Various Bhutanese Dancers (Five Designs; 2ch, 5ch, 20ch, 1nu, 1.30nu vert.)

	Perf. 14½x14, 14x14½		
1964, Apr. 16			
15	A5 2ch multicolored	.15	.15
16	A5 3ch multicolored	.15	.15
17	A5 5ch multicolored	.15	.15
18	A5 20ch multicolored	.15	.15
19	A5 33ch multicolored	.15	.15
20	A5 70ch multicolored	.20	.20
21	A5 1nu multicolored	.35	.35
22	A5 1.30nu multicolored	.40	.40
23	A5 2nu multicolored	.65	.65
	Nos. 15-23 (9)	2.35	2.35

For surcharges see Nos. 70-71, 74-75, 129A, 129G. For overprints see Nos. C1-C3, C11-C13.

Stone Throwing — A6

Sport: 5ch, 33ch, Boxing. 1nu, 3nu, Archery. 2nu, Soccer.

1964, Oct. 10	Litho.	Perf. 14½
24	A6 2ch emerald & multi	.15 .15
25	A6 5ch orange & multi	.15 .15
26	A6 15ch brt citron & multi	.15 .15
27	A6 33ch rose lil & multi	.15 .15
28	A6 1nu multicolored	.40 .40
29	A6 2nu rose lilac & multi	.60 .60
30	A6 3nu lt blue & multi	.90 .90
	Nos. 24-30 (7)	2.50 2.50

18th Olympic Games, Tokyo, Oct. 10-25. See No. B4.
Nos. 24-30 exist imperf. Value $4.

Flags of the World at Half-mast — A7

1964, Nov. 22	Unwmk.	Perf. 14½
	Flags in Original Colors	
31	A7 33ch steel gray	.15 .15
32	A7 1nu silver	.45 .45
33	A7 3nu gold	1.10 1.10
a.	Souv. sheet, perf. 13½ or imperf.	2.75 2.75
	Nos. 31-33 (3)	1.70 1.70

Issued in memory of those who died in the service of their country. Nos. 31-33 exist imperf.
No. 33a contains 2 stamps similar to Nos. 32-33.
For overprints see Nos. 44, 46.

Flowers — A8

1965, Jan. 6	Litho.	Perf. 13
34	A8 2ch Primrose	.15 .15
35	A8 5ch Gentian	.15 .15
36	A8 15ch Primrose	.15 .15
37	A8 33ch Gentian	.15 .15
38	A8 50ch Rhododendron	.15 .15
39	A8 75ch Peony	.20 .20
40	A8 1nu Rhododendron	.20 .20
41	A8 2nu Peony	.40 .40
	Nos. 34-41 (8)	1.55 1.55

For overprints see Nos. 43, 45, C4-C5, C14-C15.

Nos. 5, 40, 32, 41 and 33 Overprinted: "WINSTON CHURCHILL 1874-1965"

1965, Feb. 27		
42	A1 33ch bl grn & lilac	.15 .15
43	A8 1nu pink, grn & dk gray	.40 .40
44	A7 1nu silver & multi	.40 .40
45	A8 2nu sepia, yel & grn	.75 .75
46	A7 3nu gold & multi	1.00 1.00
	Nos. 42-46 (5)	2.70 2.70

Issued in memory of Sir Winston Churchill (1874-1965). The overprint is in three lines on Nos. 42-43 and 45; in two lines on Nos. 44 and 46.
Nos. 44 and 46 exist imperf. Value, both, $4.50.

Skyscraper, Pagoda and World's Fair Emblem — A9

Designs: 10ch, 2nu, Pieta by Michelangelo and statue of Khmer Buddha. 20ch, Skyline of NYC and Bhutanese village. 33ch, George Washington Bridge, NY, and foot bridge, Bhutan.

1965, Apr. 21	Litho.	Perf. 14½
47	A9 1ch blue & multi	.15 .15
48	A9 10ch green & multi	.15 .15
49	A9 20ch rose lilac & multi	.15 .15
50	A9 33ch bister & multi	.15 .15
51	A9 1.50nu bister & multi	.50 .50
52	A9 2nu multicolored	.65 .65
a.	Souv. sheet, perf. 13½ or imperf.	2.75 2.75
	Nos. 47-52 (6)	1.75 1.75

Nos. 47-52 exist imperf.; value $3.50.
No. 52a contains two stamps similar to Nos. 51-52.
For overprints see #87-87B, C6-C10, C16-C20.

Telstar, Short-wave Radio and ITU Emblem — A10

Designs (ITU Emblem and): 2nu, Telstar and Morse key. 3nu, Syncom and ear phones.

1966, Mar. 2	Litho.	Perf. 14½
53	A10 35ch multicolored	.15 .15
54	A10 2nu multicolored	.55 .55
55	A10 3nu multicolored	.75 .75
	Nos. 53-55 (3)	1.45 1.45

Cent. (in 1965) of the ITU. Souvenir sheets exist containing two stamps similar to Nos. 54-55, perf. 13½ and imperf. Value, 2 sheets, $5.

Leopard — A11

Animals: 1ch, 4nu, Asiatic black bear. 4ch, 2nu, Pigmy hog. 8ch, 75ch, Tiger. 10ch, 1.50nu, Dhole (Asiatic hunting dog). 1nu, 5nu, Takin (goat).

1966, Mar. 24	Litho.	Perf. 13
56	A11 1ch yellow & blk	.15 .15
57	A11 2ch pale grn & blk	.15 .15
58	A11 4ch lt citron & blk	.15 .15
59	A11 8ch lt blue & blk	.15 .15
60	A11 10ch lt lilac & blk	.15 .15
61	A11 75ch lt yel grn & blk	.20 .20
62	A11 1nu lt green & blk	.50 .50
63	A11 1.50nu lt bl grn & blk	.40 .40
64	A11 2nu dull org & blk	.50 .50
65	A11 3nu bluish lil & blk	.75 .75
66	A11 4nu lt green & blk	1.00 1.00
67	A11 5nu pink & black	1.40 1.40
	Nos. 56-67 (12)	5.50 5.50

For surcharges see Nos. 115C, 115E, 115I, 117N, 117P, 129B, 129J.

Nos. 6-9, 20-23 Surcharged

1965(?)	Perf. 14½x14, 14x14½	
68	A2 5ch on 1nu	26.00 26.00
69	A2 5ch on 2nu	26.00 26.00
70	A5 10ch on 70ch	4.25 4.25
71	A5 10ch on 1.30nu	4.25 4.25
72	A1 15ch on 70ch	6.25 6.25
73	A1 15ch on 1.30nu	6.25 6.25
74	A5 20ch on 1nu	8.25 8.25
75	A5 20ch on 1.30nu	8.25 8.25
	Nos. 68-75 (8)	89.50 89.50

The surcharges on Nos. 68-69 contain two bars at left and right obliterating the denomination on both sides of the design. Four bars on Nos. 72-73.

Simtokha Dzong A12

Tashichho Dzong — A13

BHUTAN

Daga Dzong — A14

Designs: 5ch, Rinpung Dzong. 50ch, Tongsa Dzong. 1nu, Lhuntsi Dzong.

Perf. 14½x14 (A12), 13½ (A13, A14)
1966-70				Photo.
76	A12	5ch orange brn ('67)	.15	.15
77	A13	10ch dk grn & rose vio ('68)	.15	.15
78	A12	15ch brown	.15	.15
79	A12	20ch green	.15	.15
80	A13	50ch blue grn ('68)	.25	.25
81	A14	75ch dk bl & ol gray ('70)	.25	.25
82	A14	1nu dk vio & vio bl ('70)	.40	.40
		Nos. 76-82 (7)	1.50	1.40

Sizes: 5ch, 15ch, 20ch, 37x20½mm. 10ch, 53½x28½mm. 50ch, 35½x25½mm.

King Jigme Wangchuk — A14a

Coins: 1.30nu, 3nu, 5nu, reverse.

Litho. & Embossed on Gold Foil
1966, July 8		Die Cut		Imperf.
83	A14a	10ch green	.15	.15
83A	A14a	25ch green	.25	.25
83B	A14a	50ch green	.50	.50
83C	A14a	1nu red	1.00	1.00
83D	A14a	1.30nu red	1.15	1.15
83E	A14a	2nu red	1.80	1.80
83F	A14a	3nu red	2.60	2.60
83G	A14a	4nu red	3.75	3.75
83H	A14a	5nu red	4.50	4.50
		Nos. 83-83H (9)	15.70	15.70

See Nos. 98-98B.

Abominable Snowman — A14b

1966		Photo.		Perf. 13½
84	A14b	1ch multicolored	.15	.15
84A	A14b	2ch multi, diff.	.15	.15
84B	A14b	3ch multi, diff.	.15	.15
84C	A14b	4ch multi, diff.	.15	.15
84D	A14b	5ch multi, diff.	.15	.15
84E	A14b	15ch like #84	.15	.15
84F	A14b	30ch like #84	.15	.15
84G	A14b	40ch like #84B	.15	.15
84H	A14b	50ch like #84C	.15	.15
84I	A14b	15nu like #84B	.30	.30
84J	A14b	2.50nu like #84	.65	.65
84K	A14b	3nu like #84A	.75	.75
84L	A14b	5nu like #84B	1.25	1.25
84M	A14b	6nu like #84C	1.50	1.50
84N	A14b	7nu like #84D	1.75	1.75
		Nos. 84-84N (15)	7.55	7.55

Issue dates: 1ch, 2ch, 3ch, 4ch, 5ch, 15ch, 30ch, 40ch, 50ch, Oct. 12; others, Nov. 15. Exist imperf.
For overprints see Nos. 93-93G. For surcharges see Nos. 115D, 115K, 115O, 115P, 117I, 117S.

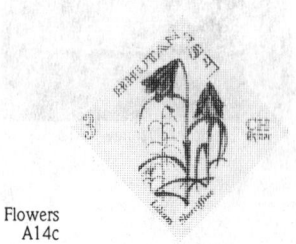

Flowers A14c

Designs: 3ch, 50ch, Lilium sherriffiae. 5ch, 2nu, Meconopsis dhwoju. 7ch, 2.50nu, Rhododendron chaetomallum. 10ch, 4nu, Pleione hookeriana. 5nu, Rhododendron giganteum.

1967, Feb. 9		Litho.		Perf. 13
85	A14c	3ch multicolored	.15	.15
85A	A14c	5ch multicolored	.15	.15
85B	A14c	7ch multicolored	.15	.15
85C	A14c	10ch multicolored	.15	.15

Gray Background
85D	A14c	50ch multicolored	.15	.15
85E	A14c	1nu multicolored	.30	.30
85F	A14c	2.50nu multicolored	.75	.75
85G	A14c	4nu multicolored	1.20	1.20
85H	A14c	5nu multicolored	1.50	1.50
		Nos. 85-85H (9)	4.50	4.50

For surcharges see Nos. 115F, 115L.

Boy Scouts — A14d

1967, Mar. 28		Photo.		Perf. 13½
86	A14d	5ch Planting tree	.15	.15
86A	A14d	10ch Cooking	.15	.15
86B	A14d	15ch Mountain climbing	.15	.15

Emblem, Border in Gold
86C	A14d	50ch like #86	.15	.15
86D	A14d	1.25nu like #86A	.60	.60
86E	A14d	4nu like #86B	1.75	1.75
f.		Souv. sheet of 2, #86D, 86E	2.50	2.50
		Nos. 86-86E (6)	2.95	2.95

Exist imperf.
See Nos. 89-89E for overprints. For surcharges see Nos. 115G, 117J, 129K.

Nos. 50-52, 52a Ovptd.

expo67

1967, May 25		Litho.		Perfs. as Before
87	A9	33ch on #50	.15	.15
87A	A9	1.50nu on #51	.45	.45
87B	A9	2nu on #52	.60	.60
c.		Souv. sheet of 4, on #52a	1.50	1.50
		Nos. 87-87B (3)	1.20	1.20

Nos. 87-87B exist imperf.

Airplanes — A14f

1967, June 26		Litho.		Perf. 13½
88	A14f	45ch Lancaster	.15	.15
88A	A14f	2nu Spitfire	.45	.45
88B	A14f	4nu Hurricane	.95	.95
c.		Souv. sheet of 2, #88A, 88B	2.00	2.00
		Nos. 88-88B (3)	1.55	1.55

Churchill and Battle of Britain. Exist imperf.
For surcharges see Nos. 117Q, 117T.

Nos. 86-86D, 86e Overprinted "WORLD JAMBOREE / IDAHO, U.S.A. / AUG. 1-9,/67"

1967, Aug. 8		Photo.		Perf. 13½
89	A14d	5ch Planting tree	.15	.15
89A	A14d	10ch Cookout	.15	.15
89B	A14d	15ch Mountain climbing	.15	.15
89C	A14d	50ch like #89	.20	.20
89D	A14d	1.25nu like #89A	.60	.60
89E	A14d	4nu like #89B	1.90	1.90
f.		Souv. sheet of 2, #89D, 89E	2.75	2.75
		Nos. 89-89E (6)	3.15	3.15

No. 89f sold for 6.25nu. Exist imperf.

Girl Scouts — A14g

1967, Sept. 28		Photo.		Perf. 13½
90	A14g	5ch Painting	.15	.15
90A	A14g	10ch Making music	.15	.15
90B	A14g	15ch Picking fruit	.15	.15

Emblem, Border in Gold
90C	A14g	1.50nu like #90	.30	.30
90D	A14g	2.50nu like #90A	.45	.45
90E	A14g	5nu like #90B	.90	.90
f.		Souv. sheet of 2, #90A, 90B	2.00	2.00
		Nos. 90-90E (6)	2.10	2.10

Exist imperf.
For surcharge see No. 266.

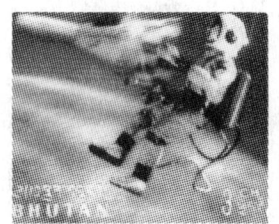

Astronaut, Space Capsule — A14h

Astronaut walking in space and: 5ch, 30ch, 4nu, Orbiter, Lunar modules docked. 7ch, 50ch, 5nu, Lunar module. 10ch, 1.25nu, 9nu, Other astronauts.

1967, Oct. 30		Litho.		Imperf.
91	A14h	3ch multi	.15	.15
91A	A14h	5ch multi	.15	.15
91B	A14h	7ch multi	.20	.20
91C	A14h	10ch multi	.25	.25
m.		Souv. sheet of 4, #91-91C	.75	.75
91D	A14h	15ch multi	.35	.35
91E	A14h	30ch multi	.75	.75
91F	A14h	50ch multi	1.25	1.25
91G	A14h	1.25nu multi	3.00	3.00
n.		Souv. sheet of 4, #91D-91G	6.75	6.75
91H	A14h	2.50nu multi	1.75	1.75
91I	A14h	4nu multi	3.00	3.00
91J	A14h	5nu multi	3.75	3.75
91K	A14h	9nu multi	6.50	6.50
o.		Souv. sheet of 4, #91H-91K		
		Nos. 91-91K (12)	21.10	21.10

Nos. 91H-91K are airmail. Simulated 3-dimensions using a plastic overlay.
For other space issues see types A15a, A15e.

Pheasants — A14i

Designs: 1ch, 2nu, Tragopan satyra. 2ch, 4nu, Lophophorus sclareti. 4ch, 5nu, Lophophorus impeyanus. 8ch, 7nu, Lophura leucomelana. 15ch, 9nu, Crossoptilon crossoptilon.

1968		Photo.		Perf. 13½
92	A14i	1ch multicolored	.15	.15
92A	A14i	2ch multicolored	.15	.15
92B	A14i	4ch multicolored	.15	.15
92C	A14i	8ch multicolored	.15	.15
92D	A14i	15ch multicolored	.15	.15

Border in Gold
92E	A14i	2nu multicolored	.40	.40
92F	A14i	4nu multicolored	.80	.80
92G	A14i	5nu multicolored	1.00	1.00
92H	A14i	7nu multicolored	1.40	1.40
92I	A14i	9nu multicolored	1.90	1.90
		Nos. 92-92I (10)	6.25	6.25

Issue dates: 1ch, 2ch, 4ch, 8ch, 15ch, 2nu, 4nu, 7nu, Jan. 20. 5nu, 9nu, Apr. 23.
Unauthorized imperfs. exist.
For surcharges see Nos. 115H, 117R, 117V, 129D, 129L.

Nos. 84G, 84I, 84K, 84M Ovptd. in Black on Silver

a    b

1968, Feb. 16	Photo.		Perfs. as Before
Overprint Type "a"
93	A14b	40ch on #84G	.15	.15
93A	A14b	1.25nu on #84I	.20	.20
93B	A14b	3nu on #84K	.50	.50
93C	A14b	6nu on #84M	1.00	1.00
Overprint Type "b"
93D	A14b	40ch on #84G	.15	.15
93E	A14b	1.25nu on #84I	.20	.20
93F	A14b	3nu on #84K	.50	.50
93G	A14b	6nu on #84M	1.00	1.00
		Nos. 93-93G (8)	3.70	3.70

Exist imperf.

Snow Lion — A14j

1968, Mar. 14		Photo.		Perf. 12½
94	A14j	2ch Elephant	.15	.15
94A	A14j	3ch Garuda	.15	.15
94B	A14j	4ch Monastery Tiger	.15	.15
94C	A14j	5ch Wind Horse	.15	.15
94D	A14j	15ch Snow Lion	.15	.15
94E	A14j	20ch like #94	.15	.15
94F	A14j	30ch like #94A	.15	.15
94G	A14j	50ch like #94B	.15	.15
94H	A14j	1.25nu like #94C	.20	.20
94I	A14j	1.50nu like #94	.25	.25
94J	A14j	2nu like #94D	.35	.35
94K	A14j	2.50nu like #94A	.40	.40
94L	A14j	4nu like #94B	.65	.65
94M	A14j	5nu like #94C	.80	.80
94N	A14j	10nu like #94D	1.65	1.65
		Nos. 94-94N (15)	5.50	5.50

Nos. 94I, 94K-94N are airmail. All exist imperf.
For surcharges see Nos. 115, 115M, 115Q, 117-117E, 129C, C35-C36.

Butterflies A14k

Designs: 15ch, Catagramma sorana. 50ch, Delias hyparete. 1.25nu, Anteos maerula. 2nu, Ornithoptera priamus urvilleanus. 3nu, Euploea mulciber. 4nu, Morpho rhetenor. 5nu, Papilio androgeous. 6nu, Troides magellanus.

1968, May 20		Litho.		Imperf.
95	A14k	15ch multi	.15	.15
95A	A14k	50ch multi	.45	.45
95B	A14k	1.25nu multi	1.10	1.10

BHUTAN

95C	A14k	2nu multi	1.75	1.75
h.		Souv. sheet of 4, #95-95C	3.50	3.50
95D	A14k	3nu multi	1.25	1.25
95E	A14k	4nu multi	1.65	1.65
95F	A14k	5nu multi	2.00	2.00
95G	A14k	6nu multi	2.50	2.50
i.		Souv. sheet of 4, #95D-95G	7.50	7.50
		Nos. 95-95G (8)	10.85	10.85

Souv. sheets issued Oct. 23. Nos. 95D-95G, 95i are airmail. Simulated 3-dimensions using a plastic overlay.

Paintings — A14m

1968 Litho. & Embossed Imperf.

96	A14m	2ch Van Gogh	.15	.15
96A	A14m	4ch Millet	.15	.15
96B	A14m	5ch Monet	.15	.15
96C	A14m	10ch Corot	.15	.15
p.		Souv. sheet of 4, #96-96C	.15	.15
96D	A14m	45ch like #96	.20	.20
96E	A14m	80ch like #96A	.35	.35
96F	A14m	1.05nu like #96B	.45	.45
96G	A14m	1.40nu like #96C	.60	.60
q.		Souv. sheet of 4, #96D-96G	1.65	1.65
96H	A14m	1.50nu like #96	.65	.65
96I	A14m	2nu like #96	.85	.85
96J	A14m	2.50nu like #96A	1.10	1.10
96K	A14m	3nu like #96A	1.25	1.25
96L	A14m	4nu like #96B	1.10	1.10
96M	A14m	5nu like #96C	1.40	1.40
r.		Souv. sheet of 4, #96I, 96K-96M	4.75	4.75
96N	A14m	6nu like #96B	1.75	1.75
96O	A14m	8nu like #96C	2.25	2.25
s.		Souv. sheet of 4, #96H, 96J, 96N-96O	6.00	6.00
		Nos. 96-96O (16)	12.55	12.55

Issue dates: Nos. 96-96G, 96I, 96K-96M, July 8. Nos. 96p, 96q, 96r, Aug. 5. Others, Aug. 28. Nos. 96H, 96J, 96N-96O are airmail.
See Nos. 114-114O, 144-144G.

Summer Olympics, Mexico, 1968 — A14n

1968, Oct. 1 Photo. Perf. 13½

97	A14n	5ch Discus	.15	.15
97A	A14n	45ch Basketball	.15	.15
97B	A14n	60ch Javelin	.15	.15
97C	A14n	80ch Shooting	.15	.15
97D	A14n	1.05nu like #97	.15	.15
97E	A14n	2nu like #97B	.20	.20
97F	A14n	3nu like #97C	.35	.35
97G	A14n	5nu Soccer	.60	.60
h.		Souv. sheet of 2, #97D, 97G	2.25	2.25
		Nos. 97-97G (8)	1.90	1.90

Exist imperf.
For surcharges see Nos. 129E, B5-B7.

Coin Type of 1966 Overprinted

HUMAN RIGHTS YEAR 1968

Embossed on Gold Foil

1968, Nov. 12 Die Cut Imperf.

98	A14a	15ch green	.15	.15
98A	A14a	33ch green	.25	.25
98B	A14a	9nu green	4.75	4.75
		Nos. 98-98B (3)	5.15	5.15

Human Rights Year.

Birds — A14p

Designs: 2ch, 20ch, 1.50nu, Crimson-winged laughing thrush. 3ch, 30ch, 2.50nu, Ward's trogon, vert. 4ch, 50ch, 4nu, Grey peacock-pheasant. 5ch, 1.25nu, 5nu, Rufous necked hornbill, vert. 15ch, 2nu, 10nu, Myzornis.

1968-69 Photo. Perf. 12½

99	A14p	2ch multicolored	.15	.15
99A	A14p	3ch multicolored	.15	.15
99B	A14p	4ch multicolored	.15	.15
99C	A14p	5ch multicolored	.15	.15
99D	A14p	15ch multicolored	.15	.15
99E	A14p	20ch multicolored	.15	.15
99F	A14p	30ch multicolored	.15	.15
99G	A14p	50ch multicolored	.15	.15
99H	A14p	1.25nu multicolored	.30	.30
99I	A14p	1.50nu multicolored	.35	.35
99J	A14p	2nu multicolored	.40	.40
99K	A14p	2.50nu multicolored	.50	.50
99L	A14p	4nu multicolored	.85	.85
99M	A14p	5nu multicolored	1.10	1.10
99N	A14p	10nu multicolored	2.00	2.00
		Nos. 99-99N (15)	6.70	6.70

Issue dates: 2ch, 3ch, 4ch, 5ch, 15ch, 30ch, 50ch, Dec. 7, 1968. 20ch, 1.25nu, 2nu, Dec. 28, 1968. Others, Jan. 29, 1969.
1.50nu, 2.50nu, 4nu, 5nu, 10nu are airmail.
Exist imperf.
For surcharges see Nos. 115A-115B, 115I, 115M, 115R, 117F-117G, 117K, 117O, 129H.

Fish A14q

1969, Feb. 27 Litho. Imperf.

100	A14q	15ch multicolored	.80	.80
100A	A14q	20ch multi, diff.	1.00	1.00
100B	A14q	30ch multi, diff.	1.50	1.50
100C	A14q	5nu multi, diff.	2.00	2.00
100D	A14q	6nu multi, diff.	2.50	2.50
100E	A14q	7nu multi, diff.	3.00	3.00
f.		Souv. sheet of 4, #100B-100E	9.00	9.00
		Nos. 100-100E (6)	10.80	10.80

Nos. 100C-100E are airmail. Simulated 3-dimensions using a plastic overlay.

Insects — A14r

1969, Apr. 10 Litho. Imperf.

101	A14r	10ch multicolored	.15	.15
101A	A14r	75ch multi, diff.	.35	.35
101B	A14r	1.25nu multi, diff.	.60	.60
101C	A14r	2nu multi, diff.	1.00	1.00
h.		Souv. sheet of 4, #101-101C	3.75	3.75
101D	A14r	3nu multi, diff.	1.10	1.10
101E	A14r	4nu multi, diff.	1.50	1.50
101F	A14r	5nu multi, diff.	1.90	1.90
101G	A14r	6nu multi, diff.	2.25	2.25
i.		Souv. sheet of 4, #101D-101G	8.00	8.00
		Nos. 101-101G (8)	8.85	8.85

Nos. 101D-101G, 101i are airmail. Stamps from souvenir sheets have inscription at lower right. Simulated 3-dimensions using a plastic overlay.

Admission to UPU — A14s

Illustration reduced.

1969, May 2 Photo. Perf. 13

102	A14s	5ch multicolored	.15	.15
102A	A14s	10ch multicolored	.15	.15
102B	A14s	15ch multicolored	.15	.15
102C	A14s	45ch multicolored	.15	.15
102D	A14s	60ch multicolored	.16	.16
102E	A14s	1.05nu multicolored	.25	.25
102F	A14s	1.40nu multicolored	.35	.35
102G	A14s	4nu multicolored	1.00	1.00
		Nos. 102-102G (8)	2.36	2.36

Exist imperf.
For surcharges see #117H, 117L, 117U, 129.

History of Steel Making — A14t

Designs: 2ch, Pre-biblical. 5ch, Damascus sword. 15ch, 3nu, Saugus Mill. 45ch, Beehive coke ovens. 75ch, 4nu, Bessemer converter. 1.50nu, 5nu, Rolling mill. 1.75nu, Steel mill. 2nu, 6nu, Future applications.

Litho. on Steel Foil

1969, June 2 Without Gum Imperf.

103	A14t	2ch multicolored	.15	.15
103A	A14t	5ch multicolored	.15	.15
103B	A14t	15ch multicolored	.15	.15
m.		Souv. sheet of 2, #103A-103B	.15	.15
103C	A14t	45ch multicolored	.15	.15
n.		Souv. sheet of 2, #103, 103C	.30	.30
103D	A14t	75ch multicolored	.20	.20
103E	A14t	1.50nu multicolored	.45	.45
103F	A14t	1.75nu multicolored	.50	.50
o.		Souv. sheet of 2, #103E-103F	.60	.60
103G	A14t	2nu multicolored	.60	.60
p.		Souv. sheet of 2, #103D, 103G	1.90	1.90
103H	A14t	3nu multicolored	.85	.85
103I	A14t	4nu multicolored	1.10	1.10
103J	A14t	5nu multicolored	1.40	1.40
q.		Souv. sheet of 2, #103I-103J	3.75	3.75
103K	A14t	6nu multicolored	1.65	1.65
r.		Souv. sheet of 2, #103H, 103K	7.35	7.35
		Nos. 103-103K (12)	7.35	7.35

Nos. 103H-103K, 103q, 103r are airmail. Souv. sheets issued June 30.

Birds A14u

1969, Aug. 5 Litho. Imperf.

104	A14u	15ch Owl	.15	.15
104A	A14u	50ch Red birds	.35	.35
104B	A14u	1.25nu Hawk	.95	.95
104C	A14u	2nu Penguin	1.50	1.50
h.		Souv. sheet of 4, #104-104C	3.25	3.25
104D	A14u	3nu Macaws	1.10	1.10
104E	A14u	4nu Bird of paradise	1.40	1.40
104F	A14u	5nu Duck	1.75	1.75
104G	A14u	6nu Pheasant	2.00	2.00
i.		Souv. sheet of 4, #104D-104G	6.75	6.75
		Nos. 104-104G (8)	9.20	9.20

Nos. 104D-104G, 104i are airmail. Simulated 3-dimensions using a plastic overlay. Souv. sheets issued Aug. 28.

Buddhist Prayer Banners — A14v

Litho. on Cloth

1969, Sep. 30 Self-adhesive Imperf.

Sizes: 15ch, 75ch, 2nu, 57x57mm, 5nu, 6nu, 70x37mm

105	A14v	15ch multicolored	.15	.15
105A	A14v	75ch multi, diff.	.25	.25
105B	A14v	2nu multi, diff.	.70	.70
105C	A14v	5nu multi, diff.	1.75	1.75
105D	A14v	6nu multi, diff.	2.25	2.25
		Nos. 105-105D (5)	5.10	5.10

Souvenir Sheet

105E		Sheet of 3	5.00	5.00

No. 105E shows denominations of 75ch, 5nu, 6nu with design elements of Nos. 105A, 105C, 105D with gray frame. Exists perf. 13½.

Mahatma Gandhi — A15

1969, Oct. 2 Litho. Perf. 13x13½

106	A15	20ch light blue & brn	.15	.15
107	A15	2nu lemon & brn olive	.75	.75

Mohandas K. Gandhi (1869-1948), leader in India's struggle for independence.

Apollo 11 Moon Landing — A15a

Designs: 3ch, Separation from third stage. 5ch, Entering lunar orbit. 15ch, Lunar module separating from orbiter. 20ch, 3nu, Astronaut standing on lunar module's foot pad. 25ch, Astronaut, flag. 50ch, 4nu, Setting up experiments. 1.75nu, Lunar module docking with orbiter. 5nu, Lift-off from Cape Canaveral. 6nu, Recovery at sea.

1969 Litho. Imperf.

108	A15a	3ch multi	.15	.15
108A	A15a	5ch multi	.15	.15
108B	A15a	15ch multi	.20	.20
108C	A15a	20ch multi	.25	.25
m.		Souv. sheet of 4, #108-108C	.60	.60
108D	A15a	25ch multi	.30	.30
108E	A15a	45ch multi	.50	.50
108F	A15a	50ch multi	.55	.55
108G	A15a	1.75nu multi	1.75	1.75
n.		Souv. sheet of 4, #108D-108G	4.00	4.00
108H	A15a	3nu multi	1.50	1.50
108I	A15a	4nu multi	2.00	2.00
108J	A15a	5nu multi	2.50	2.50
108K	A15a	6nu multi	3.00	3.00
o.		Souv. sheet of 4, #108H-108K	21.00	21.00
		Nos. 108-108K (12)	12.85	12.85

Issue dates: Nos. 108-108G, Nov. 3. Nos. 108H-108K, Nov. 20. Souv. sheets, Dec. 20.
Nos. 108H-108K, 108o are airmail. Simulated 3-dimensions using a plastic overlay.
"Aldrin" misspelled on No. 108o.

The index in each volume of the Scott Catalogue contains many listings that help identify stamps.

BHUTAN

Paintings — A15b

		1970, Jan. 19	Litho.	Imperf.
109	A15b	5ch Clouet	.15	.15
109A	A15b	10ch van Eyck	.15	.15
109B	A15b	15ch David	.15	.15
109C	A15b	2.75nu Rubens	1.75	1.75
h.		Souv. sheet of 4, #109-109C	2.50	2.50
109D	A15b	3nu Homer	1.10	1.10
109E	A15b	4nu Gentileschi	1.40	1.40
109F	A15b	5nu Raphael	1.75	1.75
109G	A15b	6nu Ghirlandaio	2.25	2.25
i.		Souv. sheet of 4, #109D-109G	7.50	7.50
		Nos. 109-109G (8)	8.70	8.70

Nos. 109D-109G, 109i are airmail. Simulated 3-dimensions using a plastic overlay. Souv. sheets issued Feb. 25.

Various Forms of Mail Transport, UPU Headquarters, Bern — A15c

		1970, Feb. 27	Photo.	Perf. 13½
110	A15c	3ch ol grn & gold	.15	.15
111	A15c	10ch red brn & gold	.15	.15
112	A15c	20ch Prus bl & gold	.15	.15
113	A15c	2.50nu dp mag & gold	.65	.65
		Nos. 110-113 (4)	1.10	1.10

New Headquarters of Universal Postal Union, Bern, Switzerland.
Exist imperf. Value $5.
For surcharge see No. 129I.

Painting Type of 1968

Paintings of flowers.

Litho. & Embossed

		1970, May 6		Imperf.
114	A14m	2ch Van Gogh	.15	.15
114A	A14m	3ch Redon	.15	.15
114B	A14m	5ch Kuroda	.15	.15
114C	A14m	10ch Renoir	.15	.15
p.		Souv. sheet of 4, #114-114C	.15	.15
114D	A14m	15ch Renoir, diff.	.15	.15
114E	A14m	75ch Monet	.30	.30
114F	A14m	80ch like #114	.20	.20
114G	A14m	90ch like #114A	.20	.20
114H	A14m	1nu La Tour	.40	.40
114I	A14m	1.10nu like #114B	.30	.30
114J	A14m	1.40nu Oudot	.60	.60
q.		Souv. sheet of 4, #114D, 114E, 114I, 114J	1.90	1.90
114K	A14m	1.40nu like #114C	.35	.35
r.		Souv. sheet of 4, #114F, 114G, 114I, 114K	1.25	1.25
114L	A14m	1.60nu like #114D	.40	.40
114M	A14m	1.70nu like #114E	.40	.40
114N	A14m	3nu like #114H	.75	.75
114O	A14m	3.50nu like #114J	.85	.85
s.		Souv. sheet of 4, #114L-114O	2.75	2.75
		Nos. 114-114O (16)	5.50	5.50

#114F-114G, 114I, 114K-114O are airmail.

Stamps of 1966-69 Surcharged

		1970, June 19		
115	A14j	20ch on 2nu, #94J	2.50	2.50
115A	A14p	20ch on 2nu, #99J	2.50	2.50
115B	A14p	20ch on 2.50nu, #99K	2.50	2.50
115C	A11	20ch on 3nu, #65	2.50	2.50
115D	A14b	20ch on 3nu, #84K	2.50	2.50
115E	A11	20ch on 4nu, #66	2.50	2.50
115F	A14c	20ch on 4nu, #85G	2.50	2.50
115G	A14d	20ch on 4nu, #86E	2.50	2.50
115H	A14i	20ch on 4nu, #92F	2.50	2.50
115I	A14p	20ch on 4nu, #99L	2.50	2.50
115J	A11	20ch on 5nu, #67	2.50	2.50
115K	A14c	20ch on 5nu, #84L	2.50	2.50
115L	A14c	20ch on 5nu, #85H	2.50	2.50
115M	A14j	20ch on 5nu, #94M	2.50	2.50
115N	A14p	20ch on 5nu, #99M	2.50	2.50
115O	A14b	20ch on 6nu, #84M	2.50	2.50
115P	A14b	20ch on 7nu, #84N	2.50	2.50
115Q	A14j	20ch on 10nu, #94N	2.50	2.50
115R	A14p	20ch on 10nu, #99N	2.50	2.50
		Nos. 115-115R (19)	47.50	47.50

Nos. 115B, 115I, 115M-115N, 115Q-115R are airmail.

Animals — A15d

		1970, Oct. 15	Litho.	Imperf.
116	A15d	5ch African elephant	.15	.15
116A	A15d	10ch Leopard	.15	.15
116B	A15d	20ch Ibex	.25	.25
116C	A15d	25ch Tiger	.30	.30
116D	A15d	30ch Abominable snowman	.35	.35
116E	A15d	40ch Water buffalo	.50	.50
116F	A15d	65ch Rhinoceros	.80	.80
116G	A15d	75ch Giant pandas	.95	.95
116H	A15d	85ch Snow leopard	1.10	1.10
116I	A15d	2nu Young deer	1.50	1.50
116J	A15d	3nu Wild boar, vert.	2.25	2.25
116K	A15d	4nu Collared bear, vert.	3.00	3.00
116L	A15d	5nu Takin	4.00	4.00
		Nos. 116-116L (13)	15.30	15.30

Nos. 116I-116L are airmail. Simulated 3-dimensions using a plastic overlay.

Stamps of 1963-69 Surcharged

		1970, Nov. 2		
117	A14j	5ch on 30ch, #94F	.60	.60
117A	A14j	5ch on 50ch, #94G	.60	.60
117B	A14j	5ch on 1.25nu, #94H	.60	.60
117C	A14j	5ch on 1.50nu, #94I	.60	.60
117D	A14j	5ch on 2nu, #94J	.60	.60
117E	A14j	5ch on 2.50nu, #94K	.60	.60
117F	A14p	20ch on 30ch, #99F	2.50	2.50
117G	A14p	20ch on 50ch, #99G	2.50	2.50
117H	A14s	20ch on 1.05nu, #102E	2.50	2.50
117I	A14b	20ch on 1.25nu, #84I	2.50	2.50
117J	A14d	20ch on 1.25nu, #86D	2.50	2.50
117K	A14p	20ch on 1.25nu, #99H	2.50	2.50
117L	A14s	20ch on 1.40nu, #102F	2.50	2.50
117M	A4	20ch on 1.50nu, #14	2.50	2.50
117N	A11	20ch on 1.50nu, #63	2.50	2.50
117O	A14p	20ch on 1.50nu, #99I	2.50	2.50
117P	A11	20ch on 2nu, #64	2.50	2.50
117Q	A14f	20ch on 2nu, #88A	2.50	2.50
117R	A14i	20ch on 2nu, #92E	2.50	2.50
117S	A14b	20ch on 2.50nu, #84J	2.50	2.50
117T	A14f	20ch on 4nu, #88B	2.50	2.50
117U	A14s	20ch on 4nu, #102G	2.50	2.50
117V	A14i	20ch on 7nu, #92H	2.50	2.50
		Nos. 117-117V (23)	46.10	46.10

Nos. 117C, 117E, 117O are airmail.

Conquest of Space — A15e

Designs: 2ch, Jules Verne's "From the Earth to the Moon." 5ch, V-2 rocket. 15ch, Vostok. 25ch, Mariner 2. 30ch, Gemini 7. 50ch, Lift-off. 75ch, Edward White during space walk. 1.50nu, Apollo 13. 2nu, View of Earth from moon. 3nu, Another galaxy. 6nu, Moon, Earth, Sun, Mars, Jupiter. 7nu, Future space station.

		1970	Litho.	Imperf.
118	A15e	2ch multicolored	.15	.15
118A	A15e	5ch multicolored	.15	.15
118B	A15e	15ch multicolored	.15	.15
118C	A15e	25ch multicolored	.20	.20
m.		Souv. sheet of 4, #118-118C	.60	.60
118D	A15e	35ch multicolored	.25	.25
118E	A15e	50ch multicolored	.35	.35
118F	A15e	75ch multicolored	.55	.55
118G	A15e	1.50nu multicolored	1.10	1.10
n.		Souv. sheet of 4, #118D-118G	3.75	3.75
118H	A15e	2nu multicolored	.65	.65
118I	A15e	3nu multicolored	1.00	1.00
118J	A15e	6nu multicolored	2.00	2.00
118K	A15e	7nu multicolored	2.25	2.25
o.		Souv. sheet of 4, #118H-118K	10.00	10.00
		Nos. 118-118K (12)	8.80	8.80

Issue dates: Nos. 118-118G, Nov. 9. Nos. 118H-118K, Nov. 30. Souv. sheets, Dec. 18. Nos. 118H-118K are airmail. Simulated 3-dimensions using a plastic overlay.
See Nos. 127-127C. For surcharge see No. 129F.

Wangdiphodrang Dzong and Bridge — A15f

		1971-72	Photo.	Perf. 13½
119	A15f	2ch gray	.15	.15
120	A15f	3ch deep red lilac	.15	.15
121	A15f	4ch violet	.15	.15
122	A15f	5ch dark green	.15	.15
123	A15f	10ch orange brown	.15	.15
124	A15f	15ch deep blue	.15	.15
125	A15f	20ch deep plum	.15	.15
		Nos. 119-125 (7)	1.05	1.05

Issued: 5ch-20ch, Feb. 22. 2ch-4ch, Apr. 1972.

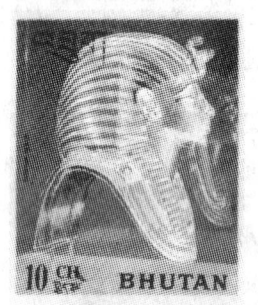

Funeral Mask of King Tutankhamen — A15g

History of Sculpture: 75ch, Winged Bull. 1.25nu, Head of Zeus. 2nu, She-wolf Suckling Romulus and Remus, horiz. 3nu, Head of Cicero. 4nu, Head of David, by Michaelangelo. 5nu, Age of Bronze, by Rodin. 6nu, Head of Woman, by Modigliani.

		1971, Feb. 27	Litho.	Imperf.
		Self-adhesive		
126	A15g	10ch multicolored	.15	.15
126A	A15g	75ch multicolored	.35	.35
126B	A15g	1.25nu multicolored	.60	.60
126C	A15g	2nu multicolored	1.00	1.00
h.		Souv. sheet of 4, #126-126C	2.50	2.50
126D	A15g	3nu multicolored	.80	.80
126E	A15g	4nu multicolored	1.10	1.10
126F	A15g	5nu multicolored	1.40	1.40
126G	A15g	6nu multicolored	1.65	1.65
i.		Souv. sheet of 4, #126D-126G	5.50	5.50
		Nos. 126-126G (8)	7.05	7.05

Stamps are plastic heat molded into three dimensions. Nos. 126D-126G are airmail.

Conquest of Space Type of 1970

Designs: 10ch, 2.50nu, Lunokhod 1. 1.70nu, 4nu, Apollo 15.

		1971, Mar. 20	Litho.	Imperf.
127	A15e	10ch multicolored	.15	.15
127A	A15e	1.70nu multicolored	1.00	1.00
127B	A15e	2.50nu multicolored	1.50	1.50
127C	A15e	4nu multicolored	2.25	2.25
d.		Souv. sheet of 4, #127-127C	5.00	5.00
		Nos. 127-127C (4)	4.90	4.90

Nos. 127B-127C are airmail. Simulated 3-dimensions using a plastic overlay.

Antique Automobiles — A15h

		1971	Litho.	Imperf.
128	A15h	2ch Mercedes Benz, Germany	.15	.15
128A	A15h	5ch Ford, US	.15	.15
128B	A15h	10ch Alfa Romeo, Italy	.15	.15
128C	A15h	15ch Cord, US	.15	.15
128D	A15h	20ch Hispano Suiza, Spain	.15	.15
128E	A15h	30ch Invicta, Britain	.15	.15
128F	A15h	60ch Renault, France	.20	.20
128G	A15h	75ch Talbot, Britain	.25	.25
128H	A15h	85ch Mercer, US	.30	.30
128I	A15h	1nu Sunbeam, Britain	.35	.35
128J	A15h	1.20nu Austrian Daimler	.40	.40
128K	A15h	1.55nu Bugatti, Italy	.55	.55
128L	A15h	1.80nu Simplex, US	.60	.60
128M	A15h	2nu Amilcar, France	.65	.65
128N	A15h	2.50nu Bentley, Britain	.85	.85
128O	A15h	4nu Morris Garage, Britain	.85	.85
128P	A15h	6nu Duesenberg, US	1.10	1.10
128Q	A15h	7nu Aston Martin, Britain	1.25	1.25
128R	A15h	9nu Packard, US	1.65	1.65
128S	A15h	10nu Rolls Royce, Britain	1.75	1.75
		Nos. 128-128S (20)	11.65	11.65

Issue dates: Nos. 128-128F, May 20. Nos. 128G-128N, June 10. Nos. 128O-128S, July 5. Nos. 128O-128S are airmail. Simulated 3-dimensions using a plastic overlay.
"Romeo" misspelled.

Stamps of 1964-71 Surcharged

		1971, July 1		
129	A14s	55ch on 60ch, #102D	.75	.75
129A	A5	55ch on 1.30nu, #22	.40	.40
129B	A11	55ch on 3nu, #65	.40	.40
129C	A14i	55ch on 4nu, #94L	.40	.40
129D	A14i	55ch on 5nu, #92G	.40	.40
129E	A14n	90ch on 1.05nu, #97D	1.90	1.90
129F	A15e	90ch on 1.70nu, #127A	4.25	4.25
129G	A5	90ch on 2nu, #23	.40	.40
129H	A14j	90ch on 2nu, #99J	.75	.75
129I	A15c	90ch on 2.50nu, #113	1.10	1.10
129J	A11	90ch on 4nu, #66	.75	.75
129K	A14d	90ch on 4nu, #86E	1.90	1.90
129L	A14i	90ch on 9nu, #92I	.75	.75
		Nos. 129-129L (13)	14.15	14.15

No. 129C is airmail. No. 129F comes with lines 8mm or 18mm long.

UN Emblem and Bhutan Flag — A16

Designs (Bhutan Flag and): 10ch, UN Headquarters, NY. 20ch, Security Council Chamber and mural by Per Krohg. 3nu, General Assembly Hall.

		1971, Sept. 21	Photo.	Perf. 13½
130	A16	5ch gold, bl & multi	.15	.15
131	A16	10ch gold & multi	.15	.15
132	A16	20ch gold & multi	.15	.15
133	A16	3nu gold & multi	.60	.60
		Nos. 130-133,C21-C23 (7)	3.60	3.60

Bhutan's admission to the UN. Exist imperf.
For overprints see Nos. 140-143. For surcharge see No. 252.

Boy Scout Crossing Stream in Rope Sling — A17

BHUTAN

Emblem & Boy Scouts: 20ch, 2nu, mountaineering. 50ch, 6nu, reading map. 75ch, as 10ch.

1971, Nov. 30 Litho. Perf. 13½

134	A17	10ch gold & multi	.15	.15
135	A17	20ch gold & multi	.15	.15
136	A17	50ch gold & multi	.15	.15
137	A17	75ch silver & multi	.16	.16
138	A17	2nu silver & multi	.40	.40
139	A17	6nu silver & multi	1.00	1.00
a.	Souv. sheet of 2, #138-139 + 2 labels		2.00	2.00
	Nos. 134-139 (6)		2.01	2.01

60th anniv. of the Boy Scouts. Exist imperf.
For overprint and surcharge see #253, 383.

UNHCR UNRWA 1971

Nos. 130-133 Overprinted in Gold

1971, Dec. 23

140	A16	5ch gold & multi	.15	.15
141	A16	10ch gold & multi	.15	.15
142	A16	20ch gold & multi	.15	.15
143	A16	3nu gold & multi	.85	.85
	Nos. 140-143,C24-C26 (7)		5.30	5.30

World Refugee Year. Exist imperf.

The Bathing Girl by Renoir — A17a

Designs: 20ch, A Bar at the Follies, by Monet, horiz. 90ch, Mona Lisa, by da Vinci. 1.70nu, Cart of Father Junier, by Rousseau, horiz. 2.50nu, The Gleaners, by Millet, horiz. 4.60nu, White Horse, by Gaugin. 5.40nu, The Dancing Lesson, by Degas. 6nu, After the Rain, by Gaillauman, horiz.

1972 Litho. & Embossed Imperf.

144	A17a	15ch multicolored	.15	.15
144A	A17a	20ch multicolored	.15	.15
144B	A17a	90ch multicolored	.35	.35
144C	A17a	1.70nu multicolored	.50	.50
144D	A17a	2.50nu multicolored	1.00	1.00
h.	Souv. sheet of 4, #144A-144B, 144D		3.50	3.50
144E	A17a	4.60nu multicolored	1.40	1.40
144F	A17a	5.40nu multicolored	1.65	1.65
144G	A17a	6nu multicolored	1.90	1.90
i.	Souv. sheet of 4, #144C, 144E-144G		6.00	6.00
	Nos. 144-144G (8)		7.10	7.10

Issued: #144-144B, 144D, 1/29; others, 2/28.
Nos. 144C, 144E-144G are airmail.

Famous Men — A17b

1972, Apr. 17 Litho. Imperf.
Self-adhesive

145	A17b	10ch John F. Kennedy	.15	.15
145A	A17b	15ch Gandhi	.15	.15
145B	A17b	55ch Churchill	.45	.45
145C	A17b	2nu De Gaulle	.50	.50
145D	A17b	6nu Pope John XVIII	1.50	1.50
145E	A17b	8nu Eisenhower	2.00	2.00
f.	Souv. sheet of 4, #145B-145E		5.00	5.00
	Nos. 145-145E (6)		4.75	4.75

Nos. 145C-145E are airmail. Stamps are plastic heat molded into three dimensions.

Book Year Emblem — A17c

1972, May 15 Photo. Perf. 13½x13

146	A17c	2ch multicolored	.15	.15
146A	A17c	3ch multicolored	.15	.15
146B	A17c	5ch multicolored	.15	.15
146C	A17c	20ch multicolored	.15	.15
	Nos. 146-146C (4)		.60	.60

International Book Year.

1972 Summer Olympics, Munich — A17d

1972, June 6 Photo. Perf. 13½

147	A17d	10ch Handball	.15	.15
147A	A17d	15ch Archery	.15	.15
147B	A17d	20ch Boxing	.15	.15
147C	A17d	30ch Discus	.15	.15
147D	A17d	35ch Javelin	.15	.15
147E	A17d	45ch Shooting	.15	.15
147F	A17d	1.35nu like #147A	.38	.38
147G	A17d	7nu like #147	1.90	1.90
h.	Souv. sheet of 3, #147D, 147F-147G		3.00	3.00
	Nos. 147-147G (8)		3.18	3.18

Nos. 147D, 147F-147G are airmail and have a gold border.
Exist imperf.
For overprint see No. 384.

Apollo 11 Type of 1969

Apollo 16: 15ch, Lift-off, vert. 20ch, Achieving lunar orbit. 90ch, Astronauts Young, Mattingly, Duke, vert. 1.70nu, Lunar module. 2.50nu, Walking on moon. 4.60nu, Gathering rock samples. 5.40nu, Apollo 16 on launch pad, vert. 6nu, Looking at earth, vert.

1972, Sept. 1 Litho. Imperf.

148	A15a	15ch multicolored	.15	.15
148A	A15a	20ch multicolored	.15	.15
148B	A15a	90ch multicolored	.18	.18
148C	A15a	1.70nu multicolored	.35	.35
148D	A15a	2.50nu multicolored	.50	.50
h.	Souv. sheet of 4, #148-148D		3.00	3.00
148E	A15a	4.60nu multicolored	.90	.90
148F	A15a	5.40nu multicolored	1.10	1.10
148G	A15a	6nu multicolored	1.20	1.20
i.	Souv. sheet of 4, #148C, 148E-148G		5.00	5.00
	Nos. 148-148G (8)		4.53	4.53

Nos. 148C, 148E-148G are airmail. Simulated 3-dimensions using a plastic overlay.

Dogs — A17f

1972-73 Photo. Perf. 13½

149	A17f	2ch Pointer	.15	.15
149A	A17f	3ch Irish Setter	.15	.15
149B	A17f	5ch Lhasa Apso, vert	.15	.15
149C	A17f	10ch Dochi	.15	.15
149D	A17f	15ch Damci	.15	.15
149E	A17f	15ch Collie	.15	.15
149F	A17f	20ch Basset hound	.15	.15
149G	A17f	25ch Damci, diff	.15	.15
149H	A17f	30ch Fox terrier	.15	.15
149I	A17f	55ch Lhasa Apso, diff.	.15	.15
149J	A17f	90ch Boxer	.22	.22
149K	A17f	2.50nu St. Bernard	.55	.55
149L	A17f	4nu Cocker Spaniel	.90	.90
o.	Souv. sheet of 3, #149J-149L, perf. 14		3.00	3.00
149M	A17f	8nu Damci, diff.	1.90	1.90
p.	Souv. sheet of 2, #149I, 149M, perf. 14		3.25	3.25
	Nos. 149-149M (14)		5.07	5.07

Souvenir Sheet
Perf. 14

149N	A17f	18nu Poodle	5.00	5.00

Issue dates: Nos. 149B-149D, 149G, 149I, 149M, 149p, Oct. 5. Nos. 149-149A, 149E-149F, 149H, 149J-149L, 149o, Jan. 1, 1973. No. 149N, Jan. 15, 1973. No. 149N is airmail. All exist imperf.
For surcharges & overprints see #268-269, 385.

Roses — A17g

1973, Jan. 30 Photo. Perf. 13½
Scented Paper

150	A17g	15ch Wendy Cussons	.15	.15
150A	A17g	25ch Iceberg	.15	.15
150B	A17g	30ch Marchioness of Urquio	.15	.15
150C	A17g	3nu Pink parfait	.70	.70
150D	A17g	6nu Roslyn	1.40	1.40
150E	A17g	7nu Blue moon	1.65	1.65
f.	Souv. sheet of 2, #150D-150E		2.50	2.50
	Nos. 150-150E (6)		4.20	4.20

#150D-150E are airmail. Exist imperf.

Apollo 11 Type of 1969

Apollo 17: 10ch, Taking photographs on moon. 15ch, Setting up experiments. 55ch, Earth. 2nu, Driving lunar rover. 7nu, Satellite. 9nu, Astronauts Cernan, Evans, Schmitt.

1973, Feb. 28 Litho. Imperf.
Size: 50x49mm

151	A15a	10ch multicolored	.15	.15
151A	A15a	15ch multicolored	.15	.15
151B	A15a	55ch multicolored	.20	.20
151C	A15a	2nu multicolored	.70	.70
f.	Souv. sheet of 4, #151-151C		2.50	2.50
151D	A15a	7nu multicolored	2.25	2.25
151E	A15a	9nu multicolored	3.25	3.25
g.	Souv. sheet of 2, #151D-151E		10.00	10.00
	Nos. 151-151E (6)		6.70	6.70

Simulated 3-dimensions using a plastic overlay. Nos. 151D-151E are airmail. No. 151g is circular, 160mm in diameter.

Phonograph Records — A17h

Recordings: 10ch, Bhutanese History. 25ch, Royal Bhutan Anthem. 1.25nu, Bhutanese History (English). 3nu, Bhutanese History (Bhutanese), Folk Song #1. 7nu, Folk Song #1. 8nu, Folk Song #2. 9nu, History in English, Folk Songs #1 & 2.

1973, Apr. 15
Self-adhesive
Diameter: #152-152B, 152D-152E, 69mm; #152C, 152F, 100mm

152	A17h	10ch yel on red	.70	.70
152A	A17h	25ch gold on grn	1.00	1.00
152B	A17h	1.25nu sil on bl	4.50	4.50
152C	A17h	3nu sil on pur	10.00	10.00
152D	A17h	7nu sil on blk	22.50	22.50
152E	A17h	8nu red on white	30.00	30.00
152F	A17h	9nu blk on yel	32.50	32.50
	Nos. 152-152F (7)		101.20	101.20

Nos. 152C, 152F are airmail.

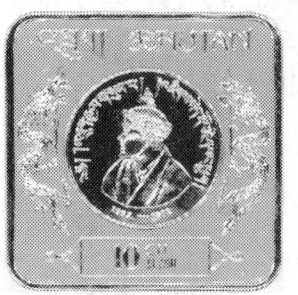

King Jigme Dorji Wangchuk (d. 1972) — A17i

Embossed on Gold Foil
1973, May 2 Die Cut Imperf.

153	A17i	10ch orange	.15	.15
153A	A17i	25ch red	.15	.15
153B	A17i	3nu green	.70	.70
153C	A17i	6nu blue	1.40	1.40
153D	A17i	8nu purple	1.90	1.90
e.	Souv. sheet of 2, #153C-153D		4.50	4.50
	Nos. 153-153D (5)		4.30	4.30

Nos. 153C-153D are airmail.

Mushrooms — A17j

Different mushrooms.

1973, Sept. 25 Litho. Imperf.

154	A17j	15ch multicolored	.15	.15
154A	A17j	25ch multicolored	.20	.20
154B	A17j	30ch multicolored	.25	.25
154C	A17j	3nu multicolored	2.50	2.50
f.	Souvenir sheet of 4, #154-154C		15.00	15.00
154D	A17j	6nu multicolored	5.75	5.75
154E	A17j	7nu multicolored	6.75	6.75
g.	Souvenir sheet of 4, #154D-154E		35.00	35.00
	Nos. 154-154E (6)		15.60	15.60

Simulated 3-dimensions using a plastic overlay. Nos. 154D-154E are airmail.

Bhutanese Mail Service — A17k

Designs: 5ch, 6nu, Letter carrier at mail box. 10ch, 5nu, Postmaster, letter carrier. 15ch, Sacking mail. 25ch, Mailtruck. 1.25nu, Sorting mail. 3nu, Hand-delivered mail.

1973, Nov. 14 Photo. Perf. 13½

155	A17k	5ch multicolored	.15	.15
155A	A17k	10ch multicolored	.15	.15
155B	A17k	15ch multicolored	.15	.15
155C	A17k	25ch multicolored	.15	.15
155D	A17k	1.25nu multicolored	.30	.30
155E	A17k	3nu multicolored	.65	.65
155F	A17k	5nu multicolored	1.10	1.10
155G	A17k	6nu multicolored	1.25	1.25
h.	Souv. sheet of 2, #155F-155G		6.00	6.00
	Nos. 155-155G (8)		3.90	3.90

Indipex '73. Nos. 155F-155G are airmail. All exist imperf.
For surcharges and overprint see Nos. 267, 382, C37-C38.

For all your stamp supply needs
www.scottonline.com

BHUTAN

A set of 15 stamps plus souvenir sheet of 3 showing paintings with reading and writing themes was not authorized.

King Jigme Singye Wangchuk and Royal Crest — A18

Designs (King and): 25ch, 90ch, Flag of Bhutan. 1.25nu, Wheel with 8 good luck signs. 2nu, 4nu, Punakha Dzong, former winter capital. 3nu, 5nu, Crown. 5ch, same as 10ch.

1974, June 2		Litho.		Perf. 13½	
157	A18	10ch maroon & multi		.15	.15
158	A18	25ch gold & multi		.15	.15
159	A18	1.25nu multi		.35	.35
160	A18	2nu gold & multi		.55	.55
161	A18	3nu multi		.75	.75
		Nos. 157-161 (5)		1.95	1.95

Souvenir Sheets
Perf. 13½, Imperf.

162		Sheet of 2	2.75	2.75
a.	A18	5ch maroon & multi		.15
b.	A18	5nu red orange & multi		2.50
163		Sheet of 2	2.75	2.75
a.	A18	90ch gold & multi		.75
b.	A18	4nu gold & multi		1.90	1.90

Coronation of King Jigme Singye Wangchuk, June 2, 1974.

Mailman on Horseback A19

Old and New Locomotives A20

Designs (UPU Emblem, Carrier Pigeon and): 3ch, Sailing and steam ships. 4ch, Old biplane and jet. 25ch, Mail runner and jeep.

1974, Oct. 9		Litho.		Perf. 14½	
164	A19	10ch grn & multi		.15	.15
165	A20	2ch lilac & multi		.15	.15
166	A20	3ch ocher & multi		.15	.15
167	A20	4ch yel grn & multi		.15	.15
168	A20	25ch salmon & multi		.15	.15
		Nos. 164-168,C27-C29 (8)		1.90	1.90

Centenary of Universal Postal Union. Issued in sheets of 50 and sheets of 5 plus label with multicolored margin. Exist imperf.

Family and WPY Emblem — A21

1974, Dec. 17			Perf. 13½	
169	A21	25ch bl & multi	.15	.15
170	A21	50ch org & multi	.15	.15
171	A21	90ch ver & multi	.30	.30
172	A21	2.50nu brn & multi	.75	.75
a.		Souvenir sheet, 10nu	2.25	2.25
		Nos. 169-172 (4)	1.35	1.35

For surcharge see No. 254.

Sephisa Chandra A22

Designs: Indigenous butterflies.

1975, Sept. 15		Litho.	Perf. 14½	
173	A22	1ch shown	.15	.15
174	A22	2ch Lethe kansa	.15	.15
175	A22	3ch Neope bhadra	.15	.15
176	A22	4ch Euthalia duda	.15	.15
177	A22	5ch Vindula erota	.15	.15
178	A22	10ch Bhutanitis Lidderdale	.15	.15
179	A22	3nu Limenitis zayla	.60	.60
180	A22	5nu Delis thysbe	1.40	1.40
		Nos. 173-180 (8)	2.90	2.90

Souvenir Sheet
Perf. 13

| 181 | A22 | 10nu Dabasa gyas | 2.50 | 2.50 |

For surcharges see Nos. 255-256.

Apollo and Apollo-Soyuz Emblem — A23

Design: No. 183, Soyuz and emblem.

1975, Dec. 1		Litho.	Perf. 14x13½	
182	A23	10nu multicolored	2.75	2.75
183	A23	10nu multicolored	2.75	2.75
a.		Souvenir sheet of 2, 15nu	7.00	7.00

Apollo Soyuz link-up in space, July 17. Nos. 182-183 printed se-tenant in sheets of 10. No. 183a contains two 15nu stamps similar to Nos 182-183. Exist imperf.
For surcharges see Nos. 257-258.

Jewelry A24

Designs: 2ch, Coffee pot, bell and sugar cup. 3ch, Container and drinking horn. 4ch, Pendants and box cover. 5ch, Painter. 15ch, Silversmith. 20ch, Wood carver with tools. 1.50nu, Mat maker. 5nu, 10nu, Printer.

1975, Dec. 17			Perf. 14½	
184	A24	1ch multicolored	.15	.15
185	A24	2ch multicolored	.15	.15
186	A24	3ch multicolored	.15	.15
187	A24	4ch multicolored	.15	.15
188	A24	5ch multicolored	.15	.15
189	A24	15ch multicolored	.15	.15
190	A24	20ch multicolored	.15	.15
191	A24	1.50nu multicolored	.40	.40
192	A24	10nu multicolored	2.50	2.50
		Nos. 184-192 (9)	3.95	3.95

Souvenir Sheet
Perf. 13

| 193 | A24 | 5nu multicolored | 1.40 | 1.40 |

Handicrafts and craftsmen.
For surcharges see No. 259, 381.

King Jigme Singye Wangchuk A25

Designs: 25ch, 90ch, 1nu, 2nu, 4nu, like 15ch. 1.30nu, 3nu, 5nu, Coat of arms. Sizes (Diameter): 15ch, 1nu, 1.30nu, 38mm. 25ch, 2nu, 3nu, 49mm. 90ch, 4nu, 5nu, 63mm.

Lithographed, Embossed on Gold Foil
1975, Nov. 11			Imperf.	
194	A25	15ch emerald	.15	.15
195	A25	25ch emerald	.15	.15
196	A25	90ch emerald	.35	.35
197	A25	1nu bright carmine	.40	.40
198	A25	1.30nu bright carmine	.45	.45
199	A25	2nu bright carmine	.65	.65
200	A25	3nu bright carmine	1.00	1.00
201	A25	4nu bright carmine	1.65	1.65
202	A25	5nu bright carmine	2.00	2.00
		Nos. 194-202 (9)	6.80	6.80

King Jigme Singye Wangchuk's 20th birthday.

Rhododendron Cinnabarinum — A28

Rhododendron: 2ch, Campanulatum. 3ch, Fortunei. 4ch, Red arboreum. 5ch, Pink arboreum. 1nu, Falconeri. 3nu, Hodgsonii. 5nu, Keysii. 10nu, Cinnabarinum.

1976, Feb. 15		Litho.	Perf. 15	
203	A28	1ch rose & multi	.15	.15
204	A28	2ch lt grn & multi	.15	.15
205	A28	3ch gray & multi	.15	.15
206	A28	4ch lil & multi	.15	.15
207	A28	5ch ol gray & multi	.15	.15
208	A28	1nu brn org & multi	.25	.20
209	A28	3nu ultra & multi	.75	.60
210	A28	5nu gray & multi	1.25	.90
		Nos. 203-210 (8)	3.00	2.45

Souvenir Sheet
Perf. 13½

| 211 | A28 | 10nu multicolored | 2.50 | 2.50 |

For surcharge see No. 260.

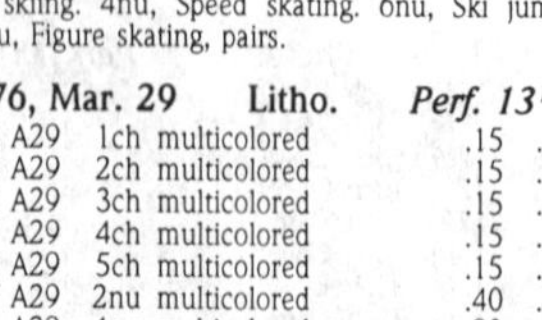

Slalom and Olympic Games Emblem — A29

Designs (Olympic Games Emblem and): 2ch, 4-men bobsled. 3ch, Ice hockey. 4ch, Cross-country skiing. 5ch, Figure skating, women's. 2nu, Downhill skiing. 4nu, Speed skating. 6nu, Ski jump. 10nu, Figure skating, pairs.

1976, Mar. 29		Litho.	Perf. 13½	
212	A29	1ch multicolored	.15	.15
213	A29	2ch multicolored	.15	.15
214	A29	3ch multicolored	.15	.15
215	A29	4ch multicolored	.15	.15
216	A29	5ch multicolored	.15	.15
217	A29	2nu multicolored	.40	.35
218	A29	4nu multicolored	.90	.75
219	A29	10nu multicolored	2.50	1.75
		Nos. 212-219 (8)	4.55	3.60

Souvenir Sheet

| 220 | A29 | 6nu multicolored | 1.50 | 1.50 |

12th Winter Olympic Games, Innsbruck, Austria, Feb. 4-15.
For surcharges see Nos. 261-262.

Ceremonial Masks A29a

Various masks.

1976, Apr. 23		Litho.	Imperf.	
220A	A29a	5ch multicolored	.15	.15
220B	A29a	10ch multicolored	.15	.15
220C	A29a	15ch multicolored	.15	.15
220D	A29a	20ch multicolored	.15	.15
220E	A29a	25ch multi, horiz.	.15	.15
220F	A29a	30ch multi, horiz.	.15	.15
220G	A29a	35ch multi, horiz.	.15	.15
220H	A29a	1nu multi, horiz.	.45	.45
220I	A29a	2nu multi, horiz.	.90	.90
220J	A29a	2.50nu multi, horiz.	1.10	1.10
220K	A29a	3nu multi, horiz.	1.40	1.40
		Nos. 220A-220K (11)	4.90	4.90

Souvenir Sheets

| 220L | A29a | 5nu like #220C | 1.65 | 1.65 |
| 220M | A29a | 10nu like #220F | 3.25 | 3.25 |

Simulated 3-dimensions using a plastic overlay. Nos. 220H-220M are airmail.
Sizes of stamps: No. 220L, 59x70mm, No. 220M, 69x57mm.

Orchid A30

Designs: Various flowers.

1976, May 29		Litho.	Perf. 14½	
221	A30	1ch multicolored	.15	.15
222	A30	2ch multicolored	.15	.15
223	A30	3ch multicolored	.15	.15
224	A30	4ch multicolored	.15	.15
225	A30	5ch multicolored	.15	.15
226	A30	2nu multicolored	.40	.35
227	A30	4nu multicolored	.80	.60
228	A30	6nu multicolored	1.25	1.00
		Nos. 221-228 (8)	3.20	2.65

Souvenir Sheet
Perf. 13½

| 229 | A30 | 10nu multicolored | 2.75 | 2.50 |

For surcharges see Nos. 263-264.

Double Carp Design A31

Designs: Various symbolic designs and Colombo Plan emblem.

1976, July 1		Litho.	Perf. 14½	
230	A31	3ch red & multi	.15	.15
231	A31	4ch ver & multi	.15	.15
232	A31	5ch multicolored	.15	.15
233	A31	25ch bl & multi	.20	.15
234	A31	1.25nu multicolored	.35	.30
235	A31	2nu yel & multi	.60	.50
236	A31	2.50nu vio & multi	.75	.60
237	A31	3nu multicolored	.90	.75
		Nos. 230-237 (8)	3.25	2.75

Colombo Plan, 25th anniversary.
For surcharge see No. 265.

BHUTAN

Bandaranaike Conference Hall — A32

1976, Aug. 16   Litho.   Perf. 13½
238	A32	1.25nu multicolored	.35	.22
239	A32	2.50nu multicolored	.65	.45

5th Summit Conference of Non-aligned Countries, Colombo, Sri Lanka, Aug. 9-19.

Elizabeth II — A33

Liberty Bell — A34

Spirit of St. Louis — A35

Bhutanese Archer, Olympic Rings — A36

Designs: No. 242, Alexander Graham Bell. No. 245, LZ 3 Zeppelin docking, 1907. No. 246, Alfred B. Nobel.

1978, Nov. 15   Litho.   Perf. 14½
240	A33	20nu multicolored	4.00	4.00
241	A34	20nu multicolored	4.00	4.00
242	A33	20nu multicolored	4.00	4.00
243	A35	20nu multicolored	4.00	4.00
244	A36	20nu multicolored	4.00	4.00
245	A33	20nu multicolored	4.00	4.00
246	A33	20nu multicolored	4.00	4.00
		Nos. 240-246 (7)	28.00	28.00

25th anniv. of coronation of Elizabeth II; American Bicentennial; cent. of 1st telephone call by Alexander Graham Bell; Charles A. Lindbergh crossing the Atlantic, 50th anniv.; Olympic Games; 75th anniv. of the Zeppelin; 75th anniv. of Nobel Prize. Seven souvenir sheets exist, each 25nu, commemorating same events with different designs. Size: 103x80mm.

Issues of 1967-1976 Surcharged with New Value and Bars
Perforations and Printing as Before
1978
252	A16	25ch on 3nu (#133)
253	A17	25ch on 6nu (#139)
254	A21	25ch on 2.50nu (#172)
255	A22	25ch on 3nu (#179)
256	A22	25ch on 5nu (#180)
257	A23	25ch on 10nu (#182)
258	A23	25ch on 10nu (#183)
259	A24	25ch on 10nu (#192)
260	A28	25ch on 5nu (#210)
261	A29	25ch on 4nu (#218)
262	A29	25ch on 10nu (#219)
263	A30	25ch on 4nu (#227)
264	A30	25ch on 6nu (#228)
265	A31	25ch on 2.50nu (#236)
266	A14g	25ch on 5nu (#90E)
267	A17k	25ch on 3nu (#155E)
268	A17f	25ch on 4nu (#149L)
269	A17f	25ch on 8nu (#149M)
		Nos. 252-269, C31-C38 (26) 80.00 80.00

Mother and Child, IYC Emblem — A37

IYC Emblem and: 5nu, Mother and two children. 10nu, Boys with blackboards and stylus.

1979, June   Litho.   Perf. 14x13½
289	A37	2nu multicolored	.50	.40
290	A37	5nu multicolored	1.40	1.00
291	A37	10nu multicolored	2.50	2.00
a.		Souv. sheet of 3, #289-291 + label, perf. 15x13½	4.25	3.25
		Nos. 289-291 (3)	4.40	3.40

International Year of the Child.
For overprints see Nos. 761-763.

Conference Emblem and Dove — A38

Design: 10nu, Emblem and Bhutanese symbols.

1979, Sept. 3   Litho.   Perf. 14x13½
292	A38	25ch multicolored	.15	.15
293	A38	10nu multicolored	3.25	2.50

6th Non-Aligned Summit Conference, Havana, August 1979.

Silver Rattle, Dorji A39

Antiques: 10ch, Silver handell, Dilbu, vert. 15ch, Cylindrical jar, Jadum, vert. 25ch, Ornamental teapot, Jamjee. 1nu, Leather container, Kem, vert. 1.25nu, Brass teapot, Jamjee. 1.70nu, Vessel with elephant-head legs, Sangphor, vert. 2nu, Teapot with ornamental spout, Jamjee. 3nu, Metal pot on claw-shaped feet, Yangtho, vert. 4nu, Dish inlaid with precious stones, Battha. 5nu, Metal circular flask, Chhap, vert.

1979, Dec. 17   Photo.   Perf. 14
294	A39	5ch multicolored	.15	.15
295	A39	10ch multicolored	.15	.15
296	A39	15ch multicolored	.15	.15
297	A39	25ch multicolored	.15	.15
298	A39	1nu multicolored	.45	.40
299	A39	1.25nu multicolored	.50	.50
300	A39	1.70nu multicolored	.70	.70
301	A39	2nu multicolored	.90	.75
302	A39	3nu multicolored	1.25	1.10
303	A39	4nu multicolored	1.65	1.50
304	A39	5nu multicolored	2.25	1.90
		Nos. 294-304 (11)	8.30	7.45

Hill, Rinpiang Dzong — A40

Hill Statue, Stamps of Bhutan and: 2nu, Dzong. 5nu, Ounsti Dzong. 10nu, Lingzi Dzong, Gt. Britain Type 81. 20nu, Rope bridge, Penny Black.

1980, May 6   Litho.   Perf. 14x13½
305	A40	1nu multicolored	.30	.25
306	A40	2nu multicolored	.60	.50
307	A40	5nu multicolored	1.60	1.25
308	A40	10nu multicolored	3.00	2.50
		Nos. 305-308 (4)	5.50	4.50

Souvenir Sheet
309	A40	20nu multicolored	5.75	4.25

Sir Rowland Hill (1795-1879), originator of penny postage.

Kichu Lhakhang Monastery, Phari — A41

Guru Padma Sambhava's Birthday: Monasteries.

1981, July 11   Litho.   Perf. 14
310	A41	1nu Dungtse, Phari, vert.	.25	.20
311	A41	2nu shown	.50	.40
312	A41	2.25nu Kurjey	.65	.45
313	A41	3nu Tangu, Thimphu	.75	.60
314	A41	4nu Cheri, Thimphu	1.00	.75
315	A41	5nu Chorten, Kora	1.50	1.00
316	A41	7nu Tak-Tsang, Phari, vert.	2.00	1.50
		Nos. 310-316 (7)	6.65	4.90

Prince Charles and Lady Diana — A42

Orange-bellied Chloropsis — A43

1981, Sept. 10   Litho.   Perf. 14½
317	A42	1nu St. Paul's Cathedral	.20	.15
318	A42	5nu like #317	1.00	.65
319	A42	20nu shown	4.00	2.50
320	A42	25nu like #319	4.50	3.50
		Nos. 317-320 (4)	9.70	6.80

Souvenir Sheet
321	A42	20nu Wedding procession	5.00	4.00

Royal wedding. Nos. 318-319 issued in sheets of 5 plus label.
For surcharges see Nos. 471-475.

1982, Apr. 19   Litho.   Perf. 14
322	A43	2nu shown	.55	.40
323	A43	3nu Monal pheasant	.80	.60
324	A43	5nu Ward's trogon	1.40	1.00
325	A43	10nu Mrs. Gould's sunbird	2.50	2.00
		Nos. 322-325 (4)	5.25	4.00

Souvenir Sheet
326	A43	25nu Maroon oriole	7.00	5.00

1982 World Cup — A44

Designs: Various soccer players.

1982, June 25   Litho.   Perf. 14½x14
327	A44	1nu multicolored	.25	.20
328	A44	5nu multicolored	.55	.40
329	A44	3nu multicolored	.80	.60
330	A44	20nu multicolored	5.25	4.00
		Nos. 327-330 (4)	6.85	5.20

Souvenir Sheets
331	A44	25nu multicolored	12.00	7.50

Nos. 331 have margins continuing design and listing finalists (Algeria, etc. or Hungary, etc.).
For surcharges see Nos. 481-485.

21st Birthday of Princess Diana — A45

1982, Aug.
332	A45	1nu St. James' Palace	.25	.20
332A	A45	10nu Diana, Charles	2.50	1.75
332B	A45	15nu Windsor Castle	4.00	4.50
333	A45	25nu Wedding	6.50	4.50
		Nos. 332-333 (4)	13.25	10.95

Souvenir Sheet
334	A45	20nu Diana	5.50	4.00

10nu-15nu issued only in sheets of 5 + label.
For overprints and surcharges see Nos. 361-363, 455-459, 476-480.

Scouting Year — A46

1982, Aug. 23   Litho.   Perf. 14
335	A46	3nu Baden-Powell, vert.	.65	.50
336	A46	5nu Eating around fire	1.10	.85
337	A46	15nu Reading map	3.50	2.50
338	A46	20nu Pitching tents	4.50	3.50
		Nos. 335-338 (4)	9.75	7.35

Souvenir Sheet
339	A46	25nu Mountain climbing	6.00	4.50

For surcharges see Nos. 450-454.

Rama and Cubs with Mowgli — A47

Scenes from Walt Disney's The Jungle Book.

1982, Sept. 1   Perf. 11
340	A47	1ch multicolored	.15	.15
341	A47	2ch multicolored	.15	.15
342	A47	3ch multicolored	.15	.15
343	A47	4ch multicolored	.15	.15
344	A47	5ch multicolored	.15	.15
345	A47	10ch multicolored	.15	.15
346	A47	30ch multicolored	.15	.15
347	A47	2nu multicolored	.50	.40
348	A47	20nu multicolored	5.50	4.25
		Nos. 340-348 (9)	7.05	5.70

Souvenir Sheets
Perf. 13½
349	A47	20nu Baloo and Mowgli in forest	5.25	4.00
350	A47	20nu Baloo and Mowgli floating	5.25	4.00

George Washington Surveying A48

1982, Nov. 15   Litho.   Perf. 15
351	A48	50ch shown	.15	.15
352	A48	1nu FDR, Harvard	.16	.15
353	A48	2nu Washington at Valley Forge	.32	.25
354	A48	3nu FDR, family	.50	.38
355	A48	4nu Washington, Battle of Monmouth	.65	.50
356	A48	5nu FDR, White House	.85	.65
357	A48	15nu Washington, Mt. Vernon	2.50	2.00
358	A48	20nu FDR, Churchill, Stalin	3.25	2.50
		Nos. 351-358 (8)	8.38	6.58

647

BHUTAN

Souvenir Sheets

| 359 | A48 | 25nu Washington, vert. | 4.25 | 3.25 |
| 360 | A48 | 25nu FDR, vert. | 4.25 | 3.25 |

Washington and Franklin D. Roosevelt.

Nos. 332-334 Overprinted: "ROYAL BABY / 21.6.82"

1982, Nov. 19   *Perf. 14½x14*

361	A45	1nu multicolored	.25	.25
361A	A45	10nu multicolored	2.50	1.75
361B	A45	15nu multicolored	3.75	3.00
362	A45	25nu multicolored	6.25	4.75
		Nos. 361-362 (4)	12.75	9.75

Souvenir Sheet

| 363 | A45 | 20nu multicolored | 5.25 | 4.25 |

Birth of Prince William of Wales, June 21.

500th Birth Anniv. of Raphael — A51

Portraits.

1983, Mar. 23   *Perf. 13½*

375	A51	1nu Angelo Doni	.25	.20
376	A51	4nu Maddalena Doni	1.00	.75
377	A51	5nu Baldassare Castiglione	1.25	.90
378	A51	20nu La Donna Velata	5.00	3.75
		Nos. 375-378 (4)	7.50	5.60

Souvenir Sheets

| 379 | A51 | 25nu Expulsion of Heliodorus | 6.25 | 4.75 |
| 380 | A51 | 25nu Mass of Bolsena | 6.25 | 4.75 |

Nos. 184, 155F, 139, 184, 147G, 149M Surchd. or Ovptd.: "Druk Air"

1983, Feb. 11

381	A24	30ch on 1ch multi	.15	.15
382	A17k	5nu multicolored	2.00	1.25
383	A17	6nu multicolored	2.25	1.50
384	A17d	7nu multicolored	2.50	1.50
385	A17f	8nu multicolored	2.50	1.75
		Nos. 381-385 (5)	9.40	6.15

Druk Air Service inauguration. Overprint of 8nu all caps. Nos. 382, 384 air mail.

Manned Flight Bicentenary A52

1983, Aug. 15   *Litho.*   *Perf. 15*

386	A52	50ch Dornier Wal	.15	.15
387	A52	3nu Savoia-Marchetti S-66	.75	.55
388	A52	10nu Hawker Osprey	2.00	1.75
389	A52	20nu Ville de Paris	4.00	3.75
		Nos. 386-389 (4)	6.90	6.20

Souvenir Sheet

| 390 | A52 | 25nu Balloon Captif | 5.00 | 3.75 |

Buddhist Symbols — A53

1983, Aug. 11   *Litho.*   *Perf. 13½*

391	A53	25ch Sacred vase	.15	.15
392	A53	50ch Five Sensory Symbols	.15	.15
393	A53	2nu Seven Treasures	.35	.30
394	A53	3nu Five Sensory Organs	.60	.45
395	A53	8nu Five Fleshes	1.50	1.10
396	A53	9nu Sacrificial cake	1.75	1.25
a.		Souv. sheet of 6, #391-396	4.50	3.50
		Nos. 391-396 (6)	4.50	3.40

Size of Nos. 393, 396: 45x40mm.

World Communications Year (1983) — A54

Various Disney characters and history of communications.

1984, Apr. 10   *Litho.*   *Perf. 14½x14*

397	A54	4ch multicolored	.15	.15
398	A54	5ch multicolored	.15	.15
399	A54	10ch multicolored	.15	.15
400	A54	20ch multicolored	.15	.15
401	A54	25ch multicolored	.15	.15
402	A54	50ch multicolored	.15	.15
403	A54	1nu multicolored	.30	.25
404	A54	5nu multicolored	1.10	.95
405	A54	20nu multicolored	4.25	3.75
		Nos. 397-405 (9)	6.55	5.85

Souvenir Sheets   *Perf. 14x14½*

| 406 | A54 | 20nu Donald Duck on phone, horiz. | 4.75 | 4.00 |
| 407 | A54 | 20nu Mickey Mouse on TV | 4.75 | 4.00 |

1984 Winter Olympics — A55

1984, June 16   *Perf. 14*

408	A55	50ch Skiing	.15	.15
409	A55	1nu Cross-country skiing	.25	.20
410	A55	3nu Speed skating	.60	.45
411	A55	20nu Bobsledding	3.75	3.00
		Nos. 408-411 (4)	4.75	3.80

Souvenir Sheet

| 412 | A55 | 25nu Hockey | 5.00 | 3.25 |

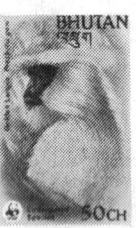

Golden Langur A56

Locomotives A57

1984, June 10   *Litho.*   *Perf. 14½*

413	A56	50ch shown	.15	.15
414	A56	1nu Group in tree, horiz.	.20	.15
415	A56	2nu Family, horiz.	.40	.30
416	A56	4nu Group walking	.80	.60
		Nos. 413-416 (4)	1.55	1.20

Souvenir Sheets

417	A56	20nu Snow leopard	4.00	2.00
418	A56	25nu Yak	4.00	2.00
419	A56	25nu Blue sheep, horiz.	4.00	2.00

1984, July 16

420	A57	50ch Sans Pareil, 1829	.15	.15
421	A57	1nu Planet, 1830	.20	.15
422	A57	3nu Experiment, 1832	.60	.45
423	A57	4nu Black Hawk, 1835	.80	.60
424	A57	5.50nu Jenny Lind, 1847	1.10	.85
425	A57	8nu Semmering-Bavaria, 1851	1.60	1.25
426	A57	10nu Great Northern #1, 1870	2.00	1.50
427	A57	25nu German Natl. Tinder, 1880	5.00	3.75
		Nos. 420-427 (8)	11.45	8.70

Souvenir Sheets

428	A57	20nu Darjeeling Himalayan Railway, 1984	4.00	3.00
429	A57	20nu Sondermann Freight, 1896	4.00	3.00
430	A57	20nu Crampton's locomotive, 1846	4.00	3.00
431	A57	20nu Erzsebet, 1870	4.00	3.00

Nos. 424-427 horiz.

Classic Cars A58

1984, Aug. 29   *Litho.*   *Perf. 14*

432	A58	50ch Riley Sprite, 1936	.15	.15
433	A58	1nu Lanchester, 1919	.20	.15
434	A58	3nu Itala, 1907	.65	.45
435	A58	4nu Morris Oxford Bullnose, 1913	.90	.60
436	A58	5.50nu Lagonda LG6, 1939	1.25	.85
437	A58	6nu Wolseley, 1903	1.40	.90
438	A58	8nu Buick Super, 1952	1.75	1.20
439	A58	20nu Maybach Zeppelin, 1933	4.50	3.00
		Nos. 432-439 (8)	10.80	7.30

Souvenir Sheets

| 440 | A58 | 25nu Simplex, 1912 | 2.50 | 1.50 |
| 441 | A58 | 25nu Renault, 1901 | 2.50 | 1.50 |

For surcharges see Nos. 537-544.

Summer Olympic Games — A59

1984, Oct. 27   *Litho.*

442	A59	15ch Women's archery	.15	.15
443	A59	25ch Men's archery	.15	.15
444	A59	2nu Table tennis	.40	.30
445	A59	2.25nu Basketball	.45	.35
446	A59	5.50nu Boxing	1.10	.85
447	A59	6nu Running	1.20	.90
448	A59	8nu Tennis	1.60	1.20
		Nos. 442-448 (7)	5.05	3.90

Souvenir Sheet

| 449 | A59 | 25nu Archery | 5.00 | 3.50 |

For overprints see Nos. 537-544.

Nos. 335-339 Surcharged with New Values and Bars in Black or Silver

1985   *Litho.*   *Perf. 14*

450	A46	10nu on 3nu multi	2.00	1.50
451	A46	10nu on 5nu multi	2.00	1.50
452	A46	10nu on 15nu multi	2.00	1.50
453	A46	10nu on 20nu multi	2.00	1.50
		Nos. 450-453 (4)	8.00	6.00

Souvenir Sheet

| 454 | A46 | 20nu on 25nu multi | 4.00 | 3.00 |

Nos. 332, 332A, 332B, 333-334 Surcharged with New Values and Bars

1985, Feb. 28

455	A45	5nu on 1nu multi	1.00	.70
456	A45	5nu on 10nu multi	1.00	.70
457	A45	5nu on 15nu multi	1.00	.70
458	A45	40nu on 25nu multi	8.00	5.25
		Nos. 455-458 (4)	11.00	7.35

Souvenir Sheet

| 459 | A45 | 25nu on 20nu multi | 5.00 | 4.00 |

50th Anniv. of Donald Duck — A60

1984, Dec. 10   *Litho.*   *Perf. 13½x14*

460	A60	4ch Magician Mickey	.15	.15
461	A60	5ch Slide, Donald, Slide	.15	.15
462	A60	10ch Donald's Golf Game	.15	.15
463	A60	20ch Mr. Duck Steps Out	.15	.15
464	A60	25ch Lion Around	.15	.15
465	A60	50ch Alpine Climbers	.15	.15
466	A60	1nu Flying Jalopy	.25	.15
467	A60	5nu Frank Duck	1.10	.75
468	A60	20nu Good Scouts	4.50	3.25
		Nos. 460-468 (9)	6.75	5.05

Souvenir Sheets

| 469 | A60 | 20nu Three Caballeros | 4.50 | 3.25 |
| 470 | A60 | 20nu Sea Scouts | 4.50 | 3.25 |

Nos. 317-321 Surcharged with New Values and Bars

1985, Feb. 28   *Litho.*   *Perf. 14½*

471	A42	10nu on 1nu multi	2.00	1.50
472	A42	10nu on 5nu multi	2.00	1.50
473	A42	10nu on 20nu multi	2.00	1.50
474	A42	10nu on 25nu multi	2.00	1.50
		Nos. 471-474 (4)	8.00	6.00

Souvenir Sheet

| 475 | A42 | 30nu on 20nu multi | 6.00 | 5.00 |

Nos. 361, 361A, 361B, 362-363 Surcharged with New Values and Bars

1985, Feb. 28   *Perf. 14½x14*

476	A45	5nu on 1nu multi	.75	.75
477	A45	5nu on 10nu multi	.75	.55
478	A45	5nu on 15nu multi	.75	.55
479	A45	40nu on 25nu multi	7.50	5.50
		Nos. 476-479 (4)	9.75	7.35

Souvenir Sheet

| 480 | A45 | 25nu on 20nu multi | 5.00 | 3.75 |

Nos. 327-331 Surcharged with New Values and Bars in Black or Silver

1985, June

481	A44	5nu on 1nu multi	1.50	1.10
482	A44	5nu on 2nu multi	1.50	1.10
483	A44	5nu on 3nu multi	1.50	1.10
484	A44	5nu on 4nu multi	1.50	1.10
		Nos. 481-484 (4)	6.00	4.40

Souvenir Sheets

| 485 | A44 | 20nu on 25nu multi | 7.50 | 5.50 |

Mask Dance of the Judgement of Death — A61

1985, Apr. 27   *Perf. 13½*

486	A61	5ch Shinje Choegyel	.15	.15
487	A61	35ch Raksh Lango	.15	.15
488	A61	50ch Druelgo	.15	.15
489	A61	2.50nu Pago	.45	.35
490	A61	3nu Telgo	.55	.40
491	A61	4nu Due Nakcung	.75	.60
492	A61	5nu Lha Karpo	.90	.70
a.		Souv. sheet of 4, #486-487, 491-492	1.90	1.50
493	A61	5.50nu Nyalbum	1.00	.75
494	A61	6nu Khimda Pelkyi	1.10	.85
		Nos. 486-494 (9)	5.20	4.10

For overprints see Nos. 764-772.

Monasteries A62

1984, Dec. 1   *Litho.*   *Perf. 12*

495	A62	10ch Domkhar	.15	.15
496	A62	25ch Shemgang	.15	.15
497	A62	50ch Chapcha	.15	.15
498	A62	1nu Tashigang	.15	.15
499	A62	2nu Pungthang Chhug	.30	.30
500	A62	5nu Dechhenphoda	.70	.70
		Nos. 495-500 (6)	1.60	1.60

Veteran's War Memorial Building, San Francisco A63

BHUTAN

1985, Oct. 24	Litho.	Perf. 14
502 A63 50ch Flags of Bhutan, UN, vert.	.15	.15
503 A63 15nu Headquarters, NY, vert.	2.75	2.00
504 A63 20nu shown	3.75	2.75
Nos. 502-504 (3)	6.65	4.90

Souvenir Sheet

505 A63 25nu UN Human Rights Declaration	4.25	3.00

UN, 40th anniv.

Audubon Birth Bicentenary A64

Illustrations of North American bird species by Audubon.

1985

506 A64 50ch Anas breweri	.15	.15
507 A64 1nu Lagopus lagopus	.20	.15
508 A64 2nu Charadrius montanus	.35	.25
509 A64 3nu Cavia stellata	.50	.40
510 A64 4nu Canachites canadensis	.70	.50
511 A64 5nu Mergus cucullatus	.85	.60
512 A64 15nu Olor buccinator	2.50	1.75
513 A64 20nu Bucephala clangula	3.50	2.50
Nos. 506-513 (8)	8.75	6.30

Souvenir Sheets

514 A64 25nu Accipiter striatus	3.75	2.25
515 A64 25nu Parus bicolor	3.75	2.25

Issue dates: Nos. 507, 510-511, 514 Nov. 15. Nos. 506, 508-509, 513, 515 Dec. 6.

A Tramp Abroad, by Mark Twain (1835-1910) A65

Walt Disney animated characters.

1985, Nov. 15

516 A65 50ch multicolored	.15	.15
517 A65 2nu multicolored	.35	.25
518 A65 5nu multicolored	.85	.60
519 A65 9nu multicolored	1.50	1.10
520 A65 20nu multicolored	3.50	2.50
Nos. 516-520 (5)	6.35	4.60

Souvenir Sheet

521 A65 25nu Goofy, Mickey Mouse	5.00	3.50

Intl. Youth Year.
For overprints see Nos. 554, 556-557.

Rapunzel, by Jacob and Wilhelm Grimm — A66

Walt Disney animated characters.

1985, Nov. 15

522 A66 1nu multicolored	.20	.15
523 A66 4nu multicolored	.70	.50
524 A66 7nu multicolored	1.25	.95
525 A66 8nu multicolored	1.40	1.05
526 A66 20nu multicolored	2.50	1.75
Nos. 522-526 (5)	6.05	4.40

Souvenir Sheet

527 A66 25nu multicolored	5.00	4.00

No. 525 printed in sheets of 8.
For overprints see Nos. 553, 555, 558.

First South Asian Regional Cooperation Summit, Dec. 7-8, Dacca, Bangladesh A67

1985, Dec. 8		Perf. 14
528 A67 50ch multicolored	.15	.15
529 A67 5nu multicolored	.85	.60

Seven Precious Attributes of the Universal King — A68

1986, Feb. 12	Litho.	Perf. 13x12½
530 A68 30ch Wheel	.15	.15
531 A68 50ch Gem	.15	.15
532 A68 1.25nu Queen	.20	.20
533 A68 2nu Minister	.30	.30
534 A68 4nu Elephant	.55	.55
535 A68 6nu Horse	.85	.85
536 A68 8nu General	1.10	1.10
Nos. 530-536 (7)	3.30	3.30

Nos. 442-443, 445-449 Ovptd. with Medal, Winners' Names and Countries. No. 449 Ovptd. for Men's and Women's Events.

1986, May 5	Litho.	Perf. 14
537 A59 15ch Hyang Soon Seo, So. Korea	.15	.15
538 A59 25ch Darrell Pace, US	.15	.15
539 A59 2.25nu US	.30	.30
540 A59 5.50nu Mark Breland, US	.80	.80
541 A59 6nu Daley Thompson, Britain	.85	.85
542 A59 8nu Stefan Edberg, Sweden	1.10	1.10
Nos. 537-542 (6)	3.35	3.35

Souvenir Sheets

543 A59 25nu Hyang Soon Seo	3.50	3.50
544 A59 25nu Darrel Pace	3.50	3.50

Kilkhor Mandalas, Deities — A69

Religious art: 10ch, 1nu, Phurpa, ritual dagger. 25ch, 3nu, Amitayus in wrath. 50ch, 5nu, Overpowering Deities. 75ch, 7nu, Great Wrathful One, Guru Rinpoche.

1986, June 17		Perf. 13½
545 A69 10ch multicolored	.15	.15
546 A69 25ch multicolored	.15	.15
547 A69 50ch multicolored	.15	.15
548 A69 75ch multicolored	.15	.15
549 A69 1nu multicolored	.15	.15
550 A69 3nu multicolored	.40	.40
551 A69 5nu multicolored	.70	.70
552 A69 7nu multicolored	1.00	1.00
Nos. 545-552 (8)	2.85	2.85

Nos. 525, 519, 526, 520, 521 and 527 Ovptd. with AMERIPEX '86 Emblem.

1986, June 16	Litho.	Perf. 14
553 A65 8nu multi	1.40	1.00
554 A65 9nu multi	1.50	1.10
555 A65 15nu multi	2.50	1.75
556 A65 20nu multi	3.50	2.50
Nos. 553-556 (4)	8.90	6.35

Souvenir Sheets

557 A65 25nu #521	4.25	3.00
558 A66 25nu #527	4.25	3.00

A70

A71

Halley's Comet A72

Designs: 50ch, Babylonian tablet fragments, 2349 B.C. sighting. 1nu, 17th cent. print, A.D. 66 sighting. 2nu, French silhouette art, 1835 sighting. 3nu, Bayeux Tapestry, 1066 sighting. 4nu, Woodblock, 684 sighting. 5nu, Illustration from Bybel Printen, 1650. 15nu, 1456 Sighting, Cancer constellation. 20nu, Delft plate, 1910 sighting. No. 572, Comet over Himalayas. No. 573, Comet over domed temple Dug-gye Jong.

1986, Nov. 4	Litho.	Perf. 15
564 A70 50ch multicolored	.15	.15
565 A70 1nu multicolored	.20	.15
566 A71 2nu multicolored	.35	.30
567 A70 3nu multicolored	.50	.35
568 A70 4nu multicolored	.70	.50
569 A71 5nu multicolored	.85	.65
570 A70 15nu multicolored	2.50	2.00
571 A70 20nu multicolored	3.50	2.50
Nos. 564-571 (8)	8.75	6.60

Souvenir Sheets

572 A72 25nu multicolored	4.25	3.00
573 A72 25nu multicolored	4.25	3.00

A73

Statue of Liberty, Cent. — A74

Statue and ships: 50ch, Mircea, Romania. 1nu, Shalom, Israel. 2nu, Leonardo da Vinci, Italy. 3nu, Libertad, Argentina. 4nu, France, France. 5nu, SS United States, US. 15nu, Queen Elizabeth II, England. 20nu, Europa, West Germany. No. 582, Statue. No. 583, Statue, World Trade Center.

1986, Nov. 4		
574 A73 50ch multicolored	.15	.15
575 A73 1nu multicolored	.20	.15
576 A73 2nu multicolored	.35	.30
577 A73 3nu multicolored	.50	.35
578 A73 4nu multicolored	.65	.50
579 A73 5nu multicolored	.85	.65
580 A73 15nu multicolored	2.50	1.90
581 A73 20nu multicolored	3.40	2.50
Nos. 574-581 (8)	8.60	6.50

Souvenir Sheets

582 A74 25nu multicolored	4.25	3.00
583 A74 25nu multi, diff.	4.25	3.00

Discovery of America, 500th Anniv. A75

1987, May 25	Litho.	Perf. 14
584 A75 20ch Santa Maria	.40	.40
585 A75 25ch Queen Isabella	.40	.40
586 A75 50ch Ship, flying fish	.40	.40
587 A75 1nu Columbus's coat of arms	.75	.60
588 A75 2nu Christopher Columbus	1.40	1.00
589 A75 3nu Landing in the New World	2.00	2.00
a. Miniature sheet of 6, #584-589	5.00	5.00
Nos. 584-589 (6)	5.35	4.80

Souvenir Sheets

590 A75 20ch Pineapple		
591 A75 25ch Indian hammock		
592 A75 50ch Tobacco plant		
593 A75 1nu Flamingo		
594 A75 2nu Navigator, astrolabe, 15th cent.		
595 A75 3nu Lizard		
596 A75 5nu Iguana	1.25	.95

All stamps are vertical except those contained in Nos. 591, 595 and 596. Stamps from No. 589a have white background.

CAPEX '87 — A76

Locomotives.

1987, June 15		
597 A76 50ch Canadian Natl. U1-f	.15	.15
598 A76 1nu Via Rail L.R.C.	.20	.15
599 A76 2nu Canadian Natl. GM GF-30t	.35	.25
600 A76 3nu Canadian Natl. 4-8-4	.50	.35
601 A76 8nu Canadian Pacific 4-6-2	1.40	1.00
602 A76 10nu Via Express passenger train	1.75	1.25
603 A76 15nu Canadian Nat. Turbotrain	2.50	1.90
604 A76 20nu Canadian Pacific Diesel-Electric Express	3.25	2.50
Nos. 597-604 (8)	10.10	7.55

Souvenir Sheet

605 A76 25nu Royal Hudson 4-6-4	4.25	3.00
606 A76 25nu Canadian Natl. 4-8-4, diff.	4.25	3.00

Two Faces, Sculpture by Marc Chagall (1887-1984) A77

Paintings: 1nu, At the Barber's. 2nu, Old Jew with Torah. 3nu, Red Maternity. 4nu, Eve of Yom Kippur. 5nu, The Old Musician. 6nu, The Rabbi of Vitebsk. 7nu, Couple at Dusk. 9nu, The Artistes. 10nu, Moses Breaking the Tablets of the Law. 12nu, Bouquet with Flying Lovers. 20nu, In the Sky of the Opera. No. 619, Romeo and Juliet. No. 620, Magician of Paris. No. 621, Maternity. No. 622, The Carnival for Aleko: Scene II. No. 623, Visit to the Grandparents. No. 624, The Smolensk Newspaper. No. 625, The Concert. No. 626, Composition with Goat. No. 627, Still Life. No. 628. The Red Gateway. No. 629, Cow with Parasol. No. 630, Russian Village.

1987, Dec. 17	Litho.	Perf. 14
607 A77 50ch multicolored	.15	.15
608 A77 1nu multicolored	.15	.15
609 A77 2nu multicolored	.35	.25
610 A77 3nu multicolored	.45	.35
611 A77 4nu multicolored	.65	.45
612 A77 5nu multicolored	.80	.60
613 A77 6nu multicolored	.95	.70
614 A77 7nu multicolored	1.10	.90
615 A77 9nu multicolored	1.50	1.10
616 A77 10nu multicolored	1.60	1.25
617 A77 12nu multicolored	1.90	1.50
618 A77 20nu multicolored	3.25	2.50

Size: 110x95mm

Imperf

619 A77 25nu multicolored	4.00	3.00
620 A77 25nu multicolored	4.00	3.00
621 A77 25nu multicolored	4.00	3.00
622 A77 25nu multicolored	4.00	3.00
623 A77 25nu multicolored	4.00	3.00

649

BHUTAN

624	A77	25nu multicolored	4.00	3.00
625	A77	25nu multicolored	4.00	3.00
626	A77	25nu multicolored	4.00	3.00
627	A77	25nu multicolored	4.00	3.00
628	A77	25nu multicolored	4.00	3.00
629	A77	25nu multicolored	4.00	3.00
630	A77	25nu multicolored	4.00	3.00
		Nos. 607-630 (24)	60.85	45.90

1988 Winter Olympics, Calgary — A78

Emblem and Disney animated characters as competitors in Olympic events.

1988, Feb. 15   Litho.   Perf. 14

631	A78	50ch Slalom	.15	.15
632	A78	1nu Downhill skiing	.16	.15
633	A78	2nu Ice hockey	.30	.25
634	A78	4nu Biathlon	.65	.50
635	A78	7nu Speed skating	1.10	.85
636	A78	8nu Figure skating	1.25	.95
637	A78	9nu Figure skating, diff.	1.50	1.10
638	A78	20nu Bobsled	3.25	2.50
		Nos. 631-638 (8)	8.36	6.45

Souvenir Sheets

639	A78	25nu Ski jumping	4.00	4.00
640	A78	25nu Ice dancing	4.00	4.00

Transportation Innovations — A79

1988, Mar. 31

641	A79	50ch Pullman Pioneer, 1865	.15	.15
642	A79	1nu Stephenson's Rocket, 1829	.15	.15
643	A79	2nu Pierre L'Allement's Velocipede, 1866	.30	.25
644	A79	3nu Benz Velocipede, 1886	.50	.35
645	A79	4nu Volkswagen Beetle, c. 1960	.65	.50
646	A79	5nu Natchez Vs. Robert E. Lee, 1870	.80	.60
647	A79	6nu American La France, 1910	1.00	.75
648	A79	7nu USS Constitution, 1787, vert.	1.15	.85
649	A79	9nu Bell Rocket Belt, 1961, vert.	1.50	1.10
650	A79	10nu Trevithick Locomotive, 1804	1.60	1.25
		Nos. 641-650 (10)	7.80	5.95

Souvenir Sheets

651	A79	25nu Concorde jet	4.00	4.00
652	A79	25nu Mallard, 1938, vert.	4.00	4.00
653	A79	25nu Shinkansen	4.00	4.00
654	A79	25nu TGV, 1981	4.00	4.00

1988 Summer Olympics, Seoul A80

7nu-20nu vert.

1989, Feb. 15   Litho.

655	A80	50ch Women's gymnastics	.15	.15
656	A80	1nu Tae kwon do	.15	.15
657	A80	2nu Shot put	.30	.25
658	A80	4nu Women's volleyball	.65	.50
659	A80	7nu Basketball	1.10	.85
660	A80	8nu Soccer	1.25	.95
661	A80	9nu Women's high jump	1.50	1.10
662	A80	20nu Running	3.25	2.50
		Nos. 655-662 (8)	8.35	6.45

Souvenir Sheets

663	A80	25nu Archery, vert.	4.00	4.00
664	A80	25nu Fencing	4.00	4.00

Paintings by Titian — A81

Designs: 50ch, *Gentleman with a Book.* 1nu, *Venus and Cupid, with a Lute Player.* 2nu, *Diana and Actaeon.* 3nu, *Cardinal Ippolito dei Medici.* 4nu, *Sleeping Venus.* 5nu, *Venus Risen from the Waves.* 6nu, *Worship of Venus.* 7nu, *Fete Champetre.* 10nu, *Perseus and Andromeda.* 15nu, *Danae.* 20nu, *Venus at the Mirror.* 25nu, *Venus and the Organ Player.* No. 677, *The Pardo Venus,* horiz. No. 678, *Venus and Cupid, with an Organist.* No. 679, *Miracle of the Irascible Son.* No. 680, *Diana and Callisto.* No. 681, *Saint John the Almsgiver.* No. 682, *Danae with the Shower of Gold,* horiz. No. 683, *Bacchus and Ariadne.* No. 684, *Venus Blindfolding Cupid.* No. 685, *Portrait of Laura Dianti.* No. 686, *Venus of Urbino.* No. 687, *Portrait of Johann Friedrich.* No. 688, *Mater Dolorosa with Raised Hands.*

Perf. 13½x14, 14x13½

1989, Feb. 15   Litho.

665	A81	50ch multicolored	.15	.15
666	A81	1nu multicolored	.15	.15
667	A81	2nu multicolored	.30	.25
668	A81	3nu multicolored	.50	.35
669	A81	4nu multicolored	.65	.50
670	A81	5nu multicolored	.80	.60
671	A81	6nu multicolored	.95	.75
672	A81	7nu multicolored	1.10	.85
673	A81	10nu multicolored	1.60	1.25
674	A81	15nu multicolored	2.50	1.75
675	A81	20nu multicolored	3.25	2.50
676	A81	25nu multicolored	4.00	3.00
		Nos. 665-676 (12)	15.95	12.10

Souvenir Sheets

677-688	A81	25nu each	4.00	4.00

Mickey Mouse, 60th Anniv. (in 1988) — A82

Movie posters.

1989, June 20   Litho.   Perf. 13½x14

689	A82	1ch Mickey Mouse, 1930s	.15	.15
690	A82	2ch Barnyard Olympics, 1932	.15	.15
691	A82	3ch Society Dog Show, 1939	.15	.15
692	A82	4ch Fantasia, 1980s re-release	.15	.15
693	A82	5ch The Mad Dog, 1932	.15	.15
694	A82	10ch A Gentleman's Gentleman, 1941	.15	.15
695	A82	50ch Symphony hour, 1942	.15	.15
696	A82	10nu The Moose Hunt, 1931	1.50	1.25
697	A82	15nu Wild Waves, 1929	2.25	1.75
698	A82	20nu Mickey in Arabia, 1932	3.00	2.50
699	A82	25nu Tugboat Mickey, 1940	3.75	3.00
700	A82	30nu Building a Building, 1933	4.25	3.50
		Nos. 689-700 (12)	15.80	13.05

Souvenir Sheets

701	A82	25nu The Mad Doctor, 1933	4.00	4.00
702	A82	25nu The Meller Drammer, 1933	4.00	4.00
703	A82	25nu Ye Olden Days, 1933	4.00	4.00
704	A82	25nu Mickey's Good Deed, 1932	4.00	4.00
705	A82	25nu Mickey's Pal Pluto, 1933	4.00	4.00
706	A82	25nu Trader Mickey, 1932	4.00	4.00
707	A82	25nu Touchdown Mickey, 1932	4.00	4.00
708	A82	25nu Steamboat Willie, 1928	4.00	4.00
709	A82	25nu The Whoopee Party, 1932	4.00	4.00
710	A82	25nu Mickey's Nightmare, 1932	4.00	4.00
711	A82	25nu The Klondike Kid, 1932	4.00	4.00
712	A82	25nu The Wayward Canary, 1932	4.00	4.00

Mushrooms — A83

1989, Aug. 22   Litho.   Perf. 14

713	A83	50ch Tricholoma pardalotum	.15	.15
714	A83	1nu Suillus placidus	.15	.15
715	A83	2nu Boletus regius	.30	.25
716	A83	3nu Gomphidius glutinosus	.50	.35
717	A83	4nu Boletus calopus	.65	.50
718	A83	5nu Suillus grevillei	.80	.60
719	A83	6nu Boletus appendiculatus	.95	.70
720	A83	7nu Lactarius torminosus	1.10	.80
721	A83	10nu Macrolepiota rhacodes	1.60	1.25
722	A83	15nu Amanita rubescens	2.50	1.75
723	A83	20nu Amanita phalloides	3.25	2.50
724	A83	25nu Amanita citrina	4.00	3.00
		Nos. 713-724 (12)	15.95	12.00

Souvenir Sheets

725	A83	25nu Russula aurata	4.00	4.00
726	A83	25nu Gyroporus castaneus	4.00	4.00
727	A83	25nu Cantharellus cibarius	4.00	4.00
728	A83	25nu Boletus rhodoxanthus	4.00	4.00
729	A83	25nu Paxillus involutus	4.00	4.00
730	A83	25nu Gyroporus cyanescens	4.00	4.00
731	A83	25nu Lepista nuda	4.00	4.00
732	A83	25nu Dentinum repandum	4.00	4.00
733	A83	25nu Lepista saeva	4.00	4.00
734	A83	25nu Hydnum imbricatum	4.00	4.00
735	A83	25nu Xerocomus subtomentosus	4.00	4.00
736	A83	25nu Russula olivacea	4.00	4.00

Intl. Maritime Organization, 30th Anniv. — A84

Ships: 50ch, Spanish galleon *La Reale,* 1680. 1nu, Submersible *Turtle,* 1776. 2nu, *Charlote Dundas,* 1802. 3nu, *Great Eastern,* c. 1858. 4nu, HMS *Warrior,* 1862. 5nu, Mississippi steamer, 1884. 6nu, *Preussen,* 1902. 7nu, USS *Arizona,* 1915. 10nu, *Bluenose,* 1921. 15nu, Steam trawler, 1925. 20nu, American liberty ship, 1943. No. 748, S.S. *United States,* 1952. No. 749, Moran tug, c. 1950. No. 750, Sinking of the *Titanic,* 1912. No. 751, U-boat, c. 1942. No. 752, Japanese warship *Yamato,* 1944. No. 753, HMS *Dreadnought.* Not 754, S.S. *Normandie,* c. 1933, and a Chinese junk. No. 755, HMS *Victory,* 1805. No. 756, USS *Monitor,* 1862. No. 757, *Cutty Sark,* 1869. No. 758, USS *Constitution.* No. 759, HMS *Resolution.* No. 760, Chinese junk.

1989, Aug. 24   Litho.   Perf. 14

737	A84	50ch multicolored	.15	.15
738	A84	1nu multicolored	.15	.15
739	A84	2nu multicolored	.30	.25
740	A84	3nu multicolored	.50	.35
741	A84	4nu multicolored	.65	.50
742	A84	5nu multicolored	.80	.60
743	A84	6nu multicolored	.95	.70
744	A84	7nu multicolored	1.10	.80
745	A84	10nu multicolored	1.60	1.25
746	A84	15nu multicolored	2.50	1.75
747	A84	20nu multicolored	3.25	2.50
748	A84	25nu multicolored	4.00	3.00
		Nos. 737-748 (12)	15.95	12.00

Souvenir Sheets

749-760	A84	25nu each	4.00	4.00

Nos. 289-291 Overprinted:
WORLD / AIDS DAY

1988, Dec. 1   Litho.   Perf. 14x13½

761	A37	2nu multicolored	.45	.35
762	A37	5nu multicolored	1.10	.90
763	A37	10nu multicolored	2.25	1.75
		Nos. 761-763 (3)	3.80	3.00

Nos. 486-494 Ovptd. in Silver:
ASIA-PACIFIC EXPOSITION FUKUOKA '89

1989, Mar. 17   Perf. 13½

764	A61	5ch multicolored	.15	.15
765	A61	35ch multicolored	.15	.15
766	A61	50ch multicolored	.15	.15
767	A61	2.50nu multicolored	.40	.30
768	A61	3nu multicolored	.50	.35
769	A61	4nu multicolored	.65	.50
770	A61	5nu multicolored	.80	.60
771	A61	5.50nu multicolored	.90	.65
772	A61	6nu multicolored	1.00	.80
		Nos. 764-772 (9)	4.70	3.65

This set exists overprinted in Japanese.

Chhukha Hydroelectric Project — A85

1988, Oct. 21   Litho.   Perf. 13½

773	A85	50ch multicolored	.15	.15

Jawaharlal Nehru (1889-1964), Indian Prime Minister — A85a

1989, Nov. 14   Photo.   Perf. 14
773A	A85a	100ch olive brown	.15	.15

Denomination is shown as 1.00ch in error.

Birds A86

Designs: 50ch, Larger goldenbacked woodpecker. 1nu, Black-naped monarch. 2nu, White-crested laughing thrush. 3nu, Blood-pheasant. 4nu, Blossom-headed parakeet. 5nu, Rosy minivet. 6nu, Chestnut-headed tit babbler. 7nu, Blue pitta. 10nu, Black-naped oriole. 15nu, Green magpie. 20nu, Indian three-toed kingfisher. No. 785, Ibisbill. No. 786, Great pied hornbill. No. 787, Himalayan red-breasted falconet. No. 788, Lammergeier. No. 789, Large racket-tailed drongo. No. 790, Fire-tailed sunbird. No. 791, Indian crested swift. No. 792, White-eared pheasant. No. 793, Satyr tragopan. No. 794, Wallcreeper. No. 795, Fairy bluebird. No. 796, Little spiderhunter. No. 797, Spotted forktail. Nos. 774-779 vert.

1989, Nov. 22   Litho.   Perf. 14

774	A86	50ch multicolored	.15	.15
775	A86	1nu multicolored	.15	.15
776	A86	2nu multicolored	.30	.25
777	A86	3nu multicolored	.50	.35
778	A86	4nu multicolored	.65	.50
779	A86	5nu multicolored	.80	.60
780	A86	6nu multicolored	.95	.70
781	A86	7nu multicolored	1.10	.80
782	A86	10nu multicolored	1.60	1.25
783	A86	15nu multicolored	2.50	1.75
784	A86	20nu multicolored	3.25	2.50
785	A86	25nu multicolored	4.00	3.00
		Nos. 774-785 (12)	15.95	12.00

Souvenir Sheets

786-797	A86	25nu each	4.00	4.00

Steam Locomotives A87

Designs: 50ch, *Best Friend of Charleston*, 1830, US 1nu, Class U, 1949, France. 2nu, *Consolidation*, 1866, US. 3nu, *Luggage Engine*, 1843, Great Britain. 4nu, Class 60-3 Shay, 1913, US. 5nu, *John Bull*, 1831, US. 6nu, *Hercules*, 1837, US. 7nu, Eight-wheel tank engine, 1874, Great Britain. 10nu, *The Illinois*, 1852, US. 15nu, German State 4-6-4, 1935. 20nu, American Standard, 1865. No. 809, Class Ps-4, 1926, US. No. 810, *Puffing Billy*, 1814, Great Britain. No. 811, Stephenson's *Rocket*, 1829, Great Britain. No. 812, *Cumberland*, 1845, US, vert. No. 813, *John Stevens*, 1849, US, vert. No. 814, No. 22 Baldwin Locomotive Works, 1873, US, No. 815, *Ariel*, 1877, US. No. 816, 1899 *No. 1301* Webb Compound Engine, Great Britain. No. 817, 1893 *No. 999* Empire State Express, US. No. 818, 1923 Class K-36, US. No. 819, 1935 Class A4, Great Britain. No. 820, 1935 Class A, US. No. 821, 1943 Class P-1, US.

1990, Jan. 30

798	A87	50ch	multi	.15	.15
799	A87	1nu	multi	.15	.15
800	A87	2nu	multi	.30	.25
801	A87	3nu	multi	.50	.35
802	A87	4nu	multi	.65	.50
803	A87	5nu	multi	.80	.60
804	A87	6nu	multi	.95	.70
805	A87	7nu	multi	1.10	.80
806	A87	10nu	multi	1.60	1.25
807	A87	15nu	multi	2.50	1.75
808	A87	20nu	multi	3.25	2.50
809	A87	25nu	multi	4.00	3.00
			Nos. 798-809 (12)	15.95	12.00

Souvenir Sheets

810-821	A87	25nu	each	4.00	4.00

Butterflies A88

1990, Jan. 30 Litho. *Perf. 14*

822	A88	50ch	*Charaxes harmodius*	.15	.15
823	A88	1nu	*Prioneris thestylis*	.15	.15
824	A88	2nu	*Sephisa chandra*	.30	.25
825	A88	3nu	*Penthema usarda*	.50	.35
826	A88	4nu	*Troides aecus*	.65	.50
827	A88	5nu	*Polyura eudamippus*	.80	.60
828	A88	6nu	*Polyura dolon*	.95	.70
829	A88	7nu	*Neope bhadra*	1.10	.80
830	A88	10nu	*Delias descombesi*	1.60	1.25
831	A88	15nu	*Childreni childrena*	2.50	1.75
832	A88	20nu	*Kallima inachus*	3.25	2.50
833	A88	25nu	*Elymnias malelas*	4.00	3.00
			Nos. 822-833 (12)	15.95	12.00

Souvenir Sheets

834	A88	25nu	Red lacewing	4.00	4.00
835	A88	25nu	Bhutan glory	4.00	4.00
836	A88	25nu	Great eggfly	4.00	4.00
837	A88	25nu	Kaiser-I-Hind	4.00	4.00
838	A88	25nu	Chestnut tiger	4.00	4.00
839	A88	25nu	Common map	4.00	4.00
840	A88	25nu	Swallowtail	4.00	4.00
841	A88	25nu	Jungle glory	4.00	4.00
842	A88	25nu	Checkered swallowtail	4.00	4.00
843	A88	25nu	Common birdwing	4.00	4.00
844	A88	25nu	Blue banded peacock	4.00	4.00
845	A88	25nu	Camberwell beauty	4.00	4.00

Nos. 822-824, 826-827, 830-831, 834-835, 844-845 are vert.

Paintings by Hiroshige A89

Designs: 10ch, Plum Estate, Kameido. 20ch, Yatsumi Bridge. 50ch, Ayase River and Kanegafuchi. 75ch, View of Shiba Coast. 1nu, Grandpa's Teahouse, Meguro. 2nu, Kameido Tenjin Shrine. 6nu, Yoroi Ferry, Koami-cho. 7nu, Sakasai Ferry. 10nu, Fukagawa Lumberyards. 15nu, Suido Bridge and Surugadai. 20nu, Meguro Drum Bridge and Sunset Hill. No. 857, Atagoshita and Yabu Lane. No. 858, Towboats Along the Yotsugi-dori Canal. No. 859, Minowa, Kanasugi, Mikawashima. No. 860, Horikiri Iris Garden. No. 861, Fukagawa Susaki and Jumantsubo. No. 862, Suijin Shrine and Massaki on the Sumida River. No. 863, New Year's Eve Foxfires at the Changing Tree, Oji. No. 864, Nihonbashi, Clearing After Snow. No. 865, View to the North from Asukayama. No. 866, Komakata Hall and Azuma Bridge. No. 867, The City Flourishing, Tanabata Festival. No. 868, Suruga-cho. No. 869, Sudden Shower over Shin-Ohashi Bridge and Atake.

1990, May 21 Litho. *Perf. 13½*

846	A89	10ch	multicolored	.15	.15
847	A89	20ch	multicolored	.15	.15
848	A89	50ch	multicolored	.15	.15
849	A89	75ch	multicolored	.15	.15
850	A89	1nu	multicolored	.15	.15
851	A89	2nu	multicolored	.30	.25
852	A89	6nu	multicolored	.95	.70
853	A89	7nu	multicolored	1.10	.85
854	A89	10nu	multicolored	1.60	1.25
855	A89	15nu	multicolored	2.50	1.75
856	A89	20nu	multicolored	3.25	2.50
857	A89	25nu	multicolored	4.00	3.00
			Nos. 846-857 (12)	14.45	11.05

Souvenir Sheets

858-869	A89	25nu	each	4.00	3.00

Hirohito (1901-1989) and enthronement of Akihito as emperor of Japan.

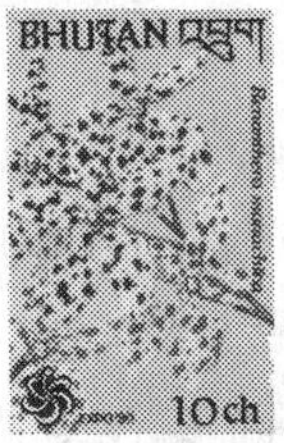

Orchids — A90

1990, Apr. 6 Litho. *Perf. 14*

870	A90	10ch	*Renanthera monachica*	.15	.15
871	A90	50ch	*Vanda coerulea*	.15	.15
872	A90	1nu	*Phalaenopsis violacea*	.15	.15
873	A90	2nu	*Dendrobium nobile*	.30	.25
874	A90	5nu	*Vandopsis lissochiloides*	.80	.60
875	A90	6nu	*Paphiopedilum rothschildianum*	.95	.70
876	A90	7nu	*Phalaenopsis schilleriana*	1.10	.80
877	A90	9nu	*Paphiopedilum insigne*	1.50	1.10
878	A90	10nu	*Paphiopedilum bellatulum*	1.60	1.25
879	A90	20nu	*Doritis pulcherrima*	3.25	2.50
880	A90	25nu	*Cymbidium giganteum*	4.00	3.00
881	A90	35nu	*Phalaenopsis mariae*	5.50	4.25
			Nos. 870-881 (12)	19.45	14.90

Souvenir Sheets

882	A90	30nu	*Vanda coerulescens*	4.75	4.75
883	A90	30nu	*Vandopsis parishi*	4.75	4.75
884	A90	30nu	*Dendrobium aphyllum*	4.75	4.75
885	A90	30nu	*Phalaenopsis amabilis*	4.75	4.75
886	A90	30nu	*Paphiopedilum haynaldianum*	4.75	4.75
887	A90	30nu	*Dendrobium lodigesii*	4.75	4.75
888	A90	30nu	*Vanda alpina*	4.75	4.75
889	A90	30nu	*Phalaenopsis equestris*	4.75	4.75
890	A90	30nu	*Vanda cristata*	4.75	4.75
891	A90	30nu	*Phalaenopsis cornu cervi*	4.75	4.75
892	A90	30nu	*Paphiopedilum niveum*	4.75	4.75
893	A90	30nu	*Dendrobium margaritaceum*	4.75	4.75

EXPO '90 Intl. Garden and Greenery Exposition, Osaka, Apr. 1-Dec. 31.

G.P.O., Thimphu — A90a

1990, May 29 Photo. *Perf. 14*

893A	A90a	1nu	multicolored	.15	.15

Penny Black, 150th Anniv. A90b

Penny Black and: 50ch, Bhutan #1. 1nu, Oldenburg #1. 2nu, Bergedorf #3. 4nu, German Democratic Republic #48. 5nu, Brunswick #1. 6nu, Basel #3L1. 8nu, Geneva #2L1. 10nu, Zurich #1L1. No. 902, France #3. 20nu, Vatican City #1. 25nu, Israel #1. No. 905, Japan #1.

Penny Black and: No. 906a, Mecklenburg-Schwerin #1. b, Mecklenburg-Strelitz #1. No. 907a, Germany #5, #9. b, Prussia #2. No. 908a, Hamburg #1. b, North German Confederation #1, #7. No. 909a, Baden #1. b, Wurttemberg #1. No. 910a, Heligoland #1. b, Hanover #1. No. 911a, Thurn & Taxis #3. b, Thurn & Taxis #42. No. 912a, Schleswig-Holstein #1. b, Lubeck #5. No. 913, Saxony #1. No. 914, Berlin #9N1. No. 915, No other stamp. No. 916, US #1. No. 917, Bavaria #1.

1990, Oct. 9 *Perf. 14*

894	A90b	50ch	multicolored	.15	.15
895	A90b	1nu	multicolored	.15	.15
896	A90b	2nu	multicolored	.30	.25
897	A90b	4nu	multicolored	.65	.50
898	A90b	5nu	multicolored	.80	.60
899	A90b	6nu	multicolored	1.00	.75
900	A90b	8nu	multicolored	1.25	1.00
901	A90b	10nu	multicolored	1.60	1.25
902	A90b	15nu	multicolored	2.50	1.75
903	A90b	20nu	multicolored	3.25	2.50
904	A90b	25nu	multicolored	4.00	3.00
905	A90b	30nu	multicolored	4.75	3.50
			Nos. 894-905 (12)	20.40	15.40

Souvenir Sheets

Sheets of 2 (#906-912) or 1

906-912	A90b	15nu	each	4.75	4.75
913-917	A90b	30nu	each	4.75	4.75

Stamp World London '90.

Giant Pandas A91

Tiger A92

Endangered wildlife of Asia.

1990 *Perf. 14*

918	A91	50ch	multi, diff.	.15	.15
919	A91	1nu	multi, diff.	.15	.15
920	A91	2nu	multi, diff.	.30	.25
921	A91	3nu	shown	.50	.35
922	A91	4nu	multi, diff.	.65	.50
923	A92	5nu	shown	.80	.60
924	A91	6nu	multi, diff.	.95	.70
925	A91	7nu	multi, diff.	1.10	.80
926	A92	10nu	Elephant	1.60	1.25
927	A91	15nu	multi, diff.	2.50	1.75
928	A92	20nu	Barking deer	3.25	2.50
929	A92	25nu	Snow leopard	4.00	3.00
			Nos. 918-929 (12)	15.95	12.00

Souvenir Sheets

930	A92	25nu	Rhinoceros	4.00	4.00
931	A92	25nu	Clouded leopard	4.00	4.00
932	A92	25nu	Asiatic wild dog	4.00	4.00
933	A92	25nu	Himalayan shou	4.00	4.00
934	A92	25nu	Golden cat	4.00	4.00
935	A92	25nu	Himalayan musk deer	4.00	4.00
936	A91	25nu	multi, diff.	4.00	4.00
937	A92	25nu	Asiatic black bear	4.00	4.00
938	A92	25nu	Gaur	4.00	4.00
939	A92	25nu	Pygmy hog	4.00	4.00
940	A92	25nu	Wolf	4.00	4.00
941	A92	25nu	Sloth bear	4.00	4.00

Nos. 919-920 and 927 vert.

Buddhist Musical Instruments — A93

1990, Sept. 29 Litho. *Perf. 13½x13*

942	A93	10ch	Dungchen	.15	.15
943	A93	20ch	Dungkar	.15	.15
944	A93	30ch	Roim	.15	.15
945	A93	50ch	Tinchag	.15	.15
946	A93	1nu	Dradu & drilbu	.15	.15
947	A93	2nu	Gya-ling	.30	.25
948	A93	2.50nu	Nga	.40	.30
	a.		Souv. sheet of 4, #943, 945, 947-948	.85	.65
949	A93	3.50nu	Kang-dung	.55	.40
	a.		Souv. sheet of 4, #942, 944, 946, 949	.85	.65
			Set value	1.65	1.25

Year of the Girl Child — A94

1990, Dec. 8

950	A94	50ch	shown	.15	.15
951	A94	20nu	Young girl	3.25	2.50

Wonders of the World A95

Walt Disney characters viewing: 1ch, Temple of Artemis, Ephesus. 2ch, Statue of Zeus, Olympia. 3ch, Egyptian pyramids. 4ch, Lighthouse, Alexandria. 5ch, Mausoleum at Halicarnassus. 10ch, Colossus of Rhodes. 50ch, Hanging gardens of Babylon. 5nu, Mauna Loa volcano, Hawaii. 6nu, Carlsbad Caverns, New Mexico. 10nu, Rainbow Bridge, Utah. 15nu, Grand Canyon of the Colorado, Arizona. 20nu, Old Faithful geyser, Wyoming. 25nu, Giant sequoias, California. 30nu, Crater Lake and Wizard Island, Oregon. 5nu, 6nu, 10nu, 15nu, 20nu, 25nu, 30nu are horiz.

Walt Disney characters viewing: No. 966, Great Wall of China, horiz. No. 967, Mosque of St. Sophia, Istanbul, Turkey. No. 968, The Leaning Tower of Pisa, Italy. No. 969, Colosseum, Rome. No. 970, Stonehenge, England. No. 971, Catacombs of Alexandria, Egypt. No. 972, Porcelain Tower, Nanking, China, horiz. No. 973, The Panama Canal, horiz. No. 974, Golden Gate Bridge, San Francisco, horiz. No. 975, Sears Tower, Chicago, horiz. No. 976, Gateway Arch, St. Louis. No. 977, Alcan Highway, Alaska and Canada, horiz. No. 978, Hoover Dam, Nevada. No. 979, Empire State Building, New York.

1991, Feb. 2 Litho. *Perf. 14*

952	A95	1ch	multicolored	.15	.15
953	A95	2ch	multicolored	.15	.15
954	A95	3ch	multicolored	.15	.15
955	A95	4ch	multicolored	.15	.15
956	A95	5ch	multicolored	.15	.15
957	A95	10ch	multicolored	.15	.15
958	A95	50ch	multicolored	.15	.15
959	A95	5nu	multicolored	.80	.60
960	A95	6nu	multicolored	.95	.70
961	A95	10nu	multicolored	1.60	1.25
962	A95	15nu	multicolored	2.50	1.75
963	A95	20nu	multicolored	3.25	2.50
964	A95	25nu	multicolored	4.00	3.00
965	A95	30nu	multicolored	4.75	3.50
			Nos. 952-965 (14)	18.90	14.35

BHUTAN

Souvenir Sheets
Perf. 14x13½, 13½x14

966-979	A95	25nu each	4.00	4.00

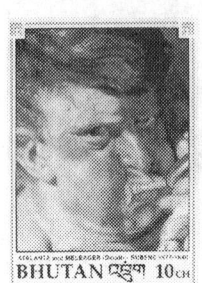

Peter Paul Rubens (1577-1640), Painter — A96

Entire paintings or different details from: 10ch, 5nu, 6nu, 10nu, No. 992, Atalanta and Meleager. 50ch, Fall of Phaethon. 1nu, No. 993, Feast of Venus Verticordia. 2nu, Achilles Slaying Hector. 3nu, No. 994, Arachne Punished by Minerva. 4nu, No. 995, Jupiter Receives Psyche on Olympus. 7nu, Venus in Vulcan's Furnace. 20nu, No. 996, Briseis Returned to Achilles. 30nu, No. 997, Mars and Rhea Sylvia. No. 998, Venus Shivering. No. 999, Ganymede and the Eagle. No. 1000, Origin of the Milky Way. No. 1001, Adonis and Venus. No. 1002, Hero and Leander. No. 1003, Fall of the Titans.

Nos. 994, 996-997, 1000-1003 are horiz.

1991, Feb. 2

980	A96	10ch multicolored	.15	.15
981	A96	50ch multicolored	.15	.15
982	A96	1nu multicolored	.15	.15
983	A96	2nu multicolored	.30	.15
984	A96	3nu multicolored	.50	.15
985	A96	4nu multicolored	.65	.15
986	A96	5nu multicolored	.80	.60
987	A96	6nu multicolored	.95	.70
988	A96	7nu multicolored	1.10	.85
989	A96	10nu multicolored	1.60	1.25
990	A96	20nu multicolored	3.25	2.50
991	A96	30nu multicolored	4.75	3.50
	Nos. 980-991 (12)		14.35	10.30

Souvenir Sheets

992-1003	A96	25nu each	4.00	4.00

Vincent Van Gogh (1853-1890), Painter — A97

Paintings: 10ch, Cottages, Reminiscence of the North. 50ch, Head of a Peasant Woman with Dark Cap. 1nu, Portrait of a Woman in Blue. 2nu, The Midwife. 8nu, Vase with Hollyhocks. 10nu, Portrait of a Man with a Skull Cap. 12nu, Agostina Segatori Sitting in the Cafe du Tambourin. 15nu, Vase with Daisies and Anemones. 18nu, Fritillaries in a Copper Vase. 20nu, Woman Sitting in the Grass. 25nu, On the Outskirts of Paris, horiz. 30nu, Chrysanthemums and Wild Flowers in a Vase.

No. 1016, Le Moulin de la Galette. No. 1017, Bowl with Sunflowers, Roses and Other Flowers, horiz. No. 1018, Poppies and Butterflies. No. 1019, Trees in the Garden of Saint-Paul Hospital. No. 1020, Le Moulin de Blute Fin. No. 1021, Le Moulin de la Galette, diff. No. 1022, Vase with Peonies. No. 1023, Vase with Zinnias. No. 1024, Fishing in the Spring, Pont de Clichy, horiz. No. 1025, Village Street in Auvers, horiz. No. 1026, Vase with Zinnias and Other Flowers, horiz. No. 2027, Vase with Red Poppies.

1991, July 22   *Litho.*   *Perf. 13½*

1004	A97	10ch multicolored	.15	.15
1005	A97	50ch multicolored	.15	.15
1006	A97	1nu multicolored	.15	.15
1007	A97	2nu multicolored	.30	.15
1008	A97	8nu multicolored	1.25	1.00
1009	A97	10nu multicolored	1.65	1.25
1010	A97	12nu multicolored	2.00	1.50
1011	A97	15nu multicolored	2.50	1.75
1012	A97	18nu multicolored	3.00	2.25
1013	A97	20nu multicolored	3.25	2.50
1014	A97	25nu multicolored	4.00	3.00
1015	A97	30nu multicolored	4.75	3.50
	Nos. 1004-1015 (12)		23.15	17.35

Size: 76x102mm, 102x76mm
Imperf

1016-1027	A97	30nu each	4.75	4.75

History of World Cup Soccer — A98

Winning team pictures, plays or possible future site: 50ch, Uruguay, 1930. 1nu, Italy, 1934. 2nu, Italy, 1938. 3nu, Uruguay, 1950. 5nu, West Germany, 1954. 10nu, Brazil, 1958. 20nu, Brazil, 1962. 25nu, England, 1966. 29nu, Brazil, 1970. 30nu, West Germany, 1974. 31nu, Argentina, 1978. 32nu, Italy, 1982. 33nu, Argentina, 1986. 34nu, West Germany, 1990. 35nu, Los Angeles Coliseum, 1994.

Players: No. 1043, Claudio Caniggia, Argentina, vert. No. 1044, Salvatore Schillaci, Italy, vert. No. 1045, Roberto Baggio, Italy, vert. No. 1046, Peter Shilton, England, vert. No. 1047, Lothar Matthaus, West Germany, vert. No. 1048, Paul Gascoigne, England, vert.

1991, Aug. 1   *Litho.*   *Perf. 13½*

1028	A98	50ch multicolored	.15	.15
1029	A98	1nu multicolored	.15	.15
1030	A98	3nu multicolored	.30	.15
1031	A98	3nu multicolored	.50	.15
1032	A98	5nu multicolored	.80	.60
1033	A98	10nu multicolored	1.65	1.25
1034	A98	20nu multicolored	3.25	2.50
1035	A98	25nu multicolored	4.00	3.00
1036	A98	29nu multicolored	4.75	3.50
1037	A98	30nu multicolored	4.75	3.50
1038	A98	31nu multicolored	5.00	3.75
1039	A98	32nu multicolored	5.25	4.00
1040	A98	33nu multicolored	5.50	4.00
1041	A98	34nu multicolored	5.50	4.25
1042	A98	35nu multicolored	5.75	4.25
	Nos. 1028-1042 (15)		47.30	35.20

Souvenir Sheets

1043-1048	A98	30nu each	4.75	4.75

Phila Nippon '91 — A99

1991, Nov. 16   *Perf. 13*

1049	A99	15nu multicolored	2.50	1.50

Education in Bhutan A100

1992, Mar. 5   *Photo.*   *Perf. 13½*

1050	A100	1nu multicolored	.20	.15

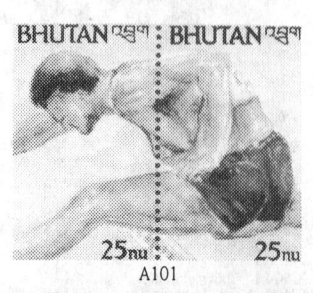

A101

1992 Summer Olympics, Barcelona — A102

1992, July 24   *Litho.*   *Perf. 12*

1051	A101	25nu Pair, #a.-b.	8.25	8.25

Souvenir Sheet

1052	A102	25nu Archer	4.00	4.00

German Reunification — A103

1992, Oct. 3   *Litho.*   *Perf. 12*

1053	A103	25nu multicolored	2.00	2.00

Souvenir Sheet

1054	A103	25nu multicolored	2.00	2.00

Stamp from No. 1054 does not have white inscription or border.

Bhutan Postal Service, 30th Anniv. A104

Designs: 1nu, Mail truck, plane. 3nu, Letter carrier approaching village. 5nu, Letter carrier emptying mail box.

1992, Oct. 9

1055	A104	1nu multicolored	.15	.15
1056	A104	3nu multicolored	.25	.25
1057	A104	5nu multicolored	.40	.40
	Nos. 1055-1057 (3)		.80	.80

Environmental Protection — A105

Designs: a, 7nu, Red panda. b, 20nu, Takin. c, 15nu, Black-necked crane, blue poppy. d, 10nu, One-horned rhinoceros.

1993, July 1   *Litho.*   *Perf. 14*

1058	A105	Sheet of 4, #b.-e.		

No. 1058 was delayed from its originally scheduled release in 1992, although some copies were made available to the trade at that time.

A106   **A107**

1992, Sept. 18   *Perf. 12*

1059	A106	15nu Ship	1.25	1.25
1060	A106	20nu Portrait	1.60	1.60

Souvenir Sheet

1061	A106	25nu like #1060	2.00	2.00

Discovery of America, 500th anniv.

Stamp from No. 1061 does not have silver inscription or white border.

1992, Nov. 11   *Litho.*   *Perf. 12*

Reign of King Jigme Singye Wangchuk, 20th Anniv.: a, 1nu, Man tilling field, factory. b, 5nu, Airplane. c, 10nu, House, well. d, 15nu, King. 20nu, People, flag, King, horiz.

1062	A107	Block of 4, #a.-d.	2.50	2.50

Souvenir Sheet

1063	A107	20nu multicolored	1.75	1.75

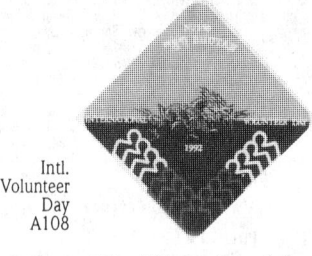

Intl. Volunteer Day A108

Designs: a, 1.50nu, White inscription. b, 9nu, Green inscription. c, 15nu, Red inscription.

1992, Dec. 5   *Litho.*   *Perf. 14*

1067	A108	Block of 4, #a.-c. + label	2.00	2.00

Medicinal Plants — A109

1993, Jan. 1   *Litho.*   *Perf. 12*

1068	A109	1.50nu Meconopsis grandis prain	.15	.15
1069	A109	7nu Meconopsis sp.	.60	.60
1070	A109	10nu Meconopsis wallichii	.80	.80
1071	A109	12nu Meconopsis horridula	1.00	1.00
1072	A109	20nu Meconopsis discigera	1.75	1.75
	Nos. 1068-1072 (5)		4.30	4.30

Souvenir Sheet

1073	A109	25nu Meconopsis horridula, diff.	2.00	2.00

Miniature Sheet

Lunar New Year — A110

1993, Feb. 22   *Litho.*   *Perf. 14*

1074	A110	25nu multicolored	2.00	2.00

No. 1074 Surcharged "TAIPEI '93" in Silver and Black

1993, Aug. 14   *Litho.*   *Perf. 14*

1075	A110	30nu on 25nu	2.50	2.50

BHUTAN

Door Gods — A112

Flowers — A113

1993, Dec. 17   Litho.   *Perf. 12*
1091	A112	1.50nu Namtheo-Say	.15	.15
1092	A112	5nu Pha-Ke-Po	.50	.50
1093	A112	10nu Chen-Mi-Jang	1.00	1.00
1094	A112	15nu Yul-Khor-Sung	1.50	1.50
		Nos. 1091-1094 (4)	3.15	3.15

1993, Jan. 1   *Perf. 13*

Designs: No. 1095a, 1nu, Rhododendron mucronatum. b, 1.5nu. Anemone rupicola. c, 2nu, Polemonium coeruleum. d, 2.5nu, Rosa marophylla. e, 4nu, Paraquilegia microphylla. f, 5nu, Aquilegia nivalis. g, 6nu, Geranium wallichianum. h, 7nu, Rhododendron campanulatum. i, 9nu, Viola suavis. j, 10nu, Cyananthus lobatus. 13nu, Red flower, horiz.

1095	A113	Strip of 10, #a.-j.	4.75	4.75

Souvenir Sheet
1096	A113	13nu multicolored	1.40	1.40

New Year 1994 (Year of the Dog) — A114

1994, Feb. 11   Litho.   *Perf. 14*
1097	A114	11.50nu multicolored	.80	.80

Souvenir Sheet
1098	A114	20nu like #1097	1.40	1.40

Hong Kong '94.

Stamp Cards — A115

Designs: 16nu, Tagtshang Monastery. 20nu, Map of Bhutan. Illustration reduced.

Rouletted 26 on 2 or 3 Sides
1994, Aug. 15   Litho.
Self-Adhesive
Cards of 6 + 6 labels
1099	A115	16nu #a.-f.	6.25	6.25
1100	A115	20nu #a.-f.	7.75	7.75

Individual stamps measure 70x9mm and have a card backing. Se-tenant labels inscribed "AIR MAIL."

Souvenir Sheet

First Manned Moon Landing, 25th Anniv. — A116

Designs: a, 30nu, Astronaut on moon. b, 36nu, Space shuttle, earth, moon. Illustration reduced.

1994, Nov. 11   Litho.   *Perf. 14x14½*
1101	A116	Sheet of 2, #a.-b.	4.25	4.25

Nos. 1101a, 1101b have holographic images. Soaking in water may affect the holograms.

Souvenir Sheet

Victory Over Tibet-Mongol Army, 350th Anniv. — A117

Battle scene: a, Mounted officer. b, Hand to hand combat, soldiers in yellow or blue armor. c, Soldier on gray horse. d, Soldiers in red, drummer, horn player.

1994, Dec. 17   Litho.   *Perf. 12½*
Granite Paper
1102	A117	15nu Sheet of 4, #a.-d.	4.00	4.00

Souvenir Sheet

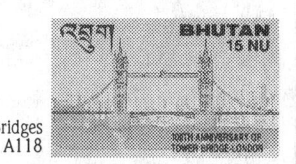

Bridges A118

Designs: a, 15nu, Tower Bridge, London, cent. b, 16nu, Wangdue Bridge, Bhutan, 250th anniv.

1994, Nov. 11   Litho.   *Perf. 12*
1103	A118	Sheet of 2, #a.-b.	2.00	2.00

1994 World Cup Soccer Championships, US — A119

1994, July 17   Litho.   *Perf. 12*
1104	A119	15nu multicolored	1.00	1.00

Souvenir Sheet

World Tourism Year A120

Scenes of Bhutan: a, 1.50nu, Paro Valley. b, 5nu, Chorten Kora. c, 10nu, Thimphu Tshechu. d, 15nu, Wangdue Tshechu.

1995, Apr. 2   Litho.   *Perf. 12*
1105	A120	Sheet of 4, #a.-d.	2.00	2.00

Miniature Sheet of 12

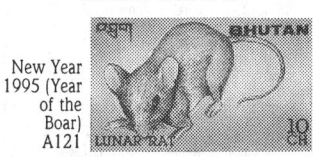

New Year 1995 (Year of the Boar) A121

Symbols of Chinese Lunar New Year: a, 10ch, Rat. b, 20ch, Ox. c, 30ch, Tiger. d, 40ch, Rabbit. e, 1nu, Dragon. f, 2nu, Snake. g, 3nu, Horse. h, 4nu, Sheep. i, 5nu, Monkey. j, 7nu, Rooster. k, 8nu, Dog. l, 9nu, Boar. 10nu, Wood Hog.

1995, Mar. 2
1106	A121	#a.-l.	2.50	2.50

Souvenir Sheet
1107	A121	10nu multicolored	.65	.65

No. 1107 is a continuous design.

A122

A123

Flowers: 9nu, Pleione praecox. 10nu, Primula calderina. 16nu, Primula whitei. 18nu, Notholirion macrophyllum.

1995, May 2   Litho.   *Perf. 12*
1108-1111	A122	Set of 4	3.50	3.50

1995, June 26   *Perf. 14*

UN, 50th Anniv.: a, 1.5nu, Human resources development. b, 9nu, Health & population. c, 10nu, Water & sanitation. d, 5nu, Transport & communications. e, 16nu, Forestry & environment. f, 18nu, Peace & security. g, 11.5nu, UN in Bhutan.

1112	A123	Strip of 7	4.75	4.75

Miniature Sheet of 6

Singapore '95 — A124

Birds: No. 1113a, 1nu, Himalayan pied kingfisher. b, 2nu, Blyth's tragopan. c, 3nu, Long-tailed minivet. d, 10nu, Red junglefowl. e, 15nu, Black-capped sibia. f, 20nu, Red-billed chough. No. 1114, Black-neck crane.

1995, June 2   Litho.   *Perf. 12*
1113	A124	#a.-f. + 3 labels	3.50	3.50

Souvenir Sheet
1114	A124	20nu multicolored	1.40	1.40

Traditional Crafts — A125

Designs: 1nu, Drying parchment. 2nu, Making tapestry. 3nu, Restoring archaeological finds. 10nu, Weaving textiles. 15nu, Sewing garments. No. 1120, 20nu, Carving wooden vessels. No. 1121, Mosaic.

1995, Aug. 15   Litho.   *Perf. 14*
1115-1120	A125	Set of 6	2.50	2.50

Souvenir Sheet
1121	A125	20nu multicolored	1.40	1.40

New Year 1996 (Year of the Rat) — A126

Designs: a, Monkey. b, Rat, fire. c, Dragon.

1996, Jan. 1   Litho.   *Perf. 14*
1122	A126	10nu Sheet of 3, #a.-c.	2.00	2.00

Butterflies A127

Designs: a, 2nu, Blue pansy. b, 3nu, Blue peacock. c, 5nu, Great Mormon. d, 10nu, Fritillary. e, 15nu, Blue duke. f, 25nu, Brown Gorgon. No. 1124, Xanthomelas. No. 1124A, Fivebar swordtail.

1996, May 2   Litho.   *Perf. 14*
1123	A127	Sheet of 6, #a.-f.	4.00	4.00

Souvenir Sheets
1124-1124A	A127	30nu each	2.00	2.00

1996 Summer Olympic Games, Atlanta — A128

5nu, Silver 300n coin, soccer. 7nu, Silver 300n coin, basketball. 10nu, Gold 5s coin, judo. 15nu, Archery.

1996, June 15   Litho.   *Perf. 14*
1125-1127	A128	Set of 3	1.50	1.50

Souvenir Sheet
1128	A128	15nu multicolored	1.00	1.00

Olymphilex '96.

Folktales — A129

Designs: a, 1nu, The White Bird. b, 2nu, Sing Sing Lhamo and the Moon. c, 3nu, The Hoopoe. d, 5nu, The Cloud Fairies. e, 10nu, The Three Wishes. f, 20nu, The Abominable Snowman.

1996, Apr. 15   Litho.   *Perf. 12*
1129	A129	Sheet of 6, #a.-f.	3.00	3.00

Souvenir Sheet
1130	A129	25nu like #1129d	1.75	1.75

Locomotives — A130

No. 1131: a, 0-6-4 Tank engine (Chile). b, First Pacific locomotive in Europe (France). c, 4-6-0 Passenger engine (Norway). d, Atlantic type express (Germany). e, 4-Cylinder 4-6-0 express (Belgium). f, Standard type "4" diesel-electric (England).
No. 1132: a, Standard 0-6-0 Goods engine (India). b, Main-line 1,900 horsepower diesel-electric (Finland). c, 0-8-0 Shunting tank engine (Russia). d, Alco "PA-1" diesel-electric (US). e, "C11" Class 2-6-4 branch passenger tank engine (Japan). f, "Settebello" deluxe high-speed electric train (Italy).
No. 1133, Class "KD" 0-6-0 Goods locomotive, 1900 (Sweden). No. 1134, Shinkansen "New Railway" series 200 (Japan).

1996, Nov. 25   Litho.   *Perf. 14*
1131-1132	A130	20nu Sheets of 6, #a.-f., each	8.00	8.00

Souvenir Sheets
1133-1134	A130	70nu each	4.75	4.75

BHUTAN

Penny Black — A131

Litho. & Embossed
1996, Dec. 17   Perf. 13½
1135 A131 140nu black & gold   9.50   9.50

A132   A133

Winter Olympic Medalists: 10nu, Vegard Ulvang, cross-country skiing, 1992. 15nu, Kristi Yamaguchi, figure skating, 1992. 25nu, Markus Wasmeier, giant slalom, 1994. 30nu, Georg Hackl, luge, 1992.
No. 1140: a, Andreas Ostler, 2-man bobsled, 1952. b, Wolfgang Hoppe, 4-man bobsled, 1984. c, Stein Eriksen, giant slalom, 1952. d, Alberto Tomba, giant slalom, 1988.
No. 1141, Henri Oreiller, downhill, 1948. No. 1142, Eduard Scherrer, 4-man bobsled, 1924.

1997, Jan. 1   Perf. 14
1136-1139 A132 Set of 4   5.50   5.50
1140 A132 15nu Strip of 4, #a.-d.   4.00   4.00
Souvenir Sheets
1141-1142 A132 70nu each   4.50   4.50
No. 1140 was issued in sheets of 8 stamps.

1997, Jan. 15   Perf. 13
Insects and Arachnids: a, 1ch, Apis laboriosa smith. b, 2ch, Neptunides polychromus. c, 3ch, Conocephalus maculctus. d, 4ch, Blattidae. e, 5ch, Dytiscus marginalis. f, 10ch, Dynastes hercules. g, 15ch, Hippodamia. h, 20ch, Sarcophaga haemorrhoidalis. i, 25ch, Lucanus cervus. j, 30ch, Caterpillar. k, 35ch, Lycia hirtaria. l, 40ch, Clytarius pennatus. m, 45ch, Ephemera denica. n, 50ch, Gryllus campestris. o, 60ch, Deilephila elpenor. p, 65ch, Gerris. q, 70ch, Agrion splendens. r, 80ch, Tachyta nana. s, 90ch, Eurydema pulchra. t, 1nu, Hadrurus hirsutus. u, 1.50nu, Vespa germanica. v, 2nu, Pyrops. w, 2.50nu, Mantis religiosa. x, 3nu, Araneus diadematus. y, 3.50nu, Atrophaneura. 15nu, Melolontha.

1143 A133 Sheet of 25, #a.-y.   1.35   1.35
Souvenir Sheet
1144 A133 15nu multicolored   1.00   1.00

Hong Kong '97 — A134

Wildlife: a, Thalarctos maritiumus. b, Phascolarctos cinereus. c, Selenarcios thibelanus. d, Ailurus fulgens.
20nu, Ailuropoda melanoleuca.

1997, Feb. 1   Litho.   Perf. 14
1145 A134 10nu Sheet of 4, #a.-d.   2.75   2.75
Souvenir Sheet
1146 A134 20nu multicolored   1.35   1.35

Signs of the Chinese Zodiac — A135

No. 1147: a, 1ch, Mouse. b, 2ch, Ox. c, 3ch, Tiger. d, 4ch, Rabbit. e, 5nu, Dragon. f, 6nu, Snake. g, 7nu, Horse. h, 8nu, Sheep. i, 90ch, Monkey. j, 10nu, Rooster. k, 11nu, Dog. l, 12nu, Pig. 20nu, Ox, diff.

1997, Feb. 8   Litho.   Perf. 14
1147 A135 Sheet of 12, #a.-l. + label   4.00   4.00
Souvenir Sheet
1148 A135 20nu multicolored   1.35   1.35

Fauna A136

Cuon alpinus: No. 1149: a, Adult, hind legs off ground. b, Adult walking right. c, Mother nursing young. d, Two seated.
Endangered species: No. 1150: a, Lynx. b, Red panda. c, Takin. d, Musk deer. e, Snow leopard. f, Golden langur. g, Tiger. h, Muntjac. i, Marmot.
No. 1151, Pseudois nayaur. No. 1152, Ursus thibetanus.

1997, Apr. 24
1149 A136 10nu Block or strip of 4, #a.-d.   2.75   2.75
1150 A136 1nu Sheet of 9, #a.-i.   6.00   6.00
Souvenir Sheets
1151-1152 A136 70nu each   4.75   4.75
World Wildlife Fund (No. 1149).
No. 1149 issued in sheets of 12 stamps.

UNESCO, 50th Anniv. A137

No. 1153: a, Mount Hungshan, China. b, Mausoleum of first Qin Emperor, China. c, Imperial Bronze Dragon, China. d, Tikal Natl. Park, Guatemala. e, Evora, Portugal. f, Shirakami-Sanchi, Japan. g, Paris, France. h, Valley Below the Falls, Plitvice Lakes Natl. Park, Croatia.
Sites in Germany: No. 1154: a, Cathedral, Bamberg. b, Bamberg. c, St. Michael's Church, Hildesheim. d, Potsdam Palace. e, Potsdam Church. f, Lubeck. g, Quedlinburg. h, Benedictine Church, Lorsch.
No. 1155, Goslar, Germany, horiz. No. 1156, Cathedral, Comenzada, Portugal, horiz.

1997, May 15
Sheets of 8 + Label
1153 A137 10nu #a.-h.   5.50   5.50
1154 A137 15nu #a.-h.   8.00   8.00
Souvenir Sheets
1155-1156 A137 60nu each   4.00   4.00

Have you found a typo or other error in this catalogue?
Inform the editors via our web site or e-mail
sctcat@
scottonline.com

Chernobyl Disaster, 10th Anniv. — A138

1997, May 2   Litho.   Perf. 13½x14
1157 A138 35nu UNESCO   2.40   2.40

Dogs — A139   Cats — A140

Designs: 10nu, Dalmatian. 15nu, Siberian husky. 20nu, Saluki. 25nu, Shar pei.
No. 1162: a, Dandie Dinmont terrier. b, Chinese crested. c, Norwich terrier. d, Basset hound. e, Cardigan welsh corgi. f, French bulldog.
60nu, Hovawart.

1997, July 15   Perf. 14
1158-1161 A139 Set of 4   4.75   4.75
1162 A139 20nu Sheet of 6, #a.-f.   8.00   8.00
Souvenir Sheet
1163 A139 60nu multicolored   4.00   4.00

1997, July 15
Designs: 10nu, Turkish angora. 15nu, Oriental shorthair. 20nu, British shorthair. 25nu, Burmese.
No. 1168: a, Japanese bobtail. b, Ceylon. c, Exotic. d, Rex. e, Ragdoll. f, Russian blue.
60nu, Tonkinese.

1164-1167 A140 Set of 4   4.75   4.75
1168 A140 15nu Sheet of 6, #a.-f.   6.00   6.00
Souvenir Sheet
1169 A140 60nu multicolored   4.25   4.25

1998 World Cup Soccer, France — A141

English players: 5nu, Pearce. 10nu, Gascoigne. 15nu, Beckham. 20nu, McManaman. 25nu, Adams. 30nu, Ince.
World Cup captains, horiz.: No. 1176: a, Maradona, Argentina, 1986. b, Alberto, Brazil, 1970. c, Dunga, Brazil, 1994. d, Moore, England, 1966. e, Fritzwalter, Germany, 1954. f, Matthaus, Germany, 1990. g, Beckenbauer, Germany, 1974. h, Passarella, Argentina, 1978.
Winning teams, horiz.: No. 1177: a, Italy, 1938. b, W. Germany, 1954. c, Uruguay, 1958. d, England, 1966. e, Argentina, 1978. f, Brazil, 1962. g, Italy, 1934. h, Brazil, 1970. i, Uruguay, 1930.
No. 1178, Philippe Albert, Belgium. No. 1179, Salvatore (Toto) Schillaci, Italy, horiz.

Perf. 13½x14, 14x13½
1997, Oct. 9   Litho.
1170-1175 A141 Set of 6   7.00   7.00
Sheets of 8 or 9
1176 A141 10nu #a.-h. + label   5.50   5.50
1177 A141 10nu #a.-i.   6.00   6.00
Souvenir Sheets
1178-1179 A141 35nu each   3.75   3.75

Friendship Between India and Bhutan — A142

3nu, Jawaharlal Nehru, King Jigme Dorji Wangchuk. 10nu, Rajiv Gandhi, King Jigme Singye Wangchuk.
20nu, Indian Pres. R. V. Venkataraman, King Jigme Singye Wangchuk.

1998   Litho.   Perf. 13x13½
1180 A142 3nu multicolored   .20   .20
1181 A142 10nu multicolored   .80   .80
Souvenir Sheet
1182 A142 20nu multicolored   1.20   1.20
No. 1182 contains one 76x35mm stamp.

A143   A144

Indepex '97: No. 1183: a, 3nu, Buddha seated with legs crossed. b, 15nu, Buddha seated with legs down. c, 7nu, Gandhi with hands folded. d, 10nu, Gandhi.
No. 1184, Buddha. No. 1185, Gandhi holding staff.

1998   Perf. 13½x13
1183 A143 Sheet of 4, #a.-d.   2.10   2.10
Souvenir Sheets
1184-1185 A143 15nu each   1.20   1.20
India's independence, 50th anniv.

1998, Feb. 28   Litho.   Perf. 14
New Year 1998 (Year of the Tiger): 3nu, Stylized tiger walking right.
Tigers: No. 1187: a, 5nu, Lying down. b, 15nu, Adult walking forward. c, 17nu, Cub walking over rocks.
20nu, Adult up close.
1186 A144 3nu multicolored   .20   .20
1187 A144 Sheet of 4, #a.-c., #1186 2.40   2.40
Souvenir Sheet
1188 A144 20nu multicolored   1.20   1.20

WHO, 50th Anniv. A145

1998, Apr. 7   Litho.   Perf. 13½
1189 A145 3nu multicolored   .20   .20
1190 A145 10nu multicolored   .60   .60
Souvenir Sheet
Perf. 14
1191 A145 15nu Mother, child   .90   .90
Safe Motherhood. No. 1191 contains one 35x35mm stamp.

Mother Teresa (1910-97) A146

No. 1192: a, Portrait (shown). b, With Princess Diana. c, Holding child. d, Holding starving infant. e, Seated among nuns. f, Looking down at sick. g, With hands folded in prayer. h, With Pope John Paul II. i, Portrait, diff.
No. 1193: a, like #1192b. b, like #1192h.

BHUTAN — BOLIVIA

1998, May 25   Litho.   Perf. 13½
1192 A146 10nu Sheet of 9, #a.-i.   5.50 5.50
Souvenir Sheet
1193 A146 25nu Sheet of 2, #a.-b.   3.00 3.00
No. 1193 contains two 38x43mm stamps.

Birds — A147

No. 1194: a, 10ch, Red-billed chough. b, 30ch, Great hornbill. c, 50ch, Singing lark. d, 70ch, Chestnut-flanked white-eye. e, 90ch, Magpie-robin. f, 1nu, Mrs. Gould's sunbird. g, 2nu, Tailorbird. h, 3nu, Duck. i, 5nu, Spotted cuckoo. j, 7nu, Gold crest. k, 9nu, Common mynah. l, 10nu, Green cochoa.
15nu, Turtle dove.

1998, July 28   Litho.   Perf. 13
1194 A147 Sheet of 12, #a.-l.   2.50 2.50
Souvenir Sheet
1195 A147 15nu multicolored   .90 .90
No. 1195 contains one 40x30mm stamp.

SEMI-POSTAL STAMPS

Nos. 10-12 Surcharged

+ 50 ch

Perf. 14x14½
1964, Mar.   Litho.   Unwmk.
B1 A3 33ch + 50ch multi   2.00 2.00
B2 A3 70ch + 50ch multi   2.00 2.00
B3 A3 1.30ch + 50ch multi   2.00 2.00
    Nos. B1-B3 (3)   6.00 6.00

9th Winter Olympic Games, Innsbruck, Jan. 29-Feb. 9, 1964.

Olympic Games Type of Regular Issue, 1964
Souvenir Sheet
1964, Oct. 10   Perf. 13½, Imperf.
B4 A6 Sheet of 2   7.50 7.50
  a. 1nu + 50ch Archery   .90 .90
  b. 2nu + 50ch Soccer   2.00 2.00

18th Olympic Games, Tokyo, Oct. 10-25.

FLOOD RELIEF

+ 5Ch

1968, Dec. 7   Photo.   Perf. 13½
B5 A14n 5ch +5ch   .15 .15
B6 A14n 80ch +25ch   .35 .35
B7 A14n 2nu +50ch   .85 .85
    Nos. B5-B7 (3)   1.35 1.35

AIR POST STAMPS

Nos. 19-21, 38-39, 63-67 Ovptd.

AIR MAIL   AIR MAIL
a   b

1967, Jan. 10   Litho.   Perfs. as Before
Overprint "a"
C1 A5 33ch on #19   .15 .15
C2 A5 70ch on #20   .30 .30
C3 A5 1nu on #21   .40 .40
C4 A8 50ch on #38   .20 .20
C5 A8 75ch on #39   .30 .30
C6 A11 1.50nu on #63   .65 .65
C7 A11 2nu on #64   .85 .85
C8 A11 3nu on #65   1.25 1.25
C9 A11 4nu on #66   1.75 1.75
C10 A11 5nu on #67   2.25 2.25
Overprint "b"
C11 A5 33ch on #19   .15 .15
C12 A5 70ch on #20   .30 .30
C13 A5 1nu on #21   .40 .40
C14 A8 50ch on #38   .20 .20
C15 A8 75ch on #39   .30 .30
C16 A11 1.50nu on #63   .65 .65
C17 A11 2nu on #64   .85 .85
C18 A11 3nu on #65   1.25 1.25
C19 A11 4nu on #66   1.75 1.75
C20 A11 5nu on #67   2.25 2.25
    Nos. C1-C20 (20)   16.20 16.20

UN Type of Regular Issue

Bhutan Flag and: 2.50nu, UN Headquarters, NYC. 5nu, Security Council Chamber and mural by Per Krohg. 6nu, General Assembly Hall.

1971, Sept. 21   Photo.   Perf. 13½
C21 A16 2.50nu silver & multi   .50 .50
C22 A16 5nu silver & multi   .95 .95
C23 A16 6nu silver & multi   1.10 1.10
    Nos. C21-C23 (3)   2.55 2.55

Bhutan's admission to the United Nations. Exist imperf.

Nos. C21-C23 Overprinted in Gold: "UNHCR / UNRWA / 1971" like Nos. 145-145C

1971, Dec. 23   Litho.   Perf. 13½
C24 A16 2.50nu silver & multi   .70 .70
C25 A16 5nu silver & multi   1.40 1.40
C26 A16 6nu silver & multi   1.90 1.90
    Nos. C24-C26 (3)   4.00 4.00

World Refugee Year. Exist imperf.

UPU Types of 1974

UPU Emblem, Carrier Pigeon and: 1nu, Mail runner and jeep. 1.40nu, 10nu, Old and new locomotives. 2nu, Old biplane and jet.

1974, Oct. 9   Litho.   Perf. 14½
C27 A19 1nu salmon & multi   .25 .25
C28 A20 1.40nu lilac & multi   .40 .40
C29 A20 2nu multicolored   .50 .50
    Nos. C27-C29 (3)   1.15 1.15
Souvenir Sheet
Perf. 13
C30 A20 10nu lilac & multi   2.75 2.75

Cent. of the UPU. Nos. C27-C29 were issued in sheets of 50 and sheets of 5 plus label with multicolored margin. Exist imperf.

Issues of 1968-1974 Surcharged 25ch and Bars

1978   Perf. & Printing as Before
C31 A16 25ch on 5nu, #C22   1.25 1.25
C32 A16 25ch on 6nu, #C23   1.25 1.25
C33 A20 25ch on 1.40nu, #C28   1.25 1.25
C34 A20 25ch on 2nu, #C29   1.25 1.25
C35 A14j 25ch on 4nu, #94L   1.25 1.25
C36 A14j 25ch on 10nu, #94N   1.25 1.25
C37 A17k 25ch on 5nu, #154F   1.25 1.25
C38 A17k 25ch on 6nu, #154G   1.25 1.25
    Nos. C31-C38 (8)   10.00 10.00

BOLIVIA

bə-'li-vē-ə

LOCATION — Central South America, separated from the Pacific Ocean by Chile and Peru.
GOVT. — Republic
AREA — 424,165 sq. mi.
POP. — 6,252,250 (est. 1984)
CAPITAL — Sucre (La Paz is the actual seat of government).
100 Centavos = 1 Boliviano
100 Centavos = 1 Peso Boliviano (1963)
100 Centavos = 1 Boliviano (1987)

Catalogue values for unused stamps in this country are for Never Hinged items, beginning with Scott 308 in the regular postage section, Scott C112 in the airpost section, Scott RA5 in the postal tax section, and Scott RAC1 in airpost postal tax section.

On Feb. 21, 1863, the Bolivian Government decreed contracts for carrying the mails should be let to the highest bidder, the service to commence on the day the bid was accepted, and stamps used for the payment of postage. On Mar. 18, the contract was awarded to Sr. Justiniano Garcia and was in effect until Apr. 29, 1863, when it was rescinded. Stamps in the form illustrated above were prepared in denominations of ½, 1, 2 and 4 reales. All values exist in black and in blue. The blue are twice as scarce as the black. Value, black, $75 each.
It is said that used copies exist on covers, but the authenticity of these covers remains to be established.

Condor — A1   A2

A3

72 varieties of each of the 5c, 78 varieties of the 10c, 30 varieties of each of the 50c and 100c.
The plate of the 5c stamps was entirely reengraved 4 times and retouched at least 6 times. Various states of the plate have distinguishing characteristics, each of which is typical of most, though not all the stamps in a sheet. These characteristics (usually termed types) are found in the shading lines at the right side of the globe. a, diagonal lines. b, diagonal lines only. c, diagonal and horizontal with traces of vertical lines. d, diagonal and horizontal lines. e, horizontal lines only. f, no lines except the curved ones forming the outlines of the globe.

1867-68   Unwmk.   Engr.   Imperf.
1 A1 5c yel grn, thin paper (a, b)   3.50 4.50
  a. 5c blue green (a)   4.50 14.00
  b. 5c deep green (a)   4.50 14.00
  c. 5c ol grn, thick paper (a)   35.00 25.00
  d. 5c yel grn, thick paper (a)   80.00 80.00
  e. 5c deep green, thick paper (b)   80.00 80.00
  f. 5c blue green (b)   4.50 14.00
2 A1 5c green (d)   4.00 7.00
  a. 5c green (c)   4.00 7.00
  b. 5c green (e)   4.00 7.00
  c. 5c green (f)   4.00 7.00
3 A1 5c vio ('68)   185.00 140.00
  a. 5c rose lilac ('68)   185.00 140.00
    Revenue cancel   28.00
4 A3 10c brown   225.00 140.00
5 A3 50c orange   20.00
6 A2 50c blue ('68)   325.00
  a. 50c dark blue ('68)   325.00
    Revenue cancel   28.00
7 A3 100c blue   60.00
    Revenue cancel   15.00
8 A3 100c green ('68)   140.00
  a. 100c pale blue grn ('68)   140.00
    Revenue cancel   28.00

Used values are for postally canceled copies. Pen cancellations usually indicate that the stamps have been used fiscally and such stamps sell for about one-fifth as much as those with postal cancellations. The 500c is an essay.
Reprints of Nos. 3, 4, 6 and 8 are common. Value, $10 each. Reprints of Nos. 2 and 5 are scarcer. Value, $25 each.

Coat of Arms
A4   A5

1868-69   Perf. 12
Nine Stars
10 A4 5c green   17.50 8.75
11 A4 10c vermilion   25.00 8.75
12 A4 50c blue   45.00 25.00
13 A4 100c orange   45.00 27.50
14 A4 500c black   475.00 375.00

Eleven Stars
15 A5 5c green   10.00 6.25
16 A5 10c vermilion   14.00 10.00
  a. Half used as 5c as cover   400.00
17 A5 50c blue   37.50 17.50
18 A5 100c dp orange   35.00 17.50
19 A5 500c black   1,750. 1,750.
See Nos. 26-27, 31-34.

Arms and "The Law" — A6

1878   Various Frames   Perf. 12
20 A6 5c ultra   9.25 4.25
21 A6 10c orange   7.50 3.25
  a. Half used as 5c on cover   50.00
22 A6 20c green   22.50 4.25
  a. Half used as 10c on cover   160.00
23 A6 50c dull carmine   110.00 12.00
    Nos. 20-23 (4)   149.25 23.75

Numerals Upright
(11 Stars)-A7   (9 Stars)-A8

1887   Rouletted
24 A7 1c rose   2.25 2.00
25 A7 2c violet   2.25 2.00
26 A5 5c blue   7.25 3.50
27 A5 10c rose   7.25 3.50
    Nos. 24-27 (4)   19.00 11.00
See No. 37.

1890   Perf. 12
28 A8 1c rose   1.65 .80
29 A8 2c violet   4.25 2.00
30 A4 5c blue   3.00 .80
31 A4 10c orange   6.25 .95
32 A4 20c dk green   12.50 1.65
33 A4 50c red   6.25 1.65
34 A4 100c yellow   12.50 3.25
    Nos. 28-34 (7)   46.40 11.10
See Nos. 35-36, 38-39.

1893   Litho.   Perf. 11
35 A8 1c rose   3.50 2.50
  a. Imperf. pair   35.00
  b. Horiz. pair, imperf. vert.   20.00
  c. Horiz. pair, imperf. btwn.   35.00
36 A8 2c violet   3.50 2.50
  a. Block of 4 imperf. vert. and horiz. through center   50.00
  b. Horiz. pair, imperf. btwn.   27.50
37 A7 5c blue   6.00 2.50
  a. Vert. pair, imperf. horiz.   27.50
  b. Horiz. pair, imperf. btwn.   35.00
38 A8 10c orange   17.00 4.00
  a. Horiz. pair, imperf. btwn.   50.00
39 A8 20c dark green   40.00 18.00
  a. Imperf. pair, vert. or horiz.   140.00
  b. Pair, imperf. btwn., vert. or horiz.   140.00
    Nos. 35-39 (5)   70.00 29.50

Coat of Arms — A9

1894   Unwmk.   Engr.   Perf. 14, 14½
Thin Paper
40 A9 1c bister   1.00 .60
41 A9 2c red orange   1.00 .60
42 A9 5c green   1.00 .60

BOLIVIA

43	A9	10c yellow brn		1.00	.60
44	A9	20c dark blue		3.00	1.25
45	A9	50c claret		7.50	1.75
46	A9	100c brown rose		17.50	6.25
		Nos. 40-46 (7)		32.00	11.65

Stamps of type A9 on thick paper were surreptitiously printed in Paris on the order of an official and without government authorization. Some of these stamps were substituted for part of a shipment of stamps on thin paper, which had been printed in London on government order. When the thick paper stamps reached Bolivia they were at first repudiated but afterwards were allowed to do postal duty. A large quantity of the thick paper stamps were fraudulently canceled in Paris with a cancellation of heavy bars forming an oval.

To be legitimate, copies of the thick paper stamps must have genuine cancellations of Bolivia. Value, on cover, each $125.

The 10c blue on thick paper is not known to have been issued.

Some copies of Nos. 40-46 show part of a papermakers' watermark "1011."

For overprints see Nos. 55-59.

President Tomas Frias — A10

President Jose M. Linares — A11

Pedro Domingo Murillo A12

Bernardo Monteagudo A13

Gen. Jose Ballivian — A14

Gen. Antonio Jose de Sucre — A15

Simon Bolivar — A16

Coat of Arms — A17

1897   Litho.   Perf. 12

47	A10	1c pale yellow grn	1.25	.80
a.		Vert. pair, imperf. horiz.	50.00	
b.		Vert. pair, imperf. btwn.	50.00	
48	A11	2c red	1.75	1.40
49	A12	5c dk green	2.50	.80
a.		Horiz. pair, imperf. btwn.	50.00	
50	A13	10c brown vio	2.50	.80
a.		Vert. pair, imperf. btwn.	50.00	
51	A14	20c lake & blk	4.75	.95
a.		Imperf., pair		150.00
52	A15	50c orange	4.75	2.50
53	A16	1b Prus blue	4.75	5.50
54	A17	2b red, yel, grn & blk	37.50	50.00
		Nos. 47-54 (8)	59.75	62.75

Excellent forgeries of No. 54, perf and imperf, exist, some postally used.

Reprint of No. 53 has dot in numeral. Same value.

Nos. 40-44 Handstamped in Violet or Blue

E.F. 1899

1899   Perf. 14½

55	A9	1c yellow bis	13.00	13.00
56	A9	2c red orange	16.00	16.00
57	A9	5c green	10.50	10.50
58	A9	10c yellow brn	13.00	10.00
59	A9	20c dark blue	21.00	21.00
		Nos. 55-59 (5)	73.50	71.00

The handstamp is found inverted, double, etc. Values twice the listed amounts. Forgeries of this handstamp are plentiful. "E.F." stands for Estado Federal.

The 50c and 100c (Nos. 45-46) were overprinted at a later date in Brazil.

Antonio José de Sucre — A18

Perf. 11½, 12
1899   Engr.   Thin Paper

62	A18	1c gray blue	2.50	.75
63	A18	2c brnsh red	1.75	.75
64	A18	5c dk green	6.00	1.50
65	A18	10c yellow org	2.50	1.25
66	A18	20c rose pink	3.00	.80
67	A18	50c bister brn	6.00	2.50
68	A18	1b gray violet	1.75	1.75
		Nos. 62-68 (7)	23.50	9.30

1901

69	A18	5c dark red	1.90	.60

Col. Adolfo Ballivian A19

Eliodoro Camacho A20

President Narciso Campero A21

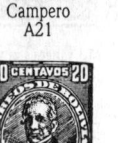

Jose Ballivian A22

Gen. Andres Santa Cruz — A23

Coat of Arms — A24

1901-02   Engr.

70	A19	1c claret	.55	.15
71	A20	2c green	.55	.20
73	A21	5c scarlet	.55	.20
74	A22	10c blue	1.40	.15
75	A23	20c violet & blk	.80	1.90
76	A24	2b brown	3.75	2.75
		Nos. 70-71,73-76 (6)	7.60	3.60

Nos. 73, 74 exist imperf. Value, pairs, each $50.
For surcharges see #95-96, 193.

1904   Litho.

77	A19	1c claret	2.25	.55

In No. 70 the panel above "CENTAVO" is shaded with continuous lines. In No. 77 the shading is of dots.

See Nos. 103-105, 107, 110.

Coat of Arms of Dept. of La Paz — A25

Murillo — A26

Jose Miguel Lanza — A27

Ismael Montes — A28

1909   Litho.   Perf. 11

78	A25	5c blue & blk	9.00	5.00
79	A26	10c green & blk	9.00	5.00
80	A27	20c orange & blk	9.00	5.00
81	A28	2b red & black	9.00	5.00
		Nos. 78-81 (4)	36.00	20.00

Centenary of Revolution of July, 1809.
Nos. 78-81 exist imperf. and tête bêche. Nos. 79-81 exist with center inverted.

Miguel Betanzos A29

Col. Ignacio Warnes A30

Murillo A31

Monteagudo A32

Esteban Arce — A33

Antonio Jose de Sucre — A34

Simon Bolivar A35

Manuel Belgrano A36

1909   Dated 1809-1825   Perf. 11½

82	A29	1c lt brown & blk	.55	.35
83	A30	2c green & blk	.55	.40
84	A31	5c red & blk	.55	.30
85	A32	10c dull bl & blk	.55	.30
86	A33	20c violet & blk	.65	.40
87	A34	50c olive bister & blk	1.00	.55
88	A35	1b gray brn & blk	1.00	.80
89	A36	2b chocolate & blk	1.65	1.10
		Nos. 82-89 (8)	6.50	4.20

War of Independence, 1809-1825.
Exist imperf. For surcharge see #97.

Warnes A37

Betanzos A38

Arce — A39

Dated 1910-1825

1910   Perf. 13x13½

92	A37	5c green & black	.40	.15
a.		Imperf., pair	5.00	
93	A38	10c claret & indigo	.40	.15
a.		Imperf., pair	5.00	
94	A39	20c dull blue & indigo	.65	.40
a.		Imperf., pair	5.00	
		Nos. 92-94 (3)	1.45	.70

War of Independence.
Nos. 92-94 may be found with parts of a papermaker's watermark: "A I & Co/EXTRA STRONG/9303."

Both perf and imperf exist with inverted centers.

Nos. 71 and 75 Surcharged in Black

5 Centavos 1911

1911   Perf. 11½, 12

95	A20	5c on 2c green	.45	.20
a.		Inverted surcharge	5.00	5.00
b.		Double surcharge	15.00	
c.		Period after "1911"	3.50	.80
d.		Blue surcharge	75.00	60.00
e.		Double dsurch., one invtd.	15.00	
96	A23	5c on 20c vio & blk	16.00	16.00
a.		Inverted surcharge	30.00	30.00
b.		Double surch., one invtd.	60.00	

20 CENTS 1911

No. 83 Handstamp Surcharged in Green

97	A30	20c on 2c grn & blk		1,100.

This provisional was issued by local authorities at Villa Bella, a town on the Brazilian border. The 20c surcharge was applied after the stamp had been affixed to the cover. Excellent forgeries of No. 96-97 exist.

"Justice"
A40   A41

1912   Black or Dark Blue Overprint On Revenue Stamps

98	A40	2c green (Bk)	.35	.25
a.		Inverted overprint	5.00	
99	A41	10c ver (Bl)	1.10	.45
a.		Inverted overprint	5.00	

A42    A43

Red or Black Overprint
Engr.

100	A42	5c orange (R)	.55	.40
a.		Inverted overprint	5.00	
b.		Pair, one without overprint	12.50	

BOLIVIA

c.	Black overprint	50.00	

Red or Black Surcharge
101	A43	10c on 1c bl (R)	.55	.20
a.		Inverted surcharge	6.00	
b.		Double surcharge	6.00	
c.		Dbl. surcharge, one invtd.	7.50	
d.		Black surcharge	100.00	100.00
e.		As "d." inverted		
f.		As "d." double surcharge		
g.		Pair, one without black surch.	400.00	

Fakes of No. 101d are plentiful.

Revenue Stamp Surcharged "CORREOS / 10 Cts. / · 1917 ·" in Red

1917			Litho.	
102		10c on 1c blue	6,000.	1,750.

Design similar to type A43. Excellent forgeries exist.

Types of 1901 and

Frias-A45 Sucre-A46 Bolivar-A47

1913		Engr.	Perf. 12	
103	A19	1c car rose	.40	.25
104	A20	2c vermilion	.40	.15
105	A21	5c green	.45	.15
106	A45	8c yellow	.80	.50
107	A22	10c gray	.80	.25
108	A46	50c dull violet	1.50	.55
109	A47	1b slate blue	2.25	1.40
110	A24	2b black	4.50	2.75
		Nos. 103-110 (8)	11.10	6.00

No. 107, litho., was not regularly issued.

Nine values commemorating the Guiqui-La Paz railroad were printed in 1915 but never issued. Typographed forgeries exist.

Monolith of Tiahuanacu A48

Mt. Potosí A49

Lake Titicaca — A50

Mt. Illimani — A51

Legislature Building — A53

FIVE CENTAVOS.
Type I - Numerals have background of vertical lines. Clouds formed of dots.
Type II - Numerals on white background. Clouds near the mountain formed of wavy lines.

1916-17		Litho.	Perf. 11½	
111	A48	½c brown	.15	.15
a.		Horiz. pair, imperf. vert.	5.00	
112	A49	1c gray green	.15	.15
a.		Imperf., pair	2.00	
113	A50	2c car & blk	.25	.15
a.		Imperf., pair	2.00	
c.		Center inverted	12.50	11.25
d.		Imperf., center inverted	17.50	
114	A51	5c dk blue (I)	.50	.18
a.		Imperf., pair	2.00	
b.		Vert. pair, imperf. horiz.	3.50	
c.		Horiz. pair, imperf. vert.	3.50	
115	A51	5c dk blue (II)	.50	.15
a.		Imperf., pair	2.50	
116	A53	10c org & bl	1.00	.15
a.		Imperf., pair	3.50	
b.		No period after "Legislativo"	1.00	.15

c.	Center inverted	40.00	40.00
d.	Vertical pair, imperf. between	5.00	
	Nos. 111-116 (6)	2.55	.93

For surcharges see Nos. 194-196.

Coat of Arms
A54 A55

Printed by the American Bank Note Co.

1919-20		Engr.	Perf. 12	
118	A54	1c carmine	.25	.20
119	A54	2c dk violet	4.75	3.00
120	A54	5c dk green	.50	.15
121	A54	10c vermilion	.50	.15
122	A54	20c dk blue	1.50	.30
123	A54	22c lt blue	.90	.75
124	A54	24c purple	.60	.50
125	A54	50c orange	4.75	.45
126	A55	1b red brown	6.00	1.75
127	A55	2b black brn	9.00	4.50
		Nos. 118-127 (10)	28.75	11.90

Printed by Perkins, Bacon & Co., Ltd.

1923-27		Re-engraved	Perf. 13½	
128	A54	1c carmine ('27)	.15	.15
129	A54	2c dk violet	.25	.15
130	A54	5c dp green	.80	.15
131	A54	10c vermilion	14.00	12.00
132	A54	20c slate blue	1.75	.20
135	A54	50c orange	2.75	.60
136	A55	1b red brown	.70	.30
137	A55	2b black brown	.50	.30
		Nos. 128-137 (8)	20.90	13.85

There are many differences in the designs of the two issues but they are too minute to be illustrated or described.

Nos. 128-137 exist imperf.

See Nos. 144-146, 173-177. For surcharges see Nos. 138-143, 160, 162, 181-186, 236-237.

Stamps of 1919-20 Surcharged in Blue, Black or Red

Habilitada 15 cts.

1924			Perf. 12	
138	A54	5c on 1c car (Bl)	.40	.20
a.		Inverted surcharge	5.00	5.00
b.		Double surcharge	5.00	5.00
139	A54	15c on 10c ver (Bk)	.70	.50
a.		Inverted surcharge	6.00	6.00
140	A54	15c on 22c lt bl (Bk)	.70	.30
a.		Inverted surcharge	5.25	5.25
b.		Double surcharge, one inverted		

No. 140 surcharged in red or blue probably are trial impressions. They appear jointly, and with black in blocks.

Same Surcharge on No. 131
			Perf. 13½	
142	A54	15c on 10c ver (Bk)	.70	.25
a.		Inverted surcharge	6.00	6.00

No. 121 Surcharged
Habilitada 15 cts.

			Perf. 12	
143	A54	15c on 10c ver (Bk)	.90	.30
a.		Inverted surcharge	6.00	6.00
b.		Double surcharge	5.00	5.00
		Nos. 138-143 (5)	3.40	1.55

Type of 1919-20 Issue Printed by Waterlow & Sons
Second Re-engraving

1925		Unwmk.	Perf. 12½	
144	A54	5c deep green	.80	.25
145	A54	15c ultra	.80	.15
146	A54	20c dark blue	.35	.15
		Nos. 144-146 (3)	1.95	.55

These stamps may be identified by the perforation.

Condor Looking Toward the Sea — A57

Designs: 2c, Sower. 5c, Torch of Eternal Freedom. 10c, National flower (kantuta). 15c, Pres. Bautista Saavedra. 50c, Liberty head. 1b, Archer on horse. 2b, Mercury. 5b, Gen. A. J. de Sucre.

1925		Engr.	Perf. 14	
150	A56	1c dark green	.75	
151	A56	2c rose	.75	
152	A56	5c red, grn	.75	.35
153	A56	10c car, yel	1.25	.75
154	A56	15c red brown	.50	.25
155	A57	25c ultra	.50	.50
156	A56	50c dp violet	.50	.50
157	A56	1b red	1.25	1.25
158	A57	2b orange	1.75	1.75
159	A56	5b black brn	2.00	2.00
		Nos. 150-159 (10)	10.00	

Cent. of the Republic. The 1c and 2c were not released for general use.

Nos. 150-159 exist imperf. Value, $60 each pair.

For surcharges see Nos. C59-C62.

1927
5 CENTAVOS

Stamps of 1919-27 Surcharged in Blue, Black or Red

1927				
160	A54	5c on 1c car (Bl)	2.50	.90
a.		Inverted surcharge	6.00	6.00
b.		Black surcharge	22.50	22.50

		Perf. 12		
162	A54	10c on 24c pur (Bk)	2.50	1.50
a.		Inverted surcharge	30.00	30.00
b.		Red surcharge	22.50	22.50

Coat of Arms — A66

Printed by Waterlow & Sons

1927		Litho.	Perf. 13½	
165	A66	2c yellow	.40	.20
166	A66	3c pink	.50	.50
167	A66	4c red brown	.40	.40
168	A66	20c lt ol grn	.65	.20
169	A66	25c deep blue	.65	.30
170	A66	30c violet	.80	.80
171	A66	40c orange	1.50	1.25
172	A66	50c dp brown	1.50	.50
173	A55	1b red	1.75	1.25
174	A55	2b plum	2.50	2.50
175	A55	3b olive grn	2.50	2.50
176	A55	4b claret	4.00	3.50
177	A55	5b bister brn	4.75	4.00
		Nos. 165-177 (13)	21.90	17.90

For overprints and surcharges see Nos. 178-180, 208, 211-212.

Type of 1927 Issue Overprinted
Octubre 9 1927

1927				
178	A66	5c dark green	.20	.15
179	A66	10c slate	.45	.15
180	A66	15c carmine	.65	.25
		Nos. 178-180 (3)	1.30	.55

Exist with inverted overprint. Value $20 each.

Stamps of 1919-27 Surcharged
15 cts. 1928

1928			Perf. 12, 12½, 13½	
		Red Surcharge		
181	A54	15c on 20c #122	9.00	9.00
182	A54	15c on 20c #132	9.00	9.00
a.		Black surcharge	30.00	
183	A54	15c on 20c #146	165.00	165.00
		Black Surcharge		
184	A54	15c on 24c #124	1.65	.90
a.		Inverted surcharge	5.00	5.00
b.		Blue surcharge	50.00	

185	A54	15c on 50c #125	50.00	42.50
186	A54	15c on 50c #135	1.25	.70
		Nos. 181-186 (6)	235.90	227.10

Condor — A67

Hernando Siles — A68

Map of Bolivia — A69

Printed by Perkins, Bacon & Co., Ltd.

1928		Engr.	Perf. 13½	
189	A67	5c green	1.50	.15
190	A68	10c slate	.30	.15
191	A69	15c carmine lake	.60	.15
		Nos. 189-191 (3)	2.40	.45

Nos. 104, 111, 113, Surcharged in Various Colors
0.03 Centavos R.S. 21-4 1930

1930			Perf. 12, 11½	
193	A20	1c on 2c (Bl)	.80	.80
a.		"0.10" for "0.01"	12.50	12.50
194	A50	3c on 2c (Br)	.80	.80
195	A48	25c on ½c (Bk)	.80	.80
196	A50	25c on 2c (V)	.80	.80
		Nos. 193-196 (4)	3.20	3.20

The lines of the surcharges were spaced to fit the various shapes of the stamps. The surcharges exist inverted, double, etc.

Trial printings were made of the surcharges on #193 and 194 in black and on #196 in brown.

Mt. Potosí — A70

Mt. Illimani — A71

Eduardo Abaroa — A72

Map of Bolivia — A73

Sucre — A74

Bolivar — A75

1931		Engr.	Perf. 14	
197	A70	2c green	1.40	.50
198	A71	5c light blue	1.40	.20
199	A72	10c red orange	1.40	.20
200	A73	15c violet	1.40	.20
201	A73	35c carmine	2.00	.85
202	A73	45c orange	2.00	.75
203	A74	50c gray	.55	.55
204	A75	1b brown	.55	.55
		Nos. 197-204 (8)	10.70	3.80

No. 198 exists imperf.

See #207, 241. For surcharges see #209-210.

BOLIVIA

Symbols of 1930 Revolution — A76

1931 Litho. Perf. 11
205 A76 15c scarlet 2.25 .40
  a. Pair, imperf. between
206 A76 50c brt violet .70 .70
  a. Pair, imperf. between 7.50

Revolution of June 25, 1930.
For surcharges see Nos. 239-240.

Map Type of 1931
Without Imprint

1932 Litho.
207 A73 15c violet 1.50 .35

Habilitada A 15 Cts.
D. S. 13-7.1933

Stamps of 1927-31 Surcharged

1933 Perf. 13½, 14
208 A66 5c on 1b red .60 .35
  a. Without period after "Cts" 1.25 1.25
209 A73 15c on 35c car .35 .35
  a. Inverted surcharge 20.00
210 A73 15c on 45c orange .35 .35
  a. Inverted surcharge 3.00 3.00
211 A66 15c on 50c dp brn 1.50 .30
212 A66 25c on 40c orange .60 .25
Nos. 208-212 (5) 3.40 1.60

The hyphens in "13-7-33" occur in three positions.

Coat of Arms — A77

1933 Engr. Perf. 12
213 A77 2c blue green .25 .15
214 A77 5c blue .25 .15
215 A77 10c red .45 .30
216 A77 15c deep violet .35 .15
217 A77 25c dark blue .65 .55
Nos. 213-217 (5) 1.95 1.30

For surcharges see Nos. 233-235, 238.

Mariano Baptista — A78
Map of Bolivia — A79 

1935
218 A78 15c dull violet .45 .20

1935
219 A79 2c dark blue .15 .15
220 A79 3c yellow .15 .15
221 A79 5c vermilion .15 .15
222 A79 5c blue grn .35 .15
223 A79 10c black brn .35 .15
224 A79 15c deep rose .35 .15
225 A79 15c ultra .35 .15
226 A79 20c yellow grn .40 .15
227 A79 25c lt blue .40 .15
228 A79 30c deep rose .80 .55
229 A79 40c orange .80 .55
230 A79 50c gray violet .80 .25
231 A79 1b yellow .55 .35
232 A79 2b olive brown .80 .70
Nos. 219-232 (14) 6.40 3.75

Regular Stamps of 1925-33 Surcharged in Black

Comunicaciones
D. S. 25-2-37
0.05

1937 Perf. 11, 12, 13½
233 A77 5c on 2c bl grn .25 .25
234 A77 15c on 25c dk bl .30 .30
235 A77 30c on 25c dk bl .50 .50
236 A55 45c on 1b red brn .60 .60
237 A55 1b on 2b plum .75 .75
  a. "1" missing 7.50 7.50
238 A77 2b on 25c dk bl .75 .75

"Comunicaciones" on one line
239 A76 3b on 50c brt vio 1.25 1.25
  a. "3" of value missing 6.00 6.00
240 A76 5b on 50c brt vio 1.25 1.25
Nos. 233-240 (8) 5.65 5.65

Exist inverted, double, etc.

President Siles — A80

1937 Unwmk. Perf. 14
241 A80 1c yellow brown .30 .30

Native School — A81
Oil Wells — A82 
Modern Factories A83 
Torch of Knowledge A84 
Map of the Sucre-Camiri R. R. — A85 
Allegory of Free Education — A86 
Allegorical Figure of Learning A87 
Symbols of Industry A88 
Modern Agriculture — A89 

1938 Litho. Perf. 10½, 11
242 A81 2c dull red .40 .40
243 A82 10c pink .45 .25
244 A83 15c yellow grn .60 .30
245 A84 30c yellow .75 .35
246 A85 45c rose red 1.40 .75
247 A86 60c dk violet 1.10 .35
248 A87 75c dull blue 1.50 .35
249 A88 1b lt brown 2.25 .35
250 A89 2b bister 2.00 .75
Nos. 242-250 (9) 10.45 3.85

For surcharge see No. 314.

Llamas — A90
Vicuna — A91 
Coat of Arms — A92 
Cocoi Herons — A93
Chinchilla — A94 
Toco Toucan — A95 
Condor — A96 
Jaguar — A97 

1939, Jan. 21 Perf. 10½, 11½x10½
251 A90 2c green .40 .30
252 A90 4c fawn .40 .30
253 A90 5c red violet .40 .25
254 A91 10c black .60 .30
255 A91 15c emerald .60 .35
256 A91 20c dk slate grn .60 .25
257 A92 25c lemon .60 .25
258 A92 30c dark blue .60 .30
259 A93 40c vermilion 1.40 .30
260 A93 45c gray 1.40 .30
261 A94 60c rose red 1.40 .55
262 A94 75c slate blue 2.75 .55
263 A95 90c orange 2.00 .55
264 A95 1b blue 2.00 .55
265 A96 2b rose lake 2.75 .55
266 A96 3b dark violet 3.50 .80
267 A96 4b brown org 4.00 1.10
268 A97 5b gray brown 5.00 1.40
Nos. 251-268 (18) 30.40 8.95

All but 20c exist imperf.
Imperf. counterfeits with altered designs exist of some values.
For surcharges see Nos. 315-317.

Flags of 21 American Republics A98

1940, Apr. Litho. Perf. 10½
269 A98 9b multicolored 1.10 1.10

Pan American Union, 150th anniversary.

Statue of Murillo — A99
Urns of Murillo and Sagarnaga — A100 
Dream of Murillo A101 
Murillo A102 

1941, Apr. 15
270 A99 10c dull vio brn .15 .15
271 A100 15c lt green .20 .15
  a. Imperf., pair 3.50
  b. Double impression 6.00
272 A101 45c carmine rose .20 .15
  a. Double impression 6.00
273 A102 1.05b dk ultra .45 .15
Nos. 270-273 (4) 1.00 .60

130th anniv. of the execution of Pedro Domingo Murillo (1759-1810), patriot.
For surcharge see No. 333.

First Stamp of Bolivia and 1941 Airmail Stamp — A103

1942, Oct. Litho. Perf. 13½
274 A103 5c pink .50 .50
275 A103 10c orange .50 .40
276 A103 20c yellow grn 1.00 .65
277 A103 40c carmine rose 1.25 .80
278 A103 90c ultra 2.50 1.00
279 A103 1b violet 3.00 1.65
280 A103 10b olive bister 10.00 8.25
Nos. 274-280 (7) 18.75 13.25

1st School Phil. Exposition held in La Paz, Oct., 1941.

Gen. Ballivian Leading Cavalry Charge, Battle of Ingavi — A104

1943 Photo. Perf. 12½
281 A104 2c lt blue grn .15 .15
282 A104 3c orange .15 .15
283 A104 25c deep plum .15 .15
284 A104 45c ultra .18 .15
285 A104 3b scarlet .38 .35
286 A104 4b brt rose lilac .55 .45
287 A104 5b black brown .80 .55
Nos. 281-287 (7) 2.36 1.95

Souvenir Sheets
Perf. 13, Imperf.
288 A104 Sheet of 4 1.50 1.50
289 A104 Sheet of 3 4.50 4.50

Centenary of the Battle of Ingavi, 1841. No. 288 contains 4 stamps similar to Nos. 281-284, No. 289 three stamps similar to Nos. 285-287.

Potosi A107
Quechisla A108 
Miner — A109
Dam A110 
Mine Interior A111 
Chaquiri Dam A112

BOLIVIA

Entrance to Pulacayo Mine — A113

1943		Engr.	Perf. 12½	
290	A107	15c red brown	.20	.15
291	A108	45c vio blue	.20	.15
292	A109	1.25b brt rose vio	.25	.30
293	A110	1.50b emerald	.25	.30
294	A111	2b brown blk	.30	.15
295	A112	2.10b lt blue	.40	.45
296	A113	3b red orange	.50	.55
		Nos. 290-296 (7)	2.10	2.25

General José Ballivián and Cathedral at Trinidad — A114

1943, Nov. 18				
297	A114	5c dk green & brn	.15	.15
298	A114	10c dull pur & brn	.15	.15
299	A114	30c rose red & brn	.15	.25
300	A114	45c brt ultra & brn	.20	.25
301	A114	2.10b dp org & brn	.30	.35
		Nos. 297-301,C91-C95 (10)	2.05	1.98

Department of Beni centenary.

"Honor, Work, Law" — A115

"United for the Country" — A116

1944		Litho.	Perf. 13½	
302	A115	20c orange	.15	.15
303	A115	90c ultra	.15	.15
304	A116	1b brt red vio	.15	.15
305	A116	2.40b dull brown	.20	.15

1945				
306	A115	20c green	.15	.15
307	A115	90c dp rose	.15	.15
		Nos. 302-307,C96-C99 (10)	1.81	1.53

Nos. 302-307 were issued to commemorate the Revolution of Dec. 20, 1943.

Catalogue values for unused stamps in this section, from this point to the end of the section, are for Never Hinged items.

Leopold Benedetto Vincenti, Joseph Ignacio de Sanjines and Bars of Anthem — A117

1946, Aug. 21		Litho.	Perf. 10½	
308	A117	5c rose vio & blk	.15	.15
309	A117	10c ultra & blk	.15	.15
310	A117	15c blue grn & blk	.15	.15
311	A117	30c vermilion & brn	.15	.15
a.		Souv. sheet of 1, imperf.	.65	.65
312	A117	90c dk blue & brn	.15	.15
313	A117	2b black & brn	.30	.15
a.		Souv. sheet of 1, imperf.	1.25	1.25
		Nos. 308-313 (6)	1.05	.90

Cent. of the adoption of Bolivia's natl. anthem.
Nos. 311a and 313a sold for 4b over face.

Nos. 248 and 262 Surcharged in Carmine, Black or Orange

1947 Habilitada Bs 1.40

1947, Mar. 12		Perf. 10½, 11	
314 A87	1.40b on 75c (C)	.15	.15
315 A94	1.40b on 75c (Bk)	.15	.15
316 A94	1.40b on 75c (C)	.15	.15
317 A94	1.40b on 75c (O)	.15	.15
Nos. 314-317,C112 (5)		.78	.78

People Attacking Presidential Palace — A118

Arms of Bolivia and Argentina — A119

1947, Sept.		Litho.	Perf. 13½	
318	A118	20c blue grn	.15	.15
319	A118	50c lilac rose	.15	.15
320	A118	1.40b grnsh bl	.15	.15
321	A118	3.70b dull org	.15	.15
322	A118	4b violet	.18	.15
323	A118	10b olive	.40	.25
		Nos. 318-323,C113-C117 (11)	2.01	1.75

1st anniv. of the Revolution of July 21, 1946. Exist imperf.

1947, Oct. 23				
324 A119	1.40b deep orange		.20	.15

Meeting of Presidents Enrique Hertzog of Bolivia and Juan D. Peron of Argentina at Yacuiba on Oct. 23, 1947. Exist imperf.
See No. C118.

Statue of Christ above La Paz — A120

2b, Child kneeling before cross of Golgotha. 3b, St. John Bosco. #328, Virgin of Copacabana. #329, Pope Pius XII blessing University of La Paz.

1948, Sept. 26		Unwmk.	Perf. 11½	
325	A120	1.40b blue & yel	.30	.15
326	A120	2b yel grn & sal	.40	.15
327	A120	3b green & gray	.65	.20
328	A120	5b violet & sal	.80	.25
329	A120	5b red brn & lt grn	1.10	.25
		Nos. 325-329,C119-C123 (10)	6.05	2.51

3rd Inter-American Cong. of Catholic Education.

Map and Emblem of Bolivia Auto Club — A125

Pres. Gregorio Pacheco, Map and Post Horn — A126

1948, Oct. 20				
330 A125	5b indigo & salmon		1.50	.15

Intl. Automobile Races of South America, Sept.-Oct. 1948. See No. C124.

1950, Jan. 2		Litho.	Perf. 11½	
331 A126	1.40b violet blue		.15	.15
332 A126	4.20b red		.15	.15
		Nos. 331-332,C125-C127 (5)	.75	.75

75th anniv. of the UPU.

No. 273 Surcharged in Black

Bs. 2.- Habilitada

D.S. 6·VII·50

1950			Perf. 10½	
333 A102	2b on 1.05b dk ultra		.16	.15

Crucifix and View of Potosi — A127

Symbols of United Nations — A128

1950, Sept. 14		Litho.	Unwmk.	
		Perf. 11½		
334	A127	20c violet	.15	.15
335	A127	30c dp orange	.15	.15
336	A127	50c lilac rose	.15	.15
337	A127	1b carmine	.15	.15
338	A127	2b blue	.30	.15
339	A127	6b chocolate	.25	.15
		Nos. 334-339 (6)	1.15	.90

400th anniv. of the appearance of a crucifix at Potosi. Exist imperf.

1950, Oct. 24				
340 A128	60c ultra		1.00	.15
341 A128	2b green		1.40	.22

5th anniv. of the UN, Oct. 24, 1945. See Nos. C138-C139.

Gate of the Sun and Llama — A129

Church of San Francisco — A130

Designs: 40c, Avenue Camacho. 50c, Consistorial Palace. 1b, Legislative Palace. 1.40b, Communications Bldg. 2b, Arms. 3b, La Gasca ordering Mendoza to found La Paz. 5b, Capt. Alonso de Mendoza founding La Paz. 10b, Arms; portrait of Mendoza.

1951, Mar.		Engr.	Perf. 12½	
		Center in Black		
342	A129	20c green	.15	.15
343	A130	30c dp orange	.15	.15
344	A129	40c bister brn	.15	.15
345	A129	50c dk red	.15	.15
346	A129	1b dp purple	.15	.15
347	A129	1.40b dk vio blue	.15	.15
348	A129	2b dp purple	.15	.15
349	A129	3b red lilac	.20	.15
a.		Sheet, Nos. 345, 346, 348, 349	1.10	1.10
b.		As "a," imperf.	1.10	1.10
350	A129	5b dk red	.22	.16
a.		Sheet, Nos. 344, 347, 350	1.10	1.10
b.		As "a," imperf.	1.10	1.10
351	A129	10b sepia	.50	.22
a.		Sheet, Nos. 342, 343, 351	1.10	1.10
b.		As "a," imperf.	1.10	1.10
		Nos. 342-351,C140-C149 (20)	4.97	4.58

400th anniv. of the founding of La Paz.
For surcharges see Nos. 393-402.

Boxing — A131

	Perf. 12½			
1951, July 1		Unwmk.	Engr.	
352	A131	20c shown	.16	.15
353	A131	50c Tennis	.16	.15
354	A131	1b Diving	.20	.15
355	A131	1.40b Soccer	.20	.15
356	A131	2b Skiing	.38	.30
357	A131	3b Handball	.80	.80
a.		Sheet, Nos. 352, 353, 356, 357	2.25	1.75
b.		As "a," imperf.	2.25	1.75
358	A131	4b Cycling	1.00	1.00
a.		Sheet, Nos. 354, 355, 358	2.00	1.50
b.		As "a," imperf.	2.00	1.50
		Nos. 352-358,C150-C156 (14)	8.15	5.85

The stamps were intended to commemorate the 5th athletic championship matches held at La Paz, October 1948.

Eagle and Flag of Bolivia — A132

1951, Nov. 5		Litho.	Perf. 11½	
		Flag in Red, Yellow and Green.		
359	A132	2b aqua	.15	.15
360	A132	3.50b ultra	.15	.15
361	A132	5b purple	.15	.15
362	A132	7.50b gray	.20	.15
363	A132	15b dp car	.25	.22
364	A132	30b sepia	.50	.50
		Nos. 359-364 (6)	1.40	1.32

Cent. of the adoption of Bolivia's natl. flag.

Eduardo Abaroa — A133

Queen Isabella I — A134

1952, Mar.			Perf. 11	
365	A133	80c dk carmine	.15	.15
366	A133	1b red orange	.15	.15
367	A133	2b emerald	.20	.15
368	A133	5b ultra	.25	.15
369	A133	10b lilac rose	.50	.16
370	A133	20b dk brown	.75	.65
		Nos. 365-370,C157-C162 (12)	5.00	4.11

73rd anniversary of the death of Eduardo Abaroa.

1952, July 16		Unwmk.	Perf. 13½	
371	A134	2b vio bl	.15	.15
372	A134	6.30b carmine	.20	.20
		Set value	.30	.30

500th anniv. of the birth of Isabella I of Spain. See Nos. C163-C164.

Columbus Lighthouse — A135

1952, July 16			Litho.	
373	A135	2b vio bl, bl	.15	.15
374	A135	5b car, sal	.50	.40
375	A135	9b emer, grn	.85	.60
		Nos. 373-375,C165-C168 (7)	2.50	1.90

Miner — A136

1953, Apr. 9				
376	A136	2.50b vermilion	.15	.15
377	A136	8b violet	.15	.15

Nationalization of the mines.

Gualberto Villarroel, Victor Paz Estenssoro and Hernan Siles Zuazo — A137

1953, Apr. 9			Perf. 11½	
378	A137	50c rose lil	.15	.15
379	A137	1b brt rose	.15	.15
380	A137	2b vio bl	.15	.15
381	A137	3b lt grn	.15	.15
382	A137	4b yel org	.15	.15
383	A137	5b dl vio	.16	.15
		Nos. 378-383,C169-C175 (13)	2.31	2.00

Revolution of Apr. 9, 1952, 1st anniv.

659

BOLIVIA

Map of Bolivia and Cow's Head — A138

25b, 85b, Map and ear of wheat.

1954, Aug. 2   Perf. 12x11½
384	A138	5b car rose	.15 .15
385	A138	17b aqua	.15 .15
386	A138	25b chalky blue	.15 .15
387	A138	85b blk brn	.25 .20
		Nos. 384-387,C176-C181 (10)	2.73 1.69

Nos. 384-385 for the agrarian reform laws of 1953-54. Nos. 386-387 for the 1st National Congress of Agronomy. Exist imperf.

Oil Refinery A139

1955, Oct. 9   Unwmk.   Perf. 12x11½
388	A139	10b ultra & lt ultra	.15 .15
389	A139	35b rose car & rose	.15 .15
390	A139	40b dk & lt yel grn	.15 .15
391	A139	50b red vio & lil rose	.15 .15
392	A139	80b brn & bis brn	.15 .15
		Nos. 388-392,C182-C186 (10)	3.28 2.85

Exist imperf.

Nos. 342-351, Surcharged with New Values and Bars in Ultramarine

1957, Feb. 14   Engr.   Perf. 12½
Center in Black
393	A129	50b on 3b red lilac	.15 .15
394	A129	100b on 2b dp pur	.15 .15
395	A129	200b on 1b dp pur	.15 .15
396	A129	300b on 1.40b dk vio bl	.16 .15
397	A129	350b on 20c green	.22 .15
398	A129	400b on 40c bis brn	.22 .15
399	A130	600b on 30c dp org	.35 .15
400	A129	800b on 50c dk red	.40 .15
401	A129	1000b on 10b sepia	.40 .15
402	A129	2000b on 5b dk red	.65 .20
		Nos. 393-402 (10)	2.85 1.55

See Nos. C187-C196.

CEPAL Building, Santiago de Chile, and Meeting Hall in La Paz — A140

1957, May 15   Litho.   Perf. 13
403	A140	150b gray & ultra	.15 .15
404	A140	350b bis brn & gray	.18 .18
405	A140	550b chlky bl & brn	.20 .20
406	A140	750b dp rose & grn	.30 .20
407	A140	900b grn & brn blk	.40 .15
		Nos. 403-407,C197-C201 (10)	5.03 3.48

7th session of the C. E. P. A. L. (Comision Economica para la America Latina de las Naciones Unidas), La Paz. Exist imperf.
For surcharges see Nos. 482-484.

Presidents Siles Zuazo and Aramburu A141

1957, Dec. 15   Unwmk.   Perf. 11½
408	A141	50b red org	.15 .15
409	A141	350b blue	.25 .15
410	A141	1000b redsh brn	.50 .15
		Nos. 408-410,C202-C204 (6)	1.97 .90

Opening of the Santa Cruz-Yacuiba Railroad and the meeting of the Presidents of Bolivia and Argentina. Exist imperf.
For surcharge see No. 699.

Flags of Bolivia and Mexico and Presidents Hernan Siles Zuazo and Adolfo Lopez Mateos A142

1960, Jan. 30   Litho.   Perf. 11½
411	A142	350b olive	.16 .16
412	A142	600b red brn	.22 .22
413	A142	1500b blk brn	.50 .50
		Nos. 411-413,C205-C207 (6)	3.03 2.18

Issued for an expected visit of Mexico's President Adolfo Lopez Mateos. On sale Jan. 30-Feb. 1, 1960.

Indians and Mt. Illimani A143

Refugee Children A144

1960, Mar. 26   Unwmk.
414	A143	500b ol bis	.50 .50
415	A143	1000b blue	.90 .30
416	A143	2000b brown	2.00 .50
417	A143	4000b green	3.75 2.50
		Nos. 414-417,C208-C211 (8)	23.90 12.90

1960, Apr. 7   Perf. 11½
418	A144	50b brown	.15 .15
419	A144	350b claret	.15 .15
420	A144	400b steel blue	.16 .16
421	A144	1000b gray brn	.50 .50
422	A144	3000b slate grn	1.00 1.00
		Nos. 418-422,C212-C216 (10)	4.26 4.21

Issued to publicize World Refugee Year, July 1, 1959-June 30, 1960.
For surcharges see Nos. 454-458, 529.

Jaime Laredo A145

Rotary Emblem and Nurse with Children A146

1960, Aug. 15   Litho.   Perf. 11½
423	A145	100b olive	.20 .15
424	A145	350b dp rose	.30 .25
425	A145	500b Prus grn	.38 .20
426	A145	1000b brown	.50 .50
427	A145	1500b vio bl	.90 .90
428	A145	5000b gray	3.00 3.00
		Nos. 423-428,C217-C222 (12)	13.03 8.70

Issued to honor violinist Jaime Laredo.
For surcharge see No. 485.

1960, Nov. 19   Perf. 11½
429	A146	350b multi	.16 .15
430	A146	500b multi	.22 .15
431	A146	600b multi	.35 .35
432	A146	1000b multi	.40 .20
		Nos. 429-432,C223-C226 (8)	6.13 3.49

Issued for the Children's Hospital, sponsored by the Rotary Club of La Paz.
For surcharges see Nos. 486-487.

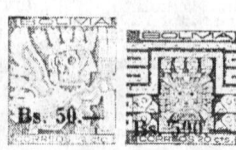

Designs from Gate of the Sun
A147   A148

Designs: Various prehistoric gods and ornaments from Tiahuanaco excavations.

1960, Dec. 16   Perf. 13x12, 12x13
Gold Background
Surcharge in Black or Dark Red
Sizes: 21x23mm, 23x21mm
433	A147	50b on ½c red	.45 .30
434	A147	100b on 1c red	.35 .15
435	A147	200b on 2c blk	.75 .35
436	A147	300b on 5c grn (DR)	.25 .20
437	A147	350b on 10c grn	.25 .75
438	A148	400b on 15c red	.35 .15
439	A148	500b on 20c red	.35 .30
440	A148	500b on 50c red	.40 .15
441	A148	600b on 22½c grn	.45 .45
442	A148	600b on 60c vio	.60 .50
443	A148	700b on 25c vio	.75 .15
444	A148	700b on 1b grn	1.00 1.00
445	A148	800b on 30c red	.60 .15
446	A148	900b on 40c grn	.45 .20
447	A148	1000b on 2b bl	.60 .50
448	A148	1800b on 3b gray	5.00 3.50

Perf. 11
Size: 49½x23mm
449	A148	4000b on 4b gray	30.00 25.00

Perf. 11x13½
Size: 49x53mm
450	A147	5000b on 5b gray	7.50 7.00
		Nos. 433-450 (18)	50.10 40.80

Nos. 433-450 were not regularly issued without surcharge. Value, set $20.
The decree for Nos. 433-450 stipulated that 7 were for air mail (500b on 50c, 600b on 60c, 700b on 1b, 1000b, 1800b, 4000b and 5000b), but the overprinting failed to include "Aereo."
The 800b surcharge also exists on the 1c red and gold. This was not listed in the decree.
For surcharges see Nos. 528, 614.

Miguel de Cervantes A149

Nuflo de Chaves A150

1961, Nov.   Photo.   Perf. 13x12½
451	A149	600b ocher & dl vio	.38 .15

Cervantes' appointment as Chief Magistrate of La Paz. See No. C230.

1961, Nov.   Unwmk.
452	A150	1500b dk bl, buff	.75 .30

Founding of Santa Cruz de la Sierra, 400th anniv. See #468, C246. For surcharge see #533.

People below Eucharist Symbol — A151

Flowers — A152

1962, Mar. 19   Litho.   Perf. 10½
453	A151	1000b gray grn, red & yel	.65 .35

4th Natl. Eucharistic Congress, Santa Cruz, 1961. See No. C231.

Nos. 418-422 Surcharged Horizontally with New Value and Bars or Greek Key Border Segment

1962, June   Perf. 11½
454	A144	600b on 50b brown	.18 .18
455	A144	900b on 350b claret	.22 .15
456	A144	1000b on 400b steel blue	.32 .15
457	A144	2000b on 1000b gray brn	.38 .22
458	A144	3500b on 3000b slate grn	.65 .65
		Nos. 454-458,C232-C236 (10)	5.15 4.45

Old value obliterated with two short bars on No. 454; four short bars on Nos. 455-456 and Greek key border on Nos. 457-458. The Greek key obliteration comes in two positions: two full "keys" on top, and one full and two half keys on top.

1962, June 28   Litho.   Perf. 10½
459	A152	200b Hibiscus	.30 .15
460	A152	400b Bicolored vanda	.45 .15
461	A152	600b Lily	.75 .15
462	A152	1000b Orchid	1.00 .18
		Nos. 459-462,C237-C240 (8)	7.50 3.18

Bolivia's Armed Forces A153

Anti-Malaria Emblem A154

1962, Sept. 5   Perf. 11½
463	A153	400b Infantry	.15 .15
464	A153	500b Cavalry	.15 .15
465	A153	600b Artillery	.16 .15
466	A153	2000b Engineers	.50 .35
		Nos. 463-466,C241-C244 (8)	3.96 2.15

1962, Oct. 4
467	A154	600b dk & lt vio & yel	.25 .25

WHO drive to eradicate malaria. See #C245.

Portrait Type of 1961

Design: 600b, Alonso de Mendoza.

1962   Photo.   Perf. 13x12½
468	A150	600b rose vio, bluish	.25 .15

Soccer and Flags — A155

Design: 1b, Goalkeeper catching ball, vert.

1963, Mar. 21   Litho.   Perf. 11½
Flags in National Colors
469	A155	60c gray	.40 .40
470	A155	1b gray	.60 .20

21st South American Soccer Championships. See Nos. C247-C248.

Globe and Wheat Emblem — A156

1963, Aug. 1   Unwmk.   Perf. 11½
471	A156	60c dk bl, bl & yel	.25 .25

"Freedom from Hunger" campaign of the FAO. See No. C249.

Oil Derrick and Chart — A157

Designs: 60c, Map of Bolivia. 1b, Students.

1963, Dec. 21   Litho.   Perf. 11½
472	A157	10c grn & dk brn	.15 .15
473	A157	60c ocher & dk brn	.22 .15
474	A157	1b dk bl, grn & yel	.28 .15
		Nos. 472-474,C251-C253 (6)	2.55 1.80

Revolution of Apr. 9, 1952, 10th anniv.

Flags of Bolivia and Peru — A158

BOLIVIA

1966, Aug. 10 Wmk. 90 Perf. 13½
Flags in National Colors
475	A158	10c blk & tan	.15	.15
476	A158	60c blk & lt grn	.20	.20
477	A158	1b blk & gray	.35	.35
478	A158	2b blk & rose	.50	.50
		Nos. 475-478,C254-C257 (8)	2.85	2.85

Marshal Andrés Santa Cruz (1792-1865), president of Bolivia and of Peru-Bolivian Confederation.

Children — A159

Perf. 13½
1966, Dec. 16 Unwmk. Litho.
| 479 | A159 | 30c ocher & sepia | .15 | .15 |

Issued to help poor children. See No. C258.

Map and Flag of Bolivia and Generals Ovando and Barrientos
A160

1966, Dec. 16 Litho. Perf. 13½
Flag in Red, Yellow and Green
| 480 | A160 | 60c vio brn & tan | .30 | .20 |
| 481 | A160 | 1b dl grn & tan | .45 | .15 |

Issued to honor Generals Rene Barrientos Ortuno and Alfredo Ovando C., co-Presidents, 1965-66. See Nos. C259-C260.

Various Issues 1957-60 and Type A161 Surcharged with New Values and Bars

A161

1966, Dec. 21
On No. 403: "Centenario de la / Cruz Roja / Internacional"
| 482 | A140 | 20c on 150b gray & ultra | .20 | .15 |

On Nos. 405-406: "Homenaje a la / Generala / J. Azurduy de / Padilla"
| 483 | A140 | 30c on 550b chky bl & brn | .30 | .15 |
| 484 | A140 | 2.80b on 750b dp rose & grn | .75 | .50 |

On No. 424: "CL Aniversario / Heroinas Coronilla"
| 485 | A145 | 60c on 350b dp rose | .50 | .15 |

Nos. 429-430 Surcharged
| 486 | A146 | 1.60b on 350b multi | .75 | .50 |
| 487 | A146 | 2.40b on 500b multi | 1.00 | .75 |

Revenue Stamps of 1946 surcharged with New Value, "X" and: "XXV Aniversario / Gobierno Busch"
| 488 | A161 | 20c on 5b red | .20 | .15 |

Overprinted: "XX Aniversario / Gob. Villaroel"
| 489 | A161 | 60c on 2b grn | .30 | .15 |

Overprinted: "Centenario do / Rurrenabaque"
| 490 | A161 | 1b on 10b brn | .50 | .15 |

Overprinted: "XXV Aniversario / Dpto. Pando"
| 491 | A161 | 1.60b on 50c vio | .50 | .16 |
| | | Nos. 482-491,C261-C272 (22) | 14.50 | 8.86 |

For surcharge see No. C272.

Sower
A162

"Macheteros"
A163

1967, Sept. 20 Litho. Perf. 13½x13
| 492 | A162 | 70c multi | .35 | .15 |

50th anniv. of Lions Intl. See #C273-C273a.

1968, June 24 Perf. 13½x13
Designs (Folklore characters): 60c, Chunchos. 1b, Wiphala. 2b, Diablada.
493	A163	30c gray & multi	.15	.15
494	A163	60c sky bl & multi	.25	.25
495	A163	1b gray & multi	.40	.15
496	A163	2b gray ol & multi	.60	.20
		Nos. 493-496,C274-C277 (8)	3.90	1.65

Issued to publicize the 9th Congress of the Postal Union of the Americas and Spain.
A souvenir sheet exists containing 4 imperf. stamps similar to #493-496. Size: 131x81½mm.

Arms of Tarija — A164

Pres. Gualberto Villaroel — A165

1968, Oct. 29 Litho. Perf. 13½x13
497	A164	20c pale sal & multi	.15	.15
498	A164	30c gray & multi	.15	.15
499	A164	40c dl yel & multi	.15	.15
500	A164	60c lt yel grn & multi	.20	.20
		Nos. 497-500,C278-C281 (8)	3.15	2.40

Battle of Tablada sesquicentennial.

1968, Nov. 6 Unwmk.
501	A165	30c sepia & org	.30	.15
502	A165	30c sepia & dl bl grn	.30	.15
503	A165	40c sepia & dl rose	.30	.20
504	A165	50c sepia & yel grn	.30	.15
505	A165	1b sepia & ol bister	.30	.15
		Nos. 501-505 (5)	1.50	.80

4th centenary of the founding of Cochabamba. See Nos. C282-C286.

ITU Emblem — A166

1968, Dec. 3 Litho. Perf. 13x13½
| 506 | A166 | 10c gray, blk & yel | .20 | .20 |
| 507 | A166 | 60c org, blk & ol | .40 | .40 |

Cent. (in 1965) of the ITU. See Nos. C287-C288.

Polychrome Painted Clay Cup, Inca Period — A167

1968, Nov. 14 Perf. 13½x13
| 508 | A167 | 20c dk bl grn & multi | .15 | .15 |
| 509 | A167 | 60c vio bl & multi | .35 | .35 |

20th anniv. (in 1966) of UNESCO. See Nos. C289-C290.

John F. Kennedy — A168

Tennis Player — A169

1968, Nov. 22 Perf. 13x13½
| 510 | A168 | 10c yel grn & blk | .15 | .15 |
| 511 | A168 | 4b vio & blk | 1.40 | 1.40 |

A souvenir sheet contains one imperf. stamp similar to No. 511. Green marginal inscription. Size: 131x81½mm.
See Nos. C291-C292.

1968, Dec. 10 Perf. 13x13½
512	A169	10c gray, blk & lt brn	.25	.25
513	A169	20c yel, blk & lt brn	.25	.25
514	A169	30c ultra, blk & lt brn	.25	.25
		Nos. 512-514 (3)	.75	.75

32nd South American Tennis Championships, La Paz, 1965. See Nos. C293-C294.
A souvenir sheet exists containing 3 imperf. stamps similar to Nos. 512-514. Size: 131x81½mm.

Issue of 1863 — A170

1968, Dec. 23 Litho. Perf. 13x13½
515	A170	10c yel grn, brn & blk	.35	.20
516	A170	30c lt bl, brn & blk	.35	.35
517	A170	2b gray, brn & blk	.35	.35
		Nos. 515-517,C295-C297 (6)	3.55	3.40

Cent. of Bolivian postage stamps. See Nos. C295-C297.
A souvenir sheet exists containing 3 imperf. stamps similar to Nos. 515-517. Yellow green marginal inscription. Size: 131x81½mm.

Rifle Shooting — A171

Sports: 50c, Equestrian. 60c, Canoeing.

1969, Oct. 29 Litho. Perf. 13x13½
518	A171	40c red brn, org & blk	.40	.40
519	A171	50c emer, red & blk	.40	.40
520	A171	60c bl, emer & blk	.40	.40
		Nos. 518-520,C299-C301 (6)	4.20	3.85

19th Olympic Games, Mexico City, 10/12-27/68.
A souvenir sheet exists containing 3 imperf. stamps similar to #518-520. Size: 130½x81mm.

Temenis Laothoe Violetta A172

Butterflies: 10c, Papilio crassus. 20c, Catagramma cynosura. 30c, Eunica eurota flora. 80c, Ituna phenarete.

1970, Apr. 24 Litho. Perf. 13x13½
521	A172	5c pale lil & multi	.70	.70
522	A172	10c pink & multi	1.40	1.40
523	A172	20c gray & multi	1.40	1.40
524	A172	30c yel & multi	1.40	1.40
525	A172	80c multicolored	1.40	1.40
		Nos. 521-525,C302-C306 (10)	20.20	20.20

A souvenir sheet exists containing 3 imperf. stamps similar to Nos. 521-523. Black marginal inscription. Size: 129½x80mm.

Boy Scout — A173

Design: 10c, Girl Scout planting rose bush.

1970, June 17 Perf. 13½x13
| 526 | A173 | 5c multicolored | .20 | .15 |
| 527 | A173 | 10c multicolored | .20 | .15 |

Issued to honor the Bolivian Scout movement. See Nos. C307-C308.

No. 437 Surcharged "EXFILCA 70 / $b. 0.30" and Two Bars in Red

1970, Dec. 6 Litho. Perf. 13x12
| 528 | A147 | 30c on 350b on 10c | .25 | .25 |

EXFILCA 70, 2nd Interamerican Philatelic Exhib., Caracas, Venezuela, Nov. 27-Dec. 6.

Nos. 455 and 452 Surcharged in Black or Red

1970, Dec. Photo. Perf. 11½
| 529 | A144 | 60c on 900b on 350b | .25 | .20 |
| 533 | A150 | 1.20b on 1500b (R) | .50 | .15 |

Amaryllis Yungacensis A174

Sica Sica Church, EXFILIMA Emblem A175

Bolivian Flowers: 30c, Amaryllis escobar uriae, horiz. 40c, Amaryllis evansae, horiz. 2b, Gymnocalycium chiquitanum.

Perf. 13x13½, 13½x13
1971, Aug. 9 Litho. Unwmk.
534	A174	30c gray & multi	.30	.30
535	A174	40c multi	.30	.30
536	A174	50c multi	.35	.35
537	A174	2b multi	1.00	.60
		Nos. 534-537,C310-C313 (8)	6.95	4.45

1971, Nov. 6 Perf. 14x13½
| 538 | A175 | 20c red & multi | .20 | .15 |

EXFILIMA '71, 3rd Inter-American Philatelic Exhibition, Lima, Peru, Nov. 6-14.

A176

A177

Design: Pres. Hugo Banzer Suarez.

1972, Jan. 24 Litho. Perf. 13½
| 539 | A176 | 1.20b blk & multi | .50 | .15 |

Bolivia's development, Aug. 19, 1971, to Jan. 24, 1972.

1972, Mar. 23 Litho. Perf. 13½x13
Folk Dances: 20c, Chiriwano de Achocalla. 40c, Rueda Chapaca. 60c, Kena-kena. 1b, Waca Thokori.
540	A177	20c red & multi	.15	.15
541	A177	40c rose lil & multi	.30	.25
542	A177	60c cream & multi	.45	.20
543	A177	1b citron & multi	.55	.22
		Nos. 540-543,C314-C315 (6)	2.60	1.14

BOLIVIA

Madonna and Child by B. Bitti — A178

Tarija Cathedral, EXFILBRA Emblem — A179

Bolivian paintings: 10c, Nativity, by Melchor Perez de Holguin. 50c, Coronation of the Virgin, by G. M. Berrio. 70c, Harquebusier, anonymous. 80c, St. Peter of Alcantara, by Holguin.

1972   Litho.   Perf. 14x13½
544	A178	10c gray & multi	.15	.15
545	A178	50c sal & multi	.25	.15
546	A178	70c lt grn & multi	.35	.15
547	A178	80c buff & multi	.40	.15
548	A178	1b multi	.50	.15
		Nos. 544-548,C316-C319 (9)	3.40	1.45

Issue dates: 1b, Aug. 17; others, Dec. 4.

1972, Aug. 26
549 A178 30c multi   .16 .15

4th Inter-American Philatelic Exhibition, EXFIL-BRA, Rio de Janeiro, Brazil, Aug. 26-Sept. 2.

Echinocactus Notocactus — A180

Designs: Various cacti.

1973, Aug. 6   Litho.   Perf. 13½
550	A180	20c crim & multi	.30	.25
551	A180	40c multi	.30	.25
552	A180	50c multi	.30	.15
553	A180	70c multi	.30	.20
		Nos. 550-553,C321-C323 (7)	2.70	1.45

Power Station, Santa Isabel A181

Designs: 20c, Tin industry. 90c, Bismuth industry. 1b, Natural gas plant.

1973, Nov. 26   Litho.   Perf. 13½
554	A181	10c gray & multi	.15	.15
555	A181	20c tan & multi	.15	.15
556	A181	90c lt grn & multi	.25	.20
557	A181	1b yel & multi	.25	.15
		Nos. 554-557,C324-C325 (6)	1.80	1.00

Bolivia's development.

Cattleya Nobilior — A182

Orchids: 50c, Zygopetalum bolivianum. 1b, Huntleya melagris.

1974, May 15   Perf. 13½
558	A182	20c gray & multi	.40	.15
559	A182	50c lt bl & multi	.40	.15
560	A182	1b cit & multi	.40	.15
		Nos. 558-560,C327-C330 (7)	7.70	1.97

For surcharge see No. 704.

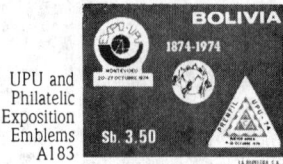

UPU and Philatelic Exposition Emblems A183

1974, Oct. 9
561 A183 3.50b grn, blk & bl   1.00 .40

Centenary of Universal Postal Union: PRENFIL-UPU Philatelic Exhibition, Buenos Aires, Oct. 1-12; EXPO-UPU Philatelic Exhibition, Montevideo, Oct. 20-27.

Gen. Sucre, by I. Wallpher — A184

1974, Dec. 9   Litho.   Perf. 13½
562 A184 5b multicolored   1.10 .50

Sesquicentennial of the Battle of Ayacucho.

Lions Emblem and Steles A185

1975, Mar.   Litho.   Perf. 13½
563 A185 30c red & multi   .35 .35

Lions Intl. in Bolivia, 25th anniv.

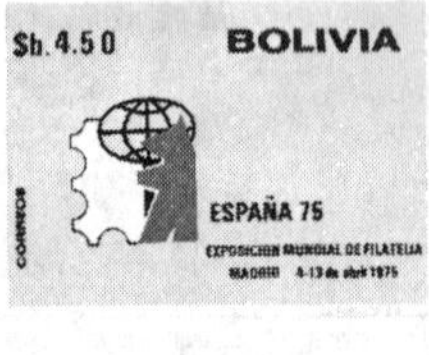

España 75 Emblem A186

1975, Mar.
564 A186 4.50b yel, red & blk   .80 .35

Espana 75 International Philatelic Exhibition, Madrid, Apr. 4-13.

Emblem A187

1975   Litho.   Perf. 13½
565 A187 2.50b lil, blk & sil   .65 .25

First meeting of Postal Ministers, Quito, Ecuador, March 1974, and for the Cartagena Agreement.

Pando Coat of Arms — A188

Designs: Departmental coats of arms.

1975, July 16   Litho.   Perf. 13½
566	A188	20c shown	.15	.15
567	A188	2b Chuquisaca	.40	.40
568	A188	3b Cochabamba	.50	.50
		Nos. 566-568,C336-C341 (9)	4.10	4.10

Sesquicentennial of Republic of Bolivia.

Simón Bolívar — A189

Presidents and Statesmen of Bolivia: 30c, Victor Paz Estenssoro. 60c, Tomas Frias. 1b, Ismael Montes. 2.50b, Aniceto Arce. 7b, Bautista Saavedra. 10b, Jose Manuel Pando. 15b, Jose Maria Linares. 50b, Simon Bolivar.

1975   Litho.   Perf. 13½

Size: 24x32mm
569	A189	30c multi	.15	.15
569A	A189	60c multi	.20	.20
570	A189	1b multi	.30	.30
571	A189	2.50b multi	.50	.50
572	A189	7b multi	1.40	.50
573	A189	10b multi	2.00	.75
574	A189	15b multi	2.50	2.50

Size: 28x39mm
575	A189	50b multi	10.00	10.00
		Nos. 569-575,C346-C353 (16)	36.05	31.15

Sesquicentennial of Republic of Bolivia.

"EXFIVIA 75" A190

1975, Dec. 1   Litho.   Perf. 13½
576	A190	3b multicolored	.75	.60
	a.	Souvenir sheet	1.50	1.50

EXFIVIA 75, first Bolivian Philatelic Exposition. No. 576a contains one stamp similar to No. 576 with simulated perforations. Sold for 5b.

A191    A192

Chiang Kai-shek, flags of Bolivia and China.

1976, Apr. 4   Litho.   Perf. 13½
577	A191	2.50b multi, red circle	1.00	1.00
578	A191	2.50b multi, bl circle	1.00	1.00

Pres. Chiang Kai-shek of China (1887-1975). Erroneous red of sun's circle on Chinese flag of No. 577 was corrected on No. 578 with a dark blue overlay.

1976, Apr.   Litho.   Perf. 13½
579 A192 50c Naval insignia   .40 .35

Navy anniversary.

Geological Map, Pickax and Lamp A193

1976, May
580 A193 4b multicolored   .80 .60

Bolivian Geological Institute.

Lufthansa Jet, Bolivian and German Colors A194

1976, May
581 A194 3b multicolored   .80 .35

Lufthansa, 50th anniversary.

Boy Scout and Scout Emblem — A195

1976, May   Litho.   Perf. 13½
582 A195 1b multicolored   .50 .50

Bolivian Boy Scouts, 60th anniversary.

Battle Scene, US Bicentennial Emblem A196

1976, May 25
583 A196 4.50b bis & multi   1.40 .65

American Bicentennial. A souvenir sheet contains one stamp similar to No. 583 with simulated perforations. Size: 130x80mm.

Family, Map of Bolivia — A197    Vicente Bernedo — A198

1976   Perf. 13½
584 A197 2.50b multicolored   .50 .40

National Census 1976.

1976, Oct.
585 A198 1.50b multicolored   .35 .30

Brother Vicente Bernedo de Potosi (1544-1619), missionary to the Indians.

Policeman with Dog, Rainbow over La Paz — A199

1976, Oct.
586 A199 2.50b multicolored   .60 .60

Bolivian Police, 150 years of service.

BOLIVIA

Emblem, Bolivar and Sucre
A200

1976, Nov. 18   Litho.   *Perf. 13½*
587 A200   1.50b multicolored   .60   .60
Intl. Congress of Bolivarian Societies.

Pedro Poveda, View of La Paz — A201

1976, Dec.
588 A201   1.50b multicolored   .35   .25
Pedro Poveda (1874-1936), educator.

A202    Boy and Girl — A203

1976, Dec. 17   *Perf. 10½*
594 A202   20c brown   .30   .15
595 A202   1b ultra   .45   .15
596 A202   1.50b green   .75   .50
     Nos. 594-596 (3)   1.50   .80

1977, Feb. 4   Litho.   *Perf. 13½*
599 A203   50c multicolored   .15   .15
Christmas 1976, and for 50th anniversary of the Inter-American Children's Institute.

Staff of Aesculapius A204    Supreme Court, La Paz A205

1977, Mar. 18   Litho.   *Perf. 13½x13*
600 A204   3b multicolored   .75   .30
National Seminar on Chagas' disease, Cochabamba, Feb. 21-26.

1977, May 3

Designs: 4b, Manuel Maria Urcullu, first President of Supreme Court. 4.50b, Pantaleon Dalence, President 1883-1889.
601 A205   2.50b multi   .30   .30
602 A205   4b multi   .42   .14
603 A205   4.50b multi   .50   .20
     Nos. 601-603 (3)   1.22   .65
Sesquicentennial of Bolivian Supreme Court.

Newspaper Mastheads A206    Map of Bolivia, Tower and Flag A207

Designs: 2.50b, Alfredo Alexander and Hoy, horiz. 3b, Jose Carrasco and El Diario, horiz. 4b, Demetrio Canelas and Los Tiempos. 5.50b, Frontpage of Presencia.

1977, June   Litho.   *Perf. 13½*
604 A206   1.50b multi   .22   .15
605 A206   2.50b multi   .35   .30
606 A206   3b multi   .42   .25
607 A206   4b multi   .50   .35
608 A206   5.50b multi   .65   .20
     Nos. 604-608 (5)   2.14   1.25
Bolivian newspapers and their founders.

1977, June
609 A207   3b multi   .50   .16
90th anniversary of Oruro Club.

Games' Poster — A208    Tin Miner and Emblem — A209

1977, Oct. 20   Litho.   *Perf. 13½*
610 A208   5b blue & multi   .75   .20
8th Bolivian Games, La Paz, Oct. 1977.

1977, Oct. 31   Litho.   *Perf. 13*
611 A209   3b multicolored   .60   .40
Bolivian Mining Corp., 25th anniv.

Miners, Globe, Tin Symbol — A210    Map of Bolivia, Radio Masts — A211

1977, Nov. 3
612 A210   6b silver & multi   .80   .25
Intl. Tin Symposium, La Paz, Nov. 14-21.

1977, Nov. 11
613 A211   2.50b blue & multi   .50   .35
Radio Bolivia, ASBORA, 50th anniversary.

No. 450 Surcharged with New Value, 3 Bars and "EXFIVIA-77"

1977, Nov. 25   Litho.   *Perf. 11x13½*
614 A147   5b on 5000b on 5b   1.00   1.25
EXFIVIA '77 Philatelic Exhibition, Cochabamba.

Eye, Compass, Book of Law — A212

1978, May 3   Litho.   *Perf. 13½x13*
615 A212   5b multi   .65   .16
Audit Department, 50th anniversary.

Mt. Illimani — A213    Pre-Columbian Monolith — A214

Design: 1.50b, Mt. Cerro de Potosi.

Perf. 11x10½, 10½x11
1978, June 1   Litho.
616 A213   50c bl & Prus bl   .15   .15
617 A214   1b brn & lemon   .20   .15
618 A213   1.50b red & bl gray   .35   .25
     Nos. 616-618 (3)   .70   .55

Andean Countries, Staff of Aesculapius — A215    Map of Americas with Bolivia — A216

1978, June 1   *Perf. 10½x11*
626 A215   2b org & blk   .35   .15
Health Ministers of Andean Countries, 5th meeting.

1978, June 1
627 A216   2.50b dp ultra & red   .35   .15
World Rheumatism Year.
For surcharges see Nos. 697, 972.

Central Bank Building — A217    Jesus and Children — A218

1978, July 26   Litho.   *Perf. 13½*
628 A217   7b multi   1.00   .25
50th anniversary of Bank of Bolivia.

1979, Feb. 20   Litho.   *Perf. 13½*
629 A218   8b multicolored   .90   .16
International Year of the Child.

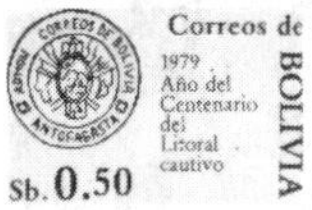

Antofagasta Cancel — A219    Eduardo Abaroa, Chain — A220

Designs: 1b, La Chimba cancel. 1.50b, Mejillones cancel. 5.50b, View of Antofagasta, horiz. 6.50b, Woman in chains, symbolizing captive province. 8b, Map of Antofagasta Province, 1876. 10b, Arms of province.

1979, Mar. 23   Litho.   *Perf. 10½*
630 A219   50c buff & blk   .30   .20
631 A219   1b pink & blk   .50   .25
632 A219   1.50b pale grn & blk   .50   .25

Perf. 13½
633 A220   5.50b multi   .60   .25
634 A220   6.50b multi   .80   .30
635 A220   7b multi   .80   .30
636 A220   8b multi   .90   .35
637 A220   10b multi   1.10   .35
     Nos. 630-637 (8)   5.50   2.25
Loss of Antofagasta coastal area to Chile, cent.
For surcharge see No. 696.

Emblem and Map of Bolivia A221    Gymnast A222

1979, Mar. 26   *Perf. 13½x13*
638 A221   3b multicolored   .75   .50
Radio Club of Bolivia.

Perf. 13x13½, 13½x13
1979, Mar. 27
6.50b, Runner and Games emblem, horiz.
639 A222   6.50b multi   .80   .50
640 A222   10b multi   1.10   .25
Southern Cross Sports Games, Bolivia, Nov. 3-12, 1978.
A souvenir sheet contains 1 stamp similar to No. 640 with simulated perforations. Sold for 20b. Size: 80x130mm.
For surcharge see No. 965.

Bulgaria No. 1 — A223    EXFILMAR Emblem — A224

1979, Mar. 30   *Perf. 10½*
641 A223   2.50b multi   .35   .25
PHILASERDICA '79 International Philatelic Exhibition, Sofia, Bulgaria, May 18-27.
For surcharge see No. 694.

1979, Apr. 2
642 A224   2b multi   .20   .20
Bolivian Maritime Philatelic Exhibition, La Paz, Nov. 18-28.
For surcharge see No. 698.

OAS Emblem, Map of Bolivia — A226

1979, Oct. 22   Litho.   *Perf. 14x13½*
644 A226   6b multi   .75   .25
Organization of American States, 9th Congress, La Paz, Oct.-Nov.

Franz Tamayo — A227    Bolivian and Japanese Flags, Hospital — A228

The Scott Catalogue value is a retail value; that is, what you could expect to pay for the stamp in a grade of Very Fine. The value listed reflects recent actual dealer selling prices.

UN Emblem and
Meeting — A229

Radio Tower and
Waves — A230

1979, Dec.
645 A227 2.80b blk & gray .35 .25
646 A228 5b multi .50 .35
648 A229 5b multi .50 .35
649 A230 6b multi .65 .25
Nos. 645-649 (4) 2.00 1.20
Franz Tamayo, lawyer, birth centenary; Japanese-Bolivian health care cooperation; CEPAL, 18th Congress, La Paz, Sept. 18-26; Bolivian National Radio, 50th anniversary.
For surcharge see No. 695.

Puerto Suarez Iron Ore Deposits A231

1979 Litho. Perf. 13½x14
650 A231 9.50b multi 1.10 .50

Bolivia No. 19, EXFILMAR Emblem, Bolivian Flag — A232

1980 Litho. Perf. 13½
651 A232 4b multi .55 .30
EXFILMAR, Bolivian Maritime Philatelic Exhibition, La Paz, Nov. 18-28, 1979.

Juana Azurduy on Horseback — A233

1980 Litho. Perf. 14x13½
652 A233 4b multi .55 .30
Juana Azurduy de Padilla, independence fighter, birth bicentenary.

La Salle and World Map A234

1980 Perf. 13½x14
653 A234 9b multi 1.10 .60
St. Jean Baptiste de la Salle (1651-1719), educator.
For surcharge see No. 966.

For all your
stamp supply needs
www.scottonline.com

"Victory" in Chariot, Madrid, Exhibition Emblem, Flags of Bolivia and Spain A235

1980, Oct. Litho. Perf. 13½x14
654 A235 14b multi 1.60 .75
ESPAMER '80 Stamp Exhibition, Madrid.

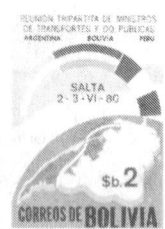

Map of South America, Flags of Argentina, Bolivia and Peru — A236

1980, Oct. Litho. Perf. 14x13½
655 A236 2b multi .25 .20
Ministers of Public Works and Transport of Argentina, Bolivia and Peru meeting.

Santa Cruz-Trinidad Railroad, Inauguration of Third Section — A237

1980, Oct.
656 A237 3b multi .35 .20

Flag on Provincial Map — A238

Parrots — A239

Perf. 14x13½, 13½x14

1981, May 11 Litho.
657 A238 1b Soldier, flag, map .15 .15
658 A238 3b Flag, map .35 .15
659 A238 40b shown 5.00 1.25
660 A238 50b Soldier, civilians, horiz. 6.00 1.25
Nos. 657-660 (4) 11.50 2.80
July 17 Revolution memorial.

1981, May 11 Perf. 14x13½
661 A239 4b Ara macao .50 .30
662 A239 7b Ara chloroptera .80 .50
663 A239 8b Ara ararauna 1.00 .60
664 A239 9b Ara rubrogenys 1.10 .65
665 A239 10b Ara auricollis 1.10 .65
666 A239 12b Anodorynchus hyacinthinus 1.50 .75
667 A239 15b Ara militaris 1.75 1.00
668 A239 20b Ara severa 2.25 1.25
Nos. 661-668 (8) 10.00 5.70

Christmas 1981 — A240

1981, Dec. 7 Litho. Perf. 10½
669 A240 1b Virgin and Child, vert. .15 .15
670 A240 2b Child, star .25 .15

American Airforces Commanders' 22nd Conference, Buenos Aires — A241

1982, Apr. 12 Litho. Perf. 13½
671 A241 14b multi 1.60 .50

75th Anniv. of Cobija — A242

Simon Bolivar Birth Bicentenary (1983) — A243

1982, July 8 Litho. Perf. 13½
672 A242 28b multi .40 .25

1982, July 12
673 A243 18b multi .25 .20

1983 World Telecommunications Day — A244

1982 World Cup — A245

1982, July 15
674 A244 26b Receiving station .40 .25

1982, July 21 Perf. 11
675 A245 4b shown .15 .15
676 A245 100b Final Act, by Picasso 1.75 .95
For surcharge see No. 701.

Girl Playing Piano — A246

1982, July 25 Perf. 13½
677 A246 16b Boy playing soccer, vert. .25 .15
678 A246 20b shown .35 .20

Bolivian-Chinese Agricultural Cooperation, 1972-1982 — A247

1982, Aug. 12
679 A247 30b multi .50 .25

First Bolivian-Japanese Gastroenterology Conference, La Paz, Jan. — A248

1982, Aug. 26
680 A248 22b multi .35 .25

A249

A250

1982, Aug. 31 Litho. Perf. 14x13½
681 A249 19b Stamps .35 .20
10th Anniv. of Bolivian Philatelic Federation.

1982, Sept. 1
682 A250 20b tan & dk brown .30 .20
Pres. Hernando Siles, birth centenary.

Scouting Year — A251

Cochabamba Philatelic Center, 25th Anniv. — A252

1982, Sept. 3 Perf. 11
683 A251 5b Baden-Powell .15 .15
For surcharge see No. 703.

1982, Sept. 14
684 A252 3b multicolored .15 .15
For surcharge see No. 700.

Cochabamba Superior Court of Justice Sesquicentennial A253

1982 Litho. Perf. 13½
685 A253 10b multicolored .20 .15
For surcharge see No. 970.

Enthronement of Virgin of Copacabana, 400th Anniv. — A254

Navy Day — A255

1982, Nov. 15 Litho. Perf. 13½
686 A254 13b multicolored .15 .15
For surcharge see No. 971.

1982, Nov. 17
687 A255 14b Port Busch Naval Base .25 .15

BOLIVIA

A256  A257

1982, Nov. 19   **Perf. 11**
688 A256 10b green & gray   .20 .15
Christmas. For surcharge see No. 702.

1983, Feb. 13   **Litho.**   **Perf. 13½**
689 A257 50b multicolored   .80 .40
10th Youth Soccer Championship, Jan. 22-Feb. 13.

EXFIVIA '83 Philatelic Exhibition — A258

1983, Nov. 5   **Litho.**   **Perf. 13½**
690 A258 150b brown carmine   1.00 .50

Visit of Brazilian Pres. Joao Figueiredo, Feb. — A259

1984, Feb. 7   **Litho.**   **Perf. 13½x14**
691 A259 150b multicolored   .40 .20

Simon Bolivar Entering La Paz, by Carmen Baptista — A260

Paintings of Bolivar: 50b, Riding Horse, by Mulato Gil de Quesada, vert.

Perf. 14x13½, 13½x14
1984, Mar. 30
692 A260 50b multi   .15 .15
693 A260 200b multi   .55 .22

Types of 1957-79 Surcharged

$b. 60.-

No. 697

1984, Mar.
694 A223 40b on 2.50b #641   .15 .15
695 A227 40b on 2.80b #645   .15 .15
696 A219 60b on 1.50b #632   .18 .15
697 A219 60b on 2.50b #627   .18 .15
698 A224 100b on 2b #642   .30 .15
699 A141 200b on 350b #409   .60 .25
       Nos. 694-699 (6)   1.56 1.00

See No. 972 for surcharge similar to No. 697.

Nos. 675, 683-684, 688, C328 Surcharged
1984, June 27   **Litho.**   **Perf. 11**
700 A252 500b on 3b #684   .75 .35
701 A245 1000b on 4b #675   1.50 .75
702 A256 2000b on 10b #688   3.00 1.25
703 A251 5000b on 5b #683   7.50 3.00

Perf. 13½
704 A182 10,000b on 3.80b #C328   10.00 6.00
      Nos. 700-704 (5)   22.75 11.35

Road Safety Education — A261

Jose Eustaquio Mendez, 200th Birth Anniv. — A262

Cartoons.
1984, Sept. 7   **Litho.**   **Perf. 11**
705 A261 80b Jaywalker   .15 .15
706 A261 120b Motorcycle policeman, ambulance   .15 .15

Perf. 14x13½, 13½x14
1984, Sept. 19
Paintings: 300b, Birthplace, by Jorge Campos. 500b, Mendez Leading the Battle of La Tablada, by M. Villegas, horiz.
707 A262 300b multi   .15 .15
708 A262 500b multi   .15 .15

1983 World Cup Soccer Championships, Mexico — A263

Chasqui, Postal Runner — A264

Sponsoring shoe-manufacturers' trademarks and: 100b, 200b, Outline map of Bolivia, national colors. 600b, World map and soccer ball, horiz.

1984, Oct. 26   **Perf. 11**
709 A263 100b multi   .15 .15
710 A263 200b multi   .15 .15
711 A263 600b multi   .15 .15
      Nos. 709-711 (3)   .45 .45

1985
712 A264 11000b vio bl   .25 .15
For surcharge see No. 962.

Intl. Year of Professional Education — A265

Intl. Anti-Polio Campaign — A266

1985, Apr. 25
713 A265 2000b Natl. Manual Crafts emblem   .15 .15
For surcharges see Nos. 721-722, 959.

1985, May 22
714 A266 20000b lt bl & vio   .25 .15

Endangered Wildlife — A267

1985, May 22
715 A267 23000b Altiplano boliviano   .20 .15
716 A267 25000b Sarcorhamphus gryphus   .22 .15
717 A267 30000b Blastocaros dichotomus   .30 .15
      Nos. 715-717 (3)   .72 .45
Nos. 716-717 vert.
For surcharge see No. 963.

Dona Vicenta Juaristi Eguino (b. 1785), Independence Heroine — A268

UN, 40th Anniv. — A269

1985, Oct.   **Litho.**   **Perf. 13½**
718 A268 300000b multi   .20 .15

1985, Oct. 24   **Perf. 11**
719 A269 1000000b bl & gold   .65 .30
For surcharge see No. 964.

A270  A271

1985, Nov.
720 A270 200000b multi   .15 .15
Soccer Team named "The Strongest," 75th anniv.

No. 713 Surcharged
1986   **Litho.**   **Perf. 11**
721 A265 200000b on 2000b   .22 .15
722 A265 5000000b on 2000b   5.25 2.50

1986
723 A271 300000 Emblems, vert.   .32 .15
724 A271 550000 Pique trademark, vert.   .58 .24
725 A271 1000000 Azteca Stadium   1.05 .50
726 A271 2500000 World cup, vert.   2.65 1.25
      Nos. 723-726 (4)   4.60 2.14
1986 World Cup Soccer Championships.
For surcharge see No. 961.

Intl. Youth Year
A272 A273

1986
727 A272 150000 brt car rose   .16 .15
728 A272 500000 bl grn   .55 .35
729 A273 3000000 multi   3.15 1.50
      Nos. 727-729 (3)   3.86 2.00
Inscribed 1985.
For surcharge see No. 958.

Alfonso Sobieta Viaduct, Carretera Quillacollo, Confital — A274

1986   **Perf. 13½**
730 A274 400000 int bl & gray   .42 .20
Inter-American Development Bank, 25th anniv.

Admission of Bolivia to the UPU, Cent. — A275

Postal Workers Soc., 50th Anniv. — A276

1986, Apr. 3   **Perf. 11**
731 A275 800000 multi   .85 .40

1986, Sept. 5
732 A276 2000000 brn & pale brn   2.10 1.00
For surcharge see No. 967.

Founding of Trinidad, 300th Anniv. — A277

1986, May 25   **Perf. 13½x14**
733 A277 1400000 Bull and Rider, by Vaca   1.50 .75
For surcharge see No. 960.

Bolivian Philatelic Federation, 15th Anniv. — A278

1986, Nov. 28
734 A278 600000b No. 19   .62 .30

Death of a Priest, by Jose Antonio Zampa — A279

Intl. Peace Year — A280

1986, Nov. 21   **Perf. 14x13½**
735 A279 400000b multi   .42 .20

1986, Sept. 16   **Perf. 11**
736 A280 200000 yel grn & pale grn   .22 .15

Natl. Oil Corp. (YPBF), 50th Anniv. — A281

1986, Dec. 22   **Litho.**   **Perf. 11**
737 A281 1000000b multi   1.50 .50

A282  A283

BOLIVIA

Photograph of a Devil-mask Dancer, by Jimenez Cordero.

1987, Feb. 13   Litho.   *Perf. 14x13½*
738 A282 20c multi   .30   .15

February 10th Society, cent. (in 1985).

1987, Mar. 20   Litho.   *Perf. 14x13½*
739 A283 30c Crossed flags   .45   .25

State Visit of Richard von Weizsacker, Pres. of Germany, Mar. 20.

State Visit of King Juan Carlos of Spain, May 20 — A284

1987, May 20   *Perf. 13½x14*
740 A284 60c Natl. arms   .90   .40

EXFIVIA '87 — A285
Mount Potosi, 18th cent. engraving.

1987, Oct.   Litho.   *Perf. 13½*
741 A285 50c multi   .72   .35

See No. 750.

1987, Oct.
742 A286 20c Condor   .30   .15
743 A286 20c Tapir   .30   .15
744 A286 30c Vicuna   .45   .25
745 A286 30c Armadillo   .45   .25
746 A286 40c Spectacled bears   .58   .30
747 A286 60c Toucans   .88   .40
       Nos. 742-747 (6)   2.96 1.50

Wildlife in danger of extinction.

ESPAMER '87, La Coruna A287

1987, Oct.   Litho.   *Perf. 14x13½*
748 A287 20c Nina, stern of Santa
               Maria   .30   .15
749 A287 20c Bow of Santa Maria,
               Pinta   .30   .15
  a.   Pair, #748-749   .60   .25

No. 749a has a continuous design.

EXFIVIA Type of 1987
Photograph of Mt. Potosi by Jimenez Cordero.

1987, Aug. 5   Litho.   *Perf. 13½*
750 A285 40c multi   .58   .30

Musical Instruments A288

1987, Dec. 3   *Perf. 13½x14, 14x13½*
751 A288 50c Zampona and quena
               (wind instruments)   .72   .35
752 A288 1b Charango, vert.   1.45   .70

A289

State Visit of Pope John Paul II A290

Pontiff, religious architecture and art: No. 753, Cathedral of Kings, Beni. No. 754, Carabuco Church. No. 755, Tihuanacu Church. No. 756, St. Francis's Church, Sucre. No. 757, St. Joseph's of Chiquitos Church. 40c, Cobija Chapel, vert. No. 759, Jayu Kcota Church. No. 760, Cochabamba Cathedral, vert. 60c, St. Francis's Basilica, La Paz, vert. No. 762, Christ of Machaca Church. No. 763, St. Lawrence's Church, Potosi, vert. No. 764, *The Holy Family*, by Rubens, vert. No. 765, *The Virgin of Copacabana*, statue, vert. No. 766, Vallegrande Church. No. 767, Tarija Cathedral, vert. No. 768, Concepcion Church.

1988   Litho.   *Perf. 13½x14, 14x13½*
753 A289 20c multi   .25   .15
754 A289 20c multi   .25   .15
755 A289 20c multi   .25   .15
756 A289 30c multi   .38   .20
757 A289 30c multi   .38   .20
758 A289 40c multi   .50   .25
759 A289 50c multi   .65   .30
760 A289 50c multi   .65   .30
761 A289 60c multi   .75   .35
762 A289 70c multi   .90   .45
763 A289 70c multi   .90   .45
764 A289 80c multi   1.00   .45
765 A289 80c multi   1.00   .45
766 A289 80c multi   1.00   .45
767 A289 1.30b multi   1.65   .75
768 A289 1.30b multi   1.65   .75
769 A290 1.50b shown   1.90   .90
       Nos. 753-769 (17)   14.06 6.50

Issue dates: 1.50b, May 9. Others, Mar. 3.

Visit of Pres. Jose Sarney of Brazil A291

1988, Aug. 2   Litho.   *Perf. 13½x14*
770 A291 50c multi   .60   .30

St. John Bosco (1815-1888) — A292

1988, Aug. 16   *Perf. 13½*
771 A292 30c multi   .42   .20

Bolivian Railways, Cent. — A293

Design: 1b, Steam locomotive from the La Paz-Beni line, made by Marca Shy Ohio, Natl. Railway Museum, Sucre.

1988, Aug. 29
772 A293 1b multi   1.20   .60

Nataniel Aguirre (b. 1888), Author — A294

Department of Pando, 50th Anniv. — A295

1988, Sept. 14   Litho.   *Perf. 13½*
773 A294 1b blk & beige   1.20   .60

1988, Sept. 26   *Perf. 13½*

Designs: 40c, Columna Porvenir, memorial to the Battle of Bahio. 60c, Siringuero rubber production (worker sapping latex from *Hevea brasiliensis*).

774 A295 40c multi   .48   .25
775 A295 60c multi   .72   .35

A296    A297

1988, Sept. 27
776 A296 1.50b multi   1.85   .90

1988 Summer Olympics, Seoul.

1988

Designs: 70c, Archbishop Bernardino de Cardenas (1579-1668). 80c, Mother Rosa Gattorno (1831-1900), founder of the Sisters of Santa Ana.

777 A297 70c multi   .90   .45
778 A297 80c multi   1.05   .50

Issue dates: 70c, Oct. 20, 80c, Oct. 14.

Ministry of Transportation & Communications A298

1988, Oct. 24   Litho.   *Perf. 14x13½*
779 A298 2b deep car, blk & pale ol-
              ive grn   2.35 1.00

Army Communications, 50th Anniv. (in 1987) — A299

1988, Nov. 29   Litho.   *Perf. 13½*
780 A299 70c multi   .95   .45

Bolivian Automobile Club, 50th Anniv. — A300

1988, Dec. 29   Litho.   *Perf. 13½*
781 A300 1.50b multi   1.45   .70

Flowering Plants and Emblems A301

Designs: 50c, Orchid, BULGARIA '89 emblem, vert. 60c, Kantuta blossoms, ITALIA '90 emblem, vert. 70c, *Heliconia humilis*, Albertville '86 emblem, vert. 1b, Hoffmanseggia, Barcelona '92 Games emblem, vert. 2b, Puya raymondi, Seoul '88 Games and five-ring emblems, vert.

1989, Feb. 17   Litho.   *Perf. 13½*
782 A301 50c multi   .58   .24
783 A301 60c multi   .70   .28
784 A301 70c multi   .80   .32
785 A301 1b multi   1.15   .45
786 A301 2b multi   2.30   .92
       Nos. 782-786 (5)   5.53 2.21

Radio FIDES, 50th Anniv. — A302

1989, Feb. 2
787 A302 80c multi   .92   .38

Gold Quarto of 1852 A303

1989, Feb. 9   *Perf. 13½x14*
788 A303 1b multi   1.20   .48

French Revolution, Bicent. — A304

1989, June 23   Litho.   *Perf. 14x13½*
789 A304 70c red, blk & blue   .90   .35

Uyuni Township, Cent. — A305

1989, July 9   Litho.   *Perf. 14x13½*
790 A305 30c blue, black & gray   .38   .15

BOLIVIA

Noel Kempff Mercado Natl. Park, Santa Cruz — A306

Designs: 1.50b, Federico Ahlfeld Falls, Pauserna River. 3b, *Ozotoceros bezcarticus* (deer).

1989, Sept. 24   Litho.   *Perf. 13½x14*
791 A306   1.50b multicolored   2.00   .75
792 A306   3b multicolored   4.00   1.50

UPAEP — A306a

1989, Oct. 12   Litho.   *Perf. 13½*
792A A306a   50c Metalworking   .52   .20
792B A306a   1b Temple of Kalasasaya   1.05   .42
See Nos. 808-809.

State Visit by Dr. Carlos Andres Perez, Pres. of Venezuela A306b

1989, Oct. 14
792C A306b   2b multi   2.05   .82
See Nos. 825-826, 832.

City of Potosi — A306c

1989, Nov. 10   Litho.   *Perf. 13½*
792D A306c   60c Cobija Arch   .75   .30
792E A306c   80c Mint   .85   .40
   f.   Pair, #792D-792E   1.60   .70

Christmas A307

Paintings: 40c, *Andean Stillwaters*, by Arturo Borda. 60c, *The Virgin of the Roses*, anonymous. 80c, *The Conquistador*, by Jorge de la Reza. 1b, *Native Harmony*, by Juan Rimsa. 1.50b, *Woman with Jug*, by Cecilio Guzman de Rojas. 2b, *Bloom of Tenderness*, by Gil Imana. Nos. 794-798 vert.

Perf. 13½x14, 14x13½
1989, Dec. 18
793 A307   40c multicolored   .42   .17
794 A307   60c multicolored   .62   .25
795 A307   80c multicolored   .82   .32
796 A307   1b multicolored   1.05   .42
797 A307   1.50b multicolored   1.55   .62
798 A307   2b multicolored   2.05   .82
   Nos. 793-798 (6)   6.51   2.60

A308   A309

1990, Jan. 23   Litho.   *Perf. 13½*
799 A308   80c multicolored   .85   .35
Fight against drug abuse.

1990, May 13   *Perf. 14x13½*
Great Britain #1, Sir Rowland Hill & Bolivia #1
800 A309   4b multicolored   4.10   1.70
Penny Black, 150th anniv.

World Cup Soccer Championships, Italy — A310

1990, June 16   *Perf. 13½*
801 A310   2b Stadium, Milan   2.00   .80
802 A310   6b Game   6.00   2.40

Organization of American States, Cent. — A311

1990, Apr. 14
803 A311   80c dark bl & brt bl   .82   .32

A312   A313

1990, Apr. 16
804 A312   1.20b multi   1.22   .62

1990   Litho.   *Perf. 14x13½*
805 A313   70c Telecommunications   .72   .55

National Chamber of Commerce, Cent. — A314

1990, June
806 A314   50c gold, blk & bl   .58   .42

Cochabamba Social Club, Cent. — A315

1990, Sept. 14   Litho.   *Perf. 13½*
807 A315   40c multicolored   .42   .32

UPAEP Type of 1989
Perf. 13½x14, 14x13½
1990, Oct. 12   Litho.
808 A306a   80c Huts   .75   .30
809 A306a   1b Mountains, lake, vert.   .95   .38

A317   A318

1990, Oct. 19   *Perf. 14x13½*
810 A317   1.20b multicolored   1.05   .42
Magistrate's District of Larecaja, 400th Anniv.

1990, Oct. 12   *Perf. 14x13½*
811 A318   2b multicolored   1.75   .70
Discovery of America, 500th anniv. (in 1992).

German Reunification A319

1990, Nov. 19   Litho.   *Perf. 14x13½*
812 A319   2b multicolored   1.70   .70

Visit of Carlos Salinas de Gortari, Pres. of Mexico — A320

Design: 80c, Visit of Rodrigo Borja Cevallos, Pres. of Ecuador.

1990, Dec. 13   Litho.   *Perf. 13½*
813 A320   60c multicolored   .75   .30
814 A320   85c multicolored   .85   .40

4th Congress of the Andean Presidents A321

1990, Nov. 29   *Perf. 13½x14*
815 A321   1.50b multicolored   1.35   .55

Exfivia '90 A322   Christmas A323

1990, Dec. 9   *Perf. 13½*
816 A322   40c dk blue   .40   .15

1990, Nov. 20   *Perf. 11*
817 A323   50c multicolored   .45   .18

Express Mail Service A324

1990, Dec. 14   *Perf. 13½x14*
818 A324   1b multicolored   .90   .35

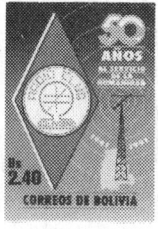

Bolivian Radio Club, 50th Anniv. — A325

1991, Mar. 1   Litho.   *Perf. 14x13½*
819 A325   2.40b multicolored   2.00   .80

End of Chaco War, 56th Anniv. — A326   National Museums — A327

Map of Heroes of Chaco Highway.

1991, June 14   Litho.   *Perf. 14x13½*
820 A326   60c multicolored   .55   .22

1991, June 13   *Perf. 13½*
821 A327   50c Archaeology   .42   .18
822 A327   50c Art   .42   .18
823 A327   1b Ethnology, Folklore   .85   .35
   a.   Strip of 3, #821-823   1.70   .70
Espamer '91.

A328   A329

Our Lady of Peace, Metropolitan Cathedral.

1991, July 15   Litho.   *Perf. 14x13½*
824 A328   1.20b multicolored   1.15   .45

Presidential State Visit Type of 1989

Jaime Paz Zamora, Pres. of Bolivia and: No. 825, Dr. Carlos Saul Menem, Pres. of Argentina. No. 826, Dr. Luis Alberto Lacalle, Pres. of Uruguay.

BOLIVIA

1991   *Perf. 13½x14*
825 A306b 1b multicolored .85 .35
826 A306b 1b multicolored .85 .35
Issue dates: #825, Aug. 5; #826, Aug. 12.

1991, May 31   *Perf. 13½*
Tremarctos ornatus.
827 A329 30c Adult, 2 cubs 1.10 .15
828 A329 30c Adult's head 1.10 .15
829 A329 30c Adult on tree limb 1.10 .15
830 A329 30c Adult, cubs on tree limb 1.10 .15
Nos. 827-830 (4) 4.40 .60
World Wildlife Fund.

A330    A331

1991, Aug. 21   Litho.   *Perf. 14x13½*
831 A330 70c multicolored .68 .28
Bolivian Philatelic Federation, 20th anniv.

Presidential State Visit Type of 1989
Design: 50c, Jaime Paz Zamora, Pres. of Bolivia and Alberto Fujimori, Pres. of Peru.

1991, Aug. 29   *Perf. 13½x14*
832 A306b 50c multicolored .45 .18

1991, Nov. 19   Litho.   *Perf. 14x13½*
833 A331 50c multicolored .45 .18
National census.

America Issue — A332

UPAEP emblem and: 60c, First Discovery of Chuquiago, 1535, by Arturo Reque M. 1.20c, Founding of the City of La Paz, 1548, by J. Rimsa, vert.

Perf. 13½x14, 14x13½
1991, Oct. 12
834 A332 60c multicolored .58 .25
835 A332 1.20b multicolored 1.15 .45

First National Grand Prix Auto and Motorcycle Race — A332a

1991, Sept. 5   Litho.   *Perf. 14x13½*
835A A332a 50c multicolored .45 .18

ECOBOL, Postal Security System A333

1991, Sept. 9   *Perf. 13½x14*
836 A333 1.40b multicolored 1.35 .52

Simon Bolivar — A334

1992, Feb. 15   Litho.   *Perf. 13½*
837 A334 1.20b buff, brn & org brn 1.15 .45
Exfilbo '92.

Scouting in Bolivia, 75th Anniv. (in 1990) and 1992 Andes Jamboree A335

1992, Jan. 13   *Perf. 13½x14*
838 A335 1.20b multicolored 1.15 .45
Dated 1991.

Christmas A336

Paintings: 2b, Landscape, by Daniel Pena y Sarmiento. 5b, Woman with Fruit, by Cecilio Guzman de Rojas. 15b, Native Mother, by Crespo Gastelu.

1991, Dec. 19   Litho.   *Perf. 13½*
839 A336 2b multicolored 1.50 .60
840 A336 5b multicolored 3.75 1.50
841 A336 15b multicolored 11.20 4.50
Nos. 839-841 (3) 16.45 6.60

Pacific Ocean Access Pact Between Bolivia and Peru A337

Designs: 1.20b, Pres. Zamora raising flag, vert. 1.50b, Pres. Jaime Paz Zamora of Bolivia and Pres. Alberto Fujimori, Peru. 1.80b, Shoreline of access zone near Ilo, Peru.

Perf. 14x13½, 13½x14
1992, Mar. 23
842 A337 1.20b multicolored .95 .40
843 A337 1.50b multicolored 1.15 .48
844 A337 1.80b multicolored 1.40 .55
Nos. 842-844 (3) 3.50 1.43

Expo '92, Seville A338

1992, Apr. 15   *Perf. 13½x14*
845 A338 30c multicolored .28 .15
846 A338 50c Columbus' ships .45 .18

Miraflores Rotary Club, District 4690, Mt. Illimani — A339

1992, Apr. 30   Litho.   *Perf. 13½*
847 A339 90c multicolored .70 .45

Prof. Elizardo Perez, Founder of Ayllu of Warisata School, Birth Cent. — A340

1992, June 6   Litho.   *Perf. 13½*
848 A340 60c multicolored .52 .22

Government Palace, Sucre A341

1992, July 10   Litho.   *Perf. 13½x14*
849 A341 50c multicolored .42 .16

A342    A343

1992, Sept. 11   *Perf. 14x13½*
850 A342 50c multicolored .42 .16
Los Tiempos Newpaper, 25th anniv.

1992, Aug. 9   *Perf. 13½*
1.50b, Mario Martinez Guzman, tennis player.
851 A343 1.50b multicolored 1.15 .48
1992 Summer Olympics, Barcelona.

First Intl. Whitewater Canoe Regatta, Bermejo River — A343a

1992, Sept. 17   Litho.   *Perf. 13½*
851A A343a 1.20b multicolored 1.10 .48

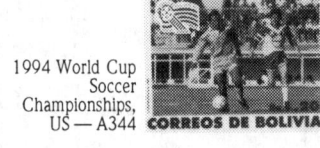

1994 World Cup Soccer Championships, US — A344

1992, Oct. 2   Litho.   *Perf. 13½*
852 A344 1.20b multicolored 1.85 .75

Oruro Technical University, Cent. — A345

1992, Oct. 15   *Perf. 13½x14*
853 A345 50c multicolored .38 .15

Interamerican Institute for Agricultural Cooperation, 50th Anniv. — A346

1992, Oct. 7   *Perf. 13½*
854 A346 1.20b Chenopodium quinoa 1.15 .48

Discovery of America, 500th Anniv. A347

Paintings: 60c, Columbus departing from Palos, vert. 2b, Columbus with Caribbean natives.

1992, Oct. 1   *Perf. 14x13½, 13½x14*
855 A347 60c multicolored .42 .18
856 A347 2b multicolored 1.40 .58

Battle of Ingavi, 150th Anniv. (in 1991) A348

1992, Nov. 18   Litho.   *Perf. 13½x14*
857 A348 1.20b sepia & black .95 .38

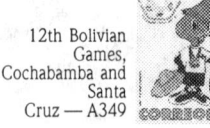

12th Bolivian Games, Cochabamba and Santa Cruz — A349

1992, Nov. 13
858 A349 2b multicolored 1.50 .60

Fauna, Events — A350

Event emblem and fauna: 20c, Beni Dept., sesquicentennial, caiman. 50c, Polska '93, paca. 1b, Bangkok '93, chinchilla. 2b, 1994 Winter Olympics, Lillehammer, Norway, anteater. 3b, Brandenburg Gate, jaguar. 4b, Brasiliana '93, hummingbird, vert. 5b, 1994 World Cup Soccer Championships, US, piranhas.

1992, Nov. 18   Litho.   *Perf. 13½*
859 A350 20c multicolored .15 .15
860 A350 50c multicolored .35 .15
861 A350 1b multicolored .75 .30
862 A350 2b multicolored 1.50 .60
863 A350 3b multicolored 2.25 .90
864 A350 4b multicolored 3.00 1.25
865 A350 5b multicolored 3.75 1.50
Nos. 859-865 (7) 11.75 4.85

Christmas A350a

Designs: 1.20b, Man in canoe, star. 2.50b, Star over churches. 6b, Flowers, church, infant on hay.

1992, Dec. 1   Litho.   *Perf. 13½*
865A A350a 1.20b multicolored .90 .35
865B A350a 2.50b multicolored 1.90 .75
865C A350a 6b multicolored 4.50 1.75
Nos. 865A-865C (3) 7.30 2.85

A351    A352

BOLIVIA

Nicolaus Copernicus (1473-1543), Polish Astronomer: 50c, Santa Ana Intl. astrometrical observatory, Tarija, horiz.

Perf. 13x13½, 13½x13
1993, Feb. 18   Litho.
866 A351 50c multicolored .38 .15
867 A351 2b black 1.50 .60

1993, Apr. 14   Litho.   Perf. 13½
868 A352 60c multicolored .58 .24

Beatification of Mother Nazaria.

12th Bolivar Games A353

1993, Apr. 24   Perf. 13½x14
869 A353 2.30b multicolored 1.65 .65

Bolivia #C240, Brazil #3 — A354

1993, May 31
870 A354 2.30b multicolored 1.65 .65

First Brazilian Stamp, 150th anniv.

A355   A356

Eternal Father, by Gaspar de la Cueva.

1993, June 9   Litho.   Perf. 13½
871 A355 1.80b multicolored 1.25 .50

1993, July 31 Litho.   Perf. 14x13½
872 A356 50c Virgin of Urkupina .35 .15

City of Quillacollo, 400th anniv.

Pedro Domingo Murillo Industrial School — A357

1993, Aug. 4   Litho.   Perf. 13½
873 A357 60c multicolored .40 .15

Butterflies A358

1993, June 4   Perf. 13½x14
874 A358 60c Archaeoprepona demophon .55 .20
875 A358 60c Morpho sp. .55 .20
876 A358 80c Papilio sp. .70 .25
877 A358 80c Historis odius .70 .25
878 A358 80c Euptoieta hegesia .70 .25
879 A358 1.80b Morpho deidamia 1.75 .55
880 A358 1.80b Papilio thoas 1.75 .55
881 A358 1.80b Danaus plexippus 1.75 .55
882 A358 2.30b Caligo sp. 2.00 .60
883 A358 2.30b Anaea marthesia 2.00 .60
884 A358 2.30b Rothschildia sp. 2.00 .60
885 A358 2.70b Heliconius sp. 2.25 .75
886 A358 2.70b Marpesia corinna 2.25 .75
887 A358 2.70b Prepona chromus 2.25 .75
888 A358 3.50b Heliconius sp., diff. 3.00 .95
889 A358 3.50b Siproeta epaphus 3.00 .95
   a. Sheet of 16, #874-889 30.00 30.00
      Nos. 874-889 (16) 27.20 8.75

Pan-American Health Organization, 90th Anniv. — A359

1993, Oct. 13   Litho.   Perf. 13½
890 A359 80c multicolored .55 .20

Archaeological Finds — A360

Location of cave paintings: No. 891, Oruro. No. 892, Santa Cruz, vert. No. 893, Beni, vert. No. 894, Chuquisaca, vert. No. 895, Chuquisaca. No. 896, Potosi. No. 897, La Paz, vert. No. 898, Tarija, vert. No. 899, Cochabamba.

1993, Sept. 28
891 A360 80c multicolored .55 .20
892 A360 80c multicolored .55 .20
893 A360 80c multicolored .55 .20
894 A360 80c multicolored .55 .20
895 A360 80c multicolored .55 .20
896 A360 80c multicolored .55 .20
897 A360 80c multicolored .55 .20
898 A360 80c multicolored .55 .20
899 A360 80c multicolored .55 .20
      Nos. 891-899 (9) 4.95 1.80

America Issue — A361

1993, Oct. 9   Litho.   Perf. 13½
900 A361 80c Saimiri sciereus .55 .20
901 A361 2.30b Felis pordalis 1.50 .60

Famous People — A361a   Christmas — A361b

Designs: 50c, Yolanda Bedregal, poet. 70c, Simon Martinic, President of Cochabamba Philatelic Center. 90c, Eugenio von Boeck, politician, President of Bolivian Philatelic Federation. 1b, Marina Nunez del Prado, sculptor.

1993, Nov. 17   Litho.   Perf. 11
901A A361a 50c sepia .32 .15
901B A361a 70c sepia .45 .18
901C A361a 90c sepia .55 .22
901D A361a 1b sepia .60 .25
      Nos. 901A-901D (4) 1.92 .80

1993, Dec. 8   Perf. 14x13½

Paintings: 2.30b, Adoration of the Shepherds, by Leonardo Flores. 3.50b, Virgin with Child and Saints, by unknown artist. 6b, Virgin of the Milk, by Melchor Perez de Holguin.

901E A361b 2.30b multicolored 1.40 .55
901F A361b 3.50b multicolored 2.25 .85
901G A361b 6b multicolored 3.75 1.50
      Nos. 901E-901G (3) 7.40 2.90

Town of Riberalta, Cent. — A362

1994, Feb. 3   Litho.   Perf. 13½
902 A362 2b multicolored 1.25 .60

World Population Day A363

1994, Feb. 17   Litho.   Perf. 13½
903 A363 2.30b multicolored 1.50 .60

A364   A365

1994, Feb. 21   Perf. 13½
904 A364 2b buff & multi 1.25 .60
905 A364 2.30b multi 1.50 .60

Inauguration of Pres. Gonzalo Sanchez de Lozada.

1994, Mar. 22

1994 World Cup Soccer Championships, US: 80c, Mascot. 1.80b, Bolivia, Uruguay. 2.30b, Bolivia, Venezuela. No. 909, Part of Bolivian team, goalies in black. No. 910, Part of Bolivian team, diff. 2.70b, Bolivia, Ecuador. 3.50b, Bolivia, Brazil.

906 A365 80c multicolored .48 .20
907 A365 1.80b multicolored 1.10 .45
908 A365 2.30b multicolored 1.40 .55
909 A365 2.50b multicolored 1.50 .60
910 A365 2.50b multicolored 1.50 .60
   a. Pair, #909-910 3.00 1.25
911 A365 2.70b multicolored 1.65 .65
912 A365 3.50b multicolored 2.25 .85
      Nos. 906-912 (7) 9.88 3.90

SOS Children's Village, Bolivia — A366

1994, Apr. 12   Litho.   Perf. 13½
913 A366 2.70b multicolored 1.65 .65

Catholic Archdiocese La Paz, 50th Anniv. — A367

Churches, priests: 1.80b, Church of San Pedro, Msgr. Jorge Manrique Hurtado. 2b, Archbishop Abel I. Antezana y Rojas, Church of the Sacred Heart of Mary, vert. 3.50b, Msgr. Luis Sainz Hinojosa, Church of Santo Domingo, vert.

1994, July 12   Litho.   Perf. 13½
914 A367 1.80b multicolored 1.10 .45
915 A367 2b multicolored 1.25 .60
916 A367 3.50b multicolored 2.25 .85
      Nos. 914-916 (3) 4.60 1.90

A368   A369

Design: 2b, Pres. Victor Paz Estenssoro.

1994, Oct. 2   Litho.   Perf. 13½
917 A368 2b multicolored 1.25 .50

1994, Oct. 9
918 A369 1.80b No. 46 1.10 .45

Battle of Ft. Boqueron A370

Col. Manuel Marzana Oroza, battle scene.

1994, Oct. 6
919 A370 80c multicolored .50 .20

San Borja, 300th Anniv. — A371

1994, Oct. 14
920 A371 1.60b Erythrina fusca 1.00 .40

America Issue — A372

Old, new methods of postal transport: 1b, Streetcar, van. 5b, Airplane, ox cart.

1994, Oct. 12
921 A372 1b multicolored .65 .25
922 A372 5b multicolored 3.25 1.25

1994 Solar Eclipse — A373   Environmental Protection — A374

1994 Oct. 21
923 A373 3.50b multicolored 2.25 .85

1994, Sept. 21

Trees: 60c, Buddleja coriacea. 1.80b, Bertholletia exelsa. 2b, Schinus molle, horiz. 2.70b, Polylepis racemosa. 3, Tabebuia chrysantha. 3.50b, Erythrina falcata, horiz.

924 A374 60c multicolored .38 .15
925 A374 1.80b multicolored 1.10 .45
926 A374 2b multicolored 1.25 .50
927 A374 2.70b multicolored 1.65 .65
928 A374 3b multicolored 1.90 .75
929 A374 3.50b multicolored 2.25 .85
      Nos. 924-929 (6) 8.53 3.35

BOLIVIA

Gen. Antonio Jose de Sucre (1795-1830)
A375

1995, Jan. 25	Litho.		*Perf. 13½*
930	A375	1.80b shown	.75 .30
931	A375	3.50b diff. background	1.50 .60

A377

A378

1994, Nov. 25	Litho.		*Perf. 13½*
933	A377	2b Tarija girl	1.10 .45
934	A377	5b High plateau child	2.75 .45
935	A377	20b Eastern girl	11.00 3.75
		Nos. 933-935 (3)	14.85 4.65

Christmas.

1994, Nov. 28	Litho.		*Perf. 13½*
936	A378	1.80b multicolored	.90 .35

Pan-American Scout Jamboree, Cochabamba

Yacuma-Beni Province, Cent. — A379

Design: 1.90b, 2.90b, Cathedral of St. Anne.

1995, Apr. 21	Litho.		*Perf. 13½*
937	A379	1.90b black & multi	1.25 .60
938	A379	2.90b blue & multi	1.75 .90

Franciscans at Copacabana Natl. Sanctuary, Cent. — A380

1995, May 2
939	A380	60c gray & multi	.40 .15
940	A380	80c bister & multi	.55 .20

A381

A382

1995	Litho.		*Perf. 13½*
941	A381	2b multicolored	1.00 .40

Peace Between Bolivia and Paraguay. Dated 1994.

1995, July 25
| 942 | A382 | 2.40b multicolored | 1.25 .50 |

Andes Development Corporation (CAF), 25th anniv.

50th Anniv. of Publication of "Nationalism and the Colonial Age," by Carlos Montenegro (1904-53) — A383

1995, Aug. 8			
943	A383	1.20b pink & black	.60 .25

A384

A385

1995, Sept. 26
| 944 | A384 | 1b multicolored | .50 .20 |

FAO, 50th anniv.

1995, Oct. 24			*Perf. 14½*
945	A385	2.90b multicolored	1.50 .60

UN, 50th anniv.

America Issue — A386

1995, Nov. 21			*Perf. 14*
946	A386	5b Condor	2.50 1.00
947	A386	5b Llamas	2.50 1.00
a.		Pair, #946-947	5.00 2.00

ICAO, 50th Anniv. — A387

1995, Dec. 4			*Perf. 13½x13*
948	A387	50c multicolored	.25 .15

Temple of Samaipata
A388

Archaeological finds and: a, 1.90b, Top of ruins. b, 1b, Top of ruins, diff. c, 2.40b, Lower excavation. d, 2b, Floor, tiers.

1995, Dec. 4			*Perf. 13x13½*
949	A388	Block of 4, #a.-d.	3.75 1.50

No. 949 is a continuous design.

Taquiña Brewery, Cent. — A389

1995, Dec. 8			*Perf. 14*
950	A389	1b multicolored	.50 .20

Christmas — A390

Paintings: 1.20b, The Annunciation, by Cima da Conegliano. 3b, The Nativity, by Hans Baldung. 3.50b, Adoration of the Magi, by Rogier van der Weyden.

1995, Dec. 15			*Perf. 14x13½*
951	A390	1.20b multicolored	.60 .25
952	A390	3b multicolored	1.50 .60
953	A390	3.50b multicolored	1.75 .70
		Nos. 951-953 (3)	3.85 1.55

Natl. Anthem, 150th Anniv. — A391

Designs: 1b, J.I. de Sanjines, lyricist. 2b, B. Vincenti, composer.

1995, Dec. 18	Litho.		*Perf. 13½*
954	A391	1b multicolored	.40 .15
955	A391	2b multicolored	.80 .30
a.		Pair, #954-955	1.20 .45

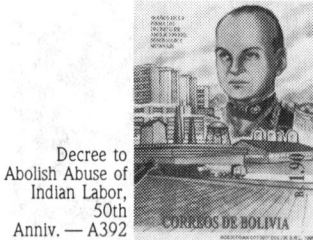

Decree to Abolish Abuse of Indian Labor, 50th Anniv. — A392

Designs: 1.90b, Modern representations of industry, Gov. Gualberto Villarroel. 2.90, Addressing labor policies, silhouettes of people rejoicing.

1996, Jan. 26			*Perf. 14*
956	A392	1.90b multicolored	.75 .30
957	A392	2.90b multicolored	1.15 .45
a.		Pair, #956-957	1.90 .75

Nos. 639, 653, 685-686, 712-713, 715, 719, 726, 729, 732-733, C332, C348 Surcharged

Bs. 0.50

Perfs. and Printing Methods as Before
1996
958	A273	50c on 3,000,000b #729	.20 .15
959	A265	60c on 2000b #713	.25 .15
960	A277	60c on 1,400,000b #733	.25 .15
961	A271	1b on 2,500,000b #726	.40 .15
962	A264	1.50b on 11,000b #712	.60 .25
963	A267	2.50b on 23,000b #715	1.00 .40
964	A269	3b on 1,000,000b #719	1.15 .45
965	A222	3.50b on 6.50b #639	1.40 .55
966	A234	3.50b on 9b #653	1.40 .55
967	A276	3.50b on 2,000,000b #732	1.40 .55
968	AP67	3.80b on 3.80b #C332	1.50 .60
969	A189	20b on 3.80b #C348	8.00 3.20
970	A253	20b on 10b #685	8.00 3.20
971	A254	20b on 13b #686	8.00 3.20
		Nos. 958-971 (14)	33.55 13.55

Size and location of surcharge varies.

Bs 0.60

No. 627 Surcharged

1996	Litho.		*Perf. 10½*
972	A216	60c on 2.50b multicolored	.40 .15

See No. 697 for similar surcharge.

10th Summit of the Chiefs of State and Government (Rio Group), Cochabamba
A393

Designs: 2.50b, Stylized person. 3.50b, Stylized globe surrounded by lines.

1996, Sept. 4			*Perf. 14*
973	A393	2.50b multicolored	1.00 .40
974	A393	3.50b multicolored	1.35 .55

Anniversaries
A394

50c, Natl. Bank of Bolivia, 125th anniv. 1b, Jose Joaquin de Lemoine (1776-1851), first postal administrator, vert.

1996, Dec. 8	Litho.		*Perf. 13½*
975	A394	50c multicolored	.20 .15
976	A394	1b multicolored	.40 .15

Summit of the Americas to Sustain Development
A395

CARE in Bolivia, 20th Anniv.
A396

1996, Dec. 8			*Perf. 14x13½*
977	A395	2.50b brown & multi	.95 .40
978	A395	5b black & multi	1.90 .75

1996, Dec. 19 *Perf. 13½*
979	A396	60c Family, horiz.	.25 .15
980	A396	70c shown	.25 .15

BOLIVIA

Natl. Symphony Orchestra, 50th Anniv. — A397

1996, Dec. 24
981	A397	1.50b shown	.60	.25
982	A397	2b String instruments	.75	.30
a.		Pair, #981-982	1.35	.55

No. 982a is a continuous design.

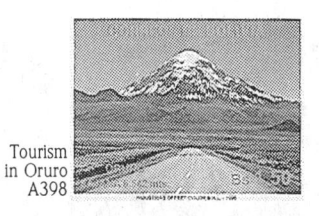

Tourism in Oruro A398

Designs: 50c, Miners' Monument, vert. 60c, Folklore costume, vert. 1b, Virgin of Socavon, vert. 1.50b, Sajama mountains. 2.50b, Chipaya child, building, vert. 3b, Raul Shaw, "Moreno."

1997, Feb. 3   Litho.   Perf. 14½
983	A398	50c multicolored	.20	.15
984	A398	60c multicolored	.25	.15
985	A398	1b multicolored	.40	.15
986	A398	1.50b multicolored	.60	.25
987	A398	2.50b multicolored	.95	.40
988	A398	3b multicolored	1.10	.45
		Nos. 983-988 (6)	3.50	1.55

Dated 1996.

Tourism in Chuquisaca A399

Designs: 60c, La Glorieta. 1b, Governor's Palace, vert. No. 991, Dinosaur tracks. No. 992, House of Liberty. 2b, Tarabaqueno, vert. 3b, Statue of Juana Azurduy of Padilla, vert.

Perf. 13½x14, 14x13½
1997, Jan. 30
989	A399	60c multicolored	.25	.15
990	A399	1b multicolored	.40	.15
991	A399	1.50b multicolored	.60	.25
992	A399	1.50b multicolored	.60	.25
993	A399	2b multicolored	.75	.30
994	A399	3b multicolored	1.10	.45
		Nos. 989-994 (6)	3.70	1.55

Dated 1996.

Tourism in Tarija A400

Designs: 50c, House of Culture, Dorada, vert. 60c, Church of Entre Rios, vert. 80c, San Luis Falls. 1b, Monument to the Chaco War. 3b, Temple, Statue of the Virgin Mary, Chaguay. 20b, Eustaquio Mendez house, monument.

Perf. 14x13½, 13½x14
1997, Jan. 24
995	A400	50c multicolored	.20	.15
996	A400	60c multicolored	.25	.15
997	A400	80c multicolored	.30	.15
998	A400	1b multicolored	.40	.15
999	A400	3b multicolored	1.10	.45
1000	A400	20b multicolored	7.75	3.00
		Nos. 995-1000 (6)	10.00	4.05

Dated 1996.

Visit of French Pres. Jacques Chirac A401

Design: Bolivian Pres. Gonzalo Sanchez de Lozada, Chirac.

1997, Mar. 15   Perf. 14
| 1001 | A401 | 4b multicolored | 1.50 | .60 |

Salesian Order in Bolivia, Cent. — A402

Designs: 1.50b, St. John Bosco (1815-88), church. 2b, Statue of St. John Bosco talking with boy, church.

1997, Apr. 29   Litho.   Perf. 13½
| 1002 | A402 | 1.50b multicolored | .60 | .25 |
| 1003 | A402 | 2b multicolored | .75 | .30 |

UNICEF, 50th Anniv. — A403

Children's drawings: 50c, Houses, children on playground. 90c, Child running, cactus, rock, lake. 1b, Boys, girls arm in arm across globe. 2.50b, Girl on swing, others in background.

1997
1004	A403	50c multicolored	.20	.15
1005	A403	90c multicolored	.35	.15
1006	A403	1b multicolored	.40	.15
1007	A403	2.50b multicolored	.95	.40
		Nos. 1004-1007 (4)	1.90	.85

Department of La Paz A404

Tourism: 50c, Mt. Chulumani, Las Yungas, vert. 80c, Inca monolith, vert. 1.50b, City, Mt. Illimani, vert. 2b, Gate of the Sun, Tiwanacu. 2.50b, Traditional dancers, vert. 10b, Virgin of Copacabana, reed boat.

1997, May 28   Litho.   Perf. 13½
1008	A404	50c multicolored	.20	.15
1009	A404	80c multicolored	.30	.15
1010	A404	1.50b multicolored	.60	.25
1011	A404	2b multicolored	.75	.30
1012	A404	2.50b multicolored	.95	.40
1013	A404	10b multicolored	3.75	1.50
		Nos. 1008-1013 (6)	6.55	2.75

1997 America Cup Soccer Championships, Bolivia — A405

1998 World Cup Soccer Championships, France — A406

1997, June 13
| 1014 | A405 | 3b multicolored | 1.20 | .50 |
| 1015 | A406 | 5b multicolored | 1.90 | .75 |

America Issue — A408

Women in traditional costumes: 5b, From valley region. 15b, From eastern Bolivia.

1997, July 14   Litho.   Perf. 13½
| 1017 | A408 | 5b multicolored | 1.90 | .75 |
| 1018 | A408 | 15b multicolored | 5.75 | 2.25 |

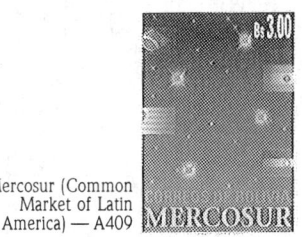

Mercosur (Common Market of Latin America) — A409

1997, Sept. 26
| 1019 | A409 | 3b multicolored | 1.10 | .45 |

See Argentina #1975, Brazil #2646, Paraguay #2565, Uruguay #1681.

Christmas — A410

Paintings: 2b, Virgin del Cerro, by unknown artist. 5b, Virgin de la Leche, by unknown artist. 10b, The Holy Family, by Melchor Pérez de Holguin.

1997, Dec. 19   Litho.   Perf. 13½
1020	A410	2b multicolored	.75	.30
1021	A410	5b multicolored	1.75	.75
1022	A410	10b multicolored	3.50	1.50
		Nos. 1020-1022 (3)	6.00	2.55

Diana, Princess of Wales (1961-97) A411

1997, Dec. 29
| 1023 | A411 | 2b Portrait, vert. | 1.25 | .50 |
| 1024 | A411 | 3b In mine field | 1.75 | .75 |

Visit of Prime Minister of Spain A412

Hugo Banzer Suarez, Pres. of Bolivia and José Maria Aznar.

1998, Mar. 16
| 1025 | A412 | 6b multicolored | 3.30 | 1.30 |

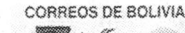

Bolivian Society of Engineers, 75th Anniv. — A413

1998, Apr. 28
| 1026 | A413 | 3.50b multicolored | 1.25 | .55 |

A144    A415

1998, Apr. 30   Litho.   Perf. 13½
| 1027 | A414 | 5b multicolored | 1.75 | .75 |

Rotary Intl. in Bolivia, 70th anniv.

1998, July 9

Letter Carriers, 1942: 3b, Postman delivering mail to woman, vert.

| 1028 | A415 | 3b multicolored | 1.10 | .45 |
| 1029 | A415 | 4b multicolored | 1.40 | .60 |

America Issue.

Famous Men — A416

1.50b, Werner Guttentag Tichauer, bibliographer. 2b, Dr. Martin Cardenas Hermosa, botanist. 3.50b, Adrian Patiño Carpio, composer.

1998, July 10
1030	A416	1.50b brown	.55	.20
1031	A416	2b green, vert	.70	.30
1032	A416	3.50b black, vert	1.25	.50
		Nos. 1030-1032 (3)	2.50	1.00

Regions in Bolivia A417

Beni: 50c, Victoria regia. 1b, Callandria. 1.50b, White Tajibo tree, vert. 3.50b, Amazon mask. 5b, Nutrea. 7b, Tropical condor.

Pando: 50c, Acre River. 1b, Sloth climbing bamboo tree, vert. 1.50b, Bahla Arroyo, vert. 4b, Boa. 5b, Family of capybaras. 7b, Houses, palm trees, vert.

1998   Litho.   Perf. 13½
1033	A417	50c black & multi	.20	.15
1034	A417	1b black & multi	.35	.15
1035	A417	1.50b black & multi	.55	.25
1036	A417	3.50b black & multi	1.25	.55
1037	A417	5b black & multi	1.75	.80
1038	A417	7b black & multi	2.50	1.10
		Nos. 1033-1038 (6)	6.60	3.00
1039	A417	50c green & multi	.20	.15
1040	A417	1b green & multi	.35	.15
1041	A417	1.50b green & multi	.55	.25
1042	A417	4b green & multi	1.40	.65
1043	A417	5b green & multi	1.75	.80
1044	A417	7b green & multi	2.50	1.10
		Nos. 1039-1044 (6)	6.75	3.10

Women of Bolivia — A418

BOLIVIA

First Lady Yolanda Prada de Banzer and: 1.50b, Women working in fields, making pottery, weaving. 2b, Women working on computer, standing at blackboard.

1998
1045	A418	1.50b multicolored	.55	.25
1046	A418	2b multicolored	.70	.30
a.		Pair, #1045-1046	1.25	.55

America Issue.

City of La Paz, 450th Anniv. A419

1998
1047	A419	2b Plaza de Laja Church	.70	.30

AIR POST STAMPS

Aviation School
AP1   AP2

1924, Dec.   Unwmk.   Engr.   Perf. 14
C1	AP1	10c ver & blk	.25	.30
a.		Inverted center	800.00	
C2	AP1	15c carmine & blk	1.50	.50
C3	AP1	25c dk bl & blk	.60	.60
C4	AP1	50c orange & blk	1.50	1.25
C5	AP2	1b red brn & blk	.95	.95
C6	AP2	2b blk brn & blk	1.75	1.75
C7	AP2	5b dk vio & blk	5.50	5.50
		Nos. C1-C7 (7)	12.05	10.85

Natl. Aviation School establishment.
These stamps were available for ordinary postage. Nos. C1, C3, C5 and C6 exist imperforate. Proofs of the 2b with inverted center exist imperforate and privately perforated.
For overprints and surcharges see Nos. C11-C23, C56-C58.

Emblem of Lloyd Aéreo Boliviano — AP3

1928   Litho.   Perf. 11
C8	AP3	15c green	1.00	1.00
a.		Imperf., pair	50.00	
C9	AP3	20c dark blue	.25	.25
C10	AP3	35c red brown	.60	.60
		Nos. C8-C10 (3)	1.85	1.85

No. C8 exists imperf. between.
For surcharges see #C24-C26, C53-C55.

Graf Zeppelin Issues
Nos. C1-C5 Surcharged or Overprinted in Various Colors:

CORREO AEREO
R. S. 6-V-1930
5 Cts.
Nos. C11, C19

CORREO AEREO
R. S.
6-V-1930
Nos. C12-C18, C20-C23

1930, May 6   Perf. 14
C11	AP1	5c on 10c ver & blk (G)	9.50	9.50
C12	AP1	10c ver & blk (Bl)	9.50	9.50
C13	AP1	10c ver & blk (Br)	600.00	875.00
C14	AP1	15c car & blk (V)	9.50	9.50
C15	AP1	25c dk bl & blk (R)	9.50	9.50
C16	AP1	50c org & blk (Br)	9.50	9.50
C17	AP1	50c org & blk (R)	475.00	600.00
C18	AP2	1b red brn & blk (gold)	150.00	150.00

Experts consider the 50c with gold or silver overprint and 5c with black to be trial color proofs.
Nos. C11-C18 exist with the surcharges inverted, double, or double with one inverted, but the regularity of these varieties is questioned.
See notes following No. C23.

Surcharged or Overprinted in Bronze Inks of Various Colors
C19	AP1	5c on 10c ver & blk (G)	77.50	80.00
C20	AP1	10c ver & blk (Bl)	67.50	67.50
C21	AP1	15c car & blk (V)	77.50	80.00
C22	AP1	25c dk bl & blk (cop)	77.50	80.00
C23	AP2	1b red brn & blk (gold)	190.00	200.00
		Nos. C19-C23 (5)	490.00	507.50

Flight of the airship Graf Zeppelin from Europe to Brazil and return via Lakehurst, NJ.
Nos. C19 to C23 were intended for use on postal matter forwarded by the Graf Zeppelin.
No. C18 was overprinted with light gold or gilt bronze ink. No. C23 was overprinted with deep gold bronze ink. Nos. C13 and C17 were overprinted with trial colors but were sold with the regular printings. The 5c on 10c is known surcharged in black and in blue.

Z   1930
No. C8-C10 Surcharged
Bs. 3.—

1930, May 6   Perf. 11
C24	AP3	1.50b on 15c	25.00	25.00
a.		Inverted surcharge	57.50	57.50
b.		Comma instead of period after "1"	35.00	35.00
C25	AP3	3b on 20c	25.00	25.00
a.		Inverted surcharge	62.50	62.50
b.		Comma instead of period after "3"	40.00	40.00
C26	AP3	6b on 35c	37.50	40.00
a.		Inverted surcharge	110.00	110.00
b.		Comma instead of period after "6"	62.50	62.50
		Nos. C24-C26 (3)	87.50	90.00

Airplane and Bullock Cart — AP6
Airplane and River Boat — AP7

1930, July 24   Litho.   Perf. 14
C27	AP6	5c dp violet	1.25	1.00
C28	AP7	15c red	1.25	1.00
C29	AP7	20c yellow	.50	.50
C30	AP6	35c yellow grn	.40	.25
C31	AP7	50c deep blue	.40	.25
C32	AP6	1b lt brown	.40	.25
C33	AP7	2b deep rose	.40	.40
C34	AP6	3b slate	1.40	1.40
		Nos. C27-C34 (8)	6.00	5.05

Nos. C27 to C34 exist imperforate.
For surcharge see No. C52.

Air Service Emblem AP8

1932, Sept. 16   Perf. 11
C35	AP8	5c ultra	.70	.55
C36	AP8	10c gray	.45	.35
C37	AP8	15c dark rose	.70	.55
C38	AP8	25c orange	.70	.55
C39	AP8	30c green	.60	.30
C40	AP8	50c violet	.60	.35
C41	AP8	1b dk brown	.60	.35
		Nos. C35-C41 (7)	4.35	3.00

Map of Bolivia — AP9

1935, Feb. 1   Engr.   Perf. 12
C42	AP9	5c brown red	.15	.15
C43	AP9	10c dk green	.15	.15
C44	AP9	20c dk violet	.15	.15
C45	AP9	30c ultra	.25	.15
C46	AP9	50c orange	.30	.15
C47	AP9	1b bister brn	.30	.25
C48	AP9	1½b yellow	.60	.15
C49	AP9	2b carmine	.60	.30
C50	AP9	5b green	1.10	.40
C51	AP9	10b dk brown	1.75	.75
		Nos. C42-C51 (10)	5.35	2.60

Nos. C1, C4, C10, C30 Surcharged in Red (#C52-C56) or Green (#C57-C58) — c

Correo Aéreo
D. S. 25-2-37
0.05

1937, Oct. 6   Perf. 11, 14
C52	AP6	5c on 35c yel grn	.40	.30
a.		"Carreo"	12.50	
b.		Inverted surcharge		
C53	AP3	20c on 35c red brn	.50	.40
a.		Inverted surcharge		
C54	AP3	50c on 35c red brn	1.50	1.25
a.		Inverted surcharge	17.50	
C55	AP3	1b on 35c red brn	1.10	.65
C56	AP1	2b on 50c org & blk	1.65	1.00
a.		Inverted surcharge		
C57	AP1	12b on 10c ver & blk	5.75	4.75
a.		Inverted surcharge	22.50	
C58	AP1	15b on 10c ver & blk	5.75	2.75
a.		Inverted surcharge		

Regular Postage Stamps of 1925 Surcharged in Green or Red — d

Correo Aéreo
D. S.
25-2-37
Bs. 4.—

Perf. 14
C59	A56 (d)	3b on 50c dp vio (G)	1.10	1.00
C60	A56 (d)	4b on 1b red (G)	1.40	1.40
C61	A57 (c)	5b on 2b org (G)	1.90	1.65
C62	A56 (d)	10b on 5b blk brn	4.50	3.25
a.		Double surcharge	35.00	
		Nos. C52-C62 (11)	25.55	18.40

No. C59-C62 exist with inverted surcharge, No. C62a with black and black and red surcharges.

Courtyard of Potosi Mint — AP10 
Miner — AP11

Emancipated Woman — AP12 
Pincers, Torch and Good Will Principles — AP15

Airplane over Field — AP13

Airplanes and Liberty Monument AP14

Airplane over River — AP16

Emblem of New Government AP17
Transport Planes over Map of Bolivia AP18 

1938, May   Litho.   Perf. 10½
C63	AP10	20c deep rose	.25	.25
C64	AP11	30c gray	.25	.25
C65	AP12	40c yellow	.25	.25
C66	AP13	50c yellow grn	.50	.25
C67	AP14	60c dull blue	.50	.25
C68	AP15	1b dull red	.75	.25
C69	AP16	2b bister	1.25	.25
C70	AP17	3b lt brown	1.25	.25
C71	AP18	5b dk violet	1.90	.25
		Nos. C63-C71 (9)	6.90	2.25

40c, 1b, 2b exist imperf.

Chalice — AP19

Virgin of Copacabana AP20 
Jesus Christ AP21

Church of San Francisco, La Paz — AP22

St. Anthony of Padua — AP23

Perf. 13½, 10½
C72	AP19	5c dull violet	.35	.35
a.		Pair, imperf. between	30.00	
C73	AP20	30c lt bl grn	.30	.20
C74	AP21	45c violet bl	.60	.20
a.		Vertical pair, imperf. between	42.50	
C75	AP22	60c carmine	.40	.25
C76	AP23	75c vermilion	.65	.60
C77	AP23	90c deep blue	.45	.25
C78	AP22	2b dull brown	.75	.25
C79	AP21	4b deep plum	1.00	.40
C80	AP20	5b lt blue	2.50	.25
C81	AP19	10b yellow	12.00	3.10
		Nos. C72-C81 (10)		

1939, July 19   Litho.

2nd National Eucharistic Congress.
For surcharge see No. C112.

Plane over Lake Titicaca — AP24
Mt. Illimani and Condor — AP25

BOLIVIA

1941, Aug. 21   *Perf. 13½*
C82	AP24	10b dull green	3.25	.38
C83	AP24	20b light ultra	3.75	.65
C84	AP25	50c rose lilac	6.50	1.00
C85	AP25	100b olive bister	16.00	6.00
		Nos. C82-C85 (4)	29.50	8.03

Counterfeits exist.

Liberty and Clasped Hands — AP26

1942, Nov. 12
C86	AP26	40c rose lake	.25	.25
C87	AP26	50c ultra	.25	.25
C88	AP26	1b orange brn	1.25	.75
C89	AP26	5b magenta	.75	.25
a.		Double impression	2.50	1.25
C90	AP26	10b dull brn vio	2.50	1.25
		Nos. C86-C90 (5)	5.00	2.75

Conference of Chancellors, Jan. 15, 1942.

General José Ballivián; Old and Modern Transportation — AP27

1943, Nov. 18   *Engr.*   *Perf. 12½*
C91	AP27	10c rose vio & brn	.15	.15
C92	AP27	20c emerald & brn	.15	.15
C93	AP27	30c rose car & brn	.18	.18
C94	AP27	3b blue & brn	.22	.18
C95	AP27	5b black & brn	.40	.30
		Nos. C91-C95 (5)	1.10	.93

Department of Beni centenary.

Condor and Sun Rising — AP28    Plane — AP29

1944, Sept. 19   *Litho.*   *Perf. 13½*
C96	AP28	40c red violet	.15	.15
C97	AP28	1b blue violet	.15	.15
C98	AP29	1.50b yellow green	.18	.15
C99	AP29	2.50b dk gray blue	.38	.18
		Nos. C96-C99 (4)	.86	.63

Revolution of Dec. 20, 1943.

Map of Natl. Airways — AP30    Map of Bolivian Air Lines — AP31

1945, May 31   *Perf. 11*
C100	AP30	10c red	.15	.15
a.		Imperf., pair	9.00	
C101	AP30	50c yellow	.15	.15
a.		Imperf., pair	27.50	
C102	AP30	90c lt green	.20	.15
a.		Imperf., pair	30.00	
C103	AP30	5b lt ultra	.35	.15
C104	AP30	20b deep brown	1.00	.45
		Nos. C100-C104 (5)	1.85	1.05

10th anniversary of first flight, La Paz to Tacha, Peru, by Panagra Airways.
For surcharges see Nos. C128-C129.

1945, Sept. 15   *Perf. 13½*
Centers in Red and Blue
C105	AP31	20c violet	.15	.15
C106	AP31	30c orange brn	.15	.15
C107	AP31	50c brt blue grn	.15	.15
C108	AP31	90c brt violet	.15	.15
C109	AP31	2b blue	.15	.15
C110	AP31	3b magenta	.20	.15
C111	AP31	4b olive bister	.35	.16
		Nos. C105-C111 (7)	1.30	1.06

Founding of Lloyd Aéreo Boliviano, 20th anniv.

> Catalogue values for unused stamps in this section, from this point to the end of the section, are for Never Hinged items.

No. C76 Surcharged in Blue — *Habilitada Bs 1.40* (1947)

1947, Mar. 23
C112	AP23	1.40b on 75c ver	.18	.18

Mt. Illimani — AP32    Arms of Bolivia and Argentina — AP33

1947, Sept. 15   *Litho.*   *Perf. 11½*
C113	AP32	1b rose car	.15	.15
C114	AP32	1.40b emerald	.15	.15
C115	AP32	2.50b blue	.15	.15
C116	AP32	3b dp orange	.18	.15
C117	AP32	4b rose lilac	.20	.15
		Nos. C113-C117 (5)	.83	.75

1st anniv. of the Revolution of July 21, 1946.
1.40b, 2.50b exist imperf.
For surcharge see No. C137.

1947, Oct. 23   *Perf. 13½*
C118	AP33	2.90b ultra	.25	.25
a.		Imperf., pair	20.00	
b.		Perf. 10½	5.00	4.00

Meeting of Presidents Enrique Hertzog of Bolivia and Juan D. Perón of Argentina at Yacuiba, Oct. 23, 1947.

Types of Regular Issue of 1948

Designs: 2.50b, Statue of Christ above La Paz. 3.70b, Child kneeling before cross. No. C121, St. John Bosco. No. C122, Virgin of Copacabana. 13.60b, Pope Plus XII blessing University of La Paz.

1948, Sept. 26   *Perf. 11½*
C119	A120	2.50b ver & yel	.45	.35
C120	A120	3.70b rose & cream	.55	.35
C121	A120	4b rose lil & gray	.55	.25
C122	A120	4b lt ultra & sal	.55	.16
C123	A120	13.60b ultra & lt grn	.70	.40
		Nos. C119-C123 (5)	2.80	1.51

Type of Regular Issue of 1948

1948, Oct.
C124	A125	10b emerald & salmon	1.60	.18

Pres. Gregorio Pacheco, Map and Post Horn — AP34    L. A. B. Plane — AP35

1950, Jan. 2   Unwmk.
C125	AP34	1.40b orange brown	.15	.15
C126	AP34	2.50b orange	.15	.15
C127	AP34	3.30b rose violet	.15	.15
		Nos. C125-C127 (3)	.45	.45

75th anniv. of the UPU.

Nos. C100 and C104 Surcharged in Black — *XV Aniversario Panagra Bs 4.- 1935-1950*

1950, May 31   *Perf. 11*
C128	AP30	4b on 10c red	.15	.15
a.		Inverted surcharge	17.50	17.50
C129	AP30	10b on 20b dp brn	.30	.22
a.		Inverted surcharge	17.50	17.50

Panagra air services in Bolivia, 15th anniv.

1950, Sept. 15   *Litho.*   *Perf. 13½*
C130	AP35	20c red orange	.15	.15
C131	AP35	30c purple	.15	.15
C132	AP35	50c green	.15	.15
C133	AP35	1b orange	.15	.15
C134	AP35	3b ultra	.25	.15
C135	AP35	15b carmine	.50	.15
C136	AP35	50b chocolate	1.00	.35
		Nos. C130-C136 (7)	2.35	1.25

25th anniv. of the founding of Lloyd Aero Boliviano. 30c, 50c, 15b exist imperforate.
No. C132 exists without imprint at bottom of stamp.

No. C116 Surcharged in Black — *Triunfo de la Democracia 24 de Sept. 49 Bs 1.40*

1950, Sept. 24   *Perf. 11½*
C137	AP32	1.40b on 3b dp orange	.25	.25

1st anniv. of the ending of the Civil War of Aug. 24-Sept. 24, 1949.
Exists with inverted and double surcharge.

Symbols of United Nations — AP36

1950, Oct. 24   Unwmk.
C138	AP36	3.60b crimson rose	.50	.16
C139	AP36	4.70b black brown	.65	.16

5th anniv. of the UN.

Gate of the Sun and Llama AP37    Church of San Francisco AP38

Designs: 40c, Avenue Camacho. 50c, Consistorial Palace. 1b, Legislative Palace. 2b, Communications Bldg. 3b, Arms. 4b, La Gasca ordering Mendoza to found La Paz. 5b, Capt. Alonso de Mendoza founding La Paz. 10b, Arms; portrait of Mendoza.

1951, Mar. 1   *Engr.*   *Perf. 12½*
Center in Black
C140	AP37	20c carmine	.15	.15
C141	AP38	30c dk vio bl	.15	.15
C142	AP37	40c dark blue	.15	.15
C143	AP37	50c blue green	.15	.15
C144	AP37	1b red	.20	.20
C145	AP37	2b red orange	.35	.35
C146	AP37	3b deep blue	.35	.35
C147	AP37	4b vermilion	.45	.45
a.		Souvenir sheet of 4	1.00	1.00
C148	AP37	5b dark green	.40	.40
a.		Souvenir sheet of 3	1.00	1.00
C149	AP37	10b red brown	.65	.65
a.		Souvenir sheet of 3	1.00	1.00
		Nos. C140-C149 (10)	3.00	3.00

400th anniv. of the founding of La Paz.
No. C147a contains C143-C145, C147; No. C148a contains C142, C146, C148; No. C149a contains C140, C141, C149. Perf. and imperf., size: 150x100mm.
For surcharges see Nos. C187-C196.

Horsemanship AP39

Designs: 30c, Basketball. 50c, Fencing. 1b, Hurdling. 2.50b, Javelin throwing. 3b, Relay race. 5b, La Paz stadium.

1951, Aug. 23   Unwmk.
Center in Black
C150	AP39	20c purple	.20	.15
C151	AP39	30c rose vio	.30	.15
C152	AP39	50c dp red org	.50	.15
C153	AP39	1b chocolate	.50	.15
C154	AP39	2.50b orange	.75	.30
C155	AP39	3b black brn	1.00	.75
a.		Souvenir sheet of 3, #C153-C155	4.00	3.50
C156	AP39	5b red	2.00	1.50
a.		Souvenir sheet of 4, C150-C152, C156	4.50	4.00
		Nos. C150-C156 (7)	5.25	3.15

The stamps were intended to commemorate the 5th South American Games and the 2nd National Sports Congress held at La Paz, October 1948.
Nos. C155a, C156a exist perf. and imperf.

Eduardo Abaroa — AP40    Queen Isabella I — AP41

1952, Mar. 24   *Litho.*   *Perf. 11*
C157	AP40	70c rose red	.15	.15
C158	AP40	2b orange yel	.25	.25
C159	AP40	3b yellow green	.25	.25
C160	AP40	4b orange	.25	.25
C161	AP40	50b rose lilac	1.00	.90
C162	AP40	100b gray black	1.10	1.10
a.		Perf. 14	10.00	
		Nos. C157-C162 (6)	3.00	2.70

73rd anniv. of the death of Abaroa.

1952, July 16   *Perf. 13½*
C163	AP41	50b emerald	.35	.25
C164	AP41	100b brown	.65	.35

500th anniversary of the birth of Queen Isabella I of Spain. Exist imperforate.

Columbus Lighthouse AP42

1952, July 16
C165	AP42	2b rose lilac, *salmon*	.20	.20
C166	AP42	3.70b blue grn, *bl*	.20	.20
C167	AP42	4.40b orange, *salmon*	.20	.20
C168	AP42	20b dk brn, *cream*	.40	.15
		Nos. C165-C168 (4)	1.00	.75

No. C168 exists imperforate.

Soldiers — AP43

Gualberto Villarroel, Victor Paz Estenssoro and Hernan Siles Zuazo — AP44

Perf. 13½ (AP43), 11½ (AP44)
1953, Apr. 9   *Litho.*
C169	AP44	3.70b chocolate	.15	.15
C170	AP43	6b red violet	.15	.15
C171	AP44	9b brown rose	.15	.15
C172	AP44	10b aqua	.15	.15
C173	AP44	16b vermilion	.15	.15
C174	AP43	22.50b dk brown	.25	.20
C175	AP44	40b gray	.40	.15
		Nos. C169-C175 (7)	1.40	1.10

1st anniv. of the Revolution of Apr. 9, 1952.
Nos. C169-C170 and C174 exist imperf.

BOLIVIA

Pres. Victor Paz Estenssoro Embracing Indian — AP45

Map and Peasant — AP46

1954, Aug. 2   Perf. 12x11½
C176 AP45 20b orange brn   .15   .15
C177 AP46 27b brt pink   .15   .16
C178 AP46 30b red org   .15   .15
C179 AP46 45b violet brn   .20   .15
C180 AP45 100b blue grn   .38   .15
C181 AP46 300b yellow grn   1.00   .28
    Nos. C176-C181 (6)   2.03 1.04

Nos. C176, C180 for 3rd Inter-American Indian Congress. Nos. C177-C179, C181 agrarian reform laws of 1953-1954.
Nos. C176-C180 exist imperf.
For surcharge see No. C261.

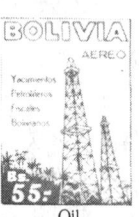

Oil Derricks — AP47

Map of South America and La Paz Arms — AP48

1955, Oct. 9   Perf. 10½
C182 AP47 55b dk & lt grnsh bl   .20   .15
C183 AP47 70b dk gray & gray   .20   .15
C184 AP47 90b dk & lt grn   .20   .15

     Perf. 13
C185 AP47 500b red lilac   .65   .40
C186 AP47 1000b blk brn & fawn   1.25   1.25
    Nos. C182-C186 (5)   2.50 2.10

For surcharge see No. C262.

Nos. C140-C149 Surcharged with New Values and Bars in Black or Carmine
1957   Engr.   Perf. 12½
    Center in Black
C187 AP37 100b on 3b (C)   .15   .15
C188 AP37 200b on 2b   .15   .15
C189 AP37 500b on 4b   .16   .15
C190 AP37 600b on 1b   .16   .15
C191 AP37 700b on 20c   .25   .15
C192 AP37 800b on 40c (C)   .35   .15
C193 AP38 900b on 30c (C)   .40   .15
C194 AP37 1800b on 50c (C)   .65   .25
C195 AP37 3000b on 5b (C)   1.00   .45
C196 AP37 5000b on 10b (C)   1.60   .75
    Nos. C187-C196 (10)   4.87 2.50

     Unwmk.
1957, May 25   Litho.   Perf. 12
C197 AP48 700b lilac & vio   .35   .35
C198 AP48 1200b pale brn   .40   .35
C199 AP48 1350b rose car   .55   .50
C200 AP48 2700b blue grn   1.10   .65
C201 AP48 4000b violet bl   1.40   .75
    Nos. C197-C201 (5)   3.80 2.60

7th session of the C. E. P. A. L. (Comision Economica para la America Latina de las Naciones Unidas), La Paz.
Exist imperf.
For surcharges see Nos. C263-C265.

Type of Regular Issue, 1957
1957, Dec. 19   Perf. 11½
C202 A141 600b magenta   .22   .15
C203 A141 700b violet bl   .35   .15
C204 A141 900b pale grn   .50   .15
    Nos. C202-C204 (3)   1.07   .45

Type of Regular Issue, 1960
1960, Jan. 30
C205 A142 400b rose claret   .50   .30
C206 A142 800b slate blue   .65   .40
C207 A142 2000b slate   1.00   .60
    Nos. C205-C207 (3)   2.15 1.30

Gate of the Sun, Tiahuanacu AP49

Uprooted Oak Emblem AP50

1960, Mar. 26   Litho.   Perf. 11½
C208 AP49 3000b gray   2.00   1.10
C209 AP49 5000b orange   3.00   1.10
C210 AP49 10,000b rose claret   4.75   2.75
C211 AP49 15,000b blue violet   7.00   4.50
    Nos. C208-C211 (4)   16.75 9.45

1960, Apr. 7   Perf. 11½
C212 AP50 600b ultra   .35   .35
C213 AP50 700b lt red brn   .35   .35
C214 AP50 900b dk bl grn   .35   .35
C215 AP50 1800b violet   .60   .60
C216 AP50 2000b gray   .65   .60
    Nos. C212-C216 (5)   2.30 2.25

WRY, July 1, 1959-June 30, 1960.
No. C215 exists with "1961" overprint in dark carmine, but was not regularly issued in this form.

Jaime Laredo — AP51

    Perf. 11½
1960, Aug. 15   Unwmk.   Litho.
C217 AP51 600b rose vio   .75   .45
C218 AP51 700b ol gray   .75   .25
C219 AP51 800b vio brn   .75   .25
C220 AP51 900b dk bl   1.00   .25
C221 AP51 1800b green   1.50   1.50
C222 AP51 4000b dk gray   3.00   1.00
    Nos. C217-C222 (6)   7.75 3.70

Issued to honor the violinist Jaime Laredo.
For surcharges see Nos. C266-C267.

Children's Hospital Type of 1960
1960, Nov. 21   Perf. 11½
C223 A146 600b multi   .40   .22
C224 A146 1000b multi   .60   .22
C225 A146 1800b multi   1.00   1.00
C226 A146 5000b multi   3.00   1.20
    Nos. C223-C226 (4)   5.00 2.64

For surcharges see Nos. C268-C269.

Pres. Paz Estenssoro and Pres. Getulio Vargas of Brazil AP52

1960, Dec. 14   Litho.   Perf. 11½
C227 AP52 1200b on 10b org & blk   .70   .70

Exists with surcharge inverted.
No. C227 without surcharge was not regularly issued, although a decree authorizing its circulation was published. Value, $2.
Postally-used counterfeits of surcharge exist.

Pres. Paz Estenssoro and Pres. Frondizi of Argentina AP53

Design: 4000b, Flags of Bolivia and Argentina.

1961, May 23   Perf. 10½
C228 AP53 4000b brn, red, yel, grn & bl   .75   .75
C229 AP53 6000b dk grn & blk   1.50   1.50

Visit of the President of Argentina, Dr. Arturo Frondizi, to Bolivia.
For surcharge see No. C309.

Miguel de Cervantes — AP54

1961, Oct.   Photo.   Perf. 13
C230 AP54 1400b pale grn & dk ol grn   .58   .22

Cervantes' appointment as Chief Magistrate of La Paz.

Virgin of Cotoca and Symbol of Eucharist AP55

Planes and Parachutes AP56

1962, Mar. 19   Litho.   Perf. 10½
C231 AP55 1400b brn, pink & yel   .65   .35

4th Natl. Eucharistic Cong., Santa Cruz, 1961.

Nos. C212-C216 Surcharged Vertically with New Value and Greek Key Border
1962, June   Unwmk.   Perf. 11½
C232 AP50 1200b on 600b   .55   .55
C233 AP50 1300b on 700b   .50   .50
C234 AP50 1400b on 900b   .55   .55
C235 AP50 2800b on 1,800b   .90   .75
C236 AP50 3000b on 2,000b   .90   .75
    Nos. C232-C236 (5)   3.40 3.10

The overprinted segment of Greek key border on Nos. C232-C236 comes in two positions: two full "keys" on top, and one full and two half keys on top.

Flower Type of 1962
Flowers: 100b, 1800b, Cantua buxifolia. 800b, 10,000b, Cantua bicolor.

1962, June 28   Litho.   Perf. 10½
    Flowers in Natural Colors
C237 A152 100b dk bl   .25   .15
C238 A152 800b green   .50   .15
C239 A152 1800b violet   1.00   .50
   a.   Souvenir sheet of 3   7.50   6.00
C240 A152 10,000b dk bl   3.25   1.75
    Nos. C237-C240 (4)   5.00 2.55

No. C239a contains 3 imperf. stamps similar to Nos. C237-C239, but with the 1,800b background color changed to dark violet blue.
For surcharges see Nos. C270-C271.

1962, Sept. 5   Litho.   Perf. 11½
1200b, 5000b, Plane and oxcart. 2000b, Aerial photography (plane over South America).
    Emblem in Red, Yellow & Green
C241 AP56 600b blk & bl   .25   .15
C242 AP56 1200b multi   .50   .20
C243 AP56 2000b multi   .75   .35
C244 AP56 5000b multi   1.50   .65
    Nos. C241-C244 (4)   3.00 1.35

Armed Forces of Bolivia.

Malaria Type of 1962
Design: Inscription around mosquito, laurel around globe.

1962, Oct. 4
C245 A154 2000b indigo, grn & yel   .80   .50

Type of Regular Issue, 1961
Design: Pedro de la Gasca (1485-1567).

1962   Unwmk.   Photo.   Perf. 13x12½
C246 A150 1200b brn, yel   .35   .20

Condor, Soccer Ball and Flags AP57

Alliance for Progress Emblem AP58

1.80b, Map of Bolivia, soccer ball, goal and flags.

1963, Mar. 21   Litho.   Perf. 11½
C247 AP57 1.40b multi   1.00   .65
C248 AP57 1.80b multi   1.00   1.00

21st South American Soccer Championships.

Freedom from Hunger Type
Design: Wheat, globe and wheat emblem.

1963, Aug. 1   Unwmk.   Perf. 11½
C249 A156 1.20b dk grn, bl & yel   .75   .75

1963, Nov. 15   Perf. 11½
C250 AP58 1.20b dl yel, ultra & grn   .80   .75

2nd anniv. of the Alliance for Progress, which aims to stimulate economic growth and raise living standards in Latin America.

Type of Regular Issue, 1963
Designs: 1.20b, Ballot box and voters. 1.40b, Map and farmer breaking chain. 2.80b, Miners.

1963, Dec. 21   Perf. 11½
C251 A157 1.20b gray, dk brn & rose   .40   .20
C252 A157 1.40b bister & grn   .50   .25
C253 A157 2.80b slate & buff   1.00   .80
    Nos. C251-C253 (3)   1.90 1.35

Andrés Santa Cruz — AP59

     Perf. 13½
1966, Aug. 10   Wmk. 90   Litho.
C254 AP59 20c dp bl   .15   .15
C255 AP59 60c dp grn   .20   .20
C256 AP59 1.20b red brn   .50   .50
C257 AP59 2.80b black   .80   .80
    Nos. C254-C257 (4)   1.65 1.65

Cent. (in 1965) of the death of Marshal Andrés Santa Cruz (1792-1865), pres. of Bolivia and of Peru-Bolivia Confederation.

Children Type of 1966
Design: 1.40b, Mother and children.

1966, Dec. 16   Unwmk.   Perf. 13½
C258 A159 1.40b gray bl & blk   1.00   .42

Co-Presidents Type of Regular Issue
1966, Dec. 16   Litho.   Perf. 12½
    Flag in Red, Yellow and Green
C259 A160 2.80b gray & tan   1.40   1.40
C260 A160 10b sep & tan   1.60   .50
   a.   Souvenir sheet of 4   6.50   6.50

No. C260a contains 4 imperf. stamps similar to Nos. 480-481 and C259-C260. Dark green marginal inscription. Size: 135x82mm.

Various Issues 1954-62 Surcharged with New Values and Bars
1966, Dec. 21
    On No. C177: "XII Aniversario / Reforma / Agraria"
C261 AP46 10c on 27b   .20   .15
   a.   Agraria/Agraria   10.00

    On No. C182: "XXV / Aniversario Paz / del Chaco"
C262 AP47 10c on 55b   .20   .15

    On No. C199: "Centenario de / Tupiza"
C263 AP48 60c on 1350b   .50   .20

On No. C200: "XXV / Aniversario / Automovil Club / Boliviano"

C264 AP48 2.80b on 2700b 2.00 1.60

On No. C201: "Centenario de la / Cruz Roja / Internacional"

C265 AP48 4b on 4000b 1.40 1.00

On No. C219: "CL Aniversario / Heroinas Coronilla"

C266 AP51 1.20b on 800b .75 .50

On No. C222: "Centenario Himno / Paceño"

C267 AP51 1.40b on 4,000b .75 .50

Nos. C224-C225 Surcharged

C268 A146 1.40b on 1,000b .60 .60
C269 A146 1.40b on 1,800b .60 .60

On Nos. C238-C239: "Aniversario / Centro Filatelico / Cochabamba"

C270 A152 1.20b on 800b 1.00 .25
C271 A152 1.20b on 1,800b 1.00 .25

Revenue Stamp of 1946 Surcharged with New Value "X" and: "XXV Aniversario / Dpto. Pando / Aéreo"

C272 A161 1.20b on 1b dk bl .50 .25
Nos. C261-C272 (12) 9.50 6.05

Lions Emblem and Pre-historic Sculptures AP60

1967, Sept. 20 Litho. *Perf. 13x13½*

C273 AP60 2b red & multi .80 .65
a. Souvenir sheet of 2 3.75 3.75

50th anniv. of Lions Intl. No. C273a contains 2 imperf. stamps similar to Nos. 492 and C273.

Folklore Type of Regular Issue

Designs (Folklore characters): 1.20p, Pujllay. 1.40p, Ujusiris. 2p, Morenada. 3p, Auki-aukis.

1968, June 24 *Perf. 13½x13*

C274 A163 1.20b lt yel grn & multi .35 .20
C275 A163 1.40b gray & multi .40 .20
C276 A163 2b dk ol bis & multi .75 .25
C277 A163 3b sky bl & multi 1.00 .25
Nos. C274-C277 (4) 2.50 .90

A souvenir sheet exists containing 4 imperf. stamps similar to Nos. C274-C277. Size: 131x81½mm.

Moto Mendez — AP61

1968, Oct. 29 Litho. *Perf. 13½x13*

C278 AP61 1b multi .35 .15
C279 AP61 1.20b multi .40 .35
C280 AP61 2b multi .75 .50
C281 AP61 4b multi 1.00 .75
Nos. C278-C281 (4) 2.50 1.75

Battle of Tablada sesquicentennial.

Pres. Gualberto Villaroel — AP62

1968, Nov. 6 *Perf. 13x13½*

C282 AP62 1.40b org & blk .30 .22
C283 AP62 3b lt bl & blk .55 .32
C284 AP62 4b rose & blk .70 .40
C285 AP62 5b gray grn & blk .90 .55
C286 AP62 10b pale pur & blk 1.60 1.10
Nos. C282-C286 (5) 4.05 2.59

4th centenary of Cochabamba.

ITU Type of Regular Issue

1968, Dec. 3 Litho. *Perf. 13x13½*

C287 A166 1.20b gray, blk & yel .60 .30
C288 A166 1.40b bl, blk & gray ol .60 .20

UNESCO Emblem — AP63

1968, Nov. 14 *Perf. 13½x13*

C289 AP63 1.20b pale vio & blk .35 .35
C290 AP63 2.80b yel grn & blk .65 .65

20th anniv. (in 1966) of UNESCO.

Kennedy Type of Regular Issue

1968, Nov. 22 Unwmk.

C291 A168 1b grn & blk .25 .15
C292 A168 10b scar & blk 2.75 2.75

A souvenir sheet contains one imperf. stamp similar to No. C291. Dark violet marginal inscription. Size: 131x81½mm.

Tennis Type of Regular Issue

1968, Dec. 10 *Perf. 13x13½*

C293 A169 1.40b org, blk & lt brn .35 .35
C294 A169 2.80b sky bl, blk & lt brn .65 .65

A souvenir sheet exists containing one imperf. stamp similar to No. C293. Size: 131x81½mm.

Stamp Centenary Type of Regular Issue

Design: 1.40b, 2.80b, 3b, Bolivia No. 1.

1968, Dec. 23 Litho. *Perf. 13x13½*

C295 A170 1.40b org, grn & blk .50 .50
C296 A170 2.80b pale rose, grn & blk 1.00 1.00
C297 A170 3b lt vio, grn & blk 1.00 1.00
Nos. C295-C297 (3) 2.50 2.50

A souvenir sheet exists containing 3 imperf. stamps similar to Nos. C295-C297. Size: 131x81½mm.

Franklin D. Roosevelt — AP64

1969, Oct. 29 Litho. *Perf. 13½x13*

C298 AP64 5b brn, blk & buff 1.75 1.10

Olympic Type of Regular Issue

Sports: 1.20b, Woman runner, vert. 2.80b, Discus thrower, vert. 5b, Hurdler.

Perf. 13½x13, 13x13½

1969, Oct. 29 Litho.

C299 A171 1.20b yel grn, bis & blk .50 .40
C300 A171 2.80b red, org & blk 1.00 .75
C301 A171 5b bl, lt bl, red & blk 1.50 1.50
Nos. C299-C301 (3) 3.00 2.65

A souvenir sheet exists containing 3 imperf. stamps similar to Nos. C299-C301. Size: 130½x81mm.

Butterfly Type of Regular Issue

Butterflies: 1b, Metamorpha dido wernichei. 1.80b, Heliconius felix. 2.80b, Morpho casica. 3b, Papilio yuracares. 4b, Heliconius melitus.

1970, Apr. 24 Litho. *Perf. 13x13½*

C302 A172 1b sal & multi 1.40 1.40
C303 A172 1.80b lt bl & multi 2.00 2.00
C304 A172 2.80b multi 3.25 3.25
C305 A172 3b multi 3.25 3.25
C306 A172 4b multi 4.00 4.00
Nos. C302-C306 (5) 13.90 13.90

A souvenir sheet exists containing 3 imperf. stamps similar to Nos. C302-C304. Black marginal inscription. Size: 129½x80mm.

Scout Type of Regular Issue

Designs: 50c, Boy Scout building brick wall. 1.20b, Bolivian Boy Scout emblem.

1970, June 17 Litho. *Perf. 13½x13*

C307 A173 50c yel & multi .15 .15
C308 A173 1.20b multi .40 .40

No. C228 Surcharged

1970, Dec. Litho. *Perf. 10½*

C309 AP53 1.20b on 4000b multi .25 .15

Flower Type of Regular Issue

Bolivian Flowers: 1.20b, Amaryllis pseudopardina, horiz. 1.40b, Rebutia kruegeri. 2.80b, Lobivia pentlandii, horiz. 4b, Rebutia tunariensis.

Perf. 13x13½, 13½x13

1971, Aug. 9 Litho. Unwmk.

C310 A174 1.20b multi .70 .40
C311 A174 1.40b multi .80 .50
C312 A174 2.80b multi 1.50 .75
C313 A174 4b multi 2.00 1.25
Nos. C310-C313 (4) 5.00 2.90

Two souvenir sheets of 4 exist. One contains imperf. stamps similar to Nos. 534-535 and C310, C312. The other contains imperf. stamps similar to Nos. 536-537, C311, C313. Size: 130x80mm.

Folk Dance Type of Regular Issue

1972, Mar. 23 Litho. *Perf. 13½x13*

C314 A177 1.20b Kusillo .50 .16
C315 A177 1.40b Taquirari .65 .16

Two souvenir sheets of 3 exist. One contains imperf. stamps similar to Nos. 542-543, C314. The other contains imperf. stamps similar to Nos. 540-541, C315. Size: 80x129mm.

Painting Type of Regular Issue

Bolivian Paintings: 1.40b, Portrait of Chola Paceña, by Cecilio Guzman de Rojas. 1.50b, Adoration of the Kings, by G. Gamarra. 1.60b, Adoration of Pachamama (mountain), by A. Borda. 2b, The Kiss of the Idol, by Guzman de Rojas.

1972 Litho. *Perf. 13½*

C316 A178 1.40b multi .40 .15
C317 A178 1.50b multi .40 .15
C318 A178 1.60b multi .40 .20
C319 A178 2b multi .55 .20
Nos. C316-C319 (4) 1.75 .70

Two souvenir sheets of 2 exist. One contains imperf. stamps similar to Nos. 548 and C318. The other contains imperf. stamps similar to Nos. C317 and C319. Size: 129x80mm.
Issue dates: 1.40b, Dec. 4. Others, Aug. 17.

Bolivian Coat of Arms AP65

1972, Dec. 4 *Perf. 13½x14*

C320 AP65 4b lt bl & multi 1.40 .50

Cactus Type of Regular Issue

Designs: Various cacti.

1973, Aug. 6 Litho. *Perf. 13½*

C321 A180 1.20b tan & multi .35 .15
C322 A180 1.90b org & multi .50 .20
C323 A180 2b multi .65 .25
Nos. C321-C323 (3) 1.50 .60

Development Type of Regular Issue

1.40b, Highway 1Y4. 2b, Rail car on bridge.

1973, Nov. 26 Litho. *Perf. 13½*

C324 A181 1.40b salmon & multi .40 .15
C325 A181 2b multi .60 .20

Santos-Dumont and 14-Bis Plane — AP66

1973, July 20

C326 AP66 1.40b yel & blk .65 .35

Centenary of the birth of Alberto Santos-Dumont (1873-1932), Brazilian aviation pioneer.

Orchid Type of 1974

Orchids: 2.50b, Cattleya luteola, horiz. 3.80b, Stanhopaea. 4b, Catasetum, horiz. 5b, Maxillaria.

1974 Litho. *Perf. 13½*

C327 A182 2.50b multi 1.00 .22
C328 A182 3.80b rose & multi 1.50 .45
C329 A182 4b multi 1.50 .40
C330 A182 5b sal & multi 2.50 .45
Nos. C327-C330 (4) 6.50 1.52

Air Force Emblem, Plane over Map of Bolivia — AP67

Designs: 3.80b, Plane over Andes. 4.50b, Triple decker and jet. 8b, Rafael Pabon and double decker. 15b, Jet and "50."

1974 Litho. *Perf. 13x13½*

C331 AP67 3b multi .65 .25
C332 AP67 3.80b multi 1.00 .25
C333 AP67 4.50b multi 1.00 .25
C334 AP67 8b multi 1.60 .40
C335 AP67 15b multi 3.50 .50
Nos. C331-C335 (5) 7.75 1.65

Bolivian Air Force, 50th anniv. Exist imperf.
For surcharge see No. 968.

Coat of Arms Type of 1975

Designs: Departmental coats of arms.

1975, July 16 Litho. *Perf. 13½*

C336 A188 20c Beni .15 .15
C337 A188 30c Tarija .15 .15
C338 A188 50c Potosi .25 .25
C339 A188 1b Oruro .50 .50
C340 A188 2.50b Santa Cruz 1.00 1.00
C341 A188 3b La Paz 1.00 1.00
Nos. C336-C341 (6) 3.05 3.05

LAB Emblem — AP68

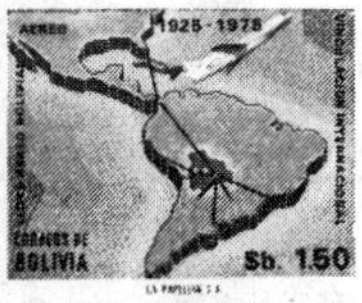

Bolivia on Map of Americas — AP69

Map of Bolivia, Plane and Kyllmann AP70

1975 Litho. *Perf. 13½*

C342 AP68 1b gold, bl & blk .40 .40
C343 AP69 1.50b multi .60 .60
C344 AP70 2b multi .75 .75
Nos. C342-C344 (3) 1.75 1.75

Lloyd Aereo Boliviano, 50th anniversary, founded by Guillermo Kyllmann.

Bolivar, Presidents Perez and Banzer, and Flags AP71

1975, Aug. 4 Litho. *Perf. 13½*

C345 AP71 3b gold & multi .75 .65

Visit of Pres. Carlos A. Perez of Venezuela.

Bolivar Type of 1975

Presidents and Statesmen of Bolivia: 50c, Rene Barrientes O. 2b, Francisco B. O'Connor. 3.80b, Gualberto Villarroel. 4.20b, German Busch. 4.50b, Hugo Banzer Suarez. 20b, José Ballivian. 30b, Andres de Santa Cruz. 40b, Antonio Jose de Sucre.

1975 Litho. *Perf. 13½*

Size: 24x33mm

C346 A189 50c multi .25 .25
C347 A189 2b multi .50 .50
C348 A189 3.80b multi .75 .75
C349 A189 4.20b multi 1.00 .75

Size: 28x39mm

C350 A189 4.50b multi 1.00 .50

Size: 24x33mm

C351 A189 20b multi 4.00 2.00
C352 A189 30b multi 5.00 5.00
C353 A189 40b multi 6.50 6.50
Nos. C346-C353 (8) 19.00 16.25

For surcharge see No. 969.

BOLIVIA — BOSNIA AND HERZEGOVINA

UPU Emblem
AP72

1975, Dec. 7   Litho.   Perf. 13½
C358 AP72 25b bl & multi 3.00 3.00
Cent. of UPU (in 1974).

POSTAGE DUE STAMPS

D1

1931   Unwmk.   Engr.   Perf. 14, 14½
J1	D1	5c ultra	1.10	1.25
J2	D1	10c red	1.10	1.25
J3	D1	15c yellow	1.75	1.90
J4	D1	30c deep green	1.75	1.90
J5	D1	40c deep violet	2.75	3.00
J6	D1	50c black brown	4.00	4.25
		Nos. J1-J6 (6)	12.45	13.55

Youth — D2   Knowledge — D3

Symbol of the Revolution of May 17, 1936 — D4

1938   Litho.   Perf. 11
J7	D2	5c deep rose	.50	.45
a.		Pair, imperf. between		
J8	D3	10c green	.50	.45
J9	D4	30c gray blue	.50	.45
		Nos. J7-J9 (3)	1.50	1.35

POSTAL TAX STAMPS

Worker — PT1

Imprint: "LITO. UNIDAS LA PAZ."
Perf. 13½x10½, 10½, 13½
1939   Litho.   Unwmk.
RA1 PT1 5c dull violet .... .70 .15
a. Double impression

Redrawn
Imprint: "TALL. OFFSET LA PAZ."
1940   Perf. 12x11, 11
RA2 PT1 5c violet .... .60 .15
a. Horizontal pair, imperf. between ... 2.00
b. Imperf. horiz., pair

Tax of Nos. RA1-RA2 was for the Workers' Home Building Fund.

Communication Symbols — PT2   Condor, Envelope and Post Horn — PT3

Communication Symbols — PT4    Postman Blowing Horn — PT5

1944-45   Litho.   Perf. 10½
RA3 PT2 10c salmon .... .40 .15
RA4 PT2 10c blue ('45) .... .40 .15

A 30c orange inscribed "Centenario de la Creacion del Departamento del Beni" was issued in 1946 and required to be affixed to all air and surface mail to and from the Department of Beni in addition to regular postage. Five higher denominations in the same scenic design were used for local revenue purposes.

Catalogue values for unused stamps in this section, from this point to the end of the section, are for Never Hinged items.

Type of 1944 Redrawn
1947-48   Unwmk.   Perf. 10½
RA5 PT2 10c carmine .... .40 .15
RA6 PT2 10c org yel ('48) .... .35 .15
RA7 PT2 10c yel brn ('48) .... .35 .15
RA8 PT2 10c emerald ('48) .... .35 .15
    Nos. RA5-RA8 (4) .... 1.45 .60

Post horn and envelope reduced in size.

1951-52
RA9 PT3 20c deep orange .... .40 .20
a. Imperf., pair 20.00
RA10 PT3 20c green ('52) .... .50 .20
a. Imperf., pair 20.00
RA11 PT3 20c blue ('52) .... .50 .20
a. Imperf., pair 20.00
    Nos. RA9-RA11 (3) .... 1.40 .60

For surcharges see Nos. RA17-RA18.

1952-54   Perf. 13½, 10½, 10½x12
RA12 PT4 50c green .... .50 .15
RA13 PT4 50c carmine .... .50 .15
RA14 PT4 3b green .... .50 .15
RA15 PT4 3b olive bister .... .50 .50
RA16 PT4 5b violet ('54) .... .50 .50
    Nos. RA12-RA16 (5) 2.50 1.45

For surcharges see Nos. RA21-RA22.

No. RA10 and Type of 1951-52 Surcharged with New Value in Black
1953   Perf. 10½
RA17 PT3 50c on 20c green .... .25 .15
RA18 PT3 50c on 20c red vio .... .25 .15

1954-55   Unwmk.   Perf. 10½
RA19 PT5 1b brown .... .20 .15
RA20 PT5 1b car rose ('55) .... .20 .15

Exist imperf.

Nos. RA15 and RA14 Surcharged in Black
"Bs. 5.-/D. S./21-IV-55"
1955   Perf. 10½, 10½x12
RA21 PT4 5b on 3b olive bister .... .25 .15
RA22 PT4 5b on 3b green .... .25 .15

Tax of Nos. RA3-RA22 was for the Communications Employees Fund.
No. RA21 is known with surcharge in thin type of different font and with comma added after "55."

Plane over Airport — PT6    Planes — PT7

Perf. 10½, 12, 13½
1955   Unwmk.   Litho.
RA23 PT6 5b dp ultra .... .25 .15
a. Vertical pair imperf. between

Perf. 11½
RA24 PT7 10b light green .... .20 .15

PT8   PT9

1955   Litho.   Perf. 10½
RA25 PT8 5b red 7.50 7.50
a. Imperf., pair 35.00

Perf. 12
RA26 PT9 20b dark brown .... .25 .15

Tax of Nos. RA23-RA26 was for the building of new airports.

General Alfredo Ovando and Three Men — PT10

1970, Sept. 26   Litho.   Perf. 13x13½
RA27 PT10 20c black & red .... .50 .15

See No. RAC1.

Pres. German Busch — PT11

1971, May 13   Litho.   Perf. 13x13½
RA28 PT11 20c lilac & black .... .50 .15

AIR POST POSTAL TAX STAMPS

Catalogue values for unused stamps in this section are for Never Hinged items.

Type of Postal Tax Issue
Design: 30c, General Ovando and oil well.
1970, Sept. 26   Litho.   Perf. 13x13½
RAC1 PT10 30c blk & grn .... .50 .15

Pres. Gualberto Villarroel, Refinery PTAP1

1971, May 25   Litho.   Perf. 13x13½
RAC2 PTAP1 30c lt bl & blk .... .50 .15

Type of 1971 Inscribed: "XXV ANIVERSARIO DE SU GOBIERNO"
1975   Litho.   Perf. 13x13½
RAC3 PTAP1 30c lt bl & blk 3.00 3.00

BOSNIA AND HERZEGOVINA
ˈbäz-nē-ə and ˌhert-sə-gō-ˈvē-nə

LOCATION — Dalmatia and Serbia
GOVT. — Provinces of Turkey under Austro-Hungarian occupation, 1879-1908; provinces of Austria-Hungary 1908-1918
AREA — 19,768 sq. mi.
POP. — 2,000,000 (approx. 1918)
CAPITAL — Sarajevo

Following World War I Bosnia and Herzegovina united with the kingdoms of Montenegro and Serbia, and Croatia, Dalmatia and Slovenia, to form the Kingdom of Yugoslavia (See Yugoslavia.)

100 Novcica (Neukreuzer) = 1 Florin (Gulden)
100 Heller = 1 Krone (1900)

Watermark

Wmk. 91- BRIEF-MARKEN or (from 1890) ZEITUNGS-MARKEN in Double-lined Capitals, Across the Sheet

Coat of Arms — A1

Type I - The heraldic eaglets on the right side of the escutcheon are entirely blank. The eye of the lion is indicated by a very small dot, which sometimes fails to print.
Type II - There is a colored line across the lowest eaglet. A similar line sometimes appears on the middle eaglet. The eye of the lion is formed by a large dot which touches the outline of the head above it.
Type III - The eaglets and eye of the lion are similar to type I. Each tail feather of the large eagle has two lines of shading and the lowest feather does not touch the curved line below it. In types I and II there are several shading lines in these feathers, and the lowest feather touches the curved line.

Varieties of the Numerals
2 NOVCICA:
A - The "2" has curved tail. All are type I.
B - The "2" has straight tail. All are type II.
15 NOVCICA:
C - The serif of the "1" is short and forms a wide angle with the vertical stroke.
D - The serif of the "1" forms an acute angle with the vertical stroke.
The numerals of the 5n were retouched several times and show minor differences, especially in the flag.

Other Varieties
½ NOVCICA:
There is a black dot between the curved ends of the ornaments near the lower spandrels.
G - This dot touches the curve at its right. Stamps of this (1st) printing are litho.
H - This dot stands clear of the curved lines. Stamps of this (2nd) printing are typo.
10 NOVCICA:
Ten stamps in each sheet of type II show a small cross in the upper section of the right side of the escutcheon.

Perf. 9 to 13½ and Compound
1879-94   Litho.   Wmk. 91
Type I
1	A1	½n blk (type II) ('94)	7.25	15.00
2	A1	1n gray	4.75	1.50
c.		1n gray lilac		1.50
4	A1	2n yellow	9.00	.90
5	A1	3n green	6.00	1.75
6	A1	5n rose red	10.00	.40
7	A1	10n blue	30.00	.75
8	A1	15n brown	32.50	4.50
9	A1	20n gray green ('93)	150.00	6.75
10	A1	25n violet	27.50	6.75
		Nos. 1-10 (9)	277.00	38.30

No. 2c was never issued. It is usually canceled by blue pencil marks and "mint" copies generally have been cleaned.

Perf. 10½ to 13 and Compound
1894-98   Typo.
1a	A1	½n black	10.00	15.00
2a	A1	1n gray	4.00	1.00
4a	A1	2n yellow	3.00	.55
5a	A1	3n green	4.00	1.00
6a	A1	5n rose red	55.00	.35
7a	A1	10n blue	5.50	.70
8a	A1	15n brown	4.75	3.25
9a	A1	20n gray green	6.75	3.50
10a	A1	25n violet	7.25	5.75
		Nos. 1a-10a (9)	100.25	31.35

Type III
| 6b | A1 | 5n rose red ('98) | 1.50 | .35 |

All the preceding stamps exist in various shades.
Nos. 1a to 10a were reprinted in 1911 in lighter colors, on very white paper and perf. 12½. Value, set $25.

BOSNIA AND HERZEGOVINA

A2   A3

Perf. 10½, 12½ and Compound

1900   Typo.

11	A2	1h gray black	.30	.15
12	A2	2h gray	.30	.15
13	A2	3h yellow	.30	.15
14	A2	5h green	.30	.15
15	A2	6h brown	.60	.15
16	A2	10h red	.25	.15
17	A2	20h rose	100.00	4.50
18	A2	25h blue	.85	.15
19	A2	30h bister brown	110.00	4.75
20	A2	40h orange	150.00	8.00
21	A2	50h red lilac	1.00	.15
22	A3	1k dark rose	1.25	.50
23	A3	2k ultra	1.50	1.25
24	A3	5k dull blue grn	3.75	3.75
		Nos. 11-24 (14)	370.40	23.65

All values of this issue except the 3h exist on ribbed paper.

Nos. 17, 19 and 20 were reprinted in 1911. The reprints are in lighter colors and on whiter paper than the originals. Reprints of Nos. 17 and 19 are perf. 10½ and those of No. 20 are perf. 12½. Value each $1.50.

Numerals in Black

1901-04   Perf. 12½

25	A2	20h pink ('02)	.55	.40
26	A2	30h bister brn ('03)	.55	.40
27	A2	35h blue	.75	.40
a.		35h ultramarine	80.00	4.75
28	A2	40h orange ('03)	1.00	.80
29	A2	45h grnsh blue ('04)	.65	.45
		Nos. 25-29 (5)	3.50	2.45

Nos. 11-16, 18, 21-29 exist imperf. Most of Nos. 11-29 exist perf. 6½; compound with 12½; part perf.; in pairs imperf. between. These were supplied only to some high-ranking officials and never sold at any P.O.

View of Deboj — A4

The Carsija at Sarajevo — A5

Designs: 2h, View of Mostar. 3h, Pliva Gate, Jajce. 5h, Narenta Pass and Prenj River. 6h, Rama Valley. 10h, Vrbas Valley. 20h, Old Bridge, Mostar. 25h, Bey's Mosque, Sarajevo. 30h, Donkey post. 35h, Jezero and tourists' pavilion. 40h, Mail wagon. 45h, Bazaar at Sarajevo. 50h, Postal car. 2k, St. Luke's Campanile, Jajce. 5k, Emperor Franz Josef.

Perf. 6½, 9½, 10½ and 12½, also Compounds

1906   Engr.   Unwmk.

30	A4	1h black	.15	.15
31	A4	2h violet	.15	.15
32	A4	3h olive	.15	.15
33	A4	5h dark green	.15	.15
34	A4	6h brown	.15	.15
a.		Perf. 13½	15.00	18.00
35	A4	10h carmine	.15	.15
36	A4	20h dark brown	.35	.20
a.		Perf. 13½	37.50	37.50
37	A4	25h deep blue	1.10	.75
38	A4	30h green	1.25	.30
39	A4	35h myrtle green	1.40	.40
40	A4	40h orange red	1.40	.30
41	A4	45h brown red	1.40	.90
42	A4	50h dull violet	1.50	.60
43	A5	1k maroon	3.75	1.25
44	A5	2k gray green	4.75	6.00
45	A5	5k dull blue	4.00	4.50
		Nos. 30-45 (16)	21.80	16.00

Nos. 30-45 exist imperf. Value, set $50 unused, $37.50 canceled.

For overprint and surcharges see #126, B1-B4.

Birthday Jubilee Issue

Designs of 1906 Issue, with "1830-1910" in Label at Bottom

1910   Perf. 12½

46	A4	1h black	.40	.15
47	A4	2h violet	.50	.15
48	A4	3h olive	.50	.25
49	A4	5h dark green	.55	.15
50	A4	6h orange brn	.55	.25
51	A4	10h carmine	.55	.15
52	A4	20h dark brown	1.25	1.25
53	A4	25h deep blue	2.50	2.50
54	A4	30h green	1.75	2.00
55	A4	35h myrtle grn	2.50	2.25
56	A4	40h orange red	2.50	2.75
57	A4	45h brown red	4.25	4.75
58	A4	50h dull violet	4.25	5.00
59	A5	1k maroon	4.25	5.00
60	A5	2k gray green	15.00	15.00
61	A5	5k dull blue	3.00	3.25
		Nos. 46-61 (16)	44.30	44.85

80th birthday of Emperor Franz Josef.

Scenic Type of 1906

Views: 12h, Jaice. 60h, Konjica. 72h, Vishegrad.

1912

62	A4	12h ultra	4.00	4.25
63	A4	60h dull blue	2.50	3.75
64	A4	72h carmine	12.00	14.00
		Nos. 62-64 (3)	18.50	22.00

Value, imperf. set, $75.

See Austria for similar designs inscribed "FELDPOST" instead of "MILITARPOST."

Emperor Franz Josef
A23   A24

A25    A26

1912-14

Various Frames

65	A23	1h olive green	.35	.15
66	A23	2h brt blue	.35	.15
67	A23	3h claret	.35	.15
68	A23	5h green	.35	.15
69	A23	6h dark gray	.35	.15
70	A23	10h rose car	.40	.15
71	A23	12h dp olive grn	1.10	.30
72	A23	20h orange brn	4.50	.15
73	A23	25h ultra	2.25	.15
74	A23	30h orange red	2.25	.15
75	A24	35h myrtle grn	2.25	.15
76	A24	40h dk violet	6.75	.15
77	A24	45h olive brn	3.00	.15
78	A24	50h slate blue	3.00	.15
79	A24	60h brown vio	2.75	.15
80	A24	72h dark blue	3.25	3.00
81	A25	1k brn vio, straw	12.50	.35
82	A25	2k dk gray, bl	7.25	.25
83	A26	3k carmine, grn	12.00	9.00
84	A26	5k dk vio, gray	22.50	20.00
85	A25	10k dk ultra, gray ('14)	82.50	70.00
		Nos. 65-85 (21)	170.00	105.00

Value, imperf. set, $450.

For overprints and surcharges see #127, B5-B8, Austria M1-M21.

A27   A28

1916-17   Perf. 12½

86	A27	3h dark gray	.15	.20
87	A27	5h olive green	.25	.35
88	A27	6h violet	.30	.35
89	A27	10h bister	1.40	1.65
90	A27	12h blue gray	.45	.45
91	A27	15h car rose	.15	.15
92	A27	20h brown	.35	.45
93	A27	25h blue	.25	.35
94	A27	30h dark green	.25	.35
95	A27	40h vermilion	.25	.35
96	A27	50h green	.25	.35
97	A27	60h lake	.25	.35
98	A27	80h orange brn	1.25	.40
a.		Perf. 11½	3.50	3.00
99	A27	90h dark violet	.75	.50
a.		Perf. 11½	450.00	675.00
101	A28	2k claret, straw	.75	.75
102	A28	3k green, bl	1.90	3.25
103	A28	4k carmine, grn	5.75	7.25
104	A28	10k dp vio, gray	15.00	20.00
		Nos. 86-104 (18)	29.70	37.50

Value, imperf. set, $175.
For overprints see Nos. B11-B12.

Emperor Karl I
A29   A30

1917   Perf. 12½

105	A29	3h olive gray	.15	.20
a.		Perf. 11½	75.00	75.00
b.		Perf. 12½x11½	13.00	21.00
106	A29	5h olive green	.15	.15
107	A29	6h violet	.30	.55
108	A29	10h orange brn	.15	.15
a.		Perf. 11½x12½	62.50	95.00
b.		Perf. 11½		
109	A29	12h blue	.50	.75
110	A29	15h brt rose	.15	.15
111	A29	20h red brown	.15	.15
112	A29	25h ultra	1.00	.50
113	A29	30h gray green	.25	.20
114	A29	40h olive bis	.25	.15
115	A29	50h dp green	.85	.50
116	A29	60h car rose	.85	.45
a.		Perf. 11½	15.00	21.00
117	A29	80h steel blue	.25	.25
118	A29	90h dull violet	1.00	1.40
119	A30	2k carmine, straw	.90	.45
120	A30	3k green, bl	13.00	16.00
121	A30	4k carmine, grn	5.25	7.25
122	A30	10k dp violet, gray	3.25	5.75
		Nos. 105-122 (18)	28.00	35.00

Value, imperf. set, $85.

Nos. 47 and 66 Overprinted in **1918** Red

1918

126	A4	2h violet	.45	.50
b.		Inverted overprint	17.50	
d.		Double overprint	37.50	
f.		Double overprint, one inverted		
127	A23	2h bright blue	.50	.60
a.		Pair, one without overprint		
b.		Inverted overprint	15.00	
c.		Double overprint	15.00	
d.		Double overprint, one inverted		

Emperor Karl I — A31

1918   Typo.   Perf. 12½, Imperf.

128	A31	2h orange	9.00
129	A31	3h dark green	9.00
130	A31	5h lt green	9.00
131	A31	6h blue green	9.00
132	A31	10h brown	9.00
133	A31	20h brick red	9.00
134	A31	25h ultra	9.00
135	A31	45h dk slate	9.00
136	A31	50h lt bluish grn	9.00
137	A31	60h blue violet	9.00
138	A31	70h ocher	9.00
139	A31	80h rose	9.00
140	A31	90h violet brn	9.00

Engr.

141	A30	1k ol grn, grnsh	2,250.
		Nos. 128-140 (13)	117.00

Nos. 128-141 were prepared for use in Bosnia and Herzegovina, but were not issued there. They were sold after the Armistice at the Vienna post office for a few days.

SEMI-POSTAL STAMPS

Nos. 33 and 35 Surcharged in Red

1914.   **7 Heller**

1914   Unwmk.   Perf. 12½

B1	A4	7h on 5h dk grn	.40	.40
B2	A4	12h on 10h car	.40	.40

Various minor varieties of the surcharge include "4" with open top, narrow "4" and wide "4."
Nos. B1-B2 exist with double and inverted surcharges. Value about $20 each.

Nos. 33 and 35 Surcharged in Red or Blue

1915.   **7 Heller**

1915   Perf. 12½

B3	A4	7h on 5h (R)	9.50	9.00
a.		Perf. 9½	140.00	140.00
B4	A4	12h on 10h (Bl)	.30	.30

Nos. B3-B4 exist with double and inverted surcharges. Value about $18.50 each.

1915

Nos. 68 and 70 Surcharged in Red or Blue

7 Heller.

1915

B5	A23	7h on 5h (R)	.80	.75
a.		"1915" at top and bottom	35.00	37.50
B6	A23	12h on 10h (Bl)	1.40	1.50
a.		Surcharged "7 Heller."	35.00	37.50

Nos. B5-B6 are found in three types differing in length of surcharge lines:
I- date 18mm, denomination 14mm.
II- date 16mm, denomination 14mm.
III- date 18mm, denomination 16mm.
Nos. B5-B6 exist with double and inverted surcharges. Value $25 each.
Nos. B5a and B6a exist double and inverted.

Bosnia/Herzegovina

New Issue Service
All Issues from 1991 available
we are an official agency
for Bosnia/Herzegovina

Delaware Valley Stamp Co.
6173 Strasburg Rd.   Atglen, PA 19310
Telephone 610-593-6684   FAX 610-593-8013
Email:devasco@epix.com

BOSNIA AND HERZEGOVINA — BOTSWANA

❖ 1916. ❖

Nos. 68 and 70 Surcharged in Red or Blue

7 Heller.

1916
B7	A23	7h on 5h (R)	.50	.65
B8	A23	12h on 10h (Bl)	.50	.65

Nos. B7-B8 exist with double and inverted surcharges. Value $12.50 each.

Wounded Soldier — SP1
Blind Soldier — SP2 

1916   **Engr.**
B9	SP1	5h (+ 2h) green	.65	.60
B10	SP2	10h (+ 2h) magenta	1.00	.90

Nos. B9-B10 exist imperf. Value, set $27.50.

Nos. 89, 91 Overprinted

WITWEN- UND WAISENWOCHE 1917

1917
B11	A27	10h bister	.15	.15
B12	A27	15h carmine rose	.15	.15

Nos. B11-B12 exist imperf. Value set, $16.
Nos. B11-B12 exist with double and inverted overprint. Value $9 each.

Design for Memorial Church at Sarajevo — SP3
Archduke Francis Ferdinand — SP4  
Duchess Sophia and Archduke Francis Ferdinand — SP5 

1917   **Typo.**   **Perf. 11½, 12½**
B13	SP3	10h violet black	.15	.20
B14	SP4	15h claret	.15	.20
B15	SP5	40h deep blue	.15	.20
		Nos. B13-B15 (3)	.45	.60

Assassination of Archduke Ferdinand and Archduchess Sophia. Sold at a premium of 2h each which helped build a memorial church at Sarajevo. Exist imperf. Value, set $2.50.

Blind Soldier — SP6
Emperor Karl I — SP8 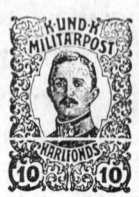

Design: 15h, Wounded soldier.

1918   **Engr.**   **Perf. 12½**
B16	SP6	10h (+ 10h) grnsh bl	.60	.55
B17	SP6	15h (+ 10h) red brn	.60	.55

#B16-B17 exist imperf. Value, set $18.50.

1918   **Typo.**   **Perf. 12½x13**

Design: 15h, Empress Zita.
B18	SP8	10h gray green	.35	.45
B19	SP8	15h brown red	.35	.45
B20	SP8	40h violet	.35	.45
		Nos. B18-B20 (3)	1.05	1.35

Sold at a premium of 10h each which went to the "Karl's Fund."
#B18-B20 exist imperf. Value, set $22.50.

POSTAGE DUE STAMPS

D1
D2 

Perf. 9½, 10½, 12½ and Compound

1904   **Unwmk.**
J1	D1	1h black, red & yel	.45	.15
J2	D1	2h black, red & yel	.45	.20
J3	D1	3h black, red & yel	.50	.15
J4	D1	4h black, red & yel	.50	.15
J5	D1	5h black, red & yel	.50	.15
J6	D1	6h black, red & yel	.15	.15
J7	D1	7h black, red & yel	2.75	2.50
J8	D1	8h black, red & yel	2.75	.50
J9	D1	10h black, red & yel	.65	.15
J10	D1	15h black, red & yel	.60	.15
J11	D1	20h black, red & yel	3.25	.20
J12	D1	50h black, red & yel	2.25	.15
J13	D1	200h black, red & grn	9.25	.70
		Nos. J1-J13 (13)	24.05	5.30

Value, imperf. set, $150.
For overprints see Western Ukraine Nos. 61-72.

1916-18   **Perf. 12½**
J14	D2	2h red ('18)	.45	.55
J15	D2	4h red ('18)	.35	.40
J16	D2	5h red	.45	.55
J17	D2	6h red ('18)	.35	.40
J18	D2	10h red	.45	.55
J19	D2	15h red	3.25	4.00
J20	D2	20h red	.50	.60
J21	D2	25h red	1.40	1.75
J22	D2	30h red	1.10	1.40
J23	D2	40h red	8.75	10.00
J24	D2	50h red	26.00	32.50
J25	D2	1k dark blue	3.25	4.00
J26	D2	3k dark blue	14.50	17.50
		Nos. J14-J26 (13)	60.80	74.20

Nos. J25-J26 have colored numerals on a white tablet.
Value, imperf. set, $110.
For surcharges see Italy Nos. NJ1-NJ7.

NEWSPAPER STAMPS

Bosnian Girl — N1

1913   **Unwmk.**   **Imperf.**
P1	N1	2h ultra	.45	.40
P2	N1	6h violet	1.75	1.50
P3	N1	10h rose	1.75	1.50
P4	N1	20h green	2.10	1.90
		Nos. P1-P4 (4)	6.05	5.30

After Bosnia and Herzegovina became part of Yugoslavia stamps of type N1 perf., and imperf. copies surcharged with new values, were used as regular postage stamps. See Yugoslavia Nos. 1L21-1L22, 1L43-1L45.

Bosnia and Herzegovina stamps can be mounted in the Scott Austria album.

SPECIAL HANDLING STAMPS

"Lightning" — SH1

1916   **Unwmk.**   **Engr.**   **Perf. 12½**
QE1	SH1	2h vermilion	.20	.20
a.		Perf. 11½x12½	250.00	250.00
QE2	SH1	5h deep green	.35	.35
a.		Perf. 11½	13.00	13.00

For surcharges see Italy Nos. NE1-NE2.

BOTSWANA

bä-'swä-nə

LOCATION — In central South Africa, north of the Republic of South Africa, east of South-West Africa and bounded on the north and east by Angola and Zimbabwe.
GOVT. — Independent republic
AREA — 222,000 sq. mi.
POP. — 941,027 (1981)
CAPITAL — Gaborone

The former Bechuanaland Protectorate became an independent republic, September 30, 1966, taking the name Botswana.

100 Cents = 1 Rand
100 Thebe = 1 Pula (1976)

Catalogue values for all unused stamps in this country are for Never Hinged items.

National Assembly Building — A1

Designs: 5c, Abattoir, Lobatsi. 15c, Dakota plane. 35c, State House, Gaborone.

Unwmk.

1966, Sept. 30   **Photo.**   **Perf. 14**
1	A1	2½c multicolored	.15	.15
a.		Imperf., pair	200.00	
2	A1	5c multicolored	.15	.15
3	A1	15c multicolored	.35	.35
4	A1	35c multicolored	.75	.75
		Nos. 1-4 (4)	1.40	1.40

Establishment of Republic of Botswana.

Bechuanaland Protectorate Nos. 180-193 Overprinted
REPUBLIC OF BOTSWANA

Perf. 14x14½, 14½x14

1966, Sept. 30   **Wmk. 314**
5	A15	1c multicolored	.15	.15
6	A15	2c multicolored	.15	.15
7	A15	2½c multicolored	.15	.15
8	A15	3½c multicolored	.15	.15
9	A15	5c multicolored	.15	.15
10	A15	7½c multicolored	.18	.18
11	A15	10c multicolored	.22	.22
12	A15	12½c multicolored	1.25	.28
13	A15	20c gray & brown	1.25	.40
14	A15	25c yel & dk brn	.55	.55
15	A15	35c dp org & ultra	.70	.70
16	A15	50c lt org & sep	1.75	1.25
17	A15	1r ocher & black	3.25	2.50
18	A15	2r blue & brown	7.00	8.00
		Nos. 5-18 (14)	16.90	14.83

European Golden Oriole — A2

Birds: 2c, African hoopoe. 3c, Groundscraper thrush. 4c, Blue waxbill. 5c, Secretary bird. 7c, Yellow-billed hornbill. 10c, Crimson-breasted shrike. 15c, Malachite kingfisher. 20c, Fish eagle. 25c, Gray lourie. 35c, Scimitar bill. 50c, Knob-billed duck. 1r, Crested barbet. 2r, Didric cuckoo.

Perf. 14x14½

1967, Jan. 3   **Photo.**   **Unwmk.**
19	A2	1c gray & multi	.20	.15
20	A2	2c lt blue & multi	.20	.15
21	A2	3c yel green & multi	.30	.15
22	A2	4c salmon & multi	.50	.25
23	A2	5c pink & multi	.50	.30
24	A2	7c slate & multi	.75	.40
25	A2	10c emerald & multi	1.00	.50
26	A2	15c lt green & multi	2.00	1.00
27	A2	20c ultra & multi	2.25	1.25
28	A2	25c green & multi	3.25	1.60
29	A2	35c multicolored	4.00	2.00
30	A2	50c dl yel & multi	6.00	3.00
31	A2	1r dl grn & multi	12.50	6.00
32	A2	2r org brn & multi	22.50	10.00
		Nos. 19-32 (14)	55.95	26.75

University Buildings and Graduates — A3

1967, Apr. 7   **Perf. 14x14½**
33	A3	3c yel, sepia & dp blue	.15	.15
34	A3	7c blue, sepia & dp bl	.15	.15
35	A3	15c dull rose, sepia & dp bl	.16	.16
36	A3	35c lt vio, sepia & dp bl	.38	.38
		Nos. 33-36 (4)	.84	.84

1st conferment of degrees by the University of Botswana, Lesotho and Swaziland at Roma, Lesotho.

Chobe Bush Bucks — A4

Designs: 7c, Sable antelopes. 35c, Fishing on the Chobe River.

1967, Oct. 2   **Photo.**   **Perf. 14**
37	A4	3c multicolored	.15	.15
38	A4	7c multicolored	.22	.22
39	A4	35c multicolored	1.10	1.10
		Nos. 37-39 (3)	1.47	1.47

Publicity for Chobe Game Reserve.

Human Rights Flame and Arms of Botswana — A5

Design elements rearranged on 15c, 25c.

1968, Apr. 8   **Litho.**   **Perf. 13½x13**
40	A5	3c brown red & multi	.15	.15
41	A5	15c emerald & multi	.25	.20
42	A5	25c yellow & multi	.40	.30
		Nos. 40-42 (3)	.80	.65

International Human Rights Year.

Rock Painting — A6

BOTSWANA

Girl Wearing Ceremonial Beads — A7

Designs: 10c, Baobab Trees, by Thomas Baines (34x25mm). 15c, National Museum and Art Gallery (71½x19mm).

Perf. 13x13½ (3c, 10c); Perf. 12½ (7c); Perf. 12½x13 (15c)

1968, Sept. 30 — Litho.
43	A6	3c multicolored	.15	.15
44	A7	7c multicolored	.25	.25
45	A6	10c multicolored	.50	.50
46	A6	15c multicolored	1.00	1.00
a.	Souv. sheet of 4, #43-46, perf. 13½		2.25	3.00
	Nos. 43-46 (4)		1.90	1.90

Opening of the National Museum and Art Gallery, Gaborone, Sept. 30, 1968.

African Nativity Scene — A8

1968, Nov. 11 Unwmk. *Perf. 13x14*
47	A8	1c car & multi	.15	.15
48	A8	2c brown & multi	.15	.15
49	A8	5c green & multi	.15	.15
50	A8	25c dp violet & multi	.55	.50
	Nos. 47-50 (4)		1.00	.95

Christmas.

Boy Scout, Botswana Scout Emblem and Lion — A9

Botswana Boy Scout Emblem, Lion and: 15c, Boy Scouts cooking, vert. 25c, Boy Scouts around campfire.

1969, Aug. 21 Litho. *Perf. 13½*
51	A9	3c emerald & multi	.15	.15
52	A9	15c lt brown & multi	.85	.85
53	A9	25c dk brown & multi	1.50	1.50
	Nos. 51-53 (3)		2.50	2.50

22nd World Scouting Conf., Helsinki, Finland, Aug. 21-27.

Mother, Child and Star of Bethlehem — A10

Diamond Treatment Plant, Orapa — A11

1969, Nov. 6 *Perf. 14½x14*
54	A10	1c dk brn & lt blue	.15	.15
55	A10	2c dk brn & apple grn	.15	.15
56	A10	4c dk brn & dull yel	.15	.15
57	A10	35c dk brn & vio blue	.80	.80
a.	Souv. sheet of 4, #54-57, perf. 14½		1.40	1.00
	Nos. 54-57 (4)		1.25	1.25

Christmas.

Perf. 14½x14, 14x14½
1970, Mar. 23

Designs: 7c, Copper and nickel mining, Selebi-Pikwe. 10c, Copper and nickel mining and metal bars, Selebi-Pikwe, horiz. 35c, Orapa diamond mine and diamonds, horiz.

58	A11	3c multicolored	.50	.25
59	A11	7c multicolored	1.10	.55
60	A11	10c multicolored	2.25	1.10
61	A11	35c multicolored	3.50	1.70
	Nos. 58-61 (4)		7.35	3.60

Botswana development program.

Mr. Micawber and Charles Dickens — A12

Charles Dickens (1812-70), English novelist and: 7c, Scrooge. 15c, Fagin. 25c, Bill Sykes.

1970, July 7 *Perf. 11*
62	A12	3c gray green & multi	.15	.15
63	A12	7c multicolored	.30	.30
64	A12	15c brown & multi	.60	.60
65	A12	25c dp violet & multi	1.00	1.00
a.	Souvenir sheet of 4, #62-65		4.50	4.50
	Nos. 62-65 (4)		2.05	2.05

UN Headquarters, Emblem — A13

1970, Oct. 24 Litho. *Perf. 11*
| 66 | A13 | 15c ultra, red & silver | .70 | .50 |

United Nations' 25th anniversary.

Toys — A14

1970, Nov. 3 Litho. *Perf. 14*
67	A14	1c Crocodile	.15	.15
68	A14	2c Giraffe	.15	.15
69	A14	7c Elephant	.20	.20
70	A14	25c Rhinoceros	.75	.75
a.	Souvenir sheet of 4, #67-70		2.00	2.00
	Nos. 67-70 (4)		1.25	1.25

Christmas.

Sorghum A15

1971, Apr. 6 Litho. *Perf. 14*
71	A15	3c shown	.15	.15
72	A15	7c Millet	.20	.20
73	A15	10c Corn	.25	.25
74	A15	35c Peanuts	1.00	1.00
	Nos. 71-74 (4)		1.60	1.60

Ox Head and Botswana Map — A16

King Bringing Gift — A17

Map of Botswana and: 4c, Cogwheels and waves. 7c, Zebra rampant. 10c, Tusk and corn. 20c, Coat of arms of Botswana.

1971, Sept. 30 *Perf. 14½x14*
75	A16	3c yel grn, blk & brn	.15	.15
76	A16	4c lt blue, blk & bl	.15	.15
77	A16	7c orange & blk	.20	.20
78	A16	10c yellow & multi	.30	.30
79	A16	20c blue & multi	.60	.60
	Nos. 75-79 (5)		1.40	1.40

5th anniversary of independence.

1971, Nov. 11 *Perf. 14*

Christmas: 2c, King bringing gift. 7c, Kneeling King with gift. 20c, Three Kings and star.

80	A17	2c brt rose & multi	.15	.15
81	A17	3c lt blue & multi	.15	.15
82	A17	7c brt pink & multi	.15	.15
83	A17	20c vio blue & multi	.50	.50
a.	Souvenir sheet of 4, #80-83		1.50	1.50
	Nos. 80-83 (4)		.95	.95

Constellation Orion — A18

Night Sky over Botswana: 7c, Scorpio. 10c, Centaur. 20c, Southern Cross.

1972, Apr. 24 Litho. *Perf. 14*
84	A18	3c dp org, bl grn & blk	.35	.35
85	A18	7c org, blue & blk	.75	.75
86	A18	10c org, green & blk	1.10	1.10
87	A18	20c emer, vio bl & blk	2.25	2.25
	Nos. 84-87 (4)		4.45	4.45

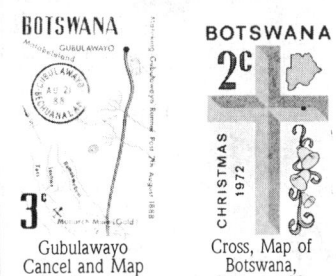

Gubulawayo Cancel and Map of Trail — A19

Cross, Map of Botswana, Bells — A20

Sections of Mafeking-Gubulawayo Trail and: 4c, Bechuanaland Protectorate No. 65. 7c, Mail runners. 20c, Mafeking 638 killer cancellation.

1972, Aug. 21 *Perf. 13½x13*
88	A19	3c cream & multi	.15	.15
89	A19	4c cream & multi	.18	.18
90	A19	7c cream & multi	.45	.45
91	A19	20c cream & multi	1.50	1.50
a.	Souvenir sheet of 4		10.00	10.00
	Nos. 88-91 (4)		2.28	2.28

84th anniv. of Mafeking to Gubulawayo runner post. No. 91a contains one each of Nos. 88-91, arranged vertically to show map of trail.
Compare with design A89.

1972, Nov. 6 Litho. *Perf. 14*

Cross, Map of Botswana and: 3c, Candle. 7c, Christmas tree. 20c, Star and holly.

92	A20	2c yellow & multi	.15	.15
93	A20	3c pale lilac & multi	.15	.15
94	A20	7c yel green & multi	.24	.24
95	A20	20c pink & multi	.60	.60
a.	Souvenir sheet of 4, #92-95		2.00	2.00
	Nos. 92-95 (4)		1.14	1.14

Christmas.

Chariot of the Sun, Trundholm, Denmark A21

WMO Emblem and: 3c, Thor, Norse thunder god, vert. 7c, Ymir, Icelandic frost giant, vert. 20c, Odin on 8-legged horse Sleipnir.

1973, Mar. 23 Litho. *Perf. 14*
96	A21	3c orange & multi	.20	.20
97	A21	4c yellow & multi	.25	.25
98	A21	7c ultra & multi	.45	.45
99	A21	20c gold & multi	1.25	1.25
	Nos. 96-99 (4)		2.15	2.15

Intl. meteorological cooperation, cent.

Livingstone and Boat on Lake Ngwami — A22

Design: 20c, Livingstone and his meeting with Henry Stanley.

1973, Sept. 10 Litho. *Perf. 13½x14*
| 100 | A22 | 3c gray & multi | .15 | .15 |
| 101 | A22 | 20c yel green & multi | .95 | .95 |

Dr. David Livingstone (1813-1873), medical missionary and explorer.

Shepherd and Flock A23

Christmas: 3c, Ass and foal, African huts, vert. 7c, African mother, child and star, vert. 20c, Tribal meeting (kgotla), symbolic of Wise Men.

1973, Nov. 12 Litho. *Perf. 14½*
102	A23	3c multicolored	.15	.15
103	A23	4c multicolored	.15	.15
104	A23	20c multicolored	.20	.20
105	A23	20c multicolored	.60	.60
	Nos. 102-105 (4)		1.10	1.10

Gaborone Campus, Botswana A24

Designs: 7c, Kwaluseni Campus, Swaziland. 20c, Roma Campus, Lesotho. 35c, Map and flags of Botswana, Swaziland and Lesotho.

1974, May 8 Litho. *Perf. 14*
106	A24	3c lt blue & multi	.15	.15
107	A24	7c yel green & multi	.15	.15
108	A24	20c yel green & multi	.20	.20
109	A24	35c brt blue & multi	.30	.30
	Nos. 106-109 (4)		.80	.80

10th anniversary of the University of Botswana, Lesotho and Swaziland.

UPU Emblem, Mail Vehicles — A25

UPU Cent.: 3c, Post Office, Palapye, c. 1889. 7c, Bechuanaland police camel post, 1900. 20c, 1920 and 1974 planes.

1974, May 22 Litho. *Perf. 13½x14*
110	A25	2c car & multi	.25	.20
111	A25	3c green & multi	.40	.30
112	A25	7c brown & multi	1.00	.75
113	A25	20c blue & multi	3.00	2.25
	Nos. 110-113 (4)		4.65	3.50

Amethyst A26

Minerals, precious and semiprecious stones.

BOTSWANA

1974, July 1 Photo. Perf. 14x13
114	A26	1c shown	.15	.15
115	A26	2c Agate	.20	.15
116	A26	3c Quartz	.25	.20
117	A26	4c Niccolite	.45	.35
118	A26	5c Moss agate	.55	.40
119	A26	7c Agate	.90	.60
120	A26	10c Stilbite	1.25	.85
121	A26	15c Moshaneng banded marble	2.00	1.25
122	A26	20c Gem diamonds	2.50	1.65
123	A26	25c Chrysotile	3.00	2.00
124	A26	35c Jasper	4.25	2.75
125	A26	50c Moss quartz	6.00	3.75
126	A26	1r Citrine	12.50	8.00
127	A26	2r Chalcopyrite	27.50	17.00
		Nos. 114-127 (14)	61.50	39.10

For surcharges see Nos. 155-168.

Stapelia Variegata — A27
Pres. Sir Seretse Khama — A28 

Flowers of Botswana: 7c, Hibiscus lunarifolius. 15c, Ceratotheca triloba. 20c, Nerine laticoma.

1974, Nov. 4 Litho. Perf. 14
128	A27	2c multicolored	.15	.15
129	A27	7c multicolored	.50	.50
130	A27	15c multicolored	1.00	1.00
131	A27	20c multicolored	1.50	1.50
a.		Souvenir sheet of 4, #128-131	4.00	4.00
		Nos. 128-131 (4)	3.15	3.15

1975, Mar. 24 Photo. Perf. 13½x13
132	A28	4c olive & multi	.15	.15
133	A28	10c yellow & multi	.15	.15
134	A28	20c ultra & multi	.30	.30
135	A28	35c brown & multi	.50	.50
a.		Souvenir sheet of 4, #132-135	1.40	1.40
		Nos. 132-135 (4)	1.10	1.10

10th anniv. of self-government.

Ostrich and Rock Painting — A29

Paintings and Animals: 10c, Rhinoceros. 25c, Hyena. 35c, Scorpion.

1975, June 23 Litho. Perf. 14x14½
136	A29	4c yel green & multi	.25	.25
137	A29	10c buff & multi	.75	.75
138	A29	25c blue & multi	1.75	1.75
139	A29	35c lilac & multi	2.75	2.75
a.		Souvenir sheet of 4, #136-139	9.00	9.00
		Nos. 136-139 (4)	5.50	5.50

Rock paintings from Tsodilo Hills.

Map of British Bechuanaland A30

Chiefs Sebele, Bathoen and Khama A31

Design: 10c, Khama the Great and antelope.

Perf. 14½x14, 14x14½ Litho.
140	A30	6c buff & multi	.25	.25
141	A30	10c rose & multi	.50	.50
142	A31	25c lt green & multi	1.25	1.25
		Nos. 140-142 (3)	2.00	2.00

Establishment of Protectorate, 90th anniv. (6c); Khama the Great (1828-1923), centenary of his accession as chief (10c); visit of the chiefs of the Bakwena, Bangwaketse and Bamangwato tribes to London, 80th anniv. (25c).

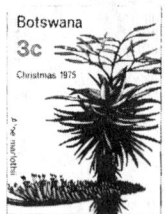

Aloe Marlothii — A32

Christmas: 10c, Aloe lutescens. 15c, Aloe zebrina. 25c, Aloe littoralis.

1975, Nov. 3 Litho. Perf. 14½x14
143	A32	3c multicolored	.25	.20
144	A32	10c multicolored	.75	.65
145	A32	15c multicolored	1.00	.90
146	A32	25c multicolored	2.00	1.75
		Nos. 143-146 (4)	4.00	3.50

Drum A33

Traditional Musical Instruments: 10c, Hand piano. 15c, Segankuru (violin). 25c, Kudu signal horn.

1976, Mar. 1 Litho. Perf. 14
147	A33	4c yellow & multi	.15	.15
148	A33	10c lilac & multi	.30	.30
149	A33	15c dull yel & multi	.50	.50
150	A33	25c lt blue & multi	.75	.75
		Nos. 147-150 (4)	1.70	1.70

1-pula Bank Note with Seretse Khama A34

Reverse of Bank Notes: 10c, Farm workers. 15c, Antelopes. 25c, National Assembly building.

1976, June 28 Litho. Perf. 14
151	A34	4c rose & multi	.15	.15
152	A34	10c brt green & multi	.25	.25
153	A34	15c yel green & multi	.35	.35
154	A34	25c blue & multi	.65	.65
a.		Souvenir sheet of 4, #151-154	2.25	2.25
		Nos. 151-154 (4)	1.40	1.40

First national currency.

Nos. 114-127 Surcharged in Black or Gold

1976, Aug. 23 Photo. Perf. 14x13
155	A26	1t on 1c multi	.30	.15
156	A26	2t on 2c multi	.30	.15
157	A26	3t on 3c multi (G)	.30	.15
158	A26	4t on 4c multi	.60	.30
159	A26	5t on 5c multi	.75	.35
160	A26	7t on 7c multi	1.00	.50
161	A26	10t on 10c multi	1.50	.65
162	A26	15t on 15c multi (G)	2.50	1.00
163	A26	20t on 20c multi	3.00	1.50
164	A26	25t on 25c multi	4.00	1.75
165	A26	35t on 35c multi	5.00	2.00
166	A26	50t on 50c multi	6.00	2.50
167	A26	1p on 1r multi	12.50	6.50
168	A26	2p on 2r multi (G)	22.50	12.50
		Nos. 155-168 (14)	60.25	30.00

Cattle Industry A35

Designs: 10t, Antelope, tourism, vert. 15t, Schoolhouse and children, education. 25t, Rural weaving, vert. 35t, Mining industry, vert.

1976, Sept. 30 Litho. Perf. 14x14½ Textured Paper
169	A35	4t multicolored	.20	.20
170	A35	10t multicolored	.40	.40
171	A35	15t multicolored	.50	.50
172	A35	25t multicolored	.75	.75
173	A35	35t multicolored	1.00	1.00
		Nos. 169-173 (5)	2.85	2.85

10th anniversary of independence.

Colophospermum Mopane — A36

Trees: 4t, Baikiaea plurijuga. 10t, Sterculia rogersii. 25t, Acacia nilotica. 40t, Kigelia africana.

1976, Nov. 1 Litho. Perf. 13
174	A36	3t multicolored	.15	.15
175	A36	10t multicolored	.15	.15
176	A36	15t multicolored	.35	.35
177	A36	25t multicolored	.75	.75
178	A36	40t multicolored	1.25	1.25
		Nos. 174-178 (5)	2.65	2.65

Christmas.

Pres. Seretse Khama and Elizabeth II — A37

Designs: 25t, Coronation coach in procession. 40t, Recognition scene.

1977, Feb. 7 Litho. Perf. 12
179	A37	4t multicolored	.15	.15
180	A37	25t multicolored	.35	.35
181	A37	40t multicolored	.50	.50
		Nos. 179-181 (3)	1.00	1.00

Reign of Queen Elizabeth II, 25th anniv.

Clawless Otter A38

Wildlife Fund Emblem and: 4t, Serval. 10t, Bat-eared foxes. 25t, Pangolins. 40t, Brown hyena.

1977, June 6 Litho. Perf. 14
182	A38	3t multicolored	1.50	.50
183	A38	4t multicolored	2.00	1.00
184	A38	10t multicolored	4.00	1.75
185	A38	25t multicolored	10.00	4.00
186	A38	40t multicolored	20.00	9.00
		Nos. 182-186 (5)	37.50	16.25

Endangered wildlife.

Khama Memorial A39

Designs: 4t, Cwihaba Caves. 15t, Green's (expedition) tree. 20t, Mmajojo ruins. 25t, Ancient morabaraba board. 35t, Matsieng's footprints.

1977, Aug. 22 Litho. Perf. 14
187	A39	4t multicolored	.15	.15
188	A39	10t multicolored	.18	.18
189	A39	15t multicolored	.45	.45
190	A39	20t multicolored	.55	.55
191	A39	25t multicolored	.80	.80
192	A39	35t multicolored	1.10	1.10
a.		Souvenir sheet of 6, #187-192	3.50	3.50
		Nos. 187-192 (6)	3.23	3.23

Historical sites and national monuments.

Hypoxis itida — A40
Black Korhaan — A41 

Lilies: 5t, Haemanthus magnificus. 10t, Boophane disticha. 25t, Vellozia retinervis. 40t, Ammocharis coranica.

1977, Oct. 31 Litho. Perf. 14
193	A40	3t sepia & multi	.15	.15
194	A40	5t gray & multi	.15	.15
195	A40	10t multicolored	.30	.30
196	A40	25t multicolored	.75	.75
197	A40	40t multicolored	1.25	1.25
		Nos. 193-197 (5)	2.60	2.60

Christmas.

1978, July 3 Photo. Perf. 14
Designs: Birds.
198	A41	1t shown	.15	.15
199	A41	2t Marabou storks	.15	.15
200	A41	3t Red-billed hoopoe	.15	.15
201	A41	4t Carmine bee-eaters	.20	.15
202	A41	5t African jacana	.20	.15
203	A41	7t Paradise flycatcher	.25	.20
204	A41	10t Bennett's woodpecker	.35	.25
205	A41	15t Red bishop	.50	.40
206	A41	20t Crowned plovers	.70	.50
207	A41	25t Giant kingfishers	.90	.65
208	A41	30t White-faced ducks	1.10	.75
209	A41	35t Green-backed heron	1.50	.90
210	A41	45t Black-headed herons	1.75	1.25
211	A41	50t Spotted eagle owl	2.00	1.50
212	A41	1p Gabar goshawk	3.75	2.50
213	A41	2p Martial eagle	7.50	5.00
214	A41	5p Saddlebill storks	15.00	10.00
		Nos. 198-214 (17)	36.15	24.65

For surcharges see Nos. 289-290.

Tawana Making Kaross (garment) A42

Designs: 5t, Map of Okavango Delta. 15t, Bushman collecting roots. 20t, Herero woman milking cow. 25t, Yei pulling mokoro (boat). 35t, Mbukushu fishing.

1978, Sept. 11 Litho. Perf. 14 Textured Paper
215	A42	4t multicolored	.15	.15
216	A42	5t multicolored	.15	.15
217	A42	15t multicolored	.20	.20
218	A42	20t multicolored	.32	.32
219	A42	25t multicolored	.40	.40
220	A42	35t multicolored	.52	.52
a.		Souvenir sheet of 6, #215-220	2.50	3.00
		Nos. 215-220 (6)	1.74	1.74

People of the Okavango Delta.

Caralluma Lutea — A43
Boy at Sip Well — A44

Flowers: 10t, Hoodia lugardii. 15t, Ipomoea transvaalensis. 25t, Ansellia gigantea.

1978, Nov. 6
221	A43	5t multicolored	.16	.16
222	A43	10t multicolored	.32	.32
223	A43	15t multicolored	.48	.48
224	A43	25t multicolored	.80	.80
		Nos. 221-224 (4)	1.76	1.76

Christmas.

BOTSWANA

1979, Feb. 12   Litho.   Perf. 14
Water Development: 5t, Watering pit. 10t, Hand-dug well and goats. 25t, Windmill, well and cattle. 40t, Modern drilling rig.
225	A44	3t multicolored	.15	.15
226	A44	5t multicolored	.15	.15
227	A44	10t multicolored	.15	.15
228	A44	25t multicolored	.40	.40
229	A44	40t multicolored	.65	.65
		Nos. 225-229 (5)	1.50	1.50

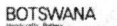

Botswana Pot — A45

Handicrafts: 10t, Clay buffalo. 25t, Woven covered basket. 40t, Beaded bag.

1979, June 4   Litho.   Perf. 14
230	A45	5t multicolored	.15	.15
231	A45	10t multicolored	.16	.16
232	A45	25t multicolored	.42	.42
233	A45	40t multicolored	.65	.65
a.		Souvenir sheet of 4, #230-233	1.65	1.65
		Nos. 230-233 (4)	1.38	1.38

Bechuanaland No. 6, Rowland Hill — A46

Sir Rowland Hill (1795-1879), originator of penny postage, and: 25t, Bechuanaland Protectorate No. 107. 45t, Botswana No. 20.

1979, Aug. 27   Litho.   Perf. 13½
234	A46	5t rose & black	.15	.15
235	A46	25t multicolored	.35	.35
236	A46	45t multicolored	.60	.60
		Nos. 234-236 (3)	1.10	1.10

Children Playing — A47

Design: 10t, Child playing with rag doll, and IYC emblem, vert.

1979, Sept. 24   Perf. 14
| 237 | A47 | 5t multicolored | .15 | .15 |
| 238 | A47 | 10t multicolored | .25 | .25 |

International Year of the Child.

Ximenia Caffra — A48

Christmas: 10t, Sclerocarya caffra. 15t, Hexalobus monopetalus. 25t, Ficus soldanella.

1979, Nov. 12   Litho.   Perf. 14
239	A48	5t multicolored	.15	.15
240	A48	10t multicolored	.20	.20
241	A48	15t multicolored	.30	.30
242	A48	25t multicolored	.50	.50
		Nos. 239-242 (4)	1.15	1.15

Flap-Necked Chameleon A49

1980, Mar. 3   Litho.   Perf. 14
243	A49	5t shown	.15	.15
244	A49	10t Leopard tortoise	.18	.18
245	A49	25t Puff adder	.45	.45
246	A49	40t White-throated monitor	.75	.75
		Nos. 243-246 (4)	1.53	1.53

Rock Breaking (Early Mining) — A50

1980, July 7   Litho.   Perf. 13½x14
247	A50	5t shown	.15	.15
248	A50	10t Ore hoisting	.18	.18
249	A50	15t Ore transport	.25	.25
250	A50	20t Ore crushing	.35	.35
251	A50	25t Smelting	.40	.40
252	A50	35t Tools, products	.60	.60
		Nos. 247-252 (6)	1.93	1.93

Chiwele and the Giant — A51

Folktales: 10t, Kgori Is Not Deceived. 30t, Nyambi's Wife and Crocodile. 45t, Clever Hare, horiz.

Perf. 14, 14½ (10t, 30t)
1980, Sept. 8
| 253 | A51 | 5t multicolored | .15 | .15 |

Size: 28x36mm
| 254 | A51 | 10t multicolored | .18 | .18 |
| 255 | A51 | 30t multicolored | .52 | .52 |

Size: 44x26mm
| 256 | A51 | 45t multicolored | .80 | .80 |
| | | Nos. 253-256 (4) | 1.65 | 1.65 |

Game Watching — A52

1980, Oct. 6   Litho.   Perf. 14
| 257 | A52 | 5t multicolored | .20 | .20 |

World Tourism Conf., Manila, Sept. 27.

Acacia Gerrardii — A53

Christmas: Flowering Trees.

1980, Nov. 3   Litho.   Perf. 14
258	A53	5t shown	.15	.15
259	A53	10t Acacia nilotica	.15	.15
260	A53	25t Acacia erubescens	.32	.32
261	A53	40t Dichrostachys cinerea	.45	.45
		Nos. 258-261 (4)	1.07	1.07

Heinrich von Stephan, Bechuanaland Protectorate No. 150, Botswana No. 111 — A55

Design: 20t, Von Stephan, Bechuanaland Protectorate No. 151, Botswana No. 112.

1981, Jan. 7   Wmk. 373   Perf. 14
| 266 | A55 | 6t multicolored | .15 | .15 |
| 267 | A55 | 20t multicolored | .45 | .45 |

Von Stephan (1831-1897), founder of UPU.

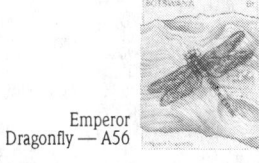

Emperor Dragonfly — A56

1981, Feb. 23   Litho.   Perf. 14
268	A56	6t shown	.15	.15
269	A56	7t Praying mantis	.15	.15
270	A56	10t Elegant grasshopper	.15	.15
271	A56	20t Dung beetle	.25	.25
272	A56	30t Citrus swallowtail butterfly	.40	.40
273	A56	45t Mopane worm	.60	.60
a.		Souv. sheet of 6, #268-273	2.00	2.00
		Nos. 268-273 (6)	1.70	1.70

Blind Basket Weaver A57

1981, Apr. 4   Litho.   Perf. 14
274	A57	6t Seamstress	.15	.15
275	A57	7t Shown	.30	.30
276	A57	30t Carpenter	.40	.40
		Nos. 274-276 (3)	.85	.85

International Year of the Disabled.

Woman Reading Letter (Literacy Campaign) — A58

1981, June 8
277	A58	6t shown	.15	.15
278	A58	7t Man sending telegram	.15	.15
279	A58	20t Boy, newspaper	.25	.25
280	A58	30t Father and daughter reading	.40	.40
		Nos. 277-280 (4)	.95	.95

Pres. Seretse Khama and Flag — A59

First death anniv. of Pres. Khama: Portrait and local buildings.

1981, July 13
281	A59	6t multicolored	.15	.15
282	A59	7t multicolored	.15	.15
283	A59	30t multicolored	.40	.40
284	A59	45t multicolored	.60	.60
		Nos. 281-284 (4)	1.30	1.30

Cattle in Agricultural Show — A60

1981, Sept. 21   Litho.   Perf. 14½
285	A60	6t Plowing	.15	.15
286	A60	20t shown	.20	.20
287	A60	30t Meat Commission	.35	.35
288	A60	45t Vaccine Institute	.50	.50
		Nos. 285-288 (4)	1.20	1.20

Nos. 209, 204 Surcharged in Black

1981, Sept.   Photo.   Perf. 14
| 289 | A41 | 25t on 35t multicolored | .30 | .30 |
| 290 | A41 | 30t on 10t multicolored | .40 | .40 |

Christmas — A61

Designs: Water lilies.

1981, Nov. 2   Litho.
291	A61	6t Nymphaea caerulea	.15	.15
292	A61	10t Nymphoides indica	.15	.15
293	A61	25t Nymphaea lotus	.30	.30
294	A61	40t Ottelia kunenensis	.50	.50
		Nos. 291-294 (4)	1.10	1.10

Children's Drawings — A62

1982, Feb. 15   Litho.   Perf. 14½x14
295	A62	6t Cattle	.15	.15
296	A62	10t Kgotla meeting	.15	.15
297	A62	30t Village	.40	.40
298	A62	45t Huts	.60	.60
		Nos. 295-298 (4)	1.30	1.30

Traditional Houses — A63

1982, May 3   Litho.   Perf. 14
299	A63	6t Common type	.15	.15
300	A63	10t Kgatleng	.15	.15
301	A63	30t Northeastern	.40	.40
302	A63	45t Sarwa	.60	.60
		Nos. 299-302 (4)	1.30	1.30

Red-billed Teals — A64

Perf. 14x14½, 14½x14
1982, July 1   Photo.
303	A64	1t Masked weaver	.15	.15
304	A64	2t Lesser double-collared sunbirds	.15	.15
305	A64	3t White-fronted bee-eaters	.15	.15
306	A64	4t Ostriches	.15	.15
307	A64	5t Grey-headed gulls	.30	.20
308	A64	6t Pygmy geese	.40	.30
309	A64	7t Cattle egrets	.50	.40
310	A64	8t Lanner falcon	.60	.45
311	A64	10t Yellow-billed storks	.75	.65
312	A64	15t shown	1.25	1.00
313	A64	20t Barn owls	1.50	1.25
314	A64	25t Hamerkops	2.00	1.40
315	A64	30t Stilts	2.25	1.65
316	A64	35t Blacksmith plovers	2.75	2.00
317	A64	45t Wattled plover	3.50	2.25
318	A64	50t Crowned guinea-fowl	3.75	2.75
319	A64	1p Cape vultures	8.00	5.50
320	A64	2p Augur bustards	15.00	11.00
		Nos. 303-320 (18)	43.15	31.40

Nos. 303-311 vert.
For surcharges see Nos. 401-403.

Christmas — A65

Endangered Species — A67

BOTSWANA

A66

Designs: Mushrooms.

1982, Nov. 2   Litho.   Perf. 14½
321	A65	7t Shaggy mane	.70	.70
322	A65	15t Orange milk	1.50	1.50
323	A65	35t Panther	3.50	3.50
324	A65	50t King boletus	4.75	4.75
		Nos. 321-324 (4)	10.45	10.45

1983, Mar. 14   Litho.   Perf. 14
325	A66	7t Pres. Quett Masire	.15	.15
326	A66	15t Dancers	.20	.20
327	A66	35t Melbourne Conference Center	.50	.50
328	A66	45t Heads of State meeting	.60	.60
		Nos. 325-328 (4)	1.45	1.45

Commonwealth Day.

1983, Apr. 19   Litho.   Perf. 14x14½
329	A67	7t Wattle crane	.40	.20
330	A67	15t Aloe lutescens	1.10	.70
331	A67	35t Roan antelope	2.75	1.65
332	A67	50t Hyphaene ventricosa	3.50	2.00
		Nos. 329-332 (4)	7.75	4.55

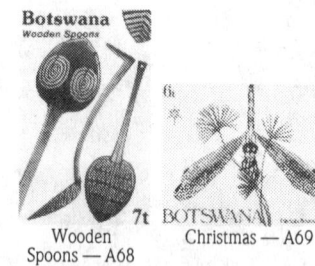

Wooden Spoons — A68

Christmas — A69

1983, July 20   Litho.   Perf. 14
333	A68	7t shown	.25	.15
334	A68	15t Jewelry	.45	.35
335	A68	35t Ox-hide milk bag	1.10	.85
336	A68	50t Decorated knives	1.25	1.00
a.		Souvenir sheet of 4, #333-336	6.00	5.00
		Nos. 333-336 (4)	3.05	2.35

1983, Nov. 7   Litho.   Perf. 14½x14

Designs: Dragonflies.
337	A69	6t Pantala flavescens	.15	.15
338	A69	15t Anax imperator	.30	.30
339	A69	25t Trithemis arteriosa	.50	.50
340	A69	45t Chlorolestes elegans	.90	.90
		Nos. 337-340 (4)	1.85	1.85

Mining Industry — A70

1984, Mar. 19   Litho.   Perf. 14½
341	A70	7t Diamonds	.40	.20
342	A70	15t Lime	1.10	.65
343	A70	35t Copper, nickel, vert.	3.00	2.00
344	A70	50t Coal, vert.	3.50	2.50
		Nos. 341-344 (4)	8.00	5.35

Traditional Transport — A71

1984, June 16   Litho.   Perf. 14½x14
345	A71	7t Man riding ox	.15	.15
346	A71	25t Sled	.42	.42
347	A71	35t Wagon	.65	.65
348	A71	50t Cart	.90	.90
		Nos. 345-348 (4)	2.12	2.12

Intl. Civil Aviation Org., 40th Anniv. — A72

1984, Oct. 8   Litho.   Perf. 14x13½
349	A72	7t Avro 504	.15	.15
350	A72	10t Westland Wessex	.15	.15
351	A72	15t Junkers 52-3M	.25	.25
352	A72	25t Dragon Rapide	.40	.40
353	A72	35t DC-3	.60	.60
354	A72	50t F27 Fokker Friendship	.80	.80
		Nos. 349-354 (6)	2.35	2.35

Christmas — A73

Butterflies.

1984, Nov. 5   Litho.   Perf. 14½x14
355	A73	7t Papilio demodocus	.40	.30
356	A73	25t Byblia acheloia	1.75	1.00
357	A73	35t Hypolimnas missipus	2.75	1.50
358	A73	50t Graphium taboranus	3.50	2.00
		Nos. 355-358 (4)	8.40	4.80

Traditional & Exotic Foods — A74

Bechuanaland No. 4 — A75

1985, Mar. 18   Litho.   Perf. 14½
359	A74	7t Man preparing seswaa	.15	.15
360	A74	15t Woman preparing bogobe	.20	.20
361	A74	35t Girl eating madilla	.32	.32
362	A74	50t Woman collecting caterpillars	.65	.65
a.		Souvenir sheet of 4, #359-362	1.40	1.40
		Nos. 359-362 (4)	1.32	1.32

Southern African Development Coordination Conference, 5th anniv.

1985, June 24

Postage stamp cent.: 15t, Bechuanaland Protectorate No. 72. 25t, Bechuanaland Protectorate No. 106. 35t, Bechuanaland No. 199, 50t, Botswana No. 1, horiz.
363	A75	7t multicolored	.15	.15
364	A75	15t multicolored	.18	.18
365	A75	25t multicolored	.30	.30
366	A75	35t multicolored	.42	.42
367	A75	50t multicolored	.62	.62
		Nos. 363-367 (5)	1.67	1.67

Police Centenary — A76

Designs: 7t, Bechuanaland Border Police, 1885-1895. 10t, Bechuanaland Mounted Police, 1894-1902. 25t, Bechuanaland Protectorate Police, 1903-1966. 50t, Botswana Motorcycle Police, 1966-1985.

1985, Aug. 5   Perf. 14½x14
368	A76	7t multicolored	.15	.15
369	A76	10t multicolored	.15	.15
370	A76	25t multicolored	.30	.30
371	A76	50t multicolored	.62	.62
		Nos. 368-371 (4)	1.22	1.22

Edible Wild Cucumbers A77

1985, Nov. 4
372	A77	7t Cucumis metuliferus	.15	.15
373	A77	15t Acanthosicyos naudinianus	.18	.18
374	A77	25t Coccinia sessifolia	.30	.30
375	A77	50t Momordica balsamina	.62	.62
		Nos. 372-375 (4)	1.25	1.25

Christmas.

Declaration of Protectorate, Cent. — A78

1985, Dec. 30   Litho.   Perf. 14x14½
376	A78	7t Heads of state meet	.15	.15
377	A78	15t Declaration reading, 1885	.18	.18
378	A78	25t Mackenzie and Khama	.30	.30
379	A78	50t Map	.62	.62
a.		Souvenir sheet of 4, #376-379	1.20	1.20
		Nos. 376-379 (4)	1.25	1.25

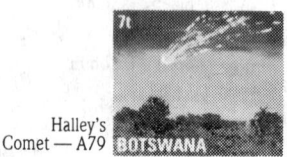

Halley's Comet — A79

1986, Mar. 24   Perf. 14½x14
380	A79	7t Comet over Serowe	.15	.15
381	A79	15t Over Bobonong	.18	.18
382	A79	35t Over Gomare swamps	.42	.42
383	A79	50t Over Thamaga, Letlhakeng	.62	.62
		Nos. 380-383 (4)	1.37	1.37

Milk Containers — A80

1986, June 23   Perf. 14½
384	A80	8t Leather bag	.15	.15
385	A80	15t Ceramic pots	.18	.18
386	A80	35t Wood pot	.42	.42
387	A80	50t Woman, pots	.62	.62
		Nos. 384-387 (4)	1.37	1.37

Souvenir Sheet

Natl. Independence, 20th Anniv. — A81

Designs: a, Map of natl. parks and reserves. b, Morupule Power Station. c, Cattle, Kgalagadi. d, Natl. Assembly.

1986, Sept. 30   Litho.   Perf. 14½x14
| 388 | | Sheet of 4 | .90 | .90 |
| a.-d. | | A81 20t any single | .22 | .22 |

Flowers of the Okavango Swamps — A82

1986, Nov. 3   Litho.   Perf. 14x14½
389	A82	8t Ludwigia stogonifera	.15	.15
390	A82	15t Sopubia manii	.16	.16
391	A82	35t Commelina diffusa	.38	.38
392	A82	50t Hibiscus diversifolius	.55	.55
		Nos. 389-392 (4)	1.24	1.24

Christmas.

Traditional Medicine A83

UN Child Survival Campaign A84

1987, Mar. 2   Litho.   Perf. 14½x14
393	A83	8t Professional diviners	.15	.15
394	A83	15t Lightning prevention	.18	.18
395	A83	35t Rainmaker	.45	.45
396	A83	50t Bloodletting	.65	.65
		Nos. 393-396 (4)	1.43	1.43

1987, June 1
397	A84	8t Oral rehydration therapy	.15	.15
398	A84	15t Growth monitoring	.18	.18
399	A84	35t Immunization	.45	.45
400	A84	50t Breast-feeding	.65	.65
		Nos. 397-400 (4)	1.43	1.43

Nos. 308, 311 and 318 Surcharged

Perf. 14x14½, 14½x14

1987, Apr. 1   Photo.
401	A64	3t on 6t No. 308	.15	.15
402	A64	5t on 10t No. 311	.15	.15
403	A64	20t on 50t No. 318	.30	.30
		Nos. 401-403 (3)	.60	.60

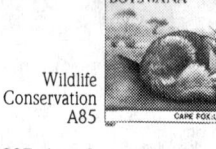

Wildlife Conservation A85

1987, Aug. 3   Perf. 14
404	A85	1t Cape fox	.15	.15
405	A85	2t Lechwe	.15	.15
406	A85	3t Zebra	.15	.15
407	A85	4t Duiker	.15	.15
408	A85	5t Banded mongoose	.15	.15
409	A85	6t Rusty-spotted genet	.15	.15
410	A85	8t Hedgehog	.15	.15
411	A85	10t Scrub hare	.15	.15
412	A85	12t Hippopotamus	.15	.15
413	A85	15t Suricate	.20	.15
414	A85	20t Caracal	.25	.20
415	A85	25t Steenbok	.35	.30
416	A85	30t Gemsbok	.45	.35
417	A85	35t Square-lipped rhino	.50	.45
418	A85	40t Mountain reedbuck	.60	.50
419	A85	50t Rock dassie	.75	.60
420	A85	1p Giraffe	1.50	1.25
421	A85	2p Tsessebe	3.00	2.50
422	A85	3p Side-striped jackal	4.75	3.75
423	A85	5p Hartebeest	8.00	6.50
		Nos. 404-423 (20)	21.70	17.90

For surcharges see Nos. 480-482, 506-509.

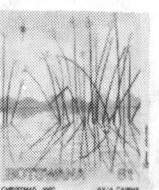

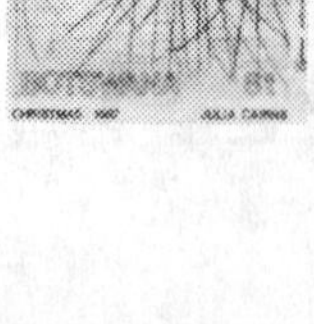

Wetland Grasses — A86

BOTSWANA

1987, Oct. 26   *Perf. 14x14½*
424	A86	8t Cyperus articulatus	.15	.15
425	A86	15t Miscanthus junceus	.15	.15
426	A86	30t Cyperus alopecuroides	.36	.36
427	A86	1p Typha latifolia	1.20	1.20
a.		Souvenir sheet of 4, #424-427	1.85	1.85
		Nos. 424-427 (4)	1.86	1.86

Christmas, preservation of the Okavango and Kuando-Chobe River wetlands.

Early Cultivation Techniques — A87

1988, Mar. 14   Litho.   *Perf. 14½x14*
428	A87	8t Digging stick	.15	.15
429	A87	15t Iron hoe	.18	.18
430	A87	35t Wooden plow	.42	.42
431	A87	50t Communal planting, Lesotla	.60	.60
		Nos. 428-431 (4)	1.35	1.35

World Wildlife Fund — A88

Designs: WWF emblem and various red lechwe, Kobus leche.

1988, June 6   Litho.   *Perf. 14½x14*
432	A88	10t Adult wading	.35	.35
433	A88	15t Adult, sun	.50	.50
434	A88	35t Cow, calf	1.10	1.10
435	A88	75t Herd	2.50	1.75
		Nos. 432-435 (4)	4.45	3.70

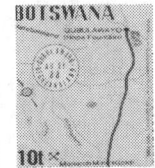

Runner Post, Cent. — A89

Routes and: 10t, Gubulawayo, Bechuanaland, cancellation dated Aug. 21 '88. 15t, Bechuanaland Protectorate No. 65. 30t, Pack traders. 60t, Mafeking killer cancel No. 638.

1988, Aug. 22   Litho.   *Perf. 14½*
436	A89	10t multicolored	.15	.15
437	A89	15t multicolored	.18	.18
438	A89	30t multicolored	.35	.35
439	A89	60t multicolored	.65	.65
a.		Souvenir sheet of 4, #436-439	1.30	1.30
		Nos. 436-439 (4)	1.33	1.33

Printed in a continuous design picturing the Mafeking-Gubulawayo route and part of the Shoshong runner post route.

State Visit of Pope John Paul II, Sept. 13 — A90

Natl. Museum and Art Gallery, Gaborone, 20th Anniv. — A91

1988, Sept. 13   Litho.   *Perf. 14x14½*
440	A90	10t Map, portrait	.15	.15
441	A90	15t Portrait	.15	.15
442	A90	30t Map, portrait, diff.	.35	.35
443	A90	80t Portrait, diff.	.85	.85
		Nos. 440-443 (4)	1.50	1.50

1988, Sept. 30   *Perf. 14½*
444	A91	8t Museum	.15	.15
445	A91	15t Pottery, c. 400-1300	.18	.18
446	A91	30t Buffalo bellows	.35	.35
447	A91	60t Children, mobile museum	.68	.68
		Nos. 444-447 (4)	1.36	1.36

A92    A93

Flowering plants of southeastern Botswana.

1988, Oct. 11   Litho.   *Perf. 14x14½*
448	A92	8t Grewia flava	.15	.15
449	A92	15t Cienfuegosia digitata	.15	.15
450	A92	40t Solanum seaforthianum	.42	.42
451	A92	75t Carissa bispinosa	.78	.78
		Nos. 448-451 (4)	1.50	1.50

Christmas.

1989, Mar. 13   Litho.   *Perf. 14x14½*

Traditional grain storage.
452	A93	8t Sesigo basket granary	.15	.15
453	A93	15t Letlole daga granary	.15	.15
454	A93	30t Sefalana bisque granary	.30	.30
455	A93	60t Serala granaries	.60	.60
		Nos. 452-455 (4)	1.20	1.20

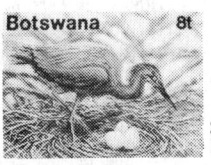

Slaty Egrets — A94

1989, July 5   *Perf. 15x14*
456	A94	8t Nesting	.15	.15
457	A94	15t Young	.45	.30
458	A94	30t Adult in flight	.75	.60
459	A94	60t Two adults	1.65	1.40
a.		Souvenir sheet of 4, #456-459	3.00	2.50
		Nos. 456-459 (4)	3.00	2.45

Children's Drawings — A95

Perf. 14½x14, 14x14½

1989, Sept. 4
460	A95	10t Ephraim Seeletso	.15	.15
461	A95	15t Neelma Bhatia, vert.	.15	.15
462	A95	30t Thabo Habana	.30	.30
463	A95	1p Thabo Olesitse	1.00	1.00
		Nos. 460-463 (4)	1.60	1.60

Star and Orchids — A96

1989, Oct. 30   Litho.   *Perf. 14x14½*
464	A96	8t Eulophia angolensis	.15	.15
465	A96	15t Eulophia hereroensis	.26	.26
466	A96	30t Eulophia speciosa	.52	.52
467	A96	60t Eulophia petersii	1.10	1.10
		Nos. 464-467 (4)	2.03	2.03

Christmas.

Anniversaries — A97

8t, Bechuanaland Protectorate #201. 15t, Voter at ballot box. 30t, Map & flags of nations at SADCC conference. 60t, Great Britain #1.

1990, Mar. 5   Litho.   *Perf. 14½*
468	A97	8t multicolored	.15	.15
469	A97	15t multicolored	.15	.15
470	A97	30t multicolored	.30	.30
471	A97	60t multicolored	.60	.60
		Nos. 468-471 (4)	1.20	1.20

25th anniv. of self government (8t); 1st elections, 25th anniv. (15t); Southern African Development Coordination Conference (SADCC), 10th anniv. (30t); and Penny Black, 150th anniv. (60t).

Stamp World London '90 — A98

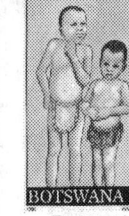

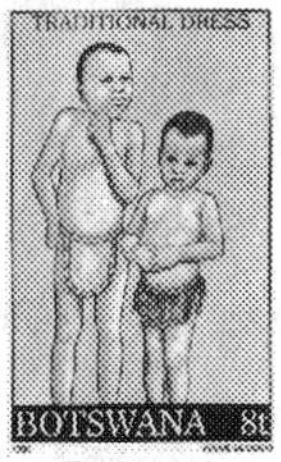

Traditional Dress — A99

Aspects of the telecommunications industry.

1990, May 3
472	A98	8t Training	.15	.15
473	A98	15t Transmission	.15	.15
474	A98	30t Public telephone	.30	.30
475	A98	2p Testing circuitry	2.00	2.00
		Nos. 472-475 (4)	2.60	2.60

1990, Aug. 1   Litho.   *Perf. 14*
476	A99	8t Children	.15	.15
477	A99	15t Young woman	.15	.15
478	A99	30t Man	.26	.26
479	A99	2p Adult woman	1.75	1.75
a.		Souvenir sheet of 4, #476-479	2.50	2.50
		Nos. 476-479 (4)	2.31	2.31

Nos. 404 and 412 Surcharged **10t**

No. 409 Surcharged **20t**

1990
480	A85	10t on 1t No. 404	.15	.15
481	A85	20t on 6t No. 409	.20	.20
482	A85	50t on 12t No. 412	.50	.50
		Nos. 480-482 (3)	.85	.85

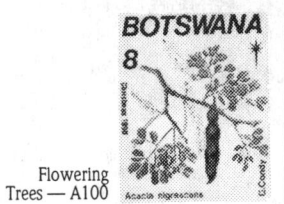

Flowering Trees — A100

1990, Oct. 30   Litho.   *Perf. 14*
483	A100	8t Acacia nigrescens	.15	.15
484	A100	15t Peltophorum africanum	.15	.15
485	A100	30t Burkea africana	.26	.26
486	A100	2p Pterocarpus angolensis	1.75	1.75
		Nos. 483-486 (4)	2.31	2.31

Christmas.

Natl. Road Safety Day — A101

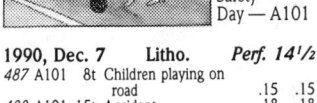

1990, Dec. 7   Litho.   *Perf. 14½*
487	A101	8t Children playing on road	.15	.15
488	A101	15t Accident	.18	.18
489	A101	30t Livestock on road	.36	.36
		Nos. 487-489 (3)	.69	.69

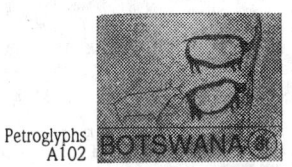

Petroglyphs — A102

Various petroglyphs.

1991, Mar. 4   Litho.   *Perf. 14x14½*
Textured Paper
490	A102	8t multicolored	.15	.15
491	A102	15t multicolored	.15	.15
492	A102	30t multicolored	.30	.30
493	A102	2p multicolored	2.00	2.00
		Nos. 490-493 (4)	2.60	2.60

Natl. Census — A103

1991, June 3   Litho.   *Perf. 14*
494	A103	8t Children playing	.15	.15

Perf. 14½
495	A103	15t Houses	.18	.18

Perf. 14x14½
496	A103	30t Children in schoolyard	.36	.36
497	A103	2p Children, hospital	2.40	2.40
		Nos. 494-497 (4)	3.09	3.09

African Tourism Year — A104

1991, Sept. 30   Litho.   *Perf. 14*
498	A104	8t Tourists, elephants	.15	.15
499	A104	15t Birds, crocodiles	.18	.18
500	A104	35t Airplane, fish eagles	.40	.40

Size 26x43mm
501	A104	2p Okavango Delta	2.40	2.40
		Nos. 498-501 (4)	3.13	3.13

No. 501 incorporates designs of #498-500.

Christmas — A105

Seed pods: 8t, Harpagophytum procumbens. 15t, Tylosema esculentum. 30t, Abrus precatorius. 2p, Kigelia africana.

1991, Nov. 4   Litho.   *Perf. 14*
502	A105	8t multicolored	.15	.15
503	A105	15t multicolored	.16	.16
504	A105	30t multicolored	.32	.32
505	A105	2p multicolored	2.25	2.25
		Nos. 502-505 (4)	2.88	2.88

Nos. 406, 409, & 412 Surcharged **8t**

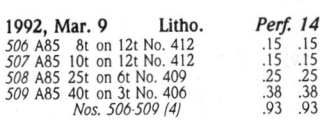

1992, Mar. 9   Litho.   *Perf. 14*
506	A85	8t on 12t No. 412	.15	.15
507	A85	10t on 12t No. 412	.15	.15
508	A85	25t on 6t No. 409	.25	.25
509	A85	40t on 3t No. 406	.38	.38
		Nos. 506-509 (4)	.93	.93

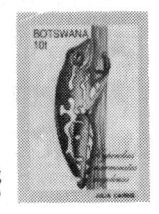

Climbing Frogs — A106

Designs: 8t, Cacosternum boettgeri, horiz. 10t, Hyperolius marmoratus angolensis. 40t, Bufo fenoulheti, horiz. 1p, Hyperolius.

Perf. 14½x14, 14x14½

1992, Mar. 23
510	A106	8t multicolored	.15	.15
511	A106	10t multicolored	.15	.15
512	A106	40t multicolored	.40	.40
513	A106	1p multicolored	.95	.95
		Nos. 510-513 (4)	1.65	1.65

BOTSWANA

Botswana Railways — A107

Designs: 10t, Deluxe air-conditioned coaches. 25t, BD1 locomotive, vert. 40t, Deluxe coach interior, vert. 2p, Locomotive pulling air-conditioned coaches.

1992, June 29   Litho.   *Perf. 14*

514	A107	10t multicolored	.15	.15
515	A107	25t multicolored	.15	.15
516	A107	40t multicolored	.20	.20
517	A107	2p multicolored	1.00	1.00
a.		Souv. sheet of 4, #514-517 + label	1.40	1.40
		Nos. 514-517 (4)	1.50	1.50

Wild Animals — A108

1992, Aug. 3   Litho.   *Perf. 14½*

518	A108	1t Cheetah	.15	.15
519	A108	2t Spring hares	.15	.15
520	A108	4t Blackfooted cat	.15	.15
521	A108	5t Striped mouse	.15	.15
522	A108	10t Oribi	.15	.15
523	A108	12t Pangolin	.15	.15
524	A108	15t Aardwolf	.15	.15
525	A108	20t Warthog	.20	.20
526	A108	25t Ground squirrels	.25	.25
527	A108	35t Honey badger	.30	.30
528	A108	40t Common mole rat	.35	.35
529	A108	45t Wild dogs	.40	.40
530	A108	50t Water mongoose	.45	.45
531	A108	80t Klipspringer	.70	.70
532	A108	1p Lesser bushbaby	.90	.90
533	A108	2p Bushveld elephant shrew	1.80	1.80
534	A108	5p Zorilla	4.50	4.50
535	A108	10p Vervet monkey	9.00	9.00
		Nos. 518-535 (18)	19.90	19.90

For surcharges see Nos. 518-520.

A109    Ferns — A110

1992, Aug. 7   *Perf. 14x15*

536	A109	10t Boxer	.15	.15
537	A109	50t Four sprinters	.45	.45
538	A109	1p Two boxers	.95	.95
539	A109	2p Three runners	1.85	1.85
a.		Souvenir sheet of 4, #536-539	3.40	3.40
		Nos. 536-539 (4)	3.40	3.40

1992 Summer Olympics, Barcelona.

1992, Nov. 23   Litho.   *Perf. 14½*

540	A110	10t Adiantum incisum	.15	.15
541	A110	25t Actiniopteris radiata	.25	.25
542	A110	40t Ceratopteris cornuta	.40	.40
543	A110	1.50p Pellaea calomelanos	1.40	1.40
		Nos. 540-543 (4)	2.20	2.20

Christmas.

Organizations — A111

Designs: 10t, Lions Intl., conquering blindness, vert. 15t, Red Cross Society. 25t, Ecumenical Decade, churches in solidarity with women, vert. 35t, Round Table supporting the deaf. 40t, Rotary Intl., vert. 50t, Botswana Christian Council.

1993, Mar. 29   Litho.   *Perf. 14*

544	A111	10t multicolored	.15	.15
545	A111	15t multicolored	.15	.15
546	A111	25t multicolored	.20	.20
547	A111	35t multicolored	.30	.30
548	A111	40t multicolored	.40	.40
549	A111	50t multicolored	.45	.45
		Nos. 544-549 (6)	1.65	1.65

Botswana Railway, Cent. A112

Designs: 10t, Engine No. 1, 6th class 4-6-0, Bechuanaland Railways. 40t, Engine No. 317, 19th class 4-8-2. 50t, Engine No. 256, 12th class 4-8-2. 1.50p, Engine No. 71, 7th class 4-8-0, Rhodesia Railways.

1993, May 24   Litho.   *Perf. 15x14*

550	A112	10t multicolored	.15	.15
551	A112	40t multicolored	.40	.40
552	A112	50t multicolored	.50	.50
553	A112	1.50p multicolored	1.45	1.45
a.		Souvenir sheet of 4, #550-553	2.50	2.50
		Nos. 550-553 (4)	2.50	2.50

Eagles — A113    Christmas — A114

1993, Aug. 30   Litho.   *Perf. 14½*

554	A113	10t Long crested eagle	.20	.20
555	A113	25t Snake eagle	.50	.50
556	A113	50t Bateleur eagle	1.00	1.00
557	A113	1.50p Secretary bird	3.00	3.00
		Nos. 554-557 (4)	4.70	4.70

1993, Oct. 25   Litho.   *Perf. 14x14½*

558	A114	12t Aloe zebrina	.15	.15
559	A114	25t Croton megalobotrys	.20	.20
560	A114	50t Boophane disticha	.45	.45
561	A114	1p Euphorbia davyi	.90	.90
		Nos. 558-561 (4)	1.70	1.70

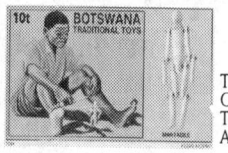

Traditional Children's Toys A115

1994, Mar. 28   Litho.   *Perf. 14½*

562	A115	10t Mantadile	.15	.15
563	A115	40t Dikgomo tsa mimopa	.30	.30
564	A115	50t Sefuu-fuu	.40	.40
565	A115	1p Mantlwane	.75	.75
		Nos. 562-565 (4)	1.60	1.60

ICAO, 50th Anniv. A116

Perf. 14½x14, 14x14½

1994, June 30   Litho.

566	A116	10t Inside control tower	.15	.15
567	A116	25t Fire engine	.25	.25
568	A116	40t Baggage carts, vert.	.40	.40
569	A116	50t Control tower, vert.	.50	.50
		Nos. 566-569 (4)	1.30	1.30

A117    A118

Environmental Protection: 10t, Flamingos, Sua Pan, vert. 35t, Makgadikgadi Pan trees. 50t, Zebra, Makgadikgadi Palm trees, vert. 2p, Map of Makgadikgadi Pans.

1994, Aug. 30   Litho.   *Perf. 14*

570	A117	10t multicolored	.15	.15
571	A117	35t multicolored	.45	.45
572	A117	50t multicolored	.65	.65
573	A117	2p multicolored	2.50	2.50
		Nos. 570-573 (4)	3.75	3.75

1994, Oct. 24

Edible fruits: 10t, Ziziphus mucronata. 25t, Strychnos cocculoides. 40t, Bauhinia petersiana. 50t, Schinziphyton rautaneii.

574	A118	10t multicolored	.15	.15
575	A118	25t multicolored	.20	.20
576	A118	40t multicolored	.30	.30
577	A118	50t multicolored	.35	.35
		Nos. 574-577 (4)	1.00	1.00

Christmas.

See Nos. 587-590.

Traditional Fishing A119

1995, Apr. 3   Litho.   *Perf. 14*

578	A119	15t Spear	.15	.15
579	A119	40t Hook	.30	.30
580	A119	65t Net	.50	.50
581	A119	80t Basket	.60	.60
		Nos. 578-581 (4)	1.55	1.55

UN, 50th Anniv. — A120

1995, Oct. 16   Litho.   *Perf. 14*

582	A120	20t FAO	.15	.15
583	A120	50t World Food Program	.35	.35
584	A120	80t Development Plan	.60	.60
585	A120	1p UNICEF	.70	.70
		Nos. 582-585 (4)	1.80	1.80

World Wildlife Fund — A121

Hyaena brunnea: a, 20t, Adult walking right. b, 50t, Two young. c, 80t, Adult finding eggs. d, 1p, Two young, adult resting.

1995, Nov. 6

586	A121	Strip of 4, #a.-d.	1.75	1.75

No. 586 was issued in miniature sheets of 4 each.

Christmas Type of 1994

1995, Nov. 27   Litho.   *Perf. 14*

587	A118	20t Adenia glauca	.15	.15
588	A118	50t Pterodiscus ngamicus	.35	.35
589	A118	80t Sesamothamnus lugardii	.60	.60
590	A118	1p Fockea multiflora	.70	.70
		Nos. 587-590 (4)	1.80	1.80

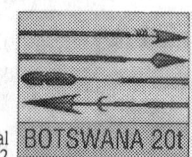

Traditional Weapons — A122

1996, Mar. 25   Litho.   *Perf. 14*

591	A122	20t Spears	.15	.15
592	A122	50t Axes	.30	.30
593	A122	80t Shield, knob-kerries	.50	.50
594	A122	1p Knives, cases	.60	.60
		Nos. 591-594 (4)	1.55	1.55

Nos. 518-520 Surcharged 20t

1996, Feb. 12   Litho.   *Perf. 14½*

595	A108	20t on 2t No. 519	.15	.15
596	A108	30t on 1t No. 518	.20	.20
597	A108	70t on 4t No. 520	.40	.40
		Nos. 595-597 (3)	.75	.75

A123 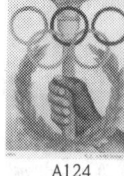   A124

Radio, Cent.: 20t, Child listening to early radio. 50t, Mobile unit, transmitter. 80t, Local police. 1p, Radio Botswana at the Kgotila.

1996, June 3   Litho.   *Perf. 14*

598	A123	20t multicolored	.15	.15
599	A123	50t multicolored	.35	.35
600	A123	80t multicolored	.60	.60
601	A123	1p multicolored	.75	.75
		Nos. 598-601 (4)	1.85	1.85

1996, July 19   Litho.   *Perf. 14*

Modern Olympic Games, Cent.: 20t, Hand holding torch, laurel wreath, Olympic rings. 50t, Pierre de Coubertin. 80t, Map, flag of Botswana, athletes. 1p, Ruins of original Olympic Stadium, Olympia.

602	A124	20t multicolored	.15	.15
603	A124	50t multicolored	.35	.35
604	A124	80t multicolored	.60	.60
605	A124	1p multicolored	.75	.75
		Nos. 602-605 (4)	1.85	1.85

A125    A126

Worthy Causes: 20t, Family planning education, Welfare Association. 30t, Skills for the blind, Pudulogong Rehabilitation Center. 50t, Collection of seeds, Forestry Association. 70t, Secretarial class, YWCA. 80t, Day care center, Council of Women. 1p, SOS Children's Village, Tlokweng.

1996, Sept. 23   Litho.   *Perf. 14*

606	A125	20t multicolored	.15	.15
607	A125	30t multicolored	.25	.25
608	A125	50t multicolored	.35	.35
609	A125	70t multicolored	.55	.55
610	A125	80t multicolored	.60	.60
611	A125	1p multicolored	.75	.75
		Nos. 606-611 (6)	2.65	2.65

1996, Nov. 4   Litho.   *Perf. 14*

Adansonia Digitata

612	A126	20t Leaf, flower	.15	.15
613	A126	50t Fruit	.35	.35
614	A126	80t Tree in leaf	.60	.60
615	A126	1p Tree without leaves	.75	.75
		Nos. 612-615 (4)	1.85	1.85

Christmas.

Francistown, Cent. — A127

20t, Tati Hotel. 50t, Railway station. 80t, Company manager's house. 1p, Monarch Mine.

1997, Apr. 21   Litho.   *Perf. 14*

616	A127	20t multicolored	.15	.15
617	A127	50t multicolored	.30	.30
618	A127	80t multicolored	.45	.45
619	A127	1p multicolored	.55	.55
		Nos. 616-619 (4)	1.45	1.45

BOTSWANA — BRAZIL

Birds — A128

5t, Pel's fishing owl, vert. 10t, Gymnogene. 15t, Meyers parrot, vert. 20t, Harlequin quail. 25t, Marico sunbird. 30t, Kurrichane thrush. 40t, Redheaded finch, vert. 50t, Buffalo weaver, vert. 60t, Sacred ibis. 70t, Cape shoveller. 80t, Greater honeyguide. 1p, Woodland kingfisher. 1.25p, Purple heron, vert. 1.50p, Yellowbilled oxpecker. 2p, Shafttailed whydah, vert. 2.50p, White stork, vert. 5p, Ovambo sparrowhawk, vert. 10p, Spotted crake, vert.

1997, Aug. 4 Litho. *Perf. 13½*
620	A128	5t multicolored	.15	.15
621	A128	10t multicolored	.15	.15
622	A128	15t multicolored	.15	.15
623	A128	20t multicolored	.15	.15
624	A128	25t multicolored	.15	.15
625	A128	30t multicolored	.20	.20
626	A128	40t multicolored	.25	.25
627	A128	50t multicolored	.30	.30
628	A128	60t multicolored	.35	.35
629	A128	70t multicolored	.40	.40
630	A128	80t multicolored	.45	.45
631	A128	1p multicolored	.55	.55
632	A128	1.25p multicolored	.70	.70
633	A128	1.50p multicolored	.85	.85
634	A128	2p multicolored	1.10	1.10
635	A128	2.50p multicolored	1.40	1.40
636	A128	5p multicolored	2.75	2.75
637	A128	10p multicolored	5.50	5.50

Nos. 620-637 (18) 15.55 15.55

Botswana Railway, Cent. — A129

Designs: 35t, Bechuanaland Rail, 1897. 50t, Elephants on the tracks. 80t, First locomotives in Bechuanaland, Cape of Good Hope 4-6-0. 1p, 4-6-4+4-6-4 Beyer Garratt. 2p, New BD3 locomotive. 2.50p, Fantuzzi Container Stacker.

1997, July 12 Litho. *Perf. 14x14½*
638	A129	35t multicolored	.20	.20
639	A129	50t multicolored	.30	.30
640	A129	80t multicolored	.50	.50
641	A129	1p multicolored	.60	.60
642	A129	2p multicolored	1.20	1.20
643	A129	2.50p multicolored	1.50	1.50

Nos. 638-643 (6) 4.30 4.30

A130 A131

Queen Elizabeth II and Prince Philip, 50th Wedding Anniv.: No. 644, Prince in casual attire. No. 645, Queen wearing white & blue hat. No. 646, Queen with horse. No. 647, Prince with horse. No. 648, Prince, Queen. No. 649, Princess Ann in riding attire.

10p, Queen, Prince riding in open carriage.

Wmk. 373
1997, Sept. 22 Litho. *Perf. 13*
644	A130	35t multicolored	.20	.20
645	A130	35t multicolored	.20	.20
a.		Pair, #644-645	.40	.40
646	A130	2p multicolored	1.20	1.20
647	A130	2p multicolored	1.20	1.20
a.		Pair, #646-647	2.40	2.40
648	A130	2.50p multicolored	1.50	1.50
649	A130	2.50p multicolored	1.50	1.50
a.		Pair, #648-649	3.00	3.00

Nos. 644-649 (6) 5.80 5.80

Souvenir Sheet
| 650 | A130 | 10p multicolored | 6.00 | 6.00 |

1997, Nov. 10 Litho. *Perf. 14*
Christmas (Combretum):, 35t, Zeyheri. 1p, Apiculatum. 2p, Molle. 2.50p, Imberbe.
651	A131	35t multicolored	.20	.20
652	A131	1p multicolored	.60	.60
653	A131	2p multicolored	1.20	1.20
654	A131	2.50p multicolored	1.50	1.50

Nos. 651-654 (4) 3.50 3.50

Tourism A132

1998, Mar. 23 Litho. *Perf. 14*
655	A132	35t Baobab trees	.20	.20
656	A132	1p Crocodile	.55	.55
657	A132	2p Stalactites, vert.	1.10	1.10
658	A132	2.50p Tourists, vert.	1.40	1.40

Nos. 655-658 (4) 3.25 3.25

Diana, Princess of Wales (1961-97)
Common Design Type

Portraits: 35t, #663a, Wearing red (without hat). 1p, #663b, Wearing red with hat. 2p, #663c, Wearing white (hand on face). #662, Greeting people.

Wmk. 373
1998, June 1 Litho. *Perf. 13*
659	CD355	35t multicolored	.20	.20
660	CD355	1p multicolored	.55	.55
661	CD355	2p multicolored	1.10	1.10
662	CD355	2.50p multicolored	1.40	1.40

Nos. 659-662 (4) 3.25 3.25

Sheet of 4
| 663 | CD355 | 2.50p #a.-c. + #662 | 5.50 | 5.50 |

Textiles — A133

35t, Tapestry of a village. 55t, Woman arranging materials on ground. 1p, Tapestry of African map, animals, huts, people. 2p, Woman seated at loom. 2.50p, Tapestry of elephants and trees, horiz.

1998, Sept. 28 Litho. *Perf. 14x13½*
664	A133	35t multicolored	.20	.20
665	A133	55t multicolored	.30	.30
666	A133	1p multicolored	.55	.55
667	A133	2p multicolored	1.10	1.10

Nos. 664-667 (4) 2.15 2.15

Souvenir Sheet
Perf. 13½
| 668 | A133 | 2.50p multicolored | 1.40 | 1.40 |

POSTAGE DUE STAMPS

Bechuanaland Protectorate Nos. J10-J12 Overprinted: "REPUBLIC OF / BOTSWANA"

Wmk. 4
1967, Mar. 1 Typo. *Perf. 14*
J1	D2	1c carmine rose	.15	1.00
J2	D2	2c dull violet	.25	1.50
J3	D2	5c olive green	.60	2.00

Nos. J1-J3 (3) 1.00 4.50

Elephant D1  Zebra D2

Perf. 13½
1971, June 9 Litho. Unwmk.
J4	D1	1c carmine rose	1.00	2.25
J5	D1	2c violet blue	1.25	3.00
J6	D1	6c sepia	2.00	5.00
J7	D1	14c green	4.00	7.00

Nos. J4-J7 (4) 8.25 17.25

1978 *Perf. 12½*
J8	D2	1t red orange & black	.70	.70
J9	D2	2t emerald & black	.70	.70
J10	D2	4t red & black	.70	.70
J11	D2	10t dark blue & black	.70	.70
J12	D2	16t brown & black	.70	.70

Nos. J8-J12 (5) 3.50 3.50

1984 *Perf. 14½x14*
J8a	D2	1t	.60	.60
J9a	D2	2t	.60	.60
J10a	D2	4t	.60	.60
J11a	D2	10t	.60	.60
J12a	D2	16t	.60	.60

Nos. J8a-J12a (5) 3.00 3.00

1989, Apr. 1 *Perf. 14½*
J8b	D2	1t	.15	.15
J9b	D2	2t	.15	.15
J10b	D2	4t	.15	.15
J11b	D2	10t	.20	.20
J12b	D2	16t	.45	.45

Nos. J8b-J12b (5) 1.10 1.10

The design is the same size on the 1984 and 1989 issues, but the grass of Nos. J8b-J12b is lower and less defined than on previous issues. The paper is wider on the 1989 issue.

1994, Dec. 1 *Perf. 14*
J8c	D2	1t	.15	.15
J9c	D2	2t	.15	.15
J10c	D2	4t	.15	.15
J11c	D2	10t	.15	.15
J12c	D2	16t	.15	.15

Nos. J8c-J12c (5) .75 .75

See note after No. J12b.

BRAZIL

brə-'zil

Brasil (after 1918)

LOCATION — On the north and east coasts of South America, bordering on the Atlantic Ocean.
GOVT. — Republic
AREA — 3,286,000 sq. mi.
POP. — 132,580,000 (est. 1984)
CAPITAL — Brasilia

Brazil was an independent empire from 1822 to 1889, when a constitution was adopted and the country became officially known as The United States of Brazil.

1000 Reis = 1 Milreis
100 Centavos = 1 Cruzeiro (1942)
100 Centavos = 1 Cruzado (1986)
100 Centavos = 1 Cruzeiro (1990)
100 Centavos = 1 Cruzeiro Real (Aug. 2, 1993)

Catalogue values for unused stamps in this country are for Never Hinged items, beginning with Scott 680 in the regular postage section, Scott B12 in the semi-postal section, Scott C66 in the airpost section, Scott RA2 in the postal tax section, and Scott RAB1 in the postal tax semi-postal section.

Values for unused stamps are for examples with original gum as defined in the catalogue introduction except for Nos. 1-38 and 42-52 which are valued without gum.

Watermarks

Wmk. 97- "CORREIO FEDERAL REPUBLICA DOS ESTADOS UNIDOS DO BRAZIL" in Sheet

Wmk. 98- "IMPOSTO DE CONSUMO REPUBLICA DOS ESTADOS UNIDOS DO BRAZIL" in Sheet

Wmk. 99- "CORREIO"

Wmk. 100- "CASA DA MOEDA" in Sheet

Because of the spacing of this watermark, a few stamps in each sheet may show no watermark.

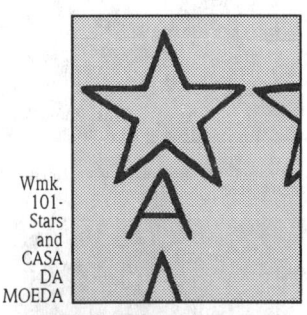

Wmk. 101- Stars and CASA DA MOEDA

Wmk. 193- ESTADOS UNIDOS DO BRASIL

Wmk. 206- Star-framed CM, Multiple

Wmk. 218- E U BRASIL Multiple, Letters 8mm High

Wmk. 221- ESTADOS UNIDOS DO BRASIL, Multiple, Letters 6mm High

BRAZIL

Wmk. 222- CORREIO BRASIL and 5 Stars in Squared Circle

Wmk. 236- Coat of Arms in Sheet

Watermark (reduced illustration) covers 22 stamps in sheet.

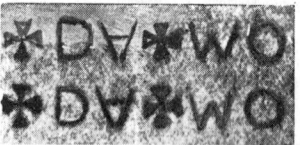

Wmk. 245- Multiple "CASA DA MOEDA DO BRASIL" and Small Formee Cross

Wmk. 249- "CORREIO BRASIL" multiple

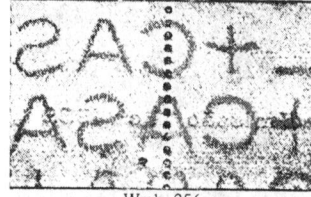

Wmk. 256- "CASA+DA+MOEDA+DO+BRAZIL" in 8mm Letters

Ordering on-line is QUICK! EASY! CONVENIENT! www.scottonline.com

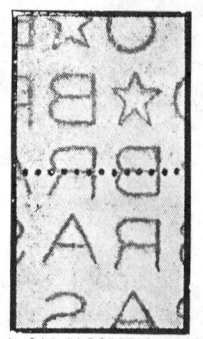

Wmk. 264- "*CORREIO*BRASIL*" Multiple, Letters 7mm High

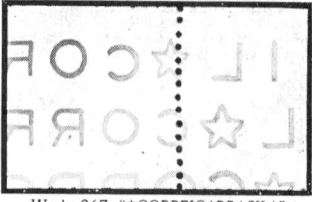

Wmk. 267- "*CORREIO*BRASIL*" Multiple in Small Letters 5mm High

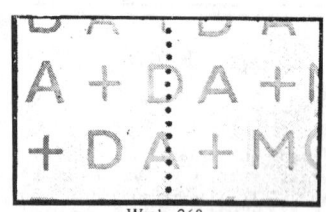

Wmk. 268- "CASA+DA+MOEDA+DO+BRASIL" in 6mm Letters

Wmk. 270- Wavy Lines and Seal

Wmk. 271- Wavy Lines

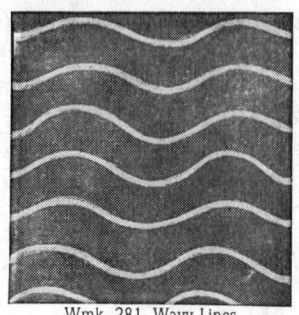

Wmk. 281- Wavy Lines

Issues of the Empire

A1

Grayish or Yellowish Paper
Fine Impressions

1843, Aug. 1   Unwmk.   Engr.   *Imperf.*
1	A1	10r black	2,250.	550.
c.	In pair with No. 2			300,000.
2	A1	60r black	600.	225.
3	A1	90r black	2,750.	1,150.

Nos. 1-3 were issued with gum, but very few unused examples retain even a trace of their original gum. Copies with original gum command substantial premiums.

Fine impressions are true black and have background lathework complete. Intermediate impressions are grayish black and have weaker lathework in the background. These sell for somewhat less than fine impressions. Worn impressions have white areas in the background surrounding the numerals due to plate wear affecting especially the lathework. These examples sell for somewhat less than intermediate impressions.

Most examples of Nos. 1-3 also exist on white paper, usually thin and somewhat translucent. Such examples are scarce and command premiums.

A2    A3

Grayish or Yellowish Paper
1844-46
7	A2	10r black	100.00	20.00
8	A2	30r black	125.00	30.00
9	A2	60r black	100.00	22.50
10	A2	90r black	750.00	100.00
11	A2	180r black	3,500.	1,300.
12	A2	300r black	5,250.	1,800.
13	A2	600r black	5,000.	2,000.

Nos. 8, 9 and 10 exist on thick paper and are considerably scarcer.

Grayish or Yellowish Paper
1850, Jan. 1
21	A3	10r black	25.00	35.00
22	A3	20r black	75.00	100.00
23	A3	30r black	10.00	3.00
24	A3	60r black	10.00	2.25
25	A3	90r black	80.00	11.50
26	A3	180r black	80.00	52.50
27	A3	300r black	325.00	60.00
28	A3	600r black	375.00	90.00

No. 22 used is generally found precanceled with a single horizontal line in pen or blue crayon. Value precanceled without gum, $75.

All values except the 90r were reprinted in 1910 on very thick paper.

1854
| 37 | A3 | 10r blue | 12.00 | 11.50 |
| 38 | A3 | 30r blue | 32.50 | 50.00 |

A4

1861
| 39 | A4 | 280r red | 140.00 | 100.00 |
| 40 | A4 | 430r yellow | 225.00 | 140.00 |

Nos. 39 and 40 have been reprinted on thick white paper with white gum. They are printed in aniline inks and the colors are brighter than those of the originals.

1866   *Perf. 13½*
42	A3	10r blue	120.00	150.00
43	A3	20r black	900.00	400.00
44	A3	30r black	300.00	150.00
45	A3	30r blue	675.00	750.00
46	A3	60r black	120.00	25.00
47	A3	90r black	575.00	275.00
48	A3	180r black	600.00	275.00
49	A4	280r red	650.00	675.00
50	A3	300r black	750.00	400.00
51	A4	430r yellow	600.00	350.00
52	A3	600r black	575.00	240.00

Fraudulent perforations abound. Purchases should be accompanied by certificates of authenticity.

A 10r black is questioned.

A5    A6

A7    A8

A8a    A9

Emperor Dom Pedro — A9a

Thick or Thin White Wove Paper
1866, July 1   *Perf. 12*
53	A5	10r vermilion	12.00	5.00
54	A6	20r red lilac	20.00	3.00
a.	20r dull violet		65.00	25.00
56	A7	50r blue	30.00	2.50
57	A8	80r slate violet	75.00	5.00
58	A8a	100r blue green	30.00	1.50
a.	100r yellow green		30.00	1.50

If you are a Collector of Brazil
Call the experts: *LIANE & SERGIO SISMONDO*
"THE CLASSIC COLLECTOR"
Visit our website:www.sismondostamps.com
BUYING, SELLING, APPRAISALS.
RARE AND CLASSIC STAMPS, POSTAL HISTORY, PROOFS.

10035 Carousel Center Drive
Syracuse, NY 13290-0001
Ph. 315-422-2331, Fax 315-422-2956
P.O. Box 6277, Station J,
Ottawa, Canada K2A 1T4.
Ph. 613-722-1621, Fax: 613-728-7305
e-mail:sismondo@dreamscape.com

BRAZIL

59	A9	200r black	100.00	8.00
a.		Half used as 100r on cover		1,500.
60	A9a	500r orange	200.00	35.00
		Nos. 53-60 (7)	467.00	60.00

The 10r and 20r exist imperf. on both white and bluish paper. Some authorities consider them proofs.
Nos. 58 and 65 are found in three types.

Bluish Paper

53a	A5	10r	500.00	425.00
54b	A6	20r	160.00	24.00
56a	A7	50r	200.00	25.00
57a	A8	80r	240.00	27.50
58b	A8a	100r	800.00	115.00

1876-77 — Rouletted

61	A5	10r vermilion ('77)	60.00	35.00
62	A6	20r red lilac ('77)	70.00	27.50
63	A7	50r blue ('77)	70.00	10.00
64	A8	80r violet ('77)	175.00	20.00
65	A8a	100r green	40.00	1.25
66	A9	200r black ('77)	80.00	7.50
a.		Half used as 100r on cover		1,000.
67	A9a	500r orange	190.00	40.00
		Nos. 61-67 (7)	685.00	141.25

1878-79 — Rouletted

68	A10	10r vermilion	12.00	3.00
69	A11	20r violet	15.00	2.50
70	A12	50r blue	24.00	2.00
71	A13	80r lake	27.50	10.00
72	A14	100r green	27.50	1.25
73	A15	200r black	140.00	17.50
a.		Half used as 100r on cover		1,200.
74	A16	260r dk brown	80.00	22.00
75	A18	300r bister	80.00	6.00
a.		One-third used as 100r on cover		10,000.
76	A19	700r red brown	160.00	85.00
77	A20	1000r gray lilac	190.00	37.50
a.		Half used as 500r on cover		10,000.
		Nos. 68-77 (10)	756.00	186.75

1878, Aug. 21 — Perf. 12

78	A17	300r orange & grn	85.00	20.00

Nos. 68-78 exist imperforate.

Small Heads
Laid Paper
Perf. 13, 13½ and Compound

1881, July 15

79	A21	50r blue	120.00	18.00
80	A22	100r olive green	500.00	30.00
81	A23	200r pale red brn	475.00	110.00
a.		Half used as 100r on cover		1,750.

On Nos. 79 and 80 the hair above the ear curves forward. On Nos. 83 and 88 it is drawn backward. On the stamps of the 1881 issue the beard is smaller than in the 1882-85 issues and fills less of the space between the neck and the frame at the left.
See No. 88.

Two types each of the 100 and 200 reis.

100 REIS:
Type I - Groundwork formed of diagonal crossed lines and horizontal lines.
Type II - Groundwork formed of diagonal crossed lines and vertical lines.

200 REIS:
Type I - Groundwork formed of diagonal and horizontal lines.
Type II - Groundwork formed of diagonal crossed lines.

Larger Heads
Laid Paper
Perf. 12½ to 14 and Compound

1882-84

82	A24	10r black	10.00	20.00
83	A25	100r ol grn, type I	35.00	3.00
a.		100r dark green, type I	37.50	3.00
b.		100r dark green, type II	200.00	12.00
84	A26	200r pale red brn, type I	85.00	22.50
a.		Half used as 100r on cover		1,100.
85	A27	200r pale rose, type II	45.00	4.50
a.		Diag. half used as 100r on cover		800.00
		Nos. 82-85 (4)	175.00	50.00

See No. 86.

Three types of A29
Type I - Groundwork of horizontal lines.
Type II - Groundwork of diagonal crossed lines.
Type III - Groundwork solid.

Perf. 13, 13½, 14 and Compound

1884-85

86	A24	10r orange	2.50	2.00
87	A28	20r slate green	30.00	3.00
a.		20r olive green	30.00	3.00
b.		Half used as 10r on newspaper		3,000.
88	A21	50r bl, head larger	30.00	3.00
90	A29	100r lilac, type I	120.00	2.50
a.		100r lilac, type II	450.00	75.00
b.		100r lilac, type III	325.00	55.00
91	A30	100r lilac	180.00	4.00
		Nos. 86-91 (5)	362.50	14.50

Southern Cross A33
Crown A34
Perf. 13, 13½, 14 and Compound

1885

92	A31	100r lilac	100.00	2.50

Compare design A31 with A35.

1887

93	A32	50r chalky blue	27.50	4.00
94	A33	300r gray blue	200.00	25.00
95	A34	500r olive	110.00	12.00
		Nos. 93-95 (3)	337.50	41.00

Entrance to Bay of Rio de Janeiro — A37

1888

96	A35	100r lilac	60.00	1.50
a.		Imperf., pair	120.00	160.00
97	A36	700r violet	65.00	100.00
98	A37	1000r dull blue	250.00	100.00
		Nos. 96-98 (3)	375.00	201.50

Issues of the Republic

Southern Cross — A38

Wove Paper, Thin to Thick
Perf. 12½ to 14, 11 to 11½, and 12½ to 14x11 to 11½, Rough or Clean-Cut
Engraved; Typographed (#102)

1890-91

99	A38	20r gray green	2.00	1.50
a.		20r blue green	2.00	1.50
b.		20r emerald	16.00	6.00
100	A38	50r gray green	5.00	1.50
a.		50r olive green	12.00	6.00
b.		50r yellow green	12.00	6.00
c.		50r dark slate green	7.00	3.50
d.		Horiz. pair, imperf. btwn.		
101	A38	100r lilac rose	360.00	4.50
102	A38	100r red lil, redrawn	25.00	1.50
a.		Tete beche pair	15,000.	16,500.
103	A38	200r purple	8.00	1.50
a.		200r violet	10.00	2.00
b.		200r violet blue	22.50	3.00
104	A38	300r slate vio	150.00	25.00
a.		300r gray	75.00	8.50
b.		300r gray blue	85.00	8.50
c.		300r dark violet	75.00	5.00
105	A38	500r olive bister	17.50	8.00
a.		500r olive gray	17.50	10.00
106	A38	500r slate	17.50	12.00
107	A38	700r chocolate	20.00	22.50
a.		700r fawn	16.00	16.00
108	A38	1000r bister	15.00	3.00
a.		1000r yellow buff	30.00	7.50
		Nos. 96-108 (10)	620.00	81.00

The redrawn 100r may be distinguished by the absence of the curved lines of shading in the left side of the central oval. The pearls in the oval are not well aligned and there is less shading at right and left of "CORREIO" and "100 REIS."

A 100 reis stamp of type A38 but inscribed "BRAZIL" instead of "E. U. DO BRAZIL" was not placed in issue but postmarked copies are known. A reprint on thick paper was made in 1910.

No. 101 exists imperf., not regularly issued.
For surcharges see Nos. 151-158.

Liberty Head A39 / A40
Perf. 12½ to 14, 11 to 11½ and 12½ to 14x11 to 11½

1891, May 1 — Typo.

109	A39	100r blue & red	32.50	1.50
a.		Head inverted	100.00	90.00
b.		Tete beche pair	675.00	750.00
c.		100r ultra & red	32.50	1.50

Perf. 11, 11½, 13, 13½, 14 and Compound

1893, Jan. 18 — Litho.

111	A40	100r rose	75.00	1.75

Sugarloaf Mountain A41 / A41a

Liberty Head A42 / A42a

Hermes — A43

Perf. 11 to 11½, 12½ to 14 and 12½ to 14x11 to 11½

1894-97 — Unwmk.

112	A41	10r rose & blue	2.00	.75
113	A41a	10r rose & blue	2.00	.75
114	A41a	20r orange & bl	1.10	.35
115	A41a	50r dk blue & blue	8.00	1.25
116	A42	100r carmine & blk	4.00	.40
a.		Vert. pair, imperf. btwn.	100.00	
118	A42a	200r orange & blk	1.00	.40
a.		Imperf. horiz., pair	80.00	
b.		Vert. pair, imperf. btwn.	80.00	
119	A42a	300r green & blk	15.00	.60
120	A42a	500r blue & blk	25.00	1.75
121	A42a	700r lilac & blk	16.00	2.00
122	A43	1000r green & vio	55.00	1.75
124	A43	2000r blk & gray lil	65.00	15.00
		Nos. 112-124 (11)	194.10	25.00

The head of No. 116 exists in five types. See Nos. 140-150A, 159-161, 166-171d.

Newspaper Stamps Surcharged:

100   **200**

1898   **1898**

100   **200** (b)

100

1898

100 (c)

Surcharged on 1889 Issue of type N1

1898 — Rouletted
Green Surcharge

125	(b)	700r on 500r yel	6.75	10.00
126	(c)	1000r on 700r yel	32.50	27.50
a.		Surcharged "700r"	675.00	775.00
127	(c)	2000r on 1000r yel	27.50	15.00
128	(c)	2000r on 1000r brn	20.00	6.00

BRAZIL

Violet Surcharge
129	(a)	100r on 50r brn yel	2.00	45.00
130	(c)	100r on 50r brn yel	65.00	45.00
131	(c)	300r on 200r blk	3.50	1.25
a.		Double surcharge	160.00	275.00

The surcharge on No. 130 is handstamped. The impression is blurred and lighter in color than on No. 129. The two surcharges differ most in the shapes and serifs of the figures "1."
Counterfeits exist of No. 126a.

Black Surcharge
132	(b)	200r on 100r violet	3.50	1.25
a.		Double surcharge	80.00	175.00
b.		Inverted surcharge	80.00	175.00
132C	(b)	500r on 300r car	5.50	3.00
133	(b)	700r on 500r green	8.00	2.00

Blue Surcharge
134	(b)	500r on 300r car	6.50	5.50

Red Surcharge
135	(c)	1000r on 700r ultra	22.50	15.00
a.		Inverted surcharge	200.00	200.00

Surcharged on 1890-94 Issues:

200 **1898**
1898 **50 RÉIS 50**
d e

Perf. 11 to 14 and Compound
Black Surcharge
136	N3(e)	20r on 10r blue	3.00	6.00
137	N2(d)	200r on 10r red lilac	20.00	15.00
a.		Double surcharge	225.00	250.00

Surcharge on No. 137 comes blue to deep black.

Blue Surcharge
138	N3(e)	50r on 20r green	8.00	10.00

Red Surcharge
139	N3(e)	100r on 50r green	18.00	20.00
a.		Blue surcharge		12.50

The surcharge on Nos. 139 and 139a exists double, inverted, one missing, etc.

Types of 1894-97
1899
Perf. 5½-7 and 11-11½x5½-7
140	A41a	10r rose & bl	4.50	2.00
141	A41a	20r orange & bl	7.50	7.50
142	A41a	50r dk bl & lt bl	9.00	30.00
143	A42	100r carmine & blk	16.00	4.50
144	A42a	200r orange & blk	9.00	3.00
145	A42a	300r green & blk	60.00	7.50
		Nos. 140-145 (6)	106.00	64.50

Perf. 8½-9½, 8½-9½x11-11½
146	A41a	10r rose & bl	4.50	3.00
147	A41a	20r orange & bl	15.00	3.00
147A	A41a	50r dk bl & lt bl	125.00	30.00
148	A42	100r carmine & blk	30.00	1.50
149	A42a	200r orange & blk	15.00	1.00
150	A42a	300r green & blk	60.00	5.00
150A	A43	1000r green & vio	125.00	12.50
		Nos. 146-150A (7)	374.50	56.00

Nos. 140-150A are valued with perfs just cut into the design on one or two sides. Expect some irregularity of the perforations.

Issue of 1890-93 Surcharged in Violet or Magenta

1899
50 RÉIS

Perf. 11 to 11½, 12½ to 14 and Compound
1899, June 25
151	A38	50r on 20r gray grn	2.00	3.00
a.		Double surcharge	125.00	125.00
152	A38	100r on 50r gray grn	2.00	3.00
b.		Double surcharge	100.00	100.00
153	A38	300r on 200r pur	7.50	12.00
a.		Double surcharge	250.00	250.00
b.		Pair, one without surcharge	425.00	—
154	A38	500r on 300r ultra, perf. 13	18.00	7.50
a.		500r on 300r gray lilac	30.00	9.00
b.		Pair, one without surcharge	425.00	500.00
c.		500r on 300r slate violet	37.50	15.00
155	A38	700r on 500r ol bis	24.00	6.00
a.		Pair, one without surcharge	425.00	—
156	A38	1000r on 700r choc	17.50	6.00
157	A38	1000r on 700r fawn	17.50	6.00
a.		Pair, one without surcharge	425.00	500.00
158	A38	2000r on 1000r yel buff	60.00	4.50
a.		2000r on 1000r bister	30.00	4.50
b.		Pair, one without surcharge	425.00	500.00
		Nos. 151-158 (8)	148.50	48.00

Types of 1894-97
Perf. 11, 11½, 13 and Compound
1900
159	A41a	50r green	10.00	.60
160	A42	100r rose	20.00	.30
a.		Frame around inner oval	100.00	4.00
161	A42a	200r blue	12.00	.35
		Nos. 159-161 (3)	42.00	1.25

Three types exist of No. 161, all of which have the frame around inner oval.

Cabral Arrives at Brazil — A44

Independence Proclaimed A45

"Emancipation of Slaves" — A46

Allegory, Republic of Brazil — A47

1900, Jan. 1 Litho. Perf. 12½
162	A44	100r red	5.50	4.50
a.		Imperf., pair	400.00	500.00
163	A45	200r green & yel	5.50	4.50
164	A46	500r blue	5.50	4.50
165	A47	700r emerald	5.50	4.50
		Nos. 162-165 (4)	22.00	18.00

Discovery of Brazil, 400th anniversary.

Types of 1894-97
Wmk. (97? or 98?)
1905 Perf. 11, 11½
166	A41a	10r rose & bl	5.75	4.00
167	A41a	20r orange & bl	10.00	2.00
168	A41a	50r green	20.00	3.00
169	A42	100r rose	27.50	1.00
170	A42a	200r dark blue	16.00	1.00
171	A42a	300r green & blk	55.00	2.00
		Nos. 166-171 (6)	134.25	13.00

Positive identification of Wmk. 97 or 98 places stamp in specific watermark groups below.

Wmk. 97
166b	A41a	10r rose & blue	30.00	16.00
167b	A41a	20r orange & blue	30.00	8.00
168b	A41a	50r green	55.00	8.00
169b	A42	100r rose	200.00	30.00
170b	A42a	200r dark blue	120.00	4.00
171b	A42a	300r green & blk	375.00	30.00
171A	A43	1000r green & vio	290.00	30.00
		Nos. 166b-171A (7)	1,100.	126.00

Wmk. 98
166c	A41a	10r rose & blue	40.00	40.00
167c	A41a	20r orange & blue	80.00	20.00
168c	A41a	50r green	160.00	30.00
169c	A42	100r rose	80.00	4.00
170c	A42a	200r dark blue	120.00	4.00
171d	A42a	300r green & blk	290.00	30.00
		Nos. 166c-171d (6)	770.00	128.00

Allegory, Pan-American Congress A48

1906, July 23 Litho. Unwmk.
172	A48	100r carmine rose	30.00	30.00
173	A48	200r blue	75.00	10.00

Third Pan-American Congress.

Aristides Lobo — A48a

Benjamin Constant — A49

Pedro Alvares Cabral — A50

Eduardo Wandenkolk — A51

Manuel Deodoro da Fonseca — A52

Floriano Peixoto — A53

Prudente de Moraes — A54

Manuel Ferraz de Campos Salles — A55

Francisco de Paula Rodrigues Alves — A56

Liberty Head — A57

A58

A59

1906-16 Engr. Perf. 12
174	A48a	10r bluish slate	.90	.20
175	A49	20r aniline vio	.90	.20
176	A50	50r green	.90	.20
a.		Booklet pane of 6 ('08)	40.00	120.00
177	A51	100r anil rose	2.00	.20
a.		Imperf. vert., coil ('16)	4.00	.35
b.		Booklet pane of 6 ('08)	80.00	120.00
178	A52	200r blue	2.00	.20
a.		Booklet pane of 6 ('08)	60.00	120.00
179	A52	200r ultra ('15)	2.00	.35
a.		Imperf. vert., coil ('16)	2.00	.35
180	A53	300r gray blk	3.00	.65
181	A54	400r olive grn	30.00	2.00
182	A55	500r dk violet	6.00	.65
183	A54	600r olive grn ('10)	3.00	1.00
184	A56	700r red brown	6.00	3.00
185	A57	1000r vermilion	32.50	1.00
186	A58	2000r yellow grn	20.00	.65
187	A58	2000r Prus blue ('15)	10.00	1.00
188	A59	5000r carmine rose	8.00	2.00
		Nos. 174-188 (15)	127.20	13.30

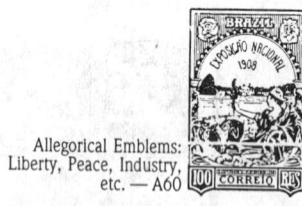

Allegorical Emblems: Liberty, Peace, Industry, etc. — A60

1908, July 14
189	A60	100r carmine	20.00	1.75

National Exhibition, Rio de Janeiro.

Emblems of Peace Between Brazil and Portugal A61

1908, July 14
190	A61	100r red	8.00	1.25

Opening of Brazilian ports to foreign commerce, cent. Medallions picture King Carlos I of Portugal and Pres. Affonso Penna of Brazil.

Bonifacio, Bolivar, Hidalgo, O'Higgins, San Martin, Washington — A62

1909
191	A62	200r deep blue	7.50	1.00

For surcharge see No. E1.

Nilo Peçanha — A63

Baron of Rio Branco — A64

1910, Nov. 15
192	A63	10,000r brown	8.00	2.00

1913-16
193	A64	1000r deep green	3.75	.35
194	A64	1000r slate ('16)	21.00	.65

Cabo Frio — A65

Perf. 11½
1915, Nov. 13 Litho. Wmk. 99
195	A65	100r dk grn, yelsh	4.00	3.50

Founding of the town of Cabo Frio, 300th anniversary.

Bay of Guajara — A66

1916, Jan. 5
196	A66	100r carmine	7.50	4.00

City of Belem, 300th anniversary.

Revolutionary Flag — A67

1917, Mar. 6
197	A67	100r deep blue	15.00	7.50

Revolution of Pernambuco, Mar. 6, 1817.

Rodrigues Alves — A68

1917, Aug. 31 Engr. Unwmk. Perf. 12
198	A68	5000r red brown	60.00	10.00

Liberty Head
A69   A70

Perf. 12½, 13, 13x13½
1918-20 Typo. Unwmk.
200	A69	10r orange brn	.50	.25
201	A69	20r slate	.50	.25
202	A69	25r ol gray ('20)	.50	.25
203	A69	50r green	27.50	3.25

BRAZIL

204	A70	100r rose	1.75	.25
a.	Imperf., pair			
205	A70	300r red orange	19.00	3.25
206	A70	500r dull violet	19.00	3.25
	Nos. 200-206 (7)		68.75	10.75

1918-20   Wmk. 100

207	A69	10r red brown	6.00	1.75
a.	Imperf., pair			
207B	A69	20r slate	1.50	1.50
c.	Imperf., pair			
208	A69	25r ol gray ('20)	.75	.50
209	A69	50r green	1.50	.50
210	A70	100r rose	47.50	.50
211	A70	200r dull blue	6.00	.50
a.	Imperf., pair			
212	A70	300r orange	47.50	3.50
213	A70	500r dull violet	47.50	7.50
214	A70	600r orange	2.50	7.50
	Nos. 207-214 (9)		150.75	23.75

Because of the spacing of this watermark, a few stamps in each sheet may show no watermark.

"Education" — A72

1918   Engr.   Perf. 11½

215	A72	1000r gray	6.00	.20
216	A72	2000r red brown	27.50	6.00
217	A72	5000r dark violet	7.50	6.00
	Nos. 215-217 (3)		41.00	12.25

Watermark note below No. 257 also applies to Nos. 215-217.

See Nos. 233-234, 283-285, 404, 406, 458, 460. For surcharge see No. C30.

Railroad A73

"Industry" A74

"Aviation" A75

Mercury A76

"Navigation" — A77

Perf. 13½x13, 13x13½

1920-22   Typo.   Unwmk.

218	A73	10r red violet	.75	.40
219	A73	20r olive green	.75	.40
220	A74	25r brown violet	.50	.40
221	A74	50r blue green	.85	.40
222	A74	50r orange brn ('22)	1.40	.40
223	A75	100r rose red	2.75	.40
224	A75	100r orange ('22)	7.50	.40
225	A75	150r violet ('21)	1.40	.40
226	A75	200r blue	4.50	.40
227	A75	200r rose red ('22)	8.00	.40
228	A76	300r olive gray	12.50	.50
229	A76	400r dull blue ('22)	22.50	3.50
230	A76	500r red brown	17.50	.70
	Nos. 218-230 (13)		80.90	8.50

See Nos. 236-257, 265-266, 268-271, 273-274, 276-281, 302-311, 316-322, 326-340, 357-358, 431-434, 436-441, 461-463B, 467-470, 472-474, 488-490, 492-494. For surcharges see Nos. 356-358, 376-377.

Perf. 11, 11½
Engr.   Wmk. 100

231	A77	600r red orange	2.00	.35
232	A77	1000r claret	5.00	.25
a.	Perf. 8½		37.50	7.50
233	A72	2000r dull violet	20.00	.75
234	A72	5000r brown	16.00	9.00
	Nos. 231-234 (4)		43.00	10.35

Nos. 233 and 234 are inscribed "BRASIL CORREIO." Watermark note below No. 257 also applies to Nos. 231-234.

See No. 282.

King Albert of Belgium and President Epitacio Pessoa A78

1920, Sept. 19   Engr.   Perf. 11½x11

235	A78	100r dull red	.65	.65

Visit of the King and Queen of Belgium.

Types of 1920-22 Issue
Perf. 13x13½, 13x12½

1922-29   Typo.   Wmk. 100

236	A73	10r red violet	.30	.15
237	A73	20r olive green	.30	.15
238	A75	20r gray violet ('29)	.30	.15
239	A74	25r brown violet	.35	.15
240	A74	50r blue grn	3.25	35.00
241	A74	50r org brn ('23)	.45	.35
a.	Booklet pane of 6			
242	A75	100r rose red	22.50	.40
243	A75	100r orange ('26)	.50	.15
a.	Booklet pane of 6			
244	A75	100r turq grn ('28)	.35	.15
245	A75	150r violet	2.50	.15
246	A75	200r blue	300.00	12.50
247	A75	200r rose red	.40	.15
a.	Booklet pane of 6			
248	A75	200r ol grn ('28)	2.50	3.00
249	A76	300r olive gray	1.90	.25
a.	Booklet pane of 6			
250	A76	300r rose red ('29)	.35	.25
251	A76	400r blue	1.90	.15
252	A76	400r orange ('29)	.75	.60
253	A76	500r red brown	7.50	.50
a.	Booklet pane of 6			
254	A76	500r ultra ('29)	8.50	.15
255	A76	600r brn org ('29)	7.50	3.00
256	A76	700r dull vio ('29)	7.50	1.75
257	A76	1000r turq bl ('29)	9.50	.70
	Nos. 236-257 (22)		379.10	59.80

Because of the spacing of the watermark, a few stamps in each sheet show no watermark.

"Agriculture" — A79

1922   Unwmk.   Perf. 13x13½

258	A79	40r orange brown	.50	.35
259	A79	80r grnsh blue	.35	2.50

See Nos. 263, 267, 275.

Declaration of Ypiranga — A80

Dom Pedro I and Jose Bonifacio — A81

National Exposition and President Pessoa — A82

Unwmk.
1922, Sept. 7   Engr.   Perf. 14

260	A80	100r ultra	5.00	.45
261	A81	200r red	6.00	.30
262	A82	300r green	6.00	.30
	Nos. 260-262 (3)		17.00	1.05

Cent. of Independence and Natl. Exposition of 1922.

Agriculture Type of 1922
Perf. 13½x12

1923   Wmk. 100   Typo.

263	A79	40r orange brown	.60	.60

Brazilian Army Entering Bahia — A83

Unwmk.
1923, July 12   Litho.   Perf. 13

264	A83	200r rose	7.50	5.00

Centenary of the taking of Bahia from the Portuguese.

Types of 1920-22 Issues
Perf. 13x13½

1924   Typo.   Wmk. 193

265	A73	10r red violet	5.50	3.75
266	A73	20r olive green	6.00	3.75
267	A79	40r orange brown	4.25	.60
268	A74	50r orange brown	3.75	18.00
269	A75	100r orange	4.25	.35
270	A75	200r rose	6.00	.25
271	A76	400r blue	3.75	3.75
	Nos. 265-271 (7)		33.50	30.45

Arms of Equatorial Confederation, 1824 — A84

Unwmk.
1924, July 2   Litho.   Perf. 11

272	A84	200r bl, blk, yel, & red	2.00	2.25
a.	Red omitted		275.00	275.00

Centenary of the Equatorial Confederation.

Types of 1920-22 Issues
Perf. 9½ to 13½ and Compound

1924-28   Typo.   Wmk. 101

273	A73	10r red violet	.45	.30
274	A73	20r olive green	.45	.30
275	A79	40r orange brn	.45	.30
276	A74	50r orange brn	.75	.30
277	A75	100r red orange	1.50	.30
278	A75	200r rose	.75	.30
279	A76	300r ol gray ('25)	7.00	1.00
280	A76	400r blue	4.00	.35
281	A76	500r red brown	9.00	.45

Engr.

282	A77	600r red orange ('26)	1.00	.30
283	A72	2000r dull vio ('26)	5.00	.30
284	A72	5000r brown ('26)	15.00	.70
285	A72	10,000r rose ('28)	17.50	.90
	Nos. 273-285 (13)		62.85	5.80

Nos. 283-285 are inscribed "BRASIL CORREIO."

Ruy Barbosa — A85

1925   Wmk. 100   Perf. 11½

286	A85	1000r claret	4.25	1.50

1926   Wmk. 101

287	A85	1000r claret	1.75	.35

"Justice" — A86

Scales of Justice and Map of Brazil — A87

Perf. 13½x13
1927, Aug. 11   Typo.   Wmk. 206

288	A86	100r deep blue	.90	.50
289	A87	200r rose	.80	.35

Founding of the law courses, cent.

Liberty Holding Coffee Leaves — A88

1928, Mar. 5

290	A88	100r blue green	1.00	.60
291	A88	200r carmine	.65	.50
292	A88	300r olive black	5.00	.40
	Nos. 290-292 (3)		6.65	1.50

Introduction of the coffee tree in Brazil, bicent.

Official Stamps of 1919 Surcharged in Red or Black   **700 Réis**

Perf. 11, 11½
1928   Wmk. 100   Engr.

293	O3	700r on 500r orange	2.25	1.50
a.	Inverted surcharge		175.00	175.00
294	O3	1000r on 100r rose red (Bk)	1.50	.30
295	O3	2000r on 200r dull bl	2.25	.45
296	O3	5000r on 50r green	2.25	.55
297	O3	10,000r on 10r ol grn	11.00	.90
	Nos. 293-297 (5)		19.25	3.70

#293-297 were used for ordinary postage. Stamps in the outer rows of the sheets are often without watermark.

Ruy Barbosa — A89

Perf. 9, 9½x11, 11, and Compound
1929   Wmk. 101

300	A89	5000r blue violet	12.50	.75

See #405, 459. For surcharge see #C29.

Types of 1920-21 Issue
Perf. 13½x12½

1929   Typo.   Wmk. 218

302	A75	20r gray violet	.25	.20
303	A75	50r red brown	.25	.20
304	A75	100r turq green	.30	.20
305	A75	200r olive green	12.50	2.25
306	A76	300r rose red	.60	.20
307	A76	400r orange	.70	.25
308	A76	500r ultra	7.00	.45
309	A76	600r brown org	8.50	.60
310	A76	700r dp violet	2.25	.20
311	A76	1000r turq blue	4.00	.20
	Nos. 302-311 (10)		36.35	4.75

Wmk. 218 exists both in vertical alignment and in echelon.

Wmk. in echelon

302a	A75	20r		.25	.35
303a	A75	50r		80.00	27.50
306a	A76	300r		.65	.30
308a	A76	500r		110.00	15.00
311a	A76	1000r		6.50	6.50

Architectural Fantasies A90   A91

Architectural Fantasy — A92

Perf. 13x13½
1930, June 20   Wmk. 206

312	A90	100r turq blue	1.25	.80
313	A91	200r olive gray	2.00	.70
314	A92	300r rose red	3.50	.80
	Nos. 312-314 (3)		6.75	2.30

Fourth Pan-American Congress of Architects and Exposition of Architecture.

Types of 1920-21 Issues

1930   Wmk. 221   Perf. 13x12½

316	A75	20r gray violet	.20	.15
317	A75	50r red brown	.20	.15
318	A75	100r turq blue	.25	.15
319	A75	200r olive green	3.00	.25
320	A76	300r rose red	.60	.25
321	A76	500r ultra	1.50	.20
322	A76	1000r turq blue	25.00	.70
	Nos. 316-322 (7)		30.75	1.90

689

BRAZIL

Imperforates
Since 1930, imperforate or partly perforated sheets of nearly all commemorative and some definitive issues have become obtainable.

Types of 1920-29 Issue
Perf. 11, 13½x13, 13x12½

1931-34		Typo.	Wmk. 222	
326	A75	10r deep brown	.15	.15
327	A75	20r gray violet	.15	.15
328	A74	25r brn vio ('34)	.15	.60
330	A75	50r blue green	.15	.15
331	A75	50r red brown	.15	.15
332	A75	100r orange	.30	.15
334	A75	200r dp carmine	.45	.15
335	A76	300r olive green	.60	.15
336	A76	400r ultra	.85	.15
337	A76	500r red brown	3.50	.15
338	A76	600r brown org	3.50	.15
339	A76	700r deep violet	3.50	.15
340	A76	1000r turq blue	12.50	.15
		Nos. 326-340 (13)	25.95	2.40

Getulio Vargas and Joao Pessoa — A93

Vargas and Pessoa — A94

Oswaldo Aranha
A95 A96

Antonio Carlos A97
Pessoa A98 

Vargas — A99

Unwmk.
1931, Apr. 29   Litho.   Perf. 14

342	A93	10r + 10r lt bl	.15	4.50
343	A93	20r + 20r yel brn	.15	3.25
344	A95	50r + 50r bl grn, red & yel	.15	.15
a.		Red missing at left	.90	.90
345	A93	100r + 50r orange	.30	.30
346	A93	200r + 100r green	.30	.30
347	A94	300r + 150r multi	.30	.30
348	A93	400r + 200r dp rose	1.00	.65
349	A93	500r + 250r dk blue	.70	.55
350	A93	600r + 300r brn vio	.50	6.50
351	A94	700r + 350r multi	.90	.55
352	A96	1000r + 500r brt grn, red & yel	2.00	.25
353	A97	2000r + 1000r gray blk & red	4.00	.55
354	A98	5000r + 2500r blk & red	17.50	4.50
355	A99	10000r + 5000r brt grn & yel	42.50	10.00
		Nos. 342-355 (14)	70.45	32.35

Revolution of Oct. 3, 1930. Prepared as semi-postal stamps, Nos. 342-355 were sold as ordinary postage stamps with stated surtax ignored.

1931
Nos. 306, 320 and 250 Surcharged
200 Réis

Wmk. E U BRASIL Multiple (218)
1931, July 20   Perf. 13½x12½

356	A76	200r on 300r rose red	.90	.90
a.		Wmk. in echelon	17.50	17.50
b.		Inverted surcharge	40.00	

Perf. 13x12½ Wmk. 221

357	A76	200r on 300r rose red	.30	.30
a.		Inverted surcharge	45.00	45.00

Perf. 13½x12½ Wmk. 100

| 358 | A76 | 200r on 300r rose red | 60.00 | 60.00 |

Map of South America Showing Meridian of Tordesillas A100

Joao Ramalho and Tibiriça A101

Martim Affonso de Souza A102

King John III of Portugal A103

Disembarkation of M. A. de Souza at Sao Vicente — A104

Wmk. 222
1932, June 3   Typo.   Perf. 13

359	A100	20r dk violet	.20	.20
360	A101	100r black	.35	.35
361	A102	200r purple	1.00	.25
362	A103	600r red brown	1.65	1.25

Engr. Wmk. 101 Perf. 9½, 11, 9½x11

363	A104	700r ultra	2.50	1.75
		Nos. 359-363 (5)	5.70	3.80

1st colonization of Brazil at Sao Vicente, in 1532, under the hereditary captaincy of Martim Affonso de Souza.

Revolutionary Issue

Map of Brazil — A105
Soldier and Flag — A106 
Allegory: Freedom, Justice, Equality — A107 
Soldier's Head — A108 
"LEX" and Sword A109 

Symbolical of Law and Order A110

Symbolical of Justice A111

Perf. 11½
1932, Sept. 13   Litho.   Unwmk.

364	A105	100r brown org	.40	2.00
365	A106	200r dk carmine	.35	.70
366	A107	300r gray green	2.00	3.50
367	A108	400r dark blue	7.25	7.25
368	A105	500r black brown	7.25	7.25
369	A107	600r red	7.25	7.25
370	A106	700r violet	3.50	7.25
371	A108	1000r orange	1.75	7.25
372	A109	2000r dark brown	14.00	20.00
373	A110	5000r yellow grn	17.50	32.50
374	A111	10000r plum	20.00	37.50
		Nos. 364-374 (11)	81.25	132.45

Issued by the revolutionary forces in the state of Sao Paulo during the revolt of September, 1932. Subsequently the stamps were recognized by the Federal Government and placed in general use.
Excellent counterfeits of Nos. 373 and 374 exist. Counterfeit cancellations abound.

City of Vassouras and Illuminated Memorial — A112

Wmk. 222
1933, Jan. 15   Typo.   Perf. 12

| 375 | A112 | 200r rose red | 1.00 | .90 |

City of Vassouras founding, cent.

Nos. 306, 320 Surcharged **200 RÉIS**

Perf. 13½x12½
1933, July 28   Wmk. 218

376	A76	200r on 300r rose red	.60	.60
a.		Wmk. 218 in echelon (No. 306a)	12.50	12.50
b.		Wmk. 100 (No. 250)	87.50	87.50

Perf. 13x12½ Wmk. 221

377	A76	200r on 300r rose red	.45	.45
a.		Inverted surcharge	35.00	
b.		Double surcharge	35.00	

Religious Symbols and Inscriptions — A113

Wmk. 222
1933, Sept. 3   Typo.   Perf. 13

| 378 | A113 | 200r dark red | .90 | .75 |

1st Natl. Eucharistic Congress in Brazil.

"Flag of the Race" A114

1933, Aug. 18

| 379 | A114 | 200r deep red | .90 | .75 |

The raising of the "Flag of the Race" and the 441st anniv. of the sailing of Columbus from Palos, Spain, Aug. 3, 1492.

Republic Figure, Flags of Brazil and Argentina — A115

Perf. 11½
1933, Oct. 7   Wmk. 101   Engr.

| 380 | A115 | 200r blue | .35 | .25 |

Thick Laid Paper Perf. 11, 11½ Wmk. 236

381	A115	400r green	.90	.80
382	A115	600r brt rose	3.00	3.25
383	A115	1000r lt violet	4.50	3.75
		Nos. 380-383 (4)	8.75	8.05

Visit of President Justo of the Argentina to Brazil, Oct. 2-7, 1933.

Allegory: "Faith and Energy" — A116
Allegory of Flight — A117 

1933   Typo.   Wmk. 222

384	A116	200r dark red	.25	.15
385	A116	200r dark violet	.30	.15

See Nos. 435, 471, 491.

Wmk. 236
1934, Apr. 15   Engr.   Perf. 12

| 386 | A117 | 200r blue | .50 | .50 |

1st Natl. Aviation Congress at Sao Paulo.

A118

Wmk. 222
1934, May 12   Typo.   Perf. 11

387	A118	200r dark olive	.30	.30
388	A118	400r carmine	1.50	1.50
389	A118	700r ultra	1.50	.90
390	A118	1000r orange	3.75	.60
		Nos. 387-390 (4)	7.05	3.30

7th Intl. Fair at Rio de Janeiro.

Christ of Corcovado — A119

1934, Oct. 20

392	A119	300r dark red	1.90	1.90
a.		Tete beche pair	6.00	7.25
393	A119	700r ultra	8.00	5.00
a.		Tete beche pair	19.00	22.50

Visit of Eugenio Cardinal Pacelli, later Pope Pius XII, to Brazil.
The three printings of Nos. 392-393, distinguishable by shades, sell for different prices.

José de Anchieta A120

BRAZIL

Thick Laid Paper
1934, Nov. 8 Wmk. 236   Perf. 11, 12
394	A120	200r yellow brown	.55	.15
395	A120	300r violet	.45	.25
396	A120	700r blue	1.75	1.40
397	A120	1000r lt green	3.50	.55
		Nos. 394-397 (4)	6.25	2.35

Jose de Anchieta, S.J. (1534-1597), Portuguese missionary and "father of Brazilian literature."

"Brazil" and "Uruguay"
A121   A122

Wmk. 222
1935, Jan. 8   Typo.   Perf. 11
398	A121	200r orange	.65	.40
399	A122	300r yellow	.80	.50
400	A122	700r ultra	3.25	3.25
401	A121	1000r dk violet	8.00	4.00
		Nos. 398-401 (4)	12.70	8.15

Visit of President Terra of Uruguay.

View of Town of Igarassu — A123

1935, July 1
| 402 | A123 | 200r maroon & brn | .85 | .45 |
| 403 | A123 | 300r vio & olive brn | .85 | .35 |

Captaincy of Pernambuco founding, 400th anniv.

Types of 1918-29
Thick Laid Paper
Perf. 9½, 11, 12, 12x11
1934-36   Engr.   Wmk. 236
404	A72	2000r violet	3.75	.40
405	A89	5000r blue vio ('36)	11.00	.50
406	A72	10000r claret ('36)	8.75	.75
		Nos. 404-406 (3)	23.50	1.65

No. 404 is inscribed "BRASIL CORREIO."

Revolutionist — A124

Bento Gonçalves da Silva — A125

Duke of Caxias A126

1935, Sept. 20   Engr.   Perf. 11, 12
407	A124	200r black	.55	.45
408	A124	300r rose lake	.55	.35
409	A125	700r dull blue	2.25	2.25
410	A126	1000r light violet	2.50	1.40
		Nos. 407-410 (4)	5.85	4.45

Centenary of the "Ragged" Revolution.

Federal District Coat of Arms A127

Wmk. 222
1935, Oct. 19   Typo.   Perf. 11
| 411 | A127 | 200r blue | 2.25 | 2.25 |

8th Intl. Sample Fair held at Rio de Janeiro.

Coutinho's Ship A128

Arms of Fernandes Coutinho — A129

1935, Oct. 25
| 412 | A128 | 300r maroon | 2.25 | 1.00 |
| 413 | A129 | 700r turq blue | 3.25 | 2.00 |

400th anniversary of the establishment of the first Portuguese colony at Espirito Santo by Vasco Fernandes Coutinho.

Gavea, Rock near Rio de Janeiro A130

1935, Oct. 12   Wmk. 245   Perf. 11
414	A130	300r brown & vio	1.75	1.50
415	A130	300r blk & turq bl	1.75	1.50
416	A130	300r Prus bl & ultra	1.75	1.50
417	A130	300r crimson & blk	1.75	1.50
		Nos. 414-417 (4)	7.00	6.00

"Child's Day," Oct. 12.

Viscount of Cairu — A131

Perf. 11, 12x11
1936, Jan. 20   Engr.   Wmk. 236
| 418 | A131 | 1200r violet | 6.00 | 2.75 |

Jose da Silva Lisboa, Viscount of Cairu (1756-1835).

View of Cametá A132

1936, Feb. 26   Perf. 11, 12
| 419 | A132 | 200r brown orange | 1.25 | 1.00 |
| 420 | A132 | 300r green | 1.25 | .80 |

300th anniversary of the founding of the city of Cameta, Dec. 24, 1635.

Coining Press A133

Thick Laid Paper
1936, Mar. 24   Perf. 11
| 421 | A133 | 300r pur brn, cr | 1.25 | .90 |

1st Numismatic Cong. at Sao Paulo, Mar., 1936.

Carlos Gomes A134

"Il Guarany" A135

Thick Laid Paper
1936, July 11   Perf. 11, 11x12
422	A134	300r dull rose	.50	.35
423	A134	300r black brown	.50	.35
424	A135	700r ocher	2.00	.90
425	A135	700r blue	1.75	.90
		Nos. 422-425 (4)	4.75	2.50

100th anniversary of the birth of Antonio Carlos Gomes, who composed the opera "Il Guarany."

Scales of Justice — A136

Wmk. 222
1936, July 4   Typo.   Perf. 11
| 426 | A136 | 300r rose | 1.25 | .45 |

First National Judicial Congress.

Federal District Coat of Arms A137

1936, Nov. 13   Typo.   Wmk. 249
| 427 | A137 | 200r rose red | .75 | .45 |

Ninth International Sample Fair held at Rio de Janeiro.

Eucharistic Congress Seal — A138

1936, Dec. 17   Wmk. 245   Perf. 11½
| 428 | A138 | 300r grn, yel bl & blk | .70 | .45 |

2nd Natl. Eucharistic Congress in Brazil.

Botafogo Bay — A139

Thick Laid Paper
Wmk. 236
1937, Jan. 2   Engr.   Perf. 11
| 429 | A139 | 700r blue | .75 | .45 |
| 430 | A139 | 700r black | .75 | .45 |

Birth cent. of Francisco Pereira Passos, engineer who planned the modern city of Rio de Janeiro.

Types of 1920-21, 1933
Perf. 11, 11½ and Compound
1936-37   Typo.   Wmk. 249
431	A75	10r deep brown	.15	.15
432	A75	20r dull violet	.15	.15
433	A75	50r blue green	.15	.15
434	A75	100r orange	.25	.15
435	A116	200r dk violet	.45	.15
436	A76	300r olive green	.25	.15
437	A76	400r ultra	.45	.15
438	A76	500r lt brown	.70	.15
439	A76	600r brn org ('37)	1.50	.15
440	A76	700r deep violet	2.75	.15
441	A76	1000r turq blue	3.00	.15
		Nos. 431-441 (11)	9.80	1.65

Massed Flags and Star of Esperanto A140

1937, Jan. 19
| 442 | A140 | 300r green | 1.00 | .50 |

Ninth Brazilian Esperanto Congress.

Bay of Rio de Janeiro A141

1937, June 9   Unwmk.   Perf. 12½
| 443 | A141 | 300r orange red & blk | .50 | .50 |
| 444 | A141 | 700r blue & dk brn | 1.25 | .50 |

2nd South American Radio Communication Conf. held in Rio, June 7-19.

Globe — A142

1937, Sept. 4   Wmk. 249   Perf. 11, 12
| 445 | A142 | 300r green | .85 | .50 |

50th anniversary of Esperanto.

Monroe Palace, Rio de Janeiro — A143

Botanical Garden, Rio de Janeiro — A144

1937, Sept. 30   Unwmk.   Perf. 12½
446	A143	200r lt brn & bl	.50	.35
447	A143	300r org & ol grn	.50	.35
448	A143	2000r grn & cerise	3.75	5.50
449	A144	10000r lake & indigo	32.50	27.50
		Nos. 446-449 (4)	37.25	33.70

Brig. Gen. Jose da Silva Paes — A145

Eagle and Shield — A146

1937, Oct. 11   Wmk. 249   Perf. 11½
| 450 | A145 | 300r blue | .75 | .30 |

Bicentenary of Rio Grande do Sul.

1937, Dec. 2   Typo.   Perf. 11
| 451 | A146 | 400r dark blue | .75 | .30 |

150th anniversary of the US Constitution.

BRAZIL

Bags of Brazilian Coffee — A147

Frame Engraved, Center Typographed
1938, Jan. 17   Unwmk.   Perf. 12½
452 A147 1200r multicolored   3.00   .40

Arms of Olinda A148

Perf. 11, 11x11½
1938, Jan. 24   Engr.   Wmk. 249
453 A148 400r violet   .50   .25
4th cent. of the founding of the city of Olinda.

Independence Memorial, Ypiranga — A149

1938, Jan. 24   Typo.   Perf. 11
454 A149 400r brown olive   .60   .25
Proclamation of Brazil's independence by Dom Pedro, Sept. 7, 1822.

Iguaçu Falls — A150

Perf. 12½
1938, Jan. 10   Unwmk.   Engr.
455 A150 1000r sepia & yel brn   1.50   .75
456 A150 5000r ol blk & grn   17.00   7.50

Couto de Magalhaes — A151

Perf. 11, 11x11½
1938, Mar. 17   Wmk. 249
457 A151 400r dull green   .50   .25
General Couto de Magalhaes (1837-1898), statesman, soldier, explorer, writer, developer.

Types of 1918-38
Perf. 11, 12x11, 12x11½, 12
1938   Engr.   Wmk. 249
458 A72   2000r blue violet   6.50   .15
459 A89   5000r violet blue   24.00   .50
  a.   5000r deep blue   20.00   .50
460 A72 10000r rose lake   27.50   1.00
     Nos. 458-460 (3)   58.00   1.65
No. 458 is inscribed "BRASIL CORREIO."

Types of 1920-22
1938   Wmk. 245   Typo.   Perf. 11
461 A75   50r blue green   .50   .75
462 A75 100r orange   .50   .75
463 A76 300r olive green   .50   .15
463A A76 400r ultra   100.00   35.00
463B A76 500r red brown   .50   10.00
     Nos. 461-463B (5)   102.00   46.65

National Archives Building A152

1938, May 20   Wmk. 249
464 A152 400r brown   .40   .25
Centenary of National Archives.

Souvenir Sheets

Sir Rowland Hill A153

1938, Oct. 22   Imperf.
465 A153   Sheet of 10   12.50   12.50
  a.   400r dull green, single stamp   .75   .75
Brazilian Intl. Philatelic Exposition (Brapex). Issued in sheets measuring 106x118mm. A few perforated sheets exist.

President Vargas A154

1938, Nov. 10   Perf. 11
Without Gum
466 A154   Sheet of 10   5.00   8.50
  a.   400r slate blue, single stamp   .40   .40
Constitution of Brazil, set up by President Vargas, Nov. 10, 1937. Size: 113x135½mm.

Types of 1920-33
1939   Typo.   Wmk. 256   Perf. 11
467 A75   10r red brown   .30   .25
468 A75   20r dull violet   .30   .15
469 A75   50r blue green   .30   .15
470 A75 100r yellow org   .45   .15
471 A116 200r dk violet   .55   .15
472 A76 400r ultra   1.00   .15
473 A76 600r dull orange   1.00   .15
474 A76 1000r turq blue   7.00   .15
     Nos. 467-474 (8)   10.90   1.30

View of Rio de Janeiro — A155

View of Santos — A156

1939, June 14   Engr.   Wmk. 249
475 A155 1200r dull violet   1.25   .25

1939, Aug. 23
476 A156 400r dull blue   .40   .20
Centenary of founding of Santos.

Chalice Vine and Blossoms — A157

Eucharistic Congress Seal — A158

1939, Aug. 23
477 A157 400r green   1.00   .25
1st South American Botanical Congress held in January, 1938.

1939, Sept. 3
478 A158 400r rose red   .40   .20
Third National Eucharistic Congress.

Duke of Caxias, Army Patron — A159

1939, Sept. 12   Photo.   Rouletted
479 A159 400r deep ultra   .40   .25
Issued for Soldiers' Day.

A159a

A159b    A159d

A159c

Designs: 400r, George Washington. 800r, Emperor Pedro II. 1200r, Grover Cleveland. 1600r, Statue of Friendship, given by US.

1939, Oct. 7   Unwmk.   Engr.   Perf. 12
480 A159a 400r yellow orange   .40   .25
481 A159b 800r dark green   .25   .15
482 A159c 1200r rose car   .50   .15
483 A159d 1600r dark blue   .50   .25
     Nos. 480-483 (4)   1.65   .80
New York World's Fair.

Benjamin Constant A160

Fonseca on Horseback A161

Manuel Deodoro da Fonseca and President Vargas — A162

Wmk. 249
1939, Nov. 15   Photo.   Rouletted
484 A160 400r deep green   .30   .20
485 A162 1200r chocolate   .75   .30

Engr.   Perf. 11
486 A161 800r gray black   .45   .30
     Nos. 484-486 (3)   1.50   .80
50th anniv. of the Proclamation of the Republic.

President Roosevelt, President Vargas and Map of the Americas A163

1940, Apr. 14
487 A163 400r slate blue   .70   .40
Pan American Union, 50th anniversary.

Types of 1920-33
1940-41   Typo.   Wmk. 264   Perf. 11
488 A75   10r red brown   .15   .15
489 A75   20r dull violet   .25   .25
489A A75   50r blue grn ('41)   .85   1.25
490 A75   100r yellow org   1.00   .15
491 A116 200r violet   .75   .15
492 A76   400r ultra   4.50   .15
493 A76   600r dull orange   4.50   .15
494 A76 1000r turq blue   11.00   .15
     Nos. 488-494 (8)   23.00   2.50

Map of Brazil — A164

1940, Sept. 7   Engr.
495 A164 400r carmine   .40   .20
  a.   Unwmk.   50.00   30.00
9th Brazilian Congress of Geography held at Florianopolis.

Victoria Regia Water Lily — A165

President Vargas — A166

Relief Map of Brazil — A167

1940, Oct. 30   Wmk. 249   Perf. 11
Without Gum
496 A165 1000r dull violet   .85   .85
  a.   Sheet of 10   8.50   25.00
497 A166 5000r red   6.75   5.00
  a.   Sheet of 10   72.50   110.00
498 A167 10,000r slate blue   7.50   2.50
  a.   Sheet of 10   100.00   110.00
     Nos. 496-498 (3)   15.10   8.35
New York World's Fair.
All three sheets exist unwatermarked and also with papermaker's watermark of large globe and "AMERICA BANK" in sheet. A few imperforate sheets also exist.

BRAZIL

Joaquim Machado de Assis — A168

Pioneers and Buildings of Porto Alegre — A169

1940, Nov. 1
499 A168 400r black .50 .20
Birth centenary of Joaquim Maria Machado de Assis, poet and novelist.

1940, Nov. 2 Wmk. 264
500 A169 400r green .40 .15
Colonization of Porto Alegre, bicent.

Proclamation of King John IV of Portugal A173

1940, Dec. 1 Wmk. 249
501 A173 1200r blue black 1.00 .25
800th anniv. of Portuguese independence and 300th anniv. of the restoration of the monarchy.
No. 501 was also printed on paper with papermaker's watermark of large globe and "AMERICA BANK." Unwatermarked copies are from these sheets.

Brazilian Flags and Head of Liberty — A175

Wmk. 256
1940, Dec. 18 Engr. Perf. 11
502 A175 400r dull violet .50 .20
 b. Unwmkd. 40.00 40.00
Wmk. 245
502A A175 400r dull violet 40.00 40.00
10th anniv. of the inauguration of President Vargas.

Calendar Sheet and Inscription "Day of the Fifth General Census of Brazil" — A176

Wmk. 256
1941, Jan. 14 Typo. Perf. 11
503 A176 400r blue & red .40 .20
Wmk. 245
504 A176 400r blue & red 3.00 .80
Fifth general census of Brazil.

King Alfonso Henriques A177

Father Antonio Vieira A178

Salvador Corrêia de Sa e Benevides — A179

President Carmona of Portugal and President Vargas A180

Wmk. 264
1940-41 Photo. Rouletted
504A A177 200r pink .15 .15
505 A178 400r ultra .20 .15
506 A179 800r brt violet .25 .15
506A A180 5400r slate grn 1.65 .70
Wmk. 249
507 A177 200r pink 5.25 3.25
507A A178 400r ultra 25.00 8.50
508 A180 5400r slate grn 2.50 1.25
Nos. 504A-508 (7) 35.00 14.15
Portuguese Independence, 800th anniv.
For surcharge and overprint see Nos. C45, C47.

Jose de Anchieta A181

Amador Bueno A182

Wmk. 264
1941, Aug. 1 Engr. Perf. 11
509 A181 1000r gray violet 1.00 .50
Society of Jesus, 400th anniversary.

1941, Oct. 20 Perf. 11½
510 A182 400r black .50 .30
300th anniv. of the acclamation of Amador Bueno (1572-1648) as king of Sao Paulo.

Air Force Emblem A183

1941, Oct. 20 Perf. 11
511 A183 5400r slate green 3.00 2.00
Issued in connection with Aviation Week, as propaganda for the Brazilian Air Force.

Petroleum — A184

Agriculture — A185

Steel Industry — A186

Commerce — A187

Marshal Peixoto — A188

Count of Porto Alegre — A189

Admiral J. A. C. Maurity — A190

"Armed Forces" — A191

Vargas — A192

1941-42 Wmk. 264 Typo. Perf. 11
512 A184 10r yellow brn .20 .20
513 A184 20r olive grn .15 .15
514 A184 50r olive bis .15 .15
515 A184 100r blue grn .20 .15
516 A185 200r brown org .45 .15
517 A185 300r lilac rose .25 .15
518 A185 400r grnsh blue .65 .15
519 A185 500r salmon .30 .15
520 A186 600r violet .65 .15
521 A186 700r brt rose .30 .15
522 A186 1000r gray 1.75 .15
523 A186 1200r dl blue 3.00 .15
524 A187 2000r gray vio 2.50 .15
 Engr.
525 A188 5000r blue 5.50 .15
526 A189 10,000r rose red 7.00 .20
527 A190 20,000r dp brown 7.00 .35
528 A191 50,000r red ('42) 27.50 21.00
529 A192 100,000r blue ('42) .60 9.00
Nos. 512-529 (18) 58.15 32.70
Nos. 512 to 527 and later issues come on thick or thin paper. The stamps on both papers also exist with three vertical green lines printed on the back, a control mark.
See Nos. 541-587, 592-593, 656-670.

Bernardino de Campos A193

Prudente de Morais A194

1942, May 25
533 A193 1000r red 1.25 .40
534 A194 1200r blue 3.00 .25
100th anniversary of the birth of Bernardino de Campos and Prudente de Morais, lawyers and statesmen of Brazil.

Head of Indo-Brazilian Bull — A195

1942, May 1 Wmk. 264 Perf. 11½
535 A195 200r blue .45 .25
536 A195 400r orange brn .45 .25
 a. Wmk. 267 45.00 45.00
2nd Agriculture and Livestock Show of Central Brazil held at Uberaba.

Outline of Brazil and Torch of Knowledge A196

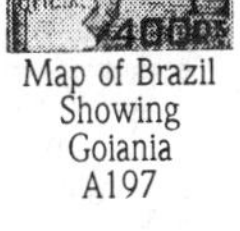

Map of Brazil Showing Goiania A197

Wmk. 264
1942, July 5 Typo. Perf. 11
537 A196 400r orange brn .30 .25
8th Brazilian Congress of Education.

1942, July 5
538 A197 400r lt violet .40 .30
Founding of Goiania city.

Seal of Congress — A198

1942, Sept. 20 Wmk. 264
539 A198 400r olive bister .25 .20
 a. Wmk. 267 25.00 12.50
4th Natl. Eucharistic Cong. at Sao Paulo.

Types of 1941-42
1942-47 Wmk. 245 Perf. 11
541 A184 20r olive green .15 .40
542 A184 50r olive bister .15 .15
543 A184 100r blue grn .40 .40
544 A185 200r brown org .65 .50
545 A185 400r grnsh blue .40 .15
546 A186 600r lt violet 3.00 .15
547 A186 700r brt rose .35 .80
548 A186 1200r dl blue 1.25 .15
549 A187 2000r gray vio ('47) 9.00 9.00
 Engr.
550 A188 5000r blue 10.00 .40
551 A189 10,000r rose red 6.00 1.50
552 A190 20,000r dp brn ('47) 4.50 .45
553 A192 100,000r blue 3.50 8.00
Nos. 541-553 (13) 39.35 22.05

Types of 1941-42
1941-47 Typo. Wmk. 268 Perf. 11
554 A184 20r olive grn .20 .15
555 A184 50r ol bis ('47) .55 .55
556 A184 100r bl grn ('43) .20 .15
557 A185 200r brn org ('43) .20 .15
558 A185 300r lilac rose ('43) .15 .15
559 A185 400r grnsh bl ('42) .30 .15
560 A185 500r salmon ('43) .20 .15
561 A186 600r violet .60 .15
562 A186 700r brt rose ('45) .35 1.75
563 A186 1000r gray .65 .15
564 A186 1200r dp blue ('44) .85 .15
565 A187 2000r gray vio ('43) 3.00 .15
 Engr.
566 A188 5000r blue ('43) 4.25 .15
567 A189 10,000r rose red ('43) 8.50 .40
568 A190 20,000r dp brn ('42) 19.00 .45
569 A191 50,000r red ('42) 21.00 3.00
 a. 50,000r dark brown red ('47) 15.00 8.50
570 A192 100,000r blue .55 .55
Nos. 554-570 (17) 60.55 8.35

Types of 1941-42
1942-47 Typo. Wmk. 267
573 A184 20r ol grn ('43) .15 .15
574 A184 50r ol bis ('43) .15 .15
575 A184 100r bl grn ('43) .20 .15
576 A185 200r brn org ('43) .25 .25
577 A185 400r grnsh blue .25 .15
578 A185 500r sal ('43) 70.00 10.00
579 A186 600r violet ('43) .45 .30
580 A186 700r brt rose ('47) .35 3.50
581 A186 1000r gray ('44) 2.10 .15
582 A186 1200r dl bl 2.50 .15
583 A187 2000r gray vio 2.50 .15
 Engr.
584 A188 5000r blue 4.25 .15
585 A189 10,000r rose red ('44) 7.00 .60
586 A190 20,000r dp brn ('45) 8.50 .45
587 A191 50,000r red ('43) 25.00 5.25
Nos. 573-587 (15) 123.65 21.55

1942 Typo. Wmk. 249
592 A184 100r bl grn 4.00 2.50
593 A186 600r violet 4.00 .80

Map Showing Amazon River — A199

1943, Mar. 19 Wmk. 267 Perf. 11
607 A199 40c orange brown .35 .35
Discovery of the Amazon River, 400th anniv.

BRAZIL

Reproduction of Brazil Stamp of 1866 — A200

1943, Mar. 28		Wmk. 267
608 A200 40c violet		.50 .25
a. Wmk. 268		650.00

Centenary of city of Petropolis.

Adaptation of 1843 "Bull's-eye" A201

1943, Aug. 1	Engr.	Imperf.
609 A201 30c black		.45 .25
610 A201 60c black		.55 .25
611 A201 90c black		.45 .25
Nos. 609-611 (3)		1.45 .75

Cent. of the 1st postage stamp of Brazil. The 30c and 90c exist unwatermarked; values $25 and $65.

Souvenir Sheet

A202

Wmk. 281 Horizontally or Vertically
1943   Engr.   Imperf.
Without Gum

612 A202 Sheet of 3	7.50 6.75
a. 30c black	1.90 1.90
b. 60c black	1.90 1.90
c. 90c black	1.90 1.90

Ubaldino do Amaral A203

"Justice" A204

	Perf. 11, 12	
1943, Aug. 27	Typo.	Wmk. 264
613 A203 40c dull slate green		.40 .20
a. Wmk. 267		20.00 15.00

Birth centenary of Ubaldino do Amaral, banker and statesman.

1943, Aug. 30		Wmk. 267
614 A204 2cr bright rose		.70 .40

Centenary of Institute of Brazilian Lawyers.

Indo-Brazilian Bull — A205

1943, Aug. 30		Engr.
615 A205 40c dk red brn		.70 .40

9th Livestock Show at Bahia.

José Barbosa Rodrigues A206

1943, Nov. 13		Typo.
616 A206 40c bluish grn		.40 .20

Birth cent. of Jose Barbosa Rodrigues, botanist.

Charity Hospital, Santos A207

1943, Nov. 7		Engr.
617 A207 1cr blue		.40 .30

400th anniv. of Charity Hospital, Santos.

Pedro Americo de Figueirido e Melo (1843-1905), Artist-hero and Statesman — A208

Wmk. 267
1943, Dec. 16	Typo.	Perf. 11
618 A208 40c brown orange		.20 .20

Gen. A. E. Gomes Carneiro A209

1944, Feb. 9		Engr.
619 A209 1.20cr rose		.50 .35

50th anniversary of the Lapa siege.

Statue of Baron of Rio Branco — A210

1944, May 13		Typo.
620 A210 1cr blue		.40 .25

Statue of the Baron of Rio Branco unveiling.

Duke of Caxias A211

1944, May 13	Unwmk.	Perf. 12
	Granite Paper	
621 A211 1.20cr bl grn & pale org		.50 .30

Centenary of pacification of Sao Paulo and Minas Gerais in an independence movement in 1842.

YMCA Seal — A212

1944, June 7	Litho.	Perf. 11
	Granite Paper	
622 A212 40c dp bl, car & yel		.30 .20

Centenary of Young Men's Christian Assn.

Chamber of Commerce Rio Grande — A213

Wmk. 268
1944, Sept. 25	Engr.	Perf. 12
623 A213 40c lt yellow brn		.30 .25

Centenary of the Chamber of Commerce of Rio Grande.

Martim F. R. de Andrada A214

1945, Jan. 30		Perf. 11
624 A214 40c blue		.30 .25

Ccentenary of the death of Martim F. R. de Andrada, statesman.

Meeting of Duke of Caxias and David Canabarro A215

1945, Mar. 19		Photo.
625 A215 40c ultra		.30 .20

Pacification of Rio Grande do Sul, cent.

Globe and "Esperanto" A216

1945, Apr. 16		
626 A216 40c lt blue grn		.50 .25

10th Esperanto Congress, Rio, Apr. 14-22.

Baron of Rio Branco's Bookplate — A217

1945, Apr. 20	Wmk. 268	Perf. 11
627 A217 40c violet		.50 .25

Cent. of the birth of Jose Maria da Silva Paranhos, Baron of Rio Branco.

Tranquility — A218   Glory — A219

Victory A220

Peace A221

Cooperation A222

	Rouletted 7	
1945, May 8	Engr.	Wmk. 268
628 A218 20c dk rose vio		.15 .15
629 A219 40c dk carmine		.15 .15
630 A220 1cr dull orange		.35 .30
631 A221 2cr steel blue		.85 .45
632 A222 5cr green		1.65 .55
Nos. 628-632 (5)		3.15 1.60

Victory of the Allied Nations in Europe. Nos. 628-632 exist on thin card, imperf. and unwatermarked.

Francisco Manoel da Silva (1795-1865), Composer (in 1831) of the National Anthem — A223

Wmk. 245
1945, May 30	Typo.	Perf. 12
633 A223 40c brt rose		.45 .30
a. Wmk. 268		6.75 6.75

Bahia Institute of Geography and History A224

1945, May 30	Wmk. 268	Perf. 11
634 A224 40c lt ultra		.25 .20

50th anniv. of the founding of the Institute of Geography and History at Bahia.

Emblems of 5th Army and B.E.F.
A225   A226

BRAZIL

US Flag and Shoulder Patches — A227

Brazilian Flag and Shoulder Patches — A228

Victory Symbol and Shoulder Patches — A229

1945, July 18   Litho.
635	A225	20c multicolored	.15 .15
636	A226	40c multicolored	.15 .15
637	A227	1cr multicolored	.70 .60
638	A228	2cr multicolored	1.00 .60
639	A229	5cr multicolored	3.00 .70
		Nos. 635-639 (5)	5.00 2.00

Honoring the Brazilian Expeditionary Force and the US 5th Army Battle against the Axis in Italy.

Radio Tower and Map — A230

1945, Sept. 3   Engr.
640 A230 1.20cr gray   .45 .25

Third Inter-American Conference on Radio Communications.

No. 640 was reproduced on a souvenir card with blue background and inscriptions. Size: 145x161mm.

A 40c lilac stamp, picturing the International Bridge between Argentina and Brazil and portraits of Presidents Justo and Vargas, was prepared late in 1945. It was not issued, but later was sold, without postal value, to collectors. Value, 15 cents.

Admiral Luiz Felipe Saldanha da Gama (1846-1895) A231

1946, Apr. 7
641 A231 40c gray black   .25 .25

Princess Isabel d'Orleans-Braganca Birth Cent. — A232

1946, July 29   Unwmk.
642 A232 40c black   .25 .25

Post Horn, V and Envelope — A233

Post Office, Rio de Janeiro — A234

Bay of Rio de Janeiro and Plane A235

             Wmk. 268
1946, Sept. 2   Litho.   Perf. 11
643 A233 40c blk & pale org   .15 .15

            Perf. 12½
       Engr.   Unwmk.
      Center in Ultramarine
644	A234	2cr slate	.50 .15
645	A234	5cr orange brn	2.50 .85
646	A234	10cr dk violet	2.75 .50

      Center in Brown Orange
647	A235	1.30cr dk green	.30 .35
648	A235	1.70cr car rose	.30 .35
649	A235	2.20cr dp ultra	.50 .50
		Nos. 643-649 (7)	7.00 2.85

5th Postal Union Congress of the Americas and Spain.
No. 643 was reproduced on a souvenir card. Size: 188x239mm. Sold for 10cr.

Liberty — A236

            Perf. 11x11½
1946, Sept. 18   Wmk. 268
650 A236 40c blk & gray   .25 .15
    a. Unwmkd.   150.00

Adoption of the Constitution of 1946.

Columbus Lighthouse, Dominican Republic A237

1946, Sept. 14   Litho.   Perf. 11
651 A237 5cr Prus grn   4.00 1.50

Orchid — A238

Gen. A. E. Gomes Carneiro — A239

1946, Nov. 8   Wmk. 268
652 A238 40c ultra, red & yel   .40 .30
    a. Unwmkd.   55.00

4th National Exhibition of Orchids, Rio de Janeiro, November, 1946.

            Perf. 10½x12
1946, Dec. 6   Engr.   Unwmk.
653 A239 40c deep green   .20 .20

Centenary of the birth of Gen. Antonio Ernesto Gomes Carneiro.

Brazilian Academy of Letters A240

1946, Dec. 14   Perf. 11
654 A240 40c blue   .25 .20

50th anniv. of the foundation of the Brazilian Academy of Letters, Rio de Janeiro.

Antonio de Castro Alves (1847-1871), Poet — A241

1947, Mar. 14   Litho.   Wmk. 267
655 A241 40c bluish green   .20 .20

Types of 1941-42, Values in Centavos or Cruzeiros

1947-54   Wmk. 267   Typo.   Perf. 11
656	A184	2c olive	.15 .15
657	A184	5c yellow brn	.15 .15
658	A184	10c green	.15 .15
659	A185	20c brown org	.15 .15
660	A185	30c dk lilac rose	.60 .15
661	A185	40c blue	.30 .15
b.		Wmk. 268	800.00 60.00
661A	A185	50c salmon	.60 .15
662	A186	60c lt violet	1.00 .15
663	A186	70c brt rose ('54)	.40 .15
664	A186	1cr gray	1.00 .15
665	A186	1.20cr dull blue	2.50 .15
a.		Wmk. 268	11.00 9.00
666	A187	2cr gray violet	4.00 .15
		Engr.	
667	A188	5cr blue	7.50 .15
668	A189	10cr rose red	7.50 .15
		Perf. 11, 13	
669	A190	20cr deep brown	15.00 .75
670	A191	50cr red	30.00 .50
		Nos. 656-670 (16)	71.00 3.35

The 5, 20, 50c also exist with perf. 12-13.

Pres. Gonzalez Videla of Chile — A242

1947, June 26   Unwmk.   Perf. 12x11
671 A242 40c dk brown orange   .20 .15

Visit of President Gabriel Gonzalez Videla of Chile, June 1947.
A souvenir folder contains four impressions of No. 671, and measures 6½x8¼ inches.

"Peace" and Western Hemisphere — A243

1947, Aug. 15   Perf. 11x12
672 A243 1.20cr blue   .20 .15

Inter-American Defense Conference at Rio de Janeiro, August-September, 1947.

Pres. Harry S Truman, Map and Statue of Liberty A244

1947, Sept. 1   Typo.   Perf. 12x11
673 A244 40c ultra   .20 .15

Visit of US President Harry S Truman to Brazil, Sept. 1947.

Pres. Eurico Gaspar Dutra — A245

Mother and Child — A246

                Wmk. 268
1947, Sept. 7   Engr.   Perf. 11
674	A245	20c green	.15 .15
675	A245	40c rose carmine	.15 .15
676	A245	1.20cr deep blue	.25 .15
		Nos. 674-676 (3)	.55 .45

The souvenir sheet containing Nos. 674-676 is listed as No. C73A. See No. 679.

1947, Oct. 10   Typo.   Unwmk.
677 A246 40c brt ultra   .20 .15

Issued to mark Child Care Week, 1947.

Arms of Belo Horizonte A247

Globe A248

1947, Dec. 12   Engr.   Wmk. 267
678 A247 1.20cr rose carmine   .30 .15

50th anniversary of the founding of the city of Belo Horizonte.

       Dutra Type of 1947
1948   Engr.   Wmk. 267
679 A245 20c green   1.50 1.50

Catalogue values for unused stamps in this section, from this point to the end of the section, are for Never Hinged items.

1948, July 10   Litho.
680 A248 40c dl grn & pale lil   .35 .15

International Exposition of Industry and Commerce, Petropolis, 1948.

Keep up to date with all new stamp issues by subscribing to the "Scott Stamp Monthly." Please call 1-800-572-6885 for more information.

BRAZIL

Arms of Paranagua — A249

Child Reading Book — A250

1948, July 29
681 A249 5cr bister brown   1.75   .50
300th anniversary of the founding of the city of Paranagua, July 29, 1648.

1948, Aug. 1
682 A250 40c green   .25   .20
National Education Campaign.
No. 682 was reproduced on a souvenir card. Size: 124x157mm.

Tiradentes A251

Symbolical of Cancer Eradication A252

1948, Nov. 12
683 A251 40c brown orange   .25   .20
200th anniversary of the birth of Joaquim José da Silva Xavier (Tiradentes).

1948, Dec. 14
684 A252 40c claret   .25   .25
Anti-cancer publicity.

Adult Student A253

1949, Jan. 3   Wmk. 267   Perf. 12x11
685 A253 60c red vio & pink   .25   .15
Campaign for adult education.

"Battle of Guararapes," by Vitor Meireles — A254

1949, Feb. 15   Perf. 11½x12
686 A254 60c lt blue   .95   .60
2nd Battle of Guararapes, 300th anniv.

Church of Sao Francisco de Paula — A255

Manuel de Nobrega — A256

1949, Mar. 8   Perf. 11x12
Unwmk.   Engr.
687 A255 60c dark brown   .20   .15
   a.   Souvenir sheet   30.00   30.00
Bicentenary of city of Ouro Fino, state of Minas Gerais.
No. 687a contains one imperf. stamp similar to No. 687, with dates in lower margin. Size: 70x89mm.

1949, Mar. 29   Imperf.
688 A256 60c violet   .25   .25
Founding of the City of Salvador, 400th anniv.

Emblem of Brazilian Air Force and Plane — A257

1949, June 18
689 A257 60c blue violet   .25   .25
Issued to honor the Brazilian Air Force.

Star and Angel — A258

1949   Wmk. 267   Litho.   Perf. 11x12
690 A258 60c pink   .20   .15
1st Ecclesiastical Cong., Salvador, Bahia.

Globe — A259

1949, Oct. 31   Typo.   Perf. 12x11
691 A259 1.50cr blue   .25   .15
75th anniv. of the UPU.

Ruy Barbosa A260

Unwmk.
1949, Dec. 14   Engr.   Perf. 12
692 A260 1.20cr rose carmine   .65   .30
Centenary of birth of Ruy Barbosa.

Joaquim Cardinal Arcoverde A. Cavalcanti, Birth Centenary — A261

1950, Feb. 27   Perf. 11x12
Litho.   Wmk. 267
693 A261 60c rose   .25   .20

Grapes and Factory A262

1950, Mar. 15   Perf. 12x11
694 A262 60c rose lake   .25   .20
75th anniversary of Italian immigration to the state of Rio Grande do Sul.

Virgin of the Globe — A263

Globe and Soccer Players — A264

1950, May 31   Perf. 11x12
695 A263 60c blk & lt bl   .25   .20
Establishment in Brazil of the Daughters of Charity of St. Vincent de Paul, cent.

1950, June 24
696 A264 60c ultra, bl & gray   .85   .50
4th World Soccer Championship.

Symbolical of Brazilian Population Growth A265

1950, July 10   Typo.   Perf. 12x11
697 A265 60c rose lake   .25   .20
Issued to publicize the 6th Brazilian census.

Dr. Oswaldo Cruz — A266

1950, Aug. 23   Litho.   Perf. 11x12
698 A266 60c orange brown   .25   .20
5th International Congress of Microbiology.

View of Blumenau and Itajai River — A267

1950, Sept. 9   Wmk. 267   Perf. 12x11
699 A267 60c bright pink   .25   .20
Centenary of the founding of Blumenau.

Amazonas Theater, Manaus A268

1950, Sept. 27
700 A268 60c light brn red   .20   .15
Centenary of Amazonas Province.

Arms of Juiz de Fora — A269

1950, Oct. 24   Perf. 11x12
701 A269 60c carmine   .25   .25
Centenary of the founding of Juiz de Fora.

Post Office at Recife — A270

1951, Jan. 10   Typo.   Perf. 12x11
702 A270 60c carmine   .20   .15
703 A270 1.20cr carmine   .30   .20
Opening of the new building of the Pernambuco Post Office.

Arms of Joinville — A271

Jean-Baptiste de La Salle — A272

1951, Mar. 9   Perf. 11x12
704 A271 60c orange brown   .25   .20
Centenary of the founding of Joinville.

1951, Apr. 30   Litho.
705 A272 60c blue   .25   .20
Birth of Jean-Baptiste de La Salle, 300th anniv.

Heart and Flowers — A273

Sylvio Romero — A274

1951, May 13   Engr.
706 A273 60c deep plum   .25   .20
Mother's Day, May 14, 1951.

1951, Apr. 21   Litho.
707 A274 60c dl vio brn   .20   .20
Romero (1851-1914), poet and author.

Joao Caetano, Stage and Masks — A275

1951, July 9   Perf. 12x11
708 A275 60c lt gray bl   .25   .20
1st Brazilian Theater Cong., Rio, July 9-13, 1951.

BRAZIL

Orville A. Derby — A276

First Mass Celebrated in Brazil — A277

1951, July 23   Perf. 11x12
709 A276 2cr slate   .35 .35
Centenary of the birth (in New York State) of Orville A. Derby, geologist.

1951, July 25
710 A277 60c dl brn & buff   .20 .16
4th Inter-American Congress on Catholic Education, Rio de Janeiro, 1951.

Euclides Pinto Martins A278

1951, Aug. 16   Perf. 12x11
711 A278 3.80cr brn & citron   1.50 .35
1st flight from NYC to Rio, 29th anniv.

Monastery of the Rock — A279

1951, Sept. 8
712 A279 60c dl brn & cream   .20 .20
Founding of Vitoria, 4th centenary.

Santos-Dumont and Model Plane Contest — A280

Dirigible and Eiffel Tower — A281

   Perf. 11x12
1951, Oct. 19   Wmk. 267   Litho.
713 A280 60c salmon & dk brn   .42 .35

   Unwmk.   Engr.
714 A281 3.80cr dk pur   1.25 .40

Week of the Wing and 50th anniv. of Santos-Dumont's flight around the Eiffel Tower.
In December 1951, Nos. 713 and 714 were privately overprinted: "Exposicao Filatelica Regional Distrito Federal 15-XII-1951 23-XII-1951." These were attached to souvenir sheets bearing engraved facsimiles of Nos. 38, 49 and 51, which were sold by Clube Filatelico do Brasil to mark its 20th anniversary. The overprinted stamps on the sheets were canceled, but 530 "unused" sets were sold by the club.

Farmers and Ear of Wheat — A282

1951, Nov. 10   Litho.   Wmk. 267
715 A282 60c dp grn & gray   .25 .25
Festival of Grain at Bage, 1951.

Map and Open Bible — A283

1951, Dec. 9   Perf. 12x11
716 A283 1.20cr brn org   .50 .35
Issued to publicize the Day of the Bible.

Queen Isabella — A284

Henrique Oswald — A285

1952, Mar. 10   Perf. 11x12
717 A284 3.80cr lt bl   .60 .30
500th anniversary of the birth of Queen Isabella I of Spain.

1952, Apr. 22
718 A285 60c brown   .25 .20
Oswald (1852-1931), composer.

Vicente Licinio Cardoso A286

Map and Symbol of Labor A287

1952, May 2
719 A286 60c gray bl   .25 .20
4th Brazilian Homeopathic Congress.

1952, Apr. 30
720 A287 1.50cr brnsh pink   .25 .20
5th International Labor Organization Conference for American Countries.

Gen. Polidoro da Fonseca — A288

Luiz de Albuquerque M. P. Caceres — A289

Portraits: 5cr, Baron de Capanema. 10cr, Minister Eusebio de Queiros.

   Unwmk.   Engr.   Perf. 11
1952, May 11
721 A288 2.40cr lt car   .35 .20
722 A288 5cr blue   2.25 .28
723 A288 10cr dk bl grn   2.25 .28
   Nos. 721-723 (3)   4.85 .76
Centenary of telegraph in Brazil.

   Perf. 11x12
1952, June 8   Litho.   Wmk. 267
724 A289 1.20cr vio bl   .25 .20
200th anniversary of the founding of the city of Mato Grosso.

Symbolizing the Glory of Sports — A290

1952, July 21   Perf. 12x11
725 A290 1.20cr dp bl & bl   .60 .40
Fluminense Soccer Club, 50th anniversary.

José Antonio Saraiva — A291

Emperor Dom Pedro — A292

1952, Aug. 16   Perf. 11x12
726 A291 60c lil rose   .25 .20
Centenary of the founding of Terezina, capital of Piaui State.

1952, Sept. 3   Wmk. 267
727 A292 60c lt bl & blk   .25 .20
Issued for Stamp Day and the 2nd Philatelic Exhibition of Sao Paulo.

Flag-encircled Globe — A293

1952, Oct. 24   Perf. 13½
728 A293 3.80cr blue   .85 .50
Issued to publicize United Nations Day.

View of Sao Paulo, Sun and Compasses A294

1952, Nov. 8   Litho.   Perf. 12x11
729 A294 60c dl bl, yel & gray grn   .25 .20
City Planning Day.

Father Diogo Antonio Feijo — A295

1952, Nov. 9   Perf. 11x12
730 A295 60c fawn   .25 .20

Rodolpho Bernardelli and His "Christ and the Adultress" A297

1952, Dec. 18   Perf. 12x11
732 A297 60c gray bl   .25 .20
Bernardelli, sculptor and painter, birth cent.

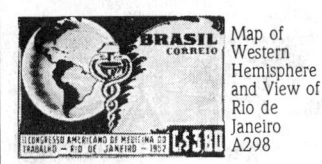

Map of Western Hemisphere and View of Rio de Janeiro A298

1952, Sept. 20
733 A298 3.80cr vio brn & lt grn   .80 .30
2nd Congress of American Industrial Medicine, Rio de Janeiro, 1952.

Arms and Head of Pioneer A299

Coffee, Cotton and Sugar Cane — A300

Designs: 2.80cr, Jesuit monk planting tree. 3.80cr and 5.80cr, Spiral, symbolizing progress.

1953, Jan. 25   Litho.   Perf. 11
734 A299 1.20cr ol brn & blk brn   .52 .35
735 A300 2cr olive grn & yel   1.75 .35
736 A300 2.80cr red brn & dp org   1.20 .20
737 A300 3.80cr dk brn & yel grn   1.00 .20
738 A300 5.80cr int bl & yel grn   .70 .20
   Nos. 734-738 (5)   5.17 1.30
400th anniversary of Sao Paulo.
Used copies of No. 734 exist with design inverted.

Ledger and Winged Cap — A301

1953, Feb. 22   Perf. 12x11
739 A301 1.20cr dl brn & fawn   .25 .20
6th Brazilian Accounting Congress.

Joao Ramalho — A302

   Perf. 11½
1953, Apr. 8   Wmk. 264   Engr.
740 A302 60c blue   .25 .20
Founding of the city of Santo Andre, 4th cent.

BRAZIL

Aarao Reis and Plan of Belo Horizonte — A303

1953, May 6   Photo.
741 A303 1.20cr red brn   .25   .20
   Aarao Leal de Carvalho Reis (1853-1936), civil engineer.

A304  / A305

1953, May 16
742 A304 1.50cr Almirante Saldanha   .40   .25
   4th globe-circling voyage of the training ship Almirante Saldanha.

1953, July 5   Photo.
   Joaquim Jose Rodrigues Torres, Viscount of Itaborai.
743 A305 1.20cr violet   .20   .16
   Centenary of the Bank of Brazil.

Lamp and Rio-Petropolis Highway — A306

1953, July 14
744 A306 1.20cr gray   .25   .20
   10th Intl. Congress of Nursing, Petropolis, 1953.

Bay of Rio de Janeiro — A307

1953, July 15
745 A307 3.80cr dk bl grn   .40   .20
   Issued to publicize the fourth World Congress of Baptist Youth, July 1953.

Arms of Jau and Map — A308

1953, Aug. 15   Engr.
746 A308 1.20cr purple   .25   .20
   Centenary of the city of Jau.

Ministry of Health and Education Building, Rio — A309

1953, Aug. 1
747 A309 1.20cr dp grn   .25   .20
   Day of the Stamp and the first Philatelic Exhibition of National Education.

1953, Aug. 21   Photo.
748 A310 60c vio bl   .25   .20
   Centenary of the death of Maria Quiteria de Jesus Medeiros (1792-1848), independence heroine.

Pres. Odria of Peru — A311  / Duke of Caxias Leading his Troops — A312

1953, Aug. 25
749 A311 1.40cr rose brn   .25   .20
   Issued to publicize the visit of Gen. Manuel A. Odria, President of Peru, Aug. 25, 1953.

Engr. (60c, 5.80cr); Photo.
1953, Aug. 25
Designs: 1.20cr, Caxias' tomb. 1.70cr, 5.80cr, Portrait of Caxias. 3.80cr, Arms of Caxias.
750 A312   60c dp grn   .32   .16
751 A312 1.20cr dp claret   .40   .16
752 A312 1.70cr slate grn   .40   .16
753 A312 3.80cr rose brn   .65   .16
754 A312 5.80cr gray vio   .65   .16
   Nos. 750-754 (5)   2.42   .80
   150th anniversary of the birth of Luis Alves de Lima e Silva, Duke of Caxias.

Quill Pen, Map and Tree — A313  / Horacio Hora — A314

1953, Sept. 12   Photo.
755 A313 60c ultra   .25   .20
   5th National Congress of Journalism.

1953, Sept. 17   Litho.   Wmk. 267
756 A314 60c org & dp plum   .25   .20
   Horacio Pinto de Hora (1853-1890), painter.

Pres. Somoza of Nicaragua — A315 / Auguste de Saint-Hilaire — A316

1953, Sept. 24   Photo.   Wmk. 264
757 A315 1.40cr dk vio brn   .25   .20
   Issued to publicize the visit of Gen. Anastasio Somoza, president of Nicaragua.

1953, Sept. 30
758 A316 1.20cr dk brn car   .25   .25
   Centenary of the death of Auguste de Saint-Hilaire, explorer and botanist.

Jose Carlos do Patrocinio — A317 / Clock Tower, Crato — A318

1953, Oct. 9   Photo.
759 A317 60c dk slate gray   .25   .20
   Jose Carlos do Patrocinio, (1853-1905), journalist and abolitionist.

1953, Oct. 17
760 A318 60c blue green   .25   .20
   Centenary of the city of Crato.

Joao Capistrano de Abreu — A319  / Allegory: "Justice" — A320

1953, Oct. 23
761 A319 60c dull blue   .20   .20
762 A319 5cr purple   .85   .85
   Joao Capistrano de Abreu (1853-1927), historian.

1953, Nov. 17
763 A320   60c indigo   .25   .20
764 A320 1.20cr dp magenta   .25   .20
   50th anniv. of the Treaty of Petropolis.

Farm Worker in Wheat Field — A321   / Teacher and Pupils — A322

1953, Nov. 29   Photo.   Perf. 11½
766 A321 60c dk green   .25   .20
   3rd Natl. Wheat Festival, Erechim, 1953.

1953, Dec. 14
767 A322 60c red   .25   .25
   First National Conference of Primary School Teachers, Salvador, 1953.

Zacarias de Gois e Vasconsellos — A323 / Alexandre de Gusmao — A324

Design: 5cr, Porters with Trays of Coffee Beans.

1953-54   Photo.
768 A323 2cr org brn & blk, buff ('54)   .65   .40
  a.   White paper   1.75   .40
769 A323 5cr dp org & blk   1.25   .40
   Centenary of the state of Parana.

1954, Jan. 13
770 A324 1.20cr brn vio   .25   .20
   Gusmao (1695-1753), statesman, diplomat and writer.

Symbolical of Sao Paulo's Growth — A325

Arms and View of Sao Paulo — A326

Designs: 2cr, Priest, settler and Indian. 2.80cr, José de Anchieta.

1954, Jan. 25   Perf. 11½x11
771 A325 1.20cr dk vio brn   .75   .50
  a.   Buff paper   1.75   1.00
Engr.
772 A325   2cr lilac rose   1.05   .60
773 A325 2.80cr pur gray   1.05   1.00
Perf. 11x11½
774 A326 3.80cr dl grn   1.25   .50
  a.   Buff paper   2.25   2.00
775 A326 5.80cr dl red   1.25   .60
  a.   Buff paper   5.00   .75
   Nos. 771-775 (5)   5.35   3.20
   400th anniversary of Sao Paulo.

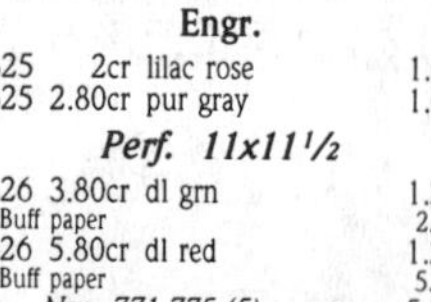

J. Fernandes Vieira, A. Vidal de Negreiros, A. F. Camarao and H. Dias — A327

BRAZIL

1954, Feb. 18   Perf. 11x11½   Photo.   Unwmk.
776 A327 1.20cr ultra   .25 .25

300th anniversary of the recovery of Pernambuco from the Dutch.

Sao Paulo and Minerva A328

1954, Feb. 24
777 A328 1.50cr dp plum   .25 .25

10th International Congress of Scientific Organizations, Sao Paulo, 1954.

Stylized Grapes, Jug and Map A329

Monument of the Immigrants A330

1954, Feb. 27   Photo.   Perf. 11½x11
778 A329 40c dp claret   .25 .20

Grape Festival, Rio Grande do Sul.

1954, Feb. 28
779 A330 60c dp vio bl   .25 .20

Unveiling of the Monument to the Immigrants of Caxias do Sul.

First Brazilian Locomotive A331

Perf. 11x11½
1954, Apr. 30   Unwmk.
781 A331 40c carmine   .25 .20

Centenary of the first railroad engine built in Brazil.

Pres. Chamoun of Lebanon — A332

1954, May 12   Photo.   Perf. 11½x11
782 A332 1.50cr maroon   .25 .25

Visit of Pres. Camille Chamoun of Lebanon.

Sao Jose College, Rio de Janeiro A333

J. B. Champagnat Marcelin A334

Apolonia Pinto A335

1954, June 6   Perf. 11x11½, 11½x11
783 A333 60c purple   .20 .15
784 A334 120c vio blue   .22 .20

50th anniversary of the founding of the Marist Brothers in Brazil.

1954, June 21   Photo.
785 A335 1.20cr bright green   .15 .15

Apolonia Pinto (1854-1937), actress.

Adm. Margues Tamandare — A336

Portraits: 2c, 5c, 10c, Admiral Margues Tamandare. 20c, 30c, 40c, Oswaldo Cruz. 50c, 60c, 90c, Joaquim Murtinho. 1cr, 1.50cr, 2cr, Duke of Caxias. 5cr, 10cr, Ruy Barbosa. 20cr, 50cr, Jose Bonifacio.

1954-60   Wmk. 267   Perf. 11x11½
786 A336 2c vio blue   .20 .15
787 A336 5c org red   .20 .15
788 A336 10c brt green   .20 .15
789 A336 20c magenta   .20 .15
790 A336 30c dk gray grn   .20 .15
791 A336 40c rose red   .35 .15
792 A336 50c violet   .25 .15
793 A336 60c gray grn   .20 .15
794 A336 90c orange ('55)   .35 .15
795 A336 1cr brown   .20 .15
796 A336 1.50cr blue   .20 .15
   a.   Wmk. 264   16.00 8.00
797 A336 2cr dk bl grn ('56)   .45 .15
798 A336 5cr rose lil ('56)   .35 .15
799 A336 10cr lt grn ('60)   .90 .15
800 A336 20cr crim rose ('59)   .90 .15
801 A336 50cr ultra ('59)   5.50 .20
   Nos. 786-801 (16)   10.65 2.45

See Nos. 890, 930-933.

Boy Scout Waving Flag (Statue) A337

Baltasar Fernandes, Explorer A338

1954, Aug. 2   Unwmk.   Perf. 11½x11
802 A337 1.20cr vio bl   .40 .25

Intl. Boy Scout Encampment, Sao Paulo.

1954, Aug. 15
803 A338 60c dk red   .25 .25

300th anniversary of city of Sorocaba.

Adeodato Giovanni Cardinal Piazza — A339

Our Lady of Aparecida, Map of Brazil — A340

1954, Sept. 2
804 A339 4.20cr red org   .50 .35

Visit of Adeodato Cardinal Piazza, papal legate to Brazil.

1954
Design: 1.20cr, Virgin standing on globe.
805 A340 60c claret   .30 .30
806 A340 1.20cr vio bl   .40 .30

No. 805 was issued for the 1st Cong. of Brazil's Patron Saint (Our Lady of Aparecida); No. 806, the cent. of the proclamation of the dogma of the Immaculate Conception. Both stamps also for the Marian Year.
Issue dates: 60c, Sept. 6; 1.20cr, Sept. 8.

Benjamin Constant and Hand Reading Braille A341

1954, Sept. 27   Photo.   Unwmk.
807 A341 60c dk grn   .25 .20

Centenary of the founding of the Benjamin Constant Institute.

River Battle of Riachuelo A342

Admiral F. M. Barroso A343

Dr. Christian F. S. Hahnemann A344

1954, Oct. 6   Perf. 11x11½, 11½x11
808 A342 40c redsh brown   .30 .20
809 A343 60c purple   .20 .20

Admiral Francisco Manoel Barroso da Silva (1804-82).

1954, Oct. 8   Perf. 11½x11
810 A344 2.70cr dk green   .30 .25

1st World Cong. of Homeopathic Medicine.

Nizia Floresta A345

Ears of Wheat A346

1954, Oct. 12
811 A345 60c lilac rose   .25 .20

Reburial of the remains of Nizia Floresta (Dio Nizia Pinto Lisboa), writer and educator.

1954, Oct. 22
812 A346 60c olive green   .20 .16

4th National Wheat Festival, Carazinho.

Basketball Player and Ball-Globe A347

Allegory of the Spring Games A348

1954, Oct. 23   Photo.
813 A347 1.40cr orange red   .30 .30

Issued to publicize the second World Basketball Championship Matches, 1954.

Perf. 11½x11
1954, Nov. 6   Wmk. 267
814 A348 60c red brown   .25 .20

Issued to publicize the 6th Spring Games.

San Francisco Hydroelectric Plant — A349

1955, Jan. 15   Perf. 11x11½
815 A349 60c brown org   .20 .15

Issued to publicize the inauguration of the San Francisco Hydroelectric Plant.

Itutinga Hydroelectric Plant — A350

1955, Feb. 3
816 A350 40c blue   .20 .15

Issued to publicize the inauguration of the Itutinga Hydroelectric Plant at Lavras.

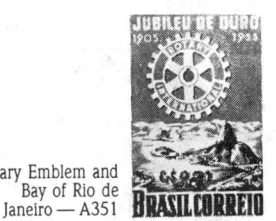

Rotary Emblem and Bay of Rio de Janeiro — A351

1955, Feb. 23   Perf. 12x11½
817 A351 2.70cr slate gray & blk   .85 .25

Rotary International, 50th anniversary.

BRAZIL

Fausto Cardoso Palace — A352

1955, Mar. 17   Perf. 11x11½
818 A352 40c henna brown   .25 .25
Centenary of Aracaju.

Aviation Symbols — A353

1955, Mar. 13   Photo.   Perf. 11½
819 A353 60c dark gray green   .16 .15
Issued to publicize the third National Aviation Congress at Sao Paulo, Mar. 6-13.

Arms of Botucatu — A354

1955, Apr. 14
820 A354   60c orange brn   .15 .15
821 A354 1.20cr brt green   .25 .15
Centenary of Botucatu.

Young Racers at Starting Line — A355

Perf. 11½
1955, Apr. 30   Photo.   Unwmk.
823 A355 60c orange brn   .25 .20
5th Children's Games.

Marshal Hermes da Fonseca — A356

Congress Altar, Sail and Sugarloaf Mountain — A357

1955, May 12   Wmk. 267
824 A356 60c purple   .20 .16
Marshal Hermes da Fonseca, birth cent.

Engraved; Photogravure (2.70cr)
1955, July 17   Unwmk.   Perf. 11½
Designs: 2.70cr, St. Pascoal. 4.20cr, Aloisi Benedetto Cardinal Masella.
825 A357 1.40cr green   .15 .15
826 A357 2.70cr deep claret   .25 .20
827 A357 4.20cr blue   .30 .15
    Nos. 825-827 (3)   .70 .50
36th World Eucharistic Cong. in Rio de Janeiro.

Girl Gymnasts — A358

1955, Nov. 12   Engr.
Granite Paper
828 A358 60c rose lilac   .20 .20
Issued to publicize the 7th Spring Games.

José B. Monteiro Lobato, Author — A359

1955, Dec. 8
Granite Paper
829 A359 40c dark green   .20 .15

Adolfo Lutz — A360

Lt. Col. Vilagran Cabrita — A361

1955, Dec. 18
Granite Paper
830 A360 60c dk green   .20 .15
Centenary of the birth of Adolfo Lutz, public health pioneer.

1955, Dec. 22   Photo.   Wmk. 267
831 A361 60c violet blue   .20 .15
First Battalion of Engineers, cent.

Salto Grande Hydroelectric Dam — A362

1956, Jan. 15   Unwmk.   Perf. 11½
Granite Paper
832 A362 60c brick red   .20 .15

Arms of Mococa — A363

"G" and Globe — A364

Perf. 11½
1956, Apr. 17   Wmk. 256   Photo.
833 A363 60c brick red   .16 .15
Centenary of Mococa, Sao Paulo.

1956, Apr. 14   Unwmk.
Granite Paper
834 A364 1.20cr violet blue   .16 .20
18th Intl. Geographic Cong., Rio, Aug. 1956.

Girls' Foot Race — A365

1956, Apr. 28   Photo.
Granite Paper
835 A365 2.50cr brt blue   .30 .20
6th Children's Games.

Plane over Map of Brazil — A366

1956, June 12   Wmk. 267   Perf. 11½
836 A366 3.30cr brt vio bl   .40 .20
National Airmail Service, 25th anniv.

Fireman Rescuing Child — A367

1956, July 2   Wmk. 264
837 A367 2.50cr crimson   .40 .25
   a. Buff paper   2.25 2.00
Centenary of the Fire Brigade.

Map of Brazil and Open Book — A368

1956, Sept. 8   Wmk. 267
838 A368 2.50cr brt vio bl   .30 .20
50th anniversary of the arrival of the Marist Brothers in Northern Brazil.

Church and Monument, Franca — A369

1956, Sept. 7   Engr.
839 A369 2.50cr dk blue   .30 .20
Centenary of city of Franca, Sao Paulo.

Woman Hurdler — A370

1956, Sept. 22   Photo.   Unwmk.
Granite Paper
840 A370 2.50cr dk car   .40 .20
Issued to publicize the 8th Spring Games.

Forest and Map of Brazil — A371

1956, Sept. 30   Wmk. 267   Perf. 11½
841 A371 2.50cr dk green   .25 .20
Issued to publicize education in forestry.

Baron da Bocaina — A372

1956, Oct. 8   Engr.   Wmk. 268
842 A372 2.50cr reddish brown   .25 .20
Centenary of the birth of Baron da Bocaina, who introduced the special delivery mail system to Brazil.

Marbleized Paper
Paper with a distinct wavy-line or marbleized watermark (which Brazilians call *marmorizado* paper) has been found on many stamps of Brazil, 1956-68, including Nos. 843-845, 847, 851-854, 858-858A, 864, 878, 880, 882, 884, 886-887, 896, 909, 918, 920-921, 925-928, 936-939, 949, 955-958, 960, 962-964, 978-979, 983, 985-987, 997-998, 1002-1003, 1005, 1009-1012, 1017, 1024, 1026, 1055, 1075, 1078, 1082, C82, C82a, C83-C87, C96, C99, C109.
Quantities are much less than those of stamps on regular paper.

Panama Stamp Showing Pres. Juscelino Kubitschek — A373

1956, Oct. 12   Photo.   Wmk. 267
843 A373 3.30cr green & blk   .40 .20
Issued on America Day, Oct. 12, to commemorate the meeting of the Presidents and the Pan-American Conference at Panama City, July 21-22.

Symbolical of Steel Production — A374

Perf. 11½
1957, Jan. 31   Wmk. 267   Photo.
844 A374 2.50cr chocolate   .25 .15
2nd expansion of the National Steel Company at Volta Redonda.

Joaquim E. Gomes da Silva — A375

1957, Mar. 1   Photo.   Unwmk.
Granite Paper
845 A375 2.50cr dk bl grn   .25 .15
Centenary of the birth (in 1856) of Joaquim E. Gomes da Silva.

Allan Kardec — A376

BRAZIL

Perf. 11½
1957, Apr. 18   Wmk. 268   Engr.
846 A376 2.50cr dk brown   .25 .15
Issued in honor of Allan Kardec, pen name of Leon Hippolyto Denizard Rivail, and for the centenary of the publication of his "Codification of Spiritism."

Boy Gymnast A377

1957, Apr. 27   Photo.   Unwmk.
Granite Paper
847 A377 2.50cr lake   .48 .25
7th Children's Games.

Pres. Craveiro Lopes — A378    Stamp of 1932 — A379

1957, June 7   Engr.   Wmk. 267
848 A378 6.50cr blue   .40 .20
Visit of Gen. Francisco Higino Craveiro Lopes, President of Portugal.

1957, July 9   Photo.
849 A379 2.50cr rose   .25 .15
25th anniv. of the movement for a constitution.

St. Antonio Monastery, Pernambuco A380

1957, Aug. 24   Engr.   Wmk. 267
850 A380 2.50cr deep magenta   .25 .15
300th anniv. of the emancipation of the Franciscan province of St. Antonio in Pernambuco State.

Volleyball A381    Basketball A382

1957, Sept. 28   Photo.   Perf. 11½
851 A381 2.50cr dull org red   .45 .25
Issued for the 9th Spring Games.

1957, Oct. 12
852 A382 3.30cr org & brt grn   .45 .25
2nd Women's International Basketball Championship, Rio de Janeiro.

Count of Pinhal and Sao Carlos A383

1957, Nov. 4   Wmk. 267   Perf. 11½
853 A383 2.50cr rose   .28 .25
Centenary of the city of Sao Carlos and honoring the Count of Pinhal, its founder.

Auguste Comte — A384

1957, Nov. 15
854 A384 2.50cr dk red brn   .25 .20
Centenary of the death of Auguste Comte, French mathematician and philosopher.

Radio Station A385

1957, Dec. 10   Wmk. 268
855 A385 2.50cr dk green   .20 .15
Opening of Sarapui Central Radio Station.

Admiral Tamandare and Warship A386

Design: 3.30cr, Aircraft carrier.

1957-58   Photo.
856 A386 2.50cr light blue   .25 .20
Engr.
857 A386 3.30cr green ('58)   .28 .20
150th anniversary of the birth of Admiral Joaquin Marques de Tamandare, founder of the Brazilian navy.

Coffee Plant and Symbolic "R" — A387

Perf. 11½
1957-58   Wmk. 267   Photo.
858 A387 2.50cr magenta   .52 .35
Unwmk.
Granite Paper
858A A387 2.50cr magenta ('58)   .45 .35
Centenary (in 1956) of the city of Ribeirao Preto in Sao Paulo state.

Dom John VI — A388

1958, Jan. 28   Engr.   Wmk. 268
859 A388 2.50cr magenta   .35 .25
150th anniversary of the opening of the ports of Brazil to foreign trade.

Bugler A389

1958, Mar. 18   Wmk. 267
860 A389 2.50cr red   .35 .25
Brazilian Marine Corps, 150th anniv.

Station at Rio and Locomotive of 1858 — A390    Court House — A391

Perf. 11½
1958, Mar. 29   Wmk. 267   Photo.
861 A390 2.50cr red brn   .35 .25
Central Railroad of Brazil, cent.

1958, Apr. 1   Engr.   Wmk. 256
862 A391 2.50cr green   .25 .15
150th anniv. of the Military Superior Court.

Emblem and Brazilian Pavilion A392

1958, Apr. 17   Wmk. 267
863 A392 2.50cr dk blue   .25 .25
World's Fair, Brussels, Apr. 17-Oct. 19.

High Jump — A393

1958, Apr. 20   Photo.   Unwmk.
Granite Paper
864 A393 2.50cr crimson rose   .25 .15
8th Children's Games.

Marshal Mariano da Silva Rondon A394

1958, Apr. 19   Engr.   Wmk. 267
865 A394 2.50cr magenta   .25 .15
Issued to honor Marshal Mariano da Silva Rondon and the "Day of the Indian."

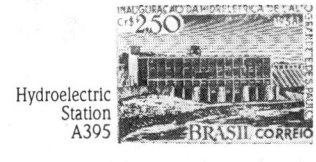

Hydroelectric Station A395

1958, Apr. 28   Wmk. 267   Perf. 11½
866 A395 2.50cr magenta   .25 .15
Opening of Sao Paulo State power plant.

National Printing Plant — A396

1958, May 22   Photo.
867 A396 2.50cr redsh brn   .20 .15
150th anniversary of the founding of the National Printing Plant.

Marshal Osorio — A397

1958, May 24
868 A397 2.50cr brt violet   .20 .15
150th anniversary of the birth of Marshal Manoel Luiz Osorio.

Pres. Ramon Villeda Morales — A398    Fountain — A399

1958, June 7   Engr.   Perf. 11½
869 A398 6.50cr dk green   1.25 .75
 a.   Wmk. 268   5.00 2.00
Visit of Pres. Ramon Villeda Morales of Honduras.

1958, June 13
870 A399 2.50cr dk green   .25 .15
Botanical Garden, Rio de Janeiro, 150th anniv.

Symbols of Agriculture A400    Prophet Joel A401

1958, June 18   Photo.
871 A400 2.50cr rose carmine   .25 .15
50th anniv. of Japanese immigration to Brazil.

1958, June 21   Engr.
872 A401 2.50cr dk blue   .25 .15
Bicentenary of the Cathedral of Bom Jesus at Matosinhos.

Stylized Globe — A402

1958, July 10   Photo.
873 A402 2.50cr dk brown   .20 .15
Intl. Investment Conference, Belo Horizonte.

Julio Bueno Brandao — A403

1958, Aug. 1   Wmk. 268   Perf. 11½
874 A403 2.50cr red brown   .25 .15
Centenary of the birth of Julio Bueno Brandao, President of Minas Gerais.

BRAZIL

Palacio Tiradentes (House of Congress) A404

1958, July 24   Engr.
875 A404 2.50cr sepia   .25 .15
47th Interparliamentary Conference, Rio de Janeiro, July 24-Aug. 1.

Presidential Palace, Brasilia A405

1958, Aug. 8   Photo.   Wmk. 267
876 A405 2.50cr ultra   .20 .15
Issued to publicize the construction of Brazil's new capital, Brasilia.

Freighters A406

1958, Aug. 22
877 A406 2.50cr blue   .25 .15
Brazilian merchant marine.

Joaquim Caetano da Silva — A407

1958, Sept. 2   Unwmk.
Granite Paper
878 A407 2.50cr redsh brn   .25 .15
Joaquim Caetano da Silva, scientist & historian.

Giovanni Gronchi — A408    Archers — A409

1958, Sept. 4   Engr.   Wmk. 268
879 A408 7cr dk blue   .50 .15
Visit of Italy's President Giovanni Gronchi to Brazil.

Perf. 11½
1958, Sept. 21   Photo.   Unwmk.
Granite Paper
880 A409 2.50cr red org   .35 .20
Issued to publicize the 10th Spring Games.

Have you found a typo or other error in this catalogue? Inform the editors via our web site or e-mail

sctcat@
scottonline.com

Elderly Couple — A410    Machado de Assis — A411

1958, Sept. 27   Wmk. 267
881 A410 2.50cr magenta   .25 .15
Day of the Old People, Sept. 27.

1958, Sept. 28   Unwmk.
882 A411 2.50cr red brn   .25 .15
50th anniversary of the death of Joaquim Maria Machado de Assis, writer.

Pres. Vargas and Oil Derrick A412

1958, Oct. 6   Wmk. 268
883 A412 2.50cr blue   .25 .15
5th anniv. of Pres. Getulio D. Vargas' oil law.

Globe — A413    Gen. Lauro Sodré — A414

Perf. 11½
1958, Nov. 14   Photo.   Wmk. 267
884 A413 2.50cr blue   .30 .15
7th Inter-American Congress of Municipalities.

1958, Nov. 15   Engr.
885 A414 3.30cr green   .25 .15
Cent. of the birth of Gen. Lauro Sodré.

UN Emblem — A415    Soccer Player — A416

1958, Dec. 26   Photo.   Perf. 11½
886 A415 2.50cr brt blue   .20 .15
10th anniv. of the signing of the Universal Declaration of Human Rights.

1959, Jan. 20
887 A416 3.30cr emer & red brn   .40 .20
World Soccer Championships of 1958.

Railroad Track and Map A417    Pres. Sukarno of Indonesia A418

1959, Apr.   Wmk. 267   Perf. 11½
888 A417 2.50cr dp orange   .25 .20
Centenary of the linking of Patos and Campina Grande by railroad.

1959, May 20
889 A418 2.50cr blue   .25 .15
Visit of President Sukarno of Indonesia.

Dom John VI — A419    Boy Polo Players — A420

Perf. 10½x11½
1959, June 12   Wmk. 267
890 A419 2.50cr crimson   .25 .15

1959, June 13   Perf. 11½
891 A420 2.50cr orange brn   .25 .15
9th Children's Games.

Loading Freighter A421    Organ and Emblem A422

1959, July 10
892 A421 2.50cr dk green   .25 .15
Issued to honor the merchant marine.

1959, July 16   Photo.
893 A422 3.30cr magenta   .25 .15
Bicentenary of the Carmelite Order in Brazil.

Joachim Silverio de Souza — A423    Symbolic Road — A424

1959, July 20   Perf. 11½
894 A423 2.50cr red brown   .25 .15
Birth centenary of Joachim Silverio de Souza, first bishop of Diamantina, Minas Gerais.

1959, Sept. 27   Wmk. 267
895 A424 3.30cr bl grn & ultra   .25 .15
11th International Roadbuilding Congress.

Woman Athlete — A425

1959, Oct. 4
896 A425 2.50cr lilac rose   .25 .15
11th Spring Games.

Map of Parana A426

1959, Sept. 27
897 A426 2.50cr dk green   .25 .15
Founding of Londrina, Parana, 25th anniv.

Globe and Snipes A427    Cross of Lusitania A428

1959, Oct. 22   Perf. 11½
898 A427 6.50cr dull grn   .20 .15
World Championship of Snipe Class Sailboats, Porto Alegre, won by Brazilian yachtsmen.

1959, Oct. 24   Engr.
899 A428 6.50cr dull blue   .25 .15
4th Intl. Conf. on Brazilian-Portuguese Studies, University of Bahia, Aug. 10-20.

Factory Entrance and Order of Southern Cross — A429    Corcovado Christ, Globe and Southern Cross — A430

1959, Nov. 19   Photo.
900 A429 3.30cr orange red   .20 .15
Pres. Vargas Gunpowder Factory, 50th anniv.

1959, Nov. 26   Perf. 11½
901 A430 2.50cr blue   .20 .15
Universal Thanksgiving Day.

Burning Bush — A431

1959, Dec. 24   Wmk. 267
902 A431 3.30cr lt grn   .20 .15
Centenary of Presbyterian work in Brazil.

BRAZIL

Piraja da Silva and Schistosoma Mansoni — A432

1959, Dec. 28
903 A432 2.50cr rose violet .20 .15
25th anniv. of the discovery and identification of schistosoma mansoni, a parasite of the fluke family, by Dr. Piraja da Silva.

Luiz de Matos — A433

1960, Jan. 3 Photo.
904 A433 3.30cr red brown .15 .15
Birth centenary of Luiz de Matos.

Zamenhof A434   Adél Pinto A435

1960, Mar. 10   Wmk. 267   Perf. 11½
905 A434 6.50cr emerald .20 .15
Lazarus Ludwig Zamenhof (1859-1917), Polish oculist who invented Esperanto in 1887.

1960, Mar. 19   Engr.   Wmk. 268
906 A435 11.50cr rose red .20 .15
Centenary of the birth of Adél Pinto, civil engineer and railroad expert.

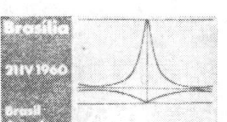

Presidential Palace, Colonnade A436

Design: 27cr, Plan of Brasilia (like #C98).

Perf. 11x11½
1960   Photo.   Wmk. 267
907 A436 2.50cr brt green .20 .15
Size: 105x46½mm
908 A436 27cr salmon .60 .60
Nos. 907-908,C95-C98 (6) 2.00 1.35
No. 907 for the inauguration of Brazil's new capital, Brasilia, Apr. 21, 1960.
No. 908 for the birthday of Pres. Juscelino Kubitschek and has a 27cr in design of No. C98, flanked by the chief design features of Nos. 907, C95-C97, with Kubitschek signature below. Issued in sheets of 4 with wide horizontal gutter.
Issued: 2.50cr, 4/21; 27cr, 9/12.

Grain, Coffee, Cotton and Cacao — A437    Paulo de Frontin — A438

Perf. 11½x11
1960, July 28   Wmk. 267
909 A437 2.50cr brown .20 .15
Centenary of Ministry of Agriculture.

1960, Oct. 12   Wmk. 268
910 A438 2.50cr orange red .20 .15
Cent. of the birth of Paulo de Frontin, engineer.

Woman Athlete Holding Torch — A439

1960, Oct. 18   Perf. 11½x11
911 A439 2.50cr blue grn .20 .15
12th Spring Games.

Volleyball and Net A440   Locomotive Wheels A441

Perf. 11½x11
1960, Nov. 12   Wmk. 268
912 A440 11cr blue .20 .15
International Volleyball Championships.

1960, Oct. 15   Perf. 11½x11
913 A441 2.50cr ultra .20 .15
10th Pan-American Railroad Congress.

Symbols of Flight A442

1960, Dec. 16   Photo.   Perf. 11½
914 A442 2.50cr brn & yel .15 .15
Intl. Fair of Industry and Commerce, Rio.

Emperor Haile Selassie — A443

1961, Jan. 31   Perf. 11½x11
915 A443 2.50cr dk brown .16 .15
Visit of Emperor Haile Selassie of Ethiopia to Brazil, Dec. 1960.

Map of Brazil, Open Book and Sacred Heart Emblem A444

Perf. 11x11½
1961, Mar. 13   Wmk. 268
916 A444 2.50cr blue .20 .15
50th anniv. of the operation in Brazil of the Order of the Blessed Heart of Mary.

Map of Guanabara A445

1961, Mar. 27   Wmk. 267
917 A445 7.50cr org brn .20 .15
Promulgation of the constitution of the state of Guanabara.

Arms of Agulhas Negras A446   Brazil and Senegal Linked on Map A447

Design: 3.30cr, Dress helmet and sword.

Perf. 11½x11
1961, Apr. 23   Wmk. 267
918 A446 2.50cr green .20 .15
919 A446 3.30cr rose car .15 .15
Sesquicentennial of the Agulhas Negras Military Academy.

1961, Apr. 28   Photo.
920 A447 27cr ultra .25 .20
Issued to commemorate the visit of Afonso Arinos, Brazilian foreign minister, to Senegal to attend its independence ceremonies.

View of Ouro Preto, 1711 A448

1961, June 6   Perf. 11x11½
921 A448 1cr orange .20 .20
250th anniversary of Ouro Preto.

War Arsenal A449

1961, June 20   Wmk. 256
924 A449 5cr dk red brn .25 .15
150th anniv. of the War Arsenal, Rio de Janeiro.

Coffee Bean and Branch A450   Rabindranath Tagore A451

Perf. 11½x11
1961, June 26   Wmk. 267
925 A450 20cr redsh brn .80 .25
8th Directorial Committee meeting of the Intl. Coffee Convention, Rio, June 26.

1961, July 28   Photo.   Wmk. 267
926 A451 10cr rose car .20 .15
Rabindranath Tagore, Indian poet, birth cent.

Stamp of 1861 and Map of English Channel A452

Design: 20cr, 430r stamp of 1861 and map of Netherlands.

1961, Aug. 1   Perf. 11x11½
927 A452 10cr rose .75 .20
928 A452 20cr salmon pink 2.00 .30
Centenary of 1861 stamp issue.

Portrait Type of 1954-60
Designs as Before
1961   Wmk. 268   Perf. 11x11½
930 A336 1cr brown .80 .50
931 A336 2cr dk bl grn 1.25 .50
932 A336 5cr red lilac 3.75 .30
933 A336 10cr emerald 7.25 .30
Nos. 930-933 (4) 13.05 1.60
1cr, 5cr and 10cr have patterned background.

Sun, Clouds, Rain and Weather Symbols — A453    Dedo de Deus Peak — A454

1962, Mar. 23   Perf. 11½x11
936 A453 10cr red brown .75 .30
World Meteorological Day, Mar. 23.

1962, Apr. 14   Photo.   Wmk. 267
937 A454 8cr emerald .20 .25
50th anniversary of the climbing of Dedo de Deus (Finger of God) peak.

Dr. Gaspar Vianna and Leishmania Protozoa A455

1962, Apr. 24   Perf. 11½x11
938 A455 8cr blue .25 .15
Discovery by Gaspar Oliveiro Vianna (1885-1914) of a cure for leishmaniasis, 50th anniv.

Henrique Dias A456

1962, June 18   Wmk. 267
939 A456 10cr dk vio brn .32 .15
300th anniversary of the death of Henrique Dias, Negro military leader who fought against the Dutch and Spaniards.

BRAZIL

Millimeter Gauge — A457

1962, June 26   *Perf. 11½x11*
940 A457 100cr car rose   .35 .20
Centenary of the introduction of the metric system in Brazil.

Sailboats, Snipe Class — A458

1962, July 21   Photo.   Wmk. 267
941 A458 8cr Prus grn   .20 .15
Issued to commemorate the 13th Brazilian championships for Snipe Class sailing.

Julio Mesquita A459

1962, Aug. 18   *Perf. 11x11½*
942 A459 8cr dull brown   .20 .15
Centenary of the birth of Julio Mesquita, journalist and founder of a Sao Paulo newspaper.

Empress Leopoldina — A460

1962, Sept. 7   *Perf. 11½x11*
943 A460 8cr rose claret   .20 .15
140th anniversary of independence.

Buildings, Brasilia A461

1962, Oct. 24   *Perf. 11x11½*   Wmk. 267
944 A461 10cr orange   .30 .15
51st Interparliamentary Conf., Brasilia.

Pouring Ladle — A462

1962, Oct. 26   *Perf. 11½x11*
945 A462 8cr orange   .20 .15
Inauguration of the Usiminas State Iron and Steel Foundry at Belo Horizonte, Minas Gerais.

UPAE Emblem A463

1962, Nov. 19   *Perf. 11x11½*
946 A463 8cr bright magenta   .20 .15
Founding of the Postal Union of the Americas and Spain, UPAE, 50th anniv.

Chimney and Cogwheel Forming "10" — A464

1962, Nov. 26   *Perf. 11x11½*
947 A464 10cr lt blue grn   .20 .15
Natl. Economic and Development Bank, 10th anniv.

Quintino Bocaiuva A465

Soccer Player and Globe A466

Perf. 11½x11
1962, Dec. 27   Photo.   Wmk. 267
948 A465 8cr brown org   .20 .15
Bocaiuva, journalist, 50th death anniv.

1963, Jan. 14
949 A466 10cr blue grn   .40 .15
World Soccer Championship of 1962.

Carrier Pigeon A467

1963, Jan.   Unwmk.   Litho.   *Perf. 14*
950 A467 8cr yel, dk bl, red & grn   .20 .15

Souvenir Sheet
Imperf
951 A467 100cr yel, dk bl, red & grn   1.25 3.00
300 years of Brazilian postal service.
Issue dates: 8cr, Jan. 25; 100cr, Jan. 31.

Severino Neiva — A468

Perf. 10½x11½
1963, Jan. 31   Photo.   Wmk. 267
952 A468 8cr brt vio   .20 .15

Radar Tracking Station and Rockets — A469

"Cross of Unity" — A470

Perf. 11½x11
1963, Mar. 15   Wmk. 268
953 A469 21cr lt ultra   .20 .15
Issued to publicize the International Aeronautics and Space Exhibition, Sao Paulo.

1963   Wmk. 267   *Perf. 11½x11*
954 A470 8cr red lilac   .20 .15
Vatican II, the 21st Ecumenical Council of the Roman Catholic Church.

"ABC" in Geometric Form — A471

Basketball Player — A472

1963, Apr. 22   Photo.   Wmk. 267
955 A471 8cr brt bl & lt bl   .16 .15
Education Week, Apr. 22-27, 3-year alphabetization program.

1963, May 15
956 A472 8cr dp lilac rose   .20 .15
4th International Basketball Championships, Rio de Janeiro, May 10-25, 1963.

Games Emblem A473

"OEA" and Map of the Americas A474

1963, May 22   *Perf. 11½x11*
957 A473 10cr car rose   .30 .15
4th Pan American Games, Sao Paulo.

1963, June 6
958 A474 10cr org & dp org   .30 .15
15th anniversary of the charter of the Organization of American States.

José Bonifacio de Andrada — A475

1963, June 13
959 A475 8cr dk brown   .15 .15
Bicentenary of the birth of José Bonifacio de Andrada e Silva, statesman.

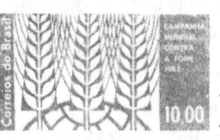

Wheat A476

Perf. 11x11½
1963, June 19   Photo.   Wmk. 267
960 A476 10cr blue   .30 .15
FAO "Freedom from Hunger" campaign.

Centenary Emblem A477

Joao Caetano A478

1963, Aug. 19   *Perf. 11½x11*
961 A477 8cr yel org & red   .25 .15
Centenary of International Red Cross.

1963, Aug. 24   *Perf. 11½x11*
962 A478 8cr slate   .20 .15
Death centenary of Joao Caetano, actor.

Symbols of Agriculture, Industry and Atomic Energy A479

Hammer Thrower A480

1963, Aug. 28
963 A479 10cr car rose   .25 .15
Atomic Development Law, 1st anniv.

1963, Sept. 13
964 A480 10cr gray   .42 .15
Intl. College Students' Games, Porto Alegre.

BRAZIL

Marshal Tito — A481

Compass Rose, Map of Brazil and View of Rio — A482

1963, Sept. 19
965 A481 80cr sepia .35 .30
Visit of Marshal Tito of Yugoslavia.

1963, Sept. 20
966 A482 8cr lt blue grn .16 .15
8th International Leprology Congress.

Oil Derrick and Storage Tank A483

1963, Oct. 3 Perf. 11x11½
967 A483 8cr dk slate grn .16 .15
10th anniv. of Petrobras, the natl. oil company.

"Spring Games" A484

1963, Nov. 5 Photo. Wmk. 267
968 A484 8cr yel & org .20 .20
1963 Spring Games.

Dr. Borges de Medeiros (1863-1962), Governor of Rio Grande do Sul — A485

1963, Nov. 29 Perf. 11½x11
969 A485 8cr red brown .16 .15

Sao Joao del Rei — A486

1963, Dec. 8 Perf. 11x11½
970 A486 8cr violet blue .16 .15
250th anniversary of Sao Joao del Rei.

Dr. Alvaro Alvim A487

1963, Dec. 19
971 A487 8cr dk gray .16 .15
Alvaro Alvim (1863-1928), X-ray specialist and martyr of science.

Viscount de Mauá A488

1963, Dec. 28 Perf. 11½x11
972 A488 8cr rose car .16 .15
Sesquicentennial of the birth of Viscount de Mauá, founder of first Brazilian railroad.

Mandacaru Cactus and Emblem A489

1964, Jan. 23 Photo. Wmk. 267
973 A489 8cr dull green .16 .15
Bank of Northeast Brazil, 10th anniv.

Coelho Netto — A490

Lauro Müller — A491

1964, Feb. 21 Perf. 11½x11
974 A490 8cr brt violet .16 .15
Birth centenary of Coelho Netto, writer.

1964, Mar. 8 Wmk. 267
975 A491 8cr dp orange .16 .15
Lauro Siverino Müller, politician and member of the Brazilian Academy of Letters, birth cent.

Child Holding Spoon A492

1964, Mar. 25 Perf. 11x11½
976 A492 8cr yel brn & yel .16 .15
Issued for "School Meals Week."

Chalice Rock — A493

Allan Kardec — A494

1964, Apr. 9 Engr. Perf. 11½x11
977 A493 80cr red orange .20 .15
Issued for tourist publicity.

1964, Apr. 18 Photo.
978 A494 30cr slate green .45 .15
Cent. of "O Evangelho" (Gospel) of the codification of Spiritism.

Heinrich Lübke — A495

Pope John XXIII — A496

Perf. 11½x11
1964, May 8 Photo. Wmk. 267
979 A495 100cr red brown .60 .18
Visit of President Heinrich Lübke of Germany.

1964, June 29 Wmk. 267
980 A496 20cr dk car rose .20 .18
a. Unwmkd. .20 .18
Issued in memory of Pope John XXIII.

Pres. Senghor of Senegal — A497

1964, Sept. 19 Wmk. 267
981 A497 20cr dk brown .25 .15
Visit of Leopold Sedar Senghor, President of Senegal.

Botafogo Bay and Sugarloaf Mountain A498

Perf. 11x11½, 11½x11
1964-65 Photo.
983 A498 15cr org & bl .30 .22
984 A498 100cr brt grn & red brn, yel .18 .16
985 A498 200cr black & red 1.75 .30
a. Souvenir sheet of 3 ('65) 4.75 4.00
Nos. 983-985 (3) 2.23 .68
4th cent. of Rio de Janeiro.
No. 985a contains three imperf. stamps similar to Nos. 983-985, but printed in brown. Sold for 320cr. Issued Dec. 30, 1965.
A souvenir card containing one lithographed facsimile of No. 984, imperf., exists, but has no franking value. Size: 100x125mm. Sold by P.O. for 250cr.

Pres. Charles de Gaulle A499

Pres. John F. Kennedy A500

1964, Oct. 13 Perf. 11½x11
986 A499 100cr orange brn .35 .15
Visit of Charles de Gaulle, President of France, Oct. 13-15.

1964, Oct. 24 Photo. Wmk. 267
987 A500 100cr slate .20 .15

"Prophet" by Lisboa — A501

1964, Nov. 18 Perf. 11½x11
988 A501 10cr slate .16 .15
150th death anniv. of the sculptor Antonio Francisco Lisboa, "O Aleijadinho" (The Cripple).

Antonio Goncalves Dias — A502

Designs: 30cr, Euclides da Cunha. 50cr, Prof. Angelo Moreira da Costa Lima. 200cr, Tiradentes. 500cr, Dom Pedro I. 1000cr, Dom Pedro II.

1965-66 Wmk. 267 Perf. 11x11½
989 A502 30cr brt bluish grn ('66) 2.00 .25
989A A502 50cr dull brn ('66) 1.50 .15
990 A502 100cr blue .60 .15
991 A502 200cr brown org 2.00 .15
992 A502 500cr red brown 6.00 .50
992A A502 1000cr sl bl ('66) 10.00 .50
Nos. 989-992A (6) 22.10 1.70

Statue of St. Sebastian, Guanataro Bay — A503

The Arches A504

Design: 35cr, Estacio de Sa (1520-67), founder of Rio de Janeiro.

1965 Photo. Perf. 11½
Size: 24x37mm
993 A503 30cr bl & rose red .30 .15

Lithographed and Engraved
Perf. 11x11½
994 A504 30cr lt bl & blk .30 .15

Photo. Perf. 11½
Size: 21x39mm
995 A503 35cr blk & org .18 .25
a. Souvenir sheet of 3 3.25 4.00
Nos. 993-995 (3) .78 .55
4th cent. of Rio de Janeiro. Issue dates: No. 993, Mar. 5. No. 994, Nov. 30. No. 995, July 28. No. 995a, Dec. 30.
No. 995a contains three imperf. stamps similar to Nos. 993-995, but printed in deep orange. Size: 130x79mm. Sold for 100cr.

Sword and Cross — A505

1965, Apr. 15 Wmk. 267 Perf. 11½
996 A505 120cr gray .30 .15
1st anniv. of the democratic revolution.

BRAZIL

Vital Brazil — A506

1965, Apr. 28 Wmk. 267 Perf. 11½
997 A506 120cr deep orange .30 .15
Centenary of birth of Vital Brazil, M.D.
A souvenir card containing one impression similar to No. 997, imperf., exists, printed in dull plum. Sold by P.O. for 250cr. Size: 114x180mm.

Shah of Iran — A507

1965, May 5 Photo.
998 A507 120cr rose claret .25 .15
Issued to commemorate the visit of Shah Mohammed Riza Pahlavi of Iran.

Marshal Mariano da Silva Rondon A508

1965, May 7 Engr.
999 A508 30cr claret .25 .15
Marshal Mariano da Silva Rondon (1865-1958), explorer and expert on Indians.

Lions' Emblem A509

1965, May 14 Photo.
1000 A509 35cr pale vio & blk .20 .15
12th convention of the Lions Clubs of Brazil, Rio de Janeiro, May 11-16.

ITU Emblem, Old and New Communication Equipment — A510

1965, May 21 Perf. 11½
1001 A510 120cr yellow & grn .30 .20
Centenary of the ITU.

Epitácio Pessoa — A511

Statue of Admiral Barroso — A512

1965, May 23 Photo.
1002 A511 35cr blue gray .20 .15
Epitácio da Silva Pessoa (1865-1942), jurist, president of Brazil, 1919-22.

1965, June 11
1003 A512 30cr blue .25 .15
Cent. of the naval battle of Riachuelo.
A souvenir card containing one lithographed facsimile of No. 1003, imperf., exists. Size: 100x139½mm.

José de Alencar and Indian Princess — A513

1965, June 24 Perf. 11½x11
1004 A513 30cr deep plum .25 .15
Centenary of the publication of "Iracema" by Josede Alencar.
A souvenir card containing one lithographed facsimile of No. 1004, printed in rose red and imperf., exists. Size: 100x141½mm.

Winston Churchill A514

1965, June 25 Perf. 11x11½
1005 A514 200cr slate .50 .25

Scout Jamboree Emblem — A515

1965, July 17 Photo.
1006 A515 30cr dull bl grn .30 .15
1st Pan-American Boy Scout Jamboree, Fundao Island, Rio de Janeiro, July 15-25.

ICY Emblem A516

1965, Aug. 25 Wmk. 267 Perf. 11½
1007 A516 120cr dl bl & blk .25 .15
International Cooperation Year, 1965.

Leoncio Correias A517

Emblem A518

1965, Sept. 1 Perf. 11½x11
1008 A517 35cr slate grn .25 .15
Leoncio Correias, poet, birth cent.

1965, Sept. 4
1009 A518 30cr brt rose .20 .15
Issued to publicize the Eighth Biennial Fine Arts Exhibition, Sao Paulo, Nov.-Dec., 1965.

Pres. Saragat of Italy — A519

1965, Sept. 11 Photo. Wmk. 267
1010 A519 100cr slate grn, *pink* .25 .15
Visit of Pres. Giuseppe Saragat of Italy.

Grand Duke and Duchess of Luxembourg — A520

1965, Sept. 17 Perf. 11x11½
1011 A520 100cr brn olive .25 .15
Visit of Grand Duke Jean and Grand Duchess Josephine Charlotte of Luxembourg.

Biplane — A521

1965, Oct. 8 Photo. Perf. 11½x11
1012 A521 35cr ultra .20 .15
3rd Aviation Week Philatelic Exhibition, Rio.
A souvenir card carries one impression of this 35cr, imperf. Size: 102x140mm. Sold for 100cr.

Flags of OAS Members A522

1965, Nov. 17 Perf. 11x11½
1013 A522 100cr brt bl & blk .25 .20
2nd meeting of OAS Foreign Ministers, Rio.

King Baudouin and Queen Fabiola of Belgium A523

1965, Nov. 18
1014 A523 100cr gray .25 .20
Visit of King and Queen of Belgium.

"Coffee Beans" — A524

Perf. 11½x11
1965, Dec. 21 Photo. Wmk. 267
1015 A524 30cr brown .30 .15
Brazilian coffee publicity.

Conveyor and Loading Crane A525

1966, Apr. 1 Perf. 11x11½
1016 A525 110cr tan & dk sl grn .25 .20
Opening of the new terminal of the Rio Doce Iron Ore Company at Tubarao.

Pouring Ladle and Steel Beam — A526

Prof. de Rocha Dissecting Cadaver — A527

Perf. 11½x11
1966, Apr. 16 Photo. Wmk. 267
1017 A526 30cr blk, dp org .25 .15
25th anniv. of the National Steel Company (nationalization of the steel industry).

1966, Apr. 26
1018 A527 30cr brt bluish grn .40 .15
50th anniv. of the discovery and description of Rickettsia prowazeki, the cause of typhus fever, by Prof. Henrique de Rocha Lima.

Battle of Tuiuti A528

Perf. 11x11½
1966, May 24 Photo. Wmk. 267
1019 A528 30cr gray grn .30 .15
Centenary of the Battle of Tuiuti.

Symbolic Water Cycle — A529

Pres. Shazar of Israel — A530

1966, July 1 Perf. 11½x11
1020 A529 100cr lt brn & bl .25 .20
Hydrological Decade (UNESCO), 1965-74.

1966, July 18 Photo. Wmk. 267
1021 A530 100cr ultra .30 .20
Visit of Pres. Zalman Shazar of Israel.

Imperial Academy of Fine Arts A531

Perf. 11½x11
1966, Aug. 12 Engr. Wmk. 267
1022 A531 100cr red brown .60 .20
150th anniversary of French art mission.

BRAZIL

Military Service Emblem — A532

1966, Sept. 6   Photo.   Perf. 11x11½
1023 A532 30cr yel, ultra & grn   .25   .15
a. With commemorative border   3.50   3.00
 New Military Service Law.
 No. 1023a issued in sheets of 4. It carries at left a 30cr, design A532, in deeper tones of yellow and ultramarine, Wmk. 264. Without gum. Sold for 100cr.

Ruben Dario — A533

Perf. 11½x11
1966, Sept. 20   Photo.   Wmk. 267
1024 A533 100cr brt rose lilac   .25   .15
 Ruben Dario (pen name of Felix Ruben Garcia Sarmiento (1867-1916), Nicaraguan poet, newspaper correspondent and diplomat.

Ceramic Candlestick from Santarém A534

1966, Oct. 6   Perf. 11x11½
1025 A534 30cr dk brn, salmon   .25   .15
 Centenary of Goeldi Museum at Belem.

Arms of Santa Cruz — A535

Perf. 11½x11
1966, Oct. 15   Photo.   Wmk. 267
1026 A535 30cr slate grn   .25   .15
 1st Natl. Tobacco Exposition, Santa Cruz.

UNESCO Emblem — A536

1966, Oct. 24   Engr.   Perf. 11½
1027 A536 120cr black   .75   .25
a. With commemorative border   6.00   2.50
 20th anniv. of UNESCO. No. 1027a issued in sheets of 4. It carries at right a design similar to No. 1027. Unwatermarked granite paper, without gum. Sold for 150cr.

Captain Antonio Correia Pinto and Map of Lages — A537

Cross of Lusitania and Southern Cross — A538

Perf. 11½x11
1966, Nov. 22   Photo.   Wmk. 267
1028 A537 30cr salmon pink   .25   .15
 Arrival of Capt. Antonio Correia Pinto, cent.

1966, Dec. 4   Perf. 11½
1029 A538 100cr blue green   .30   .15
 LUBRAPEX 1966 philatelic exhibition at the National Museum of Fine Arts, Rio.

Madonna and Child — A539

A540

Perf. 11½x11
1966, Dec.   Photo.   Wmk. 267
1030 A539 30cr blue green   .25   .15
 Perf. 11½
1031 A540 35cr salmon & ultra   .20   .20
a. 150cr salmon & ultra   2.50   3.00
 Christmas 1966.
 No. 1031a measures 46x103mm and is printed in sheets of 4. It is inscribed "Pax Hominibus" (but not "Brasil Correio") and carries the Madonna shown on No. 1031. Issued without gum.
 Issued: 30cr, 12/8; 35cr, 12/22; 150cr, 12/28.

Arms of Laguna A541

1967, Jan. 4   Engr.   Perf. 11½x11
1032 A541 60cr sepia   .20   .15
 Centenary of the Post and Telegraph Agency of Laguna, Santa Catarina.

Railroad Bridge A542

1967, Feb. 16   Photo.   Wmk. 267
1033 A542 50cr deep orange   .45   .20
 Centenary of the Santos-Jundiai railroad.

Black Madonna of Czestochowa, Polish Eagle and Cross — A543

1967, Mar. 12   Perf. 11½x11
1034 A543 50cr yel, bl & rose red   .35   .20
 Adoption of Christianity in Poland, 1,000th anniv.

Research Rocket A544

Anita Garibaldi A545

1967, Mar. 23   Perf. 11½x11
1035 A544 50cr blk & brt bl   .60   .30
 World Meteorological Day, March 23.

Perf. 11x11½
1967-69   Photo.   Wmk. 267
 Portraits: 1c, Mother Joana Angelica. 2c, Marilia de Dirceu. 3c, Dr. Rita Lobato. 6c, Ana Neri. 10c, Darcy Vargas.
1036 A545 1c dp ultra   .15   .15
1037 A545 2c red brn   .15   .15
1038 A545 3c brt grn   .18   .15
1039 A545 5c black   .35   .15
1040 A545 6c brown   .35   .15
1041 A545 10c dk slate grn   1.10   .30
   Nos. 1036-1041 (6)   2.28   1.05
 Issued: 1c, May 3; 2c, Aug. 14; 3c, June 7; 5c, Apr. 14; 6c, May 14, 1967; 10c, June 18, 1969.

VARIG Airlines A546

Madonna and Child, by Robert Feruzzi A548

Lions Emblem and Globes A547

1967, May 8   Perf. 11½x11
1046 A546 6c brt bl & blk   .30   .25
 40th anniversary of VARIG Airlines.

1967, May 9   Engr.   Perf. 11x11½
1047 A547 6c green   .30   .25
a. Souvenir sheet   2.50   3.00
 50th anniv. of Lions Intl. No. 1047a contains one imperf. stamp similar to No. 1047. Sold for 15c.

1967, May 14   Photo.   Perf. 11½x11
1048 A548 5c violet   .25   .20
a. 15c Souvenir sheet   2.25   2.25
 Mother's Day. No. 1048a contains one 15c imperf. stamp in design of No. 1048.

Prince Akihito and Princess Michiko A549

1967, May 25   Perf. 11x11½
1049 A549 10c black & pink   .30   .20
 Visit to Brazil of Crown Prince Akihito and Princess Michiko of Japan.

Carrier Pigeon and Radar Screen A550

Brother Vicente do Salvador A551

Perf. 11½x11
1967, June 20   Photo.   Wmk. 267
1050 A550 10c sl & brt pink   .25   .20
 Issued to commemorate the opening of the Communications Ministry in Brasilia.

1967, June 28   Engr.
1051 A551 5c brown   .25   .20
 400th birth anniv. of Brother Vicente do Salvador (1564-1636), founder of Franciscan convent in Rio de Janeiro, and historian.

Boy, Girl and 4-S Emblem A552

1967, July 12   Photo.   Perf. 11½
1052 A552 5c green & blk   .25   .20
 National 4-S (4-H) Day.

Möbius Strip A553

1967, July 21   Perf. 11x11½
1053 A553 5c brt bl & blk   .25   .20
 6th Brazilian Mathematical Congress.

Fish — A554

1967, Aug. 1   Perf. 11½
1054 A554 5c slate   .30   .20
 Bicentenary of city of Piracicaba.

Values quoted in this catalogue are for stamps graded Very Fine and with no faults. An illustrated guide to grade is provided in the "Catalogue Information" section of the Introduction.

Golden Rose and Papal Arms — A555

1967, Aug. 15
1055 A555 20c mag & yel   1.00   .40
Offering of a golden rose by Pope Paul VI to the Virgin Mary of Fatima (Our Lady of Peace), Patroness of Brazil.

General Sampaio A556

King Olaf of Norway A557

1967, Aug. 25   Engr.   Perf. 11½x11
1056 A556 5c blue   .25   .20
Issued to honor General Antonio de Sampaio, hero of the Battle of Tutui.

1967, Sept. 8   Photo.
1057 A557 10c brown org   .25   .20
Visit of King Olaf of Norway.

Sun over Sugar Loaf, Botafogo Bay A558

Nilo Peçanha A559

Photogravure and Embossed
1967, Sept. 25   Wmk. 267   Perf. 11½
1058 A558 10c blk & dp org   .25   .20
22nd meeting of the Intl. Monetary Fund, Intl. Bank for Reconstruction and Development, Intl. Financial Corporation and Intl. Development Assoc.

     Perf. 11½x11
1967, Oct. 1   Photo.   Wmk. 267
1059 A559 5c brown violet   .25   .20
Peçanha (1867-1924), Pres. of Brazil 1909-10.

Virgin of the Apparition and Basilica of Aparecida A560

Cockerel, Festival Emblem A561

1967, Oct. 11   Perf. 11½
1060 A560 5c ultra & dl yel   .30   .20
    a.   Souvenir sheet of 2   3.25   3.25
250th anniv. of the discovery of the statue of Our Lady of the Apparition, now in the National Basilica of the Apparition at Aparecida do Norte.
No. 1060a contains imperf. 5c and 10c stamps similar to No. 1060. Issued Dec. 27, 1967, for Christmas.

Engraved and Photogravure
1967, Oct. 16   Perf. 11½x11
1061 A561 20c black & multi   .50   .40
Second International Folksong Festival.

Balloon, Plane and Rocket A562

     Perf. 11x11½
1967, Oct. 18   Photo.   Unwmk.
1062 A562 10c blue   .50   .30
    a.   15c souvenir sheet   4.50   4.50
Week of the Wing, Oct. 18-23. No. 1062a contains one imperf. 15c stamp similar to No. 1062 and was issued Oct. 23.

Pres. Arthur Bernardes — A563

Portraits of Brazilian Presidents: 20c, Campos Salles. 50c, Wenceslau Pereira Gomes Braz. 1cr, Washington Pereira de Souza Luiz. 2cr, Castello Branco.

     Perf. 11x11½
1967-68   Photo.   Wmk. 267
1063 A563 10c blue   .24   .20
1064 A563 20c dk red brn   .75   .20
     Engr.
1065 A563 50c black ('68)   3.75   .30
1066 A563 1cr lil rose ('68)   6.00   .30
1067 A563 2cr emerald ('68)   1.10   .30
   Nos. 1063-1067 (5)   11.84   1.30

Carnival of Rio — A564

Ships, Anchor and Sailor — A565

1967, Nov. 22   Perf. 11½x11
1070 A564 10c lem, ultra & pink   .30   .20
    a.   15c souvenir sheet   3.50   4.50
Issued for International Tourist Year, 1967. No. 1070a contains a 15c imperf. stamp in design of No. 1070. Issued Nov. 24.

1967, Dec. 6
1071 A565 10c ultra   .30   .25
Issued for Navy Week.

Christmas Decorations A566

1967, Dec. 8   Perf. 11½
1072 A566 5c car, yel & bl   .25   .20
Christmas 1967.

Olavo Bilac, Planes, Tank and Aircraft Carrier A567

     Perf. 11x11½
1967, Dec. 16   Photo.   Wmk. 267
1073 A567 5c brt blue & yel   .30   .20
Issued for Reservists' Day and to honor Olavo Bilac, sponsor of compulsory military service.

Rodrigues de Carvalho — A568

1967, Dec. 18   Engr.   Perf. 11½x11
1074 A568 10c green   .25   .20
Cent. of the birth of Rodrigues de Carvalho, poet and lawyer.

Orlando Rangel A569

1968, Feb. 29   Photo.   Perf. 11x11½
1075 A569 5c lt grnsh bl & blk   .35   .25
Orlando de Fonseca Rangel, pioneer of pharmaceutical industry in Brazil, birth cent.

Virgin of Paranagua and Diver A570

Map of Brazil Showing Manaus A571

1968, Mar. 9   Perf. 11½x11
1076 A570 10c dk sl grn & brt yel grn   .35   .25
250th anniversary of the first underwater explorations at Paranagua.

1968, Mar. 13   Photo.   Wmk. 267
1077 A571 10c yel, grn & red   .35   .25
Free port of Manaus on the Amazon River.

Human Rights Flame A572

Paul Harris and Rotary Emblem A573

1968, Mar. 21   Perf. 11½x11
1078 A572 10c blue & salmon   .35   .25
International Human Rights Year.

1968, Apr. 19   Litho.   Unwmk.
     Without Gum
1079 A573 20c grn & org brn   1.25   .70
Paul Percy Harris (1868-1947), founder of Rotary International.

Pedro Alvares Cabral and his Fleet — A574

Design: 20c, First Mass celebrated in Brazil.

1968   Without Gum   Perf. 11½
1080 A574 10c multicolored   .55   .45
1081 A574 20c multicolored   .80   .60
500th anniversary of the birth of Pedro Alvares Cabral, navigator, who took possession of Brazil for Portugal.
Issue dates: 10c, Apr. 22; 20c, July 11.

College Arms — A575

1968, Apr. 22   Photo.   Wmk. 267
1082 A575 10c vio bl, red & gold   .55   .35
Centenary of St. Luiz College, Sao Paulo.

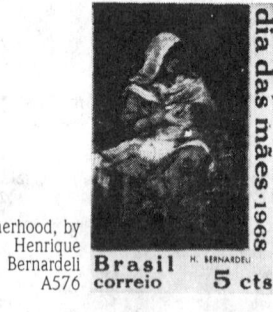

Motherhood, by Henrique Bernardelli A576

1968, May 12   Litho.   Unwmk.
     Without Gum
1083 A576 5c multicolored   .35   .25
Issued for Mother's Day.

Harpy Eagle — A577

Photogravure and Engraved
1968, May 28   Wmk. 267
1084 A577 20c brt bl & blk   1.50   .50
Sesquicentennial of National Museum.

BRAZIL

Brazilian and Japanese Women — A578

1968, June 28   Litho.   Unwmk.
Without Gum
1085 A578 10c yellow & multi   .60 .40
Issued to commemorate the inauguration of Varig's direct Brazil-Japan airline.

Horse Race A579

Perf. 11x11½
1968, July 16   Litho.   Unwmk.
Without Gum
1086 A579 10c multicolored   .35 .25
Centenary of the Jockey Club of Brazil.

Musician Wren A580

Designs: 10c, Red-crested cardinal, vert. 50c, Royal flycatcher, vert.

Perf. 11½x11, 11x11½
1968-69   Engr.   Wmk. in Sheet
Without Gum
1087 A580 10c multi ('69)   .45 .28
1088 A580 20c multicolored   .75 .28
1089 A580 50c multicolored   1.00 .55
  Nos. 1087-1089 (3)   2.20 1.11

Some stamps in each sheet of Nos. 1087-1089 show parts of a two-line papermaker's watermark: "WESTERPOST / INDUSTRIA BRASILEIRA" with diamond-shaped emblem between last two words. Entire watermark appears in one sheet margin. Issue dates: 10c, Aug. 20, 1969. 20c, July 19, 1968. 50c, Aug. 2, 1968.

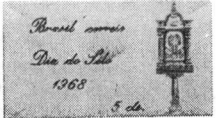

Mailbox and Envelope A581

Photogravure and Engraved
1968, Aug. 1   Wmk. 267   Perf. 11
1091 A581 5c citron, blk & grn   .20 .20
Stamp Day, 1968 and for 125th anniv. of the 1st Brazilian postage stamps.

Emilio Luiz Mallet A582

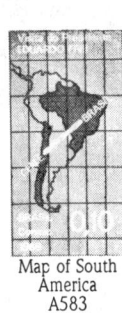

Map of South America A583

Perf. 11½x11
1968, Aug. 25   Engr.   Wmk. 267
1092 A582 10c pale purple   .20 .20
Issued to honor Marshal Emilio Luiz Mallet, Baron of Itapevi, patron of the marines.

1968, Sept. 5   Photo.
1093 A583 10c deep orange   .20 .20
Visit of President Eduardo Frei of Chile.

Seal of Portuguese Literary School — A584

Photogravure and Engraved
1968, Sept. 10   Perf. 11½
1094 A584 5c pink & grn   .20 .20
Centenary of Portuguese Literary School.

Map of Brazil and Telex Tape A585

1968, Sept.   Photo.   Perf. 11x11½
1095 A585 20c citron & brt grn   .50 .25
Linking of 25 Brazilian cities by teletype.

Soldiers' Heads on Medal — A586

Perf. 11½x11
1968, Sept. 24   Litho.   Unwmk.
Without Gum
1096 A586 5c blue & gray   .20 .25
8th American Armed Forces Conference.

Clef, Notes and Sugarloaf Mountain A587

1968, Sept. 30   Perf. 11½
Without Gum
1097 A587 6c blk, yel & red   .50 .30
Third International Folksong Festival.

Catalytic Cracking Plant — A588

1968, Oct. 4
Without Gum
1098 A588 6c blue & multi   .50 .40
Petrobras, the natl. oil company, 15th anniv.

Child Protection A589

Whimsical Girl — A590

Design: 5c, School boy walking toward the sun.

Perf. 11½x11, 11x11½
1968, Oct. 16   Litho.   Unwmk.
Without Gum
1099 A590 5c gray & lt bl   .32 .30
1100 A589 10c brt bl, dk red & blk   .40 .25
1101 A590 20c multicolored   .50 .25
  Nos. 1099-1101 (3)   1.22 .80
22nd anniv. of UNICEF.

Children with Books A591

1968, Oct. 23   Perf. 11x11½
Without Gum
1102 A591 5c multicolored   .25 .25
Issued to publicize Book Week.

UN Emblem and Flags — A592

1968, Oct. 24   Perf. 11½x11
Without Gum
1103 A592 20c black & multi   .45 .25
20th anniv. of WHO.

Jean Baptiste Debret, Self-portrait — A593

Perf. 11x11½
1968, Oct. 30   Litho.   Unwmk.
Without Gum
1104 A593 10c dk gray & pale yel   .35 .25
Jean Baptiste Debret, (1768-1848), French painter who worked in Brazil (1816-31). Design includes his "Burden Bearer."

Queen Elizabeth II A594

1968, Nov. 4   Perf. 11½
Without Gum
1105 A594 70c lt bl & multi   1.75 1.00
Visit of Queen Elizabeth II of Great Britain.

Francisco Braga — A595

Perf. 11½x11
1968, Nov. 19   Wmk. 267
1106 A595 5c dull red brn   .40 .25
Cent. of the birth of Antonio Francisco Braga, composer of the Hymn of the Flag.

Brazilian Flag — A596

1968, Nov. 19   Unwmk.   Perf. 11½
Without Gum
1107 A596 10c multicolored   .40 .30
Issued for Flag Day.

Clasped Hands and Globe A597

Perf. 11x11½
1968, Nov. 25   Typo.   Unwmk.
Without Gum
1108 A597 5c multicolored   .25 .25
Issued for Voluntary Blood Donor's Day.

Old Locomotive — A598

1968, Nov. 28   Litho.   Perf. 11½
Without Gum
1109 A598 5c multicolored   1.00 .50
Centenary of the Sao Paulo Railroad.

BRAZIL

Bell — A599

Francisco Caldas, Jr. — A600

Design: 6c, Santa Claus and boy.

1968 **Without Gum** *Perf. 11½x11*
1110 A599 5c multicolored .30 .25
1111 A599 6c multicolored .30 .25
Christmas 1968.
Issue dates: 5c, Dec. 12; 6c, Dec. 20.

1968, Dec. 13
Without Gum
1112 A600 10c crimson & blk .20 .20
Cent. of the birth of Francisco Caldas, Jr., journalist and founder of Correio de Povo, newspaper.

Map of Brazil, War Memorial and Reservists' Emblem
A601

Perf. 11x11½
1968, Dec. 16 Photo. Wmk. 267
1113 A601 5c bl grn & org brn .30 .20
Issued for Reservists' Day.

Radar Antenna
A602

Viscount of Rio Branco
A603

Perf. 11½x11
1969, Feb. 28 Litho. Unwmk.
Without Gum
1114 A602 30c ultra, lt bl & blk .70 .55
Inauguration of EMBRATEL, satellite communications ground station bringing US television to Brazil via Telstar.

1969, Mar. 16
Without Gum
1115 A603 5c black & buff .25 .25
José Maria da Silva Paranhos, Viscount of Rio Branco (1819-1880), statesman.

St. Gabriel — A604

1969, Mar. 24
Without Gum
1116 A604 5c multicolored .40 .25
Issued to honor St. Gabriel as patron saint of telecommunications.

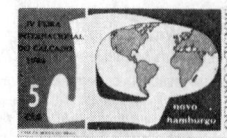

Shoemaker's Last and Globe — A605

Perf. 11x11½
1969, Mar. 29 Litho. Unwmk.
Without Gum
1117 A605 5c multicolored .25 .25
4th Intl. Shoe Fair, Novo Hamburgo.

Allan Kardec
A606

1969, Mar. 31 Photo. Wmk. 267
1118 A606 5c brt grn & org brn .25 .25
Allan Kardec (pen name of Leon Hippolyto Denizard Rivail, 1803-1869), French physician and spiritist.

Men of 3 Races and Arms of Cuiabá
A607

1969, Apr. 8 Litho. Unwmk.
Without Gum
1119 A607 5c black & multi .25 .25
250th anniversary of the founding of Cuiabá, capital of Matto Grosso.

State Mint — A608

1969, Apr. 11 *Perf. 11½*
Without Gum
1120 A608 5c olive bister & org .45 .35
Opening of the state money printing plant.

Brazilian Stamps and Emblem
A609

Perf. 11x11½
1969, Apr. 30 Litho. Unwmk.
Without Gum
1121 A609 5c multicolored .25 .25
Sao Paulo Philatelic Society, 50th anniv.

St. Anne, Baroque Statue — A610

1969, May 8 *Perf. 11½*
Without Gum
1122 A610 5c lemon & multi .50 .40
Issued for Mother's Day.

ILO Emblem
A611

Perf. 11x11½
1969, May 13 Photo. Wmk. 267
1123 A611 5c dp rose red & gold .25 .20
50th anniv. of the ILO.

Diving Platform and Swimming Pool — A612

Mother and Child at Window — A613

Lithographed and Photogravure
Perf. 11½x11
1969, June 13 Unwmk.
Without Gum
1124 A612 20c bis brn, blk & bl grn .55 .40
40th anniversary of the Cearense Water Sports Club, Fortaleza.

1969 Litho. *Perf. 11½*
Designs: 20c, Modern sculpture by Felicia Leirner. 50c, "The Sun Sets in Brasilia," by Danilo di Prete. 1cr, Angelfish, painting by Aldemir Martins.

Size: 24x36mm
1125 A613 10c orange & multi .55 .25
Size: 33x34mm
1126 A613 20c red & multi .55 .50
Size: 33x53mm
1127 A613 50c yellow & multi 1.90 1.25
Without Gum
1128 A613 1cr gray & multi 2.50 1.25
Nos. 1125-1128 (4) 5.50 3.25
Issued to publicize the 10th Biennial Art Exhibition, Sao Paulo, Sept.-Dec. 1969.

Angelfish
A614

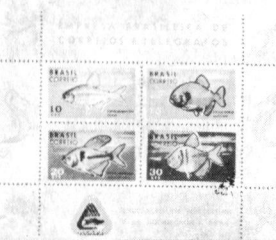

Fish — A615

Fish: 10c, Tetra. 15c, Piranha. No. 1130c, Megalamphodus megalopterus. 30c, Black tetra.

Perf. 11½
1969, July 21 Litho. Wmk. 267
1129 A614 20c multicolored .70 .40

Souvenir Sheet
1969, July 24 Unwmk. *Imperf.*
1130 A615 Sheet of 4 5.00 5.00
  a. 10c yellow & multi .90
  b. 15c bright blue & multi .90
  c. 20c green & multi .90
  d. 30c orange & multi .90
Issued to publicize the work of ACAPI, an organization devoted to the preservation and development of fish in Brazil.
No. 1130 contains 4 stamps, size: 38½x21mm.

L. O. Teles de Menezes
A616

Mailman
A617

Perf. 11½x11
1969, July 26 Photo. Wmk. 267
1131 A616 50c dp org & bl grn 1.25 1.00
Centenary of Spiritism press in Brazil.

1969, Aug. 1
1132 A617 30c blue 1.10 .90
Issued for Stamp Day.

Map of Brazil
A618

Gen. Tasso Fragoso
A620

Railroad Bridge
A619

Perf. 11½
1969, Aug. 25 Unwmk. Litho.
Without Gum
1133 A618 10c lt ultra, grn & yel .25 .20
Perf. 11x11½
1134 A619 20c multicolored .80 .40

Perf. 11½x11
Engr. Wmk. 267
With Gum
1135 A620 20c green .80 .50
Nos. 1133-1135 (3) 1.85 1.10
No. 1133 honors the Army as guardian of security; No. 1134, as promoter of development. No. 1135 the birth centenary of Gen. Tasso Fragoso.

Jupia Dam, Parana River — A621

BRAZIL

Perf. 11½
1969, Sept. 10　　Litho.　　Unwmk.
Without Gum
1136　A621　20c lt blue & multi　　.35　.35
Inauguration of the Jupia Dam, part of the Urubupunga hydroelectric system serving Sao Paulo.

Gandhi and Spinning Wheel — A622

1969, Oct. 2　　　　*Perf. 11x11½*
1137　A622　20c yellow & blk　　.40　.30
Mohandas K. Gandhi (1869-1948), leader in India's fight for independence.

Santos Dumont, Eiffel Tower and Module Landing on Moon — A623

1969, Oct. 17　　　*Perf. 11½*
Without Gum
1138　A623　50c dk bl & multi　　1.75　1.25
Man's first landing on the moon, July 20, 1969. See note after US No. C76.

Smelting Plant — A624

1969, Oct. 26　　Unwmk.　　*Perf. 11½*
Without Gum
1139　A624　20c multicolored　　.45　.40
Expansion of Brazil's steel industry.

Steel Furnace A625

1969, Oct. 31　　　　Litho.
Without Gum
1140　A625　10c yellow & multi　　.45　.40
25th anniversary of Acesita Steel Works.

Water Vendor, by J. B. Debret — A626

Design: 30c, Street Scene, by Debret.
1969-70
Without Gum
1141　A626　20c multicolored　　1.25　.50
1141A　A626　30c multicolored　　1.25　1.00
Jean Baptiste Debret (1768-1848), painter.
Issued: 20c, Nov. 5, 1969; 30c, May 19, 1970.

Exhibition Emblem — A627

1969, Nov. 15　　　*Perf. 11½x11*
Without Gum
1142　A627　10c multicolored　　.35　.20
Issued to publicize the ABUEXPO 69 Philatelic Exposition, Sao Paulo, Nov. 15-23.

Plane — A628

1969, Nov. 23
Without Gum
1143　A628　50c multicolored　　2.75　1.40
Issued to publicize the year of the expansion of the national aviation industry.

Pelé Scoring — A629

1969-70
Without Gum
1144　A629　10c multicolored　　.40　.30
Souvenir Sheet
Imperf
1145　A629　75c multi ('70)　　4.50　3.50
Issued to commemorate the 1,000th goal scored by Pele, Brazilian soccer player.
No. 1145 contains one imperf. stamp with simulated perforations.
Issued: 10c, Nov. 28, 1969; 75c, Jan. 23, 1970.

Madonna and Child from Villa Velha Monastery A630

Perf. 11½
1969, Dec.　　Unwmk.　　Litho.
Without Gum
1146　A630　10c gold & multi　　.35　.20
Souvenir Sheet
Imperf
1147　A630　75c gold & multi　　12.00　15.00
Christmas 1969.
No. 1147 has simulated perforations.
Issue dates: 10c, Dec. 8; 75c, Dec. 18.

Destroyer and Submarine A631

Perf. 11x11½
1969, Dec. 9　　Engr.　　Wmk. 267
1148　A631　5c bluish gray　　.40　.25
Issued for Navy Day.

Dr. Herman Blumenau A632

1969, Dec. 26　　　　*Perf. 11½*
1149　A632　20c gray grn　　.85　.40
Dr. Herman Blumenau (1819-1899), founder of Blumenau, Santa Catarina State.

Carnival Scene — A633

Sugarloaf Mountain, Mask, Confetti and Streamers A634

Designs: 5c, Jumping boy and 2 women, vert. 20c, Clowns. 50c, Drummer.
1969-70　　Litho.　　Unwmk.
Without Gum
1150　A633　5c multicolored　　.40　.30
1151　A633　10c multicolored　　.40　.30
1152　A633　20c multicolored　　.50　.40
1153　A634　30c multicolored　　3.00　3.00
1154　A634　50c multicolored　　2.75　2.50
　　Nos. 1150-1154 (5)　　7.05　6.50
Carico Carnival, Rio de Janeiro.
Issue dates: Nos. 1150-1152, Dec. 29, 1969. Nos. 1153-1154, Feb. 5, 1970.

Opening Bars of "Il Guarani" with Antonio Carlos Gomes Conducting A635

1970, Mar. 19　　Litho.　　*Perf. 11½*
Without Gum
1155　A635　20c blk, yel, gray & brn　　.60　.40
Centenary of the opera Il Guarani, by Antonio Carlos Gomes.

Church of Penha — A636

1970, Apr. 6　　Unwmk.　　*Perf. 11½*
Without Gum
1156　A636　20c black & multi　　.30　.20
400th anniversary of the Church of Penha, State of Espirito Santo.

Assembly Building A637

10th anniv. of Brasilia: 50c, Reflecting Pool. 1cr, Presidential Palace.
1970, Apr. 21
Without Gum
1157　A637　20c multicolored　　.90　.70
1158　A637　50c multicolored　　2.25　1.75
1159　A637　1cr multicolored　　2.25　1.75
　　Nos. 1157-1159 (3)　　5.40　4.20

Symbolic Water Design — A638

1970, May 5　　Unwmk.　　*Perf. 11½*
Without Gum
1161　A638　50c multicolored　　2.50　3.00
Issued to publicize the Rondon Project for the development of the Amazon River basin.

Marshal Manoel Luiz Osorio and Osorio Arms — A639

1970, May 8
Without Gum
1162　A639　20c multicolored　　1.50　1.00
Issued to commemorate the inauguration of the Marshal Osorio Historical Park.

Madonna, from San Antonio Monastery, Rio de Janeiro — A640

Detail from Brasilia Cathedral — A641

1970, May 10
Without Gum
1163 A640 20c multicolored .40 .40
Issued for Mother's Day.

1970, May 27 Engr. Wmk. 267
1164 A641 20c lt yellow grn .25 .25
8th National Eucharistic Congress, Brasilia.

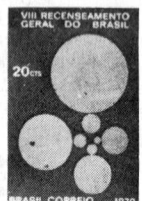

Census Symbol — A642

Perf. 11½
1970, June 22 Unwmk. Litho.
Without Gum
1165 A642 20c green & yel .60 .60
Issued to publicize the 8th general census.

Soccer Cup, Maps of Brazil and Mexico — A643

Swedish Flag and Player Holding Rimet Cup — A644

Designs: 2cr, Chilean flag and soccer. 3cr, Mexican flag and soccer.

1970
Without Gum
1166 A643 50c blk, lt bl & gold .90 .90
1167 A644 1cr pink & multi 2.75 1.50
1168 A644 2cr gray & multi 5.25 1.50
1169 A644 3cr multicolored 4.50 1.00
Nos. 1166-1169 (4) 13.40 4.90
9th World Soccer Championships for the Jules Rimet Cup, Mexico City, May 30-June 21. No. 1166 honors Brazil's victory.
Issued: #1166, June 24; #1167-1169, Aug. 4.

Corcovado Christ and Map of South America — A645

1970, July 18
Without Gum
1170 A645 50c brn, dk red & bl 2.50 2.50
6th World Cong. of Marist Brothers' Alumni.

Pandia Calogeras, Minister of War — A646

Perf. 11½x11
1970, Aug. 25 Photo. Unwmk.
1171 A646 20c blue green .50 .50

Brazilian Military Emblems and Map — A647

Perf. 11x11½
1970, Sept. 8 Litho. Unwmk.
Without Gum
1172 A647 20c gray & multi .50 .50
25th anniv. of victory in World War II.

Annunciation (Brazilian Primitive Painting) — A648

1970, Sept. 29 Perf. 11½
Without Gum
1173 A648 20c multicolored 1.25 1.00
Issued for St. Gabriel's (patron saint of communications) Day.

Boy in Library — A649

UN Emblem — A650

1970, Oct. 23
Without Gum
1174 A649 20c multicolored 1.25 1.00
Issued to publicize Book Week.

1970, Oct. 24
Without Gum
1175 A650 50c dk bl, lt bl & sil 1.25 1.25
25th anniversary of the United Nations.

Rio de Janeiro, 1820 — A651

Designs: 50c, LUBRAPEX 70 emblem. 1cr, Rio de Janeiro with Sugar Loaf Mountain, 1970. No. 1179, like 20c.

1970, Oct.
Without Gum
1176 A651 20c multicolored 1.75 1.00
1177 A651 50c yel brn & blk 3.50 2.00
1178 A651 1cr multicolored 3.50 3.75
Nos. 1176-1178 (3) 8.75 6.75
Souvenir Sheet
Imperf
1179 A651 1cr multicolored 11.00 17.00
LUBRAPEX 70, 3rd Portuguese-Brazilian Phil. Exhib., Rio de Janeiro, Oct. 24-31.
Issued: #1176-1178, Oct. 27; #1179, Oct. 31.

Holy Family by Candido Portinari — A652

1970, Dec. Litho. Perf. 11½
Without Gum
1180 A652 50c multicolored 1.50 1.50
Souvenir Sheet
Imperf
1181 A652 1cr multicolored 15.00 24.00
Christmas 1970. No. 1181 contains one stamp with simulated perforations.
Issue dates: 50c, Dec. 1; 1cr, Dec. 8.

Battleship — A653

CIH Emblem — A654

1970, Dec. 11 Litho. Perf. 11½
Without Gum
1182 A653 20c multicolored 1.25 .75
Navy Day.

1971, Mar. 28 Litho. Perf. 11½
Without Gum
1183 A654 50c black & red 1.50 1.75
3rd Inter-American Housing Congress, Mar. 27-Apr. 3.

Links Around Globe — A655

1971, Mar. 31 Litho. Perf. 12½x11
Without Gum
1184 A655 20c grn, yel, blk & red .65 .50
Intl. year against racial discrimination.

Morpho Melacheilus — A656

Design: 1cr, Papilio thoas brasiliensis.

Perf. 11x11½
1971, Apr. 28 Litho. Unwmk.
Without Gum
1185 A656 20c multicolored 1.25 .60
1186 A656 1cr multicolored 5.50 3.25

Madonna and Child — A657

1971, May 9 Litho. Perf. 11½
Without Gum
1187 A657 20c multicolored .85 .40
Mother's Day, 1971.

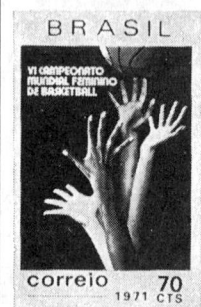

Basketball — A658

1971, May 19
Without Gum
1188 A658 70c multicolored 1.50 1.00
6th World Women's Basketball Championship.

Map of Trans-Amazon Highway — A660 A659

Perf. 11½
1971, July 1 Unwmk. Litho.
Without Gum
1189 A659 40c multicolored 5.50 2.75
1190 A660 1cr multicolored 5.50 5.50
a. Pair, #1189-1190 11.00 11.00
Trans-Amazon Highway. No. 1190a printed in sheets of 28 (4x7). Horizontal rows contain 2 No. 1190a with a label between. Each label carries different inscription.

Man's Head, by Victor Mairelles de Lima — A661

Stamp Day: 1cr, Arab Violinist, by Pedro Américo.

1971, Aug. 1
Without Gum
1191 A661 40c pink & multi 1.25 .80
1192 A661 1cr gray & multi 3.25 1.65

BRAZIL

Duke of Caxias and Map of Brazil — A662

1971, Aug. 23   Photo.
1193 A662   20c yel grn & red brn   .50   .60
Army Week.

Anita Garibaldi — A663

1971, Aug. 30   Litho.
Without Gum
1194 A663   20c multicolored   .40   .40
Anita Garibaldi (1821-1849), heroine in liberation of Brazil.

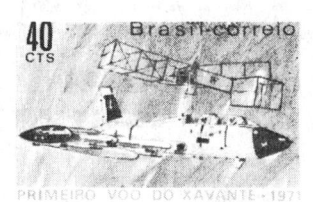

Xavante Jet and Santos Dumont's Plane, 1910 — A664

1971, Sept. 6
Without Gum
1195 A664   40c yellow & multi   1.40   .75
First flight of Xavante jet plane.

Flags and Map of Central American Nations — A665

"71" in French Flag Colors — A666

1971, Sept. 15
Without Gum
1196 A665   40c ocher & multi   1.25   .60
Sesquicentennial of the independence of Central American nations.

1971, Sept. 16
Without Gum
1197 A666   1.30cr ultra & multi   1.25   1.10
French Exhibition.

Black Mother, by Lucílio de Albuquerque A667

Archangel Gabriel A668

1971, Sept. 28
Without Gum
1198 A667   40c multicolored   .60   .50
Centenary of law guaranteeing personal freedom starting at birth.

1971, Sept. 29   Perf. 11½x11
Without Gum
1199 A668   40c multicolored   .75   .65
St. Gabriel's Day.

Bridge over River — A669

Children's Drawings: 35c, People crossing bridge. 60c, Woman with hat.

1971, Oct. 25   Perf. 11½
Without Gum
1200 A669   35c pink, bl & blk   .55   .45
1201 A669   45c black & multi   1.40   .45
1202 A669   60c olive & multi   .55   .45
    Nos. 1200-1202 (3)   2.50   1.35
Children's Day.

Werkhäuserii Superba A670

1971, Nov. 16
Without Gum
1203 A670   40c blue & multi   2.00   1.00
In memory of Carlos Werkhauser, botanist.

Greek Key Pattern "25" — A671

Design: 40c, like 20c but inscribed "sesc / servicio social / do comercio."

1971, Dec. 3
Without Gum
1204 A671   20c black & blue   1.25   1.00
1205 A671   40c black & org   1.25   1.00
  a.   Pair, #1204-1205   2.50   2.50
25th anniversary of SENAC (national apprenticeship system) and SESC (commercial social service).

Gunboat A672

1971, Dec. 8   Perf. 11
Without Gum
1206 A672   20c blue & multi   .85   .50
Navy Day.

Cross and Circles — A673

Washing of Bonfim Church, Salvador, Bahia — A674

1971, Dec. 11
1207 A673   20c car & blue   .40   .40
1208 A673   75c silver & gray   .80   3.00
1209 A673   1.30cr blk, yel, grn & bl   4.75   2.50
    Nos. 1207-1209 (3)   5.95   5.90
Christmas 1971.

1972, Feb. 18   Litho.   Perf. 11½x11
Designs: 40c, Grape Festival, Rio Grande do Sul. 75c, Festival of the Virgin of Nazareth, Belém. 1.30cr, Winter Arts Festival, Ouro Preto.
Without Gum
1210 A674   20c silver & multi   1.50   .75
1211 A674   40c silver & multi   2.75   .75
1212 A674   75c silver & multi   2.75   3.00
1213 A674   1.30cr silver & multi   6.00   3.00
    Nos. 1210-1213 (4)   13.00   7.50

Pres. Lanusse and Flag of Argentina A675

1972, Mar. 13   Perf. 11x11½
Without Gum
1214 A675   40c blue & multi   2.00   2.50
Visit of Lt. Gen. Alejandro Agustin Lanusse, president of Argentina.

Presidents Castello Branco, Costa e Silva and Garrastazu Medici A676

1972, Mar. 29
Without Gum
1215 A676   20c emerald & multi   1.25   .60
Anniversary of 1964 revolution.

Post Office Emblem — A677

1972, Apr. 10   Photo.   Perf. 11½x11   Unwmk.
1216 A677   20c red brown   2.00   .20
No. 1216 is luminescent.

Pres. Thomas and Portuguese Flag A678

1972, Apr. 22   Litho.   Perf. 11
Without Gum
1217 A678   75c ol brn & multi   1.75   1.75
Visit of Pres. Americo Thomas of Portugal to Brazil, Apr. 22-27.

Soil Research (CPRM) A679

1972, May 3   Perf. 11½
Without Gum
1218 A679   20c shown   1.50   .50
1219 A679   40c Offshore oil rig   3.50   .85
1220 A679   75c Hydroelectric dam   1.50   1.75
1221 A679   1.30cr Iron ore production   3.50   1.40
    Nos. 1218-1221 (4)   10.00   4.50
Industrial development. Stamps are inscribed with names of industrial firms.
See Nos. 1228-1229.

Souvenir Sheet

Poster for Modern Art Week 1922 — A680

1972, May 5
1222 A680   1cr black & car   26.00   26.00
50th anniversary of Modern Art Week.

Mailman, Map of Brazil and Letters A681

Designs: 45c, "Telecommunications", vert. 60c, Tropospheric scatter system. 70c, Road map of Brazil and worker.

1972, May 26
Without Gum
1223 A681   35c blue & multi   1.25   .40
1224 A681   45c silver & multi   1.50   1.50
1225 A681   60c black & multi   1.50   1.25
1226 A681   70c multicolored   1.75   1.25
    Nos. 1223-1226 (4)   6.00   4.40
Unification of communications in Brazil.

Development Type and Automobiles — A682

1972, June 21   Perf. 11x11½, 11½x11
1227 A682   35c shown   1.00   .50   Photo.
    Litho.
1228 A679   45c Ships   1.00   .60
1229 A679   70c Ingots   1.00   .40
    Nos. 1227-1229 (3)   3.00   1.50
Industrial development. The 35c is luminescent.

BRAZIL

Soccer — A683

Designs: 75c, Folk music. 1.30cr, Plastic arts.

		Perf. 11½x11		
1972, July 7		Photo.	Unwmk.	
1230	A683	20c black & yel	1.00	.50
1231	A683	75c black & ver	2.00	3.50
1232	A683	1.30cr black & ultra	4.00	3.50
	Nos. 1230-1232 (3)		7.00	7.50

150th anniversary of independence. No. 1230 publicizes the 1972 sports tournament, a part of independence celebrations. Luminescent.

Souvenir Sheet

Shout of Independence, by Pedro Americo de Figueiredo e Melo — A684

1972, July 19		Litho.	Perf. 11½	
		Without Gum		
1233	A684	1cr multicolored	4.00	9.00

4th Interamerican Philatelic Exhibition, EXFILBRA, Rio de Janeiro, Aug 26-Sept. 2.

Figurehead A685

Brazilian folklore: 60c, Gauchos dancing fandango. 75c, Acrobats (capoeira). 1.15cr, Karajá (ceramic) doll. 1.30cr, Mock bullfight (bumba meu boi).

1972, Aug. 6				
		Without Gum		
1234	A685	45c multicolored	.85	.35
1235	A685	60c orange & multi	1.65	1.50
1236	A685	75c gray & multi	.30	.30
1237	A685	1.15cr multicolored	.55	.55
1238	A685	1.30cr yellow & multi	5.00	2.00
	Nos. 1234-1238 (5)		8.35	4.70

Map of Brazil, by Diego Homem, 1568 — A686

Designs: 1cr, Map of Americas, by Nicholas Visscher, 1652. 2cr, Map of Americas, by Lopo Homem, 1519.

1972, Aug. 26		Litho.	Perf. 11½	
		Without Gum		
1239	A686	70c multicolored	.50	.50
1240	A686	1cr multicolored	9.00	1.00
1241	A686	2cr multicolored	4.50	1.50
	Nos. 1239-1241 (3)		14.00	3.00

4th Inter-American Philatelic Exhibition, EXFILBRA, Rio de Janeiro, Aug. 26-Sept. 2.

Dom Pedro Proclaimed Emperor, by Jean Baptiste Debret A687

Designs: 30c, Founding of Brazil (people with imperial flag), vert. 1cr, Coronation of Emperor Dom Pedro, vert. 2cr, Dom Pedro commemorative medal. 3.50cr, Independence Monument, Ipiranga.

1972, Sept. 4		Litho.	Perf. 11½x11	
1242	A687	30c yellow & grn	1.25	1.25
1243	A687	70c pink & rose lil	1.25	.80
1244	A687	1cr buff & red brn	8.00	1.25
1245	A687	2cr pale yel & blk	4.00	1.25
1246	A687	3.50cr gray & blk	7.25	4.00
	Nos. 1242-1246 (5)		21.75	8.55

Sesquicentennial of independence.

Souvenir Sheet

"Automobile Race" — A688

1972, Nov. 14			Perf. 11½	
1247	A688	2cr multicolored	10.00	15.00

Emerson Fittipaldi, Brazilian world racing champion.

Numeral and Post Office Emblem — A689

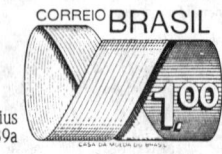

Möbius Strip — A689a

		Perf. 11½x11		
1972-75		Unwmk.	Photo.	
1248	A689	5c orange	.35	.15
a.		Wmk. 267	.20	.15
1249	A689	10c brown ('73)	.20	.15
a.		Wmk. 267	4.00	.15
1250	A689	15c brt blue ('75)	.15	.15
1251	A689	20c ultra	.35	.15
1252	A689	25c sepia ('75)	.25	.15
1253	A689	30c dp carmine	.40	.15
1254	A689	40c dk grn ('73)	.20	.15
1255	A689	50c olive	.30	.15
1256	A689	70c red lilac ('75)	.30	.15
		Engr.	Perf. 11½	
1257	A689a	1cr lilac ('74)	.45	.15
1258	A689a	2cr grnsh bl ('74)	.65	.15
1259	A689a	4cr org & vio ('75)	1.40	.20
1260	A689a	5cr brn, car & buff ('74)	2.00	.20
1261	A689a	10cr grn, blk & buff ('74)	4.50	.30
	Nos. 1248-1261 (14)		11.50	2.35

The 5cr and 10cr have beige lithographed multiple Post Office emblem underprint.
Nos. 1248-1261 are luminescent. Nos. 1248a and 1249a are not.

Hand Writing "Mobral" A690

20c, Multiracial group and population growth curve. 1cr, People and hands holding house. 2cr, People, industrial scene and upward arrow.

1972, Nov. 28		Litho.	Perf. 11½	
		Without Gum		
1262	A690	10c black & multi	.20	.50
1263	A690	20c black & multi	1.00	.75
1264	A690	1cr black & multi	8.75	.30
1265	A690	2cr black & multi	2.00	.75
	Nos. 1262-1265 (4)		11.95	2.30

Publicity for: "Mobral" literacy campaign (10c); Centenary of census (20c); Housing and retirement fund (1cr); Growth of gross national product (2cr).

Congress Building, Brasilia, by Oscar Niemeyer, and "Os Guerreiros," by Bruno Giorgi A691

1972, Dec. 4				
		Without Gum		
1266	A691	1cr blue, blk & org	10.00	6.00

Meeting of Natl. Cong., Brasilia, Dec. 4-8.

Holy Family (Clay Figurines) A692

Retirement Plan A693

1972, Dec. 13		Photo.	Perf. 11½x11	
1267	A692	20c ocher & blk	.85	.50

Christmas 1972. Luminescent.

		Perf. 11½x11, 11x11½		
1972, Dec. 20			Litho.	

#1269, School children and traffic lights, horiz. 70c, Dr. Oswaldo Cruz with Red Cross, caricature. 2cr, Produce, fish and cattle, horiz.

		Without Gum		
1268	A693	10c blk, bl & dl org	.50	.50
1269	A693	10c orange & multi	1.00	1.00
1270	A693	70c blk, red & brn	9.00	3.75
1271	A693	2cr green & multi	15.00	6.50
	Nos. 1268-1271 (4)		25.50	11.75

Publicity for: Agricultural workers' assistance program (No. 1268); highway and transportation development (No. 1269); centenary of the birth of Dr. Oswaldo Cruz (1872-1917), Director of Public Health Institute (70c); agricultural and cattle export (2cr). Nos. 1268-1271 are luminescent.

Sailing Ship, Navy A694

Designs: 10c, Monument, Brazilian Expeditionary Force. No. 1274, Plumed helmet, Army. No. 1275, Rocket, Air Force.

		Lithographed and Engraved		
1972, Dec. 28			Perf. 11x11½	
		Without Gum		
1272	A694	10c brn, dk brn & blk	1.50	1.10
1273	A694	30c lt ultra, grn & blk	1.50	1.10
1274	A694	30c yel grn, bl grn & blk	1.50	1.10
1275	A694	30c lilac, mar & blk	1.50	1.10
a.		Block of 4, #1272-1275	6.00	5.00

Armed Forces Day.

Rotary Emblem and Cogwheels A695

		Perf. 11½		
1973, Mar. 21		Litho.	Unwmk.	
1276	A695	1cr ultra, grnsh bl & yel	1.75	1.50

Rotary International serving Brazil 50 years.

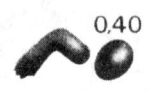

Swimming A696

#1278, Gymnastics. #1279, Volleyball, vert.

1973		Photo.	Perf. 11x11½, 11½x11	
1277	A696	40c brt bl & red brn	.35	.35
1278	A696	40c green & org brn	2.75	.70
1279	A696	40c violet & org brn	.70	.70
	Nos. 1277-1279 (3)		3.80	1.75

Issue dates: No. 1277, Apr. 19; No. 1278, May 22; No. 1279, Oct. 15.

Flag of Paraguay A697

		Perf. 11½		
1973, Apr. 27		Litho.	Unwmk.	
1280	A697	70c multicolored	1.75	1.25

Visit of Pres. Alfredo Stroessner of Paraguay, Apr. 25-27.

"Communications" — A698

1cr, Neptune, map of South America and Africa.

1973, May 5			Perf. 11x11½	
1281	A698	70c multicolored	.80	.70
1282	A698	1cr multicolored	4.25	3.00

Inauguration of the Ministry of Communications Building, Brasilia (70c); and of the first underwater telephone cable between South America and Europe, Bracan 1 (1cr).

Congress Emblem — A699

1973, May 19			Perf. 11½x11	
1283	A699	1cr orange & pur	4.00	3.00

24th Congress of the International Chamber of Commerce, Rio de Janeiro, May 19-26.

BRAZIL

Swallowtailed Manakin — A700

Birds: No. 1285, Orange-backed oriole. No. 1286, Brazilian ruby (hummingbird).

1973	Litho.		Perf. 11x11½
1284	A700	20c multicolored	.50 .20
1285	A700	20c multicolored	.50 .20
1286	A700	20c multicolored	.50 .20
		Nos. 1284-1286 (3)	1.50 .60

Issue dates: No. 1284, May 26; No. 1285, June 6; No. 1286, June 19.

Tourists A701

1973, June 28	Litho.	Perf. 11x11½
1287	A701 70c multicolored	.90 .85

National Tourism Year.

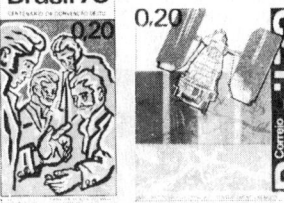

Conference at Itu — A702 Satellite and Multispectral Image — A703

1973			Perf. 11½x11
1288	A702	20c shown	.52 .35
1289	A702	20c Decorated wagon	.52 .35
1290	A702	20c Indian	.52 .35
1291	A702	20c Graciosa Road	.52 .35
		Nos. 1288-1291 (4)	2.08 1.40

Centenary of the Itu Convention (1288); sesquicentennial of the July 2 episode (1289); 400th anniversary of the founding of Niteroi (1290); centenary of Graciosa Road (1291).

Issue dates: #1291, July 29; others July 2.

1973, July 11		Perf. 11½

Designs: 70c, Official opening of Engineering School, 1913. 1cr, Möbius strips and "IMPA."

1292	A703	20c black & multi	.25 .40
1293	A703	70c dk blue & multi	2.25 1.00
1294	A703	1cr lilac & multi	3.00 1.00
		Nos. 1292-1294 (3)	5.50 2.40

Institute for Space Research (20c); School of Engineering, Itajubá, 60th anniversary (70c); Institute for Pure and Applied Mathematics (1cr).

Santos-Dumont and 14-Bis Plane — A704

Designs (Santos-Dumont and): 70c, No. 6 Balloon and Eiffel Tower. 2cr Demoiselle plane.

Lithographed and Engraved

1973, July 20		Perf. 11x11½
1295	A704 20c lt grn, brt grn & brn	.75 .25
1296	A704 70c yel, rose red & brn	1.75 1.25
1297	A704 2cr bl, vio bl & brn	1.75 1.25
	Nos. 1295-1297 (3)	4.25 2.75

Centenary of the birth of Alberto Santos-Dumont (1873-1932), aviation pioneer.

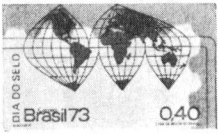

Mercator Map A705

No. 1299, Same, red border on top and at left.

Photogravure and Engraved

1973, Aug. 1		Wmk. 267
1298	A705 40c red & black	2.50 1.50
1299	A705 40c red & black	2.10 2.10
a.	Block of 4	21.00 15.00

Stamp Day. Nos. 1298-1299 are printed se-tenant horizontally and tête bêche vertically in sheets of 55. Blocks of 4 have red border all around.

Gonçalves Dias (1823-1864), Poet — A706

	Perf. 11½x11	
1973, Aug. 10		Wmk. 267
1300	A706 40c violet & blk	.70 .42

Souvenir Sheet

Copernicus and Sun — A707

	Perf. 11x11½	
1973, Aug. 15	Litho.	Unwmk.
1301	A707 1cr multicolored	4.00 5.00

500th anniversary of the birth of Nicolaus Copernicus (1473-1543), Polish astronomer.

Folklore Festival Banner — A708

1973, Aug. 22		Perf. 11½
1302	A708 40c ultra & multi	.75 .52

Folklore Day, Aug. 22.

Masonic Emblem A709

1973, Aug. 24	Photo.	Perf. 11x11½
1303	A709 1cr Prus blue	3.00 2.00

Free Masons of Brazil, 1822-1973.

Nature Protection A710

#1305, Fire protection. #1306, Aviation safety. #1307, Safeguarding cultural heritage.

1973, Sept. 20	Litho.	Perf. 11x11½
1304	A710 40c brt grn & multi	.75 .40
1305	A710 40c dk blue & multi	.75 .40
1306	A710 40c lt blue & multi	.75 .40
1307	A710 40c pink & multi	.75 .40
	Nos. 1304-1307 (4)	3.00 1.60

Souvenir Sheet

St. Gabriel and Proclamation of Pope Paul VI — A711

Lithographed and Engraved

1973, Sept. 29	Unwmk.	Perf. 11½
1308	A711 1cr bister & blk	7.50 10.00

1st National Exhibition of Religious Philately, Rio de Janeiro, Sept. 29-Oct. 6.

St. Teresa — A712

Photogravure and Engraved
Perf. 11½x11

1973, Sept. 30		Wmk. 267
1309	A712 2cr dk org & brn	3.50 2.50

St. Teresa of Lisieux, the Little Flower (1873-1897), Carmelite nun.

Monteiro Lobato and Emily A713

	Perf. 11½	
1973, Oct. 12	Litho.	Unwmk.
1310	A713 40c shown	.80 .50
1311	A713 40c Aunt Nastacia	.80 .50
1312	A713 40c Snubnose, Peter and Rhino	.80 .50
1313	A713 40c Viscount de Sabugosa	.80 .50
1314	A713 40c Dona Benta	.80 .50
a.	Block of 5 + label	4.00 4.00

Monteiro Lobato, author of children's books.

Soapstone Sculpture of Isaiah (detail) — A714

Baroque Art in Brazil: No. 1316, Arabesque, gilded wood carving, horiz. 70c, Father José Mauricio Nuñes Garcia and music score. 1cr, Church door, Salvador, Bahia. 2cr, Angels, church ceiling painting by Manoel da Costa Athayde, horiz.

1973, Nov. 5		
1315	A714 40c multicolored	.30 .30
1316	A714 40c multicolored	.30 .30
1317	A714 70c multicolored	1.50 1.40
1318	A714 1cr multicolored	9.00 3.00
1319	A714 2cr multicolored	4.00 3.00
	Nos. 1315-1319 (5)	15.10 8.00

Old and New Telephones A715

1973, Nov. 28		Perf. 11x11½
1320	A715 40c multicolored	.35 .30

50th anniv. of Brazilian Telephone Co.

Symbolic Angel — A716

1973, Nov. 30		Perf. 11½
1321	A716 40c ver & multi	.35 .30

Christmas 1973.

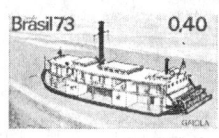

River Boats A717

1973, Nov. 30	Litho.	Perf. 11x11½
1322	A717 40c "Gaiola"	.35 .35
1323	A717 70c "Regatao"	1.05 1.05
1324	A717 1cr "Jangada"	4.50 3.00
1325	A717 2cr "Saveiro"	4.25 3.00
	Nos. 1322-1325 (4)	10.15 7.40

Nos. 1322-1325 are luminescent.

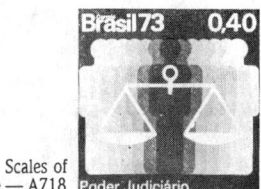

Scales of Justice — A718

	Perf. 11½	
1973, Dec. 5		
1326	A718 40c magenta & vio	.50 .32

To honor the High Federal Court, created in 1891. Luminescent.

José Placido de Castro — A719 Scarlet Ibis and Victoria Regia — A720

Lithographed and Engraved
Perf. 11½x11

1973, Dec. 12		Wmk. 267
1327	A719 40c lilac rose & blk	.60 .35

Centenary of the birth of Jose Placido de Castro, liberator of the State of Acre.

	Perf. 11½x11	
1973, Dec. 28	Litho.	Unwmk.

Designs: 70c, Jaguar and spathodea campanulata. 1cr, Scarlet macaw and carnauba palm. 2cr, Rhea and coral tree.

1328	A720 40c brown & multi	.80 .50
1329	A720 70c brown & multi	2.25 1.50
1330	A720 1cr bister & multi	3.50 .40
1331	A720 2cr bister & multi	6.25 3.50
	Nos. 1328-1331 (4)	12.80 5.90

Nos. 1328-1331 are luminescent.

Saci Perere, Mocking Goblin — A721

BRAZIL

Characters from Brazilian Legends: 80c, Zumbi, last chief of rebellious slaves. 1cr, Chico Rei, African king. 1.30cr, Little Black Boy of the Pasture. 2.50cr, Iara, Queen of the Waters.

1974, Feb. 28   Litho.   Unwmk.
Size: 21x39mm
Perf. 11½x11

1332	A721	40c multicolored	.35	.25
1333	A721	80c multicolored	.70	.60
1334	A721	1cr multicolored	1.65	.45

Perf. 11½
Size: 32½x33mm

1335	A721	1.30cr multicolored	2.50	.85
1336	A721	2.50cr multicolored	10.50	2.50
		Nos. 1332-1336 (5)	15.70	4.65

Nos. 1332-1336 are luminescent.

Pres. Costa e Silva Bridge — A722

1974, Mar. 11
1337 A722 40c multicolored   .60 .30

Inauguration of the Pres. Costa e Silva Bridge, Rio Niteroi, connecting Rio de Janeiro and Guanabara State.

"The Press" — A723

1974, Mar. 25   Perf. 11½
1338	A723	40c shown	.50	.30
1339	A723	40c "Radio"	.25	.25
1340	A723	40c "Television"	.40	.30
		Nos. 1338-1340 (3)	1.15	.85

Communications Commemorations: No. 1338, bicentenary of first Brazilian newspaper, published in London by Hipolito da Costa; No. 1339, founding of the Radio Sociedade do Rio de Janeiro by Roquette Pinto; No. 1340, installation of first Brazilian television station by Assis Chateaubriand. Luminescent.

"Reconstruction" — A724

1974, Mar. 31
1341 A724 40c multicolored   .70 .45

10 years of progress. Luminescent.

Corcovado Christ, Marconi, Colors of Brazil and Italy — A725

1974, Apr. 25   Litho.   Perf. 11½
1342 A725 2.50cr multi   6.00 3.00

Guglielmo Marconi (1874-1937), Italian physicist and inventor. Luminescent.

Stamp Printing Press, Stamp Designing — A726

1974, May 6
1343 A726 80c multicolored   1.00 .50

Brazilian mint.

World Map, Indian, Caucasian and Black Men — A727

World Map and: #1345, Brazilians. #1346, Cabin & German horseback rider. #1347, Italian farm wagon. #1348, Japanese woman & torii.

1974, May 3   Unwmk.
1344	A727	40c multicolored	.30	.30
1345	A727	40c multicolored	.20	.20
1346	A727	2.50cr multicolored	3.25	1.50
1347	A727	2.50cr multicolored	4.75	1.50
1348	A727	2.50cr multicolored	1.25	.85
		Nos. 1344-1348 (5)	9.75	4.35

Ethnic and migration influences in Brazil.

Sandstone Cliffs, Sete Cidades National Park — A728

Tourist publicity: 80c, Ruins of Cathedral of Sao Miguel das Missões.

Lithographed and Engraved
1974, June 8   Perf. 11x11½
| 1349 | A728 | 40c multicolored | .75 | .50 |
| 1350 | A728 | 80c multicolored | .75 | .50 |

Souvenir Sheet

Soccer — A729

1974, June 20   Litho.   Perf. 11½
1351 A729 2.50cr multi   3.50 6.00

World Cup Soccer Championship, Munich, June 13-July 7.

Church and College, Caraça — A730

1974, July 6   Litho.   Perf. 11x11½
1352 A730 40c multicolored   .45 .30

College (Seminary) of Caraça, bicent.

Wave on Television Screen — A731

1974, July 15   Perf. 11½
1353 A731 40c black & blue   .30 .40

TELEBRAS, Third Brazilian Congress of Telecommunications, Brasilia, July 15-20.

Fernao Dias Paes — A732

1974, July 21   Perf. 11½
1354 A732 20c green & multi   .30 .30

3rd centenary of the expedition led by Fernao Dias Paes exploring Minas Gerais and the passage from South to North in Brazil.

Mexican Flag — A733

1974, July 24   Litho.   Perf. 11½
1355 A733 80c multicolored   2.25 1.10

Visit of Pres. Luis Echeverria Alvares of Mexico, July 24-29.

Flags of Brazil and Germany — A734

1974, Aug. 5   Perf. 11x11½
1356 A734 40c multicolored   .50 .50

World Cup Soccer Championship, 1974, victory of German Federal Republic.

Souvenir Sheet

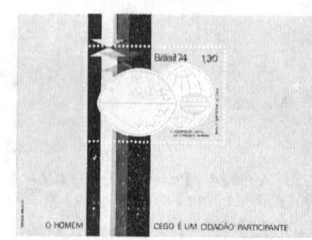

Congress Emblem — A735

1974, Aug. 7   Perf. 11½
1357 A735 1.30cr multi   .85 1.75

5th World Assembly of the World Council for the Welfare of the Blind, Sao Paulo, Aug. 7-16. Stamp and margin inscribed in Braille with name of Assembly.

Raul Pederneiras (1874-1953, Journalist, Professor of Law and Fine Arts), Caricature by J. Carlos — A736

Lithographed and Engraved
1974, Aug. 15   Perf. 11½x11
1358 A736 40c buff, blk & ocher   .30 .40

Society Emblem and Landscape — A737

1974, Aug. 19   Litho.   Perf. 11x11½
1359 A737 1.30cr multi   1.25 .90

13th Congress of the International Union of Building and Savings Societies.

Souvenir Sheet

Five Women, by Di Cavalcanti — A738

1974, Aug. 26   Litho.   Perf. 11½
1360 A738 2cr multicolored   2.50 6.00

LUBRAPEX 74, 5th Portuguese-Brazilian Phil. Exhib., Sao Paulo, Nov. 26-Dec. 4.

"UPU" and World Map — A739

1974, Oct. 9   Litho.   Perf. 11½
1361 A739 2.50cr blk & brt bl   4.50 1.75

Centenary of Universal Postal Union.

Hammock (Antillean Arawak Culture) — A740

Bilro Lace — A741

BRAZIL

Singer of "Cord" Verses — A742
Ceramic Figure by Master Vitalino — A743 

1974, Oct. 16 Litho. Perf. 11½
1362	A740	50c deep rose lilac	2.00	.40
1363	A741	50c lt & dk blue	2.50	.40
1364	A742	50c yel & red brn	.60	.40
1365	A743	50c brt yel & dk brn	.75	.40
		Nos. 1362-1365 (4)	5.85	1.60

Popular Brazilian crafts.

Branch of Coffee A744

1974, Oct. 27 Unwmk. Perf. 11
1366 A744 50c multicolored 1.00 .60

Centenary of city of Campinas.

Hornless Tabapua A745

Animals of Brazil: 1.30cr, Creole horse. 2.50cr, Brazilian mastiff.

1974, Nov. 10 Perf. 11½
1367	A745	80c multi	1.10	.75
1368	A745	1.30cr multi	1.10	.75
1369	A745	2.50cr multi	7.75	2.50
		Nos. 1367-1369 (3)	9.95	4.00

Christmas — A746

1974, Nov. 18 Perf. 11½x11
1370 A746 50c Angel .70 .30

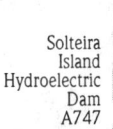

Solteira Island Hydroelectric Dam A747

1974, Nov. 11 Perf. 11½
1371 A747 50c black & yellow 1.40 .50

Inauguration of the Solteira Island Hydroelectric Dam over Parana River.

The Girls, by Carlos Reis — A748

1974, Nov. 26
1372 A748 1.30cr multi .70 .50

LUBRAPEX 74, 5th Portuguese-Brazilian Phil. Exhib., Sao Paulo, Nov. 26-Dec. 4.

Youths, Judge, Scales A749

1974, Dec. 20 Litho. Perf. 11½
1373 A749 90c yel, red & bl .30 .35

Juvenile Court of Brazil, 50th anniversary.

Long Distance Runner — A750

1974, Dec. 23
1374 A750 3.30cr multi .75 .75

Sao Silvestre long distance running, 50th anniversary.

News Vendor, 1875, Masthead, 1975 — A751

1975, Jan. 4
1375 A751 50c multicolored 1.25 .75

Newspaper "O Estado de S. Paulo," cent.

Sao Paulo Industrial Park A752

Designs: 1.40cr, Natural rubber industry, Acre. 4.50cr, Manganese mining, Amapá.

1975, Jan. 24 Litho. Perf. 11x11½
1376	A752	50c vio bl & yel	1.25	.40
1377	A752	1.40cr yellow & brn	.60	.40
1378	A752	4.50cr yellow & blk	6.00	.40
		Nos. 1376-1378 (3)	7.85	1.20

Economic development.

Fort of the Holy Cross A753

Colonial forts: No. 1380, Fort of the Three Kings. No. 1381, Fort of Montserrat. 90c, Fort of Our Lady of Help.

Litho. & Engr.
1975, Mar. 14 Perf. 11½
1379	A753	50c yel & red brn	.24	.16
1380	A753	50c yel & red brn	.40	.16
1381	A753	50c yel & red brn	.80	.16
1382	A753	90c yel & red brn	.24	.16
		Nos. 1379-1382 (4)	1.68	.64

House on Stilts, Amazon Region A754

Designs: 50c, Modern houses and plan of Brasilia. 1.40cr, Indian hut, Rondonia. 3.30cr, German-style cottage (Enxaimel), Santa Catarina.

1975, Apr. 18 Litho. Perf. 11½
1383	A754	50c yel & multi	1.25	2.25
1384	A754	50c yel & multi	8.50	6.25
a.		Pair, #1383-1384	10.00	8.50
1385	A754	1cr yel & multi	.85	1.20
1386	A754	1.40cr yel & multi	1.75	2.50
1387	A754	1.40cr yel & multi	.50	.85
a.		Pair, #1386-1387	2.25	3.50
1388	A754	3.30cr yel & multi	.75	1.25
1389	A754	3.30cr yel & multi	3.50	4.00
a.		Pair, #1388-1389	4.25	5.25
		Nos. 1383-1389 (7)	17.10	17.32

Brazilian architecture. Nos. 1383, 1386, 1388 have yellow strip at right side, others at left.

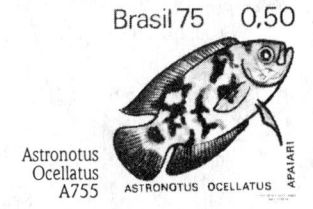

Astronotus Ocellatus A755

Designs: Brazilian fresh-water fish.

1975, May 2 Litho. Perf. 11½
1390	A755	50c shown	1.40	.40
1391	A755	50c Colomesus psitacus	.25	.25
1392	A755	50c Phallocerus caudimaculatus	.25	.40
1393	A755	50c Symphysodon discus	.48	.50
		Nos. 1390-1393 (4)	2.38	1.55

Soldier's Head in Brazil's Colors, Plane, Rifle and Ship — A756

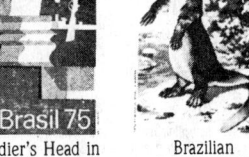

Brazilian Otter — A757

1975, May 8 Perf. 11½x11
1394 A756 50c vio bl & multi .35 .30

In honor of the veterans of World War II, on the 30th anniversary of victory.

1975, June 17 Litho. Perf. 11½

Nature protection: 70c, Brazilian pines, horiz. 3.30cr, Marsh cayman, horiz.

1395	A757	70c bl, grn & blk	1.05	.50
1396	A757	1cr multi	1.05	1.00
1397	A757	3.30cr multi	.90	.75
		Nos. 1395-1397 (3)	3.00	2.25

Petroglyphs, Stone of Ingá — A758 
Marjoara Vase, Pará — A759

Vinctifer Comptoni, Petrified Fish — A760

1975, July 8 Litho. Perf. 11½
1398	A758	70c multicolored	.55	.40
1399	A759	1cr multicolored	.35	.40
1400	A760	1cr multicolored	.35	.40
		Nos. 1398-1400 (3)	1.25	1.20

Archaeological discoveries.

Immaculate Conception, Franciscan Monastery, Vitoria — A761
Post and Telegraph Ministry — A762 

1975, July 15
1401 A761 3.30cr blue & multi .95 .95

Holy Year 1975 and 300th anniv. of establishment of the Franciscan Province in Southern Brazil.

1975, Aug. 8 Engr. Perf. 11½
1402 A762 70c dk carmine .70 .30

Stamp Day 1975.

Sword Dance, Minas Gerais — A763

Folk Dances: No. 1404, Umbrella Dance, Pernambuco. No. 1405, Warrior's Dance, Alagoas.

1975, Aug. 22 Litho. Perf. 11½
1403	A763	70c gray & multi	.35	.35
1404	A763	70c pink & multi	.35	.35
1405	A763	70c yellow & multi	.35	.35
		Nos. 1403-1405 (3)	1.05	1.05

Trees A764

1975, Sept. 15 Perf. 11x11½
1406 A764 70c multicolored .30 .25

Annual Tree Festival.

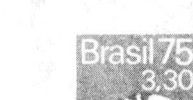

Globe, Radar and Satellite — A765

1975, Sept. 16 Perf. 11½
1407 A765 3.30cr multi .70 .75

Inauguration of 2nd antenna of Tangua Earth Station, Rio de Janeiro State.

BRAZIL

Woman Holding Flowers and Globe — A766

1975, Sept. 23
1408 A766 3.30cr multi 1.00 1.00
International Women's Year 1975.

Tile, Railing and Column, Alcantara — A767

Cross and Monastery, Sao Cristovao — A768

Historic cities: No. 1411, Jug and Clock Tower, Goiás, vert.

1975, Sept. 27   Litho.   Perf. 11½
1409 A767 70c multicolored .... .32 .45
1410 A768 70c multicolored .... .60 .45
1411 A768 70c multicolored .... .60 .45
Nos. 1409-1411 (3) 1.52 1.35

"Books teach how to live" — A769

1975, Oct. 23   Litho.   Perf. 11½
1412 A769 70c multicolored .... .25 .30
Day of the Book.

ASTA Congress Emblem — A770

1975, Oct. 27   Perf. 11x11½
1413 A770 70c multicolored .... .25 .30
American Society of Travel Agents, 45th World Congress, Rio, Oct. 27-Nov. 1.

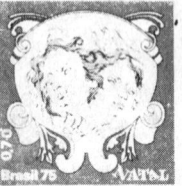

Angels — A771

1975, Nov. 11
1414 A771 70c red & brown .... .25 .20
Christmas 1975.

For all your stamp supply needs
www.scottonline.com

Map of Americas, Waves — A772

Dom Pedro II — A773

1975, Nov. 19   Perf. 11½x12
1415 A772 5.20cr gray & multi 2.75 2.00
2nd Interamerican Conference of Telecommunications (CITEL), Rio, Nov. 19-27.

1975, Dec. 2   Engr.   Perf. 12
1416 A773 70c violet brown .... .75 .45
Dom Pedro II (1825-1891), emperor of Brazil, birth sesquicentennial.

People and Cross — A774

1975, Nov. 27   Litho.   Perf. 11x11½
1417 A774 70c lt bl & dp bl .... .50 .65
National Day of Thanksgiving.

Guarapari Beach, Espirito Santo — A775

Tourist Publicity: #1419, Salt Stone beach, Piauí. #1420, Cliffs, Rio Grande Do Sul.

1975, Dec. 19   Litho.   Perf. 11½
1418 A775 70c multicolored .... .28 .28
1419 A775 70c multicolored .... .28 .28
1420 A775 70c multicolored .... .28 .28
Nos. 1418-1420 (3) .... .84 .84

Triple Jump, Games Emblem — A776

1975, Dec. 22   Perf. 11x11½
1421 A776 1.60cr bl grn & blk .... .25 .35
Triple jump world record by Joao Carlos de Oliveira in 7th Pan-American Games, Mexico City, Oct. 12-26.

UN Emblem and Headquarters — A777

1975, Dec. 29   Perf. 11½
1422 A777 1.30cr dp bl & vio bl .... .25 .30
United Nations, 30th anniversary.

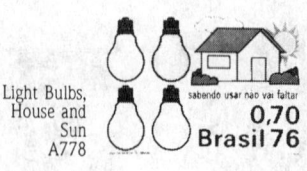

Light Bulbs, House and Sun — A778

Energy conservation: No. 1424, Gasoline drops, car and sun.

1976, Jan. 16
1423 A778 70c multicolored .... .30 .20
1424 A778 70c multicolored .... .30 .15

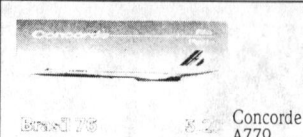

Concorde — A779

1976, Jan. 21   Litho.   Perf. 11x11½
1425 A779 5.20cr bluish black .... .50 .35
First commercial flight of supersonic jet Concorde from Paris to Rio, Jan. 21.

Souvenir Sheet

Nautical Map of South Atlantic, 1776 — A780

1976, Feb. 2   Perf. 11½
1426 A780 70c salmon & multi .... .85 1.50
Centenary of the Naval Hydrographic and Navigation Institute.

Telephone Lines, 1876 Telephone — A781

1976, Mar. 10   Litho.   Perf. 11x11½
1427 A781 5.20cr orange & blue .... .65 .48
Centenary of first telephone call by Alexander Graham Bell, March 10, 1876.

Eye and Exclamation Point — A782

Kaiapo Body Painting — A783

1976, Apr. 7   Litho.   Perf. 11½x11
1428 A782 1cr vio brn & brn .... .50 .75
World Health Day: "Foresight prevents blindness."

1976, Apr. 19   Litho.   Perf. 11½
Designs: No. 1430, Bakairi ceremonial mask. No. 1431, Karajá feather headdress.
1429 A783 1cr light violet & multi .... .16 .16
1430 A783 1cr light violet & multi .... .16 .16
1431 A783 1cr light violet & multi .... .16 .16
Nos. 1429-1431 (3) .... .48 .48
Preservation of indigenous culture.

Itamaraty Palace, Brasilia — A784

1976, Apr. 20
1432 A784 1cr multicolored .... .60 .60
Diplomats' Day. Itamaraty Palace, designed by Oscar Niemeyer, houses the Ministry of Foreign Affairs.

Watering Can over Stones, by José Tarcisio — A785

Fingers and Ribbons, by Pietrina Checcacci — A786

1976, May 14   Litho.   Perf. 11½
1433 A785 1cr multi .... .22 .20
1434 A786 1.60cr multi .... .28 .20
Modern Brazilian art.

Basketball — A787

Orchid — A788

Designs (Olympic Rings and): 1.40cr, Yachting. 5.20cr, Judo.

1976, May 21   Litho.   Perf. 11½
1435 A787 1cr emerald & blk .... .16 .15
1436 A787 1.40cr dk blue & blk .... .20 .15
1437 A787 5.20cr orange & blk .... .65 .50
Nos. 1435-1437 (3) .... 1.01 .80
21st Olympic Games, Montreal, Canada, July 17-Aug. 1.

1976, June 4   Perf. 11½x11
Nature protection: No. 1439, Golden-faced lion monkey.
1438 A788 1cr multicolored .... .22 .20
1439 A788 1cr multicolored .... .22 .20

Film Camera, Brazilian Colors — A789

1976, June 19
1440 A789 1cr vio bl, brt grn & yel .... .20 .25
Brazilian film industry.

Bahia Woman — A790

Designs: 10c, Oxcart driver, horiz. 20c, Raft fishermen, horiz. 30c, Rubber plantation worker. 40c, Cowboy, horiz. 50c, Gaucho. 80c, Gold panner. 1cr, Banana plantation worker. 1.10cr, Grape harvester. 1.30cr, Coffee picker. 1.80cr, Farmer gathering wax palms. 2cr, Potter. 5cr, Sugar cane cutter. 7cr, Salt mine worker. 10cr, Fisherman. 15cr, Coconut seller. 20cr, Lacemaker.

Perf. 11½x11, 11x11½
1976-78   Photo.
1441 A790 10c red brown ('77) .... .15 .15
1442 A790 15c brown .... .24 .32
1443 A790 20c violet blue .... .15 .15
1444 A790 30c lilac rose .... .15 .15
1445 A790 40c orange ('77) .... .15 .15
1446 A790 50c citron .... .15 .15
1447 A790 80c slate green .... .38 .15
1448 A790 1cr black .... .16 .15

BRAZIL

1449	A790	1.10cr magenta ('77)	.16 .15
1450	A790	1.30cr red ('77)	.16 .15
1451	A790	1.80cr dk vio bl ('78)	.18 .15

Engr.

1452	A790	2cr brown ('77)	.22 .15
1453	A790	5cr dk pur ('77)	.50 .15
1454	A790	7cr violet	1.50 .15
1455	A790	10cr yel grn ('77)	.55 .15
1456	A790	15cr gray grn ('78)	1.40 .15
1457	A790	20cr blue	1.40 .15
		Nos. 1441-1457 (17)	7.60 2.72

See Nos. 1653-1657.

Hyphessobrycon Innesi — A791

Designs: Brazilian fresh-water fish.

1976, July 12   Litho.   Perf. 11x11½

1460	A791	1cr shown	.42 .40
1461	A791	1cr Copeina arnoldi	.42 .40
1462	A791	1cr Prochilodus insignis	.42 .40
1463	A791	1cr Crenicichla lepidota	.42 .40
1464	A791	1cr Ageneiosus	.42 .40
1465	A791	1cr Corydoras reticulatus	.42 .40
a.		Block of 6, #1460-1465	2.50 2.50

Santa Marta Lighthouse — A792

1976, July 29   Engr.   Perf. 12x11½

1466 A792 1cr blue .20 .30

300th anniversary of the city of Laguna.

Children on Magic Carpet A793

1976, Aug. 1   Litho.   Perf. 11½x12

1467 A793 1cr multicolored .20 .20

Stamp Day.

Nurse's Lamp and Head A794

1976, Aug. 12   Litho.   Perf. 11½

1468 A794 1cr multicolored .20 .20

Brazilian Nurses' Assoc., 50th anniv.

Puppet, Soldier — A795

Winner's Medal — A796

Designs: 1.30cr, Girl's head. 1.60cr, Hand with puppet head on each finger, horiz.

1976, Aug. 20

1469	A795	1cr multi	.20 .20
1470	A795	1.30cr multi	.20 .20
1471	A795	1.60cr multi	.20 .20
		Nos. 1469-1471 (3)	.60 .60

Mamulengo puppet show.

1976, Aug. 21

1472 A796 5.20cr multi .70 .50

27th International Military Athletic Championships, Rio de Janeiro, Aug. 21-28.

Family Protection — A797

1976, Sept. 12

1473 A797 1cr lt & dk blue .20 .20

National organizations SENAC and SESC helping commercial employees to improve their living standard, both commercially and socially.

Dying Tree — A798

1976, Sept. 20   Litho.   Perf. 11½

1474 A798 1cr gray & multi .20 .20

Protection of the environment.

Atom Symbol, Electron Orbits A799

1976, Sept. 21

1475 A799 5.20cr multi .70 .50

20th General Conference of the International Atomic Energy Agency, Rio de Janeiro, Sept. 21-29.

Train in Tunnel — A800

1976, Sept. 26

1476 A800 1.60cr multi .25 .25

Sao Paulo subway, 1st in Brazil.

St. Francis and Birds A801

1976, Oct. 4

1477 A801 5.20cr multi .60 .42

St. Francis of Assisi, 750th death anniv.

Ouro Preto School of Mining — A802

1976, Oct. 12   Engr.   Perf. 12x11½

1478 A802 1cr dk vio .40 .50

Ouro Preto School of Mining, centenary.

Three Kings — A803

Designs: Children's drawings.

1976, Nov. 4   Litho.   Perf. 11½

1479	A803	80c shown	.28 .28
1480	A803	80c Santa Claus on donkey	.28 .28
1481	A803	80c Virgin and Child and Angels	.28 .28
1482	A803	80c Angels with candle	.28 .28
1483	A803	80c Nativity	.28 .28
a.		Strip of 5, #1479-1483	1.40 1.40

Christmas 1976.

Souvenir Sheet

30,000 Reis Banknote — A804

1976, Nov. 5   Litho.   Perf. 11½

1484 A804 80c multicolored .40 1.50

Opening of 1000th branch of Bank of Brazil, Barra do Bugres, Mato Grosso.

Virgin of Monte Serrat, by Friar Agostinho A805

St. Joseph, 18th Century Wood Sculpture — A806

Designs: 5.60cr, The Dance, by Rodolfo Bernadelli, 19th century. 6.50cr, The Caravel, by Bruno Giorgi, 20th century abstract sculpture.

1976, Nov. 5

1485	A805	80c multi	.15 .15
1486	A806	5cr multi	.65 .40
1487	A805	5.60cr multi	.65 .40
1488	A806	6.50cr multi	.65 .40
		Nos. 1485-1488 (4)	2.10 1.35

Development of Brazilian sculpture.

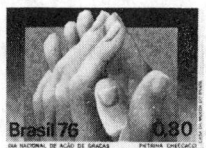

Praying Hands A807

1976, Nov. 25

1489 A807 80c multicolored .25 .25

National Day of Thanksgiving.

Sailor, 1840 — A808

Design: 2cr, Marine's uniform, 1808.

1976, Dec. 13   Litho.   Perf. 11½x11

1490	A808	80c multicolored	.22 .22
1491	A808	2cr multicolored	.32 .22

Brazilian Navy.

"Natural Resources and Development" — A809

1976, Dec. 17   Perf. 11½

1492 A809 80c multicolored .20 .16

Brazilian Bureau of Standards, founded 1940.

Wheel of Life — A810

Designs: 5.60cr, Beggar, sculpture by Agnaldo dos Santos. 6.50cr, Benin mask.

1977, Jan. 14

1493	A810	5cr multi	.55 .35
1494	A810	5.60cr multi	.55 .35
1495	A810	6.50cr multi	1.10 .35
		Nos. 1493-1495 (3)	2.20 1.05

FESTAC '77, 2nd World Black and African Festival, Lagos, Nigeria, Jan. 15-Feb. 12.

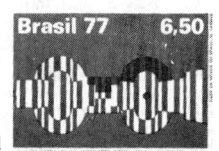

A811

1977, Jan. 20   Litho.   Perf. 11½

1496 A811 6.50cr bl & yel grn .85 .65

Rio de Janeiro International Airport.

BRAZIL

Seminar Emblem with Map of Americas — A812
Salicylate, Microphoto — A813

1977, Feb. 6
1497 A812 1.10cr gray, vio bl & bl .35 .18
6th Inter-American Budget Seminar.

1977, Apr. 10 Litho. Perf. 11½
1498 A813 1.10cr multi .20 .15
International Rheumatism Year.

Lions International Emblem — A814

1977, Apr. 16
1499 A814 1.10cr multi .20 .20
25th anniv. of Brazilian Lions Intl.

Heitor Villa Lobos — A815

1977, Apr. 26 Perf. 11x11½
1500 A815 1.10cr shown .15 .20
1501 A815 1.10cr Chiquinha Gonzaga .15 .20
1502 A815 1.10cr Noel Rosa .15 .20
Nos. 1500-1502 (3) .45 .60
Brazilian composers.

Farmer and Worker — A816
Medicine Bottles and Flask — A817

1977, May 8 Litho. Perf. 11½
1503 A816 1.10cr grn & multi .15 .20
1504 A817 1.10cr lt & dk grn .15 .20
Support and security for rural and urban workers (No. 1503) and establishment in 1971 of Medicine Distribution Center (CEME) for low-cost medicines (No. 1504).

Churchyard Cross, Porto Seguro — A818

Views, Porto Seguro: 5cr, Beach and boats. 5.60cr, Our Lady of Pena Chapel. 6.50cr, Town Hall.

1977, May 25 Litho. Perf. 11½
1505 A818 1.10cr multi .15 .15
1506 A818 5cr multi 1.40 .35
1507 A818 5.60cr multi .55 .45
1508 A818 6.50cr multi .80 .55
Nos. 1505-1508 (4) 2.90 1.50
Cent. of Brazil's membership in UPU.

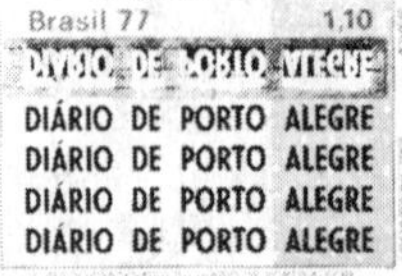

Diario de Porto Alegre — A819

1977, June 1
1509 A819 1.10cr multi .20 .20
Diario de Porto Alegre, newspaper, 150th anniv.

Blue Whale — A820

1977, June 3
1510 A820 1.30cr multi .20 .20
Protection of marine life.

"Life and Development" — A821

1977, June 20
1511 A821 1.30cr multi .20 .20
National Development Bank, 25th anniversary.

Train Leaving Tunnel — A822

1977, July 8 Engr. Perf. 11½
1512 A822 1.30cr black .20 .20
Centenary of Sao Paulo-Rio de Janeiro railroad.

Vasum Cassiforme — A823
Caduceus, Formulas for Water and Fluoride — A824

Sea Shells: No. 1514, Strombus goliath. No. 1515, Murex tenuivaricosus.

1977, July 14 Litho.
1513 A823 1.30cr blue & multi .20 .20
1514 A823 1.30cr brown & multi .20 .20
1515 A823 1.30cr green & multi .20 .20
Nos. 1513-1515 (3) .60 .60

1977, July 15 Perf. 11½x11
1516 A824 1.30cr multi .20 .20
3rd Intl. Odontology Congress, Rio, July 15-21.

Masonic Emblem, Map of Brazil — A825
"Stamps Don't Sink or Lose their Way" — A826

1977, July 18 Perf. 11½
1517 A825 1.30cr bl, lt bl & blk .20 .20
50th anniversary of the founding of the Brazilian Grand Masonic Lodge.

1977, Aug. 1
1518 A826 1.30cr multi .20 .20
Stamp Day 1977.

Dom Pedro's Proclamation — A827
Horses and Bulls — A828

1977, Aug. 11 Litho. Perf. 11½
1519 A827 1.30cr multi .20 .20
150th anniversary of Brazilian Law School.

Perf. 11½x11, 11x11½
1977, Aug. 20 Litho.
Brazilian folklore: No. 1521, King on horseback. No. 1522, Joust, horiz.
1520 A828 1.30cr ocher & multi .20 .20
1521 A828 1.30cr blue & multi .20 .20
1522 A828 1.30cr yel & multi .20 .20
Nos. 1520-1522 (3) .60 .60

2000-reis Doubloon — A829

Brazilian Colonial Coins: No. 1524, 640r pataca. No. 1525, 20r copper "vintem."

1977, Aug. 31 Perf. 11½
1523 A829 1.30cr vio bl & multi .20 .15
1524 A829 1.30cr dk red & multi .20 .15
1525 A829 1.30cr yel & multi .20 .15
Nos. 1523-1525 (3) .60 .45

Pinwheel — A830
Neoregelia Carolinae — A831

1977, Sept. 1
1526 A830 1.30cr multi .20 .15
National Week.

1977, Sept. 21 Litho. Perf. 11½
1527 A831 1.30cr multi .20 .15
Nature preservation.

Pen, Pencil, Letters — A832

1977, Oct. 15 Litho. Perf. 11½
1528 A832 1.30cr multi .20 .15
Primary education, sesquicentennial.

Dome and Telescope — A833

1977, Oct. 15
1529 A833 1.30cr multi .20 .15
National Astrophysics Observatory, Brasópolis, sesquicentennial.

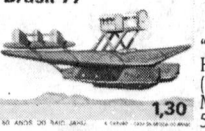

"Jahu" Hydroplane (Savoia Marchetti S-55) — A834

Design: No. 1531, PAX, dirigible.

1977, Oct. 17
1530 A834 1.30cr multi .25 .25
1531 A834 1.30cr multi .25 .25
50th anniv. of crossing of South Atlantic by Joao Ribeiro de Barros, Genoa-Sao Paulo (#1530) and 75th anniv. of the PAX airship (#1531).

A835
A836

1977, Oct. 24
1532 A835 1.30cr Il'Guarani .20 .15
Book Day and to honor Jose Martiniano de Alencar, writer, jurist.

1977, Nov. 5 Litho. Perf. 11½
1533 A836 1.30cr Waves .20 .15
Amateur Radio Operators' Day.

Nativity — A837

Christmas (folk art): 2cr, Annunciation. 5cr, Nativity.

1977, Nov. 10
1534 A837 1.30cr bister & multi .22 .15
1535 A837 2cr bister & multi .32 .15
1536 A837 5cr bister & multi .65 .25
Nos. 1534-1536 (3) 1.19 .55

BRAZIL

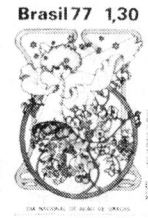

A838

A839

1977, Nov. 19
1537	A838	1.30cr Emerald	.20	.20
1538	A838	1.30cr Topaz	.20	.20
1539	A838	1.30cr Aquamarine	.20	.20
		Nos. 1537-1539 (3)	.60	.60

PORTUCALE 77, 2nd International Topical Exhibition, Porto, Nov. 19-20.

1977, Nov. 24 Litho. Perf. 11½
| 1540 | A839 | 1.30cr Angel, cornucopia | .20 | .20 |

National Thanksgiving Day.

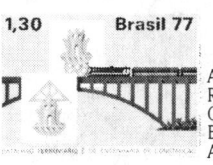

Army's Railroad Construction Battalion — A840

Civilian services of armed forces: No. 1542, Navy's Amazon flotilla. No. 1543, Air Force's postal service (plane).

1977, Dec. 5
1541	A840	1.30cr multi	.20	.20
1542	A840	1.30cr multi	.20	.20
1543	A840	1.30cr multi	.20	.20
		Nos. 1541-1543 (3)	.60	.60

Varig Emblem, Jet — A841

1977, Dec. Perf. 11x11½
| 1544 | A841 | 1.30cr bl & blk | .20 | .20 |

50th anniversary of Varig Airline.

Sts. Cosme and Damiao Church, Igaracu — A842

Woman Holding Sheaf — A843

Brazilian Architecture: 7.50cr, St. Bento Monastery Church, Rio de Janeiro. 8.50cr, Church of St. Francis of Assisi, Ouro Preto. 9.50cr, St. Anthony Convent Church, Joao Pessoa.

1977, Dec. 8
1545	A842	2.70cr multi	.30	.15
1546	A842	7.50cr multi	.90	.35
1547	A842	8.50cr multi	.90	.40
1548	A842	9.50cr multi	1.25	.45
		Nos. 1545-1548 (4)	3.35	1.35

1977, Dec. 19 Perf. 11½
| 1549 | A843 | 1.30cr multi | .20 | .20 |

Brazilian diplomacy.

Soccer Ball and Foot — A844

Designs: No. 1551, Soccer ball in net. No. 1552, Symbolic soccer player.

1978, Mar. 1 Litho. Perf. 11½
1550	A844	1.80cr multi	.28	.20
1551	A844	1.80cr multi	.28	.20
1552	A844	1.80cr multi	.28	.20
		Nos. 1550-1552 (3)	.84	.60

11th World Cup Soccer Championship, Argentina, June 1-25.

"La Fosca" on La Scala Stage and Carlos Gomes — A845

1978, Feb. 9
| 1553 | A845 | 1.80cr multi | .20 | .20 |

Bicentenary of La Scala in Milan, and to honor Carlos Gomes (1836-1893), Brazilian composer.

Symbols of Postal Mechanization — A846

1978, Mar. 15 Litho. Perf. 11½
| 1554 | A846 | 1.80cr multi | .20 | .20 |

Opening of Postal Staff College.

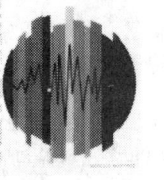

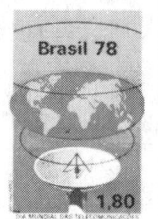

Hypertension Chart — A847

Waves from Antenna Uniting World — A848

1978, Apr. 4
| 1555 | A847 | 1.80cr multi | .20 | .20 |

World Health Day, fight against hypertension.

1978, May 17 Litho. Perf. 12x11½
| 1556 | A848 | 1.80cr multi | .20 | .20 |

10th World Telecommunications Day.

Brazilian Canary — A849

Birds: 8.50cr, Cotinga. 9.50cr, Tanager fastuosa.

1978, June 5 Perf. 11½x12
1557	A849	7.50cr multi	1.00	.75
1558	A849	8.50cr multi	1.00	.80
1559	A849	9.50cr multi	1.00	1.00
		Nos. 1557-1559 (3)	3.00	2.55

Inocencio Serzedelo Correa and Manuel Francisco Correa, 1893 — A850

1978, June 20 Litho. Perf. 11x11½
| 1560 | A850 | 1.80cr multi | .20 | .20 |

85th anniversary of Union Court of Audit.

Post and Telegraph Building — A851

1978, June 22 Perf. 11½
| 1561 | A851 | 1.80cr multi | .20 | .25 |

Souvenir Sheet
Imperf
| 1562 | A851 | 7.50cr multi | .75 | 1.50 |

Inauguration of Post and Telegraph Building (ECT), Brasilia, and for BRAPEX, 3rd Brazilian Philatelic Exhibition, Brasilia, June 23-28 (No. 1562).

Ernesto Geisel, President of Brazil — A852

1978, June 22 Engr. Perf. 11½
| 1563 | A852 | 1.80cr dull green | .20 | .15 |

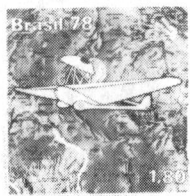

Savoia-Marchetti S-64, Map of South Atlantic — A853

1978, July 3 Litho.
| 1564 | A853 | 1.80cr multi | .20 | .20 |

50th anniv. of 1st crossing of South Atlantic by Carlos del Prete and Arturo Ferrarin.

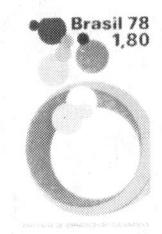

Symbolic of Smallpox Eradication — A854

Brazil No. 68 — A855

1978, July 25
| 1565 | A854 | 1.80cr multi | .20 | .20 |

Eradication of smallpox.

1978, Aug. 1
| 1566 | A855 | 1.80cr multi | .20 | .20 |

Stamp Day, centenary of the "Barba Branca" (white beard) issue.

Stormy Sea, by Seelinger — A856

1978, Aug. 4
| 1567 | A856 | 1.80cr multi | .20 | .20 |

Helios Seelinger, painter, birth centenary.

Guitar Players — A857

Musicians and Instruments: No. 1569, Flutes. No. 1570, Percussion instruments.

1978, Aug. 22 Litho. Perf. 11½
1568	A857	1.80cr multi	.20	.15
1569	A857	1.80cr multi	.20	.15
1570	A857	1.80cr multi	.20	.20
		Nos. 1568-1570 (3)	.60	.50

Children at Play — A858

1978, Sept. 1 Litho. Perf. 11½
| 1571 | A858 | 1.80cr multi | .20 | .20 |

National Week.

Collegiate Church — A859

1978, Sept. 6 Engr.
| 1572 | A859 | 1.80cr red brn | .20 | .20 |

Restoration of patio of Collegiate Church, Sao Paulo.

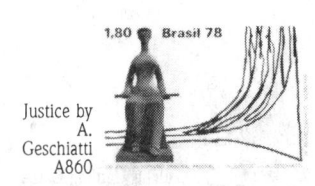

Justice by A. Geschiatti — A860

1978, Sept. 18 Litho.
| 1573 | A860 | 1.80cr blk & olive | .20 | .20 |

Federal Supreme Court, sesquicentennial.

Iguacu Falls — A861

Design: No. 1575, Yellow ipecac.

1978, Sept. 21
| 1574 | A861 | 1.80cr multi | .20 | .20 |
| 1575 | A861 | 1.80cr multi | .20 | .20 |

Iguacu National Park.

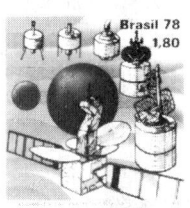

Stages of Intelsat Satellite — A862

1978, Oct. 9 Litho. Perf. 11½
| 1576 | A862 | 1.80cr multi | .20 | .20 |

Flag of Order of Christ — A863

Brazilian Flags: No. 1578, Principality of Brazil. No. 1579, United Kingdom. No. 1580, Imperial Brazil. No. 1581, National flag (current).

1978, Oct. 13
1577	A863	1.80cr multi	.65	.55
1578	A863	1.80cr multi	.65	.55
1579	A863	1.80cr multi	.65	.55
1580	A863	8.50cr multi	.65	.55
1581	A863	8.50cr multi	.65	.55
a.	Block of 5, #1577-1581 + label		4.00	6.50
	Nos. 1577-1581 (5)		3.25	2.75

7th LUBRAPEX Philatelic Exhibition, Porto Alegre.

Mail Street Car — A864

Mail Transportation: No. 1583, Overland mail truck. No. 1584, Mail delivery truck. 7.50cr, Railroad mail car. 8.50cr, Mail coach. 9.50cr, Post riders.

1978, Oct. 21 Perf. 11x11½
1582	A864	1.80cr multi	.50	.40
1583	A864	1.80cr multi	.50	.40
1584	A864	1.80cr multi	.50	.40
1585	A864	7.50cr multi	.50	.40
1586	A864	8.50cr multi	.50	.40
1587	A864	9.50cr multi	.50	.50
a.	Block of 6, #1582-1587		3.00	3.00

18th UPU Congress, Rio de Janeiro, 1979.

Gaucho Herding Cattle, and Cactus — A865

1978, Oct. 23 Perf. 11½x11
1588 A865 1.80cr multi .20 .20

Joao Guimaraes Rosa, poet and diplomat, 70th birthday.

St. Anthony's Hill, by Nicholas A. Taunay A866

Landscape Paintings: No. 1590, Castle Hill, by Victor Meirelles. No. 1591, View of Sabara, by Alberto da Veiga Guignard. No. 1592, View of Pernambuco, by Frans Post.

1978, Nov. 6 Litho. Perf. 11½
1589	A866	1.80cr multi	.20	.20
1590	A866	1.80cr multi	.20	.20
1591	A866	1.80cr multi	.20	.20
1592	A866	1.80cr multi	.20	.20
	Nos. 1589-1592 (4)		.80	.80

Angel with Harp — A867

Christmas: No. 1594, Angel with lute. No. 1595, Angel with oboe.

1978, Nov. 10
1593	A867	1.80cr multi	.20	.20
1594	A867	1.80cr multi	.20	.20
1595	A867	1.80cr multi	.20	.20
	Nos. 1593-1595 (3)		.60	.60

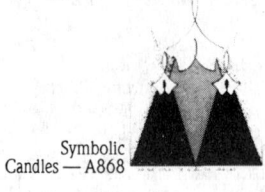

Symbolic Candles — A868

1978, Nov. 23
1596 A868 1.80cr blk, gold & car .20 .20

National Thanksgiving Day.

Red Crosses and Activities A869

1978, Dec. 5 Litho. Perf. 11x11½
1597 A869 1.80cr blk & red .20 .20

70th anniversary of Brazilian Red Cross.

Paz Theater, Belem — A870

12cr, José de Alencar Theater, Portaleza. 12.50cr, Municipal Theater, Rio de Janeiro.

1978, Dec. 6 Perf. 11½
1598	A870	10.50cr multi	.70	.25
1599	A870	12cr multi	.70	.25
1600	A870	12.50cr multi	.70	.25
	Nos. 1598-1600 (3)		2.10	.75

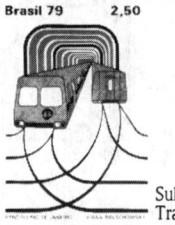

Subway Trains — A871

1979, Mar. 5 Litho. Perf. 11½
1601 A871 2.50cr multi .20 .20

Inauguration of Rio subway system.

Old and New Post Offices A872

Designs: No. 1603, Old and new mail boxes. No. 1604, Manual and automatic mail sorting. No. 1605, Old and new planes. No. 1606, Telegraph and telex machine. No. 1607, Mailmen's uniforms.

1979, Mar. 20 Litho. Perf. 11x11½
1602	A872	2.50cr multi	.25	.20
1603	A872	2.50cr multi	.25	.20
1604	A872	2.50cr multi	.25	.20
1605	A872	2.50cr multi	.25	.20
1606	A872	2.50cr multi	.25	.20
1607	A872	2.50cr multi	.25	.20
a.	Block of 6, #1602-1607		1.50	1.50

10th anniv. of the new Post and Telegraph Dept., and 18th Universal Postal Union Cong., Rio de Janeiro, Sept.-Oct., 1979.

O'Day 23 Class Yacht A873

Yachts and Stamp Outlines: 10.50cr, Penguin Class. 12cr, Hobie Cat Class. 12.50cr, Snipe Class.

1979, Apr. 18 Litho. Perf. 11x11½
1608	A873	2.50cr multi	.30	.25
1609	A873	10.50cr multi	.55	.45
1610	A873	12cr multi	.55	.35
1611	A873	12.50cr multi	.75	.35
	Nos. 1608-1611 (4)		2.15	1.40

Brasiliana '79, 3rd World Thematic Stamp Exhibition, Sao Conrado, Sept. 15-23.

Children, IYC Emblem — A874

1979, May 30 Litho. Perf. 11½
1612 A874 2.50cr multi .25 .20

Intl. Year of the Child & Children's Book Day.

Giant Water Lily — A875

12cr, Amazon manatee. 12.50cr, Arrau (turtle).

1979, June 5 Litho. Perf. 11½
1613	A875	10.50cr multi	.70	.50
1614	A875	12cr multi	.90	.60
1615	A875	12.50cr multi	.90	.60
	Nos. 1613-1615 (3)		2.50	1.70

Amazon National Park, nature conservation.

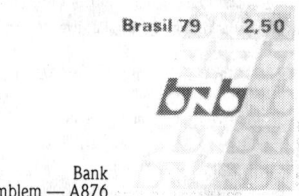

Bank Emblem — A876

1979, June 7
1616 A876 2.50cr multi .20 .15

Northwest Bank of Brazil, 25th anniversary.

Physician Tending Patient 15th Cent. Woodcut A877

1979, June 30
1617 A877 2.50cr multi .20 .15

Natl. Academy of Medicine, 50th anniv.

Flower made of Hearts — A878

1979, July 8 Litho. Perf. 11½
1618 A878 2.50cr multi .20 .15

35th Brazilian Cardiology Congress.

Souvenir Sheet

Hotel Nacional, Rio de Janeiro A879

1979, July 16
1619 A879 12.50cr multi .75 1.50

Brasiliana '79 comprising 1st Inter-American Exhibition of Classical Philately and 3rd World Topical Exhibition, Rio de Janeiro, Sept. 15-23.

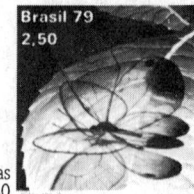

Cithaerias Aurora — A880

Moths: 10.50cr, Evenus regalis. 12cr, Caligo eurilochus. 12.50cr, Diaethria clymena janeira.

1979, Aug. 1
1620	A880	2.50cr multi	.18	.15
1621	A880	10.50cr multi	.60	.40
1622	A880	12cr multi	.70	.52
1623	A880	12.50cr multi	.70	.52
	Nos. 1620-1623 (4)		2.18	1.59

Stamp Day 1979.

EMB-121 Xingo A881

1979, Aug. 19 Litho. Perf. 11½
1624 A881 2.50cr vio blue .20 .20

Embraer, Brazilian aircraft comp., 10th anniv.

A882    A883

BRAZIL

Natl. emblem over landscape.

1979, Sept. 12
1625 A882 3.20cr multi .20 .20
National Week.

1979, Sept. 8 Litho. *Perf. 11½*
1626 A883 2.50cr multi .20 .20
Statue of Our Lady of the Apparition, 75th anniversary of coronation.

"UPU," Envelope and Mail Transport — A884

"UPU" and: No. 1628, Post Office emblems. 10.50cr, Globe. 12cr, Flags of Brazil and UN. 12.50cr, UPU emblem.

1979, Sept. 12 *Perf. 11x11½*
1627 A884 2.50cr multi .16 .16
1628 A884 2.50cr multi .16 .16
1629 A884 10.50cr multi .52 .52
1630 A884 12cr multi .70 .70
1631 A884 12.50cr multi .70 .70
Nos. 1627-1631 (5) 2.24 2.24

18th UPU Cong., Rio, Sept.-Oct. 1979.

Pyramid Fountain, Rio de Janeiro — A885

Fountains: 10.50cr, Facade, Marilia, Ouro Preto, horiz. 12cr, Boa Vista, Recife.

Perf. 12x11½, 11½x12
1979, Sept. 15
1632 A885 2.50cr multi .16 .16
1633 A885 10.50cr multi .50 .50
1634 A885 12cr multi .60 .60
Nos. 1632-1634 (3) 1.26 1.26

Brasiliana '79, 1st Interamerican Exhibition of Classical Philately.

Church of the Glory — A886

Landscapes by Leandro Joaquim: 12cr, Fishing on Guanabara Bay. 12.50cr, Boqueirao Lake and Carioca Arches.

1979, Sept. 15 *Perf. 11½*
1635 A886 2.50cr multi .16 .16
1636 A886 12cr multi .60 .60
1637 A886 12.50cr multi .60 .60
Nos. 1635-1637 (3) 1.36 1.36

Brasiliana '79, 3rd World Topical Exhibition, Sao Conrado, Sept. 15-23.

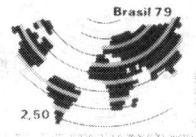

World Map — A887

1979, Sept. 20
1638 A887 2.50cr multi .20 .20

3rd World Telecommunications Exhibition, Geneva, Sept. 20-26.

"UPU" and UPU Emblem — A888

1979, Oct. 9 Litho. *Perf. 11½x11*
1639 A888 2.50cr multi .18 .18
1640 A888 10.50cr multi .55 .55
1641 A888 12cr multi .65 .65
1642 A888 12.50cr multi .65 .65
Nos. 1639-1642 (4) 2.03 2.03

Universal Postal Union Day.

IYC Emblem, Feather Toy A889

IYC Emblem and Toys: No. 1644, Bumble bee, ragdoll. No. 1645, Flower, top. No. 1646, Wooden acrobat.

1979, Oct. 12 *Perf. 11½*
1643 A889 2.50cr multi .25 .20
1644 A889 3.20cr multi .25 .25
1645 A889 3.20cr multi .25 .25
1646 A889 3.20cr multi .25 .25
Nos. 1643-1646 (4) 1.00 .95

International Year of the Child.

Adoration of the Kings — A890

Christmas 1979: No. 1648, Nativity. No. 1649 Jesus and the Elders in the Temple.

1979, Nov. 12 Litho. *Perf. 11½*
1647 A890 3.20cr multi .20 .18
1648 A890 3.20cr multi .20 .18
1649 A890 3.20cr multi .20 .18
Nos. 1647-1649 (3) .60 .54

Souvenir Sheet

Hands Reading Braille — A891

Lithographed and Embossed
1979, Nov. 20 *Perf. 11½*
1650 A891 3.20cr multi .50 1.25

Publication of Braille script, 150th anniversary. Margin shows extension of stamp design with Braille printed and embossed.

Ordering on-line is
QUICK!
EASY!
CONVENIENT!
www.scottonline.com

Wheat Harvester — A892
Steel Mill — A893 

1979, Nov. 22
1651 A892 3.20cr multi .20 .15
Thanksgiving 1979.

1979, Nov. 23
1652 A893 3.20cr multi .20 .15
COSIPA Steelworks, Sao Paulo, 25th anniversary.

Type of 1976

Designs: 70c, Women grinding coconuts. 2.50cr, Basket weaver. 3.20cr, River boatman. 21cr, Harvesting ramie (China grass). 27cr, Man leading pack mule. 3.20cr, 27cr, horiz.

Photogravure, Engraved (21cr)
1979 *Perf. 11x11½, 11½x11*
1653 A790 70c gray grn .15 .15
1654 A790 2.50cr sepia .15 .15
1655 A790 3.20cr blue .15 .15
1656 A790 21cr purple .38 .15
1657 A790 27cr sepia .45 .15
Nos. 1653-1657 (5) 1.28 .75

A894

Designs: 2cr, Coconuts. 3cr, Mangoes. 4cr, Corn. 5cr, Onions. 7cr, Oranges. 10cr, Maracuja. 12cr, Pineapple. 15cr, Bananas. 17cr, Guarana. 20cr, Sugar cane. 24cr, Beekeeping. 30cr, Silkworm. 34cr, Cacao. 38cr, Coffee. 42cr, Soybeans. 45cr, Mandioca. 50cr, Wheat. 57cr, Peanuts. 66cr, Grapes. 100cr, Cashews. 140cr, Tomatoes. 200cr, Mamona. 500cr, Cotton.

1980-83 Photo. *Perf. 11½x11*
1658 A894 2cr yel brn ('82) .15 .15
1659 A894 3cr red ('82) .15 .15
1660 A894 4cr orange .15 .15
1661 A894 5cr dk pur ('82) .15 .15
1662 A894 7cr org ('81) .15 .15
1663 A894 10cr bl grn ('82) .15 .15
1664 A894 12cr dk grn ('81) .22 .15
1665 A894 15cr gldn brn ('83) .15 .15
1666 A894 17cr brn org ('82) .24 .15
1667 A894 20cr olive ('82) .22 .15
1668 A894 24cr bis ('82) .15 .15
1669 A894 30cr blk ('82) .15 .15
1670 A894 34cr brown .35 .15
1671 A894 38cr red ('83) .15 .15
1672 A894 42cr green 5.75 .50
1673 A894 45cr sepia ('83) .55 .15
1674 A894 50cr yel org ('82) .16 .15
1675 A894 57cr brn ('83) .16 .15
1676 A894 66cr pur ('81) 3.75 .15
1677 A894 100cr dk red brn ('81) 2.25 .15
1678 A894 140cr red ('82) 2.75 .15

Engr.
1678A A894 200cr grn ('82) 2.75 .15
1679 A894 500cr brn ('82) 5.75 .15
Nos. 1658-1679 (23) 26.40 3.80

See Nos. 1934-1941.

Plant Inside Raindrop — A896

Light Bulb Containing: 17cr+7cr, Sun. 20cr+8cr, Windmill. 21cr+9cr, Dam.

1980, Jan. 2 Litho. *Perf. 12*
1680 A896 3.20cr multi .15 .15
1681 A896 24cr (17 + 7) 1.25 .65
1682 A896 28cr (20 + 8) 1.50 .75
1683 A896 30cr (21 + 9) 2.25 .85
Nos. 1680-1683 (4) 5.15 2.40

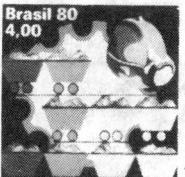

Anthracite Industry — A897

1980, Mar. 19 Litho. *Perf. 11½*
1684 A897 4cr multi .20 .15

Map of Americas, Symbols of Development — A898

1980, Apr. 14 Litho. *Perf. 11x11½*
1685 A898 4cr multi .20 .15

21st Assembly of Inter-American Development Bank Governors, Rio, Apr. 14-16.

Tapirape Mask, Mato Grosso A899

1980, Apr. 18 *Perf. 11½*
1686 A899 4cr shown .20 .15
1687 A899 4cr Tukuna mask, Amazonas, vert. .20 .15
1688 A899 4cr Kanela mask, Maranhao, vert. .20 .15
Nos. 1686-1688 (3) .60 .45

Brazilian Television, 30th Anniversary A900

1980, May 5 Litho. *Perf. 11½*
1689 A900 4cr multicolored .18 .15

Duke of Caxias, by Miranda — A901
The Worker, by Candido Partinari — A902 

1980, May 7
1690 A901 4cr multicolored .18 .15
Duke of Caxias, death centenary.

1980, May 18

Paintings: 28cr, Mademoiselle Pogany, by Constantin Brancusi. 30cr, The Glass of Water, by Francisco Aurelio de Figueiredo.

1691 A902 24cr multi 1.10 .55
1692 A902 28cr multi 1.10 .55
1693 A902 30cr multi 1.65 .55
Nos. 1691-1693 (3) 3.85 1.65

BRAZIL

Graf Zeppelin, 50th Anniversary of Atlantic Crossing
A903

1980, June   Litho.   Perf. 11x11½
1694 A903 4cr multicolored .... .20 .15

Pope John Paul II, St. Peter's, Rome, Congress Emblem
A904

Pope, Emblem and Brazilian Churches: No. 1696, Fortaleza, vert. 24cr, Apericida 28cr, Rio de Janeiro, 30cr, Brasilia.

1980, June 24   Perf. 12
1695 A904 4cr multi .... .18 .15
1696 A904 4cr multi .... .18 .15
1697 A904 24cr multi .... .90 .40
1698 A904 28cr multi .... .90 .40
1699 A904 30cr multi .... 1.75 .40
  Nos. 1695-1699 (5) 3.91 1.50

Visit of Pope John Paul II to Brazil, June 30-July 12; 10th National Eucharistic Congress, Fortaleza, July 9-16.

1st Airmail Flight across the South Atlantic, 50th Anniv.
A905

1980, June   Litho.   Perf. 11x11½
1700 A905 4cr multicolored .... .20 .15

Souvenir Sheet

Yacht Sail, Exhibition Emblem — A906

1980, June   Perf. 11½
1701 A906 30cr multi 1.00 1.50

Brapex IV Stamp Exhib., Fortaleza, June 13-21.

Rowing, Moscow '80 Emblem
A907

1980, June 30
1702 A907 4cr shown .... .20 .15
1703 A907 4cr Target shooting .... .20 .15
1704 A907 4cr Bicycling .... .20 .15
  Nos. 1702-1704 (3) .... .60 .45

22nd Summer Olympic Games, Moscow, July 19-Aug. 3.

Rondon Community Works Project
A908

1980, July 11
1705 A908 4cr multicolored .... .20 .15

Helen Keller and Anne Sullivan
A909

1980, July 28
1706 A909 4cr multicolored .... .20 .15

Helen Keller (1880-1968), blind deaf writer and lecturer taught by Anne Sullivan (1867-1936).

Souvenir Sheet

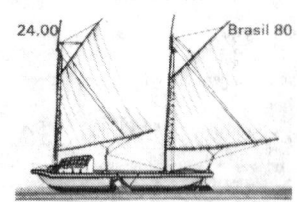

São Francisco River Canoe — A910

1980, Aug. 1   Litho.   Perf. 11½
1707 A910 24cr multi 1.00 1.50

Stamp Day.

Microscope, Red Cross, Insects, Brick and Tile Houses — A911

1980, Aug. 5   Perf. 11½x11
1708 A911 4cr multi .... .25 .15

National Health Day.

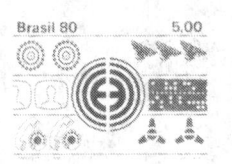

Brazilian Postal Administration, 15th Anniversary — A912

1980, Sept. 16   Litho.   Perf. 12
1709 A912 5cr multi .... .25 .20

Souvenir Sheet

St. Gabriel World Union, 6th Congress
A913

1980, Sept. 29   Perf. 11½x12
1710 A913 30cr multi 1.00 1.50

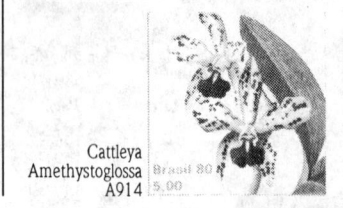

Cattleya Amethystoglossa
A914

Amazona Braziliensis
A915

Captain Rodrigo, Hero of Érico Verissimo's "O Continento"
A916

1980, Oct. 3   Perf. 11½
1711 A914 5cr shown .... .18 .15
1712 A914 5cr Laelia cinnabarina .... .18 .15
1713 A914 24cr Zygopetalum crinitum .... 1.10 .60
1714 A914 28cr Laelia tenebrosa .... 1.10 .60
  Nos. 1711-1714 (4) 2.56 1.50

Espamer 80, American-European Philatelic Exhibition, Madrid, Oct. 3-12.

Parrots: No. 1716, Amazona Vinacea. No. 1717, Touit melanonota. No. 1718, Amazona pretrei.

1980, Oct. 18   Litho.   Perf. 12
1715 A915 5cr multi .... .18 .15
1716 A915 5cr multi .... .18 .15
1717 A915 28cr multi .... 1.10 .60
1718 A915 28cr multi .... 1.10 .60
  Nos. 1715-1718 (4) 2.56 1.50

Lubrapex '80 Stamp Exhib., Lisbon, Oct. 18-26.

1980, Oct. 23
1719 A916 5cr multi .... .25 .20

Book Day.

Flight into Egypt — A917

1980, Nov. 5
1720 A917 5cr multi .... .25 .20

Christmas 1980.

Sound Waves and Oscillator Screen
A918

1980, Nov. 7
1721 A918 5cr multi .... .25 .20

Telebras Research Center inauguration.

Carvalho Viaduct, Paranagua-Curitiba Railroad — A919

1980, Nov. 10
1722 A919 5cr multi .... .25 .20

Engineering Club centenary.

A920 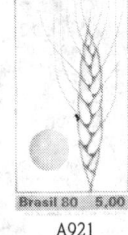   A921

1980, Nov. 18   Litho.   Perf. 11½
1723 A920 5cr Portable chess board .... .25 .50

Postal chess contest.

1980, Nov. 27   Perf. 11½x11
1724 A921 5cr Sun, wheat .... .25 .40

Thanksgiving 1980

Father Anchieta Writing "Virgin Mary, Mother of God" on Sand of Iperoig Beach — A922

1980, Dec. 8   Perf. 12
1725 A922 5cr multi .... .25 .20

Christ Carrying Cross, By O Aleijadinho
A923

Antonio Francisco Lisboa (O Aleijadinho), 250th Birth Anniv.: Paintings of the life of Christ: a, Mount of Olives. b, Arrest in the Garden. c, Flagellation. d, Crown of Thorns. f, Crucifixion.

1980, Dec. 29
1726   Block of 6 .... 1.65 1.65
a.-f. A923 5cr any single .... .24 .16

Agricultural Productivity
A924

1981, Jan. 2   Litho.   Perf. 11x11½
1727 A924 30cr shown .... 1.25 .35
1728 A924 35cr Domestic markets .... 1.10 .35
1729 A924 40cr Exports .... 1.10 .35
  Nos. 1727-1729 (3) 3.45 1.05

Boy Scout and Campfire
A925

1981, Jan. 22   Litho.   Perf. 11x11½
1730 A925 5cr shown .... .25 .20
1731 A925 5cr Scouts cooking .... .25 .20
1732 A925 5cr Scout, tents .... .25 .20
  Nos. 1730-1732 (3) .... .75 .60

4th Pan-American Scout Jamboree.

Souvenir Sheet

Mailman, 1930 — A926

BRAZIL

1981, Mar. 11   Litho.   Perf. 11
1733   Sheet of 3   4.00   4.00
   a.   A926 30cr shown   1.00   1.00
   b.   A926 35cr Mailman, 1981   1.00   1.00
   c.   A926 40cr Telegram messenger, 1930   1.00   1.00
Dept. of Posts & Telegraphs, 50th anniv.

Souvenir Sheet

The Hunter and the Jaguar, by Felix Taunay (1795-1881) A927

1981, Apr. 10   Litho.   Perf. 11
1734   A927 30cr multi   1.00   2.00

Lima Barreto and Rio de Janeiro, 1900 A928

1981, May 13   Litho.   Perf. 11½
1735   A928 7cr multi   .25   .20
Lima Barreto, writer, birth centenary.

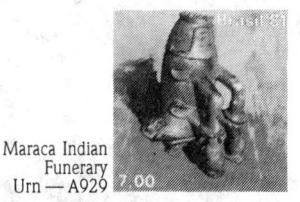

Maraca Indian Funerary Urn — A929

1981, May 18
1736   A929 7cr shown   .25   .20
1737   A929 7cr Marajoara triangular jug   .25   .20
1738   A929 7cr Tupi-Guarani bowl   .25   .20
   Nos. 1736-1738 (3)   .75   .60

Lophornis Magnifica A930

Designs: Hummingbirds.

1981, May 22   Perf. 11½
1739   A930 7cr shown   .30   .20
1740   A930 7cr Phaethornis pretrei   .30   .20
1741   A930 7cr Chrysolampis mosquitus   .30   .20
1742   A930 7cr Heliactin cornuta   .30   .20
   Nos. 1739-1742 (4)   1.20   .80

Rotary Emblem and Faces — A931

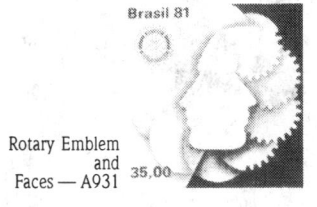

1981, May 31
1743   A931 7cr Emblem, hands   .20   .15
1744   A931 35cr shown   1.00   .80
72nd Convention of Rotary Intl., Sao Paulo.

Environmental Protection A932

1981, June 5   Perf. 12
1745   A932 7cr shown   .25   .20
1746   A932 7cr Forest   .25   .20
1747   A932 7cr Clouds (air)   .25   .20
1748   A932 7cr Village (soil)   .25   .20
   a.   Block of 4, #1745-1748   1.00   1.00

Biplane, 1931 (Airmail Service, 50th Anniv.) A933

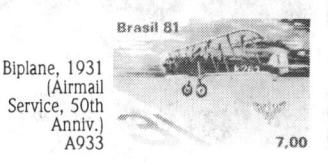

1981, June 10   Perf. 11½
1749   A933 7cr multi   .25   .20

Madeira-Mamore Railroad, 50th Anniv. of Nationalization — A934

1981, July 10   Litho.   Perf. 11x11½
1750   A934 7cr multi   .25   .20

66th Intl. Esperanto Congress, Brasilia A935

1981, July 26   Perf. 12
1751   A935 7cr green & blk   .25   .20

No. 79 A936

1981, Aug. 1
1752   A936 50cr shown   1.40   .30
1753   A936 55cr No. 80   1.40   .30
1754   A936 60cr No. 81   1.40   .30
   Nos. 1752-1754 (3)   4.20   .90
Stamp Day; cent. of "small head" stamps.

Institute of Military Engineering, 50th Anniv. — A937

1981, Aug. 11   Litho.   Perf. 11½
1755   A937 12cr multi   .25   .20

Reisado Dancers — A938

1981, Aug. 22
1756   A938 50cr Dancers, diff.   .80   .22
1757   A938 55cr Sailors   .80   .25
1758   A938 60cr shown   .80   .20
   Nos. 1756-1758 (3)   2.40   .67

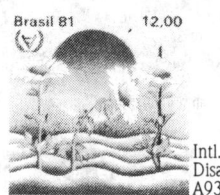

Intl. Year of the Disabled A939

1981, Sept. 17   Litho.   Perf. 11½
1759   A939 12cr multi   .25   .20

Flowers of the Central Plateau A940

1981, Sept. 21   Litho.   Perf. 12
1760   A940 12cr Palicourea rigida   .25   .20
1761   A940 12cr Dalechampia caperonioides   .25   .20
1762   A940 12cr Cassia claussseni, vert.   .25   .20
1763   A940 12cr Eremanthus sphaerocephalus, vert.   .25   .20
   Nos. 1760-1763 (4)   1.00   .80

Virgin of Nazareth Statue — A941

Christ the Redeemer Statue, Rio de Janeiro, 50th Anniv. — A942

1981, Oct. 10   Litho.   Perf. 12
1764   A941 12cr multi   .25   .20
Candle Festival of Nazareth, Belem.

1981, Oct. 12
1765   A942 12cr multi   .25   .20

World Food Day — A943

1981, Oct. 16
1766   A943 12c multi   .25   .20

75th Anniv. of Santos-Dumont's First Flight — A944

1981, Oct. 23   Litho.   Perf. 12
1767   A944 60cr multi   1.00   .35

Father José de Santa Rita Durao, Titlepage of his Epic Poem Caramuru, Diego Alvares Correia (Character) A945

1981, Oct. 29
1768   A945 12cr multi   .25   .20
Caramuru publication cent.; World Book Day.

Christmas 1981 — A946

Designs: Creches and figurines.

1981, Nov. 10   Litho.   Perf. 12
1769   A946 12cr multi   .15   .15
1770   A946 50cr multi   1.25   .25
1771   A946 55cr multi, vert.   1.25   .28
1772   A946 60cr multi, vert.   1.25   .30
   Nos. 1769-1772 (4)   3.90   .98

State Flags — A947

Designs: a, Alagoas. b, Bahia. c, Federal District. d, Pernambuco. e, Sergipe.

1981, Nov. 19
1773   Block of 5 + label   1.25   1.25
   a.-e.   A947 12cr, any single   .20   .20
Label shows arms of Brazil.

Thanksgiving 1981 — A948

1981, Nov. 26   Litho.   Perf. 11½
1776   A948 12cr multi   .25   .15

Ministry of Labor, 50th Anniv. A949

1981, Nov. 26
1777   A949 12cr multi   .20   .15

School of Engineering, Itajuba A950

1981, Nov. 30   Perf. 11x11½
1778   A950 15cr lt grn & pur   .35   .15
Theodomiro C. Santiago, founder, birth centenary.

Sao Paulo State Police Sesquicentennial A951

1981, Dec. 15   Litho.   Perf. 12
1779   A951 12cr Policeman with saxophone   .20   .15
1780   A951 12cr Mounted policemen   .20   .15

BRAZIL

Army Library Centenary A952

1981, Dec. 17
1781 A952 12cr multi .20 .15

Souvenir Sheet 
Philatelic Club of Brazil, 50th Anniv. A953

1981, Dec. 18 Perf. 11
1782 A953 180cr multi 4.50 4.50

Brigadier Eduardo Gomes A954

1982, Jan. 20 Litho. Perf. 11x11½
1783 A954 12cr blue & blk .30 .15

Birth Centenary of Henrique Lage, Industrialist A956

1982, Mar. 14 Litho. Perf. 11½
1785 A956 17cr multi .50 .16

1982 World Cup Soccer — A957   TB Bacillus Cent. — A958

Designs: Various soccer players.

1982, Mar. 19
1786 A957 75cr multi .75 .25
1787 A957 80cr multi .75 .28
1788 A957 85cr multi .75 .28
Nos. 1786-1788 (3) 2.25 .81

Souvenir Sheet
Imperf
1789   Sheet of 3 3.00 6.00
  a. A957 100cr like #1786 1.00
  b. A957 100cr like #1787 1.00
  c. A957 100cr like #1788 1.00

1982, Mar. 24 Perf. 12
1790 A958 90cr Microscope, lung 1.25 .80
1791 A958 100cr Lung, pills 1.25 .90
  a. Pair, #1790-1791 2.50 2.00

Souvenir Sheet

A959

1982, Apr. 17 Litho. Perf. 11
1792   Sheet of 3 3.50 3.25
  a. A959 75cr Laelia Purpurata 1.00 .50
  b. A959 80cr Oncidium flexuosum 1.00 .50
  c. A959 85cr Cleistes revoluta 1.25 .55
BRAPEX V Stamp Exhibition, Blumenau.

Oil Drilling Centenary A960

1982, Apr. 18 Perf. 11½
1793 A960 17cr multi .25 .15

400th Birth Anniv. of St. Vincent de Paul — A961

1982, Apr. 24 Litho. Perf. 11½
1794 A961 17cr multi .25 .15

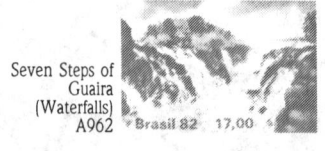

Seven Steps of Guaira (Waterfalls) A962

1982, Apr. 29
1795 A962 17cr Fifth Fall .20 .15
1796 A962 21cr Seventh Fall .30 .20

Ministry of Communications, 15th Anniv. — A963

1982, May 15
1797 A963 21cr multi .25 .20

Museology Course, Natl. Historical Museum, 50th Anniv. A964

1982, May 18
1798 A964 17cr blk & sal pink .20 .15

Vale de Rio Doce Mining Co. — A965

1982, June 1
1799 A965 17cr Gears .25 .15

Martin Afonso de Souza Reading Charter to Settlers A966

1982, June 3 Litho. Perf. 11½
1800 A966 17cr multi .25 .15
Town of Sao Vincente, 450th anniv.

Armadillo A967

1982, June 4
1801 A967 17cr shown .55 .15
1802 A967 21cr Wolves .55 .18
1803 A967 30cr Deer 1.65 .22
Nos. 1801-1803 (3) 2.75 .55

Film Strip and Award A968

1982, June 19
1804 A968 17cr multi .25 .15
20th anniv. of Golden Palm award for The Promise Keeper, Cannes Film Festival.

Souvenir Sheet

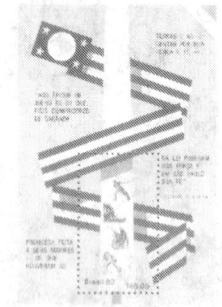

50th Anniv. of Constitutionalist Revolution — A969

1982, July 9 Litho. Perf. 11
1805 A969 140cr multi 1.75 1.75

Church of Our Lady of O'Sabara — A970   St. Francis of Assisi, 800th Birth Anniv. — A971

Baroque Architecture, Minas Gerais State: No. 1807, Church of Our Lady of the Rosary, Diamantina. No. 1808, Town Square, Mariana.

1982, July 16 Perf. 11½
1806 A970 17cr multi .25 .15
1807 A970 17cr multi, horiz. .25 .15
1808 A970 17cr multi, horiz. .25 .15
Nos. 1806-1808 (3) .75 .45

1982, July 24
1809 A971 21cr multi .20 .16

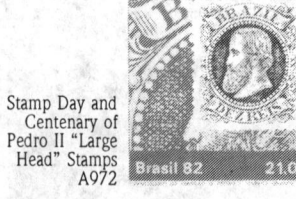

Stamp Day and Centenary of Pedro II "Large Head" Stamps A972

1982, Aug. 1
1810 A972 21cr No. 82 .25 .20

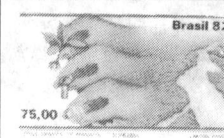

Port of Manaus Free Trade Zone A973

1982, Aug. 15 Perf. 11x11½
1811 A973 75cr multi .65 .35

Scouting Year — A974

1982, Aug. 21 Litho. Perf. 11
1812   Sheet of 2 2.75 3.75
  a. A974 85cr Baden-Powell 1.00 1.10
  b. A974 185cr Scout 1.65 2.00

Orixas Folk Costumes of African Origin — A975

1982, Aug. 21 Perf. 11½
1813 A975 20cr Iemanja .20 .16
1814 A975 20cr Xango .20 .16
1815 A975 20cr Oxumare .20 .16
Nos. 1813-1815 (3) .60 .48

10th Anniv. of Central Bank of Brazil Currency Museum A976

1982, Aug. 31
1816 A976 25cr 12-florin coin, 1645, obverse and reverse .25 .20
1817 A976 25cr Emperor Pedro's 6.40-reis coronation coin, 1822 .25 .20

National Week — A977

1982, Sept. 1
1818 A977 25cr Don Pedro proclaiming independence .38 .25

A978   A979

1982, Oct. 4
1819 A978 85cr Portrait 1.00 .60
St. Theresa of Avila (1515-1582).

BRAZIL

1982, Oct. 15   Litho.   Perf. 11½x11
1820	A979	75cr Instruments	.65	.38
1821	A979	80cr Dancers	.65	.38
1822	A979	85cr Musicians	.70	.40
a.		Souvenir sheet of 3, #1820-1822, perf. 11	2.75	2.75
		Nos. 1820-1822 (3)	2.00	1.16

Lubrapex '82, 4th Portuguese-Brazilian Stamp Exhibition. Stamps in No. 1822a are without "LUBRAPEX 82."

Aviation Industry Day — A980

1982, Oct. 17   Perf. 12
1823 A980 24cr Embraer EMB-312 trainer plane   .25   .20

Bastos Tigre, Poet, Birth Centenary, and "Saudade" Text — A981

1982, Oct. 29
1824 A981 24cr multi   .25   .20

Book Day.

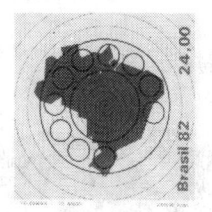

10th Anniv. of Brazilian Telecommunications Co. — A982

1982, Nov. 9   Litho.   Perf. 11½
1825 A982 24cr multi   .25   .20

Christmas 1982 — A983

Children's Drawings.

1982, Nov. 10
1826	A983	24cr Nativity	.25	.20
1827	A983	24cr Angels	.25	.20
1828	A983	30cr Nativity, diff.	.32	.45
1829	A983	30cr Flight into Egypt	.32	.45
		Nos. 1826-1829 (4)	1.14	1.30

State Flags — A984

Designs: a, Ceara. b, Espirito Santo. c, Paraiba. d, Grande de Norte. e, Rondonia.

1982, Nov. 19
| 1830 | | Block of 5 + label | 5.25 | 5.25 |
| a.-e. | | A984 24cr any single | 1.00 | .20 |

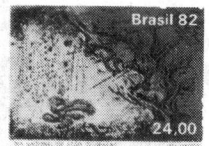

Thanksgiving 1982 — A985

1982, Nov. 25
1835 A985 24cr multi   .25   .20

Homage to the Deaf — A986

1982, Dec. 1
1836 A986 24cr multi   .25   .20

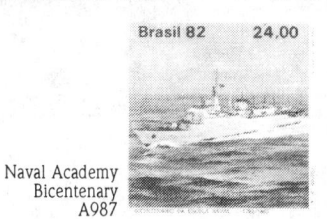

Naval Academy Bicentenary A987

Training Ships.

1982, Dec. 14
1837	A987	24cr Brazil	.35	.20
1838	A987	24cr Benjamin Constant	.35	.20
1839	A987	24cr Almirante Saldanha	.35	.20
		Nos. 1837-1839 (3)	1.05	.60

Souvenir Sheet

No. 12 — A988

1982, Dec. 18   Litho.   Perf. 11
1840 A988 200cr multi   4.00   5.00

BRASILIANA '83 Intl. Stamp Exhibition, Rio de Janeiro, July 29-Aug. 7.

Brasiliana '83 Carnival A989

1983, Feb. 9   Litho.   Perf. 11½
1841	A989	24cr Samba drummers	.20	.15
1842	A989	130cr Street parade	1.40	.50
1843	A989	140cr Dancer	1.40	.52
1844	A989	150cr Male dancer	1.40	.55
		Nos. 1841-1844 (4)	4.40	1.72

Antarctic Expedition A990

1983, Feb. 20   Litho.   Perf. 11½
1845 A990 150cr Support ship Barano de Teffe   2.00   .55

50th Anniv. of Women's Rights — A991

1983, Mar. 8
1846 A991 130cr multi   1.25   .50

Itaipu Hydroelectric Power Station Opening A992

1983, Mar.   Litho.   Perf. 12
1847 A992 140cr multi   1.90   .42

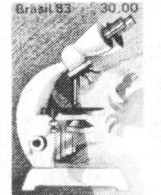

Cancer Prevention A993    Martin Luther (1483-1546) A994

30cr, Microscope. 38cr, Antonio Prudente, Paulista Cancer Assoc. founder, Camargo Hospital.

1983, Apr. 18
1848	A993	30cr multi	.30	.15
1849	A993	38cr multi	.32	.15
a.		Pair, #1848-1849	.65	.35

1983, Apr. 18
1850 A994 150cr pale grn & blk   1.25   .50

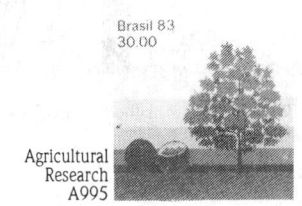

Agricultural Research A995

1983, Apr. 26   Litho.   Perf. 11½
1851	A995	30cr Chestnut tree	.20	.15
1852	A995	30cr Genetic research	.20	.15
1853	A995	38cr Tropical soy beans	.25	.15
		Nos. 1851-1853 (3)	.65	.45

Father Rogerio Neuhaus (1863-1934), Centenary of Ordination — A996

1983, May 3   Perf. 11½x11
1854 A996 30cr multi   .25   .15

30th Anniv. of Customs Cooperation Council A997

1983, May 5   Perf. 11x11½
1855 A997 30cr multi   .25   .15

World Communications Year — A998

1983, May 17   Litho.   Perf. 11½
1856 A998 250cr multi   1.50   .45

Toucans A999

1983, May 21
1857	A999	30cr Tucanucu	.15	.15
1858	A999	185cr White-breasted	1.25	.38
1859	A999	205cr Green-beaked	1.25	.40
1860	A999	215cr Black-beaked	1.25	.45
		Nos. 1857-1860 (4)	3.90	1.38

Souvenir Sheet

Resurrection, by Raphael (1483-1517) — A1000

1983, May 25   Perf. 11
1861 A1000 250cr multi   2.50   3.00

Hohenzollern 980 Locomotive, 1875 A1001

Various locomotives.

1983, June 12   Litho.   Perf. 11½
1862	A1001	30cr shown	.25	.15
1863	A1001	30cr Baldwin #1, 1881	.25	.15
1864	A1001	38cr Fowler #1, 1872	.30	.15
		Nos. 1862-1864 (3)	.80	.45

9th Women's Basketball World Championship — A1002

1983, July 24   Litho.   Perf. 11½x11
| 1865 | A1002 | 30cr Players, front view | .20 | .15 |
| 1866 | A1002 | 30cr Players, rear view | .20 | .15 |

Simon Bolivar (1783-1830) A1003

1983, July 24   Perf. 12
1867 A1003 30cr multi   .20   .15

BRAZIL

Children's Polio and Measles Vaccination Campaign — A1004

1983, July 25
| 1868 | A1004 | 30cr Girl, measles | .20 | .15 |
| 1869 | A1004 | 30cr Boy, polio | .20 | .15 |

A1005   A1006

1983, July 28 Perf. 11½x11
| 1870 | A1005 | 30cr Minerva (goddess of wisdom), computer tape | .20 | .15 |

20th Anniv. of Master's program in engineering.

1983, July 29 Engr.
Guanabara Bay.
1871	A1006	185cr No. 1	1.50	.38
1872	A1006	205cr No. 2	1.50	.40
1873	A1006	215cr No. 3	1.50	.45
		Nos. 1871-1873 (3)	4.50	1.23

Souvenir Sheet Perf. 11
1874		Sheet of 3	8.00	10.00
a.	A1006 185cr No. 1		2.00	3.00
b.	A1006 205cr No. 2		2.00	3.00
c.	A1006 215cr No. 3		2.00	3.00

BRASILIANA '83 Intl. Stamp Show, Rio de Janeiro, July 29-Aug. 7.

Stamps in No. 1874 have unframed denomination at bottom of the stamps. The background scene is enlarged to cover all 3 stamps in a continuous design.

Souvenir Sheet

The First Mass in Brazil, by Vitor Meireles (1833-1903) — A1007

1983, Aug. 18 Perf. 11
| 1875 | A1007 | 250cr multi | 3.00 | 1.50 |

EMB-120 Brasilia Passenger Plane A1008

1983, Aug. 19 Perf. 12
| 1876 | A1008 | 30cr multi | .25 | .15 |

Vision of Don Bosco Centenary A1009

1983, Aug. 30
| 1877 | A1009 | 130cr multi | .75 | .25 |

Independence Week A1010

1983, Sept. 1 Litho. Perf. 11½
| 1878 | A1010 | 50cr multi | .25 | .15 |

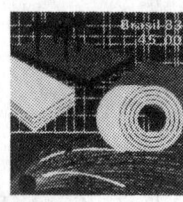

National Steel Corp., 10th Anniv. — A1011

1983, Sept. 17 Litho. Perf. 11½
| 1879 | A1011 | 45cr multi | .25 | .15 |

Cactus — A1012

1983, Sept. 12 Litho. Perf. 11½
1880	A1012	45cr Pilosocereus gounellei	.32	.15
1881	A1012	45cr Melocactus bahiensis	.32	.15
1882	A1012	57cr Cereus jamacaru	.40	.15
		Nos. 1880-1882 (3)	1.04	.45

1st National Eucharistic Congress — A1013

1983, Oct. 12 Litho. Perf. 11½
| 1883 | A1013 | 45cr multi | .25 | .15 |

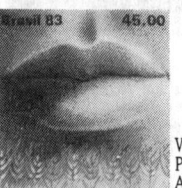

World Food Program A1014

1983, Oct. 14 Litho. Perf. 11½
| 1884 | A1014 | 45cr Mouth, grain | .30 | .15 |
| 1885 | A1014 | 57cr Fish, sailboat | .40 | .15 |

Souvenir Sheet

Louis Breguet, Death Centenary A1015

1983, Oct. 27 Litho. Perf. 11
| 1886 | A1015 | 376cr Telegraph transmitter | 4.25 | 1.50 |

Christmas 1983 — A1016

17th-18th Cent. Statues: 45cr, Our Lady of the Angels. 315cr, Our Lady of the Parturition. 335cr, Our Lady of Joy. 345cr, Our Lady of the Presentation.

1983, Nov. 10 Litho. Perf. 11½
1887	A1016	45cr multi	.25	.15
1888	A1016	315cr multi	1.65	.60
1889	A1016	335cr multi	1.65	.65
1890	A1016	345cr multi	1.65	.70
		Nos. 1887-1890 (4)	5.20	2.10

Marshal Mascarenhas Birth Centenary A1017

1983, Nov. 13 Litho. Perf. 11½
| 1891 | A1017 | 45cr Battle sites | .20 | .15 |

Commander of Brazilian Expeditionary Force in Italy.

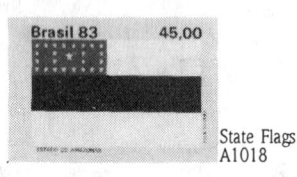

State Flags A1018

Designs: a, Amazonas. b, Goias. c, Rio. d, Mato Grosso Do Sol. e, Parana.

1983, Nov. 17 Litho. Perf. 11½
| 1892 | | Block of 5 + label | 3.00 | 3.00 |
| a.-e. | A1018 45cr any single | | .50 | .20 |

Thanksgiving A1018a

1983, Nov. 24 Litho. Perf. 12
| 1896 | A1018a | 45cr Madonna, wheat | .35 | .15 |

Manned Flight Bicentenary — A1019

1983, Dec. 15 Litho. Perf. 12
| 1897 | A1019 | 345cr Montgolfiere balloon, 1783 | 5.00 | .50 |

Ethnic Groups A1020

1984, Jan. 20 Litho. Perf. 12
| 1898 | A1020 | 45cr multi | .20 | .15 |

50th anniv. of publication of Masters and Slaves, sociological study by Gilberto Freyre.

Centenary of Crystal Palace, Petropolis A1021

1984, Feb. 2
| 1899 | A1021 | 45cr multi | .18 | .15 |

Souvenir Sheet

Flags (Sculpture with 40 Figures), by Victor Brecheret (b. 1894) A1022

1984, Feb. 22 Litho. Perf. 11
| 1900 | A1022 | 805cr multi | 1.50 | 1.00 |

Naval Museum Centenary A1023

1984, Mar. 23 Litho. Perf. 11½
| 1901 | A1023 | 620cr Figurehead, frigate, 1847 | .85 | .52 |

Slavery Abolition Centenary A1024

1984, Mar. 25
| 1902 | A1024 | 585cr Broken chain, raft | .85 | .55 |
| 1903 | A1024 | 610cr Freed slave | .90 | .60 |

Souvenir Sheet

Visit of King Carl XVI Gustaf of Sweden A1025

1984, Apr. 2 Perf. 11
| 1904 | A1025 | 2105cr multi | 3.50 | 2.50 |

1984 Summer Olympics A1026

1984, Apr. 13 Perf. 11½
1905	A1026	65cr Long jump	.15	.15
1906	A1026	65cr 100-meter race	.15	.15
1907	A1026	65cr Relay race	.15	.15
1908	A1026	585cr Pole vault	.80	.65
1909	A1026	610cr High jump	.85	.70
1910	A1026	620cr Hurdles	.90	.80
a.	Block of 6, #1905-1910		3.00	3.00

Voters Casting Ballots, Symbols of Labor A1027

Pres. Getulio Vargas Birth Centenary: Symbols of Development.

1984, Apr. 19 Litho. Perf. 11½
1911	A1027	65cr shown	.15	.15
1912	A1027	65cr Oil rig, blast furnace	.15	.15
1913	A1027	65cr High-tension towers	.15	.15
		Nos. 1911-1913 (3)	.45	.45

Columbus, Espana '84 Emblem — A1028

BRAZIL

1984, Apr. 27
1914 A1028 65cr Pedro Cabral .15 .15
1915 A1028 610cr shown 1.25 .70

Map of Americas, Heads — A1029
Lubrapex '84 — A1030

1984, May 7 Litho. Perf. 11½
1916 A1029 65cr multi .15 .15
Pan-American Association of Finance and Guarantees, 8th Assembly.

1984, May 8 Perf. 11½x11
18th Century Paintings, Mariana Cathedral.
1917 A1030 65cr Hunting scene .15 .15
1918 A1030 585cr Pastoral scene .75 .42
1919 A1030 610cr People under umbrellas .80 .50
1920 A1030 620cr Elephants .85 .50
Nos. 1917-1920 (4) 2.55 1.57

Souvenir Sheet

Intl. Fedn. of Soccer Associations, 80th Anniv. — A1031

1984, May 21 Perf. 11
1921 A1031 2115cr Globe 3.50 1.75

Matto Grosso Lowland Fauna A1032

1984, June 5 Litho. Perf. 11½
1922 Strip of 3 .60 .30
 a. A1032 65cr Deer .20 .15
 b. A1032 65cr Jaguar .20 .15
 c. A1032 80cr Alligator .20 .15

First Letter Mailed in Brazil, by Guido Mondin — A1033

1984, June 8 Perf. 12x11½
1923 A1033 65cr multi .15 .15
Postal Union of Americas and Spain, first anniv. of new headquarters.

Brazil-Germany Air Service, 50th Anniv.
A1034 A1035

1984, June 19
1924 A1034 610cr Dornier-Wal seaplane 1.00 .70
1925 A1035 620cr Steamer Westfalen 1.05 .72
 a. Pair, #1924-1925 2.05 1.50

Woolly Spider Monkey, World Wildlife Fund Emblem — A1036

1984, July 6 Perf. 11½
1926 A1036 65cr Mother, baby .48 .15
1927 A1036 80cr Monkey .32 .15

Agriculture Type of 1980
Designs: 65cr, Rubber tree. 80cr, Brazil nuts. 120cr, Rice. 150cr, Eucalyptus. 300cr, Pinha da Parana. 800cr, Carnauba. 1000cr, Babacu. 2000cr, Sunflower.

Photogravure (65, 80, 120, 150cr), Engraved

1984-85 Perf. 11x11½
1934 A894 65cr lilac .20 .15
1935 A894 80cr brn red .25 .15
1936 A894 120cr dk sl bl .35 .15
1937 A894 150cr green .15 .15
1938 A894 300cr rose mag .50 .15
1939 A894 800cr grnsh bl 1.40 .15
1940 A894 1000cr lemon 1.40 .15
1941 A894 2000cr yel org ('85) .75 .25
Nos. 1934-1941 (8) 5.00 1.30

Marajo Isld. Buffalo A1037

1984, July 9 Litho. Perf. 12
1942 Strip of 3 .50 .28
 a. A1037 65cr Approaching stream .15 .15
 b. A1037 65cr Standing on bank .15 .15
 c. A1037 80cr Drinking .18 .15
Continuous design.

Banco Economico Sesquicentenary — A1038

1984, July 13 Perf. 11½
1943 A1038 65cr Bank, coins .15 .15

Historic Railway Stations A1039

1984, July 23 Litho. Perf. 11½
1944 A1039 65cr Japeri .15 .15
1945 A1039 65cr Luz, vert. .15 .15
1946 A1039 80cr Sao Joao del Rei .16 .15
Nos. 1944-1946 (3) .46 .45

A1040 A1041

1984, Aug. 13 Perf. 11
Souvenir Sheet
1947 A1040 585cr Girl scout 1.40 1.00
Girl Scouts in Brazil, 65th anniv.

1984, Aug. 21 Litho. Perf. 11½
1948 A1041 65cr Couple sheltered from rain .15 .15
Housing project bank, 20th anniv.

Independence Week A1042

Children's Drawings.

1984, Sept. 3
1949 A1042 100cr Explorer & ship .15 .15
1950 A1042 100cr Sailing ships .15 .15
1951 A1042 100cr "BRASIL" mural .15 .15
1952 A1042 100cr Children under rainbow .15 .15
Nos. 1949-1952 (4) .60 .60

Rio de Janeiro Chamber of Commerce Sesquicentenary — A1043

1984, Sept. 10
1953 A1043 100cr Monument, worker silhouette .15 .15

Death Sesquicentenary of Don Pedro I (IV of Portugal) — A1044

1984, Sept. 23 Perf. 12x11½
1954 A1044 1000cr Portrait 1.50 1.10

Local Mushrooms — A1045
Book Day — A1046

1984, Oct. 22 Perf. 11½
1955 A1045 120cr Pycnoporus sanguineus .15 .15
1956 A1045 1050cr Calvatia sp 1.10 1.25
1957 A1045 1080cr Pleurotus sp, horiz. 1.20 1.30
Nos. 1955-1957 (3) 2.45 2.70

1984, Oct. 23 Perf. 11½
1958 A1046 120cr Girl in open book .15 .15

New State Mint Opening — A1047

1984, Nov. 1
1959 A1047 120cr multi .15 .15

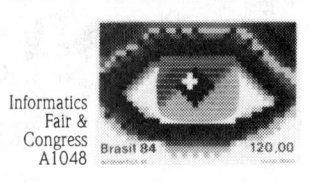

Informatics Fair & Congress A1048

1984, Nov. 5 Litho. Perf. 12
1960 A1048 120cr Eye, computer terminal .15 .15

Org. of American States, 14th Assembly — A1049

1984, Nov. 14
1961 A1049 120cr Emblem, flags .15 .15

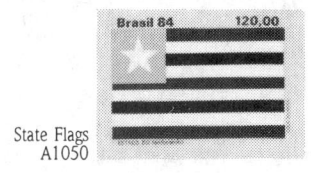

State Flags A1050

Designs: a, Maranhaio. b, Mato Grosso. c, Minas Gerais. d, Piaui. e, Santa Catarina.

1984, Nov. 19 Perf. 11½
1962 Block of 5 + label 1.00 1.00
 a.-e. A1050 120cr, any single .20 .15
See Nos. 2037, 2249.

Thanksgiving 1984 — A1051

1984, Nov. 22
1963 A1051 120cr Bell tower, Brasilia .15 .15

Christmas 1984 A1052

Paintings: No. 1964, Nativity, by Djanira. No. 1965, Virgin and Child, by Glauco Rodrigues. No. 1966, Flight into Egypt, by Paul Garfunkel. No. 1967, Nativity, by Di Cavalcanti.

1984, Dec. 3 Litho. Perf. 12
1964 A1052 120cr multi .15 .15
1965 A1052 120cr multi .15 .15
1966 A1052 1050cr multi .85 .40
1967 A1052 1080cr multi .85 .40
Nos. 1964-1967 (4) 2.00 1.10

40th Anniv., International Civil Aviation Organization A1053

1984, Dec. 7 Litho. Perf. 12
1968 A1053 120cr Aircraft, Earth globe .15 .15

BRAZIL

25th Anniv., North-Eastern Development A1054

1984, Dec. 14 Litho. Perf. 12
1969 A1054 120cr Farmer, field   .15 .15

Emilio Rouede A1055

Painting: Church of the Virgin of Safe Travels, by Rouede.

1985, Jan. 22 Litho. Perf. 12
1970 A1055 120cr multi   .15 .15

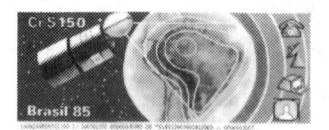

BRASILSAT — A1056

1985, Feb. 8 Litho. Perf. 11½x12
1971 A1056 150cr Satellite, Brazil   .15 .15

Metropolitan Railways — A1057

1985, Mar. 2 Litho. Perf. 11x11½
1972 A1057 200cr Passenger trains   .15 .15

Brasilia Botanical Gardens A1058

1985, Mar. 8 Litho. Perf. 11½x12
1973 A1058 200cr Caryocar brasiliense   .15 .15

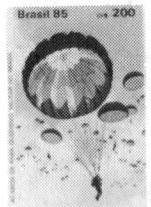

40th Anniv., Brazilian Paratroops — A1059

1985, Mar. 8 Litho. Perf. 11½x12
1974 A1059 200cr Parachute drop   .15 .15

Natl. Climate Awareness Program — A1060

1985, Mar. 18 Litho. Perf. 11½x12
1975 A1060 500cr multi   .20 .15

Thoroughbred Horses A1061

1985, Mar. 19 Litho. Perf. 12
1976 A1061 1000cr Campolina   .38 .22
1977 A1061 1500cr Marajoara   .70 .35
1978 A1061 1500cr Mangalarga marchador   .70 .35
   Nos. 1976-1978 (3)   1.78 .92

Ouro Preto — A1062

1985, Apr. 18 Litho. Perf. 11½x12
1979 A1062 220cr shown   .15 .15
1980 A1062 220cr St. Miguel des Missoes   .15 .15
1981 A1062 220cr Olinda   .15 .15
   Nos. 1979-1981 (3)   .45 .45

Polivolume, by Mary Vieira — A1063

1985, Apr. 20 Litho.
1982 A1063 220cr multi   .15 .15
Rio Branco Inst., 40th anniv.

Natl. Capital, Brasilia, 25th Anniv. — A1064

1985, Apr. 22 Litho.
1983 A1064 220cr Natl. Theater, acoustic shell   .15 .15
1984 A1064 220cr Catetinho Palace, JK Memorial   .15 .15

A1065   A1065a

1985-86 Photo. Perf. 11½
1985 A1065 50cr lake   .15 .15
1986 A1065 100cr dp vio   .15 .15
1987 A1065 150cr violet   .15 .15
1988 A1065 200cr ultra   .15 .15
1989 A1065 220cr green   .15 .15
1990 A1065 300cr royal bl   .18 .15
1991 A1065 500cr olive blk   .30 .22
1992 A1065a 1000cr brn ol ('86)   .18 .15
1993 A1065a 2000cr brt grn ('86)   .35 .22
1994 A1065a 3000cr dl vio   .42 .32
1995 A1065a 5000cr brown   .58 .42
   Nos. 1985-1995 (11)   2.76 2.23

Marshal Rondon, 120th Birth Anniv. A1066

1985, May 5 Perf. 11x11½
1996 A1066 220cr multi   .15 .15
Educator, protector of the Indians, building superintendent of telegraph lines.

Candido Fontoura (1885-1974) A1067

Brapex VI A1068

1985, May 14 Perf. 12x11½
1997 A1067 220cr multi   .15 .15
Pioneer of the Brazilian pharmaceutical industry.

1985, May 18 Perf. 11½x11
Cave paintings: No. 1998, Deer, Cerca Grande. No. 1999, Lizards, Lapa do Caboclo. No. 2000, Running deer, Grande Abrigo de Santana do Riacho.
1998 A1068 300cr multi   .15 .15
1999 A1068 300cr multi   .15 .15
2000 A1068 300cr multi   .75 .50
 a. Souvenir sheet of 3, #1998-2000, perf. 10½x11   1.00 1.00
   Nos. 1998-2000 (3)   1.05 .80

Wildlife Conservation A1069

Birds in Marinho dos Abrolhos National Park.

1985, June 5 Perf. 11½x12
2001 A1069 220cr Fregata magnificens   .15 .15
2002 A1069 220cr Sula dactylatra   .15 .15
2003 A1069 220cr Anous stolidus   .15 .15
2004 A1069 2000cr Pluvialis squatarola   .60 .25
   Nos. 2001-2004 (4)   1.05 .70

A1070   A1071

1985, June 11 Perf. 12x11½
2005 A1070 220cr Mother breastfeeding infant   .15 .15
2006 A1070 220cr Hand, eyedropper, children   .15 .15
 a. Pair, #2005-2006   .25 .25
UN infant survival campaign.

1985, June 22 Litho. Perf. 11½x11
Helicopter rescue, search ship, diver.
2007 A1071 220cr multi   .15 .15
Sea Search & Rescue.

Souvenir Sheet

World Cup Soccer, Mexico, 1986 A1072

1985, June 23 Perf. 11
2008 A1072 2000cr Player dribbling, World Cup   4.00 .85

Intl. Youth Year — A1073

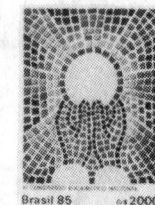

11th Natl. Eucharistic Congress — A1074

1985, June 28 Perf. 12
2009 A1073 220cr Circle of children   .15 .15

1985, July 16 Perf. 12x11½
2010 A1074 2000cr Mosaic, Priest raising host   .55 .38

Director Humberto Mauro, Scene from Sangue Mineiro, 1929 A1075

1985, July 27
2011 A1075 300cr multi   .15 .15
Cataguases Studios, 60th anniv.

Escola e Sacro Museum, Convent St. Anthony, Joao Pessoa, Paraiba A1076

1985, Aug. 5 Perf. 11½x12
2012 A1076 330cr multi   .15 .15
Paraiba State 400th anniv.

Inconfidencia Museum — A1077

Cabanagem Insurrection, 150th Anniv. — A1078

1985, Aug. 11 Perf. 12x11½
2013 A1077 300cr shown   .15 .15
2014 A1077 300cr Museum of History & Diplomacy   .15 .15

1985, Aug. 14
Design: Revolutionary, detail from an oil painting by Guido Mondin.
2015 A1078 330cr multi   .15 .15

AMX Subsonic Air Force Fighter Plane A1079

1985, Aug. 19 Perf. 11½x12
2016 A1079 330cr multi   .15 .15
AMX Project, joint program with Italy.

BRAZIL

16th-17th Century Military Uniforms — A1080

1985, Aug. 26   *Perf. 12x11½*
2017 A1080 300cr Captain, crossbowman .16 .15
2018 A1080 300cr Harquebusier, sergeant .16 .15
2019 A1080 300cr Musketeer, pikeman .16 .15
2020 A1080 300cr Fusilier, pikeman .16 .15
     Nos. 2017-2020 (4) .64 .60

Farrouphilha Insurrection, 150th Anniv. A1081

Design: Bento Goncalves and insurrectionist cavalry on Southern battlefields, detail of an oil painting by Guido Mondin.

1985, Sept. 20   *Perf. 11½x12*
2021 A1081 330cr multi .15 .15

Aparados da Serra National Park A1082

1985, Sept. 23
2022 A1082 3100cr Ravine .65 .52
2023 A1082 3320cr Mountains .70 .55
2024 A1082 3480cr Forest, waterfall .75 .60
     Nos. 2022-2024 (3) 2.10 1.67

President-elect Tancredo Neves — A1083

Design: Portrait, Natl. Congress, Alvorada Palace, Federal Supreme Court.

1985, Oct. 10   Litho.   *Perf. 11x11½*
2025 A1083 330cr multi .15 .15

FEB, Postmark A1084

1985, Oct. 10   *Perf. 11½x12*
2026 A1084 500cr multi .15 .15
Brazilian Expeditionary Force Postal Service, 41st anniv.

Rio de Janeiro-Niteroi Ferry Service, 150th Anniv. — A1085

1985, Oct. 14   *Perf. 11½x12*
2027 A1085 500cr Segunda .20 .15
2028 A1085 500cr Terceira .20 .15
2029 A1085 500cr Especuladora .20 .15
2030 A1085 500cr Urca .20 .15
     Nos. 2027-2030 (4) .80 .60

Muniz M-7 Inaugural Flight, 50th Anniv. — A1086

1985, Oct. 22
2031 A1086 500cr multi .15 .15

UN 40th Anniv. — A1087    **Natl. Press System — A1088**

1985, Oct. 24   *Perf. 11½x11*
2032 A1087 500cr multi .15 .15

1985, Nov. 7
2033 A1088 500cr Newspaper masthead, reader .15 .15
Diario de Pernambuco, newspaper, 160th anniv.

Christmas 1985 A1089

1985, Nov. 11   *Perf. 11½x12*
2034 A1089 500cr Christ in Manger .20 .15
2035 A1089 500cr Adoration of the Magi .20 .15
2036 A1089 500cr Flight to Egypt .20 .15
     Nos. 2034-2036 (3) .60 .45

State Flag Type
State Flags: a, Para. b, Rio Grande do Sul. c, Acre. d, Sao Paulo.

1985, Nov. 19   *Perf. 12*
2037   Block of 4 .80 .60
   a.-d. A1050 500cr, any single .20 .15

Thanksgiving Day — A1091

1985, Nov. 28   *Perf. 12x11½*
2038 A1091 500cr Child gathering wheat .20 .15

Economic Development of Serra dos Carajas Region A1092

1985, Dec. 11   Litho.   *Perf. 11½x12*
2039 A1092 500cr multi .15 .15

Fr. Bartholomeu Lourenco de Gusmao (1685-1724), Inventor, the Aerostat A1093

1985, Dec. 19   Litho.   *Perf. 11x11½*
2040 A1093 500cr multi .15 .15

A1094    A1095

The Trees, by Da Costa E Silva (b. 1885), poet.

1985, Dec. 20   Litho.   *Perf. 12x11½*
2041 A1094 500cr multi .15 .15

1986, Mar. 3   Litho.   *Perf. 11 Souvenir Sheet*
2042 A1095 10000cr multi 2.25 2.00
1986 World Cup Soccer Championships, Mexico. LUBRAPEX '86, philatelic exhibition.

Halley's Comet — A1096

1986, Apr. 11   Litho.   *Perf. 11½x12*
2043 A1096 50c multi .15 .15

Commander Ferraz Antarctic Station, 2nd Anniv. A1097

1986, Apr. 25
2044 A1097 50c multi .15 .15

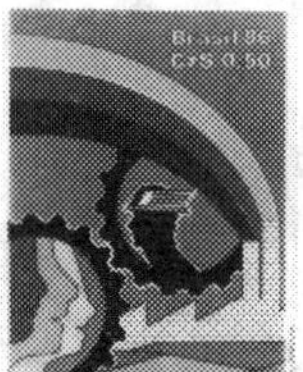

Labor Day A1098 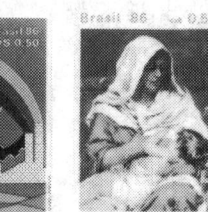   **Maternity, by Henrique Bernardelli (1858-1936) A1099**

1986, May 1   Litho.   *Perf. 12x11½*
2045 A1098 50c multi .15 .15

1986, May 8
2046 A1099 50c multi .15 .15

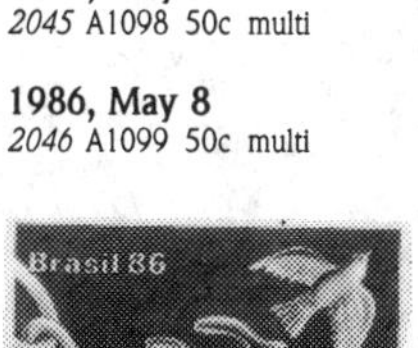

Amnesty Intl., 25th Anniv. A1100

1986, May 28   Litho.   *Perf. 11½x12*
2047 A1100 50c multi .15 .15

Butterflies — A1101

1985, June 5   *Perf. 12x11½*
2048 A1101 50c Pyrrhopyge ruficauda .15 .15
2049 A1101 50c Prepona eugenes diluta .15 .15
2050 A1101 50c Pierriballia mandel molione .15 .15
     Nos. 2048-2050 (3) .45 .45

Score from Opera "Il Guarani" and Antonio Carlos Gomes (1836-1896), Composer A1102

1986, July 11   *Perf. 11½x12*
2051 A1102 50c multi .18 .15

Natl. Accident Prevention Campaign — A1103    **Stamp Day — A1104**

1986, July 30   Litho.   *Perf. 11½x11*
2052 A1103 50c Lineman .15 .15

Souvenir Sheet
1986, Aug. 1   *Perf. 11*
2053 A1104 5cz No. 53 .85 .35
Brazilian Phil. Soc., 75th anniv., and Dom Pedro II issue, Nos. 53-60, 120th anniv.

Architecture A1105    **Famous Men A1106**

Designs: 10c, House of Garcia D'Avila, Nazare de Mata, Bahia. 20c, Church of Our Lady of the Assumption, Anchieta Village. 50c, Fort Reis Magos, Natal. 1cz, Pilgrim's Column, Alcantara Village, 1648. 2cz, Cloisters, St. Francis Convent, Olinda. 5cz, St. Anthony's Chapel, Sao Roque. 10cz, St. Lawrence of the Indians Church, Niteroi. 20cz, Principe da Beiro Fort, Mato Dentro. 50cz, Jesus of Matozinhos Church, vert. 100cz, Church of our Lady of Sorrow, Campanha. 200cz, Casa dos Contos, Ouro Preto. 500cz, Antiga Alfandega, Belem, Para.

Perf. 11½x11, 11x11½
1986-88   Photo.
2055 A1105 10c sage grn .15 .15
2057 A1105 20c brt blue .15 .15
2059 A1105 50c orange .15 .15
2064 A1105 1cz golden brn .15 .15
2065 A1105 2cz dull rose .25 .18
   a.   Litho., perf. 13 ('88) .15 .15
2067 A1105 5cz lt olive grn .60 .45
   a.   Litho., perf. 13 ('88) .15 .15
2068 A1105 10cz slate blue .50 .35
2069 A1105 20cz lt red brn .15 .15
2070 A1105 50cz brn org 2.25 1.75
2071 A1105 100cz dull grn 2.70 2.10
2072 A1105 200cz deep blue 2.50 1.85
2073 A1105 500cz dull red brn 1.30 1.00
     Nos. 2055-2073 (12) 11.45 8.76

Issued: 10c, 8/11; 20c, 12/8; 50c, 8/19; 1cz, 11/19; 2cz, 11/9; 5cz, 12/30; 10cz, 6/2/87;

20cz, 50cz, 9/18/87; 100cz, 12/21/87; 200cz, 5/9/88; 500cz, 11/22/88.
 This is an expanding set. Numbers will change if necessary.

1986   *Perf. 12x11½, 11½x12*

Designs: No. 2074, Juscelino Kubitschek de Oliveira, president 1956-61, and Alvorado Palace, Brasilia. No. 2075, Octavio Mangabeira, statesman, and Itamaraty Palace, Rio de Janeiro, horiz.

2074 A1106   50c multi   .15   .15
2075 A1106   50c multi   .15   .15

Issue dates: #2074, Aug. 21. #2075, Aug. 27.

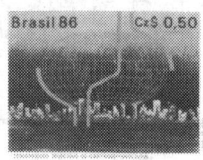

World Gastroenterology Congress, Sao Paulo — A1107

1986, Sept. 7   *Perf. 11½x12*
2076 A1107   50c multi   .15   .15

Federal Broadcasting System, 50th Anniv. — A1108

Intl. Peace Year — A1109

1986, Sept. 15   *Perf. 12x11½*
2077 A1108   50c multi   .15   .15

1986, Sept. 16
Painting (detail): War and Peace, by Candido Portinari.
2078 A1109   50c multi   .15   .15

Ernesto Simoes Filho (b. 1886), Publisher of A Tarde A1110

1986, Oct. 4   Litho.   *Perf. 11½x12*
2079 A1110   50c multi   .15   .15

Famous Men — A1111

Federal Savings Bank, 125th Anniv. — A1112

Designs: No. 2080, Title page from manuscript, c. 1683-94, by Gregorio Mattose e Guerra (b. 1636), author. No. 2081, Manuel Bandeira (1886-1968), poet, text from I'll Go Back to Pasargada.

1986, Oct. 29   *Perf. 11½x11*
2080 A1111   50c lake & beige   .15   .15
2081 A1111   50c lake & dl grn   .15   .15

1986, Nov. 4   *Perf. 12x11½*
2082 A1112   50c multi   .15   .15

Flowering Plants A1113

Glauber Rocha, Film Industry Pioneer A1114

Perf. 12x11½, 11½x12
1986, Sept. 23
2083 A1113   50c Urera mitis   .15   .15
2084 A1113   6.50cz Couroupita guyanensis   .52   .40
2085 A1113   6.90cz Bauhinia variegata, horiz.   .55   .42
   Nos. 2083-2085 (3)   1.22   .97

1986, Nov. 20   *Perf. 12x11½*
2086 A1114   50c multi   .15   .15

LUBRAPEX '86 — A1115

Cordel Folk Tales: No. 2087, Romance of the Mysterious Peacock. No. 2088, History of the Empress Porcina.

1986, Nov. 21   *Perf. 11x12*
2087 A1115   6.90cz multi   .45   .35
2088 A1115   6.90cz multi   .45   .35
  a.   Souvenir sheet of 2, #2087-2088, perf. 11   1.10   .85

Christmas A1116

Birds: 50c, And Christ child. 6.50cz, And tree. 7.30cz, Eating fruit.

1986, Nov. 10   *Perf. 11½x12*
2089 A1116   50c multi   .15   .15
2090 A1116   6.50cz multi   .65   .48
2091 A1116   7.30cz multi   .75   .58
   Nos. 2089-2091 (3)   1.55   1.21

Military Uniforms, c. 1930 — A1117

Bartolomeu de Gusmao Airport, 50th Anniv. — A1118

Designs: No. 2092, Navy lieutenant commander, dreadnought Minas Gerais. No. 2093, Army flight lieutenant, WACO S.C.O. biplane, Fortaleza Airport.

1986, Dec. 15   *Perf. 12x11½*
2092 A1117   50c multi   .15   .15
2093 A1117   50c multi   .15   .15
Fortaleza Air Base, 50th anniv. (No. 2093).

1986, Dec. 26
2094 A1118   1cz multi   .15   .15

Heitor Villa Lobos (1887-1959), Conductor — A1119

1987, Mar. 5   Litho.   *Perf. 12x11½*
2095 A1119   1.50cz multi   .15   .15

Natl. Air Force C-130 Transport Plane, Flag, the Antarctic A1120

1987, Mar. 9   *Perf. 11x11½*
2096 A1120   1cz multi   .15   .15
Antarctic Project.

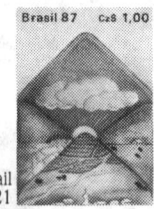

Special Mail Services — A1121

1987, Mar. 20   *Perf. 12x11½*
2097 A1121   1cz Rural delivery   .15   .15
2098 A1121   1cz Intl. express   .15   .15

TELECOM '87, Geneva A1122

1987, May 5   *Perf. 11½x12*
2099 A1122   2cz Brazilsat, wave, globe   .20   .15

10th Pan American Games, Indianapolis, Aug. 7-25 — A1123

1987, May 20   *Perf. 12x11½*
2100 A1123   18cz multi   1.00   .75

Natl. Fine Arts Museum, 150th Anniv A1124

1987, Jan. 13   *Perf. 11½x12*
2101 A1124   1cz multi   .15   .15

Marine Conservation — A1125

1987, June 5
2102 A1125   2cz Eubalaena australis   .15   .15
2103 A1125   2cz Eretmochelys imbricata   .15   .15

Federal Court of Appeal, 40th Anniv. A1126

1987, June 15
2104 A1126   2cz multi   .15   .15

Military Club, Cent. — A1127

1987, June 26   *Perf. 12x11½*
2105 A1127   3cz multi   .18   .15

Agriculture Institute of Campinas, Cent. A1128

1987, June 27   *Perf. 11½x12*
2106 A1128   2cz multi   .15   .15

Entomological Society, 50th Anniv. A1129

1987, July 17
2107 A1129   3cz Zoolea lopiceps   .15   .15
2108 A1129   3cz Fulgora servillei   .15   .15

Natl. Tourism Year A1130

Designs: No. 2109, Monuments and Sugarloaf Mountain, Rio de Janeiro. No. 2110, Colonial church, sailboats, parrot, cashews.

1987, Aug. 4
2109 A1130   3cz multi   .15   .15
2110 A1130   3cz multi   .15   .15

BRAZIL

Royal Portuguese Cabinet of Literature, 150th Anniv. — A1131

1987, Aug. 27		Perf. 12x11½
2111 A1131 30cz ver & brt grn	1.10	.85

Sport Club Intl. — A1132

Championship soccer clubs, Brazil's Gold Cup: b, Sao Paulo. c, Guarani. d, Regatas do Flamengo.

1987, Aug. 29		Perf. 11½x12
2112 Block of 4	.60	.40
a.-d. A1132 3cz any single	.15	.15

St. Francis Convent, 400th Anniv. A1133

1987, Oct. 4		
2113 A1133 4cz multi	.20	.15

Jose Americo de Almeida, Author A1134

Design: Characters from romance novel, "A Bagaceira," 1928, and portrait of author.

1987, Oct. 23	Litho.	Perf. 11x11½
2114 A1134 4cz multi	.18	.15

Spanish Galleons Anchored in Recife Port, 1537 A1135

1987, Nov. 12	Litho.	Perf. 11½x12
2115 A1135 5cz Harbor entrance	.18	.15

Recife City, 450th anniv.

Thanksgiving A1136

1987, Nov. 26		Perf. 12x11½
2116 A1136 5cz multi	.18	.15

Christmas 1987 A1137

1987, Nov. 30		Perf. 11½x12
2117 A1137 6cz Shepherd and flock	.20	.15
2118 A1137 6cz Christmas pageant	.20	.15
2119 A1137 6cz Six angels	.20	.15
Nos. 2117-2119 (3)	.60	.45

Pedro II College, 150th Anniv. — A1138

Gold pen Emperor Pedro II used to sign edict establishing the school, and Senator Bernardo Pereira de Vasconcellos, founder.

1987, Dec. 2		
2120 A1138 6cz multi	.18	.15

Natl. Orchid Growers' Soc., 50th Anniv. A1139

1987, Dec. 3		
2121 A1139 6cz Laelia lobata veitch	.20	.15
2122 A1139 6cz Cattleya guttata lindley	.20	.15

Marian Year — A1140

Statue of Our Lady and Basilica at Fatima, Portugal.

1987, Dec. 20		Perf. 12x11½
2123 A1140 50cz multi	1.10	.85

Exhibit of the Statue of Our Lady of Fatima in Brazil.

Descriptive Treatise of Brazil, by Gabriel S. de Sousa, 400th Anniv. A1141

1987, Dec. 21	Litho.	Perf. 11x11½
2124 A1141 7cz multi	.20	.16

Natl. Archives, 150th Anniv. A1142

Design: Text from illuminated Gregorian canticle and computer terminal.

1988, Jan. 5		Perf. 11½x12
2125 A1142 7cz multi	.20	.16

Opening of Brazilian Ports to Ships of Friendly Nations, 180th Anniv. A1143

1988, Jan. 28		Perf. 11x11½
2126 A1143 7cz multi	.24	.18

Souvenir Sheet

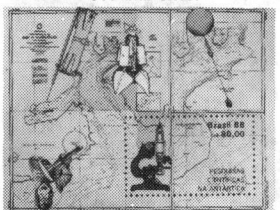

Antarctic Research — A1144

1988, Feb. 9	Litho.	Perf. 11
2127 A1144 80cz multi	2.00	2.00

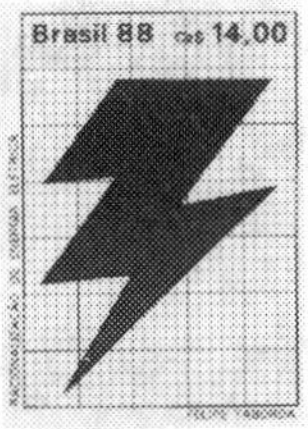

Energy Resources — A1145

1988, Mar. 15	Litho.	Perf. 12x11½
2128 A1145 14cz Electricity	.22	.16
2129 A1145 14cz Fossil fuels	.22	.16

Souvenir Sheet

Brazilians as Formula 1 World Champions in 1981, 1983, 1987 — A1146

1988, Mar. 30		Perf. 11
2130 A1146 300cz multi	4.50	4.50

Jose Bonifacio, Armorial and Masonic Emblems — A1147

1988, Apr. 6		Perf. 12x11½
2131 A1147 20cz multi	.30	.24

Jose Bonifacio de Andrada e Silva (c. 1763-1838), geologist and prime minister under Pedro I who supported the movement for independence from Portugal and was exiled for opposing the emperor's advisors.

Abolition of Slavery, Cent. — A1148

Telecom '88 — A1149

Designs: 20cz, Declaration and quill pen. 50cz, Slave ship and maps of African coastline and slave trade route between Africa and South America.

1988, May 12	Litho.	Perf. 12x11½
2132 A1148 20cz multi	.25	.18
2133 A1148 50cz multi	.65	.50

1988, May 16		Perf. 11½x11
2134 A1149 50cz multi	.60	.45

Jesus of Matosinhos Sanctuary A1150

1988, May 16		Perf. 11½x12
2135 A1150 20cz shown	.22	.15
2136 A1150 50cz Pilot plan of Brazilia	.58	.45
2137 A1150 100cz Salvador historic district	1.20	.90
Nos. 2135-2137 (3)	2.00	1.50

LUBRAPEX '88. World heritage list.

Japanese Immigrants in Brazil, 80th Anniv. — A1151

1988, June 18	Litho.	Perf. 11½x11
2138 A1151 100cz multi	.75	.55

A1152

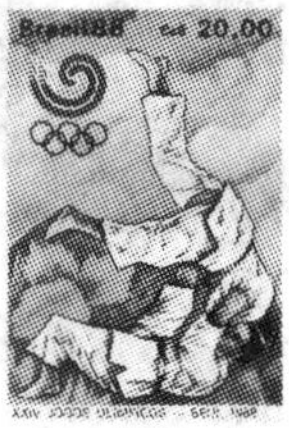

A1153

1988, July 1	Photo.	Perf. 13
2139 A1152 (A) brt blue	.22	.16

No. 2139 met the first class domestic letter postage rate (28cz).
See Nos. 2201, 2218.

1988, July 14	Litho.	Perf. 12x11½
2140 A1153 20cz Judo	.22	.16

1988 Summer Olympics, Seoul.

Wildlife Conservation A1154

733

BRAZIL

1988, July 24   *Perf. 11½x12*
2141 A1154 20cz Myrmecophaga tridactyla .15 .15
2142 A1154 50cz Chaetomys subspinosus .32 .25
2143 A1154 100cz Speothos venaticus .65 .50
Nos. 2141-2143 (3) 1.12 .90

Souvenir Sheet

The Motherland, 1919 by Pedro Bruno — A1155

1988, Aug. 1   *Litho.*   *Perf. 11*
2144 A1155 250cz multi 1.50 1.50

Stamp Day, BRASILIANA '89.

Natl. Confederation of Industries, 50th Anniv. — A1156

1988, Aug. 12   *Perf. 11½x12*
2145 A1156 50cz multi .26 .20

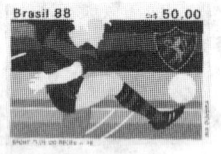

Soccer Clubs A1157

No. 2146, Recife, Pernambuco. No. 2147, Coritiba, Parana. 100cz, Gremio, Porto Alegre, Rio Grando do Sul. 200cz, Fluminense, Rio de Janeiro.

1988, Sept. 29   *Perf. 11½x12*
2146 A1157 50cz multi .16 .15
2147 A1157 50cz multi .16 .15
2148 A1157 100cz multi .32 .22
2149 A1157 200cz multi .60 .48
a. Block of 4, #2146-2149 1.25 .95

Poems, 1888 A1158

Portraits and text: 50cz, *O Ateneu*, by Raul Pompeia. 100cz, *Poesias*, by Olavo Bilac.

1988, Oct. 28   *Perf. 11x11½*
2150 A1158 50cz multi .15 .15
2151 A1158 100cz multi .26 .20

Souvenir Sheet

1988 Democratic Constitution for the Union of the People and the State — A1159

1988, Oct. 5   *Litho.*   *Perf. 11*
2152 A1159 550cz Government building 2.40 2.40

Origami Art — A1160

1988, Nov. 11   *Litho.*   *Perf. 11½x12*
2153 A1160 50cz Abbey, nuns .15 .15
2154 A1160 100cz Nativity .25 .20
2155 A1160 200cz Santa Claus, presents .52 .40
Nos. 2153-2155 (3) .92 .75

Christmas.

ARBRAFEX Philatelic Exhibition of Argentina and Brazil A1161

1988, Nov. 26
2156 A1161 400cz multi .85 .65

Fresh-water Fish — A1162

Designs: a, *Gasteropelecus*. b, *Osteoglossum ferreirai*. c, *Moenkhausia*. d, *Xavantei*. e, *Ancistrus hoplogenys*. f, *Brochis splendens*. Se-tenant in a continuous design.
Illustration reduced.

1988, Nov. 29   *Litho.*   *Perf. 11½x12*
2157 Block of 6 .90 .72
a.-f. A1162 55cz any single .15 .15

Souvenir Sheet

BRAPEX '88, Ecological Preservation — A1163

1988, Dec. 10   *Perf. 11*
2158 Sheet of 3 1.80 1.80
a. A1163 100cz Parrot .25 .25
b. A1163 250cz Plant .60 .60
c. A1163 400cz Pelican .95 .95

Satellite Dishes A1164

Performing Arts A1165

1988, Dec. 20   *Perf. 12x11½*
2159 A1164 70cz multi .18 .15

Ansat 10-Earth satellite station communication.

1988, Dec. 21
2160 A1165 70cz multi .18 .15

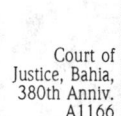

Court of Justice, Bahia, 380th Anniv. A1166

1989, Mar. 10   *Litho.*   *Perf. 11½x12*
2161 A1166 25c multi .42 .32

Public Library Year — A1167

1989, Mar. 13   *Perf. 11½*
2162 A1167 25c Library, Bahia, 1811 .42 .32

Brazilian Post & Telegraph Enterprise, 20th Anniv. A1168

Intl. and domestic postal services: a, Facsimile transmission (Post-Grama). b, Express mail (EMS). c, Parcel post (Sedex). d, Postal savings (CEFPostal).

1989, Mar. 20   *Perf. 11½x12*
2163 Block of 4 1.65 1.25
a.-d. A1168 25c any single .40 .30

Souvenir Sheet

Ayrton Senna, 1988 Formula 1 World Champion — A1169

1989, Mar. 23
2164 A1169 2cz multi 4.00 4.00

Environmental Conservation A1170

1989, Apr. 6   *Litho.*   *Perf. 12x11½*
2165 A1170 25c multi .35 .25

Mineira Inconfidencia Independence Movement, Bicent. — A1171

Designs: a, Pyramid, hand. b, Figure of a man, houses. c, Destruction of houses.

1989, Apr. 21   *Perf. 11½x12*
2166 Strip of 3 1.30 .95
a.-b. A1171 30c any single .38 .28
c. A1171 40c multi .52 .38

First rebellion against Portuguese dominion.

Military School, Rio de Janeiro, Cent. A1172

1989, May 6   *Litho.*   *Perf. 11½x12*
2167 A1172 50c multi .50 .38

Flowering Plants A1173

1989, June 5   *Perf. 11½x12, 12x11½*
2168 A1173 50c *Pavonia alnifolia* .60 .45
2169 A1173 1cz *Worsleya rayneri* 1.25 .90
2170 A1173 1.50cz *Heliconia farinosa* 1.75 1.40
Nos. 2168-2170 (3) 3.60 2.75

Nos. 2169-2170 vert.

Barreto and Recife Law School, Pedro II Square A1174

1989, June 7   *Perf. 11x11½*
2171 A1174 50c multi .65 .48

Tobias Barreto (b. 1839), advocate of Germanization of Brazil.

Cultura Broadcasting System, 20th Anniv. — A1175

1989, June 27   *Litho.*   *Perf. 11½x12*
2172 A1175 50c multi .60 .45

Aviation A1176

1989, July 7
2173 A1176 50c Ultra-light aircraft .52 .40
2174 A1176 1.50cz Eiffel Tower, Demoiselle 1.65 1.10

Flight of Santos-Dumont's *Demoiselle*, 80th anniv (1.50cz).

Indigenous Flora — A1177

1989 Photo.   *Perf. 11x11½, 11½x11*
2176 A1177 10c *Dichorisandra*, vert. .15 .15
2177 A1177 20c *Qulabentia zehnteri* .22 .16
2178 A1177 50c *Bougainvillea glabra* .52 .42
2179 A1177 1cz *Impatiens specie* 1.00 .80
2180 A1177 2cz *Chorisia crispiflora* .25 .18
2181 A1177 5cz *Hibiscus trilineatus* .60 .45
Nos. 2176-2181 (6) 2.74 2.16

Issued: 10c, July 4; 20c, June 21; 50c, June 26; 1cz, June 19; 2cz, 5cz, Dec. 4.
No. 2181 vert.
See Nos. 2259-2273.

BRAZIL

Souvenir Sheet

Largo da Carioca, by Nicolas Antoine Taunay — A1179

1989, July 7 Litho. Perf. 11
2197 A1179 3cz multi 3.00 3.00
PHILEXFRANCE '89, French revolution bicent.

Cut and Uncut Gemstones — A1180

1989, July 12 Litho. Perf. 12x11½
2198 A1180 50c Tourmaline .40 .30
2199 A1180 1.50cz Amethyst 1.20 .90

Souvenir Sheet

Paco Imperial, Rio de Janeiro, and Map — A1181

1989, July 28 Perf. 11
2200 A1181 5cz multi 3.75 3.75
BRASILANA '89.

Type of 1988 Redrawn

1989, July 26 Photo. Perf. 13
Size: 17x21mm
2201 A1152 (A) org & brt blue .18 .15
Size of type and postal emblem are smaller on No. 2201; "1e PORTE" is at lower left.
No. 2201 met the first class domestic letter postage rate (cz).

Pernambuco Commercial Assoc., 150th Anniv. A1182

1989, Aug. 1 Litho. Perf. 11½x12
2202 A1182 50c multi .40 .30

Photography, 150th Anniv. — A1183

1989, Aug. 14
2203 A1183 1.50cz multi 1.10 .85

1st Hydroelectric Power Station in South America, Marmelos-o, Cent. A1184

1989, Sept. 5 Litho. Perf. 11½x12
2204 A1184 50c multi .35 .25

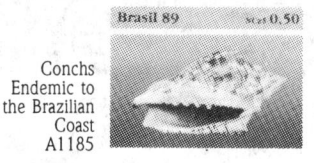

Conchs Endemic to the Brazilian Coast A1185

1989, Sept. 8
2205 A1185 50c *Voluta ebraea* .32 .22
2206 A1185 1cz *Morum matthewsi* .60 .45
2207 A1185 1.50cz *Agaronia travassosi* .90 .65
Nos. 2205-2207 (3) 1.82 1.32
Wildlife conservation.

America Issue A1186

UPAE emblem and pre-Columbian stone carvings: 1cz, Muiraquita ritual statue, vert. 4cz, Ceramic brazier under three-footed votive urn.

Perf. 12x11½, 11½x12
1989, Oct. 12 Litho.
2208 A1186 1cz multicolored .48 .35
2209 A1186 4cz shown 1.85 1.40
Discovery of America 500th anniv. (in 1992).

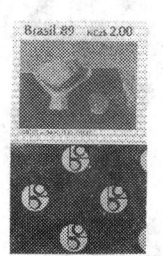

A1187 A1188

Hologram and: a. *Lemons*, by Danilo di Prete. b. *O Indio E A Suacuapara*, by sculptor Victor Brecheret. c. Francisco Matarazzo.

1989, Oct. 14 Perf. 11
Souvenir Sheet
2210 Sheet of 3 3.75 3.75
 a. A1187 2cz multicolored .72 .72
 b. A1187 3cz multicolored 1.10 1.10
 c. A1187 5cz multicolored 1.75 1.75
Sao Paulo 20th intl. art biennial.

1989, Oct. 26 Perf. 11½x11
Writers, residences and quotes: No. 2211, Casimiro de Abreu (b. 1839). No. 2212, Cora Coralina (b. 1889). No. 2213, Joaquim Machado de Assis (b. 1839).
2211 A1188 1cz shown .57 .42
2212 A1188 1cz multicolored .57 .42
2213 A1188 1cz multicolored .57 .42
Nos. 2211-2213 (3) 1.71 1.26

Federal Police Department, 25th Anniv. A1189

1989, Nov. 9 Perf. 11½x12
2214 A1189 1cz multicolored .27 .20

Christmas — A1190   Thanksgiving Day — A1191

1989, Nov. 10 Perf. 12x11½
2215 A1190 70c Heralding angel .18 .15
2216 A1190 1cz Holy family .24 .18

1989, Nov. 23
2217 A1191 1cz multicolored .24 .18

Type of 1988 Redrawn

1989, Nov. 6 Photo. Perf. 13x13½
Size: 22x26mm
2218 A1152 (B) org & dark red 2.00 1.50
Size of type and postal emblem are smaller on No. 2218; "1e PORTE" is at lower left.
No. 2218 met the first class intl. letter postage rate, initially at 9cz.

Souvenir Sheet

Proclamation of the Republic, Cent. — A1192

1989, Nov. 19 Litho. Perf. 11
2225 A1192 15cz multicolored 4.50 4.50

Bahia Sports Club, 58th Anniv. A1193

1989, Nov. 30 Perf. 11½x12
2226 A1193 50c Soccer .15 .15

Yellow Man, by Anita Malfatti (b. 1889) — A1194

1989, Dec. 2 Perf. 12x11½
2227 A1194 1cz multicolored .26 .20

Bahia State Public Archives, Cent. — A1195

1990, Jan. 16 Litho. Perf. 11½x12
2228 A1195 2cz multicolored .28 .20

Brazilian Botanical Soc., 40th Anniv. A1196

1990, Jan. 21
2229 A1196 2cz Sabia, Caatinga .22 .16
2230 A1196 13cz Pau, Brazil 1.40 1.10

Churches A1197

Designs: 2cz, St. John the Baptist Cathedral, Santa Cruz do Sul, vert. 3cz, Our Lady of Victory Church, Oeiras. 5cz, Our Lady of the Rosary Church, Ouro Preto, vert.

1990, Feb. 5 Perf. 12x11½, 11½x12
2231 A1197 2cz multicolored .16 .15
2232 A1197 3cz multicolored .25 .20
2233 A1197 5cz multicolored .42 .32
Nos. 2231-2233 (3) .83 .67

Lloyd's of London in Brazil, Cent. A1198

1990, Feb. 19 Litho. Perf. 11½x12
2234 A1198 3cz multicolored .15 .15

Souvenir Sheet

Antarctic Research Program — A1199

1990, Feb. 22 Litho. Perf. 11
2235 A1199 20cz Fauna, map 1.55 1.55

Vasco da Gama Soccer Club A1200

1990, Mar. 5
2236 A1200 10cz multicolored .48 .38

Lindolfo Collor (b. 1890), Syndicated Columnist, and Labor Monument A1201

1990, Mar. 7
2237 A1201 20cz multicolored .95 .70

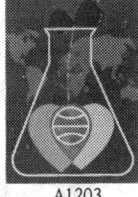

A1202 A1203

736　　　　　　　　　　　　　　　　　　　BRAZIL

Pres. Jose Sarney.

1990, Mar. 8   *Perf. 12x11½*
2238 A1202 20cz chalky blue   .95 .70

1990, Apr. 6   *Perf. 12x11½*
2239 A1203 20cz multicolored   .70 .52
AIDS prevention.

Souvenir Sheet

Penny Black, 150th Anniv. — A1204

Designs: 20cr, Dom Pedro, Brazil No. 1. 100cr, Queen Victoria, Great Britain No. 1.

1990, May 3   Litho.   *Perf. 11*
2240 A1204 Sheet of 2   2.35 1.75
   a. 20cr multicolored
   b. 100cr multicolored

Central Bank, 25th Anniv. A1205

1990, Mar. 30   Litho.   *Perf. 11½x12*
2241 A1205 20cr multicolored   .70 .52

Amazon River Postal Network, 21st Anniv. A1207

1990, Apr. 20   *Perf. 11x11½*
2243 A1207 20cr multicolored   .70 .52

Souvenir Sheet

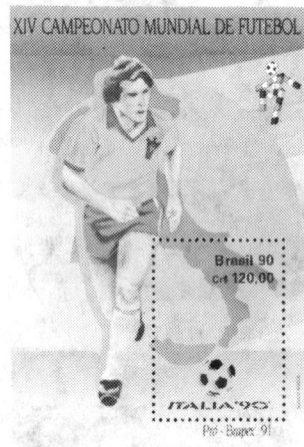

World Cup Soccer Championships, Italy — A1208

1990, May 12   Litho.   *Perf. 12x11½*
2244 A1208 120cr multicolored   3.00 3.00

22nd Congress of the Intl. Union of Highway Transportation — A1209

1990, May 14   *Perf. 11½x12*
2245 A1209 20cr multicolored   .65 .48
2246 A1209 80cr multicolored   3.00 2.25
   a. Pair, #2245-2246   3.75 2.75
No. 2246a has a continuous design.

Imperial Crown, 18th Cent. — A1210

Designs: No. 2248, Our Lady of Immaculate Conception, 18th cent.

1990, May 18   *Perf. 12x11½*
2247 A1210 20cr shown   .68 .52
2248 A1210 20cr multicolored   .68 .52
Imperial Museum, 50th anniv.(No. 2247). Mission Museum, 50th anniv. (No. 2248).

State Flags Type

1990, May 20   *Perf. 11½x12*
2249 A1050 20cr Tocantins   .68 .52

Army Geographical Service, Cent. — A1212

1990, May 30   *Perf. 11x11½*
2250 A1212 20cr multicolored   .68 .52

Film Personalities A1213

1990, June 19   *Perf. 11½x12*
2251 A1213 25cr Adhemar Gonzaga   .80 .60
2252 A1213 25cr Carmen Miranda   .80 .60
2253 A1213 25cr Carmen Santos   .80 .60
2254 A1213 25cr Oscarito   .80 .60
   a. Block of 4, #2251-2254   3.20 2.40

France-Brazil House, Rio de Janeiro A1214

1990, July 14   Litho.   *Perf. 11½x11*
2255 A1214 50cr multicolored   1.50 1.10
See France No. 2226.

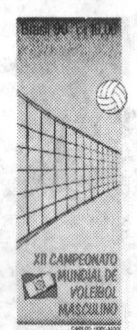

World Men's Volleyball Chmpships. A1215

Intl. Literacy Year A1217

CBA 123 — A1216

1990, July 28   Litho.   *Perf. 12x11½*
2256 A1215 10cr multicolored   .30 .24

1990, July 30   *Perf. 11½x12*
2257 A1216 10cr multicolored   .30 .24

1990, Aug. 22   *Perf. 12x11½*
2258 A1217 10cr multicolored   .30 .24

Flora Type of 1989
Perf. 11x11½, 11½x11

1989-93   Photo.

Design A1177

2259	1cr like #2179	.15	.15
2260	2cr like #2180	.15	.15
2261	5cr like #2181	.15	.15
2262	10cr Tibouchina granulosa	.15	.15
2263	20cr Cassia macranthera	.15	.15
2264	50cr Clitoria fairchildiana	.28	.15
2265	50cr Tibouchina mutabilis	.35	.35
2266	100cr Erythrina crista-galli, perf. 13	.55	.28
2267	200cr Jacaranda mimosifolia	1.10	.55
2268	500cr Caesalpinia peltophoroides	2.75	1.40
2269	1000cr Pachira aquatica	.15	.15
2270	2000cr Hibiscus pernambucensis	.15	.15
2271	5000cr Triplaris surinamensis	.85	.85
2272	10,000cr Tabebuia heptaphylla	1.65	1.65
2273	20,000cr Erythrina speciosa	2.25	2.25
	Nos. 2259-2273 (15)	10.83	8.53

Issued: 1cr, 11/8/90; 2cr, 11/12/90; 5cr, 11/16/90; #2264, 6/1/89; 10cr, 4/18/90; 20cr, 5/4/90; 100cr, 8/24/90; 200cr, 6/16/91; 500cr, 5/14/91; 1000cr, 9/2/92; 2000cr, 9/8/92; 5000cr, 10/16/92; 10,000cr, 11/16/92; 20,000cr, 4/25/93; #2265, 10/20/93.

Granbery Institute, Cent. A1218

1990, Sept. 8   Litho.   *Perf. 11½x12*
2279 A1218 13cr multicolored   .40 .28

18th Panamerican Railroad Congress A1219

1990, Sept. 9
2280 A1219 95cr multicolored   2.00 1.50

Embratel, 25th Anniv. — A1220

1990, Sept. 21
2281 A1220 13cr multicolored   .40 .30

LUBRAPEX '90 — A1221

Statues by Ceschiatti and Giorgi (No. 2283).

1990, Sept. 22
2282 A1221 25cr As Banhistas   .62 .45
2283 A1221 25cr Os Candangos   .62 .45
2284 A1221 100cr Evangelista Sao Joao   1.25 .90
2285 A1221 100cr A Justica   1.25 .90
   a. Block of 4, #2282-2285   4.00 3.00
   b. Souv. sheet of 4, #2282-2285   6.00 6.00

Praia Do Sul Wildlife Reserve A1222

1990, Oct. 12
2286 A1222 15cr Flowers   .45 .32
2287 A1222 105cr Shoreline   2.60 1.80
   a. Pair, #2286-2287   3.05 2.12
Discovery of America, 500th anniv. (in 1992).

Natl. Library, 180th Anniv. A1223

Writers: No. 2289, Guilherme de Almeida (1890-1969). No. 2290, Oswald de Andrade (1890-1954).

1990, Oct. 29   Litho.   *Perf. 11x11½*
2288 A1223 15cr multicolored   .40 .30
2289 A1223 15cr multicolored   .40 .30
2290 A1223 15cr multicolored   .40 .30
   Nos. 2288-2290 (3)   1.20 .90

Natl. Tax Court, Cent. A1224

1990, Nov. 7   Litho.   *Perf. 11½x12*
2291 A1224 15cr multicolored   .40 .30

Christmas A1225

Architecture of Brasilia: No. 2292, National Congress. No. 2293, Television tower.

1990, Nov. 20
2292 A1225 15cr multicolored   .40 .30
2293 A1225 15cr multicolored   .40 .30

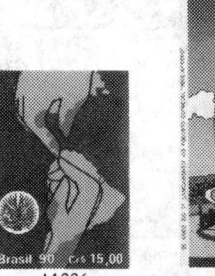

A1226   A1227

1990, Dec. 13   Litho.   *Perf. 12x11½*
2294 A1226 15cr multicolored   .18 .15
Organization of American States, cent.

1990, Dec. 14
2295 A1227 15cr multicolored   .18 .15
First Flight of Nike Apache Missile, 25th anniv.

BRAZIL

Colonization of Sergipe, Founding of Sao Cristovao, 400th Anniv. A1228

1990, Dec. 18   Litho.   Perf. 11½x12
2296 A1228 15cr multicolored   .18 .15

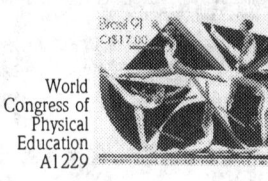

World Congress of Physical Education A1229

1991, Jan. 7   Perf. 11½x12
2297 A1229 17cr multicolored   .18 .15

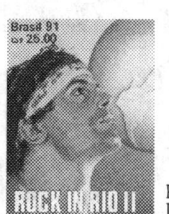

Rock in Rio II — A1230

1991, Jan. 9   Perf. 12x11½
2298 A1230 25cr Cazuza   .20 .15
2299 A1230 185cr Raul Seixas   1.65 1.00
    a. Pair, #2298-2299   2.00 1.10
Printed in sheets of 12.

Ministry of Aviation, 50th Anniv. A1231

1991, Jan. 20   Perf. 11x11½
2300 A1231 17cr multicolored   .20 .15

A1232    A1233

Carnivals.

1991, Feb. 8   Litho.   Perf. 12x11½
2301 A1232 25cr Olinda   .24 .16
2302 A1232 30cr Salvador   .28 .20
2303 A1232 280cr Rio de Janeiro   2.50 2.00
    Nos. 2301-2303 (3)   3.02 2.36

1991, Feb. 20
2304 A1233 300cr multicolored   3.00 2.25
Visit by Pres. Collor to Antarctica.

Hang Gliding World Championships — A1234

1991, Feb. 24   Perf. 11½x12
2305 A1234 36cr multicolored   .36 .28

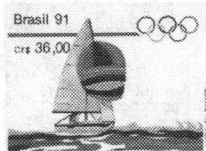

11th Pan American Games, 25th Summer Olympics A1235

1991, Mar. 30   Litho.   Perf. 11½x12
2306 A1235 36cr Sailing   .32 .24
2307 A1235 36cr Rowing   .32 .24
2308 A1235 300cr Swimming   2.50 1.90
    a. Block of 3, #2306-2308 + label   3.25 2.50

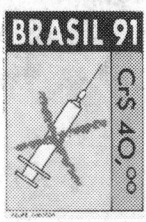

Fight Against Drugs A1236   Yanomami Indian Culture A1237

1991, Apr. 7   Litho.   Perf. 12x11½
2309 A1236 40cr Drugs   .35 .30
2310 A1236 40cr Alcohol   .35 .30
2311 A1236 40cr Smoking   .35 .30
    Nos. 2309-2311 (3)   1.05 .90

Perf. 11½x11, 11x11½
1991, Apr. 19
2312 A1237 40cr shown   .35 .28
2313 A1237 400cr Indian, horiz.   3.50 2.75

Journal of Brazil, Cent. A1238

1991, Apr. 8   Litho.   Perf. 11x11½
2314 A1238 40cr multicolored   .35 .28

Neochen Jubata (Orinoco Goose) — A1239

1991, June 5   Litho.   Perf. 12x11½
2315 A1239 45cr multi   .30 .22
UN Conference on Development.

Snakes & Dinosaurs A1240

1991, June 6   Perf. 11½x12
2316 A1240 45cr Bothrops jararaca   .30 .22
2317 A1240 45cr Corallus caninus   .30 .22
    a. Pair, #2316-2317   .60 .45
2318 A1240 45cr Teropods   .30 .22
2319 A1240 350cr Sauropods   2.10 1.60
    a. Pair, #2318-2319   2.40 1.85
    Nos. 2316-2319 (4)   3.00 2.26

Flag of Brazil — A1241

1991, June 10   Photo.   Perf. 13x13½
2320 A1241 A multicolored   .25 .20
Valued at domestic letter rate (cr) on day of issue.
Exists with inscription at lower right. Same value.

Fire Pumper A1242

1991, July 2   Litho.   Perf. 11½x12
2321 A1242 45cr multicolored   .30 .22

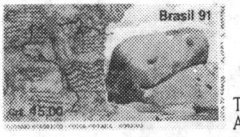

Tourism A1243

Perf. 11x11½
2322 A1243 45cr multicolored   .28 .20
2323 A1243 350cr multicolored   2.00 1.50
Map location and: 45cr, Painted stones, Roraima. 350cr, Dedo de Deus Mountain, Rio De Janeiro.

Labor Laws, 50th Anniv. A1244

1991, Aug. 11   Perf. 11½x12
2324 A1244 45cr multicolored   .30 .22

Leonardo Mota, Birth Cent. A1245

1991, Aug. 22
2325 A1245 45cr buff, blk & red   .30 .22
Folklore Festival.

Jose Basilio da Gama (1741-1795), Poet A1246

Designs: No. 2327, Fagundes Varela (b. 1841), poet. No. 2328, Jackson de Figueiredo (b. 1891), writer.

1991, Aug. 29
2326 A1246 45cr multicolored   .26 .18
2327 A1246 50cr multicolored   .30 .22
2328 A1246 50cr multicolored   .30 .22
    Nos. 2326-2328 (3)   .86 .62

12th Natl. Eucharistic Congress — A1247

1991, Oct. 6   Litho.   Perf. 12x11½
2329 A1247 50cr Pope John Paul II   .18 .15
2330 A1247 400cr Map, crosses   1.40 1.05
    a. Pair, #2329-2330   1.60 1.20
Visit by Pope John Paul II.

First Brazilian Constitution, Cent. A1248

1991, Oct. 7   Perf. 11½x12
2331 A1248 50cr multicolored   .18 .15

Telecom '91 — A1249

1991, Oct. 8   Perf. 12x11½
2332 A1249 50cr multicolored   .18 .15
Sixth World Forum and Exposition on Telecommunications, Geneva, Switzerland.

America Issue A1250

UPAEP emblem and explorers: 50cr, Ferdinand Magellan (c. 1480-1521). 400cr, Francisco de Orellana (c. 1490-c. 1546).

1991, Oct. 12   Perf. 11½x12
2333 A1250 50cr multicolored   .18 .15
2334 A1250 400cr multicolored   1.40 1.05
Discovery of America, 500th anniv. (in 1992).

A1251    A1252

BRAPEX VIII (Orchids and Hummingbirds): 50cr, Colibri serrirostris, cattleya warneri. No. 2336, Chlorostilbon aureoventris, rodrigueszia venusta. No. 2337, Clytolaema rubricauda, zygopetalum intermedium. No. 2338a, 50cr, Colibri serrirostris. b, 50cr, Chlorostilbon aureoventris. c, 500cr, Clytolaema rubricauda.

1991, Oct. 29   Litho.   Perf. 12x11½
2335 A1251 50cr multicolored   .15 .15
2336 A1251 65cr multicolored   .18 .15
2337 A1251 65cr multicolored   .18 .15
    Nos. 2335-2337 (3)   .51 .45

Souvenir Sheet
2338 A1251   Sheet of 3, #a.-c.   2.20 1.65

1991, Oct. 29   Litho.   Perf. 11½x11
2339 A1252 400cr multicolored   .90 .65
Lasar Segall, artist, birth cent.

BRAZIL

Bureau of Agriculture and Provision of Sao Paulo, Cent. — A1253

1991, Nov. 11   *Perf. 12x11½*
2340 A1253 70cr multicolored   .20   .15

First Civilian Presidents, Birth Sesquicentennials — A1254

1991, Nov. 14   *Perf. 11½x12*
2341 A1254 70cr Manuel de Campos Salles   .20   .15
2342 A1254 90cr Prudente de Moraes Barros   .25   .18
   a. Pair, #2341-2342   .45   .35

Christmas A1255
Thanksgiving A1256

1991, Nov. 20   *Perf. 12x11½*
2343 A1255 70cr multicolored   .20   .15

1991, Nov. 28
2344 A1256 70cr multicolored   .20   .15

Military Police A1257

1991, Dec. 1   *Perf. 11½x12*
2345 A1257 80cr multicolored   .22   .16

Souvenir Sheet

Emperor Dom Pedro (1825-1891) — A1258

a, 80cr, Older age. b, 800cr, Wearing crown.

Litho. & Engr.
1991, Nov. 29   *Perf. 11*
2346 A1258 Sheet of 2, #a.-b.   2.50   2.50
   BRASILIANA 93.

Churches — A1259

Designs: No. 2347, Presbyterian Church, Rio de Janeiro. No. 2348, First Baptist Church, Niteroi.

1992, Jan. 12   Litho.   *Perf. 12x11½*
2347 A1259 250cr multicolored   .30   .22
2348 A1259 250cr multicolored   .30   .22

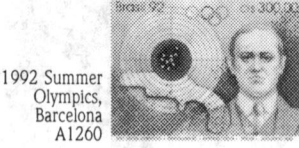

1992 Summer Olympics, Barcelona A1260

Medalists in shooting, Antwerp, 1920: 300cr, Afranio Costa, silver. 2500cr, Guilherme Paraense, gold.

1992, Jan. 28   *Perf. 11½x12*
2349 A1260 300cr multicolored   .32   .24
2350 A1260 2500cr multicolored   2.75   2.00

Port of Santos, Cent. — A1261

1992, Feb. 3   Litho.   *Perf. 11½*
2351 A1261 300cr multicolored   .45   .35

Fauna of Fernando de Noronha Island A1262

1992, Feb. 25   Litho.   *Perf. 11½x12*
2352 A1262 400cr White-tailed tropicbirds   .40   .30
2353 A1262 2500cr Dolphins   2.50   1.75
   Earth Summit, Rio de Janeiro.

Yellow Amaryllis — A1263

1992, Feb. 27   Photo.   *Perf. 13½*
2354 A1263 (A) multicolored   .25   .20

No. 2354 met the second class domestic letter postage rate of 265cr on date of issue.

ARBRAFEX '92, Argentina-Brazil Philatelic Exhibition — A1264

Designs: No. 2355, Gaucho throwing bola at rhea. No. 2356, Man playing accordion, couple dancing. No. 2357, Couple in horse-drawn cart, woman. 1000cr, Gaucho throwing lasso at steer.

No. 2358c, 250cr, like #2356. d, 500cr, like #2355. e, 1500cr, like #2358.

1992, Mar. 20   Litho.   *Perf. 11½x12*
2355 A1264 250cr multicolored   .15   .15
2356 A1264 250cr multicolored   .15   .15
2357 A1264 250cr multicolored   .15   .15
2358 A1264 1000cr multicolored   .60   .60
   a. Block of 4, Nos. 2355-2358   1.05   1.05

Souvenir Sheet
2358B A1264 Sheet of 4, #2357, 2358c-2358e   1.05   1.05

1992 Summer Olympics, Barcelona — A1265

1992, Apr. 3   *Perf. 12x11½*
2359 A1265 300cr multicolored   .18   .18

Discovery of America, 500th Anniv. A1266

1992, Apr. 24   *Perf. 11½x12*
2360 A1266 500cr Columbus' fleet   .30   .30
2361 A1266 3500cr Columbus, map   2.10   2.10
   a. Pair, #2360-2361   2.40   2.40

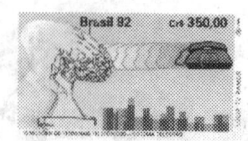

Telebras Telecommunications System — A1267

1992, May 5   *Perf. 11x11½*
2362 A1267 350cr multicolored   .20   .20
   Installation of 10 million telephones.

Langsdorff Expedition to Brazil, 170th Anniv. A1268

Designs: No. 2363, Aime-Adrien Taunay, natives. No. 2364, Johann Moritz Rugendas, monkey. No. 2365, Hercule Florence, flowering plant. 3000cr, Gregory Ivanovitch Langsdorff, map.

1992, June 2   *Perf. 11½x12*
2363 A1268 500cr multicolored   .25   .25
2364 A1268 500cr multicolored   .25   .25
2365 A1268 500cr multicolored   .25   .25
2366 A1268 3000cr multicolored   1.50   1.50
   Nos. 2363-2366 (4)   2.25   2.25
   UN Conf. on Environmental Development, Rio.

UN Conference on Environmental Development, Rio de Janeiro — A1269

Globe and: No. 2367, Flags of Sweden and Brazil. No. 2368, City, grain, mountain and tree. 3000cr, Map of Brazil, parrot, orchid.

1992, June 3   Litho.   *Perf. 11x11½*
2367 A1269 450cr multicolored   .20   .20
2368 A1269 450cr multicolored   .20   .20
2369 A1269 3000cr multicolored   1.50   1.50
   Nos. 2367-2369 (3)   1.90   1.90

Ecology A1270

Designs: No. 2370, Flowers, waterfall, and butterflies. No. 2371, Butterflies, canoe, and hummingbirds. No. 2372, Boy taking pictures of tropical birds. No. 2373, Armadillo, girl picking fruit.

1992, June 4   *Perf. 11½x12*
2370 A1270 500cr multicolored   .25   .25
2371 A1270 500cr multicolored   .25   .25
2372 A1270 500cr multicolored   .25   .25
2373 A1270 500cr multicolored   .25   .25
   a. Strip of 4, #2370-2373   1.00   1.00
   UN Conf. on Environmental Development, Rio.

Floral Paintings by Margaret Mee — A1271

1992, June 5   *Perf. 12x11½*
2374 A1271 600cr Nidularium innocentii   .35   .35
2375 A1271 600cr Canistrum exiguum   .35   .35
2376 A1271 700cr Canistrum cyathiforme   .42   .42
2377 A1271 700cr Nidularium rubens   .42   .42
   Nos. 2374-2377 (4)   1.54   1.54
   UN Conf. on Environmental Development, Rio.

Souvenir Sheet

Joaquim Jose da Silva Xavier (1748-1792), Patriot — A1272

1992, Apr. 21   Litho. & Engr.   *Perf. 11*
2378 A1272 3500cr multicolored   2.10   2.10

Souvenir Sheet

Expedition of Alexandre Rodrigues Ferreira, Bicent. A1273

Designs: a, 500cr, Sailing ships, gray and green hulls. b, 1000cr, Sailing ships, red hulls. c, 2500cr, Sailing ship at shore.

1992, May 9   Litho.   *Perf. 11½x12*
2379 A1273 Sheet of 3, #a.-c.   2.40   2.40
   Lubrapex '92.

BRAZIL

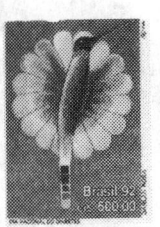

A1274

A1275

1992, June 5   Litho.   *Perf. 12x11½*
2380 A1274   600cr Hummingbird   .25   .25
Diabetes Day.

1992, July 13   Litho.   *Perf. 11½x11*
2381 A1275   550cr multicolored   .25   .25
Volunteer firemen of Joinville.

A1276

A1277

Serra da Capivara National Park: No. 2382, Leopard, animals, map of park. No. 2383, Canyon, map of Brazil.

1992, July 17   *Perf. 12x11½*
2382 A1276   550cr multicolored   .22   .22
2383 A1276   550cr multicolored   .22   .22
   a.   Pair, #2382-2383   .45   .45

1992, July 24
2384 A1277   550cr multicolored   .25   .25
Financing for studies and projects.

Natl. Service for Industrial Training, 50th Anniv. — A1278

1992, Aug. 5   *Perf. 11½x12*
2385 A1278   650cr multicolored   .35   .35

Fortresses
A1279

1992, Aug. 19   Litho.   *Perf. 11½x12*
2386 A1279   650cr Santa Cruz   .28   .28
2387 A1279   3000cr Santo Antonio   1.25   1.25

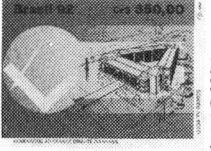

Masonic Square, Compass and Lodge
A1280

1992, Aug. 20
2388 A1280   650cr multicolored   .28   .28

Shop with Scott Publishing Co. 24 hours a day 7 days a week at www.scottonline.com

Brazilian Assistance Legion, 50th Anniv.
A1281

Hospital of Medicine and Orthopedics
A1282

1992, Aug. 28   *Perf. 12x11½*
2389 A1281   650cr multicolored   .28   .28

1992, Sept. 11
2390 A1282   800cr multicolored   .30   .30

Merry Christmas
A1283

1992, Nov. 20   *Perf. 11½*
2391 A1283 (1) multicolored   .25   .25
No. 2391 met the first class domestic letter postage rate of 1090cr on day of issue.

Writers
A1284

#2392, Graciliano Ramos (1892-1953), vert. #2393, Menotti del Picchia (1892-1988), vert. 1000cr, Assis Chateaubriand (1892-1968).

1992, Oct. 29   *Perf. 12x11½, 11½x12*   Litho.
2392 A1284   900cr multicolored   .22   .22
2393 A1284   900cr multicolored   .22   .22
2394 A1284   1000cr multicolored   .28   .28

Expedition of Luis Cruls, Cent.
A1285

1992, Nov. 11   *Perf. 11½x12*
2395 A1285   900cr multicolored   .22   .22

Brazillian Program for Quality and Productivity
A1286

1992, Nov. 12
2396 A1286   1200cr multicolored   .28   .28

Souvenir Sheet

Tourism Year in the Americas — A1287

Designs: a, 1200cr, Mountains, coastline. b, 9000cr, Sugarloaf Mt., aerial tram, Rio de Janeiro.

1992, Nov. 18   Litho.   *Perf. 11½x12*
2397 A1287   Sheet of 2, #a.-b.   2.00   2.00
Brasiliana '93.

Sister Irma Dulce
A1288

1993, Mar. 13   Litho.   *Perf. 11½x12*
2398 A1288   3500cr multicolored   .35   .35

Souvenir Sheet

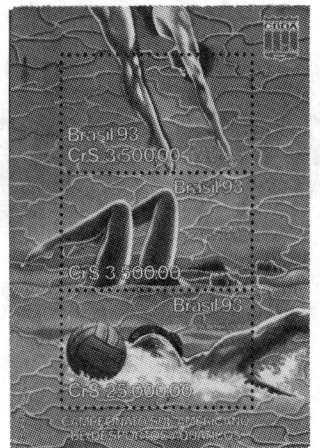

Water Sports Championships of South America — A1289

Designs: a, 3500cr, Diver. b, 3500cr, Synchronized swimmers. c, 25,000cr, Water polo.

1993, Mar. 21   Litho.   *Perf. 11*
2399 A1289   Sheet of 3, #a.-c.   2.75   2.75

Curitiba, 300th Anniv.
A1290

1993, Mar. 29
2400 A1290   4500cr multicolored   .40   .40

Health and Preservation of Life — A1291

Pedro Americo, 150th Birth Anniv. — A1292

Red Cross emblem and: No. 2401, Bleeding heart, flowers. No. 2402, Cancer symbol, breast. No. 2403, Brain waves, rainbow emerging from head.

1993, Apr. 7   Litho.   *Perf. 12x11½*
2401 A1291   4500cr multicolored   .30   .30
2402 A1291   4500cr multicolored   .30   .30
2403 A1291   4500cr multicolored   .30   .30
   a.   Strip of 3, #2401-2403   .90   .90

Perf. 12x11½, 11½x12
1993, Apr. 29

Paintings: 5500cr, A Study of Love, 1883. No. 2405, David and Abizag, 1879, horiz. No. 2406, Seated Nude, 1882.

2404 A1292   5500cr multi   .25   .25
2405 A1292   36,000cr multi   1.65   1.65
2406 A1292   36,000cr multi   1.65   1.65
   Nos. 2404-2406 (3)   3.55   3.55

Natl. Flag — A1292a

1993, May 26   Litho.   *Die Cut*   *Self-adhesive*
2407 A1292a   A multicolored   .35   .35
No. 2407 valued at first class domestic letter rate of 9570cr on day of issue.

Beetles
A1293

1993, June 5   Litho.   *Perf. 11½x12*
2408 A1293   8000cr Dynastes hercules   .35   .35
2409 A1293   55,000cr Batus barbicornis   2.25   2.25

3rd Iberian-American Conference of Chiefs of State and Heads of Government, Salvador — A1294

1993, July 15   Litho.   *Perf. 11x11½*
2410 A1294   12,000cr multi   .15   .15

1st Brazilian Postage Stamps, 150th Anniv. — A1295

BRAZIL

Perf. 12x11½
1993, July 30 Litho. & Engr.
2411 A1295 30,000cr No. 1 .30 .30
2412 A1295 60,000cr No. 2 .60 .60
2413 A1295 90,000cr No. 3 .90 .90
  a. Souvenir sheet of 3, #2411-2413, wmk. 268 2.00 2.00
  Nos. 2411-2413 (3) 1.80 1.80
  No. 2413a sold for 200,000cr.

Union of Portuguese Speaking Capitals — A1296

a, 15,000cr, Brasilia. b, 71,000cr, Rio de Janiero.

1993, July 30 Litho. **Perf. 11½x12**
2414 A1296 Pair, #a.-b. .90 .90
  No. 2414 printed in continuous design.

Monica & Friends, by Mauricio de Sousa — A1297

Monica, Cebolinha, Cascao, Magali, and Bidu: a, Engraving die. b, Reading proclamation, king, No. 1. c, Writing and sending letter, No. 2. d, Receiving letter, No. 3.

1993, Aug. 1
2415 A1297 (1) Strip of 4, #a.-d. .85 .85
  First Brazilian postage stamps, 150th anniv. Nos. 2415a-2415d paid the first class rate (9600cr) on day of issue.

Brazilian Post, 330th Anniv. A1298

Postal buildings: a, Imperial Post Office, Rio de Janeiro. b, Petropolis. c, Central office, Rio de Janeiro. d, Niteroi.

1993, Aug. 3 Litho. **Perf. 11½x12**
2416 A1298 20,000cr Block of 4, #a.-d. .45 .45

Brazilian Engineering Schools A1299

Designs: No. 2417, School of Engineering, Federal University, Rio de Janeiro. No. 2418, Polytechnical School, University of Sao Paulo.

1993, Aug. 24 Litho. **Perf. 11x11½**
2417 A1299 17cr multicolored .30 .30
2418 A1299 17cr multicolored .30 .30

Preservation of Sambaquis Archaeological Sites — A1300

1993, Sept. 19 **Perf. 12x11½**
2419 A1300 17cr Two artifacts .22 .22
2420 A1300 17cr Six artifacts .22 .22

Ulysses Guimaraes, Natl. Congress — A1301

1993, Oct. 6 Litho. **Perf. 11x11½**
2421 A1301 22cr multicolored .28 .28

A1302 A1303

1993, Oct. 8 Litho. **Perf. 12x11½**
2422 A1302 22cr multicolored .28 .28
  Virgin of Nazare Religious Festival, bicent.

1993, Oct. 13 Litho. **Perf. 11½x11**
  Endangered birds (America Issue): 22cr, Anodorhynchus hyacinthinus, anodorhynchus glaucus, anodorhynchus leari. 130cr, Cyanopsitta spixii.
2423 A1303 22cr multicolored .25 .25
2424 A1303 130cr multicolored 1.40 1.40

Composers — A1304 A1307

1993, Oct. 19 Litho. **Perf. 12x11½**
2425 A1304 22cr Vinicius de Moraes .18 .18
2426 A1304 22cr Pixinguinha .18 .18

1993, Oct. 29 Litho. **Perf. 12x11½**
  Poets: No. 2427, Mario de Andrade (1893-1945). No. 2428, Alceu Amoroso Lima (Tristao de Athayde) (1893-1983). No. 2429, Gilka Machado (1893-1980).
2427 A1307 30cr multicolored .28 .28
2428 A1307 30cr multicolored .28 .28
2429 A1307 30cr multicolored .28 .28
  Nos. 2427-2429 (3) .84 .84
  Natl. Book Day.

Brazil-Portugal Treaty of Consultation and Friendship, 40th Anniv. — A1308

1993, Nov. 3 Litho. **Perf. 11½x12**
2430 A1308 30cr multicolored .28 .28
  See Portugal No. 1980.

Image of the Republic — A1309

1993, Nov. 3 Photo. & Engr. **Perf. 13**
2431 A1309 (B) multicolored 2.50 2.50
  Valued at first class international letter rate (178.70 cr) on day of issue.

2nd Intl. Biennial of Comic Strips A1310

Cartoon drawings: No. 2432, Nho-Quim. No. 2433, Benjamin. No. 2434, Lamparina. No. 2435, Reco-Reco, Bolao, Azeitona.

1993, Nov. 11 Litho. **Perf. 11½x12**
2432 A1310 (1) multicolored .42 .42
2433 A1310 (1) multicolored .42 .42
2434 A1310 (1) multicolored .42 .42
2435 A1310 (1) multicolored .42 .42
  a. Block of 4, #2432-2435 1.75 1.75
  Valued at first class domestic letter rate (30.20 cr) on day of issue.

Launching of First Brazilian-Built Submarine — A1311

1993, Nov. 18 **Perf. 11½**
2436 A1311 240cr multicolored 1.75 1.75

Christmas A1312

1993, Nov. 20
2437 A1312 (1) multicolored .45 .45
  Valued at first class domestic letter rate (30.20 cr) on day of issue.

First Fighter Group, 50th Anniv. A1313

1993, Dec. 18 Litho. **Perf. 11½**
2438 A1313 42cr multicolored .35 .35

Convent of Merces, 340th Anniv. A1314

1994, Jan. 31 Litho. **Perf. 11½x12**
2439 A1314 58cr multicolored .32 .32

Mae Menininha of Gantois, Birth Cent. A1315

1994, Feb. 10 Litho. **Perf. 11x11½**
2440 A1315 80cr multicolored .40 .40

Intl. Olympic Committee, Cent. A1316

1994, Feb. 17 **Perf. 11½x12**
2441 A1316 (1) multicolored 2.25 2.25
  No. 2441 valued at first class international letter rate (446.30 cr) on day of issue.

Natl. Flag — A1317

1994, Jan. 31 Litho. **Die Cut**
Self-Adhesive
2442 A1317 (1) multicolored .40 .40
  No. 2442 valued at first class domestic letter rate (55.90 cr) on day of issue.

Birds — A1318

1994 Photo. **Perf. 11x11½**
2443 A1318 10cr Notiochelidon cyanoleuca .15 .15
2444 A1318 20cr Buteo magnirostris .15 .15
2445 A1318 50cr Turdus rufiventris .15 .15
2446 A1318 100cr Columbina talpacoti .15 .15
2447 A1318 200cr Vanellus chilensis .20 .20
2448 A1318 500cr Zonotrichia capensis .50 .50
  Nos. 2443-2448 (6) 1.30 1.30
  Issued: 10cr, 3/17/94. 20cr, 3/9/94. 50cr, 3/1/94. 100cr, 2/2/94. 200cr, 4/4/94. 500cr, 4/13/94. See Nos. 2484-2494.

Image of the Republic — A1318a

1994, May 10 Litho.
Self-Adhesive
Die Cut
2449 A1318a (1) blue .22 .22
2450 A1318a (3) claret .40 .40
  Size: 25x35mm
  Perf. 12x11½
2451 A1318a (4) green .80 .80
2452 A1318a (5) henna brown 1.50 1.50
  Nos. 2449-2452 (4) 2.92 2.92
  Nos. 2449, 2450, 2451, 2452 valued 131.37cr, 321.14cr, 452.52cr 905.05cr on day of issue.

BRAZIL

Prince Henry the Navigator (1394-1460) — A1319

1994, Mar. 4   Litho.   Perf. 11½x12
2463 A1319 635cr multicolored   2.25 2.25
See Macao No. 719, Portugal No. 1987.

America Issue A1320

Postal vehicles: 110cr, Bicycle, country scene. 635cr, Motorcycle, city scene.

1994, Mar. 18
2464 A1320 110cr multicolored   .20 .20
2465 A1320 635cr multicolored   1.10 1.10

Father Cicero Romao Batista, 150th Birth Anniv. A1321

1994, Mar. 24   Perf. 11x11½
2466 A1321 (1) multicolored   .35 .35
No. 2466 valued at first class domestic letter rate (98.80 cr) on day of issue.

Albert Sabin, Campaign Against Polio A1322

1994, Apr. 7   Perf. 11½x12
2467 A1322 160cr multicolored   .30 .30

Carlos Castello Branco, Journalist A1323

1994, Apr. 14
2468 A1323 160cr multicolored   .30 .30

Karl Friedrich Phillip von Martius, Naturalist — A1324

Flowers: No. 2469, Euterpe oleracea. No. 2470, Jacaranda paucifoliolata. No. 2471, Barbacernia tomentosa.

1994, Apr. 24   Perf. 12x11½
2469 A1324 (1) multicolored   .35 .35
2470 A1324 (1) multicolored   .35 .35
2471 A1324 (1) multicolored   2.00 2.00
    Nos. 2469-2471 (3)   2.70 2.70
Nos. 2469-2470 were valued at first class domestic letter rate (144 cr) on day of issue. No. 2471 valued at first class intl. letter rate (860 cr) on day of issue.

Monkeys — A1326

No. 2474, Leontopithecus rosalia. No. 2475, Saguinus imperator. No. 2476, Saguinus bicolor.

1994, May 24
2474 A1326 (1) multicolored   .35 .35
2475 A1326 (1) multicolored   .35 .35
2476 A1326 (1) multicolored   .35 .35
    Nos. 2474-2476 (3)   1.05 1.05
Nos. 2474-2476 were valued at first class domestic letter rate (207.03 cr) on day of issue.

1994 World Cup Soccer Championships, US — A1327

1994, May 19   Perf. 11½x12
2477 A1327 (1) multicolored   2.00 2.00
No. 2477 was valued at first class intl. rate (1378.32 cr) on day of issue. Soccer in Brazil, cent.

Souvenir Sheet

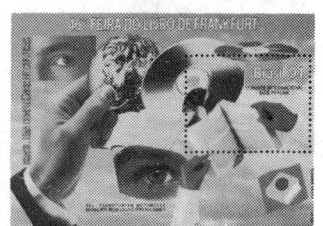

46th Frankfurt Intl. Book Fair — A1328

Illustration reduced.

1994, May 27
2478 A1328 (1) multicolored   2.00 2.00
No. 2478 was valued at first class intl. rate (1523.83 cr) on day of issue.

Natl. Literacy Program — A1329

Designs: No. 2479, Pencil, buildings. No. 2480, Pencil, people on television, people watching. No. 2481, Classroom, pencil. No. 2482, Pencils crossed over fingerprint, map of Brazil.

1994, June 3   Litho.   Perf. 12x11½
2479 A1329 (1) multicolored   .32 .32
2480 A1329 (1) multicolored   .32 .32
2481 A1329 (1) multicolored   .32 .32
2482 A1329 (1) multicolored   .32 .32
    Nos. 2479-2482 (4)   1.28 1.28
Nos. 2479-2482 were valued at first class domestic letter rate (233.05 cr) on day of issue.

Souvenir Sheet

Treaty of Tordesillas, 500th Anniv. — A1330

1994, June 7
2483 A1330 (1) multicolored   2.25 2.25
No. 2483 was valued at first class intl. letter rate (1689.02 cr) on day of issue.

Bird Type of 1994 and A1330a

Perf. 11x11½, 13 (15c), 12½x13 (22c, (22c)
1994-98   Photo.
2484 A1318 1c like No. 2443   .15 .15
2485 A1318 2c like No. 2444   .15 .15
2486 A1318 5c like No. 2445   .15 .15
2487 A1318 10c like No. 2446   .20 .20
2488 A1330a 15c Sicaris flaveola .35 .35
2489 A1318 20c like No. 2447   .42 .42
2490 A1318 22c Tyrannus savana .50 .50
2491 A1318 50c like No. 2448   1.00 1.00
2494 A1318 1r Furnarius rufus 2.25 2.25
    Nos. 2484-2494 (8)   4.67 4.67

Size: 21x26mm
Self-Adhesive
Serpentine Die Cut
2498 A1330a 22c Myiozetetes similis   .50 .50
2499 A1330a (22c) Volatinia jacarina   .50 .50
No. 2499 is inscribed "1o PORTE NATIONAL" and was valued at 22c on day of issue.
Issued: 1c, 2c, 5c, 20c, 20c, 50c, 1r, 7/1/94; 11/16/95; #2490, 10/13/97; #2498, 2/16/98; #2499, 7/22/97.
This is an expanding set. Numbers may change.

Prominent Brazilians A1331

Designs: No. 2504, Edgard Santos (1894-1962), surgeon, educator. No. 2505, Oswaldo Aranha (1894-1960), politician. No. 2507, Otto Lara Resende (1922-92), writer, educator.

1994, July 5   Litho.   Perf. 11½x12
2504 A1331 (1) multicolored   .28 .28
2505 A1331 (1) multicolored   .28 .28
2506 A1331 (1) multicolored   .28 .28
    Nos. 2504-2506 (3)   .84 .84
Nos. 2504-2506 were valued at first class domestic letter rate (12c) on day of issue.

A1332    A1333

1994, July 15   Perf. 12x11½
2507 A1332 12c multicolored   .28 .28
Petrobras, 40th anniv.

Litho. & Engr.
1994, July 26   Perf. 11½
2508 A1333 12c multicolored   .28 .28
Brazilian State Mint, 300th anniv.

Campaign Against Famine & Misery A1334

1994, July 27   Litho.   Perf. 11½x12
2509 A1334 (1) Fish   .28 .28
2510 A1334 (1) Bread   .28 .28
Nos. 2509-2510 were valued at first class domestic letter rate (12c) on day of issue.

Institute of Brazilian Lawyers, 150th Anniv. A1335

1994, Aug. 11
2511 A1335 12c multicolored   .28 .28

Intl. Year of the Family A1336

1994, Aug. 16   Perf. 11½
2512 A1336 84c multicolored   2.00 2.00

Maternity Hospital of Sao Paulo, Cent. A1337

1994, Aug. 26   Perf. 11½x12
2513 A1337 12c multicolored   .28 .28

Vincente Celestino (1894-1968), Singer A1338

1994, Sept. 12
2514 A1338 12c multicolored   .28 .28

741

BRAZIL

"Contos da Carochinha," First Brazilian Children's Book, Cent. — A1339

Fairy tales: a, Joao e Maria (Hansel & Gretel). b, Dona Baratinha. c, Puss 'n Boots. d, Tom Thumb.

1994, Oct. 5   Litho.   Perf. 11½x12
2515   Block of 4   4.75 4.75
  a.-b.   A1339 12c any single   .28   .28
  c.-d.   A1339 84c any single   2.00 2.00

Brazilian Literature — A1340

Portraits: No. 2516, Tomas Antonio Gonzaga (1744-1809?), poet. No. 2517, Fernando de Azevedo (1894-1974), author.

1994, Oct. 5   Perf. 11½
2516 A1340 12c multicolored   .28   .28
2517 A1340 12c multicolored   .28   .28

St. Clare of Assisi (1194-1253) — A1341

1994, Oct. 19   Perf. 12x11½
2518 A1341 12c multicolored   .28   .28

Ayrton Senna (1960-1994), Race Car Driver — A1342

Designs: a, McClaren Formula 1 race car, Brazilian flag. b, Fans, Senna. c, Flags, race cars, Senna.

1994, Oct. 24   Perf. 11½x12
2519   Triptych   2.75 2.75
  a.-b.   A1342 12c any single   .28   .28
  c.   A1342 84c multicolored   2.00 2.00

Institute of History & Geography of Sao Paulo, Cent. — A1343

1994, Nov. 1
2520 A1343 12c multicolored   .28   .28

Popular Music — A1344

Designs: No. 2521, Music from "The Sea," by Dorival Caymmi. No. 2522, Adoniran Barbosa (1910-82), samba composer.

1994, Nov. 5   Perf. 11½
2521 A1344 12c multicolored   .28   .28
2522 A1344 12c multicolored   .28   .28

Christmas — A1345

Folk characters: No. 2523: a, Boy wearing Santa coat, pot on head. b, Worm in apple. c, Man, animals singing. d, Shoe on tree stump, man with pipe holding pen.

1994, Dec. 1   Litho.   Perf. 11½
2523   Block of 4   2.75 2.75
  a.   A1345 84c multicolored   1.90 1.90
  b.-d. A1345 12c any single   .28   .28
  e.   Booklet pane, #2523 + 4 labels 5.50
        Complete booklet, #2523a   5.50

Souvenir Sheet

Brazil, 1994 World Cup Soccer Champions — A1346

Illustration reduced.

1994, Dec. 5   Perf. 12x11½
2524 A1346 2.14r multicolored   5.00 5.00

Louis Pasteur (1822-95) — A1347

1995, Feb. 19   Litho.   Perf. 11½x12
2525 A1347 84c multicolored   2.00 2.00

Historical Events — A1348

Designs: No. 2526, Capture of Monte Castello, 50th anniv. No. 2527, End of the Farroupilha Revolution, 150th anniv.

1995, Feb. 21
2526 A1348 12c multicolored   .28   .28
2527 A1348 12c multicolored   .28   .28

Pres. Itamar Franco — A1349   FAO, 50th Anniv. — A1350

1995, Mar. 22   Litho.   Perf. 12x11½
2528 A1349 12c multicolored   .28   .28

1995, Apr. 3   Perf. 11½x11
2529 A1350 84c multicolored   2.00 2.00

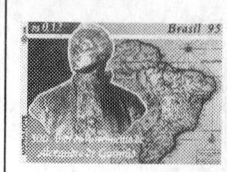

Famous Men — A1351

#2530, Alexandre de Gusmao (1695-1753), diplomat. #2531, Francisco Brandao, Viscount of Jequitinhonha (1794-1870), lawyer, abolitionist. 15c, Jose da Silva Paranhos, Jr., Baron of Rio Branco (1845-1912), politician, diplomat.

1995, Apr. 28   Perf. 11½x12
2530 A1351 12c multicolored   .28   .28
2531 A1351 12c multicolored   .28   .28
2532 A1351 15c multicolored   .35   .35
      Nos. 2530-2532 (3)   .91   .91

Radio, Cent. — A1352

Design: Guglielmo Marconi (1874-1937), transmitting equipment.

1995, May 5   Litho.   Perf. 11½x12
2533 A1352 84c multicolored   2.00 2.00

Friendship Between Brazil & Japan — A1353

1995, May 29
2534 A1353 84c multicolored   2.00 2.00

Endangered Birds — A1354

1995, June 5   Perf. 12x11½
2535 A1354 12c Tinamus solitarius   .30   .30
2536 A1354 12c Mitu mitu   .30   .30

June Festivals — A1355

Designs: No. 2537, Couples dancing at Campina Grande, "Greatest St. John's Party of the World." No. 2538, Bride, bridegroom, festivities, Caruaru.

1995, June 11   Perf. 11½x12
2537 A1355 12c multicolored   .30   .30
2538 A1355 12c multicolored   .30   .30

St. Anthony of Padua (1195-1231) — A1356

1995, June 13
2539 A1356 84c multicolored   2.00 2.00
      See Portugal No. 2054.

Souvenir Sheet

Motion Picture, Cent. — A1357

Design: Louis and Auguste Lumiere, camera.

1995, June 21
2540 A1357 2.14r multicolored 4.75 4.75

New Currency, The Real, 1st Anniv. — A1358   Volleyball, Cent. — A1359

1995, July 1   Litho.   Perf. 12x11½
2541 A1358 12c multicolored   .30   .30

1995, July 8
2542 A1359 15c multicolored   .35   .35

Dinosaurs — A1360

1995, July 23   Perf. 11½x12
2543 A1360 15c Angaturama limai   .35   .35
2544 A1360 1.50r Titanosaurus   3.25 3.25

Traffic Safety Program — A1361

Designs: 12c, Test dummy without seat belt hitting windshield. 71c, Auto hitting alcoholic beverage glass.

1995, July 25
2545 A1361 12c multicolored   .30   .30
2546 A1361 71c multicolored   1.65 1.65

Souvenir Sheet

Roberto Burle Marx, Botanist — A1362

Designs: a, 15c, Calathea burle-marxii. b, 15c, Vellozia burle-marxii. c, 1.50r, Heliconia aemygdiana. Illustration reduced.

1995, Aug. 4   Litho.   Perf. 12x11½
2547 A1362 Sheet of 3, #a.-c. 4.50 4.50
      Singapore '95.

BRAZIL

Parachute Infantry Brigade, 50th Anniv. — A1363

1995, Aug. 23
2548 A1363 15c multicolored .35 .35

Paulista Museum, Cent. — A1364

1995, Sept. 5 *Perf. 11½*
2549 A1364 15c multicolored .35 .35

Lighthouses A1365

1995, Sept. 28
2550 A1365 15c Olinda .35 .35
2551 A1365 15c Sao Joao .35 .35
2552 A1365 15c Santo Antonio da Barra .35 .35
 Nos. 2550-2552 (3) 1.05 1.05

Wilhelm Röntgen (1845-1923), Discovery of the X-Ray, Cent. — A1366

1995, Sept. 30
2553 A1366 84c multicolored 2.00 2.00

Lubrapex '95, 15th Brazilian-Portuguese Philatelic Exhibition — A1367

Wildlife scene along Tiete River: 15c, #2556a, Bird, otter with fish. 84c, #2556b, Birds, river boat.

1995, Sept. 30 *Perf. 12x11½*
2554 A1367 15c multicolored .35 .35
2555 A1367 84c multicolored 2.00 2.00
 Souvenir Sheet
2556 A1367 1.50r Sheet of 2, #a.-b. 6.50 6.50
 No. 2556 is a continuous design.

Flamengo Regatta Soccer Club A1368

1995, Oct. 6 *Perf. 11x11½*
2557 A1368 15c multicolored .35 .35

America Issue A1369

Outdoor scenes: 15c, Trees, mushrooms, alligator, lake. 84c, Black-neck swans on lake, false swans in air.

1995, Oct. 12 *Litho. Perf. 11½x12*
2558 A1369 15c multicolored .35 .35
2559 A1369 84c multicolored 2.00 2.00
 a. Pair, #2558-2559 2.35 2.25

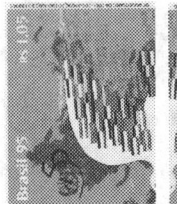

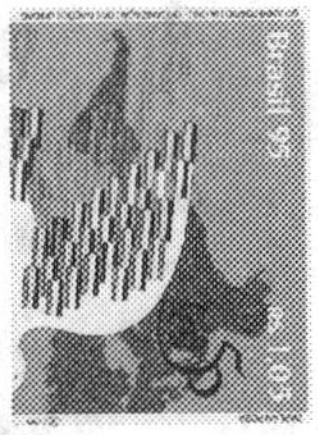

UN, 50th Anniv.
A1370   A1371

1995, Oct. 24 *Perf. 12x11½*
2560 A1370 1.05r multicolored 2.25 2.25
2561 A1371 1.05r multicolored 2.25 2.25
 a. Pair, No. 2560-2561 4.50 4.50

Writers — A1372

Designs: No. 2562, Eca de Queiroz (1845-90), village. No. 2563, Rubem Braga (1913-90), beach, Rio de Janeiro. 23c, Carlos Drummond de Andrade (1902-87), letters.

1995, Oct. 27 *Perf. 12x11*
2562 A1372 15c multicolored .35 .35
2563 A1372 15c multicolored .35 .35
2564 A1372 23c multicolored .50 .50
 Nos. 2562-2564 (3) 1.20 1.20

Souvenir Sheet

Death of Zumbi Dos Palmares, Slave Resistance Leader, 300th Anniv. — A1373

Illustration reduced.

1995, Nov. 20 *Perf. 12x11½*
2565 A1373 1.05r multicolored 2.25 2.25

2nd World Short Course Swimming Championships — A1374

Four swimmers performing different strokes: a, Freestyle. b, Backstroke. c, Butterfly. d, Breaststroke.

1995, Nov. 30 *Perf. 11½x12*
2566 A1374 23c Block of 4, #a.-d. 2.00 2.00

Christmas A1375

Designs: a, 23c, Cherub looking right, stars. b, 15c, Cherub looking left, stars.

1995, Dec. 1 *Perf. 11½*
2567 A1375 Pair, #a.-b.+2 labels .85 .85

Botafogo Soccer and Regatta Club A1376

1995, Dec. 8 *Perf. 11x11½*
2568 A1376 15c multicolored .35 .35

Diário de Pernambuco Newspaper, 170th Anniv. — A1377

1995, Dec. 14 *Litho. Perf. 12x11½*
2569 A1377 23c multicolored .50 .50

Souvenir Sheet

Amazon Theatre, Cent. — A1378

Illustration reduced.

1996, Feb. 27
2570 A1378 1.23r multicolored 2.50 2.50

Francisco Prestes Maia, Politician, Birth Cent. A1379

1996, Mar. 19 *Perf. 11½x12*
2571 A1379 18c multicolored .40 .40

Irineu Bornhausen, Governor of Santa Catarina, Birth Cent. — A1380

1996, Mar. 25 *Perf. 11x11½*
2572 A1380 27c multicolored .55 .55

Paintings — A1381

Designs: No. 2573, Boat with Little Flags and Birds, by Alfredo Volpi. No. 2574, Ouro Preto Landscape, by Alberto da Veiga Guignard.

1996, Apr. 15 *Perf. 12x11½*
2573 A1381 15c multicolored .30 .30
2574 A1381 15c multicolored .30 .30

UNICEF, 50th Anniv. A1382

1996, Apr. 16 *Perf. 11½*
2575 A1382 23c multicolored .50 .50

Portuguese Discovery of Brazil, 500th Anniv. (in 2000) — A1383

1996, Apr. 22 *Perf. 12x11½*
2576 A1383 1.05r multicolored 2.10 2.10
 See No. 2626.

Israel Pinheiro da Silva, Politician, Business Entrepeneur, Birth Cent. A1384

1996, Apr. 23 *Perf. 11½x12*
2577 A1384 18c multicolored .40 .40

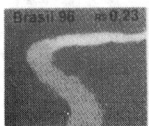

Tourism — A1385

#2578, Amazon River. #2579, Swampland area. #2580, Sail boat, northeastern states. #2581, Sugarloaf, Guanabara Bay. #2582, Iguacu Falls.

1996, Apr. 24 *Die Cut*
 Self-Adhesive
2578 A1385 23c multicolored .50 .50
2579 A1385 23c multicolored .50 .50
2580 A1385 23c multicolored .50 .50
2581 A1385 23c multicolored .50 .50
2582 A1385 23c multicolored .50 .50
 a. Strip of 5, #2578-2582 2.50

Hummingbirds A1386

Espamer '96: 15c, Topaza pella. 1.05r, Stephanoxis lalandi. 1.15r, Eupetomena macroura.

BRAZIL

1996, May 4 Litho. Perf. 11½
2583 A1386 15c multicolored .35 .35
2584 A1386 1.05r multicolored 2.40 2.40
2585 A1386 1.15r multicolored 2.60 2.60
Nos. 2583-2585 (3) 5.35 5.35

1996 Summer Olympic Games, Atlanta — A1387

1996, May 21
2586 A1387 18c Marathon .40 .40
2587 A1387 23c Gymnastics .50 .50
2588 A1387 1.05r Swimming 2.40 2.40
2589 A1387 1.05r Beach volleyball 2.40 2.40
Nos. 2586-2589 (4) 5.70 5.70

Souvenir Sheet

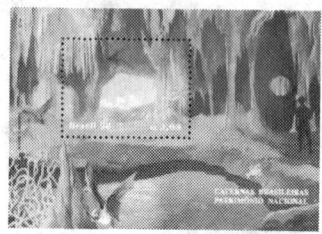

Brazilian Caverns — A1388

Illustration reduced.

1996, June 5 Perf. 11½x12
2590 A1388 2.68r multicolored 6.25 6.25

Americas Telecom '96 — A1389

1996, June 10 Perf. 11½
2591 A1389 1.05r multicolored 2.40 2.40

Souvenir Sheet

World Day to Fight Desertification — A1390

Illustration reduced.

1996, June 17 Perf. 12x11½
2592 A1390 1.23r multicolored 2.80 2.80

Fight Against Drug Abuse — A1391

1996, June 26 Perf. 11½x12
2593 A1391 27c multicolored .65 .65

Year of Education — A1392

1996, July 10 Perf. 12x11½
2594 A1392 23c multicolored .55 .55

Princess Isabel, 150th Birth Anniv. — A1393

1996, July 29 Perf. 11½x12
2595 A1393 18c multicolored .40 .40

Carlos Gomes (1836-96), Composer — A1394

1996, Sept. 16 Perf. 11½
2596 A1394 50c multicolored 1.25 1.25

15th World Orchid Conference — A1395

#2597, Promenaea stapelioides. #2598, Cattleya eldorado. #2599, Cattleya loddigesii.

1996, Sept. 17
2597 A1395 15c multicolored .35 .35
2598 A1395 15c multicolored .35 .35
2599 A1395 15c multicolored .35 .35
Nos. 2597-2599 (3) 1.05 1.05

Apparition of Virgin Mary at La Salette, 150th Anniv. — A1396

1996, Sept. 19
2600 A1396 1r multicolored 2.30 2.30

Souvenir Sheet

Popular Legends — A1397

Designs: a, 23c, "Cuca" walking from house. b, 1.05r, "Boitatá," snake of life. c, 1.15r, "Caipora," defender of ecology.

1996, Sept. 28 Perf. 11x10½
2601 A1397 Sheet of 3, #a.-c. 5.60 5.60
BRAPEX '96.

23rd Sao Paulo Intl. Biennial Exhibition — A1398

Designs: a, Marilyn Monroe by Andy Warhol, vert. b, The Scream, by Edvard Munch, vert. c, Abstract, by Louise Bourgeois, vert. d, Woman Drawing, by Pablo Picasso.

1996, Oct. 5 Perf. 12x11½
2602 A1398 55c Block of 4, #a.-d. 5.00 5.00

Traditional Costumes — A1400

America issue: 50c, Man dressed as cowboy. 1r, Woman dressed in baiana clothes.

1996, Oct. 12 Litho. Perf. 11½
2604 A1400 50c multicolored 1.15 1.15
2605 A1400 1r multicolored 2.30 2.30

Christmas — A1401

José Carlos (1884-1950), Carcicaturist — A1402

1996, Nov. 4 Litho. Perf. 12x11½
2606 A1401 1st multicolored .60 .60
No. 2606 was valued at 23c on day of issue.

1996, Nov. 22
2607 A1402 1st multicolored .60 .60
No. 2607 was valued at 23c on day of issue.

Tourism — A1403

#2608, Ipiranga Monument, Sao Paulo. #2607, Hercílio Luz Bridge, Florianópolis. #2608, Natl. Congress Building, Brasília. #2609, Pelourinho, Salvador. #2610, Ver-o-Peso Market, Belém.

Serpentine Die Cut
1996, Dec. 9 Photo.
Self-Adhesive
2608 A1403 1st multicolored .75 .75
2609 A1403 1st multicolored .75 .75
2610 A1403 1st multicolored .75 .75
2611 A1403 1st multicolored .75 .75
2612 A1403 1st multicolored .75 .75
  a. Strip of 5, #2608-2612 3.75

Nos. 2608-2612 are inscribed "1o PORTE NACIONAL," and were valued 23c on day of issue. Selvage surrounding each stamp in #2612a is rouletted.

Rio de Janeiro, Candidate for 2004 Summer Olympic Games — A1404

1997, Jan. 17 Litho. Perf. 11½
2613 A1404 1st multicolored 2.20 2.20
No. 2613 is inscribed "1o PORTE INTERNACIONAL" and was valued at 1.05r on day of issue.

The Postman — A1405

1997, Jan. 25
2614 A1405 1st multicolored .85 .85
America issue. No. 2614 is inscribed "1o PORTE NACIONAL" and was valued at 23c on day of issue.

Antonio de Castro Alves (1847-71), Poet — A1406

1997, Mar. 14
2615 A1406 15c multicolored .35 .35

Marquis of Tamandaré, Naval Officer, Death Cent. — A1407

1997, Mar. 19 Perf. 11x11½
2616 A1407 23c multicolored .50 .50

Stamp Design Contest Winner — A1408

1997, Mar. 20 Perf. 11½x12
2617 A1408 15c "Joy Joy" .35 .35

World Day of Water — A1409

1997, Mar. 22 Perf. 12x11½
2618 A1409 1.05r multicolored 2.10 2.10

Brazilian Airplanes — A1410

BRAZIL

Designs: No. 2619, EMB-145. No. 2620, AMX. No. 2621, EMB-312 H Super Tucano. No. 2622, EMB-120 Brasilia. No. 2623, EMB-312 Tucano.

1997, Mar. 27   Litho.   *Die Cut*
Self-Adhesive

2619	A1410	15c multicolored	.25	.25
2620	A1410	15c multicolored	.25	.25
2621	A1410	15c multicolored	.25	.25
2622	A1410	15c multicolored	.25	.25
2623	A1410	15c multicolored	.25	.25
a.		Strip of 5, #2619-2623	1.25	

Campaign Against AIDS — A1411

1997, Apr. 7   Litho.   *Perf. 12x11½*
2624   A1411   23c multicolored   .50   .50

Souvenir Sheet

Indian Culture — A1412
Weapons of the Xingu Indians.
Illustration reduced.

1997, Apr. 16   *Perf. 11x11½*
2625   A1412   1.15r multicolored   2.30   2.30

Portuguese Discovery of Brazil, 500th Anniv. Type of 1996

1997, Apr. 22   *Perf. 12x11½*
2626   A1383   1.05r like #2576   2.10   2.20

No. 2576 has green background and blue in lower right corner. No. 2626 has those colors reversed and is inscribed "BRASIL 97" at top.

Pixinguinha (1897-1973), Composer, Musician — A1413

1997, Apr. 23
2627   A1413   15c multicolored   .35   .35

Souvenir Sheet

Brazilian Claim to Trindade Island, Cent. — A1414

Illustration reduced.

1997, May 7   *Perf. 11½x11*
2628   A1414   1.23r multicolored   2.50   2.50

Human Rights — A1415

1997, May 13   *Perf. 12x11½*
2629   A1415   18c multicolored   .45   .45

Souvenir Sheet

Brazilian Antarctic Program — A1416

1997, May 13
2630   A1416   2.68r multicolored   5.50   5.50

Fruits and Nuts — A1417

1997-98   Litho.   *Serpentine Die Cut*
Self-Adhesive

2631	A1417	1c Oranges	.15	.15
2632	A1417	2c Bananas	.15	.15
2633	A1417	5c Papayas	.15	.15
2634	A1417	10c Pineapple, vert.	.20	.20
2635	A1417	20c Cashews, vert.	.40	.40
2636	A1417	20c Sugar apple, vert.	.40	.40
2636A	A1417	22c Grapes	.40	.40
2636B	A1417	(22c) Watermelon	.45	.45
2636C	A1417	51c Coconuts, vert.	1.00	1.00
2636D	A1417	80c Apples	1.40	1.40
2636E	A1417	82c Lemons, vert.	1.60	1.60
2636F	A1417	1r Strawberries, vert.	2.00	2.00
		Nos. 2631-2636F (10)	6.50	6.50

Issued: #2636B, 5/28/97; #2631, 6/97; #2632, 2634, 2635, 7/97; #2633, 8/97; #2636F, 8/3/97; #2636A, 10/3/97; #2636, 2636C-2636E, 1/15/98.

No. 2636B is inscribed "1o PORTE NATIONAL" and was valued at 22c on day of issue.

This is an expanding set. Numbers may change.

Amazon Flora and Fauna — A1419

Designs: No. 2637, Swietenia macrophylla. No. 2638, Arapaima gigas.

1997, June 5   Litho.   *Perf. 11½x12*
2637   A1418   27c multicolored   .55   .55
2638   A1419   27c multicolored   .55   .55

Fr. José de Anchieta (1534-97), Missionary in Brazil — A1420

Design: No. 2640, Fr. António Vieira (1608-97), missionary in Brazil, diplomat.

1997, June 9   *Perf. 12*
2639   A1420   1.05r multicolored   2.10   2.10
2640   A1420   1.05r multicolored   2.10   2.10

See Portugal Nos. 2168-2169.

Tourism A1421

Designs: No. 2641, Parnaíba River Delta. No. 2642, Lençóis Maranhenses Park.

1997, June 20   *Perf. 11½x12*
2641   A1421   1st multicolored   2.10   2.10
2642   A1421   1st multicolored   2.10   2.10

Nos. 2641-2642 are inscribed "1o PORTE INTERNACIONAL TAXE PERCUE" and were each valued at on day of issue.

Brazilian Academy of Literature, Cent. A1422

1997, July 20
2643   A1422   22c multicolored   .50   .50

Emiliano de Cavalcanti (1897-1976), Painter A1423

1997, Sept. 16   Litho.   *Perf. 11½*
2644   A1423   31c multicolored   .65   .65

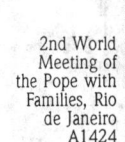

2nd World Meeting of the Pope with Families, Rio de Janeiro A1424

1997, Sept. 22   *Perf. 11½x12*
2645   A1424   1.20r multicolored   2.50   2.50

A1425   A1426

1997, Sept. 26   *Perf. 12x11½*
2646   A1425   80c multicolored   1.60   1.60

MERCOSUR (Common Market of Latin America). See Argentina #1975, Bolivia #1019, Paraguay #2565, Uruguay #1681.

1997, Sept. 27
2647   A1426   22c multicolored   .45   .45

End of Canudos War, cent.

Integration of MERCOSUR Communications by Telebras, 25th Anniv. — A1427

1997, Oct. 6   *Perf. 11½*
2648   A1427   80c multicolored   1.60   1.60

Composers — A1428

#2649, Oscar Lorenzo Fernandez (1897-1948). #2650, Francisco Mignone (1897-1986).

1997, Oct. 7   *Perf. 11x11½*
2649   A1428   22c multicolored   .45   .45
2650   A1428   22c multicolored   .45   .45

Marist Brothers Presence in Brazil, Cent. A1429

1997, Oct. 22
2651   A1429   22c multicolored   .45   .45

Christmas — A1430

1997, Nov. 5   *Perf. 12x11½*
2652   A1430   22c multicolored   .45   .45

BRAZIL

Education
and
Citizenship
A1431

1997, Dec. 10   *Perf. 11x11½*
2653 A1431 31c blue & yellow   .65 .65

City of Belo
Horizonte,
Cent.
A1432

1997, Dec. 12   *Perf. 11½x12*
2654 A1432 31c multicolored   .65 .65

Citzenship — A1433

Map of Brazil and: No. 2655, Education, stack of books. No. 2656, Employment, worker's papers. No. 2657, Agriculture, oranges. No. 2658, Health, stethoscope, vert. No. 2659, Culture, clapboard with musical notes, artist's paint brush, vert.

1997, Dec. 20   *Die Cut*
Self-Adhesive
Booklet Stamps
2655 A1433 22c multicolored   .45 .45
2656 A1433 22c multicolored   .45 .45
2657 A1433 22c multicolored   .45 .45
2658 A1433 22c multicolored   .45 .45
2659 A1433 22c multicolored   .45 .45
   a. Booklet pane, 2 each #2655-2659   4.50

The peelable paper backing of No. 2659a serves as a booklet cover.

Gems — A1434

1998, Jan. 22   *Perf. 12x11½*
2660 A1434 22c Alexandrite   .45 .45
2661 A1434 22c Cat's eye chrysoberyl   .45 .45
2662 A1434 22c Indicolite   .45 .45
   a. Strip of 3, #2660-2662   1.40 1.40

Famous
Brazilian
Women
A1435

America Issue: No. 2663, Elis Regina, singer. No. 2664, Clementia de Jesus, singer. No. 2665, Dulcina de Moraes, actress. No. 2666, Clarice Lispector, writer.

1998, Mar. 11   *Perf. 11½*
2663 A1435 22c multicolored   .45 .45
2664 A1435 22c multicolored   .45 .45
2665 A1435 22c multicolored   .45 .45
2666 A1435 22c multicolored   .45 .45
   a. Block of 4, #2663-2666   1.80 1.80

Education
A1436

1998, Mar. 19   *Perf. 12x11½*
2667 A1436 31c Children at desks   .65 .65
2668 A1436 31c Teacher at blackboard   .65 .65
   a. Pair, #2667-2668   1.30 1.30

Cruz e Sousa
(1861-98),
Poet
A1437

1998, Mar. 19   *Litho.*   *Perf. 11½x12*
2669 A1437 36c multicolored   .65 .65

Discovery of Brazil,
500th
Anniv. — A1438

#2670, 1519 map showing natives, vegetation, fauna. #2671, Caravel from Cabral's fleet.

1998, Apr. 22   *Perf. 12x11½*
2670 A1438 1.05r multicolored   1.75 1.75
2671 A1438 1.05r multicolored   1.75 1.75
   a. Pair, #2670-2671   3.50 3.50

Volunteer
Work
A1439

Designs: a, Caring for sick man. b, Caring for sick child. c, Fighting forest fire. c, Child's hand holding adult's finger.

1998, May 5   *Perf. 11½x12*
2672 A1439 31c Block of 4, #a.-d.   2.25 2.25

Brazilian
Circus — A1440

Piolin the clown: a, Looking through circle. b, Standing in ring. c, With outside of tent to the left. d, With inside of tent to the right.

1998, May 18   *Perf. 12x11½*
2673 A1440 31c Block of 4, #a.-d.   2.25 2.25

Intl. Year of
the Ocean
A1441

Pictures, drawings of marine life: a, Turtle. b, Tail fin of whale. c, Barracuda. d, Jellyfish, school of fish. e, School of fish, diver. f, Dolphins. g, Yellow round fish. h, Two whales. i, Two black-striped butterfly fish. j, Orange & yellow fish. k, Manatee. l, Yellow-striped fish. m, Blue & yellow fish. n, Several striped fish. o, Fish with wing-like fins. p, Manta ray. q, Two fish swimming in opposite directions. r, Long, thin fish, coral. s, Moray eel. t, Yellow & black butterfly fish, coral. u, Starfish, fish. v, Crab, coral. w, Black & orange fish, coral. x, Sea horse, coral.

1998, May 22   *Perf. 11½x12*
2674 A1441 31c #a.-x.   12.50 12.50
   Sheet of 24

Expo '98.

1998 World Cup Soccer Championships,
France — A1442

Stylized paintings, by: a, Gregorio Gruber. b, Mario Gruber. c, Maciej Babinski. d, Cildo Meireles, vert. e, Claudio Tozzi, vert. f, Antonio Henrique Amaral, vert. g, Jose Roberto Aguilar. h, Nelson Leirner. i, Wesley Duke Lee. j, Mauricio Nogueira Lima. k, Zelio Alves Pinto, vert. l, Aldemir Martins, vert. m, Ivald Granato. n, Carlos Vergara. o, Joao Camara, vert. p, Roberto Magalhaes, vert. q, Guto Lacaz, vert. r, Glauco Rodrigues, vert. s, Leda Catunda. t, Tomoshige Kusuno. u, Jose Zaragoza. v, Luiz Zerbine, vert. w, Antonio Peticov, vert. x, Marcia Grostein, vert.

Perf. 11½x12, 12x11½
1998, May 28
2675 A1442 22c Sheet of 24, #a.-x.   9.00 9.00

Feijoada,
Traditional
Cuisine
A1443

1998, June 1   *Perf. 11½*
2676 A1443 31c multicolored   .55 .55

Preservation
of Flora and
Fauna
A1444

Designs: No. 2677, Araucaria angustifolia. No. 2678, Cyanocorax caeruleus.

1998, June 5   *Perf. 11½x12*
2677 A1444 22c multicolored   .40 .40
2678 A1444 22c multicolored   .40 .40
   a. Pair, #2677-2678   .80 .80

Launching of
Submarine
Tapajó
A1445

1998, June 5
2679 A1445 51c multicolored   .90 .90

Luiz de Queiroz
(1849-98),
Founder of
Agricultural
School
A1446

1998, June 6   *Perf. 11½*
2680 A1446 36c multicolored   .65 .65

SEMI-POSTAL STAMPS

In 1980 three stamps that were intended to be semi-postals were issued as postage stamps at the total combined face value. See Nos. 1681-1683.

National Philatelic Exhibition Issue

SP1

Wmk. Coat of Arms in Sheet (236)
1934, Sept. 16   *Engr.*   *Imperf.*
   Thick Paper
B1 SP1 200r + 100r dp claret   1.00 2.00
B2 SP1 300r + 100r ver   1.00 2.00
B3 SP1 700r + 100r brt bl   6.00 17.50
B4 SP1 1000r + 100r blk   6.00 17.50
   Nos. B1-B4 (4)   14.00 39.00

The surtax was to help defray the expenses of the exhibition. Issued in sheets of 60, inscribed "EXPOSICAO FILATELICA NACIONAL."

Red Cross
Nurse and
Soldier
SP2

Wmk. 222
1935, Sept. 19   *Typo.*   *Perf. 11*
B5 SP2 200r + 100r pur & red   1.25 1.25
B6 SP2 300r + 100r ol brn & red   1.25 .90
B7 SP2 700r + 100r turq bl & red   8.00 7.00
   Nos. B5-B7 (3)   10.50 9.15

3rd Pan-American Red Cross Conf. Exist imperf.

Three Wise Men
and Star of
Bethlehem — SP3

Angel and
Child — SP4

Southern Cross
and Child — SP5

Mother and
Child — SP6

Perf. 10½
1939, Dec. 20   *Litho.*   *Wmk. 249*
B8 SP3 100r + 100r chlky bl & bl blk   .75 .75
   a. Horiz. or vert. pair, imperf. between   35.00
B9 SP4 200r + 100r brt grnsh bl   1.00 1.00
   a. Horizontal pair, imperf. between   35.00
B10 SP5 400r + 200r ol grn & ol   .80 .50
B11 SP6 1200r + 400r crim & brn red   3.25 1.50
   a. Vertical pair, imperf. between   35.00
   Nos. B8-B11 (4)   5.80 3.75

Surtax for charitable institutions.
For surcharges see Nos. C55-C59.

Catalogue values for unused stamps in this section, from this point to the end of the section, are for Never Hinged items.

BRAZIL

Children and Citzenship — SP7

Designs: a, Cutouts of children forming pyramid. b, Man and woman's hands holding onto girl. c, Children going into school. d, Pregnant woman in front of house. e, Children flying paper doves. f, Parent working in garden, child writing letters, g, Breastfeeding. h, Father holding birth certificate, mother holding infant. i, Disabled child on wheelchair ramp. j, Mother, father with sick child. k, Stylized child, pencil, letters. l, Hands above and below pregnant woman. m, Two families of different races. n, Small child playing large guitar. o, People looking to baby on pedestal. p, Children, book, "Statute of Children and Adolescent."

1997, Nov. 20   Litho.   Perf. 12x11½
B12   Sheet of 16   9.60 9.60
a.-p.   SP7 22c +8c any single   .60   .60

Surcharge for Natl. Fund for Children and Adolescents.

AIR POST STAMPS

Nos. O14-O29 Surcharged   **SERVIÇO AEREO 200 Rs.**

1927, Dec. 28   Unwmk.   Perf. 12
C1	O2	50r on 10r	.35	.35
a.		Inverted surcharge	325.00	
b.		Top ornaments missing	75.00	
C2	O2	200r on 1000r	2.25	2.75
a.		Double surcharge	325.00	
C3	O2	200r on 2000r	1.40	4.75
a.		Double surcharge	750.00	
b.		Double surcharge, one inverted	750.00	
C4	O2	200r on 5000r	1.50	1.00
a.		Double surcharge	325.00	
b.		Double surcharge, one inverted	350.00	
c.		Triple surcharge	450.00	
C5	O2	300r on 500r	1.50	2.00
C6	O2	300r on 600r	.75	.90
b.		Pair, one without surch.		
C6A	O2	500r on 10r	325.00	375.00
C7	O2	500r on 50r	1.50	.65
a.		Double surcharge	300.00	
C8	O2	1000r on 20r	1.00	.35
a.		Double surcharge	300.00	
C9	O2	2000r on 100r	2.25	1.40
a.		Pair, one without surcharge		
b.		Double surcharge	300.00	
C10	O2	2000r on 200r	2.75	1.40
C11	O2	2000r on 10,000r	2.25	.50
C12	O2	5000r on 20,000r	7.50	3.00
C13	O2	5000r on 50,000r	7.50	3.00
C14	O2	5000r on 100,000r	25.00	30.00
C15	O2	10,000r on 500,000r	27.50	22.50
C16	O2	10,000r on 1,000,000r	25.00	25.00
	Nos. C1-C6,C7-C16 (16)	110.00	99.55	

Nos. C1, C1b; C7, C8 and C9 have small diamonds printed over the numerals in the upper corners.

Monument to de Gusmao — AP1

Santos-Dumont's Airship — AP2

Augusto Severo's Airship "Pax" — AP3

Santos-Dumont's Biplane "14 Bis" — AP4

Ribeiro de Barros's Seaplane "Jahu" — AP5

Perf. 11, 12½x13, 13x13½
1929   Typo.   Wmk. 206
C17	AP1	50r blue grn	.35	.20
C18	AP2	200r red	1.40	.20
C19	AP3	300r brt blue	1.75	.20
C20	AP4	500r red violet	2.50	.20
C21	AP5	1000r orange brn	9.00	.40
	Nos. C17-C21 (5)	15.00	1.20	

See #C32-C36. For surcharges see #C26-C27.

Bartholomeu de Gusmao AP6

Augusto Severo AP7

Alberto Santos-Dumont — AP8

Perf. 9, 11 and Compound
1929-30   Engr.   Wmk. 101
C22	AP6	2000r lt green ('30)	7.50	.35
C23	AP7	5000r carmine	7.50	1.25
C24	AP8	10,000r olive grn	7.50	1.40
	Nos. C22-C24 (3)	22.50	3.00	

Nos. C23-C24 exist imperf. See Nos. C37, C40.

Allegory: Airmail Service between Brazil and the US — AP9

1929   Typo.   Wmk. 206
C25 AP9 3000r violet   10.00 1.75

Exists imperf. See Nos. C38, C41. For surcharge see No. C28.

Nos. C18-C19 Surcharged in Blue or Red   **2$500**

1931, Aug. 16   Perf. 12½x13½
C26 AP2 2500r on 200r (Bl)   25.00 25.00
C27 AP3 5000r on 300r (R)   30.00 30.00

No. C25 Surcharged   **2.500 REIS**

1931, Sept. 2   Perf. 11
C28 AP9 2500r on 3000r vio   27.50 27.50
a.   Inverted surcharge   160.00
b.   Surch. on front and back   160.00

Regular Issues of 1928-29 **ZEPPELIN** Surcharged   **3$500**

1932, May   Wmk. 101   Perf. 11, 11½
C29 A89 3500r on 5000r gray lil   20.00 20.00
C30 A72 7000r on 10,000r rose   20.00 20.00
b.   Horiz. pair, imperf. between   750.00

Imperforates
Since 1933, imperforate or partly perforated sheets of nearly all of the airmail issues have become available.

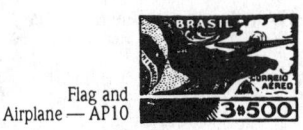

Flag and Airplane — AP10

1933, June 7   Typo.   Perf. 11
C31 AP10 3500r grn, yel & dk bl   5.00 2.00

See Nos. C39, C42.

1934   Wmk. 222
C32	AP1	50r blue grn	1.75	1.75
C33	AP2	200r red	2.25	.65
C34	AP3	300r brt blue	5.50	1.90
C35	AP4	500r red violet	2.25	.65
C36	AP5	1000r orange brn	7.50	.65
	Nos. C32-C36 (5)	19.25	5.60	

1934   Wmk. 236   Engr.   Perf. 12x11 Thick Laid Paper
C37 AP6 2000r lt green   4.50 1.50

Types of 1929, 1933
Perf. 11, 11½, 12
1937-40   Typo.   Wmk. 249
C38 AP9 3000r violet   17.50 1.75
C39 AP10 3500r grn, yel & dk bl   3.00 1.50
Engr.
C40 AP7 5000r ver ('40)   4.00 .75
Nos. C38-C40 (3)   24.50 4.00

Watermark note after #501 also applies to #C40.

Types of 1929-33
Perf. 11, 11½x12
1939-40   Typo.   Wmk. 256
C41 AP9 3000r violet   1.25 .60
C42 AP10 3500r bl, dl grn & yel ('40)   .90 .50

Map of the Western Hemisphere Showing Brazil AP11

1941, Jan. 14   Engr.   Perf. 11
C43 AP11 1200r dark brown   2.50 .65

5th general census of Brazil.

No. 506A Overprinted in Carmine   **AÉREO "10 Nov." 937-941**

1941, Nov. 10   Wmk. 264   Rouletted
C45 A180 5400r slate grn   2.50 1.25
a.   Overprint inverted   140.00

President Varges' new constitution, 4th anniv.

Nos. 506A and 508 Surcharged in Black   **AÉREO "10 Nov." 937-942 Cr.$ 5,40**

1942, Nov. 10   Wmk. 264
C47 A180 5.40cr on 5400r sl grn   2.50 1.90
a.   Wmk. 249   80.00 80.00
b.   Surcharge inverted   60.00 75.00

President Vargas' new constitution, 5th anniv. The status of No. C47a is questioned.

Southern Cross and Arms of Paraguay AP12

Perf. 12½
1943, May 11   Engr.   Wmk. 270
C48 AP12 1.20cr lt gray blue   1.75 1.00

Issued in commemoration of the visit of President Higinio Morinigo of Paraguay.

Map of South America — AP13

1943, June 30   Wmk. 271   Perf. 12½
C49 AP13 1.20cr multi   1.75 .75

Visit of President Penaranda of Bolivia.

Numeral of Value — AP14

1943, Aug. 7
C50 AP14 1cr blk & dull yel   2.00 1.50
a.   Double impression   30.00
C51 AP14 2cr blk & pale grn   2.75 1.50
a.   Double impression   40.00
C52 AP14 5cr blk & pink   3.25 2.00
Nos. C50-C52 (3)   8.00 5.00

Centenary of Brazil's first postage stamps.

Souvenir Sheet   AP15

Without Gum   Imperf.
C53 AP15 Sheet of 3   35.00 35.00
a.   1cr black & dull yellow   10.00 10.00
b.   2cr black & pale green   10.00 10.00
c.   5cr black & pink   10.00 10.00

100th anniv. of the 1st postage stamps of Brazil and the 2nd Phil. Exposition (Brapex). Printed in panes of 6 sheets, perforated 12½ between. Each sheet is perforated on two or three sides. Size approximately 155x155mm.

Law Book — AP16

1943, Aug. 13   Perf. 12½
C54 AP16 1.20cr rose & lil rose   .50 .30

2nd Inter-American Conf. of Lawyers.

No. B10 Surcharged in Red, Carmine or Black   **AÉREO 20 Cts.**

1944, Jan. 3   Wmk. 249   Perf. 10½
C55 SP5 20c on 400r+200r (R)   .85 .65
C56 SP5 40c on 400r+200r (Bk)   1.25 .65
C57 SP5 60c on 400r+200r (C)   1.25 .45
C58 SP5 1cr on 400r+200r (Bk)   1.75 .65
C59 SP5 1.20cr on 400r+200r (C)   2.25 .45
Nos. C55-C59 (5)   7.35 2.85

No. C59 is known with surcharge in black but its status is questioned.

BRAZIL

Bartholomeu de Gusmao and the "Aerostat" — AP17

Wmk. 268
1944, Oct. 23   Engr.   Perf. 12
C60 AP17 1.20cr rose carmine   .35 .15
Week of the Wing.

L. L. Zamenhof AP18

1945, Apr. 16   Litho.   Perf. 11
C61 AP18 1.20cr dull brown   .35 .25
Esperanto Congress held in Rio, Apr. 14-22.

Map of South America — AP19
Baron of Rio Branco — AP20 

1945, Apr. 20
C62 AP19 1.20cr gray brown   .35 .25
C63 AP20 5cr rose lilac   .95 .40
Centenary of the birth of José Maria de Silva Paranhos, Baron of Rio Branco.

Dove and Flags of American Republics AP21

Perf. 12x11
1947, Aug. 15   Engr.   Unwmk.
C64 AP21 2.20cr dk blue green   .30 .25
Inter-American Defense Conference at Rio de Janeiro August-September, 1947.

Santos-Dumont Monument, St. Cloud, France — AP22
Bay of Rio de Janeiro and Rotary Emblem — AP23 

1947, Nov. 15   Typo.   Perf. 11x12
C65 AP22 1.20cr org brn & ol   .30 .25
Issued to commemorate the Week of the Wing and to honor the Santos-Dumont monument which was destroyed in World War II.

Catalogue values for unused stamps in this section, from this point to the end of the section, are for Never Hinged items.

1948, May 16   Engr.   Perf. 11
C66 AP23 1.20cr deep claret   .50 .40
C67 AP23 3.80cr dull violet   1.00 .40
39th convention of Rotary Intl., Rio.

Hotel Quitandinha, Petropolis AP24

1948, July 10   Litho.   Wmk. 267
C68 AP24 1.20cr org brn   .25 .25
C69 AP24 3.80cr violet   .50 .30
International Exposition of Industry and Commerce, Petropolis, 1948.

Musician and Singers AP25

1948, Aug. 13   Engr.   Unwmk.
C70 AP25 1.20cr blue   .30 .20
National School of Music, cent.

Luis Batlle Berres AP26

1948, Sept. 2   Typo.
C71 AP26 1.70cr blue   .20 .20
Visit of President Luis Batlle Berres of Uruguay, September, 1948.

Merino Ram — AP27

1948, Oct. 10 Wmk. 267 Perf. 12x11
C72 AP27 1.20cr dp orange   .50 .30
Intl. Livestock Exposition at Bagé.

Eucharistic Congress Seal — AP28

Unwmk.
1948, Oct. 23   Engr.   Perf. 11
C73 AP28 1.20cr dk car rose   .30 .30
5th Natl. Eucharistic Cong., Porto Alegre, Oct. 24-31.

Souvenir Sheet

AP28a

1948, Dec. 14   Engr.   Imperf.
Without Gum
C73A AP28a Sheet of 3   50.00 65.00
No. C73A contains one each of Nos. 674-676. Issued in honor of President Eurico Gasper Dutra and the armed forces. Exists both with and without number on back. Measures 130x75mm.

Church of Prazeres, Guararapes — AP29

Perf. 11½x12
1949, Feb. 15   Litho.   Wmk. 267
C74 AP29 1.20cr pink   1.50 .75
Second Battle of Guararapes, 300th anniv.

Thomé de Souza Meeting Indians — AP30

Perf. 11x12
1949, Mar. 29   Engr.   Unwmk.
C75 AP30 1.20cr blue   .20 .20
Founding of the City of Salvador, 400th anniv.
A souvenir folder, issued with No. C75, has an engraved 20cr red brown postage stamp portraying John III printed on it, and a copy of No. C75 affixed to it and postmarked. Paper is laid, and size of folder front is 100x150mm. Value, $5.

Franklin D. Roosevelt AP31

1949, May 20   Unwmk.   Imperf.
C76 AP31 3.80cr deep blue   .60 .60
a. Souvenir sheet   12.00 15.00
No. C76a measures 85x110mm, with deep blue inscriptions in upper and lower margins. It also exists with papermaker's watermark.

Joaquim Nabuco (1849-1910), Lawyer and Writer — AP32

1949, Aug. 30   Perf. 12
C77 AP32 3.80cr rose lilac   .40 .32
a. Wmk. 256, imperf.   25.00

Maracaná Stadium AP33

Soccer Player and Flag — AP34

Perf. 11x12, 12x11
1950, June 24   Litho.   Wmk. 267
C78 AP33 1.20cr ultra & salmon   .95 .40
C79 AP34 5.80cr bl, yel grn & yel   2.75 .50
4th World Soccer Championship, Rio.

AP35
AP36 

Symbolical of Brazilian population growth.

1950, July 10   Perf. 12x11
C80 AP35 1.20cr red brown   .30 .15
Issued to publicize the 6th Brazilian census.

1956, Sept. 8   Engr.   Perf. 11½
Design: J. B. Marcelino Champagnat.
C81 AP36 3.30cr rose lilac   .30 .15
50th anniversary of the arrival of the Marist Brothers in Northern Brazil.

Santos-Dumont's 1906 Plane — AP37

1956   Photo.
C82 AP37 3cr dk blue grn   .85 .30
C83 AP37 3.30cr brt ultra   .20 .15
C84 AP37 4cr dp claret   .40 .15
C85 AP37 6.50cr red brown   .15 .15
C86 AP37 11.50cr orange red   .85 .35
  Nos. C82-C86 (5)   2.45 1.10

Souvenir Sheet
C86A AP37 Sheet of 4   6.00 6.00
b. 3cr dark carmine   1.50 .90
1st flight by Santos-Dumont, 50th anniv.
Issued: #C86A, 10/14; others 10/16.

Lord Baden-Powell — AP38

1957, Aug. 1   Unwmk.
Granite Paper
C87 AP38 3.30cr deep red lilac   .25 .15
Centenary of the birth of Lord Baden-Powell, founder of the Boy Scouts.

UN Emblem, Soldier and Map of Suez Canal Area — AP39

Perf. 11½
1957, Oct. 24   Wmk. 267   Engr.
C88 AP39 3.30cr dark blue   .25 .18
Brazilian contingent of the UN Emergency Force.

BRAZIL

Basketball Player — AP40

1959, May 30   Photo.   Perf. 11½
C89 AP40 3.30cr brt red brn & bl   .25 .15
Brazil's victory in the World Basketball Championships of 1959.

Symbol of Flight — AP41

1959, Oct. 21   Wmk. 267
C90 AP41 3.30cr deep ultra   .16 .15
Issued to publicize Week of the Wing.

Caravelle AP42

1959, Dec. 18   Perf. 11½
C91 AP42 6.50cr ultra   .16 .15
Inauguration of Brazilian jet flights.

Pres. Adolfo Lopez Mateos AP43

Pres. Dwight D. Eisenhower AP44

1960, Jan. 19   Photo.   Wmk. 267
C92 AP43 6.50cr brown   .16 .15
Issued to commemorate the visit of President Adolfo Lopez Mateos of Mexico.

1960, Feb. 23   Perf. 11½
C93 AP44 6.50cr deep orange   .16 .15
Visit of Pres. Dwight D. Eisenhower.

World Refugee Year Emblem — AP45

Tower at Brasilia — AP46

1960, Apr. 7   Wmk. 268
C94 AP45 6.50cr blue   .16 .15
WRY, July 1, 1959-June 30, 1960.

Type of Regular Issue and AP46
Designs: 3.30cr, Square of the Three Entities. 4cr, Cathedral. 11.50cr, Plan of Brasilia.

Perf. 11x11½, 11½x11
1960, Apr. 21   Photo.   Wmk. 267
C95 A436   3.30cr violet   .15 .15
C96 A436   4cr blue   .75 .15
C97 A436   6.50cr rose carmine   .15 .15
C98 A436   11.50cr brown   .15 .15
  Nos. C95-C98 (4)   1.20 .60
Inauguration of Brazil's new capital, Brasilia, Apr. 21, 1960.

Chrismon and Oil Lamp AP47

1960, May 16   Perf. 11x11½
C99 AP47 3.30cr lilac rose   .15 .15
7th Natl. Eucharistic Congress at Curitiba.

Cross, Sugarloaf Mountain and Emblem AP48

1960, July 1   Wmk. 267
C100 AP48 6.50cr brt blue   .15 .15
10th Cong. of the World Baptist Alliance, Rio.

Boy Scout — AP49

Caravel — AP50

1960, July 23   Perf. 11½x11
C101 AP49 3.30cr orange ver   .15 .15
Boy Scouts of Brazil, 50th anniversary.

1960, Aug. 5   Engr.   Wmk. 268
C102 AP50 6.50cr black   .15 .15
Prince Henry the Navigator, 500th birth anniv.

Maria E. Bueno AP51

1960, Dec. 15   Photo.   Perf. 11x11½
C103 AP51 60cr pale brown   .15 .15
Victory at Wimbledon of Maria E. Bueno, women's singles tennis champion.

War Memorial, Sugarloaf Mountain and Allied Flags AP52

1960, Dec. 22   Wmk. 268
C104 AP52 3.30cr lilac rose   .15 .15
Reburial of Brazilian servicemen of WW II.

Power Line and Map AP53

Malaria Eradication Emblem AP54

1961, Jan. 20   Perf. 11½x11
C105 AP53 3.30cr lilac rose   .15 .15
Inauguration of Three Marias Dam and hydroelectric station in Minas Gerais.

1962, May 24   Wmk. 267   Engr.
C106 AP54 21cr blue   .15 .15
WHO drive to eradicate malaria.

F. A. de Varnhagen — AP55

1966, Feb. 17   Photo.   Wmk. 267
C107 AP55 45cr red brown   .18 .15
Francisco Adolfo de Varnhagen, Viscount of Porto Seguro (1816-1878), historian and diplomat.

Map of the Americas and Alliance for Progress Emblem AP56

1966, Mar. 14   Perf. 11x11½
C108 AP56 120cr grnsh bl & vio bl   .40 .15
5th anniv. of the Alliance for Progress.
A souvenir card contains one impression of No. C108, imperf. Size: 113x160mm.

Nun and Globe — AP57

Face of Jesus from Shroud of Turin — AP58

1966, Mar. 25   Photo.   Perf. 11½x11
C109 AP57 35cr violet   .18 .15
Centenary of the arrival of the teaching Sisters of St. Dorothea.

1966, June 3   Photo.   Wmk. 267
C110 AP58 45cr brown org   .20 .15
Issued to commemorate Vatican II, the 21st Ecumenical Council of the Roman Catholic Church, Oct. 11, 1962-Dec. 8, 1965.
A souvenir card contains one impression of No. C110, imperf. Size: 100x39mm.

Admiral Mariz e Barros AP59

"Youth" by Eliseu Visconti AP60

1966, June 13   Photo.   Wmk. 267
C111 AP59 35cr red brown   .16 .15
Death centenary of Admiral Antonio Carlos Mariz e Barros, who died in the Battle of Itaperu.

1966, July 31   Perf. 11½x11
C112 AP60 120cr red brown   .40 .20
Birth centenary of Eliseu Visconti, painter.

SPECIAL DELIVERY STAMPS

No. 191 Surcharged **1000 REIS EXPRESSO**

1930   Unwmk.   Perf. 12
E1 A62 1000r on 200r dp blue   4.00 1.75
  a. Inverted surcharge   500.00

POSTAGE DUE STAMPS

D1   D2

1889   Unwmk.   Typo.   Rouletted
J1   D1   10r carmine   2.00   1.40
J2   D1   20r carmine   2.75   2.00
J3   D1   50r carmine   5.00   4.00
J4   D1   100r carmine   2.00   1.40
J5   D1   200r carmine   55.00 15.00
J6   D1   300r carmine   6.00   8.00
J7   D1   500r carmine   6.00   8.00
J8   D1   700r carmine   10.00 14.00
J9   D1   1000r carmine   10.00 10.00
  Nos. J1-J9 (9)   98.75 63.80
Counterfeits are common.

1890
J10 D1   10r orange   .60   .30
J11 D1   20r ultra   .60   .30
J12 D1   50r olive   1.25   .30
J13 D1   200r magenta   6.00   .60
J14 D1   300r blue green   3.00   1.50
J15 D1   500r slate   4.00   3.00
J16 D1   700r purple   4.50   7.50
J17 D1   1000r dk violet   5.50   5.00
  Nos. J10-J17 (8)   25.45 18.50

Perf. 11 to 11½, 12½ to 14 and Compound
1895-1901
J18 D2   10r dk blue ('01)   2.00   1.25
J19 D2   20r yellow grn   8.00   3.00
J20 D2   50r yellow grn ('01)   10.00   5.50
J21 D2   100r brick red   6.25   1.25
J22 D2   200r violet   6.00   .60
  a. 200r gray lilac ('98)   12.00   2.00
J23 D2   300r dull blue   3.50   2.25
J24 D2   2000r brown   12.00 12.00
  Nos. J18-J24 (7)   47.75 25.85

1906   Wmk. 97
J25 D2   100r brick red   8.00   3.00

Wmk. (97? or 98?)
J26 D2   200r violet   7.50   1.25
  a. Wmk. 97   275.00 85.00
  b. Wmk. 98   12.50 50.00

BRAZIL

D3  **D4**

1906-10 Unwmk. Engr. Perf. 12
J28	D3	10r slate	.15	.15
J29	D3	20r brt violet	.15	.15
J30	D3	50r dk green	.25	.15
J31	D3	100r carmine	1.75	.60
J32	D3	200r dp blue	1.00	.30
J33	D3	300r gray blk	.40	.60
J34	D3	400r olive grn	1.00	.90
J35	D3	500r dk violet	35.00	35.00
J36	D3	600r violet ('10)	1.25	3.00
J37	D3	700r red brown	30.00	30.00
J38	D3	1000r red	1.50	3.00
J39	D3	2000r green	4.75	5.50
J40	D3	5000r choc ('10)	1.50	14.00
		Nos. J28-J40 (13)	78.70	93.35

1919-23 Perf. 12½, 11, 11x10½ Typo.
J41	D4	5r red brown	.15	.25
J42	D4	10r violet	.25	.25
J43	D4	20r olive gray	.20	.15
J44	D4	50r green ('23)	.20	.20
J45	D4	100r red	1.10	1.00
J46	D4	200r blue	5.25	1.50
J47	D4	400r brown ('23)	1.40	1.25
		Nos. J41-J47 (7)	8.55	4.60

1924-35 Perf. 12½, 12½x13½ Wmk. 100
J48	D4	5r red brown	.25	.20
J49	D4	100r red	.75	.30
J50	D4	200r slate bl ('29)	1.00	.50
J51	D4	400r dp brn ('29)	1.50	1.00
J52	D4	600r dk vio ('29)	1.75	1.10
J53	D4	600r orange ('35)	.75	.50
		Nos. J48-J53 (6)	6.00	3.60

1924 Wmk. 193 Perf. 11x10½
J54	D4	100r red	45.00	45.00
J55	D4	200r slate blue	5.50	5.50

Perf. 11x10½, 13x13½
1925-27 Wmk. 101
J56	D4	20r olive gray	.20	.15
J57	D4	100r red	1.05	.30
J58	D4	200r slate blue	3.25	.35
J59	D4	400r brown	1.75	1.25
J60	D4	600r dk violet	4.25	2.50
		Nos. J56-J60 (5)	10.50	4.55

Wmk. E U BRASIL Multiple (218)
1929-30 Perf. 12½x13½
J61	D4	100r light red	.25	.20
J62	D4	200r blue black	.40	.25
J63	D4	400r brown	.40	.25
J64	D4	1000r myrtle green	.75	.50
		Nos. J61-J64 (4)	1.80	1.20

Perf. 11, 12½x13, 13
1931-36 Wmk. 222
J65	D4	10r lt violet ('35)	.15	.15
J66	D4	20r black ('33)	.20	.15
J67	D4	50r blue grn ('35)	.25	.20
J68	D4	100r rose violet ('35)	.25	.20
J69	D4	200r sl blue ('35)	.40	.30
J70	D4	400r blk brn ('35)	2.00	2.00
J71	D4	600r dk violet	.35	.20
J72	D4	1000r myrtle grn	.50	.35
J73	D4	2000r brown ('36)	.80	.80
J74	D4	5000r indigo ('36)	1.25	1.00
		Nos. J65-J74 (10)	6.15	5.35

1938 Wmk. 249 Perf. 11
J75	D4	200r slate blue	2.00	.75

1940 Typo. Wmk. 256
J76	D4	10r light violet	.50	.50
J77	D4	20r black	.50	.50
J79	D4	100r rose red	.50	.50
J80	D4	200r myrtle green	.50	.50
		Nos. J76-J80 (4)	2.00	2.00

1942 Wmk. 264
J81	D4	10r lt violet	.15	.15
J82	D4	20r olive blk	.15	.15
J83	D4	50r lt blue grn	.15	.15
J84	D4	100r vermilion	.40	.30
J85	D4	200r gray blue	.40	.30
J86	D4	400r claret	.40	.30
J87	D4	600r rose vio	.30	.20
J88	D4	1000r dk bl grn	.30	.20
J89	D4	2000r dp yel brn	.75	.50
J90	D4	5000r indigo	.40	.30
		Nos. J81-J90 (10)	3.40	2.55

1949 Wmk. 268
J91	D4	10c pale rose lilac	4.00	3.25
J92	D4	20r black	25.00	25.00

No. J92 exists in shades of gray ranging to gray olive.

OFFICIAL STAMPS

Pres. Affonso Penna — O1
Pres. Hermes da Fonseca — O2 

Unwmk.
1906, Nov. 15 Engr. Perf. 12
O1	O1	10r org & grn	.75	.30
O2	O1	20r org & grn	.90	.30
O3	O1	50r org & grn	1.50	.30
O4	O1	100r org & grn	.75	.30
O5	O1	200r org & grn	.90	.30
O6	O1	300r org & grn	2.75	.60
O7	O1	400r org & grn	6.00	1.75
O8	O1	500r org & grn	3.00	1.25
O9	O1	700r org & grn	4.50	3.00
O10	O1	1000r org & grn	4.50	1.25
O11	O1	2000r org & grn	5.00	2.25
O12	O1	5000r org & grn	10.00	.50
O13	O1	10,000r org & grn	10.00	1.25
		Nos. O1-O13 (13)	50.55	13.35

The portrait is the same but the frame differs for each denomination of this issue.

1913, Nov. 15 Center in Black
O14	O2	10r gray	.35	.50
O15	O2	20r ol grn	.35	.50
O16	O2	50r gray	.35	.50
O17	O2	100r ver	1.00	.35
O18	O2	200r blue	1.75	.35
O19	O2	500r orange	3.00	.65
O20	O2	600r violet	3.50	2.75
O21	O2	1000r blk brn	4.25	1.25
O22	O2	2000r red brn	6.50	1.25
O23	O2	5000r brown	7.50	3.00
O24	O2	10,000r black	15.00	7.50
O25	O2	20,000r blue	27.50	27.50
O26	O2	50,000r green	50.00	55.00
O27	O2	100,000r org red	175.00	200.00
O28	O2	500,000r brown	300.00	325.00
O29	O2	1,000,000r dk brn	325.00	350.00
		Nos. O14-O29 (16)	921.05	976.10

The portrait is the same on all denominations of this series but there are eight types of the frame.

Pres. Wenceslau Braz — O3

Perf. 11, 11½
1919, Apr. 11 Wmk. 100
O30	O3	10r olive green	.40	2.00
O31	O3	50r green	1.00	1.25
O32	O3	100r rose red	2.00	.85
O33	O3	200r dull blue	2.75	.85
O34	O3	500r orange	7.50	14.00
		Nos. O30-O34 (5)	13.65	18.95

The official decree called for eleven stamps in this series but only five were issued.
For surcharges see Nos. 293-297.

NEWSPAPER STAMPS

N1

Rouletted
1889, Feb. 1 Unwmk. Litho.
P1	N1	10r yellow	3.00	3.00
a.		Pair, imperf. between	125.00	145.00
P2	N1	20r yellow	6.00	7.50
P3	N1	50r yellow	10.00	6.00
P4	N1	100r yellow	3.75	3.00
P5	N1	200r yellow	3.00	1.50
P6	N1	300r yellow	3.00	1.50
P7	N1	500r yellow	20.00	8.00
P8	N1	700r yellow	3.00	10.00
P9	N1	1000r yellow	3.00	10.00
		Nos. P1-P9 (9)	54.75	50.50

For surcharges see Nos. 125-127.

1889, May 1
P10	N1	10r olive	2.00	.50
P11	N1	20r green	2.00	.50
P12	N1	50r brn yel	2.75	1.00
P13	N1	100r violet	3.00	2.00
a.		100r deep violet	6.50	15.00
b.		100r lilac	12.00	10.00
P14	N1	200r blue	3.00	2.00
P15	N1	300r carmine	12.00	10.00
P16	N1	500r green	50.00	50.00
P17	N1	700r pale blue	25.00	30.00
a.		100r ultramarine	65.00	75.00
b.		100r cobalt	400.00	425.00
P18	N1	1000r brown	12.00	15.00
		Nos. P10-P18 (9)	111.75	111.00

For surcharges see Nos. 128-135.

N2  N3

White Wove Paper Thin to Thick
Perf. 11 to 11½, 12½ to 14 and 12½ to 14x11 to 11½

1890 Typo.
P19	N2	10r blue	14.00	10.00
a.		10r ultramarine	14.00	10.00
P20	N2	20r emerald	40.00	15.00
P21	N2	100r violet	16.00	14.00
		Nos. P19-P21 (3)	70.00	39.00

For surcharge see No. 137.

1890-93
P22	N3	10r ultramarine	3.00	3.00
a.		10r blue	7.50	4.00
P23	N3	10r ultra, buff	3.00	3.00
P24	N3	20r green	10.00	3.00
a.		20r emerald	10.00	3.00
P25	N3	50r yel grn ('93)	17.50	10.00
		Nos. P22-P25 (4)	33.50	19.00

For surcharges see Nos. 136, 138-139.

POSTAL TAX STAMPS

Icarus from the Santos-Dumont Monument at St. Cloud, France — PT1

Perf. 13½x12½, 11
1933, Oct. 1 Typo. Wmk. 222
RA1	PT1	100r deep rose	.65	.25

Honoring the Brazilian aviator, Santos-Dumont. Its use was obligatory as a tax on all correspondence sent to countries in South America, the US and Spain. Its use on correspondence to other countries was optional. The funds obtained were used for the construction of airports throughout Brazil.

Catalogue values for unused stamps in this section, from this point to the end of the section, are for Never Hinged items.

Father Joseph Damien and Children PT2

Perf. 12x11
1952, Nov. 24 Litho. Wmk. 267
RA2	PT2	10c yellow brown	.25	.15

1953, Nov. 30
RA3	PT2	10c yellow green	.25	.15

Father Bento Dias Pacheco PT3
Eunice Weaver PT4 

1954, Nov. 22 Photo. Perf. 11½
RA4	PT3	10c violet blue	.20	.15

1955-69, Nov. 24
RA5	PT3	10c dk car rose	.20	.15
RA6	PT3	10c org red ('57)	.20	.15
RA7	PT3	10c dp emer ('58)	.15	.15
RA8	PT3	10c red lilac ('61)	.15	.15
RA9	PT3	10c choc ('62)	.15	.15
RA10	PT3	10c slate ('63)	.15	.15
RA11	PT3	2cr dp mag ('64)	.15	.15
RA12	PT3	2cr violet ('65)	.15	.15
RA13	PT3	2cr orange ('66)	.15	.15
RA14	PT3	5c brt yel grn ('68)	1.25	.15
RA15	PT3	5c deep plum ('69)	.50	.25

Issued: 11/25, #RA14; 11/28, #RA15; others, 11/24.

1971-73, Nov. 24
RA16	PT4	10c slate green	1.00	.40
RA17	PT4	10c brt rose lil ('73)	.20	.15

Father Nicodemos PT5
Father Vicente Borgard (1888-1977) PT6 

1975, Nov. 24 Litho. Unwmk.
RA18	PT5	10c sepia	.20	.15

1983, Nov. 24 Photo. Perf. 11½
RA19	PT6	10cr brown	.60	.60

Father Bento Dias Pacheco — PT7
Father Santiago Uchoa — PT8 

1984, Nov. 24 Photo. Perf. 11½
RA20	PT7	30cr deep blue	.15	.15

1985, Nov. 24 Litho.
RA21	PT7	100cr lake	.15	.15

1986, Nov. 24 Litho.
RA22	PT7	10c gray brown	.15	.15

1987, Nov. 24 Photo.
RA23	PT7	30c sage green	.15	.15

1988, Nov. 24 Litho.
RA24	PT8	1.30cz dull red brn	.15	.15

See Nos. RA29-RA30.

Fr. Joseph Damien — PT9

1989-92 Photo. Perf. 11½
RA25	PT9	2c deep lilac rose	.15	.15
RA26	PT9	50c blue	.15	.15

Perf. 12½
RA27	PT9	3cr green	.15	.15
RA28	PT9	30cr brown	.15	.15
		Nos. RA25-RA28 (4)	.60	.60

Issued: 2c, Nov. 24; 50c, Nov. 24, 1990; 3cr, Nov. 24, 1991; 30cr, Nov. 24, 1992.

Father Santiago Uchoa Type of 1988

1993, Nov. 24 Photo. Perf. 12½
RA29	PT8	50c blue	.15	.15

1994, Nov. 24
RA30	PT8	1c dull lake	.15	.15

The tax was for the care and treatment of lepers. Use of #RA2-RA30 was required for one week.

BRAZIL — BRITISH ANTARCTIC TERRITORY

POSTAL TAX SEMI-POSTAL STAMP

Catalogue values for unused stamps in this section are for Never Hinged items.

Icarus — PTSP1

Wmk. 267

	1947, Nov. 15	Typo.	Perf. 11
RA B1	PTSP1 40c + 10c brt red	.35	.20
a.	Pair, imperf. between		350.00

Aviation Week, November 15-22, 1947, and compulsory on all domestic correspondence during that week.

BRITISH ANTARCTIC TERRITORY

'bri-tish (,)ant-'ärk-tik 'ter-ə-,tōr-ē

LOCATION — South Atlantic Ocean between 20-80 degrees longitude and south of 60 degrees latitude
GOVT. — British territory
POP. — About 100 scientific staff at research stations.

This territory includes Graham Land (Palmer Peninsula), South Shetland Islands and South Orkney Islands. Formerly part of Falkland Islands Dependency.

12 Pence = 1 Shilling
20 Shillings = 1 Pound
100 Pence = 1 Pound (1971)

Catalogue values for all unused stamps in this country are for Never Hinged items.

M. V. Kista Dan — A1

Designs: 1p, Skiers hauling load. 1½p, Muskeg (tractor). 2p, Skiers. 2½p, Beaver seaplane. 3p, R.R.S. John Biscoe. 4p, Camp scene. 6p, H.M.S. Protector. 9p, Dog sled. 1sh, Otter ski-plane. 2sh, Huskies and aurora australis. 2sh6p, Helicopter. 5sh, Snocat (truck). 10sh, R.R.S. Shackleton. £1, Map of Antarctica.

Perf. 11x11½

	1963, Feb. 1	Engr.	Wmk. 314
1	A1	½p dark blue	.20 .15
2	A1	1p brown	.15 .15
3	A1	1½p plum & red	.20 .15
4	A1	2p rose violet	.30 .20
5	A1	2½p dull green	.35 .25
6	A1	3p Prus blue	.40 .30
7	A1	4p sepia	.50 .40
8	A1	6p dk blue & ol	.80 .70
9	A1	9p olive	1.00 .80
10	A1	1sh steel blue	1.35 1.10
11	A1	2sh dl vio & bis	6.75 5.50
12	A1	2sh6p blue	7.50 6.25
13	A1	5sh rose red & org	14.50 14.00
14	A1	10sh grn & vio bl	35.00 32.50
15	A1	£1 black & blue	85.00 67.50
	Nos. 1-15 (15)		154.00 130.00

See No. 24. For surcharges see Nos. 25-38.

Common Design Types pictured following the introduction.

Churchill Memorial Issue
Common Design Type

	1966, Jan. 24	Photo.	Perf. 14
16	CD319	½p bright blue	.40 .30
17	CD319	1p green	1.60 .70
18	CD319	1sh brown	16.00 15.00
19	CD319	2sh violet	21.00 16.00
	Nos. 16-19 (4)		39.00 32.00

Lemaire Channel, Iceberg and Adelie Penguins A2

Designs: 6p, Weather sonde and operator. 1sh, Muskeg (tractor) pulling tent equipment. 2sh, Surveyors with theodolite.

	1969, Feb. 6		Litho.
20	A2	3½p blue, vio bl & blk	.90 .85
21	A2	6p emer, blk & dp org	1.60 1.50
22	A2	1sh ultra, blk & ver	2.75 2.75
23	A2	2sh grnsh bl, blk & ocher	5.50 5.50
	Nos. 20-23 (4)		10.75 10.60

25 years of continuous scientific work in the Antarctic.

Type of 1963

Design: £1, H.M.S. Endurance and helicopter.

	1969, Dec. 1	Engr.	Perf. 11x11½
24	A1	£1 black & rose red	125.00 125.00

Nos. 1-14 Surcharged in Decimal Currency; Three Bars Overprinted

	1971, Feb. 15		Wmk. 314
25	A1	½p on ½p dk blue	.15 .15
26	A1	1p on 1p brown	.20 .20
27	A1	1½p on 1½p plum & red	.30 .25
28	A1	2p on 2p rose vio	.30 .30
29	A1	2½p on 2½p dl grn	.35 .40
30	A1	3p on 3p Prus bl	.65 .55
31	A1	4p on 4p sepia	.95 .90
32	A1	5p on 6p dk bl & ol	1.25 1.10
33	A1	6p on 9p olive	1.60 1.40
34	A1	7½p on 1sh steel bl	2.00 1.90
35	A1	10p on 2sh dl vio & bis	4.75 4.00
36	A1	15p on 2sh6p blue	14.00 12.00
37	A1	25p on 5sh rose red & org	27.50 24.00
38	A1	50p on 10sh grn & vio blue	62.50 60.00
	Nos. 25-38 (14)		116.50 107.15

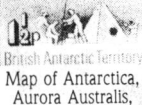

Map of Antarctica, Aurora Australis, Explorers — A3

Capt. Cook and "Resolution" — A4

Map of Antarctica, Aurora Australis and: 4p, Sea gulls. 5p, Seals. 10p, Penguins.

Litho. & Engr.

	1971, June 23		Perf. 14x13
39	A3	1½p multicolored	3.25 1.25
40	A3	4p multicolored	6.00 4.00
41	A3	5p multicolored	8.00 6.00
42	A3	10p multicolored	13.00 10.00
	Nos. 39-42 (4)		30.25 21.25

10th anniv. of the Antarctic Treaty pledging peaceful uses of and scientific cooperation in Antarctica.

Silver Wedding Issue, 1972
Common Design Type

Design: Queen Elizabeth II, Prince Philip, seals and emperor penguins.

	1972, Dec. 13	Photo.	Perf. 14x14½
43	CD324	5p rose brn & multi	2.00 2.00
44	CD324	10p olive & multi	4.00 4.00

Perf. 14½

	1975-80	Litho.	Wmk. 373

Polar Explorers and their Crafts: 1p, Thaddeus von Bellingshausen and "Vostok." 1½p, James Weddell and "Jane." 2p, John Biscoe and "Tula."

2½p, J. S. C. Dumont d'Urville and "Astrolabe." 3p, James Clark Ross and "Erebus." 4p, C. A. Larsen and "Jason." 5p, Adrien de Gerlache and "Belgica." 6p, Otto Nordenskjöld and "Antarctic." 7½p, W. S. Bruce and "Scotia." 10p, Jean-Baptiste Charcot and "Pourquoi Pas?" 15p, Ernest Shackleton and "Endurance." 25p, Hubert Wilkins and airplane "San Francisco." 50p, Lincoln Ellsworth and airplane "Polar Star." £1, John Rymill and "Penola."

45	A4	½p multi	.15 .15
46	A4	1p multi	.15 .15
47	A4	1½p multi ('78)	.15 .15
48	A4	2p multi ('79)	.15 .15
49	A4	2½p multi ('79)	.20 .20
50	A4	3p multi ('79)	.20 .20
52	A4	5p multi ('79)	.30 .30
55	A4	10p multi ('79)	.65 .65
56	A4	15p multi ('79)	1.00 1.00
57	A4	25p multi ('79)	1.60 1.60
58	A4	50p multi ('79)	3.25 3.25
59	A4	£1 multi ('78)	5.25 5.25
	Nos. 45-59 (12)		13.05 13.05

	1973, Feb. 14		Wmk. 314
45a	A4	½p multi	1.75 1.75
46a	A4	1p multi	2.00 2.10
47a	A4	1½p multi	3.50 3.50
48a	A4	2p multi	.25 .15
49a	A4	2½p multi	.30 .20
50a	A4	3p multi	.30 .20
51a	A4	4p multi	.30 .30
52a	A4	5p multi	.40 .30
53a	A4	5p multi	.40 .30
54a	A4	7½p multi	.55 .50
55a	A4	10p multi	1.05 .55
56a	A4	15p multi	1.75 1.00
57a	A4	25p multi	2.00 1.50
58a	A4	50p multi	4.00 3.00
59a	A4	£1 multi	12.00 11.00
	Nos. 45a-59a (15)		30.55 26.25

	1980		Wmk. 373	Perf. 12
51	A4	4p multi	.30 .30
53	A4	6p multi	.40 .40
54	A4	7½p multi	.50 .50
55b	A4	10p multi	.65 .65
56b	A4	15p multi	.70 .70
57b	A4	25p multi	1.25 1.25
58b	A4	50p multi	2.50 2.50
59b	A4	£1 multi	5.00 5.00
	Nos. 51-59b (8)		11.30 11.30

Princess Anne's Wedding Issue
Common Design Type

	1973, Nov. 14	Wmk. 314	Perf. 14
60	CD325	5p ocher & multi	.30 .30
61	CD325	15p blue grn & multi	.80 .80

Wedding of Princess Anne and Capt. Mark Phillips, Nov. 14, 1973.

Churchill and Map of Churchill Peninsula A5

Design: 15p, Churchill and "Trepassey" of Operation Tabarin, 1943.

	1974, Nov. 30	Litho.	Perf. 14
62	A5	5p multicolored	1.25 .80
63	A5	15p multicolored	2.50 2.50
a.	Souvenir sheet of 2, #62-63		6.75 4.50

Sir Winston Churchill (1874-1965).

Humpback Whale — A6

	1977, Jan. 4	Litho.	Wmk. 373	Perf. 14
64	A6	2p Sperm whale	2.25 1.00
65	A6	8p Fin whale	2.75 1.50
66	A6	11p shown	5.50 3.00
67	A6	25p Blue whale	6.50 4.50
	Nos. 64-67 (4)		17.00 10.00

Conservation of whales.

Prince Philip in Antarctica, 1956-57 — A7

Designs: 11p, Coronation oath. 33p, Queen before taking oath.

	1977, Feb. 7		Perf. 13½x14
68	A7	6p multicolored	.35 .35
69	A7	11p multicolored	.60 .60
70	A7	33p multicolored	2.00 2.00
	Nos. 68-70 (3)		2.95 2.95

25th anniv. of the reign of Elizabeth II.

Elizabeth II Coronation Anniversary Issue
Common Design Types
Souvenir Sheet
Unwmk.

	1978, June 2	Litho.	Perf. 15
71	Sheet of 6		5.00 5.00
a.	CD326 25p Black bull of Clarence	.75 .75
b.	CD327 25p Elizabeth II	.75 .75
c.	CD328 25p Emperor penguin	.75 .75

No. 71 contains 2 se-tenant strips of Nos. 71a-71c, separated by horizontal gutter with commemorative and descriptive inscriptions and showing central part of coronation procession with coach.

Macaroni Penguins — A8

Perf. 13½x14

	1979, Jan. 14	Litho.	Wmk. 373
72	A8	3p shown	6.25 2.00
73	A8	8p Gentoo	1.65 1.00
74	A8	11p Adelie	1.40 1.25
75	A8	25p Emperor	3.50 1.50
	Nos. 72-75 (4)		12.80 5.75

John Barrow, Tula, Society Emblem A9

Royal Geographical Society Sesquicentennial (Past Presidents and Expedition Scenes): 7p, Clement Markham 11p, Lord Curzon. 15p, William Goodenough. 22p, James Wordie. 30p, Raymond Priestley.

Perf. 13½

	1980, Dec. 1	Litho.	Wmk. 373
76	A9	3p multicolored	.15 .15
77	A9	7p multicolored	.20 .20
78	A9	11p multicolored	.30 .30
79	A9	15p multicolored	.50 .50
80	A9	22p multicolored	.75 .75
81	A9	30p multicolored	.95 .95
	Nos. 76-81 (6)		2.85 2.85

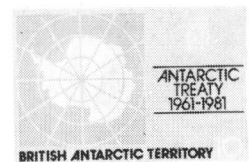

20th Anniv. of Antarctic Treaty — A10

	1981, Dec. 1		Perf. 13½x14
82	A10	10p Map	.25 .25
83	A10	13p Conservation research	.40 .40
84	A10	25p Satellite image mapping	.70 .70
85	A10	26p Global geophysics	.75 .75
	Nos. 82-85 (4)		2.10 2.10

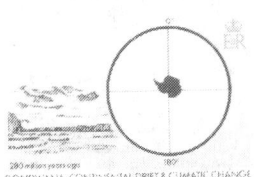

Continental Drift and Climatic Change — A11

BRITISH ANTARCTIC TERRITORY

1982, Mar. 8 Litho. Perf. 13½x14
86	A11	3p	Land, water	.15	.15
87	A11	6p	Shrubs	.15	.15
88	A11	10p	Dinosaur	.35	.35
89	A11	13p	Volcano	.40	.40
90	A11	25p	Trees	.75	.75
91	A11	26p	Penguins	.85	.85
			Nos. 86-91 (6)	2.65	2.65

Princess Diana Issue
Common Design Type

1982, July 1 Litho. Perf. 14½x14
92	CD333	5p	Arms	.15	.15
93	CD333	17p	Diana, by Bryan Organ	.55	.55
94	CD333	37p	Wedding	1.25	1.25
95	CD333	50p	Portrait	1.65	1.65
			Nos. 92-95 (4)	3.60	3.60

10th Anniv. of Convention for Conservation of Antarctic Seals — A12

1982, Nov. Litho.
96	A12	5p	shown	.15	.15
97	A12	10p	Weddell seals	.30	.30
98	A12	13p	Elephant seals	.40	.40
99	A12	17p	Fur seals	.55	.55
100	A12	25p	Ross seal	.55	.55
101	A12	34p	Crabeater seals	1.10	1.10
			Nos. 96-101 (6)	3.05	3.05

Corethron Criophilum A13 1p

1984, Mar. 15 Litho. Perf. 14
102	A13	1p	shown	.15	.15
103	A13	2p	Desmonema gaudichaudi	.15	.15
104	A13	3p	Tomopteris carpenteri	.15	.15
105	A13	4p	Pareuchaeta antarctica	.15	.15
106	A13	5p	Antarctomysis maxima	.15	.15
107	A13	6p	Antarcturus signiensis	.20	.20
108	A13	7p	Serolis comuta	.20	.20
109	A13	8p	Parathemisto gaudichaudii	.25	.25
110	A13	9p	Bovallia gigantea	.30	.30
110A	A13	10p	Euphausia superba	.35	.35
111	A13	15p	Colossendeis australis	.50	.50
112	A13	20p	Todarodes sagittatus	.65	.65
113	A13	25p	Notothenia neglecta	.85	.85
114	A13	50p	Chaenocephalus aceratus	1.65	1.65
115	A13	£1	Lobodon carcinophagus	3.25	3.25
116	A13	£3	Antarctic marine food chain	8.25	8.25
			Nos. 102-116 (16)	17.20	17.20

Manned Flight Bicentenary A14

1983, Dec. 17 Wmk. 373
117	A14	5p	De Havilland Twin Otter	.15	.15
118	A14	13p	De Havilland Single Otter	.35	.35
119	A14	17p	Consolidated Canso	.55	.55
120	A14	50p	Lockheed Vega	1.60	1.60
			Nos. 117-120 (4)	2.65	2.65

British-Graham Land Expedition, 1934-1937 — A15

Designs: 7p, M. Y. Penola in Stella Creek. 22p, Northern base, Winter Island. 27p, D. H. Fox Moth at southern base, Barry Island. 54p, Dog team near Ablation Point, George VI Sound.

1985, Mar. 23 Litho. Perf. 14½
121	A15	7p	multicolored	.20	.20
122	A15	22p	multicolored	.55	.55
123	A15	27p	multicolored	.65	.65
124	A15	54p	multicolored	1.40	1.40
			Nos. 121-124 (4)	2.80	2.80

A16  A17

Naturalists, fauna and flora: 7p, Robert McCormick (1800-1890), Catharacta Skua Maccormicki. 22p, Sir Joseph Dalton Hooker (1817-1911), Deschampsea antarctica. 27p, Jean Rene C. Quoy (1790-1869), Lagenorhynchus cruciger. 54p, James Weddell (1787-1834), Leptonychotes weddelli.

1985, Nov. 4 Litho. Perf. 14½
125	A16	7p	multicolored	.25	.25
126	A16	22p	multicolored	.85	.85
127	A16	27p	multicolored	1.00	1.00
128	A16	54p	multicolored	2.00	2.00
			Nos. 125-128 (4)	4.10	4.10

1986, Jan. 6 Wmk. 373 Perf. 14
Halley's comet.
129	A17	7p	Edmond Halley	.30	.30
130	A17	22p	Halley Station	1.00	1.00
131	A17	27p	Trajectory, 1531	1.25	1.25
132	A17	54p	Giotto space probe	2.50	2.50
			Nos. 129-132 (4)	5.05	5.05

Intl. Glaciological Society, 50th Anniv. — A18

Different snowflakes.

1986, Dec. 6 Wmk. 384 Perf. 14½
133	A18	10p	dp blue & lt bl	.30	.30
134	A18	24p	blue grn & lt bl grn	.70	.70
135	A18	29p	dp rose lil & lt lil	.85	.85
136	A18	58p	dp vio & pale vio blue	1.75	1.75
			Nos. 133-136 (4)	3.60	3.60

Capt. Robert Falcon Scott, CVO RN (1868-1912) A19

Designs: 24p, The Discovery at Hut Point, 1902-1904. 29p, Cape Evans Hut, 1911-1913. 58p, South Pole, 1912.

1987, Mar. 19 Litho. Wmk. 373
137	A19	10p	multicolored	.30	.30
138	A19	24p	multicolored	.70	.70
139	A19	29p	multicolored	.85	.85
140	A19	58p	multicolored	1.75	1.75
			Nos. 137-140 (4)	3.60	3.60

Intl. Geophysical Year, 30th Anniv. — A20

Commonwealth Trans-Antarctic Expedition — A21

1987, Dec. 25 Wmk. 384
141	A20	10p	Emblem	.40	.40
142	A20	24p	Port Lockroy	.90	.90
143	A20	29p	Argentine Islands	1.10	1.10
144	A20	58p	Halley Bay	2.25	2.25
			Nos. 141-144 (4)	4.65	4.65

1988, Mar. 19 Perf. 14
145	A21	10p	Aurora over South Ice	.35	.35
146	A21	24p	Otter aircraft	.80	.80
147	A21	29p	Seismic ice-depth sounding	.95	.95
148	A21	58p	Sno-cat over crevasse	1.90	1.90
			Nos. 145-148 (4)	4.00	4.00

Lichens A22

1989, Mar. 25 Wmk. 373
149	A22	10p	Xanthoria elegans	.40	.40
150	A22	24p	Usnea aurantiaco-atra	1.00	1.00
151	A22	29p	Cladonia chlorophaea	1.25	1.25
152	A22	58p	Umbilicaria antarctica	2.50	2.50
			Nos. 149-152 (4)	5.15	5.15

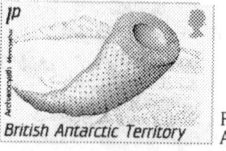

Fossils A23

1990, Apr. 2 Litho. Wmk. 384
153	A23	1p	Archaeocyath	.15	.15
154	A23	2p	Brachiopod	.15	.15
155	A23	3p	Trilobite (Triplagnostus)	.15	.15
156	A23	4p	Trilobite (Lyriaspis)	.15	.15
157	A23	5p	Gymnosperm	.15	.15
158	A23	6p	Fern	.20	.20
159	A23	7p	Belemnite	.20	.20
160	A23	8p	Ammonite (Sanmartinoceras)	.20	.20
161	A23	9p	Bivalve (Pinna)	.25	.25
162	A23	10p	Bivalve (Aucellina)	.30	.30
163	A23	20p	Bivalve (Trigonia)	.60	.60
164	A23	25p	Gastropod	.70	.70
165	A23	50p	Ammonite (Ainoceras)	1.40	1.40
166	A23	£1	Ammonite (Gunnarites)	2.75	2.75
167	A23	£3	Crayfish	8.00	8.00
			Nos. 153-167 (15)	15.35	15.35

Queen Mother, 90th Birthday
Common Design Types

1990, Aug. 4 Wmk. 384 Perf. 14x15
| 170 | CD343 | 26p | Wedding portrait, 1923 | .90 | .90 |

Perf. 14½
| 171 | CD344 | £1 | Family portrait, 1940 | 3.25 | 3.25 |

Age of Dinosaurs A24

1991, Mar. 27 Wmk. 373 Perf. 14
172	A24	12p	Late Cretaceous forest	.75	.75
173	A24	26p	Hypsilophodont dinosaur	1.50	1.50
174	A24	31p	Frilled shark	1.90	1.90
175	A24	62p	Mosasaur, plesiosaur	3.50	3.50
			Nos. 172-175 (4)	7.65	7.65

Antarctic Ozone Hole — A25

1991, Mar. 30 Perf. 14½x14
176	A25	12p	Launching weather balloon	.40	.40
177	A25	26p	Measuring ozone	.95	.95
178	A25	31p	Ozone hole over Antarctica	1.25	1.25
179	A25	62p	Airplane, chemical studies	2.40	2.40
			Nos. 176-179 (4)	5.00	5.00

Antarctic Treaty, 30th Anniv. — A26

1991, June 24 Perf. 14½
180	A26	12p	Dry valley	.40	.40
181	A26	26p	Mapping ice sheet	.95	.95
182	A26	31p	BIOMASS emblem	1.25	1.25
183	A26	62p	Ross seal	2.40	2.40
			Nos. 180-183 (4)	5.00	5.00

Royal Research Ship James Clark Ross — A27

Designs: 12p, HMS Erebus and Terror in Antarctic by John W. Carmichael. 26p, Launch of RRS James Clark Ross. 62p, Scientific research.

1991, Dec. 10 Perf. 14x14½
184	A27	12p	multicolored	.40	.40
185	A27	26p	multicolored	.95	.95
186	A27	31p	shown	1.25	1.25
187	A27	62p	multicolored	2.40	2.40
			Nos. 184-187 (4)	5.00	5.00

Inscribed in Blue
200th Anniversary M. Faraday 1791-1867

1991, Dec. 24
188	A27	12p	like #184	.40	.40
189	A27	26p	like #185	.95	.95
190	A27	31p	like #186	1.25	1.25
191	A27	62p	like #187	2.40	2.40
			Nos. 188-191 (4)	5.00	5.00

Seals and Penguins A28

1992, Oct. 20 Perf. 13½
192	A28	4p	Ross seal	.15	.15
193	A28	5p	Adelie penguin	.20	.20
194	A28	7p	Weddell seal	.30	.30
195	A28	29p	Emperor penguin	1.25	1.25
196	A28	34p	Crabeater seal	1.50	1.50
197	A28	68p	Chinstrap penguin	3.00	3.00
			Nos. 192-197 (6)	6.40	6.40

World Wildlife Fund.

Lower Atmospheric Phenomena A29

1992, Dec. 22 Litho. Perf. 14x14½
					Wmk. 373
198	A29	14p	Sun pillar at Faraday	.50	.50
199	A29	29p	Halo with iceberg	1.10	1.10
200	A29	34p	Lee wave cloud	1.25	1.25
201	A29	68p	Nacreous clouds	2.50	2.50
			Nos. 198-201 (4)	5.35	5.35

Research Ships A30

BRITISH ANTARCTIC TERRITORY — BRITISH CENTRAL AFRICA

Wmk. 373

1993, Dec. 13   Litho.   Perf. 14

202	A30	1p SS Fitzroy	.15	.15
203	A30	2p HMS William Scoresby	.15	.15
204	A30	3p SS Eagle	.15	.15
205	A30	4p MV Trepassey	.15	.15
206	A30	5p RRS John Biscoe (I)	.15	.15
207	A30	10p MV Norsel	.30	.30
208	A30	20p HMS Protector	.55	.55
209	A30	30p MV Oluf Sven	.85	.85
210	A30	50p RRS John Biscoe (II), RRS Shackleton	1.40	1.40
a.		Souvenir sheet of 1	1.75	1.75
211	A30	£1 MV Tottan	2.75	2.75
a.		Souvenir sheet of 1	3.50	3.50
212	A30	£3 MV Perla Dan	8.50	8.50
213	A30	£5 HMS Endurance (I)	14.00	14.00
		Nos. 202-213 (12)	29.10	29.10

No. 210a for Hong Kong '97. Issued 2/3/97.
No. 211a for return of Hong Kong to China. Issued 7/1/97.

Operation Taberin, 50th Anniv. — A31

Designs: 15p, Bransfield House and Post Office, Port Lockroy. 31p, Survey team, Hope Bay. 36p, Dog team, Hope Bay. 72p, SS Fitzroy, HMS William Scoresby at sea.

Wmk. 373

1994, Mar. 19   Litho.   Perf. 14

214	A31	15p multicolored	.45	.45
215	A31	31p multicolored	.90	.90
216	A31	36p multicolored	1.10	1.10
217	A31	72p multicolored	2.25	2.25
		Nos. 214-217 (4)	4.70	4.70

Old and New Transportation — A32

Designs: 15p, Huskies. 24p, DeHavilland DHC-2 Turbo Beaver, British Antarctic Survey. 31p, Dogs, cargo being taken from aircraft. 36p, DHC-6 Twin Otter, sled team. 62p, DHC-6 in flight. 72p, DHC-6 taxiing down runway.

1994, Mar. 21

218	A32	15p multicolored	.45	.45
219	A32	24p multicolored	.70	.70
220	A32	31p multicolored	.90	.90
221	A32	36p multicolored	1.10	1.10
222	A32	62p multicolored	1.75	1.75
223	A32	72p multicolored	2.25	2.25
		Nos. 218-223 (6)	7.15	7.15

Ovptd. with Hong Kong '94 Emblem

1994, Feb. 18

224	A32	15p on #218	.45	.45
225	A32	24p on #219	.70	.70
226	A32	31p on #220	.90	.90
227	A32	36p on #221	1.10	1.10
228	A32	62p on #222	1.75	1.75
229	A32	72p on #223	2.25	2.25
		Nos. 224-229 (6)	7.15	7.15

Antarctic Food Chain A33

a, Crabeater seals. b, Blue whale. c, Wandering albatross. d, Mackeral icefish. e, Krill. f, Squid.

1994, Nov. 29

230	A33	35p Sheet of 6	6.50	6.50

Geological Structures A34

Designs: 17p, Hauberg Mountains, folded sedimentary rocks. 35p, Arrowsmith Peninsula, dikes cross-cutting granite. 40p, Colbert Mountains, columnar jointing in volcanic rocks. 76p, Succession Cliffs, flat-lying sedimentary rocks.

1995, Nov. 28   Litho.   Wmk. 373   Perf. 14x14½

231	A34	17p multicolored	.55	.55
232	A34	35p multicolored	1.10	1.10
233	A34	40p multicolored	1.25	1.25
234	A34	76p multicolored	2.50	2.50
		Nos. 231-234 (4)	5.40	5.40

Scientific Committee on Antarctic Research (SCAR) A35

Designs: 17p, World map showing SCAR member countries. 35p, Earth sciences. 40p, Atmospheric sciences. 76p, Life sciences.
£1, Cambridge, August 1996.

1996, Mar. 23   Litho.   Wmk. 384   Perf. 14

235	A35	17p multicolored	.55	.55
236	A35	35p multicolored	1.10	1.10
237	A35	40p multicolored	1.25	1.25
238	A35	76p multicolored	2.50	2.50
		Nos. 235-238 (4)	5.40	5.40

Souvenir Sheet

239	A35	£1 multicolored	3.25	3.25

Queen Elizabeth II, 70th Birthday
Common Design Type

Various portraits of Queen: 17p, Pink outfit. 35p, In formal dress, tiara. 40p, Blue outfit. 76p, Red coat.

Perf. 14½

1996, Nov. 25   Litho.   Wmk. 384

240	CD354	17p multicolored	.60	.60
241	CD354	35p multicolored	1.10	1.10
242	CD354	40p multicolored	1.40	1.40
243	CD354	76p multicolored	2.50	2.50
		Nos. 240-243 (4)	5.60	5.60

Whales A36

Wmk. 373

1996, Nov. 25   Litho.   Perf. 14

244	A36	17p Killer whale	.60	.60
245	A36	35p Sperm whale	1.10	1.10
246	A36	40p Minke whale	1.40	1.40
247	A36	76p Blue whale	2.50	2.50
		Nos. 244-247 (4)	5.60	5.60

Souvenir Sheet

248	A36	£1 Humpback whale	3.50	3.50

Christmas — A37

Penguins in snow: 17p, Sledding. 35p, Caroling. 40p, Throwing snowballs. 76p, Ice skating.

Perf. 14½

1997, Dec. 22   Litho.   Wmk. 384

249	A37	17p multicolored	.55	.55
250	A37	35p multicolored	1.10	1.10
251	A37	40p multicolored	1.30	1.30
252	A37	76p multicolored	2.40	2.40
		Nos. 249-252 (4)	5.35	5.35

British Antarctic Territory stamps can be mounted in the annually supplemented Scott British Antarctic Territories album.

History of Mapping — A38

Maps of Antarctic and: 16p, Surveyor looking through theodolite, 1902-03. 30p, Cartographer, 1949. 35p, Man using radar rangefinder, 1964. 40p, Satellite, 1981. 65p, Tripod, hand held remote control device, 1993.

1998   Litho.   Wmk. 373   Perf. 14

253	A38	16p multicolored	.55	.55
254	A38	30p multicolored	1.00	1.00
255	A38	35p multicolored	1.20	1.20
256	A38	40p multicolored	1.35	1.35
257	A38	65p multicolored	2.20	2.20
		Nos. 253-257 (5)	6.30	6.30

Diana, Princess of Wales (1961-97)
Common Design Type

Designs: a, Wearing sun glasses. b, In white top. c, Up close. d, Wearing blue-green blazer.

1998, Mar. 31   Perf. 14½x14

258	CD355	35p Sheet of 4, #a.-c.	5.25	5.25

No. 258 sold for £1.40 + 20p, with surtax and 50% of profit from total sales being donated to the Princess Diana Memorial Fund.

SEMI-POSTAL STAMPS

Antarctic Heritage SP1

Designs: 17p+3p, Capt. James Cook, HMS Resolution. 35p+15p, Sir James Clark Ross, HMS Erebus, HMS Terror. 40p+10p, Capt. Robert Falcon Scott. 76p+4p, Sir Ernest Shackleton, HMS Endurance trapped in ice.

Perf. 14½

1994, Nov. 23   Litho.   Wmk. 384

B1	SP1	17p + 3p multi	.65	.65
B2	SP1	35p + 15p multi	1.50	1.50
B3	SP1	40p + 10p multi	1.50	1.50
B4	SP1	76p + 4p multi	2.50	2.50
		Nos. B1-B4 (4)	6.15	6.15

Surtax for United Kingdom Antarctic Heritage Trust.

BRITISH CENTRAL AFRICA

'bri-tish 'sen-trəl 'a-fri-kə

LOCATION — Central Africa, on the west shore of Lake Nyassa
GOVT. — Former British territory, under charter to the British South Africa Company
AREA — 37,800 sq. mi.
POP. — 1,639,329
CAPITAL — Zomba

In 1907 the name was changed to Nyasaland Protectorate, and stamps so inscribed replaced those of British Central Africa.

12 Pence = 1 Shilling
20 Shillings = 1 Pound

Rhodesia Nos. 2, 4-19 Overprinted in Black B.C.A.

1891-95   Unwmk.   Perf. 14

1	A1	1p black	2.50	2.50
2	A2	2p gray green & ver	2.50	2.50
3	A2	4p red brn & blk	5.00	5.00
4	A1	6p ultramarine	45.00	24.00
5	A1	6p dark blue	5.00	7.50
6	A2	8p rose & blue	12.00	25.00
7	A1	1sh bis brown	11.00	10.00
8	A1	2sh vermilion	20.00	40.00
9	A1	2sh6p gray lilac	45.00	55.00
10	A2	3sh brn & grn ('95)	45.00	50.00
11	A2	4sh gray & ver ('93)	45.00	65.00
12	A1	5sh yellow	45.00	55.00
13	A1	10sh green	85.00	120.00
14	A3	£1 blue	600.00	650.00
15	A3	£2 rose red	800.00	800.00
16	A3	£5 yel green	1,600.	1,700.
17	A3	£10 red brown	3,000.	3,000.
		Nos. 1-13 (13)	365.00	459.50

High values with fiscal cancellation are fairly common and can be purchased at a small fraction of the above values. This applies to subsequent issues also.

For surcharge see No. 20.

Rhodesia Nos. 13-14 Surcharged in Black B.C.A. THREE SHILLINGS.

1892-93

18	A2	3sh on 4sh gray & ver ('93)	275.00	275.00
19	A1	4sh on 5sh yellow	65.00	75.00

No. 2 Surcharged in ONE PENNY. Black, with Bar

1895

20	A2	1p on 2p	7.50	20.00
a.		Double surcharge	3,000.	2,000.

A double surcharge, without period after "Penny," and measuring 16mm instead of 18mm, is from a trial printing.

Coat of Arms of the Protectorate

A4   A5

1895   Unwmk.   Typo.   Perf. 14

21	A4	1p black	7.50	5.00
22	A4	2p green & black	12.50	10.00
23	A4	4p org & black	22.50	22.50
24	A4	6p ultra & black	35.00	7.50
25	A4	1sh rose & black	40.00	17.50
26	A4	2sh6p vio & black	100.00	125.00
27	A4	3sh yel & black	65.00	42.50
28	A5	5sh olive & blk	85.00	90.00
29	A5	£1 org & black	650.00	375.00
30	A5	£10 vert & black	3,250.	2,750.
31	A5	£25 bl grn & blk	5,750.	6,000.
		Nos. 21-28 (8)	367.50	320.00

1896   Wmk. 2

32	A4	1p black	4.50	4.50
33	A4	2p green & black	12.00	5.75
34	A4	4p org brown & blk	14.00	16.00
35	A4	6p ultra & black	15.00	8.00
36	A4	1sh rose & black	16.00	9.00

Wmk. 1 Sideways

37	A5	2sh6p vio rose & blk	75.00	90.00
38	A5	3sh yel & black	55.00	40.00
39	A5	5sh olive & blk	80.00	95.00
40	A5	£1 blue & blk	675.00	475.00
41	A5	£10 vert & blk	3,750.	2,250.
42	A5	£25 bl grn & blk	9,500.	9,500.
		Nos. 32-39 (8)	271.50	268.25

A6   A7

1897-1901   Wmk. 2

43	A6	1p ultra & black	1.00	.60
44	A6	1p rose & violet ('01)	1.25	.90
45	A6	2p yel & black	1.50	.70
46	A6	4p car rose & blk	4.50	2.50
47	A6	4p ol green & violet ('01)	5.00	6.00
48	A6	6p green & black	27.50	9.00
49	A6	6p red brown & violet ('01)	4.00	3.75
50	A6	1sh gray lilac & blk	7.50	6.25

Wmk. 1

51	A7	2sh6p ultra & blk	32.50	35.00
52	A7	3sh gray grn & blk	150.00	175.00
53	A7	4sh car rose & blk	60.00	60.00
54	A7	10sh ol & black	75.00	90.00

753

55 A7 £1 dp vio & blk 225.00 140.00
56 A7 £10 org & black 3,500. 1,600.
Nos. 43-54 (12) 369.75 384.70

No. 52 Surcharged in Red

ONE
PENNY

1897
57 A7 1p on 3s 5.00 7.50
a. "PNNEY" 1,500.
b. "PENN" 900.00
c. Double surcharge 750.00 600.00

A8

1898, Mar. 11 Unwmk. *Imperf.*
58 A8 1p ver & ultra 1,500. 50.00
a. Center inverted 10,000.
b. Double oval
c. Pair, one without oval 6,500.
d. Pair with three ovals
e. Initials of P.M. General on back 450.00

Perf. 12
59 A8 1p ver & blue 1,750. 15.00

There are two settings of Nos. 58-59, with 30 types of each.
No. 58 issued without gum.

King Edward VII
A9 A10

1903-04 Wmk. 2
60 A9 1p car & black 3.75 .75
61 A9 2p vio & dull vio 3.00 2.50
62 A9 4p blk & gray green 2.25 5.75
63 A9 6p org brn & blk 2.25 4.50
64 A9 1sh pale blue & blk ('04) 2.25 4.00

Wmk. 1
65 A10 2sh6p gray green 27.50 35.00
66 A10 4sh vio & dl vio 47.50 70.00
67 A10 10sh blk & gray green 62.50 125.00
68 A10 £1 scar & blk 175.00 135.00
69 A10 £10 ultra & blk 3,500. 2,750.
Nos. 60-68 (9) 326.00 382.50

1907 Wmk. 3
70 A9 1p car & black 2.00 .90
71 A9 2p vio & dull vio 7,250.
72 A9 4p blk & gray grn 7,250.
73 A9 6p org brn & blk 25.00 32.50

Nos. 71-72 were not issued.
British Central Africa stamps were replaced by those of Nyasaland Protectorate in 1908.

BRITISH EAST AFRICA

'bri-tish 'ēst 'a-fri-kə

LOCATION — Formerly included all of the territory in East Africa under British control.

Postage stamps were issued by the British East Africa Company in 1896. Later the territory administered by this company was incorporated in the East Africa and Uganda Protectorate which, together with Kenya, became officially designated Kenya Colony.

16 Annas = 1 Rupee

Queen Victoria
A1 A2 A3

1890 Wmk. 30 *Perf. 14*
1 A1 ½a on 1p lilac 300.00 200.00
2 A2 1a on 2p grn & car rose 400.00 250.00
3 A3 4a on 5p lilac & bl 450.00 275.00

Sun and Crown Symbolical of "Light and Liberty"
A4 A5

1890-94 Unwmk. Litho. *Perf. 14*
14 A4 ½a bister brown 1.00 2.75
b. ½a deep brown 1.00 2.50
c. As "b," horiz. pair, imperf. btwn. 1,500. 750.00
d. As "b," vert. pair, imperf. btwn. 750.00 475.00
15 A4 1a blue green 1.00 1.00
16 A4 2a vermilion 2.50 1.50
17 A4 2½a black, *yel* ('91) 3.50 3.00
b. Vert. pair, imperf. btwn. 600.00 400.00
c. Horiz. pair, imperf. btwn. 800.00 500.00
18 A4 3a black, *red* ('91) 1.25 1.40
b. Horiz. pair, imperf. btwn. 600.00 400.00
c. Vert. pair, imperf. btwn. 450.00 350.00
19 A4 4a yellow brown 2.50 2.25
20 A4 4½a brown vio ('91) 2.50 3.25
b. 4½a gray violet ('91) 25.00 7.25
c. Horiz. pair, imperf. btwn. 1,250. 1,250.
d. Vert. pair, imperf. btwn. 675.00 450.00
21 A4 5a black, *blue* ('94) 1.10 1.75
22 A4 7½a black ('94) 1.10 1.75
23 A4 8a blue 5.50 7.50
24 A4 8a gray 250.00 325.00
25 A4 1r rose 6.00 7.50
26 A4 1r gray 225.00 225.00
27 A5 2r brick red 10.00 8.00
28 A5 3r gray violet 7.50 6.25
29 A5 4r ultra 12.00 12.50
30 A5 5r gray green 30.00 25.00
Nos. 14-30 (17) 562.45 635.40

Some of the paper used for this issue had a papermaker's watermark and parts of it often can be seen on the stamps.
Values for Nos. 14c, 14d, 17b, 17c, 18b, 18c, 20c, 20d, unused, are for copies with little or no original gum. Stamps with natural straight edges are almost as common as fully perforated stamps from the early printings of Nos. 14-30, and for all printings of the rupee values. Values about the same.
For surcharges and overprints see Nos. 31-53.

1890-91 *Imperf.*

Values for Pairs except No. 19b.

14a A4 ½a bister brown 600. 350.
14e A4 ½a deep brown 650. 400.
15a A4 1a blue green 800. 475.
16a A4 2a vermilion 1,200. 550.
17a A4 2½a black, *yellow* 750. 400.
18a A4 3a black, *red* 725. 600.
19a A4 4a yel brown 1,400. 600.
19b A4 4a gray 1,400. 1,400.
20a A4 4½a dull violet 1,100. 525.
23a A4 8a blue 1,800. 600.
25a A4 1r rose 2,400. 625.

A6 A7

Handstamped Surcharges

1891 *Perf. 14*
31 A6 ½a on 2a ver ("A.D.") 2,750. 900.00
a. Double surcharge 3,250.
32 A6 1a on 4a yel brn ("A.B.") 6,000. 1,300.

Nos. 31-32 are initialed in manuscript "A.D." or "A.B." See note below No. 35.

Manuscript Surcharges

1891-95
33 A6 ½a on 2a ver ("A.B.") 3,000. 675.00
a. "½ Annas" ("A.B.") 1,200.
b. Initialed "A.D." 1,000.
c. "½ Annas" ("A.D.") 1,600.
34 A6 ½a on 3a blk, *red* ("T.E.C.R.") 200.00 50.00
b. Initialed "A.B." 2,400. 1,100.
34A A6 1a on 3a blk, *red* ("V.H.M.") 3,000. 1,200.
c. Initialed "T.E.C.R." 3,000. 1,500.
35 A6 1a on 4a yel brn ("A.B.") 2,750. 950.00

The manuscript initials on Nos. 31-35, given in parentheses, stand for Andrew Dick, Archibald Brown, Victor H. Mackenzie (1891) and T.E. C. Remington (1895).

Printed Surcharges

1894
36 A7 5a on 8a blue 52.50 72.50
37 A7 7½a on 1r rose 52.50 72.50

Stamps of 1890-94 Handstamped in Black

BRITISH
EAST
AFRICA

1895
38 A4 ½a deep brown 60.00 20.00
39 A4 1a blue green 70.00 65.00
40 A4 2a vermilion 125.00 90.00
41 A4 2½a black, *yellow* 110.00 45.00
42 A4 3a black, *red* 42.50 37.50
43 A4 4a yel brown 37.50 37.50
44 A4 4½a gray violet 125.00 85.00
a. 4½a brown violet 750.00 650.00
45 A4 5a black, *blue* 140.00 87.50
b. Inverted overprint 2,000.
46 A4 7½a black 95.00 80.00
47 A4 8a blue 80.00 75.00
b. Inverted overprint 2,000.
48 A4 1r rose 45.00 47.50
49 A5 2r brick red 250.00 175.00
50 A5 3r gray violet 140.00 125.00
b. Inverted overprint
51 A5 4r ultra 125.00 125.00
52 A5 5r gray green 325.00 350.00
Nos. 38-52 (15) 1,770. 1,445.

Double Overprints

38a A4 ½a 350. 350.
39a A4 1a 350. 350.
40a A4 2a 400. 400.
41a A4 2½a 400. 350.
43a A4 4a 375. 375.
44b A4 4½a gray violet 475. 450.
44c A4 4½a brown violet 1,500. 1,400.
45a A4 5a 700. 650.
46a A4 7½a 450. 450.
47a A4 8a 475. 475.
48a A4 1r 425. 425.
50a A5 3r 750. 750.
51a A5 4r 750. 750.
52a A5 5r 1,100. 1,100.

Surcharged in Red

2½

1895
53 A4 2½a on 4½a gray vio 90.00 55.00
a. Double overprint (#44b) 700.00 700.00

Stamps of India 1874-95 Overprinted or Surcharged

British
East
Africa

2½ 2½ 2½
a b c

1895 Wmk. Star (39)
54 A17 ½a green 3.50 4.00
55 A19 1a maroon 3.50 3.50
56 A20 1a6p bister brn 3.50 3.00
57 A21 2a ultra 3.50 2.25
58 A28 2a6p green 5.00 2.75
59 A20(a) 2½a on 1a6p bis brown 40.00 27.50
a. "½" without fraction line 70.00
d. As "a," "1" of "½" invtd. 750.00 600.00
62 A22 3a orange 7.00 7.50
63 A23 4a olive green 25.00 16.00
64 A25 8a red violet 25.00 32.50
a. 8a red lilac 45.00 50.00
65 A26 12a vio, *red* 18.00 22.50
66 A27 1r gray 55.00 47.50
67 A29 1r car & grn 32.50 55.00
a. Dbl. ovpt., one sideways 350.00 550.00
68 A30 2r bis & rose 45.00 75.00
69 A30 3r grn & brn 55.00 85.00
70 A30 5r vio & ultra 80.00 120.00
a. Double overprint 1,800.

Wmk. Elephant's Head (38)
71 A14 6a bister 21.00 30.00
Nos. 54-59,62-71 (16) 422.50 534.00

Varieties of the overprint include: "Britsh," "Bri-tish," "Bpitish" and "Biitish" for "British", "Africa" for "Africa"; "Eas" and "Easa" for "East."
No. 59 is surcharged in bright red; surcharges in brown red were prepared for the UPU, but not regularly issued as stamps. See note following No. 93.

Queen Victoria and British Lions — A8

1896-1903 Engr. Wmk. 2 *Perf. 14*
72 A8 ½a yel green .80 .70
73 A8 1a carmine 2.50 .40
a. 1a red 2.50 .40
74 A8 1a dp rose ('03) 27.50 3.25
75 A8 2a chocolate 3.75 3.25
76 A8 2½a dark blue 4.75 1.00
77 A8 3a gray 2.50 4.50
78 A8 4a deep green 5.00 2.50
79 A8 4½a orange 4.00 8.00
80 A8 5a dk ocher 6.00 3.50
81 A8 7½a lilac 4.50 16.00
82 A8 8a olive gray 2.25 4.00
83 A8 1r ultra 25.00 17.00
a. 1r pale blue 25.00 17.50
84 A8 2r red orange 42.50 22.50
85 A8 3r deep violet 42.50 22.50
86 A8 4r lake 42.50 42.50
87 A8 5r dark brown 42.50 35.00
Nos. 72-87 (16) 258.55 186.60

Zanzibar Nos. 38-40, 44-46 Overprinted in Black

British
East
Africa

1897 Wmk. Rosette (71)
88 A2 ½a yel grn & red 37.50 37.50
89 A2 1a indigo & red 75.00 75.00
90 A2 2a red brn & red 27.50 18.00
91 A2 4½a org & red 37.50 22.50
92 A2 5a bister & red 37.50 27.50
93 A2 7½a lilac & red 42.50 30.00
a. Ovptd. on front and back
Nos. 88-93 (6) 257.50 210.50

The 1a with red overprint, which includes a period after "Africa", was sent to the UPU, but never placed in use. Nos. 88, 90-93 and 95-100 also exist with period (in black) in sets sent to the UPU. Some experts consider these essays.

Black Ovpt. on Zanzibar #39, 42
New Value Surcharged in Red

1897
95 A2(a) 2½a on 1a 75.00 50.00
a. Black overprint double 6,500.
b. "2" over "1" for "½" 1,200.
96 A2(b) 2½a on 1a 140.00 90.00
97 A2(c) 2½a on 1a 85.00 55.00
98 A2(a) 2½a on 3a 65.00 45.00
a. "2" over "1" for "½" 1,200.
99 A2(b) 2½a on 3a 125.00 85.00
100 A2(c) 2½a on 3a 75.00 50.00
Nos. 95-100 (6) 565.00 375.00

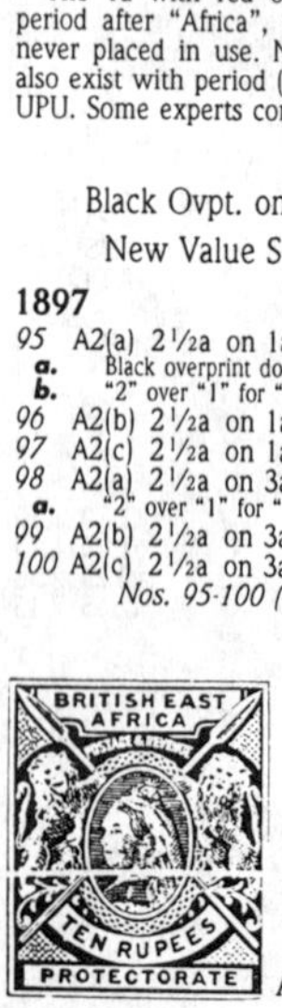
A10

1898 Wmk. 1 Engr.
102 A10 1r gray blue 27.50 17.50
a. 1r ultra 125.00 100.00
103 A10 2r orange 42.50 45.00
104 A10 3r dk violet 42.50 60.00
105 A10 4r carmine 125.00 150.00
106 A10 5r black brown 110.00 150.00
107 A10 10r bister 160.00 225.00
108 A10 20r yel green 575.00 1,000.
109 A10 50r lilac 1,900. 2,750.
Nos. 102-107 (6) 507.50 647.50

The stamps of this country were superseded in 1904 by the stamps of East Africa and Uganda Protectorate.

BRITISH GUIANA

'bri-tish gē-'a-nə, -'ä-nə

LOCATION — On the northeast coast of South America
GOVT. — Former British Crown Colony
AREA — 83,000 sq. mi.
POP. — 628,000 (estimated 1964)
CAPITAL — Georgetown

British Guiana became the independent state of Guyana May 26, 1966.

100 Cents = 1 Dollar

Catalogue values for unused stamps in this country are for Never Hinged items, beginning with Scott 242 in the regular postage section and Scott J1 in the postage due section.

Values for unused stamps are for copies with original gum except for Nos. 6-12 and 35-53, which are valued without gum. Very fine examples of all stamps from No. 6 on will have four clear margins. Inferior copies sell at much reduced prices, depending on the condition of the individual specimen.

A1

1850-51 Typeset Unwmk. Imperf.

1	A1	2c blk, *pale rose*, cut to shape ('51)	70,000.	
2	A1	4c black, *orange*	20,000.	
		Cut to shape	3,500.	
a.		4c black, *yellow*	27,500.	
		Cut to shape	4,000.	
3	A1	4c blk, *yellow* (pelure)	37,500.	
		Cut to shape	4,000.	
4	A1	8c black, *green*	13,000.	
		Cut to shape	2,500.	
5	A1	12c black, *blue*	5,250.	
		Cut to shape	1,900.	
a.		12c black, *pale blue*	11,000.	
		Cut to shape	3,000.	
b.		12c black, *indigo*	13,000.	
		Cut to shape	3,000.	
c.		"1" of "12" omitted	—	

These stamps were initialed before use by the Deputy Postmaster General or by one of the clerks of the Colonial Postoffice at Georgetown. The following initials are found:—E. T. E. D(alton); E. D. W(ight); G. B. S(mith); H. A. K(illikelley); W. H. L(ortimer). As these stamps are type-set there are several types of each value.

Ship and Motto of Colony — A2
Seal of the Colony — A3

1852 Litho.

| 6 | A2 | 1c black, *magenta* | 10,000. | 5,250. |
| 7 | A2 | 4c black, *blue* | 15,000. | 5,750. |

Both 1c and 4c are found in two types. Copies with paper cracked or rubbed sell for much less. Some copies are initialed E. D. W(ight).
The reprints are on thicker paper and the colors are brighter. They are perforated 12½ and imperforate. Value $15 each.

1853-59 Imperf.
Without Line above Value

| 8 | A3 | 1c vermilion | 4,500. | 1,150. |

Copies in reddish brown probably are proofs.

Full or Partial White Line Above Value

9	A3	1c red	2,750.	950.
10	A3	4c blue	1,100.	450.
a.		4c dark blue	1,375.	525.
b.		4c pale blue	1,000.	375.

On No. 9, "ONE CENT" varies from 11 to 13mm in width.

No. 10 Retouched; White Line above Value Removed

11	A3	4c blue	1,650.	600.
a.		4c dark blue	2,000.	650.
b.		4c pale blue	1,600.	650.

Reprints of Nos. 8 and 10 are on thin paper, perf. 12½ or imperf. The 1c is orange red, the 4c sky blue.

1860
Numerals in Corners Framed

| 12 | A3 | 4c blue | 3,250. | 450. |

A4

1856 Typeset Imperf.

13	A4	1c black, *magenta*		7,500.
14	A4	4c black, *magenta*		10,500.
a.		4c black, *rose carmine*		
15	A4	4c black, *blue*		45,000.
16	A4	4c black, *blue, paper colored through*		60,000.

These stamps were initialed before being issued and the following initials are found:—E. T. E. D.; E. D. W.; W. H. L.; C. A. W. No. 13 is unique.

A5

Wide space between value and "Cents"

1860-61 Thick Paper Litho. Perf. 12

17	A5	1c brown red ('61)	350.00	85.00
18	A5	1c pink	1,100.	165.00
19	A5	2c orange	150.00	37.50
20	A5	8c rose	300.00	45.00
21	A5	12c gray	350.00	30.00
a.		12c lilac	450.00	40.00
22	A5	24c green	950.00	75.00

All denominations of type A5 above four cents are expressed in Roman numerals.
Bisects and trisects are found on covers. These were not officially authorized.
The reprints of the 1c pink are perforated 12½; the other values have not been reprinted.

Thin Paper
1862-65

23	A5	1c brown	400.00	175.00
24	A5	1c black	100.00	45.00
25	A5	2c orange	80.00	30.00
26	A5	8c rose	110.00	45.00
27	A5	12c lilac	125.00	25.00
28	A5	24c green	750.00	85.00

Perf. 12½ and 13

29	A5	1c black	50.00	25.00
30	A5	2c orange	75.00	22.50
31	A5	8c rose	225.00	75.00
32	A5	12c lilac	475.00	110.00
33	A5	24c green	550.00	75.00

Medium Paper

33A	A5	1c black	50.00	25.00
33B	A5	2c orange	70.00	20.00
33C	A5	8c pink	145.00	50.00
33D	A5	12c lilac ('65)	425.00	90.00
33E	A5	24c green	160.00	40.00
f.		24c deep green	325.00	80.00

Perf. 10

| 34 | A5 | 12c gray lilac | 400.00 | 65.00 |

Imperfs. are proofs. See Nos. 44-62.

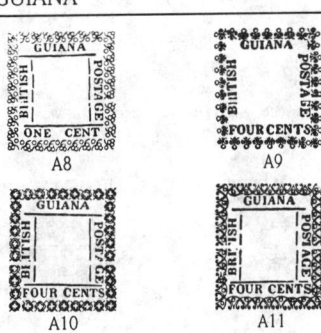

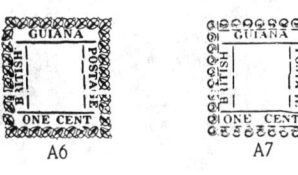

A6 A7

A8 A9

A10 A11

1862 Typeset Rouletted

35	A6	1c black, *rose*	1,650.	350.
		Unsigned	200.	
36	A7	1c black, *rose*	2,000.	450.
		Unsigned	200.	
37	A8	1c black, *rose*	3,500.	575.
		Unsigned	400.	
38	A6	2c black, *yellow*	1,600.	275.
		Unsigned	350.	
39	A7	2c black, *yellow*	2,250.	350.
		Unsigned	400.	
40	A8	2c black, *yellow*	3,250.	575.
		Unsigned	600.	
41	A9	4c black, *blue*	2,000.	475.
		Unsigned	375.	
42	A10	4c black, *blue*	3,500.	1,450.
a.		Without inner lines	600.	
		As "a", unsigned	2,000.	475.
			350.	
43	A11	4c black, *blue*	1,750.	400.
		Unsigned	350.	

Nos. 35-43 were typeset, there being 24 types of each value. They were initialed before use "R. M. Ac. R. G.," being the initials of Robert Mather, Acting Receiver General.
The initials are in black on the 1c and in red on the 2c. An alkali was used on the 4c stamps, which, destroying the color of the paper, caused the initials to appear to be written in white.
Uninitialed stamps are remainders, few sheets having been found.
Specimens with roulette on all sides are valued higher.

Narrow space between value and "Cents"
1860 Thick Paper Litho. Perf. 12

| 44 | A5 | 4c blue | 275.00 | 50.00 |
| c. | | 4c deep blue | 375.00 | 75.00 |

Thin Paper

| 44A | A5 | 4c blue | 75.00 | 20.00 |

Perf. 12½ and 13
Medium Paper

| 44B | A5 | 4c blue | 75.00 | 22.50 |

1863-68 Perf. 12½ and 13

45	A5	1c black ('66)	30.00	16.00
46	A5	2c orange	30.00	5.00
47	A5	4c blue ('64)	65.00	12.50
48	A5	8c rose ('68)	135.00	17.50
49	A5	12c lilac ('67)	375.00	22.50
		Nos. 45-49 (5)	635.00	73.50

1866 Perf. 10

50	A5	1c black	8.00	4.00
51	A5	2c orange	17.50	2.50
52	A5	4c blue	75.00	7.00
a.		Half used as 2c on cover	4,000.	
53	A5	8c rose	110.00	13.00
		Diagonal half used as 4c on cover	—	
54	A5	12c lilac	125.00	12.00
a.		Third used as 4c on cover	—	
		Nos. 50-54 (5)	335.50	38.50

1875 Perf. 15

58	A5	1c black	35.00	7.50
59	A5	2c orange	150.00	8.50
60	A5	4c blue	225.00	75.00
61	A5	8c rose	250.00	75.00
62	A5	12c lilac	525.00	47.50
		Nos. 58-62 (5)	1,185.	208.50

Seal of Colony
A12 A13

1863 Perf. 12

| 63 | A12 | 24c yellow green | 125.00 | 12.50 |
| a. | | 24c green | 250.00 | 22.50 |

Perf. 12½ to 13

64	A12	6c blue	100.00	40.00
65	A12	24c green	125.00	10.00
66	A12	48c deep red	150.00	45.00
a.		48c rose	250.00	45.00
		Nos. 63-66 (4)	500.00	107.50

1866 Perf. 10

67	A12	6c blue	100.00	22.50
a.		6c ultramarine	125.00	32.50
68	A12	24c yellow green	150.00	8.00
a.		24c green	190.00	10.00
69	A12	48c rose red	275.00	25.00
		Nos. 67-69 (3)	525.00	55.50

For surcharges see Nos. 83-92.

1875 Perf. 15

70	A12	6c ultra	375.00	80.00
71	A12	24c yellow green	525.00	35.00
a.		24c deep green	650.00	55.00

1876 Typo. Wmk. 1 Perf. 14

72	A13	1c slate	2.50	1.50
a.		Perf. 14x12½		190.00
73	A13	2c orange	30.00	2.00
74	A13	4c ultra	110.00	7.00
a.		Perf. 12½	1,300.	200.00
75	A13	6c chocolate	70.00	7.50
76	A13	8c rose	90.00	1.90
77	A13	12c lilac	50.00	3.50
78	A13	24c green	60.00	5.00
79	A13	48c red brown	110.00	17.50
80	A13	96c bister	475.00	250.00
		Nos. 72-80 (9)	997.50	295.90

See Nos. 107-111. For surcharges see Nos. 93-95, 98-101.

Stamps Surcharged by Brush-like Pen Lines

Surcharge Types:
Type a - Two horiz. lines.
Type b - Two lines, one horiz., one vert.
Type c - Three lines, two horiz., one vert.
Type d - One horiz. line.

On Nos. 75 and 67
1878 Perf. 10, 14

82	A13(a)	(1c) on 6c choc	37.50	32.50
83	A12(b)	(1c) on 6c blue	140.00	65.00
84	A13(b)	(1c) on 6c choc	175.00	85.00

On Nos. O3, O8-O10

85	A13(c)	(1c) on 4c ultra	175.00	85.00
a.		Type b		2,500.
86	A13(c)	(1c) on 6c choc	200.00	80.00
87	A5(c)	(2c) on 8c rose	750.00	175.00
88A	A13(b)	(2c) on 8c rose	250.00	90.00

On Nos. O1, O3, O6-O7

89	A5(d)	(1c) on 1c blk	150.00	75.00
89A	A5(d)	(2c) on 8c rose	—	
90	A13(d)	(1c) on 1c sl	125.00	50.00
91	A13(d)	(2c) on 2c org	250.00	60.00

The provisional values of Nos. 82 to 91 were established by various official decrees. The horizontal lines crossed out the old value, "OFFICIAL," or both.

Nos. 69 and 80 Surcharged with New Values in Black

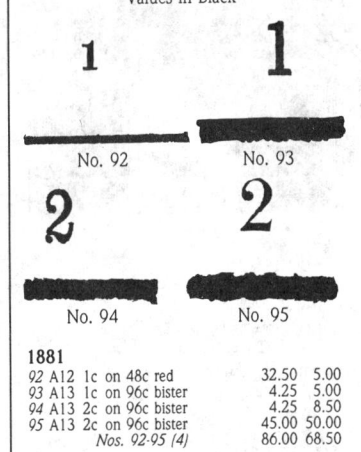

No. 92 No. 93
No. 94 No. 95

1881

92	A12	1c on 48c red	32.50	5.00
93	A13	1c on 96c bister	4.25	5.00
94	A13	2c on 96c bister	4.25	8.50
95	A13	2c on 96c bister	45.00	50.00
		Nos. 92-95 (4)	86.00	68.50

Unissued Official Stamps Surcharged with New Values

A24
No. 96 
No. 97 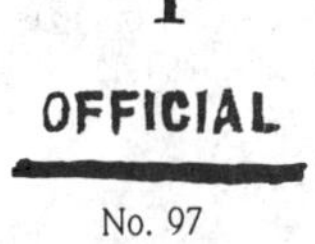
Nos. 99, 101

BRITISH GUIANA

2 OFFICIAL No. 102

1881
96	A13	1c on 12c lilac	110.00	65.00
97	A13	1c on 48c red brn	125.00	90.00
98	A24	2c on 12c lilac	325.00	225.00
99	A13	2c on 12c lilac	60.00	25.00
a.		"2" inverted		
b.		"2" double	700.00	475.00
100	A24	2c on 24c green	575.00	575.00
101	A13	2c on 24c green	70.00	37.50
a.		"2" Inverted		
d.		Double surcharge	750.00	
102	A13	3c on 24c green	200.00	125.00

A27

Typeset
ONE AND TWO CENTS.
Type I — Ship with three masts.
Type II — Brig with two masts.

"SPECIMEN"
Perforated Diagonally across Stamp

1882 Unwmk. Perf. 12
103	A27	1c black, lil rose, I	35.00	30.00
a.		Without "Specimen"	325.00	275.00
104	A27	1c black, lil rose, II	35.00	30.00
a.		Without "Specimen"	325.00	275.00
105	A27	2c black, yel, I	50.00	40.00
a.		Without "Specimen"	325.00	325.00
b.		Diagonal half used as 1c on cover		
106	A27	2c black, yel, II	50.00	42.50
a.		Without "Specimen"	325.00	325.00
		Nos. 103-106 (4)	170.00	142.50

Nos. 103-106 were typeset, 12 to a sheet, and, to prevent fraud on the government, the word "Specimen" was perforated across them before they were issued. There were 2 settings of the 1c and 3 settings of the 2c, thus there are 24 types of the former and 36 of the latter.

Type of 1876
1882 Typo. Wmk. 2 Perf. 14
107	A13	1c slate	7.00	.35
108	A13	2c orange	20.00	.45
a.		"2 CENTS" double		
109	A13	4c ultra	80.00	7.00
110	A13	6c brown	6.00	8.00
111	A13	8c rose	80.00	1.40
		Nos. 107-111 (5)	193.00	17.20

A28    A29

4 CENTS and $4
Type I — Figure "4" is 3mm high.
Type II — Figure "4" is 3½mm high.
6 CENTS
Type I — Top of "6" is flat.
Type II — Top of "6" turns downward.

"INLAND REVENUE" Overprint and Surcharged in Black

1889
112	A28	1c lilac	1.65	.70
113	A28	2c lilac	1.40	.45
114	A28	3c lilac	1.00	.45
115	A28	4c lilac, I	3.00	.45
116	A28	4c lilac, II	21.00	14.00
117	A28	6c lilac, I	20.00	5.00
118	A28	6c lilac, II	3.00	3.00
119	A28	8c lilac	1.75	.80
120	A28	10c lilac	6.00	2.00
121	A28	20c lilac	16.00	10.00
122	A28	40c lilac	20.00	15.00
123	A28	72c lilac	32.50	32.50
124	A28	$1 green	400.00	400.00
125	A28	$2 green	150.00	175.00
126	A28	$3 green	110.00	110.00
127	A28	$4 green, I	375.00	375.00
127A	A28	$4 green, II	900.00	900.00
128	A28	$5 green	225.00	200.00
		Nos. 112-128 (18)	2,287.	2,244.

For surcharges see Nos. 129, 148-151B.

No. 113 Surcharged "2" in Red
1889
129	A29	2c on 2c lilac		.80 .40

Inverted and double surcharges of "2" were privately made.

A30    A31

1889-1903 Typo.
130	A30	1c lilac & gray	1.75	1.00
131	A30	1c green ('90)	.50	.20
131A	A30	1c gray grn ('00)	3.25	1.75
132	A30	2c lilac & org	1.50	.15
133	A30	2c lil & rose ('00)	3.25	.25
134	A30	2c vio & blk, red ('01)	1.10	.90
135	A30	4c lilac & ultra	4.00	1.25
a.		4c lilac & blue	12.00	2.00
136	A30	5c ultra ('91)	2.75	.25
137	A30	6c lilac & mar	6.00	6.00
a.		6c lilac & brown	30.00	8.50
138	A30	6c gray blk & ultra ('02)	6.00	10.00
139	A30	6c lilac & rose	8.00	.75
140	A30	8c lil & blk ('90)	3.00	2.25
141	A30	12c lilac & vio	8.00	1.75
142	A30	24c lilac & grn	7.00	2.25
143	A30	48c lilac & ver	15.00	8.50
144	A30	48c dk gray & lil brn ('01)	27.50	27.50
a.		48c gray & purple brown	50.00	35.00
145	A30	60c gray grn & car ('03)	60.00	65.00
146	A30	72c lil & org brn	25.00	30.00
a.		72c lilac & yellow brown	70.00	75.00
147	A30	96c lilac & carmine	70.00	75.00
a.		96c lilac & rose	75.00	80.00
		Nos. 130-147 (19)	253.60	234.75

Stamps of the 1889-1903 issue with pen or revenue cancellation sell for a small fraction of the above quotations.
See Nos. 160-177.

Red Surcharge
1890
148	A31	1c on $1 grn & blk	1.00	.40
a.		Double surcharge	80.00	80.00
149	A31	1c on $2 grn & blk	.55	.55
a.		Double surcharge	80.00	80.00
150	A31	1c on $3 grn & blk	1.50	1.25
a.		Double surcharge	90.00	90.00
151	A31	1c on $4 grn & blk, type I	2.00	5.00
a.		Double surcharge	80.00	
151B	A31	1c on $4 grn & blk, type II	10.00	22.50
c.		Double surcharge		
		Nos. 148-151B (5)	15.05	29.70

Mt. Roraima — A32

Kaieteur (Old Man's) Falls — A33

1898 Wmk. 1 Engr.
152	A32	1c car & gray blk	2.75	.90
153	A33	2c indigo & brn	6.00	1.00
a.		Horiz. pair, imperf. between	4.500.	
b.		2c blue & brown	15.00	1.50
154	A32	5c brown & grn	25.00	5.00
155	A33	10c red & blue blk	14.00	20.00
156	A32	15c blue & red brn	22.50	15.00
		Nos. 152-156 (5)	70.25	41.90

60th anniv. of Queen Victoria's accession to the throne.

Nos. 154-156 Surcharged in Black TWO CENTS.
1899
157	A32	2c on 5c brn & grn	2.00	1.65
a.		Without period	60.00	60.00
158	A33	2c on 10c red & bl black	1.00	1.50
a.		"GENTS"	55.00	75.00
b.		Inverted surcharge	300.00	350.00
c.		Without period	22.50	45.00

159	A32	2c on 15c bl & red brown	1.50	1.50
a.		Without period	50.00	55.00
b.		Double surcharge	425.00	525.00
c.		Inverted surcharge	300.00	350.00
		Nos. 157-159 (3)	4.50	4.65

There are many slight errors in the setting of this surcharge, such as: small "E" in "CENTS"; no period and narrow "C"; comma between "T" and "S"; dash between "TWO" and "CENTS"; comma between "N" and "T."

Ship Type of 1889-1903
1905-10 Chalky Paper Wmk. 3
160	A30	1c gray green	1.50	.30
a.		1c blue green, ordinary paper ('10)	3.50	1.50
b.		Booklet pane of 6		
161	A30	2c vio & blk, red	2.50	.20
162	A30	4c lilac & ultra	12.00	8.50
163	A30	5c lil & blue, bl	7.75	3.75
164	A30	6c gray black & ultra	14.00	20.00
165	A30	12c lilac & vio	17.50	27.50
166	A30	24c lil & grn ('06)	3.50	4.25
167	A30	48c gray & vio brn	11.00	17.50
168	A30	60c gray grn & car rose	12.50	55.00
169	A30	72c lil & org brn ('07)	32.50	60.00
170	A30	96c blk & red, yel ('06)	35.00	42.50
		Nos. 160-170 (11)	149.75	239.50

The 2c-60c exist on ordinary paper.

A34    George V — A35

Black Overprint
171	A34	$2.40 grn & vio	190.00	190.00

Ship Type of 1889-1903
Ordinary Paper
TWO CENTS
Type I — Only the upper right corner of the flag touches the mast.
Type II — The entire right side of the flag touches the mast.

1907
172	A30	2c red, type I	3.75	.30
b.		2c red, type II	1.00	.25
174	A30	4c brown & vio	3.25	1.65
175	A30	5c blue	5.00	.70
176	A30	6c gray & black	12.50	5.00
177	A30	12c orange & vio	5.50	5.00
		Nos. 172-177 (5)	30.00	12.65

1913-16 Perf. 14
178	A35	1c green	1.75	.20
179	A35	2c scarlet	.85	.20
a.		2c carmine	.65	.20
180	A35	4c brn & red vio	1.10	.40
181	A35	5c ultra	1.10	.45
182	A35	6c gray & black	1.10	.95
183	A35	12c org & vio	1.50	1.50

Chalky Paper
184	A35	24c dl vio & grn	2.50	2.50
185	A35	48c blk & vio brn	6.00	6.00
186	A35	60c grn & car	13.00	19.00
187	A35	72c dl vio & org brn	24.00	30.00

Surface Colored Paper
188	A35	96c blk & red, yel	24.00	30.00

Paper Colored Through
189	A35	96c blk & red, yel ('16)	17.00	21.00
		Nos. 178-189 (12)	93.90	112.20

The 72c and late printings of the 2c and 5c are from redrawn dies. The ruled lines behind the value are thin and faint, making the tablet appear lighter than before. The shading lines in other parts of the stamps are also lighter.

1921-27 Wmk. 4
191	A35	1c green	1.75	.25
192	A35	2c rose red	1.50	.20
193	A35	2c dp vio ('23)	.90	.15
194	A35	4c brn & vio	2.00	.15
195	A35	6c ultra	1.60	.25
196	A35	12c org & vio	1.65	1.40

Chalky Paper
197	A35	24c dl vio & grn	2.75	2.75
198	A35	48c blk & vio brn ('26)	7.50	2.75
199	A35	60c grn & car ('26)	7.50	25.00
200	A35	72c dl vio & brn org	9.00	22.50
201	A35	96c blk & red, yel ('27)	12.50	20.00
		Nos. 191-201 (11)	48.65	75.40

Plowing a Rice Field — A36

Indian Shooting Fish — A37

Kaieteur Falls — A38

Georgetown, Public Buildings — A39

1931, July 21 Engr. Perf. 12½
205	A36	1c blue green	1.25	.50
206	A37	2c dk brown	1.25	.45
207	A38	4c car rose	2.75	1.75
208	A39	6c ultra	2.25	2.50
209	A38	$1 violet	24.00	30.00
		Nos. 205-209 (5)	31.50	35.20

Cent. of the union of Berbice, Demerara and Essequibo to form the Colony of British Guiana.

A40    A41

Gold Mining — A42

Shooting Logs over Falls — A44

Kaieteur Falls — A43

Stabroek Market — A45

Forest Road — A47

Sugar Cane in Punts — A46

Victoria Regia Lilies — A48

BRITISH GUIANA

Mt. Roraima — A49

Sir Walter Raleigh and Son — A50

Botanical Gardens — A51

1934, Oct. 1		Perf. 12½	
210 A40	1c green	.40	.25
211 A41	2c brown	.75	.20
212 A42	3c carmine	.30	.15
b.	Perf. 12½x13½ ('43)	.30	.15
c.	Perf. 13x13½ ('49)	.30	.15
213 A43	4c vio black	1.50	.50
a.	Vert. pair, imperf. horiz.		8,000.
214 A44	6c dp ultra	2.00	1.75
215 A45	12c orange	.15	.20
a.	Perf. 13½x13 ('51)	.20	.40
216 A46	24c rose violet	3.00	1.75
217 A47	48c black	10.50	9.25
218 A43	50c green	12.00	15.00
219 A48	60c brown	21.00	24.00
220 A49	72c rose violet	1.25	1.00
221 A50	96c black	20.00	25.00
222 A51	$1 violet	25.00	22.50
	Nos. 210-222 (13)	97.85	101.55

See Nos. 236, 238, 240.

Common Design Types pictured following the introduction.

Silver Jubilee Issue
Common Design Type

1935, May 6		Perf. 13½x14	
223 CD301	2c gray blk & ultra	.20	.20
224 CD301	6c blue & brown	.85	.40
225 CD301	12c indigo & grn	1.40	1.00
226 CD301	24c brt vio & ind	3.25	3.25
	Nos. 223-226 (4)	5.70	4.85

Coronation Issue
Common Design Type

1937, May 12		Perf. 13½x14	
227 CD302	2c brown	.15	.15
228 CD302	4c gray black	.15	.15
229 CD302	6c bright ultra	.20	.20
	Nos. 227-229 (3)	.50	.50

A52  A53
A54 A56
A55 A57
A58

Victoria Regia Lilies and Jacanas — A59

1938-52	Engr. Wmk. 4	Perf. 12½	
230 A52	1c green	.20	.15
b.	Perf. 14x13 ('49)	.20	.20
231 A53	2c violet blk, perf. 13x14 ('49)	.20	.15
b.	Perf. 12½	.45	.15
232 A54	4c black & rose, perf. 13x14 ('52)	.35	.15
a.	Perf. 12½	.55	.15
c.	Vert. pair, imperf. between	6,500.	6,000.
233 A55	6c deep ultra, perf. 13x14 ('49)	.20	.15
a.	Perf. 12½	.30	.15
234 A56	24c deep green	.95	.15
a.	Wmk. upright	20.00	8.75
235 A53	36c purple	1.40	.15
a.	Perf. 13x14 ('51)	1.90	.25
236 A47	48c orange yel	.45	.35
a.	Perf. 14x13 ('51)	1.10	1.10
237 A57	60c brown	8.50	3.00
238 A50	96c brown vio	1.90	2.25
a.	Perf. 12½x13½ ('44)	3.00	3.50
239 A58	$1 deep violet	7.75	.30
a.	Perf. 14x13 ('51)	225.00	300.00
240 A49	$2 rose vio ('45)	3.25	11.00
a.	Perf. 14x13 ('50)	6.00	11.00
241 A59	$3 orange brn ('45)	19.00	21.00
a.	Perf. 14x13 ('52)	17.50	37.50
	Nos. 230-241 (12)	44.15	38.80

The watermark on No. 234 is sideways.

Catalogue values for unused stamps in this section, from this point to the end of the section, are for Never Hinged items.

Peace Issue
Common Design Type

1946, Oct. 21		Perf. 13½x14	
242 CD303	3c carmine	.15	.15
243 CD303	6c deep blue	.15	.15

Silver Wedding Issue
Common Design Type

1948, Dec. 20	Photo.	Perf. 14x14½	
244 CD304	3c scarlet	.15	.15

Engr.
Perf. 11½x11
245 CD305 $3 orange brown   11.00 17.00

UPU Issue
Common Design Types
Engr.; Name Typo. on 6c and 12c
Perf. 13½x14, 11x11½

1949, Oct. 10		Wmk. 4	
246 CD306	4c rose carmine	.35	.15
247 CD307	6c indigo	.55	.55
248 CD308	12c orange	.70	.70
249 CD309	24c blue green	1.40	1.40
	Nos. 246-249 (4)	3.00	2.80

University Issue
Common Design Types

1951, Feb. 16	Engr.	Perf. 14x14½	
250 CD310	3c carmine & black	.30	.20
251 CD311	6c dp ultra & black	.40	.40

Coronation Issue
Common Design Type

1953, June 2		Perf. 13½x13	
252 CD312	4c carmine & black	.20	.15

G.P.O., Georgetown — A60

Indian Shooting Fish — A61

Designs: 2c, Botanical gardens. 3c, Victoria regia lilies and jacanas. 5c, Map. 6c, Rice combine. 8c, Sugar cane entering factory. 12c, Felling greenheart tree. 24c, Bauxite mining. 36c, Mt. Roraima. 48c, Kaieteur Falls. 72c, Arapaima (fish). $1, Toucan. $2, Dredging gold. $5, Coat of Arms.

Engr., Center Litho. on $1
Perf. 12½x13, 13

1954, Dec. 1		Wmk. 4	
253 A60	1c black	.15	.15
254 A60	2c dark green	.15	.15
255 A60	3c red brn & ol	2.50	.15
256 A60	4c violet	.15	.15
257 A60	5c black & red	.25	.15
258 A60	6c yellow green	.15	.15
259 A60	8c ultramarine	.15	.15
260 A61	12c brown & black	.50	.30
261 A61	24c orange & black	3.50	.15
262 A60	36c black & rose	1.25	.45
263 A61	48c red brn & ultra	.60	.35
264 A61	72c emerald & rose	9.50	2.00
265 A60	$1 blk, yel, grn & sal	10.00	1.90
266 A60	$2 magenta	10.00	3.25
267 A61	$5 black & ultra	10.50	12.00
	Nos. 253-267 (15)	49.35	21.45

See Nos. 279-287.

Clasped Hands — A62

1961, Oct. 23	Photo.	Perf. 14½x14	Wmk. 314
268 A62	5c sal pink & brown	.15	.15
269 A62	6c lt blue grn & brown	.15	.15
270 A62	30c lt orange & brown	.40	.40
	Nos. 268-270 (3)	.70	.70

Fourth annual History and Culture Week.

Freedom from Hunger Issue
Common Design Type

1963, June 4		Perf. 14x14½	
271 CD314	20c lilac	.45	.45

Red Cross Centenary Issue
Common Design Type
Wmk. 314

1963, Sept. 2	Litho.	Perf. 13	
272 CD315	5c black & red	.15	.15
273 CD315	20c ultra & red	.65	.65

Queen Types of 1954
Engr.; Center Litho. on $1
Perf. 12½x13, 13

1963-65		Wmk. 314	
279 A60	3c red brn & ol ('65)	4.75	4.75
280 A60	5c black & red ('64)	.15	.15
281 A61	12c brown & blk ('64)	.15	.15
282 A60	24c orange & black	1.50	.15
283 A60	36c black & rose	.50	.15
284 A61	48c red brn & ultra	1.00	2.00
285 A61	72c emerald & rose	3.25	16.00
286 A60	$1 blk, yel, grn & sal	5.75	.75
287 A60	$2 magenta	6.25	12.50
	Nos. 279-287 (9)	23.30	36.60

Weight Lifter A63

1964, Oct. 1	Photo.	Perf. 13x13½	
290 A63	5c orange	.15	.15
291 A63	8c blue	.15	.15
292 A63	25c carmine rose	.40	.40
	Nos. 290-292 (3)	.70	.70

18th Olympic Games, Tokyo, Oct. 10-25.

ITU Issue
Common Design Type
Perf. 11x11½

1965, May 17		Wmk. 314	
293 CD317	5c emerald & olive	.15	.15
294 CD317	25c lt blue & brt pink	.45	.45

Intl. Cooperation Year Issue
Common Design Type

1965, Oct. 25	Wmk. 314	Perf. 14½	
295 CD318	5c blue grn & claret	.15	.15
296 CD318	25c lt vio & green	.50	.50

Winston Churchill and St. George's Cathedral, Georgetown A64

1966, Jan. 24	Photo.	Perf. 14x14½	
297 A64	5c multicolored	.15	.15
298 A64	25c dp blue, blk & gold	.60	.50

Sir Winston Leonard Spencer Churchill (1874-1965), statesman and WWII leader.

Royal Visit Issue
Common Design Type

1966, Feb. 4	Litho.	Perf. 11x12	
299 CD320	3c violet blue	.25	.20
300 CD320	25c dark car rose	1.40	1.10

POSTAGE DUE STAMPS

Catalogue values for unused stamps in this section are for Never Hinged items.

D1

1940-52	Typo.	Perf. 13½x14	Wmk. 4
J1 D1	1c green	1.25	1.25
a.	Wmk. 4a (error)	40.00	
J2 D1	2c black	1.25	1.25
a.	Wmk. 4a (error)	35.00	
J3 D1	4c ultra ('52)	.80	1.50
a.	Wmk. 4a (error)	35.00	
J4 D1	12c carmine	3.50	7.00
	Nos. J1-J4 (4)	6.80	11.50

The 2c and 12c are on chalky paper as well as ordinary paper.

WAR TAX STAMP

Regular Issue No. 179 Overprinted

War Tax

1918, Jan. 4	Wmk. 3	Perf. 14	
MR1 A35	2c scarlet	.15	.15

OFFICIAL STAMPS

Counterfeit overprints exist.

No. 50 Overprinted in Red

OFFICIAL

1875	Unwmk.	Perf. 10	
O1 A5	1c black	40.00	16.00
a.	Horiz. pair, imperf btwn.		

Nos. 51, 53-54, 68 Overprinted in Black

OFFICIAL

O2 A5	2c orange	140.00	16.00
O3 A5	8c rose	375.00	125.00
O4 A5	12c lilac	1,400.	550.00
O5 A12	24c green	850.00	275.00

For surcharges see Nos. 87, 89, 89A, 96, 102.

Nos. 72-76 Overprinted "OFFICIAL" Similar to #O2-O5

1877	Wmk. 1	Perf. 14	
O6 A13	1c slate	225.00	95.00
a.	Vert. pair, imperf btwn.		
O7 A13	2c orange	90.00	16.00
O8 A13	4c ultramarine	100.00	35.00
O9 A13	6c chocolate	2,750.	625.00
O10 A13	8c rose	2,250.	500.00

The type A13 12c lilac, 24c green and 48c red brown overprinted "OFFICIAL" were never placed in use. A few copies of the 12c and 24c have been seen but the 48c is only known surcharged with new value for provisional use in 1881. See Nos. 97-101.

For surcharges see Nos. 85-86, 88A, 90-91.

BRITISH HONDURAS

'brĭ-tĭsh hän-'dŭr-əs

LOCATION — Central America bordering on Caribbean on east, Mexico on north and Guatemala on west.
GOVT. — British Crown Colony
AREA — 8,867 sq. mi.
POP. — 130,000 (est. 1972)
CAPITAL — Belmopan

Before British Honduras became a colony (subordinate to Jamaica) in 1862, it was a settlement under British influence. In 1884 it became an independent colony. In 1973 the colony changed its name to Belize.

12 Pence = 1 Shilling
100 Cents = 1 Dollar (1888)

Catalogue values for unused stamps in this country are for Never Hinged items, beginning with Scott 127 in the regular postage section, Scott J1 in the postage due section.

Values for unused stamps are for examples with original gum as defined in the catalogue introduction. Very fine examples of Nos. 1-37 will have perforations touching the design on at least one side due to the narrow spacing of the stamps on the plates. Stamps with perfs clear of the design on all four sides are extremely scarce and will command higher prices.

Queen Victoria — A1

1866 Unwmk. Typo. Perf. 14
1	A1	1p blue	50.00	50.00
a.	Horiz. pair, imperf. btwn.			
2	A1	6p rose	250.00	100.00
3	A1	1sh rose	250.00	100.00
		Nos. 1-3 (3)	550.00	250.00

The 6p and 1sh were printed only in a sheet with the 1p. The 1sh is known in se-tenant gutter pairs with the 1p and the 6p.

1872 Wmk. 1 Perf. 12½
4	A1	1p blue	60.00	18.00
5	A1	3p brown	100.00	70.00
6	A1	6p rose	190.00	30.00
7	A1	1sh green	225.00	22.50
a.	Horiz. pair, imperf. btwn.			12,500.
		Nos. 4-7 (4)	575.00	140.50

For surcharges see Nos. 18-19.
No. 7a is unique and has faults.

1877-79 Perf. 14
8	A1	1p blue	50.00	14.00
a.	Horiz. strip of 3, imperf. btwn.		4,500.	
9	A1	3p brown	85.00	17.50
10	A1	4p violet ('79)	125.00	12.50
11	A1	6p rose ('78)	300.00	175.00
12	A1	1sh green	225.00	12.50
		Nos. 8-12 (5)	785.00	231.50

For surcharges see Nos. 20-21, 29.

1882-87 Wmk. 2
13	A1	1p blue ('84)	40.00	18.00
14	A1	1p rose ('84)	20.00	12.50
a.	Diagonal half used as ½p on cover			
15	A1	4p violet	70.00	4.00
16	A1	6p yellow ('85)	250.00	175.00
17	A1	1sh gray ('87)	250.00	150.00
		Nos. 13-17 (5)	630.00	359.50

For surcharges see Nos. 22-26, 28-35.

Stamps of 1872-87 Surcharged in Black **2 CENTS**

1888 Wmk. 1 Perf. 12½
18	A1	2c on 6p rose	120.00	100.00
19	A1	3c on 3p brown	10,000.	5,250.

Perf. 14
20	A1	2c on 6p rose	70.00	65.00
a.	Diagonal half used as 1c on cover			225.00
b.	Double surcharge		1,300.	1,300.
c.	"2" with curved tail		850.00	850.00
21	A1	3c on 3p brown	60.00	55.00

Wmk. 2
22	A1	2c on 1p rose	9.00	17.50
a.	Diagonal half used as 1c on cover			250.00
b.	Double surcharge		1,000.	950.00
c.	Inverted surcharge		1,300.	1,250.
23	A1	10c on 4p violet	35.00	15.00
a.	Inverted surcharge			
24	A1	20c on 6p yellow	27.50	30.00
25	A1	50c on 1sh gray	350.00	500.00

No. 25 with Additional Surcharge in Red or Black **TWO**

26	A1	2c (R) on 50c on 1sh gray	40.00	75.00
a.	"TWO" in black		8,750.	8,500.
b.	"TWO" double (Blk + R)		8,750.	8,000.
c.	Diagonal half used as 1c on cover			325.00

Stamps of 1872-87 Surcharged in Black **2 CENTS**

1888-89
28	A1	2c on 1p rose	.50	1.25
a.	Diagonal half used as 1c on cover			110.00
29	A1	3c on 3p brown	1.25	1.50
30	A1	4c on 4p violet	2.50	1.75
31	A1	20c on 6p yel ('89)	10.00	15.00
32	A1	50c on 1sh gray	20.00	50.00
		Nos. 28-32 (5)	34.25	69.50

For other examples of this surcharge see Nos. 36, 47. For overprint see No. 51.

No. 30 with Additional Surcharge in Black or Red **6**

1891
33	A1	6c (Blk) on 10c on 4p	1.00	3.75
a.	"6" and bar inverted		3,000.	
b.	"6" only inverted			3,000.
34	A1	6c (R) on 10c on 4p	.75	2.50
a.	"6" and bar inverted		500.	500.
b.	"6" only inverted			3,000.

Stamps similar to No. 33 but with "SIX" instead of "6," both with and without bar, were prepared but not regularly issued. See No. 37.

No. 29 with Additional Surcharge in Black **FIVE**

1891
35	A1	5c on 3c on 3p brown	1.50	3.25
a.	Double surcharge of "Five" and bar		200.00	250.00

Black Surcharge, Type "c"
36	A1	6c on 3p blue	7.50	7.50

No. 36 with Additional Surcharge like Nos. 33-34 in Red

1891
37	A1	15c (R) on 6c on 3p blue	7.50	20.00
a.	Double surcharge			

A8 2c A9 5c

1891-98 Wmk. 2 Perf. 14
38	A8	1c green	1.00	1.00
39	A8	2c carmine rose	1.00	.25
40	A8	3c brown	3.75	1.50
41	A8	5c ultra ('95)	12.50	.90
42	A8	6c ultramarine	3.50	1.00
43	A8	10c vio & grn ('95)	8.50	8.50
44	A8	12c vio & green	3.50	2.50
45	A8	24c yellow & blue	6.00	12.50
46	A8	25c red brn & grn ('98)	30.00	60.00
		Nos. 38-46 (9)	69.75	88.15

Numeral tablet on Nos. 43-46 has lined background with colorless value and "c."
For overprints see Nos. 48-50.

Type of 1866 Surcharged Type "c"

1892
47	A1	1c on 1p green	.30	.80

Regular Issue Overprinted **REVENUE** in Black

1899
48	A8	5c ultramarine	4.50	2.25
a.	"BEVENUE"		70.00	80.00
49	A8	10c lilac & green	3.50	11.00
a.	"BEVENUE"		190.00	225.00
50	A8	25c red brn & grn	3.00	25.00
a.	"BEVENUE"		135.00	135.00
51	A1	50c on 1sh gray (No. 32)	135.00	275.00
a.	"BEVENUE"		2,750.	2,750.
		Nos. 48-51 (4)	146.00	313.25

The overprint is found in two lengths: 12mm (43 to the pane) and 11mm (17 to the pane). The "U" is found in both a tall, narrow type and the more common small type.

1899-1901
52	A9	5c gray blk & ultra, bl ('00)	7.50	1.50
53	A9	10c vio & grn ('01)	6.50	6.50
54	A9	50c grn & car rose	16.00	37.50
55	A9	$1 grn & car rose	35.00	60.00
56	A9	$2 green & ultra	55.00	75.00
57	A9	$5 green & black	225.00	275.00
		Nos. 52-57 (6)	345.00	455.50

Numeral tablet on Nos. 53-54 has lined background with colorless value and "c."

King Edward VII — A10

1902-04 Typo. Wmk. 2
58	A10	1c gray grn & grn ('04)	4.00	12.50
59	A10	2c vio & blk, red	2.00	.35
60	A10	5c gray blk & ultra, blue	3.00	.80
61	A10	20c dl vio & vio ('04)	5.00	12.00
		Nos. 58-61 (4)	14.00	25.65

1904-06 Chalky Paper Wmk. 3
62	A10	1c green	.30	.50
63	A10	2c vio & blk, red	1.25	.15
64	A10	5c blk & ultra, bl ('05)	1.75	.30
65	A10	10c vio & grn ('06)	4.00	9.00
66	A10	25c vio & grn ('06)	6.00	25.00
67	A10	50c grn & car rose ('06)	10.00	35.00
68	A10	$1 grn & car rose ('06)	25.00	50.00
69	A10	$2 grn & ultra ('06)	55.00	100.00
70	A10	$5 grn & blk ('06)	190.00	225.00
		Nos. 62-71 (9)	293.30	444.95

The 1c and 2c exist also on ordinary paper.

1909 Ordinary Paper
72	A10	2c carmine	3.00	.25
73	A10	5c ultramarine	3.00	.25

1911
74	A10	25c black, green	6.00	27.50

Numeral tablet on #61, 65-68, 74 has lined background with colorless value and "c."

King George V
A11   A12

1913-17 Wmk. 3 Perf. 14
75	A11	1c green	1.00	.40
76	A11	2c scarlet	1.10	.30
a.	2c carmine		.90	.95
77	A11	3c orange ('17)	.45	.20
78	A11	5c ultra	2.25	1.25

Chalky Paper
79	A12	10c dl vio & ol grn	2.50	5.00
80	A12	25c blk, gray grn	3.75	7.50
a.	25c black, emerald		2.50	12.50
b.	25c blk, bl grn, olive back		3.25	6.00
81	A10	50c vio & ultra, bl	4.50	9.00
82	A11	$1 black & scar	8.00	17.50
83	A11	$2 grn & dull vio	32.50	37.50
84	A11	$5 vio & blk, red	225.00	250.00
		Nos. 75-84 (10)	281.05	328.65

See No. 91. For overprints see Nos. MR2-MR5.

With Moire Overprint in Violet

1915
85	A11	1c green	1.50	7.50
86	A11	2c carmine	1.10	2.00
87	A11	5c ultramarine	.75	3.25
		Nos. 85-87 (3)	3.35	12.75

For overprint see No. MR1.

Peace Commemorative Issue

Seal of Colony and George V — A13

1921, Apr. 28 Engr.
89	A13	2c carmine	2.50	1.00

Similar to A13 but without "Peace Peace"

1922 Wmk. 4
90	A13	4c dark gray	2.75	.95

Type of 1913-17

1921 Typo. Wmk. 4
91	A11	1c green	2.00	5.00

A14

1922-33 Typo. Wmk. 4
92	A14	1c green ('29)	.80	1.10
93	A14	2c dark brown	.35	.35
94	A14	2c rose red ('27)	.85	.70
95	A14	3c orange ('33)	3.50	1.90
96	A14	4c gray ('29)	1.25	.25
97	A14	5c ultramarine	1.00	.20

Chalky Paper
98	A14	10c olive grn & lil	1.25	.35
99	A14	25c black, emerald	1.50	4.00
100	A14	50c ultra & vio, bl	4.00	9.00
101	A14	$1 scarlet & blk	6.50	12.50
102	A14	$2 red vio & grn	22.50	50.00

Wmk. 3
103	A14	25c black, emerald	4.25	17.50
104	A14	$5 blk & vio, red	200.00	190.00
		Nos. 92-104 (13)	247.75	286.80

For surcharges see Nos. B1-B5.

Common Design Types pictured following the introduction.

Silver Jubilee Issue
Common Design Type
Perf. 11x12

1935, May 6 Engr. Wmk. 4
108	CD301	3c black & ultra	.65	.65
109	CD301	4c indigo & grn	1.10	1.40
110	CD301	5c ultra & brn	2.00	2.00
111	CD301	25c brn vio & ind	4.00	6.00
		Nos. 108-111 (4)	7.75	10.05
		Set, never hinged	12.00	

Coronation Issue
Common Design Type

1937, May 12 Perf. 13½x14
112	CD302	3c deep orange	.15	.20
113	CD302	4c gray black	.25	.20
114	CD302	5c bright ultra	.25	.35
		Nos. 112-114 (3)	.65	.75
		Set, never hinged	1.75	

Mayan Figures — A15

British Honduras stamps can be mounted in the Scott British Honduras album.

BRITISH HONDURAS

Chicle Tapping — A16
Cohune Palm — A17 
Local Products A18 
Grapefruit Industry A19 
Mahogany Logs in River — A20 
Sergeant's Cay — A21 
Dory — A22 
Chicle Industry A23 
Court House, Belize — A24 
Mahogany Cutting — A25 
Seal of Colony — A26 

1938		Perf. 11x11½, 11½x11		
115	A15	1c green & violet	.15	.70
116	A16	2c car & black	.15	.70
a.		Perf. 12 ('47)	1.10	.75
117	A17	3c brown & dk vio	.20	.50
118	A18	4c green & black	.20	.50
119	A19	5c slate bl & red vio	.35	.30
120	A20	10c brown & yel grn	.45	.50
121	A21	15c blue & brown	.65	.50
122	A22	25c green & ultra	1.10	.85
123	A23	50c dk vio & blk	7.00	2.50
124	A24	$1 ol green & car	12.50	5.25
125	A25	$2 rose lake & ind	14.00	13.00
126	A26	$5 brn & carmine	13.00	19.00
		Nos. 115-126 (12)	49.75	44.30
		Set, never hinged	70.00	

Issued: 3c-5c, 1/10; 1c, 2c, 10c-50c, 2/14; $1-$5, 2/28.

Catalogue values for unused stamps in this section, from this point to the end of the section, are for Never Hinged items.

Peace Issue
Common Design Type
Perf. 13½x14

1946, Sept. 9	Engr.	Wmk. 4		
127	CD303	3c brown	.15	.15
128	CD303	5c deep blue	.15	.15

Silver Wedding Issue
Common Design Types

1948, Oct. 1	Photo.	Perf. 14x14½		
129	CD304	4c dark green	.20	.20

Engraved; Name Typographed
Perf. 11½x11

| 130 | CD305 | $5 light brown | 22.50 | 25.00 |

St. George's Cay — A27
H.M.S. Merlin — A28 

1949, Jan. 10	Engr.	Perf. 12½		
131	A27	1c green & ultra	.15	.15
132	A27	3c yel brn & dp blue	.20	.20
133	A27	4c purple & brn ol	.30	.30
134	A28	5c dk blue & brown	.30	.30
135	A28	10c vio brn & blue grn	.50	.50
136	A28	15c ultra & emerald	.90	.90
		Nos. 131-136 (6)	2.35	2.35

Battle of St. George's Cay, 150th anniv.

UPU Issue
Common Design Types
Perf. 13½, 11x11½

1949, Oct. 10	Engr.	Wmk. 4		
137	CD306	4c blue green	.35	.35
138	CD307	5c indigo	.55	.55
139	CD308	10c chocolate	.90	.90
140	CD309	25c blue	1.50	1.50
		Nos. 137-140 (4)	3.30	3.30

University Issue
Common Design Types

1951, Feb. 16	Engr.	Perf. 14x14½		
141	CD310	3c choc & purple	.35	.35
142	CD311	5c choc & green	.65	.65

Coronation Issue
Common Design Type

1953, June 2		Perf. 13½x13		
143	CD312	4c dk green & black	.40	.40

Arms — A29
Maya — A30 

Designs: 2c, Tapir. 3c, Legislative Council Chamber and mace. 4c, Pine industry. 5c, Spiny lobster. 10c, Stanley Field Airport. 15c, Mayan frieze. 25c, Blue butterfly. $1, Armadillo. $2, Hawkesworth Bridge. $5, Pine Ridge orchid.

1953-57		Engr.	Perf. 13½	
144	A29	1c gray blk & green	.15	.15
145	A29	2c gray blk & brn, perf. 14 ('57)	.15	.15
a.		Perf. 13½	.30	.30
146	A29	3c mag & rose lil, perf. 14 ('57)	.15	.15
		Perf. 13½	.15	.15
147	A29	4c grn & dk brn	.15	.15
148	A29	5c car & ol brn, perf. 14 ('57)	.20	.20
		Perf. 13½	.45	.45
149	A29	10c ultra & bl gray	.20	.20
150	A29	15c vio & yel grn	.35	.35
151	A29	25c brown & ultra	3.50	1.75
152	A30	50c purple & brown	4.00	1.65
153	A29	$1 red brn & sl bl	4.00	3.50
154	A29	$2 gray & car	5.50	4.00
155	A30	$5 blue gray & pur	25.00	15.00
		Nos. 144-155 (12)	43.35	27.25

Issue dates: No. 148, May 15, Nos. 145-146, Sept. 18, perf. 13½, Sept. 2.
For overprints see Nos. 159-166.

View of Belize, 1842 — A31

Designs: 10c, Public seals, 1860 and 1960. 15c, Tamarind Tree, Newtown Barracks.

Perf. 11½x11

1960, July 1		Wmk. 314		
156	A31	2c green	.15	.15
157	A31	10c carmine	.25	.25
158	A31	15c blue	.45	.45
		Nos. 156-158 (3)	.85	.85

Cent. of the establishment of a local PO.

Nos. 145-146 and 149-150 Overprinted: "NEW CONSTITUTION/1960"

1961, Mar. 1	Wmk. 4	Perf. 14, 13		
159	A29	2c gray black & brn	.15	.15
160	A29	3c mag & rose lilac	.15	.15
161	A29	10c ultra & blue gray	.35	.35
162	A29	15c violet & yel green	.50	.30
		Nos. 159-162 (4)	1.15	.85

Nos. 144, 149, 151 and 152 Overprinted: "HURRICANE/HATTIE"

1962, Jan. 15		Perf. 13		
163	A29	1c gray black & green	.15	.15
164	A29	10c ultra & blue gray	.15	.15
165	A29	25c brown & ultra	.30	.30
166	A30	50c purple & brown	.70	.70
		Nos. 163-166 (4)	1.30	1.30

Hurricane Hattie struck Belize, Oct. 31, 1961.

Great Curassow A32

Birds: 2c, Red-legged honeycreeper. 3c, American jacana. 4c, Great kiskadee. 5c, Scarlet-rumped tanager. 10c, Scarlet macaw. 15c, Massena trogon. 25c, Redfooted booby. 50c, Keel-billed toucan. $1, Magnificent frigate bird. $2, Rufoustailed jacamar. $5, Montezuma oropendola.

Perf. 14x14½

1962, Apr. 2	Photo.	Wmk. 314		

Birds in Natural Colors; Black Inscriptions

167	A32	1c yellow	.90	.70
168	A32	2c gray	1.40	.15
a.		Green omitted	175.00	
169	A32	3c lt yel green	1.40	.85
a.		Dark grn (legs) omitted	250.00	
170	A32	4c lt gray	2.75	1.25
171	A32	5c buff	1.65	.15
172	A32	10c beige	1.90	.20
a.		Blue omitted	225.00	
173	A32	15c pale lemon	.90	.30
174	A32	25c bluish gray & pink	3.50	.25
175	A32	50c pale blue	5.00	.35
b.		Blue (beak & claw) omitted		
176	A32	$1 blue	7.75	.70
177	A32	$2 pale gray	8.25	2.50
178	A32	$5 light blue	24.00	12.50
		Nos. 167-178 (12)	59.40	19.90

For overprints see Nos. 182-186, 195-199.

1967		Wmk. 314 Sideways		

Colors as 1962 Issue

167a	A32	1c	.15	.15
168b	A32	2c	.15	.15
170a	A32	4c	.30	.25
171a	A32	5c	.55	.30
172b	A32	10c	.80	.65

173a	A32	15c	1.10	.95
175a	A32	50c	4.25	3.50
		Nos. 167a-175a (7)	7.30	5.95

Issued: 1c, 4c, 5c, 50c, 2/16; 2c, 10c, 15c, 11/28.

Freedom from Hunger Issue
Common Design Type

1963, June 4		Perf. 14x14½		
179	CD314	22c green	.85	.85

Red Cross Centenary Issue
Common Design Type
Wmk. 314

1963, Sept. 2	Litho.	Perf. 13		
180	CD315	4c black & red	.15	.15
181	CD315	22c ultra & red	1.40	1.40

Nos. 167, 169, 170, 172 and 174 Overprinted: "SELF GOVERNMENT / 1964"

1964	Photo.	Perf. 14x14½		
182	A32	1c multicolored	.15	.15
a.		Yellow omitted	125.00	
183	A32	3c multicolored	.15	.15
184	A32	4c multicolored	.15	.15
185	A32	10c multicolored	.30	.30
186	A32	25c multicolored	.55	.55
		Nos. 182-186 (5)	1.30	1.30

Attainment of self-government.

ITU Issue
Common Design Type
Perf. 11x11½

1965, May 17	Litho.	Wmk. 314		
187	CD317	2c ver & green	.15	.15
188	CD317	50c yel & red lilac	1.00	1.00

Intl. Cooperation Year Issue
Common Design Type

1965, Oct. 25		Perf. 14½		
189	CD318	1c bl grn & claret	.15	.15
190	CD318	22c lt violet & green	.75	.75

Churchill Memorial Issue
Common Design Type

1966, Jan. 24	Photo.	Perf. 14		

Design in Black, Gold and Carmine Rose

191	CD319	1c bright blue	.15	.15
192	CD319	4c green	.15	.15
193	CD319	22c brown	.65	.65
194	CD319	25c violet	.90	.90
		Nos. 191-194 (4)	1.85	1.85

Bird Type of 1962 Overprinted: "DEDICATION OF SITE / NEW CAPITAL / 9th OCTOBER 1965"
Wmk. 314 Sideways

1966, July 1		Perf. 14x14½		
195	A32	1c multicolored	.15	.15
196	A32	3c multicolored	.25	.15
197	A32	4c multicolored	.25	.25
198	A32	10c multicolored	.30	.25
199	A32	25c multicolored	.50	.50
		Nos. 195-199 (5)	1.45	1.20

Citrus Grove — A33

10c, Half Moon Cay & Lighthouse Reef. 22c, Hidden Valley Falls & Mountain Pine Ridge. 25c, Xunantunich Mayan ruins in Cayo district.

Perf. 14x14½

1966, Oct. 1	Photo.	Wmk. 314		
200	A33	5c multicolored	.15	.15
201	A33	10c multicolored	.20	.20
202	A33	22c multicolored	.25	.25
203	A33	25c multicolored	.40	.40
		Nos. 200-203 (4)	1.00	1.00

1st British Honduras stamp issue, cent.

International Tourist Year — A34

BRITISH HONDURAS

1967, Dec. 4   *Perf. 12½*

204	A34	5c Sailfish	.15	.15
205	A34	10c Deer	.15	.15
206	A34	22c Jaguar	.35	.35
207	A34	25c Tarpon	.45	.45
		Nos. 204-207 (4)	1.10	1.10

Schomburgkia Tibicinis — A35

Belizean Patriots' Memorial, Belize City, and Human Rights Flame — A36

Orchids: 10c, Maxillaria tenuifolia. 22c, Bletia purpurea. 25c, Sobralia macrantha.

Inscribed: "20th Anniversary of E.C.L.A."

Perf. 14½x14

1968, Apr. 16   Photo.   Wmk. 314

208	A35	5c violet & multi	.15	.15
209	A35	10c green & multi	.20	.20
210	A35	22c multicolored	.35	.35
211	A35	25c olive & multi	.50	.50
		Nos. 208-211 (4)	1.20	1.20

20th anniv. of the Economic Commission for Latin America. See #226-229, 255-258.

Perf. 13x13½

1968, July 15   Litho.   Wmk. 314

Design: 50c, Mayan motif stele, monument at new capital site and Human Rights flame.

| 212 | A36 | 22c multicolored | .30 | .30 |
| 213 | A36 | 50c multicolored | .70 | .70 |

International Human Rights Year.

BRITISH HONDURAS Jewfish — A37

Designs: 2c, White-lipped peccary. 3c, Grouper (sea bass). 4c, Collared anteater. 5c, Bonefish. 10c, Paca. 15c, Dolphinfish. 25c, Kinkajou. 50c, Yellow-and-green-banded muttonfish. $1, Tayra. $2, Great barracudas. $5, Mountain lion.

Perf. 13x12½

1968, Oct. 15   Unwmk.

214	A37	1c yellow & multi	.15	.15
215	A37	2c brt yel & multi	.15	.15
216	A37	3c pink & multi	.15	.15
217	A37	4c brt grn & multi	.15	.15
218	A37	5c brick red & multi	.15	.15
219	A37	10c lilac & multi	.20	.15
220	A37	15c org yel & multi	.25	.20
221	A37	25c multicolored	.45	.40
222	A37	50c bl grn & multi	.95	.85
223	A37	$1 ocher & multi	1.90	1.75
224	A37	$2 violet & multi	3.75	3.50
225	A37	$5 ultra & multi	8.25	7.50
		Nos. 214-225 (12)	16.50	15.10

See Nos. 234-240, Belize 327-339.
For overprints see Nos. 251-254, 281-282.

Orchid Type of 1968
Inscribed "Orchids of Belize"

Designs: 5c, Rhyncholaetia digbyana. 10c, Cattleya bowringiana. 22c, Lycaste cochleatum. 25c, Coryanthes speciosum.

Perf. 14½x14

1969, Apr. 9   Photo.   Wmk. 314

226	A35	5c Prus blue & multi	.15	.15
227	A35	10c olive bis & multi	.30	.30
228	A35	22c yellow grn & multi	.70	.70
229	A35	25c violet blue & multi	.85	.85
		Nos. 226-229 (4)	2.00	2.00

Hardwood Trees — A38

Virgin and Child, by Giovanni Bellini — A39

1969, Sept. 1   Litho.   *Perf. 14*

230	A38	5c Ziricote	.15	.15
231	A38	10c Rosewood	.15	.15
232	A38	22c Mayflower	.30	.30
233	A38	25c Mahogany	.40	.40
		Nos. 230-233 (4)	1.00	1.00

Timber industry of British Honduras. Issued in sheets of 9 (3x3) on simulated wood background.

Fish-Animal Type of 1968

Designs: ½c, Crana (fish). Others as before.

Wmk. 314 Sideways (½c, 2c, $5),
Upright (3c, 5c, 10c)

1969-72   Litho.   *Perf. 13x12½*

234	A37	½c vio bl, yel & blk	.15	.15
235	A37	½c citron, blk & bl ('71)	.70	1.00
236	A37	2c brt yel, blk & grn ('72)	3.00	3.00
237	A37	3c pink & multi ('72)	1.00	1.65
a.		Wmk. sideways ('72)	3.00	3.00
238	A37	5c brick red & multi ('72)	1.00	1.65
239	A37	10c lilac & multi ('72)	1.00	1.65
a.		Wmk. sideways ('72)	3.50	3.50
240	A37	$5 ultra & multi ('70)	9.00	9.00
		Nos. 234-240 (7)	15.85	18.10

For overprints see Nos. 251-252.

1969, Oct. 1   Litho.   *Perf. 14*

Christmas: 22c, 25c, Adoration of the Kings, by Veronese.

247	A39	5c multicolored	.15	.15
248	A39	15c dp orange & multi	.20	.20
249	A39	22c lilac rose & multi	.40	.40
250	A39	25c emerald & multi	.50	.50
		Nos. 247-250 (4)	1.25	1.25

Nos. 238-239 and Type of 1968
Overprinted "POPULATION/ CENSUS 1970"

Wmk. 314 Sideways

1970, Feb. 2   Photo.   *Perf. 13x12½*

251	A37	5c brick red & multi	.15	.15
252	A37	10c lilac & multi	.15	.15
253	A37	15c org yel & multi	.25	.25
254	A37	25c multicolored	.40	.40
		Nos. 251-254 (4)	.95	.95

Orchid Type of 1968
Inscribed: "Orchids of Belize"

Wmk. 314

1970, Apr. 2   Litho.   *Perf. 14*

255	A35	5c Black	.15	.15
256	A35	15c White butterfly	.35	.35
257	A35	22c Swan	.50	.50
258	A35	25c Butterfly	.60	.60
		Nos. 255-258 (4)	1.60	1.60

Santa Maria Tree and Wood (Calophyllum Brasiliense) — A40

Nativity, by Arthur Hughes — A41

Hardwood Trees and Woods: 15c, Nargusta (terminalia amazonia). 22c, Cedar (cedrela mexicana). 25c, Sapodilla (achras sapota).

1970, Sept. 7   *Perf. 14*

259	A40	5c multicolored	.15	.15
260	A40	15c multicolored	.30	.30
261	A40	22c multicolored	.45	.45
262	A40	25c multicolored	.45	.45
		Nos. 259-262 (4)	1.35	1.35

1970, Nov. 2   *Perf. 14*

Christmas: 5c, 15c, 50c, Mystic Nativity, by Botticelli.

263	A41	½c black & multi	.15	.15
264	A41	5c brown & multi	.15	.15
265	A41	10c multicolored	.15	.15
266	A41	15c slate bl & multi	.25	.25
267	A41	25c dk green & multi	.40	.40
268	A41	50c black & multi	.85	.85
		Nos. 263-268 (6)	1.95	1.95

Legislative Assembly House A42

Designs: 5c, View of South Side of Belize. 10c, Government Plaza, Belmopan. 22c, Magistrates' Court. 25c, Police Headquarters. 50c, New General Post Office.

1971, Jan. 30   Litho.   *Perf. 13½x14*

Size: 59x22mm

| 269 | A42 | 5c multicolored | .15 | .15 |
| 270 | A42 | 10c multicolored | .15 | .15 |

Size: 37x21½mm

271	A42	15c multicolored	.20	.20
272	A42	22c multicolored	.30	.30
273	A42	25c multicolored	.40	.40
274	A42	50c multicolored	.70	.70
		Nos. 269-274 (6)	1.90	1.90

New capital at Belmopan.

Tabebuia Chrysantha — A43

Flowers: 5c, 22c, Hymenocallis littoralis. 10c, 25c, Hippeastrum equestre. 15c, like ½c.

1971, Mar. 27   Litho.   *Perf. 14*

275	A43	½c vio blue & multi	.15	.15
276	A43	5c olive & multi	.15	.15
277	A43	10c violet & multi	.20	.20
278	A43	15c multicolored	.30	.30
279	A43	22c multicolored	.45	.45
280	A43	25c lt brown & multi	.55	.55
		Nos. 275-280 (6)	1.80	1.80

Easter.

Type of 1968 Overprinted: "RACIAL EQUALITY / YEAR—1971"

Perf. 13x12½

1971, June 14   Litho.   Wmk. 314

| 281 | A37 | 10c lilac & multi | .15 | .15 |
| 282 | A37 | 50c blue green & multi | .70 | .70 |

Intl. year against racial discrimination.

Tubroos (Enterolobium Cyclocarpum) A44

Hardwood Trees of Belize: 15c, Yemeri (Vochysia hondurensis). 26c, Billyweb (Sweetia panamensis). 50c, Logwood (Haematoxylum campechianum).

1971, Aug. 16   *Perf. 14*

Queen's Head in Silver

283	A44	5c green, brn & blk	.15	.15
284	A44	15c multicolored	.50	.50
285	A44	26c multicolored	.85	.85
286	A44	50c multicolored	1.50	1.50
a.		Souvenir sheet of 4, #283-286	5.25	5.25
		Nos. 283-286 (4)	3.00	3.00

Verrazano-Narrows Bridge, New York, and Quebec Bridge, Canada — A45

Bridges of the World: ½c, Hawksworth Bridge connecting San Ignacio and Santa Helena and Belcan Bridge, Belize, Br. Honduras. 26c, London Bridge in 1871, and at Lake Havasu City, Ariz., in 1971. 50c, Belize-Mexico Bridge and Belize Swing Bridge.

1971, Sept. 23   Litho.

287	A45	½c multicolored	.15	.15
288	A45	5c multicolored	.15	.15
289	A45	26c multicolored	.55	.55
290	A45	50c multicolored	1.10	1.10
		Nos. 287-290 (4)	1.95	1.95

Petrae Volubis — A46

Seated Jade Figure — A47

Wild Flowers: 15c, Vochysia hondurensis. 26c, Tabebuia pentaphylla. 50c, Erythrina americana.

1972, Feb. 28
Flowers in Natural Colors; Black Inscriptions

292	A46	6c lilac & yellow	.15	.15
293	A46	15c lt blue & pale grn	.35	.35
294	A46	26c pink & lt blue	.65	.65
295	A46	50c orange & lt grn	1.25	1.25
		Nos. 292-295 (4)	2.40	2.40

Easter.

Perf. 14x13½, 13½x14

1972, May 22   Unwmk.

Mayan Carved Jade, 4th-8th centuries: 6c, Dancing priest. 16c, Sun god's head, horiz. 26c, Priest on throne and sun god's head. 50c, Figure and mask.

296	A47	3c rose red & multi	.15	.15
297	A47	6c vio bl & multi	.15	.15
298	A47	16c brown & multi	.25	.25
299	A47	26c ol grn & multi	.40	.40
300	A47	50c purple & multi	.85	.85
		Nos. 296-300 (5)	1.80	1.80

Black inscription with details of designs on back of stamps.

Banak (Virola Koschnyi) — A48

Hardwood Trees of Belize: 5c, Quamwood (Schizolobium parahybum). 16c, Waika chewstick (Symphonia globulifera). 26c, Mammee-apple (Mammea americana). 50c, My lady (Aspidosperma megalocarpon).

1972, Aug. 21   Wmk. 314   *Perf. 14*
Queen's Head in Gold

301	A48	3c brt pink & multi	.15	.15
302	A48	5c gray & multi	.15	.15
303	A48	16c green & multi	.30	.30
304	A48	26c lemon & multi	.50	.50
305	A48	50c lt violet & multi	.90	.90
		Nos. 301-305 (5)	2.00	2.00

BRITISH HONDURAS — BRITISH INDIAN OCEAN TERRITORY

Silver Wedding Issue, 1972
Common Design Type

Design: Queen Elizabeth II, Prince Philip and Belize orchids.

1972, Nov. 20   Photo.   Perf. 14x14½
| 306 | CD324 | 26c slate grn & multi | .40 | .40 |
| 307 | CD324 | 50c violet & multi | .75 | .75 |

Baron Bliss Day — A49

Festivals of Belize: 10c, Labor Day boat race. 26c, Carib Settlement Day dance. 50c, Pan American Day parade.

1973, Mar. 9   Litho.   Perf. 14½
308	A49	3c dull blue & black	.15	.15
309	A49	10c red & multi	.15	.15
310	A49	26c ver & multi	.40	.40
311	A49	50c black & multi	.75	.75
		Nos. 308-311 (4)	1.45	1.45

SEMI-POSTAL STAMPS

Regular Issue of 1921-29 Surcharged in Black or Red

BELIZE RELIEF FUND PLUS 3 CENTS

1932   Wmk. 4   Perf. 14
B1	A14	1c + 1c green	1.50	4.75
B2	A14	2c + 2c rose red	1.50	4.75
B3	A14	3c + 3c orange	2.50	6.25
B4	A14	4c + 4c gray (R)	3.25	9.50
B5	A14	5c + 5c ultra	5.00	16.00
		Nos. B1-B5 (5)	13.75	41.25

The surtax was for a fund to aid sufferers from the destruction of the city of Belize by a hurricane in Sept. 1931.

POSTAGE DUE STAMPS

Catalogue values for unused stamps in this section are for Never Hinged items.

D1 — POSTAGE DUE 1c

1923   Typo.   Wmk. 4   Perf. 14
J1	D1	1c black	.90	5.00
J2	D1	2c black	1.10	4.00
J3	D1	4c black	3.00	10.00
		Nos. J1-J3 (3)	5.00	19.00

Nos. J1-J3 were re-issued on chalky paper in 1956.

Perf. 13½x13, 13½x14
1965-72   Wmk. 314
| J4 | D1 | 2c black ('72) | 1.50 | 3.00 |
| J5 | D1 | 4c black | 1.00 | 3.50 |

WAR TAX STAMPS

Nos. 85, 75 and 77 Overprinted WAR

1916-17   Wmk. 3   Perf. 14
With Moire Overprint
| MR1 | A11 | 1c green | .15 | .35 |
| a. | | "WAR" inverted | 250.00 | 250.00 |

Without Moire Overprint
MR2	A11	1c green ('17)	.25	.75
MR3	A11	3c orange ('17)	.75	.75
a.		Double overprint	450.00	450.00
		Nos. MR1-MR3 (3)	1.15	1.85

Nos. 75 and 77 Overprinted WAR

1918
| MR4 | A11 | 1c green | .15 | .25 |
| MR5 | A11 | 3c orange | .20 | .50 |

BRITISH INDIAN OCEAN TERRITORY

'bri-tish 'in-dēən 'ō-chən 'ter-ə-tŏr-ē

LOCATION — Indian Ocean
GOVT. — British Dependency
POP. — 558 (1972)

B.I.O.T. was established Nov. 8, 1965. This island group lies 1,180 miles north of Mauritius. It consisted of Chagos Archipelago (chief island: Diego Garcia), Aldabra, Farquhar and Des Roches Islands until June 23, 1976, when the last three named islands were returned to Seychelles.

100 Cents = 1 Rupee
100 Pence = 1 Pound (1990)

Catalogue values for all unused stamps in this country are for Never Hinged items.

Seychelles Nos. 198-202, 204-212 Overprinted **B.I.O.T.**

Perf. 14½x14, 14x14½
1968, Jan. 17   Photo.   Wmk. 314
Size: 24x31, 31x24mm
1	A17	5c multicolored	.15	.15
2	A17	10c multicolored	.15	.15
3	A17	15c multicolored	.15	.15
4	A17	20c multicolored	.15	.15
5	A17	25c multicolored	.15	.15
6	A18	40c multicolored	.25	.30
7	A18	45c multicolored	.30	.30
8	A17	50c multicolored	.30	.35
9	A17	75c multicolored	.35	.35
10	A18	1r multicolored	.90	1.00
11	A18	1.50r multicolored	1.65	1.75
12	A18	2.25r multicolored	3.00	3.00
13	A18	3.50r multicolored	4.50	4.50
14	A18	5r multicolored	10.00	10.50

Perf. 13x14
Size: 22½x39mm
| 15 | A17 | 10r multicolored | 20.00 | 21.00 |
| | | Nos. 1-15 (15) | 42.00 | 43.80 |

Lascar — A1

Marine Fauna: 10c, Hammerhead shark, vert. 15c, Tiger shark. 20c, Sooty eagle ray. 25c, Butterlyfish, vert. 30c, Robber crab. 40c, Green carangue. 45c, Needlefish, vert. 50c, Barracuda. 60c, Spotted pebble crab. 75c, Parrotfish. 85c, Rainbow runner (fish). 1r, Giant hermit crab. 1.50r, Humphead. 2.25r, Rock cod. 3.50r, Black marlin. 5r, Whale shark, vert. 10r, Lionfish.

Perf. 14x13½, 13½x14; 14 (30c, 60c, 85c)
1968-73   Litho.   Wmk. 314
16	A1	5c multicolored	.40	.40
a.		Wmk. upright ('73)	.55	.55
17	A1	10c multicolored	.15	.15
18	A1	15c multicolored	.15	.15
19	A1	20c multicolored	.15	.15
20	A1	25c multicolored	.35	.35
21	A1	30c multi ('70)	.40	.40
22	A1	40c multicolored	.35	.35
23	A1	45c multicolored	2.75	2.75
24	A1	50c multicolored	.35	.35
25	A1	60c multi ('70)	.80	.80
26	A1	75c multicolored	4.00	4.00
27	A1	85c multi ('70)	1.75	1.75
28	A1	1r multicolored	1.40	1.40
29	A1	1.50r multicolored	1.75	1.75
30	A1	2.25r multicolored	14.00	14.00
31	A1	3.50r multicolored	4.00	4.00
32	A1	5r multicolored	6.00	6.00
33	A1	10r multicolored	17.00	17.00
		Nos. 16-33 (18)	55.75	55.75

No. 16 has watermark sideways.

Aldabra Atoll and Sacred Ibis — A2

1969, July 10   Litho.   Perf. 13½x13
| 34 | A2 | 2.25r vio blue & multi | 2.25 | 1.60 |

Outrigger Canoe — A3

Designs: 75c, Beaching canoe. 1r, Merchant ship Nordvaer. 1.50r, Yacht, Isle of Farquhar.

Perf. 13½x14
1969, Dec. 15   Litho.   Wmk. 314
35	A3	45c multicolored	.45	.45
36	A3	75c multicolored	.85	.75
37	A3	1r multicolored	1.25	1.10
38	A3	1.50r multicolored	2.25	1.75
		Nos. 35-38 (4)	4.80	4.05

Giant Land Tortoise — A4

Designs: 75c, Aldabra lily. 1r, Aldabra tree snail. 1.50r, Dimorphic egrets.

1971, Feb. 1   Litho.   Wmk. 314
39	A4	45c multicolored	1.90	1.10
40	A4	75c multicolored	2.50	1.65
41	A4	1r multicolored	5.00	3.25
42	A4	1.50r multicolored	6.50	4.25
		Nos. 39-42 (4)	15.90	10.25

Aldabra Nature Reserve.

Society Coat of Arms and Flightless Rail — A5

1971, June 30   Litho.   Perf. 13½
| 43 | A5 | 3.50r multicolored | 10.00 | 7.00 |

Opening of Royal Society Research Station at Aldabra.

Acropora Formosa — A6

Corals: 60c, Goniastrea pectinata. 1r, Fungia fungites. 1.75r, Tubipora musica.

1972, Mar. 1
44	A6	40c blue & multi	.95	.95
45	A6	60c brt pink & multi	1.65	1.65
46	A6	1r blue & multi	3.25	3.25
47	A6	1.75r brt pink & multi	7.25	7.25
		Nos. 44-47 (4)	13.10	13.10

Common Design Types pictured following the introduction.

Silver Wedding Issue, 1972
Common Design Type

Design: Queen Elizabeth II, Prince Philip, flightless rail and sacred ibis.

1972, Nov. 20   Photo.   Perf. 14x14½
| 48 | CD324 | 95c multicolored | 1.10 | .50 |
| 49 | CD324 | 1.50r violet & multi | 1.50 | .75 |

Crucifixion, 17th Century — A7

Upsidedown Jellyfish — A8

Paintings, Ethiopian Manuscripts, 17th Century: 75c, 1.50r, Joseph and Nicodemus burying Jesus. 1r, Like 45c.

1973, Apr. 9   Litho.   Perf. 14
50	A7	45c buff & multi	.30	.20
51	A7	75c buff & multi	.45	.35
52	A7	1r buff & multi	.65	.40
53	A7	1.50r buff & multi	1.10	.70
a.		Souvenir sheet of 4, #50-53	3.50	2.75
		Nos. 50-53 (4)	2.50	1.65

Easter.

1973, Nov. 12   Litho.   Wmk. 314
54	A8	50c shown	1.40	1.00
55	A8	1r Butterflies	2.25	1.50
56	A8	1.50r Spider	3.75	2.50
		Nos. 54-56 (3)	7.40	5.00

Nordvaer and July 14, 1969 Cancel — A9

Design: 2.50r, Nordvaer offshore and cancel.

1974, July 14
| 57 | A9 | 85c multicolored | .75 | .50 |
| 58 | A9 | 2.50r multicolored | 2.00 | 1.25 |

Nordvaer traveling post office, 5th anniv.

Terebra Maculata and Terebra Subulata — A10

Sea Shells: 75c, Turbo marmoratus. 1r, Drupa rubusidaeus. 1.50r, Cassis rufa.

1974, Nov. 12   Litho.   Perf. 13½x14
59	A10	45c multicolored	.90	.70
60	A10	75c multicolored	1.40	1.25
61	A10	1r multicolored	2.25	1.75
62	A10	1.50r multicolored	4.00	3.00
		Nos. 59-62 (4)	8.55	6.70

Aldabra Drongo — A11

Grewia Salicifolia — A12

Birds: 10c, Malagasy coucal. 20c, Red-headed forest fody. 25c, Fairy tern. 30c, Crested tern. 40c,

BRITISH INDIAN OCEAN TERRITORY

Brown booby. 50c, Noddy tern. 60c, Gray heron. 65c, Blue-faced booby. 95c, Malagasy white-eye. 1r, Green-backed heron. 1.75r, Lesser frigate bird. 3.50r, White-tailed tropic bird. 5r, Souimanga sunbird. 10r, Malagasy turtledove. Nos. 69, 71-77 horiz.

1975, Feb. 28   Wmk. 314   *Perf. 14*

63	A11	5c buff & multi	.15	.15
64	A11	10c lt ultra & multi	.15	.15
65	A11	20c dp yel & multi	.15	.15
66	A11	25c ultra & multi	.20	.15
67	A11	30c dl yel & multi	.30	.30
68	A11	40c bis & multi	.40	.40
69	A11	50c lt blue & multi	.45	.45
70	A11	60c yel & multi	.50	.50
71	A11	65c yel grn & multi	.60	.60
72	A11	95c citron & multi	.75	.75
73	A11	1r bister & multi	.95	.95
74	A11	1.75r yel & multi	1.90	1.90
75	A11	3.50r blue & multi	3.75	3.75
76	A11	5r pale sal & multi	6.25	6.25
77	A11	10r brt yel & multi	9.50	9.50
		Nos. 63-77 (15)	26.00	25.95

1975, July 10   Litho.   Wmk. 314

Native Plants: 65c, Cassia aldabrensis. 1r, Hypoestes aldabrensis. 1.60r, Euphorbia pyrifolia.

78	A12	50c multicolored	.35	.35
79	A12	65c multicolored	.50	.50
80	A12	1r multicolored	.75	.75
81	A12	1.60r multicolored	1.25	1.25
		Nos. 78-81 (4)	2.85	2.85

Nature protection.

Aldabra and Compass Rose — A13

Maps of Islands: 1r, Desroches. 1.50r, Farquhar. 2r, Diego Garcia.

1975, Nov. 8   Litho.   *Perf. 13½x14*

82	A13	50c blk, blue & grn	.30	.25
83	A13	1r green & multi	.65	.50
84	A13	1.50r blk, ultra & grn	1.00	.70
85	A13	2r blk, lilac & grn	1.40	1.00
a.		Souvenir sheet of 4, #82-85	7.50	7.50
		Nos. 82-85 (4)	3.35	2.45

British Indian Ocean Territory, 10th anniv.

Crimson Speckled Moth — A14

Insects: 1.20r, Dysdercus fasciatus. 1.50r, Sphex torridus. 2r, Oryctes rhinoceros.

1976, Mar. 22   Litho.   Wmk. 373

86	A14	65c multicolored	.40	.40
87	A14	1.20r multicolored	.65	.65
88	A14	1.50r multicolored	.90	.90
89	A14	2r multicolored	1.40	1.40
		Nos. 86-89 (4)	3.35	3.35

Exhibition Emblem and No. 37 — A15

1990, May 3   Wmk. 373   *Perf. 14*

90	A15	15p No. 62	.60	.60
91	A15	20p No. 89	.85	.85
92	A15	34p No. 85	1.25	1.25
93	A15	54p shown	2.25	2.25
		Nos. 90-93 (4)	4.95	4.95

Stamp World London '90.

Birds — A16

1990, May 3   Wmk. 384   *Perf. 14*

94	A16	15p White-tailed tropic birds	.45	.45
95	A16	20p Turtle doves	.65	.65
96	A16	24p Greater frigate birds	.75	.75
97	A16	30p Little green herons	1.00	1.00
98	A16	34p Greater sand plovers	1.10	1.10
99	A16	41p Crab plovers	1.40	1.40
100	A16	45p Crested terns	1.60	1.60
101	A16	54p Lesser crested terns	1.75	1.75
102	A16	62p Fairy terns	2.00	2.00
103	A16	71p Red-footed boobies	2.25	2.25
104	A16	80p Indian mynahs	2.75	2.75
105	A16	£1 Madagascar fodies	3.25	3.25
		Nos. 94-105 (12)	18.95	18.95

For overprints see Nos. 145-146.

Queen Mother, 90th Birthday
Common Design Types

Designs: 24p, Lady Elizabeth Bowes-Lyon, 1923. £1, Queen, Princesses Elizabeth & Margaret, 1940.

1990, Aug. 4   Wmk. 384   *Perf. 14x15*

| 106 | CD343 | 24p multicolored | 1.10 | 1.10 |

Perf. 14½

| 107 | CD344 | £1 brown & black | 4.50 | 4.50 |

British Indian Ocean Territory, 25th Anniv. — A17

1990, Nov. 8   Litho.   *Perf. 14*

| 108 | A17 | 20p Flag | .75 | .75 |
| 109 | A17 | 24p Coat of arms | .95 | .95 |

Souvenir Sheet

| 110 | A17 | £1 Map | 4.00 | 4.00 |

Govt. Services A18

1991, June 3   Litho.   Wmk. 373   *Perf. 14*

111	A18	20p Postal service	.70	.70
112	A18	24p Royal Marines	.85	.85
113	A18	34p Police station, officers	1.25	1.25
114	A18	54p Customs service	1.90	1.90
		Nos. 111-114 (4)	4.70	4.70

Visiting Ships A19

1991, Nov. 8

115	A19	20p Survey ship Experiment, 1786	.70	.70
116	A19	24p US Brig Pickering, 1819	.85	.85
117	A19	34p SMS Emden, 1914	1.25	1.25
118	A19	54p HMS Edinburgh, 1988	1.90	1.90
		Nos. 115-118 (4)	4.70	4.70

Queen Elizabeth II's Accession to the Throne, 40th Anniv.
Common Design Type

Wmk. 373

1992, Feb. 6   Litho.   *Perf. 14*

119	CD349	15p multicolored	.50	.50
120	CD349	20p multicolored	.70	.70
121	CD349	24p multicolored	.85	.85
122	CD349	34p multicolored	1.25	1.25
123	CD349	54p multicolored	1.90	1.90
		Nos. 119-123 (5)	5.20	5.20

Aircraft A20

Wmk. 384

1992, Oct. 23   Litho.   *Perf. 14*

124	A20	20p Catalina	.75	.75
125	A20	24p Nimrod	.95	.95
126	A20	34p P-3 Orion	1.25	1.25
127	A20	54p B-52	2.00	2.00
		Nos. 124-127 (4)	4.95	4.95

Christmas — A21

Paintings: 5p, The Mystical Marriage of St. Cathrin, by Correggio. 24p, Madonna and Child by unknown artist. 34p, Madonna and Child by unknown artist, diff. 54p, The Birth of Jesus, by Kaspar Jele.

1992, Nov. 27   *Perf. 14½*

128	A21	5p multicolored	.20	.20
129	A21	24p multicolored	.80	.80
130	A21	34p multicolored	1.10	1.10
131	A21	54p multicolored	1.90	1.90
		Nos. 128-131 (4)	4.00	4.00

Coconut Crab A22

Wmk. 384

1993, Mar. 3   Litho.   *Perf. 14*

132	A22	10p Crab, coconut	1.10	1.10
133	A22	10p Large crab	1.10	1.10
134	A22	10p Two crabs	1.10	1.10
135	A22	15p Crab on tree trunk	1.75	1.75
		Nos. 132-135 (4)	5.05	5.05

World Wildlife Fund.

Royal Air Force, 75th Anniv.
Common Design Type

#136, Vickers Virginia. 24p, Bristol Bulldog. 34p, Short Sunderland. 54p, Bristol Blenheim IV.
#140: a, Douglas Dakota. b, Gloster Javelin. c, Blackburn Beverley. d, Vickers VC10.

1993, Apr. 1   Wmk. 373

136	CD350	20p multicolored	.60	.60
137	CD350	24p multicolored	.70	.70
138	CD350	34p multicolored	1.00	1.00
139	CD350	54p multicolored	1.50	1.50
		Nos. 136-139 (4)	3.80	3.80

Souvenir Sheet

| 140 | CD350 | 20p Sheet of 4, #a.-d. | 2.30 | 2.30 |

Flowers — A23

Christmas: 20p, Stachytarpheta urticifolia. 24p, Ipomea pes-caprae. 34p, Sida pusilla. 54p, Catharanthus roseus.

Perf. 14½

1993, Nov. 22   Litho.   Wmk. 373

| 141-144 | A23 | Set of 4 | 3.75 | 3.75 |

Nos. 96, 105 Ovptd. with Hong Kong '94 Emblem

Wmk. 384

1994, Feb. 18   Litho.   *Perf. 14*

| 145 | A16 | 24p multicolored | .65 | .65 |
| 146 | A16 | £1 multicolored | 2.75 | 2.75 |

A24    Butterflies — A25

18th Cent. Maps and Charts: a, 20p, Sketch of Diego Garcia. b, 24p, Plan of harbor, Chagos Island or Diego Garcia, by Lt. Archibald Blair. c, 34p, Chart of Chagos Archipelago, by Lt. Blair. d, 44p, Plan of part of Chagos Island or Diego Garcia, from survey made by the Drake. e, 54p, Plan of Chagos Island or Diego Garcia, by M. Aa Fontaine.

1994, June 1   Wmk. 373

| 147 | A24 | Strip of 5, #a.-e. | 5.25 | 5.25 |

1994, Aug. 16   Wmk. 384

148	A25	24p Junonia villida	1.10	1.10
149	A25	30p Petrelaea dana	1.40	1.40
150	A25	56p Hypolimnas misippus	2.50	2.50
		Nos. 148-150 (3)	5.00	5.00

Sharks A26

1994, Nov. 1   Wmk. 373

151	A26	15p Nurse	.45	.45
152	A26	20p Silver tip	.60	.60
153	A26	24p Black tip reef	.75	.75
154	A26	30p Oceanic white tip	.95	.95
155	A26	35p Black tip	1.10	1.10
156	A26	41p Smooth hammerhead	1.25	1.25
157	A26	46p Lemon	1.40	1.40
158	A26	55p White tip reef	1.75	1.75
159	A26	65p Tiger	2.00	2.00
a.		Souvenir sheet of 1	2.00	2.00
160	A26	74p Indian sand tiger	2.25	2.25
a.		Souvenir sheet of 1	2.25	2.25
161	A26	80p Great hammerhead	2.50	2.50
162	A26	£1 Great white	3.00	3.00
		Nos. 151-162 (12)	18.00	18.00

No. 159a for Hong Kong '97. Issued 2/3/97.
No. 160a for return of Hong Kong to China. Issued 7/1/97.

End of World War II, 50th Anniv.
Common Design Types

20p, War graves, memorial cross, Diego Garcia. 24p, 6-inch naval gun, Cannon Point. 30p, Sunderland flying boat, 230 Squadron. 56p, HMIS Clive. £1, Reverse of War Medal 1939-45.

Wmk. 373

1995, May 8   Litho.   *Perf. 14*

163	CD351	20p multicolored	.50	.50
164	CD351	24p multicolored	.65	.65
165	CD351	30p multicolored	.80	.80
166	CD351	56p multicolored	1.50	1.50
		Nos. 163-166 (4)	3.45	3.45

Souvenir Sheet

| 167 | CD352 | £1 multicolored | 2.75 | 2.75 |

Game Fish A27

BRITISH INDIAN OCEAN TERRITORY — BRUNEI

BRITISH INDIAN OCEAN TERRITORY

1995, Oct. 6   Wmk. 384
68	A27	20p Dolphinfish	.60	.60
69	A27	24p Sailfish	.75	.75
70	A27	30p Wahoo	.95	.95
71	A27	56p Striped marlin	1.75	1.75
		Nos. 168-171 (4)	4.05	4.05

Sea Shells — A28

20p, Terebra crenulata. 24p, Bursa bufonia. 30p, Nassarius papillosus. 56p, Lopha cristagalli.

1996, Jan. 8   Wmk. 373   Perf. 14
172	A28	20p multicolored	.60	.60
173	A28	24p multicolored	.75	.75
174	A28	30p multicolored	.95	.95
175	A28	56p multicolored	1.75	1.75
		Nos. 172-175 (4)	4.05	4.05

Queen Elizabeth II, 70th Birthday
Common Design Type

Various portraits of Queen, scenes of British Indian Ocean Territory: 20p, View to north from south end of lagoon. 24p, Manager's House, Peros Banhos. 30p, Wireless station, Peros Banhos. 56p, Sunset scene.
£1, Wearing crown, formal dress.

1996, Apr. 22   Perf. 14x14½   Wmk. 384
176	CD354	20p multicolored	.65	.65
177	CD354	24p multicolored	.80	.80
178	CD354	30p multicolored	1.00	1.00
179	CD354	56p multicolored	1.75	1.75
		Nos. 176-179 (4)	4.20	4.20

Souvenir Sheet
180	CD354	£1 multicolored	3.25	3.25

Turtles — A29

1996, Sept. 2   Wmk. 373
181	A29	20p Loggerhead	.60	.60
182	A29	24p Leatherback	.75	.75
183	A29	30p Hawksbill	.95	.95
184	A29	56p Green	1.75	1.75
		Nos. 181-184 (4)	4.05	4.05

Uniforms — A30

Designs: 20p, British representative. 24p, Royal Marine officer. 30p, Royal Marine in camouflage. 56p, Police dog handler, female police officer.

1996, Dec.   Perf. 14
185	A30	20p multicolored	.65	.65
186	A30	24p multicolored	.80	.80
187	A30	30p multicolored	1.00	1.00
188	A30	56p multicolored	1.90	1.90
		Nos. 185-188 (4)	4.35	4.35

Queen Elizabeth II and Prince Philip, 50th Wedding Anniv. — A31

#189, Queen up close. #190, 4-horse team fording river. #191, Queen riding in open carriage. #192, Prince Philip up close. #193, Prince driving 4-horse team, Prince, Queen near jeep. #194, Queen on horseback, castle in distance.
£1.50, Queen, Prince riding in open carriage.

1997, July 10   Perf. 14½x14
189	A31	20p multicolored	.65	.65
190	A31	20p multicolored	.65	.65
a.		Pair, #189-190	1.30	1.30
191	A31	24p multicolored	.80	.80
192	A31	24p multicolored	.80	.80
a.		Pair, #191-192	1.60	1.60
193	A31	30p multicolored	1.00	1.00
194	A31	30p multicolored	1.00	1.00
a.		Pair, #193-194	2.00	2.00
		Nos. 189-194 (6)	4.90	4.90

Souvenir Sheet
195	A31	£1.50 multicolored	5.00	5.00

Ocean Wave '97, Naval Exercise — A32

Designs: a, HMS Richmond, HMS Beaver. b, HMS Illustrious. c, HMS Richmond. d, RFA Sir Percivale, HMY Britannia, HMS Beaver. e, HMY Britannia. f, HMS Richmond, HMS Beaver, HMS Gloucester. g, HMS Richmond. h, HMS Illustrious (aerial view). i, HMS Sheffield. j, RFA Diligence, HMS Trenchant. k, HMS Illustrious, RFA Fort George, HMS Gloucester. l, HMS Richmond, HMS Beaver, HMS Gloucester.

1997   Litho.   Perf. 14x14½
196	A32	24p Sheet of 12, #a.-l.	9.25	9.25

Diana, Princess of Wales (1961-97)
Common Design Type

Various portraits: a, 26p, shown. b, 26p, Close-up. c, 34p. d, 60p.

1998, Mar. 31   Perf. 14½x14
197	CD355	Sheet of 4, #a.-d.	5.50	5.50

No. 197 sold for £1.46 + 20p, with surtax and 50% of profits from total sale being donated to the Princess Diana Memorial Fund.

Royal Air Force, 80th Anniv.
Common Design Type of 1993
Re-inscribed

Designs: 26p, Blackburn Iris, 1930-34. 34p, Gloster Gamecock, 1926-33. 60p, North American Sabre F86, 1953-56. 80p, Avro Lincoln, 1945-55. No. 202: a, Sopwith Baby, 1915-19. b, Martinsyde Elephant, 1916-19. c, De Havilland Tiger Moth, 1932-55. d, North American Mustang III, 1943-47.

1998   Wmk. 384   Perf. 14
198	CD350	26p multicolored	.85	.85
199	CD350	34p multicolored	1.10	1.10
200	CD350	60p multicolored	2.00	2.00
201	CD350	80p multicolored	2.75	2.75
		Nos. 198-201 (4)	6.70	6.70

Souvenir Sheet
202	CD350	34p Sheet of 4, #a.-d.	4.50	4.50

BRUNEI

ˈbrü-ˌnī

LOCATION — On the northwest coast of Borneo
GOVT. — Independent state
AREA — 2,226 sq. mi.
POP. — 191,770 (1981)
CAPITAL — Bandar Seri Begawan

Brunei became a British protectorate in 1888. A treaty between the sultan and the British Government in 1979 provided for independence in 1983.

100 Cents (Sen) = 1 Dollar

Catalogue values for unused stamps in this country are for Never Hinged items, beginning with Scott 62.

Watermark

Wmk. 385 - CARTOR

Labuan Stamps of 1902-03 Overprinted or Surcharged in Red:

BRUNEI.

BRUNEI.   **TWO CENTS.**

1906   Unwmk.   Perf. 12 to 16
1	A38	1c violet & blk	14.00	32.50
a.		Black overprint	2,000.	2,750.
2	A38	2c on 3c brn & blk	1.50	5.00
a.		"BRUNEI." double	4,250.	3,000.
3	A38	2c on 8c org & blk	16.00	55.00
a.		"TWO CENTS." double	5,750.	
b.		"TWO CENTS." omitted, in pair with normal	6,000.	
4	A38	3c on 8c brown & blk	16.00	55.00
5	A38	4c on 12c yel & black	1.75	4.75
6	A38	5c on 16c org brn & green	20.00	42.50
7	A38	8c orange & blk	7.00	17.00
8	A38	10c on 16c org brn & green	7.00	15.00
9	A38	25c on 16c org brn & green	72.50	110.00
10	A38	30c on 16c org brn & green	72.50	100.00
11	A38	50c on 16c org brn & green	72.50	100.00
12	A38	$1 on 8c org & blk	72.50	100.00
		Nos. 1-12 (12)	373.25	636.75

The 25c surcharge reads: "25 CENTS."

Scene on Brunei River — A1

Two Types of 1908 1c, 3c:
Type I - Dots form bottom line of water shading. (Double plate.)
Type II - Dots removed. (Single plate.)

1907-21   Engr.   Wmk. 3   Perf. 14
13	A1	1c yel green & blk	1.50	2.75
14	A1	1c green (II) ('08)	.40	.40
a.		Type I ('19)	.60	1.50
15	A1	2c red & black	1.50	3.00
16	A1	2c brn & blk ('11)	.60	1.40
17	A1	3c red brn & blk	12.50	15.00
18	A1	3c car (I) ('08)	.85	1.50
a.		Type II ('17)	12.50	17.50
19	A1	4c lilac & blk	5.00	9.00
20	A1	4c claret ('12)	4.00	.50
21	A1	5c ultra & blk	37.50	50.00
22	A1	5c org & blk ('08)	3.50	4.00
23	A1	5c orange ('16)	1.75	2.25
24	A1	5c orange & blk	5.50	20.00
25	A1	8c blue ('08)	4.25	6.25
26	A1	8c ultra ('16)	2.00	2.25
27	A1	10c dk green & blk	9.00	15.00
28	A1	10c violet, yel ('12)	1.00	1.25
29	A1	25c yel brn & blue	19.00	30.00
30	A1	25c violet ('12)	1.90	4.00
31	A1	30c black & pur	19.00	30.00
32	A1	30c org & red vio ('12)	6.50	12.50
33	A1	50c brown & grn	19.00	30.00
34	A1	50c blk, grn ('12)	19.00	30.00
35	A1	50c blk, grnsh bl ('21)	5.50	13.50
36	A1	$1 slate & red	62.50	75.00
37	A1	$1 red & blk, bl ('12)	25.00	45.00
38	A1	$5 lake, grn ('08)	67.50	125.00
39	A1	$25 blk, red ('08)	450.00	450.00
		Nos. 13-38 (26)	335.75	534.55

Used value for No. 39 is for CTO. CTOs dated before Dec. 1941 cost more.

Stamps of 1908-21 Overprinted in Black:
"MALAYA-BORNEO EXHIBITION, 1922"
in Four Lines

1922
14b	A1	1c green	2.25	17.00
16a	A1	2c brown & black	5.00	21.00
18b	A1	3c carmine	6.75	30.00
20a	A1	4c claret	5.25	35.00
23a	A1	5c orange	10.00	45.00
28a	A1	10c violet, yellow	8.75	45.00
30a	A1	25c violet	19.00	67.50
35a	A1	50c greenish blue	60.00	125.00
37a	A1	$1 red & black, blue	92.50	165.00
		Nos. 14b-37a (9)	209.50	550.50

Industrial fair, Singapore, Mar. 31-Apr. 15.

Type of 1907 Issue

1924-37   Wmk. 4
43	A1	1c black ('26)	.20	.30
44	A1	2c deep brown	.70	2.75
45	A1	2c green ('33)	.25	.25
46	A1	3c green	.70	3.75
47	A1	4c claret brown	1.90	.65
48	A1	4c orange ('29)	.50	.40
49	A1	5c orange	.65	.75
50	A1	5c lt gray ('31)	3.50	5.75
51	A1	5c brown ('33)	1.75	.15
52	A1	8c ultra ('27)	2.50	4.25
53	A1	8c gray ('33)	2.75	.45
54	A1	10c violet, yel ('37)	6.25	15.00
55	A1	25c dk violet ('31)	4.00	9.00
56	A1	30c org & red vio ('31)	4.75	12.50
57	A1	50c black, grn ('31)	6.00	10.50
58	A1	$1 red & blk, bl ('31)	25.00	55.00
		Nos. 43-58 (16)	61.40	121.45

For overprints see Nos. N1-N20.

Dwellings in Town of Brunei — A2

1924-31
59	A2	6c black	3.50	8.25
60	A2	6c red ('31)	2.75	9.00
61	A2	12c blue	5.00	7.50
		Nos. 59-61 (3)	11.25	24.75

See note after Nos. N1-N19.

Catalogue values for unused stamps in this section, from this point to the end of the section, are for Never Hinged items.

Types of 1907-24

1947-51   Engr.   Perf. 14
62	A1	1c brown	.15	.15
63	A1	2c gray	.15	.15
a.		Perf. 14½x13½ ('50)	1.75	2.50
64	A2	3c dark green	.35	.35
65	A1	5c deep orange	.15	.15
a.		Perf. 14½x13½ ('50)	7.25	9.00
66	A2	6c gray black	1.75	1.75
67	A1	8c scarlet	.20	.20
a.		Perf. 13 ('51)	.20	.20
68	A1	10c violet	.20	.20
a.		Perf. 14½x13½ ('50)	1.75	3.00
69	A1	15c brt ultra	3.75	3.75
70	A1	25c red violet	.35	.35
a.		Perf. 14½x13½ ('51)	.60	1.25
71	A1	30c dp org & gray blk	.45	.45
a.		Perf. 14½x13½ ('51)	.55	1.25
72	A1	50c black	.45	.45
a.		Perf. 13 ('51)	3.50	2.00
73	A1	$1 scar & gray blk	1.25	1.25
74	A1	$5 red org & grn ('48)	15.00	15.00
75	A1	$10 dp claret & gray blk ('48)	30.00	42.50
		Nos. 62-75 (14)	54.20	66.70

Sultan Ahmed and Pile Dwellings — A3

1949, Sept. 22   Wmk. 4   Perf. 13
76	A3	8c car & black	1.60	1.60
77	A3	25c red orange & pur	1.60	1.60
78	A3	50c blue & black	2.00	2.00
		Nos. 76-78 (3)	5.20	5.20

25th anniv. of the reign of Sultan Ahmed Tajudin Akhazul Khair Wad-din.

Common Design Types pictured following the introduction.

BRUNEI

UPU Issue
Common Design Types
Engr.; Name Typo. on 15c and 25c
1949, Oct. 10   Perf. 13½, 11x11½
79	CD306	8c rose car	.50	.50
80	CD307	15c indigo	.75	.75
81	CD308	25c red lilac	1.25	1.25
82	CD309	50c slate	2.50	2.50
		Nos. 79-82 (4)	5.00	5.00

Sultan Omar Ali Saifuddin — A4

River Kampong A5

1952, Mar. 1   Engr.   Wmk. 4
Center in Black
Perf. 13½x13
83	A4	1c black	.15	.15
84	A4	2c red orange	.15	.15
85	A4	3c red brown	.15	.15
86	A4	4c green	.15	.15
87	A4	6c gray	.25	.15
88	A4	8c carmine	.30	.15
89	A4	10c olive brown	.30	.15
90	A4	12c violet	.35	.15
91	A4	15c blue	.50	.15
92	A4	25c purple	.75	.25
93	A4	50c ultramarine	1.10	.30

Perf. 13
94	A5	$1 dull green	3.00	.60
95	A5	$2 red	4.50	1.50
96	A5	$5 deep plum	15.00	5.00
		Nos. 83-96 (14)	26.65	9.00

See Nos. 101-114.

Mosque and Sultan Omar — A6

1958, Sept. 24   Wmk. 314   Perf. 13
Center in Black
97	A6	8c dull green	.25	.30
98	A6	15c carmine rose	.30	.25
99	A6	35c rose violet	.50	.75
		Nos. 97-99 (3)	1.05	1.30

Opening of the Brunei Mosque.

Freedom from Hunger Issue
Common Design Type with Portrait of Sultan Omar
1963, June 4   Photo.   Perf. 14x14½
| 100 | CD314 | 12c sepia | 1.50 | 1.50 |

Types of 1952
Wmk. 314 Upright
1964-70   Engr.   Perf. 13½x13
Center in Black
101	A4	1c black	.15	.15
102	A4	2c red orange	.15	.15
103	A4	3c red brown	.15	.15
104	A4	4c green	.15	.15
105	A4	6c black	.25	.15
106	A4	8c dk carmine	.45	.15
107	A4	10c olive brown	.35	.30
108	A4	12c violet	.60	.30
109	A4	15c blue	.60	.15
110	A4	25c purple	1.25	.40
111	A4	50c ultramarine	2.50	1.50

Perf. 13
112	A5	$1 dull green ('68)	4.75	3.00
113	A5	$2 red ('70)	16.00	10.00
114	A5	$5 deep plum ('70)	32.50	25.00
		Nos. 101-114 (14)	59.85	41.75

Nos. 101-112 were reissued in 1968-70 on whiter, glazed paper; the $2 and $5 are only on this paper.

Wmk. 314 Sideways
1972-73   Perf. 13½x13
Center in Black
102a	A4	2c red orange	.35	.35
103a	A4	3c red brown	.40	.40
104a	A4	4c green	.50	.50
105a	A4	6c black	.85	.85
106a	A4	8c dark carmine	1.10	1.10
107a	A4	10c olive brown	1.50	1.50
108a	A4	12c violet	1.75	1.75
109a	A4	15c blue	3.00	3.00
		Nos. 102a-109a (8)	9.45	9.45

The stamps with watermark sideways are on the whiter, glazed paper.
Issue dates: 2c, 8c, May 9, 1973, others, Nov. 17, 1972.

The following six sets are Common Design Types but with the portrait of Sultan Omar.

ITU Issue
Perf. 11x11½
1965, May 17   Litho.   Wmk. 314
| 116 | CD317 | 4c red lil & org brn | .15 | .15 |
| 117 | CD317 | 75c orange & emer | 1.40 | 1.40 |

Intl. Cooperation Year Issue
1965, Oct. 25   Perf. 14½
| 118 | CD318 | 4c blue grn & claret | .15 | .15 |
| 119 | CD318 | 15c lt violet & grn | .70 | .70 |

Churchill Memorial Issue
1966, Jan. 24   Photo.   Perf. 14
120	CD319	3c multicolored	.25	.15
121	CD319	12c multicolored	.65	.35
122	CD319	15c multicolored	1.00	.60
123	CD319	75c multicolored	3.50	2.50
		Nos. 120-123 (4)	5.40	3.60

World Cup Soccer Issue
1966, July 4   Litho.   Perf. 14
| 124 | CD321 | 4c multicolored | .15 | .15 |
| 125 | CD321 | 75c multicolored | 1.25 | 1.25 |

WHO Headquarters Issue
1966, Sept. 20   Litho.   Perf. 14
| 126 | CD322 | 12c multicolored | .25 | .20 |
| 127 | CD322 | 25c multicolored | .75 | .75 |

UNESCO Anniversary Issue
1966, Dec. 1   Litho.   Wmk. 314
128	CD323	4c "Education"	.15	.15
129	CD323	15c "Science"	.45	.45
130	CD323	75c "Culture"	2.25	2.25
		Nos. 128-130 (3)	2.85	2.85

State Religious Building and Sultan Hassanal Bolkiah — A7

1967, Dec. 19   Photo.   Perf. 12½
131	A7	4c violet & multi	.15	.15
132	A7	10c red & multi	.15	.15
133	A7	25c orange & multi	.35	.35
134	A7	50c lt violet & multi	.65	.65
		Nos. 131-134 (4)	1.30	1.30

A three-stamp set (12c, 25c, 50c) showing views of the new Language and Communications Headquarters was prepared and announced for release in April, 1968. The Crown Agents distributed sample sets, but the stamps were not issued. Later, Nos. 144-146 were issued instead.

Sultan Hassanal Bolkiah, Brunei Mosque and Flags — A8

Sultan Hassanal Bolkiah Installation: 12c, Sultan, Mosque and flags, horiz.
1968, July 9   Photo.   Perf. 13x14, 14x13   Unwmk.
135	A8	4c green & multi	.15	.15
136	A8	12c dp bister & multi	.30	.30
137	A8	25c violet & multi	.75	.75
		Nos. 135-137 (3)	1.20	1.20

Sultan Hassanal Bolkiah — A9

1968, July 15   Litho.   Wmk. 314   Perf. 12
138	A9	4c multicolored	.15	.15
139	A9	12c multicolored	.20	.20
140	A9	25c multicolored	.40	.50
		Nos. 138-140 (3)	.75	.85

Sultan Hassanal Bolkiah's birthday.

Coronation of Sultan Hassanal Bolkiah, Aug. 1, 1968 — A10

1968, Aug. 1   Photo.   Perf. 14½x14
141	A10	4c Prus blue & multi	.15	.15
142	A10	12c rose lilac & multi	.25	.25
143	A10	25c multicolored	.50	.50
		Nos. 141-143 (3)	.90	.90

A11

Hall of Language and Culture — A12

Perf. 13½, 12½x13½ (A12)
1968, Sept. 29   Photo.   Wmk. 314
144	A11	10c blue grn & multi	.15	.25
145	A12	15c ocher & multi	.20	.30
146	A12	30c ultra & multi	.45	.75
		Nos. 144-146 (3)	.80	1.30

Opening of the Hall of Language and Culture and of the Broadcasting and Information Department Building. Nos. 144-146 are overprinted "1968" and 4 bars over the 1967 date. They were not issued without this overprint.

Human Rights Flame and Struggling Man — A13

Unwmk.
1968, Dec. 16   Litho.   Perf. 14
147	A13	12c green, yel & blk	.15	.15
148	A13	25c ultra & blk	.35	.35
149	A13	75c dk plum, yel & blk	.90	.90
		Nos. 147-149 (3)	1.40	1.40

International Human Rights Year.

Sultan and WHO Emblem A14

1968, Dec. 19   Litho.   Perf. 14
150	A14	4c lt blue, org & blk	.15	.15
151	A14	15c brt purple, org & blk	.22	.22
152	A14	25c olive, org & blk	.38	.38
		Nos. 150-152 (3)	.75	.75

20th anniv. of the WHO.

Sultan Hassanal Bolkiah, Pengiran Shahbandar and Oil Rig — A15

Perf. 14x13
1969, July 10   Photo.   Wmk. 314
153	A15	12c green & multi	.20	.20
154	A15	40c dk rose brn & multi	.60	.60
155	A15	50c violet & multi	.75	.75
		Nos. 153-155 (3)	1.55	1.55

Installation of Pengiran Shahbandar as Second Minister (Di-Galong Sahibol Mal).

Royal Assembly Hall and Council Chamber — A16

Design: 50c, Front view of buildings.

Unwmk.
1969, Sept. 23   Litho.   Perf. 15
156	A16	12c multicolored	.15	.15
157	A16	25c multicolored	.35	.35
158	A16	50c violet & pink	.65	.65
		Nos. 156-158 (3)	1.15	1.15

Opening of the Royal Assembly Hall and Council Chamber.

Youth Center — A17

1969, Dec. 20   Litho.   Wmk. 314
159	A17	6c lt org, blk & dull vio	.15	.15
160	A17	10c cit, blk & dl Prus grn	.15	.15
161	A17	30c yel green, blk & brn	.45	.45
		Nos. 159-161 (3)	.75	.75

Opening of Youth Center, Mar. 15, 1969.

Helicopter and Emblem A18

Designs: 10c, Soldier and emblem, vert. 75c, Patrol boat and emblem.

1971, May 31   Litho.   Perf. 14
162	A18	10c green & multi	.38	.15
163	A18	15c Prus blue & multi	.45	.25
164	A18	75c lt ultra & multi	2.75	1.75
		Nos. 162-164 (3)	3.58	2.15

10th anniv. of Royal Brunei Malay Reg.

BRUNEI

50th Anniv. of the Royal Brunei Police Force — A19

1971, Aug. 14		Perf. 14½	
165 A19	10c Superintendent	.40	.25
166 A19	15c Constable	.50	.32
167 A19	50c Traffic policeman	2.25	1.60
	Nos. 165-167 (3)	3.15	2.17

Sultan, Heir Apparent and View of Brunei — A20

Portraits and: 25c, View of Brunei with Mosque. 50c, Mosque and banner.

1971, Aug. 27	Litho.	Wmk. 314	
168 A20	15c multicolored	.38	.22
169 A20	25c multicolored	.75	.55
170 A20	50c multicolored	1.40	1.10
	Nos. 168-170 (3)	2.53	1.87

Installation of Sultan Hassanal Bolkiah's brother Muda Omar Ali Saifuddin as heir apparent (Perdana Wazir).

Brass and Copper Goods A21

Designs: 12c, Basketware. 15c, Leather goods. 25c, Silverware. 50c, Brunei Museum.

1972, Feb. 29		Perf. 13½x14	
	Size: 37x21mm		
171 A21	10c brn, sal & yel grn	.15	.15
172 A21	12c org, yel & green	.18	.15
173 A21	15c dk grn, emer & org	.25	.25
174 A21	25c brown, org & slate	.70	.60
	Size: 58x21mm		
175 A21	50c dull blue & multi	1.50	1.10
	Nos. 171-175 (5)	2.78	2.22

Opening of Brunei Museum.

Queen Elizabeth II, Sultan and View — A22

Queen Elizabeth II, Sultan Hassanal Bolkiah and: 15c, View of Brunei. 25c, Mosque and barge. 50c, Royal Assembly Hall.

1972, Feb. 29	Photo.	Perf. 13x13½	
176 A22	10c lt brown & multi	.24	.20
177 A22	15c lt blue & multi	.35	.30
178 A22	25c lt green & multi	.70	.60
179 A22	50c dull purple & multi	2.00	2.00
	Nos. 176-179 (4)	3.29	3.10

Visit of Queen Elizabeth II, Feb. 29.

Bangunan Secretariat (Government Buildings) — A23

Sultans Omar Ali Saifuddin and Hassanal Bolkiah: 15c, Istana Darul Hana (Sultan's residence). 25c, View of capital. 50c, View of new Mosque.

1972, Oct. 4	Litho.	Perf. 13½	
180 A23	10c org, blk & green	.15	.15
181 A23	15c green & multi	.25	.25
182 A23	25c ultra & multi	.50	.50
183 A23	50c rose red & multi	1.00	1.00
	Nos. 180-183 (4)	1.90	1.90

Change of capital's name from Brunei to Bandar Seri Begawan, Oct. 4, 1970.

Beverley Plane Landing — A24

Design: 25c, Blackburn Beverley plane dropping supplies by parachute, vert.

1972, Nov. 15		Perf. 14x13½, 13½x14	Litho.
184 A24	25c blue & multi	1.65	1.65
185 A24	75c ultra & multi	4.00	4.00

Opening of Royal Air Force Museum, Hendon, London.

Silver Wedding Issue, 1972
Common Design Type

Design: Queen Elizabeth II, Prince Philip; girl and boy with traditional gifts.

1972, Nov. 20	Photo.	Perf. 14x14½	
186 CD324	12c multi	.40	.15
187 CD324	75c multi	1.25	1.25

INTERPOL Emblem and Headquarters, Paris — A25

Design: 50c, similar to 25c.

1973, Sept. 7	Litho.	Perf. 14x14½	
188 A25	25c emerald & multi	.75	.75
189 A25	50c multicolored	1.50	1.50

50th anniv. of Intl. Criminal Police Org. (INTERPOL).

Princess Anne and Mark Phillips — A26

1973, Nov. 14	Litho.	Perf. 13½	
190 A26	25c vio blue & multi	.20	.20
191 A26	50c red lilac & multi	.40	.40

Wedding of Princess Anne and Capt. Mark Phillips, Nov. 14, 1973.

Churchill Painting Outdoors A27

Sultan Hassanal Bolkiah A28

Design: 50c, Churchill making "V" sign.

	Perf. 14x13½		
1973, Dec. 31	Litho.	Wmk. 314	
192 A27	12c car rose & multi	.15	.15
193 A27	50c dk green & multi	.55	.55

Winston Churchill Memorial Exhibition.

Wmk. 314 Sideways

1974, July 15	Photo.	Perf. 13x15	
194 A28	4c blue grn & multi	.15	.15
195 A28	5c dull blue & multi	.15	.15
196 A28	6c olive grn & multi	.15	.15
197 A28	10c lt violet & multi	.15	.15
b.	Watermark upright ('76)	.15	.15
198 A28	15c brown & multi	.15	.15
199 A28	20c buff & multi	.16	.15
b.	Watermark upright ('76)	.16	.16
200 A28	25c olive & multi	.18	.16
b.	Watermark upright ('76)	.20	.18
201 A28	30c multicolored	.22	.20
202 A28	35c gray & multi	.25	.22
203 A28	40c multicolored	.32	.28
204 A28	50c yel brn & multi	.38	.32
205 A28	75c multicolored	.60	.50
206 A28	$1 dull org & multi	.75	.65
207 A28	$2 multicolored	1.65	1.40
208 A28	$5 silver & multi	3.50	3.25
209 A28	$10 gold & multi	8.25	8.25
	Nos. 194-209 (16)	17.01	16.13

Issue date: Nos. 197b-200b, Apr. 12.

1975, Aug. 13		Wmk. 373	
194a A28	4c	.15	.15
195a A28	5c	.15	.15
196a A28	6c	.15	.15
197a A28	10c	.15	.15
198a A28	15c	.15	.15
199a A28	20c	.16	.16
200a A28	25c	.20	.20
201a A28	30c	.24	.24
202a A28	35c	.28	.28
203a A28	40c	.32	.32
204a A28	50c	.40	.40
205a A28	75c	.60	.60
206a A28	$1	.80	.80
207a A28	$2	1.60	1.60
208a A28	$5	4.00	4.00
209a A28	$10	8.00	8.00
	Nos. 194a-209a (16)	17.35	17.35

For surcharge see No. 225.

Brunei Airport A29

Design: 75c, Sultan Hassanal Bolkiah in uniform and jet over airport.

	Perf. 14x14½, 12½x13 (75c)		
1974, July 18	Litho.	Wmk. 314	
	Size: 44x28mm		
215 A29	50c multicolored	1.00	1.00
	Size: 47x36mm		
216 A29	75c multicolored	1.35	1.35

Opening of Brunei Airport.

UPU Emblem A30

1974, Oct. 28		Perf. 14½	
217 A30	12c orange & multi	.15	.15
218 A30	50c blue & multi	.50	.50
219 A30	75c emerald & multi	.75	.75
	Nos. 217-219 (3)	1.40	1.40

Centenary of Universal Postal Union.

Winston Churchill A31

Design: 75c, Churchill smoking cigar.

1974, Nov. 30	Wmk. 373	Perf. 14	
220 A31	12c vio blue, blue & gold	.15	.15
221 A31	75c dk green, black & gold	.90	.90

Sir Winston Churchill (1874-1965).

Boeing 737 Planes at Airport A32

Designs: 35c, Boeing 737 over Bandar Seri Begawan Mosque. 75c, Boeing 737 in flight. All planes with crest of Royal Brunei Airlines.

	Perf. 12½x12		
1975, May 14		Unwmk.	
222 A32	12c multicolored	.30	.25
223 A32	35c multicolored	1.00	.75
224 A32	75c multicolored	2.00	2.00
	Nos. 222-224 (3)	3.30	3.00

Inauguration of Royal Brunei Airlines.

No. 196a Surcharged in Silver

	Perf. 13x15		
1976, Aug. 16	Photo.	Wmk. 373	
225 A28	10c on 6c multicolored	.25	.25

British Royal Coat of Arms — A33

20c, Imperial State Crown. 75c, Elizabeth II.

	Wmk. 373		
1977, June 7	Litho.	Perf. 14	
226 A33	10c dk blue & multi	.15	.15
227 A33	20c purple & multi	.20	.20
228 A33	75c yellow & multi	.65	.65
	Nos. 226-228 (3)	1.00	1.00

25th anniv. of the reign of Elizabeth II.

Coronation of Elizabeth II — A34

20c, Elizabeth II with coronation regalia. 75c, Departure from Westminster Abbey (coach).

1978, June 2	Litho.	Perf. 13½x13	
229 A34	10c multicolored	.15	.15
230 A34	20c multicolored	.20	.20
231 A34	75c multicolored	.65	.65
	Nos. 229-231 (3)	1.00	1.00

25th anniv. of coronation of Elizabeth II.

Market value for a particular scarce stamp may remain relatively low if few collectors want it.

BRUNEI

Sultan's Coat of Arms — A35

Struggling Man, Human Rights Flame — A36

Coronation of Sultan Hassanal Bolkiah, 10th Anniv.: 20c, Ceremony. 75c, Royal crown.

1978, Aug. 1   Wmk. 373   Perf. 12
232	A35	10c multicolored	.15	.15
233	A35	20c multicolored	.22	.18
234	A35	75c multicolored	.90	.75
a.		Souvenir sheet of 3, #232-234	8.50	6.00
		Nos. 232-234 (3)	1.27	1.08

1978, Dec. 10   Litho.   Perf. 14
235	A36	10c red, black & yel	.15	.15
236	A36	20c violet, black & yel	.18	.18
237	A36	75c olive, black & yel	.65	.65
		Nos. 235-237 (3)	.98	.98

Universal Declaration of Human Rights, 30th anniversary.

Children and IYC Emblem — A37

1979, June 30   Wmk. 373   Perf. 14
238	A37	10c shown	.15	.15
239	A37	$1 IYC emblem	.90	.90

Telisai Earth Satellite Station — A38

Designs: 20c, Radar screen and satellite. 75c, Cameraman, telex operator, telephone.

1979, Sept. 23   Litho.   Perf. 14½x14
240	A38	10c multicolored	.15	.15
241	A38	20c multicolored	.18	.15
242	A38	75c multicolored	.75	.75
		Nos. 240-242 (3)	1.08	1.05

Hajeer Emblem — A39

1979, Nov. 21
243	A39	10c multicolored	.15	.15
244	A39	20c multicolored	.20	.20
245	A39	75c multicolored	.75	.75
a.		Souvenir sheet of 3, #243-245	2.50	2.50
		Nos. 243-245 (3)	1.10	1.10

Hegira, 1400th anniversary.

For all your stamp supply needs
www.scottonline.com

A40    **A41**

1980   Litho.   Perf. 14
246	A40	10c Installation ceremony	.15	.15
247	A40	10c Ceremony, diff.	.15	.15
248	A40	75c Jefri Bolkiah	.60	.60
249	A40	75c Sufri Bolkiah	.60	.60
		Nos. 246-249 (4)	1.50	1.50

Installation of Jefri Bolkiah and Sufri Bolkiah as Wizars (Ministers of State for Royalty) 1st anniv. Issue dates: Nos. 246, 248, Nov. 8; others, Dec. 6.

1981, Jan. 19   Litho.   Perf. 12x11½
255	A41	10c Umbrella	.15	.15
256	A41	15c Dagger, shield	.18	.18
257	A41	20c Spears	.25	.25
258	A41	30c Gold pouch	.35	.35

Size: 22½x40mm
Perf. 14x13½
259	A41	50c Headdress	.60	.60
a.		Souvenir sheet of 5, #255-259	2.25	2.25
		Nos. 255-259 (5)	1.53	1.53

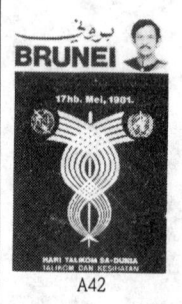

A42 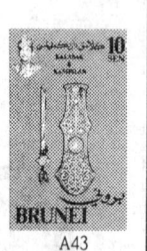   **A43**

1981, May 17   Litho.   Perf. 13x13½
260	A42	10c car rose & black	.15	.15
261	A42	75c dp violet & black	.75	.75

13th World Telecommunications Day.

Perf. 12½x12, 12 (75c)

1981, July 15   Litho.
Deep Rose Lilac Background
262	A43	10c Dagger, case	.15	.15
263	A43	15c Rifle, powder pouch	.15	.15
264	A43	20c Spears	.18	.18
265	A43	30c Sword, tunic, shield	.30	.30
266	A43	50c Horns	.50	.50

Size: 28½x45mm
267	A43	75c Gold bowl, table	.75	.75
		Nos. 262-267 (6)	2.03	2.03

See Nos. 278-289.

Royal Wedding Issue
Common Design Type

1981, July 29   Perf. 14
268	CD331	10c Bouquet	.15	.15
269	CD331	$1 Charles	.65	.65
270	CD331	$2 Couple	1.25	1.25
		Nos. 268-270 (3)	2.05	2.05

World Food Day — A44   **Intl. Year of the Disabled — A45**

1981, Oct. 16   Litho.   Perf. 12
271	A44	10c Fishermen	.15	.15
272	A44	$1 Produce	.80	.80

1981, Dec. 16   Wmk. 373   Perf. 12
273	A45	10c Blind man	.15	.15
274	A45	20c Sign language	.16	.16
275	A45	75c Man in wheelchair	.60	.60
		Nos. 273-275 (3)	.91	.91

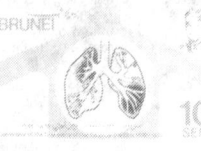

TB Bacillus Centenary A46

1982, Mar. 24   Perf. 12, 13½ (75c)
276	A46	10c Lungs	.15	.15
277	A46	75c Bacillus, microscope	.60	.60

Type of 1981
1982, May 31   Litho.   Perf. 12½x12
Deep Magenta Background
278	A43	10c shown	.15	.15
279	A43	15c Pedestal urn	.15	.15
280	A43	20c Silver bowl	.20	.20
281	A43	30c Candle	.30	.30
282	A43	50c Gold pipe	.50	.50

Size: 28x44mm
Perf. 13½
283	A43	75c Silver pointer	.75	.75
		Nos. 278-283 (6)	2.05	2.05

1982, July 15   Litho.   Perf. 12½x12
Violet Background
284	A43	10c Urn	.15	.15
285	A43	15c Crossed banners	.15	.15
286	A43	20c Golden fan	.20	.20
287	A43	30c Lid	.30	.30
288	A43	50c Sword, sheath	.50	.50

Size: 28x44mm
Perf. 12
289	A43	75c Golden chalice pole	.75	.75
		Nos. 284-289 (6)	2.05	2.05

A47

1983, Mar. 14   Litho.   Perf. 13½
290	A47	10c Flag	.15	.15
291	A47	20c Natl. palace	.20	.20
292	A47	75c Oil drilling	.75	.75
293	A47	$2 Sultan Bolkiah	2.00	2.00
a.		Block of 4, #290-293	3.05	3.05

Commonwealth Day.

World Communications Year — A48

1983, July 15   Litho.   Perf. 13½
294	A48	10c Mail delivery	.15	.15
295	A48	75c Typewriter, phone	.80	.80
296	A48	$2 Dish antenna, satellite, TV	2.00	2.00
		Nos. 294-296 (3)	2.95	2.95

Opening of Hassanal Bolkiah National Stadium A49

1983, Sept. 23   Litho.   Perf. 12
297	A49	10c Soccer, vert.	.15	.15
298	A49	75c Runners, vert.	1.00	1.00
299	A49	$1 shown	1.25	1.25
		Nos. 297-299 (3)	2.40	2.40

Size, Nos. 297-298: 26x33mm.

Fishing Industry — A50

1983, Sept. 23   Litho.   Perf. 13½
300	A50	10c Shrimp, lobster	.15	.15
301	A50	50c Pacific jacks	.60	.60
302	A50	75c Parrotfish, flatfish	.90	.90
303	A50	$1 Tuna	1.25	1.25
		Nos. 300-303 (4)	2.90	2.90

State Assembly Building — A51

Map of Southeast Asia, Flag — A52

Sultan Hassanal Bolkiah — A53

1984, Jan. 1   Litho.   Perf. 13
304	A51	10c shown	.15	.15
305	A51	20c State Secretariat building	.25	.25
306	A51	35c New Law Court	.40	.40
307	A51	50c Liquid natural gas well	.60	.60
308	A51	75c Omar Ali Saifuddin Mosque	.90	.90
309	A51	$1 Sultan's Palace	1.20	1.20
310	A52	$3 shown	3.60	3.60
a.		Souvenir sheet of 7, #304-310	7.25	7.25
		Nos. 304-310 (7)	7.10	7.10

Souvenir Sheets
311	Sheet of 4, Constitution signing, 1959	1.25	1.25
a.-d.	A53 25c any single	.25	.25
312	Sheet of 4, Brunei U.K. Friendship Agreement, 1979	1.25	1.25
a.-d.	A53 25c any single	.25	.25

Forestry Resources — A54

1984, Apr. 21   Litho.   Perf. 13½
313	A54	10c Forests, enrichment planting	.15	.15
314	A54	50c Irrigation canal	.60	.60
315	A54	75c Recreation forest	.90	.90
316	A54	$1 Wildlife	1.20	1.20
		Nos. 313-316 (4)	2.85	2.85

Philakorea 1984 — A55

BRUNEI

Litho. & Engr.
1984, Oct. 22 — Perf. 13
- 317 A55 10c No. 93 .15 .15
  - a. Souvenir sheet of 1 .15 .15
- 318 A55 75c No. 27 .90 .90
  - a. Souvenir sheet of 1 .90 .90
- 319 A55 $2 1895 local stamp 2.50 2.50
  - a. Souvenir sheet of 1 2.50 2.50
- Nos. 317-319 (3) 3.55 3.55

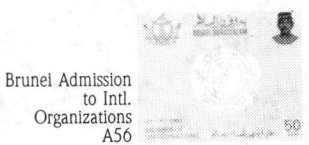

Brunei Admission to Intl. Organizations — A56

1985, Sept. 23 Litho. Perf. 13
- 320 A56 50c UN .45 .45
- 321 A56 50c Commonwealth .45 .45
- 322 A56 50c ASEAN .45 .45
- 323 A56 50c OIC .45 .45
  - a. Souv. sheet of 4, #320-323 + label 2.00 2.00
- Nos. 320-323 (4) 1.80 1.80

Intl. Youth Year — A57

1985, Oct. 17 Perf. 12
- 324 A57 10c shown .15 .15
- 325 A57 75c Industry, education .55 .55
- 326 A57 $1 Public Service .70 .70
- Nos. 324-326 (3) 1.40 1.40

Intl. Day of Solidarity with the Palestinian People — A58

1985, Nov. 29 Perf. 12x12½
- 327 A58 10c lt blue & multi .15 .15
- 328 A58 50c pink & multi .55 .55
- 329 A58 $1 lt green & multi 1.10 1.10
- Nos. 327-329 (3) 1.80 1.80

Natl. Scout Jamboree, Dec. 14-20 — A59

Sultan Hassanal Bolkiah — A60

1985, Dec. 14 Perf. 13½
- 330 A59 10c Scout handshake .15 .15
- 331 A59 20c Semaphore .18 .18
- 332 A59 $2 Jamboree emblem 1.75 1.75
- Nos. 330-332 (3) 2.08 2.08

1985-86 Wmk. 233 Perf. 13½x14½
- 333 A60 10c multi .15 .15
- 334 A60 15c multi .15 .15
- 335 A60 20c multi .18 .18
- 336 A60 25c multi .22 .22
- 337 A60 35c multi ('86) .32 .32
- 338 A60 40c multi ('86) .36 .36
- 339 A60 60c multi ('86) .45 .45
- 340 A60 75c multi ('86) .68 .68

Size: 35x42mm
Perf. 14
- 341 A60 $1 multi ('86) .90 .90
- 342 A60 $2 multi ('86) 1.75 1.75
- 343 A60 $5 multi ('86) 4.50 4.50
- 344 A60 $10 multi ('86) 9.00 9.00
- Nos. 333-344 (12) 18.66 18.66

Issued: #333-336, Dec. 23; #337-340, Jan. 15; #341-343, Feb. 23; #344, Mar. 29.

Admission to Intl. Organizations — A61

Wmk. Cartor (385)
1986, Apr. 30 Litho. Perf. 13
- 345 A61 50c WMO .45 .45
- 346 A61 50c ITU .45 .45
- 347 A61 50c UPU .45 .45
- 348 A61 50c ICAO .45 .45
  - a. Souv. sheet of 4, #345-348 + label 1.80 1.80
- Nos. 345-348 (4) 1.80 1.80

Royal Brunei Armed Forces, 25th Anniv. A62

1986, May 31 Unwmk. Perf. 13½
- 349 Strip of 4 1.40 1.40
  - a. A62 10c In combat .15 .15
  - b. A62 20c Communications .18 .18
  - c. A62 50c Air and sea defense .45 .45
  - d. A62 75c On parade, Royal Palace .68 .68

Royal Ensigns — A63

#350, Tunggul charok buritan, Pisang-pisang, Alam bernaga, Sandaran. #351, Dadap, Tunggul kawan, Ambal, Payong ubor-ubor, Sapu-sapu ayeng and Rawai lidah. #352, Ula-ula besar, Payong haram, Sumbu layang. #353, Payong ubor-ubor tiga ringkat and Payong tinggi. #354, Panji-panji, Chogan istiadat, Chogan ugama. #355, Lambang duli yang maha mulia and Mahligai.

1986 Litho. Perf. 12½
- 350 A63 10c multicolored .15 .15
- 351 A63 10c multicolored .15 .15
- 352 A63 75c multicolored .68 .68
- 353 A63 75c multicolored .68 .68
- 354 A63 $2 multicolored 1.75 1.75
- 355 A63 $2 multicolored 1.75 1.75
- Nos. 350-355 (6) 5.16 5.16

Intl. Peace Year — A64

1986, Oct. 24 Litho. Perf. 12
- 356 A64 50c Peace doves .48 .48
- 357 A64 75c Hands .68 .68
- 358 A64 $1 Peace symbols .88 .88
- Nos. 356-358 (3) 2.04 2.04

Natl. Anti-Drug Campaign Posters — A65

Brass Artifacts — A66

1987, Mar. 15 Litho. Perf. 12
- 359 A65 10c Jail .15 .15
- 360 A65 75c Noose .65 .65
- 361 A65 $1 Execution .88 .88
- Nos. 359-361 (3) 1.68 1.68

1987, July 15
- 362 A66 50c Kiri (kettle) .45 .45
- 363 A66 50c Langguai (bowl) .45 .45
- 364 A66 50c Badil (cannon) .45 .45
- 365 A66 50c Pelita (lamp) .45 .45
- Nos. 362-365 (4) 1.80 1.80

See Nos. 388-391.

Dewan Bahasa Dan Pustaka, 25th Anniv. — A67

Illustration reduced.

1987, Sept. 29 Perf. 13½x13
- 366 A67 Strip of 3 1.75 1.75
  - a. 10c multicolored .15 .15
  - b. 50c multicolored .30 .30
  - c. $2 multicolored 1.25 1.25

Language and Literature Bureau.

ASEAN, 20th Anniv. — A68

1987, Aug. 8 Litho. Perf. 14x13½
- 367 A68 20c Map .18 .18
- 368 A68 50c Year dates .45 .45
- 369 A68 $1 Flags, emblem .90 .90
- Nos. 367-369 (3) 1.53 1.53

World Food Day A70

Fruit: a, Artocarpus odoratissima. b, Canarium odontophyllum mig. c, Litsea garciae. d, Mangifera foetida lour.

1987, Oct. 31 Perf. 12½
- 370 Strip of 4 1.80 1.80
  - a.-d. A70 50c any single .45 .45

See Nos. 374, 405, 423, 457-460.

Intl. Year of Shelter for the Homeless A71

Various houses.

1987, Nov. 28 Litho. Perf. 13
- 371 A71 50c multi .48 .48
- 372 A71 75c multi, diff. .70 .70
- 373 A71 $1 multi, diff. .95 .95
- Nos. 371-373 (3) 2.13 2.13

Fruit Type of 1987
Without FAO Emblem, Dated 1988

Fruit: a, Durio. b, Durio oxleyanus. c, Durio graveolens (cross section at L). d, Durio graveolens (cross section at R).

1988, Jan. 30 Litho. Perf. 12
- 374 Strip of 4 2.00 2.00
  - a.-d. A70 50c, any single .50 .50

Opening of Malay Technology Museum — A72

1988, Feb. 29 Perf. 12½x12
- 375 A72 10c Wooden lathe .15 .15
- 376 A72 75c Water wheel, buffalo .75 .75
- 377 A72 $1 Bird caller in blind 1.00 1.00
- Nos. 375-377 (3) 1.90 1.90

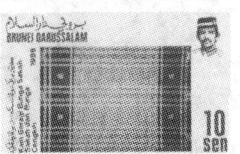

Handwoven Cloth — A73

Designs: 10c, Kain Beragi Bunga Sakah-Sakah Dan Bunga Cengkih. 20c, Kain Jong Sarat. 25c, Kain Si Pugut. 40c, Kain Si Pugut Bunga Berlapis. 75c, Kain Si Lobang Bangsi Bunga Belitang Kipas.

1988, Apr. 30 Litho. Perf. 12
- 378 A73 10c multicolored .15 .15
- 379 A73 20c org brown & blk .20 .20
- 380 A73 25c multicolored .25 .25
- 381 A73 40c multicolored .40 .40
- 382 A73 75c multicolored .75 .75
  - a. Souvenir sheet of 5, #378-382 + label 1.70 1.70
- Nos. 378-382 (5) 1.75 1.75

1988, Sept. 29 Litho. Perf. 12

Designs: 10c, Kain Beragi. 20c, Kain Bertabur. 25c, Kain Sukma Indra. 40c, Kain Si Pugut Bunga Bersusup. 75c, Kain Beragi Si Lobang Bangsi Bunga Cendera Kesuma.

- 383 A73 10c multicolored .15 .15
- 384 A73 20c multicolored .20 .20
- 385 A73 25c multicolored .25 .25
- 386 A73 40c multicolored .40 .40
- 387 A73 75c multicolored .75 .75
  - a. Souvenir sheet of 5, #383-387 1.70 1.70
- Nos. 383-387 (5) 1.75 1.75

Brass Artifacts Type of 1987
1988, June 30 Litho. Perf. 12
- 388 A66 50c Celapa (repousse box) .50 .50
- 389 A66 50c Gangsa (footed plate) .50 .50
- 390 A66 50c Periok (lidded pot) .50 .50
- 391 A66 50c Lampong (candlestick) .50 .50
- Nos. 388-391 (4) 2.00 2.00

Coronation of Sultan Hassanal Bolkiah, 20th Anniv. — A74

1988, Aug. 1 Litho. Perf. 14
- 392 A74 20c shown .20 .20
- 393 A74 75c Reading from the Koran .75 .75

Size: 26x62mm
Perf. 12½x13
- 394 A74 $2 In full regalia 2.00 2.00
  - a. Souvenir sheet of 3, #392-394 3.00 3.00
- Nos. 392-394 (3) 2.95 2.95

Eradicate Malaria, WHO 40th Anniv. A75

1988, Dec. 17 Litho. Perf. 14x13½
- 395 A75 25c Mosquito .25 .25
- 396 A75 35c Extermination .35 .35
- 397 A75 $2 Microscope, infected blood cells 2.10 2.10
- Nos. 395-397 (3) 2.70 2.70

Natl. Day — A76

1989, Feb. 23 Litho. Perf. 12
Size of 60c: 22x54½mm
- 398 A76 20c Sultan Bolkiah, officials .20 .20
- 399 A76 30c Honor guard .30 .30
- 400 A76 60c Fireworks, palace, vert. .60 .60
- 401 A76 $2 Religious ceremony 2.00 2.00
  - a. Souvenir sheet of 4, #398-401 3.20 3.20
- Nos. 398-401 (4) 3.10 3.10

Independence from Britain, 5th anniv.

BRUNEI

Solidarity with the Palestinians A77

1989, Apr. 1   Litho.   Perf. 13½
402 A77 20c shown   .20   .20
403 A77 75c Map, flag   .75   .75
404 A77 $1 Dome of the Rock   1.00 1.00
     Nos. 402-404 (3)   1.95 1.95

Fruit Type of 1987
Without FAO Emblem, Dated 1989
Designs: a, Daemonorops fissa. b, Eleiodoxa conferia. c, Salacca zalacca. d, Calamus ornatus.

1989, Oct. 31   Litho.   Perf. 12
405   Strip of 4   2.50 2.50
  a.-d. A70 60c any single   .82   .82

Oil and Gas Industry, 60th Anniv. A79

1989, Dec. 28   Perf. 13½
406 A79 20c Drill   .22   .22
407 A79 60c Tanker   .65   .65
408 A79 90c Refinery   1.00 1.00
409 A79 $1 Rail transport   1.10 1.10
410 A79 $2 Offshore rig   2.20 2.20
     Nos. 406-410 (5)   5.17 5.17

Brunei Museum, 25th Anniv. A80

1990, Jan. 1   Litho.   Perf. 12x12½
411 A80 30c Exhibits   .30   .30
412 A80 60c Official opening, 1965 .60   .60
413 A80 $1 Museum exterior   1.00 1.00
     Nos. 411-413 (3)   1.90 1.90

Intl. Literacy Year — A81

1990, July 15   Litho.   Perf. 12x12½
414 A81 15c multicolored   .16   .16
415 A81 90c multicolored   .95   .95
416 A81 $1 multicolored   1.10 1.10
     Nos. 414-416 (3)   2.21 2.21

Tarsier — A82    Fight Against AIDS — A83

1990, Sept. 29   Litho.   Perf. 12
417 A82 20c shown   .22   .22
418 A82 60c Eating leaves   .68   .68
419 A82 90c Climbing tree   1.00 1.00
     Nos. 417-419 (3)   1.90 1.90

1990, Dec. 1   Litho.   Perf. 13
420 A83 20c shown   .22   .22
421 A83 30c AIDS transmission   .35   .35
422 A83 90c Tombstone, skulls   1.00 1.00
     Nos. 420-422 (3)   1.57 1.57

Fruit Type of 1987
Without FAO Emblem, Dated 1990
Fruit: a, Willoughbea (uncut core). b, Willoughbea (core cut in half). c, Willoughbea angustifolia.

1990, Dec. 31   Perf. 12½
423   Strip of 3   2.05 2.05
  a.-c. A70 60c any single   .68   .68

Proboscis Monkey — A84

1991, Mar. 30   Litho.   Perf. 13½x14
424 A84 15c shown   .18   .18
425 A84 20c Head, facing   .22   .22
426 A84 50c Sitting on branch   .60   .60
427 A84 60c Adult with young   .70   .70
     Nos. 424-427 (4)   1.70 1.70

Teacher's Day A85

Design: 90c, Teacher at blackboard.

1991, Sept. 23   Litho.   Perf. 13½x14
428 A85 60c multicolored   .70   .70
429 A85 90c multicolored   1.05 1.05

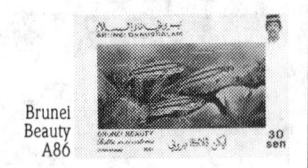

Brunei Beauty A86

1991, Oct. 1   Litho.   Perf. 13
430 A86 30c Three immature   .35   .35
431 A86 60c Female   .70   .70
432 A86 $1 Adult male   1.20 1.20
     Nos. 430-432 (3)   2.25 2.25

Happy Family Campaign — A87

1991, Nov. 30   Litho.   Perf. 13
433 A87 20c Family, graduating son .25   .25
434 A87 60c Mothers, children   .70   .70
435 A87 90c Adults, children, heart 1.05 1.05
     Nos. 433-435 (3)   2.00 2.00

World Health Day — A88

1992, Apr. 7   Litho.   Perf. 13
436 A88 20c multicolored   .25   .25
437 A88 50c multi. diff.   .58   .58

Size: 48x28mm

438 A88 75c multi. diff.   .90   .90
     Nos. 436-438 (3)   1.73 1.73

Brunei-Singapore and Brunei-Malaysia-Philippines Fiber Optic Submarine Cables — A89

1992, Apr. 28   Litho.   Perf. 12
439 A89 20c Map   .25   .25
440 A89 30c Diagram   .35   .35
441 A89 90c Submarine cable   1.05 1.05
     Nos. 439-441 (3)   1.65 1.65

Visit ASEAN Year A90

Designs: a, 20c, Sculptures. b, 60c, Judo exhibition. c, $1, Sculptures, diff.

1992, June 30   Litho.   Perf. 13½x14
442 A90 Strip of 3, #a.-c.   2.00 2.00

ASEAN, 25th Anniv. — A91

1992, Aug. 8   Litho.   Perf. 14
443 A91 20c shown   .25   .25
444 A91 60c Building   .70   .70
445 A91 90c Views of member states 1.05 1.05
     Nos. 443-445 (3)   2.00 2.00

1992, Oct. 5   Perf. 14x13½

Sultan in various forms of dress and: No. 446a, Coronation procession. b, Airport. c, New Law Court, Sultan's Palace. d, Ship and Brunei University. e, Mosque, buildings.

446 A92 25c Strip of 5, #a.-e.   1.50 1.50

Sultan Hassanal Bolkiah's Accession to the Throne, 25th Anniv.

Birds — A93

Designs: No. 447, Crested wood partridge, vert. No. 448, Long-tailed parakeet, vert. No. 449, Chestnut-breasted malkoha. No. 450, Asian paradise flycatcher, vert. No. 451, Magpie robin, vert. No. 452, White-rumped shama. No. 453, Great argus pheasant, vert. No. 454, Malay lorikeet, vert. No. 455, Black and red broadbill, vert.

Perf. 14x13½, 13½x14

1992-93   Litho.
447 A93 30c multicolored   .38   .38
448 A93 30c multicolored   .38   .38
449 A93 30c multicolored   .38   .38
450 A93 60c multicolored   .75   .75
451 A93 60c multicolored   .75   .75
452 A93 60c multicolored   .75   .75
453 A93 $1 multicolored   1.20 1.20
454 A93 $1 multicolored   1.20 1.20
455 A93 $1 multicolored   1.20 1.20
     Nos. 447-455 (9)   6.99 6.99

Issued: #447, 450, 453, 12/30/92; #448, 451, 454, 1/27/93; others, 5/3/93.

Natl. Day, 10th Anniv. — A94

10th anniv. emblem and: a, 10c, Natl. flag. b, 20c, Hands supporting inscription. c, 30c, Natl. day emblems, 1985-93. d, 60c, Emblem with star, crossed swords.

1994, June 16   Litho.   Perf. 13
456 A94 Strip of 4, #a.-d.   1.50 1.50

Fruit Type of 1987
Without FAO Emblem, Dated 1994
Designs: No. 457, Nephelium mutabile. No. 458, Nephelium xerospermoides. No. 459, Nephelium spp. No. 460, Nephelium macrophyllum.

1994, Aug. 8   Litho.   Perf. 13½x13
457 A70 60c multicolored   .75   .75
458 A70 60c multicolored   .75   .75
459 A70 60c multicolored   .75   .75
460 A70 60c multicolored   .75   .75
     Nos. 457-460 (4)   3.00 3.00

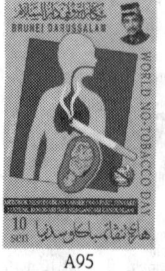

A95    A96

World Stop Smoking Day: 10c, Cigarette, lung, fetus over human figure. 15c, People throwing away tobacco, cigarettes, pipe. $2, Arms around world crushing out cigarettes.

1994, Sept. 1   Litho.   Perf. 13½x13
461 A95 10c multicolored   .15   .15
462 A95 15c multicolored   .20   .20
463 A95 $2 multicolored   2.50 2.50
     Nos. 461-463 (3)   2.85 2.85

1994, Oct. 7   Perf. 13½

Girl Guides in Brunei, 40th anniv.: a, Leader. b, Girl receiving award. c, Girl reading. d, Girls in various costumes. e, Girls camping out.

464 A96 40c Strip of 5, #a.-e.   2.50 2.50

Royal Brunei Airlines, 20th Anniv. — A97

Airplanes: 10c, Twin-engine propeller. 20c, Passenger jet attached to tow bar. $1, Passenger jet in air.

1994, Nov. 18   Litho.   Perf. 13½
465 A97 10c multicolored   .15   .15
466 A97 20c multicolored   .28   .28
467 A97 $1 multicolored   1.25 1.25
     Nos. 465-467 (3)   1.68 1.68

BRUNEI — BULGARIA

Intl. Day Against Drug Abuse — A98

Healthy people wearing traditional costumes: 20c, 60c, $1.

1994, Dec. 30   Litho.   Perf. 13½
468 A98 Strip of 3, #a.-c.   2.25 2.25
No. 468 is a continuous design.

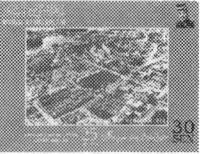

City of Bandar Seri Begawan, 25th Anniv. A100

Aerial view of city: 30c, In 1970. 50c, In 1980, with details of significant buildings. $1, In 1990.

1995, Oct. 4   Litho.   Perf. 13½
481 A100 30c multicolored   .40   .40
482 A100 50c multicolored   .70   .70
483 A100 $1 multicolored   1.40 1.40
       Nos. 481-483 (3)   2.50 2.50

A101 / A102

UN headquarters: 20c, Delegates in General Assembly. 60c, Security Council. 90c, Exterior.

1995, Oct. 24   Perf. 14½x14
484 A101 20c multicolored   .30   .30
485 A101 60c multicolored   .85   .85
       Size: 27x44mm
486 A101 90c multicolored   1.30 1.30
       Nos. 484-486 (3)   2.45 2.45
       UN, 50th anniv.

1995, Oct. 28   Perf. 13x13½

University of Brunei, 10th Anniv.: 30c, Students in classroom. 50c, Campus buildings. 90c, Sultan in procession.

487 A102 30c multicolored   .40   .40
488 A102 50c multicolored   .70   .70
489 A102 90c multicolored   1.30 1.30
       Nos. 487-489 (3)   2.40 2.40

A103 / A104

Royal Brunei Police, 25th Anniv.: 25c, Policemen in various uniforms. 50c, Various tasks performed by police. 75c, Sultan reviewing police.

1996, Feb. 10   Litho.   Perf. 13½x13
490 A103 25c multicolored   .35   .35
491 A103 50c multicolored   .75   .75
492 A103 75c multicolored   1.10 1.10
       Nos. 490-492 (3)   2.20 2.20

1996, May 17   Litho.   Perf. 13½
World Telecommunications Day: 20c, Cartoon telephone, cordless telephone. 35c, Globe, telephone dial surrounded by communication devices. $1, Signals transmitting from earth, people communicating.

493 A104 20c multicolored   .30   .30
494 A104 35c multicolored   .50   .50
495 A104 $1 multicolored   1.45 1.45
       Nos. 493-495 (3)   2.25 2.25

A105 / A106

Sultan: No. 496, Among people, in black attire. No. 497, Waving, in yellow attire. No. 498, In blue shirt. No. 499, Among people, wearing cream-colored robe.
$1, Hand raised in yellow attire.

1996, July 15   Litho.   Perf. 13
496 A105 50c multicolored   .75   .75
497 A105 50c multicolored   .75   .75
498 A105 50c multicolored   .75   .75
499 A105 50c multicolored   .75   .75
       Nos. 496-499 (4)   3.00 3.00
       Souvenir Sheet
500 A105 $1 multicolored   1.40 1.40
Sultan Paduka Seri Baginda, 50th birthday.
A souvenir sheet of five $50 stamps exists.

1996, Nov. 11   Litho.   Perf. 13½
Terns.
501 A106 20c Black-naped tern   .30   .30
502 A106 30c Roseate tern   .45   .45
503 A106 $1 Bridle tern   1.45 1.45
       Nos. 501-503 (3)   2.20 2.20
No. 502 is spelled "Roslate" on stamp.

Sultan Hassanal Bolkiah
A107 / A108

1996, Oct. 9   Litho.   Wmk. 387
Background Color
504 A107 10c yellow green   .15   .15
505 A107 15c pale pink   .20   .20
506 A107 20c lilac pink   .30   .30
507 A107 30c salmon   .45   .45
508 A107 50c yellow   .75   .75
509 A107 60c pale green   .85   .85
510 A107 75c blue   1.10 1.10
511 A107 90c lilac   1.30 1.30
512 A108 $1 pink   1.45 1.45
513 A108 $2 orange yellow   2.90 2.90
514 A108 $5 light blue   7.25 7.25
515 A108 $10 bright yellow   14.50 14.50
       Nos. 504-515 (12)   31.20 31.15

Flowers A109

1997, May 29   Litho.   Perf. 12
516 A109 20c Acanthus ebracteatus   .30   .30
517 A109 30c Lumnitzera littorea   .45   .45
518 A109 $1 Nypa fruticans   1.45 1.45
       Nos. 516-518 (3)   2.20 2.20

Marine Life A110

Designs: No. 519, Bohadschia argus. No. 520, Oxycomanthus bennetti. No. 521, Heterocentrotus mammillatus. No. 522, Linckia laevigata.

1997, Dec. 15   Litho.   Perf. 12
519 A110 60c multicolored   .85   .85
520 A110 60c multicolored   .85   .85
521 A110 60c multicolored   .85   .85
522 A110 60c multicolored   .85   .85
       Nos. 519-522 (4)   3.40 3.40

Asian and Pacific Decade of Disabled Persons (1993-2002) A111

Designs: 20c, Silhouettes of people, hands finger spelling "Brunei," children. 50c, Fireworks over city, blind people participating in arts, crafts, music. $1, Handicapped people playing sports.

1998, Mar. 31   Litho.   Perf. 13x13½
523 A111 20c multicolored   .25   .25
524 A111 50c multicolored   .65   .65
525 A111 $1 multicolored   1.25 1.25
       Nos. 523-525 (3)   2.15 2.15

ASEAN, 30th Anniv. — A112

Designs: No. 526, Night scene of Sultan's Palace, buildings, map of Brunei. No. 527, Flags of ASEAN nations. No. 528, Daytime scenes of Sultan's Palace, transportation methods, buildings in Brunei.

1998, Aug. 8   Litho.   Perf. 13½
526 A112 30c multicolored   .40   .40
527 A112 30c multicolored   .40   .40
528 A112 30c multicolored   .40   .40
       Nos. 526-528 (3)   1.20 1.20

Sultan Hassanal Bolkiah, 30th Anniv. of Coronation A113

Designs: 60c, In procession, saluting, on throne. 90c, Sultan Omar Ali Saifuddin standing, Sultan Hassanal Bolkiah on throne. $1, Procession.

1998, Aug. 1   Litho.   Perf. 12
529 A113 60c multicolored   .65   .65
530 A113 90c multicolored   1.10 1.10
531 A113 $1 multicolored   1.25 1.25
  a.   Souvenir sheet, #529-531   3.00 3.00
       Nos. 529-531 (3)   3.00 3.00

A114 / A115

Investiture of Crown Prince Al-Muhtadee Billah: $1, Signing document. $2, Formal portrait. $3, Arms of the Crown Prince.

1998, Aug. 10
532 A114 $1 multicolored   1.25 1.25
533 A114 $2 multicolored   2.50 2.50
534 A114 $3 multicolored   3.50 3.50
  a.   Souvenir sheet #532-534   7.25 7.25
       Nos. 532-534 (3)   7.25 7.25

1998, Sept. 29   Perf. 13x13½
30c, Hands clasped, woman, man. 60c, Dollar sign over book, arrows, "7.45AM." 90c, Silhouettes of people seated at table, standing, scales.

535 A115 30c multicolored   .35   .35
536 A115 60c multicolored   .70   .70
537 A115 90c multicolored   1.10 1.10
       Nos. 535-537 (3)   2.15 2.15
Civil Service Day, 5th anniv.

Kingfishers — A116

1998, Nov. 11   Litho.   Perf. 13½x13
538 A116 20c Blue-eared   .25   .25
539 A116 30c Common   .35   .35
540 A116 60c White-collared   .75   .75
       Nos. 538-540 (3)   1.35 1.35

OCCUPATION STAMPS

Issued under Japanese Occupation
Stamps and Types of 1908-37
Handstamped in Violet, Red Violet, Blue or Red

大日本帝國政府

Perf. 14, 14x11½ (#N7)
1942-44   Wmk. 4
N1   A1   1c black   6.50 11.00
N2   A1   2c green   65.00 100.00
N3   A1   2c dull orange   3.50   6.00
N4   A1   3c green   27.50 65.00
N5   A1   4c orange   5.00 14.00
N6   A1   5c brown   5.50 14.00
N7   A2   6c slate gray   65.00 140.00
N8   A2   6c red   650.00 500.00
N9   A1   8c gray (RV)   650.00 825.00
N10 A2   8c carmine   5.00 10.00
N11 A1 10c violet, *yel*   10.00 17.50
N12 A2 12c blue   10.00 17.50
N13 A2 15c ultra   10.00 17.50
N14 A1 25c dk violet   22.50 65.00
N15 A1 30c org & red vio   110.00 275.00
N16 A1 50c blk, *green*   35.00 80.00
N17 A1 $1 red & blk, *bl*   60.00 100.00
                                      Wmk. 3
N18 A1 $5 lake, *green*   800.   750.
N19 A1 $25 black, *red*   1,400. 1,500.

Overprints vary in shade. Nos. N3, N7, N10 and N13 without overprint are not believed to have been regularly issued.

大日本
郵*便
帝國*郵使

No. 43 Surcharged in Red

1944   Wmk. 4   Perf. 14
N20 A1 $3 on 1c black   3,250. 3,250.
  a.   On No. N1   3,250. 3,250.

BULGARIA

,bəl-'gar-ē-ə

LOCATION — Southeastern Europe bordering on the Black Sea on the east and the Danube River on the north
GOVT. — Republic
AREA — 42,823 sq. mi.

BULGARIA

POP. — 8,929,332 (1983)
CAPITAL — Sofia

In 1885 Bulgaria, then a principality under the suzerainty of the Sultan of Turkey, was joined by Eastern Rumelia. Independence from Turkey was obtained in 1908.

100 Centimes = 1 Franc
100 Stotinki = 1 Lev (1881)

Catalogue values for unused stamps in this country are for Never Hinged items, beginning with Scott 293 in the regular postage section, Scott B1 in the semi-postal section, Scott C15 in the airpost section, Scott CB1 in the airpost semi-postal section, Scott E1 in the special delivery section, Scott J47 in the postage due section, Scott O1 in the officials section, and Scott Q1 in the parcel post section.

Watermarks

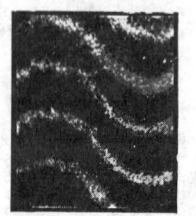

Wmk. 145- Wavy Lines

Wmk. 168- Wavy Lines and EZGV in Cyrillic

Wmk. 275- Entwined Curved Lines

Lion of Bulgaria
A1   A2   A3

Perf. 14½x15

1879, June 1   Wmk. 168   Typo.
Laid Paper

1	A1	5c black & yel	65.00	18.00
2	A1	10c black & grn	250.00	60.00
3	A1	25c black & vio	175.00	15.00
a.		Imperf.		
4	A1	50c black & blue	250.00	50.00
5	A2	1fr black & red	50.00	17.50

1881, June 10

6	A3	3s red & silver	12.50	2.50
7	A3	5s black & grn	15.00	2.50
a.		Background inverted		1,750.
8	A3	10s black & grn	60.00	6.50
9	A3	15s red & grn	60.00	6.50
10	A3	25s black & vio	250.00	30.00
11	A3	30s blue & fawn	17.50	6.50

1882, Dec. 4

12	A3	3s orange & yel	1.00	.50
a.		Background inverted	2,750.	1,400.
13	A3	5s green & pale green	6.00	.50
a.		5s rose & pale rose (error)	1,600.	1,300.
14	A3	10s rose & pale rose	8.00	.75
15	A3	15s red vio & pale lil	6.00	.40
16	A3	25s blue & pale blue	6.00	.50
17	A3	30s violet & grn	6.00	.75
18	A3	50s blue & pink	6.00	.75
		Nos. 12-18 (7)	39.00	4.15

See Nos. 207-210, 286.

A4   A5

Surcharged in Black, Carmine or Vermilion
1884, May 1   Typo. Surcharge

19	A4	3s on 10s rose (Bk)	95.00	30.00
20	A4	5s on 30s blue & fawn (C)	95.00	45.00
20A	A4	5s on 30s bl & fawn (Bk)	1,750.	1,750.
21	A5	15s on 25s blue (C)	140.00	40.00

On some values the surcharge may be found inverted or double.

1885, June   Litho. Surcharge

21B	A4	3s on 10s rose (Bk)	45.00	27.50
21C	A4	5s on 30s bl & fawn (V)	50.00	35.00
21D	A5	15s on 25s blue (V)	70.00	45.00
22	A5	50s on 1fr blk & red (Bk)	190.00	125.00

Forgeries of Nos. 19-22 are plentiful.

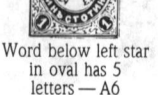

Word below left star in oval has 5 letters — A6

Third letter below left star is "A" — A7

1885, May 25

| 23 | A6 | 1s gray vio & pale gray | 12.00 | 5.00 |
| 24 | A7 | 2s sl grn & pale gray | 12.00 | 4.00 |

Word below left star has 4 letters — A8

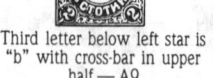

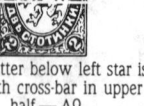

A10

Third letter below left star is "b" with cross-bar in upper half — A9

1886-87

25	A8	1s gray vio & pale gray	1.00	.20
26	A9	2s sl grn & pale gray	1.00	.20
27	A10	1 l black & red ('87)	27.50	3.00
		Nos. 25-27 (3)	29.50	3.40

For surcharge see No. 40.

A11

Perf. 10½, 11, 11½, 13, 13½
1889   Wove Paper   Unwmk.

28	A11	1s lilac	.16	.15
29	A11	2s gray	.60	.15
30	A11	3s bister brown	.40	.15
31	A11	5s yellow green	.25	.15
a.		Vert. pair, imperf. btwn.		
32	A11	10s rose	1.10	.15
33	A11	15s orange	.65	.15
34	A11	25s blue	1.00	.15
35	A11	30s dk brown	8.75	.15
36	A11	50s green	.60	.32
37	A11	1 l orange red	.52	.38
		Nos. 28-37 (10)	14.03	1.90

The 10s orange is a proof.
Nos. 28-34 exist imperforate. Value, set $225.
See Nos. 39, 41-42. For overprints and surcharges see Nos. 38, 55-56, 77-81, 113.

No. 35 Surcharged in Black   15

1892, Jan. 26

| 38 | A11 | 15s on 30s brn | 10.00 | 1.00 |
| a. | | Inverted surcharge | 70.00 | 52.50 |

1894   Perf. 10½, 11, 11½
Pelure Paper

| 39 | A11 | 10s red | 7.00 | .50 |
| a. | | Imperf. | 57.50 | |

No. 26 Surcharged in Red   01

Wmk. Wavy Lines (168)
1895, Oct. 25   Perf. 14½x15
Laid Paper

40	A9	1s on 2s	.75	.20
a.		Inverted surcharge	6.00	5.00
b.		Double surcharge	62.50	62.50
c.		Pair, one without surcharge	125.00	125.00

This surcharge on No. 24 is a proof.

Wmk. Coat of Arms in the Sheet
1896, Apr. 30   Perf. 11½, 13
Wove Paper

| 41 | A11 | 2 l rose & pale rose | 2.00 | 1.50 |
| 42 | A11 | 3 l black & buff | 3.50 | 3.00 |

Coat of Arms — A14

Cherry Wood Cannon — A15

1896, Feb. 2   Perf. 13

43	A14	1s blue green	.32	.15
44	A14	5s dark blue	.32	.15
45	A14	15s purple	.50	.18
46	A14	25s red	4.75	.85
		Nos. 43-46 (4)	5.89	1.33

Baptism of Prince Boris.
Examples of Nos. 41-46 from sheet edges show no watermark.
Nos. 43, 45-46 were also printed on rough unwatermarked paper.

1901, Apr. 20   Litho.   Unwmk.

| 53 | A15 | 5s carmine | 1.25 | .90 |
| 54 | A15 | 15s yellow green | 1.25 | .90 |

Insurrection of Independence in April, 1876, 25th anniversary.
Exist imperf. Forgeries exist.

Nos. 30 and 36 Surcharged in Black   5

1901, Mar. 24   Typo.

55	A11	5s on 3s bister brn	1.75	.75
a.		Inverted surcharge	42.50	42.50
b.		Pair, one without surcharge	70.00	70.00
56	A11	10s on 50s green	2.25	.75
a.		Inverted surcharge	50.00	50.00
b.		Pair, one without surcharge	70.00	70.00

Tsar Ferdinand A17

Fighting at Shipka Pass A18

ONE LEV
Type I - The numerals in the upper corners have, at the top, a sloping serif on the left side and a short straight serif on the right.
Type II - The numerals in the upper corners are of ordinary shape without the serif at the right.

1901-05   Typo.   Perf. 12½

57	A17	1s vio & gray blk	.15	.15
58	A17	2s brnz grn & ind	.15	.15
a.		Imperf.		
59	A17	3s orange & ind	.15	.15
60	A17	5s emerald & brn	2.25	.15
61	A17	10s rose & blk	1.50	.15
62	A17	15s claret & gray blk	.65	.15
63	A17	25s blue & blk	.65	.15
64	A17	30s bis & gray blk	15.00	.15
65	A17	50s dk blue & brn	.80	.15
66	A17	1 l red org & brnz grn, type I	2.00	.15
67	A17	1 l brn red & brnz grn, II ('05)	45.00	1.75
68	A17	2 l carmine & blk	4.00	.85
69	A17	3 l slate & red brn	5.00	1.90
		Nos. 57-69 (13)	77.30	6.00

For surcharges see Nos. 73, 83-85, 87-88.

1902, Aug. 29   Litho.   Perf. 11½

70	A18	5s lake	1.00	.35
71	A18	10s blue green	1.00	.35
72	A18	15s blue	5.25	1.25
		Nos. 70-72 (3)	7.25	2.35

Battle of Shipka Pass, 1877.
Imperf. copies are proofs.
Excellent forgeries of Nos. 70 to 72 exist.

No. 62 Surcharged in Black   10

1903, Oct. 1   Perf. 12½

73	A17	10s on 15s	5.00	.35
a.		Inverted surcharge	57.50	50.00
b.		Double surcharge	57.50	50.00
c.		Pair, one without surcharge	100.00	100.00
d.		10s on 10s rose & black	275.00	275.00

Ferdinand in 1887 and 1907 — A19

1907, Aug. 12   Litho.   Perf. 11½

74	A19	5s deep green	9.00	.90
75	A19	10s red brown	16.00	.90
76	A19	25s deep blue	24.00	1.75
		Nos. 74-76 (3)	49.00	3.55

Accession to the throne of Ferdinand I, 20th anniversary.
Nos. 74-76 imperf. are proofs. Nos. 74-76 exist in pairs imperforate between.

Stamps of 1889 Overprinted   1909

1909

77	A11	1s lilac	1.00	.50
a.		Inverted overprint	21.00	17.50
b.		Double overprint, one inverted	25.00	25.00
78	A11	5s yellow green	1.00	.50
a.		Inverted overprint	25.00	25.00
b.		Double overprint	25.00	25.00

With Additional Surcharge   5 or 10

79	A11	5s on 30s brown (Bk)	1.50	.18
a.		"5" double	700.00	550.00
80	A11	10s on 15s org (Bk)	1.50	.40
a.		Inverted surcharge	17.50	17.50
b.		"1909" omitted	27.50	27.50
81	A11	10s on 50s dk green (R)	1.50	.40
a.		"1990" for "1909"	100.00	100.00
b.		Black surcharge	52.50	52.50

Nos. 62 & 64
Surcharged with Value Only

83	A17	5s on 15s (Bl)	1.75	.60
a.		Inverted surcharge	21.00	21.00
84	A17	10s on 15s (Bl)	4.50	.40
a.		Inverted surcharge	21.00	21.00
85	A17	25s on 30s (R)	5.75	.90
a.		Double surcharge	70.00	70.00
b.		"2" of "25" omitted	87.50	87.50
c.		Blue surcharge	275.00	175.00

1910

Nos. 59 and 62 Surcharged in Blue   **5**

BULGARIA

1910, Oct.
87	A17	1s on 3s	3.50	.75
a.		"1910" omitted	21.00	
88	A17	5s on 15s	1.50	.50

Tsar Assen's Tower (Crown over lion) A20

Tsar Ferdinand A21

City of Trnovo A22

Tsar Ferdinand A23

Ferdinand A24

Isker River A25

Ferdinand A26

Rila Monastery (Crown at UR) A27

Tsar and Princes — A28

Ferdinand in Robes of Ancient Tsars — A29

Monastery of Holy Trinity — A30

View of Varna — A31

1911, Feb. 14   Engr.   Perf. 12
89	A20	1s myrtle green	.16	.15
90	A21	2s car & blk	.16	.15
91	A22	3s lake & blk	.40	.15
92	A23	5s green & blk	1.00	.15
93	A24	10s dp red & blk	1.40	.15
94	A25	15s brown bister	2.50	.15
95	A26	25s ultra & blk	.50	.15
96	A27	30s blue & blk	6.75	.16
97	A28	50s ocher & blk	16.00	.22
a.		Center inverted		2,250.
98	A29	1 l chocolate	6.00	.28
99	A30	2 l dull pur & blk	1.65	.90
100	A31	3 l blue vio & blk	6.75	3.00
		Nos. 89-100 (12)	43.27	5.61

See Nos. 114-120, 161-162. For overprints and surcharges see Nos. 104-112, 188, B8, Greece N167-N178, N182-N187, Thrace 16-21, Romania 2N1-2N4.

Tsar Ferdinand — A32

1912, Aug. 2   Typo.   Perf. 12½
101	A32	5s olive green	2.25	.70
a.		5s pale green	275.00	125.00
102	A32	10s claret	3.50	1.50
103	A32	25s slate	5.00	1.75
		Nos. 101-103 (3)	10.75	3.95

25th year of reign of Tsar Ferdinand.

ОСВОБ. ВОЙНА

Nos. 89-95 Overprinted in Various Colors

1912-1913

1913, Aug. 6   Engr.
104	A20	1s myrtle grn (C)	.15	.15
105	A21	2s car & blk (Bl)	.15	.15
107	A22	3s lake & blk (Bl Bk)	.18	.15
108	A23	5s grn & blk (R)	.15	.15
109	A24	10s dp red & blk (Bk)	.28	.15
110	A25	15s brown bis (G)	.55	.26
111	A26	25s ultra & blk (R)	2.75	.38
		Nos. 104-111 (7)	4.21	1.39

Victory over the Turks in Balkan War of 1912-1913.

10 СТ.

No. 95 Surcharged in Red

1915, July 6
112	A26	10s on 25s	.50	.15

No. 28 Surcharged in Green

3 стотинки

113	A11	3s on 1s lilac	3.50	4.50

Types of 1911 Re-engraved

1915, Nov. 7   Perf. 11½, 14
114	A20	1s dk bl grn	.15	.15
115	A23	5s grn & brn vio	1.40	.15
116	A24	10s red brn & brnsh blk	.22	.15
117	A25	15s olive green	.22	.15
118	A26	25s indigo & blk	.22	.15
119	A27	30s ol grn & red brn	.22	.15
120	A29	1 l dark brown	.32	.28
		Nos. 114-120 (7)	2.75	1.18

Widths: No. 114 is 19½mm; No. 89, 18½mm. No. 118 is 19¼mm; No. 95, 18¼mm. No. 120 is 20mm; No. 98, 19mm. The re-engraved stamps also differ from the 1911 issue in many details of design. Nos. 114-120 exist imperforate.
The 5s and 10s exist perf. 14x11½.
For Nos. 114-116 and 118 overprinted with Cyrillic characters and "1916-1917," see Romania Nos. 2N1-2N4.

Coat of Arms — A33

Peasant and Bullock — A34

Soldier and Mt. Sonichka — A35

View of Nish — A36

Town and Lake Okhrida — A37

Demir-Kapiya (Iron Gate) — A37a

View of Gevgeli — A38

Perf. 11½, 12½x13, 13x12½

1917-19   Typo.
122	A33	5s green	.28	.15
123	A34	15s slate	.15	.15
124	A35	25s blue	.15	.15
125	A36	30s orange	.15	.15
126	A37	50s violet	.52	.28
126A	A37a	2 l brn org ('19)	.52	.35
127	A38	3 l claret	.80	.75
		Nos. 122-127 (7)	2.57	1.98

Liberation of Macedonia. A 1 l dark green was prepared but not issued. Value $1.65.
For surcharges see Nos. B9-B10, B12.

View of Veles — A39

Monastery of St. Clement at Okhrida — A40

1918   Perf. 13x14
128	A39	1s gray	.15	.15
129	A40	5s green	.15	.15

Tsar Ferdinand A41

Plowing with Oxen A42

1918, July 1   Perf. 12½x13
130	A41	1s dark green	.15	.15
131	A41	2s dark brown	.15	.15
132	A41	3s indigo	.30	.16
133	A41	10s brown red	.30	.16
		Nos. 130-133 (4)	.90	.62

Ferdinand's accession to the throne, 30th anniv.

1919   Perf. 13½x13
134	A42	1s gray	.15	.15

Sobranye Palace — A43

Tsar Boris III — A44

1919   Perf. 11½x12, 12x11½
135	A43	1s black	.15	.15
137	A43	2s olive green	.15	.15

For surcharges see Nos. 186, B1.

1919, Oct. 3
138	A44	3s orange brn	.15	.15
139	A44	5s green	.15	.15
140	A44	10s rose red	.15	.15
141	A44	15s violet	.15	.15
142	A44	25s deep blue	.15	.15
143	A44	30s chocolate	.18	.15
144	A44	50s yellow brn	.18	.15
		Nos. 138-144 (7)	1.11	1.05

1st anniv. of enthronement of Tsar Boris III.
Nos. 135-144 exist imperforate.
For surcharges see Nos. 187, B2-B7.

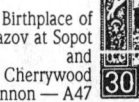

Birthplace of Vazov at Sopot and Cherrywood Cannon — A47

"The Bear Fighter"-a Character from "Under the Yoke" — A48

Ivan Vazov in 1870 and 1920 — A49

Vazov — A50

The Monk Paisii — A52

Homes of Vazov at Plovdiv and Sofia — A51

1920, Oct. 20   Photo.   Perf. 11½
147	A47	30s brown red	.15	.15
148	A48	50s dark green	.15	.15
149	A49	1 l drab	.22	.18
150	A50	2 l light brown	.60	.60
151	A51	3 l black violet	.95	.65
152	A52	5 l deep blue	1.10	.80
		Nos. 147-152 (6)	3.17	2.63

70th birthday of Ivan Vazov (1850-1921), Bulgarian poet and novelist.
Several values of this series exist imperforate and in pairs imperforate between.

Tsar Ferdinand A53

A54

Mt. Shar — A55

Bridge over Vardar River — A56

View of Ohrid — A57

Perf. 13x14, 14x13

1921, June 11   Typo.
153	A53	10s claret	.15	.15
154	A54	10s claret	.15	.15
155	A55	10s claret	.15	.15

BULGARIA

156	A56	10s rose lilac	.15	.15
157	A57	20s blue	.28	.16
		Nos. 153-157 (5)	.88	.76

Nos. 153-157 were intended to be issued in 1915 to commemorate the liberation of Macedonia. They were not put in use until 1921. A 50s violet was prepared but never placed in use. Value $1.75.

View of Sofia — A58

"The Liberator," Monument to Alexander II — A59

Monastery at Shipka Pass — A62

Tsar Boris III — A63

Harvesting Grain — A64

Tsar Assen's Tower (No crown over lion) — A65

Rila Monastery (Rosette at upper right) — A66

1921-23 Engr. Perf. 12

158	A58	10s blue gray	.15	.15
159	A59	20s deep green	.15	.15
160	A63	25s blue grn ('22)	.15	.15
161	A22	50s orange	.15	.15
162	A22	50s dk blue ('23)	2.50	2.50
163	A62	75s dull vio	.15	.15
164	A63	75s dp blue ('23)	.30	.15
165	A63	1 l carmine	.30	.16
166	A63	1 l dp blue ('22)	.30	.15
167	A64	2 l brown	.32	.15
168	A65	3 l brown vio	.38	.15
169	A66	5 l lt blue	2.50	.32
170	A63	10 l violet brn	6.75	1.10
		Nos. 158-170 (13)	14.10	5.43

For surcharge see No. 189.

Bourchier in Bulgarian Costume A67

James David Bourchier A68

View of Rila Monastery A69

1921, Dec. 31

171	A67	10s red orange	.15	.15
172	A67	20s orange	.15	.15
173	A68	30s dp gray	.15	.15
174	A68	50s bluish gray	.15	.15
175	A68	1 l dull vio	.18	.15
176	A69	1½ l olive grn	.18	.15
177	A69	2 l deep green	.18	.15
178	A69	3 l Prus blue	.45	.20
179	A69	5 l red brown	.85	.35
		Nos. 171-179 (9)	2.44	1.60

Death of James D. Bourchier, Balkan correspondent of the London Times.
For surcharges see Nos. B13-B16.

Postage Due Stamps of 1919-22 Surcharged

a **10 СТОТИНКИ**

1924

182	D6	10s on 20s yellow	.15	.15
183	D6	20s on 5s gray grn	.15	.15
a.		20s on 5s emerald	7.00	7.00
184	D6	20s on 10s violet	.15	.15
185	D6	20s on 30s orange	.15	.15
		Nos. 182-185 (4)	.60	.60

Nos. 182 to 185 were used for ordinary postage.

Regular Issues of 1919-23 Surcharged in Blue or Red:

b **1 ЛЕВЪ** c **3 ЛЕВА**

186	A43	(a) 10s on 1s black (R)	.15	.15
187	A44	(b) 1 l on 5s emer (Bl)	.15	.15
188	A22	(c) 3 l on 50s dk bl (R)	.20	.15
189	A63	(b) 6 l on 1 l car (Bl)	.60	.20
		Nos. 186-189 (4)	1.10	.65

The surcharge of No. 188 comes in three types: normal, thick and thin.
#182, 184-189 exist with inverted surcharge.

Lion of Bulgaria A70

A71

Tsar Boris III — A72

New Sofia Cathedral — A73

Harvesting — A74

1925 Typo. Perf. 13, 11½

191	A70	10s red & bl, *pink*	.15	.15
192	A70	15s car & org, *blue*	.15	.15
193	A70	30s blk & buff	.15	.15
a.		Cliche of 15s in plate of 30s		
194	A71	50s choc, *green*	.15	.15
195	A72	1 l dull green	.48	.15
196	A73	2 l dk grn & buff	1.10	.15
197	A74	4 l lake & yellow	1.10	.15
		Nos. 191-197 (7)	3.28	1.05

Several values of this series exist imperforate and in pairs imperforate between.
See #199, 201. For overprint see #C2.

Cathedral of Sveta Nedelya, Sofia, Ruined by Bomb — A75

1926 Perf. 11½

198	A75	50s gray black	.15	.15

A76

A77

Type A72 Re-engraved. (Shoulder at left does not touch frame)

1926

199	A76	1 l gray	.45	.15
a.		1 l green	.45	.15
201	A76	2 l olive brown	.52	.15

Center Embossed

202	A77	6 l dp bl & pale lemon	1.10	.15
203	A77	10 l brn blk & brn org	4.00	.75
		Nos. 199-203 (4)	6.07	1.20

For overprints see Nos. C1, C3-C4.

Christo Botev — A78

Tsar Boris III — A79

1926, June 2

204	A78	1 l olive green	.32	.15
205	A78	2 l slate violet	.90	.15
206	A78	4 l red brown	.90	.35
		Nos. 204-206 (3)	2.12	.65

Botev (1847-76), Bulgarian revolutionary, poet.

Lion Type of 1881

1927-29 Perf. 13

207	A3	10s dk red & drab	.15	.15
208	A3	15s blk & org ('29)	.15	.15
209	A3	30s dk bl & bis brn ('28)	.15	.15
a.		30s indigo & buff	.15	.15
210	A3	50s blk & rose red ('28)	.15	.15
		Nos. 207-210 (4)	.60	.60

1928, Oct. 3 Perf. 11½

211	A79	1 l olive green	.90	.15
212	A79	2 l deep brown	1.00	.15

St. Clement — A80

Konstantin Miladinov — A81

George S. Rakovski A82

Drenovo Monastery A83

Paisii — A84

Tsar Simeon — A85

Lyuben Karavelov A86

Vassil Levski A87

Georgi Benkovski A88

Tsar Alexander II A89

1929, May 12

213	A80	10s dk violet	.15	.15
214	A81	15s violet brn	.15	.15
215	A82	30s red	.15	.15
216	A83	50s olive grn	.25	.15
217	A84	1 l orange brn	.60	.15
218	A85	2 l dk blue	.70	.15
219	A86	3 l dull green	1.50	.45
220	A87	4 l olive brown	2.50	.25
221	A88	5 l brown	1.50	.35
222	A89	6 l Prus green	2.25	.90
		Nos. 213-222 (10)	9.75	2.82

Millenary of Tsar Simeon and 50th anniv. of the liberation of Bulgaria from the Turks.

Royal Wedding Issue

Tsar Boris and Fiancee, Princess Giovanna A90

Queen Ioanna and Tsar Boris — A91

1930, Nov. 12 Perf. 11½

223	A90	1 l green	.25	.24
224	A91	2 l dull violet	.22	.32
225	A90	4 l rose red	.22	.32
226	A91	6 l dark blue	.25	.38
		Nos. 223-226 (4)	.94	1.26

Fifty-five copies of a miniature sheet incorporating one each of Nos. 223-226 were printed and given to royal, governmental and diplomatic personages.

Tsar Boris III A92 A93

Perf. 11½, 12x11½, 13

1931-37 Unwmk.

227	A92	1 l blue green	.25	.15
228	A92	2 l carmine	.40	.15
229	A92	4 l red org ('34)	.75	.15
230	A92	4 l yel org ('37)	.20	.15
231	A92	6 l deep blue	.70	.15
232	A92	7 l dp bl ('37)	.20	.15
233	A92	10 l slate blk	8.75	.70
234	A92	12 l lt brown	.40	.18
235	A92	14 l brn ('37)	.28	.22
236	A93	20 l claret & org brn	1.00	.45
		Nos. 227-236 (10)	12.93	2.45

Nos. 230-233 and 235 have outer bars at top and bottom as shown on cut A92; Nos. 227-229 and 234 are without outer bars.
See Nos. 251, 279-280, 287. For surcharge see No. 252.

BULGARIA

Balkan Games Issues

Gymnast — A95
Soccer — A96 
Riding — A97 
Swimmer A100 
"Victory" A101 

Designs: 6 l, Fencing. 10 l, Bicycle race.

1931, Sept. 18		Perf. 11½	
237 A95	1 l lt green	1.75	.50
238 A96	2 l garnet	1.75	.50
239 A97	4 l carmine	4.00	.75
240 A95	6 l Prus blue	7.50	1.25
241 A95	10 l red org	20.00	3.75
242 A100	12 l dk blue	65.00	7.50
243 A101	50 l olive brn	60.00	22.50
Nos. 237-243 (7)		160.00	36.75

1933, Jan. 5			
244 A95	1 l blue grn	1.25	.95
245 A96	2 l blue	2.00	.95
246 A97	4 l brn vio	2.75	1.10
247 A95	6 l brt rose	5.00	1.65
248 A95	10 l olive brn	27.50	9.00
249 A100	12 l orange	60.00	18.00
250 A101	50 l red brown	110.00	82.50
Nos. 244-250 (7)		208.50	114.15

Nos. 244-250 were sold only at the philatelic agency.

Boris Type of 1931
Outer Bars at Top and Bottom Removed

1933		Perf. 13	
251 A92	6 l deep blue	.80	.15

Type of 1931 Surcharged in Blue 2

1934			
252 A92	2 (l) on 3 l ol brn	4.00	.25

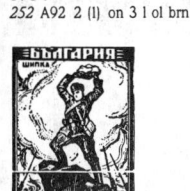

Soldier Defending Shipka Pass A102
Shipka Battle Memorial A103 
Color-Bearer A104 
Veteran of the War of Liberation, 1878 A105 

Widow and Orphans — A106

1934, Aug. 26	Perf. 10½, 11½	Wmk. 145	
253 A102	1 l green	.45	.38
254 A103	2 l pale red	.45	.24
255 A104	3 l bister brn	1.40	1.25
256 A105	4 l dk carmine	1.25	.60
257 A104	7 l dk blue	2.25	2.00
258 A106	14 l plum	6.00	5.75
Nos. 253-258 (6)		11.80	10.22

Shipka Pass Battle memorial unveiling.
An unwatermarked miniature sheet incorporating one each of Nos. 253-258 was put on sale in 1938 in five cities at a price of 8,000 leva. Printing: 100 sheets.

1934, Sept. 21			
259 A102	1 l bright green	.45	.38
260 A103	2 l dull orange	.45	.24
261 A104	3 l yellow	1.40	1.25
262 A105	4 l rose	1.25	.60
263 A104	7 l blue	2.25	2.00
264 A106	14 l olive bister	6.00	5.75
Nos. 259-264 (6)		11.80	10.22

An unwatermarked miniature sheet incorporating one each of Nos. 259-263 was issued.

Velcho A. Djamjiyata A108
Capt. G. S. Mamarchev A109 

1935, May 5		Perf. 11½	
265 A108	1 l deep blue	.95	.25
266 A109	2 l maroon	.95	.28

Bulgarian uprising against the Turks, cent.

Soccer Game — A110
Cathedral of Alexander Nevski — A111 
Soccer Team — A112 
Symbolical of Victory — A113 
Player and Trophy — A114 
The Trophy — A115 

1935, June 14			
267 A110	1 l green	1.10	.90
268 A111	2 l blue gray	2.50	1.40
269 A112	4 l crimson	4.00	2.00
270 A113	7 l brt blue	7.75	2.50
271 A114	14 l orange	7.75	3.25
272 A115	50 l lilac brn	60.00	52.50
Nos. 267-272 (6)		83.10	62.55

5th Balkan Soccer Tournament.

Gymnast on Parallel Bars — A116
Youth in "Yunak" Costume — A117 
Girl in "Yunak" Costume A118 
Pole Vaulting A119 
Stadium, Sofia — A120 
Yunak Emblem — A121 

1935, July 10			
273 A116	1 l green	2.00	1.10
274 A117	2 l lt blue	2.75	1.10
275 A118	4 l carmine	5.50	2.25
276 A119	7 l dk blue	5.50	3.00
277 A120	14 l dk brown	5.50	3.00
278 A121	50 l red	65.00	42.50
Nos. 273-278 (6)		86.25	52.95

8th tournament of the Yunak Gymnastic Organization at Sofia, July 12-14.

Boris Type of 1931

1935		Wmk. 145	Perf. 12½, 13
279 A92	1 l green	.30	.15
280 A92	2 l carmine	20.00	.15

Janos Hunyadi A122
King Ladislas Varnenchik A123 
Varna Memorial — A124
King Ladislas III — A125
Battle of Varna, 1444 — A126 

1935, Aug. 4		Perf. 10½, 11½	
281 A122	1 l brown org	1.10	.75
282 A123	2 l maroon	1.10	.75
283 A124	4 l vermilion	5.50	3.75
284 A125	7 l dull blue	2.50	1.25
285 A126	14 l green	2.50	1.25
Nos. 281-285 (5)		12.70	7.75

Battle of Varna, and the death of the Polish King, Ladislas Varnenchik (1424-44).

Lion Type of 1881

1935		Wmk. 145	Perf. 13
286 A3	10s dk red & drab	.70	.15

Boris Type of 1933
Outer Bars at Top and Bottom Removed

1935			
287 A92	6 l gray blue	.60	.15

Dimitr Monument A127
Haji Dimitr A128 
Haji Dimitr and Stefan Karaja — A129 
Taking the Oath — A130 
Birthplace of Dimitr — A131 

1935, Oct. 1	Unwmk.	Perf. 11½	
288 A127	1 l green	1.25	.35
289 A128	2 l brown	1.75	.70
290 A129	4 l car rose	3.50	2.50
291 A130	7 l blue	4.50	3.50
292 A131	14 l orange	4.50	3.50
Nos. 288-292 (5)		15.50	10.55

67th anniv. of the death of the Bulgarian patriots, Haji Dimitr and Stefan Karaja.

> Catalogue values for unused stamps in this section, from this point to the end of the section, are for Never Hinged items.

A132
A133 

1936-39		Perf. 13x12½, 13	
293 A132	10s red org ('37)	.15	.15
294 A132	15s emerald	.15	.15
295 A133	30s maroon	.15	.15
296 A133	30s yel brn ('37)	.15	.15
297 A133	30s Prus bl ('37)	.15	.15
298 A133	50s ultra	.15	.15
299 A133	50s dk car ('37)	.20	.15
300 A133	50s slate grn ('39)	.15	.15
Nos. 293-300 (8)		1.25	1.20

BULGARIA

Meteorological Station, Mt. Moussalla — A134
Peasant Girl — A135 
Town of Nessebr A136 

1936, Aug. 16   Photo.   *Perf. 11½*
301 A134   1 l purple   1.40   .65
302 A135   2 l ultra   1.40   .60
303 A136   7 l dark blue   3.75   1.50
    Nos. 301-303 (3)   6.55   2.75

4th Geographical & Ethnographical Cong., Sofia, Aug. 1936.

Sts. Cyril and Methodius A137
Displaying the Bible to the People A138 

1937, June 2
304 A137   1 l dk green   .22   .15
305 A137   2 l dk plum   .22   .15
306 A138   4 l vermilion   .45   .22
307 A137   7 l dk blue   1.75   1.10
308 A138   14 l rose red   1.75   1.10
    Nos. 304-308 (5)   4.39   2.72

Millennium of Cyrillic alphabet.

3sa

Princess Marie Louise — A139
Tsar Boris III — A140 

1937, Oct. 3
310 A139   1 l yellow green   .35   .15
311 A139   2 l brown red   .26   .15
312 A139   4 l scarlet   .35   .15
    Nos. 310-312 (3)   .96   .45

Issued in honor of Princess Marie Louise.

1937, Oct. 3
313 A140   2 l brown red   .35   .15

19th anniv. of the accession of Tsar Boris III to the throne. See No. B11.

National Products Issue

Peasants Bundling Wheat A141 
Sunflower A142

Wheat — A143
Chickens and Eggs — A144 
Cluster of Grapes — A145 
Rose and Perfume Flask — A146 
Strawberries A147 
Girl Carrying Grape Clusters A148 
Rose — A149 
Tobacco Leaves — A150 

1938   *Perf. 13*
316 A141   10s orange   .15   .15
317 A141   10s red org   .15   .15
318 A142   15s brt rose   .30   .15
319 A142   15s deep plum   .30   .15
320 A143   30s golden brn   .15   .15
321 A143   30s copper brn   .15   .15
322 A144   50s black   .15   .15
323 A144   50s indigo   .15   .15
324 A145   1 l yel grn   .65   .15
325 A145   1 l green   .65   .15
326 A146   2 l rose pink   .60   .15
327 A146   2 l rose brn   .60   .15
328 A147   3 l dp red lil   1.25   .15
329 A147   3 l brn lake   1.25   .15
330 A148   4 l plum   .80   .15
331 A148   4 l golden brn   .80   .15
332 A149   7 l vio blue   1.50   .55
333 A149   7 l dp blue   1.50   .55
334 A150   14 l dk brown   2.25   .90
335 A150   14 l red brn   2.25   .90
    Nos. 316-335 (20)   15.60   5.30

Several values of this series exist imperforate.

Crown Prince Simeon A151

Designs: 2 l, Same portrait as 1 l, value at lower left. 14 l, similar to 4 l, but no wreath.

1938, June 16
336 A151   1 l brt green   .15   .15
337 A151   2 l rose pink   .15   .15
338 A153   4 l dp orange   .16   .15
339 A151   7 l ultra   .80   .38
340 A153   14 l dp brown   .80   .38
    Nos. 336-340 (5)   2.06   1.21

First birthday of Prince Simeon.

Tsar Boris III A155
A156

Various Portraits of Tsar.

1938, Oct. 3
341 A155   1 l lt green   .15   .15
342 A156   2 l rose brown   .60   .15
343 A156   4 l golden brn   .15   .15
344 A156   7 l brt ultra   .30   .22
345 A156   14 l deep red lilac   .35   .26
    Nos. 341-345 (5)   1.55   .93

Reign of Tsar Boris III, 20th anniv.

Early Locomotive A160

Designs: 2 l, Modern locomotive. 4 l, Train crossing bridge. 7 l, Tsar Boris in cab.

1939, Apr. 26
346 A160   1 l yel green   .20   .15
347 A160   2 l copper brn   .20   .15
348 A160   4 l red orange   1.40   .16
349 A160   7 l dark blue   3.25   .85
    Nos. 346-349 (4)   5.05   1.31

50th anniv. of Bulgarian State Railways.

Post Horns and Arrows — A164
Central Post Office, Sofia — A165 

1939, May 14   Typo.
350 A164   1 l yellow grn   .16   .15
351 A165   2 l brt carmine   .24   .15

Establishment of the postal system, 60th anniv.

Gymnast on Bar — A166 
Yunak Emblem — A167
Discus Thrower — A168  
Athletic Dancer — A169

Weight Lifter — A170

1939, July 7   Photo.
352 A166   1 l yel grn & pale grn   .35   .15
353 A167   2 l brt rose   .35   .15
354 A168   4 l brn & gldn brn   .52   .22
355 A169   7 l dk bl & bl   1.25   .65
356 A170   14 l plum & rose vio   5.50   2.75
    Nos. 352-356 (5)   7.97   3.92

9th tournament of the Yunak Gymnastic Organization at Sofia, July 4-8.

Tsar Boris III — A171
Bulgaria's First Stamp — A172 

1940-41   Typo.
356A A171   1 l dl grn ('41)   .80   .15
357 A171   2 l brt crimson   .20   .15

1940, May 19   Photo.   *Perf. 13*

20 l, Similar design, scroll dated "1840-1940."

358 A172   10 l olive black   1.25   .85
359 A172   20 l indigo   1.25   .85

Cent. of 1st postage stamp. Exist imperf.

Peasant Couple and Tsar Boris — A174
Flags over Wheat Field and Tsar Boris — A175 
Tsar Boris and Map of Dobrudja A176 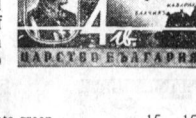

1940, Sept. 20
360 A174   1 l slate green   .15   .15
361 A175   2 l rose red   .15   .15
362 A176   4 l dark brown   .15   .15
363 A176   7 l dark blue   .60   .32
    Nos. 360-363 (4)   1.05   .77

Return of Dobrudja from Romania.

Fruit A177
Bees and Flowers A178 
Plowing A179 
Shepherd and Sheep A180

BULGARIA

Tsar Boris III — A181

Perf. 10, 10½x11½, 11½, 13

1940-44		Typo.	Unwmk.	
364	A177	10s red orange	.15	.15
365	A178	15s blue	.15	.15
366	A179	30s olive brn ('41)	.15	.15
367	A180	50s violet	.15	.15
368	A181	1 l brt green	.15	.15
369	A181	2 l rose car	.15	.15
370	A181	4 l red orange	.15	.15
371	A181	6 l red vio ('44)	.28	.15
372	A181	7 l blue	.28	.15
373	A181	10 l blue grn ('41)	.30	.15
		Nos. 364-373 (10)	1.91	1.50

See Nos. 373A-377, 440. For overprints see Nos. 455-463, C31-C32.

1940-41		Wmk. 145	Perf. 13	
373A	A180	50s violet ('41)	.15	.15
374	A181	1 l brt grn	.15	.15
375	A181	2 l rose car	.18	.15
376	A181	7 l dull blue	.45	.15
377	A181	10 l blue green	.65	.15
		Nos. 373A-377 (5)	1.58	.75

Watermarked vertically or horizontally.

P. R. Slaveikov A182

Sofronii, Bishop of Vratza A183

Saint Ivan Rilski — A184

Martin S. Drinov — A185

Monk Khrabr — A186

Kolio Ficheto — A187

1940, Sept. 23		Photo.	Unwmk.	
378	A182	1 l brt bl grn	.15	.15
379	A183	2 l brt carmine	.15	.15
380	A184	3 l dp red brn	.15	.15
381	A185	4 l red orange	.15	.15
382	A186	7 l deep blue	1.00	.60
383	A187	10 l dp red brn	1.50	.85
		Nos. 378-383 (6)	3.10	2.05

Liberation of Bulgaria from the Turks in 1878.

Johannes Gutenberg A188

N. Karastoyanov, 1st Bulgarian Printer A189

1940, Dec. 16				
384	A188	1 l slate green	.15	.15
385	A189	2 l orange brown	.15	.15

500th anniv. of the invention of the printing press and 100th anniv. of the 1st Bulgarian printing press.

Christo Botev — A190

Monument to Botev — A192

Botev with his Insurgent Band — A191

1941, May 3				
386	A190	1 l dark blue green	.15	.15
387	A191	2 l crimson rose	.20	.15
388	A192	3 l dark brown	.65	.32
		Nos. 386-388 (3)	1.00	.62

Christo Botev, patriot and poet.

Palace of Justice, Sofia — A193

1941-43		Engr.	Perf. 11½	
389	A193	14 l lt gray brn ('43)	.20	.15
390	A193	20 l gray grn ('43)	.38	.16
391	A193	50 l lt bl gray	1.90	1.25
		Nos. 389-391 (3)	2.48	1.56

20 l, Workers' hospital. 50 l, National Bank.

Macedonian Woman — A196

City of Okhrida — A200

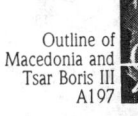

Outline of Macedonia and Tsar Boris III A197

View of Aegean Sea — A198

Poganovski Monastery A199

1941, Oct. 3		Photo.	Perf. 13	
392	A196	1 l slate grn	.15	.15
393	A197	2 l crimson	.15	.15
394	A198	3 l red org	.15	.15
395	A199	4 l org brn	.15	.15
396	A200	7 l dp gray bl	.38	.28
		Nos. 392-396 (5)	.98	.88

Issued to commemorate the acquisition of Macedonian territory from neighboring countries.

Peasant Working in a Field — A201

Designs: 15s, Plowing. 30s, Apiary. 50s, Women harvesting fruit. 3 l, Shepherd and sheep. 5 l, Inspecting cattle.

1941-44				
397	A201	10s dk violet	.15	.15
398	A201	10s dk blue	.15	.15
399	A201	15s Prus blue	.15	.15
400	A201	15s dk ol brn	.15	.15
401	A201	30s red orange	.15	.15
402	A201	30s dk slate grn	.15	.15
403	A201	50s blue vio	.15	.15
404	A201	50s red lilac	.15	.15
405	A201	3 l henna brn	.42	.25
406	A201	3 l dk brn ('44)	1.40	1.10
407	A201	5 l sepia	.52	.48
408	A201	5 l vio bl ('44)	1.40	1.10
		Nos. 397-408 (12)	4.94	4.13

Girls Singing — A207

Boys in Camp — A208

Raising Flag — A209

Folk Dancers — A211

Camp Scene — A210

1942, June 1			Photo.	
409	A207	1 l dk bl grn	.15	.15
410	A208	2 l scarlet	.15	.15
411	A209	4 l olive gray	.15	.15
412	A210	7 l deep blue	.16	.15
413	A211	14 l fawn	.32	.22
		Nos. 409-413 (5)	.93	.82

National "Work and Joy" movement.

Wounded Soldier — A212

Soldier's Farewell — A213

1942, Sept. 7				
414	A212	1 l slate grn	.15	.15
415	A213	2 l brt rose	.15	.15
416	A213	4 l yel org	.15	.15
417	A213	7 l dark blue	.15	.15
418	A213	14 l brown	.15	.15
419	A213	20 l olive blk	.22	.15
		Nos. 414-419 (6)	.97	.90

4 l, Aiding wounded soldier. 7 l, Widow & orphans at grave. 14 l, Tomb of Unknown Soldier. 20 l, Queen Ioanna visiting wounded.

Issued to aid war victims. No. 419 was printed in sheets of 50, alternating with 50 labels.

Legend of Kubrat — A218

Cavalry Charge — A219

Designs: 30s, Rider of Madara. 50s, Christening of Boris I. 1 l, School, St. Naum. 2 l, Crowning of Tsar Simeon by Boris I. 3 l, Golden era of Bulgarian literature. 4 l, Sentencing of the Bogomil Basil. 5 l, Proclamation of 2nd Bulgarian Empire. 7 l, Ivan Assen II at Trebizond. 10 l, Deporting the Patriarch Jeftimi. 14 l, Wandering minstrel. 20 l, Monk Paisii. 30 l, Monument, Shipka Pass.

1942, Oct. 12				
420	A218	10s bluish blk	.15	.15
421	A219	15s Prus blue	.15	.15
422	A219	30s dk rose vio	.15	.15
423	A219	50s indigo	.15	.15
424	A219	1 l slate grn	.15	.15
425	A219	2 l crimson	.15	.15
426	A219	3 l brown	.15	.15
427	A219	4 l orange	.15	.15
428	A219	5 l grnsh blk	.15	.15
429	A219	7 l dk blue	.15	.15
430	A219	10 l brown blk	.15	.15
431	A219	14 l olive blk	.15	.15
432	A219	20 l henna brn	.42	.28
433	A219	30 l black	.70	.42
		Nos. 420-433 (14)	2.92	2.50

Tsar Boris III — A234

Designs: Various portraits of Tsar.

1944, Feb. 28		Photo.	Wmk. 275	
		Perf. 13, Imperf.		
		Frames in Black		
434	A234	1 l olive grn	.15	.15
435	A234	2 l red brown	.16	.15
436	A234	4 l brown	.20	.15
437	A234	5 l gray vio	.28	.16
438	A234	7 l slate blue	.28	.16
		Nos. 434-438 (5)	1.07	.77

Tsar Boris III (1894-1943).

Tsar Simeon II — A239

Perf. 11½, 13

1944, June 12		Typo.	Unwmk.	
439	A239	3 l red orange	.25	.15

Shepherd Type of 1940

1944				
440	A180	50s yellow green	.20	.15

Parcel Post Stamps of 1944 Overprinted in Black or Orange

ВСИЧКО ЗА ФРОНТА

1945, Jan. 25			Perf. 11½	
448	PP5	1 l dk carmine	.15	.15
449	PP5	7 l rose lilac	.15	.15
450	PP5	20 l org brn	.15	.15
451	PP5	30 l dk brn car	.15	.15
452	PP5	50 l red orange	.25	.15
453	PP5	100 l blue (O)	.60	.16

Overprint reads: "Everything for the Front."

No. 448 with Additional Surcharge of New Value in Black

454	PP5	4 l on 1 l dk car	.15	.15
		Nos. 448-454 (7)	1.60	1.06

BULGARIA

Nos. 368 to 370
Overprinted in Black

СЪБИРАЙТЕ
СТАРО
ЖЕЛѢЗО

1945, Mar. 15   Perf. 11½, 13
455 A181 1 l brt green .25 .15
456 A181 2 l rose carmine .40 .15
457 A181 4 l red orange .60 .15

Overprint reads: "Collect old iron."

Overprinted in Black

СЪБИРАЙТЕ
ХАРТИЕНИ
ОТПАДЪЦИ

458 A181 1 l brt green .25 .15
459 A181 2 l rose carmine .40 .15
460 A181 4 l red orange .60 .15

Overprint reads: "Collect discarded paper."

Overprinted in Black

СЪБИРАЙТЕ
ВСЯКАКВИ
ПАРЦАЛИ

461 A181 1 l brt green .25 .15
462 A181 2 l rose carmine .40 .15
463 A181 4 l red orange .60 .15
    Nos. 455-463 (9) 3.75 1.35

Overprint reads: "Collect all kinds of rags."

Oak Tree — A245

1945   Imperf., Perf. 11½.
        Litho.   Unwmk.
464 A245 4 l vermilion .15 .15
465 A245 10 l blue .15 .15

Imperf
466 A245 50 l brown lake .15 .15
    Nos. 464-466 (3) .45 .45

Slav Congress, Sofia, March, 1945.

A246
A247 
A248 
A249 
A251 
A252 
A253 
A254 

2 l and 4 l:
Type I. Large crown close to coat of arms.
Type II. Smaller crown standing high.

1945-46   Photo.   Perf. 13
469 A246 30s yellow grn .15 .15
470 A247 50s peacock grn .15 .15
471 A248 1 l dk green .15 .15
472 A249 2 l choc (I) .15 .15
   a. Type II .15 .15

473 A249 4 l dk blue (I) .15 .15
   a. Type II .15 .15
475 A251 5 l red violet .15 .15
476 A251 9 l slate gray .15 .15
477 A252 10 l Prus blue .15 .15
478 A253 15 l brown .15 .15
479 A254 20 l carmine .20 .15
480 A254 20 l gray blk .20 .15
    Nos. 469-480 (11) 1.75 1.65

Breaking Chain — A255
1 Lev Coin — A256
Water Wheel — A257 
Coin and Symbols of Agriculture and Industry — A258 

1945, June 4   Unwmk.   Imperf.
        Litho.
        Laid Paper
481 A255 50 l brn red, *pink* .15 .15
482 A255 50 l org, *pink* .15 .15
483 A256 100 l gray bl, *pink* .20 .15
484 A256 100 l brn, *pink* .20 .15
485 A257 150 l dk ol gray, *pink* .35 .18
486 A257 150 l dl car, *pink* .35 .18
487 A258 200 l dp bl, *pink* .50 .30
488 A258 200 l ol grn, *pink* .50 .30
    Nos. 481-488 (8) 2.40 1.56

Souvenir Sheets
489   Sheet of 4 3.00 1.75
   a. A255 50 l violet blue .30 .18
   b. A256 100 l violet blue .30 .18
   c. A257 150 l violet blue .30 .18
   d. A258 200 l violet blue .30 .18
490   Sheet of 4 3.00 1.75
   a. A255 50 l brown orange .30 .18
   b. A256 100 l brown orange .30 .18
   c. A257 150 l brown orange .30 .18
   d. A258 200 l brown orange .30 .18

Publicizing Bulgaria's Liberty Loan.

Olive Branch — A260

1945, Sept. 1   Typo.   Perf. 13
491 A260 10 l org brn & yel grn .15 .15
492 A260 50 l dull red & dp grn .25 .15

Victory of Allied Nations, World War II.

September 9, 1944 — A261
Numeral, Broken Chain — A262 

1945, Sept. 7
493 A261 1 l gray green .15 .15
494 A261 2 l deep blue .15 .15
495 A261 5 l rose lilac .15 .15
496 A262 10 l lt blue .15 .15
497 A262 20 l brt car .18 .15
498 A261 50 l brt bl grn .42 .18
499 A261 100 l orange brn .48 .35
    Nos. 493-499 (7) 1.68 1.30

1st anniv. of Bulgaria's liberation.

Old Postal Savings Emblem — A263
Child Putting Coin in Bank — A265 
First Bulgarian Postal Savings Stamp — A264 
Postal Savings Building, Sofia — A266 

1946, Apr. 12
500 A263 4 l brown org .15 .15
501 A264 10 l dk olive .15 .15
502 A265 20 l ultra .15 .15
503 A266 50 l slate gray .52 .52
    Nos. 500-503 (4) .97 .97

50th anniv. of Bulgarian Postal Savings.

Refugee Children — A267
Nurse Assisting Wounded Soldier — A269 
Wounded Soldier — A268 

Design: 35 l, 100 l, Red Cross hospital train.

1946, Apr. 4
       Cross in Carmine
504 A267 2 l dk olive .15 .15
505 A268 4 l violet .15 .15
506 A267 10 l plum .15 .15
507 A268 20 l ultra .15 .15
508 A269 30 l brown org .15 .15
509 A268 35 l gray blk .15 .15
510 A269 50 l violet brn .22 .18
511 A268 100 l gray brn .70 .60
    Nos. 504-511 (8) 1.82 1.68

See Nos. 553-560.

Advancing Troops A271 
Grenade Thrower A272

Attacking Planes — A274

Designs: 5 l, Horse-drawn cannon. 9 l, Engineers building pontoon bridge. 10 l, 30 l, Cavalry charge.

40 l, Horse-drawn supply column. 50 l, Motor transport column. 60 l, Infantry, tanks and planes.

1946, Aug. 9   Typo.   Unwmk.
512 A271 2 l dk red vio .15 .15
513 A272 4 l dk gray .15 .15
514 A271 5 l dk org red .15 .15
515 A274 6 l black brn .15 .15
516 A271 9 l rose lilac .15 .15
517 A271 10 l dp violet .15 .15
518 A271 20 l dp blue .24 .15
519 A271 30 l red org .24 .15
520 A271 40 l dk ol bis .30 .16
521 A271 50 l dk green .30 .16
522 A271 60 l red brown .42 .28
    Nos. 512-522 (11) 2.40 1.80

Bulgaria's participation in World War II.

Arms of Russia and Bulgaria A279
Lion Rampant A280 

1946, May 23
523 A279 4 l red orange .15 .15
525 A279 20 l turq green .22 .15

Congress of the Bulgarian-Soviet Association, May 1946. The 4 l exists in dk car rose and 20 l in blue, value, set $7.

1946, May 25   Imperf.
526 A280 20 l blue .30 .22

Day of the Postage Stamp, May 26, 1946.

Alekandr Stamboliski A281
Flags of Albania, Romania, Bulgaria and Yugoslavia A282 

1946, June 13   Perf. 12
527 A281 100 l red orange 4.00 1.90

23rd anniversary of the death of Alekandr Stamboliski, agrarian leader.

1946, July 6   Perf. 11½
528 A282 100 l black brown .75 .50

1946 Balkan Games.
Sheet of 100 arranged so that all stamps are tete beche vert. and horiz., except 2 center rows in left pane which provide 10 vert. pairs that are not tete beche vert.

St. Ivan Rilski — A283
A286 
A284 
A285

BULGARIA

Views of Rila Monastery
A287

1946, Aug. 26
529	A283	1 l red brown		.15	.15
530	A284	4 l black brn		.15	.15
531	A285	10 l dk green		.15	.15
532	A286	20 l dp blue		.18	.15
533	A287	50 l dk red		.80	.50
	Nos. 529-533 (5)			1.43	1.10

Millenary of Rila Monastery.

People's Republic

A288

1946, Sept. 15   Typo.
534	A288	4 l brown lake		.15	.15
535	A288	20 l dull blue		.15	.15
536	A288	50 l olive bister		.18	.16
	Nos. 534-536 (3)			.48	.46

No. 535 is inscribed "BULGARIA" in Latin characters.

Referendum of Sept. 8, 1946, resulting in the establishment of the Bulgarian People's Republic.

Partisan Army — A289   Snipers — A290

Soldiers: Past and Present — A291

Design: 30 l, Partisans advancing.

1946, Dec. 2
537	A289	1 l violet brn		.15	.15
538	A290	4 l dull grn		.15	.15
539	A291	5 l chocolate		.15	.15
540	A290	10 l crimson		.15	.15
541	A289	20 l ultra		.24	.15
542	A290	30 l olive bister		.24	.15
543	A291	50 l black		.28	.22
	Nos. 537-543 (7)			1.36	1.12

Relief Worker and Children — A294

Child with Gift Parcels — A295

Waiting for Food Distribution A296

Mother and Child A297

1946, Dec. 30
545	A294	1 l dk vio brn		.15	.15
546	A295	4 l brt red		.15	.15
547	A295	9 l olive bis		.15	.15
548	A294	10 l slate gray		.15	.15
549	A296	20 l ultra		.15	.15
550	A297	30 l dp brn org		.15	.15
551	A296	40 l maroon		.18	.15
552	A294	50 l peacock grn		.32	.28
	Nos. 545-552 (8)			1.40	1.33

"Bulgaria" is in Latin characters on No. 548.

Red Cross Types of 1946
1947, Jan. 31   Cross in Carmine
553	A267	2 l olive bister		.15	.15
554	A268	4 l olive black		.15	.15
555	A267	10 l blue grn		.15	.15
556	A267	20 l brt blue		.15	.15
557	A269	30 l yellow grn		.30	.22
558	A268	35 l grnsh gray		.32	.24
559	A269	50 l henna brn		.48	.35
560	A268	100 l dark blue		.70	.50
	Nos. 553-560 (8)			2.40	1.91

Laurel Branch, Allied and Bulgarian Emblems — A298

Dove of Peace — A299

1947, Feb. 28
561	A298	4 l olive		.15	.15
562	A299	10 l brown red		.15	.15
563	A299	20 l deep blue		.18	.16
	Nos. 561-563 (3)			.48	.46

Return to peace at the close of World War II. "Bulgaria" in Latin characters on No. 563.

A302

Guerrilla Fighters
A303   A304

1947, Jan. 21   Perf. 11½
567	A302	10 l choc & brn org		.32	.16
568	A303	20 l dk bl & bl		.32	.16
569	A304	70 l dp claret & rose		18.00	8.00
	Nos. 567-569 (3)			18.64	8.32

Issued to honor the anti-fascists.

Hydroelectric Station — A305

Miner A306

Symbols of Industry A307

Tractor — A308

1947, Aug. 6
570	A305	4 l olive green		.15	.15
571	A306	9 l red brown		.15	.15
572	A307	20 l deep blue		.18	.18
573	A308	40 l olive brown		.42	.28
	Nos. 570-573 (4)			.90	.76

Exhibition Building A309

Former Home of Alphonse de Lamartine A310

Symbols of Agriculture and Horticulture — A311

Perf. 11x11½, 11½x11
1947, Aug. 31   Litho.   Unwmk.
574	A309	4 l scarlet		.15	.15
575	A310	9 l brown lake		.15	.15
576	A311	20 l brt ultra		.20	.15
	Nos. 574-576 (3)			.50	.45

Plovdiv Intl. Fair, 1947. See No. C54.

Basil Evstatiev Aprilov — A312

1947, Oct. 19   Photo.   Perf. 11
577	A312	40 l brt ultra		.35	.18

Cent. of the death of Basil Evstatiev Aprilov, educator and historian. See No. 603.

Bicycle Race — A313

Basketball A314

Chess A315

Balkan Games: 20 l, Soccer players. 60 l, Four flags of participating nations.

1947, Sept. 29   Typo.   Perf. 11½
578	A313	2 l plum		.18	.15
579	A314	4 l dk olive grn		.18	.15
580	A315	9 l orange brn		.42	.15
581	A315	20 l brt ultra		.80	.18
582	A315	60 l violet brn		1.65	.75
	Nos. 578-582 (5)			3.23	1.38

People's Theater, Sofia A316

National Assembly A317

Central Post Office, Sofia A318

Presidential Mansion A319

1947-48   Typo.   Perf. 12½
583	A316	50s yellow grn		.15	.15
584	A317	50s yellow grn		.15	.15
585	A318	1 l green		.15	.15
586	A319	1 l green		.15	.15
587	A316	2 l brown lake		.15	.15
588	A317	2 l lt brown		.15	.15
589	A316	4 l deep blue		.15	.15
590	A317	4 l deep blue		.15	.15
591	A316	9 l carmine		.35	.15
592	A317	20 l deep blue		.75	.30
	Nos. 583-592 (10)			2.30	1.65

On Nos. 583-592 inscription reads "Bulgarian Republic." No. 592 is inscribed in Latin characters.

Redrawn
НАРОДНА
added to inscription

593	A318	1 l green		.15	.15
594	A318	2 l brown lake		.15	.15
595	A318	4 l deep blue		.15	.15
	Nos. 593-595 (3)			.45	.45

Cyrillic inscription beneath design on Nos. 593-595 reads "Bulgarian People's Republic."

Geno Kirov — A320

Actors' Portraits: 1 l, Zlatina Nedeva. 2 l, Ivan Popov. 3 l, Athanas Kirchev. 4 l, Elena Snejina. 5 l, Stoyan Bachvarov.

Perf. 10½
1947, Dec. 8   Unwmk.   Litho.
596	A320	50s bister brn		.15	.15
597	A320	1 l lt blue grn		.15	.15
598	A320	2 l slate green		.15	.15
599	A320	3 l dp blue		.15	.15
600	A320	4 l scarlet		.15	.15
601	A320	5 l red brown		.15	.15
	Nos. 596-601,B22-B26 (11)			2.13	1.80

National Theater, 50th anniversary.

Merchant Ship "Fatherland" — A321

1947, Dec. 19
602	A321	50 l Prus bl, *cream*		.45	.15

Ordering on-line is
QUICK!
EASY!
CONVENIENT!
www.scottonline.com

BULGARIA

B. E. Aprilov — A322

Worker — A323

1948, Feb. 19   *Perf. 11*
603 A322   4 l brn car, *cream*   .15   .15
Centenary of the death of Basil Evstatiev Aprilov, educator and historian.

1948, Feb. 29   Photo.   *Perf. 11½x12*
604 A323   4 l dp blue, *cream*   .15   .15
2nd Bulgarian Workers' Congress.

Self-education — A324

Accordion Player — A325

Factory Recess A326

Girl Throwing Basketball A327

1948, Mar. 31   Photo.
605 A324   4 l red   .15   .15
606 A325   20 l deep blue   .15   .15
607 A326   40 l dull green   .20   .15
608 A327   60 l brown   .60   .35
Nos. 605-608 (4)   1.10   .80

Nicholas Vaptzarov — A328

Portraits: 9 l, P. K. Iavorov. 15 l, Christo Smirnenski. 20 l, Ivan Vazov. 45 l, P. R. Slaveikov.

1948, May 18   Litho.   *Perf. 11*
Cream Paper
611 A328   4 l brt ver   .15   .15
612 A328   9 l lt brown   .15   .15
613 A328   15 l claret   .15   .15
614 A328   20 l deep blue   .15   .15
615 A328   45 l green   .32   .32
Nos. 611-615 (5)   .92   .92

Soviet Soldier — A329

Civilians Offering Gifts to Soldiers — A330

Designs: 20 l, Soldiers, 1878 and 1944. 60 l, Stalin and Spasski Tower.

1948, July 5   Photo.
Cream Paper
616 A329   4 l brown org   .15   .15
617 A330   10 l olive grn   .15   .15
618 A330   20 l dp blue   .15   .15
619 A329   60 l olive brn   .42   .35
Nos. 616-619 (4)   .87   .80
The Soviet Army.

Demeter Blagoev — A331

Monument to Bishop Andrey — A332

9 l, Gabriel Genov. 60 l, Marching youths.

1948, Sept. 6   Litho.
Cream Paper
620 A331   4 l dk brown   .15   .15
621 A331   9 l brown org   .15   .15
622 A332   20 l dp blue   .15   .15
623 A332   60 l brown   .52   .42
Nos. 620-623 (4)   .97   .87
No. 623 is inscribed in Cyrillic characters.
Natl. Insurrection of 1923, 25th anniv.

Christo Smirnenski A333

Battle of Grivitza, 1877 A334

1948, Oct. 2   Photo.   *Perf. 11½*
Cream Paper
624 A333   4 l blue   .15   .15
625 A333   16 l red brown   .16   .15
Christo Smirnenski, poet, 1898-1923.

1948, Nov. 1
626 A334   20 l blue   .15   .15
Nos. 626,C56-C57 (3)   .89   .62
Romanian-Bulgarian friendship.

Bath, Gorna Banya — A335

Bath, Bankya — A336

Mineral Bath, Sofia A337

Maliovitza A338

1948-49   Typo.   *Perf. 12½*
627 A335   2 l red brown   .15   .15
628 A336   3 l red orange   .15   .15
629 A337   4 l deep blue   .15   .15
630 A338   5 l violet brown   .15   .15
631 A336   10 l red violet   .15   .15
632 A338   15 l olive grn ('49)   .20   .15
633 A335   20 l deep blue   .75   .16
Nos. 627-633 (7)   1.70   1.06
Latin characters on No. 633. See No. 653.

Emblem of the Republic — A339

1948-50
634 A339   50s red orange   .15   .15
634A A339   50s org brn ('50)   .15   .15
635 A339   1 l green   .15   .15
636 A339   9 l black   .15   .15
Nos. 634-636 (4)   .60   .60

Botev's Birthplace, Kalofer — A340

Christo Botev — A341

Designs: 9 l, Steamer "Radetzky." 15 l, Kalofer village. 20 l, Botev in uniform. 40 l, Botev's mother. 50 l, Pen, pistol and wreath.

Perf. 11x11½, 11½

1948, Dec. 21   Photo.
Cream Paper
638 A340   1 l dk green   .15   .15
639 A341   4 l violet brn   .15   .15
640 A340   9 l violet   .15   .15
641 A340   15 l brown   .15   .15
642 A340   20 l blue   .16   .15
643 A340   40 l red brown   .25   .16
644 A341   50 l olive blk   .35   .22
Nos. 638-644 (7)   1.36   1.13
Botev, Bulgarian natl. poet, birth cent.

Lenin — A342

Lenin Speaking — A343

1949, Jan. 24   Unwmk.   *Perf. 11½*
Cream Paper
645 A342   4 l brown   .15   .15
646 A343   20 l brown red   .30   .18
25th anniversary of the death of Lenin.

Road Construction A344

Designs: 5 l, Tunnel construction. 9 l, Locomotive. 10 l, Textile worker. 20 l, Female tractor driver. 40 l, Workers in truck.

1949, Apr. 6   *Perf. 10½*
Inscribed: "CHM"
Cream Paper
647 A344   4 l dark red   .15   .15
648 A344   5 l dark brown   .15   .15
649 A344   9 l dk slate grn   .22   .15
650 A344   10 l violet   .25   .15
651 A344   20 l dull blue   .60   .38
652 A344   40 l brown   .95   .55
Nos. 647-652 (6)   2.32   1.53
Issued to honor the Workers' Cultural Brigade.

Type of 1948
Redrawn
Country Name and "POSTA" in Latin Characters

1949   Typo.   *Perf. 12½*
653 A337   20 l deep blue   .55   .15

Miner — A345

1949   *Perf. 11x11½*
654 A345   4 l dark blue   .20   .15

A347

Prime Minister George Dimitrov, 1882-1949 — A348

1949, July 10   Photo.
656 A347   4 l red brown   .22   .15
657 A348   20 l dark blue   .52   .16

Power Station — A349

Grain Towers — A350

Farm Machinery A351

Tractor Parade A352

Agriculture and Industry — A353

1949, Aug. 5   *Perf. 11½x11, 11x11½*
658 A349   4 l olive green   .15   .15
659 A350   9 l dark red   .15   .15
660 A351   15 l purple   .18   .15
661 A352   20 l blue   .55   .38
662 A353   50 l orange brn   1.75   .85
Nos. 658-662 (5)   2.78   1.68
Bulgaria's Five Year Plan.

Grenade and Javelin Throwers A354

Hurdlers A355

BULGARIA

Motorcycle and Tractor — A356
Boy and Girl Athletes — A357 

1949, Sept. 5
663	A354	4 l brown orange		.30	.15
664	A355	9 l olive green		.60	.22
665	A356	20 l violet blue		1.25	.65
666	A357	50 l red brown		3.00	1.25
		Nos. 663-666 (4)		5.15	2.27

Frontier Guards A358 / A359

1949, Oct. 31
667	A358	4 l chestnut brn		.15	.15
668	A359	20 l gray blue		.60	.26

See No. C60.

George Dimitrov A360
Allegory of Labor A361

Laborers of Both Sexes — A362
Workers and Flags of Bulgaria and Russia — A363 

Perf. 11½
1949, Dec. 13 Photo. Unwmk.
669	A360	4 l orange brn		.15	.15
670	A361	9 l purple		.18	.15
671	A362	20 l dull blue		.32	.22
672	A363	50 l red		.65	.45
		Nos. 669-672 (4)		1.30	.97

Joseph V. Stalin — A364
Stalin and Dove — A365 

1949, Dec. 21
673	A364	4 l deep orange		.20	.15
674	A365	40 l rose brown		.60	.32

70th anniv. of the birth of Joseph V. Stalin.

Kharalamby Stoyanov — A366
Communications Strikers — A368 
Railway Strikers — A367 

1950, Feb. 15
675	A366	4 l yellow brown		.15	.15
676	A367	20 l violet blue		.22	.15
677	A368	60 l brown olive		.60	.38
		Nos. 675-677 (3)		.97	.68

30th anniv. (in 1949) of the General Railway and Postal Employees' Strike of 1919.

Miner — A369
Locomotive — A370 

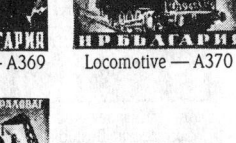

Shipbuilding A371
Tractor A372 

Stalin Central Heating Plant — A374
Textile Worker — A375 

Farm Machinery A373

1950-51 Perf. 11½, 13
678	A369	1 l olive		.15	.15
679	A370	2 l gray blk		.15	.15
680	A371	3 l gray blue		.20	.15
681	A372	4 l dk blue grn		1.75	.52
682	A373	5 l henna brn		.40	.15
682A	A373	9 l gray blk ('51)		.20	.15
683	A374	10 l dp plum ('51)		.28	.15
684	A375	15 l dk car ('51)		.40	.15
685	A375	20 l dk blue ('51)		.70	.40
		Nos. 678-685 (9)		4.23	1.97

No. 685 is inscribed in Latin characters. See Nos. 750-751A.

Vassil Kolarov (1877-1950) — A377

1950, Mar. 6 Perf. 11½
Size: 21½x31½mm
686	A377	4 l red brown		.15	.15

Size: 27x39½mm
687	A377	20 l violet blue		.26	.22

No. 687 has altered frame and is inscribed in Latin characters.

Stanislav Dospevski, Self-portrait A378
King Kaloyan and Desislava A379 

Plowman Resting, by Christo Stanchev A380

Statue of Dimtcho Debelianov, by Ivan Lazarov A381
"Harvest," by V. Dimitrov A382 

Design: 9 l, Nikolai Pavlovich, self-portrait.

1950, Apr. 15 Perf. 11½
688	A378	1 l dk olive grn		.32	.15
689	A379	4 l dk red		.90	.22
690	A378	9 l chocolate		.90	.22
691	A380	15 l brown		1.50	.25
692	A380	20 l deep blue		2.00	.80
693	A381	40 l red brown		2.75	1.25
694	A382	60 l deep orange		4.00	1.65
		Nos. 688-694 (7)		12.37	4.54

Latin characters on No. 692.

Ivan Vazov (1850-1921), Poet and Birthplace A383

1950, June 26
695	A383	4 l olive green		.15	.15

Road Building — A384
Men of Three Races and "Stalin" Flag — A385 

Perf. 11½x11, 11x11½
1950, Sept. 19
696	A384	4 l brown red		.15	.15
697	A385	20 l violet blue		.32	.16

2nd National Peace Conference.

Molotov, Kolarov, Stalin and Dimitrov — A386
Spasski Tower and Flags — A387 

Russian and Bulgarian Women — A388
Loading Russian Ship — A389 

Perf. 11½
1950, Oct. 10 Unwmk. Photo.
698	A386	4 l brown		.15	.15
699	A387	9 l rose carmine		.15	.15
700	A388	20 l gray blue		.20	.15
701	A389	50 l dk grnsh blue		1.10	.45
		Nos. 698-701 (4)		1.60	.90

2nd anniversary of the Soviet-Bulgarian treaty of mutual assistance.

St. Constantine Sanatorium — A390

2 l, 10 l, Children at seashore. 5 l, Rest home.

1950 Typo.
702	A390	1 l dark green		.15	.15
703	A390	2 l carmine		.15	.15
704	A390	5 l deep orange		.16	.15
705	A390	10 l deep blue		.42	.22
		Nos. 702-705 (4)		.88	.67

Originally prepared in 1945 as "Sunday Delivery Stamps," this issue was released for ordinary postage in 1950.

Runners — A393

1950, Aug. 21 Photo. Perf. 11
706	A393	4 l shown		.15	.15
707	A393	9 l Cycling		.15	.15
708	A393	20 l Shot put		.20	.20
709	A393	40 l Volleyball		.42	.42
		Nos. 706-709 (4)		.92	.92

Marshal Fedor I. Tolbukhin A394
Natives Greeting Tolbukhin A395 

Perf. 11½x11, 11x11½
1950, Dec. 10 Photo. Unwmk.
710	A394	4 l claret		.15	.15
711	A395	20 l dk blue		.35	.18

The return of Dobrich and part of the province of Dobruja from Romania to Bulgaria.

BULGARIA

Dimitrov's Birthplace A396

George Dimitrov
A397 A398
Various Portraits, Inscribed:
Г. ДИМИТРОВ

Design: 2 l, Dimitrov Museum, Sofia.

1950, July 2 Perf. 10½
712 A396 50s olive grn .15 .15
713 A396 50s brown .15 .15
714 A397 1 l redsh brn .22 .15
715 A396 2 l gray .22 .15
716 A397 4 l claret .40 .15
717 A397 9 l red brown .60 .25
718 A398 10 l brown red .65 .35
719 A396 15 l olive gray .65 .35
720 A396 20 l dark blue 1.75 .55
   Nos. 712-720,C61 (10) 7.79 3.35

1st anniversary of the death of George Dimitrov, statesman. No. 720 is inscribed in Latin characters.

A. S. Popov — A400

1951, Feb. 10
722 A400 4 l red brown .20 .15
723 A400 20 l dark blue .55 .15

No. 723 is inscribed in Latin characters.

Arms of Bulgaria
A401 A402

1950 Unwmk. Typo. Perf. 13
724 A401 2 l dk brown .15 .15
725 A401 3 l rose .15 .15
726 A402 5 l carmine .15 .15
727 A402 9 l aqua .15 .15
   Nos. 724-727 (4) .60 .60

Nos. 724-727 were prepared in 1947 for official use but were issued as regular postage stamps Oct. 1, 1950.

Heroes Chankova, Antonov-Malchik, Dimitrov and Dimitrova — A403

Stanke Dimitrov-Marek A404

George Kirkov A405

George Dimitrov at Leipzig — A406

Natcho Ivanov and Avr. Stoyanov — A407

9 l, Anton Ivanov. 15 l, Christo Michailov.

1951, Mar. 25 Photo. Perf. 11½
728 A403 1 l red violet .15 .15
729 A404 2 l dk red brn .15 .15
730 A405 4 l car rose .15 .15
731 A405 9 l orange brn .45 .15
732 A405 15 l olive brn .80 .22
733 A406 20 l dark blue 1.10 .55
734 A407 50 l olive gray 2.50 .90
   Nos. 728-734 (7) 5.30 2.27

First Bulgarian Tractor A408

First Steam Roller — A409

First Truck — A410

Bulgarian Embroidery — A411

15 l, Carpet. 20 l, Tobacco & roses. 40 l, Fruits.

  Perf. 11x10½
1951, Mar. 30 Photo. Unwmk.
735 A408 1 l olive brn .18 .15
736 A409 2 l violet .28 .15
737 A410 4 l red brown .50 .15
738 A411 9 l purple .70 .15
739 A409 15 l deep plum 1.00 .28
740 A411 20 l violet blue 1.50 .32
741 A410 40 l deep green 2.50 .65
  Perf. 13
  Size: 23x18½mm
742 A408 1 l purple .15 .15
743 A409 2 l Prus green .28 .15
744 A410 4 l red brown .28 .15
   Nos. 735-744 (10) 7.37 2.30

See Nos. 894, 973. For surcharge see No. 973.

Turkish Attack on Mt. Zlee Dol A412

Designs: 4 l, Georgi Benkovski speaking to rebels. 9 l, Cherrywood cannon of 1876 and Russian cavalry, 1945. 20 l, Rebel, 1876 and partisan, 1944. 40 l, Benkovski and Dimitrov.

1951, May 3 Perf. 10½
  Cream Paper
745 A412 1 l redsh brown .16 .15
746 A412 4 l dark green .16 .15
747 A412 9 l violet brown .50 .28
748 A412 20 l deep blue .65 .48
749 A412 40 l dark red 1.00 .70
   Nos. 745-749 (5) 2.47 1.76

75th anniv. of the "April" revolution.

Industrial Types of 1950

1951 Perf. 13
750 A369 1 l violet .15 .15
751 A370 2 l dk brown .15 .15
751A A372 4 l dk yel grn .75 .15
   Nos. 750-751A (3) 1.05 .45

Demeter Blagoev Addressing 1891 Congress at Busludja — A413

1951 Photo. Perf. 11
752 A413 1 l purple .24 .15
753 A413 4 l dark green .35 .15
754 A413 9 l deep claret .60 .32
   Nos. 752-754 (3) 1.19 .62

60th anniversary of the first Congress of the Bulgarian Social-Democratic Party.
See Nos. 1174-1176.

Day Nursery — A414

Designs: 4 l, Model building construction. 9 l, Playground. 20 l, Children's town.

1951, Oct. 10 Unwmk.
755 A414 1 l brown .15 .15
756 A414 4 l deep plum .20 .15
757 A414 9 l blue green .60 .22
758 A414 20 l deep blue 1.00 .55
   Nos. 755-758 (4) 1.95 1.07

Children's Day, Sept. 25, 1951.

Order of Labor
A415 A416

1952, Feb. 1 Perf. 13
  Reverse of Medal
759 A415 1 l red brown .15 .15
760 A415 4 l blue green .15 .15
761 A415 9 l dark blue .28 .15
  Obverse of Medal
762 A416 1 l carmine .15 .15
763 A416 4 l green .15 .15
764 A416 9 l purple .28 .15
   Nos. 759-764 (6) 1.16 .90

No. 764 has numeral at lower left and different background.

Workers and Symbols of Industry — A417

Design: 4 l, Flags, Dimitrov, Chervenkov.

1951, Dec. 29 Perf. 11
  Inscribed: "16 XII 1951"
765 A417 1 l olive black .15 .15
766 A417 4 l chocolate .16 .15

Third Congress of Bulgarian General Workers' Professional Union.

Dimitrov and Chemical Works — A418

George Dimitrov and V. Chervenkov A419

Portrait: 80s, Dimitrov.

  Unwmk.
1952, June 18 Photo. Perf. 11
767 A418 16s brown .35 .22
768 A419 44s brown carmine .52 .25
769 A418 80s brt blue 1.10 .52
   Nos. 767-769 (3) 1.97 .99

70th anniv. of the birth of George Dimitrov.

Vassil Kolarov Dam — A420

Republika Power Station — A421

1952, May 16 Perf. 13
770 A420 4s dark green .15 .15
771 A420 12s purple .15 .15
772 A420 16s red brown .15 .15
773 A420 44s rose brown .50 .15
774 A420 80s brt blue 1.65 .18
   Nos. 770-774 (5) 2.60 .78

No. 774 is inscribed in Latin characters.

1952, June 30 Perf. 13, Pin Perf.
775 A421 16s dark brown .20 .15
776 A421 44s magenta .75 .15

Nikolai I. Vapzarov — A422

Designs: Various portraits.

1952, July 23 Perf. 10½
777 A422 16s rose brown .16 .15
778 A422 44s dk red brn .65 .16
779 A422 80s dk olive brn 1.40 .52
   Nos. 777-779 (3) 2.21 .83

10th anniversary of the death of Nikolai I. Vapzarov, poet and revolutionary.

BULGARIA

Dimitrov and Youth Conference — A423

Designs: 16s, Resistance movement incident. 44s, Frontier guards and industrial scene. 80s, George Dimitrov and young workers.

1952, Sept. 1   *Perf. 11x11½*
780	A423	2s brown carmine	.15	.15
781	A423	16s purple	.20	.15
782	A423	44s dark green	.52	.28
783	A423	80s dark brown	1.10	.60
		Nos. 780-783 (4)	1.97	1.18

40th anniv. of the founding conference of the Union of Social Democratic Youth.

Assault on the Winter Palace — A424

Designs: 8s, Volga-Don Canal. 16s, Symbols of world peace. 44s, Lenin and Stalin. 80s, Himlay hydroelectric station.

Perf. 11½
1952, Nov. 6   Unwmk.   Photo.
Dated: "1917-1952"
784	A424	4s red brown	.15	.15
785	A424	8s dark green	.15	.15
786	A424	16s dark blue	.15	.15
787	A424	44s brown	.32	.18
788	A424	80s olive brown	.75	.35
		Nos. 784-788 (5)	1.52	.98

35th anniv. of the Russian revolution.

Vassil Levski — A425

Design: 44s, Levski and comrades.

1953, Feb. 19   Cream Paper   *Perf. 11*
789	A425	16s brown	.15	.15
790	A425	44s brown blk	.25	.15

80th anniv. of the death of Levski, patriot.

Ferrying Artillery and Troops into Battle A426

Soldier A427

Mother and Children A428

Designs: 44s, Victorious soldiers. 80s, Soldier welcomed. 1 l, Monuments.

1953, Mar. 3   *Perf. 10½*
791	A426	8s Prus green	.16	.15
792	A427	16s dp brown	.22	.15
793	A426	44s dk slate grn	.42	.15
794	A426	80s dull red brn	.85	.20
795	A426	1 l black	1.10	.32
		Nos. 791-795 (5)	2.75	.97

Bulgaria's independence from Turkey, 75th anniv.

1953, Mar. 9
796	A428	16s slate green	.15	.15
797	A428	16s bright blue	.15	.15

Women's Day.

Woodcarvings at Rila Monastery
A429   **A430**

Designs: 12s, 16s, 28s, Woodcarvings, Rila Monastery. 44s, Carved Ceilings, Trnovo. 80s, 1 l, 4 l, Carvings, Pasardjik.

1953   Unwmk.   Photo.   *Perf. 13*
798	A429	2s gray brown	.15	.15
799	A430	8s dk slate grn	.15	.15
800	A430	12s brown	.15	.15
801	A430	16s rose lake	.24	.15
802	A429	28s dk olive grn	.32	.15
803	A430	44s dk brown	.50	.15
804	A430	80s ultra	.85	.15
805	A430	1 l violet blue	1.75	.22
806	A430	4 l rose lake	3.50	.90
		Nos. 798-806 (9)	7.61	2.17

For surcharge see No. 1204.

Karl Marx A431    **"Das Kapital" A432**

1953, Apr. 30   *Perf. 10½*
807	A431	16s bright blue	.15	.15
808	A432	44s deep brown	.32	.18

70th anniv. of the death of Karl Marx.

Labor Day Parade — A433    **Joseph V. Stalin — A434**

1953, Apr. 30   *Perf. 13*
809	A433	16s brown red	.15	.15

Labor Day, May 1, 1953.

1953, May 23   *Perf. 13x13½*
810	A434	16s dark gray	.20	.15
811	A434	16s dark brown	.20	.15

Death of Joseph V. Stalin, Mar. 5, 1953.

Georgi Delchev — A435     **Battle Scene — A436**

Peasants Attacking Turkish Troops — A437

1953, Aug. 8   *Perf. 13*
812	A435	16s dark brown	.15	.15
813	A436	44s purple	.30	.15
814	A437	1 l deep claret	.45	.16
		Nos. 812-814 (3)	.90	.46

50th anniv. of the Ilinden Revolt (#812, 814) and the Preobrazhene Revolt (#813).

Soldier and Rebels — A438

44s, Soldier guarding industrial construction.

1953, Sept. 18
815	A438	16s deep claret	.15	.15
816	A438	44s greenish blue	.35	.15

Army Day.

George Dimitrov and Vassil Kolarov — A439    **Demeter Blagoev — A440**

Designs: 16s, Citizens in revolt. 44s, Attack.

1953, Sept. 22
817	A439	8s olive gray	.15	.15
818	A439	16s dk red brn	.18	.15
819	A439	44s cerise	.45	.18
		Nos. 817-819 (3)	.78	.48

September Revolution, 30th anniversary.

1953, Sept. 21

Portraits: 44s, G. Dimitrov and D. Blagoev.
820	A440	16s brown	.25	.15
821	A440	44s red brown	.38	.15

50th anniversary of the formation of the Social Democratic Party.

Railway Viaduct — A441    **Pouring Molten Metal — A442**

Designs: 16s, Welder and storage tanks. 80s, Harvesting machine.

1953, Oct. 17
826	A441	8s brt blue	.15	.15
827	A441	16s grnsh blk	.15	.15
828	A442	44s brown red	.28	.15
829	A441	80s orange	.45	.28
		Nos. 826-829 (4)	1.03	.73

Month of Bulgarian-Russian friendship.

Belladonna A443    **Kolarov Library, Sofia A444**

Medicinal Flowers: 4s, Jimson weed. 8s, Sage. 12s, Dog rose. 16s, Gentian. 20s, Poppy. 28s, Peppermint. 40s, Bear grass. 44s, Coltsfoot. 80s, Cowslip. 1 l, Dandelion. 2 l, Foxglove.

1953   Unwmk.   Photo.   *Perf. 13*
White or Cream Paper
830	A443	2s dull blue	.15	.15
831	A443	4s brown org	.15	.15
832	A443	8s blue grn	.15	.15
833	A443	12s brown org	.15	.15
834	A443	12s blue grn	.15	.15
835	A443	16s violet blue	.15	.15
836	A443	16s dp red brn	.15	.15
837	A443	20s car rose	.15	.15
838	A443	28s dk gray grn	.30	.15
839	A443	40s dark blue	.35	.15
840	A443	44s brown	.35	.18
841	A443	80s yellow brn	.60	.35
842	A443	1 l henna brn	2.25	.48
843	A443	2 l purple	3.75	1.25
		a. Souvenir sheet	27.50	20.00
		Nos. 830-843 (14)	8.80	3.79

No. 843a contains 12 stamps, one of each denomination above, printed in dark green. Size: 161x172mm. Sold for 6 leva.

1953, Dec. 16
854	A444	44s brown	.25	.15

75th anniversary of the founding of the Kolarov Library, Sofia.

Singer and Accordionist A445    **Lenin and Stalin A446**

1953, Dec. 26
855	A445	16s shown	.15	.15
856	A445	44s Dancers	.18	.15

1954, Mar. 13

Designs: 44s, Lenin statue. 80s, Lenin mausoleum, Moscow. 1 l, Lenin.

Cream Paper
857	A446	16s brown	.20	.15
858	A446	44s rose brown	.26	.15
859	A446	80s blue	.42	.15
860	A446	1 l dp olive grn	.60	.26
		Nos. 857-860 (4)	1.48	.71

30th anniversary of the death of Lenin.

Demeter Blagoev and Followers A447

Design: 44s, Blagoev at desk.

1954, Apr. 28   Cream Paper
861	A447	16s dp red brn	.15	.15
862	A447	44s black brn	.32	.15

30th anniv. of the death of Demeter Blagoev.

George Dimitrov A448    **Dimitrov and Refinery A449**

1954, June 11
863	A448	44s lake, *cream*	.22	.15
864	A449	80s brown, *cream*	.65	.15

5th anniv. of the death of George Dimitrov.

Train Leaving Tunnel — A450

1954, July 30
865	A450	44s dk grn, *cream*	.60	.15
866	A450	44s blk brn, *cream*	.60	.15

Day of the Railroads, Aug. 1, 1954.

BULGARIA

Miner at Work — A451

1954, Aug. 19
867 A451 44s grnsh blk, *cream* .20 .15
Miners' Day.

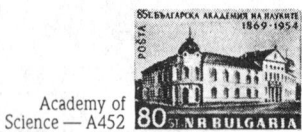

Academy of Science — A452

1954, Oct. 27
868 A452 80s black, *cream* .55 .18
85th anniversary of the foundation of the Bulgarian Academy of Science.

Horsemanship A454

16s, 44s, 2 l, vert.

1954, Dec. 21
869 A454 16s Gymnastics .52 .16
870 A454 44s Wrestling .60 .20
871 A454 80s shown 1.25 .55
872 A454 2 l Skiing 3.00 1.65
Nos. 869-872 (4) 5.37 2.56

Welcoming Liberators — A455
Soldier's Return — A456

Designs: 28s, Refinery. 44s, Dimitrov and Workers. 80s, Girl and boy. 1 l, George Dimitrov.

1954, Oct. 4
Cream Paper
873 A455 12s brown car .15 .15
874 A456 16s dp carmine .15 .15
875 A455 28s indigo .15 .15
876 A455 44s redsh brn .15 .15
877 A456 80s deep blue .55 .25
878 A456 1 l dark green .55 .25
Nos. 873-878 (6) 1.70 1.10

10th anniversary of Bulgaria's liberation.

Recreation at Workers' Rest Home — A457
Metal Worker and Furnace — A458

Portraits: 80s, Dimitrov, Blagoev, and Kirkov.

Unwmk.
1954, Dec. 28 Photo. Perf. 13
Cream Paper
879 A457 16s dark green .16 .16
880 A458 44s brown orange .16 .15
881 A457 80s dp violet blue .42 .20
Nos. 879-881 (3) .74 .50

50th anniversary of Bulgaria's trade union movement.

Geese — A459

Designs: 4s, Chickens. 12s, Hogs. 16s, Sheep. 28s, Telephone building. 44s, Communist party headquarters. 80s, Apartment buildings. 1 l, St. Kiradgieff Mills.

1955-56
882 A459 2s dk blue grn .16 .15
883 A459 4s olive green .28 .15
884 A459 12s dk red brn .42 .15
885 A459 16s brown orange .65 .15
886 A459 28s violet blue .32 .15
887 A459 44s lil red, *cream* .60 .15
a. 44s brown red 4.50 .15
888 A459 80s dk red brown .75 .15
889 A459 1 l dk blue green 1.50 .16
Nos. 882-889 (8) 4.68 1.21

Issued: #887, 4/20/56; others, 2/19/55.

Textile Worker — A460
Mother and Child — A461

Design: 16s, Woman feeding calf.

1955, Mar. 5
890 A460 12s dark brown .15 .15
891 A460 16s dark green .15 .15
892 A461 44s dk car rose .50 .15
893 A461 44s blue .50 .15
Nos. 890-893 (4) 1.30 .60

Women's Day, Mar. 8, 1955.

No. 744 Surcharged in Blue
1955, Mar. 8 Perf. 13
894 A410 16s on 4 l red brown .45 .15

May Day Demonstration of Workers A462
Sts. Cyril and Methodius A463

Design: 44s, Three workers and globe.

1955, Apr. 23 Photo.
895 A462 16s car rose .15 .15
896 A462 44s blue .30 .15

Labor Day, May 1, 1955.

1955, May 21
Designs: 8s, Paisii Hilendarski. 16s, Nicolas Karastoyanov's printing press. 28s, Christo Botev. 44s, Ivan Vazov. 80s, Demeter Blagoev and socialist papers. 2 l, Blagoev printing plant, Sofia.

Cream Paper
897 A463 4s deep blue .15 .15
898 A463 8s olive .15 .15
899 A463 16s black .15 .15
900 A463 28s henna brn .16 .15
901 A463 44s brown .32 .15
902 A463 80s rose red .50 .16
903 A463 2 l black 1.50 .42
Nos. 897-903 (7) 2.93 1.33

Creation of the Cyrillic alphabet, 1100th anniv. Latin lettering at bottom on #901-903.

Sergei Rumyantzev A464
Mother and Children A465

Portraits: 16s, Christo Jassenov. 44s, Geo Milev.

1955, June 30 Unwmk. Perf. 13
Cream Paper
904 A464 12s orange brn .16 .15
905 A464 16s lt brown .16 .15
906 A464 44s grnsh blk .42 .15
Nos. 904-906 (3) .74 .45

30th anniv. of the deaths of Sergei Rumyanchev, Christo Jassenov and Geo Milev. Latin lettering at bottom of No. 906.

1955, July 30
907 A465 44s brn car, *cream* .30 .15

World Congress of Mothers in Lausanne, 1955.

Young People of Three Races — A466
Friedrich Engels and Book — A467

1955, July 30
908 A466 44s blue, *cream* .30 .15

5th World Festival of Youth in Warsaw, July 31-Aug. 14.

1955, July 30
909 A467 44s brown .30 .15

60th anniv. of the death of Friedrich Engels.

Entrance to Fair, 1892 — A468
Statuary Group at Fair, 1955 — A469

Designs: 44s, "Fruit of our Land." 80s, Woman holding Fair emblem.

1955, Aug. 31
Cream Paper
910 A468 4s deep brown .15 .15
911 A469 16s dk car rose .15 .15
912 A468 44s olive blk .20 .15
913 A469 80s deep blue .45 .15
Nos. 910-913 (4) .95 .60

16th International Plovdiv Fair. Latin lettering on Nos. 912-913.

Friedrich von Schiller — A470

Portraits: 44s, Adam Mickiewicz. 60s, Hans Christian Andersen. 80s, Baron de Montesquieu. 1 l, Miguel de Cervantes. 2 l, Walt Whitman.

1955, Oct. 31
Cream Paper
914 A470 16s brown .15 .15
915 A470 44s brown red .38 .15
916 A470 60s Prus blue .60 .15
917 A470 80s black .60 .15
918 A470 1 l rose violet 1.40 .32
919 A470 2 l olive green 1.90 .50
Nos. 914-919 (6) 5.03 1.42

Various anniversaries of famous writers. Nos. 918 and 919 are issued in sheets alternating with labels without franking value. The labels show title pages for Leaves of Grass and Don Quixote in English and Spanish, respectively. Latin lettering on #915-919.

Karl Marx Industrial Plant — A471

Friendship Monument — A472
I. V. Michurin — A473

Designs: 4s, Alekandr Stamboliski Dam. 16s, Bridge over Danube. 1 l, Vladimir V. Mayakovsky.

1955, Dec. 1 Unwmk.
920 A471 2s slate blk .15 .15
921 A471 4s deep blue .15 .15
922 A471 16s dk blue grn .15 .15
923 A472 44s red brown .15 .15
924 A473 80s dark green .25 .15
925 A473 1 l gray blk .38 .15
Nos. 920-925 (6) 1.23 .90

Russian-Bulgarian friendship.

Library Seal — A474
Krusto Pishurka — A475

Portrait: 44s, Bacho Kiro.

1956, Feb. 10 Perf. 11x10½
926 A474 12s car lake, *cream* .15 .15
927 A475 16s dp brn, *cream* .15 .15
928 A475 44s slate blk, *cream* .22 .15
Nos. 926-928 (3) .52 .45

100th anniversary of the National Library. Latin lettering at bottom of No. 928.

Canceled to Order
Beginning about 1956, some issues were sold in sheets canceled to order. Values in second column when much less than unused are for "CTO" copies. Postally used stamps are valued at slightly less than, or the same as, unused.

Quinces — A476
Cherrywood Cannon — A477

Designs: 8s, Pears. 16s, Apples. 44s, Grapes.

1956 Photo. Perf. 13
929 A476 4s carmine .75 .15
930 A476 8s blue green .32 .15
931 A476 16s lilac rose .80 .15
932 A476 44s deep violet .80 .15
Nos. 929-932 (4) 2.67 .61

Latin lettering on #932. See #964-967. For surcharge see #1364.

BULGARIA

1956, Apr. 28   *Perf. 11x10½*
933 A477 16s shown .15 .15
934 A477 44s Cavalry attack .22 .15
April Uprising against Turkish rule, 80th anniv.

Demeter Blagoev (1856-1924), Writer, Birthplace — A478

Cherries — A479

1956, May 30   *Perf. 11*
935 A478 44s Prus blue .25 .15

1956   Unwmk.   *Perf. 13*
936 A479 2s shown .15 .15
937 A479 12s Plums .15 .15
938 A479 28s Peaches .18 .15
939 A479 80s Strawberries .55 .20
    Nos. 936-939 (4) 1.03 .65
Latin lettering on No. 939.

Gymnastics — A480

Pole Vaulting — A481

Designs: 12s, Discus throw. 44s, Soccer. 80s, Basketball. 1 l, Boxing.

Perf. 11x10½, 10½x11
1956, Aug. 29
940 A480 4s brt ultra .15 .15
941 A480 12s brick red .15 .15
942 A481 16s yellow brn .32 .16
943 A480 44s dark green .48 .25
944 A480 80s dark red brn 1.00 .50
945 A481 1 l deep magenta 1.65 .65
    Nos. 940-945 (6) 3.75 1.86
Latin lettering on Nos. 943-945.
16th Olympic Games at Melbourne, Nov. 22-Dec. 8, 1956.

Tobacco, Rose and Distillery — A482

People's Theater — A483

1956, Sept. 1   *Perf. 13*
946 A482 44s deep carmine .38 .16
947 A482 44s olive green .38 .16
17th International Plovdiv Fair.

1956, Nov. 16   Unwmk.
Design: 44s, Dobri Woinikoff and Sawa Dobroplodni, dramatists.
948 A483 16s dull red brown .15 .15
949 A483 44s dark blue green .22 .15
Bulgarian Theater centenary.

Benjamin Franklin — A484

Cyclists, Palms and Pyramids — A485

Portraits: 20s, Rembrandt. 40s, Mozart. 44s, Heinrich Heine. 60s, Shaw. 80s, Dostoevski. 1 l, Ibsen. 2 l, Pierre Curie.

1956, Dec. 29
950 A484 16s dark olive grn .15 .15
951 A484 20s brown .18 .15
952 A484 40s dark car rose .18 .15
953 A484 44s dark violet brn .22 .15
954 A484 60s dark slate .32 .15
955 A484 80s dark brown .45 .15
956 A484 1 l bluish grn .80 .30
957 A484 2 l Prus green 1.75 .52
    Nos. 950-957 (8) 4.05 1.72
Great personalities of the world.

1957, Mar. 6   Photo.   *Perf. 10½*
958 A485 80s henna brown .50 .25
959 A485 80s Prus green .50 .25
Fourth Egyptian bicycle race.

Woman Technician — A486

"New Times" Review — A487

Designs: 16s, Woman and children. 44s, Woman feeding chickens.

1957, Mar. 8
960 A486 12s deep blue .15 .15
961 A486 16s henna brown .15 .15
962 A486 44s slate green .30 .15
    Nos. 960-962 (3) .60 .45
Women's Day. Latin lettering on 44s.

1957, Mar. 8   Unwmk.
963 A487 16s deep carmine .20 .15
60th anniversary of the founding of the "New Times" review.

Fruit Type of 1956.
4s, Quinces. 8s, Pears. 16s, Apples. 44s, Grapes.

1957   Photo.   *Perf. 13*
964 A476 4s yellow green .15 .15
965 A476 8s brown orange .15 .15
966 A476 16s rose red .15 .15
967 A476 44s orange yellow .40 .15
    Nos. 964-967 (4) .85 .60
Latin lettering on #967. For surcharge see #1364.

Sts. Cyril and Methodius — A488

Basketball — A489

1957, May 22   *Perf. 11*
968 A488 44s olive grn & buff .50 .15
Centenary of the first public veneration of Sts. Cyril and Methodius, inventors of the Cyrillic alphabet.

1957, June 20   Photo.   *Perf. 10½x11*
969 A489 44s dark green .95 .30
10th European Basketball Championship at Sofia.

Dancer and Spasski Tower, Moscow — A490

1957, July 18   *Perf. 13*
970 A490 44s blue .30 .15
Sixth World Youth Festival in Moscow.

George Dimitrov (1882-1949) — A491

1957, July 18
971 A491 44s deep carmine .50 .15

Vassil Levski — A492

1957, July 18   *Perf. 11*
972 A492 44s grnsh black .30 .15
120th anniversary of the birth of Vassil Levski, patriot and national hero.

No. 742 Surcharged in Carmine
1957   Unwmk.   *Perf. 13*
973 A408 16s on 1 l purple .15 .15

Trnovo and Lazarus L. Zamenhof — A493

1957, July 27
974 A493 44s slate green .50 .15
50th anniv. of the Bulgarian Esperanto Society and the 70th anniv. of Esperanto.
For surcharge see No. 1235.

Bulgarian Veteran of 1877 War and Russian Soldier — A494

1957, Aug. 13
975 A494 16s dk blue grn .15 .15
976 A494 44s brown .32 .15
80th anniversary of Bulgaria's liberation from the Turks. Latin lettering on No. 976.

Woman Planting Tree — A495

Red Deer in Forest — A496

Designs: 16s, Dam, lake and forest. 44s, Plane over forest. 80s, Fields on edge of forest.

1957, Sept. 16   Photo.   *Perf. 13*
977 A495 2s deep green .15 .15
978 A496 12s dark brown .15 .15
979 A496 16s Prus blue .15 .15
980 A496 44s Prus green .22 .15
981 A496 80s yellow green .42 .15
    Nos. 977-981 (5) 1.09 .75
Latin lettering on Nos. 980 and 981.

Lenin — A497

Designs: 16s, Cruiser "Aurora." 44s, Dove over map of communist area. 60s, Revolutionaries and banners. 80s, Oil refinery.

1957, Oct. 29   *Perf. 11*
982 A497 12s chocolate .16 .15
983 A497 16s Prus green .32 .15
984 A497 44s deep blue .65 .15
985 A497 60s dk car rose .75 .15
986 A497 80s dark green 1.25 .22
    Nos. 982-986 (5) 3.13 .82
40th anniv. of the Communist Revolution.
Latin lettering on Nos. 984-985.

Globes — A498

1957, Oct. 4   *Perf. 13*
987 A498 44s Prus blue .30 .15
4th Intl. Trade Union Cong., Leipzig, Oct. 4-15.

Vassil Kolarov Hotel — A499

Bulgarian Health Resorts: 4s, Skis and Pirin Mountains. 8s, Old house at Koprivspitsa. 12s, Rest home at Velingrad. 44s, Momin-Prochod Hotel. 60s, Nesebr Hotel, shoreline and peninsula. 80s, Varna beach scene. 1 l, Hotel at Varna.

1958   Photo.   *Perf. 13*
988 A499 4s blue .15 .15
989 A499 8s orange brn .15 .15
990 A499 12s dk green .15 .15
991 A499 16s green .15 .15
992 A499 44s dk blue grn .15 .15
993 A499 60s deep blue .18 .15
994 A499 80s fawn .28 .15
995 A499 1 l dk red brn .35 .18
    Nos. 988-995 (8) 1.56 1.23
Latin lettering on 44s, 60s, 80s, and 1 l.
Issue dates: #991-994, Jan. 20; others, July 5.
For surcharges see Nos. 1200, 1436.

Mikhail I. Glinka — A500

Portraits: 16s, Jan A. Komensky (Comenius). 40s, Carl von Linné. 44s, William Blake. 60s, Carlo Goldoni. 80s, Auguste Comte.

1957, Dec. 30
996 A500 12s dark brown .20 .15
997 A500 16s dark green .20 .15
998 A500 40s Prus blue .20 .15
999 A500 44s maroon .20 .15
1000 A500 60s orange brown .75 .15
1001 A500 80s deep plum 2.50 .90
    Nos. 996-1001 (6) 4.05 1.65
Famous men of other countries. Latin lettering on Nos. 999-1001.

BULGARIA

Young Couple, Flag, Dimitrov — A501

People's Front Salute — A502

1957, Dec. 28   *Perf. 11*
1002 A501 16s carmine rose   .15 .15
10th anniversary of Dimitrov's Union of the People's Youth.

1957, Dec. 28
1003 A502 16s dk violet brn   .15 .15
15th anniversary of the People's Front.

Hare — A503

12s, Red deer (doe), vert. 16s, Red deer (stag). 44s, Chamois. 80s, Brown bear. 1 l, Wild boar.

1958, Apr. 5   *Unwmk.*   *Perf. 10½*   *Photo.*
1004 A503 2s lt & dk ol grn   .15 .15
1005 A503 12s sl grn & red brn   .18 .15
1006 A503 16s bluish grn & dk red brn   .20 .15
1007 A503 44s blue & brown   .24 .15
1008 A503 80s bis & dk brn   .75 .25
1009 A503 1 l stl bl & dk brn   1.00 .40
   Nos. 1004-1009 (6)   2.52 1.07
Value, imperf. set $4.

Marx and Lenin — A504

Designs: 16s, Marchers and flags. 44s, Lenin blast furnaces.

1958, July 2   *Perf. 11*
1010 A504 12s dark brown   .16 .15
1011 A504 16s dark carmine   .20 .15
1012 A504 44s dark blue   .85 .15
   Nos. 1010-1012 (3)   1.21 .45
Bulgarian Communist Party, 7th Congress.

Wrestlers — A505

1958, June 20   *Perf. 10½*
1013 A505 60s dk carmine rose   .65 .35
1014 A505 80s deep brown   1.10 .55
World Wrestling Championship, Sofia.

Chessmen and Globe — A506

1958, July 18   *Unwmk.*   *Perf. 10½*   *Photo.*
1015 A506 80s grn & yel grn   2.50 .80
5th World Students' Chess Games, Varna.

Conference Emblem — A507

1958, Sept. 24
1016 A507 44s blue   .40 .15
World Trade Union Conference of Working Youth, Prague, July 14-20.

Swimmer — A508

1958 Students' Games: 28s, Dancer, vert. 44s, Volleyball, vert.

1958, Sept. 19   *Perf. 11x10½*
1017 A508 16s bright blue   .15 .15
1018 A508 28s brown orange   .22 .15
1019 A508 44s bright green   .30 .15
   Nos. 1017-1019 (3)   .67 .45

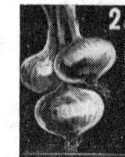

Onions — A509

Vegetables: 12s, Garlic. 16s, Peppers. 44s, Tomatoes. 80s, Cucumbers. 1 l, Eggplant.

1958, Sept. 20   *Perf. 13*
1020 A509 2s orange brown   .15 .15
1021 A509 12s Prus blue   .15 .15
1022 A509 16s dark green   .15 .15
1023 A509 44s deep carmine   .16 .15
1024 A509 80s deep green   .40 .15
1025 A509 1 l brt purple   .60 .15
   Nos. 1020-1025 (6)   1.61 .90
Value, imperf. set $4.
See No. 1072. For surcharge see No. 1201.

Plovdiv Fair Building — A510

1958, Sept. 14   *Unwmk.*   *Perf. 11*
1026 A510 44s deep carmine   .40 .15
18th International Plovdiv Fair.

Attack — A511

Design: 44s, Fighter dragging wounded man.

1958, Sept. 23   *Photo.*   *Perf. 11*
1027 A511 16s orange ver   .15 .15
1028 A511 44s lake   .35 .15
35th anniv. of the September Revolution.

Emblem, Brussels Fair — A512

1958, Oct. 13   *Perf. 11*
1029 A512 1 l blk & brt blue   5.00 1.25
Brussels World's Fair, Apr. 17-Oct. 19. Exists imperf.

Runner at Finish Line — A513

Woman Throwing Javelin — A514

60s, High jumper. 80s, Hurdler. 4 l, Shot putter.

1958, Nov. 30
1030 A513 16s red brn, *pnksh*   .40 .15
1031 A514 44s olive, *yelsh*   .40 .15
1032 A514 60s dk bl, *bluish*   .75 .20
1033 A514 80s dp grn, *grnsh*   1.00 .20
1034 A513 4 l dp rose cl, *pnksh*   6.25 1.40
   Nos. 1030-1034 (5)   8.80 2.10
1958 Balkan Games.
Latin lettering on Nos. 1032-1033.

Christo Smirnenski — A515

1958, Dec. 22
1035 A515 16s dark carmine   .15 .15
Christo Smirnenski (1898-1923), poet.

Girls Harvesting — A516

Girl Tending Calves — A517

Designs: 16s, Boy and girl laborers. 40s, Boy pushing wheelbarrow. 44s, Headquarters building.

1959, Nov. 29   *Photo.*
1036 A516 8s dk olive green   .15 .15
1037 A517 12s redsh brown   .15 .15
1038 A516 16s violet brown   .15 .15
1039 A517 40s Prus blue   .15 .15
1040 A516 44s deep carmine   .60 .15
   Nos. 1036-1040 (5)   1.20 .75
4th Congress of Dimitrov's Union of People's Youth.

UNESCO Building, Paris — A518

1959, Mar. 28   *Unwmk.*   *Perf. 11*
1041 A518 2 l dp red lilac, *cream*   1.25 1.00
Opening of UNESCO Headquarters, Paris, Nov. 3, 1958. Value imperf. $2.50

Skier — A519

Soccer Players — A520

1959, Mar. 28   *Perf. 11*
1042 A519 1 l blue, *cream*   .90 .50
Forty years of skiing in Bulgaria.

1959, Mar. 25
1043 A520 2 l chestnut, *cream*   1.25 .65
1959 European Youth Soccer Championship.

Russian Soldiers Installing Telegraph Wires — A521

First Bulgarian Postal Coach — A522

Designs: 60s, Stamp of 1879. 80s, First Bulgarian automobile. 1 l, Television tower. 2 l, Strike of railroad and postal workers, 1919.

1959, May 4
1044 A521 12s dk grn & cit   .15 .15
1045 A522 16s deep plum   .15 .15
1046 A521 60s dk brn & yel   .32 .15
1047 A522 80s hn brn & sal   .45 .15
1048 A521 1 l blue   .60 .16
1049 A522 2 l dk red brown   1.65 .80
   Nos. 1044-1049 (6)   3.32 1.56

80th anniv. of the Bulgarian post. Latin lettering on Nos. 1046-1049.
Two imperf. souvenir sheets exist with olive borders and inscriptions. One contains one copy of No. 1046 in black & ocher, and measures 92x121mm. The other sheet contains one copy each of Nos. 1044-1045 and 1047-1048 in changed colors: 12s, olive green & ocher; 16s, deep claret & ocher; 80s, dark red & ocher; 1 l, olive & ocher. Each sheet sold for 5 leva. Value, each $22.50.

Great Tits — A523

Birds: 8s, Hoopoe. 16s, Great spotted woodpecker, vert. 45s, Gray partridge, vert. 60s, Rock partridge. 80s, European cuckoo.

1959, June 30   *Photo.*
1050 A523 2s olive & sl grn   .15 .15
1051 A523 8s dp orange & blk   .15 .15
1052 A523 16s chestnut & dk brn   .22 .15
1053 A523 45s brown & blk   .28 .15
1054 A523 60s dp blue & gray   .65 .15
1055 A523 80s dp bl grn & gray   1.10 .18
   Nos. 1050-1055 (6)   2.55 .93

BULGARIA

Bagpiper — A524

Designs: 12s, Acrobats. 16s, Girls exercising with hoops. 20s, Male dancers. 80s, Ballet dancers. 1 l, Ceramic pitcher. 16s, 20s, 80s are horizontal.

1959, Aug. 29   Unwmk.   Perf. 11
Surface-colored Paper
1056	A524	4s dk olive	.15	.15
1057	A524	12s scarlet	.15	.15
1058	A524	16s maroon	.15	.15
1059	A524	20s dk blue	.25	.15
1060	A524	80s brt green	.52	.26
1061	A524	1 l brown org	.95	.42
		Nos. 1056-1061 (6)	2.17	1.28

7th International Youth Festival, Vienna. Latin inscriptions on Nos. 1060-1061.

Partisans in Truck A525

Designs: 16s, Partisans and soldiers shaking hands. 45s, Refinery. 60s, Tanks. 80s, Harvester. 1.25 l, Children with flag, vert.

1959, Sept. 8
1062	A525	12s red & Prus grn	.15	.15
1063	A525	16s red & dk pur	.15	.15
1064	A525	45s red & int bl	.15	.15
1065	A525	60s red & ol grn	.15	.15
1066	A525	80s red & brn	.26	.15
1067	A525	1.25 l red & dp brn	.65	.38
		Nos. 1062-1067 (6)	1.51	1.13

15th anniversary of Bulgarian liberation.

Soccer A526

1959, Oct. 10   Unwmk.   Perf. 11
1068 A526   1.25 l dp green, yel   3.50 2.00

50 years of Bulgarian soccer.
Set exists imperf. in changed colors. Value $7.50 unused, $4 canceled.

Batak Defenders A527

1959, Aug. 8
1069 A527   16s deep claret   .20 .15

300th anniv. of the settlement of Batak.

Post Horn and Letter — A528    Bird-shaped Lyre — A529

Design: 1.25 l, Dove and letter.

1959, Nov. 23
| 1070 | A528 | 45s emerald & blk | .30 | .15 |
| 1071 | A528 | 1.25 l lt blue, red & blk | .50 | .20 |

Intl. Letter Writing Week Oct. 5-11.

Type of 1958 Surcharged "45 CT." in Dark Blue

Design: Tomatoes.

1959   Photo.   Perf. 13
1072 A509   45s on 44s scarlet   .55 .15

1960, Feb. 23   Unwmk.   Perf. 10½
| 1073 | A529 | 80s shown | .40 | .15 |
| 1074 | A529 | 1.25 l Lyre | .70 | .18 |

50th anniv. of Bulgaria's State Opera.

N. I. Vapzarov — A530    Parachute and Radio Tower — A531

1959, Dec. 14   Perf. 11
1075 A530   80s yel grn & red brn   .35 .15

Vapzarov, poet and patriot, 50th birth anniv.

1959, Dec. 3   Photo.
1076 A531   1.25 l dp grnsh bl & yel   1.25 .45

3rd Cong. of Voluntary Participants in Defense.

Cotton Picker — A532   Harvester Combine — A533

Designs: 2s, Kindergarten. 4s, Woman doctor and child. 10s, Woman milking cow. 12s, Woman holding tobacco leaves. 15s, Woman working loom. 16s, Stalin textile mill, Dimitrovgrad. 25s, Rural electrification. 28s, Woman picking sunflowers. 40s, "Cold-well" hydroelectric dam. 45s, Miner. 60s, Foundry worker. 80s. Woman harvesting grapes. 1 l, Worker and peasant with cogwheel. 1.25 l, Industrial worker. 2 l, Party leader.

1959-61   Photo.   Perf. 13
1077	A533	2s brown org ('60)	.15	.15
1077A	A532	4s gldn brn ('61)	.15	.15
1078	A532	5s dk green	.15	.15
1079	A532	10s red brn ('61)	.15	.15
1080	A532	12s red brown	.15	.15
1081	A532	15s red lil ('61)	.15	.15
1082	A532	16s dp vio ('60)	.15	.15
1083	A533	20s orange	.15	.15
1084	A532	25s brt blue ('60)	.15	.15
1085	A532	28s brt green	.18	.15
1086	A533	40s brt grnsh bl	.30	.15
1087	A532	45s choc ('60)	.22	.15
1088	A533	60s scarlet	.42	.15
1089	A532	80s ol ('60)	.50	.15
1090	A532	1 l maroon	.50	.15
1090A	A533	1.25 l dull bl ('61)	1.75	.30
1091	A532	2 l dp car ('60)	1.10	.22
		Nos. 1077-1091 (17)	6.32	2.77

Early completion of the 5-year plan (in 1959).
For surcharges see Nos. 1192-1199, 1202-1203.

L. L. Zamenhof — A534    Path of Lunik 3 — A535

1959, Dec. 5   Unwmk.   Perf. 11
1092 A534   1.25 l dk grn & yel grn   .75 .38

Lazarus Ludwig Zamenhof (1859-1917), inventor of Esperanto.

1960, Mar. 28   Perf. 11
1093 A535   1.25 l Prus bl & brt yel   3.50 1.90

Flight of Lunik 3 around moon. Value, imperf. $5

Skier A536

1960, Apr. 15   Litho.
1094 A536   2 l ultra, blk & brn   .95 .35

8th Winter Olympics, Squaw Valley, CA, Feb. 18-29. Value, imperf. $2 unused, $1 canceled.

Vela Blagoeva — A537

Portraits: 28s, Anna Maimunkova. 45s, Vela Piskova. 60s, Rosa Luxemburg. 80s, Klara Zetkin. 1.25 l, N. K. Krupskaya.

1960, Apr. 27   Photo.   Perf. 11
1095	A537	16s rose & red brn	.15	.15
1096	A537	28s citron & olive	.15	.15
1097	A537	45s ol grn & sl grn	.20	.15
1098	A537	60s lt bl & Prus bl	.20	.15
1099	A537	80s red org & dp brn	.35	.15
1100	A537	1.25 l dull yel & olive	.60	.18
		Nos. 1095-1100 (6)	1.65	.93

International Women's Day, Mar. 8, 1960.

Lenin — A538

1960, May 12
| 1101 | A538 | 16s shown | .50 | .15 |
| 1102 | A538 | 45s Lenin sitting | 1.10 | .16 |

90th anniversary of the birth of Lenin.

A539    A541

1960, June 3   Perf. 11
1103 A539   1.25 l yel & slate grn   .85 .35

Seventh European Women's Basketball championships.

1960, June 29   Litho.
| 1105 | A541 | 16s Parachutist | .55 | .30 |
| 1106 | A541 | 1.25 l Parachutes | 1.50 | .45 |

5th International Parachute Championships.

Yellow Gentian — A542

Flowers: 5s, Tulips. 25s, Turk's-cap lily. 45s, Rhododendron. 60s, Lady's-slipper. 80s, Violets.

1960, July 27   Photo.   Perf. 11
1107	A542	2s beige, grn & yel	.15	.15
1108	A542	5s yel grn, grn & car rose	.15	.15
1109	A542	25s pink, grn & org	.20	.15
1110	A542	45s pale lil, grn & rose lil	.35	.15
1111	A542	60s yel, grn & org	.75	.15
1112	A542	80s gray, grn & vio bl	.90	.22
		Nos. 1107-1112 (6)	2.50	.97

Soccer A543

Sports: 12s, Wrestling. 16s, Weight lifting. 45s, Woman gymnast. 80s, Canoeing. 2 l, Runner.

1960, Aug. 29   Unwmk.   Perf. 11
Athletes' Figures in Pink
1113	A543	8s brown	.15	.15
1114	A543	12s violet	.15	.15
1115	A543	16s Prus blue	.15	.15
1116	A543	45s deep plum	.18	.15
1117	A543	80s blue	.30	.15
1118	A543	2 l deep green	1.25	.35
		Nos. 1113-1118 (6)	2.18	1.10

17th Olympic Games, Rome, Aug. 25-Sept. 11. Value, set imperf. in changed colors, $3.50.

Globes A544

1960, Oct. 12   Photo.   Unwmk.   Perf. 11
1125 A544   1.25 l blue & ultra   .50 .20

15th anniversary of the World Federation of Trade Unions.

Alexander Popov — A545

1960, Oct. 12
1126 A545   90s blue & blk   .75 .15

Centenary of the birth of Alexander Popov, radio pioneer.

Bicyclists A546

1960, Sept. 22
1127 A546   1 l yel, red org & blk   .90 .45

The 10th Tour of Bulgaria Bicycle Race.

Jaroslav Vésin — A547

1960, Nov. 22   Unwmk.   Perf. 11
1128 A547   1 l brt citron & ol grn   2.75 .65

Birth centenary of Jaroslav Vesin, painter.

UN Headquarters A548    Costume of Kyustendil A549

BULGARIA

1961, Jan. 14   **Photo.**   *Perf. 11*

1129	A548	1 l brown & yel	1.00	.45
a.		Souvenir sheet	4.00	2.75

15th anniv. of the UN. #1129 sold for 2 l. Value, imperf. $3.50.

No. 1129a sold for 2.50 l and contains one copy of No. 1129, imperf, in dark olive and pink.

1961, Jan. 28

Designs (Regional Costumes): 16s, Pleven. 28s, Sliven. 45s, Sofia. 60s, Rhodope. 80s, Karnobat.

1130	A549	12s salmon, sl grn & yel	.15	.15
1131	A549	16s pale lil, brn vio & buff	.15	.15
1132	A549	28s pale grn, sl grn & rose	.15	.15
1133	A549	45s blue & red	.30	.15
1134	A549	60s grnsh bl, Prus bl & yel	.48	.15
1135	A549	80s yel, sl grn & pink	.60	.25
		Nos. 1130-1135 (6)	1.83	1.00

Theodor Tiro (Fresco) A550

Designs: 60s, Boyana Church. 1.25 l, Duchess of Dessislava (fresco).

1961, Jan. 28   **Photo.**

1136	A550	60s yel grn, blk & grn	.50	.15
1137	A550	80s yel, sl grn & org	.50	.15
1138	A550	1.25 l yel grn, hn brn & buff	1.00	.22
		Nos. 1136-1138 (3)	2.00	.52

700th anniv. of murals in Boyana Church.

Clock Tower, Vratsa — A551

Wooden Jug — A552

Designs: 12s, Clock tower, Bansko. 20s, Anguchev House, Mogilitsa. 28s, Oslekov House, Koprivspitsa, horiz. 40s, Pasha's house, Melnik, horiz. 45s, Lion sculpture. 60s, Man on horseback, Madara. 80s, Fresco, Bratchkovo monastery. 1 l, Tsar Assen coin.

1961, Feb. 25   **Unwmk.**   *Perf. 11*
Denomination and Stars in Vermilion

1139	A551	8s olive grn	.15	.15
1140	A551	12s lt violet	.15	.15
1141	A552	16s dk red brn	.15	.15
1142	A551	20s brt blue	.15	.15
1143	A551	28s grnsh blue	.15	.15
1144	A551	40s red brown	.15	.15
1145	A552	45s olive gray	.16	.15
1146	A552	60s slate	.32	.15
1147	A552	80s dk olive gray	.55	.15
1148	A552	1 l green	.70	.15
		Nos. 1139-1148 (10)	2.63	1.50

Capercaillie — A553

Birds: 4s, Dalmatian pelican. 16s, Ringnecked pheasant. 80s, Great bustard. 1 l, Lammergeier. 2 l, Hazel hen.

1961, Mar. 31

1149	A553	2s blk, sal & Prus grn	.15	.15
1150	A553	4s blk, yel grn & org	.15	.15
1151	A553	16s brn, lt grn & org	.15	.15
1152	A553	80s brn, bluish grn & yel	.35	.15
1153	A553	1 l blk, lt bl & yel	.65	.15
1154	A553	2 l brn, bl & yel	1.65	.55
		Nos. 1149-1153 (5)	1.45	.75

Radio Tower and Winged Anchor — A554

1961, Apr. 1   **Unwmk.**   *Perf. 11*

| 1155 | A554 | 80s brt green & blk | .45 | .20 |

50th anniv. of the Transport Workers' Union.

T. G. Shevchenko — A555

Water Polo — A556

1961, Apr. 27

| 1156 | A555 | 1 l olive & blk | 2.50 | .65 |

Centenary of the death of Taras G. Shevchenko, Ukrainian poet.

1961, May 15

Designs: 5s, Tennis. 16s, Fencing. 45s, Throwing the discus. 1.25 l, Sports Palace. 2 l, Basketball. 5 l, Sports Palace, different view. 5s, 16s, 45s and 1.25 l, are horizontal.

Black Inscriptions

1157	A556	4s lt ultra	.15	.15
1158	A556	5s orange ver	.15	.15
1159	A556	16s olive grn	.15	.15
1160	A556	45s dull blue	.15	.15
1161	A556	1.25 l yellow brn	.60	.18
1162	A556	2 l lilac	.85	.40
		Nos. 1157-1162 (6)	2.05	1.18

Souvenir Sheet
Imperf

| 1163 | A556 | 5 l yel grn, dl bl & yel | 7.50 | 6.50 |

1961 World University Games, Sofia, Aug. 26-Sept. 3.

Value, Nos. 1157-1162 in changed colors, imperf. $4.50.

Monk Seal A557

Black Sea Fauna: 12s, Jellyfish. 16s, Dolphin. 45s, Black Sea sea horse, vert. 1 l, Starred sturgeon. 1.25 l, Thornback ray.

1961, June 19   *Perf. 11*

1164	A557	2s green & blk	.15	.15
1165	A557	12s Prus grn & pink	.15	.15
1166	A557	16s ultra & vio bl	.15	.15
1167	A557	45s lt blue & brn	.28	.15
1168	A557	1 l yel grn & Prus grn	.65	.20
1169	A557	1.25 l lt vio bl & red brn	1.10	.35
		Nos. 1164-1169 (6)	2.48	1.15

Hikers — A558

Designs: 4s, "Sredetz" hostel, horiz. 16s, Tents. 1.25 l, Mountain climber.

1961, Aug. 25   **Litho.**   *Perf. 11*

1170	A558	4s yel grn, yel & blk	.15	.15
1171	A558	12s lt bl, cr & blk	.15	.15
1172	A558	16s green, cr & blk	.15	.15
1173	A558	1.25 l bister, cr & blk	.45	.15
		Nos. 1170-1173 (4)	.90	.60

"Know Your Country" campaign.

Demeter Blagoev Addressing 1891 Congress at Busludja — A559

1961, Aug. 5   **Photo.**

1174	A559	45s dk red & buff	.20	.15
1175	A559	80s blue & pink	.30	.15
1176	A559	2 l dk brn & pale citron	.75	.25
		Nos. 1174-1176 (3)	1.25	.55

70th anniversary of the first Congress of the Bulgarian Social-Democratic Party.

The Golden Girl — A560

Fairy Tales: 8s, The Living Water. 12s, The Golden Apple. 16s, Krali-Marko, hero. 45s, Samovila-Vila, Witch. 80s, Tom Thumb.

1961, Oct. 10   **Unwmk.**   *Perf. 11*

1177	A560	2s blue, blk & org	.18	.15
1178	A560	8s rose lil, blk & gray	.24	.15
1179	A560	12s bl grn, blk & pink	.24	.15
1180	A560	16s red, blk, bl & gray	.38	.15
1181	A560	45s ol grn, blk & pink	.75	.22
1182	A560	80s ocher, blk & dk car	1.10	.28
		Nos. 1177-1182 (6)	2.89	1.10

Caesar's Mushroom A561

Miladinov Brothers and Title Page A562

Designs: Various mushrooms.

1961, Dec. 20   **Photo.**   *Perf. 11*
Denominations in Black

1183	A561	2s lemon & red	.15	.15
1184	A561	4s ol grn & red brn	.15	.15
1185	A561	12s bister & red brn	.15	.15
1186	A561	16s lilac & red brn	.15	.15
1187	A561	45s car rose & yel	.15	.15
1188	A561	80s brn org & sepia	.18	.15
1189	A561	1.25 l vio & dk brn	.40	.18
1190	A561	2 l org brn & brn	.70	.40
		Nos. 1183-1190 (8)	2.03	1.48

Value, denomination in dark grn, imperf. set $5 unused, $1.75 canceled.

1961, Dec. 21   **Unwmk.**   *Perf. 10½*

| 1191 | A562 | 1.25 l olive & blk | .60 | .20 |

Publication of "Collected Folksongs" by the Brothers Miladinov, Dimitri and Konstantin, cent.

Nos. 1079-1085, 1087, 992, 1023, 1090-1091 and 806 Surcharged with New Value in Black, Red or Violet

1962, Jan. 1

1192	A533	1s on 10s red brown	.15	.15
1193	A532	1s on 12s red brown	.15	.15
1194	A532	2s on 15s red lilac	.15	.15
1195	A533	2s on 16s dp vio (R)	.15	.15
1196	A533	2s on 20s orange	.15	.15
	a.	"2 CT." on 2 lines	.15	.15
1197	A532	3s on 25s brt bl (R)	.15	.15
	a.	Black surcharge	7.00	4.00
1198	A532	3s on 28s brt grn (R)	.15	.15
1199	A532	5s on 45s chocolate	.15	.15
1200	A499	5s on 44s dk bl grn (R)	.15	.15
1201	A509	5s on 44s dp car (V)	.15	.15
1202	A532	10s on 1 l maroon	.25	.15
1203	A532	20s on 2 l dp car	.70	.22
1204	A430	40s on 4 l rose lake (V)	1.50	.48
		Nos. 1192-1204 (13)	3.95	2.35

Freighter "Varna" A563

Designs: 5s, Tanker "Komsomoletz." 20s, Liner "G. Dimitrov."

1962, Mar. 1   **Photo.**   *Perf. 10½*

1205	A563	1s lt grn & brt bl	.15	.15
1206	A563	5s lt blue & grn	.18	.15
1207	A563	20s gray bl & grnsh bl	.70	.16
		Nos. 1205-1207 (3)	1.03	.46

Dimitrov Working as Printer — A564

Roses — A565

13s, Griffin, emblem of state printing works.

1962, Mar. 19   **Unwmk.**

1208	A564	2s ver, blk & yel	.15	.15
1209	A564	13s red org, blk & yel	.42	.15

80th anniversary (in 1961) of the George Dimitrov state printing works.

1962, Mar. 28
Various Roses in Natural Colors

1210	A565	1s deep violet	.15	.15
1211	A565	2s salmon & dk car	.15	.15
1212	A565	3s gray & car	.15	.15
1213	A565	4s dark green	.16	.15
1214	A565	5s ultra	.22	.15
1215	A565	6s bluish grn & dk car	.48	.15
1216	A565	8s citron & car	1.10	.18
1217	A565	13s blue	2.25	.60
		Nos. 1210-1217 (8)	4.66	1.68

For overprint and surcharges see Nos. 1281-1283.

Malaria Eradication Emblem and Mosquito A566

Design: 20s, Malaria eradication emblem.

1962, Apr. 19

1218	A566	5s org brn, yel & blk	.40	.15
1219	A566	20s emerald, yel & blk	.85	.35

WHO drive to eradicate malaria.
Value, imperf. $2.50 unused, $1.50 canceled.

Lenin and First Issue of Pravda A567

1962, May 4   **Unwmk.**   *Perf. 10*

| 1220 | A567 | 5s deep rose & slate | .50 | .15 |

50th anniversary of Pravda, Russian newspaper founded by Lenin.

Blackboard and Book — A568

1962, May 21   **Photo.**

| 1221 | A568 | 5s Prus bl, blk & yel | .25 | .15 |

The 1962 Teachers' Congress.

BULGARIA

Soccer Player and Globe — A569

1962, May 26   Perf. 10½
1222 A569 13s brt grn, blk & lt brn   .65 .25

World Soccer Championship, Chile, May 30-June 17. Value, imperf. in changed colors, $2.50 unused, $1.65 canceled.

George Dimitrov A570

1962, June 18   Photo.
1223 A570 2s dark green   .20 .15
1224 A570 5s turq blue   .40 .15

80th anniv. of the birth of George Dimitrov (1882-1949), communist leader and premier of the Bulgarian Peoples' Republic.

Bishop — A571

1962, July 7   Unwmk.   Perf. 10½
1225 A571 1s shown   .15 .15
1226 A571 2s Rook   .15 .15
1227 A571 3s Queen   .15 .15
1228 A571 13s Knight   .65 .22
1229 A571 20s Pawn   1.10 .42
   Nos. 1225-1229 (5)   2.20 1.09

15th Chess Olympics, Varna. Nos. 1225-1229 were also issued imperf. in changed colors. An imperf. souvenir sheet contains one 20s horizontal stamp showing five chessmen. Size: 75x66mm.

Rila Mountain A572

Designs: 2s, Pirin mountain. 6s, Nesebr, Black Sea. 8s, Danube. 13s, Vidin Castle. 1 l, Rhodope mountain.

1962-63   Perf. 13
1230 A572 1s dk blue grn   .15 .15
1231 A572 2s blue   .15 .15
1232 A572 6s grnsh blue   .15 .15
1233 A572 8c lilac   .16 .15
1234 A572 13s yellow grn   .38 .15
1234A A572 1 l dp green ('63)   3.25 .30
   Nos. 1230-1234A (6)   4.24 1.05

No. 974 Surcharged in Red

XXXV КОНГРЕС
1962

13 =

1962, July 14   Perf. 13
1235 A493 13s on 44s slate grn   2.25 .80

25th Bulgarian Esperanto Congress, Burgas, July 14-16.

Girl and Festival Emblem A573

Design: 5s, Festival emblem.

1962, Aug. 18   Photo.   Perf. 10½
1236 A573 5s green, lt bl & pink   .20 .15
1237 A573 13s lilac, lt bl & gray   .35 .15

8th Youth Festival for Peace and Friendship, Helsinki, July 28-Aug. 6, 1962.

Parnassius Apollo A574

1962, Sept. 13
Various Butterflies in Natural Colors
1238 A574 1s pale cit & dk grn   .15 .15
1239 A574 2s rose & brown   .15 .15
1240 A574 3s buff & red brn   .15 .15
1241 A574 4s gray & brown   .15 .15
1242 A574 5s lt gray & brn   .16 .15
1243 A574 6s gray & black   .18 .15
1244 A574 10s pale grn & blk   1.25 .25
1245 A574 13s buff & red brn   1.90 .40
   Nos. 1238-1245 (8)   4.09 1.55

Planting Machine A575

2s, Electric locomotive. 3s, Blast furnace. 13s, Blagoev and Dimitrov and Communist flag.

1962, Nov. 1   Perf. 11½
1246 A575 1s bl grn & dk ol grn   .15 .15
1247 A575 2s bl & Prus bl   .15 .15
1248 A575 3s carmine & brn   .18 .15
1249 A575 13s plum, red & blk   .55 .20
   Nos. 1246-1249 (4)   1.03 .65

Bulgarian Communist Party, 8th Congress.

Title Page of "Slav-Bulgarian History" — A576

Paisii Hilendarski Writing History — A577

1962, Dec. 8   Unwmk.   Perf. 10½
1250 A576 2s olive grn & blk   .15 .15
1251 A577 5s brown org & blk   .15 .15

200th anniv. of "Slav-Bulgarian History."

Aleco Konstantinov (1863-1897), Writer — A578

1963, Mar. 5   Photo.   Perf. 11½
1252 A578 5s red, grn & blk   .25 .15

Printed with alternating red brown and black label showing Bai Ganu, hero from Konstantinov's books.

A579    Sofia University — A580

Designs: No. 1255, Levski Stadium, Sofia. No. 1256, Arch, Nissaria. No. 1257, Parachutist.

1963, Feb. 20   Unwmk.   Perf. 10
1253 A579 1s brown red   .15 .15
1254 A580 1s red brown   .15 .15
1255 A580 1s blue green   .15 .15
1256 A580 1s dark green   .15 .15
1257 A580 1s brt blue   .15 .15
   Nos. 1253-1257 (5)   .75 .75

Vassil Levski — A581    Boy, Girl and Dimitrov — A582

1963, Apr. 11   Photo.
1258 A581 13s grnsh blue & buff   .75 .25

90th anniversary of the death of Vassil Levski, revolutionary leader in the fight for liberation from the Turks.

1963, Apr. 25   Unwmk.   Perf. 11½
13s, Girl with book & boy with hammer.
1259 A582 2s org, ver, red brn & blk   .15 .15
1260 A582 13s bluish grn, brn & blk   .42 .15

10th Congress of Dimitrov's Union of the People's Youth.

Red Squirrel — A583    Sun Coast Promenade — A584

2s, Hedgehog. 3s, European polecat. 5s, Pine marten. 13s, Badger. 20s, Otter. 2s, 3s, 13s, horiz.

1963, Apr. 30
Red Numerals
1261 A583 1s grn & brn, grnsh   .15 .15
1262 A583 2s grn & blk, yel   .15 .15
1263 A583 3s grn & brn, bis   .15 .15
1264 A583 5s vio & red brn, lil   .20 .15
1265 A583 13s red brn & blk, buff   .80 .16
1266 A583 20s blk & brn, blue   1.25 .20
   Nos. 1261-1266 (6)   2.70 .96

1963, Mar. 12   Unwmk.   Perf. 13
Black Sea Resorts: 2s, 3s, 13s, Views of Gold Sand. 5s, 20s, Sun Coast.
1267 A584 1s blue   .15 .15
1268 A584 2s vermilion   .26 .15
1269 A584 2s car rose   .38 .15
1270 A584 3s ocher   .18 .15
1271 A584 5s lilac   .18 .15
1272 A584 13s blue green   .52 .15
1273 A584 20s green   .95 .20
   Nos. 1267-1273 (7)   2.62 1.10

Freestyle Wrestling — A585

Design: 20s, Freestyle wrestling, horiz.

1963, May 31   Perf. 11½
1274 A585 5s yel bister & blk   .16 .15
1275 A585 20s org brn & blk   .80 .18

15th International Freestyle Wrestling Competitions, Sofia.

"Women for Peace" A586

1963, June 24   Unwmk.   Perf. 11½
1276 A586 20s blue & blk   .60 .15

World Congress of Women, Moscow, June 24-29.

Esperanto Emblem and Arms of Sofia — A587    Moon, Earth and Lunik 4 — A588

1963, June 29   Photo.
1277 A587 13s multicolored   .60 .15

48th World Esperanto Congress, Sofia, Aug. 3-10.

1963, July 22
2s, Radar equipment. 3s, Satellites and moon.
1278 A588 1s ultra   .15 .15
1279 A588 2s red lilac   .15 .15
1280 A588 3s greenish blue   .15 .15
   Nos. 1278-1280 (3)   .45 .45

Russia's rocket to the moon, Apr. 2, 1963.

MOSTRA EUROPEISTICA · 1963
13
Nos. 1211-1212 and 1215 Overprinted or Surcharged in Green, Ultramarine or Black

RICCIONE

1963, Aug. 31   Perf. 10½
1281 A565 2s (G)   .25 .15
1282 A565 5s on 3s (U)   .38 .15
1283 A565 13s on 6s   .70 .22
   Nos. 1281-1283 (3)   1.33 .52

Intl. Stamp Fair, Riccione, Aug. 31.

Women's Relay Race A589

Designs: 2s, Hammer thrower. 3s, Women's long jump. 5s, Men's high jump. 13s, Discus thrower.

Perf. 11½
1963, Sept. 13   Photo.   Unwmk.
Flags in National Colors
1284 A589 1s slate green   .15 .15
1285 A589 2s purple   .15 .15
1286 A589 3s Prus blue   .16 .15
1287 A589 5s maroon   .45 .30
1288 A589 13s chestnut brn   1.65 1.25
   Nos. 1284-1288 (5)   2.56 2.00

Balkan Games. A multicolored, 50s, imperf. souvenir sheet shows design of women's relay race. Size: 74x70mm.

BULGARIA

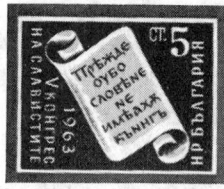

"Slav-Bulgarian History" — A590

1963, Sept. 19 Perf. 10½
1289 A590 5s salmon pink, slate & yel   .20 .15
5th International Slavic Congress.

Revolutionists A591   Christo Smirnenski A592

1963, Sept. 22 Perf. 11½
1290 A591 2s brt red & blk   .15 .15
40th anniversary of the September Revolution.

1963, Oct. 28 Perf. 10½
1291 A592 13s pale lilac & indigo   .45 .15
Christo Smirnenski, poet, 65th birth anniv.

Columbine A593   Horses A594

1963, Oct. 9 Photo. Perf. 11½
1292 A593 1s shown   .15 .15
1293 A593 2s Edelweiss   .15 .15
1294 A593 3s Primrose   .15 .15
1295 A593 5s Water lily   .15 .15
1296 A593 6s Tulips   .16 .15
1297 A593 8s Larkspur   .30 .15
1298 A593 10s Alpine clematis   .70 .16
1299 A593 13s Anemone   1.25 .25
   Nos. 1292-1299 (8)   3.01 1.31

1963, Dec. 28 Unwmk. Perf. 10½
Designs: 2s, Charioteer and chariot. 3s, Trumpeters. 5s, Woman carrying tray with food. 13s, Man holding bowl. 20s, Woman in armchair. Designs are from a Thracian tomb at Kazanlik.
1300 A594 1s gray, org & dk red   .15 .15
1301 A594 2s gray, ocher & pur   .15 .15
1302 A594 3s gray, dl yel & sl grn   .15 .15
1303 A594 5s pale grn, ocher & brn   .15 .15
1304 A594 13s pale grn, bis & blk   .42 .15
1305 A594 20s pale grn, org & dk car   .75 .30
   Nos. 1300-1305 (6)   1.77 1.05

World Map and Emblem A595

Designs: 2s, Blood transfusion. 3s, Nurse bandaging injured wrist. 5s, Red Cross nurse. 13s, Henri Dunant.

1964, Jan. 27 Perf. 10½
1306 A595 1s lem, blk & red   .15 .15
1307 A595 2s ultra, blk & red   .15 .15
1308 A595 3s gray, sl, blk & red   .15 .15
1309 A595 5s brt bl, blk & red   .15 .15
1310 A595 13s org yel, blk & red   .42 .15
   Nos. 1306-1310 (5)   1.02 .75
Centenary of International Red Cross.

Speed Skating A596

Sports: 2s, 50s, Women's figure skating. 3s, Cross-country skiing. 5s, Ski jump. 10s, Ice hockey goalkeeper. 13s, Ice hockey players.

1964, Feb. 21 Unwmk. Perf. 10½
1311 A596 1s grnsh bl, ind & ocher   .15 .15
1312 A596 2s brt pink, ol grn & dk sl grn   .15 .15
1313 A596 3s dl grn, dk grn & brn   .15 .15
1314 A596 5s bl, blk & yel brn   .18 .15
1315 A596 10s gray, org & blk   .40 .18
1316 A596 13s lil, blk & lil rose   .70 .28
   Nos. 1311-1316 (6)   1.73 1.06

Miniature Sheet
Imperf
1317 A596 50s gray, Prus grn & pink   3.75 3.00
9th Winter Olympic Games, Innsbruck, Jan. 29-Feb. 9, 1964.

Mask of Nobleman, 2nd Century — A597

2s, Thracian horseman. 3s, Ceramic jug. 5s, Clasp & belt. 6s, Copper kettle. 8s, Angel. 10s, Lioness. 13s, Scrub woman, contemporary sculpture.

1964, Mar. 14 Photo. Perf. 10½
Gray Frame
1318 A597 1s dp green & red   .15 .15
1319 A597 2s ol gray & red   .15 .15
1320 A597 3s bister & red   .15 .15
1321 A597 5s indigo & red   .16 .15
1322 A597 6s org brn & red   .22 .15
1323 A597 8s brn red & red   .38 .15
1324 A597 10s olive & red   .42 .15
1325 A597 13s gray ol & red   .65 .22
   Nos. 1318-1325 (8)   2.28 1.27
2,500 years of Bulgarian art.

"The Unborn Maid" A598

Fairy Tales: 2s, Grandfather's Glove. 3s, The Big Turnip. 5s, The Wolf and the Seven Kids. 8s, Cunning Peter. 13s, The Wheat Cake.

1964, Apr. 17 Unwmk. Perf. 10½
1326 A598 1s bl grn, red & org brn   .15 .15
1327 A598 2s ultra, ocher & blk   .15 .15
1328 A598 3s cit, red & blk   .15 .15
1329 A598 5s dp rose, brn & blk   .15 .15
1330 A598 8s yel grn, red & blk   .20 .15
1331 A598 13s lt vio bl, grn & blk   .70 .18
   Nos. 1326-1331 (6)   1.50 .93

Ascalaphus Otomanus A599

Insects: 2s, Nemoptera coa., vert. 3s, Saga natalia (grasshopper). 5s, Rosalia alpina, vert. 13s, Anisoplia austriaca, vert. 20s, Scolia flavitrons.

1964, May 16 Photo. Perf. 11½
1332 A599 1s brn org, yel & blk   .15 .15
1333 A599 2s dl bl grn, bis & blk   .15 .15
1334 A599 3s gray, grn & blk   .15 .15
1335 A599 5s lt ol grn, blk & vio   .15 .15
1336 A599 13s vio, bis & blk   .55 .16
1337 A599 20s gray bl, yel & blk   .85 .28
   Nos. 1332-1337 (6)   2.00 1.04

Soccer — A600

Designs: 13s, Women's volleyball. 60s, Map of Europe and European Women's Volleyball Championship Cup (rectangular, size: 60x69mm).

1964, June 8 Unwmk. Perf. 11½
1338 A600 2s bl, dk bl, ocher & red   .15 .15
1339 A600 13s bl, dk bl, ocher & red   .52 .22

Miniature Sheet
Imperf
1340 A600 60s ultra, ocher, red & gray   3.00 2.25
Levski Physical Culture Assoc., 50th anniv.

Peter Beron and Title Page of Primer A601

1964, June 22 Perf. 11½
1341 A601 20s red brn & dk brn, grysh   1.00 .60
140th anniversary of the publication of the first Bulgarian primer.

Robert Stephenson's "Rocket" Locomotive, 1825 — A602

Designs: 2s, Modern steam locomotive. 3s, Diesel locomotive. 5s, Electric locomotive. 8s, Freight train on bridge. 13s, Diesel locomotive and tunnel.

1964, July 1 Photo. Perf. 11½
1342 A602 1s multicolored   .15 .15
1343 A602 2s multicolored   .15 .15
1344 A602 3s multicolored   .15 .15
1345 A602 5s multicolored   .15 .15
1346 A602 8s multicolored   .32 .15
1347 A602 13s multicolored   .80 .20
   Nos. 1342-1347 (6)   1.72 .95

German Shepherd A603

1964, Aug. 22 Photo.
1348 A603 1s shown   .15 .15
1349 A603 2s Setter   .15 .15
1350 A603 3s Poodle   .15 .15
1351 A603 4s Pomeranian   .16 .15
1352 A603 5s St. Bernard   .20 .15
1353 A603 6s Terrier   .26 .15
1354 A603 10s Pointer   1.40 .22
1355 A603 13s Dachshund   2.75 .42
   Nos. 1348-1355 (8)   5.22 1.54

Partisans — A604

Designs: 2s, People welcoming Soviet army. 3s, Russian aid to Bulgaria. 4s, Blast furnace, Kremikovski. 5s, Combine. 6s, Peace demonstration. 8s, Sentry. 13s, Demeter Blagoev and George Dimitrov.

1964, Sept. 9 Unwmk. Perf. 11½
Flag in Red
1356 A604 1s lt & dp ultra   .15 .15
1357 A604 2s ol bis & dp ol   .15 .15
1358 A604 3s rose lil & mar   .15 .15
1359 A604 4s lt vio & vio   .15 .15
1360 A604 5s org & red brn   .15 .15
1361 A604 6s bl & dp bl   .15 .15
1362 A604 8s lt grn & grn   .20 .15
1363 A604 13s fawn & red brn   .42 .15
   Nos. 1356-1363 (8)   1.52 1.20
20th anniv. of People's Government of Bulgaria.

No. 967 Surcharged

1964, Sept. 13 Perf. 13
1364 A476 20s on 44s org yel   1.00 .35
International Plovdiv Fair.

Gymnast on Parallel Bars A606   Vratcata Mountain Road A607

Sports: 2s, Long jump. 3s, Woman diver. 5s, Soccer. 13s, Women's volleyball. 20s, Wrestling.

1964, Oct. 10 Perf. 11½
1366 A606 1s pale grn, grn & red   .15 .15
1367 A606 2s pale vio, vio bl & red   .15 .15
1368 A606 3s bl grn, brn & red   .15 .15
1369 A606 5s pink, pur & red   .16 .15
1370 A606 13s bl, Prus grn & red   .52 .15
1371 A606 20s yel, grn & red   .90 .22
   Nos. 1366-1371 (6)   2.03 .97
18th Olympic Games, Tokyo. Oct. 10-25. See No. B27.

1964, Oct. 26 Photo. Perf. 12½x13
Bulgarian Views: 2s, Ritlite mountain road. 3s, Pines, Malovica peak. 4s, Pobitite rocks. 5s, Erkupria. 6s, Rhodope mountain road.
1372 A607 1s dk slate grn   .15 .15
1373 A607 2s brown   .15 .15
1374 A607 3s grnsh blue   .15 .15
1375 A607 4s dk red brn   .15 .15
1376 A607 5s deep green   .20 .15
1377 A607 6s blue violet   .30 .15
   Nos. 1372-1377 (6)   1.10 .90

Mail Coach, Plane and Rocket A608

1964, Oct. 3 Unwmk. Perf. 11½
1378 A608 20s greenish blue   1.25 .48
First national stamp exhibition, Sofia, Oct. 3-18. Issued in sheets of 12 stamps and 12 labels (woman's head and inscription, 5x5) arranged around one central label showing stylized bird design.

BULGARIA

Students Holding Book — A609

1964, Dec. 30   Photo.
1379 A609   13s lt blue & blk   .45   .15
8th Intl. Students' Congress, Sofia.

500-Year-Old Walnut Tree at Golemo Drenovo A610

Designs: Various old trees.

1964, Dec. 28
1380 A610   1s blk, buff & cl brn   .15   .15
1381 A610   2s blk, pink & dp cl   .15   .15
1382 A610   3s blk, yel & dk brn   .15   .15
1383 A610   4s blk, lt bl & Prus bl   .15   .15
1384 A610   10s blk, pale grn & grn   .22   .15
1385 A610   13s blk, pale bis & dk ol grn   .42   .15
    Nos. 1380-1385 (6)   1.24   .90

Soldiers' Monument — A611

1965, Jan. 1   Unwmk.
1386 A611   2s red & black   .20   .15
Bulgarian-Soviet friendship.

Olympic Medal Inscribed "Olympic Glory" — A612

1965, Jan. 27   Photo.   Perf. 11½
1387 A612   20s org brn, gold & blk   .60   .16
Bulgarian victories in the 1964 Olympic Games.

"Victory Over Fascism" A613

Design: 13s, "Fight for Peace" (dove and globe).

1965, Apr. 16   Perf. 11½
1388 A613   5s gray, blk & ol bis   .15   .15
1389 A613   13s gray, blk & blue   .26   .16
Victory over Fascism, May 9, 1945, 20th anniv.

Vladimir M. Komarov and Section of Globe — A614

Designs: 2s, Konstantin Feoktistov. 5s, Boris B. Yegorov. 13s, Komarov, Feoktistov and Yegorov. 20s, Spaceship Voskhod.

1965, Feb. 15   Photo.
1390 A614   1s pale lil & dk bl   .15   .15
1391 A614   2s lt bl, ind & dl vio   .15   .15
1392 A614   5s pale grn, grn & ol grn   .15   .15
1393 A614   13s pale pink, dp rose & mar   .42   .15
1394 A614   20s lt bl, vio bl, grnsh bl & yel   .75   .16
    Nos. 1390-1394 (5)   1.62   .76
Russian 3-man space flight, Oct. 12-13, 1964. Imperfs. in changed colors. Four low values setenant. Value, set $2 unused, $1 canceled.

Bullfinch — A615

Birds: 2s, European golden oriole. 3s, Common rock thrush. 5s, Barn swallow. 8s, European roller. 10s, European goldfinch. 13s, Rosy pastor starling. 20s, Nightingale.

1965, Apr. 20   Unwmk.   Perf. 11½
Birds in Natural Colors
1395 A615   1s blue green   .15   .15
1396 A615   2s rose lilac   .15   .15
1397 A615   3s rose   .15   .15
1398 A615   5s brt blue   .15   .15
1399 A615   8s citron   .32   .15
1400 A615   10s gray   1.10   .15
1401 A615   13s lt vio blue   1.10   .18
1402 A615   20s emerald   2.25   .35
    Nos. 1395-1402 (8)   5.37   1.43

Black Sea Fish — A616

1965, June 10   Photo.   Perf. 11½
Gray Frames
1403 A616   1s Sting ray   .15   .15
1404 A616   2s Belted bonito   .15   .15
1405 A616   3s Hogfish   .15   .15
1406 A616   5s Gurnard   .18   .15
1407 A616   10s Scad   .75   .16
1408 A616   13s Turbot   1.10   .26
    Nos. 1403-1408 (6)   2.48   1.02

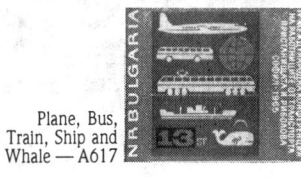

Plane, Bus, Train, Ship and Whale — A617

1965, Apr. 30
1409 A617   13s multicolored   .45   .15
4th Intl. Conf. of Transport, Dock and Fishery Workers, Sofia, May 10-14.

ITU Emblem and Communications Symbols — A618

1965, May 17
1410 A618   20s multicolored   .65   .30
Centenary of the ITU.

Col. Pavel Belyayev and Lt. Col. Alexei Leonov A619

Design: 20s, Leonov floating in space.

1965, May 20   Unwmk.
1411 A619   2s gray, dull bl & dk brn   .15   .20
1412 A619   20s multicolored   1.00   .45
Space flight of Voskhod 2 and the first man floating in space, Lt. Col. Alexei Leonov.

ICY Emblem — A620

1965, May 15   Photo.
1413 A620   20s orange, olive & blk   .65   .15
International Cooperation Year, 1965.

Corn A621    Marx and Lenin A622

1965, Apr. 1   Perf. 12½x13
1414 A621   1s shown   .15   .15
1415 A621   2s Wheat   .15   .15
1416 A621   3s Sunflowers   .15   .15
1417 A621   4s Sugar beet   .15   .15
1418 A621   5s Clover   .15   .15
1419 A621   10s Cotton   .42   .15
1420 A621   13s Tobacco   .60   .15
    Nos. 1414-1420 (7)   1.77   1.05

1965, June   Perf. 10½
1421 A622   13s red & dk brn   .65   .15
6th Conference of Postal Ministers of Communist Countries, Peking, June 21-July 15.

Film and UNESCO Emblem A623

1965, June 30
1422 A623   13s dp bl, blk & lt gray   .50   .15
Balkan Film Festival, Varna.

Ballerina — A624

1965, July 10   Photo.
1423 A624   5s dp lil rose & blk   .60   .25
2nd Intl. Ballet Competition, Varna.

Map of Balkan Peninsula and Dove with Letter — A625

Col. Pavel Belyayev and Lt. Col. Alexei Leonov — A626

2s, Sailboat and modern buildings. 3s, Fish and plants. 13s, Symbolic sun and rocket. 40s, Map of Balkan Peninsula and dove with letter (like 1s).

1965   Perf. 10½
1424 A625   1s sil, dp ultra & yel   .15   .15
1425 A625   2s sil, pur & yel   .15   .15
1426 A625   3s gold, grn & yel   .15   .15
1427 A625   13s gold, hn brn & yel   .55   .50
1428 A626   20s sil, bl & brn   .70   .55
    Nos. 1424-1428 (5)   1.70   1.50
Miniature Sheet
Imperf
1429 A625   40s gold & brt bl   1.75   1.00
Balkanphila 1965 Philatelic Exhibition, Varna, Aug. 7-15, and visit of Russian astronauts Belyayev and Leonov.
Value, No. 1428 imperf. in changed colors, 90 cents.
Issued: 20s, 40s, 8/7; others, 7/23.

Woman Gymnast — A627

Designs: 2s, Woman gymnast on parallel bars. 3s, Weight lifter. 5s, Automobile and chart. 10s, Women basketball players. 13s, Automobile and map of rally.

1965, Aug. 14   Perf. 10½
1430 A627   1s crim, brn & blk   .15   .15
1431 A627   2s rose vio, dp cl & blk   .15   .15
1432 A627   3s dp car, brn & blk   .15   .15
1433 A627   5s fawn, red brn & blk   .15   .15
1434 A627   10s dp lil rose, dp cl & blk   .52   .15
1435 A627   13s lilac, claret & blk   .65   .16
    Nos. 1430-1435 (6)   1.77   .91
Sports events in Bulgaria during May-June, 1965.

No. 989 Surcharged

1965, Aug. 12   Perf. 13
1436 A499   2s on 8s orange brn   .75   .26
1st Natl. Folklore Competition, Aug. 12-15.

BULGARIA

Escaping Prisoners
A628

Fruit
A629

1965, July 23   Perf. 10½
1437 A628 2s slate   .20 .15
40th anniversary of the escape of political prisoners from Bolshevik Island.

1965, July 1   Perf. 13
1438 A629 1s Apples   .15 .15
1439 A629 2s Grapes   .15 .15
1440 A629 3s Pears   .15 .15
1441 A629 4s Peaches   .15 .15
1442 A629 5s Strawberries   .20 .15
1443 A629 6s Walnuts   .32 .15
     Nos. 1438-1443 (6)   1.12 .90

Horsemanship — A630

1965, Sept. 30   Unwmk.   Perf. 10½
1444 A630 1s Dressage   .15 .15
1445 A630 2s Three-day test   .15 .15
1446 A630 3s Jumping   .15 .15
1447 A630 5s Race   .15 .15
1448 A630 10s Steeplechase   .75 .20
1449 A630 13s Hurdle race   1.40 .28
     Nos. 1444-1449 (6)   2.75 1.08
     See No. B28.

Smiling Children — A631

Designs: 2s, Two girl Pioneers. 3s, Bugler. 5s, Pioneer with model plane. 8s, Two singing girls in national costume. 13s, Running boy.

1965, Oct. 24   Photo.
1450 A631 1s dk bl grn & yel grn   .15 .15
1451 A631 2s vio & deep rose   .15 .15
1452 A631 3s olive & lemon   .15 .15
1453 A631 5s dp blue & bister   .15 .15
1454 A631 8s olive bister & org   .28 .15
1455 A631 13s rose car & vio   .65 .24
     Nos. 1450-1455 (6)   1.53 .99
Dimitrov Pioneer Organization.

U-52 Plane over Trnovo
A632

Designs: 2c, IL-14 over Plovdiv. 3s, Mi-4 Helicopter over Dimitrovgrad. 5s, Tu-104 over Ruse. 13s, IL-18 over Varna. 20s, Tu-114 over Sofia.

1965, Nov. 25   Perf. 10½
1456 A632 1s gray, blue & red   .15 .15
1457 A632 2s gray, lilac & red   .15 .15
1458 A632 3s gray, grnsh bl & red   .15 .15
1459 A632 5s gray, orange & red   .15 .15
1460 A632 13s gray, bister & red   .70 .15
1461 A632 20s gray, lt grn & red   1.00 .28
     Nos. 1456-1461 (6)   2.30 1.03
Development of Bulgarian Civil Air Transport.

IQSY Emblem, and Earth Radiation Zones
A633

Designs (IQSY Emblem and): 2s, Sun with corona. 13s, Solar eclipse.

1965, Dec. 15   Photo.   Perf. 10½
1462 A633 1s grn, yel & ultra   .15 .15
1463 A633 2s yel, red lil & red   .15 .15
1464 A633 13s bl, yel & blk   .32 .15
     Nos. 1462-1464 (3)   .62 .45
International Quiet Sun Year, 1964-65.

"North and South Bulgaria"
A634

"Martenitsa" Emblem
A635

1965, Dec. 6
1465 A634 13s brt yel grn & blk   .50 .25
Union of North and South Bulgaria, cent.

1966, Jan. 10   Photo.   Perf. 10½
"Spring" in Folklore: 2s, Drummer. 3s, Bird ornaments. 5s, Dancer "Lazarka." 8s, Vase with flowers. 13s, Bagpiper.
1466 A635 1s rose lil, vio bl & gray   .15 .15
1467 A635 2s gray, blk & crim   .15 .15
1468 A635 3s red, vio & gray   .15 .15
1469 A635 5s lil, blk & crimson   .15 .15
1470 A635 8s rose lil, brn & pur   .22 .15
1471 A635 13s bl, blk & rose lilac   .50 .20
     Nos. 1466-1471 (6)   1.32 .95

Church of St. John the Baptist, Nessebr
A636

Designs: 1s, Christ, fresco from Bojana Church. 2s, Ikon "Destruction of Idols," horiz. 3s, Bratchkovo Monastery. 4s, Zemen Monastery, horiz. 13s, Nativity, ikon from Arbanassi. 20s, Ikon "Virgin and Child," 1342.

1966, Feb. 25   Litho.   Perf. 11½
1472 A636 1s gray & multi   3.50 1.25
1473 A636 2s gray & multi   .25 .15
1474 A636 3s multicolored   .25 .15
1475 A636 4s multicolored   .25 .15
1476 A636 5s multicolored   .25 .15
1477 A636 13s gray & multi   .50 .15
1478 A636 20s multicolored   .95 .35
     Nos. 1472-1478 (7)   5.95 2.35
2,500 years of art in Bulgaria.

Georgi Benkovski and T. Kableshkov
A637

1s, Proclamation of April Uprising, Koprivstitsa. 3s, Dedication of flag, Panaguriste. 5s, V. Petleshkov, Z. Dyustabanov. 10s, Botev landing at Kozlodui. 13s, P. Volov, Ilarion Dragostinov.

1966, Mar. 3   Photo.   Perf. 10½
     Center in Black
1479 A637 1s red brn & gold   .15 .15
1480 A637 2s brt red & gold   .15 .15
1481 A637 3s ol grn & gold   .15 .15
1482 A637 5s steel bl & gold   .15 .15
1483 A637 10s brt rose lil & gold   .20 .15
1484 A637 13s lt vio & gold   .48 .15
     Nos. 1479-1484 (6)   1.28 .90
April Uprising against the Turks, 90th anniv.

Sofia Zoo Animals
A638

1966, May 23   Litho.
1485 A638 1s Elephant   .15 .15
1486 A638 2s Tiger   .15 .15
1487 A638 3s Chimpanzee   .15 .15
1488 A638 4s Siberian ibex   .18 .15
1489 A638 5s Polar bear   .25 .15
1490 A638 8s Lion   .25 .15
1491 A638 13s Bison   .80 .20
1492 A638 20s Kangaroo   1.50 .30
     Nos. 1485-1492 (8)   3.43 1.40

WHO Headquarters, Geneva — A639

1966, May 3   Photo.
1493 A639 13s deep blue & silver   .60 .25
Inauguration of the WHO Headquarters, Geneva.

Worker
A640

1966, May 9   Photo.   Perf. 10½
1494 A640 20s gray & rose   .65 .15
Sixth Trade Union Congress.

Yantra River Bridge, Biela — A641

#1496, Maritsa River Bridge, Svilengrad. #1497, Fountain, Samokov. #1498, Ruins of Fort, Kaskovo. 8s, Old Fort, Ruse. 13s, House, Gabrovo.

1966, Feb. 10   Perf. 13
1495 A641 1s Prus blue   .15 .15
1496 A641 1s brt green   .15 .15
1497 A641 2s olive green   .15 .15
1498 A641 2s dk red brown   .15 .15
1499 A641 8s red brown   .25 .15
1500 A641 13s dark blue   .42 .15
     Nos. 1495-1500 (6)   1.27 .90

     Souvenir Sheet

Moon Allegory — A642

1966, Apr. 29   Imperf.
1501 A642 60s blk, plum & sil   2.50 1.25
1st Russian soft landing on the moon by Luna 9, Feb. 3, 1966.

Steamer Radetzky and Bugler
A643

1966, May 28   Perf. 10½
1502 A643 2s multicolored   .15 .15
90th anniv. of the participation of the Danube steamer Radetzky in the uprising against the Turks.

Standard Bearer Nicola Simov-Kuruto
A644

1966, May 30
1503 A644 5s bister, green & olive   .25 .15
Hero of the Turkish War.

UNESCO Emblem — A645

1966, June 8
1504 A645 20s gold, blk & ver   .60 .16
20th anniv. of UNESCO.

Youth Federation Badge — A646

1966, June 6   Photo.   Perf. 10½
1505 A646 13s silver, bl & blk   .40 .15
7th Assembly of the Intl. Youth Federation.

Soccer — A647

Various soccer scenes. 50s, Jules Rimet Cup.

1966, June 27
1506 A647 1s gray, yel brn & blk   .15 .15
1507 A647 2s gray, crim & blk   .15 .15
1508 A647 5s gray, ol bis & blk   .15 .15
1509 A647 13s gray, ultra & blk   .35 .15
1510 A647 20s gray, Prus bl & blk   .60 .20
     Nos. 1506-1510 (5)   1.40 .80
     Miniature Sheet
     Imperf
1511 A647 50s gray, dp lil rose & gold   2.25 1.50
World Soccer Cup Championship, Wembley, England, July 11-30. Size of No. 1511: 60x64mm.

Woman Javelin Thrower — A648

Designs: No. 1513, Runner. No. 1514, Young man and woman carrying banners, vert.

BULGARIA

1966	Photo.	Perf. 10½
1512 A648	2s grn, yel & ver	.15 .15
1513 A648	13s dp grn, yel & sal pink	.40 .15
1514 A648	13s bl, lt bl & salmon	.40 .15
	Nos. 1512-1514 (3)	.95 .45

Nos. 1512-1513: 3rd Spartacist Games; issued Aug. 10. No. 1514: 3rd congress of the Bulgarian Youth Federation; issued May 25.

Wrestlers Nicolas Petrov and Dan Kolov — A649

1966, July 29
1515 A649 13s bis brn, dk brn & lt ol grn   .40 .20

3rd International Wrestling Championships.

Map of Balkan Countries, Globe and UNESCO Emblem — A650

1966, Aug. 26   Perf. 10½x11½
1516 A650 13s ultra, lt grn & pink   .40 .15

First Congress of Balkanologists.

Children with Building Blocks — A651

2s, Bunny & teddy bear with book. 3s, Children as astronauts. 13s, Children with pails & shovel.

1966, Sept. 1		Perf. 10½
1517 A651	1s dk car, org & blk	.15 .15
1518 A651	2s emerald, blk & red brn	.15 .15
1519 A651	3s ultra, org & blk	.15 .15
1520 A651	13s blue, rose & blk	.60 .15
	Nos. 1517-1520 (4)	1.05 .60

Children's Day.

Yuri A. Gagarin and Vostok 1 — A652

Designs: 2s, Gherman S. Titov, Vostok 2. 3s, Andrian G. Nikolayev, Pavel R. Popovich, Vostoks 3 & 4. 5s, Valentina Tereshkova, Valeri Bykovski, Vostoks 5 & 6. 8s, Vladimir M. Komarov, Boris B. Yegorov, Konstantin Feoktistov, Voskhod 1. 13s, Pavel Belyayev, Alexei Leonov, Voskhod 2.

1966, Sept. 29 Photo.		Perf. 11x11½
1521 A652	1s slate & gray	.15 .15
1522 A652	2s plum & gray	.15 .15
1523 A652	3s yel brn & gray	.15 .15
1524 A652	5s brn red & gray	.15 .15
1525 A652	8s ultra & gray	.15 .15
1526 A652	13s Prus bl & gray	.48 .15
	Nos. 1521-1526,B29 (7)	2.23 1.25

Russian space explorations.

St. Clement, 14th Century Wood Sculpture — A653

1966, Oct. 27   Photo.   Perf. 11½x11
1527 A653 5s red, buff & brown   .20 .15

1050th anniversary of the birth of St. Clement of Ochrida.

Metodi Shatorov A654

Portraits: 3s, Vladimir Trichkov. 5s, Valcho Ivanov. 10s, Raiko Daskalov. 13s, General Vladimir Zaimov.

1966, Nov. 8   Perf. 11x11½
Gold Frame, Black Denomination

1528 A654	2s crimson & bl vio	.15 .15
1529 A654	3s magenta & blk	.15 .15
1530 A654	5s car rose & dk bl	.15 .15
1531 A654	10s orange & olive	.28 .15
1532 A654	13s red & brown	.40 .15
	Nos. 1529-1532 (4)	.98 .60

Fighters against fascism.

George Dimitrov — A655    Steel Worker — A656

1966, Nov. 14   Photo.   Perf. 11½x11
1533 A655 2s magenta & blk   .15 .15
1534 A656 20s fawn, gray & blk   .70 .15

Bulgarian Communist Party, 9th Congress.

Deer's Head Drinking Cup A667

Gold Treasure: 2s, 6s, 10s, Various Amazon's head jugs. 3s, Ram's head cup. 5s, Circular plate. 8s, Deer's head cup. 13s, Amphora. 20s, Ram drinking horn.

1966, Nov. 28   Perf. 12x11½
Vessels in Gold and Brown; Black Inscriptions

1535 A667	1s gray & violet	.15 .15
1536 A667	2s gray & green	.15 .15
1537 A667	3s gray & dk bl	.15 .15
1538 A667	5s gray & red brn	.15 .15
1539 A667	6s gray & Prus bl	.15 .15
1540 A667	8s gray & brn ol	.85 .15
1541 A667	10s gray & sepia	.85 .18
1542 A667	13s gray & dk vio bl	.85 .28
1543 A667	20s gray & vio brn	.95 .32
	Nos. 1535-1543 (9)	4.25 1.68

The gold treasure from the 4th century B.C. was found near Panagyurishte in 1949.

Tourist House, Bansko — A668

Tourist Houses: No. 1545, Belogradchik. No. 1546, Triavna. 20s, Rila.

1966, Nov. 29   Photo.   Perf. 11x11½
1544 A668 1s dark blue   .15 .15
1545 A668 2s dark green   .15 .15
1546 A668 2s brown red   .15 .15
1547 A668 20s lilac   .42 .15
 Nos. 1544-1547 (4)   .87 .60

Decorated Tree — A669

Design: 13s, Jug with bird design.

1966, Dec. 12   Perf. 11
1548 A669 2s grn, pink & gold   .18 .15
1549 A669 13s brn lake, rose, emer & gold   .38 .15

New Year, 1967.

Pencho Slavikov, Author — A670    Dahlia — A671

Portraits: 2s, Dimcho Debeljanov, author. 3s, P. H. Todorov, author. 5s, Dimitri Dobrovich, painter. 8s, Ivan Markvichka, painter. 13s, Ilya Bezhkov, painter.

1966, Dec. 15   Perf. 10½x11
1550 A670 1s blue, olive & org   .15 .15
1551 A670 2s orange, brn & gray   .15 .15
1552 A670 3s olive, bl & org   .15 .15
1553 A670 5s gray, red brn & org   .15 .15
1554 A670 8s lilac, dk gray & bl   .30 .15
1555 A670 13s blue, vio & lil   .38 .15
 Nos. 1550-1555 (6)   1.28 .90

1966, Dec. 29
Flowers: No. 1557, Clematis. No. 1558, Foxglove. No. 1559, Narcissus. 3s, Snowdrop. 5s, Petunia. 13s, Tiger lily. 20s, Bellflower.

Flowers in Natural Colors
1556 A671 1s gray & lt brn   .15 .15
1557 A671 1s gray & dull bl   .15 .15
1558 A671 3s gray & dull lil   .15 .15
1559 A671 2s gray & brown   .15 .15
1560 A671 3s gray & dk grn   .16 .15
1561 A671 5s gray & dp ultra   .22 .15
1562 A671 8s gray & brown   .60 .15
1563 A671 20s gray & ultra   .95 .15
 Nos. 1556-1563 (8)   2.53 1.20

Ringnecked Pheasant A672

Game: 2s, Rock partridge. 3s, Gray partridge. 5s, Hare. 8s, Roe deer. 13s, Red deer.

1967, Jan. 28   Perf. 11x10½
1564 A672 1s lt ultra, dk brn & ocher   .15 .15
1565 A672 2s pale yel grn & dk grn   .15 .15
1566 A672 3s lt bl, blk & cr   .16 .15
1567 A672 5s lt grn & blk   .16 .15
1568 A672 8s pale bl, dk brn & ocher   .70 .15
1569 A672 13s bl & dk brn   1.25 .25
 Nos. 1564-1569 (6)   2.57 1.00

Bulgaria No. 1, 1879 — A673    Thracian Coin, 6th Century, B.C. — A674

1967, Feb. 4   Photo.   Perf. 10½
1570 A673 10s emerald, blk & yel   .75 .22

Bulgarian Philatelic Union, 10th Congress.

1967, Mar. 30   Perf. 11½x11
Coins: 2s, Macedonian tetradrachma, 2nd cent. B.C. 3s, Tetradrachma of Odessus, 2nd cent. B.C. 5s, Philip II of Macedonia, 4th cent. B.C. 13s, Thracian King Seuthus VII, 4th cent., B.C., obverse and reverse. 20s, Apollonian coin, 5th cent., B.C., obverse and reverse.

Size: 25x25mm
1571 A674 1s brn, blk & sil   .15 .15
1572 A674 2s red lil, blk & sil   .15 .15
1573 A674 3s grn, blk & sil   .15 .15
1574 A674 5s brn org, blk & sil   .16 .15

Size: 37½x25mm
1575 A674 13s brt bl, blk & brnz   .70 .24
1576 A674 20s vio, blk & sil   1.25 .45
 Nos. 1571-1576 (6)   2.56 1.29

Partisans Listening to Radio — A675

Design: 20s, George Dimitrov addressing crowd and Bulgarian flag.

1967, Apr. 20   Perf. 11x11½
1577 A675 1s red, gold, buff & sl grn   .15 .15
1578 A675 20s red, gold, dl red, grn & blk   .55 .15

25th anniversary of the Union of Patriotic Front Organizations.

Nikolas Kofardjiev A676

Portraits: 2s, Petko Napetov. 5s, Petko D. Petkov. 10s, Emil Markov. 13s, Traitcho Kostov.

1967, Apr. 24   Perf. 11½x11
1579 A676 1s brn red, gray & blk   .15 .15
1580 A676 2s ol grn, gray & blk   .15 .15
1581 A676 5s brn, gray & blk   .15 .15
1582 A676 10s dp bl, gray & blk   .20 .15
1583 A676 13s mag, gray & blk   .42 .15
 Nos. 1579-1583 (5)   1.07 .75

Fighters against fascism.

Symbolic Flower and Flame — A677

1967, May 18   Photo.   Perf. 11x11½
1584 A677 13s gold, yel & lt grn   .45 .15

First Cultural Congress, May 18-19.

BULGARIA

Gold Sand Beach and ITY Emblem — A678

20s, Hotel, Pamporovo. 40s, Nessebr Church.

1967, June 12	Photo.	Perf. 11x11½
1585 A678	13s ultra, yel & blk	.28 .15
1586 A678	20s Prus bl, blk & buff	.42 .15
1587 A678	40s brt grn, blk & ocher	1.00 .28
	Nos. 1585-1587 (3)	1.70 .58

International Tourist Year, 1967.

Angora Cat — A679

Cats: 2s, Siamese, horiz. 3s, Abyssinian. 5s, Black European. 13s, Persian, horiz. 20s, Striped domestic.

Perf. 11½x11, 11x11½

1967, June 19		
1588 A679	1s dl vio, dk brn & buff	.15 .15
1589 A679	2s ol, sl & brt bl	.15 .15
1590 A679	3s dull blue & brn	.15 .15
1591 A679	5s grn, blk & yel	.20 .15
1592 A679	13s dl red brn, sl & org	.90 .15
1593 A679	20s gray grn, brn & buff	1.65 .25
	Nos. 1588-1593 (6)	3.20 1.00

Scene from Opera "The Master of Boyana" by K. Iliev — A680

Songbird on Keyboard — A681

1967, June 19		
1594 A680	5s gray, vio bl & dp car	.38 .15
1595 A681	13s gray, dp car & dk bl	1.10 .15

3rd Intl. Competition for Young Opera Singers.

George Kirkov (1867-1919), Revolutionist A682

1967, June 24	Perf. 11x11½
1596 A682	2s rose red & dk brn .15 .15

Symbolic Tree and Stars — A683

1967, July 28	Photo.	Perf. 11½x11
1597 A683	13s dp bl, car & blk	.30 .15

11th Congress of Dimitrov's Union of the People's Youth.

Roses and Distillery A684

Designs: No. 1599, Chick and incubator. No. 1600, Cucumbers and hothouse. No. 1601, Lamb and sheep farm. 3s, Sunflower and oil mill. 4s, Pigs and pig farm. 5s, Hops and hop farm. 6s, Corn and irrigation system. 8s, Grapes and Bolgar tractor. 10s, Apples and cultivated tree. 13s, Bees and honey. 20s, Bee, blossoms and beehives.

1967		Perf. 11x11½
1598 A684	1s multicolored	.15 .15
1599 A684	1s dk car, yel & blk	.15 .15
1600 A684	2s vio, lt grn & blk	.15 .15
1601 A684	2s brt grn, gray & blk	.15 .15
1602 A684	3s yel grn, yel & blk	.15 .15
1603 A684	4s brt pur, yel & blk	.15 .15
1604 A684	5s ol bis, yel grn & blk	.15 .15
1605 A684	6s ol, brt grn & blk	.15 .15
1606 A684	8s grn, bis & blk	.15 .15
1607 A684	10s multicolored	.25 .15
1608 A684	13s grn, bis brn & blk	.42 .15
1609 A684	20s grnsh bl, brt pink & blk	.55 .15
	Nos. 1598-1609 (12)	2.57 1.80

Issue dates: Nos. 1598-1601, 1607, 1609, July 15; Nos. 1602-1606, 1608, July 24.

Map of Communist Countries, Spasski Tower A685

2s, Lenin speaking to soldiers. 3s, Fighting at Wlodaja, 1918. 5s, Marx, Engels & Lenin. 13s, Oil refinery. 20s, Molniya communication satellite.

1967, Aug. 25		Perf. 11
1610 A685	1s multicolored	.15 .15
1611 A685	2s magenta & olive	.15 .15
1612 A685	3s magenta & dull vio	.15 .15
1613 A685	5s magenta & red	.15 .15
1614 A685	13s magenta & ultra	.25 .15
1615 A685	20s magenta & blue	.45 .15
	Nos. 1610-1615 (6)	1.30 .90

50th anniv. of the Russian October Revolution.

Rod, "Fish" and Varna — A686

1967, Aug. 29	Photo.	Perf. 11
1616 A686	10s multicolored	.35 .15

7th World Angling Championships, Varna.

Skiers and Winter Olympics' Emblem — A687

Sports and Emblem: 2s, Ski jump. 3s, Biathlon. 5s, Ice hockey. 13s, Figure skating couple.

1967, Sept. 20	Photo.	Perf. 11
1617 A687	1s dk bl grn, red & blk	.15 .15
1618 A687	2s ultra, blk & ol	.15 .15
1619 A687	3s vio brn, bl & blk	.15 .15
1620 A687	5s green, yel & blk	.15 .15
1621 A687	13s vio bl, blk & buff	.35 .15
	Nos. 1617-1621, B31 (6)	2.05 1.03

10th Winter Olympic Games, Grenoble, France, Feb. 6-18, 1968.

Mountain Peaks — A688

1967, Sept. 25	Engr.	Perf. 11½
1622 A688	1s Bogdan	.15 .15
1623 A688	2s Czerny	.15 .15
1624 A688	3s Ruen, vert.	.15 .15
1625 A688	5s Persenk	.15 .15
1626 A688	10s Botev	.15 .15
1627 A688	13s Rila, vert.	.25 .15
1628 A688	20s Vihren	.55 .15
	Nos. 1622-1628 (7)	1.55 1.05

George Rakovski A689

1967, Oct. 20	Photo.	Perf. 11
1629 A689	13s yellow grn & blk	.40 .15

Centenary of the death of George Rakovski, revolutionary against Turkish rule.

Yuri A. Gagarin, Valentina Tereshkova and Alexei Leonov — A690

Designs: 2s, Lt. Col. John H. Glenn, Jr., and Maj. Edward H. White. 5s, Earth and Molniya 1. 10s, Gemini 6 and 7. 13s, Luna 13 moon probe. 20s, Gemini 10 and Agena rocket.

1967, Nov. 25		
1630 A690	1s Prus bl, blk & yel	.15 .15
1631 A690	2s dl bl, blk & dl yel	.15 .15
1632 A690	5s vio bl, grnsh bl & blk	.15 .15
1633 A690	10s dk bl, blk & red	.35 .15
1634 A690	13s grnsh bl, brt yel & blk	.55 .15
1635 A690	20s dl bl, blk & red	.75 .20
	Nos. 1630-1635 (6)	2.10 .95

Achievements in space exploration.

Various Views of Trnovo — A691

1967, Dec. 5	Photo.	Perf. 11
1636 A691	1s multicolored	.15 .15
1637 A691	2s multicolored	.15 .15
1638 A691	3s multicolored	.15 .15
1639 A691	5s multicolored	.16 .15
1640 A691	13s multicolored	.32 .15
1641 A691	20s multicolored	.50 .15
	Nos. 1636-1641 (6)	1.43 .90

Restoration of the ancient capital Veliko Trnovo.

Ratchenitza Folk Dance, by Ivan Markvichka — A692

1967, Dec. 9
1642 A692 20s gold & gray green 1.00 .80

Belgo-Bulgarian Philatelic Exposition, Brussels, Dec. 9-10. Printed in sheets of 8 stamps and 8 labels.

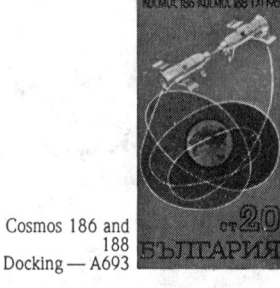

Cosmos 186 and 188 Docking — A693

40s, Venus 4 and orbits around Venus, horiz.

1968, Jan.		
1643 A693	20s vio, gray & pink	.55 .15
1644 A693	40s multicolored	1.00 .24

Docking maneuvers of the Russian spaceships Cosmos 186 and Cosmos 188, Nov. 1, 1967, and the flight to Venus of Venus 4, June 12-Nov. 18, 1967.

Crossing the Danube, by Orenburgski A694

Paintings: 2s, Flag of Samara, by J. Veschin, vert. 3s, Battle of Pleven by Orenburgski. 13s, Battle of Orlovo Gnezdo, by N. Popov, vert. 20s, Welcome for Russian Soldiers, by D. Gudienov.

1968, Jan. 25	Photo.	Perf. 11
1645 A694	1s gold & dk green	.15 .15
1646 A694	2s gold & dk blue	.15 .15
1647 A694	3s gold & chocolate	.15 .15
1648 A694	13s gold & dk vio	.32 .15
1649 A694	20s gold & Prus grn	.48 .18
	Nos. 1645-1649 (5)	1.25 .78

90th anniv. of the liberation from Turkey.

Shepherds, by Zlatyn Boyadjiev — A695

Paintings: 2s, Wedding dance, by V. Dimitrov, vert. 3s, Partisans' Song, by Ilya Petrov. 5s, Portrait of Anna Penchovich, by Nikolai Pavlovich, vert. 13s, Self-portrait, by Zachary Zograf, vert. 20s, View of Old Plovdiv, by T. Lavrenov. 60s, St. Clement of Ochrida, by A. Mitov.

1967, Dec.   Litho.   Perf. 11½
Size: 45x38mm, 38x45mm
1650 A695 1s gray & multi .15 .15
1651 A695 2s gray & multi .15 .15
Size: 55x35mm
1652 A695 3s gray & multi .22 .15

BULGARIA

Size: 38x45mm, 45x38mm
1653	A695 5s gray & multi	.40	.15
1654	A695 13s gray & multi	.90	.22
1655	A695 20s gray & multi	1.25	.40
	Nos. 1650-1655 (6)	3.07	1.22

Miniature Sheet
Size: 65x84mm
Imperf
1656	A695 60s multicolored	3.25	1.90

Marx Statue, Sofia — A696

Maxim Gorky — A697

1968, Feb. 20   Photo.   Perf. 11
1657	A696 13s black & red	.35	.15

150th anniversary of birth of Karl Marx.

1968, Feb. 20
1658	A697 13s ver & grnsh blk	.40	.15

Maxim Gorky (1868-1936), Russian writer.

Folk Dancers — A698

Designs: 5s, Runners. 13s, Doves. 20s, Festival poster, (head, flowers and birds). 40s, Globe and Bulgaria No. 1 under magnifying glass.

1968, Mar. 20
1659	A698 2s multicolored	.15	.15
1660	A698 5s multicolored	.15	.15
1661	A698 13s multicolored	.22	.15
1662	A698 20s multicolored	.48	.20
1663	A698 40s multicolored	1.10	.40
	Nos. 1659-1663 (5)	2.10	1.05

9th Youth Festival for Peace and Friendship, Sofia, July 28-Aug. 6.

Bellflower — A699

1968, Apr. 25   Perf. 11
1664	A699 1s shown	.15	.15
1665	A699 2s Gentian	.15	.15
1666	A699 3s Crocus	.15	.15
1667	A699 5s Iris	.16	.15
1668	A699 10s Dog-tooth violet	.20	.15
1669	A699 13s Sempervivum	.70	.15
1670	A699 20s Dictamnus	.95	.22
	Nos. 1664-1670 (7)	2.46	1.12

"The Unknown Hero," Tale by Ran Bosilek A700

Design: 20s, The Witch and the Young Man (Hans Christian Andersen fairy tale.)

1968, Apr. 25   Photo.   Perf. 10½
1671	A700 13s black & multi	.35	.15
1672	A700 20s black & multi	.52	.20

Bulgarian-Danish Philatelic Exhibition.

Memorial Church, Shipka — A701

Steeplechase — A702

1968, May 3
1673	A701 13s multicolored	.60	.20

Bulgarian Stamp Exhibition in Berlin.

1968, June 24   Photo.   Perf. 10½
1674	A702 1s red & black	.15	.15
1675	A702 2s gray, blk & rose brn	.15	.15
1676	A702 3s magenta, gray & blk	.15	.15
1677	A702 10s grnsh bl, blk & lem	.15	.15
1678	A702 13s vio bl, gray & pink	.55	.18
	Nos. 1674-1678, B33 (6)	2.15	1.10

Olympic Rings and: 1s, Gymnast on bar. 3s, Fencer. 10s, Boxer. 13s, Woman discus thrower.

19th Olympic Games, Mexico City, Oct. 12-27.

Battle of Buzluja A703

Design: 13s, Haji Dimitr and Stefan Karaja.

1968, July 1
1679	A703 2s silver & red brn	.15	.15
1680	A703 13s gold & sl grn	.32	.15

Centenary of the death of the patriots Haji Dimitr and Stefan Karaja.

Lakes of Smolian — A704

Sofia Zoo, Cent. — A705

Bulgarian Scenes: 2s, Ropotamo Lake. 3s, Erma-Idreloto mountain pass. 8s, Isker River dam. 10s, Slanchev Breg (sailing ship). 13s, Cape Caliacra. 40s, Old houses, Sozopol. 2 l, Chudnite Skali ("Strange Mountains").

1968   Photo.   Perf. 13
1681	A704 1s Prus green	.15	.15
1682	A704 3s dark green	.15	.15
1683	A704 3s dark brown	.15	.15
1684	A704 8s olive green	.15	.15
1685	A704 10s redsh brown	.15	.15
1686	A704 13s dk olive grn	.22	.15
1687	A704 40s Prus blue	.60	.25
1688	A704 2 l sepia	3.75	.85
	Nos. 1681-1688 (8)	5.32	2.00

1968, July 29   Perf. 10½
1689	A705 1s Cinereous vulture	.15	.15
1690	A705 2s Crowned crane	.15	.15
1691	A705 3s Zebra	.22	.15
1692	A705 5s Cheetah	.38	.15
1693	A705 13s Indian python	.70	.15
1694	A705 20s African crocodile	1.25	.30
	Nos. 1689-1694 (6)	2.85	1.05

Human Rights Flame — A706

1968, July 8
1695	A706 20s dp blue & gold	.60	.15

International Human Rights Year, 1968.

Congress Hall, Varna, and Emblem A707

1968, Sept. 17   Photo.   Perf. 10½
1696	A707 20s bister, grn & red	.50	.15

56th International Dental Congress, Varna.

Flying Swans — A708

Rose A709

Stag Beetle A710

Designs: 2s, Jug. 20s, Five Viking ships.

1968   Photo.   Perf. 10½
1697	A709 2s green & ocher	.75	.50
1698	A708 5s dp blue & gray	.75	.50
1699	A709 13s dp plum & lil rose	.75	.50
a.	Pair, #1698, 1699 + label	1.50	1.00
1700	A708 20s dp vio & gray	.75	.50
a.	Pair, #1697, 1700 + label	1.50	1.00
	Nos. 1697-1700 (4)	3.00	2.00

Cooperation with the Scandinavian countries.
Issued: 5s, 13s, Sept. 12; 2s, 20s, Nov. 22.

Perf. 12½x13, 13x12½
1968, Aug. 26

#1702, Ground beetle (Procerus scabrosus). #1703, Ground beetle (Calosoma sycophania). #1704, Scarab beetle, horiz. #1705, Saturnid moth, horiz.

1701	A710 1s brown olive	.15	.15
1702	A710 1s dark blue	.15	.15
1703	A710 1s dark green	.15	.15
1704	A710 1s orange brown	.15	.15
1705	A710 1s magenta	.15	.15
	Nos. 1701-1705 (5)	.75	.75

Turks Fighting Insurgents, 1688 A711

1968, Aug. 22   Perf. 10½
1706	A711 13s multicolored	.45	.15

280th anniversary of the Tchiprovtzi insurrection.

Christo Smirnenski (1898-1923), Poet — A712

1968, Sept. 28   Litho.   Perf. 10½
1707	A712 13s gold, red org & blk	.40	.15

Dalmatian Pelican A713

Birds: 2s, Little egret. 3s, Crested grebe. 5s, Common tern. 13s, European spoonbill. 20s, Glossy ibis.

1968, Oct. 28   Photo.
1708	A713 1s silver & multi	.15	.15
1709	A713 2s silver & multi	.15	.15
1710	A713 3s silver & multi	.15	.15
1711	A713 5s silver & multi	.15	.15
1712	A713 13s silver & multi	.52	.15
1713	A713 20s silver & multi	1.10	.32
	Nos. 1708-1713 (6)	2.22	1.07

Srebirna wild life reservation.

Carrier Pigeon A714

1968, Oct. 19
1714	A714 20s emerald	.70	.25
a.	Sheet of 4 + labels	5.00	1.65

2nd Natl. Stamp Exhib. in Sofia, Oct. 25-Nov. 15. No. 1714a contains 4 No. 1714 and 5 labels.

Man and Woman from Lovetch — A715

Regional Costumes: 1s, Silistra. 3s, Jambol. 13s, Chirpan. 20s, Razgrad. 40s, Ihtiman.

1968, Nov. 20   Perf. 13½
1715	A715 1s dp org & multi	.15	.15
1716	A715 2s Prus bl & multi	.15	.15
1717	A715 3s multicolored	.16	.15
1718	A715 13s multicolored	.28	.15
1719	A715 20s multicolored	.55	.25
1720	A715 40s green & multi	1.40	.45
	Nos. 1715-1720 (6)	2.69	1.30

St. Arsenius A716

10th cent. Murals & Icons: 2s, Procession with relics of St. Ivan Rilsky, horiz. 3s, St. Michael Torturing the Soul of the Rich Man. 13s, St. Ivan Rilski. 20s, St. John. 40s, St. George. 1 l, Procession meeting relics of St. Ivan Rilsky, horiz.

BULGARIA

Perf. 11½x12½, 12½x11½
1968, Nov. 25   Photo.
1721	A716	1s gold & multi	.15	.15
1722	A716	2s gold & multi	.15	.15
1723	A716	3s gold & multi	.15	.15
1724	A716	13s gold & multi	.42	.16
1725	A716	20s gold & multi	.95	.28
1726	A716	40s gold & multi	1.40	.60
		Nos. 1721-1726 (6)	3.22	1.49

Souvenir Sheet
Imperf
| 1727 | A716 | 1 l gold & multi | 3.75 | 2.75 |

Millenium of Rila Monastery. No. 1727 also: Sofia 1969 Intl. Phil. Exhib., May 31-June 8, 1969. No. 1727 contains one stamp, size: 57x51mm.

Medlar — A717

Herbs: No. 1729, Camomile. 2s, Lily-of-the-valley. 3s, Belladonna. 5s, Mallow. 10s, Buttercup. 13s, Poppies. 20s, Thyme.

1969, Jan. 2   Litho.   *Perf. 10½*
1728	A717	1s black, grn & org red	.15	.15
1729	A717	1s black, grn & yel	.15	.15
1730	A717	2s black, emer & grn	.15	.15
1731	A717	3s black & multi	.15	.15
1732	A717	5s black & multi	.15	.15
1733	A717	10s black, grn & yel	.16	.15
1734	A717	13s black & multi	.30	.15
1735	A717	20s black, lil & grn	.65	.15
		Nos. 1728-1735 (8)	1.86	1.20

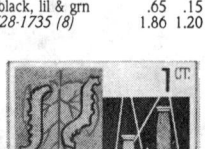

Silkworms and Spindles A718

Designs: 2s, Silkworm, cocoons and pattern. 3s, Cocoons and spinning wheel. 5s, Cocoons, woof-and-warp diagram. 13s, Silk moth, Cocoon and spinning frame. 20s, Silk moth, eggs and shuttle.

1969, Jan. 30   Photo.   *Perf. 10½*
1736	A718	1s bl, grn, sil & blk	.15	.15
1737	A718	2s dp car, sil & blk	.15	.15
1738	A718	3s Prus bl, sil & blk	.15	.15
1739	A718	5s pur, ver, sil & blk	.15	.15
1740	A718	13s red lil, ocher, sil & blk	.25	.15
1741	A718	20s grn, org, sil & blk	.45	.15
		Nos. 1736-1741 (6)	1.30	.90

Bulgarian silk industry.

Attack and Capture of Emperor Nicephorus — A719

Sts. Cyril and Methodius, Mural, Troian Monastery — A720

Designs (Manasses Chronicle): No. 1742, Death of Ivan Asen. 3s, Khan Kroum feasting after victory. No. 1748, Invasion of Bulgaria by Prince Sviatoslav of Kiev. No. 1750, Russian invasion and campaigns of Emperor John I Zimisces, c. 972 A.D. 40s, Tsar Ivan Alexander, Jesus and Constantine Manasses.

Horizontal designs: No. 1743, Kings Nebuchadnezzar, Balthazar, Darius and Cyrus. No. 1745, Kings Cambyses, Gyges and Darius. 5s, King David and Tsar Ivan Alexander. No. 1749, Persecution of Byzantine army after battle of July 26, 811. No. 1751, Christening of Bulgarian Tsar Boris, 865. 60s, Arrival of Tsar Simeon in Constantinople and his succeeding surprise attack on that city.

1969   Photo.   *Perf. 14x13½, 13½x14*
1742	A719	1s multicolored	.15	.15
1743	A719	1s multicolored	.15	.15
1744	A719	2s multicolored	.15	.15
1745	A719	2s multicolored	.15	.15
1746	A719	3s multicolored	.15	.15
1747	A719	5s multicolored	.15	.15
1748	A719	13s multicolored	.38	.15
1749	A719	13s multicolored	.38	.15
1750	A719	20s multicolored	.80	.15
1751	A719	20s multicolored	.80	.15
1752	A719	40s multicolored	1.25	.38
1753	A719	60s multicolored	2.25	.42
		Nos. 1742-1753 (12)	6.76	2.30

1969, Mar. 23
| 1754 | A720 | 28s gold & multi | .75 | .45 |

Post Horn — A721

Designs: 13s, Bulgaria Nos. 1 and 534. 20s, Street fighting at Stackata, 1919.

1969, Apr. 15   Photo.   *Perf. 10½*
1755	A721	2s green & yel	.15	.15
1756	A721	13s multicolored	.40	.15
1757	A721	20s dk bl & lt bl	.48	.18
		Nos. 1755-1757 (3)	1.03	.48

Bulgarian postal administration, 90th anniv.

The Fox and the Rabbit A722

Children's Drawings: 2s, Boy reading to wolf and fox. 13s, Two birds and cat singing together.

1969, Apr. 21
1758	A722	1s emer, org & blk	.15	.15
1759	A722	2s org, lt bl & blk	.15	.15
1760	A722	13s lt bl, ol & blk	.38	.15
		Nos. 1758-1760 (3)	.68	.45

Issued for Children's Week.

ILO Emblem — A723

1969, Apr. 28
| 1761 | A723 | 13s dull grn & blk | .30 | .15 |

50th anniv. of the ILO.

St. George and SOFIA 69 Emblem — A724

Designs: 2s, Virgin Mary and St. John Bogoslov. 3s, Archangel Michael. 5s, Three Saints. 8s, Jesus Christ. 13s, Sts. George and Dimitrie. 20s, Christ, the Almighty. 40s, St. Dimitrie. 60s, The 40 Martyrs. 80s, The Transfiguration.

1969, Apr. 30   *Perf. 11x12*
1762	A724	1s gold & multi	.15	.15
1763	A724	2s gold & multi	.15	.15
1764	A724	3s gold & multi	.15	.15
1765	A724	5s gold & multi	.15	.15
1766	A724	8s gold & multi	.16	.15
1767	A724	13s gold & multi	.32	.15
1768	A724	20s gold & multi	.65	.22
1769	A724	40s gold & multi	1.40	.42
	a.	Sheet of 4	5.75	6.00
1770	A724	60s gold & multi	1.75	.85
1771	A724	80s gold & multi	2.75	1.00
		Nos. 1762-1771 (10)	7.63	3.39

Old Bulgarian art from the National Art Gallery. No. 1769a contains 4 of No. 1769 with center gutter showing Alexander Nevski Shrine. See note on SOFIA 69 after Nos. C112-C120.

St. Cyril Preaching — A725

Design: 28s, St. Cyril and followers.

1969, June 20   Litho.   *Perf. 10½*
1772	A725	2s sil, grn & red	.16	.15
1773	A725	28s sil, dk bl & red	.75	.22

St. Cyril (827-869), apostle to the Slavs, inventor of Cyrillic alphabet. Issued in sheets of 25 with se-tenant labels; Cyrillic inscription on label of 2s, Glagolitic inscription on label of 28s.

St. Sophia Church — A726

Sofia Through the Ages: 1s, Roman coin with inscription "Ulpia Serdica." 2s, Roman coin with Aesculapius Temple. 4s, Bojana Church. 5s, Sobranic Parliament. 13s, Vasov National Theater. 20s, Alexander Nevski Shrine. 40s, Clement Ochrida University. 1 l, Coat of arms.

1969, May 25   *Perf. 13x12½*
1774	A726	1s gold & blue	.15	.15
1775	A726	2s gold & ol grn	.15	.15
1776	A726	3s gold & red brn	.15	.15
1777	A726	4s gold & purple	.15	.15
1778	A726	5s gold & plum	.15	.15
1779	A726	13s gold & brt grn	.28	.15
1780	A726	20s gold & vio bl	.45	.15
1781	A726	40s gold & dp car	1.10	.25
		Nos. 1774-1781 (8)	2.58	1.30

Souvenir Sheet
Imperf
| 1782 | A726 | 1 l grn, gold & red | 2.25 | 2.00 |

Historic Sofia in connection with the International Philatelic Exhibition, Sofia, May 31-June 8.
#1782 contains one 43½x43½mm stamp. Emblems of 8 preceding philatelic exhibitions in metallic ink in margin; gold inscription.
No. 1782 was overprinted in green "IBRA 73" and various symbols, and released May 4, 1973, for the Munich Philatelic Exhibition. The overprint also exists in gray.

St. George — A727

1969, June 9   Litho.   *Perf. 11½*
| 1783 | A727 | 40s sil, blk & pale rose | 1.25 | .50 |

38th FIP Congress, June 9-11.

Hand Planting Sapling A728

1969, Apr. 28   Photo.   *Perf. 11*
| 1784 | A728 | 2s ol grn, blk & lilac | .15 | .15 |

25 years of the reforestation campaign.

Partisans A729

Designs: 2s, Combine harvester. 3s, Dam. 5s, Flutist and singers. 13s, Factory. 20s, Lenin, Dimitrov, Russian and Bulgarian flags.

1969, Sept. 9
1785	A729	1s blk, pur & org	.15	.15
1786	A729	2s blk, ol bis & org	.15	.15
1787	A729	3s blk, bl grn & org	.15	.15
1788	A729	5s blk, brn red & org	.15	.15
1789	A729	13s blk, bl & org	.30	.15
1790	A729	20s blk, brn & org	.50	.15
		Nos. 1785-1790 (6)	1.40	.90

25th anniversary of People's Republic.

Women Gymnasts A730

1969, Sept.   Photo.   *Perf. 11*
| 1791 | A730 | 2s shown | .15 | .15 |
| 1792 | A730 | 20s Wrestlers | .42 | .22 |

Third National Spartakiad.

Tchanko Bakalov Tcherkovski, Poet. Birth Cent. — A731

1969, Sept.
| 1793 | A731 | 13s multicolored | .35 | .15 |

Woman Gymnast A732

Designs: 2s, Two women with hoops. 3s, Woman with hoop. 5s, Two women with spheres.

1969, Oct.
Gymnasts in Light Gray
1794	A732	1s green & dk blue	.15	.15
1795	A732	2s blue & dk blue	.15	.15
1796	A732	3s emer & sl grn	.15	.15
1797	A732	5s orange & pur	.15	.15
		Nos. 1794-1797,B35-B36 (6)	1.70	1.05

World Championships for Artistic Gymnastics, Varna.

BULGARIA

The Priest Rilski, by Zachary Zograf — A733

Paintings from the National Art Gallery. 2s, Woman at Window, by Vasil Stoilov. 3s, Workers at Rest, by Nenko Balkanski, horiz. 4s, Woman Dressing (Nude), by Ivan Nenov. 5s, Portrait of a Woman, by N. Pavlovich. 13s, Falstaff, by Duzunov Kr. Sarafov. No. 1804, Portrait of a Woman, by N. Mihajlov, horiz. No. 1805, Workers at Mealtime, by Stojan Sotirov, horiz. 40s, Self-portrait, by Tcheno Togorov.

Perf. 11½x12, 12x11½
1969, Nov. 10
1798	A733	1s gold & multi	.15	.15
1799	A733	2s gold & multi	.15	.15
1800	A733	3s gold & multi	.15	.15
1801	A733	4s gold & multi	.15	.15
1802	A733	5s gold & multi	.15	.15
1803	A733	13s gold & multi	.32	.15
1804	A733	20s gold & multi	.70	.22
1805	A733	20s gold & multi	.70	.22
1806	A733	40s gold & multi	1.40	.60
		Nos. 1798-1806 (9)	3.87	1.94

Roman Bronze Wolf A734

Design: 2s, Roman statue of woman, found at Silistra, vert.

1969, Oct. Photo. Perf. 11
| 1807 | A734 | 2s sil, ultra & gray | .15 | .15 |
| 1808 | A734 | 13s sil, dk grn & gray | .42 | .15 |

City of Silistra's 1,800th anniversary.

Worker and Factory — A735

1969 Perf. 13
| 1809 | A735 | 6s ultra & blk | .15 | .15 |

25th anniversary of the factory militia.

European Hake — A736

Designs: No. 1811, Deep-sea fishing trawler. Fish: 2s, Atlantic horse mackerel. 3s, Pilchard. 5s, Dentex macrophthalmus. 10s, Chub mackerel. 13s, Otolithes macrognathus. 20s, Lichia vadigo.

1969 Perf. 11
1810	A736	1s ol grn & blk	.15	.15
1811	A736	1s ultra, ind & gray	.15	.15
1812	A736	2s lilac & blk	.15	.15
1813	A736	3s vio bl & blk	.15	.15
1814	A736	5s rose cl, pink & blk	.24	.15
1815	A736	10s gray & blk	.48	.15
1816	A736	13s ver, sal & blk	.70	.15
1817	A736	20s ocher & black	1.25	.18
		Nos. 1810-1817 (8)	3.27	1.23

Marin Drinov A737

1969, Nov. 10 Litho. Perf. 11
| 1818 | A737 | 20s black & red org | .35 | .15 |

Centenary of the Bulgarian Academy of Science, founded by Marin Drinov.

Trapeze Artists A738    **Pavel Bania Sanatorium A739**

Circus Performers: 2s, Jugglers. 3s, Jugglers with loops. 5s, Juggler and bear on bicycle. 13s, Woman and performing horse. 20s, Musical clowns.

1969 Photo. Perf. 11
1819	A738	1s dk blue & multi	.15	.15
1820	A738	2s dk green & multi	.15	.15
1821	A738	3s dk violet & multi	.15	.15
1822	A738	5s multicolored	.15	.15
1823	A738	13s multicolored	.30	.15
1824	A738	20s multicolored	.55	.20
		Nos. 1819-1824 (6)	1.45	.95

1969, Dec. Photo. Perf. 10½-14

Health Resorts: 5s, Chisar Sanatorium. 6s, Kotel Children's Sanatorium. 20s, Narechen Polyclinic.

1825	A739	2s blue	.15	.15
1826	A739	5s ultra	.15	.15
1827	A739	6s green	.15	.15
1828	A739	20s emerald	.32	.15
		Nos. 1825-1828 (4)	.77	.60

G. S. Shonin, V. N. Kubasov and Spacecraft — A740

Designs: 2s, A. V. Filipchenko, V. N. Volkov, V. V. Gorbatko and spacecraft. 3s, Vladimir A. Shatalov, Alexei S. Yeliseyev and spacecraft. 28s, Three spacecraft in orbit.

1970, Jan. Photo. Perf. 11
1829	A740	1s rose car, ol grn & blk	.15	.15
1830	A740	2s bl, dl cl & blk	.15	.15
1831	A740	3s grnsh bl, vio & blk	.15	.15
1832	A740	28s vio bl, lil rose & lt bl	.70	.16
		Nos. 1829-1832 (4)	1.15	.61

Russian space flights of Soyuz 6, 7 and 8, Oct. 11-13, 1969.

Khan Krum and Defeat of Emperor Nicephorus, 811 — A741

Bulgarian History: 1s, Khan Asparuch and Bulgars crossing the Danube (679). 3s, Conversion of Prince Boris to Christianity, 865. 5s, Tsar Simeon and battle of Akhelo, 917. 8s, Tsar Samuel defeating the Byzantines, 976. 10s, Tsar Kaloyan defeating Emperor Baldwin, 1205. 13s, Tsar Ivan Assen II defeating Greek King Theodore Komnine, 1230. 20s, Coronation of Tsar Ivailo, 1277.

1970, Feb. Perf. 10½
1833	A741	1s gold & multi	.15	.15
1834	A741	2s gold & multi	.15	.15
1835	A741	3s gold & multi	.15	.15
1836	A741	5s gold & multi	.15	.15
1837	A741	8s gold & multi	.18	.15
1838	A741	10s gold & multi	.30	.15
1839	A741	13s gold & multi	.40	.15
1840	A741	20s gold & multi	.70	.15
		Nos. 1833-1840 (8)	2.18	1.20

See Nos. 2126-2133.

Bulgarian Pavilion, EXPO '70 — A742

1970 Perf. 12½
| 1841 | A742 | 20s brown, sil & org | .75 | .50 |

EXPO '70 International Exposition, Osaka, Japan, Mar. 15-Sept. 13, 1970.

Soccer A743

Designs: Various views of soccer game.

1970, Mar. 4 Photo. Perf. 12½
1842	A743	1s blue & multi	.15	.15
1843	A743	2s rose car & multi	.15	.15
1844	A743	3s ultra & multi	.15	.15
1845	A743	5s green & multi	.15	.15
1846	A743	20s emerald & multi	.55	.15
1847	A743	40s red & multi	1.25	.28
		Nos. 1842-1847 (6)	2.40	1.03

9th World Soccer Championships for the Jules Rimet Cup, Mexico City, May 30-June 21, 1970. See No. B37.

Lenin (1870-1924) A744

1970, Apr. 22
1848	A744	2s shown	.15	.15
1849	A744	13s Portrait	.32	.15
1850	A744	20s Writing	.70	.15
		Nos. 1848-1850 (3)	1.17	.45

Tephrocactus Alexanderi V. Bruchii — A745

Cacti: 2s, Opuntia drummondii. 3s, Hatiora cilindrica. 5s, Gymnocalycium vatteri. 8s, Heliantho cereus grandiflorus. 10s, Neochilenia andreaeana. 13s, Peireskia vargasii v. longispina. 20s, Neobesseya rosiflora.

1970 Photo. Perf. 12½
1851	A745	1s multicolored	.15	.15
1852	A745	2s dk green & multi	.15	.15
1853	A745	3s multicolored	.15	.15
1854	A745	5s blue & multi	.15	.15
1855	A745	8s brown & multi	.28	.15
1856	A745	10s vio bl & multi	1.00	.16
1857	A745	13s brn red & multi	1.00	.16
1858	A745	20s purple & multi	1.40	.32
		Nos. 1851-1858 (8)	4.28	1.39

Rose — A746

Designs: Various Roses.

1970, June 8 Litho. Perf. 13½
1859	A746	1s gray & multi	.15	.15
1860	A746	2s gray & multi	.15	.15
1861	A746	3s gray & multi	.15	.15
1862	A746	5s gray & multi	.15	.15
1863	A746	5s gray & multi	.15	.15
1864	A746	13s gray & multi	.16	.15
1865	A746	20s gray & multi	1.10	.25
1866	A746	28s gray & multi	1.90	.42
		Nos. 1859-1866 (8)	3.91	1.57

Gold Bowl — A747

Designs: Various bowls and art objects from Gold Treasure of Thrace.

1970, June 15 Photo. Perf. 12½
1867	A747	1s blk, bl & gold	.15	.15
1868	A747	2s blk, lt vio & gold	.15	.15
1869	A747	3s blk, ver & gold	.15	.15
1870	A747	5s blk, yel grn & gold	.15	.15
1871	A747	13s blk, org & gold	.70	.15
1872	A747	20s blk, lil & gold	.85	.18
		Nos. 1867-1872 (6)	2.15	.93

EXPO Emblem, Rose and Bulgarian Woman — A748

Designs (EXPO Emblem and): 2s, Three women. 3s, Woman and fruit. 28s, Dancers. 40s, Mt. Fuji and pavilions.

1970, June 20
1873	A748	1s gold & multi	.15	.15
1874	A748	2s gold & multi	.15	.15
1875	A748	3s gold & multi	.15	.15
1876	A748	28s gold & multi	.70	.22
		Nos. 1873-1876 (4)	1.15	.67

Miniature Sheet
Imperf
| 1877 | A748 | 40s gold & multi | 1.00 | .60 |

EXPO '70 International Exposition, Osaka, Japan, Mar. 15-Sept. 13. No. 1877 contains one stamp with simulated perforations.

Ivan Vasov — A749

1970, Aug. 1 Photo. Perf. 12½
| 1878 | A749 | 13s violet blue | .40 | .15 |

120th anniv. of the birth of Ivan Vasov, author.

BULGARIA

UN Emblem — A750

1970, Aug. 1
1879 A750 20s Prus bl & gold .50 .20
25th anniversary of the United Nations.

George Dimitrov A751
Retriever A752

1970, Aug.
1880 A751 20s blk, gold & org .60 .15
BZNC (Bulgarian Communist Party), 70th anniv.

1970   Photo.   Perf. 12½

Dogs: 1s, Golden retriever, horiz. 3s, Great Dane. 4s, Boxer. 5s, Cocker spaniel. 13s, Doberman pinscher. 20s, Scottish terrier. 28s, Russian greyhound, horiz.

1881	A752	1s multicolored	.15	.15
1882	A752	2s multicolored	.15	.15
1883	A752	3s multicolored	.15	.15
1884	A752	4s multicolored	.15	.15
1885	A752	5s multicolored	.15	.15
1886	A752	13s multicolored	.52	.15
1887	A752	20s multicolored	1.10	.26
1888	A752	28s multicolored	1.65	.32
	Nos. 1881-1888 (8)	4.02	1.48

Volleyball — A753

Designs: No. 1890, Two women players. No. 1891, Woman player. No. 1892, Man player.

1970, Sept.   Photo.   Perf. 12½
1889 A753 2s dk red brn, bl & blk .15 .15
1890 A753 2s ultra, org & blk .15 .15
1891 A753 20s Prus bl, yel & blk .48 .15
1892 A753 20s grn, yel & blk .48 .15
  Nos. 1889-1892 (4) 1.26 .60

World Volleyball Championships.

Enrico Caruso and "I Pagliacci" by Ruggiero Leoncavallo — A754

Opera Singers and Operas: 2s, Christina Morfova and "The Bartered Bride" by Bedrich Smetana. 3s, Peter Reitchev and "Tosca" by Giacomo Puccini. 10s, Svetana Tabakova and "The Flying Dutchman" by Richard Wagner. 13s, Katia Popova and "The Masters" by Paroshkev Hadjev. 20s, Feodor Chaliapin and "Boris Godunov" by Modest Musorgski.

1970, Oct. 15   Photo.   Perf. 14
1893 A754 1s black & multi .15 .15
1894 A754 2s black & multi .15 .15
1895 A754 3s black & multi .15 .15
1896 A754 10s black & multi .20 .15
1897 A754 13s black & multi .28 .16
1898 A754 20s black & multi 1.00 .25
  Nos. 1893-1898 (6) 1.93 1.01

Honoring opera singers in their best roles.

Ivan Assen II Coin — A755

Coins from 14th Century with Ruler's Portrait: 2s, Theodor Svetoslav. 3s, Mikhail Chichman. 13s, Ivan Alexander and Mikhail Assen. 20s, Ivan Sratsimir. 28s, Ivan Chichman (initials).

1970, Nov.   Perf. 12½
1899 A755 1s buff & multi .15 .15
1900 A755 2s gray & multi .15 .15
1901 A755 3s multicolored .15 .15
1902 A755 13s multicolored .22 .15
1903 A755 20s lt blue & multi .60 .15
1904 A755 28s multicolored .85 .22
  Nos. 1899-1904 (6) 2.12 .97

Fire Protection A756

1970   Litho.   Perf. 12½
1905 A756 1s Fireman .15 .15
1906 A756 3s Fire engine .15 .15

Bicyclists — A757
Congress Emblem — A758

1970   Photo.
1907 A757 20s grn, yel & pink .50 .20
20th Bulgarian bicycle race.

1970
1908 A758 13s gold & multi .35 .15
7th World Congress of Sociology, Varna, Sept. 14-19.

Ludwig van Beethoven — A759
Friedrich Engels — A760

1970
1909 A759 28s lil rose & dk bl .90 .40
Beethoven (1770-1827), composer.

1970   Photo.   Perf. 12½
1910 A760 13s ver, tan & brn .30 .15
Friedrich Engels (1820-1895), German socialist, collaborator of Karl Marx.

Miniature Sheets

Luna 16 A761

Russian moon mission: 80s, Lunokhod 1, unmanned vehicle on moon, horiz.

1970   Photo.   Imperf.
1911 A761 80s plum, sil, blk & bl 2.00 2.00
1912 A761 1 l vio bl, sil & red 4.00 2.75

No. 1911, Lunokhod 1, Nov. 10-17. No. 1912, Luna 16 mission, Sept. 12-24.
Issue dates: 80s, Dec. 18; 1 l, Nov. 10.

Snowflake A762

1970, Dec. 15   Photo.   Perf. 12½x13
1913 A762 2s ultra & multi .15 .15
New Year 1971.

Birds and Flowers A763

Folk Art: 2s, Bird and flowers. 3s, Flying birds. 5s, Birds and flowers. 13s, Sun. 20s, Tulips and pansies.

1971, Jan. 25   Perf. 12½x13½
1914 A763 1s multicolored .15 .15
1915 A763 2s multicolored .15 .15
1916 A763 3s multicolored .15 .15
1917 A763 5s multicolored .15 .15
1918 A763 13s multicolored .16 .15
1919 A763 20s multicolored .55 .15
  Nos. 1914-1919 (6) 1.31 .90

Spring 1971.

Girl, by Zeko Spiridonov A764

Modern Bulgarian Sculpture: 2s, Third Class (people looking through train window), by Ivan Funev. 3s, Bust of Elin Pelin, by Marko Markov. 13s, Bust of Nina, by Andrej Nikolov. 20s, Monument to P. K. Yavorov (kneeling woman), by Ivan Lazarov. 28s, Engineer, by Ivan Funev. 1 l, Refugees, by Sekul Krimov, horiz.

1971, Feb.   Perf. 12½
1920 A764 1s gold & vio .15 .15
1921 A764 2s gold & dk ol grn .15 .15
1922 A764 3s gold & rose brn .15 .15
1923 A764 13s gold & dk grn .30 .15
1924 A764 20s gold & red brn .52 .15
1925 A764 28s gold & dk brn .80 .20
  Nos. 1920-1925 (6) 2.07 .95

Souvenir Sheet
Imperf
1926 A764 1 l gold, dk brn & buff 2.00 1.75

Runner A765

Design: 20s, Woman putting the shot.

1971, Mar. 13   Photo.   Perf. 12½x13
1927 A765 2s brown & multi .15 .15
1928 A765 20s dp grn, org & blk .90 .22

2nd European Indoor Track and Field Championships.

Bulgarian Secondary School, Bolgrad — A766

Educators: 20s, Dimiter Mitev, Prince Bogoridi and Sava Radoulov.

1971, Mar. 16   Perf. 12½
1929 A766 2s silver, brn & grn .15 .15
1930 A766 20s silver, brn & vio .52 .15

First Bulgarian secondary school, 1858, in Bolgrad, USSR.

Communards — A767

1971, Mar. 18   Photo.   Perf. 12½x13
1931 A767 20s rose magenta & blk .50 .20
Centenary of the Paris Commune.

Dimitrov Facing Goering, Quotation, FIR Emblem A768

1971, Apr. 11   Perf. 12½
1932 A768 2s grn, gold, blk & red .15 .15
1933 A768 13s plum, gold, blk & red .70 .15

Intl. Fed. of Resistance Fighters (FIR), 20th anniv.

George S. Rakovski (1821-1867), Revolutionary Against Turkish Rule — A769

1971, Apr. 14
1934 A769 13s olive & blk brn .30 .15

Edelweiss Hotel, Borovets — A770

Designs: 2s, Panorama Hotel, Pamporovo. 4s, Boats at Albena, Black Sea. 8s, Boats at Rousalka. 10s, Shtastlivetsa Hotel, Mt. Vitosha.

BULGARIA

1971			Perf. 13	
1935	A770	1s brt green	.15	.15
1936	A770	2s olive gray	.15	.15
1937	A770	4s brt blue	.15	.15
1938	A770	8s blue	.15	.15
1939	A770	10s bluish green	.25	.15
		Nos. 1935-1939 (5)	.85	.75

Technological Progress — A771

Designs: 1s, Mason with banner, vert. 13s, Two men and doves, vert.

1971, Apr. 20	Photo.	Perf. 12½	
1940 A771	1s gold & multi	.15	.15
1941 A771	2s gray blue & multi	.15	.15
1942 A771	13s lt green & multi	.52	.16
	Nos. 1940-1942 (3)	.82	.46

10th Cong. of Bulgarian Communist Party.

Panayot Pipkov and Anthem A772

1971, May 20
1943 A772 13s sil, blk & brt grn   .45 .15
Panayot Pipkov, composer, birth cent.

Mammoth A773

Prehistoric Animals: 2s, Bear, vert. 3s, Hipparion (horse). 13s, Platybelodon. 20s, Dinotherium, vert. 28s, Saber-tooth tiger.

1971, May 29		Perf. 12½	
1944 A773	1s dull bl & multi	.15	.15
1945 A773	2s lilac & multi	.15	.15
1946 A773	3s multicolored	.15	.15
1947 A773	13s multicolored	.48	.15
1948 A773	20s dp grn & multi	.80	.18
1949 A773	28s multicolored	1.40	.28
	Nos. 1944-1949 (6)	3.13	1.06

Khan Asparuch Crossing Danube, 679 A.D., by Boris Angelushev — A774

Historical Paintings: 3s, Reception at Trnovo, by Ilya Petrov. 5s, Chevartov's Troops at Benkovsky, by P. Morozov. 8s, Russian Gen. Gurko and People in Sofia, 1878, by D. Gudjenko. 28s, People Greeting Red Army, by S. Venov.

1971, Mar. 6		Perf. 13½x14	
1950 A774	2s gold & multi	.15	.15
1951 A774	3s gold & multi	.15	.15
1952 A774	5s gold & multi	.16	.15
1953 A774	8s gold & multi	.32	.15
a.	Souv. sheet of 4, #1950-1953	1.00	.50
1954 A774	28s gold & multi	2.75	.85
	Nos. 1950-1954 (5)	3.53	1.45

In 1973, No. 1953a was surcharged 1 lev and overprinted "Visitez la Bulgarie," airline initials and emblems, and, on the 5s stamp, "Par Avion."

Freed Black, White and Yellow Men — A775

1971, May 20   Photo.   Perf. 12½
1955 A775 13s blue, blk & yel   .35 .15
Intl. Year against Racial Discrimination.

Map of Europe, Championship Emblem — A776

"XXX" Supporting Barbell — A777

1971, June 19
1956 A776 2s lt blue & multi   .15 .15
1957 A777 13s yellow & multi   .60 .18
30th European Weight Lifting Championships, Sofia, June 19-27.

Facade, Old House, Koprivnica A778

Designs: Decorated facades of various old houses in Koprivnica.

1971, July 10	Photo.	Perf. 12½	
1958 A778	1s green & multi	.15	.15
1959 A778	2s brown & multi	.15	.15
1960 A778	6s violet & multi	.15	.15
1961 A778	13s dk red & multi	.42	.15
	Nos. 1958-1961 (4)	.87	.60

Frontier Guard and German Shepherd A779

1971, July 31   Perf. 13
1962 A779 2s green & ol grn   .15 .15
25th anniversary of the Frontier Guards.

Congress of Busludja, Bas-relief — A780

1971, July 31   Perf. 12½
1963 A780 2s dk red & ol grn   .15 .15
80th anniversary of the first Congress of the Bulgarian Social Democratic party.

Young Woman, by Ivan Nenov — A781

Paintings: 2s, Lazarova in Evening Gown, by Stefan Ivanov. 3s, Performer in Dress Suit, by Kyril Zonev. 13s, Portrait of a Woman, by Detchko Uzunov. 20s, Woman from Kalotina, by Vladimir Dimitrov. 40s, Gorjanin (Mountain Man), by Stoyan Venev.

1971, Aug. 2		Perf. 14x13½	
1964 A781	1s green & multi	.15	.15
1965 A781	2s green & multi	.15	.15
1966 A781	3s green & multi	.15	.15
1967 A781	13s green & multi	.38	.15
1968 A781	20s green & multi	.75	.30
1969 A781	40s green & multi	1.65	.45
	Nos. 1964-1969 (6)	3.23	1.35

National Art Gallery.

Wrestlers A782

Designs: 13s, Wrestlers.

1971, Aug. 27		Perf. 12½	
1970 A782	2s green, blk & bl	.15	.15
1971 A782	13s red org, blk & bl	.48	.15

European Wrestling Championships.

Young Workers A783

Post Horn Emblem A784

1971   Photo.   Perf. 13
1972 A783 2s dark blue   .15 .15
25th anniv. of the Young People's Brigade.

1971, Sept. 15   Perf. 12½
1973 A784 20s dp green & gold   .45 .20
8th meeting of postal administrations of socialist countries, Varna.

FEBS Waves Emblem — A785

1971, Sept. 20
1974 A785 13s black, red & mar   .50 .20
7th Congress of European Biochemical Association (FEBS), Varna.

Statue of Republic — A786

Design: 13s, Bulgarian flag.

1971, Sept. 20   Perf. 13x12½
1975 A786 2s gold, yel & dk red   .15 .15
1976 A786 13s gold, grn & red   .38 .20
Bulgarian People's Republic, 25th anniv.

Cross Country Skiing and Winter Olympics Emblem A787

Sport and Winter Olympics Emblem: 2s, Downhill skiing. 3s, Ski jump and skiing. 4s, Women's figure skating. 13s, Ice hockey. 28s, Slalom skiing. 1 l, Torch and stadium.

1971, Sept. 25		Perf. 12½	
1977 A787	1s dk green & multi	.15	.15
1978 A787	2s vio blue & multi	.15	.15
1979 A787	3s ultra & multi	.15	.15
1980 A787	4s dp plum & multi	.15	.15
1981 A787	13s dk blue & multi	.40	.15
1982 A787	28s multicolored	.90	.35
	Nos. 1977-1982 (6)	1.90	1.10

Miniature Sheet
Imperf
1983 A787 1 l multicolored   3.50 1.65
11th Winter Olympic Games, Sapporo, Japan, Feb. 3-13, 1972.

Factory, Botevgrad A788

Industrial Buildings: 2s, Petro-chemical works, Pleven, vert. 10s, Chemical works, Vratsa. 13s, Maritsa-Istok Power Station, Dimitrovgrad. 40s, Electronics works, Sofia.

1971	Photo.	Perf. 13	
1984 A788	1s violet	.15	.15
1985 A788	2s orange	.15	.15
1986 A788	10s deep purple	.18	.15
1987 A788	13s lilac rose	.22	.15
1988 A788	40s deep brown	.70	.15
	Nos. 1984-1988 (5)	1.40	.75

UNESCO Emblem A789

1971, Nov. 4   Perf. 12½
1989 A789 20s lt bl, blk, gold & red   .45 .15
25th anniv. of UNESCO.

Soccer Player, by Kyril Zonev (1896-1971) A790

Paintings by Kyril Zonev: 2s, Landscape, horiz. 3s, Self-portrait. 13s, Lilies. 20s, Landscape, horiz. 40s, Portrait of a Young Woman.

1971, Nov. 10 *Perf. 11x12*
1990	A790	1s gold & multi	.15	.15
1991	A790	2s gold & multi	.15	.15
1992	A790	3s gold & multi	.15	.15
1993	A790	13s gold & multi	.22	.15
1994	A790	20s gold & multi	.85	.24
1995	A790	40s gold & multi	1.25	.35
		Nos. 1990-1995 (6)	2.77	1.19

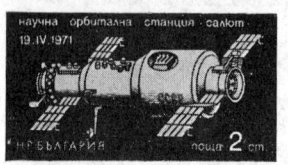

Salyut Space Station — A791

Astronauts Dobrovolsky, Volkov and Patsayev — A792

Designs: 13s, Soyuz 11 space transport. 40s, Salyut and Soyuz 11 joined.

1971, Dec. 20 *Perf. 12½*
1996	A791	3s dk grn, yel & red	.15	.15
1997	A791	13s multicolored	.22	.16
1998	A791	40s dk blue & multi	1.25	.40
		Nos. 1996-1998 (3)	1.62	.71

Souvenir Sheet
Imperf
1999 A792 80s multicolored 2.00 1.50

Salyut-Soyuz 11 space mission, and in memory of the Russian astronauts Lt. Col. Georgii T. Dobrovolsky, Vladislav N. Volkov and Victor I. Patsayev, who died during the Soyuz 11 space mission, June 6-30, 1971.

Oil Tanker Vihren A793

1972, Jan. 8 Photo. *Perf. 12½*
2000 A793 18s lil rose, vio & blk .75 .25

Bulgarian shipbuilding industry.

Goce Delchev A794

Portraits: 5s, Jan Sandanski. 13s, Damjan Gruev.

1972, Jan. 21 Photo. *Perf. 12½*
2001	A794	2s brick red & blk	.15	.15
2002	A794	5s green & blk	.15	.15
2003	A794	13s lemon & blk	.35	.15
		Nos. 2001-2003 (3)	.65	.45

Centenary of the births of Bulgarian patriots Delchev (1872-1903) and Sandanski, and of Macedonian Gruev (1871-1906).

Gymnast with Ball, Medals — A795

Designs: 18s, Gymnast with hoop, and medals. 70s, Gymnasts with hoops, and medals.

1972, Feb. 10
| 2004 | A795 | 13s multicolored | .42 | .15 |
| 2005 | A795 | 18s multicolored | .55 | .16 |

Miniature Sheet
Imperf
2006 A795 70s multicolored 2.25 2.00

5th World Women's Gymnastic Championships, Havana, Cuba.

View of Melnik, by Petar Mladenov — A796

Paintings from National Art Gallery: 2s, Plower, by Pencho Georgiev. 3s, Funeral, by Alexander Djendov. 13s, Husband and Wife, by Vladimir Dimitrov. 20s, Nursing Mother, by Nenko Balkanski. 40s, Paisii Hilendarski Writing History, by Koio Denchev.

1972, Feb. 20 *Perf. 13½x14*
2007	A796	1s green & multi	.15	.15
2008	A796	2s green & multi	.15	.15
2009	A796	3s green & multi	.15	.15
2010	A796	13s green & multi	.42	.15
2011	A796	20s green & multi	.75	.20
2012	A796	40s green & multi	1.25	.35
		Nos. 2007-2012 (6)	2.87	1.15

Paintings from National Art Gallery.

Worker — A797

1972, Mar. 7 *Perf. 12½*
2013 A797 13s silver & multi .20 .15

7th Bulgarian Trade Union Congress.

Singing Harvesters A798

Designs: Paintings by Vladimir Dimitrov.

Perf. 11½x12, 12x11½
1972, Mar. 31
2014	A798	1s shown	.15	.15
2015	A798	2s Harvester	.15	.15
2016	A798	3s Women Diggers	.15	.15
2017	A798	13s Fabric Dyers	.35	.15
2018	A798	20s "My Mother"	.70	.15
2019	A798	40s Self-portrait	1.40	.32
		Nos. 2014-2019 (6)	2.90	1.07

Vladimir Dimitrov, painter, 90th birth anniv.

"Your Heart is your Health" — A799

St. Mark's Basilica and Wave — A800

1972, Apr. 30 *Perf. 12½*
2020 A799 13s red, blk & grn .70 .30

World Health Day.

1972, May 6 *Perf. 13x12½*
Design: 13s, Ca' D'Oro and wave.
| 2021 | A800 | 2s ol grn, bl grn & lt bl | .15 | .15 |
| 2022 | A800 | 13s red brn, vio & lt grn | .52 | .18 |

UNESCO campaign to save Venice.

Dimitrov in Print Shop, 1901 — A801

Designs: Life of George Dimitrov.

1972, May 8 Photo. *Perf. 12½*
2023	A801	1s shown	.15	.15
2024	A801	2s Dimitrov as leader of 1923 uprising	.15	.15
2025	A801	3s Leipzig trial, 1933	.15	.15
2026	A801	5s As Communist functionary, 1935	.15	.15
2027	A801	13s As leader and teacher, 1948	.15	.15
2028	A801	18s Addressing youth rally, 1948	.42	.15
2029	A801	28s With Pioneers, 1948	.65	.16
2030	A801	40s Mausoleum	1.00	.32
2031	A801	80s Portrait	2.75	.45
a.		Souvenir sheet	4.25	2.50
		Nos. 2023-2031 (9)	5.57	1.83

90th anniversary of the birth of George Dimitrov (1882-1949), communist leader.
No. 2031a contains one imperf. stamp similar to No. 2031, but in different colors.
Value, No. 2031 imperf. in slightly changed colors, $5.

Paisii Hilendarski — A802

Design: 2s, Flame and quotation.

1972, May 12
| 2032 | A802 | 2s gold, grn & brn | .15 | .15 |
| 2033 | A802 | 13s gold, grn & brn | .50 | .15 |

Paisii Hilendarski (1722-1798), monk, writer of Bulgarian-Slavic history.

Canoeing, Motion and Olympic Emblems — A803

Designs (Motion and Olympic emblems and): 2s, Gymnastics. 3s, Swimming, women's. 13s, Volleyball. 18s, Jumping. 40s, Wrestling. 80s, Stadium and sports.

1972, June 25
Figures of Athletes in Silver & Black
2034	A803	1s lt blue & multi	.15	.15
2035	A803	2s orange & multi	.15	.15
2036	A803	3s multicolored	.15	.15
2037	A803	13s yellow & multi	.15	.15
2038	A803	18s multicolored	.42	.18
2039	A803	40s pink & multi	1.25	.30
		Nos. 2034-2039 (6)	2.27	1.08

Miniature Sheet
Imperf
Size: 62x60mm
2040 A803 80s gold, ver & yel 1.75 1.00

20th Olympic Games, Munich, Aug. 26-Sept. 11.

Angel Kunchev A804

1972, June 30 Photo. *Perf. 12½*
2041 A804 2s magenta, dk pur & gold .15 .15

Centenary of the death of Angel Kunchev, patriot and revolutionist.

Zlatni Pyassatsi — A805

1972, Sept. 16
2042	A805	1s shown	.15	.15
2043	A805	2s Drouzhba	.15	.15
2044	A805	3s Slunchev Bryag	.15	.15
2045	A805	13s Primorsko	.15	.15
2046	A805	28s Roussalka	.60	.24
2047	A805	40s Albena	.85	.30
		Nos. 2042-2047 (6)	2.05	1.14

Bulgarian Black Sea resorts.

Bronze Medal, Olympic Emblems, Canoeing A806

Olympic Emblems and: 2s, Silver medal, broad jump. 3s, Gold medal, boxing. 18s, Gold medal, wrestling. 40s, Gold medal, weight lifting.

1972, Sept. 29
2048	A806	1s Prus bl & multi	.15	.15
2049	A806	2s dk green & multi	.15	.15
2050	A806	3s orange brn & multi	.15	.15
2051	A806	18s olive & multi	.50	.16
2052	A806	40s multicolored	1.00	.30
		Nos. 2048-2052 (5)	1.95	.91

Bulgarian victories in 20th Olympic Games.
For overprint see No. 2066.

Stoj Dimitrov — A807

Resistance Fighters: 2s, Cvetko Radoinov. 3s, Bogdan Stivrodski. 5s, Mirko Laiev. 13s, Nedelyo Nikolov.

1972, Oct. 30 Photo. *Perf. 12½x13*
2053	A807	1s olive & multi	.15	.15
2054	A807	2s multicolored	.15	.15
2055	A807	3s multicolored	.15	.15
2056	A807	5s multicolored	.15	.15
2057	A807	13s multicolored	.28	.15
		Nos. 2053-2057 (5)	.88	.75

BULGARIA

"50 Years USSR" — A808

1972, Nov. 3   Photo.   Perf. 12½x13
2058 A808 13s gold, red & yellow   .35 .15
50th anniversary of Soviet Union.

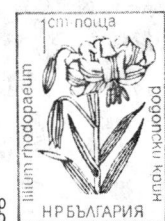

Turk's-cap Lily — A809

Protected Plants: 2s, Gentian. 3s, Sea daffodil. 4s, Globe flower. 18s, Primrose. 23s, Pulsatilla vernalis. 40s, Snake's-head.

1972, Nov. 25   Perf. 12½
Flowers in Natural Colors
2059 A809 1s olive bister   .15 .15
2060 A809 2s olive bister   .15 .15
2061 A809 3s olive bister   .15 .15
2062 A809 4s olive bister   .15 .15
2063 A809 18s olive bister   .28 .15
2064 A809 23s olive bister   .75 .20
2065 A809 40s olive bister   1.40 .35
       Nos. 2059-2065 (7)   3.03 1.30

No. 2052 Overprinted in СВЕТОВЕН ПЪРВЕНЕЦ Red

1972, Nov. 27
2066 A806 40s multicolored   .95 .24
Bulgarian weight lifting Olympic gold medalists.

Dobri Chintulov — A810

1972, Nov. 28   Photo.   Perf. 12½
2067 A810 2s gray, dk & lt grn   .20 .15
Dobri Chintulov, writer, 150th birth anniversary.

Forehead Band — A811

Designs (14th-19th Century Jewelry): 2s, Belt buckles. 3s, Amulet. 8s, Pendant. 23s, Earrings. 40s, Necklace.

1972, Dec. 27   Engr.   Perf. 14x13½
2068 A811 1s red brn & blk   .15 .15
2069 A811 2s emerald & blk   .15 .15
2070 A811 3s Prus bl & blk   .15 .15
2071 A811 8s dk red & blk   .15 .15
2072 A811 23s red org & multi   .50 .20
2073 A811 40s violet & blk   1.10 .42
       Nos. 2068-2073 (6)   2.20 1.22

Skin Divers A812

Designs: 2s, Shelf-1 underwater house and divers. 18s, Diving bell and diver, vert. 40s, Elevation balloon and divers, vert.

1973, Jan. 24   Photo.   Perf. 12½
2074 A812 1s lt bl, blk & yel   .15 .15
2075 A812 2s blk, bl & org yel   .15 .15
2076 A812 18s blk, Prus bl & dl org   .42 .15
2077 A812 40s blk, ultra & bister   .95 .30
       Nos. 2074-2077 (4)   1.67 .75

Bulgarian deep-sea research in the Black Sea. A souvenir sheet of four contains imperf. 20s stamps in designs of Nos. 2074-2077 with colors changed. Sold for 1 l. Value $3.50 unused, $3 canceled.

Execution of Levski, by Boris Angelushev — A813

Design: 20s, Vassil Levski, by Georgi Danchev.

1973, Feb. 19   Perf. 13x12½
2078 A813 2s dull rose & Prus grn   .15 .15
2079 A813 20s dull grn & brn   .90 .18

Centenary of the death of Vassil Levski (1837-1873), patriot, executed by the Turks.

Kukersky Mask, Elhovo Region A814

Nicolaus Copernicus A815

Kukersky Masks at pre-Spring Festival: 2s, Breznik. 3s, Hissar. 13s, Radomir. 20s, Karnobat. 40s, Pernik.

1973, Feb. 26   Perf. 12½
2080 A814 1s dp rose & multi   .15 .15
2081 A814 2s emerald & multi   .15 .15
2082 A814 3s violet & multi   .15 .15
2083 A814 13s multicolored   .35 .15
2084 A814 20s multicolored   .38 .15
2085 A814 40s multicolored   2.25 1.10
       Nos. 2080-2085 (6)   3.43 1.85

1973, Mar. 21   Photo.   Perf. 12½
2086 A815 28s ocher, blk & claret   1.25 .60

500th anniversary of the birth of Nicolaus Copernicus (1473-1543), Polish astronomer.

Vietnamese Worker and Rainbow — A816

1973, Apr. 16
2087 A816 18s lt blue & multi   .35 .15
Peace in Viet Nam.

A817

A818

Wild flowers.

1973, May   Photo.   Perf. 13
2088 A817 1s Poppy   .15 .15
2089 A817 2s Daisy   .15 .15
2090 A817 3s Peony   .15 .15
2091 A817 13s Centaury   .25 .15
2092 A817 18s Corn cockle   2.75 1.10
2093 A817 28s Ranunculus   .60 .22
       Nos. 2088-2093 (6)   4.05 1.92

1973, June 2
2094 A818 2s pale grn, buff & brn   .15 .15
2095 A818 18s pale brn, gray & grn   .65 .42

Christo Botev (1848-1876), poet.

"Suffering Worker" — A819

Design: 1s, Asen Halachev and revolutionists.

1973, June 6   Photo.   Perf. 13
2096 A819 1s gold, red & blk   .15 .15
2097 A819 2s gold, org & dk brn   .15 .15

50th anniversary of Pleven uprising.

Muskrat A820

Perf. 12½x13, 13x12½
1973, June 29   Litho.
2098 A820 1s shown   .15 .15
2099 A820 2s Racoon   .15 .15
2100 A820 3s Mouflon, vert.   .15 .15
2101 A820 13s Fallow deer, vert.   .22 .15
2102 A820 18s European bison   .50 .15
2103 A820 40s Elk   2.50 1.00
       Nos. 2098-2103 (6)   3.67 1.75

Aleksandr Stamboliski A821

1973, June 14   Photo.   Perf. 12½
2104 A821 18s dp brown & org   .35 .18
   a.   18s orange   2.50 .75

Aleksandr Stamboliski (1879-1923), leader of Peasants' Party and premier.

Have you found a typo or other error in this catalogue?
Inform the editors via our web site or e-mail

sctcat@ scottonline.com

Trade Union Emblem — A822

Stylized Sun, Olympic Rings — A823

1973, Aug. 27   Photo.   Perf. 12½
2105 A822 2s yellow & multi   .15 .15

8th Congress of World Federation of Trade Unions, Varna, Oct. 15-22.

1973, Aug. 29   Perf. 13

28s, Emblem of Bulgarian Olympic Committee & Olympic rings. 80s, Soccer, emblems of Innsbruck & Montreal 1976 Games, horiz.

2106 A823 13s multicolored   .70 .32
2107 A823 28s multicolored   1.25 .40

Souvenir Sheet
2108 A823 80s multicolored   3.25 1.75

Olympic Congress, Varna. No. 2108 contains one stamp. It also exists imperf.; also with violet margin, imperf.

Revolutionists with Communist Flag — A824

Designs: 5s, Revolutionists on flatcar blocking train. 13s, Raising Communist flag, vert. 18s, George Dimitrov and Vassil Kolarov.

1973, Sept. 22   Photo.   Perf. 12½
2109 A824 2s magenta & multi   .15 .15
2110 A824 5s magenta & multi   .15 .15
2111 A824 13s magenta & multi   .30 .15
2112 A824 18s magenta & multi   .85 .32
       Nos. 2109-2112 (4)   1.45 .77

50th anniv. of the September Revolution.

Warrior Saint — A825

Murals from Boyana Church: 1s, Tsar Kaloyan and 2s, his wife Dessislava. 5s, "St. Wystratti." 10s, Tsar Constantine Assen. 13s, Deacon Laurentius. 18s, Virgin Mary. 20s, St. Ephraim. 28s, Jesus. 80s, Jesus in the Temple, horiz.

1973, Sept. 24
2113 A825 1s gold & multi   .15 .15
2114 A825 2s gold & multi   .15 .15
2115 A825 3s gold & multi   .15 .15
2116 A825 5s gold & multi   .15 .15
2117 A825 10s gold & multi   .35 .15
2118 A825 13s gold & multi   .45 .15
2119 A825 18s gold & multi   .70 .15
2120 A825 20s gold & multi   .95 .18
2121 A825 28s gold & multi   3.50 .35
       Nos. 2113-2121 (9)   6.55 1.58

Miniature Sheet
Imperf
2122 A825 80s gold & multi   3.75 2.25

No. 2122 contains one stamp with simulated perforations.

BULGARIA

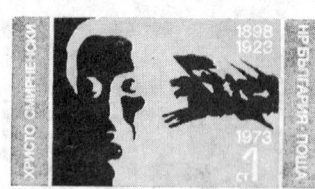

Christo Smirnenski — A826

1973, Sept. 29   Photo.   Perf. 12½
2123 A826 1s multicolored   .15 .15
2124 A826 2s vio blue & multi   .18 .15
Christo Smirnenski (1898-1923), poet.

Human Rights Flame — A827

1973, Oct. 10
2125 A827 13s dk blue, red & gold   .30 .16
Universal Declaration of Human Rights, 25th anniv.

Type of 1970

History of Bulgaria: 1s, Tsar Theodor Svetoslav receiving Byzantine envoys. 2s, Tsar Mihail Shishman's army in battle with Byzantines. 3s, Tsar Ivan Alexander's victory at Russocastro. 4s, Patriarch Euthimius at the defense of Turnovo. 5s, Tsar Ivan Shishman leading horsemen against the Turks. 13s, Momchil attacking Turks at Umour. 18s, Tsar Ivan Stratsimir meeting King Sigismund's crusaders. 28s, The Boyars Balik, Theodor and Dobrotitsa, meeting ship bringing envoys from Anne of Savoy.

1973, Oct. 23   Perf. 13
Silver and Black Vignettes
2126 A741 1s olive bister   .15 .15
2127 A741 2s Prus blue   .15 .15
2128 A741 3s lilac   .15 .15
2129 A741 4s green   .15 .15
2130 A741 5s violet   .15 .15
2131 A741 13s orange & brn   .22 .15
2132 A741 18s olive green   .40 .18
2133 A741 28s yel brn & brn   1.10 .48
     Nos. 2126-2133 (8)   2.47 1.56

Finn Class — A828

Sailboats: 2s, Flying Dutchman. 3s, Soling class. 13s, Tempest class. 20s, Class 470. 40s, Tornado class.

1973, Oct. 29   Litho.   Perf. 13
2134 A828 1s ultra & multi   .15 .15
2135 A828 2s green & multi   .15 .15
2136 A828 3s dk blue & multi   .15 .15
2137 A828 13s dull vio & multi   .28 .15
2138 A828 20s gray bl & multi   .60 .32
2139 A828 40s dk blue & multi   2.50 2.00
     Nos. 2134-2139 (6)   3.83 2.92
Value, set imperf. in changed colors, $10.

Village, by Bencho Obreshkov — A829

Paintings: 2s, Mother and Child, by Stoyan Venev. 3s, Rest (woman), by Tsenko Boyadjiev. 13s, Flowers in Vase, by Sirak Skitnik. 18s, Meri Kuneva (portrait), by Ilya Petrov. 40s, Winter in Plovdiv, by Zlatyu Boyadjiev. 13s, 18s, 40s, vert.

Perf. 12½x12, 12x12½
1973, Nov. 10
2140 A829 1s gold & multi   .15 .15
2141 A829 2s gold & multi   .15 .15
2142 A829 3s gold & multi   .15 .15
2143 A829 13s gold & multi   .22 .15
2144 A829 18s gold & multi   .42 .20
2145 A829 40s gold & multi   2.25 .75
     Nos. 2140-2145 (6)   3.34 1.55

Souvenir Sheet
Paintings by Stanislav Dospevski: a, Domnica Lambreva. b, Self-portrait. Both vert.
2146   Sheet of 2   2.75 1.75
  a. A829 50s gold & multi   .70   .52
  b. A829 50s gold & multi   .70   .52
Bulgarian paintings. No. 2146 commemorates the 150th birth anniv. of Stanislav Dospevski.

Souvenir Sheet

Soccer A830

1973, Dec. 10   Photo.   Perf. 13
2147 A830 28s multicolored   4.00 3.50
No. 2147 sold for 1 l. Exists overprinted for Argentina 78.

Angel and Ornaments — A831

Designs: 1s, Attendant facing right. 2s, Passover table and lamb. 3s, Attendant facing left. 8s, Abraham and ornaments. 13s, Adam and Eve. 28s, Expulsion from Garden of Eden.

1974, Jan. 21   Photo.   Perf. 13
2148 A831 1s fawn, yel & brn   .15 .15
2149 A831 2s fawn, yel & brn   .15 .15
2150 A831 3s fawn, yel & brn   .15 .15
  a. Strip of 3, #2148-2150   .25 .20
2151 A831 5s slate grn & yel   .15 .15
2152 A831 8s slate grn & yel   .20 .15
  a. Pair, #2151-2152   .30 .25
2153 A831 13s lt brown, yel & ol .28 .24
2154 A831 28s lt brown, yel & ol .52 .32
  a. Pair, #2153-2154   .80 .35
     Nos. 2148-2154 (7)   1.60 1.31
Woodcarvings from Rozhen Monastery, 19th century.

Lenin, by N. Mirtchev — A832

18s, Lenin visiting Workers, by W. A. Serov.

1974, Jan. 28   Litho.   Perf. 12½x12
2155 A832 2s ocher & multi   .15 .15
2156 A832 18s ocher & multi   .48 .22
50th anniversary of the death of Lenin.

1974, Jan. 28
Demeter Blagoev at Rally, by G. Kowachev.
2157 A832 2s multicolored   .15 .15
50th anniversary of the death of Demeter Blagoev, founder of Bulgarian Communist Party.

Domestic Animals A833

1974, Feb. 1   Photo.   Perf. 13
2158 A833 1s Sheep   .15 .15
2159 A833 2s Goat   .15 .15
2160 A833 3s Pig   .15 .15
2161 A833 5s Cow   .16 .15
2162 A833 13s Buffalo cow .30 .15
2163 A833 20s Horse   .80 .28
     Nos. 2158-2163 (6)   1.71 1.03

Comecon Emblem A834

1974, Feb. 11   Photo.   Perf. 13
2164 A834 13s silver & multi   .40 .15
25th anniversary of the Council of Mutual Economic Assistance.

Soccer — A835

Designs: Various soccer action scenes.

1974, Mar.   Photo.   Perf. 13
2165 A835 1s dull green & multi   .15 .15
2166 A835 2s brt green & multi   .15 .15
2167 A835 3s slate grn & multi   .15 .15
2168 A835 13s olive & multi   .15 .20
2169 A835 28s blue grn & multi   .65 .42
2170 A835 40s emerald & multi   1.50 .70
     Nos. 2165-2170 (6)   2.75 1.77

Souvenir Sheet
2171 A835 1 l green & multi   3.00 1.65
World Soccer Championship, Munich, June 13-July 7. No. 2171 exists imperf.

Salt Production A836

Children's Paintings: 1s, Cosmic Research for Peaceful Purposes. 3s, Fire Dancers. 28s, Russian-Bulgarian Friendship (train and children). 60s, Spring (birds).

1974, Apr. 15   Photo.   Perf. 13
2172 A836 1s lilac & multi   .15 .15
2173 A836 2s lt green & multi   .15 .15
2174 A836 3s blue & multi   .15 .15
2175 A836 28s slate & multi   1.75 .95
     Nos. 2172-2175 (4)   2.20 1.40

Souvenir Sheet
Imperf
2176 A836 60s blue & multi   2.25 1.75
Third World Youth Philatelic Exhibition, Sofia, May 23-30. No. 2176 contains one stamp with simulated perforations.

Folk Singers — A837

Designs: 2s, Folk dancers (men). 3s, Bagpiper and drummer. 5s, Wrestlers. 13s, Runners (women). 18s, Gymnast.

1974, Apr. 25   Perf. 13
2178 A837 1s vermilion & multi   .15 .15
2179 A837 2s orange brn & multi   .15 .15
2180 A837 3s brn red & multi   .15 .15
2181 A837 5s blue & multi   .15 .15
2182 A837 13s ultra & multi   .75 .25
2183 A837 18s violet bl & multi   .42 .17
     Nos. 2178-2183 (6)   1.77 1.00
4th Amateur Arts and Sports Festival

Flowers A838

1974, May   Photo.   Perf. 13
2184 A838 1s Aster   .15 .15
2185 A838 2s Petunia   .15 .15
2186 A838 3s Fuchsia   .15 .15
2187 A838 18s Tulip   .28 .15
2188 A838 20s Carnation   .60 .22
2189 A838 28s Pansy   1.65 .55
     Nos. 2184-2189 (6)   2.98 1.37

Souvenir Sheet
2190 A838 80s Sunflower   1.75 .85

Automobiles and Emblems A839

1974, May 15   Photo.   Perf. 13
2191 A839 13s multicolored   .30 .15
International Automobile Federation (FIA) Spring Congress, Sofia, May 20-24.

Old and New Buildings, UNESCO Emblem A840

1974, June 15
2192 A840 18s multicolored   .30 .15
UNESCO Executive Council, 94th Session, Varna.

Postrider A841

Designs: 18s, First Bulgarian mail coach. 28s, UPU Monument, Bern.

1974, Aug. 5
2193 A841 2s ocher, blk & vio   .15 .15
2194 A841 18s ocher, blk & grn   .38 .15

Souvenir Sheet
2195 A841 28s ocher, blk & bl   2.00 1.50
UPU cent. No. 2195 exists imperf.

BULGARIA

Pioneer and Komsomol Girl — A842

Designs: 2s, Pioneer and birds. 60s, Emblem with portrait of George Dimitrov.

1974, Aug. 12
2196 A842 1s green & multi   .15 .15
2197 A842 2s blue & multi   .15 .15

Souvenir Sheet
2198 A842 60s red & multi   1.65 1.10

30th anniversary of Dimitrov Pioneer Organization, Septemvrilche.

"Bulgarian Communist Party" — A843

Symbolic Designs: 2s, Russian liberators. 5s, Industrialization. 13s, Advanced agriculture and husbandry. 18s, Scientific and technical progress.

1974, Aug. 20
2199 A843 1s blue gray & multi   .15 .15
2200 A843 2s blue gray & multi   .15 .15
2201 A843 5s gray & multi   .15 .15
2202 A843 13s gray & multi   .26 .15
2203 A843 18s gray & multi   .35 .15
       Nos. 2199-2203 (5)   1.06 .75

30th anniversary of the People's Republic.

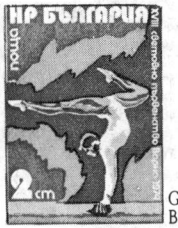

Gymnast on Parallel Bars — A844

Design: 13s, Gymnast on vaulting horse.

1974, Oct. 18   Photo.   Perf. 13
2204 A844 2s multicolored   .15 .15
2205 A844 13s multicolored   .28 .20

18th Gymnastic Championships, Varna.

Souvenir Sheet

Symbols of Peace — A845

1974, Oct. 29   Photo.   Perf. 13
2206 A845 Sheet of 4   2.50 1.10
  a. 13s Doves   .18 .15
  b. 13s Map of Europe   .18 .15
  c. 13s Olive Branch   .18 .15
  d. 13s Inscription   .18 .15

1974 European Peace Conference. "Peace" in various languages written on Nos. 2206a-2206c. Sold for 60s. Exists imperf.

Nib and Envelope — A846

1974, Nov. 20
2207 A846 2s yellow, blk & grn   .15 .15

Introduction of postal zone numbers.

Flowers A847

1974, Dec. 5
2208 A847 2s emerald & multi   .15 .15

St. Todor, Ceramic Icon — A848

Fruit Tree Blossoms — A849

Designs: 2s, Medallion, Veliko Turnovo. 3s, Carved capital. 5s, Silver bowl. 8s, Goblet. 13s, Lion's head finial. 18s, Gold plate with Cross. 28s, Breastplate with eagle.

1974, Dec. 18   Photo.   Perf. 13
2209 A848 1s orange & multi   .15 .15
2210 A848 2s pink & multi   .15 .15
2211 A848 3s blue & multi   .15 .15
2212 A848 5s lt vio & multi   .15 .15
2213 A848 8s brown & multi   .15 .15
2214 A848 13s multicolored   .22 .15
2215 A848 18s red & multi   .32 .16
2216 A848 28s ultra & multi   1.00 .60
       Nos. 2209-2216 (8)   2.29 1.66

Art works from 9th-12th centuries.

1975, Jan.   Photo.   Perf. 13
2217 A849 1s Apricot   .15 .15
2218 A849 2s Apple   .15 .15
2219 A849 3s Cherry   .15 .15
2220 A849 19s Pear   .28 .15
2221 A849 28s Peach   .70 .25
       Nos. 2217-2221 (5)   1.43 .85

Tree and Book A850

1975, Mar. 25   Photo.   Perf. 13
2222 A850 2s gold & multi   .15 .15

Forestry High School, 50th anniversary.

Souvenir Sheet

Farmers' Activities (Woodcuts) — A851

1975, Mar. 25
2223 A851 Sheet of 4   .80 .48
  a. 2s Farmer with ax and flag
  b. 5s Farmers on guard
  c. 13s Dancing couple
  d. 18s Woman picking fruit

Bulgarian Agrarian Peoples Union, 75th anniv.

Michelangelo, Self-portrait A852

13s, Night, horiz. 18s, Day, horiz. Both designs after sculptures from Medici Tomb, Florence.

1975
2224 A852 2s plum & dk blue   .15 .15
2225 A852 13s vio bl & plum   .24 .15
2226 A852 18s brown & green   .52 .15
       Nos. 2224-2226 (3)   .91 .45

Souvenir Sheet
2227 A852 2s olive & red   1.25 1.25

Michelangelo Buonarotti (1475-1564), Italian sculptor, painter and architect. No. 2227 issued to publicize ARPHILA 75 Intl. Phil. Exhib., Paris, June 6-16. Sheet sold for 60s.
Issued: #2224-2226, 3/28; #2227, 3/31.

Souvenir Sheet

Spain No. 1 and España 75 Emblem A853

1975, Apr. 4
2228 A853 40s multicolored   3.75 3.00

Espana 75 International Philatelic Exhibition, Madrid, Apr. 4-13.

Gabrov Costume — A854

Regional Costumes: 3s, Trnsk. 5s, Vidin. 13s, Gocedelchev. 18s, Risen.

1975, Apr.   Photo.   Perf. 13
2229 A854 2s blue & multi   .15 .15
2230 A854 3s emerald & multi   .15 .15
2231 A854 5s orange & multi   .15 .15
2232 A854 13s olive & multi   .35 .15
2233 A854 18s multicolored   .80 .24
       Nos. 2229-2233 (5)   1.60 .84

Red Star and Arrow — A855

Standard Kilogram and Meter — A856

Design: 13s, Dove and broken sword.

1975, May 9
2234 A855 2s red, blk & gold   .15 .15
2235 A855 13s blue, blk & gold   .32 .15

Victory over Fascism, 30th anniversary.

1975, May 9   Perf. 13x13½
2236 A856 13s silver, lil & blk   .35 .15

Cent. of Intl. Meter Convention, Paris, 1875.

IWY Emblem, Woman's Head — A857

Ivan Vasov — A858

1975, May 20   Photo.   Perf. 13
2237 A857 13s multicolored   .35 .15

International Women's Year 1975.

1975, May

Design: 13s, Ivan Vasov, seated.
2238 A858 2s buff & multi   .15 .15
2239 A858 13s gray & multi   .32 .15

125th birth anniversary of Ivan Vasov.

Nikolov and Sava Kokarechkov — A859

Designs: 2s, Mitko Palaouzov and Ivan Vassilev. 5s, Nicolas Nakev and Stevtcho Kraychev. 13s, Ivanka Pachkoulova and Detelina Mintcheva.

1975, May 30
2240 A859 1s multicolored   .15 .15
2241 A859 2s multicolored   .15 .15
2242 A859 5s multicolored   .15 .15
2243 A859 13s multicolored   .28 .15
       Nos. 2240-2243 (4)   .73 .60

Teen-age resistance fighters, killed during World War II.

BULGARIA

Mother Feeding Child, by John E. Millais — A861

Etchings: 2s, The Dead Daughter, by Goya. 3s, Reunion, by Beshkov. 13s, Seated Nude, by Renoir. 20s, Man in a Fur Hat, by Rembrandt. 40s, The Dream, by Daumier, horiz. 1 l, Temptation, by Dürer.

Photogravure and Engraved
1975, Aug.   Perf. 12x11½, 11½x12
2248 A861 1s yel grn & multi   .15   .15
2249 A861 2s orange & multi   .15   .15
2250 A861 3s lilac & multi   .15   .15
2251 A861 13s lt blue & multi   .26   .15
2252 A861 20s ocher & multi   .40   .18
2253 A861 40s rose & multi   1.10 .28
       Nos. 2248-2253 (6)   2.21 1.06
Souvenir Sheet
2254 A861 1 l emerald & multi   2.00 1.25
World Graphics Exhibition.

Letter "Z" from 12th Century Manuscript A862

Initials from Illuminated Manuscripts: 2s, "B" from 17th cent. prayerbook. 3s, "V" from 16th cent. Bouhovo Gospel. 8s, "B" from 14th cent. Turnovo collection. 13s, "V" from Dobreisho's Gospel, 13th cent. 18s, "E" from 11th cent. Enina book of the Apostles.

1975, Aug.   Litho.   Perf. 11½
2255 A862 1s multicolored   .15   .15
2256 A862 2s multicolored   .15   .15
2257 A862 3s multicolored   .15   .15
2258 A862 8s multicolored   .15   .15
2259 A862 13s multicolored   .25   .15
2260 A862 18s multicolored   .65   .16
       Nos. 2255-2260 (6)   1.50 .91
Bulgarian art.

Whimsical Globe — A863

1975, Aug.   Photo.   Perf. 13
2261 A863 2s multicolored   .15   .15
Festival of Humor and Satire.

Lifeboat Dju IV and Gibraltar-Cuba Route — A864

1975, Aug. 5   Photo.   Perf. 13
2262 A864 13s multicolored   .25   .15
Oceanexpo 75, 1st Intl. Ocean Exhib., Okinawa, July 20, 1975-Jan. 18, 1976.

Sts. Cyril and Methodius A865

Sts. Constantine and Helena A866

St. Sophia Church, Sofia, Woodcut by V. Zahriev — A867

1975, Aug. 21
2263 A865 2s ver, yel & brn   .15   .15
2264 A866 13s green, yel & brn   .25   .15
Souvenir Sheet
2265 A867 50s orange & multi   1.25 .80
Balkanphila V, philatelic exhibition, Sofia, Sept. 27-Oct. 5.

Peace Dove and Map of Europe — A868

1975, Nov.   Photo.   Perf. 13
2266 A868 18s ultra, rose & yel   .45   .22
European Security and Cooperation Conference, Helsinki, Finland, July 30-Aug. 1. No. 2266 printed in sheets of 5 stamps and 4 labels, arranged checkerwise.

Acherontia Atropos A869

Designs: Moths.

1975   Photo.   Perf. 13
2267 A869 1s shown   .15   .15
2268 A869 2s Daphnis nerii   .15   .15
2269 A869 3s Smerinthus ocellata   .15   .15
2270 A869 10s Deilephila nicea   .20   .15
2271 A869 13s Choerocampa elpenor   .24   .15
2272 A869 18s Macroglossum fuciformis .90 .25
       Nos. 2267-2272 (6)   1.79 1.00

Soccer Player — A870

1975, Sept. 21
2273 A870 2s multicolored   .15   .15
8th Inter-Toto (soccer pool) Soccer Championships, Varna.

Constantine's Rebellion Against the Turks, 1403 — A871

Designs (Woodcuts): 2s, Campaign of Vladislav III, 1443-1444. 3s, Battles of Turnovo, 1598 and 1686. 10s, Battle of Liprovsko, 1688. 13s, Guerrillas, 17th century. 18s, Return of exiled peasants.

1975, Nov. 27   Photo.   Perf. 13
2274 A871 1s bister, grn & blk   .15   .15
2275 A871 2s blue, car & blk   .15   .15
2276 A871 3s yellow, lil & blk   .15   .15
2277 A871 10s orange, grn & blk   .16   .15
2278 A871 13s green, lil & blk   .22   .15
2279 A871 18s pink, grn & blk   .45   .18
       Nos. 2274-2279 (6)   1.28 .93
Bulgarian history.

Red Cross and First Aid — A872

Design: 13s, Red Cross and dove.

1975, Dec. 1
2280 A872 2s red brn, red & blk   .15   .15
2281 A872 13s bl grn, red & blk   .22   .15
90th anniversary of Bulgarian Red Cross.

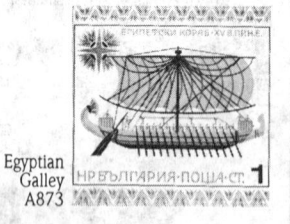

Egyptian Galley A873

Historic Ships: 2s, Phoenician galley. 3s, Greek trireme. 5s, Roman galley. 13s, Viking longship. 18s, Venetian galley.

1975, Dec. 15   Photo.   Perf. 13
2282 A873 1s multicolored   .15   .15
2283 A873 2s multicolored   .15   .15
2284 A873 3s multicolored   .15   .15
2285 A873 5s multicolored   .15   .15
2286 A873 13s multicolored   .32   .15
2287 A873 18s multicolored   .60   .16
       Nos. 2282-2287 (6)   1.52 .91
See Nos. 2431-2436, 2700-2705.

Souvenir Sheet

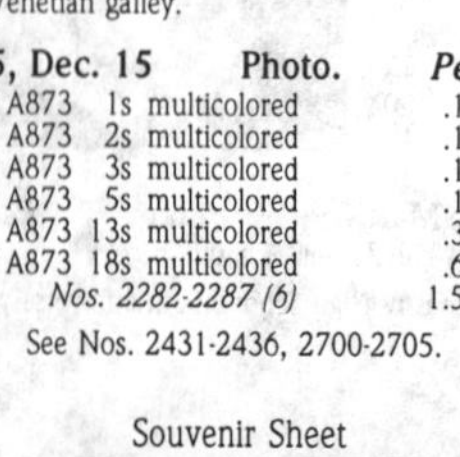

Ethnographical Museum, Plovdiv — A874

1975, Dec. 17
2288 Sheet of 3   4.50 2.50
  a. A874 80s green, yellow & dark brown 1.25 .65
European Architectural Heritage Year. No. 2288 contains 3 stamps and 3 labels showing stylized bird.

Dobri Hristov — A875

1975, Dec.   Perf. 13
2289 A875 5s brt green, yel & brn   .15   .15
Dobri Hristov, musician, birth centenary.

United Nations Emblem — A876

1975, Dec.
2290 A876 13s gold, blk & mag   .20   .15
United Nations, 30th anniversary.

Glass Ornaments A877

Design: 13s, Peace dove, decorated ornament.

1975, Dec. 22   Photo.   Perf. 13
2291 A877 2s brt violet & multi   .15   .15
2292 A877 13s gray & multi   .20   .15
New Year 1976.

Downhill Skiing — A878

Designs (Winter Olympic Games Emblem and): 2s, Cross country skier, vert. 3s, Ski jump. 13s, Biathlon, vert. 18s, Ice hockey, vert. 23s, Speed skating, vert. 80s, Figure skating, pair, vert.

1976, Jan. 30   Perf. 13½
2293 A878 1s silver & multi   .15   .15
2294 A878 2s silver & multi   .15   .15
2295 A878 3s silver & multi   .15   .15
2296 A878 13s silver & multi   .22   .15
2297 A878 18s silver & multi   .32   .15
2298 A878 23s silver & multi   .80   .30
       Nos. 2293-2298 (6)   1.79 1.05
Souvenir Sheet
2299 A878 80s silver & multi   1.65 1.10
12th Winter Olympic Games, Innsbruck, Austria, Feb. 4-15.

Electric Streetcar, Sofia, 1976 — A879

Design: 13s, Streetcar and trailer, 1901.

BULGARIA

1976, Jan. 12   Photo.   Perf. 13½x13
2300 A879 2s gray & multi   .15 .15
2301 A879 13s gray & multi   .38 .15
75th anniversary of Sofia streetcars.

Stylized Bird — A880

1976, Mar. 1   Perf. 13
2302 A880 2s gold & multi   .15 .15
2303 A880 5s gold & multi   .15 .15
2304 A880 13s gold & multi   .25 .15
  Nos. 2302-2304 (3)   .55 .45
Souvenir Sheet
2305 A880 50s gold & multi   1.00 .45
11th Bulgarian Communist Party Congress.

A. G. Bell and Telephone, 1876 — A881

1976, Mar. 10
2306 A881 18s dk brn, yel & ocher   .25 .15
Centenary of first telephone call by Alexander Graham Bell, Mar. 10, 1876.

Mute Swan — A882

Waterfowl: 2s, Ruddy shelduck. 3s, Common shelduck. 5s, Garganey teal. 13s, Mallard. 18s, Red-crested pochard.

1976, Mar. 27   Litho.   Perf. 11½
2307 A882 1s vio bl & multi   .15 .15
2308 A882 2s yel grn & multi   .15 .15
2309 A882 3s blue & multi   .15 .15
2310 A882 5s multicolored   .22 .15
2311 A882 13s purple & multi   .65 .15
2312 A882 18s green & multi   .90 .15
  Nos. 2307-2312 (6)   2.22 .90

Guerrillas — A883

Designs (Woodcuts by Stoev): 2s, Peasants with rifle and proclamation. 5s, Raina Knaginia with horse and guerrilla. 13s, Insurgents with cherrywood cannon.

1976, Apr. 5   Photo.   Perf. 13
2313 A883 1s multicolored   .15 .15
2314 A883 2s multicolored   .15 .15
2315 A883 5s multicolored   .15 .15
2316 A883 13s multicolored   .24 .15
  Nos. 2313-2316 (4)   .69 .60
Centenary of uprising against Turkey.

Guard and Dog — A884

13s, Men on horseback, observation tower.

1976, May 15
2317 A884 2s multicolored   .15 .15
2318 A884 13s multicolored   .20 .15
30th anniversary of Border Guards.

Construction Worker — A885

1976, May 20
2319 A885 2s multicolored   .15 .15
Young Workers Brigade, 30th anniversary.

Busludja, Bas-relief — A886    AES Complex — A887

Design: 5s, Memorial building.

1976, May 28   Photo.   Perf. 13
2320 A886 2s green & multi   .15 .15
2321 A886 5s violet bl & multi   .15 .15
First Congress of Bulgarian Social Democratic Party, 85th anniversary.

1976, Apr. 7
Designs: 8s, Factory. 10s, Apartment houses. 13s, Refinery. 20s, Hydroelectric station.
2322 A887 5s green   .15 .15
2323 A887 8s maroon   .16 .15
2324 A887 10s green   .20 .15
2325 A887 13s violet   .32 .15
2326 A887 20s brt green   .42 .15
  Nos. 2322-2326 (5)   1.25 .75
Five-year plan accomplishments.

Children Playing Around Table — A888

Kindergarten Children: 2s, with doll carriage & hobby horse. 5s, playing ball. 23s, in costume.

1976, June 15
2327 A888 1s green & multi   .15 .15
2328 A888 2s yellow & multi   .15 .15
2329 A888 5s lilac & multi   .15 .15
2330 A888 23s rose & multi   .42 .15
  Nos. 2327-2330 (4)   .87 .60

Demeter Blagoev — A889    Christo Botev — A890

1976, May 28
2331 A889 13s bluish blk, red & gold .25 .15
Demeter Blagoev (1856-1924), writer, political leader, 120th birth anniversary.

1976, May 25
2332 A890 13s ocher & slate grn   .25 .15
Christo Botev (1848-1876), poet, death centenary. Printed se-tenant with yellow green and ocher label, inscribed with poem.

Boxing, Montreal Olympic Emblem — A891    Belt Buckle — A892

Designs (Montreal Olympic Emblem): 1s, Wrestling, horiz. 3s, 1 l, Weight lifting. 13s, One-man kayak. 18s, Woman gymnast. 28s, Woman diver. 40s, Woman runner.

1976, June 25
2333 A891 1s orange & multi   .15 .15
2334 A891 2s multicolored   .15 .15
2335 A891 3s lilac & multi   .15 .15
2336 A891 5s multicolored   .18 .15
2337 A891 18s multicolored   .28 .15
2338 A891 28s blue & multi   .38 .16
2339 A891 40s lemon & multi   .75 .30
  Nos. 2333-2339 (7)   2.04 1.21
Souvenir Sheet
2340 A891 1 l orange & multi   1.65 1.10
21st Olympic Games, Montreal, Canada, July 17-Aug. 1.

1976, July 30   Photo.   Perf. 13
Thracian Art (8th-4th Centuries): 2s, Brooch. 3s, Mirror handle. 5s, Helmet cheek cover. 13s, Gold ornament. 18s, Lion's head (harness decoration). 20s, Knee guard. 28s, Jeweled pendant.
2341 A892 1s brown & multi   .15 .15
2342 A892 2s blue & multi   .15 .15
2343 A892 3s multicolored   .15 .15
2344 A892 5s claret & multi   .15 .15
2345 A892 13s purple & multi   .24 .15
2346 A892 18s multicolored   .32 .15
2347 A892 20s multicolored   .42 .15
2348 A892 28s multicolored   .60 .18
  Nos. 2341-2348 (8)   2.18 1.23

Souvenir Sheet 
Composite of Bulgarian Stamp Designs A893

1976, June 5
2349 A893 50s red & multi   1.65 .65
International Federation of Philately (F.I.P.), 50th anniversary and 12th Congress.

Partisans at Night, by Ilya Petrov — A894

Paintings: 5s, Old Town, by Tsanko Lavenov. 13s, Seated Woman, by Petrov, vert. 18s, Seated Boy, by Petrov, vert. 28s, Old Plovdiv, by Lavenov, vert. 80s, Ilya Petrov, self-portrait, vert.

1976, Aug. 11   Photo.   Perf. 14
2350 A894 2s multicolored   .15 .15
2351 A894 5s multicolored   .15 .15
2352 A894 13s ultra & multi   .32 .15
2353 A894 18s multicolored   .45 .15
2354 A894 28s multicolored   .65 .18
  Nos. 2350-2354 (5)   1.72 .78
Souvenir Sheet
2354A A894 80s multicolored   1.25 .95

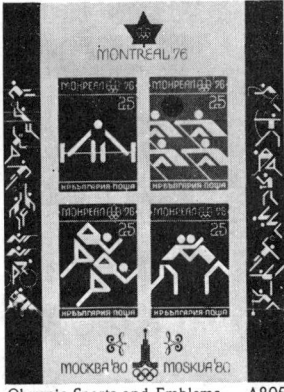

Olympic Sports and Emblems — A895

1976, Sept. 6   Photo.   Perf. 13
2355 A895 Sheet of 4   1.65 1.00
  a. 25s Weight Lifting   .35 .18
  b. 25s Rowing   .35 .18
  c. 25s Running   .35 .18
  d. 25s Wrestling   .35 .18
Medalists, 21st Olympic Games, Montreal.

Have you found a typo or other error in this catalogue?

Inform the editors via our web site or e-mail

sctcat@
scottonline.com

BULGARIA

Souvenir Sheet

Fresco and UNESCO Emblem — A896

1976, Dec. 3
2356 A896 50s red & multi   1.25   .55
UNESCO, 30th anniv.

"The Pianist" by Jendov — A897

Fish and Hook — A898

Designs (Caricatures by Jendov): 5s, Imperialist "Trick or Treat." 13s, The Leader, 1931.

1976, Sept. 30   Photo.   Perf. 13
2357 A897 2s green & multi   .15 .15
2358 A897 5s purple & multi   .15 .15
2359 A897 13s magenta & multi .32 .15
       Nos. 2357-2359 (3)   .62 .45
Alex Jendov (1901-1953), caricaturist.

1976, Sept. 21   Photo.   Perf. 13
2360 A898 5s multicolored   .15 .15
World Sport Fishing Congress, Varna.

St. Theodore A899

Frescoes: 3s, St. Paul. 5s, St. Joachim. 13s, Melchizedek. 19s, St. Porphyrius. 28s, Queen. 1 l, The Last Supper.

1976, Oct. 4   Litho.   Perf. 12x12½
2361 A899 2s gold & multi   .15 .15
2362 A899 3s gold & multi   .15 .15
2363 A899 5s gold & multi   .15 .15
2364 A899 13s gold & multi   .32 .15
2365 A899 19s gold & multi   .35 .15
2366 A899 28s gold & multi   .65 .20
       Nos. 2361-2366 (6)   1.77 .95

Miniature Sheet
Perf. 12
2367 A899 1 l gold & multi 1.50 .95
Zemen Monastery frescoes, 14th cent.

Document — A900

1976, Oct. 5
2368 A900 5s multicolored   .15 .15
State Archives, 25th anniversary.

Cinquefoil — A901

1976, Oct. 14   Photo.   Perf. 13
2369 A901 1s Chestnut   .15 .15
2370 A901 2s shown   .15 .15
2371 A901 5s Holly   .15 .15
2372 A901 8s Yew   .15 .15
2373 A901 13s Daphne   .32 .15
2374 A901 13s Judas tree   .60 .18
       Nos. 2369-2374 (6)   1.52 .93

Dimitri Polianov — A902

1976, Nov. 19
2375 A902 2s dk purple & ocher .15 .15
Dimitri Polianov (1876-1953), poet.

Christo Botev, by Zlatyu Boyadjiev A903

Paintings: 2s, Partisan Carrying Cherrywood Cannon, by Ilya Petrov. 3s, "Necklace of Immortality" (man's portrait), by Detchko Uzunov. 13s, "April 1876," by Georgi Popoff. 18s, Partisans, by Stoyan Venev. 60s, The Oath, by Svetlin Ruseff.

1976, Dec. 8
2376 A903 1s bister & multi   .15 .15
2377 A903 2s bister & multi   .15 .15
2378 A903 3s bister & multi   .15 .15
2379 A903 13s bister & multi .24 .15
2380 A903 18s bister & multi .35 .15
       Nos. 2376-2380 (5)   1.04 .75

Souvenir Sheet
Imperf
2381 A903 60s gold & multi   .95 .55
Uprising against Turkish rule, centenary.

"Pollution" and Tree A904

Design: 18s, "Pollution" obscuring sun.

1976, Nov. 10   Perf. 13
2382 A904 2s ultra & multi   .15 .15
2383 A904 18s blue & multi   .30 .15
Protection of the environment.

Congress Emblem — A904a    Flags — A904b

1976, Nov. 28   Photo.   Perf. 13
2384   A904a 2s multicolored   .15 .15
2384A A904b 13s multicolored .26 .15
33rd BSIS Cong. (Bulgarian Socialist Party).

Tobacco Workers, by Stajkov A905

Paintings by Stajkov: 2s, View of Melnik. 13s, Shipbuilder.

1976, Dec. 16   Photo.   Perf. 13
2385 A905 1s multicolored   .15 .15
2386 A905 2s multicolored   .15 .15
2387 A905 13s multicolored   .28 .15
       Nos. 2385-2387 (3)   .58 .45
Veselin Stajkov (1906-1970), painter.

Snowflake A906

1976, Dec. 20
2388 A906 2s silver & multi   .15 .15
New Year 1977.

Zachary Stoyanov (1851-1889), Historian — A907

1976, Dec. 30
2389 A907 2s multicolored   .15 .15

Bronze Coin of Septimus Severus — A908

Roman Coins: 2s, 13s, 18s, Bronze coins of Caracalla, diff. 23s, Copper coin of Diocletian.

1977, Jan. 28   Photo.   Perf. 13½x13
2390 A908 1s gold & multi   .15 .15
2391 A908 2s gold & multi   .15 .15
2392 A908 13s gold & multi   .20 .15
2393 A908 18s gold & multi   .26 .15
2394 A908 23s gold & multi   .45 .20
       Nos. 2390-2394 (5)   1.21 .80
Coins struck in Serdica (modern Sofia).

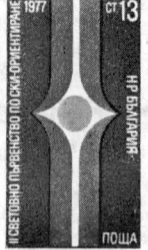

Skis and Compass — A909    Tourist Congress Emblem — A910

1977, Feb. 14   Perf. 13
2395 A909 13s ultra, red & lt bl .25 .15
2nd World Ski Orienteering Championships.

1977, Feb. 24   Photo.   Perf. 13
2396 A910 2s multicolored   .15 .15
5th Congress of Bulgarian Tourist Organization.

Bellflower — A911

Designs: Various bellflowers.

1977, Mar. 2
2397 A911 1s yellow & multi   .15 .15
2398 A911 2s rose & multi   .15 .15
2399 A911 3s lt blue & multi .15 .15
2400 A911 13s multicolored   .30 .15
2401 A911 43s yellow & multi 1.10 .28
       Nos. 2397-2401 (5)   1.85 .88

Vasil Kolarov — A912   Union Congress Emblem — A913

1977, Mar. 21   Photo.   Perf. 13
2402 A912 2s blue & black   .15 .15
Vasil Kolarov (1877-1950), politician.

1977, Mar. 25
2403 A913 2s multicolored   .15 .15
8th Bulgarian Trade Union Cong., Apr. 4-7.

Wolf A914

Wild Animals: 2s, Red fox. 10s, Weasel. 13s, European wildcat. 23s, Jackal.

1977, May 16   Litho.   Perf. 12½x12
2404 A914 1s multicolored   .15 .15
2405 A914 2s multicolored   .15 .15
2406 A914 10s multicolored   .18 .15
2407 A914 13s multicolored   .35 .15
2408 A914 23s multicolored   .60 .18
       Nos. 2404-2408 (5)   1.43 .78

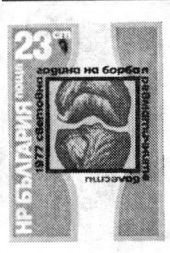

BULGARIA

Diseased Knee — A915

1977, Mar. 31   Photo.   Perf. 13
2409 A915 23s multicolored   .40 .15
World Rheumatism Year.

Writers' Congress Emblem A916

1977, June 7
2410 A916 23s lt bl & yel grn   .65 .20
International Writers Congress: "Peace, the Hope of the Planet." No. 2410 printed in sheets of 8 stamps and 4 labels with signatures of participating writers.

Old Testament Trinity, Sofia, 16th Century A917

Icons: 1s, St. Nicholas, Nessebur, 13th cent. 3s, Annunciation, Royal Gates, Veliko Turnovo, 16th cent. 5s, Christ Enthroned, Nessebur, 17th cent. 13s, St. Nicholas, Elena, 18th cent. 23s, Presentation of the Virgin, Rila Monastery, 18th cent. 35s, Virgin and Child, Tryavna, 19th cent. 40s, St. Demetrius on Horseback, Provadia, 19th cent. 1 l, The 12 Holidays, Rila Monastery, 18th cent.

1977, May 10   Photo.   Perf. 13
2411 A917 1s black & multi   .15 .15
2412 A917 2s green & multi   .15 .15
2413 A917 3s brown & multi   .15 .15
2414 A917 5s blue & multi   .15 .15
2415 A917 13s olive & multi   .30 .15
2416 A917 23s maroon & multi   .50 .15
2417 A917 35s green & multi   .80 .25
2418 A917 40s dp ultra & multi   1.10 .38
       Nos. 2411-2418 (8)   3.30 1.53

Miniature Sheet
Imperf.
2419 A917 1 l gold & multi   2.25 1.10
Bulgarian icons. See Nos. 2615-2619.

Souvenir Sheet

St. Cyril A918

1977, June 7   Photo.   Perf. 13
2420 A918 1 l gold & multi   1.75 .90
1150th anniversary of the birth of St. Cyril (827-869), reputed inventor of Cyrillic alphabet.

Congress Emblem — A919

1977, May 9
2421 A919 2s red, gold & grn   .15 .15
13th Komsomol Congress.

Newspaper Masthead A920

1977, June 3   Photo.   Perf. 13
2422 A920 2s multicolored   .15 .15
Cent. of Bulgarian daily press and 50th anniv. of Rabotnichesko Delo newspaper.

Patriotic Front Emblem — A921

Weight Lifting — A922

1977, May 26
2423 A921 2s gold & multi   .15 .15
8th Congress of Patriotic Front.

1977, June 15
2424 A922 13s dp brown & multi   .25 .15
European Youth Weight Lifting Championships, Sofia, June.

Women Basketball Players — A923

1977, June 15   Perf. 13
2425 A923 23s multicolored   .50 .18
7th European Women's Basketball Championships.

Wrestling — A924

Designs (Games Emblem and): 13s, Running. 23s, Basketball. 43s, Women's gymnastics.

1977, Apr. 15
2426 A924 2s multicolored   .15 .15
2427 A924 13s multicolored   .20 .15
2428 A924 23s multicolored   .38 .15
2429 A924 43s multicolored   .70 .26
       Nos. 2426-2429 (4)   1.43 .71
UNIVERSIADE '77, University Games, Sofia, Aug. 18-27.

TV Tower, Berlin — A925

1977, Aug. 12   Litho.   Perf. 13
2430 A925 25s blue & dk blue   .50 .16
SOZPHILEX 77 Philatelic Exhibition, Berlin, Aug. 19-28.

Ship Type of 1975

Historic Ships: 1s, Hansa cog. 2s, Santa Maria, caravelle. 3s, Golden Hind, frigate. 12s, Santa Catherina, carrack. 13s, La Corone, galleon. 43s, Mediterranean galleass.

1977, Aug. 29   Photo.   Perf. 13
2431 A873 1s multicolored   .15 .15
2432 A873 2s multicolored   .15 .15
2433 A873 3s multicolored   .15 .15
2434 A873 12s multicolored   .25 .15
2435 A873 13s multicolored   .25 .15
2436 A873 43s multicolored   1.00 .25
       Nos. 2431-2436 (6)   1.95 1.00

Ivan Vasov National Theater — A926

Buildings, Sofia: 13s, Party Headquarters. 23s, House of the People's Army. 30s, Clement Ochrida University. 80s, National Gallery. 1 l, National Assembly.

1977, Aug. 30   Photo.   Perf. 13
2437 A926 12s red, gray   .18 .15
2438 A926 13s red brn, gray   .18 .15
2439 A926 23s blue, gray   .30 .15
2440 A926 30s olive, gray   .40 .15
2441 A926 80s violet, gray   1.10 .42
2442 A926 1 l claret, gray   1.40 .52
       Nos. 2437-2442 (6)   3.56 1.54

Map of Europe A927

1977, June 10
2443 A927 23s brown, bl & grn   .40 .18
21st Congress of the European Organization for Quality Control, Varna.

Union of Earth and Water, by Rubens A928

Rubens Paintings: 23s, Venus and Adonis. 40s, Pastoral Scene (man and woman). 1 l, Portrait of a Lady in Waiting.

1977, Sept. 23   Litho.   Perf. 12
2444 A928 13s gold & multi   .45 .15
2445 A928 23s gold & multi   .65 .15
2446 A928 40s gold & multi   1.10 .25
       Nos. 2444-2446 (3)   2.20 .55

Souvenir Sheet
2447 A928 1 l gold & multi   2.50 1.65
Peter Paul Rubens (1577-1640).

George Dimitrov A929

1977, June 17   Photo.   Perf. 13
2448 A929 13s red & deep claret   .35 .15
George Dimitrov (1882-1947).

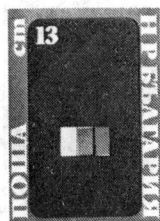

Flame with Star — A930

Smart Pete on Donkey, by Ilya Beshkov — A931

1977, May 17
2449 A930 13s gold & multi   .25 .15
3rd Bulgarian Culture Congress.

1977, May 19
2450 A931 2s multicolored   .15 .15
11th National Festival of Humor and Satire Gabrovo.

Elin Pelin — A932

Dr. Pirogov — A934

13th Canoe World Championships — A933

Albena, Black Sea A933a

Writers: 2s, Pelin (Dimitur Ivanov Stojanov, (1877-1949). 5s, Peju K. Jaworov (1878-1914).
Artists: 13s, Boris Angelushev (1902-1966), 23s, Ceno Todorov (Ceno Todorov Dikov, 1877-1953). Each printed with label showing scenes from authors' works or illustrations by the artists.

BULGARIA

1977, Aug. 26 Photo. *Perf. 13*
2451 A932   2s gold & brown   .15 .15
2452 A932   5s gold & gray grn   .15 .15
2453 A932 13s gold & claret   .22 .15
2454 A932 23s gold & blue   .45 .15
       Nos. 2451-2454 (4)   .97 .60

1977, Sept. 1 Photo. *Perf. 13*
2455 A933   2s shown   .15 .15
2456 A933 23s 2-man canoe   .42 .18

1977, Oct. 5 Photo. *Perf. 13*
2456A A933a 35s shown   .65 .15
2456B A933a 43s Rila Monastery   .80 .30
       Sheet contains 4 each plus label.

1977, Oct. 14 Photo. *Perf. 13*
2457 A934 13s olive, ocher & brown   .25 .15
  Centenary of visit by Russian physician N. J. Pirogov during war of liberation from Turkey.

Peace Decree, 1917 — A935
Old Soldier with Grandchild — A936 

  13s, Lenin, 1917. 23s, "1917" as a flame.

1977, Oct. 21
2458 A935   2s black, buff & red   .15 .15
2459 A935 13s multicolored   .24 .15
2460 A935 23s multicolored   .45 .15
       Nos. 2458-2460 (3)   .84 .45
  60th anniv. of Russian October Revolution.

1977, Sept. 30
  Designs (Festival Posters): 13s, "The Bugler." 23s, Liberation Monument, Sofia (detail). 25s, Samara flag.
2461 A936   2s multicolored   .15 .15
2462 A936 13s multicolored   .25 .15
2463 A936 23s multicolored   .42 .15
2464 A936 25s multicolored   .52 .22
       Nos. 2461-2464 (4)   1.34 .67
  Liberation from Turkish rule, centenary.

Souvenir Sheet

Games' and Sports Emblems — A937

1977, Aug. 10 Photo. *Perf. 13½x13*
2465 A937 1 l multicolored   1.50 1.25
  University Games '77, Sofia.

Conference Building — A938

1977, Sept. 12 *Perf. 13½*
2466 A938 23s multicolored   .40 .18
  64th Interparliamentary Union Conference, Sofia.

Bulgarian Worker's Newspaper, Anniversaries A939

1977, Sept. 12 Photo. *Perf. 13*
2467 A939   2s yel grn, blk & red   .15 .15

Ornament A940

  New Year 1978: 13s, Different ornament.

1977, Dec. 1
2468 A940   2s gold & multi   .15 .15
2469 A940 13s silver & multi   .26 .15

Railroad Bridge — A941

1977, Nov. 9
2470 A941 13s green, yel & gray   .30 .15
  Transport Organization, 50th anniversary.

A942  A943

1977, Nov. 15
2471 A942   8s gold & vio brn   .15 .15
  Petko Ratchev Slaveikov (1827-95), poet, birth sesquicentennial. No. 2471 printed in sheets of 8 stamps and 8 labels in 4 alternating vertical rows.

1978, Jan. 30 Photo. *Perf. 13*
  Designs: 23s, Soccer player and Games' emblem. 50s, Soccer players.
2472 A943 13s multicolored   .24 .15
2473 A943 23s multicolored   .45 .15

Souvenir Sheet
2474 A943 50s ultra & multi   1.00 .85
  11th World Cup Soccer Championship, Argentina, June 1-25.

Todor Zhivkov and Leonid I. Brezhnev — A944
Ostankino Tower, Moscow, Bulgarian Post Emblem — A945 

1977, Sept. 7 Photo. *Perf. 13*
2475 A944 18s gold, car & brn   .30 .15
  Bulgarian-Soviet Friendship. No. 2475 issued in sheets of 3 stamps and 3 labels.

1978, Mar. 1
2476 A945 13s multicolored   .25 .15
  20th anniversary of the Comecon Postal Organization (Council of Mutual Economic Assistance).

Leo Tolstoy — A946
Shipka Pass Monument — A947 

  5s, Fedor Dostoevski. 13s, Ivan Sergeevich Turgenev. 23s, Vasili Vasilievich Vershchagin. 25s, Giuseppe Garibaldi. 35s, Victor Hugo.

1978, Mar. 28 Photo. *Perf. 13*
2477 A946   2s yellow & dk grn   .15 .15
2478 A946   5s lemon & brown   .15 .15
2479 A946 13s tan & sl grn   .22 .15
2480 A946 23s gray & vio brn   .35 .15
2481 A946 25s yel grn & blk   .40 .15
2482 A946 35s lt bl & vio bl   .80 .38
       Nos. 2477-2482 (6)   2.07 1.13

Souvenir Sheet
2483 A947 50s multicolored   .80 .60
  Bulgaria's liberation from Ottoman rule, cent.

Bulgarian and Russian Colors A948

1978, Mar. 18
2484 A948   2s multicolored   .15 .15
  30th anniv. of Russo-Bulgarian co-operation.

Heart and WHO Emblem A949

1978, May 12
2485 A949 23s gray, red & org   .32 .15
  World Health Day, fight against hypertension.

Goddess A950

  Ceramics (2nd-4th Centuries) and Exhibition Emblem: 5s, Mask of bearded man. 13s, Vase. 23s, Vase. 35s, Head of Silenus. 53s, Cock.

1978, Apr. 26
2486 A950   2s green & multi   .15 .15
2487 A950   5s multicolored   .15 .15
2488 A950 13s multicolored   .26 .15
2489 A950 23s multicolored   .48 .16
2490 A950 35s multicolored   .75 .24
2491 A950 53s carmine & multi   1.25 .32
       Nos. 2486-2491 (6)   3.04 1.17
  Philaserdica Philatelic Exhibition.

Nikolai Roerich, by Svyatoslav Roerich — A951
"Mind and Matter," by Andrei Nikolov — A952 

1978, Apr. 5
2492 A951   8s multicolored   .16 .15
2493 A952 13s multicolored   .28 .15
  Nikolai K. Roerich (1874-1947) and Andrei Nikolov (1878-1959), artists.

Bulgarian Flag and Red Star — A953

1978, Apr. 18
2494 A953   2s vio blue & multi   .15 .15
  Bulgarian Communist Party Congress.

Young Man, by Albrecht Dürer A954

  Paintings: 23s, Bathsheba at Fountain, by Rubens. 25s, Portrait of a Man, by Hans Holbein the Younger. 35s, Rembrandt and Saskia, by Rembrandt. 43s, Lady in Mourning, by Tintoretto. 60s, Old Man with Beard, by Rembrandt. 80s, Knight in Armor, by Van Dyck.

1978, June 19 Photo. *Perf. 13*
2495 A954 13s multicolored   .16 .15
2496 A954 23s multicolored   .30 .15
2497 A954 25s multicolored   .32 .15
2498 A954 35s multicolored   .45 .15
2499 A954 43s multicolored   .55 .20
2500 A954 60s multicolored   .85 .26
2501 A954 80s multicolored   1.10 .38
       Nos. 2495-2501 (7)   3.73 1.44
  Dresden Art Gallery paintings.

Doves and Festival Emblem — A955

1978, May 31
2502 A955 13s multicolored   .25 .15
  11th World Youth Festival, Havana, 7/28-8/5.

BULGARIA

Fritillaria Stribrnyi — A956

Rare Flowers: 2s, Fritillaria drenovskyi. 3s, Lilium rhodopaeum. 13s, Tulipa urumoffii. 23s, Lilium jankae. 43s, Tulipa rhodopaea.

1978, June 27			
2503 A956	1s multicolored	.15	.15
2504 A956	2s multicolored	.15	.15
2505 A956	3s multicolored	.15	.15
2506 A956	13s multicolored	.26	.15
2507 A956	23s multicolored	.45	.15
2508 A956	43s multicolored	.90	.30
	Nos. 2503-2508 (6)	2.06	1.05

Yacht Cor Caroli and Map of Voyage — A957

1978, May 19 Photo. *Perf. 13*
2509 A957 23s multicolored .50 .18

First Bulgarian around-the-world voyage, Capt. Georgi Georgiev, Dec. 20, 1976-Dec. 20, 1977.

Market, by Naiden Petkov — A958

Views of Sofia: 5s, Street, by Emil Stoichev. 13s, Street, by Boris Ivanov. 23s, Tolbukhin Boulevard, by Nikola Tanev. 35s, National Theater, by Nikola Petrov. 53s, Market, by Anton Mitov.

1978, Aug. 28		Litho.	*Perf. 12½x12*
2510 A958	2s multicolored	.15	.15
2511 A958	5s multicolored	.15	.15
2512 A958	13s multicolored	.18	.15
2513 A958	23s multicolored	.30	.15
2514 A958	35s multicolored	.52	.18
2515 A958	53s multicolored	.85	.28
	Nos. 2510-2515 (6)	2.15	1.06

Miniature Sheet

Sleeping Venus, by Giorgione — A959

1978, Aug. 7 Photo. *Imperf.*
2516 A959 1 l multicolored 2.00 .85

View of Varna — A960

1978, July 13 Photo. *Perf. 13*
2517 A960 13s multicolored .25 .15

63rd Esperanto Cong., Varna, July 29-Aug. 5.

Black Woodpecker — A961

Woodpeckers: 2s, Syrian. 3s, Three-toed. 13s, Middle spotted. 23s, Lesser spotted. 43s, Green.

1978, Sept. 1			
2518 A961	1s multicolored	.15	.15
2519 A961	2s multicolored	.15	.15
2520 A961	3s multicolored	.15	.15
2521 A961	13s multicolored	.26	.15
2522 A961	23s multicolored	.42	.15
2523 A961	43s multicolored	1.10	.25
	Nos. 2518-2523 (6)	2.23	1.00

"September 1923" — A962

1978, Sept. 5
2524 A962 2s red & brn .25 .15

55th anniversary of September uprising.

Souvenir Sheet

National Theater, Sofia — A963

Photogravure and Engraved
1978, Sept. 1 *Perf. 12x11½*
2525 Sheet of 4 2.50 1.00
 a. A963 40s shown .60 .16
 b. A963 40s Festival Hall, Sofia .60 .16
 c. A963 40s Charles Bridge, Prague .60 .16
 d. A963 40s Belvedere Palace, Prague .60 .16

PRAGA '78 and PHILASERDICA '79 Philatelic Exhibitions.

Black and White Hands, Human Rights Emblem — A964

1978, Oct. 3 Photo. *Perf. 13x13½*
2526 A964 13s multicolored .25 .15

Anti-Apartheid Year.

Gotse Deltchev — A965

Bulgarian Calculator — A966

1978, Aug. 1 Photo. *Perf. 13*
2527 A965 13s multicolored .25 .15

Gotse Deltchev (1872-1903), patriot.

1978, Sept. 3
2528 A966 2s multicolored .15 .15

International Sample Fair, Plovdiv.

Guerrillas — A967

1978, Aug. 1
2529 A967 5s blk & rose red .15 .15

Ilinden and Preobrazhene revolts, 75th anniv.

"Pipe Line" and Flags — A968

1978, Oct. 3
2530 A968 13s multicolored .25 .15

Construction of gas pipe line from Orenburg to Russian border.

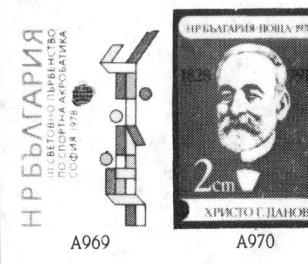

A969   A970

1978, Oct. 4 *Perf. 13x13½*
2531 A969 13s Three acrobats .25 .15

3rd World Acrobatic Championships, Sofia, Oct. 6-8.

1978, Sept. 18 Photo. *Perf. 13*
2532 A970 2s dp claret & ocher .15 .15

Christo G. Danov (1828-1911), 1st Bulgarian publisher. No. 2532 printed with se-tenant label showing early printing press.

Insurgents, by Todor Panajotov — A971

1978, Sept. 20
2533 A971 2s multicolored .15 .15

Vladaja mutiny, 60th anniversary.

A972   A973

1978, Oct. 11 Photo. *Perf. 13*
2534 A972 13s dk brn & org red .25 .15

Salvador Allende (1908-1973), president of Chile.

1978, Oct. 18
2535 A973 23s Human Rights flame .50 .20

Universal Declaration of Human Rights, 30th anniversary.

A974   A975

Burgarian Paintings: 1s, Levski and Matei Mitkaloto, by Kalina Tasseva. 2s, "Strength for my Arm" by Ziatyu Boyadjiev. 3s, Rumena, woman military leader, by Nikola Mirchev, horiz. 13s, Kolju Ficeto, by Elza Goeva. 23s, Family, National Revival Period, by Naiden Petkov.

		Perf. 12x12½, 12½x12	
1978, Oct. 25			Litho.
2536 A974	1s multicolored	.15	.15
2537 A974	2s multicolored	.15	.15
2538 A974	3s multicolored	.15	.15
2539 A974	13s multicolored	.24	.15
2540 A974	23s multicolored	.42	.15
	Nos. 2536-2540 (5)	1.11	.75

1300th anniversary of Bulgaria (in 1981).

1978, Nov. 1 Photo. *Perf. 13*

Designs: a, Tourism building, Plovdiv. b, Chrelo Tower, Rila Cloister.

Souvenir Sheet
2541 Sheet of 5 + label 4.00 2.00
 a. A975 43s multicolored .70 .28
 b. A975 43s multicolored .70 .28

Conservation of European architectural heritage. No. 2541 contains 3 No. 2541a & 2 No. 2541b.

Ferry, Map of Black Sea with Route — A976

1978, Nov. 1 Photo. *Perf. 13*
2542 A976 13s multicolored .25 .15

Opening of Ilychovsk-Varna Ferry.

Bird, from Marble Floor, St. Sofia Church — A977

1978, Nov. 20
2543 A977 5s multicolored .15 .15

3rd Bulgaria '78, National Philatelic Exhibition, Sofia. Printed se-tenant with label showing emblems of Bulgaria '78 and Philaserdica '79.

BULGARIA

Initial, 13th Century Gospel — A978

Designs: 13s, St. Cyril, miniature, 1567. 23s, Book cover, 16th century. 80s, St. Methodius, miniature, 13th century.

1978, Dec. 15   Photo.   *Perf. 13*
2544	A978	2s multicolored	.15	.15
2545	A978	13s multicolored	.20	.15
2546	A978	23s multicolored	.35	.15
	Nos. 2544-2546 (3)		.70	.45

Souvenir Sheet
2547	A978	80s multicolored	1.25	1.00

Cent. of the Cyril and Methodius Natl. Library.

Bulgaria No. 53 A979

Bulgarian Stamps: 13s, #534. 23s, #968. 35s, #1176, vert. 53s, #1223, vert. 1 l, #1.

1978, Dec. 30
2548	A979	2s ol grn & red	.15	.15
2549	A979	13s ultra & rose car	.18	.15
2550	A979	23s rose lil & ol grn	.32	.15
2551	A979	35s brt bl & blk	.48	.20
2552	A979	53s ver & sl grn	.90	.32
	Nos. 2548-2552 (5)		2.03	.97

Souvenir Sheet
2553	A979	1 l multicolored	1.50	1.25

Philaserdica '79, International Philatelic Exhibition, Sofia, May 18-27, 1979, and centenary of Bulgarian stamps. No. 2553 exists imperf. See Nos. 2560-2564.

St. Clement of Ochrida — A980

1978, Dec. 8
2554	A980	2s multicolored	.15	.15

Clement of Ochrida University, 90th anniv.

Ballet Dancers A981

1978, Dec. 22
2555	A981	13s multicolored	.30	.15

Bulgarian ballet, 50th anniversary.

Get free stamps every month! A subscription to the "Scott Stamp Monthly" entitles you to write in for each month's free offer. The value of the free stamps more than offsets the subscription cost. For more information, please call 1-800-572-6885.

Nikola Karastojanov A982

1978, Dec. 12
2556	A982	2s multicolored	.15	.15

Nikola Karastojanov (1778-1874), printer. No. 2556 printed se-tenant with label showing printing press.

Christmas Tree Made of Birds A983

1978, Dec. 22
2557	A983	2s shown	.15	.15
2558	A983	13s Post horn	.20	.15

New Year 1979.

COMECON Building, Moscow, Members' Flags — A984

1979, Jan. 25   Photo.   *Perf. 13*
2559	A984	13s multicolored	.25	.15

Council for Mutual Economic Aid (COMECON), 30th anniversary.

Philaserdica Type of 1978
Designs as Before

1979, Jan. 30
2560	A979	2s brt bl & red	.15	.15
2561	A979	13s grn & dk car	.18	.15
2562	A979	23s org brn & multi	.32	.15
2563	A979	35s dl red & blk	.50	.22
2564	A979	53s vio & dk ol	.90	.35
	Nos. 2560-2564 (5)		2.05	1.02

Philaserdica '79.

Bank Building, Commemorative Coin — A985

1979, Feb. 13
2565	A985	2s yel, gray & silver	.15	.15

Centenary of Bulgarian People's Bank.

Aleksandr Stamboliski A986

1979, Feb. 28
2566	A986	2s orange & dk brn	.15	.15

Aleksandr Stamboliski (1879-1923), leader of peasant's party and premier.

Flower with Child's Face, IYC Emblem — A987

1979, Mar. 8
2568	A987	23s multicolored	.40	.15

International Year of the Child.

Stylized Heads, World Association Emblem — A988

1979, Mar. 20
2569	A988	13s multicolored	.25	.15

8th World Cong. for the Deaf, Varna, June 20-27.

"75" and Trade Union Emblem — A989

1979, Mar. 20
2570	A989	2s slate grn & org	.15	.15

75th anniversary of Bulgarian Trade Unions.

Souvenir Sheet

Sculptures in Sofia — A990

Designs: 2s, Soviet Army Monument (detail). 5s, Mother and Child, Central Railroad Station. 13s, 23s, 25s, Bas-relief from Monument of the Liberators.

1979, Apr. 2   Photo.   *Perf. 13*
2571	A990	Sheet of 5 + label	1.25	.60
a.		2s multicolored		.15
b.		5s multicolored		.15
c.		13s multicolored		.22
d.		23s multicolored		.38
e.		25s multicolored		.48

Centenary of Sofia as capital.

Rocket Launch, Space Flight Emblems — A991

Designs (Intercosmos and Bulgarian-USSR Flight Emblems and): 25s, Link-up, horiz. 35s, Parachute descent. 1 l, Globe, emblems and orbit, horiz.

1979, Apr. 11
2572	A991	12s multicolored	.20	.15
2573	A991	25s multicolored	.45	.15
2574	A991	35s multicolored	.60	.22
	Nos. 2572-2574 (3)		1.25	.52

Souvenir Sheet
2575	A991	1 l multicolored	1.50	.75

1st Bulgarian cosmonaut on Russian space flight. A slightly larger imperf. sheet similar to No. 2575 with control numbers at bottom and rockets at sides exists.

Nicolai Rukavishnikov — A992

Design: 13s, Rukavishnikov and Soviet cosmonaut Georgi Ivanov.

1979, May 14   Photo.   *Perf. 13*
2576	A992	2s multicolored	.15	.15
2577	A992	13s multicolored	.32	.15

Col. Rukavishnikov, 1st Bulgarian astronaut.

Souvenir Sheet

Thracian Gold-leaf Collar — A993

1979, May 16
2578	A993	1 l multicolored	2.00	1.50

48th International Philatelic Federation Congress, Sofia, May 16-17.

Post Horn, Carrier Pigeon, Jet, Globes and UPU Emblem — A994

Designs (Post Horn, Globes and ITU Emblem): 5s, 1st Bulgarian and modern telephones. 13s, Morse key and teleprinter. 23s, Old radio transmitter and radio towers. 35s, Bulgarian TV tower and satellite. 50s, Ground receiving station

BULGARIA

1979, May 8   *Perf. 13½x13*
2579	A994	2s multicolored	.15 .15
2580	A994	5s multicolored	.15 .15
2581	A994	20s multicolored	.20 .15
2582	A994	23s multicolored	.38 .15
2583	A994	35s multicolored	.60 .22
		Nos. 2579-2583 (5)	1.48 .82

Souvenir Sheet
Perf. 13
2584 A994 50s vio, blk & gray   1.00 .65

Intl. Telecommunications Day and cent. of Bulgarian Postal & Telegraph Services. Size of stamp in #2584: 39x28mm. #2584 exists imperf.

Hotel Vitosha-New Otani — A996

1979, May 20
2586 A996 2s ultra & pink   .15 .15

Philaserdica '79 Day.

Horseman Receiving Gifts, by Karellia and Boris Kuklievi — A997

1979, May 23
2587 A997 2s multicolored   .15 .15

Bulgarian-Russian Friendship Day.

A998   A999

Design: Man on Donkey, by Boris Angeloushev.

1979, May 23   *Photo.*   *Perf. 13½*
2588 A998 2s multicolored   .15 .15

12th National Festival of Humor and Satire, Gabrovo.

Lithographed and Engraved
1979, May 31   *Perf. 14x13½*

Durer Engravings: 13s, Four Women. 23s, Three Peasants. 25s, The Cook and his Wife. 35s, Portrait of Helius Eobanus Hessus. 80s, Rhinoceros, horiz.

2589	A999	13s multicolored	.24 .15
2590	A999	23s multicolored	.40 .15
2591	A999	25s multicolored	.45 .15
2592	A999	35s multicolored	.65 .18
		Nos. 2589-2592 (4)	1.74 .63

Souvenir Sheet
Imperf
2593 A999 80s multicolored   1.50 1.25

Albrecht Durer (1471-1528), German engraver and painter.

R. Todorov (1879-1916) — A1000

Bulgarian Writers: No. 2595, Dimitri Dymov (1909-1966). No. 2596, S. A. Kostov (1879-1939).

1979, June 26   *Photo.*   *Perf. 13*
2594	A1000	2s multicolored	.15 .15
2595	A1000	2s slate grn & yel grn	.15 .15
2596	A1000	2s dp claret & yel	.15 .15
		Nos. 2594-2596 (3)	.45 .45

Nos. 2594-2596 each printed se-tenant with label showing title page or character from writer's work.

Moscow '80 Emblem, Runners — A1001

Moscow '80 Emblem and: 13s, Pole vault, horiz. 25s, Discus. 35s, Hurdles, horiz. 43s, High jump, horiz. 1 l, Long jump.

1979, May 15   *Perf. 13*
2597	A1001	2s multicolored	.15 .15
2598	A1001	13s multicolored	.20 .15
2599	A1001	25s multicolored	.40 .15
2600	A1001	35s multicolored	.80 .24
2601	A1001	43s multicolored	1.00 .30
2602	A1001	1 l multicolored	2.25 .65
		Nos. 2597-2602 (6)	4.80 1.64

Souvenir Sheet
2602A A1001 2 l multicolored   6.00 3.25

22nd Summer Olympic Games, Moscow, July 19-Aug. 3, 1980.

Rocket — A1002

5s, Flags of USSR and Bulgaria. 13s, "35."

1979, Sept. 4   *Photo.*
2603	A1002	2s multicolored	.15 .15
2604	A1002	5s multicolored	.15 .15
2605	A1002	13s multicolored	.18 .15
		Nos. 2603-2605 (3)	.48 .45

35th anniversary of liberation.

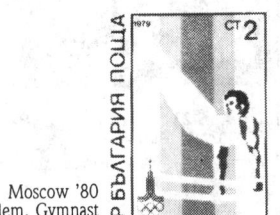

Moscow '80 Emblem, Gymnast — A1003

Moscow '80 Emblem & gymnasts. 13s horiz.

1979, July 31   *Photo.*   *Perf. 13*
2606	A1003	2s multicolored	.15 .15
2607	A1003	13s multicolored	.20 .15
2608	A1003	25s multicolored	.48 .15
2609	A1003	35s multicolored	.75 .22
2610	A1003	43s multicolored	1.00 .25
2611	A1003	1 l multicolored	2.25 .80
		Nos. 2606-2611 (6)	4.83 1.72

Souvenir Sheet
2612 A1003 2 l multicolored   6.00 3.25

22nd Summer Olympic Games, Moscow, July 19-Aug. 3, 1980.

A1004   A1005

1979, July 8   *Photo.*   *Perf. 13*
2613 A1004 13s ultra & blk   .18 .15

Theater Institute, 18th Congress.

1979, July 17
2614 A1005 8s multicolored   .15 .15

Journalists' Vacation House, Varna, 20th Anniv.

Icon Type of 1977

Virgin and Child by: 13s, 23s, Nesebar, 16th cent., diff. 35s, 43s, Sozopol, 16th cent., diff. 53s, Samokov, 19th cent. Inscribed 1979.

1979, Aug. 7   *Litho.*   *Perf. 12½*
2615	A917	13s multicolored	.20 .15
2616	A917	23s multicolored	.35 .15
2617	A917	35s multicolored	.50 .15
2618	A917	43s multicolored	.60 .16
2619	A917	53s multicolored	.85 .24
		Nos. 2615-2619 (5)	2.50 .85

A1006   A1007

1979, Aug. 9   *Photo.*   *Perf. 13x13½*
2620 A1006 2s Anton Besenschek   .15 .15

Bulgarian stenography centenary.

1979, Aug. 28   *Perf. 13*
2621 A1007 2s multicolored   .15 .15

Bulgarian Alpine Club, 50th anniv.

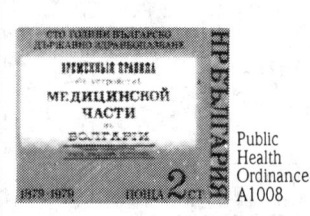

Public Health Ordinance — A1008

1979, Aug. 31   *Perf. 13½*
2622 A1008 2s multicolored   .15 .15

Public Health Service centenary. No. 2622 printed with label showing Dimitar Mollov, founder.

Isotope Measuring Device — A1009

1979, Sept. 8   *Perf. 13½x13*
2623 A1009 2s multicolored   .15 .15

International Sample Fair, Plovdiv.

Games' Emblem — A1010

1979, Sept. 20   *Perf. 13*
2624 A1010 5s multicolored   .15 .15

Universiada '79, World University Games, Mexico City, Sept.

Sofia Locomotive Sports Club, 50th Anniversary — A1011

1979, Oct. 2
2625 A1011 2s blue & org red   .15 .15

Ljuben Karavelov (1837-1879), Poet and Freedom Fighter — A1012

1979, Oct. 4   *Photo.*   *Perf. 13*
2626 A1012 2s blue & slate grn   .15 .15

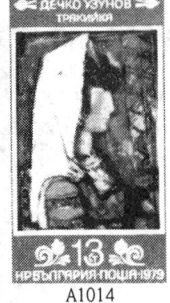

A1013   A1014

1979, Oct. 20
2627	A1013	2s Biathlon	.15 .15
2628	A1013	13s Speed skating	.22 .15
2629	A1013	23s Downhill skiing	.38 .15
2630	A1013	43s Luge	.75 .22
		Nos. 2627-2630 (4)	1.50 .67

Souvenir Sheet
Imperf
2631 A1013 1 l Slalom   1.75 1.10

13th Winter Olympic Games, Lake Placid, NY, Feb. 12-24.

BULGARIA

1979, Oct. 31 *Perf. 14*
Decko Uzunov, 80th Birthday: 12s, Apparition in Red. 13s, Woman from Thrace. 23s, Composition.

2632	A1014	12s multicolored	.24	.15
2633	A1014	13s multicolored	.24	.15
2634	A1014	23s multicolored	.38	.15
		Nos. 2632-2634 (3)	.86	.45

Swimming, Moscow '80 Emblem — A1016

1979, Nov. 30 *Photo.* *Perf. 13*

2636	A1016	2s Two-man kayak, vert.	.15	.15
2637	A1016	13s Swimming, vert.	.18	.15
2638	A1016	25s shown	.40	.15
2639	A1016	35s One-man kayak	.80	.20
2640	A1016	43s Diving, vert	1.00	.40
2641	A1016	1 l Diving, vert., diff.	2.25	.70
		Nos. 2636-2641 (6)	4.78	1.75

Souvenir Sheet

| 2642 | A1016 | 2 l Water polo, vert. | 6.00 | 3.25 |

22nd Summer Olympic Games, Moscow, July 19-Aug. 3, 1980.

Nikola Vapzarov — A1017

1979, Dec. 7 *Photo.* *Perf. 13*

| 2643 | A1017 | 2s claret & rose | .15 | .15 |

Vapzarov (1909-1942), poet and freedom fighter. No. 2643 printed with label showing smokestacks.

The First Socialists, by Bojan Petrov — A1018

Paintings: 13s, Demeter Blagoev Reading Newspaper, by Demeter Gjudshenov, 1892. 25s, Workers' Party March, by Sotir Sotirov, 1917. 35s, Dawn in Plovdiv, by Johann Leviev, vert.

Perf. 12½x12, 12x12½

1979, Dec. 10 *Litho.*

2644	A1018	2s multicolored	.15	.15
2645	A1018	13s multicolored	.22	.15
2646	A1018	25s multicolored	.38	.15
2647	A1018	35s multicolored	.55	.15
		Nos. 2644-2647 (4)	1.30	.60

Sharpshooting, Moscow '80 Emblem — A1019

1979, Dec. 22 *Photo.* *Perf. 13*

2648	A1019	2s shown	.15	.15
2649	A1019	13s Judo, horiz.	.20	.15
2650	A1019	25s Wrestling, horiz.	.40	.16
2651	A1019	35s Archery	.80	.25
2652	A1019	43s Fencing, horiz.	1.00	.50
2653	A1019	1 l Fencing	2.25	.90
		Nos. 2648-2653 (6)	4.80	2.11

Souvenir Sheet

| 2654 | A1019 | 2 l Boxing | 6.00 | 4.00 |

Procession with Relics, 11th Century Fresco — A1020

Frescoes of Sts. Cyril and Methodius, St. Clement's Basilica, Rome: 13s, Reception by Pope Hadrian II. 23s, Burial of Cyril the Philosopher, 18th century. 25s, St. Cyril. 35s, St. Methodius.

1979, Dec. 25

2655	A1020	2s multicolored	.15	.15
2656	A1020	13s multicolored	.24	.15
2657	A1020	23s multicolored	.42	.15
2658	A1020	25s multicolored	.45	.15
2659	A1020	35s multicolored	.65	.18
		Nos. 2655-2659 (5)	1.91	.78

Bulgarian Television Emblem — A1021

1979, Dec. 29 *Perf. 13½*

| 2660 | A1021 | 5s violet bl & lt bl | .15 | .15 |

Bulgarian television, 25th anniversary. No. 2660 printed with label showing Sofia television tower.

Doves in Girl's Hair — A1022

Design: 2s, Children's heads, mosaic, vert.

1979 *Perf. 13*

| 2661 | A1022 | 2s multicolored | .15 | .15 |
| 2662 | A1022 | 13s multicolored | .16 | .15 |

International Year of the Child. Issue dates: 2s, July 17; 13s, Dec. 14.

Puppet on Horseback, IYC Emblem — A1023

Thracian Rider, Votive Tablet, 3rd Century — A1024

1980, Jan. 22 *Photo.* *Perf. 13*

| 2663 | A1023 | 2s multicolored | .15 | .15 |

UNIMA, Intl. Puppet Theater Organization, 50th anniv. (1979); Intl. Year of the Child (1979).

1980, Jan. 29 *Photo.* *Perf. 13x13½*

National Archaeological Museum Centenary; 13s, Deines stele, 5th century B.C.

| 2664 | A1024 | 2s brown & gold | .15 | .15 |
| 2665 | A1024 | 13s multicolored | .20 | .15 |

Dimitrov Meeting Lenin in Moscow, by Alexander Poplilov — A1026

1980, Mar. 28 *Perf. 12x12½*

| 2667 | A1026 | 13s multicolored | .20 | .15 |

Lenin, 110th birth anniversary.

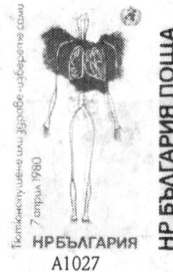

A1027   A1027a

Circulatory system, lungs enveloped in smoke.

1980, Apr. 7 *Perf. 13*

| 2668 | A1027 | 5s multicolored | .15 | .15 |

World Health Day fight against cigarette smoking.

1980, Apr. 10 *Photo.* *Perf. 13*

2669	A1027a	2s Basketball	.15	.15
2670	A1027a	13s Soccer	.18	.15
2671	A1027a	25s Hockey	.40	.15
2672	A1027a	35s Cycling	.80	.20
2673	A1027a	43s Handball	1.00	.40
2674	A1027a	1 l Volleyball	2.25	.70
		Nos. 2669-2674 (6)	4.78	1.75

Souvenir Sheet

| 2675 | A1027a | 2 l Weightlifting | 6.50 | 4.25 |

Intercosmos Emblem, Cosmonauts — A1028

1980, Apr. 22 *Perf. 12*

| 2676 | A1028 | 50s multicolored | 1.00 | .45 |

Intercosmos cooperative space program.

Penio Penev (1930-1959), Poet — A1029

1980, Apr. 22 *Photo.* *Perf. 13*

| 2677 | A1029 | 5s multicolored | .15 | .15 |

Se-tenant with label showing quote from author's work.

Penny Black — A1030

1980, Apr. 24 *Perf. 13*

| 2678 | A1030 | 25s dark red & sepia | .60 | .45 |

London 1980 International Stamp Exhibition, May 6-14; printed se-tenant with label showing Rowland Hill between every two stamps.

Demeter H. Tchorbadjiiski, Self-portrait — A1031

1980, Apr. 29

| 2679 | A1031 | 5s shown | .15 | .15 |
| 2680 | A1031 | 13s "Our People" | .18 | .15 |

Nikolai Giaurov — A1032   Raising Red Flag Reichstag Building, Berlin — A1033

1980, Apr. 30

| 2681 | A1032 | 5s multicolored | .15 | .15 |

Nikolai Giaurov (b. 1930), opera singer; printed se-tenant with label showing Boris Godunov.

1980, May 6 *Perf. 13x13½*

Armistice, 35th Anniversary: 13s, Soviet Army memorial, Berlin-Treptow.

| 2682 | A1033 | 5s multicolored | .15 | .15 |
| 2683 | A1033 | 13s multicolored | .18 | .15 |

Numeral — A1034

1979 *Perf. 14*

| 2684 | A1034 | 2s ultra | .15 | .15 |
| 2685 | A1034 | 5s rose car | .15 | .15 |

BULGARIA

A1034a   A1035

1980, May 12   Photo.   Perf. 13
2685A A1034a 5s multicolored .15 .15
75th Anniv. of Teachers' Union.

1980, May 14   Photo.   Perf. 13
2686 A1035 13s multicolored .20 .15
Warsaw Pact, 25th anniv.

A1036   A1037

Statues.

1980, June 10
2687 A1036 2s multicolored .15 .15
2688 A1036 13s multicolored .18 .15
2689 A1036 25s multicolored .40 .15
2690 A1036 35s multicolored .80 .30
2691 A1036 43s multicolored 1.00 .60
2692 A1036 1 l multicolored 2.25 1.10
Nos. 2687-2692 (6) 4.78 2.45

Souvenir Sheet
2693 A1036 2 l multicolored 6.00 3.25
22nd Summer Olympic Games, Moscow, July 19-Aug. 3.

1980, Sept.   Photo.   Perf. 13
2694 A1037 13s multicolored .25 .15
10th Intl. Ballet Competition, Varna.

Hotel Europa, Sofia A1038

Hotels: No. 2696, Bulgaria, Burgas, vert. No. 2697, Plovdiv, Plovdiv. No. 2698, Riga, Russe, vert. No. 2699, Varna, Djuba.

1980, July 11
2695 A1038 23s lt ultra & multi .30 .15
2696 A1038 23s orange & multi .30 .15
2697 A1038 23s gray & multi .30 .15
2698 A1038 23s blue & multi .30 .15
2699 A1038 23s yellow & multi .30 .15
Nos. 2695-2699 (5) 1.50 .75
See No. 2766.

Ship Type of 1975

Ships of 16th, 17th Centuries: 5s, Christ of Lubeck, galleon. 8s, Roman galley. 13s, Eagle, Russian galleon. 23s, Mayflower. 35s, Maltese galley. 53s, Royal Louis, galleon.

1980, July 14
2700 A873 5s multicolored .15 .15
2701 A873 8s multicolored .15 .15
2702 A873 13s multicolored .25 .15
2703 A873 23s multicolored .45 .18
2704 A873 35s multicolored .70 .20
2705 A873 53s multicolored 1.10 .35
Nos. 2700-2705 (6) 2.80 1.18

Int'l Year of the Child, 1979 — A1040

Designs: Children's drawings and IYC emblem. 43s, Tower. 5s, 25s, 43s, vert.

1980 Litho.   Perf. 12½x12, 12x12½
2708 A1040 3s multicolored .15 .15
2709 A1040 5s multicolored .15 .15
2710 A1040 13s multicolored .20 .15
2711 A1040 13s multicolored .20 .15
2712 A1040 25s multicolored .38 .15
2713 A1040 35s multicolored .52 .15
2714 A1040 43s multicolored .65 .18
Nos. 2708-2714 (7) 2.20 1.08

Helicopter, Missile Transport, Tank — A1041

1980, Sept. 23   Photo.   Perf. 13
2715 A1041 3s shown .15 .15
2716 A1041 5s Jet, radar, rocket .15 .15
2717 A1041 8s Helicopter, ships .16 .15
Nos. 2715-2717 (3) .46 .45
Bulgarian People's Army, 35th anniversary.

St. Anne, by Leonardo da Vinci A1042

Da Vinci Paintings: 8s, 13s, Annunciation (diff.). 25s, Adoration of the Kings. 35s, Lady with the Ermine. 50s, Mona Lisa.

1980, Nov.
2718 A1042 5s multicolored .15 .15
2719 A1042 8s multicolored .15 .15
2720 A1042 13s multicolored .20 .15
2721 A1042 25s multicolored .38 .15
2722 A1042 35s multicolored .55 .18
Nos. 2718-2722 (5) 1.43 .78

Souvenir Sheet
Imperf
2723 A1042 50s multicolored 1.00 .35

International Peace Conference, Sofia — A1043

1980, Sept. 4   Photo.   Perf. 13
2724 A1043 25s multicolored .35 .15

Jordan Jowkov (1880-1937), Writer — A1044

1980, Sept. 19
2725 A1044 5s multicolored .15 .15
Se-tenant with label showing scene from Jowkov's work.

International Samples Fair, Plovdiv — A1045

1980, Sept. 24   Perf. 13½x13
2726 A1045 5s multicolored .15 .15

Blooming Cacti — A1045a

1980, Nov. 4   Photo.   Perf. 13
2726A A1045a 5s multicolored .15 .15
2726B A1045a 13s multicolored .20 .15
2726C A1045a 25s multicolored .42 .16
2726D A1045a 35s multicolored .60 .25
2726E A1045a 53s multicolored 1.00 .32
Nos. 2726A-2726E (5) 2.37 1.03

Souvenir Sheet

25th Anniv. of Bulgarian UN Membership — A1045b

1980, Nov. 25
2726F A1045b 60s multicolored 2.25 2.00

World Ski Racing Championship, Velingrad — A1046

1981, Jan. 17   Photo.   Perf. 13
2727 A1046 43s multicolored .60 .22

Hawthorn — A1047   Slalom — A1048

Designs: Medicinal herbs.

1981, Jan.
2728 A1047 3s shown .15 .15
2729 A1047 5s St. John's wort .15 .15
2730 A1047 13s Common elder .20 .15
2731 A1047 25s Blackberries .38 .15
2732 A1047 35s Lime .55 .20
2733 A1047 43s Wild briar .65 .24
Nos. 2728-2733 (6) 2.08 1.04

1981, Feb. 27   Photo.   Perf. 13
2734 A1048 43s multicolored .60 .25
Evian Alpine World Ski Cup Championship, Borovets.

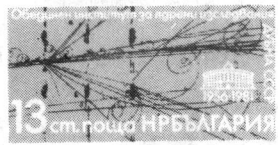

Nuclear Traces, Research Institute — A1049

1981, Mar. 10   Perf. 13½x13
2735 A1049 13s gray & blk .20 .15
Nuclear Research Institute, Dubna, USSR, 25th anniversary.

Congress Emblem A1050

1981, Mar. 12   Perf. 13½
2736 A1050 5s shown .15 .15
2737 A1050 13s Stars .20 .15
2738 A1050 23s Teletape .35 .15
Nos. 2736-2738 (3) .70 .45

Souvenir Sheet
2739 A1050 50s Demeter Blagoev, George Dimitrov .80 .48
12th Bulgarian Communist Party Congress. Nos. 2736-2738 each printed se-tenant with label.

Paintings by Zachary Zograf — A1050a

1981, Mar. 23   Photo.   Perf. 12x12½
2739A A1050a 5s multicolored .15 .15
2739B A1050a 13s multicolored .22 .15
2739C A1050a 23s multicolored .42 .15
2739D A1050a 25s multicolored .48 .15
2739E A1050a 35s multicolored .70 .18
Nos. 2739A-2739E (5) 1.97 .78

Nos. 2739A-2739C are vert.

811

BULGARIA

EXPO '81, Plovdiv — A1050b

1981, Apr. 7
2739F	A1050b	5s multicolored	.15	.15
2739G	A1050b	8s multicolored	.15	.15
2739H	A1050b	13s multicolored	.25	.15
2739J	A1050b	25s multicolored	.45	.15
2739K	A1050b	53s multicolored	1.00	.24
	Nos. 2739F-2739K (5)		2.00	.84

Centenary of Bulgarian Shipbuilding — A1050c

1981, Apr. 15 Photo. Perf. 13
2739L	A1050c	35s Georgi Dimitrov, liner	.55	.20
2739M	A1050c	43s 5th from RMS, freighter	.65	.25
2739N	A1050c	53s Khan Asparuch, tanker	.80	.28
	Nos. 2739L-2739N (3)		2.00	.73

Arabian Horse — A1051

1980, Nov. 27 Litho. Perf. 12½x12
2740	A1051	3s multicolored	.15	.15
2741	A1051	5s multicolored	.15	.15
2742	A1051	13s multicolored	.30	.15
2743	A1051	23s multicolored	.45	.15
2744	A1051	35s multicolored	.75	.20
	Nos. 2740-2744 (5)		1.80	.80

Vassil Stoin, Ethnologist, Birth Centenary — A1052

1980, Dec. 5 Photo. Perf. 13½x13
| 2745 | A1052 | 5s multicolored | .15 | .15 |

12th Bulgarian Communist Party Congress — A1052a

1980, Dec. 26 Photo. Perf. 13x13½
| 2745A | A1052a | 5s Party symbols | .15 | .15 |

New Year — A1053

1980, Dec. 8 Perf. 13
| 2746 | A1053 | 5s shown | .15 | .15 |
| 2747 | A1053 | 13s Cup, date | .18 | .15 |

Culture Palace, Sofia — A1053a

1981, Mar. 13 Photo. Perf. 13
| 2747A | A1053a | 5s multicolored | .15 | .15 |

Vienna Hofburg Palace — A1054

1981, May 15 Photo. Perf. 13
| 2748 | A1054 | 35s multicolored | .45 | .18 |

WIPA 1981 Intl. Philatelic Exhibition, Vienna, May 22-31.

34th Farmers' Union Congress — A1055

1981, May 18 Perf. 13½
2749	A1055	5s shown	.15	.15
2750	A1055	8s Flags	.15	.15
2751	A1055	13s Flags, diff.	.20	.15
	Nos. 2749-2751 (3)		.50	.45

Wild Cat — A1056

1981, May 27
2752	A1056	5s shown	.15	.15
2753	A1056	13s Boar	.22	.15
2754	A1056	23s Mouflon	.40	.15
2755	A1056	25s Mountain goat	.45	.15
2756	A1056	35s Stag	.60	.18
2757	A1056	53s Roe deer	1.00	.26
	Nos. 2752-2757 (6)		2.82	1.04

Souvenir Sheet Perf. 13½x13
| 2758 | A1056 | 1 l Stag, diff. | 1.65 | .85 |

EXPO '81 Intl. Hunting Exhibition, Plovdiv. Nos. 2752-2757 each se-tenant with labels showing various hunting rifles. No. 2758 contains one stamp, size: 48½x39mm.

25th Anniv. of UNESCO Membership — A1057

1981, June 11 Perf. 13
| 2759 | A1057 | 13s multicolored | .20 | .15 |

Hotel Type of 1980

1981, July 13 Photo. Perf. 13
| 2766 | A1038 | 23s Veliko Tirnovo Hotel | .35 | .15 |

Flying Figure, Sculpture by Velichko Minekov — A1059

Bulgarian Social Democratic Party Buzludja Congress, 90th Anniv. (Minkov Sculpture): 13s, Advancing Female Figure.

1981, July 16 Perf. 13½
| 2767 | A1059 | 5s multicolored | .15 | .15 |
| 2768 | A1059 | 13s multicolored | .18 | .15 |

Kukeri, by Georg Tschapkanov — A1060

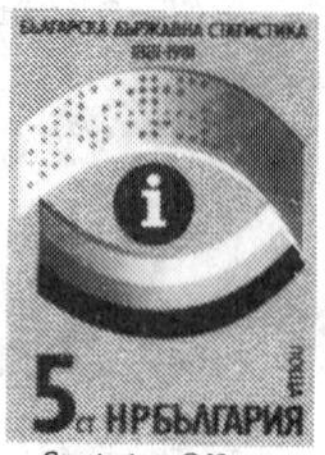

Statistics Office Centenary — A1061

1981, May 28 Photo. Perf. 13
| 2769 | A1060 | 5s multicolored | .15 | .15 |

13th Natl. Festival of Humor and Satire.

1981, June 9
| 2770 | A1061 | 5s multicolored | .15 | .15 |

Gold Dish — A1063

Designs: Goldsmiths' works, 7th-9th cent.

1981, July 21
2772	A1063	5s multicolored	.15	.15
2773	A1063	13s multicolored	.20	.15
2774	A1063	23s multicolored	.35	.22
2775	A1063	25s multicolored	.40	.25
2776	A1063	35s multicolored	.55	.35
2777	A1063	53s multicolored	.90	.38
	Nos. 2772-2777 (6)		2.55	1.50

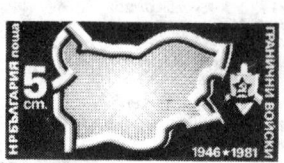

35th Anniv. of Frontier Force — A1064

1981, July 28 Perf. 13½x13
| 2778 | A1064 | 5s multicolored | .15 | .15 |

1300th Anniv. of First Bulgarian State — A1065

Designs: No. 2779, Sts. Cyril and Methodius. No. 2780, 9th cent. bas-relief. 8s, Floor plan, Round Church, Preslav, 10th cent. 12s, Four Evangelists of King Ivan Alexander, miniature, 1356. No. 2783, King Ivan Asen II memorial column. No. 2784, Warriors on horseback. 16s, April uprising, 1876. 23s, Russian liberators, Tirnovo. 25s, Social Democratic Party founding, 1891. 35s, September uprising, 1923. 41s, Fatherland Front. 43s, Prime Minister George Dimitrov, 5th Communist Party Congress, 1948. 50s, Lion, 10th cent. bas-relief. 53s, 10th Communist Party Congress. 55s,

Kremikovski Metalurgical Plant. 1 l, Brezhnev, Gen. Todor Zhivkov.

1981, Aug. 10
2779	A1065	5s multicolored	.15	.15
2780	A1065	5s multicolored	.15	.15
2781	A1065	8s multicolored	.15	.15
2782	A1065	12s multicolored	.18	.15
2783	A1065	13s multicolored	.18	.15
2784	A1065	13s multicolored	.18	.15
2785	A1065	16s multicolored	.22	.15
2786	A1065	23s multicolored	.30	.15
2787	A1065	25s multicolored	.35	.15
2788	A1065	35s multicolored	.48	.20
2789	A1065	41s multicolored	.55	.22
2790	A1065	43s multicolored	.60	.24
2791	A1065	53s multicolored	.75	.30
2792	A1065	55s multicolored	.75	.30
	Nos. 2779-2792 (14)		4.99	2.61

Souvenir Sheets
| 2793 | A1065 | 50s multicolored | .90 | .55 |
| 2794 | A1065 | 1 l multicolored | 1.90 | 1.10 |

European Volleyball Championship — A1066

1981, Sept. 16 Perf. 13
| 2795 | A1066 | 13s multicolored | .20 | .15 |

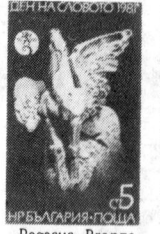

Pegasus, Bronze Sculpture (Word Day) — A1067

World Food Day — A1068

1981, Oct. 2
| 2796 | A1067 | 5s olive & cream | .15 | .15 |

1981, Oct. 16
| 2797 | A1068 | 13s multicolored | .16 | .15 |

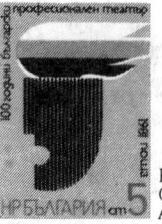

Professional Theater Centenary — A1069

1981, Oct. 30
| 2798 | A1069 | 5s multicolored | .15 | .15 |

Anti-Apartheid Year — A1070

1981, Dec. 2
| 2799 | A1070 | 5s multicolored | .15 | .15 |

BULGARIA

Espana '82 World Cup Soccer — A1071

Designs: Various soccer players.

1981, Dec.
2800	A1071	5s multicolored	.15	.15
2801	A1071	13s multicolored	.24	.18
2802	A1071	43s multicolored	.70	.24
2803	A1071	53s multicolored	.95	.35
		Nos. 2800-2803 (4)	2.04	.92

Heritage Day A1072

1981, Nov. 21   Photo.   Perf. 13
| 2804 | A1072 | 13s multicolored | .20 | .15 |

Souvenir Sheet
| 2804A | A1072 | 60s multicolored | 4.25 | 1.10 |

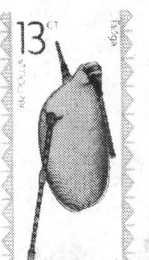

Bagpipe — A1073   Public Libraries and Reading Rooms, 125th Anniv — A1074

1982, Jan. 14
2805	A1073	13s shown	.20	.15
2806	A1073	25s Flutes	.40	.18
2807	A1073	30s Rebec	.50	.20
2808	A1073	35s Flute, recorder	.55	.24
2809	A1073	44s Mandolin	.75	.30
		Nos. 2805-2809 (5)	2.40	1.07

1982, Jan. 20
| 2810 | A1074 | 5s dk grn | .15 | .15 |

Souvenir Sheet

Intl. Decade for Women (1975-1985) — A1075

1982, Mar. 8
| 2811 | A1075 | 1 l multicolored | 1.65 | 1.00 |

New Year 1982 A1076

1981, Dec. 22   Photo.   Perf. 13
| 2812 | A1076 | 5s Ornament | .15 | .15 |
| 2813 | A1076 | 13s Ornament, diff. | .18 | .15 |

The Sofia Plains, by Nicolas Petrov (1881-1916) — A1077

1982, Feb. 10   Perf. 12½
2814	A1077	5s shown	.15	.15
2815	A1077	13s Girl Embroidering	.20	.15
2816	A1077	30s Fields of Peshtera	.48	.20
		Nos. 2814-2816 (3)	.83	.50

25th Anniv. of UNICEF (1981) — A1078

Mother and Child Paintings.

1982, Feb. 25   Perf. 14
2817	A1078	53s Vladimir Dimitrov	.80	.32
2818	A1078	53s Basil Stoilov	.80	.32
2819	A1078	53s Ivan Milev	.80	.32
2820	A1078	53s Liliana Russeva	.80	.32
		Nos. 2817-2820 (4)	3.20	1.28

Figures, by Vladamir Dimitrov (1882-1961) — A1079

1982, Mar. 8   Litho.
2821	A1079	5s shown	.15	.15
2822	A1079	8s Landscape	.15	.15
2823	A1079	13s View of Istanbul	.22	.15
2824	A1079	25s Harvesters, vert.	.42	.16
2825	A1079	30s Woman in a Landscape, vert.	.50	.20
2826	A1079	35s Peasant Woman, vert.	.60	.25
		Nos. 2821-2826 (6)	2.04	1.06

Souvenir Sheet
| 2827 | A1079 | 50s Self-portrait | .80 | .65 |

No. 2827 contains one stamp, size: 54x32mm.

Trade Union Congress A1080

1982, Apr. 8   Photo.   Perf. 13½
| 2828 | A1080 | 5s Dimitrov reading union paper | .15 | .15 |
| 2829 | A1080 | 5s Culture Palace | .15 | .15 |

#2828-2829 se-tenant with label showing text.

Marsh Snowdrop — A1081

Designs: Medicinal plants.

1982, Apr. 10   Photo.   Perf. 13
2830	A1081	3s shown	.15	.15
2831	A1081	5s Chicory	.15	.15
2832	A1081	8s Chamaenerium angustifolium	.15	.15
2833	A1081	13s Solomon's seal	.25	.15
2834	A1081	25s Violets	.50	.20
2835	A1081	35s Centaury	.70	.26
		Nos. 2830-2835 (6)	1.90	1.06

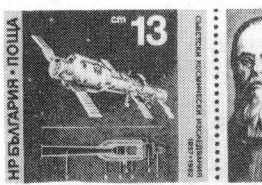

Cosmonauts' Day — A1082

1982, Apr. 12   Perf. 13½
| 2836 | A1082 | 13s Salyut-Soyuz link-up | .20 | .15 |

Se-tenant with label showing K.E. Tsiolkovsky (space pioneer).

Souvenir Sheet

SOZFILEX Stamp Exhibition — A1083

1982, May 7   Perf. 13
| 2837 | A1083 | 50s Dimitrov, emblems | .80 | .45 |

14th Komsomol Congress (Youth Communists) — A1084

1982, May 25
| 2838 | A1084 | 5s multicolored | .15 | .15 |

PHILEXFRANCE '82 Intl. Stamp Exhibition, Paris, June 11-21 — A1085

1982, May 28
| 2839 | A1085 | 42s France #1, Bulgaria #1 | .65 | .25 |

19th Cent. Fresco A1086

Designs: Various floral pattern frescoes.

1982, June 8   Perf. 11½
2840	A1086	5s red & multi	.15	.15
2841	A1086	13s green & multi	.25	.15
2842	A1086	25s violet & multi	.40	.15
2843	A1086	30s ol grn & multi	.50	.20
2844	A1086	42s blue & multi	.75	.25
2845	A1086	60s brown & multi	1.00	.40
		Nos. 2840-2845 (6)	3.05	1.30

Souvenir Sheet

George Dimitrov (1882-1949), First Prime Minister — A1087

1982, June 15   Perf. 13
| 2846 | A1087 | 50s multicolored | 1.00 | .45 |

9th Congress of the National Front — A1088

1982, June 21   Photo.   Perf. 13
| 2847 | A1088 | 5s Dimitrov | .15 | .15 |

35th Anniv. of Balkan Bulgarian Airline A1089

1982, June 28   Perf. 13½x13
| 2848 | A1089 | 42s multicolored | .65 | .26 |

Shop with Scott Publishing Co. 24 hours a day 7 days a week at www.scottonline.com

A1090   A1091

1982, July 15   *Perf. 13*
2849 A1090 13s multicolored   .25 .15
Nuclear disarmament.

1982, July   *Photo.*   *Perf. 13*
2850 A1091 5s multicolored   .15 .15
2851 A1091 13s multicolored   .18 .15
Souvenir Sheet
2852 A1091 11 multicolored   1.50 .75
Ludmila Zhivkova (b. 1942), artist.

5th Congress of Bulgarian Painters — A1092

1982, July 27   *Perf. 13½*
2853 A1092 5s multicolored   .20 .15
Se-tenant with label showing text.

Flag of Peace Youth Assembly — A1093

Various children's drawings.

1982, Aug. 10   *Perf. 14*
2853A A1093 3s multicolored   .15 .15
2853B A1093 5s multicolored   .15 .15
2853C A1093 8s multicolored   .15 .15
2853D A1093 13s multicolored   .22 .15
Nos. 2853A-2853D (4)   .67 .60
Souvenir Sheet
Perf. 14, Imperf.
2853E A1093 50s In balloon   3.00 .35
See Nos. 2864-2870, 3052-3058, 3321-3327.

10th Anniv. of UN Conference on Human Environment, Stockholm — A1093a

1982, Nov. 10   *Perf. 13*
2854 A1093a 13s dk blue & grn   .20 .15

A1094 A1095

Designs: No. 2855, Park Hotel Moskva, Sofia. No. 2856, Tchernomore, Varna.

1982, Oct. 20   *Photo.*   *Perf. 13*
2855 A1094 32s lt blue & multi   .42 .18
2856 A1094 32s pink & multi   .42 .18

1982, Nov. 4
2857 A1095 13s Cruiser Aurora, Sputnik II   .16 .15
October Revolution, 65th anniv.

60th Anniv. of Institute of Communications A1096

1982, Dec. 9
2858 A1096 5s ultra   .15 .15

60th Anniv. of USSR A1097

1982, Dec. 9
2859 A1097 13s multicolored   .18 .15

The Piano, by Pablo Picasso (1881-1973) A1098

Perf. 11½x12½
1982, Dec. 24   *Litho.*
2860 A1098 13s shown   .20 .15
2861 A1098 30s Portrait of Jacqueline   .40 .18
2862 A1098 42s Maternity   .60 .26
Nos. 2860-2862 (3)   1.20 .59
Souvenir Sheet
2863 A1098 11 Self-portrait   2.50 .75

Children's Drawings Type of 1982
Various children's drawings. 8s, 13s, 50s vert.

1982, Dec. 28   *Perf. 14*
2864 A1093 3s multicolored   .15 .15
2865 A1093 5s multicolored   .15 .15
2866 A1093 8s multicolored   .15 .15
2867 A1093 13s multicolored   .20 .15
2868 A1093 25s multicolored   .35 .15
2869 A1093 30s multicolored   .40 .18
Nos. 2864-2869 (6)   1.40 .93
Souvenir Sheet
Perf. 14, Imperf.
2870 A1093 50s Shaking hands   2.50 .35

New Year A1100

1982, Dec. 28   *Photo.*   *Perf. 13*
2872 A1100 5s multicolored   .15 .15
2873 A1100 13s multicolored   .18 .15

A1101 A1102

1982, Dec. 28
2874 A1101 25s Robert Koch   .38 .15
2875 A1101 30s Simon Bolivar   .42 .18
2876 A1101 30s Rabindranath Tagore (1861-1941)   .42 .18
Nos. 2874-2876 (3)   1.22 .51
No. 2874 also for TB bacillus cent.

1983, Jan. 10   *Photo.*   *Perf. 13x13½*
2877 A1102 5s olive & brown   .15 .15
Vassil Levski (1837-73), revolutionary.

Universiade Games — A1103

1983, Feb. 15   *Perf. 13*
2878 A1103 30s Downhill skiing   .35 .18

Fresh-water Fish — A1104

1983, Mar. 24   *Photo.*   *Perf. 13½x13*
2879 A1104 3s Pike   .15 .15
2880 A1104 5s Sturgeon   .15 .15
2881 A1104 13s Chub   .20 .15
2882 A1104 25s Perch   .38 .15
2883 A1104 30s Catfish   .42 .18
2884 A1104 42s Trout   .55 .24
Nos. 2879-2884 (6)   1.85 1.02

Karl Marx (1818-1883) A1105

1983, Apr. 5   *Perf. 13x13½*
2885 A1105 13s multicolored   .20 .15

Jaroslav Hasek (1883-1923) — A1106

1983, Apr. 20   *Photo.*   *Perf. 13*
2886 A1106 13s multicolored   .20 .15

Martin Luther (1483-1546) A1107

1983, May 10
2887 A1107 13s multicolored   .20 .15

55th Anniv. of Komsomol Youth Movement — A1108

1983, May 13
2888 A1108 5s "PMC"   .15 .15

A1109 A1111

National costumes.

1983, May 17   *Litho.*   *Perf. 14*
2889 A1109 5s Khaskovo   .15 .15
2890 A1109 8s Pernik   .15 .15
2891 A1109 13s Burgas   .20 .15
2892 A1109 25s Tolbukhin   .35 .15
2893 A1109 30s Blagoevgrad   .40 .15
2894 A1109 42s Topolovgrad   .50 .20
Nos. 2889-2894 (6)   1.75 .95

1983, May 20
6th Intl. Satire and Humor Biennial, Gabrovo: Old Man Feeding Chickens.
2900 A1111 5s multicolored   .15 .15

Christo Smirnensky (1898-1983), Poet — A1112

1983, May 25
2901 A1112 5s multicolored   .15 .15

17th Intl. Geodesists' Congress — A1113

1983, May 27
2902 A1113 30s Emblem   .45 .20

Interarch '83 Architecture Exhibition, Sofia — A1114

1983, June 6
2903 A1114 30s multicolored   .45 .20

BULGARIA

8th European Chess
Championships,
Plovdiv — A1115

1983, June 20 Photo. Perf. 13
2904 A1115 13s Chess pieces, map of Europe .20 .15

Souvenir Sheet

BRASILIANA '83 Philatelic Exhibition — A1116

1983, June 24
2905 A1116 1 l Brazilian and Bulgarian stamps 1.50 .95

Social Democratic Party Congress of Russia, 80th Anniv. A1118

Design: Lenin addressing congress.

1983, July 29 Photo. Perf. 13
2907 A1118 5s multicolored .15 .15

Ilinden-Preobrazhensky Insurrection, 80th Anniv. — A1119

1983, July 29
2908 A1119 5s Gun, dagger, book .15 .15

Institute of Mining and Geology, Sofia, 30th Anniv. — A1120

1983, Aug. 10
2909 A1120 5s multicolored .15 .15

60th Anniv. of September 1923 Uprising — A1121

1983, Aug. 19
2910 A1121 5s multicolored .15 .15
2911 A1121 13s multicolored .18 .15

Angora Cat A1123

1983, Sept. 26 Perf. 13
2917 A1123 5s shown .15 .15
2918 A1123 13s Siamese .22 .15
2919 A1123 20s Abyssinian, vert. .38 .15
2920 A1123 25s Persian .45 .18
2921 A1123 30s European, vert. .55 .22
2922 A1123 42s Indochinese .75 .30
     Nos. 2917-2922 (6) 2.50 1.15

Animated Film Festival — A1124

1983, Sept. 15 Photo. Perf. 14x13½
2923 A1124 5s Articulation layout .15 .15

Trevethick's Engine, 1804 — A1125

Locomotives: 13s, Blenkinsop's Prince Royal, 1810. 42s, Hedley's Puffing Billy, 1812. 60s, Adler (first German locomotive), 1835.

1983, Oct. 20 Perf. 13
2924 A1125 5s multicolored .15 .15
2925 A1125 13s multicolored .32 .15
2926 A1125 42s multicolored .95 .30
2927 A1125 60s multicolored 1.40 .42
     Nos. 2924-2927 (4) 2.82 1.02
     See Nos. 2983-2987.

Souvenir Sheet

Liberation Monument, Plovdiv — A1126

1983, Nov. 4
2928 A1126 50s multicolored .80 .60
Philatelic Federation, 90th anniv.

Sofia Opera, 75th Anniv. — A1127

Composers' Assoc., 50th Anniv. — A1128

1983, Dec. 2 Perf. 13x13½
2929 A1127 5s Mask, lyre, laurel .15 .15

1983, Dec. 5
Composers: 5s, Ioan Kukuzel (14th cent.) 8s, Atanasov. 13s, Petko Stainov. 20s, Veselin Stodiov. 25s, Liubomir Pipkov. 30s, Pancho Vladigerov. Setenant with labels showing compositions.
2930 A1128 5s multicolored .15 .15
2931 A1128 8s multicolored .15 .15
2932 A1128 13s multicolored .18 .15
2933 A1128 20s multicolored .30 .15
2934 A1128 25s multicolored .38 .16
2935 A1128 30s multicolored .48 .20
     Nos. 2930-2935 (6) 1.64 .96

New Year 1984 A1129

1983, Dec. 10 Perf. 13
2936 A1129 5s multicolored .15 .15

Angelo Donni, by Raphael — A1130

1983, Dec. 22 Perf. 14
2937 A1130 5s shown .15 .15
2938 A1130 13s Cardinal .20 .15
2939 A1130 30s Baldassare Castiglioni .45 .20
2940 A1130 42s Donna Belata .68 .30
     Nos. 2937-2940 (4) 1.48 .80

Souvenir Sheet
2941 A1130 1 l Sistine Madonna 1.65 1.25

Bat, World Wildlife Emblem A1131

Various bats and rodents.

1983, Dec. 30 Perf. 13
2942 A1131 12s multicolored .16 .15
2943 A1131 13s multicolored .18 .15
2944 A1131 20s multicolored .28 .15
2945 A1131 30s multicolored .45 .22
2946 A1131 42s multicolored .65 .30
     Nos. 2942-2946 (5) 1.72 .97

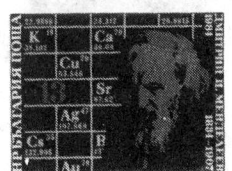

Dmitri Mendeleev (1834-1907), Russian Chemist — A1132

1984, Mar. 14
2947 A1132 13s multicolored .22 .15

Ljuben Karavelov, Poet and Freedom Fighter, Birth Sesquicentenary A1133

1984, Jan. 31 Perf. 13x13½
2948 A1133 5s multicolored .15 .15

Tanker Gen. V.I. Zaimov A1137

1984, Mar. 22 Perf. 13½
2959 A1137 5s shown .15 .15
2960 A1137 13s Mesta .20 .15
2961 A1137 25s Veleka .40 .15
2962 A1137 32s Ferry .55 .20
2963 A1137 42s Cargo ship Rossen .70 .30
     Nos. 2959-2963 (5) 2.00 .95

Souvenir Sheet

World Cup Soccer Commemorative of 1982, Spain No. 2281 — A1137a

1984, Apr. 18 Photo. Perf. 13x13½
2963A A1137a 2 l multicolored 3.00 2.50
ESPANA '84.

Dove with Letter over Globe — A1138

Berries — A1139

1984, Apr. 24 Perf. 13
2964 A1138 5s multicolored .15 .15
World Youth Stamp Exhibition, Pleven, Oct. 5-11.

1984, May 5
2965 A1139 5s Cherries .15 .15
2966 A1139 8s Strawberries .15 .15
2967 A1139 13s Blackberries .20 .15
2968 A1139 20s Raspberries .35 .15
2969 A1139 42s Currants .70 .32
     Nos. 2965-2969 (5) 1.55 .92

A1140   A1142

1984, May 23
2970 A1140 13s Athlete, doves .20 .15
6th Republican Spartikiade games,

1984, June 12
2972 A1142 5s Folk singer, drum .15 .15
6th amateur art festival.

BULGARIA

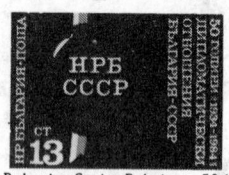

Bulgarian-Soviet Relations, 50th Anniv. — A1143

1984, June 27
2973 A1143 13s Initialed seal .15 .15

Doves and Pigeons — A1144

1984, July 6   Litho.   Perf. 14
2974 A1144 5s Rock dove .15 .15
2975 A1144 13s Stock dove .20 .15
2976 A1144 20s Wood pigeon .35 .15
2977 A1144 30s Turtle dove .48 .20
2978 A1144 42s Domestic pigeon .70 .28
Nos. 2974-2978 (5) 1.88 .93

1st Natl. Communist Party Congress, 60th Anniv. — A1145

1984, May 18   Photo.   Perf. 13½x13
2979 A1145 5s multicolored .15 .15

Souvenir Sheet

Intl. Stamp Exhibition, Essen, May 26-31 — A1146

Europa Conference stamps: No. 2980a, 1980. No. 2980b, 1981.

1984, May 22   Perf. 13x13½
2980 A1146 Sheet of 2 12.00 10.00
    a.-b.   1.50 l multi 6.00 5.00

Mount Everest — A1147

1984, May 31   Perf. 13
2981 A1147 5s multicolored .15 .15
1st Bulgarian Everest climbing expedition, Apr. 20-May 9.

Souvenir Sheet

UPU Congress, Hamburg — A1148

1984, June 11   Perf. 13½x13
2982 A1148 3 l Sailing ship 12.00 10.00

Locomotives Type of 1983

1984, July 31   Perf. 13
2983 A1125 13s Best Friend of Charleston, 1830, US .24 .15
2984 A1125 25s Saxonia, 1836, Dresden .42 .25
2985 A1125 30s Lafayette, 1837, US .52 .30
2986 A1125 42s Borsig, 1841, Germany .75 .42
2987 A1125 60s Philadelphia, 1843, Austria 1.10 .65
Nos. 2983-2987 (5) 3.03 1.77

September 9 Revolution, 40th Anniv. — A1149

1984, Aug. 4
2988 A1149 5s K, production quality emblem .15 .15
2989 A1149 20s Victory Monument, Sofia .35 .20
2990 A1149 30s Star, "9" .55 .30
Nos. 2988-2990 (3) 1.05 .65

Paintings by Nenko Balkanski (1907-1977) — A1150

1984, Sept. 17   Perf. 14
2991 A1150 5s Boy Playing Harmonica, vert. .15 .15
2992 A1150 30s A Paris Window, vert. .55 .30
2993 A1150 42s Double Portrait .80 .42
Nos. 2991-2993 (3) 1.50 .87

Souvenir Sheet
2994 A1150 1 l Self-portrait, vert. 1.75 1.25

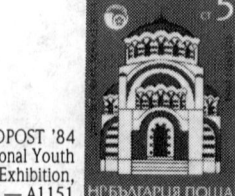

MLADPOST '84 International Youth Stamp Exhibition, Pleven — A1151

Buildings in Pleven: 5s, Mausoleum to Russian soldiers, 1877-78 Russo-Turkish War. 13s, Panorama Building.

1984, Sept. 20   Perf. 13
2995 A1151 5s multicolored .15 .15
2996 A1151 13s multicolored .28 .15

Septembrist Young Pioneers Org., 40th Anniv. A1152

1984, Sept. 21   Photo.   Perf. 13
2997 A1152 5s multicolored .15 .15

Nikola Vapzarov A1153

1984, Oct. 2
2998 A1153 5s maroon & pale yel .15 .15

Natl. Soccer, 75th Anniv. A1154

1984, Oct. 3
2999 A1154 42s multicolored .75 .42

Souvenir Sheet

MLADPOST '84 — A1155

1984, Oct. 5   Photo.   Perf. 13
3000 A1155 50s multicolored 1.00 .50

Bridges and Maps — A1156

1984, Oct. 5   Photo.   Perf. 13½x13
3001 A1156 5s Devil's Bridge, Arda River .15 .15
3002 A1156 13s Koljo-Fitscheto, Bjala .25 .15
3003 A1156 30s Asparuchowa, Warna .60 .30
3004 A1156 42s Bebresch Highway Bridge, Botevgrad .75 .40
Nos. 3001-3004 (4) 1.75 1.00

Intl. Olympic Committee, 90th Anniv. A1158

1984, Oct. 24   Photo.   Perf. 13
3007 A1158 13s multicolored .25 .15

A1159   A1160

Pelecanus crispus.

1984, Nov. 2
3008 A1159 5s Adult, young .15 .15
3009 A1159 13s Two adults .28 .15
3010 A1159 20s Adult in water .40 .20
3011 A1159 32s In flight .65 .32
Nos. 3008-3011 (4) 1.48 .82
World Wildlife Fund.

1984, Nov. 2
3012 A1160 5s multicolored .15 .15
Anton Ivanov (1884-1942), labor leader.

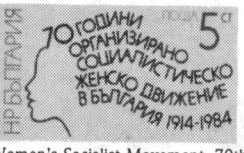

Women's Socialist Movement, 70th Anniv. — A1161

1984, Nov. 9
3013 A1161 5s multicolored .15 .15

Telecommunication Towers — A1162

1984, Nov. 23
3014 A1162 5s Snezhanka .15 .15
3015 A1162 1 l Orelek 1.90 1.00

Snowflakes, New Year 1985 — A1163

1984, Dec. 5
3016 A1163 5s Doves, posthorns .15 .15
3017 A1163 13s Doves, blossom .22 .15

Paintings by Stoyan Venev (b. 1904) — A1164

1984, Dec. 10   Litho.
3018 A1164 5s September Nights .15 .15
3019 A1164 30s Man with Three Medals .48 .30
3020 A1164 42s The Best .70 .42
Nos. 3018-3020 (3) 1.33 .87

BULGARIA

Butterflies A1165

1984, Dec. 14   Perf. 11½
3021	A1165	13s Inachis io	.25 .15
3022	A1165	25s Papilio machaon	.42 .25
3023	A1165	30s Brintesia circe	.52 .30
3024	A1165	42s Anthocaris cardamines	.75 .42
3025	A1165	60s Vanessa atalanta	1.00 .60
		Nos. 3021-3025 (5)	2.94 1.72

Souvenir Sheet
3026 A1165   1 l Limenitis populi   2.00 1.00

A1166   A1167

1984, Dec. 18   Photo.   Perf. 13x13½
3027 A1166 13s multicolored   .25 .15
Cesar Augusto Sandino (1895-1934), Nicaraguan freedom fighter.

1984, Dec. 28   Litho.   Perf. 14
3028	A1167	5s The Three Graces	.15 .15
3029	A1167	13s Cupid and the Graces	.28 .15
3030	A1167	30s Original Sin	.55 .30
3031	A1167	42s La Fornarina	.80 .42
		Nos. 3028-3031 (4)	1.78 1.02

Souvenir Sheet
3032 A1167   1 l Galatea   2.00 1.00
Raphael, 500th birth anniv. (1983).

Cruise Ship Sofia, Maiden Voyage — A1168

1984, Dec. 29   Photo.   Perf. 13
3033 A1168 13s blue, dk bl & yel   .25 .15

Predators A1170

1985, Jan. 17
3035	A1170	13s Conepatus leuconotus	.25 .15
3036	A1170	25s Prionodon linsang	.42 .25
3037	A1170	30s Ictonix striatus	.52 .30
3038	A1170	42s Hemigalus derbyanus	.75 .42
3039	A1170	60s Galidictis fasciata	1.00 .60
		Nos. 3035-3039 (5)	2.94 1.72

Nikolai Liliev (1885-1960), Poet, UNESCO Emblem — A1171

1985, Jan. 25
3040 A1171 30s multicolored   .50 .30

Zviatko Radojnov (1895-1942), Labor Leader — A1172

1985, Jan. 29
3041 A1172 5s dk red & dk brn   .15 .15

Dr. Assen Zlatarov (1885-1936), Chemist — A1173

1985, Feb. 14
3042 A1173 5s multicolored   .15 .15

Souvenir Sheet

Akademik, Research Vessel — A1174

1985, Mar. 1
3043 A1174 80s multicolored   1.25 .80
UNESCO Intl. Oceanographic Commission, 25th anniv.

Souvenir Sheet

Lenin — A1175

1985, Mar. 12
3044 A1175 50s multicolored   .85 .50

A1176   A1177

1985, Mar. 19
3045 A1176 13s multicolored   .25 .15
Warsaw Treaty Org., 30th anniv.

1985, Mar. 25
Composers.
3046	A1177	42s Bach	.50 .30
3047	A1177	42s Mozart	.50 .30
3048	A1177	42s Tchaikovsky	.50 .30
3049	A1177	42s Mussorgsky	.50 .30
3050	A1177	42s Verdi	.50 .30
3051	A1177	42s Tenev	.50 .30
		Nos. 3046-3051 (6)	3.00 1.80

Children's Drawings Type of 1982
Inscribed 1985. Various children's drawings.

1985, Mar. 26   Litho.   Perf. 14
3052	A1093	5s multicolored	.15 .15
3053	A1093	8s multicolored	.15 .15
3054	A1093	13s multicolored	.20 .15
3055	A1093	20s multicolored	.30 .20
3056	A1093	25s multicolored	.40 .25
3057	A1093	30s multicolored	.50 .30
		Nos. 3052-3057 (6)	1.70 1.20

Souvenir Sheet
3058 A1093 50s Children dancing, vert.   1.00 .50
3rd Flag of Peace Intl. Assembly, Sofia. No. 3058 exists imperf. with blue control number, same value.

St. Methodius, 1100th Death Anniv. — A1179

1985, Apr. 6   Photo.   Perf. 13
3059 A1179 13s multicolored   .25 .15

Victory Parade, Moscow, 1945 A1180

13s, 11th Infantry on parade, Sofia. 30s, Soviet soldier, orphan. 50s, Soviet flag-raising, Berlin.

1985, Apr. 30   Perf. 13½
3060	A1180	5s multicolored	.15 .15
3061	A1180	13s multicolored	.24 .15
3062	A1180	30s multicolored	.52 .30
		Nos. 3060-3062 (3)	.91 .60

Souvenir Sheet
Perf. 13
3063 A1180 50s multicolored   1.00 .50
Defeat of Nazi Germany, end of World War II, 40th anniv. Nos. 3060-3062 printed se-tenant with labels picturing Soviet (5s, 30s) and Bulgarian medals of honor.

7th Intl. Humor and Satire Biennial A1181

1985, Apr. 30   Perf. 13½
3064 A1181 13s yel, sage grn & red   .25 .15
No. 3064 printed se-tenant with label picturing Gabrovo Cat emblem.

Intl. Youth Year — A1182

1985, May 21   Perf. 13
3065 A1182 13s multicolored   .25 .15

Ivan Vasov (1850-1921), Poet — A1183

1985, May 30   Perf. 13½
3066 A1183 5s tan & sepia   .15 .15
No. 3066 printed se-tenant with label picturing Vasov's birthplace in Sopot.

Soviet War Memorial, Haskovo City Arms A1184

1985, June 1   Perf. 13
3067 A1184 5s multicolored   .15 .15
Haskovo millennium.

12th World Youth Festival, Moscow — A1185

1985, June 25
3068 A1185 13s multicolored   .25 .15

Indira Gandhi (1917-1984), Prime Minister of India — A1186

1985, June 26
3069 A1186 30s org yel, sepia & ver   .60 .30

BULGARIA

Vasil Aprilov, Founder — A1187

1985, June 30
3070 A1187 5s multicolored .15 .15
1st secular school, Gabrovo, 150th anniv.

INTERSTENO '85 — A1188

1985, June 30
3071 A1188 13s multicolored .25 .15
Congress for the Intl. Union of Stenographers and Typists, Sofia.

Alexander Nevski Cathedral A1189

1985, July 9
3072 A1189 42s multicolored .80 .42
World Tourism Org., general assembly, Sofia.

UN, 40th Anniv. A1190

1985, July 16
3073 A1190 13s multicolored .25 .15

A1191   **Roses — A1192**

1985, July 16
3074 A1191 13s multicolored .25 .15
Admission of Bulgaria to UN, 30th anniv.

1985, July 20   Litho.
3075 A1192 5s Rosa damascena .15 .15
3076 A1192 13s Rosa trakijka .24 .15
3077 A1192 20s Rosa radiman .35 .20
3078 A1192 30s Rosa marista .50 .30
3079 A1192 42s Rosa valentina .75 .42
3080 A1192 60s Rosa maria 1.00 .60
  a. Min. sheet of 6, #3075-3080 3.50 2.00
    Nos. 3075-3080 (6) 2.99 1.82

Helsinki Conference, 10th Anniv. — A1193

1985, Aug. 1   Photo.
3081 A1193 13s multicolored .25 .15

European Swimming Championships, Sofia — A1194

1985, Aug. 2   Litho.   Perf. 12½
3082 A1194 5s Butterfly stroke .15 .15
3083 A1194 13s Water polo, vert. .20 .20
3084 A1194 42s Diving, vert. .60 .35
3085 A1194 60s Synchronized swimming .75 .40
    Nos. 3082-3085 (4) 1.70 1.05
The 60s exists with central design inverted.

Natl. Tourism Assoc., 90th Anniv. A1195

1985, Aug. 15   Photo.   Perf. 13
3086 A1195 5s multicolored .15 .15

1986 World Cup Soccer Championships, Mexico — A1196

Various soccer plays. Nos. 3087-3090 vert.

1985, Aug. 29   Perf. 13
3087 A1196 5s multicolored .15 .15
3088 A1196 13s multicolored .20 .15
3089 A1196 30s multicolored .40 .20
3090 A1196 42s multicolored .50 .25
    Nos. 3087-3090 (4) 1.25 .75

Souvenir Sheet
3091 A1196 1 1 multicolored 1.25 .75

Union of Eastern Rumelia and Bulgaria, 1885 — A1197

1985, Aug. 29   Perf. 14x13½
3092 A1197 5s multicolored .15 .15

Computer Design Portraits — A1198

1985, Sept. 23   Perf. 13
3093 A1198 5s Boy .15 .15
3094 A1198 13s Youth .24 .15
3095 A1198 30s Cosmonaut .52 .30
    Nos. 3093-3095 (3) .91 .60
Intl. Exhibition of the Works of Youth Inventors, Plovdiv.

St. John the Baptist Church, Nessebar — A1199

Natl. restoration projects: 13s, Tyrant Hreljo Tower, Rila Monastery. 35s, Soldier, fresco, Ivanovo Rock Church. 42s, Archangel Gabriel, fresco, Bojana Church. 60s, Thracian Woman, fresco, Tomb of Kasanlak, 3rd century B.C. 1 l, The Horseman of Madara, bas-relief.

1985, Sept. 25   Litho.   Perf. 12½
3096 A1199 5s multicolored .15 .15
3097 A1199 13s multicolored .22 .15
3098 A1199 35s multicolored .60 .32
3099 A1199 42s multicolored .75 .40
3100 A1199 60s multicolored 1.10 .60
    Nos. 3096-3100 (5) 2.82 1.62

Souvenir Sheet
Imperf
3101 A1199 1 1 multicolored 1.75 1.00
UNESCO, 40th anniv.

Souvenir Sheet

Ludmila Zhishkova Cultural Palace, Sofia — A1200

1985, Oct. 8   Perf. 13
3102 A1200 1 1 multicolored 1.75 1.00
UNESCO 23rd General Assembly, Sofia.

Colosseum, Rome A1201

1985, Oct. 15   Photo.   Perf. 13½
3103 A1201 42s multicolored .75 .42
ITALIA '85. No. 3103 printed se-tenant with label picturing the exhibition emblem.

Souvenir Sheet

Cultural Congress, Budapest — A1202

Designs: No. 3104a, St. Cyril, patron saint of Europe. No. 3104b, Map of Europe. No. 3104c, St. Methodius, patron saint of Europe.

Perf. 13, 13 Vert. (#3104b)
1985, Oct. 22   Photo.
3104 A1202 Sheet of 3 2.75 1.50
  a.-c. 50s, any single .90 .50
Helsinki Congress, 10th anniv.

Flowers — A1203

1985, Oct. 22   Photo.   Perf. 13x13½
3105 A1203 5s Gladiolus hybridy .15 .15
3106 A1203 5s Iris germanica .15 .15
3107 A1203 5s Convolvulus tricolor .15 .15
    Nos. 3105-3107 (3) .45 .45
See Nos. 3184-3186.

Historic Sailing Ships A1204

1985, Oct. 28   Photo.   Perf. 13
3108 A1204 5s Dutch .15 .15
3109 A1204 12s Sea Sovereign, Britain .22 .15
3110 A1204 20s Mediterranean .35 .20
3111 A1204 25s Royal Prince, Britain .45 .25
3112 A1204 42s Mediterranean .75 .42
3113 A1204 60s British battleship 1.10 .60
    Nos. 3108-3113 (6) 3.02 1.77

Souvenir Sheet

PHILATELIA '85, Cologne — A1205

Designs: a, Cologne Cathedral. b, Alexander Nevski Cathedral, Sofia.

1985, Nov. 4   Imperf.
3114 A1205 Sheet of 2 1.25 .65
  a.-b. 30s, any single .60 .30

Conspiracy to Liberate Bulgaria from Turkish Rule, 150th Anniv. — A1206

BULGARIA

Freedom fighters and symbols: #3115, Georgi Stojkov Rakowski (1820-76). #3116, Batscho Kiro (1835-76). #3117, Sword, Bible & hands.

1985, Nov. 6		Perf. 13	
3115	A1206	5s multicolored	.15 .15
3116	A1206	5s multicolored	.15 .15
3117	A1206	13s multicolored	.22 .15
	Nos. 3115-3117 (3)		.52 .45

Liberation from Byzantine Rule, 800th Anniv. — A1207

Paintings: 5s, The Revolt 1185, by G. Bogdanov. 13s, The Revolt 1185, by Alexander Tersiev. 30s, Battle Near Klokotnitza, by B. Grigorov and M. Ganowski. 42s, Velika Tarnovo Town Wall, by Zanko Lawrenov. 1 l, St. Dimitriev Church, 12th cent.

1985, Nov. 15		Litho.	
3118	A1207	5s multicolored	.15 .15
3119	A1207	13s multicolored	.22 .15
3120	A1207	30s multicolored	.52 .30
3121	A1207	42s multicolored	.75 .42
	Nos. 3118-3121 (4)		1.64 1.02

Souvenir Sheet
Imperf

3122 A1207 1 l multicolored 2.00 1.00

Souvenir Sheet

BALKANPHILA '85 — A1208

1985, Nov. 29	Photo.	Perf. 13
3123 A1208 40s Dove, posthorn		.75 .40

Intl. Post and Telecommunications Development Program — A1209

1985, Dec. 2
3124 A1209 13s multicolored .25 .15

Anton Popov (1915-1942), Freedom Fighter — A1210

1985, Dec. 11	Photo.	Perf. 13
3125 A1210 5s lake		.15 .15

New Year 1986 A1211

1985, Dec. 11	Photo.	Perf. 13
3126 A1211 5s Doves, snowflake		.15 .15
3127 A1211 13s Doves		.22 .15

Hunting Dogs and Prey — A1212

Designs: 5s, Pointer and partridge. 8s, Irish setter and pochard. 13s, English setter and mallard. 20s, Cocker spaniel and woodcock. 25s, German pointer and rabbit. 30s, Balkan hound and boar. 42s, Shorthaired dachshund and fox.

1985, Dec. 27		Litho.	Perf. 13x12½
3128	A1212	5s multicolored	.15 .15
3129	A1212	8s multicolored	.16 .15
3130	A1212	13s multicolored	.28 .15
3131	A1212	20s multicolored	.40 .20
3132	A1212	25s multicolored	.50 .25
3133	A1212	30s multicolored	.60 .30
3134	A1212	42s multicolored	.85 .42
	Nos. 3128-3134 (7)		2.94 1.62

Intl. Year of the Handicapped — A1213

1985, Dec. 30	Photo.	Perf. 13
3135 A1213 5s multicolored		.15 .15

George Dimitrov (1882-1949) — A1214

1985, Dec. 30	Photo.	Perf. 13
3136 A1214 13s brn lake		.25 .15

7th Intl. Communist Congress, Moscow.

UN Child Survival Campaign — A1215

1986, Jan. 21	Photo.	Perf. 13
3137 A1215 13s multicolored		.25 .15

UNICEF, 40th anniv.

Demeter Blagoev (1856-1924) — A1216

1986, Jan. 28	Photo.	Perf. 13
3138 A1216 5s dk lake, car & dk red		.15 .15

Intl. Peace Year — A1217

1986, Jan. 31		Perf. 13½
3139 A1217 5s multicolored		.15 .15

Orchids — A1218

1986, Feb. 12		Litho.	Perf. 13x12½
3140	A1218	5s Dactylorhiza romana	.15 .15
3141	A1218	13s Epipactis palustris	.20 .15
3142	A1218	30s Ophrys cornuta	.40 .30
3143	A1218	32s Limodorum abortivum	.40 .30
3144	A1218	42s Cypripedium calceolus	.50 .40
3145	A1218	60s Orchis papilionacea	1.00 .50
a.	Min. sheet of 6, #3140-3145		3.00 1.50
	Nos. 3140-3145 (6)		2.65 1.80

Hares and Rabbits A1219

1986, Feb. 24		Perf. 12½x12
3146	A1219 5s multicolored	.15 .15
3147	A1219 25s multicolored	.45 .25
3148	A1219 30s multicolored	.55 .30
3149	A1219 32s multicolored	.60 .32
3150	A1219 42s multicolored	.75 .42
3151	A1219 60s multicolored	1.00 .60
	Nos. 3146-3151 (6)	3.50 2.04

Bulgarian Eagle, Newspaper, 140th Anniv. — A1220

Front page of 1st issue & Ivan Bogorov, journalist.

1986, Feb. 2	Photo.	Perf. 13
3152 A1220 5s multicolored		.15 .15

Souvenir Sheet

Halley's Comet A1221

Comet's orbit in the Solar System: a, 1980. b, 1910-86. c, 1916-70. d, 1911.

1986, Mar. 7		Perf. 13½x13
3153	Sheet of 4	1.75 1.25
a.-d.	A1221 25s, any single	.42 .30

A1222 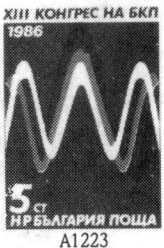 A1223

1986, Mar. 12		Perf. 13x13½
3154 A1222 5s dp bl & bl		.15 .15

Vladimir Bachev (1935-1967), poet.

1986, Mar. 17		Perf. 13
3155	A1223 5s Wavy lines	.15 .15
3156	A1223 8s Star	.15 .15
3157	A1223 13s Worker	.24 .15
	Nos. 3155-3157 (3)	.54 .45

Souvenir Sheet

3158 A1223 50s Scaffold, flags .90 .50

13th Natl. Communist Party Congress.

Souvenir Sheet

1st Manned Space Flight, 25th Anniv. — A1224

Designs: a, Vostok I, 1961. b, Yuri Gagarin (1934-68), Russian cosmonaut.

1986, Mar. 28		Perf. 13½x13
3159	Sheet of 2	1.75 1.00
a.-b.	A1224 50s, any single	1.00 .50

April Uprising against the Turks, 110th Anniv. — A1225

Monuments: 5s, 1876 Uprising monument, Panagjuriste. 13s, Christo Botev, Vraca.

1986, Mar. 30		Perf. 13
3160	A1225 5s multicolored	.15 .15
3161	A1225 13s multicolored	.26 .15

A1225a

BULGARIA

Levsky-Spartak Sports Club, 75th
Anniv. — A1226

1986			Perf. 13
3161A	A1225a	5s multicolored	.15 .15

Souvenir Sheet
Imperf
3162 A1226 50s Rhythmic gymnastics .80 .50

Issue dates: 5s, Dec. 50s, May 12.

A1227   A1228

1986, May 19		Perf. 13
3163 A1227	5s Congress emblem	.15 .15
3164 A1227	8s Emblem on globe	.15 .15
3165 A1227	13s Flags	.24 .15
	Nos. 3163-3165 (3)	.54 .45

35th Congress of Bulgarian farmers, Sofia.

1986, May 27		Perf. 13x13½
3166 A1228	13s multicolored	.25 .15

Conference of Transport Ministers from Socialist Countries.

17th Intl. Book Fair, Sofia — A1229

1986, May 28
3167 A1229 13s blk, brt red & grysh blk .25 .15

1986 World Cup Soccer Championships, Mexico — A1230

Various soccer plays; attached labels picture Mexican landmarks.

1986, May 30		Perf. 13½
3168 A1230	5s multi, vert.	.15 .15
3169 A1230	13s multicolored	.25 .15
3170 A1230	20s multicolored	.35 .20
3171 A1230	30s multicolored	.55 .30
3172 A1230	42s multicolored	.75 .42
3173 A1230	60s multi, vert.	1.10 .60
	Nos. 3168-3173 (6)	3.15 1.82

Souvenir Sheet
Perf. 13
3174 A1230 1 l Azteca Stadium 1.75 1.00

Treasures of Preslav — A1231

Gold artifacts: 5s, Embossed brooch. 13s, Pendant with pearl cross, vert. 20s, Crystal and pearl pendant. 30s, Embossed shield. 42s, Pearl and enamel pendant, vert. 60s, Enamel shield.

1986, June 7	Perf. 13½x13, 13x13½
3175 A1231	5s multicolored	.15 .15
3176 A1231	13s multicolored	.25 .15
3177 A1231	20s multicolored	.35 .20
3178 A1231	30s multicolored	.55 .30
3179 A1231	42s multicolored	.75 .42
3180 A1231	60s multicolored	1.00 .60
	Nos. 3175-3180 (6)	3.05 1.82

World Fencing Championships, Sofia, July 25-Aug. 3 — A1232

1986, July 25	Photo.	Perf. 13
3181 A1232	5s Head cut, lunge	.15 .15
3182 A1232	13s Touche	.25 .15
3183 A1232	25s Lunge, parry	.45 .25
	Nos. 3181-3183 (3)	.85 .55

Flower Type of 1985

1986, July 29		Perf. 13x13½
3184 A1203	8s Ipomoea tricolor	.15 .15
3185 A1203	13s Anemone coronaria	.15 .15
3186 A1203	32s Lilium auratum	.55 .32
	Nos. 3184-3186 (3)	.85 .62

A1233   A1234

1986, Aug. 25
3187 A1233 42s sepia, sal brn & lake .75 .42

STOCKHOLMIA '86. No. 3187 printed in sheets of 3 + 3 labels picturing folk art.

Miniature Sheet
Environmental Conservation: a, Ciconia ciconia. b, Nuphar lutea. c, Salamandra salamandra. d, Nymphaea alba.

1986, Aug. 25	Litho.	Perf. 14
3188	Sheet of 4 + label	2.00 .90
a.-d.	A1234 30s any single	.50 .22

No. 3188 contains center label picturing the oldest oak tree in Bulgaria, Granit Village.

Natl. Arms, Building of the Sobranie — A1235

1986, Sept. 13	Photo.	Perf. 13
3189 A1235	5s Prus grn, yel grn & red	.15 .15

People's Republic of Bulgaria, 40th anniv.

15th Postal Union Congress — A1236

1986, Sept. 24
3190 A1236 13s multicolored .25 .15

Natl. Youth Brigade Movement, 40th Anniv. A1237

Intl. Organization of Journalists, 10th Congress A1238

1986, Oct. 4
3191 A1237 5s multicolored .15 .15

1986, Oct. 13
3192 A1238 13s blue & dark blue .25 .15

Sts. Cyril and Methodius, Disciples A1239

1986, Oct. 23		Perf. 13½
3193 A1239	13s dark brown & buff	.25 .15

Sts. Cyril and Methodius in Bulgaria, 1100th anniv. No. 3193 se-tenant with inscribed label.

Telephones in Bulgaria, Cent. A1240

1986, Nov. 5		Perf. 13
3194 A1240	5s multicolored	.15 .15

World Weight Lifting Championships — A1241

1986, Nov. 6
3195 A1241 13s multicolored .25 .15

Ships A1242

1986, Nov. 20
3196 A1242	5s King of Prussia	.15 .15
3197 A1242	13s East Indiaman, 18th cent.	.25 .15
3198 A1242	25s Shebek, 18th cent.	.45 .25
3199 A1242	30s St Paul	.55 .30
3200 A1242	32s Topsail schooner, 18th cent.	.60 .32
3201 A1242	42s Victory	.80 .42
	Nos. 3196-3201 (6)	2.80 1.59

Souvenir Sheet

European Security and Cooperation Congress, Vienna — A1243

Various buildings and emblems: a, Bulgaria. b, Austria. c, Donau Park, UN.

	Perf. 13, Imperf. x13 (#3202b)
1986, Nov. 27	
3202	Sheet of 3	3.00 1.50
a.-c.	A1243 50s any single	1.00 .50

Exists imperf. bearing control number.

Rogozen Thracian Pitchers A1244

1986, Dec. 5		Perf. 13
3203 A1244	10s Facing left	.18 .15
3204 A1244	10s Facing right	.18 .15

Union of Bulgarian Philatelists, 14th Congress. Nos. 3203-3204 printed se-tenant with labels picturing carved figures on pitchers in blocks of 4.

New Year 1987 A1245

1986, Dec. 9
3205 A1245 5s shown .15 .15
3206 A1245 13s Snow flakes .26 .15

Home Amateur Radio Operators in Bulgaria, 60th Anniv. — A1246

1986, Dec. 10
3207 A1246 13s multicolored .25 .15

Miniature Sheet

Paintings by Bulgarian Artists — A1247

Designs: a, Red Tree, by Danail Dechev (1891-1962). b, Troopers Confront Two Men, by Ilya Beshkov (1901-58). c, View of Melnik, by Veselin Stajkov (1906-70). d, View of Houses through Trees, by Kyril Zonev (1896-1961).

BULGARIA

1986, Dec. 10 Litho. *Perf. 14*
3208 Sheet of 4   2.25 1.10
a.-b. A1247 25s any single   .50   .25
c.-d. A1247 30s any single   .60   .30

Sofia Academy of Art, 90th anniv.

Augusto Cesar Sandino (1893-1934), Nicaraguan Revolutionary, and Flag — A1248

1986, Dec. 16 Photo. *Perf. 13*
3209 A1248 13s multicolored   .25   .15

Sandinista movement in Nicaragua, 25th anniv.

Smoyan Mihylovsky (b. 1856), Writer — A1249

Ran Bossilek (b. 1886) — A1250

Title Page from Bulgarian Folk Songs of the Miladinov Brothers — A1251

Annivs. and events: No. 3211, Pentcho Slaveyckov (b. 1861), writer. No. 3212, Nickola Atanassov (b. 1886), musician.

1986, Dec. 17
3210 A1249 5s multicolored   .15   .15
3211 A1249 5s multicolored   .15   .15
3212 A1249 8s multicolored   .16   .15
3213 A1250 8s multicolored   .16   .15
3214 A1251 10s multicolored   .20   .15
       Nos. 3210-3214 (5)   .82   .75

A1252

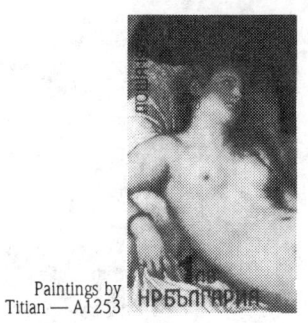

Paintings by Titian — A1253

Various portraits.

1986, Dec. 23 Litho. *Perf. 14*
3215 A1252 5s multicolored   .15   .15
3216 A1252 13s multicolored   .28   .15
3217 A1252 20s multicolored   .40   .20
3218 A1252 30s multicolored   .60   .30
3219 A1252 32s multicolored   .65   .35
3220 A1252 42s multicolored   .85   .42
  a.   Min. sheet of 6, #3215-3220 3.00 1.50
       Nos. 3215-3220 (6)   2.93 1.54
       Souvenir Sheet
3221 A1253 1 1 multicolored   2.25 1.00

Rayko Daskalov (b. 1886), Politician A1254

1986, Dec. 23 Photo. *Perf. 13*
3222 A1254 5s deep claret   .15   .15

Sports Cars — A1255

1986, Dec. 30 Litho. *Perf. 13 1/2*
3223 A1255 5s 1905 Fiat   .15   .15
3224 A1255 10s 1928 Bugatti   .15   .15
3225 A1255 25s 1936 Mercedes   .40   .25
3226 A1255 32s 1952 Ferrari   .50   .30
3227 A1255 40s 1985 Lotus   .60   .40
3228 A1255 42s 1986 McLaren   .65   .40
       Nos. 3223-3228 (6)   2.45 1.65

Varna Railway Inauguration, 120th Anniv. — A1257

1987, Jan. 19   Photo.
3229 A1257 5s multicolored   .15   .15

Dimcho Debelianov (1887-1916), Poet — A1258

1987, Jan. 20 Photo. *Perf. 13*
3230 A1258 5s blue, dull yel & dp blue .15 .15

L.L. Zamenhof, Creator of Esperanto A1259

1987, Feb. 12
3231 A1259 13s multicolored   .15   .15

Mushrooms A1260

10th Natl. Trade Unions Congress A1261

1987, Feb. 6 Litho. *Perf. 11 1/2*
3232 A1260 5s Amanita rubescens   .15   .15
3233 A1260 20s Boletus regius   .35   .25
3234 A1260 30s Leccinum aurantiacum .50 .35
3235 A1260 32s Coprinus comatus   .55   .40
3236 A1260 40s Russula vesca   .75   .50
3237 A1260 60s Cantharellus cibarius 1.00 .60
  a.   Min. sheet of 6, #3232-3237 5.00
       Nos. 3232-3237 (6)   3.30 2.25

1987, Mar. 20   Photo. *Perf. 13*
3238 A1261 5s dark red & violet   .15   .15

Rogozen Thracian Treasure A1262

Embossed and gilded silver artifacts: 5s, Plate, Priestess Auge approaching Heracles. 8s, Pitcher, lioness attacking stag. 20s, Plate, floral pattern. 30s, Pitcher, warriors on horseback dueling. 32s, Urn, decorative pattern. 42s, Pitcher (not gilded), winged horses.

1987, Mar. 31
3239 A1262 5s multicolored   .15   .15
3240 A1262 8s multicolored   .20   .15
3241 A1262 20s multicolored   .45   .35
3242 A1262 30s multicolored   .70   .45
3243 A1262 32s multicolored   .75   .50
3244 A1262 42s multicolored   .90   .60
       Nos. 3239-3244 (6)   3.15 2.15

Miniature Sheet

Modern Architecture — A1263

Designs: a, Ludmila Zhivkova conf. center, Varna. b, Ministry of Foreign Affairs, Sofia. c, Interpred Building, Sofia. d, Hotel, Sandanski.

1987, Apr. 7   *Perf. 13 1/2x13*
3245 Sheet of 4   3.00 1.80
a.-d. A1263 30s any single   .75   .45

Exists imperf. with black control number.

European Freestyle Wrestling Championships A1264

1987, Apr. 22   *Perf. 13*
3246 A1264 5s multicolored   .15   .15
3247 A1264 13s multi, diff.   .38   .18

CAPEX '87, Toronto A1265

1987, Apr. 24
3248 A1265 42s multicolored   1.00   .42

10th Congress of the Natl. Front — A1266

1987, May 11
3249 A1266 5s multicolored   .15   .15

15th Communist Youth Congress A1267

1987, May 13
3250 A1267 5s George Dimitrov   .15   .15

8th Intl. Humor and Satire Biennial, Gabrovo — A1268

1987, May 15   *Perf. 13x13 1/2*
3251 A1268 13s multicolored   .35   .15

13th World Rhythmic Gymnastics Championships, Varna — A1269

Gymnasts.

1987, Aug. 5 Photo. *Perf. 13*
3252   A1269 5s Maria Gigova   .15   .15
3252A A1269 8s Iliana Raeva   .18   .15
3252B A1269 13s Anelia Ralenkova   .28   .16
3252C A1269 25s Pilyana Georgieva .55   .32

BULGARIA

3252D	A1269	30s Lilia Ignatova	.65 .38
3252E	A1269	42s Bianca Panova	.90 .52
	Nos. 3252-3252E (6)		2.71 1.68

Souvenir Sheet
Perf. 13x13½

3252F	A1269	1 1 Neshka Robeva, coach	2.25 1.50

Exists imperf. with black control number.

Vassil Kolarov — A1270

1987, June 3 *Perf. 13*

3253	A1270	5s dk red, yel & dk bl	.15 .15

Stela Blagoeva (b. 1887) — A1271

1987, June 4

3254	A1271	5s pink & sepia	.15 .15

Rabotnichesko Delo Newspaper, 60th Anniv. — A1272

1987, May 28

3255	A1272	5s black & lake	.15 .15

Deer
Alces alces A1273

1987, June 23 *Litho.*

3256	A1273	5s Capreolus capreolus, vert.	.15 .15
3257	A1273	10s Alces alces	.25 .15
3258	A1273	32s Dama dama, vert.	.75 .25
3259	A1273	40s Cervus nippon, vert.	1.10 .30
3260	A1273	42s Cervus elaphus	1.10 .32
3261	A1273	60s Rangifer tarandus, vert.	1.40 .45
a.		Min. sheet of 6, #3256-3261, imperf.	5.50 2.85
	Nos. 3256-3261 (6)		4.75 1.62

Vassil Levski (1837-73) A1274

Various portraits.

1987, June 19 *Photo.*

3262	A1274	5s red brn & dark grn	.15 .15
3263	A1274	13s dark grn & red brn	.35 .20

Namibia Day A1275

1987, July 8

3264	A1275	13s org, blk & dark red	.30 .20

Georgi Kirkov (1867-1919), Revolutionary A1276

1987, July 17 *Perf. 13x13½*

3265	A1276	5s claret & deep claret	.15 .15

Bees and Plants — A1277

1987, July 29 *Litho. Perf. 13*

3266	A1277	5s Phacelia tanacetifolia	.15 .15
3267	A1277	10s Helianthus annuus	.20 .15
3268	A1277	30s Robinia pseudoacacia	.60 .35
3269	A1277	32s Lavandula vera	.65 .40
3270	A1277	42s Tilia parvifolia	.90 .50
3271	A1277	60s Onobrychis sativa	1.10 .70
a.		Min. sheet of 6, #3266-3271	4.50 2.75
	Nos. 3266-3271 (6)		3.60 2.25

BULGARIA '89 — A1278

1987, Sept. 3 *Perf. 13½x13*

3272	A1278	13s No. 1	.40 .20

HAFNIA '87 — A1279

1987, Sept. 8 *Perf. 13*

3273	A1279	42s multicolored	1.00 .62

No. 3273 issued in sheets of 3 plus 2 labels picturing emblems of the HAFNIA '87 and BULGARIA '89 exhibitions, and 1 label with background similar to Denmark Type A32 with castle instead of denomination.

Portrait of a Girl, by Stefan Ivanov — A1280

Paintings in the Sofia City Art Galler: 8s, Grapegatherer, by Bencho Obreshkov. 20s, Portrait of a Lady with a Hat, by David Perets. 25s, Listeners of Marimba, by Kiril Tsonev. 32s, Boy with an Harmonica, by Nenko Balkanski. 60s, Rumyana, by Vasil Stoilov.

1987, Sept. 15 *Litho. Perf. 14*

3274	A1280	5s shown	.15 .15
3275	A1280	8s multicolored	.20 .15
3276	A1280	20s multicolored	.50 .30
3277	A1280	25s multicolored	.60 .35
3278	A1280	32s multicolored	.75 .45
3279	A1280	60s multicolored	1.25 .80
	Nos. 3274-3279 (6)		3.45 2.20

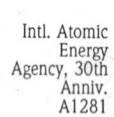

Intl. Atomic Energy Agency, 30th Anniv. A1281

1987, Sept. 15 *Photo. Perf. 13½x13*

3280	A1281	13s red, lt blue & emer	.35 .20

Songbirds A1282

1987, Oct. 12 *Litho. Perf. 12½x12*

3281	A1282	5s Troglodytes troglodytes	.15 .15
3282	A1282	13s Emberiza citrinella	.35 .16
3283	A1282	20s Sitta europaea	.55 .25
3284	A1282	30s Turdus merula	.80 .35
3285	A1282	42s Coccothraustes coccothraustes	1.10 .50
3286	A1282	60s Cinclus cinclus	1.50 .75
a.		Min. sheet of 6, #3281-3286	5.00 2.25
	Nos. 3281-3286 (6)		4.45 2.16

Balkan War, 75th Anniv. A1283

1987, Sept. 15 *Photo. Perf. 13½*

3287	A1283	5s buff, blk & brt org	.15 .15

Newspaper Anniversaries — A1283a

1987, Sept. 24 *Photo. Perf. 13*

3287A	A1283a	5s multicolored	.15 .15

Rabotnik, 95th anniv., Rabotnicheski Vstnik, 90th anniv. and Rabotnichesko Delo, 60th anniv.

October Revolution, Russia, 70th Anniv. A1284

Lenin and: 5s, Revolutionary. 13s, Cosmonaut.

1987, Oct. 27 *Photo. Perf. 13*

3288	A1284	5s rose brn & red org	.15 .15
3289	A1284	13s brt ultra & red org	.35 .20

1988 Winter Olympics, Calgary — A1285

1987, Oct. 27 *Litho. Perf. 13x13½*

3290	A1285	5s Biathlon	.15 .15
3291	A1285	13s Slalom	.38 .20
3292	A1285	30s Women's figure skating	.85 .45
3293	A1285	42s 4-Man bobsled	1.10 .62
	Nos. 3290-3293 (4)		2.48 1.42

Souvenir Sheet

3294	A1285	1 1 Ice hockey	2.75 1.50

No. 3294 exists imperf.

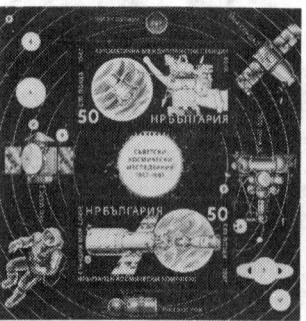

Soviet Space Achievements, 1937-87 — A1286

Designs: No. 3295a, Vega probe. No. 3295b, Mir-Soyuz Space Station.

1987, Dec. 24 *Photo. Perf. 13½x13*

3295	A1286	Sheet of 2	2.75 1.50
a.-b.		50s any single	1.25 .75

Exists imperf.

New Year 1988 A1287

Sofia stamp exhibition emblem within folklore patterns.

1987, Dec. 25 *Perf. 13*

3296	A1287	5s multicolored	.15 .15
3297	A1287	13s multi, diff.	.35 .20

BULGARIA

Souvenir Sheet

European Security Conferences — A1288

Conferences held in Helsinki, 1973, and Vienna, 1987: a, Helsinki Conf. Center. b, Map of Europe. c, Vienna Conf. Center.

Perf. 13x13½ on 2 or 4 Sides
1987, Dec. 30
3298   Sheet of 3   4.00 3.00
a.-c. A1288 50s any single   1.50   .75
Exists imperf.

A1289 / A1290

1988, Jan. 20
3299 A1289 5s multicolored   .15   .15

Christo Kabaktchiev (b. 1878), party leader.

1988, Jan. 25 *Litho.* *Perf. 12*
Marine flowers.
3300 A1290   5s Scilla bythynica   .15 .15
3301 A1290 10s Geum rhodopaeum   .20 .15
3302 A1290 13s Caltha polypetala   .30 .20
3303 A1290 25s Nymphoides peltata   .50 .30
3304 A1290 30s Cortusa matthioli   .60 .40
3305 A1290 42s Stratiotes aloides   .75 .60
  a.   Min. sheet of 6, #3300-3305 3.00 2.00
       Nos. 3300-3305 (6)   2.50 1.70

Liberation of Bulgaria, 110th Anniv. A1291

1988, Feb. 15 *Photo.* *Perf. 13*
3306 A1291   5s Officer, horse   .15 .15
3307 A1291 13s Soldiers   .35 .20

8th Intl. Civil Servants Congress, Sofia A1292

1988, Mar. 22 *Photo.* *Perf. 13*
3308 A1292 13s multicolored   .30 .16

State Railways, Cent. — A1293

Locomotives: 5s, Jantra, 1888. 13s, Christo Botev, 1905. 25s, 0-10-1, 1918. 32s, 4-12-1 heavy duty, 1943. 42s, Diesel, 1964. 60s, Electric, 1979.

1988, Mar. 25 *Litho.* *Perf. 11*
3309 A1293   5s multicolored   .15   .15
3310 A1293 13s multicolored   .25   .15
3311 A1293 25s multicolored   .50   .30
3312 A1293 32s multicolored   .65   .35
3313 A1293 42s multicolored   .80   .45
3314 A1293 60s multicolored   1.00   .60
  a.   Min. sheet of 6, #3309-3314 3.50 2.00
       Nos. 3309-3314 (6)   3.35 2.00

Ivan Nedyalkov (1880-1925) A1294

Postal workers, heroes of socialism: 8s, Delcho Spasov (1918-43). 10s, Nikola Ganchev (1915-43). 13s, Ganka Stoyanova Rasheva (1921-44).

1988, Mar. 31 *Photo.* *Perf. 13½x13*
3315 A1294   5s buff & dark rose brn   .15 .15
3316 A1294   8s pale ultra & violet
                blue   .16 .15
3317 A1294 10s pale olive grn & ol-
                ive grn   .22 .15
3318 A1294 13s pale pink & lake   .26 .16
       Nos. 3315-3318 (4)   .79 .61

Georgi Traikov (b. 1898), Statesman A1295

Intl. Red Cross and Red Crescent Organizations, 125th Anniv. A1296

1988, Apr. 8 *Litho.* *Perf. 13x13½*
3319 A1295   5s orange & brn   .15 .15

1988, Apr. 26 *Photo.* *Perf. 13*
3320 A1296 13s multicolored   .25 .16

Children's Drawings Type of 1982

Designs: 5s, Girl wearing a folk costume, vert. 8s, Painter at easel, vert. 13s, Children playing. 20s, Ringing bells for peace. 32s, Accordion player, vert. 42s, Cosmonaut, vert. 50s, Assembly emblem.

1988, Apr. 28 *Litho.* *Perf. 14*
3321 A1093   5s multicolored   .15 .15
3322 A1093   8s multicolored   .18 .15
3323 A1093 13s multicolored   .28 .16
3324 A1093 20s multicolored   .42 .25
3325 A1093 32s multicolored   .65 .40
3326 A1093 42s multicolored   .90 .52
       Nos. 3321-3326 (6)   2.58 1.63

Souvenir Sheet
3327 A1093 50s multicolored   1.00   .62

4th Intl. Children's Assembly, Sofia. No. 3327 exists imperf.

Karl Marx A1297

1988, May 5 *Perf. 13*
3328 A1297 13s multicolored   .30 .16

Birds — A1297a

1988, May 6 *Litho.* *Perf. 13x13½*
3328A A1297a   5s Ciconia ciconia   .15 .15
3328B A1297a   5s Larus argentatus   .15 .15
3328C A1297a   8s Ardea cinerea   .18 .15
3328D A1297a   8s Corvus corone
                    cornix   .18 .15
3328E A1297a 10s Accipiter gentil-
                    lis   .22 .15
3328F A1297a 42s Bubo bubo   .90 .50
       Nos. 3328A-3328F (6)   1.78 1.25
Dated 1987.

Sofia Zoo, Cent. A1298

1988, May 20
3329 A1298   5s Loxodonta africana   .15 .15
3330 A1298 13s Ceratotherium
                simum   .25 .16
3331 A1298 25s Lycaon pictus   .50 .30
3332 A1298 30s Pelecanus onocrota-
                lus   .65 .36
3333 A1298 32s Bucorvus abissinicus .70 .40
3334 A1298 42s Nyctea scandiaca   .90 .52
  a.   Min. sheet of 6, #3329-3334   3.60 1.80
       Nos. 3329-3334 (6)   3.15 1.89

FINLANDIA '88 — A1299

1988, June 7
3335 A1299 30s Finland No. 1   .70 .35
No. 3335 printed in miniature sheets of 3 plus 3 labels picturing skyline, SOFIA '89 and FINLANDIA '88 exhibition emblems.
Exists imperf.

2nd Joint USSR-Bulgaria Space Flight — A1300

1988, June 7
3336 A1300   5s shown   .15 .15
3337 A1300 13s Rocket, globe   .30 .16

EXPO '91, Plovdiv — A1301

1988, June 7 *Perf. 13½x13*
3338 A1301 13s multicolored   .30 .16

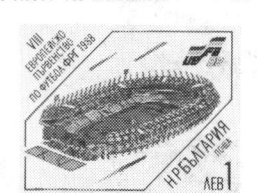

1988 European Soccer Championships — A1302

1988, June 10 *Perf. 13*
3339 A1302   5s Corner kick   .15 .15
3340 A1302 13s Heading the ball   .25 .16
3341 A1302 30s Referee, player   .55 .36
3342 A1302 42s Player holding tro-
                phy   .85 .55
       Nos. 3339-3342 (4)   1.80 1.22

Souvenir Sheet
3343 A1302 1 1 Stadium   2.25 1.25

Paintings by Dechko Usunov (1899-1986) A1303

Designs: 5s, Portrait of a Young Girl. 13s, Portrait of Maria Wassilewa. 30s, Self-portrait.

1988, June 14 *Perf. 13x13½*
3344 A1303   5s multicolored   .15 .15
3345 A1303 13s multicolored   .32 .16
3346 A1303 30s multicolored   .72 .36
       Nos. 3344-3346 (3)   1.19 .67

Souvenir Sheet

1st Woman in Space, 25th Anniv. — A1304

1988, June 16 *Perf. 13½x13*
3347 A1304 1 1 multicolored   2.50 1.50

Valentina Tereshkova's flight, June 16-19, 1963.

Kurdzhali Region Religious Art — A1305

Designs: 5s, St. John the Baptist, 1592. 8s, St. George Slaying the Dragon, 1841.

1988, June 27 *Perf. 13x13½*
3348 A1305   5s multicolored   .15 .15
3349 A1305   8s multicolored   .20 .15

1988 Summer Olympics, Seoul — A1306

1988, July 25 *Litho.* *Perf. 13*
3350 A1306   5s High jump   .15 .15
3351 A1306 13s Weight lifting   .28 .16
3352 A1306 30s Greco-Roman wres-
                tling   .65 .38
3353 A1306 42s Rhythmic gymnas-
                tics   .90 .52
       Nos. 3350-3353 (4)   1.98 1.21

Souvenir Sheet
3354 A1306 1 1 Volleyball   2.50 1.25
No. 3354 exists imperf.

BULGARIA

Dimitr and Karaja — A1307

1988, July 25 Litho. Perf. 13
3355 A1307 5s blk, dark olive bister & grn .15 .15

120th anniv. of the deaths of Haji Dimitr and Stefan Karaja, patriots killed during the Balkan Wars.

Problems of Peace and Socialism, 30th Anniv. A1308

1988, July 26 Photo.
3356 A1308 13s multicolored .25 .16

Paintings in the Ludmila Zhivkova Art Gallery — A1309

Paintings: No. 3357, *Harbor, Algiers*, by Albermarke (1875-1947). No. 3358, *Portrait of Ermin David in the Studio*, by Jul Pasken (1885-1930). No. 3359, *Madonna with Child and Sts. Sebastian and Roko*, by Giovanni Rosso (1494-1540). No. 3360, *The Barren Tree*, by Roland Udo (1879-1982).

1988, July 27 Litho. Perf. 14
3357 A1309 30s multicolored .65 .38
3358 A1309 30s multicolored .65 .38
3359 A1309 30s multicolored .65 .38
3360 A1309 30s multicolored .65 .38
Nos. 3357-3360 (4) 2.60 1.52

St. Clement of Ohrid University, Sofia, 100th Anniv. A1310

1988, Aug. 22 Perf. 13
3361 A1310 5s blk & pale yel .15 .15

PRAGA '88 A1311

1988, Aug. 22
3362 A1311 25s Czechoslovakia #2 in vermilion .60 .30

Printed in miniature sheets of 3 plus 3 labels picturing skyline, PRAGA '88 and SOFIA '89 exhibition emblems.
Exists imperf.

OLYMPHILEX '88 — A1312

1988, Sept. 1
3363 A1312 62s Korea No. 1 1.25 .75

Printed in miniature sheets of 3 plus 3 labels picturing skyline, OLYMPHILEX '88 and SOFIA '89 exhibition emblems.
Exists imperf.

A1313    A1314

1988, Sept. 15
3364 A1313 5s deep blue, lt blue & red .15 .15

Kremikovtsi steel mill, 25th anniv.

1988, Sept. 16 Perf. 13½x13
3365 A1314 13s dark red & ultra .25 .16

80th Interparliamentary Conference.

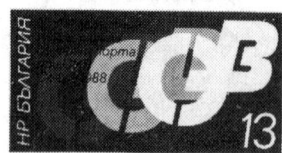

Transportation Commission 80th Congress — A1315

1988, Oct. 17
3366 A1315 13s deep lil rose & blk .25 .16

Kurdzhali Region Artifacts A1316

5s, Earthenware bowl, 13th-14th cent. 8s, Medieval fortification, Gorna Krepost Village, vert.

1988, Sept. 20 Perf. 13
3367 A1316 5s multicolored .15 .15
3368 A1316 8s multicolored .20 .15

Chiprovo Uprising, 300th Anniv. — A1317

1988, Sept. 23
3369 A1317 5s multicolored .15 .15

Bears A1318

1988, Sept. 26 Perf. 12½
3370 A1318 5s *Ursus arctos* .15 .15
3371 A1318 8s *Thalassarctos maritimus* .18 .15
3372 A1318 13s *Melursus ursinus* .30 .16
3373 A1318 20s *Helarctos malayanus* .45 .25
3374 A1318 32s *Selenarctos thibetanus* .70 .40
3375 A1318 42s *Tremarctos ornatus* .95 .52
a.   Min. sheet of 6, #3370-3375 3.00 1.50
Nos. 3370-3375 (6) 2.73 1.63

ECOFORUM for Peace — A1319

1988, Oct. 29 Perf. 13
3376 A1319 20s multicolored .50 .25

PLOVDIV '88 A1320

Design: Amphitheater ruins, PRAGA '88 and PLOVDIV '88 emblems.

1988, Nov. 2
3377 A1320 5s multicolored .15 .15

Exists in imperf. sheet of six.

Radio & Television Authority, 25th Anniv. — A1321

1988, Nov. 17 Litho. Perf. 13
3378 A1321 5s multicolored .15 .15

BULGARIA '89 A1321a

1988, Nov. 22 Litho. Perf. 13
3379 A1321a 42s No. 1 1.10 .58

Printed in miniature sheets of 3+3 labels picturing exhib. emblem and conf. center.
Exists imperf.

Souvenir Sheet

Danube Cruise Excursion Industry, 40th Anniv. — A1321b

1988, Nov. 25 Perf. 13½x13
3380   Sheet of 2 4.75 2.75
a. A1321b 1 l *Russia* 2.50 1.35
b. A1321b 1 l *Aleksandr Stamboliski* 2.50 1.35

Traffic Safety A1321c

1988, Nov. 28
3381 A1321c 5s multicolored .15 .15

New Year 1989 — A1321d

1988, Dec. 20 Perf. 13
3382 A1321d 5s shown .15 .15
3383 A1321d 13s multi, diff. .35 .25

Hotels in Winter A1322

1988, Dec. 19 Litho. Perf. 13½x13
3384 A1322 5s shown .15 .15
3385 A1322 8s multi, diff. .18 .15
3386 A1322 13s multi, diff. .28 .16
3387 A1322 30s multi, diff. .70 .40
Nos. 3384-3387 (4) 1.31 .84

Souvenir Sheet

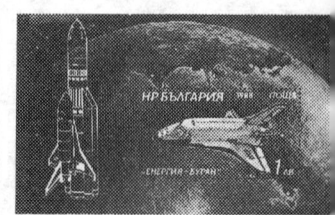

Soviet Space Shuttle *Energija-Buran* — A1322a

1988, Dec. 28 Perf. 13½x13
3387A A1322a 1 l dark blue 2.75 1.50

BULGARIA '89 — A1322b

Traditional modes of postal conveyance.

1988, Dec. 29 Perf. 13½x13
3387B A1322b 25s Mail coach .50 .30
3387C A1322b 25s Biplane .50 .30
3387D A1322b 25s Truck .50 .30
3387E A1322b 25s Steam packet .50 .30
Nos. 3387B-3387E (4) 2.00 1.20

Philatelic Exhibitions A1323

1989 Litho. Perf. 13
3388 A1322 42s France No. 1 1.00 .52
3389 A1322 62s India No. 200 1.50 .78

BULGARIA '89 and PHILEXFRANCE '89 (42s) or INDIA '89 (62s).
Nos. 3388-3389 each printed in sheets of 3 + 3 labels picturing skylines, BULGARIA '89 and

BULGARIA

PHILEXFRANCE or INDIA exhibition labels. Exist in sheets of 4 also. Exist imperf. Issue dates: 42s, Feb. 23; 62s, Jan. 14.

Souvenir Sheet

Universiade Winter Games, Sofia — A1324

Designs: a, Downhill skiing. b, Ice hockey. c, Cross-country skiing. d, Speed skating.

1989, Jan. 30   Litho.   Imperf.
Simulated Perforations
3390 Sheet of 4   2.25 1.25
a.-d. A1324 25s multicolored   .55   .30
No. 3390 exists imperf. without simulated perforations and containing black control number.

Humor and Satire Festival, Gabrovo A1325

1989, Feb. 7   Perf. 13½x13
3391 A1325 13s Don Quixote   .30   .16

Endangered Plant Species — A1326

1989, Feb. 22   Perf. 13x13½
3392 A1326 5s Ramonda serbica   .15   .15
3393 A1326 10s Paeonia maskula   .20   .15
3394 A1326 25s Viola perinensis   .50   .30
3395 A1326 30s Dracunculus vulgaris .60 .35
3396 A1326 42s Tulipa splendens   .85   .50
3397 A1326 60s Rindera umbellata   1.25 .70
a. Min. sheet of 6, #3392-3397   4.00 2.50
    Nos. 3392-3397 (6)   3.55 2.15

World Wildlife Fund A1327

Bats.
1989, Feb. 27   Perf. 13
3398 A1327 5s Nyctalus noctula   .15   .15
3399 A1327 13s Rhinolophus ferrumequinum .30 .15
3400 A1327 30s Myotis myotis   .70   .35
3401 A1327 42s Vespertilio murinus 1.00 .50
a. Min. sheet of 4, #3398-3401   2.25 1.25
    Nos. 3398-3401 (4)   2.15 1.15

Aleksandr Stamboliski (1879-1923), Premier — A1328

1989, Mar. 1   Perf. 13½x13
3402 A1328 5s brt org & blk   .15   .15

Souvenir Sheet

Soviet-Bulgarian Joint Space Flight, 10th Anniv. — A1329

Designs: a, Liftoff. b, Crew.

1989, Apr. 10   Perf. 13
3403 A1329 Sheet of 2   2.25 1.25
a.-b. 50s any single   1.10   .62

Exists imperf.

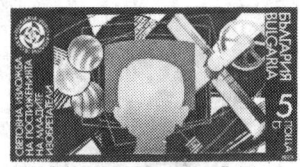

EXPO '91 Young Inventors Exhibition, Plovdiv — A1330

1989, Apr. 20   Perf. 13½x13
3404 A1330 5s multicolored   .15   .15

Petko Enev (b. 1889) A1331

Stanke Dimitrov Marek (b. 1889) — A1332

Perf. 13½x13, 13x13½
1989, Apr. 28
3405 A1331 5s scarlet & black   .15   .15
3406 A1332 5s scarlet & black   .15   .15

Icons A1333

Photocopier A1334

Paintings by Bulgarian artists: No. 3407, Archangel Michael, by Dimiter Molerov. No. 3408, Mother and Child, by Toma Vishanov. No. 3409, St. John, by Vishanov. No. 3410, St. Dimitri, by Ivan Terziev.

1989, Apr. 28   Perf. 13x13½
3407 A1333 30s multicolored   .65   .35
3408 A1333 30s multicolored   .65   .35
3409 A1333 30s multicolored   .65   .35
3410 A1333 30s multicolored   .65   .35
    Nos. 3407-3410 (4)   2.60 1.40

Nos. 3408, 3410 exist in sheets of four. Nos. 3407-3410 exist in souvenir sheets of four and together in one sheet of four, imperf.

1989, May 5
3411 A1334 5s shown   .15   .15
3412 A1334 8s Computer   .18   .15
3413 A1334 35s Telephone   .80   .45
3414 A1334 42s Dish receiver   .90   .52
    Nos. 3411-3414 (4)   2.03 1.27

Bulgarian Communications, 110th anniv. Nos. 3411-3413 exist in imperf. sheets of six.

Souvenir Sheet

58th FIP Congress — A1335

1989, May 22
3415 A1335 1 l Charioteer   2.00 1.00

Exists imperf.

1st Communist Party Congress in Bulgaria, 70th Anniv. — A1336

Famous Men — A1337

1989, June 15
3416 A1336 5s mar, blk & dk red   .15   .15

1989
#3417, Ilya Blaskov. #3418, Sofronii, Bishop of Vratza. #3419, Vassil Aprilov (b. 1789), educator, historian. #3420, Christo Jassenov (1889-1925). 10s, Stoyan Zagorchinov (1889-1969).

3417 A1337 5s black & gray olive   .15   .15
3418 A1337 5s blk, brn blk & pale green .15 .15
3419 A1337 8s lt blue, blk & vio blk .28 .15
3420 A1337 8s tan, blk & dark red brown .22 .15
3421 A1337 10s blk, pale pink & gray blue .28 .15
    Nos. 3417-3421 (5)   1.08   .75

Issued: #3417-3418, June 15; #3419, Aug. 1; #3420, Sept. 25; 10s, Aug. 5.

French Revolution, Bicent. — A1338

1989, June 26   Perf. 13½x13
3422 A1338 13s Anniv. emblem   .26   .15
3423 A1338 30s Jean-Paul Marat   .60   .35
3424 A1338 85s Robespierre   .85   .50
    Nos. 3422-3424 (3)   1.71 1.00

7th Army Games A1339

1989, June 30   Perf. 13
3425 A1339 5s Gymnast   .15   .15
3426 A1339 13s Equestrian   .28   .16
3427 A1339 30s Running   .65   .38
3428 A1339 42s Shooting   .95   .52
    Nos. 3425-3428 (4)   2.03 1.21

22nd World Canoe and Kayak Championships, Plovdiv — A1340

1989, Aug. 11   Litho.   Perf. 13
3429 A1340 13s Woman paddling   .28   .15
3430 A1340 40s Man rowing   .60   .25

Photography, 150th Anniv. — A1341

1989, Aug. 29   Perf. 13½x13
3431 A1341 42s blk, buff & yellow .85   .45

September 9 Revolution, 45th Anniv. — A1342

1989, Aug. 30   Perf. 13
3432 A1342 5s Revolutionaries   .15   .15
3433 A1342 8s Couple embracing   .16   .15
3434 A1342 13s Faces in a crowd   .25   .16
    Nos. 3432-3434 (3)   .56   .46

BULGARIA

Natural History Museum, Cent. A1343

1989, Aug. 31
3435 A1343 13s multicolored .30 .16

Postal Workers Killed in World War II — A1343a

Designs: 5s, L.D. Dardjikov. 8s, I.B. Dobrev. 10s, N.P. Antonov.

1989, Sept. 22 Litho. *Perf. 13*
3436 A1343a 5s multicolored .15 .15
3437 A1343a 8s multicolored .18 .15
3438 A1343a 13s multicolored .32 .18
   Nos. 3436-3438 (3) .65 .48

12th Shipping Unions Congress (FIATA) A1344

1989, Sept. 25 Litho. *Perf. 13½x13*
3439 A1344 42s light blue & dark blue .85 .45

Jawaharlal Nehru, 1st Prime Minister of Independent India — A1346

1989, Oct. 10
3440 A1346 13s blk, pale yel & brn .32 .16

Souvenir Sheet

European Ecology Congress — A1347

1989, Oct. 12 *Perf. 13*
3441 A1347 Sheet of 2 3.50 1.75
   a. 50s multicolored 1.20 .60
   b. 1 l multicolored 2.25 1.15

Snakes A1368

1989, Oct. 20 Litho. *Perf. 13*
3491 A1368 5s *Eryx jaculus turcicus* .15 .15
3492 A1368 10s *Elaphe longissima* .22 .15
3493 A1368 25s *Elaphe situla* .55 .30
3494 A1368 30s *Elaphe quatuor-lineata* .65 .35
3495 A1368 42s *Telescopus fallax* .90 .50
3496 A1368 60s *Coluber rubriceps* 1.25 .70
   a. Min. sheet of 6, #3491-3496 4.00 2.05
   Nos. 3491-3496 (6) 3.72 2.15

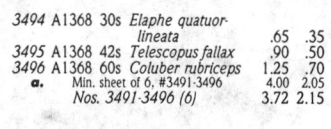

Intl. Youth Science Fair, Plovdiv, 1989 — A1369

1989, Nov. 4
3497 A1369 13s multicolored .25 .15

1990 World Soccer Championships, Italy — A1370

Various athletes: No. 3502a, Athletes facing right. No. 3502b, Athletes facing left.

1989, Dec. 1
3498 A1370 5s shown .15 .15
3499 A1370 13s multi, diff. .30 .15
3500 A1370 30s multi, diff. .70 .35
3501 A1370 42s multi, diff. .98 .50
   Nos. 3498-3501 (4) 2.13 1.15

Souvenir Sheet
3502   Sheet of 2 2.30 1.15
 a.-b. A1370 50s any single 1.15 .57

Air Sports A1371

1989, Dec. 8
3503 A1371 5s Glider planes .15 .15
3504 A1371 13s Hang glider .30 .15
3505 A1371 30s Sky diving .70 .35
3506 A1371 42s Three sky divers .98 .50
   Nos. 3503-3506 (4) 2.13 1.15

82nd General conference of the FAI, Varna.

Traffic Safety A1372

1989, Dec. 12
3507 A1372 5s multicolored .15 .15

New Year 1990 — A1373

1989, Dec. 25 Litho. *Perf. 13*
3508 A1373 5s Santa's sleigh .15 .15
3509 A1373 13s Snowman .32 .16

Cats — A1374

Designs: No. 3510, Persian. No. 3511, Tiger. 8s, Tabby. No. 3513, Himalayan. No. 3514, Persian, diff. 13s, Siamese. Nos. 3511 and 3514-3515 vert.

Perf. 13½x13, 13x13½
1989, Dec. 26 Background Color
3510 A1374 5s gray .15 .15
3511 A1374 5s yellow .15 .15
3512 A1374 8s orange .20 .15
3513 A1374 10s blue .24 .15
3514 A1374 10s brown orange .24 .15
3515 A1374 13s red .30 .15
   Nos. 3510-3515 (6) 1.28 .90

Explorers and Their Ships A1375

1990, Jan. 17 *Perf. 13*
3516 A1375 5s Christopher Columbus .15 .15
3517 A1375 8s Vasco da Gama .15 .15
3518 A1375 13s Fernando Magellan .25 .15
3519 A1375 32s Sir Francis Drake .60 .35
3520 A1375 42s Henry Hudson .75 .50
3521 A1375 60s James Cook 1.00 .70
   a. Min. sheet of 6, #3516-3521 3.50 1.75
   Nos. 3516-3521 (6) 2.90 2.00

Natl. Esperanto Movement, Cent. — A1376

1990, Feb. 23 Litho. *Perf. 13*
3522 A1376 10s multicolored .25 .15

Paintings by Foreign Artists in the Natl. Museum — A1377

Artists: No. 3523, Suzanna Valadon (1867-1938). No. 3524, Maurice Brianchon (1899-1978). No. 3525, Moise Kisling (1891-1953). No. 3526, Giovanni Beltraffio (1467-1516).

1990, Mar. 23 *Perf. 14*
3523 A1377 30s multicolored .65 .38
3524 A1377 30s multicolored .65 .38
3525 A1377 30s multicolored .65 .38
3526 A1377 30s multicolored .65 .38
   Nos. 3523-3526 (4) 2.60 1.52

1990 World Soccer Championships, Italy — A1378

Various athletes.

1990, Mar. 26 *Perf. 13*
3527 A1378 5s multicolored .15 .15
3528 A1378 13s multi, diff. .28 .15
3529 A1378 30s multi, diff. .70 .38
3530 A1378 42s multi, diff. .95 .50
   Nos. 3527-3530 (4) 2.08 1.18

Souvenir Sheet
3531   Sheet of 2 2.25 1.20
 a. A1378 50s Three players 1.10 .60
 b. A1378 50s Two players 1.10 .60

Bavaria No. 1 A1379

1990, Apr. 6 Litho. *Perf. 13*
3532 A1379 42s vermilion & blk 1.00 .50

ESSEN '90, Germany, Apr. 12-22. No. 3532 printed in sheets of 3 + 3 labels.

Souvenir Sheet

Penny Black, 150th Anniv. A1380

1990, Apr. 10
3533   Sheet of 2 2.25 1.20
 a. A1380 50s Great Britain #1 1.10 .60
 b. A1380 50s Sir Rowland Hill 1.10 .60

Cooperative Farming in Bulgaria, Cent. — A1381

1990, Apr. 17
3534 A1381 5s multicolored .15 .15

Dimitar Chorbadjiski-Chudomir (1890-1967) — A1382

1990, Apr. 24
3535 A1382 5s multicolored .15 .15

Labor Day, Cent. — A1383

1990, May 1 *Perf. 13x13½*
3536 A1383 10s multicolored .25 .15

BULGARIA

ITU, 125th Anniv. — A1384

1990, May 13		Litho.		Perf. 13½x13	
3537	A1384	20s blue, red & black		.45	.24

Belgium No. 1 — A1385

1990, May 23				Perf. 13	
3538	A1385	30s multicolored		.75	.38

Belgica '90. No. 3538 printed in sheets of 3 + 3 labels.

Lamartine (1790-1869), French Poet — A1386

1990, June 15				Perf. 13½x13	
3539	A1386	20s multicolored		.45	.25

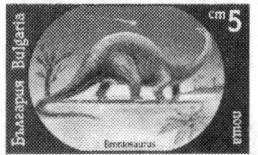

Dinosaurs — A1387

1990, June 19				Perf. 12½	
3540	A1387	5s Brontosaurus		.15	.15
3541	A1387	8s Stegosaurus		.20	.15
3542	A1387	13s Edaphosaurus		.32	.16
3543	A1387	25s Rhamphorhynchus		.62	.30
3544	A1387	32s Protoceratops		.80	.40
3545	A1387	42s Triceratops		1.05	.55
a.		Min. sheet of 6, #3540-3545		3.25	1.60
		Nos. 3540-3545 (6)		3.14	1.71

1992 Summer Olympic Games, Barcelona — A1388

1990, July 13				Perf. 13½x13	
3546	A1388	5s Swimming		.15	.15
3547	A1388	13s Handball		.32	.16
3548	A1388	30s Hurdling		.75	.38
3549	A1388	42s Cycling		1.05	.55
		Nos. 3546-3549 (4)		2.27	1.24

Souvenir Sheet

3550		Sheet of 2		2.50	1.25
a.	A1388	50s Tennis, forehand		1.25	.62
b.	A1388	50s Tennis, backhand		1.25	.62

Butterflies — A1389

1990, Aug. 8		Litho.		Perf. 13	
3551	A1389	5s Zerynthia Polyxena		.15	.15
3552	A1389	10s Panaxia quadripunctaria		.22	.15
3553	A1389	20s Proserpinus proserpina		.45	.24
3554	A1389	30s Hyles lineata		.65	.36
3555	A1389	42s Thecla betulae		.95	.55
3556	A1389	60s Euphydryas cynthia		1.25	.72
a.		Min. sheet of 6, #3551-3556		4.00	2.10
		Nos. 3551-3556 (6)		3.67	2.17

Airplanes — A1390

1990, Aug. 30		Litho.		Perf. 13½x13	
3557	A1390	5s Airbus A-300		.15	.15
3558	A1390	10s Tu-204		.15	.15
3559	A1390	25s Concorde		.30	.25
3560	A1390	30s DC-9		.40	.20
3561	A1390	42s Il-86		.55	.40
3562	A1390	60s Boeing 747		.75	.55
a.		Min. sheet of 6, #3557-3562		3.00	2.00
		Nos. 3557-3562 (6)		2.30	1.80

Exarch Joseph I (1840-1915), Religious Leader — A1391

1990, Sept. 27				Perf. 13	
3563	A1391	5s blk, pur & grn		.15	.15

Intl. Traffic Safety Year — A1392

1990, Oct. 9		Litho.		Perf. 13	
3564	A1392	5s multicolored		.15	.15

Olymphilex '90, Varna — A1393

1990, Oct. 16				Perf. 13x13½	
3565	A1393	5s Shot put		.15	.15
3566	A1393	13s Discus		.25	.15
3567	A1393	42s Hammer throw		.90	.55
3568	A1393	60s Javelin		1.25	.72
a.		Souv. sheet of 4, #3565-3568, imperf.		12.00	1.50
		Nos. 3565-3568 (4)		2.55	1.57

Space Exploration — A1394

Designs: 5s, Sputnik, 1957, USSR. 8s, Vostok, 1961, USSR. 10s, Voshkod 2, 1965, USSR. 20s, Apollo-Soyuz, 1975, US-USSR. 42s, Space Shuttle Columbia, 1981, US. 60s, Galileo, 1989-1996, US. 1 l, Apollo 11 Moon landing, 1969, US.

1990, Oct. 22				Perf. 13½x13	
3569	A1394	5s multicolored		.15	.15
3570	A1394	8s multicolored		.16	.15
3571	A1394	10s multicolored		.20	.15
3572	A1394	20s multicolored		.40	.24
3573	A1394	42s multicolored		.90	.55
3574	A1394	60s multicolored		1.25	.72
		Nos. 3569-3574 (6)		3.06	1.96

Souvenir Sheet

3575	A1394	1 l multicolored		2.75	1.50

St. Clement of Okhrida — A1395

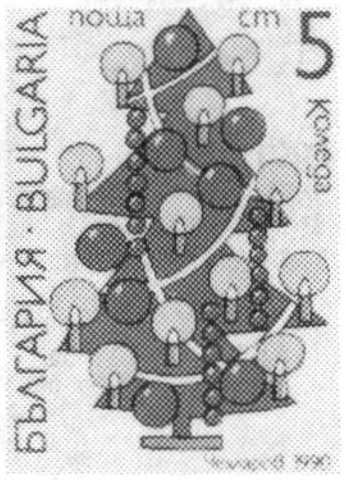

1990, Nov. 29		Litho.		Perf. 13	
3576	A1395	5s multicolored		.15	.15

Christmas — A1396

1990, Dec. 25		Litho.		Perf. 13	
3577	A1396	5s Christmas tree		.15	.15
3578	A1396	20s Santa Claus		.40	.24

European Figure Skating Championships, Sofia — A1397

1991, Jan. 18				Perf. 13½x13	
3579	A1397	15s multicolored		.35	.18

Farm Animals — A1398

1991-92				Perf. 14x13½	
3581	A1398	20s Sheep		.30	.15
3582	A1398	25s Goose		.35	.15
3583	A1398	30s Hen, chicks		.40	.20
3584	A1398	40s Horse		.55	.30
3585	A1398	62s Goat		.85	.40
3586	A1398	86s Sow		1.25	.60
3587	A1398	95s Goat		.70	.35
3588	A1398	1 l Donkey		1.40	.50
3589	A1398	2 l Bull		2.75	.60
3590	A1398	5 l Turkey		7.00	1.50
3591	A1398	10 l Cow		14.00	2.00
		Nos. 3581-3591 (11)		29.55	6.75

Issued: 20s, 25s, 40s, 86s, 1 l, Aug. 21; 10 l, Feb. 22; 95s, May 5, 1992; others, Feb. 11, 1991.

Mushrooms — A1399

1991, Mar. 19				Perf. 12½x13	
3597	A1399	5s Amanita phalloides		.15	.15
3598	A1399	10s Amanita verna		.15	.15
3599	A1399	20s Amanita pantherina		.30	.15
3600	A1399	32s Amanita muscaria		.50	.30
3601	A1399	42s Gyromitra esculenta		.60	.35
3602	A1399	60s Boletus satanas		.80	.50
a.		Min. sheet of 6, #3597-3602		3.00	1.50
		Nos. 3597-3602 (6)		2.50	1.60

French Impressionists — A1400

Designs: 20s, Good Morning, by Gauguin. 43s, Madame Dobini, by Degas. 62s, Peasant Woman, by Pissarro. 67s, Woman with Black Hair, by Manet. 80s, Blue Vase, by Cezanne. 2 l, Jeanny Samari, by Renoir. 3 l, Self portrait, by Van Gogh.

1991, Apr. 1				Perf. 13	
3603	A1400	20s multicolored		.22	.18
3604	A1400	43s multicolored		.50	.38
3605	A1400	62s multicolored		.70	.55
3606	A1400	67s multicolored		.80	.60
3607	A1400	80s multicolored		1.00	.75
3608	A1400	2 l multicolored		2.25	1.75
		Nos. 3603-3608 (6)		5.47	4.21

Miniature Sheet

3609	A1400	3 l multicolored		4.50	2.65

Swiss Confederation, 700th Anniv. — A1401

1991, Apr. 11					
3610	A1401	62s multicolored		.90	.55

Philatelic Review, Cent. — A1402

1991, May 7		Litho.		Perf. 13	
3611	A1402	30s multicolored		.45	.25

Europa — A1403

1991, May 10				Perf. 13x13½	
3612	A1403	43s Meteosat		.70	.38
3613	A1403	62s Ariane rocket		1.00	.55

Horses — A1404

1991, May 21				Perf. 13x12½	
3614	A1404	5s Przewalski's horse		.15	.15
3615	A1404	10s Tarpan		.15	.15
3616	A1404	25s Arabian		.35	.20
3617	A1404	35s Arabian		.45	.30
3618	A1404	42s Shetland pony		.55	.35
3619	A1404	60s Draft horse		.80	.50
a.		Min. sheet of 6, #3614-3619		3.00	1.50
		Nos. 3614-3619 (6)		2.45	1.65

BULGARIA

EXPO 91, Plovdiv — A1405

1991, June 6		Litho.	Perf. 13½x13
3620	A1405	30s multicolored	.45 .28

Wolfgang Amadeus Mozart — A1406

1991, July 2			Perf. 13
3621	A1406	62s multicolored	.95 .55

Space Shuttle Missions, 10th Anniv. — A1407

1991, July 23		Litho.	Perf. 13
3622	A1407	12s Columbia	.15 .15
3623	A1407	32s Challenger	.30 .15
3624	A1407	50s Discovery	.40 .20
3625	A1407	86s Atlantis, vert.	.75 .40
3626	A1407	1.50 l Buran, vert.	1.25 .60
3627	A1407	2 l Atlantis, diff., vert.	1.50 .75
		Nos. 3622-3627 (6)	4.35 2.25

Souvenir Sheet

3628	A1407	3 l US shuttle, earth	4.00 2.00

1992 Winter Olympics, Albertville — A1408

1991, Aug. 7		Litho.	Perf. 13x13½
3629	A1408	30s Luge	.40 .28
3630	A1408	43s Slalom skiing	.52 .38
3631	A1408	67s Ski jumping	.85 .60
3632	A1408	2 l Biathlon	2.50 1.75
		Nos. 3629-3632 (4)	4.27 3.01

Souvenir Sheet

3633	A1408	3 l Two-man bobsled	4.50 2.65

Sheraton Sofia Hotel Balkan A1409

1991, Sept. 6		Litho.	Perf. 13
3634	A1409	62s multicolored	1.10 .55

Printed in sheets of 3 + 3 labels.

For all your stamp supply needs
www.scottonline.com

Dogs — A1410

1991, Oct. 11			Perf. 13x13½
3635	A1410	30s Japanese	.25 .15
3636	A1410	43s Chihuahua	.40 .20
3637	A1410	62s Pinscher	.55 .30
3638	A1410	80s Yorkshire terrier	.70 .35
3639	A1410	1 l Chinese	.90 .45
3640	A1410	3 l Pug	2.50 1.25
a.		Min. sheet of 6, #3635-3640	5.50 2.75
		Nos. 3635-3640 (6)	5.30 2.70

Cologne '91, Intl. Philatelic Exhibition A1411

1991, Oct. 21			Perf. 13
3641	A1411	86s multicolored	1.50 .75

Printed in sheets of 3 + 3 labels.

Souvenir Sheet

Brandenburg Gate, Bicent. — A1412

1991, Oct. 23			
3642	A1412	4 l multicolored	7.00 3.50

Exists imperf.

Phila Nippon '91 A1413

1991, Nov. 11			
3643	A1413	62s Japan #1	1.10 .55

Printed in sheets of 3 + 3 labels.

Bulgarian Railroad, 125th Anniv. — A1414

1991, Nov. 30			
3644	A1414	30s Locomotive	.55 .28
3645	A1414	30s Passenger car	.55 .28

Medicinal Plants A1415

Designs: 30s, Pulsatilla vernalis. 40s, Pulsatilla pratensis. 55s, Pulsatilla halleri. 60s, Aquilegia nigricans. 1 l, Hippophae rhamnoides. 2 l, Ribes nigrum.

1991, Nov. 20		Litho.	Perf. 13
3646	A1415	30s +15s label	.40 .20
3647	A1415	40s multicolored	.35 .20
3648	A1415	55s multicolored	.50 .25
3649	A1415	60s multicolored	.55 .30
3650	A1415	1 l multicolored	.90 .45
3651	A1415	2 l multicolored	1.75 .90
a.		Min. sheet of 6, #3646-3651	4.50 2.50
		Nos. 3646-3651 (6)	4.45 2.30

No. 3646 printed se-tenant with label. No. 3651a sold for 5 l, but does not contain the 15s label printed with No. 3646.

Basketball, Cent. A1416

1991, Dec. 6			Perf. 13½x13
3652	A1416	43s Ball below rim	.50 .25
3653	A1416	62s Ball at rim	.75 .40
3654	A1416	90s Ball in cylinder	1.10 .55
3655	A1416	1 l Ball in basket	1.25 .65
		Nos. 3652-3655 (4)	3.60 1.85

El Greco, 450th Birth Anniv. — A1417

Paintings: 43s, Christ Carrying the Cross. 50s, Holy Family with St. Anne. 60s, St. John the Evangelist and St. John the Baptist. 62s, St. Andrew and St. Francis. 1 l, Holy Family with St. Mary Magdalene. 2 l, Cardinal Nino de Guevara. 3 l, Holy Family with St. Anne (detail).

1991, Dec. 13			Perf. 13
3656	A1417	43s multicolored	.45 .25
3657	A1417	50s multicolored	.55 .30
3658	A1417	60s multicolored	.65 .35
3659	A1417	62s multicolored	.70 .40
3660	A1417	1 l multicolored	1.10 .55
3661	A1417	2 l multicolored	2.00 1.00
		Nos. 3656-3661 (6)	5.45 2.85

Souvenir Sheet

3662	A1417	3 l multicolored	4.00 2.00

No. 3662 contains one 43x53mm stamp.

Christmas A1418

1991, Dec. 18			
3663	A1418	30s Snowman, candle, bell, heart	.55 .28
3664	A1418	62s Star, angel, flower, house, tree	1.10 .55

Marine Mammals — A1419

Designs: 30s, Phogophoca graenlandica. 43s, Orcinus orca. 62s, Odobenus rosmarus. 68s, Tursiops truncatus. 1 l, Monachus monachus. 2 l, Phocaena phocaena.

1991, Dec. 24			
3665	A1419	30s multicolored	.35 .20
3666	A1419	43s multicolored	.50 .25
3667	A1419	62s multicolored	.75 .40
3668	A1419	68s multicolored	.80 .40
3669	A1419	1 l multicolored	1.25 .65
3670	A1419	2 l multicolored	2.50 1.25
a.		Min. sheet of #3665-3670	6.25 3.25
		Nos. 3665-3670 (6)	6.15 3.15

Settlement of Jews in Bulgaria, 500th Anniv. — A1420

1992, Mar. 5		Litho.	Perf. 13
3671	A1420	1 l multicolored	1.75 .90

Gioacchino Rossini (1792-1868), Composer — A1421

1992, Mar. 11			
3672	A1421	50s multicolored	.88 .45

Plovdiv Fair, Cent. A1422

1992, Mar. 25			
3673	A1422	1 l buff & black	1.75 .90

Fiat Croma — A1423

Automobiles.

1992, Mar. 26			Perf. 13½x13
3674	A1423	30s Volvo 740	.35 .20
3675	A1423	45s Ford Escort	.55 .30
3676	A1423	50s shown	.60 .30
3677	A1423	50s Mercedes 600	.60 .30
3678	A1423	1 l Peugeot 605	1.10 .55
3679	A1423	2 l BMW 316	1.75 .90
		Nos. 3674-3679 (6)	4.95 2.55

Francisco de Orellana — A1424

Explorers: No. 3681, Vespucci. No. 3682, Magellan. No. 3683, Gonzalo Jimenez de Quesada (1509-1579). 2 l, Drake. 3 l, Pedro de Valdivia (1500-1553). 4 l, Columbus.

1992, Apr. 22		Litho.	Perf. 13
3680	A1424	50s multicolored	.45 .22
3681	A1424	50s multicolored	.45 .22
3682	A1424	1 l multicolored	.90 .45
3683	A1424	1 l multicolored	.90 .45
3684	A1424	2 l multicolored	1.80 .90
3685	A1424	3 l multicolored	2.70 1.35
		Nos. 3680-3685 (6)	7.20 3.59

Souvenir Sheet

3686	A1424	4 l multicolored	3.50 1.75

BULGARIA

Granada '92 — A1425

1992, Apr. 23
3687 A1425 62s multicolored .55 .28
No. 3687 printed in sheets of 3 + 3 labels.

Discovery of America, 500th Anniv. A1426

1992, Apr. 24
3688 A1426 1 l Ships, map .90 .45
3689 A1426 2 l Columbus, ship 1.80 .90
a. Pair, #3688-3689 2.60 1.30

Europa.

SOS Children's Village A1427

1992, June 15 Litho. Perf. 13
3690 A1427 1 l multicolored .90 .45

1992 Summer Olympics, Barcelona A1428

1992, July 15 Perf. 13½x13
3691 A1428 50s Swimming .45 .22
3692 A1428 50s Long jump .45 .22
3693 A1428 1 l High jump .90 .45
3694 A1428 3 l Gymnastics 2.70 1.35
Nos. 3691-3694 (4) 4.50 2.24

Souvenir Sheet
Perf. 13x13½
3695 A1428 4 l Torch, vert. 3.60 1.80

Motorcycles A1429

Designs: 30s, 1902 Laurin & Klement. No. 3697, 1928 Puch 200 Luxus. No. 3698, 1931 Norton CS1. 70s, 1950 Harley Davidson. 1 l, 1986 Gilera SP 01. 2 l, 1990 BMW K1.

1992, July 30 Perf. 13
3696 A1429 30s multicolored .20 .15
3697 A1429 50s multicolored .30 .15
3698 A1429 50s multicolored .30 .15
3699 A1429 70s multicolored .40 .20
3700 A1429 1 l multicolored .60 .30
3701 A1429 2 l multicolored 1.25 .65
Nos. 3696-3701 (6) 3.05 1.60

Genoa '92 Intl. Philatelic Exhibition A1430

1992, Sept. 18 Perf. 13
3702 A1430 1 l multicolored .90 .45
This is a developing set. Numbers may change.

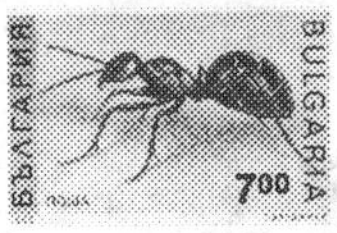

Insects — A1431

1992 Litho. Perf. 14x13½
3710 A1431 1 l Dragonfly .15
3711 A1431 2 l Mayfly .22
3712 A1431 3 l Locust .32
3713 A1431 4 l Stag beetle .45
3714 A1431 5 l Carrion beetle .55
3715 A1431 7 l Ant .75
3718 A1431 20 l Bee 2.25
3718A A1431 50 l Praying mantis 5.75
Nos. 3710-3718A (8) 10.44

Issued: 7, 20 l, Sept. 25; 3, 50 l, Nov. 30; 1, 2, 4, 5 l, Dec. 15, 1993.
This is a developing set. Numbers may change.

Based on available currency exchange rates the face value of No. 3718A was about $2. It appears that many Bulgarian stamps are appearing in the market at significantly higher prices than face values would indicate.

A1432   A1433

1992, Sept. 30 Perf. 13
3719 A1432 1 l blk, pink & rose .90 .45
Higher Institute of Architecture and Building, 50th anniv.

1992, Oct. 16 Litho. Perf. 13
Trees: No. 3720, Quercus mestensis. No. 3721, Aesculus hippocastanum. No. 3722, Quercus thracica. No. 3723, Pinus peuce. 2 l, Acer heldreichii. 3 l, Pyrus bulgarica.
3720 A1433 50s multicolored .30 .15
3721 A1433 50s multicolored .30 .15
3722 A1433 1 l multicolored .60 .30
3723 A1433 1 l multicolored .60 .30
3724 A1433 2 l multicolored 1.25 .65
3725 A1433 3 l multicolored 2.00 1.00
Nos. 3720-3725 (6) 5.05 2.55

Ethnographical Museum, Cent. — A1434

1992, Oct. 23
3726 A1434 1 l multicolored .90 .45

Tanker Bulgaria — A1435

1992, Oct. 30 Litho. Perf. 13
3727 A1435 30s Freighter Bulgaria .20 .15
3728 A1435 50s Castor .30 .15
3729 A1435 1 l Hero of Sevastopol .60 .30
3730 A1435 2 l shown 1.25 .65
3731 A1435 2 l Aleko Constantinov 1.25 .65
3732 A1435 3 l Varna 2.00 1.00
Nos. 3727-3732 (6) 5.60 2.90

Bulgarian Merchant Fleet, Cent.

Bulgaria, Member of the Council of Europe — A1436

1992, Nov. 6 Litho. Perf. 13
3733 A1436 7 l multicolored 6.30 3.15

Souvenir Sheet

4th World Congress of Popular Sports, Varna — A1437

1992, Nov. 17 Litho. Perf. 13
3734 A1437 4 l multicolored 4.00

Christmas A1438

1992, Dec. 1 Perf. 13½x13
3735 A1438 1 l Santa Claus .75
3736 A1438 7 l Madonna & Child 5.25

Wild Cats — A1439

1992, Dec. 18 Litho. Perf. 13
3737 A1439 50s Panthera pardus .25
3738 A1439 50s Acinonyx jubatus .25
3739 A1439 1 l Panthera onca .50
3740 A1439 2 l Panthera tigris 1.00
3741 A1439 2 l Felis concolor 1.00
3742 A1439 3 l Panthera leo 1.50
Nos. 3737-3742 (6) 4.50

Sports A1440

1992, Dec. 18
3743 A1440 50s Baseball .35
3744 A1440 50s Cricket .35
3745 A1440 1 l Polo .75
3746 A1440 1 l Harness racing .75
3747 A1440 2 l Field hockey 1.50
3748 A1440 3 l Football 2.25
Nos. 3743-3748 (6) 5.95

Owls A1441

1992, Dec. 23
3749 A1441 30s Aegolius funereus .20
3750 A1441 50s Strix aluco .25
3751 A1441 1 l Asio otus .50
3752 A1441 1 l Otus scops 1.00
3753 A1441 2 l Asio flammeus 1.00
3754 A1441 3 l Tyto alba 1.50
Nos. 3749-3754 (6) 4.45

Nos. 3749, 3751, 3753-3754 are vert.

Paintings Depicting History of Bulgaria A1442

Artists: 50s, Dimiter Gyudzhenov. 1 l, 3 l, Nikolai Pavlovich. 2 l, Dimiter Panchev. 4 l, Mito Ganovski.

1992, Dec. 28
3755 A1442 50s multicolored .38
3756 A1442 1 l multicolored .75
3757 A1442 2 l multicolored 1.50
3758 A1442 3 l multicolored 2.25
Nos. 3755-3758 (4) 4.88

Souvenir Sheet
3759 A1442 4 l multicolored, vert. 3.00

Archeological Museum, Cent. — A1443

1993 World Biathlon Championships, Borovetz — A1444

1993, Jan. 1 Litho. Perf. 13x13½
3760 A1443 1 l multicolored .75

1993, Feb. 5
3761 A1444 1 l Woman aiming rifle .75
3762 A1444 7 l Skiing 5.25

Neophit Rilski, Birth Bicent. A1445

1993, Apr. 22 Litho. Perf. 13½x13
3763 A1445 1 l henna brn & ol bis .75

829

BULGARIA

Contemporary Art — A1446

Europa: 3 l, Sculpture of centaur, by Georgi Chapkinov. 8 l, Painting of geometric forms, by D. Bujukliski.

1993, Apr. 29   Perf. 13x13½
3764 A1446 3 l multicolored   2.25
3765 A1446 8 l multicolored   6.00

Fish — A1447

1993, June 29   Litho.   Perf. 13
3766 A1447 1 l C.a.j. bicaudatus   .75
3767 A1447 2 l Mollienesia velifera   1.50
3768 A1447 2 l Aphyosemion bivittatum   2.25
3769 A1447 3 l Pterophyllum eimekei   2.25
3770 A1447 4 l Symphysodon discus   3.00
3771 A1447 8 l Trichogaster leeri   6.00
    Nos. 3766-3771 (6)   15.75

Fruit — A1448

1993, July 8   Perf. 13x13½
3772 A1448 1 l Malus domestica   .35
3773 A1448 2 l Pyrus sativa   .70
3774 A1448 2 l Persica vulgaris   .70
3775 A1448 3 l Cydonia oblonga   1.00
3776 A1448 5 l Punica granatum   1.75
3777 A1448 7 l Ficus carica   2.50
    Nos. 3772-3777 (6)   7.00

Claudio Monteverdi (1567-1643), Composer A1449

1993, July 20   Litho.   Perf. 13½x13
3778 A1449 1 l multicolored   .75

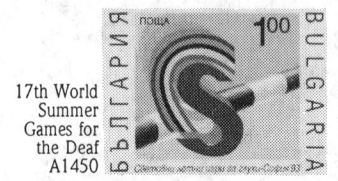

17th World Summer Games for the Deaf A1450

1993, July 20   Perf. 13
3779 A1450 1 l shown   .75
3780 A1450 2 l Swimming   1.50
3781 A1450 3 l Cycling   2.25
3782 A1450 4 l Tennis   3.00
    Nos. 3779-3782 (4)   7.50

Souvenir Sheet
3783 A1450 5 l Soccer

Miniature Sheet 
A1451

Council of Preslav, Cyrillic Alphabet in Bulgaria, 1100th Anniv.: a, Baptism of Christian convert. b, Tsar Boris I (852-889). c, Tsar Simeon (893-927). d, Battle between Bulgarians and Byzantines.

1993, Sept. 16   Litho.   Perf. 13½x13
3784 A1451 5 l Sheet of 4, #a.-d.   3.50

Alexander of Battenberg (1857-93), Prince of Bulgaria — A1452

1993, Sept. 23   Perf. 13x13½
3785 A1452 3 l multicolored   .50

Peter I. Tchaikovsky (1840-93) A1453

1993, Sept. 30   Perf. 13½x13
3786 A1453 3 l multicolored   .50

Small Arms A1454    Isaac Newton (1643-1725) A1455

1993, Oct. 22   Litho.   Perf. 13½x14
3787 A1454 1 l Crossbow, 16th cent.   .18
3788 A1454 2 l Pistol, 18th cent.   .35
3789 A1454 3 l Luger, 1908   .50
3790 A1454 3 l Pistol, 1873   .50
3791 A1454 5 l Rifle, 1938   .85
3792 A1454 7 l Kalashnikov, 1947   1.25
    Nos. 3787-3792 (6)   3.63

1993, Oct. 29   Perf. 13½x13
3793 A1455 1 l multicolored   .18

Organized Philately in Bulgaria, Cent. A1456

1993, Nov. 16
3794 A1456 1 l multicolored   .18

Ecology A1457

1993, Nov. 17
3795 A1457 1 l shown   .18
3796 A1457 7 l Ecology   1.25

Game Animals A1458

1993, Nov. 25
3797 A1458 1 l Anas platrhynchos   .18
3798 A1458 1 l Phasianus colchicus   .18
3799 A1458 2 l Vulpes vulpes   .35
3800 A1458 3 l Capreolus capreolus   .50
3801 A1458 6 l Lepus europaeus   1.00
3802 A1458 7 l Sus scrofa   1.40
    Nos. 3797-3802 (6)   3.61

Christmas A1459

Signs of Zodiac on sundial: No. 3803a, Taurus, Gemini, Cancer. b, Libra, Virgo, Leo. No. 3804a, Aquarius, Pisces, Aries. b, Capricorn, Sagittarius, Scorpio.

1993, Dec. 1
3803 A1459 1 l Pair, #a.-b.   .35
3804 A1459 7 l Pair, #a.-b.   2.50

When placed together, Nos. 3803-3804 form a complete sundial.

Regional Folk Costumes for Men
A1460   A1461

1993, Dec. 16   Litho.   Perf. 13½x14
3805 A1460 1 l Sofia   .15
3806 A1461 1 l Plovdiv   .15
3807 A1460 2 l Belogradchik   .22
3808 A1460 3 l Shumen   .32
3809 A1461 3 l Oryakhovitsa   .32
3810 A1461 8 l Kurdzhali   .90
    Nos. 3805-3810 (6)   2.06

1994 Winter Olympics, Lillehammer A1462

1994, Feb. 8   Perf. 13
3811 A1462 1 l Freestlye skiing   .15
3812 A1462 2 l Speed skating   .22
3813 A1462 3 l 2-Man luge   .32
3814 A1462 4 l Hockey   .45
    Nos. 3811-3814 (4)   1.14

Souvenir Sheet
3815 A1462 5 l Downhill skiing   .55

Nikolai Pavlovich (1835-94) A1463

1994, Feb. 16   Perf. 13½x13
3816 A1463 3 l multicolored   .32

Dinosaurs A1464

1994, Apr. 27   Litho.   Perf. 13
3817 A1464 2 l Plesiosaurus   .15
3818 A1464 3 l Iguanodon   .15
3819 A1464 3 l Archaeopteryx   .15
3820 A1464 4 l Edmontonia   .16
3821 A1464 5 l Styracosaurus   .20
3822 A1464 7 l Tyrannosaurus Rex   .28
    Nos. 3817-3822 (6)   1.09

1994 World Cup Soccer Championships, US — A1465

Players in championships of : 3 l, Chile, 1962. 6 l, England, 1966. 7 l, Mexico, 1970. 9 l, West Germany, 1974. No. 3827a, Mexico, 1986, vert. b, US, 1994.

1994, Apr. 28
3823 A1465 3 l multicolored   .15
3824 A1465 6 l multicolored   .22
3825 A1465 7 l multicolored   .28
3826 A1465 9 l multicolored   .35
    Nos. 3823-3826 (4)   1.00

Souvenir Sheet
3827 A1465 5 l Sheet of 2, #a.-b.   .40

For No. 3827 with inscription reading up along the left margin, see No. 3851.

Europa — A1466

European Discoveries: 3 l, Axis of symmetry. 15 l, Electrocardiogram.

1994, Apr. 29   Litho.   Perf. 13½
3828 A1466 3 l multicolored   .15
3829 A1466 15 l multicolored   .60

Boris Hristov (1914-93) — A1467

1994, May 18   Litho.   Perf. 13
3830 A1467 3 l brown & bister   .15

Cricetus Cricetus — A1468

Designs: 3 l, In nest. 7 l, Emerging from burrow. 10 l, Standing on hind legs. 15 l, Finding berry.

1994, Sept. 23   Litho.   Perf. 13
3831 A1468 3 l multicolored   .15
3832 A1468 7 l multicolored   .28
3833 A1468 10 l multicolored   .40
3834 A1468 15 l multicolored   .60
    Nos. 3831-3834 (4)   1.43

World Wildlife Fund.

BULGARIA

Space Program — A1469

Intl. Olympic Committee, Cent. — A1470

1994, Nov. 4   Litho.   *Perf. 13*
3835 A1469   3 l multicolored   .15

1994, Nov. 7
3836 A1470   3 l multicolored   .15

Icons A1471

Christmas A1472

1994, Nov. 24   Litho.   *Perf. 13x13½*
3837 A1471   2 l Christ   .15
3838 A1471   3 l Christ, the healer   .15
3839 A1471   5 l Crucifixion   .16
3840 A1471   7 l Archangel Michael   .22
3841 A1471   8 l Sts. Cyril, Methodius   .25
3842 A1471   15 l Madonna & Child   .45
Nos. 3837-3842 (6)   1.38

1994, Dec. 1
3843 A1472   3 l Ancient coin   .20
3844 A1472   15 l Coin, diff.   1.00

Roses A1473

1994, Dec. 12   *Perf. 13*
Color of Rose
3845 A1473   2 l yellow   .15
3846 A1473   3 l rose red   .15
3847 A1473   5 l white   .15
3848 A1473   7 l salmon   .20
3849 A1473   10 l carmine   .30
3850 A1473   15 l orange & yellow   .40
Nos. 3845-3850 (6)   1.35

Souvenir Sheet
No. 3827 with Additional Inscription in Left Sheet Margin

1994, Dec. 15   Litho.   *Perf. 13*
3851 A1465   5 l Sheet of 2, #a.-b.   .40

Trams A1474

1994, Dec. 29
3852 A1474   1 l Model 1912   .15
3853 A1474   2 l Model 1928   .15
3854 A1474   3 l Model 1931   .15
3855 A1474   5 l Model 1942   .16
3856 A1474   8 l Model 1951   .25
3857 A1474   10 l Model 1961   .32
Nos. 3852-3857 (6)   1.18

Vassil Petleshkov (1845-76), Revolutionary A1475

1995, Feb. 27   Litho.   *Perf. 13½x13*
3858 A1475   3 l multicolored   .15

End of World War II, 50th Anniv. — A1476

Europa: 15 l, Dove holding olive branch standing on gun barrel.

1995, May 3   Litho.   *Perf. 13*
3859 A1476   3 l multicolored   .15
3860 A1476   15 l multicolored   .45

Souvenir Sheet

Men's World Volleyball League, Cent. A1477

Designs: a, 10 l, Player digging ball. b, 15 l, Player spiking ball, vert.

1995, May 25   Litho.   *Perf. 13*
3861 A1477   Sheet of 2, #a.-b.   .75

Souvenir Sheet

European Nature Conservation Year — A1478

Designs: a, 10 l, Pancratium maritimum. b, 15 l, Aquila heliaca. Illustration reduced.

1995, June 23   Litho.   *Perf. 13*
3862 A1478   Sheet of 2, #a.-b.   .75

Antarctic Wildlife — A1479

1 l, Euphausia superba. 2 l, Chaenocephalus. 3 l, Physeter catodon. 5 l, Leptonychotes weddelli. 8 l, Stercorarius skua. 10 l, Aptenodytes forsteri, vert.

1995, June 29
3863 A1479   1 l multicolored   .15
3864 A1479   2 l multicolored   .15
3865 A1479   3 l multicolored   .15
3866 A1479   5 l multicolored   .15
3867 A1479   8 l multicolored   .25
3868 A1479   10 l multicolored   .30
Nos. 3863-3868 (6)   1.15

Stephan Stambolov (1854-95), Revolutionary Leader, Politician — A1480

1995, July 6   Litho.   *Perf. 13*
3869 A1480   3 l multicolored   .15

1996 Summer Olympics, Atlanta A1481

Designs: 3 l, Pole vault. 7 l, High jump. 10 l, Women's long jump. 15 l, Track.

1995, July 17
3870 A1481   3 l multicolored   .15
3871 A1481   7 l multicolored   .20
3872 A1481   10 l multicolored   .30
3873 A1481   15 l multicolored   .45
Nos. 3870-3873 (4)   1.10

Legumes — A1482

1995, July 31
3874 A1482   2 l Pisum sativum   .15
3875 A1482   3 l Glicine   .15
3876 A1482   3 l Cicer arietinum   .15
3877 A1482   4 l Spinacia oleracea   .15
3878 A1482   5 l Arachis hypogaea   .15
3879 A1482   15 l Lens esculenta   .45
Nos. 3874-3879 (6)   1.20

Organized Tourism in Bulgaria, Cent. A1483

1995, Aug. 21   Litho.   *Perf. 13*
3880 A1483   3 l multicolored   .15

Vassil Zahariev (1895-1971), Graphic Artist — A1484

Designs: 2 l, Woodcut of a man. 3 l, Woodcut of building in valley. 5 l, Self-portrait. 10 l, Carving of two women.

1995, Sept. 4   Litho.   *Perf. 13*
3881 A1484   2 l multicolored   .15
3882 A1484   3 l multicolored   .15
3883 A1484   5 l multicolored   .15
3884 A1484   10 l multicolored   .30
Nos. 3881-3884 (4)   .75

UN, 50th Anniv. A1485

1995, Sept. 12
3885 A1485   3 l multicolored   .15

Airplanes — A1486

1995, Sept. 26   Litho.   *Perf. 13*
3886 A1486   3 l PO-2   .15
3887 A1486   5 l Li-2   .15
3888 A1486   7 l JU52-3M   .20
3889 A1486   10 l FV-58   .30
Nos. 3886-3889 (4)   .80

Motion Pictures, Cent. — A1487

Designs: 2 l, Charlie Chaplin, Mickey Mouse. 3 l, Marilyn Monroe, Marlene Dietrich. 5 l, Humphrey Bogart. 8 l, Sophia Loren, Liza Minnelli. 10 l, Toshiro Mifune. 15 l, Katya Paskaleva.

1995, Oct. 16
3890 A1487   2 l multicolored   .15
3891 A1487   3 l multicolored   .15
3892 A1487   5 l multicolored   .15
3893 A1487   8 l multicolored   .25
3894 A1487   10 l multicolored   .30
3895 A1487   15 l multicolored   .45
Nos. 3890-3895 (6)   1.45

Minerals A1488

1995, Nov. 20   Litho.   *Perf. 13*
3896 A1488   1 l Agate   .15
3897 A1488   2 l Sphalerite   .15
3898 A1488   5 l Calcite   .15
3899 A1488   7 l Quartz   .20
3900 A1488   8 l Pyromorphite   .25
3901 A1488   10 l Almandine   .30
Nos. 3896-3901 (6)   1.20

Christmas A1489

1995, Dec. 8   Litho.   *Perf. 13*
3902 A1489   3 l shown   .15
3903 A1489   15 l Magi   .45

BULGARIA

Southern Fruit, by Cyril Tsonev (1896-1961) — A1490

1996, Jan. 25 Litho. *Perf. 13*
3904 A1490 3 l multicolored .15

Martin Luther (1483-1546) — A1491

1996, Feb. 5
3905 A1491 3 l multicolored .15

Historic Buildings A1492

Monasteries: 3 l, Preobragenie. 5 l, Arapovsky. 10 l, Drianovo. 20 l, Bachkovo. 25 l, Troyan. 40 l, Zografski.

1996, Feb. 28 *Perf. 14x13½*
3906 A1492 3 l green .15
3907 A1492 5 l red .15
3908 A1492 10 l blue .30
3909 A1492 20 l yellow orange .60
3910 A1492 25 l brown .75
3911 A1492 40 l purple 1.20
  Nos. 3906-3911 (6) 3.15

5th Meeting of European Bank for Reconstruction and Development A1493

1996, Apr. 15 Litho. *Perf. 13*
3912 A1493 7 l shown .15
3913 A1493 30 l Building, diff. .50

Conifers A1494

Designs: 5 l, Taxus baccata. 8 l, Abies alba. 10 l, Picea abies. 20 l, Pinus silvestris. 25 l, Pinus heldreichii. 40 l, Juniperus excelsa.

1996, Apr. 23 *Perf. 13½x13*
3914 A1494 5 l multicolored .15
3915 A1494 8 l multicolored .15
3916 A1494 10 l multicolored .15
3917 A1494 20 l multicolored .30
3918 A1494 25 l multicolored .40
3919 A1494 40 l multicolored .65
  Nos. 3914-3919 (6) 1.80

A1495   A1496

Designs: 10 l, People in distress. 40 l, Khristo Botev (1848-1876), poet, patriot, horiz.

1996, May 1 *Perf. 13*
3920 A1495 10 l multicolored .15
3921 A1495 40 l multicolored .65
  April Uprising, death of Khristo Botev, 120th anniv.

1996, May 6
Uniforms: 5 l, Light brown dress uniform. 8 l, Brown combat, helmet. 10 l, Brown uniform, holding gun with fixed bayonet. 20 l, Early red, blue dress uniform. 25 l, Officer's early green dress uniform. 40 l, Soldier's green uniform.

1996, May 6
3922 A1496 5 l multicolored .15
3923 A1496 8 l multicolored .15
3924 A1496 10 l multicolored .15
3925 A1496 20 l multicolored .30
3926 A1496 25 l multicolored .40
3927 A1496 40 l multicolored .65
  Nos. 3922-3927 (6) 1.80

Republic of Bulgaria, 50th Anniv. — A1497

1996, May 13 Litho. *Perf. 13½*
3928 A1497 10 l multicolored .15

Famous Women A1498

Europa: 10 l, Elisaveta Bagriana (1893-1990), poet. 40 l, Katia Popova (1924-66), opera singer.

1996, May 29 Litho. *Perf. 13*
3929 A1498 10 l multicolored .25
  Complete booklet, 5 #3929 1.25
3930 A1498 40 l multicolored .95
  Complete booklet, 5 #3930 4.75

A1499   A1500

10 l, Soccer player. 15 l, Soccer player, diff.

1996, June 4
3931 A1499 Sheet of 2, #a.-b. .60
  Euro '96, European Soccer Championships, Great Britain.

1996, July 4
3932 A1500 5 l Wrestling .15
3933 A1500 8 l Boxing .20
3934 A1500 10 l Women's shot put .25
3935 A1500 25 l Women sculling .60
  Nos. 3932-3935 (4) 1.20

Souvenir Sheet
3936 A1500 15 l Pierre de Coubertin .35
  1996 Summer Olympic Games, Atlanta. Olymphilex '96 (#3936).

Crabs A1501

Designs: 5 l, Gammarus arduus. 10 l, Asellus aquaticus. 12 l, Astacus astacus. 25 l, Palaemon serratus. 30 l, Cumella limicola. 40 l, Carcinus mediterraneus.

1996, July 30
3937 A1501 5 l multicolored .15
3938 A1501 10 l multicolored .25
3939 A1501 12 l multicolored .30
3940 A1501 25 l multicolored .60
3941 A1501 30 l multicolored .70
3942 A1501 40 l multicolored .95
  Nos. 3937-3942 (6) 2.95

Francisco Goya (1746-1828) — A1502

Entire paintings or details: 8 l, Young Woman with a Letter. 26 l, The Second of May, 1808. 40 l, Neighboring Women on a Balcony.
No. 3947: a, 10 l, The Clothed Maja. b, 15 l, The Naked Maja.

1996, July 9 Litho. *Perf. 13*
3943 A1502 5 l multicolored .15
3944 A1502 8 l multicolored .20
3945 A1502 26 l multicolored .65
3946 A1502 40 l multicolored 1.00
  Nos. 3943-3946 (4) 2.00

Souvenir Sheet
Perf. 13½x13
3947 A1502 Sheet of 2, #a.-b. .60
  No. 3947 contains two 54x29mm stamps.

Souvenir Sheet

St. John of Rila (876-946), Founder of Rila Monastery — A1503

1996, Sept. 3
3948 A1503 10 l multicolored .25

Bulgarian Renaissance Houses — A1504

Various multi-level houses.

1996, Sept. 12 Litho. *Perf. 14x13½*
Background Color
3949 A1504 10 l buff .15
3950 A1504 15 l orange yellow .15
3951 A1504 30 l yellow green .30
3952 A1504 50 l red lilac .45
3953 A1504 60 l apple green .55
3954 A1504 100 l green blue .95
  Nos. 3949-3954 (6) 2.55

Steam Locomotives A1505

1996, Sept. 24 *Perf. 13*
3955 A1505 5 l 1836 .15
3956 A1505 10 l 1847 .15
3957 A1505 12 l 1848 .15
3958 A1505 26 l 1876 .25
  Nos. 3955-3958 (4) .70

Natl. Gallery of Art, Cent. A1506

1996, Oct. 14 Litho. *Perf. 13*
3959 A1506 15 l multicolored .15

Defeat of Byzantine Army by Tsar Simeon, 1100th Anniv. — A1507

Designs: 10 l, Sword hilt, soldiers on horseback. 40 l, Sword blade, dagger, fallen soldiers.

1996, Oct. 21
3960 A1507 10 l multicolored .15
3961 A1507 40 l multicolored .35
  a. Pair, #3960-3961 .50
  No. 3961 is a continuous design.

UNICEF, 50th Anniv. — A1508

Children's drawings: 7 l, Diver, fish. 15 l, Circus performers. 20 l, Boy, artist's pallete. 60 l, Women seated at table.

1996, Nov. 18 Litho. *Perf. 13*
3962 A1508 7 l multicolored .15
3963 A1508 15 l multicolored .30
3964 A1508 20 l multicolored .40
3965 A1508 60 l multicolored 1.25
  Nos. 3962-3965 (4) 2.10

A1509   A1510

1996, Nov. 26
3966 A1509 15 l Candles on tree .30
3967 A1509 60 l Church 1.20
  Christmas.

1996, Dec. 11 Litho. *Perf. 13*
Painting of Old Bulgarian Town, by Tsanko Lavrenov (1896-1978).
3968 A1510 15 l multicolored .30

BULGARIA

Puppies
A1511
ПОЙНТЕР • POINTER

1997, Feb. 25   Litho.   Perf. 13
3969	A1511	5 l Pointer	.15
3970	A1511	7 l Chow chow	.15
3971	A1511	25 l Carakachan dog	.30
3972	A1511	50 l Basset hound	.60
		Nos. 3969-3972 (4)	1.20

Alexander Graham Bell (1847-1922) — A1512

1997, Mar. 10
| 3973 | A1512 | 30 l multicolored | .40 |

Ivan Milev (1897-1927), Painter — A1513

Stories and Legends — A1514

Paintings: 5 l, Boy drinking from jar. 15 l, Person with head bowed holding up hand. 30 l, Woman. 60 l, Woman carrying child.

1997, Mar. 20
3974	A1513	5 l multicolored	.15
3975	A1513	15 l multicolored	.20
3976	A1513	30 l multicolored	.40
3977	A1513	60 l multicolored	.80
		Nos. 3974-3977 (4)	1.55

1997, Apr. 14

Europa: 120 l, "March" lady in folk costume, symbol of spring. 600 l, St. George.
| 3978 | A1514 | 120 l multicolored | 1.60 |
| 3979 | A1514 | 600 l multicolored | 7.75 |

Konstantin Kissimov (1897-1965), Actor — A1515

1997, Apr. 16
| 3980 | A1515 | 120 l multicolored | 1.60 |

A1516   A1517

1997, Apr. 21
| 3981 | A1516 | 60 l multicolored | .80 |

Heinrich von Stephan (1831-97).

1997, May 2   Perf. 13½

Historical Landmarks: 80 l, Nessebar. 200 l, Ivanovo Rock Churches. 300 l, Boyana Church. 500 l, Madara horseman. 600 l, Tomb of Sveshtari. 1000 l, Tomb of Kazanlak.
3982	A1517	80 l browm & multi	1.00
3983	A1517	200 l purple & multi	2.50
3984	A1517	300 l bister & multi	4.00
3985	A1517	500 l green & multi	6.50
3986	A1517	600 l yellow & multi	7.75
3987	A1517	1000 l orange & multi	13.00
		Nos. 3982-3987 (6)	34.75

Composers A1518

Designs: a, Gaetano Donizetti (1797-1848). b, Franz Schubert (1797-1828). c, Felix Mendelssohn (1809-1847). d, Johannes Brahms (1833-1897).

1997, May 29   Litho.   Perf. 13½x13
| 3988 | A1518 | 120 l Sheet of 4, #a.-d. | 6.50 |

Plants in Bulgaria's Red Book A1519

Designs: 80 l, Trifolium rubens. 100 l, Tulipa hageri. 120 l, Inula spiraeifolia. 200 l, Paeonia tenuifolia.

1997, June 24   Perf. 13
3989	A1519	80 l multicolored	1.00
3990	A1519	100 l multicolored	1.25
3991	A1519	120 l multicolored	1.60
3992	A1519	200 l multicolored	2.50
		Nos. 3989-3992 (4)	6.35

A1520   A1521

1997, June 29   Litho.   Perf. 13
| 3993 | A1520 | 120 l multicolored | 1.60 |

Civil aviation in Bulgaria, 50th anniv.

1997, July 3
| 3994 | A1521 | 120 l multicolored | 1.60 |

Evlogy Georgiev (1819-97), banker, philanthopist.

Sofia '97, Modern Pentathlon World Championship — A1522

Designs: 60 l, Equestrian cross-country, running. 80 l, Fencing, swimming. 100 l, Running, women's fencing. 120 l, Men's shooting, diving. 200 l, Equestrian jumping, women's shooting.

1997, July 25
3995	A1522	60 l multicolored	.75
3996	A1522	80 l multicolored	1.00
3997	A1522	100 l multicolored	1.25
3998	A1522	120 l multicolored	1.60
3999	A1522	200 l multicolored	2.50
		Nos. 3995-3999 (5)	7.10

City of Moscow, 850th Anniv. — A1523

1997, July 30
| 4000 | A1523 | 120 l multicolored | 1.60 |

No. 4000 is printed se-tenant with label for Moscow '97 Intl. Philatelic Exhibition.

Diesel Engine, Cent. A1524

1997, Sept. 8   Litho.   Perf. 13½x13
4001	A1524	80 l Boat	.15
4002	A1524	100 l Tractor	.15
4003	A1524	120 l Truck	.15
4004	A1524	200 l Forklift	.30
		Nos. 4001-4004 (4)	.75

43rd General Assembly of Atlantic Club of Bulgaria — A1525

Designs: a, Goddess Tyche. b, Eagle on sphere. c, Building, lion statue, denomination UL. d, Building, denomination UR.

1997, Oct. 2   Perf. 13
| 4005 | A1525 | 120 l Sheet of 4, #a.-d. | .55 |

Miguel de Cervantes (1547-1616) — A1526

1997, Oct. 15
| 4006 | A1526 | 120 l multicolored | .15 |

Asen Raztsvetnikov (1897-1951), Poet, Writer — A1527

1997, Nov. 5
| 4007 | A1528 | 120 l multicolored | .15 |

Tsar Samuel (d. 1014), Ascension to Throne, 1000th Anniv. A1528

1997, Nov. 18   Perf. 13½x13
4008	A1528	120 l Inscription	.15
4009	A1528	600 l Tsar, soldiers	.85
a.		Pair, #4008-4009	1.00

Christmas — A1529

Designs: 120 l, Snow-covered houses, stars inside shape of Christmas tree, animals. 600 l, Nativity scene.

1997, Dec. 8   Perf. 13x13½
| 4010 | A1529 | 120 l multicolored | .15 |
| 4011 | A1529 | 600 l multicolored | .85 |

1998 Winter Olympic Games, Nagano A1530

Designs: 60 l, Speed skating. 80 l, Skiing. 120 l, Biathlon. 600 l, Pairs figure skating.

1997, Dec. 17   Perf. 13½x13
4012	A1530	60 l multicolored	.15
4013	A1530	80 l multicolored	.15
4014	A1530	120 l multicolored	.15
4015	A1530	600 l multicolored	.85
		Nos. 4012-4015 (4)	1.30

For overprint see No. 4029.

Coat of Arms of Bulgaria A1531

1997, Dec. 22   Litho.   Perf. 13½x13
| 4016 | A1531 | 120 l multicolored | .35 |

Bulgarian Space Program, 25th Anniv. — A1532

Illustration reduced.

1997, Dec. 22   Perf. 13
| 4017 | A1532 | 120 l multicolored | .35 |

Christo Botev (1848-76), Revolutionary, Poet A1533

Bertolt Brecht (1898-1956), Playwright A1534

1998, Jan. 6   Litho.   Perf. 13
| 4018 | A1533 | 120 l multicolored | .15 |

1998, Feb. 10
| 4019 | A1534 | 120 l multicolored | .15 |

BULGARIA

Bulgarian Telegraph Agency, Cent. — A1535

1998, Feb. 13
4020 A1535 120 l multicolored .15

Illustrations by Alexander Bozhinov (1878-1968) A1536

Designs: a, Bird wearing bonnet. b, Black bird wearing hat. c, Grandfather Frost, children. d, Girl among flowers looking upward at rain.

1998, Feb. 24 *Perf. 13½x13*
4021 A1536 120 l Sheet of 4, #a.-d. .55

A1537

Easter — A1538

1998, Feb. 27 *Perf. 13*
4022 A1537 120 l Prince Alexander .15
4023 A1537 600 l Monument .65
  a. Pair, #4022-4023 .80
Bulgarian independence from Turkey, 120th anniv.

1998, Mar. 27 *Litho. Perf. 13*
4024 A1538 120 l multicolored .15

Bulgarian Olympic Committee, 75th Anniv. — A1539

1998, Mar. 30
4025 A1539 120 l multicolored .15

PHARE (Intl. Post and Telecommunications Program) — A1540

1998, Apr. 24 *Litho. Perf. 13*
4026 A1540 120 l multicolored .35

National Days and Festivals — A1541

Europa: 120 l, Girls with flowers, "Enyovden." 600 l, Masked men with bells, "Kukery."

1998, Apr. 27
4027 A1541 120 l multicolored .35
4028 A1541 600 l multicolored 1.65

No. 4014 Ovptd.

1998, Apr. 29 *Perf. 13½x13*
4029 A1530 120 l multicolored .35

Dante and Virgil in Hell, by Eugène Delacroix (1798-1863) A1542

1998, Apr. 30
4030 A1542 120 l multicolored .35

A1543   A1544

1998, May 15 *Perf. 13*
4031 A1543 120 l multicolored .15
Soccer Team of Central Sports Club of the Army, 50th anniv.

1998, May 25
Cats: 60 l, European tabby. 80 l, Siamese. 120 l, Exotic shorthair. 600 l, Birman.
4032 A1544 60 l multicolored .15
4033 A1544 80 l multicolored .15
4034 A1544 120 l multicolored .35
4035 A1544 600 l multicolored 1.65
  Nos. 4032-4035 (4) 2.30

Are You Jealous?, by Paul Gauguin (1848-1903) — A1545

1998, June 4
4036 A1545 120 l multicolored .35

Neophit Hylendarsky-Bozvely (1745-1848), Priest, Author — A1546

1998, June 4
4037 A1546 120 l multicolored .35

1998 World Cup Soccer Championships, France — A1547

Lion mascot with soccer ball, various stylized soccer plays.

1998, June 10
4038 A1547 60 l multicolored .15
4039 A1547 80 l multicolored .15
4040 A1547 120 l multicolored .35
4041 A1547 600 l multicolored 1.65
  Nos. 4038-4041 (4) 2.30
  Souvenir Sheet
4042 A1547 120 l Mascot, Eiffel Tower .35

A. Aleksandrov's Flight on Mir, 10th Anniv. — A1548

1998, June 17 *Litho. Perf. 13*
4043 A1548 120 l multicolored .15

Lisbon '98 A1549

Designs: a, Map showing route around Cape of Good Hope, Vasco da Gama (1460-1524). b, Sailing ship, map of Africa.

1998, June 23
4044 A1549 600 l Sheet of 2, #a.-b. + 2 labels 1.40

Helicopters — A1550

Designs: 80 l, Focke Wulf FW61, 1937. 100 l, Sikorsky R-4, 1943. 120 l, Mil Mi-12 (V-12), 1970. 200 l, McDonnell-Douglas MD-900, 1995.

1998, July 7 *Litho. Perf. 13*
4045 A1550 80 l multicolored .20 .20
4046 A1550 100 l multicolored .25 .25
4047 A1550 120 l multicolored .30 .30
4048 A1550 200 l multicolored .45 .45
  Nos. 4045-4048 (4) 1.20 1.20
  Souvenir Sheet

Intl. Year of the Ocean — A1551

Monachus monachus. Illustration reduced.

1998, July 14 *Litho. Perf. 13*
4049 A1551 120 l multicolored .30 .30

Dimitr Talev (1898-1966), Writer — A1552

1998, Sept. 14
4050 A1552 180 l multicolored .20 .20

A1553   A1554

1998, Sept. 22
4051 A1553 180 l multicolored .20 .20
Declaration of Bulgarian Independence, 90th anniv.

1998, Sept. 24
Butterflies, flowers: 60 l, Limenitis redukta, ligularia sibirica. 180 l, Vanessa cardui, anthemis macrantha. 200 l, Vanessa atalanta, trachelium jacquinii. 600 l, Anthocharis gruneri, geranium tuberosum.
4052 A1554 60 l multicolored .15 .15
4053 A1554 180 l multicolored .20 .20
4054 A1554 200 l multicolored .25 .25
4055 A1554 600 l multicolored .75 .75
  Nos. 4052-4055 (4) 1.35 1.35

BULGARIA & EASTERN EUROPE

Albania
Czechoslovakia
Hungary
Poland
Romania
Russia & Assoc. Territories

YEARLY UNITS
WANTLISTS INVITED

Lists available on request at 50¢ for each country.

R.J.B. Mail Sales
25958 Genesee Trail Rd.
#424
Golden, CO 80401

BULGARIA

Christo Smirnenski
(1898-1923),
Poet — A1555

1998, Sept. 29
4056 A1555 180 l multicolored .20 .20

Universal
Declaration
of Human
Rights, 50th
Anniv.
A1556

1998, Oct. 26 Litho. *Perf. 13*
4057 A1556 180 l multicolored .20 .20

Giordano Bruno (1548-1600),
Philosopher — A1557

1998, Oct. 26
4058 A1557 180 l multicolored .20 .20

Greetings
Stamps
A1558

#4059, Man diving through flaming heart, "I Love You." #4060, Baby emerging from chalice, "Happy Birthday." #4061, Grape vine, bird, wine coming from vat, "Happy Holiday." #4062, Waiter carrying tray with glass & ttle of wine, "Happy Name Day."

1998, Nov. 11
4059	A1558	180 l multi	.20	.20
4060	A1558	180 l multi, vert.	.20	.20
4061	A1558	180 l multi, vert.	.20	.20
4062	A1558	180 l multi, vert.	.20	.20
		Nos. 4059-4062 (4)	.80	.80

Christmas
A1559

1998, Dec. 2 Litho. *Perf. 13½x13*
4063 A1559 180 l multicolored .15 .15

SEMI-POSTAL STAMPS

Catalogue values for unused stamps in this section are for Never Hinged items.

Regular Issues of 1911-20 Surcharged:

a. ЗА НАШИТѢ
b. ЗА НАШИТѢ ПЛѢННИЦИ 5
c. ЗА НАШИТѢ ПЛѢННИЦИ 50

Perf. 11½x12, 12x11½

1920, June 20 Unwmk.
B1	A43 (a)	2s + 1s ol grn	.15	.15
B2	A44 (b)	5s + 2½s grn	.15	.15
B3	A44 (b)	10s + 5s rose	.15	.15
B4	A44 (b)	15s + 7½s vio	.15	.15
B5	A44 (b)	25s + 12½s dp bl	.15	.15
B6	A44 (b)	30s + 15s choc	.15	.15
B7	A44 (b)	50s + 25s yel brn	.15	.15
B8	A29 (c)	1 l + 50s dk brn	.15	.15
B9	A37a (a)	2 l + 1 l brn org	.25	.25
B10	A38 (a)	3 l + 1½ l claret	.55	.45
		Nos. B1-B10 (10)	2.00	1.90

Surtax aided ex-prisoners of war. Value, Nos. B1-B7 imperf., $7.75.

Tsar Boris Type of 1937
Souvenir Sheet

1937, Nov. 22 Photo. *Imperf.*
B11 A140 2 l + 18 l ultra 4.50 2.50

19th anniv. of the accession of Tsar Boris III to the throne.

Наводненнето 1939
1+1 лева

Stamps of 1917-21
Surcharged in Black

1939, Oct. 22 *Perf. 12½, 12*
B12	A34	1 l + 1 l on 15s slate	.15	.15
B13	A69	2 l + 1 l on 1½ l ol grn	.15	.15
B14	A69	4 l + 2 l on 2 l dp grn	.18	.15
B15	A69	7 l + 4 l on 3 l Prus bl	.50	.28
B16	A69	14 l + 7 l on 5 l red brn	.85	.48
		Nos. B12-B16 (5)	1.83	1.21

Surtax aided victims of the Sevlievo flood. The surcharge on #B13-B16 omits "leva."

Map of
Bulgaria — SP2

1947, June 6 Typo. *Perf. 11½*
B17 SP2 20 l + 10 l dk brn red & grn .45 .30

30th Jubilee Esperanto Cong., Sofia, 1947.

Postman — SP3

Radio
Towers — SP6

#B19, Lineman. #B20, Telephone operators.

1947, Nov. 5
B18	SP3	4 l + 2 l ol brn	.15	.15
B19	SP3	10 l + 5 l brt red	.15	.15
B20	SP3	20 l + 10 l dp ultra	.15	.15
B21	SP6	40 l + 20 l choc	.70	.55
		Nos. B18-B21 (4)	1.15	1.00

Christo Ganchev — SP7

Actors' Portraits: 10 l+6 l, Adriana Budevska. 15 l+7 l, Vasil Kirkov. 20 l+15 l, Sava Ognianov. 30 l+20 l, Krostyu Sarafov.

1947, Dec. 8 Litho. *Perf. 10½*
B22	SP7	9 l + 5 l Prus grn	.15	.15
B23	SP7	10 l + 6 l car lake	.20	.15
B24	SP7	15 l + 7 l rose vio	.20	.15
B25	SP7	20 l + 15 l ultra	.20	.15
B26	SP7	30 l + 20 l vio brn	.48	.30
		Nos. B22-B26 (5)	1.23	.90

National Theater, 50th anniversary.

Souvenir Sheet

Olympic Emblem — SP8

1964, Oct. 10 Litho. *Imperf.*
B27 SP8 40s + 20s bis, red & bl 2.75 1.40

18th Olympic Games, Tokyo, Oct. 10-25.

Horsemanship Type of 1965
Miniature Sheet

1965, Sept. 30 Photo. *Imperf.*
B28 A630 40s + 20s Hurdle race 2.00 1.00

Space Exploration Type of 1966

Designs: 20s+10s, Yuri A. Gagarin, Alexei Leonov and Valentina Tereshkova. 30s+10s, Rocket and globe.

1966, Sept. 29 Photo. *Perf. 11½x11*
B29 A652 20s + 10s pur & gray 1.00 .35

Miniature Sheet
B30 A652 30s + 10s gray, fawn & blk 2.00 .95

Winter Olympic Games Type of 1967
Sports and Emblem: 20s+10s, Slalom. 40s+10s, Figure skating couple.

1967, Sept. Photo. *Perf. 11*
B31 A687 20s + 10s multi 1.10 .28

Souvenir Sheet
Imperf
B32 A687 40s + 10s multi 2.00 .85

Type of Olympic Games Issue, 1968
Designs: 20s+10s, Rowing. 50s+10s, Stadium, Mexico City, and communications satellite.

1968, June 24 Photo. *Perf. 10½*
B33 A702 20s + 10s vio bl, gray & pink 1.00 .32

Miniature Sheet
Imperf
B34 A702 50s + 10s gray, blk & Prus bl 2.25 1.50

Sports Type of Regular Issue, 1969
Designs: 13s+5s, Woman with ball. 20s+10s, Acrobatic jump.

1969, Oct. Photo. *Perf. 11*
Gymnasts in Light Gray
B35 A732 13s + 5s brt rose & vio .40 .15
B36 A732 20s + 10s citron & bl grn .70 .30

Miniature Sheet

Soccer
Ball — SP9

1970, Mar. 4 Photo. *Imperf.*
B37 SP9 80s + 20s multi 2.25 1.40

9th World Soccer Championships for the Jules Rimet Cup, Mexico City, May 30-June 21, 1970.

Souvenir Sheet

Yuri A. Gagarin — SP10

1971, Apr. 12 Photo. *Imperf.*
B38 SP10 40s + 20s multi 2.00 1.10

10th anniversary of the first man in space.

SP11  SP12

Bulgarian lion, magnifying glass, stamp tongs

1971, July 10 Photo. *Perf. 12½*
B39 SP11 20s + 10s brn org, blk & gold .90 .40

11th Congress of Bulgarian Philatelists, Sofia, July, 1971.

1989, Nov. 10 Litho. *Perf. 13x13½*
Toys: a, Skateboarding. b, Doll, ball. c, Rope. d, Train set.

Souvenir Sheet
B40 Sheet of 4 2.75 1.40
a.-d. SP12 30s +15s any single .65 .35

For the benefit of the Children's Foundation.

AIR POST STAMPS

Regular Issues of 1925-26 Overprinted in Various Colors

1927-28 Unwmk. *Perf. 11½*
C1	A76	2 l ol (R) ('28)	1.10	.70
C2	A74	4 l lake & yel (Bl)	1.10	.70
C3	A77	10 l brn blk & brn org (G) ('28)	17.00	13.00

Overprinted Vertically and Surcharged with New Value

C4 A77 1 l on 6 l dp bl & pale lem (C) 1.10 .70
a. Inverted surcharge 325.00 275.00
b. Pair, one without surcharge 425.00
Nos. C1-C4 (4) 20.30 15.10

Nos. C2-C4 overprinted in changed colors were not issued, value set $10.50.

BULGARIA

Dove Delivering Message — AP1

Junkers Plane, Rila Monastery — AP2

1931, Oct. 28   Typo.
C5	AP1	1 l dk green	.18	.15
C6	AP1	2 l maroon	.18	.15
C7	AP1	6 l dp blue	.28	.20
C8	AP1	12 l carmine	.28	.30
C9	AP1	20 l dk violet	.70	.55
C10	AP1	30 l dp orange	1.10	1.25
C11	AP1	50 l orange brn	2.25	1.40
		Nos. C5-C11 (7)	4.97	4.00

Counterfeits exist. See Nos. C15-C18.

1932, May 9
C12	AP2	18 l blue grn	14.00	11.00
C13	AP2	24 l dp red	14.00	11.00
C14	AP2	28 l ultra	14.00	11.00
		Nos. C12-C14 (3)	42.00	33.00

Catalogue values for unused stamps in this section, from this point to the end of the section, are for Never Hinged items.

1938, Dec. 27
C15	AP1	1 l violet brown	.24	.15
C16	AP1	2 l green	.18	.15
C17	AP1	6 l deep rose	.70	.28
C18	AP1	12 l peacock blue	.85	.32
		Nos. C15-C18 (4)	1.97	.90

Counterfeits exist.

Mail Plane — AP3

Plane over Tsar Assen's Tower — AP4

Designs: 4 l, Plane over Bachkovski Monastery. 6 l, Bojurishte Airport, Sofia. 10 l, Plane, train and motorcycle. 12 l, Planes over Sofia Palace. 16 l, Plane over Pirin Valley. 19 l, Plane over Rila Monastery. 30 l, Plane and Swallow. 45 l, Plane over Sofia Cathedral. 70 l, Plane over Shipka Monument. 100 l, Plane and Royal Cipher.

1940, Jan. 15   Photo.   Perf. 13
C19	AP3	1 l dk green	.15	.15
C20	AP4	2 l crimson	1.10	.15
C21	AP4	4 l red orange	.15	.15
C22	AP3	6 l dp blue	.20	.15
C23	AP4	10 l dk brown	.30	.15
C24	AP3	12 l dull brown	.52	.18
C25	AP3	16 l brt bl vio	.55	.24
C26	AP3	19 l sapphire	.75	.32
C27	AP4	30 l rose lake	1.10	.48
C28	AP4	45 l gray violet	2.75	.95
C29	AP4	70 l rose pink	2.75	1.25
C30	AP4	100 l dp slate bl	9.00	3.75
		Nos. C19-C30 (12)	19.32	7.92

Nos. 368 and 370 Overprinted in Black

1945, Jan. 26
C31	A181	1 l bright green	.15	.15
C32	A181	4 l red orange	.15	.15

A similar overprint on Nos. O4, O5, O7 and O8 was privately applied.

Type of Parcel Post Stamps of 1944 Surcharged or Overprinted in Various Colors

Imperf
C37	PP5	10 l on 100 l dl yel (Bl)	.18	.15
C38	PP5	45 l on 100 l dl yel (C)	.28	.15
C39	PP5	75 l on 100 l dl yel (G)	.38	.25
C40	PP5	100 l dl yel (V)	.70	.35
		Nos. C37-C40 (4)	1.54	.90

Plane and Sun — AP16

Pigeon with Letter — AP17

Plane, Letter — AP18

Wings, Posthorn — AP19

Winged Letter — AP20

Plane, Sun — AP21

Pigeon, Posthorn — AP22

Mail Plane — AP23

Conventionalized Figure Holding Pigeon — AP24

1946, July 15   Litho.   Perf. 13
C41	AP16	1 l dull lilac	.15	.15
C42	AP16	2 l slate gray	.15	.15
C43	AP17	4 l violet blk	.15	.15
C44	AP18	6 l blue	.15	.15
C45	AP19	10 l turq green	.15	.15
C46	AP19	12 l yellow brn	.15	.15
C47	AP20	16 l rose violet	.15	.15
C48	AP19	19 l carmine	.15	.15
C49	AP21	30 l orange	.15	.15
C50	AP22	45 l lt ol grn	.18	.15
C51	AP22	75 l red brown	.24	.15
C52	AP23	100 l slate blk	.65	.24
C53	AP24	100 l red	.65	.24
		Nos. C41-C53 (13)	3.07	2.13

No. C47 exists imperf. Value $90.

People's Republic

Plane over Plovdiv AP25

1947, Aug. 31   Photo.   Imperf.
C54	AP25	40 l dull olive grn	.60	.50

Plovdiv International Fair, 1947.

Baldwin's Tower — AP26

1948, May 23   Litho.   Perf. 11½
C55	AP26	50 l ol brn, cr	.75	.60

Stamp Day and the 10th Congress of Bulgarian Philatelic Societies, June 1948.

Romanian and Bulgarian Parliament Buildings AP27

Romanian and Bulgarian Flags, Bridge over Danube AP28

1948, Nov. 3   Photo.
C56	AP27	40 l ol gray, cr	.22	.15
C57	AP28	100 l red vio, cr	.52	.32

Romanian-Bulgarian friendship.

Mausoleum of Pleven — AP29

1949, June 26
C58	AP29	50 l brown	2.00	1.25

7th Congress of Bulgarian Philatelic Associations, June 26-27, 1949.

Symbols of the UPU — AP30

Frontier Guard and Dog — AP31

1949, Oct. 10   Perf. 11½
C59	AP30	50 l violet blue	1.50	.75

75th anniv. of the UPU.

1949, Oct. 31
C60	AP31	60 l olive black	1.25	.90

Dimitrov Mausoleum AP32

1950, July 3   Perf. 10½
C61	AP32	40 l olive brown	3.00	1.10

1st anniv. of the death of George Dimitrov.

Belogradchic Rocks — AP33

Air View of Plovdiv Fair — AP34

Designs: 16s, Beach, Varna. 20s, Harvesting grain. 28s, Rila monastery. 44s, Studena dam. 60s, View of Dimitrovgrad. 80s, View of Trnovo. 1 l, University building, Sofia. 4 l, Partisans' Monument.

1954, Apr. 1   Unwmk.   Perf. 13
C62	AP33	8s olive black	.15	.15
C63	AP34	12s rose brown	.15	.15
C64	AP33	16s brown	.15	.15
C65	AP33	20s brn red, cream	.15	.15
C66	AP33	28s dp bl, cream	.18	.15
C67	AP33	44s vio brn, cream	.18	.15
C68	AP33	60s red brn, cream	.26	.15
C69	AP34	80s dk grn, cream	.26	.18
C70	AP33	1 l dk bl grn, cream	1.25	.35
C71	AP34	4 l deep blue	3.00	.80
		Nos. C62-C71 (10)	5.73	2.38

Glider on Mountainside AP35

1956, Oct. 15   Photo.
C72	AP35	44s brt blue	.16	.15
C73	AP35	60s purple	.30	.15
C74	AP35	80s dk blue grn	.48	.15
		Nos. C72-C74 (3)	.94	.45

30th anniv. of glider flights in Bulgaria.

60s, Glider over airport. 80s, Three gliders.

Passenger Plane AP36

1957, May 21   Unwmk.   Perf. 13
C75	AP36	80s deep blue	.60	.32

10th anniv. of civil aviation in Bulgaria.

Sputnik 3 over Earth — AP37

1958, Nov. 28   Perf. 11
C76	AP37	80s brt grnsh blue	3.00	2.25

International Geophysical Year, 1957-58. Value, imperf. $7.50.

Lunik 1 Leaving Earth for Moon — AP38

1959, Feb. 28   Perf. 10½
C77	AP38	2 l brt blue & ocher	3.00	2.75

Launching of 1st man-made satellite to orbit moon. Value, imperf. in slightly different colors, $7.50 unused, $5.25 canceled.

Statue of Liberty and Tu-110 Airliner AP39

BULGARIA

Perf. 10½
1959, Nov. 11 Photo. Unwmk.
C78 AP39 1 l violet bl & pink 1.75 1.50
Visit of Khrushchev to US. Value, imperf. $5.

Lunik 2 and Moon — AP40

1960, June 23 Litho. **Perf. 11**
C79 AP40 1.25 l blue, blk & yel 3.50 1.65
Russian rocket to the Moon, Sept. 12, 1959.

Sputnik 5 and Dogs Belka and Strelka AP41

1961, Jan. 14 Photo. **Perf. 11**
C80 AP41 1.25 l brt grnsh bl & org 4.00 2.50
Russian rocket flight of Aug. 19, 1970.

Maj. Yuri A. Gagarin and Vostok 1 AP42

1961, Apr. 26 Unwmk.
C81 AP42 4 l grnsh bl, blk & red 2.50 1.50
First manned space flight, Apr. 12, 1961.

Soviet Space Dogs — AP43

1961, June 28 **Perf. 11**
C82 AP43 2 l slate & dk car 2.00 1.00

Venus-bound Rocket — AP44

1961, June 28
C83 AP44 2 l brt bl, yel & org 4.00 2.50
Soviet launching of the Venus space probe, 2/12/61.

Maj. Gherman Titov — AP45

Design: 1.25 l, Spaceship Vostok 2.

1961, Nov. 20 Photo. **Perf. 11x10½**
C84 AP45 75s dk ol grn & gray grn 1.75 1.25
C85 AP45 1.25 l vio bl, lt bl & pink 2.25 1.75
1st manned space flight around the world, Maj. Gherman Titov of Russia, Aug. 6-7, 1961.

Iskar River Narrows — AP46

Designs: 2s, Varna and sailboat. 3s, Melnik. 10s, Trnovo. 40s, Pirin mountains.

1962, Feb. 3 Unwmk. **Perf. 13**
C86 AP46 1s bl grn & gray bl .15 .15
C87 AP46 2s blue & pink .15 .15
C88 AP46 3s brown & ocher .22 .15
C89 AP46 10s black & lemon .45 .15
C90 AP46 40s dk green & green 1.10 .28
Nos. C86-C90 (5) 2.07 .88

Ilyushin Turboprop Airliner AP47

1962, Aug. 18 **Perf. 11**
C91 AP47 13s blue & black .60 .25
15th anniversary of TABSO airline.

Konstantin E. Tsiolkovsky and Rocket Launching AP48

Design: 13s, Earth, moon and rocket on future flight to the moon.

1962, Sept. 24 **Perf. 11**
C92 AP48 5s dp green & gray 1.90 .85
C93 AP48 13s ultra & yellow 1.10 .35
13th meeting of the International Astronautical Federation.

Maj. Andrian G. Nikolayev — AP49

Designs: 2s, Lt. Col. Pavel R. Popovich. 40s, Vostoks 3 and 4 in orbit.

1962, Dec. 9 Photo. Unwmk.
C94 AP49 1s bl, sl grn & blk .15 .15
C95 AP49 2s bl grn, grn & blk .24 .15
C96 AP49 40s dk bl grn, pink & blk 1.65 .85
Nos. C94-C96 (3) 2.04 1.15
First Russian group space flight of Vostoks 3 and 4, Aug. 12-15, 1962.

Spacecraft "Mars 1" Approaching Mars — AP50

Design: 13s, Rocket launching spacecraft, Earth, Moon and Mars.

1963, Feb. 25 Unwmk. **Perf. 11**
C97 AP50 5s multicolored .50 .28
C98 AP50 13s multicolored 1.00 .45
Launching of the Russian spacecraft "Mars 1," Nov. 1, 1962.

Lt. Col. Valeri F. Bykovski AP51

Designs: 2s, Lt. Valentina Tereshkova. 5s, Globe and trajectories.

1963, Aug. 26 Unwmk. **Perf. 11½**
C99 AP51 1s pale vio & Prus bl .15 .15
C100 AP51 2s citron & red brn .15 .15
C101 AP51 5s rose & dk red .15 .15
Nos. C99-C101 (3) .45 .45
The space flights of Valeri Bykovski, June 14-19, and Valentina Tereshkova, first woman cosmonaut, June 16-19, 1963. An imperf. souvenir sheet contains one 50s stamp showing Spasski tower and globe in lilac and red brown. Light blue border with red brown inscription. Size: 77x67mm. Value $2.50. See No. CB3.

Nos. C99-C100 Surcharged in Magenta or Green

1964, Aug. 22
C102 AP51 10s on 1s (M) .32 .18
C103 AP51 20s on 2s .65 .22
International Space Exhibition in Riccione, Italy. Overprint in Italian on No. C103.

St. John's Monastery, Rila — AP52

13s, Notre Dame, Paris; French inscription.

1964, Dec. 22 Photo. **Perf. 11½**
C104 AP52 5s pale brn & blk .18 .15
C105 AP52 13s lt ultra & sl bl .65 .20
The philatelic exhibition at St. Ouen (Seine) organized by the Franco-Russian Philatelic Circle and philatelic organizations in various People's Democracies.

Paper Mill, Bukijovtz AP53

10s, Metal works, Plovdiv. 13s, Metal works, Kremikovtsi. 20s, Oil refinery, Stara-Zagora. 40s, Fertilizer plant, Stara-Zagora. 1 l, Rest home, Meded.

1964-68 Unwmk. **Perf. 13**
C106 AP53 8s grnsh blue .15 .15
C107 AP53 10s red lilac .15 .15
C108 AP53 13s brt violet .22 .15
C109 AP53 20s slate blue .70 .15
C110 AP53 40s dk olive grn 1.10 .15
C111 AP53 1 l red ('68) 1.90 .32
Nos. C106-C111 (6) 4.22 1.10
Issue dates: 1 l, May 6. Others, Dec. 7.

Three-master — AP54  Veliko Turnovo — AP55

Means of Communication: 2s, Postal coach. 3s, Old steam locomotive. 5s, Early cars. 10s, Montgolfier balloon. 13s, Early plane. 20s, Jet planes. 40s, Rocket and satellites. 1 l, Postrider.

1969, Mar. 31 Photo. **Perf. 13x12½**
C112 AP54 1s gray & multi .15 .15
C113 AP54 2s gray & multi .15 .15
C114 AP54 3s gray & multi .15 .15
C115 AP54 5s gray & multi .15 .15
C116 AP54 10s gray & multi .15 .15
C117 AP54 13s gray & multi .25 .15
C118 AP54 20s gray & multi .50 .22
C119 AP54 40s gray & multi .90 .38
Nos. C112-C119 (8) 2.40 1.50

Miniature Sheet
Imperf
C120 AP54 1 l gold & org 2.25 1.50
SOFIA 1969 Philatelic Exhibition, Sofia, May 31-June 8.

1973, July 30 Photo. **Perf. 13**
Designs: Historic buildings in various cities.
C121 AP55 2s shown .15 .15
C122 AP55 13s Roussalka .25 .15
C123 AP55 20s Plovdiv 1.50 .80
C124 AP55 28s Sofia .65 .18
Nos. C121-C124 (4) 2.55 1.28

Aleksei A. Leonov and Soyuz AP56

Designs: 18s, Thomas P. Stafford and Apollo. 28s, Apollo and Soyuz over earth. 1 l, Apollo Soyuz link-up.

1975, July 15
C125 AP56 13s blue & multi .30 .15
C126 AP56 18s purple & multi .40 .15
C127 AP56 28s multicolored 1.00 .28
Nos. C125-C127 (3) 1.70 .58

Souvenir Sheet
C128 AP56 1 l violet & multi 2.00 1.25
Apollo Soyuz space test project (Russo-American cooperation), launching July 15; link-up July 17.

Balloon Over Plovdiv — AP57

1977, Sept. 3
C129 AP57 25s yellow, brn & red .50 .20

Alexei Leonov Floating in Space — AP58

Designs: 25s, Mariner 6, US spacecraft. 35s, Venera 4, USSR Venus probe.

1977, Oct. 14 Photo. **Perf. 13½**
C130 AP58 12s multicolored .20 .15
C131 AP58 25s multicolored .42 .15
C132 AP58 35s multicolored .60 .22
Nos. C130-C132 (3) 1.22 .52
Space era, 20 years.

Ordering on-line is
QUICK!
EASY!
CONVENIENT!
www.scottonline.com

BULGARIA

TU-154, Balkanair
Emblem — AP59

1977   *Perf. 13*
C133 AP59 35s ultra & multi   .75 .35

30th anniv. of Bulgarian airline, Balkanair. Issued in sheets of 6 stamps + 3 labels (in lilac) with inscription and Balkanair emblem.

Baba Vida
Fortress
AP60

Design: 35s, Peace Bridge, connecting Rousse, Bulgaria, with Giurgiu, Romania.

1978   *Photo.*   *Perf. 13*
C134 AP60 25s multicolored   .40 .40
C135 AP60 35s multicolored   .55 .55

The Danube, European Intercontinental Waterway. Issued in sheets containing 5 each of Nos. C134-C135 and 2 labels, one showing course of Danube, the other hydrofoil and fish.

Red Cross
AP61

1978, Mar.   *Photo.*   *Perf. 13*
C136 AP61 25s multicolored   .50 .16

Centenary of Bulgarian Red Cross.

AP62    AP63

Clock towers.

1979, June 5   *Litho.*   *Perf. 12x12½*
C137 AP62 13s Byalla Cherkva   .16 .15
C138 AP62 23s Botevgrad   .30 .15
C139 AP62 25s Pazardgick   .32 .15
C140 AP62 35s Grabovo   .42 .18
C141 AP62 53s Tryavna   .75 .30
   Nos. C137-C141 (5)   1.95 .93

1980, Oct. 22   *Photo.*   *Perf. 12x12½*
C142 AP62 13s Bjala   .20 .15
C143 AP62 23s Rasgrad   .35 .22
C144 AP62 25s Karnabat   .40 .18
C145 AP62 35s Serlievo   .52 .25
C146 AP62 53s Berkovitza   .80 .35
   Nos. C142-C146 (5)   2.27 1.15

1980
C147 AP63 13s shown   .20 .15
C148 AP63 25s Parachutist   .40 .15

15th World Parachute Championships, Kazanluk.

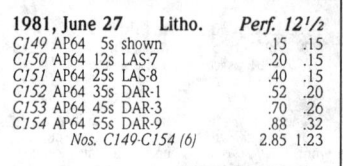

DWVY-1 Aircraft — AP64

1981, June 27   *Litho.*   *Perf. 12½*
C149 AP64 5s shown   .15 .15
C150 AP64 12s LAS-7   .20 .15
C151 AP64 25s LAS-8   .40 .15
C152 AP64 35s DAR-1   .52 .20
C153 AP64 45s DAR-3   .70 .26
C154 AP64 55s DAR-9   .88 .32
   Nos. C149-C154 (6)   2.85 1.23

AP65    AP66

1983, June 28
C155   Sheet of 2   1.50 1.00
   a. AP65 50s Valentina Tereshkova   .75 .50
   b. AP65 50s Svetlana Savitskaya   .75 .50

Women in space, 20th anniv.

1983, July 20   *Photo.*   *Perf. 13*
C156 AP66 5s TV tower, Tolbukhin   .15 .15
C157 AP66 13s Postwoman   .25 .15
C158 AP66 35s TV tower, Mt. Botev   .60 .30
   a. Strip of 3, #C156-C158   .95 .60

World Communications Year. Emblems of World Communications Year, Bulgarian Post, UPU and ITU on attached margins.

Souvenir Sheet

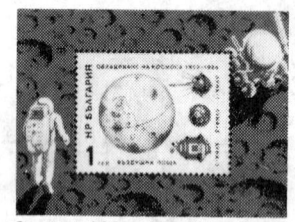

Geophysical Map of the Moon, Russia's
Luna I, II and III Satellites — AP67

1984, Oct. 24   *Photo.*   *Perf. 13*
C159 AP67 1 l multicolored   2.00 1.00

Conquest of Space.

Intl. Civil Aviation Org., 40th
Anniv. — AP68

1984, Dec. 21   *Photo.*   *Perf. 13*
C160 AP68 42s Balkan Airlines jet   .85 .42

Balkan Airlines — AP69

Design: Helicopter MU-8, passenger jet TU-154 and AN-21 transport plane.

1987, Aug. 25   *Photo.*
C161 AP69 25s multicolored   .75 .35

2nd Joint Soviet-Bulgarian Space
Flight — AP70

Cosmonauts: A. Aleksandrov, A. Solovov and V. Savinich.

1989, June 7   *Litho.*   *Perf. 13½x13*
C162 AP70 13s multicolored   .35 .18

AIR POST SEMI-POSTAL STAMPS

Catalogue values for unused stamps in this section are for Never Hinged items.

Statue of Liberty,
Plane and
Bridge — SPAP1

Perf. 11½.
1947, May 24   *Unwmk.*   *Litho.*
CB1 SPAP1 70 l + 30 l red brown   .95 .95

5th Philatelic Congress, Trnovo, and CIPEX, NYC, May, 1947.

Bulgarian Worker
SPAP2

1948, Feb. 28   *Photo.*   *Perf. 12x11½*
CB2 SPAP2 60 l henna brn, *cream*   .45 .35

2nd Bulgarian Workers' Congress, and sold by subscription only, at a premium of 16 l over face value.

Type of Air Post Stamps, 1963
Valeri Bykovski & Valentina Tereshkova.

1963, Aug. 26   *Unwmk.*   *Perf. 11½*
CB3 AP51 20s + 10s pale bluish grn & dk grn   1.25 .45

See note after No. C101.

SPECIAL DELIVERY STAMPS

Catalogue values for unused stamps in this section are for Never Hinged items.

Postman on   Mail Car — SD2
Bicycle — SD1

Postman on
Motorcycle — SD3

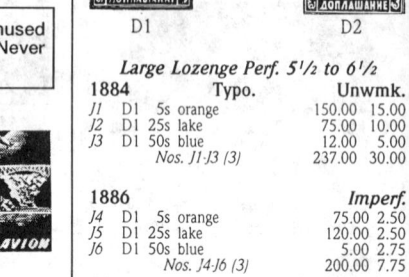

1939   *Unwmk.*   *Photo.*   *Perf. 13*
E1 SD1 5 l deep blue   .60 .15
E2 SD2 6 l copper brn   .24 .15
E3 SD3 7 l golden brn   .35 .15
E4 SD1 8 l red orange   .60 .15
E5 SD1 20 l bright rose   1.25 .30
   Nos. E1-E5 (5)   3.04 .98

POSTAGE DUE STAMPS

D1    D2

Large Lozenge Perf. 5½ to 6½
1884   *Typo.*   *Unwmk.*
J1 D1 5s orange   150.00 15.00
J2 D1 25s lake   75.00 10.00
J3 D1 50s blue   12.00 5.00
   Nos. J1-J3 (3)   237.00 30.00

1886   *Imperf.*
J4 D1 5s orange   75.00 2.50
J5 D1 25s lake   120.00 2.50
J6 D1 50s blue   5.00 2.75
   Nos. J4-J6 (3)   200.00 7.75

1887   *Perf. 11½*
J7 D1 5s orange   9.50 1.00
J8 D1 25s lake   9.50 1.00
J9 D1 50s blue   3.50 1.00
   Nos. J7-J9 (3)   22.50 3.00

Same, Redrawn
24 horizontal lines of shading in upper part instead of 30 lines
1892   *Perf. 10½, 11½*
J10 D1 5s orange   7.50 1.25
J11 D1 25s lake   7.50 1.25

1893
Pelure Paper
J12 D2 5s orange   10.00 3.50

D3    D4

1895   *Imperf.*
J13 D3 30s on 50s blue   7.00 2.00
Perf. 10½, 11½
J14 D3 30s on 50s blue   7.00 2.00

Wmk. Coat of Arms in the Sheet
1896   *Perf. 13*
J15 D4 5s orange   3.00 .75
J16 D4 10s purple   2.00 .75
J17 D4 30s green   1.40 .45
   Nos. J15-J17 (3)   6.40 1.95

Nos. J15-J17 are also known on unwatermarked paper from the edges of sheets.

In 1901 a cancellation, "T" in circle, was applied to Nos. 60-65 and used provisionally as postage dues.

D5    D6

1901-04   *Unwmk.*   *Perf. 11½*
J19 D5 5s dl rose   .20 .15
J20 D5 10s yel grn   .42 .15
J21 D5 20s dl bl ('04)   3.25 .16
J22 D5 30s vio brn   .35 .16
J23 D5 50s org ('02)   5.50 4.00
   Nos. J19-J23 (5)   9.72 4.62

Nos. J19-J23 exist imperf. and in pairs imperf. between. Value, imperf., $250.

BULGARIA — BURKINA FASO

1915		Unwmk.	Perf. 11½
Thin Semi-Transparent Paper			
J24	D6	5s purple	.15 .15
J25	D6	10s purple	.20 .15
J26	D6	20s dl rose	.20 .15
J27	D6	30s dp org	1.10 .20
J28	D6	50s dp bl	.35 .17
		Nos. J24-J28 (5)	2.00 .82

1919-21			Perf. 11½, 12x11½
J29	D6	5s emerald	.15 .15
a.		5s gray green ('21)	.30 .15
J30	D6	10s violet	.15 .15
J31	D6	20s salmon	.15 .15
a.		20s yellow	.15 .15
J32	D6	30s orange	.15 .15
a.		30s red orange ('21)	.65 .65
J33	D6	50s blue	.15 .15
J34	D6	1 l emerald ('21)	.18 .15
J35	D6	2 l rose ('21)	.18 .15
J36	D6	3 l brown org ('21)	.30 .15
		Nos. J29-J36 (8)	1.41 1.20

Stotinki values of the above series surcharged 10s or 20s were used as ordinary postage stamps. See Nos. 182-185.

The 1919 printings are on thicker white paper with clean-cut perforations, the 1921 printings on thicker grayish paper with rough perforations.

Most of this series exist imperforate and in pairs imperforate between.

Heraldic Lion — D7

1932, Aug. 15
Thin Paper
J37	D7	1 l olive bister	.24 .20
J38	D7	2 l rose brown	.24 .20
J39	D7	6 l brown violet	.75 .35
		Nos. J37-J39 (3)	1.23 .75

Lion of Trnovo — D8    National Arms — D9

1933, Apr. 10
J40	D8	20s dk brn	.15 .15
J41	D8	40s dp bl	.15 .15
J42	D8	80s car rose	.15 .15
J43	D9	1 l org brn	.24 .18
J44	D9	2 l olive	.30 .25
J45	D9	6 l dl vio	.15 .15
J46	D9	14 l ultra	.24 .15
		Nos. J40-J46 (7)	1.38 1.18

Catalogue values for unused stamps in this section, from this point to the end of the section, are for Never Hinged items.

National Arms — D10

1947, June   Typo.   Perf. 10½
J47	D10	1 l chocolate	.15 .15
J48	D10	2 l deep claret	.15 .15
J49	D10	8 l deep orange	.15 .15
J50	D10	20 l blue	.22 .15
		Nos. J47-J50 (4)	.67 .60

Arms of the People's Republic — D11

1951   Perf. 11½x10½
J51	D11	1 l chocolate	.15 .15
J52	D11	2 l claret	.15 .15
J53	D11	8 l red orange	.22 .15
J54	D11	20 l deep blue	.60 .32
		Nos. J51-J54 (4)	1.12 .77

OFFICIAL STAMPS

Catalogue values for unused stamps in this section are for Never Hinged items.

Bulgarian Coat of Arms
O1   O2

1942   Unwmk.   Typo.   Perf. 13
O1	O1	10s yel grn	.15 .15
O2	O1	30s red	.15 .15
O3	O1	50s bister	.15 .15
O4	O2	1 l vio bl	.15 .15
O5	O2	2 l dk grn	.15 .15
O6	O2	3 l lilac	.15 .15
O7	O2	4 l rose	.15 .15
O8	O2	5 l carmine	.16 .15
		Nos. O1-O8 (8)	1.21 1.20

1944   Perf. 10½x11½
| O9 | O2 | 1 l blue | .20 .15 |
| O10 | O2 | 2 l brt red | .20 .15 |

Lion Rampant
O3   O4

O5

1945   Imperf.
| O11 | O5 | 1 l pink | .15 .15 |

Perf. 10½x11½, Imperf.
O12	O3	2 l blue green	.15 .15
O13	O4	3 l bister brown	.15 .15
O14	O4	4 l light ultra	.15 .15
O15	O5	5 l brown lake	.15 .15
		Nos. O11-O15 (5)	.75 .75

In 1950, four stamps prepared for official use were issued as regular postage stamps. See Nos. 724-727.

PARCEL POST STAMPS

Catalogue values for unused stamps in this section are for Never Hinged items.

Weighing Packages — PP1   Parcel Post — PP2

Designs: 3 l, 8 l, 20 l, Parcel post truck. 4 l, 6 l, 10 l, Motorcycle.

Perf. 12½x13½, 13½x12½
1941-42   Photo.   Unwmk.
Q1	PP1	1 l slate grn	.15 .15
Q2	PP2	2 l crimson	.15 .15
Q3	PP2	3 l dull brn	.15 .15
Q4	PP2	4 l red org	.15 .15
Q5	PP1	5 l deep blue	.15 .15
Q6	PP1	5 l slate grn ('42)	.15 .15
Q7	PP2	6 l red vio	.15 .15
Q8	PP1	6 l henna brn ('42)	.15 .15
Q9	PP1	7 l dark blue	.15 .15
Q10	PP1	7 l dk brn ('42)	.15 .15
Q11	PP2	8 l brt bl grn	.15 .15
Q12	PP2	8 l green ('42)	.15 .15
Q13	PP2	9 l olive gray	.15 .15
Q14	PP2	9 l dp olive ('42)	.15 .15
Q15	PP2	10 l orange	.15 .15
Q16	PP2	20 l gray vio	.42 .15
Q17	PP2	30 l dull blk	.55 .15
Q18	PP2	30 l sepia ('42)	.50 .15
		Nos. Q1-Q18 (18)	3.72 2.70

Arms of Bulgaria — PP5

1944   Litho.   Imperf.
Q21	PP5	1 l dk carmine	.15 .15
Q22	PP5	3 l blue grn	.15 .15
Q23	PP5	5 l dull bl grn	.15 .15
Q24	PP5	7 l rose lilac	.15 .15
Q25	PP5	10 l deep blue	.15 .15
Q26	PP5	20 l orange brn	.15 .15
Q27	PP5	30 l dk brn car	.15 .15
Q28	PP5	50 l red orange	.30 .15
Q29	PP5	100 l blue	.52 .22
		Nos. Q21-Q29 (9)	1.87 1.42

For overprints and surcharges see Nos. 448-454, C37-C40.

POSTAL TAX STAMPS

The use of stamps Nos. RA1 to RA18 was compulsory on letters, etc., to be delivered on Sundays and holidays. The money received from their sale was used toward maintaining a sanatorium for employees of the post, telegraph and telephone services.

View of Sanatorium PT1

Sanatorium, Peshtera PT2

1925-29   Unwmk.   Typo.   Perf. 11½
RA1	PT1	1 l blk, grnsh bl	2.75 .15
RA2	PT1	1 l chocolate ('26)	2.75 .15
RA3	PT1	1 l orange ('27)	3.00 .15
RA4	PT1	1 l pink ('28)	4.50 .15
RA5	PT1	1 l vio, pnksh ('29)	4.25 .15
RA6	PT2	2 l blue green	.35 .15
RA7	PT2	2 l violet ('27)	.35 .16
RA8	PT2	5 l deep blue	3.00 .80
RA9	PT2	5 l rose ('27)	3.75 .40
		Nos. RA1-RA9 (9)	24.70 2.26

St. Constantine Sanatorium PT3

1930-33
RA10	PT3	1 l red brn & ol grn	4.00 .16
RA11	PT3	1 l ol grn & yel ('31)	.50 .16
RA12	PT3	1 l red vio & ol brn ('33)	.50 .16
		Nos. RA10-RA12 (3)	5.00 .48

Trojan Rest Home — PT4

Sanatorium PT5

1935   Wmk. 145   Perf. 11, 11½
RA13	PT4	1 l choc & red org	.32 .15
RA14	PT4	1 l emer & indigo	.32 .15
RA15	PT5	5 l red brn & indigo	1.40 .35
		Nos. RA13-RA15 (3)	2.04 .65

St. Constantine Sanatorium PT6

2 l, Children at seashore. 5 l, Rest home.

1941   Unwmk.   Photo.   Perf. 13
RA16	PT6	1 l dark olive green	.15 .15
RA17	PT6	2 l red orange	.15 .15
RA18	PT6	5 l deep blue	.30 .15
		Nos. RA16-RA18 (3)	.60 .45

See Nos. 702-705 for same designs in smaller size issued as regular postage.

BURKINA FASO

bùr-'kē-nə-'fä-sō

Upper Volta

LOCATION — Northwestern Africa, north of Ghana
GOVT. — Republic
AREA — 105,869 sq. mi.
POP. — 6,695,500 (est. 1984)
CAPITAL — Ouagadougou

In 1919 the French territory of Upper Volta was detached from the southern section of Upper Senegal and Niger and made a separate colony. In 1933 the colony was divided among its neighbors: French Sudan, Ivory Coast, and Niger Territory. The Republic of Upper Volta was proclaimed December 11, 1958; the name was changed to Burkina Faso on August 4, 1984.

100 Centimes = 1 Franc

Catalogue values for unused stamps in this country are for Never Hinged items, beginning with Scott 70 in the regular postage section, Scott B1 in the semi-postal section, Scott C1 in the airpost section, Scott J21 in the postage due section, and Scott O1 in the official section.

Stamps and Types of Upper Senegal and Niger, 1914-17, Overprinted in Black or Red

HAUTE-VOLTA

1920-28   Unwmk.   Perf. 13½x14
1	A4	1c brn vio & vio	.15 .15
2	A4	2c gray & brn vio (R)	.15 .15
3	A4	4c blk & bl	.15 .15
4	A4	5c yel grn & bl grn	.60 .25
5	A4	5c ol brn & dk brn ('22)	.15 .15
6	A4	10c red org & rose	1.00 .50
7	A4	10c yel grn & bl grn ('22)	.15 .15
8	A4	10c claret & bl ('25)	.25 .25
a.		Overprint omitted	80.00
9	A4	15c choc & org	.40 .30
10	A4	20c brn vio & blk (R)	.65 .55
11	A4	25c ultra & bl	.80 .25
12	A4	25c blk & bl grn ('22)	.45 .40
a.		Overprint omitted	65.00
13	A4	30c brn & brn (R)	1.50 1.25
14	A4	30c red org & rose ('22)	.40 .35
15	A4	30c vio & brn ('25)	.40 .35
16	A4	30c dl grn & bl grn ('27)	.70 .60
17	A4	35c* car rose & vio	.45 .30
18	A4	40c gray & car rose	.45 .35
19	A4	45c bl & brn (R)	.35 .20
20	A4	50c blk & grn	1.75 1.25
21	A4	50c ultra & bl ('22)	.50 .50
22	A4	50c red org & bl ('25)	.60 .60
23	A4	60c org red ('26)	.15 .15
24	A4	65c bis & pale bl ('28)	.80 .60
25	A4	75c org & brn	.30 .30
26	A4	1fr brn & brn vio	.80 .70
27	A4	2fr grn & bl	1.25 .80
28	A4	5fr vio & blk (R)	2.50 2.25
		Nos. 1-28 (28)	17.80 14.05

No. 9 Surcharged in Various Colors   **0,01 = 0,01**

BURKINA FASO

1922
29	A4	0,01c on 15c (Bk)	.40	.40
a.		Double surcharge	50.00	50.00
30	A4	0,02c on 15c (Bl)	.40	.40
31	A4	0,05c on 15c (R)	.40	.40
		Nos. 29-31 (3)	1.20	1.20

Type of 1920 Surcharged **60 = 60**

1922
32	A4	60c on 75c vio, pnksh	.35	.35

Stamps and Types of 1920 Surcharged with New Value and Bars

1924-27
33	A4	25c on 2fr grn & bl	.45	.45
34	A4	25c on 5fr vio & blk	.45	.45
35	A4	65c on 45c bl & brn ('25)	.50	.50
36	A4	85c on 75c org & brn ('25)	.70	.70
37	A4	90c on 75c brn red & sal pink ('27)	.70	.70
38	A4	1.25fr on 1fr dp bl & lt bl (R) ('26)	.45	.45
39	A4	1.50fr on 1fr dp bl & ultra ('27)	1.25	1.25
40	A4	3fr on 5fr dl red & brn org ('27)	1.65	1.65
41	A4	10fr on 5fr ol grn & lil rose ('27)	7.25	7.25
42	A4	20fr on 5fr org brn & vio ('27)	10.00	10.00
		Nos. 33-42 (10)	23.40	23.40

Hausa Chief — A5
Hausa Woman — A6 
Hausa Warrior A7 

1928 Typo. Perf. 13½x14
43	A5	1c indigo & grn	.15	.15
44	A5	2c brn & lil	.15	.15
45	A5	4c blk & yel	.15	.15
46	A5	5c indigo & gray bl	.20	.20
47	A5	10c indigo & pink	.50	.50
48	A5	15c brn & bl	.90	.90
49	A5	20c brn & grn	.90	.90
50	A6	25c brn & yel	1.10	1.10
51	A6	30c dp grn & grn	1.10	1.10
52	A6	40c blk & pink	1.10	1.10
53	A6	45c brn & blue	1.10	1.10
54	A6	50c blk & grn	1.10	1.10
55	A6	65c indigo & bl	1.65	1.65
56	A6	75c blk & lil	1.10	1.10
57	A6	90c brn red & lil	1.10	1.10

Perf. 14x13½
58	A7	1fr brn & grn	1.10	1.10
59	A7	1.10fr indigo & lil	1.10	1.10
60	A7	1.50fr ultra & grysh	1.75	1.75
61	A7	2fr blk & bl	2.25	2.25
62	A7	3fr brn & yel	2.25	2.25
63	A7	5fr brn & lil	2.25	2.25
64	A7	10fr blk & grn	9.00	9.00
65	A7	20fr blk & pink	13.00	13.00
		Nos. 43-65 (23)	45.00	45.00

Common Design Types pictured following the introduction.

Colonial Exposition Issue
Common Design Types
1931 Engr. Perf. 12½
Country Name Typo. in Black
66	CD70	40c dp grn	1.75	1.75
67	CD71	50c violet	2.00	2.00
68	CD72	90c red org	2.00	2.00
69	CD73	1.50fr dull blue	2.50	2.50
		Nos. 66-69 (4)	8.25	8.25

Catalogue values for unused stamps in this section, from this point to the end of the section, are for Never Hinged items.

Republic

President Ouezzin Coulibaly — A8
Deer Mask and Deer — A9 

1959 Unwmk. Engr. Perf. 13
70	A8	25fr black & magenta	.25	.15

1st anniv. of the proclamation of the Republic; Ouezzin Coulibaly, Council President, who died in December, 1958.

Imperforates
Most Upper Volta stamps from 1959 onward exist imperforate in issued and trial colors, and also in small presentation sheets in issued colors.

1960
Animal Masks: 1fr, 2fr, 4fr, Wart hog. 5fr, 6fr, 8fr, Monkey. 10fr, 15fr, 20fr, Buffalo. 25fr, Coba (antelope). 30fr, 40fr, 50fr, Elephant. 60fr, 85fr, Secretary bird.

71	A9	30c rose & violet	.15	.15
72	A9	40c buff & dp claret	.15	.15
73	A9	50c bl grn & gray ol	.15	.15
74	A9	1fr red, blk & red brn	.15	.15
75	A9	2fr emer, yel grn & dk grn	.15	.15
76	A9	4fr bl, vio & ind	.15	.15
77	A9	5fr ol bis, red & brn	.15	.15
78	A9	6fr grnsh bl & vio brn	.15	.15
79	A9	8fr org & red brn	.15	.15
80	A9	10fr lt yel grn & plum	.15	.15
81	A9	15fr org, ultra & brn	.15	.15
82	A9	20fr green & ultra	.22	.15
83	A9	25fr bl, emer & dp claret	.25	.15
84	A9	30fr dk bl grn, blk & brn	.30	.15
85	A9	40fr ultra, ind & dk car	.38	.15
86	A9	50fr brt pink, brn & grn	.42	.18
87	A9	60fr org brn & bl	.55	.25
88	A9	85fr gray ol & dk bl	.80	.32
		Nos. 71-88 (18)	4.57	3.00

C.C.T.A. Issue
Common Design Type
1960 Engr. Perf. 13
89	CD106	25fr vio bl & slate	.35	.35

Emblem of the Entente — A9a
Pres. Maurice Yameogo — A10 

1960 Photo. Perf. 13x13½
90	A9a	25fr multicolored	.40	.35

Council of the Entente.

1960, May 1 Engr. Perf. 13
91	A10	25fr dk vio brn & slate	.25	.16

Flag, Village and Couple — A11

1960, Aug. 5 Unwmk. Perf. 13
92	A11	25fr red brn, blk & red	.35	.25

Proclamation of independence, Aug. 5, 1960.

World Meteorological Organization Emblem — A12

1961, May 4
93	A12	25fr blk, bl & red	.30	.25

First World Meteorological Day.

Arms of Republic — A13

1961, Dec. 8 Photo. Perf. 12x12½
94	A13	25fr multicolored	.25	.25

The 1961 independence celebrations.

WMO Emblem, Weather Station and Sorghum Grain — A14

1962, Mar. 23 Unwmk. Perf. 13
95	A14	25fr dk bl, emer & brn	.30	.25

UN 2nd World Meteorological Day, Mar. 23.

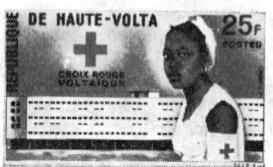

Hospital and Nurse — A15

1962, June 23 Perf. 13x12
96	A15	25fr multicolored	.35	.35

Founding of Upper Volta Red Cross.

Buffalos at Water Hole — A16

Designs: 10fr, Lions, horiz. 15fr, Defassa waterbuck. 25fr, Arly reservation, horiz. 50fr, Diapaga reservation, horiz. 85fr, Buffon's kob.

Perf. 12½x12, 12x12½
97	A16	5fr sepia, bl & grn	.15	.15
98	A16	10fr red brn, grn & yel	.16	.15
99	A16	15fr sepia, grn & yel	.25	.16
100	A16	25fr vio brn, bl & grn	.45	.20
101	A16	50fr vio brn, bl & grn	.80	.55
102	A16	85fr red brn, bl & grn	1.20	.80
		Nos. 97-102 (6)	3.01	2.01

Abidjan Games Issue
Common Design Type
Designs: 20fr, Soccer. 25fr, Bicycling. 85fr, Boxing. All horiz.

1962, July 21 Photo. Perf. 12½x12
103	CD109	20fr multicolored	.25	.18
104	CD109	25fr multicolored	.30	.25
105	CD109	85fr multicolored	.60	.40
		Nos. 103-105 (3)	1.15	.83

African-Malgache Union Issue
Common Design Type
1962, Sept. 8 Unwmk.
106	CD110	30fr red, bluish grn & gold	.70	.65

Weather Map and UN Emblem A17

1963, Mar. 23 Perf. 12x12½
107	A17	70fr multicolored	.60	.45

3rd World Meteorological Day, Mar. 23.

Friendship Games, Dakar, Apr. 11-21 — A18

1963, Apr. 11 Engr. Perf. 13
108	A18	20fr Basketball	.22	.15
109	A18	25fr Discus	.25	.15
110	A18	50fr Judo	.55	.25
		Nos. 108-110 (3)	1.02	.55

Amaryllis A19

Flowers: 50c, Hibiscus. 1fr, Oldenlandia grandiflora. 1.50fr, Rose moss (portulaca). 2fr, Tobacco. 4fr, Morning glory. 5fr, Striga senegalensis. 6fr, Cowpea. 8fr, Lepidagathis heudelotiana. 10fr, Spurge. 25fr, Argyreia nervosa. 30fr, Rangoon creeper. 40fr, Water lily. 50fr, White plumeria. 60fr, Crotalaria retusa. 85fr, Hibiscus. Nos. 111-119 are vert.

1963 Photo.
111	A19	50c multicolored	.15	.15
112	A19	1fr multicolored	.15	.15
113	A19	1.50fr multicolored	.15	.15
114	A19	2fr multicolored	.15	.15
115	A19	4fr multicolored	.15	.15
116	A19	5fr multicolored	.15	.15
117	A19	6fr multicolored	.15	.15
118	A19	8fr multicolored	.15	.15
119	A19	10fr multicolored	.16	.15
120	A19	15fr multicolored	.20	.15
121	A19	25fr multicolored	.30	.16
122	A19	30fr multicolored	.35	.20
123	A19	40fr multicolored	.40	.30
124	A19	50fr multicolored	.55	.38
125	A19	60fr multicolored	.65	.42
126	A19	85fr multicolored	.90	.55
		Nos. 111-126 (16)	4.71	3.51

Centenary Emblem and Globe — A20
Scroll — A21 

1963, Oct. 21 Unwmk. Perf. 12
127	A20	25fr multicolored	.50	.40

Centenary of International Red Cross.

1963, Dec. 10 Photo. Perf. 13x12½
128	A21	25fr dp claret, gold & bl	.30	.20

15th anniv. of the Universal Declaration of Human Rights.

BURKINA FASO

Sound Wave Patterns — A22

1964, Jan. 16   Perf. 12½x13
129 A22 25fr multicolored   .25 .20
Upper Volta's admission to the ITU.

Barograph and WMO Emblem — A23

1964, Mar. 23   Engr.   Perf. 13
130 A23 50fr dk car rose, grn & bl   .55 .40
4th World Meteorological Day, Mar. 23.

World Connected by Letters and Carrier Pigeon — A24

60fr, World connected by letters and jet plane.

1964, Mar. 29   Photo.   Perf. 13x12
131 A24 25fr gray brn & ultra   .25 .20
132 A24 60fr gray brn & org   .60 .42
Upper Volta's admission to the UPU.

IQSY Emblem and Seasonal Allegories — A25

1964, Aug. 17   Engr.   Perf. 13
133 A25 30fr grn, ocher & car   .35 .25
International Quiet Sun Year.

Cooperation Issue
Common Design Type

1964, Nov. 7   Unwmk.   Perf. 13
134 CD119 70fr dl bl grn, dk brn & car   .65 .42

Hotel Independance, Ouagadougou — A26

1964, Dec. 11   Litho.   Perf. 12½x13
135 A26 25fr multicolored   1.00 .35

Pigmy Long-tailed Sunbird — A27    Comoe Waterfall — A28

1965, Mar. 1   Photo.   Perf. 13x12½
Size: 22x36mm
136 A27 10fr shown   .20 .16
137 A27 15fr Olive-bellied Sunbird   .25 .20
138 A27 20fr Splendid Sunbird   .40 .25
Nos. 136-138,C20 (4)   6.35 3.11

1965   Engr.   Perf. 13
Design: 25fr, Great Waterfall of Banfora, horiz.
139 A28 5fr yel grn, bl & red brn   .15 .15
140 A28 25fr dk red, brt bl & grn   .25 .16
Nos. 139-140 (2)   .40 .31

Soccer — A29    Abraham Lincoln — A30

Designs: 25fr, Boxing gloves and ring. 70fr, Tennis rackets, ball and net.

1965, July 15   Unwmk.   Perf. 13
141 A29 15fr brn, red & dk grn   .16 .15
142 A29 25fr pale org, bl & brn   .28 .18
143 A29 70fr dk car & brt grn   .60 .32
Nos. 141-143 (3)   1.04 .65
1st African Games, Brazzaville, July 18-25.

1965, Nov. 3   Photo.   Perf. 13x12½
144 A30 50fr green & multi   .50 .38
Centenary of death of Abraham Lincoln.

Pres. Maurice Yameogo — A31

1965, Dec. 11   Photo.   Perf. 13x12½
145 A31 25fr multicolored   .25 .16

Mantis A32

Wart Hog A33    Headdress A34

1966   Perf. 13x12½, 12½x13
146 A33 1fr Nemopistha imperatrix   .15 .15
147 A33 2fr Ball python   .15 .15
148 A32 3fr shown   .15 .15
149 A32 4fr Grasshopper   .15 .15
150 A33 5fr shown   .15 .15
151 A32 6fr Scorpion   .15 .15
152 A33 8fr Green monkey   .15 .15
153 A32 10fr Dromedary   .15 .15
154 A33 15fr Leopard   .20 .15
155 A32 20fr Cape buffalo   .22 .16
156 A33 25fr Hippopotamus   .30 .16
157 A32 30fr Agama lizard   .38 .20
158 A33 45fr Common puff adder   .55 .22
159 A33 50fr Chameleon   .60 .35
160 A33 60fr Ugada limbata   .70 .42
161 A33 85fr Elephant   .90 .50
Nos. 146-161 (16)   5.05 3.36

1966, Apr. 9   Photo.   Perf. 13x12½
25fr, Plumed headdress. 60fr, Male dancer.
162 A34 20fr yel grn, choc & red   .20 .15
163 A34 25fr multicolored   .25 .16
164 A34 60fr org, dk brn & red   .60 .35
Nos. 162-164 (3)   1.05 .66
Intl. Negro Arts Festival, Dakar, Senegal, 4/1-24.

Pô Church A35

Design: No. 166, Bobo-Dioulasso Mosque.

1966, Apr. 15   Perf. 12½x13
165 A35 25fr multicolored   .22 .16
166 A35 25fr bl, cream & red brn   .22 .16

The Red Cross Helping the World — A36

1966, June   Photo.   Perf. 13x12½
167 A36 25fr lemon, blk & car   .22 .15
Issued to honor the Red Cross.

Boy Scouts in Camp — A37

15fr, Two Scouts on a cliff exploring the country.

1966, June 15   Photo.   Perf. 12½x13
168 A37 10fr multicolored   .15 .15
169 A37 15fr blk, bis brn, & dl yel   .16 .15
Issued to honor the Boy Scouts.

Cow Receiving Injection A38

1966, Aug. 16   Photo.   Perf. 12½x13
170 A38 25fr yel, blk & blue   .25 .20
Campaign against cattle plague.

Plowing with Donkey A39

Design: 30fr, Crop rotation, Kamboince Experimental Station.

1966, Sept. 15   Photo.   Perf. 12½x13
171 A39 25fr multicolored   .22 .15
172 A39 30fr multicolored   .25 .16
Natl. and rural education; 3rd anniv. of the Kamboince Experimental Station (No. 172).

UNESCO Emblem and Map of Africa — A40

UNICEF Emblem and Children A41

1966, Dec. 10   Engr.   Perf. 13
173 A40 50fr brt bl, blk & red   .50 .25
174 A41 50fr dk vio, dp lil & dk red   .50 .25
20th anniv. of UNESCO and of UNICEF.

Arms of Upper Volta — A42    Symbols of Agriculture, Industry, Men and Women — A43

1967, Jan. 2   Photo.   Perf. 12½x13
175 A42 30fr multicolored   .22 .15

Europafrica Issue
1967, Feb. 4   Photo.   Perf. 12½
176 A43 60fr multicolored   .50 .30

Scout Handclasp and Jamboree Emblem A44

5fr, Jamboree emblem and Scout holding hat.

1967, June 8   Photo.   Perf. 12½x13
177 A44 5fr multicolored   .20 .15
178 A44 20fr multicolored   .55 .40
12th Boy Scout World Jamboree, Farragut State Park, Idaho, Aug. 1-9. See No. C41.

Bank Book and Hands with Coins — A45

1967, Aug. 22   Engr.   Perf. 13
179 A45 30fr slate grn, ocher & olive   .25 .15
National Savings Bank.

Mailman on Bicycle — A46

1967, Oct. 15   Engr.   Perf. 13
180 A46 30fr dk bl, emer & brn   .30 .16
Stamp Day.

Monetary Union Issue
Common Design Type

1967, Nov. 4   Engr.   Perf. 13
181 CD125 30fr dk vio & dl bl   .25 .15

View of Nizier — A47

Olympic Emblem and: 50fr, Les Deux-Alps, vert. 100fr, Ski lift and view of Villard-de-Lans.

1967, Nov. 28
182 A47 15fr brt bl, grn & brn   .16 .15
183 A47 50fr brt bl & slate grn   .45 .20
184 A47 100fr brt bl, grn & red   .90 .45
Nos. 182-184 (3)   1.51 .80
10th Winter Olympic Games, Grenoble, France, Feb. 6-18, 1968.

BURKINA FASO

White and Black Men Holding Human Rights Emblem — A48

1968, Jan. 2   Photo.   Perf. 12½x13
185 A48 20fr brt bl, gold & dp car   .20 .15
186 A48 30fr grn, gold & dp car   .30 .16
International Human Rights Year.

Administration School and Student — A49

1968, Feb. 2   Engr.   Perf. 13
187 A49 30fr ol bis, Prus bl & brt grn   .25 .15
National School of Administration.

WHO Emblem and Sick People — A50

1968, Apr. 7   Engr.   Perf. 13
188 A50 30fr ind, brt bl & car rose   .30 .16
189 A50 50fr brt bl, sl grn & lt brn   .45 .22
WHO, 20th anniversary.

Telephone Office, Bobo-Dioulasso — A51

1968, Sept. 30   Photo.   Perf. 12½x12
190 A51 30fr multicolored   .28 .15
Opening of the automatic telephone office in Bobo-Dioulasso.

Weaver A52

1968, Oct. 30   Engr.   Perf. 13
Size: 36x22mm
191 A52 30fr magenta, brn & ocher   .30 .16
See No. C58.

Grain Pouring over World, Plower and FAO Emblem — A53

1969, Jan. 7   Engr.   Perf. 13
192 A53 30fr slate, vio bl & maroon   .25 .15
UNFAO world food program.

Automatic Looms and ILO Emblem A54

1969, Mar. 15   Engr.   Perf. 13
193 A54 30fr brt grn, mar & indigo   .25 .15
ILO, 50th anniversary.

Smith — A55

1969, Apr. 3   Engr.   Perf. 13
Size: 36x22mm
194 A55 5fr magenta & blk   .15 .15
See No. C64.

Blood Donor — A56

1969, May 15   Engr.   Perf. 13
195 A56 30fr blk, bl & car   .25 .16
League of Red Cross Societies, 50th anniv.

Nile Pike — A57

Fish: 20fr, Nannocharax gobioides. 25fr, Hemigrammocharax polli. 55fr, Alestes luteus. 85fr, Micralestes voltae.

1969   Engr.   Perf. 13
Size: 36x22mm
196 A57 20fr brt bl, brn & yel   .32 .20
197 A57 25fr slate, brn & dk brn   .32 .20
198 A57 30fr dk olive & blk   .45 .25
199 A57 55fr dk grn, yel & ol   .60 .42
200 A57 85fr slate brn & pink   1.25 .90
    Nos. 196-200,C66-C67 (7)   5.24 3.01

Development Bank Issue
Common Design Type
1969, Sept. 10   Engr.   Perf. 13
201 CD130 30fr sl grn, grn & ocher   .22 .15

Millet — A58

Design: 30fr, Cotton.

1969, Oct. 30   Photo.   Perf. 12½x13
202 A58 15fr dk brn, grn & yel   .16 .15
203 A58 30fr dp claret & brt bl   .30 .16
See Nos. C73-C74.

ASECNA Issue
Common Design Type
1969, Dec. 12   Engr.   Perf. 13
204 CD132 100fr brown   .80 .50

Niadale Mask — A59

Carvings from National Museum: 30fr, Niaga. 45fr, Man and woman, Iliu Bara. 80fr, Karan Weeba figurine.

1970, Mar. 5   Engr.   Perf. 13
207 A59 10fr dk car rose, org & dk brn   .15 .15
209 A59 30fr dk brn, brt vio & grnsh bl   .22 .15
211 A59 45fr yel grn, brn & bl   .32 .15
212 A59 80fr pur, rose lil & brn   .60 .25
    Nos. 207-212 (4)   1.29 .70

African Huts and European City — A60

1970, Apr. 25   Engr.   Perf. 13
213 A60 30fr dk brn, red & bl   .25 .15
Issued for Linked Cities' Day.

Mask for Nebwa Gnomo Dance — A61

Designs: 8fr, Cauris dancers, vert. 20fr, Gourmantchés dancers, vert. 30fr, Larilé dancers.

1970, May 7   Photo.   Perf. 13
214 A61 5fr lt brn, vio bl & blk   .15 .15
215 A61 8fr org brn, car & blk   .15 .15
216 A61 20fr dk brn, sl grn & ocher   .16 .15
217 A61 30fr dp car, dk gray & brn   .25 .15
    Nos. 214-217 (4)   .71 .60

Education Year Emblem, Open Book and Pupils — A62

Design: 90fr, Education Year emblem, telecommunication and education symbols.

1970, May 14   Perf. 12½x12
218 A62 40fr black & multi   .35 .20
219 A62 90fr olive & multi   .65 .35
International Education Year.

UPU Headquarters Issue
Abraham Lincoln, UPU Headquarters and Emblem — A63 

1970, May 20   Engr.   Perf. 13
220 A63 30fr dk car rose, ind & red brn   .30 .16
221 A63 60fr dk bl grn, vio & red brn   .50 .25
See note after CD133, Common Design section.

Ship-building Industry A64

45fr, Chemical industry. 80fr, Electrical industry.

1970, June 15
222 A64 15fr brt pink, red brn & blk   .15 .15
223 A64 45fr emerald, dp bl & blk   .35 .20
224 A64 80fr red brn, claret & blk   .65 .35
    Nos. 222-224 (3)   1.15 .70
Hanover Fair.

Cattle Vaccination A65

1970, June 30   Photo.   Perf. 13
225 A65 30fr Prus bl, yel & sepia   .30 .15
National Veterinary College.

Vaccination and Red Cross — A66

1970, Aug. 28   Engr.   Perf. 12½x13
226 A66 30fr chocolate & car   .25 .16
Issued for the Upper Volta Red Cross. For surcharge see No. 252.

Europafrica Issue

Nurse with Child, by Frans Hals — A67

Paintings: 30fr, Courtyard of a House in Delft, by Pieter de Hooch. 150fr, Christina of Denmark, by Hans Holbein. 250fr, Courtyard of the Royal Palace at Innsbruck, Austria, by Albrecht Dürer.

1970, Sept. 25   Litho.   Perf. 13x14
227 A67 25fr multicolored   .22 .15
228 A67 30fr multicolored   .30 .16
229 A67 150fr multicolored   1.40 .65
230 A67 250fr multicolored   2.00 1.00
    Nos. 227-230 (4)   3.92 1.96

Citroen — A68

Design: 40fr, Old and new Citroen cars.

1970, Oct. 16   Engr.   Perf. 13
231 A68 25fr ol brn, mar & sl grn   .22 .15
232 A68 40fr brt grn, plum & sl   .40 .20
57th Paris Automobile Salon.

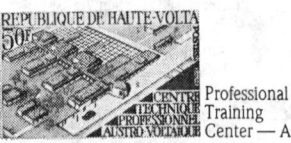

Professional Training Center — A69

1970, Dec. 10   Engr.   Perf. 13
233 A69 50fr grn, bis & brn   .38 .16
Opening of Professional Training Center under joint sponsorship of Austria and Upper Volta.

Upper Volta Arms and Soaring Bird — A70

1970, Dec. 10   Photo.
234 A70 30fr lt blue & multi   .22 .15
Tenth anniversary of independence, Dec. 11.

BURKINA FASO

Political Maps of Africa — A71

1970, Dec. 14   Litho.   Perf. 13½
235 A71 50fr multicolored   .40 .20
10th anniv. of the declaration granting independence to colonial territories and countries.

Beingolo Hunting Horn — A72

Musical Instruments: 15fr, Mossi guitar, vert. 20fr, Gourounsi flutes, vert. 25fr, Lunga drums.

1971, Mar. 1   Engr.   Perf. 13
236 A72 5fr blue, brn & car   .15 .15
237 A72 15fr green, crim rose & brn   .15 .15
238 A72 20fr car rose, bl & gray   .16 .15
239 A72 25fr brt grn, red brn & ol gray   .20 .15
    Nos. 236-239 (4)   .66 .60
Voltaphilex I, National Phil. Exhibition.

Four Races — A73

1971, Mar. 21   Engr.   Perf. 13
240 A73 50fr rose cl, lt grn & dk brn   .40 .22
Intl. year against racial discrimination.

Telephone and Globes — A74

1971, May 17   Engr.   Perf. 13
241 A74 50fr brn, gray & dk pur   .40 .20
3rd World Telecommunications Day.

Cane Field Worker, Banfora Sugar Mill — A75

Cotton and Voltex Mill Emblem — A76

1971, June 24   Photo.   Perf. 13
242 A75 10fr multicolored   .15 .15
243 A76 35fr multicolored   .25 .15
Industrial development.

Gonimbrasia Hecate A77

Butterflies and Moths: 2fr, Hamanumida daedalus. 3fr, Ophideres materna. 5fr, Danaus chyrsippus. 40fr, Hypolimnas misippus. 45fr, Danaus petiverana.

1971, June 30
244 A77 1fr blue & multi   .15 .15
245 A77 2fr lt lilac & multi   .15 .15
246 A77 3fr multicolored   .15 .15
247 A77 5fr gray & multi   .15 .15
248 A77 40fr ocher & multi   .60 .35
249 A77 45fr multicolored   .80 .50
    Nos. 244-249 (6)   2.00 1.45

Kabuki Actor — A78

Design: 40fr, African mask and Kabuki actor.

1971, Aug. 12   Photo.   Perf. 13
250 A78 25fr multicolored   .20 .15
251 A78 40fr multicolored   .30 .15
Philatokyo 71, Philatelic Exposition, Tokyo, Apr. 19-29.

No. 226 Surcharged

100F

1971   Engr.   Perf. 12½x13
252 A66 100fr on 30fr choc & car   .65 .40
10th anniversary of Upper Volta Red Cross.

Seed Preparation A79

Designs: 75fr, Old farmer with seed packet, vert. 100fr, Farmer in rice field.

1971, Sept. 30   Photo.   Perf. 13
253 A79 35fr ocher & multi   .22 .15
254 A79 75fr lt blue & multi   .50 .20
255 A79 100fr brown & multi   .65 .35
    Nos. 253-255 (3)   1.37 .70
National campaign for seed protection.

Outdoor Classroom A80

Design: 50fr, Mother learning to read.

1971, Oct. 14
256 A80 35fr multicolored   .22 .15
257 A80 50fr multicolored   .38 .16
Women's education.

Joseph Dakiri, Soldiers Driving Tractors — A81

Children and UNICEF Emblem — A84

Spraying Lake, Fly, Man Leading Blind Women A82

40fr, Dakiri & soldiers gathering harvest.

1971, Oct. 13   Perf. 12x12½
258 A81 15fr blk, yel & red brn   .15 .15
259 A81 40fr blue & multi   .25 .16
Joseph Dakiri (1938-1971), inaugurator of the Army-Aid-to-Agriculture Program.

1971, Nov. 26   Photo.   Perf. 13
260 A82 40fr dk brn, yel & bl   .25 .16
Drive against onchocerciasis, roundworm infestation.
For surcharge see No. 295.

1971, Dec. 11   Perf. 13
262 A84 45fr red, bister & blk   .35 .16
UNICEF, 25th anniv.

Peulh House — A85

Upper Volta Houses: 20fr, Gourounsi house. 35fr, Mossi houses. 45fr, Bobo house, vert. 50fr, Dagari house, vert. 90fr, Bango house, interior.

Perf. 13x13½, 13½x13
1971-72   Photo.
263 A85 10fr ver & multi   .15 .15
264 A85 20fr multicolored   .16 .15
265 A85 35fr brt grn & multi   .22 .15
266 A85 45fr multi ('72)   .35 .16
267 A85 50fr multi ('72)   .40 .20
268 A85 90fr multi ('72)   .60 .35
    Nos. 263-268 (6)   1.88 1.16

Town Halls of Bobo-Dioulasso and Chalons-sur-Marne — A86

1971, Dec. 23   Perf. 13x12½
269 A86 40fr yellow & multi   .25 .15
Kinship between the cities of Bobo-Dioulasso, Upper Volta, and Chalons-sur-Marne, France.

Louis Armstrong — A87

1972, May 17   Perf. 14x13
270 A87 45fr multicolored   .45 .25
Black musician. See No. C104.

Red Crescent, Cross and Lion Emblems A88

1972, June 23   Perf. 13x14
271 A88 40fr yellow & multi   .35 .16
World Red Cross Day. See No. C105.

Coiffure of Peulh Woman — A89

Designs: Various hair styles.

1972, July 23   Litho.   Perf. 13
272 A89 25fr blue & multi   .20 .15
273 A89 35fr emerald & multi   .22 .15
274 A89 75fr yellow & multi   .45 .18
    Nos. 272-274 (3)   .87 .48

Classroom A90

Designs: 15fr, Clinic. 20fr, Factory. 35fr, Cattle. 40fr, Flowers. 85fr, Road building machinery.

1972, Oct. 30   Engr.   Perf. 13
275 A90 10fr sl grn, lt grn & choc   .15 .15
276 A90 15fr brt grn, brn org & brn   .15 .15
277 A90 20fr bl, lt brn & grn   .15 .15
278 A90 35fr grn, brn & brt bl   .18 .15
279 A90 40fr choc, pink & sl grn   .22 .16
    Nos. 275-279, C106 (6)   1.30 .98
2nd Five-Year Plan.

West African Monetary Union Issue
Common Design Type
1972, Nov. 2
280 CD136 40fr brn, bl & gray   .25 .15

Lottery Office and Emblem — A91

1972, Nov. 6   Litho.
281 A91 35fr multicolored   .22 .15
5th anniversary of National Lottery.

Domestic Animals — A92

1972, Dec. 4   Litho.   Perf. 13½x12½
282 A92 5fr Donkeys   .15 .15
283 A92 10fr Geese   .15 .15
284 A92 30fr Goats   .20 .15
285 A92 50fr Cow   .35 .15
286 A92 65fr Dromedaries   .42 .20
    Nos. 282-286 (5)   1.27 .80

Mossi Woman's Hair Style, and Village — A93

1973, Jan. 24   Engr.   Perf. 13
287 A93 5fr slate grn, org & choc   .15 .15
288 A93 40fr bl, org & chocolate   .22 .15

BURKINA FASO

Eugene A.
Cernan and
Lunar Module
A94

65fr, Ronald E. Evans & splashdown. 100fr, Capsule, in orbit & interior, horiz. 150fr, Harrison H. Schmitt & lift-off. 200fr, Conference & moon-buggy. 500fr, Moon-buggy & capsule, horiz.

	Perf. 12½x13½, 13½x12½		
1973, Mar. 29		Litho.	
289 A94	50fr multi	.32	.16
290 A94	65fr multi	.38	.18
291 A94	100fr multi	.60	.30
292 A94	150fr multi	.90	.45
293 A94	200fr multi	1.25	.60
	Nos. 289-293 (5)	3.45	1.69
Souvenir Sheet			
294 A94	500fr multi	3.50	1.60

Apollo 17 moon mission.

No. 260 Surcharged in Red

O. M. S.
25ᵉ Anniversaire
45ᶠ
=

1973, Apr. 7	Photo.	Perf. 13	
295 A82	45fr on 40fr multi	.25	.16

WHO, 25th anniversary.

Scout
Bugler — A95

1973, July 18	Litho.	Perf. 12½x13	
296 A95	20fr multicolored	.15	.15
	Nos. 296,C160-C163 (5)	3.30	1.70

African Postal Union Issue
Common Design Type

1973, Sept. 12	Engr.	Perf. 13	
297 CD137	100fr brt red, mag & dl yel	.65	.25

Pres.
Kennedy,
Saturn 5 on
Assembly
Trailer — A96

Pres. John F. Kennedy (1917-1963) and: 10fr, Atlas rocket carrying John H. Glenn. 30fr, Titan 2 rocket and Gemini 3 capsule.

1973, Sept. 12	Litho.	Perf. 12½x13	
298 A96	5fr multicolored	.15	.15
299 A96	10fr multicolored	.15	.15
300 A96	30fr multicolored	.20	.15
	Nos. 298-300,C167-C168 (5)	3.90	2.10

Cross-examination — A97

Designs: 65fr, "Diamond Ede." 70fr, Forensic Institute. 150fr, Robbery scene.

1973, Sept. 15		Perf. 13x12½	
301 A97	50fr multicolored	.32	.16
302 A97	65fr multicolored	.38	.18
303 A97	70fr multicolored	.40	.20
304 A97	150fr multicolored	.90	.45
	Nos. 301-304 (4)	2.00	.99

Interpol, 50th anniversary. See No. C170.

Market Place, Ouagadougou — A98

1973, Sept. 30			
305 A98	35fr multicolored	.22	.15
306 A98	40fr multicolored	.25	.15

Tourism. See Nos. C171-C172.

Protestant Church — A99

Design: 40fr, Ouahigouya Mosque.

1973, Sept. 28		Perf. 13x12½	
307 A99	35fr multicolored	.22	.15
308 A99	40fr multicolored	.25	.15

Houses of worship. See No. C173.

Kiembara
Dancers
A100

Design: 40fr, Dancers.

1973, Nov. 30	Litho.	Perf. 12½x13	
309 A100	35fr multicolored	.22	.15
310 A100	40fr multicolored	.25	.15

Folklore. See Nos. C174-C175.

Yuri Gagarin and Aries — A101

Famous Men and their Zodiac Signs: 10fr, Lenin and Taurus. 20fr, John F. Kennedy, rocket and Gemini. 25fr, John H. Glenn, orbiting capsule and Cancer. 30fr, Napoleon and Leo. 50fr, Goethe and Virgo. 60fr, Pelé and Libra. 75fr, Charles de Gaulle and Scorpio. 100fr, Beethoven and Sagittarius. 175fr, Conrad Adenauer and Capricorn. 200fr, Edwin E. Aldrin, Jr. (Apollo XI) and Aquarius. 250fr, Lord Baden-Powell and Pisces.

1973, Dec. 15	Litho.	Perf. 13x14	
311 A101	5fr multicolored	.15	.15
312 A101	10fr multicolored	.15	.15
313 A101	20fr multicolored	.15	.15
314 A101	25fr multicolored	.15	.15
315 A101	30fr multicolored	.16	.15
316 A101	50fr multicolored	.30	.15
317 A101	60fr multicolored	.38	.18
318 A101	75fr multicolored	.42	.20
319 A101	100fr multicolored	.60	.30
320 A101	175fr multicolored	1.10	.55
321 A101	200fr multicolored	1.20	.55
322 A101	250fr multicolored	1.50	.70
	Nos. 311-322 (12)	6.26	3.38

See Nos. C176-C178.

Rivera with Italian Flag and Championship
'74 Emblem — A102

40fr, World Cup, soccer ball, World Championship '74 emblem & Pelé with Brazilian flag.

1974, Jan. 15		Perf. 13x12½	
323 A102	5fr multicolored	.15	.15
324 A102	40fr multicolored	.25	.15
	Nos. 323-324,C179-C181 (5)	3.15	1.70

10th World Cup Soccer Championship, Munich, June 13-July 7.

Charles de
Gaulle
A103

40fr, De Gaulle memorial. 60fr, Pres. de Gaulle.

1974, Feb. 4	Litho.	Perf. 12½x13	
325 A103	35fr multicolored	.20	.15
326 A103	40fr multicolored	.20	.15
327 A103	60fr multicolored	.35	.16
a.	Strip of 3, Nos. 325-327	.75	.45
	Nos. 325-327,C183 (4)	2.75	1.46

Gen. Charles de Gaulle (1890-1970), president of France. See #C184.

N'Dongo and
Cameroun
Flag — A104

World Cup, Emblems and: 20fr, Kolev and Bulgarian flag. 50fr, Keita and Mali flag.

1974, Mar. 19			
328 A104	10fr multicolored	.15	.15
329 A104	20fr multicolored	.15	.15
330 A104	50fr multicolored	.35	.16
	Nos. 328-330,C185-C186 (5)	2.90	1.59

10th World Cup Soccer Championship, Munich, June 13-July 7.

Map and Flags
of Members
A105

1974, May 29	Photo.	Perf. 13x12½	
331 A105	40fr blue & multi	.22	.15

15th anniversary of the Council of Accord.

UPU Emblem and Mail Coach — A106

1974, July 23	Litho.	Perf. 13½	
332 A106	35fr shown	.22	.15
333 A106	40fr Steamship	.25	.15
334 A106	85fr Mailman	.55	.28
	Nos. 332-334,C189-C191 (6)	4.02	2.08

Universal Postal Union centenary.
For overprints see #339-341, C197-C200.

Soccer Game, Winner Italy, in France,
1938 — A107

World Cup, Game and Flags: 25fr, Uruguay, in Brazil, 1950. 50fr, East Germany, in Switzerland, 1954.

1974, Sept. 2	Litho.	Perf. 13½	
335 A107	10fr multicolored	.15	.15
336 A107	25fr multicolored	.16	.15
337 A107	50fr multicolored	.35	.16
	Nos. 335-337,C193-C195 (6)	4.66	2.41

World Cup Soccer winners.

Shop with
Scott Publishing Co.
24 hours a day
7 days a week at
www.scottonline.com

BURKINA FASO

Map and Farm Woman — A108

1974, Oct. 2　Litho.　Perf. 13x12½
338　A108　35fr yellow & multi　.20　.15
Kou Valley Development.

Nos. 332-334 Overprinted in Red "100e ANNIVERSAIRE DE L'UNION POSTALE UNIVERSELLE / 9 OCTOBRE 1974"

1974, Oct. 9
339　A106　35fr multicolored　.22　.15
340　A106　40fr multicolored　.25　.15
341　A106　85fr multicolored　.55　.28
　Nos. 339-341,C197-C199 (6)　5.07　2.58
Universal Postal Union centenary.

Flowers, by Pierre Bonnard — A109

Flower Paintings by: 10fr, Jan Brueghel. 30fr, Jean van Os. 50fr, Van Brussel.

1974, Oct. 31　Litho.　Perf. 12½x13
342　A109　5fr multicolored　.15　.15
343　A109　10fr multicolored　.15　.15
344　A109　30fr multicolored　.16　.15
345　A109　50fr multicolored　.25　.15
　Nos. 342-345,C201 (5)　2.71　1.60

Churchill as Officer of India Hussars — A110

Churchill: 75fr, As Secretary of State for Interior. 100fr, As pilot. 125fr, meeting with Roosevelt, 1941. 300fr, As painter. 450fr, and "HMS Resolution."

1975, Jan. 11　　Perf. 13½
346　A110　50fr multicolored　.30　.15
347　A110　75fr multicolored　.42　.20
348　A110　100fr multicolored　.55　.28
349　A110　125fr multicolored　.70　.38
350　A110　300fr multicolored　1.60　.80
　Nos. 346-350 (5)　3.57　1.81

Souvenir Sheet
351　A110　450fr multicolored　2.50　1.25
Sir Winston Churchill, birth centenary.

US No. 619 and Minutemen — A111

US Stamps: 40fr, #118 and Proclamation of Independence. 75fr, #798 and Signing the Constitution. 100fr, #703 and Surrender at Yorktown. 200fr, #1003 and George Washington. 300fr, #644 and Surrender of Burgoyne at Saratoga. 500fr, #63, 68, 73, 157, 179, 228 and 1483a.

1975, Feb. 17　Litho.　Perf. 11
352　A111　35fr multicolored　.20　.15
353　A111　40fr multicolored　.22　.15
354　A111　75fr multicolored　.42　.20
355　A111　100fr multicolored　.55　.28
356　A111　200fr multicolored　1.20　.55
357　A111　300fr multicolored　1.60　.80
　Nos. 352-357 (6)　4.19　2.13

Souvenir Sheet
Imperf
358　A111　500fr multicolored　3.00　1.50
American Bicentennial.

"Atlantic" No. 2670, 1904-12 — A112

Locomotives from Mulhouse, France, Railroad Museum: 25fr, No. 2029, 1882. 50fr, No. 2129, 1882.

1975, Feb. 28　Litho.　Perf. 13x12½
359　A112　15fr multicolored　.15　.15
360　A112　25fr multicolored　.16　.15
361　A112　50fr multicolored　.35　.16
　Nos. 359-361,C203-C204 (5)　2.71　1.46

French Flag and Renault Petit Duc, 1910 — A113

Flags and Old Cars: 30fr, US and Ford Model T, 1909. 35fr, Italy and Alfa Romeo "Le Mans," 1931.

1975, Apr. 6　　Perf. 14x13½
362　A113　10fr multicolored　.15　.15
363　A113　30fr multicolored　.20　.15
364　A113　35fr multicolored　.22　.15
　Nos. 362-364,C206-C207 (5)　2.97　1.60

Washington and Lafayette — A114

American Bicentennial: 40fr, Washington reviewing troops at Valley Forge. 50fr, Washington taking oath of office.

1975, May 6　Litho.　Perf. 14
365　A114　30fr multicolored　.20　.15
366　A114　40fr multicolored　.25　.15
367　A114　50fr multicolored　.35　.16
　Nos. 365-367,C209-C210 (5)　4.20　2.11

Souvenir Sheet
367A　A114　500fr multicolored　3.50　1.60

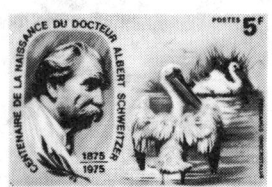

Schweitzer and Pelicans — A115

15fr, Albert Schweitzer and bateleur eagle.

1975, May 25　Litho.　Perf. 13½
368　A115　5fr multicolored　.15　.15
369　A115　15fr multicolored　.15　.15
　Nos. 368-369,C212-C214 (5)　3.90　2.00
Albert Schweitzer, birth centenary.

Apollo and Soyuz Orbiting Earth — A116

Design: 50fr, Apollo and Soyuz near link-up.

1975, July 18
370　A116　40fr multicolored　.25　.15
371　A116　50fr multicolored　.35　.16
　Nos. 370-371,C216-C218 (5)　4.65　2.31
Apollo-Soyuz space test project, Russo-American cooperation, launched July 15, link-up July 17.

Maria Picasso Lopez, Artist's Mother — A117

Paintings by Pablo Picasso (1881-1973): 60fr, Self-portrait. 90fr, First Communion.

1975, Aug. 7
372　A117　50fr multicolored　.35　.16
373　A117　60fr multicolored　.40　.20
374　A117　90fr multicolored　.60　.30
　Nos. 372-374,C220-C221 (5)　4.60　2.36

Expo '75 Emblem and Tanker, Idemitsu Maru — A118

Oceanographic Exposition, Okinawa: 25fr, Training ship, Kaio Maru. 45fr, Firefighting ship, Hiryu. 50fr, Battleship, Yamato. 60fr, Container ship, Kamakura Maru.

1975, Sept. 26　Litho.　Perf. 11
375　A118　15fr multicolored　.15　.15
376　A118　25fr multicolored　.16　.15
377　A118　45fr multicolored　.30　.15
377A　A118　50fr multicolored　.35　.16
378　A118　60fr multicolored　.40　.20
　Nos. 375-378,C223 (6)　2.11　1.19

Woman, Globe and IWY Emblem — A119

1975, Nov. 20　Photo.　Perf. 13
379　A119　65fr multicolored　.38　.22
International Women's Year.

Msgr. Joanny Thevenoud and Cathedral — A120

65fr, Father Guillaume Templier & Cathedral.

1975, Nov. 20　Engr.　Perf. 13x12½
380　A120　55fr grn, blk & dl red　.20　.15
381　A120　65fr blk, org & dl red　.26　.16
75th anniv. of the Evangelization of Upper Volta.

Farmer's Hat, Hoe and Emblem A121

1975, Dec. 10　Photo.　Perf. 13x13½
382　A121　15fr buff & multi　.15　.15
383　A121　50fr lt green & multi　.18　.15
Development of the Volta valleys.

Sledding and Olympic Emblem — A122

Innsbruck Background, Olympic Emblem and: 45fr, Figure skating. 85fr, Skiing.

1975, Dec. 16　Litho.　Perf. 13½
384　A122　35fr multicolored　.18　.15
385　A122　45fr multicolored　.22　.15
386　A122　85fr multicolored　.45　.22
　Nos. 384-386,C225-C226 (5)　2.90　1.52
12th Winter Olympic Games, Innsbruck, Austria, Feb. 4-15, 1976.

Gymnast and Olympic Emblem — A123

1976, Mar. 17
387　A123　40fr shown　.20　.15
388　A123　50fr Sailing　.25　.15
389　A123　100fr Soccer　.55　.28
　Nos. 387-389,C228-C229 (5)　2.40　1.26
21st Olympic Games, Montreal, Canada, July 17-Aug. 1.

Olympic Emblem and Sprinters A124

Olympic Emblem and: 55fr, Equestrian. 75fr, Hurdles.

BURKINA FASO

1976, Mar. 25	Litho.		Perf. 11	
390	A124	30fr multicolored	.16	.15
391	A124	55fr multicolored	.30	.15
392	A124	75fr multicolored	.42	.20
	Nos. 390-392,C231-C232 (5)		2.63	1.38

21st Olympic Games, Montreal.
For overprints see #420-422, C245-C247.

Blind Woman and Man — A125

1976, Apr. 7	Engr.		Perf. 13	
393	A125	75fr dk brn, grn & org	.40	.25
394	A125	250fr dk brn, ocher & org	1.40	.80

Drive against onchocerciasis, roundworm infestation.

"Deutschland" over Friedrichshafen — A126

Airships: 40fr, "Victoria Louise" over sailing ships. 50fr, "Sachsen" over German countryside.

1976, May 11	Litho.		Perf. 11	
395	A126	10fr multicolored	.70	.15
396	A126	40fr multicolored	.25	.15
397	A126	50fr multicolored	.35	.16
	Nos. 395-397,C234-C236 (6)		5.35	2.46

75th anniversary of the Zeppelin.

Viking Lander and Probe on Mars — A127

Viking Mars project: 55fr, Viking orbiter in flight. 75fr, Titan rocket start for Mars, vert.

1976, June 24			Perf. 13½	
398	A127	30fr multicolored	.15	.15
399	A127	55fr multicolored	.22	.15
400	A127	75fr multicolored	.32	.16
	Nos. 398-400,C238-C239 (5)		3.19	1.71

World Map, Arms of Upper Volta — A128

Design: 100fr, World map, arms and dove.

1976, Aug. 19	Litho.		Perf. 12½	
401	A128	55fr brown & multi	.22	.16
402	A128	100fr blue & multi	.42	.30

5th Summit Conference of Non-aligned Countries, Colombo, Sri Lanka, Aug. 9-19.

Bicentennial, Interphil 76 Emblems and Washington at Battle of Trenton — A129

Design: 90fr, Bicentennial, Interphil 76 emblems and Seat of Government, Pennsylvania.

1976, Sept. 30			Perf. 13½	
403	A129	60fr multicolored	.40	.16
404	A129	90fr multicolored	.55	.22
	Nos. 403-404,C241-C243 (5)		5.00	2.38

American Bicentennial, Interphil 76, Philadelphia, Pa., May 29-June 6.

UPU and UN Emblems — A130

1976, Dec. 8	Engr.		Perf. 13	
405	A130	200fr red, olive & blue	1.00	.60

UN Postal Administration, 25th anniv.

Arms of Tenkodogo A131

Bronze Statuette A132

Coats of Arms: 20fr, 100fr, Ouagadougou.

1977, May 2	Litho.		Perf. 13	
406	A131	10fr multicolored	.15	.15
407	A131	20fr multicolored	.15	.15
408	A131	65fr multicolored	.35	.25
409	A131	100fr multicolored	.55	.40
	Nos. 406-409 (4)		1.20	.95

1977, June 13	Photo.		Perf. 13	
410	A132	55fr multicolored	.30	.20
411	A132	65fr multicolored	.35	.20

#410-411 issued in sheets and coils with black control number on every 5th stamp.

Granaries — A133

Handbags — A134

1977, June 20	Photo.		Perf. 13½x13	
412	A133	5fr Samo	.15	.15
413	A133	35fr Boromo	.20	.15
414	A133	45fr Banfora	.22	.15
415	A133	55fr Mossi	.30	.20
	Nos. 412-415 (4)		.87	.65

1977, June 20

416	A134	30fr Gouin	.16	.15
417	A134	40fr Bissa	.20	.15
418	A134	60fr Lobi	.35	.20
419	A134	70fr Mossi	.38	.22
	Nos. 416-419 (4)		1.09	.72

Nos. 390-392 Overprinted in Gold:
a. VAINQUEUR 1976 / LASSE VIREN / FINLANDE
b. VAINQUEUR 1976 / ALWIN SCHOCKEMOHLE / R.F.A.
c. VAINQUEUR 1976 / JOHANNA SCHALLER / R.D.A.

1977, July 4	Litho.		Perf. 11	
420	A124 (a)	30fr multicolored	.16	.15
421	A124 (b)	55fr multicolored	.30	.15
422	A124 (c)	75fr multicolored	.40	.20
	Nos. 420-422,C245-C246 (5)		3.26	1.65

Winners, 21st Olympic Games.

Crinum Ornatum — A135

Haemanthus Multiflorus — A136

Hannoa Undulata — A137

Designs: Flowers, flowering branches and wild fruits. 175fr, 300fr, horiz.

1977	Litho.		Perf. 12½	
423	A137	2fr Cordia myxa	.15	.15
424	A137	3fr Opilia celtidifolia	.15	.15
425	A135	15fr shown	.15	.15
426	A136	25fr shown	.15	.15
427	A137	50fr shown	.25	.20
428	A135	90fr Cochlospermum planchonii	.45	.35
429	A135	125fr Clitoria ternatea	.65	.50
430	A136	150fr Cassia alata	.80	.60
431	A136	175fr Nauclea latifolia	.90	.65
432	A136	300fr Bombax costatum	1.60	1.20
433	A135	400fr Eulophia cucullata	2.00	1.60
	Nos. 423-433 (11)		7.25	5.70

Issued: 25fr, 150fr, 175fr, 300fr, Aug. 1; 2fr, 3fr, 50fr, Aug. 8; 15fr, 90fr, 125fr, 400fr, Aug. 23.

De Gaulle and Cross of Lorraine A138

Designs: 200fr, King Baudouin of Belgium.

1977, Aug. 16			Perf. 13½x14	
434	A138	100fr multicolored	.55	.22
435	A138	200fr multicolored	1.10	.42

Elizabeth II A139

Designs: 300fr, Elizabeth II taking salute. 500fr, Elizabeth II after Coronation.

1977, Aug. 16

| 436 | A139 | 200fr multicolored | .80 | .32 |
| 437 | A139 | 300fr multicolored | 1.20 | .50 |

Souvenir Sheet

| 438 | A139 | 500fr multicolored | 2.00 | .90 |

25th anniv. of reign of Queen Elizabeth II.
For overprints see Nos. 478-480.

Lottery Tickets, Cars and Map of Upper Volta in Flag Colors — A140

1977, Sept. 16	Photo.		Perf. 13	
439	A140	55fr multicolored	.30	.22

10th anniversary of National Lottery.

Selma Lagerlöf, Literature — A141

Nobel Prize Winners: 65fr, Guglielmo Marconi, physics. 125fr, Bertrand Russell, literature. 200fr, Linus C. Pauling, chemistry. 300fr, Robert Koch, medicine. 500fr, Albert Schweitzer, peace.

1977, Sept. 22	Litho.		Perf. 13½	
440	A141	55fr multicolored	.30	.15
441	A141	65fr multicolored	.38	.15
442	A141	125fr multicolored	.65	.25
443	A141	200fr multicolored	1.10	.45
444	A141	300fr multicolored	1.60	.65
	Nos. 440-444 (5)		4.03	1.63

Souvenir Sheet

| 445 | A141 | 500fr multicolored | 2.50 | 1.20 |

The Three Graces, by Rubens A142

Paintings by Peter Paul Rubens (1577-1640): 55fr, Heads of Black Men, horiz. 85fr, Bathsheba at the Fountain. 150fr, The Drunken Silenus. 200fr, 300fr, Life of Maria de Medicis, diff.

1977, Oct. 19	Litho.		Perf. 14	
446	A142	55fr multicolored	.30	.15
447	A142	65fr multicolored	.38	.16
448	A142	85fr multicolored	.45	.22
449	A142	150fr multicolored	.80	.40
450	A142	200fr multicolored	1.10	.45
451	A142	300fr multicolored	1.60	.60
	Nos. 446-451 (6)		4.63	1.98

Lenin in His Office A143

85fr, Lenin Monument, Kremlin. 200fr, Lenin with youth. 500fr, Lenin & Leonid Brezhnev.

BURKINA FASO

1977, Oct. 28 Litho. Perf. 12
452	A143	10fr multicolored	.15	.15
453	A143	85fr multicolored	.45	.25
454	A143	200fr multicolored	1.10	.65
455	A143	500fr multicolored	2.50	1.60
		Nos. 452-455 (4)	4.20	2.65

Russian October Revolution, 60th anniv.

Stadium and Brazil No. C79 — A144

Stadium and: 65fr, Brazil #1144. 125fr, Gt. Britain #458. 200fr, Chile #340. 300fr, Switzerland #350. 500fr, Germany #1147.

1977, Dec. 30 Litho. Perf. 13½
456	A144	55fr multicolored	.30	.15
457	A144	65fr multicolored	.38	.16
458	A144	125fr multicolored	.65	.25
459	A144	200fr multicolored	1.10	.42
460	A144	300fr multicolored	1.60	.65
		Nos. 456-460 (5)	4.03	1.63

Souvenir Sheet
| 461 | A144 | 500fr multicolored | 2.50 | 1.20 |

11th World Cup Soccer Championship, Argentina. For overprints see Nos. 486-491.

Jean Mermoz and Seaplane — A145

History of Aviation: 75fr, Anthony H. G. Fokker. 85fr, Wiley Post. 90fr, Otto Lilienthal, vert. 100fr, Concorde. 500fr, Charles Lindbergh and "Spirit of St. Louis."

1978, Jan. 2 Litho. Perf. 13½
462	A145	65fr multicolored	.38	.16
463	A145	75fr multicolored	.40	.20
464	A145	85fr multicolored	.45	.20
465	A145	90fr multicolored	.50	.20
466	A145	100fr multicolored	.55	.22
		Nos. 462-466 (5)	2.28	.98

Souvenir Sheet
| 467 | A145 | 500fr multicolored | 2.50 | 1.25 |

Crataeva Religiosa — A146

1978, Feb. 28 Litho. Perf. 12½
| 468 | A146 | 55fr shown | .30 | .22 |
| 469 | A146 | 75fr Fig tree | .40 | .30 |

Souvenir Sheet

Virgin and Child, by Rubens A147

1978, May 24 Litho. Perf. 13½x14
| 470 | A147 | 500fr multicolored | 2.50 | 1.20 |

Peter Paul Rubens (1577-1640).

Antenna and ITU Emblem A148

1978, May 30 Perf. 13
| 471 | A148 | 65fr silver & multi | .38 | .16 |

10th World Telecommunications Day.

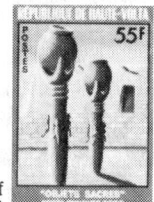

Fetish Gate of Bobo — A149

1978, July 10 Litho. Perf. 13½
| 472 | A149 | 55fr shown | .30 | .15 |
| 473 | A149 | 65fr Mossi fetish | .38 | .16 |

Capt. Cook and "Endeavour" — A150

Capt. James Cook (1728-1779) and: 85fr, Death on Hawaiian beach. 250fr, Navigational instruments. 350fr, "Resolution."

1978, Sept. 1 Litho. Perf. 14½
474	A150	65fr multicolored	.38	.16
475	A150	85fr multicolored	.45	.20
476	A150	250fr multicolored	1.40	.65
477	A150	350fr multicolored	1.90	.80
		Nos. 474-477 (4)	4.13	1.81

Nos. 436-438 Overprinted Vertically in Silver: "ANNIVERSAIRE DU COURONNEMENT 1953-1978"

1978, Oct. 24 Litho. Perf. 13½x14
| 478 | A139 | 200fr multicolored | 1.10 | .42 |
| 479 | A139 | 300fr multicolored | 1.60 | .65 |

Souvenir Sheet
| 480 | A139 | 500fr multicolored | 2.50 | 1.20 |

25th anniversary of Coronation of Queen Elizabeth II. Overprint in 3 lines on 200fr, in 2 lines on 300fr and 500fr.
#478-480 exist with overprint in metallic red.

Trent Castle, by Dürer A151

Paintings by Albrecht Dürer (1471-1528): 150fr, Virgin and Child with St. Anne. 250fr, Sts. George and Eustachius, vert. 350fr, Hans Holzschuher, vert.

Perf. 14x13½, 13½x14

1978, Nov. 20 Litho.
481	A151	65fr multicolored	.38	.16
482	A151	150fr multicolored	.80	.38
483	A151	250fr multicolored	1.40	.65
484	A151	350fr multicolored	1.90	.65
		Nos. 481-484 (4)	4.48	1.84

Human Rights Emblem A152

1978, Dec. 10 Litho. Perf. 12½
| 485 | A152 | 55fr multicolored | .30 | .15 |

Universal Declaration of Human Rights, 30th anniv.

Nos. 456-461 Overprinted in Silver
a, VAINQUEURS 1950 URUGUAY / 1978 / ARGENTINE
b, VAINQUEURS 1970 BRESIL / 1978 ARGENTINE
c, VAINQUEURS 1966 GRANDE BRETAGNE / 1978 ARGENTINE
d, VAINQUEURS / 1962 BRESIL / 1978 ARGENTINE
e, VAINQUEURS 1954 ALLEMAGNE (RFA) / 1978 ARGENTINE
f, VAINQUEURS 1974 ALLEMAGNE (RFA) / 1978 ARGENTINE

1979, Jan. 4 Litho. Perf. 13½
486	A144(a)	55fr multicolored	.30	.15
487	A144(b)	65fr multicolored	.38	.16
488	A144(c)	125fr multicolored	.65	.25
489	A144(d)	200fr multicolored	1.10	.40
490	A144(e)	300fr multicolored	1.60	.65
		Nos. 486-490 (5)	4.03	1.61

Souvenir Sheet
| 491 | A144(f) | 500fr multicolored | 2.50 | 1.20 |

Winners, World Soccer Cup Championships 1950-1978.

Radio Station A153

Design: 65fr, Mail plane at airport.

1979, Mar. 30 Litho. Perf. 12½
| 492 | A153 | 55fr multicolored | .30 | .15 |
| 493 | A153 | 65fr multicolored | .38 | .16 |

Post and Telecommunications Org., 10th anniv.

Teacher and Pupils, IYC Emblem — A154

1979, Apr. 9 Perf. 13½
| 494 | A154 | 75fr multicolored | .40 | .20 |

International Year of the Child.

Telecommunications A155

1979, May 17 Litho. Perf. 13
| 495 | A155 | 70fr multicolored | .45 | .20 |

11th Telecommunications Day.

Basketmaker and Upper Volta No. 111 — A156

Design: No. 497, May of Upper Volta, Concorde, truck and UPU emblem.

1979, June 8 Photo.
| 496 | A156 | 100fr multicolored | .65 | .35 |
| 497 | A156 | 100fr multicolored | .65 | .35 |

Philexafrique II, Libreville, Gabon, June 8-17. Nos. 496, 497 each printed in sheets of 10 and 5 labels showing exhibition emblem.

Synodontis Voltae A157

Fresh-water Fish: 50fr, Micralestes comoensis. 85fr, Silurus.

1979, June 10 Litho. Perf. 12½
498	A157	20fr multicolored	.15	.15
499	A157	50fr multicolored	.35	.16
500	A157	85fr multicolored	.55	.30
		Nos. 498-500 (3)	1.05	.61

Rowland Hill, Train and Upper Volta No. 60 — A158

Sir Rowland Hill (1795-1879), originator of penny postage, Trains and Upper Volta Stamps: 165fr, #59. 200fr, #57. 300fr, #56. 500fr, #55.

1979, June Litho. Perf. 13½
501	A158	65fr multicolored	.42	.20
502	A158	165fr multicolored	1.10	.55
503	A158	200fr multicolored	1.40	.65
504	A158	300fr multicolored	2.00	1.00
		Nos. 501-504 (4)	4.92	2.40

Souvenir Sheet
| 505 | A158 | 500fr multicolored | 3.50 | 1.60 |

Wildlife Fund Emblem and Protected Animals — A159

BURKINA FASO

1979, Aug. 30   Litho.   Perf. 14½
506	A159	30fr Waterbuck	.20	.15
507	A159	40fr Roan antelope	.25	.15
508	A159	60fr Caracal	.40	.20
509	A159	100fr African bush elephant	.65	.35
510	A159	175fr Hartebeest	1.20	.80
511	A159	250fr Leopard	1.60	.80
		Nos. 506-511 (6)	4.30	2.20

Adult Students and Teacher — A160

Design: 55fr, Man reading book, vert.

Perf. 12½x13, 13x12½
1979, Sept. 8
512	A160	55fr multicolored	.38	.18
513	A160	250fr multicolored	1.60	.85

World Literacy Day.

Map of Upper Volta, Telephone Receiver and Lines, Telecom Emblem — A161

1979, Sept. 20   Perf. 13x12½
514	A161	200fr multicolored	1.40	.65

3rd World Telecommunications Exhibition, Geneva, Sept. 20-26.

King Vulture — A162

1979, Oct. 26   Litho.   Perf. 13
515	A162	5fr shown	.15	.15
516	A162	10fr Hoopoe	.15	.15
517	A162	15fr Bald vulture	.15	.15
518	A162	25fr Herons	.16	.15
519	A162	35fr Ostrich	.22	.15
520	A162	45fr Crowned crane	.30	.15
521	A162	125fr Eagle	.80	.40
		Nos. 515-521 (7)	1.93	1.30

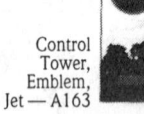

Control Tower, Emblem, Jet — A163

1979, Dec. 12   Photo.   Perf. 13x12½
| 522 | A163 | 65fr multicolored | .42 | .20 |

ASECNA (Air Safety Board), 20th anniv.

Central Bank of West African States — A164

1979, Dec. 28   Litho.   Perf. 12½
| 523 | A164 | 55fr multicolored | .38 | .18 |

Eugene Jamot, Map of Upper Volta, Tsetse Fly — A165

1979, Dec. 28   Perf. 13x13½
| 524 | A165 | 55fr multicolored | .38 | .18 |

Eugene Jamot (1879-1937), discoverer of sleeping sickness cure.

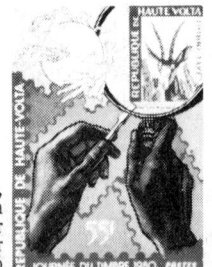

UPU Emblem, Upper Volta Type D4 under Magnifier A166

1980, Feb. 26   Litho.   Perf. 12½x13
| 525 | A166 | 55fr multicolored | .38 | .18 |

Stamp Day.

World Locomotive Speed Record, 25th Anniversary A167

1980, Mar. 30   Litho.   Perf. 12½
526	A167	75fr multicolored	.50	.25
527	A167	100fr multicolored	.65	.35

Pres. Sangoule Lamizana, Pope John Paul II, Cardinal Pau Zoungrana, Map of Upper Volta — A168

1980, May 10   Litho.   Perf. 12½
| 528 | A168 | 65fr shown | .42 | .20 |

Size: 21x36mm
| 529 | A168 | 100fr Pope John Paul II | .65 | .35 |

Visit of Pope John Paul II to Upper Volta.

A169    A170

1980, May 17   Perf. 13x12½
| 530 | A169 | 50fr multicolored | .35 | .16 |

12th World Telecommunications Day.

1980, June 12   Litho.   Perf. 13
531	A170	65fr Sun and earth	.42	.20
532	A170	100fr Solar energy	.65	.35

Downhill Skiing, Lake Placid '80 Emblem A171

1980, June 26   Perf. 14½
533	A171	65fr shown	.35	.15
534	A171	100fr Women's downhill	.55	.30
535	A171	200fr Figure skating	1.25	.55
536	A171	350fr Slalom, vert.	1.90	1.00
		Nos. 533-536 (4)	4.05	2.00

Souvenir Sheet
| 537 | A171 | 55fr Speed skating | 3.50 | 1.60 |

12th Winter Olympic Game Winners, Lake Placid, NY, Feb. 12-24.

Map of Europe and Africa, Jet — A172    Hand Holding Back Sand Dune — A173

Europafrica Issue
1980, July 14   Litho.   Perf. 13
| 538 | A172 | 100fr multicolored | .65 | .35 |

1980, July 18
Operation Green Sahel: 55fr, Hands holding seedlings.
539	A173	50fr multicolored	.35	.16
540	A173	55fr multicolored	.38	.20

Gourmantche Chief Initiation — A174

1980, Sept. 12   Litho.   Perf. 14
541	A174	30fr shown	.20	.15
542	A174	55fr Moro Naba, Mossi Emperor	.38	.18
543	A174	65fr Princess Guimbe Quattara, vert.	.42	.20
		Nos. 541-543 (3)	1.00	.53

A175    A176

Gourounsi mask, conference emblem.

1980, Oct. 6   Perf. 13½x13
| 544 | A175 | 65fr multicolored | .42 | .20 |

World Tourism Conf., Manila, Sept. 27.

1980, Nov. 5   Litho.   Perf. 12½
545	A176	55fr Agriculture	.40	.20
546	A176	65fr Transportation	.45	.20
547	A176	75fr Dam, highway	.50	.25
548	A176	100fr Industry	.65	.35
		Nos. 545-548 (4)	2.00	1.00

West African Economic Council, 5th anniv.

20th Anniv. of Independence — A177

1980, Dec. 11   Perf. 13
| 549 | A177 | 500fr multicolored | 3.50 | 1.60 |

Madonna and Child, by Raphael — A178    West African Postal Union, 5th Anniv. — A179

Christmas: Paintings of Madonna and Child, by Raphael.

1980, Dec. 22   Perf. 12½
550	A178	60fr multicolored	.40	.20
551	A178	150fr multicolored	1.00	.50
552	A178	200fr multicolored	1.60	.80
		Nos. 550-552 (3)	3.00	1.50

1980, Dec. 24   Photo.   Perf. 13½
| 553 | A179 | 55fr multicolored | .38 | .20 |

Dung Beetle — A180

Perf. 13x13½, 13½x13
1981, Mar. 10   Litho.
554	A180	5fr shown	.15	.15
555	A180	10fr Crickets	.15	.15
556	A180	15fr Termites	.15	.15
557	A180	20fr Praying mantis, vert.	.15	.15
558	A180	55fr Emperor moth	.38	.25
559	A180	65fr Locust, vert.	.42	.20
		Nos. 554-559 (6)	1.40	1.05

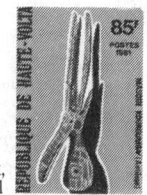

BURKINA FASO

Antelope Mask,
Kouroumba — A181

Designs: Various ceremonial masks.

1981, Mar. 20   Litho.   Perf. 13
560 A181   45fr multicolored   .26   .15
561 A181   55fr multicolored   .32   .16
562 A181   85fr multicolored   .48   .15
563 A181   105fr multicolored   .60   .30
       Nos. 560-563 (4)   1.66   .86

Notre Dame of Kologh'
Naba College, 25th Anniv.
A182

1981, Mar. 30
564 A182   55fr multicolored   .32   .18

Heinrich von Stephan, UPU Founder, Birth Sesquicentennial — A183

1981, May 4   Litho.   Perf. 13
565 A183   65fr multicolored   .35   .18

13th World Telecommunications Day — A184

1981, May 17   Perf. 13½x13
566 A184   90fr multicolored   .52   .25

Diesel Train, Abidjan-Niger Railroad A185

Designs: Trains.

1981, July 6   Litho.   Perf. 13
567 A185   25fr shown   .16   .15
568 A185   30fr Gazelle   .20   .15
569 A185   40fr Belier   .25   .15
       Nos. 567-569 (3)   .61   .45

Tree Planting Month — A186

1981, July 15
570 A186   70fr multicolored   .45   .22

Natl. Red Cross, 20th Anniv. A187

1981, July 31   Perf. 12½x13
571 A187   70fr multicolored   .45   .22

Intl. Year of the Disabled — A188

1981, Aug. 20   Litho.   Perf. 13x12½
572 A188   70fr multicolored   .45   .22

View of Koudougou A189

1981, Sept. 3   Litho.   Perf. 12½
573 A189   35fr shown   .22   .15
574 A189   45fr Toma   .30   .15
575 A189   85fr Volta Noire   .55   .28
       Nos. 573-575 (3)   1.07   .58

World Food Day A190

1981, Oct. 16   Perf. 13
576 A190   90fr multicolored   .60   .30

Elephant A191

Designs: Various protected species.

1981, Oct. 21   Photo.   Perf. 14
577 A191   5fr multicolored   .15   .15
578 A191   15fr multicolored   .15   .15
579 A191   40fr multicolored   .25   .15
580 A191   60fr multicolored   .40   .20
581 A191   70fr multicolored   .45   .22
       Nos. 577-581 (5)   1.40   .87

Fight Against Apartheid — A192    Mangoes — A193

1981, Dec. 9   Litho.   Perf. 12½
582 A192   90fr red orange   .60   .30

Perf. 13x13½, 13½x13
1981, Dec. 15
583 A193   20fr Papayas, horiz.   .15   .15
584 A193   35fr Fruits, vegetables,
              horiz.   .22   .15
585 A193   75fr shown   .50   .25
586 A193   90fr Melons, horiz.   .60   .30
       Nos. 583-586 (4)   1.47   .85

Guinea Hen — A194    West African Rice Development Assoc., 10th Anniv. — A195

Designs: Breeding animals. 10fr, 25fr, 70fr, 250fr, 300fr horiz.

1981, Dec. 22   Perf. 13
587 A194   10fr Donkey   .15   .15
588 A194   25fr Pig   .16   .15
589 A194   70fr Cow   .45   .22
590 A194   90fr shown   .60   .30
591 A194   250fr Rabbit   1.60   .80
       Nos. 587-591 (5)   2.96 1.62

Souvenir Sheet
592 A194   300fr Sheep   2.00 1.00

1981, Dec. 29
593 A195   90fr multicolored   .60   .30

20th Anniv. of World Food Program — A196

1982, Jan. 18
594 A196   50fr multicolored   .35   .16

Traditional Houses — A197

1982, Apr. 23   Litho.   Perf. 12½
595 A197   30fr Morhonaba Palace,
              vert.   .20   .15
596 A197   70fr Bobo   .45   .22
597 A197   100fr Gourounsi   .65   .35
598 A197   200fr Peulh   1.40   .65
599 A197   250fr Dagari   1.60   .80
       Nos. 595-599 (5)   4.30 2.17

14th World Telecommunications Day — A198

1982, May 17
600 A198   125fr multicolored   .85   .40

Water Lily — A199    25th Anniv. of Cultural Aid Fund — A201

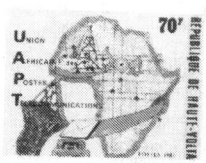

African Postal Union A200

1982, Sept. 22   Perf. 13x12½
601 A199   25fr shown   .15   .15
602 A199   40fr Kapoks   .20   .15
603 A199   70fr Frangipani   .35   .18
604 A199   90fr Cochlospermum
              planchonii   .60   .22
605 A199   100fr Cotton   .50   .25
       Nos. 601-605 (5)   1.80   .95

1982, Oct. 7
606 A200   70fr multicolored   .45   .22
607 A200   90fr multicolored   .60   .30

1982, Nov. 10   Perf. 12½x13
608 A201   70fr multicolored   .45   .22

Map, Hand Holding Grain, Steer Head — A202

1982   Perf. 12½
609 A202   90fr multicolored   .60   .30

Traditional Hairstyle A203

1983, Jan.   Litho.   Perf. 12½
610 A203   90fr lt green & multi   .52   .25
611 A203   120fr lt blue & multi   .70   .35
612 A203   170fr pink & multi   .95   .48
       Nos. 610-612 (3)   2.17 1.08
       For overprints see Nos. 884-886.

8th Film Festival, Ouagadougou — A204

1983, Feb. 10   Litho.   Perf. 13x12½
613 A204   90fr Scene   .60   .30
614 A204   500fr Filmmaker Dumarou
              Ganda   3.50 1.60

UN Intl. Drinking Water and Sanitation Decade, 1981-90 — A205

1983, Apr. 21   Litho.   Perf. 13½x13
615 A205   60fr Water drops   .40   .20
616 A205   70fr Carrying water   .45   .22

Manned Flight Bicentenary A206

Portraits and Balloons: 15fr, J.M. Montgolfier, 1783. 25fr, Etienne Montgolfier's balloon, 1783, Pilatre de Rozier. 70fr, Charles & Roberts flight, 1783, Jacques Charles. 90fr, Flight over English Channel, John Jeffries. 100fr, Testu-Brissy's horseback flight, Wilhemine Reichardt. 250fr, Andree's Spitzbergen flight, 1897, S.A. Andree. 300fr, Piccard's stratosphere flight, 1931, August Piccard.

1983, Apr. 15   Litho.   Perf. 13½
617 A206   15fr multicolored   .15   .15
618 A206   25fr multicolored   .16   .15
619 A206   70fr multicolored   .45   .22
620 A206   90fr multicolored   .60   .30

849

BURKINA FASO

621	A206	100fr multicolored	.65	.35
622	A206	250fr multicolored	1.60	.80
		Nos. 617-622 (6)	3.61	1.97

Souvenir Sheet

| 623 | A206 | 300fr multicolored | 2.00 | 1.00 |

No. 623 contains one stamp 38x47mm. Nos. 621-623 airmail.

World Communications Year — A207

1983, May 26   Litho.   Perf. 12½

624	A207	30fr Man reading letter	.16	.15
625	A207	35fr Like No. 624	.18	.15
626	A207	45fr Aircraft over stream	.25	.15
627	A207	90fr Girl on telephone	.50	.25
		Nos. 624-627 (4)	1.09	.70

Fishing Resources A208

1983, July 28   Litho.   Perf. 13

628	A208	20fr Synadontis gambiensis	.15	.15
629	A208	30fr Palmotochromis	.15	.15
630	A208	40fr Boy fishing, vert.	.15	.15
631	A208	50fr Fishing with net	.16	.15
632	A208	75fr Fishing with basket	.25	.15
		Nos. 628-632 (5)	.86	.75

Anti-deforestation — A209

1983, Sept. 13   Litho.   Perf. 13

633	A209	10fr Planting saplings	.15	.15
634	A209	50fr Tree nursery	.16	.15
635	A209	100fr Prevent forest fires	.35	.16
636	A209	150fr Woman cooking	.50	.25
637	A209	200fr Prevent felling, vert.	.65	.35
		Nos. 633-637 (5)	1.81	1.06

Fresco Detail, by Raphael — A210

Paintings: 120fr, Self-portrait, by Pablo Picasso, 1901, vert. 185fr, Self-portrait at the palette, by Manet, 1878, vert. 350fr, Fresco Detail, diff., by Raphael. 500fr, Goethe, by George Oswald May, 1779, vert.

1983, Nov.   Litho.   Perf. 13

638	A210	120fr multicolored	.40	.20
639	A210	185fr multicolored	.62	.32
640	A210	300fr multicolored	1.00	.50
641	A210	350fr multicolored	1.20	.60
642	A210	500fr multicolored	1.60	.80
		Nos. 638-642 (5)	4.82	2.42

25th Anniv. of the Republic A211

1983, Dec. 9   Litho.   Perf. 14

| 643 | A211 | 90fr Arms | .30 | .15 |
| 644 | A211 | 500fr Family, flag | 1.60 | .80 |

A212 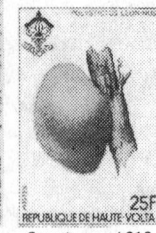   Scouting — A213

1984, May 29   Litho.   Perf. 12½

| 645 | A212 | 90fr multicolored | .30 | .15 |
| 646 | A212 | 100fr multicolored | .35 | .16 |

Council of Unity, 25th anniv.

1984, June 15   Litho.   Perf. 13½

647	A213	25fr Polystictus leoninus	.15	.15
648	A213	185fr Pterocarpus Lucens	.90	.45
649	A213	200fr Phlebopus colossus sudanicus	1.10	.50
650	A213	250fr Cosmos sulphureus	1.25	.62
651	A213	300fr Trametes versicolor	1.50	.80
652	A213	400fr Ganoderma lucidum	2.00	1.10
		Nos. 647-652 (6)	6.90	3.62

Souvenir Sheet

| 653 | A213 | 600fr Leucocoprinus cepaestipes | 3.25 | 1.60 |

Nos. 651-653 are airmail. For overprints see Nos. 669-674.

Wildlife — A214    Wildlife — A215

1984, July 19

654	A214	15fr Cheetah, four cubs	.15	.15
655	A214	35fr Two adults	.15	.15
656	A214	90fr One adult	.35	.16
657	A214	120fr Cheetah, two cubs	.45	.22
658	A214	300fr Baboons	1.20	.55
659	A214	400fr Vultures	1.50	.80
		Nos. 654-659 (6)	3.80	2.03

Souvenir Sheet

| 660 | A215 | 1000fr Antelopes | 4.00 | 1.90 |

World Wildlife Fund (Nos. 654-567); Rotary Intl. (Nos. 658, 660); Natl. Boy Scouts (No. 659). Nos. 658-660 are airmail.

Sailing Ships and Locomotives — A216

1984, Aug. 14   Perf. 12½

661	A216	20fr Maiden Queen	.15	.15
662	A216	40fr CC 2400 ch	.16	.15
663	A216	60fr Scawfell	.22	.15
664	A216	100fr PO 1806	.38	.18
665	A216	120fr Harbinger	.45	.22
666	A216	145fr Livingstone	.55	.28
667	A216	400fr True Briton	1.50	.80
668	A216	450fr Pacific C51	1.60	.85
		Nos. 661-668 (8)	5.01	2.78

Natl. Defense — A216a

Design: 120fr, Capt. Sankara, crowd, horiz.

1984, Nov. 21   Litho.   Perf. 13½

| 668A | A216a | 90fr multicolored | | |
| 668B | A216a | 120fr multicolored | | |

Nos. 647-652 Ovptd. with Two Bars and "BURKINA FASO"

1985, Mar. 5   Litho.   Perf. 13½

669	A213	25fr multicolored	.15	.15
670	A213	185fr multicolored	.55	.25
671	A213	200fr multicolored	.60	.30
672	A213	250fr multicolored	.75	.38
673	A213	300fr multicolored	.90	.45
674	A213	400fr multicolored	1.20	.60
		Nos. 669-674 (6)	4.15	2.13

A217

Designs: 5fr, 120fr, Flag. 15fr, 150fr, Natl. Arms, vert. 90fr, 185fr, Map.

1985, Mar. 8   Litho.   Perf. 12½

675	A217	5fr multicolored		
676	A217	15fr multicolored		
677	A217	90fr multicolored		
678	A217	120fr multicolored		
679	A217	150fr multicolored		
680	A217	185fr multicolored		

Nos. 678-680 are airmail.

1986 World Cup Soccer Championships, Mexico — A218

1985, Apr. 20   Litho.   Perf. 13

681	A218	25fr multicolored	.15	.15
682	A218	45fr multicolored	.16	.15
683	A218	90fr multicolored	.35	.16
684	A218	100fr multicolored	.38	.18
685	A218	150fr multicolored	.55	.25
686	A218	200fr multicolored	.70	.38
687	A218	250fr multicolored	.90	.45
		Nos. 681-687 (7)	3.19	1.72

Souvenir Sheet

| 688 | A219 | 500fr multicolored | 1.90 | 1.20 |

Nos. 681-685 vert. No. 684-688 are airmail.

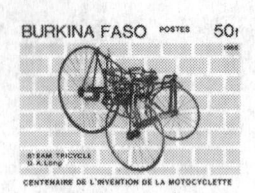

Motorcycle, Cent. — A220

1985, May 26

689	A220	50fr Steam tricycle, G.A. Long	.18	.15
690	A220	75fr Pope	.28	.15
691	A220	80fr Manet-90	.30	.15
692	A220	100fr Ducati	.38	.18
693	A220	150fr Jawa	.55	.28
694	A220	200fr Honda	.70	.38
695	A220	250fr B.M.W.	.90	.45
		Nos. 689-695 (7)	3.29	1.74

Nos. 692-695 are airmail.

Reptiles A221

1985, June 20

696	A221	5fr Chamaeleon dilepis	.15	.15
697	A221	15fr Agama stellio	.15	.15
698	A221	35fr Lacerta Lepida	.15	.15
699	A221	85fr Hiperolius marmoratus	.32	.16
700	A221	100fr Echis leucogaster	.38	.18
701	A221	150fr Kinixys erosa	.55	.28
702	A221	250fr Python regius	.90	.45
		Nos. 696-702 (7)	2.60	1.52

#696-697 vert. #700-702 are airmail.

British Queen Mother, 85th Birthday A222

1985, June 21   Perf. 13½

703	A222	75fr On pony bobs	.22	.15
704	A222	85fr Wedding, 1923	.25	.15
705	A222	500fr Holding infant Elizabeth, 1926	1.60	.80
706	A222	600fr Coronation of King George VI, 1937	1.90	.90
		Nos. 703-706 (4)	3.97	2.00

Souvenir Sheet

| 707 | A222 | 1000fr Christening of Prince William, 1982 | 3.25 | 1.60 |

Nos. 705-707 are airmail.

Vintage Autos and Aircraft — A223

1985, June 21

708	A223	5fr Benz Victoria, 1893	.15	.15
709	A223	25fr Peugeot 174, 1927	.15	.15
710	A223	45fr Louis Bleriot	.16	.15
711	A223	50fr Breguet 14	.18	.15
712	A223	500fr Bugatti Coupe Napoleon T41 Royale	1.90	.90
713	A223	500fr Airbus A300-P4	1.90	.90
714	A223	600fr Mercedes-Benz 540K, 1938	2.25	1.20
715	A223	600fr Airbus A300B	2.25	1.20
		Nos. 708-715 (8)	8.96	4.80

Souvenir Sheet

| 716 | A223 | 1000fr Louis Bleriot, Karl Benz | 4.00 | 1.90 |

Automobile, cent. Nos. 712-716 are airmail.

Audubon Birth Bicent. A224

Illustrations of No. American bird species by Audubon and scouting trefoil.

1985, June 21
717	A224	60fr	Aix sponsa	.22	.15
718	A224	100fr	Mimus polyglotos	.38	.18
719	A224	300fr	Icterus galbula	1.20	.60
720	A224	400fr	Sitta carolinensis	1.50	.80
721	A224	500fr	Asyndesmus lewis	1.50	.90
722	A224	600fr	Buteo cagopus	2.25	1.10
			Nos. 717-722 (6)	7.05	3.73

Souvenir Sheet
| 723 | A224 | 1000fr | Columba leucocephala | 4.00 | 1.90 |

Nos. 721-723 are airmail.

ARGENTINA '85, Buenos Aires — A225

Various equestrians.

1985, July 5 Perf. 13
724	A225	25fr	Gaucho, piebald	.15	.15
725	A225	45fr	Horse and rider, Andes Mountains	.16	.15
726	A225	90fr	Rodeo	.32	.16
727	A225	100fr	Hunting gazelle	.38	.18
728	A225	150fr	Gauchos, 3 horses	.55	.25
729	A225	200fr	Rider beside mount	.70	.35
730	A225	250fr	Contest	.90	.42
			Nos. 724-730 (7)	3.16	1.66

Souvenir Sheet
| 731 | A225 | 500fr | Foal | 1.90 | .70 |

Nos. 727-731 are airmail.

Locomotives — A226

1985, July 23
732	A226	50fr	105-30 electric, tank wagon	.15	.15
733	A226	75fr	Diesel shunting locomotive	.25	.15
734	A226	80fr	Diesel locomotive	.25	.15
735	A226	100fr	Diesel railcar	.35	.15
736	A226	150fr	No. 6093	.50	.25
737	A226	200fr	No. 105 diesel railcar	.60	.35
738	A226	250fr	Diesel, passenger car	.75	.40
			Nos. 732-738 (7)	2.85	1.60

Nos. 735-738 are airmail.

Artifacts — A227   Fungi — A228

1985, July 27 Perf. 13x12½
739	A227	10fr	4-legged jar, Tikare	.15	.15
740	A227	40fr	Lidded pot with bird handles, P. Bazega	.15	.15
741	A227	90fr	Mother and child, bronze statue, Ouagadougou	.35	.16
742	A227	120fr	Drummer, bronze statue, Ouagadougou	.42	.20
			Nos. 739-742 (4)	1.07	.66

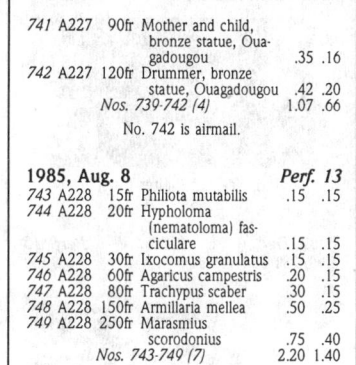

No. 742 is airmail.

1985, Aug. 8 Perf. 13
743	A228	15fr	Philiota mutabilis	.15	.15
744	A228	20fr	Hypholoma (nematoloma) fasciculare	.15	.15
745	A228	30fr	Ixocomus granulatus	.15	.15
746	A228	60fr	Agaricus campestris	.20	.15
747	A228	80fr	Trachypus scaber	.30	.15
748	A228	150fr	Armillaria mellea	.50	.25
749	A228	250fr	Marasmius scorodonius	.75	.40
			Nos. 743-749 (7)	2.20	1.40

Nos. 748 is airmail.

ITALIA '85 — A228a

Paintings by Botticelli: 25fr, Virgin and Child. 45fr, Portrait of a Man. 90fr, Mars and Venus. 100fr, Birth of Venus. 150fr, Allegory of the Calumny. 200fr, Pallas and the Centaur. 250fr, Allegory of Spring. 500fr, The Virgin of Melagrana.

1985, Oct. 25 Litho. Perf. 12½x13
749A	A228a	25fr	multicolored	.15	.15
749B	A228a	45fr	multicolored	.22	.15
749C	A228a	90fr	multicolored	.45	.22
749D	A228a	100fr	multicolored	.50	.25
749E	A228a	150fr	multicolored	.70	.38
749F	A228a	200fr	multicolored	1.00	.50
749G	A228a	250fr	multicolored	1.25	.60
			Nos. 749A-749G (7)	4.27	2.25

Souvenir Sheet
| 749H | A228a | 500fr | multicolored | 2.50 | 1.25 |

No. 749D-749H are airmail.

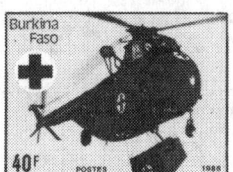

Intl. Red Cross in Burkina Faso, 75th Anniv. A229

1985, Nov. 10
750	A229	40f	Helicopter	.15	.15
751	A229	85fr	Ambulance	.30	.15
752	A229	150fr	Henri Dunant	.55	.25
753	A229	250fr	Physician, patient	.90	.42
			Nos. 750-753 (4)	1.90	.97

Nos. 752-753 are vert. and airmail.

Child Survival — A230

1986, Jan. 6
| 754 | A230 | 90fr | Breast-feeding | .48 | .25 |

Dated 1985.

Dodo Carnival A231

1986, Jan. 6 Perf. 12½
755	A231	20fr	Three children, drummer	.15	.15
756	A231	25fr	Lion, 4 dancers	.15	.15
757	A231	40fr	Two dancers, two drummers	.22	.15
758	A231	45fr	Three dancers	.25	.15
759	A231	90fr	Zebra, ostrich, dancers	.48	.25
760	A231	90fr	Elephant, dancer	.48	.25
			Nos. 755-760 (6)	1.73	1.10

Dated 1985.

Christopher Columbus (1451-1506) — A232

Columbus: 250fr, At Court of King of Portugal, the Nina. 300fr, Using astrolable, the Santa Maria. 400fr, Imprisonment at Hispanicola, 1500, the Santa Maria. 450fr, At San Salvador, 1492, the Pinta. 1000fr, Fleet departing Palos harbor, 1492.

1986, Feb. 10 Perf. 13½
761	A232	250fr	multicolored	1.35	.68
762	A232	300fr	multicolored	1.65	.82
763	A232	400fr	multicolored	2.25	1.15
764	A232	450fr	multicolored	2.50	1.25
			Nos. 761-764 (4)	7.75	3.90

Souvenir Sheet
| 765 | A232 | 1000fr | multicolored | 5.50 | 2.75 |

Nos. 764-765 are airmail. Dated 1985.

Railroad Construction — A233

1986, Feb. 10
766	A233	90fr	Man, woman carrying rail	.50	.25
767	A233	120fr	Laying rails	.65	.32
768	A233	185fr	Diesel train on new tracks	1.00	.50
769	A233	500fr	Adler locomotive, 1835	2.75	1.40
			Nos. 766-769 (4)	4.90	2.47

Souvenir Sheet
| 770 | A233 | 1000fr | Electric train, Series 290 diesel | 5.00 | 2.75 |

German Railways, sesquicentennial. Nos. 769-770 are airmail. Dated 1985.

Intl. Peace Year — A234   World Health by the Year 2000 — A235

1986, Oct. 10 Photo. Perf. 12½x13
| 771 | A234 | 90fr | blue | 1.10 | .55 |

1986, Aug. 8 Litho. Perf. 13
Designs: 100fr, Primary care medicine. 150fr, Mass inoculations.
| 772 | A235 | 90fr | multicolored | .65 | .32 |

Size: 26x30mm
Perf. 12½x13
773	A235	100fr	multicolored	.72	.35
774	A235	150fr	multicolored	.85	.42
			Nos. 772-774 (3)	2.22	1.09

Insects — A236   World Post Day — A237

1986, Sept. 10 Litho. Perf. 12½x13
775	A236	15fr	Phryneta aurocincta	.15	.15
776	A236	20fr	Sternocera interrupta	.18	.15
777	A236	40fr	Prosopocera lactator	.36	.18
778	A236	45fr	Gonimbrasia hecate	.42	.20
778A	A236	85fr	Charaxes epijasius	.78	.36
			Nos. 775-778A (5)	1.89	1.04

1986, Oct. 9 Perf. 13
| 779 | A237 | 120fr | multicolored | .68 | .35 |

UN Child Survival Campaign — A238

Designs: 30fr, Mother feeding child. 60fr, Adding medicines to food. 90fr, Nurse vaccinating child.

1986, Oct. 8 Litho. Perf. 11½x12
780	A238	30fr	multicolored		
781	A238	60fr	multicolored		
782	A238	90fr	multicolored		

No. 783 has been reserved for a 120fr stamp.

Mammals A239

Designs: 50fr, Warthog. 65fr, Hyena. 90fr, Antelope. 100fr, Gazelle. 120fr, Bushbuck. 145fr, Kudu. 500fr, Gazelle, diff.

1986, Nov. 3 Litho. Perf. 13x12½
784	A239	50fr	multicolored		
784A	A239	65fr	multicolored		
784B	A239	90fr	multicolored		
784C	A239	100fr	multicolored		
784D	A239	120fr	multicolored		
784E	A239	145fr	multicolored		
784F	A239	500fr	multicolored		

Traditional Dances — A240

Designs: 10fr, Namende. 25fr, Mouhoun. 90fr, Houet. 105fr, Seno. 120fr, Ganzourgou.

1986, Nov. 3 Litho. Perf. 12½x13
785	A240	10fr	multicolored		
785A	A240	25fr	multicolored		
785B	A240	90fr	multicolored		
785C	A240	105fr	multicolored		
785D	A240	120fr	multicolored		

BURKINA FASO

Hairstyles — A241

1986, Nov. 4   Litho.   Perf. 12½x13
788	A241	35fr Peul	.28	.15
789	A241	75fr Dafing	.60	.30
790	A241	90fr Peul, diff.	.70	.35
791	A241	120fr Mossi	.95	.48
792	A241	185fr Peul, diff.	1.50	.75
	Nos. 788-792 (5)		4.03	2.03

10th African Film Festival — A242

Intl Women's Day — A243

1987, Feb. 21   Litho.   Perf. 12x12½
793	A242	90fr Maps, cameras		
794	A242	120fr Jolson, cameramen		
795	A242	185fr Charlie Chaplin		

60th Anniv. of the film *The Jazz Singer* (120fr); 10th anniv. of the death of Charlie Chaplin (185fr).

1987, Mar. 8   Perf. 13½
| 796 | A243 | 90fr multicolored | | |

Flora — A244

Fight Against Leprosy — A245

1987, June 6   Litho.   Perf. 12½x13
797	A244	70fr Calotropis procera	.48	.24
798	A244	75fr Acacia seyal	.52	.25
799	A244	85fr Parkia biglobosa	.60	.30
800	A244	90fr Sterospermum kunthianum	.62	.30
801	A244	100fr Dichrostachys cinerea	.70	.35
802	A244	300fr Combretum paniculatum	2.10	1.05
	Nos. 797-802 (6)		5.02	2.49

1987, Aug. 6   Perf. 13

Raoul Follereau (1903-1977) and: 90fr, Doctors examining African youth. 100fr, Laboratory research. 120fr, Gerhard Hansen (1841-1912), microscope, bacillus under magnification. 300fr, Follereau embracing cured leper.

803	A245	90fr multicolored	.62	.30
804	A245	100fr multicolored	.70	.35
805	A245	120fr multicolored	.85	.42
806	A245	300fr multicolored	2.10	1.05
	Nos. 803-806 (4)		4.27	2.12

World Environment Day — A246

1987, Aug. 18   Litho.   Perf. 13x12½
| 807 | A246 | 90fr shown | .68 | .35 |
| 808 | A246 | 145fr Emblem, huts | 1.10 | .55 |

Pre-Olympic Year — A247

1987, Aug. 31   Perf. 12½
809	A247	75fr High jump	.55	.28
810	A247	85fr Tennis, vert.	.62	.30
811	A247	90fr Ski jumping	.68	.35
812	A247	100fr Soccer	.75	.38
813	A247	145fr Running	1.10	.55
814	A247	350fr Pierre de Coubertin, tennis, vert.	2.60	1.30
	Nos. 809-814 (6)		6.30	3.16

Pierre de Coubertin (1863-1937).

World Post Day — A248

1987, Oct. 5   Litho.   Perf. 12½x13
| 815 | A248 | 90fr multicolored | | |

Fight Against Apartheid — A249

1987, Nov. 11   Litho.   Perf. 13
| 816 | A249 | 90fr shown | 1.00 | .50 |
| 817 | A249 | 100fr Luthuli, book, 1962 | 1.10 | .55 |

Albert John Luthuli (1898-1967), South African reformer, author and 1960 Nobel Peace Prize winner. No. 817 incorrectly inscribed "1899-1967."

Traditional Costumes — A250

1987, Dec. 4   Litho.   Perf. 11½x12
818	A250	10fr Dagari		
819	A250	30fr Peul		
820	A250	90fr Mossi		
821	A250	200fr Senoufo		

No. 822 has been reserved for a 500fr stamp.

Traditional Musical Instruments A251

Perf. 12x11½, 11½x12
1987, Dec. 4   Litho.
823	A251	20fr Xylophone	.18	.15
824	A251	25fr 3-Stringed lute, vert.	.22	.15
825	A251	35fr Zither	.30	.15
826	A251	90fr Conical drum	.78	.40
827	A251	1000fr Calabash drum, vert.	8.50	4.25
	Nos. 823-827 (5)		9.98	5.10

Intl. Year of Shelter for the Homeless — A252

1987, Dec. 4   Litho.   Perf. 13
| 828 | A252 | 90fr multicolored | .65 | .32 |

Five-year Natl. Development Plan — A253

1987, Dec. 15   Perf. 13½
829	A253	40fr Small businesses	.30	.15
830	A253	55fr Agriculture	.40	.20
831	A253	60fr Constructing schools	.45	.22
832	A253	90fr Transportation and communications	.65	.32
833	A253	100fr Literacy	.72	.35
834	A253	120fr Animal husbandry	.88	.45
	Nos. 829-834 (6)		3.40	1.69

World Health Organization, 40th Anniv. — A254

1988, Mar. 31   Litho.   Perf. 12½x13
| 835 | A254 | 120fr multicolored | .78 | .40 |

1988 Summer Olympics, Seoul — A255

1988, May 5   Perf. 13x12½
836	A255	30fr shown	.20	.15
837	A255	160fr Torch, vert.	1.05	.52
838	A255	175fr Soccer	1.15	.58
839	A255	235fr Volleyball, vert.	1.50	.75
840	A255	450fr Basketball, vert.	2.90	1.45
	Nos. 836-840 (5)		6.80	3.45

Souvenir Sheet
Perf. 12½x13
| 841 | A255 | 500fr Runners | 3.25 | 1.65 |

No. 841 contains one stamp, size: 40x52mm plus two labels.

Ritual Masks A256

1988, May 30   Litho.   Perf. 13
842	A256	10fr Epervier, Houet	.15	.15
843	A256	20fr Jeunes Filles, Oullo	.15	.15
844	A256	30fr Bubale, Houet	.20	.15
845	A256	40fr Forgeron, Mouhoun	.28	.15
846	A256	120fr Nounouma, Ouri	.80	.40
847	A256	175fr Chauve-souris, Ouri	1.20	.60
	Nos. 842-847 (6)		2.78	1.60

Nos. 842-846 vert.

Handicrafts A257

1988, Aug. 22   Litho.   Perf. 13½
848	A257	5fr Kieriebe ceramic pitcher, vert.	.15	.15
849	A257	15fr Mossi basket	.15	.15
850	A257	25fr Gurunsi chair	.18	.15
851	A257	30fr Bissa basket	.20	.15
852	A257	45fr Ougadougou leather box	.35	.18
853	A257	85fr Ougadougou bronze statue, vert.	.68	.35
854	A257	120fr Ougadougou leather valise	.80	.40
	Nos. 848-854 (7)		2.51	1.53

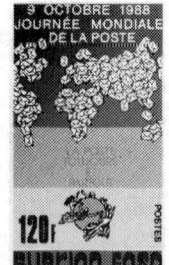

World Post Day — A258

1988, Oct. 9   Litho.   Perf. 13
| 855 | A258 | 120fr multicolored | .80 | .40 |

Aquatic Fauna — A259

1988, Oct. 31   Perf. 12
856	A259	70fr Angler martin	.48	.25
857	A259	100fr Mormyrus rume	.68	.35
858	A259	120fr Frog	.80	.40
859	A259	160fr Duck	1.10	.55
	Nos. 856-859 (4)		3.06	1.55

Civil Rights and Political Activists A260

Designs: 80fr, Mohammed Ali Jinnah (1876-1948), 1st Governor General of Pakistan. 120fr, Mahatma Gandhi (1869-1948), India. 160fr, John F. Kennedy. 235fr, Martin Luther King, Jr.

1988, Nov. 22   Litho.   Perf. 14
860	A260	80fr multicolored	.52	.25
861	A260	120fr multicolored	.78	.40
862	A260	160fr multicolored	1.00	.50
863	A260	235fr multicolored	1.50	.75
	Nos. 860-863 (4)		3.80	1.90

A261   A262

Christmas: Stained-glass windows.

1988, Dec. 2   Perf. 12
864	A261	120fr Adoration of the shepherds	.78	.40
865	A261	160fr Adoration of the Magi	1.00	.50
866	A261	450fr Madonna and child	2.90	1.45
867	A261	1000fr Flight into Egypt	6.35	3.15
	Nos. 864-867 (4)		11.03	5.50

1989, Feb. 25   Litho.   Perf. 14
868	A262	75fr shown	.24	.15
869	A262	500fr Ababacar Makharam	1.60	.80
870	A262	500fr Jean Tchissoukou	1.60	.80
871	A262	500fr Paulin Vieyra	1.60	.80
	Nos. 868-871 (4)		5.04	2.55

BURKINA FASO

Souvenir Sheet
872 Sheet of 3 9.00 4.50
a.-c. A262 500fr like #869-871, inscribed in gold 3.00 1.50
Panafrican Film Festival (FESPACO), 20th anniv. Nos. 869-872 are airmail.

World Fight Against AIDS — A263

1989, Apr. 7   Litho.   Perf. 13
873 A263 120fr multicolored   .78 .40

Council for Rural Development, 30th Anniv. — A264

1989, May 3   Litho.   Perf. 15x14
874 A264 75fr multicolored   .48 .25

Parasitic Plants — A265

Legumes and cereals.

1989, Oct. 9   Litho.   Perf. 11½
Granite Paper
875 A265 20fr Striga generiodes   .15 .15
876 A265 50fr Striga hermonthica   .32 .16
877 A265 235fr Striga aspera   1.50 .78
878 A265 450fr Alectra vogelii   3.00 1.50
   Nos. 875-878 (4)   4.97 2.59

Dogs — A266

1989, Oct. 9   Litho.   Perf. 15x14½
879 A266 35fr Sahel   .24 .15
880 A266 50fr Puppy   .35 .18
881 A266 60fr Hunting dog   .40 .20
882 A266 350fr Guard dog   2.30 1.15
   Nos. 879-882 (4)   3.29 1.68

Solidarity with the Palestinian People — A267

1989, Nov. 15   Perf. 13
883 A267 120fr Monument, Place de la Palestine   .80 .40

Nos. 610-612 Overprinted

1988, Dec. 21   Litho.   Perf. 12½
884 A203 90fr multicolored   .62 .30
885 A203 120fr multicolored   .85 .42
886 A203 170fr multicolored   1.20 .60
   Nos. 884-886 (3)   2.67 1.32

Visit of Pope John Paul II — A268

1990, Jan. 1   Litho.   Perf. 15x14
887 A268 120fr Our Lady of Yagma   .85 .42
888 A269 160fr Pope, crowd   1.20 .60

150th Anniv. of the Postage Stamp — A269

1990, Mar. 20   Litho.   Perf. 15x14
889 A269 120fr multicolored   1.00 .50
Souvenir Sheet   Perf. 14x15
890 A269 500fr Penny Black, ship   4.00 2.00
Stamp World London '90.

World Cup Soccer Championships, Italy — A270

1990, Apr. 26   Litho.   Perf. 11½
891 A270 30fr multicolored   .22 .15
892 A270 150fr multi. diff.   1.10 .55
Souvenir Sheet
893 A270 1000fr multi, horiz.   7.25 3.65

Intl. Literacy Year — A271

1990, July 10   Litho.   Perf. 13
894 A271 40fr multicolored   .28 .15
895 A271 130fr multicolored   .90 .45

Mushrooms — A272

1990, May 17   Litho.   Perf. 11½
896 A272 10fr Cantharellus cibarius   .15 .15
897 A272 15fr Psalliota bispora   .15 .15
898 A272 60fr Amanita caesarea   .48 .24
899 A272 190fr Boletus badius   1.50 .75
a.   Souv. sheet of 4, #896-899   2.25 1.10
   Nos. 896-899 (4)   2.28 1.29

Intl. Exposition of Handicrafts — A273

1990, Sept. 25   Litho.   Perf. 13
900 A273 35fr Masks, fans, vert.   .30 .15
901 A273 45fr shown   .40 .20
902 A273 270fr Rattan chair, vert.   2.35 1.20
   Nos. 900-902 (3)   3.05 1.55

Gen. Charles de Gaulle (1890-1970) — A274

1990, Nov. 22   Litho.   Perf. 13
903 A274 200fr multicolored   1.75 .90

Minerals A275

1991, Feb. 4   Litho.   Perf. 15x14
904 A275 20fr Quartz   .15 .15
905 A275 50fr Granite   .40 .20
906 A275 280fr Amphibolite   2.25 1.12
   Nos. 904-906 (3)   2.80 1.47

African Film Festival — A276    Fight Against Drugs — A277

1991, Feb. 20   Perf. 11½
907 A276 150fr multicolored   1.20 .60
Souvenir Sheet
908 A276 1000fr Award   8.00 4.00

1991, Feb. 20
909 A277 130fr multicolored   1.05 .55

Samuel F.B. Morse (1791-1872), Inventor — A278

1991, May 17   Litho.   Perf. 13
910 A278 200fr multicolored   1.60 .80

Native Girl — A279    Flowers — A280

1991-93   Litho.   Perf. 14½x15
911 A279 5fr gray & multi   .15 .15
912 A279 10fr yellow & multi   .15 .15
913 A279 25fr lilac rose & multi   .15 .15
914 A279 50fr red lilac & multi   .28 .15
915 A279 130fr blue & multi   1.10 .55
916 A279 150fr multicolored   1.20 .60
920 A279 200fr multicolored   1.60 .80
922 A279 330fr orange & multi   2.75 1.40
   Nos. 911-922 (8)   7.38 3.95
Issued: 150fr, 200fr, 6/20/91; 130fr, 330fr, 1/15/93; 5-50fr, 1994.
This is an expanding set. Numbers may change.

1991, July 31   Litho.   Perf. 11½
926 A280 5fr Grewia tenax   .15 .15
927 A280 15fr Hymenocardia acide   .15 .15
928 A280 60fr Cassia sieberiana, vert.   .48 .24
929 A280 100fr Adenium obesum   .78 .40
930 A280 300fr Mitragyna inermis   2.40 1.20
   Nos. 926-930 (5)   3.96 2.14

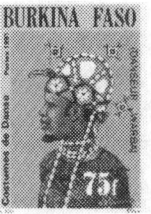

Traditional Dance Costumes — A281    World Post Day — A282

1991, Aug. 20   Perf. 12½
931 A281 75fr Warba   .60 .30
932 A281 130fr Wiskamba   1.05 .52
933 A281 280fr Pa-zenin   2.20 1.10
   Nos. 931-933 (3)   3.85 1.92

1991, Oct. 9   Perf. 13½
934 A282 130fr multicolored   1.05 .52

Cooking Utensils — A283

1992, Jan. 8   Litho.   Perf. 11½
935 A283 45fr Pancake fryer   .35 .18
936 A283 130fr Cooking pot, vert.   1.00 .50
937 A283 310fr Mortar & pestle, vert.   2.40 1.20
938 A283 500fr Ladle, calabash   4.00 2.00
   Nos. 935-938 (4)   7.75 3.88

1992 African Soccer Championships, Senegal — A284

1992, Jan. 17   Perf. 13½
939 A284 50fr Yousouf Fofana   .40 .20
940 A284 100fr Francois-Jules Bocande   .78 .40
Souvenir Sheet   Perf. 13x12½
941 A284 500fr Trophy   4.00 2.00

BURKINA FASO

UN Decade For the Handicapped A285

1992, Mar. 31 Litho. Perf. 12½
942 A285 100fr multicolored .85 .42

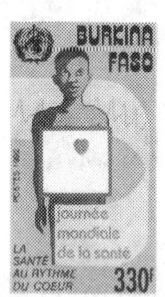

World Health Day — A286

1992, Apr. 7 Perf. 13
943 A286 330fr multicolored 2.70 1.35

Discovery of America, 500th Anniv. A287

1992, Aug. 12 Litho. Perf. 12½
944 A287 50fr Columbus, Santa Maria .42 .22
945 A287 150fr Ships, natives 1.25 .65

Souvenir Sheet
946 A287 350fr Map 3.00 1.50

Genoa '92. No. 946 contains one 52x31mm stamp.

A288    A289

Insects.

1992, Aug. 17 Perf. 15x14
947 A288 20fr Dysdercus voelkeri .18 .15
948 A288 40fr Rhizopertha dominica .35 .18
949 A288 85fr Orthetrum microstigma .75 .35
950 A288 400fr Apis mellifera 4.25 2.25
  Nos. 947-950 (4) 5.53 2.93

1992, Dec. 21 Litho. Perf. 11½
Christmas: 10fr, Boy, creche. 130fr, Children decorating creche. 1000fr, Boy holding painting of Madonna and Child.
951 A289 10fr multicolored .15 .15
952 A289 130fr multicolored 1.00 .50
953 A289 1000fr multicolored 8.00 4.00
  Nos. 951-953 (3) 9.15 4.65

Invention of the Diesel Engine, Cent. A290

1993, Jan. 25 Litho. Perf. 11½
954 A290 1000fr multicolored 8.00 4.00

The date of issue is in question.

Paris '94, Philatelic Exhibition A291

1993, July 15
955 A291 400fr multicolored 3.50 1.75
956 A291 650fr multi, diff. 5.50 2.75

African Film Festival — A292    Birds — A293

Designs: 250fr, Monument to the cinema. 750fr, M. Douta (1919-1991), comedian, horiz.

Perf. 11½x12, 12x11½ Litho.
1993, Feb. 16
957 A292 250fr multicolored 2.00 1.00
958 A292 750fr multicolored 6.00 3.00

1993, Mar. 31 Perf. 11½x12
100fr, Mycteria ibis. 200fr, Leptoptilos crumeniferus. 500fr, Ephippiorhynchus senegalensis.
959 A293 100fr multicolored .80 .40
960 A293 200fr multicolored 1.60 .80
961 A293 500fr multicolored 4.00 2.00
  a. Souvenir sheet of 3, #959-961 9.60 4.80
  Nos. 959-961 (3) 6.40 3.20

No. 961a sold for 1200fr.

1994 World Cup Soccer Championships, US — A294

1993, Apr. 8 Perf. 15
962 A294 500fr shown 4.00 2.00
963 A294 1000fr Players, US flag 8.00 4.00

Fruit Trees — A295

150fr, Saba senegalensis, vert. 300fr, Butyrospermum parkii. 600fr, Adansonia digitata, vert.

1993, June 2 Litho. Perf. 11½
964 A295 150fr multicolored 1.25 .65
965 A295 300fr multicolored 2.50 1.25
966 A295 600fr multicolored 5.00 2.50
  Nos. 964-966 (3) 8.75 4.40

Traditional Jewelry — A296

1993, Sept. 25 Litho. Perf. 11½
967 A296 200fr Ring for hair 1.65 .85
968 A296 250fr Agate necklace, vert. 2.00 1.00
969 A296 500fr Bracelet 4.00 2.00
  Nos. 967-969 (3) 7.65 3.85

Gazella Rufifrons A297

1993, Dec. 10 Litho. Perf. 14½
970 A297 30fr shown .25 .15
971 A297 40fr Two facing left .32 .16
972 A297 60fr Two standing .50 .25
973 A297 100fr Young gazelle .80 .40
  a. Souvenir sheet, #970-973 3.25 1.65
  Nos. 970-973 (4) 1.87 .96

World Wildlife Fund (#970-973). No. 973a sold for 400fr.

Kingfishers — A298

1994, Mar. 8 Litho. Perf. 11½
974 A298 600fr Halcyon senegalensis 2.00 1.00
975 A298 1200fr Halcyon chelicuti 4.25 2.25

Souvenir Sheet
976 A298 2000fr Ceyx picta 7.00 3.50

1994 World Cup Soccer Championships, US — A299

1994, Mar. 28
977 A299 1000fr Players, US map 3.50 1.75
978 A299 1800fr Soccer ball, players 6.50 3.25
  a. Souvenir sheet of 1 7.00 3.50

No. 978a sold for 2000fr.

First Manned Moon Landing, 25th Anniv. — A300

1994, July 15 Litho. Perf. 11½
979 A300 750fr Astronaut, flag 3.75 1.90
980 A300 750fr Lunar module, earth 3.75 1.90
  a. Pair, #979-980 7.50 3.75

No. 980a is a continuous design.

First Stamp Exhibition, Paris, 1994 A301

1994, Apr. 28
981 A301 1500fr Dogs 7.75 3.75
  a. Souvenir sheet of 1 7.75 3.75

Legumes — A302

Designs: 40fr, Hibiscus sabdariffa. 45fr, Solanum aethiopicum. 75fr, Solanum melongena. 100fr, Hibiscus esculentus.

1994 Litho. Perf. 11½
982 A302 40fr multicolored .20 .15
983 A302 45fr multicolored .22 .15
984 A302 75fr multicolored .38 .15
985 A302 100fr multicolored .50 .25
  Nos. 982-985 (4) 1.30 .75

Intl. Olympic Committee, Cent. — A303    Domestic Animals — A304

1994, Oct. 10 Perf. 15
986 A303 320fr multicolored 1.65 .80

1994, Oct. 10 Perf. 11½
987 A304 150fr Pig, horiz. .75 .35
988 A304 1000fr Capra hircus 4.75 2.50
989 A304 1500fr Ovis aries, horiz. 7.25 3.75
  Nos. 987-989 (3) 12.75 6.60

Elvis Presley (1935-77) A305

A305a

Portraits in feature films: 300fr, Loving You. 500fr, Jailhouse Rock. 1000fr, Blue Hawaii. 1500fr, Marilyn Monroe, Presley. 0

1995 Litho. Perf. 13½
990-992 A305 Set of 3 7.50 3.75

Souvenir Sheets
993 A305 1500fr multicolored 6.00 3.00

Litho. & Embossed
993A A305a 3000fr gold & multi

Nos. 990-992 exist in souvenir sheets of one. No. 993 contains one 51x42mm stamp with continuous design. No. 993A, exists in souvenir sheets of silver & multi with different designs in sheet margin.
Issued: No. 993A, 2/24/95.
See Nos. 1012-1015A.

Crocodile — A306

1995, Feb. 6 Litho. Perf. 15x14½
994 A306 10fr brown & multi .15 .15
995 A306 20fr lilac & multi .15 .15
996 A306 25fr olive brn & multi .15 .15
997 A306 30fr green & multi .15 .15
998 A306 40fr red brown & multi .20 .15
999 A306 50fr gray & multi .25 .15
1000 A306 75fr gray violet & multi .38 .18
1001 A306 100fr gray brown & multi .50 .25
1002 A306 150fr olive & multi .75 .38
1003 A306 175fr gray blue & multi .90 .45

BURKINA FASO

1004	A306	250fr brown lake & multi	1.25	.65
1005	A306	400fr blue green & multi	2.00	1.00
	Nos. 994-1005 (12)		6.83	3.81

World Tourism Organization, 20th Anniv. — A307

Designs: 150fr, Man riding donkey, vert. 350fr, Bobo-Dioulasso railroad station. 450fr, Grand Mosque, Bani. 650fr, Gazelle, map.

1995, Jan. 26   Litho.   Perf. 11½

1006	A307	150fr multicolored	.75	.38
1007	A307	350fr multicolored	1.75	.90
1008	A307	400fr multicolored	2.25	1.10
1009	A307	650fr multicolored	3.25	1.65
	Nos. 1006-1009 (4)		8.00	4.03

FESPACO '95 — A308

Motion pictures: 150fr, "Rabi," Gaston Kabore. 250fr, "Tilai," Idrissa Ouedraogo.

1995   Perf. 13½

1010	A308	150fr multicolored	.80	.40
1011	A308	250fr multicolored	1.40	.70

Nos. 1010-1011 exist in souvenir sheets of one. Motion pictures, cent.

Stars of Motion Pictures Type of 1995

Marilyn Monroe in feature films: 400fr, The Joyful Parade. 650fr, The Village Tramp. 750fr, Niagara.
1500fr, The Seven Year Itch. 3000fr, Marilyn Monroe (1926-62).

1995   Litho.   Perf. 13½

1012-1014	A305	Set of 3	7.50	3.75

Souvenir Sheets

1015	A305	1500fr multicolored	6.00	3.00

Litho. & Embossed

1015A A305a 3000fr gold & multi

Nos. 1012-1014 exist in souvenir sheets of 1. No. 1015 contains one 42x51mm stamp with continuous design. No. 1015A exists in souvenir sheets of silver & multi with different designs in sheet margin.

Birds — A309

Designs: 450fr, Laniarius barbarus. 600fr, Estrilda bengala. 750fr, Euplectes afer.

1995, Apr. 5   Litho.   Perf. 11½

1016	A309	450fr multicolored	2.00	1.00
1017	A309	600fr multicolored	2.75	1.40
1018	A309	750fr multicolored	3.50	1.75
a.	Souvenir sheet of 3, #1016-1018		9.00	4.50
	Nos. 1016-1018 (3)		8.25	4.15

No. 1018a sold for 2000fr.

Reptiles A310

Designs: 450fr, Psammophis sibilans. 500fr, Eryx muelleri. 1500fr, Turtle.

1995

1019	A310	450fr multicolored	2.00	1.00
1020	A310	500fr multicolored	2.25	1.10
1021	A310	1500fr multicolored	6.75	3.50
	Nos. 1019-1021 (3)		11.00	5.60

1996 Summer Olympics, Atlanta — A311

Design: 3000fr, Tennis, diff.

1995   Litho.   Perf. 13½

1022	A311	150fr Basketball	.70	.35
1023	A311	250fr Baseball	1.25	.60
1024	A311	650fr Tennis	3.00	1.50
1025	A311	750fr Table tennis	3.50	1.75
a.	Souv. sheet of 4, #1022-1025		8.45	4.20
	Nos. 1022-1025 (4)		8.45	4.20

Souvenir Sheets

1026	A311	1500fr Equestrian event	7.00	7.00

Litho. & Embossed

1026A A311 3000fr gold & multi

No. 1026A also exists as a silver & multi souvenir sheet with different design in sheet margin. Both the gold & silver stamps also exist together in a souvenir sheet of 2.

Sports Figures — A312

Ayrton Senna (1960-94), World Driving Champion A313

Designs: 300fr, Juan Manuel Fangio, race car driver, 1955 Mercedes W 196. 400fr, Andre Agassi, US tennis player. 500fr, Ayrton Senna (1960-94), race car driver, McLaren MP 4/6 Honda. 1000fr, Michael Schumacher, race car driver, 1995 Benetton B 195.
1500fr, Enzo Ferrari, 412 TR, F40.

1995

1027	A312	300fr multicolored	2.25	1.10
1028	A312	400fr multicolored	3.25	1.65
1029	A312	500fr multicolored	4.00	2.00
1030	A312	1000fr multicolored	8.00	4.00
a.	Souvenir sheet of 3, #1027, 1029-1030		14.50	7.25
	Nos. 1027-1030 (4)		17.50	8.75

Souvenir Sheets

1031	A312	1500fr multicolored	7.00	3.50

Litho. & Embossed

1032 A313 3000fr gold & multi

Nos. 1027-1030 exist in souvenir sheets of 1. No. 1031 contains one 55x48mm stamp.
No. 1032 also exists as a silver & multi souvenir sheet with different design in sheet margin. Both the gold and silver stamps also exist together in a souvenir sheet of 2.
For surcharge see No. 1078.

Souvenir Sheets

John Lennon (1940-1980) — A314

Designs: No. 1033, With guitar, circular pattern with name "LENNON," portrait. No. 1034, With guitar, emblem, portrait.

1995   Litho. & Embossed   Perf. 13½

1033	A314	3000fr gold & multi		
1034	A314	3000fr gold & multi		

Nos. 1033-1034 each exist in souvenir sheets of silver & multi. Souvenir sheets of one gold and one silver exist in same designs and one of each design.

1995 Boy Scout Jamboree, Holland A315

Mushrooms: 150fr, Russula nigricans. 250fr, Lepiota rhacodes. 300fr, Xerocomus subtomentos. 400fr, Boletus erythropus. 500fr, Russula sanguinea. 650fr, Amanita rubescens. 750fr, Amanita vaginata. 1000fr, Geastrum sessil.
No. 1043, Amanita muscaria. No. 1044, Morchella esculenta.

1995   Litho.   Perf. 13½

1035-1042	A315	Set of 8	16.00	8.00
1041a		Sheet of 4, #1035, 1037, 1040-1041	7.30	3.70
1042a		Sheet of 4, #1036, 1038-1039, 1042	8.50	4.25

Souvenir Sheets

1043-1044	A315	1500fr each	6.00	3.00

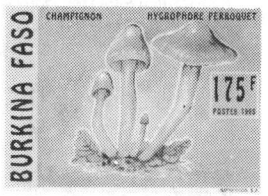

Mushrooms — A316

Designs: 175fr, Hygrophore perroquet. 250fr, Pleurote en huitre. 300fr, Pezize (oreille d'ane). 450fr, Clavaire jolie.

1996

1045-1048	A316	Set of 4	4.60	2.30
1048a		Souvenir sheet of 4, #1045-1048	4.60	2.30

#1045-1048 each exist in souvenir sheets of 1.

UN, 50th Anniv. — A317

Designs: 500fr, UN headquarters, New York. 1000fr, UN emblem, people, vert.

1995   Perf. 11½

1049	A317	500fr multicolored	2.70	1.30
1050	A317	1000fr multicolored	5.30	2.70

Christmas A318

Designs: 150fr, Christmas tree, children pointing to picture of nativity scene. 450fr, Yagma Grotto. 500fr, Flight into Egypt. 1000fr, Adoration of the Magi.

1995

1051	A318	150fr multicolored	.80	.40
1052	A318	450fr multicolored	2.40	1.20
1053	A318	500fr multicolored	2.70	1.30
1054	A318	1000fr multicolored	5.30	2.70
	Nos. 1051-1054 (4)		11.20	5.60

Butterflies and Insects A320

Designs: 100fr, Epiphora bauhiniae, vert. 150fr, Kraussella amabile, vert. 175fr, Charaxes epijasius, vert. 250fr, Locusta migratoria.

1996   Litho.   Perf. 13½

1065	A320	100fr multicolored	.45	.20
1066	A320	150fr multicolored	.70	.35
1067	A320	175fr multicolored	.80	.40
1068	A320	250fr multicolored	1.15	.60
	Nos. 1065-1068 (4)		3.10	1.55

Two souvenir sheets containing Nos. 1065, 1067 and Nos. 1066, 1068, respectively, exist.

Butterflies A321

Designs: 150fr, Morpho rega. 250fr, Hypolymnas misippus. 450fr, Pseudacraea boisduvali. 600fr, Charaxes castor.
1500fr, Antanartia delius.

1996   Litho.   Perf. 13½

1069	A321	150fr multicolored	.70	.35
1070	A321	250fr multicolored	1.10	.55
1071	A321	450fr multicolored	2.00	1.00
1072	A321	600fr multicolored	2.70	2.70
	Nos. 1069-1072 (4)		6.50	4.60

Souvenir Sheet

1073	A321	1500fr multicolored	6.75	6.75
a.	Ovptd. in sheet margin		6.30	6.30

Overprint in silver in sheet margin of No. 1073a contains Hong Kong '97 Exhibition emblem and two line inscription in Chinese. Issued in 1997.

1998 World Cup Soccer Championships, France — A322

Various soccer plays.

1996   Litho.   Perf. 13

1074	A322	50fr multi	.20	.15
1075	A322	150fr multi, vert.	.65	.30
1076	A322	250fr multi, vert.	1.10	.55
1077	A322	450fr multi, vert.	1.90	1.00
	Nos. 1074-1077 (4)		3.85	2.00

No. 1028 Ovptd. in Metallic Red

1996	**Litho.**	**Perf. 13½**
1078 A312 400fr multicolored		1.65 .80

No. 1078 exists in souvenir sheet of 1.

Wild Cats — A323

Designs: 100fr, Panthera leo. 150fr, Acinonyx jubatus. 175fr, Lynx caracal. 250fr, Panthera pardus.
Illustration reduced.

1996		**Perf. 12½x12**
1079 A323 100fr multicolored		.40 .20
1080 A323 150fr multicolored		.55 .30
1081 A323 175fr multicolored		.65 .35
1082 A323 250fr multicolored		.95 .45
Nos. 1079-1082 (4)		2.55 1.30

Orchids — A324

Various orchids.

1996	**Litho.**	**Perf. 12½x13**
1083 A324 100fr blue & multi		1.10 .55
1084 A324 175fr lilac & multi		1.90 .95
1085 A324 250fr orange & multi		2.75 1.30
1086 A324 300fr olive & multi		3.25 1.60
Nos. 1083-1086 (4)		9.00 4.40

Birds A325

Designs: 500fr, Falco peregrinus. 750fr, Crossoptilon mantchuricum. 1000fr, Branta canadensis. 1500fr, Pelecanus crispus.

1996		**Perf. 12½x12**
1087 A325 500fr multicolored		2.00 1.00
1088 A325 750fr multicolored		2.60 1.30
1089 A325 1000fr multicolored		3.75 1.90
1090 A325 1500fr multicolored		5.75 2.90
Nos. 1087-1090 (4)		14.10 7.10

#1087-1090 each printed se-tenant with labels.

See French West Africa Nos. 67, 84 for additional stamps inscribed "Haute Volta" and "Afrique Occidentale Francaise."

A326   A327

Various portraits, color of sheet margin: No. 1091, Pale pink. No. 1092, Pale blue. No. 1093, Pale yellow.

No. 1094, In white dress, serving food to child (in sheet margin). No. 1095, Wearing wide-brimmed hat.

1998	**Litho.**	**Perf. 14**
1091 A326 425fr Sheet of 6, #a.-f.		8.75 4.50
1092 A326 530fr Sheet of 6, #a.-f.		11.00 5.50
1093 A326 590fr Sheet of 6, #a.-f.		12.00 6.00
Souvenir Sheets		
1094-1095 A326 1500fr each		5.00 2.50

Diana, Princess of Wales (1961-97).

1998	**Litho.**	**Perf. 14**
1096 A327 260fr shown		.60 .30
Souvenir Sheet		
1097 A327 1500fr Portrait, diff.		5.00 2.50

Mother Teresa (1910-97). No. 1096 was issued in sheets of 6. Nos. 1096-1097 have birth date inscribed "1907."

Birds — A328

5fr, White-winged triller. 10fr, Golden sparrow. 100fr, American goldfinch. 170fr, Red-legged thrush. 260fr, Willow warbler. 425fr, Blue grosbeak.
No. 1104: a, Bank swallow. b, Kirtland's warbler. c, Long-tailed minivet. d, Blue-gray gnatcatcher. e, Reed-bunting. f, Black-collared apalis. g, American robin. h, Cape long-claw. i, Wood thrush.
No. 1105: a, Song sparrow. b, Dartford warbler. c, Eastern bluebird. d, Rock thrush. e, Northern mockingbird. f, Northern cardinal. g, Eurasian goldfinch. h, Varied thrush. i, Northern oriole.
No. 1106, Golden whistler. No. 1107, Barn swallow, horiz.

1998, Oct. 1	**Litho.**	**Perf. 13½**
1098-1103 A328 Set of 6		3.50 1.75
Sheets of 9		
1104 A328 260fr #a.-i.		8.25 4.00
1105 A328 425fr #a.-i.		14.00 7.00
Souvenir Sheets		
1106-1107 A328 1500fr each		5.50 2.75

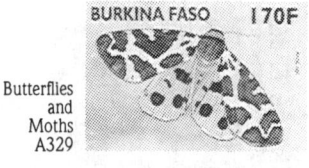

Butterflies and Moths A329

No. 1108: a, Arctia caja. b, Nymphalis antiopa. c, Brahmaea wallichii. d, Issoria lathonia. e, Speyeria cybele. f, Vanessa virginiensis. g, Rothchildia orizaba. h, Cethosia hypsea. i, Marpesia petreus.
No. 1109: a, Agraulis vanillae. b, Junonia coenia. c, Danaus gilippus. d, Polygonia comma. e, Anthocharis cardamines. f, Heliconius aoede. g, Atlides halesus. h, Mesosemia croseus. i, Automeris io.
No. 1110, Papilio xuthus. No. 1111, Pteourus multicaudatus. No. 1112, Pterourus troilus. No. 1113, Papilio machaon.

1998, Oct. 25		
Sheets of 9		
1108 A329 170fr #a.-i.		5.25 2.75
1109 A329 530fr #a.-i.		16.00 8.00
Souvenir Sheets		
1110-1113 A329 1500fr each		5.50 2.75

#1110-1113 each contain one 56x42mm stamp.

Christmas A330

Fauna, flora with Christmas items: 100fr, Tersina viridis, holly, vert. 170fr, Citherias menander, present, vert. 260fr, Chrysanthemum, reindeer, sleigh, vert. 425fr, Swallowtail butterfly, greeting card. 530fr, European bee eater, Santa Claus, snowman.
No. 1119, Anthemis tinctoria, sleigh. No. 1120, Papilio ulysses, greeting card.

1998, Dec. 1	**Litho.**	**Perf. 14**
1114-1118 A330 Set of 5		5.50 2.75
Souvenir Sheets		
1119-1120 A330 1500fr each		5.50 2.75

Trains A331

No. 1121: a, CDR No. 19, Ireland. b, EMD "F" Series Bo-Bo, US. c, Class 72000, France. d, Class AE 4/4 Bo-Bo, Switzerland. e, Class 277, Spain. f, ET 403 four car train, West Germany. g, Class EM2 Co-Co, UK. h, Europe Dutch Swiss Tee.
No. 1122: a, DF 4 East Wind IV Co-Co, China. b, Union Pacific Railroad, US. c, No. 3.641, Norway. d, Class GE 4/4 Bo-bo, Switzerland. e, Class GE Bo-Bo, South Africa. f, WDM-2 Co-Co, India. g, Kraus Mafeei Co-Co, US. h, RTG Four-car transit, France.
No. 1123, ETR 401 Pendolino, Italy. No. 1124, No. 12 Sarah Siddons, UK.

1998, Nov. 10		
Sheets of 8		
1121 A331 170fr #a.-h.		5.00 2.50
1122 A331 425fr #a.-h.		12.50 6.25
Souvenir Sheets		
1123-1124 A331 1500fr each		5.50 2.75

SEMI-POSTAL STAMPS

Catalogue values for unused stamps in this section are for Never Hinged items.

Anti-Malaria Issue
Common Design Type
Perf. 12½x12

1962, Apr. 7	**Engr.**	**Unwmk.**
B1 CD108 25fr + 5fr red org		.50 .50

Freedom from Hunger Issue
Common Design Type

1963, Mar. 21		**Perf. 13**
B2 CD112 25fr + 5fr dk grn, bl & brn		.50 .50

CAN '96 (African Nations) Soccer Championships — SP1

Designs: 150fr+25fr, Stallions, soccer ball. 250fr+25fr, Map of Africa, soccer player.

1996	**Litho.**	**Perf. 11½**
B3 SP1 150fr +25fr multi		.95 .45
a. Souvenir sheet of 1		2.75 1.40
B4 SP1 250fr +25fr multi		1.50 .75

No. B3a sold for 500fr.

AIR POST STAMPS

Catalogue values for unused stamps in this section are for Never Hinged items.

Plane over Map Showing Air Routes — AP1

Designs: 200fr, Plane at airport, Ouagadougou. 500fr, Champs Elysees, Ouagadougou.

		Unwmk.
1961, Mar. 4	**Engr.**	**Perf. 13**
C1 AP1 100fr multicolored		.85 .28
C2 AP1 200fr multicolored		1.65 .55
C3 AP1 500fr multicolored		4.00 1.50
Nos. C1-C3 (3)		6.50 2.33

Air Afrique Issue
Common Design Type

1962, Feb. 17		
C4 CD107 25fr brt pink, dk pur & lt grn		.30 .18

UN Emblem and Upper Volta Flag — AP2

	Perf. 13½x12½	
1962, Sept. 22		**Photo.**
C5 AP2 50fr multicolored		.42 .22
C6 AP2 100fr multicolored		.85 .48

Admission to UN, second anniversary.

Post Office, Ouagadougou — AP3

1962, Dec. 11		**Perf. 13x12**
C7 AP3 100fr multicolored		.75 .42

Jet Over Map AP4

1963, June 24		
C8 AP4 200fr multicolored		1.65 .65

First jet flight, Ouagadougou to Paris.
For surcharge see No. C10.

African Postal Union Issue
Common Design Type

1963, Sept. 8		**Perf. 12½**
C9 CD114 85fr dp vio, ocher & red		.70 .48

No. C8 Surcharged in Red

AIR AFRIQUE
19-11-63
50F

1963, Nov. 19		**Perf. 13x12**
C10 AP4 50fr on 200fr multi		.52 .42

See note after Mauritania No. C26.

Europafrica Issue
Common Design Type

50fr, Sunburst & Europe linked with Africa.

1964, Jan. 6		**Perf. 12x13**
C11 CD116 50fr multicolored		.75 .52

BURKINA FASO

Ramses II, Abu Simbel — AP5

Greek Sculptures — AP6

1964, Mar. 8   Engr.   Perf. 13
C12 AP5 25fr dp green & choc   .35 .30
C13 AP5 100fr brt bl & brn   1.40 1.20
UNESCO world campaign to save historic monuments of Nubia.

1964, July 1   Unwmk.   Perf. 13
C14 AP6 15fr Greek Portrait Head   .20 .15
C15 AP6 25fr Seated boxer   .25 .20
C16 AP6 85fr Victorious athlete   .80 .60
C17 AP6 100fr Venus of Milo   1.10 .70
  a. Min. sheet of 4, #C14-C17   3.50 3.50
    Nos. C14-C17 (4)   2.35 1.65
18th Olympic Games, Tokyo, Oct. 10-25.

West African Gray Woodpecker AP7

President John F. Kennedy (1917-1963) AP8

1964, Oct. 1   Engr.   Perf. 13
C18 AP7 250fr multicolored   2.75 1.90

1964, Nov. 25   Photo.   Perf. 12½
C19 AP8 100fr orange, brn & lil   .70 .70
  a. Souvenir sheet of 4   4.50 4.50

Bird Type of Regular Issue, 1965
1965, Mar. 1   Photo.   Perf. 13
Size: 27x48mm
C20 A27 500fr Abyssinian roller   5.50 2.50

Earth and Sun AP9

1965, Mar. 23   Engr.
C21 AP9 50fr multicolored   .45 .16
5th World Meteorological Day.

Hughes Telegraph, ITU Emblem and Dial Telephone — AP10

1965, May 17   Unwmk.   Perf. 13
C22 AP10 100fr red, sl grn & bl grn   .80 .40
ITU, centenary.

Intl. Cooperation Year — AP10a

1965, June 21   Photo.   Perf. 13
C23 AP10a 25fr multicolored   .20 .15
C24 AP10a 100fr multicolored   .55 .26
  a. Min. sheet, each #C23-C24   1.90 1.90

Sacred Sabou Crocodile — AP11

1965, Aug. 9   Engr.   Perf. 13
C25 AP11 60fr shown   .60 .30
C26 AP11 85fr Lion, vert.   .80 .42

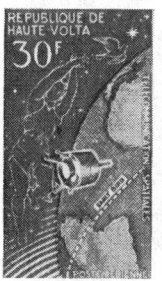

Early Bird Satellite over Globe — AP12

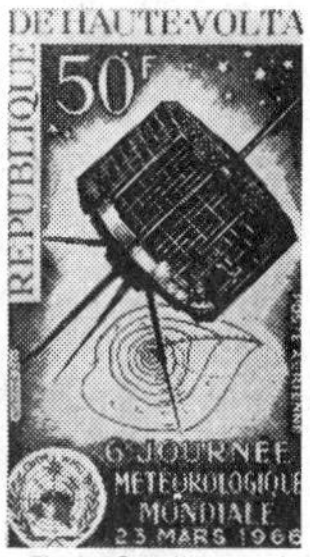

Tiros Satellite and Weather Map — AP13

1965, Sept. 15   Unwmk.   Perf. 13
C27 AP12 30fr brt bl, brn & brn red   .28 .16
Space communications.

1966, Mar. 23   Engr.   Perf. 13
C28 AP13 50fr dk car, brt bl & blk   .40 .28
6th World Meteorological Day.

FR-1 Satellite over Ouagadougou Space Tracking Station AP14

1966, Apr. 28   Perf. 13
C29 AP14 250fr mag, ind & org brn   2.00 .90

Inauguration of WHO Headquarters, Geneva — AP15

1966, May 3   Photo.
C30 AP15 100fr yel, blk & bl   .80 .45

Air Afrique Issue
Common Design Type
1966, Aug. 31   Photo.   Perf. 13
C31 CD123 25fr tan, blk & yel grn   .30 .15

Sir Winston Churchill, British Lion and "V" Sign — AP16

1966, Nov. 5   Engr.   Perf. 13
C32 AP16 100fr slate grn & car rose   1.00 .55
Sir Winston Spencer Churchill (1874-1965), statesman and WWII leader.

Pope Paul VI, Peace Dove, UN General Assembly and Emblem — AP17

1966, Nov. 5
C33 AP17 100fr dk blue & pur   1.00 .55
Pope Paul's appeal for peace before the UN General Assembly, Oct. 4, 1965.

Blind Man and Lions Emblem — AP18

1967, Feb. 28   Engr.   Perf. 13
C34 AP18 100fr dk vio bl, brt bl & dk brn   1.40 .55
50th anniversary of Lions Intl.

UN Emblem and Rain over Landscape — AP19

Diamant Rocket — AP20

1967, Mar. 23   Engr.   Perf. 13
C35 AP19 50fr ultra, dk grn & bl grn   .50 .22
7th World Meteorological Day.

1967, Apr. 18   Engr.   Perf. 13
French Spacecraft: 20fr, FR-1 satellite, horiz. 30fr, D1-C satellite. 100fr, D1-D satellite, horiz.
C36 AP20 5fr brt bl, sl grn & org   .15 .15
C37 AP20 20fr lilac & slate blue   .20 .15
C38 AP20 30fr red brn, brt bl & emer   .32 .16
C39 AP20 100fr emer & dp claret   .90 .45
    Nos. C36-C39 (4)   1.57 .91
For overprint see No. C69.

Albert Schweitzer (1875-1965), Medical Missionary and Organ Pipes — AP21

1967, May 12   Engr.   Perf. 13
C40 AP21 250fr claret & blk   1.75 .95

World Map and 1967 Jamboree Emblem — AP22

1967, June 8   Photo.
C41 AP22 100fr multicolored   1.00 .55
12th Boy Scout World Jamboree, Farragut State Park, Idaho, Aug. 1-9.

Madonna and Child, 15th Century AP23

Paintings: 20fr, Still life by Paul Gauguin. 50fr, Pietà, by Dick Bouts. 60fr, Anne of Cleves, by Hans Holbein the Younger. 90fr, The Money Lender and his Wife, by Quentin Massys (38x40mm). 100fr, Blessing of the Risen Christ, by Giovanni Bellini. 200fr, The Handcart, by Louis Le Nain, horiz. 250fr, The Four Evangelists, by Jacob Jordaens.

Perf. 12½x12, 12x12½, 13½ (90fr)
1967-68   Photo.
C42 AP23 20fr multi ('68)   .25 .15
C43 AP23 30fr multicolored   .30 .15
C44 AP23 50fr multi ('68)   .50 .25
C45 AP23 60fr multi ('68)   .60 .25
C46 AP23 90fr multi ('68)   .85 .42
C47 AP23 100fr multicolored   1.00 .38
C48 AP23 200fr multi ('68)   2.00 .70
C49 AP23 250fr multicolored   2.75 1.00
    Nos. C42-C49 (8)   8.25 3.30
See Nos. C70-C72.

African Postal Union Issue, 1967
Common Design Type
1967, Sept. 9   Engr.   Perf. 13
C50 CD124 100fr multicolored   .80 .35

Caravelle "Ouagadougou" — AP24

1968, Feb. 29   Engr.   Perf. 13
C51 AP24 500fr bl, dp claret & blk   3.75 1.40

WMO Emblem, Sun, Rain, Wheat — AP25

1968, Mar. 23 Engr. Perf. 13
C52 AP25 50fr dk red, ultra & gray grn .45 .22
8th World Meteorological Day.

Europafrica Issue

Clove Hitch — AP25a

1968, July 20 Photo. Perf. 13
C53 AP25a 50fr yel bis, blk & dk red .40 .20
See note after Niger No. C89.

Vessel in Form of Acrobat with Bells, Colima Culture — AP26

Mexican Sculptures: 30fr, Ballplayer, Veracruz, vert. 60fr, Javelin thrower, Colima, vert. 100fr, Seated athlete with cape, Jalisco.

1968, Oct. 14 Engr. Perf. 13
C54 AP26 10fr dk red, ocher & choc .15 .15
C55 AP26 30fr bl grn, brt grn & dk brn .22 .15
C56 AP26 60fr ultra, ol & mar .45 .22
C57 AP26 100fr brt grn, bl & mar .65 .35
Nos. C54-C57 (4) 1.47 .87
19th Olympic Games, Mexico City, Oct. 12-27.

Artisan Type of Regular Issue
1968, Oct. 30 Engr. Perf. 13
Size: 48x27mm
C58 A52 100fr Potter .70 .32

PHILEXAFRIQUE Issue

Too Late or The Letter, by Armand Cambon AP27

1968, Nov. 22 Photo. Perf. 12½
C59 AP27 100fr multicolored 1.00 .75
PHILEXAFRIQUE, Phil. Exhib., Abidjan, Feb. 14-23, 1969. Printed with alternating rose claret label.

Albert John Luthuli — AP28

Design: No. C61, Mahatma Gandhi.
1968, Dec. 16 Photo. Perf. 12½
C60 AP28 100fr dk grn, yel grn & blk .75 .40
C61 AP28 100fr dk grn, yel & blk .75 .40
a. Min. sheet, 2 each #C60-C61 3.00 3.00
Exponents of non-violence.

2nd PHILEXAFRIQUE Issue
Common Design Type
50fr, Upper Volta #59, dancers & musicians.
1969, Feb. 14 Engr. Perf. 13
C62 CD128 50fr pur, bl car & brn .55 .55

Weather Sonde, WMO Emblem, Mule and Cattle in Irrigated Field — AP29

1969, Mar. 24 Engr. Perf. 13
C63 AP29 100fr dk brn, brt bl & grn .90 .50
9th World Meteorological Day.

Artisan Type of Regular Issue
Design: 150fr, Basket weaver.
1969, Apr. 3 Engr. Perf. 13
Size: 48x27mm
C64 A55 150fr brn, bl & blk 1.20 .60

Lions Emblem, Eye and Blind Man — AP30

1969, Apr. 30 Photo.
C65 AP30 250fr red & multi 2.50 1.00
12th Congress of District 403 of Lions Intl., Ouagadougou, May 2-3.

Fish Type of Regular Issue
Designs: 100fr, Phenacogrammus pabrensis. 150fr, Upside-down catfish.
1969 Engr. Perf. 13
Size: 48x27mm
C66 A57 100fr slate, pur & yel .90 .42
C67 A57 150fr org brn, gray & slate 1.40 .62

Earth and Astronaut — AP31

Embossed on Gold Foil
1969 Die-cut Perf. 10½x10
C68 AP31 1000fr gold 8.25 8.25
Apollo 8 mission, which put the first man into orbit around the moon, Dec. 21-27, 1968.

No. C39 Overprinted in red with Lunar Landing Module and: "L'HOMME SUR LA LUNE / JUILLET 1969 / APOLLO 11"
1969, July 25 Engr. Perf. 13
C69 AP20 100fr emer & dp claret 2.25 1.90
See note after Mali No. C80.

Painting Type of 1967-68
Paintings: 50fr, Napoleon Crossing Great St. Bernard Pass, by Jacques Louis David. 150fr, Napoleon Awarding the First Cross of the Legion of Honor, by Jean-Baptiste Debret. 250fr, Napoleon Before Madrid, by Carle Vernet.

1969, Aug. 18 Photo. Perf. 12½x12
C70 AP23 50fr carmine & multi .45 .35
C71 AP23 150fr violet & multi 1.10 .80
C72 AP23 250fr green & multi 2.25 1.40
Nos. C70-C72 (3) 3.80 2.55
Napoleon Bonaparte (1769-1821).

Agriculture Type of Regular Issue
1969, Oct. 30 Photo. Perf. 12½x13
Size: 47½x27mm
C73 A58 100fr Peanuts .75 .28
C74 A58 200fr Rice 1.65 .55

AP32   AP33

Tree of Life, symbols of science, agriculture and industry.
1969, Nov. 21 Photo. Perf. 12x13
C75 AP32 100fr multicolored .65 .35
See note after Mauritania No. C28.

1970, Apr. 22 Photo. Perf. 12½
Designs: 20fr, Lenin. 100fr, Lenin Addressing Revolutionaries in Petrograd, by V. A. Serov, horiz.
C76 AP33 20fr ocher & brn .15 .15
C77 AP33 100fr blk, lt grn & red .65 .38
Lenin (1870-1924), Russian communist leader.

Pres. Roosevelt with Stamp Collection — AP34

Design: 10fr, Franklin Delano Roosevelt, vert.
1970, June 4 Photo. Perf. 12½
C78 AP34 10fr dk brn, emer & red brn .15 .15
C79 AP34 200fr vio bl, gray & dk car 1.40 .45
Set value .50

Soccer Game and Jules Rimet Cup — AP35

100fr, Goalkeeper catching ball, globe.
1970, June 4 Engr. Perf. 13
C80 AP35 40fr olive, brt grn & brn .40 .20
C81 AP35 100fr blk, lil, brn & grn .90 .40
9th World Soccer Championships for the Jules Rimet Cup, Mexico City, May 30-June 21, 1970.

EXPO Emblem, Monorail and "Cranes at the Seashore" — AP36

UN Emblem, Dove and Star — AP37

Design: 150fr, EXPO emblem, rocket, satellites and "Geisha."
1970, Aug. 7 Photo. Perf. 12½
C82 AP36 50fr multicolored .35 .16
C83 AP36 150fr green & multi 1.00 .60
Issued to publicize EXPO '70 International Exhibition, Osaka, Japan, Mar. 15-Sept. 13.

1970, Oct. 2 Engr. Perf. 13
Design: 250fr, UN emblem and doves, horiz.
C84 AP37 60fr dk bl, bl & grn .40 .20
C85 AP37 250fr dk red brn, vio bl & ol 1.60 .65
25th anniversary of the United Nations.

Holy Family AP38

Silver Embossed
1970, Nov. 27 Die-Cut Perf. 10
C86 AP38 300fr silver 2.50 2.50
Gold Embossed
C87 AP38 1000fr gold 9.00 9.00
Christmas.

Family and Upper Volta Flag — AP39

Gamal Abdel Nasser — AP41

UN "Key to a Free World" — AP40

Litho.; Gold Embossed
1970, Dec. 10 Perf. 12½
C88 AP39 500fr gold, blk & red 2.50 1.50
10th anniversary of independence, Dec. 11.

1970, Dec. 14 Engr. Perf. 13
C89 AP40 40fr red, bister & blue .35 .16
UN Declaration of Independence for Colonial Peoples, 10th anniv.

1971, Jan. 30 Photo. Perf. 12½
C90 AP41 100fr green & multi .65 .30
Nasser (1918-1970), president of Egypt.

BURKINA FASO

Herons, Egyptian Art, 1354 — AP42

250fr, Page from Koran, Egypt, 1368-1388.

1971, May 13	Photo.	Perf. 13
C91 AP42 100fr multi		.55 .25
C92 AP42 250fr multi, vert.		1.40 .70

Olympic Rings and Various Sports — AP43

1971, June 10	Engr.	Perf. 13
C93 AP43 150fr vio bl & red		1.00 .60

Pre-Olympic Year.

Boy Scout and Buildings — AP44

1971, Aug. 12	Photo.	Perf. 12½
C94 AP44 45fr multicolored		.35 .16

13th Boy Scout World Jamboree, Asagiri Plain, Japan, Aug. 2-10.

De Gaulle, Map of Upper Volta, Cross of Lorraine — AP45

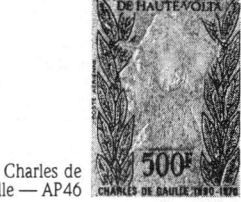

Charles de Gaulle — AP46

1971, Nov. 9	Photo.	Perf. 13x12
C95 AP45 40fr lt brn, grn & blk		.40 .35

Lithographed; Gold Embossed
Perf. 12½

C96 AP46 500fr gold & grn	4.00 3.75

Gen. Charles de Gaulle (1890-1970), president of France.

African Postal Union Issue, 1971
Common Design Type

Design: 100fr, Mossi dancer and UAMPT building, Brazzaville, Congo.

1971, Nov. 13	Photo.	Perf. 13x13½
C97 CD135 100fr bl & multi		.65 .35

Gen. Sangoule Lamizana — AP47

Kabuki Actor and Ice Hockey — AP48

1971, Dec. 11		Perf. 12½
C98 AP47 35fr sep, blk, gold & ultra		.22 .15

Inauguration of 2nd Republic of Upper Volta.

1972, Feb. 15	Engr.	Perf. 13
C99 AP48 150fr red, bl & pur		1.00 .60

11th Winter Olympic Games, Sapporo, Japan, Feb. 3-13.

Music, by Pietro Longhi AP49

Design: 150fr, Gondolas and general view, by Ippolito Caffi, horiz.

1972, Feb. 28	Photo.	Perf. 13
C100 AP49 100fr gold & multi		.65 .35
C101 AP49 150fr gold & multi		1.10 .40

UNESCO campaign to save Venice.

Running and Olympic Rings — AP50

Design: 200fr, Discus and Olympic rings.

1972, May 5	Engr.	Perf. 13
C102 AP50 65fr dp bl, brn & grn		.35 .15
C103 AP50 200fr dp bl & brn		1.10 .35
a. Min. sheet of 2, #C102-C103		1.65 1.65

20th Olympic Games, Munich, Aug. 26-Sept. 10.

Musician Type of Regular Issue
Design: 500fr, Jimmy Smith and keyboard.

1972, May 17	Photo.	Perf. 14x13
C104 A87 500fr green & multi		4.00 1.90

Red Crescent Type of Regular Issue

1972, June 23		Perf. 13x14
C105 A88 100fr yellow & multi		.65 .25

2nd Plan Type of Regular Issue
Design: 85fr, Road building machinery.

1972, Oct. 30	Engr.	Perf. 13
C106 A90 85fr brick red, bl & blk		.45 .22

Presidents Pompidou and Lamizana — AP51

Design: 250fr, Presidents Pompidou and Lamizana, different design.

1972, Nov. 20	Photo.	Perf. 13
Size: 48x37mm		
C107 AP51 40fr gold & multi		.45 .35

Photogravure; Gold Embossed
Size: 56x36mm

C108 AP51 250fr yel grn, dk grn & gold	2.50 2.50

Visit of Pres. Georges Pompidou of France, Nov. 1972.

Skeet-shooting, Scalzone, Italy — AP52

Gold-medal Winners: 40fr, Pentathlon, Peters, Great Britain. 45fr, Dressage, Meade, Great Britain. 50fr, Weight lifting, Talts, USSR. 60fr, Boxing, light-weight, Seales, US. 65fr, Fencing, Ragno-Lonzi, Italy. 75fr, Gymnastics, rings, Nakayama, Japan. 85fr, Gymnastics, Touritcheva, USSR. 90fr, 110m high hurdles, Milburn, US. 150fr, Judo, Kawaguchi, Japan. 200fr, Sailing, Finn class, Maury, France. 250fr, Swimming, Spitz, US (7 gold). 300fr, Women's high jump, Meyfarth, West Germany. 350fr, Field Hockey, West Germany. 400fr, Javelin, Wolfermann, West Germany. No. C124, Women's diving, King, US. No. C125, Cycling, Morelon, France. No. C126, Individual dressage, Linsenhoff, West Germany.

1972-73	Litho.	Perf. 12½
C109 AP52 35fr multi ('73)		.18 .15
C110 AP52 40fr multicolored		.20 .15
C111 AP52 45fr multi ('73)		.22 .15
C112 AP52 50fr multi ('73)		.25 .15
C113 AP52 60fr multi ('73)		.30 .15
C114 AP52 65fr multicolored		.35 .16
C115 AP52 75fr multi ('73)		.40 .20
C116 AP52 85fr multicolored		.42 .20
C117 AP52 90fr multi ('73)		.45 .22
C118 AP52 150fr multi ('73)		.80 .40
C119 AP52 200fr multicolored		1.10 .50
C120 AP52 250fr multi ('73)		1.40 .65
C121 AP52 300fr multicolored		1.60 .80
C122 AP52 350fr multi ('73)		1.90 .90
C123 AP52 400fr multi ('73)		2.00 1.10
Nos. C109-C123 (15)		11.57 5.88

Souvenir Sheets

C124 AP52 500fr multicolored	2.25 1.60
C125 AP52 500fr multi ('73)	2.25 1.60
C126 AP52 500fr multi ('73)	2.25 1.60

20th Olympic Games, Munich.

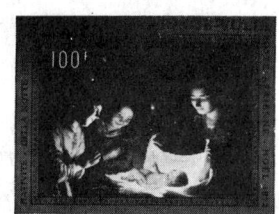

Nativity, by Della Notte — AP53

Christmas: 200fr, Adoration of the Kings, by Albrecht Dürer.

1972, Dec. 23	Photo.	Perf. 13
C127 AP53 100fr gold & multi		.50 .22
C128 AP53 200fr gold & multi		1.10 .65

Madonna and Child, by Albrecht Dürer — AP54

Christmas: 75fr, Virgin Mary, Child and St. John, by Joseph von Führich. 100fr, The Virgin of Grand Duc, by Raphael. 125fr, Holy Family, by David. 150fr, Madonna and Child, artist unknown. 400fr, Flight into Egypt, by Gentile da Fabriano, horiz.

1973, Mar. 22	Litho.	Perf. 12½x13
C129 AP54 50fr multi		.35 .16
C130 AP54 75fr multi		.50 .25
C131 AP54 100fr multi		.65 .35
C132 AP54 125fr multi		.80 .40
C133 AP54 150fr multi		1.00 .50
Nos. C129-C133 (5)		3.30 1.66

Souvenir Sheet

C134 AP54 400fr multi	2.50 1.40

Manned Lunar Buggy on Moon — AP55

Moon Exploration: 65fr, Lunakhod, Russian unmanned vehicle on moon. 100fr, Lunar module returning to orbiting Apollo capsule. 150fr, Apollo capsule in moon orbit. 200fr, Space walk. 250fr, Walk in Sea of Tranquillity.

1973, Apr. 30	Litho.	Perf. 13x12½
C135 AP55 50fr multi		.35 .16
C136 AP55 65fr multi		.42 .20
C137 AP55 100fr multi		.65 .35
C138 AP55 150fr multi		1.00 .50
C139 AP55 200fr multi		1.40 .65
Nos. C135-C139 (5)		3.82 1.86

Souvenir Sheet

C140 AP55 250fr multi	1.60 .80

Giraffes AP56

African Wild Animals: 150fr, Elephants. 200fr, Leopard, horiz. 250fr, Lion, horiz. 300fr, Rhinoceros, horiz. 500fr, Crocodile, horiz.

Perf. 12½x13, 13x12½

1973, May 3		Litho.
C141 AP56 100fr multi		65 .35
C142 AP56 150fr multi		1.00 .50
C143 AP56 200fr multi		1.40 .65
C144 AP56 250fr multi		1.60 .80
C145 AP56 500fr multi		3.50 1.60
Nos. C141-C145 (5)		8.15 3.90

Souvenir Sheet

C146 AP56 300fr multi	2.00 1.00

Europafrica Issue

Girl Reading Letter, by Jan Vermeer AP57

Paintings: 65fr, Portrait of a Lady, by Roger van der Weyden. 100fr, Young Lady at her Toilette, by Titian. 150fr, Jane Seymour, by Hans Holbein. 200fr, Mrs. Williams, by John Hoppner. 250fr, Milkmaid, by Jean-Baptiste Greuze.

1973, June 7	Litho.	Perf. 12½x13
C147 AP57 50fr multi	.35	.16
C148 AP57 65fr multi	.42	.20
C149 AP57 100fr multi	.65	.35
C150 AP57 150fr multi	1.00	.50
C151 AP57 200fr multi	1.40	.65
Nos. C147-C151 (5)	3.82	1.86

Souvenir Sheet

C152 AP57 250fr multi 1.60 .80

For overprint see No. C165-C166.

Africa Encircled by OAU Flags — AP58

1973, June 7

C153 AP58 45fr multi .30 .15

10th anniv. of Org. for African Unity.

Locomotive "Pacific" 4546, 1908 — AP59

Locomotives from Railroad Museum, Mulhouse, France: 40fr, No. 242, 1927. 50fr, No. 2029, 1882. 150fr, No. 701, 1885-92. 250fr, "Coupe-Vent" No. C145, 1900. 350fr, Buddicomb No. 33, Paris to Rouen, 1884.

1973, June 30	Perf. 13x12½
C154 AP59 10fr multi	.15 .15
C155 AP59 40fr multi	.25 .15
C156 AP59 50fr multi	.35 .16
C157 AP59 150fr multi	1.00 .50
C158 AP59 250fr multi	1.60 .80
Nos. C154-C158 (5)	3.35 1.76

Souvenir Sheet

C159 AP59 350fr multi 2.25 1.20

Boy Scout Type of 1973

40fr, Flag signaling. 75fr, Skiing. 150fr, Cooking. 200fr, Hiking. 250fr, Studying stars.

1973, July 18	Litho.	Perf. 12½x13
C160 A95 40fr multi	.25	.15
C161 A95 75fr multi	.50	.25
C162 A95 150fr multi	1.00	.50
C163 A95 200fr multi	1.40	.65
Nos. C160-C163 (4)	3.15	1.55

Souvenir Sheet

C164 A95 250fr multi 1.60 .80

Nos. C148 and C150 Surcharged in Silver New Value and "SECHERESSE / SOLIDARITE AFRICAINE / ET INTERNATIONALE"

1973, Aug. 16		
C165 AP57 100fr on 65fr multi	.65	.35
C166 AP57 on 150fr multi	1.40	.65

Drought relief.

Kennedy Type, 1973

John F. Kennedy and: 200fr, Firing Saturn 1 rocket, Apollo program. 300fr, First NASA manned space capsule. 400fr, Saturn 5 countdown.

1973, Sept. 12	Litho.	Perf. 12½x13
C167 A96 200fr multi	1.40	.65
C168 A96 300fr multi	2.00	1.00

Souvenir Sheet

C169 A96 400fr multi 2.50 1.40

10th death anniv. of Pres John F. Kennedy.

Interpol Type of 1973
Souvenir Sheet

Design: Victim in city street.

1973, Sept. 15	Perf. 13x12½
C170 A97 300fr multi	2.00 1.00

Tourism Type of 1973

1973, Sept. 30		
C171 A98 100fr Waterfalls	.65	.35

Souvenir Sheet

C172 A98 275fr Elephant 1.90 .90

House of Worship Type of 1973

Cathedral of the Immaculate Conception.

1973, Sept. 28		
C173 A99 200fr multi	1.40	.65

Folklore Type of 1973

100fr, 225fr, Bobo masked dancers, diff.

1973, Nov. 30	Litho.	Perf. 12½x13
C174 A100 100fr multi	.65	.35
C175 A100 225fr multi	1.50	.70

Zodiac Type of 1973
Souvenir Sheets

Zodiacal Light and: #C176, 1st 4 signs of Zodiac. #C177, 2nd 4 signs. #C178, Last 4 signs.

1973, Dec. 15	Perf. 13x14
C176 A101 250fr multi	1.60 .80
C177 A101 250fr multi	1.60 .80
C178 A101 250fr multi	1.60 .80

Nos. C176-C178 have multicolored margin showing night sky and portraits: No. C176, Louis Armstrong; No. C177, Mahatma Gandhi; No. C178, Martin Luther King.

Soccer Championship Type, 1974

Championship '74 emblem and: 75fr, Gento, Spanish flag. 100fr, Bereta, French flag. 250fr, Best, British flag. 400fr, Beckenbauer, West German flag.

1974, Jan. 15	Litho.	Perf. 13x12½
C179 A102 75fr multi	.50	.25
C180 A102 100fr multi	.65	.35
C181 A102 250fr multi	1.60	.80
Nos. C179-C181 (3)	2.75	1.40

Souvenir Sheet

C182 A102 400fr multi 2.50 1.40

De Gaulle Type, 1974

Designs: 300fr, De Gaulle and Concorde, horiz. 400fr, De Gaulle and French space shot.

	Perf. 13x12½, 12½x13
1974, Feb. 4	Litho.
C183 A103 300fr multi	2.00 1.00

Souvenir Sheet

C184 A103 400fr multi 2.50 1.40

Soccer Cup Championship Type, 1974

World Cup, Emblems and: 150fr, Brindisis, Argentinian flag. No. C186, Kenko, Zaire flag. No. C187, Streich, East German flag. 400fr, Cruyff, Netherlands flag.

1974, Mar. 19	Perf. 12½x13
C185 A104 150fr multi	.75 .38
C186 A104 300fr multi	1.50 .75

Souvenir Sheets

| C187 A104 300fr multi | 1.50 .75 |
| C188 A104 400fr multi | 2.00 1.00 |

UPU Type, 1974

UPU Emblem and: 100fr, Dove carrying mail. 200fr, Air Afrique 707. 300fr, Dish antenna. 500fr, Telstar satellite.

1974, July 23	Perf. 13½
C189 A106 100fr multi	.50 .25
C190 A106 200fr multi	1.00 .50
C191 A106 300fr multi	1.50 .75
Nos. C189-C191 (3)	3.00 1.50

Souvenir Sheet

C192 A106 500fr multi 2.50 1.25

For overprint see No. C197-C200.

Soccer Cup Winners Type, 1974

World Cup, Game and Flags: 150fr, Brazil, in Sweden, 1958. 200fr, Brazil, in Chile, 1962. 250fr, Brazil, in Mexico, 1970. 450fr, England, in England, 1966.

1974, Sept. 2		
C193 A107 150fr multi	1.00	.50
C194 A107 200fr multi	1.40	.65
C195 A107 250fr multi	1.60	.80
Nos. C193-C195 (3)	4.00	1.95

Souvenir Sheet

C196 A107 450fr multi 3.00 1.50

Nos. C189-C192 Overprinted in Red "100e ANNIVERSAIRE DE L'UNION POSTALE UNIVERSELLE / 9 OCTOBRE 1974"

1974, Oct. 9		
C197 A106 100fr multi	.65	.35
C198 A106 200fr multi	1.40	.65
C199 A106 300fr multi	2.00	1.00
Nos. C197-C199 (3)	4.05	2.00

Souvenir Sheet

C200 A106 500fr multi 3.00 1.40

Universal Postal Union, centenary.

Flower Type of 1974

Flower Paintings by: 300fr, Auguste Renoir. 400fr, Carl Brendt.

1974, Oct. 31	Litho.	Perf. 12½x13
C201 A109 300fr multi	2.00	1.00

Souvenir Sheet

C202 A109 400fr multi 2.50 1.40

Locomotive Type of 1975

Locomotives from Railroad Museum, Mulhouse, France: 100fr, Crampton No. 80, 1852. 200fr, No. 701, 1885-92. 300fr, "Forquenot", 1882.

1975, Feb. 28	Litho.	Perf. 13x12½
C203 A112 100fr multi	.65	.35
C204 A112 200fr multi	1.40	.65

Souvenir Sheet

C205 A112 300fr multi 2.00 1.00

Old Cars Type, 1975

Flags and Old Cars: 150fr, Germany and Mercedes-Benz, 1929. 200fr, Germany and Maybach, 1936. 400fr, Great Britain and Rolls Royce Silver Ghost, 1910.

1975, Apr. 6	Perf. 14x13½
C206 A113 150fr multi	1.00 .50
C207 A113 200fr multi	1.40 .65

Souvenir Sheet

C208 A113 400fr multi 2.50 1.40

American Bicentennial Type of 1975

200fr, Washington crossing Delaware. 300fr, Hessians Captured at Trenton.

1975, May 6	Litho.	Perf. 14
C209 A114 200fr multi	1.40	.65
C210 A114 300fr multi	2.00	1.00

Schweitzer Type of 1975

Albert Schweitzer and: 150fr, Toucan. 175fr, Vulturine guinea fowl. 200fr, King vulture. 450fr, Crested corythornis.

1975, May 25	Litho.	Perf. 13½
C212 A115 150fr multi	1.00	.50
C213 A115 175fr multi	1.20	.55
C214 A115 200fr multi	1.40	.65
Nos. C212-C214 (3)	3.60	1.70

Souvenir Sheet

C215 A115 450fr multi 3.00 1.50

Apollo Soyuz Type of 1975

Designs: 100fr, Apollo and Soyuz near link-up. 200fr, Cosmonauts Alexei Leonov and Valeri Kubasov. 300fr, Astronauts Donald K. Slayton, Vance Brand and Thomas P. Stafford. 500fr, Apollo Soyuz emblem, US and USSR flags.

1975, July 18	Litho.	Perf. 13½
C216 A116 100fr multi	.65	.35
C217 A116 200fr multi	1.40	.65
C218 A116 300fr multi	2.00	1.00
Nos. C216-C218 (3)	4.05	2.00

Souvenir Sheet

C219 A116 500fr multi 3.50 1.60

Picasso Type of 1975

Picasso Paintings: 150fr, El Prado, horiz. 350fr, Couple in Patio. 400fr, Science and Charity.

1975, Aug. 7		
C220 A117 300fr multi	1.00	.50
C221 A117 350fr multi	2.25	1.20

Souvenir Sheet

C222 A117 400fr multi 2.50 1.40

EXPO '75 Type of 1975

Expo '75 emblem and: 150fr, Passenger liner Asama Maru. 300fr, Future floating city Aquapolis.

1975, Sept. 26	Litho.	Perf. 11
C223 A118 150fr multi	.75	.38

Souvenir Sheet
Perf. 13½

C224 A118 300fr multi 1.50 .75

Winter Olympic Games Type of 1975

Innsbruck Background, Olympic Emblem and: 100fr, Ice hockey. 200fr, Ski jump. 300fr, Speed skating.

1975, Dec. 15	Litho.	Perf. 13½
C225 A122 100fr multi	.65	.35
C226 A122 200fr multi	1.40	.65

Souvenir Sheet

C227 A122 300fr multi 2.00 1.00

Olympic Games Type of 1976

Olympic Emblem and: 125fr, Heavyweight judo. 150fr, Weight lifting. 500fr, Sprint.

1976, Mar. 17	Litho.	Perf. 13½
C228 A123 125fr multi	.65	.30
C229 A123 150fr multi	.75	.38

Souvenir Sheet

C230 A123 500fr multi 2.50 1.25

Summer Olympic Games Type of 1976

Olympic emblem and: 150fr, Pole vault. 200fr, Gymnast on balance beam. 500fr, Two-man sculls.

1976, Mar. 25	Perf. 11
C231 A124 150fr multi	.75 .38
C232 A124 200fr multi	1.00 .50

Souvenir Sheet

C233 A124 500fr multi 2.50 1.25

For overprint see No. C245-C247.

Zeppelin Type of 1976

Airships: 100fr, Graf Zeppelin over Swiss Alps. 200fr, LZ-129 over city. 300fr, Graf Zeppelin. 500fr, Zeppelin over Bodensee.

1976, May 11		
C234 A126 100fr multi	.65	.35
C235 A126 200fr multi	1.40	.65
C236 A126 300fr multi	2.00	1.00
Nos. C234-C236 (3)	4.05	2.00

Souvenir Sheet

C237 A126 500fr multi 3.50 1.60

Viking Mars Type of 1976

Designs: 200fr, Viking lander assembly. 300fr, Viking orbiter in descent on Mars. 450fr, Viking in Mars orbit.

1976, June 24	Litho.	Perf. 13½
C238 A127 200fr multi	1.00	.50
C239 A127 300fr multi	1.50	.75

Souvenir Sheet

C240 A127 450fr multi 2.25 1.10

American Bicentennial Type of 1976

Bicentennial and Interphil '76 Emblems and: 100fr, Siege of Yorktown. 200fr, Battle of Cape St. Vincent. 300fr, Peter Francisco's bravery. 500fr, Surrender of the Hessians.

1976, Sept. 30	Litho.	Perf. 13½
C241 A129 100fr multi	.65	.35
C242 A129 200fr multi	1.40	.65
C243 A129 300fr multi	2.00	1.00
Nos. C241-C243 (3)	4.05	2.00

Souvenir Sheet

C244 A129 500fr multi 3.50 1.60

Nos. C231-C233 Overprinted in Gold:
a. VAINQUEUR 1976 / TADEUSZ SLUSARSKI / POLOGNE

BURKINA FASO

b. VAINQUEUR 1976 / NADIA COMANECI / ROUMANIE
c. VAINQUEUR 1976 / FRANK ET ALF HANSEN / NORVEGE

1976, July 4   Litho.   *Perf. 11*
C245 A124(a) 150fr multi   1.00   .50
C246 A124(b) 200fr multi   1.40   .65
       Souvenir Sheet
C247 A124(c) 500fr multi   3.50 1.60
Winners, 21st Olympic Games.

UPU Emblem over Globe — AP60

1978, Aug. 8   Litho.   *Perf. 13*
C248 AP60 350fr multi   2.25 1.50
Congress of Paris, establishing UPU, cent.

Jules Verne, Apollo 11 Emblem, Footprint on Moon, Neil Armstrong — AP61

Space Conquest: 50fr, Yuri Gagarin and moon landing. 100fr, Montgolfier hot air balloon and memorial medal, 1783; Bleriot's monoplane, 1909.

1978, Sept. 27   Litho.   *Perf. 13x12½*
C249 AP61 50fr multi   .35 .16
C250 AP61 80fr multi   .40 .20
C251 AP61 100fr multi   .65 .35
   Nos. C249-C251 (3)   1.40 .71

Anti Apartheid Year — AP62

1978, Oct. 12   Litho.   *Perf. 13*
C252 AP62 100fr blue & multi   .65 .35

Philexafrique II-Essen Issue
Common Design Types
Designs: #C253, Hippopotamus and Upper Volta #C18. #C254, Hummingbird and Hanover #1.

1978, Nov. 1   Litho.   *Perf. 12½*
C253 CD138 100fr multi   .65 .35
C254 CD139 100fr multi   .65 .35
Nos. C253-C254 printed se-tenant.

Sun God Horus with Sun — AP63
Jules Verne and Balloon — AP64 

300fr, Falcon with cartouches, UNESCO emblem.

1978, Dec. 4
C255 AP63 200fr multi   1.40 .65
C256 AP63 300fr multi   2.00 1.00
UNESCO Campaign to safeguard monuments at Philae.

1978, Dec. 10   Engr.   *Perf. 13*
C257 AP64 200fr multi   1.40 .65
Verne (1828-1905), science fiction writer.

Bicycling, Olympic Rings AP65

Designs: Bicycling scenes.

1980   *Perf. 14½*
C258 AP65 65fr multi   .65 .32
C259 AP65 150fr multi, vert.   1.00 .50
C260 AP65 250fr multi   1.60 .80
C261 AP65 350fr multi   2.25 1.20
   Nos. C258-C261 (4)   5.50 2.82
       Souvenir Sheet
C262 AP65 500fr multi   3.50 1.60
22nd Summer Olympic Games, Moscow, July 19-Aug. 3.

Nos. C258-C262 Overprinted with Name of Winner and Country

1980, Nov. 22   Litho.   *Perf. 14½*
C263 AP65 65fr multi   .42 .20
C264 AP65 150fr multi   1.00 .50
C265 AP65 250fr multi   1.60 .80
C266 AP65 350fr multi   2.25 1.20
   Nos. C263-C266 (4)   5.27 2.70
       Souvenir Sheet
C267 AP65 500fr multi   3.50 1.60

1982 World Cup — AP66

Designs: Various soccer players.

1982, June 22   Litho.   *Perf. 13½*
C268 AP66 70fr multi   .45 .22
C269 AP66 90fr multi   .60 .30
C270 AP66 150fr multi   1.00 .50
C271 AP66 300fr multi   2.00 1.00
   Nos. C268-C271 (4)   4.05 2.02
       Souvenir Sheet
C272 AP66 500fr multi   3.50 1.60

Anniversaries and Events — AP67

1983, June   Litho.   *Perf. 13½*
C273 AP67 90fr Space Shuttle   .30 .15
C274 AP67 120fr World Soccer Cup   .40 .20
C275 AP67 300fr Cup, diff.   1.00 .50
C276 AP67 450fr Royal Wedding   1.50 .70
   Nos. C273-C276 (4)   3.20 1.55
       Souvenir Sheet
C277 AP67 500fr Prince Charles, Lady Diana   1.60 1.60

Pre-Olympics, 1984 Los Angeles AP68

1983, Aug. 1   Litho.   *Perf. 13*
C278 AP68 90fr Sailing   .30 .15
C279 AP68 120fr Type 470   .40 .20
C280 AP68 300fr Wind surfing   1.00 .50
C281 AP68 400fr Wind surfing, diff.   1.40 .65
   Nos. C278-C281 (4)   3.10 1.50
       Souvenir Sheet
C282 AP68 500fr Soling Class, Wind surfing   1.60 1.60

Christmas AP69

Rubens Paintings.

1983   Litho.   *Perf. 13*
C283 AP69 120fr Adoration of the Shepherds   .40 .20
C284 AP69 350fr Virgin of the Garland   1.20 .60
C285 AP69 500fr Adoration of the Kings   1.60 .80
   Nos. C283-C285 (3)   3.20 1.60

1984 Summer Olympics — AP70

1984, Mar. 26   Litho.   *Perf. 12½*
C286 AP70 90fr Handball, vert.   .30 .15
C287 AP70 120fr Volleyball, vert.   .40 .20
C288 AP70 150fr Handball, diff.   .50 .25
C289 AP70 250fr Basketball   .80 .42
C290 AP70 300fr Soccer   1.00 .50
   Nos. C286-C290 (5)   3.00 1.52
       Souvenir Sheet
C291 AP70 500fr Volleyball, diff.   1.60 .80

Local Birds AP71

1984, May 14   Litho.   *Perf. 12½*
C292 AP71 90fr Phoenicopterus roseus   .30 .15
C293 AP71 185fr Choriotis kori, vert.   .62 .32
C294 AP71 200fr Buphagus erythrorhynchus, vert.   .65 .35
C295 AP71 300fr Bucorvus leadbeateri   1.00 .50
   Nos. C292-C295 (4)   2.57 1.32

AP72

Famous Men — AP73

Designs: 5fr, Houari Boumediene (1927-1978), president of Algeria 1965-78. 125fr, Gottlieb Daimler (1834-1900), German automotive pioneer, and 1886 Daimler. 250fr, Louis Bleriot (1872-1936), French aviator, first to fly the English Channel in a heavier-than-air craft. 300fr, Abraham Lincoln. 400fr, Henri Dunant (1828-1910), founder of the Red Cross. 450fr, Auguste Piccard (1884-1962), Swiss physicist, inventor of the bathyscaphe Trieste, 1948. 500fr, Robert Baden-Powell (1856-1941), founder of Boy Scouts. 600fr, Anatoli Karpov, Russian chess champion. 1000fr, Paul Harris (1868-1947), founder of Rotary Intl.

1984, May 21   Litho.   *Perf. 13½*
C296 AP72 5fr multi   .15 .15
C297 AP72 125fr multi   .50 .25
C298 AP72 250fr multi   1.00 .50
C299 AP72 300fr multi   1.20 .60
C300 AP72 400fr multi   1.60 .80
C301 AP72 450fr multi   1.90 .90
C302 AP72 500fr multi   2.00 1.00
C303 AP72 600fr multi   2.25 1.20
   Nos. C296-C303 (8)   10.60 5.40
       Souvenir Sheet
C304 AP73 1000fr multi   4.00 2.00
No. C304 contains one 51x30mm stamp.

Burkina Faso

Butterflies — AP73a

1984, May 23   *Perf. 13½*
C305 AP73a 10fr Graphium pylades   .15 .15
C306 AP73a 120fr Hypolimnas misippus   .50 .22
C307 AP73a 400fr Danaus chrysippus   1.60 .80
C308 AP73a 450fr Papilio demodocus   1.90 .90
   Nos. C305-C308 (4)   4.15 2.07

Philexafrica '85, Lome — AP74

1985, May 20   Litho.   *Perf. 13*
C309 AP74 200fr Solar & wind energy   .55 .25
C310 AP74 200fr Children   .55 .25
Nos. C309-C310 se-tenant with center label picturing a map of Africa or the exhibition emblem.

PHILEXAFRICA '85, Lome — AP75

National development: No. C311, Youth. No. C312, Communications and transportation.

1985, Nov. 16   Litho.   *Perf. 13*
C311 AP75 250fr multi   .90 .45
C312 AP75 250fr multi   .90 .45
Intl. Youth Year (No. C311). Nos. C311-C312 printed se-tenant with center label picturing

PHILEXAFRICA '85 emblem or outline map of Africa.

French Revolution, Bicent. — AP76

Designs: 150fr, *Oath of the Tennis Court*, by David. 200fr, *Storming of the Bastille*, by Thevenin. 600fr, *Rouget de Lisle Singing La Marseillaise*, by Pils.
Illustration reduced.

1989, May 3		Litho.		Perf. 13	
C313	AP76	150fr multi		.90	.45
C314	AP76	200fr multi		1.20	.60
C315	AP76	600fr multi		3.60	1.80
		Nos. C313-C315 (3)		5.70	2.85

PHILEXFRANCE '89. Printed se-tenant with label containing the exhibition emblem.

POSTAGE DUE STAMPS

Postage Due Stamps of Upper Senegal and Niger, 1914, Overprinted in Black or Red

HAUTE-VOLTA

1920		Unwmk.	Perf. 14x13½	
J1	D2	5c green	.30	.30
J2	D2	10c rose	.30	.30
J3	D2	15c gray	.30	.30
J4	D2	20c brown (R)	.40	.40
J5	D2	30c blue	.45	.45
J6	D2	50c black (R)	.65	.65
J7	D2	60c orange	.65	.65
J8	D2	1fr violet	.90	.90
		Nos. J1-J8 (8)	3.95	3.95

Type of 1914 Issue Surcharged **2F.**

1927				
J9	D2	2fr on 1fr lilac rose	2.25	2.25
J10	D2	3fr on 1fr orange brn	2.50	2.50

D3

Red-fronted Gazelle — D4

1928			Typo.	
J11	D3	5c green	.30	.30
J12	D3	10c rose	.30	.30
J13	D3	15c dark gray	.40	.40
J14	D3	20c dark brown	.40	.40
J15	D3	30c dark blue	.50	.50
J16	D3	50c black	1.75	1.75
J17	D3	60c orange	2.00	2.00
J18	D3	1fr dull violet	3.50	3.50
J19	D3	2fr lilac rose	6.00	6.00
J20	D3	3fr orange brn	6.50	6.50
		Nos. J11-J20 (10)	21.65	21.65

Catalogue values for unused stamps in this section, from this point to the end of the section, are for Never Hinged items.

Republic

1962, Jan. 31		Perf. 14x13½	
	Denomination in Black		
J21	D4	1fr bright blue	.15	.15
J22	D4	2fr orange	.15	.15
J23	D4	5fr brt vio blue	.15	.15
J24	D4	10fr red lilac	.20	.20
J25	D4	20fr emerald	.45	.45
J26	D4	50fr rose red	1.10	1.10
		Nos. J21-J26 (6)	2.20	2.20

OFFICIAL STAMPS

Catalogue values for unused stamps in this section are for Never Hinged items.

Elephant O1

1963, Feb. 1		Perf. 12½	
		Unwmk.	Photo.
	Center in Sepia		
O1	O1	1fr red brown	.15	.15
O2	O1	5fr yel green	.15	.15
O3	O1	10fr deep vio	.20	.20
O4	O1	15fr red org	.25	.25
O5	O1	25fr brt rose lilac	.35	.35
O6	O1	50fr brt green	.55	.55
O7	O1	60fr brt red	.70	.70
O8	O1	85fr dk slate grn	1.10	1.10
O9	O1	100fr brt blue	1.75	1.75
O10	O1	200fr bright rose	3.00	3.00
		Nos. O1-O10 (10)	8.20	8.20

BURMA

ˈbər-mə

Myanmar

LOCATION — Bounded on the north by China; east by China, Laos and Thailand; south and west by the Bay of Bengal, Bangladesh and India.
GOVT. — Republic
AREA — 261,789 sq. mi.
POP. — 35,313,905 (1983)
CAPITAL — Yangon (Rangoon)

Burma was part of India from 1826 until April 1, 1937, when it became a self-governing unit of the British Commonwealth and received a constitution. On January 4, 1948, Burma became an independent nation.

12 Pies = 1 Anna
16 Annas = 1 Rupee
100 Pyas = 1 Kyat (1953)

Catalogue values for unused stamps in this country are for Never Hinged items, beginning with Scott 35 in the regular postage section and Scott O28 in the official section.

Watermarks

Wmk. 254 — Elephant Heads

Wmk. 257 — Curved Wavy Lines

Stamps of India 1926-36 Overprinted **BURMA**

1937, Apr. 1		Wmk. 196	Perf. 14	
1	A46	3p slate	.15	.15
2	A71	½a green	.15	.15
3	A68	9p dark green	.20	.20
4	A72	1a dark brown	.15	.15
5	A49	2a ver (small die)	.15	.15
6	A57	2a6p buff	.15	.15
7	A51	3a carmine rose	.40	.15
8	A70	3a6p deep blue	.40	.15
9	A52	4a olive green	.45	.15
10	A53	6a bister	.40	.25
11	A54	8a red violet	.90	.15
12	A55	12a claret	1.50	.50

Overprinted **BURMA**

13	A56	1r green & brown	5.00	.75
14	A56	2r brn org & car rose	7.50	2.50
15	A56	5r dk violet & ultra	10.00	3.00
16	A56	10r car & green	27.50	6.00
17	A56	15r ol green & ultra	125.00	60.00
18	A56	25r blue & ocher	250.00	150.00
		Nos. 1-18 (18)	430.00	224.50

For overprints see #1N1-1N3, 1N25-1N26, 1N47.

King George VI
A1   A2

Royal Barge — A3

Elephant Moving Teak Log — A4

Farmer Plowing Rice Field — A5

Sailboat on Irrawaddy River — A6

Peacock — A7   George VI — A8

1938-40		Perf. 13½x14		
		Litho.	Wmk. 254	
18A	A1	1p red orange ('40)	.85	.30
19	A1	3p violet	.15	.15
20	A1	6p ultramarine	.15	.15
21	A1	9p yel green	.55	.35
22	A2	1a brown violet	.15	.15
23	A2	1½a turquoise green	.15	.15
24	A2	2a carmine	.30	.15
		Perf. 13		
25	A3	2a6p rose lake	.80	.45
26	A4	3a dk violet	2.50	.50
27	A5	3a6p dp blue & brt bl	1.50	2.75
28	A2	4a slate blue, perf. 13½x14	.15	.15
29	A6	8a slate green	1.50	.15
		Perf. 13½		
30	A7	1r brt ultra & dk violet	2.25	.30
31	A7	2r dk vio & red brown	5.50	1.50
32	A8	5r car & dull vio	22.50	9.00
33	A8	10r gray grn & brn	45.00	35.00
		Nos. 18A-33 (16)	84.00	51.20
		Set, never hinged	110.00	

See Nos. 51-65. For overprints and surcharges see Nos. 34-50, O15-O27, 1N4-1N11, 1N28-1N30, 1N37-1N46, 1N48-1N49.

No. 25 Surcharged in Black

COMMEMORATION
POSTAGE STAMP
6th MAY 1840

ONE ANNA   1A

1940, May 6			Perf. 13	
34	A3	1a on 2a6p rose lake	1.00	.80
		Never hinged	4.00	

Centenary of first postage stamp.

Catalogue values for unused stamps in this section, from this point to the end of the section, are for Never Hinged items.

Nos. 18A to 33 Overprinted in Black:

MILY ADMN   MILY ADMN
a   b

1945				
35	A1(a)	1p red orange	.15	.15
36	A1(a)	3p violet	.15	.15
37	A1(a)	6p ultramarine	.15	.15
38	A1(a)	9p yel green	.15	.15
39	A2(a)	1a brown violet	.15	.15
40	A2(a)	1½a turq green	.15	.15
41	A2(a)	2a carmine	.15	.15
42	A3(b)	2a6p rose lake	.45	.45
43	A4(a)	3a dk violet	.75	.15
44	A5(b)	3a6p dp bl & brt bl	.15	.15
45	A2(a)	4a slate blue	.15	.15
46	A6(b)	8a slate green	.15	.20
47	A7(b)	1r brt ultra & dk violet	.30	.40
48	A7(b)	2r dk vio & red brown	.30	.25
49	A8(b)	5r car & dull vio	.75	.80
50	A8(b)	10r gray grn & brn	1.50	1.50
		Nos. 35-50 (16)	5.55	5.60

Types of 1938
Perf. 13½x14

1946, Jan. 1		Litho.	Wmk. 254	
51	A1	3p brown	.15	.15
52	A1	6p violet	.15	.15
53	A1	9p dull green	.15	.15
54	A2	1a deep blue	.15	.15
55	A2	1½a salmon	.15	.15
56	A2	2a rose lake	.15	.15
		Perf. 13		
57	A3	2a6p greenish blue	.25	.15
58	A4	3a blue violet	6.75	1.50
59	A5	3a6p ultra & gray blk	.15	.15
60	A2	4a rose lil, perf. 13½x14	.15	.15
61	A6	8a deep magenta	2.25	.20
		Perf. 13½		
62	A7	1r dp mag & dk vio	1.25	.25
63	A7	2r salmon & red brn	7.50	1.75
64	A8	5r red brn & dk grn	7.50	7.50
65	A8	10r dk vio & car	7.50	7.50
		Nos. 51-65 (15)	34.20	20.05

For overprints see Nos. 70-84, O28-O42.

Burmese Man — A9

Burmese Woman — A10

Mythological Chinze — A11

Elephant Hauling Teak — A12

BURMA

1946, May 2 Perf. 13
66	A9	9p peacock green	.20	.20
67	A10	1½a brt violet	.20	.20
68	A11	2a carmine	.20	.20
69	A12	3a6p ultramarine	.20	.20
		Nos. 66-69 (4)	.80	.80

Victory of the Allied Nations in WWII.

Nos. 51-65 Overprinted in ကြား ဖြတ် အစိုးရ။ Black

1947, Oct. 1 Perf. 13½x14, 13, 13½
70	A1	3p brown	.45	.45
71	A1	6p violet	.15	.25
72	A1	9p dull green	.15	.25
	a.	Inverted overprint	12.50	12.50
73	A2	1a deep blue	.15	.25
74	A2	1½a salmon	1.25	.15
75	A2	2a rose lake	.30	.15
76	A3	2a6p greenish bl	1.40	.75
77	A4	3a blue violet	2.50	1.25
78	A5	3a6p ultra & gray blk	.50	.75
79	A2	4a rose lilac	1.60	.25
80	A6	8a dp magenta	1.60	.70
81	A7	1r dp mag & dk vio	2.25	.30
82	A7	2r sal & red brn	2.50	2.50
83	A8	5r red brn & dk grn	3.50	3.75
84	A8	10r dk vio & car	3.50	3.75
		Nos. 70-84 (15)	21.80	15.50

The overprint is slightly larger on Nos. 76 to 78 and 80 to 84. The Burmese characters read "Interim Government."

Other denominations are known with the overprint inverted or double.

Issues of the Republic

U Aung San Map and Chinze — A13

Martyrs' Memorial — A14

Perf. 12½x12

1948, Jan. 6 Litho. Unwmk.
85	A13	½a emerald	.15	.15
86	A13	1a deep rose	.15	.15
87	A13	2a carmine	.15	.15
88	A13	3½a blue	.15	.15
89	A13	8a lt chocolate	.20	.20
		Nos. 85-89 (5)	.80	.80

Attainment of independence, Jan. 4, 1948.

1948, July 19 Engr. Perf. 14x13½
90	A14	3p ultramarine	.15	.15
91	A14	6p green	.15	.15
92	A14	9p dp carmine	.15	.15
93	A14	1a purple	.15	.15
94	A14	2a lilac rose	.15	.15
95	A14	3½a dk slate green	.15	.15
96	A14	4a yel brown	.15	.15
97	A14	8a orange red	.15	.15
98	A14	12a claret	.16	.15
99	A14	1r blue green	.20	.15
100	A14	2r deep blue	.48	.35
101	A14	5r chocolate	1.25	.80
		Nos. 90-101 (12)	3.29	2.66

1st anniv. of the assassination of Burma's leaders in the fight for independence.

Ball Game (Chinlon) A15

Bell A16

Mythical Bird — A17

Rice Planting — A18

Throne — A19

Designs: 6p, Dancer. 9p, Musician. 3a, Spinning. 3a6p, Royal Palace. 4a, Cutting teak. 8a, Plowing rice field.

Perf. 12½ (A15-A17), 12x12½ (A18), 13 (A19)

1949, Jan. 4
102	A15	3p ultramarine	.15	.15
103	A15	6p green	.15	.15
104	A15	1a carmine	.15	.15
105	A16	1a red orange	.15	.15
106	A17	2a orange	.15	.15
107	A18	2a6p lilac rose	.15	.15
108	A18	3a purple	.15	.15
109	A18	3a6p dk slate grn	.15	.15
110	A16	4a chocolate	.15	.15
111	A18	8a carmine	.25	.15
112	A19	1r blue green	.40	.20
	a.	Perf. 14		2.50
113	A19	2r deep blue	.90	.32
114	A19	5r chocolate	1.75	.70
115	A19	10r orange red	4.00	1.00
		Nos. 102-115 (14)	8.65	3.72

See Nos. 122-135, 139-152, O56-O67.

UPU Monument, Bern — A20

1949, Oct. 9 Unwmk. Perf. 13
116	A20	2a orange	.15	.15
117	A20	3½a olive grn	.15	.15
118	A20	6a lilac	.30	.15
119	A20	8a crimson	.40	.20
120	A20	12½a ultra	.50	.20
121	A20	1r blue green	.75	.50
		Nos. 116-121 (6)	2.25	1.35

75th anniv. of the UPU.

Types of 1949

Designs as before.

Perf. 13½x14, 14x13½, 13

1952-53 Litho. Wmk. 254
122	A15	3p brown orange	.15	.15
123	A15	6p deep plum	.15	.15
124	A15	9p blue	.15	.15
125	A16	1a violet bl	.15	.15
126	A17	2a green ('52)	.15	.15
127	A18	2a6p green	.15	.15
128	A18	3a sal pink ('52)	.15	.15
129	A18	3a6p brown orange	.15	.15
130	A16	4a vermilion	.15	.15
131	A18	8a lt blue ('52)	.15	.15
132	A19	1r rose violet	.25	.15
133	A19	2r yel green	.55	.25
134	A19	5r ultramarine	1.75	.85
135	A19	10r aquamarine	3.25	1.65
		Nos. 122-135 (14)	7.30	4.40

Map of Burma and Monument — A21

1953, Jan. 4 Perf. 14
| 136 | A21 | 14p green | .15 | .15 |

Perf. 13

Size: 36½x26mm
| 137 | A21 | 20p salmon pink | .15 | .15 |
| 138 | A21 | 25p ultramarine | .15 | .15 |

Fifth anniversary of independence.
For surcharge see No. 166.

Types of 1949

Designs: 2p, Dancer. 3p, Musician. 20p, Spinning. 25p, Royal Palace. 30p, Cutting teak. 50p, Plowing rice field.

1954, Jan. 4 Perf. 14x13½, 13, 14
139	A15	1p brown orange	.15	.15
140	A15	2p plum	.15	.15
141	A15	3p blue	.15	.15
142	A16	5p ultramarine	.15	.15
143	A18	10p yel green	.15	.15
144	A17	15p green	.15	.15
145	A18	20p vermilion	.15	.15
146	A18	25p lt red org	.15	.15
147	A16	30p vermilion	.15	.15
148	A19	50p blue	.24	.15
149	A19	1k rose violet	.50	.15
150	A19	2k green	1.00	.15
151	A19	5k ultramarine	2.75	.15
152	A19	10k light blue	5.00	.26
		Nos. 139-152 (14)	10.84	2.21

For overprints and surcharges see Nos. 163-165, 173-175, O68-O79, O80-O81, O83, O85, O87.

Peace Pagoda, Monks' Hostels and Meeting-cave A22

Designs: 10p, Sangha (community) of Cambodia. 15p, Council meeting. 50p, Sangha of Thailand. 1k, Sangha of Ceylon. 2k, Sangha of Laos.

1954 Typo. Perf. 13
153	A22	10p deep blue	.15	.15
154	A22	15p deep claret	.15	.15
155	A22	35p dark brown	.15	.15
156	A22	50p green	.16	.15
157	A22	1k carmine	.32	.16
158	A22	2k violet	.60	.40
		Nos. 153-158 (6)	1.53	1.16

6th Buddhist Council, Rangoon, 1954-56.

Marble Markers of 5th Buddhist Council A23

Designs: 40p, Thatbyinnyu Pagoda. 60p, Shwedagon Pagoda, Rangoon. 1.25k, Aerial View of 6th Buddhist Council, Yegu.

Perf. 11x11½

1956, May 24 Litho. Unwmk.
159	A23	20p blue & gray olive	.15	.15
160	A23	40p blue & brt yel grn	.15	.15
161	A23	60p green & lemon	.16	.15
162	A23	1.25k gray blue & yel	.32	.20
		Nos. 159-162 (4)	.78	.65

2500th anniv. of the Buddhist Era.

Nos. 146, 149-150 Surcharged or Overprinted

မြန်မာ့လာ-နှင့်တရာ ၁၇၁-၁၇၁ 15 P ၁၅ပ

1959, Nov. 9 Wmk. 254 Perf. 13, 14
163	A18	15p on 25p lt red org	.15	.15
164	A19	1k rose violet	.30	.16
165	A19	2k green	.55	.45
		Nos. 163-165 (3)	1.00	.76

Centenary of Mandalay, former capital.
The two lines of overprint are 4mm apart on No. 163; 7mm on Nos. 164-165.

No. 136 Surcharged:

၁၅ိ

1961, June Perf. 14
| 166 | A21 | 15p on 14p green | .32 | .16 |

Children — A24

Unwmk.

1961, Dec. 11 Litho. Perf. 13
| 167 | A24 | 15p claret & rose claret | .15 | .15 |

15th anniversary of UNICEF.

Runner with Torch — A25

Soccer, Pole Vault and Shot Put — A26

Designs: 50p, Women runners. 1k, Hurdling, weight lifting, boxing, bicycling and swimming.

1961, Dec. 11 Photo. Perf. 14x13
168	A25	15p red & ultra	.15	.15
169	A26	25p dk green & ocher	.15	.15
170	A26	50p vio blue & pink	.20	.15
171	A25	1k brt green & yel	.35	.25
		Nos. 168-171 (4)	.85	.70

2nd South East Asia Peninsular Games, Rangoon.

Map and Flag of Burma — A27

Wmk. 254

1963, Mar. 2 Engr. Perf. 13
| 172 | A27 | 15p red | .20 | .15 |

First anniversary of new government.

Nos. 143 and 148 Overprinted in Violet or Red: "FREEDOM FROM HUNGER"

1963, Mar. 21 Litho.
| 173 | A18 | 10p yel green (V) | .15 | .15 |
| 174 | A18 | 50p blue (R) | .20 | .15 |

FAO "Freedom from Hunger" campaign.

No. 145 Overprinted အလုပ်သမားနေ့ ၁၉၆၃

1963, May 1
| 175 | A18 | 20p vermilion | .15 | .15 |

Issued for May Day.

White-browed Fantail — A28

Indian Roller — A29

Birds: 20p, Red-whiskered bulbul. 25p, Crested serpent eagle. 50p, Sarus crane. 1k, Malabar pied hornbill. 2k, Lineated kalij pheasant. 5k, Green peafowl.

Unwmk.

1964, Apr. 16 Photo. Perf. 13
Size: 25x21mm
176	A28	1p gray	.15	.15
177	A28	2p carmine rose	.15	.15
178	A28	3p blue green	.15	.15

Size: 22x26½mm
179	A29	5p violet blue	.15	.15
180	A29	10p orange brn	.15	.15
181	A29	15p olive	.15	.15

Size: 35x25mm
| 182 | A28 | 20p rose & brn | .16 | .15 |

Size: 27x36½mm, 36½x27mm
183	A29	25p yel & brown	.20	.15
184	A29	50p red, blk & gray	.50	.15
185	A29	1k gray, ind & yel	1.00	.15
186	A28	2k pale ol, ind & red	2.00	.32
187	A29	5k citron, dk bl & red	4.75	.65
		Nos. 176-187 (12)	9.51	2.47

See Nos. 197-208. For overprints see Nos. O82, O84, O86, O88-O93, O94-O115.

BURMA

ITU Emblem, Old and New Communication Equipment — A30

1965, May 17   Litho.   Perf. 15
Size: 32x22mm
188 A30 20p bright pink .... .15 .15

Perf. 13
Size: 34x24½mm
189 A30 50p dull green .... .25 .25
Centenary of the ITU.

ICY Emblem A31

1965, July 1   Unwmk.   Perf. 13
190 A31 5p violet blue .... .15 .15
191 A31 10p brown orange .... .15 .15
192 A31 15p olive .... .15 .15
　　Nos. 190-192 (3) .... .45 .45
International Cooperation Year.

Rice Farmer — A32
Cogwheel and Hammer — A33 

1966, Mar. 2
193 A32 15p multicolored .... .15 .15
Issued for Farmers' Day.

1967, May 1   Litho.   Unwmk.
194 A33 15p lt blue, yel & black .... .15 .15
Issued for Labor Day, May 1.

Aung San, Tractor and Farmers A34

1968, Jan. 4   Unwmk.   Perf. 13
195 A34 15p sky blue, black & ocher .... .15 .15
20th anniversary of independence.

Largest Burmese Pearl — A35

1968, Mar. 4   Litho.   Perf. 13½x13
196 A35 15p blue, ultra, gray & yel .... .15 .15
Burmese pearl industry.

Bird Types of 1964 in Changed Sizes;
Designs as Before
Unwmk.

1968, July 1   Photo.   Perf. 14
Size: 21x17mm
197 A28 1p gray .... .15 .15
198 A28 2p carmine rose .... .15 .15
199 A28 3p blue green .... .15 .15

Size: 23½x28mm
200 A29 5p violet blue .... .15 .15
201 A29 10p orange brown .... .15 .15
202 A29 15p olive .... .15 .15
Size: 38½x21, 21x38½mm
203 A28 20p rose & brown .... .15 .15
204 A29 25p yel & brown .... .16 .15
205 A29 50p ver, blk, & gray .... .32 .15
206 A29 1k gray, ind & yel .... .65 .15
207 A28 2k dull cit, ind & red .... 1.40 .24
208 A29 5k yel, dk blue & red .... 3.25 .55
　　Nos. 197-208 (12) 6.83 2.29
For overprints see Nos. O92-O102.

Wheat — A36

1969, Mar. 2   Litho.   Perf. 13
209 A36 15p blue, emerald & yel .... .15 .15
Issued for Peasant's Day.

ILO Emblem A37

1969, Oct. 29   Photo.   Wmk. 254
210 A37 15p dk blue grn & gold .... .15 .15
211 A37 50p dp carmine & gold .... .15 .15
50th anniv. of the ILO.

Soccer — A38

Designs: 25p, Runner, horiz. 50p, Weight lifter. 1k, Women's volleyball.

Perf. 12½x13, 13x12½
1969, Dec. 1   Litho.   Wmk. 254
212 A38 15p brt olive & multi .... .15 .15
213 A38 25p brown & multi .... .15 .15
214 A38 50p brt green & multi .... .25 .15
215 A38 1k blue, yel grn & blk .... .45 .30
　　Nos. 212-215 (4) .... 1.00 .75
5th South East Asia Peninsular Games, Rangoon.

Burmese Flags and Marching Soldiers — A39

1970, Mar. 27   Perf. 13
216 A39 15p multicolored .... .15 .15
Issued for Armed Forces Day.

Solar System and UN Emblem A40

1970, June 26   Photo.   Unwmk.
217 A40 15p lt ultra & multi .... .15 .15
25th anniversary of the United Nations.

Scroll, Marchers, Peacock Emblem A41

Designs: 25p, Students' boycott demonstration. 50p, Banner and marchers at Shwedagon Camp.

1970, Nov. 23   Litho.   Perf. 13x13½
218 A41 15p ultra & multi .... .15 .15
219 A41 25p multicolored .... .15 .15
220 A41 50p lt blue & multi .... .24 .15
　　Nos. 218-220 (3) .... .54 .45
50th National Day (Students' 1920 uprising).

Workers, Farmers, Technicians — A42

15p, Burmese of various races, & flags. 25p, Hands holding document. 50p, Red party flag.

1971, June 28   Litho.   Perf. 13½
221 A42 5p blue & multi .... .15 .15
222 A42 15p blue & multi .... .15 .15
223 A42 25p blue & multi .... .15 .15
224 A42 50p blue & multi .... .22 .15
　a. Souvenir sheet of 4, #221-224 .... .45 .45
　　Nos. 221-224 (4) .... .67 .60
1st Congress of Burmese Socialist Program Party.

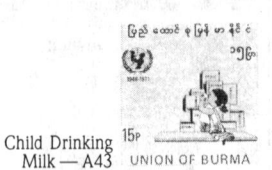

Child Drinking Milk — A43

UNICEF, 25th Anniv.: 50p, Marionettes.

1971, Dec. 11   Perf. 14½
225 A43 15p lt ultra & multi .... .15 .15
226 A43 50p emerald & multi .... .30 .15

Aung San, Independence Monument, Pinlon — A44

Union Day, 25th Anniv.: 50p, Bogyoke Aung San and people in front of Independence Monument. 1k, Map of Burma with flag pointing to Pinlon, vert.

1972, Feb. 12   Perf. 14
227 A44 15p ocher & multi .... .15 .15
228 A44 50p blue & multi .... .24 .15
229 A44 1k green, ultra & red .... .40 .20
　　Nos. 227-229 (3) .... .79 .50

Burmese and Double Star A45

1972   Litho.   Perf. 14
230 A45 15p bister & multi .... .15 .15
Revolutionary Council, 10th anniversary.

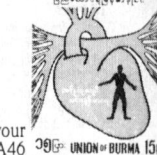

"Your Heart is your Health" — A46

1972, Apr. 7   Perf. 14x14½
231 A46 15p yellow, red & black .... .15 .15
World Health Day.

Burmese of Various Ethnic Groups A47

1973, Feb. 12   Litho.   Perf. 14
232 A47 15p multicolored .... .15 .15
1973 census.

Casting Vote — A48

Natl. Referendum: 10p, Voters holding map of Burma. 15p, Farmer & soldier holding ballots.

Perf. 14x14½, 14½x14
1973, Dec. 15   Litho.
233 A48 5p deep org & black .... .15 .15
234 A48 10p blue & multi .... .15 .15
235 A48 15p blue & multi, vert. .... .15 .15
　　Nos. 233-235 (3) .... .45 .45

Open-air Meeting A49

Designs: 15p, Regional flags. 1k, Scales of justice and Burmese emblem.

1974, Mar. 2   Photo.   Perf. 14
Size: 80x26mm
236 A49 15p blue & multi .... .15 .15
Size: 37x25mm
237 A49 50p blue & multi .... .20 .15
238 A49 1k lt blue, bis & blk .... .40 .20
　　Nos. 236-238 (3) .... .75 .50
First meeting of People's Parliament.

Messenger Bird and UPU Emblem A50

UPU Cent.: 20p, Mother reading letter to child, vert. 50p, Simulated block of stamps, vert. 1k, Burmese doll, vert. 2k, Mailman delivering letter to family.

1974, May 22
239 A50 15p grn, lt grn & org .... .15 .15
240 A50 20p multicolored .... .15 .15
241 A50 50p green & multi .... .22 .15
242 A50 1k ultra & multi .... .48 .20
243 A50 2k blue & multi .... .95 .50
　　Nos. 239-243 (5) 1.95 1.20

Children A51

Man and Woman A52

BURMA

Designs: 3p, Girl. 5p, 15p, Man and woman. 10p, Children (like 1p). 50p, Woman with fan. 1k, Seated woman. 5k, Drummer.

Perf. 13, 13x13½ (#248-251)

1974-78   **Photo.**
244	A51	1p rose & lilac rose		.15	.15
245	A51	3p dk brown & pink		.15	.15
246	A51	5p pink & violet		.15	.15
246A	A51	10p Prus blue ('76)		.15	.15
247	A51	15p lt green & olive ('75)		.15	.15
248	A52	20p lt blue & multi		.15	.15
249	A52	50p ocher & multi		.24	.15
250	A52	1k brt rose & multi		.48	.28
251	A52	5k ol green & multi		2.00	1.40
		Nos. 244-251 (9)		3.62	2.73

For different country names see Nos. 298-303.

IWY Emblem, Woman and Globe — A53

IWY: 2k, Symbolic flower, globe and IWY emblem, vert.

1975, Dec. 15   **Photo.**   **Perf. 13½**
252	A53	50p green & black		.18	.15
253	A53	2k black & blue		.70	.48

Burmese with Raised Fists — A54

Constitution Day: 50p, Demonstrators with banners and emblem. 1k, People and map of Burma, emblem.

1976, Jan. 3   **Perf. 14**
254	A54	20p blue & black		.15	.15
255	A54	50p blue, blk & brn		.22	.15

Size: 56x20mm
256	A54	1k blue & multi		.45	.20
		Nos. 254-256 (3)		.82	.50

Students, Campaign Emblem A55

Abacus A56

Intl. Literacy Year: 50p, Campaign emblem. 1k, Emblem, book and globe.

1976, Sept. 8   **Photo.**   **Perf. 14**
257	A55	10p salmon & black		.15	.15
258	A56	15p blue grn & multi		.15	.15
259	A56	50p ultra, org & blk		.24	.15
260	A55	1k multicolored		.60	.30
		Nos. 257-260 (4)		1.14	.75

Steam Locomotive — A57

Diesel Train Emerging from Tunnel — A58

Cent. of Burma's Railroad: 20p, Early train and oxcart. 25p, Old and new trains approaching station. 50p, Railroad bridge.

1977, May 1   **Perf. 13½**
261	A57	15p multicolored		.15	.15

Size: 38x26, 26x38mm
262	A57	20p multicolored		.15	.15
263	A57	25p multicolored		.15	.15
264	A57	50p multicolored		.26	.15
265	A58	1k multicolored		.52	.25
		Nos. 261-265 (5)		1.23	.85

Karaweik Pagoda A59

Design: 1k, Karaweik Pagoda, front view.

1977
266	A59	50p light brown		.20	.15

Size: 78x25mm
267	A59	1k multicolored		.35	.25

Jade Dragon — A60

Precious Jewelry: 20p, Gold bird with large pearl. 50p, Hand holding pearl necklace with pendant. 1k, Gold dragon, horiz.

1978   **Photo.**   **Perf. 13**
268	A60	15p green & yel grn		.15	.15
269	A60	25p multicolored		.15	.15
270	A60	50p multicolored		.30	.20

Size: 55x20mm
Perf. 14
271	A60	1k multicolored		.50	.30
		Nos. 268-271 (4)		1.10	.80

Satellite over Map of Asia — A61

1979, Feb., 12   **Photo.**   **Perf. 13**
272	A61	25p multicolored		.15	.15

IYC Emblem in Map of Burma — A62

Weather Balloon, WMO Emblem — A63

1979, Dec.   **Photo.**   **Perf. 13½**
273	A62	25p multicolored		.16	.15
274	A62	50p multicolored		.32	.16

International Year of the Child.

1980, Mar. 23   **Photo.**   **Perf. 13½**
275	A63	25p shown		.16	.15
276	A63	50p Weather satellite, cloud		.32	.16

World Meteorological Day.

Weight Lifting, Olympic Rings A64

1980, Dec.   **Litho.**   **Perf. 14**
277	A64	20p shown		.15	.15
278	A64	50p Boxing		.20	.15
279	A64	1k Soccer		.40	.25
		Nos. 277-279 (3)		.75	.55

22nd Summer Olympic Games, Moscow, July 19-Aug. 3.

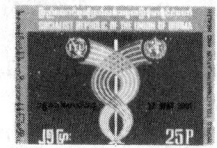

13th World Telecommunications Day — A65

1981, May 17   **Photo.**   **Perf. 13½**
280	A65	25p orange & black		.15	.15

World Food Day — A66

1981, Oct. 16   **Photo.**   **Perf. 13½**
281	A66	25p Livestock, produce		.15	.15
282	A66	50p Farmer, rice, produce		.20	.15
283	A66	1k Emblems		.40	.25
		Nos. 281-283 (3)		.75	.55

Intl. Year of the Disabled A67

1981, Dec. 12
284	A67	25p multicolored		.15	.15

World Communications Year — A68

1983, Sept. 15   **Litho.**   **Perf. 14½x14**
285	A68	15p pale blue & black		.15	.15
286	A68	25p dull lake & black		.15	.15
287	A68	50p pale brn, blk & lake		.30	.20
288	A68	1k buff, blk, beige & yel grn		.60	.40
		Nos. 285-288 (4)		1.20	.90

Fish, Ship, Globe, FAO Emblem — A69

1983, Oct. 16   **Photo.**   **Perf. 14½x14**
289	A69	15p brt blue, bister & blk		.15	.15
290	A69	25p yel grn, pale org & blk		.15	.15
291	A69	50p org, pale grn & blk		.30	.20
292	A69	1k yel, ultra & black		.60	.40
		Nos. 289-292 (4)		1.20	.90

World Food Day.

Stylized Trees, Hemispheres and Log — A70

1984, Oct. 16   **Perf. 14½x14**
293	A70	15p org, black & blue		.15	.15
294	A70	25p pale yel, blk & lt vio		.15	.15
295	A70	50p pale pink, blk & lt grn		.30	.20
296	A70	1k yel, blk, red & lt rose vio		.60	.40
		Nos. 293-296 (4)		1.20	.90

World Food Day.

Intl. Youth Year — A71

1985, Oct. 15   **Perf. 14x14½**
297	A71	15p multicolored		.15	.15

Types of 1974
Inscribed: Union of Burma

1989   **Photo.**   **Perf. 13½**
298	A51	15p olive & lt green		.15	.15
299	A52	50p violet & brown		.25	.25
300	A52	1k multicolored		.52	.52
		Nos. 298-300 (3)		.92	.92

Issued: 15p, June 26; 50p, June 12; 1k, Sept. 6.

Inscribed: Union of Myanmar

1990   **Photo.**   **Perf. 13½**
301	A51	15p olive & lt green		.15	.15
301A	A51	20p			
302	A52	50p violet & brown		.25	.25
303	A52	1k multicolored		.52	.52

Issued: 15p, May 26; 50p, May 12.

Fountain, Natl. Assembly Park — A74

Illustration reduced.

1990, May 27   **Litho.**   **Perf. 14½x14**
304	A74	1k multicolored		.52	.52

State Law and Order Restoration Council.

A75    A76

1990, Dec. 20   **Litho.**   **Perf. 14x14½**
305	A75	2k multicolored		.82	.82

UN Development Program, 40th anniv.

1991, Jan. 26
306	A76	50p Nawata ruby		.28	.28

Painting of Freedom Fighters — A77

Bronze Statue — A78

1992, Jan. 4   **Litho.**   **Perf. 14x14½**
307	A77	50p multicolored		.20	.20
308	A78	2k multicolored		.80	.80

BURMA

A79 — 50p — National Sports Festival
A80 — 50p — World Campaign Against AIDS

1992, Apr. 10 Litho. Perf. 14x14½
309 A79 50p multicolored .52 .52
National Sports Festival.

1992, Dec. 1 Litho. Perf. 14x14½
310 A80 50p red .35 .35
World Campaign Against AIDS.

A81 — 50p — Background Color
A82 — K10 — Artifacts

1992, Dec. 5 Litho. Perf. 14x14½
Background Color
311 A81 50p pink .20 .20
312 A81 1k yellow .42 .42
313 A81 3k orange 1.25 1.25
314 A81 5k green 2.05 2.05
  Nos. 311-314 (4) 3.92 3.92
Intl. Conference on Nutrition, Rome.

1993, Sept. 1 Litho. Perf. 14x14½
315 A82 5k Bird 1.65 1.65
316 A82 10k shown 3.25 3.25

A83 — 50p — Natl. Assembly

1993, Jan. 1 Litho. Perf. 14x14½
317 A83 50p multicolored .16 .16
318 A83 3k multicolored 1.00 1.00

A84 — K3 — Equestrian Festival

1993, Oct. 23 Litho. Perf. 14½x14
319 A84 3k multicolored 1.00 1.00

Have you found a typo or other error in this catalogue? Inform the editors via our web site or e-mail
sctcat@scottonline.com

A85 — K4
A86 — K3

1994, June 5 Litho. Perf. 14
320 A85 4k multicolored 1.50 1.50
Environment day.

1994, Sept. 15 Litho. Perf. 14
321 A86 3k multicolored 1.25 1.25
Union of Solidarity & Development, 1st anniv.

A87 — 50p — Armed Forces, 50th Anniv.

1995, Mar. 27 Litho. Perf. 14½x14
322 A87 50p multicolored .22 .22

A88 — K2
A89 — 50p

1995, June 26 Litho. Perf. 14
323 A88 2k multicolored .80 .80
Prevent drug abuse.

1995, Oct. 17 Litho. Perf. 14x14½
324 A89 50p multicolored .40 .40
Myanmar motion pictures, 60th anniv.

A90 — K4
A91 — 50p

1995, Oct. 24
325 A90 4k UN, 50th Anniv. 2.00 2.00

1995, Nov. 1
326 A91 50p pink & multi .25 .25
327 A91 2k green & multi 1.00 1.00
University of Yangon (Rangoon), 75th anniv.

A92 — Visit Myanmar Year

Designs: 50p, Couple in boat on Inlay Lake with food bowl for Buddha, Buddhist monks. 4k, Decorated royal barge on Kandawgyi (Royal Lake), Yangoon. 5k, Royal moat, entrance of Yadanabon (Mandalay), vert.

Perf. 14½x14, 14x14½
1996, Mar. 1 Litho.
328 A92 50p multicolored .20 .20
329 A92 4k multicolored 1.75 1.75
330 A92 5k multicolored 2.20 2.20
  Nos. 328-330 (3) 4.15 4.15

A93 — K1 — UNICEF, 50th Anniv.

Stylized designs: 1k, Mother breastfeeding. 2k, Vaccinating child. 4k, Girls going to school.

1996, Dec. 11 Litho. Perf. 14x14½
331 A93 1k multicolored .40 .40
332 A93 2k multicolored .85 .85
333 A93 4k multicolored 1.70 1.70
  Nos. 331-333 (3) 2.95 2.95

A94 — K2 — Intl. Letter Writing Week

Designs: 2k, Men in canoe. 5k, Stylized figures forming pyramid, flag, map, vert.

1996, Oct. 7 Perf. 14½x14, 14x14½
334 A94 2k multicolored .85 .85
335 A94 5k multicolored 2.00 2.00

A95 — K2
A96 — K2

1997, July 24 Litho. Perf. 14x14½
336 A95 1k blue & multi .40 .40
337 A95 2k yellow & multi .85 .85
Assoc. of Southeast Asian Nations (ASEAN), 30th anniv.

1998 Litho. Perf. 14x14½
338 A96 2k multicolored .90 .90
Independence, 50th anniv.

A97 — K5 — Musical Instruments

1998 Litho. Perf. 13
339 A97 5k Xylophone 1.90 1.90
Issued: 5k, 8/28/98. Numbers have been reserved for additional values in this set.

OFFICIAL STAMPS

BURMA

Stamps of India, 1926-34, Overprinted in Black

SERVICE

1937 Wmk. 196 Perf. 14
O1 A46 3p gray .40 .20
O2 A71 ½a green 2.25 .25
O3 A68 9p dark green 1.50 .40
O4 A72 1a dark brown 1.50 .25
O5 A49 2a vermilion 2.25 .55
O6 A57 2a6p buff 2.25 .90
O7 A52 4a olive grn 1.50 .90
O8 A53 6a bister 2.25 3.50
O9 A54 8a red violet 1.40 1.00
O10 A55 12a claret 1.40 1.75

BURMA

Overprinted **SERVICE**

O11 A56 1r green & brown 11.00 3.25
O12 A56 2r buff & car rose 20.00 17.50
O13 A56 5r dk vio & ultra 47.50 32.50
O14 A56 10r car & green 140.00 85.00
  Nos. O1-O14 (14) 235.20 147.90
For overprint see No. 1N27.

Regular Issue of 1938 Overprinted in Black **SERVICE**

Perf. 13½x14, 13, 13½
1939 Wmk. 254
O15 A1 3p violet .15 .15
O16 A1 6p ultramarine .15 .15
O17 A1 9p yel green 3.25 .15
O18 A2 1a brown violet .15 .15
O19 A2 1½a turquoise green 3.00 .15
O20 A2 2a carmine .80 .15
O21 A2 4a slate blue 3.50 .15

Overprinted **SERVICE**

O22 A3 2a6p rose lake 16.00 2.50
O23 A6 8a slate green 16.00 3.00
O24 A7 1r brt ultra & dk vio 25.00 3.00
O25 A7 2r dk vio & red brn 30.00 5.00
O26 A8 5r car & dull vio 27.50 32.50
O27 A8 10r gray grn & brn 80.00 42.50
  Nos. O15-O27 (13) 205.50 89.80
For overprints see Nos. 1N12-1N16, 1N31-1N36, 1NO1.

Catalogue values for unused stamps in this section, from this point to the end of the section, are for Never Hinged items.

Nos. 51-56, 60 Overprinted Like Nos. O15-O21

1946 Perf. 13½x14
O28 A1 3p brown .15 .15
O29 A1 6p violet .15 .15
O30 A1 9p dull green .15 .15
O31 A2 1a deep blue .15 .15
O32 A2 1½a salmon .15 .15
O33 A2 2a rose lake .15 .15
O34 A2 4a rose lilac .15 .15

Nos. 57, 61-65 Ovptd. Like Nos. O22-O27
Perf. 13, 13½
O35 A3 2a6p greenish blue .15 .15
O38 A6 8a deep magenta .15 1.50
O39 A7 1r dp mag & dk vio .75 2.25
O40 A7 2r salmon & red brn 5.00 20.00
O41 A8 5r red brn & dk grn 10.00 22.50
O42 A8 10r dk violet & car 17.50 35.00
  Nos. O28-O42 (13) 34.60 82.45

Nos. O28 to O42 Overprinted in Black

1947
O43 A1 3p brown .15 .15
O44 A1 6p violet .15 .15
O45 A1 9p dull green .15 .15
O46 A2 1a deep blue .15 .15
O47 A2 1½a salmon .15 .15

BURMA

O48 A2	2a rose lake	.15	.15
O49 A3	2a6p greenish bl	.15	.15
O50 A2	4a rose lilac	3.00	1.25
O51 A6	8a dp magenta	3.50	2.25
O52 A7	1r dp mag & dk vio	6.50	2.25
O53 A7	2r sal & red brn	12.50	9.00
O54 A8	5r red brn & dk grn	17.50	17.50
O55 A8	10r dk vio & car	25.00	25.00
Nos. O43-O55 (13)		69.05	58.30

The overprint is slightly larger on Nos. O49 and O51 to O55. The Burmese characters read "Interim Government."

Issues of the Republic

Nos. 102 to 106 and 109 to 115 Overprinted in Carmine or Black

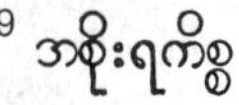

a. Overprint 13mm long.
b. Overprint 15mm long.

1949 Unwmk. Perf. 12½, 13

O56 A15(a)	3p ultra (C)	.15	.15
O57 A15(a)	6p green (C)	.15	.15
O58 A15(a)	9p carmine	.15	.15
O59 A16(a)	1a red orange	.15	.15
O60 A17(a)	2a orange	.15	.15
O61 A18(b)	3a6p dk sl grn (C)	.15	.15
O62 A16(a)	4a chocolate	.15	.15
O63 A18(b)	8a carmine	.20	.15
O64 A19(b)	1r blue green (C)	.35	.25
O65 A19(b)	2r dp blue (C)	.65	.40
O66 A19(b)	5r chocolate	1.65	1.25
O67 A19(b)	10r orange red	3.25	2.50
Nos. O56-O67 (12)		7.15	5.60

Same Overprint in Black on Nos. 139-142, 144-152

1954-57 Perf. 14x13½, 13, 14 Wmk. 254

O68 A15(a)	1p brown org	.15	.15
O69 A15(a)	2p plum	.15	.15
O70 A15(a)	3p blue	.15	.15
O71 A16(a)	5p ultra	.15	.15
O72 A17(a)	15p green	.15	.15
O72A A18(b)	20p ver ('57)	.15	.15
O73 A18(b)	25p lt red org	.15	.15
O74 A16(a)	30p vermilion	.15	.15
O75 A18(b)	50p blue	.20	.15
O76 A19(b)	1k rose violet	.40	.15
O77 A19(b)	2k green	.85	.20
O78 A19(b)	5k ultra	1.65	.30
O79 A19(b)	10k light blue	3.25	.45
Nos. O68-O79 (13)		7.55	2.45

No. 141 Ovptd. **Service**

1964 Litho. Perf. 14

| O80 A15 | 3p blue | 10.00 | 7.00 |

Nos. 139, 141-142, 144, 177-179, 181, 183 Ovptd.

1964-65 Overprint: 11½mm

O81 A15	1p brown orange	3.00	.75
O82 A28	2p carmine rose ('65)	2.50	.60
O83 A15	3p blue	3.00	.75
O84 A28	3p blue green ('65)	2.50	.60
O85 A28	5p ultramarine	3.00	.75
O86 A28	5p violet blue ('65)	2.50	.60
O87 A17	15p green	3.00	.75
O88 A28	15p olive ('65)	2.50	.60
O89 A29	25p yel & brn ('65)	2.60	.60
Nos. O81-O89 (9)		24.60	6.00

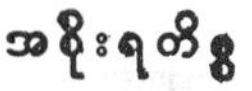

#176-178 Ovptd. #181 Ovptd.

1966 Overprint: 15mm

O90 A28	1p black		
O91 A28	2p carmine rose		
O92 A28	3p blue green		

Overprint: 12mm

| O93 A28 | 15p olive | | |

Nos. 176-179, 181-187 Overprinted in Black or Red

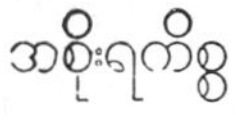

1967 Unwmk. Photo. Perf. 13

Overprint: 15mm
Size: 25x21mm

O94 A28	1p gray	.15	.15
O95 A28	2p carmine rose	.15	.15
O96 A28	3p blue green	.15	.15

Size: 22x26½mm

| O97 A29 | 5p violet blue | .15 | .15 |
| O98 A29 | 15p olive | .15 | .15 |

Size: 35x25mm

| O99 A28 | 20p rose & brown | .15 | .15 |

Size: 27x36½mm, 36½x27mm

O100 A29	25p yel & brown (R)	.15	.15
O101 A29	50p red, blk & gray	.26	.15
O102 A29	1k gray, ind & yel	.52	.15
O103 A28	2k pale ol, ind & red (R)	1.10	.30
O104 A29	5k cit, dk bl & red (R)	2.75	.65
Nos. O94-O104 (11)		5.68	2.30

Similar Overprint on Nos. 197-200, 202-208 in Black or Red

1968 Unwmk. Perf. 14
Size: 21x17mm
Overprint: 13mm

O105 A28	1p gray	.15	.15
O106 A28	2p carmine rose	.15	.15
O107 A28	3p blue green	.15	.15

Size: 23½x28mm
Overprint: 15mm

| O108 A29 | 5p violet blue | .15 | .15 |
| O109 A29 | 15p olive | .15 | .15 |

Size: 38½x21mm, 21x38½mm
Overprint: 14mm

O110 A28	20p rose & brn	.15	.15
O111 A29	25p yel & brown (R)	.15	.15
O112 A29	50p ver, blk & gray	.26	.15
O113 A29	1k gray, ind & yel (R)	.52	.15
O114 A28	2k dl cit, ind & red (R)	1.10	.24
O115 A29	5k yel, dk bl & red (R)	2.75	.55
Nos. O105-O115 (11)		5.68	2.14

OCCUPATION STAMPS

Issued by Burma Independence Army (in conjunction with Japanese occupation officials)

Stamps of Burma, 1937-40, Overprinted in Blue, Black Blue, Black or Red

Henzada Issue
#1, 3, 5 Overprinted in Blue or Black

Henzada Type I

1942, May Wmk. 196 Perf. 14

1N1 A46	3p slate	5.00	7.50
1N2 A68	9p dark green	17.50	17.50
1N3 A49	2a vermilion	50.00	75.00

On 1938-40 George VI Issue
Perf. 13½x14
Wmk. 254

1N4 A1	1p red orange	150.00	87.50
1N5 A1	3p violet	17.50	35.00
1N6 A1	6p ultra	15.00	30.00
1N7 A1	9p yel green	200.00	
1N8 A2	1a brown violet	5.00	7.50
1N9 A2	1½a turq green	12.50	17.50
1N10 A2	2a carmine	15.00	17.50
1N11 A2	4a slate blue	30.00	37.50

On Official Stamps of 1939

1N12 A1	3p violet	50.00	62.50
1N13 A1	6p ultra	45.00	62.50
1N14 A2	1½a turq green	65.00	87.50
1N15 A2	2a carmine	150.00	150.00
1N16 A2	4a slate blue	200.00	250.00

Authorities believe this overprint was officially applied only to postal stationery and that the adhesive stamps existing with it were not regularly issued. It has been called "Henzada Type II."

Myaungmya Issue
1937 George V Issue Overprinted in Black

Myaungmya Type I

1942, May Wmk. 196 Perf. 14

| 1N25 A68 | 9p dk green | 50.00 | 62.50 |
| 1N26 A70 | 3a6p deep blue | 25.00 | 32.50 |

On Official Stamp of 1937, No. O8

| 1N27 A53 | 6a bister | 50.00 | 62.50 |

On 1938-40 George VI Issue
Perf. 13½x14
Wmk. 254

1N28 A1	9p yel green	100.00	125.00
1N29 A2	1a brown vio	175.00	225.00
1N30 A2	4a sl blue (blk ovpt. over red)	100.00	125.00

On Official Stamps of 1939

1N31 A1	3p violet	15.00	15.00
1N32 A1	6p ultra	7.50	10.00
1N33 A2	1a brown vio	7.50	10.00
1N34 A2	1½a turq green	400.00	
1N35 A2	2a carmine	15.00	20.00
1N36 A2	4a slate blue	12.50	17.50

1938-40 George VI Issue Overprinted

Myaungmya Type II

1942, May

1N37 A1	3p violet	12.50	20.00
1N38 A1	6p ultra	25.00	30.00
1N39 A1	9p yel green	10.00	15.00
1N40 A2	1a brown vio	10.00	12.50
1N41 A2	2a carmine	15.00	20.00
1N42 A2	4a slate blue	15.00	25.00

Myaungmya Type III

Nos. 30-31 Overprinted

| 1N43 A7 | 1r brt ultra & dk vio | 150.00 | |
| 1N44 A7 | 2r dk vio & red brn | 110.00 | |

Pyapon Issue

No. 5 and 1938-40 George VI Issue Overprinted

1942, May

1N45 A1	6p ultra	75.00	
1N46 A2	1a brown vio	65.00	50.00
1N47 A49	2a vermilion	75.00	
1N48 A2	2a carmine	45.00	62.50
1N49 A2	4a slate blue	150.00	200.00
Nos. 1N45-1N49 (5)		410.00	

Counterfeits of the peacock overprints exist.

OCCUPATION OFFICIAL STAMP

Myaungmya Issue
Burma No. O23 Overprinted in Black

1942, May Wmk. 254 Perf. 13

| 1NO1 A6 | 8a slate green | 50.00 | 62.50 |

Overprint characters translate: "Office use." Two types of overprint differ mainly in base of peacock which is either 5mm or 8mm.

ISSUED UNDER JAPANESE OCCUPATION

Yano Seal — OS1

Wmk. ABSORBO DUPLICATOR and Outline of Elephant in Center of Sheet Handstamped

1942, June 1 Perf. 12x11
Without Gum

| 2N1 OS1 | 1(a) vermilion | 30.00 | 37.50 |

This stamp is the handstamped impression of the personal chop or seal of Shizuo Yano, chairman of the committee appointed to re-establish the Burmese postal system. It was prepared in Rangoon on paper captured from the Burma Government Offices. Not every stamp shows a portion of the watermark.

Farmer Plowing — OS2

Vertically Laid Paper
Without Gum
Wmk. ELEPHANT BRAND and Outline of Trumpeting Elephant Covering Several Stamps

1942, June 15 Litho. Perf. 11x12

| 2N2 OS2 | 1a scarlet | 20.00 | 25.00 |

See illustration OS4.

Same, Surcharged with New Value

1942, Oct. 15

| 2N3 OS2 | 5c on 1a scarlet | 12.50 | 10.50 |

Rice Harvest — A83
General Nogi — A84 
Power Plant — A85 
Admiral Togo — A86 
Diamond Mountains, Korea — A89 
Meiji Shrine, Tokyo — A90 
Yomei Gate, Nikko — A91 
Mount Fuji and Cherry Blossoms — A94 
Torii of Miyajima Shrine — A96

BURMA — BURUNDI

Stamps of Japan, 1937-42, Handstamp Surcharged with New Value in Black

1942, Sept.   Wmk. 257   Perf. 13

2N4	A83	¼a on 1s fawn	12.50	15.00
2N5	A84	½a on 2s crim	12.50	15.00
2N6	A85	¾a on 3s green	20.00	20.00
2N7	A86	1a on 5s brn lake	17.50	20.00
2N8	A89	3a on 7s dp green	30.00	32.50
2N9	A90	4a on 4s dk green	22.50	27.50
a.		4a on 4s + 2s dk green (#B5)	75.00	87.50
2N10	A90	8a on 8s dk pur & pale vio	100.00	100.00
a.		Red surcharge	140.00	150.00
2N11	A91	1r on 10s lake	12.50	15.00
2N12	A94	2r on 20s ultra	30.00	35.00
a.		Red surcharge	37.50	37.50
2N13	A96	5r on 30s pck bl	10.00	10.00
a.		Red surcharge	15.00	15.00
		Nos. 2N4-2N13 (10)	267.50	290.00

Numerous double, inverted, etc., surcharges exist.

Re-surcharged in Black

1942, Oct. 15

2N14	A83	1c on ¼a on 1s	25.00	25.00
2N15	A84	2c on ½a on 2s	25.00	25.00
2N16	A85	3c on ¾a on 3s	30.00	32.50
a.		"3C." in blue	75.00	100.00
2N17	A86	5c on 1a on 5s	40.00	40.00
a.		"3C." in blue	125.00	
2N18	A89	10c on 3a on 7s	45.00	45.00
2N19	A86	15c on 4a on 4s	19.50	10.50
2N20	A90	20c on 8a on 8s (#2N10)	110.00	90.00
a.		On #2N10a	125.00	100.00
		Nos. 2N14-2N20 (7)	285.50	268.00

No. 2N16a was issued in the Shan States. Done locally, numerous different handstamps of each denomination can exist.

Stamps of Japan, 1937-42, Handstamp Surcharged with New Value in Black

1942, Oct. 15

2N21	A83	1c on 1s fawn	10.00	12.50
2N22	A84	2c on 2s crim	17.50	20.00
2N23	A85	3c on 3s green	20.00	25.00
a.		"3C." in blue	75.00	87.50
2N24	A86	5c on 5s brn lake	20.00	25.00
a.		"5C." in violet	87.50	100.00
2N25	A89	10c on 7s dp grn	25.00	30.00
2N26	A86	15c on 4s dk grn	10.00	12.50
2N27	A90	20c on 8s dk pur & pale vio	70.00	60.00
		Nos. 2N21-2N27 (7)	172.50	185.00

Nos. 2N23a and 2N24a were issued in the Shan States.

Burma State Government Crest — OS3

1943, Feb. 15   Unwmk.   Litho.   Perf. 12
Without Gum

2N29	OS3	5c carmine	10.00	12.50
a.		Imperf.	12.50	15.00

This stamp was intended to be used to cover the embossed George VI envelope stamp and generally was sold affixed to such envelopes. It is also known used on private envelopes.

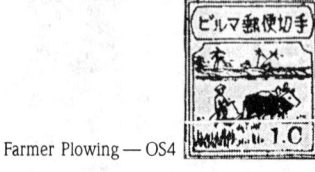

Farmer Plowing — OS4

1943, Mar.   Typo.
Without Gum

2N30	OS4	1c deep orange	1.00	1.00
2N31	OS4	2c yel green	1.00	1.50
2N32	OS4	3c blue	1.00	1.00
a.		Laid paper	10.00	10.00
2N33	OS4	5c carmine	.50	.65
a.		Small "5c"	3.00	4.00
b.		Imperf.		
2N34	OS4	10c violet brown	.75	.90
2N35	OS4	15c red violet	.25	.25
a.		Laid paper	10.00	
2N36	OS4	20c dull purple		.75
2N37	OS4	30c blue green	.25	.75
		Nos. 2N30-2N37 (8)	5.00	6.80

Small "c" in Nos. 2N34 to 2N37.

Burmese Soldier Carving "Independence" OS5

Farmer Rejoicing OS6

Boy with Burmese Flag — OS7

Hyphen-hole Perf., Pin-Perf. x Hyphen-hole Perf.
1943, Aug. 1   Typo.

2N38	OS5	1c orange	1.00	2.00
a.		Perf. 11	3.50	4.00
2N39	OS6	3c blue	1.00	2.00
a.		Perf. 11	3.50	4.00
2N40	OS7	5c rose	1.00	2.00
a.		Perf. 11	3.50	4.00
		Nos. 2N38-2N40 (3)	3.00	6.00

Declaration of the independence of Burma by the Ba Maw government, Aug. 1, 1943.

Burmese Girl Carrying Water Jar — OS8

Elephant Carrying Teak Log — OS9

Watch Tower of Mandalay Palace — OS10

1943, Oct. 1   Litho.   Perf. 12½

2N41	OS8	1c dp salmon	17.00	10.00
2N42	OS8	2c yel green	.60	1.25
2N43	OS8	3c violet	.60	1.00
2N44	OS9	5c rose	.65	1.00
2N45	OS9	10c blue	.80	.60
2N46	OS9	15c vermilion	.80	1.00
2N47	OS9	20c yel green	.80	1.25
2N48	OS9	30c brown	.80	1.25
2N49	OS10	1r vermilion	.35	3.00
2N50	OS10	2r violet	.35	5.00
		Nos. 2N41-2N50 (10)	22.75	25.35

No. 2N49 exists imperforate. Canceled to order copies of Nos. 2N42-2N50 same values as unused.

Bullock Cart — OS11

Shan Woman — OS12

1943, Oct. 1   Perf. 12½

2N51	OS11	1c brown	22.50	35.00
2N52	OS11	2c yel green	22.50	35.00
2N53	OS11	3c violet	20.00	30.00
2N54	OS11	5c ultra	4.50	12.00
2N55	OS12	10c blue	20.00	35.00
2N56	OS12	20c rose	22.50	35.00
2N57	OS12	30c brown	22.50	35.00
		Nos. 2N51-2N57 (7)	134.50	217.00

For use only in the Shan States. Perak No. N34 also used in Shan States. CTO's ½ used value.

Surcharged in Black

1944, Nov. 1

2N58	OS11	1c brown	4.00	5.00
2N59	OS11	2c yel green	.20	1.25
		Inverted surcharge	150.00	200.00
2N60	OS11	3c violet	2.50	4.00
2N61	OS11	5c ultra	1.25	1.50
2N62	OS12	10c blue	2.50	3.50
2N63	OS12	20c rose	.60	1.50
2N64	OS12	30c brown	.75	1.50
		Nos. 2N58-2N64 (7)	11.80	18.25

Top line of surcharge reads: "Bama naing ngan daw" (Burma State). Bottom line repeats denomination in Burmese. Surcharge applied when the Shan States came under Burmese government administration, Dec. 24, 1943. CTO's same value as unused.

BURUNDI

bü-'rün-dē

LOCATION — Central Africa, adjoining the ex-Belgian Congo Republic, Rwanda and Tanzania
GOVT. — Republic
AREA — 10,759 sq. mi.
POP. — 4,920,000 (est. 1983)
CAPITAL — Bujumbura

Burundi was established as an independent country on July 1, 1962. With Rwanda, it had been a UN trusteeship territory (Ruanda-Urundi) administered by Belgium. A military coup overthrew the monarchy November 28, 1966.

100 Centimes = 1 Franc

Catalogue values for all unused stamps in this country are for Never Hinged items.

Flower Issue of Ruanda-Urundi, 1953 Overprinted:

Royaume du Burundi

Perf. 11½
1962, July 1   Unwmk.   Photo.
Flowers in Natural Colors

1	A27	25c dk grn & dull org	.15	.15
2	A27	40c green & salmon	.15	.15
3	A27	60c blue grn & pink	.20	.15
4	A27	1.25fr dk green & blue	7.00	6.50
5	A27	1.50fr vio & apple grn	.30	.25
6	A27	5fr dp plum & lt bl grn	.42	.30
7	A27	7fr dk green & fawn	.85	.55
8	A27	10fr dp plum & pale ol	1.20	.85
		Nos. 1-8 (8)	10.27	8.90

Animal Issue of Ruanda-Urundi, 1959-61 with Similar Overprint or Surcharge in Black or Violet Blue

Size: 23x33mm, 33x23mm

9	A29	10c brn, crim & blk brn	.15	.15
10	A30	20c gray, ap grn & blk	.15	.15
11	A29	40c mag, blk & gray grn	.15	.15
12	A30	50c grn, org yel & brn	.15	.15
a.		Larger overprint and bar	.15	.15
13	A29	1fr brn, ultra & blk	.15	.15
14	A30	1.50fr blk, gray & org (VB)	.15	.15
15	A29	2fr grnsh bl, ind & brn	.15	.15
16	A30	3fr brn, dp car & blk	.15	.15
17	A30	3.50fr on 3fr brn, dp car & blk	.15	.15
18	A30	4fr on 10fr multi ("XX" 6mm wide)	.15	.15
a.		"XX" 4mm wide	.45	.45
19	A30	5fr multicolored	.15	.15
20	A30	6.50fr red, org yel & brn	.25	.18
21	A30	8fr bl, mag & blk	.30	.22
a.		Violet blue overprint	.65	.65
22	A30	10fr multicolored	.30	.30

Size: 45x26½mm

23	A30	20fr multicolored	.65	.65
24	A30	50fr multi (ovpt. bars 2mm wide)	1.25	1.10
a.		Overprint bars 4mm wide	1.90	1.10
		Nos. 9-24 (16)	4.40	4.10

On #12a, "Burundi" is 13mm long; bar is continuous line across sheet. On #12, "Burundi" is 10mm; bar is 29mm. #12a was issued in 1963.

Two types of overprint exist on 10c, 40c, 1fr and 2fr: I, "du" is below "me"; bar 22½mm. II, "du" below "oy"; bar 20mm.

The 50c and 3fr exist in two types, besides the larger 50c overprint listed as No. 12: I, "du" is closer to "Royaume" than to "Burundi"; bar is less than 29mm; wording is centered above bar. II, "du" is closer to "Burundi"; bar is more than 30mm; wording is off-center leftward.

King Mwami Mwambutsa IV and Royal Drummers — A1

Flag and Arms of Burundi — A2

Design: 2fr, 8fr, 50fr, Map of Burundi and King.

Unwmk.
1962, Sept. 27   Photo.   Perf. 14

25	A1	50c dull rose car & dk brn	.15	.15
26	A2	1fr dk green, red & emer	.15	.15
27	A1	2fr brown ol & dk brn	.15	.15
28	A1	3fr vermilion & dk brn	.22	.15
29	A2	4fr Prus blue, red & emer	.18	.15
30	A1	8fr violet & dk brn	.32	.15
31	A1	10fr brt green & dk brn	.50	.15
32	A2	20fr brown, red & emer	1.25	.40
33	A1	50fr brt pink & dk brn	2.25	.40
		Nos. 25-33 (9)	5.17	1.65

Burundi's independence, July 1, 1962.
See #47-50. For overprints see #45-46, 51-52.

Ruanda-Urundi Nos. 151-152 Surcharged:

HOMMAGE A DAG HAMMARSKJÖLD 3.50F ROYAUME DU BURUNDI

Photogravure, Surcharge Engraved
1962, Oct. 31   Perf. 11½
Inscription in French

34	A31	3.50fr on 3fr ultra & red	.15	.15
35	A31	6.50fr on 3fr ultra & red	.20	.15
36	A31	10fr on 3fr ultra & red	.30	.25

Inscription in Flemish

37	A31	3.50fr on 3fr ultra & red	.15	.15
38	A31	6.50fr on 3fr ultra & red	.20	.15
39	A31	10fr on 3fr ultra & red	.30	.25
		Nos. 34-39 (6)	1.30	1.10

Dag Hammarskjold, Secretary General of the United Nations, 1953-61.

King Mwami Mwambutsa IV, Map of Burundi and Emblem — A3

1962, Dec. 10   Photo.   Perf. 14

40	A3	8fr yel, bl grn & blk brn	.65	.15
41	A3	50fr gray grn, bl grn & blk brn	1.75	.35

WHO drive to eradicate malaria.
Stamps of type A3 without anti-malaria emblem are listed as Nos. 27, 30 and 33.

BURUNDI

Sowing Seed over Africa — A4

1963, Mar. 21			Perf. 14x13	
42	A4	4fr olive & dull pur	.15	.15
43	A4	8fr dp org & dull pur	.15	.15
44	A4	15fr emerald & dull pur	.20	.15
		Nos. 42-44 (3)	.50	.45

FAO "Freedom from Hunger" campaign.

Nos. 27 and 33 Overprinted in Dark Green

1963, June 19		Unwmk.	Perf. 14	
45	A1	2fr brn olive & dk brn	1.65	1.25
46	A1	50fr brt pink & dk brn	1.90	1.25

Conquest and peaceful use of outer space.

Types of 1962 Inscribed: "Premier Anniversaire" in Red or Magenta

1963, July 1			Photo.	
47	A1	4fr olive, red & emer (R)	.15	.15
48	A1	8fr orange & dk brn (M)	.15	.15
49	A1	10fr lilac & dk brn (M)	.20	.15
50	A2	20fr gray, red & emer (R)	.40	.25
		Nos. 47-50 (4)	.90	.70

First anniversary of independence.

Nos. 26 and 32 Surcharged in Brown

1963, Sept. 24		Unwmk.	Perf. 14	
51	A2	6.50fr on 1fr multi	.38	.15
52	A2	15fr on 20fr multi	.75	.25

Red Cross Flag over Globe with Map of Africa — A5

1963, Sept. 26			Perf. 14x13	
53	A5	4fr emer, car & gray	.15	.15
54	A5	8fr brn ol, car & gray	.25	.15
55	A5	10fr blk, car & gray	.38	.18
56	A5	20fr lilac, car & gray	.75	.30
		Nos. 53-56 (4)	1.53	.78

Centenary of International Red Cross. See No. B7.

"1962", Arms of Burundi, UN and UNESCO Emblems — A6

UN Agency Emblems: 8fr, ITU. 10fr, World Meteorological Organization. 20fr, UPU. 50fr, FAO.

1963, Nov. 4		Unwmk.	Perf. 14	
57	A6	4fr yel, ol grn & blk	.15	.15
58	A6	8fr pale lil, Prus bl & blk	.15	.15
59	A6	10fr blue, lil & blk	.20	.15
60	A6	20fr yel grn, grn & blk	.35	.15
61	A6	50fr yel, red brn & blk	.90	.30
a.		Souvenir sheet of 2	3.00	3.00
		Nos. 57-61 (5)	1.75	.90

1st anniv. of Burundi's admission to the UN. No. 61a contains two imperf. stamps with simulated perforations similar to Nos. 60-61. The 20fr stamp shows the FAO and the 50fr the WMO emblems.

UNESCO Emblem, Scales and Map — A7

Designs: 3.50fr, 6.50fr, Scroll, scales and "UNESCO." 10fr, 20fr, Abraham Lincoln, broken chain and scales.

1963, Dec. 10		Litho.	Perf. 14x13½	
62	A7	50c pink, lt bl & blk	.15	.15
63	A7	1.50fr org, lt bl & blk	.15	.15
64	A7	3.50fr fawn, lt grn & blk	.18	.15
65	A7	6.50fr lt vio, lt grn & blk	.18	.15
66	A7	10fr blue, bis & blk	.30	.15
67	A7	20fr pale brn, ocher, bl & blk	.60	.18
		Nos. 62-67 (6)	1.53	.93

15th anniv. of the Universal Declaration of Human Rights and the cent. of the American Emancipation Proclamation (Nos. 66-67).

Ice Hockey — A8   Impala — A9

Designs: 3.50fr, Women's figure skating. 6.50fr, Torch. 10fr, Men's speed skating. 20fr, Slalom.

		Unwmk.		
1964, Jan. 25		Photo.	Perf. 14	
68	A8	50c olive, blk & gold	.15	.15
69	A8	3.50fr lt brown, blk & gold	.15	.15
70	A8	6.50fr pale gray, blk & gold	.38	.15
71	A8	10fr gray, blk & gold	.50	.15
72	A8	20fr tan, blk & gold	1.00	.32
		Nos. 68-72 (5)	2.18	.92

Issued to publicize the 9th Winter Olympic Games, Innsbruck, Jan. 29-Feb. 9, 1964.
A souvenir sheet contains two stamps (10fr+5fr and 20fr+5fr) in tan, black and gold.

Canceled to Order
Starting about 1964, values in the used column are for "canceled to order" stamps. Postally used copies sell for much more.

1964		Litho.	Perf. 14x13, 13x14	

Animals: 1fr, 5fr, Hippopotamus, horiz. 1.50fr, 10fr, Giraffe. 2fr, 8fr, Cape buffalo, horiz. 3fr, 6.50fr, Zebra, horiz. 15fr, Defassa waterbuck. 20fr, Cheetah. 50fr, Elephant. 100fr, Lion.

Size: 21½x35mm, 35x21½mm

73	A9	50c multi	.15	.15
74	A9	1fr multi	.15	.15
75	A9	1.50fr multi	.15	.15
76	A9	2fr multi	.15	.15
77	A9	3fr multi	.18	.15
78	A9	3.50fr multi	.20	.15

Size: 26x42mm, 42x26mm

79	A9	5fr multi	.22	.15
80	A9	5fr multi	.28	.15
81	A9	6.50fr multi	.32	.15
82	A9	8fr multi	.40	.15
83	A9	10fr multi	.50	.15
84	A9	15fr multi	.65	.18

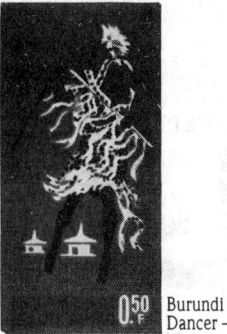

Perf. 14
Size: 53x33mm

85	A9	20fr multi	.85	.20
86	A9	50fr multi	2.25	.32
87	A9	100fr multi	4.00	.65
		Nos. 73-87, C1-C7 (22)	13.12	4.28

Burundi Dancer — A10

Designs: Various Dancers and Drummers.

		Unwmk.		
1964, Aug. 21		Litho.	Perf. 14	
88	A10	50c gold & emerald	.15	.15
89	A10	1fr gold & vio blue	.15	.15
90	A10	4fr gold & brt blue	.15	.15
91	A10	6.50fr gold & red	.20	.15
92	A10	10fr gold & brt blue	.30	.15
93	A10	15fr gold & emerald	.45	.15
94	A10	20fr gold & red	.65	.22
a.		Souvenir sheet of 3, #92-94	1.50	1.50
		Nos. 88-94 (7)	2.05	1.12

1965, Sept. 10		Dancers Multicolored		
88a	A10	50c silver & emerald	.15	.15
89a	A10	1fr silver & violet blue	.15	.15
90a	A10	4fr silver & bright blue	.15	.15
91a	A10	6.50fr silver & red	.15	.15
92a	A10	10fr silver & bright blue	.18	.15
93a	A10	15fr silver & emerald	.20	.18
94b	A10	20fr silver & red	.30	.30
c.		Souvenir sheet of 3, #92a-94b	1.50	1.50
		Nos. 88a-94b (7)	1.28	1.23

New York World's Fair, 1964-65.

Pope Paul VI and King Mwami Mwambutsa IV — A11

22 Sainted Martyrs — A12

4fr, 14fr, Pope John XXIII and King Mwami.

1964, Nov. 12		Photo.	Perf. 12	
95	A11	50c brt bl, gold & red brn	.15	.15
96	A12	1fr mag, gold & slate	.15	.15
97	A11	4fr pale rose lil, gold & brn	.18	.15
98	A12	8fr red, gold & brn	.18	.15
99	A11	14fr lt grn, gold & brn	.42	.15
100	A11	20fr red brn, gold & grn	.65	.30
		Nos. 95-100 (6)	1.73	1.05

Canonization of 22 African martyrs, 10/18/64.

Shot Put — A13   African Purple Gallinule — A14

Sports: 1fr, Discus. 3fr, Swimming. 4fr, Running. 6.50fr, Javelin, woman. 8fr, Hurdling. 10fr, Broad jump. 14fr, Diving, woman. 18fr, High jump. 20fr, Vaulting.
3fr, 8fr, 10fr, 18fr, 20fr are horiz.

1964, Nov. 18		Litho.	Perf. 14	
101	A13	50c olive & multi	.15	.15
102	A13	1fr brt pink & multi	.15	.15
103	A13	3fr multi	.15	.15
104	A13	4fr multi	.15	.15
105	A13	6.50fr multi	.15	.15
106	A13	8fr lt bl & multi	.16	.15
107	A13	10fr multi	.20	.15
108	A13	14fr multi	.26	.15
109	A13	18fr bister & multi	.32	.15
110	A13	20fr gray & multi	.35	.22
		Nos. 101-110 (10)	2.04	1.60

18th Olympic Games, Tokyo, Oct. 10-25, 1964. See No. B8.

1965		Unwmk.	Perf. 14	

Birds: 1fr, 5fr, Little bee eater. 1.50fr, 6.50fr, Secretary bird. 2fr, 8fr, Yellow-billed stork. 3fr, 10fr, Congo peacock. 3.50fr, 15fr, African anhinga. 20fr, Saddle-billed stork. 50fr, Abyssinian ground hornbill. 100fr, Crowned crane.

Birds in Natural Colors
Size: 21x35mm

111	A14	50c tan, grn & blk	.15	.15
112	A14	1fr pink, mag & blk	.15	.15
113	A14	1.50fr blue & blk	.15	.15
114	A14	2fr yel grn, dk grn & blk	.15	.15
115	A14	3fr yellow, brn & blk	.15	.15
116	A14	3.50fr yel grn, dk grn & blk	.15	.15

Size: 26x43mm

117	A14	4fr grn, dk grn & blk	.15	.15
118	A14	5fr pink, mag & blk	.15	.15
119	A14	6.50fr blue & blk	.15	.15
120	A14	8fr yel grn, dk grn & blk	.15	.15
121	A14	10fr yel, brn & blk	.20	.15
122	A14	15fr yel grn, dk grn & blk	.38	.15

Size: 33x53mm

123	A14	20fr rose lilac & blk	.50	.30
124	A14	50fr yellow, brn & blk	1.25	.20
125	A14	100fr green, yel & blk	2.75	.40
		Nos. 111-125 (15)	6.58	2.70

Issue dates: Nos. 111-116, Mar. 31. Nos. 117-122, Apr. 16. Nos. 123-125, Apr. 30.
For overprints see #174-184, C35A-C35I.

Relay Satellite and Morse Key — A15

Designs: 3fr, Telstar and old telephone handpiece. 4fr, Relay satellite and old wall telephone. 6.50fr, Orbiting Geophysical Observatory and radar screen. 8fr, Telstar II and headphones. 10fr, Sputnik II and radar aerial. 14fr, Syncom and transmission aerial. 20fr, Interplanetary Explorer and tracking aerial.

1965, July 3		Litho.	Perf. 13	
126	A15	1fr multi	.15	.15
127	A15	3fr multi	.15	.15
128	A15	4fr multi	.15	.15
129	A15	6.50fr multi	.15	.15
130	A15	8fr multi	.15	.15
131	A15	10fr multi	.18	.15
132	A15	14fr multi	.25	.15
133	A15	20fr multi	.30	.18
		Nos. 126-133 (8)	1.48	1.23

Cent. of the ITU. Perf. and imperf. souv. sheets of 2 contain Nos. 131, 133. Size: 120x86mm. Value, both sheets, $7.50.

BURUNDI

Globe and ICY Emblem — A16

Designs: 4fr, Map of Africa and UN development emblem. 8fr, Map of Asia and Colombo Plan emblem. 10fr, Globe and UN emblem. 18fr, Map of the Americas and Alliance for Progress emblem. 25fr, Map of Europe and EUROPA emblems. 40fr, Map of Outer Space and satellite with UN wreath.

1965, Oct. 1		Litho.	Perf. 13	
134	A16	1fr ol green & multi	.15	.15
135	A16	4fr dull blue & multi	.15	.15
136	A16	8fr pale yellow & multi	.15	.15
137	A16	10fr lilac & multi	.16	.15
138	A16	18fr salmon & multi	.25	.15
139	A16	25fr gray & multi	.50	.15
140	A16	40fr blue & multi	.75	.16
a.		Souvenir sheet of 3, #138-140	1.65	1.65
		Nos. 134-140 (7)	2.11	1.06

International Cooperation Year.

Protea A17

Flowers: 1fr, 5fr, Crossandra. 1.50fr, 6.50fr, Ansellia. 2fr, 8fr, Thunbergia. 3fr, 10fr, Schizoglossum. 3.50fr, 15fr, Dissotis. 4fr, 20fr, Protea. 50fr, Gazania. 100fr, Hibiscus. 150fr, Markhamia.

1966		Unwmk.	Perf. 13½	
		Size: 26x26mm		
141	A17	50c multi	.15	.15
142	A17	1fr multi	.15	.15
143	A17	1.50fr multi	.15	.15
144	A17	2fr multi	.15	.15
145	A17	3fr multi	.15	.15
146	A17	3.50fr multi	.15	.15
		Size: 31x31mm		
147	A17	4fr multi	.15	.15
148	A17	5fr multi	.15	.15
149	A17	6.50fr multi	.15	.15
150	A17	8fr multi	.15	.15
151	A17	10fr multi	.15	.15
152	A17	15fr multi	.30	.15
		Size: 39x39mm		
153	A17	20fr multi	.38	.15
154	A17	50fr multi	1.00	.25
155	A17	100fr multi	1.90	.38
156	A17	150fr multi	2.75	.55
		Nos. 141-156,C17-C25 (25)	12.02	4.75

Issue dates: Nos. 141-147, Feb. 28; Nos. 148-153, May 18; Nos. 154-156, June 15.

For overprints see Nos. 159-173, C27-C35.

Souvenir Sheets

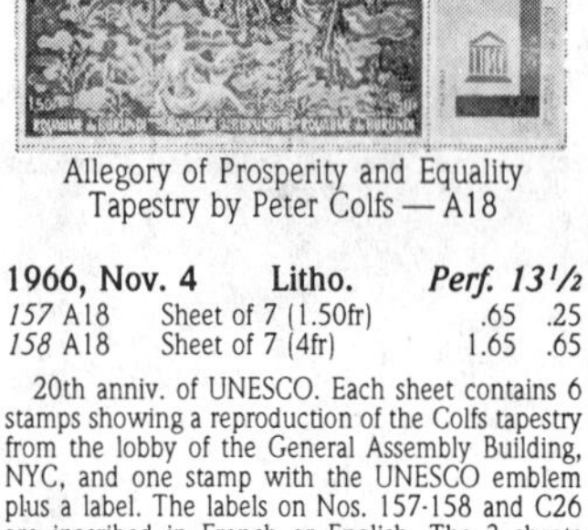

Allegory of Prosperity and Equality Tapestry by Peter Colfs — A18

1966, Nov. 4		Litho.	Perf. 13½	
157	A18	Sheet of 7 (1.50fr)	.65	.25
158	A18	Sheet of 7 (4fr)	1.65	.65

20th anniv. of UNESCO. Each sheet contains 6 stamps showing a reproduction of the Colfs tapestry from the lobby of the General Assembly Building, NYC, and one stamp with the UNESCO emblem plus a label. The labels on Nos. 157-158 and C26 are inscribed in French or English. The 3 sheets with French inscription have light blue marginal border. The 3 sheets with English inscription have pink border. See No. C26.

Republic

Nos. 141-152, 154-156 Overprinted

REPUBLIQUE DU BURUNDI

1967		Litho.	Perf. 13½	
		Size: 26x26mm		
159	A17	50c multi	.15	.15
160	A17	1fr multi	.15	.15
161	A17	1.50fr multi	.15	.15
162	A17	2fr multi	.15	.15
163	A17	3fr multi	.15	.15
164	A17	3.50fr multi	.15	.15
		Size: 31x31mm		
165	A17	4fr multi	.80	.30
166	A17	5fr multi	.16	.15
167	A17	6.50fr multi	.20	.15
168	A17	8fr multi	.25	.15
169	A17	10fr multi	.32	.15
170	A17	15fr multi	.38	.15
		Size: 39x39mm		
171	A17	50fr multi	3.75	1.25
172	A17	100fr multi	6.25	2.50
173	A17	150fr multi	5.00	2.25
		Nos. 159-173,C27-C35 (24)	29.24	10.98

Nos. 111, 113, 116, 118-125 Overprinted "REPUBLIQUE DU BURUNDI" and Horizontal Bar

1967		Litho.	Perf. 14	
		Birds in Natural Colors		
		Size: 21x35mm		
174	A14	50c multi	1.25	.65
175	A14	1.50fr blue & black	.15	.15
176	A14	3.50fr multi	.15	.15
		Size: 26x43mm		
177	A14	5fr multi	.15	.15
178	A14	6.50fr blue & black	.15	.15
179	A14	8fr multi	.18	.15
180	A14	10fr yel, brn & blk	.32	.15
181	A14	15fr multi	.65	.15
		Size: 33x53mm		
182	A14	20fr multi	2.00	.38
183	A14	50fr multi	4.00	1.40
184	A14	100fr multi	6.00	2.75
		Nos. 174-184 (11)	15.00	6.23

Haplochromis Multicolor — A19

Various Tropical Fish.

1967		Photo.	Perf. 13½	
		Size: 42x19mm		
186	A19	50c multi	.15	.15
187	A19	1fr multi	.15	.15
188	A19	1.50fr multi	.15	.15
189	A19	2fr multi	.15	.15
190	A19	3fr multi	.15	.15
191	A19	3.50fr multi	.15	.15
		Size: 50x25mm		
192	A19	4fr multi	.16	.15
193	A19	5fr multi	.20	.15
194	A19	6.50fr multi	.25	.15
195	A19	8fr multi	.28	.15
196	A19	10fr multi	.32	.15
197	A19	15fr multi	.50	.15
		Size: 59x30mm		
198	A19	20fr multi	.65	.15
199	A19	50fr multi	1.40	.18
200	A19	100fr multi	3.00	.30
201	A19	150fr multi	4.25	.45
		Nos. 186-201,C46-C54 (25)	17.27	4.35

Issue Dates: Nos. 186-191, Apr. 4; Nos. 192-197, Apr. 28; Nos. 198-201, May 18.

Ancestor Figures, Ivory Coast — A20

African Art: 1fr, Seat of Honor, Southeast Congo. 1.50fr, Antelope head, Aribinda Region. 2fr, Buffalo mask, Upper Volta. 4fr, Funeral figures, Southwest Ethiopia.

1967, June 5		Photo.	Perf. 13½	
202	A20	50c silver & multi	.15	.15
203	A20	1fr silver & multi	.15	.15
204	A20	1.50fr silver & multi	.15	.15
205	A20	2fr silver & multi	.15	.15
206	A20	4fr silver & multi	.15	.15
		Nos. 202-206,C36-C40 (10)	1.84	1.60

Scouts on Hiking Trip — A21

Designs: 1fr, Cooking at campfire. 1.50fr, Lord Baden-Powell. 2fr, Boy Scout and Cub Scout giving Scout sign. 4fr, First aid.

1967, Aug. 9		Photo.	Perf. 13½	
207	A21	50c silver & multi	.15	.15
208	A21	1fr silver & multi	.15	.15
209	A21	1.50fr silver & multi	.15	.15
210	A21	2fr silver & multi	.15	.15
211	A21	4fr silver & multi	.15	.15
		Nos. 207-211,C41-C45 (10)	2.52	1.56

60th anniv. of the Boy Scouts and the 12th Boy Scout World Jamboree, Farragut State Park, Idaho, Aug. 1-9.

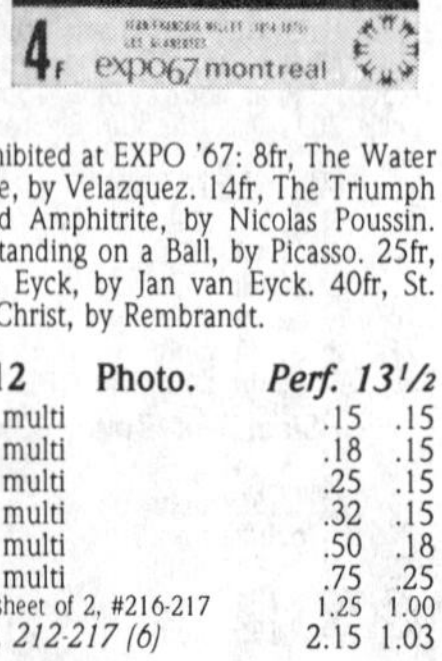

The Gleaners, by François Millet A22

Paintings Exhibited at EXPO '67: 8fr, The Water Carrier of Seville, by Velazquez. 14fr, The Triumph of Neptune and Amphitrite, by Nicolas Poussin. 18fr, Acrobat Standing on a Ball, by Picasso. 25fr, Marguerite van Eyck, by Jan van Eyck. 40fr, St. Peter Denying Christ, by Rembrandt.

1967, Oct. 12		Photo.	Perf. 13½	
212	A22	4fr multi	.15	.15
213	A22	8fr multi	.18	.15
214	A22	14fr multi	.25	.15
215	A22	18fr multi	.32	.15
216	A22	25fr multi	.50	.18
217	A22	40fr multi	.75	.25
a.		Souvenir sheet of 2, #216-217	1.25	1.00
		Nos. 212-217 (6)	2.15	1.03

EXPO '67 International Exhibition, Montreal, Apr. 28-Oct. 27. Printed in sheets of 10 stamps and 2 labels inscribed in French or English. No. 217a exists imperf.

Place de la Revolution and Pres. Michel Micombero — A23

Designs: 5fr, President Michel Micombero and flag. 14fr, Formal garden and coat of arms. 20fr, Modern building and coat of arms.

1967, Nov. 23			Perf. 13½	
218	A23	5fr multi	.15	.15
219	A23	14fr multi	.20	.15
220	A23	20fr multi	.30	.15
221	A23	30fr multi	.45	.22
		Nos. 218-221 (4)	1.10	.67

First anniversary of the Republic.

Madonna by Carlo Crivelli — A24

Designs: 1fr, Adoration of the Shepherds by Juan Bautista Mayno. 4fr, Holy Family by Anthony Van Dyck. 14fr, Nativity by Maitre de Moulins.

1967, Dec. 7		Photo.	Perf. 13½	
222	A24	1fr multi	.15	.15
223	A24	4fr multi	.15	.15
224	A24	14fr multi	.25	.15
225	A24	26fr multi	.60	.25
		Nos. 222-225 (4)	1.15	.70

Christmas 1967. Printed in sheets of 25 and one corner label inscribed "Noel 1967" and giving name of painting and painter.

Slalom — A25

10fr, Ice hockey. 14fr, Women's skating. 17fr, Bobsled. 26fr, Ski jump. 40fr, Speed skating. 60fr, Hand holding torch, and Winter Olympics emblem.

1968, Feb. 16		Photo.	Perf. 13½	
226	A25	5fr silver & multi	.15	.15
227	A25	10fr silver & multi	.20	.15
228	A25	14fr silver & multi	.25	.15
229	A25	17fr silver & multi	.30	.15
230	A25	26fr silver & multi	.50	.15
231	A25	40fr silver & multi	.75	.20
232	A25	60fr silver & multi	1.25	.20
		Nos. 226-232 (7)	3.40	1.10

Issued to publicize the 10th Winter Olympic Games, Grenoble, France, Feb. 6-18. Issued in sheets of 10 stamps and label.

BURUNDI

The Lacemaker, by Vermeer — A26

Paintings: 1.50fr, Portrait of a Young Man, by Botticelli. 2fr, Maja Vestida, by Goya, horiz.

1968, Mar. 29   Photo.   Perf. 13½
233	A26	1.50fr gold & multi	.15	.15
234	A26	2fr gold & multi	.15	.15
235	A26	4fr gold & multi	.15	.15
		Nos. 233-235,C59-C61 (6)	1.80	.98

Issued in sheets of 6.

Moon Probe — A27

Designs: 6fr, Russian astronaut walking in space. 8fr, Weather satellite. 10fr, American astronaut walking in space.

1968, May 15   Photo.   Perf. 13½   Size: 35x35mm
236	A27	4fr silver & multi	.15	.15
237	A27	6fr silver & multi	.15	.15
238	A27	8fr silver & multi	.20	.15
239	A27	10fr silver & multi	.22	.15
		Nos. 236-239,C62-C65 (8)	2.42	1.23

Issued to publicize peaceful space explorations.
A souvenir sheet contains one 25fr stamp in Moon Probe design and one 40fr in Weather Satellite design. Stamp size: 41x41mm. Value $2. Sheet exists imperf. Price $3.

Salamis Aethiops — A28

Butterflies: 1fr, 5fr, Graphium ridleyanus. 1.50fr, 2.50fr, Cymothoe. 2fr, 8fr, Charaxes eupale. 3fr, 10fr, Papilio bromius. 3.50fr, 15fr, Teracolus annae. 20fr, Salamis aethiops. 50fr, Papilio zonobia. 100fr, Danais chrysippus. 150fr, Salamis temora.

1968   Size: 30x33½mm
240	A28	50c gold & multi	.15	.15
241	A28	1fr gold & multi	.15	.15
242	A28	1.50fr gold & multi	.15	.15
243	A28	2fr gold & multi	.15	.15
244	A28	3fr gold & multi	.15	.15
245	A28	3.50fr gold & multi	.15	.15

Size: 33½x37½mm
246	A28	4fr gold & multi	.15	.15
247	A28	5fr gold & multi	.15	.15
248	A28	6.50fr gold & multi	.55	.15
249	A28	8fr gold & multi	.65	.15
250	A28	10fr gold & multi	.75	.15
251	A28	15fr gold & multi	.90	.15

Size: 41x46mm
252	A28	20fr gold & multi	1.50	.15
253	A28	50fr gold & multi	3.00	.15
254	A28	100fr gold & multi	5.00	.30
255	A28	150fr gold & multi	7.50	.60
		Nos. 240-255,C66-C74 (25)	30.85	4.30

Issue dates: Nos. 240-245, June 7; Nos. 246-251, June 28. Nos. 252-255, July 19.

Women, Along the Manzanares, by Goya — A29

Paintings: 7fr, The Letter, by Pieter de Hooch. 11fr, Woman Reading a Letter, by Gerard Terborch. 14fr, Man Writing a Letter, by Gabriel Metsu.

1968, Sept. 30   Photo.   Perf. 13½
256	A29	4fr multi	.15	.15
257	A29	7fr multi	.15	.15
258	A29	11fr multi	.20	.15
259	A29	14fr multi	.30	.15
		Nos. 256-259,C84-C87 (8)	2.74	1.23

International Letter Writing Week.

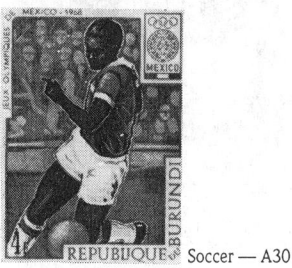

Soccer — A30

1968, Oct. 24
260	A30	4fr shown	.15	.15
261	A30	7fr Basketball	.15	.15
262	A30	13fr High jump	.18	.15
263	A30	24fr Relay race	.35	.15
264	A30	40fr Javelin	.60	.30
		Nos. 260-264,C88-C92 (10)	3.98	1.85

19th Olympic Games, Mexico City, Oct. 12-27. Printed in sheets of 8.

Virgin and Child, by Fra Filippo Lippi — A31

Paintings: 5fr, The Magnificat, by Sandro Botticelli. 6fr, Virgin and Child, by Albrecht Durer. 11fr, Madonna del Gran Duca, by Raphael.

1968, Nov. 26   Photo.   Perf. 13½
265	A31	3fr multi	.15	.15
266	A31	5fr multi	.15	.15
267	A31	6fr multi	.15	.15
268	A31	11fr multi	.22	.15
a.		Souvenir sheet of 4, #265-268	1.00	1.00
		Nos. 265-268,C93-C96 (8)	1.72	1.20

Christmas 1968. For overprints see Nos. 272-275, C100-C103.

WHO Emblem and Map of Africa — A32

1969, Jan. 22
269	A32	5fr gold, dk grn & yel	.15	.15
270	A32	6fr gold, vio & ver	.15	.15
271	A32	11fr gold, pur & red lil	.22	.15
		Nos. 269-271 (3)	.52	.45

20th anniv. of WHO in Africa.

Nos. 265-268 Overprinted in Silver

1969, Feb. 17   Photo.   Perf. 13½
272	A31	3fr multi	.15	.15
273	A31	5fr multi	.15	.15
274	A31	6fr multi	.15	.15
275	A31	11fr multi	.22	.15
		Nos. 272-275,C100-C103 (8)	2.00	1.27

Man's 1st flight around the moon by the US spacecraft Apollo 8, Dec. 21-27, 1968.

Map of Africa, and CEPT Emblem — A33

Designs: 14fr, Plowing with tractor. 17fr, Teacher and pupil. 26fr, Maps of Europe and Africa and CEPT (Conference of European Postal and Telecommunications Administrations) emblem, horiz.

1969, Mar. 12   Photo.   Perf. 13
276	A33	5fr multi	.15	.15
277	A33	14fr multi	.20	.15
278	A33	17fr multi	.25	.15
279	A33	26fr multi	.32	.15
		Nos. 276-279 (4)	.92	.60

5th anniv. of the Yaounde (Cameroun) Agreement, creating the European and African-Malgache Economic Community.

Resurrection, by Gaspard Isenmann — A34

Paintings: 14fr, Resurrection by Antoine Caron. 17fr, Noli me Tangere, by Martin Schongauer. 26fr, Resurrection, by El Greco.

1969, Mar. 24
280	A34	11fr gold & multi	.15	.15
281	A34	14fr gold & multi	.20	.15
282	A34	17fr gold & multi	.25	.15
283	A34	26fr gold & multi	.38	.15
a.		Souvenir sheet of 4, #280-283	1.50	1.50
		Nos. 280-283 (4)	.98	.60

Easter 1969.

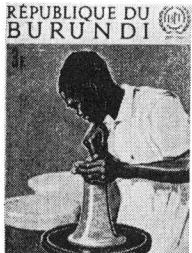

Potter — A35

ITU Emblem and: 5fr, Farm workers. 7fr, Foundry worker. 10fr, Woman testing corn crop.

1969, May 17   Photo.   Perf. 13½
284	A35	3fr multicolored	.15	.15
285	A35	5fr multicolored	.15	.15
286	A35	7fr multicolored	.15	.15
287	A35	10fr multicolored	.20	.15
		Nos. 284-287 (4)	.65	.60

50th anniv. of the ILO.

Industry and Bank's Emblem — A36

Designs (African Development Bank Emblem and): 17fr, Communications. 30fr, Education. 50fr, Agriculture.

1969, July 29   Photo.   Perf. 13½
288	A36	10fr gold & multi	.18	.15
289	A36	17fr gold & multi	.30	.15
290	A36	30fr gold & multi	.50	.15
291	A36	50fr gold & multi	.80	.25
a.		Souvenir sheet of 4, #288-291	1.90	1.90
		Nos. 288-291 (4)	1.78	.70

5th anniversary of the African Development Bank.

Girl Reading Letter, by Vermeer — A37

Paintings: 7fr, Graziella (young woman), by Auguste Renoir. 14fr, Woman writing a letter, by Gerard Terborch. 26fr, Galileo Galilei, painter unknown. 40fr, Ludwig van Beethoven, painter unknown.

1969, Oct. 24   Photo.   Perf. 13½
292	A37	4fr multicolored	.15	.15
293	A37	7fr multicolored	.15	.15
294	A37	14fr multicolored	.32	.15
295	A37	26fr multicolored	.55	.15
296	A37	40fr multicolored	.75	.20
a.		Souvenir sheet of 2, #295-296	1.75	1.75
		Nos. 292-296 (5)	1.92	.80

Intl. Letter Writing Week, Oct. 7-13.

Rocket Launching — A38

Moon Landing: 6.50fr, Rocket in space. 7fr, Separation of landing module from capsule. 14fr, 26fr, Landing module landing on moon. 17fr, Capsule in space. 40fr, Neil A. Armstrong leaving landing module. 50fr, Astronaut on moon.

1969, Nov. 6   Photo.   Perf. 13½
297	A38	4fr blue & multi	.15	.15
298	A38	6.50fr vio blue & multi	.22	.15
299	A38	7fr vio blue & multi	.22	.15
300	A38	14fr black & multi	.35	.20
301	A38	17fr vio blue & multi	.55	.25
		Nos. 297-301,C104-C106 (8)	3.64	1.95

Souvenir Sheet
302		Sheet of 3	3.00	3.00
a.	A38	26fr multicolored	.50	.50
b.	A38	40fr multicolored	.75	.75
c.	A38	50fr multicolored	1.00	1.00

See note after Algeria No. 427.

BURUNDI

Madonna and Child, by Rubens — A39

Paintings: 6fr, Madonna and Child with St. John, by Giulio Romano. 10fr, Magnificat Madonna, by Botticelli.

1969, Dec. 2		Photo.	
303	A39	5fr gold & multi	.15 .15
304	A39	6fr gold & multi	.15 .15
305	A39	10fr gold & multi	.25 .15
a.	A39	Souvenir sheet of 3, #303-305	.75 .75
		Nos. 303-305,C107-C109 (6)	2.33 1.03

Christmas 1969.

Sternotomis Bohemani A40

Designs: Various Beetles and Weevils.

1970		Perf. 13½	
		Size: 39x28mm	
306	A40	50c multicolored	.15 .15
307	A40	1fr multicolored	.15 .15
308	A40	1.50fr multicolored	.15 .15
309	A40	2fr multicolored	.15 .15
310	A40	3fr multicolored	.15 .15
311	A40	3.50fr multicolored	.15 .15
		Size: 46x32mm	
312	A40	4fr multicolored	.15 .15
313	A40	5fr multicolored	.15 .15
314	A40	6.50fr multicolored	.15 .15
315	A40	8fr multicolored	.20 .15
316	A40	10fr multicolored	.25 .15
317	A40	15fr multicolored	.38 .15
		Size: 52x36mm	
318	A40	20fr multicolored	.50 .15
319	A40	50fr multicolored	1.00 .18
320	A40	100fr multicolored	1.90 .35
321	A40	150fr multicolored	2.75 .50
		Nos. 306-321,C110-C118 (25)	19.11 4.78

Issue dates: Nos. 306-313, Jan. 20; Nos. 314-318, Feb. 17; Nos. 319-321, Apr. 3.

Jesus Condemned to Death — A41

Stations of the Cross, by Juan de Aranoa y Carredano: 1.50fr, Jesus carries His Cross. 2fr, Jesus falls the first time. 3fr, Jesus meets His mother. 3.50fr, Simon of Cyrene helps carry the cross. 4fr, Veronica wipes the face of Jesus. 5fr, Jesus falls the second time.

1970, Mar. 16		Photo.	Perf. 13½
322	A41	1fr gold & multi	.15 .15
323	A41	1.50fr gold & multi	.15 .15
324	A41	2fr gold & multi	.15 .15
325	A41	3fr gold & multi	.15 .15
326	A41	3.50fr gold & multi	.15 .15
327	A41	4fr gold & multi	.15 .15
328	A41	5fr gold & multi	.15 .15
a.		Souv. sheet of 7, #322-328 + label	.60 .60
		Nos. 322-328,C119-C125 (14)	3.10 2.25

Easter 1970.

Parade and EXPO '70 Emblem — A42

Designs (EXPO '70 Emblem and): 6.50fr, Aerial view. 7fr, African pavilions. 14fr, Pagoda, vert. 26fr, Recording pavilion and pool. 40fr, Tower of the Sun, vert. 50fr, Flags of participating nations.

1970, May 5		Photo.	Perf. 13½
329	A42	4fr gold & multi	.15 .15
330	A42	6.50fr gold & multi	.15 .15
331	A42	7fr gold & multi	.15 .15
332	A42	14fr gold & multi	.22 .15
333	A42	26fr gold & multi	.38 .15
334	A42	40fr gold & multi	.55 .15
335	A42	50fr gold & multi	.80 .20
		Nos. 329-335 (7)	2.40 1.10

EXPO '70 Intl. Exhibition, Osaka, Japan, Mar. 15-Sept. 13, 1970. See No. C126.

White Rhinoceros — A43

Designs, FAUNA: Camel, dromedary, okapi, addax, Burundi cow (2 stamps of each animal in 2 different poses). MAP OF THE NILE: Delta and pyramids, dhow, cataract, Blue Nile and crowned crane, Victoria Nile and secretary bird, Lake Victoria and source of Nile on Mt. Gikizi.

1970, July 8			Perf. 13½
336		Sheet of 18	7.00 1.50
a.		A43 7fr any single	.38 .15

Issued in sheets of 18 (3x6) stamps of different designs, to publicize the southernmost source of the Nile on Mt. Gikizi in Burundi. See No. C127.

Winter Wren, Firecrest, Skylark and Crested Lark — A44

Birds: 2fr, 3.50fr, 5fr, vert.; others horiz.

1970, Sept. 30		Photo.	Perf. 13½
		Stamp Size: 44x33mm	
337	A44	Block of 4	.60 .15
a.		2fr Northern shrike	.15
b.		2fr European starling	.15
c.		2fr Yellow wagtail	.15
d.		2fr Bank swallow	.15
338	A44	Block of 4	.90 .15
a.		3fr Winter wren	.20
b.		3fr Firecrest	.20
c.		3fr Skylark	.20
d.		3fr Crested lark	.20
339	A44	Block of 4	1.25 .15
a.		3.50fr Woodchat shrike	.30
b.		3.50fr Common rock thrush	.30
c.		3.50fr Black redstart	.30
d.		3.50fr Ring ouzel	.30
340	A44	Block of 4	1.50 .15
a.		4fr European Redstart	.35
b.		4fr Hedge sparrow	.35
c.		4fr Gray wagtail	.35
d.		4fr Meadow pipit	.35
341	A44	Block of 4	1.75 .15
a.		5fr Eurasian hoopoe	.40
b.		5fr Pied flycatcher	.40
c.		5fr Great reed warbler	.40
d.		5fr Eurasian kingfisher	.40
342	A44	Block of 4	2.00 .15
a.		6.50fr House martin	.50
b.		6.50fr Sedge warbler	.50
c.		6.50fr Fieldfare	.50
d.		6.50fr European Golden oriole	.50
		Nos. 337-342,C132-C137 (12)	38.50 3.30

Nos. 337-342 are printed in sheets of 16.

Library, UN Emblem — A45

Designs: 5fr, Students taking test, and emblem of University of Bujumbura. 7fr, Students in laboratory and emblem of Ecole Normale Superieure of Burundi. 10fr, Students with electron-microscope and Education Year emblem.

1970, Oct. 23			
343	A45	3fr gold & multi	.15 .15
344	A45	5fr gold & multi	.15 .15
345	A45	7fr gold & multi	.15 .15
346	A45	10fr gold & multi	.15 .15
		Nos. 343-346 (4)	.60 .60

Issued for International Education Year.

Pres. and Mrs. Michel Micombero — A46

Designs: 7fr, Pres. Michel Micombero and Burundi flag. 11fr, Pres. Micombero and Revolution Memorial.

1970, Nov. 28		Photo.	Perf. 13½
347	A46	4fr gold & multi	.15 .15
348	A46	7fr gold & multi	.15 .15
349	A46	11fr gold & multi	.20 .15
a.		Souvenir sheet of 3	.50 .50
		Nos. 347-349 (3)	.50 .45

4th anniv. of independence. No. 349a contains 3 stamps similar to Nos. 347-349, but inscribed "Poste Aerienne." Exists imperf.
See Nos. C140-C142.

Lenin with Delegates A47

Designs (Lenin, Paintings): 5fr, addressing crowd. 6.50fr, with soldier and sailor. 15fr, speaking from balcony. 50fr, Portrait.

1970, Dec. 31		Photo.	Perf. 13½
		Gold Frame	
350	A47	3.50fr dk red brown	.15 .15
351	A47	5fr dk red brown	.15 .15
352	A47	6.50fr dk red brown	.15 .15
353	A47	15fr dk red brown	.32 .15
354	A47	50fr dk red brown	1.10 .18
		Nos. 350-354 (5)	1.87 .78

Lenin's birth centenary (1870-1924).

Lion — A48

1971, Mar. 19		Photo.	Perf. 13½
		Size: 38x38mm	
355		Strip of 4	.35 .15
a.	A48	1fr Lion	.15
b.	A48	1fr Cape buffalo	.15
c.	A48	1fr Hippopotamus	.15
d.	A48	1fr Giraffe	.15
356		Strip of 4	.40 .15
a.	A48	2fr Hartebeest	.15
b.	A48	2fr Black rhinoceros	.15
c.	A48	2fr Zebra	.15
d.	A48	2fr Leopard	.15
357		Strip of 4	.50 .15
a.	A48	3fr Grant's gazelles	.15
b.	A48	3fr Cheetah	.15
c.	A48	3fr African white-backed vultures	.15
d.	A48	3fr Johnston's okapi	.15
358		Strip of 4	.75 .20
a.	A48	5fr Chimpanzee	.15
b.	A48	5fr Elephant	.15
c.	A48	5fr Spotted hyenas	.15
d.	A48	5fr Beisa	.15
359		Strip of 4	1.00 .4
a.	A48	6fr Gorilla	.25
b.	A48	6fr Gnu	.25
c.	A48	6fr Wart hog	.25
d.	A48	6fr Cape hunting dog	.25
360		Strip of 4	2.00 .4
a.	A48	11fr Sable antelope	.50
b.	A48	11fr Caracal lynx	.50
c.	A48	11fr Ostriches	.50
d.	A48	11fr Bongo	.50
		Nos. 355-360,C146-C151 (12)	24.25 3.4

For overprints and surcharges see Nos. C152 CB15-CB18.

The Resurrection, by Il Sodoma — A49

Paintings: 6fr, Resurrection, by Andrea del Castagno. 11fr, Noli me Tangere, by Correggio.

1971, Apr. 2			
361	A49	3fr gold & multi	.15 .15
362	A49	6fr gold & multi	.15 .15
363	A49	11fr gold & multi	.28 .15
a.		Souvenir sheet of 3, #361-363	.60 .6
		Nos. 361-363,C143-C145 (6)	1.30 .9

Easter 1971. No. 363a exists imperf.

Young Venetian Woman, by Dürer — A50

Dürer Paintings: 11fr, Hieronymus Holzschuher 14fr, Emperor Maximilian I. 17fr, Holy Family from Paumgartner Altar. 26fr, Haller Madonna 31fr, Self-portrait, 1498.

1971, Sept. 20			
364	A50	6fr multicolored	.15 .15
365	A50	11fr multicolored	.22 .15
366	A50	14fr multicolored	.38 .15
367	A50	17fr multicolored	.45 .22
368	A50	26fr multicolored	.65 .35
369	A50	31fr multicolored	.80 .5
a.		Souvenir sheet of 2, #368-369	1.60 1.60
		Nos. 364-369 (6)	2.65 1.42

International Letter Writing Week. Albrech Dürer (1471-1528), German painter and engraver. No. 369a exists imperf.

Nos. 364-369, 369a Overprinted in Black and Gold: "VIème CONGRES / DE L'INSTITUT INTERNATIONAL / DE DROIT D'EXPRESSION FRANCAISE"

1971, Oct. 8			
370	A50	6fr multicolored	.15 .15
371	A50	11fr multicolored	.22 .15
372	A50	14fr multicolored	.28 .15
373	A50	17fr multicolored	.35 .15
374	A50	26fr multicolored	.50 .15

BURUNDI

375 A50 31fr multicolored .65 .18
a. Souvenir sheet of 2 1.25 1.25
Nos. 370-375 (6) 2.15 .93

6th Congress of the Intl. Legal Institute of the French-speaking Area, Bujumbura, Aug. 10-19.

Madonna and Child, by Il Perugino — A51

Paintings of the Madonna and Child by: 5fr, Andrea del Sarto. 6fr, Luis de Morales.

1971, Nov. 2   Photo.   Perf. 13½

376 A51 3fr dk green & multi .15 .15
377 A51 5fr dk green & multi .15 .15
378 A51 6fr dk green & multi .15 .15
a. Souvenir sheet of 3, #376-378 .38 .38
Nos. 376-378,C153-C155 (6) 1.55 .95

Christmas 1971. No. 378a exists imperf.
For surcharges see #B49-B51, CB19-CB21.

Lunar Orbiter — A52

Designs: 11fr, Vostok. 14fr, Luna 1. 17fr, Apollo 11 astronaut on moon. 26fr, Soyuz 11. 40fr, Lunar Rover (Apollo 15).

1972, Jan. 15

379 A52 6fr gold & multi .18 .15
380 A52 11fr gold & multi .22 .15
381 A52 14fr gold & multi .28 .15
382 A52 17fr gold & multi .40 .20
383 A52 26fr gold & multi .40 .32
384 A52 40fr gold & multi .62 .32
a. Souvenir sheet of 6 2.25 1.25
Nos. 379-384 (6) 2.10 1.29

Conquest of space. See No. C156.
No. 384a contains one each of Nos. 379-384 inscribed "APOLLO 16."

Slalom and Sapporo '72 Emblem — A53

Designs (Sapporo '72 Emblem and): 6fr, Figure skating, pairs. 11fr, Figure skating, women's. 14fr, Ski jump. 17fr, Ice hockey. 24fr, Speed skating, men's. 26fr, Snow scooter. 31fr, Downhill skiing. 50fr, Bobsledding.

1972, Feb. 3

385 A53 5fr silver & multi .15 .15
386 A53 6fr silver & multi .15 .15
387 A53 11fr silver & multi .18 .15
388 A53 14fr silver & multi .22 .15
389 A53 17fr silver & multi .28 .15
390 A53 24fr silver & multi .38 .15
391 A53 26fr silver & multi .40 .15
392 A53 31fr silver & multi .50 .15
393 A53 50fr silver & multi .80 .20
Nos. 385-393 (9) 3.06 1.40

11th Winter Olympic Games, Sapporo, Japan, Feb. 3-13. Printed in sheets of 12. See No. C157.
Issued: #385-390, Feb. 1; #391-393, Feb. 21.

Ecce Homo, by Quentin Massys — A54

Paintings: 6.50fr, Crucifixion, by Rubens. 10fr, Descent from the Cross, by Jacopo da Pontormo. 18fr, Pieta, by Ferdinand Gallegos. 27fr, Trinity, by El Greco.

1972, Mar. 20   Photo.   Perf. 13½

394 A54 3.50fr gold & multi .15 .15
395 A54 6.50fr gold & multi .15 .15
396 A54 10fr gold & multi .15 .15
397 A54 18fr gold & multi .25 .15
398 A54 27fr gold & multi .65 .15
a. Souv. sheet of 5, #394-398 + label 1.50 1.25
Nos. 394-398 (5) 1.35 .75

Easter 1972. Printed in sheets of 8 with label.
No. 398a exists imperf.

Gymnastics, Olympic Rings and "Motion" A55

1972, May 19

399 A55 5fr shown .15 .15
400 A55 6fr Javelin .15 .15
401 A55 11fr Fencing .22 .15
402 A55 14fr Bicycling .25 .15
403 A55 17fr Pole vault .32 .15
Nos. 399-403,C158-C161 (9) 2.94 1.40

Souvenir Sheet

404 Sheet of 2 1.75 1.25
a. A55 31fr Discus .45 .45
b. A55 40fr Soccer .60 .60

20th Olympic Games, Munich, Aug. 26-Sept. 11.

Prince Rwagasore, Pres. Micombero, Burundi Flag, Drummers A56

Designs: 7fr, Rwagasore, Micombero, flag, map of Africa, globe. 13fr, Micombero, flag, globe.

1972, Aug. 24   Photo.   Perf. 13½

405 A56 5fr silver & multi .15 .15
406 A56 7fr silver & multi .15 .15
407 A56 13fr silver & multi .22 .15
a. Souvenir sheet of 3, #405-407 .50
Nos. 405-407,C162-C164 (6) 1.52 .90

10th anniversary of independence.

Madonna and Child, by Andrea Solario — A57

Paintings of the Madonna and Child by: 10fr, Raphael. 15fr, Botticelli.

1972, Nov. 2

408 A57 5fr lt blue & multi .15 .15
409 A57 10fr lt blue & multi .15 .15
410 A57 15fr lt blue & multi .22 .15
a. Souvenir sheet of 3, #408-410 .50
Nos. 408-410,C165-C167 (6) 1.80 .93

Christmas 1972. Sheets of 20 stamps + label.
For surcharges see #B56-B58, CB26-CB28.

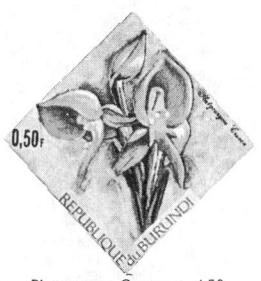

Platycoryne Crocea — A58

1972

Size: 33x33mm

411 A58 50c shown .15 .15
412 A58 1fr Cattleya trianaei .15 .15
413 A58 2fr Eulophia cucullata .15 .15
414 A58 3fr Cymbidium hamsey .15 .15
415 A58 4fr Thelymitra pauciflora .15 .15
416 A58 5fr Miltassia .15 .15
417 A58 6fr Miltonia .15 .15

Size: 38x38mm

418 A58 7fr Like 50c .15 .15
419 A58 8fr Like 1fr .20 .15
420 A58 9fr Like 2fr .20 .15
421 A58 13fr Like 3fr .30 .15
Nos. 411-421,C168-C174 (18) 10.65 2.70

Orchids. Issued: #411-417, 11/6; #418-421, 11/29.

Henry Morton Stanley — A59

Designs: 7fr, Porters, Stanley's expedition. 13fr, Stanley entering Ujiji.

1973, Mar. 19   Photo.   Perf. 13½

422 A59 5fr gold & multi .15 .15
423 A59 7fr gold & multi .15 .15
424 A59 13fr gold & multi .20 .15
Nos. 422-424,C175-C177 (6) 1.40 .90

Exploration of Africa by David Livingstone (1813-1873) and Henry Morton Stanley (John Rowlands; 1841-1904).

Crucifixion, by Roger van der Weyden — A60

Easter (Paintings): 5fr, Flagellation of Christ, by Caravaggio. 13fr, The Burial of Christ, by Raphael.

1973, Apr. 10

425 A60 5fr gold & multi .15 .15
426 A60 7fr gold & multi .15 .15
427 A60 13fr gold & multi .20 .15
a. Souvenir sheet of 3, #425-427 .60 .60
Nos. 425-427,C178-C180 (6) 1.63 .90

INTERPOL Emblem, Flag — A61

Design: 10fr, INTERPOL flag and emblem. 18fr, INTERPOL Headquarters and emblem.

1973, May 19   Photo.   Perf. 13½

428 A61 5fr silver & multi .15 .15
429 A61 10fr silver & multi .15 .15
430 A61 18fr silver & multi .28 .15
Nos. 428-430,C181-C182 (5) 1.46 .81

Intl. Criminal Police Organization, 50th anniv.

Signs of the Zodiac, Babylon — A62

Designs: 5fr, Greek and Roman gods representing planets. 7fr, Ptolemy (No. 433a) and Ptolemaic solar system. 13fr, Copernicus (No. 434a) and heliocentric system.
a, UL. b, UR. c, LL. d, LR.

1973, July 27   Photo.   Perf. 13½

431 A62 3fr Block of 4, #a.-d. .20 .15
432 A62 5fr Block of 4, #a.-d. .25 .15
433 A62 7fr Block of 4, #a.-d. .32 .15
434 A62 13fr Block of 4, #a.-d. .75 .20
a. Souvenir sheet of 4, #431-434 2.75 1.40
Nos. 431-434,C183-C186 (8) 9.32 2.50

500th anniversary of the birth of Nicolaus Copernicus (1473-1543), Polish astronomer.

Flowers and Butterflies — A63

Designs: Each block of 4 contains 2 flower and 2 butterfly designs. The 1fr, 2fr, 5fr and 11fr have flower designs listed as "a" and "d" numbers, butterflies as "b" and "c" numbers; the arrangement is reversed for the 3fr and 6fr.

1973, Sept. 3   Photo.   Perf. 13
Stamp Size: 34x41½mm

435 A63 Block of 4 .35 .15
a. 1fr Protea cynaroides .15 .15
b. 1fr Precis octavia .15 .15
c. 1fr Epiphora bauhiniae .15 .15
d. 1fr Gazania longiscapa .15 .15
436 A63 Block of 4 .35 .15
a. 2fr Kniphofia .15 .15
b. 2fr Cymothoe coccinata .15 .15
c. 2fr Nudaurelia zambesina .15 .15
d. 2fr Freesia refracta .15 .15
437 A63 Block of 4 .40 .15
a. 3fr Calotis eupompe .15 .15
b. 3fr Narcissus .15 .15
c. 3fr Cineraria hybrida .15 .15
d. 3fr Cyrestis camillus .15 .15

BURUNDI

438	A63	Block of 4	.65 .15
a.		5fr Iris tingitana	.15 .15
b.		5fr Pappilio demodocus	.15 .15
c.		5fr Catopsila avelaneda	.15 .15
d.		5fr Nerine sarniensis	.15 .15
439	A63	Block of 4	.80 .20
a.		6fr Hypolimnas dexithea	.20 .15
b.		6fr Zantedeschia tropicalis	.20 .15
c.		6fr Sandersonia aurantiaca	.20 .15
d.		6fr Drurya antimachus	.20 .15
440	A63	Block of 4	1.75 .22
a.		11fr Nymphaea capensis	.40 .15
b.		11fr Pandoriana pandora	.40 .15
c.		11fr Precis orythia	.40 .15
d.		11fr Pelargonium domestica	.40 .15
		Nos. 435-440,C187-C192 (12)	34.80 4.22

Virgin and Child, by Giovanni Bellini — A64

Virgin and Child by: 10fr, Jan van Eyck. 15fr, Giovanni Boltraffio.

1973, Nov. 13   Photo.   *Perf. 13*

441	A64	5fr gold & multi	.15 .15
442	A64	10fr gold & multi	.15 .15
443	A64	15fr gold & multi	.22 .15
a.		Souvenir sheet of 3, #441-443	.50 .50
		Nos. 441-443,C193-C195 (6)	1.80 .91

Christmas 1973.
For surcharges see #B59-B61, CB29-CB31.

Pietá, by Paolo Veronese — A65

Paintings: 10fr, Virgin and St. John, by van der Weyden. 18fr, Crucifixion, by van der Weyden. 27fr, Burial of Christ, by Titian. 40fr, Pietá, by El Greco.

1974, Apr. 19   Photo.   *Perf. 14x13½*

444	A65	5fr gold & multi	.15 .15
445	A65	10fr gold & multi	.15 .15
446	A65	18fr gold & multi	.28 .15
447	A65	27fr gold & multi	.42 .15
448	A65	40fr gold & multi	.65 .15
a.		Souvenir sheet of 5, #444-448	1.65 1.65
		Nos. 444-448 (5)	1.65 .75

Easter 1974.

Fish — A66

1974, May 30   Photo.   *Perf. 13*
Stamp Size: 35x35mm

449	A66	Block of 4	.30 .20
a.		1fr Haplochromis multicolor	.15 .15
b.		1fr Pantodon buchholzi	.15 .15
c.		1fr Tropheus duboisi	.15 .15
d.		1fr Distichodus sexfasciatus	.15 .15
450	A66	Block of 4	.30 .15
a.		2fr Pelmatochromis kribensis	.15 .15
b.		2fr Nannaethiops tritaeniatus	.15 .15
c.		2fr Polycentropsis abbreviata	.15 .15
d.		2fr Hemichromis bimaculatus	.15 .15
451	A66	Block of 4	.30 .20
a.		3fr Ctenopoma acutirostre	.15 .15
b.		3fr Syndontis angelicus	.15 .15
c.		3fr Tilapia melanopleura	.15 .15
d.		3fr Aphyosemion bivittatum	.15 .15
452	A66	Block of 4	.50 .15
a.		5fr Monodactylus argenteus	.15 .15
b.		5fr Zanclus canescens	.15 .15
c.		5fr Pygoplites diacanthus	.15 .15
d.		5fr Cephalopholis argus	.15 .15
453	A66	Block of 4	.60 .15
a.		6fr Priacanthus arenatus	.15 .15
b.		6fr Pomacanthus arcuatus	.15 .15
c.		6fr Scarus guacamala	.15 .15
d.		6fr Zeus faber	.15 .15
454	A66	Block of 4	1.00 .20
a.		11fr Lactophrys quadricornis	.20 .15
b.		11fr Balistes vetula	.20 .15
c.		11fr Acanthurus bahianus	.20 .15
d.		11fr Holocanthus ciliaris	.20 .15
		Nos. 449-454,C207-C212 (12)	18.75 2.65

Soccer and Cup A67

Designs: Various soccer scenes and cup.

1974, July 4   Photo.   *Perf. 13*

455	A67	5fr gold & multi	.15
456	A67	6fr gold & multi	.15
457	A67	11fr gold & multi	.16
458	A67	14fr gold & multi	.22
459	A67	17fr gold & multi	.25
a.		Souvenir sheet of 3	1.40
		Nos. 455-459,C196-C198 (8)	2.23

World Soccer Championship, Munich, June 13-July 7. No. 459a contains 3 stamps similar to Nos. C196-C198 without "Poste Aerienne."
Nos. 455-459 and 459a exist imperf.

Flags over UPU Headquarters, Bern — A68

#461, G.P.O., Bujumbura. #462, Mailmen ("11F" in UR). #463, Mailmen ("11F" in UL). #464, UPU emblem. #465, Means of transportation. #466, Pigeon over globe showing Burundi. #467, Swiss flag, pigeon over map showing Bern.

1974, July 23

460	A68	6fr gold & multi	.18
461	A68	6fr gold & multi	.18
462	A68	11fr gold & multi	.30
463	A68	11fr gold & multi	.30
464	A68	14fr gold & multi	.38
465	A68	14fr gold & multi	.38
466	A68	17fr gold & multi	.45
467	A68	17fr gold & multi	.50
a.		Souvenir sheet of 8, #460-467	2.75
		Nos. 460-467,C199-C206 (16)	9.97
		Set, used	1.00

Cent. of UPU. Stamps of same denomination printed se-tenant (continuous design).

St. Ildefonso Writing Letter, by El Greco — A69

Paintings: 11fr, Lady Sealing Letter, by Chardin. 14fr, Titus at Desk, by Rembrandt. 17fr, The Love Letter, by Vermeer. 26fr, The Merchant G. Gisze, by Holbein. 31fr, Portrait of Alexandre Lenoir, by David.

1974, Oct. 1   Photo.   *Perf. 13*

468	A69	6fr gold & multi	.15
469	A69	11fr gold & multi	.16
470	A69	14fr gold & multi	.22
471	A69	17fr gold & multi	.25
472	A69	26fr gold & multi	.40
473	A69	31fr gold & multi	.45
a.		Souvenir sheet of 2, #472-473	1.10
		Nos. 468-473 (6)	1.63

International Letter Writing Week, Oct. 6-12.
No. 473a exists imperf.

Virgin and Child, by Bernaert van Orley — A70

Paintings of the Virgin and Child: 10fr, by Hans Memling. 15fr, by Botticelli.

1974, Nov. 7   Photo.   *Perf. 13*

474	A70	5fr gold & multi	.15
475	A70	10fr gold & multi	.15
476	A70	15fr gold & multi	.22
a.		Souvenir sheet of 3, #474-476	.50
		Nos. 474-476,C213-C215 (6)	1.80

Christmas 1974. Sheets of 20 stamps and one label. No. 476a exists imperf.

Apollo-Soyuz Space Mission and Emblem — A71

1975, July 10   Photo.   *Perf. 13*

477	A71	Block of 4	.80
a.		26fr A.A. Leonov, V.N. Kubasov, Soviet flag	.20
b.		26fr Soyuz and Soviet flag	.20
c.		26fr Apollo and American flag	.20
d.		26fr D.K. Slayton, V.D. Brand, T.P. Stafford, American flag	.20
478	A71	Block of 4	1.25
a.		31fr Apollo-Soyuz link-up	.28
b.		31fr Apollo, blast-off	.28
c.		31fr Soyuz, blast-off	.28
d.		31fr Kubasov, Leonov, Slayton, Brand, Stafford	.28
		Nos. 477-478,C216-C217 (4)	4.35

Apollo Soyuz space test project (Russo-American cooperation), launching July 15; link-up, July 17.

Addax — A72

1975, July 31   Photo.   *Perf. 13½*

479		Strip of 4	.20
a.	A72	1fr shown	.15
b.	A72	1fr Roan antelope	.15
c.	A72	1fr Nyala	.15
d.	A72	1fr White rhinoceros	.15
480		Strip of 4	.20
a.	A72	2fr Mandrill	.15
b.	A72	2fr Eland	.15
c.	A72	2fr Salt's dik-dik	.15
d.	A72	2fr Thomson's gazelles	.15
481		Strip of 4	.20
a.	A72	3fr African small-clawed otter	.15
b.	A72	3fr Reed buck	.15
c.	A72	3fr Indian civet	.15
d.	A72	3fr Cape buffalo	.15
482		Strip of 4	.35
a.	A72	5fr White-tailed gnu	.15
b.	A72	5fr African wild asses	.15
c.	A72	5fr Black-and-white colobus monkey	.15
d.	A72	5fr Gerenuk	.15
483		Strip of 4	.36
a.	A72	6fr Dama gazelle	.15
b.	A72	6fr Black-backed jackal	.15
c.	A72	6fr Sitatungas	.15
d.	A72	6fr Zebra antelope	.15
484		Strip of 4	.65
a.	A72	11fr Fennec	.16
b.	A72	11fr Lesser kudus	.15
c.	A72	11fr Biesbok	.16
d.	A72	11fr Serval	.16
		Nos. 479-484,C218-C223 (12)	12.61

For overprints see Nos. C224-C227.

Jonah, by Michelangelo — A73

Designs: Paintings from Sistine Chapel.

1975, Dec. 3   Photo.   *Perf. 13*

485	A73	5fr shown	.15
486	A73	5fr Libyan Sybil	.15
487	A73	13fr Prophet Isaiah	.20
488	A73	13fr Delphic Sybil	.20
489	A73	27fr Daniel	.40
490	A73	27fr Cumaean Sybil	.40
a.		Souvenir sheet of 6, #485-490	2.00
		Nos. 485-490,C228-C233 (12)	5.10

Michelangelo Buonarotti (1475-1564), Italian sculptor, painter and architect. Stamps of same denominations printed se-tenant in sheets of 18 stamps and 2 labels.
For surcharges see Nos. B65-B70, CB35-CB40.

Speed Skating — A74   Basketball — A75

Designs (Innsbruck Games Emblem and): 24fr, Figure skating, women's. 26fr, Two-man bobsled. 31fr, Cross-country skiing.

1976, Jan. 23   Photo.   *Perf. 14x13½*

491	A74	17fr dp bl & multi	.30
492	A74	24fr multi	.45
493	A74	26fr multi	.48
494	A74	31fr plum & multi	.55
a.		Souvenir sheet of 3, perf. 13½	2.25
		Nos. 491-494,C234-C236 (7)	3.70

12th Winter Olympic Games, Innsbruck, Austria, Feb. 4-15.
No. 494a contains stamps similar to #C234-C236, without "POSTE AERIENNE."

1976, May 3   Litho.   *Perf. 13½*

Montreal Games Emblem and: #496, 499, 503b, Pole vault. #497, 500, 503d, Running. #498, 501, 503a, Soccer. #502, 503c, Basketball.

495	A75	14fr blue & multi	.25
496	A75	14fr olive & multi	.25
497	A75	17fr magenta & multi	.30
498	A75	17fr vermilion & multi	.30
499	A75	28fr olive & multi	.48
500	A75	28fr magenta & multi	.48
501	A75	40fr vermilion & multi	.70
502	A75	40fr blue & multi	.70
		Nos. 495-502,C237-C242 (14)	7.20

Souvenir Sheet

503		Sheet of 4	1.65
a.	A75	14fr red & multi	.22
b.	A75	17fr olive & multi	.25
c.	A75	28fr blue & multi	.40
d.	A75	40fr magenta & multi	.60

21st Olympic Games, Montreal, Canada, July 17-Aug. 1. Stamps of same denomination printed se-tenant in sheets of 20.

BURUNDI

Virgin and Child, by Dirk Bouts — A76

Virgin and Child by: 13fr, Giovanni Bellini. 27fr, Carlo Crivelli.

1976, Oct. 18   Photo.   Perf. 13½
504	A76	5fr gold & multi	.15
505	A76	13fr gold & multi	.20
506	A76	27fr gold & multi	.40
a.		Souvenir sheet of 3, #504-506	.75
		Nos. 504-506,C250-C252 (6)	2.05

Christmas 1976. Sheets of 20 stamps and descriptive label.
For surcharges see #B71-B73, CB41-CB43.

St. Veronica, by Rubens A77

Paintings by Rubens: 21fr, Christ on the Cross. 27fr, Descent from the Cross. 35fr, The Deposition.

1977, Apr. 5   Photo.   Perf. 13
507	A77	10fr gold & multi	.15
508	A77	21fr gold & multi	.32
509	A77	27fr gold & multi	.40
510	A77	35fr gold & multi	.55
a.		Souvenir sheet of 4	1.50
		Nos. 507-510 (4)	1.42

Easter 1977. Sheets of 30 stamps and descriptive label. No. 510a contains 4 stamps similar to Nos. 507-510 inscribed "POSTE AERIENNE."

Alexander Graham Bell — A78

Intelsat Satellite, Modern and Old Telephones — A79

Designs: No. 513, Switchboard operator, c. 1910, and wall telephone. No. 514, Intelsat and radar. No. 515, A.G. Bell and first telephone. No. 516, Satellites around globe and videophone.

1977, May 17   Photo.   Perf. 13
511	A78	10fr multi	.15
512	A79	10fr multi	.15
513	A78	17fr multi	.15
514	A79	17fr multi	.15
515	A78	26fr multi	.22
516	A79	26fr multi	.22
		Nos. 511-516,C253-C256 (10)	1.84

Centenary of first telephone call by Alexander Graham Bell, Mar. 10, 1876. Stamps of same denomination printed se-tenant in sheets of 32.

Buffon's Kob — A80

1977, Aug. 22   Photo.   Perf. 14x14½
517		Strip of 4	.30
a.	A80	2fr shown	.15
b.	A80	2fr Marabus	.15
c.	A80	2fr Brindled gnu	.15
d.	A80	2fr River hog	.15
518		Strip of 4	.50
a.	A80	5fr Zebras	.15
b.	A80	5fr Shoebill	.15
c.	A80	5fr Striped hyenas	.15
d.	A80	5fr Chimpanzee	.15
519		Strip of 4	.75
a.	A80	8fr Flamingos	.15
b.	A80	8fr Nile crocodiles	.15
c.	A80	8fr Green mamba	.15
d.	A80	8fr Greater kudus	.15
520		Strip of 4	1.00
a.	A80	11fr Hyrax	.25
b.	A80	11fr Cobra	.25
c.	A80	11fr Jackals	.25
d.	A80	11fr Verreaux's eagles	.25
521		Strip of 4	2.00
a.	A80	21fr Honey badger	.50
b.	A80	21fr Harnessed antelopes	.50
c.	A80	21fr Secretary bird	.50
d.	A80	21fr Klipspringer	.50
522		Strip of 4	2.00
a.	A80	27fr African big-eared fox	.50
b.	A80	27fr Elephants	.50
c.	A80	27fr Vulturine guineafowl	.50
d.	A80	27fr Impalas	.50
		Nos. 517-522,C258-C263 (12)	22.70

The Goose Girl, by Grimm — A81

Fairy Tales: 5fr, by Grimm Brothers. 11fr, by Aesop. 14fr, by Hans Christian Andersen. 17fr, by Jean de La Fontaine. 26fr, English fairy tales.

1977, Sept. 14   Perf. 14
523		Block of 4	.38
a.	A81	5fr shown	.15
b.	A81	5fr The Two Wanderers	.15
c.	A81	5fr The Man of Iron	.15
d.	A81	5fr Snow White and Rose Red	.15
524		Block of 4	.85
a.	A81	11fr The Quarreling Cats	.20
b.	A81	11fr The Blind and the Lame	.20
c.	A81	11fr The Hermit and the Bear	.20
d.	A81	11fr The Fox and the Stork	.20
525		Block of 4	1.00
a.	A81	14fr The Princess and the Pea	.25
b.	A81	14fr The Old Tree Mother	.25
c.	A81	14fr The Ice Maiden	.25
d.	A81	14fr The Old House	.25
526		Block of 4	1.25
a.	A81	17fr The Oyster and the Suitors	.30
b.	A81	17fr The Wolf and the Lamb	.30
c.	A81	17fr Hen with the Golden Egg	.30
d.	A81	17fr The Wolf as Shepherd	.30
527		Block of 4	2.00
a.	A81	26fr Three Heads in the Well	.50
b.	A81	26fr Mother Goose	.50
c.	A81	26fr Jack and the Beanstalk	.50
d.	A81	26fr Alice in Wonderland	.50
		Nos. 523-527 (5)	5.48

Security Council Chamber, UN Nos. 28, 46, 37, C7 — A82

Designs (UN Stamps and): 8fr, UN General Assembly, interior. 21fr, UN Meeting Hall.

1977, Oct. 10   Photo.   Perf. 13½
528	A82	Block of 4	.65
a.		8fr No. 25	.15
b.		8fr No. C5	.15
c.		8fr No. 23	.15
d.		8fr No. 2	.15
529	A82	Block of 4	.75
a.		10fr No. 28	.18
b.		10fr No. 46	.18
c.		10fr No. 37	.18
d.		10fr No. C7	.18
530	A82	Block of 4	1.50
a.		21fr No. 45	.35
b.		21fr No. 42	.35
c.		21fr No. 17	.35
d.		21fr No. 13	.35
e.		Souvenir sheet of 3	.65
		Nos. 528-530,C264-C266 (6)	10.05

25th anniv. (in 1976) of the UN Postal Administration. No. 530e contains 8fr in design of No. 529d, 10fr in design of No. 530b, 21fr in design of No. 528c.

Virgin and Child — A83

Designs: Paintings of the Virgin and Child.

1977, Oct. 31   Photo.   Perf. 14x13
531	A83	5fr By Meliore Toscano	.15
532	A83	13fr By J. Lombardos	.20
533	A83	27fr By Emmanuel Tzanes, 1610-1680	.40
a.		Souvenir sheet of 3, #531-533	.75
		Nos. 531-533,C267-C269 (6)	2.11

Christmas 1977. Sheets of 24 stamps with descriptive label.
For surcharges see #B74-B76, CB44-CB46.

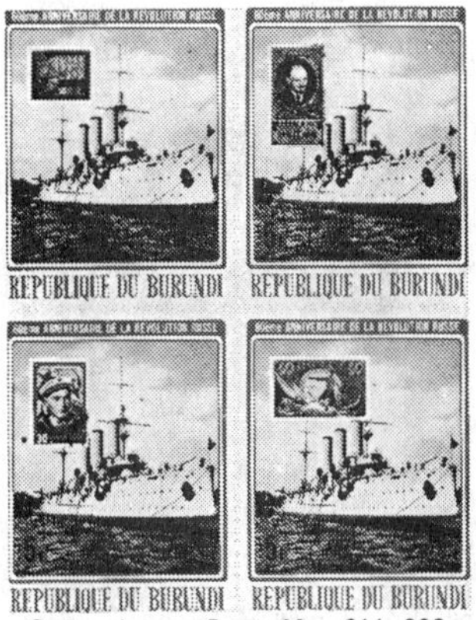

Cruiser Aurora, Russia Nos. 211, 303, 1252, 187 — A84

Russian Stamps and: 8fr, Kremlin, Moscow. 11fr, Pokrovski Cathedral, Moscow. 13fr, Labor Day parade, 1977 and 1980 Olympic Games emblem.

1977, Nov. 14   Photo.   Perf. 13
534	A84	Block of 4	.38
a.		5fr No. 211	.15
b.		5fr No. 303	.15
c.		5fr No. 1252	.15
d.		5fr No. 187	.15
535	A84	Block of 4	.65
a.		8fr No. 856	.15
b.		8fr No. 1986	.15
c.		8fr No. 908	.15
d.		8fr No. 2551	.15
536	A84	Block of 4	.85
a.		11fr No. 3844b	.20
b.		11fr No. 3452	.20
c.		11fr No. 3382	.20
d.		11fr No. 3837	.20
537	A84	Block of 4	1.00
a.		13fr No. 4446	.25
b.		13fr No. 3497	.25
c.		13fr No. 2926	.25
d.		13fr No. 2365	.25
		Nos. 534-537 (4)	2.88

60th anniv. of Russian October Revolution.

Ship at Dock, Arms and Flag — A85

Burundi Arms and Flag and: 5fr, Men at lathes. 11fr, Male leopard dance. 14fr, Coffee harvest. 17fr, Government Palace.

1977, Nov. 25   Photo.   Perf. 13½
538	A85	1fr sil & multi	.15
539	A85	5fr sil & multi	.15
540	A85	11fr sil & multi	.16
541	A85	14fr sil & multi	.20
542	A85	17fr sil & multi	.25
		Nos. 538-542 (5)	.91

15th anniversary of independence.

A86    A87

Paintings of the Virgin and Child by: 13fr, Rubens. 17fr, Solario. 27fr, Tiepolo. 31fr, Gerard David. 40fr, Bellini.

1979, Feb.   Photo.   Perf. 14x13
543	A86	13fr multi	.20
544	A86	17fr multi	.25
545	A86	27fr multi	.40
546	A86	31fr multi	.48
547	A86	40fr multi	.60
		Nos. 543-547 (5)	1.93

Christmas 1978. See No. C270.

1979   Photo.   Perf. 13½x13
548	A87	1fr Abyssinian hornbill	.15
549	A87	2fr Snakebird	.15
550	A87	3fr Melittophagus pusillus	.15
551	A87	5fr Flamingo	.15
552	A87	8fr Afropavo congenis	.15
553	A87	10fr Gallinule	.35
554	A87	20fr Martial eagle	.65
555	A87	27fr Ibis	.85
556	A87	50fr Saddle-billed stork	1.75
		Nos. 548-556,C273-C281 (18)	13.20

Mother and Infant, IYC Emblem A88

IYC Emblem and: 20fr, Infant. 27fr, Girl with doll. 50fr, Children in Children's Village.

1979, July 19   Photo.   Perf. 14
557	A88	10fr multi	.15
558	A88	20fr multi	.25
559	A88	27fr multi	.32
560	A88	50fr multi	.55
		Nos. 557-560 (4)	1.27

Intl. Year of the Child. See No. B82.

A89    A90

Virgin and Child by: 20fr, del Garbo. 27fr, Giovanni Penni. 31fr, G. Romano. 50fr, Jacopo Bassano.

1979, Oct. 12
561	A89	20fr multi	.30
562	A89	27fr multi	.40
563	A89	31fr multi	.48
564	A89	50fr multi	.75
		Nos. 561-564,B83-B86 (8)	3.95

Christmas 1979. See Nos. C271, CB48.

1979, Nov. 6

Designs: 20fr, Rowland Hill, Penny Black. Stamps of Burundi: 27fr, German East Africa Nos. 17, N17. 31fr, Nos. 4, 24. 40fr, Nos. 29, 294. 60fr, Heinrich von Stephan, Nos. 464-465.

565	A90	20fr multi	.30
566	A90	27fr multi	.40
567	A90	31fr multi	.48
568	A90	40fr multi	.60
569	A90	50fr multi	.90
		Nos. 565-569 (5)	2.68

Sir Rowland Hill (1795-1879), originator of penny postage. See No. C272.

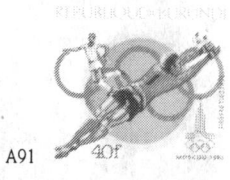

BURUNDI

A91

1980, Oct. 24   Photo.   Perf. 13x13½
570	A91	20fr	110-meter hurdles	.38
571	A91	20fr	Hurdles, Thomas Munkelt	.38
572	A91	20fr	Hurdles, R.D.A.	.38
573	A91	30fr	Discus	.55
574	A91	30fr	Discus, V. Rasshchupkin	.55
575	A91	30fr	Discus, U.R.S.S.	.55
576	A91	40fr	Soccer, Tchecoslovaquie	.75
577	A91	40fr	"Football"	.75
578	A91	40fr	shown	.75

Nos. 570-578 (9)   5.04

22nd Summer Olympic Games, Moscow, July 19-Aug. 3. Stamps of same denomination se-tenant.
See No. C282.

Virgin and Child, by Mainardi — A92

Christmas 1980 (Paintings): 30fr, Holy Family, by Michelangelo. 40fr, Virgin and Child, by di Cosimo. 45fr, Holy Family, by Fra Bartolomeo.

1980, Dec. 12   Photo.   Perf. 13½x13
579	A92	10fr multi	.15
580	A92	30fr multi	.30
581	A92	40fr multi	.42
582	A92	45fr multi	.45

Nos. 579-582,B87-B90 (8)   2.71

UPRONA Party National Congress, 1979 — A93

1980, Dec. 29   Perf. 14x13½
583	A93	10fr multi	.15
584	A93	40fr multi	.60
585	A93	45fr multi	.65

Nos. 583-585 (3)   1.40

Johannes Kepler, Dish Antenna A94

1981, Feb. 12   Perf. 14
586	A94	10fr shown	.15
587	A94	40fr Satellite	.60
588	A94	45fr Satellite, diff.	.65
a.		Souvenir sheet of 3, #586-588	1.50

Nos. 586-588 (3)   1.40

350th death anniv. of Johannes Kepler and 1st earth satellite station in Burundi.

Lion
RÉPUBLIQUE DU BURUNDI   A95

1983, Apr. 22   Photo.   Perf. 13
589	A95	2fr shown	
590	A95	3fr Giraffes	
591	A95	5fr Rhinoceros	
592	A95	10fr Water buffalo	
593	A95	20fr Elephant	
594	A95	25fr Hippopotamus	
595	A95	30fr Zebra	
596	A95	50fr Warthog	
597	A95	60fr Oryx	
598	A95	65fr Wild dog	
599	A95	70fr Cheetah	
600	A95	75fr Wildebeest	
601	A95	85fr Hyena	

Nos. 589-601 (13)   50.00

Nos. 589-601 Overprinted in Silver with World Wildlife Fund Emblem

1983   Photo.   Perf. 13
589a	A95	2fr multi	
590a	A95	3fr multi	
591a	A95	5fr multi	
592a	A95	10fr multi	
593a	A95	20fr multi	
594a	A95	25fr multi	
595a	A95	30fr multi	
596a	A95	50fr multi	
597a	A95	60fr multi	
598a	A95	65fr multi	
599a	A95	70fr multi	
600a	A95	75fr multi	
601a	A95	85fr multi	

Nos. 589a-601a (13)   600.00

Apparently there is speculation in these two sets.

20th Anniv. of Independence, July 1, 1982 — A96

Flags, various arms, map or portrait.

1983   Perf. 14
602	A96	10fr multi	.15
603	A96	25fr multi	.38
604	A96	30fr multi	.45
605	A96	50fr multi	.75
606	A96	65fr multi	1.00

Nos. 602-606 (5)   2.73

Christmas 1983 — A97

Virgin and Child paintings: 10fr, by Luca Signorelli (1450-1523). 25fr, by Esteban Murillo (1617-1682). 30fr, by Carlo Crivelli (1430-1495). 50fr, by Nicolas Poussin (1594-1665).

1983, Oct. 3   Litho.   Perf. 14½x13½
607	A97	10fr multi	.15
608	A97	25fr multi	.38
609	A97	30fr multi	.45
610	A97	50fr multi	.75

Nos. 607-610,B91-B94 (8)   3.52

See Nos. C285, CB50.

Butterflies A98

1984, June 29   Photo.   Perf. 13
611	A98	5fr Cymothoe coccinata	.20
612	A98	5fr Papilio zalmoxis	.20
613	A98	10fr Asterope pechueli	.40
614	A98	10fr Papilio antimachus	.40
615	A98	30fr Papilio hesperus	1.00
616	A98	30fr Bebearia mardania	1.00
617	A98	35fr Euphaedra neophron	1.25
618	A98	35fr Euphaedra perseis	1.25
619	A98	65fr Euphaedra imperialis	2.25
620	A98	65fr Pseudocraea striata	2.25

Nos. 611-620 (10)   10.20

Stamps of the same denomination printed horizontally se-tenant.
For surcharges see Nos. 654D-654E.

19th UPU Congress, Hamburg A99

UPU emblem and: 10fr, German East Africa, #17, N17. 30fr, #4, 24. 35fr, #294, 595. 65fr, Dr. Heinrich von Stephan, #464-465.

1984, July 14   Litho.   Perf. 13x13½
621	A99	10fr multi	.15
622	A99	30fr multi	.45
623	A99	35fr multi	.50
624	A99	65fr multi	1.00

Nos. 621-624 (4)   2.10

See No. C286.

1984 Summer Olympics A100

Gold medalists: 10fr, Jesse Owens, US, track and field, Berlin, 1936. 30fr, Rafer Johnson, US, decathlon, 1960. 35fr, Bob Beamon, US, long jump, 1968. 65fr, Kipchoge Keino, Kenya, 3000-meter steeplechase, 1972.

1984, Aug. 6   Perf. 13½x13
625	A100	10fr multi	.25
626	A100	30fr multi	.70
627	A100	35fr multi	.85
628	A100	65fr multi	1.50

Nos. 625-628 (4)   3.30

See No. C287.

Christmas 1984 — A101

Paintings: 10fr, Rest During the Flight into Egypt, by Murillo (1617-1682). 25fr, Virgin and Child, by R. del Garbo. 30fr, Virgin and Child, by Botticelli (1445-1510). 50fr, The Adoration of the Shepherds, by Giacomo da Bassano (1517-1592).

1984, Dec. 15   Perf. 13½
629	A101	10fr multi	.15
630	A101	25fr multi	.38
631	A101	30fr multi	.45
632	A101	50fr multi	.75

Nos. 629-632,B95-B98 (8)   3.52

See Nos. C288, CB51.

Flowers — A102

1986, July 31   Photo.   Perf. 13½x13½
633	A102	2fr Thunbergia	.15
634	A102	3fr Saintpaulia	.15
635	A102	5fr Clivia	.15
636	A102	10fr Cassia	.15
637	A102	20fr Strelitzia	.25
638	A102	35fr Gloriosa	.55

Nos. 633-638,C289-C294 (12)   8.20

Intl. Peace Year — A103

1986, May 1   Litho.   Perf. 14
639	A103	10fr Rockets as housing	.15
640	A103	20fr Atom as flower	.18
641	A103	30fr Handshake	.28
642	A103	40fr Globe, chicks	.35
a.		Souvenir sheet of 4, #639-642	.90

Nos. 639-642 (4)   .96

No. 642a exists imperf.

Great Lake Nations Economic Community (CEPGI), 10th Anniv. — A104

Outline maps of Lake Tanganyika, CEPGI emblem and: 5fr, Aviation. 10fr, Agriculture. 15fr, Industry. 25fr, Electrification. 35fr, Flags of Burundi, Rwanda and Zaire.

1986, May 1   Photo.   Perf. 13½x14½
643	A104	5fr multi	.15
644	A104	10fr multi	.15
645	A104	15fr multi	.20
646	A104	25fr multi	.32
647	A104	35fr multi	.45
a.		Souv. sheet of 5, #643-647 + label	1.25

Nos. 643-647 (5)   1.27

Intl. Year of Shelter for the Homeless A105

1987, June   Litho.   Perf. 14
648	A105	10fr Hovel	.28
649	A105	20fr Drain pipe shelter	.55
650	A105	80fr Shoveling sand	2.15
651	A105	150fr Children, house model	4.00
a.		Souvenir sheet of 4, #648-651	7.00

Nos. 648-651 (4)   6.98

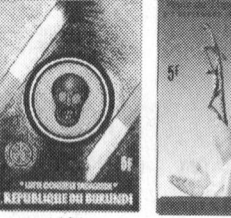

A106    A107

1987(?)   Litho.   Perf. 14
652	A106	5fr shown	.15
653	A106	20fr Skull, lungs	.30
654	A106	80fr Cigarette, face	1.25

Nos. 652-654 (3)   1.70

WHO Anti-smoking campaign.

Nos. 615-616 Surcharged 80f

1989   Photo.   Perf. 13
| 654D | A98 | 80fr on 30fr #615 | |
| 654E | A98 | 80fr on 30fr #616 | |

Numbers have been reserved for additional values in this set.

1990   Litho.   Perf. 14
655	A107	5fr red lil & multi	.15
656	A107	10fr blue & multi	.24
657	A107	20fr gray & multi	.48
658	A107	30fr ol grn & multi	.72
659	A107	50fr brt blue & multi	1.20

BURUNDI

660	A107	80fr grn bl & multi	1.95
a.		Souv. sheet of 6, #655-660, perf. 13½	4.75
		Nos. 655-660 (6)	4.74

Visit of Pope John Paul II.

Animals — A108

1991, Oct. 4   Litho.   Perf. 14

661	A108	5fr Hippopotamus	.15
662	A108	10fr Chickens	.15
663	A108	20fr Lion	.32
664	A108	30fr Elephant	.48
665	A108	50fr Guinea fowl	.80
666	A108	80fr Crocodile	1.25
a.		Souv. sheet of 6, #661-666, perf. 13½	3.15
		Nos. 661-666 (6)	3.15

No. 666a exists imperf.

Flowers — A108a

1992, June 2   Litho.   Perf. 14

666B	A108a	15fr Impatiens petersiana	.40
666C	A108a	20fr Lachenalia aloides	.50
666D	A108a	30fr Nymphaea lotus	.80
666E	A108a	50fr Clivia miniata	1.30
f.		Souvenir sheet of 4, #666B-666E, perf. 13½	3.00
		Nos. 666B-666E (4)	3.00

Native Music and Dancing — A110

1992, Apr. 2   Litho.   Perf. 14

667	A109	15fr multicolored	.25
668	A109	30fr multicolored	.48
669	A110	115fr multicolored	1.80
670	A110	200fr multicolored	3.10
a.		Souvenir sheet	5.65
		Nos. 667-670 (4)	5.63

No. 670a contains one each of Nos. 667-668, perf. 13x13½, and Nos. 669-670, perf. 13½x13.

Independence, 30th Anniv. — A111

Designs: 30fr, 140fr, People with flag. 85fr, 115fr, Natl. flag. 110fr, 200fr, Monument, vert. 120fr, 250fr, Map, vert.

1992, June 30   Litho.   Perf. 15

671	A111	30fr multicolored	.35
672	A111	85fr multicolored	1.00
673	A111	110fr multicolored	1.25
674	A111	115fr multicolored	1.35
675	A111	120fr multicolored	1.40
676	A111	140fr multicolored	1.65
677	A111	200fr multicolored	2.35
678	A111	250fr multicolored	3.00
		Nos. 671-678 (8)	12.35

Discovery of America, 500th Anniv. — A112

Columbus' fleet, globe and: 200fr, Pre-Columbian artifacts. 400fr, Fruits and vegetables.

1992, Oct. 12   Litho.   Perf. 15

679	A112	200fr multicolored	3.00
680	A112	400fr multicolored	6.25

Felis Serval — A113

1992, Oct. 16

681	A113	30fr shown	.48
682	A113	130fr Two seated	2.00
683	A113	200fr One standing, one lying	3.10
684	A113	220fr Two faces	3.40
		Nos. 681-684 (4)	8.98

World Wildlife Fund.

Mushrooms — A114

1992 Summer Olympics, Barcelona — A115

Designs: 10fr, Russula ingens. 15fr, Russula brunneorigida. 20fr, Amanita zambiana. 30fr, Russula subfistulosa. 75fr, 85fr, Russula meleagris. 100fr, Russula immaculata. 110fr, like #685. 115fr, like #686. 120fr, 130fr, Russula sejuncta. 250fr, Afroboletus luteolus.

1992-93   Perf. 11½x12   **Granite Paper**

685	A114	10fr multicolored	.15
686	A114	15fr multicolored	.24
687	A114	20fr multicolored	.32
688	A114	30fr multicolored	.48
689	A114	75fr multicolored	1.15
690	A114	85fr multicolored	1.35
691	A114	100fr multicolored	1.55
691A	A114	110fr multicolored	1.65
691B	A114	115fr multicolored	1.75
692	A114	120fr multicolored	1.90
693	A114	130fr multicolored	2.00
694	A114	250fr multicolored	3.75
		Nos. 685-694 (12)	16.29

Issued: 110fr, 115fr, 1993; others, 9/30/92.

1992, Nov. 6   Perf. 15

695	A115	130fr Runners	2.00
696	A115	500fr Hurdler	7.75

Christmas (Details of Adoration of the Kings, by Gentile da Fabriano): a, 100fr, Crowd, horses. b, 130fr, Kings. c, 250fr, Nativity scene.

1992, Dec. 7   Litho.   Perf. 11½

697	A116	Strip of 3, #a.-c.	5.25
d.		Souvenir sheet of 3, #697a-697c	6.50

Nos. 697a-697c have white border. No. 697d has continuous design and sold for 580fr.

1992, Dec. 5   Litho.   Perf. 15

Designs: 200fr, Emblems. 220fr, Profile of person made from fruits and vegetables.

697E	A116a	200fr multicolored	5.25
697F	A116a	220fr multicolored	5.75

Intl. Conference on Nutrition, Rome.

European Common Market — A117

Designs: 130fr, Flags, stars. 500fr, Europe, Africa, clasped hands, stars.

1993, Mar. 29   Litho.   Perf. 15

698	A117	130fr multicolored	1.50
699	A117	500fr multicolored	5.75

1994 World Cup Soccer Championships, US — A118

Players, stadium, US flag and: 130fr, Statue of Liberty. 200fr, Golden Gate Bridge.

1993, July 5   Litho.   Perf. 15

700	A118	130fr multicolored	1.50
701	A118	200fr multicolored	2.30

Traditional Musical Instruments — A119

1993, Apr. 30   Litho.   Perf. 15

702	A119	130fr Indonongo	2.30
703	A119	220fr Ingoma	2.50
704	A119	250fr Ikembe	2.75
705	A119	300fr Umuduri	3.50
		Nos. 702-705 (4)	11.05

1993, June 4   Litho.   Perf. 11½

706	A120	130fr Papilio bromius	1.50
707	A120	200fr Charaxes eupale	2.25
708	A120	250fr Cymothoe caenis	2.75
709	A120	300fr Graphium ridleyanus	3.50
a.		Souvenir sheet of 4, #706-709	11.50
		Nos. 706-709 (4)	10.00

No. 709a sold for 980fr.

1993, Dec. 9   Perf. 14

710	A121	100fr Cattle	1.10
711	A121	120fr Sheep	1.40
712	A121	130fr Pigs	1.50
713	A121	250fr Goats	2.75
		Nos. 710-713 (4)	6.75

Christmas — A122   Rock Stars — A123

Natives adoring Christ Child: a, 100fr, Woman carrying baby, two people kneeling. b, 130fr, With Christ Child. 250fr, c, Woman carrying baby, three other people.

1993, Dec. 10   Perf. 11½

714	A122	Strip of 3, #a.-c.	5.00
d.		Souvenir sheet of 3, #714a-714c	6.00

Nos. 714a-714c have white border. No. 714d has continuous design and sold for 580fr.

1994   Litho.   Perf. 15

715	A123	60fr Elvis Presley	.65
716	A123	115fr Mick Jagger	1.25
717	A123	120fr John Lennon	1.25
718	A123	200fr Michael Jackson	2.25
a.		Souvenir sheet of #715-718	6.50
		Nos. 715-718 (4)	5.40

No. 718a sold for 600fr.

1994, Oct. 10   Litho.   Perf. 15

719	A124	150fr multicolored	1.10

Intl. Olympic Committee, cent.

1994, Dec. 14   Photo.   Perf. 15

Christmas (Madonna and Child): a, 115fr, Chinese. b, 120fr, Japanese. c, 250fr, Polish.

720	A125	Strip of 3, #a.-c.	5.00
d.		Souvenir sheet of 1, #720c	2.75

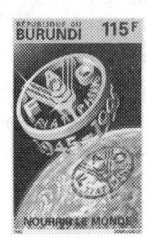

115fr, FAO, 50th anniv. 120fr, UN, 50th anniv.

1995, Feb. 21   Litho.   Perf. 11½

721	A126	115fr multicolored	1.25
722	A126	120fr multicolored	1.25

1995   Litho.   Perf. 11½

Flowers: 15fr, Cassia didymobotrya. 20fr, Mitragyna rubrostipulosa. 30fr, Phytolacca dodecandra. 85fr, Acanthus pubescens. 100fr, Bulbophyllum comatum. 110fr, Angraecum evradianum. 115fr, Eulophia burundiensis. 120fr, Habenaria adolphii.

Granite Paper

723	A127	15fr multicolored	.15
724	A127	20fr multicolored	.20
725	A127	30fr multicolored	.30
726	A127	85fr multicolored	.80
727	A127	100fr multicolored	.90
728	A127	110fr multicolored	1.00
729	A127	115fr multicolored	1.00
730	A127	120fr multicolored	1.10
		Nos. 723-730 (8)	5.45

BURUNDI

Transportation Methods — A128

30fr, Otraco bus. 115fr, Transintra semi truck. 120fr, Arnolac tugboat. 250fr, Air Burundi airplane.

1995, Nov. 16   Litho.   Perf. 11½
731	A128	30fr multicolored	.45
732	A128	115fr multicolored	1.70
733	A128	120fr multicolored	1.75
734	A128	250fr multicolored	3.60
		Nos. 731-734 (4)	7.50

A129   A130

Christmas (African sculpture): a, 100fr, Boy with panga, basket on head. b, 130fr, Boy carrying sheaf of wheat. c, 250fr, Mother, children.

1995, Dec. 26   Litho.   Perf. 11½x12
735	A129	Strip of 3, #a.-c.	2.25
d.		Souvenir sheet of 3, #735a-735c	2.25

1996, June 28   Litho.   Perf. 14

Athlete, national flag: 130fr, Venuste Niyongabo. 500fr, Arthemon Hatungimana.
736	A130	130fr multicolored	.65
737	A130	500fr multicolored	2.50

1996 Summer Olympic Games, Atlanta.

Birds A131

Designs: 15fr, Hagedashia hagedash. 20fr, Alopochen aegyptiacus. 30fr, Haliaeetus vocifer. 120fr, Ardea goliath. 165fr, Balearica regulorum. 220fr, Actophilornis africana.

1996   Litho.   Perf. 14
740	A131	15fr multicolored	.15
741	A131	20fr multicolored	.20
742	A131	30fr multicolored	.30
743	A131	120fr multicolored	1.15
744	A131	165fr multicolored	1.60
745	A131	220fr multicolored	2.00
		Nos. 740-745 (6)	5.40

SEMI-POSTAL STAMPS

Prince Louis Rwagasore — SP1

Prince and Stadium SP2

Design: 1.50fr+75c, 6.50fr+3fr, Prince and memorial monument.

Perf. 14x13, 13x14

1963, Feb. 15   Photo.   Unwmk.
B1	SP1	50c + 25c brt vio	.15 .15
B2	SP2	1fr + 50c red org & dk bl	.15 .15
B3	SP2	1.50fr + 75c lem & dk vio	.15 .15
B4	SP1	3.50fr + 1.50fr lil rose	.15 .15
B5	SP2	5fr + 2fr rose pink & dk bl	.15 .15
B6	SP2	6.50fr + 3fr gray ol & dk vio	.15 .15
		Nos. B1-B6 (6)	.90 .90

Issued in memory of Prince Louis Rwagasore (1932-61), son of King Mwami Mwambutsa IV and Prime Minister. The surtax was for the stadium and monument in his honor.

Red Cross Type of Regular Issue Souvenir Sheet

1963, Sept. 26   Litho.   Imperf.
B7		Sheet of 4	2.00 2.00
a.	A5	4fr + 2fr fawn, red & black	.32 .32
b.	A5	8fr + 2fr green, red & black	.38 .38
c.	A5	10fr + 2fr gray, red & black	.42 .42
d.	A5	20fr + 2fr ultra, red & black	.65 .65

Surtax for Red Cross work in Burundi.

Olympic Type of Regular Issue Souvenir Sheet

Designs: 18fr+2fr, Hurdling, horiz. 20fr+5fr, Vaulting, horiz.

1964, Nov. 18   Perf. 13½
B8		Sheet of 2	3.00 2.75
a.	A13	18fr + 2fr yel grn & multi	1.25 1.00
b.	A13	20fr + 5fr brt pink & multi	1.25 1.00

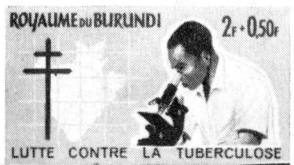

Scientist with Microscope and Map of Burundi — SP3

Lithographed and Photogravure

1965, Jan. 28   Unwmk.   Perf. 14½
B9	SP3	2fr + 50c multi	.15 .15
B10	SP3	4fr + 1.50fr multi	.15 .15
B11	SP3	5fr + 50fr multi	.20 .15
B12	SP3	8fr + 3fr multi	.25 .15
B13	SP3	10fr + 5fr multi	.38 .16
		Nos. B9-B13 (5)	1.13 .76

Souvenir Sheet   Perf. 13x13½
B14	SP3	10fr + 10fr multi	.85 .85

Issued for the fight against tuberculosis.

Coat of Arms, 10fr Coin, Reverse SP4

Designs (Coins of Various Denominations): 4fr+50c, 8fr+50c, 15fr+50c, 40fr+50c, King Mwambutsa IV, obverse.

Lithographed; Embossed on Gilt Foil
1965, Aug. 9   Imperf.

Diameter: 39mm
B15	SP4	2fr + 50c crimson & org	.15 .15
B16	SP4	4fr + 50c ultra & ver	.15 .15

Diameter: 45mm
B17	SP4	6fr + 50c org & gray	.15 .15
B18	SP4	8fr + 50c bl & magenta	.15 .15

Diameter: 56mm
B19	SP4	12fr + 50c lt grn & red lil	.25 .25
B20	SP4	15fr + 50c yel grn & lt lil	.30 .30

Diameter: 67mm
B21	SP4	25fr + 50c vio lol & buff	.50 .50
B22	SP4	40fr + 50c brt pink & red brn	.75 .75
		Nos. B15-B22 (8)	2.40 2.40

Stamps are backed with patterned paper in blue, orange and pink engine-turned design.

Prince Louis Rwagasore and Pres. John F. Kennedy SP5

Designs: 4fr+1fr, 20fr+5fr, Prince Louis and memorial. 20fr+2fr, 40fr+5fr, Pres. John F. Kennedy and library shelves. 40fr+2fr, King Mwambutsa IV at Kennedy grave, Arlington, vert.

1966, Jan. 21   Photo.   Perf. 13½
B23	SP5	4fr + 1fr gray bl & dk brn	.15 .15
B24	SP5	10fr + 1fr pale grn, ind & brn	.18 .15
B25	SP5	20fr + 2fr lil & dp grn	.38 .15
B26	SP5	40fr + 2fr gray grn & dk brn	.65 .15
		Nos. B23-B26 (4)	1.36 .60

Souvenir Sheet
B27		Sheet of 2	1.50 1.00
a.		SP5 20fr + 5fr gray blue & multi	.50 .45
b.		SP5 40fr + 5fr lilac & deep green	.75 .50

Issued in memory of Prince Louis Rwagasore and President John F. Kennedy.

Republic

Winston Churchill and St. Paul's, London SP6

Designs: 15fr+2fr, Tower of London and Churchill. 20fr+3fr, Big Ben and Churchill.

1967, Mar. 23   Photo.   Perf. 13½
B28	SP6	4fr + 1fr multi	.15 .15
B29	SP6	15fr + 2fr multi	.35 .15
B30	SP6	20fr + 3fr multi	.45 .18
		Nos. B28-B30 (3)	.95 .48

Issued in memory of Sir Winston Churchill (1874-1965), statesman and World War II leader. A souvenir sheet contains one airmail stamp, 50fr+5fr, with Churchill portrait centered. Size: 80x80mm. Exists perf. and imperf. Value, each sheet, $3.50.

Nos. B28-B30 Overprinted

1967, July 14   Photo.   Perf. 13½
B31	SP6	4fr + 1fr multi	.15 .15
B32	SP6	15fr + 2fr multi	.42 .20
B33	SP6	20fr + 3fr multi	.65 .30
		Nos. B31-B33 (3)	1.22 .65

50th anniversary of Lions International. Exist with dates transposed. The souvenir sheets described below No. B30 also received this Lions overprint. Value, each $3.50.

Blood Transfusion and Red Cross — SP7

Designs: 7fr+1fr, Stretcher bearers and wounded man. 11fr+1fr, Surgical team. 17fr+1fr, Nurses tending blood bank.

1969, June 26   Photo.   Perf. 13½
B34	SP7	4fr + 1fr multi	.15 .15
B35	SP7	7fr + 1fr multi	.15 .15
B36	SP7	11fr + 1fr multi	.30 .15
B37	SP7	17fr + 1fr multi	.32 .15
		Nos. B34-B37,CB9-CB11 (7)	2.50 1.10

League of Red Cross Societies, 50th anniv.

Pope Paul VI and Map of Africa — SP8

3fr+2fr, 17fr+2fr, Pope Paul VI. 10fr+2fr, Flag made of flags of African Nations. 14fr+2fr, View of St. Peter's, Rome. 40fr+2fr, 40fr+5fr, Martyrs of Uganda. 50fr+2fr, 50fr+5fr, Pope on Throne.

1969, Sept. 12   Photo.   Perf. 13½
B38	SP8	3fr + 2fr multi, vert.	.15 .15
B39	SP8	5fr + 2fr multi	.15 .15
B40	SP8	10fr + 2fr multi	.30 .15
B41	SP8	14fr + 2fr multi	.42 .15
B42	SP8	17fr + 2fr multi, vert.	.50 .15
B43	SP8	40fr + 2fr multi	1.00 .18
B44	SP8	50fr + 2fr multi	1.10 .20
		Nos. B38-B44 (7)	3.62 1.13

Souvenir Sheet
B45		Sheet of 2	2.00 1.75
a.		SP8 40fr + 5fr multi	.90 .90
b.		SP8 50fr + 5fr multi	1.00 .90

Visit of Pope Paul VI to Uganda, July 31-Aug. 2.

Virgin and Child, by Albrecht Dürer — SP9

Christmas (Paintings): 11fr+1fr, Madonna of the Eucharist, by Sandro Botticelli. 20fr+1fr, Holy Family, by El Greco.

1970, Dec. 14   Photo.   Perf. 13½
Gold Frame
B46	SP9	6.50fr + 1fr multi	.15 .15
B47	SP9	11fr + 1fr multi	.22 .15
B48	SP9	20fr + 1fr multi	.42 .15
a.		Souvenir sheet of 3B46-B48	.90 .90
		Nos. B46-B48,CB12-CB14 (6)	2.14 .95

Nos. 376-378 Surcharged in Gold and Black

1971, Nov. 27
B49	A51	3fr + 1fr multi	.15 .15
B50	A51	5fr + 1fr multi	.15 .15
B51	A51	6fr + 1fr multi	.18 .15
a.		Souvenir sheet of 3	.55 .55
		Nos. B49-B51,CB19-CB21 (6)	1.78 .91

UNICE, 25th anniv. #B51a contains 3 stamps similar to #B49-B51 with 2fr surtax each.

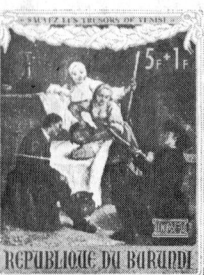

"La Polenta," by Pietro Longhi SP10

Designs: 3fr+1fr, Archangel Michael, Byzantine icon from St. Mark's 6fr+1fr, "Gossip," by Pietro Longhi. 11fr+1fr, "Diana's Bath," by Giovanni Batista Pittoni. All stamps inscribed UNESCO.

1971, Dec. 27
B52 SP10 3fr + 1fr gold & multi .15 .15
B53 SP10 5fr + 1fr gold & multi .15 .15
B54 SP10 6fr + 1fr gold & multi .18 .15
B55 SP10 11fr + 1fr gold & multi .30 .15
a. Souvenir sheet of 4 .75 .50
Nos. B52-B55,CB22-CB25 (8) 2.26 1.21

The surtax was for the UNESCO campaign to save the treasures of Venice. No. B55a contains 4 stamps similar to Nos. B52-B55, but with 2fr surtax. Sheet exists imperf.

Nos. 408-410 Surcharged "+1F" in Silver

1972, Dec. 12 Photo. *Perf. 13½*
B56 A57 5fr + 1fr multi .15 .15
B57 A57 10fr + 1fr multi .22 .15
B58 A57 15fr + 1fr multi .32 .15
a. Souvenir sheet of 3 .75 .70
Nos. B56-B58,CB26-CB28 (6) 2.02 .93

Christmas 1972. No. B58a contains 3 stamps similar to Nos. B56-B58, but with 2fr surtax.

Nos. 441-443 Surcharged "+1F" in Silver

1973, Dec. 14 Photo. *Perf. 13*
B59 A64 5fr + 1fr multi .15 .15
B60 A64 10fr + 1fr multi .20 .15
B61 A64 15fr + 1fr multi .30 .15
a. Souvenir sheet of 3 .65 .65
Nos. B59-B61,CB29-CB31 (6) 1.93 .95

Christmas 1973. No. B61a contains 3 stamps similar to Nos. B59-B61 with 2fr surtax each.

Christmas Type of 1974

1974, Dec. 2 Photo. *Perf. 13*
B62 A70 5fr + 1fr multi .15 .15
B63 A70 10fr + 1fr multi .20 .15
B64 A70 15fr + 1fr multi .30 .18
a. Souvenir sheet of 3 .75 .75
Nos. B62-B64,CB32-CB34 (6) 2.17 1.40

No. B64a contains 3 stamps similar to Nos. B62-B64 with 2fr surtax each.

Nos. 485-490 Surcharged "+ 1F" in Silver and Black

1975, Dec. 22 Photo. *Perf. 13*
B65 A73 5fr + 1fr #485 .15
B66 A73 5fr + 1fr #486 .15
B67 A73 13fr + 1fr #487 .28
B68 A73 13fr + 1fr #488 .28
B69 A73 27fr + 1fr #489 .50
B70 A73 27fr + 1fr #490 .50
a. Souvenir sheet of 6 2.50
Nos. B65-B70,CB35-CB40 (12) 5.16

Michelangelo Buonarroti (1475-1564), 500th birth anniversary. No. B70a contains 6 stamps similar to Nos. B65-B70 with 2fr surcharge each.

Nos. 504-506 Surcharged "+1f" in Silver and Black

1976, Nov. 25 Photo. *Perf. 13½*
B71 A76 5fr + 1fr multi .15
B72 A76 13fr + 1fr multi .22
B73 A76 27fr + 1fr multi .42
a. Souvenir sheet of 3 .85
Nos. B71-B73,CB41-CB43 (6) 2.19

Christmas 1976. No. B73a contains 3 stamps similar to Nos. B71-B73 with 2fr surtax each.

Nos. 531-533 Surcharged "+1fr" in Silver and Black

1977 Photo. *Perf. 14x13*
B74 A83 5fr + 1fr multi .15
B75 A83 13fr + 1fr multi .22
B76 A83 27fr + 1fr multi .42
a. Souvenir sheet of 3 .85
Nos. B74-B76,CB44-CB46 (6) 2.17

Christmas 1977. No. B76a contains 3 stamps similar to Nos. B74-B76 with 2fr surtax each.

Christmas Type of 1979

1979, Feb. Photo. *Perf. 14x13*
B77 A86 13fr + 1fr multi .22
B78 A86 17fr + 1fr multi .28
B79 A86 27fr + 1fr multi .42
B80 A86 31fr + 1fr multi .50
B81 A86 40fr + 1fr multi .60
Nos. B77-B81 (5) 2.02

IYC Type of 1979

1979, July 19 Photo. *Perf. 14*
B82 Sheet of 4 1.25 1.00
a. A88 10fr + 2fr like #557 .15 .15
b. A88 20fr + 2fr like #558 .24 .15
c. A88 27fr + 2fr like #559 .28 .20
d. A88 50fr + 2fr like #560 .55 .32

Christmas Type of 1979

1979, Dec. 10 Photo. *Perf. 13½*
B83 A89 20fr + 1fr like #561 .32
B84 A89 27fr + 1fr like #562 .42
B85 A89 31fr + 1fr like #563 .48
B86 A89 50fr + 2fr like #564 .80
Nos. B83-B86 (4) 2.02

Christmas Type of 1980

1981, Jan. 16 Photo. *Perf. 13½x13*
B87 A92 10fr + 1fr like #579 .15
B88 A92 30fr + 1fr like #580 .32
B89 A92 40fr + 1fr like #581 .42
B90 A92 50fr + 1fr like #582 .50
Nos. B87-B90 (4) 1.39

Christmas Type of 1983

1983, Nov. 2 Litho. *Perf. 14½x13½*
B91 A97 10fr + 1fr like #607 .16
B92 A97 25fr + 1fr like #608 .40
B93 A97 30fr + 1fr like #609 .48
B94 A97 50fr + 1fr like #610 .75
Nos. B91-B94 (4) 1.79

Christmas Type of 1984

1984, Dec. 15 *Perf. 13½*
B95 A101 10fr + 1fr like #629 .16
B96 A101 25fr + 1fr like #630 .40
B97 A101 30fr + 1fr like #631 .48
B98 A101 50fr + 1fr like #632 .75
Nos. B95-B98 (4) 1.79

Multi-party Elections, 1st Anniv.
SP11 SP12

Designs: 30fr+10fr, Pres. Buyoya handing Baton of Power to Pres. Ndadaye. 110fr+10fr, Pres. Ndadaye giving inauguration speech. 115fr+10fr, Arms, map of Burundi. 120fr+10fr, Warrior, flag of Burundi, trees, map of Burundi.

1994, Oct. 20 Litho. *Perf. 15*
B99 SP11 30fr +10fr multi .30
B100 SP11 110fr +10fr multi .90
B101 SP12 115fr +10fr multi .95
B102 SP12 120fr +10fr multi 1.00
Nos. B99-B102 (4) 3.15

AIR POST STAMPS

Animal Type of Regular Issue

6fr, Zebra. 8fr, Cape buffalo (bubalis). 10fr, Impala. 14fr, Hippopotamus. 15fr, Defassa waterbuck. 20fr, Cheetah. 50fr, Elephant.

Unwmk.

1964, July 2 Litho. *Perf. 14*
Size: 42x21mm, 21x42mm
C1 A9 6fr multi .15 .15
C2 A9 8fr multi .16 .15
C3 A9 10fr multi, vert. .22 .15
C4 A9 14fr multi .30 .15
C5 A9 15fr multi, vert. .32 .15
Size: 53x32½mm
C6 A9 20fr multi .42 .15
C7 A9 50fr multi 1.10 .38
Nos. C1-C7 (7) 2.67 1.28

Bird Type of Regular Issue

Birds: 6fr, Secretary bird. 8fr, African anhinga. 10fr, African peacock. 14fr, Bee eater. 15fr, Yellow-billed stork. 20fr, Saddle-billed stork. 50fr, Abyssinian ground hornbill. 75fr, Martial eagle. 130fr, Lesser flamingo.

1965, June 10 Litho. *Perf. 14*
Size: 26x43mm
C8 A14 6fr multi .15 .15
C9 A14 8fr multi .15 .15
C10 A14 10fr multi .20 .15
C11 A14 14fr multi .25 .15
C12 A14 15fr multi .30 .15
Size: 33x53mm
C13 A14 20fr multi .35 .15
C14 A14 50fr multi .90 .20
C15 A14 75fr multi 1.25 .25
C16 A14 130fr multi 2.25 .38
Nos. C8-C16 (9) 5.80 1.73

For overprints see Nos. C35A-C35I.

Flower Type of Regular Issue

Flowers: 6fr, Dissotis. 8fr, Crossandra. 10fr, Ansellia. 14fr, Thunbergia. 15fr, Schizoglossum. 20fr, Gazania. 50fr, Protea. 75fr, Hibiscus. 130fr, Markhamia.

1966, Oct. 10 Unwmk. *Perf. 13½*
Size: 31x31mm
C17 A17 6fr multi .15 .15
C18 A17 8fr multi .15 .15
C19 A17 10fr multi .18 .15
C20 A17 14fr multi .22 .15
C21 A17 15fr multi .22 .15
Size: 39x39mm
C22 A17 20fr multi .22 .15
C23 A17 50fr multi .60 .18
C24 A17 75fr multi .80 .22
C25 A17 130fr multi 1.50 .32
Nos. C17-C25 (9) 4.04 1.62

For overprints see Nos. C27-C35.

Tapestry Type of Regular Issue
Souvenir Sheet

1960, Nov. 4 Unwmk. *Perf. 13½*
C26 A18 Sheet of 7 (14fr) 1.25 .65

See note after No. 158.

Republic
Nos. C17-C25 Overprinted

1967 Litho. *Perf. 13½*
Size: 31x31mm
C27 A17 6fr multi .20 .15
C28 A17 8fr multi .22 .15
C29 A17 10fr multi .25 .15
C30 A17 14fr multi .48 .15
C31 A17 15fr multi .48 .15
Size: 39x39mm
C32 A17 20fr multi .70 .18
C33 A17 50fr multi 1.90 .50
C34 A17 75fr multi 3.00 .50
C35 A17 130fr multi 4.00 1.10
Nos. C27-C35 (9) 11.23 3.03

Nos. C8-C16 Overprinted "REPUBLIQUE / DU / BURUNDI" and Horizontal Bar

1967 Litho. *Perf. 14*
Size: 26x43mm
C35A A14 6fr multi *.15*
C35B A14 8fr multi *.18*
C35C A14 10fr multi *.20*
C35D A14 14fr multi *.30*
C35E A14 15fr multi *.48*
Size: 33x53mm
C35F A14 20fr multi *.75*
C35G A14 50fr multi *1.90*
C35H A14 75fr multi *3.00*
C35I A14 130fr multi *3.50*
Nos. C35A-C35I (9) *10.46*

African Art Type of Regular Issue

African Art: 10fr, Spirit of Bakutu figurine, Equatorial Africa. 14fr, Pearl throne of Sultan of the Bamum, Cameroun. 17fr, Bronze head of Mother Queen of Benin, Nigeria. 24fr, Statue of 109th Bakouba king, Kata-Mbula, Central Congo. 26fr, Baskets and lances, Burundi.

1967, June 5 Photo. *Perf. 13½*
C36 A20 10fr gold & multi .15 .15
C37 A20 14fr gold & multi .15 .15
C38 A20 17fr gold & multi .15 .15
C39 A20 24fr gold & multi .22 .15
C40 A20 26fr gold & multi .42 .25
Nos. C36-C40 (5) 1.09 .85

Boy Scout Type of Regular Issue

10fr, Scouts on hiking trip. 14fr, Cooking at campfire. 17fr, Lord Baden-Powell. 24fr, Boy Scout & Cub Scout giving Scout sign. 26fr, First aid.

1967, Aug. 9 *Perf. 13½*
C41 A21 10fr gold & multi .15 .15
C42 A21 14fr gold & multi .22 .15
C43 A21 17fr gold & multi .28 .15
C44 A21 24fr gold & multi .42 .18
C45 A21 26fr gold & multi .70 .18
Nos. C41-C45 (5) 1.77 .81

A souvenir sheet of 2 contains one each of Nos. C44-C45 and 2 labels in the designs of Nos. 208-209 with commemorative inscriptions was issued Jan. 8, 1968. Size: 100x100mm

Fish Type of Regular Issue

Designs: Various Tropical Fish

1967, Sept. 8 Photo. *Perf. 13½*
Size: 50x23mm
C46 A19 6fr multi .15 .15
C47 A19 8fr multi .16 .15
C48 A19 10fr multi .18 .15
C49 A19 14fr multi .25 .15
C50 A19 15fr multi .25 .15
Size: 58x27mm
C51 A19 20fr multi .32 .15
C52 A19 50fr multi .80 .15
C53 A19 75fr multi 1.25 .16
C54 A19 130fr multi 2.00 .26
Nos. C46-C54 (9) 5.36 1.47

Boeing 707 of Air Congo and ITY Emblem — AP1

Designs: 14fr, Boeing 727 of Sabena over lake. 17fr, Vickers VC10 of East African Airways over lake. 26fr, Boeing 727 of Sabena over airport.

1967, Nov. 3 Photo. *Perf. 13*
C55 AP1 10fr blk, yel brn & sil .15 .15
C56 AP1 14fr blk, org & sil .20 .15
C57 AP1 17fr blk, brt bl & sil .25 .15
C58 AP1 26fr blk, brt rose lil & sil .42 .15
Nos. C55-C58 (4) 1.02 .60

Opening of the jet airport at Bujumbura and for International Tourist Year, 1967.

Paintings Type of Regular Issue

Paintings: 17fr, Woman with Cat, by Renoir. 24fr, The Jewish Bride, by Rembrandt, horiz. 26fr, Pope Innocent X, by Velazquez.

1968, Mar. 29 Photo. *Perf. 13½*
C59 A26 17fr multi .35 .15
C60 A26 24fr multi .45 .18
C61 A26 26fr multi .55 .20
Nos. C59-C61 (3) 1.35 .53

Issued in sheets of 6.

Space Type of Regular Issue

Designs: 14fr, Moon Probe. 18fr, Russian astronaut walking in space. 25fr, Weather satellite. 40fr, American astronaut walking in space.

1968, May 15 Photo. *Perf. 13½*
Size: 41x41mm
C62 A27 14fr sil & multi .25 .15
C63 A27 18fr sil & multi .30 .15
C64 A27 25fr sil & multi .45 .15
C65 A27 40fr sil & multi .70 .18
Nos. C62-C65 (4) 1.70 .63

Butterfly Type of Regular Issue

Butterflies: 6fr, Teracolus annae. 8fr, Graphium ridleyanus. 10fr, Cymothoe. 14fr, Charaxes eupale. 15fr, Papilio bromius. 20fr, Papilio zenobia. 50fr, Salamis aethiops. 75fr, Danais chrysippus. 130fr, Salamis temora.

1968, Sept. 9 Photo. *Perf. 13½*
Size: 38x42mm
C66 A28 6fr gold & multi .15 .15
C67 A28 8fr gold & multi .15 .15
C68 A28 10fr gold & multi .35 .15
C69 A28 14fr gold & multi .40 .15
C70 A28 15fr gold & multi .40 .15
Size: 44x49mm
C71 A28 20fr gold & multi .60 .15
C72 A28 50fr gold & multi 1.25 .15
C73 A28 75fr gold & multi 2.50 .15
C74 A28 130fr gold & multi 4.00 .20
Nos. C66-C74 (9) 9.80 1.40

Painting Type of Regular Issue

Paintings: 17fr, The Letter, by Jean H. Fragonard. 26fr, Young Woman Reading Letter, by Jan Vermeer. 40fr, Lady Folding Letter, by Elisabeth Vigée-Lebrun. 50fr, Mademoiselle Lavergne, by Jean Etienne Liotard.

1968, Sept. 30 Photo. *Perf. 13½*
C84 A29 17fr multi .22 .15
C85 A29 26fr multi .42 .15
C86 A29 40fr multi .60 .15
C87 A29 50fr multi .70 .18
Nos. C84-C87 (4) 1.94 .63

Olympic Games Type

1968, Oct. 24
C88 A30 10fr Shot put .15 .15
C89 A30 17fr Running .22 .15
C90 A30 26fr Hammer throw .38 .15

BURUNDI

C91 A30 50fr Hurdling .70 .20
C92 A30 75fr Broad jump 1.10 .30
Nos. C88-C92 (5) 2.55 .95

Christmas Type of 1968

Paintings: 10fr, Virgin and Child, by Correggio. 14fr, Nativity, by Federigo Barocchio. 17fr, Holy Family, by El Greco. 26fr, Adoration of the Magi, by Maino.

1968, Nov. 26 Photo. Perf. 13½
C93 A31 10fr multi .15 .15
C94 A31 14fr multi .22 .15
C95 A31 17fr multi .28 .15
C96 A31 26fr multi .40 .15
a. Souv. sheet of 4, #C93-C96 1.10
Nos. C93-C96 (4) 1.05 .60

For overprints see Nos. C100-C103.

Human Rights Flame, Hand and Globe — AP2

1969, Jan. 22
C97 AP2 10fr multi .15 .15
C98 AP2 14fr multi .22 .15
C99 AP2 26fr lil & multi .40 .15
Nos. C97-C99 (3) .77 .45

International Human Rights Year, 1968.

Nos. C93-C96 Overprinted in Silver

1969, Feb. 17 Photo. Perf. 13½
C100 A31 10fr multi .20 .15
C101 A31 14fr multi .28 .15
C102 A31 17fr multi .35 .15
C103 A31 26fr multi .50 .22
Nos. C100-C103 (4) 1.33 .67

Man's 1st flight around the moon by the US spacecraft Apollo 8, Dec. 21-27, 1968.

Moon Landing Type of 1969

Designs: 26fr, Neil A. Armstrong leaving landing module. 40fr, Astronaut on moon. 50fr, Splashdown in the Pacific.

1969, Nov. 6 Photo. Perf. 13½
C104 A38 26fr gold & multi .50 .25
C105 A38 40fr gold & multi .75 .38
C106 A38 50fr gold & multi .90 .42
Nos. C104-C106 (3) 2.15 1.05

Christmas Type of 1969

Paintings: 17fr, Madonna and Child, by Benvenuto da Garofalo. 26fr, Madonna and Child, by Jacopo Negretti. 50fr, Madonna and Child, by Il Giorgione. All horizontal.

1969, Dec. 2 Photo.
C107 A39 17fr gold & multi .38 .15
C108 A39 26fr gold & multi .50 .15
C109 A39 50fr gold & multi .90 .28
a. Souv. sheet of 3, #C107-C109 1.90 1.50
Nos. C107-C109 (3) 1.78 .58

Insect Type of Regular Issue

Designs: Various Beetles and Weevils.

1970 Perf. 13½
Size: 46x32mm
C110 A40 6fr gold & multi .15 .15
C111 A40 8fr gold & multi .15 .15
C112 A40 10fr gold & multi .18 .15
C113 A40 14fr gold & multi .25 .15
C114 A40 15fr gold & multi .30 .15
Size: 52x36mm
C115 A40 20fr gold & multi 1.00 .15
C116 A40 50fr gold & multi 2.00 .25
C117 A40 75fr gold & multi 3.00 .15
C118 A40 130fr gold & multi 3.75 .40
Nos. C110-C118 (9) 10.78 1.80

Issued: #C110-C115, 1/20; $C116-C118, 2/27.

Easter Type of 1970

Stations of the Cross, by Juan de Aranoa y Carredano: 8fr, Jesus meets the women of Jerusalem. 10fr, Jesus falls a third time. 14fr, Jesus stripped. 15fr, Jesus nailed to the cross. 18fr, Jesus dies on the cross. 20fr, Descent from the cross. 50fr, Jesus laid in the tomb.

1970, Mar. 16 Photo. Perf. 13½
C119 A41 8fr gold & multi .15 .15
C120 A41 10fr gold & multi .15 .15
C121 A41 14fr gold & multi .22 .15
C122 A41 15fr gold & multi .25 .15
C123 A41 18fr gold & multi .28 .15
C124 A41 20fr gold & multi .30 .15
C125 A41 50fr gold & multi .70 .15
a. Souv. sheet of 7, #C119-C125 + label 2.25 1.75
Nos. C119-C125 (7) 2.05 1.20

EXPO '70 Type of Regular Issue Souvenir Sheet

Designs: 40fr, Tower of the Sun, vert. 50fr, Flags of participating nations, vert.

1970, May 5 Photo. Perf. 13½
C126 Sheet of 2 1.40 1.40
a. A42 40fr multi .50 .50
b. A42 50fr multi .60 .60

Rhinoceros Type of Regular Issue

FAUNA: Camel, dromedary, okapi, rhinoceros, addax, Burundi cow (2 stamps of each animal in 2 different poses). MAP OF THE NILE: Delta and pyramids, dhow, cataract, Blue Nile and crowned crane, Victoria Nile and secretary bird, Lake Victoria and source of Nile on Mt. Gikizi.

1970, July 8 Photo. Perf. 13½
C127 Sheet of 18 5.25
a. A43 14fr any single .28 .15

Issued in sheets of 18 (3x6) stamps of different designs, to publicize the southernmost source of the Nile on Mt. Gikizi in Burundi.

UN Emblem and Headquarters, NYC — AP3

25th Anniv. of the UN (UN Emblem and): 11fr, Security Council and mural by Per Krohg. 26fr, Pope Paul VI and U Thant. 40fr, Flags in front of UN Headquarters, NYC.

1970, Oct. 23 Photo. Perf. 13½
C128 AP3 7fr gold & multi .15 .15
C129 AP3 11fr gold & multi .18 .15
C130 AP3 26fr gold & multi .40 .15
C131 AP3 40fr gold & multi .60 .15
a. Souv. sheet of 2 1.10 .90
Nos. C128-C131 (4) 1.33 .60

No. C131a contains 2 stamps similar to Nos. C130-C131 but without "Poste Aerienne." Exists imperf.

Bird Type of Regular Issue

8fr, 14fr, 30fr, vert.; 10fr, 20fr, 50fr, horiz.

1970 Photo. Perf. 13½
Stamp size: 52x44mm
C132 A44 Block of 4 2.00 .15
a. 8fr Northern shrike .50 .15
b. 8fr European starling .50 .15
c. 8fr Yellow wagtail .50 .15
d. 8fr Bank swallow .50 .15
C133 A44 Block of 4 2.50 .20
a. 10fr Winter wren .60 .15
b. 10fr Firecrest .60 .15
c. 10fr Skylark .60 .15
d. 10fr Crested lark .60 .15
C134 A44 Block of 4 3.00 .25
a. 14fr Woodchat shrike .75 .15
b. 14fr Common rock thrush .75 .15
c. 14fr Black redstart .75 .15
d. 14fr Ring ouzel .75 .15
C135 A44 Block of 4 5.00 .35
a. 20fr European redstart 1.25 .15
b. 20fr Hedge sparrow 1.25 .15
c. 20fr Gray wagtail 1.25 .15
d. 20fr Meadow pipit 1.25 .15
C136 A44 Block of 4 7.00 .55
a. 30fr Eurasian hoopoe 1.75 .15
b. 30fr Pied flycatcher 1.75 .15
c. 30fr Great reed warbler 1.75 .15
d. 30fr Eurasian kingfisher 1.75 .15
C137 A44 Block of 4 11.00 .90
a. 50fr House martin 2.75 .20
b. 50fr Sedge warbler 2.75 .20
c. 50fr Fieldfare 2.75 .20
d. 50fr European Golden oriole 2.75 .20
Nos. C132-C137 (6) 30.50 2.40

Queen Fabiola and King Baudouin of Belgium AP4

Designs: 20fr, Pres. Michel Micombero and King Baudouin. 40fr, Pres. Micombero and coats of arms of Burundi and Belgium.

1970, Nov. 28 Photo. Perf. 13½
C140 AP4 6fr multicolored .15 .15
C141 AP4 20fr multicolored .45 .15
C142 AP4 40fr multicolored .90 .30
a. Souvenir sheet of 3 1.50 1.50
Nos. C140-C142 (3) 1.50 .60

Visit of the King and Queen of Belgium. No. C142a contains 3 stamps similar to Nos. C140-C142, but without "Poste Aerienne." No. C142a exists imperf.

Easter Type of Regular Issue

Paintings of the Resurrection: 14fr, by Louis Borrassá. 17fr, Piero della Francesca. 26fr, Michel Wohlgemuth.

1971, Apr. 2 Photo. Perf. 13½
C143 A49 14fr gold & multi .20 .15
C144 A49 17fr gold & multi .22 .15
C145 A49 26fr gold & multi .30 .15
a. Souv. sheet of 3, #C143-C145 1.00 .75
Nos. C143-C145 (3) .72 .45

Easter 1971. No. C145a sheet exists imperf.

Animal Type of Regular Issue

1971 Photo. Perf. 13½
Size: 44x44mm
C146 Strip of 4 1.50 .15
a. A48 10fr Lion .35 .15
b. A48 10fr Cape buffalo .35 .15
c. A48 10fr Hippopotamus .35 .15
d. A48 10fr Giraffe .35 .15
C147 Strip of 4 2.25 .25
a. A48 14fr Hartebeest .55 .15
b. A48 14fr Black rhinoceros .55 .15
c. A48 14fr Zebra .55 .15
d. A48 14fr Leopard .55 .15
C148 Strip of 4 3.00 .25
a. A48 17fr Grant's gazelles .75 .15
b. A48 17fr Cheetah .75 .15
c. A48 17fr African white-backed vultures .75 .15
d. A48 17fr Johnston's okapi .75 .15
C149 Strip of 4 3.50 .35
a. A48 24fr Chimpanzee .85 .15
b. A48 24fr Elephant .85 .15
c. A48 24fr Spotted Hyenas .85 .15
d. A48 24fr Beisa .85 .15
C150 Strip of 4 4.00 .40
a. A48 26fr Gorilla 1.00 .15
b. A48 26fr Gnu 1.00 .15
c. A48 26fr Warthog 1.00 .15
d. A48 26fr Cape hunting dog 1.00 .15
C151 Strip of 4 5.00 .50
a. A48 31fr Sable antelope 1.25 .15
b. A48 31fr Caracal lynx 1.25 .15
c. A48 31fr Ostriches 1.25 .15
d. A48 31fr Bongo 1.25 .15
Nos. C146-C151 (6) 19.25 1.90

For overprint and surcharges see Nos. C152, CB15-C18.

No. C146 Overprinted in Gold and Black

1971, July 20 Photo. Perf. 13½
C152 Strip of 4 .60 .15
a. A48 10fr Lion .15 .15
b. A48 10fr Cape buffalo .15 .15
c. A48 10fr Hippopotamus .15 .15
d. A48 10fr Giraffe .15 .15

Intl. Year Against Racial Discrimination.

Christmas Type of Regular Issue

Paintings of the Madonna and Child by: 14fr, Cima de Conegliano. 17fr, Fra Filippo Lippi. 31fr, Leonardo da Vinci.

1971, Nov. 2 Photo. Perf. 13½
C153 A51 14fr red & multi .28 .15
C154 A51 17fr red & multi .32 .15
C155 A51 31fr red & multi .50 .20
a. Souv. sheet of 3, #C153-C155 1.10 1.10
Nos. C153-C155 (3) 1.10 .50

Christmas 1971. No. C155a exists imperf. For surcharges see Nos. CB19-CB21.

Spacecraft Type of Regular Issue Souvenir Sheet

1972, Jan. 15 Photo. Perf. 13½
C156 Sheet of 6 1.50 1.00
a. A52 6fr Lunar Orbiter .15 .15
b. A52 11fr Vostok .15 .15
c. A52 14fr Luna I .18 .15
d. A52 17fr Apollo 11 astronaut on moon .22 .15
e. A52 26fr Soyuz 11 .35 .18
f. A52 40fr Lunar rover (Apollo 15) .50 .25

Sapporo '72 Type of Regular Issue Souvenir Sheet

Designs (Sapporo '72 Emblem and): 26fr, Snow scooter. 31fr, Downhill skiing. 50fr, Bobsledding.

1972, Feb. 3
C157 Sheet of 3 1.50 1.25
a. A53 26fr silver & multi .35 .20
b. A53 31fr silver & multi .40 .30
c. A53 50fr silver & multi .65 .45

No. C157 contains 3 stamps, arranged vertically.

Olympic Games Type of 1972

1972, July 24 Photo. Perf. 13½
C158 A55 24fr Weight lifting .35 .15
C159 A55 26fr Hurdles .40 .15
C160 A55 31fr Discus .50 .15
C161 A55 40fr Soccer .60 .20
Nos. C158-C161 (4) 1.85 .65

Independence Type of 1972

Designs: 15fr, Prince Rwagasore, Pres. Micombero, Burundi flag, drummers. 18fr, Rwagasore, Micombero, flag, map of Africa, globe. 27fr, Micombero, flag, globe.

1972, Aug. 24 Photo. Perf. 13½
C162 A56 15fr gold & multi .25 .15
C163 A56 18fr gold & multi .30 .15
C164 A56 27fr gold & multi .45 .15
a. Souv. sheet of 3, #C162-C164 1.10 1.10
Nos. C162-C164 (3) 1.00 .45

Christmas Type of 1972

Paintings of the Madonna and Child by: 18fr, Sebastiano Mainardi. 27fr, Hans Memling. 40fr, Lorenzo Lotto.

1972, Nov. 2 Photo. Perf. 13½
C165 A57 18fr dk car & multi .28 .15
C166 A57 27fr dk car & multi .40 .15
C167 A57 40fr dk car & multi .60 .18
a. Souv. sheet of 3, #C165-C167 1.40 1.40
Nos. C165-C167 (3) 1.28 .48

For surcharges see Nos. CB26-CB28.

Orchid Type of Regular Issue

1973, Jan. 18 Photo. Perf. 13½
Size: 38x38mm
C168 A58 13fr Thelymitra pauciflora .80 .15
C169 A58 14fr Miltassia .80 .15
C170 A58 15fr Miltonia .90 .15
C171 A58 18fr Platycoryne crocea 1.00 .15
C172 A58 20fr Cattleya trinaei 1.25 .15
C173 A58 27fr Eulophia cucullata 1.75 .15
C174 A58 36fr Cymbidium hamsey 2.25 .15
Nos. C168-C174 (7) 8.75 1.05

African Exploration Type of 1973

Designs: 15fr, Livingstone writing his diary. 18fr, "Dr. Livingstone, I presume." 27fr, Livingstone and Stanley discussing expedition.

1973, Mar. 19 Photo. Perf. 13½
C175 A59 15fr gold & multi .22 .15
C176 A59 18fr gold & multi .28 .15
C177 A59 27fr gold & multi .40 .15
a. Souv. sheet of 3 1.10 1.10
Nos. C175-C177 (3) .90 .45

#C177a contains 3 stamps similar to #C175-C177, but without "Poste Aerienne."

Easter Type of 1973

Paintings: 15fr, Christ at the Pillar, by Guido Reni. 18fr, Crucifixion, by Mathias Grunewald. 27fr, Descent from the Cross, by Caravaggio.

1973, Apr. 10
C178 A60 15fr gold & multi .28 .15
C179 A60 18fr gold & multi .35 .15
C180 A60 27fr gold & multi .50 .15
a. Souv. sheet of 3, #C178-C180 1.25 1.25
Nos. C178-C180 (3) 1.13 .45

INTERPOL Type of Regular Issue

Designs: 27fr, INTERPOL emblem and flag. 40fr, INTERPOL flag and emblem.

1973, May 19 Photo. *Perf. 13½*

C181 A61 27fr gold & multi .40 .16
C182 A61 40fr gold & multi .48 .20

Copernicus Type of Regular Issue

Designs: 15fr, Copernicus (C183a), Earth, Pluto, and Jupiter. 18fr, Copernicus (No. C184a), Venus, Saturn, Mars. 27fr, Copernicus (No. C185a), Uranus, Neptune, Mercury. 36fr, Earth and various spacecrafts.

a, UL. b, UR. c, LL. d, LR.

1973, July 27 Photo. *Perf. 13½*

C183 A62 15fr Block of 4, #a.-d. 1.40 .30
C184 A62 18fr Block of 4, #a.-d. 1.65 .35
C185 A62 27fr Block of 4, #a.-d. 2.00 .50
C186 A62 36fr Block of 4, #a.-d. 2.75 .70
e. Souv. sheet of 4, #C183-C186 7.00 7.00
Nos. C183-C186 (4) 7.80 1.85

Flower-Butterfly Type of 1973

Designs: Each block of 4 contains 2 flower and 2 butterfly designs. The 10fr, 14fr, 24fr and 31fr have flower designs listed as "a" and "d" numbers, butterflies as "b" and "c" numbers; the arrangement is reversed for the 17fr and 26fr.

1973, Sept. 28 Photo. *Perf. 13*
Stamp Size: 35x45mm

C187 A63 Block of 4 3.00 .40
a. 10fr *Protea cynaroides* .75 .15
b. 10fr *Precis octavia* .75 .15
c. 10fr *Epiphora bauhiniae* .75 .15
d. 10fr *Gazania longiscapa* .75 .15
C188 A63 Block of 4 4.00 .50
a. 14fr *Kniphofia* 1.00 .15
b. 14fr *Cymothoe coccinata* 1.00 .15
c. 14fr *Nudaurelia zambesina* 1.00 .15
d. 14fr *Freesia refracta* 1.00 .15
C189 A63 Block of 4 5.00 .60
a. 17fr *Calotis eupompe* 1.25 .15
b. 17fr *Narcissus* 1.25 .15
c. 17fr *Cineraria hybrida* 1.25 .15
d. 17fr *Cyrestis camillus* 1.25 .15
C190 A63 Block of 4 5.50 .50
a. 24fr *Iris tingitana* 1.25 .15
b. 24fr *Papilio demodocus* 1.25 .15
c. 24fr *Catopsilia avelaneda* 1.25 .15
d. 24fr *Nerine sarniensis* 1.25 .15
C191 A63 Block of 4 6.00 .55
a. 26fr *Hypolimnas dexithea* 1.50 .15
b. 26fr *Zantedeschia tropicalis* 1.50 .15
c. 26fr *Sandersonia aurantiaca* 1.50 .15
d. 26fr *Drurya antimachus* 1.50 .15
C192 A63 Block of 4 7.00 .65
a. 31fr *Nymphaea capensis* 1.75 .15
b. 31fr *Pandoriana pandora* 1.75 .15
c. 31fr *Precis orythia* 1.75 .15
d. 31fr *Pelargonium domestica* 1.75 .15
Nos. C187-C192 (6) 30.50 3.20

Christmas Type of 1973

Virgin and Child by: 18fr, Raphael. 27fr, Pietro Perugino. 40fr, Titian.

1973, Nov. 19

C193 A64 18fr gold & multi .28 .15
C194 A64 27fr gold & multi .40 .15
C195 A64 40fr gold & multi .60 .16
a. Souv. sheet of 3, #C193-C195 1.40 1.40
Nos. C193-C195 (3) 1.28 .46

For surcharges see Nos. CB239-CB31.

Soccer Type of Regular Issue

Designs: Various soccer scenes and cup.

1974, July 4 Photo. *Perf. 13*

C196 A67 20fr gold & multi .30
C197 A67 26fr gold & multi .40
C198 A67 40fr gold & multi .60
Nos. C196-C198 (3) 1.30

For souvenir sheet see No. 459a.

UPU Type of 1974

Designs: No. C199, Flags over UPU Headquarters, Bern. No. C200, G.P.O., Usumbura. No. C201, Mailmen ("26F" in UR). No. C202, Mailmen ("26F" in UL). No. C203, UPU emblem. No. C204, Means of transportation. No. C205, Pigeon over globe showing Burundi. No. C206, Swiss flag, pigeon over map showing Bern.

1974, July 23

C199 A68 24fr gold & multi .65
C200 A68 24fr gold & multi .65
C201 A68 26fr gold & multi .75
C202 A68 26fr gold & multi .75
C203 A68 31fr gold & multi 1.00
C204 A68 31fr gold & multi 1.00
C205 A68 40fr gold & multi 1.25
C206 A68 40fr gold & multi 1.25
a. Souv. sheet of 8, #C199-C206 7.50
Nos. C199-C206 (8) 7.30

Stamps of same denomination printed setenant (continuous design) in sheets of 40.

Fish Type of 1974

1974, Sept. 9 Photo. *Perf. 13*
Size: 35x35mm

C207 A66 Block of 4 1.50 .15
a. 10fr *Haplochromis multicolor* .35 .15
b. 10fr *Pantodon buchholzi* .35 .15
c. 10fr *Tropheus duboisi* .35 .15
d. 10fr *Distichodus sexfasciatus* .35 .15
C208 A66 Block of 4 1.75 .20
a. 14fr *Pelmatochromis kribensis* .40 .15
b. 14fr *Nannaethiops tritaeniatus* .40 .15
c. 14fr *Polycentropsis abbreviata* .40 .15
d. 14fr *Hemichromis bimaculatus* .40 .15
C209 A66 Block of 4 2.50 .20
a. 17fr *Ctenopoma acutirostre* .60 .15
b. 17fr *Synodontis angelicus* .60 .15
c. 17fr *Tilapia melanopleura* .60 .15
d. 17fr*Aphyosemion bivittatum* .60 .15
C210 A66 Block of 4 3.00 .30
a. 24fr *Monodactylus argenteus* .75 .15
b. 24fr *Zanclus canescens* .75 .15
c. 24fr *Pygoplites diacanthus* .75 .15
d. 24fr *Cephalopholis argus* .75 .15
C211 A66 Block of 4 3.00 .35
a. 26fr *Priacanthus arenatus* .75 .15
b. 26fr *Pomacanthus arcutus* .75 .15
c. 26fr *Scarus guacamaia* .75 .15
d. 26fr *Zeus faber* .75 .15
C212 A66 Block of 4 4.00 .40
a. 31fr *Lactophrys quadricornis* 1.00 .15
b. 31fr *Balistes vetula* 1.00 .15
c. 31fr *Acanthurus bahianus* 1.00 .15
d. 31fr *Holocanthus ciliaris* 1.00 .15
Nos. C207-C212 (6) 15.75 1.60

Christmas Type of 1974

Paintings of the Virgin and Child: 18fr, by Hans Memling. 27fr, by Filippino Lippi. 40fr, by Lorenzo di Gredi.

1974, Nov. 7 Photo. *Perf. 13*

C213 A70 18fr gold & multi .28 .22
C214 A70 27fr gold & multi .40 .32
C215 A70 40fr gold & multi .60 .48
a. Souv. sheet of 3, #C213-C215 1.50 1.50
Nos. C213-C215 (3) 1.28 1.02

Christmas 1974. Sheets of 20 stamps and one label. No. C215a exists imperf.

Apollo-Soyuz Type of 1975

1975, July 10 Photo. *Perf. 13*

C216 A71 Block of 4 .90
a. 27fr A.A. Leonov, V.N. Kubasov, Soviet flag .22
b. 27fr Soyuz and Soviet flag .22
c. 27fr Apollo and American flag .22
d. 27fr Slayton, Brand, Stafford, American flag .22
C217 A71 Block of 4 1.40
a. 40fr Apollo-Soyuz link-up .32
b. 40fr Apollo, blast-off .32
c. 40fr Soyuz, blast-off .32
d. 40fr Kubasov, Leonov, Slayton, Brand, Stafford .32

Nos. C216-C217 are printed in sheets of 32 containing 8 blocks of 4.

Animal Type of 1975

1975, Sept. 17 Photo. *Perf. 13½*

C218 Strip of 4 .90
a. A72 10fr Addax .22
b. A72 10fr Roan antelope .22
c. A72 10fr Nyala .22
d. A72 10fr White rhinoceros .22
C219 Strip of 4 1.25
a. A72 14fr Mandrill .30
b. A72 14fr Eland .30
c. A72 14fr Salt's dik-dik .30
d. A72 14fr Thomson's gazelles .30
C220 Strip of 4 1.50
a. A72 17fr African small-clawed otter .35
b. A72 17fr Reed buck .35
c. A72 17fr Indian civet .35
d. A72 17fr Cape buffalo .35
C221 Strip of 4 2.00
a. A72 24fr White-tailed gnu .50
b. A72 24fr African wild asses .50
c. A72 24fr Black-and-white colobus monkey .50
d. A72 24fr Gerenuk .50
C222 Strip of 4 2.25
a. A72 26fr Dama gazelle .55
b. A72 26fr Black-backed jackal .55
c. A72 26fr Sitatungas .55
d. A72 26fr Zebra antelope .55
C223 Strip of 4 2.75
a. A72 31fr Fennec .65
b. A72 31fr Lesser kudus .65
c. A72 31fr Blesbok .65
d. A72 31fr Serval .65
Nos. C218-C223 (6) 10.65

Nos. C218-C219 Overprinted in Black and Silver with IWY Emblem and: "ANNEE INTERNATIONALE / DE LA FEMME"

1975, Nov. 19 Photo. *Perf. 13½*

C224 Strip of 4 .60 .15
a. A72 10fr Addax .15 .15
b. A72 10fr Roan antelope .15 .15
c. A72 10fr Nyala .15 .15
d. A72 10fr White rhinoceros .15 .15
C225 Strip of 4 .80 .20
a. A72 14fr Mandrill .20 .15
b. A72 14fr Oryx .20 .15
c. A72 14fr Dik-dik .20 .15
d. A72 14fr Thomson's gazelles .20 .15

International Women's Year 1975.

Nos. C222-C223 Overprinted in Black and Silver with UN Emblem and: "30ème ANNIVERSAIRE DES/ NATIONS UNIES"

1975, Nov. 19

C226 Strip of 4 1.65 .30
a. A72 26fr Dama gazelle .38 .15
b. A72 26fr Wild dog .38 .15
c. A72 26fr Sitatungas .38 .15
d. A72 26fr Striped duiker .38 .15
C227 Strip of 4 1.90 .32
a. A72 31fr Fennec .45 .15
b. A72 31fr Lesser kudus .45 .15
c. A72 31fr Blesbok .45 .15
d. A72 31fr Serval .45 .15

United Nations, 30th anniversary.

Michelangelo Type of 1975

Designs: Paintings from Sistine Chapel.

1975, Dec. 3 Photo. *Perf. 13*

C228 A73 18fr Zachariah .35
C229 A73 18fr Joel .35
C230 A73 31fr Erythrean Sybil .65
C231 A73 31fr Prophet Ezekiel .65
C232 A73 40fr Persian Sybil .80
C233 A73 40fr Prophet Jeremiah .80
a. Souv. sheet of 6, #C228-C233 3.75
Nos. C228-C233 (6) 3.60

Stamps of same denominations printed se-tenant in sheets of 18 stamps and 2 labels.

For surcharges see Nos. CB35-CB40.

Olympic Games Type, 1976

Designs (Olympic Games Emblem and): 18fr, Ski jump. 36fr, Slalom. 50fr, Ice hockey.

1976, Jan. 23 Photo. *Perf. 14x13½*

C234 A74 18fr ol brn & multi .32
C235 A74 36fr grn & multi .70
C236 A74 50fr pur & multi .90
a. Souvenir sheet of 4 2.00
Nos. C234-C236 (3) 1.92

No. C236a contains 4 stamps similar to Nos. 491-494, perf. 13½, inscribed "POSTE AERIENNE."

Hurdles — AP5

Montreal Games Emblem and: #C238, C241, C243b, High jump. #C239, C242, C243a, Athlete on rings. #C240, C243c, Hurdles.

1976, May 3 Litho. *Perf. 13½*

C237 AP5 27fr grn & multi .42
C238 AP5 27fr dk bl & multi .42
C239 AP5 31fr ocher & multi .55
C240 AP5 31fr grn & multi .55
C241 AP5 50fr dk bl & multi .90
C242 AP5 50fr ocher & multi .90
Nos. C237-C242 (6) 3.74

Souvenir Sheet

C243 Sheet of 3 1.75
a. AP5 27fr ocher & multi .38
b. AP5 31fr dark blue & multi .45
c. AP5 50fr green & multi .75

21st Olympic Games, Montreal, Canada, July 17-Aug. 1. Stamps of same denomination printed se-tenant in sheets of 20.

Battle of Bunker Hill, by John Trumbull
AP6 AP7

Paintings: 26fr, Franklin, Jefferson and John Adams. 36fr, Declaration of Independence, by John Trumbull.

1976, July 16 Photo. *Perf. 13*

C244 AP6 18fr gold & multi .35
C245 AP7 18fr gold & multi .35
C246 AP6 26fr gold & multi .45
C247 AP7 26fr gold & multi .45
C248 AP6 36fr gold & multi .75
C249 AP7 36fr gold & multi .75
a. Souv. sheet of 6, #C244-C249 3.25
Nos. C244-C249 (6) 3.10

American Bicentennial. Stamps of same denomination printed se-tenant in sheets of 50.

Christmas Type of 1976

Paintings: 18fr, Virgin and Child with St. Anne, by Leonardo da Vinci. 31fr, Holy Family with Lamb, by Raphael. 40fr, Madonna of the Basket, by Correggio.

1976, Oct. 18 Photo. *Perf. 13½*

C250 A76 18fr gold & multi .25
C251 A76 31fr gold & multi .45
C252 A76 40fr gold & multi .60
a. Souv. sheet of 3, #C250-C252 1.40
Nos. C250-C252 (3) 1.30

Christmas 1976. Sheets of 20 stamps and descriptive label.

For surcharges see Nos. CB41-CB43.

A.G. Bell Type of 1977

Designs: 10fr, A.G. Bell and first telephone. Nos. C253, 17fr, A.G. Bell speaking into microphone. Nos. C254, C257e, Satellites around globe and videophone. No. C255, Switchboard operator, c.1910, and wall telephone. Nos. C256, 26fr, Intelsat satellite, modern and old telephones. No. C257c, Intelsat and radar.

1977, May 17 Photo. *Perf. 13*

C253 A78 18fr multi .15
C254 A79 18fr multi .15
C255 A78 36fr multi .25
C256 A79 36fr multi .25
C257 Sheet of 5 1.75 1.00
a. A78 10fr multi .15 .15
b. A78 17fr multi .25 .15
c. A79 18fr multi .25 .15
d. A79 26fr multi .40 .22
e. A79 36fr multi .52 .25

No. C257 contains 3 postage (10fr, 17fr, 26fr) and 2 air post stamps (18fr, 36fr).

Animal Type of 1977

1977, Aug. 22 Photo. *Perf. 14x14½*

C258 Strip of 4 .80
a. A80 9fr Buffon's kob .20
b. A80 9fr Marabous .20
c. A80 9fr Brindled gnu .20
d. A80 9fr River hog .20
C259 Strip of 4 1.10
a. A80 13fr Zebras .25
b. A80 13fr Shoebill .25
c. A80 13fr Striped hyenas .25
d. A80 13fr Chimpanzee .25
C260 Strip of 4 2.25
a. A80 30fr Flamingos .55
b. A80 30fr Nile Crocodiles .55
c. A80 30fr Green mamba .55
d. A80 30fr Greater kudus .55
C261 Strip of 4 2.75
a. A80 35fr Hyrax .65
b. A80 35fr Cobra .65
c. A80 35fr Jackals .65
d. A80 35fr Verreaux's eagles .65
C262 Strip of 4 4.25
a. A80 54fr Honey badger 1.00
b. A80 54fr Harnessed antelopes 1.00
c. A80 54fr Secretary bird 1.00
d. A80 54fr Klipspringer 1.00
C263 Strip of 4 5.00
a. A80 70fr African big-eared fox 1.25
b. A80 70fr Elephants 1.25
c. A80 70fr Vulturine guineafowl 1.25
d. A80 70fr Impalas 1.25
Nos. C258-C263 (6) 16.15

UN Type of 1977

Designs (UN Stamps and): 24fr, UN buildings by night. 27fr, UN buildings and view of Manhattan. 35fr, UN buildings by day.

1977, Oct. 10 Photo. *Perf. 13½*

C264 A82 Block of 4 1.90
a. 24fr No. 77 .45
b. 24fr No. 78 .45
c. 24fr No. 40 .45
d. 24fr No. 32 .45
C265 A82 Block of 4 2.00
a. 27fr No. 50 .50
b. 27fr No. 21 .50
c. 27fr No. 30 .50
d. 27fr No. 44 .50
C266 A82 Block of 4 3.25
a. 35fr No. C6 .75
b. 35fr No. 105 .75
c. 35fr No. 4 .75
d. 35fr No. 1 .75
e. Souvenir sheet of 3 1.40
Nos. C264-C266 (3) 7.15

No. C266e contains 24fr in design of No. C265b, 27fr in design of No. C266a, 35fr in design of No. C264c.

Christmas Type of 1977

Designs: Paintings of the Virgin and Child.

1977, Oct. 31 Photo. *Perf. 14x13*

C267 A83 18fr Master of Moulins .28
C268 A83 31fr Workshop of Lorenzo de Credi .48
C269 A83 40fr Palma Vecchio .60
a. Souv. sheet of 3, #C267-C269 1.50
Nos. C267-C269 (3) 1.36

Sheets of 24 stamps and descriptive label.

For surcharges see Nos. CB44-CB46.

BURUNDI

Christmas 1978 Type of 1979
Souvenir Sheet

1979, Feb.	Photo.	Perf. 14x13½
C270	Sheet of 5	2.00
a.	A86 13fr like #543	.20
b.	A86 17fr like #544	.25
c.	A86 27fr like #545	.40
d.	A86 31fr like #546	.48
e.	A86 40fr like #547	.60

Christmas Type of 1979
Souvenir Sheet

1979, Oct. 12		Perf. 13½	
C271	Sheet of 4	2.00	1.25
a.	A89 20fr like #561	.30	.16
b.	A89 27fr like #562	.40	.22
c.	A89 31fr like #563	.48	.28
d.	A89 50fr like #564	.75	.42

Hill Type of 1979
Souvenir Sheet

1979, Nov. 6			
C272	Sheet of 5	3.50	1.75
a.	A90 20fr like #565	.40	.16
b.	A90 27fr like #566	.55	.22
c.	A90 31fr like #567	.60	.28
d.	A90 40fr like #568	.80	.35
e.	A90 50fr like #569	1.00	.50

Sir Rowland Hill (1795-1879), originator of penny postage.

Bird Type of 1979

1979	Photo.	Perf. 13½x2x3
C273	A87 6fr like #548	.20
C274	A87 13fr like #549	.40
C275	A87 18fr like #550	.55
C276	A87 26fr like #551	.75
C277	A87 31fr like #552	1.00
C278	A87 36fr like #553	1.10
C279	A87 40fr like #554	1.25
C280	A87 54fr like #555	1.60
C281	A87 70fr like #556	2.00
	Nos. C273-C281 (9)	8.85

Olympic Type of 1980
Souvenir Sheet

1980, Oct. 24	Photo.	Perf. 13½
C282	Sheet of 9	4.25
a.	A91 20fr like #570	.30
b.	A91 20fr like #571	.30
c.	A91 20fr like #572	.30
d.	A91 30fr like #573	.45
e.	A91 30fr like #574	.45
f.	A91 30fr like #575	.45
g.	A91 40fr like #576	.60
h.	A91 40fr like #577	.60
i.	A91 40fr like #578	.60

22nd Summer Olympic Games, Moscow, July 19-Aug. 3.

Christmas Type of 1980
Souvenir Sheet

1980, Dec. 12	Photo.	Perf. 13½x13	
C283	Sheet of 4	1.90	1.40
a.	A92 10fr like #579	.15	.15
b.	A92 30fr like #580	.45	.30
c.	A92 40fr like #581	.60	.40
d.	A92 45fr like #582	.65	.45

UPRONA Type of 1980
Souvenir Sheet

1980, Dec. 29		Perf. 14½x13½
C284	Sheet of 3	1.50
a.	A93 10fr like #583	.15
b.	A93 40fr like #584	.60
c.	A93 45fr like #585	.65

Christmas Type of 1983
Souvenir Sheet

1983, Oct. 3	Litho.	Perf. 14½x13½
C285	Sheet of 4	1.75
a.	A97 10fr like #607	.15
b.	A97 25fr like #608	.38
c.	A97 30fr like #609	.45
d.	A97 50fr like #610	.75

UPU Congress Type of 1984
Souvenir Sheet

1984, July 14		Perf. 13x13½
C286	Sheet of 4	2.25
a.	A99 10fr like #621	.15
b.	A99 30fr like #622	.45
c.	A99 35fr like #623	.50
d.	A99 65fr like #624	1.00

Summer Olympics Type of 1984
Souvenir Sheet

1984, Aug. 6		Perf. 13½x13
C287	Sheet of 4	2.25
a.	A100 10fr like #625	.15
b.	A100 30fr like #626	.45
c.	A100 35fr like #627	.50
d.	A100 65fr like #628	1.00

Christmas Type of 1984
Souvenir Sheet

1984, Dec. 15		Perf. 13½
C288	Sheet of 4	1.75
a.	A101 10fr like #629	.15
b.	A101 25fr like #630	.38
c.	A101 30fr like #631	.45
d.	A101 50fr like #632	.75

Flower Type of 1986 with Dull Lilac Border

1986, July 31	Photo.	Perf. 13x13½
C289	A102 70fr like #633	.80
C290	A102 75fr like #634	.90
C291	A102 80fr like #635	1.00
C292	A102 85fr like #636	1.10
C293	A102 120fr like #637	1.25
C294	A102 150fr like #638	1.75
	Nos. C289-C294 (6)	6.80

Animals AP8

1992, June 2	Litho.	Perf. 14
C298	AP8 100fr M. nemestrina	1.55
C299	AP8 115fr Equus grevyi	1.75
C300	AP8 200fr Long horn cattle	3.10
C301	AP8 220fr Pelecanus onocrotalus	3.40
a.	Souvenir sheet of 4, #C298-C301, perf. 13½	10.00
	Nos. C298-C301 (4)	9.80

AIR POST SEMI-POSTAL STAMPS

Coin Type of Semi-Postal Issue

Designs (Coins of Various Denominations): 3fr+1fr, 11fr+1fr, 20fr+1fr, 50fr+1fr, Coat of Arms, reverse. 5fr+1fr, 14fr+1fr, 30fr+1fr, 100fr+1fr, King Mwambutsa IV, obverse.

Lithographed; Embossed on Gilt Foil

1965, Nov. 15		Imperf.	
	Diameter: 39mm		
CB1	SP4 3fr + 1fr lt & dk vio	.15	.15
CB2	SP4 5fr + 1fr pale grn & red	.15	.15
	Diameter: 45mm		
CB3	SP4 11fr + 1fr org & lilac	.25	.25
CB4	SP4 14fr + 1fr red & emer	.30	.30
	Diameter: 56mm		
CB5	SP4 20fr + 1fr ultra & blk	.40	.40
CB6	SP4 30fr + 1fr dp org & mar	.60	.60
	Diameter: 67mm		
CB7	SP4 50fr + 1fr bl & vio bl	1.00	1.00
CB8	SP4 100fr + 1fr rose & dp cl	2.25	2.25
	Nos. CB1-CB8 (8)	5.10	5.10

Stamps are backed with patterned paper in blue, orange, and pink engine-turned design.

Red Cross Type of Semi-Postal Issue

Designs: 26fr+3fr, Laboratory. 40fr+3fr, Ambulance and thatched huts. 50fr+3fr, Red Cross nurse with patient.

1969, June 26	Photo.	Perf. 13½	
CB9	SP7 26fr + 3fr multi	.38	.15
CB10	SP7 40fr + 3fr multi	.55	.15
CB11	SP7 50fr + 3fr multi	.65	.20
	Nos. CB9-CB11 (3)	1.58	.50

Perf. and imperf. souvenir sheets exist containing 3 stamps similar to Nos. CB9-CB11, but without "Poste Aerienne." Size: 90½x97mm

Christmas Type of Semi-Postal Issue

Paintings: 14fr+3fr, Virgin and Child, by Velázquez. 26fr+3fr, Holy Family, by Joos van Cleve. 40fr+3fr, Virgin and Child, by Rogier van der Weyden.

1970, Dec. 14	Photo.	Perf. 13½	
CB12	SP9 14fr + 3fr multi	.25	.15
CB13	SP9 26fr + 3fr multi	.45	.15
CB14	SP9 40fr + 3fr multi	.65	.20
a.	Souv. sheet of 3, #CB12-CB14	1.50	1.50
	Nos. CB12-CB14 (3)	1.35	.50

No. C147 Surcharged in Gold and Black

+2F UNESCO LUTTE CONTRE L'ANALPHABETISME

1971, Aug. 9	Photo.	Perf. 13½	
CB15	Strip of 4	.80	.20
a.	A48 14fr+2fr Hartebeest	.20	.15
b.	A48 14fr+2fr Black rhinoceros	.20	.15
c.	A48 14fr+2fr Zebra	.20	.15
d.	A48 14fr+2fr Leopard	.20	.15

UNESCO campaign against illiteracy.

No. C148 Surcharged in Gold and Black

+1F AIDE INTERNATIONALE AUX REFUGIES

1971, Aug. 9			
CB16	Strip of 4	1.00	.20
a.	A48 17fr+1fr Grant's gazelles	.22	.15
b.	A48 17fr+1fr Cheetah	.22	.15
c.	A48 17fr+1fr African white-backed vultures	.22	.15
d.	A48 17fr+1fr Johnston's okapi	.22	.15

International help for refugees.

Nos. C150-C151 Surcharged in Black and Gold

a **+1F 75eme ANNIVERSAIRE DES JEUX OLYMPIQUES MODERNES (1896-1971)**

b **+1F JEUX PRE-OLYMPIQUES MUNICH 1972**

1971, Aug. 16			
CB17	Strip of 4	2.25	.45
a.	A48(a) 26fr+1fr Gorilla	.55	.15
b.	A48(a) 26fr+1fr Gnu	.55	.15
c.	A48(a) 26fr+1fr Warthog	.55	.15
d.	A48(a) 26fr+1fr Cape hunting dog	.55	.15
CB18	Strip of 4	3.00	.60
a.	A48(b) 31fr+1fr Sable antelope	.75	.15
b.	A48(b) 31fr+1fr Caracal lynx	.75	.15
c.	A48(b) 31fr+1fr Ostriches	.75	.15
d.	A48(b) 31fr+1fr Bongo	.75	.15

75th anniv. of modern Olympic Games (#CB17); Olympic Games, Munich, 1972 (#CB18).

Nos. C153-C155 Surcharged

+1F UNICEF

1971, Nov. 27	Photo.	Perf. 13½	
CB19	A51 14fr + 1fr multi	.32	.15
CB20	A51 17fr + 1fr multi	.38	.15
CB21	A51 31fr + 1fr multi	.60	.16
	Nos. CB19-CB21 (3)	1.30	.46

25th anniv. of UNICEF.

Casa D'Oro, Venice SPAP1

Views in Venice: 17fr+1fr, Doge's Palace. 24fr+1fr, Church of Sts. John and Paul. 31fr+1fr, Doge's Palace and Piazzetta at Feast of Ascension, by Canaletto.

1971, Dec. 27			
CB22	SPAP1 10fr + 1fr multi	.16	.15
CB23	SPAP1 17fr + 1fr multi	.32	.15
CB24	SPAP1 24fr + 1fr multi	.45	.15
CB25	SPAP1 31fr + 1fr multi	.55	.16
a.	Souvenir sheet of 4	1.50	1.50
	Nos. CB22-CB25 (4)	1.48	.61

Surtax for the UNESCO campaign to save the treasures of Venice. No. CB25a contains 4 stamps similar to Nos. CB22-CB25, but with 2fr surtax.

Nos. C165-C167, C193-C195 Surcharged "+1F" in Silver

1972, Dec. 12	Photo.	Perf. 13½	
CB26	A57 18fr + 1fr multi	.28	.15
CB27	A57 27fr + 1fr multi	.45	.15
CB28	A57 40fr + 1fr multi	.60	.18
a.	Souvenir sheet of 3	1.50	1.50
	Nos. CB26-CB28 (3)	1.33	.48

Christmas 1972. No. CB28a contains 3 stamps similar to Nos. CB26-CB28 but with 2fr surtax.

1973, Dec. 14	Photo.	Perf. 13	
CB29	A64 18fr + 1fr multi	.28	.15
CB30	A64 27fr + 1fr multi	.40	.15
CB31	A64 40fr + 1fr multi	.60	.18
a.	Souvenir sheet of 3	1.50	1.50
	Nos. CB29-CB31 (3)	1.28	.50

Christmas 1973. No. CB31 contains 3 stamps similar to Nos. CB29-CB31 with 2fr surtax each.

Christmas Type of 1974

1974, Dec. 2	Photo.	Perf. 13	
CB32	A70 18fr + 1fr multi	.32	.20
CB33	A70 27fr + 1fr multi	.50	.30
CB34	A70 40fr + 1fr multi	.70	.42
a.	Souvenir sheet of 3	1.75	1.75
	Nos. CB32-CB34 (3)	1.52	.92

Christmas 1974. No. CB34a contains 3 stamps similar to Nos. CB32-CB34 with 2fr surtax.

Nos. C228-C233 Surcharged "+1F" in Silver and Black

1975, Dec. 22	Photo.	Perf. 13
CB35	A73 18fr + 1fr #C228	.35
CB36	A73 18fr + 1fr #C229	.35
CB37	A73 31fr + 1fr #C230	.55
CB38	A73 31fr + 1fr #C231	.55
CB39	A73 40fr + 1fr #C232	.75
CB40	A73 40fr + 1fr #C233	.75
a.	Souvenir sheet of 6	4.25
	Nos. CB35-CB40 (6)	3.30

Michelangelo Buonarroti (1475-1564). No. CB40a contains 6 stamps similar to Nos. CB35-CB40 with 2fr surtax each.

Nos. C250-C252 Surcharged "+1f" in Silver and Black

1976, Nov. 25	Photo.	Perf. 13½
CB41	A76 18fr + 1fr multi	.30
CB42	A76 31fr + 1fr multi	.50
CB43	A76 40fr + 1fr multi	.60
a.	Souvenir sheet of 3	1.50
	Nos. CB41-CB43 (3)	1.40

Christmas 1976. No. CB43a contains 3 stamps similar to Nos. CB41-CB43 with 2fr surtax each.

Nos. C267-C269 Surcharged "+1fr" in Silver and Black

1977		Perf. 14x13
CB44	A83 18fr + 1fr multi	.28
CB45	A83 31fr + 1fr multi	.50
CB46	A83 40fr + 1fr multi	.60
a.	Souvenir sheet of 3	1.50
	Nos. CB44-CB46 (3)	1.38

Christmas 1977. No. CB46a contains 3 stamps similar to Nos. CB44-CB46 with 2fr surtax each.

Christmas 1978 Type
Souvenir Sheet
1979, Feb.   *Photo.*   *Perf. 14x13*
CB47		Sheet of 5	3.00
a.	A86	13fr + 2fr multi	.30
b.	A86	17fr + 2fr multi	.36
c.	A86	27fr + 2fr multi	.55
d.	A86	31fr + 2fr multi	.70
e.	A86	40fr + 2fr multi	.85

Christmas Type of 1979
Souvenir Sheet
1979, Dec. 10   *Photo.*   *Perf. 13½*
CB48		Sheet of 4	2.75
a.	A89	20fr + 2fr like #561	.45
b.	A89	27fr + 2fr like #562	.55
c.	A89	31fr + 2fr like #563	.70
d.	A89	50fr + 2fr like #564	1.00

Christmas Type of 1980
Souvenir Sheet
1981, Jan. 16   *Photo.*   *Perf. 13½x13*
CB49		Sheet of 4	2.50
a.	A92	10fr + 2fr like #579	.20
b.	A92	30fr + 2fr like #580	.55
c.	A92	40fr + 2fr like #581	.75
d.	A92	50fr + 2fr like #582	.90

Christmas Type of 1983
Souvenir Sheet
1983, Nov. 2   *Litho.*   *Perf. 14½x13½*
CB50		Sheet of 4	1.90
a.	A97	10fr + 2fr like #607	.16
b.	A97	25fr + 2fr like #608	.38
c.	A97	30fr + 2fr like #609	.50
d.	A97	50fr + 2fr like #610	.75

Christmas Type of 1984
Souvenir Sheet
1984, Dec. 15   *Perf. 13½*
CB51		Sheet of 4	1.90
a.	A101	10fr + 2fr like #629	.16
b.	A101	25fr + 2fr like #630	.38
c.	A101	30fr + 2fr like #631	.50
d.	A101	50fr + 2fr like #632	1.00

BUSHIRE
bü-'shir

LOCATION — On Persian Gulf

Bushire is a Persian port which British troops occupied Aug. 8, 1915.

20 Chahis (or Shahis) = 1 Kran
10 Krans = 1 Toman

Watermark

Wmk. 161 - Lion

ISSUED UNDER BRITISH OCCUPATION

Basic Iranian Designs

Shah Ahmed — A32 
Imperial Crown — A33

King Darius, Ahura-Mazda Overhead — A34
Ruins of Persepolis — A35 

BUSHIRE
Iranian Stamps of 1911-13 Overprinted in Black — Under British Occupation.

Perf. 11½, 11½x11
Typo. & Engr.

1915, Aug. 15   Unwmk.
N1	A32	1c green & org	27.50	27.50
N2	A32	2c red & sepia	27.50	27.50
N3	A32	3c gray brn & grn	30.00	27.50
N4	A32	5c brown & car	300.00	300.00
N5	A32	6c green & red brn	22.50	22.50
N6	A32	9c yel brn & vio	25.00	27.50
a.		Double overprint		
N7	A32	10c red & org brn	25.00	25.00
N8	A32	12c grn & ultra	32.50	32.50
N9	A32	1k ultra & car	45.00	27.50
a.		Double overprint	5,250.	
N10	A32	24c vio & grn	50.00	30.00
N11	A32	2k grn & red vio	175.00	140.00
N12	A32	3k vio & blk	150.00	165.00
N13	A32	5k red & ultra	82.50	75.00
N14	A32	10k ol bis & cl	75.00	75.00
		Nos. N1-N14 (14)	1,067.	1,002.

Nos. N1-N14, except No. N4, exist without period after "Occupation." This variety sells for more.

Forged overprints exist of Nos. N1-N29.

The Bushire overprint exists on Iran No. 537 but is considered a forgery.

On Iranian Stamps of 1915
Perf. 11, 11½

1915, Sept.   Wmk. 161
N15	A33	1c car & indigo	350.	350.
N16	A33	2c blue & car	4,750.	6,000.
N17	A33	3c dk grn	350.	400.
N18	A33	5c red	4,000.	4,250.
N19	A33	6c ol grn & car	3,000.	3,500.
N20	A33	9c yel brn & vio	500.	525.
N21	A33	10c bl grn & yel brn	800.	900.
N22	A33	12c ultra	950.	1,250.
N23	A34	1k sil, yel brn & gray	350.	375.
N24	A34	24c yel brn & dk brn	450.	400.
N25	A34	2k sil, bl & rose	300.	350.
N26	A34	3k sil, vio & brn	400.	425.
N27	A34	5k sil, brn & grn	450.	450.
a.		Inverted overprint		
N28	A35	1t gold, pur & blk	325.	375.
N29	A35	3t gold, cl & red brn	2,500.	2,750.

Persia resumed administration of Bushire post office Oct. 16, 1915.

For all your stamp supply needs
www.scottonline.com

Value Priced Stockbooks

Stockbooks are a classic and convenient storage alternative for many collectors. These German-made stockbooks feature heavyweight archival quality paper with 9 pockets on each page. The 8½" x 11⅞" pages are bound inside a handsome leatherette grain cover and include glassine interleaving between the pages for added protection. The Value Priced Stockbooks are available in two page styles, the white page stockbooks feature glassine pockets while the black page variety includes clear acetate pockets

BLACK PAGE STOCKBOOKS ACETATE POCKETS

WHITE PAGE STOCKBOOKS GLASSINE POCKETS

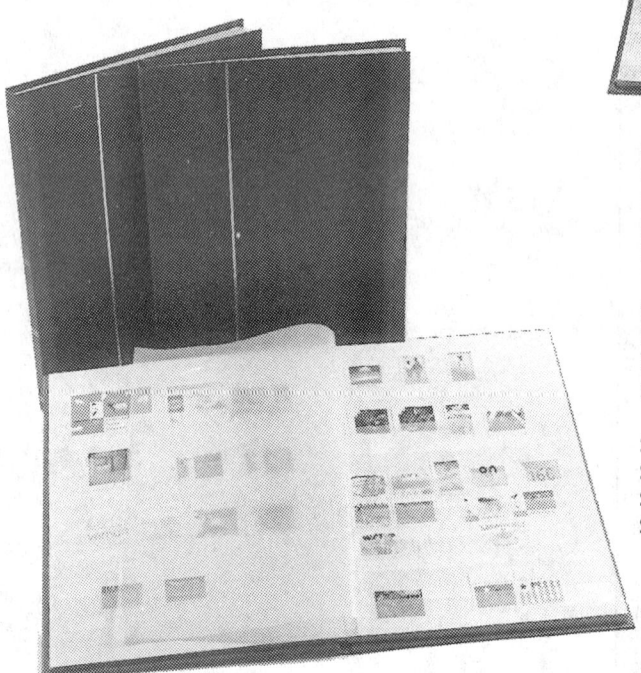

Item	Color	Pages	Retail
ST16RD	Red	16 pages	$9.95
ST16GR	Green	16 pages	$9.95
ST16BL	Blue	16 pages	$9.95
ST16BK	Black	16 pages	$9.95
ST32RD	Red	32 pages	$14.95
ST32GR	Green	32 pages	$14.95
ST32BL	Blue	32 pages	$14.95
ST32BK	Black	32 pages	$14.95
ST64RD	Red	64 pages	$27.95
ST64GR	Green	64 pages	$27.95
ST64BL	Blue	64 pages	$27.95
ST64BK	Black	64 pages	$27.95

Item	Description		Retail
SW16BL	Blue	16 pages	$5.95
SW16GR	Green	16 pages	$5.95
SW16RD	Red	16 pages	$5.95

The black page stockbook is available in three sizes:
16 pages
32 pages
64 pages.

Scott Value Priced Stockbooks are available from your favorite dealer or direct from:

SCOTT
P.O. Box 828
Sidney OH 45365-0828
www.scottonline.com

1-800-572-6885

2000 Vol. 1 Number Additions, Deletions & Changes

Number in 1999 Catalogue	Number in 2000 Catalogue

United States
1999	2000
250a, 250b	250c, 250d
new	250a, 250b
new	251a
252a, 252b	252b, 252c
new	252a
new	267a, 267b, 267c
new	279Bg, 279Bh, 279Bi
new	406c
new	416a
new	510a
new	573a
new	657a
1331a	1332b
new	1338s, 1338Ft
new	1362c
1421a	1422a
new	1423b
1434a, 1434b	1435b, 1435d
1569a, 1569b	1570a, 1570c
1577a-1577c	1578a-1578c
new	1556d
new	1629a
1723a	1724a
new	1726b, 1726c
1732a-1732b	1733b-1733c
new	1757j, 1757k
new	1951d
new	2035c
new	2037b
new	2171b, 2179a
new	2188a
2429b	deleted
new	2429b
2429c	2429d
new	2429c, 2429e
new	2443c
new	2453b
new	2466a-2466b
new	2485c
new	2521b
2527b	deleted
new	2527b
2527c	2527d
new	2527c
new	2542a
footnoted	2544b
new	2595d
new	2624d, 2626d, 2628d
new	2778b
new	2877a
2904b	2904c
new	2915AI
2921b-2921c	2921d-2921e
new	2921b-2921c
new	2943a-2943b
new 3054a, 3054b, 3054c,	3054d, 3054e
new	3111b
new	3112b-3112c
new	3122e
new	3122b-3123d
new	3136p
C108a, C108b	C108b, C108d
new	E6a, E9a, E10a
reinstated	O116a

Envelopes
1999	2000
new	U448a-U448c
new	U449a-U449c
new	U450-U450c
new	U451b-U451d
U452a	U452b
new	U452a
U453	U453a
U453a	U453
U454	U454a
new	U454, U454b, U454c
new	U455a, U455b
U456a	U456
new	U456a, U456b
new	U457a, U457b
U458a-U458d	U458d-U458g
new	U458h-U458m
U459a	U459h
U459b	U459g
new	U459a-U459c
new	U459d-U459f

Envelopes
1999	2000
U460a	U460c
U460b	U460f
new	U460a, U460b
new	U460d, U460e
U461a	U461d
new	U461a-U461c
new	U461e-U461g
new	U465a
new	U466Ad, U466Ae
U468a, U468b	U468d, U468e
U468c	U468k
U468d	U468f
U468e	U468l
new	U468a-U468c
new	U468g-U468j
U469a	U469e
new	U469a-U469c
new	U469d, U469f-U469g
U470a	U470d
U470b	U470e
new	U470a-U470c
new	U470f, U470g
U471a	U471d
U471b	U471e
new	U471a-U471c
new	U471d, U471f
new	U474a-U474b
U476a	U476b
new	U476a
new	U477a-U477c
new	U479a, U479b
U490b	U490c
new	U490b
U491	U491c
U491a	U491b
new	U491
new	U491d
new	U491b
new	U494a
U495a-U495c	U495b-U495d
new	U495a, U495e-U495f
new	U496a, U496b
new	U497a
new	U498a, U498b
new	U502a, U502b
new	U503b
new	U504a
U510a	U510e
U515a-U515d	U515d-U515g
new	U515a-U515c
new	U515h-U515l
new	U516a
new	U517a
U518a	U518c
new	U518a, U518b
new	U520a-U520c
new	U632b

Revenue
1999	2000
R155	R155b, R155Ag
R155a	R155c, R155Ah
R155b	R155d, R155e
R155c	R155f
new	R155, R155A
new	R624a
new	RW26a

Confederate States
1999	2000
new	20XU1a

Canal Zone
1999	2000
new	16c

Cuba
1999	2000
222	222, 222A
222a	222b, 222Ac
222c	222Ad
223	223, 223A
223a	223b, 223Ac

Philippines
1999	2000
new	214c, 214d
new	O25b

Puerto Rico
1999	2000
216a	deleted

Ryukyu Islands
1999	2000
new	C19b, C19c, C19d, C19e

United Nations
1999	2000
new	C3a

Aden
Kathiri State of Seiyun
1999	2000
new	13b

Angola
1999	2000
991A	989E
991Ab-991Ad	989Ef-989Eh

Antigua
1999	2000
new	4b
new	21a

Argentina
1999	2000
2a	2f
3a	3c

Ascension
1999	2000
40	40a
40a	40
42	42b
42b	42
43	43b
43b	43
44A	44Ac
44Ac	44A
new	55b

Australia
1999	2000
new	622a
new	1246g
1277-1281	1271-1276
1282f	1276a
1282A-1282B	1277-1279
1282Cd, 1282Cf	1279a, 1279b
1283	1280
1286-1290	1281-1285
1292-1295	1286-1289
1295A-1295D	1290-1293
1295De, 1295Df	1293a, 1293b
new	O10a, O11a

Austria
1999	2000
new	11b
40b	footnoted
121a	121a, 121b
122a	122a, 122b
124a	124a, 124b
new	290b, 291b, 292b
new	294b, 294c, 295a
new	338a, 338b, 339a
new	347a, 376a, 376b
B50	B50a
B50a	B50
N2b, N6c, N7b, N8b	deleted
new	N29a, N29b, N30a
new	N52b

Offices in Crete
1999	2000
8	8a
8a	8

Offices in the Turkish Empire
1999	2000
new	5c
6	6b
new	6
21a, 37a	deleted

Bahamas
1999	2000
new	12a, 12b
new	104Ab

Bangladesh
1999	2000
O45A	O47A

Barbados
1999	2000
21a, 21b	21b, 21c

Barbuda
1999	2000
1637H	1637B
1637Ab-1637Ag	1637Ac-1637Ah
1619-1621	1620-1621A

Belgium
1999	2000
16a	deleted
18a, 20a	18b, 20b
25a	deleted
new	127a, 128a
new	139b
141b	deleted
151	151a
new	151

Bermuda
1999	2000
21	21a
21a	21

Bhutan
1999	2000
1074A	1058

Brazil
1999	2000
C82a	C86A
C82b	C86Ab

British East Africa
1999	2000
102	102a
102a	102

Cover & Mint Sheet Storage

Cover Box
Keep your collection organized in a 7 ½" x 10 ½" x 4 ¼" cover box. Box will hold hundreds of covers. Available in classic marble styling.

Item		Retail
CVBOX	Marble Cover Box	$6.95

Cover Binders & Pages
Padded, durable, 3-ring binder will hold up to 100 covers. Features the "D" ring mechanism on the right hand side of album so you don't have to worry about creasing or wrinkling covers when opening or closing binder.

Cover pages sold separately.

Item		Retail
CBRD	Cover Binder - Red	$7.95
CBBL	Cover Binder - Blue	$7.95
CBGY	Cover Binder - Gray	$7.95
CBBK	Cover Binder - Black	$7.95
T2	Cover Pages Black (25 per pack)	$4.95
T2C	Cover Pages Clear (25 per pack)	$4.95

Mint Sheet Binders & Pages

Keep those mint sheets intact in a handsome, 3-ring binder. Just like the cover album, the Mint Sheet album features the "D" ring mechanism on the right hand side of binder so you don't have to worry about damaging your stamps when turning the pages. Mint Sheet binder available in four colors.

Mint sheet pages sold separately.

Item		Retail
MBRD	Mint Sheet Binder - Red	$9.95
MBBL	Mint Sheet Binder - Blue	$9.95
MBGY	Mint Sheet Binder - Gray	$9.95
MBBK	Mint Sheet Binder - Black	$9.95
MS1	Mint Sheet Pages (25 per pack)	$5.95

Mint Sheet and Plate Block Storage

Item		Retail
191A000	Regular Plate Block File 24 pockets	$2.50
193A000	Mint Sheet File 24 pockets	$5.50

Available from your favorite stamp dealer direct from:

SCOTT

P.O. Box 828
Sidney OH 45365-0828
1-800-572-6885
www.scottonline.com

Dies of British Colonial Stamps Referred to in the Catalogue

DIE A

DIE B

DIE I

DIE II

DIE A:
1. The lines in the groundwork vary in thickness and are not uniformly straight.
2. The seventh and eighth lines from the top, in the groundwork, converge where they meet the head.
3. There is a small dash in the upper part of the second jewel in the band of the crown.
4. The vertical color line in front of the throat stops at the sixth line of shading on the neck.

DIE B:
1. The lines in the groundwork are all thin and straight.
2. All the lines of the background are parallel.
3. There is no dash in the upper part of the second jewel in the band of the crown.
4. The vertical color line in front of the throat stops at the eighth line of shading on the neck.

DIE I:
1. The base of the crown is well below the level of the inner white line around the vignette.
2. The labels inscribed "POSTAGE" and "REVENUE" are cut square at the top.
3. There is a white "bud" on the outer side of the main stem of the curved ornaments in each lower corner.
4. The second (thick) line below the country name has the ends next to the crown cut diagonally.

DIE Ia.
1 as die II.
2 and 3 as die I.

DIE Ib.
1 and 3 as die II.
2 as die I.

DIE II:
1. The base of the crown is aligned with the underside of the white line around the vignette.
2. The labels curve inward at the top inner corners.
3. The "bud" has been removed from the outer curve of the ornaments in each corner.
4. The second line below the country name has the ends next to the crown cut vertically.

Wmk. 1 Crown and C C

Wmk. 2 Crown and C A

Wmk. 3 Multiple Crown and C A

Wmk. 4 Multiple Crown and Script C A

Wmk. 4a

Wmk. 314 St. Edward's Crown and C A Multiple

Wmk. 373

Wmk. 384

British Colonial and Crown Agents Watermarks

Watermarks 1 to 4, 314, 373, and 384, common to many British territories, are illustrated here to avoid duplication.

The letters "CC" of Wmk. 1 identify the paper as having been made for the use of the Crown Colonies, while the letters "CA" of the others stand for "Crown Agents." Both Wmks. 1 and 2 were used on stamps printed by De La Rue & Co.

Wmk. 3 was adopted in 1904; Wmk. 4 in 1921; Wmk. 314 in 1957; Wmk. 373 in 1974; and Wmk. 384 in 1985.

In Wmk. 4a, a non-matching crown of the general St. Edwards type (bulging on both sides at top) was substituted for one of the Wmk. 4 crowns which fell off the dandy roll. The non-matching crown occurs in 1950-52 printings in a horizontal row of crowns on certain regular stamps of Johore and Seychelles, and on various postage due stamps of Barbados, Basutoland, British Guiana, Gold Coast, Grenada, Northern Rhodesia, St. Lucia, Swaziland and Trinidad and Tobago. A variation of Wmk. 4a, with the non-matching crown in a horizontal row of crown-CA-crown, occurs on regular stamps of Bahamas, St. Kitts-Nevis and Singapore.

Wmk. 314 was intentionally used sideways, starting in 1966. When a stamp was issued with Wmk. 314 both upright and sideways, the sideways varieties usually are listed also — with minor numbers. In many of the later issues, Wmk. 314 is slightly visible.

Wmk. 373 is usually only faintly visible.

Illustrated Identifier

This section pictures stamps or parts of stamp designs that will help identify postage stamps that do not have English words on them.

Many of the symbols that identify stamps of countries are shown here as well as typical examples of their stamps.

See the Index and Identifier on the previous pages for stamps with inscriptions such as "sen," "posta," "Baja Porto," "Helvetia," "K.S.A.," etc.

Linn's Stamp Identifier is now available. The 144 pages include more 2,000 inscriptions and over 500 large stamp illustrations. Available from Linn's Stamp News, P.O. Box 29, Sidney, OH 45365-0029.

1. HEADS, PICTURES AND NUMERALS

GREAT BRITAIN

Great Britain stamps never show the country name, but, except for postage dues, show a picture of the reigning monarch.

Victoria

Edward VII   George V   Edward VIII

George VI

Elizabeth II

Some George VI and Elizabeth II stamps are surcharged in annas, new paisa or rupees. These are listed under Oman.

Silhouette (sometimes facing right, generally at the top of stamp)

The silhouette indicates this is a British stamp. It is not a U.S. stamp.

VICTORIA

Queen Victoria

INDIA

Other stamps of India show this portrait of Queen Victoria and the words "Service" and "Annas."

AUSTRIA

YUGOSLAVIA

(Also BOSNIA & HERZEGOVINA if imperf.)

BOSNIA & HERZEGOVINA

Denominations also appear in top corners instead of bottom corners.

HUNGARY

Another stamp has posthorn facing left

BRAZIL

AUSTRALIA

Kangaroo and Emu

GERMANY

Mecklenburg-Vorpommern

ILLUSTRATED IDENTIFIER

SWITZERLAND

2. ORIENTAL INSCRIPTIONS

CHINA

Any stamp with this one character is from China (Imperial, Republic or People's Republic). This character appears in a four-character overprint on stamps of Manchukuo. These stamps are local provisionals, which are unlisted. Other overprinted Manchukuo stamps show this character, but have more than four characters in the overprints. These are listed in People's Republic of China.

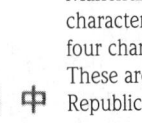

中　中

Some Chinese stamps show the Sun.

中華民國郵票

Most stamps of Republic of China show this series of characters.

Stamps with the China character and this character are from People's Republic of China.　人

中国人民邮政　8分
中国人民邮政

Calligraphic form of People's Republic of China

Chinese stamps without China character

REPUBLIC OF CHINA

PEOPLE'S REPUBLIC OF CHINA

ILLUSTRATED IDENTIFIER

Mao Tse-tung

MANCHUKUO

Temple    Emperor Pu-Yi

The first 3 characters are common to many Manchukuo stamps.

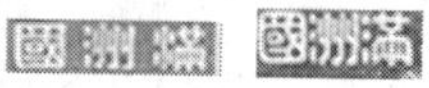

The last 3 characters are common to other Manchukuo stamps.

Orchid Crest

Manchukuo stamp without these elements

JAPAN

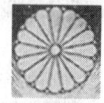

Chrysanthemum Crest 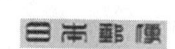   Country Name

Japanese stamps without these elements

The number of characters in the center and the design of dragons on the sides will vary.

RYUKYU ISLANDS

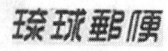

Country Name

PHILIPPINES
(Japanese Occupation)

Country Name

NORTH BORNEO
(Japanese Occupation)

Indicates Japanese Occupation    Country Name

MALAYA
(Japanese Occupation)

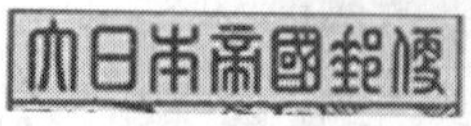

Indicates Japanese Occupation 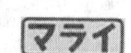   Country Name

BURMA
(Japanese Occupation)

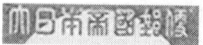

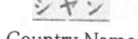

Indicates Japanese Occupation   Country Name

Other Burma Japanese Occupation stamps without these elements

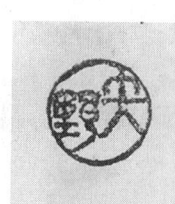

ILLUSTRATED IDENTIFIER

Burmese Script

KOREA

These two characters, in any order, are common to stamps from the Republic of Korea (South Korea) or the unlisted stamps of the People's Democratic Republic of Korea (North Korea).

This series of four characters can be found on the stamps of both Koreas.

Yin Yang appears on some stamps.

Indicates Republic of Korea (South Korea)

South Korean postage stamps issed after 1952 do not show currency expressed in Latin letters. Stamps wiith "HW," "HWAN," "WON," "WN," "W" or "W" with two lines through it, if not illustrated in listings of stamps before this date, are revenues. North Korean postage stamps do not have currency expressed in Latin letters.

THAILAND

Country Name

King Chulalongkorn

King Prajadhipok and Chao P'ya Chakri

3. CENTRAL AND EASTERN ASIAN INSCRIPTIONS

INDIA - FEUDATORY STATES

Alwar

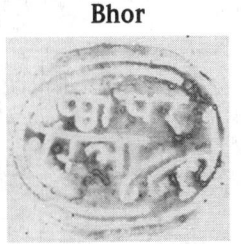

Bhor

Bundi

Similar stamps come with different designs in corners and differently drawn daggers (at center of circle).

Dhar

Faridkot

Hyderabad

Similar stamps exist with straight line frame around stamp, and also with different central design which is inscribed "Postage" or "Post & Receipt."

Indore

Jhalawar

A similar stamp has the central figure in an oval.

Nandgaon

Nowanuggur

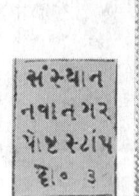

Poonch

Similar stamps exist in various sizes

Rajpeepla

Soruth

BANGLADESH

বাংলাদেশ
Country Name

NEPAL

Similar stamps are smaller, have squares in upper corners and have five or nine characters in central bottom panel.

TANNU TUVA

ISRAEL

GEORGIA

This inscription is found on other pictorial stamps.

Country Name

ARMENIA

The four characters are found somewhere on pictorial stamps. On some stamps only the middle two are found.

4. AFRICAN INSCRIPTIONS

ETHIOPIA

5. ARABIC INSCRIPTIONS

AFGHANISTAN

Many early Afghanistan stamps show Tiger's head, many of these have ornaments protruding from outer ring, others show inscriptions in black.

ILLUSTRATED IDENTIFIER

893

Arabic Script

Mosque Gate & Crossed Cannons
The four characters are found somewhere on pictorial stamps. On some stamps only the middle two are found.

BAHRAIN

EGYPT

Postage

INDIA - FEUDATORY STATES

Jammu & Kashmir

Text and thickness of ovals vary. Some stamps have flower devices in corners.

India-Hyderabad

894　ILLUSTRATED IDENTIFIER

IRAN

Country Name

Royal Crown

Lion with Sword

Symbol

IRAQ

JORDAN

LEBANON

Similar types have denominations at top and slightly different design.

LIBYA

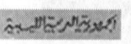

Country Name in various styles

Other Libya stamps show Eagle and Shield (head facing either direction) or Red, White and Black Shield (with or without eagle in center).

SAUDI ARABIA

ILLUSTRATED IDENTIFIER

Palm Tree and Swords

SYRIA

THRACE   YEMEN

PAKISTAN

Tughra (Central design)

PAKISTAN - Bahawalpur

Country Name in top panel, star and crescent

TURKEY

Star & Crescent is a device found on many Turkish stamps, but is also found on stamps from other Arabic areas (see Pakistan-Bahawalpur)

Tughra (similar tughras can be found on stamps of Turkey in Asia, Afghanistan and Saudi Arabia)

Mohammed V

ILLUSTRATED IDENTIFIER

Mustafa Kemal

Plane, Star and Crescent

TURKEY IN ASIA

Other Turkey in Asia pictorials show star & crescent.
Other stamps show tughra shown under Turkey.

6. GREEK INSCRIPTIONS

GREECE
Country Name in various styles
(Some Crete stamps overprinted with the Greece country name are listed in Crete.)

Lepta

ΔΡΑΧΜΗ ΔΡΑΧΜΑΙ ΛΕΠΤΟΝ
Drachma Drachmas Lepton
Abbreviated Country Name ΕΛΛ

Other forms of Country Name

No country name

CRETE

Country Name

These words are on other stamps

Grosion

Crete stamps with a surcharge that have the year "1922" are listed under Greece.

EPIRUS
Country Name

IONIAN ISLANDS

ILLUSTRATED IDENTIFIER

7. CYRILLIC INSCRIPTIONS

RUSSIA

Postage Stamp

Imperial Eagle

Postage in various styles

Abbreviation for Kopeck

Abbreviation for Ruble

Russia

Abbreviation for Russian Soviet Federated Socialist Republic
RSFSR stamps were overprinted (see below)

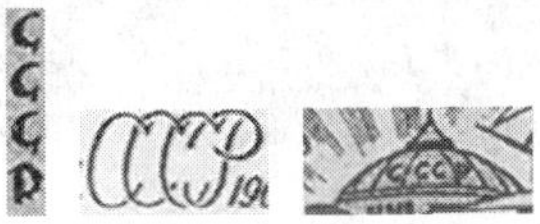

Abbreviation for Union of Soviet Socialist Republics

This item is footnoted in Latvia

RUSSIA - Army of the North

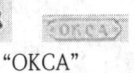

"OKCA"

RUSSIA - Wenden

RUSSIAN OFFICES IN THE TURKISH EMPIRE

These letters appear on other stamps of the Russian offices.

The unoverprinted version of this stamp and a similar stamp were overprinted by various countries (see below).

ARMENIA

BELARUS

FAR EASTERN REPUBLIC

Country Name

ILLUSTRATED IDENTIFIER

SOUTH RUSSIA
Country Name

Forms of Country Name

FINLAND
Circles and Dots on stamps similar to Imperial Russia issues 

BATUM
Forms of Country Name

TRANSCAUCASIAN FEDERATED REPUBLICS
Abbreviation for Country Name

KAZAKHSTAN
ҚАЗАҚСТАН
Country Name

KYRGYZSTAN
КЫРГЫЗСТАН
КЫРГЫЗСТАН
Counrty Name

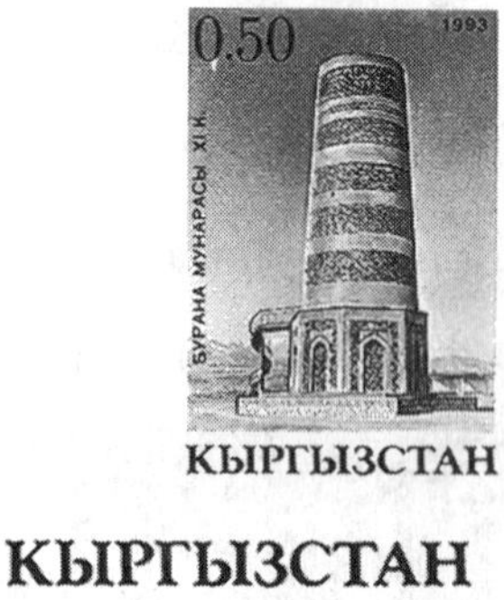

ROMANIA

TADJIKISTAN
Counrty Name & Abbreviation 

UKRAINE
Пошта України України
України України
Country Name in various forms

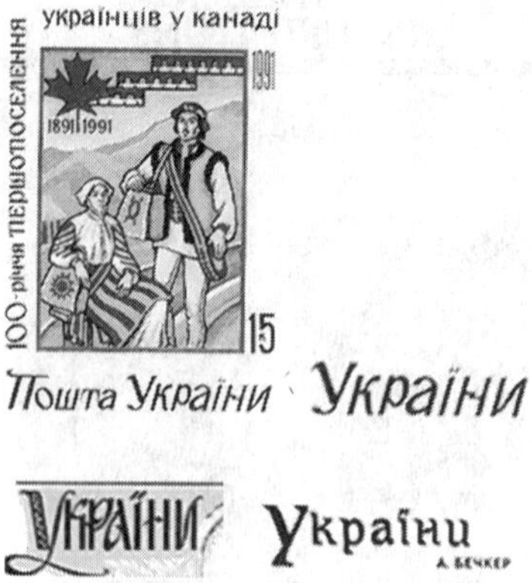

The trident appears on many stamps, usually as an overprint.

Abbreviation for Ukrainian Soviet Socialist Republic

WESTERN UKRAINE
Abbreviation for Country Name

AZERBAIJAN
AZƏRBAYCAN
AZƏRBAYCAN
Country Name

ILLUSTRATED IDENTIFIER

899

A.C.C.P. Abbreviation for Azerbaijan Soviet Socialist Republic

MONTENEGRO

ЦРНА ГОРА
Country Name in various forms

Abbreviation for country name

No country name (A similar Montenegro stamp without country name has same vignette.)

SERBIA

СРПСКА СРБИЈА
Country Name in various forms

Abbreviation for country name

No country name

YUGOSLAVIA

ЈУГОСЛАВИЈА
Showing country name

No Country Name

MACEDONIA

МАКЕДОНИЈА
Country Name

МАКЕДОНСКИ
Different form of Country Name

BULGARIA

Country Name | Postage

Stotinka

Stotinki (plural) | Abbreviation for Stotinki

Country Name in various forms and styles

НР България

ILLUSTRATED IDENTIFIER

No country name

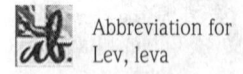

Abbreviation for
Lev, leva

MONGOLIA

Country name in   Tugrik in Cyrillic
one word

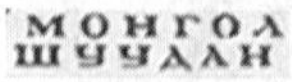

Country name in   Mung in Cyrillic
two words

Mung
in Mongolian

Tugrik
in Mongolian

Arms

No Country Name

Specialty Series

Scott produces album pages for more than 160 different countries. Scott Specialty pages are renowned for their quality and detail. There are spaces for every major variety of postage stamp within each country or specialty area. Each space is identified by Scott number and many of the spaces are illustrated. Pages are printed on one side only on chemically neutral paper that will not harm your stamps.

Below is complete list of the entire line of foriegn pages produced by Scott. Albums are updated annually. For page and price breakouts see your favorite dealer or visit the Scott Publishing web site at www.scottonline.com

Scott Produces Album Pages for more than 160 countries.

ADEN	EQUATORIAL GUINEA	LEBANON	RUSSIA
AFGHANISTAN	ERITREA	LESOTHO	SALVADOR
ALBANIA	ETHIOPIA	LIBERIA	SAMOA
ALGERIA	FALKLAND ISLANDS	LIECHTENSTEIN	SAN MARINO
ANTIGUA	FAROE ISLANDS	LUXEMBOURG	SAUDI ARABIA
AUSTRALIA	FIJI	MACEDONIA	SENEGAL
AUSTRALIA DEPENDENCIES	FINLAND & ALAND ISLANDS	MADAGASCAR	SEYCHELLES
AUSTRIA	FRANCE	MALAWI	SIERRA LEONE
BAHAMAS	FRENCH OFFICES ABROAD	MALAYSIA	SLOVENIA
BAHRAIN	FRENCH POLYNESIA	MALDIVE ISLANDS	SOLOMON ISLANDS
BALTIC STATES	FRENCH SOUTH. & ANTARCTIC TERRIT.	MALI	SOUTH AFRICA
BANGLADESH	GABON	MAURITIUS	SPAIN & SPANISH ANDORRA
BARBADOS	GAMBIA	MEXICO	SRI LANKA
BELGIUM	GERMANY	MONACO & FRENCH ANDORRA	ST LUCIA
BELIZE	EAST GERMANY	MONTSERRAT	ST PIERRE & MIQUELON
BERMUDA	GHANA	MOROCCO	ST THOMAS & PRINCE ISLANDS
BHUTAN	GILBERT & ELLICE ISLANDS	NAMIBIA	ST VINCENT
BOLIVIA	GREAT BRITAIN	NAURU	SUDAN
BOTSWANA	GREAT BRITAIN OFFICES ABROAD	NEPAL	SWAZILAND
BRAZIL	GREECE	NEW CALEDONIA	SWEDEN
BRITISH AFRICA	GREENLAND	NEW HEBRIDES (BRITISH)	SWITZERLAND
BRITISH ANTARCTIC TERRITORIES	GRENADA	NEW HEBRIDES (FRENCH)	SYRIA
BRITISH EUROPE	GUATEMALA	NEW ZEALAND	TAIWAN
BRITISH HONDURAS	GUINEA	NEW ZEALAND DEPENDENCIES	TANZANIA
BRITISH ORIENT	GUINEA-BISSAU	NEVIS/ST KITTS	THAILAND
BRITISH SOUTH ATLANTIC	HAITI	NICARAGUA	TOGO
BRUNEI	HONDURAS	NIGER	TONGA
BULGARIA	HUNGARY	NIGERIA	TRINIDAD
BURKINA FASO	ICELAND	NORWAY	TUNISIA
BURMA	INDIA	OMAN	TURKEY
BURUNDI	INDONESIA	PAKISTAN	TURKS & CAICOS ISLANDS
CANADA	IRELAND	PANAMA	TUVALU
CAYMAN ISLANDS	ISRAEL	PARAGUAY	UGANDA
CENTRAL AFRICA	ISRAEL TABS	PAKISTAN	UNITED ARAB EMIRATES
CHANNEL ISLANDS	ITALIAN COLONIES	PANAMA	URUGUAY
CHILE	ITALY	PARAGUAY	VANUATU
CHINA	IVORY COAST	PEOPLE'S REPUBLIC OF CHINA	VATICAN CITY
COLOMBIA	JAMAICA	PERU	VENEZUELA
COM. OF INDEPENDENT STATES	JAPAN	PHILIPPINES	VIRGIN ISLANDS
COMORO ISLANDS	JORDAN	PITCAIRN ISLANDS	WALLIS & FUTUNA
CONGO	KENYA	POLAND	YEMEN
COSTA RICA	KIRIBATI	PORTUGAL	YUGOSLAVIA
CROATIA	KOREA	PORTUGUESE COLONIES	ZAIRE
CZECHOSLOVAKIA	KUWAIT	QATAR	ZAMBIA
DENMARK	LAOS	ROMANIA	ZIMBABWE
DOMINICA			
DOMINICAN REPUBLIC			
ECUADOR			
EGYPT			

SCOTT

www.scottonline.com

Index and Identifier

All page numbers shown are those in this Volume 1.
Postage stamps that do not have English words on them are shown in the Identifier which begins on page 888.

A & T ovptd. on French Colonies ... 301
Aberdeen, Miss. ... 121
Abingdon, Va. ... 121
Abu Dhabi ... 167, Vol. 6
Abyssinia (Ethiopia) ... Vol. 2
A.C.C.P., A.D.C.P. ... 489
A Certo ovptd. on stamps of Peru ... Vol. 5
Acores ... 489, Vol. 5
Aden ... 168
AEF ... Vol. 2
Aegean Islands (Greek Occupation) .. Vol. 3
Aegean Islands (Italian Occupation) .. Vol. 3
Aeroport International de Kandahar (Afghanistan #679) ... 182
Afars and Issas ... 170
AFF EXCEP ... Vol. 2
Afghanistan, Afghan, Afghanes ... 173
AFR ... Vol. 5
Africa Occidental Espanola ... Vol. 6
Africa, British Offices ... Vol. 3
Africa, German East ... Vol. 3
Africa, German South-West ... Vol. 3
Africa Orientale Italiana ... Vol. 3
Africa, Portuguese ... Vol. 5
Afrique Equatoriale Francaise ... Vol. 2
Afrique Francaise ... Vol. 2
Afrique Occidentale Francaise ... Vol. 2
Aguera, La ... 200
AHA (Confed. 44X1) ... 124
Aitutaki ... 200
Ajman ... 208
Aland Islands ... Vol. 2
Alaouites ... 208
Albania ... 209
Albania, Greek Occupation ... Vol. 3
Albania, Italian Offices ... Vol. 3
Albany, Ga. ... 121
Alderney ... Vol. 3
Alerta ovptd. on stamps of Peru ... Vol. 5
Alexandretta, Alexandrette ... 241
Alexandria, Alexandrie, French Offices ... Vol. 2
Alexandria, Va. ... 1
Alexandroupolis ... Vol. 3
Algeria, Algerie ... 242
Allemagne Duitschland ... Vol. 3
Allenstein ... 263
Allied Military Government (Austria) ... 482
Allied Military Government (France) . Vol. 2
Allied Military Gov. (Germany) ... Vol. 3
Allied Military Government (Italy) ... Vol. 3
Allied Military Government (Trieste) Vol. 3
Allied Occupation of Azerbaijan ... 489
Allied Occupation of Thrace ... Vol. 6
Alsace ... Vol. 2
Alsace and Lorraine ... Vol. 2
Alwar ... Vol. 3
A.M.G. ... 482, Vol. 2, Vol. 3
A.M.G./F.T.T. ... Vol. 3
A.M.G./V.G. ... Vol. 3
AM Post ... Vol. 3
Anatolia ... Vol. 6
Ancachs ... Vol. 5
Andalusia ... Vol. 6
Anderson Court House, S.C. ... 121
Andorra, Andorre ... 264
Angola ... 279
Angra ... 291
Anguilla ... 291, Vol. 5
Anhwei ... Vol. 2
Anjouan ... 300
Anna surcharged on France ... Vol. 2
Anna, Annas ... Vol. 3
Annam ... Vol. 3
Annam and Tonkin ... 301
Annapolis, Md. ... 1
Antigua ... 301, Vol. 5
Antioquia ... Vol. 2
A.O. ovptd. on Congo ... Vol. 3
AOF on France ... Vol. 2
A.O.I. ovpt. on Italy ... Vol. 3
A percevoir (see France, French colonies, postage due) ... 603, Vol. 2, Vol. 3

Apurimac ... Vol. 5
A R ... Vol. 4
A.R. ovptd. on stamps of Colombia ... Vol. 5
Arabie Saoudite ... Vol. 5
Arad ... Vol. 5
A receber (See Portuguese Colonies) . Vol. 5
Arequipa ... Vol. 5
Argentina ... 324
Argyrokastron ... Vol. 2
Arica ... Vol. 5
Armenia ... 374
Armenian stamps ovptd. ... Vol. 3, Vol. 5
Army of the North ... Vol. 5
Army of the Northwest ... Vol. 5
Aruba ... 379
Arwad ... Vol. 5
Ascension ... 382
Assistencia Nacionalaos Tuberculosos Vol. 5
Assistencia Publica ... Vol. 4
Asturias ... Vol. 6
Athens, Ga. ... 121
Atlanta, Ga. ... 121
Augusta, Ga. ... 121
Aunus, ovptd. on Finland ... Vol. 5
Austin, Miss. ... 121
Austin, Tex. ... 121
Australia ... 402
Australia, Occupation of Japan ... 430
Australian Antarctic Territory ... 430
Australian States ... 390
Austria ... 431
Austria, Allied Military Govt. ... 482
Austria, Adm. of Liechtenstein ... Vol. 4
Austria, Lombardy-Venetia ... 483
Austria-Hungary ... 432
Austrian Occupation of Italy ... Vol. 3
Austrian Occupation of Montenegro . Vol. 4
Austrian Occupation of Romania ... Vol. 5
Austrian Occupation of Serbia ... Vol. 5
Austrian Offices Abroad ... 482
Austrian stamps surcharged or overprinted ... Vol. 3, Vol. 6
Autaugaville, Ala. ... 121
Autopaketti, Autorahti ... Vol. 2
Avisporto ... Vol. 2
Ayacucho ... Vol. 5
Azerbaijan, Azarbaycan, Azerbaycan, Azerbaidjan ... 484, Vol. 3
Azirbayedjan ... 489
Azores ... 489, Vol. 5

B ... 606, Vol. 4
B ovptd. on Straits Settlements ... 509
Baden ... Vol. 3
Baghdad ... Vol. 4
Bahamas ... 491
Bahawalpur ... Vol. 5
Bahrain ... 502
Bajar Porto ... Vol. 3
Baku ... 485
Baltimore, Md. ... 1, 98
Bamra ... Vol. 3
Banat, Bacska ... Vol. 3
Bangkok ... 509
Bangladesh ... 509
Bani ovptd. on Hungary ... Vol. 3
Baranya ... Vol. 3
Barbados ... 520
Barbuda ... 308, 531
Barcelona ... Vol. 6
Barranquilla ... Vol. 2
Barwani ... Vol. 3
Basel ... Vol. 6
Bashahr ... Vol. 3
Basutoland ... 540
Batavia ... Vol. 4
Baton Rouge, La. ... 121
Batum, batym (British Occupation) ... 541
Bavaria ... Vol. 3
Bayar Porto ... Vol. 3
Bayer., Bayern ... Vol. 3
B.C.A. ovptd. on Rhodesia ... 753
B.C.M. ... Vol. 4
B.C.O.F. ... 430
Beaumont, Tex. ... 122
Bechuanaland ... 542
Bechuanaland Protectorate ... 542
Beckmann's City Post ... 99
Behie ... Vol. 6

Belarus ... 544
Belgian (Belgisch) Congo ... 548
Belgian East Africa ... Vol. 5
Belgian Occ. of German East Africa ... Vol. 3
Belgian Occupation of Germany ... Vol. 3
Belgien ... 607
Belgium, Belgique, Belgie ... 552
Belgium (German Occupation) ... 607
Belize ... 608
Belize, Cayes of ... 617
Benadir ... Vol. 6
Bengasi ... Vol. 3
Benin ... 617
Bequia ... Vol. 5
Bergedorf ... Vol. 3
Berlin ... Vol. 3
Berlin-Brandenburg ... Vol. 3
Bermuda ... 632
Besetztes Gebiet Nordfrankreich ... Vol. 2
Beseiged ovptd. On Cape of Good Hope ... Vol. 6
Beyrouth, French Offices ... Vol. 2
Beyrouth, Russian Offices ... Vol. 5
B. Guiana ... 755
Bhopal ... Vol. 3
Bhor ... Vol. 3
Bhutan ... 641
Bijawar ... Vol. 3
B.I.O.T. ovptd. on Seychelles ... 761
Bishop's City Post ... 99
Blagoveshchensk ... Vol. 2
Bluefields ... Vol. 4
B.M.A. Eritrea ... Vol. 3
B.M.A. Somalia ... Vol. 3
B.M.A. Tripolitania ... Vol. 3
Bocas del Toro ... Vol. 5
Boer Occupation ... Vol. 6
Bogota ... Vol. 2
Bohemia and Moravia ... Vol. 2
Bohmen and Mahren ... Vol. 2
Bolivar ... Vol. 2
Bolivia ... 655
Boletta, Bollettino ... Vol. 3, Vol. 5, Vol. 6
Bollo ... Vol. 3
Bollo Postale ... Vol. 5
Bophuthatswana ... Vol. 6
Borneo ... Vol. 4
Boscawen, N.H. ... 1
Bosna i Hercegovina ... Vol. 6
Bosnia and Herzegovina ... 676, Vol. 6
Bosnia stamps surcharged ... Vol. 6
Bosnien Herzegowina ... 677
Boston, Mass. ... 99
Botswana ... 678
Boyaca ... Vol. 2
Brattleboro, Vt. ... 1
Braunschweig ... Vol. 3
Brazil, Brasil ... 685
Bremen ... Vol. 3
Bridgeville, Ala. ... 122
British Antarctic Territory ... 751
British Bechuanaland ... 542
British Central Africa ... 753
British Colonies - Dies I & II ... See table of contents
British Columbia & Vancouver Is. ... Vol. 2
British Consular Mail ... Vol. 4
British Dominion of Samoa ... Vol. 5
British East Africa ... 754
British Guiana ... 755
British Honduras ... 758
British Indian Ocean Territory ... 761
British Levant ... Vol. 3
British New Guinea ... Vol. 5
British North Borneo ... Vol. 4
British Occupation (of Batum) ... 541
British Occupation of Bushire ... 883
British Occupation of Cameroun ... Vol. 2
British Occupation of Crete ... Vol. 2
British Occ. of German East Africa ... Vol. 3
British Occupation of Iraq ... Vol. 3, Vol. 4
British Occupation of Mesopotamia ... Vol. 4
British Occ. of Orange River Colony . Vol. 4
British Occupation overprint ... 541
British Occupation of Palestine ... Vol. 5
British Occupation of Persia ... 883
British Occupation of Togo ... Vol. 6
British Occ. of Transvaal ... Vol. 6
British Offices in Africa ... Vol. 3

British Offices in China ... Vol. 3
British Offices in Morocco ... Vol. 3
British Offices in Tangier ... Vol. 3
British Off. in the Turkish Empire ... Vol. 3
British Samoa ... Vol. 5
British Solomon Islands ... Vol. 6
British Somaliland (Somaliland Protectorate) ... Vol. 6
British South Africa (Rhodesia) ... Vol. 5
British Vice-Consulate ... Vol. 4
British Virgin Islands ... Vol. 6
British Zone (Germany) ... Vol. 3
Brunei ... 763
Brunei (Japanese Occupation) ... 769
Brunswick ... Vol. 3
Buchanan ... 1, Vol. 4
Buenos Aires ... 373
Bulgaria, Bulgarie ... 769
Bulgarian Occupation of Romania ... Vol. 5
Bulgarian stamps overprinted or surcharged ... Vol. 3, Vol. 5, Vol. 6
Bundi ... Vol. 3
Bundi stamps overprinted ... Vol. 3
Bureau International ... Vol. 6
Burgenland ... 435, 436
Burgos ... Vol. 6
Burkina Faso ... 839
Burma ... 862
Burma (Japanese Occupation) ... 867
Burundi ... 868
Bushire ... 883
Bussahir ... Vol. 3
Buu-Chinh ... Vol. 6
Buu-Bien ... Vol. 6
Byelorussia ... 544

Cabo, Cabo Gracias a Dios ... Vol. 4
Cabo Juby, Jubi ... Vol. 2
Cabo Verde ... Vol. 5
Cadiz ... Vol. 6
Caicos ... Vol. 6
Calchi ... Vol. 3
Cali ... Vol. 2
Calino, Calimno ... Vol. 3
Callao ... Vol. 5
Camb. Aust. Sigillum Nov. ... 390
Cambodia, (Int. Com., India) ... Vol. 3
Cambodia, Cambodge ... Vol. 2, Vol. 3
Cameroons (U.K.T.T.) ... Vol. 2
Cameroun (Republique Federale) ... Vol. 2
Campeche ... Vol. 4
Canada ... Vol. 2
Canadian Provinces ... Vol. 2
Canal Zone ... 127
Canary Islands, Canarias ... Vol. 6
Candia ... Vol. 2
Canton, French Offices ... Vol. 2
Canton, Miss. ... 122
Cape Juby ... Vol. 2
Cape of Good Hope stamps surchd. (see Griqualand West) ... Vol. 3
Cape of Good Hope ... Vol. 2
Cape Verde ... Vol. 5
Carchi ... Vol. 3
Carinthia ... 482, Vol. 6
Carlist ... Vol. 6
Carolina City, N.C. ... 122
Caroline Islands ... Vol. 2
Carpatho-Ukraine ... Vol. 2
Carriers Stamps ... 98
Cartagena ... Vol. 2
Carupano ... Vol. 6
Caso ... Vol. 3
Castellorizo, Castelrosso ... Vol. 2
Cataluna ... Vol. 6
Cauca ... Vol. 2
Cavalla (Greek) ... Vol. 3
Cavalle, Cavalla (French) ... Vol. 2
Cayes of Belize ... 617
Cayman Islands ... Vol. 2
CCCP ... Vol. 5
C.CH on French Colonies ... Vol. 2
C.E.F. ovptd. on Cameroun ... Vol. 2
C.E.F. ovptd. on India ... Vol. 3
Cefalonia ovptd. on Greece ... Vol. 3
Celebes ... Vol. 4
Cent ... Vol. 2
Centavos overprinted on Japan . 139, Vol. 5
Centenaire Algerie RF ... Vol. 2

INDEX AND IDENTIFIER 903

Centenary-1st Postage Stamp (Pakistan #63-64) … Vol. 5
Centesimi overprinted on Austria or Bosnia … Vol. 3
Centesimi di corona … 482, Vol. 2
Centimes … Vol. 2
Centimes ovptd. on Austria … 482
Centimes ovptd. on Germany … Vol. 3
Centimos (no country name) … Vol. 6
Centimos ovptd. on France … Vol. 2
Central Africa (Centrafricaine) … Vol. 2
Central China … Vol. 2
Central Lithuania … Vol. 2
Cephalonia … Vol. 3
Cerigo … Vol. 3
Cervantes … Vol. 6
Ceska Republica … Vol. 2
Ceskoslovenska, Ceskoslovensko … Vol. 2
Ceylon … Vol. 2
CFA … Vol. 2
C.G.H.S. … Vol. 6
Ch … Vol. 3, Vol. 4
Chachapoyas … Vol. 5
Chad … Vol. 2
Chahar … Vol. 2
Chala … Vol. 5
Chamba … Vol. 3
Channel Islands … Vol. 3
Chapel Hill, N.C. … 122
Charkhari … Vol. 3
Charleston, S.C. … 99, 122
Chattanooga, Tenn. … 122
Chekiang … Vol. 2
Cherifien … Vol. 2
Chiapas … Vol. 4
Chiclayo … Vol. 5
Chiffre (see France and French colonies, postage due) … Vol. 6
Chihuahua … Vol. 4
Chile … Vol. 2
Chilean Occupation of Peru … Vol. 5
Chimarra … Vol. 2
China, Chinese … Vol. 2
China (Japanese Occupation) … Vol. 2
China Expeditionary Force (India) … Vol. 3
China, Formosa … Vol. 2, Vol. 4
China, British Offices … Vol. 3
China, French Offices … Vol. 2
China, German Offices … Vol. 3
China, Italian Offices … Vol. 3
China, Japanese Offices … Vol. 4
China, Northeastern Provinces … Vol. 2
China, Offices in Manchuria … Vol. 2
China, Offices in Tibet … Vol. 2
China, People's Republic … Vol. 2
China, People's Republic Regional Issues … Vol. 2
China, People's Republic Hong Kong Vol. 3
China, Russian Offices … Vol. 5
China, United States Offices … 95
Chine … Vol. 2
Chios … Vol. 3
Chita … Vol. 2
Chosen … Vol. 4
Christiansburg, Va. … 122
Christmas Island … Vol. 2
Chungking … Vol. 2
C.I.H.S. … Vol. 6
Cilicia, Cilicie … Vol. 2, Vol. 5
Cincinnati, O. … 99
Cirenaica … Vol. 2
Ciskei … Vol. 6
City Post … 99
Cleveland, O. … 99
Cluj … Vol. 3
c/m … Vol. 2
C.M.T. … Vol. 6
Coamo … 140, Vol. 5
Cochin … Vol. 3
Cochin China … Vol. 2
Cochin, Travancore … Vol. 3
Co. Ci. ovptd. on Yugoslavia … Vol. 6
Cocos Islands … Vol. 2
Colaparchee, Ga. … 122
Colis Postaux … 605
Colombia … Vol. 2, Vol. 5
Colombian Dominion of Panama … Vol. 5
Colon … Vol. 5
Colonie (Coloniali) Italiane … Vol. 3
Colonies de l'Empire Francaise … Vol. 2
Columbia, S.C. … 122
Columbia, Tenn. … 122
Columbus Archipelago … Vol. 2
Columbus, Ga. … 122
Comayagua … Vol. 3
Common Designs … See table of contents
Commissioning of Maryan Babangida (Nigeria #607) … Vol. 4
Communicaciones … Vol. 6
Communist China … Vol. 2
Comores, Archipel des … Vol. 2
Comoro Islands (Comores, Comorien) … Vol. 2
Compania Colombiana … Vol. 2
Confederate States … 121, 127
Congo … 548, Vol. 2
Congo Democratic Republic … Vol. 2
Congo People's Republic (ex-French) Vol. 2
Congo, Belgian (Belge) … 548
Congo Francais … Vol. 2
Congo, Indian U.N. Force … Vol. 3
Congo, Portuguese … Vol. 5
Congreso … Vol. 6
Conseil de l'Europe … Vol. 2
Constantinople, Italian Offices … Vol. 3
Constantinople, Romanian Offices … Vol. 5
Constantinople, Russian Offices … Vol. 5
Constantinople, Turkey … Vol. 6
Contribucao Industrial (Macao A14, P. Guinea WT1) … Vol. 4, Vol. 5
Convention States (India) … Vol. 3
Coo … Vol. 3
Cook Islands … Vol. 2
Cordoba … 373
Corea … Vol. 4
Corfu … Vol. 2, Vol. 3, Vol. 5
Corona … 482, Vol. 2
Correio, Correios e Telegraphos … Vol. 5
Correo Submarino … Vol. 6
Correo, Correos (no name) … 140, Vol. 2, Vol. 5, Vol. 6
Corrientes … 373
Cos … Vol. 3
Costa Atlantica … Vol. 4
Costa Rica … Vol. 2
Costantinopoli … Vol. 3
Cote d'Ivoire … Vol. 3
Cote des Somalis … Vol. 6
Council of Europe … Vol. 2
Cour Permanente de Justice Internationale … Vol. 4
Courtland, Ala. … 122
Cracow … Vol. 5
Crete … Vol. 2, Vol. 3
Crete, Austrian Offices … 482
Crete, French Offices … Vol. 2
Crete, Italian Offices … Vol. 3
Crimea … Vol. 5, Vol. 6
Croatia … Vol. 2
Croatia-Slavonia … Vol. 6
C.S.A. Postage … 127
Ct … 771
Cuautla … Vol. 4
Cuba … 132, Vol. 2
Cuba stamps overprinted … Vol. 5
Cuba, U.S. Administration … 132, Vol. 2
Cucuta … Vol. 2
Cuernavaca … Vol. 4
Cundinamarca … Vol. 2
Curacao … Vol. 4
Cuzco … Vol. 5
C.X.C. on Bosnia and Herzegovina … Vol. 6
Cyprus … Vol. 2
Cyprus, Turkish Republic of Northern Vol. 6
Cyrenaica … Vol. 2, Vol. 3, Vol. 4
Czechoslovakia, Czech Rep. … Vol. 2
Czechoslovak Legion Post … Vol. 2

Dahomey … 617, Vol. 2
Dakar-Abidjan … Vol. 2
Dalmatia … Vol. 2
Dalton, Ga. … 122
Danish West Indies … 133, Vol. 2
Danmark … Vol. 2
Dansk-Vestindien … 133, Vol. 2
Dansk-Vestindiske … 133, Vol. 2
Danville, Va. … 122
Danzig … Vol. 2
Danzig, Polish Offices … Vol. 5
Dardanelles … Vol. 5
Datia (Duttia) … Vol. 3
D.B.L. ovptd. on Siberia and Russia .. Vol. 2
D.B.P. (Dalni Vostochini Respoublika) Vol. 2
D. de A. … Vol. 2
DDR … Vol. 3
Debrecen … Vol. 3
Deccan (Hyderabad) … Vol. 3
Dedeagatch (Greek) … Vol. 3
Dedeagh, Dedeagatch (French) … Vol. 2
Deficit … Vol. 5
Demopolis, Ala. … 122
Denikin … Vol. 5, Vol. 6
Denmark … Vol. 2
Denmark stamps surcharged … Vol. 2
Denver Issue, Mexico … Vol. 4
Den Waisen ovptd. on Italy … Vol. 6
Despatch (US 1LB, 5LB) … 98
Deutsch-Neu-Guinea … Vol. 3
Deutsch-Ostafrika … Vol. 3
Deutsch-Sudwest Afrika … Vol. 3
Deutsche Bundespost … Vol. 3
Deutsche Demokratische Republik … Vol. 3
Deutsche Nationalversammlung … Vol. 3
Deutsche Post … Vol. 3
Deutsche Reich … Vol. 3
Deutsche Reich, Nr.21, Nr.16 … Vol. 3
Deutschland … Vol. 3
Deutschosterreich … 433
Dhar … Vol. 3
Diego-Suarez … Vol. 2
Diego-Suarez stamps surcharged … Vol. 4
Dienftmarke (Dienstmarke) … Vol. 3
Dies I & II, British Colonies … See table of contents
Diligencia … Vol. 6
Dispatch (US 1LB) … 99
Distrito ovptd. on Arequipa … Vol. 5
DJ ovptd. on Obock … Vol. 6
Djibouti (Somali Coast) … Vol. 2, Vol. 6
Dobruja District … Vol. 5
Dodecanese Islands … Vol. 3
Dominica … Vol. 2
Dominican Republic, Dominicana … Vol. 2
Don Government … Vol. 6
Dorpat … Vol. 2
Drzava SHS … Vol. 6
Dubai … Vol. 2, Vol. 6
Duck Stamps (Hunting Permit) … 120
Dulce et Decorum est Pro Patria Mori (Nepal O1) … Vol. 4
Durazzo … Vol. 3
Dutch Guiana (Surinam) … Vol. 6
Dutch Indies … Vol. 4
Dutch New Guinea … Vol. 4
Duttia … Vol. 3

E.A.F. overprinted on stamps of Great Britain … Vol. 3
East Africa (British) … 754, Vol. 3
East Africa (German) … Vol. 3
East Africa (Italian) … Vol. 3
East Africa and Uganda Protectorates … Vol. 2, Vol. 4
East Africa Forces … Vol. 3
East China … Vol. 2
Eastern Rumelia … Vol. 2
Eastern Silesia … Vol. 2
Eastern Szechwan … Vol. 2
Eastern Thrace … Vol. 6
East India … Vol. 3
East Saxony … Vol. 3
Eatonton, Ga. … 122
Ecuador … Vol. 2
E.E.F. … Vol. 5
Eesti … Vol. 2
Egeo … Vol. 3
Egiziane (A9-A10) … Vol. 2
Egypt, Egypte, Egyptiennes … Vol. 2, Vol. 5
Egypt, French Offices … Vol. 2
Eire (Ireland) … Vol. 3
Ekaterinodar … Vol. 6
11/2/1917 … Vol. 2
Elobey, Annobon and Corisco … Vol. 2
El Salvador … Vol. 5
Elsas … Vol. 2
Elua Keneta … 134
Emory, Va. … 122
Empire, Franc, Francais … Vol. 2
Epirus … Vol. 2
Equateur (Ecuador #19-21) … Vol. 2
Equatorial Guinea … Vol. 2
Eritrea … Vol. 2
Eritrea (British Military Administration) … Vol. 3
Escuelas … Vol. 6
Espana, Espanola … Vol. 6
Estado da India … Vol. 5
Est African Allemand overprinted on Congo … Vol. 3
Estensi … Vol. 3
Estero … Vol. 3
Estland … Vol. 2
Estonia … Vol. 2, Vol. 5
Etablissments Francais dans l'Inde … Vol. 2
Ethiopia, Etiopia, Ethiopie, Ethiopiennes … Vol. 2, Vol. 3
Eupen … Vol. 3

F. A. F. L. … Vol. 6
Falkland Dependencies … Vol. 2
Falkland Islands … Vol. 2
Far Eastern Republic … Vol. 2
Far Eastern Republic surcharged or ovptd. … Vol. 5
Faridkot … Vol. 3
Faroe Islands … Vol. 2
FCFA ovptd. on France … Vol. 2
Federacion … Vol. 6
Federal Republic (Germany) … Vol. 3
Federated Malay States … Vol. 4
Fen, Fn. (Manchukuo) … Vol. 4
Fernando Po, Fdo. Poo … Vol. 2
Feudatory States … Vol. 3
Fezzan, Fezzan-Ghadames … Vol. 4
Fiera Campionaria Tripoli … Vol. 4
15 August 1947 (Pakistan #23) … Vol. 5
Fiji … Vol. 2
Filipinas, Filipas. … Vol. 5
Fincastle, Va. … 122
Finland … Vol. 2
Finnish Occupation of Karelia … Vol. 4
Finnish Occupation of Russia … Vol. 5
Fiume … Vol. 2
Fiume-Kupa Zone (Fiumano Kupa) … Vol. 6
Five Cents (Confed. 53X) … 124
Florida … Vol. 6
Foochow, Chinese … Vol. 2
Foochow, German … Vol. 3
Formosa … Vol. 2, Vol. 4
Foroyar … Vol. 2
Forsyth, Ga. … 123
Franc … Vol. 2
Franc ovptd. on Austria … 482
Franca ovptd. on stamps of Peru … Vol. 5
Francais, Francaise … (see France and French colonies)
France … Vol. 2
France (Allied Military Gov't.) … Vol. 2
France (German occupation) … Vol. 2
France D'Outre Mer … Vol. 2
Franco Bollo … Vol. 3
Franco Marke … Vol. 3
Franco Scrisorei … Vol. 5
Franklin, N.C. … 123
Franqueo … Vol. 5
Franquicia … Vol. 6
Fredericksburg, Va. … 123
Frei Durch Ablosung … Vol. 3
Freimarke (No Country Name) … Vol. 3
French Administration of Andorra … 269
French Administration of Saar … Vol. 5
French Colonies … Vol. 2
French Colonies surcharged … Vol. 2, Vol. 3, Vol. 4, Vol. 5, Vol. 6
French Commemoratives Index … Vol. 2
French Congo … Vol. 2
French Equatorial Africa … Vol. 2
French Guiana … Vol. 2
French Guinea … Vol. 2
French India … Vol. 2
French Levant … Vol. 2, Vol. 6
French Mandate of Alaouites … 208
French Mandate of Lebanon … Vol. 4
French Morocco … Vol. 2
French Occupation of Cameroun … Vol. 2
French Occupation of Castellorizo … Vol. 2

French Occupation of Crete .... Vol. 2
French Occupation of Germany .... Vol. 3
French Occupation of Hungary .... Vol. 3
French Occupation of Libya .... Vol. 4
French Occupation of Syria .... Vol. 6
French Occupation of Togo .... Vol. 6
French Oceania .... Vol. 2
French Offices Abroad .... Vol. 2
French Offices in China .... Vol. 2
French Offices in Crete .... Vol. 2
French Offices in Egypt .... Vol. 2
French Offices in Madagascar .... Vol. 4
French Offices in Morocco .... Vol. 2
French Offices in Tangier .... Vol. 2
French Offices in Turkish Empire ...... Vol. 2
French Offices in Zanzibar .... Vol. 2
French Polynesia .... Vol. 2
French Saar .... Vol. 5
French Southern and Antarctic
Territories .... Vol. 2
French stamps inscribed CFA .... Vol. 2
French stamps surcharged ..... Vol. 2, Vol. 4
French Sudan .... Vol. 2
French West Africa .... Vol. 2
French Zone (Germany) .... Vol. 3
Frimarke, Frmrk (No Country
Name) .... Vol. 2, Vol. 4, Vol. 6
Fujeira .... Vol. 2
Fukien .... Vol. 2
Funafuti .... Vol. 6
Funchal .... Vol. 2

G or GW overprinted on Cape of Good Hope .... Vol. 3
GAB on French Colonies .... Vol. 3
Gabon, Gabonaise .... Vol. 3
Gainesville, Ala. 123
Galapagos Islands .... Vol. 2
Galveston, Tex. 123
Gambia .... Vol. 3
Gaza .... Vol. 3
G & D overprinted on French Colonies Vol. 3
G.E.A. ovptd. .... Vol. 3, Vol. 6
General Gouvernement (Poland) ...... Vol. 5
Geneva, Geneve .... Vol. 6
Georgetown, S.C. 123
Georgia .... Vol. 3
Georgienne, Republique .... Vol. 3
German Administration of Albania 212
German Administration of Danzig .... Vol. 2
German Administration of Saar .... Vol. 5
German Democratic Republic .... Vol. 3
German Dominion of Cameroun ...... Vol. 2
German Dominion of Mariana Is. ..... Vol. 4
German Dominion of Marshall Is. ..... Vol. 4
German Dominion of Samoa .... Vol. 5
German Dominion of Togo .... Vol. 6
German East Africa .... Vol. 3
German East Africa (Belgian occ.) ..... Vol. 3
German East Africa (British occ.) ...... Vol. 3
German New Guinea .... Vol. 3
German New Guinea (New Britain) .. Vol. 4
German Occupation of Belgium 607
German Occupation of Estonia .... Vol. 2
German Occupation of France .... Vol. 2
German Occupation of Guernsey ...... Vol. 3
German Occupation of Ionian Is. ...... Vol. 3
German Occupation of Jersey .... Vol. 3
German Occupation of Latvia .... Vol. 4
German Occupation of Lithuania ...... Vol. 4
German Occupation of Ljubljana ...... Vol. 6
German Occupation of Luxembourg . Vol. 4
German Occupation of Montenegro .. Vol. 4
German Occupation of Poland .... Vol. 5
German Occupation of Romania .... Vol. 5
German Occupation of Russia .... Vol. 5
German Occupation of Serbia .... Vol. 5
German Occupation of Ukraine .... Vol. 5
German Occupation of Yugoslavia .... Vol. 6
German Occupation of Zante .... Vol. 3
German Offices in China .... Vol. 3
German Offices in Morocco .... Vol. 3
German Offices in Turkish Empire .... Vol. 3
German Protectorate of Bohemia
and Moravia .... Vol. 2
German South-West Africa .... Vol. 3
German stamps surchd. .... Vol. 2,
Vol. 3, Vol. 4, Vol. 5
German States .... Vol. 3
Germany .... Vol. 3
Germany (Allied Military Govt.) .... Vol. 3
Gerusalemme .... Vol. 3
Ghadames .... Vol. 4
Ghana .... Vol. 3
Gibraltar .... Vol. 3
Gilbert and Ellice Islands .... Vol. 3
Gilbert Islands .... Vol. 3
Giumulzina District .... Vol. 6
Gjirokaster .... Vol. 2
Gniezno .... Vol. 5
Gold Coast .... Vol. 3
Golfo del Guinea .... Vol. 6
Goliad, Tex. 123
Gonzales, Tex. 123
Gorny Slask .... Vol. 6
Government (U.S. 1LB) 99
Governo Militare Alleato .... Vol. 3
G.P.E. ovptd. on French Colonies ..... Vol. 3
Graham Land .... Vol. 2
Granadine Confederation,
Granadina .... Vol. 2
Grand Comoro, Grande Comore ...... Vol. 3
Grand Liban, Gd Liban .... Vol. 4
Great Britain .... Vol. 3
Great Britain, Gaelic ovpt. .... Vol. 3
Great Britain, Offices in Africa .... Vol. 3
Great Britain, Offices in China .... Vol. 3
Great Britain, Offices in Morocco ...... Vol. 3
Great Britain, Offices in
Turkish Empire .... Vol. 3
Greater Rajasthan Union .... Vol. 3
Greece .... Vol. 3
Greek Occupation of Albania, North
Epirus, Dodecanese Islands .... Vol. 3
Greek Occupation of Epirus .... Vol. 2
Greek Occ. of the Aegean Islands ..... Vol. 3
Greek Occupation of Thrace .... Vol. 6
Greek Occupation of Turkey . Vol. 3, Vol. 6
Greek stamps overprinted .... Vol. 6
Greenland .... Vol. 3
Greensboro, Ala. 123
Greensboro, N.C. 123
Greenville, Grenville .... Vol. 4
Greenville, Ala. 123
Greenville Court House, S.C. 123
Greenwood Depot, Va. 123
Grenada .... Vol. 3
Grenadines of Grenada .... Vol. 3
Grenadines of St. Vincent .... Vol. 5
G.R.I. overprinted on German
New Guinea .... Vol. 4
G.R.I. overprinted on German
Samoa .... Vol. 5
G.R.I. overprinted on Marshall Is. ..... Vol. 4
Griffin, Ga. 123
Griqualand West .... Vol. 3
Grodno District .... .Vol. 4
Gronland .... Vol. 3
Grossdeutsches Reich ....Vol. 3
Groszy .... Vol. 5
Grove Hill, Ala. 123
Gruzija (Georgia) .... Vol. 3
Guadalajara .... Vol. 4
Guadeloupe .... Vol. 3
Guam 134
Guanacaste .... Vol. 2
Guatemala .... Vol. 3
Guayana .... Vol. 6
Guernsey .... Vol. 3
Guernsey, German Occupation .... Vol. 3
Guiana, British 755
Guiana, Dutch .... Vol. 6
Guiana, French .... Vol. 2
Guine .... Vol. 5
Guinea .... Vol. 3, Vol. 6
Guinea Ecuatorial............................. Vol. 2
Guinea, French .... Vol. 2
Guinea, Portuguese .... Vol. 5
Guinea, Spanish .... Vol. 6
Guinea-Bissau, Guine-Bissau .... Vol. 3
Guinee .... Vol. 2, Vol. 3
Guipuzcoa .... Vol. 6
Gultig 9, Armee .... Vol. 5
Guyana .... Vol. 3
Guyane, Guy. Franc. .... Vol. 2
G. W. ovptd. On Cape of
Good Hope.................................... Vol. 3
Gwalior .... Vol. 3

Habilitado-1/2 (Tlacotalpan #1) . Vol. 4
Habilitado on Stamps of Cuba 132,
Vol. 2, Vol. 5
Habilitado on Telegrafos or
revenues .... Vol. 5, Vol. 6
Hadhramaut 170
Hainan Island .... Vol. 2
Haiti .... Vol. 3
Hall, A. D. (Confed. 27XU1)................. 123
Hallettsville, Tex. 123
Hamburg .... Vol. 3
Hamburgh, S.C. 123
Hamilton, Bermuda 632
Hangchow .... Vol. 2
Hankow .... Vol. 2
Hanover, Hannover .... Vol. 3
Harper .... Vol. 4
Hatay .... Vol. 3
Hatirasi (Design PT44) .... Vol. 6
Haute Silesie .... Vol. 6
Haute Volta 839
Haut Senegal-Niger .... Vol. 6
Hawaii, Hawaiian 134
H B A ovptd. on Russia .... Vol. 5
Hebrew inscriptions .... Vol. 3
H.E.H. The Nizam's (Hyderabad) ..... Vol. 3
Heilungkiang .... Vol. 2
Hejaz .... Vol. 5
Hejaz-Nejd .... Vol. 5
Hejaz overprinted .... Vol. 4
Helena, Tex. 123
Heligoland .... Vol. 3
Hellas .... Vol. 3
Helsinki (Helsingfors) .... Vol. 2
Helvetia, Helvetica (Switzerland) ...... Vol. 6
Heraklion .... Vol. 2
Herzegovina 676
Herzogth .... Vol. 3
H.H. Nawabshah Jahanbegam .... Vol. 3
H.I. Postage 134
Hillsboro, N.C. 123
Hoi Hao, French Offices .... Vol. 2
Holkar (Indore) .... Vol. 3
Holland (Netherlands) .... Vol. 4
Holstein .... Vol. 3
Honan .... Vol. 2
Honda .... Vol. 2
Honduras .... Vol. 3
Honduras, British 758
Hong Kong .... Vol. 2, Vol. 3
Hong Kong (Japanese Occupation) .... Vol. 3
Hong Kong Special Admin. Region..... Vol. 3
Hong Kong ovptd. China .... Vol. 3
Honour's (Hondur's) City 99
Hopeh .... Vol. 2
Hopei .... Vol. 2
Horta .... Vol. 3
Houston, Tex. 123
Hrvatska .... Vol. 2, Vol. 6
Hrzgl. .... Vol. 3
Huacho .... Vol. 5
Hunan .... Vol. 2
Hungary .... 432, Vol. 3
Hungary (French Occupation) .... Vol. 3
Hungary (Romanian Occupation) ...... Vol. 3
Hungary (Serbian Occupation) .... Vol. 3
Huntsville, Tex. 123
Hupeh .... Vol. 2
Hyderabad (Deccan) .... Vol. 3

I.B. (West Irian) .... Vol. 6
Icaria .... Vol. 3
ICC ovptd. on India .... Vol. 3
Iceland .... Vol. 3
Idar .... Vol. 3
I.E.F. ovptd. on India .... Vol. 3
I.E.F. D ovptd. on Turkey .... Vol. 4
Ierusalem .... Vol. 5
Ifni .... Vol. 3
Ile Rouad .... Vol. 5
Imperio Colonial Portugues .... Vol. 5
Impuesto (Impto) de Guerra .... Vol. 6
Inde. Fcaise .... Vol. 2
Independence, Tex. 123
Index of U.S. Issues 84
India .... Vol. 3, Vol. 5
India, China Expeditionary Force ...... Vol. 3
India, Convention States .... Vol. 3
India, Feudatory States .... Vol. 3
India, French .... Vol. 2
India, Portuguese .... Vol. 5
India, Stamps overprinted ...... Vol. 3, Vol. 4
India, surcharge and crown .... Vol. 6
Indian Custodial Unit, Korea .... Vol. 3
Indian Expeditionary Force .... Vol. 3
Indian U.N. Force, Congo .... Vol. 3
Indian U.N. Force, Gaza .... Vol. 3
Indian Postal Administration of
Bahrain 502
Indo-China, Indo-chine .... Vol. 3
Indo-China stamps surcharhged......... Vol. 6
Indo-China, Int. Commission .... Vol. 3
Indonesia .... Vol. 3, Vol. 4
Indore .... Vol. 3
Industrielle Kriegswirschaft .... Vol. 6
Inhambane .... Vol. 3
Inini .... Vol. 3
Inland (Liberia #21) .... Vol. 4
Inner Mongolia (Meng Chiang) .... Vol. 2
Insufficiently prepaid .... Vol. 6
Instruccion .... Vol. 6
International Bureau of Education .... Vol. 6
International Commission in
Indo-China .... Vol. 3
International Court of Justice .... Vol. 4
International Labor Bureau .... Vol. 6
International Refugee Organization ... Vol. 6
International Telecommunication
Union .... Vol. 6
Ionian Islands, IONIKON KPATOE ... Vol. 3
I.O.V.R. .... Vol. 5
Iran, Iraniennes .... Vol. 3
Iran (Bushire) 883
Iraq .... Vol. 3
Iraq (British Occupation) .... Vol. 4
Ireland .... Vol. 3
Ireland, Northern .... Vol. 3
Irian Barat .... Vol. 6
Island .... Vol. 3
Isle of Man .... Vol. 3
Isole Italiane dell'Egeo .... Vol. 3
Isole Jonie .... Vol. 3
Israel .... Vol. 3
Istria .... Vol. 6
Itaca ovptd. on Greece .... Vol. 3
Ita-Karjala .... Vol. 4
Italia, Italiano, Italiane .... Vol. 3
Italian Colonies .... Vol. 3
Italian Dominion of Albania 211
Italian Dominion of Castellorizo .... Vol. 2
Italian East Africa .... Vol. 3
Italian Jubaland .... Vol. 4
Italian Occ. of Aegean Islands .... Vol. 3
Italian Occupation of Austria 482
Italian Occupation of Corfu .... Vol. 2
Italian Occupation of Crete .... Vol. 2
Italian Occupation of Dalmatia .... Vol. 2
Italian Occupation of Ethiopia .... Vol. 2
Italian Occupation of Fiume-Kupa ..... Vol. 6
Italian Occupation of Ionian Islands .. Vol. 3
Italian Occupation of Ljubljana .... Vol. 6
Italian Occupation of Montenegro .... Vol. 4
Italian Occupation of Yugoslavia .... Vol. 6
Italian Offices Abroad .... Vol. 3
Italian Offices in Africa .... Vol. 3
Italian Offices in Albania .... Vol. 3
Italian Offices in China .... Vol. 3
Italian Offices in Constantinople .... Vol. 3
Italian Offices in Crete .... Vol. 3
Italian Offices in the Turkish Empire . Vol. 3
Italian Social Republic .... Vol. 3
Italian Somaliland .... Vol. 6
Italian Somaliland (E.A.F.) .... Vol. 3
Italian stamps surcharged ...... Vol. 2, Vol. 3
Italian States .... Vol. 3
Italy (Allied Military Govt.) .... Vol. 3
Italy (Austrian Occupation) .... Vol. 3
Italy .... Vol. 3
Ithaca .... Vol. 3
Iuka, Miss. 123
Ivory Coast .... Vol. 3
Izmir .... Vol. 6

J. ovptd. on stamps of Peru .... Vol. 5
Jackson, Miss. 124
Jacksonville, Ala. 124
Jaffa .... Vol. 5
Jaipur .... Vol. 3

INDEX AND IDENTIFIER 905

Jamaica ... Vol. 4
Jamhuri ... Vol. 6
Jammu ... Vol. 3
Jammu and Kashmir ... Vol. 3
Janina ... Vol. 3
Japan, Japanese ... Vol. 4
Japan (Australian Occ.) ... 430
Japan (Taiwan) ... Vol. 2, Vol. 4
Japanese Offices Abroad ... Vol. 4
Japan Occupation of Brunei ... 769
Japan Occupation of Burma ... 867
Japan Occupation of China ... Vol. 2
Japan Occupation of Dutch Indies ... Vol. 4
Japan Occupation of Hong Kong ... Vol. 3
Japan Occupation of Johore ... Vol. 4
Japan Occupation of Kedah ... Vol. 4
Japan Occupation of Kelantan ... Vol. 4
Japan Occupation of Malacca ... Vol. 4
Japan Occupation of Malaya ... Vol. 4
Japan Occupation of Negri Sembilan . Vol. 4
Japan Occupation of North Borneo ... Vol. 4
Japan Occupation of Pahang ... Vol. 4
Japan Occupation of Penang ... Vol. 4
Japan Occupation of Perak ... Vol. 4
Japan Occupation of Philippines 139, Vol. 5
Japan Occupation of Sarawak ... Vol. 5
Japan Occupation of Selangor ... Vol. 4
Japan Occupation of Sts. Settlements Vol. 6
Japan Occ. of Trengganu ... Vol. 4
Other Japanese Stamps
Overprinted ... Vol. 2, Vol. 4
Jasdan ... Vol. 3
Java ... Vol. 4
Jedda ... Vol. 5
Jeend ... Vol. 3
Jehol ... Vol. 2
Jersey ... Vol. 3
Jersey, German Occupation ... Vol. 3
Jerusalem, Italian Offices ... Vol. 3
Jerusalem, Russian Offices ... Vol. 5
Jetersville, Va. ... 124
Jhalawar ... Vol. 3
Jhind, Jind ... Vol. 3
Johore, Johor ... Vol. 4
Jonesboro, Tenn. ... 124
J. P. Johnson ... 125
Jordan ... Vol. 4
Jordan (Palestine Occ.) ... Vol. 4
Journaux ... Vol. 2
Juan Fernandez Islands (Chile) ... Vol. 2
Jubile de l'Union Postale Universelle
(Switzerland #98) ... Vol. 6
Jugoslavia, Jugoslavija ... Vol. 6
Junagarh ... Vol. 3

K ... 374, 677
КАЗАКСТАН ... Vol. 4
Kabul ... 173, 175
Kalaallit Nunaat, Kalatdlit Nunat ... Vol. 3
Kamerun ... Vol. 2
Kampuchea ... Vol. 2
Kansu ... Vol. 2
Karelia, Karjala ... Vol. 4
Karki ... Vol. 3
Karolinen ... Vol. 2
Kashmir ... Vol. 3
Katanga ... Vol. 4
Kathiri State of Seiyun ... 169
Kaunas ... Vol. 4
Kazakhstan, Kazahstan ... Vol. 4
Kedah ... Vol. 4
Keeling Islands ... Vol. 2
Kelantan ... Vol. 4
Kentta Postia ... Vol. 2
Kenya ... Vol. 4
Kenya and Uganda ... Vol. 4
Kenya, Uganda, Tanzania ... Vol. 4
Kenya, Uganda, Tanganyika ... Vol. 4
Kenya, Uganda, Tanganyika,
Zanzibar ... Vol. 4
Kerassunde ... Vol. 5
K.G.C.A. ovptd. on Yugoslavia ... Vol. 6
K.G.L. ... 133, Vol. 2
Khmer Republic ... Vol. 2
Khor Fakkan ... Vol. 5
Kiangsi ... Vol. 2
Kiangsu ... Vol. 2
Kiauchau, Kiautschou ... Vol. 4
Kibris ... Vol. 6
Kibris Cumhuriyeti (Cyprus #198-
200) ... Vol. 2
Kilis ... Vol. 6
King Edward VII Land ... Vol. 4
Kingman's City Post ... 99
Kingston, Ga. ... 124
Kionga ... Vol. 4
Kirghizia ... Vol. 4
Kiribati ... Vol. 4
Kirin ... Vol. 2
Kishangarh, Kishengarh ... Vol. 3
Kithyra ... Vol. 3
K.K. Post Stempel ... 432, 483
Klaipeda ... Vol. 4
Knoxville, Tenn. ... 124
Kolomyya ... Vol. 6
Kolozsvar ... Vol. 3
Kon ... 541, 544,
Vol. 2, Vol. 4, Vol. 5, Vol. 6
Kongeligt ... Vol. 2
Kop Koh ... Vol. 2
Korca, Korce (Albania) ... 210
Korea ... Vol. 4
Korea (Japanese Offices) ... Vol. 4
Korea, Indian Custodial Unit ... Vol. 3
Koritsa ... Vol. 2
Korytsa ... 210
Kos ... Vol. 3
Kouang Tcheou-Wan ... Vol. 2
KPHTH (Crete) ... Vol. 2
Kr. ... Vol. 3
Kr., Kreuzer ... 432
Kraljevstvo, Kraljevina ... Vol. 6
K.S.A. ... Vol. 5
Kuban Government ... Vol. 6
K.U.K., K. und K. ... 480, 677,
Vol. 3, Vol. 5
Kunming ... Vol. 2
Kupa Zone ... Vol. 6
Kurland, Kurzeme ... Vol. 4
Kuwait, Koweit ... Vol. 4
Kwangchowan ... Vol. 2
Kwangsi ... Vol. 2
Kwangtung ... Vol. 2
Kweichow ... Vol. 2
K. Wurtt. Post ... Vol. 3
Kyrgyzstan ... Vol. 4

La Aguera ... 200
Labuan ... Vol. 4
La Canea ... Vol. 3
Lady McLeod ... Vol. 6
La Georgie ... Vol. 3
Lagos ... Vol. 4
La Grange, Tex. ... 124
Laibach ... Vol. 6
Lake City, Fla. ... 124
Lanchow ... Vol. 2
Land Post ... Vol. 3
Lao, Laos ... Vol. 4
Laos (Int. Com., India) ... Vol. 3
L.A.R. ... Vol. 4
Las Bela ... Vol. 3
Latakia, Lattaquie ... Vol. 4
Latvia, Latvija ... Vol. 4, Vol. 5
Laurens Court House, S.C. ... 124
Lavaca ... 125
League of Nations ... Vol. 6
Lebanon ... Vol. 4, Vol. 5
Leeward Islands ... Vol. 4
Lefkas ... Vol. 3
Lemnos ... Vol. 3
Lenoir, N.C. ... 124
Lero, Leros ... Vol. 3
Lesbos ... Vol. 3
Lesotho ... Vol. 4
Lesser Sundas ... Vol. 4
Lettland, Lettonia ... Vol. 4
Levant, British ... Vol. 3
Levant, French ... Vol. 2, Vol. 6
Levant, Italian ... Vol. 3
Levant, Polish ... Vol. 5
Levant, Romanian ... Vol. 5
Levant, Russian ... Vol. 5
Levant, Syrian (on Lebanon) ... 288
Lexington, Miss. ... 124
Liaoning ... Vol. 2
Liban, Libanaise ... Vol. 4
Libau ovptd. on German ... Vol. 4
Liberia ... Vol. 4
Liberty, Va. ... 124
Libya, Libia, Libye ... Vol. 4
Liechtenstein ... Vol. 4
Lietuva, Lietuvos ... Vol. 4
Ligne Aeriennes de la France
Libre (Syria #MC5) ... Vol. 6
Lima ... Vol. 5
Limestone Springs, S.C. ... 124
Linja-Autorahti Bussfrakt ... Vol. 2
Lipso, Lisso ... Vol. 3
Lisboa ... Vol. 5
Lithuania ... Vol. 4, Vol. 5
Lithuania, Central ... Vol. 2
Lithuanian Occupation of Memel ... Vol. 4
Litwa Srodkowa, Litwy Srodkowej ... Vol. 2
Livingston, Ala. ... 124
Livonia ... Vol. 5
Ljubljana ... Vol. 6
L McL ... Vol. 6
Local ... 495
Local Post ... Vol. 2
Lockport, N.Y. ... 1
Lombardy-Venetia ... 483
Lorraine ... Vol. 2
Losen ... Vol. 6
Lothringen ... Vol. 2
Louisville, Ky. ... 99
Lourenco Marques, L. Marques ... Vol. 4
Lower Austria ... 435, 436
L P overprinted on Russian stamps ... Vol. 4
LTSR on Lithuania ... Vol. 4
Lubeck, Luebeck ... Vol. 3
Lubiana ... Vol. 6
Lublin ... Vol. 5
Luminescence ... 24
Luxembourg ... Vol. 4
Lviv ... Vol. 6
Lydenburg ... Vol. 6
Lynchburg, Va. ... 124

Macao, Macau ... Vol. 4
Macedonia ... Vol. 4
Macon, Ga. ... 124
Madagascar, Madagasikara ... Vol. 4
Madagascar (British) ... Vol. 4
Madeira ... Vol. 4, Vol. 5
Madrid ... Vol. 6
Madura ... Vol. 4
Mafeking ... Vol. 2
Magdalena ... Vol. 2
Magyar, Magyarorszag ... Vol. 3
Magy. Kir. ... Vol. 3
Majunga ... Vol. 4
Makedonija ... Vol. 4
Malacca ... Vol. 4
Malaga ... Vol. 6
Malagasy ... Vol. 4
Malawi ... Vol. 4
Malaya ... Vol. 4
Malaya (Japanese Occ.) ... Vol. 4
Malaya (Thai Occ.) ... Vol. 4
Malaya, Federation of ... Vol. 4
Malaysia ... Vol. 4
Malay States ... Vol. 4
Maldive Islands, Maldives ... Vol. 4
Malgache Republique ... Vol. 4
Mali ... Vol. 4
Malmedy ... Vol. 3
Malta ... Vol. 4
Maluku Selatan (So. Moluccas) ... Vol. 6
Man, Isle of ... Vol. 3
Manchukuo ... Vol. 4
Manchuria ... Vol. 2
Manizales ... Vol. 2
Mapka, Mapok ... Vol. 2, Vol. 5, Vol. 6
Mariana Islands, Marianen ... Vol. 4
Marienwerder ... Vol. 4
Marietta, Ga. ... 124
Marion, Va. ... 124
Markka, Markkaa ... Vol. 2
Maroc, Marocco ... Vol. 2, Vol. 3, Vol. 4
Marruecos ... Vol. 4, Vol. 6
Marshall Islands, Marshall-Inseln ... Vol. 4
Marshall Islands (G.R.I. surch.) ... Vol. 4
Martinique ... Vol. 4
Martin's City Post ... 99
Mauritania, Mauritanie ... Vol. 4
Mauritania stamps surcharged ... Vol. 2
Mauritius ... Vol. 4
Mayotte ... Vol. 4
M. B. D. ... Vol. 3
Mecklenburg-Schwerin ... Vol. 3
Mecklenburg-Strelitz ... Vol. 3
Mecklenburg-Vorpomm ... Vol. 3
Mecklenburg-Vorpommern ... Vol. 3
Medellin ... Vol. 2
Medina ... Vol. 5
Medio Real ... Vol. 2
M.E.F. ovptd on Great Britain ... Vol. 3
Mejico ... Vol. 4
Melaka ... Vol. 4
Memel, Memelgebiet ... Vol. 4
Memphis, Tenn. ... 124
Meng Chiang ... Vol. 2
Menge ... Vol. 4
Mengtsz ... Vol. 2
Merida ... Vol. 4
Mesopotamia (British Occupation) ... Vol. 4
Metelin ... Vol. 5
Mexico, Mexicano ... Vol. 4
Micanopy, Fla. ... 125
Micronesia ... Vol. 4
Middle Congo ... Vol. 4
Middle East Forces ... Vol. 3
Mil ... Vol. 4
Militarpost (Milit. Post) ... 677
Millbury, Mass. ... 1
Milledgeville, Ga. ... 125
Miller, Gen. ... Vol. 5
Mitau ... Vol. 4
M. Kir. ... Vol. 3
Mn. ... Vol. 4
Mobile, Ala. ... 125
Mocambique ... Vol. 4
Modena, Modones ... Vol. 3
Moheli ... Vol. 4
Moldavia ... Vol. 4, Vol. 5
Moldova ... Vol. 4
Moluccas ... Vol. 4
Monaco ... Vol. 4
Monastir ... Vol. 6
Mongolia ... Vol. 4
Mongtseu, Mongtze ... Vol. 2
Monrovia ... Vol. 4
Mont Athos ... Vol. 5
Montenegro ... Vol. 4
Monterrey ... Vol. 4
Montevideo ... Vol. 6
Montgomery, Ala. ... 125
Montserrat ... Vol. 4
Moquea, Moquegua ... Vol. 5
Morelia ... Vol. 4
Morocco ... Vol. 3, Vol. 4
Morocco (German Offices) ... Vol. 3
Morocco, French ... Vol. 2
Morocco, Spanish ... Vol. 6
Morvi ... Vol. 3
Mosul ... Vol. 4
Mount Athos (Turkey) ... Vol. 6
Mount Athos, Russian Offices ... Vol. 5
Mount Lebanon, La. ... 125
Moyen-Congo ... Vol. 4
Mozambique ... Vol. 4
Mozambique Co. ... Vol. 4
MQE ovptd. on French Colonies ... Vol. 4
Muscat and Oman ... Vol. 4
M.V.iR ... Vol. 5
Myanmar (Burma) ... 862, 865
Mytilene ... Vol. 3

Nabha ... Vol. 3
Nagyvarad ... Vol. 3
Namibia ... Vol. 4, Vol. 6
Nandgaon ... Vol. 3
Nanking ... Vol. 2
Nanumaga ... Vol. 6
Nanumea ... Vol. 6
Naples, Napoletana ... Vol. 3
Nashville, Tenn. ... 125
Natal ... Vol. 4
Nations Unies ... 160, Vol. 6
Native Feudatory States, India ... Vol. 3
Nauru ... Vol. 4
Navanagar ... Vol. 3
N.C.E. ovptd. on French Colonies ... Vol. 4
Neapolitan Provinces ... Vol. 3
Ned. Antillen ... Vol. 4

Ned. (Nederl) Indie	Vol. 4	Nueva Granada	Vol. 2
Nederland	Vol. 4	Nui	Vol. 6
Negeri Sembilan	Vol. 4	Nukufetau	Vol. 6
Negri Sembilan	Vol. 4	Nukulaelae	Vol. 6
Nejd	Vol. 5	Nyasaland (Protectorate)	Vol. 4
Nejdi Administration of Hejaz	Vol. 5	Nyasaland and Rhodesia	Vol. 5
Nepal	Vol. 4	Nyassa	Vol. 4
Netherlands	Vol. 4	N.Z.	Vol. 4
Netherlands Antilles	Vol. 4		
Netherlands Indies	Vol. 4	**Oakway, S.C.**	**125**
Netherlands New Guinea	Vol. 4	Oaxaca	Vol. 4
Nevis	Vol. 4, Vol. 5	Obock	Vol. 4
New Britain	Vol. 4	Ob. Ost ovptd. on Germany	
New Brunswick	Vol. 2	(Lithuania)	Vol. 4
New Caledonia	Vol. 4	Occupation Francaise	Vol. 3
Newfoundland	Vol. 2	Oceania, Oceanie	Vol. 2
New Granada	Vol. 2	Oesterr. Post, Ofterreich	432
New Greece	Vol. 3	Offentlig Sak, Off. Sak	Vol. 4
New Guinea	Vol. 4	Oil Rivers	Vol. 4
New Guinea, British	Vol. 5	O K C A (Russia)	Vol. 5
New Guinea, western	Vol. 4	Oldenburg	Vol. 3
New Haven, Conn.	1	Olonets	Vol. 5
New Hebrides (British)	Vol. 4	Oltre Giuba	Vol. 4
New Hebrides (French)	Vol. 4	Oman, Sultanate of	Vol. 4
New Orleans, La.	125	Oradea	Vol. 3
New Republic	Vol. 4	Orange River Colony	Vol. 4
New Smyrna, Fla.	125	Oranje Vrij Staat	Vol. 4
New South Wales	390	Orchha, Orcha	Vol. 3
New York	1, 99	Orense	Vol. 6
New Zealand	Vol. 4	Organisation Mondiale	Vol. 6
Nezavisna	Vol. 2	Oriental	Vol. 6
N.F. overprinted on Nyasaland Pro.	Vol. 3	Orts-Post	Vol. 3
Nicaragua	Vol. 4	O.S.	Vol. 4
Nicaria	Vol. 3	Osten	Vol. 5
Nieuwe Republiek	Vol. 4	Osterreich	432
Nieuw Guinea	Vol. 4	Ostland	Vol. 5
Niger	Vol. 4	Ottoman, Ottomanes	Vol. 2, Vol. 6
Niger and Senegambia	Vol. 5	Oubangi Chari	Vol. 6
Niger and Upper Senegal	Vol. 6	Outer Mongolia	Vol. 6
Niger Coast Protectorate	Vol. 4	Oizbekiston	Vol. 6
Nigeria	Vol. 4		
Nikolaevsk	Vol. 5	**P on Straits Settlements**	**Vol. 4**
Ningsia	Vol. 2	P	Vol. 2, Vol. 6
Nippon	Vol. 4	Pacchi Postali	Vol. 3, Vol. 5, Vol. 6
Nisiro, Nisiros	Vol. 3	Pacific Steam Navigation Co.	Vol. 5
Niuafo'ou	Vol. 6	Packhoi, Pakhoi	Vol. 2
Niue	Vol. 4	Pahang	Vol. 4
Niutao	Vol. 6	Paid (Confed. 35X, etc.)	123
Nlle. Caledonie	Vol. 4	Paid 5 (US 4X1, many Confed.)	1
No Hay Estampillas	Vol. 2	Paid 10 (Confed. 76XU, 101XU, 80XU)	126
N. O. P. O. (Confed. 62XU1)	125	Paid 2 Cents (Confed. 2XU)	121
Norddeutscher Postbezirk	Vol. 3	Paita	Vol. 5
Noreg	Vol. 4	Pakistan	Vol. 5
Norfolk Island	Vol. 4	Pakke-porto	Vol. 3
Norge	Vol. 4	Palau	Vol. 5
North Borneo	Vol. 4	Palestine	Vol. 2, Vol. 5
North China	Vol. 2	Palestine (British Administration)	Vol. 5
Northeast China	Vol. 2	Palestine (Jordan Occ.)	Vol. 4
Northeastern Provinces (China)	Vol. 2	Palestine overprinted	Vol. 4
North Epirus (Greek Occupation)	Vol. 3	Palestinian Authority	Vol. 5
Northern Cook Islands	Vol. 5	Panama	Vol. 5
Northern Cyprus, Turkish Rep. of	Vol. 6	Panama (Colombian Dom.)	Vol. 2, Vol. 5
Northern Ireland	Vol. 3	Panama Canal Zone	127
Northern Kiangsu	Vol. 2	Papua	Vol. 5
Northern Nigeria	Vol. 4	Papua New Guinea	Vol. 5
Northern Poland	Vol. 5	Para	Vol. 2
Northern Rhodesia	Vol. 4	Para ovptd. on Austria	483
Northern Zone, Morocco	Vol. 4	Para ovptd. on France	Vol. 3
North German Confederation	Vol. 3	Para ovptd. on Germany	Vol. 3
North Ingermanland	Vol. 4	Para ovptd. on Italy	Vol. 3
North Viet Nam	Vol. 6	Paraguay	Vol. 5
Northwest China	Vol. 2	Paras	210, Vol. 6
North West Pacific Islands	Vol. 4	Paras	Vol. 4, Vol. 6
Norway	Vol. 4	Paras ovpt. on Great Britain	Vol. 3
Nossi-Be	Vol. 4	Paras ovpt. on Romania	Vol. 3
Nouvelle Caledonie	Vol. 4	Parma, Parm., Parmensi	Vol. 3
Nouvelle Hebrides	Vol. 4	Pasco	Vol. 5
Nova Scotia	Vol. 2	Patiala	Vol. 3
Novocherkassk	Vol. 6	Patmo, Patmos	Vol. 3
Nowa	770	Patzcuaro	Vol. 4
Nowa Bb ovptd. on Bulgaria	Vol. 5	Paxos	Vol. 2, Vol. 3
Nowanuggur	Vol. 3	PC CP	Vol. 5
Nowta	Vol. 5, Vol. 6	PD	Vol. 5
Noyta 541, Vol. 3, Vol. 4, Vol. 5, Vol. 6		P.E. (Egypt #4, etc.)	Vol. 2
Nr.21, Nr.16	Vol. 3	Pechino, Peking	Vol. 2
N S B ovptd. on French Colonies	Vol. 4	Pen, Penna	Vol. 2
N. Sembilan	Vol. 4	Penang	Vol. 4
N.S.W.	393	Penny Post (US 3LB)	99
		Penrhyn Island	Vol. 5
		Pensacola, Fla.	125

People's Republic of China	Vol. 2	Prussia	Vol. 3
Perak	Vol. 4	PS	Vol. 2, Vol. 3
Perlis	Vol. 4	P.S.N.C. (Peru)	Vol. 5
Persekutuan Tanah Melayu (Malaya)	Vol. 4	Puerto Principe	132, Vol. 2
Persia (British Occupation)	883	Puerto Rico, Pto. Rico	Vol. 2, Vol. 5
Persia, Persanes	Vol. 3	Puerto Rico (US Admin.)	140, Vol. 5
Peru, Peruana	Vol. 5	Pul	175
Pesa ovpt. on Germany	Vol. 3	Pulau Pinang	Vol. 4
Peso overprinted on Japan	139, Vol. 5	Puno	Vol. 5
Petersburg, Va.	125	Puttialla State	Vol. 3
Pfennig, Pfg., Pf.	Vol. 2, Vol. 3, Vol. 4		
P.G.S. (Perak)	Vol. 4	**Qatar**	**Vol. 5**
Philadelphia, Pa.	99	Qu'aiti State in Hadhramaut	170
Philippines	Vol. 2, Vol. 5	Qu'aiti State of Shihr and Mukalla	169
Philippines (US Admin.)	136, Vol. 5	Queensland	393
Philippines (Japanese Occ.)	139, Vol. 5	Quelimane	Vol. 5
Piast., Piaster ovptd. on Austria	483		
Piaster ovptd. on Germany	Vol. 3	**R (Armenia)**	**374**
Piaster ovptd. on Romania	Vol. 3	R (Jind)	Vol. 3
Piastre, Piastra ovptd. on Italy	Vol. 3	R ovptd. on French Colonies	Vol. 2
Piastre	Vol. 2, Vol. 4, Vol. 6	Rajasthan	Vol. 3
Piastre ovpt. on France	Vol. 2	Rajpeepla, Rajpipla	Vol. 3
Piastres ovpt. on Great Britain	Vol. 3	Raleigh, N.C.	125
Pies	Vol. 3	Rappen	Vol. 6
Pietersburg	Vol. 6	Rarotonga	Vol. 5
Pilgrim Tercentenary (US 548)	12	Ras Al Khaima	Vol. 6
Pilipinas	139, Vol. 5	R.A.U.	Vol. 6
Pisco	Vol. 5	Rayon	Vol. 6
Piscopi	Vol. 3	Republique Arab Unie	Vol. 6
Pitcairn Islands	Vol. 5	Regatul	Vol. 3
Pittsylvania C.H., Va.	125	Reichspost	Vol. 3
Piura	Vol. 5	Reis (Portugal)	Vol. 5
Pleasant Shade, Va.	125	Repubblica Sociale Italiana	Vol. 3
Pobres (#RA11)	Vol. 6	Resistance overprinted on France	Vol. 6
Poczta Polska	Vol. 2, Vol. 5	Rethymnon, Retymno	Vol. 2
Pohjois Inkeri	Vol. 4	Reunion	Vol. 5
Pokutia	Vol. 6	R.F. (see France or French Colonies)	
Poland	Vol. 5	RF - Solidarite Francaise	Vol. 2
Poland, exile government in		R H	Vol. 3
Great Britain	Vol. 5	Rheatown, Tenn.	125
Polish Offices in Danzig	Vol. 5	Rheinland-Pfalz	Vol. 3
Polish Offices in Turkish Empire	Vol. 5	Rhine Palatinate	Vol. 3
Polska	Vol. 5	Rhodes	Vol. 3
Polynesia, French (Polynesie)	Vol. 2	Rhodesia	Vol. 5
Ponce	140, Vol. 5	Rhodesia (formerly So. Rhodesia)	Vol. 5
Ponta Delgada	Vol. 5	Rhodesia and Nyasaland	Vol. 5
Poonch	Vol. 3	Riau, Riouw Archipelago	Vol. 3
Popayan	Vol. 2	Ricevuta	Vol. 3, Vol. 5, Vol. 6
Port Arthur and Dairen	Vol. 2	Richmond, Tex.	125
Porte de Conduccion	Vol. 5	Rigsbank Skilling	Vol. 2
Porte de Mar	Vol. 4	Ringgold, Ga.	125
Porte Franco	Vol. 3	Rio de Oro	Vol. 5
Port Gdansk	Vol. 5	Rio Muni	Vol. 5
Port Hood, Nova Scotia	Vol. 2	RIS on Netherlands Indies	Vol. 3
Port Lagos	Vol. 2	Rizeh	Vol. 5
Port Lavaca, Tex.	125	RNS	Vol. 3
Porto	479, Vol. 6	R. O. ovptd. on Turkey	Vol. 2
Porto Gazetei	Vol. 3	Robertsport	Vol. 4
Porto Pflichtige	Vol. 3	Rodi	Vol. 3
Porto Rico	140, Vol. 2, Vol. 5	Romagna, Romagne	Vol. 3
Port Said, French Offices	Vol. 2	Romana	Vol. 3, Vol. 5
Portugal, Portuguesa	Vol. 5	Romania, Roumania	Vol. 5
Portuguese Africa	Vol. 5	Romania, Occupation, Offices	Vol. 5
Portuguese Congo	Vol. 5	Romanian Occupation of Hungary	Vol. 5
Portuguese East Africa (Mozambique)	Vol. 4	Romanian Occupation of	
Portuguese Guinea	Vol. 5	Western Ukraine	Vol. 6
Portuguese India	Vol. 5	Roman States	Vol. 3
Posen (Poznan)	Vol. 5	Romina	Vol. 3
Post	Vol. 3	Ross Dependency	Vol. 4
Post (Postage) & Receipt	Vol. 3	Rossija	Vol. 5
Posta	210, Vol. 6	Rostov	Vol. 6
Postage(s)	390, 429, Vol. 3, Vol. 4, Vol. 5	Rouad, Ile	Vol. 5
Postas le hioc	Vol. 3	Roumelie Orientale	Vol. 2
Poste Locale	Vol. 6	RSA	Vol. 6
Postes	553, Vol. 2, Vol. 4, Vol. 5	R S M (San Marino)	Vol. 3
Postes Serbes ovptd. on France	Vol. 5	Ruanda ovptd. on Congo	Vol. 3
Postgebiet Ob. Ost.	Vol. 4	Ruanda-Urundi	Vol. 3
Postmarke	Vol. 3	Rumania, Roumania	Vol. 5
Post Office (US 7X, 9X)	1, 98	Rumanien on Germany	Vol. 5
Postzegel	Vol. 4	Rupee on Great Britain	Vol. 4
P.P. ovptd. on French postage dues	Vol. 2	Russia	Vol. 5
Pre	Vol. 5	Russia (Finnish Occupation)	Vol. 5
P.P.C. ovptd. on Poland	Vol. 5	Russia (German Occupation)	Vol. 5
Preussen	Vol. 3	Russian Dominion of Poland	Vol. 5
Priamur	Vol. 5	Russian Empire, Finland	Vol. 5
Prince Edward Island	Vol. 2	Russian Occupation of Crete	Vol. 5
Pristina	Vol. 6	Russian Occupation of Germany	Vol. 5
Province of Canada	Vol. 2	Russian Occupation of Latvia	Vol. 4
Providence, R.I.	1	Russian Occupation of Lithuania	Vol. 4

Russian Offices	Vol. 5	Silesia, Eastern	Vol. 2	St. Kitts	Vol. 5	Thailand, Thai	Vol. 6
Russian stamps surch. or ovptd. .. 374, 541, Vol. 2, Vol. 3, Vol. 4, Vol. 5, Vol. 6		Silesia, Upper	Vol. 6	St. Kitts-Nevis	Vol. 5	Thailand (Occupation of Malaya)	Vol. 4
		Simi	Vol. 3	St. Louis, Mo.	1, 99	Thessaly	Vol. 6
Russian Turkestan	Vol. 5	Sinaloa	Vol. 4	St. Lucia	Vol. 5	Thomasville, Ga.	126
Russisch-Polen ovptd. on Germany	Vol. 5	Singapore	Vol. 5	St. Pierre and Miquelon	Vol. 5	Thrace	Vol. 6
Rustenburg	Vol. 6	Sinkiang	Vol. 2	Straits Settlements overprinted	Vol. 6	Thuringia, Thuringen	Vol. 3
Rutherfordton, N.C.	125	Sirmoor, Sirmur	Vol. 3	Straits Settlements overprinted	Vol. 4	Thurn and Taxis	Vol. 3
Rwanda, Rwandaise	Vol. 5	Sld.	483	St. Thomas and Prince Islands	Vol. 5	Tibet	Vol. 6
Ryukyu Islands	140	Slesvig	Vol. 5	STT Vuja	Vol. 6	Tibet (Chinese province)	Vol. 2
		Slovakia	Vol. 2, Vol. 5	St. Vincent	Vol. 5	Tibet, Chinese Offices	Vol. 2
S on Straits Settlements	Vol. 4	Slovene Coast	Vol. 6	St. Vincent and the Grenadines	Vol. 5	Tical	Vol. 6
S A, S.A.K. (Saudi Arabia)	Vol. 5	Slovenia, Slovenija	Vol. 5, Vol. 6	St. Vincent Grenadines	Vol. 5	Tientsin (Chinese)	Vol. 2
Saar, Saargebiet, Saar Land	Vol. 5	Slovenia, Italian	Vol. 6	Styria	436, 482	Tientsin (German)	Vol. 3
Sabah	Vol. 4	Slovensko, Slovenska	Vol. 2, Vol. 5	S.U. on Straits Settlements	Vol. 4	Tientsin (Italian)	Vol. 3
Sachsen	Vol. 3	S. Marino	Vol. 5	Submarine mail (Correo Submarino)	Vol. 6	Tiflis	Vol. 3
Sahara Occidental (Espanol)	Vol. 6	Smirne, Smyrna	Vol. 3	Sudan	Vol. 6	Timbre ovptd. on France	Vol. 2
Saint	see St.	Smyrne	Vol. 5	Sudan, French	Vol. 2	Timor	Vol. 6
Salamanca	Vol. 6	S O ovptd. on Czechoslovakia, Poland	Vol. 2	Suid Afrika	Vol. 6	Tin Can Island	Vol. 6
Salem, N.C.	125			Suidwes-Afrika	Vol. 6	Tjedan Solidarnosti (#RA82)	Vol. 6
Salem, Va.	124	Sobreporte	Vol. 2	Suiyuan	Vol. 2	Tjenestefrimerke	Vol. 2, Vol. 4
Salisbury, N.C.	126	Sociedad Colombo-Alemana	Vol. 2	Sultanate of Oman	Vol. 4	Tlacotalpan	Vol. 4
Salonicco, Salonika	Vol. 3	Sociedade de Geographia de Lisboa	Vol. 5	Sumatra	Vol. 6	Tobago	Vol. 6
Salonika (Turkish)	Vol. 5	Societe des Nations	Vol. 6	Sumter, S.C.	126	Toga	Vol. 5
Salonique	Vol. 5	Soldi	484	Sungei Ujong	Vol. 4	Togo, Togolaise	Vol. 5
Salvador, El	Vol. 5	Solomon Islands	Vol. 6	Suomi (Finland)	Vol. 2	Tokelau Islands	Vol. 6
Salzburg	482	Somali, Somalia, Somaliya	Vol. 6	Supeh	Vol. 2	Tolima	Vol. 2
Samoa	Vol. 5	Somalia, B.M.A.	Vol. 3	Surinam, Suriname	Vol. 6	Tonga	Vol. 6
Samos	Vol. 2, Vol. 3	Somalia, E.A.F.	Vol. 6	Suvalki	Vol. 4	Tongareva	Vol. 5
San Antonio, Tex.	126	Somali Coast (Djibouti)	Vol. 6	Sverige	Vol. 6	To Pay	Vol. 3
San Marino	Vol. 5	Somaliland Protectorate	Vol. 6	S.W.A.	Vol. 6	Toscano	Vol. 3
San Sebastian	Vol. 6	Sonora	Vol. 4	Swaziland, Swazieland	Vol. 6	Tou	Vol. 3
Santa Cruz de Tenerife	Vol. 6	Soomaaliya, Sooomaliyeed	Vol. 6	Sweden	Vol. 6	Touva, Tovva	Vol. 6
Santa Maura	Vol. 6	Soruth, Sorath	Vol. 3	Switzerland	Vol. 6	Transcaucasian Federated Republics	Vol. 6
Santander	Vol. 2	Soudan	Vol. 2, Vol. 6	Switzerland, Administration of Liechtenstein	Vol. 4	Trans-Jordan	Vol. 4, Vol. 5
Sao Tome and Principe	Vol. 5	Souraahtra	Vol. 3			Trans-Jordan (Palestine Occ.)	Vol. 4
SAR	Vol. 6	South Africa	Vol. 6	Syria, Syrie, Syrienne	Vol. 5, Vol. 6	Transkei	Vol. 6
Sarawak	Vol. 5	South African Republic (Transvaal)	Vol. 6	Syria (Arabian Government)	Vol. 6	Transvaal	Vol. 6
Sardinia	Vol. 3	South Arabia	Vol. 6	Syrie-Grand Liban	Vol. 6	Transylvania	Vol. 3
Sarre overprinted on Germany and Bavaria	Vol. 5	South Australia	395	Szechwan	Vol. 2	Trasporto Pacchi	Vol. 3
		South Bulgaria	Vol. 2	Szechwan Province	Vol. 2	Travancore	Vol. 3
Saseno	Vol. 5	South China	Vol. 2	Szeged	Vol. 3	Travancore-Cochin, State of	Vol. 3
Saudi Arabia	Vol. 5	Southern Nigeria	Vol. 6			Trebizonde	Vol. 5
Saudi Arabia overprinted	Vol. 4	Southern Poland	Vol. 5	T	603, Vol. 2	Trengganu	Vol. 4
Saurashtra	Vol. 3	Southern Rhodesia	Vol. 6	T ovptd. on stamps of Peru	Vol. 5	Trentino	482
Savannah, Ga.	126	Southern Yemen	Vol. 6	Tacna	Vol. 5	Trieste	482, Vol. 3, Vol. 6
Saxony	Vol. 3	South Georgia	Vol. 2, Vol. 6	Tadjikistan, Tadzikistan	Vol. 6	Trinidad	Vol. 6
SCADTA	Vol. 2	South Georgia and South Sandwich Islands	Vol. 6	Tae Han (Korea)	Vol. 4	Trinidad and Tobago	Vol. 6
Scarpanto	Vol. 3			Tahiti	Vol. 6	Trinidad Society	Vol. 6
Schleswig	Vol. 3, Vol. 5	South Kasai	Vol. 6	Taiwan (ROC)	Vol. 2	Tripoli di Barberia (Tripoli)	Vol. 3
Schleswig-Holstein	Vol. 3	South Korea	Vol. 4	Taiwan (Formosa)	Vol. 4	Tripoli, Fiera Campionaria	Vol. 4
Schweizer Reneke	Vol. 6	South Lithuania	Vol. 4	Taiwan, Japanese	Vol. 2, Vol. 4	Tripolitania	Vol. 4, Vol. 6
Scinde	Vol. 3	South Moluccas	Vol. 6	Takca	838	Tripolitania (B.M.A.)	Vol. 3
Scotland	Vol. 3	South Orkneys	Vol. 2	Talbotton, Ga.	126	Tristan da Cunha	Vol. 6
Scutari, Italian Offices	Vol. 3	South Russia	Vol. 6	Talca	Vol. 2	Trucial States	Vol. 2
Segnatasse, Segna Tassa	Vol. 3	South Shetlands	Vol. 2	Tanganyika	Vol. 6	Tsinghai	Vol. 2
Seiyun	169	South Viet Nam	Vol. 6	Tanganyika and Zanzibar	Vol. 6	Tsingtau	Vol. 2, Vol. 4
Selangor	Vol. 4	South West Africa	Vol. 6	Tanganyika (Tanzania), Kenya, Uganda	Vol. 2, Vol. 6	T. Ta. C	Vol. 6
Selma, Ala.	126	Southwest China	Vol. 2			Tullahoma, Tenn.	126
Semenov	Vol. 2	Soviet Union (Russia)	Vol. 5	Tanger	Vol. 2, Vol. 6	Tumbes (Peru #129-133)	Vol. 5
Sen, Sn.	140, Vol. 4	Sowjetische Besatzungs Zone	Vol. 3	Tangier, British Offices	Vol. 3	Tunisia, Tunisie, Tunis, Tunisienne	Vol. 6
Senegal	Vol. 5	Spain	Vol. 6	Tangier, French Offices	Vol. 3	Turkestan, Russian	Vol. 5
Senegal stamps surcharged	Vol. 5	Spain, Dominion of Cuba	Vol. 2	Tangier, Spanish Offices	Vol. 6	Turkey, Turkiye	Vol. 6
Senegambia and Niger	Vol. 5	Spanish Administration of Andorra	264	Tannu Tuva	Vol. 6	Turkey (Greek Occupation)	Vol. 3, Vol. 6
Serbia, Serbien	Vol. 5	Spanish Dominion of Mariana Islands	Vol. 4	Tanzania	Vol. 6	Turkey in Asia	Vol. 6
Serbian Occupation of Hungary	Vol. 5	Spanish Dominion of Philippines	Vol. 5	Tanzania-Zanzibar	Vol. 6	Turk Federe Devleti	Vol. 6
Service	Vol. 5	Spanish Dominion of Puerto Rico	Vol. 5	Tartu	Vol. 2	Turkish Empire, Austrian Offices	483
Seville, Sevilla	Vol. 6	Spanish Guinea	Vol. 6	Tasmania	397	Turkish Empire, British Offices	Vol. 3
Seychelles	Vol. 5	Spanish Morocco	Vol. 6	Tassa Gazzette	Vol. 3	Turkish Empire, French Offices	Vol. 2
S.H.	Vol. 3	Spanish Sahara	Vol. 6	Taxa de Guerra	Vol. 4, Vol. 5	Turkish Empire, German Offices	Vol. 3
Shanghai	Vol. 2, Vol. 5	Spanish West Africa	Vol. 6	Taxyapom	Vol. 2	Turkish Empire, Italian Offices	Vol. 3
Shanghai (U.S. Offices)	95	Spanish Western Sahara	Vol. 6	Tchad	Vol. 2	Turkish Empire, Polish Offices	Vol. 5
Shanghai and Nanking	Vol. 2	Sparta, Ga.	126	Tchongking	Vol. 2	Turkish Empire, Romanian Offices	Vol. 5
Shansi	Vol. 2	Spartanburg, S.C.	126	T.C. overprinted on Cochin	Vol. 3	Turkish Empire, Russian Offices	Vol. 5
Shantung	Vol. 2	SPM ovptd. on French Cols.	Vol. 5	T.C., Postalari	Vol. 6	Turkish Republic of Northern Cyprus	Vol. 6
Sharjah	Vol. 5, Vol. 6	Sri Lanka	Vol. 6	Te Betalen	603, Vol. 4, Vol. 6	Turkish stamps surcharged or overprinted	Vol. 2, Vol. 3, Vol. 6
Shensi	Vol. 2	Srodkowa Litwa	Vol. 2	Tegucigalpa	Vol. 3		
Shihr and Mukalla	169	Stamp (Tibet #O1)	Vol. 6	Teheran	Vol. 6	Turkmenistan, Turkmenpocta	Vol. 6
Shqipenia, Shqiptare, Shqiperija, Shqiperise (Albania)	209	Stampalia	Vol. 3	Tellico Plains, Tenn.	126	Turks and Caicos Islands	Vol. 6
		Stanislav	Vol. 6	Temesvar	Vol. 3	Turks Islands	Vol. 6
Shri Lanka	Vol. 6	Statesville, N.C.	126	Tenaire on French Colonies	Vol. 4	Tuscaloosa, Ala	126
S.H.S. on Bosnia and Herzegovina	Vol. 6	St. Christopher	Vol. 5	T.E.O. ovptd. on Turkey or France	Vol. 2, Vol. 6	Tuscany	Vol. 3
S.H.S. on Hungary	Vol. 6	St. Christopher-Nevis-Anguilla	Vol. 5			Tuscumbia, Ala.	1, 126
Siam (Thailand)	Vol. 6	Steinmeyer's City Post	99	Terres Australes et Antarctiques Francaises	Vol. 2	Tuva Autonomous Region	Vol. 6
Siberia	Vol. 5	Ste. Marie de Madagascar	Vol. 5			Tuvalu	Vol. 6
Sicily, Sicilia	Vol. 3	Stellaland	Vol. 6	Territorio Insular Chileno (Chile #1011)	Vol. 2	Two Cents (Confed. 53X5)	124
Siege de la Ligue Arabe (Morocco #44)	Vol. 4	Stempel	432, 483			Two Sicilies	Vol. 3
		St. Georges, Bermuda	632	Teruel	Vol. 6	Tyosen (Korea)	Vol. 4
Sierra Leone	Vol. 5	St. Helena	Vol. 5	Tete	Vol. 6	Tyrol	482
Sikang	Vol. 2	S. Thome (Tome) E Principe	Vol. 5	Tetuan	Vol. 6		

Entry	Reference
UAE ovptd. on Abu Dhabi	Vol. 6
U.A.R.	Vol. 2, Vol. 6
Ubangi, Ubangi-Shari	Vol. 6
Uganda, U.G.	Vol. 6
Uganda, and Kenya	Vol. 4
Uganda, Tanganyika, Kenya	Vol. 4
Ukraine (Ukrainia)	Vol. 6
Ukraine (German Occupation)	Vol. 5
Uku Leta	134
Ultramar	Vol. 2
Umm al Qiwain	Vol. 6
UNEF ovptd. on India	Vol. 3
UNESCO	Vol. 2
U.N. Force in Congo or Gaza (India)	Vol. 3
Union City, Tenn.	126
Union Island, St. Vincent	Vol. 5
Union Islands	Vol. 6
Union of South Africa	Vol. 6
Union of Soviet Socialist Republics	Vol. 5
Uniontown, Ala.	126
Unionville, S.C.	126
United Arab Emirates	Vol. 6
United Arab Republic (UAR)	Vol. 2, Vol. 6
United Arab Republic, Egypt	Vol. 2
United Arab Republic Issues for Syria	Vol. 6
United Kingdom	Vol. 3
United Nations	146
United Nations European Office	Vol. 6
United Nations Offices in Geneva	160
United Nations Offices in Vienna	164
United Nations - West Irian	Vol. 6
United State of Saurashtra	Vol. 3
United States Adm. of Canal Zone	127
United States Adm. of Cuba	132, Vol. 2
United States Adm. of Guam	134
U. S. Adm. of Philippines	136, Vol. 5
U. S. Adm. of Puerto Rico	140, Vol. 5
U. S. Military Rule of Korea	Vol. 4
United States of America	1
United States of Indonesia	Vol. 3
United States of New Granada	Vol. 2
United States, Offices in China	95
U. S. P. O.	99
U.S. Zone (Germany)	Vol. 3
Universal Postal Union, Intl. Bureau	Vol. 6
UNTEA ovptd. on Netherlands New Guinea	Vol. 6
UPHA ROPA	Vol. 4
Upper Austria	482
Upper Senegal and Niger	Vol. 6
Upper Silesia	Vol. 6
Upper Volta	839
Urgente	Vol. 6
U.R.I. ovptd. on Yugoslavia	Vol. 6
Uruguay	Vol. 6
Urundi ovptd. on Congo	Vol. 3
Uskub	Vol. 6
U.S.P.O Despatch	99
U. S. T.C. overprinted on Cochin	Vol. 3
Uzbekistan	Vol. 6
Vaitupu	**Vol. 6**
Valdosta, Ga.	126
Valladolid	Vol. 6
Valona	Vol. 3
Valparaiso	Vol. 2
Vancouver Island	Vol. 2
Van Diemen's Land (Tasmania)	397
Vanuatu	Vol. 6
Varldspost Kongress (Sweden #197)	Vol. 6
Vasa	Vol. 2
Vathy	Vol. 2
Vatican City, Vaticane, Vaticano	Vol. 6
Venda	Vol. 6
Venezia Giulia	482, Vol. 3
Venezia Tridentina	482
Venezuela, Veneza., Venezolana	Vol. 6
Venizelist Government	Vol. 3
Vereinte Nationen	164
Vetekeverria	210
Victoria	398
Victoria, Texas	126
Victoria Land	Vol. 4
Vienna	435, 436
Viet Minh	Vol. 6
Viet Nam	Vol. 6
Viet Nam, (Int. Com., India)	Vol. 3
Viet Nam, North	Vol. 6
Viet Nam, South	Vol. 6
Vilnius	Vol. 4
Virgin Islands	Vol. 6
Vladivostok	Vol. 2
Vojna Uprava	Vol. 6
Volksrust	Vol. 6
Vom Empfanger	Vol. 2, Vol. 3
Vorarlberg	482
V.R. ovptd. on Transvaal	Vol. 2, Vol. 6
Vryburg	Vol. 2
Vuja-STT	Vol. 6
Wadhwan	**Vol. 3**
Walachia	Vol. 5
Wales & Monmouthshire	Vol. 3
Wallis and Futuna Islands	Vol. 6
Walterborough, S.C.	126
War Board of Trade	Vol. 6
Warrenton, Ga.	126
Warsaw, Warszawa	Vol. 5
Washington, Ga.	126
Watermarks (British Colonies)	See table of contents
Weatherford, Texas	127
Wenden, Wendensche	Vol. 5
Western Australia	401
Western Samoa	Vol. 5
Western Szechwan	Vol. 2
Western Thrace (Greek Occupation)	Vol. 6
Western Ukraine	Vol. 6
West Irian	Vol. 6
West New Guinea	Vol. 6
West Saxony	Vol. 3
Wet and dry printings	24, 129
White Russia	544
Wiederaufbauspende	Vol. 3
Wilayah Persekutuan	Vol. 4
William's City Post	99
Winnsborough, S.C.	127
Wir sind frei	Vol. 2
Wn.	Vol. 4
Wolmaransstad	Vol. 6
World Health Organization	Vol. 6
World Intellectual Property Organization	Vol. 6
World Meteorological Organization	Vol. 6
Wrangel Issues	Vol. 5
Wuhu	Vol. 2
Wurttemberg	Vol. 3
Wytheville, Va.	127
Xeimappa	**Vol. 2**
Yambo	**Vol. 5**
Y.A.R.	Vol. 6
Yca	Vol. 5
Yemen	Vol. 6
Yemen Arab Republic	Vol. 6
Yemen People's Republic	Vol. 6
Yemen, People's Democratic Rep.	Vol. 6
Yen, Yn.	140, Vol. 4
Ykp. H.P., Ykpaiha	Vol. 6
Yksi Markka	Vol. 2
Yuan	Vol. 2
Yucatan	Vol. 4
Yudenich, Gen.	Vol. 5
Yugoslavia	Vol. 6
Yugoslavia (German Occupation)	Vol. 6
Yugoslavia (Italian Occupation)	Vol. 6
Yugoslavia (Trieste)	Vol. 6
Yugoslavia (Zone B)	Vol. 6
Yugoslavia Offices Abroad	Vol. 6
Yunnan (China)	Vol. 2
Yunnan Fou, Yunnansen	Vol. 2
Za Crveni Krst (Yugoslavia #RA2)	**800**
Z. Afr. Republiek, Z.A.R.	Vol. 6
Zaire	Vol. 6
Zambezia	Vol. 6
Zambia	Vol. 6
Zante	Vol. 3
Zanzibar	Vol. 6
Zanzibar, French Offices	Vol. 2
Zanzibar (Kenya, Uganda, Tanganyika)	Vol. 4
Zanzibar-Tanzania	Vol. 6
Z.A.R. ovptd. on Cape of Good Hope	Vol. 2
Zelaya	Vol. 4
Zentraler Kurierdienst	Vol. 3
Zil Eloigne Sesel	Vol. 5
Zil Elwagne Sesel	Vol. 5
Zil Elwannyen Sesel	Vol. 5
Zimbabwe	Vol. 6
Zimska Pomoc ovptd. on Italy	Vol. 6
Zone A (Trieste)	Vol. 3
Zone B (Istria)	Vol. 6
Zone B (Trieste)	Vol. 6
Zone Francaise	Vol. 3
Zuidafrikaansche Republiek	Vol. 6
Zuidwest Afrika	Vol. 6
Zululand	Vol. 6
Zurich	Vol. 6

Stock Pages

Hagner-style stock pages offer convenience and flexibility. Pages are produced on thick, archival-quality paper with acetate pockets glued from the bottom of each pocket. They're ideal for the topical collector who may require various page styles to store a complete collection. Multi-hole punch fits most binder types. Available in 9 different page formats. 8 1/2" x 11" size accomodates every size stamp.

Sold in packages of 10.
Available with pockets on one side or both sides.
"D" in item number denotes two-sided page.

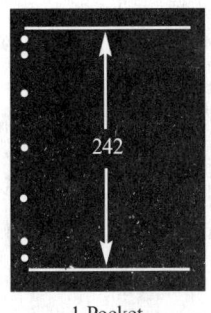

1 Pocket (242 mm)
Item	Retail
S1	$8.95
S1D	$13.95

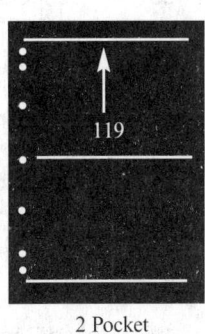

2 Pocket (119 mm)
Item	Retail
S2	$8.95
S2D	$13.95

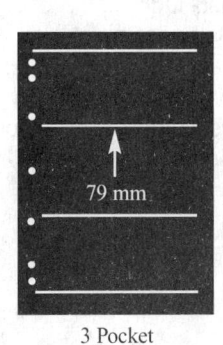

3 Pocket (79 mm)
Item	Retail
S3	$8.95
S3D	$13.95

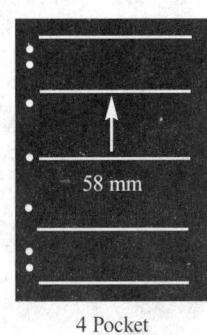

4 Pocket (58 mm)
Item	Retail
S4	$8.95
S4D	$13.95

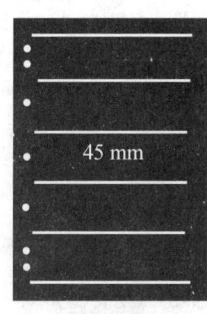

5 Pocket (45 mm)
Item	Retail
S5	$8.95
S5D	$13.95

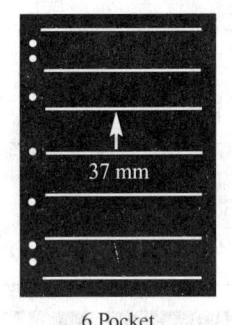

6 Pocket (37 mm)
Item	Retail
S6	$8.95
S6D	$13.95

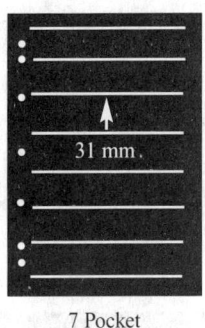

7 Pocket (31 mm)
Item	Retail
S7	$8.95
S7D	$13.95

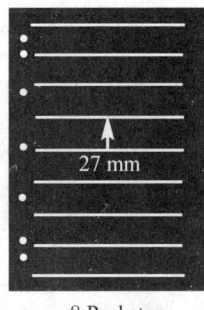

8 Pocket (27 mm)
Item	Retail
S8	$8.95
S8D	$13.95

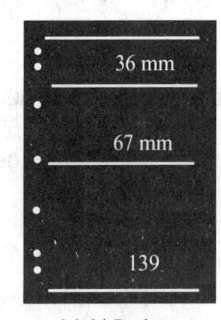

Multi-Pockets (36 mm, 67 mm, 139 mm)
Item	Retail
S9	$8.95
S9D	$13.95

STOCK PAGE BINDER AND SLIPCASE

Keep all your stock pages neat and tidy with binder and accompanying slipcase. Available in two colors.

Item	Color	Retail
SSBSRD	Red	$19.95
SSBSBL	Blue	$19.95

Available from your favorite dealer or direct from:

SCOTT

Box 828 Sidney OH 45365-0828
1-800-572-6885
www.scottonline.com

INDEX TO ADVERTISERS – 2000 VOLUME 1

ADVERTISER	PAGE
– A –	
Almaz Co.	Yellow Pages
American Stamp Dealers Assoc., Inc	Yellow Pages
Antarctic Philatelic Exchange	430
– B –	
Robert E. Barker	Yellow Pages
Belgian Philatelic Specialists, Inc.	549
Belgian Philatelic Specialists, Inc.	553
Belgian Philatelic Specialists, Inc.	581
Brewart Stamps	Yellow Pages
Budget Stamps	406
– C –	
Campo Rodan	581
Central Philatelic	583
City Stamp Montreal	3
The Classic Collector	391
The Classic Collector	399
The Classic Collector	433
The Classic Collector	484
The Classic Collector	686
Colonial Stamp Co.	Yellow Pages
County Stamp Center	Yellow Pages
– D –	
Dallas Stamp Gallery	Yellow Pages
Delaware Valley Stamp Co.	677
Lowell S. Donald Co.	Yellow Pages
– E –	
Joseph Eder	434
– G –	
Henry Gitner Philatelists, Inc.	159
Henry Gitner Philatelists, Inc.	435
Henry Gitner Philatelists, Inc.	553
Ercole Gloria	Yellow Pages
Golden Philatelics	113
– H –	
Aron R. Halberstam Philatelists Ltd.	405
Aron R. Halberstam Philatelists Ltd.	633
Aron R. Halberstam Philatelists Ltd.	Yellow Pages
John B. Head	143
– J –	
Michael Jaffe Stamps, Inc.	121
Don Joss	501
– L –	
Guy Lestrade	171
Robin Linke	405
– M –	
Steve Malack	4
– P –	
The Perf Gauge	404
Pittwater Philatelic	404
– Q –	
Quality Investors	95
– R –	
R.J.B. Mail Sales	239
R.J.B. Mail Sales	834
– S –	
Sam Houston Duck Company	120
Sandafayre Limited	Insert
Jacques C. Schiff, Jr. Inc.	Yellow Pages
R. Schneider	434
Shreves Philatelic Galleries	Back Cover
Shull Service	141
Juan N. Simona	325
Jay Smith	133
Stanley Gibbons	403
Max Stern	428
Superior Stamp & Coin	2A
– U –	
United Postal Stationery Society	100
– V –	
Victoria Stamp Company	633
Victoria Stamp Company	Yellow Pages
– W –	
Warren T. Wasson	Yellow Pages
Raymond H. Weill	Inside Front cover
Winter Park Stamp Shop	Yellow Pages
Laurence Winum	90

DEALERS...TAKE ADVANTAGE OF SCOTT'S ADVERTISING OPPORTUNITIES!

SCOTT GIVES YOU THE AMERICAN MARKET...AND AN EVER INCREASING WORLD MARKET!
Present Your Buying or Selling Messages, in Your Specialty Area, to Serious Collectors by placing Your Advertisements in Scott Products!

2001 SCOTT CATALOGUES
Call now to reserve ad space and to receive advertising information. If you're interested in specific positions...call or write as soon as possible.

SCOTT STAMP MONTHLY
Whether you're buying or selling, our readership of active mail-order collectors offers you a perfect opportunity for increased sales and contacts.

SCOTT U.S. FDC CATALOGUE
The First Day Cover reference collectors of all levels have come to depend on. Call now for advertising information.

SCOTT U.S. POCKET CAT.
Now a full-color reference, this popular annual catalogue can bring you many new customers. Thousands are sold each year to active and beginning collectors.

For Information Call 1-800-895-9881, Fax 1-800-488-5349,
Visit our web site at www.scottonline.com
or write SCOTT, P.O. Box 828, Sidney, OH 45365-0828 USA.

2000 VOLUME 1 DEALER DIRECTORY YELLOW PAGE LISTINGS

This section of your Scott Catalogue contains advertisements to help you conveniently find what you need, when you need it...!

Accessories 912	British Pacific 914	Lots & Collections 915	US - Mint 919
Aitutaki 912	Brunei 914	Mail Bid Auctions 915	United States - Plate
Albania 912	Bulgaria 914	Mail Bid Sales 915	Blocks 919
Albums & Accessories 912	Burma 914	Mail Order 915	US - Price Lists 919
Antarctic 912	Bushire 914	Major Errors 915	US - Rare Stamps 919
Appraisals 912	Buying 914	New Issues 915	US Singles - Classic &
Approvals - Personalized	Canada 914	New Issues - Retail 916	Modern 919
Worldwide & U.S. 912	Canada - Duck Stamps 914	New Issues - Wholesale ... 916	US - Stamps 920
Approvals - Worldwide 912	Canada - Postal Bid Sales . 914	Proofs & Essays 916	US - State Duck Stamps ... 920
Approvals - Worldwide -	Canada - Worldwide 914	Publications - Collector 916	US - Transportation Coils . 920
Collections 912	China 914	Spain 916	US - Used 920
Argentina - New Issues 912	China, Peoples Republic .. 914	Stamp Shows 916	US - Want Lists 920
Asia 912	Classics 914	Stamp Stores ... 916, 917, 918	Want Lists 920
Auction House 912	Collections 914, 915	Supplies & Accessories 918	Want Lists - British Empire
Auctions 912, 913	Conservation Stamps 915	Supplies - Mail Order 918	1840-1935 German
Auctions - Public 913	Czechoslovakia 915	Supplies - Stamps &	Col./Offices 920
Australia 913	Disney 915	Coins 918	Wanted - Estates 920
Australia - New Issues 913	Duck Stamps 915	Topicals 918	Wanted - US 920
Austria 913	Egypt 915	Topicals - Columbus 918	Websites 920
Bahamas 913	Errors, Freaks & Oddities . 915	Topicals - Miscellaneous .. 918	Wholesale 920
Bangkok 913	Errors - Major 915	United Nations 918	Wholesale - Collections 920
Barbados 913	Exchange 915	United Nations - New	Wholesale - Philatelic &
Belgium 913	FDC's 915	Issues 918	Numismatic
Belgium - New Issues 913	France 915	United States 918, 919	Accessories 920
Bermuda 913	German Areas 915	US - Booklet Panes 919	Wholesale - Supplies 920
Brazil - New Issues 913	Great Britain 915	US - Classics 919	Wholesale - US 920
British Colonies 913	Imperial China 915	United States -	Worldwide 920
British	Insurance 915	Classics/Modern 919	Worldwide - Collections .. 920
Commonwealth 913, 914	Israel - New Issues 915	US - Duck Stamps 919	Worldwide - Romania 920
British East Africa 914	Latin America 915	US - EFOs 919	Worldwide - Year Sets 920
British Guiana 914	Literature 915		

Collectors:
Buying – Selling – Appraisals – The ASDA Can Help

The American Stamp Dealers Association, Inc., serving the needs of the collecting community for over 80 years, is ready to assist you. Our members represent all segments of the philatelic marketplace. We are the leader in establishing the highest standards of professionalism for the rest of the industry to emulate. As a collector, you are guaranteed absolute satisfaction with every transaction.

Contact Us Today For:
1.) A list of ASDA dealers in your geographic area.
2.) A list of ASDA dealers by your collecting area.
3.) The brochure, "Selling a stamp collection, - what you need to know."
4.) The brochure, "Expertizing Philatelic Materials."

Please send a #10 SASE, including 55¢ postage if ordering all of the above.

Professionals Serving Philately Since 1914
- Integrity • Honesty • Expertise
- Dedication • Hobby Builders • Reliability

AMERICAN STAMP DEALERS ASSOCIATION, INC.
3 School St. Dept. SC, Glen Cove, NY 11542
email:asda@inx.net   web:www.amerstampdlrs.com

Accessories

BROOKLYN GALLERY COIN & STAMP
8725 4th Ave.
Brooklyn, NY 11209
718-745-5701
718-745-2775 Fax
Web:http://www.brooklyngallery.com

Aitutaki

OVPT PHILATELICS
P.O. Box 36217
Los Angeles, CA 90036
818-893-4603 Telephone & Fax
Email:OVPTphmc@aol.com

Albania

HUNGARIA STAMP EXCHANGE
P.O. Box 3024
Andover, MA 01810
508-682-0242
508-794-2567 Fax

Albums & Accessories

THE KEEPING ROOM
P.O. Box 257
Trumbull, CT 06611-0257
203-372-8436

Antarctic

ANTARCTIC PHILATELIC EXCHANGE
1208A-280 Simco St.
Toronto, ON M5T 2Y5
Canada
416-593-7849
Email:jporter@interlog.com
Web:http://www.interlog.com/~jporter

Appraisals

KUKSTIS AUCTIONS, INC.
P.O. Box 130
Scituate, MA 02066
800-649-0083 or 781-545-8494
781-545-4610 Fax
Email:paulk@dreamcom.net
Web:http://www.kukstis.com

RANDY SCHOLL STAMP COMPANY
Southhampton Square
7460 Jager Court
Cincinnati, OH 45230-4344
513-624-6800
513-624-6440 Fax

UNIQUE ESTATE APPRAISALS
1937 NE Broadway
Portland, OR 97232
503-287-4200 or
800-646-1147
Email:uea@stampsandcoins.com
Web:www.stampsandcoins.com

Approvals - Personalized Worldwide & U.S.

THE KEEPING ROOM
P.O. Box 257
Trumbull, CT 06611-0257
203-372-8436

Approvals Worldwide

ROSS WETREICH INC.
P.O. Box 1300
Valley Stream, NY 11582-1300
516-825-8974

Approvals Worldwide - Collections

S. R. L. STAMPS
P.O. Box 296
Huguenot, NY 12746
800-369-4617 pin 3429 Phone &Fax

Argentina - New Issues

VICTOR R. OSTOLAZA LTD.
P.O. Box 4664
Wayne, NJ 07474-4664
973-720-5884
Email:vroltd@worldnet.att.net

Asia

ALLKOR STAMP COMPANY
Box 1346
Port Washington, NY 11050
516-883-3296 Telephone & Fax

MICHAEL ROGERS, INC.
199 E. Welbourne Ave.
Winter Park, FL 32789
407-644-2290
407-645-4434 Fax
Web:http://www.michael-rogersinc.com

THE STAMP ACT
P.O. Box 1136
Belmont, CA 94002
650-592-3315
650-508-8104 Fax
Email:Bchang@IX.NETCOM.COM

SOUTHEAST STAMPS
P.O. Box 6768
Shreveport, LA 71106

Auction House

B TRADING CO.
114 Quail Street
Albany, NY 12206
518-465-3497 Telephone & Fax
Email:btradeco@wizvax.net

Auctions

CHARLES G. FIRBY AUCTIONS
6695 Highland Road Suite #107
Waterford, MI 48327-1967
248-666-5333
248-666-5020 Fax
Email:Firbystamps@prodigy.net

Auctions

Schiff Auctions

Buyers, Auctioneers & Appraisers of U.S. & Worldwide Stamps & Covers

We have been catering to the individual buyer and seller since 1947. Let us put our **52 years** of experience to work for you when selling your stamps, covers or your collection. Whether you prefer consigning to public auction or selling outright, call us first. Describe your material before sending. Please include your address and telephone numbers.

CATALOG SUBSCRIPTIONS	N. AMERICA	OVERSEAS
1 Year Catalogs & Prices Realized	$10.00	$18.00
1 Year Catalog Only	$7.50	$15.00
1 Catalog with Prices Realized	$1.50	$2.50
1 Catalog Only	$1.00	$1.50

JACQUES C. SCHIFF, JR., INC.

195 Main St., Ridgefield Park, NJ 07660 USA
Telephone 201-641-5566 from NYC 662-2777
FAX 201-641-5705

OFFICIAL AUCTIONEERS:
AMERIPEX 1986.
WORLD STAMP EXPO 1989.
WORLD COLUMBIAN STAMP EXPO 1992.
YEARLY: COMPEX-CHICAGO

QUALIFIED AUCTIONEER

Auctions

DANIEL F. KELLEHER CO., INC.
24 Farnsworth St.
Ste. 605
Boston, MA 02210
617-443-0033
617-443-0789 Fax

KUKSTIS AUCTIONS, INC.
P.O. Box 130
Scituate, MA 02066
800-649-0083 or 781-545-8494
781-545-4610 Fax
Email:paulk@dreamcom.net
Web:http://www.kukstis.com

LAKESIDE PHILATELIC AUCTIONS
3935 Lakeside Rd.
Penticton, BC V2A 8W1
CANADA
250-493-5239
250-493-3324 Fax
Web:http://vvv.com/~greek
Email:greek@tnet.net

SAM HOUSTON PHILATELICS
13310 Westheimer #150
Houston, TX 77077
281-493-6386
281-496-1445 Fax
Email:BDHOUDUCK@AOL.COM

JACQUES C. SCHIFF, JR., INC.
195 Main St.
Ridgefield Park, NJ 07660
201-641-5566 from NYC 662-2777
201-641-5705 Fax

STAMP CENTER / DUTCH COUNTRY AUCTIONS
4115 Concord Pike
Wilmington, DE 19803
302-478-8740
302-478-8779 Fax
Web:http://www.thestampcenter.com

Auctions - Public

ALAN BLAIR STAMPS / AUCTIONS
5520A Lakeside Avenue
Richmond, VA 23228
800-689-5602 Telephone & Fax

CEE-JAY STAMP AUCTIONS
P.O. Box 1707
Glen Burnie, MD 21060
800-360-2022
410-590-9033 Fax
Email:ceejayauc@aol.com

CONNEXUS
P.O. Box 130
Tryon, NC 28782
828-859-5882
828-859-2702 Fax
Email:Connexus1@worldnet.att.net

SUBURBAN STAMPS INC.
176 Worthington St.
Springfield, MA 01103
413-785-5348
413-746-3788 Fax

Australia

COLONIAL STAMP COMPANY
5757 Wilshire Blvd. PH #8
Los Angeles, CA 90036
323-933-9435
323-939-9930 Fax
Web:http://www.colonialstamps.com

Australia - New Issues

AUSTRALIA STAMP AGENCY IN NORTH AMERICA
One Unicover Center
Cheyenne, WY 82008-0010
800-443-4225
800-628-3132 Fax
Web:http://www.unicover.com

Austria

AMEEN STAMPS
8831 Long Point Rd.
Houston, TX 77055
713-468-0644
713-468-2420 Fax

JOSEPH EDER
P.O. Box 5517
Hamden, CT 06518
203-281-0742
203-230-2410 Fax
Email:jeder@nai.net

HUNGARIA STAMP EXCHANGE
P.O. Box 3024
Andover, MA 01810
508-682-0242
508-794-2567 Fax

HENRY GITNER PHILATELISTS INC.
P.O. Box 3077-S
Middletown, NY 10940
914-343-5151 or 800-947-8267
914-343-0068
Email:hgitner@hgitner.com
Web:http://www.hgitner.com

Bahamas

COLONIAL STAMP COMPANY
5757 Wilshire Blvd. PH #8
Los Angeles, CA 90036
323-933-9435
323-939-9930 Fax
Web:http://www.colonialstamps.com

Bangkok

COLONIAL STAMP COMPANY
5757 Wilshire Blvd. PH #8
Los Angeles, CA 90036
323-933-9435
323-939-9930 Fax
Web:http://www.colonialstamps.com

Barbados

COLONIAL STAMP COMPANY
5757 Wilshire Blvd. PH #8
Los Angeles, CA 90036
323-933-9435
323-939-9930 Fax
Web:http://www.colonialstamps.com

Belguim

LEON FISCHER
P.O. Box 1338, Gracie Station
New York, NY 10028

HENRY GITNER PHILATELISTS INC.
P.O. Box 3077-S
Middletown, NY 10940
914-343-5151 or 800-947-8267
914-343-0068
Email:hgitner@hgitner.com
Web:http://www.hgitner.com

Belgium - New Issues

BELGIUM STAMP AGENCY IN NORTH AMERICA
One Unicover Center
Cheyenne, WY 82008-0026
800-443-4225
800-628-3132 Fax
Web:http://www.unicover.com

Bermuda

COLONIAL STAMP COMPANY
5757 Wilshire Blvd. PH #8
Los Angeles, CA 90036
323-933-9435
323-939-9930 Fax
Web:http://www.colonialstamps.com

Brazil - New Issues

VICTOR R. OSTOLAZA LTD.
P.O. Box 4664
Wayne, NJ 07474-4664
973-720-5884
Email:vroltd@worldnet.att.net

British Colonies

EMPIRE STAMP COMPANY
P.O. Box 19248
Encino, CA 91416
818-880-6764
818-880-6864 Fax
Email:empirestamps@msn.com

British Colonies

HUNT & COMPANY
3933 Spicewood Springs Rd.
Ste. E-400
Austin, TX 78759
512-346-4830 or 800-458-5745
512-346-4984 Fax

British Commonwealth

BRITISH COMMONWEALTH STAMP CO.
P.O. Box 10218 S-4
Wilmington, NC 28404
Email:bcstamp@stamp-mall.com
Web:http://www.stamp-mall.com
910-256-0971 Fax

British Commonwealth

Aron R. Halberstam Philatelists, Ltd.
POB 150168, Van Brunt Station
Brooklyn, NY 11215-0168
Tel: 718-788-3978
Fax: 718-965-3099
Toll Free: 800-343-1303

British Commonwealth Pre-1960

Call or write to request our free Price List, or send us your Want Lists.

We are also eager buyers of better Commonwealth collections and singles or sets. Let us know what you have to offer.

VISA MasterCard AMERICAN EXPRESS
Accepted on all orders.

PTS   APS   ASDA

The British Empire
(A-Z 1840-1935 Mint & Used)
The Largest & Most Valuable Stock in America.

Want Lists (per Scott or S. G.) prompt expert service, 30 volumes in all price ranges, stocked individually so you can acquire exactly those you need on approval or per quotations (references appreciated).

For decades we have had the great pleasure of working closely with our clients in the formation of many fine private or international exhibition standard collections. I will be pleased to place our expertise at your disposal.

George W. Holschauer

COLONIAL STAMP CO.
5757 WILSHIRE BLVD., PH #8
LOS ANGELES, CA 90036
Ph. (323) 933-9435 • Fax (323) 939-9930
VISA MasterCard AMERICAN EXPRESS
www.colonialstamps.com
CCNY, CSDA, IFSDA, INTERNATIONAL SOCIETY OF APPRAISERS

British Commonwealth

BRITISH EMPIRE EXCLUSIVELY

Request a catalogue for our next Public Auction.
Please specify your interests.

Want lists invited from serious collectors of the
BRITISH EMPIRE. References please.

Selling? Ask us about consigning
your collection to a future sale.

Victoria Stamp Co.
Established 1962

PHOEBE A. MacGILLIVARY
P.O. BOX 745, RIDGEWOOD, NJ 07451
PHONE 201-652-7283 • FAX 201-612-0024

British Commonwealth

CENTURY STAMP COMPANY LTD.
Century House
1723 Lakeshore Rd. West
Mississauga, ON L5J 1J4
Canada
905-822-5464 Telephone & Fax

JAY'S STAMP COMPANY
Box 28484 Dept. S
Philadelphia, PA 19149
215-743-0207 Telephone & Fax
Email:JASC@Juno.com
Web:http://www.jaysco.com

LAKESIDE PHILATELIC AUCTIONS
3935 Lakeside Rd.
Penticton, BC V2A 8W1
CANADA
250-493-5239
250-493-3324 Fax
Web:http://vvv.com/~greek
Email:greek@tnet.net

SOUTHEAST STAMPS
P.O. Box 6768
Shreveport, LA 71106

VICTORIA STAMP COMPANY
P.O. Box 745
Ridgewood, NJ 07451
201-652-7283
201-612-0024 Fax

British East Africa

COLONIAL STAMP COMPANY
5757 Wilshire Blvd. PH #8
Los Angeles, CA 90036
323-933-9435
323-939-9930 Fax
Web:http://www.colonialstamps.com

British Guiana

COLONIAL STAMP COMPANY
5757 Wilshire Blvd. PH #8
Los Angeles, CA 90036
323-933-9435
323-939-9930 Fax
Web:http://www.colonialstamps.com

British Pacific

OVPT PHILATELICS
P.O. Box 36217
Los Angeles, CA 90036
818-893-4603 Telephone & Fax
Email:OVPTphmc@aol.com

Brunei

COLONIAL STAMP COMPANY
5757 Wilshire Blvd. PH #8
Los Angeles, CA 90036
323-933-9435
323-939-9930 Fax
Web:http://www.colonialstamps.com

Bulgaria

HUNGARIA STAMP EXCHANGE
P.O. Box 3024
Andover, MA 01810
508-682-0242
508-794-2567 Fax

Burma

COLONIAL STAMP COMPANY
5757 Wilshire Blvd. PH #8
Los Angeles, CA 90036
323-933-9435
323-939-9930 Fax
Web:http://www.colonialstamps.com

Bushire

COLONIAL STAMP COMPANY
5757 Wilshire Blvd. PH #8
Los Angeles, CA 90036
323-933-9435
323-939-9930 Fax
Web:http://www.colonialstamps.com

Canada

CENTURY STAMP COMPANY LTD.
Century House
1723 Lakeshore Rd. West
Mississauga, ON L5J 1J4
Canada
905-822-5464 Telephone & Fax

LAKESIDE PHILATELIC AUCTIONS
3935 Lakeside Rd.
Penticton, BC V2A 8W1
CANADA
250-493-5239
250-493-3324 Fax
Web:http://vvv.com/~greek
Email:greek@tnet.net

Canada - Duck Stamps

METROPOLITAN STAMP COMPANY
P.O. Box 1133
Chicago, IL 60690-1133
815-439-0142
815-439-0143 Fax

Canada - Postal Bid Sales

BOW CITY PHILATELICS LTD.
P.O. Box 6444 Central P.O.
Suite 614 206 7th Ave. SW
Calgary, AB T2P 2E1
CANADA
403-237-5828
403-264-5287 Fax
Email:bow.city@necleus.com
Web:http://www.necleus.com/~bowcity

Canada - Worldwide

BOB'S STAMP DEPT.
P.O. Box 1621
Rossland, BC V0G 1Y0
Canada
250-362-9162
Web:http://www.welcome.to/bsd

China

MICHAEL ROGERS, INC.
199 E. Welbourne Ave.
Winter Park, FL 32789
407-644-2290
407-645-4434 Fax
Web:http://www.michaerogersinc.com

China - Peoples Republic

GUANLUN HONG
P.O. Box 12623
Toledo, OH 43606
419-382-6096
419-382-0203
Email:guanlun@163.net
Email:guanlun@toledolink.com

Classics

KUKSTIS AUCTIONS, INC.
P.O. Box 130
Scituate, MA 02066
800-649-0083 or 781-545-8494
781-545-4610 Fax
Email:paulk@drcamcom.net
Web:http://www.kukstis.com

Collections

BOB & MARTHA FRIEDMAN
624 Homestead Place
Joliet, IL 60435
815-725-6666
815-725-4134

Buying

BUYING & SELLING
Stamps & Coins Since 1970
HIGH PRICES PAID U.S.-WORLDWIDE
Collections, Accumulations, Dealer Stocks, Postage Lots
Send your collection for a prompt cash offer.
We carry a full-line of Albums & Accessories.
Stamps for beginner to specialists
Open Mon. thru Fri. 9 am - 5 pm
Sat. 9 am - 4 pm

Visit our new location!

Brewart Stamps
1725 West Chapman Ave., Unit A
Orange, CA 92868
Phone: 714-533-2521 • Fax: 714-939-0643

Collections

★★★ STOP ★★★
WORLDWIDE COLLECTIONS AT LOW, LOW PRICES!

If you spend over $25.00 per month you should
subscribe to the "Money's Worth" list.
For 3 free issues, write or call:

WARREN T. WASSON
DALLAS STAMP GALLERY
1002 N. Central, Suite 501, Richardson, TX 75080
Fax: 972-669-4742
Call TOLL FREE 1-800-759-9109

Collections

HUNT & COMPANY
3933 Spicewood Springs Rd.
Ste. E-400
Austin, TX 78759
512-346-4830 or 800-458-5745
512-346-4984 Fax

Conservation Stamps

SAM HOUSTON DUCK COMPANY
P.O. Box 820087
Houston, TX 77282
281-493-6386 or 800-231-5926
281-496-1445 Fax
Email:BDHOUDUCK@AOL.COM

Czechoslovakia

SOCIETY FOR CZECHOSLOVAK PHILATELY, INC.
Tom Cossaboom, SCP Secretary
Box 25332
Scott Air Force Base, IL 62225
USA

HUNGARIA STAMP EXCHANGE
P.O. Box 3024
Andover, MA 01810
508-682-0242
508-794-2567 Fax

Disney

BROOKMAN STAMP COMPANY
P.O. Box 90
Vancouver, WA 98666
360-695-1391 or 888-545-4871
360-695-1616 Fax
Email:brookman@stampdealers.com
Web:http://www.brookmanstamps.com

Duck Stamps

MICHAEL JAFFE STAMPS, INC.
P.O. Box 61484
Vancouver, WA 98666
360-695-6161 or 800-782-6770
360-695-1616 Fax
Email:mjaffe@brookmanstamps.com
Web:http://www.brookmanstamps.com

SAM HOUSTON DUCK CO.
P.O. Box 820087
Houston, TX 77282
281-493-6386 or 800-231-5926
281-496-1445 Fax
Email:BDHOUDUCK@AOL.COM

METROPOLITAN STAMP COMPANY
P.O. Box 1133
Chicago, IL 60690
815-439-0142
815-439-0143 Fax

TRENTON STAMP & COIN CO. - THOMAS DeLUCA
Forest Glen Plaza
1804 Route 33
Hamilton Square, NJ 08690
800-446-8664
609-587-8664 Fax

Egypt

KAMAL SHALABY
3 Aly Basha Fahmy St.
Gleem, Alexandria
Egypt
20-3-5880254 Telephone & Fax

Errors, Freaks & Oddities

STEVE CRIPPE
Box 236
Bothell, WA 98041-0236
425-487-2789
Email:Stamp@SteveCrippe.com
Web:http://www.SteveCrippe.com/

SAM HOUSTON PHILATELICS
13310 Westheimer #150
Houston, TX 77077
281-493-6386
281-496-1445 Fax
Email:BDHOUDUCK@AOL.COM

Errors - Major

SUBURBAN STAMP INC.
176 Worthington Street
Springfield, MA 01103
413-785-5348
413-746-3788 Fax

Exchange

ROBERT'S STAMP EXCHANGE/Robert LeFrancois
250 Skylane Dr.
Lake Geneva, WI 53147
414-248-8159 or 847-695-6568

FDC'S

ROSS WETREICH, INC.
P.O. Box 1300
Valley Stream, NY 11582-1300
516-825-8974

France

JOSEPH EDER
P.O. Box 5517
Hamden, CT 06518
203-281-0742
203-230-2410 Fax
Email:jeder@nai.net

LEON FISCHER
P.O. Box 1338 Gracie Sta.
New York, NY 10028

German Areas

JOSEPH EDER
P.O. Box 5517
Hamden, CT 06518
203-281-0742
203-230-2410 Fax
Email:jeder@nai.net

Great Britain

COLONIAL STAMP COMPANY
5757 Wilshire Blvd. PH #8
Los Angeles, CA 90036
213-933-9435
213-939-9930 Fax
Web:http://www.colonialstamps.com

NOVA PHILATELIC SALES
Box 161
Lakeside, N.S. B3T 1M6
Canada
902-826-2165
902-826-1049 Fax
Email:novafil@ns.sympatico.ca

Imperial China

TREASURE -HUNTERS LIMITED
G.P.O. Box 11446
Hong Kong
852-2507-3773 or 2507-5770
852-2519-6820 Fax

Insurance

COLLECTIBLES INSURANCE AGENCY, INC.
P.O. Box 1200 SSC
Westminster, MD 21158-0299
888-837-9537 or 410-876-8833
410-876-9233 Fax
Email:collectinsure@pipeline.com

Israel - New Issues

ISRAEL PHILATELIC AGENCY
535 Fifth Ave.
Suite 300
New York, NY 10017
212-818-9160 or 800-607-2799
212-818-9012 Fax

Latin America

JUAN N. SIMONA
Ventas Filatelicas
Casilla de Correo #40-7311
Chillar Buenos Aires
Argentina
54-281-97281 Telephone & Fax
Email:simonafilatelia@simoanfilatelia.com.ar
Web:http://www.simonafilatelia.com.ar

Literature

OVPT PHILATELICS
P.O. Box 36217
Los Angeles, CA 90036
818-893-4603 Telephone & Fax
Email:OVPTphmc@aol.com

Lots & Collections

BOB & MARTHA FRIEDMAN
624 Homestead Place
Joliet, IL 60435
815-725-6666
815-725-4134 Fax

RANDY SCHOLL STAMP COMPANY
Southhampton Square
7460 Jager Court
Cincinnati, OH 45230-4344
513-624-6800
513-624-6440 Fax

Mail Bid Auctions

HUNT & COMPANY
3933 Spicewood Springs Rd.
Ste. E-400
Austin, TX 78759
512-346-4830 or 800-458-5745
512-346-4984 Fax

Mail Bid Sales

DALE ENTERPRISES INC.
P.O. Box 539-C
Emmaus, PA 18049
610-433-3303
610-965-6089 Fax
Email:daleent@fast.net
Web:http://www.dalestamps.com

Mail Order

ALMAZ CO., DEPT. VY
P.O. Box 100-812
Vanderveer Station
Brooklyn, NY 11210
718-241-6360 Telephone & Fax

HUNT & COMPANY
3933 Spicewood Springs Rd.
Ste. E-400
Austin, TX 78759
512-346-4830 or 800-458-5745
512-346-4984 Fax

SHARI'S STAMPS
104-3 Old Highway 40 #130
O'Fallon, MO 63366
800-382-3597
314-980-1552 Fax
Email:sharistmps@aol.com
Web:http://www.stampdealers.com/shari/

Major Errors

SUBURBAN STAMPS INC.
176 Worthington St.
Springfield, MA 01103
413-785-5348
413-746-3788 Fax

New Issues

DALE ENTERPRISES INC.
P.O. Box 539-C
Emmaus, PA 18049
610-433-3303
610-965-6089 Fax
Email:daleent@fast.net
Web:http://www.dalestamps.com

DAVIDSON'S STAMP SERVICE
P.O. Box 36355
Indianapolis, IN 46236-0355
317-826-2620
Email:davidson@in.net
Web:http://www.creativedirection.com/dss

New Issues

Extensive Coverage - New Issues from the Entire World

NEW ISSUE SERVICE

Remember Our Specialty:
All Topicals and New Issues
Want Lists for Older Issues Serviced
Top Prices Paid for Collections & Accumulations

MONTHLY NEW ISSUE LIST WITH ILLUSTRATIONS
AVAILABLE AT www.stampcenter.com/csc/

COUNTY STAMP CENTER
CALL TOLL FREE 1-800-245-7597
FAX (410) 757-5800   email:abirman@erols.com
P.O. Box 3373, Annapolis, MD 21403

New Issues - Retail

BOMBAY PHILATELIC CO., INC.
P.O. Box 7719
Delray Beach, FL 33482-7719
561-499-7990
561-499-7553 Fax
Email:sales@bombaystamps.com
Web:http://www.bombaystamps.com

New Issues - Wholesale

BOMBAY PHILATELIC CO., INC.
P.O. Box 7719
Delray Beach, FL 33482-7719
561-499-7990
561-499-7553 Fax
Email:sales@bombaystamps.com
Web:http://www.bombaystamps.com

KUKSTIS AUCTIONS, INC.
P.O. Box 130
Scituate, MA 02066
800-649-0083 or 781-545-8494
781-545-4610 Fax
Email:paulk@dreamcom.net
Web:http://www.kukstis.com

Proofs and Essays

SUBURBAN STAMP INC.
176 Worthington St.
Springfield, MA 01103
413-785-5348
413-746-3788 Fax

Publications / Collector

AMERICAN PHILATELIST
Dept. TZ
P.O. Box 8000
State College, PA 16803
814-237-3803
814-237-6128 Fax
Email:flsente@stamps.org
Web:http://www.west.net/~stamps1/aps.html

GLOBAL STAMP NEWS
P.O. Box 97
Sidney, OH 45365-0097
937-492-3183
937-492-6514 Fax
Email:global@bright.net

Spain

STAMPTRACKS
P.O. Box 70
Holtsville, NY 11742
516-289-6359 Telephone & Fax

Stamp Shows

ATLANTIC COAST EXHIBITIONS
Divison of Beach Philatelics
42 Baltimore Lane
Palm Coast, FL 32137-8850
904-445-4550
904-447-0811 Fax
Email:mrstamp2@aol.com
Web:http://www.beachphilatelics.com

STAMP STORES

Arizona

AMERICAN STAMP & COIN CO.
7225 N. Oracle Rd., Ste. 102
Tucson, AZ 85704
520-297-3456
email:stamps@azstarnet.com

B. J.'s STAMPS / BARBARA J. JOHNSON
6342 W. Bell Road
Glendale, AZ 85308
602-878-2080
602-412-3456 Fax
Email:info@bjstamps.com
Web:http://www.bjstamps.com

MOLNAR'S STAMP & COIN SHOP
7118 E. Sahuaro Dr.
Scottsdale, AZ 85254
602-948-9672 or 800-516-4850
602-948-8425 Fax
Email:molnar7118@aol.com

California

ASHTREE STAMP & COIN
2410 N. Blackstone
Fresno, CA 93703
559-227-7167

BROSIUS STAMP & COIN
2105 Main Street
Santa Monica, CA 90405
310-396-7480
310-396-7455 Fax

COLONIAL STAMP COMPANY/BRITISH EMPIRE SPECIALIST
5757 Wilshire Blvd. PH #8
(appt. only)
Los Angeles, CA 90036
213-933-9435
213-939-9930 Fax
Web:http://www.colonialstamps.com

FISCHER - WOLK PHILATELICS
24771 "G" Alicia Parkway
Laguna Hills, CA 92653
949-837-2932

NATICK STAMPS & HOBBIES
405 S. Myrtle Avenue
Monrovia, CA 91016
626-305-7333
Email:natickco@earthlink.net
Web:http://www.natickco.com

STANLEY M. PILLER
3351 Grand Ave.
Oakland, CA 94610
510-465-8290
510-465-7121 Fax
Email:stmpdlr@aol.com

THE STAMP GALLERY
1515 Locust Street
Walnut Creek, CA 94596
925-944-9111

STAMPCRAFT
P.O. Box 2425
Santa Clara, CA 95055
800-245-5389
408-241-4440 Fax

Colorado

ACKLEY'S ROCKS & STAMPS
3230 N. Stone Ave.
Colorado Springs, CO 80907
719-633-1153

SHOWCASE STAMPS
3865 Wadsworth Blvd.
Wheat Ridge, CO 80033
303-425-9252
303-425-7410 Fax

Connecticut

SILVER CITY COIN & STAMP
41 Colony Street
Meriden, CT 06451
203-235-7634
203-237-4915 Fax

Florida

CORBIN STAMP & COIN
115-A East Brandon Blvd.
Brandon, FL 33511
813-651-3266

HAUSER'S COIN & STAMP
3425 S. Florida Ave.
Lakeland, FL 33803
941-647-2052
941-644-5738 Fax
Email:hausercoin@aol.com
Web:http://www.coinsandgifts.com

INTERCONTINENTAL / RICARDO DEL CAMPO
7379 Coral Way
Miami, FL 33155-1402
305-264-4983
305-262-2919 Fax
Email:rdcstamp@worldnet.att.net

ROBERT LEVINE STAMPS, INC.
2219 South University Dr.
Davie, FL 33324
954-473-1303
954-473-1305 Fax

NEW ENGLAND STAMP
4987 Tamiami Trail East
Village Falls Professional Ctr
Naples, FL 34113
941-732-8000
941-732-7701 Fax
Email:STAMPS@SPRINTMAIL.COM

JERRY SIEGEL / STAMPS FOR COLLECTORS
1920 E. Hallandale Beach Blvd.
Suite 507
Hallandale, FL 33009
954-457-0422 Telephone & Fax
Email:stampman@herald.infi.net

THE STAMP PLACE
576 First Avenue North
St. Petersburg, FL 33701
727-894-4082

SUNCOAST STAMP COMPANY
4223 Bee Ridge Rd.
Sarasota, FL 34233
941-377-6909 or 800-927-3351
941-377-6604 Fax

Florida

WINTER PARK STAMP SHOP
Ranch Mail (17-92)
325 S. Orlando Ave., Suite 1-2
Winter Park, FL 32789-3608
407-628-1120 or 800-845-1819
407-628-0091 Fax

Georgia

STAMPS UNLIMITED OF GEORGIA
133 Carnegie Way
Room 250
Atlanta, GA 30303
404-688-9161

Illinois

DON CLARK'S STAMPS
937 1/2 W. Galena Blvd.
Aurora, IL 60506
630-896-4606

DR. ROBERT FRIEDMAN & SONS
2029 West 75th St.
Woodridge, IL 60517
630-985-1515
630-985-1588 Fax

MARSHALL FIELD'S STAMP DEPT.
111 N. State Street
Chicago, IL 60602
312-781-4237

Indiana

J & J COINS & STAMPS
7019 Calumet Avenue or
6526 Indianapolis Blvd.
Hammond, IN 46324
219-932-5818
219-845-2003 Fax

KNIGHT STAMP & COIN COMPANY
237 Main Street
Hobart, IN 46342
219-942-7529 or
800-634-2646
Email:knight@knightcoin.com
Web:http://www.knightcoin.com

Florida

When visting Central Florida be sure to stop by. Send 33¢ long SASE for our Monthly Newsletter of stamps for sale!

MasterCard   AMERICAN EXPRESS   VISA

WINTER PARK STAMP SHOP
Ranch Mall (17-92)
325 S. Orlando Avenue, Suite 1-2
Winter Park, FL 32789-3608
Phone 407-628-1120 • Fax 407-628-0091
1-800-845-1819
Mon. through Sat. 10 am-6 pm (4 miles North of Orlando)

STAMP STORES

Kentucky

COLLECTORS STAMPS LTD.
4012 DuPont Circle #313
Louisville, KY 40207
502-897-9045
Email:csl/aye.net

TREASURE ISLAND COINS & STAMPS
232 W. Broadway
Louisville, KY 40202
502-583-1222

Maryland

BALTIMORE COIN & STAMP EXCHANGE, INC.
10194 Baltimore National Pike
Unit 104
Ellicott City, MD 21042
410-418-8282
410-418-4813 Fax

BULLDOG STAMP CO.
4641 Montgomery Ave.
Bethesda, MD 20814
301-654-1138

Massachusetts

FALMOUTH STAMP & COIN
11 Town Hall Square
Falmouth, MA 02540
508-548-7075 or 800-341-3701
Email:falstamp@capecod.net
Web:http://www.coinsandstamps.com

J & N FORTIER COIN, STAMPS & ANTIQUES
484 Main St.
Worcester, MA 01608
508-757-3657
508-852-8329 Fax

KAPPY'S COINS & STAMPS
534 Washington St.
Norwood, MA 02062
781-762-5552
781-762-3292 Fax

SUBURBAN STAMP INC.
176 Worthington St.
Springfield, MA 01103
413-785-5348
413-746-3788 Fax

Michigan

BIRMINGHAM COIN AND JEWELRY
33802 Woodward
Birmingham, MI 48009
248-642-1234
248-642-4207 Fax

THE MOUSE AND SUCH
696 N. Mill Street
Plymouth, MI 48170
734-454-1515

Nebraska

TUVA ENTERPRISES
209 So. 72nd Street
Omaha, NE 68114
402-397-9937

New Jersey

AALLSTAMPS & COLLECTABLES
38 North Main Street
P.O. Box 249
Milltown, NJ 08850
732-247-1093
732-247-1094 Fax
Email:larry.aall@cwix.com

A.D.A STAMP CO., INC.
910 Boyd Street
Toms River, NJ 08753 or
P.O. Drawer J
Island Heights, NJ 08732
732-240-1131
732-240-2620 Fax

BERGEN STAMPS & COLLECTABLES
717 American Legion Dr.
Teaneck, NJ 07666
201-836-8987

CHARLES STAMP SHOP
47 Old Post Road
Edison, NJ 08817
732-985-1071
732-819-0549 Fax
Email:cerratop@aol.com

FAIRIDGE STAMP INC.
447 Broadway
Westwood, NJ 07675
201-666-8869

RON RITZER STAMPS & COLLECTIBLES
Millburn Mall
2933 Vauxhall Road
Vauxhall, NJ 07088
908-687-0007
908-687-0795 Fax
Email:ritzerstamps@usa.net

TRENTON STAMP & COIN CO. - THOMAS DeLUCA
Forest Glen Plaza
1804 Route 33
Hamilton Square, NJ 08690
800-446-8664
609-587-8664 Fax

New York

CHAMPION STAMP CO.
432 West 54th Street
New York, NY 10019
212-489-8130
212-581-8130 Fax

THE FIFTH AVENUE STAMP GALLERY
535 Fifth Ave.
Suite 300
New York, NY 10017
212-818-9160 or 800-607-2799
212-818-9012 Fax

LINCOLN COIN & STAMP
33 West Tupper Street
Buffalo, NY 14202
716-856-1884
716-856-4727 Fax

Ohio

FEDERAL COIN INC. AND ARCADE STAMP & COIN
39 The Arcade
Cleveland, OH 44114
216-861-1160
216-861-5960 Fax

Ohio

HILLTOP STAMP SERVICE
P.O. Box 626
Wooster, OH 44691
330-262-8907 or 330-262-5378
Telephone & Fax
Email:hilltop@bright.net

J L F STAMP STORE
3041 E. Waterloo Road
Akron, OH 44312
330-628-8343

THE LINK STAMP CO.
3461 E. Livingston Ave.
Columbus, OH 43227
614-237-4125
or 800-546-5726

NEWARK STAMP COMPANY
49 North Fourth Street
Newark, OH 43055
740-349-7900

RANDY SCHOLL STAMP COMPANY
Southhampton Square
7460 Jager Court
Cincinnati, OH 45230-4344
513-624-6800
513-624-6440 Fax

Oregon

UNIQUE ESTATE APPRAISALS
1937 NE Broadway
Portland, OR 97232
503-287-4200
or 800-646-1147
Email:uea@stampsand coins.com
Web:http://www.stampsandcoins.com

Pennsylvania

DAVE ALLEGO
648 Merchant St.
Ambridge, PA 15003
724-266-4237 Telephone & Fax

LARRY LEE STAMPS
322 S. Front Street
Greater Harrisburg Area
Wormleysburg, PA 17043
717-763-7605

PHILLY STAMP & COIN CO. INC.
1804 Chestnut Street
Philadelphia, PA 19103
215-563-7341
215-563-7382 Fax
Email:adelphia@uscom.com

TREASURE HUNT COLLECTABLE COINS & STAMPS
1687 Washington Road Suite 200
Pittsburgh, PA 15228
412-851-9991 or
800-259-4727

TREASURE HUNT COLLECTABLE COINS & STAMPS
10925 Perry Hwy., Ste. 11
Wexford, PA 15090
724-934-7771 or 800-545-6604

TRENTON STAMP & COIN CO. - THOMAS DeLUCA
Forest Glen Plaza
1804 Route 33
Hamilton Square, NJ 08690
800-446-8664
609-587-8664 Fax

Rhode Island

PODRAT COIN EXCHANGE INC.
769 Hope Street
Providence, RI 02906
401-861-7640
401-272-3032 Fax
Email:kpodrat@aol.com

South Carolina

THE STAMP OUTLET
Oakbrook Center #9
4650 Ladson Road
Summerville, SC 29485
843-873-4655
843-871-6704 Fax
Email:stamps4u@quik.com

Tennessee

HERRON HILL, INC.
5007 Black Road
Suite 140
Memphis, TN 38117-4505
901-683-9644

Texas

ALAMO HEIGHTS STAMP SHOP
1201 Austin Hwy
Suite 128
San Antonio, TX 78209
800-214-9526

DALLAS STAMP GALLERY
1002 North Central Expressway
Suite 501
Richardson, TX 75080
972-669-4741
972-669-4742 Fax

HUNT & COMPANY
3933 Spicewood Springs Rd.
Ste. E-400
Austin, TX 78759
512-346-4830 or 800-458-5745
512-346-4984 Fax

SAM HOUSTON PHILATELICS
13310 Westheimer #150
Houston, TX 77077
281-493-6386
281-496-1445 Fax
Email:BDHOUDUCK@AOL.COM

Virginia

KENNEDY'S STAMPS & COINS
7059 Brookfield Plaza
Springfield, VA 22150
703-569-7300
703-569-7644 Fax

LATHEROW & CO. INC.
5054 Lee Highway
Arlington, VA 22207
703-538-2727

PRINCE WILLIAM STAMP & COIN CO.
14011-H St. German Dr.
Centreville, VA 20121
703-830-4669

Washington

THE STAMP & COIN PLACE
1310 Commercial
Bellingham, WA 98225
360-676-8720
360-647-6947 Fax
Email:stmpcoin@az.com

STAMP STORES

Washington

THE STAMP & COIN SHOP
725 Pike St. #6
Seattle, WA 98101
206-624-1400
206-621-8975 Fax
Web:http://www.Stamp-Coin.com

TACOMA MALL BLVD. COIN & STAMP
5225 Tacoma Mall Blvd. E-101
Tacoma, WA 98409
253-472-9632
253-472-8948 Fax
Email:kfeldman01@sprynet.com

West Virginia

DAVID HILL LTD.
6433 U.S. Route 60 E
Barboursville, WV 25504
304-736-4383

Wisconsin

JIM LUKES' STAMP & COIN
815 Jay Street
P.O. Box 1780
Manitowoc, WI 54221
920-682-2324

Supplies & Accessories

BEACH PHILATELICS
42 Baltimore Lane
Palm Coast, FL 32137-8850
904-445-4550
904-447-0811 Fax
Email:mrstamp2@aol.com
Web:http://www.beachphilatelics.com

Supplies - Mail Order

GOPHER SUPPLY CO.
2525 Nevada Ave. N. Ste 102
Minneapolis, MN 55427
800-815-3868
612-525-1750
Email:gopher@pclink.com

STAMPCRAFT
P.O. Box 2425
Santa Clara, CA 95055
800-245-5389
408-241-4440 Fax

Topicals

TOPICALS- ALL TOPICS

For many years (first as Filatelia Pampa) we have been a leader in this field. ANY sub-topic is Not Strange for us!

VERY LARGE WORLDWIDE STOCK
... including varieties, cancels, covers, etc.

WANT LISTS WELCOME
... any Catalogue #, any main language.

ERCOLE GLORIA - Gregorio Zuskis
Piazza Pio Xi 1, 20123 Milan, ITALY
PH. +39-02-804106 • FAX +39-02-864217
email: gloria@iol.it

Supplies - Stamps & Coins

ECONOMICAL SUPPLY CO.
6 King Philip Road
Worcester, MA 01606
508-853-3127
508-852-8329 Fax

M.A. STORCK CO.
651 Forest Ave.
Portland, ME 04101
800-734-7271
207-774-7272 Fax
Email:mastork@comuserve.com

Topicals - Columbus

MR. COLUMBUS
Box 1492
Frankenmuth, MI 48734

Topicals - Miscellaneous

BOMBAY PHILATELIC CO., INC.
P.O. Box 7719
Delray Beach, FL 33482-7719
561-499-7990
561-499-7553 Fax
Email:sales@bombaystamps.com
Web:http://www.bombaystamps.com

MINI - ARTS
P.O. Box 457
Estherville, IA 51334
712-362-4710

United Nations

BEACH PHILATELICS
42 Baltimore Lane
Palm Coast, FL 32137-8850
904-445-4550
904-447-0811 Fax
Email:mrstamp2@aol.com
Web:http://www.beachphilatelics.com

United Nations - New Issues

VICTOR R. OSTOLAZA LTD.
P.O. Box 4664
Wayne, NJ 07474-4664
973-720-5884
Email:vroltd@worldnet.att.net

United States

BEACH PHILATELICS
42 Baltimore Lane
Palm Coast, FL 32137-8850
904-445-4550
904-447-0811 Fax
Email:mrstamp2@aol.com
Web:http://www.beachphilatelics.com

DALE ENTERPRISES INC.
P.O. Box 539-C
Emmaus, PA 18049
610-433-3303
610-965-6089 Fax
Email:daleent@fast.net
Web:http://www.dalestamps.com

United States

BOB & MARTHA FRIEDMAN
624 Homestead Place
Joliet, IL 60435
815-725-6666
815-725-4134 Fax

DR. ROBERT FRIEDMAN & SONS
2029 West 75th St.
Woodridge, IL 60517
630-985-1515
630-985-1588 Fax

HUNT & COMPANY
3933 Spicewood Springs Rd.
Ste. E-400
Austin, TX 78759
512-346-4830 or 800-458-5745
512-346-4984 Fax

United States

LARGE SELECTION OF U.S. AND WORLDWIDE STAMPS

Over 400 Countries & Colonies in stock, A-Z. Mint and Used. Fast Service and Low Prices.
FOR A PRICE LIST WRITE TO:

ALMAZ CO., Dept. V1
P.O. Box 100-812, Vanderveer Station
Brooklyn, NY 11210
Phone/Fax (718) 241-6360

★ U.S.A. ★ BELOW MARKET PRICES!!
- USED
- UNUSED

MOST GRADES & PRICE RANGES!

Here is your opportunity to have the older and scarcer stamps of our country at low, reasonable prices. Issues prior to the year 1950 worth anywhere from 25¢ up to several hundred dollars each.

JUST SEND 33¢ POSTAGE for complete price list. Compare for PROOF OF LOWEST PRICES before ordering, and find out what you have missed until you discovered us!!!

LOWELL S. DONALD CO.
P.O. BOX 728,
RUTLAND, VERMONT 05702

United States

STEVE MALACK STAMPS
P.O. Box 5628
Endicott, NY 13763
607-862-9441 Telephone & Fax
Email:Malackweb@aol.com
Web:http://www.members.aol.com/MALACKWEB

GARY POSNER
6340 Ave. N., Ste. 121
Brooklyn, NY 11234
800-323-4279
718-241-2801

United States - Booklet Panes

DALE ENTERPRISES INC.
P.O. Box 539-C
Emmaus, PA 18049
610-433-3303
610-965-6089 Fax
Email:daleent@fast.net
Web:http://www.dalestamps.com

United States - Classics

DALE ENTERPRISES INC.
P.O. Box 539-C
Emmaus, PA 18049
610-433-3303
610-965-6089 Fax
Email:daleent@fast.net
Web:http://www.dalestamps.com

BOB & MARTHA FRIEDMAN
624 Homestead Place
Joliet, IL 60435
815-725-6666
815-725-4134 Fax

United States - Classics

GARY POSNER
6340 Ave. N., Ste. 121
Brooklyn, NY 11234
800-323-4279
718-241-2801

United States - Classics / Modern

JIM'S CAN-AM SPECIALTIES
3110 Cannongate
Fort Wayne, IN 46808-4511
219-471-2469 Telephone & Fax
Email:stamp@gte.net

SUBURBAN STAMP INC.
176 Worthington St.
Springfield, MA 01103
413-785-5348
413-746-3788 Fax

United States - Duck Stamps

SAM HOUSTON DUCK COMPANY
P.O. Box 820087
Houston, TX 77282
281-493-6386 or 800-231-5926
281-496-1445 Fax
Email:BDHOUDUCK@AOL.COM

United States - EFO's

GARY POSNER
6340 Ave. N., Ste. 121
Brooklyn, NY 11234
800-323-4279
718-241-2801

United States - Mint

BOB & MARTHA FRIEDMAN
624 Homestead Place
Joliet, IL 60435
815-725-6666
815-725-4134 Fax

HUNT & COMPANY
3933 Spicewood Springs Rd.
Ste. E-400
Austin, TX 78759
512-346-4830 or 800-458-5745
512-346-4984 Fax

United States - Plate Blocks

BEACH PHILATELICS
42 Baltimore Lane
Palm Coast, FL 32137-8850
904-445-4550
904-447-0811 Fax
Email:mrstamp2@aol.com
Web:http://www.beachphilatelics.com

BOB & MARTHA FRIEDMAN
624 Homestead Place
Joliet, IL 60435
815-725-6666
815-725-4134 Fax

GARY POSNER
6340 Ave. N., Ste. 121
Brooklyn, NY 11234
800-323-4279
718-241-2801

United States - Price Lists

ROBERT E. BARKER
P.O. Box 888063
Dunwoody, GA 30356
770-395-1757
770-671-8918 Fax
Email:rebarker@rebarker.com

DALE ENTERPRISES INC.
P.O. Box 539-C
Emmaus, PA 18049
610-433-3303
610-965-6089 Fax
Email:daleent@fast.net
Web:http://www.dalestamps.com

United States - Rare Stamps

GARY POSNER
6340 Ave. N., Ste. 121
Brooklyn, NY 11234
800-323-4279
718-241-2801

United States - Singles Classic & Modern

BOB & MARTHA FRIEDMAN
624 Homestead Place
Joliet, IL 60435
815-725-6666
815-725-4134 Fax

UNITED STATES & WORLDWIDE
ACCUMULATIONS, COLLECTIONS, ETC.

• BUYING •
PAYING HIGH PRICES SINCE 1955. WRITE TO US OR CALL FIRST TO DISCUSS YOUR HOLDINGS, PROMPT, CASH OFFERS AND PROMPT RETURNS SHOULD OUR OFFER BE DECLINED. WE WILL TRAVEL TO INSPECT LARGE HOLDINGS! ACT TODAY!

• SELLING •
EXCELLENT STOCK OF UNITED STATES AND WORLDWIDE MATERIAL! WRITE TO RECEIVE OUR FREE "FULL-OF-BARGAINS" PRICE LIST UNITED STATES or FOREIGN... (PLEASE INCLUDE 55¢ POSTAGE).

• ESTATE SERVICES •
INHERITED A COLLECTION AND FRUSTRATED WITH HOW TO DISPOSE OF THE STAMPS? LET ME HELP. REPUTABLE SERVICE SINCE 1955. OUT RIGHT PURCHASE, APPRAISALS, AND ADVISORY SERVICES AVAILABLE. CALL WITH CONFIDENCE.

CALL TOLL FREE 1-800-833-0217 (24 HOURS)
NO PRICELIST CALLS PLEASE

ROBERT E. BARKER
BOX 888244, ATLANTA, GA 30356
Phone/Fax • 770-395-1757 • 770-671-8918
Email:rebarker@rebarker.com
Website:www.rebarker.com

United States - Stamps

GARY'S STAMP SHOP
120 E. Broadway
Box 6011
Enid, OK 73701
580-233-0007

United States - State Duck Stamps

SAM HOUSTON DUCK COMPANY
P.O. Box 820087
Houston, TX 77282
281-493-6386 or 800-231-5926
281-496-1445 Fax
Email:BDHOUDUCK@AOL.COM

United States - Transportation Coils

DALE ENTERPRISES INC.
P.O. Box 539-C
Emmaus, PA 18049
610-433-3303
610-965-6089 Fax
Email:daleent@fast.net
Web:http://www.dalestamps.com

United States - Used

BOB & MARTHA FRIEDMAN
624 Homestead Place
Joliet, IL 60435
815-725-6666
815-725-4134 Fax

United States - Want Lists

GARY POSNER
6340 Ave. N., Ste. 121
Brooklyn, NY 11234
800-323-4279
718-241-2801

Want Lists

BROOKMAN INTERNATIONAL
P.O. Box 450
Vancouver, WA 98666
360-695-4311 or Toll Free 888-695-4311
360-695-1616 Fax
Email:brookman@stampdealers.com

CHARLES P. SCHWARTZ
P.O. Box 165
Mora, MN 55051
320-679-4705

Want Lists - British Empire/1840-1935 German Col./Offices

COLONIAL STAMP COMPANY
5757 Wilshire Blvd. PH #8
Los Angeles, CA 90036
213-933-9435
213-939-9930 Fax
Web:http://www.colonialstamps.com

Wanted - Estates

FRED BOATWRIGHT
P.O. Box 695
Sullivan, MO 63080
Ph & Fax 573-860-4057

DALE ENTERPRISES INC.
P.O. Box 539-C
Emmaus, PA 18049
610-433-3303
610-965-6089 Fax
Email:daleent@fast.net
Web:http://www.dalestamps.com

Wanted - United States

GARY POSNER
6340 Ave. N., Ste. 121
Brooklyn, NY 11234
800-323-4279
718-241-2801

Websites

MILLER'S STAMP SHOP
41 New London Turnpike
Uncasville, CT 06382
860-848-0468
860-848-1926 Fax
Email:millstamps@aol.com
Web:http://www.millerstamps.com

Wholesale

HENRY GITNER PHILATELISTS, INC.
P.O. Box 3077-S
Middletown, NY 10940
914-343-5151 or 800-947-8267
914-343-0068 Fax
Email:hgitner@hgitner.com
Web:http://www.hgitner.com

Wholesale Collections

A.D.A STAMP CO., INC.
910 Boyd Street
Toms River, NJ 08753 or
P.O. Drawer J
Island Heights, NJ 08732
732-240-1131
732-240-2620 Fax

Wholesale Philatelic & Numismatic Accessories

CHARLES R. HEISLER INC.
500 Oak Grove Drive
Lancaster, PA 17601
800-784-6886
717-299-2366 Fax

M.A. STORCK CO.
651 Forest Ave.
Portland, ME 04101
800-734-7271
207-774-7272 Fax
Email:mastork@comuserve.com

Wholesale Supplies

JOHN VAN ALSTYNE STAMPS & SUPPLIES
1787 Tribute Rd. Suite J
Sacramento, CA 95815
916-565-0600 or 800-297-3929
916-565-0539 Fax
Email:sherjohn@softcom.net

Wholesale - United States

GARY POSNER
6340 Ave. N., Ste. 121
Brooklyn, NY 11234
800-323-4279
718-241-2801

Worldwide

GARY'S STAMP SHOP
120 E. Broadway
Box 6011
Enid, OK 73701
405-233-0007

EDWARD J. MCKIM
1373 Isabelle
Memphis, TN 38122
901-327-8959

Worldwide Collections

BOB & MARTHA FRIEDMAN
624 Homestead Place
Joliet, IL 60435
815-725-6666
815-725-4134 Fax

Worldwide - Romania

GEORGE ARGHIR, PHILATELISTS
Detunata Str. 17-27
P.O. Box 521
RO-3400 Cluj-Napoca 9
Romania
Ph. & Fax: 40-64-414036

Worldwide - Year Sets

BOMBAY PHILATELIC CO., INC.
P.O. Box 7719
Delray Beach, FL 33482-7719
561-499-7990
561-499-7553 Fax
Email:sales@bombaystamps.com
Web:http://www.bombaystamps.com

WALLACE STAMPS
Box 82
Port Washington, NY 11050
516-883-5578

Looking for some of stamp collecting's most fascinating and entertaining issues?

Subscribe to Scott Stamp Monthly

Every month you'll find a wide variety of articles, columns and departments for all collecting interests. Whether it's a tale about an amazing stamp find, a feature about some of your favorite stamps or the latest listing of stamp releases from around the world, you'll find it on the pages of *Scott Stamp Monthly*.

Scott Stamp Monthly offers a level of entertainment not found in a news publication. With features such as "Fun in Philately," "Lesser Known Rarities," "Snapshots," "Amazing Stamp Stories," and "Free For All".

For instance, our monthly "Free For All" column allows you to add stamps, covers and products to your collection simply by sending us a stamped, self-addressed envelope. This feature alone usually covers the cost of your subscription.

In addition, as a subscriber, you'll enjoy huge savings on the entire line of Scott products through the *Scott Stamp Monthly* Advantage Program.

Original and intriguing articles, listings of all the new issues, free stamps and huge savings all add up to a great magazine. You won't find a better deal in stamp collecting. Save more than $18 off the cover price. To subscribe, call:

12 Issues Only $17.95

1-800-572-6885
Subscribe today!

SCOTT
P.O. Box 828 Sidney OH 45365-0828
www.scottonline.com

ScottMounts

For stamp presentation unequaled in beauty and clarity, insist on ScottMounts. Made of 100% inert polystyrol foil, ScottMounts protect your stamps from the harmful effects of dust and moisture. Available in your choice of clear or black backs, ScottMounts are center-split across the back for easy insertion of stamps and feature crystal clear mount faces. Double layers of gum assure stay-put bonding on the album page. Discover the quality and value ScottMounts have to offer.

ScottMounts are available from your favorite stamp dealer or direct from:

Scott Publishing Co.
P.O. Box 828 Sidney OH 45365-0828
www.scottonline.com

Discover the quality and value ScottMounts have to offer.
For a complete list of ScottMount sizes or a free sample pack call or write Scott Publishing Co.

SCOTT
1-800-572-6885

ScottMounts

HOW TO ORDER THE RIGHT SIZE:

Pre-cut ScottMounts come in sizes labeled as stamp width by stamp height, measured in millimeters. Strips of mount material come in three different lengths: 215mm, 240mm and 265mm. The strip you should use is based on the height of the stamp you wish to mount.

ScottMounts are available with clear or black backs. Please indicate color choice when ordering.

Pre-Cut Single Mounts

Size	Description	# Mounts	Item	Price
40 x 25	U.S. Standard Commemorative–Horizontal	40	901	$2.75
25 x 40	U.S. Standard Commemorative–Vertical	40	902	2.75
25 x 22	U.S. Regular Issue–Horizontal	40	903	2.75
22 x 25	U.S. Regular Issue–Vertical	40	904	2.75
41 x 31	U.S. Semi-Jumbo–Horizontal	40	905	2.75
31 x 41	U.S. Semi-Jumbo–Vertical	40	906	2.75
50 x 31	U.S. Jumbo–Horizontal	40	907	2.75
31 x 50	U.S. Jumbo–Vertical	40	908	2.75
25 x 27	U.S. Famous Americans	40	909	2.75
33 x 27	United Nations	40	910	2.75
40 x 27	United Nations	40	911	2.75
67 x 25	PNC, Strips of Three	40	976	4.75
67 x 34	Pacific '97 Triangle	10	984	2.25
111 x 25	PNC, Strips of Five	25	985	4.75
51 x 36	U.S. Hunting Permit/Express Mail	40	986	4.75

Pre-Cut Plate Block, FDC & Postal Card Mounts

Size	Description	# Mounts	Item	Price
57 x 55	Regular Issue Plate Block	25	912	$4.75
73 x 63	Champions of Liberty	25	913	4.75
106 x 55	Rotary Press Standard Commemorative	20	914	4.75
105 x 57	Giori Press Standard Commemorative	20	915	4.75
165 x 94	First Day Cover	10	917	4.75
140 x 90	Postal Card Size	10	918	4.75

Strips 215mm Long

Size	Description	# Mounts	Item	Price
20	U.S. 19th Century/Horizontal Coil	22	919	$5.95
22	U.S. Early Air Mail	22	920	5.95
24	U.S., Canada, Great Britain	22	921	5.95
25	U.S. Comm. and Regular	22	922	5.95
27	U.S. Famous Americans	22	923	5.95
28	U.S. 19th Century	22	924	5.95
30	U.S. 19th Century	22	925	5.95
31	U.S. Jumbo and Semi-Jumbo	22	926	5.95
33	United Nations	22	927	5.95
36	U.S. Hunting Permit, Canada	15	928	5.95
39	U.S. Early 20th Century	15	929	5.95
41	U.S. Semi-Jumbo	15	930	5.95
	Multiple Assortment: one strip of each size 22-41 (Two 25mm strips)	12	931	5.95
44	U.S. Vertical Coil Pair	15	932	5.95
48	U.S. Farley, Gutter Pair	15	933	5.95
50	U.S. Jumbo	15	934	5.95
52	U.S. Standard Commemorative Block	15	935	5.95
55	U.S. Century of Progress	15	936	5.95
57	U.S. Famous Americans Block	15	937	5.95
61	U.S. Blocks, Israel Tab	15	938	5.95

Strips 240mm Long

Size	Description	# Mounts	Item	Price
63	U.S. Jumbo Commemorative–Horizontal Block	10	939	$6.75
66	Israel Tab Block	10	940	6.75
68	U.S. Farley, Gutter Pair & Souvenir Sheets	10	941	6.75
74	U.S. TIPEX Souvenir Sheet	10	942	6.75
80	U.S. Standard Commemorative–Vertical Block	10	943	6.75
82	U.S. Blocks of Four	10	944	6.75
84	Israel Tab Block/Mars Pathfinder	10	945	6.75
89	U.S. Postal Card Size	10	946	6.75

Strips 265mm Long

Size	Description	# Mounts	Item	Price
100	U.N. Margin Inscribed Block	7	947	6.75
120	Various Souvenir Sheets and Blocks	7	948	6.75
40	Standard Commemorative Vertical	10	949	$6.75
55	U.S. Regular Plate Block Strip 20	10	950	6.75
59	U.S. Double Issue Strip	10	951	6.75
70	U.S. Jumbo Com. Plate Block	10	952	9.75
91	Great Britain Souvenir Sheet/Norman Rockwell	10	953	9.75

Strips 265mm Long Con't'd.

Size	Description	# Mounts	Item	Price
105	U.S. Standard Plate Number Strip	10	954	9.75
107	Same as above–Wide Margin	10	955	9.75
111	U.S. Gravure-Intaglio Plate Number Strip	10	956	11.25
127	U.S. Jumbo Commemorative Plate Number Strip	10	957	13.75
137	Great Britain Coronation	10	958	14.50
158	U.S. Apollo-Soyuz Plate Number Strip	10	959	15.25
231	U.S. Full Post Office Pane Regular and Commemorative	5	961	14.25

Souvenir Sheets/Small Panes

Size	Description	# Mounts	Item	Price
111 x 25	PNC, Strips of Five	25	985	4.75
204 x 153	U.S. Bicent. White Plains	5	962	$6.95
187 x 144	U.N. Flag Sheet	10	963	12.25
160 x 200	New U.N., Israel Sheet	10	964	12.25
120 x 207	AMERIPEX President Sht.	4	965	4.75
229 x 131	World War II Commemorative Sheet	5	968	6.95
111 x 91	Columbian Souvenir Sheet	6	970	2.95
148 x 196	Apollo Moon Landing	4	972	5.95
129 x 122	U.S. Definitive Mini-Sheet	8	989	7.95
189 x 151	Chinese New Year	5	990	7.95
150 x 185	Dr. Davis/World Cup	5	991	7.95
198 x 151	Cherokee	5	992	7.95
198 x 187	Postal Museum	4	994	7.95
156 x 187	Sign Lang., Statehood	5	995	7.95
188 x 197	Country-Western	4	996	7.95
151 x 192	Olympic	5	997	7.95
174 x 185	Buffalo Soldiers	5	998	7.95
130 x 198	Silent Screen Stars	5	999	7.95
190 x 199	Leg. West, Civil, Comic	4	1000	7.95
178 x 181	Cranes	4	1001	7.95
183 x 212	Wonders of the Sea	3	1002	7.95
156 x 264	$14 Eagle	4	1003	7.95
159 x 270	$9.95 Moon Landing	4	1004	7.95
159 x 259	$2.90 Priority/$9.95 Express Mail	4	1005	7.95
223 x 187	Marilyn Monroe	3	1006	7.95
185 x 181	Challenger Shuttle	4	1007	7.95
152 x 228	Indian Dances/Antique Autos	5	1008	7.95
165 x 150	River Boat/Hanukkah	6	1009	7.95
275 x 200	Large Gutter Blocks/Aircraft/Dinosaurs	2	1010	7.95
161 x 160	Pacific '97 Triangle Block of 16	6	1011	7.95
174 x 130	Bugs Bunny	6	1012	7.95
196 x 158	Football Coaches	4	1013	7.95
184 x 184	American Dolls	4	1014	7.95
186 x 230	Classic Movie Monsters	3	1015	7.95
187 x 160	Trans-Mississippi Sheet	4	1016	7.95
192 x 230	Celebrate the Century	3	1017	7.95

Available from your favorite stamp dealer or direct from:

SCOTT
P.O. Box 828 Sidney OH 45365-0828

For more information on Scott products visit our web site at:
www.scottonline.com

National Albums

SCOTT NATIONAL SERIES

The National series offers a panoramic view of our country's heritage through postage stamps. It is the most complete and comprehensive U.S. album series you can buy. There are spaces for every major U.S. stamp listed in the Scott Catalogue, including Special Printings, Newspaper stamps and much more.

* Pages printed on one side.
* All spaces identified by Scott numbers.
* All major variety of stamps or either illustrated or described.
* Chemically neutral paper protects stamps.

Item			Retail
100NTL1	1845-1934	97 pgs	$29.95
100NTL2	1935-1976	108 pgs	$29.95
100NTL3	1977-1993	110 pgs	$29.95
100NTL4	1994-1998	101 pgs	$29.95

Supplemented in March. Back supplements available.

Computer Vended Postage
103CVP0 1989-1994 11 pgs $3.95

National Blank Pages (Border B)
ACC120 20 per pack $6.95

National Quad Blank Pages (Border B)
ACC121 20 per pack $6.95

National Album Package

Get everything you need to house and value your collection in one convenient and affordable package. There's never been a better or more economical way to get the album pages, accessories and catalogues you need to build a better collection for one low price.

The National Album Package Include

1	National Pages Part 1 1845 - 1934 97 pgs.
1	National Pages Part 2 1935 - 1976 108 pgs.
1	National Pages Part 3 1977 - 1993 110 pgs.
1	National Pages Part 4 1994 - 1997 81 pgs.
4	Large three-ring binders
4	Large Slipcases
4	Black Protector Fly Sheets
4	National Album Labels
1	ScottMount Assortment (Item 966B)
1	Current U.S. Specialized Catalogue

SET PRICE $259.00

SCOTT
1-800-572-6885
www.scottonline.com

Scott albums are available from your favorite stamp dealer or direct from:

Scott Publishing Co.
P.O. Box 828
Sidney OH 45365-0828

National Albums

U.S. BOOKLET PANES
Includes slogan types and tagging varieties.

Item			Retail
101BKP1	1900-1993	103 pgs	$54.95
101BKP2	1994-1997	49 pgs	$29.95

Supplemented in April.

U.S. COMMEMORATIVE AND COMMEMORATIVE AIR PLATE BLOCKS
Divided chronologically into seven parts. Begins with the Pan American issue of 1901.

Item			Retail
120CPB1	1901-1940	80 pgs	$29.95
120CPB2	1940-1959	78 pgs	$29.95
120CPB3	1959-1968	70 pgs	$29.95
120CPB4	1969-1973	47 pgs	$24.95
120CPB5	1973-1979	83 pgs	$29.95
120CPB6	1980-1988	97 pgs	$39.95
120CPB7	1989-1995	97 pgs	$39.95
120S096	1996	14 pgs	$11.95
120S097	1997	14 pgs	$11.95

U.S. COMPREHENSIVE PLATE NUMBER COILS
Provides spaces for every coil issue where the plate number is part of the design, and for every existing plate number for each issue. Space provided for strips of 3. Accommodates strips of 5. Includes precancels.

Item			Retail
114PNC1	1981-1988	114 pgs	$49.95
114PNC2	1989-1994	146 pgs	$59.95
114S095	1995	36 pgs	$18.95
114S096	1996	28 pgs	$16.95
114S097	1997	20 pgs	$13.95

Supplemented in April.

U.S. COMPREHENSIVE PLATE NUMBER SINGLES
Provides space for every single issue where the plate number is part of the design. Includes spaces for every existing plate number.

Item			Retail
117PNC1	1981-1993	147 pgs	$44.95
117PNC2	1994-1997	89 pgs	$29.95

Supplemented in April.
Note: Pages are three-hole punched to fit Scott 3-ring binder.

U.S. FEDERAL DUCK STAMP PLATE BLOCKS
Contains spaces for all federal migratory bird hunting stamps in plate block form.

Item			Retail
116DKB0	1934-1996	42 pgs	$29.95

Supplemented in April.

U.S. FEDERAL AND STATE DUCK SINGLES
Extra space for future issues and blank pages for collateral material.

Item			Retail
115DUK1	1934-1988	83 pgs	$49.95
115DUK2*	1989-1994	189 pgs	$49.95
115S095	1995	12 pgs	$9.95
115S096	1996	14 pgs	$11.95
115S097	1997	20 pgs	$14.95

* Part 2 includes many replacement pages which are used to update your album. These are included at no charge. Supplemented in April.

U.S. GUTTER PAIRS AND BLOCKS
An album and series of National supplements that includes spaces for vertical and horizontal gutter pairs and blocks from uncut sheets. Pages for cross-gutter blocks consistent with listings in the *U.S. Specialized*.

Item			Retail
123GPR1	1994-1996	30 pgs	$19.95
123GP97	1997	22 pgs	$14.95
123GP98	1998	22 pgs	$15.95

U.S. GUTTER PAIRS AND BLOCKS 1935 FARLEY
Pages exclusively for the gutter pairs and blocks for Scott numbers 752 - 771

Item			Retail
123FAR0		28 pgs	$18.95

U.S. OFFICIAL JOINT ISSUES ALBUM
Features illustrations and descriptive stories for 29 joint issues of the United States and 19 foreign countries. Pages are organized chronologically beginning with the 1959 Canada - U.S. official joint issue commemorating the opening of the St. Lawrence seaway.

Item			Retail
119JNT0	1959-1996	36 pgs	$19.95

Supplemented as needed.

U.S. POSSESSIONS
Pages for all postage, airpost, postage due and special delivery from Canal Zone, Guam, Hawaii and Danish West Indies, as well as those from periods of U.S. administration of Cuba, Phillipines and Puerto Rico. No supplement necessary. Pages complete through 1978.

Item			Retail
112POS0	1851-1978	67 pgs	$39.95

U.S. POSTAL CARD
Includes spaces for all major number postal cards listed in the Scott *U.S. Specialized Catalogue*. Heavyweight paper of the finest quality supports the extra weight of the cards.

Item			Retail
110PCD1	1873-1981	95 pgs	$49.95
110PCD2	1982-1995	126 pgs	$69.95
110S096	1996	38 pgs	$19.95
110S097	1997	12 pgs	$10.95

Supplemented in April.

110Z000	Postal Card Blank Pgs	$6.95
	(20 per pack)	

U.S. POSTAL STATIONERY
Provides spaces for cut squares of every major postal stationery item in the Scott *U.S. Specialized Catalogue* and entires of airletter sheets.

Item			Retail
105PST0	1853-1992	104 pgs	$59.95
105S095	1993-1995	6 pgs	$5.95

Supplemented as needed.

U.S. REGULAR AND REGULAR AIR PLATE BLOCKS
Begins with the first airpost issue of 1918 (Scott C1-C3) and the 1922-25 regulars (beginning with Scott 551).

Item			Retail
125RPB0	1918-1991	111 pgs	$49.95
125S095	1992-1995	8 pgs	$7.95

Supplemented as needed.

U.S. REVENUE PAGES
Contains spaces for: Documentary, War Savings, Tobacco Sales Tax, Proprietary, Treasury Savings, Narcotic Tax, Future Delivery, Cordials & Wines, Consular Service Fee, Stock Transfer, Playing Cards, Customs Fee, Postal Note, Silver Tax, Motor Vehicle Use Postal Savings, Cigarette Tubes, Boating Savings, Potato Tax, Firearms Transfer Tax

Item			Retail
160RVN0		134 pgs	$49.95

U.S. SIMPLIFIED PLATE NUMBER COILS
Provides space for each stamp design. Lets you mount one plate number example of each issue. Designed for strips of 3. Precancels spaces are included.

Item			Retail
113PNC0	1981-1996	108 pgs	$54.95
113S097	1997	6 pgs	$5.95

Supplemented in April.

U.S. SMALL PANES ALBUM
Features spaces for small panes as listed in the *Scott Specialized Catalogue*. The small pane format for U.S. stamps was introduced in 1987.

Item			Retail
118SMP0	1987-1995	40 pgs	$39.95
118S096	1996	20 pgs	$13.95
118S097	1997	26 pgs	$14.95

Supplemented in April.

U.S. TAGGED VARIETY ALBUM
Includes spaces for the listed varieties of all U.S. stamps that were issued tagged and untagged. A specialized section that belongs in all National albums.

Item			Retail
102TAG0	1963-1987	11 pgs	$7.95
102S093	1988-1993	8 pgs	$5.95

U.S. TRUST TERRITORIES
MARSHALL ISLANDS
Stamps of the Marshall Islands.

Item			Retail
111MAR0	1897-1994	64 pgs	$34.95
111MA95	1995	18 pgs	$12.95
111MA96	1996	8 pgs	$7.95
111MA97	1997	14 pgs	$11.95

MICRONESIA
Stamps of Micronesia.

Item			Retail
111MIC0	1984-1994	48 pgs	$29.95
111MI95	1995	10 pgs	$9.95
111MI96	1996	8 pgs	$7.95
111MI97	1997	12 pgs	$10.95

PALAU
Stamps of Palau.

Item			Retail
111PAL0	1983-1994	79 pgs	$39.95
111PA95	1995	20 pgs	$12.95
111PA96	1996	14 pgs	$11.95
111PA97	1997	20 pgs	$13.95

Available from your local dealer or direct from:

Scott Publishing Co.
Box 828 Sidney OH 45365-0828
1-800-572-6885
www.scottonline.com

Pronunciation Symbols

ə	banana, collide, abut		ȯ	saw, all, gnaw, caught
ˈə, ˌə	humdrum, abut		œ	French bœuf, German Hölle
ə	immediately preceding \l\, \n\, \m\, \ŋ\, as in battle, mitten, eaten, and sometimes open \ˈō-pᵊm\, lock and key \-ᵊŋ-\; immediately following \l\, \m\, \r\, as often in French table, prisme, titre		œ̄	French feu, German Höhle
			ȯi	coin, destroy
			p	pepper, lip
			r	red, car, rarity
ər	further, merger, bird		s	source, less
ˈər-, ˈə-r	as in two different pronunciations of hurry \ˈhər-ē, ˈhə-rē\		sh	as in shy, mission, machine, special (actually, this is a single sound, not two); with a hyphen between, two sounds as in grasshopper \ˈgras-ˌhä-pər\
a	mat, map, mad, gag, snap, patch			
ā	day, fade, date, aorta, drape, cape		t	tie, attack, late, later, latter
ä	bother, cot, and, with most American speakers, father, cart		th	as in thin, ether (actually, this is a single sound, not two); with a hyphen between, two sounds as in knighthood \ˈnīt-ˌhu̇d\
ȧ	father as pronounced by speakers who do not rhyme it with bother; French patte		th	then, either, this (actually, this is a single sound, not two)
au̇	now, loud, out		ü	rule, youth, union \ˈyün-yən\, few \ˈfyü\
b	baby, rib		u̇	pull, wood, book, curable \ˈkyu̇r-ə-bəl\, fury \ˈfyu̇r-ē\
ch	chin, nature \ˈnā-chər\			
d	did, adder		ue	German füllen, hübsch
e	bet, bed, peck		ūe	French rue, German fühlen
ˈē, ˌē	beat, nosebleed, evenly, easy		v	vivid, give
ē	easy, mealy		w	we, away
f	fifty, cuff		y	yard, young, cue \ˈkyü\, mute \ˈmyüt\, union \ˈyün-yən\
g	go, big, gift			
h	hat, ahead		ʸ	indicates that during the articulation of the sound represented by the preceding character the front of the tongue has substantially the position it has for the articulation of the first sound of yard, as in French digne \dēnʸ\
hw	whale as pronounced by those who do not have the same pronunciation for both whale and wail			
i	tip, banish, active		z	zone, raise
ī	site, side, buy, tripe		zh	as in vision, azure \ˈa-zhər\ (actually, this is a single sound, not two); with a hyphen between, two sounds as in hogshead \ˈhȯgz-ˌhed, ˈhägz-\
j	job, gem, edge, join, judge			
k	kin, cook, ache		\	slant line used in pairs to mark the beginning and end of a transcription: \ˈpen\
ḵ	German ich, Buch; one pronunciation of loch			
l	lily, pool		ˈ	mark preceding a syllable with primary (strongest) stress: \ˈpen-mən-ˌship\
m	murmur, dim, nymph			
n	no, own		ˌ	mark preceding a syllable with secondary (medium) stress: \ˈpen-mən-ˌship\
ⁿ	indicates that a preceding vowel or diphthong is pronounced with the nasal passages open, as in French un bon vin blanc \œⁿ-bōⁿ-vaⁿ-bläⁿ\		-	mark of syllable division
			( )	indicate that what is symbolized between is present in some utterances but not in others: factory \ˈfak-t(ə-)rē\
ŋ	sing \ˈsiŋ\, singer \ˈsiŋ-ər\, finger \ˈfiŋ-gər\, ink \ˈiŋk\			
ō	bone, know, beau		÷	indicates that many regard as unacceptable the pronunciation variant immediately following: cupola \ˈkyü-pə-lə, ÷-ˌlō\

The system of pronunciation is used by permission from Merriam-Webster's Collegiate® Dictionary, Tenth Edition ©1993 by Merriam-Webster Inc., publisher of the Merriam-Webster® dictionaries.